Who's Who in the East

Biographical Titles Currently Published by Marquis Who's Who

Who's Who in America
Who's Who in America derivatives:
  Who's Who in America Junior & Senior High School Version
  Geographic/Professional Index
  Supplement to Who's Who in America
  Who's Who in America Classroom Project Book
Who Was Who in America
  Historical Volume (1607-1896)
  Volume I (1897-1942)
  Volume II (1943-1950)
  Volume III (1951-1960)
  Volume IV (1961-1968)
  Volume V (1969-1973)
  Volume VI (1974-1976)
  Volume VII (1977-1981)
  Volume VIII (1982-1985)
  Volume IX (1985-1989)
  Index Volume (1607-1989)
Who's Who in the World
Who's Who in the East
Who's Who in the Midwest
Who's Who in the South and Southwest
Who's Who in the West
Who's Who in Advertising
Who's Who in American Law
Who's Who of American Women
Who's Who of Emerging Leaders in America
Who's Who in Entertainment
Who's Who in Finance and Industry
Who's Who in Religion
Who's Who in Science and Engineering
Index to Who's Who Books
Directory of Medical Specialists
Supplement to Directory of Medical Specialists

Who's Who
in the East ®

Including Connecticut, Delaware, Maine, Maryland,
Massachusetts, New Hampshire, New Jersey, New York,
Pennsylvania, Rhode Island, Vermont, Washington, D.C.,
and in Canada, the provinces of New Brunswick,
Newfoundland, Nova Scotia, Prince Edward Island, Quebec,
and the eastern half of Ontario.

24th edition
1993 - 1994

MARQUIS
Who'sWho

A Reed Reference Publishing Company
121 Chanlon Road
New Providence, N.J. 07974

Published by Marquis Who's Who, a Reed Reference Publishing company. Copyright © 1992 by Reed Publishing (USA) Inc. All rights reserved. No part of this publication may be reproduced, stored in a retrieval system or transmitted in any form or by any means—including, but not limited to, electronic, mechanical, photocopying, recording or otherwise—or used for any commercial purpose whatsoever without the prior written permission of the publisher and, if publisher deems necessary, execution of a formal license agreement with publisher. For information, contact Marquis Who's Who, 121 Chanlon Road, New Providence, New Jersey 07974, 1-800/621-9669.

Sandra S. Barnes—Publisher
Peter E. Simon—Vice President, Database Publishing
Leigh Yuster—Associate Publisher
Paul Canning—Editorial Director
Frederick M. Marks—Senior Managing Editor
Samuel J. Dempsey—Managing Editor

Library of Congress Catalog Card Number 43–18522
International Standard Book Numbers 0–8379–0624–5 (classic edition)
0–8379–0625–8 (deluxe edition)

WHO'S WHO IN THE EAST is a registered trademark of Reed Publishing (Nederland) B.V., used under license.

Manufactured in the United States of America

Table of Contents

Preface

The twenty-fourth edition of *Who's Who in the East* is our most recent compilation of biographical information on men and women of distinction whose influence is concentrated in the eastern sector of North America. Such individuals are of reference interest locally, and to a degree, nationally.

The volume contains approximately 26,750 names from the eastern region of the United States including Connecticut, Delaware, Maine, Maryland, Massachusetts, New Hampshire, New Jersey, New York, Pennsylvania, Rhode Island, Vermont, and Washington, D.C. (the metropolitan area of which may include residents of Virginia). The Canadian provinces of New Brunswick, Newfoundland, Nova Scotia, Prince Edward Island, Quebec, and the eastern section of Ontario are also included in this book. Reviewed, revised, and amended, the twenty-fourth edition offers current coverage of a broad range of Easterners based on position or individual achievement.

The persons sketched in this volume represent virtually every important field of endeavor. Included are executives and officials in government, business, education, religion, the press, law, and other fields. This edition also includes significant contributors in such areas as contemporary art, music, and science.

In most cases, biographees have furnished their own data, thus assuring a high degree of accuracy. In some cases where individuals failed to supply information, Marquis staff members compiled the data through careful, independent research. Sketches compiled in this manner are denoted by an asterisk. As in previous editions, biographees were given the opportunity to review prepublication proofs of their sketches to make sure they were correct.

The question is often asked, "How do people get into a Marquis Who's Who volume?" Name selection is based on one fundamental principle: reference value.

Biographees of *Who's Who in the East* can be classified in two basic categories: (1) Persons who are of regional reference importance to colleagues, librarians, researchers, scholars, the media, historians, biographers, participants in business and civic affairs, and others with specific or general inquiry needs; (2) Individuals of national reference interest who are also of such regional or local importance that their inclusion in the book is essential.

In the editorial evaluation that resulted in the ultimate selection of the names appearing in this directory, an individual's desire to be listed was not sufficient reason for inclusion; rather it was the person's achievement that ruled. Similarly, neither wealth nor social position was a criterion; only occupational stature or achievement in a field within the eastern region of North America influenced selection.

Marquis Who's Who editors exercise the utmost care in preparing each biographical sketch for publication. Occasionally, however, errors occur. Users of this directory are requested to draw the attention of the publisher to any errors found so that corrections can be made in a subsequent edition.

The twenty-fourth edition of *Who's Who in the East* carries on the tradition of excellence established in 1899 with the publication of the first edition of *Who's Who in America*. The essence of that tradition is reflected in our continuing effort to produce reference works that are responsive to the needs of their users throughout the world.

Board of Advisors

Marquis Who's Who gratefully acknowledges the following distinguished individuals who have made themselves available for review, evaluation, and general comment with regard to the publication of the twenty-fourth edition of *Who's Who in the East*. The advisors have enhanced the reference value of this edition by the nomination of outstanding individuals for inclusion. However, the Board of Advisors, either collectively or individually, is in no way responsible for the final selection of names appearing in this volume, nor does the Board of Advisors bear responsibility for the accuracy or comprehensiveness of the biographical information or other material contained herein.

Board of Nominators

Marquis Who's Who gratefully acknowledges the following distinguished individuals for their assistance with regard to the publication of the twenty-fourth edition of *Who's Who in the East*. As nominators they have enhanced the reference value of this edition by the recommendation of outstanding persons from their respective states or local areas. The Board of Nominators, either collectively or individually, is in no way responsible for the final selection of names appearing in this volume, nor does the Board of Nominators bear responsibility for the accuracy or comprehensiveness of the biographical information or other material contained herein.

John M. Burris
President
Delaware State Chamber of Commerce
Wilmington, Delaware

Frank D. Fulco
President
Waterbury Chamber of Commerce
Waterbury, Connecticut

Thomas T. Mooney
President
Rochester Area Chamber of Commerce
Rochester, New York

William C. Wyer
Former President
Delaware State Chamber of Commerce
Wilmington, Delaware

Standards of Admission

The foremost consideration in selecting biographees for *Who's Who in the East* is the extent of an individual's reference interest. Such reference interest is judged on either of two factors: 1) the position of responsibility held, or 2) the level of achievement attained by the individual.

Admissions based on the factor of position include:

Members of the U.S. Congress

Federal judges

Governors of states covered by this volume

Premiers of Canadian provinces covered by this volume

State attorneys general

Judges of state and territorial courts of highest appellate jurisdiction

Mayors of major cities

Heads of major universities and colleges

Heads of leading philanthropic, educational, cultural, and scientific institutions and associations

Chief ecclesiastics of the principal religious denominations

Others chosen because of incumbency or membership

Admission for individual achievement is based on objective qualitative criteria. To be selected, a person must have attained conspicuous achievement. The biographee may scarcely be known in the local community but may be recognized in some field of endeavor for noteworthy accomplishment.

Key to Information

[1] **KILLBROOK, WALTER BOSTON,** [2] lawyer; [3] b. Topeka, Kans., Aug. 3, 1922; [4] s. Samuel Taylor and Bertha (Hanson) K.; [5] m. Nancy Roudebush, June 20, 1943; [6] children: Theodore Murray, Abbe Gail, William Frank. [7] BA, Pa. State U., 1943; JD, Syracuse U., 1948. [8] Bar: N.Y. 1948. [9] Assoc. firm Prine, Belden & Coates, Rochester, N.Y., 1948-55; mem. firm Johnson, Randolph, Sikes and Bord, Rochester, 1955-82, ptnr., 1961-82; sr. ptnr. Randolph, Killbrook & Gere, Rochester, 1982—; [10] legal cons. Rochester Urban League, 1968—. [11] Author: Urban Renewal and the Law, 1969; contbr. articles to profl. jours. [12] Commr. Monroe County Park Dist., 1978-79; mem. planning com. Genesee-Crossroads Redevel. Project, Rochester, 1974—; bd. dirs. Eastman Sch. Music, 1985—. [13] Served with U.S. Army, 1944-45. [14] Named Man of Yr., Rochester Times-Union, 1984. [15] Mem. ABA, N.Y. Bar Assn., Rochester Bar Assn., Am. Judicature Soc., Order of Coif, Rochester Country Club, Tuesday Luncheon Club, Lions. [16] Democrat. [17] Episcopalian. [18] Home: 3080 Grant St Rochester NY 14650 [19] Office: Randolph Killbrook & Gere 10 St Paul Ave Rochester NY 14606

KEY

[1]	Name
[2]	Occupation
[3]	Vital statistics
[4]	Parents
[5]	Marriage
[6]	Children
[7]	Education
[8]	Professional certifications
[9]	Career
[10]	Career Related
[11]	Writings and creative works
[12]	Civic and political activities
[13]	Military
[14]	Awards and fellowships
[15]	Professional and association memberships, Clubs and Lodges
[16]	Political affiliation
[17]	Religion
[18]	Home address
[19]	Office address

Table of Abbreviations

The following abbreviations and symbols are frequently used in this book.

*An asterisk following a sketch indicates that it was researched by the Marquis Who's Who editorial staff and has not been verified by the biographee.

A Associate (used with academic degrees only)
AA, A.A. Associate in Arts, Associate of Arts
AAAL American Academy of Arts and Letters
AAAS American Association for the Advancement of Science
AACD American Association for Counseling and Development
AACN American Association of Critical Care Nurses
AAHA American Academy of Health Administrators
AAHP American Association of Hospital Planners
AAHPER Alliance for Health, Physical Education and Recreation
AAS Associate of Applied Science
AASL American Association of School Librarians
AASPA American Association of School Personnel Administrators
AAU Amateur Athletic Union
AAUP American Association of University Professors
AAUW American Association of University Women
AB, A.B. Arts, Bachelor of
AB Alberta
ABA American Bar Association
ABC American Broadcasting Company
AC Air Corps
acad. academy, academic
acct. accountant
acctg. accounting
ACDA Arms Control and Disarmament Agency
ACHA American College of Hospital Administrators
ACLS Advanced Cardiac Life Support
ACLU American Civil Liberties Union
ACP American College of Physicians
ACS American College of Surgeons
ADA American Dental Association
a.d.c. aide-de-camp
adj. adjunct, adjutant
adj. gen. adjutant general
adm. admiral
adminstr. administrator
adminstrn. administration
adminstrv. administrative
ADN Associate's Degree in Nursing
ADP Automatic Data Processing
adv. advocate, advisory
advt. advertising
AE, A.E. Agricultural Engineer

A.E. and P. Ambassador Extraordinary and Plenipotentiary
AEC Atomic Energy Commission
aero. aeronautical, aeronautic
aerodyn. aerodynamic
AFB Air Force Base
AFL-CIO American Federation of Labor and Congress of Industrial Organizations
AFTRA American Federation of TV and Radio Artists
AFSCME American Federation of State, County and Municipal Employees
agr. agriculture
agrl. agricultural
agt. agent
AGVA American Guild of Variety Artists
agy. agency
A&I Agricultural and Industrial
AIA American Institute of Architects
AIAA American Institute of Aeronautics and Astronautics
AICPA American Institute of Certified Public Accountants
AID Agency for International Development
AIDS Acquired Immune Deficiency Syndrome
AIEE American Institute of Electrical Engineers
AIM American Institute of Management
AIME American Institute of Mining, Metallurgy, and Petroleum Engineers
AK Alaska
AL Alabama
ALA American Library Association
Ala. Alabama
alt. alternate
Alta. Alberta
A&M Agricultural and Mechanical
AM, A.M. Arts, Master of
Am. American, America
AMA American Medical Association
amb. ambassador
A.M.E. African Methodist Episcopal
Amtrak National Railroad Passenger Corporation
AMVETS American Veterans of World War II, Korea, Vietnam
ANA American Nurses Association
anat. anatomical
ANCC American Nurses Credentialing Center
ann. annual
ANTA American National Theatre and Academy
anthrop. anthropological
AP Associated Press
APA American Psychological Association
APGA American Personnel Guidance Association

APHA American Public Health Association
APO Army Post Office
apptd. appointed
Apr. April
apt. apartment
AR Arkansas
ARC American Red Cross
archeol. archeological
archtl. architectural
Ariz. Arizona
Ark. Arkansas
ArtsD, ArtsD. Arts, Doctor of
arty. artillery
AS American Samoa
AS Associate in Science, Associate of Applied Science
ASCAP American Society of Composers, Authors and Publishers
ASCD Association for Supervision and Curriculum Development
ASCE American Society of Civil Engineers
ASHRAE American Society of Heating, Refrigeration, and Air Conditioning Engineers
ASME American Society of Mechanical Engineers
ASNSA American Society for Nursing Service Administrators
ASPA American Society for Public Administration
ASPCA American Society for the Prevention of Cruelty to Animals
assn. association
assoc. associate
asst. assistant
ASTD American Society for Training and Development
ASTM American Society for Testing and Materials
astron. astronomical
astrophys. astrophysical
ATSC Air Technical Service Command
AT&T American Telephone & Telegraph Company
atty. attorney
Aug. August
AUS Army of the United States
aux. auxiliary
Ave. Avenue
AVMA American Veterinary Medical Association
AZ Arizona

B. Bachelor
b. born
BA, B.A. Bachelor of Arts
BAgr, B.Agr. Bachelor of Agriculture
Balt. Baltimore

Bapt. Baptist
BArch, B.Arch. Bachelor of Architecture
BAS, B.A.S. Bachelor of Agricultural Science
BBA, B.B.A. Bachelor of Business Administration
BBC British Broadcasting Corporation
BC, B.C. British Columbia
BCE, B.C.E. Bachelor of Civil Engineering
BChir, B.Chir. Bachelor of Surgery
BCL, B.C.L. Bachelor of Civil Law
BCLS Basic Cardiac Life Support
BCS, B.C.S. Bachelor of Commercial Science
BD, B.D. Bachelor of Divinity
bd. board
BE, B.E. Bachelor of Education
BEE, B.E.E. Bachelor of Electrical Engineering
BFA, B.F.A. Bachelor of Fine Arts
bibl. biblical
bibliog. bibliographical
biog. biographical
biol. biological
BJ, B.J. Bachelor of Journalism
Bklyn. Brooklyn
BL, B.L. Bachelor of Letters
bldg. building
BLS, B.L.S. Bachelor of Library Science
BLS Basic Life Support
Blvd. Boulevard
BMW Bavarian Motor Works (Bayerische Motoren Werke)
bn. battalion
B.& O.R.R. Baltimore & Ohio Railroad
bot. botanical
BPE, B.P.E. Bachelor of Physical Education
BPhil, B.Phil. Bachelor of Philosophy
br. branch
BRE, B.R.E. Bachelor of Religious Education
brig. gen. brigadier general
Brit. British, Brittanica
Bros. Brothers
BS, B.S. Bachelor of Science
BSA, B.S.A. Bachelor of Agricultural Science
BSBA Bachelor of Science in Business Administration
BSChemE Bachelor of Science in Chemical Engineering
BSD, B.S.D. Bachelor of Didactic Science
BSN Bachelor of Science in Nursing
BST, B.S.T. Bachelor of Sacred Theology
BTh, B.Th. Bachelor of Theology
bull. bulletin
bur. bureau
bus. business
B.W.I. British West Indies

CA California
CAA Civil Aeronautics Administration
CAB Civil Aeronautics Board
CAD-CAM Computer Aided Design-Computer Aided Model
Calif. California
C.Am. Central America

Can. Canada, Canadian
CAP Civil Air Patrol
capt. captain
CARE Cooperative American Relief Everywhere
Cath. Catholic
cav. cavalry
CBC Canadian Broadcasting Company
CBI China, Burma, India Theatre of Operations
CBS Columbia Broadcasting Company
CCC Commodity Credit Corporation
CCNY City College of New York
CCU Cardiac Care Unit
CD Civil Defense
CE, C.E. Corps of Engineers, Civil Engineer
cen. central
CEN Certified Emergency Nurse
CENTO Central Treaty Organization
CERN European Organization of Nuclear Research
cert. certificate, certification, certified
CETA Comprehensive Employment Training Act
CFL Canadian Football League
ch. church
ChD, Ch.D. Doctor of Chemistry
chem. chemical
ChemE, Chem.E. Chemical Engineer
Chgo. Chicago
chirurg. chirurgical
chmn. chairman
chpt. chapter
CIA Central Intelligence Agency
Cin. Cincinnati
cir. circuit
Cleve. Cleveland
climatol. climatological
clin. clinical
clk. clerk
C.L.U. Chartered Life Underwriter
CM, C.M. Master in Surgery
CM Northern Mariana Islands
CMA Certified Medical Assistant
CNA Certified Nurse's Aide
CNOR Certified Nurse (Operating Room)
C.&N.W.Ry. Chicago & North Western Railway
CO Colorado
Co. Company
COF Catholic Order of Foresters
C. of C. Chamber of Commerce
col. colonel
coll. college
Colo. Colorado
com. committee
comd. commanded
comdg. commanding
comdr. commander
comdt. commandant
commd. commissioned
comml. commercial
commn. commission
commr. commissioner
compt. comptroller
condr. conductor
Conf. Conference
Congl. Congregational, Congressional

Conglist. Congregationalist
Conn. Connecticut
cons. consultant, consulting
consol. consolidated
constl. constitutional
constn. constitution
constrn. construction
contbd. contributed
contbg. contributing
contbn. contribution
contbr. contributor
contr. controller
Conv. Convention
coop. cooperative
coord. coordinator
CORDS Civil Operations and Revolutionary Development Support
CORE Congress of Racial Equality
corp. corporation, corporate
corr. correspondent, corresponding, correspondence
C.&O.Ry. Chesapeake & Ohio Railway
coun. council
C.P.A. Certified Public Accountant
C.P.C.U. Chartered Property and Casualty Underwriter
CPH, C.P.H. Certificate of Public Health
cpl. corporal
C.P.R. Cardio-Pulmonary Resuscitation
C.P.Ry. Canadian Pacific Railway
CRT Cathode Ray Terminal
C.S. Christian Science
CSB, C.S.B. Bachelor of Christian Science
C.S.C. Civil Service Commission
CT Connecticut
ct. court
ctr. center
CWS Chemical Warfare Service
C.Z. Canal Zone

D. Doctor
d. daughter
DAgr, D.Agr. Doctor of Agriculture
DAR Daughters of the American Revolution
dau. daughter
DAV Disabled American Veterans
DC, D.C. District of Columbia
DCL, D.C.L. Doctor of Civil Law
DCS, D.C.S. Doctor of Commercial Science
DD, D.D. Doctor of Divinity
DDS, D.D.S. Doctor of Dental Surgery
DE Delaware
Dec. December
dec. deceased
def. defense
Del. Delaware
del. delegate, delegation
Dem. Democrat, Democratic
DEng, D.Eng. Doctor of Engineering
denom. denomination, denominational
dep. deputy
dept. department
dermatol. dermatological
desc. descendant
devel. development, developmental
DFA, D.F.A. Doctor of Fine Arts
D.F.C. Distinguished Flying Cross
DHL, D.H.L. Doctor of Hebrew Literature
dir. director

dist. district
distbg. distributing
distbn. distribution
distbr. distributor
disting. distinguished
div. division, divinity, divorce
DLitt, D.Litt. Doctor of Literature
DMD, D.M.D. Doctor of Dental Medicine
DMS, D.M.S. Doctor of Medical Science
DO, D.O. Doctor of Osteopathy
DON Director of Nursing
DPH, D.P.H. Diploma in Public Health
DPhil, D.Phil. Doctor of Philosophy
D.R. Daughters of the Revolution
Dr. Drive, Doctor
DRE, D.R.E. Doctor of Religious Education
DrPH, Dr.P.H. Doctor of Public Health, Doctor of Public Hygiene
D.S.C. Distinguished Service Cross
DSc, D.Sc. Doctor of Science
D.S.M. Distinguished Service Medal
DST, D.S.T. Doctor of Sacred Theology
DTM, D.T.M. Doctor of Tropical Medicine
DVM, D.V.M. Doctor of Veterinary Medicine
DVS, D.V.S. Doctor of Veterinary Surgery

E, E. East
ea. eastern
E. and P. Extraordinary and Plenipotentiary
Eccles. Ecclesiastical
ecol. ecological
econ. economic
ECOSOC Economic and Social Council (of the UN)
ED, E.D. Doctor of Engineering
ed. educated
EdB, Ed.B. Bachelor of Education
EdD, Ed.D. Doctor of Education
edit. edition
EdM, Ed.M. Master of Education
edn. education
ednl. educational
EDP Electronic Data Processing
EdS, Ed.S. Specialist in Education
EE, E.E. Electrical Engineer
E.E. and M.P. Envoy Extraordinary and Minister Plenipotentiary
EEC European Economic Community
EEG Electroencephalogram
EEO Equal Employment Opportunity
EEOC Equal Employment Opportunity Commission
E.Ger. German Democratic Republic
EKG Electrocardiogram
elec. electrical
electrochem. electrochemical
electrophys. electrophysical
elem. elementary
EM, E.M. Engineer of Mines
EMT Emergency Medical Technician
ency. encyclopedia
Eng. England
engr. engineer
engring. engineering
entomol. entomological
environ. environmental
EPA Environmental Protection Agency
epidemiol. epidemiological

Episc. Episcopalian
ERA Equal Rights Amendment
ERDA Energy Research and Development Administration
ESEA Elementary and Secondary Education Act
ESL English as Second Language
ESPN Entertainment and Sports Programming Network
ESSA Environmental Science Services Administration
ethnol. ethnological
ETO European Theatre of Operations
Evang. Evangelical
exam. examination, examining
Exch. Exchange
exec. executive
exhbn. exhibition
expdn. expedition
expn. exposition
expt. experiment
exptl. experimental
Expwy. Expressway

F.A. Field Artillery
FAA Federal Aviation Administration
FAO Food and Agriculture Organization (of the UN)
FBI Federal Bureau of Investigation
FCA Farm Credit Administration
FCC Federal Communications Commission
FCDA Federal Civil Defense Administration
FDA Food and Drug Administration
FDIA Federal Deposit Insurance Administration
FDIC Federal Deposit Insurance Corporation
FE, F.E. Forest Engineer
FEA Federal Energy Administration
Feb. February
fed. federal
fedn. federation
FERC Federal Energy Regulatory Commission
fgn. foreign
FHA Federal Housing Administration
fin. financial, finance
FL Florida
Fl. Floor
Fla. Florida
FMC Federal Maritime Commission
FNP Family Nurse Practitioner
FOA Foreign Operations Administration
found. foundation
FPC Federal Power Commission
FPO Fleet Post Office
frat. fraternity
FRS Federal Reserve System
Frwy. Freeway
FSA Federal Security Agency
Ft. Fort
FTC Federal Trade Commission

G-1 (or other number) Division of General Staff
GA, Ga. Georgia
GAO General Accounting Office
gastroent. gastroenterological

GATE Gifted and Talented Educators
GATT General Agreement of Tariff and Trades
GE General Electric Company
gen. general
geneal. genealogical
geod. geodetic
geog. geographic, geographical
geol. geological
geophys. geophysical
gerontol. gerontological
G.H.Q. General Headquarters
GM General Motors Corporation
GMAC General Motors Acceptance Corporation
G.N.Ry. Great Northern Railway
gov. governor
govt. government
govtl. governmental
GPO Government Printing Office
grad. graduate, graduated
GSA General Services Administration
Gt. Great
GTE General Telephone and Electric Company
GU Guam
gynecol. gynecological

HBO Home Box Office
hdqrs. headquarters
HEW Department of Health, Education and Welfare
HHD, H.H.D. Doctor of Humanities
HHFA Housing and Home Finance Agency
HHS Department of Health and Human Services
HI Hawaii
hist. historical, historic
HM, H.M. Master of Humanics
HMO Health Maintenance Organization
homeo. homeopathic
hon. honorary, honorable
Ho. of Dels. House of Delegates
Ho. of Reps. House of Representatives
hort. horticultural
hosp. hospital
HUD Department of Housing and Urban Development
Hwy. Highway
hydrog. hydrographic

IA Iowa
IAEA International Atomic Energy Agency
IBM International Business Machines Corporation
IBRD International Bank for Reconstruction and Development
ICA International Cooperation Administration
ICC Interstate Commerce Commission
ICCE International Council for Computers in Education
ICU Intensive Care Unit
ID Idaho
IEEE Institute of Electrical and Electronics Engineers
IFC International Finance Corporation
IGY International Geophysical Year

IL Illinois
Ill. Illinois
illus. illustrated
ILO International Labor Organization
IMF International Monetary Fund
IN Indiana
Inc. Incorporated
Ind. Indiana
ind. independent
Indpls. Indianapolis
indsl. industrial
inf. infantry
info. information
ins. insurance
insp. inspector
insp. gen. inspector general
inst. institute
instl. institutional
instn. institution
instr. instructor
instrn. instruction
internat. international
intro. introduction
IRE Institute of Radio Engineers
IRS Internal Revenue Service
ITT International Telephone &
    Telegraph Corporation

JAG Judge Advocate General
JAGC Judge Advocate General Corps
Jan. January
Jaycees Junior Chamber of Commerce
JB, J.B. Jurum Baccalaureus
JCB, J.C.B. Juris Canoni Baccalaureus
JCD, J.C.D. Juris Canonici Doctor, Juris
    Civilis Doctor
JCL, J.C.L. Juris Canonici Licentiatus
JD, J.D. Juris Doctor
jg. junior grade
jour. journal
jr. junior
JSD, J.S.D. Juris Scientiae Doctor
JUD, J.U.D. Juris Utriusque Doctor
jud. judicial

Kans. Kansas
K.C. Knights of Columbus
K.P. Knights of Pythias
KS Kansas
K.T. Knight Templar
KY, Ky. Kentucky

LA, La. Louisiana
L.A. Los Angeles
lab. laboratory
lang. language
laryngol. laryngological
LB Labrador
LDS Church Church of Jesus Christ of
    Latter Day Saints
lectr. lecturer
legis. legislation, legislative
LHD, L.H.D. Doctor of Humane Letters
L.I. Long Island
libr. librarian, library
lic. licensed, license
L.I.R.R. Long Island Railroad
lit. literature
LittB, Litt.B. Bachelor of Letters
LittD, Litt.D. Doctor of Letters

LLB, LL.B. Bachelor of Laws
LLD, L.L.D. Doctor of Laws
LLM, L.L.M. Master of Laws
Ln. Lane
L.&N.R.R. Louisville & Nashville Railroad
LPGA Ladies Professional Golf Association
LPN Licensed Practical Nurse
LS, L.S. Library Science (in degree)
lt. lieutenant
Ltd. Limited
Luth. Lutheran
LWV League of Women Voters

M. Master
m. married
MA, M.A. Master of Arts
MA Massachusetts
MADD Mothers Against Drunk Driving
mag. magazine
MAgr, M.Agr. Master of Agriculture
maj. major
Man. Manitoba
Mar. March
MArch, M.Arch. Master in Architecture
Mass. Massachusetts
math. mathematics, mathematical
MATS Military Air Transport Service
MB, M.B. Bachelor of Medicine
MB Manitoba
MBA, M.B.A. Master of Business
    Administration
MBS Mutual Broadcasting System
M.C. Medical Corps
MCE, M.C.E. Master of Civil Engineering
mcht. merchant
mcpl. municipal
MCS, M.C.S. Master of Commercial
    Science
MD, M.D. Doctor of Medicine
MD, Md. Maryland
MDiv Master of Divinity
MDip, M.Dip. Master in Diplomacy
mdse. merchandise
MDV, M.D.V. Doctor of Veterinary
    Medicine
ME, M.E. Mechanical Engineer
ME Maine
M.E.Ch. Methodist Episcopal Church
mech. mechanical
MEd., M.Ed. Master of Education
med. medical
MEE, M.E.E. Master of Electrical
    Engineering
mem. member
meml. memorial
merc. mercantile
met. metropolitan
metall. metallurgical
MetE, Met.E. Metallurgical Engineer
meteorol. meteorological
Meth. Methodist
Mex. Mexico
MF, M.F. Master of Forestry
MFA, M.F.A. Master of Fine Arts
mfg. manufacturing
mfr. manufacturer
mgmt. management
mgr. manager
MHA, M.H.A. Master of Hospital

Administration
M.I. Military Intelligence
MI Michigan
Mich. Michigan
micros. microscopic, microscopical
mid. middle
mil. military
Milw. Milwaukee
Min. Minister
mineral. mineralogical
Minn. Minnesota
MIS Management Information Systems
Miss. Mississippi
MIT Massachusetts Institute of Technology
mktg. marketing
ML, M.L. Master of Laws
MLA Modern Language Association
M.L.D. Magister Legnum Diplomatic
MLitt, M.Litt. Master of Literature,
    Master of Letters
MLS, M.L.S. Master of Library Science
MME, M.M.E. Master of Mechanical
    Engineering
MN Minnesota
mng. managing
MO, Mo. Missouri
moblzn. mobilization
Mont. Montana
MP Northern Mariana Islands
M.P. Member of Parliament
MPA Master of Public Administration
MPE, M.P.E. Master of Physical Education
MPH, M.P.H. Master of Public Health
MPhil, M.Phil. Master of Philosophy
MPL, M.P.L. Master of Patent Law
Mpls. Minneapolis
MRE, M.R.E. Master of Religious
    Education
MS, M.S. Master of Science
MS, Ms. Mississippi
MSc, M.Sc. Master of Science
MSChemE Master of Science in Chemical
    Engineering
MSF, M.S.F. Master of Science of Forestry
MSN Master of Science in Nursing
MST, M.S.T. Master of Sacred Theology
MSW, M.S.W. Master of Social Work
MT Montana
Mt. Mount
MTO Mediterranean Theatre of Operation
MTV Music Television
mus. museum, musical
MusB, Mus.B. Bachelor of Music
MusD, Mus.D. Doctor of Music
MusM, Mus.M. Master of Music
mut. mutual
mycol. mycological

N. North
NAACOG Nurses Association of the
    American College of Obstetricians and
    Gynecologists
NAACP National Association for the
    Advancement of Colored People
NACA National Advisory Committee for
    Aeronautics
NACU National Association of Colleges
    and Universities
NAD National Academy of Design
NAE National Academy of Engineering,

National Association of Educators
NAESP National Association of Elementary School Principals
NAFE National Association of Female Executives
N.Am. North America
NAM National Association of Manufacturers
NAMH National Association for Mental Health
NAPA National Association of Performing Artists
NARAS National Academy of Recording Arts and Sciences
NAREB National Association of Real Estate Boards
NARS National Archives and Record Service
NAS National Academy of Sciences
NASA National Aeronautics and Space Administration
NASP National Association of School Psychologists
NASW National Association of Social Workers
nat. national
NATAS National Academy of Television Arts and Sciences
NATO North Atlantic Treaty Organization
NATOUSA North African Theatre of Operations
nav. navigation
NB, N.B. New Brunswick
NBA National Basketball Association
NBC National Broadcasting Company
NC, N.C. North Carolina
NCAA National College Athletic Association
NCCJ National Conference of Christians and Jews
ND, N.D. North Dakota
NDEA National Defense Education Act
NE Nebraska
NE, N.E. Northeast
NEA National Education Association
Nebr. Nebraska
NEH National Endowment for Humanities
neurol. neurological
Nev. Nevada
NF Newfoundland
NFL National Football League
Nfld. Newfoundland
NG National Guard
NH, N.H. New Hampshire
NHL National Hockey League
NIH National Institutes of Health
NIMH National Institute of Mental Health
NJ, N.J. New Jersey
NLRB National Labor Relations Board
NM New Mexico
N.Mex. New Mexico
No. Northern
NOAA National Oceanographic and Atmospheric Administration
NORAD North America Air Defense
Nov. November
NOW National Organization for Women
N.P.Ry. Northern Pacific Railway
nr. near

NRA National Rifle Association
NRC National Research Council
NS, N.S. Nova Scotia
NSC National Security Council
NSF National Science Foundation
NSTA National Science Teachers Association
NSW New South Wales
N.T. New Testament
NT Northwest Territories
numis. numismatic
NV Nevada
NW, N.W. Northwest
N.W.T. Northwest Territories
NY, N.Y. New York
N.Y.C. New York City
NYU New York University
N.Z. New Zealand

OAS Organization of American States
ob-gyn obstetrics-gynecology
obs. observatory
obstet. obstetrical
Oct. October
OD, O.D. Doctor of Optometry
OECD Organization of European Cooperation and Development
OEEC Organization of European Economic Cooperation
OEO Office of Economic Opportunity
ofcl. official
OH Ohio
OK Oklahoma
Okla. Oklahoma
ON Ontario
Ont. Ontario
oper. operating
ophthal. ophthalmological
ops. operations
OR Oregon
orch. orchestra
Oreg. Oregon
orgn. organization
ornithol. ornithological
OSHA Occupational Safety and Health Administration
OSRD Office of Scientific Research and Development
OSS Office of Strategic Services
osteo. osteopathic
otol. otological
otolaryn. otolaryngological

PA, Pa. Pennsylvania
P.A. Professional Association
paleontol. paleontological
path. pathological
PBS Public Broadcasting System
P.C. Professional Corporation
PE Prince Edward Island
P.E.I. Prince Edward Island
PEN Poets, Playwrights, Editors, Essayists and Novelists (international association)
penol. penological
P.E.O. women's organization (full name not disclosed)
pers. personnel
pfc. private first class
PGA Professional Golfers' Association of

America
PHA Public Housing Administration
pharm. pharmaceutical
PharmD, Pharm.D. Doctor of Pharmacy
PharmM, Pharm.M. Master of Pharmacy
PhB, Ph.B. Bachelor of Philosophy
PhD, Ph.D. Doctor of Philosophy
PhDChemE Doctor of Science in Chemical Engineering
PhM, Ph.M. Master of Philosophy
Phila. Philadelphia
philharm. philharmonic
philol. philological
philos. philosophical
photog. photographic
phys. physical
physiol. physiological
Pitts. Pittsburgh
Pk. Park
Pkwy. Parkway
Pl. Place
Pla. Plaza
P.&L.E.R.R. Pittsburgh & Lake Erie Railroad
PNP Pediatric Nurse Practitioner
P.O. Post Office
PO Box Post Office Box
polit. political
poly. polytechnic, polytechnical
PQ Province of Quebec
PR, P.R. Puerto Rico
prep. preparatory
pres. president
Presbyn. Presbyterian
presdl. presidential
prin. principal
proc. proceedings
prod. produced (play production)
prodn. production
prof. professor
profl. professional
prog. progressive
propr. proprietor
pros. atty. prosecuting attorney
pro tem pro tempore
PSRO Professional Services Review Organization
psychiat. psychiatric
psychol. psychological
PTA Parent-Teachers Association
ptnr. partner
PTO Pacific Theatre of Operations, Parent Teacher Organization
pub. publisher, publishing, published
pub. public
publ. publication
pvt. private

quar. quarterly
qm. quartermaster
Q.M.C. Quartermaster Corps
Que. Quebec

radiol. radiological
RAF Royal Air Force
RCA Radio Corporation of America
RCAF Royal Canadian Air Force
RD Rural Delivery
Rd. Road

R&D Research & Development
REA Rural Electrification Administration
rec. recording
ref. reformed
regt. regiment
regtl. regimental
rehab. rehabilitation
rels. relations
Rep. Republican
rep. representative
Res. Reserve
ret. retired
Rev. Reverend
rev. review, revised
RFC Reconstruction Finance Corporation
RFD Rural Free Delivery
rhinol. rhinological
RI, R.I. Rhode Island
RISD Rhode Island School of Design
Rm. Room
RN, R.N. Registered Nurse
roentgenol. roentgenological
ROTC Reserve Officers Training Corps
RR Rural Route
R.R. Railroad
rsch. research
Rte. Route
Ry. Railway

S. South
s. son
SAC Strategic Air Command
SAG Screen Actors Guild
SALT Strategic Arms Limitation Talks
S.Am. South America
san. sanitary
SAR Sons of the American Revolution
Sask. Saskatchewan
savs. savings
SB, S.B. Bachelor of Science
SBA Small Business Administration
SC, S.C. South Carolina
SCAP Supreme Command Allies Pacific
ScB, Sc.B. Bachelor of Science
SCD, S.C.D. Doctor of Commercial Science
ScD, Sc.D. Doctor of Science
sch. school
sci. science, scientific
SCLC Southern Christian Leadership
    Conference
SCV Sons of Confederate Veterans
SD, S.D. South Dakota
SE, S.E. Southeast
SEATO Southeast Asia Treaty Organization
SEC Securities and Exchange Commission
sec. secretary
sect. section
seismol. seismological
sem. seminary
Sept. September
s.g. senior grade
sgt. sergeant
SHAEF Supreme Headquarters Allied
    Expeditionary Forces
SHAPE Supreme Headquarters Allied
    Powers in Europe
S.I. Staten Island
S.J. Society of Jesus (Jesuit)
SJD Scientiae Juridicae Doctor
SK Saskatchewan

SM, S.M. Master of Science
SNP Society of Nursing Professionals
So. Southern
soc. society
sociol. sociological
S.P. Co. Southern Pacific Company
spl. special
splty. specialty
Sq. Square
S.R. Sons of the Revolution
sr. senior
SS Steamship
SSS Selective Service System
St. Saint, Street
sta. station
stats. statistics
statis. statistical
STB, S.T.B. Bachelor of Sacred Theology
stblzn. stabilization
STD, S.T.D. Doctor of Sacred Theology
Ste. Suite
subs. subsidiary
SUNY State University of New York
supr. supervisor
supt. superintendent
surg. surgical
svc. service
SW, S.W. Southwest

TAPPI Technical Association of the Pulp
    and Paper Industry
Tb. Tuberculosis
tchr. teacher
tech. technical, technology
technol. technological
Tel. & Tel. Telephone & Telegraph
temp. temporary
Tenn. Tennessee
Ter. Territory
Terr. Terrace
Tex. Texas
ThD, Th.D. Doctor of Theology
theol. theological
ThM, Th.M. Master of Theology
TN Tennessee
tng. training
topog. topographical
trans. transaction, transferred
transl. translation, translated
transp. transportation
treas. treasurer
TT Trust Territory
TV television
TVA Tennessee Valley Authority
TWA Trans World Airlines
twp. township
TX Texas
typog. typographical

U. University
UAW United Auto Workers
UCLA University of California at Los
    Angeles
UDC United Daughters of the Confederacy
U.K. United Kingdom
UN United Nations
UNESCO United Nations Educational,
    Scientific and Cultural Organization
UNICEF United Nations International
    Children's Emergency Fund

univ. university
UNRRA United Nations Relief and
    Rehabilitation Administration
UPI United Press International
U.P.R.R. United Pacific Railroad
urol. urological
U.S. United States
U.S.A. United States of America
USAAF United States Army Air Force
USAF United States Air Force
USAFR United States Air Force Reserve
USAR United States Army Reserve
USCG United States Coast Guard
USCGR United States Coast Guard Reserve
USES United States Employment Service
USIA United States Information Agency
USMC United States Marine Corps
USMCR United States Marine Corps
    Reserve
USN United States Navy
USNG United States National Guard
USNR United States Naval Reserve
USO United Service Organizations
USPHS United States Public Health Service
USS United States Ship
USSR Union of the Soviet Socialist
    Republics
USTA United States Tennis Association
USV United States Volunteers
UT Utah

VA Veterans Administration
VA, Va. Virginia
vet. veteran, veterinary
VFW Veterans of Foreign Wars
VI, V.I. Virgin Islands
vice pres. vice president
vis. visiting
VISTA Volunteers in Service to America
VITA Volunteers in Technical Service
vocat. vocational
vol. volunteer, volume
v.p. vice president
vs. versus
VT, Vt. Vermont

W, W. West
WA Washington (state)
WAC Women's Army Corps
Wash. Washington (state)
WAVES Women's Reserve, US Naval
    Reserve
WCTU Women's Christian Temperance
    Union
we. western
W. Ger. Germany, Federal Republic of
WHO World Health Organization
WI Wisconsin
W.I. West Indies
Wis. Wisconsin
WSB Wage Stabilization Board
WV West Virginia
W.Va. West Virginia
WY Wyoming
Wyo. Wyoming

YK Yukon Territory
YMCA Young Men's Christian Association
YMHA Young Men's Hebrew Association
YM & YWHA Young Men's and Young
    Women's Hebrew Association

Alphabetical Practices

Names are arranged alphabetically according to the surnames, and under identical surnames according to the first given name. If both surname and first given name are identical, names are arranged alphabetically according to the second given name.

Surnames beginning with De, Des, Du, however capitalized or spaced, are recorded with the prefix preceding the surname and arranged alphabetically under the letter D.

Surnames beginning with Mac and Mc are arranged alphabetically under M.

Surnames beginning with Saint or St. appear after names that begin Sains, and are arranged according to the second part of the name, e.g. St. Clair before Saint Dennis.

Surnames beginning with Van, Von or von are arranged alphabetically under letter V.

Compound hyphenated surnames are arranged according to the first member of the compound. Compound unhyphenated surnames are treated as hyphenated names.

Parentheses used in connection with a name indicate which part of the full name is usually deleted in common usage. Hence Abbott, W(illiam) Lewis indicates that the usual form of the given name is W. Lewis. In such a case, the parentheses are ignored in alphabetizing and the name would be arranged as Abbott, William Lewis. However, if the name is recorded Abbott, (William) Lewis, signifying that the entire name William is not commonly used, the alphabetizing would be arranged as though the name were Abbott, Lewis. If an entire middle or last name is enclosed in parentheses, that portion of the name is used in the alphabetical arrangement. Hence Abbott, William (Lewis) would be arranged as Abbott, William Lewis.

Who'sWho in the East

AARESTAD, JAMES HARRISON, educational administrator, retired; b. Mpls., Dec. 3, 1924; s. Selmer Emil and Myrthel Perline (Olson) A.; m. Mary-Jo Finn, Oct. 20, 1951; 1 child, Elizabeth Boe. BA, U. Minn., 1949; MA, Georgetown U., 1959; postgrad., Commd. and Gen. Staff Coll., Ft. Leavenworth, Kans., 1960-61, Nat. War Coll., Washington, 1970-71. Commd. 2d lt. U.S. Army, 1949, advanced through grades to col., 1970; comdr. 2d Squadron, 11th Cav., U.S. Army, Vietnam, 1969; dir. strategy and policy War Plans Div., Washington, 1970; chief staff Hdqrs. 1st Armored Div., Fed. Republic Germany, 1971-72; comdr. 2d Brigade, 3d Armored Div., Fed. Republic Germany, 1972-74; dir. nat. security seminar Army War Coll., Carlisle Barracks, Pa., 1974-76; ret., 1976; dep. dir. indsl. devel. N.C. Dept. Commerce, Raleigh, 1976-79; sec., bus. mgr. Dover (Pa.) Area Sch. Dist., 1979-92; ret., 1992; sr. strategy cons. Ketron Corp., Malvern, Pa., 1980—. Bd. dirs., vice chmn. York County Indsl. Devel. Corp., 1980-85, chmn. bd., 1986-88, treas., 1988—; chmn. mgmt. com. CYBER Ctr., York, 1980—; bd. dirs. Small Enterprise Devel. Co., York. Decorated Silver Star, Legion of Merit, DFC, Bronze Star, Air medal; recipient cert. of appreciation Gov. State of N.C., 1976, 79, resolution of appreciation York County Indsl. Devel. Corp., 1988. Mem. Nat. Assn. Sch. Bus. Ofcls. (registered sch. bus. adminstr.), Pa. Assn. Sch. Bus. Ofcls. (regional pres. 1982-83, citation 1986), Ends of Earth Club (N.Y.C.), Cavalry and Guards Club (London), Arm-Navy Country Club (Arlington, Va.), Sigma Alpha Epsilon. Republican. Episcopalian. Home: 922 McKenzie St York PA 17403-3712 Office: Dover Area Sch Dist School Ln Dover PA 17315-1498

AARON, EVALYN WILHELMINA, artist; b. N.Y.C.; d. John J. and Anna (Horowitz) Keisler; m. Paul Aaron (dec. 1987); children: Ellen, Barry. Student, Art Students League, N.Y.C., 1960-62, New Sch. Social Research, N.Y.C., 1975-80, Parsons Sch. Design, N.Y.C., 1975-80. Pres., instr. Workshops for Art, Inc., Port Washington, N.Y., 1964-73; instr. Sumi-E Great Neck, N.Y., 1964-74, 89-90; cons. in field; lectr. in field. One woman show Unitarian Ch., Plandome, N.Y., 1968, Mirage Gallery, N.Y.C. and others; exhibited in groups shows at Mirage Gallery, Nippon Club, N.Y.C., Japan House, N.Y.C., Sun Yat Sen Gallery, Queens, Trade Ctr. N.Y.C., Seamen's Ch., N.Y.C., North Shore Community Arts Ctr., L.I., Port Washington Libr., L.I., Great Neck Libr., Gallery Soho-7 Ltd., L.I., North Hempstead Town Hall; represented in permanent collections. Recipient Poplar award, Internat. Platform Assn., 1974 80, first prize, Art League Nassau County, 1977, Town of N. Hempstead, 1973, others. Mem. Art League Nassau County, Internat. Platform Assn. (bd. govs.), Sumi-e Soc. Am. (pres. emeritus, founder, judge exhbns. 1972, 73), also others. Address: 270-20K Grand Central Pkwy Floral Park NY 11005

AARON, JUDITH GLASS, college dean; b. N.Y.C., Jan. 10, 1951; d. Harold and Jean (Feldman) Fiedler; m. Elliot Glass, 1972 (div. 1983); m. Mitchell Keith Aaron; 1 child, Alexandra. BA, Queens Coll., 1972, MLS, 1974. Media specialist York Coll., Jamaica, N.Y., 1974-77, coord. continuing edn., 1980-81, dir. spl. svcs., 1981-84; coord. rsch. adminstrn. Chancellor's Office CUNY, N.Y.C., 1977-79; dir. continuing edn. Pratt Inst., Bklyn., 1984-87, assoc. dean continuing edn., 1987-89, dean Sch. Continuing Edn., 1989-91, assoc. provost, dean Sch. Profl. Studies, 1991—. Author: Building Maintenance and Repairs, 1980. Office: Pratt Inst 200 Willoughby Ave Brooklyn NY 11205-3899

AARON, M. EUGENE, diplomat; b. Sebring, Fla., Oct. 2, 1944; s. Joseph Ernest and Annie Mae (Grady) A.; m. Daphne Diane Page, July 24, 1971. BA, Fla. A&M U., 1965; MBA, U. Pa., 1973. Supr. credit Procter and Gamble, Cin., 1970-71; fin. analyst E.I. Dupont de Nemours, Wilmington, Del., 1973-76; sr. fin. analyst Hercules Inc., Wilmington, 1976-82; mgr. credit Hercules Inc., 1982-87; fgn. svc. officer U.S. Dept. State, Washington, 1988—; 1st sec. U.S. Embassy, Asuncion, Paraguay, 1989-91; consul U.S. Consulate Gen., Monterrey, Mex., 1991—; pres. MidAtlantic Fin. Cons., Wilmington, 1983-87. Contbr. photography to various publs. and exhbns. Advisor Jr. Achievement, 1973, 74; co-chair allocations panel United Way Del., 1979-82, loaned exec., 1981; bd. dirs. Friends of the Wilmington Library, 1982-83, Del. Guidance Svcs. for Children and Youth, 1986; mem. fundraising com. New Med. Ctr. of Del., 1982; vestry mem. St. Mathews Episcopal Ch., 1987—. Capt. U.S. Army, 1966-70. Mem. Am. Fgn. Svc. Assn., Nat. Black MBA Assn. (v.p. Phila. chpt. 1978-79), Brandywine Profl. Assn. (co-founder, bd. dirs. 1982-84), Alpha Phi Alpha (exec. com. Gamma Theta Lambda chpt.). Home: PO Box 3098 Laredo TX 78044-3098 Office: US Consulate Gen PO Box 3098 Laredo TX 78044-3098

AARON, RONALD, physics educator; b. Phila., June 14, 1935; s. Isadore and Mary (Mill) A.; m. Marilyn Berlin, June 17, 1962; children: Robin, Arthur. BA, Temple U., 1956; PhD, U. Pa., 1961. Rsch. assoc. U. Md., College Park, 1961-62, Ind. U., Bloomington, 1962-63; asst. prof. Northeastern U., Boston, 1963-66, assoc. prof., 1967-72, prof. physics, 1972—; vis. scientist Lawrence Radiation Lab., Livermore, Calif., 1964-67; vis. staff mem. Los Alamos (N.Mex.) Sci. Lab., 1967-74; rsch. assoc. NAS, NASA/Goddard Space Flight Ctr., 1965-66. Fellow Am. Phys. Soc. Home: 50 West Boulevard Rd Newton Center MA 02159-1348 Office: Northeastern U Physics Dept Boston MA 02115

AASLESTAD, HALVOR GUNERIUS, academic dean; b. Birmingham, Ala., Sept. 6, 1937; s. Knut and Geraldine (Dobson) A.; m. Barbara Wohn, July 30, 1960; children: Katherine, Karen, Peter, Lauren. BS, La. State U., 1960, PhD, 1965; MS, Pa. State U., 1961. Asst. prof. U. Ga., Athens, 1968-70; rsch. scientist Wistair Inst., Phila., 1970-73; sr. scientist Frederick (Md.) Cancer Rsch. Ctr., 1973-76; exec. sec. NIH, Bethesda, Md., 1976-81, rev. chief, 1981-85; dir. rsch. grants Sch. Medicine Yale U., New Haven, 1985—, asst. dean Sch. Medicine, 1987—, assoc. dean Sch. Medicine, 1989—; cons. NIH, Bethesda, 1985—. NIH rsch. grantee and fellow, 1965—. Mem. Assn. Univ. Tech. Mgrs., Am. Soc. for Virology, Nat. Coun. Univ. Rsch. Adminstrs., Soc. Rsch. Adminstrs. Office: Yale U 333 Cedar St New Haven CT 06510-3289

ABANY, ALBERT CHARLES, art educator, artist; b. Boston, Mar. 30, 1921; s. Charles and Sophie A.; m. Helen Barbara Prifty, Apr. 28, 1963; 1 child, Lisa Ellen. BS in Edn., Tufts U., 1949. Art tchr. Art Inst. of Boston, 1965-73, Quincy (Mass.) Jr. Coll., 1975-76, South Shore Art Ctr., Cohasset, Mass., 1983—. One man show at Carl Siembab Gallery, Boston, 1956, Tufts U., 1971, Art Inst. of Boston, 1972, Babson Coll., Wellesley, Mass., 1977. With U.S. Army, 1942-46; ETO. Mary O. Longstreth scholar, 1942. Mem. Coll. Art Assn., Boston Visual Artists Union, Artists Equity. Methodist. Home: 42 Macarthur Rd Natick MA 01760-2938 Office: South Shore Art Ctr 119 Ripley Rd Cohasset MA 02025-1744

ABBOTT, CHRISTOPHER CUNNINGHAM, marketing professional; b. Boston, Oct. 22, 1956; s. Gordon Jr. and Katharine (Stanley-Brown) A.; m. Lexanne Johnson, June 24, 1989. BA cum laude, St. Lawrence U., 1980; postgrad., NYU, 1981-84. Corp. intern Merrill Lynch & Co., N.Y.C., 1981-82; regional mktg. mgr. Merrill Lynch Econs., N.Y.C., 1982-84; asst. v.p. Merrill Lynch Capital Markets, N.Y.C. and Boston, 1984-86; v.p. Merrill Lynch Capital Markets, N.Y.C., 1986-90; sr. v.p. The Putnam Cos., Inc., Boston, 1990—. Mem. Mass. State Rep. Fin. Com., Boston, 1985. Mem. Brooks Sch. Alumni Assn. (bd. dirs. 1984—), St. Lawrence U. Alumni Assn. (exec. coun. 1982-88), N.Y. Yacht Club. Episcopalian.

ABBOTT, GEORGE, playwright, producer; b. Forestville, N.Y., June 25, 1887; s. George Burwell and May (McLaury) A.; m. Ednah Levis, July 9, 1914 (dec. 1930); 1 dau., Judith Ann; m. Mary Sinclair, Apr. 1946 (div. 1951); m. Joy Valderrama, Nov. 1983. A.B., U. Rochester, 1911, H.H.D., 1961; postgrad., Harvard U., 1912; H.H.D., U. Miami, Fla., 1974. Became an actor, 1913; appeared 48th St. Theatre, 1915; actor: The Queen's Enemy, 1916; asst. stage mgr.: Three Wise Fools, 1918; writer, dir. plays and films, 1919; co-author and dir.: plays including Love 'Em and Leave 'Em; dir. Broadway plays: Too Many Girls, 1940, Broadway, Coquette, Four Walls, Three Men on a Horse, On Your Toes, The Boys From Syracuse, Best Foot Forward, Where's Charley?, A Tree Grows in Brooklyn, The Pajama Game, 1957, Damn Yankees, 1958, New Girl in Town, Chicago, Boy Meets Girl, Brother Rat, Room Service, What a Life, Primrose Path, Pal Joey, Kiss and Tell, On The Town, Billion Dollar Baby, High Button Shoes, Call Me Madam, Wonderful Town, Never Too Late, A Funny Thing Happened on the Way to the Forum, Take Her, She's Mine, Flora, The Red Menace, Fade Out-Fade In, Help Stamp Out Marriage, Agatha Sue, I Love You, How Now, Dow Jones, 1967, The Education of Hyman Kaplan, 1968, The Fig Leaves Are Falling, 1968, Three Men on a Horse, 1969, Norman, Is That You?, 1970, Not Now Darling, 1970; dir. others; revival (musical) On Your Toes, 1983; also dir. of: motion pictures Damn Yankees; Author: Try-Out, 1979. Co-recipient Pulitzer Prize for Fiorello, 1960; N.Y. Drama Critics Circle award, 1960; Tony award, 1955, 56, 60, 63; Donaldson award, 1946, 48, 53, 55; Lawrence Langner award, 1976; Handel medallion City of N.Y., 1976; Kennedy Ctr. honoree, 1983. Clubs: Coffee House, Dutch Treat (N.Y.C.); Indian Creek Country (Fla.); Merriewold (N.Y.). Office: 10 Rockefeller Pla Room 1009 New York NY 10020*

ABBOTT, IRA RICHMOND, III, pediatric neurosurgeon, educator; b. Schenectady, N.Y., Aug. 31, 1950; s. Ira Richmond Jr. and Anne Elizabeth (Shellabarger) A.; m. Elaine Luckadoo, June 7, 1975; children: Ira Richmond IV, John Hampton. BA, Colo. Coll., 1972; MD, Baylor U., 1980. Intern Baylor Affiliated Hosps., Houston, 1980-81, resident in neurosurgery, 1981-86; fellow in pediatric neurosurgery NYU Med. Ctr., N.Y.C., 1986-87, instr. dept. neurosurgery, 1987-88, asst. prof. dept. neurosurgery, 1988—, also mem. surg. case rev., 1990—; lectr. in field. Editor, author: Neurosurgery for Spasticity, 1991; contbr. articles to profl. jours. Sgt. USAF, 1973-77. Fellow Am. Assn. Neurol. Surgens; mem. Congress Neurol. Surgeons, Internat. Soc. Pediatric Neurosurgeons. Office: Div Pediatric Neurosurgery 550 1st Ave New York NY 10016

ABBOTT, JOSEPH, author, publisher; b. Jersey City, Aug. 9, 1937. Author: Absolute Power, 1986, How to Awaken Your Occult Powers, 1989. Office: Directions Unltd PO Box 343 Wood Ridge NJ 07075-0343

ABBOTT, MURIEL MACPHERSON, psychometrician; b. Montclair, N.J.; d. Graham and Muriel Margaret (Burleigh) Macpherson; B.A., Brown U.; M.A., Newark State Coll., 1961; Ph.D. (NDEA fellow), Columbia U., 1968; m. Charles F. Abbott (div.). Adj. prof. Tchrs. Coll., Columbia U., 1965-75; asst. dir. spl. projects Harcourt Brace Jovanovich Inc. (Psychol. Corp.), N.Y.C., 1965-76, asst. dir. profl. exams., 1976-78; dir. test devel. N.Y.C. Bd. Edn., 1978—; summer fellow in measurement Ednl. Testing Service, 1963. Mem. bd. mgrs. Vanderbilt YMCA, N.Y.C., 1977—, named Woman of Yr., 1982. Mem. Am. Psychol. Assn., Am. Ednl. Research Assn., Nat. Council Measurement in Edn., Nat. Assn. Test Dirs., Brown U. Alumni Assn., Columbia U. Alumni Assn., Sigma Xi. Clubs: Brown U., New Eng. Soc. Contbr. articles to profl. jours. Home: 249 E 48th St New York NY 10017-1526 Office: 110 Livingston Brooklyn NY 11201

ABBOTT, THOMAS EDWARD, college administrator; b. Sanford, Maine, June 1, 1949; s. Marshall Lincoln and Rose Marie Louise (Shalhoup) A.; m. Judith Bain MacDougal, June 12, 1971; 1 child, Jacob Thomas. BA, U. Maine, 1972; MS, U. South Maine, 1976; PhD, Boston Coll., 1989. Coord. coop. edn. U. Maine, Augusta, 1974-76, asst. dean adult edn., 1976-78, asst. dean acad. affairs, 1978-80, assoc. dean acad. affairs, 1980-82, acting acad. dean, 1983-84, dir. learning resources, 1986—, dir. equal opportunity, 1986—; exec. v.p. U. Maine Found. U. Maine at Augusta Found., Augusta, 1990—; ednl. cons.; guest lectr. U. Maine, Augusta, 1986—. Editor/pubr. book: Through the Years, 1990; co-designer TV course: Bibliographic Instruction, 1990. Trustee Gardiner Pub. Libr., 1988—; dir. West Gardiner Fire Fighting Assn., 1989—; tng. officer West Gardiner Fire Dept., 1989-92 (named Firefighter of Yr. 1990). Mem. Alpha Sigma Nu. Office: U Maine at Autusta University Dr Augusta ME 04330

ABBOTT, WILLIAM M., vascular surgeon; b. San Francisco, Apr. 14, 1936; s. William and Elizabeth A.; m. Cynthia Davison; children: Sarah, Wallace. AB, Stanford U., 1958, MD, 1961; MA (hon.), Harvard U., 1990. Diplomate Am. Bd. Surgery, Am. Bd. Vascular Surgery. Surg. intern Mass. Gen. Hosp., Boston, 1961-62, asst. resident in surgery, 1962-65, fellow in transplant biology, 1965-66, sr. resident in surgery, 1969-70, chief resident in surgery, 1970-71, asst. in surg., 1971-74, asst. surgeon, 1975-79, chief vascular surgery, 1977—; rsch. fellow in surgery Med. Sch. Harvard U., 1965-66, instr. in surgery Med. Sch., 1971-73, from asst. prof. to assoc. prof., 1973-89, prof., 1989—; asst. dir. Tissue Bank, Naval Med. Rsch. Inst., Bethesda, Md., 1966-69; rsch. affiliate MIT, 1978—; mem. U.S. tech. adv. group Internat. Standards Orgn., 1980; mem. surgery and bioengring. study sect. NIH, 1983-87; mem. ad hoc com. on reimbursement for non invasive peripheral vascular diagnostic studies Blue Shield Mass., 1987; mem. emergency ward com. Mass. Gen. Hosp., 1973, mem. house officer tng. com. Dept. Surgery, 1974—, mem. surg. rsch. fellowship com., 1980—, mem. bllod transfusion svc. com., 1990—, others, assoc. vis. surgeon, 1980-85, vis. surgeon, 1986—, dir. vascular rsch. lab., 1972—, dir. clin. vascular lab. and vascular lab. unit, 1976—; supr. rsch. activities, thesis preparation of rsch. fellows Med. Sch. Harvard U., 1975, adv. core clin. program, 1976—; co-dir. Conf. on Vascular Disorders, Palm Beach, Fla., 1980. Contbr. 163 articles and 25 book chpts. to profl. publs. Lt. comdr. USMC, 1966-69, Vietnam, USNR. Recipient Merck Award, Stanford U., 1961. Fellow Am. Heart Assn. Coun. on Cardiovascular Surgery; mem. AAAS, ACS (com. on operating rm. environment 1977-78, surg. forum program com. 1988-90), Internat. Soc. Applied Cardiovascular Biology, Internat. Soc. Parenteral Nutrition, Internat. Cardiovascular Soc., Am. Surg. Assn., Assn. Acad. Surgery (com. on issues 1977-78), Assn. Advancement of Med. Instrumentation, Am. Physiol. Soc., Am. Trauma Soc., Soc. Vascular Surgery, Soc. for Cryobiology, New Eng. Soc. Vascular Surgery (charter). Office: Mass Gen Hosp 15 Parkman St # 458 Boston MA 02114-3139

ABBOUD, G. JASON, telecommunications executive, consultant, engineer; b. Tripoli, Lebanon, May 28, 1955; came to U.S., 1973; s. Nassry and Minerva (Keyrouz) A. BSME, Lehigh U., 1977; MBA, Columbia U., 1992. With tech. sales and mktg. Worthington Group, Mountainside, N.J., 1977-81; project engr. Badger Am., Tampa, Fla., 1981-82; sales mgr. Dorr-Oliver, Stamford, Conn., 1982-84; mgr. internat. rels. div. MCI Internat., Rye Brook, N.Y., 1984-85, dir. internat. rels., 1985-87; v.p. mktg. devel. Internat. 800 Telecom, Stamford, 1987, with office of the pres., 1987-88; mng. dir. Concepts in Tech., Stamford, 1988-89; dir. global strategy NYNEX Corp., White Plains, N.Y., 1989—. Mem. Columbia Club N.Y., Planning Forum, Landmark Club, Beta Gamma Sigma. Republican. Roman Catholic. Office: Nynex Corp 1113 Westchester Ave White Plains NY 10604-3510

ABBRECHT, PETER HERMAN, medical educator; b. Toledo, Nov. 27, 1930; s. Hermann Richard and Paula Katherine (Schwenk) A.; m. Anne Patterson Lampman, Feb. 16, 1957; children—Elaine, Brian. B.S., Purdue U., 1952; M.S., U. Mich., 1953, Ph.D. in Chem. Engring, 1957, M.D., 1962. Diplomate: Am. Bd. Internal Medicine, Am. Bd. Pulmonary Disease. Sr. chem. engr. Minn. Mining & Mfg. Co., Detroit, 1956-58; intern U. Calif. Hosp., L.A., 1962-63; mem. faculty U. Mich. Med. Sch., Ann Arbor, 1963-80; prof. physiology U. Mich. Med. Sch., 1972-80; resident in internal medicine U. Mich. Hosp., 1971-72, fellow in pulmonary disease, 1974-75; chmn. bioengring. program U. Mich. Med. Sch., 1972-77, prof. medicine, 1976-80; prof. medicine and physiology Uniformed Svcs. U. of Health Scis., Bethesda, Md., 1980—, chmn. dept. physiology, 1987—; cons. physician Walter Reed Army Med. Ctr., 1980—; guest scientist Naval Med. Rsch. Inst., 1980-82; vis. prof. bioengring. U. Calif., San Diego, 1973; dir. physiology and biomed. engring. program NIGMS, NIH, 1977-78; cons. VA, NASA, Air Force Office Sci. Rsch.; cons. NSF, mem. nat. rsch. resources adv. coun., 1975-78; cons., mem. biomed. rsch. tech. com. NIH, 1986-90, chmn., 1989-90. Editor in chief Internat. Jour. Biomed. Engring, 1972-74, Annals Biomed. Engring., 1978-84; mem. editorial bd. Jour. Biomechanics; contbr. articles to profl. jours. Recipient outstanding research award Mich. Heart Assn., 1960; research career devel. award NIH, 1969-73. Fellow ACP, Am. Coll. Chest Physicians; mem. Biomed. Engring. Soc. (dir. 1970-72); mem. Am. Physiol. Soc., Am. Thoracic Soc. Home: 2806 Spencer Rd Bethesda MD 20815-3877

ABDELNOUR, ZIAD KHALIL, international investment banker, financier; b. Beirut, Jan. 8, 1961; came to U.S., 1981; s. Khalil I. and Rose S. (Salha) A.; m. Nada S. Sahyoun, Dec. 23, 1983; children: Karl, Mark. BA, Am. U. of Beirut, 1981; MBA, The Wharton Sch. Fin., 1984. Fin. cons. Am. Express Bank, N.Y.C., 1984-86; asst. v.p. Drexel Burnham Lambert, N.Y.C., 1986-88, v.p., 1988-89, sr. v.p., 1989-90; ptnr. Laidlaw Holdings, Inc., N.Y.C., 1990—. Contbr. articles to profl. jours. Mem. Assn. for Corp. Growth, N.Y.C., Rep. Senatorial Inner Circle, Washington, Rep. Presdl. Task Force, Am. Task Force for Lebanon Policy, Coun. for the Nat. Interest, Arab Am. Leadership Coun.; bd. dirs. Arab Am. Inst. Mem. Arab Bankers Assn. N.Am. (bd. dirs.), Coun. on Fgn. Rels., Met. Club, Century Club, Jr. Internat. Club. Roman Catholic. Office: Laidlaw Holdings Inc 275 Madison Ave 12th Fl New York NY 10016

ABDELRAHMAN, TALAAT AHMAD MOHAMMAD, financial executive; b. Kafr Saqr, Sharkia, Egypt, Sept. 13, 1940; came to U.S., 1970; s. Ahmad Mohammad and Zeen Elmahdi (Hassan) A.; m. Soher T. Ali, May 7, 1941 (dec. Feb. 1979); children: Manar, Neven, Nancy, Amon; m. Ekram T. Kandil, Jan. 25, 1954. BS in Mgmt., Cairo U., 1965, BA in Law, 1969, PhD in Fin., 1987; MBA in Acctg., NYU, 1974. Fin. analyst Nat. Bank Egypt, Cairo, 1965-70; Euro-dollar specialist Bankers Trust Co., N.Y.C., 1970-74; sr. cost acct. Phelps Dodge Cable & Wire, Yonkers, N.Y., 1974-75; fin. cons. East Orange, N.J., 1975-76; asst. treas. ITT Fed. Electric, Paramus, N.J., 1976-82; fin. mgr. ITT Fed. Electric, Jed, Saudi Arabia, 1982-86; corp. fin. mgr. ITT Fed. Electric, Paramus, 1987-91; bd. dirs. ITT Howard/Egypt, Cairo, Talkan USA Inc., Morganville, N.J.; owner 7-Eleven Franchise, Wood Ridge, N.J., 1991—, Hackensack, N.J., 1992—. Contbr. articles to profl. jours. Home: 34 Van Blarcom Ln Wyckoff NJ 07481-3444

ABDOO, HELEN THERESA, public relations specialist; b. Utica, N.Y., Dec. 2, 1956; d. Louis Albert and Helen Theresa Abdoo. AAS, Mohawk Valley Community Coll., Utica, 1977; BA, Trinity Coll., 1990. Adminstrv. asst. U.S. Dept. Treasury, Washington, 1981-82; staff asst. White House, Washington, 1982-87; confidential asst. U.S. Dept. Edn., Washington, 1987-88; exec. asst. White House, Washington, 1988-89; press sec. U.S. Mint, Washington, 1989-90; news mgr. George Washington U. Med. Ctr., Washington, 1990—. Rec. sec. Our Lady of Lebanon Parish Coun., Washington, 1990-91. Mem. Wash. Met. Soc. for Health Care Pub. Rels. and Mktg., D.C. Hosp. Assn. (communications com. 1990—). Republican. Maronite Catholic. Home: 2606 Tunlaw Rd NW Washington DC 20007 Office: George Washington U Med Ctr 2300 I St NW Washington DC 20037

ABDULLAH, MOHAMMAD ISLAM, international business executive, consultant; b. Lahore, Punjab, Pakistan, June 6, 1959; came to U.S., 1980; s. Mohammad Abdullah and Fatina (Bagum) Mian. Diploma quality control and inspection, Pakistan Tech. Inst., Lahore; degree in mech. engring., Inst. Engrs., Pakistan; diploma procurement mgmt., NYU. Dy. asst. dir. mech. Pakistan Standards Inst., Karachi, 1980; mgr. procurement Keneth Designing, N.Y., 1981-86; tech. coord., bd. dirs. Rumi Internat., Bklyn., 1986—; coord. tech. and sales Global Products, N.Y., 1986—, Rumi Internat., N.Y., 1986—; coord. feasibility studies in field, 1980. With Pakistani armed forces, 1976-80. Mem. Assn. MBA Execs., Assn. Purchasing Mgmt. Moslem. Home and Office: 1671 E 17th St Apt 5I Brooklyn NY 11229-1266

ABEL, FRED HERMAN, economist; b. Remus, Mich., Nov. 21, 1936; s. Herman John and Ruth Edna (May) A.; m. Marguerite Mary Carroll, May 28, 1937; children: Paul, Steven, Mark. BS in Agrl. Edn. with honors, Mich. State U., 1959; MS in Agrl. Econs., U. Del., 1961; PhD in Agrl. Econs., Mich. State U., 1967. Rsch. economist prodn. USDA, Washington, 1965-68; rsch. economist rural devel. USDA, 1968-71; chief econs. br. U.S. Environ. Protection Agy., Washington, 1971-75; sr. economist fossil engery U.S. Dept. Energy, Washington, 1975-78; sr. economist geothermal U.S. Dept. Energy, 1978-81, sr. economist conservation, 1981—. Contbr. articles to profl. jours. Mem. Internat. Assn. Energy Economists, Am. Econs. Assn. Home: 19101 Willow Grove Rd Olney MD 20832-1232 Office: US Dept Energy CE 72 1000 Independence Ave SW Washington DC 20585-0001

ABELES, JOSEPH HY, physicist; b. N.Y.C., Apr. 14, 1955; s. Fred and Charlotte (Garten) A. SBc, MIT, 1976; AM, Princeton (N.J.) U., 1978, PhD, 1982. Mem. tech. staff Bell Labs., Murray Hill, N.J., 1982-83, Bellcore, Red Bank, N.J., 1984-89, David Sarnoff Rsch. Ctr., Princeton, 1989—. Contbr. numerous articles to profl. jours.; inventee in field. Mem. IEEE, Am. Phys. Soc., Laser and Electroptics Soc. (chmn. Princeton chpt. 1991-92), Optical Soc. Am. (patent rev. panel applied optics, 1989—, tech. com. ann. integrated photonics rsch. mtgs., 1990—). Office: David Sarnoff Rsch Ctr 201 Washington Rd Princeton NJ 08540-6492

ABELL, MILLICENT DEMMIN, university library administrator; b. Wichita, Kans., Feb. 15, 1934; d. Frederic Albert and Euphemia Millicent (Brown) Demmin; m. Julian Leo Abell, June 16, 1962; 1 son, Frederic Julian. B.A. in Psychology, Colo. Coll., 1956; M.A. in Personnel, Columbia U., 1958; M.L.S., SUNY, Albany, 1965; M.A. in Polit. Sci, U. Colo., 1969. Reference librarian U.S. Mil. Acad., West Point, N.Y., 1964-65, Penrose Public Library, Colorado Springs, Colo., 1966-68; asst. librarian Bus. Adminstrn. Library, U. Wash., Seattle, 1969-71; asst. dir. libraries U. Wash., 1971-73; assoc. dir. univ. libraries SUNY, Buffalo, 1973-76; univ. librarian U. Calif., San Diego, 1977-85, Yale U., 1985—; bd. dirs. Center for Research Libraries, 1979-86, chmn., 1984-85; bd. govs. Research Libraries Group, 1985— , mem. exec. com., 1986-91. Mem. editorial bd.: Jour. Acad. Librarianship, 1974-76; asso. editor: Library Research, 1978-82; contbr. articles to profl. jours. Trustee Conn. Pub. Broadcasting, Inc., 1988—. Mem. Assn. Coll. and Research Libraries (dir. 1976-78, 79-86, pres. 1980-81), Assn. Research Libraries (dir. 1979-83, pres. 1981-82), ALA (council 1983-86). Office: Yale U Sterling Meml Libr PO Box 1603A New Haven CT 06520

ABELL, RICHARD BENDER, lawyer, federal official; b. Phila., Dec. 2, 1943; s. Ernest George and Charlotte Amelia (Bender) A.; m. Lucia del Carmen Lombana-Cadavid, Dec. 2, 1968; children: David, Christian, Rachel. BA in Internat. Affairs, George Washington U., 1966, JD, 1974. Bar: Pa. 1974. Vol. Peace Corps, Colombia, 1967-69; assoc. Reilly & Fogwell, West Chester, Pa., 1974-80; asst. dist. atty. Chester County, Pa., 1974-79; staff mem. U.S. Senator Richard Schweiker, Washington, 1979-80; dir. Office of Program Devel. Peace Corp., Washington, 1981-83; dep. asst. atty. gen. U.S. Dept. Justice, Washington, 1983-86, asst. atty. gen., 1986-90; special master U.S. Claims Ct., 1991—; mem. adj. faculty Del. Law Sch., Wilmington, 1975-77, West Chester State U., 1976; bd. dirs. Fed. Prison Industries, Inc., 1985-91; chmn. Nat. Crime Prevention Coalition, 1986-90; mem. adv. bd. Nat. Inst. Corrections, 1986-90; co-chmn. adv. com. Nat. Ctr. for State and Local Law Enforcement Tng., 1987-90; vice chmn. rsch. and devel. rev. bd. Dept. Justice, 1987-89; mem. nat. drug policy bd. Enforcement Coordinating Group and Coordinating Group for Drug Abuse Prevention and Health, 1988-89. Chmn. Young Rep. Nat. Fedn., Washington, 1979-81; mem. exec. com. Rep. Nat. Com., 1979-81; mem. fed. coordinating coun. on Juvenile Justice and Delinquency Prevention, 1986-90; mem. Pres.'s Task Force on Adoption, 1987-88; mem. Pres.'s Commn. on Agrl. Workers, 1988—. With U.S. Army, 1969-71. Decorated Purple Heart, Army Commendation medal, Air medal, Combat Infantryman's Badge. Mem. Pa. Bar Assn., Order of Scarlet. Episcopalian. Home: 8209 Chancery Ct Alexandria VA 22308-1514

ABELL, RICHARD GURLEY, psychiatrist; b. Phila., Jan. 24, 1904; s. Edward W. Bertha (Halsey) A.; m. Ellen Yersley, 1935 (div. 1959); 1 child, Margaret Lessing Ditmars; m. Liese Baerwald, Sept. 1, 1945 (div. 1961); m. Corlis Wilber, June 15, 1962 (dec. 1977); m. Nan Scallon, June 16, 1979. AB, Swarthmore Coll., 1926; MA, U. Pa., 1930, PhD, 1933, MD, 1947. Intern Bryn Mawr (Pa.) Hosp., 1948; resident in psychiatry N.Y. State Psychiat. Inst., 1949, Bellevue Hosp., N.Y.C., 1950-51; psychiatrist Full Grade VA, N.Y.C., 1952-53; pvt. practice psychiatry, psychoanalysis N.Y.C., 1950—; mem. faculty, U. Pa. Med. Sch., 1935-47, New Sch. Social Rsch., N.Y.C., 1950, Barnard Coll., Columbia U., 1960-64, William Alanson White Inst., 1965—, NYU, 1981-83; dir. group therapy svcs., Roosevelt Hosp., N.Y.C., 1965-72; chief attending psychiatrist, Areba-Casriel Inst., N.Y.C., 1987. Author (with Corlis Wilber): Own Your Own Life, 1976; contbg. editor, Greenwich (Conn.) Time, 1982—; contbr. to med. publs. Fellow AMA, Am. Psychiat. Assn., Am. Acad. Psychoanalysis; mem. Am. Transactional Analysis Assn. (founding mem.), Assn. Med. Group Psychoanalysts (pres. 1960-61), William Alanson White Psychoanalytic Soc. (sec. 1960, chmn. program com. 1961), Am. Group Psychotherapy Assn. (com. mem. 1960-65), Ea. Group Psychotherapy Assn. (Lifetime award 1987), Internat. transactional Analysis Assn. (clin. teaching mem., trustee, 1981-84, mem. tng. com. 1981, liaison between tng. com. and cert. bd. 1986). Home: 15 Fairgreen Ln Old Greenwich CT 06870-2006 Office: 220 Central Park S New York NY 10019-1417

ABELS, DORIS HOLLOWAY, mental health counselor; b. Providence, Oct. 28, 1925; d. John William and Cecelia May (Peckenham) Holloway; m. Howard Earl Birman, June 1949 (div. 1964); children: Kerry, Kathie, John; m. J. Lester, June 17, 1979. BA, U. R.I., 1971; MA, U. Conn., 1974; cert. advanced tudy, R.I. Coll., 1982; DEd, Boston U., 1986. Lic. mental health counselor, R.I.; cert. nat. mental health counselor; approved clin. supr. Theatre, profl. dancer (Doris and Joan) Ed Sullivan Show, Holloway Sisters, Eddie Cantor, others, 1944-49; dir., mgr. Doris Holloway Sch. Dance, R.I., 1950-85; therapist Norwich (Conn.) Hosp., 1974-75, Inst. Mental Health, R.I., 1978-79; mental health counselor, ednl. advisor Providence, 1977—; adj. prof. Brown U., R.I., 1985, R.I. Coll., 1990—. Mem. adv. bd. R.I. Coun. on Arts, Providence, 1970-85; vice chmn. Internat. House R.I., Providence, 1986—; bd. dirs. R.I. Grand Opera, Inc., Providence, 1986—, Vols. in Providence Schs., 1990-91, R.I. Coll. Found. Corp., 1992—; bd. dirs., tchr. Langston Hughes Ctr. for Arts, Providence, 1986—. Grantee R.I. State Coun. on Arts, U. Utah, 1969; apptd. to R.I. Coll. Found., 1992. Mem. AACD, R.I. Assn. Counseling and Devel. (pres. 1990-92), R.I. Assn. Women in Edn., Am. Mental Health Counselors Assn., Internat. Cult Edn. Program (adv. bd. 1988—), Am. Family Found. (mem. com. 1983—). Office: 52 Armstrong Ave Providence RI 02903-4446

ABELSON, ALAN, editor, columnist; b. N.Y.C., Oct. 12, 1925; s. Harry Carl and Vivian (Finkelstein) A.; m. Virginia Eloise Peterson, Sept. 1, 1951; children—Justin Adams, Reed Vivian. B.S. in Chemistry and English, Coll. City N.Y., 1946; M.A. in Creative Writing, U. Iowa, 1947. Reporter N.Y. Jour. Am., N.Y.C., 1949-56; stock market columnist N.Y. Jour. Am., 1952-56; with Barron's Mag., N.Y.C., 1956—; mng. editor Barron's Mag., 1965-81, editor, 1981—; columnist Up & Down Wall St., 1966—. Office: Barron's Mag 200 Liberty St New York NY 10281-1003

ABELSON, ELIAS, lawyer; b. N.Y.C., Nov. 17, 1932; s. Harry and Lucille (Margulies) A.; m. Isobel Faith Schiffman, Sept. 8, 1957; children: Adam Samuel, Joshua Tobin, Matthew Noah. BA, U. Pa., 1954; JD, Columbia U., 1959. Bar: N.J. 1960, U.S. Dist. Ct. N.J. 1960, U.S. Ct. Appeals (3d cir.) 1969, U.S. Ct. Appeals (7th cir.) 1973, U.S. Claims Ct. 1969, U.S. Tax Ct. 1969, U.S. Supreme Ct. 1965. Dep. atty. gen. State of N.J., Trenton, 1960-63, 64-68, asst. atty. gen., 1968-88; assoc. Green, Robinson & Deitz, Trenton, 1963-64; gen. counsel Bucknell U., Lewisburg, Pa., 1988—; mem. N.J. Supreme Ct. Dist. Ethics Com., 1985-88; lectr. in field. Contbr. articles to legal pubs. Sec. Princeton Folk Music Soc., 1976-78; vice chmn. Princeton U. Concerts Com., 1978-82; trustee Gr. Princeton Youth Orch., 1984-88, vice-chmn., 1985-86, chmn., 1986-88. Served to 1st lt. U.S. Army, 1954-56. Mem. Nat. Assn. Coll. & Univ. Attys., N.J. Bar Assn., Pa. Bar Assn., Union County Bar Assn., Columbia Law Sch. Alumni Assn. N.J. (sec. 1982-84, trustee 1984-88). Jewish. Home: 40 S Front St Lewisburg PA 17837-1916 Office: Bucknell U 209 Marts Hall Lewisburg PA 17837

ABER, STANLEY IRWIN, real estate developer; b. N.Y.C., June 14, 1939; s. Abraham and Mollie (Ashkenazy) A.; m. Lise Aber, Sept. 27, 1974 (div. Feb. 1986); 1 child, Eric. AB, Columbia U., 1959, MBA, 1960. Real estate associate Pearce, Mayer Greer, N.Y.C., 1960-67; v.p. Goodrich Assocs., N.Y.C., 1967-70, N.K. Winston, N.Y.C., 1970-71; chmn. bd., pres. IBEC Realty Internat., N.Y.C. and San Juan, 1971-76; exec. v.p. Cadillac Fairview Shopping Ctrs., Inc., N.Y.C., 1976-78; pres. Saber Devel. Corp., N.Y.C., 1978—. With U.S. Army, 1961-62. Mem. Internat. Coun. of Shopping Ctrs., Real Estate Bd. of N.Y., Columbia U. Alumni Assn. Home: 145 E 92d St New York NY 10128 Office: Saber Devel Corp 123 E 54th St New York NY 10022

ABERE, ANDREW EVAN, economist; b. N.Y.C., June 16, 1961; s. Frank Joseph and Ruth (Mofenson) A.; m. Lisa Joy Watine, Nov. 5, 1989; 1 child, Spencer David. BA, Columbia U., 1983, MA in Econs., 1986, PhD in Econs., 1991. Economist Skadden, Arps, N.Y.C., 1987-91, Ernst & Young, N.Y.C., 1991—; instr. dept. econs. Columbia U., N.Y.C., 1987-89, lectr., 1989-90, adj. asst. prof. econs., 1991—; adj. asst. prof. dept. econs. NYU, 1991. Columbia U. fellow, 1985-87, 89-91. Mem. ABA, Am. Econ. Assn.

ABIKOFF, WILLIAM, mathematician; b. N.Y.C., Aug. 18, 1944; s. Allen and Hanna (Krotin) A.; m. Joan Thorne, Aug. 13, 1966 (Div. Feb. 1973); m. S. Christine Krieger, Sept. 30, 1978 (div. Nov. 1991). BSEE, Polytech Inst., 1965, MSEE, 1966, PhD in Math., 1971. Tech. staff Bell Telephone Lab., Holmdel, N.J., 1965-70; asst. prof. Columbia U., N.Y.C., 1970-75; asst. prof. U. Ill., Urbana, 1975-76, assoc. prof., 1976-81; prof. U. Conn., Storrs, 1981—. Author: Real Analytic Theory of Teichmuller Space, 1981; contbr. articles to profl. jours. Sloan Found. fellow, 1976-77. Mem. Am. Math. Soc., Inst. for Advanced Study. Home: 280 Perry Hill Rd Ashford CT 06278-1024 Office: U Conn Math Dept 196 Auditorium Rd Storrs Mansfield CT 06269

ABIRI, MOHAMMED, surgeon; b. Teheran, Iran, Mar. 16, 1933; came to U.S., 1959; s. Majid and Esmath (Farhoumand) A.; m. Terry Campbell, Sept. 1963 (div. 1975); children: Mark, Paul, Leila, David; m. Katherine Bradford, Dec. 1980; 1 child, Matthew. MD, Teheran U., Teheran, 1958. Diplomate Am. Bd. Surgery. Intern Beth David Hosp., N.Y.C., 1959-60; resident Seydenham Hosp., N.Y.C., 1960-61, Bklyn. Hosp., 1961-64; fellow Sloan-Kettering Meml. Hosp., N.Y.C., 1964-65; mem. surg. staff St. Joseph's Hosp., Cranston, R.I., 1969—; mem. surgery staff Fatima Hosp., Cranston, R.I., 1969—, Miriam Hosp., Cranston, R.I., 1969—, Roger Williams Hosp., Cranston, R.I., 1969—, Cranston (R.I.) Gen. Hosp., 1969—. Mem. ACS, Providence Surg. Soc. Office: 725 Reservoir Ave Cranston RI 02910

ABKARIAN, EDWARD, insurance manager, consultant; b. Tabriz, Iran, May 18, 1951; came to U.S., 1979; s. Vahan and Olga (Kabrelian) A.; m. Solanj Kniaz Melikoff, June 27, 1980; children: Elcid, Elita. BS in Chemistry, Nat. U. Iran, Tehran, 1973; MBA, Harvard U., Tehran, 1977. CLU, ChFC. Assoc. office mgr. Neypras Industries, Tehran, 1970-73; sales mgr. Asirco Chem. Industry, Tehran, 1973-76; chmn. bd. dirs. EDCHRIS Co. Ltd., Tehran, 1975-77; v.p. Coca Cola Bottling Co., Tehran, 1977-79; sr. dist. mgr. Equitable Life, N.Y.C., 1980—. Bd. dirs. Armenian Soc. of N.Y., Little Neck, 1991—. Inducted to Hall of Fame, 1989. Office: Equitable Life 1 Penn Plz Ste 400 New York NY 10119-0139

ABLOW, JOSEPH, artist, educator; b. Salem, Mass., Aug. 16, 1928; s. Benjamin and Eva (Smith) A.; m. Roselyn Karol, June 23, 1956; 1 child, Rachel. BA, Bennington Coll., 1954; MA, Harvard U., 1955. Instr. Middlebury (Vt.) Coll., 1955-58; asst. prof. Bard Coll., Annandale, N.Y., 1959-61, Wellesley (Mass.) Coll., 1962-63; assoc. prof. Boston (Mass.) Univ., 1963-72, chmn. div. of art, 1964-67, prof. of art, 1972—; vis. assoc. prof. MIT, Cambridge, 1969-70; vis. prof. Amherst (Mass.) Coll., 1975-76; vis. scholar Cambridge (Mass.) Humanities Seminar, MIT, 1973-82; mem. adv. com. Bunting Inst., Radcliffe Coll., Cambridge, 1984-87; lectr. Amherst Coll., 1975, 78, 82, Univ. N.H., 1980, 82, Inst. of Contemporary ARt, Boston, 1980, Nieman Found., Harvard Univ., 1982, 83, MIT, 1984, St. John's Univ., Collegeville, Minn., 1986, Fitchburg Art Mus., 1987, Salve Regina Coll., Newport, R.I., 1990, and others. One-man shows include Boris Mirski Gallery, Boston, 1961, 65, 69, Pucker/Safari Gallery, Boston, 1979, 81, 83, 87, 91, The Trustman Art Gallery, Simmons Coll., Boston, 1983, Fitchburg Art Mus., 1987, and others; represented in permanent collections Bard Coll., Middlebury Coll., DeCordova and Dana Mus., Univ. Mass. Harbor Campus, Mead Art Gallery Amherst Coll., Rose Art Mus., Brandeis U. and others; contbg. editor: Boston Mag., Boston, 1986-89; contbr. articles to profl. jours. Mem. bd. dirs. Jewish Cultural Endowment, Boston Univ., 1988—. Recipient Paige Traveling fellowship Mus. Fine Arts, Boston, 1951, Fulbright grant in painting, Paris, 1958-59, Silver medal award for best article of the yr. Coun. for Advancement and Support of Edn., 1987. Home: 16 Monmouth Ct Brookline MA 02146-5634 Office: Boston U Sch Visual Art 855 Commonwealth Ave Boston MA 02215-1303

ABNEY, RAY CHANDLER, psychiatrist; b. Athens, Ga., July 27, 1947; s. Howard Teasley and Mary(Ray) A.; m. Mary Ann McMahon, Oct. 10, 1980; children: Ryan Christopher, Michael James, Julie Elaine. BS in Zoology, U. Ga., Athens, 1969; MD, Vanderbilt U., Nashville, 1973. Diplomate Am. Bd. Psychiatry and Neurology. Resident in psychiatry U. Vt., Burlington, 1976; staff psychiatrist Brattleboro (Vt.) Retreat, 1976-80, 82-92, dir. Rockwell Ctr., 1978-80, acting dir., 1979, dir. outpatient div., 1982-92; staff psychiatrist VA Med. Ctr., Dallas, 1980-82; asst. chief psychiatry VA Med. Ctr., 1981-82; pvt. practice Brattleboro, 1992—; asst. prof. clin. psychiatry Dartmouth Med. Sch., Hanover, 1978-80, 82-92, U. Tex. S.W. Med. Sch., Dallas, 1980-82; cons. NIMH, 1982-87; psychiat. cons. Marlboro (Vt.) Coll., 1983-88. Bd. dirs. Vt. and Irish Kids, Brattleboro, 1985-89, Brattleboro Nursery Sch., 1986-87. Fellow Am. Psychiatric Assn.; mem. Vt. Psychiatric Assn. (pres.-elect 1980), Vt. Med. Soc., Windham County Med. Soc. (councilor 1983-89, vice speaker-Ho. of Dels. 1990). Office: PO Box 1616 Brattleboro VT 05301

ABRAHAM, ABRAM KENNETH, pastor, author; b. Indiana, Pa., Sept. 3, 1951; s. Howard George and Minnie Bryce (Clayton) A.; m. Angela Reneé Koppelberger, Sept. 25, 1982; children: Ashleigh Anne, Alyssa Reneé. BA, Asbury Coll., 1973. Ordained to ministry Christian Fellowship Ctr., 1985. V.p. Watchmen Ministries, Clymer, Pa., 1976-85, pres., 1991—; sr. pastor Christian Fellowship Ctr., Greensburg, Pa., 1985-90; bd. dirs. Doorkeepers Christian Outreach, Spring Creek, Pa., 1980—. Author: Don't Bite the Apple Til You Check for Worms, 1985, Designer Genes, 1986, Hot Trax for Guys, Hot Trax for Girls, 1987, Positive Holiness, 1988, Promises of the Messiah, 1989, Unmasking the Myths of Marriage, 1990, The Disillusioned Christian, 1991, This Isn't the Trip I Signed Up For, 1991, Armed and Dangerous, 1991, The King and the Beast, 1991; contbr. to Contemporary English Version of New Testament, 1991. Mem. ASCAP, Nat. Speakers Assn., Christian Holiness Assn., Wesleyan Theol. Soc., Country Music Assn. Republican. Home: 6153 Firelight Trl Antioch TN 37013-5650 Office: Watchmen Ministries PO Box 218 Clymer PA 15728-0218

ABRAHAM, CARL JOEL, safety specialist, inventor, consultant; b. N.Y.C., Dec. 31, 1937; s. Sol. and Mildred (Siegal) A.; m. Sharon Abraham; children: Carl Joel, Elizabeth Jean, Carrie Anne, Scott Ross, Lauren Jena, Gillian Rachel. BS, Hofstra U., 1959, postgrad., 1972, JD, 1978; postgrad., U. Oreg., 1959-60, U. N.C., 1961-63; MS, U. Pacific, 1961; PhD, Clayton U., 1975. Cert. chemistry, math. and biology tchr., N.Y.; cert. in food tech. and processing; registered profl. engr., N.Y.; diplomate Am. Acad. Environ. Engrs.; cert. in CPR, emergency cardiac care. Rsch. engr. Aerojet Gen. Corp., Sacramento, 1961, rsch. engr. and chemist, 1963-65; materials specialist corp. rsch. lab. J.P. Stevens & Co., Inc., Garfield, N.J., 1966-67; dir. rsch. and devel. Mansol Ceramics Co., Belleville, N.J., 1967-69; v.p., tech. dir. Polyphase Chem. Svc., Inc., West Hempstead, N.Y., 1968-70; chmn. bd. Inter-City Testing & Cons. Corp., Mineola, N.Y., 1971—, Athletics Safety Products Inc., 1984—; pres. Carmal Ltd.; sec., treas. Jesse H. Bidanset and Assocs., Inc.; prof. chemistry Nassau Community Coll., Garden City, N.Y., 1973-75; adj. faculty physics Empire State Coll., Old Westbury, N.Y., 1975-78; adj. faculty engring. Hofstra Univ., 1974-79, adj. prof. continuing edn. programs. Contbr. articles to profl. jours.; patentee high temperature carbonaceous and siliceous materials, sports safety equipment, storage batter explosion containment, football face mask, copyright registration on battery warnings and toxic materials. Mem. exec. bd., treas., cons. in engring. and human factors areas Hockey Equipment Cert. Coun. Recipient Civilian award for Outstanding Police Assistance, Police Dept. County of Nassau, 1974. Fellow Am. Inst. Chem. Engrs. (cert. chem. engring.), Am. Inst. Chemists (cert. profl. chemist), Royal Soc. Chemistry (chartered chemist), Textile Inst. (Manchester, Eng.); mem. AAAS, ASTM, Am. nat. Standards Inst., Am. Chem. Soc., Am. Acad. Law and Medicine, Soc. Auto. Engrs., Am. Indsl. Hygiene Assn., Am. Acad. Environ. Engrs. (diplomate), Am. soc. Safety Engrs., Soc. Plastics Engrs., Systems Safety Soc. (sr. grade environ. profl.), Elks, Alpha Chi Sigma, others. Home: 3 Baker Hill Rd Great Neck NY 11023-1413 Office: 167 Willis Ave Mineola NY 11501-2621

ABRAHAM, JOHN, mechanical engineer; b. Quilom, Kerala, India, Dec. 14, 1956; came to U.S., 1981; s. Poovannal John and Sosamma Abraham; m. Regi Sara Varghese, Jan. 12, 1986. BTech with honors, Indian Inst. Tech., Kharagpur, West Bengal, 1981; MA, Princeton U., 1984, PhD, 1986. Sr. engr. John Deere Techs. Internat., Woodridge, N.J., 1986—; vis. rsch. collaborator dept. mech. and aerospace engring. Princeton (N.J.) U., 1989—. Contbr. articles to profl. jours.; inventor rotary value for natural gas rotary engine. Mem. ASME, AIAA, Soc. Automotive Engrs., Soc. Indsl. and Applied Math., The Combustion Inst. Home: 9 Hidden Glen Dr Parsippany NJ 07054

ABRAHAM, NICHOLAS ALBERT, lawyer, real estate developer; b. Boston, Sept. 17, 1941; s. Nicholas and Ida (Ghiz) A.; m. Evie Stathopoulos, June 30, 1968; children: Annise, Nicholas. BS, Boston U., 1963, JD, 1966. Bar: Mass. 1966, U.S. Dist. Ct. Mass. 1968, U.S. Ct. Appeals (1st cir.) 1971. Sr. ptnr. Abraham-Hanna, P.C., Boston, 1968-88; chief exec. officer Boston Investors Fund, 1972—. Author: Doing Business in Egypt, 1979, Doing Business in Saudi Arabia, 1980, Doing Business in Kuwait, 1982. Bd. of trustees Boston U. Coll. of Bus. Adminstrn., 1968; chmn. fund raising com. Boy Scouts Am., 1968; coach Weston Little League; founder of Weston Youth Hockey League, 1985. Served with U.S. Army, 1966-67; to lt. comdr. USN, 1967-74. Republican. Eastern Orthodox. Home: 21 Buckskin Dr Weston MA 02193-1129 Office: Abraham Boston Investors 581 Boylston St 3d Fl Boston MA 02116

ABRAHAMS, PAUL WILLIAM, computer scientist; b. Bkyn., Nov. 17, 1935; s. Abraham Judah and Evelyn (Hirshberg) A.; m. Sheila Beryl Nemser, Mar. 9, 1980 (div. Mar. 1983); 1 child, Jodi. SB, MIT, 1956, ScD, 1963. Sect. supr. ITT Data and Info. Systems, Paramus, N.J., 1962-64; sr. rsch. scientist Info. Internat. Inc., N.Y.C., 1964-67; assoc. prof. NYU, 1967-80; cons. computer scientist Deerfield, Mass., 1980—; cons. IBM TJ Watson Rsch. Lab., Yorktown Heights, 1986-90; mem. Am. Nat. Standards Inst. com. X3J1, N.Y.C., 1968-76. Author: TeX for the Impatient, 1990, UNIX for the Impatient, 1992. Dir. Music in Deerfield, 1982-86. Mem. Assn. for Computing Machinery (v.p. 1982-84, pres. 1986-88). Democrat.

ABRAHAMSEN, DAVID, psychiatrist, psychoanalyst, author; b. Trondheim, Norway, June 23, 1903; came to U.S., 1940, naturalized, 1946; s. Salomon and Marie (Fischer) A.; m. Lova Katz, May 5, 1932; children: Inger Abrahamsen Elliott, Anne-Marie Abrahamsen Foltz. M.D., Royal Frederick U., Oslo, 1929; postgrad., Tavistock Clinic and Nat. Hosp., London, London Sch. Econs., 1936-37; M.D., SUNY, 1943. Diplomate Am. Bd. Psychiatry and Neurology. Dist. pub. health officer, pvt. practice medicine Norway, 1929-31; intern Royal Norwegian Clinics, Oslo U., 1931-32; resident, asst. physician neurology and psychiatry Psychiat. Clinic, Oslo, 1932-36; dir., supr. Children's Home, Oslo, 1934-36; psychiatrist Dept. Justice, Oslo, 1938-40, St. Elizabeth's Hosp., Washington, 1940-41, Ill. State Penitentiary, 1941-42; research asso. psychiatry Menninger Clinic, Southard Sch., Topeka, 1942-43; psychiatrist Bellevue Hosp., 1943-44; research asso. dept. psychiatry Columbia U., 1944-53, research dir. child guidance and mental hygiene, 1950-53; dir. research, treatment behavior disorders in children Psychiat. Inst., N.Y.C., 1944-48; dir. sci. research N.Y. State Dept. Mental Hygiene, 1948-52, cons., 1955-65; vis. prof. grad. faculty polit. and social sci. New Sch. for Social Research, 1959-61; research psychiat. cons. dept. psychiatry Roosevelt Hosp., N.Y.C., 1968—; organizer, dir. Psychiat. Forum, Inc., 1946—; mem. bd. Home Adv. Council, Home Term Ct., N.Y.C., 1953—; mem. bd., adv. bd. Mus. Therapy Orgn., 1954—; mem. N.Y. Gov's Com to Propose New Legislation on Definition Legal Insanity, 1957—; bd. overseers Lemberg Center for Study of Violence, Brandeis U. Author: I am a Jew (in Norwegian), 1935, new expanded edit. (in Norwegian), 1985, Crime and the Human Mind, 1944, Men, Mind and Power, 1945, The Mind and Death of a Genius, 1946, Report on Study of 102 Sex Offenders at Sing Sing Prison as Submitted to Governor Thomas E. Dewey, 1950, Who Are the Guilty?-A Study of Education and Crime, 1962, The Road to Emotional Maturity, 1958, The Psychology of Crime, 1960, The Emotional Care of Your Child, 1969, Our Violent Society, 1970, The Murdering Mind, 1973, Nixon vs. Nixon: An Emotional Tragedy, 1977, The Mind of the Accused: A Psychiatrist in the Courtroom, Confessions of Son of Sam, 1985, Murder Madness—The Secret Life of Jack the Ripper, 1992; also numerous reports.; contbr. articles to sci., med. jours. Served with Norwegian Army, 1940. Fellow AMA, Am. Psychiat. Assn., N.Y. Acad. Medicine; mem. Norwegian Med. Assn., N.Y. County Med. Soc., Am. Soc. Criminology, N.Y. Soc. Clin. Psychiatry, Am. Coll. Psychoanalysts, Authors League, PEN. Club: Harmonies. Address: 860 Fifth Ave New York NY 10021

ABRAHAMSON, WARREN GENE, II, biology educator, ecologist; b. Ludington, Mich., Mar. 26, 1947; s. Warren Gene and Alice Enid (Johnson) A.; m. Christy Raye Harmon, Aug. 16, 1969; 1 child, Jill Raye. BS in Botany, U. Mich., 1969; MA in Biology, Harvard U., 1971, Ph.D. in Biology, 1973. Asst. prof. biology Bucknell U., Lewisburg, Pa., 1973-79, assoc. prof., 1979-83, prof., 1983—; vis. asst. prof. Mich. State U., East Lansing, 1976; rsch. fellow Archbold Biol. Sta., Lake Placid, Fla., 1980-81, rsch. assoc., 1976—; panelist NSF, Washington, 1983, 85, 90, Nat. Rsh. Coun., 1992; Colo. Plateau Distinguished scholar in residence No. Ariz. U. and Mus. No. Arizona, Flagstaff, 1986-87; Editor: Plant-Animal Interactions. Contbr. articles to sci. publs. Recipient Lindback award Bucknell U., 1975, Class of 1956 Lectureship award, 1982; William Dutcher award Nat. Audubon Soc., 1984. Mem. Ecol. Soc. Am. (coun. 1987—), Bot. Soc. Am. (chmn. ecology sect. 1980-81), Soc. for Study of Evolution, Torrey Bot. Club, Seven Mountains Audubon Soc. (program chmn. 1978-80, pres. 1981-83), Sigma Xi. Democrat. Avocations: natural history, photography, sailing. Home: RD 1 PO Box 466 D Stein Ln Lewisburg PA 17837-1781 Office: Bucknell U Dept Biology Lewisburg PA 17837

ABRAM, RUTH JACOBETH, museum administrator and founder; b. Orange County, Calif., Sept. 19, 1945; d. Morris B. and Jane (Maguire) A.; m. Herbert Teitelbaum, June 4, 1967; children: Anna Mara Teitelbaum, Noah Abram Teitelbaum. BA, Sarah Lawrence Coll., 1967; MSW, Brandeis U., 1970; MA in Am. History, NYU, 1983. Exec. dir. Norman Found., N.Y.C., 1971-72; program dir. ACLU Found., N.Y.C., 1972-74; exec. dir. Women's Action Alliance, N.Y.C., 1974-79; pres., founder Paraphrase, Inc., N.Y.C., 1983—, Lower East Side Hist. Conservancy, N.Y.C., 1984-88, Lower East Side Tenement Mus., N.Y.C., 1988—. Mem. Am. Assn. State and Local History, Am. Mus. Assn.

ABRAMOVITZ, MAX, architect; b. Chgo., May 23, 1908; s. Benjamin and Sophia (Maimon) A.; m. Anne Marie Causey, Sept. 4, 1937 (div.); children: Michael John, Katherine Paul; m. Anita Zeltner Brooks, Feb. 29, 1964. B.S., U. Ill., 1929; M.S., Columbia U., 1931; postgrad., Ecole des Beaux Arts, 1932-34; D.F.A. (hon.), U. Pitts., 1961, U. Ill., 1970. Partner firm Harrison & Abramovitz, architects, 1945-76, Abramovitz-Harris-Kingsland, architects, N.Y.C., 1976-85, Abramovitz-Kingsland-Schiff, N.Y.C., 1985—; asso. prof. Yale U. Sch. Fine Arts, 1939-42; dep. dir. UN Hdqrs. Planning Office, 1947-52; Cons. Brandeis U., U. Pitts. Prin. works include U.S. Steel Bldg, Pitts., Nationwide Ins, Columbus, Ohio, Assembly Hall and Krannert Center Performing Arts, U. Ill.-Urbana; chapels Brandeis U; major campus devel. La Banque Rothschild, Paris, France, Groupe des Assurances Nationales, LaDefense, France, Jewish Chapel, U.S. Mil. Acad., West Point, N.Y. Trustee Mt. Sinai Med. Center, N.Y.C. Served with C.E. AUS, 1942-45; col. 1950-52; spl. asst. to asst. sec. air force Mar. 1952-July 1952. Recipient Legion of Merit fellow Brandeis U., 1963; Achievement award U. Ill. Alumni Assn., 1963. Fellow AIA; mem. Am. Soc. C.E., Regional Plan Assn. (chmn. bd. 1966-68, dir. 1968—), Archtl. League N.Y., N.Y. Bldg. Congress (gov. 1957-64). Club: Century Assn. (N.Y.C.). Home: Honey Rd # 77A Pound Ridge NY 10576 Office: 51 Madison Ave New York NY 10010-1603

ABRAMS, ELLIOT, meteorologist, consultant; b. Phila., May 31, 1947; s. Ellis and Bernice (Braderman) A.; m. Bonnie Debra Felkoff, Aug. 31, 1969; children: Michael Steven, Randy I. BS, Pa. State U., 1969, MS, 1971. Meteorologist, sr. v.p. Accu-Weather Inc., State College, Pa., 1976—; also bd. dirs. Accu-Weather Inc., State College; TV meteorologist Pa. State U., University Park, Pa., 1968—; educator Nat. Youth Sci. Camp, Bartow, W.Va., 1989-92. Author: OnLine with Accu Weather, 1989. Member Centre County Planning Commn., Bellefonte, Pa., 1988—; twp. supr. Patton Twp., State College, 1982—; chmn. Centre Region Coun. of Govts., State College, 1985, 91. 1st lt. Air N.G., 1972-75. Named one of Best of Phila., Phila. mag., 1978. Mem. Am. Meteorol. Soc. (bd. dirs. broadcasting bd. 1987-90), Nat. Weather Assn., Am. Assn. Weather Observers, Elks. Home: 591 Melissa Ln State College PA 16803-1250 Office: Accu Weather Inc 619 W College Ave State College PA 16801-3797

ABRAMS, GARY MICHAEL, pharmacist; b. Lowell, Mass., Dec. 8, 1955; s. John C. and Dolores K. (Monbleau) A.; 1 child, Meghan. BS, Northeastern U., 1978. Registered Pharmacist. Staff pharmacist Cen. Maine Med. Ctr., Lewiston, ME, 1978-81; dir. of pharmacy Miles Meml. Hosp., Damariscotta, ME, 1981-83; outpatient pharmacy supr. New England Med. Ctr., Boston, 1983-85; dir. pharmacy and material mgmt. Northeast Rehab. Hosp., Salem, N.H., 1985-87; dir. pharmacy Winchester (Mass.) Hosp., 1987—; pres. ME Soc. Hosp. Pharmacists, 1985, N.H. Soc. Hosp. Pharmacists, 1986-87; lectr., speaker bur. Winchester (Mass.) 1987—. Mem. Durham (ME) Sch. Com., 1982-83. Mem. Am. Sc. Hos. Pharmacists, Mass. Soc. of Hosp. Pharmacists, Acad. Med. Arts and Scis. Roman Catholic. Home: 31 Stevens Ave Lawrence MA 01843

ABRAMS, IRVING, real estate appraiser, treasurer; b. Aug. 31, 1928; s. Isaac and Gertrude (Alter) Abramowitz; m. Marilyn Factor, Dec. 14, 1969; 1 child, Mark. BS, CUNY, 1949; MA, Bklyn. Coll., 1952. Appraiser HUD, N.Y.C., 1978—; treas. Ardsley Tenants Corp., N.Y.C., 1985—. Home: 320 Central Park W New York NY 10025-7659

ABRAMS, KENNETH THEODORE, administrator; b. Paterson, N.J., Nov. 24, 1928; s. Joseph and Ruth (Rosenberg) A.; m. Madeline Laura

Cantor, Dec. 26, 1954; children: Pamela, Ursula, Joshua. BA, Washington & Jefferson Coll., 1949; PhD, Cornell U., 1965. Lectr. english lit. CUNY, Queens Coll., Flushing, 1961-65; dir. experimental coll. SUNY, Stony Brook, 1969-71, assoc. prof. English lit., 1965-71; dir. London program Empire State Coll., London, 1971-74; dir. Israel program Empire State Coll., Jerusalem, 1977-79; prof. cultural studies Empire State Coll., Saratoga Springs, N.Y., 1973—; exec. dir. Coll. Consortium Internat. Studies, N.Y.C., 1985-86; dean, Met. regional ctr. Empire State Coll., N.Y.C., 1980-87; dean internat. programs Empire State Coll., Saratoga Springs, 1987—; bd. dirs. Coll. Consortium Internat. Studies, Yardley, Pa., 1980-86, Partnership Svc. Learning, N.Y.C., 1986—; book reviewer in field. Contbr. articles to profl. jours. Ednl. advisor Mate Yehudah Regional Coun., Jeruselam, 1979-81. With U.S. Army, 1951-53. SUNY Rsch. fellow, 1966, 67, Martin Sampson fellow, 1960-61. Jewish. Home: 34 Circular St Saratoga Springs NY 12866-4212 Office: Empire State Coll 1 Union Ave Saratoga Springs NY 12866-4309

ABRAMS, LLOYD, chemist; b. N.Y.C., June 9, 1939; s. Richard and Claire (Feigenbaum) A.; m. Virginia Mai Austin, May 29, 1971; children: Elizabeth Tonia, Laura Morrell. BChE, CCNY, 1961; PhD, Rutgers U., 1967. Analytical engr. Nuclear Engine Lab. Conn. Aircraft, Meriden, 1961; exptl. engr. Apollo Fuel Cells Pratt & Whitney Aircraft, East Hartford, Conn., 1961-63; teaching asst., rsch. asst. dept. chemistry Rutgers U., New Brunswick, N.J., 1963-64, 65-66; rsch. asst. chem. dept. Brookhaven Nat. Lab., Upton, N.Y., 1966-68; rsch. chemist pigments dept. Exptl. Sta. DuPont Co., Wilmington, Del., 1968-72, sr. rsch. chemist, 1972-77, rshc. assoc., 1977-79, staff scientist Cen. Rsch., Exptl. Sta., 1979—; chmn. Gordon Rsch. Conf., Chemistry at Interfaces, 1987. Contbr. numerous articles to profl. jours.; patentee in field. Mem. fin. adv. com. Red Clay Sch. Dist., Wilmington, 1990-91; bd. dirs., treas. Team Del. (Swim Team), Wilmington, 1985-90; coach, event supr. Sci. Olympiad, A.I. DuPont High Sch., Wilmington, 1985-91; treas. William C. Lewis PTA, Wilmington, 1978-82. Brookhaven Nat. Lab. fellow, 1966, Sun Oil rsch. fellow. Mem. AAAS, Am. Chem. Soc., DuPont Country Club (tennis com. 1981-91), Westminster Swim Club (swim team rep. 1984-86), Suburban Swim League (pres. 1986), Sigma Xi, Phi Lambda Upsilon. Home: 555 Holly Knolls Rd Hockessin DE 19707-9749 Office: DuPont Co Cen Rsch Exptl Sta Bldg 262 Wilmington DE 19880

ABRAMS, MARK ALAN, information systems designer; b. Eglin AFB, Fla., May 19, 1957; s. David Lee and Marcia (Finkelstein) A.; m. Ellen Gabrielle Gittleson, June 11, 1989; children: Jennifer, Stephanie. Student, Nat. Cryptologic Inst., Ft. Mead, Md., 1982-85, Community Coll. of Air Force, 1978-82. Programmer/analyst USAF/Nat. Security Agy., Ft. Meade, 1982-85; sr. programmer/analyst Martin Marietta, Denver, 1985-86; cons. New Eng. Telephone, Boston, 1986-87, N.Y.State Office of Gen. Svcs., Albany, 1987-88, N.Y.State Div. of Housing and Community Renewal, Albany, 1988-91; dir. tech. svcs. Coll. Mktg. Group, Wilmington, Mass., 1992—; cons., presenter North East Model 204 User Group, Albany, 1991. Designer info. system: Data Fox, 1986, Oetis, 1988, Event Tracking and Scheduling, 1990. Office: CMG Info Svcs PO Box 7000 187 Ballardvale St Ste B110 Wilmington MA 01887

ABRAMS, MARY LOUISE, library director; b. N.Y.C., Oct. 31, 1934; d. Clarence Joseph and Mary Eymard (Morrissey) Johnson; m. Sam Sottosanti, Feb. 6, 1960 (div. 1975); children: Sioux, William, Lisa, Robert, Margaret; m. Allan Gerald Abrams, July 18, 1985. BA, Marymount Coll., 1958; MLS, Columbia U., 1971. Libr. Johnson Libr., Hackensack, N.J., 1971-74; asst. dir. Englewood (N.J.) Libr., 1975-89; dir. Paramus (N.J.) Libr., 1989—; pres. Bergen County Coop. Libr. System, Hackensack, N.J., 1991. Mem. Am. Libr. Assn., N.J. Libr. Assn. Roman Catholic. Office: Paramus Pub Libr 116 E Century Rd Paramus NJ 07652-4398

ABRAMS, ROBERT, state official, lawyer; b. Bronx, N.Y., July 4, 1938; s. Benjamin and Dorothy (Kaplan) A.; m. Diane B. Schulder, Sept. 15, 1974; children: Rachel Schulder, Becky Schulder. B.A., Columbia U., 1960; J.D., NYU, 1963; LL.D. (hon.), Hofstra U., 1979; Lugum Doctoris (hon.), Yeshiva U., 1984. Mem. N.Y. State Assembly, 1965-69; pres. Borough of Bronx, 1970-78; atty. gen. State of N.Y., 1979—. Contbr. articles to newspapers, legal jours. Del. Dem. Nat. Conv., 1972, 76, 80, 84, mem. platform com., 1988; elector Electoral Coll., 1988. Recipient Adam Clayton Powell Pub. Svc. award, Interfaith award Coun. Chs., N.Y.C., 1969, Bronx Community Coll. medallion for Svc., 1970, Scroll of Honor plaque United Jewish Appeal, 1970, Benjamin Cardozo award for legal excellence Jewish Lawyers Guild, Interfaith award Coun. of Chs. of N.Y.C., Brotherhood award B'nai B'rith, 1970, Man of Yr. award NAACP, , Alumni Achievement award NYU Sch. Law, Environmentalist of Yr. award Environ. Planning Lobby N.Y., Disting. Pub. Svc. Citation Bus. Coun. N.Y. State, N.Y. State Sheriff's Assn. award. Nat. Crime Victims award. Mem. N.Y. State Bar Assn. (Environ. Achievement award), Assn. Bar City N.Y., Bronx County Bar Assn., Nat. Assn. Attys. Gen. (past pres., past chmn. antitrust and environ. protection coms., Atty. Gen. of Yr. award 1991), Eastern Regional Conf. Attys. Gen. (past chmn.). Democrat. Office: 120 Broadway New York NY 10271-0002 also: Rm 221 State Capitol Dept Law Albany NY 12224

ABRAMSON, BRUCE S., food products executive; b. Bronx, N.Y., July 23, 1936; s. Moe A. and Anna Rose (Abrams) A.; m. June 17, 1961; children: Todd, Seth, Craig. B.S.C., Ohio U., 1958. Exec. Continental Cheese, N.Y.C., 1963—; assoc. Coldwell Banker Schlott Realtors, Chatham, N.J., 1991—; treas. B'nai B'rith Watchung Mountain Lodge, Summit, N.J., 1974. Mem. Cheese Importers Assn. Am., Cheese Importers Assn. Am., S. Mountain Lodge Bnai Brith. Home: 54 Woodwild Way Berkeley Heights NJ 07922-2033

ABRAMSON, CLARENCE ALLEN, lawyer; b. Ft. Worth, Oct. 15, 1932; s. Samuel and Katherine (Berg) A.; m. Maureen L. Foley, May 15, 1982; children: Steven T., Eric M., Katherine M. BBA, U. Tex., 1952, JD, 1954. Bar: Tex. 1954, N.Y. 1963, N.J. 1972, Pa. 1974. Ptnr. Wynne & Wynne, Dallas, 1954-61; atty. SEC, Washington, 1961-62; of counsel Mobil Oil Corp., N.Y., The Hague and London, 1962-69; internat. counsel Merck & Co., Inc., Rahway, N.J., 1970-86, assoc. gen. counsel, 1986-89, sec., assoc. gen. counsel, 1989-90, v.p., sec., 1991—; bd. dirs. Handy & Harman Inc. Mem. adv. bd. Southwestern Legal Found., Dallas, 1986—; chmn. Merck Polit. Action Com., Rahway, 1990—. Mem. ABA, Tex. Bar Assn., N.J. Bar Assn., Pa. Bar Assn., N.Y. State Bar Assn. Office: Merck & Co Inc PO Box 2000 Rahway NJ 07065-0900

ABRAMSON, IRWIN BARRY, retail executive; b. Newark, July 31, 1939; s. Philip J. and Freida (Belsky) A.; m. Jessica S. Farber (dec. 1985; 1 child, Eric Peter. Student, Babson Coll., Wellesley, Mass., 1961. Pres. Tiny Tots Stores, Greenbrook, N.J., 1961—; mng. dir. Pfim Realty, Greenbrook, N.J., 1980—; bd. dirs. Indian Hill Farm, Great Meadow, N.J., 1987—, 273 Main Assocs., Gladstone, N.J., 1989—, Happyrock Mgmt., Inc., Gladstone, 1989—. Bd. dirs., strutee Philharmonic Orch. of N.J., Warren, 1987—; trustee United Way of Somerset Hills, Basking Ridge, N.J., 1987—, United Way of Somerset Valley, 1988—, Bonnie Brae Sch. With USNG, 1961-66. Mem. Far Hills Yacht Club (vice commodore). Republican. Home: Hidden Pond Farm PO Box 487 Oldwick NJ 08858-0487 Office: Tiny Tots Stores 199 Rte 22 Green Brook NJ 08810

ABRAMSON, LEONARD, healthcare organization executive; b. 1938. BS, Pa. State U., 1954. V.p. Spectro Industries, Jenkintown, Pa., 1969-72, R H Med. Svcs., Inc., Phila., 1972-76; with Health Maintenance Orgn. of Pa., Phila., 1976-81; dir. U.S. Health Care Systemof Pa., Inc., Blue Bell, 1981—. Office: US Healthcare Inc 980 Jolly Rd/ Box 1109 Blue Bell PA 19422*

ABRAMSON, MORRIS BARNET, chemistry educator, researcher; b. N.Y.C., July 8, 1910; s. Barnet and Dora (Hartzmark) A.; widowed; children: Edward E., Robert J. MS, NYU, 1934, PhD, 1939. Chmn. sci. dept. Dept. Edn., N.Y.C., 1950-65; assoc. prof. Albert Einstein Coll. Medicine, Bronx, N.Y., 1965-79; adj. prof. Hofstra U., Hempstead, N.Y., 1979-90. Contbr. over 50 articles to profl. jours. Recipient postdoctoral fellowships Cambridge U., Eng., 1961, NIH, Poly. U., Bklyn., 1963, Einstein Coll. Medicine, N.Y.C., NYU. Mem. Am. Chem. Soc., Sigma Xi. Home: 53-35 Hollis Ct Blvd Flushing NY 11365

ABRAMSON, NORMAN S., critical care medicine educator, researcher; b. N.Y.C., May 22, 1944; s. Charles and Edith Abramson. BA, Cornell U., 1965; MD, NYU, 1969. Assoc. prof. div. critical care medicine Resuscitation Rsch. Ctr., U. Pitts. Sch. Medicine, 1991—, assoc. dir. clin. affairs, 1991—; rsch. cons. Neurex Corp., Menlo Park, Calif., 1991—, Marion Merrill-Dow Pharms., 1990—, C.R. Bard Co., Tewksburg, Mass., 1983-85, 90—, Sterling Pharms., 1988. Author: Medico-Legal Aspects of Critical Care, 1986, (chpt.) Code Blue: Cardiac Arrest and Resuscitation, 1987. With USAF, 1971-73. Recipient Rsch. grant NIH, 1989-93. Mem. Am. Coll. Emergency Physicians, Soc. Critical Care Medicine, Am. Heart Assn., Soc. for Acad. Emergency Medicine. Office: Internat Resuscitation Rsch Ctr 3434 5th Ave 2d Floor Pittsburgh PA 15260

ABRAMSON, ROBERT M., musician, educator. Certificate and license, Dalcroze Sch. Music; postgrad. diplome, Inst. Jacques-Dalcroze, Switzerland; MM, Manhattan Sch. Music; student, Juilliard Sch., Peabody Sch. Internat. clinician in Dalcroze Eurythmics. Prof. eurythmics and performance Juilliard Sch., N.Y.C.; prof. theory Manhattan Sch. of Music, N.Y.C. Author: Rhythm Games, 1973, Teaching Music in 20th-Century America, 1986; composer with Glanville Hicks, Wald, Lybbert, Diamond; harpsichordist with Weiss-Mann; condr. with Monteaux; recs. for Elektra, Columbia, Serenus, Tradition. Mem. Music Theory Soc. N.Y. (past officer), Dalcroze Soc. Am. (past pres.). Office: The Juilliard Sch Lincoln Ctr New York NY 10023

ABRAMSON, WARREN BLAKE, automotive sales and leasing company executive; b. Long Beach, Calif., Jan. 3, 1953; s. Herbert Allen and Harriet Ruth (Benson) A.; m. Karen Lee Carlin, Aug. 11, 1974; children: Alyson, David. BS, Boston U., 1975. Salesperson Silver Lake Dodge, Wellesley, Mass., 1975-81; gen. mgr. Silver Lake Leasing, Wellesley, 1981-87, Silver Lake Dodge & Leasing, Wellesley, 1987—; guest speaker for leasing and renting Chrysler Motors Corp., Detroit, 1983—. Dir. Harriet Abramson Cancer Found., Newton, Mass., 1989, Catrala of Mass., Inc., Lakeville; fellow mentor B'nai B'rith Sports Lodge, 1989. Jewish. Home: 10 Maple Rd Randolph MA 02368 Office: Silver Lake Dodge & Leasing 234 Worcester St Wellesley MA 02181

ABRAMSON, WILLIAM EDWARD, psychiatrist; b. Bklyn., Mar. 25, 1935; s. Joseph Louis and Rose (Lichter) A.; m. Madeline R. Reich, June 29, 1958; children: Cynthia M., Andrea L. AB, Cornell U., 1956; MD, SUNY, Buffalo, 1960. Cert. Am. Bd. Psychiatry and Neurology. Med. intern Jewish Hosp. Ctr., Bklyn., 1960-61; resident psychiatry Kings County Hosp. Ctr., Bklyn., 1961-62, Sheppard Pratt Hosp., Towson, Md., 1964-66; staff psychiatrist Sheppard Pratt Hosp., 1966-84, sr. psychiatrist, 1984—; dir. comprehensive drug abuse program Sheppard Pratt Hosp., Towson, 1972-87, pres. med. staff, 1978-80; pres. Drug Abuse Doctors Assn., Md., 1984-86. Mem. Physicians for Social Responsibility, Md., 1980, Corp. for the Advancement Psychiatry, 1984. Lt. USNR, 1962-64. Fellow Am. Psychiat. Assn.; mem. AMA, Md. Psychiat. Soc., Am. Soc. Addiciton Medicine, Med Chi Md. (com. physician rehab. 1986), Balt. County Med. Assn., Phi Lambda Kappa. Democrat. Jewish. Office: Sheppard Pratt Hosp 6501 N Charles St Baltimore MD 21204-6819

ACE, DREXEL MAURICE, JR., communications executive; b. Osaka, Japan, July 22, 1950; came to U.S, 1950; s. Drexel Maurice and Edna L. (McNamee) A. BA in Communications, U. Notre Dame, Ind., 1972. Sr. writer, editor The MITRE Corp., Bedford, Mass., 1977-83; mgr. editorial svcs. Computervision Corp., Bedford, 1983-85; dir. mktg. communications Aries Tech., Inc., Lowell, Mass., 1985—. Author: Symposium Planning Guide, 1980. Served to lt. USN, 1972-76. Mem. Internat. Platform Assn. Roman Catholic. Office: Aries Tech Inc 600 Suffolk St Lowell MA 01854

ACETO, VINCENT JOHN, librarian, educator; b. Schenectady, N.Y., Feb. 5, 1932; s. Henry and Gilda (Maietta) A.; m. Jean Louise Rasey, Aug. 27, 1955 (div. 1974); children: David, Paul, Andrew. A.B., SUNY, 1953, M.A., 1953, M.L.S., 1959; postgrad. Case Western Res. U., 1959, 62, 65-66. Tchr., Scotia (N.Y.)-Glenville Central Schs., 1956-57; high sch. librarian Burnt Hills (N.Y.)-Ballston Lake Central Schs., 1957-59; library dir. Town Ballston Pub. Library, Burnt Hills, 1958-60; Fulbright lectr. U. Dacca, East Pakistan, 1964-65; asst. prof. Sch. Library Sci., SUNY, Albany, 1959-62, assoc. prof. library sci., 1963-69, prof., 1969—, assoc. dean, 1987—. Joint editor: Film Lit. Index; contbr. articles to profl. jours. Pres., Filmdex Part II, Inc., 1973-90; library cons. various pub. schs. Govt. Cypress, 1992, dir. U.S. Office Edn. insts. and traineeships; bd. dirs. Freedom Forum, Schenectady, 1970-78, chmn., 1976-78. Served with AUS, 1954-56. Mem. Am. Library Assn., Pakistan Library Assn., East Pakistan Library Assn., N.Y. Library Assn., Hudson-Mohawk Library Assn. (v.p. 1964-66), NEA, Am. Soc. Indexers, Am. Soc. Info. Scis., Soc. Cinema Studies, Idaka Forum, Kappa Phi Kappa, Phi Delta Kappa. Democrat. Unitarian. Home: 1 Lincoln Town Dr Clifton Park NY 12065 Office: SUNY Sch Info Sci & Policy Albany NY 12222

ACEVEDO, DOMINGO ELIO, lawyer, international organization official; b. Formosa, Argentina, Jan. 5, 1936; came to U.S., 1966; s. Atenor Eduardo and Petrona (Pintos) A.; m. Patricia Walton Kennedy, Aug. 3, 1962; children: Gabriel Patricio, Mariana Teresa. JD, U. Catolica, Buenos Aires, 1964; MCL, Georgetown U., 1976; PhD, Cambridge U., 1986. Bar: Buenos Aires 1965, U.S. Dist. Ct. (fed. dist.), 1988. Legal officer Argentine Senate, Buenos Aires, 1964-65; sr. legal officer dept. legal affairs OAS, Washington, 1970-75, chief adv. svcs. div. Secretariat for Legal Affairs, 1975-80, prin. legal advisor, 1981—; adj. prof. law Am. U., Washington, 1984—. Contbr. articles to legal publs. OAS fellow, 1966-68. Mem. Fed. Bar Assn., Buenos Aires Bar Assn., Am. Soc. Internat. Law (exec. bd. 1984-87). Roman Catholic. Home: 10304 Gainsborough Rd Rockville MD 20854 Office: OAS Secretariat Legal Affairs 19th St and Constitution NW Washington DC 20006

ACEVEDO, MANUEL RAUL, surgeon; b. Santo Domingo, Dominican Republic, Mar. 3, 1945; came to U.S., 1970; s. Ezequiel Calzado and Delfina Acevedo; m. Carmen R. Perdomo, May 5, 1969 (dec. 1981); children: Enver R., Cicelia, Vladimir. BS, Liceo Juan Pablo Duarte, Santo Domingo, 1962; MD, U. de Santo Domingo, 1969. Intern Dr. Robert Reid Pediatric Hosp., Santo Domingo, 1969-70; intern Sydenham Hosp., N.Y.C., 1971, resident, 1971-76; fellow in gen. surgery LaGuardia Hosp., Forest Hill, N.Y., 1976-77; attending surgeon Hosp. for Joint Diseases, N.Y.C., 1977-78, Sydenham Hosp., N.Y.C., 1978-83, Harlem Hosp. Ctr., N.Y.C., 1983—. Fellow Hispanic Am. Med. Soc.; mem. Sociedad Medica Dominicana (sec. 1987-89). Office: Harlem Hosp Ctr 610 W 145th St New York NY 10031

ACHACOSO, THEODORE BORROMEO, computational neuroethologist; b. Iba, Zambales, Philippines, Sept. 2, 1961; s. Soliman Dimain and Graciosa (Borromeo) A. BS in Biology magna cum laude, U. Philippines, 1980, MD, 1984. Diplomate Philippine Bd. Medicine. Med. intern Philippine Gen. Hosp., Manila, 1984-85; rural health physician Dept. Health, Zambales, Philippines, 1985-86; neuroradiology fellow Makati Med. Ctr., Philippines, 1986-88; sci. rsch. specialist in pharmacology Dept. of Pharmacology, U. Philippines Coll. of Medicine, Manila, 1986-88; clin. asst. prof. neurology Philippine Gen. Hosp., Manila, 1988; vis. asst. prof. med. informatics George Washington U., Washington, 1988-92, asst. rsch. prof. computer medicine, 1992—; exec. dir. Brain Found. of Philippines, Manila, 1986-88; cons. Philippine Bur. of Food and Drugs, 1987-88. Author: AY's Neuroanatomy of C. elegans for Computation, 1992; contbr. articles to profl. jours. Sci. and tech. resource person Philippine Embassy, Washington, 1988—. Mem. ACM, IEEE, Am. Med. Informatics Assn., Internat. Neural Network Soc. Office: George Washington U Dept Computer Medicine 2300 K St NW Washington DC 20037

ACHARYA, SAGRI VASUDEVA, controller, consultant; b. Udipi, India, July 24, 1943; came to U.S., 1972; s. S. Laxminarayana and S. Padmavathi Amma; m. Nirmala S. Rao, June 3, 1971; children: Vasanth, Prasad. BS in Acctg., U. Mysore, India, 1964; chartered acct., Inst. Chartered Accts., New Delhi, India, 1967. Asst. controller City Colleges Chgo., 1973-77, OFT Exploration Inc., San Francisco, 1981; acct. mgr. North Pole (Alaska) Refining, 1977-80; internat. acctg. mgr. Comind Internat. Banking Corp., Houston, 1982; controller Petra Internat. Banking Corp., Washington, 1983—; pres. Acharya Consulting Svcs., Rockville, Md., 1983—. Editorial advisor CPA Monthly, 1984-87. Sec., treas. Ophthalmic Mission Trust, Rockville, 1988—. Fellow Am. Inst. CPAs (cert.), Assn. MBA Execs., Toastmasters Club. Home: 14613 Pommel Dr Rockville MD 20850-3542

ACHATZ, JOHN, lawyer; b. Detroit, Jan. 11, 1948. AB, U. Mich., 1975, JD, 1978. Bar: Mass. 1978, U.S. Dist. Ct. Mass. 1979. Assoc. Brown, Rudnick, Freed & Gesmer, Boston, 1978-85, ptnr., 1986—. Co-author: Massachusetts Condominium Law. Dir. Coop. Housing Task Force, Inc., Boston, 1981—; trustee Boston Lyric Opera, Inc., 1989—. Office: Brown Rudnick Freed Gesmer 1 Financial Ctr Boston MA 02111-2621

ACHENBAUM, ALVIN ALLEN, advertising agency executive; b. N.Y.C., Dec. 11, 1925; s. Benjamin and Dora (Dworin) A.; m. Barbara Ann Greenwald, June 24, 1951; children: Jonathan Peter, Lisa Jane, Martha Beth. BS, UCLA, 1950; MS, Columbia U., 1951. Mgr. market rsch. McCann-Erickson, N.Y.C., 1951-57; exec. v.p., sec., dir. Grey Advt., Inc., N.Y.C., 1957-71; exec. v.p. J. Walter Thompson Co., 1971-74; chmn. bd. dirs. Canter, Achenbaum, Assocs., Inc., N.Y.C., 1974-89; vice chmn. bd. dirs. Backer, Spielvogel, Bates Worldwide, N.Y.C., 1989—; bd. dirs. MARC, Inc. Mem. edit. bd. Jour. Advt. Rsch. Mem. Citizens Adv. Com. of Irvington, 1970—; mem. Middle Eastern affairs com. Anti-Defamation League; adv. com. Assn. Consumer Research.; Trustee Mktg. Sci. Inst. With USAAF, 1944-46. Named to Market Research Hall of Fame. Mem. Market Rsch. Coun. N.Y., Copy Rsch. Coun. N.Y., Am. Mktg. Assn. (v.p.-elect global mktg. div., bd. dirs.), Am. Econ. Assn., Assn. Pub. Opinion Rsch., Beta Gamma Sigma. Home: 34 Mallard Rise Irvington NY 10533-1033 Office: Backer Spielvogel Bates 405 Lexington Ave New York NY 10174-0002

ACHIN, MILOS KOSTA, historian, writer; b. Knjazevac, Yugoslavia, Feb. 28, 1915; came to U.S., 1950; s. Kosta Sava and Vuka (Vujic) A.; divorced; children: Vuka, Kosta. Student, Mil. Acad., Belgrade, 1934, Air Force Sch., Pancevo, 1938. Capt., editor Yugoslav Guerrila, Free Mountains, 1941-44; dir. UN IRO Ctr., Trieste, Gorica, 1948-50; writer Free Serbian Press, 1950—. Author: Prolog Buducnosti, 1963, Kosovski Kristali, 1976, Koreni & Iskorenjeni, 1982, General Mihailovic and Ravna Gora, 1976-92, Tales of Socialist Yugoslavia, Yugoslavia in Our Time, 1991, Yugoslavia Dismembered, 1992, numerous other books, essays, short stories and articles. Capt. Royal Yugoslav Air Force, 1938-41. Rankovich Charitable and Ednl. Fund grantee, 1988, 89. Mem. Soc. Serbian Writers and Artists Abroad, N.Am. Soc. Serbian Studies. Home and Office: 6221 Walhonding Rd Bethesda MD 20816-2138

ACHUTHAN, RADH M., physics educator; b. Madras, Kerala, India, Nov. 19, 1935; came to U.S., 1960; s. Radhakrishna and Sree Devi Menon; m. Joy Achuthan, July 31, 1965 (div. 1978); children: Lakshman, Arjun; m. Nisha Sahai, May 28, 1981; 1 child, Mahima. BEE, U. Madras, 1956; MSEE, U. Mo., 1962, MS in Physics, 1964; PhD in Social Psychology and Planning, Union Inst., Cin., 1976. Instr. physics NW Mo. State Coll., Maryville, 1964-65, Wis. State U., Platteville, 1966; instr. physics L.I. U., Southampton, 1966-69, asst. prof., 1969-76, assoc. prof., 1976-82, prof., 1982—; mem. core rsch. and cons. Goals for Mankind, 1975-77. Pres. League for Human Rights in Divorce, Southampton, 1979—; organizer 1st human rights in divorce nat. march, Washington, 1979; lobbyist for presumption joint custody in divorce N.Y. State Assembly, 1980. Grantee Utter Pradesh Planning Commn., 1986, State of Karnataka, 1987, India Delmia Charitable Truste, 1987, UNICEF, 1991-92. Hindu. Home: 90 Sebonac Inlet Rd Southampton NY 11968-2730 Office: LI U Southampton NY 11968

ACKERBERG, ROBERT CYRIL, chemical engineering educator, researcher; b. Mpls., Sept. 14, 1934; s. David and Eva (Fefercorn) A.; children: Daniel, Anna. BSChemE, MIT, 1956; MSE, U. Mich., 1957; MA in Applied Math., Harvard U., 1960, PhD in Applied Math., 1963. Sr. rsch. assoc. Raytheon Corp., Waltham, Mass., 1962-63; asst. prof. aerospace enging. Poly. U. (formerly Poly. Inst. N.Y., Poly. Inst. Bklyn.), Bklyn., 1963-66, assoc. prof. aerospace engring., 1966-72, assoc. prof. chem. engring., 1972-73, prof. chem. engring., 1973—. Contbr. 23 papers to internat. jours. Founder, pres. Massapequa (N.Y.) Philharm. Orch., 1983—; mem. Nassau County decentralization panel and bd. N.Y. State Coun. on Arts, 1990—, Water Authority S.E. Nassau County, 1992—. NSF fellow, 1956-59; NSF grantee, 1971-72, 74-79, Army Rsch. Office grantee, 1964-72, Sci. Rsch. Coun. of Gt. Britain grantee, 1971-72. Mem. Am. Inst. Chem. Engrs., Am. Symphony Orch. League, Sigma Xi, Tau Beta Pi, Phi Lambda Upsilon, Sigma Gamma Tau, Omega Xi Epsilon. Home: One Highland St W Massapequa NY 11758 Office: Poly U RR 10 Farmingdale NY 11735

ACKERMAN, ALLAN JAY, accountant; b. N.Y.C., Nov. 1, 1931; s. Samuel and Elizabeth (Roth) A.; m. Doris Lewis Ackerman, Feb. 19, 1955; children: Kenneth R., Michael D., Marc E. Student, NYU, 1949-50; BBA magna cum laude, Pace U., 1955. CPA, N.Y.; cert. fraud examiner. Ptnr. KMG Main Hurdman, N.Y.C., 1955-87, KPMG Peat Marwick, 1987-91; dir. litigation and bankruptcy svcs. Bennett, Kielson, Storch & Kremer, White Plains, N.Y., 1991—. Mem. AICPAs, N.Y. State Soc. CPAs (dir. 1983-85), Am. Arbitration Assn. (comml. arbitration panel), Am. Acctg. Assn., Old Oaks Country Club (sec. 1989-91). Home: 23 Rockinghorse Trl Rye Brook NY 10573-1006 Office: Bennett Kielson Storch & Kramer One Barker Ave White Plains NY 10601-1503

ACKERMAN, F. KENNETH, JR., health facility administrator; b. Mansfield, Ohio, Apr. 2, 1939; m. Patricia Ackerman, Dec. 17, 1960; children: Franklin Kenneth III, Robert Christian, Peter Jonathan. BS in Biology, Denison U., 1961; MHA, U. Mich., 1963. Adminstrv. resident Henry Ford Hosp., Detroit, 1963-64; asst. adminstrv. dir. Geisinger Med. Ctr., Danville, Pa., 1964-69, assoc. adminstrv. dir., 1969-70, sr. v.p., adminstrv. dir., 1970-90, pres., 1990—; sr. v.p. adminstrv. affairs Geisinger Found., Danville, Pa., 1981—; bd. dirs. 1st Nat. Bank Danville, 1974—, Pa. Millers Mut. Ins. Co., Wilkes-Barre, 1979—. Bd. dirs. Pa. Chamber of Bus. and Industry, Harrisburg, 1977-90, Nat. Com. for Quality Healthcare, Washington, 1985—, Hosp. R&D Inst., Pensacola, Fla., 1990—; mem. Nat. Adv. Com. on Rural Health, Washington, 1988—. Recipient Adminstr. Yr. award Am. Group Practice Assn., 1988, Polit. Action Com. award Hosp. Assn. Pa., 1982, 85, 86, 88, 90, 91, Nat. Award of Merit, Duke U. Hosp. and Health Adminstrn. Alumni Assn., 1991. Mem. Am. Coll. Healthcare Execs. (regents adv. coun. 1989—, Hudgens' Meml. Award 1975). Office: Geisinger Med Ctr 100 N Academy Ave Danville PA 17822

ACKERMAN, GARY L., congressman; b. Bklyn., Nov. 19, 1942; s. Max and Eva (Barnett) A.; m. Rita Tewel, May 27, 1967; children: Lauren Meredith, Corey Brian, Ari David. B.A., Queens Coll., 1965. Tchr. N.Y.C. Pub. Schs., 1966-72; founder Queens (N.Y.) Tribune, 1970—; owner Multi Media, Queens, 1972—; mem. N.Y. Senate, 1979-83, 98th-102nd Congresses. Mem. Queens Coll. Alumni Assn. Democrat. Club: B'nai B'rith. Office: Cannon House Office Bldg Rm 238 Washington DC 20515*

ACKERMAN, HAROLD A., judge; b. 1928. Student, Seton Hall U., 1945-46, 48; LL.B., Rutgers U., 1951. Bar: N.J. 1951. Adminstrv. asst. to Commr. of Labor and Industry, State of N.J., 1955-56; judge of compensation State of N.J., 1956-62, supervising judge of compensation, 1962-65; judge Union County Dist. Ct., 1965-70, presiding judge, 1966-70; judge Union County Ct., 1970-73, Superior Ct. law div., 1973-75, Superior Ct. Chancery div., 1975-79, U.S. Dist. Ct., Dist. of N.J., 1980—; mem. Supreme Ct. Com. on Revision of Rules, 1967; chmn. Supreme Ct. Com. on County Dist. Cts., 1968; mem. faculty Nat. Jud. Coll., 1978. Recipient Disting. Alumni award Rutgers U. Sch. Law, 1980. Fellow ABA; mem. Order of Coif. Office: US Dist Ct US PO & Courthouse PO Box 999 Newark NJ 07101-0999

ACKERMAN, LISA MARILYN, foundation administrator, consultant; b. Danville, Pa., May 19, 1960; d. Bruce David and Jean May (Pedevill) A. BA, Middlebury Coll., 1982; MBA, NYU, 1986. Intern Internat. Found. for Art Rsch., N.Y.C., 1982; adminstrv. asst. Samuel H. Kress Found., N.Y.C., 1982-84, program adminstr., 1984-87, chief adminstrv. officer, 1987—; cons. Internat. Found. for Art Rsch., N.Y.C., 1985-86; rsch. cons. survey on art-deco comml. architecture, 1987—. Contbr. articles profl. publs. Vol. Planned Parenthood, N.Y.C., 1982-83, Middlebury Coll. Alumni Assn., 1982-86, edn. dept. Mus. Modern Art, N.Y.C., 1989—. Mem. Coll. Art Assn., Middlebury Coll. Alumni Assn. (vol. 1982-88). Office: Samuel H Kress Found 174 E 80th St New York NY 10021-0439

ACKERMAN, ROBERT JON, broadcast executive; b. Passaic, N.J., Nov. 8, 1948; s. James White and Bertha (Faure) A.; m. Kathleen Appleton Ackerman, June 7, 1975; children: William, David. BFA, NYU, 1971. Prin. Plus-Sound Ideas, Huntington, N.Y., 1971-73; producer, dir. Creative Prodns., Orange, N.J., 1973-78; dir. communications Ayerst Labs., N.Y.C., 1978-80; pres. Mediamerica Corp., Cedar Grove, N.J., 1980—; pres. Image Three Media Group, Cedar Grove, N.J., 1988—. Mem. Morris County Rep. Orgn., Denville, N.J., 1992—. Sgt. 1st class USNG, 1970-76. Recipient Gold Med. Film award John Muir Med. Film Festival, Walnut Creek, Ga., 1990. Republican. Methodist. Office: Mediamerica Corp 371 Little Falls Rd Cedar Grove NJ 07009

ACKERMANN, BARBARA BOGEL, counselor; b. Bay Shore, N.Y., Nov. 16, 1940; d. Charles Henry Jurgens and Marjorie (Stevens) Bogel; children: Erika, Stefan. BS in Polit. Sci., Ursinus Coll., 1962; MS in Counseling Edn., Long Island U., 1978, profl. diploma in counseling, 1982, postgrad. Lic. sch. adminstr., N.Y. Child protective worker Suffolk County (N.Y.) Social Svc., 1962-65; med. social worker St. Joseph's Hosp., Syracuse, N.Y., 1965-69; child protective worker Tallahassee (Fla.) Social Svc., 1967-68; RSVP coord. Suffolk County Ret. Sr. Vol. Program, 1975; sch. counselor Hampton Bays (N.Y.) High Sch., 1978-86; guidance dir., counselor Southold (N.Y.) High Sch., 1986—; treas. Human Understanding and Growth Seminars, Laurel, N.Y., 1987-89, bd. dirs., 1984-90. Alt. committeewoman Southold Town Rep. Com., 1976-83; deacon Presbyn. Ch., Mattituck, N.Y., 1977—. Mem. East End Counselors Assn. (pres. 1982, bd. dirs. 1979—), L.I. Counselors Ann. Conf. (co-chair 1985), N.Y. State Assn. for Counseling and Devel. (v.p. 1983-85, North Atlantic region rep. 1985-87), Am. Sch. Counselor Assn., N.Y. State Sch. Counselors Assn. (dist. gov. 1989-92), Rotary (bd. dirs.). Home: Azalea Rd # 330 Mattituck NY 11952-1951 Office: Southold High Sch Oaklawn Ave Southold NY 11971-1701

ACKERSON, JEFFREY TOWNSEND, computer systems executive; b. Waynesboro, Pa., June 20, 1944; s. Kenneth Townsend and Charlotte (Zucker) A.; m. Sharon Gail Dawkins, Feb. 24, 1968; children: Kenneth Wayne, Craig Townsend. BME, Rensselaer Poly. Inst., 1966; MS Computer Systems Mgmt., Naval Postgrad. Sch., 1976. Commd. ensign USN, 1966, advanced to Comdr., 1980; air/missile analyst Fleet Ocean Surveillance Info. Ctr., London, 1971-75; head programming div. Fleet Intelligence Ctr., Pearl Harbor, Hawaii, 1976-80; head info. mgmt. dept. Naval Intelligence Processing Systems Support Activity, Suitland, Md., 1980-84; instr. data communications Charles County Community Coll., La Plata, Md., 1983-87; chief communications systems software Def. Intelligence Agy., Washington, 1984-86; ret. USN, 1986; program dir. Integrated Microcomputer Systems, Inc., Dahlgren, Va., 1986-89; v.p. Integrated Microcomputer Systems, Inc., Rockville, Md., 1990—. Author papers in field. Data processing coord. Am. Youth Soccer Orgn., Aiea, Hawaii, 1977-80. Mem. Armed Forces Communications and Electronics Assn. Republican. Presbyterian. Home: 2548 Snow Hill Ct Waldorf MD 20602-2035 Office: Integrated Microcomputer Systems Inc 2 Research Pl Rockville MD 20850-3214

ACKERSON, NELS J(OHN), lawyer; b. Indpls., Apr. 12, 1944; s. Ralph D. and Mariel F. (Maze) A.; m. Sharon Carroll Ackerson, June 11, 1983; children by previous marriage: Betsy Virginia, Peter Nels; stepchildren: Stacia Carroll Loveall, Joshua Michael Loveall. BS with distinction, Purdue U., 1967, M in Pub. Policy, 1971; JD cum laude, Harvard U., 1971. Bar: Ind. 1971, U.S. Dist. Ct. (so. dist.) Ind. 1971, U.S. Ct. Appeals (7th cir.) 1971, D.C. 1985, U.S. Ct. Appeals (D.C. cir.) 1985, U.S. Supreme Ct. 1989. Advisor Harvard Adv. Mission to Republic of Columbia, 1970; assoc. Barnes, Hickam, Pantzer & Boyd, Indpls., 1971-76; chief counsel U.S. Senate Subcom. Constl. Amendments, Washington, 1976-77; chief counsel, exec. dir. U.S. Senate Subcom. on Constn., Washington, 1977-79; ptnr. Campbell, Kyle & Proffitt, Noblesville, Ind., 1979-82, Sidley & Austin, Cairo, Washington, 19823-91; chmn. Ackerson & Assocs., Chartered, Washington, 1991—, Ackerson & Bishop Chartered, Washington, 1991—. Bd. editors Harvard Law Rev., 1968-71. Dem. nominee for U.S. Congress, 5th dist., Ind., 1980. Mem. ABA (litigation sect., bus. and banking sect., internat. law sect.), Am. Soc. Internat. Law, Am. Agrl. Law Assn., Nat. Planning Assn., Am. C. of C. in Egypt (pres. 1984). Presbyterian. Office: 901 15th St NW Ste 1250 Washington DC 20005-2327

ACKLIN, THOMAS PATRICK, priest, seminary rector; b. Sewickley, Pa., Jan. 6, 1950; s. Thomas and Doris Lenore (Hallisey) A. BA in Philosophy, Duquesne U., 1971, MA, 1975; MDiv, St. Vincent Sem., 1978; Licentiate of Sacred Theology, U. Louvain, 1980, PhD, 1982, STD, 1983; postgrad., Belgian Sch. Psychoanalysis, 1980-82; diploma, Pitts. Psychoanalytic Ctr., 1985; postgrad., Pitts. Psychoanalytic Inst., 1985—. Ordained priest Roman Cath. Ch., 1980. Tchr. Seton High Sch., Balt., 1972-74, St. Mary of the Mt. High Sch., Pitts., 1974-75; lectr. St. Vincent Coll., Latrobe, Pa., 1976-78; asst. prof. St. Vincent Sem. and St. Vincent Coll., Latrobe, 1982-87, assoc. prof., 1987—; acting rector St. Vincent Sem., Latrobe, 1987-88, rector, 1989—; staff announcer, engr. Sta. WBJC-FM, Sta. WITH-AM-FM, Balt., 1973-74, host program Sta. WEDO-AM, 1988—, Sta. WTAE-TV, 1991—; grad. asst. Louvain U., 1980-82; pvt. practice, 1982—; psychotherapist Pitts. Psychoanalytic Ctr., 1983-85, Latrobe Psychotherapy Assocs. Inc., 1990—; dir. formation for jr.-professed monks St. Vincent Archabbey, 1983-87; psychoanalytic psychotherapist Latrobe Psychotherapy Assocs. Inc., 1991—. Contbr. articles to religious jours. Mem. Belgian Sch. Psychoanalysis (corr.), Nat. Assn. for Advancement Psychoanalysis (cert.), European Soc. for Psychology of Religion, Pitts. Psychoanalytic Soc. (assoc.), Soc. for Sci. Study of Religion, Menninger Found., Cath. Theol. Soc. Am., Ea. Conf. Maj. Sem. Rectors, Internat. Psychoanalytical Studies Orgn. Democrat. Home: St Vincent Archabbey Latrobe PA 15650 Office: St Vincent Sem Rector's Office Latrobe PA 15650 also: Latrobe Psychotherapy Assocs Inc PO Box QQ Fraser Purchase Rd Latrobe PA 15650

ACZEL, TAMAS, English educator; b. Budapest, Hungary, Dec. 16, 1921; came to U.S., 1966; s. Joseph and Cornelia (Fabian) A.; m. Eva Kadar, Sept. 3, 1948 (div. 1957); m. Olga Anna Gyarmati, Aug. 5, 1959; children: Julia, Thomas G. BA, Peter Pazmany U., Budapest, Hungary, 1948; MA, Eotvos Lorant U., Budapest, Hungary, 1950, DLitt, 1992. Journalist Budapest, Hungary, 1945-51; editor-in-chief Csillag, Budapest, 1951-54; sec. Hungarian Writers Assn., Budapest, 1953-54; freelance writer Budapest, 1954-55; editor Hungarian Lit. Gazette, London, 1957-66; sr. rsch. fellow Centre de Recherches et d'Etudes des Institutions Religieuse, Geneva, Switzerland, 1967-73; prof. English U. Mass., Amherst, 1966—. Author: In The Shadow of Liberty, 1949, Storm and Sunshine, 1951, The Ice Age, 1965, Illuminations, 1981, The Hunt, 1991. V.p. PEN-in-Exile, N.Y.C., 1982—. Recipient Kossuth prize for poetry Govt. of Hungary, 1949, Stalin prize for lit. Govt. of USSR, 1952; fellow Nat. Endowment for Arts, 1982; Fulbright scholar, Hungary, 1991-92. Home: 34 Amity Pl Amherst MA 01002-2255 Office: U Mass Dept of English Amherst MA 01003

ADAIR, WILLIAM B., conservator, historian; b. Takoma Park, Md., Nov. 5, 1949; s. James Franklin and Anne (Clark) A.; divorced; m. Kathryn Jackson, Apr. 4, 1985; 1 child, Anne Janvier Adair. BFA, U. Md., 1972. Art conservator Smithsonian Instn., Washington, 1972-82; frame historian, gilded surfaces specialist Gold Leaf Studios, Washington, 1982—. Author: The Frame in America, 1700-1900, 1983. Recipient Rome prize Am. Acad. in Rome, 1992. Mem. Am. Inst. Conservation Hist. Works Art, Am. Assn. Mus. Office: Gold Leaf Studios PO Box 50156 Washington DC 20091

ADAM, JOHN, translator; b. La Hulpe, Brabant, Belgium, Mar. 6, 1942; came to U.S., 1971; s. William and Elisabeth Anna (Aalders) A.; m. Marie Mickie, July 5, 1969; children: Philippe, Serge, Stephane. Student, U. Libre Brussels, 1960-62; MA in Translation, Inst. Superieur Traducteurs, Brussels, 1966. Prof. English, Spanish and translation Inst. Nat. Langs., Conakry, Guinea, 1966-70; translator Pres.' Office and Ministry Fgn. Affairs, Conakry, 1966-70; freelance translator Adia, Brussels, 1970-71; translator UN, N.Y.C., 1971-75, 76-77; translator UN, Addis Ababa, Ethiopia, 1975-76, translator, reviser, 1977-78, chief tng. officer, 1978-80, chief translation svcs., 1980-85; sr. translator UN, N.Y.C., 1985—. Trustee UN Internat. Sch. Bd., 1989—. Mem. Assn. for Promotion of Study of Modern Langs., Internat. Assn. Conf. Translators, Assn. Culturelle Francophone (dep. sec. gen. 1986—). Home: Apt 11J 560 W 43d St New York NY 10036 Office: UN UN Plz New York NY 10017

ADAMAKOS, ARTHUR LOUIS, educational administrator; b. Nashua, N.H., Mar. 9, 1956; s. Louis G. and Ann (Giotas) A. BA, Boston U., 1978; MEd, Rivier Coll., Nashua, N.H., 1984. Cert. prin., N.H. Tchr. Hillside Jr. High Sch., Manchester, N.H., 1979-81, Meml. High Sch., Manchester, 1981-88; asst. prin. West High Sch., Manchester, 1988—. Mem. Nat. Assn. Secondary Sch. Prins., N.H. Assn. Sch. Prins., Columbia Scholastic Press Assn., Phi Delta Kappa. Republican. Greek Orthodox. Home: 1196 Union St Manchester NH 03104 Office: Manchester High Sch West 9 Notre Dame Ave Manchester NH 03102-3999

ADAMCHEK, JANICE LYNN, personnel director; b. Seattle, Sept. 11, 1949; d. Vernon Wayne and Hazel Kathleen (Butcher) Beranek; m. Stacy Richard Mattox, July 8, 1967 (div. Oc. 1972); 1 child, Michael Sean; m. Thomas Bruce Adamchek, Aug. 4, 1979. Student, Montgomery Coll. and U. Md., 1971-78. Adminstrv. aide Dept. Transpn. Montgomery County, Silver Spring, Md., 1967-74; adminstrv. aide to asst. Community Service Ctr. Program Montgomery County, Silver Spring, 1974-79; various positions John Brown Engrs. & Constructors Inc. Trafalgar House Co., Stamford, Conn., 1979—; mgr. personnel John Brown Engrs. & Constructors Inc. Trafalgar House Co., Stamford, 1983—; rep. Coll. Placement Council, Bethlehem, Pa., 1982—. Active United Way, Silver Spring and Stamford 1968—. Mem. Nat. Constructors Assn. (employee rels. com. 1982-85, exec. com. 1986-87, 92—), Engring. Assocs. (exec. com. 1986-87, 92—). Home: 5 Boulder Ct Norwalk CT 06854-1704 Office: John Brown E & C PO Box 1432 333 Ludlow St Stamford CT 06904

ADAMO, MARY-ELLEN MCCANN, educator; b. Bristol, Conn., Aug. 22, 1942; d. Frank and Eleanor (Riccio) McCann; m. Michael Adamo Jr., Feb. 12, 1971; children: Mary Patricia, Michele Ellen. AB, Albertus Magnus Coll., 1964; MS, Cen. Conn. State U., 1976, postgrad., 1989; postgrad., U. Mass., 1989—. Substitute tchr. Torrington Region 7/Winsted (Conn.) Schs., 1966-67; tchr. English Pearson Sch., Winsted, 1967-68, 70-71, Orme Sch., Mayer, Ariz., 1968-69; tchr. 1st grade Ctr. Sch., Norfolk, Conn., 1969-70; tchr. Kindergarten and pre-sch. Hinsdale Sch., Winsted, 1971-73; tchr. kindergarten Batcheller Sch., Winsted, 1973-74, Title I reading and math. tchr., 1974-75; Title I reading and math. tchr. St. Anthony's Sch., Winsted, 1976-81; tchr. 5th grade Antolini Sch., New Hartford, Conn., 1981-82; computer coord. Talcott Mt. Sci. Ctr., Avon, Conn., 1982-84, asst. dir., 1984-86; mem. adj. faculty U. Hartford, West Hartford, Conn., 1985-86, Cen. Conn. State U., New Britain, 1989; prodn. supr. Nutmeg Ballet Co., Torrington, Conn., 1986—; presenter workshops; systems analyst Logical Syst Inc., Canton, Conn., 1986-88; real estate cons., Torrington, 1978—. Program dir., social worker YWCA, New Haven, 1964-65, instr. in adult edn., Phoenix, Ariz., 1965-66; mem. Peace Corps, Tucson, 1965. Mem. Phi Delta Kappa, Delta Kappa Gamma. Home: 606 W Hill Rd Winsted CT 06098-3052 Office: Nutmeg Ballet Co 21 Water St Torrington CT 06790-5319

ADAMS, ARLIN MARVIN, retired judge, counsel to law firm; b. Phila., Apr. 16, 1921; s. Aaron M. and Mathilda (Landau) A.; m. Neysa Cristol, Nov. 10, 1942; children: Carol (Mrs. Howard Kirshner), Judith A., Jane C. BS in Econs., Temple U., 1941; LLB, U. Pa., 1947, MA, 1950, DHL, 1964; DSc, Phila. Coll., 1965; LLD, Phila. Coll. Textiles, 1966, Susquehanna U., 1985, Muhlenberg Coll., 1986, Villanova U., 1987, Hebrew Union Coll., 1988. Bar: Pa. 1947. Law clk. Chief Justice Horace Stern, Pa. Supreme Ct., 1947; assoc. firm Schnader, Harrison, Segal & Lewis, Phila., 1947-50, sr. partner, 1950-63, 66-69; sec. pub. welfare Commonwealth of Pa., Phila., 1963-66; judge U.S. Ct. Appeals (3d cir.), Phila., 1969-87; counsel Schnader, Harrison, Segal & Lewis, Phila., 1987—; apptd. ind. counsel to investigate dept. HUD, 1990—; instr. Am. Inst. Banking, Phila., 1948-50; lectr. fed. practice Law Sch., U. Pa., Phila., 1952-56, lectr. constl. law, 1972—. Author: Law and Religion, 2 vols., 1991, A Nation Dedicated to Religious Liberty, 1990; contbr. articles to profl. jours. V.p. Fed. Jewish Agys., 1969-71, mem. exec. com. and cabinet, 1969-76; chmn. Albert Einstein Med. Ctr., Phila., 1984-87, Annenberg Inst., 1988-91; chmn. bd. dirs. Moss Rehab. Hosp., Phila., 1962-63; trustee U. Pa., 1985—; chmn. U.S. Supreme Ct. Jud. Fellows Comm., 1987—, Fels Inst. Govt., Phila., 1967-77, Sch. of Social Work, Bryn Mawr (Pa.) Coll., 1967-78, Diagnostic and Rehab. Ctr., Phila., 1971-72; chmn. overseers U. Pa. Law Sch., 1985-92; trustee Med. Coll. of Pa., 1974-80, German Marshall Meml. Fund, 1972-84, Lewis H. Stevens Trust, Bryn Mawr Coll., Med. Coll. of Pa., Columbia U. Ctr. for Law and Econ. Studies, U. of Pa. Inst. for Law and Econs., William Penn Found., Oliver Wendell Holmes Devise, 1992—. Lt. USNR, 1942-46, PTO. Recipient Disting. Service award U. Pa. Law Sch., 1981, Justice award Am. Jud. Soc., 1982, Cresset award Rosemont Coll., Gold Medallion award Chapel of Four Chaplains. Mem. Am. Law Inst., Am. Bar Found., ABA (del. ho. of dels. 1966-67, 75-77, chmn. trade assn. com.), Pa. Bar Assn. (del. ho. of dels. 1967-71) Phila. Bar Assn. (chancellor 1967), Am. Judicature Soc. (pres. 1975-77), Am. Philos. Soc. (sec. 1980-82, v.p. 1987—), Order of Coif, Beta Gamma Sigma. Clubs: Philadelphia, Locust, Union League, Sunday Breakfast, Legal (pres. 1986-91), Jr. Legal.

ADAMS, ARVIL VAN, educator, consultant, economist; b. Cape Girardeau, Mo., Jan. 31, 1943; s. Arvil V. and Evelyn G. (Liles) A.; m. Mary Benn Ammerman, May 26, 1968; children: Gregory Edwards, Christopher Conner, Cynthia Liles. Student, William Jewell Coll., 1961-63; BA, Memphis State U., 1965, MBA, 1966; MA, U. Ky., 1968, PhD, 1970. Asst. prof. U. Ky., Lexington, 1970-72, Ohio State U., Columbus, Ohio, 1972-73; rsch. assoc. Ohio State U., Columbus, 1972-74; prof., assoc. dir. Human Resources Inst. U. Utah, Salt Lake City, 1974-77; exec. dir. Nat. Commn. on Employment and Unemployment Statis., Washington, 1977-79; prof., dir. Grad. Inst. George Washington U., Washington, 1979-89; sr. economist The World Bank, Washington, 1989—. Author: monograph Toward Fair Employment and the EEOC, 1971; author: Lingering Crisis of Youth Employment, 1978. Trustee Bluefield (Va.) Coll., 1987—; treas. West Springfield Little League, Springfield, Va., 1981-86; pres. Rhygate Civic Orgn., Springfield, 1982; bd. dirs. Springfield Babe Ruth, 1985-88. Mem. Am. Econ. Assn., Assn. for Pub. Policy Analysis and Mgmt., Springfield Country Club. Democrat. Baptist. Home: 6431 Eastleigh Ct Springfield VA 22152-2425 Office: The World Bank Ste S6-051 1818 H St NW Washington DC 20433

ADAMS, BRENT LARSEN, metallurgical engineer; b. Provo, Utah, Sept. 26, 1949; s. Mack Spencer and Margaret (Larsen) A.; m. Hilary Jill Trunnell, May 28, 1971; children: Christian, Isaac, Benjamin. BS in Physics, U. Utah, 1974; MS in Metall. Engring., Ohio State U., 1976, PhD, 1979. Sr. rsch. engr. Lynchburg Rsch. Ctr., Babcock & Wilcox Co., Lynchburg, Va., 1976-79; advanced scientist Hanford Engring. Devel. Lab., Richland, Wash., 1979-80; asst. prof. Dept. Matls. Sci. and Engring., U. Fla., Gainesville, 1980-83; assoc. prof. Dept. Mech. Engring., Brigham Young U., Provo, Utah, 1984-88, Dept. Mech. Engring., Yale U., New Haven, 1988—; dir. Ctr. for Applied Mechanics, Yale U., 1989—. Contbr. articles to profl. jours. NSF Presdl. Young Investigator award, 1985, Henry Marion Howe medal, ASM Internat., 1987. Mem. Metall. soc. of AIME (chmn. shaping and forming com. 1987-89), ASM Internat. (chmn. texture com. 1986-88). Mem. Ch. of Jesus Christ of Latter Day Saints.

ADAMS, BRENT RAY, investment banker, bond salesperson; b. Dallas, Aug. 8, 1967; s. Roger Ray and Ella Jo (Zahn) A. BBA, Tex. A&M U., 1990. Fin. analyst Rainwater Inc./RS Holdings, Ft. Worth, 1990-91; assoc. Goldman Sachs & Co., N.Y.C., 1991—. Organizer, Sam Johnson for U.S. Congress Campaign, Dallas, 1991; mentor I Have A Dream Found., Ft. Worth, 1991; fundraiser Am. Heart Assn., Ft. Worth, 1991. Gathright scholar Tex. A&M U., 1990. Republican. Christian. Home: Apt 2H 730 Columbus Ave New York NY 10025

ADAMS, CHARLES SIEGEL, university program director, researcher; b. Lawrence, Mass., May 16, 1936; s. Claude Everman and Lorena (Siegel) A.; m. Maurianne Schifren, June 11, 1961 (div. May, 1978); m. Patricia Ann Harrison, Apr. 21, 1984. BA, Haverford Coll., 1958; MA, Ind. U., 1968, PhD, 1972. Lectr. Marlboro (Vt.) Coll., 1960-61; teaching asst. Ind. U., Bloomington, 1961-64; instr. U. Mass., Amherst, 1964-70, asst. prof., 1970-76, dir., 1972—, dir. higher edn., 1988—; cons. N.J. Dept. Higher Edn., 1985, 89, 90, USAID, Malawi, 1988, 89. U.S.-Scandinavian Found. fellow, 1959, Ford Found. fellow, 1962. Mem. Am. Assn. for Higher Edn., Am. Assn. for Study of Higher Edn., Am. Ednl. Rsch. Assn., Am. Folklore Soc. Home: 271 Old Greenfield Rd Shelburne Falls MA 01370-9664 Office: U Mass Amherst Ednl Policy Adminstrn Dept Amherst MA 01003

ADAMS, (LEWIS) DEAN, theater director; b. Seattle, July 22, 1957; s. Brockman and Mary Elizabeth (Scott) A.; m. Kristin Cook Gilbert, June 20, 1981. BA in Drama and English, Tufts U., 1980; MA in TV-Film, U. Md., 1986. Stage prodn. mgr. Shakespeare and Co., Washington, 1975-79; asst. stage mgr. Arena Stage, Washington, 1976; tech. dir. St. Albans Sch., Washington, 1980-82; dir. theater Loomis Chaffee Sch., Windsor, Conn., 1982-88, Westminster Sch., Simsbury, Conn., 1989—; artistic dir. Centennial Theater Festival, Simsbury, 1989—. Dir. (U.K. tour) Dining Room, 1985; dir., producer (1st Chinese tour of Am. mus.) Once Upon a Mattress, 1987. Grantee Ford Found., 1984; scholar Tufts U., 1978-80. Mem. Internat. Brotherhood Magicians, Soc. Am. Magicians, Soc. of Stage Dirs. and Choreographers. Democrat. Episcopalian. Home: PO Box 342 Weatogue CT 06089-0342 Office: Westminster Sch Weatogue CT 06089

ADAMS, DENNIS PAUL, artist; b. Des Moines, Nov. 15, 1948; s. Paul Thomas Adams and Stella Vernita (Bushman) MacGregor; 1 child, Todd Dennis Haffner; m. Jody Rodman Walker, Oct. 8, 1981; 1 child, Jack Walker Adams. BFA, Drake U., 1969; MFA, Tyler Sch. Art, Phila., 1971. vis. artist Parsons Sch., N.Y.C., 1990, Cooper Union, N.Y.C., 1988; asst. prof. Tyler Sch. Art, 1976, Ohio Sch. Art, Athens, 1972-75. Numerous one-man shows include de Appel Found., Amsterdam, The Netherlands, 1988, The Clocktower, N.Y.C., 1988, Galerie Meert-Rihoux, Brussels, 1989, John Weber Gallery, N.Y.C., 1989, Galerie Gabrielle Maubrie, Paris, 1990, Kent Fine Art, N.Y.C., 1990, Hirschhorn Mus., Washington, 1990, Mus. Modern Art, N.Y.C., 1991, Fundacio la Caixa, Barcelona, Spain, 1992, Portikus, Frankfurt, Germany, 1992; contbr. articles to profl. jours. Bd. govs. N.Y. Found. for Arts, N.Y.C., 1989-92. NEA fellowship grantee, 1984, 88; recipient Visual Artists Project award N.Y. State Coun. on Arts, 1984. Home: 42 Walker St New York NY 10013-3588

ADAMS, DIANE LORETTA, physician; b. St. Louis, Nov. 3, 1948; m. William McKinley Adams; children: Kareem McKinley, Dawn Caron, Akeem Michael. BS, Howard U., 1969; MD, N.J. Med. Sch., 1976; MPH, resident in gen. preventive medicine, Johns Hopkins U., 1980. Resident in family practice Howard U. Hosp., Washington, 1976-79; chief med. officer USCG Shipyard, Curtis Bay, Md., 1980-83, Bur. Engraving and Printing, Washington, 1983-85; med. officer St. Elizabeth Hosp., Washington, 1985-86; rsch. analyst Office Asst. Sec. Health, Rockville, Md., 1987-90; chief minority health svcs. rsch. program Agy. Health Care Policy and Rsch., Rockville, 1990—; congl. fellow office of Congressman Louis Stokes U.S. Ho. of Reps., Washington, 1990; cons. rep. AIDS Task Force, Rockville, 1987—; pres. Scholarship Search, Inc., 1991—; lectr. intensive bioethics Georgetown U. Kennedy Inst. Ethics, 1991—. Mem. Commd. Officers Assn., Alpha Kappa Alpha (Outstanding Community Svc. award 1981-85). Home: 17032 Barn Ridge Dr Silver Spring MD 20906-1106

ADAMS, FRANCES GRANT, II, lawyer; b. Wheeling, W.Va., Nov. 30, 1955; d. Jack Richard and Frances Irene (Grant) A. BA, W.Va. U., 1976, JD, 1979; MA, Webster U., 1983. Bar: W.Va. 1979, U.S. Dist. Ct. (so. dist.) W.Va. 1979, U.S. Ct. Mil. Appeals 1979, U.S. Supreme Ct. 1988, D.C. 1989. Asst. staff judge advocate armament div. USAF, Eglin AFB, Fla., 1979-82; dep. staff judge advocate USAF, Keflavik, Iceland, 1982-83; staff judge advocate 71st Air Base Group USAF, Vance AFB, Okla., 1984-86; chief gen. torts sect. claims and tort litigation staff hdqrs. USAF, Washington, 1986-88; chief mgmt. and analysis br. claims and tort litigation div. Air Force Legal Svcs. Agy., Washington, 1988-92, sr. tort atty. claims and tort litigation div., 1992—. Procedures manual chmn. DAR, W.Va., 1989-92. Mem. Fed. Bar Assn. (program chmn. Pentagon chpt. 1989-90), DAR (W.Va. procedures manual chmn. 1989-92), Lions (sec. Annandale club 1990—).

ADAMS, GEORGE GABRIEL, mechanical engineering educator; b. Bklyn., Sept. 12, 1948; s. George Gabriel and Sally Mary (Saydah) A.; m. Janet Hope Magenheim, Apr. 29, 1984; children: Juliana Sally, Daniel Gabriel. BS, Cooper Union U., 1969; MS, U. Calif., Berkeley, 1972, PhD, 1975. Asst. prof. Clarkson U., Potsdam, N.Y., 1975-78; rsch. assoc. IBM Rsch. Lab., San Jose, Calif., 1978-79; asst. prof. Northeastern U., Boston, 1979-81, assoc. prof., 1981-86, prof. mech. engring., 1986—, dir. grad. studies mech. engring. dept., 1989-91; vis. scholar U. Calif., Berkeley, 1979. Assoc. editor jour. Tribology Transactions, 1989-91; contbr. articles to profl. jours. NSF fellow, 1970-73; NSF grantee, 1975-76, 76-78. Mem. ASME (exec. com. Boston sect. 1989-91), Soc. Engring. Sci., Am. Acad. Mechanics, Am. Soc. Engring. Educators, Soc. Tribologists and Lubrication Engrs. Office: Northeastern U Mech Engring Dept Boston MA 02115

ADAMS, GEORGE HAROLD, hospital and health executive; b. N.Y.C., July 19, 1926; s. George Harold and Charlotte (Dunbar) A.; m. Lorette Christine Johnson, Oct. 14, 1950; children: Douglas, Lori. BA, NYU, 1950; MS, Columbia U., 1955; HHD, Capitol U., 1983, LHD, 1988. Adminstr. Meth. Hosp. of Bklyn., 1955-66; pres. Luth. Med. Ctr., Bklyn., 1966—; adj. prof. NYU, 1982—, mem. adv. bd., 1984—; pres. Shore Rd. Community Svcs., Bklyn., 1985—. Contbr. articles to profl. jours. Pres. Shore Hill Housing Co., Bklyn., 1977; chmn. governing coun. Health Sci. Ctr. at Bklyn., 1983. Sgt. U.S. Army, 1944-47, ETO. Fellow Am. Coll. Healthcare Execs. (Adminstr. of the Yr. 1984); mem. Am. Hosp. Assn. (ho. of dels. 1981—), Hempstead (N.Y.) Country Club. Office: Luth Med Ctr 150 55th St Brooklyn NY 11220-2559

ADAMS, JAMES MILLS, chemical executive; b. Sioux Falls, S.D., Aug. 4, 1936; m. Sherrell D.; 2 children. BSChemE, S.D. Sch. Mines and Tech., 1958; MS in Engring., U. Wash., 1961, PhD in Chem. Nuclear Engring., 1962. Sr. engring specialist aerophysics research Aerojet-Gen. Corp., Sacramento, Calif., 1962-68; sr. spectroscopist Hoffmann La Roche, Inc., Nutley, N.J., 1968-70, sr. scientist applied scis. dept., 1970-73, mgr. CVA engring., 1974-76; plant mgr. aroma chem. plant Haarmann and Reimer Corp., Springfield, N.J., 1976-79, v.p., gen. mgr. aroma chem. div., 1978-85, exec. v.p., 1979-80, pres., chief exec. officer, 1980—, chief exec. officer, 1985—; mem. adv. bd. Cook Coll., Rutgers U., 1985-92; corp. v.p. Miles, Inc., 1989-91; chmn. bd. Creations Aromatiques, Inc., 1990—. Assoc. editor Pyrodynamics, 1966-69; contbr. over 40 articles to profl. jours.; patentee in fields of med. instrumentation, emission spectrometry, pyrometry, remote sensing, others. Mem. Charleston County Aviation Commn., 1978-79; internat. adv. coun. Monell Ctr., 1990—. H.L. Doherty Ednl. Found. scholar 1954-58; W. Alton Jones fellow, 1959-60; recipient Centennial 100 Alumni award, S.D. Sch. Mines and Tech., 1985. Mem. AAAS, Am. Phys. Soc., Am. Mgmt. Assn., Flavor and Extract Mfrs. Assn. (bd. govs. 1985—, v.p., sec. 1989—, pres. elect 1990, pres. 1992), Fragrance Materials Assn. (bd. dirs. 1985—, pres. 1988—92, Rsch. Inst. for Fragrance Materials (chmn. bd. dirs. 1984-89, vice chmn. 1989-90), N.J. C. of C., Pres. Assn., Optimists Club (pres. Watchung chpt. 1984-85), Sigma Xi (pres. Roche Rsch. club 1973-74). Home: 171 Hillcrest Rd Wachung NJ 07060-6005 Office: Haarmann & Reimer Corp PO Box 175 Springfield NJ 07081-0175

ADAMS, JOHN LAURENCE, information systems specialist; b. Reading, Pa., Feb. 24, 1943; s. Charles Anthony and Edith May (Frame) A. BS, Lehigh U., 1965, MBA, 1978. Data processing trainee IBM, Bethlehem, Pa., 1966-67, mktg. rep. data processing div., 1967-72, adv. mktg. rep., 1973-76, internat. account mgr., 1976-84; v.p. info. systems Caesars Atlantic City Casino/Hotel, 1984-91; pres. ACT Inc., Malvern, Pa., 1991—; v.p. AGSA INYNEX Svcs. Inc., Phila., 1991—. Bd. dirs., mem. fin. com., chmn. mgmt. assistance program, v.p. long range planning, v.p. community instns., exec. com. United Way of Atlantic County; trustee Atlantic Mental Health Ctrs. With U.S. Army, 1965-71. Mem. Data Processing Mgmt. Assn., Pa. Soc. Republican. Roman Catholic. Home: 4038 4th Ave Avalon NJ 08202-1444 Office: 880 First Ave 175 W King St King of Prussia PA 19406

ADAMS, JOHN WILLIAM, psychology educator; b. McKeesport, Pa., Nov. 4, 1956; s. William and Mary Ann (Ragan) A. BS in Edn., Pa. State U., 1978; MA in Edn., UCLA, 1982, PhD in Edn., 1986. Lic. sch. psychologist. Tchr. emotionally disturbed children Armstrong-Indiana County Intermediate Unit, Shelocta, Pa., 1978-79, Monrovia (Calif.) Unified Sch. Dist., 1979-80; sch. psychologist L.A. County Schs., Downey, Calif., 1984-85; teaching assoc. UCLA Grad. Sch. Edn., 1983-85, lectr., 1985-86; sch. psychologist, counselor Tripod, A Presch. for Deaf Children, L.A.,

1984-86; coord. of counseling program Calif. State U., San Bernardino, 1987-89, asst. prof. edn., 1986-89; assoc. prof. psychology Rochester (N.Y.) Inst. Tech., 1989—, also dir. sch. psychology and deafness program; cons. Tchr. Edn. Lab., UCLA, 1982-83, rsch. asst. Grad. Sch. Edn., 1981-83; psychology technician VA, L.A., 1981-92. Author: You and Your Hearing Impaired Child, 1988; contbr. articles to profl. jours. Recipient James J. Pessas Meml. award govt. internship program UCLA, 1982; fellow UCLA, 1982-86, dissertation rsch. grantee, 1985; mini-grantee Rochester Inst. Tech., 1990-91, grantee U.S. Dept. Edn., 1992. Mem. APA, Am. Assn. Counseling and Devel., Am. Ednl. Rsch., Nat. Assn. Sch. Psychologists, Coun. for Exceptional Children, N.Y. State Assn. of Edn. of the Deaf, N.Y. Assn. of Sch. Psychologists, Pa. State U. Alumni Assn., UCLA Alumni Assn., Pi Lambda Theta. Office: Rochester Inst Tech One Lomb Meml Dr Rochester NY 14623

ADAMS, JULIUS GREGG, educational psychologist; b. Buffalo, Oct. 4, 1957; s. Peter William and Evalyn (Stanley) A.; m. Carmon Grigsby, July 29, 1991. BA, SUNY, Buffalo, 1978, MA, 1985, PhD, 1988. Cert. sch. psychologist, N.Y. Psychometrician Clarence (N.Y.) Cen. Schs., summers 1980-82; instr. Millard Fillmore Coll. SUNY, Buffalo, 1986; asst. prof. edn. SUNY, Fredonia, 1988—; sch. psychologist Buffalo Pub. Schs., 1982-87; psychologist Mobile Mental Health Team, West Seneca, N.Y., 1987-88; edn. specialist Liberty Ptnrship. Program, Fredonia, 1990; cons. ARC, Buffalo, 1986. Co-author: How Much Do Future Teachers Know About AIDS?; contbr. articles to profl. jours. Mem. Am. Ednl. Rsch. Assn., Psychol. Assn. Western N.Y., Ea. Ednl. Rsch. Assn., Calif. Ednl. Rsch. Assn. Office: SUNY Coll at Fredonia 236E Thompson Hall Fredonia NY 14063

ADAMS, KAREN COOPER, scholar exchange program director; b. Electra, Tex., Sept. 11, 1941; d. Samuel A. M. and Mabel Opal (Toby) Cooper; m. Jerry Lee Adams, Mar. 16, 1974; children: Alaina, Alicia, Lori. MusB, Hardin-Simmons U., 1964; MusM, Tex. Christian U., 1965; PhD, Ohio U., 1975. Visiting prof. art Denison U., Granville, Ohio, 1976-78; arts adminstr. S.E. Ohio Cultural Arts Ctr., Athens, 1978-79; chmn., fine arts dept. Roanoke Coll., Salem, Va., 1979-85; dir. programs Nat. Coun. Internat. Health, Washington, 1985-86; arts cons. Artworks, Columbia, Md., 1986-87; mng. dir. Arna Vodenos Prodns., Rockville, Md., 1987-89; arts dir. U. Coll., U. Md., College Park, 1989-90; area chief of Western Europe Coun. for Internat. Exchange Scholars, Washington, 1990—; exec. com. Internat. Coun. Fine Arts Deans, 1983-85. Mem. arts grants com. Howard County Arts Coun., Ellicott City, Md., 1987—. Fellow Danforth Fellows; mem. Soc. Values Edn., Coll. Music Soc. (life), Sigma Alpha Iota (life, chpt. pres. 1963-64, Leadership award 1964). Home: 9639 Cold Star Ct Columbia MD 21046-2064 Office: Coun for Internat Exch of Scholars 3007 Tilden St NW Ste 5M Washington DC 20008-3009

ADAMS, KATHLEEN MARGARET, principal; b. Providence, Aug. 9, 1952; d. Chester E. and Marie R. (Hannon) A. BA, Mt. St. Joseph Coll., 1974; MEd, Providence Coll., 1984. Cert. elem. sch. tchr., R.I., cert. in religion in the Diocese of Providence, 1987; notary public, 1988. Elem. tchr. St. Brendan Sch., East Providence, R.I., 1974-78; jr. high sch. tchr. St. Rose of Lima Sch., Warwick, R.I., 1981-85; asst. prin. St. Kevin Sch., Warwick, 1985-86; prin. Cranston-Johnston Cath. Region, Cranston, R.I., 1986—; park ranger Dept. of Environ. Mgmt., Narragansett, R.I., 1984-85. Mem. accreditation com. Bayview Acad.; mem. ad hoc com. for parish tax assessment program Diocese of Providence. Named Outstanding Coll. Athlete Am., 1974. Mem. ASCD, Nat. Cath. Ednl. Assn. (mem. exec. com. of dept. elem. schs. N.E. chpt. 1990—), Internat. Reading Assn., Delta Kappa Gamma. Roman Catholic. Home: 50 Deacon Ave Warwick RI 02886-5104 Office: Cranston-Johnston Cath Region 43 Poplar Dr Cranston RI 02920-5788

ADAMS, LAURIE MARIE, art historian, psychoanalyst, educator; b. N.Y.C., Sept. 29, 1941; d. Daniel Edward and Helen Louise (Nelson) Schneider; m. John Brett Adams, July 24, 1970; children: Alexa, Caroline. MA in Art History, Tulane U., 1962; MA in Psychology, Columbia U., 1963, PhD in Art History, 1967. Prof. art history John Jay Coll. and Grad. Ctr., CUNY, . N.Y., 1966—; vis. asst. prof. U. Fla., Gainesville, 1967, Sarah Lawrence Coll., Bronxville, N.Y., 1967, Mt. Holyoke Coll., 1972; lectr. Columbia U., N.Y.C., 1968, instr. Sch. of Visual Arts, N.Y.C., 1976; pvt. psychoanalytic practice N.Y.C., 1978—. Recipient CUNY summer travel grantee, 1967, 68; Columbia summer travel grantee, 1967, 86. Mem. PEN, Mystery Writers Am., Am. Psychol. Assn. (assoc.), Coll. Art Assn., N.Y. Center for Psychoanalytic Tng. Author children's books. Editor: Giotto in Perspective, 1974, Source: Notes in the History of Art; author: Art Cop, 1974, Art on Trial, 1976; contbr. articles to profl. jours. Office: 899 10th Ave New York NY 10019-1029

ADAMS, LOWELL WILLIAM, wildlife biologist; b. Harrisonburg, Va., Aug. 8, 1946; s. David Martin and Vesta (Landis) A.; m. Patricia Ann Ruhlman, July 25, 1970; 1 child, Christopher. BS, Va. Poly. Inst., 1968; MS, Ohio State U., 1973, PhD, 1976. Cert. wildlife biologist. Wildlife biologist Urban Wildlife Rsch. Ctr., Columbia, Md., 1976-80, rsch. dir., 1980-83; v.p. rsch. Nat. Inst. for Urban Wildlife, Columbia, 1983—; instr. U. Md., College Park, 1987—. Co-author: Wildlife Reserves and Corridors in the Urban Environment, 1989; co-editor: Integrating Man and Nature in the Metropolitan Environment, 1987, Wildlife Conservation in Metropolitan Environments, 1991. Recipient Conservation award Chevron U.S.A., Inc., 1987. Mem. The Wildlife Soc., Am. Ornithologists Union, Am. Soc. Mammalogists, Wilson Ornithol. Soc. Office: Nat Inst Urban Wildlife 10921 Trotting Ridge Way Columbia MD 21044-2831

ADAMS, LYNDA CHUCHKO, internal auditor; b. Pitts., Mar. 21, 1961; d. Edward C. and Betty Jane (Dzombak) Chuchko; m. Ciro E. Adams, Dec. 17, 1988; 1 child, Tyler Edward. BA, Franklin & Marshall Coll., 1983. CPA, Pa. Sr. auditor Pannell Kerr Forster, Phila., 1983-86; internal auditor Underwood Meml. Hosp., Woodbury, N.J., 1986—. Treas. Gloucester County Young Reps., 1990-91, commiteewoman Gloucester County Rep. Exec. com., 1991. Mem. AICPA, Healthcare Fin. Mgmt. Assn., Healthcare Internal Audit Group, Pa. Inst. of CPAs. Mem. Assembly of God. Home: 2 Barry Dr Mantua NJ 08051-1170 Office: Underwood Meml Hosp 509 N Broad St Woodbury NJ 08096-1617

ADAMS, MICHAEL R., marketing director; b. Frederick, Md., Oct. 18, 1954; s. Frank R. Jr. and Joan E. (Lipps) A.; m. Theresa Mary O'Connell, Apr. 1, 1978; children: Alexis Theresa, Henry Maxwell. BA in Biology, U. Va., 1976; postgrad., Mt. St. Mary's Coll. Rsch. assoc. Frederick Cancer Rsch. Facility, 1976-83; sales rep. BioWhittaker, Inc., Walkersville, Md., 1983-86, product mgr., 1986-88; dir. mktg. BioWhittaker, Inc., Walkersville, 1988—. Contbr. articles to profl. jours. Mem. Internat. Embryo Transfer Soc., Am. Mgmt. Assn., Am. Acad. Sci., Biomed. Mktg. Assn. Office: BioWhittaker Inc 8830 Biggs Ford Rd A08 Walkersville MD 21793

ADAMS, MIGNON STRICKLAND, library director; b. Chickasha, Okla.; d. Augustus and Donna Vea (Forehand) S.; children: Melinda Bartscherer, Benjamin Adams. BS, Eastern Ill. U., 1962; MSLS, U. Ill., 1966, postgrad., 1968-70. Coord. media svcs. Sch. Dist. #7, Tolono, Ill., 1962-66; campus sch. libr. Eastern Ill. U., Charleston, 1966-67; libr. dir. Lake Land Coll., Mattoon, Ill., 1967-69; coord. libr. instruction SUNY, Oswego, 1971-82, assoc. dir. info. svcs., 1981-85; dir. libr. svcs. Phila. Coll. Pharmacy and Sci., 1985—; bd. dirs. Health Scis. Libr. Consortium, Phila., Tri-State Coll. Libr. Coop., Phila. Author: Teaching Library Skills for Academic Credit, 1985; contbr. articles to profl. jours. Overseer Phila. Monthly Meeting of Friends, Phila., 1989—. Mem. ALA, Assn. of Coll. and Rsch. Librs. (chair coll. libr. sect. 1992-93), Am. Assn. Colls. and Pharmacy (chair librs. and ednl. resources sect. 1989-91), Del. Valley Assn. of Coll. and Rsch. Librs. (bd. dirs., chair 1989-91). Mem. Soc. of Friends.

ADAMS, NOAH, broadcaster; b. Ashland, Ky.. With WCMI/Ashland, WSAZ/Huntington and WCYB/Bristol, 1963-65, constrn. co., automobile dealership and advt. agy., 1965-71; part-time rock 'n' roll announcer Sta. WBKT-FM U. Ky., 1971-74, host morning news and music program, 1974-75; editor, writer Nat. Pub. Radio, Washington, 1975-78, co-host of weekend All Things Considered newsmag., 1978-82, weekday co-host, 1982-88, host All Things Considered newsmag., 1989—; host Minn. Pub. Radio's Good Evening, 1988; host Am. West series Nat. Pub. Radio, Boise, Idaho, 1989. Author: A Radio Journal, 1992; collector essays from Good Evening Saint Croix Notes: River Mornings, Radio Nights. Recipient Prix Italia, Alfred I. duPont-Columbia U., Major Armstrong, Cindy and Clarion awards. Office: Nat Pub Radio All Things Considered 2025 M St NW Washington DC 20036-3309*

ADAMS, PAT, artist, educator; b. Stockton, Calif., July 8, 1928; d. Roy Alanson and Minerva Matilda (Smith) A.; m. Vincent John Longo, Apr.21, 1951 (div. 1969); children: Matthew Adams, Jason Rice; m. R. Arnold Ricks III, June 24, 1972. B.A., U. Calif.-Berkeley, 1949; student, Calif. Coll. Arts and Crafts, 1945, Chgo. Art Inst., 1947, Bklyn. Mus. Art Sch., 1950-51. Mem. art faculty Bennington Coll., Vt., 1964—; vis. critic of painting Yale U. Sch. Art, New Haven, Conn., 1971-72, 76, 79, 82-83, Yale/Norfolk, Conn., 1987, vis. prof. painting, 1990—; vis. lectr. Queens Coll., N.Y.C., 1972; vis. artist U. Iowa, 1976, U. N. Mex., 1978, U. Western Ky., 1978, Columbia U., 1979, Cornell U., 1984, Mills Coll., Calif., 1987, R.I. Sch. Design, 1989, U. Mass., Amherst, 1989, Skidmore Coll., Saratoga Springs, N.Y., 1992. One-woman shows Zabriskie Gallery, N.Y.C., biannually 1954—, Rutgers U. Art Mus., 1978, Contemporary Art Ctr., Cin., 1979, Columbia Mus. Art and Sci., S.C., 1982, Va. Commonwealth U., 1982, Haggin Mus., Stockton, Calif., 1986, U. Va., 1986, N.Y. Acad. Scis., 1988, AAAS, Washington, 1988, Addison-Ripley Galleries, Washington, 1988, Pat Adams Paintings 1968-88, Berkshire Mus., 1988-89; exhibited in group travelling show New Eng. Art Now (De Cordova Mus., Mass., 1987, Bowdoin Art Mus., Maine, 1988, List Gallery, 1988, Currier Gallery, N.H., New Britain Contemporary Art Mus., Conn., 1988, Fleming Mus., Vt., 1989); also exhibited in group shows, Montclair Art Mus., N.J., Berkshire Mus., Pittsfield, Mass., 1981, Boston Mus. Fine Arts., 1982, Mus. Fine Arts, Houston, 1982, U. Hawaii-Hilo, 1983, Lehigh U., 1983, Chrysler Mus., Norfolk, Va., 1983, Hassam Purchase Fund of Am. Acad. and Inst. Arts and Letters, 1983, 85, 89, Md. Inst. Coll. Art Meyerhoff Gallery, 1986, Yale Sch. Art Faculty, 1950-90, Marilyn Pearl Gallery, N.Y.C., 1990, Brattleboro Art Ctr., 1991, Webb-Parsons Gallery, Burlington, Vt., 1991. Mem. Yaddo Found., 1972—, bd. dirs., 1980-92, vice chmn., 1985-88; trustee Vt. Council for Arts, 1977-81, Williamstown Regional Art Conservation Lab., 1985-86. Recipient award Nat. Council for Arts, 1968, Achievement award Stockton Arts Commn., 1985; award in art Am. Acad. and Inst. Arts and Letters, 1986; Fulbright scholar, 1956; grantee Yaddo Found., 1954, 64, 69, 70, McDowell Colony, 1968, 72, Nat. Endowment Arts, 1976, 87. Fellow Vt. Acad. Arts and Scis.; mem. Coll. Art Assn. (bd. dirs. 1986-90, Disting. Teaching of Art award 1984), Phi Beta Kappa, Delta Epsilon. Home: 370 Elm St Bennington VT 05201-2214

ADAMS, RICHARD GLENN, marketing executive; b. Johnson City, N.Y., Apr. 21, 1951; s. Charles Albert and Audrey Jane (Bennett) A.; m. Rosalie Eva Strickland, Aug. 21, 1971; 1 child, Alicia Rose. Student, U. Ill., 1969-70; BA in History, Syracuse U., 1973, BA in Journalism, 1973; MA in History, Bob Jones U., Greenville, S.C., 1975. Writer Binghamton (N.Y.) Sun Bull., 1968-69, Urbana (Ill.) Courier, 1969-70; writer/intern Binghamton Press, 1971; news dir. WMHR-FM, Syracuse, N.Y., 1971-73; editor BJU Press, Greenville, 1973-77; dir. mktg. IBM Credit Union, Endicott, N.Y., 1977-80; sr. v.p. LRK, Binghamton, 1980-81; pres., owner Adams Communications, Vestal, N.Y., 1981-85; dir. mktg. svcs. CAE-Link Corp., Binghamton, 1985—. Author: Who Owns Your Child, 1975; editor Faith for the Family, 1973-77, Real Time, 1990—. Cons. YMCA of Broome County, Binghamton, 1984-90; sec. B.C. Open PGA Golf Tourney, Endicott, 1971; pres. Parent-Tchr. Group, 1983-86; mem. adv. bd., trustee Calvary Bapt. Tabernacle, Vestal, N.Y., 1990—. Mem. Army Aviation Assn. Am. (chpt. v.p. 1988—), Nat. Security Indsl. Assn. (MPTcom. 1989—), Fin. Mktg. Assn., Assn. U.S. Army, Navy League, Am. Def. Preparedness Assn., Nat. Tng. Systems Assn., Naval Helicopter Assn. Office: CAE-Link Corp PO Box 1237 Binghamton NY 13902-1237

ADAMS, ROBERT ARTHUR, JR., insurance agent; b. Rochester, N.Y., Feb. 2, 1959; s. Robert A. and Joan F. (Bacon) A. BA, Boston Coll., 1981; postgrad., Am. Coll., 1982. Ins. broker John Hancock Life, Wellesley, Mass., 1981-87, Adams Fin., Lowell, Mass., 1988—. Mem. Million Dollar Round Table, Merrimack C. of C. Republican. Roman Catholic. Office: Adams Fin 191 Pawtucket Blvd Lowell MA 01854

ADAMS, ROBERT MCCORMICK, anthropologist, educator; b. Chgo., July 23, 1926; s. Robert McCormick and Janet (Lawrence) A.; m. Ruth Salzman Skinner, July 24, 1953; 1 dau., Megan. PhB, U. Chgo., 1947, MA, 1952, PhD, 1956; DSc (hon.), U. Pitts., 1985, Dartmouth Coll., 1989; LHD (hon.), Hunter Coll., CUNY, 1986, Coll. William and Mary, 1989. Archaeol. field tng. in Jarmo, Iraq, 1950-51, Yucatan, Mex., 1953; field studies history irrigation and urban settlement Iraq, Saudi Arabia and Iran, 1956-77; reconnaissance and excavation ancient Mayan settlement patterns Chiapas, Mex., 1958-61; mem. faculty dept. anthropology Oriental Inst., U. Chgo., 1955-84, assoc. prof. Oriental Inst., 1961-62, prof., 1962-84, dir. Oriental Inst., 1962-68, 81-83, dean div. social scis., 1970-74, 79-80, provost, 1982-84; sec. Smithsonian Instn., Washington, 1984—; adj. prof. Johns Hopkins U., 1984—; resident dir. Baghdad Sch., Am. Schs. Oriental Research, 1968-69; chmn. assembly behavioral and social scis. NRC, 1972-76, chmn. commn. on behavioral and social scis. and edn., 1987—. Author: Land Behind Baghdad, 1965, The Evolution of Urban Society, 1966, (with H.J. Nissen) The Uruk Countryside, 1972, Heartland of Cities, 1981; Editor: (with C. H. Kraeling) City Invincible: A Symposium on Urbanization and Cultural Development in the Ancient Near East, 1960, (with C.S. Schelling) Corners of a Foreign Field, 1979, (with N.J. Smelser and D.J. Treiman) Behavioral and Social Science Research: A National Resource, 1982. Trustee Nat. Opinion Ctr., 1970—, Nat. Humanities Ctr., 1976-83, Russell Sage Found., 1978-91, Santa Fe Inst., 1984—, Am. U. Beirut, 1989—, Morehouse Coll., 1989—. Served with USNR, 1944-46. Recipient medal UCLA, 1989. Fellow Am. Acad. Arts and Scis., Mid. East Studies Assn., Iraqi Acad. (asso.). AAAS, Am. Anthrop. Assn.; mem. NAS, Soc. Am. Archaeology, German Archaeol. Inst., Am. Philos. Soc., Coun. Fgn. Rels., Soc. Antiquaries of London, Sigma Xi. Office: Smithsonian Inst Office of Sec 1000 Jefferson Dr SW Washington DC 20560

ADAMS, ROGER JAMES, art history educator; b. Ogden, Utah, Feb. 3, 1935; s. Claude Leroy and Hazel Lavon (Wood) A.; m. Sharon Hatch, Dec. 8, 1954 (div. July 1959); children: Eve, Timothy; m. Diane K. Adams, Nov. 21, 1964; children: Benjamin, Rachel, Mark, Peter, Suzanne, Elizabeth. BA, Brigham Young U., 1961, MA, 1965; PhD, Pa. State U., 1971. Asst. animator Walt Disney Prodns., Burbank, Calif., 1955-58; asst. prof. Dixie Coll., St. George, Utah, 1965-68; assoc. prof. SUNY, Brockport, 1971-81; prof. Nazareth Coll., Rochester, 1981—; bd. dirs. Meml. Art Gallery, Rochester. Author: Eastern Portal of North Transept at Chartres, 1982; contbr. articles to profl. jours. Producer Hill Cumorah Pageant, Palmyra, N.Y., 1987-91. With U.S. Army, 1959-61. Office: Nazareth Coll 9245 East Ave Rochester NY 14618-3829

ADAMS, THELMA MICHELLE, fundraising executive, writer, critic, consultant; b. L.A., Feb. 7, 1959; d. Lawrence Julius and Rosalie (Vinocor) Schwartz; m. Ranald Trevor Adams, Nov. 29, 1986. BA, U. Calif., Berkeley, 1981; MBA in Arts Mgmt., UCLA, 1985; postgrad., Columbia U., 1990—. Program asst. Am. Film Inst., Washington, 1981; asst. editor Am. Hist. Assn., Washington, 1982-83; managerial intern Lincoln Ctr. for Performing Arts, Inc., N.Y.C., 1984; devel. dir. Ind. Feature Project, N.Y.C., 1985-87; fin. officer N.Y. Coun. for Humanities, N.Y.C., 1987-90; devel. assoc. Studio Mus. in Harlem, N.Y.C., 1990; juror Am. Film Festival, N.Y.C., 1986, Student Acad. Awards, N.Y.C., 1986—; cons. Blum and O'Hara, N.Y.C. and L.A., 1987-89, The Studio Mus. in Harlem, N.Y.C., 1988—, other art orgns. Contbg. editor Berkeley Poetry Rev., 1976-77, 80; editor: Grants and Fellowship of Interest to Historians, 1982-83, Censorship and First Amendment Rights: A Primer, 1991. Pres. bd. dirs. Asian Am. Arts Alliance, 1990-91. Mem. UCLA Arts Mgmt. Alumni, Asian-Am. Arts Alliance (bd. dirs. 1990—). Democrat. Jewish. Home: 1121 8th Ave Brooklyn NY 11215-4337

ADAMS, THOMAS TILLEY, lawyer; b. Orchard Park, N.Y., Oct. 9, 1929; s. Floyd Tilley and Clara Elizabeth (Potter) A.; m. Virginia Rives Smith, Sept. 1, 1956; children: Julia, Janet, Claire, Douglas. BA, U. Buffalo, 1951; JD, Cornell U., 1957. Bar: N.Y. 1957, U.S. Ct. Appeals (2d cir.) 1962, U.S. Supreme Ct. 1962, Conn. 1964. Tchr. Lake Shore Cen. Sch., Angola, N.Y., 1953-54; assoc. Davies, Hardy & Schenck, N.Y.C., 1957-63; ptnr. Gregory & Adams, Wilton, Conn. and N.Y.C., 1963—; lectr. Cornell U. Law Sch., Ithaca, N.Y., 1962-65, emeritus mem. adv. coun., 1990—; adj. assoc. prof. law Fordham U., N.Y.C., 1973-76; adviser Dana Fund Internat. and Comparative Legal Studies, Toledo, 1976-91; assoc. bd. dirs. Union Trust Co., Stamford, Conn., 1982—; corporator Norwalk Savs. Soc., 1975—. Counsel Town of Wilton, 1966-71; pres. Five Town Found., Norwalk, Conn., 1983-85, trustee, 1989-91; chmn. bldg. com. Wilton High Sch., 1966. Recipient Silver Beaver award Boy Scouts Am., 1980, Disting. Alumnus award Cornell Law Sch., 1990. Mem. ABA, Am. Judicature Soc. (dir. 1991-92), Stamford/Norwalk Regional Bar Assn. (dir.), Conn. Bar Assn. (ethics com. 1970-75, mem. coun. bar pres.'s 1988-90), N.Y. State Bar Assn., City Midday Club, Silver Spring Country Club, Cornell Club (N.Y.), Phi Delta Phi. Republican. Episcopalian. Home: 55 Deer Run Rd Wilton CT 06897-1204 Summer: Rogers Rock Club Ticonderoga NY 12883 Office: Gregory & Adams 190 Old Ridgefield Rd Wilton CT 06897-4023

ADAMS, WILLIAM WHITE, manufacturing company executive; b. Dubuque, Iowa, May 14, 1934; s. Waldo and Therese (White) A.; m. Susan Joanne Cole, Dec. 29, 1956; children: Nancy, Sara, Mark, Catherine. B.S. in Indsl. Adminstrn., Iowa State U., 1956. With Armstrong World Industries, Inc., Lancaster, Pa., 1956—, gen. sales mgr. residential ceiling systems div., 1975-80, group v.p. bldg. products ops., 1981, exec. v.p., 1982-88, chmn., pres., chief exec. officer, 1988—; dir. Bell Telephone Co. of Pa., 1986—. Chmn. adv. bd. Lancaster-Lebanon council Boy Scouts Am., 1970—; bd. dirs. United Way Lancaster County, (Pa.), 1977-82, WITF Pub. Broadcasting, 1986-88; bd. dirs. Lancaster Symphony Assn., 1978-87, pres., 1983-84. Recipient Silver Beaver award Boy Scouts Am., 1979. Mem. Pa. C. of C. (dir.), Pa. Bus. Roundtable (dir.), Nat. Assn. Mfgrs. (dir.), Bus. Roundtable. Club: Lancaster Country (dir. 1978-84). Office: Armstrong World Industries Inc 313 W Liberty St # 3001 Lancaster PA 17603-2717

ADAMSONS, ULDIS, government official; b. Zwittau, Czechoslovakia, Jan. 2, 1945; s. Osvalds V. and Austra Agnes (Osis) A.; m. Janene Adelle Sward; children: Kari Lee, Ryan Erik. BA in Econs., U. Minn., Duluth, 1973; student, DePaul U., 1969-70; grad., Nat. Def. U., 1984. Cert. mgmt. acct. Supr. GAO, Chgo., 1968-75; team leader GAO, Honolulu, 1975-79; group dir. GAO, Washington, 1980-91, asst. dir. def. environ. issues, 1992—; chmn. bd. dirs. Muse Inc., Rockville, Md.; broadcaster classical music radio program worldwide. Mem. Congl. Squadron, Civil Air Patrol. Recipient Outstanding Achievement award, 1987, Exceptional Svc. award, 1988. Mem. Nat. Assn. Accts., World Affairs Coun., Inst. Cert. Mgmt. Accts., Internat. Platform Assn. Lutheran. Home: 7230 Ashview Dr Springfield VA 22153-1520 Office: GAO 441 G St NW Rm 5832 Washington DC 20548-0002

ADDANKI, SOMASUNDARAM, industrial hygienist; b. Lakkavakam, India, Mar. 7, 1932; s. Veeraraghavaiah and Subbaraju (Kancherla) A.; m. Sathyavathi Addanki, May 4, 1954; children: Rathna, Usha, Sharon-Sheila. BVSc, U. Madras, India, 1957; MSc, Ohio State U., 1962, PhD, 1964. Instr. Ohio State U., Columbus, 1964-66, asst. prof., 1966-70, assoc. prof., 1970-86; toxicologist Walter Reed Army Med. Ctr., Washington, 1987; cons. Vigyan Rsch. Assn., Falls Church, Va., 1988-89; indsl. hygienist Def. Pers. Support Ctr., Phila., 1989—. Author: Diabetes Breakthrough, 1982; contbr. articles to profl. publs. Pres. Rockville Toastmasters, Columbus, 1977. Grantee NSF, 1968-72, Am. Heart Assn., 1968-85, NIH, 1969-73; named Disting. Toastmaster, 1981. Democrat. Home: 1991 Shadeview Ct Dublin OH 43017

ADE, JEROME CARROLL, agent; b. N.Y.C., Mar. 1, 1950; s. Erwin Jerome and MaryJane (Carroll) A.; m. Marcia Pegeen Sweeney, Feb. 21, 1980; children: Erin Michael, Jerome Sweeney. BA in Speech, Emerson U., 1971. V.p. Gen. Talent Internat., N.Y.C., 1971-89; pres. Famous Artists Agy, N.Y.C., 1989—. Named Agt. of Yr., Performance Mag., Dallas, 1989, one of 100 Most Influential People in Music Bus., BAM Mag., Oakland, Calif., 1989, 90. Mem. Friars, N.Y. Athletic Club, Pelham Country Club. Home: 667 Esplanade Pelham NY 10803-2405 Office: Famous Artists Agy 1700 Broadway New York NY 10019-5905

ADEGBITE, SAMSON G., psychiatrist; b. Aiyetoro, Ogun, Nigeria, Nov. 22, 1952; came to U.S. 1971; s. Joseph Dare and Alice (Shikeola (Ajayi) A.; m. Victoria Johnny, Oct. 30, 1971; children: Stephen A., Michelle A. BS in Chem. & Biochem., Richmond Coll., S.I., N.Y., 1976; MS in Healthcare Adminstr, Bklyn. Coll., 1989; MD, Universidad Central Deleste, Dominican Republic, 1981; RN, Bap. Nursing Sch., Eku, Nigeria, 1970. Sr. supr. Manhattan Psychiatric Ctr., N.Y.C., 1973-74; nurse adminstr. Manhattan Psychiatric Ctr., 1974-77, 81-83; resident psychiatry Bronx-Lebanon Hosp., 1985-88; fellow in child psychiatry Met. Hosp., N.Y.C., 1988-90; instr. psychiatry adj. Albert Einstein Coll. Medicine, Bronx, 1989; instr. child psychiatry adj. N.Y. Med. Coll., Valhalla, N.Y., 1989; fellow child psychiatry Met. Hosp., N.Y.C., 1988-90; assoc. dir. nursing Manhattan Psychiatric Ctr., N.Y.C., 1983-85. Active Dem. Party. Mem. Am. Psychiatric Assn., AMA, Kings County Med. Soc., N.Y. Med. Soc., Bronx County Psychiatric Soc. Baptist. Home: 23019 138th Ave Jamaica NY 11413-2806

ADELMAN, IRVING, librarian; b. New London, Conn., Feb. 22, 1926; s. Joseph and Yetta (Broady) A.; m. Florence Less Adelman, Sept. 6, 1953; children: Steven, Marc. BA, Northeastern U., 1948; MA, Columbia U., 1951, MS in Libr. Sci., 1954. Libr. Long Beach (Calif.) Pub. Libr., 1954-56; sr. libr. Bklyn. Pub. Libr., 1956-58; head reference, asst. dir. East Meadow (N.Y.) Pub. Libr., 1958—; mem. nat. adv. bd., cons. McGraw-Hill Ency. and Subscription Book Div., N.Y.C., 1970-80; mem. index com. H.W. Wilson Co., Bronx, 1973-74; reference cons. pub. librs. in Nassau County, N.Y., 1970—. Co-author: Modern Drama, 1967 (Outstanding Ref. award 1967), Contemporary Novel, 1972 (Outstanding Ref. Book listing ALA 1972). Mem. Nassau County Libr. Assn. Democrat. Jewish. Home: 73 Autumn Ln Hicksville NY 11801-6333 Office: East Meadow Pub Libr Front St and East Meadow Dr East Meadow NY 11554

ADELMAN, KENNETH ALLAN, podiatrist; b. Jersey City, Apr. 12, 1959; s. Herbert W. and Sylvia (Endlich) A. BA, Rutgers U., 1981; D Podiatric Medicine magna cum laude, N.Y. Coll. Podiatric Medicine, 1985. Diplomate Am. Bd. Podiatric Orthopedics. Resident in podiatric medicine and surgery Gouverneur Hosp. and affiliated hosps.; pvt. practice, Passaic, N.J. Contbr. articles to profl. jours. Fellow Am. Coll. Foot Orthopedists, Am. Soc. Podiatric Medicine, Am. Soc. Podiatric Dermatology; mem. Am. Coll. Foot Surgeons (assoc.), Am. Coll. Podiatric Sports Medicine (assoc.), Am. Coll. Podopediatrics (assoc.).

ADELMAN, MILTON HARRIS, anesthesiologist; b. N.Y.C., Dec. 19, 1910; s. Samuel D. Adelman and Sadye (S.) A.; married, Jan. 15, 1950 (dec. 1990); 1 child, Samuel R. BS cum laude, NYU, 1931; MD, U. Md., Balt., 1935. Diplomate Am. Bd. Anesthesiology. Intern Hosp. for Joint Diseases, N.Y.C., 1936-38, assoc. attending anesthesiologist, 1941-46; resident in anesthesiology Michael Reese Hosp., Chgo., 1939-41; resident in medicine Mt. Sinai Hosp., N.Y.C., 1938-39, anesthesiologist, 1942-79, cons., clin. prof. emeritus, 1979—; clin. prof. anesthesiology NYU, N.Y.C., 1991—. Contbr. pubis. to profl. jours. Maj. M.C., 1942-46, ETO. Fellow Am. Coll. Anesthesiology, N.Y. Acad. Medicine; mem. Am. Soc. Anesthesiology, N.Y. Soc. Anesthesiology (life). Republican. Jewish. Home: 29 Shawnee Rd Scarsdale NY 16583 Office: NYU Sch Medicine 560 1st Ave New York NY 10016-6402

ADELMANN, PENELOPE OWENS, financial analyst; b. Bklyn.; d. Philip Cromwell and Virginia (Raebeck) Owens; m. Richard Lewis Adelmann, Sept. 11, 1965. BA, Swarthmore Coll., 1966; MBA, NYU, 1981. Chartered fin. analyst. Rating analyst Standard & Poor's, N.Y.C., 1979-81, rating specialist, 1981; asst. v.p. Bankers Trust, N.Y.C., 1981-83, v.p., 1983; v.p. AG Becker Paribas, N.Y.C., 1983-84; v.p./mgr Dean Witter, N.Y.C., 1984-87; v.p. mgr. Nomura Securities Internat., N.Y.C., 1987—. Fin. trustee Scarsdale Congregational Ch., 1989—. Mem. Fixed Income Analysts Soc. Inc. (program chmn., pres. 1984-85), N.Y. Soc. Security Analysts (membership com. 1985—, bd. dirs., membership chair 1989-91, sec., 1991-92). Republican. Congregationalist. Office: Nomura Securities Internat 180 Maiden Ln New York NY 10038-4925

ADELSON, ALAN MERRILL, cultural organization administrator, writer; b. Newton, Mass., Nov. 7, 1943; s. Herman S. and Annette Beatrice (Kahn) A.; m. Judith D. Adelman, June 25, 1966 (div. Nov. 1977); 1 child, Kerin B.; m. Kathryn Taverna, Dec. 19, 1986. BA, Case Western Res. U., 1965; MA, Columbia U., 1967. Feature writer The Wall St. Jour., N.Y.C., 1967-70; instr. CUNY, N.Y.C., 1972-78; exec. dir. The Jewish Heritage Project, N.Y.C., 1983—. Producer, dir., editor: Lodz Ghetto, 89 (Internat. Critics award 1989); author: SDS, 1972; contbr. articles to profl. jours. Recipient Best First Film award Leipzig (Federal Republic of Germany) Internat. Film Fest., 1989.

ADELSTEIN, PETER Z., chemist; b. Quebec, Can., Sept. 1, 1924; s. Harry Mitchell and Edith (Matts) A.; m. Rose Magid, May 27, 1947; children: David, Diane, Debra. B Engring., McGill U., Montreal, Que., Can., 1946; PhD in Chemistry, McGill U., Can., 1949. Lab. supr. Eastman Kodak Co., Rochester, N.Y., 1949-86; rsch. cons. Rochester Inst. Tech., 1986—. Contbg. author: Handbook of Photography, 1972, Neblette's Photography and Reprography, 1977, Manual of Photogrammetry, 1966; editor: Preservation of Historical Records, 1986; contbr. articles to profl. jours. Mem. ASTM, NAS (com. chmn. 1985), Am. Nat. Standards Inst. (com. chmn. 1960—), Internat. Standards Orgn. (com. chmn. 1960—, conf. chmn. 1989). Jewish. Home: 1629 Clover St Rochester NY 14618-2515

ADER, ROBERT, psychology educator; b. N.Y.C., Feb. 20, 1932; s. Nathan and Mae (Levine) A.; m. Gayle Simon, June 2, 1957; children: Deborah, Janet, Norine, Leslie. BS, Tulane U., 1953; PhD, Cornell U., 1957; MD (hc), U. Trondheim, Norway, 1992. Rsch. instr. dept. of psychiatry Sch. of Medicine and Dentistry, U. Rochester, N.Y., 1957-61, asst. prof. dept. psychiatry, 1961-64, assoc. prof. dept. psychiatry, 1964-68, prof. dept. psychiatry, 1968-83, dir. div. behavioral and psychosocial medicine, 1982—, George L. Engel prof. dept. psychiatry, 1983—; vis. prof. Rudolf Magnus Inst. for Pharmacology, Utrecht, Netherlands, 1970-71; Salmon lectr. N.Y. Acad. Medicine, N.Y.C., 1989. Editor: Psychoneuroimmunology, 1981, 2d edit., 1991, Experimental Foundations of Behavioral Medicine: Conditioning Approaches, 1988; editor-in-chief Brain, Behavior and Immunity, 1986—; contbr. numerous articles to profl. jours. Fellow Acad. Behavioral Medicine Rsch. (pres. 1984-85), Soc. for Behavioral Medicine; mem. Am. Psychosomatic Soc. (pres. 1979-80), Internat. Soc. Devel. Psychobiology (pres. 1981-82). Home: 9 Park Acre Dr Pittsford NY 14534-2735 Office: U Rochester Dept Psychiatry Rochester NY 14642

ADIKES, JAMES D., engineering technician; b. Manhasset, N.Y., Apr. 12, 1962; 0. William and Marian (Sommers) A.; m. Allison Lee Robitaille, Dec. 2, 1989; children: Alyssa, Ashley, Desiree Marllaj. Student, Digital Computers, Hempstead, N.Y., 1983-84. Field technician L.I. Bus. Products, Hauppauge, N.Y., 1984-89; product supr., color laser specialist Omni Bus. Systems, Melbourne, Fla., 1989-91; field engr. Delson Bus. Systems, New Hyde Park, N.Y., 1991—. Mem. Moose. Home: 18 W Scudder Pl Northport NY 11768 Office: Delson Bus Systems 101 5th Ave New Hyde Park NY

ADLAND, MARVIN LEON, psychiatrist, educator; b. Chgo., Dec. 24, 1919; s. Isadore Jack and Anna Rella (Falk) A.; m. Marilyn Friend, Oct. 22, 1947; children: Peter F., Susan F., Jonathan F., Elizabeth F. BS, U. Chgo., 1940, MD, 1943. Diplomate Am. Bd. Psychiatry and Neurology; cert. Am. Psychoanalytic Assn. Intern Milw. (Wis.) County Hosp., 1944; resident psychiatry Sheppard-Pratt Hosp., Towson, Md., 1944-46; resident to assoc. med. dir. Chestnut Lodge Hosp., Rockville, Md., 1948-63; pvt. practice Chevy Chase, Md., 1963—; supervising and tng. psychoanalyst Washington (D.C.) Psychoanalytic Inst., 1957—; clin. prof. psychiatry Georgetown Univ., Washington, 1971—. Contbr. articles to profl. jours. Capt. U.S. Army, 1946-48. Fellow Am. Psychiat. Assn. (life); mem. Washington Psychoanalytic Soc. (pres. 1991—). Home and Office: 5521 Uppingham St Bethesda MD 20815-5507

ADLE, RICHARD S., educational administrator; b. Auburn, N.Y., Jan. 28, 1946; s. Jay E. and margaret E. (Coeny) A.; m. Kathleen M. Borschel, June 29, 1967; children: Scott C., Jamie M., Dustin L. BA, SUNY, Geneseo, 1968; postgrad., Syracuse U., 1968-74; BA, Daemen Coll., 1985; MS summa cum laude, SUNY, Buffalo, 1986. Tchr. Waterville (N.Y.) Sr. High Sch., 1968-74; owner Bookstore, West Seneca, N.Y., 1976-81; text book mgr. Daemen Coll., Amherst, N.Y., 1982-87, career planning staff mem., 1986-87; dir. placement Hilbert Coll., Hamburg, N.Y., 1987-91, asst. v.p. for student life, 1991—; admissions counselor Consortium of Niagara Frontier, Amherst, 1987. Author rsch. bibliography SPA-GASPA, 1986. Facilitator Fisher Price, East Aurora, N.Y., 1990-91; creator job devel. network program, 1988. Mem. Nat. Assn. Student Pers. Adminstrs., Niagara Frontier Coll. Placement Assn. (treas. 1989), Coll. Student Pers. Assn., Nat. Assn. Student Employment Adminstrs. Democrat. Office: Hilbert Coll 5200 S Park Ave Hamburg NY 14075-1597

ADLER, EARL, insurance executive; b. N.Y.C., Apr. 5, 1932; s. Louis and Jenny (Fischman) A; m. June Cohen, June 28, 1954; children: Greg, Gary, Mitchell. BSBA, Lehigh U., 1954. CLU. Life ins. supr. Bergen Agy., Mut. Trust Life Ins. Co., N.Y.C., 1959-62; ptnr., v.p. Weinshel Inc., ins. brokers, N.Y.C., 1962-70; v.p. Brokerage Resources, Inc., N.Y.C., 1962-70; pres. Congl. Life Ins. Co., N.Y.C., 1969-70, EACO, Inc., N.Y.C., 1971—. Trustee Columbia Grammar and Prep Sch., N.Y.C., 1974-82. Served to 1st lt. inf. AUS, 1955-57. Mem. Internat. Forum, Million Dollar Round Table, Assn. Advanced Life Underwriting, Friars (gov., 1974-78), Alpine Country Club (gov.), Masons. Home: 501 E 87th St New York NY 10128-7619 Office: EACO Inc 2200 Fetcher Ave Fort Lee NJ 07024

ADLER, EDWARD I., media and entertainment company executive; b. N.Y.C., Jan. 12, 1954; s. Walter S. and Justine (Rosenberg) A. BA, Vassar Coll., 1976; MA in Journalism, NYU, 1979. Copy desk asst. People Mag. subs. Time Inc., N.Y.C., 1974-76; resporter Time Mag. subs. Time Inc, N.Y.C., 1976-79; sports programming exec. Home Box Office Inc. subs. Time Inc., N.Y.C., 1979-81; news editor TV-Calbe Week Mag. subs. TV Cable Week Mag. subs. Time Inc., N.Y.C., 1981-83; sr. assoc. corp. pub. affairs Time Inc., N.Y.C., 1983-88; mgr. media rels. corp. communications Time Warner Inc., N.Y.C., 1989—. Democrat. Jewish. Office: Time Warner Inc 75 Rockefeller Plz New York NY 10019

ADLER, ESTELLE CAROLINE, finance company executive; b. Montreal, Can., Oct. 27, 1951; d. Adam and Jadwiga (Katz) Wygnanski; m. Howard Bruce Adler, June 4, 1972 (div. Dec. 1980). BA in Psychology, McGill U., 1971; MS in Libr. Svc., Columbia U. Sch. Libr. Svc., 1975; MS in Bus., Columbia U. Grad. Sch. Bus., 1986. Asst. libr. Unicef United Nations, N.Y.C., 1971-75; French document analyst Dag Hammarskjold Libr. United Nations, N.Y.C., 1975-76, ref. libr., 1977; head libr., pub. affairs officer Canadian Consulate Gen., N.Y.C., 1977-80; mgr. bus. rsch. and strategic planning Am. Can Co., Greenwich, Conn., 1980-84; mgr. corp. and fin. svcs. audit Primerica (formerly Am. Can), Greenwich, Conn., 1984-88; v.p. bus. analysis Dollar Dry Dock Bank, White Plains, N.Y., 1988-90, first v.p. corp. fin. and strategic planning, 1990-91, first v.p. strategic planning, chief auditor, 1991—. Mem. bus. women's com. MS Found., N.Y.C., 1989—. Mem. Columbia U. Club, Fin. Women's Assn. N.Y. Home: 412 E 55th St New York NY 10022-5104 Office: Dollar Dry Dock Bank 50 Main St White Plains NY 10606-1920

ADLER, HELMUT ERNEST, psychology educator; b. Nuremberg, Fed. Republic Germany, Nov. 25, 1920; came to U.S., 1940, naturalized, 1943; s. Paul and Lola (Offenbacher) A.; m. Leonore Loeb, May 22, 1943; children—Barry Peter, Beverly Sharmaine, Evelyn Renee. B.S., Columbia U., 1948, A.M., 1949, Ph.D., 1952. Mem. sci. staff Columbia U., N.Y.C., 1952-55, vis. asst. prof., 1955, lectr., 1955-60; mem. faculty Yeshiva U., N.Y.C., 1950—, prof. psychology, 1964-91, prof. emeritus, 1991—; research fellow Am. Mus. Natural History, 1955-69, research assoc., 1969-84; research assoc. Mystic Marinelife Aquarium, Conn., 1976-85; cons. N.Y. Aquarium, 1972-73. Author: (with J.D. McDonald and Derek Goodwin) Bird Behavior, 1962, Bird Life, 1969; Fish Behavior, 1975; also articles, book chpts. Editor: Orientation: Sensory Basis, 1971, (with others) Comparative Psychology at Issue, 1973; sect. editor, contbr.: Ency. Judaica, 1972. Translator: Elements of Psychophysics (G.T. Fechner), 1966. Served with U.S. Army, 1942-46, PTO. Rsch grantee NSF; recipient Wilhelm Wundt award N.Y. State Psychol. Assn., 1991. Fellow Am. Psychol. Assn., N.Y. Acad. Scis. (chmn. sect. 1978-80); mem. Eastern Psychol. Assn., Internat. Orgn. Study of Group Tensions (asst. editor 1980-84, editorial bd. 1984-86, 88—), Internat. Council Psychologists, Internat. Soc. Comparative Psychology, Internat. Soc. History of Behavioral and Social Scis., Internat. Union Biol. Scis. (sec.-gen. sect. comparative psychology and animal behavior 1972-86), Queens County Psychol. Assn., Psi Chi. Jewish. Home: 16214 86th Ave Jamaica NY 11432-3422 Office: Yeshiva U 500 W 185th St New York NY 10033

ADLER, IRVING, mathematician; b. N.Y.C., Apr. 27, 1913; s. Marcus and Celia (Kress) A.; m. Ruth Relis, June 2, 1935 (dec. 1968); children: Stephen L., Peggy Adler Robohm; m. Joyce Lifshutz, Sept. 16, 1968. BS, CCNY, 1931; MA, Columbia U., 1938, PhD, 1961; DSc (hon.), St. Michael's Coll., 1990. Tchr. pub. high schs., N.Y.C., 1932-46; chmn. dept. math. Textile High Sch., N.Y.C., 1946-52; instr. math. Columbia U., N.Y.C., 1957-60, Bennington Coll., North Bennington, Vt., 1961, So. Vt. Coll., Bennington, 1983; researcher in math. biology North Bennington, 1972—; lectr. in field. Author 49 books; co-author 34 books; contbr. numerous articles to profl. jours.; contbg. editor Sci. and Society, 1981—; mem. editorial bd. Sci. and Nature, 1978-89. Recipient awards for outstanding sci. books for children Children's Book Coun. and Nat. Sci. Tchrs. Assn., 1972, 75, 80, 90, and others. Fellow AAAS, Vt. Acad. Arts and Sci.; mem. Am. Math. Soc., Math. Assn. Am., Nat. Council Tchrs. Math., Soc. for Indsl. and Applied Math., Authors League, Phi Beta Kappa, Sigma Xi. Democrat. Jewish. Home: RR 1 Box 532 North Bennington VT 05257-9748

ADLER, JANE EVE, internationally syndicated columnist, cartoonist and illustrator; b. Providence, Oct. 8, 1944; d. Frank Kozlov and Ruth Cohen; m. Edwin I. Adler, Feb. 19, 1961; children: Lindsay, Steven. B.A., U. R.I., 1971. Art dir. Trinity Sq. Theatre, 1971-72; T.V. talk show hostess, writer, artistic dir. original plays PBS 1971-72; weekly columnist/illustrator Boston Herald, Providence Journal, National Observer, 1972-77; syndicated columnist, illustrator News Am. Syndicate, 1977-88, Whitegate Features Syndicate, 1988—; tchr., lectr., TV and radio guest in horticulture and writing. Author monthly nat. mag. columns; writer of books on children, 1982—; columnist for Boston Herald on child healthcare, 1984—; travel writer for Whitegate News Syndicate, 1987—. Participant in numerous one woman and group art shows, 1965—. Organizer of free painting course for women at U. R.I.; active in numerous charity and cultural activities. Recipient awards for writing from various groups such as R.I. Fed. Garden Clubs. Mem. R.I. Horticulture Soc. (organizer), Garden Writers of Am., N.Y. Art Dirs. Club, Childhood and Adult Devel. Resources Inst. (founder, bd. dirs.), Nat. Orgn. Earth Care (founder, bd. dirs.) Jewish. Lodges: Masons, B'nai Brith. Office: Whitegate Features Syndicate 71 Faunce Dr Providence RI 02906-4805

ADLER, LAWRENCE JOEL, technical writer; b. White Plains, N.Y., July 10, 1939; s. David Irving and Dora (Tomin) A.; m. Celestina Do Nascimento, Apr. 13, 1989. BS in Sociology, U. Wis., 1961; diploma bus. adminstrn., London Sch. Econs., 1964. Copy writer various advt. agys., London, N.Y.C., 1965-82; rsch. cons. Quantum Sci. Corp., N.Y.C., 1985-87; computer salesman The Computer Factory, N.Y.C., 1990-91; tech. writer Switchco Inc., Englewood, N.J., 1982-85, ABR Cons., Paramus, N.J., 1988-89, Control Data Corp., Hackensack, N.J., 1991—. Author: Pele: Man With a Mission, 1976, Young Women in the World of Race Horses, 1978, Famous Horses in America, 1979, The Texas Rangers, 1979, Heros of Soccer, 1981, Help Wanted, 1990, Football Coach Quotes, 1991. With U.S. Army, 1961-62. Home: 324 E 74th St New York NY 10021-3727

ADLER, PEGGY See ROBOHM, PEGGY ADLER

ADLER, VERDA VIRGINIA, marketing executive; b. Atlanta, Sept. 18, 1956; d. Raymond and Sarah Alice (Montgomery) Forehand; m. Alan Thomas Adler, Aug. 17, 1985. Grad. with honors, Gulf Coast Community Coll., Panama City, Fla., 1975; BS with honors, U. Fla., 1977. Div. mgr. Sears Roebuck Co., Richmond, Va., 1978-79; mgmt. trainee AT&T-Southern Bell, Atlanta, 1979; industry cons. AT&T, Atlanta, 1980-83, nat. acct. mgr., 1983-84; staff mgr. bus. sales div. AT&T, Morristown, N.J., 1985-87; mktg. cons. Touch Tone Access, Inc., Whippany, N.J., 1987-89; internat. mktg. mgr. Nynex Info. Solutions Group, Pearl River, N.Y., 1989—; Contbr. articles, short story to profl. publs. Asst. Atlanta Commrs. campaign, 1980. Recipient Disting. Sales award Sales and Mktg. Execs., Internat., 1982, 83. Mem. NAFE, U. Fla. Alumni Assn., Keyettes Club, Phi Beta Kappa. Democrat. Presbyterian.

ADOLPHI, RONALD LEE, government official; b. Bremerton, Wash., Aug. 8, 1946; s. Robert L. and Margaret May (Hitland) A.; m. Sherry Lee Klepach, Oct. 5, 1968 (div. Jan. 1974), Celia Louise Fields, May 10, 1975; 1 child, Christina Lani. BA in Bus. Adminstrn., U. Wash., 1968; MS in Ednl. Adminstrn., Butler U., 1974; MBA, Syracuse U., 1976; grad., Indsl. Coll. of Armed Forces, 1984; PhD in Mgmt., Calif. Coast U., 1986. Cert. cost analyst, cert. cash mgr. Br. chief, capt. U.S. Army Fin. Sch., Indpls., 1972-73; fin. analyst Continental Steel Corp., Kokomo, Ind., 1973-74; fin. svcs. officer hdqrs. U.S. Army Pacific, Honolulu, 1974; fiscal specialist Office of Comptroller of Army, Washington, 1974-76; internat. economist Office Sec. of Def., Washington, 1976-82, asst. dir. for overseas banking, 1982-86, asst. dir. policy analysis and spl. studies, 1987-88, asst. dir. policy analysis and disbursing systems, 1988-89, dep. dir. fin. svcs. policy, 1989-91; dep. dir. acctg. policy Office of Sec. of Def., Washington, 1991—. Editorial bd. Armed Forces Comptroller Jour., 1979-83; contbr. articles to profl. publs. Treas. St. John's Luth. Ch., Alexandria, 1978-80, fin. sec., 1980-81, v.p. 1982-84, pres. 1984-86, comptroller, 1986-89, lay minister 1987—, sr. choir mem. 1976—, parliamentarian & chmn. publs., 1987—, Nat. Luth. Assn. Scouters, pres. 1980-82, regional v.p., 1983-84, sec., 1984-86; exec. bd. Capital Luth. Assn. Scouters, 1983—, pres., 1977-80, newsletter editor, 1983—; chmn. Troop 1107 com. Nat. Capital Area Coun. Boy Scouts Am., 1979—, chmn. Protestant com. on scouting, 1980-92, nat. coun. mem. at large, 1980—. Served to capt. U.S. Army, Vietnam, col. Res. Decorated Bronze Star with oak leaf cluster, Meritorious Svc. medal with oak leaf cluster, Air medal, Army Commendation medal with silver oak leaf cluster, others; recipient Encased George Washington Honor medal Freedoms Found. at Valley Forge, 1964, Silver beaver award Boy Scouts Am., 1979, Lamb award Luth. Coun. in USA, 1981, U.S. Treasury Dept. award for excellence in cash mgmt., 1985. Mem. Assn. Syracuse Army Comptrs. (1st v.p. 1978-83), Res. Officers Assn., Treasury Mgmt. Assn., Sr. Execs. Assn., Am. Soc. Mil. Comptrs. (chmn. nat. rsch. com. 1987—), Assn. Govt. Accts. (bd. dirs. Washington chpt. 1992—), Fed. Exec. Inst. Alumni Assn., Fin. Corps. Assn., Am. Legion, Phi Theta Kappa, Beta Gamma Sigma. Republican.

ADOM, EDWIN NII AMALAI, psychiatrist; b. Accra, Ghana, West Africa, Jan. 12, 1941; came to U.S., 1960; s. Isaac Quaye and Julianna Adorkor (Brown) Adom; m. Margaret Odarkor Lamptey; children: Edwin Nii Nortey Jr., Isaac Michael Nii Nortei. BA, U. Pa., 1963; MD, Meharry Med. Coll., 1968; FRSH (Eng.), Royal Soc. Health, 1974. Diplomate Am. Bd. Psychiatry and Neurology. Intern Pa. Hosp., Phila., 1968-69; resident in psychiatry Thomas Jefferson U. Med. Ctr., Phila., 1969-72; cons. psychiatrist St. Joseph Hosp., Phila., 1976-80, Stephen Smith Home for the Aged, Phila., 1976-85, Mercy Douglas Human Svcs. Ctr., Phila., 1977-79, St. Ignatius Home for the Aged, Phila., 1978-85; attending psychiatrist Phila. Psychiat. Ctr., 1987—; cons. psychiatrist psycho-social dept. Horizon House Rehab. Ctr., Phila., 1987-89; also cons. psychiatrist Phila. Psychiat. Ctr.; cons. psychiatrist U.S. Dept. Labor, Workmen's Compensation Div., Phila., 1987—, House Staff of the U. Pa. Hosp., Phila., 1989—; cons. The Grad. Hosp., Phila., 1976—; faculty clin. assoc. psychiatry U. Pa.Sch. Medicine, Phila., 1972—; active State of Pa. Bur. Disability Determination, 1975—; attending psychiatrist West Phila. Mental Health Consortium, 1972—, med. dirs., 1991—. Ghana Govt. scholar U. Pa., 1960-68; recipient Citizen Citation Chapel of the Four Chaplains, 1974. Mem. Fellow Royal Soc. Health (Eng.); mem. Am. Psychiatric Assn., Am. Acad. Psychiatry and the Law, Nat. Med. Assn., Black Psychiatrists Am. (exec. mem. 1975-77), Pa. Psychiatric Soc., Med. Soc. Ea. Pa., Phila. Psychiatric Soc., N.Y. Acad. Sci., World Fedn. Mental Health, Psychiatric Alliance, Phila. Acad. Family Psychiatrists, Nat. Geographic Soc. Presbyterian. Office: Med Towers 255 S 17th St #2704 Philadelphia PA 19103

ADONIZIO, ANN MARIE CATHERINE, retail executive; b. Pittston, Pa., May 3, 1945; d. Crucian Russell and Anna Marie (Ross) Perrone; m. John W. Adonizio, June 29, 1968; children: John W. Jr., Melissa, Maria. BS in Sociology, Coll. Misercordia, Dallas, Pa., 1967; postgrad., Marywood Coll., 1978, Wilkes Coll., 1979-80. Case worker Luz County Bd. of Assistance, Wilkes-Barre, Pa., 1967-69; substitute tchr. Pittston Area Sch. Dist., 1983-86; pres., treas. Maria's Shoe Designs, Inc., West Pittston, 1985-91; bd. dirs. Community Counseling Services, Wilkes-Barre. Bd. dirs. YMCA, Pittston, 1979-86; mem. adv. bd. Luzerno Wyo. County Mental Health/Mental Retardation, Wilkes-Barre, 1979-83; De,. committeewoman, Pittston, 1982-86; apointed Deutsch Inst. Applied Rsch. Ctrs. for Handicapped Bd.; co-chair parents exec. coun. Kings Coll., Wilkes-Barre; appointed project dir. Parents as Tchrs. program Pittston Area Sch. Dist.; program dir. Jr. Achievement of Northeast Pa.; mem., vice chmn. Luzerne County Commn. for Women; nominated to Luz County Bd. of Assistance. Recipient Am. Heart Assn. award, 1982-84, St. John Neimann award Diocese of Scranton, Pa., 1979, Pope Pius XII award Diocese of Scranton, 1984. Mem. Insalaco's Mall Mchts. Assn. (pres. 1986-88), Italian-Am. Assn. Roman Catholic. Home: 118 Parnell St Pittston PA 18640-3342 Office: Maria's Shoe Designs 118 Parnell St Pittston PA 18640-3342

ADOVASIO, J. M., anthropologist, archeologist, educator; b. Youngstown, Ohio. BA in Anthropology magna cum laude, U. Ariz., 1965, postgrad., 1965-66; PhD in Anthropology, U. Utah, 1970; DSc (hon.), Washington & Jefferson U., 1983. From instr. to asst. prof. anthropology Youngstown State U., 1966-68, 70-71; from asst. prof. to prof. anthropology, Latin Am. studies U. Pitts., Pa., 1972-90; chmn. dept. anthropology U. Pitts., 1980-89, dir. Cultural Resource Mgmt. Program, 1976-89, prof. geology and planetary scis., 1985-90; John E. Boyle prof. anthropology and archaeology, prof. geology Mercyhurst Coll., Erie, Pa., 1990—, dir. anthropology and archaeology dept., 1990—, dir. geology dept., 1991—, dir. Mercyhurst Archeol. Inst., 1990—; adj. assoc. prof. Youngstown State U., 1976-78; rsch. assoc. Smithsonian Instn., 1974—, Carnegie Mus., 1978—; expert witness ARPA cases U.S. Govt., Ariz., N.Mex., 1987—; exec. dir. archaeology rsch. program So. Meth. U., 1990—; presenter in field. Reviewer Libr. Jour., 1973—; contbr. numerous book revs. and articles to profl. jours. N.D.E.A. fellowship, U. Utah, 1968-70, Smithsonian Instn. Post-Doctoral Rsch. fellowship, 1971-72, Cert. for Acad. Achievement, Smithsonian Instn., 1972, numerous grants from 1969 to present. Fellow Am. Anthrop. Assn.; mem. AAAS, Soc. for Am. Archaeology, Current Anthropology, Am. Quaternary Assn., Soc. for Pa. Archaeology, N.Y. Acad. Scis., Phi Eta Sigma, Phi Beta Kappa, Sigma Xi. Home: 4676 White Pine Dr Erie PA 16506

ADRION, WILLIAM RICHARDS, university administrator, computer and information sciences educator; b. Alexandria, La., Nov. 2, 1943; s. Vernon Richards and Mary Leone (Carlock) A.; m. Jacqueline Cotner, July 3, 1971; children: Carrie Buchanan, Emily Richards. BS, Cornell U., 1966, ME, 1967; PhD, U. Tex., 1971. Computer engr. Honeywell EDP, Waltham, Mass., 1969-70; asst. prof. U. Tex., Austin, 1971-72; area chmn., asst. prof. Oreg. State U., Corvallis, 1972-78; program dir. NSF, Washington, 1976-78, 80-85; group mgr. Nat. Bur. Standards, 1978-80; dep. div. dir., 1985-86, chief scientist computer research, 1986; prof., chmn. computer and info. scis. U. Mass, Amherst, 1986—; chmn. adv. com. NSF/CDA, 1989—, chmn. bd. Acsiom, Inc., 1989—, Acsiom Labs., 1990—; cons. Applied Theory Assocs., Corvallis, 1973-78, Tektronix, Portland, Oreg., 1974-76, Lawrence Livermore Labs., 1985—, Radio Free Europe/Radio Liberty, Munich, Fed. Republic Germany, 1981-82; prof., lectr. Am. U., Washington, 1976-77; lectr. George Washington U., Washington, 1978; vis. prof. U. Calif.-Berkeley, 1984-85, U. Paris-Sud, 1992—; adj. research prof. Georgetown U., 1985-86. Contbr. articles to profl. jours. Named Outstanding Young Faculty, Am. Soc. Engring. Edn., 1973. Mem. AAAS, IEEE, Assn. Computing Machinery (vice-chmn. SIGSOFT 1981-85, chmn. 1985-89, past chmn. 1989—, editor-in-chief ACM Trans. on Software Engring. and Methodology 1989—), , Soc. Indsl. and Applied Math., N.Y. Acad. Scis., Computer Rsch. Assn. (dir. 1988—, chmn. govt. ops. 1990—), CSNET (exec. com. 1986-89), Sigma Xi, Phi Kappa Phi. Home: 104 Wildflower Dr Amherst MA 01002-3447 Office: U Mass Dept Computer Info Sci 307 LGRC Amherst MA 01003

ADUBATO, SUSAN ANN, psychologist, children's program director; b. Newark, Aug. 20, 1954; d. Michael C. and Angela Antonia (DiFino) Adubato. MA in Psychology, U. Nebr., 1978; PhD in Psychology, No. Ill. U., 1984. Lic. psychologist, N.J.; cert. for assessment of newborns, cert. in interdisciplinary studies. Teaching asst. No. Ill. U., DeKalb, 1980-82; intern, rsch. assoc. U. Nebr. MCRI, Omaha, 1982-84; rsch. assoc. Boy's Town Inst., Omaha, 1983-84; clinician-infant toddler parent program Community Mental Health Ctr., U. Medicine and Dentistry N.J., Newark, 1984-86, coord. infant toddler parent program, 1986-89, dir. infant toddler parent program, 1989-90; mem. depts. psychiatry and pediatrics U. Medicine and Dentistry N.J., Newark, 1986—, dir. Project B.A.B.I.E.S., 1990—; cons. for various social svc. agys., N.J., 1984—; pvt. practice child psychology, 1984—; co-founder, v.p. Baby CAMS Video Prodn. Co., N.J., 1985—; co-founder, pres. N.J. Assn. for Infant Mental Health, 1990—; mem. adv. com. Teen Progress, 1988-90, Teen Power House, 1988—, N.J. Adoption Adv. Com., 1987—; mem. adv. com. infant specialist program Rutgers U., 1986-91. Author, scriptwriter, producer (videos) The Little Babies That Could, 1986, The Little Premies That Could, 1989; contbr. articles to profl. jours. Grantee Rutgers Health Care Grant, N.J., 1989. Mem. APA, Nat. Ctr. Clin. Infant Programs, Soc. for Pediatric Psychology, Child Clin. Psychology, Assn. for Orthopsychology, ParentCare Inc., Nat. Black Child Devel. Inst., Assn. for Children in N.J., Essex County Network/N.J. Network for Adolescent Porgrams, Essex County Network for AIDS. Office: Project BABIES 256 N 7th St Newark NJ 07107-1623

AFFINITO, MONA GUSTAFSON, psychologist; b. Bristol, Conn., Oct. 28, 1929; d. Carl Arthur and Jennie Alida (Anderson) Gustafson; m. Louis A. Affinito, Oct. 3, 1955 (div. Dec. 1976); children: Douglas Anthony, Lisa Marie Affinito Neun. BA, Conn. Coll., 1951; MA, Boston U., 1952, PhD, 1964. Lic. psychologist, Conn. Instr. Johnson (Vt.) State Coll., 1952-53, U. Vt., Burlington, 1953-55; mem. faculty So. Conn. State U., New Haven, 1959—, prof. psychology, 1969-87, prof. emeritus, 1987—, chmn. dept., 1974-80, dir. grad. program in psychology, 1982-84; pvt. practice, Cheshire, Conn., 1980—; mem. staff New Haven Ctr. for Human Rels., 1976-80; psychologist Assocs. in Counseling & Therapy, New Haven, 1978-80; frequent lectr., workshop condr.; presenter in field. Contbr. articles to profl. jours. Past pres. ch. women Christ Luth. Ch., Hamden, Conn. Mem. APA, Assn. for Advancement Behavior Therapy, Conn. Psychol. Assn. (past chmn. acad. affairs com., editor Conn. Psychologist 1977-78). Office: 1358 S Main St Cheshire CT 06410-3421

AFFRONTI, LEWIS FRANCIS, microbiologist, educator; b. Rochester, N.Y., Aug. 12, 1928; s. John and Mary (Least) A.; m. Aileen Ledford, June 2, 1956; children—John, Lewis, Mary Louise, Eileen. B.A., U. Buffalo, 1950, M.A., 1951; Ph.D., Duke, 1958. Rsch. assoc. Buffalo VA Hosp., 1951-52, Roswell Meml. Cancer Inst., 1954, TB Henry Phipps Inst. U. Pa., 1957-58; asst. prof. Sch. Medicine George Washington U., Washington, 1962-65; assoc. prof. Sch. Medicine George Washington U., 1965-72, prof. microbiology Sch. Medicine, 1972—, chmn. dept. microbiology Sch. Medicine, 1973—; cons. AVCO Research Corp., VA Hosp., Martinsburg, W.Va., VA Hosp. Ctr., Wilmington, Del.; U.S. rep. WHO Conf. on Skin Test Antigens and Vaccines, Geneva, 1966; mem. med. adv. bd. VA, Wilmington, Del. Editorial bd. Infection and Immunity, 1972-78. Bd. dirs. Washington br. Nat. Found. Infectious Diseases, 1984—. Commd. officer USPHS, 1958-62; served with USAF, 1952-54. NIH Spl. fellow, 1969; Nat. Tb fellow for Internat. Conf. on Tb Moscow, 1971; Nat. Tb fellow for Internat. Conf. on Tb Tokyo, 1973; Washington Acad. Sci. fellow; Recipient WHO Exchange Research Workers award, 1970; interacad. exchange program award Nat. Acad. Sci., 1980. Fellow Am. Acad. Microbiology, Assn. Med. Sch. Microbiology Chmn. (sec.-treas. 1976-86, bd. dirs. 1976-86); mem. Am. Soc. Microbiology, Am. Assn. for Immunologists, Reticuloendothelial Soc., Am. Thoracic Soc., Assembly on Microbiologists and Immunologists (sec. 1971-72), Wash. Acad. Sci., Sigma Xi (local pres. 1986-87). Clubs: K.C; Toastmasters Internat. (Atlanta). Office: George Washington U Med Ctr Dept Microbiology 2300 I St NW Washington DC 20037-2337

AFSHAR, KAMRAN, economics educator, business consultant; b. Paris, Nov. 13, 1948; came to U.S. 1974, naturalized 1984; s. Hassan and Pouran

Afchar; m. Mahta Mojtahedi, July 6, 1972; children: Faraz, Kimya. BS in Econs. and Bus. Adminstrn., Pahlavi U., Shiraz, Iran, 1972; student U. Cambridge, 1972-73; Diploma in Econ. Devel., U. Oxford, 1974; PhD in Econs., Fla. State U., 1977. pres. Indsl. Internat., Inc., Tallahassee, Fla., 1977-78; asst. prof. Wofford Coll., Spartanburg, S.C., 1978-82, Moravian Coll., Bethlehem, Pa., 1982-88, pres., Kamran Afshar Assocs., 1988, dir. MBA, 1984-86, Lehigh Valley Consumer Rsch. Ctr., 1988—, dir. C.P.I. Project, 1984—; cons., Bethlehem, 1982—. Co-author: (with G.A. Sears) Money, Banking, Financial Markets and the Economy, 1984. Author, chief editor newsletter: A Lehigh Valley Economic Review, 1982—; contbr. articles to profl. jours. Ben Franklin Partnership grantee, 1983-84; Pvt. Industry Coun. grantee, 1986-87. Mem. Am. Econ. Assn., So. Econ. Assn., Western Econ. Assn., Pa. Conf. Economists. Moslem. Lodge: Rotary. Avocations: flying, bicycle riding. Office: PO Box 283 Bethlehem PA 18016-0283

AGAR, JOHN RUSSELL, JR., school district supervisor; b. Camden, N.J., July 25, 1949; s. John R. and Evva L. (Wilhelm) A.; m. Beatrice A. B.; 1 child, Rebekah A. BA with high honors, Rutgers U., 1971; MS, U. Pa., 1973, MS in Edn., 1975; EdD with distinction, Temple U., 1983; postgrad., U. Pa., 1989. Cert. secondary educator, supr., prin., dist. supt., Pa., N.J. Lectr. in chemistry U. Pa., Phila., 1974-75; sci. dept. head West Cath. Girls' High Sch., Phila., 1974-79; chemistry tchr. Moorestown (N.J.) Friends' Sch., 1979-82, West Deptford High Sch., Westville, N.J., 1982-84; visiting asst. prof. Temple U., Phila., 1983-88; lectr. in edn. U. Pa., Phila., 1988—; sci. supr. Marple Newtown Sch. Dist., Newtown Sq., Pa., 1984—. NIH fellow U. Pa., 1973-74, CEPUP/CHEM/NSF fellow U. Calif., Berkeley, 1990-91; recipient Nat. Tchr. award CEPUP, U. Calif., Berkeley, 1992. Mem. ASCD, Nat. Sci. Suprs. Assn., Nat. Sci. Tchrs. Assn., Phi Lambda Upsilon, Phi Delta Kappa, Mensa.

AGAR, SHARON VERED, business executive; b. Haifa, Israel, July 28, 1959; d. Joram and Ilana (Bornstein) A.; m. Richard Philip Johnson, Nov. 5, 1989. BS in Applied Math., Yale U., 1982; MBA, Harvard U., 1986. Assoc. banker Goldman, Sachs & Co., N.Y.C., 1986-89; mgr., cons. Task Force on Co. Assistance, Warsaw, Poland, 1990; mgr. bus. devel., Latin Am. Philip Morris Internat., 1991—. Bd. dirs. Chelsea Chamber Ensemble, N.Y.

AGARD, DAVID LEON, conductor; b. Binghamton, N.Y., Aug. 31, 1941; s. Richard Lynn and Martha (Davis) A.; B.S. in Music, Ithaca Coll., 1960; m. Betty Lou Dubben, Mar. 25, 1961; 1 dau., Amelia Dubben. Concertmaster, asst. condr. Amsterdam (N.Y.) Symphony, 1963-66; asst. condr. Tri-Cities Opera, Binghamton,, 1966-70; founder, artistic dir., condr. B.C. Pops Orch., Binghamton, N.Y., 1975—; free-lance violinist. Mem. Am. Fed. Musicians (past pres. local).

AGASAR, RONALD JOSEPH, mortgage banker; b. Phila., Nov. 27, 1946; s. Francis Robert and Penny Dolores (Alahverde) A.; m. Eleanor Joan Smith, Aug. 30, 1969 (div. Jan. 1982); m. Elizabeth Katherine Muhr, Apr. 20, 1989. BS, La Salle Coll., Phila., 1970; MBA in Mortgage Banking, Northwestern U., 1978. Regional v.p. Colonial Mortgage Svc. Co., Elkins Park, Pa., 1976-80, City Fed. Mortgage Corp., Cherry Hill, N.J., 1980-83; sr. v.p. Am. Residential Mortgage Corp., Cherry Hill, 1983—. Mem. Mortgage Bankers Assn. N.J., Pa. Mortgage Bankers Assn., Phila. Young Mortgage Bankers Assn. (chmn. 1983-84). Republican. Roman Catholic. Office: Am Residential Mortgage Corp 51 Haddonfield Rd Cherry Hill NJ 08002

AGATHOS, SPYROS NICHOLAS, biochemical engineer; b. Zante, Greece, July 31, 1950; came to U.S., 1975; s. Nicholas Demetrios and Kallirroe (Stamatelos) A.; m. Helene Skikos, July 27, 1985; children: Kallirroe Irene, Catherine Persephone. Diploma, Nat. Tech. U., Athens, Greece, 1973; M in Engring., McGill U., Montreal, Can., 1976; PhD, MIT, 1983. Registered profl. engr., Greece. Teaching asst. chem. engr. dept. McGill U., Montreal, 1973-75; rsch. asst. Naval Rsch. Lab. Boston City Hosp., 1975-77; teaching asst. applied biol. sci. dept. MIT, Cambridge, 1978-82; lectr. faculty engring. sci. U. Western Ont., London, Can., 1982-83; asst. prof. U. Western Ont., London, 1983-85; asst. prof. dept. chem. & biochem. engring. Rutgers U., Piscataway, N.J., 1985—; cons. to various biotech. industries nationwide. Editorial bd. Appl. Biochem. Biotechnol., Humana Press, 1986—; patent pending in field; contbr. articles to profl. jours., chpts. to books. Bd. trustees Elytis Chair Fund, Rutgers U. Found., 1989—. Fellow NATO, 1978-81; grantee NSF, 1987—, Can. Natural Scis. & Engring. Rsch. Coun., 1983-86. Fellow Tech. Chamber of Greece; mem. AAAS, Am. Chem. Soc., Am. Inst. Chem. Engrs., Soc. Indsl. Microbiology, Am. Hellenic Edn!. & Progressive Assn., N.Y. Acad. Sci., Sigma Xi. Home: 54 Agate Rd East Brunswick NJ 08816-1303 Office: Rutgers U Busch Campus Dept Chem & Biochem Engring Brett & Bowser Rds Piscataway NJ 08855

AGER, DAVID SCOTT, landscape architect; b. Poughkeepsie, N.Y., Dec. 21, 1957; s. Donald Ralph and Martha Frances (Laidlaw) A.; m. Patricia Ann Reynolds, Sept. 12, 1981; children: Steven David, Gina Patricia. B.Landscape Arch., La. State U., 1980. Registered landscape architect; cert. planner. Landscape designer Hayward & Pakan Assocs., Poughkeepsie, N.Y., 1980-81; civil designer Burns & Roe Inc., Oradell, N.J., 1981-83; land design specialist Frederick County Planning Commn., Frederick, Md., 1983-84; sr. planner Dewberry & Davis, Gaithersburg, Md., 1984-86, Rodgers & Assocs., Inc., Rockville, Md., 1986—. Mem. Frederick County Land Use Coun., 1989, Frederick County Affordable Housing Commn. Mem. Am. Soc. Landscape Architects (Md. Chpt. Honor award 1991), Am. Planning Assn., Frederick County Builders Assn., Frederick County C. of C. Republican. Episcopalian. Home: 4905 Old Swimming Pool Rd Frederick MD 21702-5821

AGNE, PHYLLIS G., artist, educator; b. N.Y.C., May 20, 1932; d. John J. and Anna (Rosen) Gross; 1 child, Wendy Agne Reed. Student, Art Students League, 1950-51; BA, Hunter Coll., CUNY, 1970; MFA, Columbia U., 1972. Lectr. Wagner Coll., Staten Island, N.Y., 1971-72, Fairleigh Dickinson U., Madison, N.J., 1972; assoc. prof. U. Conn., Waterbury, 1973-92; artist, 1992—; vis. faculty fellow Yale U./Carnegie Mellon Inst.. Solo exhbns. include The Waterbury (Conn.) Club, 1986, William Benton Mus. Art, Storrs, Conn., others; group exhbns. include Conn. Women Artists Juried Exhbns., New Haven, Norwich and Hartford, 1976-86, Slater Meml. Mus., Norwich, 1986, 88, 89, CUNY Grad. Ctr., N.Y.C., 1978, L'Atelier Gallery, Essex, Conn., 1985, Nat. Drawing Assn., N.Y.C., 1989, Galerie Triangle, Washington, 1988, Erector Sq. Gallery, New Haven, 1990, Aetna Gallery, Hartford, 1991, many others; represented in permanent collections Am. Brands, Anco Wood Specialties, Inc., The Delong Corp., The New Haven Paint and Clay Club, Tarlow, Levy, Harding and Droney, A.M. Sachs, Fulton Gallery, Mimi Kazon, Ted Hook, Peter Agostini, Mr. and Mrs. Alfred Berman, Edward Fitzgerald, Leland Sandifur, Prof. Richard Kuhns, Frank Surace, Mr. and Mrs. L. Robinson, Mr. and Mrs. Joel Lehrer, Mr. and Mrs. Wendel Agne, Irena Urdang, Victoria Read, Eugene Fracchia, Mr. and Mrs. George Chamlin. William Graf scholar Women's Trade Union League; U. Conn. Rsch. Found. grantee. Mem. Am. Artists Profl. League, Nat. Drawing Assn., Conn. Women Artists, New Haven Paint and Clay Club.

AGNEW, CHARLES ROBERT, academic administrator; b. Pitts., July 29, 1955; s. Robert Johnston and Esther (Hall) A.; m. Anne Stright, June 24, 1978; children: Charles R. Jr., Sarah Jean. BA, Edinboro State Coll., 1977; MS, Gannon U., 1981. Admissions rep. Erie (Pa.) Bus. Ctr., 1977-79; program counselor Gannon-Hahnemann B.S./M.D. program Gannon U., Erie, 1979-81, dir. admissions Villa Maria Coll., 1981-82, devel. officer, 1982-83; dir. devel. Edinboro (Pa.) U., 1983-85; v.p. external affairs Gannon U., Erie, 1985-88; v.p. for advancement Quinnipiac Coll., Hamden, Conn., 1987—; lectr. presentations to various profl. assns. Bd. dirs. United Meth. Homes of Conn., Inc., Shelton, 1989—; mem. exec. com. Quinnipiac Coun., Boy Scouts Am., Hamden, 1988—; participant Greater New Haven (Conn.) Walk Against Hunger, 1988—; coach Little League, North Haven, 1991—; chmn. adminstrv. coun. United Meth. Ch. Hamden Plains. Recipient Disting. Svc. award Edinboro Found., 1977. Mem. Nat. Soc. Fund Raising Execs., Coun. for Advancement and Support of Edn., Devel. Assn. So. Conn., Newcomen Soc. U.S., Ctr. for the Study of the Presidency, Greater New Haven C. of C., New Haven Lawn Club, Quinnipiack Club, Rotary, Phi Kappa Delta, Pi Delta Epsilon. Republican. Methodist. Home: 75 Wayland St North Haven CT 06473-4353 Office: Quinnipiac Coll Mount Carmel Ave New Haven CT 06518

AGNEW, FRANKLIN RAYMOND, development executive, musical consultant; b. Elizabethtown, NY, May 14, 1957; s. Franklin Clark and Betty Zane (Corson) A.; m. Sue Ann Charlton, July 26, 1980 (div. 1989); m. Patricia Ann Herrick, Dec. 29, 1990. MusB, Crane Sch. Music, Potsdam, N.Y., 1980. Program coord. alumni assn. SUNY, Geneseo, 1980-82; asst. dir. alumni-parent rels. SUNY, Binghamton, 1983-87, dir. ann. giving, 1987-90; asst. v.p. for devel. SUNY-Empire State Coll., Saratoga Springs, N.Y., 1990—; bd. dirs. Adirondack Home Health Aids, Glens Falls, N.Y. Composer: (mus. scores for Olympic Games in Lake Placid, N.Y.) Awards March, 1980, Fanfares, 1980; composer, producer (compact disk) Ray Agnew, 1989. Cons. United Way of Broome County, Binghamton, 1988; vol. sta. WSKG pub. radio and TV, Binghamton, 1983-90; dir. Saratoga County Arts Coun., Saratoga Springs, N.Y., 1991. Mem. ASCAP, Coun. for Advancement and Support Edn., Nat. Soc. Fund Raising Execs., Saratoga Springs C. of C. (leadership program 1990), Rotary (bd. dirs. Saratoga Springs club). Democrat. Methodist. Home: 4 Clinton Pl Saratoga Springs NY 12866-2110 Office: SUNY Empire State Coll One Union Ave Saratoga Springs NY 12866

AGNEW, JEFFREY STEVEN ANTHONY, lawyer; b. Camden, N.J., Oct. 11, 1962; s. Harrison Hatch and Patricia Clare (McKinley) A. BA, Northwestern U., 1985; JD, NYU, 1988. Bar: N.J. 1988, N.Y. 1989. Assoc. Hughes Hubbard & Reed, N.Y.C., 1987-88, Shearman & Sterling, N.Y.C., 1988—. Mem. ABA, N.Y. Bar Assn., N.J. Bar Assn., Phi Beta Kappa, Pi Sigma Alpha. Republican. Roman Catholic. Office: 599 Lexington Ave New York NY 10022-6030

AGNEW, JOHN ALEXANDER, education educator; b. Millom, Cumbria, Eng., Aug. 29, 1949; s. Herbert and Anne (MacPherson) A.; m. Susan J. Baillie, Nov. 24, 1976; children: Katherine, Christine. BA, Exeter U., Eng., 1970; Cert. Edn., Liverpool U., Eng., 1971; MA, Ohio State U., 1973, PhD, 1976. Asst. prof. Syracuse (N.Y.) U., 1975-81, assoc. prof., 1981-87, prof., 1987—; dir. social sci. prog., Syracuse U., 1981-88. Author: Place and Politics, 1987, The U.S. in World Economy, 1987; co-author: The Geography of World Economy, 1989; editor: The City in Cultural Context, 1984, The Power of Place, 1989. Mem. Assn. of Am. Geographers, Inst. of British Geographers. Office: Syracuse U 303 HB Crouse Hall Syracuse NY 13244

AGNEW, NANCY LONGLEY, educational administrator; b. Iowa City, Iowa, June 5, 1928; d. Harry Sherman and Agnes (Fulton) Longley; m. Seth Marshall Agnew, Jan. 15, 1966 (dec.); children: Lydia Agnew Speller, Rosanna Agnew LaBonte. BA, Wellesley Coll., 1950; MBA, NYU, 1968. Copywriter N.Y. Herald Tribune, N.Y.C., 1952-56; asst. to pres. Am. Heritage Pub. Co., Inc., N.Y.C., 1956-59, dir. pub. rels. and asst. mgr. Book div., 1959-69; head upper sch., advisor to devel. office Nightingale-Bamford Sch., N.Y.C., 1969-79, dir. devel., 1979-80; dir. corp. and found. giving Wellesley (Mass.) Coll., 1981-85, v.p. for pub. affairs, 1985—; speaker Coun. for Advancement and Study of Edn. confs. Contbr. articles to Glamour, Boston Globe, Wellesley Alumnae Mag., others. Vol. Boston Symphony Orch., 1985—. Mem. Cosmopolitan Club (N.Y.C.). Democrat. Episcopalian. Home: 204 Grove St Wellesley MA 02181-7409 Office: Wellesley Coll Wellesley MA 02181

AGNEW, PETER TOMLIN, employee benefit consultant; b. Orange, N.J., Nov. 20, 1948; s. William Harold and Janet Elisabeth (Gittinger) A.; m. Linda W. Seyffarth; children: Jonathan, Stephen, Douglas, Karen; 1 step child, Kristin Seyffarth. BA cum laude, Amherst Coll., 1971; MBA, NYU, 1976. CLU. Asst. investment officer Mutual Benefit Life, Newark, 1971-78; exec. v.p., bd. dir., prin. Post & Kurtz, Inc., N.Y.C., 1978-85; sr. regional dir. Minet, N.Y.C., 1985—; pres. P. Tomlin Agnew Assocs., Glen Ridge, N.J., 1982—; mem. pension com. Croda, Inc. Contbr. articles to profl. jours. Capt. United Way, Newark, 1978; assoc. class agt. Amherst Coll. Alumni Fund, 1980—; mem. exec. bd. Rep. Congl. Leadership Coun., 1988-92. Fellow Life Mgmt. Inst.; mem. Soc. CLU (com. chmn. N.Y. chpt. 1984), Assn. Advanced Life Underwriters, Yale Ins. Group (chmn. 1988-90), Glen Ridge Country Club, Downtown Assn., Williams Club. Presbyterian. Home: 503 Ridgewood Ave Glen Ridge NJ 07028-1821

AGNONE, ANTHONY MICHAEL, engineering professor, consultant; b. Naples, Campania, Italy, July 27, 1941; came to U.S., 1954; s. Serafino and Maria (Baglivo) A.; m. Maria Mercogliano, Dec. 29, 1973; 1 child, Serafino. BS in Aerospace Engring., Polytech. Inst. Bklyn., 1963; MS in Astronautics, Polytech. Inst. Bklyn., Farmingdale, N.Y., 1967; PhD, NYU, 1973. Propulsion engr. Gen. Applied Sci. Labs., Westbury, N.Y., 1963-68; sr. rsch. scientist NYU, N.Y.C., 1968-82, assoc. prof., 1983-87; sr. cons. scientist Avco Corp., Lowell, Mass., 1982-83; sr. scientist Eloret Inst., Palo Alto, Calif., 1987; assoc. prof. Hofstra U., Hempstead, N.Y., 1987—. Mem. AIAA (sr., ground test com. 1985-88, coun. mem. LI sect., chair student activities), Combustion Inst., Am. Soc. Engring. Educators. Home: 5 Pleasantview Dr Bayville NY 11709-1503 Office: Hofstra U Dept Engring 1000 Fulton Ave Hempstead NY 11550-1009

AGONAFER, DEREJE, engineer; b. Addis Ababa, Ethiopia, Jan. 16, 1950; came to U.S. 1968; s. Yemiru and Guetenesh A.; m. Carolyn T., Mar. 5, 1982; children: Damena, Senayet. BS, U. Colo., 1972; MS, Howard U., 1978, PhD, 1984. Teaching asst. Univ. Colo., Boulder, 1970-72, Howard U., Washington, 1976-79; part-time instr. Howard U., 1980-83, instr., 1983-84; sr. assoc. engr. IBM, Poughkeepsie, N.Y., 1984-85; staff engr, 1985-88, adv. engr., 1988-92; sr. engr. IBM, Poughkeepsie, N.Y., 1992—. Patentee, Circuit Package Cooling Technique 1987; author: numerous articles in profl. jours. Named Most Outstanding Student Grad., Howard U., 1984, Instr. of Yr., 1983, Most Outstanding Tchr., 1983; recipient Outstanding Tech. Achievement award Computer Aided Thermal Modeling, 1991, 1st Level Invention Achievement award, 1992. Mem. ASME (program chmn. 1987— Mid-Hudson chpt., mem. K-16 com.), Sigma Xi. Office: IBM Dept B02 Bldg 701 PO Box 950 Poughkeepsie NY 12602

AGRES, THEODORE JOEL, editor; b. Chgo., July 6, 1949; s. Morris A. and Lee (Frank) A.; m. Rosetta Maria Agres, Aug. 22, 1982; children: Jason Maxwell, Michael Antonio. BA, U. Chgo., 1971; postgrad., Johns Hopkins U., 1989—. Asst. editor Research & Devel. Mag., Chgo., 1973-75; features editor The News World, N.Y.C., 1976-78; news editor The News World, 1978-79, Washington Bur. chief, 1979-82; asst. mng. editor The Washington Times, 1982—; pres., bd. dirs. Investment & Trading Network, Cheverly, Md., 1983—. Contbr. articles to profl. jours. Mem. Soc. Profl. Journalists (pres. Washington chpt. 1985-86), Am. Soc. Newspaper Editors, Investigative Reporters and Editors, Nat. Assn. Sci. Writers, Am. Mgmt. Assn. Unificationist. Office: The Washington Times 3600 New York Ave NE Washington DC 20002-1996

AGUD, ROGER, city official; b. Bklyn., Nov. 11, 1926; s. Alfred Caravaca and Mary Rose (Momparlar) A.; student pub. schs., N.Y.C.; m. Carole Ackerman, Nov. 30, 1973; children: Linda, Steven, Nancy, Diane. Electrician, Roseland Ballroom, N.Y.C., 1945-50; carpenter H.C. Bohack, Bklyn., 1950-56; mechanic Pan Am World Airways, Kennedy Airport, N.Y.C., 1956-64; founder Agud Elec. Svc., Merrick, N.Y., 1964-67; bldg. insp. Town of Hempstead (N.Y.), 1967—. Pres. North Merrick Rep. Club, 1967; founder scoutmaster troop 455 Boy Scouts Am., 1965; v.p. Make A Wish Found. Nassau County. Served with USN, 1943-45. Recipient Charles Schlimm award Nassau County Bldg. Ofcls., 1973, Francis Klaess award, 1978. Mem. Assn. Towns N.Y. State (pres. 1990), N.Y. State Bldg. Ofcls. (pres. 1980-82), Ea. States Bldg. Ofcls. Fedn. (dir. 1979—), Kiwanis, Mason. Republican. Lutheran. Home: 6132 Greenspointe Dr Boynton Beach FL 33437-4912

AGUIAR, ADAM MARTIN, chemist, educator; b. Newark, Aug. 11, 1929; s. Joaquim Ramahlo and Emilea Andrada (Nunes) A.; m. Laura E. Brand, Sept. 2, 1980; children: Justine Diane, David Laurence, Adam Albert, Erick Arthur, Aaron Benjamin. B.S., Fairleigh Dickinson U., 1955; M.A., Columbia U., 1957, Ph.D., 1960. Chemist Otto B. May, Newark, 1948-55; asst. prof. Fairleigh Dickinson U., Rutherford, N.J., 1959-63; asst. prof. chemistry Tulane U., New Orleans, 1963-65, assoc. prof., 1965-67, prof., 1967-72, head dept. chemistry Newcomb Coll. div., 1970; dean grad. and research programs William Paterson Coll., Wayne, N.J., 1972-73; research prof. Rutgers U., Newark, 1973-75; prof. chemistry Fairleigh Dickinson U., Madison, N.J., 1975—, chmn. dept. chemistry/geol. scis., 1984-89; pres. Seltox Corp., N.J., 1980—; cons. chem. firms in, La. and N.J. Contbr. articles to profl. jours. Union Carbide fellow, 1957; NIH fellow, 1959; recipient other grants. Mem. AAUP, Am. Chem. Soc., AAAS, N.Y. Acad. Sci., Ctr. for Profl. Advancement, Sigma Xi, Phi Lambda Epsilon, Phi Omega Epsilon. Home: 37 Wyncrest Ln Neptune NJ 07753-7421 Office: Fairleigh Dickinson U 285 Madison Ave Madison NJ 07940-1099

AGUINAGA, PENELOPE ANNE, data processing executive; b. Lutcher, La., Nov. 11, 1958; d. Irby Joseph Louque and Cefronia Joyce Caldwell Zavoyna; m. Eduardo Aguinaga, Dec. 31, 1987; children: Eduardo Louque, Victoria Anne. Sec. Westinghouse Elec. Corp., Balt., 1978-89; pres. Qualified System Support, Inc., Hanover, Md., 1990—. Office: Qualified System Support 1321C Mercedes Dr Hanover MD 21076

AHEARN, ROBERT JOHN, lawyer; b. Milford, Mass., Aug. 7, 1961; s. James R. and Phyllis A. (Lombardi) A. BA in Bus., Boston U., 1983; cert. in emergency med. tech., Northeastern U., 1983; JD, Suffolk U., 1986; LLM in Tax, Boston U., 1989. Bar: Mass. 1986. Cost acct. Johnson & Johnson Products, Braintree, Mass., 1983; tax specialist Laventhol & Horwath, CPAs, Boston, 1986-87; tax atty. Hutchings & Levy, P.C., Framingham, Mass., 1987—. Mem. Am. Mensa, Nat. Acad. of Elder Law Attys. Roman Catholic. Office: Hutchings & Levy PC 205 Walnut St Framingham MA 01701

AHERN, BARBARA ANN, secondary school educator; b. Worcester, Mass., Sept. 11, 1940; d. Bernard Francis and Alice Marion (Signor) Forand; m. Ronald Joseph Ahern, Aug. 7, 1965; children: Stephen Patrick, Deborah Louise. BS, Emmanuel Coll., 1975; MEd, Boston State Coll., 1982; MSN, Anna Maria Coll., 1986. RN, Mass. Oper. rm. nurse Tufts-N.E. Med. Ctr., Boston, 1961-63; rsch./open heart nurse Harvard Med. Sch., Boston, 1963-66; spl. care nurse Mass. Gen. Peter Bent Hosp., Boston, 1966-75; mental health coord. Middlesex County Hosp., Waltham, Mass., 1975-77; crisis counselor Billerica (Mass.) High Sch., 1978-79; instr. health tech. Shawsheen Valley Tech. High Sch., Billerica, 1979—, chmn. dept., 1986—. Author curriculum in field. Fellow Inst. Critical and Creative Thinking in Scis., 1982, Donahue Inst. for Gov. Svcs., 1989; recipient Exemplary Tchr. award Order of Demolay. Mem. NEA, Mass. Tchrs. Assn., Shawsheen Tchrs. Assn. (exec. com. 1983-85, sec. 1985-86, negotiating com.), Mass. Vocat. Assn. (sec./treas. health occupational divsn. 1984-87), Mass. Voc. Leadership Assn., Psi Chi. Democrat. Roman Catholic. Home: 1 Vincent Rd Burlington MA 01803-1217 Office: Shawsheen Valley Regional Tech High Sch 100 Cook St Billerica MA 01821-5499

AHERN, MAUREEN, university art gallery administrator; m. William Knorr. BFA cum laude, U. Mass., 1969; MA in Painting, SUNY, Albany, 1972. Undergrad. teaching resident U. Mass., Amherst, 1968-69; dir. art Jewish Community Ctr. of Boston, Brighton, Mass., 1969-71; instr. painting and drawing Albny Inst. History and Art, 1975-79, curator of exhibits, 1974-81; dir. Thorne-Sagendorph Art Gallery Keene (N.H.) State Coll., 1981—; lectr. edn. programs Albany Inst. History and Art, 1975-79; instr. drawing and design SUNY, Albany, 1972; design instr. Mt. Wachusett C.C., Gardner, Mass., 1982; pres. N.H. Visual Arts Coalition, 1986—. Exhibited art works, 1979-89. Bd. dirs. Arts 1000, N.H. Citizens for Art, Concord, 1989-90, N.H. Seacoast Cultural Alliance, 1989-91, Grand Monadnock Arts Coun., 1987-89, Ox-Fam Am., 1987-89; founder, mem. Art in Pub. Places, 1987—. N.H. State Coun. on Arts grantee, 1987—. Mem. Am. Assn. State and Local History, Am. Assn. Mus., New England Mus. Assn., Am. Craft Coun. Home: 80 Eaton Rd West Swanzey NH 03469-3613 Office: Keene State Coll Thorne-Sagendorph Gallery 229 Main St Keene NH 03431

AHLEN, STEVEN PAUL, physicist, educator; b. Oak Park, Ill., Dec. 24, 1949; s. John William and Helen Beatrice (Damaske) A.; m. Susan Ann Lopez, Jan. 21, 1978 (div. Mar. 1990). BS, U. Ill., Chgo., 1970; PhD, U. Calif., Berkeley, 1976. Physicist Lawrence Berkeley Lab., Berkeley, 1976-78; asst. rsch. physicist Space Scis. Lab., Berkeley, 1979-81, assoc. rsch. physicist, 1981-83; lectr. physics dept. U. Calif., Berkeley, 1981; asst. prof. physics Ind. U., Bloomington, 1983-85; vis. sr. physicist Gran Sasso Lab., Assergi, Italy, 1988-89; prof. Boston U., 1985—; mem. Cosmic Ray Program Group NASA, Washington, 1987-90, Balloon Borne Magnet Adv. Com., 1989—. Contbr. over 30 articles to Rev. of Modern Physics, Sci., Phys. Rev., others. NDEA fellow, 1971, Alfred P. Sloan fellow, 1984. Mem. Am. Phys. Soc. Home: 83 Ivy St Apt 12 Brookline MA 02146-4071 Office: Boston U Dept Physics 590 Commonwealth Ave Boston MA 02215-2507

AHLERS, B. ORWIN, marketing executive; b. Bremen, Germany, Aug. 10, 1926; came to U.S., 1953, naturalized, 1962; s. Richard G. and Lillie (Pflueger) A.; B.A. summa cum laude, Bklyn. Coll., 1957; M.B.A., N.Y.U., 1959; m. Ellen Roser, Apr. 11, 1959; children—Eve Doris, Suzanne Ellen. With Ferrostaal A.G., Essen, W. Ger., 1950-53; with Ferrostaal Overseas Corp., N.Y.C., 1953-91, pres. Ferrostaal Corp., N.Y.C., 1973-91, also bd. dirs.; pres. Heavy Duty Equipment Inc., Irvington, N.J., also bd. dirs.; pres. Ferrostaal Machine Tool Corp., also bd. dirs.; bd. dirs. Ferrostaal Metals Corp., San Mateo, Calif.; ret. Mem. ASME. Lutheran. Home: 26 Soundview Dr Port Washington NY 11050-1726

AHLFELD, WILLIAM JOSEPH, editor; b. Benton, Ill., Aug. 18, 1922; s. Walter W. and Perna (Whittington) A.; married, Oct. 16, 1944; children: Kathy, Kevin, Kerry. Student, Northwestern U., 1940, Wright Jr. Coll., 1941-42, Ind. U., 1960-61. Reporter Chgo. Daily Times, 1941-47; account exec. Harry Coleman & Co., Chgo., 1947-48; speech writer U.S. Steel Corp., N.Y.C., 1948-63; v.p. The Mead Corp., Dayton, Ohio, 1963-80; v.p. communications Am. Forest Inst., Washington, 1980-82; dir. office pub. affairs EPA, Washington, 1983-84; cons., owner Ahlfeld & Assocs., Inc., Washington, 1984-85; pres., pub. Forest Industry Affairs Letter, Washington, 1985—. Served to lt. comdr. USNR, 1942-46, PTO. Mem. Soc. Profl. Journalists. Republican. Methodist. Club: Army-Navy (Washington); Kenwood Country (Bethesda, Md.). Home and Office: 6004 Plainview Rd Bethesda MD 20817-6155

AHLGREN, ROY BERTIL, artist; b. Erie, Pa., July 6, 1927; s. Agnar Cornelius and Annie Pauline (Lovendal) A.; m. Martha Ann Nemeth, June 28, 1952; children: Deborah Sue, Alan Roy, David Bruce, Brian Douglas. BSEd, U. Pitts., 1981. Artist, designer Marx Toy Co., Erie, Pa., 1959-70; tchr. art Tech. Meml. High Sch., Erie, 1970-90. Exhibited in group shows including N.W. Printermakers, Seattle, Portland Art Mus., Seattle Art Mus., USIA, Tokyo, 1971, World's Fair, Osaka, Japan, 1970, 8th Norwegian Internat. Print Biennale, 1986; prints exhibited in numerous internat. juried and invitational shows, Brazil, Japan, India, Germany, Poland, Israel, Yugoslavia, Romania, Italy. With USN, 1944-46. Lutheran. Home: 1012 Boyer Rd Erie PA 16511-2516

AHMAD, M. ABRAHAM, lawyer, entrepreneur; b. Tehran, Iran, Apr. 19, 1953; came to U.S., 1970; s. Mehdi and Gity (Tehranchi) A.; m. Bridget Marie Sanna, Oct. 4, 1986; children: M.J. Brendan, M.R. Cameron. B in Mech. Engring., Cath. U. Am., 1974, M in Mech. Engring., 1974, PhD, 1978; JD, Georgetown U., 1986. Bar: Pa. 1987, Md. 1987. Ptnr. Ahmad & Ahmad, L.C., Rockville, Md., 1977—, Scott & Ahmad, Rockville, Md., 1987—; assoc. Weinberg & Green, Balt., 1985-87. Home: 11212 Hurdle Hill Dr Potomac MD 20854-2529 Office: Scott & Ahmad 6110 Executive Blvd Ste 605 Rockville MD 20852-3903

AHMED, ALI, psychiatrist; b. Hyderabad, India, July 10, 1934; came to U.S., 1975; s. Mohammed Abdul and Yaseen Rahim. BSc, D.J. Coll., Karachi, Pakistan, 1957; MB, BS, Dow Med. Coll., Karachi, 1963. Resident U. Mo., Columbia, asst. prof. Dept. Psychiatry, 1980-83; chief of staff Fulton (Mo.) State Hosp., 1980-82, supt., 1983; attending psychiatrist Harrisburg (Pa.) Hosp., 1983-87, Holy Spirit Hosp., Camp Hill, Pa., 1987—, Edgewater Psychiat. Ctr., Harrisburg, 1989—; cons. psychiatrist Setven Mental Health Ctr., Carlisle, Pa., 1987—. Mem. AMA, Am. Psychiat. Assn., Pakistan Psychiat. Soc. Home: 838 Kiehl Dr Lemoyne PA 17043-1205 Office: Ste 309 890 Poplar Church Rd Camp Hill PA 17011

AHMED, IQBAL, psychiatrist, consultant; b. Tumkur, Karnataka, India, Aug. 23, 1951; came to U.S., 1976; s. Rahimuddin Ahmed and Arifa (Banu) Rahimuddin; m. Lisa Suzanne Rose, Oct. 9, 1983; children: Yasmin, Jihan. BS, MB, St. John's Med. Coll., Bangalore, India, 1975. Diplomate in gen. psychiatry and geriatric psychiatry Am. Bd. Psychiatry and Neurology. Intern St. Martha's Hosp., Bangalore, India, 1974-75; resident in psychiatry U. Nebr. Med. Ctr., Omaha, 1976-79; fellowship in consultation Boston U. Sch. Medicine, 1979-81; staff psychiatrist in consultation liaison psychiatry Boston City Hosp., 1981-87, staff psychiatrist, geriatric psychiatry, 1983-85, dir. geriatric neuropsychiatry unit, 1985-87, dir. geriatric psychiatry, 1988-92; assoc. dir. consultation liaison psychiatry New England Med. Ctr., Boston, 1989-92; asst. prof. psychiatry Sch. Medicine, Boston U., 1981-87, Sch. Medicine, Tufts U., Boston; dir. med. student edn. in psychiatry Boston City Hosp.; chief spl. svcs. Hawaii State Hosp., 1992—; assoc. prof. John A. Burn's Sch. Medicine, U. Hawaii, 1992—. Contbr. articles to profl. jours. Mem. Mass. State Dem. Party Minority Caucus, Boston, 1983. Mem. AMA, Am. Psychiat. Assn., Mass. Psychiat. Soc. (mem. coms. on aging and fgn. med. grads.), Royal Coll. Psychiatrists, Acad. Psychosomatic Medicine, Am. Acad. Geriatric Psychiatry. Democrat. Office: Hawaii State Hosp 45-710 Keaahala Rd Kaneohe HI 96744

AHMED, JAVED, consumer products company executive; b. Karachi, Pakistan, Feb. 10, 1960; came to U.S., 1986; s. Ziauddin and Haseena Ahmed; m. Talat Naila Hasan, July 11, 1985; 1 child, Sara Unzila. BA magna cum laude, Williams Coll., Williamstown, Mass., 1982; MBA, Stanford U., 1984. Directeur du marche Procter & Gamble AG, Geneva, 1984-86; mgr. Bain & Co., Inc., Boston, 1986-90, Bain & Co., U.K. Ltd., London, 1990-91; sr. mgr. Bain & Co., Inc., Boston, 1991-92; gen. mgr. Benckiser Consumer Products, Inc., Danbury, Conn., 1992—. Patron Afganistan Refugee Relief Fund, Chgo., 1986—. Haystack scholar Williams Coll, 1978-81, Harry A. Garfield scholar Williams Coll., 1981-82, Rhodes scholarship electee, 1982; fellowship grantee Stuart Found., 1982. Mem. Phi Beta Kappa. Mem. Moslem faith. Home: 277 Beacon St Boston MA 02116

AHMED, SHAIKH SULTAN, cardiologist, educator; b. Delhi, India, Sept. 13, 1937; came to U.S., 1965; s. Mohammed Rafee and Sughra Jan (Yaseen) S.; m. Shaheen K. Elley, Mar. 18, 1967; children—Salman, Sohaib. B.Sc., D.J. Sci. Coll., Karachi, Pakistan, 1958; M.B.B.S., Dow Med. Coll., Karachi, 1963. Diplomate Am. Bd. Internal Medicine, Royal Coll. Physicians of Can., 1971. Registrar Dow Med. Coll., 1964-65; intern Samaritan Hosp., Troy, N.Y., 1965-66; resident Tucson Hosp. Med. Ednl. Program, 1966-68; cardiology fellow U. Medicine and Dentistry N.J.-N.J. Med. Sch., Newark, 1968-70, mem. faculty, 1970—, prof. medicine, 1980—, co-dir. catheterization lab., 1976—, dir. stress testing lab., 1975—, chief medicine Firm C., 1983-91; cons. cardiology St. Joseph Hosp., Patterson, N.Y., St. Michael's Hosp., Newark. Contbr. articles to med. jours., chpts. to books. Sec., Pakistan Edn. Found., 1976-79; pres. Islamic Sch. Bergen County, Teaneck, N.J., 1980-81, Muslim Community of Bergen County, Teaneck. Recipient Exceptional Merit award U. Medicine and Dentistry of N.J., 1982. Fellow Royal Coll. Physicians (Can.), ACP, Am. Coll. Chest Physicians, Am. Coll. Cardiology, Am. Coll. Angiology, Royal Soc. Medicine (U.K.). Islam. Home: 40 Greentree Ter Tenafly NJ 07670-2406 Office: U Medicine and Dentistry NJ Med Sch 100 Bergen St Newark NJ 07103

AHN, HO-SAM, pharmacologist; b. Seoul, Korea, Feb. 25, 1940; came to U.S., 1965; s. Dae-Sun and Do-Nam (Kwon) A.; m. Young-Hee Im, Aug. 11, 1969; children: Mary Miwon, Katherine Misook. BS in Zoology, Seoul Nat. U., 1963, MS in Zoology and Physiology, 1965; MA in Cell Biology, Princeton U., 1967; PhD in Zoology, Rutgers U., 1972. Rsch. biochemist Merck & Co. Inc., Rahway, N.J., 1970-73; postdoctoral fellow Albert Einstein Coll. of Medicine, Yeshiva U., Bronx, 1973-77, rsch. asst. prof., 1977-78; sr. scientist Schering-Plough Corp., Bloomfield, N.J., 1978-83; prin. scientist Shering-Plough Corp., Bloomfield, N.J., 1983-92, sr. prin. scientist, 1992—; adj. assoc. prof. Fairleigh Dickinson U. Teaneck, N.J., 1986-90; expert on mission UN Indsl. Devel. Orgn., Geneva, Austria, winter 1987, spring 1989. Author: (chpt.) The Biology of Phosphodiesterase, 1992; co-author: (chpt.) Growth, Nutrition and Metabolism of Cells in Culture, vol. 4, 1977, New Cardiovascular Drugs, 1985. Coord. Korean Biosci. Club of N.Y., N.Y.C., 1983-84, founding mem.; v.p. We Search Club chpt. Toastmasters Club Internat., Bloomfield, 1987. With Korean Army, 1960-62. NIMH/NIH fellow, 1974-77; recipient Svc. award We Search chpt. Toastmasters, 1987. Mem. AAAS, Am. Soc. Pharmacology and Exptl. Therapeutics, Korean Scientists and Engrs. Assn. in Am. (pres. N.Y.C. chpt. 1983-84), NYAS Pharmacology Discussion Group. Roman Catholic. Office: Schering-Plough Rsch Inst 60 Orange St Bloomfield NJ 07003

AHN, JAEHOON, Journalist; b. P'Yang, Korea, May 13, 1941; came to U.S., 1968; s. Heung-Yul and Eunrae (Park) A.; m. Soonhoon L. Ahn, Feb. 22, 1969; children: Soomie L., Yoomie L. BA, Seoul (Korea) Nat. U., 1965. Fgn. corr. Joong-Ang Ilbo, Seoul, 1966-67; on-line editor Washington Post, Washington, 1969—; columnist Newspaper & Broadcasting KPI, Seoul, 1989—; contbr. editor Sisa-Jour., Seoul, 1989-91, 1989-90; commentator internat. news MBC Radio, Seoul, 1990—; guest columnist Korea Times, L.A., 1988—; lectr. in field. Contbr. articles to profl. jours. Mem. Asian Am. Journalists Assn., Sigma Delta Chi. Home: 8013 Quarry Ridge Way Bethesda MD 20817 Office: Washington Post 1150 15th St NW Washington DC 20071

AHO, JEAN, family counselor; b. Boston, Aug. 31, 1942; d. Glenn Gordon and Evelyn Louise (Simpson) MacNutt; children: Sara Lee Beller, Leslee Karen McKay, Glenn Edward. BA with distinction, U. Maine, 1989, postgrad. Foster care provider Div. Child Guardianship, Boston, 1969-82, Bur. Mental Retardation, Presque Isle, Maine, 1983-87; asst. instr. psychology U. Maine, Presque Isle, 1988-89; instr. Presque Isle Adult Edn., 1989, Div. Confs. and Insts., Orono, Maine, 1990; family counselor Devel. Ctr., Orono, Maine, 1190—; with statis. analysis dept. edn. U. Maine, Orono, 1991; individual counselor Personal Growth and Devel. Ctr., Orono, 1990; real estate investor, Mass., Maine, 1965—; TV lectr. dept. human devel. U. Maine, Orono, 1990, group therapy leader div. behavioral sci., Presque Isle, 1987, contbg. researcher dept. human devel., Orono, 1990. Vol. art tchr. Bridgewater (Maine) Grammar Sch., 1983; pres. Presque Isle Farmers Market, 1980-82, Houlton (Maine) Farmers Market, 1979-87; trustee MacNutt Art Trust, Dorchester, Mass., 1988-91. Harry S. Truman scholar, 1987. Mem. Am. Assn. for Counseling and Devel., Internat. Assn. Marriage and Family Counselors, Assn. for Specialists in Group Work, Am. Mental Health Counselors Assn., Internat. Assn. Addictions and Offender Counselors. Home: PO Box 94 Bridgewater ME 04735-0094 Office: 27 Congress St Old Town ME 04468-1811

AHRENS, HENRY WILLIAM, art educator, consultant, puppeteer; b. Bklyn., Apr. 11, 1918; s. Otto Conrad and Caroline Johanna (Schoneck) A.; B.F.A., Pratt Inst., Bklyn., 1941; M.A., Columbia U., 1943; Ed.D., N.Y. U., 1964; m. Marjorie June Brooks, Dec. 18, 1965. Art tchr. Lincoln Sch., Tchrs. Coll., Columbia U., N.Y.C., 1941-42; art supr. Bd. Edn., South River, N.J., 1946-47; art tchr. Bd. Edn., Elizabeth, N.J., 1947-52; asso. prof. SUNY, Buffalo, 1952-57; prof. art Trenton State Coll. (N.J.), 1957-83 chmn. art dept., 1965-70, 72-75, ret., 1983, prof. emeritus, 1987—; cons. Thomas A. Edison State Coll., Trenton, 1975—; exchange prof. U. Frankfurt, Frankfurt Am Main, W. Ger., 1970-71. Served alt. mil. duty Civilian Public Service, 1943-46. Recipient Frank A. Rexford medal for Cooperation in Govt., 1937. Mem. Art Educators N.J. (hon. life, 1st v.p., pres.), Puppeteers Am. (religious cons. 1969-76), Mercer County Ret. Tchrs. Assn., N.J. Edn. Assn., NEA, Union Internat. Del La Marionettes, Phi Delta Kappa (life). Clubs: Quaker Village Puppeteers, Pa. Guild, Puppeteers Am. Original puppet prodns. in Can., Europe and U.S., 1947—; lectr. in field. Mem. Soc. Friends. Home and Office: 139 N Main St Yardley PA 19067-1322

AHRENS, JOHN FREDERICK, physiologist, consultant; b. Bellmore, N.Y., Nov. 21, 1929; s. William Harry and Martha Elizabeth (Schneider) A.; m. Phyllis Marilyn Carle, Sept. 14, 1952; children: William, John Jr., Timothy, Karl. BSA, U. Ga., 1954; MS, Iowa State U., 1955, PhD, 1957. Conservation aide soil conservation svc. USDA, Millbrook, N.Y., 1949-50, 52; asst. plant physiologist Conn. Agr. Experiment Station, Windsor, Conn., 1957-63, assoc. plant physiologist, 1963-70, plant physiologist, 1970—; cons. in weed sci., Bloomfield, Conn., 1970—. Author: (with others) Manual North American Nut Trees; editor: (with others) Southern New England Christmas Tree Growers Manual; contbr. over 200 articles to profl. jours. Bd. dirs. Bloomfield Inland Wetlands Commn., Wintonbury Land Trust, Bloomfield, 1988—. Sgt. USMC, 1950-52, Korea. Named Man of the Year Gonn. Nurserymen's Assn., 1962, Outstanding Man in Agr. Conn. State Grange, 1974; recipient Merit award Conn. Christmas Tree Growers Assn., 1988, Extension award Am. Assn. Nurserymen, 1989, Special Recognition award N.Y. Christmas Tree Growers Assn., 1991. Fellow Weed Sci. Soc. Am. (pres. 1988-89), Northeastern Weed Sci. Soc. (pres. 1970-71, disting. mem. 1980), Plant Propagator's Soc., Coun. for Agr. Sci. and Tech., Plant Growth Regulator Soc., Sigma Xi, Alpha Zeta. Home: 32 Hoskins Rd Bloomfield CT 06002-1135 Office: Conn Agr Experiment Sta PO Box 248 Cook Hill Rd Windsor CT 06095

AHRENS, KENT, museum director, art historian; b. Martinsburg, W.Va.; s. Fred E. and Mary C. (Routzahn) A. A.B., Dartmouth Coll., 1961; M.A., U. Md., 1966; Ph.D., U. Del., 1972. Mem. faculty Fla. State U., Tallahassee, 1971-74, Randolph-Macon Woman's Coll., Lynchburg, Va., 1974-77; mem. curatorial staff Wadsworth Atheneum, Hartford, Conn., 1977-78; mem. faculty Georgetown U., Washington, 1979-82; dir. Everhart Mus., Scranton, Pa., 1982-90, The Rockwell Mus., 1990—; mem. task force on art activities Lynchburg Bicentennial Commn., 1975-76; project evaluator Md. Com. Humanities, 1980-82; adv. panel The Lucan Ctr., Scranton, Pa., 1983-84; mem. mus. adv. com. Pa. Hist. and Mus. Commn., 1984-86; trustee Williamstown Regional Art Conservation Lab., Inc., Mass., 1984-92; mem. art mus. adv. panel Pa. Council on Arts, 1984-87, Pa. Fedn. Mus. and Hist. Orgns., 1989-90; mem. adv. com. on exhbns. at Pa. Gov.'s residence, 1987-90; juror Regional Art '89, Marywood Coll. Art Galleries, Scranton, 1989, Regional 1991, Arnot Art Mus., Elmira, 1991; bd. dirs. Mus. West. Author: (with others) Rembrandt in the National Gallery of Art, 1969; contbg. author: Wadsworth Atheneum Paintings: The Netherlands and German-speaking Countries, 1969, The Drawings and Watercolors by Truman Seymour (1824-1891), Everhart Mus., 1986; co-author: Frederic C. Knight (1898-1979), Everhart Mus., 1987, The Oils and Watercolors by Edward D. Boit (1840-1915), Everhart Mus., 1990; contbr. articles on Am. art history to profl. jours. Served as 1st lt. U.S. Army, 1962-64. Recipient grant-in-aid Am. Philos. Soc., 1975; Samuel H. Kress fellow Nat. Gallery of Art, 1970-71; NEH fellow, 1973-74, Mus. Mgmt. Inst., J. Paul Getty Trust, 1991. Mem. Am. Coll. Art Assn., Am. Assn. Mus. (on-site surveyor mus. assessment program 1984-89, accreditation com. 1986), Mus. Assn. Pa. (chmn. 1984-90), Mid-Atlantic Assn. Mus., Scranton Area Found. Office: The Rockwell Mus 111 Cedar St Corning NY 14830-2694

AHSANULLAH, MOHAMMAD, statistics educator; b. Tangra, Bengal, India, Aug. 31, 1936; s. Sam Ali and Nazmun Nesa; m. Masuda Gowas; children: Omar, Tabassum, Nisar. BS with honors, Presidency Coll., Calcutta, India, 1957; MS, Calcutta U., 1959; PhD, N.C. State U., 1969. Asst. prof. N.D. State U., Fargo, 1968-69; rsch. scientist Nat. Health and Welfare Can., Ottawa, 1969-74; prof. U. Brasilia (Brazil), 1974-76; rsch. scientist Nat. Health and Welfare, Ottawa, 1976-79; prof. U. Brasilia, 1979-81; vis. prof. Nat. U. of Mex., Mexico City, 1981-82; assoc. prof. Temple U., Phila., 1982-84; prof. stats. Rider Coll., Lawrenceville, N.J., 1984—. Author: Introduction to Record Values, 1988; editor. Jour. Applied Statis. Sci.; contbr. more than 125 articles to profl. jours. Fellow Royal Statis. Soc.; mem. Inst. Math. Stats., Am. Statis. Assn., Internat. Statis. Inst. Home: 124 Independence Dr Southampton PA 18966-2785 Office: Rider Coll 2083 Lawrenceville Rd Trenton NJ 08648-3099

AIA, MICHAEL ALFRED, marketing executive; b. Boston, Oct. 13, 1933; s. Michele and Maria (Umana) A.; m. Bette J. Silva; 1 child, Steven M. BS in Chem. Engring., Northeastern U., 1956; MA in Chemistry, Queens Coll., 1965. Phosphor chemist GTE/Sylvania, Towanda, Pa., 1956-62; rsch. specialist GTE Labs., Bayside, N.Y., 1962-67; engring. mgr. gen. tech. div. IBM, Hopewell Junction, N.Y., 1967-81; faculty mem. corp. tech. inst. IBM, N.Y.C. and Thornwood, N.Y., 1981-87; securities industry mktg. exec. IBM, N.Y.C., 1987—. Patentee phosphor and battery materials. V.p. high sch. and elem. sch. bds., Towanda, 1960-62. 1st lt. Signal Corps, USAR, 1957-62. Recipient Senate Productivity award U.S. Senate, 1984. Mem. N.Y. Acad. Scis. Home: Apt LJ 333 E 49th St New York NY 10017 Office: IBM Corp 12th Fl 909 3rd Ave New York NY 10022

AIDELSON, DEBORAH ADELE, actuary, consultant; b. Savannah, Ga., Dec. 8, 1968; d. Sidney and Ruth Fay (Kosover) S. BA, Yeshiva U., N.Y.C., 1989. Actuary Kwasha Lipton, Inc., Ft. Lee, N.J., 1989-90, Am. Internat. Group, N.Y.C., 1990—. Home: 104-60 Queens Blvd Apt 4H Forest Hills NY 11375

AIELLO, EDWARD LAWRENCE, biological sciences educator; b. N.Y.C., June 12, 1928; s. James J. and Marguerite (Parry) A.; m. Ann Stassi, July 25, 1953; children: Mary Ann, Laura, Janet. BS in Biology, St. Peter's Coll., 1953; MA in Zoology, Columbia U., 1954, PhD in Zoology, 1960. Instr. Flint (Mich.) Jr. Coll., 1957-58; instr. to assoc. prof. N.Y. Med. Coll., N.Y.C., 1958-65; assoc. prof. to prof. biol. scis. Fordham U., Bronx, N.Y., 1965—, dept. chair, 1979-82. With USN, 1946-49. Mem. Am. Soc. Zoologists, Am. Soc. for Pharmacology and Exptl. Therapeutics. Home: 432 White Rd Mineola NY 11501-1022 Office: Fordham U Bronx NY 10458

AIELLO, GENNARO C., insurance company executive; b. Ridgway, Pa., Dec. 16, 1953; s. Victor C. and Victoria I. (Bevacqua) A.; m. Cynthia K. Medvid, Sept. 20, 1975; children: Erin M., Kathryn T. BS, Gannon U., 1975; postgrad., Pa. State U, 1974-76. Lic. ins. agt., real estate agt. Sales rep. Met. Ins. Co., DuBois, Pa., 1975-80; owner, agt. Ins. Mktg. Assocs., Ridgway, 1980-86; acct. exec. The Pa. Mfrs. Assn. Group, Ridgway, 1986—; gen. mgr. Wolf Run Marina, Warren, Pa., 1978-79; controller U.S. Coal, Inc., Ridgway, 1981-83; realtor Anderson and Kime, St. Marys, Pa., 1983—. Bd. dirs., v.p. Ridgway Action for Community Enhancement, 1986—; chmn. St. Leo's Home and Sch. Assn., Ridgway, 1989-91; bd. dirs. St. Leo's Parish Coun., 1986-90, pres. sports assn., 1988-91; pres. Elk County Coun. on the Arts, 1991-92, v.p., 1990-91, pres., 1991-92; pres. Ridgway Independence Festival Inc., 1990—; bd. dirs. Ridgway Community Nurses Svc. Inc., 1991—, Outdoor Companions Inc., 1991, Citizens Against Phys., Sexual and Emotional Abuse, 1992—. Mem. Johnsonburg C. of C. (bd. dirs., pres. 1989—), Elk-Cameron Bd. Realtors, Jaycees (pres. local chpt. 1986-87), Ducks Unltd. (spons. chmn. 1987-88), Elk County Country Club (bd. dirs. 1991—, v.p. 1992—), Rotary (pres. Johnsonburg lodge 1980-81, K.C. (3d deg.). Home: 220 Montmorenci Ave Ridgway PA 15853-1615 Office: The PMA Group PO Box I Mfr's Bldg Ridgway PA 15853

AIELLO, JOHN R., psychologist, consultant; b. New Rochelle, N.Y., June 14, 1946; s. John V. and Elsie R. Aiello; m. Donna Elaine Thompson, July 20, 1979; children: Lauren, Ryan. MA, CUNY, 1970; PhD, Mich. State U., 1972. Asst. prof. psychology Rutgers State U., New Brunswick, N.J., 1972-78, assoc. prof. psychology, 1978—; assoc. prof. Vanderbilt U., Nashville, 1977-79; cons. AT&T Bell Labs., Holmdel, N.J., 1980—; regional cons. State Farm Ins. Co., Wayne, N.J., 1983-88. Editor: Residential Crowding and Design, 1979; author (with others) Handbook of Environmental Psychology, 1987; Contbr. more than 100 chpts. to books and articles to profl. jours. including Jour. of Applied Social Psychology, Jour. of Personality and Social Psychology. Charter mem. Citizens for Quality Edn., Metuchen, N.J., 1989—. Grantee Nat. Inst. Child Health and Human Devel., 1974, NIH, 1977, William H. Donner Found., 1979, Nat. Sci. Found., 1981. Fellow Am. Psychol. Assn., Am. Psychol. Soc. (charter fellow); mem. Soc. Exptl. Social Psychology. Home: 77 Carson Ave Metuchen NJ 08840-2539 Office: Rutgers State U Psychology Dept Tillett Hall New Brunswick NJ 08903

AIELLO, TINA MARIE, mathematics educator; b. Medford, Mass., Aug. 16, 1963; d. Antonio and Olga (Raffa) A. BA magna cum laude, Emmanuel Coll., 1985; MA, Boston Coll., 1985. Teaching fellow Boston Coll., Chestnut Hill, Mass., 1986-88, Ahana instr., summer 1988, adj. faculty mem., 1988-89; instr. Emmanuel Coll., Boston, 1989—; text answer book cons. Brown Pub. Co., Wellesley, Mass., 1989-90. Mem. walk for hunger Project Bread, Boston. Mem. Math. Assn. Am., Nat. Coun. Tchrs. of Math., Kappa Gamma Pi. Home: 35 E Cross St Somerville MA 02145 Office: Emmanuel Coll 400 The Fenway Boston MA 02115

AIGEN, BETSY PAULA, psychotherapist; b. N.Y.C., Sept. 13, 1938; d. Abraham H. and Gertrude (Rosenblum) Wasserman; m. Ronald Aigen, Dec. 7, 1957 (div. Jan. 1979); m. Isadore Schumukler, June 20, 1982; 1 child, Jennifer Loren. BA, New Sch. Social Research, 1971; MA, Columbia U., 1972; D of Psychology, Rutgers U., 1980. Group co-leader, asst. psychotherapist Inst. Rational Psychotherapy, N.Y.C., 1967-72; asst. course instr. Columbia U., N.Y.C., 1971-72; psychotherapist Mt. Carmel Guild, Englewood, N.J., 1980-82, SELF Edn. Learning and Feeling, N.Y.C., 1982—; founder, dir. Surrogate Mother Program, N.Y.C., 1985—; cons. Police Chief Tng. Community Workshops Assn., N.Y.C., 1973-74, Richmond Fellowship Mental Health Halfway Houses, Eng. and U.S., 1970-75. Contbr. articles to profl. jours. Chmn. Tenants Com., N.Y.C., 1975-85; active Profl. Theatre, 1956-67. Mem. Nat. Orgn. Women, RESOLVE, Adoptive Parents Com., Am. Psychol. Assn., N.Y. St. Psychol. Assn., N.J. St. Psychol. Assn., N.Y. Assn. Feminist Therapists. (co-founder, charter), Am. Orgn. Surrogate Parenting Practitioners (founder, charter). Democrat. Jewish. Home: 220 W 93rd Ste 1A New York NY 10025 Office: Surrogate Mother Program Ste 3D 640 W End Ave New York NY 10024

AIKEN, LAWRENCE JAMES, cosmetics company executive, consultant; b. Toledo, Nov. 26, 1944; s. James R. and Mary (Heilner) A.; children: Amy, Monica, Nicholas. BBA, U. Toledo, 1966. Pres., chief exec. officer Sanofi Beauté, Inc., N.Y.C. Republican. Roman Catholic. Lodge: Rotary (v.p. Charlotte, N.C. chpt. 1981). Home: 1969 Cross Hwy Fairfield CT 06430-1706

AIKEN, ROBERT DENNIS, physician; b. Detroit, Sept. 4, 1950; s. Max Gordon and Hope (Collins) A.; m. Ellen Jayne Warren, Nov. 25, 1980; children: David, Caroline. BS, U. Mich., 1972; MD, Wayne State U., 1976. Med. resident Baylor Coll. Med., Houston, 1976-78; resident in Neurology Columbia Presbyn. Med. Ctr., N.Y.C., 1978-81; fellow in neuroncology Meml. Sloan Kettering Cancer Ctr., N.Y.C., 1981-83; asst. prof. Jefferson Med. Coll., Phila., 1983—. Fellow Coll. Physicians Phila.; mem. Am. Acad. Neurology, Assn. Rsch. Nervous and Mental Diseases. Office: Thomas Jefferson U Hosp Ste 617 1015 Chestnut St Philadelphia PA 19107

AIKEN, WILLIAM ERIC, securities research executive; b. Cambridge, Mass., Feb. 8, 1935; s. William Edward and Elizabeth (Polson) A.; m. Barbara Joan Rizzi, May 28, 1958 (div. Sept. 1963); 1 dau., Elizabeth Stewart; m. Yvonne P. Kane, June 1, 1985. BA in English, UCLA, 1960. Assoc. editor Bus. Week mag., Los Angeles, Chgo., N.Y.C., 1960-63; editor RIA Investors Service, N.Y.C., 1963-67; mng. editor Electronics mag., N.Y.C., 1967-69; exec. editor Value Line Investment Survey, N.Y.C., 1969-73; assoc. editor Barron's, N.Y.C., 1973-74; freelance writer and editor, N.Y.C., 1974-78; sr. v.p., dir. research Daniels & Cartwright, N.Y.C., 1978-84; founder, chief exec. officer, pub. The Proxy Monitor Inc., 1984—; cons. in field. Contbr. articles to various publs. Served with USMC, 1952-56. Mem. Sigma Delta Chi. Republican. Episcopalian. Club: Princeton (N.Y.C.). Home: 20 Haven Esplanade Staten Island NY 10301-2717

AIKMAN, WILLIAM FRANCIS, venture capitalist; b. Darby, Pa., Aug. 1, 1945; s. John Earl and Phyllis Rose (Miller) A. AB, Brown U., 1967; student, Harvard Law Sch., 1970-72; JD, U. Pa., Phila., 1972. Bar: Mass. 1972. Mem. counsel Mass. Law Reform Inst., Boston, 1969-73; pres. Mass. Ctr. for Pub. Interest Law, Boston, 1973-76, Mass. Tech. Devel. Corp., Boston, 1979-84, Gryphon Mgmt. Co., Boston, 1984—; under sec. of econ. affairs Commonwealth of Mass., Boston, 1976-79; bd. dirs. Advanced Ceramic Tech., Inc., Somerset, N.J., Optex Corp., Rockville, md., Geltech, Inc., Alachua, Fla., Maxdem Corp., San Dimas, Calif. Bd. dirs. Fedn. for Children with Spl. Needs, Boston, Mass. Cert. Devel. Corp., Boston. Mem. Harvard Club Boston, Brown Club Boston. Presbyterian. Home: 179 Beacon St Boston MA 02116-1423 Office: Gryphon Mgmt Co 545 Boylston St Boston MA 02116-3606

AILLONI-CHARAS, MIRIAM CLARA, interior designer, consultant; b. Veere, The Netherlands, July 31, 1935; came to U.S., 1958; d. Maurits and Elzina (De Groot) Taytelbaum; m. Dan Ailloni-Charas, Oct. 8, 1957; children: Ethan Benjamin, Orrin, Adam. Degree in Interiors, Pratt Inst., 1962; BSc, SUNY, Albany, 1978. Interior designer S.J. Miller Assocs., N.Y.C., 1960-63; interior design cons. Rye Brook, N.Y., 1963-88, 90—; exec. v.p. Contract 2000 Inc., Port Chester, N.Y., 1988-90. Treas. Temple Guild, Congregation Emanu-El, Rye, N.Y., 1979-88, co-chair, 1988—, trustee, 1986—. Recipient Cert. of Merit, U.S. Jaycees, 1962, March of Dimes, 1989, 91. Mem. Am. Soc. Interior Designers, Allied Bd. Trade, Westchester Assn. Women Bus. Owners (bd. dirs. 1988—), Nat. Trust for Historic Preservation, Westchester C. of C. (area devel. coun. 1988-90). Home and Office: 23 Woodland Dr Port Chester NY 10573-1797

AIN, MARK STUART, manufacturing company executive; b. N.Y.C., Apr. 23, 1943; s. Jacob and Pearl (Poneman) A.; m. Lillian Sober; children: Joshua, Adam, Rebecca. MBA, U. Rochester, N.Y., 1967; BSEE, MIT, 1964. With mktg. div. Esso Internat., N.Y.C., 1967-69; sales tng. mgr. Digital Equipment Corp., Maynard, Mass., 1969-71; cons. Billings & Reese, Concord, Mass., 1971-74; freelance cons. Newton, Mass., 1974-78; pres., chief exec. officer Kronos Inc., Waltham, Mass., 1978—; bd. advisors Prospect Hill Entrepreneur Ctr., Waltham, 1989—; bd. dirs. Managistics, Echo Lab., Gentech, etc. Inventee in field; contbr. articles to profl. jours. Coach YMCA Sports Team, Newton, 1989—. Mem. AEA LaNet Chief Exec. Officer Group. Office: Kronos Inc 62 Fourth Rd Waltham MA 02154

AINSWORTH, KENNETH GEORGE, economist, educator, consultant; b. Shawano, Wis., July 13, 1923; s. Henry and Pauline (DeSwarte) A.; m. Audrey Lacroix; children: Thomas Lee, Leslie Karen, Scott Henry. BS, U. Wis., 1948, MS, 1949; PhD, Brown U., 1957. Instr. econs. Bowdoin Coll., Brunswick, Maine, 1953-57; from asst. to assoc. prof. Allegheny Coll., Meadville, Pa., 1957-67, prof., 1967—, sec. of faculty, 1985-89; economist U.S. Congress Com. on Judiciary, Washington, 1961-63, cons., 1963-67; sr. resident Adv. Commn. Intergovtl. Rels., 1979-80; cons. in field. Contbr. articles to profl. jours. Mem. Am. Econs. Assn., Nat. Tax Assn. (mem. various coms.), Pa. Econs. Assn. (pres. 1985-86). Office: Allegheny Coll N Main Meadville PA 16335

AISENBERG, IRWIN MORTON, lawyer; b. Worcester, Mass., Aug. 8, 1925; s. William and Esther (Lewis) A.; m. Lois P., Sept. 4, 1955 (div. Apr. 1986); children: Karen Sue Portner, Sondra Lee, David Craig, Steven Bennett. BS in Chem Engring., Carnegie Mellon U., 1946; JD, Georgetown U., 1957. Bar: D.C. 1958, U.S. Ct. Customs and Patent Appeals, 1958, N.J. 1965, Va. 1969, U.S. Supreme Ct. 1964, U.S. Ct. Appeals (Fed. cir.) 1982; registered profl. engr., Mass. Patent examiner U.S. Patent and Trademark Office, Washington, 1954-57; assoc. atty. Wenderoth, Lind & Ponack, Washington, 1957-63; chief patent counsel Sandoz, Inc., Hanover, N.J., 1963-67; pvt. practice Washington, 1967-75; ptnr. Berman & Aisenberg, Washington, 1975-91; mng. ptnr. Berman, Aisenberg & Platt, Washington, 1980-85; ptnr. Jacobson, Price, Holman & Stern, Washington, 1991—; lectr. Franklin Pierce Law Sch., Concord, N.H., 1980-88; mem. appeal bd. Nat. Register of Health Svc. Providers in Psychology, 1987-89. Mem. editorial adv. bd. IDEA, Jour. Law and Tech., 1981—; author: Attorney's Dictionary of Patent Claims, 1985, Patent Law Precedent, 1991; contbr. articles to profl. jours.; patentee in field. Served to cpl. U.S. Army, 1950-52. Mem. ABA, Internat. Assn. Protection Indsl. Property, Am. Intellectual Property Law Assn., Am. Arbitration Assn. (mem. panel arbitrators). Jewish. Club: Kenwood Golf and Country, Am. Contract Bridge League (life master). Home: 6402 Kirby Rd Bethesda MD 20817-5524 Office: Jacobson Price Holman & Stern Jenifer Bldg 400 7th St NW Washington DC 20004

AISNER, MARK, internist; b. Boston, Feb. 27, 1910; s. Jacob and Sadie (Solomon) A.; m. Helen Cashman, June 27, 1948; children: Jonathan Alan, Susan Jane. AB, Harvard Coll., 1931; MD, Tufts U., 1935. Diplomate Am. Bd. Internal Medicine. Rsch. fellow physiology Tufts U. Sch. Medicine, Boston, 1935; residency Boston City Hosp., 1936-38; asst. prof. medicine Tufts U. Sch. Medicine, Boston, 1942-55, assoc. clin. prof. medicine, 1955-77, head course in phys. diagnosis, 1946-75; head course in physiology Tufts Dental Sch., Boston, 1938-43; chief cardiology Hahnemann Hosp., Boston, 1975-90; cons. staff Newton-Wellesley Hosp., Newton, Mass., 1991—, Faulkner Hosp., Boston, 1991—, Beth Israel Hosp., Boston, 1991—; vis. physician Holy Ghost Hosp. (now Yonville Hosp.), Cambridge, Mass., 1943-53; attending physician Boston VA Hosp., 1947-75; chief cardiology Winthrop Community Hosp., 1950-75; active staff to consulting staff Faulkner

Hosp., 1963—, Newton-Wellesley Hosp., 1938—; assoc. staff to consulting staff Beth ISrael Hosp., 1938—. Mem. editorial bd. New Eng. Jour. of Medicine, 1954-73; editor Disease-A-Month, 1954-59, editor emeritus, 1959—; contbr. articles to profl. jours. Trustee Countway Med. Libr., Boston, 1991—; mem. Bd. of Registration in Medicine, Boston, 1981-84. Maj. Army Med. Corps, 1943-46. Recipient Bronze star U.S. Army, 1945, Army Commendation medal U.S. Army, 1946. Fellow Mass. Med. Soc., Am. Coll. Physicians; mem. Am. Coll. Physicians (Mass. Internist of Yr. 1991), Coun. Clin. Cardiology, Am. Heart Assn., AOA Honor Med. Soc. Home: 35 Evelyn Rd Waban MA 02168

AISTARS, JOHN, artist, educator; b. Riga, Latvia, June 9, 1938; came to U.S., 1949; s. Ernest and Lidija (Sulte) A.; m. Mara Ruta Germanis, June 20, 1964; children: Sandra, Guntra. BFA, Sch. of Art Inst. Chgo., 1961; MFA, Syracuse (N.Y.) U., 1964. Faculty Cazenovia (N.Y.) Coll., 1965—, chmn. Ctr. for Art and Design Studies, 1981—, dir. Chapman Art Ctr. Gallery, 1979—. Artist: group exhbns. include: Art Inst., Chgo., Everson Mus., Syracuse, N.Y. (regional exhbn.), Meml. Art Gallery, Rochester, N.Y. (regional exhbn.), Munson-Williams-Proctor Inst., Utica, N.Y., Roberson Ctr. Arts & Sci., Binghamton, N.Y., Cooperstown (N.Y.) Art Assn. Nat.; one or two man shows include Columbus, Ohio, Syracuse, Rockville, Md., Chgo., Grand Rapids, Mich., Cleve., Utica, N.Y., Toronto, Can., others; also contbr. articles to various publs. Recipient 1st Nat. Bank award, Binghamton, N.Y., 1975, 1st prize N.Y. Regional Exhbn., Kirkland, N.Y., 1989, M. Bevier Meml. prize Cooperstown (N.Y.) Art Assn., 1989, M. Mahoney Meml. award Norwich (N.Y.) Fine Arts Guild, 1991. Mem. AAUP, Cooperstown (N.Y.) Art Assn. Home: Oran Delphi Rd Manlius NY 13104-9338 Office: Cazenovia Coll Cazenovia NY 13105

AK, DOGAN, lawyer; b. Istanbul, Turkey, Mar. 2, 1928; came to U.S., 1979; s. Mustafa Sevket and Ayse (Akat) A.; m. Aliye Aydagül, May 15, 1970; children: Ayse, Asli, Osman. Grad., Coll. St. Joseph, Turkey, 1948; lic. in law, Istanbul (Turkey) U. Law, 1952; cert., N.Y. Law Sch.; student, Bridgeport U. Law Sch., 1972, NYU, 1972. Bar: N.Y. 1978. Ptnr. Dogan Ak & Yuda Reyna Attys. at Law, Istanbul, 1955-78; assoc. Ira J. Sands Atty. at Law, N.Y.C., 1979-81; ptnr. Frankel, Russo & Ak Attys. at Law, N.Y.C., 1981-83; proprietor Dogan Ak Law Offices, N.Y.C., 1983—; legal consul Fedn. Am. & Turkish Socs., N.Y.C., 1985—. Chmn. Am. Turkish Islamic and Cultural Ctr., N.Y.C., 1985—. Served to capt. Turkish Army, 1954-55, Korea. Mem. N.Y.C. Bar Assn. Democrat. Office: 299 Broadway Ste 1200 New York NY 10007-1901

AKALAITIS, JOANNE, theater director, writer; b. Chgo., June 29, 1937; d. Clement and Estelle (Mattis) A.; m. Philip Grass, July 15, 1965 (div. 1974); children: Juliet, Zachary. BA in Philosophy, U. Chgo., 1960. Founding mem., performer, designer and dir. Mabou Mines, 1970—; co. works incluce Lee Breuer's Animations, Samuel Beckett's Cascando, Dressed Like an Egg (based on writings of Colette), Franz Xaver Kroetz's Through the Leaves (5 Obie awards); writer, dir. play and film: Dead End Kids, A History of Nuclear Power; other works include Request Concert (Drama Desk award), The Photographer at Bklyn. Acad. Mus. Next Wave Festival, Samuel Beckett's Endgame, Jean Genet's The Balcony at Am. Repertory Theater in Cambridge; writer, dir. Green Card; Leon and Lena (Georg Buchner), The Screens (Jean Genet) at Guthrie Theater, Mpls.; 'Tis Pity She's a Whore, Goodman Theater, Chgo., Cymbeline and Henry IV, Parts 1 and 2, Pub. Theater, N.Y.C.; artistic dir. N.Y. Shakespeare Festival, 1991. Recipient 4 Obie awards for disting. direction and prodn., Rosamund Gilder award; Guggenheim fellow, Rockefeller Playwright fellow Mark Taper Forum; grantee Rockefeller Found., Nat. Endowment for Arts. *

AKELL, ROBERT BERRY, chemical engineering consultant; b. Boston, May 14, 1921; s. Joseph William and Elizabeth (Posner) A.; m. Josephine Gelb, June 3, 1942 (dec. July 1985); children: Paul S., Sandra, June; m. Dorothy Margaret Hirzel, Sept. 25, 1988. BS, Northeastern U., 1942; MChemE, U. Louisville, 1946. Registered profl. engr., Del. With Joseph E. Seagrams & Sons, Louisville and Balt., 1942-56, chief chemist; from cons. engr. to prin. cons. E. I. duPont de Nemours, Wilmington, Del., 1956-82; pres. Fresno Enterprises, Inc., Wilmington, 1982—; cons. in field, 1982—. Editor: New Directions in Extraction, 1984; contbr. articles to profl. jours., chpt. to book. Dist. commr. Boy Scouts Am., Balt., 1955; bd. dirs. Wilmington Civic Assn., 1957, Wilmington Recreation Assn., 1980; trustee, v.p. Congregation Beth Emeth, Wilmington, 1966; trustee Wilmington Jewish Community Ctr., 1988-92. Fellow Am. Inst. Chem. Engrs. (mem. internat. com. for solvent extraction and tech., chmn. internat. solvent extraction conf. 1983). Republican. Home and Office: 1506 Fresno Rd Wilmington DE 19803-5124

AKERS, JOHN FELLOWS, information processing company executive; b. Boston, Dec. 28, 1934; s. Kenneth Fellows and Mary Joan (Reed) A.; m. Susan Davis, Apr. 16, 1960; children: Scott, Pamela, Anne. B.S., Yale U., 1956. With IBM Corp., Armonk, N.Y., 1960—, v.p., 1976-82, v.p., asst. group exec., 1978-81, sr. v.p., 1982-83, group exec. Info. Systems and Communications Group, 1982-83, pres., 1983-89, also bd. dirs., chief exec. officer, 1985—, chmn. bd., 1986—; bd. dirs. N.Y. Times Co., PepsiCo. Trustee Met. Mus. Art, Calif. Inst. Tech.; mem. bd. govs. United Way of Am. Lt. USNR, 1956-60. Office: IBM Corp Old Orchard Rd Armonk NY 10504-1709

AKERS, OTTIE CLAY, lawyer, publisher; b. Huntsville, Ala., Sept. 4, 1949; s. Merrideth Townsend Akers and Mary Lois (Reed) Fulford; m. Marcia Bradley Ligon, Mar. 21, 1971; 1 child, Katie Virginia. BA, U. Alabama, Birmingham, 1972, MA, 1976; JD, Samford U., Birmingham, 1985. Bar: Ala. 1985. Assoc. Haskell, Slaughter, Young & Lewis, Birmingham, 1985-86; pub., chief exec. officer Clay-Bradley, Washington, 1986-90. Mem. ABA, Am. Judicature Soc., Assn. Trial Lawyers Am., Ala. Bar Assn., Exch. Club (bd. dirs. Birmingham chpt. 1986, child abuse prevention ctr. 1985-86) Friends of Ala. Sch. Fine Arts Theatre (pres. 1989-90). Home: 120 Roebuck Dr Birmingham AL 35215-8035

AKERS, SHELDON BUCKINGHAM, JR., electrical and computer engineering educator; b. Washington, Oct. 22, 1926; s. Sheldon Buckingham and Ina (Graham) A.; m. Jean Ellen Daniel, May 30, 1953; children: Janet, Karen, Steven, David. BSEE, U. Md., 1948, MA in Math., 1952. Electronics scientist Nat. Bureau of Standards, Washington, 1948-50, computer engr., 1953-54; radio engr. USCG Hdqrs., Washington, 1950-53; mathematician Avion div. ACF Industries, Alexandria, Va., 1954-56; computer engr. Electronics Lab. GE Co., Syracuse, N.Y., 1956-85; prof. elec. and computer engring. U. Mass., Amherst, 1985—; adj. prof. Syracuse U., 1975-85. Co-author: Design Automation of Digital Systems, 1974. Grantee Tektronix Corp., 1986, NSF, 1987-89. Fellow IEEE (guest editor jour. 1986); mem. Math. Assn. Am., Sigma Xi. Presbyterian. Home: 78 Larkspur Dr Amherst MA 01002-3439 Office: U Mass Elec Engring Dept Amherst MA 01003

AKIN, GWENDOLYN, photographer; b. N.Y.C., July 26, 1950; d. John Akin and Dorothy (Forbes) Thorne. BFA, Sch. of Mus. Fine Arts, Boston, 1972. One woman shows include White Columns, N.Y.C., 1987-88, Shaidai Gallery, Tokyo O'Kane Gallery, Houston, 1988, XYZ Gallery, Ghent, Belgium, 1989, No. Light Gallery, Ariz. State U., Tempe, 1990, Galerie Farideh Cadot, Paris, 1990, Pamela Auchincloss Gallery, 1992others; exhibited in numerous group shows including Mus. fur Geologie and Minerologie, Leiden, Holland, 1989, Farideh Cadot Gallery, N.Y.C., 1989, The Alternative Mus., N.Y.C., 1989, Mus. Contemporary Art, Chgo., 1989-90, Walter Art Ctr., Mpls., 1990, Montserrat Coll. Art Gallery, Beverly, Mass., 1990, Musee Zoologique de l'Univ. Louis Pasteur, Strasbourg, France, 1990, Houston Ctr. Photography, 1990, Hallwalls, Buffalo, 1990, Boston Athenaeum, 1990, Akin Gallery, Boston, 1990, Natur Mus. Senckenberg Forschungsinstitut, Frankfort, Germany, Ctr. Creative Photography, Barcelona and Madrid, Spain, Addison Gallery Am . Art, Andover, Mass., 1991, Nat. Mus. Am. Art., Washington, 1991, Mus. Fine Art, Houston, 1992, Long Beach (Calif.) Mus. Art, 1992; others; represented in permanent collections at San Francisco Mus. Modern Art, Mus. Photographic Arts, San Diego, Tokyo Inst. Tech., Espace Photographique Paris, Mus. Fine Art, Houston, Amerada Hess Corp., N.Y.C., Afga Corp. Collection, Los Angeles County Mus. Art, Ctr. Creative Photography, Tucson; contbr. photographs to jours., books, catalogues, newspapers and brochures. Home and Studio: 55 Prince St New York NY 10012

AKIN, WILLIAM ERNEST, college administrator; b. Chambers County, Ala., Dec. 15, 1936; s. William Dewey Akin and Emily Lowery (Williams) Smith; m. Suzanne A. Winford, June 5, 1961 (div. 1970); m. Kathryn Elizabeth Teter, Aug. 27, 1971; children: Lynn Suzanne, William E. Jr. BA, U. Md., 1961, MA, 1963; PhD, U. Rochester, 1970. Instr. history SUNY, Binghamton, 1966-69; assoc. prof. history Loyola Coll., Montreal, Can., 1969-77; asst. dean of arts Concordia U., Montreal, Can., 1975-77, dean of humanities, 1977-79; dean of coll. Ursinus Coll., Collegeville, Pa., 1979-88; v.p. acad. affairs Ursinus Coll., Collegeville, 1988—; dir. Montgomery Sci. Rsch. Inc., Blue Bell, Pa., 1985—; mem. editorial bd. Small Coll. Creativity, 1989—. Author: Faculty Development in Liberal Arts Colleges, 1985, Technocracy and the American Dream, 1977. Mem. AAUP, Soc. for Am. Baseball Rsch., Am. Assn. Acad. Adminstrs., Am. Hist. Assn. Democrat. Methodist. Office: Ursinus Coll PO Box 1000 Collegeville PA 19426-1000

AKKAPEDDI, KAUSHIK SHARMA, engineer; b. Secunderabad, Andhra, India, June 26, 1954; came to U.S., 1976; s. Suryaprakasa Rao and Swarajya Laxmi (Addepalli) A.; m. Nirmala Gollapudi, Nov. 25, 1980; 1 child, Naveen. BSME, Osmania U., Hyderabad, India, 1976; MSME, N.J. Inst. Tech., 1977. Mem. tech. staff AT&T Bell Labs., Whippany, N.J., 1978—; chmn. affirmative action com. AT&T Bell Labs, Whippany, 1985-87. Contbr. articles to IEEE Transactions, Jour. Soc. Photo Instrumentation Engrs. Mem. Soc. Photo Instrumentation Engrs. Office: AT&T Bell Labs Whippany Rd Whippany NJ 07981-1508

AKMAN, JEFFREY SCOTT, psychiatrist; b. Balt., May 7, 1956; s. Alvin and Marion (Blumberg) A. BS, Duke U., 1977; MD, George Wash. U., 1981. Diplomate Am. Bd. Psychiatry and Neurology. Resident in psychiatry George Washington U., Washington, 1981-85, instr. chief resident in psychiatry, 1984-85, asst. prof. psychiatry and behavioral scis., 1985-90, assoc. prof. psychiatry and behaviorl scis., 1990-91; asst. dean for student ednl. policies George Washington Univ. Sch. Medicine, 1991—; prin. investigator AIDS edn. project NIMH/George Wash. U., 1986-89; dir. med. edn. George Washington U. Dept. Psychiatry. Contbr. articles to profl. jours. Cons. Whitman-Walker Clinic, Inc., Washington, 1986—, ARC, D.C. chpt., 1986—, D.C. Commn. of Pub. Health, 1986-89. Recipient Jr. Faculty Devel. award NIMH, 1985-86. Mem. Med. Soc. D.C., Washington Psychiat. Soc. (pres. D.C. chpt.), Med. Soc. D.C. (pres. psychiatry sect.), Am. Assn. Physicians for Human Rights, Am. Psychiat. Asns. (commn. on AIDS 1988—, C.A. Roeske award). Democrat. Jewish. Home: 1936 Calvert St NW Washington DC 20009-1502 Office: George Washington U Dept Psychiatry 2150 Pennsylvania Ave NW Washington DC 20037-2396

ALAFOUZO, ANTONIA, marketing professional; b. Cairo, Egypt, Oct. 13, 1952; came to U.S., 1982; d. Pano Antony and Agni-Maria (Ranos) A.; m. Thomas D'Ambola Jr., May 29, 1988; 1 child. BSC in Econs., Brunel U., London, 1975; Diploma in Econs. and Politics, Oxford (Eng.) U., 1977, M of Philosophy, PhD, 1980. Staff reporter The Economist, London, 1973-75, contbg. writer, 1975-82; communications exec. Rubenstein, Wolfson Co., N.Y.C., 1982-87; founder, pres. Markcom Ltd., N.Y.C., 1987—; contbg. writer Fin. Report, London, 1975-82; cons. writer Fin. Times, London, 1980-82; cons. communications and econs. World Gold Council, N.Y.C., 1982—. Contbr. reports to fin. publs. Mem. Inst. Journalism Internat., Oxford Union Soc. Office: Markcom Ltd 277 Broadway New York NY 10007

ALAIE, BELINDA JEAN, technical writer; b. Orlando, Fla., Nov. 21, 1954; d. Hugh Edwin and Emily Vinez (Whaley) Furr; m. Hossein Alaie, May 18, 1974; 1 child, Shala Michelle. AS, Henderson County Jr. Coll., Athens, Tex., 1974; BS, Tex. Tech U., 1975. Mktg. services supr. Tex. Instruments, Lubbock, 1976-79; tech. writer, redactor Waverly Press (Williams & Wilkins), Balt., 1986—. Tech. writer for Cancer Rsch., Jour. Immunology, Jour. Nuclear Medicine, Proceedings of Am. Assn. Cancer Rsch., Transplantation, Lab. Investigation. Home: 205 Norman Ave Glen Burnie MD 21060-7721 Office: Waverly Press Inc Mount Royal and Guilford Aves Baltimore MD 21202

ALAIMO, ANTHONY LOUIS, management consultant; b. Bronx, N.Y., Sept. 13, 1954; s. Louis Peter and Agatha (Trimarchi) A.; m. Laurie Leigh Kerns, Apr. 2, 1988. BS in Acctg., Fordham U., 1976; MBA, Harvard U., 1981; M in Pub. Policy, Georgetown U., 1987. Acct. Dalt Internat., Englewood, N.J., 1970-74; controller Uddeholm Steel Corp., Totowa, N.J., 1974-79; exec. v.p. Dalt Internat., Englewood, N.J., 1981-88; pres. Naturama, Inc., Fairfax, Va., 1988-90; assoc. Phoenix Northeast Corp., Franklin Lakes, N.J., 1988—; prin. Coloney Von Oosten & Assocs., Inc., Tallahassee, Fla., 1990—. Scoutmaster, Boy Scouts Am., Arlington, 1987-88, asst. scoutmaster, 1988—. Home: 12003 Settle Ct Fairfax VA 22033-2600 Office: Coloney Von Oosten Assocs 194 N Adams St Tallahassee FL 32302

ALAMAR, PAUL, consulting engineer; b. Scranton, Pa., Oct. 7, 1924; s. I.C. and Rose (Perilstein) A.; m. Naomi Weiner, Nov. 9, 1946; children Frances Alamar Gelb, Hope Alamar Morris. BS in Mech. Engring., Cornell U., 1944. Registered profl. engr., Pa., Calif.; cert. safety profl. Dist. mgr., corp. sec. H. Perilstein Glass Co., Scranton and Okmulgee, Okla., 1946-71, Scranton Plate Glass Co., 1946-71; cons. engr. Paul Alamar, P.E., Scranton, 1971—; endowment dir. Scranton-Lackawanna Jewish Fedn., 1983-85; lectr.-instr. Pa. State U., Scranton, Wilkes-Barre, Hazleton, Williamsport, 1979-83; pres. Saga Enterprises Inc., Scranton, 1980—, Webster Towers Realty Co., Scranton, 1977—, Wave Oak Realty Co., Scranton, 1973—. Pres., Jewish Fedn., Scranton, 1970-73, Planning Coun. Social Svcs., Scranton, 1981-83; treas. Scranton-Lackawanna Jewish Coun., 1969; bd. dirs. Jewish Home of Eastern Pa., Scranton, 1972—, United Way of Lackawanna County, 1975—; bd. dirs., asst. treas. Vis. Nurse Assn., 1979, pres., 1986-88 . Lt. (J.g.), USNR, 1943-46, PTO. Recipient citation of merit Scranton-Lackawanna Jewish Coun., 1967, Joel Svc. award Jewish Community Ctr., 1989; named Man of Yr., Jewish Community Ctr., 1977. Mem. Nat. Soc. Profl. Engrs. (pres. N.E. chpt. 1976-77, svc. award 1977), Am. Soc. Safety Engrs. (chmn. N.E. sect. 1977-78, leadership award 1978), Glen Oak Country Club, (v.p. 1970-72), Masons, Lions, Elks. Home: 620 Colfax Ave Scranton PA 18510-1942 Office: PO Box 134 Scranton PA 18501-0134

AL-ASSAF, IBRAHIM ABDULAZIZ, banker; b. Ayon Al-Jawa, Gassim, Saudi Arabia, Jan. 28, 1949; s. Abdulaziz Abdulla and Hussah (Al-Mante) Al-A.; m. Rogayah Al-Manie, Sept. 8, 1978; children: Abdulaziz, Moneerah, Mai, Faisal. BA in Econs. and Polit. Scis., Riyadh (Saudi Arabia) U., 1971; MA in Econs., U. Denver, 1976; PhD in Econs., Colo. State U., 1982. Teaching asst. King Abdulaziz Mil. Acad., Riyadh, 1971-82; chmn. dept. adminstrv. scis., asst. prof. econs. Saudi Fund for Devel., Riyadh, 1982-86, econ. advisor, 1982-86; alt. exec. dir. IMF, Washington, 1986-89; exec. dir. World Bank Group, Washington, 1989—; vis. lectr. Staff's Acad., Riyadh, 1982-83; bd. trustees Saudi Islamic Acad., Washington, 1986—. Mem. Arab Internat. Studies Assn. of Washington, Saudi Econ. Assn., Arab Soc. for Econ. Rsch. Office: World Bank Group 1818 H St NW Washington DC 20433-0002

ALATIS, JAMES EFSTATHIOS, university dean; b. Weirton, W.Va., July 13, 1926; s. Efstathios and Vasiliki (Galanoudis) A.; m. Penelope Mastorides, Dec. 30, 1951; children: William, Stephen, Anthony. B.A., W.Va. U., 1948; M.A., Ohio State U., 1953; Ph.D., 1966. Fulbright lectr. English U., Athens, 1955-57; English testing and teaching specialist Dept. State, 1959-61; specialist for lang. research U.S. Office Edn., 1961-65, chief lang. sect., 1965-66; asso. dean Sch. Langs. and Linguistics, Georgetown U., Washington, 1966-73; dean Sch. Langs. and Linguistics, Georgetown U., 1973—, assoc. prof. linguistics, 1966-75, prof., 1975—; exec. sec. Tchrs. of English to Speakers of Other Langs., 1966-82, exec. dir., rrom 1982; pres. Joint Nat. Com. for Langs., from 1981; Mem. adv. council ERIC Clearinghouse on Linguistics, 1966-71, from 73; bd. dirs. CONPASS, 1966-70. Editor: Studies in Honor of Albert H. Marckwardt, 1972, (with Kristie Twaddell) English as a Second Language in Bilingual Education, 1976, (with Ruth Crymes) Human Factors in ESL, 1977, (with Gerli and Brod) Language in American Life, 1978, Internat. Dimensions of Bilingual Education, 1978, (with G. R. Tucker) Language in Public Life, 1979, Current Issues in Bilingual Education, 1980, (with others) The Second Language Classroom: Directions for the 1980s, 1981, Applied Linguistics and the Preparation of Second Language Teachers: Toward a Rationale, 1983, (with John J. Staczek) Perspectives on Bilingualism and Bilingual Education, 1985, (with Deborah Tannen) Language and Linguistics: The Interdependence of Theory, Data, and Application, 1986, Language Teaching, Testing, and Technology: Lessons from the Past with a View Toward the Future, 1989, Linguistics, Language Teaching and Language Acquisition: The Interdependence of Theory, Practice, and Research, 1990, Quest for Quality: The First 21 Years of TESOL, 1991, Linguistics and Language Pedagogy: The State of the Art, 1991; contbr. articles to profl. jours. Served with USNR, 1944-46. Recipient Mary Glide Goethe prize Am. Name Soc., 1954, North East Conf. award, 1985, President's award Nat. Assn. for Bilingual Edn., 1987; Am. Council Learned Socs. summer study grantee in linguistics U. Mich., 1954. Mem. Am. Council on Teaching Fgn. Langs. Linguistic Soc. Am. (del. 1966-69), Nat. Council Tchrs. English, MLA, Nat. Assn. Fgn. Student Affairs (dir. 1965-66), Def. Language Inst. (bd. visitors), Fedn. Internationale des Professeurs de Langues Vivantes (exec. com.), Phi Beta Kappa. Home: 5108 Sutton Pl Alexandria VA 22304-2704 Office: Georgetown U Sch Lang and Linguistics Washington DC 20057

ALBALA, MARK CRAIG, computer scientist; b. Bklyn., Apr. 16, 1955; s. Albert and Phyllis (Landy) A.; m. Lynn L. Simon, May 10, 1980; 1 child, Samantha Julia. BA, Syracuse U., 1977, MA, 1978. Rsch. analyst Input, Saddle Brook, N.J., 1978-79; mem. engring. staff RCA Globcom, N.Y.C., 1979-81, adminstr. project control, 1981-83; info. analyst Home Box Office, N.Y.C., 1983-84; mem. Info. Ctr. Am. Cyanamid, Wayne, N.J., 1983-84, group leader data and data base adminstrn., 1984-87, mgr. exec. support, 1987—. Contbr. articles to profl. jours. Alumni rep. Syracuse U., 1979—. Mem. Pilot EIS Users Group (pres. 1989-90, conf. chair 1990-91), Data Processing Mgmt. Assn. (pres. 1983-84), N.J. PC Users Group (disk libr. 1986-90). Republican. Jewish. Home: 34 Academy Cir Oakland NJ 07436-2625 Office: Am Cyanamid 697 Route 46 Clifton NJ 07013-1552

ALBANESE, STEPHEN ANTHONY, union official; b. Boston, Oct. 1, 1947; s. Guy And Mary (Costa) A.; m. Camille Dombrowski, Oct. 18, 1970; children: Kristin, Andrea. BA, U. Mass., Boston, 1983. Notary pub. Commonwealth of Mass. Steward Am. Postal Workers Union, Boston, 1971-77, area v.p., 1975-77, state v.p., 1972—, gen. pres. Boston Local, 1977-92; nat. bus. agt. Clerk Craft, 1992—; arbitrator Mass. Lemon Law Panel, Boston, 1988—; field instr. in arbitration U. Mass., Boston, 1988—. Editor union publs. Bostonian, 1977—. Mem. adv. bd. U. Mass., Boston, 1987—, Labor Guild, Boston, 1980—; trustee Salem (Mass.) State Coll., 1990—. Mem. Postal Press Assn. (editor 1972—, Braxton Bates award 1988, Best Editor 1975, 89). Democrat. Roman Catholic. Office: Am Postal Workers Union 137 South St Boston MA 02111

ALBANO, ANNE MARIE, clinical psychologist; b. S.I., N.Y., Aug. 18, 1957; d. Joseph James and Kathleen Anne (Duggan) A. AA, Broward Community Coll., Pompano, Fla., 1976; BS, Fla. State U., Tallahassee, 1979; MA, U. Richmond, 1983; PhD, U. Miss., 1991. Substance abuse counselor Human Resources, Inc., Richmond, Va., 1981-82; psychologist Med. Coll. Va., Richmond, 1982-83; adolescent therapist Adolescents in Distress, Inc., Ft. Lauderdale, Fla., 1983-84; child and family therapist KIDS in Distress, Inc., Oakland Park, Fla., 1984-85; rsch. asst. U. Miss., Oxford, 1985-89, grad. instr., 1987-89; predoctoral intern Dept. Vets. Affairs Med. Ctr., Tufts U. Sch. Medicine, Boston, 1989-90; postdoctoral fellow Phobia and Anxiety Clinic, SUNY, Albany, 1990-92, asst. dir., 1992—; program coord. Ctr. for Stress and Anxiety Disorders, Child and Adolescent Fear and Anxiety Treatment Program, Albany, 1991—; rsch. assoc. faculty SUNY, Albany, 1991—. Mem. APA, Assn. for Advancement of Behavior Therapy. Roman Catholic. Office: Ctr for Stress & Anxiety 1535 Western Ave Albany NY 12203-3513

ALBANO, ANTHONY WILLIAM, career officer; b. Atlanta, Dec. 6, 1953; s. Rocco Louis and Ida Elizabeth (White) A. AA, Monatee Jr. Coll., 1973; BA, U. Fla., 1975; MA, Cen. Mich. U., 1979. Commd. 2d lt. USAF, 1975, advanced through grades to maj., 1979—. Scoutmaster Boy Scouts Am., Rochester, N.H., 1984-86, Ramstein AB, Germany, 1986-88, asst. dist. commr., Mt. Holly, N.J., 1988-92; vestry mem. St. Albans Episcopal. Congregation, Ramstein AB, 1986-88. Mem. Air Force Assn., Order Daedalians, Mil Order of World Wars, Elks. Republican. Home: 62 Dover Rd Mount Holly NJ 08060 Office: McGuire AFB 438 AW/SEF Trenton NJ 08641

ALBEE, EDWARD FRANKLIN, author, playwright; b. Mar. 12, 1928; s. Reed A. and Frances (Cotter) Albee. Student, Trinity Coll., 1946-47. Messenger Western Union, 1955-58; lectr. Brandeis U., Johns Hopkins U., Webster U., others. Plays written include The Zoo Story, 1958, The Death of Bessie Smith, 1959, The Sandbox, 1959, The American Dream, 1960, Who's Afraid of Virginia Woolf?, 1961-62, The Ballad of the Sad Cafe (adaption of Carson McCullers' novella), 1963, Tiny Alice, 1964, Malcolm, 1966, A Delicate Balance, 1966 (Pulitzer Prize winner 1967), Everything in the Garden, 1968, Box, Quotations from Chairman Mao, 1970, All Over, 1971, Seascape, 1975 (Pulitzer prize 1975), Counting the Ways, 1976, Listening, 1977, The Man Who Had Three Arms, 1983, The Lady from Dubuque, 1978-79; adaptation of Lolita (Nabokov), 1980, Finding the Sun, 1982, Marriage Play, 1986-87, Three Tall Women, 1990-91; dir. plays, including Krapp's Last Tape by Samuel Beckett, Alley Theatre, Houston, 1991. pres. Edward F. Albee Found. Recipient Pulitzer prize, 1967, 75; Gold medal in Drama Am. Acad. and Inst. Arts and Letters, 1980; inducted Theater Hall of Fame, 1985. Mem. Nat. Inst. Arts and Letters, Dramatists Guild Coun., PEN Am. Address: 14 Harrison St New York NY 10013*

ALBERT, DOUGLAS MITCHELL, editor, gallery director; b. N.Y.C., Sept. 17, 1956; s. Sheldon Albert and Barbara Helene (Albaum) Auerbach. BA in theatre, SUNY, Albany, 1973. Theatre critic/journalist New Style Mag., London, 1979-85; gen. mgr. Stonewall Repertory Co., N.Y.C., 1985-87; mng. editor ESM Documentations, N.Y.C. and Weissport, Pa., 1985—; gallery dir. Schoolhouse Fine Arts Exhibition Ctr., Weissport, 1987—; curator Schoolhouse Fine Arts Exhbn. Ctr., Weissport, 1987—; arts cons. Lehihton (Pa.) Area C. of C., 1989—. Editor: ESM Documentations Catalogue, 1985. Donor Bucknell U., Lewisburg, Pa., 1989, Webster Coll., St. Louis, 1991, WVLA-T V Channel 44, Pittston, Pa., 1987—. Mem. Whitney Mus. of Am. Art.

ALBERT, GERALD, clinical psychologist; b. N.Y.C., Nov. 13, 1917; s. Andrew I. and Eleanor (Walder) A.; divorced; m. Norma Holm Haskell, 1983; children: Jay Harvey, Laurie Ellen Albert Moxham. BA, CCNY, 1938; MA, New Sch. for Social Research, 1958; EdD, Columbia U., 1964; Cert. psychoanalytic tng. program, L.I. Inst. Mental Health, Queens, N.Y., 1964. Editor Vulcan and Creston Pubs., N.Y.C., 1939-45; nat. dir. advt., pub. relations Universal Pictures, div. ednl. films, N.Y.C., 1945-50; exec. dir. Advt. Enterprises and Continental Research Inst., Queens, N.Y., 1951-64; asst. to full prof. LIU, 1964-85, prof. Emeritus, 1985—; dir. L.I.U. C.W. Post Counseling Ctr., 1964-70; supervising psychologist, clin. dir. L.I. Consultation Ctr., until 1986—, clin. cons., 1986—; pvt. practice marriage and individual therapy, 1958—. Author: (cassette) How to Choose and Keep a Marriage Partner, 1980, The Wonderful Magic of No-Fault Living, 1990; editor-in-chief Jour. Contemporary Psychotherapy, 1985-87; contbr. articles to profl. jours., author booklets. Recipient 1st prize Most Effective Communications/Newsletters Community Agys. Pub. Rels. Assn., 1983. Fellow Am. Assn. for Marriage and Family Therapy; mem. Am. Psychol. Assn., N.Y. Soc. Clin. Psychologists, Soc. Clin. and Exptl. Hypnosis. Office: 271 Merrick Ave East Meadow NY 11554-1549

ALBERT, HARRY FRANCIS, investments executive; b. Phila., Mar. 14, 1935; s. James J. Albert and Mary A. (Miller) Mannes; m. Anna Cosmina Rago, Sept. 5, 1955; children: Anne Marie Borneman, Harry F. Jr., Steven J. Student, Drexel Inst. Tech., 1952-56; student, U. Pa., 1958. Exec. v.p. Health Corp. Am., Wayne, Pa., 1975-80; pres., chmn. Annin, Inc., Berwyn, Pa., 1980—; bd. dirs. Sixteen Corps. Dir. Del. Right to Life, Wilmington, 1975-78; mem. Nat. Right to Life, Delaware County, Pa., 1978—; mem., officer Rotary Internat., Springfield, Pa., 1966-71; bd. dirs., chmn. Ann. Walk for the Homeless, Trevor's Campaign for the Homeless. Recipient Thomas Lovejoy Cup, Manhattan Cos., N.Y., 1985. Mem. Internat. assn. Fin. Planners, Nat. Assn. Variable Annuities (founder), World Trade Club N.Y.C. Republican. Roman Catholic. Home and Office: Annin Inc PO Box 1030 472 Lantern Ln Berwyn PA 19312-2048

ALBERT, IRA BERNARD, social sciences educator; b. Balt., Aug. 8, 1944; s. Milton Albert and Augusta (Hillman) Poltilove; m. Sharon Eve, Dec. 23, 1970; 1 child, Mindi Lauren. BA, Johns Hopkins U., 1966; MA, U. Del., 1968, PhD, 1970. Asst. prof. Old Dominion Univ., Norfolk, Va., 1970-76; asst. prof. Jefferson Community Coll., Louisville, 1977-79, assoc. prof., 1979-81; assoc. prof. Dundalk Community Coll., Balt., 1981-89, prof., 1989—; adj. prof. Ea. Va. Med. Sch., Norfolk, 1974-76; cons. V.A. Hosp., Hampton, 1975-76, Louisville, 1977-81; sr. lectr. Towson State U., Balt., 1985-89; psychology assoc. Taylor Mental Health System, Balt., 1988-91. Contbr. articles to profl. jours. Home: 9213 Turnbull Rd Randallstown MD 21133-3307 Office: Dundalk Community Coll 7200 Sollers Point Rd Baltimore MD 21222-4649

ALBERT, JANET SUE, merchandising educator; b. Bklyn., Feb. 18, 1947; d. Raymond and Myrna (Lisker) Sharenow; m. Martin Jay Albert, Aug. 19, 1973; children: Elizabeth, Andrew. BS, Syracuse U., 1968; MA, NYU, 1975. Mkt. rsch. analyst textiles Dunn & Bradstreet, N.Y.C., 1968-72; fashion dir. Gen. Tire & Rubber Co., N.Y.C., 1972-74; asst. prof. merchandising U. Bridgeport (Conn.), 1974—; fashion dir. fashion sows on cable TV, 1974—. Bd. dirs. United Jewish Appeal, Westport/Bridgeport, 1974-77; bd. dirs., treas. PTA, Westport, 1977—; v.p. sisterhood-Temple Israel, Westport, 1985-89. Mem. AAUP, Am. Assn. Textiles, Shoe Women's Execs., Brandeis Nat. women's Com. (v.p. 1976-77). Democrat. Home: 21 Silver Brook Rd Westport CT 06880-1524 Office: U Bridgeport 10 Hazel St Bridgeport CT 06604-5715

ALBERT, JOHN (JACK ALBERT), communications executive; b. Bklyn., Apr. 16, 1942; s. John and Therse (Mitchell) A.; m. Eileen Hodder, Jan. 4, 1964; children: Terryann, John. AA, Fairleigh Dickinson U., 1960, BS in Bus. Mgmt., 1973, MBA, 1977, M in Mktg., 1983. Cons. engr. Western Electric, Newark, 1961-66, Alta. Govt. Telephone Co., Edmonton, Can., 1961-66; cons. engr. ITT, Nutley, N.J., 1961-66, systems engr., 1966-69; asst. v.p. Western Union, Upper Saddle River, N.J., 1969-81, 1983-85; v.p. Warner Amex Cable Communications Co., Piscataway, N.J., 1981-83; exec. v.p., chief ops. officer Visnews Internat., N.Y.C., 1985-88; v.p. Alpha Lyracom satellite com. Pam Am. Satellite, Greenwich, Conn., 1988—; bd. dirs. Brightstar Communications, London. Patentee in field; contbr. articles to profl. jours. Mem. Soc. Satellite Profls., Radio TV News Dirs. Assn., Internat. Teleprodn. Assn., Soc. Motion Picture & TV Engrs., Nat. Assn. Broadcasters, Nat. Cable TV Assn., Internat. Assn. Satellite Users and Suppliers, Am. C. of C. Office: Alpha Lyracom 1 Pickwick Plz Greenwich CT 06830-5531

ALBERTI, DONALD WESLEY, artist; b. Ft. Eustis, Va., Dec. 25, 1950; s. Donald Wesley and Johnsie Elizabeth (Knight) A. BA, Coll. William and Mary, 1971. One man-shows include Condeso-Lawler Gallery, N.Y.C., 1986, 88, Brownstone Gallery, Paris, 1988, others; exhibited in group shows at Kunsthalle Bielefeld, Germany, 1986, Musee St. Perre, Lyon, France, 1988, Inst. Francaise, Naples, Italy, 1992; author, producer: (film) Pollock/Beaubourg: 1982, 1986. Recipient purchase award Igor Found., 1990; fellow N.Y. Found. for Arts, 1987. Mem. Nat. Artists Equity Assn. Home and Studio: 93 Crosby St New York NY 10012

ALBERTINE, KURT H., anatomist, physiologist, educator; b. Newark, Nov. 29, 1952. BA, Lawrence U., 1975; PhD, Loyola U., Chgo., 1979. Asst. prof. anatomy U. South Fla., Tampa, 1984-86; rsch. asst. prof. pathology U. Pa., Phila., 1986-87, dir. pulmonary morphology lab. Inst. Environ. Medicine, 1986-88; asst. prof. medicine and physiology Jefferson Med. Coll., Phila., 1987-90, assoc. prof., 1990—, dir. microscopy lab., 1987—. NIH fellow, 1980-82; recipient New Investigator Rsch. award NIH, 1984-86. Mem. Am. Assn. Anatomists, Am. Thoracic Soc., Am. Physiol. Soc., N.Y. Acad. Scis., Electron Microscopy Soc. Am., Sigma Xi. Office: Jefferson Med Coll 804 College Bldg 1025 Walnut St Philadelphia PA 19107-5083

ALBERTS, ANDREA MAXINE, fashion and portrait photographer; b. L.A., Aug. 17, 1951; d. Maxwell Sergis and Ruth Laura (Cathey) A. BA in Art History, U. Calif., Berkeley, 1968; MA in Photography, NYU, 1975. Photo asst. N.Y.C., 1969-73; prof. photography U. Mass., Amherst, 1974-77; assoc. beauty editor Seventeen Mag., N.Y.C., 1977-78; freelance photographer, 1969—; owner Fashion Photography, N.Y.C., 1979—; main fashion photographer Gitano advt. campaign, 1984—. Office: 121 W 17th St New York NY 10011-5436

ALBIN, RRAN AHSKENAZY, marketing communications executive, consultant; b. N.Y.C., Feb. 14, 1952; d. Marvin Stanley and Natalie (Ashkenazy) A. BA in English, U. Vt., 1974. Freelance projections designer N.Y.C., 1975-80; corp. communications cons. F. Allison Prodns., N.Y.C., 1980-84; advt. account exec. Rosenfeld, Sirowitz, Humphrey & Strauss, N.Y.C., 1985-87, Saatchi & Saatchi Worldwide, N.Y.C., 1987-89; dir. of advt. Western Devel. Corp., Washington, 1989-90; mgr. communications Smart House, Upper Marlboro, Md., 1990-91; devel. dir. , photographer all women's river expedition, Luangua River, Zambia, 1982; devle. cons. D.C. chpt. Young Audiences, 1991-92; U. S. mktg. cons. to Lord Fairfax, 1992—. Mem. editorial bd. Currents mag., 1990-92; contbg. editor Remodeling News, 1991-92. Media and ad dir. Dukakis-Bentsen presidential campaign, 1988; mem. Advising Neighborhood Com., Washington, 1991; pres. condominium bd. dirs. 1991. NYSCA grant finalist, 1985; recipient Internat. Tv and Film Festival Gold award, 1982, '83, Am. Motion Picture Inst. Gold award, 1983, Golden Shopping Bag award, Bantam Books and Excellence in Print award, 1989. Mem. Advt. Women of N.Y. (com. chair N.Y.C. chpt. 1987-88), D.C. Ad Club (chair Addy's com. 1988-90), Washington Ind. Writers. Home and Office: 1230 23d St NW Washington DC 20037

ALBINAK, MARVIN JOSEPH, chemist, educator; b. Detroit, June 21, 1928; s. Alfred S. and Katherine (Smulson) A.; m. Gloria Ann Galamb, Aug. 26, 1961; children: Stephen, Anne, Alexandra. AB, U. Detroit, 1949, MS, 1952; PhD, Wayne State U., 1959. Rsch. chemist Ethyl Corp., Detroit, 1952-54; instr. to asst. prof. U. Detroit, 1954-58, 59-61; rsch. fellow Wayne State U., Detroit, 1958-59; sr. rsch. scientist Elec. Autolite Corp., Toledo, Ohio, 1961-62; rsch. chemist Owens-Ill., Inc., Toledo, 1962-65; asst. to assoc. prof. Wheeling (W.Va.) Coll., 1965-68; assoc. prof. to prof. chemistry and adminstr. Essex Community Coll., Balt., 1968—. Contbr. articles to profl. jurs. Mem. Am. Chem. Soc., Sigma Xi, Phi Lambda Upsilon. Democrat. Home: 819 Providence Rd Baltimore MD 21286-2964 Office: Essex Community Coll 7201 Rossville Blvd Baltimore MD 21237-3855

ALBOM, MICHAEL JONATHAN, surgeon, educator; b. Hartford, Conn., Oct. 2, 1944; s. Milton Jeramiah and Clare (Marcus) A.; m. Lia Shuster, Jan. 22, 1983; children: Blair Ruth, Mark Jeffrey. BA, U. Conn., 1966; MD, Boston U., 1970. Diplomate Am. Bd. Med. Examiners, Am. Bd. Dermatology. Med. intern Hartford Hosp., 1970-71; resident in dermatology Boston U., 1971-74; skin cancer surgery fellow NYU, 1974-75; asst. prof. dermatology dept. dermatology NYU Med. Ctr., 1976-83, head surgery sect., skin and cancer unit, 1979-85, clin. assoc. prof., 1983—; attending surgeon dept. plastic surgery Manhattan Eye Ear & Throat Hosp.; co-dir. Interspecialty Facial Surgery Congress, N.Y.C., 1983, 85. Contbr. articles to profl. jours., chpts. to med. books. Fellow Am. Soc. Dermatologic Surgery (bd. dirs. 1980-83, 1988-91), Am. Coll. Mohs Micrographic Surgery and Cutaneous Oncology (bd. dirs. 1987-90, sec.-treas. 1990-92), Am. Acad. Dermatology (mem. task force dermatol. surgery 1979—, advanced surgery course dir. 1979-86, dir. surg. forum 1986-91), Internat. Ophthalmoplastic Surgery Soc. (bd. dirs. 1981—); mem. AMA. Office: 33 E 70th St New York NY 10021

ALBRECHT, ALLAN JAMES, computer scientist; b. Pittston, Pa., Feb. 6, 1927; s. Arthur Carl and Edna Louise (Boldt) A.; m. Jean Carol Herman, Jan. 30, 1949; children: Drew Edward, Dale Allan. Student, Bucknell U. Jr. Coll., Wilkes-Barre, Pa., 1944-45, Wilkes Coll., 1947-48; BSEE, Bucknell U., 1949. Field engr. IBM, York, Pa., 1949-52; design engr. IBM Engring. Lab., Poughkeepsie, N.Y., 1952-55; devel. engr. IBM Fed. Systems Div., Kingston, N.Y., 1955-60; sr. engr. IBM Fed. Systems Div., L.A., 1960-69; project mgr. IBM Data Processing Svcs., L.A., 1969-72, Portland, Oreg., 1972-74; program mgr. IBM Data Processing Svcs., White Plains, N.Y., 1974-79; sr. tech. staff mem. IBM Corp., Armonk, N.Y., 1980-89; cons. Orleans, Mass., 1989—; study group mem. Pa. State U., State College, 1956, USAF/Mitre Corp., McLean, Va., 1968. Author: Function Points Definition, 1984; inventor: Function Points Analysis, 1979. Pres. Mayflower Point Assn., Orleans, 1990—. With USN, 1945-46.

ALBRECHT, RONALD LEWIS, financial services executive; b. Derby, Conn., Dec. 30, 1935; s. Lewis Davis and Gladys Imogene (Spear) A.; m. Mikyong Kim, Dec. 28, 1968; children: Rondi Kim, Kathryn Lynn, Karen Ann. BS in Agr., U. Vt., 1957; BBA in Bus. Mgmt., Baylor U., 1966; MA in Bus. Mgmt., Cen. Mich. U., 1975. Commd. 2d lt. USAF, 1957, advanced through grades to lt. col., 1973; comdr. detachment USAF, Sioux City AB, Iowa, 1957-60; air traffic control officer USAF, Cheveston, Eng., 1960-62; dir. air traffic control HQ12 USAF, Waco, Tex., 1962-66; comdr. detachment USAF, Kimpo AB, Korea, 1967-68; comdr. squadron Sewart AFB USAF, Tenn., 1969-70; comdr. squadron Holloman AFB USAF, N.Mex., 1970-73; staff officer, air traffic control HQ air force systems command USAF, Andrews AFB, 1973-75; dep. comdr. group USAF, Pentagon, 1975-77; staff officer electronics HQ joint staff USAF, Yongson, Korea, 1977-79; staff officer air traffic control communications area USAF, Rome, N.Y., 1979-80; retired USAF, 1980; real estate broker Bangor, Maine, 1980—; retirement, investment and fin. planning exec. Bangor (Maine) Savs. Bank, 1981-87; pres. Maine Fin. Services Inc., Bangor, 1987—; instr. Los Angeles Community Coll., Seoul, Korea, 1977-79, Husson Coll. Bangor, 1981-84. Mem. loaned exec. bd. div. planning com. United Way of Penobscot Valley, Bangor, 1981—, Rep. Party, Bangor, 1981—. Hood Dairy scholar U. Vt., 1955. Mem. Internat. Assn. Fin. Planning (v.p. programs, co-founder 1985, pres. Maine chpt. 1988-89), Inst. Cert. Fin. Planners, Internat. Cert. Fin. Planners (bd. standards and practices), Ret. Officers Assn., Am. Assn. Ret. Persons, Air TrafficControl Assn., Armed Forces Communications Electronics Assn., Kiwanis (2d and 1st v.p. Bangor Club, pres. 1987-88), Masons, Anah Temple, Valley of Tokyo, Orientof Japan and Korea. Home: 98 Judson Blvd Bangor ME 04401-2542

ALBRETHSEN, ADRIAN EDYSEL, metallurgist, consultant; b. Carey, Idaho, June 20, 1929; s. Norman Carl and Dollie Gustina (Brown) A.; m. Joan Alice Phelan, July 8, 1961; children: Thomas, Eric, Carl. BS in Mining Engring., U. Idaho, 1952, MSMetE, 1958; PhD in Mineral Engring., MIT, 1963. Analytical chemist Bunker Hill Co., Kellogg, Idaho, 1954-55; mining engr. Anaconda Co., Butte, Mont., 1955-57; rsch. asst. MIT, Cambridge, 1958-63; sr. engr. GE, Richland, Wash., 1963-65; sr. rsch. engr. Battelle Meml. Inst., Richland, Wash., 1965-66, ASARCO, Inc., South Plainfield, N.J., 1966-86; plant metallurgist Nord Ilmenite Corp., Jackson, N.J., 1989-92; cons. pvt. practice, Bridgewater, N.J., 1992—; cons. Bridgewater, N.J., 1986—. 1st lt. USAF, 1952-54, Korea. Mem. ASM Internat., Soc. Mining Engrs., Electrochem. Soc. (chmn. met. N.Y. sect. 1987-88), Sigma Xi. Home: 485 Vicki Dr Bridgewater NJ 08807-1941

ALBRIGHT, JAMES MICHAEL, sports information coordinator; b. Albany, N.Y., Feb. 3, 1940; s. Ernest D. and Evelyn E. (Aldrich) A.; m. Dorothy Kosik; children: Jessica, Rebecca, Kasey. BS in Physics, Syracuse U., 1962, MS in Communications, 1964, postgrad. Tech. writer Gen. Electric Corp., Syracuse, Utica, N.Y., 1962-64; publicist plastics div. Gen. Electric Corp., Pittsfield, Mass., 1964-66; grad. asst. Syracuse (N.Y.) U., 1966-68; with various publicist agys., 1968-70; publicist sci. div. Eastman Kodak Co., Rochester, N.Y., 1970-73, co. spokesperson, 1973-80, coordinator sports info., 1980—. Editor Event mag., 1966-67; contbr. more than 200 articles to profl. jours. Am. Football Coaches Assn., Coll. Sports Info. Dirs. Am., Basketball Writers Am., Football Writers Am., Track and Field Writers Am., Nat. Assn. Stock Car Auto Racing, Rochester Press and Radio Club, Women in Communication (Rochester chpt. pres. 1981-82). Republican. Club: Downtown Athletic (N.Y.C.). Office: Eastman Kodak Co 343 State St Rochester NY 14650-0001

ALBRIGHT, PAUL HERMAN, architect, consultant; b. Bel Air, Md., May 25, 1948; s. George Herman and Mary Helen (Conklin) A.; m. Carman Jean Franz; children: Jerimiah Justin, Nathanial Arrone. Cert. Nat. Coun. Archtl. Registration Bds. Architect Gerald A. Baxter, Inc., Bel Air, 1970-75, Mark Beck Assocs., Inc., Towson, Md., 1975-80, Kidde Cons., Inc., Towson, 1980-81; architect, v.p. Frederick Ward Assocs., Inc., Bel Air, 1981—. Chmn. Harford County (Md.) Solar Devices Com., 1984; mem. Harford County Energy Commn., 1984—, Harford County Bd. Elec. Ex., 1985-88; chmn. Harford County Bldg. Code Appeal Bd., 1985—; subcom. chmn. Blue Ribbon Com. for Sch. Constrn., 1991. Recipient award for solar prototype system design Dept. Energy, 1978. Mem. AIA. Lutheran. Office: Frederick Ward Assocs Inc PO Box 727 Bel Air MD 21014-0727

ALBRIGHT, RICHARD SHELDON, II, systems analyst; b. Harrisburg, Pa., July 11, 1951; s. Richard Sheldon and Iona Madrienne (Booth) A.; m. Marcia Anne Zimmers, Aug. 17, 1974; children: Christopher Erik, Courtney Elizabeth. BA in English, Lehigh U., 1973; postgrad., Harrisburg Area Community Coll. Substitute tchr. Susquenita High Sch., Duncannon, Pa., 1973-74; postal clk. U.S. Postal Svc., Harrisburg, 1974-77; supply mgmt. intern U.S. Navy Ships Parts Control Ctr., Mechanicsburg, Pa., 1977-78, supply mgmt. rep., 1978-81; fin. systems analyst U.S. Navy Fleet Material Support Office, Mechanicsburg, 1981-86, supervisory systems analyst, 1986—. Contbr. articles to profl. publs. Sunday sch. tchr. Wesley United Meth. Ch., Marysville, Pa., 1981—, lay leader, 1988—; mem. community liaison com. Susquenita Sch., 1987—. Recipient Dir.'s award U.S. Office Personnel Mgmt., 1985. Mem. Navl Supply Systems Command Managerial Cadre. Democrat. Home: 67 Fleisher Rd Marysville PA 17053-9789 Office: US Navy Fleet Material PO Box 2010 5450 Carlisle Pike Mechanicsburg PA 17055

ALBURGER, DAVID ELMER, nuclear physicist; b. Phila., Oct. 6, 1920; s. Elmer R. and Josephine (Reid) A.; m. Mary Mickle, Oct. 6, 1945; children: David R., Mary Jo, Eve A., Andrew R. BA, Swarthmore Coll., 1942; MA, Yale U., 1946, PhD, 1948. Radio engr. Naval Rsch. Lab., Washington, 1942-45; lab. asst. Yale U., New Haven, Conn., 1946-47; sr. physicist Brookhaven Nat. Lab., Upton, N.Y., 1948-90. Contbr. over 250 articles to sci. jours. Mem. Cen. Dist. #4 Sch. Bd., Bellport, N.Y., 1958-70, pres 3 yrs. With USNR, 1944-45. Sterling fellow Yale U., 1947-48. Fellow Nat. Sci. Found. (fellowship com. 1960-63); mem. Am. Phys. Soc. (phys. rev. editorial bd. 1985-88). Home: 290 Beaver Dam Rd Brookhaven NY 11719-9621 Office: Brookhaven Nat Lab Upton NY 11973

AL-CHOKHACHY, MODHAFFER KHALAF, surgeon; b. Baghdad, Iraq, Apr. 10, 1930; came to U.S., 1948; m. Carolyn Ann Coombs, Apr. 10, 1964; children: Heather, David, Robert, Evan, Elissa. BS, Boston U., 1953-56. Cert. Am. Nat. Bd. Medicine, 1956, Am. Bd. Surgery, 1963. Internship Boston City Hosp., 1956-61; residency Western Mass. Hosp., Westfield, 1961-62; fellow in surgery Harvard Med. Sch., Boston, 1962-63; teaching fellow in surgery Newton (Mass.) Wellesley Hosp., 1963-64; pvt. practice, 1965—. Mem. Mass. Med. Soc., Plymouth Dist. Med. Soc., Am. Coll. Surgeons, Mass. Chpt. Am. Coll. Surgeons, New England Endoscopy Soc., Fly Caster's. Home: Ruffini Terr Box 3357 Plymouth MA 02361 Office: 143 Court St Plymouth MA 02360

ALDERMAN, WALTER ARTHUR, JR., computer company, corporate rescue executive; b. Stoneham, Mass., July 29, 1945; s. Walter Arthur and Ida Ellen (Patchett) A.; m. Sandra May Johnston, Aug. 23, 1969; children: Walter Arthur III, Deborah Ellen. BSBA with honors, Northeastern U., 1968; MBA, Harvard U., 1971. Divisional controller Anken Industries, Williamstown, Mass., 1971-73; treas., controller James Hunter Machine Co., North Adams, Mass., 1973-78; gen. mgr. Petricca Industries, Pittsfield, Mass., 1978-80; chmn., pres. Alderman Assocs. Inc., Coral Springs, Fla., 1980-85, Bedford Computer Corp., 1985-90; owner, pres. Paragon Pub. Systems, Bedford, 1990—; bd. dirs. Mahoney and Assocs., Inc., Springfield, Mass.; instr., mem. adv. bd. North Adams (Mass.) State Coll., 1976-78; registered rep. First New England Securities, Stockbridge, Mass., 1968-74. Bd. dirs., pres. Mass. C. of C., 1976-78, YMCA, 1976-78; commr. Indsl. Devel. Commn., Mass., 1976-78; section leader United Fund, Mass., 1977. Served to lt. U.S. Army Res., 1968-74. Named Turnaround Entrepreneur of Yr., Arthur Young/Venture Mag., Boston, 1987; recipient Outstanding Svc. award C. of C., 1978, Community Svc. award United Fund, 1977. Mem. Turnaround Mgmt. Assn., Phi Kappa Phi, Beta Gamma Sigma. Office: Bedford Computer Corp 10 Corporate Dr Bedford NH 03110-5956

ALDERSON, THOMAS, retired chemist; b. N.Y.C., Aug. 18, 1917; s. Thomas Broker and Florence Amelia (Perry) A.; m. Ruthmary Mason, June 23, 1942; children: Thomas V, James Mason, Susan Elizabeth. BA, Ripon Coll., 1939; MA, Ohio State U., 1941, PhD, 1947. Rsch. chemist DuPont Co., Wilmington, Del., 1947-61, rsch. assoc., 1961-82; ret., 1982; pvt. practice cons., Wilmington, 1982—. Contbr. articles to profl. publs.; patentee in field. Mem. vestry Calvary Episcopal Ch., Wilmington. Maj. U.S. Army, 1941-45, ETO. Mem. Am. Chem. Soc., Phi Beta Kappa. Home: 522 Brighton Rd Wilmington DE 19809-2821

ALDIN, PETER, psychiatrist, educator; b. Schwerin, Germany, Oct. 29, 1931; came to U.S., 1952; m. Michèle Kenneth (div.). PhB, U. Paris, 1951; BA, CCNY, 1954, MA in Psychology, 1955; PhD Clin. Psychology, Clark U., 1957; MD, Boston U., 1964. Diplomate Am. Bd. Psychiatry and Neurology. Intern Maimonides Hosp., Bklyn., 1964-65; resident Hillside Hosp., Glen Oaks, N.Y., 1965-68, chief resident, 1966-67; attending staff St. Luke's-Roosevelt Hosp., N.Y.C.; teaching staff Columbia U. Sch. of Med., N.Y.C. Fellow Am. Psychiat. Assn. (chmn. various coms., past mem. exec. com., N.Y. County Dist. Br.), Am. Acad. Legal & Indsl. Medicine (sec. 1992—); mem. AMA. Office: 225 E 47th St Apt 1C New York NY 10017-2113

ALDISSI, MAHMOUD ALI YOUSEF, research chemist; b. Jalameh, Jordan, Sept. 15, 1952; came to U.S., 1981.; s. Ali and Amneh (Hussein) A.; m. Barbara E. Townsend, Sept. 16, 1983; children Andrew A.T., Alexandra Y. BS in Chemistry, U. Scis. et Techniques du Languedoc, Montpellier, France, 1976, MS in Polymer Chemistry, 1978, PhD in Polymer Sci., 1981. Postdoctoral fellow U. Pa., Phila., 1981-83; postdoctoral fellow Los Alamos (N.Mex.) Nat. Lab., 1983-84, rsch. chemist, 1984-90; rsch. fellow Champlain Cable Corp., Winooski, Vt., 1990—; instr. Ctr. Profl. Advancement, E. Brunswick, N.J., 1982—; cons. in field of polymer sci. and tech. Contbr. articles on polymer sci. to profl. jours.; patentee in field. Mem. Am. Chem. Soc. (mem. polymer and polymeric materials sci. and engring. divs.), Materials Rsch. Soc. Home: 22 Pine Meadow Dr Colchester VT 05446-1637 Office: Champlain Cable Corp PO Box 7 Winooski VT 05404-0007

ALDREDGE, THEONI VACHLIOTIS, costume designer; b. Athens, Greece, Aug. 22, 1932; d. Gen. Athanasios and Meropi (Gregoriades) Vachliotis; m. Thomas E. Aldredge, Dec. 10, 1953. Student, Am. Sch., Athens, 1949-53, Goodman Theatre, Chgo.; LHD, De Paul U., 1985. Mem. design staff Goodman Theatre, 1951-53; head designer N.Y. Shakespeare Festival, 1962—. Designer numerous Broadway and off Broadway shows, ballet, opera, TV spls.; films include Girl of the Night, You're a Big Boy Now, No Way To Treat a Lady, Uptight, Last Summer, I Never Sang for My Father, Promise at Dawn, The Great Gatsby (Brit. Motion Picture Acad. award 1976), Network, The Cheap Detective, The Fury, The Eyes of Laura Mars (Acad. Sci. Fiction Films award), The Champ, Semi-Tough, The Rose, Monsignor, Annie, Ghostbusters, Moonstruck, We're No Angels, Stanley and Iris, Other People's Money, Night and the City; Broadway shows include A Chorus Line (Theatre World award 1976), Annie (Tony award 1977), Barnum (Tony award 1979), Dream Girls, Woman of the Year, Onward Victoria, La Cage Aux Folles (Tony award 1984), 42nd Street, A Little Family Business, Merlin, Private Lives, The Corn Is Green, The Rink, Blithe Spirit, Chess, Gypsy (1989 revival), Oh, Kay, The Secret Garden, Nick and Nora, High Rollers. Recipient Obie award for Disting. Svc. to Off-Broadway Theatre Village Notice, Maharam award for Peer Gynt, N.Y.C. Liberty medal, 1986, numerous Drama Desk and Critic awards; inducted into Theatre Hall of Fame. Mem. United Scenic Artists, Costume Designers Guild, Acad. Motion Picture Arts Scis. (Oscar award Great Gatsby 1975). Office: 350 W 50th St New York NY 10019

ALDRICH, ALEXANDER, lawyer; b. N.Y.C., Mar. 14, 1928; s. Winthrop Williams and Harriet (Alexander) A.; m. Elizabeth Bayard Hollins, Aug. 11, 1951 (div.); children—Elizabeth, Winthrop, Amanda, Alexander; m. Phyllis W. Watts, July 28, 1971; children—William, Sarah. A.B., Harvard, 1950, LL.B., 1953; M. Pub. Adminstrn., N.Y. U., 1960. Bar: N.Y. bar 1955. Practiced N.Y.C., 1955-56; sec. N.Y.C. Police Dept., 1956-58, dep. commr. charge youth program, 1958-60; dir. N.Y. State Div. Youth, Albany, 1960-63; exec. asst. to gov. State of N.Y., Albany, 1963-66; exec. dir. Hudson River Valley Commn., 1966-69; pres. L.I.U., 1969-71; commr. Parks and Recreation State N.Y., Albany, 1971-75; atty. firm Helm, Shapiro, Anito & Aldrich, Saratoga Springs, N.Y., 1975—; exec. in residence Bus. Sch., SUNY, Albany, 1986-88; dir. Ctr. for Urban and Environ. Studies, Rensselaer Poly. Tech. Inst. Trustee Am. U., Cairo, Egypt; chmn. Nat. Adv. Coun. on Historic Preservation, 1981-85. Home and Office: 104 Union Ave Saratoga Springs NY 12866-4369

ALDRICH, FRANK NATHAN, banker; b. Jackson, Mich., June 8, 1923; s. Frank Nathan and Marion (Butterfield) A.; m. Edna Dora DeJan, Nov. 21, 1956; children: Marion Dolores, Clinton Pershing. Student, U. Md., summer 1943; A.B. in Govt, Dartmouth Coll., 1948; postgrad., Harvard U., summer 1948. Sub-mgr. First Nat. Bank of Boston, Havana, Cuba, 1949-60, Rio de Janeiro, Brazil, 1961-62; sub-mgr. First Nat. Bank of Boston, Sao Paulo, Brazil, 1963-64, mgr., 1965, exec. mgr. Rio de Janeiro, 1966, v.p. Brazilian brs., 1966-69; v.p. overseas ops. First Nat. Bank of Boston, Boston, 1969-70; v.p. Latin Am.-Asia-Africa-Middle East div., Boston, 1970-73; sr. v.p. Latin Am. div., Boston, 1973-88; pres., chief exec. officer McLaughlin Bank N.V., Netherland Antilles, 1989—. Trustee Pan Am. Devel. Found., Washington. With USAAF, 1943-46. Decorated Air medal with 4 oak leaf clusters, D.F.C. U.S.; Medalha Marechal Candido Mariano da Silva Rondon (Brazil); Ordem Nacional do Cruzeiro do Sul (Brazil). Fellow Brit. Interplanetary Soc.; mem. Air Force Assn., Res. Officers Assn., Confederate Air Force, Inst. Navigation, Royal Inst. Navigation (London), Royal Astron. Soc. Canada, Md. Hist. Soc., Am. C. of C., Rio de Janeiro, Am. C. of C. Sao Paulo, Sphinx Soc., Vets of Battle of the Bulge, Squadron A Assn. of N.Y., Beta Theta Pi. Clubs: Harvard (Boston), Dartmouth College, Yale (N.Y.C.), Army and Navy (Washington), Wellesley (Mass.) Country, Wellesley Coll. Lodges: Masons, Shriners. Home: 3 Indian Spring Rd Dover MA 02030-2331

ALDRICH, JAMES LEONARD, association executive; b. Boston, Feb. 6, 1932; s. George Leonard and Catherine Margaret (Kelley) A.; m. Ida Justina Foster, Oct. 30, 1956 (div.); children: Stephen, Cynthia, Mark; m. Anne McAvoy Blackburn, Nov. 28, 1981; stepchildren: Carol, Barbara. BA cum laude, Northeastern U., 1960. Deputy dir. Edn. Devel. Ctr., Newton, Mass., 1959-70; cons. Pres. Coun. on Environ. Quality, Washington, 1970; dir. edn. Conservation Found., Washington, 1970-76; founder and treas. Threshold, Inc., Washington, 1976-78; v.p. Mass. Audubon Soc., Lincoln, 1978-84; exec. dir. Internat. Inst. Boston, 1984—; dir. Internat. Inst. Boston, 1984—; cons. UNESCO, Paris, 1976-78, NASA Office Edn., Washington, 1976-78; dir. U.S. Com. Refugees, Washington, 1990—, Am. Coun. for Nationalities Svc., N.Y.C., 1990—. Editor: Trends in Environmental Education, 1977; founder and editor: The Environmentalist, 1979-84. Founder and pres. Friends of UN Environ. Program, Washington, 1984-86; chmn. Govs. Advisory Coun. on Refugees and Immigrants, Boston, 1985—. With U.S. Army, 1951-53. Recipient Cert. of Appreciation Friends of UNEP, Washington, 1989, Outstanding Alumni award Northeastern U., Boston, 1990. Home: 5 Brackett Rd Wayland MA 01778-2202 Office: Internat Inst Boston 287 Commonwealth Ave Boston MA 02115-2099

ALDRICH, NANCY ARMSTRONG, psychotherapist; b. Taylorville, Ill., Oct. 4, 1925; d. Guy L. and Alice Irene (Hicks) Armstrong; m. Paul Harwood Aldrich, Sept. 30, 1949; children: Gregory Paul, Mark Douglas, Alice Ann Aldrich White, Ruth Lynn Aldrich Sammis. AB with highest honors, U. Ill., 1947, BS in Chemistry, 1948, MS in Chemistry, 1949; MSS, Bryn Mawr Coll., 1986. Lic. clin. social worker, Del., Pa. Parole bd. mem. State of Del., Dover, 1970-74; instr. continuing edn. U. Del., Newark, 1976-78, program specialist, 1978-83; founder Acad. Lifelong Learning; v.p. Aldrich Assocs. Inc., Landenberg, Pa., 1983—, psychotherapist, 1987—; psychotherapist Family Community Service Del. County, Media, Pa., 1986, Tressler Ctr. for Human Growth, Wilmington, Del., 1987—; clin. affiliate Personal Performance Cons., 1990—, Acorn, 1990—, CMG Health, 1991—, DuPont EAP Program, 1992—; coord. human resources devel. program Tressler Ctr. for Human Growth, 1983-84. Pres. YWCA New Castle County, Wilmington, 1974-76; mem. Statewide Health Coordinating Council, Del., 1978-79; bd. dirs., com. mem. United Way Del., Wilmington, 1975-84;

trustee Unitarian Universalist House, Phila., 1992—. Mem. NASW, AAUW (pres. Wilmington br. 1968-70, nat. resolutions com. 1971-72, Fellowship gift named in her honor 1970), Del. Soc. Lic. Clin. social Workers (pres. 1990-91), Assn. for Humanistic Psychology, Del. Gerontol. Soc., Mental Health Assn. Del., N.Y. Soc. for Bioenergetic Analysis, Phi Beta Kappa, Phi Kappa Phi, Iota Sigma Pi. Office: 625 Chambers Rock Rd Landenberg PA 19808

ALDRICH, ROBERT ADAMS, agricultural engineer; b. Veteran Twp., N.Y., Apr. 25, 1924; s. Luman Woodbridge and Mabel Hastings (Gibbs) A.; m. Roberta Ann Bowlby, Aug. 27, 1946; children—Susan Carol, Gail Jessica, Kathleen Lois, Margaret Louise. B.S. in Agrl. Engring, Wash. State U., 1950, M.S., 1952; Ph.D., Mich. State U., 1958. Instr., then asso. prof. agrl. engring. Wash. State U., 1951-58; asso. prof. U. Ky., 1958-59, Mich. State U., 1959-62; asso. prof., then prof. Pa. State U., 1962-79; prof. agrl. engring., head dept. U. Conn., Storrs, 1979-88, prof. dept. nat. rsch., mgmt. and engring., 1988-89, ret., 1989; prin. Aldrich Engring., Mansfield Center, Conn., 1989—. Author papers in field. Served with C.E. AUS, 1942-46. Mem. Am. Soc. Agrl. Engrs., Nat. Soc. Profl. Engrs., ASHRAE. Home: 295 Wormwood Hill Rd Mansfield Center CT 06250-1033

ALDRIDGE, MYRON ANTHONY, mechanical engineer; b. Greenwood, S.C., Dec. 16, 1953; s. Henry Clay and Betty Ruth A.; m. Robin Aulton, May 21, 1977; children: Nykkol, Myron Anthony. BSME, Howard U., 1983. Mech. engr. David Taylor Naval Ship Research and Devel Ctr., Bethesda, Md., 1983-84, Naval Sea Systems Command, Washington, 1984—; mentor and coord. advanced math. program Paint Br. High Sch., Silver Spring, 1992—; part owner Classy Coiffs Salon; v.p., founding mem. Thormacal, Inc. Founding mem. University Park Civic Assn., Washington, 1978-80; mem. Iverleigh Civic Assn., Silver Spring, Md., 1987—. Mem. Assn. Scientists and Engrs., Benjamin Banneker Honors Math. and Sci. Soc. Democrat. Baptist. Home: 1609 Featherwood St Silver Spring MD 20904-6640

ALDWINCKLE, HERB SANDERS, plant pathologist; b. Stamford, Eng., July 16, 1942; s. Bartholomew William and Kathleen (Sanders) A.; m. Bernadine Verenski, Oct. 22, 1970; 1 child, David Aldwinckle. BA, Cambridge U., 1963; PhD, London U., 1967. Asst. rsch. plant pathologist U. Calif., Davis and Berkeley, Calif., 1967-70; asst., assoc., prof. Cornell U., Geneva, N.Y., 1970—, dept. chmn., 1982—. Editor: Apple Diseases, 1990; inventor, author in field. Adv. coun. Geneva (N.Y.) Sch. Bd., 1991. Grantee USDA N.Y. Apple Growers, 1975-91, Colombian Coffee Growers, 1991. Mem. Apple and Pear Disease Workers Am., Station Club, Thomas Young Club. Episcopalian. Office: Cornell U 650 W North St Geneva NY 14456-1320

ALECOCK, DAVID ANDREW, publisher; b. Long Beach, Calif., Nov. 20, 1955; s. Don William and Betty Louise (Dillingno) A.; m. Bernadette Elizabeth Noe, Oct. 27, 1990; children: Tabiatha, Daniel. BA, UCLA, 1978. Asst. prodn. mgr. Dow Jones & Co., Inc., Palo Alto, Calif., 1979-80, Federal Way, Wash., 1980-81; account exec. Sasquatch Pub., Inc., Seattle, 1981-82; bus. mgr. Info. Resources, Seattle, 1983; dir. mktg. Capitol Publs., Inc., Alexandria, Va., 1984-87; sr. mktg. mgr. Phillips Pub., Inc., Potomac, Md., 1988; v.p. mktg. The Taft Group, Inc., Rockville, Md., 1989; pub. Newsletter Svcs., Inc., Washington, 1990—. Mem. Direct Mktg. Assn. Washington, Newsletter Pubs. Assn. Office: Newsletter Svcs Inc 1545 New York Ave NE Washington DC 20002-1765

ALEGADO, ROLANDO BALADAD, orthopaedic surgeon; b. Nasipit, Agusan, Philippines, Aug. 16, 1946; s. Cesario and Florentina (Baladad) A.; m. Isabel Deleon Megado, June 28, 1978; 1 child, Ala Deleon. BS in Preparatory Medicine, Fareastern U., Manila, 1967, MD, 1972. Intern St. Joseph Hosp., Lorain, Ohio, 1974-75; resident gen. surgery Sinai Hosp., Balt., 1975-77, sr. resident orthopaedic surgery, 1979-80; resident orthopaedic surgery Balt. City Hosp., 1977-78; resident-fellow orthopaedic surgery Johns Hopkins Hosp., Balt., 1978; resident orthopaedic surgery Lawrence Kernan Childrens Hosp., Balt., 1980; mem. attending med. staff orthopaedic surgery Sinai Hosp., Balt., 1980—, Harbor Hosp. Ctr., Balt., 1980—, Md. Gen. Hosp., Balt., 1981—, Liberty Med. Ctr., Balt., 1981—, Lawrence Kernan Hosp., Balt., 1980—. Fellow Am. Acad. Orthopaedic Surgeons. Office: 3001 S Hanover St G100 Baltimore MD 21225

ALEPIAN, TARO, engineering and construction executive; b. Nicosia, Cyprus, Sept. 28, 1945; arrived in Can., 1963; s. Melcon and Anahid (Melikian) A.; m. Anahid Manoukian, July 14, 1968; children: Ronald, Norma, Alida. BE with honors, McGill U., Montreal, Que., Can., 1967. Cert. engr., Que., Alta. Process engr. Shell Can. Ltd., Montreal, 1967-72, project mgr., 1972-73; sr. analyst Shell Can. Ltd., Toronto, Ont., Can., 1973-74; dir. mktg. SNC Inc., Montreal, 1974-77, v.p. mktg., 1977-79, sr. v.p., 1979-88, sr. group v.p., 1988-91; group pres. SNC-Lavalin Inc., Montreal, 1991—; bd. dirs., chmn., chief exec. officer several subs. SNC-Lavalin Inc., Montreal, 1979—. Mem. St. James's Club. Mem. Christian Orthodox Ch. Office: SNC-Lavalin Inc, 2 Place Felix Martin, Montreal, PQ Canada H2Z 1Z3

ALESSANDRI, RICARDO WILLIAM, sports information executive; b. Mt. Vernon, N.Y., Aug. 4, 1962; s. Ricardo Francis and Rose Ann (Molle) A.; m. Patricia Ann Morello, Sept. 11, 1988. BA, Fordham U., 1984. Sales mgr., 1984-87; dir. customer svc. SportsTicker, Jersey City, 1987-89, v.p. adminstrn., 1989—. Pres. N.E. Yonkers Kids Against Dystrophy, 1974-85. Office: SportsTicker 600 Plaza Two Jersey City NJ 07311

ALESSI, GEORGE ANTHONY, financial advisor, consultant; b. N.Y.C., May 30, 1926; s. Anthony and Anna Cecilia (Li Greci) A.; m. Madeline Costanza, Nov. 21, 1953; 1 child, Anthony. BBA in Indsl. Mgmt., CCNY, 1949; cert. in elec. engring., Oreg. State U., 1945, MBA, 1952; cert., Ohio State U., 1960. Cert. profl. contract mgr., Washington. Employment interviewer City of N.Y. Dept. Social Svcs., 1949-52; various mgmt. and exec. positions U.S. Govt. Dept. of Def., 1952-86; cons., fin. advisor Galessi Enterprises, Yonkers, N.Y., 1986—. Mem. Archdiocesan Pastoral coun., N.Y., 1985-91; chmn. Vicariate of N.E. Bronx, N.Y., 1983-91; cooperator Opus Dei, 1990; mem. Cath. League for Religious and Civil Rights. With U.S. Army, 1944-46. Decorated Knight of the Holy Sepulchre, Pope John Paul II, 1984; recipient Disting. Svc. award Archdiocesan Union of Holy Name, 1985, Insignus Jesuit Community at Loyola Retreat House, Morristown, N.J., 1966. Fellow Profl. Contracts Mgmt. Assn. (cert. 1976), Cardinal Spellman Retreat League (pres. Riverdale, N.Y. 1980-82), Archdiocesan Union of Holy Name Soc. (pres. 1977-79), Male Glee Club Yonkers (v.p. 1986-87), Serra Internat. (dist. gov. 1989-92), Internat. Platform Assn., Westchester P.C. Users Group. Republican. Roman Catholic. Home and Office: 10 Massitoa Rd Yonkers NY 10710-5016

ALEXANDER, ANDREW LAMAR (LAMAR ALEXANDER), secretary of education; b. Knoxville, Tenn., July 3, 1940; s. Andrew Lamar and Genevra Floreine (Rankin) A.; m. Leslee Kathryn Buhler, Jan. 4, 1969; children: Drew, Leslee, Kathryn, Will. B.A., Vanderbilt U., 1962; J.D., NYU, 1965. Bar: Tenn. Law clk. to Hon. John Wisdom U.S. Ct. Appeals (5th cir.), New Orleans; assoc. Fowler, Rountree, Fowler & Robertson, Knoxville, 1965; legis. asst. to Senator Howard Baker, 1967-68; exec. asst. to Bryce Harlow, White House Congl. Liaison Office, 1969-70; ptnr. Dearborn and Ewing, Nashville, 1971-78; gov. State of Tenn., Nashville, 1979-87; chmn. Leadership Inst. Belmont Coll., Nashville, 1987-88; pres. U. Tenn., 1988-91; sec. Dept. Edn., Washington, 1991—; mem. Pres.'s Task Force on Federalism; chmn. Nat. Govs. Assn., 1985-86, Pres.'s Commn. on Ams. Outdoors, 1985-87. Author: Steps Along the Way, 1986, Six Months Off, 1988. Mgr. Winfield Dunn for Gov. Campaign, 1970, chief transition, 1970-71; Rep. nominee for Gov. of Tenn., 1974. Recipient Nat. Disting. Svc. to Edn. award Burger King, 1988, James B. Conant award Edn. Commn. of the States, 1988, Disting. State Leadership award Am. Assn. State Colls. and Univs., 1989; honored as Silver Anniversary scholar-athlete NCAA, 1987; NYU Law Sch. Root-Tilden scholar. Mem. Phi Beta Kappa. Republican. Presbyterian. Office: Dept Edn Office of Secretary 400 Maryland Ave SW Washington DC 20202-0002

ALEXANDER, CHRISTINA LILLIAN, pharmacist; b. N.Y.C., Dec. 25, 1942; d. Stanley Urich and Roselyn Helen (Joseph) A. BS in Pharmacy, Fordham U., 1965; MS in Pharmacology, St. John's U., Jamaica, N.Y., 1977. Chief pharmacist Holy Family Hosp., Bklyn., 1966; asst. chief pharmacist N.Y. Polyclinic Hosp., N.Y.C., 1967-69; pharmacist Mt. Sinai Hosp. Med. Ctr., N.Y.C., 1969; night pharamcist Maimonides Med. Ctr., N.Y.C., 1969-71; pharmacist N.Y. U. Hosp. and Med. Ctr., 1971-72; night pharamcist, drug info. specialist Brookdale (N.Y.) Med. Ctr. and Hosp., 1972-80; asst. clin. prof. St. John's U. Coll. Pharmacy and Allied Health Professions, 1981-82; dir. drug info. ctr. St. John's U. and L.I. Jewish-Hillside Med. Ctr., N.Y.C., 1981-82; pres. Internat. Pharm. Cons., 1982—; asst. dir. pharmacy Burke Rehab. Ctr., White Plains, N.Y., 1984-89, dir., 1989-90; pres., dir. pharm. svcs. Alexander Assocs. Health Cons., 1990—; editor, pub. Internat. Pharm. Cons. Newsletter, 1984—; clin. instr. in pharmacy Rutgers U., New Brunswick, N.J., 1975, clin. cons. Coll. Pharmacy, 1977-79; sec. internat. adv. coun. Am. Bd. Pharmacy, Internat. Contbr. to N.Y. Carib. News. Recipient The Assembly of the State of N.Y. Citation, 1986, Scholarship Incentive award N.Y. State, 1960-65. Mem. AAAS, Am. Mus. Natural History (life), Am. Bd. Diplomates in Pharmacy, Internat., Federation Internationale Pharmaceutique, Fedn. Am. Scientists, Am. Pharm. Assn., Am. Soc. Hosp. Pharmacists, Fordham U. Coll. Pharmacy Alumni Fedn. (dir., pres. 1987—), Caribbean Cultural Ctr. N.Y.C., Lambda Kappa Sigma, Rho Chi. Democrat. Roman Catholic. Home: 3333 Henry Hudson Pky # F Bronx NY 10463-3224

ALEXANDER, DANIEL SAUNDERS, mathematics historian, mathematics educator; b. Washington, Sept. 8, 1953; s. Harold Bell and Janice Fairfield (Saunders) A.; m. Rebecca Alter, Aug. 11, 1990. AB in English Lit., Colby Coll., 1975; MS in Journalism, Boston U., 1979, PhD in Math., 1992; postgrad., U. Mass., 1982-85. Freelance writer Boston, 1979-84; instr. math. U. Mass., Boston, 1984-86; instr. math., fellow Boston U., 1985-92; vis. prof. math. Colby Coll., Waterville, Maine, 1992—. Mem. Am. Math. Soc. Office: Colby Coll Dept MAth Boston MA 04901-2411

ALEXANDER, DOROTHEA DANAS, college administrator; b. Lowell, Mass.; d. Charles and Helen (Chimiklis) Danas; m. Richard J. Alexander, Nov. 5, 1960; 1 child, Richard C. BS in Edn., Salem State, 1960, MA in Edn., 1965; EdD in Ednl. Adminstrn., U. Mass., 1981. Faculty bus. div. Endicott Coll., Beverly, Mass., 1960-67; faculty bus. div. North Shore Community Coll., Danvers, Mass., 1967-76, chmn. div. bus., 1976-86, asst. dean acad. adminstrn., 1986—; ednl. cons. U.S. Dept. Edn., Washington, 1980-91, ednl. instns., 1975-91; curriculum devel. specialist, 1980-91; adminstr. devel. specialist, 1980-91. Author: Academic Chairperson: Reward and Regret; Unravelling the Paradox, 1987, The Agony and the Ecstasy of Faculty Evaluations, 1988, First-Level Academic Administrators Analysis of the Role with Implications for Staff Development. Reports officer UN WHO, Geneva; bd. dirs. Lynn (Mass.) Vis. Nurses Assn. Recipient Pride in Performance award Commonwealth of Mass., 1991, Cert. of Recognition 22d World Health Assembly. Mem. Mass. Women in Pub. Higher Edn. (pres. 1990-91), Mass. Adminstrs. in Community Colls., Am. Ednl. Rsch. Assn., ASCD, Nat. Coun. on Staff, Program and Organizational Devel. Home: 29 Mansion Dr Topsfield MA 01983-1109 Office: North Shore Community Coll 1 Ferncroft Rd Danvers MA 01923-4093

ALEXANDER, DUANE FREDERICK, pediatrician, research administrator; b. Balt., Aug. 11, 1940; s. Fred Lucas and Christiana H. (Showacre) A.; m. Marianne Ellis, June 23, 1963; children: Keith Duane, Kristin Marianne. B.S., Pa. State U., 1962; M.D., Johns Hopkins U., 1966. Diplomate: Am. Bd. Pediatrics. Intern Johns Hopkins Hosp., Balt., 1966-67, resident, 1967-68, fellow, 1970-71; commd. officer USPHS, 1968—, now rear adm.; clin. assoc. Nat. Inst. Child Health and Human Devel., NIH, Bethesda, Md., 1968-70, asst. to sci. dir., 1971-74, asst. to dir., 1978-82, dep. dir., 1982-86; dir. Nat. Inst. Child Health and Human Devel., NIH, 1986—; staff pediatrician Nat. Commn. for Protection of Human Subjects of Research, 1974-78. Contbr. articles to profl. jours. Recipient Commendation medal USPHS, 1970, Meritorious Service medal USPHS, 1985, Spl. Recognition medal USPHS, 1985, Surgeon Gen's. Exemplary Svc. medal, 1990, Irving B. Harris Lectureship award, 1991. Fellow Am. Acad. Pediatrics, Soc. Devel. Pediatrics, Am. Pediatric Soc., Assn. for Retarded Citizens. Methodist. Office: Nat Inst Child Health & Human Devel Bldg 31 9000 Rockville Pike Rm 2A03 Bethesda MD 20892-0001

ALEXANDER, EUGENE MORTON, electronics engineer; b. Phila., Aug. 15, 1926; s. Morris and Jennie (Weisbein) A.; m. Marcia Geer, Dec. 18, 1949; children: Susan, Amy. Student Swarthmore Coll., 1944-45. BSEE, U. Pa., 1949, MSEE, 1961. Electronic engr. Philco Corp., Phila., 1949-54; with RCA Corp., 1955-87, mgr. communications systems design, Camden and Paramus, N.J., Tucson, Ariz., 1961-65, mgr. med. electronic design, Camden and Nutley, N.J., 1966-68, mgr. communication and electronic mail systems design, Camden, 1969-79, mgr. electronic computer-originated mail project for U.S. Postal Service, Camden, 1980-84, mgr. robotic vision and adaptive robotics programs, RCA Advanced Tech. Labs., Moorestown, N.J., 1984-87; mgr. technical program mgmt. GE/RCA Advanced Tech Labs, Moorestown; ind. cons. in tech. mgmt., 1988— . Served to ensign USNR, 1944-46. Recipient Engring. Achievement award Philco Corp., 1953. Sr. mem. IEEE. Home and Office: 309 Cranford Rd Cherry Hill NJ 08003-3147

ALEXANDER, FERNANDE GARDNER, writer, photographer; b. Peoria, Ill., Jan. 22, 1910; d. Laurence Vaughn and Percita (West) Gardner; m. David Crampton, Feb. 1934 (div. July 1950); 1 child, Gail Vaughn Wesson; m. W. Alanson Alexander Jr., Oct. 1953; 1 stepchild, Will A. Alexander III. Student, Stuyvesant Secretarial Sch., 1927, Am. Acad. of Dramatic Art, 1928-29, Columbia U., 1930-31. Actress various stock cos., N.Y. and N.J., 1931-32; asst. editor R.R. Bowker Co., N.Y.C., 1932-36; playwright, dir. Montclair (N.J.) Cosmopolitan Club, 1930-1950, Montclair Operetta Club, 1930-50, Upper Montclair Women's Club, 1930-50; bd. dirs. Whole Theatre Co., Montclair, 1978-85; with publicity dept. Essex County Opera Co., N.J., 1936-77, Yard Sch. of Art, Montclair, 1966-67; dir. Children's Theatre, Montclair, 1940-43. Author: Doll House, 1987, Collection 6 Plays, 1991 (short story) The Brink, 1933, (operetta) Tawya, 1946; writer numerous one act plays for women. Dir. Brownies scouts Girl Scouts U.S., Montclair, 1949-52; mem. county Rep. com., Montclair, 1948-77; vol. arboretum photographer Montclair Art Mus., 1989—. Recipient 1st prize N.J. State Fedn. of Womens Clubs. Mem. Montclair Golf Club, Bay Head Yacht Club. Republican. Unitarian. Home: 68 Woodmont Rd Montclair NJ 07043-2536

ALEXANDER, GEORGE JAY, toxicologist; b. Paris, June 27, 1925; came to U.S., 1946; s. Max and Salome (Rubin) A.; m. Rita Birnbaum, Apr. 29, 1958; 1 child, Mark. BS, Hobart Coll., 1949; PhD, Rutgers U., 1953. Rsch. fellow Rutgers Endowment Found., New Brunswick, N.Y., 1951-53; staff scientist Worcester Found., Shrewsbury, Mass., 1953-58; rsch. assoc. Columbia U., N.Y.C., 1958-60, from asst. prof. to assoc. prof. biochem. psychiatry, 1960—; head behavioral toxicology N.Y. State Psychiat. Inst., N.Y.C., 1987—; rsch. scientist V N.Y. State Dept. Mental Hygiene, N.Y.C., 1977—. Contbr. chpts. in books and articles to profl. jours. Exec. bd. mem. Pub. Employees Fedn., N.Y.C., 1989—; nat. exec. bd. mem. Jewish Labor Com., N.Y.C., 1986—. Fellow Am. Philatelic Soc.; mem. Am. Soc. Chemistry and Molecular Biology, Soc. Exptl. Biology and Medicine, N.Y. Acad. Scis. Office: NY State Psychiat Inst 722 W 168th St New York NY 10583

ALEXANDER, HAROLD LUCHSINGER, engineering educator; b. Santa Barbara, Calif., Feb. 23, 1957; s. Harold Burton and Kathryn Claire (Ogler) A.; m. Patricia Michelle Varga, June 20, 1987. BA, Harvard U., 1979; MS, Stanford U., 1982, PhD, 1988. Rsch. asst. Stanford U., Palo Alto, Calif., 1982-87, rsch. assoc., 1987-88; asst. prof. aero. and astronautics MIT, Cambridge, 1988—; cons. NASA Ames Rsch. Ctr., Mountain View, Calif., 1989, Univ. Faculty Assocs., Newton, Mass., 1990. Mem. AIAA, IEEE. Democrat. Office: MIT Rm 33 119 77 Massachusetts Ave Cambridge MA 02139

ALEXANDER, JONATHAN, cardiologist, consultant; b. N.Y.C., Nov. 29, 1947; s. Josef and Hannah (Margolis) A.; m. Karen Deborah Einhorn, Aug. 8, 1971; children: Jessica Beth, Daniel Lewis, Benjamin Joel. BA, Harvard U., 1968; MD, Albert Einstein Coll. Medicine, 1973. MD. Intern, resident Yale-New Haven Hosp., 1973-76; fellow dept. cardiology Sch. Medicine Yale U., New Haven, 1976-78, asst. clin. prof. medicine, 1978-83, assoc. clin. prof. medicine, 1983—; attending physician Danbury (Conn.) Hosp., 1978—, West Haven (Conn.) Vets. Hosp., 1978—, New Milford (Conn.) Hosp., 1980; dir. cardiac rehab. unit and nuclear cardiology Danbury (Conn.) Hosp., 1978—. Recipient Samuel Kushlan award Yale-New Haven Hosp., 1974, Revlon award 11th Internat. Congress Chemotherapy, 1983. Fellow ACP, Am. Coll. Cardiology (gov.-elect for Conn. 1992—), Am. Coll. Chest Physicians, Am. Heart Assn. (coun. clin. cardiology); mem. Soc. Nuclear Medicine, Alpha Omega Alpha. Jewish.

ALEXANDER, LAMAR See **ALEXANDER, ANDREW LAMAR**

ALEXANDER, LINCOLN MACCAULEY, Canadian provincial official; b. Toronto, Ont., Can., Jan. 21, 1922; s. Lincoln MacCauley and May Rose (Royale) A.; m. Yvonne Harrison, Sept. 10, 1948; 1 son, Keith. BA, McMaster U., 1949; grad., Osgoode Hall Law Sch., 1953; LLD, McMaster U., 1987, U. Western Ont., 1988. Bar: Ont. 1953, Queen's Counsel 1966. Ptnr. Millar Alexander Tokiwa & Isaacs, Hamilton, Ont.; elected to House of Commons, 1968, 72, 74, 79, 80; Minister of Labour Can., 1979-80; chmn. Ont. Workers Compensation Bd., 1980-85; lt.-gov. Province of Ont., 1985—; UN observer, 1976, 78. Past pres. Assn. Workers Compensation Bds. Can., 1980-85. Served with RCAF, 1942-45. Decorated knight Order St. John, knight of the mil. and hospitaller Order St. Lazarus of Jerusalem; recipient St. Ursula award, 1969; named Man of Yr., Ethnic Press Council, 1982; recipient Cultural Achievement award Caribana Cultural Com., 1984, Cert. of Service award House of Commons, 1984, Silver Acorn Boy Scouts of Can., 1988, Outstanding Citizen award Kiwanis Found., 1989; Mel Osborne fellow Kiwanis Found., 1989. Mem. Hamilton Lawyers Club, Wentworth County Law Assn., Can. Bar Assn. Conservative. Baptist. Club: Optimists, Hamilton Cricket. Office: Office of Lt Gov, Main Parliament Bldg Rm 131, Toronto, ON Canada M7A 1A1

ALEXANDER, MELVIN TAYLOR, quality engineer, statistician; b. Greensboro, N.C., June 2, 1949; s. Melvin Taylor and Sabina Mae (Anglin) A.; m. Karen Gwendolyn Davenport, Aug. 22, 1973 (div. 1982); children: Asia Trinicia, Sabina, Melvin Taylor III; m. Lucia Antoinette Ward, Apr. 23, 1983. Student, Guilford Coll., 1967-70; BS in Math., N.C. A&T State U., 1972; MSPH in Biostats., U. N.C., 1979. Registered quality engr. Instr. math. N.C. A&T State U., Greensboro, 1975-77; grad. asst. biostatis. dept. U. N.C., Chapel Hill, 1977-79; rsch. assoc. Sch. Pub. Health, Chapel Hill, 1980-81, jr. statis. analyst, 1981-82; engring. staff asst. Westinghouse Def. Ctr., Balt., 1982-83, sr. engr., 1983—; cons. N.C. Dept. Adminstrn., Raleigh, 1979-80, S.C. Conf. Black Mayors, Gifford, 1980. Co-author: Managing Industrial Processes, 1984. USPHS grantee, 1977; U. N.C. Minority Student fellow, 1978. Mem. Am. Statis. Assn., Am. Soc. Quality Control (chmn. Balt. sect. 1991-93, vice chmn. 1991-92, sec. 1990-91), Internat. Soc. for Hybrid Microelectronics. Democrat. Presbyterian. Office: Westinghouse Electronic Systems Grp 7323 Aviation Blvd Baltimore MD 21203-1693

ALEXANDER, PATRICK LEE, investment executive; b. Chgo., Oct. 1, 1945; s. Sterling Edward and Marianne Florence (Dieker) A.; m. Suzanne Lynn Bayer, June 7, 1968; children: Sean Patrick, Heather Lynn. BS, U. Tulsa, 1968; MBA, MS, U. Ill., 1973; postgrad., Stanford U., 1980. Portfolio mgr. Ford Motor Co., Dearborn, Mich., 1973-75; v.p. Bank of Am., San Francisco, 1975-80; mng. dir. Bankers Trust Co., N.Y.C., 1980-90; sr. v.p. Discount Advisors, N.Y.C., 1990—. With U.S. Army, 1969-70, Vietnam. Home: 10 Butternut Rd Allendale NJ 07401-1818

ALEXANDER, ROBERT JACKSON, economist, educator; b. Canton, Ohio, Nov. 26, 1918; s. Ralph S. and Ruth (Jackson) A.; m. Joan O. Powell, Mar. 26, 1949; children: Anthony, Margaret. B.A., Columbia U., 1940; M.A., Columnbia U., 1941; Ph.D., Columbia U., 1950. Asst. economist Bd. Econ. Warfare, 1942, Office Inter-Am. Affairs, 1945-46; mem. faculty Rutgers U., 1947—, prof. econs., 1961-89, prof. emeritus, 1989—; mem. Pres.-elect Kennedy's Latin Am. Task Force, 1960-61. Author 33 books including Juan Domingo Peron: A History, 1979, Romulo Betancourt and the Transformation of Venezuela, 1982, Bolivia: Past, Present and Future of its Politics, 1982, Biographical Dictionary of Latin American and Caribbean Politics, 1988, Juscelino Kubitschek and the Development of Brazil, 1991, International Trotskvism 1929-85, 1991. Mem. nat. bd. League Indsl. Democracy, 1955—; mem. nat. exec. com. Socialist Party-Social Dem. Fedn., 1957-66. Served with USAAF, 1942-45. Decorated officer Order Condor of the Andes Bolivia. Mem. Am. Econ. Assn., Latin Am. Studies Assn., Mid. Atlantic Coun. Latin Am. Studies (v.p. 1986-87, pres. 1987-88), Coun. Fgn. Rels., Interam. Assn. Democracy and Freedom (chmn. N.Am. com. 1970-87), Phi Gamma Delta. Home: 944 River Rd Piscataway NJ 08854-5504 Office: Rutgers U Econs Dept New Brunswick NJ 08903

ALEXANDER, SAMUEL ALLEN, JR., electronics company executive; b. Washington, Oct. 9, 1938; s. Samuel Allen and Mary Pearl (Last) A.; m. Susan Karinch, Aug. 25, 1973; children: Carolyn, Samuel Allen, Emily, Jonathan, David, Susan M. B.S. and B.A., Tufts U., 1962; postgrad. in biochemistry, George Washington U., 1963. Investment banker, registered rep. Ferris & Co., Washington, 1966-69; pres. Command Fin., Washington, 1969-72, Potomac Fed. Corp., Washington, 1973-75; v.p. adminstrn. and ops. officer Potter Instrument Co., Gonic, N.H., 1975-78, pres., chief exec. officer, 1978-83; pres. successor firm Precision Magnetics and Ceramics, 1984-85; chmn. bd., chief exec. officer ETI Techs., 1986-87; chmn. bd., sec. CEI, 1989—; participant investment banking seminar Wharton Sch. Bus., U. Pa., 1968-69. Mem. Delta Tau Delta, Chevy Chase Club (Md.), Lake Sunapee Yacht Club (Sunapee, N.H.). Roman Catholic.

ALEXANDER, SAUNDRA WEISBAND, registered nurse, health care facilities designer; b. Pitts., July 25, 1944; d. Benjamin Jerome and Marion Ruth (Weiss) Weisband; children: Jennifer Lynn, Tiffany Hope, Alexis Brooke. Diploma, Presbyn. U. Sch. Nursing, Pitts., 1965; student, Internat. Inst Interior Design, 1965-67; BS in Design, La Roche Coll., Pitts., 1988; postgrad., Harvard U., 1985. RN, Pa., Ky. Mgr., nurse supr. Barbourville (Ky.) Gen. Hosp., 1965-66; office coordinator, staff nurse Group Health Assn., Washington, 1966-68; staff nurse McKeesport (Pa.) Hosp., 1974-82; founder, exec. dir. Forms Unltd., McKeesport, 1978-82, Ambulance Audit Assn., McKeesport, 1978-82; staff nurse Magee-Women's Hosp., Pitts., 1982-87, Shadyside Hosp., Pitts., 1987—; healthcare design and equipment specialist Mahan Assocs., Pitts., 1989—; prin. Healthcare Design Assocs., Pitts., 1989—; instr. prenatal classes McKeesport Hosp., 1981-82; guest instr. various schs.; coordinator diabetes in early pregnancy rsch. program NIH, Washington, 1983-87. Mem. Am. Soc. Interior Designers (allied). Home: 2704 Tilbury Ave Pittsburgh PA 15217-2517 Office: Healthcare Design Assocs Med Ctr East 911 N Whitfield St Pittsburgh PA 15206-3039

ALEXANDER, THEODORE WILLIAM, III, investor; b. Auburn, Ala., Dec. 26, 1945; s. Theodore William Jr. and Dorothy Nell (Zachry) A.; m. Sharon Williams, July 11, 1970; children: Christina Anne, Jessica Leigh, Douglas Wright. BS in Econs., Auburn U., 1970; MA in Internat. Rels., Boston U., 1974; MPhil. in Polit. Econs., Columbia U., 1978. Bank officer Chase Manhattan Bank, N.Y.C., 1979-80, asst. treas., 1980-82, second v.p., 1982-84; v.p. Can. Imperial Bank, N.Y.C., 1984-86, Citibank, N.A., Harrison, N.Y., 1986-88; dir. acquisition fin., pres. CIBC Capital Corp. Can. Imperial Bank, N.Y.C., 1988-89, dir. strategic devel., 1989-90; pres. M & T Capital Corp., Buffalo, N.Y., 1990—; bd. dirs. Nova Am. Group, Inc., Buffalo, City Matress, Inc., Amherst, N.Y., TYS, Inc., Washington, Elan, Inc., Buffalo; bd. mem. Canisius Coll. Ctr. for Entrepreneurship, Buffalo, 1991-92. Coach Amherst (N.Y.) Youth Football League, 1991-92. Maj. U.S. Army, 1970-74, USAR, 1974—. Recipient Army ROTC scholarship U.S. Army, 1967; named Disting. Mil. grad. U.S. Army, 1970. Mem. Nat. Assn. Small Bus. Investment Cos., Nat. Venture Capital Assn., Park Country Club Buffalo, Sigma Chi, Omicron Delta Kappa. Home: 8100 Floss Ln East Amherst NY 14051 Office: M & T Capital Corp One M & T Plz Buffalo NY 14240

ALEXANDER, WYNNE, writer, journalist, composer; b. Lower Merion, Pa.; d. Robert Allen Klein and Sonia Louise (Leon) Gilbert. Broadcast journalist Sta. WDAS AM & FM Radio, Phila., 1975-84; adminstr., info. officer to Chief Justice of Pa., 1984-88; TV producer Sta. WCAU TV, CBS Broadcast Div., Phila., 1988; speechwriter to elected officials, corps. Phila., 1989—; cons. Azuricom Inc., Devon, Pa., 1989—. Contbr. articles on culture and gemology to publs. Recipient Citation of Merit, Senate of Pa.,

1986, Citation of Honor, City Coun. of Phila., 1985. Office: Lapidary Jour 60 Chestnut Ave Ste 201 Devon PA 19333-1312

ALEXANDRE, DEWITT LOOMIS, JR., investment company executive; b. Morristown, N.J., Sept. 17, 1949; s. DeWitt Loomis Alexandre and Cynthia Lenox (Banks) Foshay; m. Priscilla Baker Hill, Oct. 2, 1976 (div. Jan. 1986); children: Priscilla, Anthony; m. Kristin Kalgon Kuhns, Sept. 10, 1988; 1 child, James Andrew. BA, U. Denver, 1971. Salesperson Bache & Co., N.Y.C., 1974-75; v.p. sales dept. Kidder Peabody, N.Y.C., 1975—; dir. Bates Mfg., Hackettstown, N.J. Chmn. fundraising Boy Scouts Am., Watchung, N.J., 1989-92. Office: Kidder Peabody 10 Hanover Sq New York NY 10005

ALEXIS, MARCUS L., II, management consultant; b. St. Paul, Dec. 14, 1959; s. Marcus and Marilyn Yvonne (Varlack) A. AB, Stanford U., 1983; MBA, Northwestern U., 1990. Comml. banking rep. Harris Trust and Savs. Bank, Chgo., 1983-85, investment officer, 1986-88; assoc. cons. McKinsey & Co., N.Y.C., 1990—. Chmn. Harris Bank chpt. Chgo. Jr. Assn. of Commerce and Industry, 1985; pres. Kellogg Black Mgmt. Assn., Evanston, Ill., 1989-90. 1st Nat. Bank Chgo. fellow, 1988-90. Mem. Stanford Alumni Assn., Kellogg Alumni Assn.

ALEY, CHARLES R., lawyer; b. Beaver Falls, Pa., Apr. 3, 1956; s. Charles L. and Lois E. (Teckemeyer) A.; m. Harriet M. Baker, June 21, 1986. BA in Econs., BSBA in Acctg., Bus, Adminstrn. and Data Processing, BS in Info. Systems, Geneva Coll., 1978; JD, U. Pitts., 1981; LLD (hon.), London Inst. Applied Rsch., 1990. Bar: Pa. 1981, U.S. Dist. Ct. (we. dist.) Pa. 1981, U.S. Tax Ct. 1981, U.S. Ct. Appeals (3d cir.) 1981, U.S. Ct. Appeals (fed. cir.) 1985, U.S. Supreme Ct. 1985, Ohio 1987. Tax atty. Arthur Young & Co., Pitts., 1981-82, Edward J. DeBartolo Corp., Youngstown, 1982-86, Alcan Aluminum Corp., Warren, Ohio, 1986—. Mem. Internat. Parliament for Safety and Peace, 1991—. Recipient Disting. Svc. award Geneva Coll., 1991. Mem. ABA, Pa. Bar Assn., Allegheny County Bar Assn., Beaver County Bar Assn., Fed. Cir. Bar Assn., Trumbull County Bar Assn., Assn. Trial Lawyers Am., Internat. Platform Soc., Phi Alpha Delta. Mem. United Meth. Ch. Home: 1212 6th Ave Beaver Falls PA 15010-4423 Office: Alcan Aluminum Corp 280 N Park Ave Warren OH 44481-1109

ALFANO, ANGEL ROSARIO, artist; b. Calabria, Italy, 1940; came to U.S., 1971; One man shows include Studio 45, Rome, 1968, Studio A 246, Rome, 1970, Columbus Ave. Gallery, Tuckahoe, N.Y., 1981; group shows include Interregionale Giovanile Belfiore D'Adige Ve, Italy, 1957, Di Nuoro Nuoro, Italy, 1960, Arte Contemporanea Italiana, St. Louis, 1962, Giovani Pittori Galleria, Stagny, Rome, 1964, Key Biscayne (Fla.) Art Festival, 1965, Premio Internat. Europa Arte, Bologna, Italy, 1965, Il paesaggio Italiano, Toronto, Can., 1967, Salon Internat. Del'art Libre, Paris, 1968, Pittori Italiani, N.Y., 1969, Galleria Il Coscile, Castrovillari, Italy, 1971, Mostra Internat. Della Giovane Pittura, Budapest, 1973, 10th Ann. Art Exhbn. N.Y., N.Y.C., 1975, Sinson Collection, London, 1976, Cristhin Gallery, Eastchester, 1977, Gabbiano Gallery, Firenze, Italy, 1978, C. Mason Gallery, N.Y.C., 1983, Alternate Space Gallery, N.Y.C., 1984, West Broadway Gallery, N.Y.C., 1984, Galleria Magna Graecia, Taranto, Italy, 1985, Fine Art Gallery Westchester Community Coll., Valhalla, N.Y., 1986, Robbins Collection, Rye Brook, N.Y., 1987, Galleria Il Grifo, Reggio Calabria, Italy, 1988, De La Ligue Int. Fraternitè U. Tunis, Tunisia, 1988, Nuevo Centro Cultural de Arte, Santiago, Chile, 1989; represented in numerous pvt. collections; illustrator: (by A. Staffa) Pensieri Sparsi, (by T. Pereira) Poezie, (by D. Maffia) Poesie, (by. K.S. Young) Concoa de Armor. Recipient Gold Medal award, 1965, prize Spl. Au Salon Internat. De L'ar Libre, 1965, 1st prize Internat. Art Show San Remo, 1968, prize Spl. al XVI Premio Di Pittura Pizzo, 1969, 1st Prize Nat. Art Show, 1970, Spl. award Minister Pub. Sch. Rome, 1971. Address: 44 Merritt Ave Eastchester NY 10709

ALFIERO, SALVATORE HARRY, manufacturing company executive; b. Westerly, R.I., Nov. 11, 1937; s. Charles and Ann Rose (Augeri) A.; m. Victoria Margarita Blanco, Oct. 17, 1959 (div. 1986); children: Victor S., Charles C., James J. BS in Engring., Rensselaer Poly. Inst., 1964; MBA, Harvard U., 1966. Founder, chmn., chief exec. officer Mark IV Industries, Inc., Williamsville, N.Y., 1969—; bd. dirs. Phoenix Mut. Ins. Co., Hartford, Conn., Marine Midland Bank-Western, Buffalo. Trustee Children's Hosp. Buffalo, 1987—; bd. dirs. Greater Buffalo Devel. Found., 1988—; advisor Sch. Mgmt., SUNY, Buffalo, 1989, trustee univ. found. Capt. USMCR, 1958-67. Named Entrepreneur of Yr. Medaille Coll., Buffalo, 1988. Mem. Marine Corps Res. Officers Assn., Beta Gamma Sigma. Republican. Office: Mark IV Industries Inc 501 John James Audubon Pkwy PO Box F10 Amherst NY 14226-0810*

ALFORD, BRAD ALAN, psychology educator; b. Tylertown, Miss., May 1, 1953; s. C.A. and Marilyn (Jackson) a.; m. Emily Cheryl Higgs, June 5, 1982; 1 child, Jason Alan Jackson. BA, Millsaps Coll., Jackson, Miss., 1976; MA, U. Miss., 1981, PhD, 1984. Lic. psychologist, Pa., Colo. Program dir. Western Mental Health Inst., Bolivar, Tenn., 1984-85; clin. dir. N.W. Mental Health Ctr., Martin, Tenn., 1985-87; postdoctoral fellow U. Pa., Phila., 1987-88; asst. prof. psychology U. Ky., Lexington, 1988-89, U. Scranton, Pa., 1989—; prog. cons. Charter Psychiat. Hosp., Lexington, 1988-89. Contbr. chpts. to books and articles to profl. jours. Fellow Behavior Therapy and Rsch. Soc.; mem. AAAS, Assn. for Advancement of Behavior Therapy, Am. Psychol. Soc., Psi Chi. Home: Tanglewood Lakes 716 Timber Ridge Cir Greentown PA 18426 Office: U Scranton Dept Psychology Scranton PA 18510-4596

ALFORD, ROBERT ROSS, sociologist; b. Stockton, Calif., Apr. 18, 1928; s. Ellsworth and Grace (Ross) A.; m. Gloria Kramer, June 18, 1949 (div. 1987); children: Heidi, Jonathan, Elissa; m. Nayra Atiya, Dec. 1, 1989. A.B., U. Calif., Berkeley, 1950, M.A., 1952, Ph.D., 1961. Lectr. sociology U. Calif., Berkeley, 1959-61; mem. faculty U. Wis., 1961-74, prof. sociology, 1966-74; asso. dir. Survey Research Lab., 1961-63; vis. prof. govt. U. Essex, Eng., 1966-67; vis. fellow Netherlands Inst. Advanced Study, 1981-82; vis. prof. sociology Columbia U., 1970-71, 80-81, NYU, 1987-88; prof. sociology U. Calif.-Santa Cruz, 1974-88, chmn. bd. studies in sociology, 1974-76, dir. Interdisciplinary Grad. Program in Sociology, 1976-79, acad. adminstr. research unit in instl. analysis and social policy, 1982-88; Disting. prof. sociology CUNY Grad. Ctr., 1988—; exec. officer grad. program in sociology CUNY, 1988-92. Author: Party and Society, 1963, Bureaucracy and Participation: Political Cultures in Four Wisconsin Cities, 1969, Health Care Politics, 1975, Powers of Theory, 1985; editor: Stress and Contradiction in Advanced Capitalist Societies, 1975. Mem. Am. Sociol. Assn., Am. Polit. Sci. Assn. (Woodrow Wilson Found. award 1976). Office: CUNY Grad Ctr Rm 801 33 W 42d St New York NY 10036

ALIG, ROGER CASANOVA, physicist, engineer; b. Indpls., Nov. 7, 1941; s. Daniel Bell and Glen Dora (Frank) A.; m. Marcia F. Pritchard, Dec. 22, 1963; children: Paul, Graham, Heidi. BA, Wabash Coll., 1963; MS in Physics, Purdue U., 1965, PhD in Physics, 1967. Mem. tech. staff David Sarnoff Rsch. Ctr., Princeton, N.J., 1967—; adj. prof. Rider Coll., Lawrenceville, N.J., 1990—; vis. prof. Princeton U., 1974-75, U. São Paulo, Brazil, 1970-71. Patentee television display devices; contbr. numerous articles to scientific and profl. jours. Chmn. bd. dirs. Family Svc. Princeton Area, 1987-89. Recipient David Sarnoff medal RCA Corp., N.Y.C., 1983. Mem. Soc. for Info. Display, Am. Phys. Soc., Phi Beta Kappa. Presbyterian. Office: David Sarnoff Rsch Ctr CN 5300 Princeton NJ 08543

ALITO, SAMUEL ANTHONY, JR., judge; b. Trenton, N.J., Apr. 1, 1950; s. Samuel Alfred and Rose (Fradusco) A.; m. Martha-Ann Bomgardner, Feb. 9, 1985; children: Philip Samuel, Laura Claire. AB, Princeton U., 1972; JD, Yale U., 1975. Bar: N.J. 1975, N.Y. 1982, U.S. Dist. Ct. N.J. 1975, U.S. Ct. Appeals (3d cir.) 1977, U.S. Ct. Appeals (2d cir.) 1980, U.S. Ct. Appeals (D.C. cir.) 1987, U.S. Supreme Ct. 1979. Law clk. to judge U.S. Ct. Appeals (3d cir.), Newark, 1976-77; asst. U.S. atty. U.S. Atty.'s Office, Newark, 1977-81, U.S. atty., 1987-90; asst. to solicitor gen. Office of Solicitor Gen. Dept. Justice, Washington, 1981-85; dep. asst. atty. gen. Office of Legal Counsel Dept. Justice, Washington, 1985-87; judge U.S. Ct. Appeals (3d cir.), Newark, 1990—. Contbr. articles to law revs. Fellow Am. Bar Found.; mem. ABA, N.J. Bar Assn., Assn. Fed. Bar N.J., Phi Beta Kappa. Roman Catholic. Office: US Courthouse PO Box 999 Newark NJ 07101

ALIX, SISTER JACQUELYN J., nursing home adminstrator; b. Webster, Mass., Oct. 30, 1940; d. Leonard P. and Janet E. (Fournier) A. AS, Becker Coll., 1960; BSBA, Annhurst Coll., 1970; LHD (hon.), Assumption Coll., 1984. Exec. sec. Bates Shoe Co., Webster, 1961-65; asst. adminstr. St. Francis Home, Worcester, Mass., 1970-75; adminstr. St. Francis Home, 1975—. Trustee Becker Coll., Worcester, 1984—, Elder Home Care of Worcester, 1991—; mem. Little Franciscans of Mary, Worcester, 1965—, formation com., 1990—, strategic planning com. Recipient Disting. Alumnus award Becker Coll. Alumni Assn., 1986. Fellow Am. Coll. Health Care Adminstrs.; mem. New Eng. Cath. Health Assn. , Am. Assn. Homes for the Aging, Assn. Mass. Homes for the Aging (trustee 1984—), Conf. of Religious Treas. Home and Office: 101 Plantation St Worcester MA 01604-3077

ALIZZI, ANTHONY JOSEPH, trust company executive; b. Pawtucket, R.I., June 23, 1953; s. Anthony and Eleonora Dorothy Alizzi. BSBA, Boston U., 1975, MBA, 1976. CPA, Mass. Staff acct. Price Waterhouse, Boston, 1976-79, sr. acct., 1979; sr. cons. Price Waterhouse, N.Y.C., 1979-81, mgr., 1981-84, sr. mgr., 1984-86; v.p. Bankers Trust Co., N.Y.C., 1986-87; dir. Depository Trust Co., N.Y.C., 1987-90, group dir., 1990—. Co-author: Money and Your Business, 1982. Youth coach Syosset (N.Y.) Soccer Club, 1991. Mem. AICPA, N.Y. State Soc. CPA's, Plainview-Old Bethpage Roadrunners Club.

ALLAIRE, PAUL ARTHUR, office equipment company executive; b. Worcester, Mass., July 21, 1938; s. Arthur E. Allaire and Elodie (LePrade) Murphy; m. Kathleen Buckley, Jan. 26, 1963; children: Brian, Christina. BSEE, Worcester Poly. Inst.,, 60; MSIA, Carnegie-Mellon U., 1966. Fin. analyst Xerox Corp., Rochester, N.Y., 1966-70; dir. fin. analysis Rank Xerox Ltd., London, N.Y., 1970-73; dir. internat. ops. fin. Xerox Corp., Stamford, Conn., 1973-75; chief staff officer Rank Xerox Ltd., London, 1975-79, mng. dir., 1979-83; sr. v.p., chief staff officer Xerox Corp., Stamford, Conn., 1983-86, pres., 1986-91, chmn., 1991, chmn. bd., 1991—; also bd. dirs. Rank Xerox Ltd., London, Conn.; mem. investment policy adv. com. U.S. Trade Rep.; bd. dirs. Rank Xerox Ltd., Fuji Xerox Co. Ltd., Sara Lee Corp., Crum & Forster, Morristown, N.J. Nat. Planning Assn., Washington, 1986SCIVbd. dirs., mem. bus. adv. coun., trustee Grad. Sch. Indsl. Adminstrn. Carnegie Mellon U.; trustee Worchester Poly. Inst. Mem. Tau Beta Pi, Eta Kappa Nu. Democrat. Office: Xerox Corp PO Box 1600 Stamford CT 06904-1600

ALLARD, JUDITH LOUISE, biology educator; b. Rutland, Vt., Feb. 21, 1945; d. William Edward and Orilla Marion (Trombley) A. BA, U. Vt., 1967, MS, 1969. Tchr. math., sci. Edmunds Jr. High Sch., Burlington, Vt., 1969-73; biology tchr. Edmunds Jr. High Sch., Burlington, 1973-78, sci. dept. chair, 1975-78; biology tchr. Burlington (Vt.) High Sch., 1978—; instr. environ. studies U. Vt., Burlington, 1988—; adviser Nat. Honor Soc., 1986—. Contbg. author Favorite Labs of Outstanding Tchrs., 1991. Active Amnesty Internat., 1985—; mem. Discovery Mus., Essex Junction, Vt., 1986—, Lake Champlain Com., Burlington, 1987—. Recipient Presdl. Sci. Teaching award NSF, 1983; named Outstanding Vt. Educator, U. Vt., 1983, Outstanding Vt. Sci. Tchr., Sigma Xi Soc., 1984; Tandy Tech. scholar, 1990. Mem. ASCD, NEA (bd. dirs. Vt. chpt.), Vt. Sci. Tchrs. Assn. (bd. dirs. 1980—, treas. 1985—), Burlington Edn. Assn. (exec. bd.), Burlington Profl. Standards Bd. (chair 1991—), Parents and Friends of Edn. (trustee), Nat. Assn. Biology Tchrs. (bd. dirs. Vt. Outstanding Biology Tchr. award program 1977—, Outstanding Biology Tchr. award 1975), Assn. Presdl. Awardees in Sci. Roman Catholic. Home: 221 Woodlawn Rd Burlington VT 05401-2453 Office: Burlington High Sch 52 Institute Rd Burlington VT 05401-2789

ALLARD, MARVEL JUNE, psychology educator; b. Detroit; d. Adrian Clarence and Marvel Claudia (Tremper) A.; m. James Donald Widmayer, Mar. 22, 1970 (div. Mar. 1982). AB, Mich. State U., MA, PhD. Rsch. assoc. Mich. State U., East Lansing, 1965-66; project dir., rsch. scientist Am. U., Washington, 1966-67; sr. staff Ops. Rsch., Inc., Silver Spring, Md., 1967-70; rsch. cons., 1970—; prof. psychology Worcester (Mass.) State Coll., 1973—; cons. Leasco Systems, Yankelovich Co., Middlesex County, others. Mem. editorial bd. Chronic Mental Illness and Aging newletter; contbr. rsch. articles to profl. jours. Mem. Worcester County Hort. Soc.; bd. dirs. Girls, Inc., Worcester; trustee Worcester State Hosp. NSF fellow Mich. State U., 1959-64, Nat. fellow Assn. Am. Colls., 1985; scholar Mich. State U. and pvt. orgns., 1954-58, Phi Kappa Phi scholar Mich. State U.. Mem. APA (site visitor, mem. undergrad. cons. svc.). Home: 24 Curtis St Auburn MA 01501-3149 Office: Worcester State Coll 486 Chandler St Worcester MA 01602-2597

ALLARDICE, JOHN MCCARRELL, coatings manufacturing company executive; b. Balt., May 30, 1940; s. James Barclay and Rebecca Jane (McCarrell) A.; m. J. Ann Benjamin, May 30, 1962 (div. 1979); children: John McCarrell Jr., Scott, Julie; m. Susan Bryson Miller, Aug. 15, 1981; stepchildren: Ben, Ted. Student, Washington and Jefferson Coll., 1958-61; BS in Chemistry, U. Pitts., 1963. Salesman chem. div. PPG, Pitts., 1964; silicone div. GE, Waterford, N.Y., 1965; salesman Stuaffer Chem. Co., Adrian, Mich., 1965-69; salesman, sales mgr. Fre Kote, Inc., Boca Raton, Fla., 1969-78; pres. Releasomers, Inc., Bradford Woods, Pa., 1978—. Patentee bladder lubricants. Republican. Mem. Ch. of Religious Science. Office: Releasomers Inc PO Box 82 Brackenridge PA 15014-0082

ALLEE, DEBRA COLE, environmental consultant; b. N.Y.C., Apr. 26, 1939; d. Loeb and Tilly (D.) Cole; m. John Sellier Allee, Mar. 7, 1964 (div. Feb. 1986); children: John Cole, David Sellier. AB, Radcliffe Coll., 1959; student, Yale U., 1960-62, NYU, 1973-74. Planner/sr. planner Parsons Brinckerhoff Quade & Douglas, Inc., N.Y.C., 1965-67, 68-72, sr. planner, asst. v.p., 1973-77, tech. dir., v.p., 1977-81, bd. dirs., 1980-81; pres. Allee King Rosen & Fleming, Inc., N.Y.C., 1981—; adj. assoc. prof. Grad. Sch. Architecture, Planning and Preservation, Columbia U., N.Y.C., 1984—; bd. dirs., mem. exec. com. Citizens Housing and Planning Coun., N.Y.C.; instr. continuing edn. ASCE, 1970s, Am. Law Inst./ABA, U. Colo. Law Sch., Boulder, 1980; speaker in field. Contbr. articles to profl. jours. Office: Allee King Rosen & Fleming 117 E 29th St New York NY 10016

ALLEGRANTE, JOHN PHILIP, public health educator; b. Poughkeepsie, N.y., Mar. 8, 1952; s. John Ralph and Lois Elaine (Hanlowich) A.; m. Andrea Joan Samuels, July 24, 1976; 1 child, Jason Paul. BS, SUNY, Cortland, 1974; MS, U. Ill., 1976, PhD, 1979; postgrad., RAND Corp., Santa Monica, Calif., 1987-88. Asst. prof. health edn. Columbia U. Tchrs. Coll., N.Y.C., 1979-81, dept. chmn., 1980-90, assoc. prof. health edn. (tenured), 1981—; sr. fellow Nat. Ctr. for Health Edn., N.Y.C., 1983-84; ctr. dir. Columbia U. Tchr. Coll., N.Y.C., 1984—; assoc. prof. clin. pub. health (sociomed. sci.) Columbia U. Sch. Pub. Health, N.Y.C., 1987—; edn. dir. Cornell Arthritis Ctr., N.Y.C., 1988—; div. dir. Columbia U. Tchrs. Coll., N.Y.C., 1989—; cons. NIH, Bethesda, Md., 1983—; cons. to numerous govt. agencies, founds., and univs. Mem. editorial bd. Am. Jour. Health Promotion, 1987—, Tchrs. Coll. Press, 1989—; co-author: Investing in Employee Health, 1987; contbr. essays and articles to profl. publs. Mem. N.Y. State Citizens Task Force on Child Abuse and Neglect, 1984—, N.Y. State Nutrition for Life Adv. Com., 1987-89; vol. prof. Am. Cancer Soc. Nat. Office, Atlanta, 1985-88. Kellogg Found. fellow W.K. Kellogg Found., 1985-88, Pew Health Policy fellow RAND/UCLA Ctr. for Health Policy Study, 1987-88; named Disting. Young Alumnus SUNY, Cortland, 1985; recipient Disting. Writer's award Eta Sigma Gamma, 1985; grantee NIH, 1988—. Fellow Soc. for Pub. Health Edn., N.Y. Acad. Medicine; mem. APHA (sec. 1982-83), Am. Sch. Health Assn. (rsch. coun. 1975—), Arthritis Health Professions Assn. Home: 172 Surrey Ct Ramsey NJ 07446-1270 Office: Columbia U Tchrs Coll 525 W 120th St New York NY 10027-6625

ALLEN, BARRY MORGAN, corporate communications executive; b. N.Y.C., June 3, 1939; s. Robert Mitchell and Edna B. (Feldman) A.; m. Carol Joyce Applestein, Sept. 20, 1961 (div. June 1974);1 child, Sheri; m. Rena Susan Garfinkle, June 16, 1974; children: Belinda Krasno, David Krasno. BS in Journalism, U. Md., 1961. Account mgr. Burson-Marsteller, Washington, 1967-71; dir. communications Archon Pure Products Corp., Beverly Hills, Calif., 1971-73; v.p. communications Glass Packaging Inst., Washington, 1973-77; 1st v.p., corp. communications Bank of Boston, 1977-86; sr. v.p. corp. affairs Hartford (Conn.) Nat. Corp., 1986-88, Manning, Selvage & Lee, N.Y.C., 1988—; charter mem. Evanston Group, 1985-87. Mem. Gov.'s Alliance Against Drugs, Mass., 1985-86; bd. dirs. Morgan Meml. Good Will, Boston, 1986, Bay State Games, Mass., 1986. Lt. USNR, 1961-67, Vietnam. Scholar Montgomery County, Md., 1960. Mem. Pub. Rels. Soc. Am., Phi Delta Epsilon. Home: 282 Senese Dr Fairfield CT 06430-2256 Office: Manning Selvage & Lee 79 Madison Ave New York NY 10016-7802

ALLEN, BEATRICE, piano educator; b. N.Y.C., June 30, 1917; d. Samuel and Rose (Krell) Hyman; m. Eugene Murray Allen, Jan. 23, 1937; children: Marlene Allen Galzin, Julian Lewis. Student NYU, 1933-36; diploma (scholar), Inst. Musical Arts, N.Y.C., 1939, postgrad. (scholar), 1939-40; diploma (fellow, letter commendation), Juilliard Grad. Sch., N.Y.C., 1943; BA magna cum laude Cedar Crest Coll., 1980. Mem. faculty prep. div. Juilliard Sch. Music, 1957-69, Moravian Coll., 1967-68, Northampton County Area Community Coll., 1968-70, Manhattan Sch. Music, 1969—; mem. founding faculty Community Music Sch., Allentown, Pa., 1982—; artist-in-residence, condr. Tchrs. Workshop, Antioch Coll., Yellow Springs, Ohio, 1966; Bach lectr., recitals various univs.; concert appearances Town Hall, N.Y.C., Chautauqua, N.Y., others. Winner N.J. Artists contest, 1936. Mem. Music Tchrs. Nat. Assn. (program chmn. Lehigh Valley chpt. 1981-82), Pa. Music Tchrs. Assn. Address: 2100 Main St Bethlehem PA 18017

ALLEN, CLAXTON EDMONDS, III, investment banker; b. N.Y.C., Aug. 27, 1944; s. C. Edmonds and Helen (McCreery) A. A.B., Washington and Lee U., 1964, J.D., 1967. Bar: N.Y. 1969. Assoc. Simpson Thacher & Bartlett, N.Y.C. 1967-70; assoc. gen. counsel Gen. Electric Credit Corp., 1970-71; investment banker Merrill Lynch, Pierce, Fenner & Smith, Inc., N.Y.C., 1971-72; pres. Gloucester Internat. Ltd., N.Y.C., 1972—, Comanche Exploration Corp., 1981-86, Compass Internat. Corp., 1982—, Horizon Coal Corp., Mineral Res. Corp., 1982-85, Compass Coal Corp., 1986-91, Overseas & Fgn. Investors, Inc., 1990—; mgr. dir. Elm Realty Investment Corp., 1990—; dir. Warren Resources, Inc., 1991—. Clubs: Players, Canadian, Met. Home: 405 E 54th St New York NY 10022-5123

ALLEN, DAVID, federal agency administrator; b. York, Maine, May 15, 1942; s. Pliny Arunah and Tillie (MacQuinn) A.; m. JoAnn Moeckly, 1968 (div. 1975); children: Torrie, Heather; m. Robin Lee Perry, Mar. 11, 1983; children: Rebecca, Patrick. BA, Lake Forest Coll., 1965; MA, U. Ariz., 1967, PhD, 1968. Asst. prof. dept. psychology S.D. State U., Brookings, 1968-71; rsch. psychologist U.S. Govt., Washington, 1971-78; chief rsch. br. U.S. Govt., 1978-85, dep. chief psychol. svcs. div., 1985-87; chief rsch. and info. systems div. CIA, Washington, 1987-90; investigator Office of Insp. Gen., CIA, 1990-92; chief ADP staff Latin Am. Div. CIA, 1992—. Contbr. articles to profl. jours. Rsch. fellow USPHS, 1967-68; rsch. grantee NSF, 1970-71. Mem. Apple Programmers & Developers Assn. Republican. Home: 905 N Emerson St Arlington VA 22205-2562

ALLEN, DAVID CHRISTOPHER, chemical company executive; b. Pitts., Feb. 7, 1933; s. Richard Congden and Grace Barber (Leonard) A.; m. Mary Rogers Miles, Sept. 10, 1955 (div. 1976); children: David Christopher, Peter James, Stephen Miles, Perry Elizabeth Allen Soognamillo. BS in Chem. Engring., Tufts U., 1954; MBA in Mktg., Fairleigh Dickinson U., 1973. Engr. E.I. DuPont de Nemours & Co., Wilmington, Del., 1954-60, tech. engr., 1960-66, tech. supr., 1966-74, mktg. specialist, 1974-77, sr. bus. specialist, 1977-83, bus. cons., 1983—; chmn. bd. J.A. of Del., Inc., Wilmington, 1986—. Contbr. articles to profl. jours. Pres. Red Clay Consol. Sch. Dist., Wilmington, 1986-91, Del. Sch. Bd. Assn., Dover, 1987-91, Heritage-Grendon Civic Assn., Wilmington, 1985-87; v.p. Del. State PTA, 1991—; co-chair Gov.'s Com. on Mentoring, 1991—. Recipient Bronze Nat. Leadership, Jr. Achievement, 1985, Silver Nat. Leadership, 1988. Republican. Home: 2518 Emerson Dr Wilmington DE 19808-3706 Office: E I DuPont Co Imaging Systems Dept Wilmington DE 19898

ALLEN, DAVID WOODROFFE, computer scientist; b. Hampton, Iowa, Sept. 20, 1944; s. Edward DeWalt and Julia Woodroffe (Lamb) A.; m. Barbara Ann Schneider, Sept. 15, 1973. BA, Grinnell Coll., 1967; MS, U. Pitts., 1974. Assoc. engr. Westinghouse Electric Corp., Sharon, Pa., 1967-70, engr., 1970-79, sr. engr., 1979-84; sr. computer scientist Westinghouse Electric Corp., Pitts., 1984-90, prin. engr., 1990—. Contbr. articles to profl. jours.; patentee in field. Mem. IEEE (sect. sec.-treas. 1981-82, referee tech. papers for Computer jour.), Assn. for Computing Machinery, Silicon Graphics User's Group We. Pa. (treas. 1991—), Digital Equipment Computer User's Soc. Democrat. Home: 2637 Rossmoor Dr Pittsburgh PA 15241-2572 Office: Westinghouse Electric Corp PO Box 18249 Pittsburgh PA 15236-0249

ALLEN, EDITH AGNES, economist; b. Detroit, July 2, 1939; d. Augustine Oliver and Agnes (Robinson) A.; m. Roy Louis Schult, July 26, 1958 (div. 1973); children: Rick, Daniel, Julia. BS in Physics, U. Rochester, N.Y., 1959; MA in Econs., SUNY, Stony Brook, 1974, PhD in Econs., 1978. Dir. Champaign-Urban Montessori Sch., Champaign, Ill., 1966-73; econs. asst. Econs. Dept. SUNY, Stony Brook, 1973-76; lectr., asst. prof. Soc. Sci. Dept. Mich. State U., East Lansing, 1977-83; vis. prof. Bus. and Econ. Dept. Ind. U. N.W., Gary, 1983-85; assoc. economist N.Y. State Pub. Svc. Commn., Albany, 1985—; mem. People-to-People econs. and bus. del. to Russia, Ukraine, 1992. Contbr. articles to profl. jours. Bd. dir. Day of the Child Celebration, Champaign, 1972; mem. United Way, Champaign, Ill., 1970-73. Mem. AAUW (Comstock fellow 1976-77), LWV, Econometric Soc., Am. Econ. Assn., Internat. Assn. Energy Econ., Assn. Environ. and Resource Econs., Am. Statis. Assn., Phi Beta Kappa. Episcopalian. Office: NY State Dept Pub Svc 3 Empire State Albany NY 12223

ALLEN, FRANCES JESSICA, business owner; b. Jersey City, June 17, 1961; d. Milan and Sonja (Roncevic) Zagar; m. Mark J. Allen, June 19, 1982. BA, Rutgers U., 1983. Regional mgr. Dunkin Donuts, Jersey City, 1983-86; tchr. Wallington (N.J.) High Sch., 1986-90; pres. Crafty Critters, Oakland, N.J., 1986-89, Finishing Touch Boutique, Ringwood, N.J., 1989—. Mem. Nat. Assn. Women Bus. Owners, Nat. Assn. Profl. Salespeople, Gift Assn., N.J. Assn. Women Bus. Owners (fund raiser 1990-91, recording sec. 1991-92). Office: Finishing Touch Boutique PO Box 231 Ringwood NJ 07456-0231

ALLEN, GENE ALFRED, public relations executive, consultant; b. Utica, N.Y., Nov. 2, 1953; s. Alfred Eugene and Columbia Barbara (Velocci) A.; m. Mary Beth Rider, Aug. 14,1976; children: Rebecca Anne, Andrew Damien, Daniel Alexander. BS, Utica Coll., 1981. Exec. dir. Bagg's Square Assn., Utica, N.Y., 1982-86; media cons. various, Utica, 1980—; pub. rels./devel. dir. Assn. for Retarded Citizens, Utica, 1982—. Author, chief editor: (training manual) Take Your Show On The Road, 1990. Bd. dirs. Cornhill Sr. Ctr., Utica, 1982—. Mem. Mohawk Valley Ad Club. Home: 1546 Seymour Ave Utica NY 13501-5014 Office: Assn for Retarded Citizens 925 Stark St Utica NY 13502-4122

ALLEN, HARRY FRANKLIN, finance educator; b. Amersham, Eng., Mar. 6, 1956; came to U.S., 1980.; s. Harry Cranbrook and Mary Kathleen (Andrews) A.; m. Sally Elizabeth Riley, July 9, 1977; children: James Franklin, Toby Thomas. BA, U. East Anglia, Norwich, Eng., 1977; M of Philosophy, Oxford (Eng.) U., 1979, D of Phil., 1980; MA, U. Pa., 1987. Asst. prof. fin. Wharton Sch. U. Pa., Phila., 1980-86, assoc. prof. fin. and econs., 1986-90, prof., vice dean, dir. doctoral programs, 1990—. Home: 929 Merion Square Rd Gladwyne PA 19035-1509 Office: U Pa Wharton Sch Fin Philadelphia PA 19104

ALLEN, HENRY JOSEPH, management consultant; b. Passaic, N.J., Sept. 6, 1931; s. Edward J. and Mary B. Allen; ed. Fairleigh Dickinson U., 1952, Am. Grad. U., 1975—; MBA, Met. Collegiate Inst., 1986; m. Clare B. Reardon, Jan. 21, 1956 (dec. Dec. 1983); children: Patricia Ann, Mark Terrence; m. Donna L. O'Hearn, Sept. 22, 1990. Svc. engr. Curtiss-Wright Corp., Woodridge, N.J., 1952-56, customer svc. rep, 1956-60, mil. salesman, 1960-64, sr. sales engr., 1964-66, mgr. mktg., 1966-77, dir. mil.-govt. mktg., 1977-79; corp. dir. mktg. and bus. devel. Advanced Tech., Inc., McLean, Va., 1979-80; prin. Challenger Assocs., Elmwood Park, N.J., 1980—. Served with U.S. Army, 1952-55. Mem. Tech. Mktg. Soc. Am., Assn. U.S. Army, U.S. Naval Inst., Am. Mktg. Assn., Soc. Automotive Engrs., Am. Soc. Profl.

Cons., Remotely Piloted Vehicle Assn., Am. Def. Preparedness Assn. Republican. Roman Catholic. Home: 18 Dresser St Newport RI 02840 Office: Challenger Assocs 21 Roosevelt Ave Elmwood Park NJ 07407-1023

ALLEN, HERBERT, investment banker; b. N.Y.C., Feb. 13, 1908; s. Charles and Francis (Mayer) A.; m. Kathleen Heffernan (dec.); children—Herbert Anthony, Susan Kathleen Wilson; m. Ethel Strong. D.C.S. (hon.), Ithaca Coll. Ptnr. Allen & Co., N.Y.C., 1927—; dir. emeritus Irvine Co., Newport Beach, Calif. Trustee, v.p. Hackley Sch., Tarrytown, N.Y. Clubs: Deepdale Golf; Indian Creek Golf (Fla.); Mark's (London); Saratoga Golf and Polo; Bal Harbour; Surf (Fla.). Office: Allen & Co Inc 711 5th Ave New York NY 10022-3109

ALLEN, HOWARD J., cancer research scientist; b. Gloversville, N.Y., Mar. 11, 1941; s. Howrd Joseph and Beatrice Leona (Fisher) A.; m. June Ellen Lansing, Dec. 17, 1959; children: Tina, Theresa, Howard III, Scott, Craig. BS, Albany State Coll., 1965; PhD, SUNY, Buffalo, 1970. Postdoctoral fellow Fla. State U., Tallahassee, 1970-72; cancer rsch scientist Roswell Park Cancer Inst., Buffalo, 1972—; asst. rsch. prof. SUNY, Buffalo, 1974—; rsch. prof. Niagara U., Niagara Falls, N.Y., 1977—, Canisius Coll., Buffalo, 1991—. Contbr. articles to profl. jours. NIH grantee. Republican. Roman Catholic. Home: 372 Fletcher St Tonawanda NY 14150-1930 Office: Roswell Park Cancer Inst Elm & Carlton Sts Buffalo NY 14263

ALLEN, JANE GOULD, retired bank executive; b. Lyons Falls, N.Y., Dec. 4, 1925; d. Gordon H.P. and Helen Greeley (Bowman) Gould; m. Harold Clifford Allen, Sept. 29, 1946; children: Carol Allen, Marcia A. Owen, Mary A. Dixon, Stephen H. Student, Skidmore Coll., 1943-46. Pres. Lyons Falls (N.Y.) Nat. Bank, 1977-82; ret., 1982—. Pres. Lewis County Hist. Soc., Lyons Falls, 1989-92; bd. visitors Rome (N.Y.) Devel. Disabilities, N.Y. State, 1973-93. Home: PO Box 335 Snugsboro Rd Lyons Falls NY 13368 Office: Lewis County Hist Soc High St Lyons Falls NY 13368

ALLEN, JENNIE ELIZABETH, advertising executive; b. Bryn Mawr, Pa., May 11, 1962; d. Frederick William and Patricia Jean (Snyder) Held; m. Parker Spaulding Allen, Sept. 16, 1988; 1 child, Emily Elizabeth. BA in Communications, Bethany (W.Va.) Coll., 1984. Advt. mgr. So. Lock & Supply, Pinellas Park, Fla., 1984-85; mktg. rep. Citizens & So. Bank, St. Petersburg, Fla., 1985-87, Am. Electromedics, Hudson, N.H., 1987-88; pub. rels. and advt. mgr. Micro Communications, Inc., Manchester, N.H., 1988—; pub. rels. cons. Free-Kuwait Telecommunications, Manchester, 1991. Vol. United Way, St. Petersburg, 1985-87. Home: 7 Pulaski Dr Epping NH 03042-3239 Office: Micro Communications Inc Grenier Field 438 Kelly Ave Manchester NH 03108

ALLEN, JONATHAN, physicist, electronics engineer; b. Fall River, Mass., Dec. 29, 1942; s. Mordecai and Edith (Hurwitz) A.; m. Shirley Eisenman, Nov. 21, 1971; 1 child, Laura. AB in Physics, Colby Coll., 1964; MS in Physics, Southeastern Mass. U., 1971; PhD in Physics, Washington U., St. Louis, 1977. Jr. engr. Trans-Sonics, Inc., Burlington, Mass., 1964-65; exptl. engr. United Techs. Corp., Windsor Locks, Conn., 1965-68; physicist High Energy Processing Corp., New Bedford, Mass., 1968-71; rsch. asst. physics dept. Washington U., 1972-77; scientist AeroChem Rsch. Labs., Inc., Princeton, N.J., 1978-83; sr. scientist Chronar Corp., Princeton, 1983-90; physicist Advanced Photovoltaic Systems, Inc., Princeton, 1990—; instrumentation cons., Titusville, N.J., 1983-90. Contbg. editor N.J. Hazardous Waste News, 1982-84; also articles; patentee on spectral analysis, thin film scribing. Tech. advisor Stoney-Brook-Millstone Watersheds Assn., Pennington, N.J., 1979. Mem. IEEE, Am. Phys. Soc. (life), Fedn. Am. Scientists, Greenpeace, Sierra Club. Democrat. Home: 3 Creek Rim Dr Titusville NJ 08560-1303 Office: Advanced Photovoltaic Systems Inc PO Box 7093 Princeton NJ 08543-7093

ALLEN, JUDITH, academic administrator; b. Norwood, Mass., Dec. 13, 1938; d. Joshua Allen and Helen (Gibbs) Studley. BLS, Boston U., 1970; MEd, Salem (Mass.) State Coll., 1975. Asst. dir. fin. aid Boston U., 1964-70; dir. fin. aid Regis Coll., Weston, Mass., 1970-79, dir. admissions and dir. fin. aid, 1976-79; asst. to the pres. Williams Coll., Williamstown, Mass., 1979-83; exec. dir. The Coll. Bd., Waltham, Mass., 1983—; chmn. adv. com. Higher Edn. Info. Ctr., Boston, 1989-91. Active Lowell (Mass.) Futures Adv. Coun., Lowell Statewide Youth Early Awareness Com. Mem. Nat. Assn. Coll. Admissions Counselors, New Eng. Assn. Coll. Admissions Counselors, Mass. Assn. Student Fin. Aid Adminstrs., Eastern Assn. Student Fin. Aid Adminstrs., Nellie Mae Loan Mktg. Assn. (bd. dirs. Braintree, Mass. chpt. 1981-87). Home: 35 Casey Cir Waltham MA 02154-2171 Office: New Eng Office Coll Bd 470 Totten Pond Rd Fl 5 Waltham MA 02154-1905

ALLEN, MARIETTE PATHY, photographer; b. Alexandria, Egypt, June 22, 1940; d. George Stephan and Margaret Mary Pathy; m. Kenneth Phillip Allen, Dec. 6, 1969; children: Cordelia, Julia. BA, Vassar Coll., 1962; MFA in Painting, U. Pa., Phila., 1965. Photographer, graphic artist N.J. State Mus., Trenton, 1966-67; coord. for documentation N.Y.C. Dept. Cultural Affairs, 1972-75; self-employed photographer, 1975—; speaker on gender issues. Author: Transformations: Crossdressers and Those Who Love Them, 1989; represented in permanent collections at Bklyn. Mus., N.Y.C., Bibliotheque Nationale, Paris; represented by Simon Lowinsky Gallery, N.Y.C. Participant in pilot study Equal Justice Inst., N.Y.C., 1974-75. Recipient grant N.Y. State Coun. on Arts, 1987, Thornton-Oakley scholarship U. Pa., 1965. Mem. Am. Soc. Mag. Photographers, Profl. Women Photographers (chmn. 1984-92). Home: 100 Riverside Dr New York NY 10024-4822

ALLEN, MARK PAUL, antiques dealer, consultant, appraiser; b. N.Y.C., Jan. 10, 1944; s. Merton Stone and Regina (Gartstien) A.; m. Marjorie Lee Sokoloff, Oct. 19, 1965; children: Stephanie Rebecha, Samantha Jean. BA, CUNY Lehmann Coll., 1970; MS, CUNY Hunter Coll., 1972; PhD, CUNY Grad. Ctr. Rsch. asst. Gen. Food Corp., Tarrytown, N.Y., 1965-67; rsch. assoc. Geigy Pharmaceuticals, Ardsley, N.Y., 1967-71; antiques dealer Mark & Marjorie Allen Antiques, Putnam Valley, N.Y., 1968—. Mem. Am. Ceramics Circle, Am. Soc. Appraisers (assoc.).

ALLEN, PATRICIA, English educator; b. Keene, N.H., Dec. 5, 1942; d. Robert Edward and M. Katherine (Jelley) Doody; m. Paul Frank Allen, Aug. 19, 1967; children: Kathleen, Barbara Jean, Susan Maureen. BEd, U. N.H., Keene, 1964; MEd, U. Maine, Orono, 1983. Tchr. secondary schs. Keene, 1964-67, Central, Mass., 1967-81, Woodland, Maine, 1981-86; tchr. secondary schs. Colebrook (N.H.) Acad., 1986—; prof. English N.H. Vocat.-Tech. at Berlin, Colebrook, 1989—; curriculum coord. K-12 Woodland Sch. Dist., 1983-86. Bd. dirs. Calais (Maine) Regional Hosp., 1982-86. Mem. Colebrook Ednl. Assn., Nat. Edn. Assn., N.H. Ednl. Assn., ASCD. Democrat. Roman Catholic. Home: 23 Bridge St Colebrook NH 03576-1001 Office: Colebrook Acad 1 Academy St Colebrook NH 03576-1198

ALLEN, PAUL HOWARD, financial institutions investor; b. Aldershot, Eng., Apr. 5, 1954; came to U.S., 1979; s. William and Frances Elva (Mason) A.; m. Marissa Celeste Wesely, Sept. 17, 1983; 1 child, Emma Elizabeth Wesely Allen. BA in Jurisprudence, Oxford (Eng.) U., 1976; MA in Jurisprudence, Oxford U., 1988; MBA, Harvard U., 1981. Bar: solicitor Eng. and Wales 1977. Solicitor of Supreme Ct. London, Freshfields, Eng., 1977-79; lectr. law Exeter Coll. Oxford U., 1978-79; assoc. McKinsey and Co. Inc., London, 1981-84; assoc. McKinsey and Co. Inc., N.Y.C., 1984-87, ptnr., 1987-89; co-founder ALTA Ltd. Ptnrs., L.P., N.Y.C., 1989—. Contbr. articles to profl. publs. Cons. CARE, N.Y.C., 1987—. McKinnon scholar Magdalen Coll. Oxford U., 1976; Harkness Fellow Commonwealth Fund N.Y., 1979-81; Baker scholar Harvard U., 1981. Mem. Brit. Inst. Mgmt. Office: Aston Ltd Ptnrs LP 950 3d Ave 30th Fl New York NY 10022

ALLEN, PHILLIP STEPHEN, lawyer; b. Washington, Nov. 20, 1952; s. Robert Mitchell and Edna Beverly (Feldman) A. BA with honors, U. Md., 1974; JD, George Washington U., 1978; LLM in Taxation, Georgetown U., 1982. Bar: D.C. Ct. Appeals, U.S. Dist. Ct., U.S. Tax Ct., U.S. Ct. Claims, U.S. Supreme Ct. Atty. office assoc. chief counsel IRS, Washington, 1978-84; asst. v.p. Met. Life Ins. Co., N.Y.C., 1984—; lectr. World Trade Inst., N.Y.C., 1987—. Mem. ABA (tax sect.), Fed. Bar Assn. (tax sect.), Union League Club of N.Y. Republican. Jewish. Home: 329 Franklin Tpke Ridgewood NJ 07450-1907 Office: Met Life Ins Co One Madison Ave New York NY 10010

ALLEN, RANDY LEE, management consulting executive; b. Ithaca, N.Y., June 24, 1946; d. Richard Hallstead and Mary Elizabeth (Howe) Hallstead Baker; m. John James Meehan, Apr. 24, 1983 (div. Aug. 1987); 1 child, Scott Hallstead. BA in Physics, Cornell U., 1968; postgrad., Syracuse U., 1968, Seattle U., 1973-74. Cert. mgmt. cons., cert. systems profl. Programmer IBM, Endicott, N.Y., 1968-69; product and industry mgr. Boeing Computer Svc., Seattle, 1969-74; dir. mktg. Androcor subs. Boeing Computer, Calumet City, Ill., 1974-76; ptnr. Touche Ross & Co., Newark, 1976—; ptnr.-in-charge Mgmt. cons. Trade Office, N.Y.C., 1988—; prin. Deloitte & Touche, N.Y.C., 1990—; trustee N.J. Inst. Tech., Newark, 1984-87, bd. overseers, 1988—, vice chmn. fin., 1991, mem. adv. bd. computer info. scis. dept. Author: OCR-A Cost/Benefit Guide; Pos Trends in the '80s; Bottom Line Issues in Retailing; Pos Current Trends and Beyond, 1987; also articles. Regional fund raiser Cornell U., 1983-84, 87-88, mem. Cornell Coun., 1989—; mem. Pres.'s Coun. Cornell Women, 1989—, chair, 1991—; bd. dirs. Chamber Music Am., 1989—. Recipient Acad. Women Achievers award YWCA, 1984. Mem. Inst. Mgmt. Cons., Am. Mgmt. Assn., Am. Arbitration Assn., Exec. Women of N.J. (pres. 1979-81, bd. dirs. 1981-85), Cornell Club, Basking Ridge Golf Club, Cornell U. Alumni Ambs. Office: Deloitte & Touche 1633 Broadway New York NY 10019-6708

ALLEN, RAY WALLACE, fruit grower; b. Burlington, Vt., Nov. 27, 1936; s. Ray R. and Catharine (Robinson) A.; m. Judy McBride, July 6, 1962 (div. 1984); m. Pamela Dobson Allen, Jan. 5, 1985; 1 child, Ray C. BS, U. Vt., 1959, Dr. Laws (hon.), 1991. Owner, operator Allenholm Farm, South Hero, Vt., 1960—; vice chmn. Vt. Apple Mktg. Bd., Montpelier, 1986—; dir. New Eng. Apple Coun., Shelburne, Mass., 1986—, N.Y. N.E. Apple Inst., Westfield, Mass., 1989—. Chief South Hero Rescue Inc., 1973—; dir. Champlain Valley Exposition, Essex Junction, 1965—; trustee U. Vt., 1984-90; sch. dir. Folsom Sch., South Hero, 1982-84. Mem. Vt. Tree Fruit Growers. Home and Office: PO Box 300 South Hero VT 05486

ALLEN, ROBERT ERWIN, physiologist; b. Lufkin, Tex., Oct. 9, 1941; s. John Franklin and Bonnie Mae (Smith) A.; B.A., Stephen F. Austin State Coll., 1963; Ph.D., Vanderbilt Med. Sch., 1969; m. Roma Leah Trobaugh, Oct. 18, 1970; children: Jennifer Kay, David Whitfield. With NASA Marshall Space Flight Center, Huntsville, Ala., 1969-76, chief biometrics, 1972-74, chief biotech. br., 1975-76; spl. asst. to v.p. U. Ala. Med. Sch. System, 1976; exec. sec. NIH, Bethesda, 1976-78; spl. asst. to dir. med. research service VA, Washington, 1978-87; dep. dir. AIDS Program Office VA Cen. Office, Washington, 1987-91; spl. asst. ACMD Environ. Medicine and Pub. Health Dept. Vet. Affairs, Washington, 1991—. Home: 8 Jeb Stuart Ct Rockville MD 20854-6216 Office: Central Office VA Washington DC 20420

ALLEN, ROBERT EUGENE, communications company executive; b. Joplin, Mo., Jan. 25, 1935; s. Walter Clark and Frances (Patton) A.; m. Elizabeth Terese Pfeffer, Aug. 4, 1956; children: Jay Robert, Daniel Scott, Katherine Louise, Ann Elizabeth, Amy Susan. B.A., Wabash Coll., 1957, LL.D (hon.), 1984; postgrad., Harvard Bus. Sch., 1965; hon. degree, Wabash Coll., 1984, Rutgers U., 1989, Ill. Inst. Tech., 1990, Babson Coll., 1991. With Ind. Bell Telephone Co. Inc., Indpls., 1957-74, traffic student, 1957-58, asst. traffic supr. operator svcs., 1958-61, asst. traffic supr. costs, operator svcs., 1961; dist. traffic supr. Ind. Bell Telephone Co. Inc., Bloomington, 1961-64, dist. comml. mgr., 1964-65; div. comml. mgr. Ind. Bell Telephone Co. Inc., Bloomington, Indpls., 1965-68, asst. to operations v.p., 1969, gen. comml. mgr., 1969-72, v.p., sec., treas., 1972-74; v.p., gen. mgr. Bell Telephone Co. of Pa., Phila., 1974-76; v.p., chief operating officer, dir. Ill. Bell Telephone Co., Phila., 1976-78; v.p. AT&T, Basking Ridge, N.J., 1978-81; pres., chmn. bd. C&P Telephone Cos., Washington, 1981-83, exec. v.p. corp. adminstrn. and fin., 1983-84; chmn., chief exec. officer AT&T Info. Systems, Morristown, N.J., 1985; pres., chief operating officer AT&T, N.Y.C., 1986-88, chmn., chief exec. officer, 1988—, also bd. dirs.; bd. dirs. Bristol Myers Squibb Co., PepsiCo, Inc., Bus. Coun. N.Y. State Inc., Japan Soc., Fed. Res. Bank of N.Y., New Am. Schs. Devel. Corp. Bd. govs. United Way of Am.; trustee Wabash Coll.; bd. dirs. Am.-China Soc. Mem. Nat. Assn. Wabash Men, Conf. Bd., Bus. Roundtable (policy com.), Bus. Coun., US-Japan Bus. Coun. Presbyterian. Clubs: Short Hills, Baltusrol Golf, Burning Tree, Congressional Country; Bay Head Yacht; Country of Fla. Home: 60 Stewart Rd Short Hills NJ 07078-1924 Office: AT&T 295 N maple Ave Basking Ridge NJ 07920

ALLEN, ROCELIA J., retired educator; b. Cin., Oct. 19, 1924; married; 1 child. BS cum laude in Instrumental Mus., Chgo. Conservatory Music, 1948; MEd in Spl. Edn., U. Del., Newark, 1966; PhD, Union Grad. Sch., Newark, 1979. Certified in spl. and elementary edn., music, Del.; specialist in lang. arts, behavior modification, using the operatta to teach lang. arts to educable mentally retarded. Tchr. exceptional children Colonial Sch. Dist., New Castle, Del., 1960-85; chmn. dept. spl. edn. George Read Sch., New Castle, Del., to 1985; ass.t prof. English and reading Del. Tech. Community Coll., Stanton, 1967—. Recipient Another Dream award, 1986, spl. award for Outstanding and Significant Contbn. in Edn., 1987. Mem. AAUW, NEA, Del. Edn. Assn., Nat. Music Educators Assn., Del. Music Educators Assn., Coun. Exceptional Children, Nat. Assn. Univ. Women (Woman of Yr. 1989, Wilmington Woman of Yr. 1989), Phi Delta Kappa (Book award 1991), Zeta Phi Beta. Home and Office: Tanglewood 712 S Harmony Rd Newark DE 19711

ALLEN, RODNEY DESVIGNE, music educator; b. Dover, Del., June 7, 1957; s. Emmitt and Rocelia (Jones) A.; m. Belinda Price, June 2, 1984. BS, Ind. State U., 1979; MusM in violin, West Chester U., 1981. Cert. music tchr., Del., Ind., N.J. Violinist Terre Haute (Ind.) Symphony Orch., 1975-79; tchr. piano and violin theory Christina Cultural Arts Ctr., Wilmington, Del., 1980—; tchr. band and orch. Caravel Acad., Bear, Del., 1981-85; tchr. piano theory Jewish Community Ctr., Wilmington, Del., 1985-86; chmn. string dept. Chri' Cult' Arts Ctr., 1980-88, 1st violin John Hopkins Symphony Orch., 1988—; 2d trumpet, 287th Army Band, 1987—, St. Paul String Quintet, 1988—; instr. Hartford Heights Elem. Balt. County PUb. Sch., 1988—; testing supr. student tchrs. Morgan State, 1988—; Suzuki Cert. Viola, 1922. Served with Del. N.G., 1987—. Music scholar Wilmington Music Sch., 1973. Mem. Del. Music Tchrs. Assn., NAACP. Episcopalian. Home: 712 S Harmony Rd Newark DE 19713-3343

ALLEN, STUART (STUART ALLEN SUP), film and television company executive; b. N.Y.C., July 24, 1943; s. Rudolph and Rita Geraldine (Tellez) Sup; m. Carol Ann Terminelli, June 30, 1982. A in Engring., NYU, 1961; BA in Communications, Pace U., 1963. Free-lance photographer, photojournalist N.Y.C., 1963—; producer, dir. Stuart Allen Assocs., Iselin, N.J., 1967-76; pres., chief exec. officer Internat. Media Svcs., Inc., Plainfield, N.J., 1976—. Spl. producer ABC-TV Evil Knievel Snake River Canyon Jump, 1974; author, producer Counterattack, 1978 (One to One Media award 1979), producer, dir. Eagle in the Wind, 1980 (Best Film award 1984). Chmn. Plainfield, N.J. Cultural and Heritage Commn., 1982—; mcpl. liaison Union County, N.J. Cultural and Heritage Adv. Bd., 1982—; trustee Drake House Mus., Plainfield Hist. Soc., 1982-92; dir. Plainfield Econ. Devel. Corp., 1984—; trustee DuCret Sch. of Arts, 1990—. N.J. State Council Arts grantee, 1979, 86. Mem. Indsl. Photographers Assn. N.J. (pres. 1976-77, award of Excellence), Internat. TV Assn., Am. Film Inst., Cen. Jersey C. of C., Internat. Platform Assn. Club: Marco Polo (Chgo.). Home and Office: 718 Sherman Ave Plainfield NJ 07060-2232

ALLEN, THOMAS E., obstetrician-gynecologist; b. Bairdford, Pa., July 2, 1919; s. Emerson Ray and Lillie Mabel (McIntyre) A.; children: Catherine, Christine, Cynthia, Carolyn, Thomas J. Candace. BS, U. Pitts., 1940, MD, 1943. Diplomate Am. Bd. Ob-Gyn. Rotating intern U. Pitts., 1944, assoc. clin. prof. ob-gyn. Sch. Medicine; resident in gynegology Magee Hosp., Pitts., 1944-45, resident in ob-gyn., 1948-51; gen. practice medicine Oakmont, Pa., 1947-48; practice medicine specializing in ob-gyn. Pitts., 1951—; med. dir., co-founder Women's Health Service, Inc., Pitts., 1973—; cons. ob-gyn Russelton Med. Group, New Kensington, Pa., 1953-73. Pres. Oakmont Sch. Bd., 1962-71; pres. bd. dirs. Am. Wateways Wind Orch., Pitts., 1972—; bd. dirs. ACLU, Pitts., 1972-90. Served to capt. U.S. Army, 1945-47. Am. Legion and Buhl scholar, 1937. Fellow ACS, Am. Coll. Obstetricians and Gynecologists, Pan Pacific Surg. Assn., Pitts. Ob-gyn. Soc.; mem. AMA, county and state med. assns. Democrat. Club: Oakmont Country. Home: 301 Halket St Pittsburgh PA 15213-3104 Office: 3433 Bates St Pittsburgh PA 15213-3900

ALLEN, VIRGINIA ANN, military officer; b. Phoenixville, Pa., Sept. 29, 1953; d. Eugene Womack and Claire Ruth (Reno) A. B in Music Edn., Catholic U., 1976, MusM, 1977. Commd. 2d lt. U.S. Army, 1977, advanced through grades to maj., 1989; adminstrv. officer U.S. Army Element, Sch. of Music, Norfolk, 1978, student company cmdr., 1978-79, tng. officer, 1979; cmdr. and conductor U.S. Army Forces Command Band, Ft. McPherson, Ga., 1979-82; pub. relations officer U.S. Army Field Band, Ft. Meade, Md., 1982-84, assoc. conductor, 1982-85; pub. affairs officer Dept. of Army, The Pentagon, Washington, 1985-86; staff band officer U.S. Forces Command, Ft. McPherson, 1986-88; dep. comdr. U.S. Mil. Acad. Band, West Point, N.Y., 1988—. Mem. Nat. Band Assn., Assn. of U.S. Army, Coll. Band Dirs. Nat. Assn. Office: US Mil Acad Band West Point NY 10996

ALLEN, WOODY, actor, filmmaker, author; b. N.Y.C., Dec. 1, 1935; s. Martin and Nettie (Cherry) Konigsberg; m. Louise Lasser (div.); 1 child (with Mia Farrow), Satchel. Student, NYU, 1953, CCNY, 1953. Writer TV comedy for Sid Caesar, 1957, Art Carney, 1958-59, Herb Shriner, 1953; appeared in numerous nightclubs, TV shows, from 1961; author screenplay, also appeared in motion picture What's New Pussycat?, 1964-65; screenplay, dir., actor Take the Money and Run, 1969, Bananas, 1971, What's Up Tiger Lily?, 1966, Everything You Always Wanted to Know About Sex But Were Afraid to Ask, 1972, Sleeper, 1973, Love and Death, 1975, The Front, 1976, Manhattan (Brit. Acad. award 1979, N.Y. Film Critics award), Stardust Memories, 1980; writer, dir., producer, actor films Annie Hall (N.Y. Film Critics Circle award for Best Dir. and Best Screenplay 1977, Acad. awards for best film, best direction, Nat. Soc. Film Critics Screenwriting award), Zelig, 1983, Broadway Danny Rose, 1984, Hannah and Her Sisters, 1986 (Acad. award for best screenplay, D.W. Griffith award for best dir. Nat. Bd. Rev. of Motion Pictures), Oedipus Wrecks, 1989; writer, dir., narrator film Radio Days, 1987; screenplay, dir. films Interiors, 1978, Purple Rose of Cairo, 1985, A Midsummer Night's Sex Comedy, 1982, September, 1987, Another Woman, 1988, Crimes and Misdemeanors, 1989, Alice, 1990, Shadows and Fog, 1992, Husbands and Wives, 1992; author play: Don't Drink the Water, 1966; play, screenplay Play It Again, Sam, 1969, film, 1972; actor, film King Lear, 1988, Scenes From a Mall, 1990; author: Getting Even, 1971, Without Feathers, 1975, Side Effects, 1980; play The Floating Lightbulb, 1981; contbr. numerous pieces to Playboy, New Yorker, other mags. Recipient Sylvania award, 1957; Spl. award Berlin Film Festival, 1975; nominated for Emmy award as TV writer, 1957. Democrat. *

ALLENDER, JULIE ANN, psychologist; b. Elmhurst, Ill., Feb. 27, 1950; d. Frank and Edith (Gluklick) A.; m. Louis Zivic, May 18, 1980; 1 child, Jonathan Ephriam Allender-Zivic. BS in Psychology, U. Ill., 1973; MEd in Psychoednl. Processes, Temple U., 1974, EdD in Psychoednl. Processes, 1978. Lic. psychologist, Pa., Mass.; cert. sch. psychologist, Pa. Asst. prin. Beth Or Congregation Religious Sch., Spring House, Pa., 1977-78; dir. Homebased Businesswomen's Network, Lebanon, Pa., 1983-88; pvt. practice psychologist Lebanon, 1980—; former adj. faculty Community Coll. Phila., Temple U., Phila., Phila. Coll. Textile & Scis., Thomas Jefferson U. Med. Sch., Phila., Wheelock Coll., Boston, Pa. State U., Hershey, Reading; cons. med. staff Good Samaritan Hosp.; pvt. practice therapy, consultation and testing Pa. Coll. Optometry, Phila., Headstart, Chgo., Peabody (Mass.) Pub. Schs., Lynn (Mass.) Hist. Soc., Mich. Edn. Assn., Lansing, Dept. Agr. Extension Program, Lebanon, Pa., Lebanon Valley Coll., Annville, Pa., other orgns. Contbr. articles to profl. jours. and newspapers, chpts. to books; participant media programs Sta. WRKO, Boston, 1983, Sta. WVLV, Lebanon, 1983-84, Sta. WAHT, Lebanon, 1988-90. Active Potential Reentry Opportunities in Bus. and Edn., 1986—, Homebased Businesswomen's Network of the Lebanon Valley, 1983-88; mem. women in bus. com. Lebanon C. of C., 1985-87; bd. dirs. Assn. for Humanistic Edn., 1983-87; mem. women's pavilion adv. bd. Lebanon Valley Gen. Hosp., 1986-90. Mem. APA, ASTD, Pa. Psychol. Assn., Lancaster-Lebanin Psychol. Assn. (treas. 1990—), Orthopsychiat. Assn., Assn. for Humanistic Psychology. Jewish.

ALLEN-NOBLE, ROSIE ELIZABETH, academic administrator, biology educator; b. Americus, Ga., June 22, 1938; d. Ulysses Grant Allen and Velma Douglas; m. Daniel Bernard Noble, Apr., 1964 (div. Apr. 1968); 1 child, Antoinette Celine Noble-Webb. BS, Albany State Coll., 1960; MS, Atlanta U., 1967, Rutgers U., 1974; EdD, Rutgers U., 1991; postgrad., Bryn Mawr Coll., 1987—. Cert. tchr., Ga. Tchr. biology Vienna (Ga.) High and Indsl. Sch., 1960-61, West Point (Ga.) High Sch., 1962-63, Carver Sch. Sch., Columbus, Ga., 1963-64; lab. instr. Spelman Coll., Atlanta, 1965-66; tchr., chmn. biology dept. Columbia High Sch., Dacatur, Ga., 1965-70; instr. Rutgers U., Newark, 1970-76; asst. prof. Fairleigh U., Madison, N.J., 1976-80; adminstrv. dir. Montclair State Coll., Upper Montclair, N.J., 1979—; vis. asst. prof. Seton Hall U., South Orange, N.Y., 1972-78; instr. U. Med. and Dentistry, Newark, 1972—, Women in Higher Edn. Adminstrn., Bryn Mawr Coll., 1988. Contbr. articles to prfol. jours. Bd. dirs. Gladys Dickinson Health Ctr., NAMME, 1985—. NSF fellow 1961, 64-65; NSF grantee, 1978-79, Luth. Ch. Am., 1979-80, Dept. Higher Edn., N.J., 1979-88, HHS, 1983-87; recipient Outstanding Service award Upsala Coll., 1982, Montclair State Coll., 1984, 85, 87, Merit award Montclair State Coll., 1983, 87, Career Development award, 1988, Professional Development award, 1989. Mem. Am. Assn. of Women in Sci., Am. Assn. for Higher Edn., Nat. Assn. for Biology Tchrs., Nat. Assn. for Rsch. in Sci. Teaching, Nat. Assn. of Women in Edn., Middle State Assn. (commn. higher edn. 1984-88), Nat. Assn. Advisors to Health Professions, Nat. Assn. Med. Minority Educators (coord. NE region 1988—, treas. 1985-87, dir. 1980), Soroptimist, Alpha Kappa Alpha. Democrat. Roman Catholic. Home: 364 Orange Rd Apt 5C Montclair NJ 07042-4341 Office: Montclair State Coll Valley Rd Montclair NJ 07042-2709

ALLERTON, JOSEPH, chemical engineer; b. N.Y.C., Mar. 17, 1919; s. Moses Alexander and Rebecca (Stephens) A.; m. Muriel Jobst, July 16, 1944; children: Peter, Steven, Paul, Martha. BChemE, NYU, 1941, MChemE, 1944; PhD, U. Mich., 1948. Registered profl. engr. N.Y. Engr. Office of Sci. Rsch. and Devel., N.Y.C., 1942-43, Manhattan Project, N.Y.C., 1943-45; sr. engr. Nat. Dairy Co., Oakdale, N.Y., 1948-51; sect. head Gen. Foods, Tarrytown, N.Y., 1951-63; mgr. tech. svcs. The Nestle Co., Fulton, N.Y., 1963-84; pvt. cons. Fulton, N.Y., 1984—. Co-chmn. Oswego Rivr RAP Com., Syracuse, N.Y., 1990—, Lake Neatahwanta Reclamation Com., Fulton, 1988—trustee Fulton YMCA. Mem. Fulton Rotary (pres. 1979-80, Paul Harris award 1986), Sigma Xi, Phi Lambda Upsilon, Tau Beta Pi. Methodist. Home and Office: 827 Forest Ave Fulton NY 13069-3337

ALLEY, WILLIAM JACK, holding company executive; b. Vernon, Tex., Dec. 27, 1929; s. W. H. and Opal M. (Cater) A.; m. Deborah Bunn, Dec. 28, 1979; children: Susan Jane, Pamela Jean, Patricia Ann, Sarah Elizabeth, Brayton. AA, Northeastern A&M Coll., 1949; BBA, U. Okla., 1951, JD, 1954. Bar: Okla. 1954; CLU. Atty. State Ins. Bd. Okla., 1956-57; asst. v.p. Pioneer Am. Ins. Co., 1957-59, v.p., 1959-60, v.p., agy. dir., 1960-66, dir., 1961, sr. v.p. mktg., 1966; v.p. Franklin Life Ins. Co., 1967-69, sr. v.p. agy., 1969-74, exec. v.p., 1974-75, pres., chief exec. officer, 1976-85, chmn. bd., 1977-87; dir. Am. Brands Inc., 1979, sr. v.p. strategic planning, 1983-85; sr. v.p., chief fin. officer Am. Brands, Inc., Old Greenwich, Conn., 1985-86, vice chmn., 1986-87, chmn., chief exec. officer, 1987—; bd. dirs. subs. cos.; bd. dirs. Cen. Ill. Pub. Svc. Co., Bunn-o-matic Corp., Southwestern Area Commerce and Industry Assn. Conn.; mem. bd. govs. Internat. Ins. Soc. Inc.; emeritus elector Ins. Hall of Fame; mem. bd. trustees Nat. Sales Hall of Fame; mem. adv. bd. govs. Nat. Women's Econ. Alliance Found. Bd. dirs. Cooperation Ireland, United Way Tri-State, The Silvermine Guild Arts Ctr., Conn. Bus. for Edn. Coalition; bd. overseers Exec. Coun. Fgn. Diplomats; mem. The Bus. Roundtable, The Conf. Bd. and The Ambassadors' Roundtable adv. coun.; mem. adv. bd. govs. Nat. Women's Econ. Alliance Found. Capt. USAF, 1954-56. Mem. Okla. Bar Assn., Illini Country Club, Sangamo Club, Northport Point, New Canaan Country Club, Econ. Club (N.Y.C., mem. bd. govs.), Masons, Shriners, Delta Sigma Pi, Phi Kappa Sigma, Phi Alpha Delta. Office: Am Brands Inc 1700 E Putnam Ave PO Box 819 Old Greenwich CT 06870-0819

ALLEY-BARROS, ELIZABETH DALEIN, police training instructor; b. New Bedford, Mass., Oct. 18, 1958; d. Olga (Soubassis) Marden; children: Vincent, Lisa. AS in Criminal Justice, Bristol Community Coll., 1979; BS in Adminstrn. of Criminal Justice, Roger Williams Coll., 1982. Court transp. officer New Bedford 3rd Dist. Ct., 1980-81; police officer U.S. Dept. Defense Police, Mass. and R.I., 1981-86; corrections officer S.E. Correctional Ctr., Bridgewater, Mass., 1986-87; police instr. Police Survival Defensive Tactics Training, New Bedford, 1983—; specialized training include Training Rsch. Validation, 1989, Use of Force Reporting Systems, 1989, Monadnock PR-24 Police Baton instr., 1988, Court Room Survival, 1989, Edges Weapon Defense, 1989, Street Survival, 1982-87 and others. Author: Who's Who in Law Enforcement Collecting and Police Trainers, 1988. Office: Police Survival Defense PO Box 7366 New Bedford MA 02742-7366

ALLING, JANET DICKEY, painter; b. N.Y.C., Dec. 19, 1939; d. Stanley Joseph and Susan Matilda (Jones) A. BFA, Yale U., 1962, MFA, 1964. Art instr. Bklyn. Mus. Art Sch., 1973-77, Bronxville (N.Y.) Adult Sch., 1989—; Exhibited paintings in numerous one-woman shows including Vassar Coll. Ctr. Gallery, Poughkeepsie, N.Y., 1990, St. Mary's Coll., Md., 1990, Princeton (N.J.) Day Sch., 1987, Kornblee Gallery, N.Y.C., 1974, 79, 55 Mercer Gallery, N.Y.C., 1972; prin. works represented in numerous pub. and pvt. collections including U. Va. Art Mus., Security Pacific Inc., Brown & Wood, N.Y., Morgan Stanley, Florists Transworld Deliveries, North Cen. Bronx Hosp., Rochester Hosp., Bellevue, Hosp., N.Y.C. NEA grantee, 1989, grantee Adolph and Esther Gottleib Found., 1988; recipient CAPS award N.Y. State Coun. for Arts, 1973, Adolphe Berle award Berkshire Art Mus., 1964. Mem. Coll. Art Assn. Home and Office: 652 Broadway New York NY 10012-2316

ALLISON, ADRIENNE AMELIA, voluntary organization administrator; b. Toronto, Ont., Can., Nov. 2, 1940; d. Harold Whitfield and Emmeline Amelia (Banister) Hedley; m. Stephen Vyvyan Allison, Jan. 2, 1960 (div. 1984); children: Mark Hedley, Myles Stephen, Alexander Andrew; m. Armin U. Kuder, Aug. 26, 1989. BA, George Washington U., 1978; MA, Georgetown U., 1980; MPA, Harvard U., 1986. Social sci. analyst Agy. Internat. Devel., Washington, 1980-85, project mgr., 1986-89, mem. staff, presdl. com. on HIV epidemic, 1987-88; program dir. Centre for Devel. and Population Activities, 1988-91; v.p. Centre for Devel. and Population Activities, 1991—. Co-author: Vegetable Gardening in Bangladesh, 1975. Vestry mem. St. Albans Parish, Washington, 1988; mem. commn. on peace Diocese of Washington, 1989. Mem. Am. Pub. Health Assn., Soc. Internat. Devel., Population Assn. Am. Home: 3801 Fulton St NW Washington DC 20007-1345

ALLISON, JONATHAN, lawyer; b. Washington, Pa., Apr. 17, 1916; s. Albert Johnson and Etta (Tucker) A.; B.S., Washington and Jefferson Coll., 1937; J.D., U. Pa., 1940; postgrad. Harvard Grad. Sch. Bus. Adminstrn., 1940-41. Admitted to Pa. bar, 1942; practiced in Washington, 1946—. Served to maj., AUS, 1941-46. Mem. Am., Pa., Washington County bar assns. Republican. Presbyn. Clubs: Duquesne (Pitts.); Club Internationale, Lone Pine Golf (Washington). Home: 20 Fairmont Ave Washington PA 15301-3509 Office: 438 Washington Trust Bldg Washington PA 15301

ALLISTER, PAMELA JEFFCOCK, social service administrator; b. Syracuse, N.Y., May 5, 1941; d. Howard Walter Jeffcock and Jeanette Hovey Tifft; m. Paul Stuart Clark, June 26, 1964 (div. July 1976); children: Paul Jeffrey Clark, Jennifer Rebecca Clark, Tamara Lynn Clark; m. Robert Misavage Allister, Oct. 6, 1976. BS, Cornell U., 1963; MA, Syracuse U., 1964; AA in Nursing, U. Minn., 1975; Masters, Grad. Sch. of Political Mgmt., N.Y., 1988. RN. Instr., counselor Bklyn. Coll., 1964-66; instr. Cleve. Pub. Schs., 1966-67, Rochester Pub. Schs., Minn., 1970-73, Rochester Methodist Hosp., 1974-75; health dir. State of Nevada, 1975-77; maternal child health dir. State of Montana, 1977-80; instr. Flathead Community Coll., 1980-84; with WorldWorks Found., N.J., 1985—, Somerset County Coalition on Affordable Housing, N.J., 1991—; internat. devel. cons. Tanzania and Indonesia, 1987-91; treas. Somerset Family Planning Svc., 1986-90; mem. bd. trustees Resource Ctr. for Women and Their Families, 1991—. Contbr. articles to profl. jours. Fin. dir. Chandler for Congress, 1990, Somerset County Dem. Com. Women, 1991—. Mem. Am. Nurses Assn., Nat. Edn. Assn. Democrat. Home: 10 Fremont St Somerville NJ 08876-3914 Office: WorldWorks Found 120 Finderne Ave Bridgewater NJ 08807-3149

ALLISTON, APRIL, comparative literature educator; b. New Orleans, Apr. 4, 1959. BA, Yale U., 1980, PhD, 1988. Lectr. Columbia U., N.Y.C., 1988-89; asst. prof. Princeton (N.J.) U., 1989—. Lurcy Grad. fellow Whitney Humanities Ctr., 1987, Mellon Postdoctoral fellow Columbia U., 1988-89; rsch. grantee Am. Coun. Learned Socs., 1991-92. Fellow Columbia U. Soc. Fellows in the Humanities (alumna); mem. MLA, Am. Soc. for Eighteenth-Century Studies. Office: Princeton U Dept Comparative Lit 326 E Pyne Princeton NJ 08544

ALLMAN, WILLIAM BERTHOLD, musician, engineer, consultant; b. Phila., Feb. 16, 1927; s. Drue Nunez and Blanche (Oppenheimer) A.; m. Margo Hutz, Feb. 19, 1954; children: Avis Louise, David Drue. BSEE, Drexel U., 1949; MBA, U. Pa., 1951. Registered profl. engr., Pa. Contract engr. Atlantic Refining, Phila., 1951-55, E.I. DuPont de Nemours & Co., Inc., Wilmington, Del., 1955-58; constrn. engr. Niagra Falls, N.Y., 1958-59; cons. engr. Wilmington, 1959-82, Allman Assocs., West Grove, Pa., 1982—; owner, mgr. Allman Bldgs., Phila., 1965-87. Contbr. numerous articles on plastic pipe to profl. mags.; drummer, washboard player with Allman, Melton and Co. band; performed with various musicians including Lionel Hampton, Brownie McGhee, Mississippi Fred McDowell, Sonny Terry. Mem. Bi-racial com. City of Newark, Del., 1963-71, chmn. 1965, London Grove Township Mcpl. Authority, Chester County, Pa., 1985-89, chmn. 1986; Dem. committeeman, Del., 1964-71, chmn., 1968; candidate Mayor City of Newark, 1970; adv. coun. Neighborhood Svcs. Ctr., Oxford, Pa., 1989—. With USNR, 1945-46. ETO. Mem. Am. Assn. Individual Investors, Del. Ctr. Contemporary Arts, Del. Art Mus., The Nature Conservancy. Democrat. Unitarian. Home and Office: 202 State Rd West Grove PA 19390-8906

ALLOWAY, ROBERT MALCOMBE, computer consulting executive; b. Cleve., Apr. 15, 1944; s. Robert Malcombe and May (Tingley) A.; divorced; children: Megan, Brook. BA, Brown U., 1967; MBA, Boston Coll., 1972; D in Bus. Adminstrn., Harvard U., 1975. Cert. data processor. Project mgr. Sealtest Foods, Rocky River, Ohio, 1968-70; with spl. projects staff First Nat. Stores, Summerville, Mass., 1970-72; research assoc. Boston Coll., Chestnut Hill, Mass., 1972-73; asst. prof. mgmt. sci. MIT, Cambridge, 1975-76, 77-84; pres. Alloway Inc., Lexington, Mass., 1984—; guest prof. Stockholm Sch. Econs., 1976-77; research faculty Ctr. for Info. Systems Research MIT, 1976-84. Contbr. articles to profl. jours. Pres. World Future Soc., Boston, 1973-75. Mem. Soc. for Mgmt. Info. (reviewer) 1983—). Office: Alloway Inc 250 E Emerson Rd Lexington MA 02173-2134

ALLREAD, WILLIAM O., business owner; b. Jackson, Mich.; s. Leon O. and Willa Jean (Fritage) A.; married; children: Dean Allen, Jane Allen, Virginia Lynn, Nancy Ann. BS in Metallurgy, Mich. Tech., 1958, BS in Bus., 1959, MS in Metallurgy, 1961. Metallurgisty rsch. engr. GM, Warren, Mich., Saginaw, Mich., 1960-66; metallurgisty rsch. engr. various cos., 1966-74; owner Allread Products, Terryville, Conn., 1974—. Chmn. Indsl. Commn., Terryville; mem. Bd. of Edn., Terryville. Mem. Metal Powder Indsl. Fedn., Am. Powder Metal Internat. (chmn. 1974), Chippens Hill Repeater Assn. (pres. 1984), Elks (chaplain Houghton 1957-58), Lions. Office: Allread Products 22 S Main St Terryville CT 06786-1449

ALLYN, JERRI, artist; b. Paterson, N.J., Feb. 21, 1952; d. Charles Kennedy McCracken and Maria Beatriz Diaz Alvarz; 1 child. Cert., Feminist Studio Workshop, L.A., 1978; MA in Art and Soc., Goddard Coll., 1978. Artist in residence Women's Graphic Ctr., L.A., 1983, Yellow Springs (Pa.) Inst., 1986, U. Ill., Champaign/Urbana, 1987, Calif. Coll. Arts and Crafts, Oakland, 1988, Humboldt (Calif.) Coll., 1988, Centrum Ctr. for Arts, Port Townsend, Wash., 1989, U. Wash., Pullman, 1990; vis. faculty Fairhaven Coll./Western Wash. U., Bellingham, 1987-90, New Sch. Social Rsch., N.Y.C., 1988—; co-cons. performance studies program Syracuse (N.Y.) U., 1986, Franklin and Marshall Coll., Lancaster, Pa., 1989; grant panelist NEA/Interarts Panel, Washington, 1988-90, Seattle Arts Commn., 1990, N.Y. Found. for Arts, N.Y.C., 1990; mem. Bessies Dance and Performance Arts Awards Commn., N.Y.C., 1987—. Artist: Love Novellas, 1983, American Dining: A Working Woman's Moment, 1988, Angels Have Been Sent to Me, 1991, interactive art works, radio programs. Artist bd. mem. New Mus. Contemporary Art, N.Y.C., 1989-91. Interarts grantee Nat. Endowment for Arts, Washington, 1985, 89, Art Matters grantee, N.Y.C., 1986, 90, media grantee Nat. Endowment for Arts, 1989, N.Y. State Coun. for Arts, 1989, 91; conceptual and new genres fellow Nat. Endowment for Arts, 1983, 90. Mem. Alliance for Cultural Democracy, Adoptees Liberty Movement, Nat. Campaign for Freedom of Expression, Coll. Art Assn., Women's Art Caucus, Franklin Furnace Archives. Quaker. Home: 118 Forsyth St #1 New York NY 10002-5126

ALMEIDA, VICTORIA MARTIN, lawyer; b. Pawtucket, R.I., Oct. 9, 1951; d. Antonio Sanches And Lillian (Martin) A. BA, Salve Regina U., Newport, R.I., 1973; JD, Suffolk U., 1976. Bar: Mass. 1976, R.I. 1976, U.S. Dist. Ct. R.I. 1976, U.S. Ct. Appeals (1st cir.) Mass. 1984, U.S. Supreme Ct. 1987. Law clk. to sr. assoc. justice R.I. Supreme Ct., Providence, 1976; asst. legal counsel to gov. Gov.'s Office, Providence, 1977-82; assoc. Gunning, LaFazia & Gnys, Inc., Providence, 1980-87; ptnr. Adler Pollock & Sheehan, Inc., Providence, 1987—; mem. R.I. Parole Bd., Providence, 1984—. Chair bd. trustees R.I. chpt. Nat. Multiple Sclerosis Soc., Cranston, 1989-91; mem. corp. Roger Williams Coll., Bristol, R.I., 1977—; mem. devel. com. St. Mary Acad.-Bay View, East Providence, R.I., 1988—; mem. retirement fund for religious Roman Cath. Diocese of Providence, 1988—. Named Woman of Yr., Prince Henry Club, 1977; recipient Disting. Alumna award St. Mary Acad.-Bay View, 1982, appreciation award Am. Cancer Soc., 1979. Mem. R.I. Bar Assn. (pub. rels. com., ho. of dels., young lawyers clerkship com. 1985—), Am. Arbitration Assn. (panel of arbitrators 1984—). Democrat. Office: Adler Pollock & Sheehan Inc 2300 Hospital Trust Providence RI 02903-2438

ALMGREN, NANCY WELCH, stockbroker; b. Detroit, Feb. 11, 1948; d. Robert Richard Welch and Marian Harriet (Swiney) Misenheimer; m. Kenneth David Almgren II, Sept. 23, 1978; 1 child, Kristian Drew. BA, Mich. State U., 1970. Registered investment advisor, series 65. Owner, pres. Kent Mktg. Svc. Co., Southfield, Mich., 1972-78; stockbroker Paine Webber, Clearwater, Fla., 1978-80, Washington, 1980-82; stockbroker Merrill Lynch, Annapolis, Md., 1982-84, Dean Witter, Annapolis, 1984—; tchr. Anne Arundel Community Coll., Arnold, Md., 1981—. Mem. City Cen. Com. Rep. party, Annapolis, Md., 1982-85; mem. Civil Svc. Bd. City Govt., Annapolis, 1986-88. Home: 1860 Old Annapolis Blvd Annapolis MD 21401 Office: Dean Witter 410 Severn Ave Annapolis MD 21403

ALMOND, GARY ROBERT, telecommunications company executive; b. Arlington, Va., Feb. 18, 1958; s. Alvin Ray and Bonnie Joyce (Smith) A.; m. Carol Jean Rowton, Feb. 8, 1980; children: Dustin, Candace, Gregory. Student, Brigham Young U., 1975-76, U. Md., 1991. Technician Logetronics, Inc., Springfield, Va., 1980-81; sr. technician Marsh-McBirney, Gaithersburg, Md., 1981; tech. assoc. Watkins-Johnson Co., Gaithersburg, 1981-82; assoc. mem. tech. staff Dama Telecommunications, Rockville, Md., 1982-84, mem. tech. staff, 1984-86, sr. mem. tech. staff, 1986-87; mgr. hardware engring. Data Gen. Telecommunications, Rockville, 1987-91; dir. hardware engring. COMSAT Corp., Clarksburg, Md., 1991-92; product devel mgr. Loral Western Devel. Labs., Hanover, Md., 1992—; staff researcher Byte mag., Glastonbury, Conn., 1984; cons. Transdigital Systems, Inc., Germantown, Md., 1985-88. Patentee digital communications field. Missionary LDS Ch., Germany, 1977-79. Mem. Brigham Young U. Mgmt. Soc. Republican. Home: 6259 Derby Dr Frederick MD 21701 Office: Loral Western Devel Labs 7100 Standard Dr Hanover MD 21076

ALNE, DENNIS JAMES, psychologist; b. Bklyn., Sept. 10, 1947; s. Olaf John and Clara Rose (Cebulski) A.; m. Doreen Mary Boros, June 28, 1981; children: Christina, Maria, Thomas. BS magna cum laude, Bklyn. Coll., 1976, MS, 1978; PhD, CUNY, 1984. Diplomate Am. Bd. Med. Psychotherapists; lic. psychologist, N.Y., lic. sch. psychologist, N.Y. Reporter Am. Stock Exch., N.Y.C., 1967-71; asst. supr. Dean Witter & Co., N.Y.C., 1971-74; rsch. asst. Ctr. Advanced Study in Edn., N.Y.C., 1978-81; sch. psychologist N.Y.C. Bd. Edn., N.Y.C., 1981—; psychologist, clin. dir. Ave. U. Family Counseling Ctr., Bklyn., 1985—. Contbr. articles to profl. jours. Fellow Am. Assn. Profl. Hypnotherapists; mem. Nat. Assn. Sch. Psychologists (cert.), Am. Psychol. Assn., N.Y. Psychol. Assn., Bklyn. Psychol. Assn. (bd. dirs. 1989—), Alpha Sigma Lambda, Psi Chi. Lutheran. Office: Ave U Family Counseling Ctr 2151 E 22nd St Brooklyn NY 11229-3642

ALOIA, RICHARD PAUL, JR., writer; b. Montclair, N.J., Sept. 16, 1967; s. Richard Paul Sr. and Virginia Marie (Lanahan) A. BA in English, Coll. Misericordia, 1989; postgrad., U. So. Calif., 1991-92. Master profl. writing program U. So. Calif., 1991-92. Mng. editor 10th anniversary edit. The Southern California Anthology, 1992; editor-in-chief: (newspaper) The Misericordian, Dallas, Pa., 1987-88; editor, staff poet Instress literary mag., Dallas, 1987-89; stage mgr., actor Misericordia Players, 1987-88; writer: (fiction) 18 Miles to Manhattan, 1992, (poems) Outside the Liquor Store, 1992. Founder Coll. Media Advt., Dallas, 1988. Recipient The Sister Miriam Gallagher and Mary Santopolo Meml. award Coll. Misericordia, 1989. Mem. Lambda Iota Tau. Home: 20 Andrea Dr North Caldwell NJ 07006-4727

ALPERIN, IRWIN EPHRAIM, clothing company executive; b. Scranton, Pa., Apr. 29, 1925; s. Louis I. and Bessie (Wickner) A.; m. Francine Leah Friedman, Dec. 5, 1948; children: Barbara Joy, Jane Leslie. Cert. Mech. Engring., Pa. State U., 1945; BS in Indsl. Engring., Lehigh U., 1947; DHL (hon.), U. Scranton, Pa., 1991. Mgmt. trainee Mayflower Mfg. Co., Scranton, 1947-49, sec., 1952-79, pres., 1980-91; with Triple A Trouser Mfg. Co., Inc., Scranton, 1952, v.p., treas., 1958-79, pres. 1980-91; with Gold Star Mfg. Co., Inc., Scranton, 1956, pres., 1956-91; sec. Astro Warehousing, Inc., Scranton, 1962-91; sec.-treas. Bondeal, Inc., Scranton, 1978-89, pres. 1989—; v.p. RCO, Inc., 1989-91; vice chmn. Montage, Inc., (1979-92; sec. Alperin, Inc., 1982-91, pres., 1991—; sec. All Star Industries, (n.c., 1989—; bd. dirs. Sacquoit Industries, Inc., Scranton, 1980—. Bd. dirs. Econ. Devel. Council N.E. Pa., Avoca, 1974—, v.p., 1978-83; bd. dirs. ARC, Scranton, 1968-88, pres. spl. adv. bd., 1988—; bd. dirs. Jewish Home Eastern Pa., Scranton, 1970—, treas., 1981—; bd. dirs. Jewish Community Ctr., Scranton, 1971-86, now life mem.; bd. dirs. Pa. United Way, Harrisburg, Pa., 1973-78, Scranton Counseling Ctr., 1975-78, trustee, 1979—; pres. Planning Council Social Svcs. Lackawanna County, 1972-74, now life mem.; pres. Jewish Family Svc. of Lackawanna County, 1967-70, now life bd. mem.; v.p. United Way Lackawanna County, 1974-78, exec. com., 1978-86; pres. Alperin Found., Scranton, 1962—; treas. Scranton-Lackawanna Jewish Fedn., 1973-75, life mem. bd. dirs.; trustee Amos Lodge Found., 1982—, v.p., 1989-91, Found. Jewish Elderly, 1984—, v.p. 1985—; trustee Pocono N.E. Devel. Fund, 1983-86, sec. 1986—; pres. Temple Hesed, 1969-71, life mem., bd. dirs., Scranton, Pa.; mem. Lackawanna County Libr. Bd., 1983-85; treas. Lackawanna Regional Cultural Coun., 1988-91, bd. dirs. 1988—; bd. dirs. Broadway Theatre League Lackawanna County, 1989—, Masonic Temple Civic Ctr. Found., 1989—; trustee U. Scranton, 1991—. Served with C.E., AUS, 1944-46. Recipient Americanism award, 1982; named Man of Year, Jewish Community Ctr., 1973, Disting. Pennsylvanian, Phila. C. of C., 1982. Mem. Am. Inst. Indsl. Engrs. (sr.), Glen Oak Country Club (Clarks Summit, Pa.), Wave Oak Realty (Clarks Summit) (v.p. 1989-91), Masons, Shriners, Elks, B'nai B'rith (trustee, Man of Yr. 1982). Home: 1010 Victoria Ln Clarks Summit PA 18411-9248

ALPERIN, RICHARD MARTIN, clinical social worker, psychoanalyst; b. Mt. Vernon, N.Y., Oct. 16, 1946; s. Israel and Sara A.; children: Heather Nicole, Alexander Scott. BBA, Western Mich. U., 1968; MSW, Fordham U., 1974; DSW, Columbia U., 1982; postdoctoral diploma in psychotherapy and psychoanalysis, Adelphi U., 1988. Cert. social worker, N.Y.; diplomate Am. Bd. Examiners in Clin. Social Work. Cons. Mt. Vernon Youth Bd., 1972-76; adj. faculty Marymount Manhattan Coll., N.Y.C., 1974-76; psychotherapist Riverdale Mental Health Clinic, N.Y.C., 1974-77; psychol. counselor, psychotherapist Ctr. Counseling and Psychol. Svcs. Ramapo (N.J.) Coll., 1976-81, adj. faculty, 1977-86, moderator evening forums, 1978, 80; counselor, psychotherapist Ctr. Counseling and Psychol. Svcs. SUNY, Purchase, 1981-82, 84-85, acting dir., 1982-84; clin. cons. Westside Ctr. for Family Svcs., N.Y.C., 1985-87; guest lectr. Cabrini Med. Ctr., 1979; pvt. practice psychotherapy and psychoanalysis Riverdale, N.Y., 1977—, Teaneck, N.J., 1980—, N.Y.C., 1984—; field instr. Columbia U. Sch. Social Work, 1983-85; adj. assoc. prof. Fordham U. Sch. Social Svc., 1985—; adj. asst. prof. NYU Grad. Sch. Social Work, 1989—; faculty, dean. curriculum Rockland Inst. for Psychoanalysis & Psychotherapy, 1990—; faculty Advanced Inst. Analytic Psychotherapy and Object Rels. Inst. Psychoanalysis Psychotherapy. Contbr. articles to profl. jours.; rsch. on psychotherapy, suicide and provision of preventative svcs. Nat. Jewish Welfare Bd. fellow Fordham U., 1972-74. Trainee NIMH Columbia U., 1978. Mem. NASW, N.Y. State Soc. Clin. Social Work Psychotherapists, (chair, com. on psychoanalysis), Adelphi Soc. Psychoanalysis and Psychotherapy, Am. Group Psychotherapy Assn., Inc., Ea. Group Psychotherapy Soc., Acad. Cert. Social Workers (cert.), Nat. Fedn. Soc. Clin. Social Work (treas., com. psychoanalysis). Office: 121 Cedar Ln Teaneck NJ 07666

ALPERN, MILTON, civil engineer, consultant; b. N.Y.C., June 25, 1925; s. Nathan and Rae (Kraft) A.; m. Beverly Katzman, May 30, 1946; children: Warren Deems, Barbara Lynn. BSCE, Cooper Union, 1945; MSCE, Columbia U., 1951; postgrad., Poly. Inst. Bklyn., 1957-63. Registered profl. engr., N.Y., N.J., Pa., Conn., Mass., Ill., Tex., Ky., Mo., Fla., Okla., Colo., N.C.; also nat. certification. Test engr. Edo Aircraft Co., Flushing, N.Y., 1945; design engr. Frederick Snare Corp., N.Y.C., 1947-49; asst. prof. civil engring. Cooper Union, N.Y.C., 1948-60; prin. Milton Alpern cons. engr., Wantagh, N.Y., 1960-71; prin. Alpern & Soifer, cons. engrs., Massapequa, N.Y., 1971-83, Bellmore, N.Y., 1983-92; mgr. spl. projects div. Shah Assocs., P.C., Bellmore, N.Y., 1992—; mem. N.Y. State Bd. Engring. and Land Surveying, 1978-87, chmn., 1984-86; vis. prof. civil engring. N.Y. Inst. Tech., 1977-78, Pratt Inst., 1986—. Contbr. articles to profl. jours. Chmn. bldg. com. Union Free Sch. Dist. 5, Nassau County, 1955-56; pres. Wantagh Oaks Civic Assn., 1957; mem. steering com. Am. Cancer Soc. Theatre Party, 1968-76. Served with C.E., AUS, 1945-47. Recipient Engr. of Yr. award Nassau County Profl. Engring. Soc., 1972, Lincoln Arc Welding Design awards, , 1961, 69. Fellow ASCE (life, Engr. of Yr. award L.I. chpt. 1974); mem. ASTM, Am. Arbitration Assn., Soc. Am. Mil. Engrs., Am. Welding Soc., Am. Acad. Forensic Scis., Am. Concrete Inst., N.Y. State Soc. Profl. Engrs. (pres. 1972-73), Nat. Soc. Profl. Engrs. (dir. 1967-77), Prestressed Concrete Inst., Constrn. Specifications Inst., N.Y. Cons. Engrs. Coun. (pres. L.I. chpt. 1970-71, chmn. edn., long range planning, ethics coms. 1965-74), Internat. Assn. Bridge and Structural Engrs., Nat. Acad. Forensic Engrs., Nat. Coun. Engring. Examiners (chmn. ABET com. 1981-83, dir. accreditation bd. for engring. and tech. 1981-83, dir. engring. manpower commn. 1978-79), Chi Epsilon, Tau Beta Pi. Home: 153 Biltmore Blvd Massapequa NY 11758-7244 Office: Shah Assocs P C Spl Projects Div 2635 Pettit Ave Bellmore NY 11710-3630

ALPERN, RAMONA LENNY, speech and language consultant; b. Bklyn.; d. Joseph Arthur and Cecile (Marks) Lenny; m. A. Melvin Alpern, Mar. 28, 1950; children: Carlin Jill, Edward Lenny, Kyle Meridith. BS, NYU, 1948; MA, Northwestern U., 1949. Speech tchr. N.Y.C. Sch. System, 1953-55; speech, pub. speaking tchr., speech therapist Baldwin (N.Y.) Sch. System, 1959-64; speech therapist, instructional adviser Intermediate Unit, Delaware County, Pa., 1974-75; clin. supr. Temple U., Phila., 1976; prin. Alpern & Assocs. Communications Specialists, Radnor, Pa., 1976—; therapy specialist, facilitator Magee Rehab. Hosp., Phila., 1991—. Contbr. articles to profl. jours. Pres. Town Watch, Gulph Mills, Pa.; bd. dirs. Civic Assn., Gulph Mills. Mem. AFTRA, Am. Speech, Hearing and Language Assn. (cert.), Pa. Speech and Hearing Assn., Screen Actors Guild. Home: PO Box 8214 Radnor PA 19087-8214 Office: Alpern & Assocs Box 8214 Radnor PA 19087-8214

ALPERT, ALLEN SIDNEY, patent and licensing executive, lawyer; b. Miami, Fla., Nov. 14, 1938; s. Dorothy (Schwartz) Andersen; m. Jo Ann Roskin, Apr. 4, 1959; children: David, Caren. BS in Indsl. Engring., U. Fla., 1961; LLB, George Washington U., 1965. Patent examiner U.S. Patent and Trademark Office, Washington, 1961-65; patent atty. G.E. Co., 1965-67; patent and licensing atty. IBM, 1967-72; v.p. ops., sec. University Patents Inc., Norwalk, Conn., 1972-82, pres., chief operating officer, 1982-88, pres., chief exec. officer, 1988—; chmn. bd. dirs. University Communications Inc., Westport, Conn.; bd. dirs. Plasmaco Inc., Highland, N.Y.; lectr. univs., profl. assns. Mem. Am. Intellectual Property Law Assn., Licensing Execs. Soc., Order of Coif. Office: University Patents Inc 1465 Post Rd E Westport CT 06880-5528

ALPERT, CAROLINE EVELYN, nurse; b. Bklyn., June 18, 1926; d. Harry Noah and Anna Fanny (Walfish) Spalter; m. Meyer Alpert, Jan. 21, 1951; children: Robert, Linda, Mark, David, Steven. Diploma, Jewish Hosp. Bklyn., 1947; AAS in Human Services, Westchester Community Coll., 1988. RN, N.Y. Staff nurse Jewish Hosp. Bklyn., 1947-51, 53, Burbank Hosp., Fitchburg, Mass., 1952-53; substitute sch. nurse Westchester County Schs., N.Y., 1974-85; sch. nurse Yonkers (N.Y.) Bd. Edn., 1985—; nurse Westchester Summer Day Camp, Mamaroneck, N.Y., summers, 1976-86. Mem. Jewish Hosp. Bklyn. Alumni Assn. Democrat. Home: 80 Avondale Rd Yonkers NY 10710-2021

ALPERT, JEFFREY STUART, real estate broker; b. New Haven, Conn., Dec. 3, 1944; s. Abraham Aaron and Beatrice (Gurman) A.; m. Bonnie Lunt, Aig. 1, 1987. BA in Bus., Edn., U. Miami, Fla., 1968. Notary Pub. N.Y. Prin. Alpert Realty Co., New Haven, N.Y.C., 1976—. Contbr. articles to Golf World, Golf News. Vol. Lenox Hill (N.J.) Hosp., Pawling (N.Y.) Youth Hockey. Named All Fla. Golfer, U. Miami, 1966-67, to All Am. Golf Team, U. Miami, NCAA, 1967, Golfer of Yr. N.Y. Real Estate Bd., 1989, '90; won N.J. State Amateur GolfChampionship, 1971. Mem. N.Y. State Real Estate Bd., Samoset Golf CLub, Rancocas Golf Club. Office: Alpert Realty Co 240 E 76th St New York NY 10021

ALPERT, MARK ZACHARY, performing arts executive; b. New Haven, Mar. 22, 1946; s. Aaron Lewis and Ann Shirley (Lichstein) A.; m. Cornelia Ruehlicke, Jul. 8, 1985. BA, NYU, 1969; MA, Columbia U., 1971. Asst. to pres. Am. Ballet Theatre, N.Y.C., 1970-71; gen. mgr. Erick Hawkins Dance Co., N.Y.C., 1971-75; exec. dir. Dennis Wayne's Dancers, N.Y.C., 1976-79; v.p. Columbia Artists Mgmt., N.Y.C., 1979—; bd. dirs. Matthew Nash Dance Co., N.Y.C., Saeko Ichinoe Dance Co., N.Y.C., 1985—. Office: Columbia Artists 165 W 57th St New York NY 10019

ALPERT, NELSON LEIGH, physicist, consultant; b. New Haven, June 14, 1925; s. Samuel and Frances Mark (Schupack) A.; m. Ruth Leah Sachs, Mar. 19, 1950; children: Stephen H., Nancy J. Alpert Halpert. BS, Yale U., 1945; PhD, MIT, 1948. Asst. prof. physics Rutgers U., New Brunswick, N.J., 1948-52; physicist White Devel., Stamford, Conn., 1952-58; dir. product devel. Perkin-Elmer, Norwalk, Conn., 1958-67; dir. instruments Becton Dickinson, Hackensack, N.J., 1967-68; cons. Stamford, 1968—; instr. area com. Nat. Commn. Clin. Lab. Standards, Villanova, Pa., 1969-85. Author: Clinical Instrument Reports, 1976; co-author: Theory and Practice of Infrared Spectroscopy, 1970; editor, author: Clinical Instrument Systems, 1980—; patentee in field. Mem. Am. Assn. for Clin. Chemistry (chmn. Connecticut Valley sect. 1982, founding chmn. alliance Northeastern sects. 1982-87, Seligson-Golden award 1988, Disting. Svc. award 1988), Internat. Fedn. Clin. Chemistry (instr., expert panel 1983-86). Jewish. Office: Instrument Cons 447 Glenbrook Rd Stamford CT 06906-1836

ALPERT, WILLIAM HAROLD, artist; b. N.Y.C., Dec. 21, 1934; s. Jacob Joseph and Fannie (Leff) Alperovicz. BA, UCLA, 1963, MA, 1965. adj. prof. painting Cooper Union Sch. Art, N.Y.C., 1979-82; adj. instr. drawing Parsons Sch. Design, N.Y.C., 1981-82, Pratt Inst. Summer Program, 1981; instr. painting, drawing and watercolor Sch. Visual Arts, 1989-92. Exhbns. include Constructs Orgn. Ind. Artists, Bleecker Renaissance, N.Y., 1978, Orgn. Ind. Artists Postcard Show, Bologna Art Fair, Italy, 1978, Indpls. Mus. Art, 1978, Albright-Knox Mus., 1978, Joe & Emily Loew Art Gallery, Syracuse U., 1980, W. Paterson Collection of N.J., 1981, others; public collections include Power Gallery Contemporary Art, Sydney, Australia. Contbr. to N.Y. Art Yearbook, 1975-76. Home: 64 Grand St # 5 New York NY 10013-2217

ALPIAR, HAL, marketing and management development consultant to medical practices and healthcare services; b. New Rochelle, N.Y., Apr. 29,

1941; s. Harold Peter and Vernetta (Roth) A.; (div. 1972); children: Haley Anne, Christopher Kennedy and Melissa Monica (twins); m. Kathleen Ann Marshall, Oct. 10, 1987. BBA, Iona Coll., 1964; MBA, L.I. U., 1965; cert., Inst. Advanced Advt. Studies, 1971, New Sch. for Entrepreneurs, 1979. Account exec. Young & Rubicam, Inc., N.Y.C., 1965-68, Foote, Cone, Belding, Inc., N.Y.C., 1968; account supr. Lake Spiro Shurman, Inc., Memphis, 1968-69; mktg. and new bus. dir. Friedlich, Fearon, Strohmeier, Inc., N.Y.C., 1969-71; account supr. Wells, Rich, Greene, Inc., N.Y.C., 1971-73; mktg. and promotion mgr. Guidance Assocs. div. Harcourt, Brace Jovanovich, Inc., Pleasantville, N.Y., 1973-74; dir. coop. edn., asst. prof. bus. Ocean County Coll., Toms River, N.J., 1974-79; exec. dir. Mgmt. Tng. Ctr., Point Pleasant Beach, N.J., 1979-82; pres., chief exec. officer A&B Businessworks, Inc., Lakewood, N.J., 1982—; adj. prof. bus. Pace U., 1971-73, Georgian Ct. Coll., 1980-83; pub. rels. dir. Pharm. Soc. State N.Y., 1970-72; trustee, bus. cons. Ocean County First Aid Acad., Toms River, 1979-81; two fed. appointments to region II adv. coun. SBA, 1987-91. Author, editor: Job Hunter, 1971; author, producer, host: 700 daily radio seminars for bus. and profl. practice mgmt.; designer, presenter: 2000 mgmt. skill devel. seminars and workshops; editor-in-chief Bus. Talk Mag., 1988; contbg. editor (cassette newsletter) M.D. Memo. Office: Businessworks Inc MidLantic Bank Pla 1091 River Ave Rte 9 Lakewood NJ 08701-5641

AL-SAWWAF, MONQIDH MOHAMMED, surgeon; b. Baghdad, Iraq, 1950; s. Mohammed Mahmmod and Noria (Najmaldeen) Al-S. Student, Pahlavi U. Coll. of Medicine, Shiraz, Iran, 1967-70, MD, 1976. Diplomate Am. Bd. Surgery, Am. Bd. Surg. Critical Care. Resident Harlem Hosp., N.Y.C., 1976-81, fellow, 1981-83, asst. attending physician, 1983-86, assoc. attending physician, 1986-88, attending physician, 1988—, co-chief surgury ICU, 1987-89, chief surgery ICU, 1989—; instr. surgery Columbia U., N.Y.C., 1983—, asst. clin. prof., 1989—; researcher in clin. critical care Harlem Hosp., N.Y.C., Columbia U., N.Y.C., 1983—; lectr. in critical care. Contbr. articles to profl. jours. V.p. United Drs. Assn., 1990—. Mem. Am. Soc. Gastrointestinal Endoscopy, Internat. Coll. Surgeons, Soc. Critical Care Medicine. Office: Harlem Hosp Dept Surgery 506 Lenox Ave New York NY 10037

ALSON, ELI, psychologist; b. N.Y.C., Aug. 1, 1929; s. David and Katie (Beller) A.; m. Annette Shiffman, Oct. 28, 1956; children: Beth Fay, Amy Ruth. BA, Bklyn. Coll., 1952; PhD, U. Buffalo, 1959. Lic. psychologist, N.J.; cert. in biofeedback. Rsch. psychologist VA Med. Ctr., Lyons, N.J., 1959-69, clin. psychologist, 1969-75, dir. psychology tng., 1975-84; dir. Biofeedback Clinic of Bernardsville (N.J.), 1980-87, Behavioral Medicine Clinic of VA Med. Ctr., Lyons, 1982-86; med. advisor Office of Hearings & Appeals, Social Security Adminstrn., Newark, 1986—; dir. Stress & Pain Mgmt. Ctr., St. Clares Riverside Med. Ctr., Boonton, N.J., 1987-91; cons. in behavioral medicine Life Performance Ctr., Denville, N.J., 1991—; adj. clin. prof. psychology L.I. U., Bklyn., 1976-84; adj. field supervisory faculty Rutgers U., Piscataway, N.J., 1976-84. Mem. profl. adv. com. Gov.'s Commn. for Study of Post-Traumatic Stress Disorders, 1990—. Mem. Am. Psychol. Assn., N.J. Psychol. Assn., Biofeedback Soc. N.J. (pres. 1980, 91), Assn. for Applied Psychophysiology and Biofeedback (ethics com.). Home: 25 Kitchell Rd Denville NJ 07834-1321 Office: Life Performance Ctr 16 Pocono Rd Denville NJ 07834

ALTAMURA, CARMELA ELIZABETH, concert artist, philanthropist; b. San Piero Patti, Sicily, Italy, Apr. 7, 1939; d. Salvatore and Mary (Butto) Bucceri; m. Leonard John Altamura, Apr. 15, 1938; children: Christina Chiara Maria, Leonard Anthony. Student, Caldwell Coll., 1957-59; artistic diploma, Giuseppe Verdi Conservatory, Milan, 1964. Founder, dir. Altamura Sch. Fine and Performing Arts, Union City, N.J., 1972-84, Inter-Cities Performing Arts, Inc., Union City, 1984—; founder, dir. adjudicator Enrico Caruso Internat. Voice Competition, U.S.A., Union City, 1988—; concert artist U.S., Europe, Middle East; recording artist Jericho Label & Olympia Arts, Ltd., N.Y.C., 1984-90; adjudicator Enrico Caruso Internat. Voice Composition, N.Y.C., 1988—; lectr. seminars Wagner Coll., Staten Island, N.Y., 1989—. Appeared as solo artist in numerous halls including Weill Hall at Carnegie Hall, Merkin Concert Hall, Tully Hall at Lincoln Ctr., Town Hall, Marymount Concert Hall, Symphony Hall, Newark, N.J., War Meml. Bldg., Trenton, N.J., Teatro dei Filodrammatici, Milan, Piccolo Teatro di Strehler, Milan, Ambroseaum Concert Hall, Milan, Teatro Ducale, Parma, Italy, Teatro Fraschini di Pavia, Italy, Teatro Communale di Bologna, Teatro G. Rossini, Pesaro, Italy and various others; bd. editors La Follia cultural Pub., 1990-91, Il Ponte, 1990-91; commd. bronze sculpture of Giulietta Simionato by Domenico Mazzone for Met. Opera Founder's Hall, Fanfare for the Americas orchestral work commd. from composer Rodrigo Henao and performed at Carnegie Hall Gala Salute to Italy and the Americas, 1991; performed in quincentennial celebrations Carlo Felice Opera House, Genoa, Italy, 1992; creator, author, researcher, narrator, enterpreter Commemorative Concert on the Life of Christopher Columbus; producer Third Enrico Caruso International Voice competition, USA, Caldwell Coll., N.J. Concert series founder, dir. Fomento Cultural Orgn., Union City, 1984-86; founder, dir. Italian Cultural Soc. of St. Peter's Coll., Jersey City, 1986-87; mem. Leonardo Da Vinci Cultural Soc. Recipient Gold medal Fano Opera Festival, William Matthew Sullivan Found. award, Barga Opera Festival, Cert. of Recognition as "Better World Builder" Italian Am. Hist. Soc., 1991, recipient award 1992. Mem. Nat. Orgn. Italian Am. Women, Nat. Italian Am. Found. Democrat. Roman Catholic.

ALTAMURA, ROBERT JAMES, geologist; b. Norwich, Conn., Nov. 10, 1953; s. Frank and Marie Louise (Derease) A.; m. Mary Anne Danyluk, June 2, 1979 (div. 1986). B in Environ. Earth Sci., Conn. State U., 1978; M in Geology, Wesleyan U., Middletown, Conn., 1984; postgrad., Pa. State U., 1990—. Sci. tchr. East Hampton (Conn.) High Sch., 1978-80; rsch. asst. geology Miami U., Oxford, Ohio, 1980, instr. geology, 1980-81; teaching asst. geology Wesleyan U., Middletown, 1981-83, vis. prof. geology, 1990; adj. faculty geology Conn. State U., Willimantic, 1986-90, Danbury, 1983; geol. environ. cons. State College, Pa., 1982—; geologist State Geol. Survey, Hartford, Conn., 1984—; cons. Geo-Environ. Cons., 1982—. Co-editor: State Geological Map, Conn., 1985; author: Connecticut Mining Map, 1987; editor geol. reports and maps, 1989—. Mem. AAUP, Am. Assn. Profl. Geologists, Geol. Soc. Am., Sigma Xi, Sigma Gamma Epsilon. Democrat. Roman Catholic. Home: 322A W Fairmount Ave State College PA 16801-4604 Office: Pa State U Dept Geoscis State College PA 16802

ALTCHEK, EDWARD MYER, neurosurgeon, educator; b. N.Y.C., Mar. 9, 1931; s. Isaac David and Fanny (Horowitz) A.; m. Florence Zeleznik, 1960 (div. 1968); children: Leslie Rachel, Glenn David, Michael Geoffrey; m. Roberta Louise Walsh, June 7, 1968; 1 child, Alexandra. BA in Psychology, NYU, 1951; BS in Biomed. Engring., N.Y. Inst. Tech., 1984; MD, Chgo. Med. Sch., 1955. Diplomate Am. Bd. Neurologic Soc. Intern L.I. Jewish Hosp., New Hyde Park, N.Y., 1955-56; resident neurosurgery Montefiore & Bronx Mcpl. Hosps., 1956-61; neurologic surgeon pvt. practice N.Y.C., L.I., 1961-76; prof. neuroanatomy St. George's Coll. of Medicine, Grenada, W.I., 1979-80; prof. engring. technology N.Y. Inst. Technology, Old Westbury, N.Y., 1984-91; asst. dir. rsch. inst. N.Y. Chiropractic Coll., Old Brookville, N.Y., 1987-90; assoc. prof. Touro Coll., 1992—. Patentee in field; contbr. articles to profl. jours. Mem. Soc. Automotive Engrs., Am. Assn. Med. Instrumentation. Republican. Jewish. Home and Office: 181 Woodhull Ave Riverhead NY 11901-3508

ALTER MURI, SIMONE BERNETTE, art therapist, educator; b. N.Y.C., Mar. 17, 1954; d. George Alter and Harriet (Marshall) Graicerstein; m. Samuel Muri, July 15, 1984; children: Georgina, Francesco. BA, U. Mass., Boston, 1976; MEd, Lesley Coll., 1979; EdD, U. Mass., Amherst, 1990. Registered art therapist; lic. mental health counselor. Art educator Framingham (Mass.) Art Mus., 1981-85, Talented and Gifted Program, Greenfield, Mass., 1985-88; art therapist Family Counseling Ctr., Newton, Mass., 1982-85, Northampton (Mass.) Ctr. for Children, 1987; asst. prof. art Our Lady of the Elms, Chicopee, Mass., 1990—; dir. art therapy programs Springfield Coll., 1986-91, asst. prof. art therapy, 1991—; cons. in art therapy edn. Wellesley (Mass.) Ctr. Rsch. on Women, 1990; cons. in art therapy, multicultural art Mass. Art Tchrs. Assn., Pittsfield, 1989-91, Nat. Coalition Creative Arts Therapies, Washington, 1990, New Eng. Assn. Edn. of Young Child, Newport, R.I., 1991; presenter at profl. confs. Bd. dirs. Very Spl. Arts Western Mass., Holyoke, 1990—, Gan Kenshet Pre-Sch., Northampton, 1991—. Bd. dirs. Very Spl. Arts Mass., Holyoke, 1990—, Gan Kenshet Pre-Sch., Northampton, 1991—. Mem. Am. Art Therapy Assn., Assn. Edn. Young Children, Nat. Art Edn. Assn., New Eng. Art Therapy Assn. (edn1. chair 1991). Office: Springfield Coll Dept Art Alden St Springfield MA 01109-3702

ALTHEIMER, JOSEPH, not-for-profit human services executive. BBA, CCNY, 1964; MSW, Adelphi U., 1971. Supr., caseworker child protective and family svcs. unit Spl. Svcs. for Children, N.Y.C., 1965-71, dep. dir. Office Programm Planning, asst. to commr., 1971-77; exec. dir. Good Shepherd Svcs., N.Y.C., 1977-80; pvt. practice cons., 1980-83; exec. dir. Inst. for Families and Children, N.Y.C., 1983—. With USANG, 1964-70. N.Y. State Regents scholar. Mem. NASW, Coun. for Human Svcs. in N.J. (pres.), Child Welfare League Am. (steering com. Mid Atlantic chpt., nat. task force on day care steering com.), N.Am. Commn. on Chem. Dependency and Child Welfare (steering com., subcom. on practice and tng., co-chair).

ALTHOUSE, JANET MARIE, consultant, legal assistant; b. Phila., Jan. 30, 1940; d. Elmer C. and Dolores (Windish) A. AA in Pub. Adminstrn., Phila. Community Coll., 1983; BS in Pub. Adminstrn., St. Joseph U., 1989. Cert. profl. sec., profl. cons., union steward. Various clerical positions Phila., 1958-70; acting claims supr. City Solicitor's Office, Phila., 1970-71; various legal sec. positions Phila., 1971-81; various paralegal positions, prosecution asst. I Dist. Atty.'s Office, Phila., 1981-86, prosecution asst. II, 1986-89; legal asst., cons. Phila., 1989—. Author: History of Philadelphia City Solicitor's Office 1952 to 1980, Defense of Philadelphia Home Rule Charter. Police advocate Mayfair Town Watch; adv. bd. N.E. Victim Assistance; active Mayfair Optimist, Women for Greater Phila. (Outstanding Svc. award 1983), Friends of N.E. Regional Libr., N.E. Cultural Coun., SSS Local Draft Bd. #133. Recipient Christian R. and Mary F. Lindback Found. scholarship, 1983. Mem. ABA (legal asst. assoc.), NAFE, Am. Mgmt. Assn., Am. Cons. League, Bus. and Profl. Women's Club, Delaware Valley Profl. Network, Profl. Secs. Internat. (past v.p., pres.), Nat. Assn. Legal Secs. (past. gov., corr. sec.), John Peter Zenger Law Soc., Phila. World Affairs Coun., Am. Diabetes Assn. (govt. rels. com.), Nat. Peace Inst. Found., Consumer Edn. Protection Assn., Greater N.E. Phila. C. of C., Catholic Daus., Alpha Sigma Lambda, Pi Sigma Alpha. Roman Catholic. Home and Office: 3407 Englewood St Philadelphia PA 19149-1611

ALTHUIS, THOMAS HENRY, science policy administrator; b. Kalamazoo, June 21, 1941; s. Anthony and Clara (Botma) A.; m. RoseMarie Zabbia, Mar. 18, 1967; children: Christopher, Michelle, Caroline. BS, Western Mich. U., 1963, MA in Chemistry, 1965; Dow summer fellowship, Mich. State U., 1967, NIH predoctoral fellowship, 1967, PhD in Organic Chemistry, 1968. Rsch. scientist Pfizer Cen. Rsch., Groton, Conn., 1968-74, sr. rsch. scientist, 1974-78; profl. staff sci. and tech. com. U.S. Ho. of Reps., Washington, 1978-79; sr. assoc. pub. affairs Pfizer Inc., N.Y.C., 1980-81, mgr. pub. affairs, 1981-82, asst. dir. pub. affairs, 1982-83, dir. sci. policy affairs, 1983-91; dir. sci. policy U.S. Pharms. Group, Pfizer, Inc., N.Y.C., 1992—. Co-author: Drugs Affecting the Respiratory System, 1980, Orphan Drugs, 1982; contbr. more than 30 articles to profl. jours. Pres. bd. dirs. Ea. Conn. Symphony Inc., New London, 1976-78; pres., cofounder Groton Bank Hist. Soc., 1971-82; counsellor Groton Town Coun., 1971-75; mem. City of Groton Republican Com., 1973-78, program adv. com. Found. Biomed. Rsch., Washington, 1985—, tech. task force Coun. on Competitiveness, Washington, 1987-88. Fellow Am. Inst. Chemists (chair govt. affairs com. 1989—, bd. dirs. 1991—); mem. AAAS, Am. Chem. Soc. (congl. fellowship 1978, com. on chem. and pub. affairs 1984-90), N.Y. Acad. Scis., N.Y. Sci. Policy Assn. Office: Pfizer Inc 235 E 42nd St New York NY 10017-5703

ALTIER, WILLIAM JOHN, management consultant; b. Drexel Hill, Pa., July 22, 1935; s. William John and Gertrude (Soule) A.; m. Mileen Rishel Bower, June 21, 1958: children: William Clark, Dwight Douglas. BA, Lafayette Coll., 1958; MBA, Pa. State U., 1962. Cert. mgmt. cons. Assoc., Kepner-Tregoe Inc., Princeton, N.J., 1964-68; gen. mgr. div. Princeton Rsch. Press, 1970-75, sr. assoc., 1975-76; assoc. Applied Synergetics Ctr., Waltham, Mass., 1968-69; dir. mktg. Comstock & Wescott Inc., Cambridge, Mass., 1969-70; pres. Princeton Assocs. Inc., Buckingham, Pa., 1976—; grad. asst. Dale Carnegie Courses; lectr. Assn. for Media-Based Continuing Edn. for Engrs.; guest lectr. Grad. Sch. Mgmt., New Sch. for Social Rsch.; bd. dirs., vice-chmn. Inst. Mgmt. Cons., also exec. editor IMC Newsletter; editor, pub. PA perspective; abstractor Jour. Product Innovation Mgmt.; mem. editorial rev. bd. Jour. Managerial Issues. Co-chmn. indsl. div. United Community Fund, Carlisle, Pa., 1963; elder Doylestown Presbyn. Ch.; exec. v.p. Bucks County br. ARC, also mem. planning com. Southeastern Pa. chpt.; vol. worker civic orgns. Mem. Acad. Mgmt., Am. Chem. Soc., Am. Vacuum Soc., Armed Forces Communications and Electronics Assn., Am. Mgmt. Assn., Product Devel. and Mgmt. Assn. (v.p.), Indsl. Mgmt. Club, Inst. Mgmt. Cons. (participative process cons. spl. interest group), Am. Arbitration Assn. (panel arbitrators), U. So. Calif. Ctr. for Futures Rsch., Assn. Mng. Cons. (trustee, editor newsletter UPDATE II), Mensa, Exchange Club (bd. control 1960-64), 1000 Club, Kappa Sigma Alumni Corp. (chpt. pres.). Clubs: Exchange (bd. control 1960-64) (Carlisle); 1000. Research and devel. fundamental analytical thinking processes relative to change; patentee, author articles in field. Home: 4233 York Dr Doylestown PA 18901-1752 Office: PO Box 820 Buckingham PA 18912-0820

ALTIMARI, FRANK X., federal judge; b. N.Y.C., Sept. 4, 1928; s. Antonio and Elvira (Stumpo) A.; m. Angela Scavuzzo, Sept. 23, 1951; children: Anthony, Nicholas, Vera, Michael. Student, St. Francis Coll., 1946-48, LLD (hon.), 1951; LLB, Bklyn. Law Sch., 1951. Bar: N.Y. 1951, U.S. Dist. Ct. (so. and ea. dists.) N.Y. 1955, U.S. Supreme Ct. 1959, U.S. Ct. Appeals (2d cir.) 1962. Assoc. Austin & Dupont, 1951-56; ptnr. Hoffmann & Altimari, 1956-65; dist. ct. judge Nassau County, N.Y., 1966-70, acting county ct. judge, 1969-70, county ct. judge, 1970-73, adminstrv. judge, 1973, acting surrogate, 1975-77, supervising judge, 1981, adminstrv. judge, 1982; justice N.Y. State Supreme Ct., 1974-82; judge U.S. Dist. Ct. (ea. dist.) N.Y., 1982-85, U.S. Ct. Appeals (2d cir.), 1985—; faculty St. Francis Coll., 1954-64, 72-73, St. John's Sch. Law, 1992—; lectr. Hofstra Law Sch., St. John's Sch. Law, Queens Coll.; also lectr., participant numerous panels. Former Westbury chmn. Am. Cancer Soc.; former dist. chmn. Cerebral Palsy Soc.; former regent, mem. speakers bur. St. Francis Coll.; former gen. counsel Westbury Bd. Edn., Lutheran High Sch. Assn., St. Francis Coll., St. Francis Monastery. Recipient Disting. Service award Alumni Assn. St. Francis Coll., 1967, 85, Pax et Bonum medal 1969, Norman F. Lent award Criminal Cts. Bar Assn., 1976, award Am. Acad. for Law Enforcement, 1981. Mem. N.Y. State Bar Assn., Nassau County Bar Assn. (Disting. Svc. Medallion award 1992), Jamaica Lawyers Club (past pres.). Roman Catholic. Office: US Ct Appeals Uniondale Ave at Hempstead Tnpk Hempstead NY 11553

ALTMAN, ALLAN, lawyer; b. Holyoke, Mass., Sept. 4, 1929; s. Leo and Elsie Eleanor (Siegel) A.; m. Marcia Ann Edelman, Dec. 6, 1959; children: Steven Lawrence, Michael Jay. AB, Bklyn. Coll., 1951; LLB, Bklyn. Law Sch., 1956. Bar: N.Y. 1957, U.S. Dist. Ct. (so. and ea. dists.) N.Y. 1957., U.S. Ct. Appeals (2nd cir.) 1968. Asst. mng. clk. Messrs. Cravath, Swaine & Moore, N.Y.C., 1953-56; assoc. Henry F. Dressel, N.Y.C., 1957-65; ptnr. Dressel & Altman, N.Y.C., 1965-86; ptnr. Berger & Steingut, N.Y.C., 1987—. Trustee, Temple Beth Elohim. With USMC, 1951-53. Mem. ABA, N.Y. State Bar Assn., Assn. of Bar of City of N.Y., N.Y. County Lawyers Assn., Am. Judicature Soc. Home: 330 E 38th St New York NY 10016-2759 Office: 600 Madison Ave New York NY 10022-1615

ALTMAN, DAN NIXON, business executive; b. Uniontown, Pa., June 23, 1952; s. H. Wesley and Millys N. (Nixon) A.; m. Susan Patton, Aug. 5, 1983; children: Wesley, Kirk, Andrew. BA, U. Pa., 1974, BS, 1974; JD, Harvard U., 1977. Bar: Pa. Assoc. Buchanan Ingersoll, Pitts., 1977-84, shareholder, 1984-89; pres. Elmhurst Corp., Pitts., 1989—; bd. dirs. Sporran, Inc., Pitts., Electronic Security Svcs. Co., Nashville, Calif. U. of Pa. Found.; speaker Pa. Bar Inst., 1986-88; arbitrator NASD, Pitts., 1987—. Mem. Rep. State Com., Pa., 1980-84, Young Pres. Orgn., 1991—; chmn. Fox Chapel (Pa.) Civil Svc. Mem. ABA, Pa. Bar Assn., Allegheny County Bar Assn., Assn. Corp. Growth, Duquesne Club. Home: 102 Shadow Ridge Dr Pittsburgh PA 15238-2124 Office: Elmhurst Corp 1 Bigelow Sq Ste 630 Pittsburgh PA 15219

ALTMAN, LAWRENCE GENE, biologist; b. Flushing, N.Y., July 4, 1952; s. Mark Eugene and Roberta Mercedes (Baron) A. B.A. in Biology, Fordham U., 1972, M.S., 1974, Ph.D., 1982. Mem. faculty Fordham U., N.Y.C., part-time 1979-81, Adelphi U., Garden City, N.Y., 1981-82; research biologist VA, West Haven, Conn., 1982-85; chmn. biology dept. Coll. of St. Elizabeth, Convent Station, N.J., 1985-86; asst. prof. div. sci. and math. Fordham U., N.Y.C., 1986-87; postdoctoral assoc. in pathology Yale U. Med. Sch., New Haven, 1982-85; cons. Coll. of New Rochelle, N.Y., 1980-81, Polyscis., Inc., Warrington, Pa., 1985-89, Columbia U. Coll. Physicians and Surgeons Dept. Microbiology, N.Y.C., 1986-88; part-time faculty Western Conn. State U., Danbury, 1990—; curriculum cons. Sacred Heart U., Fairfield, Conn., 1990—. Contbr. articles to profl. jours. Recipient Most Valuable Staff Mem. Faculty award Dowling Coll., 1975; Outstanding Performance award West Haven VA Med. Ctr., 1983; Fordham U. fellow, 1975-77. Mem. N.Y. Acad. Scis., Am. Soc. for Cell Biology, Electron Microscopy Soc. Am., AAAS, Conn. Electron Microscopy Soc., Sigma Xi. Avocations: Eagle scout; swimming; theater. Home and Office: 304 Lansdowne Westport CT 06880-5649

ALTMAN, RICHARD L., aeronautical engineer; b. Bklyn., Nov. 25, 1946; s. Lawrence and Helen (Namm) A.; m. Carole J. Gotham, Aug. 13, 1978; children: David Harrison, Benjamin Ian. BS in Aero. Engring., Bklyn. Poly. Inst., 1967; MSME, Rensselaer Poly. Inst., Troy, 1971; MBA, U. Conn., 1974. Aeronautical engr. United Tech./Pratt & Whitney, East Hartford, Conn., 1967-68; analytical engr. United Tech./Pratt & Whitney, 1968-71, sr. analytical engr., 1971-74, asst. project engr., 1974-77; mgr. Washington ops. United Tech./Pratt & Whitney, Washington, 1977-81; mgr. new product applications PW2000 program United Tech./Pratt & Whitney, East Hartford, 1981-83; mgr. bus. devel., adv. engines United Tech./Pratt & Whitney, 1983—, program mgr. Japanese super/hypersonic propulsion program, 1990—. Contbr. articles to profl. jours. Mem. Bd. Fin., Cromwell, Conn., 1976, Capital Expenditures Commn., Cromwell, 1975-76, others. Mem. AIAA, Coalition for Intelligent Mfg. Systems (intellectual property rights subcom. 1991—), Beta Gamma Sigma. Democrat. Jewish. Office: Pratt & Whitney 400 Main St East Hartford CT 06118-1873

ALTMAN, SIDNEY, biology educator; b. Montreal, Que., Can., May 7, 1939. BS, MIT, 1960; PhD in Biophys., U. Colo., 1967; DSc (hon.), McGill U., Montreal, 1991. Teaching asst. Columbia U., 1960-62; Damon Runyon Meml. Fund cancer rsch. fellow in molecular biology Harvard U., 1967-69; Anna Fuller Fund fellow, then Med. Rsch. Coun. fellow Med. Rsch. Coun. Lab. Molecular Biology, 1969-71; from asst. to assoc. prof. Yale U., New Haven, 1971-80, prof. biology, 1980—, chmn. dept., 1983-85; dean Yale Coll., from 1985; tutor Radcliffe Coll., 1968-69; researcher effects of acidrines on T4 DNA replications, mutants, precursors of tRNA, RNA processing by catalytic RNA and ribonuclease function. Recipient Nobel prize in chemistry, 1989. Fellow AAAS; mem. Am. Soc. Biol. Chemists, Genetics Soc. Am. Office: Yale U Dept Biology PO Box 6666 New Haven CT 06511-8161*

ALTMANN, MICHAEL STEWART, medical marketing executive; b. N.Y.C., July 12, 1952; s. Ben and Minnie (Ehrlich) A.; m. Sherri Ellen Kolomer, Oct. 7, 1972; children: Jennifer, Scott, Amanda. BA, Bklyn. Coll., 1973; postgrad., Va. Poly. Inst. and State U., 1973-75. Rsch. libr. Kallir, Philips, Ross, Inc., N.Y.C., 1975-76; med. sales rep. Alcon Labs., Inc., Ft. Worth, 1976-78; area mgr. Hydrocurve Soft Lenses, Inc., San Diego, 1978-79; dir. sales tng. Danker Labs., Inc., Parsippany, N.J., 1979; dir. mktg. and sales Copeland Intra Lenses, Inc., N.Y.C., 1979-81; account exec. Gross, Townsend, Frank, Inc., N.Y.C., 1981-82, Grey Med. Advt., N.Y.C., 1982-84; v.p., mgmt. supr. S.J. Weinstein Assocs., Inc., N.Y.C., 1984-91; v.p., account group supr. RWR Advt. Inc., N.Y.C., 1991-92; pres. Altmann Cons., Hauppauge, N.Y., 1990—; v.p. strategic devel. The AUMD Group, N.Y.C., 1992—; pres. Altmann & Assocs., Central Islip, N.Y., 1981-87; adj. prof. N.Y. Inst. Tech., Central Islip, 1989—. Pres. Heatherwood Civic Assn., Inc., Central Islip, 1982-84; v.p. Temple Beth Chai, Hauppauge, N.Y., 1986. Recipient Vol. Svc. award YM-YWHA N.Y., N.Y.C., 1970, Disting. Svc. award Heatherwood Civic Assn., Inc., 1985. Mem. AAAS, Am. Mgmt. Assn., Pharm. Advt. Coun., Am. Med. Writers Assn., Biomed. Mktg. Assn., N.Y. Acad. Scis., Sales Mktg. Exec. Intern. Home: 16 Town Line Ct Smithtown NY 11788

ALTSCHULER, BRUCE ROBERT, research dentist; b. Bklyn., Feb. 17, 1947; s. Frank Philip and Sarah Gertrude (Cloder) A.; m. Ruth Phyllis Gass, Oct. 27, 1974; children: Joan Ellen, Wendy Karen, Cheryl Miriam. BA, Bklyn. Coll., 1967; DDS, Temple U., 1971. Lic. dentist, Md., Pa., Conn., Maine, N.Y. Commd. capt. USAF, 1971, advanced through grades to col., 1986; project scientist dental holography Dental Scis. Br., Brooks AFB, Tex., 1971-74, chief dental consultation, 1975-76; chief dental laser holography USAF Dental Investigation Svc., Brooks AFB, Tex., 1976-80; chief dental computer/laser tech. USAF Aerospace Medicine, Brooks AFB, Tex., 1980-82; chief avionics advanced systems rsch. group Info. Processing Br., Wright-Patterson AFB, Ohio, 1982-84; dep. optical processing Systems Avionics Div., Wright-Patterson AFB, 1985; dental resident Advanced Clin. Dentistry Residence Program, Eglin AFB, Fla., 1985-86; Air Force rsch. liaison, chief laser imaging U.S. Army Inst. Dental Rsch., Ft. Meade, Md., 1986—; clin. asst. prof. dept. diagnosis/roentgenology U. Tex. Health Sci. Ctr., San Antonio, 1976-80, dept. dental diagnostic svc., 1980-82; mem. dental x-ray subcom. 26 Am. Nat. Standards Inst., Washington, 1980-85; reviewer NIH Computer Aided Dentistry, Washington, 1987. Editor 3-D Machine Perception; patentee in field. Bd. dirs. Am. Cancer Soc., Bexar County, Tex., 1980-82, mem. pub. edn. com., 1980-82; campaign coord. Avionics Lab. Combined Fed. Campaign, Dayton, Ohio 1984; spl. award judge Alamo Regional Sci. Fair, San Antonio, 1980-82. Mem. ADA, Internat. Assn. Dental Rsch., Soc. Photo Optical Instrumentation Engrs., Air Force Assn., Armed Forces Communications, Electronics Assn., Tex. Dental Assn., Am. Mensa. Republican. Jewish. Home: PO Box 1151 Fort George G Meade MD 20755-3151 Office: US Army Inst Dental Rsch SGRD UDR USAF Fort George G Meade MD 20755

ALTSHULLER, MARK GREGORY, philologist, Slavic languages educator; b. Leningrad, USSR, July 20, 1929; s. Gerz and Bronia (Shkolnikov) A.; m. Elena Dryzhakova, May 12, 1931; 1 child, Dmitry. MA, Leningrad U., 1952, PhD, 1966. Lectr. SUNY, Albany, 1979-80, U. Calif., Irvine, 1980-84; asst. prof. U. Va., Charlottesville, 1984-85, Washington U., St. Louis, 1985-86; prof. Slavic langs. dept. U. Pitts., 1986—. Author: Precursors of Slavophilism, 1984; co-author: The Path of Renunciation, 1985; contbr. articles to profl. jours., chpts. to books. Mem. Am. Assn. for Advancement Slavic Studies, Am. Assn. Tchrs. Slavic and East European Langs. Office: U Pitts Slavic Dept CL1417 Pittsburgh PA 15260

ALTSTADT, AUDREY L., history educator. BA, U. Ill., 1975; AM, U. Chgo., 1977, PhD, 1983. Asst. prof. history U. Mass., Amherst, 1990—. Author: Azerbaijani Turks: Power and Identity Under Russian Rule, 1992. Fellow Harvard Russian Rsch. Ctr., 1983-84, Internat. Rsch. and Exchanges Bd., 1980-81, 84-85, AAUW, 1982-83. Mem. Assn. for Advancement of Cen. Asian Rsch. (pres. 1991—). Office: U Mass Dept History Amherst MA 01003

ALUTTO, JOSEPH ANTHONY, university dean, management educator; b. Bronx, N.Y., June 3, 1941; s. Anthony and Concetta (Del Prete) A.; m. Rosemary Kerr, May 15, 1942; children: Patricia, Christina, Kerrie. BBA, Manhattan Coll., Riverdale, N.Y., 1962; MA, U. Ill., 1965; Ph.D., Cornell U., 1968. Asst. prof. orgnl. behavior SUNY, Buffalo, 1966-72, assoc. prof., 1972-75, prof., 1975-91, dean Sch. Mgmt., 1976-91; dean Coll. of Bus., Ohio State U., Columbus, 1991—; vis. prof. Carnegie-Mellon U., Pitts., 1974-75; arbitrator Fed. Mediation and Concilliation Service, 1971—; bd. dirs. Bank Pre Trust Co., Comptek, Inc. Author: (with others) Theory Testing in Organizational Behavior: The Varient Approach, 1983; contbr. 60 articles to profl. jours. Bd. dirs. United Way, Buffalo, 1982-91; pres. Amherst Cen. Sch. Bd., 1982-86. Mem. APA, AAAS, Acad. Mgmt. (pres. Ea. div. 1980-81), Am. Sociol. Assn., Capital Club, Univ. Club. Home: 2030 Cambridge Blvd Columbus OH 43221 Office: Ohio State U Coll Bus 1775 College Rd Columbus OH 43210-1399

ALVAREZ, THOMAS PETER, periodical publication company executive; b. Roslyn, N.Y., Feb. 6, 1967; s. Ernest Leonard and Theresa (DeFonsi) A.;

m. Doreen Regina Hatch, Nov. 30, 1990. BFA, L.I. U., 1989. Art dir. Bic Printing, East Meadow, N.Y., 1989-90; art tchr. East Meadow High Sch., 1989—; freelance illustrator East Meadow, 1989—; pres., cartoonist, writer Magic Comics, East Meadow, 1989—. Author: (comic books) Last Case of Sherlock Holmes, 1992, Master of Magic, 1992; artist: (comic book) Last Case of Sherlock Holmes, 1992; creator cartoon character Young Merlin, 1992. Mem. Nat. Cartoonist Soc., Berndt Toast Gang. Republican. Roman Catholic.

ALVAREZ-CULLEN, MARTHA, social worker; b. Bogota, Colombia, June 4, 1955; came to U.S., 1969; d. Silverio and Isabel (Bazurto) Alvarez; m. Dan Cullen, Feb. 14, 1985; children: Daniel Michael, Natalie Anne. BA in Edn., Queens Coll., 1978; MSW, Hunter Coll., 1982; postgrad., Fordham U., 1990. Cert. in child and adolescent therapy; cert. social worker. Drug counselor SCANT, N.Y.C. Bd. Edn., 1979-80; social worker Pius XII Non-Secure Detention, Bklyn., 1980-81, Puerto Rican Assn. for Community Affairs, N.Y.C., 1984-85, N.Y.C. Bd. Edn., Bronx, 1982—; phone vol. Victim Svcs. Orgn., Queens, 1983—. Mem. Nat. Assn. Social Workers. Home: 2035 Midland Dr Yorktown Heights NY 10598

ALVES, JOSEPH THOMAS, priest, mental health clinic executive; b. Boston, Oct. 4, 1921; s. Joseph Francis and Mary (McDermott) A.; A.B., Boston Coll., 1944, M.S.W., 1948; M.A., St. John's Sem., 1953, M.Div., 1977; Dr. Social Work, Catholic U. Am., 1959. Diplomate in Clin. Social Work; ordained priest Roman Cath. Ch., 1953. Assoc. dir. Pittsfield (Mass.) Community Chest and Berkshire County Council Social Agys., 1948-49; parish priest, Everett, Mass., 1953-56; elevated to domestic prelate by Pope, 1965; exec. dir. Family Counseling and Guidance Centers Inc., Boston, 1958-86; pastor St. Philip Neri Ch., Newton, Mass., 1986—; pres. Samaritans, Inc., 1977-84, dir., 1971—. Bd. dirs., exec. com. Nat. Council on Aging, 1969—, chmn. membership com., 1974-77, v.p., 1978-79; treas. Family Counseling Endowment Fund, Inc., 1980—; bd. dirs. Pastoral Service Commn., Mass. Council Chs., 1971-75; del. White House Conf. on Aging, 1961, 81; mem. adv. com. on services Mass. Dept. Pub. Welfare; mem. Health Planning Council for Greater Boston; chmn. adv. council for Community Mental Health Center Constrn.; mem. Beth Israel Hosp. com. on pub. responsibility in medicine and research, pres.'s coun. St. Margaret's Hosp.; trustee Third Century Found., Archdiocese Boston; bd. dirs. Assn. Psychiat. Outpatient Centers Am., 1978—, sec., 1979—, pres.-elect 1980; bd. dirs. Nat. Conf. Cath. Charities, 1959—; mem. affiliates council United Way Mass. Bay; mem. Gov.'s Com. on Children and the Family, 1979-82. Served as 1st lt., pilot USAAF, 1942-45. Decorated D.F.C., Air medal with oak leaf clusters. Mem. Nat. Assn. Social Workers (chmn. social policy and action com. Eastern Mass. chpt. 1967—), Acad. Religion and Mental Health, Gerontol. Soc. Inc., Nat. Council on Family Relations, Mass. Conf. on Social Welfare, Council Social Work Edn., Nat. Conf. Social Welfare, Nat. Conf. Catholic Charities, Am. Acad. Clin. Sociologists, Inst. Soc., Ethics and Life Scis., Internat. Council Social Welfare (U.S. com.), Am. Sociol. Assn., Acad. Polit. and Social Sci., Boston Soc. Gerontol. Psychiatry, Citizens for Decent Housing, Soc. Family Therapy and Research, Internat. Soc. Existential Psychology and Psychiatry, AAAS, Mass. Pub. Welfare Council, Am. Acad. Psychotherapists, Am. Arbitration Assn. (nat. panel arbitrators), AAAS, Mass. Assn. to Advance Human Scis., Am. Acad. Arts and Scis., Boston Latin Sch. Assn., South Shore C. of C., New Directions, Common Cause, World Federalist Assn., 73d Bomb Wing Assn. U.S. Air Force. Clubs: St. Botolph (Boston); Windsor (Newton). Author: Confidentiality in Social Work, 1959. Contbr. articles to profl. and popular jours. and mags. Home: 229 Adams St Milton MA 02186-4232

ALVINE, ROBERT, industrialist, entrepreneur, manufacturing company executive; b. Newark, Aug. 25, 1938; s. James C. and Marie Alvine; m. Diane C. Marzulli, May 6, 1961; children: Robert James, Laurie Anne. BS, Rutgers U., 1960; postgrad., Syracuse U., 1968-69; grad. PMD, Harvard Bus. Sch., 1972. With Celanese Corp., 1960-77; bus. mgr. Celanese Plastics Co., Newark, 1969-72; dir. mktg. and ops. Celanese Piping Systems and Fabricated Products Co., Hilliard, Ohio, 1972-75; v.p. comml. Celanese Polymer Spltys. Co., Louisville, 1975-77, Uniroyal Inc., 1977-87; dir. strategy planning and bus. devel. Uniroyal-Chem., Naugatuck, Conn., 1977; v.p. corp. planning and devel. Uniroyal Inc., Middlebury, Conn., 1978; v.p., gen. mgr. Uniroyal Tire Co., 1979-80; pres. Uniroyal Merchandising Co., 1979-82; pres., chief exec. officer Uniroyal Devel. Co., 1980-82; chief exec. and oper. officer, group v.p. Engineered Products & Svcs., Worldwide, 1982-87; pres. Uniroyal Plastics Co., Uniroyal Footware Columbia, Uniroyal Power Transmission Co., Uniroyal Indsl. Products Cos., 1982-87; also corp. sr. v.p. and officer responsible for mergers and acquisitions Uniroyal, Inc., 1979-87; and sr. corp. officer and major prin. in mgmt. leverage buy-out of Uniroyal, Inc., 1985; founder, chmn., chief exec. officer i-Ten Mgmt. Corp., Woodbridge, Conn., 1987—, Aim Capital Group, Woodbridge, 1987—; chmn., chief exec. officer Charter Power Systems, Plymouth Meeting, Pa., 1988—; prin. Charterhouse Group Internat., Inc., N.Y.C., 1988—; vice chmn., chief exec. officer AP Parts Mfg. Co., Toledo, 1989; prin. Uniroyal Holdings, Waterbury, Conn., 1985—; bd. dirs. Wedge Computer, Boston, Charter Power Systems, AP Parts. Mem. Rep. Presdl. Task Force, Citizens Against Govt. Waste. Served with AUS, 1962-68. Recipient numerous citations and recognitions including Disting. Bus. Achievement and Svcs. to the Nations award; Honor grad. Southeastern Signal Sch., 1962; named Ky. Col., 1976. Mem. Nat. Assoc. Corp. Dirs., Pres.'s Assn., Am. Inst. Mgmt., Nat. Planning Inst., N.Am. Planning Soc., Nat. Assn. Corp. Growth, Rubber Mfrs. Assn., Battery Coun. Internat., Newcomen Soc. Am., Soc. Plastics Industry, Soc. Plastics Engrs. (past dir.), Mfg. Chemists Assn., Nat. Paint and Coatings Assn., Coun. of Ams., Rutgers Alumni Assn., Harvard Bus. Sch. Club Greater N.Y., Ellis Island Found., U.S. Navy Meml. Found., Oaklane Country Club, Renaissance Club, Chi Phi. Mem. Ch. of Christ. Home: 55 N Racebrook Rd Woodbridge CT 06525-1407

ALVINO, GLORIA DORA, small business owner, consultant; b. Revere, Mass., June 27, 1931; d. Alfonso and Mary (Scotti) A. Student, Boston U., 1949-51; BS in Pharmacy, Mass. Coll. Pharmacy and Allied Health Services, 1955; MS in Health and Human Svcs., 1992. Registered pharmacist, Mass. Pharmacy mgr. Pierce Apothecary and Chester Baker, Inc., Brookline, Mass., 1955-59; owner Med. Ctr. Surg. Supply, Medi-Rents, Med. Ctr. Fitting Svc., Boston, 1959—; guest lectr. Med. Sch. Boston U., Northeastern U., Harvard Med. Sch., various hosps., elem. schs., 1959—, Mass. Coll. Pharmacy and Allied Health Services, Boston, 1987—; freelance cons., 1987—. Fellow Am. Coll. Apothecaries; mem. Sierra Club, NOW, Audubon Soc., Health Industry Distbn. Assn., Am. Pharm. Assn. Avocations: horseback riding, writing, reading, sketching, gardening. Home: 32 Clark Rd Brookline MA 02146-6030

ALYEA, HUBERT NEWCOMBE, chemistry educator; b. Clifton, N.J., Oct. 10, 1903; s. Joseph Pascal Strong and Sarah May (Dinsmore) A.; 1 child, Frederick Newcombe. AB, Princeton U., 1925, MA, 1926, PhD, 1928; DSc, Beaver Coll., 1970. Instr. chemistry Princeton (N.J.) U., 1930-34, asst. prof., 1934-40, assoc. prof., 1940-54, prof., 1954-72, prof. emeritus, 1972—; vis. prof. U. Hawaii, Honolulu, 1949-50; lectr. Expo-58, Brussels, 1958, Internat. Exposition, Seattle, 1952, Montreal, Que., Can., 1957; presenter 300 workshops on teaching techniques to chemistry tchrs. and 5600 demonstration lectures in 80 countries; inventor automatic slide-changer. Author 10 book on chemistry teaching; contbr. articles to profl jours. Am.-Scandinavian and GE fellow, Sweden, 1925-26, Sayre fellow, Princeton, 1927-29, Nat. Res. fellow, Minn., 1928-29, Int. Res. fellow, Berlin, 1929-30; recipient N.J. Sci. Tchr. award, 1954, 57, Chem. Mfg. Assn. award, 1970, ACS award in Chem. Edn, 1984, NSTA Carleton award, 1991. Recipient James Flack Norris award N.E. section Am. Chem. Soc., Boston, 1970, Priestley award Dickinson Coll., 1984, Robert Carleton award Nat. Assn. Sci. Tchrs., 1991. Home: 337 Harrison St Princeton NJ 08540-5649

AMABILE, JOHN LOUIS, lawyer; b. N.Y.C., Oct. 13, 1934; s. John A. and Rose (Singer) A.; m. Christina M. Leary, Nov. 23, 1963; children: Tracy Ann, John Christopher. BS cum laude, Coll. Holy Cross, 1956; LLB, St. John's Sch. Law, 1959. Bar: N.Y. 1959, U.S. Dist. Ct. (so. and ea. dists.) N.Y. 1961, U.S. Supreme Ct. 1964, U.S. Ct. Claims 1964, U.S. Ct. Appeals (2d cir.) 1970, U.S. Tax Ct. 1984, U.S. Ct. Appeals (9th cir.) 1984. Assoc. Law Office of Allen Taylor, N.Y.C., 1959-62; assoc. Schwartz & Frohlich, N.Y.C., 1963-69, ptnr., 1970; ptnr. Summit, Solomon & Feldesman (predecessor firms), N.Y.C., 1971—; faculty mem. ann. seminar Practising Law Inst. Editor St. John Law Rev. 1958-59. Regional commr. Am. Youth Soccer Orgn., Chappaqua, N.Y., 1975-84; mem. New Castle Recreation and Parks Commn., 1984-90, chairperson, 1987-89. Mem. ABA, N.Y. State Bar Assn., Assn. of Bar of City of N.Y. (com. on state legis. 1971-78, com. of grievances 1979-80, com. on judiciary 1989-92, chmn. com. on gender bias in fed. cts. 1991—), Fed. Bar Coun. (panel chairperson appellate div. disciplinary com. 1980-85, 87—). Democat. Roman Catholic. Home: 73 Orchard Rd Chappaqua NY 10514-1003 Office: Summit Solomon & Feldesman 445 Park Ave New York NY 10022-2606

AMADEI, DEBORAH LISA, librarian; b. Jersey City, June 13, 1952; d. Joseph and Thelma (Pugach) Irgon; m. Albert E. Amadei, July 19, 1987. BA, Northeastern U., 1975; MS, Pratt Inst., 1985. Cert. profl. librarian. Tech. libr. asst. Tracor Jitco, Dover, N.J., 1977-84, lead tech. libr. asst., 1984-85; sr. libr. East Orange (N.J.) Pub. Libr., 1986—. Mem. N.J. Libr. Assn., Toastmasters (ednl. v.p. Essex County, N.J. chpt. 1990-91, pres. 1992—). Office: East Orange Pub Libr 21 S Arlington Ave East Orange NJ 07018-3892

AMATO, JOSEPH JOHN, priest, psychologist; b. N.Y.C., Aug. 16, 1952; s. Salvatore and Mary (Sapienza) A. BA in Philosophy, Cathedral Coll., 1974; MA in Theology, Cath. U. Am., 1980; MA in Psychology, NYU, 1983, PhD in Counseling Psychology, 1990. Lic. psychologist, Ariz. Priest Diocese of Bridgeport, Conn., 1980—; pre-doctoral psychology intern Mary Hosp. & Med. Ctr., San Diego, 1988-89, postdoctoral psychology fellow, 1989-90; postdoctoral psychology fellow Newington (Conn.) Children's Hosp., 1990—. Recipient Conn. Outstanding Young Citizens award Conn. Jaycees, 1985-86. Roman Catholic. Home: 30 Old Stone Bridge Rd Cos Cob CT 06807-1510

AMATO, MICHELE AMATEAU, artist, educator; b. Flushing, N.Y., July 29, 1945; d. Harold Amateau and Ann (Resnick) A.; m. Albert Alhadeff, May 28, 1969 (div.); 1 child, Cara Judea; m. Don K. Schule, Nov. 22, 1978. BFA, Boston U., 1968; MFA, U. Colo., 1973. Chairperson, prof. of art Wichita (Kans.) State U., 1977-78; vis. prof. art Mpls. (Minn.) Coll. of Art and Design, 1978-79, U. Tex., San Antonio, 1982-83; curator of exhbns. Patrick Gallery, Austin, 1983-84; vis. artist U. Colo., Boulder, 1984-85; prof. art U. Tex., Austin, 1985; vis. artist East Carolina U., Greenville, N.C., 1986; prof. art S.W. Tex. State U., San Marcos, 1987-88; area head, prof. art Pa. State U. Sch. of Visual Arts, University Park, 1988—; mem. editorial adv. bd. Collegiate Press, Alta Loma, Calif., 1990—. Mem. editorial bd. Ocular mag., 1972-79; art and dance columnist Straight Creek Jour., 1971-76, Boulder Daily Camera, 1971-74; exhibited in group shows Kornblee Gallery, N.Y.C., 1975, 78, 85, Mus. Contemporary Hispanic Art, 1989, Nahan Gallery, N.Y.C., 1990, Freedman Gallery, Albright Coll., 1991, El Museo del Barrio, N.Y.C., 1992; represented in permanent collections Chase Manhattan Bank, N.Y.C., Denver Art Mus., Rose Art Mus., Brandeis U.; represented by Sandra Gering Gallery, N.Y.C. Fellow Nat. Endowment for Arts, 1988; rsch. grantee Pa. State U., 1989, travel grantee Pa. State U. Inst. for Arts and Humanistic Studies, 1991. Mem. Coll. Art Assn., Women's Caucus for Art. Democrat. Jewish. Home: 1721 Linden Hall Rd Boalsburg PA 16827-1720 Office: 102VAB Pa State U Sch Visual Arts University Park PA 16827

AMBLER, TIMOTHY FELIX JOHN, management science researcher; b. London, May 30, 1937; s. Dennis Bernard and Patricia Mary (Swabey) A.; m. Catherine Audrey Preston, June 4, 1966; 1 child, Augustine James. MA, Oxford U., 1960; MS, MIT, 1969. Clk. Peat Marwick Mitchell, London, 1960-63; acct. City Cellars Ltd., London, 1963-68; mktg. dir. IDV, Harlow, 1969-76, mng. dir., 1977-82, mktg. dir. worldwide, 1982-87, joint mgr. dir., 1987-90; fellow London Bus. Sch., 1991—; cons. Aptimus Tng. Systems Ltd., London, 1990—. Lt. British Army, 1955-57. Mem. Hurlingham. Roman Catholic. Office: London Bus Sch, Sussex Pl Regents Park, London NW1, England

AMBROSE, MARILYN MILLER, educational administrator; b. Pottsville, Pa., Feb. 7, 1946; d. Warren G. and Betty (Stout) Miller; m. Irvin Michael Ambrose, Aug. 9, 1969; children: Jennifer, Amy. BS, Bloomsburg U., 1968; MA in Mgmt., Cen. Mich. U., 1983; postgrad., U. Del., 1972-77. Tchr. Blue Mountain Sch. Dist., Orwigsburg, Pa., 1968-69, Capital Sch. Dist., Dover, Del., 1969-70; lang. arts specialist Harris Elem. Sch., Dover, 1977-79; parent sch. coord. Capital Sch. Dist., Dover, 1979-81; admissions counselor Wesley Coll., Dover, 1981-82, asst. dir. admissions, 1982-85, fin. aid. dir., 1985—; mem. exec. bd. Coll. Bd. Fin. Aid Div., 1991-93. Co-author guide book: Think College, 1989; co-editor video: Financial Aid 101, 1988. Mem. Foster Care Rev. Bd., State of Del., 1987—; pres. Friends of Milford (Del.) Pub. Libr., 1982; mem. Women's Aux. Milford Meml. Hosp., 1979—, chair hosp. fair, 1981; chair Fresh Aid Fund of Milford and Harrington, 1977-80. Mem. Del.-D.C.-Md. Assn. Student Fin. Aid Adminstrs. (chair elect 1989-90, chair 1990-91), Del. Assn. Student Fin. Aid Adminstrs. (pres. 1987-89), Nat. Assn. Student Fin. Aid Adminstrs. (membership coord. 1989—, ea. assn. chpt. bd. dirs. 1987-91, tng. com. 1989-90, presenter conf. 1992). Office: Wesley Coll 120 N State St Dover DE 19901-3835

AMBRUS, LYNDA, language educator; b. Santa Ana, Calif., July 5, 1963; d. Frederick Arnold Benson and Marilyn Mary (Lazenko) B.; m. Neil Gifford Ambrus, Aug. 18, 1991. BA in French, Stetson U., 1985; MA in French, Rutgers U., 1989. Prof. French Brevard Community Coll., Indialantic, Fla., 1985-87; adj. prof. French Montclair (N.J.) State Coll., 1990, Middlesex County Coll., Edison, N.J., 1990—; mgr. Alliance Internat. Mktg., Inc., Fanwood, N.J., 1990—. Vol. United Way, 1990-91. Mem. Modern Lang. Assn., Am. Assn. Tchrs. French, French Grad. Students Assn., La Societe Francaise, Phi Beta Kappa.

AMEEN, LANE, psychiatrist; b. Hopewell, Va., Aug. 23, 1923; m. May Sams; children: Nancy, Robert. BA, U. Va., 1943, MD, 1946. Intern Phila. Gen. Hosp., 1947, resident, 1948; resident Menninger Sch., Topeka, 1952; chief acute psychiatry VA Hosp., West Haven, Conn., 1953-79; assoc. clin. prof. Jonathan Edwards Coll., Yale U., New Haven, 1970—; sr. cons. Elmcrest Psychiat. Inst., Portland, Conn., 1971-81, med. dir., 1981—; vis. prof. U. Kuwait, 1980-81. Capt. U.S. Army, 1948-50. Fellow Am. Psychiat. Assn.; mem. Jonathan Edwards Coll., Yale U. Alumni Assn. Office: Elmcrest Psychiat Inst 25 Marlborough St Portland CT 06480-1875

AMELIO, RAYMOND CARMINE, employee relations executive; b. Pitts., Aug. 5, 1945; s. Salvatore Hugo and Minnie (Zerillla) A.; m. Paula Kay Dell, Aug. 4, 1972; children: Kaylyn Rae, Marc Raymond. BA, Duquesne U., 1971; MA, LaRoche Coll., 1986. Mem. staff ops. div. Pitts. Nat. Bank, 1972-86, tng. coord., 1987-89, mgr. tng. and employee rels., 1989—. Chmn. bd. dirs. North Hills YMCA, Pitts., 1991—; bd. dirs. Children's Coun. of West Pa., Pitts., 1990—; bd. dirs. Vietnam Vets. Leadership Program. With USN, 1966-69, Vietnam. Mem. ASTD (pres. Pitts. chpt. 1991-92). Office: Pitts Nat Bank 5th Avenue St Pittsburgh PA 15229-1250

AMENDOLA, CARL FRANCIS, bank executive; b. Bklyn., Sept. 20, 1963; s. Francesco and Domenica (Riggio) A.; m. Elizabeth Trapp, June 15, 1991. BA in Econs., NYU, 1985, postgrad., 1992—. Mgmt. trainee The Bank of N.Y., N.Y.C., 1985-86, asst. treas., 1986-89, asst. v.p., 1989-90; asst. v.p. Bayerische Hypotheken und Wechsel Bank, Ag, N.Y.C., 1990—. Mem. Assn. Cambiste Internat.-Internat. Fgn. Exch. Assn. Home: 302 W 12th St #3B New York NY 10014 Office: Bayerische Hypotheken und Wechsel Bank Ag Financial Sq 32 Old Ship New York NY 10005

AMENDOLA, SAL JOHN, artist, educator, writer; b. Fiumefreddo, Calabria, Italy, Mar. 8, 1948; came to U.S., 1948; s. Joseph and Mary (Amendola) A. Grad. high sch., Bklyn.; 3-yr. cert., Sch. Visual Arts, N.Y.C., 1966-69. Illustrator, writer DC Comics, Archie Comics, Marvel, N.Y.C., 1969-86; asst. editor, prodn. DC Comics, N.Y.C., 1970; talent coord., editor DC Comics, Warner Communications, N.Y.C., 1983-86; illustration instr. Sch. Visual Arts, Fashion Inst., N.Y.C., 1974—; founder SRV plus 1, 1990; lectr., cons., instr. seminars at librs., mus., schs., U.S., Can., 1983-86; freelance illustrator, 1987—. Writer, illustrator: (comic book) Batman Night of the Stalker, 1972 (Best Story Nominee 1973); editor: (comic books) Elvira Mistress of the Dark, Talent Showcase, 1984-86; co-artist: (movie adaptation) Superman III, 1983, (comic book) Star Trek, 1984; author, artist: (book) Perspective for Artists, 1984, (book) Other Intelligences/A Sociopolitical View, 1990; artist: (comic book) Archie, 1987 (Best Artist nominee 1988); designer toys and games. Contbr., vol. animal and human rights, environ. orgns., liberal polit. candidates. Mem. Nat. Cartoonist Soc. (profl. com. 1987). Liberal Democrat. Home: 1028 67th St Brooklyn NY 11219-5923

AMERO, ROBERT CLAYTON, chemical engineer; b. Rochester, N.Y., Oct. 25, 1917; s. Philip James and Luise (Baumann) A.; m. Grace Kunselman, Nov. 7, 1942; children: Robert Stephen, Sally Ann. BSChemE with distinction, U. Rochester, 1939. Registered profl. engr., Pa. Rsch. engr. Floridin Co., Warren, Pa., 1939-45, asst. tech. dir., 1945-46, v.p., tech. dir., 1946-48; sr. rsch. engr. Johns-Manville Rsch. Ctr., Finderne, N.J., 1948-51; staff asst. Gulf Rsch. and Devel. Co., Harmarville, Pa., 1951-58, acting sect. head fuels, 1958-60, sr. project engr. mktg. tech. div., 1960-65, staff engr. mktg. tech. div., 1965-82; cons. in fuels Glenshaw, Pa., 1982—; cons. Biennial Fuels and Lubes Conf., Am., British, Canadian, Australian Navies, London, Ottawa, Sydney, Washington, 1967-81. Patentee desulfurizing absorbent, axial intake and exhaust turbine, apparatus for skimming oil from water; contbr. articles to profl. jours. Mem. ASME (chmn. fuels div. 1974-75), Am. Inst. Chem. Engrs., Am. Soc. Energy Engrs. (cert. cogeneration specialist). Republican. Presbyterian. Home and Office: 212 Lucille St Glenshaw PA 15116-2033

AMES, CHRISTOPHER NORMAN, lawyer; b. Mesa, Ariz., Oct. 5, 1953; s. Norman and Muriel (Combs) A.; m. JoAnn E. Manson, June 12, 1979; children: Jennifer Lisa, Jeffrey Manson. AB, Harvard U., 1975; JD, Case Western Res. U., 1979; LLM, Boston U., 1980. Bar: Mass. 1979. Tax mgr. Prime Computer, Inc., Natick, Mass., 1980-86, Symbolics, Inc., Cambridge, Mass., 1986-87; v.p., dir. corp. tax, fin. svcs. Houghton Mifflin Co., Boston, 1987—. Home: 14 Washington St Beverly MA 01915-5820 Office: Houghton Mifflin Co 1 Beacon St Boston MA 02108-3106

AMES, DAVID ATWATER, religious organization administrator, chaplain; b. Glendale, Ohio, Sept. 12, 1938; m. Carol Landau, Jan. 30, 1982; children: John, Robert. BA, Miami U., Oxford, Ohio, 1960; MDiv, Episcopal Theol. Sch., 1966; D of Ministry, Episcopal Div. Sch., 1984. Ordained deacon, 1966, ordained priest, 1967. Asst. min. Ch. of St. Edward, Columbus, Ohio, 1966-68; priest-in-charge Ch. of St. Edward, Columbus, 1968-69; asst. min. Grace Ch., Providence, 1969-71; Ecumenical chaplain R.I. Coll., Providence, 1971-74; Episcopal chaplain Brown U., Providence, 1974—; clin. asst. prof. of community health Brown U. Sch. of Medicine, 1992—; Protestant chaplain Patrick I. O'Rourke Children's Ctr., 1971-74; bd. mem. div. ministries in higher edn. R.I. State Coun. Chs., 1974—; field edn. supr. Episcopal Div. Sch., Cambridge, 1975—; vicar St. Andrew's By-the-Sea, Little Compton, R.I., 1983; mem. Diocesan Coun., Diocese of R.I., Providence, 1986-89; lectr. in Christian ethics Episcopal Div. Sch., Cambridge, Mass., 1988; convenor Faculty Discussion Group, Providence, 1990-91; pres. Project Com. for Aging 2000, Providence, 1992—; others. Author: Good Genes? Emerging Values for Science, Religion and Society, 1984; contbr. articles to profl. jours. Mem. rsch. and human rights com. Women and Infants Hosp. R.I., 1974-88, bioethics com., 1985-88; bd. dirs. Interfaith Health Care Ministry, R.I., 1983—, pres., 1986-89; health profl. adv. com. R.I. Chpt. March of Dimes, 1985—; bd. dirs. Planned Parenthood, R.I., 1989—, Hospice Care of R.I., Inc., 1988—; others. With U.S. Army, 1961-63, Korea. Mem. ACLU, Assn. for Religion and Intellectual Life (exec. dir. 1989—), Episcopal Peace Fellowship, Episcopal Soc. for Ministry in Higher Edn., Nat. Conf. for Christians and Jews (resource scholar 1989), Soc. for Health and Human Values, Amnesty Internat. Home: 130 Slater Ave Providence RI 02906 Office: Brown Univ Box 1931 Providence RI 02912

AMES, LOUISE BATES, child psychologist; b. Portland, Maine, Oct. 29, 1908; d. Samuel Lewis and Annie Earle (Leach) Bates; m. Smith Whittier Ames, May 22, 1930 (div. 1937); 1 child, Joan Ames Chase. A.B., U. Maine, 1930, M.A., 1933, Sc.D., 1957; Ph.D., Yale U., 1936; D.Sc., Wheaton Coll., 1967. Cert. psychologist, Conn. Research sec., personal asst. to Dr. Gesell Yale Clinc Child Devel., Yale Med. Sch., 1933-36, instr., 1940-44, asst. prof., 1944-50; curator Yale Films of Child Devel., 1944-50; co-founder Gesell Inst. Child Devel., dir. research, sec.-treas., 1950-65, asso. dir., chief psychologist, 1968, co-dir., 1971-77, acting dir., 1978, assoc. dir., 1978—; lectr. Child Study Ctr., Yale U., 1991—. Syndicated newspaper columnist Parents Ask; host weekly TV broadcast on child behavior, WBZ, Boston, 1952-55; author 36 books including: (with others) The Gesell Institute's Child from One to Six; editorial bd. Jour. Learning Disabilities, Jour. Genetic Psychology. Mem. Conn. Psychol. Soc., Am. Psychol. Soc., Soc. Rsch. Child Devel., Internat. Coun. Psychologists (dir. 1945-47), Soc. Projective Techniques (pres. 1970), Sigma Xi. Home: 283 Edwards St New Haven CT 06511-3719 Office: Gesell Inst Child Devel 310 Prospect St New Haven CT 06511-2188

AMES, MARC L., lawyer; b. Bklyn., Mar. 14, 1943; s. Arthur L. and Ray (Sardas) A.; m. Eileen Moll, July 12, 1970. JD, Bklyn. Law Sch., 1967; LLM, NYU, 1968. Bar: N.Y. 1967, U.S. Dist. Ct. (ea. and so. dist.) N.Y. 1973, U.S. Ct. Appeals (2nd cir.) 1973, U.S. Supreme Ct. 1973, U.S. Ct. Appeals (3rd cir.) 1982; cert. arbitrator U.S. Dist. Ct. (ea. dist.) N.Y., 1986, Pa. 1988. Mem. faculty L.I. U., 1968-69, N.Y.C. Community Coll., 1969-70; pvt. practice, 1967—; arbitrator U.S. Dist. Ct. (ea. dist.) N.Y., 1986—; cons. disability retirement and pensions; arbitrator Am. Arbitration Assn.; chmn., chief exec. officer A&J Enterprises, Inc.; bd. dirs. Internat. Communications Concepts, Inc. Contbr. articles to profl. jours.; patentee bridge for billiards, storage materials for sport card collections, auto mirror. Recipient cert. appreciation N.Y. State Trial Lawyers, commendation for disting. svc. as arbitrator. Mem. N.Y. State Trial Lawyers Assn., N.Y. County Lawyers, N.Y. State Bar Assn., Electronic Technol. Soc. N.J. Inc. Office: 225 Broadway Rm 3005 New York NY 10007-3034

AMES, PETER JOHN, museum administrator; b. Rome, May 13, 1945; married; 2 children. AB in European History magna cum laude, Harvard U., 1967, JD, 1971; postgrad. internat. studies, Johns Hopkins U., Italy, 1968. Bar: Conn. 1971, N.Y. 1972, Mass. 1974. Asst. to asst. sec. internat. affairs U.S. Treasury, 1971; asst. counsel, sec. Met. Mus. Art, N.Y.C., 1971-73; staff counsel AAUP, 1973-75; counsel, sec. NYU, N.Y.C., 1975-79; dir. fin. and adminstrn. Assn. for Voluntary Surg. Construction, N.Y.C., 1986-92, New England Aquarium, 1982-86; v.p. edn. and special programs Boston Mus. Sci., 1986—; cons. Ford Found., 1979, Worldpaper, Boston, 1979, Mus. Trustees Corp., 1987, Arthur D. Little, Inc., 1987-89; corporator Brookline Savs. Bank, 1983—; mem. Am. Assn. Musicians Accreditation Vis. Com. Roster, 1989—; lectr. in field. Contbr. articles to profl. jours. Trustee Internat. Union for Conservation of Nature, 1987—, cons., 1986; trustee, chmn. Coolidge Ctr. Environ. Leadership, 1985-89; trustee, treas. Cambridge (Mass.) Multicultural Arts Ctr., 1983-88, Young Audiences Mass., 1984-86; trustee, chmn. program com. New England Sports Mus., 1987—; trustee, chmn. exec. com. Assn. Vol. Surg. Contraception, 1976—; alumni dir. St. Paul's Sch., 1979-84; gen. fifts chmn. Harvard Class 1967, 1980-84. Kellogg resident in Mus. Edn., Smithsonian Inst., 1985. Address: 90 Ivy St Brookline MA 02146

AMES, STANLEY RICHARD, biochemist; b. Madison, Wis., Dec. 18, 1918; s. Walter Ray and Mary Ellen (Fruit) A.; m. Edwina Gray Powers, Aug. 19, 1943; children: Edwina Marie, Stanley Richard Jr., Suzanne Claire, Judith Ann. BA, U. Mont., 1940; AM in Chemistry, Columbia U., 1942, PhD in Chemistry, 1944. Postdoctoral fellow in biochemistry U. Wis., Madison, 1943-46; from sr. rsch. chemist to dir. biochem. rsch. lab. Eastman Kodak Co., Rochester, N.Y., 1946-70; from biochem. rsch. lab. supr. to rsch. fellow Tenn. Eastman Rsch. Lab., Rochester, 1970-82; cons. Nutritional Biochemistry, Rochester, 1982—. Contbr. chpts. in books, articles to profl. jours. Leader and adminstr. Boy Scouts Am., Rochester, 1950-64. Fellow AAAS, Am. Inst. Nutrition (chmn. nomenclature com. 1964-71, nominating com. mem. 1971); mem. Am. Chem. Soc. (Rochester sect. editor 1956-57, editorial advisor 1958-59, mgr. 1959-60, vice chmn. 1961, chmn. 1962, councilor, 1965-68), Am. Soc. Biol. Chemists, Assn. Ofcl. Analytical Chemists (assoc. referee 1972-82), Internat. Union Nutritional Scis. (acting chmn. nomenclature com. 1969, 75, chmn. 1976-86), Internat. Union of Pure and Applied Chemistry (interdiv. com. Nomenclature and symbols 1976-84), Animal Nutrition Rsch. Coun. (chmn. tech. projects com. 1958-60, vice-chmn. 1959-60, chmn. 1960-61), Rochester Acad. Sci., Nutrition Soc. Grt.

Britain, Phi Mu Epsilon, Phi Sigma, Sigma Xi, Phi Lambda Upsilon. Home: 61 Biltmore Dr Rochester NY 14617-3107

AMES, STEVEN REEDE, financial planner; b. Washington, Aug. 15, 1951; s. Reede Maughan and Mary (Soderberg) A. BS in Bus. Adminstrn., U. Md., 1973; MPA, Am. U., 1976; cert., Fin. Planning Coll., Denver, 1986. CFP. Specialist bus. financing Gov.'s Office State Del., Dover, 1978-83; exec. v.p. Econ. and Bus. Devel. Corp. Montgomery County, Rockville, Md., 1983-85; owner, operator Scarborough Ames and Assocs., Annapolis, Md., 1986—; instr. Anne Arundel Community Coll., Annapolis, 1987—. Mem. Anne Arundel County Drug and Alcohol Adv. Coun.; steering com. Annapolis Com. Partnership; bd. dirs. Annapolis Boys and Girls Club, Alliance for Drug Free Annapolis, Cen. Md. chpt. ARC, 1990—. Mem. Nat. Assn. Personal Fin. Advisors, Annapolis C. of C. (Mem. of Yr. 1990, bd. dirs.), Hist. Annapolis Found., Kiwanis (bd. dirs. 1986—, pres. 1989-90), Md. Soc. Accts.

AMES, THOMAS-ROBERT HOWLAND, educator, psychotherapist; b. Daytona Beach, Fla., Feb. 22, 1930; s. Orris Kingsley and Helen-Margarett Geraldine (Reed) A. AA, U. Fla., Gainesville, 1951, BA, 1952; MA, NYU, 1960, EdD, 1981. Diplomate Am. Bd. Sexology; cert. sex educator, counselor, therapist Am. Assn. Sex Educators, Counselors and Therapists, rehab. counselor. Purchasing asst. Beckman-Downtown Hosp., N.Y.C., 1954-56; claims adjuster Liberty Mutual Ins. Co., N.Y.C., 1956-58; dir. programs for mentally disabled The Eastern Sch., N.Y.C., 1960-66; dir. of programs The Young Adult Inst., N.Y.C., 1966-67, exec. dir., 1967-71; dir. day camp for retarded children The Mental Retardation Inst. of N.Y. Med. Coll., N.Y.C., 1971; dir. community residence program Nassau County Assn. for Children with Learning Disabilities, Hempstead, N.Y., 1974-80; prof. human svcs. Borough of Manhattan Community Coll., CUNY, N.Y.C., 1970—; mem. steering com. CUNY consortium for developmental disabilities studies, N.Y.C., 1991—; reviewer Nat. Info. Ctr. for Children and Youth with Handicaps, 1989—; examiner Am. Bd. Sexology; cons., task force on developmental disabilities Nat. Coun. of the Chs. of Christ in U.S., 1986-88; pres. Coalition on Sexuality and Disability, 1984-88. Author: (with others) Modification of Behavior of the Mentally Ill, 1974, Handbook on Learning Disabilities, 1974; mem. editorial bd. Compendium of Sexology, 1980—; cons. editor Jour. of Sex and Marital Therapy; contbr. numerous articles to profl. jours. Chmn. bd. dirs. The N.Y. League for Early Learning, Inc., N.Y.C., 1992—; v.p., vice chair, bd. trustees Young Adult Inst., N.Y.C., 1983—; v.p., sec. United World Partnership on D.D., Inc., N.Y.C., 1988—. Recipient Citation for Outstanding Vol. Svcs., Gov. Cuomo, 1987, Disting. Svc. award Young Adult Inst., 1981, Leadership and Svc. award Nassau County ACLD, 1979, Meritorious Svcs. award Nat. Rehab. Assn., 1973, Community Mental Health Soc. of B.M.C.C. award, 1981, Anne H. Berkman Meml. award Coalition on Sexuality and Disability, 1989. Fellow Am. Assn. on Mental Retardation (region 10 exec. bd. 1973-74, Profl. award 1991), Am. Orthopsychiat. Assn., Am. Acad. Clin. Sexologists (clin.), Royal Soc. Health, Nat. Rehab. Counseling Assn. (pres. met. N.Y.C. chpt. 1974, exec. bd. N.E. region 1974, leadership award 1974), Am. Soc. Group Psychotherapy and Psychodrama; mem. Halifax Hist. Soc., Order of Crown of Charlemagne in U.S.A., Gen. Soc. Mayflower Descs., N.Y. Geneal. and Biographical Soc., Hereditary Order of Descs. of Colonial Govs. Democrat. Episcopalian. Office: BMCC CUNY 199 Chambers St # N614 New York NY 10007

AMESTOY, JEFFREY LEE, lawyer, state official; b. Rutland, Vt., July 24, 1946; s. William Joseph and Diana (Wood) A.; m. Susan Claire Lonergan, May 24, 1980; children: Katherine Leigh, Christina Elizabeth, Nancy Claire. B.A., Hobart Coll., 1968; J.D., U. Calif., San Francisco, 1972; M.P.A., Harvard U., 1982. Bar: Vt. 1973, U.S. Dist. Ct. Vt. 1973. Assoc. Mahady & Klevana, Windsor, Vt., 1973-74; legal counsel Gov.'s Justice Commn., Montpelier, Vt., 1974-77; asst. atty. gen., chief of Medicaid fraud div. State of Vt., Montpelier, 1978-81, commr. labor and industry, 1982-84, atty. gen., 1985—; mem. Vt. Criminal Rules Adv. Com., Montpelier, 1985—, Vt. Bd. Forests and Parks, Montpelier, 1985—; chmn. Ea. Regional Conf. Attys. Gen., 1988-90. Trustee Thomas Waterman Wood Gallery, Montpelier, 1986—. With USAR, 1968-74. Mem. Nat. Assn. Attys. Gen.(pres. 1992), Vt. Bar Assn. Republican. Congregationalist. Home: RR 2 Box 170 Waterbury VT 05676-9727 Office: Office of Atty Gen 109 State St Montpelier VT 05602-2700

AMIRAN, MINDARAE, English educator, consultant; b. Gary, Ind., Oct. 22, 1932; m. Nahum Amiran; children: Edoh, Eyal. AB in Gen. Edn., U. Chgo., 1951; BA in Psychology, Swarthmore Coll., 1953; MA in English, Radcliffe Coll., 1954; PhD, Hebrew U., Jerusalem, 1968. Lectr. Hebrew U., 1956-66; sr. lectr. Tel Aviv U., 1966-76, acting chair English dept., 1969-70, 75-76; cons. Bd. Edn. Chgo. Pub. Schs., 1978-81; dean spl. programs and gen. studies SUNY, Fredonia, N.Y., 1981-90, prof. English Dept., 1981—; cons. assessment various colls., 1987—; proposal reviewer Fund for the Improvement Postsecondary Edn., Dept. Edn., Washington, 1988—; evaluator Mid. States Assn. Schs. and Colls., Phila., 1986. Editor: English for Speakers of Hebrew, 1974, literature volumes in series; contbr. articles to profl. jours. Letterwriter Amnesty Internat., USA, 1983—. Mem. AAUW (scholarship chair Dunkirk-Fredonia br. 1983—), Modern Lang. Assn., Am. Ednl. Rsch. Assn., Wallace Stevens Soc., Phi Beta Kappa. Office: English Dept SUNY Coll at Fredonia Fredonia NY 14063

AMMERMAN, ROBERT THOMPSON, clinical psychologist; b. Madison, Wis., Mar. 4, 1959; s. Robert Ray and Joyce (Thompson) A.; m. Caroline Helm Bennett, June 1, 1985; 1 child, Patrick Bennett. AB, Vassar Coll., 1981; MS, U. Pitts., 1984, PhD, 1986. Supr. rsch. and clin. psychology Western Pa. Sch. for Blind Children, Pitts., 1986—; asst. prof. psychiatry U. Pitts. Sch. Medicine, 1989—; lectr. in psychology U. Pitts., 1986—; pvt. practice Sewickley, Pa., 1988—. Editor: (books) Children at Risk, 1990, Treatment of Family Violence, 1990, Case Studies in Family Violence., 1991. Grantee Nat. Inst. on Disabilities and Rehab. Rsch., U.S. Dept. Edn., 1987-90, 91-94, Vira I. Heinz Endowment, Pitts., 1988-91. Mem. Am. Psychol. Assn., Assn. for Advancement of Behavior Therapy, Internat. Soc. for the Prevention of Child Abuse and Neglect. Home: 1304 Beaver Rd Sewickley PA 15143-2008 Office: Western Pa Sch for Blind Children 201 N Bellefield Ave Pittsburgh PA 15213-1499

AMON PARISI, CRISTINA HORTENSIA, mechanical engineering educator, researcher; b. Montevideo, Uruguay, Oct. 12, 1956; came to U.S., 1983; d. Mirko Miroslav and Marisa (Kovacic) A.; m. Carmelo Parisi, Dec. 6, 1980; children: Andreina, Gabriel. Student, Universidad Simon Bolivar, Caracas, Venezuela, 1981; MSME, MIT, 1985, DSc in Mech. Engring., 1988. Instr., researcher Universidad Simon Bolivar, Caracas, 1981-83; rsch. and teaching asst. MIT, Cambridge, Mass., 1984-88; asst. prof. Carnegie-Mellon U., Pitts., 1988—; cons. Aavid, Laconia, N.H., 1986, Vanzetti Systems, Stoughton, Mass., 1986, Tex. Instruments, Calif., 1987, Bally Design, Inc., Pitts., 1988. Recipient Rsch. Initiation award NSF, G.T. Ladd award. Mem. ASME, AIAA, SAE, Sci. Rsch. Soc., Am. Soc. Engring. Educators, Venezuelan Soc. Mech. and Elec. Engrs., Soc. Women Engrs., Sigma Xi. Office: Carnegie Mellon U Dept Mech Engring Pittsburgh PA 15213

AMORE, MICHAEL JOSEPH, financial executive; b. N.Y.C., Dec. 13, 1947; s. Leonard Ralph and Bianca (Vettori) A.; BS, St. John's U., 1969; MBA, Hofstra U., 1983; m. Arlene Frances Fasullo, Sept. 19, 1970. Asst. controller Olympus Corp., Lake Success, N.Y., 1979-80, controller, 1980-83, dir. fin., 1984— , also mem. exec. com. CPA, N.Y. Mem. Am. Inst. CPAs, N.Y. Soc. CPAs. Home: 149 Cornell Dr Commack NY 11725-2526 Office: Olympus Corp 4 Nevada Dr New Hyde Park NY 11042-1179

AMOROSO, ALISON MARIA, social services executive; b. N.J., July 7, 1965; d. Joseph Anthony and Antonette Dorothy (Marchese) A. BS in Human Devel., Duke U., 1987; MEd in Counseling, Harvard U., 1990. Counselor, tchr. Md. Leadership Workshop, 1983-85; research aide Found. for Rsch. of Nature of Man, Durham, N.C., 1984-86; recreation therapist Duke U. Med. Ctr., Durham, 1984-87; student counselor Duke U. Psychology Clinic, Durham, 1985-87; executive assistant; school clinician Robert White Sch., Boston, 1988-90; social worker III Dept. Social Svcs., Dorchester, Mass., 1991—; founder, exec. dir. Women Express, Inc., Boston, 1988—. Editor: Teen Voices mag., 1988—; contbr. articles to profl. jours. Recipient Citizenship award DAR, 1983. Mem. NOW. Democrat. Home: 145 Chestnut Ave Jamaica Plain MA 02130 Office: Women Express Inc 14 Beacon St Ste 604 Boston MA 02108 also: PO Box 6009 JFK Boston MA 02114

AMOROSO, MARIE DOROTHY, retired EEG technologist; b. Phila., Jan. 16, 1924; d. Salvatore and Clorinda (Gaudio) A. Med. Lab. Tech., Hahnemann Hosp., Phila., 1943; postgrad., Temple U., Phila., 1945-48, U. Pa., Phila., 1947-48, 1950. Registered EEG Technologist; cert. registered EEG Technologist. EEG technician Hahnemann Med. Coll., Phila., 1943-53, Phila. Gen. Hosp., 1953-62; histology technician Temple Med. Coll. Temple U., Phila., 1962-63; allergy technician Harry Rogers, M.D., Phila., 1963; EEG technologist Haverford (Pa.) State Hosp., 1963-85, Irvin M. Gerson, MD, Haverford, 1985-88; EEG technologist to pvt. physician Haverford State Hosp., 1985-88; ret., 1988; instr. EEG Osteopathic Med. Ctr. Sch. Allied Health, Phila., 1978-85. Editor: The Eastern Breeze, 1977-79; contbr. articles to profl. jours.; patentee in field. Mem. Am. Soc. Electroneurodiagnostic Technologists Inc., Western Soc. Electrodiagnostic Technologists, So. Soc. EEG Technicians Inc., Ea. Soc. EEG and Neurodiagnostic Technicians (sec. 1977-79), Phila. Regional EEG Technician's Assn. (exec. bd. 1967, sec., 1969), Electro-Physiological Technologists Assn. Gt. Britain (subscriber mem.), Ea. Ass. Electroencephalographers (subscriber mem.). Home: 477 Brookfield Rd Drexel Hill PA 19026-1198

AMOROSO, VINCENT, accounting company executive; b. Caserta, Campagna, Italy, Oct. 28, 1947; s. Salvatore and Madelina (Cristillo) A.; m. Mary E. Gleason, Mar. 28, 1968 (div. 1971); m. Tamson W. Milton, Mar. 14, 1981; 1 child, Michael V. BS in Maths., SUNY, Albany, 1970. Actuarial trainee Aetna Life & Cos., Hartford, Conn., 1970-73; sr. actuary IRS, Washington, 1973-76, 79-81; cons. actuary Wyatt Co., Washington, 1976-79; chief actuary Pension Benefitr Guaranty Corp., Washington, 1981-85; ptnr., actuary KPMG Peat Marwick, Washington, 1985—. Contbr. articles to profl. jours. Trustee Arlington (Va.) Unitarian Ch., 1984-86. Fellow Soc. Actuaries (chair pension sect. 1987-90, pension rsch. coun. 1982—), Conf. Cons. Actuaries; mem. Am. Acad. Actuaries. Office: KPMG Peat Marwick 2001 M St NW Washington DC 20036

AMORUSO, DONALD JOSEPH, electronics company executive, consultant; b. Mt. Vernon, N.Y., July 15, 1937; s. Frank and Carmella (Triano) A.; m. Marie Z. Zuzzolo, Dec. 25, 1960; children: Donna-Marie, Donald J., Michael. BSEE, Manhattan Coll., 1959; MSEE, Poly. U. N.Y., 1965. V.p. adv. programs United Technologies Corp./Norden Systems, Inc., Norwalk, Conn., 1978-81, v.p. program mgmt. and contracts, 1981-84, sr. v.p., gen. mgr., 1984-88; sr. v.p. L.I. ops. United Technologies Corp./Norden Systems, Inc., Melville, N.Y., 1988-91; pres. DMA Assocs., Pleasantville, 1992—. Inventor of monopulse radar system of high accuracy and resolution, 1969. Trustee, pres. Pocantico Hills (N.Y.) Cen. Sch. Bd. Edn., 1972-82; trustee U.S. Marine Corps Command & Staff Coll. Found., 1985-91; campaign chmn. United Way, 1988-90. Poly. U. fellow, 1985. Mem. Assn. of U.S. Army (trustee 1981-91, Leadership award 1985). Home: 463 Old Sleepy Hollow Rd Pleasantville NY 10570-3809 Office: DMA Assocs 463 Old Sleepy Hollow Rd Pleasantville NY 10570-3809

AMPARADO, KEITH D., communications company executive; b. Bklyn., Oct. 5, 1952; m. Arcadeo and Sadie J. (Browne) A. BS, SUNY, Saratoga Springs. Supr. data processing Franklin Nat. Bank/European Am. Bank, 1974-78; mgr. Ctr. for Computing Activity Columbia U., N.Y.C., 1978-80; systems analyst Morgan Guaranty Trust Co., 1980-81; programmer, analyst Europen Am. Bank, 1981-83; sr. editor Mfrs. Hanover Trust, 1983-85; founder, pres. KDA Communications, Bklyn., 1985—; cons. Siloam Presbyn. Ch., Bklyn., 1988—. Mem. Soc. for Tech. Communication (sr.), Am. Mgmt. Assn., Am. Mktg. Assn., Mktg. Rsch. Assn., Nat. Assn. Desktop Pubs., Qualitative Rsch. Cons. Assn., Internat. Assn. of Bus. Communicators.

AMROD, PAUL JOSEPH, counselor; b. Saugerties, N.Y., Nov. 9, 1926; s. Ablen and Mary (Lahoud) A.; m. Jennifer Delores Mosquera, June 4, 1966. BS, SUNY, Cortland, 1950; MEd, St. Lawrence U., 1957; EdD, Nova U., 1977. Dir. athletics Chateaugay (N.Y.) Pub. Schs., 1950-58, dir. guidance, 1958-60; chmn. guidance Spring Valley (N.Y.) Sr. High Sch., 1960-86; coord. counseling Ft. Lee (N.J.) High Sch., 1987—; cons. City of Boston, 1985, Coll. Bds., N.Y.C., 1975-79; conductor workshops in field. Contbr. articles to profl. jours. Cubmaster Boy Scouts Am., Chateaugay, 1955-58, scoutmaster, 1950-55. With U.S. Army, 1944-46. Mem. Bergen County Dirs. of Guidance (pres. 1990—), Bergen County Profl. Counselors (1st v.p. 1989—), N.J. Profl. Counselors (exec. bd. 1987-89), Rotary. Democrat. Roman Catholic. Office: Fort Lee High Sch 3000 Lemoine Ave Fort Lee NJ 07024-6105

AMRON, IRVING, physical chemist, consultant; b. Bayonne, N.J., Jan. 18, 1921; s. Abe and Bertha (Fradin) A.; m. Bernice Beispel, Mar. 21, 1942; children: Arlene Joy (dec.), Steven Carl (dec.). BA, NYU, 1941, MS, 1944, PhD, 1949. Sr. chemist Manhattan Project, N.Y.C., 1944-46; instr. chemistry NYU, N.Y.C., 1946-47; rsch. assoc. Textile Found., Princeton, N.J., 1947-49; rsch. assoc. engring. div. NYU, N.Y.C., 1949-50; sr. chemist GE, Schenectady, 1950-52, Sylvania Electric Products, N.Y.C., 1952-54; mem. tech. staff AT&T Bell Labs., Murray Hill, N.J., 1954-87; cons. Amron Cons. Svc., Inc., Livingston, N.J., 1987—. Contbr. articles to Jour. Electrochem. Soc., Electrochem. Tech., Jour. Am. Chem. Soc., Jour. Chem. Edn. Fellow Am. Inst. Chemists; mem. AAAS, Am. Chem. Soc., Assn. Cons. Chemists and Chem. Engrs., Electrochem. Soc., Assn. for Computing Machinery, Sigma Xi, Phi Lambda Upsilon (pres. N.Y. chpt. 1941-42). Office: Amron Cons Svc Inc 19 Lexington Dr Livingston NJ 07039-4303

AMSLER, JOSEPH WILLIAM, JR., poet; b. Wilkinsburg, Pa., Mar. 13, 1954; s. Joseph William Amsler Sr. and Lorraine Lee (Hipple) Van Horne; m. Elizabeth A. Borandi (div. 1984). Student, Community Coll. Allegheny County, Boyce, 1975-76, 83-84. Author (poems): Pausings: Over & Under the World, 1989, 90, A Collection of 14 Poems of Comment, 1990, Seasonal Living...Spring Through Autumn & Winter...Seasonal Living, 1990.

AMY-MORENO DE TORO, ANGEL ALBERTO, social sciences educator, writer, oral historian; b. San Juan, P.R., Jan. 10, 1945; s. Alberto Sadi Amy-Ramirez and Maria de los Angelews Moreno Ledesma; m. Ana E. Cordero-Amy, May 30, 1973; children: Denise Yahara, Elberto Enrique, Juan Carlos. BA, U. P.R., Rio Piedras, 1968; MA, SUNY, Fredonia, 1972; EdD, Boston U., 1982, postgrad. in history, 1982—. Asst. librarian U. P.R., Rio Piedras, 1968-69; tchr. social studies Juan José Osuna Middle Sch., Hato Rey, P.R., 1969, Mother Cabrini Cath. Sch., Caparra Heights, P.R., 1969-70; instr. humanities U. P.R., Arecibo, 1970-74; lectr. in history Interam. U. P.R., San Juan, 1974-75; elem. tchr. Newton (Mass.) Pub. Schs., 1975—; prof., chair social scis. Roxbury Community Coll., Boston, 1975—; photography curator Galeria Labiosa, Boston and San Juan, 1984—. Writer, photographer El Mundo Newspaper, Cambridge, Mass., 1980-90; corr., photographer El Carrillon Newspaper, Andover, Mass., 1991—, Galeria Art Mag., San Juan, 1992—. Chair edn. com. State Adv. Bd. on Affirmative Action, Boston, 1988-91; chair Affirmative Action, Ward 19 Democratic Party, Boston, 1990-92; mem. history com. Commn. for Celebration of 500 Yr. Anniversary Discovery of P.R., 1986—. Recipient Puerto Rican Art Excellence award Mass. P.R. Festival, Inc., 1987, Outstanding Recognition award Senate of Commonwealth of P.R., 1990, others. Mem. New Eng. Spanish Inst., Oficina Hispana de la Comunidad (pres. bd. dirs. 1985-87), Jamaica Plain Arts Coun. (sec. bd. dirs. 1986-87), Oral History Assn. Am. (publs. com. 1987—), Hispanic Lions Club Boston (v.p. 1986-88). Roman Catholic. Home: 12 Holbrook St Boston MA 02130 Office: Roxbury Community Coll 1234 Columbus Ave Boston MA 02120

ANABLE, DAVID JOHN, educator; b. Exeter, Devon, England, June 7, 1939; came to U.S., 1966; s. Arthur and Joan Winifred (Bruford) A.; m. Isobel Anne Peacock, Sept. 4, 1965; children: Alexandra, Tessa, Perryn. MA, Cambridge (England) U., 1962; diploma in agrl. econs., Oxford (England) U., 1963. Rsch. officer Conservative Party, London, 1963-65; fgn. coor. Christian Sci. Monitor, London, 1965-66; fgn. desk Christian Sci. Monitor, Boston, 1966-73; UN coor., bureau chief Christian Sci. Monitor, N.Y.C., 1974-78; fgn. editor Christian Sci. Monitor, Boston, 1978-86, managing editor, 1986-88; prof., chmn. Boston U., 1989—; exec. sec. Mass Press Assn., Boston, 1989—; cons. Maine Times, Topsham, 1990; juror Pulitzer Prizes, N.Y.C., 1989, 90, Sigma Delta Chi Nat. Awards; speaker in field. Contbr. articles to profl. jours. Mem. adv. bd. Camden (Maine) Conf. Fgn. Affairs, 1989—, Cambridge (Mass.) Forum, 1991—; bd. dirs. Young Authors Found., Newton, Mass., 1990—. Mem. New England Press Assn., Assn. Educators in Journalism & Mass Communication, Com. to Protect Journalists, Soc. Profl. Journalists, Associated Press Managing Editors, Trustees of Reservations. Office: Boston U Sch Journalism 640 Commonwealth Ave Boston MA 02215-2422

ANAGNOSTOPOULOS, CONSTANTINE NICHOLAS, electrical engineer, scientist, researcher; b. Patras, Greece, July 4, 1944; came to U.S., 1963; s. Nicholas C. and Efrosyne (Bisgounis) A.; m. Eleni Stavrinoudis, Aug. 31, 1969; children: Effie K., Athena T. BSEE, Merrimack Coll., 1967; MS in Elec. Sci., Brown U., 1971; PhDEE, U. R.I., 1975. Rsch. physicist Rsch. Labs. Eastman Kodak Co., Rochester, N.Y., 1975-79; sr. rsch. physicist Rsch. Labs, Eatman Kodak Co., Rochester, N.Y., 1979-82, rsch. asst., mem. sr. staff, 1982—; mgr. ASIC design group Microelectronics Tech. div. Eastman Kodak Co., Rochester, N.Y., 1985-90, chmn. fuzzy logic coun., 1991—; founder Custom Integrated Cirs. Conf., Rochester, 1979—. Contbr. numerous articles to profl. jours.; numerous patents in field. Chmn. fund raising com., co-founder Mendon Dem. Com., 1991. Mem. IEEE (sr., chmn. Rochester sect. 1982-83, assoc. editor Jour. Solid State Circuits 1989—, Elec. Engr. of the Yr. 1988, Centenial Medal 1984), Hellenic Cultural Soc. Rochester. Greek Orthodox. Home: 100 Drumlin View Dr Mendon NY 14506-9708 Office: Eastman Kodak Co Rsch Labs Rochester NY 14650

ANANIA, WILLIAM CHRISTIAN, podiatrist; b. Long Branch, N.J., May 11, 1958; s. Joseph John and Marie (Forgione) A.; m. Pamela Capone, Dec. 18, 1982; 1 child, William Christian Jr. BS in Biology, Villanova U., 1980; D of Podiatric Medicine, Ohio Coll. Podiatric Medicine, 1984. Diplomate Nat. Bd. Podiatry Examiners. Resident James C. Giuffré Med. Ctr., Phila., 1984-86; pvt. practice Middletown, N.J., 1986—; cons. Fern Med., Boston, 1991. Chmn. editorial review bd. The Contemporary Podiatric Physician; assoc. editor: Jour. Current Podiatric Medicine, 1986-89; contbr. numerous articles to profl. jours. Dir. Middletown (N.J.) Area C. of C., 1988-90, 2d v.p., 1990-91. Named Dr. of the Month Jour. Current Podiatric Medicine, 1986. Fellow Am. Soc. Podiatric Medicine, Am. Soc. Podiatric Dermatology, Nat. Soc. Concious Sedation (med. advisor 1989—); mem. Am. Coll. Foot Surgeons, Am. Podiatric Med. Assn. Home: 112 Tindall Rd Middletown NJ 07748-2327 Office: 112 Tindall Rd # 673 Middletown NJ 07748-2327

ANANIAN, JOYCE LUCILLE, guidance counselor; b. Newburyport, Mass., May 28, 1948; d. Meron and Roxie (Dasdagulian) A.; m. Kevin Rowe Currie, July 28, 1984. MEd, Boston Coll., 1972; MLS, Simmons Coll., 1979. Guidance counselor Natick (Mass.) Pub. Schs., 1972—. Deacon First Congl. Ch. of Waverley, Belmont, Mass., 1991. Mem. AACD. Office: Wilson Middle Sch 24 Rutledge Rd Natick MA 01760-1764

ANASTASI, ANNE (MRS. JOHN PORTER FOLEY, JR.), psychology educator; b. N.Y.C., Dec. 19, 1908; d. Anthony and Theresa (Gaudiosi) A.; m. John Porter Foley, Jr., July 26, 1933. A.B., Barnard Coll., 1928; Ph.D., Columbia U., 1930; Litt.D. (hon.), U. Windsor, Can., 1967; Sc.D. (hon.), Cedar Crest Coll., 1971, La Salle Coll., 1979, Fordham U., 1979; Paed.D. (hon.), Villanova U., 1971. Instr. psychology Barnard Coll., N.Y.C., 1930-39; asst. prof., chmn. dept. Queens Coll., N.Y.C., 1939-46; assoc. prof. psychology Fordham U., N.Y.C., 1947-51; prof. Fordham U., 1951-79, prof. emeritus, 1979—, chmn. dept. psychology, 1968-74; mem. NRC, 1952-55; pres. Am. Psychol. Found., 1965-67. Author: Differential Psychology, 1937, rev. edit., 1949, 58, Psychological Testing, 1954, 6th edit., 1988, Fields of Applied Psychology, 1964, 2d edit., 1979; also articles in field.; editor: Individual Differences, 1965, Testing Problems in Perspective, 1966; Contributions to Differential Psychology, 1982. Recipient award for disting. service to measurement Ednl. Testing Service, 1977, award disting. contbns. to research Am. Ednl. Research Assn., 1983, Gold medal Am. Psychol. Found., 1984, Nat. Medal of Science, 1987. Mem. APA (rec. sec. 1952-55, pres. div. gen. psychology 1956-57, bd. dirs. 1956-59, 68-70, pres. div. evaluation and measurement 1965-66, pres. 1971-72, Disting. Sci. award 1981, E. L. Thorndike medal div. ednl. psychology 1984), Ea. Psychol. Assn. (pres. 1946-47, dir. 1948-50), Psychonomic Soc., Am. Psychol. Soc., Phi Beta Kappa, Sigma Xi.

ANCES, I. G(EORGE), obstetrician/gynecologist, educator; b. Balt., July 3, 1935; s. Harry and Fanny A.; m. Marlene Roth, Oct. 23, 1966; 1 son, Beau Mark. B.S., U. Md., 1956, M.D., 1959. Diplomate: Am. Bd. Obstetrics and Gynecology. Intern Ohio State U. Hosp., 1959-60; resident in obstetrics and gynecology Univ. Hosp., Balt., 1960-61, 63-65; mem. faculty U. Md. Med. Sch., Balt., 1966—; prof. obstetrics and gynecology U. Md. Med. Sch., 1975-83, dir. labs. obstetrics and gynecol. research and clin. labs., 1967-83, dir. div. adolescent obstetrics and gynecology and family planning, 1981-83;; prof. ob-gyn. Rutgers U. Sch. Medicine,, Camden,, N.J.,, 1983—; chmn. dept., 1983—. Contbr. chpts. to books, articles to profl. jours. Capt. sustaining fund drive Balt. Symphony Orch., Opera Co. Phila.; med. adv. com. Fire Dept. Balt. City. Served with USAF, 1961-63. Fellow Am. Coll. Obstetrics and Gynecology; mem. Endocrine Soc., Soc. Gynecol. Investigation, Soc. Study Reprodn. (charter), Internat. Soc. Rsch. in Biology Reprodn. (charter), Md. Obstetrics and Gynecol. Soc. (sec. 1978-81, dir. 1979—), Med. and Chirurgical Soc. Md., Soc. Adolescent Medicine, Douglas Obstet. and Gynecol. Soc. (pres. 1984—), N.J. State Med. Soc. (chmn. neo-natal coop. So. Jersey 1986—), English Speaking Union, Cooper Found., N.J. Conservation Coun., Harbour League Club, Sigma Xi. Clubs: Maryland, Towson Golf and Country. Home: 1 Lane Of Acres Haddonfield NJ 08033-3504 Office: Rutgers U Sch Medicine Dept Ob-Gyn 3 Cooper Plz Camden NJ 08103-1438

ANCHLIA, THAN MAL, executive; b. Bikaner, Rajasthan, India, Oct. 18, 1918; s. Deokaran and Goura (Nahta) A.; m. Jethi Dey Sethia, Feb. 22, 1938; children: Kanchan, Chandra, Ratna. B in Commerce, St. Xavier Coll., Calcutta, India, 1938. Exec. dir. IMC, N.Y.C., 1975-90. Author: New Dictionary System, 1988. Mem. Rep. Task Force, Washington, 1979-80. Mem. Jain. Office: IMC PO Box 20028 New York NY 10017-0001

ANDERS, ARTHUR FRETZ, III, leasing company executive; b. Norristown, Pa., May 29, 1948; s. Arthur Nice and Emma Louise (Hilderbrand) A.; m. Linda Hallman, Aug. 2, 1969; children: Arthur F. IV, Melissa Dawn. BS in Truck Transp., Ind. U., 1970. Exec. v.p. North Penn Transfer, Lansdale, Pa., 1972-87; pres. White Circle Truck Leasing, Lansdale, 1987—; dir. Middle Atlantic Conf., Washington, 1986-91, Amtralease, St. Louis, 1991—. Dir. North Pa. C. of C., Lansdale, 1974-86, pres., 1975-76; dir. North Pa. United Way, Lansdale, 1980-88, North Pa. YMCA, Lansdale, 1976-82, 88-90. 1st lt. U.S. Army, 1970-72. Recipient Disting. Svc. award Lansdale (Pa.) Jaycees, 1978. Mem. Shiloh Masonic Lodge, Lehigh Consistory, Rajah Shrine. Republican. Home: 697 Godshall Rd Telford PA 18969-2212 Office: White Circle Truck Leasing Rt 202 & 63 PO Box 385 Lansdale PA 19446

ANDERS, GEOFFREY TAYLOR, health care management executive, consultant, lawyer; b. Phila., Oct. 3, 1950; s. W. Marshall and Edna L (O'Hara) A.; m. Dorian L. Strayer, May 22, 1971; children: Geoffrey T., Jason C. BS, LaSalle Coll., 1972; JD, Temple U., 1978. Bar: Pa. 1978; CPA, Pa.; cert. prof. bus. cons. Sr. auditor Arthur Young & Co., Phila., 1971-76; pres., ptnr. Beck and Anders Law Assocs., Inc., Plymouth Meeting, Pa., 1977—; pres., cons. The Health Care Group, Plymouth Meeting, 1977—; guest lectr. U. Pa. Hosp., Pa., 1979-83, U. Calif. , 1982-85, other univ. med. schs.; editorial cons. Pension Investment Strategies, Whitehall, N.Y., 1981—, Physicians' Adv., 1978—. Contbr. articles to profl. jours. Acad. scholar La Salle Coll., 1968-71, senatorial scholar Pa. Legislature, 1976; named Outstanding Young Man of Am., Kiwanis Club, 1982. Mem. ABA, Soc. Med. Dental Cons. (bd. dirs. 1984-90, pres. 1988-89), Found. For Edn. In Healthcare Mgmt. (trustee 1987-90), Inst. Cert. Prof. Bus. Cons. (trustee 1985-87), Soc. Profl. Bus. Cons., Nat. Health Lawyer's Assn., Am. Inst. C.P.A.s, U.S. Chess Fedn. Republican. Home: 505 Beacon Hill Ln Norristown PA 19401-2365 Office: The Health Care Group Inc 140 W Germantown Pike Ste 200 Plymouth Meeting PA 19462-1434

ANDERSEN, JANET LINDA, molecular biologist; b. Jacksonville, Fla., Mar. 3, 1947; d. William D. Free and Sarah Rebeccah (Kempner) Dohanich;

m. Robert Erik Andersen, Apr. 13, 1968; children: Erik Jon, Jennifer Lynn, Karl Robert. BA in English, SUNY, Stony Brook, 1969, MA in Biology, 1985, PhD in Molecular Biology, 1989. Tchr. Half Hollow HIlls Pub. Schs., Dix Hills, 1969-72; rsch. asst. SUNY, Stony Brook, 1980-85, rsch. assoc., 1989-90; asst. prof. SUNY, 1991—. Contbr. articles to profl. jours. Recipient Alpha Omicron Pi award, 1989, 90; Arthritis Found. postdoctoral fellow, 1989-90. Mem. Sigma Xi (awards 1984, 87, 88), Sigma Delta Epsilon. Office: SUNY Stony Brook Dept Ob/Gyn Stony Brook NY 11794

ANDERSEN, KENNETH JOSEPH, pharmaceutical company executive; b. Bklyn., Dec. 24, 1936; s. Conrad Joseph and Evelyn (Olsen) A.; m. Judith Gail Lamb, June 9, 1962; children: David J., Mark A. AA, Kendall Coll., 1956; BS, Davis & Elkins Coll., 1959; MS, Syracuse U., 1962, PhD, 1965. Assoc. chief biol. sci. Battelle Meml. Inst., Columbus, Ohio, 1965-72; assoc. dir. diagnostic svcs. Johnson & Johnson Internat., New Brunswick, N.J., 1972-73; dir. biol. rsch. Norwich (N.Y.)-Eaton Pharm. Inc., 1973-82; pres. Andersen Labs., Inc., Norwich, 1982—. Pres. South New Berlin Bd. Edn., 1984-85, Chenango Ednl. Opportunities, Norwich, 1988—, Rotary Internat., Norwick, 1987. Fellow AAAS. Republican. Methodist. Home: RR 2 Box 165A South New Berlin NY 13843-9529 Office: Andersen Labs Inc PO Box 848 Norwich NY 13815-0848

ANDERSEN, KENNETH KAAE, chemistry educator; b. Perth Amboy, N.J., May 13, 1934; s. Anton Carl and Kristine (Kaae) A.; m. Barbara Estelle Fowler, July 20, 1957; children—David Kaae, Peter Carl, Joyce Karen. B.S., Rutgers U., 1955; Ph.D., U. Minn., 1959; student, Pa. State U., 1959-60. Prof. chemistry U. N.H., 1960—; vis. prof. Tech. U. Denmark, Lyngby, Denmark, 1971, 88, U. East Anglia, Norwich, Eng., 1966-67, Colo. State U., Ft. Collins, 1979. NIH postdoctoral fellow, 1959-60, NSF fellow, 1966-67; Fulbright lectr., 1971. Fellow AAAS; mem. Am. Chem. Soc. Home: 16 Garden Ln Durham NH 03824-3041

ANDERSEN, K(ENT) TUCKER, investment executive; b. Manchester, Conn., June 5, 1942; s. Alfred Hans and Dorothy Emily (Ray) A.; m. Karen Ann Kirchofer, Oct. 11, 1963; children: Heather Michele, Kristen Eileen. Student, Phillips Exeter Acad., N.H., 1957-59; BA, Wesleyan U., 1963. Chartered fin. analyst. Actuarial student Travelers Ins. Co., Hartford, Conn., 1963-66; security analyst Smith Barney & Co., N.Y.C., 1968-69; ptnr. Rudman Assocs., N.Y.C., 1969-72; ptnr. Cumberland Assocs., N.Y.C., 1972—, mng. ptnr., 1982—. Bd. dirs. Cato Inst., Washington, 1987—; trustee YWCA of Montclair, North Essex, N.J., 1980—, 1st United Meth. Ch. Montclair, 1976—, Martin Luther King Scholarship Fund of Montclair, 1989—; trustee Phillips Exeter Acad., N.H., 1989—, exec. com., chmn. investment com., 1992—, admission rep. for N.J. area, 1983—. With USPHS, 1966-68. Recipient Disting. Alumnus award Wesleyan U., 1988. Mem. Soc. Actuaries, N.Y. Soc. Security Analysts, Inst. Chartered Fin. Analysts, Polit. Club for Growth (mem. exec. com. 1984—), Kappa Nu Kappa (pres. 1963). Republican. Office: Cumberland Assocs 1114 Ave Of The Americas New York NY 10036-7703

ANDERSEN, MARIANNE SINGER, clinical psychologist; b. Baden nr. Vienna, Austria; came to U.S., 1940, naturalized, 1946; d. Richard L. and Jolanthe (Garda) Singer; 1 son, Richard Esten. BA, CUNY, 1950, MA, 1974; PhD, Fla. Inst. Tech., 1980. Rsch. assoc. Inst. for Rsch. in Hypnosis, N.Y.C., 1974-76, fellow in clin. hypnosis, 1976, dir. seminars, 1978-82, dir. edn., 1982—; psychotherapist specializing in hypnotherapy Morton Prince Ctr. for Hypnotherapy, 1976—, dir. weight control clinic, 1980—, dir. clin. services, 1981-82; dir. adminstrn. Internat. Grad. U., N.Y.C., 1974-77; pvt. practice psychotherapy, 1977—; adminstrv. coordinator Internat. Grad. Sch. Behavior Sci., Fla. Inst. Tech., 1978; co-dir. The Melbourne Group, 1983—; lectr. hypnosis and hypnotherapy to mental and phys. health profls., 1977—. Author: (with Louis Savary) Passages: A Guide for Pilgrims of the Mind, 1972; rsch. on treatment obesity with hypnotherapy; book editor specializing in psychology and psychiatry including W.W. Norton Co., Sterling Pub. Co., E.P. Dutton Co., 1950-71. Fellow Soc. for Clin. and Exptl. Hypnosis; mem. Internat. Soc. for Clin. and Exptl. Hypnosis, Am. Psychol. Assn., N.Y. Acad. Scis. Address: 60 W 57th St New York NY 10019

ANDERSEN, RENE, human resources administrator; b. N.Y.C., Apr. 10, 1946; d. John Mark and Catherine (Coronis) Colonas; m. Leonard Andersen, Jan., 1973 (div. June 1979); 1 child, Neti. AA, Colby-Sawyer Coll., 1966; MEd, Antioch U., 1979. Lic. social worker, Mass. Buyer, mgr. Harvard Coop. Soc., Cambridge, Mass., 1967-69; project coord. Mental Health Assocs., Springfield, Mass., 1977; program coord. The Cancer Coop., Springfield, 1977-84; asst. v.p. Cambridge Coll., 1976-86; co-owner Andersen/Kohler-Gray, Assocs., Northampton, Mass., 1982-85; cons. Mass. Dept. of Edn., Quincy, 1986-89; dir. Human Resource Assn. of N.E., Holyoke, Mass., 1986—; mem. Nat. Human Resource Devel. Assembly, 1989, 90. Editor (newsletter) RESOURCEs, 1990—. Member Northampton Dem. Com., 1985—, Nat. Women's Caucus for Human Resources Devel., 1988—, Nat. Minority Caucus for Human Resources Devel., 1988—. Mem. ASTC, Orgn. Devel. Network, Nat. Conf. on Gender and Diversity (planning com. 1991—). Home: 24 Winter St Northampton MA 01060-2235 Office: Human Resource Assoc 187 High St # 302 Holyoke MA 01040-6527

ANDERSEN, RICHARD ESTEN, lawyer; b. N.Y.C., Oct. 26, 1957; s. Arnold and Marianne (Singer) A.; m. Patricia Anne Woods, May 9, 1987; 1 child, Benjamin. BA, Columbia U., 1978, JD, 1981; LLM, NYU, 1987. Bar: N.Y. 1982, U.S. Tax Ct. 1982. Assoc. Jones, Day, Reavis & Pogue, N.Y.C., 1989—; mem. bd. advisors Jour. Internat. Tapafion. Mem. ABA, N.Y. State Bar Assn., Internat. Fiscal Assn. Office: Jones Day Reavis & Pogue 599 Lexington Ave New York NY 10022-6030

ANDERSEN, ROY STUART, physicist; b. Springfield, Mass., Oct. 16, 1921; s. O. William and Gladys (Merry) A.; m. Barbara Anne Norris, June 11, 1944; children: Karen Jana, Loring Dodd, Scott William. BA, Clark U., 1943; AM, Darmouth U., 1948; PhD, Duke U., 1951. Rsch. engr. Stanford Rsch. Inst., Palo Alto, Calif., 1951-52; from asst. prof. physics to assoc. prof. U. Md., College Park, 1952-60; prof. physics Clark U., Worcester, Mass., 1960-92, chmn. dept. phnysics, 1960-70, 71-72, dean grad. sch., 1970-71, prof. emeritus, 1992—; rsch. assoc. Duke U., Durham, N.C., 1951, 53, 54, U. Calif., Berkeley, 1958-59, Woods Hole (Mass.) Oceangraphic Inst., 1961. Researcher of microwave spectroscopy of atoms and molecules, radiation damage; contbr. articles to profl. jours. Lt. USNR, 1943-46, PTO. Named Sr. Fellow in Sci., NATO, 1973. Fellow Am. Phys. Soc.; mem. Am. Assn. Physics Tchrs., N.Am. Soc. Ocean History, History Sci. Soc. Office: Dept Physics Clark U Worcester MA 01610

ANDERSON, ALAN REINOLD, real estate executive; b. Danbury, Conn., Nov. 14, 1949; s. Charles Reinold and Lila Mae (Truesdale) A. BBA, Western Conn. State U., 1975, postgrad., 1977-82. Researcher, clk. Law Offices of Gemza & Daly, Danbury, Conn., 1972-77; prin. Anderson-Ricards & Co., Danbury, 1981-86, A.R. Anderson & Co., Danbury, Conn., 1977—. Conn. liaison Courageous Challenge 1987 America's Cup, 1985-87; town coord. steering and fin. com. Bush/Quayle 88, 92; alternate Conn., Rep. Nat. Conv., New Orleans, 1988; town coord. Weicker Gov., Conn., 1991; vice chmn. Environ. Impact Commn., Danbury, 1985-86. With USN, 1967-73, Vietnam. Decorated Air medals, DFC, Navy Commendation with Combat V, Vietnam Compaign with Silver Star. Mem. Milford Yacht Club, U.S. Yacht Racing Union, Assn. Naval Aviation (life), Tailhook Assn. (life), Naval Helicopter Assn., Yale Club Greater Danbury. Congregationalist. Home: 60 Miry Brook Rd Danbury CT 06810-7411

ANDERSON, ALAN STEWERT, lawyer; b. Rockville Centre, N.Y., Feb. 26, 1948; s. Donald A. Sr. and Rose (Russo) A.; m. Barbara Lynn Sattler, May 18, 1974; children: Christopher Stewert, Brian Ross. BA, Colgate U., 1970; JD with Honors, George Washington U., 1973. Bar: D.C. Ct. Appeals 1973, Md. Ct. Appeals 1985, U.S. Dist. Ct. D.C. 1974, U.S. Dist. Ct. (ea. dist.) Va., 1975, U.S. Ct. Appeals (D.C. cir.) 1974, U.S. Ct. Appeals (4th cir.) 1975; Va. Supreme Ct., 1975; U.S. Tax Ct., 1978; U.S. Supreme Ct., 1977, U.S. Dist. Ct. Md. 1985. Asst. county atty. Fairfax County, Fairfax, Va., 1975-77; ptnr. Tucker, Flyer & Lewis, Washington, 1977—. Elder Westminster Presbyn. Ch., Alexandria, Va., 1987-89, trustee, 1992—; den leader Webelos Cub Scouts Boy Scouts Am., Alexandria, 1989-91, asst. cubmaster, 1990—. Mem. ABA (litigation sect.), Va. Trial Lawyers Assn., Am. Arbitration Assn. (panel arbitrators), Alexandria Bar Assn., Va. Bar Assn., D.C. Bar Assn., Md. State Bar Assn., Nat. Inst. Trial Advocacy (cert. 1980). Office: Tucker Flyer & Lewis 1615 L St NW Ste 400 Washington DC 20036-5610

ANDERSON, ALEXA JOHANNA, retail executive; b. Ft. Monmouth, N.J., Aug. 26, 1961; d. Edward William and Heidi (Hildebrandt) Magenheimer. Student, Kean Coll., Union, N.J., 1980-81, Brookdale Coll., Lincroft, N.J., 1981. Mgr. Marshalls Dept. Store, Toms River, N.J., 1982-84; salesman Century Office Products, Scotch Plains, N.J., 1984-85; owner Jersey Shore Office Systems, Shrewsbury, N.J., 1985—. Mem. N.J. Women Bus. Owners, Nat. Assn. Female Execs., Am. Littoral Soc. Republican. Lutheran. Home: 344 Crawford St Eatontown NJ 07724-2954 Office: Jersey Shore Office Systems 555 Shrewsbury Ave Shrewsbury NJ 07702-4165

ANDERSON, ALFRED OLIVER, mathematician, consultant; b. Marmon, N.D., May 18, 1928; s. Frederick Gustav and Minnie Petrine (Jensen) A. BS, Ore. State U., 1953. Systems programmer U.S. Army Ballistics Research Lab., Aberdeen (Md.) Proving Ground, 1953-83; cons. Aberdeen, 1983—; investment specialist, Aberdeen, 1983—. Mem. Pi Mu Epsilon. Democrat. Lutheran. Home and Office: 717 Plater St Aberdeen MD 21001-3023

ANDERSON, ALLAMAY EUDORIS, health educator, home economist; b. N.Y.C., July 18, 1933; d. John Samuel and Charlotte Jane (Harrigan) Richardson; B.A., Queens Coll., CUNY, 1975; profl. mgmt. cert. Adelphi U., 1978; M.S. in Edn., Fordham U., 1984; m. Edgar Leopold Anderson, Jr., Apr. 14, 1957; 1 son, David Lancelot. Mem. staff sch. food service, dietitian Bd. Edn., N.Y.C., 1968-88; tchr. home and career skills Louis Armstrong Middle Sch., 1988; spl. edn. tchr. Manhattan High Sch., N.Y.C., 1989—; profl. devel. cons., N.Y.C., 1978—; ptnr. Masiba Bldg. Corp., Corona, N.Y., 1975-82; adj. lectr. home econs. Queens Coll., 1987; owner AEA Devel. Svc., 1987—. Devel. coord. League for Better Community Life, Inc., 1977; treas. exec. bd., 1970-76; officer N.Y.C. Community Devel. Agy., 1980-83; mem. Kwanzaa Adv. Com. (P.R.) Urban Coalition, 1983, L.I. # 28 Episcopal Cursillo, 1991; vestry mem. youth ministries Grace Episcopalian Ch., 1982-85; mem. NAACP. Recipient Elmcor Community Svc. award Elmcor Youth and Adult Activities, Inc., 1989. Mem. United Fedn. Tchrs. N.Y.C., Nat. Soc. Fund Raising Execs., Langston Hughes Libr. Action Com. (bd. dirs. 1987—, treas. 1989), Queens Coll. Home Econs. Alumni Assn. (v.p., chmn. bylaws com. 1982), Phi Delta Kappa. Office: 10013 34th Ave Flushing NY 11368-1052

ANDERSON, ARLO C., orthopedic surgeon; b. Jamestown, N.Y., Apr. 27, 1932; s. Conrad A. and Clara (Fluck) A.; m. Marjorie R. Anderson, June 4, 1964; children: John, Richard, Catherine. AB, Anderson (Ind.) U., 1955; MD, Jefferson U., 1961. Diplomate Am. Bd. Orthopedic Surgery, Am. Acad. Orthopedic Surgery, ACS. Chief orthopedic surgery dept. Sacred Heart Hosp., Norristown, Pa., 1990—; mem. attending staff orthopedic surgery dept. Sacred Heart Hosp., Norristown, 1966—, Montgomery Hosp., 1966—. Home: 1660 Williams Way Norristown PA 19403 Office: Norristown Orthopedic Assocs 1308 DeKalb St Norristown PA 19401

ANDERSON, AUSTIN CORBIN, III, college program director; b. Camden, N.J., Feb. 17, 1965; s. Austin Corbin and Marion Rose (Ohme) A.; m. Kathleen Susan Farrow, Dec. 29, 1990. Assoc. in Occupational Sci., Johnson and Wales U., Providence, 1985, BS, 1987, MS, 1989. Resident dir. Johnson and Wales U., 1987-89, dir. residential faciilties, 1989-90; dir. student life Keuka Coll., Keuka Park, N.Y., 1990-91; asst. dean residence life The Culinary Inst. Am., Hyde Park, N.Y., 1991—. Mem. ACUHO-I, Assn. Coll. Pers. Adminstrs., N.E. Assn. Coll. and Univ. Housing Officers, Assn. Student Jud. Affairs, Coll. Student Pers. Assn. N.Y. Home: 51-71 Creek Rd # 1103 Poughkeepsie NY 12601 Office: The Culinary Inst Am 433 Albany Post Rd Hyde Park NY 12538

ANDERSON, BERNARD E., economist; b. Phila.; s. William and Dorothy (Gideon) A.; children: Melinda D., Bernard E. II. BA with highest honors, Livingstone Coll., 1959; MA, Mich. State U., 1961; PhD, U. Pa., 1969; LHD (hon.), Shaw U., 1984. Economist U.S. Bur. Labor Stats., Washington, 1963-65; successively asst. prof., assoc. prof., prof. Wharton Sch. U. Pa., Phila., 1969-79, sr. economist, 1985-87; dir. social sci. The Rockefeller Found., N.Y.C., 1979-85; vis. fellow Woodrow Wilson Sch., Princeton U., N.J., 1985; mng. ptnr. The Urban Affairs Partnership, Phila., 1987-91; pres. The Anderson Group, Phila., 1991—; bd. dirs. Manpower Demonstration Rsch. Co., N.Y.C., Pa. Econ. Devel. Partnership, Harrisburg, Provident Mut. Life Ins. Co. Author: Youth Employment and Public Policy, 1980; co-author: Black Managers in American Business, 1978, Impact of Government Training and Employment Programs, 1975, Managing Growth in American Business, 1978; mem. editorial bd. Rev. Black Polit. Economy. Trustee Livingstone Coll., Salisbury, N.C., 1980—; chmn. bd. trustees Lincoln U., Oxford, Pa., 1987—; mem. Pres.'s Commn. on Employment Stats., Washington, 1979; mem. Nat. Commn. Jobs and Small Bus., Washington, 1986; bd. dirs. Com. Fgn. Rels., Phila., 1983—; chmn. Pa. Intergovtl. Cooperation Authority, Phila., 1991—. With U.S. Army, 1961-63. Recipient Alumni Disting. Svc. award Wharton Grad. Sch., U. Pa., 1992. Mem. Am. Econ. Assn., Indsl. Rels. Rsch. Assn. (mem. exec. com. 1979-82), Nat. Econ. Assn. (pres. 1982), Union League, U. Pa. Faculty Club, Princeton Club. Democrat. A.M.E. Zion. Office: The Anderson Group 1201 Fl 1528 Walnut St Philadelphia PA 19102-3616

ANDERSON, BRUCE KENNETH, information technology executive, computer engineer; b. New Britain, Conn., Jan. 9, 1943; s. Willard Herbert and Lillian (Ross) A.; m. Pearlann Carroll, July 3, 1973 (div. Mar. 1987); 1 child, Tracie-Lee. BS in Chem. Engring., U. Conn., 1965; MS in Computer Sci., Rensselaer Polytech. Inst., 1971. With Uniroyal, Inc., Middlebury, Conn., 1964-86, dir., 1973-82, dir. mgmt. info. systems, 1983-86; sr. v.p. info. tech. div., chief info. officer ADVO, Inc., Windsor, 1987—; lectr. U. N.H., New Haven, 1973-74, Tech. Tng. Corp., Torrance, Calif., 1986. Mem. Assn. for System Mgmt., Data Processing Mgmt. Assn., Assn. Computing Machinery, IEEE, Soc. Info. Mgrs., Sigma Six Flying Club. Home: 202 Candlewyck Dr Newington CT 06111-5217 Office: ADVO Inc 1 Univac Ln Windsor CT 06095-2662

ANDERSON, BRUCE MORGAN, computer scientist; b. Battle Creek, Mich., Oct. 8, 1941; s. James Albert and Beverly Jane (Morgan) A.; m. Jeannie Marie Hignight, May 24, 1975; children: Ronald, Michael, Valerie, John, Carolyn. BEE, Northwestern U., 1964; MEE, Purdue U., 1966; PhD in Elec. Engring., Northwestern U., 1973. Rsch. engr. Zenith Radio Corp., Chgo., 1965-66; assoc. engr. Ill. Inst. Tech. Rsch. Inst., Chgo., 1966-68; sr. electronics engr. Rockwell Internat., Downers Grove, Ill., 1973-75; computer scientist Argonne (Ill.) Nat. Lab., 1975-77; mem. group tech. staff Tex. Instruments, Dallas, 1977-88; sr. scientist BBN Systems and Techs., Cambridge, Mass., 1988-90; sr. systems engr. Martin Marietta, Denver, 1990—; lectr. computer sci. U. Tex.-Arlington and Dallas; adj. prof. computer sci. N. Tex. State U.; vis. indsl. prof. So. Meth. U.; computer systems cons. Info. Internat., Culver City, Calif., HCM Graphic Systems, Gt. Neck, N.Y.; computer cons. depts. geography, transp., econs., sociology and computer sci. Northwestern U., also instr. computer sci.; expert witness for firm Burleson, Pate and Gibson. Contbr. articles to tech. jours. NASA fellow Northwestern U., 1973. Mem. IEEE Computer Soc. (chmn. Dallas 1984-85), Am. Assn. Artificial Intelligence, Assn. Computing Machinery (publs. chmn. 1986 fall joint computer conf. IEEE and Assn. Computing Machinery), Toastmasters Internat., Sigma Xi, Eta Kappa Nu, Theta Delta Chi. Home: 3473 E Euclid Ave Littleton CO 80121-3663 Office: Martin Marietta Mail Stop XL4370 700 W Mineral Ave Littleton CO 80120-4511

ANDERSON, BRYCE OTIS, furniture and industrial company executive; b. Jamestown, N.Y., July 21, 1936; s. Melvin D. E. and Irene (Nelson) A.; m. Emma L. Schramm; children: Bruce Otis, Michelle Nicole. B in Profl. Arts, Art Ctr. Coll. of Design, 1959. Designer Molded Fiberglass Corp., Astubula, Ohio, 1959-60, Studebaker-Packard, South Bend, Ind., 1960-62, Radio Corp. Am., Indpls., 1962-70; mgr. of design Gen. Telephone Electronics-Sylvania Div., Batavia, N.Y., 1970-78; dir. design Gen. Telephone Electronics-Sylvania Div., Batavia, 1978-81, N.Am. Philips-Sylvania Div., Knoxville, Tenn., 1981-85, Bush Ind., Inc., Jamestown, N.Y., 1985-91; pres. Anderson Design, Lakewood, N.Y., 1991—, Talbott, Tenn., 1991—. Contbr. articles to profl. jours.; patentee in field. Recipient First Pl. Annual Exhibit, R.C.A., Ind., 1967. Mem. Am. Soc. Furniture Designers, Indsl. Designers Soc. Am., Art Ctr. Alumni, Elks, Vikings, Rod and Gun Club. Republican. Lutheran. Home: 27 Marvin Ave Lakewood NY 14750 Office: 7366 Circle Point Dr PO Box 307 Talbott TN 37877

ANDERSON, CLIFFORD HUGO, quality assurance consultant; b. West New York, N.J., Apr. 14, 1924; s. Frans Hugo and Signe (Selander) A.; m. Dorothy C. O'Neill, Apr. 3, 1949; children: Nancy L. Krause, Neil C. Anderson. Grad. high sch., North Arlington, N.J. Apprentice machinist Standard Tool and Die Co., Kearny, N.J., 1942; exptl. engine tester Curtiss Wright Corp., Woodbridge, N.J., 1953; enlisted USAF, 1953; advanced through grades to master sgt.; quality control rep. USAF Contract Mgmt., Phila., 1953-58, quality control commodity specialist, 1958-59; quality assurance specialist USAF Contract Mgmt., 1959-62; indsl. specialist McGuire AFB, Mgmt. Office, 1959-62; quality assurance specialist Def. Contract Adminstn. Region, Phila., 1963-79; quality assurance cons. Clifford H. Anderson & Assocs., Beverly, N.J., 1979—; bd. dirs. Occupational Tng. Ctr. of Burlington County, Inc., pres. Mem. ch. coun. St. Luke Luth. Ch., Willingboro, N.J. Recipient awards for contbrn. to Apollo program NASA, 1962-79. Mem. Am. Soc. for Quality Control (sr.). Office: Clifford H Anderson & Assoc PO Box 405 Beverly NJ 08010-0405

ANDERSON, CYNTHIA HARVEY, digital equipment corporation trainer, writer; b. Glen Cove, N.Y., Dec. 16, 1950; d. Vance Russell and Victoria Barbara (Kajenski) Ramskill; m. Rodney Peter Anderson, Mar. 15, 1986. AS, Beverly (Mass.) Endicott, 1970; BS cum laude, Boston U., 1974; MS, Suffolk U., 1982, cert. advanced study, 1986. Instr. Briscoe Jr. High Sch., Beverly, Mass., 1974-75, Spaulding High Sch., Rochester, N.H., 1975-81; exec. sec. to pres. Suffolk U., Boston, 1982-85; program dir. Bay State Jr. Coll., Boston, 1985-87; corp. trainer Digital Equipment Corp., Maynard, Mass., 1987—; sec. N.H. Fedn. Tchrs., Manchester, 1980-81, Rochester Fedn. Tchrs., 1978-81. Mem. Nat. Bus. Edn. Assn., Profl. Secs. Internat., N.E. Bus. Edn. Assn., Mass. Bus. Edn. Assn., Pi Lambda Theta. Democrat. Lutheran. Home: 156A Frost Rd Tyngsboro MA 01879-1142 Office: Digital Equipment Corp 129 Parker St Maynard MA 01754-2122

ANDERSON, DAVID GILROY, forestry educator, college official; b. Skaneateles, N.Y., Aug. 3, 1930; s. Edwin G. and Laura L. (Wickham) A.; m. Judith B. Valentine, Dec. 2, 1978; children: Linda, David Andrew, Timothy; stepchildren: Timothy Wadsworth, Duane Wadsworth. A.A.S., N.Y. State Ranger Sch., 1950; B.S., N.Y. State Coll. Forestry, 1953; M.S., U. Utah, 1958; M.P.A., Syracuse U., 1977, postgrad., 1979. Instr. N.Y. State Ranger Sch., Wanakena, 1959-62, asst. prof., 1963-65; asst. dean, assoc. prof. forestry SUNY-Syracuse, 1965-70; prof., univ. v.p. SUNY-Coll. Environ. Sci. and Forestry, Syracuse, 1970-88, prof., exec. asst. to pres., 1988—; dir. Univ. Hill Corp. Bd. dirs., v.p. N.Y. State Coll. Forestry Found., Inc., 1978—. Served with USNR, 1953-59. Am. Council Edn. fellow, 1970-71. Mem. Am. Forestry Assn., AAAS, Soc. Am. Foresters, N.Y. Forest Owners Assn., Nat. Audubon Soc., Nature Conservancy, Am. Soc. for Pub. Adminstrn., Am. Legion, Syracuse U. Alumni Assn., U. Utah Alumni Assn., Sigma Xi. Republican. Presbyterian. Club: Clayton Yacht. Home: 3938 Derby Dr Syracuse NY 13215-1004 Office: SUNY Coll Environ Sci and Forestry Syracuse NY 13210

ANDERSON, DAVID MARTIN, chemical engineer; b. Boston, July 19, 1930; s. Martin Jens and Dorothy (Finnin) A.; grad. Boston Latin Sch., 1948; B.S., Northeastern U., 1953; S.M., Harvard U., 1955, Ph.D., 1958; m. Marjorie Gilbert, July 19, 1958; children—David, Michael, Anne, Stephen. Research fellow Harvard Sch. Pub. Health, 1953-58; pub. health engr. USPHS, Cin., 1958-60; indsl. health engr. Bethlehem Steel Corp. (Pa.), 1960-67; asst. mgr. environ. quality control, 1967-71, mgr., 1971-80, corp. dir. environ. affairs, 1980-84, dir. environ. and govtl. affairs, 1984-87, gen. mgr. environ. affairs, 1987—; lectr. Pa. State U., 1966-71; vis. lectr. Harvard U., 1969-81; chmn. council tech. advisers Pa. Dept. Environ. Resources, 1964-70, N.Y. Dept. Environ. Conservation, 1974-75; mem. Pa. Gov.'s Task Force on Occupational Health and Safety, 1975-76; mem. com. on biol. effects of atmospheric pollutants Nat. Acad. Scis., 1971-74; mem. nat. air quality criteria adv. com. EPA, 1971-76; mem. Sec. Health, Edn. and Welfare Coal Mine Health Research Adv. Council, 1972-76; mem. U.S. Dept. Commerce Adv. Com. on Indsl. Innovation, 1978-79, Ctr. for Risk Analysis Harvard U., 1989—. Registered profl. engr., Pa. Diplomate Am. Acad. Environ. Engrs. Mem. Am. Iron and Steel Inst. (com. on environ. 1971—, chmn. 1978-80, 87-89), Internat. Iron and Steel Inst. (com. on environ. 1980—), Am. Chem. Soc., Am. Indsl. Hygiene Assn. (dir. 1968-71), Air Pollution Control Assn. (dir. 1971-74), Sigma Xi, Delta Omega. Contbr. articles to profl. jours. Research, patentee air cleaning tech. Home: 1037 Westgate Cir Bethlehem PA 18017-3637 Office: Bethlehem Steel Corp Bethlehem PA 18016

ANDERSON, DEAN WILLIAM, educational administrator; b. Mpls., Aug. 28, 1946; s. Edward Marvin and Mabel (Gilland) A.; children: Erik Wheeler, Matthew Edward. B.A., Macalester Coll., 1968; M.A., U. Calif.-Berkeley, 1970. Examiner Office Mgmt. and Budget, Washington, 1970-73; adminstrv. officer Smithsonian Instn., Washington, 1973-84, asst. sec. history and art, 1984-85, under sec., 1985-90; dep. dir. mgmt. and planning Woodrow Wilson Ctr., Washington, 1990—. Recipient Robert Brooks award Smithsonian Instn., 1983; Minn. SPAN Assn. scholar, Israel, 1967; MacPherson Found. scholar, Mpls., 1967. Mem. Phi Beta Kappa. Office: Woodrow Wilson Ctr 1000 Jefferson Dr SW Washington DC 20560

ANDERSON, DONALD MORGAN, entomologist; b. Washington, Dec. 27, 1930; s. John Kenneth and Alice Cornelia (Morgan) A. B.A., Miami U., Oxford, Ohio, 1953; Ph.D., Cornell U.l, 1958. Grad. teaching asst. Cornell U., 1954-57; asst. prof. sci. SUNY-Buffalo, 1959-60, rsch. fellow, 1960; rsch. entomologist Dept. Agrl., Washington, 1960-90, rsch. collaborator, 1990—; rsch. assoc. Buffalo Mus. Sci., 1972—, Smithsonian Instn., 1978—. Contbr. articles to profl. jours., chpts to books. Sigma Xi grantee, 1959. Mem. Entomol. Soc. Washington (corr. sec. 1963-65, pres. 1985), Entomol. Soc. Am., Soc. Systematic Zoology, Coleoperists Soc., Am. Inst. Biol. Sci., St. Andrews Soc. Washington, Clan Anderson Soc. (editor 1979-84, treas. 1985-90, pres. 1990-92), Sigma Xi, Phi Kappa Phi. Home: 1900 Lyttonsville Rd Apt 804 Silver Spring MD 20910-2238 Office: Systematic Entomology Lab Dept Agr Nat Mus Natural History Washington DC 20560

ANDERSON, DOUGLAS DEWAYNE, transportation company executive; b. June 11, 1957; s. Orville DeWayne and Dorotha Agnes (Elder) A.; m. Lori A. Anderson. BA in Bus. Adminstrn., Edinboro U., 1981. Mgr. Anderson Bus & Tour, Greenville, Pa., 1981-88, v.p., 1988-90, pres., 1990-92; mgr. Sterling Stages, Inc., Greenville, Pa., 1981-85, v.p., 1985—. Mem. Nat. Tour Assn., Am. Bus. Assn., United Bus Owners Am. (Safety award, 1988), Am. Soc. Travel Agts. (assoc.), Greenville (Pa.) C. of C. (pres. 1992), Masons, Shriners. Office: O D Anderson Inc 1 Anderson Plz Greenville PA 16125

ANDERSON, DOUGLAS SCRANTON HELMSLEY, investment banker; b. Springfield, Mass., Aug. 23, 1929; s. Lloyd Douglas Hesley and Alice Scranton (Eastman) Anderson; m. Elizabeth Bartram Radley, Sept. 20, 1969 (dissolved 1991); 1 child, Katherine Scranton. Grad. Deerfield Acad., 1947; AB, Harvard U., 1951; cert. investment banking Northwestern U., 1959. Gen. ptnr. The Anderson Co., Greenwich, Conn., 1953—, MAH Co., Greenwich, 1979—; investment banker Lehman Bros., Salomon Bros. & Hutzler, Legg & Co. and Sterling, Grace & Co., Inc., N.Y.C., 1960-81. Pres., Pecksland Rd. Assn., 1977-78; bd. dirs. Indian Harbor Dist. & Assn., 1979-91, treas., 1986-92, hon. police chief, 1991—; rep. Greenwich Town Meeting, 1979—, legis. com., 1979—, vice chmn., 1986-87, chmn., 1988—, founder, mem. spl. cost containment com., 1984-86, sec., 1986, claims com., 1982—, clk., 1992—; assoc. Rep. town com., 1984-87, mem., 1988—; sec. Greenwich Selectman's Utility Watch Com., 1982-90; trustee Round Hill Community Ch., Greenwich, 1980-85, treas., 1982-85; mem. fin. commn. Christ Episcopal Ch., 1991—; mem. Parents Coun. Ohio Wesleyan U., 1990—; mem. Fin. Commn. Christ Episcopal Ch., 1992—. Lt. USNR, 1951-53. Mem. Assn. Former Intelligence Officers, Conn. Police Chiefs Assn., Soc. Colonial Wars (coun. 1984—, gov. 1988-90, dep. gov. gen. 1990-92, nominating com. 1992—), Mayflower Descs., Order Founders and Patriots, Soc. Cin., Baronial Order of Magna Charta, Round Hill Club, Fox Club, Harvard Varsity Club, Harvard Club of Boston, Army and Navy Club (Washington), West Palm

Beach Fishing Club, Edgartown (Mass.) Yacht Club. Home: 40 Bruce Park Dr Greenwich CT 06830-1199

ANDERSON, DOUGLAS WILLIAMS, lawyer; b. Mount Vernon, N.Y., June 8, 1932; s. Carl O. and Alicia Tell (Williams) A.; m. Patricia J. Belcher, July 14, 1958 (div. July 1980); children—Arlan P., Merryl L., Lindsey C., Jevan F. AB, Columbia U., 1954, JD, 1957; student, U.S. Naval Acad., 1950-53. Bar: N.Y. 1958, U.S. Dist. Ct. (so. dist.) N.Y. 1960, U.S. Ct. Claims 1978. Atty. Haight, Gardner, Poor & Havens, N.Y.C., 1957-59, Sinclair Refining Co., N.Y.C., 1960-64; v.p. Am. Express Co., N.Y.C., 1964-70; assoc. Neale & Wilson, Scarsdale, N.Y., 1970-78; pvt. practice Scarsdale, 1978—; gen. counsel Amrox Internat. Corp., N.Y.C., 1975—, Scarsdale Improvement Corp., 1980—, Carmine Cabriola Inc., 1980—; adj. prof. Columbia U., 1983-90. Bd. dirs. Nat. Orchestral Assn., N.Y.C., 1980-87, treas. Mem. ABA, AA Alumni Assn. (pres., bd. dirs.), Westchester County Bar Assn., Princeton U. Club, Scarsdale Golf Club (gen. counsel 1979—). Republican. Episcopalian. Home: Scarswold Scarsdale NY 10583 Office: Harwood Bldg Scarsdale NY 10583

ANDERSON, EVA JEAN, nurse; b. Bobo Dioulasso, Burkina Fasso, Dec. 31, 1939; d. Andrew and Laura (Reutter) Hyndman; m. Rockne Stephen Anderson, Mar. 25, 1967; children: R. Stephen, Jr., Drew V.E. BS, Nyack Coll., 1962; ASN, Rockland Community College, 1964. RN. Pediatrics nurse Good Samaritan Hosp., Suffern, N.Y., 1964-65, asst. head nurse, pediatrics, 1965-67; hospice nurse Chandler Hall, Newtown, Pa., 1983-86; vis. nurse Homecall of Delaware Valley, Feasterville, Pa., 1986-88; supr., tng. coord. Healing Arts, Feasterville, Pa., 1988-90; field supr. Olsten Health Care, Trevose, Pa., 1990—; mem. utilization rev. com., Chandler Hall, 1985-86. Pres. Heritage Estates Women's Club, Slidell, La., 1980; v.p. Christian Women's Club, Slidell, 1979; mem. Moral Concerns Com. of Wycombe (Pa.) Bapt. Ch., 1989-91. Democrat. Home: 1067 Temperance Ln Richboro PA 18954-1101 Office: Olsten Health Care 6 Neshaminy Langhorne PA 19053-3630

ANDERSON, G. ERNEST, JR., education educator; b. Newark, July 24, 1929; s. George E. and Gladys (Pomeroy) A.; BA, Amherst Coll., 1950; M.A.T., Harvard U., 1955, EdD, 1964; m. Patricia Ruth Mottram, Dec. 28, 1957; children: Russell, Carol R. Tchr., coord. data processing Newton Pub. Schs. (Mass.), 1957-63; rsch. assoc., teaching asst. Harvard U., Cambridge, Mass., 1959-64; asst. prof., project mgr. adminstrv. data systems U. Del., Newark, 1965-67; mem. faculty U. Mass., Amherst, 1967—, prof. edn., 1974—; cons. Gen. Learning Corp., Yale U., U. R.I., others, 1977—. Troop leader Boy Scouts Am., also chmn. com.; leader Girl Scouts U.S.A. Served with U.S. Navy, 1951-54. Mem. Assn. Ednl. Data Systems (founder, pres.), Am. Ednl. Rsch. Assn., Psychometric Soc., Assn. Computing Machinery, Internet Soc. (sec. 1979-88), Mass. Soc. Profs. (sec. 1979—), Conn. Electric Ry. Assn. (dir. 1978-85, treas. 1979-82). Congregationalist. Clubs: Adirondack Mountain; Green Mountain. Editor Ednl. Data Processing Newsletter, 1963-65; editorial bd. Jour. Assn. Ednl. Data Systems, 1965—; contbr. articles to various publs. Home: 316 Alpine Dr Amherst MA 01002-1656 Office: U Mass Sch Edn Amherst MA 01003

ANDERSON, GARY WILLIAM, physician; b. Summit, N.J., Nov. 10, 1951; s. Gotfried and Elise (Koch) A.; divorced; 1 child, Eric William George. BA, Seton Hall U., 1974; MA in Psychology, Fairleigh Dickinson U., 1977; MD, Autonomous U. Guadalajara, Mex., 1983. Intern Rutgers Med. Sch., New Brunswick, N.J., 1984; resident St. Joseph's Med. Ctr., Paterson, N.J., 1985; med. dir., dir. med. writing office of v.p. Sandoz Rsch. Inst., East Hanover, N.J., 1985—. Vol. med. dir., bd. trustees, exec. com. Sussex County (N.J.) Domestic Abuse Program, 1986—. Mem. AMA, Am. Med. Writers Assn., Am. Fedn. Clin. Rsch., Nat. Honor Soc. Psychology, Am. Acad. Family Physicians, N.J. Med. Soc., Morris County Med. Soc. Republican. Office: Sandoz Rsch Inst RR 10 East Hanover NJ 07936

ANDERSON, GORDON WOOD, physicist, electrical engineer; b. Evanston, Ill., Mar. 8, 1936; s. Gordon Hilmer and Avis Elizabeth (Hillman) A.; B.E.E. (univ. scholar 1954-57, Sloan Found. scholar 1957-59), Cornell U., 1959; M.S. (Ford Found. fellow 1959-61), U. Ill., Urbana-Champaign, 1961, Ph.D., 1969; m. Gillian Anne Bunshaft, Aug. 23, 1969. Rsch. asst. U. Ill., 1960-69; instr. Tougaloo (Miss.) Coll., 1965; NRC rsch.assoc. U.S. Naval Rsch. Lab., 1969-70, rsch. physicist, 1971—; cons. Planning & Human Systems, Inc., Washington, 1978-79, Office Naval Rsch., naval systems commands, Def. Advanced Rsch. Projects Agy. Bd. dirs. Epilepsy Found. Am., 1979-85, affiliate pres., 1976-78, affiliate bd. dirs., 1972-73, 74-86, sec. affiliate profl. adv. bd., 1972-76, mem. affiliate profl. adv. bd. 1972-76, 78—; affiliate hon. bd. dirs., 1989—; bd. dirs., sec.-treas. Colonial Singers and Players, 1973—; bd. dirs. D.C. Ctr. for Ind. Living, 1981—, v.p., 1982-83, treas., 1989-90, pres., 1990—; bd. dirs. Capitol Hill Restoration Soc., 1988-89; mem. Mono Lake com. Chesapeake Bay Found. Contbr. articles to profl. jours., chpt. to book; patentee in field. NSF grantee, 1963; NRC postdoctoral rsch. assoc., 1969-70; recipient Naval Rsch. Lab. award, 1980, 83, 85, 86, 88, 89, 91. Mem. AAAS, IEEE, Am. Phys. Soc., Assn. Old Crows, Found. Sci. and Handicapped, Fedn. Am. Scientists, Union Concerned Scientists, U. Ill. Alumni Assn., ACLU, Amnesty Internat., Capitol Hill Restoration Soc., Sierra Club, Wilderness Soc., Natural Resources Def. Council, Environ. Def. Fund, Sigma Xi, Tau Beta Pi, Eta Kappa Nu, Alpha Delta Phi. Democrat. Episcopalian. Clubs: Alpine of Can., Oesterreichischer Alpenverein; Cornell (Washington), U. Ill. (Washington). Achievements include the development of channelizer technology for RF, microwave and millimeterwave receivers; research on and development of high-speed, high-dynamic-range photodetectors and arrays for optical processing; development of insulators for metal-insulator-semiconductor infrared focal plane arrays; determination of structure of vanadium phosphate semiconducting glasses. Home: 1320 N Carolina Ave NE Washington DC 20002-6424 Office: Naval Rsch Lab Code 6813 Washington DC 20375-5000

ANDERSON, HENRY FITZGERALD (JERRY ANDERSON), music producer; b. N.Y.C., Apr. 28, 1951; s. Henry Louis and Madeline Anderson; m. Deborah Todmann, Sept. 17, 1983. Student, Bronx Community Coll., 1969-71. Songwriter E.B. Marks Pub., N.Y.C., 1977-78, Screen Gems, N.Y.C., 1978-79; recording artist Capitol Records, N.Y.C., 1979-81; producer, owner Bull By the Horns Prodn., N.Y.C., 1981—. Musician, songwriter (albums) Mystic Merlin, 1979, 60 Thrills a Minute, 1980, Full Moon, 1981. Democrat. Office: Bull By the Horns Prodn 3467 Dekalb Ave Ste 4I New York NY 10467

ANDERSON, JAMES ALLEN, marketing professional; b. Bassett, Nebr., June 12, 1959; s. James D. and Mary C. (Huelle) A.; m. Beth Frederick, June 23, 1983; children: Bradley, Jared. BS in Fin., Fort Hays State U., 1981. Med. rep. Lederle Labs., Hays, Kans., 1982-83; coord. spl. projects Lederle Labs., Wayne, N.J., 1983-84, calls system mgr., 1984-85; dist. sales mgr. Lederle Labs., Columbus, Ohio, 1986-89; nat. accounts mgr. Managed Health Care (Lederle Labs.), Chgo., 1989-90; mktg. mgr. Managed Health Care Group (Lederle Labs.), Wayne, 1990-91; mgr. group purchasing markets and sales contracts Lederle Labs., Wayne, N.J., 1991—, dir. sales adminstrn., 1992—. Sec. Luth. Ch. Coun., Vernon, N.J., 1985; mem. Luth. Ch. Stewardship com., Cary, Ill., 1990. Mem. Ill. Assn. HMOs. Republican. Office: Lederle Labs Div Cyanamid Plz M2/2021A Wayne NJ 07470

ANDERSON, JAMES ARTHUR, humanities educator, academic director; b. Providence, Aug. 9, 1955; s. Arthur Charles and Ruth M. (Marshall) A.; m. Patricia A. Braza, Aug. 27, 1977; children: Erik James, Nicholas Perry. BA, R.I. Coll., 1977, MA in English, 1987; PhD, U. R.I., 1992. Assoc. editor R.I. Rev., Providence, 1981-84; instr. Johnson & Wales U., Providence, 1984-88; asst. prof. humanities Johnson & Wales U., 1988—, devel. publs./rsch. coord., 1987-90, dir. rsch. and grants, 1990—; presenter in field. Author: The Illustrated Bradbury: A Structuralist Reading of Bradbury's "The Illustrated Man", 1990; columnist, writer East Side Monthly, Providence, 1984—; contbr. articles, revs., poems to profl. jours. Coach Warwick (R.I.) Firefighters Soccer Club, 1990; fundraiser Friends of H.P. Lovecraft, Brown U., Providence, 1990. Mem. MLA, Nat. Soc. Fund Raising Execs., Horror Writers Am., Small Press Writers and Artists Orgn. (Gene Day award 1982), New Eng. Devel. Rsch. Assn., Am. Prospect Rsch. Assn. Home: 111 Whitford St Warwick RI 02886-3738 Office: Johnson & Wales U 8 Abbott Park Pl Providence RI 02903-3703

ANDERSON, JAMES BRENT, venture capitalist; b. Waterbury, Conn., Apr. 10, 1950; s. Gordon Arthur and Irene (Gustafson) A.; m. Carol Patricia Anderson, Sept. 9, 1978. BS, Worcester Polytech. Inst., 1972; MS, U. Conn., 1976, PhD, 1981. Ptnr. Anderson Assocs., Mystic, Conn., 1978-87; v.p. Advest, Inc., Hartford, Conn., 1983-87; investment officer Travelers Ins. Co., Hartford, 1987—; bd. dirs. Hampshire Instruments, Inc., Molten Metal Techs., Inc., Voxel, Inc., Fuisz Techs., Ltd. Author 2 books; contbr. articles to profl. jours. Mem. TPC at River Highlands. Republican. Home: 143 Pequot Ave Mystic CT 06355-1728 Office: Travelers Ins Co One Tower Sq Hartford CT 06183

ANDERSON, JAMES LAVALETTE, JR., resource economist, educator; b. Phila., Apr. 5, 1954; s. James Lavalette and Anne Christine (Powell) A.; m. Joan Kay Gray, July 3, 1982; children: Amy Kerr, Alyssa Gray, James Lavalette III. BS, Coll. of Wm.& Mary, 1976; MS in Agrl. Econs., U. Ariz., 1978; PhD in Agrl. Econs., U. Calif., 1983. Assoc. prof. resource econs. U. R.I., Kingston, 1983-89, 1989—; pres. J.L. Anderson Assocs., Inc., Narragansett, R.I., 1989—; com. mem. Nat. Rsch. Coun. Aqua Study, Washington, 1989-91; mem. tech. adv. com. N.E. Regional Aqua Ctr., North Dartmouth, Mass., 1989-92. Mem. editorial coun. Jour. of Environ., Econs. & Mgmt., 1989-92; assoc. editor Trans. of Am. Fisheries Soc., 1990-92, Marine Resource Econs., 1992—; contbr. articles to profl. jours. Grantee: Sea Grant, USDA, Norwegian Ctr. for Applied Rsch., Canadian Dept. of Fisheries and Oceans and others. Mem. Am. Agrl. Econs. Assn. (Outstanding PhD Thesis award 1983), Assn. Environ. and Resource Economists, World Aquaculture Soc., Am. Fisheries Soc., So. Agrl. Econs. Assn., Western Agrl. Econs. Assn., Carribean Aqua Assn. Office: U RI Dept Resource Econs Kingston RI 02881

ANDERSON, JAMES WARREN, III, scientific company executive; b. Pitts., Oct. 7, 1958; s. James Warren Jr. and Mary Louise (Hudson) A.; m. Stephanie Ann Simpson, Jan., 1987 (div. Oct. 1989); 1 child, Vanessa Ann. Student, U. Pitts., 1980-85. Rsch. computer scientist Carnegie Mellon Robotics Inst., Pitts., 1982-87; ind. cons., 1988-90; chief exec. officer Baron's Haven, Duquesne, Pa., 1990-92; lectr. at various sci. conventions, 1987—; founder, pres. PC Help!. Author: Moonflower, Greyscale Vision, 1991; actor (films) What She Doesn't Know, Lorenzo's Oil; patentee modified heat pump, pulp recycling process; contbr. articles to profl. publs. Mayoral candidate City of Duquesne, 1989. With USAF, 1976-80. Mem. German Beneficial Union, Nat. Space Soc. (v.p. Pitts. chpt. 1988-91), Moose, Pi Kappa Alpha.

ANDERSON, JEFFREY ALAN, construction company executive; b. Butler, Pa., Apr. 6, 1953; s. Kenneth Oliver and Georgia (Staff) A.; m. Susan Jean Randolph, June 20, 1981; 1 child, Lacey Michele. BSCE, U. Cin., 1976. Registered profl. engr., Pa., Fla., N.J.; lic. gen. contractor, Fla. From field engr. to project engr. Mellon-Stuart Co., Pitts., 1976-84; project mgr. Mellon-Stuart Co., Dallas, 1984-87, Morse Diesel Internat., N.Y.C., 1987—. Mem. NSPE, ASCE, Am. Arbitration Assn. (arbitrator 1985—), Soc. Christian Design Profls. Presbyterian. Home: 5160 Leatherman Walk Pipersville PA 18947 Office: Morse Diesel Internat 120 Wood Ave S Ste 500 Iselin NJ 08830-2709

ANDERSON, JERRY ALLEN, financial analyst; b. Ashland, Wis., Feb. 10, 1947; s. Elmer and Thelma Louise (Fallis) A.; m. Anne Marie Brown, June 7, 1975; 1 child, Kristen Marie. BBA, Temple U., 1969, MBA, 1975. Sr. investment officer Girard Bank, Phila., 1970-80; sr. investment analyst Sanford C. Bernstein, N.Y.C., 1980-83; dir. planning Sperry New Holland (Pa.), Inc., 1983-85, mgr. ops. analysis, 1985-87; fin. mgr. spl. markets Ford New Holland (Pa.), Inc., 1987-91; Mex. market mgr. Ford New Holland (Pa.) Inc., 1991—; cons. in fin.; instr. sch. bus. Temple U., 1976-79, sch. bus. and govt. svcs., 1979-80. Recipient Cert. of Recognition Am. Mktg. Assn., 1968, 69, Outstanding Performance award Ford New Holland, 1987. Mem. Assn. for Investment Mgmt. and Rsch., Fin. Analysts of Phila., N.Y. Soc. Security Analysts, Model A Ford Club Am., Beta Gamma Sigma, Theta Chi. Home: 544 Norwyck Dr Kng Of Prussa PA 19406-1583 Office: Ford New Holland Inc 500 Diller Ave New Holland PA 17557-9301

ANDERSON, KATHLEEN M. REX, college divison dean; b. Phila., Nov. 2, 1944; d. John Henry and Julia Monica (Gallagher) Rex; m. John M. Anderson, Aug. 20, 1966; children: D. Scott, Jill M. AB, Chestnut Hill Coll., Phila., 1966; MA in History, Villanova (Pa.) U., 1972, MA in Adminstrn., 1984; postgrad., Widener U., Chester, Pa. Tchr. Cheltenham Twp. Schs., Wyncote, Pa., 1966-71, Internat. Sch. London, 1972-74, Rosemont (Pa.) Sch., 1979-83; dir. lower sch. Agnes Irwin Sch., Rosemont, 1983-87; grad. asst. Widener U., Chester, Pa., 1988-89; grad. dean Chestnut Hill Coll., Phila., 1990—; faculty grad. mgmt. Pa. State U., Great Valley, Pa., 1990—; participant Inst. for Prins., Harvard U., Cambridge, 1987; adv. bd. Coun. for Women in Ind. Schs., Phila., 1982—. Mem. Phila. Area Coun. for Excellence, Consortium of Grad. Schs. Democrat. Roman Catholic. Office: Chestnut Hill Coll 9701 Germantown Ave Philadelphia PA 19118

ANDERSON, KENNETH NORMAN, editor, author; b. Omaha, July 10, 1921; s. Duncan McDonald and Letitia Jane (Steed) A.; m. Lois Elaine Harman, Jan. 12, 1945; children: Eric Stephen, Randi Laine, Jani Jill, Douglas Duncan. Student, U. Omaha, 1939-41, Oreg. State Coll., 1943-44, Stanford U., 1944-45, Northwestern U. Coll. Medicine, 1945-46, U. Chgo., 1958-60. With U.S. Army Fin. Office, Nebr. and Mont., 1941-42; engring. aid U.S. Army C.E., Omaha, 1946; radio news editor Sta. KOIL, Omaha, 1946-47; bur. mgr. Internat. News Service, Omaha, 1947-56, Kansas City, Mo., 1947-56; spl. features editor Better Homes and Garden mag., 1956-57; assoc. editor Popular Mechanics mag., 1957-59; editor Today's Health mag., pub. by AMA, Chgo., 1959-65, Holt, Rinehart & Winston, N.Y.C., 1965-70; exec. dir. Coffee Info. Inst., N.Y.C., 1970-81; pres. Pubs. Editorial Svcs., Inc., Katonah, N.Y., 1981-90, The Editorial Guild, Inc., Katonah, N.Y., 1981-90; lectr. mag. writing New Sch. Social Research, 1959, NYU, 1960, Omaha U., 1961, Rennselaer Poly. Inst., 1964; cons. med. editor Ferguson Pub. Co., 1971-76. Author: (with others) Lawyers' Medical Cyclopedia, 1962, The Family Physician, 1963, Today's Health Guide, 1965, Pictorial Medical Guide, 1967, Field and Stream Guide to Physical Fitness, 1969, New Concise Family Medical and Health Guide, 1971, Complete Illustrated Book of Better Health, 1973, The New Complete Medical and Health Ency., 4 vols., 1977, The Sterno Guide to the Outdoors, 1977, Eagle Claw Fish Cookbook, 1978, Guide to Weight Control and Fitness, 1978, Newsweek Ency. of Family Health, 1980, Urdang Dictionary of Current Medical Terms, 1981, Pocket Guide to Coffee and Teas, 1982, Bantam Medical Dictionary, 1982, Mosby's Medical and Nursing Dictionary, 1982, Longman's Dictionary of Psychology and Psychiatry, 1983; editor: Hudson Health Newsletter, 1982—, Orphan Drugs, 1983, Gourmet Guide to Fish and Shellfish, 1984, Prentice-Hall Dictionary of Nutrition and Health, 1984, U.S. Military Operations, 1945-84, 1984, Mosby's Medical Encyclopedia, 1985, The Language of Sex, 1986, Industrial Medicine Desk Reference, 1986, New Pediatric Guide to Drugs & Vitamins, 1987, Symptoms after 40, 1987, Signet/Mosby Medical Encyclopedia, 1987, Consumer Guide Illustrated Medical Dictionary, 1988, Sex A to Z, 1989, Mosby's Medical, Nursing and Allied Health Dictionary, 3d edit., 1989, New York Public Library Desk Reference, 1989, Mosby's Pocket Dictionary of Medicine, Nursing and Allied Health, 1990, U.S. Military Operations: 1945-91, 1991, History of the U.S. Marines, 1992; contbr. Grolier, Funk & Wagnalls Encys.; adv. editor Nutrition Today, 1965-75. Home and Office: Kingswood Estates RR 5 Box 222 Mountain Home AR 72653-9262

ANDERSON, KENNETH PATRICK, management consultant; b. Winter Park, Fla., May 10, 1966; s. John Maurice and Julie Delores (Staggers) A. BS in Acctg., Hampton U., 1988. Acct. F.S. Taylor and Assocs., Washington, 1985, 86; cons. intern Price Waterhouse, Bethesda, Md., 1987; mktg. analyst Xerox Corp., McLean, Va., 1988, contract pricing analyst, 1989-91; sr. cost acct. GTE Govt. Systems, Rockville, Md., 1991-92; exec. v.p. ICYPB, Inc., Washington, 1992—; acctg. supr. Ogden Govt. Svcs., 1992—; cons. Washington D.C. Success Guide, 1990. Mentor, dir. Jr. Achievement, Washington, 1990—; assoc. dir. People's Youth Ministry, Washington, 1990-92; planning com. Washington D.C. Countdown to 2000, 1991-92. Mem. NAACP, Alpha Phi Alpha. Congregationalist. Home: 1608 Longfellow St NW Washington DC 20011 Office: ICYBP Inc 639-B 10th St NE Washington DC 20002

ANDERSON, KENT LEE, electronics engineer; b. Crawfordsville, Ind., Oct. 23, 1949; s. Everett Hershall and Frances Elisabeth (Handy) A. BS, Rose Hulman Inst. Tech., 1971, MS, 1973. Engr. Naval Surface Weapons Ctr., Silver Spring, Md., 1971-83, Astro Space Div. GE, Princeton, N.J., 1983—. Patentee in field of acousto-optical detection, 1985. Bd. dirs. Christian Prison Ministry, Frederick, Md., 1981—. Mem. IEEE, AIAA. Home: 26 Kelly Ct Trenton NJ 08690-3616 Office: GE Astro Space Div PO Box 800 Princeton NJ 08543-0800

ANDERSON, LAURIE, performance artist; b. Wayne, Ill., 1947; d. Arthur T. and Mary Louise (Rowland) A. BA in Art History magna cum laude, Barnard Coll., 1969; MFA in Sculpture, Columbia U., 1972. Art history instr. CCNY, 1973-75; freelance critic Art News, Art Forum. Composer and performer of multi-media exhbns. consisting of music, photography, film, drawings, animation and accompanying text; works include Story Show, 1972, Automotive, 1972, O-Range, 1973, Duets on Ice, 1973, Songs and Stories for the Insomniac, 1975, Refried Beans for Instants, 1976, For Instants Part 5, The Kitchen, N.Y.C., 1977, Handphone Table, Mus. Modern Art, N.Y.C., 1978, Americans on the Move, The Kitchen, 1979, United States I-IV, Bklyn. Acad. Music, 1983, Home of the Brave, 1986, Like a Stream-3, Born, Never Asked, It's Cold Outside; recs. include O Superman, 1981, Big Science, 1982, Let X=X, Artforum Flexi-disc, 1982, United States Live, 1985; contbr.: (album anthology) You're the Guy I Want to Share My Money With, 1982, (album) Mister Heartbreak, 1984; writer, dir., performer: (film) Home of the Brave, 1986, (album) Strange Angels, 1989; one woman shows include Barnard Coll., 1970, Harold Rivkin Gallery, Washington, 1973, Artists Space, N.Y.C., 1974, Holly Solomon Gallery, N.Y.C., 1977, 80-81, Mus. Modern Art, 1978, Queens (N.Y.) Mus., 1984, Empty Places, Spoleto Festival, Charleston, 1989, and other locations; numerous group shows since 1972 including Mrs. Contemporary Art, Chgo., 1977, Los Angeles County mus Art, 1987; artist-in-residence ZBS Media, 1975; host: Live from Off Center, 1987; author: The Package, 1971, October, 1972, Transportation, Transportation, 1973, The Rose and The Stone, 1974, Notebook, 1976, Typisch Frac, 1981. (with John Perreault) Artifacts at The End of a Decade, 1981. Grantee N.Y. State Council on Arts, 1975, 77, Nat. Endowment for Arts, 1977, 79; Guggenheim fellow, 1983. Mem. Phi Beta Kappa. Office: care Liz Rosenberg Warner Bros Records 3 E 54th St New York NY 10022-3108

ANDERSON, LEA E., lawyer; b. Clarksburg, W.Va., May 25, 1954; d. Jackson Lawler and Barbara Jean (Sanford) A.; m. Templeton Smith Jr., Aug. 20, 1980; children: Templeton Smith III, Suzanne Lea Smith. BA, W.Va. U., 1976, JD, 1979. Bar: W.Va. 1979, U.S. Dist. Ct. (so. dist.) W.Va. 1979, Pa. 1981, U.S. Supreme Ct. 1982. Assoc. Bowles, McDavid, Graff & Love, Charleston, W.Va., 1979-80; assoc. Goehring, Rutter & Boehm, Pitts., 1980-84, ptnr., 1984-89, mem., 1990—; mem. credit com. Alcobar Fed. Credit Union, 1985-87, mem. supervisory com., 1981; mem. vis. com. W.Va. Coll. Law, 1986-89. Vol. March of Dimes, 1986, neighborhood coord., 1987-91; chmn. fundraising com. Southminster Nursery Sch., 1989; bd. deacons Southminster Presbyn. Ch., Lebanon, Pa., 1990-93; chmn. Windy Ridge, 1991—; active Family Ministries Commn., 1991; mem. Performing Arts for Children, South, 1991—. Mem. W.Va. Bar Assn., Pa. Bar Assn., Allegheny County Bar Assn. (past mem. Young Lawyers' exec. com., chmn. edn. com. 1983-84, treas. 1984-85), Child Study Club of Mt. Lebanon (pres. 1989-91), Phi Beta Kappa, Phi Kappa Phi, Phi Delta Phi. Republican. Office: Goehring Rutter & Boehm 1424 Frick Bldg 437 Grant Ave Pittsburgh PA 15219

ANDERSON, LEONARD LOUIS, laboratory administrator; b. Boston, Sept. 20, 1934; s. Everett Frank and Concetta (Vozzeilla) A.; m. M. Bernadette Judge, June 3, 1961; children: Christine, Eric, Lauren. BA, Harvard U., 1956; MA, Boston U., 1963; DSc, Sussex U., Brighton, Eng., 1974. Biochemist Gen. Foods Corp., Boston, 1956-57, Boston U. Med. Sch., 1959-60; rsch. biochemist Mass. Gen. Hosp., Boston, 1960-63, Tufts U., Boston, 1963-66; clin. researcher Lahey Clinic Found., Boston, 1966-79; biochemist Goddard Med. Assocs., Brockton, Mass., 1979-81; clin. rsearcher, supr. gen. lab. Biostat Lab., Brockton, 1981-84; lab. dir. New Eng. Sinai Hosp., Stoughton, Mass., 1984-88, St. John of God Hosp., Brookline, Mass., 1988—. Contbr. articles to sci. jours., chpt. to book. Soccer coach Bridgewater (Mass.) Youth Soccer Assn., 1980-86. With U.S. Army, 1957-59. Mem. Am. Fedn. for Clin. Rsch., Am. Soc. for Med. Tech., N.Y. Acad. Scis., Mass. Archaeol. Soc. (field archaeologist 1979—), Sigma Xi. Roman Catholic. Home: 353 Hayward St Bridgewater MA 02324-1912 Office: St John of God Hosp 296 Allston St Brookline MA 02146-1659

ANDERSON, LESLIE BRIAN, corporate executive, marketing professional; b. Hanover, Pa., Nov. 30, 1948; s. Francis Gerald and Dorothy (Sawyer) A.; m. Linda Katzenstein, Aug. 12, 1972; children: David, Shauna, Kerra. BSBA, U. Richmond, Va., 1971; JD, U. Balt., 1976. Asst. David M. Milton Assocs., N.Y.C., 1971-72; owner Vendomatics, Inc., Washington, 1972-77; fin. and ins. mgr. Pat Ryan Ins. Co., Chgo., 1977; dist. sales mgr. Holton Industries, Little Silver, N.J., 1978-79, plant mgr., 1979-82, v.p. mktg. div., 1982-84; pres. Medico Internat., Inc., Easton, Pa., 1984—; cons. Lab Products, Maywood, N.J., 1985—. Inventor 1st pre-saturated disinfectant wipe cide-swipes. With U.S. Army, 1971-77. Republican. Baptist. Office: Medico Internat Inc PO Box 3092 Easton PA 18043-3092

ANDERSON, LESTER WILLIAM, marketing professional; b. San Francisco, Oct. 7, 1943; s. Lester Fraver and Sarah Frances (Williams) A.; m. Linda Jean Vause, Sept. 1, 1967; children: William A., Christopher M. Student, East Carolina U., 1967-70; MBA, Wake Forest U., 1976; postgrad., U. Pa. From dir. salesman and regional v.p. Renn Enterprises Ltd., Winston-Salem, N.C., 1967-74; regional mgr. Mini-Skools Ltd., Winston-Salem, N.C., 1976-79; assoc., cons. Hayes & Assoc., Inc., Winston-Salem, N.C., 1979-82; sr. v.p. Nat. Energy Assn., Norcress, Ga., 1982-85; v.p. Corp. Resource Devel., Atlanta, 1985-87; v.p. resource devel. Delaware Group, Phila., 1987—; guest speaker on numerous TV and radio shows worldwide. Coach Pop Warner Football, Clemmon, N.C., 1974-82. Sgt. USMC, 1963-67, Vietnam. Decorated two Purple Hearts, Vietnam Cross of Gallantry. Mem. Soc. for Tng. and Devel., Nat. Speakers Assn., Univ. Club. Home: 5155 Cralyn Ct Duluth GA 30136-2450 Office: Delaware Group One Commerce Sq Philadelphia PA 19103

ANDERSON, MARGERY LAWRENCE, consultant; b. Summit, N.J., Dec. 28, 1949; d. John R. and Margaret (Wiley) A. B of Music, Coll. Wooster, 1971; MEd, Xavier U., 1976. Analyst Cin. Bell, 1977-87; sr. cons. Circorp, Pitts., 1987—. Pres. Parkview Condo West Assn., Pitts., 1988-91; chmn. Sunday divsn. Tuesday Mus. Club, Pitts., 1992—. Mem. Toastmasters. Presbyterian. Office: Circorp Penn Ctr West 2 Pittsburgh PA 15276

ANDERSON, MARK RANSOM, English educator; b. Wichita, Kans., Sept. 3, 1951; s. Berthold Sanden and Opal Marie (Ransom) A.; m. Susan Aileen Grimes, July 29, 1984; 1 child, Miles Berthold. BA, Cornell U., 1973, MFA, 1977, PhD, 1983, postgrad., 1983-84; MA, U. Minn., 1976. Postdoctoral fellow Cornell U., 1983-84; asst. prof. English, R.I. Coll., Providence, 1985-91, assoc. prof., 1991—; vis. asst. prof. Emory U., Atlanta, 1984-85. Author: The Broken Boat, 1978, Serious Joy, 1990; author numerous poems. Recipient Corson-Bishop poetry prize Cornell U., 1978. Mem. MLA, Nat. Coun. Tchrs. English, Assoc. Writing Programs, Poetry Soc. Am., Acad. Am. Poets (prize 1981). Office: RI College English Dept Providence RI 02908

ANDERSON, MICHAEL THOMAS, mathematics researcher, educator; b. Boulder, Colo., Nov. 17, 1950; s. Julian Thompson and Elinor Elizabeth (Uhl) A.; m. Myong-Hi Kim, Aug. 15, 1986. BA, U. Calif., Santa Barbara, 1975; MA, U. Calif., Berkeley, 1977, PhD, 1981. Research instr. Rice U., Houston, 1981-84; asst., then assoc., prof. Calif. Inst. Tech., Pasadena, 1984-88; assoc. prof. SUNY, Stony Brook, 1988-90, prof., 1990—. Editor Jour. Geometric and Functional Analysis, Duke Math. Jour.; contbr. articles to profl. jours. NSF grantee, 1982-84, 86—, postdoctoral fellow, 1984-86. Mem. Am. Math. Soc. (fellow 1990-91). Democrat. Office: SUNY Dept Math Stony Brook NY 11797

ANDERSON, PAUL GUSTAVUS, secondary school educator; b. Brockton, Mass., July 8, 1935; s. Ralph Gustavus and Naomi B. (Olander) A.; m. Julia Frances Cheek, Aug. 9, 1959; children: Jennifer, Stephen. MusB, Westmin-

ster Choir Coll., Princeton, N.J., 1959. Tchr. Neshaminy Sch. Dist., Langhorne, Pa., 1961—; chair lang. arts Neshaminy Sch. Dist., 1962-88, dir. humanities, 1964-69. Co-author: Writing to be Read, 1978. Trustee Village Libr., Wrightstown, Pa., 1980-83. Mem. Masons (comdr.-in-chief A.A.S.R. 1992-93, mem. supreme coun. no. jurisdiction), Royal Order Scotland. Republican. Lutheran. Home: 192 Williams Ave Newton PA 18940 Office: Neshaminy Sch Dist Langhorne PA 19047

ANDERSON, PETER IRVING, marketing executive; b. Worcester, Mass., Dec. 8, 1950; s. Robert I. and Nancy M. (Estabrook) A.; m. Cathy Williams, July 8, 1950; children: Kate Williams, Elizabeth Williams. BA in Chemistry, St. Anselm Coll., 1972; MS in Chemistry, John Carroll U., 1974; MBA, U. Conn., 1978; grad., Nat. Inst. Golf Mgmt., Wheeling, W.Va., 1990. Chemist corp. rsch. and devel. Ensign Bickford Industries, Inc., Simsbury, Conn., 1974-77, tech. devel. supr., 1977-78, tech. supr., 1980-82, mgr. rsch. and devel., 1982-86, mgr. mktg. and sales, 1986—; market devel. specialist Albany Internat. Corp., Johnston, R.I., 1978-79, Leesona Corp., Warwick, R.I., 1979-80. V.p. Spring Glen Homeowners Assn., Granby, Conn., 1986, pres., 1987-89; advisor Jr. Achievement, Simsbury, Conn., 1980-81, cons., 1980-82. Mem. Am. Chem. Soc., Soc. Palstic Engrs. (bd. dirs. 1981-87, treas. 1983-85, v.p. 1985-86, pres. 1986-87, bd. dirs. plastics edn. found. 1992—), Am. Concrete Inst., Nat. Golf Found. Roman Catholic. Office: Ensign Bickford Industries Inc Fil Fibers Div 630 Hopmeadow St Simsbury CT 06070-2420

ANDERSON, PHILIP WARREN, physicist; b. Indpls., Dec. 13, 1923; s. Harry W. and Elsie (Osborne) A.; m. Joyce Gothwaite, July 31, 1947; 1 dau., Susan Osborne. B.S., Harvard U., 1943, M.A., 1947, Ph.D., 1949; D.Sc. (hon.), U. Ill., 1979; DSc (hon.), Rutgers U., 1991, U. Ill., 1991. Mem. staff Naval Research Lab., 1943-45; mem. tech. staff Bell Telephone Labs., Murray Hill, N.J., 1949-84; chmn. theoretical physics dept. Bell Telephone Labs., 1959-60, asst. dir. phys. research lab., 1974-76, cons. dir., 1976-84; researcher in quantum theory, especially theoretical physics of solids, spectral line broadening, magnetism, superconductivity; Fulbright lectr. U. Tokyo, 1953-54; Loeb lectr. Harvard U., 1964; prof. theoretical physics Cambridge (Eng.) U., 1967-75; prof. physics Princeton U., 1975—; Overseas fellow Churchill Coll., Cambridge U., 1961-62; fellow Jesus Coll., 1969-75, hon. fellow, 1978—; Bethe lectr., 1984; external prof., Santa Fe Inst., 1990—. Author: Concepts in Solids, 1963, Basic Notions of Condensed Matter Physics, 1984. Recipient Oliver E. Buckley prize Am. Physical Soc., 1964; Dannie Heinemann prize Göttingen (Ger.) Acad. Scis., 1975; Nobel prize in physics, 1977; Guthrie medal Inst. of Physics, 1978; Nat. Medal Sci., 1982. Fellow AAAS, Am. Phys. Soc., Am. Acad. Arts and Scis., Japan Acad. Scis. (fgn.), Indian Acad. Scis. (fgn.); mem. Nat. Acad. Scis., Royal Soc. (fgn.), Accademia Lincei, Am. Philos. Soc., N.Y. Acad. Scis. (hon. life). Office: Princeton U Dept Physics Princeton NJ 08544

ANDERSON, R. QUINTUS, diversified company executive; b. Jamestown, N.Y., Nov. 27, 1930; s. Paul N. and Cecille (Ogren) A.; m. Sondra Rumsey, June 5, 1954; children: Heidi, Kristin, Gerrit, Mitchell, Tracy, Brooks. Grad., Phillips Acad., Andover, Mass., 1949; BS in Engring., Princeton U., 1953; postgrad., Grad. Sch. Indsl. Mgmt., MIT. With Dahlstrom Corp., Jamestown, 1957-76, exec. v.p., 1965, pres., 1968-76; founder, pres. Aarque Steel Corp., Jamestown, 1976-78, Aarque Mgmt. Corp., Jamestown, 1978—; founder, chmn. Aarque Cos., Jamestown, 1980—; bd. dirs. Chase Lincoln 1st Bank, N.A., Bus. Council N.Y. State, Inc.; chmn. Aarque Office Systems, Inc., Aarque Holdings Ltd., Cold Metal Products Co., Inc., Aarque Steel Group, Kardex Systems, Inc.; trustee Northwestern Mut. Life Ins. Co. Patentee in field. Chmn. Jamestown United Fund drive, 1964, 74; bd. dirs. N.Y. State Dept. Environ. Conservation; trustee Bethany Coll., Roger Tory Peterson Inst., Chautauqua Found. Inc.; civilian aide to Sec. of the U.S. Army; mem. adv. bd. World Econ. Forum. Served with USNR, 1954-57. Mem. Mfrs. Assn. Jamestown Area (pres. 1967-68), Empire State C. of C. (pres. 1974-76), Royal Round Table of Swedish Coun. Am., U.S. Can. Trade Coun., U.S. Dept. Commerce Ind. Sector Adv. Com., Tau Beta Pi. Republican. Episcopalian. Clubs: Moon Brook Country (Jamestown); Sportsmen's (Chautaqua, N.Y.); Union League Met. (N.Y.C.). Office: Aarque Cos 111 W 2d St Jamestown NY 14701

ANDERSON, RANDALL KEITH, lawyer; b. Iowa City, Nov. 11, 1952; s. Layton Paul and Viola Margaret (Brown) A.; m. Judith Esta Hollander, Aug. 14, 1982; 1 child, Kerstin Shulamit. BA, Am. U., 1974; JD, Georgetown U., 1980. Bar: N.Y. 1980. Analyst Foster Assocs., Washington, 1974-76; sr. analyst Am. Gas Assn., Rosalyn, Va., 1976-78; clk. U.S. Dist. Ct. Balt., 1980-81; assoc. Cravath, Swaine & Moore, N.Y.C., 1981-85; ptnr. Anderson, Raymond & Lowenthal, N.Y.C., 1985-87, Anderson & Raymond (merger Wachtell, Manheim & Grouf), N.Y.C., 1988-91; pvt. practice N.Y.C., 1991—. Mem. ABA, Internat. Assn. Young Lawyers (v.p. U.S. 1987—). Democrat. Methodist. Home and Office: 395 Broadway Apt 11B New York NY 10013-3541

ANDERSON, REID BRYCE, ballet company artistic director; b. New Westminister, B.C., Can., Apr. 1, 1949; s. Warren Nels and Phyllis Jessie Bryce (Purser) A. Student dance, Dolores Kirkwood, Burnaby, B.C., Royal Ballet Sch., 1967, 68. Dancer Stuttgart (Fed. Republic Germany) Ballet, 1969-86, prin. dancer, 1975-86, ballet master, 1982-86; artistic dir. Ballet B.C., Vancouver, 1987-89, Nat. Ballet Can., Toronto, Ont., 1989—. Choreographer numerous works for performing cos. Decorated Order of Fed. Republic Germany, 1986. Office: Nat Ballet of Can, 157 King St E, Toronto, ON Canada M5C 1G9

ANDERSON, RICHARD ALAN, mechanical engineer; b. N.Y.C., Mar. 7, 1933; s. Douglas Alexander and Alice Katrina (Wenning) A. BSME, CCNY, 1955. Engr. Raytheon Corp., Wayland, Mass., 1955-59, CDI, Needham, Mass., 1959-79, GE, Wilmington, Mass., 1979-92. Inventor LCD packaging, circuit interconnect to liquid crystal display. Home: 4356 LakeShore Dr Santa Clara CA 95054-1333

ANDERSON, RICHARD ALLEN, biochemist, consultant, nutritionist; b. Middle River, Minn., May 28, 1946; s. Frank William and Harriet Elizabeth (Von Wald) A.; m. Sylvia Griffin, Aug. 20, 1966; children: Brent G., Deborah D. BS, Concordia Coll., Moorhead, Minn., 1968; PhD, Iowa State U., 1973. Rsch. assoc. Harvard Med. Sch., Boston, 1973-75; lead scientist Beltsville (Md.) Human Nutrition Ctr., 1975—; mem. program com. 2d Internat. Symposium on Trace Elements, Tokyo, 1987; mem. sci. com. Trace Elements in Medicine and Biology, Grenoble, France, 1989. Author: (with others) Exercise, Nutrition & Energy Metabolism, 1988, Metal Ions, 1990, Essential & Toxic Trace Elements in Health, 1991; mem. editorial bd. Jour. Trace Elements Exptl. Medicine, 1985—. Recipient Merit award USDA, 1983, 85, Disting. Alumnus award Iowa State U., 1991, Labcatral Trace Metal prize Labcatral Enterprises, Grenoble, 1991. Mem. Am. Inst. Nutrition. Office: Beltsville Human Nutrition Ctr Bldg 307 Rm 224 Beltsville MD 20705

ANDERSON, RICHARD EUGENE, marketing professional; b. Grand Rapids, Mich., Jan. 16, 1930; s. Delmar N. and Mildred E. (Peterson) A.; m. Jean Spencer, June, 1952 (div. 1981); children: Richard, Susan, Robert, Linda; m. Janine Onimus, May 30, 1981. MS in Chemistry, U. Mich., 1953, MS in Math., 1954, PhD, 1957; MBA, NYU, 1960. Rsch. chemist Am. Cyanamid, Stamford, Conn., 1957-60; comml. devel. mgr. Allied Chem., Morristown, N.J., 1961-65; tech. dir. Chase Manhattan Bank, N.Y.C., 1965-71; v.p. chems. Amax, Inc., Greenwich, Conn., 1971-81; v.p. mktg. Atalanta/Sosnoff Capital, N.Y.C., 1981—; adj. prof. mktg. CUNY, 1967-86. Author: Administration of the Chemical Enterprise, 1972. Pres. Aldrich Mus. Contemporary Art, 1978-91, treas., 1991—, trustee, 1976—. Republican. Presbyterian. Home: 107 River Run Greenwich CT 06831-4149 Office: Atalanta/Sosnoff Capital 101 Park Ave New York NY 10178-0002

ANDERSON, ROBERT ROGER, company executive; b. Worcester, Mass., July 14, 1959; s. Curtis Winthrop and Muriel (Carlos) A.; 1 child, Marques. Student, Quinsigamond Community Coll., 1981-82. Pres. W.E.C. Prodns., Worcester, 1984—; cons. Prospect House, Worcester, 1988-91, City Mgrs. Office, Worcester, 1990, Phoenix Multi Svcs., Worcester, 1991; mem. minority adv. com. Quinsigamond Community Coll., 1991—. Cons. Com. to Elect Lynn Symonds, Worcester, 1989-90, Com. to Elect Dave Lionett, Worcester, 1990; co-chairperson AIDS/Homeless Com., Worcester, 1988-90. Home and Office: 11 Laurel St Apt 27 Worcester MA 01608-1058

ANDERSON, ROBERT SIMPERS, educator, comparative immunologist; b. Bryn Mawr, Pa., Jan. 4, 1939; s. Paul Alexander and Ella Trew Simpers Anderson; m. Lucy Anne MacDonald, Aug. 29, 1964; children: Robert S. Jr., Donald Paul. BS, Drexel U., 1961; MS, Hahnemann Med. U., 1968; PhD, U. Del., 1971. Postdoctoral fellow U. Minn., Mpls., 1970-73; rsch. lab. head Sloan-Kettering Inst. Cancer Rsch., Rye, N.Y., 1973-82; rsch. biologist U.S. Army Chem. R&D Ctr., Aberdeen Proving Ground, Md., 1982-86; prof. U. Md., Solomons, Md., 1986—; asst. prof. Cornell U. Grad. Sch. of Med. Sci., N.Y.C., 1975-82; adj. prof. Sloan-Kettering Inst. for Cancer Rsch., N.Y., 1982-84. Editor Revs. in Aquatic Scis.; editorial bd. Devel. and Comparative Immunology, Jour. Invertebrate Pathology. Grantee NIH, Dept. Def., NSF, NOAA, EPA, Whitehall Found., Griffis Found., Md. Sea Grant and others. Mem. Am. Assn. of Immunologists, Am. Soc. Zoologists (program officer 1981-83, pub. affairs com. 1991—), Soc. for Invertebrate Pathology (sec. 1989-91, chair membership com. 1986-88, trustee 1992-96), N.Y. Acad. Scis., Soc. Toxicology, Sigma Xi. Republican. Episcopalian. Office: Chesapeake Biol Lab U Md PO Box 38 Solomons MD 20688-0038

ANDERSON, ROLPH ELY, marketing educator; b. Buchanan, Mich., Aug. 27, 1936; s. Eugene Jefferson and Susanna (James) A.; m. Sallie Durkee Warner; children: Rachel Elizabeth, Stuart James. BA, Mich. State U., 1958, MBA, 1964; Ph.D., U. Fla., 1971. Mgr. new product devel. Quaker Oats Co., Chgo., 1964-67; prof., chmn. dept. bus. mgmt. Old Dominion U., Norfolk, Va., 1971-75; prof., chmn. dept. mktg. Drexel U., Phila., 1975—. Co-author: Introduction to Multivariate Data Analysis, 1974, Multivariate Data Analysis, 1979, 3d edit., 1992, Sales Management, 1983, Professional Sales Management, 1988, 2d edit., 1992; author: Professional Personal Selling, 1991; contbr. numerous articles to profl. and acad. jours. Served to capt. USNR (Ret.). Mem. S.E. Am. Inst. Decision Scis. (pres. 1977-78), Am. Inst. Decision Scis. (nat. council 1977-79), Am. Mktg. Assn. (internat. conf. co-chmn. 1978; v.p. programming Phila. chpt. 1984-85, bd. dirs. 1986-87, 92—), Sales and Mktg. Execs. Internat., So. Mktg. Assn., Acad. Mktg. Sci. (sec. 1984-86), Naval Res. Assn., N.E. Am. Inst. Decision Scis. (bd. dirs. 1977-78), Res. Officers Assn., Beta Gamma Sigma. Office: Drexel Univ Coll Bus and Adminstrn Philadelphia PA 19104

ANDERSON, ROSS BARRETT, health science facility administrator; b. Toronto, Ont., Aug. 25, 1951; came to U.S., 1956; s. John Ross and Constance (Nielson) A.; m. Gladys Jeanette Vincent, Aug. 26, 1972; children: Christopher Matthew, John Ross II, Josiah Dan. Student, Boston U., 1970-73. Housekeeping supr. Parker Hill Med. Ctr., Roxbury, Mass., 1973-76; housekeeping mgr. Union Hosp., Lynn, Mass., 1976-77, Quincy (Mass.) City Hosp., 1977-78, St. Joseph's Hosp., Lowell, Mass., 1978-79; housekeeping mgr. Waltham Weston Hosp. and Med. Ctr., Waltham, Mass., 1979-86, support services mgr., 1986-90, dir. environ. svcs., 1991—, chmn. customer svcs. bd., 1992. Active Boston Latin Sch. Assn., 1985—, Scots Charitable Soc. Boston, 1989—, Free Evang. Fellowship, Easton, Mass., 1991—. Home: 389 Crescent St West Bridgewater MA 02379-1425 Office: Waltham Weston Hosp & Med Ctr Hope Ave Waltham MA 02154-2712

ANDERSON, RUSSELL KARL, JR., physicist, horse breeder; b. Passaic, N.J., Jan. 5, 1943; s. Russell Karl and Hilda (Bartles) A.; m. Jane Louise Blair, Apr. 20, 1973; children: Christina Lynn, Melissa Jane. BS in Physics, Fairleigh Dickinson U., 1965; MS in Physics, Rensselaer Poly. Inst., 1967; cert., Penn Tech. Inst., Pitts., 1969; MBA, Duquesne U., 1973. Scientist Westinghouse Bettis Atomic Power Lab., West Mifflin, Pa., 1967-73; engr. Westinghouse Nuclear & Advanced Tech. Div., Ctr., Westinghouse Energy Systems Div., Energy Ctr., Monroeville, Pa., 1973—. NSF grantee, 1969. Mem. Am. Quarter Horse Assn., Nat. Snaffle Bit Assn., Western Pa. Quarter Horse Assn., Phi Omega Epsilon. Home: Fern Valley Farm PO Box 12 Fenelton PA 16034 Office: Westinghouse Electric Corp PO Box 355 Pittsburgh PA 15230-0355

ANDERSON, THEODORE ROBERT, physicist; b. Lodi, Ohio, Jan. 30, 1949; s. Robert Anderson and LaVaughn (Mitchell) Gillotti. BS in Physics, Fla. State U., 1971; postgrad. in math. physics, U. Geneva, Switzerland, 1973, 75; MS in Physics, NYU, 1979, MS in Applied Sci., 1983, PhD in Physics, 1986. Nuclear engr. Gibbs & Hill Inc., N.Y.C., 1980-83; rsch. physicist elec. boat div. Gen. Dynamics, Groton, Conn., 1983-88; rsch. physicist Naval Underwater Systems Ctr., New London, Conn., 1988—; adj. prof. mech. engring., ocean engring., astronomy U. Conn., Storrs, Groton, 1983—, Mitchell Coll., Manchester, Conn., 1985, Rensselaer Poly. Inst., Hartford, 1986—, U. New Haven Sch. Bus., Conn., 1989—, mech. engring., 1983—, elec. engring., 1983—, U. Hartford, 1990—, U. Bridgeport, 1989—, CUNY Hunter Coll., 1979-83, Long Island U., 1980-83; instr. Cooper Union Sch. Engring., N.Y.C., 1980. Active Met. Opera Guild, N.Y.C., 1986—, Mus. Modern Art, N.Y.C., 1985—, Met. Mus. Art, N.Y.C., 1984—, Am. Mus. Natural History, N.Y.C., 1987—, N.Y. Shakespeare Festival, 1987—, N.Y. Zool. Soc., 1988—, Ea. Nat. Park and Monument Assn., 1990—. Recipient Spl. Achievement award USN, 1989, 90. Mem. Am. Phys. Soc., AIAA, Soc. Rheology. Home: 2 Lake Dr Old Lyme CT 06371-1211

ANDERSON, THEODORE WELLINGTON, portfolio strategist; b. Napa, Calif., Apr. 30, 1941; s. Theodore William and Donna Elorita (Dove) A.; children: Thomas Wellington, Hilary Dove. Student, Princeton U., 1959-60; BA, Stanford U., 1963; MBA, U. Calif., Berkeley, 1966. Portfolio mgr., v.p. John W. Bristol Inc., N.Y.C., 1968-77; assoc. rsch. dir., sr. v.p. Argus Rsch., N.Y.C., 1977-82; portfolio strategist The Ford Found., N.Y.C., 1982—. Mem. Fin. Analysts Fedn., N.Y. Soc. Security Analysts, Angler's Club of N.Y. (treas.), Princeton Club of N.Y., Theodore Gordon Flyfishers, Trout Unltd. Episcopalian. Home: PO Box 432 Chappaqua NY 10514-0432 Office: The Ford Found 320 E 43rd St New York NY 10017-4816

ANDERSON, THOMAS CARYL, financial and administrative systems professional; b. St. Paul, Sept. 3, 1944; s. Willis Cecil and Mary Lou (Kaun) A.; m. Catherine Sophia Hofstede, Apr. 20, 1968; children: Nicole, Jennifer, Karilyn. BS, U. Minn., 1966, MS, 1970. Asst. prof. Northeastern U., Boston, 1971-74; lectr. SUNY-Albany, 1974-87, dir. grad. program Sch. Bus., 1976-81, dir. fin. and adminstrv. svcs., 1981-85, exec. officer adminstrn. and fin., 1985-87; dir. adminstrv. svcs. MGH Inst. Health Professions, Boston, 1987-90, v.p. adminstrn. and fin., 1990—; cons. various state govt. agys., Albany, 1978-87, GM, CPC Tarrytown, N.Y.,1 988-89, U. Mass., Lowell, 1990—; asst. sec. MGH Inst. Bd. Trustees, Boston, 1987—. Co-author: Elements of Organizational Behavior, 1972; contbr. articles to profl. publs. Mem. exec. com. Cen. Mass. Regional Planning Commn., 1990—. Home: 19 Plain St Hopedale MA 01747-1407 Office: MGH IHP 15 15 River St Boston MA 02108-3413

ANDERSON, THOMAS PATRICK, mechanical engineer, educator; b. Chgo., Oct. 22, 1934; s. Clarence Kenneth and Anne (Moran) A.; m. Elizabeth Ann Toof, July 9, 1960; children—Patricia, James. B.S. in Mech. Engring., Northwestern U., 1956, M.S., 1958, Ph.D., 1961. Registered profl. engr., Ill., Iowa. Engr. Askania Regulator Co., Chgo., 1953-55; research engr. Cook Research Labs., Skokie, Ill., summer, 1956; rsch. engr. ARO Inc., Tullahoma, Tenn., summers 1958, 59; asst. prof., then assoc. prof. Northwestern U., 1960-66; prof. mech. engring. U. Iowa, 1966-75, chmn. dept., 1966-70; program mgr. Office Systems Integration and Analysis, NSF, 1974-75, program mgr. div. intergovtl. sci. and pub. tech., 1975-78, acting dir. indsl. program, 1976-78; dean Sch. Sci. and engring., So. Ill. U., Edwardsville, 1978-83; prof. Sch. Engring. So. Ill. U., 1978—; cons., assoc. dep. dir. interdeptl. energy study Office Sci. and Tech., 1963-65. Contbr. numerous articles to profl. jours. Named One of Ten Outstanding Young Men Chgo. Jr. Assn. Commerce and Industry, 1964. Fellow Iowa Acad. Sci.; mem. AAUP, Am. Geophys. Union, AIAA, Am. Phys. Soc., Am. Soc. Engring. Edn., ASME, N.Y. Acad. Scis., Sigma Xi.

ANDERSON, TOM SHERIDAN, safety professional; b. Chgo., Dec. 19, 1954; s. Leo S. and Phyllis A. (Doherty) A.; m. Laura Rae Menzel, Dec. 28, 1982; children: Ray, Kathleen, Margaret. BS in Nautical Sci., Maine Maritime Acad., 1979. Cert. safety profl. Deck officer Crowley Maritime Corp., Seattle, 1979-81; dir. safety and health Am. Steamship Co., Buffalo, 1985—. Lt. USCG, 1981-85, 90-91. Mem. Nat. Safety Coun. (gen. chmn. marine sect. 1989-90), Am. Soc. Safety Engrs., Soc. Naval Architects and Marine Engrs. Office: 3200 Marine Midland Ctr Buffalo NY 14203-2832

ANDERSON, VALERIE LEE, educator; b. Worcester, Mass., Dec. 9, 1955; d. John Willard and Shirley Anne (Enman) A. BS summa cum laude, Worcester State Coll., 1977, MEd summa cum laude, 1983, postgrad., 1987; EdD, Calif. Coast U., 1992. Cert. elem. tchr., prin., supt., Mass. Tchr. elem. grades Worcester Pub. Schs., 1977-80; resource tchr. high sch. Northbridge Pub. Schs., Whitinsville, Mass., 1980-81; supr. grade sch. programs Kindercare Learning Ctrs., Inc., Westboro, Mass., 1981-83; reading tchr. Millbury (Mass.) Pub. Schs., 1983-87, 89—, tchr. 3rd grade, 1987-88, tchr. 1st grade, 1988-89. Mem. Worcester Art Mus. Mem. Internat. Reading Assn., Mass. Reading Assn., Cen. Mass. Reading Coun. (rec. sec. 1985-87, 92—), Cen. Mass. Coun. for Social Studies, Whole Lang. Tchrs. Assn., Old Sturbridge Village, New Eng. Sci. Ctr., Psychol. Honor Soc., Kappa Delta Pi (treas.). Methodist. Home: 11 Ash St Spencer MA 01562-2246

ANDERSON, WALTER DIXON, trade association management consultant; b. Elizabeth, N.J., July 22, 1932; s. Charles Michael and Hazel Mildred (Fieldstad) A. B.A., Emory U., 1954; M.A., U. Ga., 1958. State rep. Nat. Found. March of Dimes, Jacksonville, Fla., 1958-61; exec. sec. Fla. Turf-Grass Assn., Jacksonville, 1961-69; exec. dir. Irrigation Assn., Silver Spring, Md., 1969-80; exec. v.p. Irrigation Assn., 1980-85; exec. dir. Contractors Pump Bur., 1972—; mng. dir. Resilient Floor Covering Inst., 1987—. Served with U.S. Army, 1954-56. Mem. ASTM, Am. Soc. Assn. Execs., Washington Soc. Assn. Execs., Sigma Delta Chi. Republican. Methodist. Home: 6700 Heatherford Ct Rockville MD 20855-1521 Office: PO Box 5858 Rockville MD 20850

ANDERSON, WALTER HERMAN, magazine editor; b. Mt. Vernon, N.Y., Aug. 31, 1944; s. William Henry and Ethel Magdalena (Crolly) A.; m. Loretta Gritz, Sept. 9, 1967; children: Eric Christian, Melinda Christe. AA, Westchester Community Coll., 1970; BS summa cum laude, Mercy Coll., 1972; DHL (hon.), St. Ambrose U., 1988, Clemson U., 1990, Mercy Coll., 1989, U. of the Pacific, 1990. Reporter Reporter Dispatch, White Plains, N.Y., 1967-68, night city editor, 1968-69, editor, gen. mgr., 1975-77; police reporter Westchester Rockland Newspapers, White Plains, N.Y., 1969-70, help editor for action line, 1970-71, investigative reporter, 1971-72; editor, gen. mgr. Standard Star, New Rochelle, N.Y., 1974-75; sr. editor Parade mag., N.Y.C., 1977-78, mng. editor, 1978-80, editor, 1980—; guest lectr. Columbia U., NYU, U. Mass.; adj. prof. psychology, sociology Westchester Community Coll., 1972—. Author: Courage is a Three-Letter Word, 1986, The Greatest Risk of All, 1988, Read With Me, 1990, Read With Me, 1990. Chmn. bd. trustees Mercy Coll., Dobbs Ferry, N.Y., 1980-88; bd. dirs. St. Vincent's Hosp., 1975-80, N.Y. Vietnam Vets. Leadership Program Inc., 1984—, Dropout Prevention Fund, 1987—, Nat. Ctr. for Family Literacy, 1990—, Pub. Broadcasting Svc., 1992—; nat. spokesman GED, 1985—; mem. Nat. Com. for Lit. Arts; bd. advisors Naval Postgrad. Sch., 1988—; mem. nat. adv. bd. Lit. Vols., 1990—; bd. trustees Phelps Stokes Fund. With USMC, 1961-66. Recipient Valedictory award Westchester Community Coll., 1970, Frank Tripp Meml. award Gannett Group, 1971, Tree of Life award Jewish Nat. Fund, 1988, Spirit of Am. award, 1988, Napoleon Hill Gold award 1989, Literacy Vols. of Am. Stars in Literacy cert., 1990, and others. Mem. Soc. Silurians, Sigma Delta Chi, Psi Chi. Club: Overseas Press. Office: 750 3d Ave New York NY 10017

ANDERSON, WENDELL LOWRIE, retired civilian military employee; b. Altoona, Pa., Sept. 8, 1922; s. Robert G. and Elizabeth C. (Bulick) A.; m. Shirley Mae Smith, May 27, 1945; children: Wendell Lee, Larry Bruce. BS, Pa. State U., 1944, postgrad., 1945; postgrad., U. Md., 1948-50, 58-60, Va. Polytech. VPI, 1975-79. Rsch. engr. Naval Rsch. Lab., Washington, 1945-60, sect. head, 1960-71; br. head Naval Surface Warfare Ctr., Dahlgren, Va., 1971-73, dept. head, 1973-80, assoc. tech. dir., 1980-83; vis. lectr. Harvard Grad. Sch. Pub. Health, Boston, 1965—; cons. various industry and acad. firms. Author: (with others) Man-Made Textile Encyclopedia, 1959, Closed Ecological Systems, 1963, Place Filter Testing, 1969, Nuclear Air Cleaning Handbook, 1990; contbr. articles to profl. jours. With USN, 1944-45, PTO. Recipient Kratel award European Contamination Assn., 1970. Mem. Am. Filtration Soc., Am. Chem. Soc., Washington Acad. Scis., Internat. Soc. Nuclear Air Treatment Techs. (bd. dirs. 1989-91). Home and Office: RR 4 Box 4172 La Plata MD 20646-9804

ANDERSON, WILLIAM ALBERT, counselor; b. Springfield, Mass., Nov. 1, 1949; s. Herbert Carl Frederick and Jean Marie (Bishop) A.; m. Christine Margaret Russell, July 3, 1971; children: Amber Marisa, Lincoln Eli. BS, U. Mass., 1990. Chief exec. officer Neptune, Inc., West Springfield, Mass., 1973-81, ProHealth, Inc., Springfield, 1982—; counselor Wing Meml. Hosp., Palmer, Mass., 1989-91, Coastal Recovery Ctrs., Sarasota, Fla., 1991—. Author: Mind Diet, 1987. Deacon 1st Ch. of Monson, 1987-90. Mem. AACD, Internat. Assn. Eating Disorder Profls., Assn. Humanistic Edn. and Devel., Am. Mental Health Counselors Assn. Home: 4017 Crockers Lake Blvd Sarasota FL 34238-5515

ANDERSON-CHERRY, SHERRI LYNN, counselor; b. Washington, Sept. 3, 1965; d. Carl Edwin and Ida Lillian (Bass) Anderson; m. Xavier Carmichael Cherry, June 1, 1991. BA, Howard U., 1988, MEd, 1990. Lic. rape crisis counselor. U.S. Capitol page U.S. Ho. of Reps., Washington, 1981-83, Dem. overseer, 1982-83; telephone operator Howard U., Washington, 1984-86, grad. asst., 1988-90; manpower devel. specialist Dept. Employment Svcs., Washington, 1990—; Hotline counselor D.C. Rape Crisis Ctr., Washington, 1990—. Mem. AACD, Am. Coll. Pers. Assn., Nat. Employment Counselors Assn., Pub. Offenders Counselors Assn., Alpha Kappa Alpha. Democrat. Home: 2100 Yorktown Rd NW Washington DC 20012-2249 Office: Dept Employment Svcs 605 G St NW Washington DC 20001-3754

ANDERSSON, YERKER JOHAN OLOF, sociology educator; b. Vallentuna, Sweden, Nov. 29, 1929; came to U.S. 1955; s. Josef Martin Olof and Estrid Margareta (Olsson) A.; m. Ann Marie Timko, July 4, 1959. BA, Gallaudet U., 1960; MA, Columbia U., 1962; PhD, U. Md., 1981. Guidance counselor N.Y. Sch. for the Deaf, White Plains, 1960-64; asst. prof. Sociology Gallaudet U., Washington, 1964-70, assoc. prof. Sociology, 1970-81, prof. Sociology, 1981—. Editor The Deaf Am. fgn. news. V.p. World Fedn. of the Deaf, Rome, 1975-83, pres., Helsinki, Finland, 1983—. Mem. Am. Sociol. Assn. (co-chmn. Com. for Soc. and Persons with Disabilities), Nat. Assn. of Deaf. Office: Gallaudet U Dept Sociology Washington DC 20002

ANDES, CHARLES LOVETT, technology association executive; b. Phila., Sept. 23, 1930; s. Charles Lovett and Gladys (Stead) A.; m. Dorothea Roberta Abbott, Aug. 25, 1961; children: Elizabeth, Susan, Karen, Page. Student, Swarthmore Coll., 1948-50; B.A., Syracuse U., 1952. Pres. Adtech Industries, Phila., 1954-68; exec. v.p., dir. The Franklin Mint Corp., Franklin Ctr., Pa., 1969-73, pres., 1972-73, chmn. bd., 1973-85; chmn., chief exec. officer The Franklin Inst., Phila., 1985-91, chair, 1991—; pres. Tech. Coun. Greater Phila., 1991—; bd. dirs. O'Brien Environ. Energy Systems, Tech. Ptnrs., Fidelity Bank. Pres. Tech. Coun. Greater Phila.; chmn. Inst. Biotech. and Advanced Molecular Medicine; bd. dirs. Pa. Acad. Fine Arts, Clin. Nutritional Found.; mem. Pa. Intergovtl. Coop. Authority. Presbyterian. Clubs: Phila. Country (Phila.), Union League (Phila.), Merion Cricket (Phila.); Johns Island (Fla.). Office: The Franklin Inst 20th & The Benjamin Philadelphia PA 19103 also: Tech Coun Greater Phila 435 Devon Park Dr Wayne PA 19087-1900

ANDOE, JOE MICHAEL, artist; b. Tulsa, Dec. 5, 1955; s. Joe Edwin and Lois Ann (Oliver) A.; m. Karen June Cantrell, July 25, 1980; children: Samual Truman, Lilly Cantrell. BFA, Okla. U., 1980, MFA, 1981. One-person shows include Dart Gallery, Chgo., 1988, Tom Cugliani Gallery, N.Y.C., 1988, Blum Helman Gallery, L.A., 1990, Yodo Gallery, Japan, 1991, others; exhibited in group shows Blum Helman Gallery, N.Y.C., 1989, Rastovsky Gallery, N.Y.C., 1989, A/D Gallery, N.Y.C., 1990, Mus. of Fine Arts, Boston, 1990, Runkel Hue Williams, London, 1990, Templon Gallery, Paris, 1990, Blum Helman Gallery, N.Y.C., 1991, Rubell Gallery, Palm Beach, Forsblom Gallery, Helsinki, Finland, and many others; represented in permanent collections The Met. Mus. of Art, N.Y.C., Okla. U. Mus. of Art. Home: PO Box 2086 New York NY 10008-2086

ANDRE, HARVIE, Canadian government official; b. Edmonton, Alta., Can., July 27, 1940; s. John and Doris (Ewasiuk) A.; m. Joan Roberta Smith, May 15, 1965; children—Coryn, Lauren, Peter Harvie. B.Sc., U. Alta., 1962; M.S., Calif. Inst. Tech., 1963; Ph.D., U. Alta., 1966. Assoc. prof. chem. engring. U. Calgary, 1966-72; mem. Ho. of Commons, Ottawa, Ont., Can., 1972—, minister of supply and services, 1984, assoc. minister nat. defense, 1985, former minister consumer and corporate affairs, from 1986, minister regional indsl. expansion, minister of state for sci., 1989—, leader of govt. in Ho. of Commons; sworn to Queen's Privy Council, 1984. Past bd. dirs. Clifford E. Lee Found.; past v.p. Social Planning Council Calgary. Mem. Chem. Inst. Can. (chmn. Calgary sect. 1970). Mem. United Church. Clubs: Calgary Petroleum, Calgary Commerce. Office: House of Commons, Parliament Bldgs, Ottawa, ON Canada K1A 0A6

ANDRE, (KENNETH) MICHAEL, writer, editor, publisher; b. Halifax, N.S., Can., Aug. 31, 1946; s. Kenneth Bailey and Kathleen Mary (Warburton) A.; m. Erika Rothenberg, 1974 (div. 1983); m. Jane Adler; 1 child, Benjamin Eyton. BA, McGill U., 1968; MA, U. Chgo., 1969; PhD, Columbia U., 1973. Lectr. CCNY, N.Y.C., 1973, Baruch Coll., N.Y.C., 1974; editorial assoc. Art News, N.Y.C., 1973-77; treas. SoHo Baroque Opera Co., N.Y.C., 1980—; exec. dir. Unmuzzled Ox, N.Y.C., 1971—. Grantee Nat. Endowment Arts, Coordinating Coun. Lit. Mags., N.Y. State Coun. on Arts; grad. fellow Can. Coun. Fellow PEN; mem. MLA.

ANDREA, MARIO IACOBUCCI, engineer, gemologist, appraiser; b. Haverhill, Mass., May 21, 1917; s. Andrea and Lucia (Antolini) Iacobucci; m. Muriel Grace Litchfield, June 30, 1940 (div. Dec. 1947); children: Gail, Patricia; m. Elizabeth Dwight (Bowes) Bray, Dec. 31, 1949 (div. Jan. 1986); children: Marjorie, Lucia, Janet; m. Elma Williams, Nov. 29, 1986. BSc, Webb Inst., Glen Cove, N.Y., 1939; MSE, Cath. U. Am., 1967; PhD, Pacific Western U., 1984. Grad. gemologist; registered profl. engr., Md. Applicaiton engr. GE Co., Schenectady, 1948-52; marine engr. Mil. Sea Transp. Svc., Washington, 1952-54, supervisory naval architect, Yokosuka, Japan, 1954-56; gen. engr. R & D, Maritime Adminstrn., Washington, 1956-74; grad. gemologist, appraiser The Gem Tree, Bethesda, Md., 1974—; pres. Devel. Enterprises, Inc. and Nat. Inst. Gemology, Inc. Patentee helical ship hull form. Pres., treas. Maritime Recreation Assn., Washington, 1970. Lt. comdr. USNR, 1941-61. Decorated naval medals. Mem. Nat. Assn. Jewelry Appraisers (sr.), Gemol. Inst. Am. Alumni Assn. (life). Republican. Episcopalian. Avocations: chess, bridge, golf, gardening.

ANDREA, RONALD KENT, director pupil services, educator, psychologist; b. Akron, Ohio, Sept. 11, 1946; s. Nicholas J. and Margaret L. (Parsons) A.; m. Patricia J. Hoffmann, July 24, 1976; children: Brian K., Bret C. BA, U. Akron, 1968, MA, 1971; EdD, SUNY, Buffalo, 1979. Cert. psychologist, N.Y. Tchr. Boston (Ohio) Northampton Schs., 1968-69, Coventry (Ohio) Schs., 1969-70; psychology intern Summit County Bd. Edn., Akron, 1970-71; sch. psychologist Niagara Falls (N.Y.) Schs., 1971-72, West Seneca (N.Y.) Schs., 1972-79; dir. pupil svcs. East Aurora (N.Y.) Schs., 1979—; leadership cons. Nat. Ski Patrol, Denver, 1984-86. Pres. youth bd. Town of Aurora, East Aurora; bd. dirs. Anorexia-Bulimia Assn., Buffalo, 1989, Nat. Ski Patrol, Denver, 1991—. Mem. APA, Western N.Y. Assn. Sch. Psychologists (pres.), Western N.Y. Assn. Pupil Svc. Adminstrs. (pres.). Home: 5508 George Dr Hamburg NY 14075-7112 Office: 430 Main St East Aurora NY 14052-1786

ANDREADIS, THEODORE GEORGE, research entomologist; b. Chelsea, Mass., Mar. 22, 1950; s. Anthony Theodore Andreadis and Rita Mary (Stella) Tindall; m. Margaret Ann McManus, Sept. 7, 1976; children: Timothy, Katherine. BS, U. Mass., 1972, MS, 1975; PhD, U. Fla., 1978. Grad. rsch. asst. U. Mass., Amherst, 1973-74; field naturalist, edn. instr. Cape Cod Mus. Natural History, Brewster, Mass., 1975; grad. rsch. asst. U. Fla., Gainesville, 1975-78; asst. entomologist Conn. Agrl. Expt. Sta., New Haven, 1978-82, assoc. entomologist, 1982-86, entomologist, 1986-92, head dept. soil and water, 1992—; lectr. Yale U. Sch. Medicine, New Haven, 1987—. Mem. editorial bd. Jour. Invertebrate Pathology, San Diego, 1986-89; bd. reviewers Jour. Protozoology, Lawrence, Kans., 1991—; contbr. articles to profl. jours. Mem. salt-marsh mgmt. com. State of Conn., 1985—, mosquito control adv. bd., 19886—. Mem. Am. Mosquito Control Assn., Conn. Entomol. Soc., Entomol. Soc. Am. (chmn. subsect. 1991), Soc. Invertebrate Pathology (chmn. div. micropoedia, 1986-88), Soc. Protozoologist, Sigma Xi (v.p. 1981-82). Home: 306 Greenbriar Dr Cheshire CT 06410-2224 Office: Conn Agrl Expt Sta 123 Huntington St New Haven CT 06511-2000

ANDREASEN, CHARLES PETER, electronics executive; b. Bklyn., Mar. 18, 1930; s. Peter Kristian and Marie Paulene (Pedersen) A; m. Julia Kerekes, Nov. 27, 1952; 1 child; Jane Andreasen Della Grotta. Student in agrl. engring., Rutgers U., 1948-49; student in statis. quality control, Middlesex County Coll., 1970-71. Quality control engr. Gorn Aircraft Controls Co., Stamford, Conn., 1962-63; quality control supr. Lily-Tulip Cup Corp., Holmdel, N.J., 1963-70; corp. quality control lab. supr. Purolator Products Co., Rahway, N.J., 1970-73; mgr. quality control Scovill Mfg. Co., Waterbury, Conn., 1973-78; qualtiy assurance mgr. All-State Legal Supply Co., Mountainside, N.J., 1979-81, Durex, Inc., Union, N.J., 1981-82; quality and reliability engr., asst. quality mgr. Triangle Microwave, Inc., East Hanover, N.J., 1982—. Mem. Bd. Edn., Edison, N.J., 1982-91. Mem. Am. Soc. for Quality Control (met. section exec. bd. dirs.). Democrat. Roman Catholic. Lodge: Elks (audit chmn. 1970-78). Home: 24 Burchard St Edison NJ 08837-3351 Office: Triangle Microwave Inc 31 Faranella Dr East Hanover NJ 07936-2099

ANDREL, PETER A., data processing executive; b. Darby, Pa., July 22, 1955; s. Peter Anthony and Bertha (Smith) A.; m. Joan Theresa Pilla, Sept. 7, 1976; 1 child, Samantha. BA in Theology, St. Joseph's U., Phila., 1978. Programmer Wm. H. Vaughan Ins. Co., Upper Darby, Pa., 1975-79, Exide Electronics, Phila., 1979-80; cons. Nat. Systems Analysts, Cherry Hill, N.J., 1981-82; dir. IS The Arbitron Co., West Chester, Pa., 1982—. Recipient Patriotism award VFW, 1973, Laughlin award St. Joseph's U., 1978. Mem. Am. Mgmt. Assn., Data Processing Mgr. Assn. Republican. Office: The Arbitron Co 1385 Enterprise Dr West Chester PA 19380-5959

ANDREOZZI, SHARON ELAINE, school counselor; b. Norwalk, Conn., Dec. 28, 1944; d. Theodore Smith and Kathleen Patricia (Gordon) Tolles; m. Robert S. Andreozzi, Aug. 2, 1969; children: Lynn Heather, Brian Lee. BS, Western Conn. U., 1966; MS, U. Bridgeport, 1970; postgrad., So. Conn. State U., 1988—. Cert. elem. tchr. N-grade 8, sch. counselor K-grade12. Tchr. Marvin Sch., Norwalk, Conn., 1966-69, West Broad St. Sch., Stonington, Conn., 1969-77; tchr. Essex Elem. Sch., Centerbrook, Conn., 1985-86, sch. counselor, 1986—. Mem. NEA, Am. Assn. Counseling and Devel., Conn. Assn. Counseling and Devel., Conn. Sch. Counselors Assn., Conn. Assn. for Children with Learning Disabilities, Conn. Edn. Assn., Region 4 Edn. Ass., Dalta Kappa Gamma. Office: Essex Elem Sch 108 Main St Centerbrook CT 06409-1099

ANDRES, REUBIN, gerontologist; b. Dallas, June 13, 1923; s. Harry and Ida Ray (Klejman) A.; m. Amelia Martin Cristol, Dec. 19, 1948; children: Julie, Clay, Laurence, Thomas. Student, So. Meth. U., 1939-41, Coll. Medicine Baylor U., 1941-43; MD, Southwestern Med. Coll., 1944. Diplomate Am. Bd. Internal Medicine. Intern Gallinger Mcpl. Hosp., Washington, 1945; resident VA Hosp., McKinney, Tex., 1947-50; from rsch. fellow to prof. dept. medicine Johns Hopkins U., 1950—; asst. chief medicine Balt. City Hosps., 1958-62, Francis Scott Key Med. Ctr.; asst. chief Gerontology Rsch. Ctr., NIH, 1962—; clin. dir. Nat. Inst. Aging, NIH, 1976—. Served with AUS, 1945-47. Recipient Superior Svc. award HEW, 1973, NIH Dirs. award, 1978, Award of Distinction Am. Fedn. Aging Rsch., 1986, Allied-Signal Achievement award in aging, 1986, Rsch. award Am. Aging Assn., 1989, Enrico Greppi prize Italian Soc. Gerontology, 1987. Fellow Am. Geriatrics Soc. (Henderson award 1986), Gerontol. Soc. Am. (Kleemeier award 1974); mem. Assn. Am. Physicians, Am. Physiol. Soc., Am. Soc. Clin. Investigation, Endocrine Soc., Am. Diabetes Assn. Home: 6010 Lake Manor Dr Baltimore MD 21210 Office: Gerontology Rsch Ctr Francis Scott Key Med Ctr Baltimore MD 21224

ANDRESEN, MALCOLM, lawyer; b. Medford, Wis., July 26, 1917; s. Thomas Whelen and Ethel (Malkson) A.; m. Ann Kimball, 1942 (div. 1968); children: Anthony M., Susan A. Bridges, Abbott K.; m. Barbara Brown, 1971 (div. 1976); m. Nigi Sato, 1979. BA, U. Wis., 1940, LLB, 1941. Bar: Wis. 1941, N.Y. 1946, U.S. Supreme Ct. 1958. Acct., J.D. Miller & Co., N.Y.C., 1946-47; jr. tax acct. Peat Marwick Mitchell & Co., N.Y.C., 1947-48; assoc. Davis Wagner Hallett & Russell, N.Y.C., 1948-52; tax counsel, then sr. tax counsel, then sr. govt. relations adviser Mobil Oil Corp., N.Y.C., 1952-70; dir. tax legal affairs Nat. Fgn. Trade Council, N.Y.C., 1970-73; of counsel Delson & Gordon, N.Y.C., 1973-77, Whitman & Ransom, N.Y.C., 1977-86; pvt. practice, 1986—. Trustee, Cathedral Ch. of St. John the Divine, N.Y.C., 1977-84. Served to capt. USMCR, 1942-46. Decorated Bronze Star medal. Mem. Assn. of Bar of City of N.Y., Internat. Fiscal Assn. (coun. U.S.A. br.), Univ. Club (N.Y.C.). Democrat. Episcopalian. Home: Apt 24D 2 Lincoln Square Plz New York NY 10023-6214 Office: Ste 3004 675 3d Ave New York NY 10017

ANDRESON, CHARLES JEREMIAH, municipal government official; b. Worcester, Mass., Nov. 7, 1947; s. Nicholas Charles and Helen Marie (Murphy) A.; m. Cynthia Ann Osborn, June 28, 1969; children: Christine, Charles Jr., Jennifer. BSCE, Worcester Poly. Inst., 1970, postgrad., 1973-75. Registered profl. engr., Maine. Jr. civil engr. Anderson/Nichols Engring. Cons., Boston, 1970-71; jr. planner Worcester Planning Dept., 1971-72; planner City Mgr.'s Office Planning & Community Devel., Worcester, 1972-73; grad. rsch. asst. Worcester Poly. Inst., 1973-74, grad. teaching asst., 1974-75; town engr./planner Scarborough, Maine, 1975-85; supt. Scarborough Sanitary Dist., 1985—. Mem. tech. com. Portland (maine) Area Comprehensive Transp. Study, 1978—; dir. Regional Waste Systems, Portland, 1979-87; mem. Scarborough Long Range Planning Commn., 1985—; dir. Greater Portland Christian Sch., S. Portland, 1981-86. Mem. ASCE, Am. Planning Assn., Am. Inst. Cert. Planners, Maine Wastewater Control Assn. Home: 4 Val Ter Scarborough ME 04074-8738 Office: Scarborough Sanitary Dist 415 Black Point Rd Scarborough ME 04074-8660

ANDREUCCI, DEBORAH ANN, retailer art and computer supplies; b. Denville, N.J., Mar. 29, 1955; d. Nicholas D. and Florence (Benacqua) A.; divorced; 1 child, Nicholas Angelo Corby. Student, Morris County Vocat. Tech., Denville, N.J., 1973, DuCret Sch. of the Arts, North Plainfield, N.J., 1976, Centenary Coll., Hackettstown, N.J., 1982-83. Art dir. Diversi Comm, Boonton, N.J., 1976-86; owner DAR Graphics, Boonton, Parsippany, N.J., 1977-83; art. dir. Beneficial Mgmt., Peapack, N.J., 1980-83; owner Pro-Graphix Art & Computer Supply, Morris Plains, N.J., 1990—. Recipient 1st place award N.J. Craftsman Fair, 1979, League of Women Voters Cover Contest, 1979, Eberhard Fabers New Techniques Contest, 1980; Presdl. award, 1982. Mem. N.J. Women Bus. Owners Assn., Nat. Art Material Assn., Chronic Fatigue Syndrome Assn. (adv. com. Morris County Voc./Tech.). Home: 235 Lake Shore Dr Parsippany NJ 07054-2651 Office: Pro-Graphix Art & Computer Supply 1081 State Route 53 Morris Plains NJ 07950-2860

ANDREWS, DAVID BRUCE, psychology educator; b. Indpls., July 30, 1943; s. Leonard Otwell and Ruth Almyra (McGinnis) A.; m. Delina R. Hickey, May 29, 1982; children: Jon R., Ethan J. AB, Oberlin Coll., 1965; PhD, Ohio State U., 1986. Prof. psychology Keene (N.H.) State Coll., 1970—. Pres. RISE Early Intervention Bd., Keene, 1987—; vice chair Keene Bd. Edn., 1990—, Martin Luther King Human Rights Day Com., Keene, 1991. Mem. Am. Ednl. Rsch. Assn., Am. Assn. Higher Edn. Home: 429 Old Walpole Rd Keene NH 03431 Office: Dept Psychology Keene State Coll Keene NH 03431

ANDREWS, LAWRENCE DONALD, banker; b. Winchester, Mass., Sept. 11, 1960; s. Donald Lawrence and Hazel Emilie (Martin) A.; m. Sharon Pease, July 7, 1984; children: Rachel Elizabeth, Donald Lawrence. BA in Econs., Gordon Coll., Wenham, Mass., 1982; MBA in Fin., Bentley Coll., Waltham, Mass., 1984; postgrad. Stonier Grad. Sch. Banking, U. Del., 1990. Cert. Small Bus. Adminstrn. Leader, 1986. Real estate mgr. J. Linzee Coolidge, Boston, 1982-84; credit analyst Essex Bank, Peabody, Mass., 1984-85, loan officer, 1985-86, asst. v.p., 1986; asst. v.p. First Nat. Bank Boston, 1986-87; v.p., team leader Bank of New Eng., N.A., Boston, 1987-90; v.p., regional mgr. Bank of New Eng., N.A., 1990-91; v.p. regional mgr. Fleet Bank Mass., N.A., Boston, 1991—; instr. New Eng. Banking Inst., Boston, 1986-87. Mem. governing bd. Hope Alliance Ch., Wakefield, Mass., 1987—; rep. Alumni Career Exploration Program, Bentley Coll., Waltham, 1988—; seminar participant Vis. Exec. Seminar Series, Gordon Coll., Wenham, Mass., 1989—; patriot div. exec. United Ways of Ea. New Eng., 1988-89, account exec., 1990. Mem. Smaller Bus. Assn. of New Eng. (co-chair legis. breakfast com., Mass. legis. com. 1991—), Robert Morris Assocs., Japan Soc. Boston, North Shore C. of C. (com. mem. econ. devel. 1988—). Republican. Mem. Christian and Missionary Alliance Ch. Home: 98 Cedar St Wakefield MA 01880-2757 Office: Fleet Bank of Mass NA PO Box 2197 MABOS3ZCBD Boston MA 02106

ANDREWS, MARY ELLEN, travel executive; b. Corning, N.Y., Nov. 10, 1931; d. Edwin Hardy and Edith Marie (Lowe) Ober; Student, U. Paris, 1951-52; B.A., Mt. Holyoke Coll., 1953; postgrad. Syracuse U., 1974-75; m. James A. Reynolds, Jan. 28, 1962; m. 2d, Richard Hale Andrews, July 14, 1970; 1 child, Amy Elizabeth; stepchildren: R. Hale, D. Gage, Philadelphia M. French/English translator Les Ateliers de Construction Electrique de Charleroi, N.Y.C., 1954-55, French Nat. R.R., N.Y.C., 1955-56; public rels. asst. Steuben Glass, N.Y.C., 1956-64; French/English translator Corning (N.Y.) Internat. Corp., 1964-67; rsch. asst. Corning Glass Wks. Found., 1967-70; French/English translator Corning Internat. Corp., 1972-75; office mgr. Beak Assos., Ithaca, N.Y., 1975-77; corp. rels. staff, devel. office, Cornell U., Ithaca, 1977-79; staff asst. evening programs, Elmira Coll., N.Y., 1979-80, dir. public rels., 1980-84, advisor student newspaper, The Octagon, 1980-84; exec. dir. Schuyler County C. of C., 1984-91; nat. mktg. and sales dir. Finger Lakes Cen. Reservation Svc., 1991—; bd. dirs., pres. Bethany Retirement Home, 1988—. Bd. dirs. Elmira Symphony and Choral Soc., 1982-84, Chemung Valley Arts Coun., 1984-87. Mem. LWV (bd. dirs. Schuyler County), N.Y. State Coun. of Chamber Execs. (steering com., Finger Lakes Assn. spl. project com., bd. dirs. 1985-91). Democrat. Presbyterian. Editor-in-chief Campus Mag., 1980-84. Home: 2661 County Rte 17 Watkins Glen NY 14891 Office: Finger Lakes Cen Reservation Svc PO Box 249 Watkins Glen NY 14891-0249

ANDREWS, MICHAEL WILLIAM, librarian, information specialist; b. Rome, N.Y., Mar. 22, 1948; s. Martin Joseph and Mary (Dublanica) A.; m. Karen Lynn Mauro, July 23, 1982. AB in History, Cornell U., 1970; MS in Libr. Sci., Syracuse U., 1972. Libr. govt. documents SUNY, Plattsburgh, 1971-76, L.I. U., Bklyn., 1977-79; rsch. asst. Health Info. Sharing Project, Syracuse (N.Y.) U., 1979-80; readers svcs. libr. Elizabethtown (Pa.) Coll., 1980-85; online data base libr. U. D.C., Washington, 1986-87; dir. rsch. Korn/Ferry Internat., Washington, 1987—. Editor: Proceeding of the Second Annual Government Documents Workshop, 1976. contbr. articles to profl. jours. Mem. Spl. Librs. Assn. Home: 3825 Wagon Wheel Ln Woodbridge VA 22192 Office: Korn/Ferry Internat 900 19th St NW Ste 200 Washington DC 20006-2183

ANDREWS, RICHARD LOUIS, procurement coordinator; b. Washington, Oct. 12, 1951; s. Louis Gribble and Margaret Frances (Wright) A. BS, Towson State U., 1976; postgrad., U. Balt., 1977-79, 79-81. Asst. mgr. Nicoll's Sporting Goods, Towson, 1969-83; edn. aide U.S. Dept. Edn., Washington, 1984; procurement coord. Md. Dept. Budget and Fiscal Planning, Annapolis, 1985—; chmn. State Pricing Com. for Sheltered Workshops, Balt., 1988—; mem. Minority Bus. Enterprise Certification Com., 1992—. Editor: Towson State U. Student Govt. Assn. Manual, 1977. State committeeman Rep. Party, Md., 1978—; alt. del. Rep. Nat. Conv., Detroit, New Orleans, 1980, 88; nominee for state comptroller Rep. Party, Md., 1982; active Gov.'s Commn. on Legal Svcs. Mem. NRA (life). Roman Catholic. Office: State Md Budget Dept 45 Calvert St Annapolis MD 21404

ANDREWS, ROBERT E., congressman; b. Camden, N.J., Aug. 4, 1957. BA magna cum laude, Bucknell U., 1979; JD summa cum laude, Cornell U., 1982. Bar: N.J. 1982. Assoc. Archer & Greiner, Haddonfield, N.J., 1982-84, Charles J. Clarke & Assocs., Haddonfield, 1984-85, Kenney & Kearney, Cherry Hill, N.J., 1985-88; mem. Camden County (N.J.) Bd. Chosen Freeholders, 1987-90, freeholder dir., 1988-90; mem. U.S. Ho. of Reps. 1st Dist. from N.J., Washington, 1990—. Contbr. articles to law jours. Bd. dirs. Camden County March of Dimes; mem. Children's Caucus, Women's Polit. Caucus, Task Force on Govt. Waste. Mem. N.J. Bar Assn., Camden County Bar Assn., Phi Beta Kappa. Democrat. Episcopalian. Office: US House of Reps 1005 Longworth Bldg Washington DC 20515-3001*

ANDREWS, STEPHEN FRANCIS, aerospace engineer; b. Manchester, Conn., May 4, 1966; s. William J. and Irene C. (Chetwynd) A.; m. Diana L. Calusdian, July 21, 1990. BS in Aerospace Engring., U. Notre Dame, 1988; MS in Aerospace Engring., Ga. Inst. Tech., 1990. Aerospace technologist, guidance, navigation & control Goddard Space Flight Ctr., NASA, Greenbelt, Md., 1990—. Mem. AIAA. Roman Catholic.

ANDREWS, THOMAS H., congressman; b. North Easton, Mass., Mar. 23, 1953. BA, Bowdoin Coll. Organizer Maine Health and Hazardous Waste Task Force; exec. dir. Maine Assn. Handicapped Persons; founder, exec. dir. Maine Studies Ctr.; state rep., 1983-84, state senator, 1985-90; mem. 102nd Congress from 1st Dist. Maine, 1991—. Democrat. Office: 177 Commercial St Portland ME 04101*

ANDREWS, WALLACE HENRY, microbiologist; b. Biloxi, Miss., Oct. 6, 1943; s. Wallace Henry and Rita Louise (Wentzell) A. BA, U. Miss., 1965, MS, 1967, PhD, 1969. Microbiologist FDA, Dauphin Island, Ala., 1969-71; rsch. microbiologist FDA, Washington, 1971—; cons. FAO, Rome, 1983—, Pan Am. Health Orgn., WHO, 1989—. Mem. editorial bd. Jour. Food Protection, 1984—; contbr. articles to profl. jours. NASA fellow, 1966-69. Mem. Am. Soc. for Microbiology, Assn. Ofcl. Analytical Chemists (Gen. Referee of Yr. 1986, 91), Internat. Assn. Milk, Food, and Environ. Sanitarians, Inc., Phi Kappa Phi. Office: FDA 200 C St SW Washington DC 20204-0002

ANDREWS, WILLIAM PERNELL, corrections psychotherapist, management consultant; b. Richmond, Va., Mar. 24, 1947; s. William and Rena (Thompson) A.; m. Brenda Hughes, Sept. 30, 1966 (div. Jan. 1976); m. Michele Evans, Dec. 10, 1983; children: Oronde Kareem, Joshua Thompson. AA, Am. River Coll., Sacramento, Calif., 1977; BA, U. Calif., Santa Cruz, 1980; postgrad., Boston U., 1980-81; MEd, Cambridge Coll., 1989. Pharm. sales rep. Progress Labs, Inc., 1970-74; staff asst. constrn. budget program Pacific Telephone Co.; counsellor intern Santa Cruz Counseling Ctr., 1979-80; counseling psychologist intern Boston State Hosp.; staff psychologist dept. narcotics addiction Boston City Hosp., 1981-84; clin. coord. Mass. Dept. Corrections, Walpole, 1984-86, Concord, 1986—; instr. in psychology, Middlesex Community Coll., 1989—. Mem. disorder mgmt. team, tng. adv. bd. MCI-Concord, 1990—. Mem. Assn. Black Psychologists, Mass. Nurses Assn. (unit chair). Baptist. Home: 18 Curve St Newton MA 02165-2207 Office: Mass Correctional Inst PO Box 00 West Concord MA 01742

ANDRIOLA, ROCCO F., lawyer, workout specialist; b. Astoria, N.Y., Mar. 24, 1958; s. Pasquale and Lena (Dituri) A.; m. Susan A. Andriola; 1 child, Patrick Nicholas. BA summa cum laude, Fordham U., 1979; JD, NYU, 1982; LLM (corp. law), NYU, 1986. Bar: N.Y. 1983, D.C. 1985, U.S. Dist. Ct. (so., ea., no. and we. dists.), U.S. Ct. Appeals (2d cir.) 1983, U.S. Ct. Internat. Trade 1983, U.S. Tax Ct. 1983, U.S. Ct. Mil. Appeals 1983, U.S. Ct. Claims 1983, U.S. Supreme Ct. 1986. Legal asst. Am. Clerical Services, N.Y.C., summers 1978-79; assoc. Ford Marrin Esposito & Witmeyer, N.Y.C., summer 1980; summer assoc. Donovan Leisure Newton & Irvine, N.Y.C., 1981, corp. and securities assoc., 1982-86; v.p., assoc. gen. counsel Shearson Lehman Bros., Inc., N.Y.C., 1986-89, sr. v.p. Capital Preservation and Restructuring Group, 1989—. Projects editor NYU Moot Ct. Bd., 1981-82. Bd. dirs. Symphony for UN, 1985-89, Playing-to-Win, 1988—; bd. advisors Fordham U., 1987—; founder, exec. dir. St. Francis Home Visitors Program, Astoria, 1983-85; v.p. St. Francis Parish Council, Astoria, 1983-84, chair civic affairs com., 1981-82; mem. Queens Citizens Orgn., 1979-86, Astoria Civic Assn., 1983-86, Residents for a More Beautiful Port Washington, 1992—, Am. Liver Found. of L.I.; pres. Port Washington Sr. Basketball League, 1990-91; mem. L.I. chpt. MADD, 1991—. Mem. ABA (lt. gov. law student div. 1981-82), N.Y. State Bar Assn. (rep. 1980-82), Am. Corp. Counsel Assn. (bd. dirs. 1988-92, v.p. 1989-90, chmn. mergers and acquisitions com. N.Y. chpt., 1987-89), Order of Barristers, Homeowners Assn. Port Washington (pres. gen. coun. 1992—, gen. coun.), Morewood Oaks Homeowners Assn. (pres. 1991—), Order Sons of Italy in Am. Republican. Roman Catholic. Home: 45 Morewood Oaks Port Washington NY 11050-1603 Office: Shearson Lehman Bros Inc 388 Greenwich St Fl 28 New York NY 10013-2396

ANDRUS, JOHN STEBBINS, military-political affairs consultant; b. Ft. Riley, Kans., Jan. 18, 1927; s. Burton Curtis and Katharine Elizabeth (Stebbins) A.; m. Jane Braham, Apr. 3, 1954; children: Priscilla Hinchey, Marcella Lewis, Drucilla Haugh. BS, U.S. Mil. Acad., 1949; disting. grad., Squadron Officer Sch., Maxwell AFB, Ala., 1955; grad., Air Command and Staff Coll., Maxwell AFB, Ala., 1963; MPA, George Washington U., 1963. USAF internat. politico-mil. affairs officer, command pilot, parachutist. Commd. 2d lt. USAF, 1949, advanced through grades to lt col., 1968; airlift pilot Mil. Air Transport USAF, Westover AFB, Mass., 1951-52; combat control team leader Tactical Air Command USAF, Ft. Bragg, N.C., 1953; instr. Squadron Officer Sch. Air U. Command USAF, Maxwell AFB, 1955-58; comdr. nuclear weapon site USAF, Italy, 1960; action officer spl. air warfare policy hdqrs. The Pentagon USAF, Washington, 1963-65; air ops. officer 606 Air Commando Wing USAF, Nakom Phanom, Thailand, 1966-67; polit./mil. liaison Hdqrs. 13th Air Force, Clark Air Base USAF, Phila., 1967-70; chief Okinawa area field office U.S. Forces, Japan, Zukiran, Okinawa, 1972-74; dir. mgmt. seminar Dale Carnegie, Honolulu, 1978-79; cons. mil./polit. affairs Andrus Enterprises Internat., Prides Crossing, Mass., 1980—; lectr. polit./mil. subjects, various colls., 1975-91; pres. Andrus Enterprises Internat., Prides Crossing, 1986—. Author: AirForce Military Doctrine (Air Power award 1955); author essay, My Vote--Freedom's Privilege (Freedom Found. award 1960); author numerous poems; inventor hand calculators. Vice chmn. (facilities) N.J. Spl. Olympics, McGuire Air Force Base, 1975; adult friend Big Brother Program, East Providence, R.I., 1984; charter mem. Republican Presdl. Task Force, Washington, 1980-92; sponsor Nat. Rep. Congl. Com., Washington, 1980-91, chmn. 8th congl. dist. Citizens for Am., Rehoboth, Mass., 1982-85; mem. speakers bur. High Frontier, 1975-85; active in the 300th anniversary re-enactment of Waldensians Glorious Return, 1989. Decorated Bronze Star, Meritorious Svc. medal. Mem. Am. Security Coun., Internat. Platform Assn., Air Force Assn., West Point Soc. New Eng., Friends of West Point Libr., Mil. Order of World Wars (life companion), Acad. Am. Poets, Boston Computer Soc., Lions, Appalachian Mountain Club (Boston), Alpine Club of Italy (Torre Pellice). Home: 7 Hillcrest Rd Beverly MA 01915-2130 Office: Andrus Enterprises Internat PO Box 28 Prides Crossing MA 01965-0028

ANDRUSHKIW, ROMAN IHOR, mathematics educator; b. Lviv, Ukraine, May 3, 1937; came to U.S., 1949; s. Joseph Wasyl and Sofia Andrushkiw; m. Svitlana Maria Lutsky, Nov. 22, 1975; 1 child, Pavlo M. B in Engring., Stevens Inst. Tech., 1959, PhD in Math., 1973; MSEE, Newark Coll. Engring., 1964; MS in Math., U. Chgo., 1967. Data analyst Linde Div. Union Carbide Corp., Newark, 1957; sr. elec. engr. Weston Instruments & Electronics Inc., Newark, 1959-64; rsch. asst. U. Chgo., 1966-68; instr. Newark Coll. Engring., 1964-66, 68-70; asst. prof. N.J. Inst. Tech., Newark, 1970-78, assoc. prof., 1978-84, prof., 1984—; cons., instr. Bendix Corp., Teterboro, N.J., 1981-82; reviewer Math. Rev., 1977—, Centralblatt für Mathematik, 1984. Contbr. articles to Math. and Computer Modeling, Jour. Math. Physics, Bull. of Am. Math. Soc. Bd. dirs. Plast Found., Newark, 1978—; chmn. Com. for the Def. of Religious Freedom in Ukraine, Newark, 1989-90; pres. Friends of RUKH, No. N.J. Br., Newark, 1990—; v.p. Plast Inc., Newark, 1989-91. Named Union Carbide scholar, 1955-59; grantee NSF, 1966. Mem. Am. Math. Soc., Soc. for Indsl. and Applied Math., Internat. Assn. for Math. and Computers in Simulation (Citation 1985), Ukrainian Engrs. Soc. Am. (exec. coun. 1978-80), Shevchenko Sci. Soc. (bd. dirs. 1974—). Republican. Byzantine Catholic. Office: NJ Inst Tech 323 King Blvd Newark NJ 07102

ANEIRO, RICHARD JOHN, small business owner; b. Bklyn., Oct. 25, 1930; s. Edwardo Aneiro and Olivia (Suarez) A.; m. Marie LaBarbara, June 8, 1955; children: Karen, Steven, Susan, Maria. BSIE, NYU, 1950-57, MBA, 1960; SMG, Harvard U., 1979. Model cities adminstr. N.Y.C., 1957-

80; pres., chief exec. officer Devel. Corp. Bklyn. (N.Y.) Navy Yard, 1980—, pres., chief exec. officer Indsl. Coalition, 1990—; vice-chmn. Bklyn. Econ. Devel. Co., 1980—; dir. Regional Econ. Devel. Partnership Program, N.Y.C., 1992—. Contbr. articles to profl. jours. Organizer Polit. Election Campaigns, 1980, 86, 88, 90. 2d sgt. USAR, 1950-52, Korea. Recipient Presdl. Recognition award for svc. White House, 1985, 87. Roman Catholic. Home: RD 3 208 Boonton Ave Boonton NJ 07005 Office: Bklyn Navy Yard Brooklyn NY 11205

ANEROUSIS, JOHN PETER, chemical and computer software executive; b. Riverside, N.J., Aug. 29, 1949; s. Peter G. and Georgia (Batlis) A.; m. Sally Melinda Fillman, May 30, 1981. BSChemE, BS Chem. Engring. Adminstrn., U. Del., 1972; MBA, Drexel U., 1978. Registered profl. engr., Calif., Tex. Specialist, staff engr. Betz Labs., Inc., Trevose, Pa., 1972-75, project supr., 1976-78; resident project engr. Betz Labs., Inc., Los Angeles, 1975-76; dir. tech. mgmt. Betz Process Chems., Inc., The Woodlands, Tex., 1978-81; v.p. engring. Betz Energy Chems., Inc., Carpinteria, Calif., 1981-83; exec. v.p. Coastal Flow Measurement, Inc., Pasadena, Tex., 1983-88; pres., chief exec. officer Physichem Techs., Inc., Austin, Tex., 1983-88, CompuDrug USA Inc., Austin, 1988-89; pres. Symvex, Inc., South Plainfield, N.J., 1989—; speaker in field. Contbr. articles to profl. jours. Mem. Am. Inst. Chem. Engrs., Am. Mgmt. Assn., Nat. Assn. Corrosion Engrs., Soc. Petroleum Engrs., Am. Gas Assn., Am. Chem. Soc., Drug Info. Assn. Home: 9311 Rolling Oaks Trl Austin TX 78750-3810 Office: Symvex Inc 40 Cragwood Rd South Plainfield NJ 07080-2480

ANESTOS, HARRY PETER, lawyer; b. Savannah, Ga., May 21, 1917; s. Peter Tash and Catherine (Constantine) A.; m. Xanthippe Apostolakos, Jan. 25, 1953; children: Peter H., Michael H. BA, Wayne U., 1946; JD, Columbia U., 1947. Bar: Ga. 1946, U.S. Supreme Ct. 1951, D.C. 1961, Md. 1965. Pvt. practice Savannah, Ga., D.C., and Bethesda, Md., 1946—; chief comml. intelligence U.S. Dept. of Commerce Bur. Internal Commerce, Washington, 1961-62; U.S. atty. for gov't of Greece Washington, 1967-71. Author: Patent Law Article U.S. Patent Office 1962. Candidate for U.S. Congress, Savannah, 1958. Named Outstanding Am. of Greek Descent by Gov't of Greece, 1972. Mem. ABA (coun. sr. lawyers div.), Ga. Trial Lawyers Asns. (charter), Columbia Country Club, Barrister's Inn Phi Delta Phi. Democrat. Greek Orthodox. Home: 3514 Glenmoor Dr Bethesda MD 20815-5638 Office: 4809 St Elmo Ave Bethesda MD 20814-3009

ANFINSEN, CHRISTIAN BOEHMER, biochemist; b. Monessen, Pa., Mar. 26, 1916; s. Christian Boehmer and Sophie (Rasmussen) A.; m. Florence Bernice Kenenger, Nov. 29, 1941 (div. 1978); children: Carol Bernice, Margot Sophie, Christian Boehmer; m. Libby Shulman Ely, 1979. B.A., Swarthmore Coll., 1937, D.Sc., 1965; M.S., U. Pa., 1939; Ph.D., Harvard, 1943; D.Sc. (hon.), Georgetown U., 1967, N.Y. Med. Coll., 1969, Gustavus Adolphus Coll., 1975, Brandeis U., 1977, Providence Coll., 1978; M.D. (hon.), U. Naples Med. Sch., 1980, Adelphi U., 1987. Asst. prof. biol. chemistry Harvard Med. Sch., 1948-50, prof. biochemistry, 1962-63; chief lab. cellular physiology and metabolism Nat. Heart Inst., Bethesda, Md., 1950-62; chief lab. chem. biology Nat. Inst. Arthritis and Metabolic Diseases, Bethesda, 1963-82; prof. biology Johns Hopkins U., Balt., 1982—; vis. prof. Weizmann Inst. Sci., Rehovot, Israel, 1981-82, bd. govs. 1962. Author: The Molecular Basis of Evolution, 1959; contbr. articles to profl. jours. Am. Scandinavian fellow Carlsberg Lab., Copenhagen 1939; sr. cancer research fellow Nobel Inst., Stockholm, 1947; Markle scholar 1948; Guggenheim fellow Weizmann Inst., 1958; recipient Rockefeller Pub. Service award, 1954-55, Nobel prize in chemistry, 1972. Mem. Am. Soc. Biol. Chemists (pres. 1971-72), Am. Acad. Arts and Scis., Nat. Acad. Scis., Washington Acad. Scis., Am. Philos. Soc., Fedn. Am. Scientists (treas. 1958-59, vice chmn. 1959-60, 73-76), Pontifical Acad. Sci. Home: 4 Tanner Ct Baltimore MD 21208-1332 Office: Johns Hopkins U Dept Biology 34th Charles St Baltimore MD 21201-3707

ANGAROLA, ROBERT JOSEPH, banker; b. N.Y.C., Nov. 25, 1950; s. Joseph Alfred and Agnes Alice (DeLorenzo) A.; m. June 24, 1972 (div. Mar. 1987); children: Mark, Brian; m. Ilene Ackner, Dec. 17, 1988. BS, Fordham U., 1972; MBA, U. Ga., 1976. Asst. treas. J.P. Morgan & Co., N.Y.C., 1975-82; asst. v.p. Midland Montagu, N.Y.C., 1982-85; v.p. Bank of Am., N.Y.C., 1985-87; v.p., dir. Creditanstalt, N.Y.C., 1987-90; 1st v.p., chief info. officer Bank Julius Baer, N.Y.C., 1990—; prof. N.Y. Inst. Fin., N.Y.C., 1983-86. Vice pres. Bd. of Edn., New Rochelle, N.Y., 1989-91, pres., 1991—; chmn. Human Rights Commn., New Rochelle, 1980-85. Capt. USAF, 1972-75. Mem. Coun. on Internat. Banking (chmn. FX com. N.Y.C. chpt. 1982-85, bd. dirs. 1985-87). Roman Catholic. Home: 389 Pinebrook Blvd New Rochelle NY 10804 Office: Bank Julius Baer 330 Madison Ave New York NY 10017

ANGEL, ALLEN ROBERT, mathematics educator, author, consultant; b. N.Y.C., Oct. 13, 1942; s. Isaac and Sylvia (Budnick) A.; m. Kathryn Mary Pollinger, Feb. 14, 1966; children: Robert Allen, Steven Scott. AAS in Electrical Tech., N.Y.C. Community Coll., 1962; BS in Physics, SUNY, New Paltz, 1965; MS in Math., SUNY, 1967; postgrad., Rutgers U., 1969. Tchr. physics Rhineback (N.Y.) Cen. Sch., 1965-66; instr. physics, math. Sullivan County Community Coll., Loch Sheldrake, N.Y., 1967-70; prof. math. Monroe Community Coll., Rochester, N.Y., 1970—; chmn. math./computer sci. Monroe Community Coll., Rochester, 1988—; asst. dir. nat. sci. found., math. summer insts. Rutgers U., New Brunswick, N.J., 1970-72; cons. reviewer various pub. cos. including Prentice-Hall Pub. Co., Englewood Cliffs, N.J., 1983—, Addison-Wesley Pub. Co., Reading, Mass., 1978—. Author: (textbooks) A Survey of Mathematics with Applications, 3d edit., 1988, Elementary Algebra--A Practical Approach, 1985, Intermediate Algebra--A Practical Approach, 1986, Elementary Algebra for College Students, 3d edit., 1992, Intermediate Algebra for College Students, 3d edit., 1992, Algebra for College Students, 1988. Recipient Excellence award Nat. Inst. for Staff and Organizational Devel., 1991. Mem. Am. Math. Assn. of Two Yr. Colls. (v.p. 1985—, chmn. conv. 1984, Pres.'s award), N.Y. State Math. Assn. of Two Yr. Colls. (pres. 1978-80, chmn. summer inst. 1976-78, Outstanding Contributions award), Math. Assn. of Am., Nat. Council of Tchrs. of Math., Assn. Math. Tchrs. of N.Y. State, New England Math. Assn. of Two Yr. Colls., Nat. Inst. Staff & Organizational Devel. (Excellence award 1991). Home: 125 Holley Ridge Cir Rochester NY 14625-1313 Office: Monroe Community Coll 1000 E Henrietta Rd Rochester NY 14623-5780

ANGEL, ELIZABETH JOURET, publishing executive; b. Port Chester, N.Y., May 10, 1933; d. George Edward amd Carmela Marguerite (Gregory) Jouret; m. Palmer Shannon, Jan. 10, 1954 (div. 1970); children: Elizabeth Palmer, Ann Ives; m. James Leonard Angel, Sept. 1, 1972. BA, Am. U., Washington, 1980, student, 1980-82. Spot sales asst. Nat. Broadcasting Co., N.Y.C., 1954-57; freelance editor to authors Greenwich, Conn., 1957-62; staff reporter The Village Gazette, Old Greenwich, Conn., 1962-67; campaign press sec. local candidates Rep. Party, Greenwich, 1967-68; editor, print prodn. mgr. Ednl. Records Bur., Greenwich and Darien, Conn., 1968-72, Health Professions Ednl. Svc., Bethesda, Md., 1980-82; pres. Betz Pub. Co., Inc., Bethesda, 1982—. Editor: A Complete Preparation for the MCAT, 5 edits., 1980, 83, 85, 88, 91, Premedical Planning Guide, 2 edits., 1985, 90, Preveterinary Planning Guide, 2 edits., 1987, 90, Veterinary Medical School Admission Requirements in U.S. and Canada, 6 edits., 1986-91; newsletter editor Ednl. Records Bur., Darien, 1970-72. Staff aide ARC blood svcs., Greenwich, 1958-64, press release writer, 1964-72, caseworker svc. to mil. families, Montgomery County, Md. chpt., 1991. Mem. Am. Booksellers Assn., Nat. Assn. Advisors to Health Professions, Washington Book Pubs. Assn., Jr. Woman's Club (com. chair 1962-67). Republican. Methodist. Office: Betz Pub Co Inc PO Box 34631 Bethesda MD 20827-0631

ANGELAKIS, MANOS G., filmmaker, communications executive; b. Athens, Mar. 27, 1941; came to U.S., 1967; s. George E. and Urania M. (Hadjioannou) A.; m. Barbara D. Pinkus, Sept. 7, 1969. Student, Athens (Greece) Coll., 1960, Ecole des Arts Decoratif, Paris, 1962-64. Sr. photographer R. Crandall Assocs., N.Y.C., 1970-72; owner Manos Angelakis Photography, N.Y.C., 1972-75; pres. EuroConference Mgmt., London, 1983-89; pres., creative dir. Trident Communications, N.Y.C., 1975—; dir. Indsl. Strength Video, Ltd., N.Y.C., London, 1990—. Dir. (films) The Papermakers, 1983 (Gold award Internat. Film and TV Festival 1984), Impressions, 1986 (Silver award Visual Media Festival 1988); contbr. articles to profl. jours. Sgt. Royal Hellenic Airforce, 1960-62. Recipient Eagle award Visual Communications Congress, 1984, Best of Show award for video Visual Media Festival, 1988. Mem. Indsl. Photographers' Assn. of N.Y. (pres. 1977-79), Assn. for Multi-Image Internat. (treas. N.Y. chpt. 1984-88, pres. 1988-90, Best of Show award 1986). Republican. Home: 69 Fifth Ave New York NY 10003 Office: Trident Communications 31 W 21st St New York NY 10010-6806

ANGELAKOS, EVANGELOS THEODOROU, physician, physiologist, pharmacologist, educator; b. Tripolis, Greece, July 15, 1929; came to U.S., 1948, naturalized, 1966; s. Theodore A. and Aglaia (Tsiverioti) A.; m. Eleanor Pell, Aug. 28, 1954; 1 son, Theodore. Student, Athens (Greece) U., 1947-48, Cornell U., 1950-51; MA, Boston U., 1953, PhD, 1956; MD, Harvard, 1959. Mem. faculty sch. medicine Boston U., 1955-68, prof. physiology, 1963-68; prof. dept. physiology and biophysics Hahnemann U., Phila., 1968—, chmn. dept., 1968-85, prof. dept. pharmacology and medicine, 1982—, interim dean sch. medicine, 1982-83, dean Grad. Sch., 1983-92, dep. dean sch. medicine, 1985-86, dir. Med. Sci. Track Program, 1982—; chmn. adv. com. biomed. research inst. Center for Research and Advanced Studies, U. Maine, Portland, 1971-80; dir. Med. Sci. Track Program, Portland, 1982—; research assoc. biomath. MIT, 1959-60; vis. scientist Karolinska Inst., Stockholm, 1962-63; cons. U.S. Army Labs. Environ. Medicine, Natick, Mass., 1964-72, NASA Electronics Research Center, Cambridge, Mass., 1966-68; Trustee, sec. bd. Hahnemann Med. Coll. and Hosp., Phila., 1977-81. Contbr. articles to sci. jours. and textbooks. Med. Found. Research fellow, 1959-60; USPHS Research and Career Devel. grantee, 1960-68. Home: 602 Washington Sq Philadelphia PA 19106-4118 Office: Hahnemann U Med Sci Track MS 344 Philadelphia PA 19102-1192

ANGELL, JEANNE SIMON, college administrator; b. Buffalo, Nov. 10, 1961; d. Roy Charles and Esther Mary (Pearson) S.; m. Samuel John Bowne Angell, Oct. 19, 1991. BA in Psychology, Earlham Coll., 1984; MS in Social Svc. Mgmt., Bryn Mawr Coll., 1989, postgrad., 1990—. Resident advisor, counselor The Devereux Found., Devon, Pa., 1984-85; social worker Big Sisters of Phila., 1985-86, Bryn Mawr (Pa.) Hosp., 1987-88; rsch. intern Bryn Mawr & Haverford Colls., 1988-89; resident dir. A Better Chance in Lower Merion, Ardmore, Pa., 1985-89; assoc. dir. career devel. Bryn Mawr Coll., 1989—; accessibility coord. Bryn Mawr Coll., 1990—. Bd. dirs. A Better Chance in Lower Merion, Ardmore, Pa., 1989—. Mem. Am. Coll. Pers. Assn., Assn. Multi-Cultural Counseling and Devel., Mid-Atlantic Placement Assn. Quaker. Office: Career Devel Bryn Mawr Coll Bryn Mawr PA 19010

ANGELO, GIRARD FRANCIS, priest, religion consultant; b. Hazleton, Pa., Apr. 9, 1929; s. John and Julia (Gigliotti) A. AA, Belmont Abbey Coll., 1949; BA, U. Western Ont., Can., 1952; postgrad., St. Peter's Sem., London, Ont., Can., 1955. Pastor Ch. of the Sacred Heart, Hazleton, 1972—; founder, dir. Nat. Shrine of the Sacred Heart, Hazleton, 1975—; pres. Bishop Hafey High Sch., Hazleton, 1989—, Hazleton Cath. Prep. Sch., 1990—; diocesan dir. Apostleship of Prayer, Scranton, Pa., 1990—. Planning commr. Hazle Twp., Hazleton. With USN, 1945-47. Mem. Knights of Columbus (4th degree), Sons of Italy (hon. life). Home and Office: 1 Church Pl Harleigh PA 18225

ANGELO, PETER GREGORY, English and physical education educator; b. N.Y.C., July 1, 1947; s. Vincent Peter and Stella (Elizabeth (Galasso) A. BA in Psychology, SUNY, Stony Brook, 1969, MA in English, 1972, PhD in English, 1978. Dir. aquatics Cath. Child Care Soc., Shoram, N.Y., 1968-69; coord. of recreational swimming programs Cath. Child Care Soc., 1969-87; dir. aquatics N.Y. Assn. for Brain Injured Children, Suffolk, N.Y., 1971-72; asst. prof. phys. edn., coord. aquatics, instr. water safety SUNY, Stony Brook, 1977—, coord. of aquatics instr. and safety, 1977—; asst. prof. English dept. SUNY, 1978-84; asst. prof. English dept. Hofstra U., Hempstead, N.Y., 1979-80, C.W. Post Coll., L.I. U., Brentwood, N.Y., 1984—; dir. fitness and aquatics N.Y. Inst. Tech., Central Islip, 1988-90; instr., trainer water safety Northport (N.Y.) Va. Hosp., 1980-88. Author: Fall to Glory: Theological Reflections on Milton's Epics, 1988. Instructor, trainer 7 safety areas ARC, Suffolk County, N.Y., 1968—; instr. in sculpture and theology Roman Cath. Diocese Rockville Centre (N.Y.), 1982—; co-founder, mem. steering com. Hartsell Cancer Fund, Hauppauge, 1984-86; chmn. adapted aquatics Suffolk County chpt. ARC, 1984—. Republican. Roman Catholic. Home: 21 Glen Hollow Dr Apt G-14 Holtsville NY 11742 Office: SUNY Dept Phys Edn Stony Brook NY 11794

ANGELO, PRISCILLA J., academic administrator. Student, U. Vienna, Austria, 1964; BS, SUNY, Oswego, 1965; MS, Ind. U., 1968; EdD, U. Mass., 1977. Tchr. Hoover Dr. Jr. High Sch., Greece, N.Y., 1965-66, Niskayuna High Sch., Schenectady, N.Y., 1966-67; asst. dean students St. Lawrence U., Canton, N.Y., 1968-71, assoc. dir. student svcs., 1971-78, assoc. dean acad. affairs, dir. internat. affairs, 1978-87, dir. pers., 1984-85; special asst. to pres. Bryant Coll., Smithfield, R.I., 1987—, v.p. instl. advancement, 1987, dir. Internat. Affairs and World Trade Ctr., 1988—; dir. student affairs World Campus Afloat Chapman Coll., Orange, Calif., 1974; vis. adminstr. Semester at Sea U. Pitts., 1982; cons. internationalizing curriculum Ctr. Internat. Edn. U. Mass., Amherst, 1974-77; tchr. Mater Dei Coll., Empire State Coll., 1969-87. Dir. econ. devel. commn. Adirondack North Country Assn., N.Y.; treas., exec. com. Friends of Owen D. Young Lib., N.Y.; chair United Way Campaign, N.Y., St. Lawrence County Hist. Assn., N.Y., trustee; bd. dirs. E.J. Noble Guild Canton-Postdam Hosp., N.Y.; dir. Internat. Inst. R.I.; active Internat. House R.I., Leadership R.I., Bus. Vols. Arts, R.I. Fulbright scholar, 1984, 89; fellow Ctr. Internat. Edn. U. Mass., 1974-77, Bus. and Profl. Women's Club N.Y. Fellow Nat. Assn. Women Deans, Adminstrs., and Counselors (internat. affairs com.); mem. Am. Coun. Edn. (N.Y. State coord. women's nat. identification project, nat. forum). Am. Assn. Higher Edn. (nat. coord. women's caucus), N.Y. Commn. Ind. Colls. and Univs. (state legis. com.), Commn. Higher Edn. (mid. states accreditation teams), C. of C. Task Force Arts, R.I. Hist. Soc., Internat. Trade Task Force (small bus. adminstrn.), World Trade Club. Home: 165 Arnold Ave Cranston RI 02905 Office: Bryant Coll PO Box 53 Smithfield RI 02917

ANGERT, STUART HENRY, bank executive, consultant; b. Buffalo, Jan. 31, 1941; s. Henry and Gertrude (Shleser) A.; m. Joyce Asher, Nov. 19, 1967; children: Joshua, Meredith. BA, Colgate U., 1962; MBA, U. Pa., 1966. V.p. Angert Auto Parts Co. Inc., Buffalo, 1966-79, pres., 1980-85; v.p. Marine Midland Bank, Buffalo, 1986-91; exec. v.p. Remktg. Svcs. Am. Inc., Buffalo, 1991—. Contbr. articles to automotive, fin. publs. Trustee Nichols Sch., 1984-91 (pres. alumni bd. 1982); bd. dirs. SUNY, Buffalo, 1980—; exec. bd. Erie County Pvt. Industry Coun., 1980-85; bd. dirs. Everywoman's Opportunity Ctr., 1991—; mem. leadership coun. Colgate U., 1980—. Mem. Amherst C. of C. (v.p. 1982). Home: 179 Greenaway Rd Buffalo NY 14226-4165 Office: Remktg Svcs Am Inc 3380 Sheridan Dr Ste 160 Amherst NY 14226

ANGERVILLE, EDWIN DUVANEL, accountant, educator; b. St. Marc, Haiti, May 22, 1961; came to U.S., 1974; s. Joseph Aniel and Marie Cecile (Phillip-August) A. BS, CUNY, 1984. CPA, N.Y. Coll. acct. CUNY, Jamaica, 1984-87; staff acct. F.S. Todman & Co., CPAs, N.Y.C., 1987; sr. acct. Zucker & Shernicoff, CPAs, N.Y.C., 1988-89; pvt. practice Jamaica, 1990—; adj. lectr. CUNY, Jamaica, 1986—. Contbr. articles to profl. jours. Recipient Superior scholarships N.Y. State Soc. CPAs, 1984. Mem. Nat. Assn. Black Accts., York Coll. Alumni (bd. dirs. 1990—), York Coll. Acctg. Soc. (hon.). Home: 10745 142nd St Jamaica NY 11435-5219 Office: 94-20 Guy R Brewer Blvd Jamaica NY 11451

ANGIER, NATALIE MARIE, science journalist; b. N.Y.C., Feb. 16, 1958; d. Keith and Adele Bernice (Rosenthal) A.; m. Richard Steven Weiss, July 27, 1991. Student, U. Mich., 1974-76; BA, Barnard Coll., 1978. Staff writer Discover Mag., N.Y.C., 1980-83, Time Mag., N.Y.C., 1984-86; editor Savvy Mag., N.Y.C., 1983-84; journalism educator NYU, N.Y.C., 1987-89; reporter N.Y. Times, N.Y.C., 1990—. Author: Natural Obsessions, 1988. Recipient Pulitzer prize Columbia U., 1991, Journalism award GM Ind. Bd., 1991, Lewis Thomas award Marine Biol. Labs., 1990. Mem. Nat. Assn. Sci. Writers. Office: NY Times 229 W 43d St New York NY 10036

ANGILERI, ANTONIO, property manager; b. Cosoleto, Italy, Jan. 2, 1950; arrived in U.S., 1973; s. Vito and Saveria (Rositani) A.; m. Lisa Mottola, Aug. 16, 1973 (div. Feb. 1984); children: Mary, Patrizia; m. Elena Radulescu, Sept. 12, 1988. Degree in liberal arts, Turin (Italy) U., 1970; cert. in property mgmt., N.Y.C. U., 1989. Cert. property mgr. Tchr. Turin Pub. Schs., 1970-73; property mgr. Crown Bldg., N.Y.C., 1974-78, F.M. Ring Associated, Inc., N.Y.C., 1979-83, Rizzoli Internat. Corp., N.Y.C., 1983-85, El Dorado, Salzberger-Rolfe, N.Y.C., 1985-86, Kennedy House, Salzberger-Rolfe, N.Y.C., 1986-88; supr. bldgs. and grounds Haworth (N.J.) Pub. Sch. Dist., 1978-79; security cons. Comsat Security Inc., N.Y.C., 1989—; property mgr. United Charities, N.Y.C., 1989—; mgmt. cons. Children's Aid Soc., N.Y.C., 1989—, N.Y.C. Mission, 1990—, Community Svc. Soc., N.Y.C., 1989—. Author: Quelli Erano Tempi, 1990. With Italian army, 1968-69. Republican. Roman Catholic. Home: 120 Roosevelt Ave Hasbrouck Heights NJ 07604-1012 Office: United Charities 105 E 22d St New York NY 10010

ANGLE, JOHN CHARLES, retired life insurance company executive; b. N.Y.C., Aug. 22, 1923; s. Everett Edward and Catharine Elizabeth (Dodge) A.; m. Catherine Anne Sellers, Oct. 4, 1945; children: Margaret Susan, James Sellers. S.B., U. Chgo., 1944. With Union Nat. Life Ins. Co., Lincoln, Nebr., 1948-51; v.p., actuary Woodmen Accident and Life Co., Lincoln, 1953-73; dir. Woodmen Accident and Life Co., 1969-73; sr. v.p., chief actuary Guardian Life Ins. Co. Am., N.Y.C., 1973-77; exec. v.p. Guardian Life Ins. Co. Am., 1977-80, pres., 1980-84, chmn. bd., chief exec. officer, 1985-88, also bd. dirs.; pres. Probe, Inc. (ins. newsletter), 1990—; bd. dirs. Guardian Ins. & Annuity Co., Guardian Park Ave. Fund, Guardian Cash Fund, Guardian Investor Svcs. Corp. Consulting editor: Life and Health Insurance Handbook, 2d edit., 1964. Pres. Lincoln Community Chest, 1965. Lincoln Community Coun., 1966-68, 14th St-Union Sq. Bus. Improvement Dist., 1985-88; trustee Am. Coll., 1987-92; bd. dirs. Lincoln Gen. Hosp., 1970-73. 1st lt. USAF, 1943-46, capt. USAF, 1951-52. Fellow Soc. Actuaries (dir. publs. 1975-79, bd. govs. 1980-83, 84-87); mem. Am. Acad. Actuaries (bd. dirs. 1977-79), Internat. Actuarial Assn. (v.p. U.S. sect.), Health Ins. Assn. Am. (bd. dirs. 1985-88), Life Office Mgmt. Assn. (bd. dirs. 1983-89, chmn. 1987), Am. Coun. Life Ins. (bd. dirs. 1986-88), Life Ins. Coun. N.Y. (bd. dirs. 1985-88), Union League Club, Lincoln Country Club, Lincoln Univ. Club.

ANGRILLI, ALBERT, psychology educator; b. N.Y.C., Dec. 4, 1917; s. Peter and Antoinette (Levant) A.; m. Dorothy Sevush, Sept. 15, 1945 (dec. Aug. 1971); 1 child, Robert M.; m. Alma Shapiro, Aug., 1977. BS, NYU, 1949, MA, 1950, PhD, 1958. Lic. psychologist, N.Y.; diplomate Am. Bd. Profl. Psychology. Rsch. investigator Bellevue Hosp. Rapid Treatment Ctr., N.Y.C., 1945-49; clin. psychologist N.Y. State Traveling Child Guidance Clinics, Albany and Binghamton, N.Y., 1949-53; lectr. Queens Coll., CUNY, Flushing, 1953-58, asst. prof. edn., assoc. prof., prof., 1958-84, dir. Ednl. Clinic, 1946-76, prof. emeritus, 1984—, resident prof., adj. prof. grad. program in sch. psychology, 1984—; exam. asst. N.Y.C. Bd. Edn., 1962—; cons., mem. faculty, vis. prof. Internat. Grad. Sch., Lugano, Switzerland, 1962, Bar Ilan U., Israel, 1972, P.R., 1979; cons. psychologist Sherut La'am, Israel, 1972, sch. systems, N.Y. State, 1951; adj. prof. Fla. Inst. Tech. Sch. Profl. Psychology, Melbourne, 1979-90. Co-author: Child Psychology, 1981, Psychologia Infantil, 1984; also articles. Past pres. and bd. dirs. Queens County Mental Health Soc.; past liaison supr. Ferrini League; past bd. dirs. N.Y. State Mental Health Assn. Staff sgt. USAAF, 1942-45. Recipient cert. of merit N.Y.C. Dept. Health, 1957, cert. of honors contbn. Queens Coll. Sch. Edn., 1987. Fellow Am. Orthopsychiat. Assn. (life); mem. APA, N.Y. State Psychol. Assn. Home: 105 Stone Oaks Dr Hartsdale NY 10530-1148 Office: Queens Coll Dept Edn and Community Programs Kissena Blvd Flushing NY 11367

ANGULO, CHARLES BONIN, foreign service officer, lawyer; b. N.Y.C., Aug. 6, 1943; s. Manuel R. and Carolyn C. (Bonin) A.; m. Penelope Snare, June 28, 1986. BA, U. Va., 1966; cert., U. Madrid, 1966; JD, Tulane U., 1969. Bar: Va. 1969. Assoc. Michael & Dent, Charlottesville, Va., 1969-73; assoc. editor The Michie Pub. Co., Charlottesville, 1973; fgn. svc. officer U.S. Dept. State, Washington, 1973-75; fgn. svc. officer Am. Embassy U.S. Dept. State, Brussels, 1976-78; fgn. svc. officer legal advisor's office U.S. Dept. State, Washington, 1978-81; fgn. svc. officer Am. Embassy U.S. Dept. State, Santo Domingo, 1981-85; exec. dir. office of insp. gen. U.S. Dept. State, Washington, 1985-86, asst. chief protocol, 1986-88; Am. Consulate Gen. U.S. Dept. State, Jeddah, Saudi Arabia, 1988—. Mem. Coun. Fgn. Rels. Home: 200 N Pickett St Apt 1107 Alexandria VA 22304 Office: Am Consulate Gen Unit 62112 APO AE 09811-2112

ANJUM, ILYAS MOHAMMAD, mechanical engineer; b. Lahore, Punjab, Pakistan, Apr. 3, 1955; came to U.S., 1982; s. Zainab Bibi; m. Azra Ilyas, Dec. 21, 1989; 1 chld, Adeel. Diploma assoc. engring., Poly. Inst., Lahore, 1974; BS, U. Engring., Lahore, 1981; MS, George Washington U., 1984, DSc, 1988. Registered profl. engr., D.C. Rsch. asst. George Washington U., Washington, 1982-88, grad. teaching asst., 1984-88, rsch. assoc., professorial lectr., 1988, vis. asst. prof. aero. engring., 1988-91; vis. asst. prof. mech. engr. ABB, Edison, N.J., 1991—; cons. engr., Arlington, Va., 1987-89. Contbr. articles to profl. jours. Mem. AIAA, ASME (advisor), Am. Soc. Engring. Edn., Sigma Xi. Home: 2318 Strawberry Ct Edison NJ 08817-2760

ANKERSON, ROBERT WILLIAM, management consultant; b. Mt. Vernon, N.Y., Sept. 23, 1933; s. Paul Gustav and Virginia (Roberts) A.; m. Carol Ann Smith, Mar. 17, 1962 (div. Jan. 1987); children: Robert William Jr., Samuel B. AB, Dartmouth Coll., 1955. Indsl. rels. asst. Texaco Inc., N.Y.C., 1959-60; successively mktg. svcs. mgr., advt. sales rep., pub. affairs dir. Time Inc., N.Y.C., 1960-73; sr. v.p. Devine, Baldwin and Assocs., N.Y.C., 1973-75; v.p. and prin. Spencer Stuart and Assocs. Inc., N.Y.C., 1975-80; sr. v.p. and dir. Billington, Fox and Ellis, Inc., N.Y.C., 1980-82; sr. v.p. Haley Assocs. Inc., N.Y.C., 1982-86; ptnr. Ward Howell Internat. Inc., N.Y.C., 1986—. With USNR, 1956-59. Home: Seashore Ave PO Box 1202 East Quogue NY 11942 Office: Ward Howell Internat Inc 99 Park Ave New York NY 10016-1699

ANNASWAMY, ANURADHA MANDAYAM, control theorist, mechanical engineering educator; b. Bangalore, Karnataka, India, June 11, 1956; came to U.S., 1979; d. Mandayam Annaswamy and Sharada (Jayaram) Varadarajan; m. Srinivasan Mandayam, May 31, 1987. BSc in Maths., Stella Maris Coll., Madras, India, 1976; B in Engring., Indian Inst. Sci., 1979; PhD in Elec. Engring., Yale U., 1985. Postdoctoral assoc. Yale U., New Haven, 1985-87, vis. asst. prof., 1988; asst. prof. Boston U., 1988—, 1988-91; asst. prof. mech. engring. MIT, Cambridge, 1991—; cons. Yale U., 1990—. Author: Stable Adaptive Systems, 1989. Mem. IEEE, AIAA . Home: 31 Cross St Newton MA 02165-2101 Office: MIT Dept Mech Engring Cambridge MA 02139

ANSBACHER, MAX GEORGE, stockbroker; b. N.Y.C., Dec. 16, 1935; s. Heinz L. and Rowena (Ripin) A. BA, U. Vt., 1957; LLB, Yale U., 1960; LLM, NYU, 1963. Bar: Vt. 1961, D.C. 1961, N.Y. 1962. Tax lawyer IRS, N.Y.C. and Washington, 1961-65, Breed, Abbott & Morgan, N.Y.C., 1965; atty. Bristol-Myers Co., N.Y.C., 1966-70, Colgate Palmolive Co., N.Y.C., 1970-74, Campbell Soup Co., Camden, N.J., 1974-75; assoc. dir. Bear, Stearns & Co., Inc., N.Y.C., 1975—; creator The Ansbacher Index. Author: The New Options Market, 1975, How to Profit From the Coming Bull Market, 1981, The New Stock Index Market, 1983; many appearances on FNN and CNBC. Capt. USANG, 1961-67. Mem. Yale Club, West Side Tennis Club. Home: 20 Park Ave New York NY 10016-3893 Office: 245 Park Ave New York NY 10167-0002

ANSBRO, JOHN JOSEPH, philosophy educator; b. N.Y.C., Nov. 16, 1932; s. Thomas and Katherine (Reilly) A. BA, St. Joseph's Sem., Yonkers, N.Y., 1954, postgrad., 1955; MA, Fordham U., 1957, PhD, 1964. Lectr. philosophy Manhattan Coll., Riverdale, N.Y., 1958-59, instr., 1959-63, asst. prof., 1963-68, assoc. prof., 1968-79, prof., 1979—; curriculum guidance supr. of faculty counselors Sch. Arts & Scis. Manhattan Coll., 1962-73, chmn. co-curricular interdisciplinary arts program, 1962-70, chmn. com. faculty rsch. projects and grants, 1976-78, 89-92, chmn. dept. philosophy, 1977-81, chmn. sabbatical leave com., 1989-91, mem. com. faculty rsch. projects, mem. instnl. rev. bd. human subjects, mem. task force acad. programs, liaison officer Danforth Found., others; adj. asst. prof. philos. resources for contemporary problems program Grad. Sch. Arts & Scis., Fordham U., 1975; chmn. Met. Round Table Philosophy, 1972-75; project field coord. N.Y. State Dept. Edn., 1965-67. Author: Martin Luther King,

Jr.: The Making of a Mind, 1982, Mex. translator, 1985; contbr. numerous articles and critical revs. to publs. including N.Y. Times. Fordham U. Grad. Sch. scholar in Philosophy, 1956-57; Travel and Study grantee Ford Found., 1973, summer grantee Am. Can. Co. Found., 1985, Samuel Rubin Found., 1985; recipient Internat. Order Merit award Cambridge U., 1991.c. Mem. AAUP, Soc. Advancement Am. Philosophy, Am. Philos. Assn., Hegel Soc. Am., Soc. Ancient Greek Philosophy, Gandhi-King Soc. Office: Manhattan Coll Manhattan Coll Pkwy Riverdale NY 10471

ANSEN, DAVID B., critic, writer; b. Los Angeles, Apr. 21, 1945; s. Joseph and Dorothy (Blum) A. BA, Harvard U., 1967. Film critic, editor Real Paper, Cambridge, Mass., 1975-77; film critic, sr. writer Newsweek, N.Y.C., 1977—; host, writer cable TV show Bravo International Film Show, 1983-87. Writer documentaries include The Divine Garbo, 1990, The One The Only...Groucho, 1991. Recipient Page One award Newspaper Guild N.Y., 1983, Headliner award, 1984, Page One award, 1986, 88. Mem. N.Y. Film Critics Circle, Nat. Society Film Critics. Office: Newsweek 11835 W Olympic Blvd Los Angeles CA 90064-5001

ANSPACH, ERNST, economist, lawyer; b. Glogau, Germany, Feb. 4, 1913; came to U.S., 1936, naturalized, 1943; s. Hermann and Margarete (Gurassa) A.; m. Ruth Pietsch, Dec. 20, 1950; children: Paul David, Margaret Louise. Js.D., U. Freiburg, Berlin, Munich, Breslau, 1935; M.Sc., New Sch. Social Research, N.Y.C., 1943. With German jud. service, 1934-36; fin. analyst Loeb, Rhoades & Co., N.Y.C., 1936-43; reorgn. of adminstrn. Justice in Bavaria and Hesse, 1946-49; gen. counsel and polit. adviser Dept. State, U.S. Land Commr. for Hesse, 1949-52; chief economist, gen. ptnr. Loeb, Rhoades & Co., Investment Bankers, N.Y.C., 1952-79; cons., 1980—; tchr. adult edn. program Henry St. Settlement, N.Y.C., 1939-43; lectr. Univs. Munich, Marburg, Frankfurt, 1948-52; lectr. fields econs., polit. sci., theology and primitive art, 1955—. Contbr. articles to sci. jours.; collection African Tribal Art; exhibited, Mus. Primitive Art, N.Y.C., 1967-68. Trustee Bleuler Psychotherapy Ctr., 1953-85, chmn. bd., 1956-65; trustee Nightingale-Bamford Sch., 1971-77; trustee Madison Ave. Presbyn. Ch., 1966—, chmn. bd. trustees, 1975-80; mem. vis. com. dept. primitive art Met. Mus. Art, N.Y.C.; bd. dirs. Ctr. for African Art, 1982—, treas., 1982-87. Capt. AUS, 1943-46. Recipient Army commendation ribbon. Mem. Conf. Bus. Economists. Home: 118 W 79th St New York NY 10024-6445

ANSPON, HARRY DAVIS, plastics researcher; b. Washington, Sept. 25, 1917; s. Berthold Winfried and Emma Bascomb (Davis) A.; m. C. Nannette Green, Jan. 28, 1956; children: Catherine Davis, Ellen Graham. BS, U. Md., 1939, PhD, 1942. Registered patent agt., U.S. Patent Office. Teaching fellow, rsch. fellow, rsch. asst. U. Md., College Park, 1940-46; rsch. chemist Uniroyal, Passaic, N.J., 1946-48; rsch. chemist, rsch. fellow, plant chemist Gen. Aniline & Film Corp., 1948-59; sect. leader Gulf Rsch. and Devel., Merriam, Kans., 1959-68; mgr. process and product devel. U.S. Steel (USS Chems.), Pitts., 1968-69, tech. dir. plastics, 1969-75, asst. mgr. new polymer planning, 1976-78; pvt. practice cons. HDA Cons., Sewickley, Pa., 1978—; patent agt. U.S. Patent Office, Sewickley, 1979—. Contbr. chpt. to book: Manufacture of Plastics, 1964; patentee in field. Pres. Harmonie Assocs., Ambridge, Pa., 1985-86. Mem. Am Chem. Soc. (emeritus), Soc. Plastics Engrs., Plastics and Rubber Inst., Sigma Xi, Phi Kappa Phi. Home: 29 Beaver St Sewickley PA 15143-1244 Office: HDA Cons 29 Beaver St Sewickley PA 15143-1244

ANSTADT, GEORGE W., occupational medicine physician; b. Williamsport, Pa., Aug. 17, 1947; s. Vern Eugene and Jane Ann (Treon) A.; m. Nancy Jane Conrad, 1980; children: Jonathan, Jennifer. BS, Pa. State U., 1968; MD, Jefferson Med. Coll., 1970. Diplomate Am. Bd. Preventive Medicine (Occupational Medicine). Rotating intern Northwestern U., 1970-71; occupational medicine resident U. Cin., 1974-76; area physician Eastman Kodak Co., Rochester, N.Y., 1976—. Lt. comdr. M.C., USN, 1971-74. Mem. Am. Coll. Occupational Med. (nat. 2d v.p.). Home: 75 Panorama Trl Rochester NY 14625-1507 Office: Eastman Kodak Co 901 Elmgrove Rd Rochester NY 14653-0001

ANSTATT, PETER JAN, marketing services company executive; b. Haworth, N.J., Feb. 9, 1942; s. Herman E. and Margaret (Dunham) A.; m. Jean Ann Sorchiotti, Aug. 13, 1966; children: Christopher Ryan, Holley Elizabeth. B.S. in Printing Mgmt., Carnegie Mellon U., 1963; grad. program for mgmt. devel., Harvard U. Bus. Sch., 1977. Estimator Einson Freeman Inc., N.Y.C., 1963, project mgr., 1965-66; account exec. Einson Freeman Inc., Fairlawn, N.J., 1966-71; gen. mgr. Einson Freeman Inc., Fairlawn, 1971-76, pres., chief exec. officer, 1977-78; chmn., chief exec. officer Einson Freeman Inc., Paramus, N.J., 1978—; v.p. ops. EAC Industires, Paramus, 1978. Mem. alumni bd. govs. Blair Acad., 1974-77; bd. dirs. Ridgewood YMCA, 1981-90, bd. trustees, 1991—. Served with C.E., U.S. Army, 1963-65, Korea. Recipient Jacob Van Dyke award for Outstanding Service, Ridgewood YMCA, 1985. Mem. Point of Purchase Advt. Inst. (chmn. trade ethics com. 1973-78, chmn. ann. exhibit com. 1979, dir. 1973-81, vice chmn. bd. 1979, chmn. 1980, speaker ann. industry seminar 1977-88, Producer/Supplier of Yr. 1984), Beta Theta Pi (pres. 1962-63). Republican. Methodist. Home: 365 Annette Ct Wyckoff NJ 07481-3126 Office: Einson Freeman Inc 305 State Route 17 S Paramus NJ 07652-2913

ANTELL, DARRICK EUGENE, plastic surgeon; b. Cleve., Feb. 22, 1991; s. E. James and Wanda H. (Kociecki) An.; m. Elizabeth Ann Sobottka, July 14, 1984; children: Gillian Elizabeth Antell, Darrick Eugene Antell, Jr. BS in Biology, Hobart Coll., 1973; DDS, Case Western Res. U. Dental, 1978; MD, Med. Coll. of Ohio, 1982. Cert. Am. Bd. Plastic Surgery. Surgery intern Stanford (Calif.) U. Med. Ctr., 1982-83, surgery resident, 1983-85; plastic surgery resident N.Y. Hosp. Cornell, N.Y.C., 1985-87; plastic and reconstructive surgeon St. Luke's/Roosevelt, N.Y.C., 1987—. Author: Plastic Surgery, 1991; contbr. articles to profl. jours. Bd. trustees East Side House Settlement, N.Y.C., 1991; bd. trustees adv. Girl Scouts of North Am., N.Y.C., 1991. Grantee Facial Proportions AM. Soc. for Aesthetic Plastic Surgery, 1987; recipient Pres. Citizenship award N.Y. State Med. Soc., 1992. Am. Soc. Plastic and Reconstructive Surgeons, Am. Soc. Maxillofacial Surgeons Parliamentarian, N.Y. Regional Soc., Plastic and Reconstructive Surgeons, AMA, Med. Soc. of State of N.Y., N.Y. County Med. Soc., Am. Cleft Palate Assn., ADA, Am. Acad. Cosmetic Dentistry, Interplast, Lipoplasty Soc., Herbert Conway Soc., Univ. Sch. Alumni Adv. Coun., Union Club. Office: 50 E 69th St New York NY 10021

ANTHONY, ADAM, physiology educator; b. Buffalo, Oct. 19, 1923; s. John and Rozalia (Piechowicz) Chmielowski; m. Barbara Oakes, June 20, 1949 (div. Oct. 1986); children: Heather Lee, Brian Adam. BA, SUNY, Buffalo, 1943; MS, Marquette U., 1948; PhD, U. Chgo., 1952. Asst. prof. Pa. State U., University Park, 1952-57, assoc. prof., 1957-61, prof., 1961—. Contbr. and co-contbr. numerous articles to profl. jours. With U.S. Army, 1943-46. John M. Prather scholar U. Chgo., 1950-52; recipient Darbaker award Pa. Acad. Scis., 1966, 68,69, C.I. Noll Outstanding Teaching award, 1990, Pa. State U., 1990. Mem. AAAS, Am. Physiol. Soc., Phi Lambda Upsilon, Phi Sigma, Sigma Xi. Office: Pa State U 418 Mueller University Park PA 16802

ANTHONY, EDWARD MASON, linguistics educator; b. Cleve., Sept. 1, 1922; s. Edward Mason and Elsie (Haas) A.; m. Ann Louise Terbrueggen, Sept. 18, 1946; children: Lynn Diane Anthony Higgins, Janice Louise, Edward Mason, 4th. A.B., U. Mich., 1944, M.A., 1946, Ph.D., 1954. From instr. English to prof. linguistics U. Mich., 1945-64; prof. U. Pitts., 1964-90, prof. emeritus, 1990—, chmn. dept. gen. linguistics, 1964-74; dir. Lang. Acquisition Inst., 1970, dir. lang. orientation programs, 1974-82, dir. Asian Studies program, 1977-82, dir. Lang. and Culture Inst, 1982-90; vis. lectr., Afghanistan, 1951, Thailand, 1955-57, Mexico, 1964-65, Poland, 1977, Greece and Yugoslavia, 1981, Singapore and Thailand, 1984, Hong Kong, 1985, 86; dir. S.E. Asian English Project, Thailand, Laos, Vietnam, 1958-61, Rockefeller Found. Thai Project, 1967-72; vis. prof. Regional English Lang. Centre, Singapore, 1974-75, Peking Inst. Fgn. Lang., 1979-80; cons. in field; mem. Nat. Adv. Council Teaching English as a Fgn. Lang.; resource person Detroit Bd. Edn., 1964, Pitts. Bd. Edn., 1965; mem. adv. screening com. in linguistics Council for Internat. Exchange of Scholars, 1976; mem. adv. panel in English teaching to dir. USIA, 1987—. Author: Reading Thai Syllables, 1962, (with others) Foundations of Thai, 2 vols, 1968, Towards a Theory of Lexical Meaning, 1975; book rev. editor: Lan. Learning, 1948; editor, 1949. Smith- Mundt grantee, 1951; recipient Fulbright award, 1955-57; NDEA lang. Research grantee, 1965-67; State Dept. grantee, 1964, 65, 77, 81, 84, 90; plaque of Honor Ramkhamhaeng U., Bangkok, Thailand, 1986. Mellon fellow Nat. Fgn. Language Ctr. Washington, 1990; mem. Linguistic Soc., Am. Assn. Applied Linguists, Assn. Asian Studies, Siam Soc. (life), Assn. Tchrs. English to Speakers of Other Langs. (pres. 1967), Nat. Council Tchrs. English. Democrat. Presbyterian. Home: 4118 Northampton Dr Allison Park PA 15101-1532 Office: Dept Gen Linguistic U Pitts Pittsburgh PA 15260

ANTHONY, ETHAN, architect; b. Iowa City, Oct. 14, 1950; s. Frank and Carol (Kessler) A.; m. Luz Eugenia, Feb. 18, 1984; children: Winston Eugene, Alexandra Luce. Student, Boston Arch. Ctr., 1971-77; BArch, U. Oregon, 1980. Project architect Payette Assocs., Boston, 1980-83; prin. Anthony Assocs., Boston, 1983-90; ptnr. Hoyle, Doran and Berry, Inc., Boston, 1991—; cons. architect Springfield (Vt.) Hosp., 1984—; instr. design Roger Williams Coll., Bristol, R.I., 1984-89; thesis advisor Boston Arch. Ctr., 1985-87. Mem. World Affairs Coun., 1987—. Mem. AIA, S.Am. Explorers Club, Platform Assn., U. Oreg. Alumni Assn. Home: 51 Highland Ter Brockton MA 02401-3208 Office: Hoyle Doran and Berry Inc 585 Boylston St Boston MA 02116-3609

ANTHONY, JANE MARIE, state official; b. Providence, Feb. 20, 1950; d. Henry N. and Mary (Walsh) Thacher; m. Ernest Anthony, Jr., Mar. 29, 1970; children: Nicole, Ernest Anthony III, Daniel, Brian. Student, U. R.I. Exec. sec. Art Mold Products, Cranston, R.I., 1979-81; edn. coord. St. Mark Ch., Jamestown, R.I., 1981-84; jai alai judge R.I. Racing and Athletics Commn., Providence, 1984—. Mem. Jamestown Sch. Com., 1983-89; mem. Jamestown Town Coun., 1989-91; campaign mgr. for state rep., 1986, for state senator, 1988; mem. exec. bd. ARC, Jamestown, 1987-89, So. R.I. Regional Collaborative, 1988-89; chmn. Substance Abuse Prevention, Jamestown, 1988—; bd. dirs. New Visions Newport County, Newport, R.I., 1988—; mem. Narragansett coun. Boy Scouts Am., 1984-89; mem. policy coun. Family Community Leadership Program, 1991—. Mem. St. Mark Women's Club (pres. 1973-76), Alpha Sigma Lambda. Republican. Roman Catholic. Home: 8 Shady Ln Jamestown RI 02835-1233

ANTHONY, MICHAEL THOMAS, consulting firm executive; b. Schenectady, N.Y., June 9, 1959; s. Michael Joseph and Patricia (Dempsey) A.; m. Susan Anthony, May 25, 1986; 1 child, Michael Gopoian Anthony. BS in Engring., Wentworth Inst., 1984; MBA, Boston, U., 1987. Engr. Honeywell, Billerica, Mass., 1984-87; dir. Pittiglio Rabin Todd & McGrath, Weston, Mass., 1987—; adv. bd. Wentworth Inst. of Tech., Boston, 1986—; staff advisor Endicott Coll., Beverly, 1987—. Mem. IEEE, SME. Office: Pittiglio Rabin Todd & McGrath 9 Riverside Rd Weston MA 02193-2281

ANTHONY, PAUL BARRIE, international real estate counselor; b. Portsmouth, Hampshire, Eng., Feb. 14, 1934; came to U.S., 1966; s. John Edward and Maisie L. (MacAuley) A.; m. Elizabeth Craig, Dec. 10, 1960; 1 child, Nicholas. Intermediate Degree, Inst. Med. Lab. Tech., London, 1956, BS, 1957, MS, 1960. Mgr. Community Health Services (Sask.) Ltd., Regina, Can., 1964-66; dir. rehab. Hupp Corp., Inc. div. Gibson, Greenville, Mich., 1966-67; adminstr. Pipp Community Hosp., Inc., Plainville, Mich., 1967-70; administr. HEW grants Reynolds Meml. Hosp., Winston-Salem, N.C., 1970-72; supt. Oil Industry Med. Soc., Tripoli, Libya, 1972-73; pres. Antco Internat., N.Y.C., 1973—; pres. Antco Internat., assoc. co. Goddard & Smith Internat., Teaneck, N.J., 1985-87, N.Y.C., 1987—; broker, salesperson Weichert Realtors, Jersey City, 1984-87; sr. v.p. Internat. Property Counselors, N.Y., 1987-88; cons. hosp. adminstr. Al-Hanouf Med. Svcs., Saudi Arabia, 1991-92. Author: Medical Group Practice, 1967, British Health Service After 25 Years, 1970. Mem. polit. com. Malvern (Eng.) Conservative Party, 1974-75, steering com. South Cen. Mich. Helath Planning Coun., Lansing, 1968-70, Smaller Hosp. Adv. Com. Mich., Lansing, 1968-70, Hosp. Design and Constrn., Lansing, 1968-70; dir. E.M. Erith Trust, London, 1974—; sr. v.p. Fedn. Internationale des Professions Immobilieres, N.Y.C., 1986-89; owners' rep. Future Vision, New City Brazil; project dir. Knowlton Village Green Project N.J. Mem. Nat. Bd. Realtors, Internat. Real Estate Fedn., N.J. Assn. Realtors (legis. com. 1987—), Real Estate Bd. N.Y., Inst. Med. Sci., Hudson County Bd. Realtors, Internat. Platform Assn., Rotary. Republican. Episcopalian. Home: PO Box 4166 Clifton NJ 07012-0999

ANTHONY GULDEN, KATHY ANN, special education educator; b. Greensburg, Pa., June 17, 1963; d. Orville Scott and Alice Helen (Bailley) Anthony; m. Martin Lynn Gulden, Dec. 31, 1988. Cert. child care with high honors, Westmoreland County Coll., 1982; BS in Spl. Edn., Clarion U. Pa., 1985; Ms in Secondary Counseling Edn., Shippensburg U. Pa., 1990. Cert. counselor of mental and phys. handicapped and secondary counselor, Pa. Learning support tchr. Lincoln Ind. Unit 12, New Oxford, Pa., 1985-91, instrnl. support tchr., 1991—; softball coach Upper Adams Sch. Dist., Biglerville, Pa., 1986-92. Mem., leader, counselor Girl Scouts U.S.A., Greensburg, Pa., 1973-83; counselor Nazarene Ch. Camp, Butler, Pa., 1984—. Mem. NEA, AACD, Coun. Exceptional Children, Pa. Edn. Assn., Pa. Counseling Assn., Upper Adams Edn. Assn., Kappa Delta Pi. Home: PO Box 371 Bendersville PA 17306-0371

ANTIN, ANTHONY LENARD, advertising consultant, educator; b. Newark, June 7, 1923; s. John and Rochina (Barasso) A.; m. Jean Clark McKersie, Oct. 25, 1947; children: Elizabeth Burns, Parker Bruce, Meredith McKersie. LittB, Rutgers U., 1947. Asst. editor news service Carnegie Inst. of Tech., Pitts., 1947-48, editor news service, 1948-50; publicity dir. Ketchum, Inc., Pitts., 1950-53; advt. mgr. Mellon Bank, Pitts., 1953-56; asst. promotional dir. Reader's Digest Sales and Service, N.Y.C., 1956-58, internat. promotional dir., 1958-62, creative dir., 1962-71, v.p., dir. of creative services, U.S. and internat., 1971-86; cons., lectr., adj. prof. Brigham Young U., Provo, Utah, 1986—. Author: Great Print Advertising, 1992; editor: Educational Philosophy of Robert E. Dougherty, 1949. Trustee Nat. Rowing Found., Arlington, Va., 1970—. Served with U.S. Army, 1943-45. Recipient Silver Beaver award Boy Scouts Am., 1978. Mem. Phi Beta Kappa. Club: Darien Country. Home and Office: 92 Five Mile River Rd Darien CT 06820-6234

ANTLE, RICKY LEE, educator; b. Tulsa, Oct. 10, 1953; s. James Thearl and Rosalea (Durkee) A.; m. Nancy Lee Thompson, Aug. 10, 1974; children: Elizabeth Ann, Benjamin Thearl. BS, Okla. State U., 1975; PhD, Stanford (Calif.) U., 1981. Staff acct. Arthur Andersen & Co., Tulsa, 1975; asst. prof. U. Chgo., 1980-84, assoc. prof., 1984-85; assoc. prof. Sch. of Orgn. and Mgmt. Yale U., New Haven, 1985-89, prof., 1989—; lectr. Yale Exec. Mgmt. Program, 1990; presenter faculty devel. workshops U. N.C., U. Mich, McMaster U. Contbr. articles to profl. jours. Grantee Peat Marwick, 1988. Mem. Am. Acctg. Assn. mgmt. acctg. com. 1982, rsch. adv. com. 1984-85, chmn. screening subcom. of com. on notable contbn. to acctg. lit. award 1986-87, planning com., mem. resident faculty for 1988 doctoral consortium, rsch. com. 1990-91), Econometric Soc. Office: Sch Orgn and Mgmt Yale U 135 Prospect St New Haven CT 06511-3729

ANTOLIK, MICHAEL RAYMOND, political science educator; b. Yonkers, N.Y., Jan. 15, 1948; s. Michael Edward and Helen Anna (Wilhelm) A. BA, Cath. U., 1970; MA, NYU, 1973, NYU, 1977; PhD, Columbia U., 1986. Tchr. Christian Bros. Acad., Lincroft, N.J., 1970-74, La Salle Acad., N.Y.C., 1974-77; asst. prof. De La Salle U., Manila, Philippines, 1977-80; assoc. prof. polit. sci. Manhattan Coll., N.Y.C., 1986—. Author: Asean and the Diplomacy of Accomodation, 1990; contbr. articles to profl. jours. mem. Assn. Asian Studies, Conf. Third World Studies, Am. Polit. Sci. Assn., Acad. Polit. Sci. Roman Catholic. Home: 910 W End Ave Apt 6D New York NY 10025-3569 Office: Govt Dept Manhattan Coll Bronx NY 10471

ANTON, HARVEY, textile company executive; b. N.Y.C., Nov. 10, 1923; s. Abraham J. and Byrdie (Casin) A.; student Western State Coll. Colo., 1941, Savage Sch. Edn., 1941-42; B.S., N.Y. U., 1949; m. Betty L. Weintraub, Dec. 18, 1949; children: Bruce Norman, Lynne Beth. Pres., Anton Yarn Corp. (merged with Robison Textile Co. to form Robison-Anton Textile Co. 1959), N.J., 1949-50, chmn. bd., 1989—; v.p. Arrow Spinning, Susquehanna, Pa.; adv. bd. 1st Jersey Nat. Bank; v.p.Mid-Valley Textile; sec. Bloomsburg Dye; chmn. bd. Robison-Anton Textile Co. Trustee Erza Charitable Found.; pres. Anton Found. Served to 1st lt. AUS, 1943-46. Clubs: Masons, KP; Leonia Tennis; N.Y. Univ. Letter (N.Y.C.). Home: 41 Longview Dr Emerson NJ 07630-1507 Office: Robison Anton Textile Co 175 Bergen Blvd Fairview NJ 07022-1619

ANTON, MACE DAMON, loan officer; b. N.Y.C., Mar. 18, 1961; s. Morris J. and Alice (Macy) A.; m. Anna Kang, June 10, 1990; 1 child, Joshua Benjamin. BA, Yeshiva U., 1982; MA, Columbia U., 1984. Cert. notary pub., N.Y. Credit investigator, analyst trainee James Talcott, Inc., N.Y.C., 1985-86; credit analyst commodity credit dept. Bear Stearns & Co. Inc., N.Y.C., 1986; comml. loan officer, asst. cashier Merchants Bank of N.Y., N.Y.C., 1986—; pres. Profl. Image Consultants, Inc., Jamaica Estates, N.Y., 1988—; ptnr. Morris Anton Assocs., N.Y.C., 1977—. Mem. Nat. Rifle Assn., Nat. Geog. Soc., Smithsonian Inst., Kappa Delta Pi, Phi Delta Kappa. Republican. Jewish. Home: PO Box 1642 Cathedral Sta New York NY 10025

ANTONACCI, LORI (LORETTA MARIE ANTONACCI), marketing executive, consultant; b. Riverton, Ill., Mar. 31, 1947; d. Antonio and Gena Marie A. BA, Bradley U., 1969. Broadcast copywriter Sta. WIRL-TV, Peoria, Ill., 1969; communications specialist Walgreen Co., Chgo., 1970-72; creative supr. Nat. Assn. Realtors, Chgo., 1973; creative dir., producer Steve Sohmer, Inc., N.Y.C., 1974-77; owner, exec. producer Antonacci Prodns., N.Y.C., 1977-79; promotion specialist Ziff-Davis Publs., 1979-80; promotion mgr. Psychology Today, 1980-81; pres. Antonacci & Assocs., N.Y.C., 1982—; adj. prof. Gallatin div. NYU, 1986—. Bd. advisors Wildcare, Inc., Artists Talk on Art, Inc.; founder Artists Talk on Art panel series, 1974. Recipient Golden Eagle award CINE, 1976; award U.S. Indsl. Film Festival, 1977; CEBA award, 1979; Bronze medal Internat. Film and TV Festival N.Y., 1979. Mem. Advt. Women N.Y. (profl. devel. com. 1983-85, program com. 1986-90, chmn. speakers bur. 1988-90, chmn. pub. policy com. 1991—), Women in Communications, Am. Women in Radio and TV, N.Y.C. Women's Agenda, Women's City Club of N.Y., N.Y.C. Women's Agenda. Address: 15 E 10th St New York NY 10003

ANTONACCIO, MARIO AMERICO, manufacturing executive, retired; b. Harrison, N.J., Nov. 21, 1930; s. Antonio and Carmella (Comparelli) A.; m. Sonja Brunvatne, Apr. 24, 1954; 1 child, Carol. BSBA, Fairleigh Dickinson U., 1962. Billing clerk Worthington Pump Corp., Harrison, 1948-51, asst. supr., 1952-62, surp. payables, 1962-70; controller Worthington Div. Taneyton (Md.) Operation, 1970-74, mgr. fin., 1974-80, mgr. ops., 1980-81; gen. mgr. Worthington-Weir Joint Venture and Taneytown Operation, 1981-90; retired, 1991; dir. Worthington-Weir Ltd., Glascow, Scotland, 1981-90. Sgt. USAF, 1950-52. Mem. Am. Assn. Retired Persons, Am. Legion, U.S. Hist. Soc., Nat. Geographic Soc., DAV Commdrs. Club, The Statue of Liberty Ellis Island Found. Inc. (charter), Smithsonian Inst. Roman Catholic. Home: Box 544 R D #6 Hanover PA 17331

ANTONIO, SUSAN RICCIO, mathematics educator; b. West Hartford, Conn., July 17, 1963; d. Louis A. and Jennie (Moccia) Riccio; m. Ronald Harry Antonio, Aug. 13, 1988. BA, Gettysburg Coll., 1985; BS, U. Nebr., 1988. Cert. tchr., Conn. Tutor Tutoring Svcs., Omaha, 1987-88; math tchr. Masuk High Sch., Monroe, Conn., 1988—; tutor, Omaha, 1986-88; substitute tchr. Derby (Conn.) Pub. Schs., 1988; math tutor, Derby, Conn., 1988—. Mem. NEA, Nat. Coun. Tchrs. of Math., Conn. Edn. Assn., Monroe Edn. Assn., Gamma Phi Beta, Kappa Delta Pi. Republican. Roman Catholic. Home: 24 Mcveagh Rd Westbrook CT 06498 Office: Masuk High Sch 1014 Monroe Tpke Monroe CT 06468-1967

ANTONSSON, STEFAN, pharmaceutical company executive, writer; b. Reykjavik, Iceland, Apr. 13, 1960; came to U.S., 1962; s. Stefan and Johanna Sigridur (Jonsdottir) A.; m. Mary Lynn Ashley, Oct. 20, 1984 (div. Apr. 1989). BA, Columbia Coll., 1983; postgrad., NYU, 1987—. Sales rep. First Investors Corp., N.Y.C., 1983-84; asst. to nat. sales mgr. Pharmacia, Inc., Piscataway, N.J., 1984-85; sales rep. Pharmacia, Inc., Walnut Creek, Calif., 1985; product mgr. Pharmacia, Inc., Piscataway, N.J., 1986-87, sr. product mgr., 1987-88, new product mktg. mgr., 1989; sr. product mgr. Forest Labs., N.Y.C., 1989—. Author short stories.

ANTONUCCI, FRANK RALPH, chemist; b. Auburn, N.Y., Sept. 8, 1946; s. Frank R. and Mary M. (Guszcza) A.; m. Mary Ellen Antonucci, Aug. 24, 1968; children: Donald, Philip. BA, St. Michael's Coll., Winooski, Vt., 1968; MS, Coll. of Holy Cross, Worcester, Mass., 1969; PhD in Chemistry, Rensselaer Poly. Inst., 1972. Chemist Addressograph-Multigraph Corp., Cleve., 1975-77; sr. chemist St. Regis Corp., W. Nyack, N.Y., 1977-85; mgr. analytical scis. Champion Internat. Corp., W. Nyack, N.Y., 1985—. Capt. USAF, 1972-75. Mem. TAPPI, Am. Chem. Soc. Home: 3 North Dr Washingtonville NY 10992-1903 Office: Champion Internat West Nyack Rd Nyack NY 10994

ANTOSIK, STANLEY JOSEPH, history educator; b. Bratislava, Slovakia, Czechoslovakia, Mar. 11, 1943; came to U.S., 1955; s. Joseph and Otilia (Jungwirt) A.; m. Idaehla F. Cribari, Aug. 11, 1968; children: Erika, Kristina. BA, U. Ill., 1965; MA, Columbia U., 1966, PhD, 1975. Vis. asst. prof. Coll. Charleston (S.C.), summer 1979; adj. lectr. NYU, N.Y.C., 1979, 83-85, adj. asst. prof., 1985-87, adj. assoc. prof., 1987-89; legis. aide N.Y.C. Coun., 1981-83; asst. prof. St. John's U., N.Y.C., 1989—; cons. The Germanic Rev., N.Y.C., 1991—. Author: The Question of Elites, 1978; contbr. articles and revs. to profl. jours. Woodrow Wilson Ctr. fellow, 1965, Columbia U. honors fellow, 1966, N.Y.State Herbert Lehman fellow, 1966-70; recipient award for teaching excellence NYU, 1988. Mem. AAUP, Am. Hist. Assn., Internat. Leibniz Soc., N.Am. Nietzsche Soc., Soc. for Study of Crusades, Phi Beta Kappa. Republican. Lutheran. Office: St John's U 300 Howard Ave Staten Island NY 10301-4496

ANTZIS, ERROL RICHARD, banker; b. Mt. Kisco, N.Y., Feb. 17, 1958; s. Eli and Norma Joy A.; m. Deborah Leigh. BSEE, MIT, 1980; MBA in Fin., NYU, 1982. 2d v.p. Chase Manhattan Bank, N.Y.C., 1982-87; v.p. Bank of N.Y., N.Y.C., 1987-90; v.p., dir. Banque Paribas, N.Y.C., 1990—. Author: (industry study) Nat. Foundries Corp., 1980. Home: 250 W 27th St # 6E New York NY 10001 Office: Banque Paribas 787 7th Ave 32nd Fl New York NY 10019

ANYANWU, CHUKWUKRE, alcohol/drug abuse facility administrator; b. Ogbor-Ugiri, Nigeria, Apr. 14, 1943; came to U.S., 1963; s. Peter Ebo and Eunice Ikwuaha (Madu) A.; m. Ngozi G. Nwaike, Jan. 10, 1980; children: Okechukwu-Pat, Adaku Cathy, Ikechukwu-Uzo, Uremegbulem, Kingsley-Ugo, Ucheckukwu. BS in Biology and Chemistry, St. Joseph's Coll., 1971; MS in Biochemistry, Fairleigh Dickenson U., 1972; postgrad., Temple U., 1979; MD, Cetec U., Dominican Republic, 1981. Postdoctorate Temple Hosp.; diplomatic envoy Nigeria, 1973-75; extern various hosps., Phila. area, 1977-79; obstetrician-gynecologist, cons. Lagos U. Teaching Hosp., Nigeria, 1983-84; cons. psychiatry St. Mary's Hosp., Phila., 1981-82; rsch. nuclear medicine Temple U. Hosp., Phila., 1980-81; chmn. A-B Assocs. Inc., Phila., 1970—; chief exec. officer, owner, founder A-B Assocs., Inc., Phila., 1989—; virolog rsch. A-B Assocs. Inc., Phila., 1979-82, owner, chief exec. officer, dir.; mem. staff dept. of psychiatry JFK Mental Health/Retardation, Phila., 1985-88; mem. staff dept. of drug and alcohol addiction Giuffré Med. Ctr., 1988-89; counselor in psychiatry Misericordia Hosp., Phila., 1987-88; mem. staff addiction svcs. Guiffre Med. Ctr., Phila., 1988—; founder, chief exec. officer AB Assocs. Am. Beats Addiction, Inc., Phila., 1989—. Author numerous poems; contbr. articles profl. jours. Senate candidate Imo State Govt., Nigeria, 1983; Olympian competing in pole vault, 1500 meters 400 hurdles, Mex., 1968. Mem. Pa. Cet. Addiction Counselors, Orgn. NIgerian Profs. USA (chmn. jud. com.), Fedn. Police Law Enforement, Phila Fraternal Order Police, Interagency Coun. Homeless. Democrat. Roman Catholic. Office: A-B Assocs Inc PO Box 38127 Philadelphia PA 19140-0127

ANZINI, ANN ELIZABETH URBAN, art director; b. Bklyn., Oct. 6, 1962; d. Joseph and Elise Gertrude (Monauni) Urban; m. David Joseph Anzini, June 23, 1984; 1 child, Elise Marie. BFA in Graphic Design, U. Conn., 1984. Art dir. Advernomics, Sussex, N.J., 1984-85; artist Ingersoll-Rand Advt. Svcs., Washington, N.J., 1985-86; owner, art dir. A&D Graphic Design, Hampton Twp., N.J., 1986-88, Ann-Elizabeth Anzini Graphic Design, Sodus, N.Y., 1988—; coord. graphics prodn. Mobil Chem. Co., 1991—. Wayne County Rep. Committeeman, Sodus, 1989—. Mem. Wayne

County Rep. Chmn. Club. Lutheran. Home: 5610 S Geneva Rd Sodus NY 14551-9535

APCZYNSKI, JOHN, theology educator; b. Chgo., Aug. 25, 1942; s. John W. and Julia F. (Janik) A.; m. Elaine Apczynski, Aug. 2, 1969; 1 child, John V. Jr. BA, St. John's Coll., Little Rock, 1964; MA, U. Dayton, 1967; PhD, McGill U., Montreal, 1972. Prof. theology St. Bonaventure (N.Y.) U., 1970—. Author: Doers of the Word, 1977, Theology and the University, 1990; contbr. articles to profl. jours. NEH grantee, 1977, 84, 88. Mem. Am. Acad. Religion, Coll. Theology Soc. (bd. dirs. 1984-87), Cath. Theol. Soc. Am., Soc. for Sci. Study of Religion, Can. Theol. Soc., Polanyi Soc. Office: St Bonaventure Univ PO Box 12 Saint Bonaventure NY 14778-0012

APEL, BARBARA JEAN, artist; b. Falls City, Nebr., June 16, 1935; d. Orville Henry and Frances Artellia (Oberst) A.; 1 child, Kem Morehead. BFA, Kansas City Art Inst., 1965; MFA, U. Ill., 1967. Instr. Cambridge (Mass.) Ctr. for Adult Edn., 1968-69, DeCordova & Dana Mus., Lincoln, Mass., 1972-74; instr. Art Inst. of Boston, 1967-81, developer, head printmaking dept., 1969-81, dir. continuing edn., 1978-81; profl. artist Boston, 1981—; recording sec. Boston Visual Artists Union, 1976-77; lectr. in field; profl. painter. Represented in permanent collections in Mus. of Fine Arts, Boston, Hood Mus. of Art, Dartmouth Coll., Worcester Fine Arts Mus., Univ. of Wis.; exhibited in group shows at Impressions Gallery, 1977-83, Smithsonian, 1978-80, Keene State Coll., 1978. MacDowell Colony fellow, 1979; recipient First prize Prints award 7th Annual Juried Art Show, 1977. Office: Goldstein & Manello 265 Franklin St Boston MA 02110-3113

APEL, DONALD MATTHEW, educational foundation administrator; b. Rockville, Conn., Apr. 25, 1957; s. George Frederick and Joan (Dresser) A. BS, Pa. State U., 1981. Sales engr. Borg Warner Corp., Chgo., 1981-82; co-founder, owner Sturbridge (Mass.) Florist, 1983-86; assoc. mdse. mgr. New Eng. Aquarium, Boston, 1987-90; found. dir. Theta Delta Chi Ednl. Found., Boston, 1990—. Editor The Shield of Theta Delta Chi, 1990—. United Techs. Corp. scholar, 1976. Mem. Friends of New Eng. Aquarium, Nat. Assn. Self-Employed, Fraternity Execs. Assn., Pa. State U. Alumni Assn. (life), Theta Delta Chi. Office: Theta Delta Chi 135 Bay State Rd Boston MA 02215

APELIAN, VIRGINIA MATOSIAN, psychologist, assertiveness training instructor, lecturer, consultant; b. Yoghun-Oluk, Turkey, Dec. 3, 1934; came to U.S., 1950; d. Hagop M. and Christina (Atamian) Matosian; m. Henry M. Apelian, Apr. 4, 1959; children: Arminee, Gregory, Christopher and David (twins). AA in Liberal Arts, Union County Coll., 1973; BA in Psychology, Douglass Coll., Rutgers U., 1975. From clk. to v.p. N.J. Bank & Trust Co., Paterson, N.J., 1955-59; freelance artist, 1966—; adminstrv. aide dist. 22 N.J. State Assembly, Clark, Trenton, N.J., 1976-78; elected councilwoman Township Coun., Clark, 1978; office supr. Electronic Corp. Am., Springfield, N.J., 1979-81; pres. Township Council, Clark, 1979-82; dir. sr. citizens group Union County Dept. Parks, Clark, 1983-84; coord. youth programming Cen. Presbyn. Ch., Summit, N.J., 1984-85; tchr., cons. Union County Adult Edn. System, Clark, 1975-87; psychologist, assertiveness trainer, lectr. Union County Coll., Cranford, N.J., 1987—; elected to bd. govs. Union County Coll., 1992; mem. Juvenile Conf. Com., Clark, N.J., 1983-86, 90—, chair, 1990-92; N.J. Coun. for the Social Studies, 1990-92; lectr. in field. Co-editor The Presbyn., 1987-90; contbr. articles to profl. jours. Apptd. mem. Ethnic Adv. Coun., State of N.J., 1992—; tchr. Christian edn. various Presbyn. chs., Clark and Paterson, 1955-91; mem., tchr., budget and evangelism com. mem., pulpit nominating com., mediator counselor, chmn. mission and Christian edn. coms. Osceloa Presbyn. Ch., Clark; Christian edn. commr. Fanwood (N.J.) Presbyn. Ch.; liaison Eliabeth Presbytery and Armenian Missionary Assn. Am. for Armenian Earthquake Relief Fund of Dec. 1988 Catastrophe; co-chair Heart Fund Drive, Clark, 1977; chair and coord. cancer crusade Am. Cancer Soc., Clark, 1978; legis. com., chair local pub. schs. and high schs., Clark, 1975-80; lectr. on drug abuse at local schs., Clark, 1975-80; lectr. on human rights issues; mem. pub. rels. coord., lectr. fund raiser Mayor's Com. on Drug Abuse, Clark, 1973-80; mem. Clark Little League Aux., 1970-80; mem., research chair environ. health bd. Union County, 1983-84, consumer affairs bd., 1980-84; mem., sec. Union County Juvenile Adv. Bd., Elizabeth Superior Ct., 1983-86, 90—, elected chair, 1990; trustee Clark Pub. Libr. Bd., 1988-89; commr. Christian edn. dept. Fanwood (N.J.) Presbyn. Ch. Recipient spl. plaque Mayor and Township Council, Clark, 1982, Disting. Alumna award Union County Coll., 1983; named in N.J. State Assembly resolution in honor of continued disting. svc. to the community, 1984. Mem. Profl. Women's Assn. (spl. cert. recognition 1988), N.J. Assn. for Elected Women Ofcls. (charter, treas., 1st v.p.), Armenian Relief Soc. (adv. bd. mem. 1955—, sec. 1955-60, pres. 1960-70, Gold Pin 1985), N.J. Coun. for the Social Studies, Gov.'s Ethnic Adv. Coun. N.J., Clark Hist. Soc. (cultural programs 1980—), Clark Rep. Club (v.p. 1970-75, pres. 1976-82). Republican. Home: 85 Rutgers Rd Clark NJ 07066-2729

APGAR, MAHLON, IV, real estate management counselor; b. Paterson, N.J., Jan. 14, 1941; s. Mahlon III and Dorothea (Tipper) A.; m. Anne Demarest Nelson, May 30, 1970; children: Frederick Clayton Demarest, Sarah Elisabeth Tipper, James Campbell Nelson. AB, Dartmouth Coll., 1962; postgrad., Oxford U., Eng., 1965; MBA, Harvard U., 1968. Assoc. McKinsey and Co., Inc., N.Y.C. and London, 1968-74; prin., London and Washington, 1974-80; prin. Apgar & Co., Inc., Washington, Balt., 1980—; pres., chief exec. officer Wellington Real Estate, Washington, 1985-87; sr. v.p. Wellington Mgmt. Co./Thorndike, Doran, Paine & Lewis, Boston, 1985-87; mng. dir. Alex Brown Realty Services, Balt., 1987-90; rsch. assoc. Harvard Program on Tech. and Soc., 1968-69; vis. lectr. City and Regional Planning Harvard U., Cambridge, Mass., 1968-69; prin. advisor Sec. State Environment, London, 1972-74; urban advisor Minister Mcpl. and Rural Affairs, Saudi Arabia, 1974-78; devel. advisor Summa Corp. (Estate of Howard Hughes), L.A., 1983-84. Author: Tackling Urban Problems, 1973, Succeeding in Saudi Arabia, 1977; author, editor New Perspectives on Community Development, 1976; contbr. articles to profl. jours. Dir. World Affairs Coun., Washington, 1982-87; mem. investment com. Magdalen Coll., Oxford, 1986—; mem. adv. coun. Am. Ditchley Found., N.Y.C., 1979—; trustee, chmn. nominating com. Nat. Bldg. Mus., 1990—. Recipient Arthur May award Am. Inst. Real Estate Appraisers, 1970. Fellow Royal Soc. Arts; mem. Am. Soc. Real Estate Counselors (cert.), Urban Land Inst. (trustee 1990—, chmn. comml. and retail coun. 1988—, internat. com. 1987—), Met. Club (Washington), Brook's (London), Harvard Club (N.Y.C.), Pilgrims (N.Y.C.). Republican. Episcopalian. Home: 7321 Brightside Rd Baltimore MD 21212-1012

APLAN, FRANK FULTON, engineering educator; b. Boulder, Colo., Aug. 11, 1923; s. Frank Fulton Sr. and Helen Elizabeth (Fischer) A.; m. Clare Marie Donaghue, July 30, 1955; children: Susan M., Peter D., Lucy A. BS, S.D. Sch. Mines and Tech., 1948; MS, Mont. Sch. Mines, 1950; ScD, MIT, 1957; hon. degree in mineral engring., Mont. Coll. Mineral Sci. and Tech., 1968. Mill engr. Climax Molybdenum Co., Climax, Colo., 1950-51, 53; asst. prof. U. Wash., Seattle, 1951-53; sr. scientist Kennecott Copper Corp., Salt Lake City, 1957; group mgr. mineral engring. R & D Mining and Metals div., Union Carbide Corp., Niagara Falls, Tuxedo, N.Y., 1957-67; prof. metallurgy and mineral processing Pa. State U., University Park, 1968—, Disting. prof., 1990, head dept. mineral preparation, 1968-71; chmn. mineral processing sect. Pa. State U., University Pk., 1971-77; chmn. metallurgy sect. Pa. State U., University Park, 1973-75; bd. dirs. Engring. Found., N.Y.C., 1977-90, chmn. 1985-87. Contbr. articles to profl. jours.; patentee in field. T/Sgt. U.S. Army, 1942-46, ETO. Decorated Bronze Star; recipient Robert H. Richards award AIME, N.Y.C., 1978, Mineral Industry Edn. award, 1992. Mem. NAE (hon.), Am. Chem. Soc., Soc. Mining Engrs. (bd. dir. 1973-76, chmn. mineral processing div. 1972-73, Arthur F. Taggart award 1985, Disting. Mem. award 1978, Antoine M. Gaudin award 1991), Metall. Soc., Am. Inst. Chem. Engrs., Am. Soc. for Metals, Archeol. Inst. Am., Am. Filtration Soc., Sigma Xi. Home: 432 W Fairmount Ave State College PA 16801-4612 Office: Pa State U Dept Mineral Engring 115 Mineral Scis Bldg University Park PA 16802

APLAN, PETER DONAGHUE, pediatric oncologist; b. Salt Lake City, Aug. 10, 1957; s. Frank Fulton and Clare Marie (Donaghue) A.; m. Debra J. Hoffman, May 2, 1987; children: Kurt Matthew, Melissa Paige. BS in Biophysics, Pa. State U., 1979, MD, 1983. Diplomate, Am. Bd. Pediatrics. Resident, then chief resident in pediatrics Children's Hosp. Buffalo, 1983-87; pediatric oncologist NIH, Bethesda, Md., 1987—. Contbr. articles to med. jours. NIH grantee, 1989. Mem. AMA, AAAS, Am. Assn. Cancer Rsch., Am. Soc. Pediatric Hematology-Oncology (named Young Investigator of the Yr. 1991). Roman Catholic. Home: 40 Starboard Ct Gaithersburg MD 20877-3482 Office: NIH Bldg 10 900 Rockville Pike Rm 13N240 Bethesda MD 20892

APOSTOLOS, PAUL MICHAEL, librarian; b. Verona, Pa., July 7, 1936; s. Michael and Sophia (Chimbides) A.; m. Margaret Ann Morris, Aug. 17, 1974. BA, U. Pitts., 1963, MLS, 1966; MS in Edn., Temple U., 1978; AS, United Wesleyan Coll., 1982; DRE, Evangel Christian U. & Sem., 1989. With Sennot Svc. Sta., Pitts., 1950-55; with Blossom Restaurant, Verona, 1959-60, co-owner, 1960-86; caseworker I Pa. Dept. Pub. Assistance, Pitts., 1964; rep. Allegheny County Dept. Health, Pitts., 1966-70; librarian I Kutztown (Pa.) State Coll., 1970-72; evening librarian Kutztown U., 1972-89, evening periodicals microtext lab., 1989—; sec. faculty senate Kutztown U., 1978-79, chair subcom. internat. students affairs, 1981-85, co-advisor to power lifting club 1981-82 nat. champions, 1981-88. Translator: The Happy Onion, 1978; contbr. articles to profl. jours. Vice pres. Greek Orthodox Ch., Oakmont, Pa., 1968. With U.S. Army, 1957-59. Mem. Berks County Library Assn., Friends of Pa. Libraries, Kutztown Hist. Soc. (life), Pa. Dutch Folk Life and Culture Soc., Am. Legion (sr. vice comdr. Pitts. chpt. 1969-70), Masons (jr. master ceremonies 1969-70), Kutztown U. Alumni Assn. Democrat. Home: 356 College Blvd Kutztown PA 19530-1428 Office: Kutztown U College Hill Kutztown PA 19530

APOSTOLOU, PAUL CHARLES, architect; b. Pitts., Apr. 25, 1942; s. Charles Stanley and Elizabeth Mary (Seprich) A.; m. Marilyn Winafred Adams, Sept. 14, 1968; children: Christian, Alexandra, Stephanie. BArch, U. Notre Dame, 1965. Registered architect, Pa., Fla. Project architect Johnstone McMillian Assoc., Pitts., 1965-70; project mgr. Diesel Constrn., Pitts. and Chgo., 1970-72; prin. Apostolou Assocs., Pitts., 1972—; bd. dirs. St. Francis Med. Ctr., Pitts. Mem. dinner com. Catholic Youth Assn., Pitts., 1985—. Recipient Bellemy Design award Pa. Assn. Housing and Devel., 1981, 89. Mem. AIA, Pitts. Legatus (v.p. 1992-93), Serra Club Pitts. (pres. bd. 1974-76), South Hills Country Club, St. Clair Country Club, Notre Dame Club Pitts. (adv. com. 1986—). Office: Apostolou Assocs 47 Bailey Ave Pittsburgh PA 15211

APPEL, IRVING H(AROLD), optical manufacturing company executive; b. N.Y.C., Jan. 8, 1917; s. Ralph and Ada (Ader) A.; m. Gertrude Matlin, Jan. 16, 1938; children: Michael E., Bonnie A., Kathy S. Grad. U.S. Army Air Force Aviation Cadet Sch., 1943. Inventory clk. Nat. Container Corp., Long Island City, N.Y., 1935-36; prodn. mgr. Kraft Corrugated Containers, Inc., Bayonne, N.J., 1936-42; gen. mgr. Republic Container Corp., Jersey City, 1945-49; gen. mgr. San Miguel Brewery Carton Plant, Manila, 1949-56; v.p. Cleghorn Folding Box Co., Lowell, Mass., 1957-64; pres. Lowell Corrugated Container Corp., 1959-64; exec. v.p. Prince Macaroni, Lowell, 1960-64, also bd. dirs.; pres., founder Welling Internat. Corp., Milford, Conn., 1964-79, chmn. bd. dirs., 1979-84, chmn. emeritus, 1984—; cons. Darier Asia Ltd. div. of Darier & Co, Geneva, 1988; bd. dirs. Conn. Bank & Trust Co., New Haven, Orange (Conn.) Nat. Bank. Trustee Conn. Visual Health Ctr. (chmn. 1984), Bridgeport; bd. dirs. Lake Copake Conservation Soc., Copake Lake, N.Y., pres. ARMDI, Golan; bd. trustees New Eng. Coll. Optometry, Boston, 1988. 1st lt. USAAF, 1943-45, ETO, NATOUSA. Decorated D.F.C. Air medal with 5 oak leaf clusters; recipient cert. Appreciation Conn. Visual Health Ctr., Inc., 1975, Pres.'s award, 1977, Recognition award Flying Tigers, 1975, Recognition award Ambassador's Soc. Bd. Trustees, 1981, Recognition award State of Israel, 1980, Pub. Health award Conn. Visual Health Ctr., 1987, Mission of Mercy award Mogen David Adam, 1987; named Largest Individual Fund Raiser, Korea/Vietnam Meml., 1987. Mem. Aircraft Owners and Pilots Assn., 8th Air Force Hist. Soc., 2d Air Div. Assn., Air Force Assn. Home: 911 W Cypress Ln Hallandale FL 33009-6153 Office: 65 Caswell St Milford CT 06460

APPEL, ROBERT EUGENE, lawyer, educator; b. Cleve., Oct. 18, 1958; s. Robert Donald and Jean Ann (Crites) A.; m. Margaret Rose Curley, Aug. 24, 1985. BS, Cen. Conn. State U., 1980; JD, U. Bridgeport, Conn., 1982; MBA, U. Conn., 1984; LLM, Boston U., 1984. Bar: Conn. 1983. Asst. mgr. fin. services Lexington Ins. Co., Boston, 1984-85; tax. cons. Touche Ross and Co., Stamford, Conn., 1985-86; asst. dir. nat. design CIGNA Corp., Bloomfield, Conn., 1986-88; dir. nat. design CIGNA Corp., Bloomfield, 1988—; lectr. Real Estate Tng. and Ednl. Svcs., Bridgeport, 1985-88; lectr. real estate Dare Inst., Southbury, 1991—. Div. coord. United Way, 1988, annual solicitor, 1988—. Mem. ABA, Conn. Bar Assn. Republican. Roman Catholic. Home: 80 Kingston Dr East Hartford CT 06118-2433 Office: CIGNA Corp 900 Cottage Grove Rd Hartford CT 06152-0001

APPEL, STUART DAVID, land planner; b. Oceanside, N.Y., May 9, 1954; s. Irving Maurice and Bette (Seidman) A.; m. Ruth Bluethenthal, Nov. 12, 1983; children: Benjamin, Jessica. B in Environ. Sci., SUNY, Syracuse, 1978, B in Landscape Arch., 1979; MBA, LaSalle U., 1990. Registered landscape architect, Pa., N.J., Del. Landscape architect Leaver, Anthony., Holman & Assoc., Saratoga Springs, N.Y., 1978-79, Cope Linder Assocs., Phila., 1979-82; v.p., land planner, landscape architect Roger Wells, Inc., Haddonfield, N.J., 1982-88, Wells-Larson-Appel, Haddonfield, 1988—; guest lectr., design juror Harvard U., Cambridge, Mass., 1988, 89; panelist nat. real estate investment symposium U. Pa., Phila., 1988; presenter, lectr. Urban Land Inst., Princeton, N.J., 1989; guest lectr. Cornell U., Ithaca, N.Y., 1988, 89, 90, Syracuse U., 1988, Phila. Coll. Art, 1987; design juror Temple U., PHila., 1988; tchr. Rutgers U., New Brunswick, N.J., 1985—. Co-author: Greenfield Heritage Resource Inventory, 1979. Bd. dirs. young leadership coun. Jewish Fedn. Greater Phila., 1984-90, mem. cabinet, 1985-91; mem. young leadership cabinet United Jewish Appeal, Phila., 1987-91; bd. dirs. Jewish Family and Children's Agy., Phila., 1991—, Jewish Community High Sch., Melrose Park, Pa., 1991—; mem. coms. Fedn. Greater Phila. Mem. Am. Soc. Landscape Architects (Design Honor award 1990, Design Merit award 1985, 89), Nat. Trust Hist. Preservation, Nature Conservancy, Phila. Acad. Natural Scis., Mus. Early So. Decorative Arts. Office: Wells-Larson-Appel 132 N Haddon Ave Haddonfield NJ 08033-2306

APPELL, KATHLEEN MARIE, management consultant, legal administrator; b. Phila., Apr. 20, 1943; d. Joseph F. and Catherine (Laing) Hudson; m. Vincent M. Mandes (div. Apr. 1968); children: Carren Lee, Vincent, Lori. Cert., Phila. Modeling Sch., 1960-61, Horsham Found., 1979-81, Behavioral Acad., 1981, Fashion Acad., 1984. Adminstr. Phila. Modeling and Career Sch., 1965-68; pres. K.M. Appell Enterprises Ltd., Warwick, Pa., 1968-76, 1988—; exec. asst. Horsham Psychiat. Hosp., Ambler, Pa., 1976-84; cons. Horsham Psychiat. Hosp., Ambler, 1976-84; dir. admissions Career Inst., Phila., 1986-87; legal adminstr. Howson & Howson, Spring House, Pa., 1990—; cons. Resource Spectrum, Ambler, 1979-82, Horsham Mgmt. Corp., Ambler, 1978-84. Contbr. articles to profl. jours. Mem. Rep. Task Force Com., Washington, 1981; mem. Ch. of Bethesda-By-the-Sea Episcopal Ch. Mem. Women's Econ. Devel., Assn. Fashion and Image Cons., Profl. and Exec. Women. Home: PO Box 237 Danboro PA 18916-0237 Office: 321 Norristown Rd Box 457 Spring House PA 19477

APPERSON, POLLY MERRILL, physical therapist, educator; b. Norwalk, Conn., Apr. 29, 1910; d. Frank Herbert and Clara (Ryder) Merrill; m. Van Doren Apperson, June 25, 1938 (dec.). BS in Phys. Edn., Arnold Coll., 1930; BS in Phys. Therapy, NYU, 1954. Lic. real estate salesperson, Conn., N.Y. Tchr. phys. edn. Norwalk Jr. High Schs., 1930-38, Norwalk High Sch., 1938-62, 63-64; phys. therapist N.Y. Hosp.-Cornell Med. Coll., N.Y.C., 1954—, Inst. Phys. Medicine and Rehab., 1962-63, 64-65, Inst. Rehab. Medicine, N.Y.C., 1967-68, 70, Silver Hill Found., New Canaan, Conn., 1971, outpatient dept. U.S. VA, 1972-73; instr. English, An-Lac Orphanage, Saigon, Vietnam, 1967; real estate agt. Montgomery Agy., 1987-88, 89; staff mem. Sivananda Yoga Vedanta Ashram, Paradise Island, Bahamas, 1969. Asst. troop leader Girl Scouts U.S.A., 1926-27, troop capt., 1944-45; life saving examiner ARC, Norwalk, 1930-33, active fund drives, 1941-46, first aid instr., 1941-44, 54-57, tchr. sponsor Jr. Red Cross at Norwalk High Sch., 1961-62, also sponsor exchange visit with St. John, N.B., Can. Jr. Red Cross, 1961-62; vol. counselor Sivananda Vedanta Children's Yoga Camp, Valmorin, Que., Can., summer 1983; active fund drive Community Chest, Norwalk, 1932; mem. Norwalk Recreation Commn., 1939-41; mem. adv. com. Norwalk Park Comn., 1941-43; air raid warden Silvermine Sector 1, Norwalk, 1941-45; active fundraising drive Silvermine Vol. Fire Co. 1, 1942-43; bd. dirs., 1943-50; mem. common interest group Preservation Mathews Mansion, 1961-62; mem. subcom. edn. Mid-Fairfield County Com. Alcoholism, 1958-59; mem. New Horizons Club; mem. Congregation Temple Emanu-el, N.Y.C., 1973—; mem. senatorial commn. Rep. Senatorial Inner Circle, 1991—. Recipient cert. for 500 hours service CD, 1945. Mem. Conn. Edn. Assn., AAHPERD, Conn. Assn. Health, Phys. Edn. and Recreation, Am. Registry Phys. Therapists, Am. Phys. Therapist Assn., N.Y.U. Alumni Assn. Divine Life Soc., True World Order, Am. Soc. Dowsers (founder, first pres. Norman Leighton chpt. Manhattan Dowsers 1978), Nat. Trust Hist. Preservation, Pacifica Found., Spiritual Frontiers Fellowship, Sivananda Yoga Vedanta Center, Silvermine Community Assn., Silvermine River Conservation, Am. Soc. Psychical Rsch., Nat. Ret. Tchrs. Assn., Conn. Ret. Tchrs. Assn., NYU Alumni Club. Baptist (Sunday Sch. tchr. 1930-33, social chmn. Am. Soc. Dowsers, Young Peoples United Ch. League 1931-32). Home: 130 Silvermine Ave Norwalk CT 06850-2033

APPLE, DAINA DRAVNIEKS, resource information analyst; b. Kuldiga, July 6, 1944; came to U.S., 1951; d. Albins Dravnieks and Alina A. (Bergs) Zelmenis; divorced; 1 child, Almira Moronne; m. Martin A. Apple, Sept. 2, 1986. BSc, U. Calif., Berkeley, 1977, MA, 1980. Economist USDA Pacific S.W. Rsch., Berkeley, 1976-85; mgr. regional land use appeals USDA Forest Svc., San Francisco, 1986-88, program analysis officer, engring., 1988-90; asst. regulatory officer USDA Forest Svc., 1990—. Author: Public Involvement In the Forest Service-Methodologies, 1977, Public Involvement-Selected Abstracts for Natural Resources, 1979, The Management of Policy and Direction in the Forest Service, 1982, An Analysis of the Forest Service Human Resource Management Program, 1984, Organization Design-Abstracts for Natural Resources Users, 1985; sect. editor, contbr. Jour. of Women in Natural Resources. Mem. Am. Forestry Assn., Assn. Women in Sci., Soc. Am. Foresters, Phi Beta Kappa Assocs. (nat. sec. 1985-88, pres. No. Calif. chpt. 1982-84, lst v.p. 1981), Commonwealth Club Calif., Sigma Xi. Office: USDA Forest Svc Info Sys PO Box 96090 Washington DC 20090-6090

APPLE, JAMES GLENN, government lawyer; b. Huntington, W.Va., Sept. 20, 1937; s. David French and Bernice (Stewart) A.; m. Emory O'Shee, June 9, 1959 (div. May 15, 1990); children: Meredith Ellen, Miles Stewart; m. Elizabeth Fitzpatrick Jones, Nov. 10, 1990. BA (with honors), U. Va., 1959, JD, 1962; LLM, U. Edinburgh, Scotland, 1990. Bar: Va. 1962, Ky. 1962, U.S. Dist Ct. (ea. and we. dists.) Ky, U.S. Ct. Appeals (6th cir.). Pvt. practice law Wheeler & Marshall, Paducah, Ky., 1964-67; adminstrv. asst. Gov. of Ky., Frankfort, 1967-69; exec. asst. Ky. Commr. of Hwys., Frankfort, 1969-70; assoc. Stites & Harbison Law Firm, Louisville, 1970-72, ptnr., 1972-90; spl. asst., counsel to dir. Fed. Jud. Ctr., Washington, 1990-92; chief Office of Interjudicial Affairs, Fed. Jud. Ctr., 1992—; adj. prof. Bellarmine Coll., Louisville, 1988-90. Contbr. articles to profl. jours. Bd. dirs. Ky. Authority for Ednl. TV, Lexington, Ky., 1971-75; chmn. bd. Transit Authority of River City, Louisville, 1981-85; pres. Louisville Bar Found., 1986-87; mem. Leadership Louisville, 1983-84. Lt. USAR, 1962-68. Recipient Award of Merit, Louisville Bar Assn., 1980, Citation, U.S. Senate, 1988, Pres.'s award Washington Combined Fed. Co., 1990, Spl. Svc. award, 1990. Office: Fed Jud Ctr 1520 H St NW Washington DC 20005-1003

APPLEBY, ALAN, radiation science educator; b. Newcastle upon Tyne, Eng., Apr. 25, 1937; came to U.S., 1963; s. Henry James and Gladys Evelyn (Simpson) A.; m. Kathleen Anne Shippen, July 25, 1960; children: Sarah Kathleen, Emily Jane. BSc, U. Durham, Newcastle, Eng., 1958, PhD, 1963. Rsch. assoc. Brookhaven Nat. Lab., Upton, N.Y., 1963-65; sr. sci. officer Radiochem. Ctr., Amersham, Eng., 1965-67; asst. prof. radiation sci. Rutgers U., New Brunswick, N.J., 1967-71, assoc. prof., 1971-77, prof., 1977—; dir. Ea. Regional Radon Tng. Ctr., New Brunswick, 1989—. Contbr. over 50 arcitles to sci. jours. Grantee EPA, 1973, 89, NIH, 1976, Monsanto Rsch. Co., 1980, GPU Nuclear, 1981, N.J. Commn. on Cancer Rsch., 1988. Mem. Health Physics Soc., Sigma Xi. Episcopalian. Office: Rutgers U Livingston Campus Bldg 4087 New Brunswick NJ 08903

APPLEBY, AUDREY JANE, small business owner; b. Boston, Oct. 6, 1952; d. Leonard Willis Appleby and Mabel Green; m. James David McNitt III, July 17, 1982. 1 child, Eliza Helen Appleby McNitt. BS in Psychology, BA in Drama, Tufts U., 1975; MBA, NYU, 1981. Asst. acct. exec. advt. dept. J. Walter Thompson, N.Y.C., 1981-82; dir., owner MagicDance on the Water, Cos Cob, Greenwich, Stamford, Conn., 1983—; instr. ballroom dance and creative movement Whitby Sch., Greenwich, 1984—, North St. Sch., Putnam Indian Field Sch., Greeniwch, 1990—; workshop dir. Whitney Mus. Art, Stamford, 1991. Office: MagicDance on the Water 551 Boston Post Rd Cos Cob CT 06807

APPLEBY, MARJORY LU, retired school counselor; b. Pitts., Mar. 16, 1930; d. Robert Phelps and Mabel Elizabeth (Myers) Dean; m. John Malcom Appleby, Mar. 22, 1975; stepchildren: Jarrett, Brian. BS, West Chester State Coll., 1952; MEd, West Chester U., 1970. Cert. music edn. guidance and counseling, Pa. Music supr. Nether Providence Sch. Dist., Rose Valley, Pa., 1952-56; music tchr. West Chester Area Sch. Dist., West Chester, Pa., 1956-58, elem. tchr., 1958-59, elem. substitute tchr., 1959-68; guidance counselor Downingtown Area Sch. Dist., Downingtown, Pa., 1968-92; student assistance cons. Mirmont Treatment Ctr., Downingtown, 1992—. Contbr. article to Jour. of Coll. Admissions, 1986. Mem. Pa. School Counselors Assn. (Sch. Counselor of Yr. 1987-88), Am. Assn. for Counseling & Devel., NEA, Pa. Sch. Educators Assn., Downingtown Area Ednl. Assn. Home: 53 Ponds Edge Dr Downingtown PA 19335-1027

APPLEGATE, DONALD JAY, funeral director; b. Utica, N.Y., Oct. 13, 1944; s. Charles Pliny and Beatrice (Shaver) A.; m. Judy Ann Gonyea, Oct. 23, 1982; children: Jay, Justin, Suzette; stepchildren: Mark, John. Diploma in funeral svc. edn., Cin. Coll. Mortuary Sci., 1967; BS in Funeral Svc., Cen. State U., Edmond, Okla., 1969; cert. in forensic medicine, Colby Coll., Waterville, Maine, 1986. Cert. coroner, county coroner, medicolegal death investigator. Funeral dir. C.J. Applegate & Sons, Inc., Ilion, N.Y., 1967-91; pres. C.J. Applegate & Sons, Inc., 1982-91; asst. county coroner Herkimer County 4th Dist., Ilion, 1971-84; county coroner Herkimer County 4th Dist., 1985-91; owner, pres. Applegate Monument Svc., 1984-91; owner, ptnr. Day and Applegate Monument Svc., 1992—; advisor Salvation Army Exec. Bd., 1967-77, herkimer County Community Coll., 1979-91; sponsor, advisor PrePlan Program, Ilion, 1988-91. promoter Auriesville Men's Retreats, Auriesville-Ilion, 1970-91; educator, promoter Community DWI Program, Herkimer County, 1983-91; rep., sponsor New Eyes for Needy, Short Hills, N.J., Ilion, 1966-91; sponsor Stop DWI/Free No-Drive Meters, Herkimer County, Ilion, 1988-91; advanceman to elect senator Robert Kennedy for pres., Syracuse, N.Y., 1966-68, advanceman to gov. John Gilligan, Cin., 1966-67, advanceman to elect Hubert Humprey for v.p., Washington, 1966-67; mem. bd. water commrs. Village of Ilion. Recipient Cert. of Merit award Amateur Softball Assn. Am., 1989, Quality and Community Svc. award Order of Golden Rule Svc. Orgn., 1986-91, Disting. Svc. award Amvets Post, 1990. Mem. Nat. Funeral Dirs. Assn., N.Y. State Funeral Dir. Assn., N.Y. State County Coroners Med. Examiners Assn. (exec. bd.), Nat. Monument Builders Assn., N.Y. State Monument Builders Assn., Tri-County Funeral Dirs., Internat. Order of Golden Rule, Ilion Winter Club, KC (past pres. 4th degree assembly), Moose, Kiwanis, Elks (past lecturing knight). Republican. Roman Catholic. Home and Office: C J Applegate & Sons Inc 102 West St Ilion NY 13357-2299

APPLEGATE, ROBERT, computer programmer, author; b. Milw., Apr. 22, 1954; s. William and Elizabeth A.; m. Violetta Dale, October 19, 1979; 1 child, Christina Kelly. BA in Computer Sci., Beloit Coll., 1976; BA in English Lit., Marquette U., 1978; MA in English Lit., Manhattan Coll., 1980. Aide Liberal Arts and Scis. Libr. Beloit (Wis.) Coll., 1972-74, computer programmer bus. libr. reference ctr., 1974-78; computer programming cons. Werik Systems, N.Y.C., 1978—; cons. IBM, N.Y.C., 1980—; part-time instr. mythology, NYU, 1982—. Author: The Jersey Devil in Modern Times, 1982, Urban Folklore in The Northeast U.S., 1983, Abominable Snowmen to Yeti: Mythical Creatures from A to (almost) Z., 1986. Vol. Bklyn. Jr. Achievement, N.Y.C., 1987—. Mem. Nat. Office: Werik Systems 204 W 20th St New York NY 10011-3592

APPLETON, DANIEL RANDOLPH, JR., optometrist; b. Boston, June 24, 1942; s. Daniel Randolph and Dorothy (Cheney) A.; m. Sandra Marshall Appleton; children: Carole Lee, Deborah Ann, Danielle Marie, Suzanne Estelle, Seth Marshall. BS, Tufts U., 1965; OD, Mass. Coll. Optometry, 1969. Pvt. practice optometry Newburyport, Mass., 1965—; dir. pediatric clinic Mass. Coll. Optometry, 1969-71, clin. cons., 1971-72; bd. dirs. 1st and Ocean Nat. Bank. Mem. bd. incorporators Anna Jacques Hosp., Newburyport, Sch. Com., 1975-79, Newburyport sewer commn., 1972-79; 2d v.p. ARC. Recipient Com. Svc. award United Fund, 1983, Disting. Svc. award Lions Club, 1989. Mem. Am. Optometric Found., Am. Optometric Assn., Mass. Soc. Optometrists (past dist. chmn., exec. bd. dirs.), Jaycees (past pres.). Lodges: Rotary (pres. 1988), Shriners. Home: 89 Scotland Rd Newburyport MA 01951-1002 Office: 39 Green St Newburyport MA 01950-2685

APPLETON, KATHY ALLEN, elementary educator, director of children's plays; b. Racine, Wis., Nov. 14, 1950; d. William Wallace and Rita Louise (Mezera) Allen; m. Joseph Hayden Appleton, June 24, 1978; 1 child, Jeremiah Joseph. BMus, Fla. State U., 1972; M in Reading, Glassboro State Coll., 1981. Music and drama tchr. Prince George County Bd. Edn., Landover, Md., 1972-75, Glouester Twp. Bd. Edn., Blackwood, N.J., 1976—; assat. dir. Pineland Players, Medford, N.J., 1981; lighting and constrn. crew Found. Theater, Burlington County Coll., 1986-88; actor Gloucester Twp. Plays and Players, Blackwood, 1977-85; dir. Walnut St. Theatre Sch., Phila., 1989-90. Writer, dir. children's musicals Grumpy Claus, 1985, Shoes, 1990. Treas., Medford (N.J.) Rescue Squad, 1979-81. Mem. NEA, N.J. Edn. Assn., Music Educators Nat. Conf., Orff Schulwerk Assn. Home: 7 Teddington Way Mount Laurel NJ 08054-6201 Office: Erial Elem Sch Essex Ave Sicklerville NJ 08081-1210

APPLETON, WILLIAM JAMES, video production company executive; b. Audubon, N.J., Dec. 21, 1928; s. Paul Eugene and Frances Margaret (Maher) A.; m. Brenda Frances Wall, Oct. 16, 1954 (dec. 1967); children: Kathleen, Lizabeth, William Jr., Eileen; m. Jeanne Louise Armstrong, Sept. 14, 1968; 1 child, Julie. BS in Polit. Sci., Seton Hall U., 1951; postgrad., NYU, 1952-54. Advt. and mktg. coord. Goodyear Tire and Rubber Co., Akron, Ohio, 1956-62; asst. edn. and tng. dir. Ethan Allen Furniture, Stamford, Conn., 1962-70; pres. travel advt. Tra-Vel Advt. Co., Montvale, N.J., 1970-86; v.p., mng. ptnr. Video Tech. Prodns., Inc., Livingston, N.J., 1986—. Roman Catholic. Home: 83 Jean St Ramsey NJ 07446-1705

APPLEWHITE, HARRIET BRANSON, political science educator; b. Cleve., June 5, 1940; d. Robert Lees and Eleanor (Verdier) Branson; m. Philip B. Applewhite, Aug. 10, 1963; children: Eleanor, Kate, Douglas. AB, Smith Coll., Northampton, Mass., 1962; MA, Stanford U., 1964, PhD, 1972. Lectr. Smith Coll., Northampton, Mass., 1965-66; asst. prof. So. Conn. State Coll., New Haven, 1967-76; assoc. prof. So. Conn. State Coll. (now So. Conn. State U.), New Haven, 1976-82, prof. polit. sci., 1982—. Co-editor: Women in Revolutionary Paris, 1979, Women and Politics in Age of Democratic Revolution, 1990; contbr. articles to profl. jours. Rockefeller Found. grantee, 1985; Am. Coun. Learned Socs. fellow, 1983-84; NEH fellow, 1973-74. Mem. AAUP, Am. Polit. Sci. Assn., Phi Beta Kappa. Democrat. Office: So Conn State U Dept Polit Sci New Haven CT 06518

APRIL, PAUL KENNETH, engineering educator; b. Williamsport, Pa., Dec. 4, 1939; s. Stanley William and Nedra Margaret (Hehle) A.; m. Shirley Mary Quadrini, Apr. 1, 1967; children: Kenneth S., Douglas P. BS in Aerospace Engring., Pa. State U., 1961; MS in Aerospace Engring., U. Tenn., 1969; BA in Liberal Arts, Pa. State U., 1990. Commd. 2d lt. USAF, 1962, advanced through grades to lt. col., 1979, retired, 1985, various positions, 1962-71; project engr. Air Force Logistics Command, Sacramento, Calif., 1971-75; area engr. USAF-Europe, Ramstein, Germany, 1975-79; technical intelligence analyst Def. Intelligence Agy., Washington, 1979-81; chief, missile test Air Force Logistics Command, Hill AFB, Utah, 1981-83; dep. program mgr. logistics MX missile system Air Force Logistics Command, Hill AFB, 1983-85; gen. engring. faculty Pa. State Univ., Altoona, 1985—. Contbr. articles to profl. publs. Recipient L. Perez Student Adv. award Pa. State Engring. Soc., University Park, 1991. Mem. Am. Soc. Engring. Educators, Alpha Sigma Lambda. Republican. Roman Catholic. Office: Pa State U Altoona Campus Ivyside Park Altoona PA 16601-5319

APSTEIN, CARL STEPHEN, cardiologist, educator; b. N.Y.C., Oct. 14, 1941; s. Martha Apstein; m. Barbara Apstein; children: Daniel, Andrew. AB, Cornell U., 1963; MD, NYU, 1967. Prof. medicine, physiology Boston U. Sch. Medicine, 1985—; chief cardiology Boston City Hosp., 1982—; lectr. Harvard Med. Sch., Boston, 1988—; bd. dirs. BV-Cardiovascular Rsch. Tng., Boston, Cardiac Muscle Rsch. Lab, Boston; co-dir. Cardiology Fellowship Program, Boston, 1982—. Author: (chpt.) Cardiac Hypertrophy and Failure, 1990 and 15 other book chpts.; contbr. over 80 articles to profl. jours. Named Disting. Visiting Prof., British Heart Found., 1991. Fellow Am. Heart Assn., Internat. Soc. for Heart Rsch., Am. Coll. Cardiology, Am. Soc. for Clin. Investigation, Assn. Univ. Cardiologists; mem. New Eng. Cardiovascular Soc. (pres. 1989-90). Office: Boston Univ Sch Medicine 80 E Concord St R2D Boston MA 02118

APT, LESLEY A(NN), lawyer; b. N.Y.C., Feb. 20, 1946; d. Warner F. and Hedi B. (Oppenheimer) A.; m. Douglas B. Dudfield, Nov. 6, 1977; children: Eric Apt-Dudfield, Olga Apt-Dudfield. AB, Cornell U., 1967; MAT, Harvard U., 1970; JD magna cum laude, Temple U., 1979. Bar: Pa. 1979. Assoc. Fox, Rothschid, O'Brien & Fox, Phila., 1980-83; counsel GE Capital Corp., Danbury and Stamford, Conn., 1983—. Office: GE Capital 55 Federal Rd Danbury CT 06810-3199

AQUAVELLA, JAMES VINCENT, ophthalmologist; b. N.Y.C., May 2, 1932; s. Charles and Loretta Marie (Sorrentino) A.; m. Constance E., May 1, 1960; children: John, Constance, Mary, Thomas. BA, Johns Hopkins U., Balt., 1952; MD, U. Naples, Italy, 1958. Diplomate Am. Bd. Ophthalmology. Pvt. practice specializing in ophthalmology Rochester, N.Y., 1963—; dir. Dept. Ophthalmology Park Ridge Hosp., Rochester, N.Y., 1974-84, chief of staff, 1972-74; med. dir. ROA Ambulatory Ctr., Rochester, 1980-90, chief ophthalmology, 1980-89; clin. prof. ophthalmology U. Rochester Med. Ctr., 1982—, dir. cornea rsch. lab., 1982—; cons. N.Y. State Dept. Health, 1987—. Contbr. over 200 articles to profl. jours. Bd. dirs. Meml. Art Gallery, Rochester, 1972—, Rochester Eye & Human Parts Bank, 1968-80. Recipient Commendation award, Cen. N.Y. Eye Bank, 1989, Rochester Eye Bank, 1980. Fellow Internat. Coll. Surgeons; mem. AMA, Am. Coll. Physician Execs., Assn. for Rsch. and Vision in Ophthalmology, Contact Lens Assn. of Ophthalmologists (dir. 1972-82, Eye Bank Assn. Am., Pan Am. Assn. Ophthalmology (Honor award 1980, Sr. Honor award 1991), Castroviejo Soc. (dir. 1980-88, Commendation award 1985). Home: 1286 East Ave Rochester NY 14610-1554 Office: 919 Westfall Rd Rochester NY 14618-2670

AQUILINO, THOMAS JOSEPH, JR., judge, law educator; b. Mt. Kisco, N.Y., Dec. 7, 1939; s. Thomas Joseph and Virginia Burr (Doughty) A.; m. Edith Luise Berndt, Oct. 27, 1965; children: Christopher T., Philip A., Alexander B. Student, Cornell U., 1957-59, U. Munich, 1960-61; BA, Drew U., 1962; postgrad., Free U., Berlin, 1965-66; JD, Rutgers U., 1969. Bar: N.Y. 1972, U.S. Dist. Ct. (so., ea. and no. dists.) N.Y. 1973, U.S. Ct. Appeals (2d cir.) 1973, U.S. Supreme Ct. 1976, U.S. Ct. Appeals (3d cir.) 1977, Interstate Commerce Commn. 1978, U.S. Ct. Claims 1979, U.S. Ct. Internat. Trade 1984. Law clk. to judge U.S. Dist. Ct. (so. dist.) N.Y., N.Y.C., 1969-71; atty. Davis Polk & Wardwell, N.Y.C., 1971-85; judge U.S. Ct. Internat. Trade, N.Y.C., 1985—; adj. prof. law Benjamin N. Cardozo Sch. of Law, 1984—. Served with U.S. Army, 1962-65. Mem. N.Y. State Bar Assn., Fed. Bar Council. Roman Catholic. Office: US Ct Internat Trade 1 Federal Pla New York NY 10007*

AQUINO, JOSEPH MARIO, clinical psychologist; b. N.Y.C., Nov. 21, 1947; s. Joseph and Rose (Nasi) A.; m. Kathleen Ann Ryan, Oct. 6, 1990. BA in English, So. Ill. U., 1969, MS in Secondary Edn., 1976; PhD in Clin. Psychology, St. John's U., Jamaica, N.Y., 1987. Lic. psychologist, N.Y. Tchr. English Wappingers Cen. Schs., Wappingers Falls, N.Y., 1969-79; intern psychology Maimonides Med. Ctr., Bklyn., 1983-84; specialist in applied behavior sci. Builders for Family and Youth, Bklyn., 1984-85; trainee psychology and psychologist St. Vincent's Svcs., Bklyn., 1984-89; psychologist St. Christopher-Ottilie Svcs., Sea Cliff, N.Y., 1989—; pvt. practice psychology N.Y.C., 1988—; guest lectr. St. John's U., 1990. Co-author: Situational Leadership for Principals, 1983; mem. editorial bd. Jour. Urban Psychiatry, 1982-84; contbr. articles to profl. jours. Recipient citation VFW, Wappingers Falls, N.Y., 1977; Bethany House Achievement award Bethany House II, 1991; psychology teaching fellow St. John's U., 1981; cited in article Emergency mag., 1991. Mem. Am. Psychol. Assn. (div. 12). Office: 10 Rye Ridge Plz Ste 213 Port Chester NY 10573-2828

ARAGNO, ANNA, psychoanalyst, author; b. Rome, Lazio, Italy, Apr. 20, 1945; came to U.S., 1965; d. Riccardo and Anna-Rosa (Canitano) A.; m. Justino Edgardo Diaz, Oct. 3, 1967 (div. 1983); children: Natascia, Katya. BA, Empire State Coll., 1983; MA, New Sch. Social Rsch., N.Y., 1986; PhD, Union Inst., 1992. Cert. psychoanalyst, N.Y. Grad. staff Washington Square Inst., N.Y.C., 1986—. Contbr. articles to profl. jours. Mem. APA, AACD, Nat. Assn. for Advancement of Psychoanalysis. Home: 140 West End Ave New York NY 10023-6131

ARAGOSA, EMANUEL JOSEPH, small business owner; b. Schenectady, N.Y., Nov. 5, 1931; s. Joseph and Rafaela (Mauro) A.; m. Marilyn Adelaide Thimineur, Apr. 30, 1955; children: Anne Marie, Joseph Emmanuel, Mary Grace, Lynne Marie, Michael E., Theresa. BS in Econs., Siena U., 1953. Cost acct. GE, Schenectady, 1949-55; sales rep. Nat. Cash Register Co., Schenectady, Amsterdam, N.Y., 1958-74; owner Marty's True Value Hardware, Schenectady, 1974—. With USN, 1955-58. Mem. N.Y. State Order Sons of Italy (fin. sec. 1989, Family of Yr. 1990). Republican. Roman Catholic. Home: 2149 Foster Ave Schenectady NY 12308 Office: Marty's True Value Hardware 1559 Van Vranken Ave Schenectady NY 12308

ARAIZ, JOSEPH MICHAEL, securities company executive; b. Mexico City, Mex., Feb. 2, 1961; came to U.S., 1965; s. Francisco and Myra Hilda (Kagan) A.; m. Sandra Ramirez, May 25, 1990. BA, Brandeis U., 1983. Corp. bond trader Cowen & Co., Inc., 1983-85; v.p. corp. bd. Gruntal & Co. Inc., 1985-88; v.p. M.J. Whitman & Co., 1988—; v.p., ptnr., head of trading M.J. Whitman, 1989—; v.p. Whitman Security corp., 1988—, M.J. Whitman Sr. Debt Corp., 1988—; v.p. Whitman Securities Corp., exec. v.p., sr. debt corp. Mem. Nat. Trust for Historic Preservation, Whitney Mus., Guggenheim Mus. Mem. Am. Fine Arts Soc., Guggenheim Mus., Whitney Mus., B'nai Brith. Office: M J Whitman & Co Inc 767 Third Ave 5th Fl New York NY 10017

ARAKELIAN, MAUREEN, nursing educator; b. Bklyn., June 21, 1934; d. Cornelius and Catherine (O'Connell) Kerrigan; m. William E. Arakelian, Apr. 24, 1960; children: Susan Marie, William Edward. Diploma, Mass. Gen. Hosp., Boston, 1955; BS, Boston U., 1957, MS, 1972, DNSc, 1984. Staff nurse New Eng. Med. Ctr., Boston, Boston Vis. Nurse Assn., Beth Israel Hosp., Boston; prof. nursing Salem (Mass.) State Coll. Contbr. articles to profl. jours. Soc. for Nursing Rsch. grantee, 1989. Mem. ANA, NLN, Eastern Nursing Rsch. Soc., Boston Assn. Theory Devel. (sec.-treas.), Sigma Theta Tau.

ARANCIA, LOUIS JOHN, podiatrist; b. Stamford, Conn., Dec. 31, 1928; s. John A. and Frances (Arena) A. D.Podiatry cum laude, L.I.U., 1954; m. Elaine S. Taormina, May 12, 1957; 1 dau., Carol Ann. B.A., N.Y.U., 1950. Diplomate Am. Acad. of Pain Mgmt. Practice podiatry, Bklyn., 1954—; adj. clin. prof. N.Y. Coll. Podiatric Medicine; mem. surg. staff Luth. Med. Ctr., Bklyn.; guest lectr. in field. Diplomate Am. Bd. Podiatric Surgery (a founder). Fellow Am. Coll. Foot Surgeons (pres. N.Y. div. 1971-73), Am. Soc. Podiatric Medicine, Am. Assn. Hosp. Podiatrist (pres. 1964-66, exec. dir., 1966—), Am. Podiatric Med. Assn., Acad. Podiatry, N.Y. Podiatric Med. (dir. 1974-79), Kings County Podiatry Soc. (pres. 1974-76, sec. 1982-87). Republican. Roman Catholic. Masons (Bay Ridge-Minerna). Co-author: Atlas of Rearfoot Surgery, 1978; contbr. articles in field to profl. jours. Address: 420 74th St Brooklyn NY 11209

ARASKOG, RAND VINCENT, diversified multinational company executive; b. Fergus Falls, Minn., Oct. 30, 1931; s. Randolph Victor and Hilfred Mathilda A.; m. Jessie Marie Gustafson, July 29, 1956; children: William Roy, Julie Kay, Kathleen Melinda. BSME, U.S. Mil. Acad., 1953; postgrad., Harvard U., 1953-54; LHD (hon.), Hofstra U., 1990. With Def. Dept., Washington, 1954-59, Spl. asst. to dir., 1958-59; dir. mktg. aero. div. Honeywell, Inc., Mpls., 1960-66; v.p. ITT Corp., 1971-76; exec. v.p. ITT Aerospace, Electronics, Components and Energy Group, Nutley, N.J., 1976-79; pres., chief exec. officer ITT Corp., N.Y.C., 1979—, chmn. bd., chmn. exec. and policy coms., 1980—; chmn., pres., chief exec. officer ITT Holdings Inc., N.Y.C.; bd. dirs. ITT Corp., Hartford Ins., Dayton-Hudson Corp., Shell Oil Corp., Dow Jones and Co., N.Y. Stock Exchange, Fed. Res. Bank of N.Y.; mem. Nat. Security Telecommunications Adv. Com., 1983%. Author: ITT Wars, 1989; contbr. articles to jours. including Reader's Digest, The New York Times. Mem. Bus. Coun., Trilateral Commn., Competitiveness Policy Coun.; bd. advisors N.Y. Zool. Soc.; mem. Rockefellow U. Coun. Served with U.S. Army, 1954-56. Decorated Officer of Nat. Order of Legion of Honor (France), Order of Merit of the Republic of Italy in the level of grand officer. Mem. The Bus. Coun., Aerospace Industries Assn. (bd. govs.), Air Force Assn. (mem. exec. coun.), Econ. Cub (chmn.), Bus. Roundtable, Coun. Fgn. Rels., Competitiveness Policy Coun., Trilateral Commn., Bus.-Higher Edn. Forum, West Point Soc. N.Y., N.Y.C. Partnership (bd. dirs.), Links Club, River Club, Meadow Club, Knickerbocker Club, Coun. U.S.-Italy (co-chmn.). Episcopalian. Office: ITT Corp 1330 Ave Of The Americas New York NY 10019-5422

ARBEITMAN, YOËL L., research ancient languages and linguistics; b. Bronx, N.Y., June 30, 1941; s. Chaim Shimshon-Mendel and Anne (Wolf) Arbeitman. BA, CUNY, Bronx, 1972; MA, SUNY, Buffalo, 1975, NYU, 1979; PhD, U. Mich., 1985. Latin tchr. Stuart Country Sch. of the Sacred Heart, Princeton, N.J., 1990; fellow Inst. of Semitic Studies, Princeton, 1987—. Editorial assoc. Jour. of Afroasiatic Languages. Gedenkschriften: conceiver, executior Bono Homini Donum in Memory of J. Alexander Kerns, 1979-81, A Linguistic Happening in Memory of Ben Schwartz, 1983-88, Focus: Semitic and Afrasian Essays in Memory of Albert Ehrman, 1983-88, The Asia Minor Connexion: Linguistic Essays in Memory of Charles Carter, 1988-92; contbr. articles to profl. jours. Mem. Am. Oriental Soc., Cath. Bibl. Soc. Am., Soc. of Bibl. Lit., Indogermanische Gesellschaft, Am. Sch. of Oriental Rsch., Am. Philol. Assn., Assn. for the Study of Lang. in Prehistory. Jewish. Office: Inst of Semitic Studies 195 Nassau St Princeton NJ 08542-7004

ARBUCKLE, ROBERT DEAN, university administrator; b. New Kensington, Pa., Jan. 5, 1940; s. Roy Anthony and Connie (Santa Maria) A.; m. Lorraine C. Donati, Aug. 8, 1964; children: Lisa, Robert, Jeffrey. BS, Clarion State U., 1964; MS, Pa. State U., 1966, PhD, 1972. Teaching asst. Pa. State U., University Park, 1964-65, 66-67; from instr. to assoc. prof. Pa. State U., New Kensington, 1968—, assoc. dir. for acad. affairs, 1974-77, campus exec. officer, 1977—; tchr. Burrell Sr. High Sch., Lower Burrell, Pa., 1965-66; asst. prof. history U. Pitts., 1967-68. Author: John Nicholson, 1975; co-author: Pennsylvania History, 1983; contbr. articles to profl. jours. Trustee Allegheny Valley Hosp., Natrona Heights, Pa., 1990—; pres. New Kensington Area C. of C., 1985, Higher Edn. Coun. W. Pa., Pitts., 1982, United Way of Westmoreland County, 1984. Recipient Profl. of Yr. award Arnold Area C. of C., 1984, J. Harry Fisher Community Svc. award, C. of C. and area newspaper, 1984. Mem. Strongland Area C. of C. (bd. dirs. 1986—), Rotary (dist. gov. Pitts. area 1986-87, bd. dirs. New Kensington club 1982-83, Rotarian of Yr. 1982, Meritorious citation 1991, chair found.). Democrat. Roman CAtholic. Home: 42 Indian Flds Tr Lower Burrell PA 15068 Office: Pa State U 3550 7th Street Rd New Kensington PA 15068-1798

ARCA, EMIL, lawyer; b. Athens, Greece, Dec. 31, 1960; s. Bernard and Julia (Constantinides) A.; m. Denise Seutter, Aug. 4, 1990. BA, U. Mich., 1982, JD, 1985. Bar: Mich. 1985, U.S. Dist. Ct. (ea. dist.) Mich. 1986, N.Y. 1991. Assoc. Miller, Canfield, Paddock & Stone, Detroit, 1985-90, Winston & Strawn, N.Y.C., 1990—. Editor: The Triumph of the American Spirit: The Presidential Speeches of Ronald Reagan, 1984; contbr. articles to profl. jours. Mem. hon. adv. bd. Am. Remembers Campaign, San Diego, 1986—; mem. Econ. Policy Com. Econ. Enterprise Found. Detroit, 1988, Detroit Com. on Fgn. Rels., 1985-90. Mem. French-Am. C. of C., Pi Sigma Alpha. Republican. Roman Catholic. Home: 52 Sagamore Rd Bronxville NY 10708-1544 Office: Winston & Strawn 175 Water St New York NY 10038-4918

ARCAND, ANTHONY ARTHUR, accountant, tax manager; b. Woonsocket, R.I., Oct. 31, 1961; s. Armand Aldor and Irene Frances (Mauricio) A.; m. Carol Ann Joyal, June 4, 1983; 1 child, Caitlin Marie. BSBA summa cum laude, Bryant Coll., 1983, MS, 1991. CPA, R.I. Staff acct. Pascarella & Trench, CPA's, Providence, 1983-85; sr. tax acct. Ernst & Young, Providence, 1985-90; tax mgr. Batchelor, Frechette, McCrory & Michael, CPA's, Providence, 1990—. Dir. Sanwood Estates Condo. Assn., Harrisville, R.I., 1988-91; treas., dir. Southside Community Land Trust, Providence, 1989-90. Mem. AICPA, R.I. Soc. CPA's, Rotary Internat., Delta Mu Delta. Roman Catholic. Home: 56 Sanwood Dr Harrisville RI 02830-1329 Office: Batchelor Frechette McCrory & Michael 1115 Hospital Trust Bldg Providence RI 02903-2448

ARCARA, JAMES PAUL, broadcasting company executive; b. Buffalo, Sept. 21, 1934; s. Philip Anthony and Angeline (Lipomi) A.; 1 child, David James. BSBA in Econs. and Philosophy, St. Bonaventure U., 1956. Account exec. Sta. WKBW subs. Capital Cities Communications, Inc., Buffalo, 1956-61, gen. sales mgr., 1961-67; v.p., gen. mgr. Sta. WPRO-AM-FM subs. Capital Cities Communications, Inc., Providence, 1967-70, Sta. WPAT-AM-FM subs. Capital Cities Communications, Inc., Clifton, N.J., 1970-80; exec. v.p. radio Capital Cities Communications, Inc., N.Y.C., 1980-85; pres. radio div. Capital Cities/ABC, Inc., N.Y.C., 1985—; chmn. Radio Advt. Bur., N.Y.C., 1987-88; bd. dirs. Advt. Coun., Inc., N.Y.C. Bd. dirs. Providence C. of C., 1966-70, Paterson C. of C., N.J., 1973-79, Boys Club Paterson, 1973-79. Mem. Nat. Assn. Broadcasters (bd. dirs. 1988-89), R.I. State Broadcasters (pres. 1970), R.I. Advt. Club (pres. 1970), N.Y. Radio Broadcasters (chmn. 1974-75). Roman Catholic. Office: Capital Cities/ABC Inc 77 W 66th St New York NY 10023-6201

ARCHER, RICHARD JOHN, theatre educator, consultant; b. Bklyn., June 8, 1948; s. Inglis and Margaret (Coen) A.; m. Noreen A. McGuckin, Dec. 28, 1980; children: Laura, Lisa. AB, Boston Coll., 1970; MA, U. Mo., Kansas City, 1974; postgrad., U. Wis., 1976-78. Asst. tech. dir. Mo. Repertory Theatre, Kansas City, 1971-74; with Mo. Vanguard Theatre, Kansas City, 1973-74; asst. tech. dir. N.C. Sch. of the Arts, Winston Salem, 1974-75; tech. dir. Ind. Repertory Theatre, Indpls., 1975-76, Great Lakes Theatre Festival, Cleve., 1976-88; assoc. prof. dept. theatre arts Cornell U., Ithaca, N.Y., 1979—. Mem. U.S. Inst. Theatre Tech. Home: 1449 Elmira Rd Newfield NY 14867-9280 Office: Cornell U Dept Theatre 430 College Ave Ithaca NY 14850-4696

ARCHIBALD, FRED JOHN, newspaper executive; b. Lincoln, Nebr., Sept. 10, 1922; s. Fred Irwin and Edna Esther (Olson) A. B.S., U.S. Mil. Acad., 1945. Commd. 2d lt. U.S. Army, 1945, advanced through grades to capt., 1951, served various assignments, U.S., Philippines, Japan, resigned, 1955; various exec. and managerial pub. relations positions in media and community relations Gen. Motors Corp., Detroit, Cleve., N.Y.C. and Washington, 1956-78; mng. editor Frederick News-Post, Md., 1978-85, assoc. pub., 1982-85; gen. mgr., editor News-Post News Service, Frederick, 1985-87, dir. industry relations, 1987—; lectr. journalism and pub. relations, various instns., 1947—; cattle breeder Armadale Farms, Frederick, 1964—. Gen. vice chmn., producer Frederick Arts Council Beaux Arts Ball, 1984-85. Decorated Army Commendation medal, Bronze Star medal. Mem. Airedale Terrier Club Am. (treas. 1959-61), Md. Polled Hereford Assn. (pres. 1979-81), Mil. Order Carabao, Am. Legion, Sigma Delta Chi, Sigma Alpha Epsilon. Clubs: Nat. Press, Army and Navy, Georgetown (Washington); Overseas Press (N.Y.C.). Democrat. Episcopalian. Avocations: theatrical producer, experimental gardening, art collecting, press and garden photography. Home: Armadale Farms PO Box 74 Frederick MD 21701-0074 Office: Frederick News-Post PO Box 578 Frederick MD 21701-0578

ARCHIBALD, JULIUS A., JR., computer science educator; b. N.Y.C., May 9, 1931; s. Julius A. and Edzie Valerie (Fair) A.; m. Arola Loree Howard, Mar. 27, 1954; children: Julius III, Phyllis Valerie, Edzie Gladys. AB, NYU, 1952, MS, 1953. With GE, Schenectady, N.Y., 1955-68, cons. computer scientist, 1966-68; cons. systems specialist GE, Bethesda, Md., 1968-70; assoc. prof. SUNY, Plattsburg, 1970-74, prof. computer sci., 1974—. 1st lt. USAF, 1953-55. Mem. SIAM, Assn. for Computing Machinery, Computer Soc., Soc. Computer Simulation, Math. Assn. Am., Am. Math. Soc. Democrat. Methodist. Office: SUNY Plattsburg PA 12901

ARCHIBALD, NOLAN D., power tools and home improvement, household and industrial products company executive; b. Ogden, Utah, June 22, 1943; m. Margaret Hafen, June 8, 1967. AA, Dixie Coll., 1966; BS, Weber State Univ., 1968; MBA, Harvard U., 1970. Exec. v.p., gen. mgr. Sno Jet, Inc. div. Conroy, Inc., Burlington, Vt., 1970-77; sr. v.p., and pres. non-foods cos. Beatrice Foods, Chgo., 1977-85; chmn., pres., chief exec. officer The Black & Decker Corp., Towson, Md., 1985—; former All Am. basketball player. Named One of 10 Most Wanted Execs in U.S., Fortune Mag., Six Best Mgrs. in U.S., Bus. Week Mag.

ARDIA, STEPHEN VINCENT, pump manufacturing company executive; b. Hackensack, N.J., Aug. 3, 1941; s. Vincent Henry and Anita Deborah A.; m. Virginia Ellis, July 11, 1964; children: David, Daniel, Deborah. B.S., U.S. Merchant Marine Acad., 1963; M.B.A., Rutgers U., 1969. Gen. mgr. Standard Pump Div., Worthington Pump Co., East Orange, N.J., 1976-79; v.p. internat. ops. Goulds Pumps Inc., Seneca Falls, N.Y., 1979-82, v.p. sales, 1982-84, pres., 1984-85, pres., chief exec. officer, 1985—; bd. dirs. Bus. Coun. N.Y. State. Bd. dirs. Women's Hall of Fame, Seneca Falls, N.Y., Cayuga Community Coll., N.Y. Chiropractic Coll.; bd. dirs., found. bd. N.Y. State Chiropractic Coll. Mem. Skaneateles Country Club. Home: 3 W Lake St Skaneateles NY 13152-1403 Office: Goulds Pumps Inc 240 Fall St Seneca Falls NY 13148-1590

ARENA, ALBERT A., museum director; b. Waltham, Mass., Nov. 12, 1929; s. John Giovanni and Jennie (Inferrera) A.; m. Jean Marie MacDonald, Dec. 29, 1935; children: Albert A., Andrew A., Arthur A. BS, Mass. Maritime Acad., 1952. Licensed Chief Marine Engr. Marine engr. Farrell Lines Inc., Bklyn., 1952-54; naval engr. officer USS New Jersey, Norfolk, Va., 1954-56; engr. Harvard U., Roxbury, Mass., 1957-60; marine engr. SS America, N.Y.C., 1960-62; boiler and machine inspector Factory Mutual Ins., Norwood, Mass., 1963-70; assoc. prof. Mass. Maritime Acad., Buzzards Bay, Mass., 1970-72; engr. instr. Raytheon Co., Lexington, Mass., 1973-74; chief stationary engr. Allied Maintenance Corp., Boston, 1974-80; museum dir. Waltham (Mass.) Museum, 1971—. Producer, narrator This Was Waltham for Waltham Cable Access TV, 1989-91. Recipient Ship Safety Achievement Award Am. Merchant Marine Inst., 1962. Roman Catholic. Home: 17 Noonan St Waltham MA 02154-4212 Office: Waltham Mus 194 Charles St Waltham MA 02154-4206

ARENDT, RONALD HENRY, chemist; b. Chgo., Apr. 20, 1941; m. Elinor Irene Wade, June 12, 1964; children: Barbara Helen, Michael Frederick. BS, U. Chgo., 1963, MS, 1965, PhD, 1968. Staff chemist GE, Schenectady, N.Y., 1968—. Contbr. articles to profl. jours.; patentee in field. Mem. Am. Chem. Soc., Electrochem. Soc., Materials Rsch. Soc., Sigma Xi. Office: GE CR & D PO Box 8 Schenectady NY 12301-0008

ARENELLA, ROY EDWARD, photographer; b. Bklyn., July 3, 1939; s. John James and Antoinette (Aguanno) a.; m. Christine Annastas, Oct. 6, 1962 (div. May 1971); m. Martine Hahn, Dec. 14, 1973; 1 child, Kenneth René. BA, Columbia Coll., 1961. Photographer, illustrator: City Talk, 1970, The Age of Rock, Two, 1970; one-man shows include The Am. Cultural Ctr., Paris, 1976, Galleria Fotografica Nadar, Pisa, Italy, 1977, Yen Lui Gallery, Seattle, 1979, Foto Gallery, N.Y.C., 1982, East End Arts Coun., Riverhead, N.Y., 1990; exhibited in group shows at Kensington Arts Assn., Toronto, 1975, Le Museé Francais Photographie, Versailles, France, 1976, Ctr. for Photography, Woodstock, N.Y., 1988, Islip Art Mus., East Islip, N.Y., 1990, 91. Office: PO Box 1777 Riverhead NY 11901-0961

ARENS, NICHOLAS HERMAN, bank executive; b. N.Y.C., Apr. 24, 1937; s. Nicholas and Sarah (Woods) A.; m. Eileen M. Casey, Jan. 27, 1960;

children: Nicholas Jr., Steven, Cynthia, Linda. BBA, Pace U., 1969; postgrad., U. Wis., 1974. Audit officer Morgan Bank, N.Y.C., 1970-77, asst. auditor, 1978-80; chief auditor Algemene Bank Nederland, N.Y.C., 1981, sr. v.p., 1982-84; auditor Nat. Bank Kuwait, N.Y.C., 1984, mgr. ops. div., 1985-88, mgr. human resources/adminstrn. div., 1988—. Served with U.S. Army, 1958-60. Mem. Council on Internat. Banking. Home: 95 Kime Ave North Babylon NY 11703-3316 Office: Nat Bank Kuwait 299 Park Ave New York NY 10171-0002

ARESKOG, DONALD CLINTON, chiropractor; b. Bklyn., Aug. 6, 1926; s. Andrew Albert and Jennie Margaret (Dickson) A.; m. Julia Catherine Koskela, May 15, 1954. D Chiropractic, Logan Coll., St. Louis, 1950; Philosopher of Chiropractic, Atlantic States Chiropractic Coll. Pvt. practice Bklyn., 1952-56, Wappingers Falls, Bklyn., Poughkeepsie, N.Y., 1956-61, Poughkeepsie, N.Y., 1961-89; retired, 1989; bd. govs. Atlantic States Chiropractic Coll., Bklyn., 1954; research in field. Mem. Am. Chiropractic Assn. (speakers bur. 1964), Ednl. Rsch. Soc., Internat. Basic Rsch. Inst., Internat. Platform Assn., Wappingers Falls C. of C. (treas. 1959), Toastmasters. Home: 330 SE 20th Ave Apt 514 Deerfield Beach FL 33441-5181

ARESON, PETER DEWITT, surgeon; b. Montclair, N.J., July 14, 1950; s. Robert H. and Lois R. Areson; married, Oct. 20, 1975; children: Brooks, Robin. AB, Dartmouth Coll., 1972, BE, 1973; MS, Tufts U., 1977, MD, 1982. Diplomate Am. Bd. Surgery. Resident in surgery Maine Med. Ctr., Portland, 1982-87, chief resident in surgery, 1987-88; mem. staff in surgery Regional Meml. Hosp., Brunswick, Maine, 1988—, Parkton Meml. Hosp., Brunswick, 1988—, Bath (Maine) Meml. Hosp., 1988—. Office: 66 Baribeau Dr Brunswick ME 04011

ARFIELD, GEORGE, communications executive; b. Buenos Aires, Nov. 7, 1937; s. Paul and Pia (Nahm) A.; m. Carolyn C. Blackburn. BSc, Ind. U., 1960. Bur. chief The Associated Press, various fgn. cities, 1961-73; mgr. European pub. rels. Chase Manhattan Bank, London, 1973-77; mgr. internat. pub. rels. Booz, Allen & Hamilton, N.Y.C., 1977-78; account exec. Carl Byoir and Assocs., N.Y.C., 1978-81; v.p. Hill & Knowlton, Inc., N.Y.C., 1981-85; dir. pub. rels. Trintex, White Plains, N.Y., 1986-87; dir. corp. communications Akzo Am., Inc., N.Y.C., 1988-91; cons. Akzo Am. Inc., 1992—; bd. dirs. 35 Park Ave. Corp., N.Y.C., Chem. Communicators Assn., N.Y.C. Contbr. articles to jours. Mem. Soc. Profl. Journalists, Internat. Assn. Bus. Communicators, Pub. Rels. Soc. N.Y., Chem. Communicators Assn. (dir. 1990-92). Home: 35 Park Ave New York NY 10016-3838

ARGETSINGER, GERALD SCOTT, drama educator; b. Klamath Falls, Oreg., May 6, 1946; s. John Clifford and Doris June (Brooks) A.; m. Gail Bishop, June 6, 1970; children: Brandon, Erik. BA, Brigham Young U., 1971; PhD, Bowling Green State U., 1975. Chair theatre Nat. Tech. Inst. for Deaf at Rochester (N.Y.) Inst. Tech., 1975-78, asst. prof. gen. edn., 1978-87, assoc. prof. dramatic lit., 1987—; assoc. producer Hill Cumorah Pageant, Palmyra, N.Y., 1987-90; chmn. Am. Theatre Assn. Program on Drama/Theatre and the Handicapped, Washington, 1980-82. Dir. several univ. and local plays, 1975—, Hill Cumorah Pageant, 1990—; author: Ludvig Holberg's Comedies, 1983, (play) Signs of the Times, 1978; translator: Jeppe of the Hill and Other Comedies by Ludvig Holberg, 1990; entertainer Comedy Magic Show, 1970—. Active Rochester Susquicentennial, 1984; bd. dirs. Rochester Community Theatre, 1979-83. Mem. Soc. for Advancement Scandinavian Studies, Internat. Brotherhood Magicians (hist. com. 1975-88, best article award 1972), Soc. Am. Magicians, Dramatists Guild, Assn. Theatre in Higher Edn. Mormon. Home: 91 Saddlehorn Dr Rochester NY 14626-3162 Office: Nat Tech Inst for Deaf Dept Gen Edn 1 Lomb Memorial Dr Rochester NY 14623-5603

ARIAS, IRWIN MONROE, physician, educator; b. N.Y.C., Sept. 4, 1926; s. Henry Robert and Sylvia (Hirsh) A.; m. Lyuba Varticouski; children: Jonathan, Linda, Wendy, Nancy. B.S., Harvard U., 1947; M.S., Columbia U., 1948; M.D. cum laude, State U., N.Y. Med. Center, 1952. Diplomate: Am. Bd. Internal Medicine. Intern Fourth Med. Svc. (Harvard) Boston City Hosp., 1952-54, asst. resident, 1954-55; USPHS fellow gastroenterology/liver disease Second and Fourth Med. Svc., 1955-56; fellow hematology Boston VA Hosp., 1954-55; rsch. fellow N.Y. Heart Assn.; sr. rsch. fellow Albert Einstein Coll. Medicine, 1956-58, asst. prof., 1960-64, assoc. prof., 1964-69; asst. vis. physician Bronx Mcpl. Hosp. Center, 1956-64, assoc., 1964-67, attending physician, 1969-84; prin. investigator USPHS GI tng. program; dir. program and chief div. gastroenterology-liver disease Albert Einstein Coll. Medicine, Bronx, 1967-84; prof. medicine Albert Einstein Coll. Medicine, 1969-84, vice chmn. dept. medicine, 1973-84; dir. Liver Rsch. Ctr., 1973-84, asso. chmn. academic devel., dept. medicine, 1980-84; prof., chmn. dept. physiology-pathophysiology Tufts U. Sch. Medicine, 1984—, prof. medicine; cons. Rockefeller Found., 1958-60, Pan Am. Union, 1959-63. Founding editor: Hepatology; editor: (with others) Glutathione: Metabolism and Function, 1976; author: The Liver: Biology and Pathobiology, 1980; contbr. (with others) numerous articles to sci. publs. Mem. overseas med. adv. bd. Tel Aviv U. Sch. Medicine, 1963-69; mem. nat. adv. bd. La Leche League, 1970—; trustee Mount Desert Island Biol. Lab., 1969-71; mem. adv. bd. Children's Med. Rsch. Ctr., Cin., 1976-81. Recipient numerous awards including Disting. Achievement awards Am. Gastroenterologic Assn., 1970, Disting. Achievement awards Am. Coll. Gastroenterologists, 1971, Disting. Achievement award Can. Gastroenterologic Assn., 1972; B.B. Vincent Lyons award Am. Gastroenterologic Assn., 1965; San Diego-Spl. fellow. E.B. Scripps Inst. for Comparative Biology, 1967; Disting. Commendation medal medicine U. Recife, Brazil, 1972; NIH Fogarty Found. scholar, 1985. Mem. AAAS, Am. Soc. Clin. Investigation (v.p.), Am. Assn. Study Liver Disease, Am. Fedn. Clin. Rsch., Am. Gastroenterol. Assn., The Harvey Soc., Am. Physiol. Soc., Internat. Assn. Clin. Investigation, Internat. Assn. Study of Liver, Assn. Am. Physicians, Alpha Omega Alpha. Home: 55 Fay Ln Needham MA 02194-2105 Office: Tufts U Sch Medicine Dept Physiology 136 Harrison Ave Boston MA 02111-1800

ARIK, BAHA ENGIN, engineering executive; b. Turgutlu, Manisa, Turkey, June 4, 1956; came to U.S., 1974; s. Mustafa Fethi and Nevzer (Ulug) A.; m. Leyla Gucer, May 6, 1962. BA in Econs., Brown U., 1979, BSME, 1979; MS in Engring., Harvard U., 1986, PhD in Engring., 1986. Mech. engr. and economist MIGROS, Zurich, Switzerland, 1978; teaching asst. Brown U., Providence, 1977-79; rsch. asst. Inst. Exptl. Fluid Mechanics, Goettingen, Fed. Republic of Germany, 1979, Von Karman Inst., Rhode-St.-Genese, Belgium, 1980-81; systems engr. Dantec Electronics, Inc., Allendale, N.J., 1986-87, sr. product applications specialist, 1987-88; mgr. software devel. Dantec Electronics, Inc., Mahwah, N.J., 1989-91, v.p., 1990—; rsch. asst. Harvard U., Cambridge, Mass., 1981-86, teaching fellow, 1982-85; lectr. numerous colls., bus. seminars, and confs. worldwide. Author: Classical Approach to Modern Fluid Mechanics, 1988. Recipient Belgian Govt. prize, Von Karman Inst., Rhode-St.-Genese, Belgium, 1981. Mem. ASTM, Am. Phys. Soc., Evelyn Wood Reading Dynamics Inst., Sigma Xi. Home: 479 Oak Ave Maywood NJ 07607 Office: Dantec Electronics Inc 777 Corp Dr Mahwah NJ 07430

ARKIN, JOSEPH, mathematician, lecturer; b. Bklyn., May 25, 1923; s. Ben and Helen (Heller) A.; m. Judith H. Lobel, Aug. 28, 1954; children: Helen, Aviva, Jessica, Sarah. Ph.D. (hon.), Brantridge Sch., Eng., 1967. Vis. lectr. Orange Community Coll., Middletown, N.Y., 1962-67; lectr. Nanuet Pub. Schs., Rockland County, N.Y., 1962-67; sr. lectr. U.S. Mil. Acad.; researcher various profs., 1965—; math. reviewer Am. Math. Soc., R.I., 1976—. Contbr. articles to profl. jours. Active Mus. Village, Monroe, N.Y., 1978. Served with U.S. Army, 1942-43. Mem. N.Y. Acad. Scis., Internat. Congress Math (Can.), AAAS, Fibonacci Assn. (charter mem.), Math. Assn. Am., Am. Math. Soc., Can. Math. Soc., Calcutta Math Soc., Soc. Indsl. and Applied math., Am. Legion, DAV, NCO Club (West Point). Home: 197 Old Nyack Tpke Spring Valley NY 10977-5304 Office: US Mil Acad Dept Math West Point NY 10996

ARLING, BRYAN JEREMY, internist; b. Mpls., Dec. 10, 1944; s. Leonard Swenson and Marion (Schroeder) A.; m. Donna Dickson; children: Elissa, Jeremy, Timothy. BA summa cum laude, U. Minn., 1965; MD, Harvard U., 1969. Diplomate, Am. Bd. Internal Medicine. Intern Stanford (Calif.) Affiliated Hosps., 1969-70, resident in medicine, 1970-71; spl. asst. to adminstr. Health Sci. Mental Health Adminstrn. USPHS, Rockville, Md., 1971-73; instr., chief resident medicine George Washington U. Hosp., Washington, 1973-74; asst. prof. medicine George Washington U. Hosp., 1974-77; pvt. practice gen. internal medicine Washington, 1977—; clin. prof. medicine George Washington U., 1988—. Mem. adminstrv. bd., Chevy Chase United Meth. Ch.; mem. devel. com., Maret Sch., 1985—, co-chair ann. giving campaign, 1986-87, 87-88, bd. trustees 1991—; question relevance reviewer ABIM, 1991—. Mem. ACP, Am. Soc. Internal Medicine, AMA, D.C. Med. Soc., Smithsonian Assocs., Friends of Kennedy Ctr., Harvard Club Washington, Nat. Trust for Historic Preservation, Friends of nat. Zoo, Common Cause, ACLU, Physicians for Social Responsibility, Columbia Country Club, Bahamas Air-Sea Rescue Assn. Home: 3803 Taylor St Bethesda MD 20815-4117 Office: 2440 M St NW Ste 817 Washington DC 20037-1404

ARMACOST, JOHN COOPER, packaging company executive; b. Balt., Sept. 5, 1936; s. George Francis and Doris Rayne (Cooper) A.; m. Marianne Tarr, Oct. 24, 1959; children—Lisa, Beth, John, Timothy, Christopher, Suzanne. B.S. in Marine Engring., U.S. Coast Guard Acad., New London, Conn., 1958; Program Mgmt. Devel., Harvard Bus. Sch., Cambridge. Vice pres. ops. Simplex Wire & Cable, Newington, N.H., 1971-75; v.p., gen. mgr. ITT Wire & Cable Ltd., St. Jerome, Que., Can., 1975-77; pres. ITT Surprenant Div., Clinton, Mass., 1977-83, ITT Pumps & Equipment Div., Midland Park, N.J., 1983-85; pres., chief exec. officer Ludlow Corp., Exeter, N.H., 1985—; corp. v.p. Tycolabs., Inc., 1988—. Served to lt. US Coast Guard, 1958-63. Recipient Mil. Leadership award, Adminstrn. and Mgmt. award, award for highest class standing academically Highest Standing in Applied Sci. award U.S. Coast Guard Acad., 1958. Mem. Am. Paper Inst., Flexible Packaging Assn. (bd. dirs.), Nat. Elect. Mfrs. Assn. (former chmn. High Temp. Wire sect.). Republican. Roman Catholic.

ARMANT, TERRY LEE, telecommunications executive; b. Johnson City, N.Y., Aug. 7, 1948; s. Gordon M. and Marjorie (Johnson) A.; m. Bernice M. Malewiacki, Aug. v14, 1971; 1 child, Jeffrey S. AAS, State U. Agrl. & Tech. Coll., Farmingdale, N.Y., 1968; BS, State U. Coll., Oswego, N.Y., 1970. Cert. secondary tchr., N.Y. Tchr., dept. chmn. Vestal (N.Y.) Sch. Dist., 1971-80; v.p. McKilligan Indsl. Supply, Johnson City, N.Y., 1980-85; gen. mgr. Fabricon Devel. Corp., Johnson City, 1985-87; v.p. U.S. CommStruct Inc., Vestal, 1987—. Democrat. Presbyterian. Home: 3104 Knapp Rd Vestal NY 13850-3037

ARMATO, DAVID N., process engineer; b. Winchester, Mass., Sept. 15, 1961; s. Nicholas Paul (dec.) and Mary Claire (Morley) A. BA, Northeastern U., 1984; postgrad., U. Lowell, 1987-91. Chemist Polyvinyl Chem. Industries, Wilmington, Mass., 1983-85, Bemis Assocs., Watertown, Mass., 1985-86, KRC Northern, Andover, Mass., 1986-87; devel. chemist L&CP Corp., Newton, Mass., 1987-88; process cons. Webster Packaging, Peabody, Mass., 1988; process engr. A.W. Chesterton, Stoneham, Mass., 1988-89, Dan-Kar Corp., Reading, Mass., 1991—; cons. in field. Chmn. Stoneham (Mass.) Conservation Commn., 1982. Recipient Himalayan Expedition Grant Polyvinyl Chem. Co., 1984. Mem. Soc. Plastics Engrs., Am. Chem. Soc., Am. Soc. for Quality Control, Am. Alpine Club, Nat. Geog. Soc., Internat. Freelance Photographers Orgn.

ARMATO, PETER, corporate professional, consultant; b. Houston, Dec. 19, 1953; s. Jasper Joseph and Leona (Cuilla) A. BA, Rice U., 1982. Computer programmer Citibank Internat., Houston, 1976-77; area coordinator Houston Community Devel. Program, 1977; area mgr. Mickey Leland for Congress Campaign, Houston, 1978; special asst. Congressman Mickey Leland, Houston, 1979-80; mgr. Ft. Bend County Mike Andrews for Congress Campaign, Houston, 1980; candidate for Tex. Ho. of Reps., 1980; assoc. dir. S. Main Ctr. Assn., Houston, 1980-82; exec. dir. E. End Progress Assn., Houston, 1982-86; dir. govt. rels. Greater Houston Hosp. Coun., 1986-88; govt. rels. dir. Am. Coll. Cardiology, Bethesda, Md., 1988-90; exec. dir. Bus. & Profl. Assn. Georgetown, 1990—; mem. revitalization subcom. Houston Com. for Pvt. Sector Initiatives, 1984-86. Sec. Polit. Assn. Spanish-Speaking Org., 1977-79; v. pres. Harris County Democrats, 1978-79; alternate Houston/Harris County Acquired Immune Deficiency Syndrome Panel, 1987; regional convenor St. Debate Health Care, Austin 1987. Recipient Rising Star of Tex. award, Tex. Bus. Mag., 1986; named One of 5 Outstanding Young Houstonians, Jr. C. of C., 1987. Mem. Buffalo Bayou Coalition (v.p. 1987-88), Cultural Arts Coun. Houston (adv. bd. 1982-86), Tex. Hosp. Assn. (govt. rels. coun. 1986-88), Greater Houston C. of C. (govt. rels. adv. com. 1985-88), Nat. Congress Commn. Econ. Devel., Devel. Tng. Inst. (nat. intern 1984-85), Leadership Houston Club, Sierra Club, Internat. Downtown Assn. Office: PO Box 25765 Washington DC 20007-5765

ARMENAKAS, ANTHONY EMMANUEL, education educator; b. Mytilene, Greece, Aug. 23, 1924; came to U.S., 1946; s. Emmanuel Anthony and Efterpe (Sakis) A.; m. Stella Dimitri Petroutsa, Jan. 3, 1950 (dec. Jan. 1988); children: Alexandra Daphne, Noel Anthony, Melina Cybel. BSCE, Ga. Inst. Tech., 1950; MSCE, Ill. Inst. Tech., 1951; PhD in Applied Mechanics, Columbia U., 1959. Registered profl. engr., N.Y., N.J., Greece. Instr. Ill. Inst. Tech., Chgo., 1950-52; sr. structural engr. Edwards Kelcey and Beck Cons. Engrs., Newark, 1952-54; ptnr. Rynar Armenakas and McCann Cons. Engrs., Newark, 1954-59; lectr. civil engring. CUNY, N.Y.C., 1954-57; assoc. prof. civil engring. Cooper Union for the Advancement Sci. and Art, N.Y.C., 1958-64; prof. engring. sci. U. Fla., Gainesville, 1965-67; prof. aerospace Poly. U., Bklyn., 1967—; prof., dir. Inst. Structural Analysis, Nat. Tech. U., Athens, Greece, 1977-84; vis. prof. div. engring. Brown U., Providence, 1964-65; cons. Vector Engring., Springfield, N.J., 1954-59; rsch. cons. Poly. Inst., Bklyn., 1962-67, Northwestern U., Evanston, Ill., 1962-65; pres. Stress-Optics, Inc., Queens, N.Y., 1970-72; vice-chmn. bd. dirs. Greek agy. for design and rsch. earthquake protection, 1989—. Author: Free Vibrations of Circular Cylindrical Shells, 1969, Classical Structural Analysis-A Modern Approach, 1988, Modern Structural Analysis-The Matrix Method Approach, 1991; patentee in field; contbr. articles to profl. jours. Chmn. bd. dirs. Poulos Philanthropic Found., Athens, Greece. Fellow ASCE, ASME, AIAA (assoc.). Home: 52 Clark St Brooklyn NY 11201-2424 Office: Polytechnic Univ 333 Jay St Brooklyn NY 11201-2990

ARMENANTE, PIERO M., chemical engineering educator; b. Avezzano, Aquila, Italy, June 2, 1953; came to U.S., 1979; s. Euclide and Maria (Antonini) A.; m. Annemarie Aigner, Oct. 21, 1983. Laurea in chem. engring., U. Rome, 1977; PhD in Chem. Engring., U. Va., 1983. Rsch. asst. Internat. Inst. for Applied Systems Analysis, Laxenburg, Austria, 1978, U. Lund (Sweden), 1978-79; engring. specialist UN Indsl. Devel. Orgn., Vienna, Austria, 1979-87; process engr. Farmitalia Carlo Erba, Milan, Italy, 1985-87; asst. prof. N.J. Inst. Tech., Newark, 1984-91, assoc. prof., 1991—; cons. UN Indsl. Devel. Orgn., Vienna, 1978-86; presenter in field. Author: Contingency Planning for Industrial Emergencies, 1991; author: (with others) Risk Assessment and Risk Management for the Chemical Process Industry, 1991; editor: Biotechnology Applications in Hazardous Treatment, 1989; contbr. articles to profl. jours.; author reports; peer reviewer Chem. Engring. Sci., Can. Jour. Chem. Engring., Biotech. Progress, Chem. Engring. Communications. Sec. North Am. Mixing Forum, 1990—. Grantee NSF, 1991, EPA, 1989-90, 91-93, Exxon Edn. Found., 1991, Schering-Plough, Inc., 1992-93, Hazardous Substance Mgmt. Rsch. Ctr., 1988-91, 91-92, Ctr. for Mfg. Engring. Systems, Schering-Plough, Inc., 1990, 90-91, Industry/Univ. Coop. Ctr. for Hazardous Substance Mgmt., 1986-89, P.M. Armenant Inst. Tech., 1989, N.J. Inst. Tech., 1984-85. Mem. Am. Inst. Chem. Engrs. (chmn. north Jersey sect. 1992—), Am. Chem. Soc., Am. Soc. Engring. Edn., Order of the Engr., Tau Beta Pi, Sigma Xi. Office: NJ Inst Tech Dept Chem Engring Chemistry and Environ Sci Newark NJ 07102

ARMENTI, JOSEPH ROCCO, lawyer, writer; b. Neptune, N.J., Sept. 11, 1950; s. Rocco Carmen and Lucie (Taranta) A.; m. Maria Elizabeth Masters, June 6, 1982. BA, Villanova U., 1972; PhD, Dropsie U., 1982; JD, Temple U., 1986. Bar: Pa. 1986, U.S. Dist. Ct. (ea. dist.) Pa. 1986, U.S. Ct. Appeals (3d cir.) 1986, N.J. 1987. Ptnr. Joseph R. Armenti & Assoc., Phila., 1987—. Author: Elements of Divine Power, 1983; author, editor: Transcendence and Immanence, 1972, Wisdom and Knowledge, 1976, The Human Religious Quest, I-IV, 1986—; contbr. articles to profl. jours. Mem. ARC Disaster Relief Team; mem. ACLU, A.H.E.P.A. Fellow Dropsie U. for Hebrew and Cognate Studies, Phila., 1974-80. Mem. ABA, N.J. Bar Assn., Pa. Bar Assn., Phila. Bar Assn. (edn. com. criminal div. 1989—), Assn. Trial Lawyers Am., Pa. Trial Lawyers Assn., Phila. Trial Lawyers Assn., Nat. Assn. Criminal Def. Lawyers, Internat. Soc. for Neo-Platonic Studies, Am. Acad. Religion, Soc. Bibl. Lit. (pres.), Lions. Roman Catholic. Office: 12 S 12th St Ste 2001 Philadelphia PA 19107-3920 also: 601 Haddon Ave Ste 117 Collingswood NJ 08108

ARMILLEI, RAYMOND JOSEPH, psychotherapist; b. Balt., June 29, 1954; s. Raymond Robert and Rose Ann (Benzi) A.; m. Sherry Ann Burruss, Apr. 28, 1984. BA in Philosophy, Towson State U., 1983, MA in Psychology, 1982; MSW, Md. Sch. of Social Work, 1990; postgrad., Calif. Coast U., 1991—. Lic. social worker; cert. chem. dependency counselor, nat. cert. addictions counselor. Restaurant mgr. Foodmaker, Inc., Balt., 1976-80; clinician Southeastern Community Mental Health Ctr., Balt., 1980-84; drug and alcohol counselor Eastern Community Mental Health Ctr., Balt., 1984-85; mental health coord. Addict Referral and Counseling Ctr., Balt., 1985-86; psychologist II Montebello Rehab. Hosp., U. Md. Med. Systems, 1986-89, addictions specialist, 1986-89; pvt. practice Balt., 1986—; employee assistance program practitioner Sheppard Pratt Hosp., Balt., 1989—; treatment cons. for design and implementation, Balt., 1986—; workshop presenter Sheppard Pratt Hosp., Balt., 1986—, Aberdeen Proving Grounds, and others. Dacum staff Dundalk Community Coll., Balt., 1981; lead tenor choir St. Francis de Sales Ch., Abingdon, Md. Mem. Employee Assistance Profls. Assn., Cert. Addictions Counselors of Md., Md. Addictions Counselors Cert. Bd., Md. Soc. of Clin. Social Workers, Nat. Assn. of Alcoholism and Drug Abuse Counselors, Nat. Certification Reciprocity Consortium (nat. cert. alcohol and drug abuse counselor). Democrat. Roman Catholic. Home: 309 Regal Dr Abingdon MD 21009-1518 Office: Sheppard-Pratt Hosp EAP 6501 N Charles St Box 6815 Baltimore MD 21285-6815

ARMKNECHT, PAUL ANTHONY, economist, government official, educator; b. Shamokin, Pa., July 10, 1945; s. Paul Anthony and June Millicent (Bamford) A.; m. Jeanne Ansley Brennan, May 13, 1967 (div. Dec. 1980); children: Lauren, Patrick; m. Cherie Reed Lavier, Jan. 1, 1982. BS, Loyola Coll., Balt., 1967; MA, Cath. U. Am., 197l, PhD, 1982. Economist U.S. Bur. Labor Stats., Washington, 1967-72, supervisory economist, 1972-83, chief br. consumer prices, 1984-88, asst. commr., 1988—; instr. econs. Montgomery Coll., Rockville, Md., 1977-82, adj. prof., 1983—; instr. Univ. Coll., U. Md., College Park, 1984—. Contbr. articles to profl. jours. V.p. Montgomery Village Sports Assn., Gaithersburg, Md., 1984-89. Mem. Am. Econ. Assn., Am. Statis. Assn., Pi Gamma Mu. Mem. United Ch. of Christ. Office: US Bur Labor Stats Washington DC 20212-0001

ARMSTEAD, GEORGE BROOKS, JR., sewing machine manufacturing company executive; b. Hartford, Conn., Nov. 26, 1927; s. George Brooks and Frances Josephine (Lakin) A.; m. Doris Edith Field, July 29, 1950; children: Sarah, Faith, George Brooks III, Daniel. BSME, U. Conn., 1950. Engr. Remington-Rand Inc., Norwalk, Conn., 1950-51; engr. The Merrow Machine Co., Hartford, 1951-63, product mgr., 1963—; sec. The Merrow Machine Co., Newington, Conn., 1978—. Patentee in field. Chmn. com. Fourth Congregational Ch., Glastonbury, Conn., 1957-59; chmn. bd. Glastonbury br. Greater Hartford YMCA, 1960-64; skipper, scout leader Sea Scout Ship 66 and Troop 34, Wethersfield and Glastonbury, 1946-80; pres., bd. dirs. Hist. Soc. Glastonbury, 1973—. With USN, 1945. Leader mem. Acad. Model Aeronautics (contest dir. 1973-91, Disting. Svc. award 1986), Am. Soc. Materials, Nat. Free Flight Soc., Soc. Antique Modelers (life, nat. contest dir. 1982-90, Contest Dir. award 1982, 86, 90, Hall of Fame 1992), Antique Tools and Trades in Conn. (charter, publ. chair), Conn. Hist. Soc., Glastonbury Aero Modelers (pres. 1970-75). Republican. Home: 89 Harvest Ln Glastonbury CT 06033-1721 Office: The Merrow Machine Co 240 Day St Newington CT 06111-1241

ARMSTRONG, DENISE GRACE, association executive. Diploma, Briarcliffe Secretarial Sch., L.I., N.Y., 1974. Sec. Klar, Klar & Tifford, law office, East Meadow, N.Y., 1974-76; exec. sec. Nassau Acad. Medicine and Nassau County Med. Soc., Garden City, N.Y., 1976-80; adminstr. Suffolk County Dental Soc., Hauppauge, N.Y., 1980-87, exec. dir., 1988-89; dir. dept. mktg. svcs. Med. Soc. of State of N.Y., 1989-90, asst. dir. div. mktg./mktg. svcs., 1990—. Mem. NAFE, Am. Soc. Assn. Execs., Am. Assn. Med. Soc. Execs. Office: 420 Lakeville Rd New Hyde Park NY 11042-1121

ARMSTRONG, GARRY HERBERT EMILE, news reporter; b. N.Y.C., Apr. 7, 1942; s. William and Esther (Holder) A.; m. Marilyn Friedman Kraus, Sept. 15, 1990. Student, Hofstra U., 1960-65. Various positions Hempstead, N.Y., 1961-67; writer, producer ABC Radio Network, N.Y.C., 1967-70; co-anchor Sta. WHCT-TV, Hartford, Conn., 1970; reporter Channel 7 Stas. WNEV/WHDH-TV, Boston, 1971—. Lecturer Nat. Lupus Found., Boston, 1977, ARC, Boston, 1990—; lectr., role model Big Bros., Boston, 1986—. With USMC, 1959—. Recipient Clarion award Greater Boston YWCA, 1977. Mem. Nat. Acad. TV, Arts and Scis. of New Eng. (bd. dirs. 1976-80, Emmy 1976, 77, 78). Office: Sta WHDH-TV Channel 7 7 Bulfinch Pl Boston MA 02114-2913

ARMSTRONG, JAMES FRANCIS, III, educator; b. Penn Yan, N.Y., Mar. 17, 1945; s. James Francis Armstrong Jr. and Frances (Grady) Armstrong-Barden. BA in Eglish Edn. cum laude, Hobart-William Smith, 1983; cert., Kellogg Inst., 1989. Cert. English tchr.; cert. devel. educator. Audio tech. Brighton Sound, Inc., Rochester, N.Y., 1964-75; owner JFA Mgmt., Penn Yan, 1975-86; English tchr. Penn Yan Jr. High Sch., 1984-85; learning specialist Community Coll. of Finger Lakes, Geneva, N.Y., 1986-87, dir. learning ctr. and libr., 1987—; substitute tchr. Finger Lakes Schs., N.Y., 1980-84; G.E.D. instr. Bd. of Coop. Ednl. Svcs., Stanley, N.Y., 1986-87. Singer/musician (album) Feels Like Spyders, 1975; author: Adam Blast, 1983; contbr. articles to profl. jours.; film maker for Kodak, 1970. Office: Finger Lakes C C 361 Main St Geneva NY 14456-2601

ARMSTRONG, JAN MARIA, association executive; b. Washington, May 20, 1950; d. John Joseph Sr. and Helen (Phillips) Bobinger; m. Ronald Dennis Armstrong. BA in German with honors, U. Md., 1972. Grad. asst. U. Md., College Park, 1972-74; sr. specialist in health benefits U.S. Office of Pers. Mgmt., Washington, 1974-83; from mgr. div. tng. to dir. legis. and regulations CNA Ins. Cos., Rockville, Md., 1983-86; dir. edn. Group Health Assn. Am., Washington, 1986-87; exec. v.p. Am. Car Rental Assn., Washington, 1988—; pres. Armstrong Assocs., Inc., Washington, 1990—; cons. health policies, Washington, 1988. Contbr. articles to mags. Mem. Am. Soc. Assn. Execs., Greater Washington Soc. Assn. Execs., Women in Govt. Rels., Delta Phi Alpha. Office: Am Car Rental Assn 927 15th St NW Ste 1000 Washington DC 20005

ARMSTRONG, JOHN KREMER, lawyer, artist; b. Washington, Apr. 15, 1934; s. Stuart Morton and Marion Louise (Kreutzer) A.; m. A.M.E. (Mieke) van Haersma Buma, Apr. 1963; children: Marca Carine van Heloma, Jeb Stuart. BA with honors, Haverford Coll., 1956; postgrad., U. Delhi, 1956-57; LLB, Yale U., 1960. Bar: N.Y. 1961. Assoc. Davies, Hardy and Schenck, N.Y.C., 1960-68; ptnr. Davies, Hardy, Ives and Lawther, N.Y.C., 1968-72, Armstrong and Ulrich, N.Y.C., 1973-81, Cole and Deitz, N.Y.C., 1981-85, Carter, Ledyard & Milburn, N.Y.C., 1985—; dir. Kinney Can., Inc., 1973—; lectr. Longwood Garden Fellows Program, 1987. Works exhibited N.Y.C., Salisbury and Bar Harbor, Maine. Trustee Bklyn. Bot. Garden, chmn. bd., 1982-89; trustee Westchester Land Trust, 1991—; bd. regents L.I. Coll. Hosp., 1968-72, asst. sec., 1973—; fellow Rotary Found., 1956-57. Mem. ABA, N.Y. State Bar Assn. (co-chmn. com. health law 1987-89), Assn. Bar City N.Y., Lawrence Park West Assn. (dir.), Bronxville Field Club, Pilgrims Soc., Ch. Club of N.Y. (trustee 1990—, sec. 1991—), N.W. Conn. Rod and Gun Club, India House, Phi Beta Kappa. Episcopalian. Republican. Home: 14 Carlton Rd Bronxville NY 10708-5404

ARMSTRONG, ROBERT EDDY, foundation admininistrator; b. Omaha, Sept. 10, 1932; s. Paul Everett and Esther Vernelia (Eddy) A. BA in Polit. Sci. summa cum laude, U. Ill., Urbana, 1954; student, Princeton U., N.J., 1955. Budget examiner Exec. Office of Pres., Washington, 1955, 59-60; fgn. svc. officer Dept. State, Am. Embassy, Kathmandu, Nepal, 1960-62; 1st lt. U.S. Army Intelligence, Japan, 1956-59; forgn. svc. officer Dept. State Am. Embassy, Moscow, 1962-64; assoc. Rockefeller Bros. fund, N.Y.C., 1965-70; program dir. Henry Luce Found., N.Y.C., 1970-83, exec. dir., 1983-89, pres., 1989—. Bd. mem. Arts Info. Svc., N.Y.C., 1980-84, Chelsea Theatre Ctr., N.Y.C., 1968-74, Nat. Theatre of Deaf, Chester, Conn., 1991—. Mem. The Hemisphere Club, Phi Beta Kappa, Phi Kappa Phi. Episcopalian. Home:

411 W End Ave New York NY 10024-5719 Office: Henry Luce Foundation 111 W 50th St New York NY 10020-1204

ARMSTRONG, SCOTT MICHAEL, management consultant, industrial engineer; b. Newton, N.J., Aug. 17, 1964; s. Robert Van Clief and Carolyn Adelaide (Nugent) A.; m. Sue Ann Ellis, Dec. 9, 1989. BS in Ops. Rsch. and Indsl. Engring., Cornell U., 1987. Indsl. engr. Standard Tech., Inc., Rockville, Md., 1987-90; sr. cons. Birch & Davis Assocs., Inc., Silver Spring, Md., 1990—; prin. investigator Office of Asst. Sec. of Dev., Health Affairs, Washington, 1990. Contbr. articles to profl. jours. Campaign staff mem. for Monte Davis, Rep. Party, Arlington, Va., 1990, John Marshall, 1991. Mem. Inst. Indsl. Engrs. (sr. mem.), Cornell Soc. Engr., Ops. Rsch. Soc. Am. (assoc. mem.), Soc. for Health Systems, Mid-Atlantic Soc. for Health Systems (membership dir.), Arlington County Taxpayers Assn., Arlington County Young Reps. Home: 518 S Spring St Falls Church VA 22046 Office: Birch & Davis Assocs Inc 8905 Fairview Rd. Silver Spring MD 20910

ARMSTRONG, WILLIS COBURN, management consultant, former government official; b. N.Y.C., Apr. 2, 1912; s. James Claude and Hattie Amelia (Fairchild) A.; m. Martha Louise Schaffner, May 2, 1959; 1 child, Ian Coburn. BA, Swarthmore Coll., 1933; MA, Columbia U., 1934. Tchr. Horace Mann Sch., N.Y.C., 1934-39; mem. staff Am. Embassy, Moscow, 1939-41; officer Lend Lease and Fgn. Econs. Adminstrn., 1941-45, War Shipping Adminstrn., Washington, 1945-46; officer Econ. Bur., U.S. Dept. State, Washington, 1946-58; counselor, minister Am. Embassy., Ottawa, Ont., Can., 1958-62; dir. Brit. Commonwealth and No. Europe Affairs U.S. Dept. of State, Washington, 1962-64; econ. minister U.S. Embassy U.S. Embassy, London, 1964-67; asst. sec. state U.S. Dept. of State, Washington, 1972-74; assoc. dean Columbia U. Sch. Internat. Affairs, N.Y.C., 1967-69; pres. U.S. Council Internat. Bus., N.Y.C., 1969-72; Washington rep. U.S. Council Internat. Bus., 1974-82; mem. sr. rev. panel CIA, Washington, 1982-85; mem. U.S. Can. Permanent Joint Bd. on Def., 1962-64; cons. in internat. bus., 1974-82, 85—; bd. dirs. Atlantic Coun. U.S., Washington; profl., lectr. grad courses Am. U., Columbia U., Johns Hopkins U., Georgetown U. Bd. dirs. English Speaking Union U.S., N.Y.C., 1978—. Mem. Cosmos Club, Nassau Club. Republican. Presbyterian. Home: 3226 Broad Branch Ter NW Washington DC 20008-2016

ARNABOLDI, JOSEPH PAUL, retired veterinarian; b. Union City, N.J., Dec. 2, 1920; s. Joseph Paul and Gladys Ellen (Wheeler) A.; m. Mary Louise Shoemaker, Aug. 24, 1944; children: Allan Charles, Sally-Jo Ann, Loren Joseph. DVM, Cornell U., 1943; postgrad., Liberty U., 1989—. Ordained to ministry African Meth.-Episcopal Ch. Veterinarian Port Jeff Animal Hosp., Port Jefferson, N.Y., 1946-81; min. Bethel AME Ch., Setauket, N.Y., 1966-84; bishop Eglise de Dieu Montagne de Sinai, Haiti, 1982—; free-lance writer. Featured in L.I. sect. A Vet. Centennial in N.Y. State, 1890-1990; contbr. several articles to mags. Life mem., trustee Rep. Presdl. Task Force, Rep. Senatorial Inner Circle. Capt. U.S. Army, 1943-46. Paul Harris fellow Rotary Internat., 1972. Mem. ASCAP, AVMA, L.I. Vet. Med. Assn. (pres. 1952), N.Y. State Vet. Med. Soc., Christian Vet. Mission, World Concern (charter 1984—), Solar Box Cookers Internat. (founding mem. 1987—), Rotary Internat. (pres. Port Jefferson chpt. 1959-60, gov. L.I. dist. 725 1970-71), No. Brookhaven Club of Toastmasters Internat. (life; founder 1959-60, charter pres., area gov. dist. 46 1962-63). Republican. Home and Office: 520 W Broadway PO Box 3 Port Jefferson NY 11777-0003

ARNATT, RONALD KENT, musician, educator; b. London, Jan. 16, 1930; came to U.S., 1947; s. Josiah Henry and Elizabeth Christina (Kent) A.; m. Carol Freeman Woodward, June 28, 1952; children: Ronlyn, Sylvia W. MusB, Durham (Eng.) Univ., 1954; MusD, Westminster Choir Coll., 1970. Lectr., instr. Am. Univ., Washington, 1951-54; dir. of music Mary Inst., St. Louis, 1954-68; prof. music, dir. choral activities Univ. Mo., St. Louis, 1968-80; dir. music, organist Christ Ch. Cathedral, St. Louis, 1954-80; founder, conductor St. Louis Chamber Orchestra and Chorus, 1956-78; conductor, music dir. Bach Soc. of St. Louis, 1974-80; dir. music, organist Trinity Ch., Boston, 1980-82, St. John's Episcopal Ch., Beverly, Mass., 1984-87; prof. of church music Westminster Choir Coll., Princeton, N.J., 1987-91; mem. staff ECS Pub., Boston, Mass., 1992—. Composer more than 400 compositions, more than 160 of which published, including choral, liturgical, keyboard and brass ensemble pieces; composer: (opera) The Boy With a Cart; others. Chmn. religious music com. St. Louis Bicentennial Commn., 1974-76; mem. standing comm. on ch. music, Episcopal Ch. U.S.A., 1964-76, Young Audiences, Inc., St. Louis, 1969-72. Trinity Coll. fellow; recipient Anthem award Ch. of the Ascension, 1950, Composition award Nat. Assn. Am. Composers and Condrs., 1951, Kindler Meml. Found. award, 1982; Danforth Found. grantee, 1967. Fellow Trinity Coll. Music (London), Royal Coll. Organists, Am. Guild Organists (pres. 1986-90, v.p. 1979-86, Avis Blewett award 1990), Royal Coll. Organists; mem. ASCAP, Assn. Anglican Musicians (pres. 1973-74, v.p. 1972-73). Home: 109 School St Manchester MA 01944-1232 Office: ECS Pub 138 Ipswich St Boston MA 02215

ARNHEIM, FALK KANTOR, physician; b. Pitts., June 18, 1917; s. Raymond F. and Bessie (Kantor) A.; m. Marian Louise Lambie, Nov. 17, 1943; children: David, Daniel, Louise. BS, U. Pitts., 1939, MD, 1943. Diplomate Am. Bd. Urology. Intern St. Francis Hosp., Pitts., 1943-44; resident in surgery Montefiore Hosp., Pitts., 1944-47; resident in urology Michael Reese Hosp., Chgo., 1947-50; mem. staff Montefiore Hosp., Pitts., 1950—, Passavant Hosp., Pitts., 1955-60; mem. staff St. Clair Meml. Hosp., Pitts., 1955—, cons. quality assurance program, 1986—; mem. staff West Pa. Hosp., Pitts., 1970-80. Capt. U.S. Army, 1944-46, CBI. Fellow ACS, AMA, Am. Urol. Assn., AACU. Office: 1050 Bower Hill Rd Pittsburgh PA 15243

ARNICK, JOHN STEPHEN, lawyer, legislature staff member; b. Balt., Nov. 27, 1933; s. John and Josephine (Gaillardo) A. BS, U. Balt., 1956; LLD, U. Balt. Law Sch., 1961. Bar Assn. U.S. Marine Corps., 1956-69; magistrate Balt. County, 1966-67; del. Md. Gen. Assembly, Annapolis, 1967-79; atty. pvt. practice, Dundalk, Md., 1962—; del. Md. Gen. Assembly, Annapolis, 1983—. Mem. Twin Dist. Dem. Club, Battle Grove Dem. Club, Sons of Italy. Mem. Ea. Balt. C. of C., Moose Lodge, New 7th Dem. Club, South East Dem. Club. Democratic. Roman Catholic. Home: 7918 Diehlwood Rd Dundalk MD 21222 Office: Arnick & Evans 2 N Dundalk Ave Dundalk MD 21222

ARNOLD, ALICE MARIE, executive real estate management; b. Beverly, Mass., Oct. 28, 1958; d. Donald Peyton and Barbara Marie (Maihos) Hayes; m. Mark McKay Arnold, July 12, 1986. Student, Salem State Coll., 1976-78, North Shore Community Coll., 1985-86. Art supr. Beverly (Mass.) Elem. Schs., 1976-78; clk. acctg. dept. Holyoke Mutual Insur. Co., Salem, Mass., 1978-80; asst. buyer Appleseeds, Inc., Beverly, Mass., 1980-82; property mgr. Battistelli Constr. Co., Beverly, 1982-87; prin. AMA Mgmt. Co., Beverly, 1986—. Mem. Beverly Hist. Soc., 1982—. Mem. Beverly Real Estate Bd., 1987—. Home and Office: AMA Mgmt Inc 38 Pemberton Rd Topsfield MA 01983

ARNOLD, BRUCE ROBERT, investment banker; b. N.Y.C., Mar. 22, 1955; s. Edmund and Viola (Burtzloff) A. BA, Syracuse U., 1976; JD, U. Va., 1979. Bar: N.Y., D.C., Va. Assoc. atty. Reid & Priest, N.Y.C., 1979-80, Leboeuf Lamb Leiby & MacRae, N.Y.C., 1980-82; cons. N.Y.C., 1982-85; v.p. The First Boston Corp., N.Y.C., 1985-89; bd. dirs. CS First Boston, Darling Point, NSW, Australia, 1989—. Vol. Holy Trinit Men's Shelter, N.Y.C., 1983—; council mem. Holy Trinity Luth. Ch., N.Y.C., 1986-87. Mem. Phi Beta Kappa, Phi Kappa Phi. Lutheran. Office: The First Boston Corp, 6C/55 Darling Point Rd, Darling Point 2027, Australia

ARNOLD, DAVID BROWN, educator; b. Hackensack, N.J., Oct. 24, 1940; s. Robert Brown and Virginia Louise (Bunn) A.; m. Georgia Louise Carss, Dec. 28, 1963 (div. 1971); 1 child, Christopher Carss; m. Mary Helen Tryson, Dec. 23, 1971 (div. Dec. 1985); children: Phoebe Lynn, Jennifer Suzanne. BSc in Chemistry, U. Pa., 1963; PhD in Chemistry, Bryn Mawr Coll., 1970. Asst. prof. Widener U. (formerly Widener Coll., then PMC Colls.), Chester, Pa., 1968-75; assoc. prof. Widener U., Chester, Pa., 1975—; vis. prof. U. Del., Newark, 1982-83; part-time vis. prof. Bryn Mawr (Pa.) Coll., 1981; head judge Del. County Sci. Fair, 1976—. Mem. Am. Chem. Soc., Royal Soc. Chemistry, Nat. Sci. Tchrs. Assn., Penn. Sci. Tchrs. Assn. (bd. dirs. 1976—), Del. County Sci. Tchrs. Assn. (bd. dirs. 1970—, past pres.), Catalysis Club of Phila. Home: 3 Scott Ave Upland PA 19015-3013 Office: Widener U Sci Div One University Pl Chester PA 19013

ARNOLD, ELLEN HOLT, college development officer; b. Jamestown, N.Y., Jan. 3, 1943; d. Everett W. and Segrid (Lindbeck) Holt; m. Richard B. Arnold, June 20, 1964; children: Catherine Lee, Barbara Diane. AB, Bucknell U., 1964. Cert. fund raising exec. Blood svc. coord. ARC, Williamsport, Pa., 1978-82, exec. dir., 1982-84; exec. dir. Allied Arts Fund, Harrisburg, Pa., 1984-88; dir. ann. giving Lebanon Valley Coll., Annville, Pa., 1988-91, dir. devel., 1991—. Bd. dirs. OPEN STAGE of Harrisburg, 1989-91, Hemlock Girl Scouts U.S. Coun., Harrisburg, v.p., 1988—; life mem. Pa. PTA. Recipient Community Svc. award Pine Run Grange, Williamsport, 1979, Hemlock award Hemlock Girl Scouts U.S. Coun., Harrisburg, 1991. Mem. ARC (bd. dirs., Lebanon, Pa., vice chair 1988—), AAUW, Nat. Soc. Fund Raising Execs. (Cen. Pa. chpt. bd. dirs., treas. 1987-90, v.p. 1991—), Coun. Advancement and Support of Edn., Kiwanis. Presbyterian. Home: 427 W Sheridan PO Box # 189 Annville PA 17003 Office: Lebanon Valley Coll 101 N College Ave Annville PA 17003-1400

ARNOLD, J. DAVID, academic administrator, dean; b. Lancaster, Pa., Mar. 15, 1955; s. John Rosenberger and Carolyn Fay (Stauffer) A.; m. Barbara J. Dillman, Apr. 25, 1986; 1 child, J.G. Andrew. BA in Psychology, Bloomsburg (Pa.) U., 1978; MA in Social Psychology, U. N.H., 1980, PhD in Social Psychology, 1982. Asst. prof. St. Lawrence U., Canton, N.Y., 1982-88, assoc. prof., 1988-90, assoc. dean, 1989-90; assoc. dean Clarion (Pa.) U., 1990—; cons. PS Assocs., McGraw-Hill, Boston, N.Y., 1986, 89. Contbr. articles to profl. jours. Mem. APA, Phi Kappa Phi, Psi Chi. Home: 302 Ridgewood Rd Shippenville PA 16254-8708 Office: Clarion U 204 Founders Hall Clarion PA 16214

ARNOLD, JACK, fine arts dealer, graphics consultant; b. N.Y.C., Jan. 21, 1927; s. Harold and sally (Halpert) Abrahams; m. Nancy Wolnstein, June 4, 1950 (div. 1967); 1 child, Keith Michael; m. Tazuko Fujiwara, Nov. 10, 1983. BS, Syracuse U., 1950. Dir. advt. and pub. rels. Transogram Co., Inc., N.Y.C., 1955-63; dir. advt. and mktg. Remco, Inc., N.Y.C., 1963-66; pres. Motivational Devices, Inc., N.Y.C., 1966-72; v.p. Shorewood Atelier, Inc., N.Y.C., 1972-76; v.p., graphics cons. Gallery Hawaii, Inc., Honolulu, 1976-79; owner Jack Arnold Fine Arts, N.Y.C., 1979—; ptnr. Laurence Ettinger Fine Arts, Las Vegas, Nev., 1983-84; graphics cons. Gottesman Fine Arts, Monsey, N.Y., 1988-89. With USMC, 1944-46. Home and Office: 5 E 67th St New York NY 10021-5823

ARNOLD, JAY, engineering executive; b. Balt., Jan. 1, 1936; s. Otto Joseph and Margaret (Flannery) A.; m. Harriet Mary Metzbower, July 4, 1959; children: Kelly Marie Arnold Wood, Philip Driscoll Arnold, Michael Flannery Arnold. BS, Loyola Coll., Balt., 1965; MBA, Loyola Coll., Potomac, Md., 1977; postgrad., George Washington U., 1980-81, Berlitz Inst., Washington, 1987-90. Software and systems engring. positions including mgt. NASA's Manned Space Program IBM, 1962-78; vis. IBM prof. Morgan State U., Balt., 1978-79; planner of automation strategy Fed. Systems div. IBM, Gaithersburg, Md., 1979-81; sr. mgr. systems design depts. USAF Data Systems Modernization Fed. Systems div. IBM, Gaithersburg, 1981-83, sr. mgr. systems design depts. FAA Advanced Automation System, 1983-87; dir. network mgmt. and control Comsat Systems div. Communications Satellite Corp., Clarksburg, Md., 1987-88, sr. dir. Deutsche Fermelde Satellite program, 1988-90, sr. dir. MOSCOM program, 1990, sr. dir. engring. advanced systems, 1991—; speaker, instr. and lectr. in computer and communication field, 1973—. Caregiver Frederick County Hospice, 1984-87; club leader Frederick County 4-H, 1975-80; pres./v.p. Frederick County Sheep Breeders Assn., 1983-84; chmn. bd. govs. Am. Bouviers Des Flandres Club, 1981-82; mem. St. Peter's Ch. Parish Coun., 1991—, St. Peter's Parish Men's Club, 1990-91. With USAF, 1958-62. Recipient parenting awards Future Farmers of Am., 1978-80, Award for Advancement of Human Rights UN Assn., 1984; named Alumni of Yr. Mt. St. Joseph Coll. High Sch., 1989. Mem. Am. Assn. for Retired Persons, Armed Forces Communications and Electronics Assn., Johnsville Ruritan Club. Democrat. Roman Catholic. Home: Heaven Sent Farm 11131 Repp Rd Union Bridge MD 21791 Office: COMSAT 22300 Comsat Dr Clarksburg MD 20871-9470

ARNOLD, JEANNE GOSSELIN, communications executive; b. Rutland, Vt., Dec. 19, 1917; d. Eugene Arthur and Eleanor (Ranberg) Gosselin; children: Eugene Van Rensselaer Arnold, Linda Krull Beattie. Student, SUNY, Albany, 1935-38, 45-47, Russell Sage Coll., 1964-65. Reporter, women's editor, columnist, feature writer Albany Times Union, N.Y., 1945-79; dir. Media Svcs. Unltd., Westerlo, N.Y., 1979—. Author: (poetry) The Flesh Recalls, 1956, Ballad of Witches Hill, 1988; (biography) A Man of Faith, 1983; (children's book) Little Cloud That Couldn't, 1990; contbr.: Things that Go Bump in the Night, by Louis C. Jones, 1959. Chmn. Westerlo Planning Bd., 1978-86. Recipient ann. Journalism award N.Y. State Bar Assn., 1975, Outstanding Woman award Coll. St. Rose, Albany, 1976, Albany YMCA, 1977. Mem. The Newspaper Guild. Roman Catholic. Home: RR 1 Box 265 Westerlo NY 12193-9754 also: PO Box 335 Frogmore SC 29920

ARNOLD, JOHN DAVID, management counselor and consultant; b. Boston, May 14, 1933; s. Israel and Edith (Gordon) A.; B.A. cum laude in Social Relations, Harvard U., 1955; children: Derek, Keith, Craig. Prodn. supr., dealer service mgr. Arnold Stretch Mates Corp., Boston, 1957-59; asst. dir. manpower and orgn. devel. Polaroid Corp., Waltham, Mass., 1959-63; dir. internat. ops. Kepner-Tregoe & Assocs., Princeton, N.J., 1963-68; pres. John Arnold ExecuTrak Systems Inc., Waltham, 1968—; conf. leader numerous firms; speaker in field. Served to 1st lt. U.S. Army, 1955-57. Author: Make Up Your Mind, 1978; The Art of Decision Making, 1978; Shooting the Executive Rapids, 1981; How to Make the Right Decisions, 1982; Trading Up-A Career Guide: How to Get Ahead Without Getting Out, 1984; How to Protect Yourself Against a Takeover, 1986, The Complete Problem Solver! A Total System of Competitive Decision Making, 1992, When The Sparks Fly: Resolving Organizational Conflict, 1992; contbr. articles to bus. mags. Office: John Arnold Execu Trak Systems Inc 125 Technology Dr Waltham MA 02154-8901

ARNOLD, JOHN P., state attorney general; b. Boston, Nov. 11, 1946; m. Ellen; 2 children. BA, U Vermont, 1969; JD, Northeastern U, 1972. Rep. New Hampshire Gen. Ct., Concord, 1974-78; atty. Brighton Fernald Taft & Hampsey, Peterough, N.H., 1973-89; atty. gen. State of N.H., Peterough, 1989—. Office: Office of Atty Gen 208 State House Annex Concord NH 03301*

ARNOLD, MARC BENJAMIN, lawyer; b. Syracuse, N.Y., Jan. 31, 1948; s. Allen Richard and Frances Harriet (Solomon) A.; m. Iris J. Goodman, July 2, 1972 (div. Mar. 1982); 1 child, Sacha Daniel. AB, Columbia U., 1970; JD, New Eng. Sch. of Law, 1977. Bar: N.J. 1977. Law clk. Hudson County Counsel, Jersey City, 1975; law clk. U.S. Atty.'s Office State of Mass., Boston, 1976; law clk. to hon. judge T.L. Franklin Superior Ct. of N.J., Hackensack, 1977-78; dep. atty. gen. div. law State of N.J., Newark, 1978-81; assoc. Friedman, Carney & Wilson, Newark, 1981-83; owner, prin. Marc Arnold, Hoboken, N.J., 1983—. Pool atty. Hudson County Pub. Defender, Jersey City, 1988-89; pro-bono atty. Hudson County Legal Svcs., Jersey City, 1991—. New Eng. Sch. of Law scholar, 1975-76, 76-77. Mem. Assn. Trial Lawyers Am., Hoboken Bar Assn. (v.p. 1985-86), Hudson County Bar Assn. Democrat. Office: 51 Newark St # 305 Hoboken NJ 07030-4543

ARNOLD, PETER GORDON, communications consultant; b. Newton, Mass., Jan. 25, 1943; s. Israel Isaac and Edith (Gordon) A.; m. Kirsten Ellen Arnold, July 25, 1966 (div. 1979); 1 child, Jeremy Gordon; m. Margery Loewenberg, July 27, 1980; 1 child, Jessica Beth. BA, U. Mich., 1966; MA, U. So. Calif., 1969. Writer, producer Universal Studios, Hollywood, Calif., 1969-70; exec. v.p. Cameo Pictures, Hollywood, 1971-72; devel. writer Calif. Inst. Tech., Pasadena, 1973; dir. spl. projects Occidental Coll., Los Angeles, 1974-75; exec. dir. Hugh O'Brian Youth Found., Los Angeles, 1976; pres. Peter Arnold Assocs., Boston, 1977—. Author: Lady Beware, 1973, Emergency Handbook, 1980 (Literary Guild selection 1980), Job and Career Building, 1980, Packaging Your House for Profit, 1986 and seven other books. Mem. Writers Guild Am., Authors League, Advt. Club Greater Boston. Office: 1 Hollis St # 211 Wellesley MA 02181-4631

ARNOLD, PHILIP WILLARD, manufacturing company executive; b. Hastings, Mich., May 6, 1949; s. Willard Henry and Velma Marie (Kellogg) A.; m. Kathleen Atkinson, Sept. 16, 1972; children: Leslie, Lindsay, Laura. BS in Edn., Taylor U., 1971; MA in Edn., Ball State U., 1974. Tchr., coach Tipton (Ind.) Community Schs., 1971-79; sales agt. R.J. Atkinson Co., Inc., Indpls., 1979-80; sub. pres. Best Locking Systems N.Y., Inc., North Salem, N.Y., 1980—; largest rep. sales volume, 1987-91. Elder Hillside Ch., Armonk, N.Y., 1984-86, 87-90, deacon, 1982-83. Mem. Am. Soc. Indsl. Security. Mem. Christian and Missionary Alliance Ch. Office: Best Locking Systems NY Inc RD 2 Fields Ln North Salem NY 10560

ARNOLD, ROBERT H., lawyer, investment banker, consultant; b. Adams, Mass., Dec. 22, 1918; s. Edward Henry and Sylvia Jeanette (Haff) A.; m. Nancy Day Colegrove, June 5, 1948; children: Richard S., Steven E., Lois E. Arnold-Caffrey. AB, Wesleyan U., 1941; LLB, Boston U., 1948. Bar: Mass. 1948, Conn. 1957, U.S. Dist. Ct. 1957. Corp. atty. Liberty Mut. Ins. Co., Boston, 1948-52; trial atty. New England Factory Mut. Ins. Co., Boston, 1953-55; corp. sr. counsel United Aircraft Corp. (named changed to United Techs. Corp.), Hartford, Conn., 1956-86; pvt. practice, cons., 1986—, investment banker, 1989—; cons. United Techs. Corp., Hartford, 1986-89; lectr., 1976-90. Author: Dangers of Punitive Awards, 1982, Hartford, Yesterday and Today (350 Years), 1987, 3d edit., 1989; contbr. articles to profl. jours. Chmn. Community Chest Drive, Glastonbury, Conn., 1958, 59; founder Hist. Area, Glastonbury, 1960; mem. Affordable Housing Com., Glastonbury, 1989—. Capt. U.S. Army, 1942-46. Decorated Bronze Star. Mem. Glastonbury Exchange Club, Civitan Club Hartford, Hartford Club, Orchard Hill Club. Home: 45 Farmcliff Dr Glastonbury CT 06033

ARNOLD, ROGER JAMES, financial services executive; b. Syracuse, N.Y., Nov. 2, 1955; s. Roger Frederick and Audrey Virginia (Viele) A.; m. Margo C. Scaringi, Aug. 15, 1987; children: Eric, Michael, Sean, Joshua. BS in Bus. Adminstr., Siena Coll., 1977. Sales assoc. The New Eng., Syracuse, N.Y., 1977-83; exec. v.p. Empire of Am. PSB, Buffalo, 1983-85; pres., chief exec. officer Empire Agy., Inc., Buffalo, 1985-90; pres., prin. Empire Fin. Svcs., Amherst, N.Y., 1991—; project cons. Bank Mark Nat. Westchester Bank, Long Island, 1990-91. Author: (industry newsletter) Banks and Insurance. Fund raising coord. Uptowners, Easter Seals, Syracuse, 1981-85; contbr. Kids Escaping Drugs, Buffalo, 1988-91. Office: Empire Fin Svcs 350 Essjay Rd Ste 304 Williamsville NY 14221

ARNONE, MARY GRACE, radiology technologist; b. Bronx, N.Y., Dec. 28, 1961; d. Anthony Rocco and Mary Helen (Doring) A. Grad., Acad. Health Sci., U.S. Army, 1982. Lic. radiologist. With U.S. Army, 1982-86. Republican. Lutheran. Office: PO Box 566 Yonkers NY 10704-0566

ARNOTT, RICHARD JAMES, economics educator; b. London, Jan. 23, 1949; came to U.S., 1988; s. David Charles and Ruth Margaret (Burt) A. SB, MIT, 1969; MA, U. Toronto, Ont., Can., 1971; MPhil, Yale U., 1973, PhD, 1975. Prof. econs. Queen's U., Kingston, Ont., 1975-88, Boston Coll., Chestnut Hill, Mass., 1988—; vis. prof. Tel Aviv U., 1981, 83, 85, Stanford (Calif.) U., fall 1990; spl. advisor dept. fin. Govt. Can., Ottawa, Ont., 1987-88; cons. HUD, Washington, 1988-89. Author: Rent Control, 1981; mem. editorial bd. 6 jours., 1979—; field editor Urban Econs., 1983-90; also over 60 articles. Rsch. grantee NATO, 1987, NSF, 1989. Mem. Am. Econ. Assn., Can. Econs. Assn. (sec.-treas. 1981-84, Harry Johnson prize 1983), Econometric Soc. Office: Boston Coll Dept Econs Chestnut Hill MA 02167

ARNOW, LESLIE EARLE, scientist; b. Micanopy, Fla., June 22, 1909; s. Joseph Leslie and Mable Annie (Thrasher) A.; m. Jennie Martin, July 17, 1933 (dec. Sept. 1976); 1 son, Peter Leslie. Ph.G. and B.S., U. Fla., 1930; Ph.D., U. Minn., 1934, M.B. and M.D., 1940. Grad. asst. in physiol. chemistry and biophysics U. Minn., 1931-34, instr. physiol. chemistry, 1934-40, asst. prof., 1940-42; dir. biochem. research, med.-research div. Sharp and Dohme div. Merck & Co., Inc., 1942-44, dir. research, 1944-53, v.p., dir. research, 1953-56; v.p. Merck Sharp & Dohme Research Labs. div. Merck & Co., Inc.; exec. dir. Merck Inst. for Therapeutic Research, 1956-58; pres. Warner-Lambert Research Inst., 1958-65, sr. scientific cons., 1965-74; v.p. Warner-Lambert Pharm. Co., 1958-65; sec. Drexel Hill Assocs., comml. firm owning and operating 2 radio stas. and photography bus. Author, Introduction to Physiological and Pathological Chemistry, 1976, Introduction to Laboratory Chemistry, 1976, Introduction to Organic and Biological Chemistry, (with H.C. Reitz), 1949, Health In A Bottle, 1970, Food Power, 1972, also articles in tech. publs. Past pres. bd. trustees Morris County Easter Seal Soc. Recipient Centennial award U. Fla., 1953, Outstanding Achievement award U. Minn., 1955. Fellow AAAS, N.Y. Acad. Sci.; mem. Morris County Med. Soc., AMA, Med. Soc. N.J., Am. Chem. Soc., Am. Soc. for Biochemistry and Molecular Biology, Am. Soc. for Clin. Pharmacology and Therapeutics, Soc. Exptl. Biology and Medicine, Phi Beta Kappa, Sigma Xi, Alpha Omega Alpha, Phi Beta Pi, Gamma Sigma Epsilon, Rho Chi, Phi Sigma, Alpha Epsilon Delta, Gamma Alpha, Sigma Chi. Club: Morris County Golf. Home: 14 Fairfield Dr Morristown NJ 07960-6143

ARNY, LOUIS WAYNE, III, government relations executive; b. Phila., Oct. 21, 1942; s. L. Wayne Jr. and Marjorie Benton (Haviland) A.; m. Sydney Beth Lynn, Dec. 29, 1965; children: L. Wayne IV, Matthew L. BS, U.S. Naval Acad., 1964; MA in Internat. Rels., Cath. U., 1979. Commd. ensign USN, 1964, advanced through grades to comdr., 1979; fighter pilot USN, numerous locations, including Vietnam, 1964-76; naval planner Office Chief Naval Ops. USN, Washington, 1976-79; mil. fellow Am. Enterprise Inst., Washington, 1979-80; mil. analyst Dept. State, Washington, 1980-81; retired USN, 1981; profl. staff mem. Senate Armed Svcs. Com., Washington, 1981-84; prin. dep. asst. sec. Dept. Navy, Washington, 1984-86; assoc. dir. Office Mgmt. and Budget, Exec. Office Pres., Washington, 1986-89; sr. v.p. TFG, Inc., Alexandria, Va., 1989-90; pres. L. Wayne Arny & Co. Inc., Washington, 1990—; bd. dirs. Designers & Planners, Inc., Alexandria. Capt. USNR, 1984—. Decorated Air medal; recipient Disting. Civilian Svc. medal Dept. Navy, 1986. Mem. Model A Club Am., Sovereign Mil. Order of the Temple of Jerusalem, Hupmobile Club, Porsche Club Am. Republican. Office: L Wayne Arny & Co Inc 600 New Hampshire Ave NW Washington DC 20037-2403

AROGYASWAMY, BERNARD ANTHONY, management educator; b. Annamalai, Madras, India, Aug. 20, 1945; came to U.S., 1980; s. Royapuram Paul Arogyaswamy and Maria Theresa Ruthnaswamy; m. Lalita Ursula Manchanda, Mar. 25, 1973; 1 child, Tarini Melissa. BE, Coll. Engring., Madras, India, 1969; MBA, Kent State U., 1982, DBA, 1987. Asst. engr. Crompton Engring., Madras, India, 1970-75; sr. engr. Bharat Heavy Elecs., Delhi, India, 1975-80; teaching fellow Kent State U., Ohio, 1980-84; prof. mgmt. Le Moyne Coll., Syracuse, N.Y., 1986—; vis. prof. U. Akron, Ohio, 1984-85, Baldwin Wallace Coll., Berea, Ohio, 1985-86. Contbr. articles to profl. jours. Office: Le Moyne Coll Syracuse NY 13214

ARON, JOEL EDWARD, management consultant; b. Bklyn., May 4, 1928; s. Samuel and Bertha (Kallish) A.; m. Eve G. Serenson, Dec. 13, 1964; children: Jennifer, Joshua, Eric. BS, Queens Coll., Flushing, N.Y., 1950; MA, Columbia U., 1951. Personnel mgr. Sun Chem. Corp., L.I.C., 1951-56; v.p., dir. rsch. Personnel Psychology Ctr., N.Y.C., 1957-64; exec. v.p. Personnel Data Systems, N.Y.C., 1964-74; adj. prof. mgmt. NYU, 1967—; sr. v.p. Right Assocs., N.Y.C., 1974—; dir. profl. svcs. Right Assocs., Phila., 1989-91. Author: Interviewing Techniques, 1966. Commr. Human Rights, Rye, N.Y., 1980. Mem. Am. Psychol. Assn., Ea. Psychol. Assn., Internat. Assn. Outplacement Cons. Home: 470 Park Ave Rye NY 10580-1213 Office: Right Assocs 640 5th Ave New York NY 10019-6102

ARONIN, LEWIS RICHARD, metallurgical engineer; b. Norwood, Mass., Aug. 4, 1919; s. Samuel and Celia (Acoff) A.; B.S., M.I.T., 1940; m. Natalie Eleanor Wolfson, June 19, 1947; children—Marlene Aronin Sigel, Terry Aronin Dubow. Asst. to research dir. Waltham Watch Co. (Mass.), 1940-48; staff mem. M.I.T. Metall. Project, Cambridge, 1949-54; mgr. research and devel. dept. Nuclear Metals, Inc., Concord, Mass., 1954-65; cons. Kennecott Copper Corp., Lexington, Mass., 1966-67; materials engr. Army Materials Tech. Lab., Watertown, Mass., 1967-90; pvt. cons. advanced materials devel., 1990—. Registered profl. engr., Mass. Mem. AIME, Am. Soc. Metals, AIAA, Soc. Advancement Materials and Process Engring. (treas. Boston chpt. 1976-89), Engring. Socs. New Eng. (dir. 1984-87), Sigma Xi. Lodges:

Lions, Masons. Research and publs. on nuclear materials, radiation effects, beryllium, refractory materials, and advanced structural composites; patentee in field. Home and Office: 20 Ingleside Rd Lexington MA 02173-2522

ARONIN, MARC JACOB, playwright, artistic director, director; b. Queens, N.Y., July 24, 1964; s. Carl and Phyllis (Montesano) A. BFA in Theatre, MA in Ednl. Theatre magna cum laude, Adelphi U., 1987. Prof. Adelphi U., Garden City, N.Y., 1986-91; gen. mgr. Larkspur Dance Theatre, N.Y.C., 1986—; lit. agt. Profl. Artists Unltd., N.Y.C., 1987-1988; mng. dir. Olmsted Theatre, Garden City, 1990—; asst. dir. Joyce Trisler Danscompany, N.Y.C., 1991—; artistic dir. E.M. Arrow Prodns., N.Y.C., 1991—; freelance prodn. mgr. Amblin/Putnam, Talking Books, N.Y.C.; theatre cons. Vanishing Glory, Vicksburg, Miss., 1991—. Author: (drama) State of Mind, 1990, Best Laid Plans, 1991, Minstrel Melodies, 1991, Party Time, 1992, (fiction) Marking Time, Bohemia Bound. Fundraiser Family Health Ctr., Garden City, 1990-91. Named Alexander Barnes Scholar, Adelphi. U., 1982-86. Home: 240 E 30th St New York NY 10016

ARONOFF, JONATHAN ROSS, psychologist; b. Albany, N.Y., Mar. 7, 1953; s. Arthur and Eleanore (Press) A.; m. Valorie Kay, June 23, 1985; children: Jenessa, Summer. BA in Psychology, Hampshire Coll., 1975; MS in Experimental Psychology, Ohio U., 1977; MA in Clin. Psychology, Calif. Sch. Profl. Psychology, 1981; PhD in Clin. Psychology, Brighton Young U., 1984. Psychology intern Cambridge Hosp., Harvard Med. Sch., Mass., 1983-84; psychology cons. Conn. Jr. Republic, Litchfield, Conn., 1986-88; rsch. cons. Asuten Riggs Ctr., Stockbridge, Mass., 1988-89; sr. staff psychology Inst. of Living, Hartford, Conn., 1988-89; psychology cons. Eagleton Residential Treatment Ctr., Great Barnington, Mass., 1987-90; staff psychologist Austrn Riggs Ctr., 1989—; clin. dir. Eagleton Residential Treatment Ctr., 1991—. Contbr. articles to profl. jours. Water and sewer commr. Town of Stockbridge, 1988-90; asst. dir. admissions Austen Riggs Ctr., 1992—. Postdoctoral fellow Austen Riggs Ctr., 1984-86, Advanced Postdoctoral fellow, 1986-88. Mem. Am. Psychoanalytic Assn. (affiliate mem.), Am. Psychol. Assn., Ea. Psychol. Assn. Western Mass. Albany Assn. (pres. elect 1991—), Western Mass. Psychoanalytic Psychology Assn. (sec., chmn. mem. com. 1988-91, pres. 1992—), Mass. Psychol. Assn., Mass. Assn. Psychoanalytic Psychology. Home: Park St Stockbridge MA 01262-9999 Office: Austen Riggs Ctr Inc Main St Stockbridge MA 01262-9999

ARONOW, EDWARD, psychologist, educator; b. N.Y.C., Dec. 22, 1945; s. Hyman and Gertrude (Bakst) A.; B.A. in Psychology, Queens Coll., CUNY, 1967; M.A. in Psychology, Fordham U., 1969, Ph.D. in Clin. Psychology, 1973; m. Audrey Susan Gimpelson, Dec. 25, 1967; children—David, Rebecca. Psychology trainee VA, N.Y.C., 1968-72; assoc. prof. psychology Montclair (N.J.) State Coll., 1972—; sr. clin. psychologist St. Vincent's Hosp., N.Y.C., 1972-79; clin. psychologist, Montclair, N.J., 1974—. Mem. Am. Psychol. Assn., Eastern Psychol. Assn., N.J. Psychol. Assn., Soc. Personality Assessment, Sigma Xi. Author: Rorschach Content Interpretation, 1976; A Rorschach Introduction: Content and Perceptual Approaches, 1982. Home and Office: 59 Gordonhurst Ave Montclair NJ 07043-2415

ARONS, MICHAEL EUGENE, science administrator; b. N.Y.C., Mar. 29, 1939; s. Saul and Molly (Glickstein) A.; m. Rose Marie Davoli, Oct. 1, 1961; children: David, Jennifer. BEE, Cooper Union, 1959; PhD, U. Rochester, 1964. Research scientist NYU, N.Y.C., 1964-66; prof. physics CCNY, 1966—, dean sci. div., 1987—. Office: CCNY Convent Ave at 138th St J1320 New York NY 10031

ARONS, MICHAEL JEROME, social worker; b. Newark, June 22, 1942; s. Harry and Ruth (Krinzman) A.; m. Norma Gebhardt, Apr. 22, 1979; children: Robert Gebhardt, Jason Michael. BA in Sociology, Ky. Wesleyan U., Owensboro, 1965. Social worker N. Princeton (N.J.) Devel. Ctr., 1965—. Chmn. recycling Twp. of Montgomery, Bellemead, N.J., 1980-84, mem. Local Assistance Bd., 1980-90. Mem. NASW (chmn. unit 1976-78, chmn. licensing com. 1980-83), Elks. Republican. Jewish. Home: 198 Opossum Rd Skillman NJ 08558-2602

ARONSON, JAMES RIES, physical chemistry consultant; b. Chgo., Sept. 1, 1932; s. Alfred Clarence and Lucille Natalie (Ries) A.; m. Rita Marie Cronin, Jan. 27, 1963; children: James, Audrey, Kathy, Diane, Christopher. BS, Northwestern U., 1954; PhD, MIT, 1958. Rsch. assoc. MIT, Cambridge, 1958-59; scientist Arthur D. Little, Inc., Cambridge, 1959-86; rsch. prof. applied optics Fairleigh Dickinson U., Teaneck and Hackensack, N.J., 1987-88; cons. James R. Aronson, PhD & Co., Winchester, Mass., 1987—; chmn. radiation properties session AIAA Thermophys. Specialist Conf., Monterey, Calif., 1965; gen. chmn., mem. steering com. Fourier Transform Users Group, Houston, 1974; chmn. physics session Diffuse Reflectance Spectroscopy Conf., Chambersburg, Pa., 1982. Contbr. over 40 articles to profl. jours., chpts. to books. Recipient cert. of special recognition NASA, 1979. Fellow Optical Soc. Am. (tech. editor Optics and Spectroscopy 1959); mem. Boston Computer Soc. Home and Office: 20 Ridgefield Rd Winchester MA 01890-3951

ARONSON, MARK BERNE, consultant, real estate broker; b. Pitts., Aug. 24, 1941; s. Richard J. and Jean (DeRoy) A.; m. Ellen Jane Askin, July 20, 1970; children: Robert M., Andrew A., Michael D. BS in Econs., U. Pa., 1962; JD, U. Pitts., 1965. Lic. real estate broker, 1972. Pvt. practice law Pitts., 1965-66, 83-90; sr. ptnr. Behrend & Aronson, Pitts., 1967-80, Behrend, Aronson & Morrow, Pitts., 1980-83; real estate broker, cons. to attys. Past pres. Community Day Sch., Pitts., Rodef Shalom Jr. Congregation; past trustee Rodef Shalom Congregation, Pitts., 1979-87, trustee Pitts. Child Guidance Found., 1987-90; mem., Pitts. Coun. on Edn., 1986-89. Mem. Am. Arbitration Assn. (mem. nat. panel arbitrators), Masons (master). Republican. Jewish. Address: Box 8195 Pittsburgh PA 15217

ARONSON, PAUL ROBERT, company executive; b. Lynn, Mass., Jan. 12, 1927; s. Nathan and Gertrude (Goldberg) A.; m. Lenore Halper Apr. 15, 1951; children: Lisa Newmann, Steffi Karp, Michael, Nancy. AB, Bowdoin Coll., 1948. Buyer Goldberg Farm, Lynn, 1948-62; broker Tucker Anthony, Boston, 1963-80, Alex Brown, Boston, 1980-87; assoc. dir. Bear Stearns, Boston, 1987—; dir. Exec. Life, N.Y.C., Aegis Co., N.J.; chmn. bd. Getting Married Pub., Boston. Bd. dirs. Temple Emanuel, Marblehead, Mass., 1970; bd. overseers Temple Israel, Boston, 1980-89; mem. Am. Jewish Com. With USMS, 1944-45. Mem. Stockbridge Golf Club, University Club. Home: 246 Eliot St Chestnut Hill MA 02167-1447 Office: 1 Federal St Boston MA 02110-2003

ARPIN, GARY QUINTIN, editor; b. San Francisco, Aug. 30, 1944; s. Quintin Roy and Jaurata Winifred (Schneider) A.; m. Susan Jane Whittemore, Aug. 9, 1967; 1 child, Sarah Ann. BA, Northwestern U., 1966; MA, U. Va., 1967, PhD, 1971. Assoc. prof. dept. English Western Ill. U., Macomb, 1971-80; editor Harcourt, Brace, Jovanovich, N.Y.C., 1980-81, Reader's Digest, Pleasantville, N.Y., 1981—. Author: Poetry of John Berryman, 1977; contbg. author: Elements of Literature, 1988. Office: Readers Digest Assn Pleasantville NY 10708

ARPINO, GERALD PETER, performing company executive; b. Staten Island, N.Y., Jan. 14, 1928; s. Luigi and Anna (Santanastasio) A. Student, Wagner Coll., PhD (hon.), 1980; student ballet under Mary Ann Wells, student modern dance under May O'Donnell and Gertrude Shurr. Dancer Ballet Russe, 1951-52; co-founder Joffrey Ballet, 1956, dancer, to 1962, former assoc. artistic dir., now artistic dir., resident choreographer, until 1990; with faculty Joffrey Ballet Sch. N.Y.C., from 1953, now artistic dir., assoc. dir., to 1988, prin. choreographer, to 1988; bd. dirs. Dance Notation Bur., Dancers in Transition; mem. adv. coun. to dept. dance Calif. State U., Long Beach, also mem. Disting. Artists Forum. Choreographer ballets including Incubus, 1962, Viva Vivaldi!, 1965, Olympics, Nightwings, both 1966, Cello Concerto, Arcs and Angels, Elegy, all 1967, Secret Places, The Clowns, Fanfarita, A Light Fantastic, 1968, Animus, The Poppet, 1969, Confetti, Solarwind, Trinity, all 1970, Reflections, Valentine, Kettentanz, all 1971, Chabriesque, Sacred Grove on Mount Talmalpais, both 1972, Jackpot, 1973, The Relativity of Icarus, 1974, Drums, Dreams on Banjos, 1975, Orpheus Times Light 2, 1976, Touch Me, 1977, Choura, L'Air d 'Esprit, Suite Saint-Saens, all 1978, Epode, 1979, Celebration, 1980, Ropes, Partita for Four, Sea Shadow, Diverdissement, 1980, Light Rain, 1981, Round of Angels, 1982, Italian Suite, Quarter-Tones, 1983, Jamboree (commd. by City of San Antonio). Adv. Sportsmedicine Edn. & Rsch. Found., L.A.; mem. adv. com. N.Y. Internat. Festival of the Arts; mem. nat. adv. coun. ITI/USA Internat. Ballet Competition; mem. hon. com. The Yard Benefit-Vineyard Celebration, 1989; mng. dir., bd. dirs. Found. for Joffrey Balllet, Inc. Served with USCG, 1945-48. Recipient Dancemagazine award, 1974, Bravo award San Antonio Performing Arts Assn., 1984, Disting. Achievement award Nat. Orgn. Italian-Am. Women, 1987, Tiffany award Internat. Soc. Performing Arts Adminstrs., 1989, Outstanding Artistic Achievement award Staten Island Coun. on Arts, 1990, Ammy award Am. Express Corp. Office: Joffrey Ballet 130 W 56th St New York NY 10019-3818*

ARREDONDO, DAVID ERNEST, psychiatrist; b. Presque Isle, Maine, Sept. 23, 1953; s. Manuel and Fantina Graciela (Chapa) A.; children: Pablo David, William Arturo Manuel. AB cum laude, Harvard Coll., 1975; MD, Harvard Med. Sch., 1980. Cert. Am. Bd. Psychiatry and Neurology. Research instr. Dept. Psychology, Rice U., Houston, 1972; neurology asst. Baylor Coll. of Medicine, Houston, 1973; secondary research asst. neuropharmacology Mass. Gen. Hosp., Boston, 1974; neurosurgical research assoc. Beth Israel Hosp., Boston, 1975; researcher Latin Am. Health care Delivery, Amazon Basin, Peru, 1978-79; fellow Harvard Sch. Pub. Health Cardiology, Boston, 1979, various psychiat. orgns., Washington and Boston, 1982-84; attending physician Hampstead (N.H.) Hosp., 1984-90; dir. adolescent affective disorders clinic Nashua Brookside Hosp., 1990—; med. dir. dept. of psychiatry Nashua (N.H.) Meml. Hosp.; v.p. Falk Fellows, Washington, 1983-84; rep. Joint Commn. on Pub. Affair, Am. Psychiat. Assn., Washington, 1982-84. Patentee in field. Mem. Amnesty Internat., Nat. Resources Def. Coun. Mem. Am. Psychiat. Assn., Mass. Psychiat. Soc., Mass. Med. soc., Harvard Med. Sch. Alumni Assn., AAAS. Home and Office: 132 Wash Pond Rd Hampstead NH 03841-2162

ARRINGTON, GERALD LYNN, logistics management specialist; b. Montgomery, Ala., Mar. 29, 1955. BA in Biology, Chemistry, Ala. State U., 1976; MS in Human Resource Mgmt, Golden Gate U., 1986. Commd. 2d lt. USAF, 1979, advanced through grades to capt., 1981; missile combat crew comdr., safety officer USAF, McConnell AFB, Kans., 1979-82; asst. chief, chief resource plans div. USAF, Holloman AFB, N.Mex., 1982-85; spl. asst. comdr. resource mgmt. USAF, Holloman AFB, 1985-86, chief plans and programs div., 1986-87, dep. chief logistics plans div., 1987-89; logistics mgmt. specialist naval sea systems command USN, Washington, 1989—. Mem. Assn. Naval Engrs., Soc. Logistics Engrs., Logistics Edn. Found., Lions, Assn. of Soc. of Transp. and Logistics, Ret. Officers Assn. Democrat. Baptist. Office: Naval Sea Systems Command SEA 04E Washington DC 20306

ARRISON, CLEMENT R., manufacturing company executive; b. 1930; married. BS, U. Mich., 1953. Engr. Bell Aircraft Corp., 1953-59, Am. Machine and Foundry; mfrs.' rep., 1959-62; v.p. Radatron Corp., Buffalo, 1962-69; pres., dir. Mark IV Industries Inc., Amherst, N.Y., 1970—. Office: Mark IV Industries Inc 501 John James Audobon Pkwy Box 450 Amherst NY 14228*

ARSENAULT, KATE WHITMAN, artist, counselor, art therapist; b. Camden, N.J., Oct. 25, 1922; d. William Wallace and Katherine (Williamson) Chalmers; m. Frederick Grinnell Whitman, Sept. 12, 1953 (div. May 1977); children: William Wallace, Frederick Grinnell, Susan Whitman Durant; m. Ernest Steven Arsenault, Feb. 9, 1980. BA, Wellesley Coll., 1944; MS, U. Bridgeport, 1978. Registered art therapist. Adminstrv. sec. Hoover, Curtis & Ruby, N.Y.C., 1944-46; field supr., researcher Alderson & Sessions, Phila., 1949-53; art therapist variious facilities including Child Guidance Ctr., Norwalk, Conn., 1976-80, Geriatric Ctr., Darien, Conn., 1976-80; pvt. practice art therapy, 1977-80; cons. Pocasset (Mass.) Mental Health, 1987-89; tchr. painting to pvt. students; instr. watercolor Falmouth (Mass.) Artist Guild. Exhibited paintings in shows Rowayton (Conn.) Art Ctr., 1970-78, Stamford Art Assn., 1975, Cape Cod Art Assn., Barnstable, Mass., 1990, Falmouth Artists Guild, 1982, Salmagundi Club, N.Y.C., 1981, Cape Code Art Assn.; one-woman show Grey Seal Gallery, West Falmouth, Mass.; works represented in pvt. collections and reproduced in mags. Active in community affairs, 1950s and 60s; mem. Cahoon Mus. of Fine Arts, Cotuit, Mass. Recipient numerous awards for paintings. Mem. Salmagundi Club, Copley Soc., Wellesley Friends of Art, Cape Cod Art Assn., Plymouth Guild of Artists, Falmouth Artists' Guild. Republican. Home: Box 710 9 Red Brook Pond Dr Cataumet MA 02534

ARSENOVIC, ALEXANDER, family physician; b. Beograd, Yugoslavia, Dec. 19, 1928; s. Ilija and Anna (Muk) A.; v. Vukosava Dokovic, Oct. 4, 1954; children: Ilija, Nanka Arsenovic Schneider. MD, U. Beograd, 1953. Diplomate Am. Bd. Family Practice, Am. Bd. Quality Assurance; lic. physician, Pa. Internist/infectologist Univ. Clinics, Beograd, 1954-58; specialist-infectologist, chief of clin. lab. Health Ctr. Vracar, Beograd, 1958-68; resident in family practice Edgewater Hosp., Chgo., 1969-70; internist VA Hosps., various locations, 1970-86; pvt. practice family practitioner and geriatritian Community Med. Ctr. of Burgettstown, Pa., 1986—. Fellow Am. Geriatrics Soc.; mem. Am. Acad. Family Practice. Home: PO Box 371 Hickory PA 15340

ARSTARK, LESTER D., advertising agency executive; b. Hoboken, N.J., Sept. 7, 1924; s. Maurice T. and Sophia L. (Solomon) A.; m. Janice M. Corn, June 29, 1952; children: Kim A. (dec.), Dru A. AB, Brown U., 1948; postgrad. in bus., Columbia U., 1951-52. News editor Bristol (R.I.) Phoenix, 1948-49, New Bedford (Mass.) Standard-Times radio stas., 1949-51; account exec. Kenyon & Eckhardt, N.Y.C., 1951-53, supr. promotion food products, 1954-57; mgr. advt. and sales promotion Hudson Pulp and Paper Corp., 1957-59, dir. communications, 1959-60; pres. L.D. Arstark & Co., N.Y.C., 1961—; lectr. pub. rels. C.W. Post Coll., 1960-61; lectr. mktg. Bernard Baruch Sch., CCNY, 1959-61; adj. prof. N.Y. Inst. Tech., Old Westbury, 1985-91; dir., exec. com. Programming & Systems, Inc., 1961-70. Bd. dirs. Nat. Parkinson Found., exec. com., 1962-64; trustee Roslyn Landmark Soc., 1981—; mem. Roslyn Preservation Corp., 1981—; pres. Roslyn Village Civic Assn., 1985-87. Served with USAAF, 1943-46. Mem. Brown Club of L.I. (pres. 1979-81, bd. dirs. 1979-86). Home: 190 Main St Roslyn NY 11576-2131 Office: PO Box 72 Roslyn NY 11576-0072

ARTHUR, ALAN THORNE, pharmaceutical executive; b. Evanston, Ill., Feb. 26, 1942; s. Leland Thorne and Elizabeth (Campbell) A.; m. Sharon Sims, July 31, 1965; children: Katherine L., Jennifer J., Anne E. BA, Hanover (Ind.) Coll., 1964; MA, Drake U., 1966; PhD, U. Colo., 1971. NIH fellow in physiology reprodn. Worcester Found., Shrewsbury, Mass., 1971-73; asst. prof. ob./gyn. M.S. Hershey (Pa.) Med. Ctr., 1973-77; dir. endocrinology labs. Hahneman Hosp., Phila., 1977-78; mgr. reprodn. Pharms. Div. Ciba-Geigy, Ardsley, N.Y., 1978-82; assoc. dir. reprodn. Pharms. Div. Ciba-Geigy, Summit, N.J., 1982-86; head clin. studies div. Pharms. Div. Ciba-Geigy, Manchester, Eng., 1986-88; dir. gen. toxicology Ciba-Geigy, Summit, N.J., 1988—, mem. facility mgmt. com. and steering com. mgmt. forum, 1988—. Referee Am. Youth Soccer Assn., N.Y., 1978-82, Bridgewater (N.J.) Recreation Dept., 1982—. Mem. Mid-Atlantic Reprodn. and Teratology Assn. (steering com. 1982-84, pres. 1984-86), J.L. Swim Club (pres. Bridgewater 1989-92). Home: 227 Great Hills Rd Bridgewater NJ 08807 Office: Ciba-Geigy Pharm Div SEF 556 Morris Ave Summit NJ 07901

ARTURI, ANTHONY JOSEPH, engineering executive, consultant; b. Paterson, N.J., Sept. 6, 1937; s. Emanuel and Mary (Territo) A.; m. Betty Jane Hanner, July 14, 1962; children: Anthony David, Dawn Elizabeth. BSME, Stevens Inst. Tech., 1959, MS in Math., 1966. Registered profl. engr., N.J. Project engr. Gen. Precision-Kearfott, Wayne, N.J., 1962-64, Bendix Corp., Teterboro, N.J., 1964-66; engr. supr. Singer Kearfott Div., Wayne, 1966-74; project mgr. Lummus Co., Bloomfield, N.J., 1974-77, GE Info. Svcs., N.Y.C., 1977-82; pres. ARTECH Assocs., Wayne, 1982—; trustee Stevens Inst. Tech., Hoboken, N.J., 1986-88; adj. faculty Fairleigh Dickinson U., Teaneck, N.J., 1968-75. Presenter in field. Organizer, panelist Stevens Enterprise Forum, 1985-90. Recipient Alumni Achievement award Stevens Alumni Assn., 1979. Mem. IEEE, Nat. Security Indsl. Assn. (v.p. dir. 1985—, sec. 1990—), Drug Info. Assn., Stevens Entrepreneurs Club (organizer small bus. network 1986), Lions. Home: 13 Miller Rd Wayne NJ 07470-3620 Office: ARTECH Assocs 1341 Hamburg Tpke Wayne NJ 07470-4042

ARVANITIS, CYRIL STEVEN, surgeon, educator; b. Long Branch N.J., Sept. 16, 1926; s. Samuel and Sassa Alexandra (Nelopoulos) A.; m. Victoria Pappaylion, Dec. 26, 1950 (div. Jan. 1976); children:Samuel James, Hope Alexandra; m. Eva Blomberg, Aug. 8, 1976. BS, Ursinus Coll., 1949; MD, Hahnemann Med. Coll., 1953. Diplomate Am. Bd. Surgery. Intern, Hahnemann Hosp., 1953-54, resident, 1954-58; teaching fellow Hahnemann Med. Coll., Phila., 1957-58, prof. surgery, 1979—; attending surgeon Monmouth Med. Ctr., Long Branch, N.J., 1968-80, attending surgeon, 1958—, chmn. dept. surgery 1978—, also program dir. surgery, acting dir. med. edn.; acting asst. dean Hahnemann U. Sch. Medicine; vis. specialist Care-Medico, Afghanistan, 1975. Contbr. to profl. jours. Served with USN, 1944-46. Recipient Hathaway award Hahnemann Med. Coll., Phila., 1953, surg. award, 1953. Fellow ACS (councillor, pres. elect N.J. chpt., pres. 1989, com. oper. room environment), Hellenic Surg. Soc. (hon.), N.J. Soc. Surgeons, South Eastern Surg. Soc., Hahnemann Surg. Soc.; mem. Assn. Program Dirs. Surgery (nat. steering com.), AGHIA Olga Soc., Deal Country Club (N.J.), Sea Bright Beach Club, Shrewsbury Sailing And Yacht Club. Greek Orthodox. Home: 3 Laurel Ln Rumson NJ 07760-1004 Office: 279 3D Ave Long Branch NJ 07740

ARY, T S, federal official; b. Eldorado, Ill., Mar. 30, 1925; s. McKinley and Emma (Busby) A.; m. Martha K. Metz, Dec. 23, 1945; 1 child, David Metz. Student, Evansville (Ind.), 1942-43; BS in Mineral Sci., Stanford U., 1947. Registered geologist, Calif. Football, basketball, baseball coach Jacksonville (Fla.) Naval Air Sta., 1946-47; asst. football coach jr. varsity Stanford (Calif.) U., 1947-49; shift boss, asst. supt. Anaconda Copper Co., Butte, Mont., 1951-53; mining engr. Union Carbide Corp. (U.S. Vanadium Co.), Rifle, Colo., 1953-55; asst. mgr. exploration Union Carbide Corp. (U.S. Vanadium Co.), Grand Juction, Colo., 1955-57, mgr. domestic exploration, 1957-62; land mgr. Union Carbide Nuclear Co., N.Y.C., 1962-67, v.p. mineral exploration mining and metals div., 1967-74; mgr. devel., v.p. mineral exploration Utah Internat. Inc., San Francisco, 1974-80; pres. mineral exploration, pres. resource div. Kerr-McGee Corp., Oklahoma City, 1980-87; dir. Bur. Mines, U.S. Dept. Interior, Washington, 1988—; counselor Nat. Critical Materials Coun., 1989—; bd. dirs. Mineral Info. Inst., Denver; mem. Dept. State Adv. Com. to Task Force Com. of UN Law of the Sea, Washington, 1966-77, Internat. Atomic Energy Program Adv. Com., Vienna, Austria, 1970-75, Nat. Strategic Materials and Minerals Program Adv. Com., Washington, 1984-88; com. chmn. Am. Mining Congress, Washington, 1960-88. Assoc. editor, mem. editorial bd. Jour. Resource Mgmt. and Tech., 1982-88; author over 100 published articles on mineral resources, pub. lands mgmt., pub. land law, pub. policy, internat. bus. mgmt., fly fishing techniques, sports, religion. Sec.-treas. Lakehurst Homeowners Assn., Oklahoma City, 1983-88; dir. Last Frontier Coun. Boy Scouts Am., Oklahoma City, 1980-86; trustee Westminister Presbyterian Ch., Oklahoma City, 1984-87; telethon chmn. Oklahoma Soc. for Crippled Children, 1985-86; pres. Lido Isle Homeowners Assn., Foster City, Calif., 1978-80, sec. 1976-78; dir. Internat. Student Svcs. Internat. YMCA, N.Y.C., 1973-75, Sch. Bd. Dist. 51, Grand Junction, Colo., 1959-65; committeeman We. Colo. Boy Scout Coun., Grand Junction, Colo., 1960-64; dir. Grand Mesa Ski Corp., Grand Junction, 1960-65, pres. 1963-64; regional dir. Nat. Ski Patrol Assn., Denver, 1952-65; dir. Colo. Expenditure Coun., Denver, 1961-65, South Rocky Mountain Ski Assn., Denver, 1955-65, Butte (Mont.) Ski Club, 1952-53; active Boy Scouts Am., 1935-65. Lt. (j.g.) USN, 1943-47, ETO. Recipient numerous athletic awards USN, AP, Nat. Coaches Assn., Nat. Athletic Scholastic Soc., 1938-48. Mem. Am. Inst. Profl. Geologists, Circum-Pacific Coun. Energy and Mineral Resources (program chmn. 1978-80), Am. Assn. Profl. Landmen, Wyo. Mining Assn., Colo. Mining Assn., N.W. Mining Assn., Calif. Mining Assn., N.Mex. Mining Assn., Ariz. Mining Assn., AIME (sec., treas., vice-chmn., chm. 1955-65), Rocky Mountain Mineral Law Found., Mining Club of N.Y., Commonwealth Club of San Francisco, Forum on Fgn. Affairs (San Francisco), Sigma Nu. Republican. Home: 3301 N Nottingham St Arlington VA 22207-1345 Office: Bur Mines 810 7th St NW MS 1000 Washington DC 20241-9999

ARZAC, ADRIANA MARIA, association executive; b. Mexico City, Mar. 26, 1947; came to U.S., 1970; d. Jose Pedro and Amalia A. (Palumbo) A.; 1 child, Adriana Ruiz de Velasco de Solorzano. MA in Psychology, U. Ibero Americana, Mexico City, 1969; DrPH, U. Tex., Houston, 1982. Sch. psychologist Hamilton Sch., Mexico City, 1968-70; child psychologist Childrens' Hosp., Houston, 1970-72, Austin (Tex.) State Hosp., 1972-74; dir. Instituto Nacional de Proteccion a la Niñez, Nuevo Leon, 1974-76; assoc. Transactional Analysis Assn., 1976-77; dir. communications S.W. Voter Registration Project, Tex., 1983; coord. Nat. Hispanic Voter Registration Conf. SVRP, Tex., 1983; psychotherapist, orgn. cons. Tex., 1983-85; coord. Employee Assistance Program for City Employees, San Antonio, 1985-87; exec. dir. Internat. Soc. Intercultural Edn. and Tng., Washington, 1989—; cons. Youth for Understanding, Washington, 1990—, AED, Washington, 1989—, Fulbright Exch. Program, Washington, 1984-90; mem. faculty Georgetown U., Washington, 1989—. Author: Comunidad Terapeutica Infantil, 1975. Advance person Dem. Party V.P. Campaign, 1984; campaign mgr. Dem. Party, Tex. Coun., San Antonio, 1985; main rep. UN, N.Y.C., 1991. Named Profl Woman of Yr. UN Conf. Women, Mexico, 1975. Mem. APHA, Am. Soc. Assn. Exec., Internat. Transactional Analysis Assn. (coord. N.Am. exam bd. cert. 1975—). Home: 5270 Duke St Apt 215 Alexandria VA 22304-2945 Office: Internat Soc Intercultural Edn and Tng 733 15th St NW Ste 900 Washington DC 20005-2112

ASANUMA, HIROSHI, physician, educator; b. Kobe, Japan, Aug. 17, 1926; s. Kisaburo and Yukiko (Takahashi) A.; m. Reiko Shimazu, Dec. 15, 1953; children—Chisato, Mari. M.D., Keio U., Tokyo, 1952; D.M.S., Kobe Med. Coll., 1959. Instr., Kobe Med. Coll., 1953-59; asst. prof. Osaka City U., Japan, 1959-65; guest investigator Rockefeller Inst., N.Y.C., 1961-63; assoc. prof. N.Y. Med. Coll., N.Y.C., 1965-71, prof., 1971-72; prof. Rockefeller U., N.Y.C., 1972—. Contbr. articles to profl. jours. and books. Mem. Am. Physiol. Soc., Soc. for Neurosci., Harvey Soc., Japanese Physiol. Soc. Home: 505 E 79th St New York NY 10021-0709 Office: Rockefeller U Dept of Motorphysiology 1230 York Ave New York NY 10021-6341

ASCALON, DAVID, artist; b. Tel Aviv, Mar. 8, 1945; came to U.S., 1957; s. Maurice and Ziporah (Kartujinski) A.; m. Ronit Mayrowitz, Mar. 24, 1968; children: Eric, Bradley, Josh. Student, U. Calif. San Fernando Valley, 1963-65; BS in Architecture, Pratt Inst., 1974; postgrad., Bernard Baruch Coll., 1973-74. Designer Daniel Schwartzmann/Architect, N.Y.C., 1965-66; archtl. designer Arie El-Hannani/Architects, Tel Aviv, 1967-68, William A. Hall/Architects, N.Y.C., 1969-70; owner Ascalon Jewelry Co., N.Y.C., 1971-77; product mgr. Fantasia Jewelry Co., Phila., 1977-80; owner, pres. Ascalon Art Studios, Berlin, N.J., 1981—; lectr., cons. in field. Designer synagogues, holocaust meml. sculptures, stained glass windows, tapestries, ceremonial art objects, other works. Trustee Temple Beth Sholom, Haddon Heights, N.J., 1986—. Mem. Am. Soc. Interior Designers (cert.), Interfaith Forum Religion Art Architecture (merit award 1982, 87), Nat. Coun. Art in Jewish Life (4 merit awards 1983), Accredited Artists Union Am. Hebrew Congregations, B'nai B'rith. Democrat. Office: Ascalon Art Studios 115 Atlantic Ave Berlin NJ 08009-9300

ASCHNER, MICHAEL, pharmacology and toxicology educator; b. Jerusalem, Nov. 11, 1955; came to U.S., 1979; s. Marian and Maja (Bramer) A.; m. Judy L. Arbit, Aug. 5, 1979; children: Yael, Eitan, Nadav, Amir. BS, U. Rochester, 1980, MS in Anatomy, 1983, PhD in Neurobiology and Anatomy, 1985. Postdoctoral fellow U. Rochester (N.Y.), 1985-87; asst. prof. pharmacology and toxicology Albany (N.Y.) Med. Coll., 1988—. Reviewer Jour. Neurochemistry, Brain Rsch.; contbr. articles to profl. jours. Recipient New Rsch. Svc. award NIH, 1985-87, 1st award, 1989-94, rsch. award PHS, 1987, EPA Rsch. award, 1992—. Mem. Internat. Neurotoxicology Assn., Teratology Soc., Soc. Toxicology, AAAS, N.Y. Acad. Scis. Jewish. Office: Albany Med Coll 47 New Scotland Ave Albany NY 12208-3412

ASCHOFF, LORRAINE MARIE, computer information scientist; b. N.Y.C., Feb. 14, 1950; d. Edward William and Marie Louise (Marshall) A.; m. John Morgan Roquemore III, Feb. 23, 1973 (div. June 1976). BA in Art History, U. Fla., 1971; MBA in Fin., NYU, 1984, advanced profl. cert. in computer applications and info. systems, 1988. Sales rep. VIP Fabrics, N.Y.C., 1978-81; asst. to v.p. mktg. RAM Data, N.Y.C., 1981-82; sales agt. Equitable Life Assurance Soc., N.Y.C., 1982; programmer/analyst Drexel

Burnham Lambert, N.Y.C., 1984-86, sr. programmer/analyst, 1986-88, project leader, 1988-89, project mgr., asst. v.p., 1989-90; project mgr. retail banking svcs. application architecture Chem. Banking Corp. (formerly Mfrs. Hanover Trust), N.Y.C., 1990-91, officer, 1991—. Clin. assoc. Suicide and Crisis Prevention Ctr., Gainesville, Fla., 1972. Mem. Mensa, L.I. Alumni Assn., Phi Beta Kappa (sec. 1985-87, pres. 1987—), Alpha Lambda Delta. Democrat. Home: Apt A-8 64-85 Saunders St Rego Park NY 11374 Office: Chem Banking Corp 130 John St New York NY 10038

ASFOUR, WILDA, high school counselor; b. Bklyn., Dec. 21, 1931; d. Michael Elias and Alma (Hajjar) A. BA, Mount St. Vincent, 1962; MEd, Boston Coll., 1969; postgrad., Creighton Coll., 1973, U. Maine, 1982-83. 1st grade tchr. St. Gabriel Sch., Bronx, N.Y., 1954-57; 3rd grade tchr. SS Peter and Paul Sch., Bronx, 1957-61, 5th grade tchr., 1961-64; 6th grade tchr. St. John the Bapt., Bklyn., 1964-67; 7th and 8th grade tchr. St. Mary Sch., Wappingers Falls, N.Y., 1967-69; counselor, dir. York (Pa.) Cath. High Sch., 1969-78; admissions counselor Coll. of Mt. St. Vincent, Bronx, 1978-79; counselor St. Francis Prep, Fresh Meadows, N.Y., 1979—; cons. in field; developer primary drug prevention program York Cath. High Sch., 1969-78; developer parenting program St. Francis Prep High Sch., 1981—. Mem. AACD, Am. Sch. Counselors Assn., Assn. for Psychol. Type. Democrat. Roman Catholic. Office: St Francis Prep 6100 Francis Lewis Blvd Flushing NY 11365-2893

ASH, BARBARA LEE, education and human services educator; b. Boston, Sept. 2, 1940; d. Charles Edward and Helen Barbara (Elwell) Fox; m. Robert Irvin Ash, July 31, 1971;. AS, Norwich U., 1960; BS, Boston U., 1962, MEd, 1966, EdD, 1982. Cert. bus. tchr., Mass. Tchr. Chatham (Mass.) Pub. Schs., 1962-63, Braintree (Mass.) Pub. Schs., 1963-66; asst. prof. Simmons Coll., Boston, 1966-73; prof., dept. chair Bunker Hill Community Coll., Charlestown, Mass., 1973-77; prof. edn. and human svcs., dir. bus. edn. Suffolk U., Boston, 1977—; mem. adv. bd. Aquinas Coll., Newton, Mass., 1985—, Bunker Hill C.C., 1985—, LaSell Coll., Newton, 1985—, Mt. Ida Coll., 1985—; disting. lectr. Rider Coll., N.J., 1992. Contbr. articles to profl. jours. Recipient Suffolk U. Evening div. assoc. Outstanding Faculty Mem. award, 1991. Mem. Mass. Bus. Educators Assn. (pres. 1992, Tchr. of Yr. award 1990), New Eng. Bus. Educators Assn. (pres. 1988), Phi Delta Kappa, Delta Pi Epsilon (pres. 1966). Office: Suffolk U Beacon Hill Boston MA 02114

ASH, ERIN MCNERNEY, educator, case worker; b. Bradford, Pa., Jan. 21, 1953; d. Edward Augustine and Alice Frances (Hane) McNerney; m. Emil John Ash, June 11, 1976; children: Emilia Anne, Anna Elizabeth, Aaron Edward. BA, St. Bonaventure U., 1974, MS in edn., 1991. Owner, operator Family Tree Toys, Olean, N.Y., 1983-87; educator, program developer Parent Edn. Program, Inc., Olean, N.Y., 1988-91; caseworker dept. social svcs. Cattaragus County, Olean, N.Y., 1989—; cons. C-H Healthcare Ltd., Olean, 1987; part-time faculty Jamestown Community Coll., Olean, 1990; evaluator Parent Edn. Program, Inc., 1991; bd. dirs. Olean Child Devel. Ctr. Group facilitator Effective Parenting Info. for Children, Olean, 1988-90. Mem. APA (affiliate), Internat. Assn. Marriage and Family Counselors, Nat. Career Devel. Assn., Am. Assn. Counseling & Devel., Am. Mental Health Counselors Assn., N.Y. Assn. Edn. Young Children (exec. com. 1988-89), Assn. for Measurement and Devel. in Counseling and Devel., Cattaragus Allegany Assn. for Edn. of Young Children (v.p. 1989-90). Republican. Roman Catholic. Home: 121 S Barry St Olean NY 14760-3626 Office: Cattaragus County Dept Social Svcs 1707 Lincoln Ave Olean NY 14760-1121

ASH, HIRAM NEWTON, graphic designer; b. Paterson, N.J., Dec. 9, 1934; s. Newton Britain Todd and Ellen Sproule (Bowman) A.; m. Marilyn Ruth Robinson, June 29, 1957 (div. 1972); children: Erica Robinson, Jennifer Hamilton; m. Elinor Carolyn Reynolds, June 29, 1975 (div. 1981); m. Elizabeth Ruth Horton, Apr. 24, 1981 (div. 1992). Student, Hobart Coll., 1952-56, Columbia U., 1956-58; BFA, Yale U., 1960. Graphic designer Styling div. GM Tech. Ctr., Warren, Mich., 1959; art dir. N.W. Ayer & Sons, Phila., 1960-61; graphic designer George Nelson & Co., N.Y.C., 1961-62; ptnr. Ash/Reller Assocs., N.Y.C., 1962-63; pres. Hiram Ash, Inc., N.Y.C., 1963-70; prin. Hiram Ash, Colebrook, Conn., 1970—; asst. in instrn. Sch. Art and Arch., Yale U., New Haven, 1959-60; adj. instr. graphic design Cooper Union, N.Y.C., 1965-67; designer TriVers Exhbn. Systems, 1964; designer numerous album covers Caedmon Records, N.Y.C., 1960s; designer theatre posters Rugoff Theatres, N.Y.C., 1960s; designer set and program graphics Pub. Broadcast Lab., N.Y.C., 1966-67; designer signature trademark and graphics implementation Am. Shakespeare Theatre, Stratford, Conn., 1980; mktg. and product devel. cons. Indian jewelry Zuni Community Action Program, Zuni Pueblo, N.Mex., 1967-68. Designer numerous books; work presented in Graphis Anns., Indsl. Design, Trademarks & Symbols of the World, Trade Marks U.S.A. Recipient Design and Printing for Commerce and 50 Books of Yr. awards Am. Inst. Graphic Arts, N.J. Art Dirs. Club awards. Mem. Colebrook Hist. Soc. (pres. 1987-90, v.p. 1990—), Colebrook Land Conservancy, Inc. (trustee 1991—), Milbrook Music Assembly, Sandanona Harehounds, Yale Club (N.Y.C.). Republican. Episcopalian. Home and Office: Phelps Corners Colebrook CT 06021

ASH, PAUL B., public school administrator; b. Boston, Mar. 11, 1950; s. Norman and Dorothy (Cooperman) A.; m. Beverly Stone, Nov. 22, 1973; 1 child, Dawn. BS, Worcester Polytech Inst., 1971; MAT, U. Mass., 1972; CAS, Harvard Grad. Sch. Edn., 1977; PhD, Boston Coll., 1982. Cert. supt., prin., tchr. Tchr. sci. Dover (Mass.)-Sherborn High Sch., 1972-79; dir. personnel Wellesley (Mass.) Pub. Schs., 1979-86, asst. supt., 1986—. Mem. sch. com. Newton (Mass.) Sch., 1976-78. Jewish. Home: 48 Greenwood St Newton MA 02159

ASHAR, DEV, architect, consultant; b. Bombay, India, Nov. 18, 1942; came to U.S., 1969; s. Girdharlal and Diwaliben (Chhichhia) A.; m. Nalini Udeshi, Oct. 1, 1973; 1 child, Anand. Diploma in architecture, J.J. Sch. of Architecture, Bombay, 1966; BS in Architecture, U. Nebr., 1970; postgrad., Union Coll., 1976. Architect Builders Assocs., Bombay, 1965-68, Indian Navy, Bombay, 1968-69; chief estimator Allstate Drywall Systems, Briarcliff, N.Y., 1971-73; project mgr. T.J. McGlone & Co., Rahway, N.J., 1973-75, Germinario & Sons, Palisades Park, N.J., 1975-77; pres. Dev Anand Inc., Linden, N.J., 1986—; owner, operator Interior Estimating Svc., Linden, N.J., 1977—; pres. Sona Constrn., Linden, N.J., 1991—. Mem. Indian Inst. Architects (assoc.), Am. Soc. Profl. Estimators (assoc.), Am. Soc. Plastic Engrs. Home: 421 Livingston Rd Linden NJ 07036 Office: Dev Anand Inc 1526 E Elizabeth Ave Linden NJ 07036

ASHBY, ROGER ARTHUR, pulp and paper products company executive; b. Marieville, P.Q., Can., Nov. 2, 1940; s. Emmett Ashby and Aurore Ledoux; m. Marguerite Kelly, Feb. 12, 1966; children: Eric, Alexandre. BSc in Commerce, U. Montreal, Can., 1963; cert. mgmt. acctg., 1966. Registered indsl. and cost acct.; cert. gen. acct.; cert. mgmt. acct.; fellow cert. gen. acct. Acct., then dir. of adminstrn. Kimberly-Clark of Can., 1963-69; dir. adminstrv. svcs., then compt. Sopalin, S.A. subs. Kimberly-Clark Corp., Paris, 1969-71, dir. fin., 1971-72, v.p., mng. dir., bd. dirs., 1972-76; pres., chief exec. officer Spruce Falls Power & Paper Co. Ltd. subs. Kimberly-Clark Corp., Kapuskasing, Ont., Can., 1976-78; exec. v.p., chief oper. officer, bd. dirs. Rolland Inc., 1978-80; exec. v.p. then pres. Domtar, Inc. Pulp & Paper, Montreal, 1980-90; pres., chief exec. officer Rolland Inc., Montreal, 1990—; bd. dirs. Sintra Inc., Quebec Forest Industries Assn., Forest Engrng. Rsch. Inst. Can., Can. Pulp and Paper Assn., Rolland Inc. Mem. St. James Club, Mont Bruno Country Club. Office: Rolland Inc Ste 1400, 2000 Ave McGill College, Montreal, PQ Canada H3A 3H3

ASHDOWN, MARIE MATRANGA (MRS. CECIL SPANTON ASHDOWN, JR.), writer, lecturer; b. Mobile, Ala.; d. Dominic and Ave (Mallon) Matranga; m. Cecil Spanton Ashdown Jr., Feb. 8, 1958; children: Cecil Spanton III, Charles Coster; children by previous marriage: John Stephen Gartman, Vivian Marie Gartman. Student, Maryville Coll. Sacred Heart; student, Springhill Coll. Feature artist, women's program dir. daily program Sta. WALA, WALA-TV, Mobile, 1953-58; v.p., dir. Met. Opera Guild, N.Y.C., 1970-78, opera instr. in-svc. program, 1970-80; opera instr. in-svc. program Marymount Coll., N.Y.C., 1979-85; exec. dir. Musicians Emergency Fund, Inc., N.Y.C., 1985—; cons. No. Ill. U. Coll. of Visual and Performing Arts, 1985—; lectr. in field. Author: Opera Collectables, 1979, contbr. articles to profl. jours. Recipient Extraordinary Service award March of Dimes, 1958, Medal of Appreciation award Harvard Bus. Sch. Club N.Y.C., 1974, Cert. Appreciation, Kiwanis Internat., 1975, Arts Excellence award N.J. State Opera, 1986. Mem. Successful Meetings Directory, Nat. Inst. Social Scis., Com. for U.S.-China Relations. Home: 25 Sutton Pl S Apt 16K New York NY 10022-2441 Office: Musicians Emergency Fund Inc 820 2d Ave Ste 203 New York NY 10017

ASHE, ARTHUR ROBERT, JR., tennis player, sports consultant; b. Richmond, Va., July 10, 1943; s. Arthur Robert Sr. and Mattie C. (Cunningham) A.; m. Jeanne-Marie Moutoussamy, Feb. 20, 1977; 1 child, Camera Elizabeth. BS in Bus. Adminstrn., UCLA, 1966; LHD (hon.), Princeton U., Dartmouth U., Le Moyne U., Va. Union U., Bryant Coll., Trinity U., Hartford, Conn. Profl. tennis player, 1969-79; mem. U.S. Davis Cup Team, capt., 1981; dir. tennis Doral Country Club, Miami, Fla.; bd. dirs. Aetna Life and Casualty; chmn. adv. staff Head Sports USA; v.p. internat. mktg. LE COQ Sportif USA; sports cons., 1979—. Author: (with Frank DeFord) Portrait in Motion, 1973, (with Neil Amdur) Off the Court, 1981, A Hard Road To Glory, (3 vols) 1988; creator video (with Stan Smith and Vic Braden) Tennis Our Way, 1986. Campaign chmn. Am. Heart Assn., Dallas, 1981-82. Served to 1st lt. U.S. Army, 1967-69. Named Player of Yr. Assn. Tennis Profls., 1975; winner two U.S. Intercollegiate championships during coll.; winner U.S. Men's Hard Court championship, 1963; U.S. Men's Clay Ct., 1967, U.S. Amateur title, 1968, U.S. Open championship, 1968, Australian Open, 1970, French Open Doubles, 1971, Wimbledon Singles, 1975, World Championship Tennis Singles, 1975, Australian Open Doubles, 1970, 77. Mem. U.S. Tennis Assn., Kappa Alpha Psi, Sigma Pi Phi. Office: care Pro Serve 888 17th St NW Washington DC 20006-3939

ASHE, BERNARD FLEMMING, lawyer; b. Balt., Mar. 8, 1936; s. Victor Joseph Ashe and Frances Cecelia (Johnson) Flemming; m. Grace Nannette Pegram, Mar. 23, 1963; children: Walter Joseph, David Bernard. BA, Howard U., 1956, JD, 1961. Bar: Va. 1961, D.C. 1963, Mich. 1964, N.Y. 1971. Tchr. Balt. Pub. Schs., 1956-58; atty. NLRB, Washington, 1961-63; asst. gen. counsel Internat. Union United Auto Workers, Detroit, 1963-71; gen. counsel N.Y. State United Tchrs., Albany, 1971—; mem. adj. faculty Cornell Sch. Indsl. and Labor Rels., Albany div., 1981, 87. Bd. dirs. Urban League Albany, 1979-85, 1st v.p., 1981-85; trustee N.Y. Lawyers Fund for Client Protection, 1981—. Fellow Am. Bar Found. (life); mem. ABA (chmn. sect. labor and employment law sect. 1982-83, consortium on legal svcs. and the pub. 1979-84, commn. on pub. understanding of law 1987—, Ho. of Dels. 1985—, nominating com. 1988-91, bd. govs. 1991-94), Nat. Bar Assn., Am. Arbitration Assn. (bd. dir. 1982—, Whitney North Seymour Sr. medal 1989), Assn. of Bar of City of N.Y., N.Y. State Bar Assn., Nat. Lawyers Club, Albany County Bar Assn. Contbr. articles on labor and constl. law to profl. jours. Office: NY State United Tchrs 159 Wolf Rd Box 15-5008 Albany NY 12212

ASHE, DOUGLAS FULTON, construction executive; b. Boston, Mar. 25, 1953; s. Charles Fulton and Arlene Frances (Carroll) A.; m. Cheryl Ann Albano, June 1976 (div. 1979); m. Susan Theresa Boone, Apr. 12, 1980. Student, Newton (Mass.) Jr. Coll., 1972-74, Holliston (Mass.) Jr. Coll., 1978. Lic. constrn. supr., Mass., EMT, Mass. Founder, pres. H-A Constrn., Millville, Mass., 1974—. Bd. dirs. Lincoln Hill Camp, Foxboro, Mass., 1976-78; vol. patrolman Natick (Mass.) Aux. Police, 1976-81; chmn. Millville Housing Authority, 1987—; candidate for Millville Bd. Selectman, 1991; trustee Lincoln Hill Charitable Trust, Foxboro, 1988—. Recipient 50 Mem. Recruiter award U.S. Jaycees, 1981. Mem. Mass. Jaycees (dist. dir. 1979-80, regional dir. 1980-81, state v.p. 1981-82, state program mgr. 1991—, Dist. Dir. of Yr. 1980, Regional Dir. of Yr. 1981, State V.P. of yr. 1982, State Program Mgr. of Qtr. 1991), R.I. Jaycees (state v.p. 1981-83), Riverside (Mass.) Jaycees, Millville Lions (pres. 1989-90, Lion of Yr. 1989, 91, 100% Presdl. award 1990, Number One Club award 1990). Roman Catholic. Home and Office: H-A Constrn 12 Preston St Millville MA 01529-0516

ASHEN, PHILIP, chemist; b. Bklyn., Nov. 5, 1915; s. Joel and Fannie (Hirt) A. BA in Chemistry, Bklyn. Coll., 1936; MBA, NYU, 1957, PHD, 1968. Cert. profl. chemist. Chief chemist Alco Mfg. Corp., Bklyn., 1936-48; mgr. chem. div. M.W. Hardy & Co., Inc., N.Y.C., 1948-63, v.p., 1963-77, pres., chief exec. officer, 1977—; lectr. grad. sch. NYU, N.Y.C., 1954-56; lectr. chem. warfare U.S. Citizens Def. Corps., 1940-45, gas reconnaissance officer, 1940-45; cons. in field, 1957—. Author: Foreign Chemical Companies Engaged in International Trade, 1957, The American Selling Price Method of Valuation in U.S. Chemical Imports, 1969. Bd. dirs. Bklyn. Coll. Alumni Assn., Bklyn., 1969-86. Recipient citation, U.S. Treasury Dept., 1944, Nat. War Fund Commn., 1945, Civilian Def. Vol. Office, 1945, War Finance Com. U.S. Treasury Dept., 1945, award ARC, 1945, Founders Day award NYU, 1969, Roosevelt medal Theodore Roosevelt Assn.. Fellow Am. Inst. Chemists (chmn. profl. accreditation com. N.Y. chpt. 1964-68, treas. N.Y. chpt. 1970-76, councillor N.Y. chpt. 1964-70), AAAS; mem. SACI, Am. Chem. Soc., N.Y. Acad. Sci., Chemistry Alumni Soc.-Bklyn. Coll. (pres. 1966—), Chemists Club (resident). Home: 2315 Avenue I Brooklyn NY 11210-2825 Office: M W Hardy & Co Inc 111 Broadway New York NY 10006-1901

ASHER, BERNARD WOLFF, surgeon; b. Hamburg, Germany, Apr. 27, 1936; came to U.S., 1937; s. Frederick and Herta (Bechof) A.; m. Lilian L. Orba, Aug. 28, 1967; children: Robert, Elizabeth, Katherine. AB, Brown U., Providence, R.I., 1958; MD, SUNY, 1963. Diplomat Am. Bd. Surgery, 1969; recertified 1980. Intern New England Ctr. Hosp., Boston, 1963-64; surgical resident Boston City Hosp., 1964-66; chief surgical resident Bronx Lebanon Hosp. Ctr., N.Y.C., 1966-69; gen. surgeon Cuba (N.Y.) Meml. Hosp., 1969-70; gen. surgeon, chief of surgery Jones Meml. Hosp., Willsville, N.Y., 1970-71; gen. surgeon St. James Hosp., Hornell, N.Y., 1971-72, Genesee Meml. Jerome Hosp., Batavia, N.Y., 1972—. Bd. mem. Batavia (N.Y.) YMCA, 1976-80, Genesee County Bd. Health, Batavia, N.Y., 1984—; city councilman, Batavia, N.Y., 1978-82. Fellow ACS, Am. Coll. Gastroenterology; mem. Am. Soc. Gastrointestinal Endoscopy, Flying Physicians Assn., Aircraft Owners and Pilots Assn. Office: 190 Washington Ave Batavia NY 14020

ASHER, LILA OLIVER, artist; b. Phila., Nov. 15, 1921; d. Benjamin O. and Mollie (Finkelstein) Oliver; m. Sydney S. Asher, Jr., May 5, 1946 (dec.); children: Bonnie Asher-Doar, Warren Oliver; m. Kenneth P. Crawford. Student, Fleischer Art Meml., 1933-38, Frank B. A. Linton, 1938-42; cert., Phila. Coll. Art (now U. of Arts), 1943. Faculty Wilson Tchrs. Coll., Washington, 1953-54; instr. art dept. Howard U., 1947-51, lectr., 1961-64, asst. prof., 1964-66, assoc. prof., 1966-71, prof., 1971—. Artist in sculpture, graphics, watercolor, oil including murals, one-woman shows include Barnett-Aden Gallery, Washington, 1951, William C. Blood Gallery, Phila., 1955, Arts Club, Washington, 1957, Potters' House, Washington, 1963, Burr Galleries, N.Y.C., 1963, Gallery 222, El Paso, Tex., 1965, Thomson Gallery, N.Y.C., 968, B'nai B'rith Nat. Hdqrs. Gallery, 1969, U. Va., Charlottesville, 1970, Green-Field Gallery, El Paso, 1972, Northwestern Mich. Coll., 1972, Am. Club, Tokyo, 1973, Govt. Coll. Arts and Crafts, Madras, India, 1974, (retrospective) Franz Bader, 1972, Fisk U., 1974, Am. Cultural Ctr., Bombay, India, 1975, Am. U. Ctr., Calcutta, India, 1975, USIS, Pakistan, 1975, Turkey, 1976, Gallery Kormendy, Alexandria, Va., 1978, Northeastern U., Boston, 1980, Nat. Mus. History, Taiwan, 1982, KastrupgÅrdsamlingen Kunst Mus., Denmark, 1982, Gallaudet U., Washington, 1985, Mickelson Gallery, Washington, 1986, UCLA, 1986, U. Va., Charlottesville, 1988, Howard U., Washington, 1981, 91, Cosmos Club, 1992, Rockville Md. Art Mansion, 1992; exhibited in group shows World's Fair, N.Y.C., 1965, Pa. Acad. Fine Arts, Smithsonian Instn., Washington, 1950, 54-58, 60-63, Libr. of Congress, 1954, Corcoran Gallery Art, Washington, 1949, 51, 52, 55, 57-59, Howard U., 1949—, George Washington U., 1968, Pan-Am. Union, Woodmere Gallery, 1949-50, Phila. Print Club, Washington Printmaker's Soc., Balt. Mus. Art, 1959, Hood Coll., U. Va., Maine, 1959, Riverside Mus., N.Y.C., 1959, Rochester, (N.Y.) Meml. Art Gallery, 1954, Franz Bader Gallery, Washington, 1955, 71, Graphic Arts Soc., N.Y.C., 1959, Va. Intermont Coll., Nat. Collection Fine Arts, Washington Water Color Assn., Arts Club Washington, Soc. Washington Artists Ann., 1971, 72, Soc. Washington Printmakers, Dimock Gallery, George Washington U., numerous others; retrospective shows Franz Bader Gallery, Washington, 1972, Fisk U., Nashville, 1974, Howard U., 1978, 91, Northeastern U., Boston, 1980, Howard U., 1991; represented in permanent collections Howard U., Georgetown U., Corcoran Gallery, U. Va., U. Tex., Sweetbriar (Va.) Coll., Superior Ct. D.C., B'nai B'rith Washington, City of Wolfsburg, Germany, U.S. Mediation and Conciliation Service Bur., Nat. Ctr. for Research in Edn. Disadvantaged, Jerusalem, Am. Embassy, Tel Aviv, Montgomery County (Md.) Contemporary Print Collection, Nat. Mus. History, Taipei, Nat. Mus. Am. Art, Nat. Mus. of Women in the Arts, also pvt. collections; guest artist U. Tex. print program, 1972. Recipient prize for print Corcoran Gallery Art 10th Area Exhbn., 1956; U. Va. award, 1963, 70; guest artist City of Wolfsburg, 1968, 71, 75, 80; honoree Nat. Mus. Am. Art, 1981; Bd. edn. scholar Phila. Coll. Art, 1943. Mem. Soc. Washington Artists (past pres.), Soc. Washington Printmakers (past treas. and rec. sec.), Washington Water Color Club, Artist's Equity (past treas.), Print Consortium, Md. Printmakers, Cosmos Club. Address: 4100 Thornapple St Chevy Chase MD 20815

ASHER, RENEE, music publishing executive; b. Pitts., June 1, 1964; d. Gerald Simon and Dorothy Louise (Magnes) Gudukas. BA in Journalism and Communications, Point Pk. Coll., 1988. Lic. radio broadcast operator. Asst. mgr. E.T. Promotions, Pitts., 1983-87; dir. pub. rels. and advt. dir. Cape Cod Melody Tent, Hyannis, Mass., 1988-89; prin. Astron Music Pub., Pitts., 1989—. Song writer, project designer Children Care, 1990; author poems. News and prodn. vol. Sta. WDUQ-Nat. Pub. Radio, Pitts., 1987. Golden Key scholar Point Pk. Coll., Pitts., 1986. Mem. The Reggae Soc. Office: Astron Music Pub PO Box 22174 Pittsburgh PA 15222-0174

ASHGRIZ, NASSER, mechanical and aerospace engineer, educator; b. Tehran, Iran, June 21, 1957; came to U.S., 1975; s. R. Ashgriz and Kobra Khosrowshahi. BS, Carnegie Mellon U., 1979, MS in Mech. Engring., 1981, PhD, 1984. Asst. prof. SUNY, Buffalo, 1984-90, assoc. prof., 1990—; pres. Gen. Thermal Research, Pitts., 1984—; vis. prof. Tehran U., Iran, 1991. Inventor, patentee monodispersed spray generaton, 1984. NSF Rsch. Initiation grantee, 1990. Mem. AIAA (chmn. 1985—), Am. Soc. Mech. Engrs, Soc. Automotive Engring. (Ralph Teetor award), Am. Phys. Soc. (1988 Best Picture award), Combustion Inst., Sigma Xi. Home: 314 Lasalle Ave Buffalo NY 14215-1010 Office: SUNY Dept Mech Engring and Aerospace Buffalo NY 14260

ASHIZAWA, THEODORE, music educator; b. San Francisco, Dec. 6, 1934; s. Isamu Hidenori and Hideko Ashizawa; m. Martha M. Takeda, June, 1960 (div. Jan. 1981); m. Janis Diane De Palma, Mar. 21, 1987; children: Christopher, Timothy, Kristin, Andrew. BA, San Jose (Calif.) State U., 1956, MA in Music, 1960; Diploma in Choral Conducting, Juilliard Sch. of Music, 1965; DMA, U. Wash., 1976. Tchr. music Santa Clara (Calif.) County Schs., 1960-62; choral dir. Portland (Oreg.) Pub. Schs., 1965-69; prof. Genesee Community Coll., Batavia, N.Y., 1971—. ch. dir. in field. Mem. Batavia Players, 1987; bd. dirs. Guitar Soc. Rochester, N.Y., 1989; condr. Genesee Chorale, 1971-91, Ars Nova Singers. With U.S. Army, 1957-59, Korea. Recipient SUNY Chancellor's award for excellence in teaching, 1976. Mem. NEA. Home: 51 Ellicott Ave Batavia NY 14020-2030 Office: Genesee Community Coll 1 College Rd Batavia NY 14020-9703

ASHKENAZI, ELLIOTT URIEL, historian, lawyer; b. N.Y.C., July 1, 1941; s. Joshua and Katherine Millie (Doubchon) A.; m. Sandra Isaacs, Aug. 22, 1976; children: Erica Tema, Jennifer Kayle. Student, London Sch. Econs., 1961-62; BA, U. Pa., 1962; JD, Harvard U., 1965; PhD, George Washington U., 1983. Bar: N.Y. 1966. Assoc. Burlingham, Underwood & Lord, N.Y.C., 1966-69; atty. Ctr. for Automobile Safety, Washington, 1970-73; pvt. practice Washington, 1974-83, historian, 1984—; cons. documentary history project U.S. Supreme Ct., Washington, 1983-84, Bicentennial Commn., Georgetown U., Washington, 1986-88; lectr. in history George Mason U., 1991. Author: The Business of Jews in Louisiana 1840-75, 1988; contbr. articles to hist. jours. Trustee St. John's Child Devel. Ctr., Washington, 1983-89; dir. Kesher Israel Congregation, Washington, 1983-86. Mem. Am. Hist. Assn., Orgn. Am. Historians, Bus. History Conf., Am. Jewish Hist. Soc., So. Hist. Assn., George Washington U. Club, Pisces Club. Democrat. Home and Office: 5059 Sedgewick St NW Washington DC 20016-1939

ASHKINAZY, LARRY ROBERT, dentist; b. N.Y.C., Feb. 12, 1952; s. Philip and Kate (Scherer) A. BS, Bklyn. Coll., 1973; DDS, NYU, 1976. Cert. Nat. Bd. Dental Examiners. Gen. dental practice residency Cabrini Health Care Ctr., 1977; pvt. practice dentistry N.Y.C., 1977—; assoc. attending dentist Cabrini Healthcare Ctr., 1984—, assoc. attending in implantology, 1983-86, postgrad. instr. Inst. for Grad. Dentists, 1981-82; guest lectr. various pub. and profl. edn. instns.; health and sci. corr. Sta. WWOR-TV. Author: Dentistry, 1982; contbr. articles to profl. jours.; mem. editorial bd. Internat. Congress Oral Implantologists newsletter, 1982; various radio and TV appearances; patentee in field; trademarks Bionic Tooth, Tooth Plant. Health care providor Drs. with a Heart, N.Y.C., 1987; health care spokesman Jr. League, N.Y.C., 1978, Community Fair, N.Y.C., 1983. Recipient Cert. of Appreciation Greater N.Y. Dental Meeting, 1981, 87, Cert. of Appreciation NYU Dental Ctr., 1981. Fellow Acad. Gen. Dentistry, Acad. Dentistry Internat., Acad. Implants and Transplants, Am. Endodontic Soc., Internat. Congress Oral Implantologists; mem. Am. Dental Assn. (cert. appreciation 1980), Am. Acad. Oral Medicine, Internat. Analgesia Soc. , 1st Dist. Dental Soc. (oral health clinician 1978, speakers bur. subcom.chmn. 1984pub. and profl. relations com. 1982), Am. Prosthodontic Soc., Sociedad Venezolana de Implantodontologos, Am. Acad. Implant Dentistry (chmn. sci. exhibit com., 1984, edn. com. 1984, library com. 1984, membership com. 1983, N.Y. chmn. 1983 ann. meeting and world assembly. Dentistry Alumni, Alpha Omega. Club: Greater N.Y. Implant Study (pres. 1981—). Home and Office: 200 Central Park S New York NY 10019-1415

ASHLEY, MERRILL, ballerina; b. St. Paul; m. Kibbe Fitzpatrick. Student, Sch. Am. Ballet. Joined N.Y.C. Ballet, 1967, prin. dancer, 1977—. Created prin. roles in Balanchine's Ballo della Regina and Ballade, Jerome Robbins' Four Chambers Works, Robbins'/Tharp's Brahms/Handel, Peter Martins' Barber Violin Concerto, Fearful Symmetries; TV appearances include roles in Emeralds, Four Temperaments, Divertimento #15, Bournonville Divertissements, Midsummer Night's Dream and Barber Violin Concerto for Dance in America (PBS); also appeared on PBS Gala of Stars, 1980, 82, 84; author: Dancing for Balanchine, 1984. Recipient Dance Mag. award, 1987. Office: care NYC Ballet Inc Lincoln Center Pla New York NY 10023

ASHMEN, BARRY DENNIS, business educator; b. Trenton, N.J., Sept. 8, 1947; s. Gerald H. and Dorothy (Krupecki) A.; m. Sally Ann Goodwin, Sept. 24, 1971. BS in Commerce, Rider Coll., 1969, MA in Edn., 1970; EdD, Temple U., 1981. Gen. mgr. Jerry Ashmen Motors, Trenton, 1965-77; asst. prof. Rider Coll., Lawrenceville, N.J., 1978-82; prof. Bucks County Community Coll., Newtown, Pa., 1982—; adj. instr. Rider Coll., Lawrenceville, 1971-78, adj. asst. prof., 1983—; test reviewer Ednl. Testing Svc.-DANTES Exam., Princeton, N.J., 1991; lectr. Atlantic City (N.J.) Hotel Sales Mktg. Assn., 1983, NWL Industries, Bordenton, N.J., 1981, Bucks County (Pa.) Courier Times, 1988, Phila. Fed. Credit Union, 1989. Coauthor: DECA National Handbook, 1981; contbr. articles to profl. jours.; editorial reviewer numerous coll. bus. textbooks. Bd. dirs. Vis. Nurse Assn., Inc., Trenton, 1991—. Staff sgt. N.J. Nat. Guard, 1968-74. Named one of Outstanding Young Men of Am., U.S. Jaycees, 1977, 78. Mem. Omicron Delta Kappa, Alpha Epsilon Zeta. Home: 13 Taylor Way Washington Crossing PA 18977 Office: Bucks County Community Coll Swamp Rd Newtown PA 18940

ASHTON, BETSY FINLEY, broadcast journalist, author, lecturer; b. Wilkes-Barre, Pa., May 13, 1944; d. Charles Leonard Hancock Jones and Margaretta Betty (Hart) Jones Layton; m. Arthur Benner Ashton, Nov. 5, 1966 (div. 1972); m. Robert Clarke Freed, May 18, 1974 (div. 1981); m. Jacob B. Underhill III, Oct. 17, 1987. BA, Am. U., 1966, postgrad. in fine arts, 1969-71; student in painting, Corcoran Sch. Art, 1968. Tchr. art Fairfax County (Va.) Pub. Schs., 1967-70; reporter, anchor Sta. WWDC, Washington, 1972-73, Sta. WMAL-AM-FM, Washington, 1973-75; corr. Sta. WTTG-TV, Washington, 1975-76, Sta. WJLA-TV, Washington, 1976-82; consumer corr. CBS News and Sta. WCBS-TV, N.Y.C., 1982-86; sr. corr. Today's Bus., 1986-87; personal fin. contbr. CBS Morning Program, 1987,

Lifetime Cable TV, 1988—; anchor FNN Money Talk, 1989; bd. dirs. Lowell E. Mellett Fund for a Free and Responsible Press, Washington, 1979-82; courtroom artist numerous trials, Washington, 1978-81. Reporter TV news report Caffeine, 1981 (AAUW award 1982); reporter spot news 6 P.M. News, 1979 (Emmy award); author: Betsy Ashton's Guide to Living on Your Own, 1988. Concert master of ceremonies Beethoven Soc., Washington, 1979-82. Recipient Laurel award Columbia Journalism Rev., 1984, Outstanding Alumna award Am. U., 1985, Outstanding Media award Am. U., 1986, Best Consumer Journalism citation Nat. Press Club, 1983. Mem. Soc. Profl. Journalists (pres. Washington chpt. 1980-81, bd. dirs. N.Y. chpt. 1989—), Alpha Chi Omega (v.p. chpt. 1964-66), Liberty Club N.Y.C. Episcopalian.

ASHTON, JOHN K., JR., computer engineering executive; b. New Paltz, N.Y., Jan. 28, 1927; s. John K. and Elizabeth Ellen (Elliott) A.; B.A., State U. N.Y., New Paltz, 1965; m. Gloria Margaret Seidel, Nov. 20, 1953; children—Laurence, Linda, Robert. Designer, Pratt & Whitney Div., United Aircraft Corp., East Hartford, Conn., 1950-51; with IBM, Poughkeepsie, N.Y., 1951-85, Kingston, N.Y., 1985-87 . Trustee New Paltz Central Schs. Bd. Edn., 1956-62, 72-75. Served with USAAF, 1945-47. Mem. IEEE (internat. tech. com. on fault tolerant computing), Am. Inst. Aeronautics and Astronautics. Home: 230 Sawmill Rd Lake Katrine NY 12449-5230

ASHWORTH, WILLIS LOUIS, investment and insurance executive, consultant; b. Birmingham, Ala., Aug. 30, 1945; s. Willis Louis and Glenda (Collins) A.; m. Margaret Rodgers As (div.); children: Philip Rodgers, Margaret Collins. BS, Am. U., 1966. Fin. cons., stock market timer McLean, Va. Mem. Internat. Game Fishing Assn., Mercedes Benz Motor Club. Home: PO Box 2775 Lake Ridge VA 22193 Office: 2010 Corporate Ridge 6404 Ivy Ln Mc Lean VA 22102

ASIM, MOHAMMED, manufacturing engineer; b. Karachi, Sind, Pakistan, Jan. 7, 1954; came to U.S., 1978; s. Ahmed Nabi and Riffat (Saroor) Khan; m. Doreen Yvette Battle, Aug. 25, 1979; children: Mohammed Jr., Saira Nicole. HSC, Pakistan Shipowners Coll., 1972; AE, Pak-Swiss Tng. Ctr., 1975; BS, Karachi U., 1978; BSME, Manhattan Coll. Mfg. engr. Edo Corp., N.Y.C., 1980—. Home: 655 E 14th St Apt Me New York NY 10009-3139

ASKEW, THOMAS ADELBERT, history educator; b. Lorain, Ohio, Oct. 8, 1931; s. Thomas Adelbert and Mildred (Slote) A.; m. Jean Mary Askew, Dec. 15, 1931; children: Thomas Rendall, Robyn Jean, Timothy Christopher. BA in History, Wheaton Coll., 1953, MA, 1958; MA in History, Northwestern U., 1962, PhD in History, 1969. Instr. social sci. Wheaton Acad., West Chgo., 1956-60; instr. hist. and polit. sci. Wheaton (Ill.) Coll., 1960-62, asst. prof. history and polit. sci., 1962-68; prof. social sci. Nat. Coll. Edn., Evanston, Ill., 1968-72; assoc. dean undergrad. studies Nat. Coll. Edn., Evanston, 1970-72; prof. history Gordon Coll., Wenham, Mass., 1972—, asst. dean coll., 1975-76, chair history dept., 1976—; vis. faculty history U. Ill., Chgo., 1970-71. Co-author: Berverly, Massachusetts and The American Revolution, 1975, The Churches and The American Experience, 1984, A Faithful Past: An Expectant Future: Gordon Centennial History, 1988; co-editor: Literty and Law: On The Constitution, 1987; pub. Christian Scholar's Rev., 1977-87. Mem. Am. Revolution BiCentennial Com., Beverly, 1974-76; trustee Essex Inst. Mus. and Libr., Salem, Mass., 1979-87; mem. steering com. Beverly Hosp. Capital Campaign, 1980-83; mem. long range planning com. House Seven Gables, Salem, 1990—. Grantee Danforth Found., 1963-66, Commonwealth Mass., 1973-74, faculty Gordon Coll., 1981, 91. Mem. Am. Hist. Assn., Beverly Hist. Soc. (program chair 1974-75), Conf. Faith and History (editorial bd. 1982—), Essex Inst. (planning com. 1979). Home: 18 Daniels Rd Wenham MA 01984 Office: Gordon Coll 255 Grapevine Rd Wenham MA 01984

ASKINS, WALLACE BOYD, manufacturing company executive; b. Chgo., June 2, 1930; s. Wallace Fay and Evelyn Mae (Baker) A.; m. Trieste M. Olivieri, May 20, 1954; 1 child, Justin Wallace. B.A., Lake Forest (Ill.) Coll., 1952; J.D. with honors, John Marshall Law Sch., Chgo., 1961. Bar: Ill. 1961; CPA, Ill. Sr. accountant Ernst & Young (CPAs), Chgo., 1952-55; controller, house counsel Nat. Lock Co., Rockford, Ill., 1955-65; asst. corp. controller Xerox Corp., Stamford, Conn., 1965-77; exec. v.p., chief fin. officer White Motor Corp., Cleve., 1977-81, chmn. bd., chief exec. officer, 1981-84; exec. v.p., chief fin. officer Armco Inc., Parsippany, N.J., 1984—, also bd. dirs.; bd. dirs. Enviro Source, Trump's Castle. Mem. ABA, Am. Inst. CPA's, Fin. Execs. Inst., Ill. Soc. CPA's, N.Y. Soc. CPA's, Conn. Soc. CPA's, Ill. Bar Assn. Office: Armco Inc 300 Interpace Pky Parsippany NJ 07054-1100

ASSAEL, MICHAEL, lawyer, accountant; b. N.Y.C., July 20, 1949; s. Albert and Helen (Hope) A.; m. Eiko Sato. B.A., George Washington U., 1971; M.B.A., Columbia U. Grad. Sch. Bus., 1973; J.D., St. John's Law Sch., 1977. Bar: N.Y. 1978, U.S. Dist. Ct. (so. and ea. dists.) N.Y. 1980, U.S. Supreme Ct. 1982; CPA, N.Y. Tax sr. Price Waterhouse & Co., N.Y.C. and Tokyo, 1977-78; pvt. practice law, N.Y.C., 1978—; pvt. practice acctg., N.Y.C., 1978—. Author: Money Smarts, 1982. Pres. bd. dirs. 200 Block East 74th Street Assn., 1982; bd. dirs. 200 E 74 Owners Corp., 1981—, treas., 1983-84, pres., 1984-85; mem. Yorkville Civic Council, tenant adv. com. Lenox Hill Neighborhood Assn., 1981-82. Recipient N.Y. Habitat/Citibank mgmt. achievement award, 1985. Mem. ABA, N.Y. State Bar Assn., N.Y. County Lawyers Assn., Am. Inst. CPA's, Am. Assn. Atty. CPA's, Inc., Nat. Assn. Accts., N.Y. State Soc. CPA's, Aircraft Owners and Pilots Assn. Clubs: N.Y. Road Runners, Columbia Bus. Sch. (N.Y.).

ASSEF, SHERIF TAHSIN, portfolio manager; b. Cairo, Oct. 31, 1960; s. Tahsin and Gladys (Hakim)A. BA in Econs., Fordham U., 1981, MA in Econs., 1982, PhD in Econs., 1992. Teaching fellow Fordham U., N.Y.C., 1983-85; adj. lectr. Iona Coll., New Rochelle, N.Y., 1984-86; economist Equitable Life, N.Y.C., 1986-91; portfolio mgr. Equitable Capital Mgmt. Corp., N.Y.C., 1991—. Fordham U. grad. assistantship, 1981, grad. fellow, 1983. Mem. Am. Econ. Assn., Nat. Assn. Bus. Economists. Democrat. Roman Catholic. Home: 801 Bronx River Rd Apt 4I Bronxville NY 10708-7023 Office: Equitable Capital 1285 Ave of The Americas 19th Flr New York NY 10019

ASSELIN, MARTIAL, Canadian government official; b. La Malbaie, P.Q., Feb. 3, 1924; s. Martial and Eugenie (Tremblay) A.; m. Pierrette Bouchard, Feb. 14, 1953; children: Bernard, Louis; m. Ginette d'Auteuil, Sept. 17, 1976; 1 child, Jean-Louis. BA, Sem. Chicoutimi; LLB, Laval U. Bar: Que., 1951. Mayor Malbaie, 1957-63, 65, 68; apptd. min. of forestry Diefenbaker Cabinet, 1963; summoned to Senate of Can., 1972-79; apptd. min. of state Can. Internat. Devel. Agy. and Francophonie, 1979-80; ptnr. Jolin, Fournier, Morrisset, 1980-90; lt. gov. of Que., 1990—; del. of Can. to NATO Parliamentary Assembly, London, 1959; rep. of Can. Commonwealth and internat. confs., 1960-61; del. of UN to Africa, 1961. Pres. Internat. Assn. of French Speaking Parliamentarians, 1988; dir. La Laurentienne Generale, Banque Laurentienne, Sphyynx et Memisca and La Laurentienne-Vie, 1976-90. Named Grand de Charlevoix Assn. des Anciens de Charlevoix, 1989. Mem. KC (3d degree), Lions Club, Clermont-La Malbaie-Pointe-au-Pic. Mem. Conservative Party. Roman Catholic. Office: Andre Laurendeau Bldg, 1050 rue St Augustin, Quebec, PQ Canada G1A 1A1*

ASTILL, BERNARD DOUGLAS, chemist, environment health and safety consultant; b. Nottingham, Eng., Feb. 11, 1925; came to U.S., 1952; s. Bernard and Constance (Harriet) A.; m. Norma Sarah Di Lauro, Apr. 9, 1955; children: Paul, Alexandra. BS, U. Nottingham, Eng., 1950, PhD, 1953. Postdoctoral Fulbright fellow U. Rochester, N.Y., 1952-55; biochemist Eastman Kodak Co., Rochester, N.Y., 1955-64; clin. instr. U. Rochester Med. Sch., Rochester, N.Y., 1960-74; rsch. assoc. Eastman Kodak Co., Rochester, 1964-72, supr. biochemistry health & environ. lab., 1972-85, dir. regulatory affairs, life scis., 1985-87; cons. Bernard D. Astill Assocs., Rochester, 1987—; cons. in field; com. mem. NAS/NRC Div. Toxicology, Washington, 1980-85, 88-91. Author: (book chpt.) Patty's Toxicology & Indsl. Hygiene, 1981; contbr. articles to profl. jours. Chmn. Rochester Cosmopolitan Club, 1957-59; co-chmn. new mem. campaign Rochester Philharmonic Orch., 1976-78. Petty officer Royal Navy, 1943-46, South Pacific. Mem. Soc. Toxicology, Am. Guild Organists. Home and Office: 195 Lyell St Spencerport NY 14559-9536

ASTOR, BROOKE, foundation executive, civic worker; b. Portsmouth, N.H.; d. John Henry and Mabel (Howard) Russell; m. Vincent Astor. LLD (hon.), Columbia U., 1971, Brown U., 1980; LHD (hon.), Fordham U., 1980, NYU, 1986; PhD in Biomed. Sci. (honoris causa), The Rockefeller U., 1986. Feature editor House and Garden mag., N.Y.C., 1946-56, cons. editor, 1956—; pres., trustee Vincent Astor Found., N.Y.C.; corp. bd. mem. Astor Home for Children; trustee Marconi Internat. Fellowship; trustee and hon. chmn., mem. devel. com., mem. exec. com. N.Y. Pub. Libr., N.Y.C.; trustee, mem. conservation com., mem. exec. com., hon. chmn. women's com. N.Y. Zool. Soc.; trustee emeritus, mem. council of fellows Pierpont Morgan Libr.; trustee emeritus, chmn. vis. com. dept. Asian art, mem. acquisitions com., exec. com. ex officio Met. Mus. Art, N.Y.C.; life trustee Rockefeller U. Author: Patchwork Child, 1962, The Bluebird Is At Home, 1965, Footprints, 1980, The Last Blossom on the Plum Tree, 1986; feature editor House and Garden, 1946-56, cons. editor, 1992—. Mem. N.Y. State Pk. Commn., 1967-69. Decorated dame Venerable Order of St. John of Jerusalem; recipient Anniversary medal Astor, Lenox and Tilden Founds. of N.Y. Pub. Libr., 1961, award Sisters of Good Shepherd and Children of Madonna Heights Sch. for Girls, 1963, Client Award cert. N.Y. State Assn. Architects, 1964, award Pk. Assn. N.Y.C. Inc., 1965, Honor award HUD, 1966, cert. of appreciation City of N.Y., 1967, Albert S. Bard merit award City Club N.Y., 1967, Award of Honor women's aux. N.Y. chpt. AIA, 1968, Rector's award St. Phillip's Ch., 1968, Michael Friedsam medal Archtl. League N.Y., 1968, award Brotherhood-In-Action, Inc., 1968, Outstanding Contbn. award Am. Soc. Landscape Architects, 1968, Spirit of Achievement award Albert Einstein Coll. Medicine, Yeshiva U., 1969, Good Samaritan award P. Ballentine & Sons, 1969, Good Samaritan award Prospect Block Civic Assn., 1969, Disting. Svc. award N.Y. region Rotary, 1970, honor YWCA, 1970, Housing award N.Y. Met. chpt. Nat. Assn. Housing and Redevel. Officials, 1971, $24 award Mus. City of N.Y., award N.Y. Pub. Libr., 1972, Albert Gallatin medal NYU, 1972, spl. citation AIA, 1973, Medal of Merit award Lotos Club, 1973, commendation Neighborhood Com. for the Asphalt Green, 1975, commendation ARCS Found., 1976, Pres.'s medal Mcpl. Art Soc. N.Y., 1976; Gold Medal award N.Y. Zool. Soc., 1978; Elizabeth Seton Humanitarian award N.Y. Foundling Hosp., 1978, Little Apple award Met. Mus. Art; Little Apple award Morgan Library; Little Apple award N.Y. Public Library; Little Apple award N.Y. Zool. Soc.; Little Apple award Rockefeller U.; Little Apple award South St. Seaport and Sta. WNET-TV/Channel 13, 1978, New Yorker for N.Y. award Citizens Com. for N.Y.C., 1980, Myer Myers Cultural award City of N.Y., award Citizens Housing and Planning Coun., 1980, Bishop's Cross Diocese of N.Y.1980, Forsythia award Bklyn. Bot. Garden, 1981, award Pks. Coun., 1981, Woman of Conscience award Appeal of Conscience Found., 1981, commendation Lower Manhattan Cultural Coun., 1984, Disting. New Yorkers award Bowery Savs. Bank, 1984, Gov.'s Arts award State of N.Y., 1985, Am. Acad. and Inst. Arts and Letters award, 1986, Marconi Internat. Fellowship Coun. award, 1986, landmark plaque and medallion N.Y. Landmarks Preservation Found., 1987, Gold medal St. Nicholas Soc., N.Y.C., 1987, Fashion Industry award Coun. of Fashion Designers Am., 1988, Presdl. Citizen's medal Pres. Reagan, 1988, Nat. Medal of Arts Nat. Endowment for the Arts, 1988, World Monuments Fund The Hadrian award, 1991, others; named a hon. trustee and friend, Boys Brotherhood Republic, 1972; honoree 150th anniversary dinner Seamen's Ch. Inst. N.Y. & N.J., 1984; honoree Cen. Pk. Conservancy, 1985; Brooke Astor Day Proclaimed by Mayor of N.Y.C., Mar. 5, 1992. Fellow Am. Acad. Arts and Scis.; mem. Mcpl. Art Soc. N.Y., Pilgrims U.S., Venerable Order of St. John of Jerusalem (dame), The Boardroom Club, The Century Assn.Colony Club, Knickerbocker Club, N.Y. Yacht Club, Sleepy Hollow Country Club. Clubs: Colony, Grolier, Sleepy Hollow, N.Y. Yacht, Coffee House, Knickerbocker, River. Office: Astor (The Vincent) Found 405 Park Ave New York NY 10022-4405

ASTWOOD, WILLIAM PETER, psychotherapist; b. N.Y.C., May 18, 1940; s. Henry Kenneth and Rose Margit (Eastby) A.; m. Sharon Lisa Sprung, June 10, 1979; 1 child, Jesse Jack. BA, CUNY, 1962; MA, NYU, 1967, PhD, 1975. Case worker, supr. dept. social services City N.Y., 1964-67; community orgn. trainer Block Communities, Inc., N.Y.C., 1967-68; field rep. Office Econ. Opportunity, N.Y.C., 1968-70, U.S. Dept. Health, Edn., Welfare, N.Y.C., 1970-71; pvt. practice Bklyn., 1971—; bd. dirs. South Beach Psychiat. Ctr., Bklyn., 1976-78, N.Y. Group for Comprehensive Family Therapy, Mineola, 1988—; exec. bd. Met. Ctr. for Psychotherapy, N.Y.C., 1969-72. Co-author: Practicing Psychotherapy, 1980. Exec. bd. Social Service Employees Union, N.Y.C., 1965-67. Staff sgt. USANG, 1963-69. Mem. N.Y. Acad. Scis., Assn. for Humanistic Psychology. Home: 394 Atlantic Ave Brooklyn NY 11217-1703 Office: 163 Clinton St Brooklyn NY 11201-4601

ASWAD, RICHARD NEJM, lawyer; b. Niagara Falls, N.Y., Apr. 23, 1936; s. Nejm M. and Najla A. (Anton) A.; m. Betsy Becker, Sept. 22, 1962; children—Richard N., Kristin D. B.A., SUNY-Binghamton, 1958; J.D., Cornell U., 1961. Bar: N.Y. 1962, U.S. Ct. Claims 1981, U.S. Dist. Ct. (no. and we. dists.) N.Y. 1982, U.S. Supreme Ct. Assoc. firm Twining & Fischer, Binghamton, N.Y., 1962; confidential law clk. to Justice Daniel J. McAvoy, N.Y. Supreme Ct., 1963-65; assoc. firm Rosefsky & D'Esti, Binghamton, 1965-68; solo practice, Binghamton, 1968-76; ptnr. firm Aswad & Ingraham, Binghamton, 1976—. Served with Army N.G., 1961-67. Mem. ABA, N.Y. State Bar Assn., Broome County Bar Assn., Am. Judicature Soc. Presbyterian. Office: Aswad & Ingraham 46 Front St Binghamton NY 13905-4704

ATAIIFAR, ALI AKBAR, economist, educator; b. Khoy, Azerbijan, Iran, July 2, 1952; came to U.S., 1970; s. Ayoob and Khadijeh Ataiifar. BS, Internat. Iranzamin Coll., Tehran, 1977; MBA, Northrop U., 1979; MA, New Sch. for Social Rsch., N.Y.C., 1989; ABD, New Sch. for Social Rsch., 1990. Lectr. Kean Coll. N.J., Union, 1983-87, NYU, 1988-89; asst. prof. Delaware County Community Coll., Media, Pa., 1990—. Office: Delaware County CC Media PA 19063

ATHEY, LOUIS LEE, historian, educator; b. Irving, Ill., Oct. 29, 1929; s. Ralph A. and Esther Ruth (Hutchins) A.; m. Jean Murray Pursell, June 21, 1952; children: Janette Ruth, Linda Lee, Bruce Alan, Eric Nathan. BA, Trenton State Coll., 1960; PhD, U. Del., 1965. Instr. history Franklin and Marshall Coll., Lancaster, Pa., 1963-65, asst. prof., 1965-70, assoc. prof., 1970-81, prof. history, 1981-88, Charles A. Dana prof. history, 1988—; historian, cons. W.Va. Film Project, Charleston, 1991—; reviewer, evaluator NEH, Washington, 1980-88; editor Social Welfare History Group, Mpls., 1978-83. Author: Kaynoor: A New River Community, 1987; contbr. articles to profl. jours. With USN, 1947-56. Recipient summer stipend NEH, Washington, 1970. Mem. AAUP (pres. local chpt. 1985-86), So. Hist. Assn., W.Va. Labor History Group. Democrat. Home: 922 Virginia Ave Lancaster PA 17603-3116 Office: Franklin & Marshall Coll PO Box 3003 Lancaster PA 17604-3003

ATIGBI, KOFITUNDE JOLOMI, telecommunications professional; b. Bklyn., July 10, 1961; s. Ignatius Amaduwa and Joan Akwasiba (Derby) A.; m. Sondra Denise Page, Oct. 5, 1990; children: Jovan Burton, Kandon Burton. Student, Thomas Edison State Coll., Trenton, N.J. Mktg. rep. Radio Shack Computers, N.Y.C., 1984-86; dir. recruitment Robert Fiance Co., N.Y.C., 1986-88; ptnr. Ednl. Vocat. Alliance, Bklyn., 1987-89; rep. N.Y. Telephone, N.Y.C., 1988—; sales adminstr. Wireless Cable of N.Y., L.I., 1989-90; mem. network mktg. staff KT Svcs., East Orange, N.J., 1991—; cons. Higher Ednl. Devel. Fund, Bronx, N.Y., 1988-90. Recipient Community Svc. award Holy Spirit Ch., Bronx, 1979, St. Augustine Ch., Bronx, 1981. Mem. Internat. Assn. Approved Basketball Officials, Sports United Boro-Wide Alliance Inc. (Most Improved Official 1989). Home: 36 Ampere Pky East Orange NJ 07017-5428 Office: NY Telephone 5030 Broadway Rm 106 New York NY 10034-1655

ATILGAN, TIMUR FAIK, structural engineer; b. Adana, Turkey, July 15, 1943; came to U.S., 1972; s. Faik Ahmet and Sacide (Togman) A.; m. Gulsum Z. Kuzuoglu, Dec. 7, 1977 (div. 1980). BS in Civil Engring., Aegean U., Izmir, Turkey, 1967; MS in Structural Engring., U. Md., 1979. Registered profl. engr., Va. Civil engr. NATO/Infrastructure Dept., Ankara, Turkey, 1970-72; structural engr. Bendix Field Engring., Columbia, Md., 1977-79; sr. design engr. Northrop Svcs. Inc., NASA, GSFC, Greenbelt, Md., 1979-82; sr. antenna engr. COMSAT Gen. Corp., Washington, 1982-83; sr. structural engr. OAO Corp., Greenbelt, 1983-84; engring. specialist PRC-Kentron, Inc., Hampton, Va., 1984-86; prin. engr. Fairchild Space Co., Greenbelt, 1986-91; sr. engr. Def. Systems, Inc., McLean, Va., 1991—. Mem. AIAA, Turkish Architects, Engs. and Treas. Scientists in Am., Am. Turkish Assn. (bd. dirs. Washington chpt. 1981-83). Home: 7806 Cloister Pl Greenbelt MD 20770-3030 Office: Def Systems Inc 1521 Westbranch Dr Mc Lean VA 22102-3201

ATKINS, CHESTER GREENOUGH, congressman; b. Geneva, Apr. 14, 1948; s. Henry Hornblower and Karkilie (Withington) A.; m. Corrine Hobbs, 1975; children—Casey, Dean. B.A., Antioch Coll., 1970. Mem. Mass. Ho. of Reps., 1970-71, Mass. Senate, 1972-84, 99th-102d Congresses from 5th Mass. dist., Washington, 1985—; guest lectr. Concord Acad., Middlesex Sch., Kennedy Inst. for Politics, Harvard U., Antioch Coll., Boston Coll. Ex-officio mem. Mass. Dem. State Com. Office: 123 Cannon House Office Bldg Washington DC 20515*

ATKINS, RICHARD BART, film, television producer; b. Paterson, N.J., May 11, 1951; s. S. Stephen and Alice B. (Stein) A.; m. Joanna Pang; 1 child, David. AB in Polit. Sci., Princeton U., 1973. With Cadence Industries, N.Y.C., 1973-74; mgr. TV program devel. Benton & Bowles, N.Y.C., 1977-79, mgr. daytime programming, 1980; v.p. prodn. Telecom Entertainment, N.Y.C., 1981-83; pres. Atkins Pictures Inc., Florham Park, N.J., 1984—; programming and prodn. cons. Hearst Entertainment, Whittle Communications, D'Arcy Masius Benton & Bowles, King World Prodns., 1989-91, Quartier Latin, Paris, 1992. Producer TV films: Murder in Coweta County, 1983, The Gift of Love: A Christmas Story, 1983, Trapped in Silence, 1986; producer, writer videocassette: Knowing Childbirth, 1985; producer, writer feature film Forced March, 1989; author: Method to the Madness: Hollywood Explained, 1975. Democrat. Jewish. Clubs: Friar's, Princeton. Home and Office: Atkins Pictures Inc 149 Ridgedale Ave Florham Park NJ 07932-1789

ATKINS, WILLIAM ALLEN, academic administrator; b. St. Louis, Sept. 19, 1934; s. William Allen and Nancy Lou (Hunter) A.; m. Joan Markmann, Feb. 6, 1954 (div. Feb. 25, 1977); children: Andrew Bennett, Stephen Hunter; m. Maxine Stegman, Apr. 6, 1977. BA, U. Denver, 1955; MA in Edn., Washington U., 1958; CAS, Harvard U., 1962, EdD, 1965. Cert. Supt., N.Y., Mass., Vt. Elem. tchr. Univ. (Mo.) City Pub. Schs., 1956-61; asst. supt. Williamstown (Mass.) Pub. schs., 1963-65; supt. Rutland (Vt.) Pub. Schs., 1965-68; mgr. Gen. Learning Corp., Washington, 1968-71; assoc. dean Hofstra U. Sch. Edn., Hempstead, N.Y., 1971-77; exec. dir. Sexton Ednl. Ctr., Massapequa, N.Y., 1977-82; dir. Queensborough Community Coll., Bayside, N.Y., 1982-85; exec. dir. S.I. Continuum of Edn., Inc., 1985-89; asst. dean Nassau Community Coll., Garden City, N.Y., 1989-92; v.p. Nassau Community Coll., Garden City, 1992—; adj. prof. in field; edn. dir. Episcopal Diocese L.I., Garden City, N.Y., 1973-77. Co-author: Developing An Educationally Accountable Program, 1973. Chair United Way, Garden City, 1972-77; bd. dirs. St. Mary's & St. Paul Episcopal Schs., Garden City, 1973-77, Rutland, Vt. Hosp., 1965-68. Recipient Faculty Disting. Svc. award Hofstra U., 1977, Internat. Reading Assn., 1987, Presdl. award L.I. Univ., 1989, Disting. Kappan award, 1989. Mem. NEA, Am. Assn. Sch. Adminstrs., Kappa Delta Pi (faculty sponsor 1971-77), Phi Delta Kappa (pres. 1989-90). Democrat. Jewish. Home: 3725 Sandra Ct Wantagh NY 11793-1628 Office: Nassau Community Coll Garden City NY 11530-6793

ATKINSON, HOLLY GAIL, physician, journalist, author, lecturer; b. Detroit, Oct. 20, 1952; m. R. Grant Tate, Mar. 3, 1983. BA in Biology magna cum laude, Colgate U., 1974; MD, U. Rochester, 1978; MS in Journalism, Columbia U., 1981. Diplomate Nat. Med. Bds. Intern in internal medicine Strong Meml. Hosp., Rochester, N.Y., 1978-79; researcher Walter Cronkite's Universe show CBS News, N.Y.C., 1981-82; med. reporter CBS Morning News, CBS Network, N.Y.C., 1982-83; on-air co-host Bodywatch, PBS health show; contbg. editor and health columnist New Woman mag., 1983—; on-air corr., med. editor Lifetime Med. TV, 1985-89, sr. v.p. programming and med. affairs, 1989—; med. corr. The Today Show; assoc. editor Jour. Watch, 1986-90; med. corr. Today show NBC News, N.Y.C., 1991—; mem. trustee's com. U. Rochester, 1983-90. Author: Women and Fatigue, 1986; med. corr. Today Show NBC News, N.Y.C., 1991—. Vol. nat. and local level Am. Heart Assn., 1984-91, bd. dirs., chairperson nat. communications com., 1987-91. Commd. officer USPHS, 1979-80. Recipient Young Achievers award Nat. Coun. of Women, 1986. Phi Beta Kappa. Office: Lifetime Med TV 36-12 35th Ave Long Island City NY 11106

ATKINSON, JOHN SCOTT, college financial aid director; b. Rochester, N.Y., Oct. 4, 1951; s. John S. and June L. (Beeson) A.; m. Susan P. Atkinson, May 22, 1982; 1 child, Sherie. BS, Roberts Wesleyan Coll., 1973; MS, SUNY, Brockport, 1982. Payroll clk. student employment Roberts Wesleyan Coll., Rochester, N.Y., 1973-74; dir. fin. aid Roberts Wesleyan Coll., Rochester, 1974-82; dir. fin. aid, bursar U. Rochester Sch. Medicine and Dentistry, 1982-86; dir. fin. aid SUNY, Brockport, 1986—; chmn. N.Y. State Fin. Aid Adminstrn. Com., 1986-90. Mem. adv. bd. SUNY Brockport Co-op., Minority Honors, Student Support Svcs., McNair Program, 1988-92, N.Y. State Higher Edn. Svcs. Corp., 1990-92. Recipient Quality Control Leadership award U.S. Dept. Edn., 1990, Cert. of Appreciation Ednl. Opportunity Program, SUNY, Brockport, 1988, McNair Appreciation award, 1990. Mem. Nat. Assn. Fin. Aid Adminstrs., Ea. Assn. Fin. Aid Adminstrs., N.Y. State Fin. Aid Adminstrs. (conf. program com. 1990, cert. appreciation 1990, 91, Father Joseph Dunne Svc. award 1990), SUNY Fin. Aid Profls. (treas. 1990-92).

ATKINSON, PETER ALAN, mortgage banker; b. Needham, Mass., Jan. 24, 1952; s. Robert Earl and Phyllis Jeannette (Daly) A.; m. Linda Priscilla Gustafsun, July 15, 1972 (div. Dec. 1980); children: Kelly, Shawn; m. Shelley Rose Lupe, Feb. 17, 1990. BA in Econs., Union Coll., Schenectady, 1973. Bank mgr. Mohawk Nat. Bank, Schenectady, 1973-79; account exec., br. mgr. 1st Investors Corp., Albany N.Y., Tampa, Fla., 1979-84; pres. Innovative Mortgage Brokers, Tampa, 1984-89; mgr. Affordable Mortgage Co., Latham, N.Y., 1989-90; regional v.p.. Prudential Mortgage Co. Inc., Schenectady, 1990—. Home: 1061 Teviot rd Schenectady NY 12308 Office: Prudential Mortgage Co Inc 670 Franklin St Schenectady NY 12305

ATKINSON, ROBERT CHARLES, investment manager; b. Pitts., Feb. 1, 1953; s. Charles Melvin and Betty Ann (McGovern) A.; m. Rita Ann Showalter, Sept. 9, 1978; children: Rachel Elizabeth, Sarah Marie. BA, John Carroll U., 1975; MBA, Duquesne U., 1977. Asst. to v.p. Schneider, Inc., Pitts., 1977-82; fin. analyst Cabot Corp., Pitts., 1982-84; finance analyst Equitable Resources, Inc., Pitts., 1984-88, mgr. investor rels., 1988—. Mem. Petroleum Investor Rels. Assn. Roman Catholic. Office: Equitable Resources Inc 420 Blvd Of The Allies Pittsburgh PA 15219-1393

ATKINSON, ROBERT G., educator; b. Amityville, N.Y., Aug. 5, 1945; s. Leon B. and Helen (Waldorf) A.; m. cynthia Deroche. BA, L.I. U., Southampton, 1967; MA, SUNY, Cooperstown, 1968, U. N.H., 1981; PhD, U. Pa., 1985. Researcher Hudson R. Sloop Restoration, Cold Spring, N.Y., 1969-71; instr. L.I. U., 1971, Oceanics Sch., 1971, Furman U., Greenville, S.C., 1974-75, U. N.H., Durham, 1980-81; teaching fellow Harvard U., Cambridge, Mass., 1981-82; clin. researcher U. Chgo., 1985-87; assoc. prof. human devel. U. So. Maine, Gorham, 1987—, dir. Ctr. for Study Lives,, 1988—. Author: (with Offer, Ostrov and Howard) The Teenage World: Adolescents' Self Image in Ten Countries, 1987; editor: Songs of the Open Road: The Poetry of Folk-Rock and Journey of the Hero, 1974; also articles. Mem. Assn. for Humanistic Psychology, Gerontol. Soc. Am., Oral History Assn., Am. Folklore Soc. Baha'i Faith. Office: U So Maine 400 Bailey Hall Gorham ME 04038

ATKINSON, THEODORE EDWARD, III, career officer, physician; b. Atlanta, Aug. 3, 1955; s. Theodore Edward, Jr. and Theresa Marguerite (Charlot) A.; m. Anita Gail Turner, Oct. 29, 1982; children: Rebecca, Danielle. BS, Xavier U., 1978; MD, U. Miss., Jackson, 1980. Diplomate Am. Bd. of Pediatrics. Commd. capt. U.S. Army, 1980, advanced through grades to lt. col., 1992; pediatric resident Letterman Army Hosp., San Francisco, 1980-83; staff pediatrician R.W. Bliss Army Hosp., Ft. Huachuca, Ariz., 1983-86; pediatric fellow Beaumont Army Med. Ctr., El Paso, Tex., 1986-88; chief, exceptional family mem. dept. Army Regional Med. Ctr., Frankfurt, Fed. Republic of Germany, 1988—. Mem. AMA, AAAS, Am.

Acad. Pediatrics, Nat. Med. Assn. Office: 97 Gen Hosp EFMD Unit 25710 Box 60 APO AE 09242

ATKYNS, ROBERT LEE, advertising professional; b. Boston, Jan. 20, 1948; s. Glenn C. and Syme M. (Vataja) A.; m. Virgina Ginger Arispe, 1989; BA, Rutgers U., 1971; MA, U. Conn., 1974; PhD, Temple U., 1986. Grad. asst. communication div. U. Conn., Storrs, 1971-73; communications researcher drug abuse info. rsch. project, 1971-74; instr. U. Conn., Hartford, 1973-74; health care analyst The Phila. Health Plan, 1974-76, asst. dir. rsch. and evaluation, 1976-78, dir. rsch. and evaluation, 1978-80; mktg. scientist mktg. rsch. and forecasting div. AT&T Long Lines, Bedminster, N.J., 1980-82, mktg. rsch. staff mgr. AT&T Gen. Depts., Basking Ridge, N.J., 1982-83, mktg. staff mgr. AT&T Communications, Basking Ridge, N.J., 1984-85, advt. staff mgr., 1985—; cons. Chmn., Cheltenham Twp. Drug, Alcohol and Mental Health Com. Mem. Flenington Presbyn. Ch. Recipient Community Svc. award Cheltenham Twp., AT&T Eagle award, 1986, AT&T Spirit Communication awards 1990, 91. Mem. AAAS, Internat. Communication Assn., Am. Assn. Pub. Opinion Rsch., Am. Mktg. Assn., Am. Pub. Health Assn., Am. Acad. Polit. and Social Sci. Contbr. to profl. jours. and confs. Home: 263 Kingwood Station Rd Frenchtown NJ 08825 Office: AT&T Hdqrs 295 N Maple Ave Basking Ridge NJ 08720

ATLAS, ARTHUR, architectural firm executive; b. N.Y.C., Nov. 4, 1945; s. Isidor and Pauline (Gershman) A.; m. Janet Elkhaus, Mar. 27, 1988. BArch, Pratt Inst., 1968, MArch, 1989. Lic. profl. architect, N.Y.; cert. Nat. Coun. Archtl. Bd. Designer, draftsman Zion & Breen & Assocs., N.Y.C., 1968-70; archtl. designer CNI Internat., Inc., N.Y.C., 1970-73; staff architect Ulrich Franzen & Assocs., N.Y.C., 1973-74; pres. Arthur Atlas Architect, N.Y.C., 1974—; asst. prof. CUNY, 1982—. Author: Energy Efficiency in Loft Buildings, 1985. Steering com. Lower Manhattan (N.Y.) Loft Tenants, 1981-87, exec. com., 1984-87; steering com. Green Guerillas, N.Y., 1974-76. Democrat. Jewish. Home: 15 West 18th St New York NY 10011 Office: 15 West 18th St New York NY 10011

ATLAS, LIANE WIENER, publishing company executive; b. N.Y.C.; d. Louis and Frances (Ferne) Wiener; m. Martin Atlas, Mar. 5, 1944; children: Stephen Terry, Jeffrey L. AB, Vassar Coll., 1943; postgrad., Johns Hopkins U., 1953-55. Cert. fin. planner. Fgn. affairs officer Dept. State, Washington, 1962-68; sr. economist U.S. Commerce Dept., Washington, 1968-75, U.S. Treasury Dept., Washington, 1975-79, Riggs Nat. Bank, Washington, 1980-82; v.p. Fintapes Inc., Washington, 1984-87, pres., 1987—; mem. U.S. delegation UN Econ. Orgns., N.Y.C., Geneva, 1963, 64, 68, 79. Author: Middle East Financial Institutions, 1977, (audio cassettes) What Every Wife Should Know, 1986, rev., 1992, Financial Planning for Divorce, 1987; freelance writer Changing Times and other mags., 1982-87. Treas. Entertaining People/Washington Home, 1986-90. Fellow in econs. Johns Hopkins U., Balt., 1954-55; recipient Cert. of Appreciation U.S. Treasury Dept., Washington, 1977. Mem. Nat. Assn. Women Bus. Owners, Inst. Cert. Fin. Planners, Washington Ind. Writers, City Tavern Club, Vassar Club. Home: 2254 48th St NW Washington DC 20007-1035 Office: Fintapes Inc PO Box 9754 Friendship Sta Washington DC 20016

ATTANASIO, VIRGINIA, clinical psychologist; b. Newark, Sept. 1, 1958; d. John Anthony and Anna (Villani) A. BA, Seton Hall U., 1980; PhD, SUNY, Albany, 1985. Fellow Brown U. Program in Medicine, Providence, 1985-87; clin. asst. prof. psychiatry U. Medicine and Dentistry N.J., Newark, 1987—; pvt. practice, Summit, N.J., 1989—. Author: (with others) Advances in Developmental Behavioral Pediatrics, 1985; contbr. articles to profl. jours. Mem. Am. Psychol. Assn., Assn. for Advancement of Behavior Therapy, Soc. of Behavioral Medicine, Am. Assn. for Study of Headache, Assn. for Applied Psychophysiology and Biofeedback, Am. Pain Soc. Office: Summit Psychiat & Counseling Assocs 47 Maple St Ste 401 Summit NJ 07901

ATTIAS, SHEILA TELANOFF, educational administrator; b. Phila., Nov. 8, 1935; d. Rudolph M. and Gertrude (Rudolph) Telanoff; m. William Attias, June 19, 1960; children: Erik, Lori. BS in Edn., Temple U., 1957, MEd equivalency, 1960; grad., Gratz Coll., 1957. Cert. tchr., Pa. Tchr. Wissahickon Sch. Dist., Ambler, Pa., 1957-61, Fairfax County Sch. Dist., McLean, Va., 1961-63, Sch. Dist. Phila., 1963-64; owner, dir. Hawthorne Country Day Sch., Wyndmoor, Pa., 1973-81; office mgr. Germantown Window Cleaning Co., Glenside, Pa., 1981-83; admissions officer McCarrie Sch., Phila., 1983; fin. aid adminstr., registrar Gordon Phillips Beauty Sch., Phila., 1983-86; dir. student fin. svcs. Art Inst. Phila., 1986; ops. mgr. Career Inst., Phila., 1987-89; dir. fin. aid Passaic County Community Coll., Paterson, N.J., 1989—. Mem. NAFE, Nat. Assn. Student Fin. Adminstrs., N.J. Assn. Student Fin. Adminstrs. Democrat. Jewish.

ATTWOOD, JAMES ALBERT, JR., investment banker; b. Lake Forest, Ill., Apr. 20, 1958; s. James Albert and Pauline Veryl (Ellwood) A.; m. Leslie Kim Williams. BA, MA, Yale U., 1980; MBA, JD, Harvard U., 1985. Bar: Mass., N.Y., D.C. Assoc. Hewitt Assocs., Rowayton, Conn., 1980-81; v.p. Goldman, Sachs & Co., N.Y.C., 1985—. Mem. Am. Soc. Actuaries, Siwanoy Country Club, Harvard Club of N.Y.C. Democrat. Mem. Reformed Ch. of Am. Office: Goldman Sachs & Co 85 Broad St New York NY 10004-2434

ATWATER, JOHN RICHARD, artist; b. Worcester, Mass., June 8, 1954; s. Samuel Shipley and Marion Books (Sturtevant) A. BFA, Washington U., St. Louis, 1977. Artist (book) Yacht Portraits, 1987, Marine Painting, 1991, (poster) Blue Stair and Begonias, 1988. Bd. dirs. Conn. Acad. Fine Arts, 1984—, West Hartford Art League, 1990—. Mem. Conn. Watercolor Soc. (pres. 1983-91), Canton Artists Guild (chmn. bd. dirs. 1991, bd. dirs. 1981-91), Am. Watercolor Soc. (Ford Motor Co. award 1988, Paul Remmey award 1989, Edgar Whitney award 1985, Mystic Seaport Mus. Purchase award 1985).

ATWATER, MARSHALL ANDERSON, meteorological researcher, educator; b. New Haven, Conn., Feb. 14, 1940; s. Charles Lewis and Alice Linnea (Anderson) A.; m. Angela Lucia Falcetta, July 6, 1968; children: Cynthia Frances, Matthew Charles. BS, Pa. State U., 1962; MS, NYU, 1965, PhD, 1970. Cert. cons. meteorologist, Conn. Research assoc. Travelers Research Ctr., Hartford, Conn., 1962-70; div. dir. Ctr. for Environment & Man, Hartford, 1970-81; prin. scientist TRC Environ. Cons., East Hartford, Conn., 1981-86; prin. Thor Analytics, Vernon, Conn., 1986—; asst. prof. Ea. Conn. State U., Willimantic, 1986—. Contbr. 25 articles to profl. jours. Mem. Am. Geophys. Union, Am. Meteorol. Soc., Air Waste Mgmt. Assn., Conn. Acad. Sci. and Engring. Mem. United Ch. of Christ. Office: Thor Analytics PO Box 2060 Vernon Rockville CT 06066-1460

ATWELL, ROBERT HERRON, association executive; b. Washington, Pa., Jan. 26, 1931; s. R. Boice and Elsie (Herron) A.; m. Suzanne Fogg, Apr. 22, 1989; children by previous marriages: Mary, Robert, John, Nancy, Carl, Catherine, Cynthia. B.A., Coll. Wooster, 1953; M.A. in Pub. Adminstrn, U. Minn., 1957. Budget examiner U.S. Bur. Budget, Washington, 1957-60; fiscal economist, loan officer U.S. Devel. Loan Fund, Dept. State, 1960; budget examiner, program analyst for higher edn. and med. research programs U.S. Bur. Budget, 1961-62; program planning officer, asst. chief Community Mental Health Centers br. NIMH, HEW, 1962-65; vice chancellor for adminstrn. U. Wis., Madison, 1965-70; pres. Pitzer Coll., Claremont, Calif., 1970-78; v.p. Am. Council Edn., 1978-84; pres. Am. Council Edn., 1984—; chmn. coun. Claremont Coll., 1971-72; pres. Ind. Colls. So. Calif., 1974-75; trustee Tchrs. Ins. Annuity Assn./Coll. Retirement Equities, Conn. Coll., St. Norber Coll. Served with AUS, 1953-55. Home: 1505 Dumbarton Rock Ct NW Washington DC 20007-3049 Office: Am Coun Edn 1 Dupont Cir NW Ste 800 Washington DC 20036-1193

ATWOOD, JEFFREY NELSON, investment company manager; b. Rochester, N.Y., Nov. 7, 1950; s. Eugene Francis and Mary Aileen (Coleman) A.; m. Karen Heather Scott, June 12, 1982; 1 stepchild, Jennifer Heather Thompson; 1 child, Jeffrey Coleman. BS in Edn., Ohio State U., 1972. Cert. fin. planner. Investment broker E.F. Hutton, Rochester, 1978-83, Paine Webber, Rochester, 1983-89; br. mgr. A.G. Edwards, Rochester, 1989—. Mem. All Am. Team Am. Funds Group Pres. Adv. Coun., Rochester Funds. 1st lt. USMC, 1972-75. Mem. Lambda Chi Alpha (treas. Gamma Tau chpt.).

AU, WILLIAM AUGUST, III, priest, public relations director; b. Phillipsburg, N.J., Jan. 12, 1949; s. William August Au and Annabell Agnes (Lawler) Penyak. BA in Philosophy, St. Mary's Seminary, Balt., 1971; STM, St. Mary's Sch. Theology, Balt., 1975; PhD in Ch. History, The Cath. U. Am., 1983. Assoc. pastor SS Philip & James Ch., Balt., 1975-78; doctoral student The Catholic U. Am., Washington, 1978-83; resident asst. St Dominic's Ch., Balt., 1978-80; chaplain Cardinal Shehan Ctr. for the Aging, Balt., 1980-83; assoc. pastor Most Precious Blood Ch., Balt., 1983-84, St. Clare Ch., Balt., 1984-86; cons. justice and peace commn. Archdiocese of Balt., 1983-84, asst. chancellor, 1984-86, dir. pub. rels., 1986-92, 1992—; pastor S.S. Philip & James Ch., Balt.; mem. editorial bd. The U.S. Cath. Historian. Author: (book) The Cross, The Flag and the Bomb, 1984; author:(with others) Papal Teaching on War and Peace, 1985. Recipient Thomas Shahan award The Catholic Univ. Am., Washington, 1983. Mem. Am. Cath. Hist. Soc., Pub. Relations Soc. Am., Balt. Pub. Relations Soc. Democrat. Roman Catholic. Home and Office: 2801 N Charles St Baltimore MD 21218

AUBIN, GARY PAUL, tooling engineer; b. Burlington, Vt., June 10, 1945; s. Gerald Charles and Clara Sara (Morrison) A.; m. Patricia Ann Wheeler, Aug. 12, 1967; children: Bryan Paul, Erik David. BS in Music Edn., Lyndon (Vt.) State Coll., 1972. Draftsman Fairbanks-Morse Scales, St. Johnsbury, Vt., 1963-68; tchr. music Concord (Vt.) High Sch., 1972-78; tooling engr. Newport (Vt.) Plastics Corp., 1978—; mus. condr. St. Johnsbury Town Band, 1982—; pres. Lyndonville (Vt.) Mil. Band, 1988. Mem. alumni coun. Lyndon State Coll., 1984-89; trustee Colbeigh Pub. Library, Lyndonville, 1989—. Home: PO Box 505 Lyndonville VT 05851-0505 Office: Newport Plastics Corp PO Box 466 Newport VT 05855-0466

AUBIN, WILLIAM MARK, computer applications executive; b. Detroit, Dec. 17, 1929; s. Hector M. and Alice C. (Nittinger) A.; m. Joyce N. Gauthier; children: Mark R., Julie M., Denise F., Brian J., Bruce W., Allison M., Elaine A. B Aero. Engring., U. Detroit, 1953; MS, Adelphi U., 1957. Rsch. engr. Grumman Aircraft Systems, Bethpage, N.Y., 1953-62, dir., materials and mechanics, 1962-82, tech. staff asst., 1982-87, dir. computer applications, 1987—. Trustee West Islip (N.Y.) Library, 1962-71. Mem. AIAA, ASME (computer and automated systems). Republican. Roman Catholic. Home: 9 Pansmith Ln West Islip NY 11795-4724 Office: Grumman Aircraft Systems MS A30-005 Bethpage NY 11714

AUBUT, MARCEL, lawyer, sports association official; b. St. Hubert de Riviere-du-Loup, Que., Can., Jan. 5, 1948; s. Roland and Omerine (Proulx) A.; m. Francine Vallée, Aug. 15, 1970; children: Melanie, Julie, Catherine. BA, Academie de Québec, Que., 1968; LLB, U. Laval, 1970, LLM, 1975. Bar: Que. 1971; appointed Queen's Counsel, 1987. Assoc. Tremblay, Beauvais, Bouchard, Truchon & Morisset, Québec, 1972-76, sr. ptnr., 1976-83; legal advisor, sec., treas. Que. Nordiques Hockey Club, Charlesbourg, Que., 1976-78; pres., chief exec. officer Que. Nordiques Hockey Club, 1978—, chmn. bd. govs., 1980—; gov. NHL, Que., 1979—; sr. ptnr., dir. Aubut & Chabot, Québec, 1983—; prof. civil law Bar, Que., 1976-86; pres., chief exec. officer Trans-Am. Prodns., Montreal, 1984—; bd. dirs. Major Can. Corps.; dir. various corps. Chmn. bd., chief exec. officer internat. festival sports, culture and arts Rendez-Vouz 87, Que.; pres. La fête du Can., 1985. Recipient Order of Can., 1986; recipient Exec. of Yr. award NHL, 1987. Mem. Can. Bar Assn., Que. Bar Assn., Que. Jr. Bar Assn., Que. C. of C., Industry and Constrn., Que. Jr. C. of C., Garnison Club, Lions (Sillery and St.-Foy chpts.), Royal 22d Regiment Club (hon.). Office: Quebec Nordiques, 2205 Ave du Colisee, Quebec, PQ Canada G1L 4W7

AUCHINCLOSS, LOUIS STANTON, writer; b. Lawrence, N.Y., Sept. 27, 1917; s. Joseph Howland and Priscilla (Stanton) A.; m. Adele Lawrence, Sept. 1957; children: John, Blake, Andrew. Student, Yale U., 1939; LL.B., U. Va., 1941; Litt.D., N.Y. U., 1974, Pace U., 1979, U. of the South, 1986. Bar: N.Y. bar 1941. Assoc. Sullivan & Cromwell, 1941-51; assoc. Hawkins, Delafield & Wood, N.Y.C., 1954-58, ptnr., 1958-86. Author: The Indifferent Children, 1947, The Injustice Collectors, 1950, Sybil, 1952, A Law for the Lion, 1953, The Romantic Egoists, 1954, The Great World and Timothy Colt, 1956, Venus in Sparta, 1958, Pursuit of the Prodigal, 1959, The House of Five Talents, 1960, Reflections of a Jacobite, 1961, Portrait in Brownstone, 1962, Powers of Attorney, 1963, The Rector of Justin, 1964, Pioneers and Caretakers, 1965, The Embezzler, 1966, Tales of Manhattan, 1967, A World of Profit, 1968, Motiveless Malignity, 1969, Second Chance, 1970, Edith Wharton, 1971, I Came As a Thief, Richelieu, 1972, The Partners, A Writer's Capital, 1974, Reading Henry James, 1975, The Winthrop Covenant, 1976, The Dark Lady, 1977, The Country Cousin, 1978, Persons of Consequence, 1979, Life, Law and Letters, 1979, The House of the Prophet, 1980, The Cat and the King, 1981, Watchfires, 1982, Exit Lady Masham, 1983, The Book Class, 1984, Honorable Men, 1985, Diary of a Yuppie, 1986, Skinny Island, 1987, The Golden Calves, 1988, Fellow Passengers, 1989, The Vanderbilt Era, 1989, The Lady of Situations, 1991, False Gods, 1992. Trustee Josiah Macy, Jr., Found.; chmn. Mus. City of N.Y. Lt. USNR, 1941-45. Mem. Nat. Acad. Arts and Letters, Assn. Bar City N.Y., Century Assn. Episcopalian. Home: 1111 Park Ave New York NY 10128-1234

AUDET, DAVID ARTHUR, transportation manager; b. Woonsocket, R.I., Apr. 19, 1957; s. Arthur Joseph and Rose Marie (De Salvo) A.; m. Carmencita Almoguez Duque, Jan. 19, 1981 (div. Apr. 1988). Student, Coll. of Oceaneering, Wilmington, Calif., 1983-84. Cert. comml. diver. Asst. mgr. Steward Towers, Laurel, Md., 1972-76; enlisted USMC, 1977, advanced through grades to staff sgt., resigned, 1987; warehouse mgr. Bell Industries, Anaheim, Calif., 1984-88; ops. mgr. Automatic Equipment Sales, Alexandria, Va., 1988-89; warehouse svcs., safety and transp. mgr. Ga.-Pacific, Washington, 1989—; pres. Sign Impressions, Laurel, 1988—. Inventor specialty tools, 1987; composer 25 copywrighted songs. Active H.M.B. Boys and Girls Club, Hyattsville, Md., 1991, First Bapt. Ch., Hyattsville, 1991. Mem. Am. Soc. of Non-Destructive Testing. Republican. Home: 14611 Shiloh Ct Laurel MD 20708-1081 Office: Butler Paper Ga-Pacific 331 Prince Georges Blvd Upper Marlboro MD 20772-7410

AUERBACH, PHILIP B., electronics consultant; b. N.Y.C., Dec. 20, 1923; s. Kasril and Mollie (Rosenberg) A.; m. Augusta Silverstein, June 28, 1943; children: Howard M., Richard M. BME, Cooper Union, 1951; MME, Poly. Inst., Bklyn., 1957; postgrad., Adelphi U., 1957-62. Registered profl. engr., N.Y. Program mgr. Arma div. Am. Bosch Arma Corp., Garden City, N.Y., 1953-65; v.p., gen. mgr. tactical systems Sperry Corp., Gt. Neck, N.Y., 1965-86; pres. Paramax Electronics Inc. subs. sperry Can. Inc., Montreal, Que., 1983-86; exec. cons., New Hyde Park, N.Y., 1987—. Trustee Cooper Union, N.Y.C., 1980-83. Recipient citation Cooper Union, 1981. Fellow AIAA (assoc.); mem. IEEE (sr.), Nat. Security Indsl. Assn. (com. 1983-86), U.S. Navy League, Cooper Union Alumni Assn. (v.p. 1970-80, Gano Dunn medal 1987). Home and Office: 14 Laurel Dr New Hyde Park NY 11040-2144

AUERBACH, RED (ARNOLD JACOB AUERBACH), professional basketball team executive; b. N.Y.C., Sept. 20, 1917; s. Hyman and Marie (Thompson) A.; m. Dorothy Lewis, June 6, 1941; children: Nancy, Randy. BS in Phys. Edn., George Washington U., 1940, MA in Edn., 1941; LHD (hon.), Franklin Pierce Coll., 1981, U. Mass., 1982, Boston U., 1984; D in Bus. Adminstrn. (hon.), Cen. New Eng. Coll., 1986; ArtsD (hon.), Stonehill Coll., 1988; HHD (hon.), Am. Internat. Coll., 1988. Coach Washington Capitols, 1946-49, Tri-Cities Blackhawks, 1949-50; coach Boston Celtics Basketball Team, 1950-66, gen. mgr., 1966-84, pres., from 1984; rep. State Dept. for clinics, demonstrations, exhbns.; dir. basketball sch. Camp Milbrooks, Marshfield, Mass.; sports commentator, lectr.; dir. Seacrest Hotel, North Falmouth, Mass. Author: Fan and Coach, 1953, (with Paul Sann) Red Auerbach: Winning the Hard Way; (with Joe Fitzgerald) Red Auerbach: An Autobiography, Red Auerbach On and Off the Court; producer: (instructional video) Winning Basketball, 1987. Chmn. Mass. chpt. Easter Seal Soc. Served to lt. USN, 1943-46. Recipient Arch McDonald Achievement award, 1962, Boston's Disting. Achievement medal, 1965, Sports Achievement award B'nai B'rith; named Nat. Basketball Assn. Coach of Year, 1965; named to Nat. Basketball Hall of Fame, 1968, Naismith Meml. Basketball Hall of Fame, 1968; chosen All-Time NBA Coach; coach 11 consecutive all star games; winner 10 Ea. div. titles, 9 world titles. Mem. Nat. Coaches Assn., Omicron Delta Kappa, Colonials (George Washington U.). Club: Touchdown (award) (Washington). Office: care Boston Celtics 151 Merrimac 5th Fl Boston MA 02114

AUERBACH, SYLVIA, author, freelance writer; b. Phila.; d. Meyer Schwartz and Edith Frankel; m. Albert Auerbach, Feb. 28, 1942; children: Steven, Carl. BA, U. Pa.; MS in Journalism, Columbia U., 1960; grad. cert., London Sch. Econs., 1970. Assoc. editor Fact mag., N.Y.C., 1983-84; editor Physicians Fin. News, N.Y.C., 1985; adj. prof. journalism St. John's U., N.Y.C., 1986-88; dir. Pub. Inst., U. Pa., Phila., 1988-90; adj. prof. journalism Temple U., Phila., 1989—. Author: Your Money: How To Make It Stretch, 1974, A Woman's Book of Money, 1976, An Insider's Guide to Auctions, 1981; contbr. articles to Barron's, Cosmopolitan, Rx Being Well, Sylvia Porter's Personal Fin. mag., others. Helen Slade Sanders fellow Columbia U., 1960; recipient Achievement award in Geriatric Edn., Temple U., 1989. Mem. Am. Soc. Journalists and Authors, Authors Guild, Phila. Writers Orgn. Jewish.

AUERBACH, VICTOR, management and licensing consultant; b. Phila., July 4, 1917; s. Samuel and Pauline (Steinberg) A.; m. Leona Fishkin, Mar. 3, 1946; children: Burt J., Paul S., Janet L. Sherman. BA magna cum laude, Bklyn. Coll., 1940; PhD, Poly. Inst. Bklyn., 1945. Chemist Bakelite Co., Bound Brook, N.J., 1942-43, 45-46, group leader, 1946-55; rsch. assoc. Nat. Def. Rsch. Coun., Bklyn., 1943-45; assoc. coord. patents Union Carbide Plastics Co., Bound Brook, 1955-62; coord. patents plastics div. Union Carbide Corp., Bound Brook, 1962-67, patent mgr. chems. and plastics, 1967-79, patent mgr. polyolefins div., 1979-81; pvt. practice cons. Plainfield, N.J., 1981—; instr. organic chemistry Poly. Inst. Bklyn., 1942-46. Inventor new resins, resinous compositions, dermatologically benign hardeners, soil conditioners, printing plates. Co-founder, mem. adv. bd. Youth Orgn. of North Plainfield, N.J., 1967-75; co-founder, mem. steering com. Hot Line, Plainfield, N.J., 1970-73; mem. Citizen's Adv. Com. North Plainfield Bd. of Edn., 1972, '78; co-founder, bd. dirs. Voluntary Action Ctr., Plainfield, 1981-85; counselor Somerset County Chaplaincy Coun., 1981-82, Tax Counseling for Elderly, Plainfield, 1986—. Poly. Inst. Bklyn. fellow, 1941-42. Mem. North Plainfield Creative Arts League (co-founder, exec. bd. 1966-68). Home and Office: 1218 Stillman Ave Plainfield NJ 07060-2729

AUERBACH, VICTOR HUGO, biochemist, researcher; b. N.Y.C., Oct. 2, 1928; s. Leo and Goldie (Ratner) A.; m. Helen M. Matalas, June 1, 1956. AB, Columbia U., 1951; AM, Harvard U., 1955, PhD, 1957. Instr. Med. Sch., U. Wis., Madison, 1957-58; asst. prof. Sch. Medicine, Temple U., Phila., 1958-64, assoc. prof., 1964-68, rsch. prof., 1968-85, sr. rsch. prof., 1985-92, emeritus rsch. prof., 1992—; dir., enzyme lab. St. Christopher's Hosp. for Children, 1958-85, dir. of labs., 1976-85; dir. enzyme lab. St. Christopher's Hosp. for Children, Phila., 1958-85, dir. of labs., 1978-85; pres. Child Health Assn., Inc., 1975-81. Mem. AAAS, Am. Chem. Soc., Am. Assn. Cancer Rsch., Am. Assn. Clin. Chemists, Am. Soc. Human Genetics, Am. Soc. Biochemists and Molecular Biologists, Soc. Pediatric Rsch., Coll. of Physicians Phila., Nat. Acad. Clin. Biochemistry, Am. Inst. Nutrition, Am. Fedn. Clin. Rsch., Soc. Exptl. Biology and Medicine, Biochem. Soc. (London), Sigma Xi. Home: 1244 Hoffman Rd Ambler PA 19002-5033

AUFDERHEIDE, PATRICIA ANN, mass communications educator; b. Badcanstast, Fed. Republic of Germany, Oct. 31, 1948; (parents Am. citizens); d. Arthur Carl and Mary Aufderheide; m. Stephan Lane Schwartzman, Jan. 11, 1988; children: Elias, Gabriel. BA, U. Minn., 1969, MA, 1973, PhD, 1976. Organizer South Mpls. Community Credit Union, Mpls., 1977; cultural editor In These Times, Chgo., 1978-84; sr. editor In These Times, Washington, 1984—, Am. Film Mag., Washington, 1982-83; policy analyst United Ch. of Christ, Office of Communication, Washington, 1986-87; vis. prof. Duke U., Durham, N.C., 1986, 87; asst. prof. Am. U., Washington, 1989—; mem. film adv. bd. Nat. Gallery of Art, 1987—; cons. Labor Inst. Pub. Affairs, AFL-CIO, Washington, 1984-85. Assoc. editor Black Film Rev., 1988—; editor Latin American Visions, 1989, Beyond PC: Toward a Politics of Understanding, 1992; contbr. articles to profl. jours. Local chair Nat. Writers Union, 1986-87; bd. dirs. Mt. Pleasant Montessori Sch., Washington, 1991. Recipient Nondaily Criticism award Chgo. Newspaper Guild, 1989, Environ. Writing award World Hunger Media Project, 1989, Investigative Journalism award Project Censored, 1979. Mem. Assn. Edn. in Journalism and Mass Communication (Teaching Standards award 1991), Soc. for Cinema Studies, Internat. Visual Literacy Assn., Internat. Communications Assn. (Woodrow Wilson hon. scholar), Phi Beta Kappa. Office: The Am U Sch Communication 4400 Massachusetts Ave NW Washington DC 20016-8017

AUG, STEPHEN M., business journalist; b. N.Y.C., June 4, 1936; s. Joseph and Mollie (Perlmutter) A.; m. Harriet J. Fazekas, Aug. 28, 1965 (dec. 1988); children: Jeffrey, Suzanne, Michael; m. Marjorie Levine, Feb. 16, 1991. BA, NYU, 1956; MS, Columbia U., 1958. Editor Home News of North Yonkers, N.Y., 1956-57; editorial asst. Candy Industry, N.Y.C., 1957; newsman AP, Denver, 1961-64, N.Y.C., 1965, Washington, 1966-68; with Bell Telephone Labs., Murray Hill, N.J., 1964; bus. reporter Washington Star, 1968-78, bus. editor, asst. mng. editor, 1978-81; corr. ABC News, Washington, 1981—, bus. editor, 1988. Author: (with others) Who's Watching the Airways, 1971; contbr. articles to popular mags. Lt. USCG, 1958-61, capt. USCGR, 1961-82. Recipient G.M. Loeb award U. Conn., 1973, Bus. Journalism award U. Mo., 1975. Mem. Nat. Press Club, Soc. Am. Bus. and Econ. Writers. Jewish. Home: 8815 Churchfield Ln Laurel MD 20708-2428 Office: ABC News 1717 Desales St NW Washington DC 20036-4407

AUGELLO, PAUL JOHN, JR., accountant; b. Rockville Centre, N.Y., Oct. 13, 1966; s. Paul J. and Marie P. (Raffaele) A.; m. Joanne Gioia, May 28, 1989. BS in Acctg., Villanova U., 1988. CPA, N.Y. Sr. acct. Deloitte & Touche, N.Y.C., 1988-91, Random House, Inc., N.Y.C., 1991—. Mem. AICPA, N.Y. State CPA Soc., Moose. Republican. Roman Catholic. Home: 217 Nassau Blvd S Garden City NY 11530-5532 Office: Random House Inc 201 E 50th St New York NY 10022-7703

AUGSBURGER, MYRON S., minister; b. Delphos, Ohio, Aug. 20, 1929; s. Clarence A. and Estella (Shenk) A.; m. Esther Kniss, Nov. 28, 1950; children: John M., Michael D., Marcia A. AB, Ea. Mennonite Coll., 1955, ThB, 1958; MDiv, Goshen Bibl. Sem., 1959; ThM, Union Theol. Sem., 1961, ThD, 1964; LittD (hon.), Houghton Coll., 1966; LLD (hon.), Alderson Broadas Coll., 1967, Anderson U., 1988; DD (hon.), North Western Coll., Orange City, Iowa, 1982; DHL (hon.), Roberts Wesleyan U., Rochester, N.Y., 1988, Bethel Coll., 1988. Ordained to ministry Mennonite Ch., 1951. Pastor Mennonite Ch., Sarasota, Fla., 1951-54; campus pastor Ea. Mennonite Coll., Harrisonburg, Pa., 1954-58; evangelist Inter Ch. Inc., New Holland, Pa., 1955-65; pres. Ea. Mennonite Coll. and Sem., Harrisonburg, 1965-80; pastor Washington Community Fellowship, 1981—; pres. Christian Coll. Coalition, Washington, 1988—; adj. prof., theology Ea. Mennonite Sem., 1981—; speaker and cons. in field. Author: Pilgrim Aflame, 1967 (filmed The Radicals 1988). Bd. dirs. Presbyn. Mins. Fund, Phila., 1978—, Evang. Coun. Fin. Accountability, Washington, 1990—, Choose Peace, Washington, 1985-87; moderator Mennonite Ch., Elkhart, Ind., 1983-85. Office: Christian Coll Coalition 329 8th St NE Washington DC 20002-6158

AUGUSTINE, NORMAN RALPH, industrial executive; b. Denver, July 27, 1935; s. Ralph Harvey and Freda Irene (Immenga) A.; m. Margareta Engman, Jan. 20, 1962; children: Gregory Eugen, René Irene. B.S.E. magna cum laude, Princeton U., 1957, M.S.E., 1959; D of Engring. (hon.), Rensselaer Poly. Inst., 1988; DSc (hon.), U. Colo., 1989; ED(hon.), W. Maryland Coll., 1990. Research asst. Princeton U., 1957-58; program mgr., chief engr. Douglas Aircraft Co., Inc., Santa Monica, Calif., 1958-65; asst. dir. def. research and engring. U.S. Govt., Office of Sec. Def., Washington, 1965-70; v.p. advanced systems Missiles and Space Co., LTV Aerospace Corp., Dallas, 1970-73; asst. sec. army The Pentagon, Washington, 1973-75; undersec. army The Pentagon, 1975-77; v.p. ops. Martin Marietta Aerospace Corp., Bethesda, Md., 1977-82; pres. Martin Marietta Denver Aerospace Co., 1982-85, sr. v.p., info. systems, 1985, pres., chief operating officer, 1986-87, vice chmn., chief exec. officer, 1987-88, chmn., chief exec. officer, 1988—, also bd. dirs.; bd. dirs. Phillips Petroleum Co., Procter & Gamble Co., Riggs Nat. Bank Corp., N.Am. Schs. Devel. Corp.; cons. office Sec. of Def., 1971—, Exec. Office Pres., 1971-73, Dept. Army, Dept. Air Force, Dept. Navy, FAA, Dept. Energy, Dept. Transp.; mem. USAF Sci. Adv. Bd.; chmn.

Def. Sci. Bd.; mem. NATO Group Experts on Air Def., 1966-70, NASA Rsch. and Tech. Adv. Coun., 1973-75; chmn. NASA Space Sytems and Tech. Adv. Bd., 1985—; mem. Chief of Naval Ops. Exec. Bd., 1989—; chmn. def. policy adv. com. on trade, 1988—. Author: Augustine's Laws; co-author: The Defense Revolution, 1990; mem. adv. bd. Jour. Def. Rsch., 1970—; assoc. editor Def. Systems Mgmt. Rev., 1977-82; mem. editorial bd. Astronautics and Aeros.; contbr. articles to profl. jours. Trustee Johns Hopkins U., Princeton U.; chmn. nat. program evaluation com., coun. v.p., nat. v.p. Boy Scouts Am., 1990—; chmn. bd. govs. ARC; mem. Immanuel Presbyn. Ch., McLean, Va., Policy Coun. Bus. Roundtable, 1988—, Bus. Coun., 1989—. Recipient Meritorious Svc. medal Dept. Def., 1970, 4 Disting. Civilian Svc. medals Dept. Def., James Forrestal medal Nat. Security Indsl. Assn., 1988, Nat. Engring. Award, Am. Assn. Engring. Socs., 1991. Fellow IEEE, AIAA (hon., bd. dirs. 1978-85, pres. 1983-84, Goddard medal 1988), Am. Astron. Soc., Am. Helicopter Soc. (dir. 1974-75); mem. AAAS, NAE, Internat. Acad. Astronautics, Assn. U.S. Army (pres. 1980-84, chmn. 1990—), Nat. Security Indsl. Assn. (Forrestal medal 1988), Indsl. Coll. Armed Forces (Eisenhower award 1990), Armed Forces Communications and Electronics Assn. (Sarnoff medal 1990), Nat. Space Club (Goddard Trophy 1991), Rotary (Nat. Space Trophy 1992), Phi Beta Kappa, Sigma Xi, Tau Beta Pi. Office: Martin Marietta Corp 6801 Rockledge Dr Bethesda MD 20817-1836

AUGUSTINE, ROBERT LEO, chemistry educator; b. Omaha, Nov. 15, 1932; s. Anthony Charles and Bernice (Czerniak) A.; m. Marilyn Filippella, Aug. 31, 1957; children: Theresa Marie, Mary Suzanne. BS, Creighton U., 1954; MA, Columbia U., 1955, PhD, 1957. Instr. U. Tex., Austin, 1957-59, asst. prof., 1959-61; asst. prof. Seton Hall U., South Orange, N.J., 1961-62, assoc. prof., 1962-69, prof. chemistry, 1969—, chmn. chemistry dept., 1988-91. Author: Catalytic Hydrogenation, 1965, Selective Hydrogenations, 1989; editor: Reduction, 1968, Oxidation, Vol. I, 1969, Vol. II, 1971, Carbon-Carbon Bond Formation, 1979, Catalysis of Organic Reactions, 1985, 2d edit., 1988; contbr. articles to profl. publs. NIH fellow, 1955-57; grantee Rsch. Corp., 1958-59, U. Tex. Rsch. Inst., 1958-61, NIH, 1959-68, Petroleum Rsch. Fund, 1965-67, NSF, 1982-83, U.S. Dept. Energy, 1984-91. Mem. Am. Chem. Soc., Royal Chem. Soc., N.Am. Catalysis Soc. (exec. bd. 1988—), Met. Catalysis Soc. (bd. dirs. 1979-80, 82-83, 86-87), Organic Reactions Catalysis Soc. (chmn. 1982-86, exec. bd. 1986—). Office: Seton Hall U Chemistry Dept South Orange NJ 07079

AUGUSTYN, FREDERICK JOHN, JR., librarian; b. Stamford, Conn., Aug. 4, 1951; s. Fred John and Helen Josephine (Bienkowski) A. BA, Boston U., 1973; student, U. Wis., 1973-77; MA, MLS, U. Md., 1983. Tchg./research asst. Dept. Hist. U. Md., College Park, 1979-83; librarian Libr. of Congress, Washington, 1984—. Book reviewer, editorial asst.: The Md. Historian, 1981-82. Mem. Am. Econ. Assn., Am. Hist. Assn., Am. Libr. Assn., Orgn. Am. Historians, Am. Polit. Sci. Assn., Phi Alpha Theta, Beta Phi Mu. Roman Catholic. Home: 7800 Hanover Pky # 301 Greenbelt MD 20770-2620 Office: Libr of Congress Washington DC 20540

AUKERMAN, DALE H., writer, peace advocate; b. West Alexandria, Ohio, June 16, 1930; s. Willard Henry and Lucille (Miller) A.; m. Ruth Maria Seebass, July 24, 1965; children: Daniel Chris, Miriam Jane, Maren Songmy. AB, U. Chgo., 1949, postgrad., 1949-52; postgrad., Glasgow U., 1961-62. Ordained minister Ch. of the Brethren, 1956. Pastor Ch. of the Brethren, Rodney, Mich., 1956-59; coord. Puidoux Theol. Peace Confs., Europe, 1960-62; peace rep. Ch. of the Brethren, various locations, 1962-65; dir. studies Internat. Friendship House, West Germany, 1966-68; coord. Brethren Action Movement, North Manchester, Ind., 1968-69; pastor Ch. of the Brethren, Sunfield, Mich., 1970-72; peace evangelist Ch. of the Brethren, Union Bridge, Md., 1973-77; writer Union Bridge, 1978—. Author: Darkening Valley: A Biblical Perspective on Nuclear War, 1981, Dawn at Midnight: Terminal Politics and the Messianic Hope, 1993; co-author: On the Ground Floor of Heaven, 1980; contbr. articles to newspapers. Coord. Brethren Peace Fellowship, eastern U.S., 1973—; lectr., conf. organizer; mem. gen. bd. Ch. of the Brethren, 1975-80. Named Peacemaker of the Yr., Leona Row Eller Found., 1991. Home: 191 Stem Rd Union Bridge MD 21791 Office: Brethren Peace Fellowship PO Box 455 New Windsor MD 21776

AULT, NEIL NORMAN, engineering consultant; b. Dunkirk, Ohio, Mar. 31, 1922; s. Russell William and Agnes Elizabeth (Meeks) A.; m. Ruth Anne Hoffman, June 16, 1946; children: Nancy, William, Brian. B in Ceramic Engring., Ohio State U., 1947, MSc in Ceramic Engring., 1948, PhD in Ceramic Engring., 1950. Registered profl. engr., Mass. Rsch. engr. Norton Co., Worcester, Mass., 1950-87, various positions, 1987; pvt. practice cons. Holden, Mass., 1987—; chmn. materials adv. com. on export controls U.S. Dept. Commerce, Washington, 1987—. Inventee in field. Capt. USAF, 1944-46, Africa and ETO. Mem. Am. Ceramic Soc. (disting. life mem., Disting. Ceramist award 1976). Congregationalist. Home: 52 Holden St Holden MA 01520-1734

AUMILLER, GARY STEVEN, psychologist; b. Washington, July 27, 1956; s. Roy Edward and Marie Agnes (LaPorte) A. AB, U. Notre Dame, 1978; MA, Hofstra U., 1981, PhD, 1983. Lic. psychologist. Dir. psychology Suffolk Devel. Ctr., Smithtown, N.Y., 1988-89; owner, dir. Ctr. for Profl. Counseling, Hauppauge, N.Y., 1985-89, Psychol. Svcs., Hauppauge, 1989—; psychology cons. to film Small Kill. Actor, assoc. producer (film) Murdered Innocence; syndicated columnist The Hometown Psychologist. Vol. Interfaith Nutrition Network-Soup Kitchen, N.Y., 1990—. Mem. Am. Psychol. Assn., Suffolk Psychol. Assn., Am. Brewers Assn., Notre Dame Club N.Y. Republican. Roman Catholic. Office: 760 Veterans Hwy Hauppauge NY 11788-2300

AUNE, THOMAS MARTIN, immunologist; b. Winona, Minn., Apr. 23, 1951; s. Henrik Joakin and Edna Mae (Crisp) A.; m. Patricia Ann Hurt, Dec. 8, 1978; children: Jessica Phillips, Zachary Thomas. BS, Rhodes Coll., 1973; PhD, U. Tenn., 1976. Postdoctoral fellow Stanford U., Palo Alto, Calif., 1977-78; postdoctoral fellow Washington U., St. Louis, 1979-80, asst. prof. immunology, 1981-86; scientist Genentech, Inc., San Francisco, 1986-88; sect. head Miles, Inc., West Haven, Conn., 1988—. Contbr. over 50 articles to sci. jours. Recipient Jr. Faculty Rsch. award Am. Cancer Soc., 1982, Rsch. Career Devel. award, Nat. Cancer Inst., 1985. Mem. Am. Assn. Pathology, Am. Assn. Immunology. Office: Miles Inc 400 Morgan Ln West Haven CT 06516-4175

AUNGST, BRUCE JEFFREY, pharmaceutical company scientist; b. Pottsville, Pa., Nov. 22, 1952; s. Roy Stewart and Grace M. (Rupp) A.; m. Judith M. Smith, Aug. 23, 1980; children: Matthew, Colleen, Christopher, Keenan. BS, Pa. State U., 1974, MS, 1977; PhD, SUNY, Buffalo, 1982. Rsch. pharmacist DuPont, Wilmington, Del., 1981-85, sr. rsch. pharmacist, 1985-91; prin. rsch. scientist DuPont Merck, Wilmington, 1991—. Contbr. articles to profl. jours.; patentee in field. Mem. AAAS, Am. Assn. Pharm. Scientists. Office: DuPont Merck PO Box 80400 Wilmington DE 19880-0400

AURNER, ROBERT RAY, II, oil company and restaurant development executive; b. Madison, Wis., Mar. 24, 1927; s. Robert Ray and Kathryn (Dayton) A.; m. Phyllis Barrett, 1951 (div. 1966); children: Sheryl, Roxanne, Kathryn, Suzanne, Robert III; m. Deborah Marion Lucas, Jan. 31, 1976; children: William Lucas, Christopher Ray. AA, Monterey (Calif.) Peninsula Coll., 1948; BA, Calif. State U., Fresno, 1950; postgrad., U. Calif., U. Iowa, Duquesne U., Pitts. Lic. real estate broker, Calif., Pa., N.Y.; registered investment advisor. Sr. sales rep. retail svc. stas. Shell Oil Co., San Francisco, 1957-62; mgr. regional real estate Gulf Oil Corp., San Francisco and Oakland, Calif., 1962-67; real estate mgr., dir. Midwest ops. Sunray DX Oil Co. (merger Sunoco), Tulsa, 1967-71, Milex Auto Diagnostic Franchise, Inc., Plymouth Meeting, Pa., 1972-76; real estate adminstr. Steak and Ale Restaurants div. Pillsbury Cos., Dallas, 1978-80; real estate mgr. div. N.Y. and Phila. regions Phillsbury Cos. and Burger King Corp., 1980-86; real estate mgr. Pizza Hut div. Pepsi-Cola Inc., N.Y.C. Metro and SMSA, 1986-88; corp. dir. real estate and franchising Nathan's Famous Restaurant, N.Y.C., 1989-90; pres., CEO Aurner and Assocs., Mktg. Cons., 1990—; chmn. bd. dirs. Bristlecone Trading and Devel. Inc., Carmel, Calif., Surf City, N.J. With USNR, PTO. Named to Hon. Order Ky. Col., Gov. of Ky., Commodore in Okla. Navy Gov. of Okla. Mem. USS Yellowstone Assn. (USNR), U. Iowa and Calif. State U. Fraternity, Sigma Alpha Epsilon, Buccaneer Club (N.Y. and Conn.) (pres.), Elks. Republican. Episcopalian. Home and Office: 908 Long Beach Blvd Surf City NJ 08008 also: PO Box 222018 Carmel-By-The-Sea Carmel CA 93922

AUSTAD, VIGDIS, computer software company executive; b. Utica, N.Y., Sept. 26, 1954; d. Helge and Viola (Hammervold) A. BS in Econs., U. Pa., 1981; postgrad., NYU, 1982-84. Cert. employee benefit specialist. Asst. to pres. Almet, Inc., Bernardsville, N.J., 1973-81; mgr. info. systems Buck Consultants, Inc., N.Y.C., 1981-86; v.p., mktg. mgr. Cascade Techs. Inc., N.Y.C., 1986-88, pres., chief exec. officer, 1988—; treas., dir. Cascade Techs., Inc., 1985—. Contbr. articles to profl. publs. Fundraiser, Rep. Club, N.J., 1988-89. Recipient scholarship, U. Pa., Phila., 1979-81. Mem. Info. Tech. Assn. Am., Am. Soc. Pension Actuaries, Internat. Found. Cert. Employee Benefit Specialists, Cert. Employee Benefit Specialists (found., dir. 1986-88), Am. Mgmt. Assn. Republican. Lutheran. Home: 19 Indian Spring Rd Cranford NJ 07016-1615 Office: Cascade Techs Inc 1001 Ave Of The Americas New York NY 10018-5411

AUSTEN, K(ARL) FRANK, physician; b. Akron, Ohio, Mar. 14, 1928; s. Karl and Bertle (Jehle) A.; m. Joycelyn Chapman, Apr. 11, 1959; children: Leslie Marie, Karla Ann, Timothy Frank, Jonathan Arthur. AB, Amherst Coll., 1950; MD, Harvard U., 1954. Intern in medicine Mass. Gen. Hosp., 1954-55, asst. resident, 1955-56, sr. resident, 1958-59, chief resident, 1961, asst. in medicine, 1962-63, asst. physician, 1963-66, chief pulmonary unit, 1964-66; also cons. in medicine; practice medicine, specializing in internal medicine, allergy and immunology Mass. Gen. Hosp., Boston, 1962-66; USPHS postdoctoral research fellow Nat. Inst. Med. Research, Mill Hill, London, 1959-61; asst. in medicine Harvard Med. Sch., 1961, instr., 1961-62, asso. in medicine, 1962-64, asst. prof., 1965-66, assoc. prof., 1966-68, prof., 1969-72, Theodore B. Bayles prof., 1972—; physician-in-chief Robert B. Brigham Hosp., 1966-80; chmn. dept. rheumatology and immunology Brigham and Women's Hosp., 1980—; mem. fellowship subcom. Arthritis Found., 1968-71, chmn., 1971; mem. council Infectious Disease Soc. Am., 1969-71; mem. arthritis tng. grants com. Nat. Inst. Arthritis and Metabolic Diseases, NIH, 1970-73; mem. directing group, task force on immunology and disease Nat. Inst. Allergy and Infectious Diseases, 1972-73; bd. dirs. Arthritis Found., 1972-75, chmn. manpower study com., 1972-73, chmn. research com. Multipurpose Arth. Ctr., 1972-76; chmn. research com. Med. Found., Inc., 1972-76; mem. Am. Bd. Allergy and Immunology, 1973-78, Nat. Commn. on Arthritis and Related Musculoskeletal Diseases, 1975-76, Allergy and Immunology Research com., NIAID, 1975-79, chmn., 1976-79; chmn. nomenclature com. Internat. Union Immunological Socs., 1983—; mem. adv. com. to the dir. NIH, 1986-90; physician Peter Bent Brigham Hosp., 1966-80. Mem. editorial bd. Arthritis and Rheumatism, 1968-81, Proc. of Transplantation Soc., 1968-82, Jour. Infectious Diseases, 1969-79, Jour. Exptl. Medicine, 1971—, Immunol. Communications, 1972-85, Clin. Immunology and Immunopathology, 1972-89, Proc. of Nat. Acad. Scis, 1978-83, Clin. and Exptl. Immunology, 1978-88, Immunopharmacology, 1979—, Internat. Jour. Immunopharmacology, 1984, Advances in Immunology, 1985—, Advances in Pharmacology, 1989—; contbr. articles to profl. jours. Trustee Amherst Coll., 1981—. Served to capt., M.C. U.S. Army, 1956-58. Mem. NAS (chmn. sect. on med. microbiology and immunology 1983-86), Inst. Medicine, Am. Soc. Pharm. and Exptl. Therapeutics, Am. Soc. Exptl. Pathology, Am. Assn. Immunologists (pres. 1977-78), Am. Acad. Allergy and Immunology (pres. 1981), Brit. Soc. Immunology, Am. Soc. Clin. Investigation, Am. Rheumatism Assn., ACP, Transplantation Soc., Am. Acad. Arts and Scis., Assn. Am. Physicians (recorder 1978-84, pres. 1989-90), Am. Acad. Allergy (exec. com. 1970-72, sec. 1977-80, pres. 1981), Interurban Clin. Club, Fedn. Am. Soc. Exptl. Biology, Internat. Assn. Allergology and Clin. Immunology. Office: Brigham & Women's Hospital PBB-B-2 75 Francis St Boston MA 02115-6195 also: 250 Longwood Ave Rm 604 Boston MA 02115

AUSTIN, ALAN DOUGLAS, arts foundation executive, consultant; b. Ocala, Fla., Aug. 17, 1939; s. Hugh Stewart and Helen Dearmin (Clark) A.; m. Judith Ann Phelps, Jan. 28, 1961; children: Jennifer Carol, Sara Denise. AB, Duke U., 1961. Assoc. editor Duke U. Press, Durham, N.C., 1961-62; sr. editor MOTIVE Mag., Nashville, 1962-69; dir. publs. Inst. for Policy Studies, Washington, 1969-70; pres. The New Classroom, Washington, 1970-77; exec. dir. The Watershed Found., Washington, 1978—; publ. lectr. Libr. of Congress, Washington, 1974; panelist, lectr. The Radio Found., N.Y.C., 1984; media grants panelist NEH, Washington, 1985-86. Editor: (book) The Revolutionary Imperative, 1968, (cassette mag.) Black Box, 1972-78; producer: (radio series) Poem That Never Ends, 1980. Pres. ACLU of Tenn., Nashville, 1967-68. Recipient grants Nat. Endowment Arts, Washington, 1972-88, D.C. Commn. on the Arts, Washington, 1974-89, Witter Bynner Found., Santa Fe, 1980, The Lannan Found., L.A., 1991. Mem. Poetry Soc. Am., Modern Lang. Assn., Direct Mail Mktg. Assn. D.C., The Writer's Ctr. (treas. 1979-84, dir. 1978-90). Democrat. Episcopalian. Office: The Watershed Found 6925 Willow St NW Ste 201 Washington DC 20012-2023

AUSTIN, ALLEN EARLE, entrepreneur, consultant; b. Enfield, Maine, Feb. 16, 1942; s. Raymond Lamont and Bertha Virginia (Bagley) A.; m. Mary Lee Young, Apr. 20, 1963; children: Stephen Fuller, Mary Elizabeth, Mary Kathleen, Mary Victoria, Young Jack. Student, Bononos Inst., 1968, Charles County Community Coll., 1974, Mich. State U., 1984. Cert. dir. of safety. Pawnbroker Suitland (Md.) Pawnbrokers, 1964-75; owner A&M Assocs., Charlotte Hall, Md., 1972-76, Cedar City (Utah) Trading Post, 1976, Big Al's Family Diner, Farmington, Maine, 1977; v.p. LUKO Express, Bryan's Road, Md., 1977-79; mgr. govt. and safety regulations Embassy Dairies The Southland Corp., Waldorf, Md., 1979-90; owner, sr. cons. ALMA Assocs., Port Tobacco, Md., 1985—; instr. Md. State Police, Waldorf, 1983; cons. Md. Safety Coun., Balt., 1985—; employment specialist LDS Ch., Suitland, 1979—. Pres. Parent, Tchr. and Student Assns. of Margaret Brent Sch., Chaptico, Md., 1978-79, of Picowaxen Sch., 1982-84, Newburg, Md.; fundraiser Charles County Rep. Com., 1985. With U.S. Army, 1961-63. Recipient recognition Picowaxen Sch., 1984, The Md. Ind. newspaper, Waldorf, 1989. Mem. Am. Soc. Safety Engrs. (cons.), Assn. Employee Assistance Practitioners. Mem. LDS Ch.

AUSTIN, JON NICHOLAS, museum director; b. Peoria, Ill., Aug. 12, 1959; s. Harold Hutchison and Marjorie Elizabeth (Johnson) A. BA cum laude, Bradley U., 1981; MA, NYU, 1984, cert., 1985. Registrar Peoria Hist. Soc., 1978-82; asst. to dir. Peoria Pub. Libr., 1985-87; dir. St. Lawrence County Hist. Assn., Canton, N.Y., 1987; exec. dir. Rome (N.Y.) Hist. Soc., 1988—. Active Hist. and Scenic Preservation Commn., Rome, 1988—; chmn. workship and fine art com. 1st Unitedd Meth. Ch., Rome, 1989—, layleader, 1992—. Mem. Am. Assn. Mus., Am. Assn. for State and Local History (standards, tenure and ethics com. 1991—), Soc. Mayflower Descendants, Sons Am. Revolution, Regional Coun. Hist. Agys. (sec. 1991—, bd. dirs. 1990—), Cen. N.Y. Libr. Resources Coun. (documentary heritage program com. 1991—), Phi Alpha Theta. Republican. Home: 312 N Washington St Apt 1 Rome NY 13440-5121 Office: Rome Hist Soc 200 Church St Rome NY 13440-5872

AUSTIN, MARION RUSSELL, education educator, consultant; b. Keene, N.H., May 28, 1927; d. Edward John and Bessie (Merrifield) Russell; m. Donald Stevens Austin, Apr. 9, 1951. BEd, Keene State Coll., 1951, MEd, 1970; nursery cert., St. Nicholas Montessori Sch., London, 1975, jr. cert., 1976. Tchr. pub. schs. N.H., Va., 1951-60; dir. pvt. kindergarten Troy, N.H., 1960-71; chair dept. edn. Franklin Pierce Coll., Rindge, N.H., 1971—, founder, dir. Project Soar for gifted students, 1979—; cons. in gifted edn. N.H. Dept. Edn., 1980—, mem. com. on gifted edn.; bd. dirs. Keene (N.H.) Montessori Sch., 1986—. Author: Instructor History in the Curriculum, 1981. Trustee Gay-Kimball Libr., Troy, 1970-75. Mem. N.Am. Montessori Tchrs. Assn., Internat. Montessori Soc. Republican. Episcopalian. Office: Dept Edn Franklin Pierce Coll Rindge NH 03461

AUSTIN, MARSHALL EDWARD, financial planner; b. Rochester, N.Y., Aug. 3, 1957; s. Delmer Edward and Betty Janet (Watt) A.; m. Janet Marie LaRosa, Feb. 16, 1980; children: Craig Thomas, Christine Mae Austin. BBA, Cleve. State U., 1979. Cert. fin. planner. Mgr. Toys R Us, Saginaw, Mich., 1980-84; cons. Creative Employee Benefits, Grand Blanc, Mich., 1984-87; fin. planner Eagle Equities, Glen Burnie, Md., 1987-89, Comprehensive Fin. Svcs., Severna Park, Md., 1989—. Named one of Outstanding Young Men of Am., 1988. Mem. Inst. Fin. Planners, Internat. Assn. Fin. Planners. Republican. Baptist. Club: Exchange (Glen Burnie). Home: 10477 Greenbrier Dr Brighton MI 48116-9618 Office: Comprehensive Fin Svcs 811 Governor Ritchie Hwy Ste 25 Severna Park MD 21146

AUSTIN, MICHAEL CHARLES, insurance company executive; b. Syracuse, N.Y., Dec. 7, 1955; s. Harold Ernest and Helen (Sanderson) A.; m. Patricia Farrell, Aug. 12, 1978; children: Bryan, Michael. AA in Liberal Arts, Mohawk Valley Community Coll., 1974; BA in English, SUNY, Oswego, 1976. Dir. pub. rels. United Way of Greater Utica, N.Y., 1976-79; asst. mgr. advt. and pub. relations Utica Nat. Ins. Group, 1979-81, asst. dir. corp. communications, 1981-89, dir. corp. communications, 1989—; asst. sec. Utica Mut. Ins. Co.; adj. faculty Mohawk Valley Community Coll., Utica, 1982. Contbr. articles to profl. jours. Bd. dirs. United Cerebral Palsy Found., Utica, 1987—, pres., 1992—, v.p. 1989-92, treas., 1988-89; pres. bd. trustees Mohawk Valley Community Coll. Found., 1990—; vice chmn. Mohawk Valley Stop-DWI, Utica, 1985—, mem. exec. com., 1988—; dir. Mohawk Valley Coun. on Alcoholism, Utica, 1987—, United Way, Utica, 1982. Recipient Alumni Merit award Mohawk Valley C.C., 1989. Mem. Ins. Consumer Affairs Exch., Ins. Mktg. Communications Assn. (bd. dirs.), Mohawk Valley Advt. Club (pres. 1989-90, dir. 1982—, editor newsletter 1982, awards excellence, Ad Person of Yr. award 1992), Syracuse and Ad Club, MV Ad Club, Profl. Ins. Communications Am. Roman Catholic. Office: Utica Nat Ins Group 180 Genesee St Utica NY 13502-4324

AUSTIN, PATRICIA QUINN, nurse; b. Springfield, Mass., Mar. 28, 1958; d. Philip Richard and Averill Mary (Smith) Q. BSN, St. Anselm Coll., 1980. Cert. oncology nurse. Clin. nurse I-II Beth Israel Hosp., Boston, 1980-82; vis. nurse Vis. Nurse Assn. Boston, 1982-84, home health aide field supr., 1984-85; clin. nurse III Beth Israel Hosp., Boston, 1985-88; clin. nurse III-IV ambulatory hematology-oncology unit Beth Israel Hosp., 1988—. Mem. Oncology Nursing Soc., Boston Oncology Nursing Soc. Democrat. Roman Catholic. Home: 77 Adams St # 709 Quincy MA 02169-2025 Office: Beth Israel Hosp 330 Brookline Ave Boston MA 02215-5491

AUSTIN, THOMAS HOWARD, chemist; b. Mt. Pleasant, Tex., Aug. 12, 1937; s. Thomas Leon and Lillian Lucille (Fletcher) A.; m. Lucille Carroll Austin, Aug. 1, 1982; children: Janet Lynn Austin Lumpkin, Jeffrey Scott. BS, Cen. Okla. State U., 1961; PhD, Okla. State U., 1965. Teaching asst. Okla. State U., Stillwater, 1961-62, rsch. asst., 1962-65; sr. project chemist Texaco Chem. Co., Austin, Tex., 1965-87; prin. chemist Arco Chem. Co., Newtown Square, Pa., 1987—. Contbr. sci. articles to profl. jours.; patentee in field. Mem. AAAS, Am. Chem. Soc., Soc. Automotive Engrs., Sigma Xi, Phi Lambda Upsilon. Office: Arco Chemical Co 3801 W Chester Pike Newtown Square PA 19073-2387

AUSTIN, VICTOR LEE, priest; b. Oklahoma City, Mar. 29, 1956; s. Marshall Lee and Dorothy Jeane (Canada) A.; m. Susan Lanier Gavahan, Sept. 29, 1978; children: Michael Lee, Emily Parker. BA, St. John's Coll., Santa Fe, N.Mex., 1978; MA, U. N.Mex., 1982; MDiv, Gen. Theol. Seminary, N.Y.C., 1985. Ordained priest Episcopal Ch., 1986. Tchr. math. Santo Domingo Indian Reservation, Bernalillo, N.Mex., 1979-81, Santa Fe Pub. Schs., 1981-82; curate Zion Episcopal Ch., Wappingers Falls, N.Y., 1985-89; rector Ch. of Resurrection, Hopewell Junction, N.Y., 1989—. Editor Care and Community; book rev. editor Episcopal New Yorker; contbr. articles to ch. mags. Sec. Ecumenical Commn. of Episcopal Diocese of N.Y., 1989—. Mem. Rotary. Office: Ch of Resurrection PO Box 148 Hopewell Junction NY 12533-0148

AUSTRIAN, ROBERT, physician, educator; b. Balt., Apr. 12, 1916; s. Charles Robert and Florence (Hochschild) A.; m. Babette Friedmann Bernstein, Dec. 29, 1963; stepchildren: Jill Bernstein, Toni Bernstein. AB, Johns Hopkins U., 1937, MD, 1941; DSc honoris causa, Hahnemann Med. Coll., 1980, Phila. Coll. Pharmacy and Sci., 1981, U. Pa., 1987. Diplomate: Am. Bd. Internal Medicine. House officer Johns Hopkins Hosp., 1941-50, asst. dir. med. out-patient dept., 1951-52; assoc. prof. medicine, then prof. medicine SUNY Coll. Medicine, 1952-62; John Herr Musser prof., chmn. rsch. medicine U. Pa. Sch. Medicine, 1962-86, prof. emeritus, chmn. emeritus, 1986—; attending physician Hosp. U. Pa.; Tyndale vis. lectr. and prof. Coll. Medicine U. Utah, 1964; spl. research on infectious diseases, bacterial genetics; mem. Meningococcal Infections Com., 1964-72, Commn. on Acute Respiratory Disease, 1965-72, Commn. Streptococcal and Staphylococcal Diseases, 1970-72, Armed Forces Epidemiol. Bd.; cons. surg. gen. U.S. Army Research and Devel. Command, 1966-69; mem. subcom. streptococcus and pneumococcus Internat. Com. Bacteriol. Nomenclature; mem. allergy and immunology study sect. Nat. Inst. Allergy and Infectious Diseases, 1965-69, mem. bd. sci. counselors, 1967-70, chmn., 1969-70. Mem. editorial bd.: Jour. Bacteriology 1964-69, Am. Rev. Respiratory Diseases, 1963-66, Bacteriol. Rev., 1967-71, Jour. Infectious Diseases, 1969-74, Antimicrobial Agents and Chemotherapy, 1972-86, Infection and Immunity, 1973-81, Revs. of Infectious Diseases, 1979-89, Vaccine, 1983—. Trustee Johns Hopkins U., 1963-69. Served to capt. M.C. AUS, 1943-45. Recipient U.S. Typhus Commn. medal, 1947; Albert Lasker Clin. Med. Research award, 1978; Phila. award, 1979; Willard O. Thompson award Am. Geriatric Soc., 1981, others. Fellow ACP (master, James D. Bruce Meml. award 1979), N.Y. Acad. Scis., Am. Acad. Microbiology, AAAS (chmn. sect. on med. scis. 1975); mem. Assn. Am. Physicians, Am. Soc. Clin. Investigation, Am. Clin. and Climatol. Assn. (pres. 1984), Am. Soc. Microbiology (v.p. N.Y. br. 1961-62), Am. Philos. Soc., Nat. Acad. Scis., Soc. Exptl. Biology and Medicine, Harvey Soc., Am. Fedn. Clin. Research, Inst. Medicine (sr.), Balt. Med. Soc., Am. Assn. Immunologists, N.Y. Acad. Medicine (sec. sect. microbiology 1961-62), Phila. County Med. Soc. (Strittmatter award 1979), Coll. Physicians Phila. (Meritorious Service award 1980, pres.-elect 1986, pres. 1988-90), Interurban Clin. Club (pres. 1970), Infectious Disease Soc. Am. (pres. 1971, Maxwell Finland lecture award 1974, Bristol award 1986), Johns Hopkins Soc. Scholars, Phi Beta Kappa, Sigma Xi, Alpha Omega Alpha, Omicron Delta Kappa. Club: 14 W. Hamilton Street (Balt.). Office: U Pa Sch Medicine Dept Rsch Medicine Philadelphia PA 19104-6088

AUTERI, ROSE MARY PATTI, school system administrator; b. N.Y.C., June 6, 1928; d. Francesco and Stefana (Patti) A. BS, Hunter Coll., 1950; MA, Columbia U., 1962; EdD, Nova U., 1975; postdoctoral, Columbia U., 1976-77. Tchr. Howell Rd Sch., Valley Stream, N.Y., 1951-58, asst. prin., 1958-64; prin. Centennial Ave Sch., Roosevelt, N.Y., 1964-69, Northside Sch., Levittown, N.Y., 1969-83, Abbey Ln. Sch., Levittown, 1983-89; adminstr. in charge elem. schs. Levittown Pub. Schs., 1989-90; prin. Abbey Ln. Sch., Levittown, 1990—. Recipient Disting. Prin. award State of N.Y., 1988, 89, Disting. Svc. award Nat. PTA; named Italian Am. Woman of Yr., 1990. Mem. Am. Assn. Sch. Adminstrs., Nat. Assn. Elem. Sch. Prins., Nat. Assn. Supervision and Curriculum Devel., Nassau County Elem. Prins. Assn. (pres.), L.I. Assn. Supervision and Curriculum Devel. (bd. dirs.), N.Y. State Assn. Devel., Am. Assn. Electroencephalographic Technologists, Am.-Italian Hist. Assn. (sec. 1988—, pres., editor L.I. regional chpt.). Home: 1816 Thomas St Merrick NY 11566-2652 Office: Levittown Pub Schs Abbey Ln Levittown NY 11756-4007

AUTH, TONY, artist; b. Akron, Ohio, May 7, 1942; s. William Anthony and Julia Kathleen (Donnally) A. B.A., U. Calif. at Los Angeles, 1965. Chief med. illustrator Rancho Los Amigos Hosp., Downey, Calif., 1964-70. Author/illustrator: children's book Sleeping Babies', 1989; editorial cartoonist, Phila. Inquirer, 1971—; anthologies of drawings: Behind the Lines, 1978, Lost in Space - The Reagan Years, 1988. Recipient awards Overseas Press Club, 1975, 76, 84, 86, Sigma Delta Chi, 1976; Pulitzer prize, 1976. Office: Phila Inquirer 400 N Broad St Philadelphia PA 19130-4099

AUTORINO, ANNE TURNBULL, retired social worker; b. Tampa, Dec. 27, 1914; d. Stockton Graeme and Mary Barney (Walker) Turnbull; m. Frank Berlin Holt, Mar. 27, 1943 (div. 1948); m. Michael Autorino, Mar. 26, 1960. BS in Social Sc., Coll. William and Mary, 1936; MS, Psychiat. Social Work, Columbia U., 1947. Diplomate, Am. Bd. Examiners in Clin. Social Work. Med. social worker social svc. dept. N.Y. Infirmary, N.Y.C., 1948-49; sr. social worker, foster home dept. Edwin Gould Found., N.Y.C., 1949-55; med. social worker, polio epidemic emergency worker Boston City Hosp., 1955-56; dir. social svc. dept. Wyckoff Heights Hosp., Bklyn., 1954-55; social worker N.Y. Sch. for Deaf, White Plains, 1956-58; clin. social worker VA,

Newark, 1958-61; sch. social worker Div. Child Guidance, Bd. Edn., Newark, 1961-88; ret., 1988. Mem. Nat. Assn. Social Workers, N.J.Assn. Social Workers, AAUW, Ret. Educators Assn.

AVAKIAN, LAURA ANN, hospital administrator; b. DeSoto, Mo., July 6, 1945; d. Edward Ernest and Elizabeth (Gamel) McClary; m. Stephen Avakian, Dec. 30, 1969. BA, U. Mo., 1967; MA, Northwestern U., 1968. Instr. Sacramento (Calif.) State Coll., 1968-69; English tchr. Hathaway Brown Sch., Cleve., 1969-73; pers. profl. Huron Rd. Hosp., Cleve., 1974-76, dir. human resources, 1978-80; dir. employment Cleve. Clinic Found., 1976-78; v.p. human resources Beth Israel Hosp., Boston, 1980—. Assoc. editor Yearbook of Healthcare Management, 1990, 91. Mem. Mayor's Commn. on Comparable Worth, Boston, 1989-90. Mem. Am. Soc. Healthcare Human Resources Adminstrn. (bd. dirs. 1989—, Pres. Leadership award 1989), Soc. Human Resource Mgmt., Mass. Health Care Human Resources Assn. (pres. 1987-88). Office: Beth Israel Hosp 330 Brookline Ave Boston MA 02215-5491

AVALLONE, MICHAEL NICHOLAS, accountant; b. Hartford, Conn., Nov. 19, 1951; s. Arthur Nicholas and Constance (Giardini) A.; m. Lynda G. Miller, Sept. 22, 1979. BSBA, Boston Coll., 1973; MS in Fin., Bentley Coll., 1987. CPA, Mass. Supr. audit staff Coopers & Lybrand CPA's, Boston, 1973-78; supr., internal auditor Boston Edison Co., 1978-82, mgr. fin. reports, 1982—. Mem. AICPA, Mass. Soc. CPAs, Inst. Mgmt. Accts. Roman Catholic. Home: 188 Central St Rowley MA 01969 Office: Boston Edison Co 800 Boylston St # 344P Boston MA 02199-8001

AVEDISIAN, ARCHIE HARRY, community organization executive; b. Binghamton, N.Y., June 22, 1928; s. Harry and Charlotte (Charkjian) A.; m. Gloria Ann Rogers; children: Debra Ann, Anthony Joseph. BS in Edn., SUNY, Cortland, 1951; MA in Orgn. and Adminstrn., NYU, 1954, post-grad. Phys. dir. Jamestown Boys Club, N.Y.C., 1951-53; program dir. Flatbush Boys Club, Bklyn., 1953-56; exec. dir. Boys Clubs of East St. Louis, Ill., 1956-59, Columbia Park Boys Club, San Francisco, 1959-60, Santa Rosa Boys Clubs, Calif., 1960-67, Boys Clubs of Seattle and King County, 1967-72; exec. v.p. Boys and Girls Clubs of Greater Washington, D.C., 1972—; cons. Boys Clubs of Am. tng. program, 1974-75. Chmn. Seattle-King County Youth Commn., 1967-72, Congress for Community Programs, Santa Rosa, 1964, Calif. Youth Authority Sch. for Girls, 1961-66; United Way of Am., Washington, San Francisco, East St. Louis, Seattle, 1957—; bd. govs. Congress for Community Progress, East St. Louis, 1958; active Nat. Partnership Alcohol and Drug Abuse, 1986—, Greater Washington Billy Graham Crusade Adv. Com., 1986, Met. Washington Bd. Trade, 1973—, Montgomery County Employment Devel. Commn., 1978-82, Sonoma County Community Action Council, 1969, Govs. Conf. on Youth, Sonoma County, 1965, Gen. Plan Program, Santa Rosa, 1964. Recipient Disting. Service award Jr. C. of C., 1958, various gov. commd. awards, 1970-73, various United Way Am. awards, 1974-79, H. Roe Bartle Am. Humanities Recruiting award, 1979, Community Service award Sales and Mktg. Execs. of Met. Washington, 1985, Chmns. award Greater Washington Soc. Assn. Execs., 1986, community leadership award FBI Dirs., 1990; named one of Outstanding Young Men Am., 1965; named Outstanding Young Man of Yr., East St. Louis, 1958, Businessman of Day, Santa Rosa, 1967; presented key to San Francisco, 1959. Mem. NAACP, Boys Clubs Profl. Assn. (numerous local and nat. offices 1953—), Boys Clubs Am. (numerous local and nat. offices 1951—), Nat. Soc. Fund Raisers (mem. membership com.), Greater Washington Soc. Assn. Execs. (chmn. various coms.), Am. Soc. Assn. Execs., Internat. Platform Assn., D.C. C. of C. (various com. memberships, mem. bd. dirs. 1985—), Upper Montgomery County C. of C., 1986—, Jr. League of Washington Community (mem. adv. bd. 1991—). Republican. Roman Catholic. Clubs: Washington, D.C. Touchdown, Montgomery Village Golf (Gaithersburg, Md.), Tam O'Shanter Country (Bellevue, Wash.). Lodges: Rotary, Elks, Lions. Home: 9832 Meadowcroft Ln Gaithersburg MD 20879-1337

AVEDON, RICHARD, photographer; b. N.Y.C., May 15, 1923; s. Jack and Anna (Polonsky) A.; m. Dorcas Nowell, 1944; m. Evelyn Franklin, Jan. 29, 1951; 1 child, John. Student, Columbia U., 1941-42; hon. doctorate, Royal Coll. Art, London, 1989. Staff photographer Jr. Bazaar, 1945-47, Harper's Bazaar, 1945-65; photographer French collections, 1947-84; staff photographer Theatre Arts, 1952, Vogue mag., 1966-90. Author: (comments by Truman Capote) Observations, 1959, (text by James Baldwin) Nothing Personal, 1964, (intro. by Harold Rosenberg) Portraits, 1976, (essay by Harold Brodkey) Avedon Photographs, 1947-1977, 1978, In the American West, 1985; author spl. bicentennial edit. Rolling Stone mag. The Family, 1976; editor: Diary of a Century (photographs by Jacques Henri Lartigue), 1970, (with Doon Arbus) Alice in Wonderland: The Forming of a Company, The Making of a Play, 1973; photographs in permanent collections: Smithsonian Instn., Met. Mus. Art, N.Y.C., Mus. Modern Art, N.Y.C., Amon Carter Mus., Fort Worth, San Francisco Mus. Modern Art, Mus. Fine Arts, Houston, Victoria and Albert Mus., London, Nat. Portrait Gallery, Washington, Nat. Portrait Gallery, London, Ctr. for Creative Photography U. Ariz., Tucson, Kunstaus Zurich, Switzerland, Kunstaus, Basel, Switzerland, Andreas Reinhart Found., Winterthur, Switzerland; one-man retrospective exhbn. Smithsonian Instn., Washington, 1962, Mpls. Inst. Arts, 1970, Univ. Art Mus., Berkeley, Calif., 1980, one-man shows: Mus. Modern Art, 1974, Marlborough Gallery, 1975, Met. Mus. Art, N.Y.C., 1978, Amon Carter Mus., 1985, tour through 1987; group shows include: Mus. Modern Art, 1955, Met. Mus. Art, 1959, 60, 63, 67, Musée Réattu, Arles, France, 1965, N.Y. World's Fair, 1965-66, Fogg Art Mus., Cambridge, Mass., 1967, Mus. Modern Art, N.Y.C., 1964, 65, 69, Expo '70, Osaka, Japan, 1970, Whitney Mus. Am. Art, 1974, Corcoran Gallery Art, Washington, 1985, Nat. Gallery Art, Washington, 1989; photographed civil rights movement in the South, 1963, anti-war movement across U.S., 1969, Vietnam, 1971, Am. Working Class, 1978-84. With USMC, 1942-44. Recipient highest achievement medal awards Art Dirs. Show, 1950—; voted one of world's ten greatest photographers Popular Photography, 1958; citation of dedication to fashion photography Pratt Inst., 1976; Nat. Mag. award Visual Excellence, 1976; Pres.'s fellow R.I. Sch. Design, 1978; Chancellor's citation U. Calif., Berkeley, 1980; named to Hall of Fame Art Dirs. Club, 1982; Photographer of Yr., Am. Soc. Mag. Photographers, 1985; Best Photog. Book of Yr. award Maine Photog. Workshop, 1985; Dir. of Yr., Adweek mag., 1985; Comml. Dir. of Yr. award of excellence Eastman Kodak, 1985; Lifetime Achievement award Coun. Fashion Designers Am., 1989. Address: 407 E 75th St New York NY 10021

AVERBACH, BENJAMIN L., materials engineering educator; b. Rochester, N.Y., Aug. 12, 1919; s. George and Lillian (Yves) A.; m. Gertrude Mary McCarthy, Sept. 6, 1947; children: Paul, Anne, Clare. BS, Rensselaer Poly. U., 1940, MS, 1942; DSc, MIT, 1947. Registered profl. engr., Mass., Conn. Chief metallurgist U.S. Radiator Corp., Geneva, N.Y., 1942-43; metallurgist GE, Schenectady, N.Y., 1943-44; asst. prof. MIT, Cambridge, Mass., 1947-52; assoc. prof. MIT, Cambridge, 1952-60, prof., 1960—; cons. in field. Editor: Fracture, 1959. Chmn. Belmont (Mass) Rep. Town Com., 1978—. Recipient Howe medal Am. Soc. Metals, 1952. Fellow Am. Soc. Metals, Inst. Metals Brit.; mem. Internat. Inst. Welding (del. 1972), Internat. Conf. on Fracture (past pres. 1982), Am. Arbitration Assn. Republican. Home: 165 Somerset St Belmont MA 02178-2006

AVERETT-SHORT, GENEVA EVELYN, college administrator; b. Boston, Mar. 12, 1938; d. William Pinkney and Geneva Zepplyn (Stepp) A.; m. Roger Inman Blackwell, Dec. 19, 1959 (div. 1975); children: Thomas, LaVerne, Constance; m. Floyd J. Short Jr., July 3, 1984. BA in Social Sci., Bennett Coll., Greensboro, N.C., 1958; EdM, SUNY, Buffalo, 1972. Social caseworker Erie County Dept. Pub. Welfare, Buffalo, 1958-59; substitute tchr. Buffalo Bd. Edn., 1959-60; employment inteviewer N.Y. Dept. Labor, Div. Employment, Buffalo, 1967-69; admissions counselor SUNY, Buffalo, 1969-72; assoc. dean students U. Utah, Salt Lake City, 1972-74; coordinator counseling svcs. Ednl. Devel. Prog., SUNY, Fredonia, 1974-77; acting dir. Ednl. Devel. Prog., SUNY, 1976-77; substitute tchr. Greensboro (N.C.) pub. schs., 1977-78; prog. asst. D.C. Dept. Human Svcs. Commn. on Pub. Health, 1978-89; assessment counselor, coord. Prince Georges Community Coll., Largo, Md., 1989—; cons. in field. Active in past various charitable orgns. Mem. Nat. Alumnae Assn. Bennett Coll., Pierians, Inc. Democrat. Episcopalian. Address: 3301 Accolade Dr Clinton MD 20735

AVERSA, DOLORES SEJDA, educational administrator; b. Phila., Mar. 26, 1932; d. Martin Benjamin and Mary Elizabeth (Esposito) Sejda; BA, Chestnut Hill Coll., 1953; m. Zefferino A. Aversa, May 3, 1958; children: Dolores Elizabeth, Jeffrey Martin, Linda Maria. Owner, Personal Rep. and Pub. Rels., Phila., 1965-68; ednl. cons. Franklin Sch. Sci. and Arts, Phila., 1968-72; pres., owner, dir. Martin Sch. of Bus., Inc., Phila., 1972—; file reader, cons. for ct. reporting and travel tng. Southwestern Pub. Co., 1990; mem. ednl. planning com. Ravenhill Acad., Phila., 1975-76. Active Phila. Mus. of Art, Phila. Drama Guild. Mem. Nat. Bus. Edn. Assn., Pa. Bus. Edn. Assn., Am. Bus. Law Assn., Pa. Sch. Counselors Assn., Am.-Italy Soc., Am. Soc. Travel Agts. (edn. chmn. Del. Valley chpt.), Phila. Hist. Soc., World Affairs Coun. Phila., Hist. Soc. Pa., Phila. Orch. Mem. ASTA (sch. div.), Chestnut Hill Coll. Alumnae Assn. Roman Catholic. Home: 2111 Locust St Philadelphia PA 19103-4802 Office: 2417 Welsh Rd Philadelphia PA 19114

AVERY, JEANNE, astrologer, writer; b. Pinehurst, Ga., Oct. 24, 1931; d. Bolin Ivey Leaptrot and Lucy Mae Hawkins; m. Thomas Joseph Henesy, Aug. 5, 1927 (div. June 1964); children: Sharon Andrews, Diane Henesy, David. BA, George Washington U., Washington, 1952. Author: The Rising Sign, 1982, Astrological Aspects, 1985, Astrology and Your Past Lives, 1987, Astrology and Your Health, 1989. Mem. Am. Fedn. Astrologers (tchr., lectr. 1972-90). Democrat. Presbyterian. Office: Jupiter Pluto Communication 204 E 77th St New York NY 10021-2105

AVIADO, DOMINGO M., pharmacologist, toxicologist; b. Manila, Aug. 28, 1924; came to U.S., 1946, naturalized, 1990.; s. Domingo Gatus and Severina O. (Mariano) A.; m. Asuncion Palma Guevara, Aug. 15, 1953; children: Maria Cristina Aviado Gentile, Carlos G., Domingo G., Maria Asuncion. Student, U. Philippines, 1940-46; M.D., U. Pa., 1948. From asst. instr. pharmacology to assoc. prof. U. Pa. Med. Sch., 1948-65, prof., 1965-77, acting chmn. dept., 1969-70; sr. dir. biomed. research Allied Chem. Corp., Morristown, N.J., 1977-80; pres. Atmospheric Health Scis., Inc., 1980—; founder, pres. Orphan Pharms. Inc., 1984-87; adj. prof. pharmacology Coll. Medicine and Dentistry N.J., Newark, 1977-84; vis. lectr. anesthesiology Albert Einstein Med. Center, 1955-77; vis. prof. pharmacology U. of East Med. Center, Philippines, 1959-77; vis. lectr. physiology Women's Med. Coll., Phila., 1961-62, Rutgers U., 1966-67; cons. Council for Drug Research, 1972-73, Poison Control Program of Phila., 1964-70; mem. clean air sci. adv. com. EPA, 1978-80. Author textbook, 9 monographs, 2 med. dictionaries; editorial bd.: Cardiology, 1967-79, Drug Info. Jour, 1974-77, Jour. Cardiovascular Pharmacology, 1978-84, Biol. Abstracts, 1984—; La Riforma Medica, 1987—; adv. editorial bd. Archives Internationales de Pharmacodynamie et de Therapie, 1965—; editor inhalation sect. Jour. Pathology and Environ. Toxicology, 1978-80; interim editor Jour. Clin. Pharmacology, 1984-85; contbr. articles to profl. jours. Recipient Linnaeus medal Stockholm, 1961, Purkinje medal Prague, 1963; Presdl. trophy for most outstanding Filipino, 1975; named Physician of Yr., Philippine Med. Assn., 1969, numerous other awards; Guggenheim fellow, 1962-63. Fellow Acad. Medicine N.J.; mem. AMA, Physiol. Soc. Phila. (pres. 1959-60), Am. Soc. Pharmacology and Exptl. Therapeutics (fin. com. 1965-70), Am. Physiol Soc., AAAS, Am. Heart Assn., Internat. Union Pharmacology (treas. 1965-66), Am. Soc. Tropical Medicine and Hygiene, Internat. Leprosy Assn., Am. Coll. Clin. Pharmacology (bd. regents 1978-83), Soc. Toxicology, Coll. Physicians Phila., Drug Info. Assn., Sigma Xi. Home: 225 Hartshorn Dr Short Hills NJ 07078-3225 Office: 152 Parsonage Hill Rd PO Box 307 Short Hills NJ 07078

AVIDAN, AMOS ANDREW, engineering executive; b. Poland, Aug. 7, 1952; came to U.S., 1977; s. Tal and Deva (Olma) A.; m. Susan Patricia Donnelly, Jan. 1, 1985; children: Alia, Shane, Cullen. MEChemE, CUNY, 1980, PhD in Chem. Engring., 1980. Sr. engr. Mobil R & D Corp., Paulsboro, N.Y., 1980-89, mgr. catalytic crudeing, 1989—; pres. Circulating Fluidized Bed Internat. Soc., 1991—; lectr. Am. Inst. of Chem. Engrs., N.Y.C., 1987—. Author: (with others) Fluidization, 1985; contbr. articles to profl. jours. Mem. Am. Inst. of Chem. Engrs. Office: Mobil R&D Corp 600 Billingsport Rd 600 Billingsport Rd Paulsboro NJ 08066

AVILES, ALICE ALERS, psychologist; b. N.Y.C; d. Jose Oscar and Pauline (Irizarry) Alers.; m. Jose A. Aviles, Aug. 13, 1954 (div. Oct. 1981); children: Jeffrey, Brian, Gregory. BS magna cum laude, SUNY, Oswego, 1955; MA, Queens Coll., 1978; PhD, Yeshiva U., 1984; postdoctoral diploma in psychoanalysis, Adelphi U., 1991. Lic. psychologist, N.Y. Tchr. elem. schs. Spring Valley, N.Y., 1955, Erlangen (Fed. Republic Germany) Am. Sch., 1955-56; tchr. elem. schs. Uniondale, N.Y., 1956, Freeport, N.Y., 1957-58, Island Park, N.Y., 1973-75; psychology clk. Fifth Ave. Ctr. for Counseling and Psychotherapy, N.Y.C., 1978-80; psychology intern St. Vincent's Hosp. and Med. Ctr., N.Y.C., 1980-81; psychologist Kingsboro Psychiat. Ctr., Bklyn., 1981-84; psychologist to assoc. psychologist South Beach Psychiat. Ctr., Bklyn., 1984-86; pvt. practice Valley Stream, N.Y., 1985—; from staff psychologist to sr. psychologist Luth. Med. Ctr., Bklyn., 1986—; mem. adv. com. Hispanic Counseling Ctr. of Family Svc. Assn. of Nassau County, Hempstead, N.Y., 1978-80. Ford found. grad. fellow, 1978-81. Mem. Am. Psychol. Assn., N.Y. State Psychol. Assn., Nassau County Psychol. Assn., Adelphi Soc. Psychoanalysis and Psychotherapy. Office: 218 Gibson Blvd Valley Stream NY 11581-3324 also: Luth Med Ctr 514 49th St Brooklyn NY 11220

AVRETT, ROZ (ROSALIND CASE), author, advertising creative director; b. Upper Montclair, N.J., Apr. 19, 1933; d. William Lyon and Doris Edna (Clift) Case; m. William thoman Reynolds, Feb. 20, 1960 (div. 1968); 1 child, Gerald William Thomas; m. John Glenn Avrett, Dec. 31, 1972. BA in Creative Writing, Chatham Coll., 1951-55. Copy trainee Young & Rubicam, Inc., N.Y.C., 1955-56; copy writer Hicks & Greist, Inc., N.Y.C., 1958-61; sr. copy writer Dancer-Fitzgerald-Sample, N.Y.C., 1961-63; creative supr. The Marschalk Co., N.Y.C., 1963-68; assoc. creative dir. BBDO Internat., N.Y.C., 1968-78; author N.Y.C., 1978—; advt. lectr. Sch. of Visual Arts, 1970, 71. Author: My Turn, 1983, 72nd and Rodeo, 1983; author short stories. Patron Met. Opera. Recipient Leadership award Am. Biog. Inst., Raleigh, N.C. Mem. PEN, Author's Guild, People for Ethical Treatment of Animals, Met. Opera Club, Confederation of Chivalry, Creek Club. Republican. Episcopalian.

AWALT, ELIZABETH GRACE, artist, educator; b. Balt., Jan. 20, 1956; d. Richard and Hazel Elizabeth (Clary) A.; m. John Gilliam Conley, Aug. 27, 1988. Student, Skowhegan Sch., 1977; BA, Boston Coll., 1978; MFA, U. Pa., 1981. Part-time instr. Boston Coll., Chestnut Hill, Mass., 1984-86, asst. prof. fine arts dept., 1986—; resident Yaddo, Saratoga Springs, N.Y., 1984, MacDowell Colony, Peterborough, N.H., 1982. One-person shows include G.W. Einstein Gallery, Inc., N.Y.C., 1988, 90; exhibited in group shows at Mus. Fine Arts, Boston, 1984, Decordova Mus., Lincoln, Mass., 1989. Mem. Millis (Mass.) Conservation Commn., 1991. NEA grantee, 1987; recipient Major award Mass. Artists Fellowship, 1983.

AWERBUCH, SHIMON, research consultant; b. Tel Aviv, Israel, May 19, 1946; s. Erich Eli and Lilly Leah (Drabin) A.; came to U.S., 1956, naturalized, 1963; BS, Rensselaer Poly. Inst., 1968, MS in Urban and Environ. Studies, 1969, PhD in Urban and Environ. Studies, 1975. Ops. rsch. analyst asst. chief of staff, USAF, Washington, 1969-71; com. counsel Standing Com. on Environ. Conservation, N.Y. State Assembly, Albany, 1971-73; sr. cons. Mgmt. Cons. Svc., Ernst & Whinney, Washington, 1974-75; dir. policy analysis and planning project N.Y. State Edn. Dept., Albany, 1975-76; policy analyst Gov.'s Econ. Devel. Bd., Albany, 1976-77; mng. ptnr. and co-founder Tibbits Assocs., Troy, 1977-80; chief econ. and policy studies Exec. Dept., Utility Intervention Office, State of N.Y., 1980-86; prof. fin. Coll. Mgmt. Sci., U. Lowell, Mass., 1986—; cons. in utility rate-case prcoeedings; rsch. cons. Mass. Energy Dept., 1986—, Sandia Nat. Labs. U.S. Dept. Energy, Nat. Renewable Energy Lab, various regional telephone cos., 1988—. With USAF, 1969-71. Mem. Am. Fin. Assn., Fin. Mgmt. Assn., Inst. Mgmt. Sci., Sigma Xi. Author: (with William A. Wallace) Policy Evaluation for Community Development: Decision Tools for Local Government, 1976, (with D. Freireich) Nuclear Cancellations, Award Papers in Public Utility Economics and Regulations, 1983, Efficient Income Measures and the Partially Regulated Firm: Deregulating Utilities, 1989; contbr. articles on fin., regulatory econs., public policy to profl. jours. Office: U Mass Coll Mgmt Sci 1 University Ave Lowell MA 01854-2881

AWOJOODU, SAMSON OLALEKAN, architect; b. Ile Ife, Oyo, Nigeria, Oct. 15, 1955; came to U.S., 1978; s. Richard Olabisi and Akanke (Gbadamosi) A.; m. Florence T. Mepaiyeda, Apr. 20, 1985; children: Bola, Joycee, Anthony. BArch, Howard U., 1983; MArch in Urban Design, Morgan State U., 1989. Project architect Ministry of Defense, Lagos, Nigeria, 1983-85; architect Leo A. Daly, Washington, 1986-89; v.p. ops. Lyttos, Inc., Hyattsville, Md., 1987—; ptnr. Lyttos Internat., Inc., Hyattsville, Md., 1987—. Mem. AIA (assoc. mem.), Orgn. of Nigerian Profls. Office: Lyttos Internat Inc PO Box 4258 Hyattsville MD 20787-0258 also: 11703 Roby Ave Beltsville MD 20705

AXELRAD, CHARLES STEVEN, dentist; b. N.Y.C., Oct. 7, 1949; s. Nathaniel Richard and Betty (Nathanson) A.; m. Lorraine R Goldstein, June l0, 1972; children: Marisa Lauren, Jordan Eric. BS, SUNY, Stony Brook, l970; DDS, NYU, 1974. Resident in gen. practice dentistry Bronx (N.Y.)-Lebanon Hosp. Ctr., 1974-75; pvt. practice Farmingdale, N.Y., 1975—. Contbr. articles to profl. jours. Vol. dentist United Cerebral Palsy, Roosevelt, N.Y., 1980. Nat. Inst. Dental Rsch. grantee, 1974. Fellow Acad. Gen. Dentistry; mem. ADA, Am. Assn. Endodontists, N.Y. State Dental Soc., Nassau County Dental Soc., Mid Island Study Club. Office: Farmingdale Dental Group PC 260 Merritts Rd Farmingdale NY 11735-3291

AXELROD, LISA, marriage, family and child counselor, play therapist; b. Chgo., May 29, 1945; d. Eugene and Jane Alice (Machlis) Rotwein. BA, U. Calif., Berkeley, 1967, MA, 1968; Cert. Phonetique, Sorbonne, Paris, 1969. Lic. marriage, family and child counselor. Tchr. Pershing Hall Elem. Sch., Paris, 1969-70, San Francisco Schs., 1970-82; marriage, family and child counselor OMI Family Ctr., San Francisco, 1980-82, West Coast Children's Ctr., Albany, Calif., 1982-83; family counselor Ctr. for Addictive Illnesses, Morristown, N.J., 1987-89; pvt. practice therapist to children, families N.Y.C., 1992—; family counselor specializing in addictions recovery Somerset (N.J.) Med. Ctr., Somerville, N.J., 1992—. Vol. Family Dynamics, Inc., N.Y.C. Recipient HEW fellowship U.S. Dept. HEW, 1967-68, Nat. Disting. Svc. Registry award for Counseling and Devel., 1990. Mem. Am. Assn. Marriage and Family Therapy, Calif. Assn. Marriage and Family Therapists, Am. Assn. Counseling and Devel., NAFE. Office: PO Box 736 Chatham NJ 07928-0736

AXELROD, NORMAN N(ATHAN), high technology consultant; b. N.Y.C., Aug. 26, 1934; s. Louis E. and Sadie (Katz) A.; m. Victoria Ann Grant, Mar. 21, 1975; children: Lauren Grant, Brian George. AB, Cornell U., 1954; postgrad., U. Paris, France, 1958; PhD in Optics and Physics, U. Rochester, 1959. Aerospace scientist NASA, Goddard Space Flight Ctr., Washington, 1959-60; rsch. fellow U. London, 1960-61; asst. prof. U. Del., 1961-65; mem. tech. staff Bell Labs., Murray Hill, N.J., 1965-72; prin. Axelrod Assocs., N.Y.C., 1972—; bd. dirs. World Resources Devel. Co., Input-Output Tech., Inc.; mem. adv. bd. Del. Dept. Edn., 1963-64; cons. Met. Mus. Art, N.Y.C., 1969-72, French Ministry Nat. Def. and War, 1971, Bausch & Lomb, Compuscan, CPC, GE, IBM, ITT, Konishiroku, Johnson & Johnson, Medtronic, Recognition Equipment Inc., Perkin-Elmer, Sharp, Proctor & Gamble, RCA, Teradyne, Timken Co., Wall St. Jour.; participant vis. scientist program. Am. Inst. Physics, 1963-64. Editor: Optical Properties of Dielectric Films, 1968; book reviewer, cons. John Wiley & Sons, 1965-68, Rheinhold-Van Nostrand, 1968-70, Pergamon Press, 1969-70; contbr. articles to profl. jours. Patentee in field. Recipient Tech. Team Contbn. of Yr. award Fortune 500, 1990. Fellow AAAS; mem. IEEE, Am. Phys. Soc., Am. Optical Soc., Soc. Mfg. Engrs., Machine Vision Assn. (cert. mfg. engr.), Del., N.Y. Acads. Sci., Electrochem. Soc., Sigma Xi, Sigma Pi Sigma, Pi Mu Epsilon. Home: 445 E 86th St New York NY 10028-6433 Office: Norman Axelrod Assocs 28 W 44th St New York NY 10036-6603

AXELROD, STEVEN JOSEPH, literary agent; b. N.Y.C., Feb. 27, 1950; s. Herman and Sylvia (Schwartz) Z.; m. Gwenn Mayers, Dec. 17, 1978; 1 child, Nicholas Mayers. BA, Colgate U., 1972. Mng. editor Harcourt Brace Jovanovich, N.Y.C., 1974-75; editor Lit. Guild, N.Y.C., 1975-77; lit. agt. Paul R. Reynolds, Inc., N.Y.C., 1977-78, Curtis Brown Ltd., N.Y.C., 1978-81, Sterling Lord Agy., N.Y.C., 1981-83; pres. The Axelrod Agy., N.Y.C., 1983—. Office: Axelrod Agy 66 Church St Lenox MA 01240-2554

AXLINE, ROBERT PAUL, electronics executive; b. Warren, Ohio, Dec. 21, 1935; s. Robert Paul and Elizabeth L. (Knoedler) A.; m. Jean Elaine Bowers, Mar. 26, 1961; children: David Robert, Donald William. BS, Ohio U., 1957; grad., Harvard Bus. Sch., 1966. Lic. real estate broker, Mass. Mgr. RCA Computer Systems, Marlboro, Mass., 1969-70, plant mgr., 1971-73; pres., founder Polyform Corp., Northboro, Mass., 1971-73; v.p. mfg. ops. Bowmar Ali Inc., Acton, Mass., 1973-75; v.p. ops. Dymo Bus. Systems, Randolph, Mass., 1975-78; v.p. corp. devel. Addressograph Farrington, Inc. (now Data Card), Randolph, Mass., 1978-86, v.p. internat., 1986-87; pres., chief exec. officer FIMA USA, Inc., 1988—; chmn. Plastic Card Systems, Inc. Chmn., Northboro Mcpl. Housing Com. (Mass.), 1974-79; vis. prof. Ohio U. Coll. Bus. Adminstrn., 1987; bd. dirs. Progenator Corp. Pres. nat. alumni bd. Ohio U., 1980-81, alumni trustee, 1980-81; trustee Ohio U. Found., 1978—, vice chmn. 1987-92, chmn., 1992—; co-chmn. Third Century Campaign, Ohio U. , 1987-93; bd. dir. Innovation Ctr., Ohio U., Research Park, 1990—. 1st lt. U.S. Army, 1957-58. Recipient Disting. Svc. award Ohio U. Alumni, 1983, Outstanding Svc. award Jaycees, Zanesville, Ohio, 1960, Medal of Merit Ohio U., 1987. Mem. New Eng. Coun., Japan Soc. Boston, Am. Assn. Med. Systems and Informatics, Recognition Technologies Users Assns., Am. Inst. Indsl. Engrs. (sr.), Harvard Business School Club (pres. 1973-74, Worcester, Mass.), Jaycees (v.p. 1959-60, 64-65). Republican. Mem. United Ch. of Christ. Home: 10 Cherlyn Dr Northborough MA 01532-1132 Office: 85 Hayes Memorial Dr Marlborough MA 01752-1831

AYA, RODERICK HONEYMAN, retired corporate tax executive; b. Portland, Oreg., Sept. 17, 1916; s. Alfred Anthony and Grace Myrtle (Honeyman) A.; student U. Oreg., 1935-36, Internat. Accts. Soc., 1937-39, LaSalle Extension U., 1940-42, Walton Sch. Commerce, 1942, U. Calif. Extension, 1945, Nat. Grad. U., 1973; m. Helen Marjorie Riddle, June 16, 1945 (dec. Dec. 1983); children: Roderick Riddle, Deborah Aya Reynolds, Ronald Honeyman; m. Kathryn Rehnstrom Chatalas, June 22, 1986; stepchildren: John Todd, Paul Seth, Elizabeth Kate. Chief statistician Hotel Employers Assn., San Francisco, 1939-42; acct. Pacific Tel. & Tel. Co., San Francisco, 1942-52, spl. acct., 1952-63; tax acct., 1963-65; spl. acct. AT&T, N.Y.C., 1965-68, mgr. tax studies, 1968-73, div. mgr. tax rsch. and planning, 1973-80; pub. acct., San Francisco, 1940-90; music tchr., 19[illegible]—; v.p., treas., dir. Snell Rsch. Assocs., Inc., 1974-79; guest lectr. on taxes Westchester County Adult Edn. Program. Committeeman, Marin County (Calif.) coun. Boy Scouts Am., 1959-60, com. chmn., 1959-61; mem. Marin County Sheriffs' Reserve, 1962-65; law enforcement liaison com. on Juvenile Control; sec. Am. Nat. Standards Inst. Z90 Com. on Protective Headgear, 1967-80. V.p., treas., bd. dirs. Snell Meml. Found., 1957-80, dir. emeritus, 1990—; trustee Snell Meml. Found. (U.K.), Ltd., 1972-88; mem. chmn.'s com. U.S. Senatorial Bus. Adv. Bd.; mem. Rep. Presdl. Task Force; fin. com. Seaside (Oreg.) United Meth. Ch.; dir., past pres. Stuart Highlanders Pipe Band of San Francisco. Recipient Wisdom award of honor Wisdom Soc., 1970; Winston Churchill Medal of Wisdom, 1989; Pres.'s Medal of Merit, 1981; Eminent Wisdom fellow Hall of Fame, 1989, Eminent Churchill fellow Winston Churchill Medal of Wisdom Soc., 1989. Fellow Anglo Am. Soc. (hon.); mem. Nat. Soc. Pub. Accts., St. Andrews Soc. San Francisco, Telephone Pioneers Am., Soc. for Ethnomusicology (contbr. to jour.), U.S. Naval Inst., Phi Chi, Sigma Nu. Clubs: Corinthian Yacht (Tiburon, Calif.); Astoria Golf & Country; Sports Car of Am. (San Francisco region treas. 1957-58, dir. 1957-59); U.S. Yacht Racing Union. Author: The Legacy of Pete Snell, 1965; Determination of Corporate Earnings and Profits for Federal Income Tax Purposes, 2 vols., 1966.

AYCOTH, JOHN EDWARD, public relations executive, consultant; b. High Point, N.C., July 16, 1956; s. Sherman Luther and Helen (Gibson) A. Grad., USN Cryptologic Sch., 1976. Pres., chief exec. officer Edward Aycoth & Co., Inc., Washington, 1988—, Edward Aycoth Worldwide, Inc., Washington, 1990—, Edward Aycoth Worldwide, Bhd, Sdn, Kuala Lumpur, Malaysia, 1991—; bd. dirs. Hemdale Picture Corp., Hemdale Film Corp., Hemdale Malaysian Berhad. Polit. cons. Reagan-Bush Com., Fla., 1980. With USN, 1975-79. Mem. Asia Soc., Brit. Automobile Mfrs. Assn. (bd. dirs. 1988—), Brit.-Am. Bus. Assn. Republican. Office: 1667 K St NW # 340 Washington DC 20006

AYERS, CRIMORA WITTEN, sales consultant; b. Charlottesville, Va., Apr. 13, 1942; d. James Wilkerson McKenzie and Sarah Yancey (Ratrie) Witten; m. Larry Taylor Ayers, Nov. 3, 1962; children: Heather Lynn, Gregory Witten. Student, U. Va., 1960-62. Bus. owner Interior Design Co., Balt., 1974-80, Nutrition Sales Co., Balt., 1980-83, Art Sales Co., Balt., 1982-84; computer sales cons. Bell Atlantic, Benchmark-Entre, MBI, Balt., 1984-87; office furniture sales Scan, Balt., 1987-88, Internat. Import Design, Balt., 1988—; dir., sec. Ayers Investment Mgmt. Inc., Balt., 1985-92. Recipient Runnerup Club championship Balt. (Md.) Country Club, 1990. Fellow Execs. Assn., Sales Promotion Club, Woman's Golf Assn. Presbyterian. Home: 337 Warren Ave Baltimore MD 21230 Office: Internat Import Design 6625 B Dobbin Rd Columbia MD 21045

AYLWARD, JAMES FRANCIS, library director; b. Fall River, Mass., Nov. 6, 1942; s. James F. and Helen C. (Deterra) A.; m. Maria C. Abbatomarco, Nov. 19, 1944; children: Kristin, Gretchen, James, Patrick. BA, Calvin Coolidge Coll., 1966; MLS, Univ. R.I., 1968. Cert. librarianship, Mass. Head classified libr. Naval War Coll., Newport, R.I., 1968-70; head libr. Naval Air Station, Quonset Point, R.I., 1970-73; dir. Middletown (R.I.) Pub. Libr., Middletown, R.I., 1973-76, Naval Edn. and Tng. Ctr. Librs., Newport, 1976—. Mem. ALA (sec. armed forces libr. sect. 1986, v.p. armed forces librs. roundtable 1990-91, pres. 1991-92, cert. of merit 1989, fed. librs. round table), Pa. Libr. Assn. (sec. armed forces libr. sect. 1985). Roman Catholic. Home: 95 Echo Ln Portsmouth RI 02871-3218 Office: NETC Main Libr Bldg 114 Newport RI 02841-5002

AYOTTE, GASTON ARTHUR, JR., accountant; b. Woonsocket, R.I., Dec. 30, 1933; s. Gaston Arthur Sr. and Idalie (Donneau) A.; m. Diana Aurore Beauregard, Sept., 26, 1953; children: Paul Charles, Peter John. AS, Bryant Coll., 1975. Cost acct. Whitins Machine Works, Whitinsville, Mass., 1951-56; sales mgr. I. Medoff Co., Woonsocket, 1956-64; salesperson Marcoux Bros. Inc., Woonsocket, 1964-67; pub. acct. Gaston A. Ayotte & Sons, Inc., Woonsocket, 1968—. Mayor City of Woonsocket, 1981-85, mem. city coun., 1961-81, mem. sch. com., 1989-91; gen. chmn. Autumnfest, Woonsocket, 1982-88. Democrat. Roman Catholic. Home: 104 Nancy Ct Woonsocket RI 02895-5620

AYOUB, CATHERINE C., mental health nurse, psychologist; b. Chgo., Jan. 31, 1949; d. Carl R. and Alice Jane (Forester) Cook; m. John E. Ayoub, Jan. 30, 1971; children: Phillip John, James Carl. BSN, Duke U., 1971; M in Nursing, Emory U., 1973; EdD, Harvard U., 1990. Cert. child/adolescent mental health nurse, RN, Ga., Okla., Mass. Clin. specialist child-adolescent mental health Hillcrest Med. Ctr., 1973-83; exec. dir. At Risk Parent Child Program, Tulsa, 1976-83; psychology extern family devel. unit Children's Hosp., Boston, 1986-88; nursing cons. Andover, Mass.; clin. fellow in psychology Children's Hosp./Judge Baker Chilren's Ctr., Boston, 1988-90; rsch. fellow Harvard Grad. Sch. of Edn., Harvard U. Med. Sch., Cambridge, Mass., 1989-92; staff psychologist Children & The Law program Judge Baker Children's Ctr., Boston, 1991—; instr. Harvard Grad. Sch. of Edn. and Harvard Med. Sch., 1991—; instr. Harvard U. Med. Sch., Harvard U. Grad. Sch. Edn.; researcher, lectr. in field. Editorial bd. Internat. Jour. on Child Abuse; contbr. articles to profl. jours. and books. Named Okla. March of Dimes Nurses, 1979; recipient grant Nat. Ctr. on Child Abuse and Neglect, 1978-82, others. Mem. ANA (Creative Nursing award 1978), Ga. Nurses Assn., Okla. Nurses Assn. (bd. dirs. Dist. 2, 1977-80), Assn. for the Care of Children's Health, Internat. Soc. for Prevention of Child Abuse and Neglect, Mass. Nurses Assn., Ambulatory Pediatric Assn., Am. Psychol. Assn., Soc. for Rsch. in Child Devel., Am. Orthopsychiatric Assn., Sigma Theta Tau. Office: Judge Baker Childrens Ctr 295 Longwood Ave Boston MA 02115

AYRES, BARBARA JOAN, secretary; b. Binghamtom, N.Y., Dec. 2, 1937; d. Harry and Anna Stephanie (Hudec) Levene; m. Charles Francis Ayres, Apr. 4, 1958 (dec. Apr. 1992); children: Robin Ann, Nicola Maire, Stephen Randall. AS, Endicott Coll., 1957; BA, SUNY, Binghamton, 1982. Real estate broker, mall mgr. Rupe Konecny Real Estate, Stephens Sq. Mall, Binghamton, 1968-77; sec. SUNY, Binghamton, 1981—; mem. grievance com. SUNY, Binghamton, 1987—, excellence award com., 1990; pers. chair Fed. Credit Union. Bd. dirs. Binghamton Dist. N.Y. State Employees, 1991—. Mem. Profl. Secs. Internat. Home: 204 William St Vestal NY 13950

AYRES, ELIZABETH PATRICIA, poet, art center director; b. Washington, Sept. 16, 1950. BA summa cum laude, U. Md., 1972; MA, Syracuse U., 1974. Poet, cons. Md. Poets-in-the-Schs., 1972-73, N.Y. State Poets-in-the-Schs., 1973-78; workshop leader in creative writing N.Y. Pub. Libr., other instns., 1978-88; adj. asst. prof. English Coll. of New Rochelle, N.Y., 1990-91; owner Imago Ctr. for Arts, N.Y.C., 1991—; radio personality WBAI, Voice of America, N.Y., 1973; mem. adv. panel Cultural Coun. Found., N.Y., 1978. Editor: Wrestling Free, 1990; contbr. poems to profl. publs. Recipient 1st Pl. Poetry award Nat. Soc. Arts and Letters, 1973; Cornelia Ward fellow Syracuse U., 1973-74. Mem. Internat. Women's Writing Guild (workshop leader 1991), Pen and Brush Club (Sussman award 1987), Phi Kappa Phi. Home: 16 E 10th St New York NY 10003-5958

AYRES, JOHN JAMES BREVARD, psychologist; b. Ocean City, Md., Aug. 2, 1939; s. Denward Collins and Irma White (Pointer) A.; m. Sheila Anne Petera, Sept. 9, 1961; children: Julie, John. BA, Coll. William and Mary, 1961; MA, U. Ky., 1963, PhD, 1965. Rsch. asst. Pub. Health Svc. Hosp., Addiction Rsch. Ctr., Lexington, Ky., 1963-64; instr. psychology Boston U., 1966-67; from asst. to assoc. prof. U. Mass., Amherst, 1967-78, prof., 1978—; vis. prof. Western Wash. State Coll., Bellingham, 1973, U. Hawaii, Honolulu, 1982; vis. scholar U. Wash., Seattle, 1974. Assoc. editor Animal Learning and Behavior, 1980-84; contbr. articles to profl. jours. Capt. U.S. Army, 1965-67. Grantee DHEH, 1970-71, NSF, 1976-91; NSF fellow, 1963. Mem. Am. Psychol. Soc., Psychonomic Soc., Ea. Psychol. Soc. Home: 8 Laurel Ln Amherst MA 01002-2811 Office: U Mass Dept Psychology Amherst MA 01003

AYRES, ROBERT UNDERWOOD, educator; b. Plainfield, N.J., June 29, 1932; s. John Underwood and Alice Conrow (Hutchinson) A.; m. Leslie Wentz, June 26, 1954; 1 dau., Jennifer Leigh. B.S. in Math., U. Chgo., 1954; M.S. in Physics, U. Md., 1956; Ph.D., U. London, 1958. Research assoc. Hudson Inst., Croton-on-Hudson, N.Y., 1962-67; vis. scholar Resources for Future, 1967-68; v.p., dir. Internat. Research & Tech. Corp., Washington, 1968-76, Delta Research Corp., Arlington, Va., 1976—; prof. engring. and pub. policy Carnegie-Mellon U., 1979-92; chmn. bd. Variflex Corp., Pitts., 1969-87; cons. in field; mem. tech. and water com. Nat. Acad. Scis., 1971, new transp. systems and tech. com., 1971—, strategic and critical materials com., 1971-72, com. steel research, 1978, com. alts. for reduction chlorofluorocarbon emissions, 1979; mem. com. on engring. edn. Nat. Acad. Engring., 1984; dep. program leader, project leader Internat. Inst. Applied Systems Analysis, 1986-90; prof. environ. econs., Sandoz prof. environ. mgmt. INSEAD, Fontainebleu, France, 1992—. Author: Technological Forecasting and Long Range Planning, 1969, (with others) Economics and the Environment, 1971, Alternatives to the Internal Combustion Engine, 1972, Resources, Environment and Economics, 1978, Uncertain Futures, 1979, (with others) Robotics: Applications and Social Implications, 1983, The Next Industrial Revolution: Reviving Industry Through Innovation, 1984, CIM: Revolution in Progress, 1991, Information Evolution and Economics, 1992; contbr. articles to profl. jours.; assoc. editor: Jour. Transp. Tech. and Planning, 1970-74. Fellow AAAS (coun., com.-at-large sect. indsl. sci. 1972-74); mem. Am. Econ. Assn., Assn. Environ. and Resource Economists, Schumpeter Soc. Office: INSEAD, Fontainebleu France

AYRES, VIRGINIA MARIAN, physicist; b. Camden, N.J., May 14, 1954; d. Alexander Robinson and Mary Rosalie (O'Keefe) A. BA, The Johns Hopkins U., 1977; MS, Purdue U., 1982, PhD, 1985. Rsch. physicist Naval Surface Warfare Ctr. White Oak Lab., Silver Spring, Md., 1985—; vis. scholar dept. physics Dartmouth Coll., Hanover, N.H., 1989-90; sci. and tech. agt., program mgr. Interactive Space Techs. Consortium Strategic Def. Initiative, Washington, 1992—; referee NSF, Washington, 1988—; panel mem. Presdl. Young Investigator Award, 1989. Contbr. articles on lab. and space plasma physics to profl. jours., chpts. to books. Keyworker combined Fed. campaign United Way, Silver Spring, 1988. Mem. Am. Phys. Soc. (plasma physics, particles and fields, internat. group), IEEE (nuclear and plasma scis.), Assn. for Women in Sci., Am. Assn. Physics Tchrs., N.Y. Acad. Scis., Nat. Speleological Soc. Office: Naval Surface Warfare Ctr White Oak Lab Code R42 Silver Spring MD 20903-5000

AYYAGARI, KAMALAKAR RAO, surgeon; b. Mogallu, India, Aug. 16, 1944; came to U.S., 1971; s. Satyanarayana Rao and Mahalakshmi (A-treyapurapu) A.; m. Kalavathi Isola, Feb. 4, 1973; children: Subhadra, Sunil. MB, BS, Gandhi Med. U., Hyderabad, India, 1967. Diplomate Am. Bd. Surgery. Intern St. John's Riverside Hosp., Yonkers, N.Y., 1971-72; resident in gen. surgery Misericordia Hosp., Bronx, N.Y., 1973-77; chmn. dept. surgery Irvington (N.J.) Gen. Hosp., 1991—. Fellow ACS; mem. AMA, N.J. Med. Soc., ECMS. Office: K Ayyagari MD PA 2010 Springfield Ave Maplewood NJ 07040

AZACETA, LUIS CRUZ, artist; b. Havana, Cuba, Apr. 5, 1942; came to U.S., 1960; s. Salvador Cruz and Maria A.; m. Ada Perez, Oct. 11, 1969 (div. 1980); 1 child: Emile; m. Sharon A. Jacques, May 15, 1982. Student, Sch. Visual Arts, N.Y.C., 1969. One-man shows include Sette Gallery, Scottsdale, Ariz., 1987, Kunst Sta., Sankt Peter, Cologne, Fed. Rep. Germany, Frumkin/Adams Gallery, N.Y.C., 1988, Paul Anglim Gallery, San Francisco, Mus. Contemporary Hispanic Art, N.Y.C., Anderson Gallery, Richmond, Va., Fondo Del Sol Visual Arts, Washington, 1986-87, Allan Frumkin Gallery, N.Y.C., 1986, 85, 84, 82, 79, 75; exhibited in group shows at The Mus. Modern Art, N.Y.C., 1988, Met. Mus. Art, N.Y.C. 1987, numerous others; represented in numerous collections including Mus. Modern Art, Met. Mus. Art, Huntington Art Gallery, Delaware Art Mus., RISD Mus. Collection, Va. Mus. Fine Arts, Tuscon U. Art Collection. Grantee Cintas Found.- Inst. Internat. Edn., 1972-73, 75-76, Nat. Endowment For Arts, 1980-81, Creative Artist Pub. Svc., 1981-82, Mira! Can. Club Hispanic Art Tour, 1984, Nat. Endowment of Arts, Guggenheim Meml. Found. N.Y. Found. For Arts, 1985. Home: 1729 Greene Ave Flushing NY 11385-1728

AZADIAN, HARRY Y., physician; b. Somerville, Mass., Dec. 21, 1934; s. Vahan and Grace B. (Emanatian) A.; m. Carol Ann Fitzpatrick, June 24, 1956; children: Lynn, Jeffrey, Todd. BS, Tufts U., 1956; MD, Harvard Med. Sch., 1960. Intern U. Calif. Hosps., San Francisco, 1960-61; resident in surgery Boston City Hosp. Harvard Surg. Svc., 1964-68, Harvard Svc., Boston, 1964-68; pvt. practice Cambridge, Mass., 1969-89; occupational physician Raytheon Co., Tewksbury, Mass., 1989—. Fellow Am. Coll. Surgeons, Am. Coll. Occupational Medicine. Republican. Office: Raytheon Co Med Dept 50 Apple Hill Dr Tewksbury MA 01876

AZAR, RICHARD THOMAS, financial management consultant; b. Bklyn., June 3, 1954; s. Denis Anthony and Marie Elizabeth (Shakal) A. BA in Polit. Sci., U. S. Fla., 1976; MBA with honors, Pace U., 1979. CPA, N.Y. Sr. auditor, cons. Pannell Kerr Forster, N.Y.C., 1979-81; mgr. fin. systems and analysis, cons. svcs. group Ernst & Young, N.Y.C., 1982-85; mgr. fin. planning and controls, cons. svcs. group Price Waterhouse, N.Y.C., 1985-86; v.p., chief fin. officer N.Y. Real Estate Devel. Co., N.Y.C., 1986-87; cons. small bus. devel. ctr. Pace U., N.Y.C., 1987; prin. R.T. Azar and Assocs., N.Y.C., 1987-88; pres., founder CFO Resources Inc., N.Y.C., 1988-91; mgr. real estate mgmt. cons. svcs. group Kenneth Leventhal & Co., N.Y.C., 1991—. Bd. dirs. Pace U. Lubin Grad. Sch. of Bus. Alumni Assn. Mem. AICPA, N.Y. State Soc. CPA's (hotel, restaurant and club acctg. com. 1987, com. on fin. execs. in publicly held cos. 1990-91), Nat. Assn. Accts., Met. Club. Republican. Roman Catholic. Home: PO Box 135 335 E 51st St Apt 4F New York NY 10150-0135 Office: Kenneth Leventhal & Co PO Box 135 805 3d Ave New York NY 10022

AZARA, NANCY JEAN, sculptor, book artist, educator; b. N.Y.C., Oct. 13, 1939; d. Joseph Frank and Nancy Ann (Como) A.; children—Nana Olivas, Maximilian M. Olivas. A.A.S., Finch Coll., 1959; postgrad. Lester Polokav Studio of Stage Design, 1960-62, Art Students League N.Y., 1964-67; B.S., Empire State Coll., 1974. Theatrical costume designer, 1959-66; tchr. visual arts Jewish Guild for the Blind, N.Y.C., 1966-67; tchr. art Community Edn. program N.Y.C. Bd. Edn., 1967-68, art cons., 1969-70, tchr. fine arts, summer session, 1970; mem. faculty Bklyn. Coll., 1973-75, 75, 76; ind. studies instr. Empire State Coll., 1975; mem. faculty Bklyn. Mus. Art Sch., 1975-77, Coll. New Rochelle, 1979-81, 81-82; exec. dir., founding mem. Women's Ctr. for Learning N.Y. Feminist Art Inst., 1979-90, also mem. faculty; guest lectr. in field. One women shows include: Fourteen Sculptors Gallery, N.Y.C., 1976, WARM Gallery, Mpls., 1986, Bard Coll., N.Y.C., 1977, Soho 20 Gallery, N.Y.C., 1984, 87, John Jay Coll., N.Y.C., 1984, Artemisia Gallery, Chgo., 1985, A.I.R. Gallery, N.Y.C., 1992, Lannon Gallery, Chgo., 1990; exhibited in group shows at Picola Formata Galelria Numero, Florence, Italy, 1968, Queens Coll., N.Y.C., 1975, Gallery 10 Ltd., Washington, 1978, Sculpture Ctr., N.Y.C., 1980, Landmark Gallery, N.Y.C., 1980, Franklin Furnace, N.Y.C., 1980, Tweed Gallery, Plainfield N.J., 1982, William Patterson Coll., N.J., 1982, Kathryn Markel Gallery, N.Y.C., 1982, Jack Tilton Gallery, N.Y.C., 1983, Ceres Gallery, N.Y.C., 1984, Rotunda Gallery, N.Y.C., 1984, 80 Washington Sq. East Gallery, N.Y.C., 1984, Hand In Hand Gallery, N.Y.C., 1985, Janco Dada Mus., Israel, 1985, Del. Ctr. Contemporary Arts, Wilmington, 1991, The Arch. Grand Army Pla., Bklyn., 1991, Muse Gallery, Phila., 1991, Rempire Gallery, N.Y.C., 1991, numerous others. Adolph and Esther Gottlieb Found. grantee, 1985. Mem. Women's Caucus for Art (adv. bd. 1980-83). Home: 91 Franklin St New York NY 10013-3408

AZARIAN, MARDIROS, communications executive; b. Aleppo, Syrian Arab Republic, Feb. 24, 1929; came to U.S., 1937; s. Azar and Victoria (Arzouhaljian) A.; m. Hermine Yazejian, July 16, 1961: children: Gregory, Victoria Mary. BA, Russell Sage Coll., 1959. Br. mgr. Rochester (N.Y.) Germicide Co., 1962-72; pres. M. Azarian Shoes, Inc., Albany, N.Y., 1960-62, Executone-Fairfield Inc., Norwalk, Conn., 1972-86, Telephone Communications ONE, Inc., Norwalk, 1986—. Mem. Rep. Senate Inner Circle, Washington, 1988; bd. dirs. St. Peter Armenian Ch., Watervliet, N.Y., 1970; chmn. bd. dirs. Armenian Ch. Holy Ascension, Trumbull, Conn., 1988. With U.S. Army, 1951-53. Mem. N.Am. Telephone Assn., Norwalk C. of C., Kiwanis. Office: Telco ONE Inc 35 Harbor Ave Norwalk CT 06850-4229

AZIE, SCOTT DAVID, podiatrist; b. Bklyn., Aug. 6, 1951; s. Robert and Rose (Epstein) A.; m. Stephanie Kay Kruger, July 30, 1977; children: Lauren, Rebecca. Student, SUNY, Albany, 1969-72; D of Podiatric Medicine, 1976. Diplomate Am. Bd. Podiatric Orthopedics. Resident The Kensington Hosp., Phila., 1976-77; pvt. practice Newport, R.I., 1977-80, Flushing, N.Y., 1981—; mem. podiatry peer rev. com. St. Joseph's Hosp.; staff mem. St. Joseph's Hosp., Deepdale Gen. Hosp., The Jamaica Hosp. Fellow Am. Bd. Podiatric Orthopedics; mem. Am. Assn. Hosp. Podiatrists, Acad. Podiatric Sports Medicine, N.Y. State Podiatric Med. Assn. (trustee 1991—, editor Queens div. 1985-87, sec. 1987-89, v.p. 1989-91, pres. 1991—, Podiatrist of Yr. 1986-87, Soc. Am. Baseball Rsch., BMW Car Club Am. Jewish. Home: 23 Theodore Dr Plainview NY 11803-6427 Office: 72-03 164th St Flushing NY 11365

BABAH, MOHAMMED S., accountant; b. Kumasi, Ashanti, Ghana, Nov. 22, 1944; came to U.S., 1973; s. Yakub and Halimat Babah; m. Zainab Babah, Feb. 16, 1975; children: Saleem Mohammed, Jamal Mohammed, Rashad Mohammed, Omar Mohammed. AS, No. Va. Community Coll., 1975; BS, George Mason U., 1979. Tax mgr. Brown and Assocs., Washington, 1979-80; staff acct. U.S. C. of C., Washington, 1980-83, sr. staff acct., 1983-89, mgr., gen. acct., 1989—; founder, co-owner G-10 Convenience Store, Inc., Suitland, Md., 1991—, pres., 1992—. Mem. Nat. Assn. Accts. Democrat. Muslim. Home: 2225 Charleston Pl Hyattsville MD 20783-4930 Office: US C of C 1615 H St NW Washington DC 20062-0002

BABAYAN, VIGEN KHACHIG, nutrionist, chemist; b. Erivan, Armenia, Jan. 1, 1913; came to U.S., 1922; naturalized, 1929; s. Khosrov and Nectar (Kouroumdjian) B.; m. Kanre Edgarian, Nov. 15, 1942; children: Tamar, Richard, Sona. BA, NYU, 1938, PhD, 1943. Chemist E.F. Drew & Co., Boonton, N.J., 1938-41; dir. R & D Ridbo Labs, Patterson, N.J., 1941-48; chief chemist Theobold Industries, Kearny, N.J., 1948-49; v.p., dir. R & D Drew Chem. Corp., N.Y.C., 1949-64; v.p., dir. R & D and quality control Stokely-Van Camp, Inc., Indpls., 1964-78, v.p. sci. and tech., 1978-82; asst. prof. medicine Ind. U. Med. Sch., Indpls., 1968-77; sr. rsch. assoc. New Eng. Deaconess Hosp. Harvard Med. Sch., Boston, 1979-82, dir. rsch., nutrition/metabolism lab. Cancer Rsch. Inst., 1983—; vis. scientist St. Luke's Hosp. Columbia U. Med. Sch., N.Y.C., 1979—; mem. adv. com. NRC. Contbr. sects. to ency., numerous articles to profl. jours.; patentee in field. Mem. cen. exec. com. Armenian Apostolic Ch., 1972-80; active Armenian Cultural Assn. Am., 1976—, Armenian Folk Festival Com., 1962-65, Armenian Nat. Com., 1976—, Armenian Relief Soc., 1932—. Recipient award Glycerine Assn., 1964, U.S. Army Appreciation award for Patriotic Civilian Svc., 1976. Fellow Am. Coll. Nutrition, Inst. Food Technologists (Sci. Achievement award 1977); mem. AAAS, Am. Assn. Candy Technologists, Am. Assn. Cereal Chemists, Am. Chem. Soc., Am. Frozen Food Inst., Am. Inst. Nutrition, Am. Oil Chemists Soc., Am. Oil Chemists Soc. Found., Am. Soc. Clin. Nutrition, Am. Soc. Parenteral and Enteral Nutrition, Assn. Rsch. Dirs., Fedn. Am. Socs. Exptl. Biology, Grocery Mfrs. Assn., Inst. Shortening and Edible Oils, Nat. Confectioners Assn., Nat. Food Processors Assn., N.Y. Acad. Scis., N.Am. Assn. Study Obesity, Nutrition Today Soc., R & D Assocs., Soap and Detergent Assn. Home: 865 Central Ave Needham MA 02192 Office: Harvard U Med Sch Deaconess Hosp Cancer Rsch Inst 194 Pilgrim Rd Boston MA 02215

BABBAGE, JOAN DOROTHY, journalist; b. Montclair, N.J., Jan. 10, 1926; d. Laurence Washburn and Dorothy A. (Davenport) Babbage; m. Vernon H. Ellsworth, Mar. 6, 1971. B.A. in English, Mt. Holyoke Coll., 1948; postgrad. Art Students League, New Sch. for Social Research. Publicist Paramount Internat. Films, N.Y.C., 1952-58; reporter Newark News, 1960-67, food editor, 1967-72; feature writer, reporter Star-Ledger, Newark, 1972—. Author: (with others) Past and Present Lives of New Jersey Women, 1990; contbr. bus. articles to New Jersey Business mag., articles to Official Dog mag. Operator rescue orgn. SaintSaver, N.J., N.Y., Pa.; v.p. jr. group Women's Nat. Republican Club, N.Y.C., 1955. Recipient recommendation award N.J. br. Humane Soc. U.S., PICA Club N.J. award, 1980, Community Media award Assn. Retarded Citizens, Morris County Unit, N.J., 1987, Willard H. Allen Agrl. Communications Media award, N.J. Agrl. Soc., 1988, Communicator of Yr. award N.J. Dept. Agriculture, 1990. Appeared on NBC-TV to demonstrate dog tng. Home: Washington St Montclair NJ 07042-4522 Office: Star-Ledger Court St Newark NJ 07101

BABIJ, MARK JOHN, financial executive; b. Binghamton, N.Y., Sept. 13, 1956; s. Stephan and Nina B.; m. Kelly Ann Kita, June 16, 1979. BS in Econs., SUNY, Albany, 1978; MBA, U. Minn., 1983. With IDS Fin. Services, Mpls., 1979—, product mgr. life ins., 1985-86, asst. to pres., 1986-87, dir. corp. strategy and devel., 1987-89, v.p. corp. planning and analysis, 1989-91; v.p. fin. analysis and planning Am. Express Co., N.Y.C., 1991—. Mem. Planning Forum, Fin. Execs. Inst. Home: 2 South End Ave Apt 9F New York NY 10280-6405 Office: American Express Co 200 Vesey St # 4650 New York NY 10285-0001

BABITZ, BRENDA LIPTON, college administrator, educator; b. Rochester, N.Y., June, 20, 1940; d. Theodore Harris Lipton and Frieda H. (Kroll) Levine; m. Paul Barry Babitz, July 2, 1962; children: Roberta, Theodore. BS, SUNY-Syracuse, 1961. English tchr. Rochester City Schs., N.Y., 1961-64, to fgn. born. 1965-68; instr. Rochester Inst. Tech., 1969-74; dir. U. Rochester Med. Ctr. Dept. Strong Childrens Fund, N.Y., 1983, dir. devel. and community affairs Strong Children's Med. Ctr., also mem. faculty, 1979-90; chief devel. officer Monroe C.C., 1990—; pres. Monroe C.C. Found., 1991. Editor health column Times-Union, Rochester, 1978-79; bd. dirs., pres. Community Ptnrs. for Youth, Rochester, 1973-78. V.p. Nat. Coun. Jewish Women, 1978-81; bd. dirs. Genesee Valley coun. Girls Scouts U.S., 1990—, Mt. Hope Family Ctr., 1990—. Mem. Pub. Rels. Soc. Am., Women in Communications, Nat. Soc. Fund Raising Execs., Rotary. Home: 210 Bonnie Brae Ave Rochester NY 14618-2133 Office: Monroe Community Coll 1000 E Henrietta Rd Rochester NY 14623-5780

BABU, SURESH CHANDRA, economist, researcher; b. Madras, Tamil Nadu, India, May 9, 1961; came to U.S., 1984; s. Narayanasamy Bhakthavatsalam and Govindasamy Suseela; m. Chitra Jayachandran, Jan. 18, 1989; 1 child, Sabrini Sai. BS, Annamalai U., India, 1982; MS, Tamil Nadu Agri U., India, 1984, Iowa State U., 1988; PhD, Iowa State U., 1989. Agrl. reporter South Madras News, India, 1978-82; rsch. specialist Annamalai U., India, 1980-82; technologist Murugappa Chettiar Rsch. Ctr., India, 1982-83; rsch. economist Tamil Nadu U., India, 1983-84; rsch. economist Iowa State U., Ames, 1984-89, instr., 1986-89; researcher World Bank, Washington, 1987-88; rsch. assoc. Iowa Devel. Assocs., Ames, 1988-89; sr. adv. Govt. Malawi, 1989—; visiting lectr. U. Malawi, Lilongwe, 1989—; economist Cornell U., Ithaca, N.Y., 1989—; rsch. fellow Inrenat. Food Policy Rsch. Inst., Washington, 1992—; jr. cons. World Bank, Washington, 1987-88; cons. UN Orgn., Bogor, Indonesia, 1988-89, FAO, Rome, 1990—, UN Children's Fund, Malawi, 1990—. Author: Economics of Biotechnology, 1988; editor: Cultvate-Agrl. mag., 1981-82, Studies in Economic Analysis, 1985-88, Iowa Agriculture, 1986-87; contbr. articles to profl. jours. Sec. Agrl. Assn. Annamalai: Univ., Cosmopolitan Club, Ames, 1986; mem. Assn. Consumer Protection, Ames, 1984; grad. student senator, Ames, 1985; rep. Internat. Assn. Survey Statisticians, Paris. Recipient profl. advancement grant, Iowa State U., 1985, spl. course teaching grant, Honor's Program, 1987, academic excellence award, 1984, High scholarship and Outstanding Achievement award Honor Soc. Agr., 1987. Mem. Am. Econ. Assn., Am. Statis. Assn., Am. Agrl. Econs. Assn., Internat. Assn. Agribus., Econometric Soc., Assn. Survey Statisticians (rep.), Assn. Farming Systems Rsch. and Extension (charter). Hindu. Home and Office: Cornell U 307 Savage Hall Ithaca NY 14853-6301

BABU, UMA MAHESH, health/medical products executive; b. Mysore, Karnataka, India, Mar. 29, 1947; came to U.S., 1963; s. Chinnaswamy and Rajalakshmi (Kusuma) Setty; m. Vimala Govindaraj, Nov. 16, 1975; 1 child, Ravi K. BS, U. Mysore, India, 1968; PhD, U. Nebr., 1974. Postdoctoral fellow U. Manitoba, Winnipeg, Manitoba, Can., 1974-77; postdoctoral fellow Thomas Jefferson U., Phila., 1977-78, rsch. assoc. prof., 1978-84, adj. asst. prof., 1984—; sr. scientist Pittman-Moore, Hashington Crossing, N.J., 1984-86; prin. scientist Ortho Pharm. Corp., Raritan, N.J., 1986-88; asst. dir. Immunobiology Rsch. Inst., Annandale, N.J., 1988—. Named to Exch. program Am. Field Svc., 1963; named Regent's scholar U. Nebr., 1969. Mem. Triveni-Kannada Assn. (cultural sec. 1982-83), Telugu Assn. North Am. Hindu. Home: 1737 Crocker Ln Jamison PA 18929 Office: Immunobiology Rsch Inst Box 999 Rte 22 E Annandale NJ 08801

BACARISSE, PAMELA, Spanish educator; b. Cardiff, Wales; came to U.S., 1989; d. David and Nellie Mary (Jones) Phillips. BA, U. Wales, Cardiff, 1969; PhD, U. Aberdeen, Scotland, 1976. Mem. faculty U. Aberdeen, 1969-89; prof. Spanish, U. Pitts., 1989—. Author: A Alma Amortalhada, 1984, The Necessary Dream, 1988; editor: Wit of the Golden Age, 1986; contbr. articles to profl. jours. Home: 220 N Dithridge St Apt 1001 Pittsburgh PA 15213-1425 Office: U Pitts Dept Hispanic Langs & Lit 1309CL Pittsburgh PA 15260

BACCARI, CARMELLA, public relations professional; b. Wilmerding, Pa., Aug. 20, 1945. AA, Robert Morris Coll., 1965; BA, U. Md., 1973. Legis. asst. U.S. Congress, Washington, 1967-76; mgr. U. San Francisco, 1976-77; legis. asst. Wells Fargo Bank, San Francisco, 1977-78; exec. dir. Allied Florists Assn., Washington, 1978-81; editor Am. Israel Pub. Affairs Com., Washington, 1985-89; pub. rels. exec., found. mgr. Am. Assn. Clin. Chemistry, Washington, 1989—. Vol. presdl. and congl. campaigns. Mem. Pub. Rels. Soc. Am., Am. Soc. Assn. Execs. (communications cert.), Toastmasters Internat. (best speaker award). Office: Am Assn Clin Chemistry 2029 K St NW 7th Fl Washington DC 20006

BACCI, DIANA SHAWHAN HARRIS, college registrar; b. Ridley Park, Pa., Nov. 14, 1948; d. Elbert Neil and Ena Maxine (Burdine) Shawhan; m. John Kenneth Harris, Nov. 28, 1970 (div. Nov. 1981); m. Raymond R. Bacci, Jr., Oct. 21, 1989. BA, Ohio Wesleyan U., 1970; MBA, Eastern Coll., 1984. Asst. dir. admissions Eastern Coll., St. Davids, Pa., 1974-77, assoc. dir. admissions, 1977-79, assoc. registrar, 1979-88, coll. registrar, 1988—. Mem. Am. Assn. Collegiate Registrars and Admissions Officers, Mid. States Assn. Collegiate Registrars and Admissions Officers, Delaware Valley Registrar's Assn., Phi Beta Kappa, Delta Mu Delta. Republican. Presbyterian. Home: 574 Brookwood Rd Wayne PA 19087-2352 Office: Eastern Coll 10 Fairview Dr Wayne PA 19087-3696

BACH, CHARLES L., JR., lawyer; b. N.Y.C., Aug. 28, 1952; s. Charles L. and Carolyn Ann (Sidoti) B.; m. Robin Dolsky (div.); children: Alison Rose, Christina Anne. BA magna cum laude, St. John's U., 1974; JD, Union U., 1977. Bar: N.Y. 1978, U.S. Dist. Ct. (so. dist.) N.Y. 1978, (ea. dist.) N.Y. 1979, U.S. Ct. Appeals (2d cir.) 1979. Asst. dist. atty. Office of Dist. Atty., Bronx (N.Y.) County, 1977-81; assoc. Heidell, Pittoni & Moran, P.C., N.Y.C., 1981-85; ptnr. Heidell, Pittoni, Murphy & Bach, P.C., N.Y.C., 1985—. Mem. Def. Rsch. Inst., N.Y. County Lawyers Assn., N.Y. State Def. Lawyers Assn., Assn. for Hosp. Risk Mgmt. Roman Catholic. Office: Heidell Pittoni Murphy & Bach PC 99 Park Ave New York NY 10016-1503

BACH, MATT HOWARD, cardiologist; b. Fort Lee, N.J., Mar. 16, 1957; s. George and Sara (Zywotow) B.; m. Nancy Lavnick, Mar. 14, 1987; 1 child, Gregory. BS, Brandeis U., 1979; MD, U. Medicine and Dentistry N.J., 1984. Intern, resident medicine Beth Israel Med. Ctr., N.Y.C., 1984-87, fellow cardiology, 1987-91, attending cardiologist, 1991—, assoc. dir. coronary care unit, 1991—. Contbr. articles on cardiology to profl. jours. Fellow Am. Coll. Cardiology; mem. ACP, AMA. Office: Beth Israel Med Ctr 1st Ave at 16th St New York NY 10003

BACHE, THEODORE STEPHEN, recording company executive; b. N.Y.C., Dec. 19, 1936; s. Max Isselbacher and Leona (Rose) Hammel; m. Sheila Gottehrer, Oct. 18, 1959 (div. 1967); children: Mona Sharon, Caryl Michelle; m. Suellyn Kaplan, Feb. 18, 1968; children: Paul Michael, David Eric. BBA, Pace U., 1957, MBA, 1970; cert. in bus. adminstrn., Columbia U., Harriman, N.Y., 1973. CPA, N.Y. Auditor Orenstein & Bernstein, 1956-58; sr. auditor Klein, Katcher & Co., 1958-61; sr. internal auditor Rexall Drug and Chem. Co., 1961-64; supervising internal auditor CBS Inc., 1964-65, asst. to dir. acctg. TV network div., 1965-66, asst. dir. acctg. TV network div., 1966-68, dir. acctg. TV network div., 1968-69, asst. contr. TV network div., 1969-71, asst. contr., 1971-76, v.p. fin. specialty stores div., 1976-79; v.p. fin. and adminstrn. records div. CBS Inc. (changed to Sony Music Entertainment Inc.), 1979—. Mem. adv. bd. Mt. Sinai Diabetes Edn. Svc. Mem. AICPA, FIn. Exec. Inst., N.Y. Soc. CPAs, Country Music Assn., Acad. Country Music. Republican. Jewish. Office: Sony Music 1285 Ave Of The Americas New York NY 10019-4452

BACHELIS, LEONARD, psychologist. Lic. psychology, N.Y. Pvt. practice psychology N.Y.C. Office: Behavior Therapy Ctr NY PC 115 E 87th St New York NY 10128-1136

BACHENHEIMER, RALPH JAMES, merchant banker; b. Frankfurt, Fed. Republic Germany, Jan. 24, 1928; came to U.S., 1946; s. Ferdinand and Louise (Felber) B.; m. Clare Conway (dec. Feb. 1991); children: Lisa Clare, Cara Conway; m. Brith Bore. Student, Coll. Marianum, Vaduz, Liechtenstein, Switzerland, U. Zürich, Switzerland, Columbia U. V.p. Iselin-Jefferson Co., Inc., N.Y.C., 1946-66; pres., chief exec. officer Indian Head Yarn Co., N.Y.C., 1966-69; v.p. Europe Internat. Standard Brands Inc., N.Y.C., 1970-71; corp. v.p. Genesco, Inc., Nashville, 1971-76; exec. v.p., dir. Corland Corp., N.Y.C., 1976-84; mng. dir. E. S. Jacobs & Co., N.Y.C., 1985—; bd. dirs., past v.p. N.Y. Bd. Trade; bd. dirs., officer numerous corps. Founding mem. Rep. Nat. Senatorial Inner Cir., Washington; mem. Nat. Panel Arbitrators, N.Y.C. Named to Jaycees Hall of Fame, 1983. Mem. Vets. the 7th Regiment, Met. Club, Union League Club, Fripp Island Club, Greenwich Country Club, Dataw Island Club. Republican. Home: 5 Hill Rd Greenwich CT 06830-4024 Office: E S Jacobs & Co 375 Park Ave New York NY 10152-0002

BACHER, JUDITH ST. GEORGE, executive search consultant; b. New Rochelle, N.Y., July 14, 1946; d. Thomas A. and Rose-Marie (Martocci) Baiocchi; B.S., Georgetown U., 1968; M.L.S., Columbia U., 1971; m. Albert Bacher, Jan. 2, 1972; 1 son, Alexander Michael. Researcher, Time mag., N.Y.C., 1968-71; librarian Mus. Modern Art, N.Y.C., 1971-72; cons. Informaco Inc., N.Y.C., 1972-74, Booz-Allen & Hamilton, N.Y.C., 1974-79; prin. Nordeman Grimm/MBA Resources, N.Y.C., 1979—; mem. White House Adv. Com. on Personnel, Exec. Office of Pres., 1979-81; co-founder Research Roundtable, pres. 1981-83. Mem. Phi Beta Kappa. Office: Nordeman Grimm Inc 717 5th Ave New York NY 10022-8101

BACHMAN, JOHN B., city director of finance and administration; b. Harrisburg, Pa., July 18, 1955; s. Leonard J. and Darlene G. (Becker) B.; m. Judith L. Gartside, July 31, 1976; children: Kristin Lynn, Eric Thomas. BA in Biology, U. Del., 1977, BS in Chemistry, 1977; MBA in Health Care Adminstrn., U. Pa., 1980. Assoc. exec. dir. Delmarva Health Care Plan, Inc., Easton, Md., 1980-83, Delmarva Found. for Med. Care Inc., Easton, 1980-83; exec. dir. Western Mass. P.S.R.O. Inc., West Springfield, 1984, Mass. Peer Rev. Inc., Waltham, 1984; dir. adminstrv. svcs. Covenant House Health Svcs., Phila., 1985-87; asst. dir. fin. Temple U. Sch. Medicine, Phila., 1987-89; dir. fin. and adminstrn. City of Erie (Pa.), 1990—; adj. faculty Gannon U., Erie, 1991—. Mem. Govt. Fin. Officers' Assn. (budget reviewer 1991—), Am. Assn. PSROs (legis. com., long term care rev. com.), Hosp. Fin. Mgmt. Assn., Am. Hosp. Assn. Office: City of Erie 626 State St Erie PA 16501-1128

BACHMANN, PETER JOSEPH, college vice president; b. Szombathely, Hungary, June 2, 1949; came to U.S., 1956; s. Tibor and Eva Piroska (Arvay) B. BS, Villanova U., 1971; MA, Swarthmore Coll., 1973; PhD, Pa. State U., 1978. Cert. tchr. math. and sci., dir., supr., Pa., Del., N.J. Continuing edn. adminstr. Pa. State U., Media, 1973-75; instr., supr. Pa. State U., University Park, 1975-78; state ednl. statistician Del. Dept. Pub. Instrn., Dover, 1978-79, state specialist, program facilitator, 1979-82; dir. instrn. Salem Community Coll., Carneys Point, N.J., 1982-87, acting dean acad./student svcs., 1987; dean instrn. Harcum Jr. Coll., Bryn Mawr, Pa., 1987-88, v.p., dean acad. affairs, 1988—; scholar, diplomat U.S. Dept. State, Washington, 1981-82; mem. Acad. Leadership Inst., Carnegie-Mellon U., Pitts., 1991; accreditation evaluator Mid. States Assn. Colls./Schs., Phila., 1989—; nat. validator, trainer U.S. Dept. Edn., Washington, 1980-82; mem. faculty interchange program Pa. State U., University Park, 1977. Contbr. articles to profl. jours. Mem. World Affairs Coun. Phila., Winterthur Mus. Guild, Washington; bd. mem. Bela Bartok Soc. Am., Media. Grantee U.S. Dept. Edn., Dept. Inst. Dover (Del.), 1980-82. Mem. Nat. Assn. Acad. Affairs Adminstrs., Am. Assn. Community and Jr. Colls., Pa. Acad. Deans Assn., Continuing Edn. Assn. Pa.. Office: Harcum Jr Coll Montgomery And Morris Ave Bryn Mawr PA 19010-3476

BACHNER, JOHN PHILIP, business consultant; b. Boston, Nov. 8, 1944; s. Barnard and Bertha (Bellar) B.; AB, Harvard, 1966; m. Marcia L. Davis, Aug. 7, 1966; children: Barnard David, Lissa Suzanne. Screenplay writer Screen Presentations, Inc., film prodn. co. Washington, 1967-68; account exec. Hoffman Assocs., Inc., Silver Spring, Md., 1968-71; pres. Bachner Communications, Inc., communications-mktg. co., Silver Spring, 1971—; pres. Bachner Mgmt. Systems, multiple assn. mgmt. co. Silver Spring, 1973—; exec. v.p. Cons. Engrs. Council of Met. Washington, Silver Spring, 1971—, Property Mgmt. Assn., Silver Spring, 1973—, Washington Area Council Engring. Labs., Silver Spring, 1975—; exec. v.p. ASFE/The Assn. of Engring. Firms Practicing in the Geoscis.; pres., chmn. bd. Constrn. Industry Tech., Inc., Silver Spring, 1973—. Pres. Most for the Lease, 1982—; v.p. Bachner Real Estate, 1985—; exec. v.p. Mid-Atlantic Council of Shopping Ctr. Mgrs., 1986—; exec. v.p. Inst. Profl. Practice, Silver Spring, 1988—, Coll. Property Mgmt. Found., Silver Spring, 1988—; exec. v.p. CEC-MW Ednl. Found., Inc., 1990—, Profl. Liability Agts. Network, Inc., 1991—, Mid-Atlantic Cancer Rsch. Found., Silver Spring, 1992—, Internat. Found. Advancement of Thrombosis and Hematosis Rsch., Inc. Silver Spring, 1992—. Author: Marketing and Promotion for Design Professionals, 1977, PMA Guide to Practical Property Management, 1991, Practice Management for Design Professionals, 1991; writer 25 motion pictures; contbr. numerous articles to profl. publs., popular mags., profl. jours. Home: 9206 Sterling Montague Dr Great Falls VA 22066-4002

BACHNER, MARCIA LYNN, communications firm executive; b. Washington, Sept. 7, 1946; d. Milton and Libbey (Cohen) Davis; m. John Philip Bachner, Aug. 4, 1966; children: Barnard David, Lissa S. BA, Boston U., 1966. Pres. Great Equitations, Inc., Great Falls, Va., 1977-82, Lodzared, Inc., Great Falls, 1983-87; v.p. Bachner Communications, Inc., Silver Spring, Md., 1988—; exec. dir. Cons. Engrs. Coun. Met. Washington, Silver Spring, 1991—, CEC/MW Ednl. Found., Inc. Office: Bachner Communications Inc 8811 Colesville Rd Ste 6106 Silver Spring MD 20910-4343

BACKE, JOHN ELLIOTT, marketing executive; b. Cin., May 16, 1960; s. John David and Katherine Ann (Elliott) B.; m. Laura Caroline Gerndt, Sept. 20, 1986; 1 child, Emma Louise. BA in History, Duke U., 1982. Sales rep. Procter & Gamble, Phila., 1982; tchr., coach Friends Cen. Sch., Phila., 1983-84; asst. account exec. Saatchi & Saatchi Compton, N.Y.C., 1984-85; personnel mgr. SSC & B Lintas Worldwide, N.Y.C., 1985-86; mktg. mgr., v.p. The Backe Group, N.Y.C., 1987-89, exec. v.p., 1992—; v.p., pub. Andrews Communications Inc., Phila., 1989-90; pres., pub. Andrews Communications, Phila., 1990—; exec. v.p. The Backe Group, N.Y.C., 1992—; pres. Gulfshore Pub. Co., Naples, Fla., 1990—, v.p., 1987-89; v.p. Gulfstream Newspapers, Inc., Pompano, Fla., 1987-89, Sta. WDKY-TV, Inc., Lexington, Ky., 1987-89. Office: Andrews Communications Inc PO Box 1000 1646 W Chester Pike Westtown PA 19395-1000

BACKENSTOSS, HENRY BRIGHTBILL, electrical engineer, consultant; b. Washington, Sept. 28, 1912; s. Ross Elwood and Susan Catherine (Brightbill) B.; m. Violet Pentleton, Jan. 23, 1942 (div. 1952); m. Bernadette Humbert, Sept. 24, 1954; 1 child, Martine Susan. BSEE, MSEE, MIT, 1935. Registered profl. engr., Pa., Mass., Conn. Project mgr. Jackson & Moreland, Engrs., Boston, 1945-59; prof. power tech. Am. U. Beirut (Lebanon), 1959-61; spl. cons. Gen. Pub. Utilities Corp., N.Y.C., 1961-62; v.p. Jackson & Moreland Internat., Beirut, 1962-68; sr. cons. Gen. Pub. Utilities Svc. Corp., Reading, Pa., 1970-77; cons. Devel. Analysis Assocs., Cambridge, Mass., 1977-82; Govt. Saudi Arabia, 1962-69; panelist fuel crisis and power industry IEEE Tech. Conf., 1973. Contbr. articles to profl. publs. Bd. dirs. Reading Symphony Orch. (Pa.), 1975-86, Berks County Conservancy (Pa.), 1984—, Reading Mus. Found., 1986—, pres., 1988-91, chmn., 1991—, Am. Soc. Utility Investors, New Cumberland, Pa., 1989—. Mem. IEEE (life sr., power system engring. com. 1952-87, system econs. subcom. 1952-76), Am. Soc. Utility Investors (New Cumberland chpt. 1982—), Nat. Soc. Profl. Engrs., Pa. Soc. Profl. Engrs., Sigma Xi (assoc.), Tau Beta Pi. Congregationalist. Achievements include research in preparing economic studies leading to bulk power generation at mine-mouth in western Pennsylvania with transmission at 500 kv. to eastern markets. Home: 408 S Tulpehocken Rd Reading PA 19601-1030

BACKER, WILLIAM MONTAGUE, advertising agency executive; b. N.Y.C., June 9, 1926; s. Bill and Ferdinanda (Legare) B.; m. Ann Allderdice Mudge, June 11, 1983. B.A., Yale U., 1950. Creative dir., vice chmn. McCann-Erickson, N.Y.C., 1954-79; pres. Backer & Spielvogel Inc., N.Y.C., 1979-87; former vice chmn., exec. creative dir. Backer Spielvogel Bates Worldwide Inc., N.Y.C., from 1987, now pres., exec. creative dir. Composer: (with others) Teach the World to Sing, 1975. Served with USNR, 1944-46. Mem. ASCAP, Orange County Hunt Club (Va.), Yale Club. Episcopalian. Office: Backer Spielvogel Bates 405 Lexington Ave New York NY 10174-0002*

BACKES, RUTH EMERSON, counseling psychologist; b. Mt. Vernon, N.Y., Aug. 25, 1918; d. Robert Stewart and Harriett Elizabeth (Crofut) Emerson; m. Frederick Tregonning Backes (div. 1968, dec. 1981); children: Peter Frederick, Jill, Kim. BS, NYU, 1939; MEd, U. Mass., 1978, EdD, 1985. Asst. dir. health edn. YWCA, Balt., 1939-41, New Haven, 1941-44; program dir. USO, Newfoundland, 1944-46; women's dir. YMCA, Wallingford, Conn., 1947-49; coord., vol. Mental Health Ctr., Meriden, Conn., 1964-66; coord. edn. and info. Conn. Mental Health Ctr., New Haven, 1966-74; pvt. practice Amherst, Mass., 1980—; faculty Antioch Grad. Sch., Keene, N.H., 1976-81; vis. rsch. scholar Ctr. for Rsch. on Women, Wellesley (Mass.) Coll., 1991-93. Author: Bookstores of Amherst, 1989; contbr. articles to profl. jours.; mem. editorial bd. Workplace Democracy, Amherst, 1987-89, Mus. Insights, Amherst, 1989-90. Bd. dirs. Amherst Club,1987-90, Hampshire Choral Soc., Northampton, Mass., 1984-87, Helen Mitchell House for Homeless Women and Children, Amherst, 1987-90; rep. Town Meeting, Amherst, 1986—; trustee 1st Congl. Ch., Amherst, 1992—. Mem. Western Mass. Assn. for Psychoanalytic Psychology, Group for Psychoanalytic Studies. Democrat. Home and Office: 58 Cottage St Amherst MA 01002-2125

BACKMAN, ALAN GREGORY, health sciences technologist; b. Bklyn., Sept. 11, 1950; s. Gustav Adolf and Maude Therese (Darcy) B.; m. Mary Rose Vincent, Aug. 18, 1978; children: Gregory Alan, Lynsey Ann. Student, L.I. U., 1971, Thomas Edison Coll. Cert. respiratory therapy technician; cert. and registered cardiopulmonary technician; registered polysomnographic technologist. Respiratory technician St. Peter's Hosp., New Brunswick, N.J., 1969-71; biomed. engr. and dir. pulmonary Raritan Valley Hosp., Greenbrook, N.J., 1971-80; respiratory therapist NYU Hosp., N.Y.C., 1980-81; supr. pulmonary lab. Middlesex Gen. Hosp., New Brunswick, 1981-85; tech. dir., pulmonary diagnostics Deborah Heart and Lung Ctr., Browns Mills, N.J., 1985—; cons. Rutgers Occupational Health Div., New Brunswick, N.J., 1980—, Environ. Health Insp., Lakewood, N.J., 1988—, N.J. State Dept. Health, Trenton, 1987—; educator Rutgers U., Piscataway, N.J., 1981—, EOSHI/UMDNJ; adj. prof. Sch. Allied Health Profs. UMDNJ; rschr. air pollution and effects Deborah Heart and Lung Rsch. Ctr. Contbr. articles to profl. jours. Lector Mt. Virgin Ch., Middlesex, 1988-89; speaker's bur. Deborah Heart and Lung Ctr., 1985-88. With USAF, 1968-69. Recipient Contbr. award, Nat. Bd. Respiratory Care, Kans., 1987. Mem. Nat. Bd. Respiratory Care, Assn. Polysomnographic Tech., Am. Sleep Disorders Assn., Am. Inventors Soc., Am. Assn. Respiratory Care, Acad. Med. Arts and Scis. Democrat. Roman Catholic. Office: Deborah Heart and Lung Ctr 200 Trenton Rd Browns Mills NJ 08015-1799

BACKMAN, ROBERT EMIL, graphological research librarian; b. Wallace, Idaho, Nov. 13, 1917; s. Emil J. and Anna C. (Hendrickson) B.; m. Joanne M. Garland, 1980. Student, Hamilton Coll., 1946-49. Examiner captured documents U.S. Army, 1942-45; tech. info. specialist DOD, 1950-57; rsch. libr. Handwriting Analysis Rsch. Libr., New Hartford, N.Y., 1958-64, Passiac, N.J., 1964-69, Northfield, Mass., 1970, Royalston, Mass., 1971-76; Greenfield, Mass., 1977—; rsch. cons. Ea. Assn. Handwriting Analysts, 1963-65. Editor-compiler (reference books) Needles in Haystacks, 1973, Graphological Abstracts, 1975; (monographs) Poe's Autography, 1991, Graphomancy Revisited, 1991. Office: Handwriting Analysis Rsch Libr 91 Washington St Greenfield MA 01301-3411

BACKUS, DEBRA MARIE, quality assurance nurse; b. Gouveneur, N.Y., Oct. 16, 1955; d. George J. and June M. (Halladay) Gilbert; m. Paul J. Backus, July 19, 1975; children: Alicia Marie, Peter James. Nursing diploma, St. Lawrence Psychiat. Ctr., 1976; BS magna cum laude, SUNY, Utica, 1986, MS, 1989. Staff nurse Canton-Potsdam (N.Y.) Hosp., 1976-89, coord. program advancement and tng. in healthcare, 1989-90; quality assurance coord. A. Barton Hepburn Hosp., Ogdensburg, N.Y., 1990—. EMT III Canton (N.Y.) Fire Dept., 1976-91. Recipient Internat. Order of Oddfellows scholar Odd Fellows, Ogdensburg, 1973, Mary S. Goodale award St. Lawrence Psychiat. Ctr. Sch. Nursing, Ogdensburg, 1976. Mem. Am. Nurses Assn., N.Y. State Nurses Assn. (bd. dirs. dist. 6), Sigma Theta Tau (Iota Delta chpt.). Home: RR 3 Box 274A Canton NY 13617-9803 Office: A Barton Hepburn Hosp 214 King St Ogdensburg NY 13669-1142

BACON, GEORGE HUGHES, consultant and community leader; b. Phila., Mar. 4, 1935; s. George Hughes and Alice Olive (Campbell); divorced; children: Christopher Scott, Melissa Anne Bacon Hinkle. BA in English Lit. and Music, Temple U., 1957; MS in Ednl. Adminstrn., U. Pa., 1968. Cert. info. scis., tchr., Pa. Computer programmer 1st Pa. Bank, Phila., 1960-62; tchr. Bucks County, Pa., 1962-72; assoc. dir. Kranzley and Co., Cherry Hill, N.J., 1973-74; computer programmer Phila. Nat. Bank, 1975-77; cons. facilities mgmt. Sci. and Computer Tech. Inc., Malvern, Pa., 1978-79; lead systems analyst Ednl. Testing Svc., Princeton, N.J., 1979-86, ednl. and corp. analyst, 1987—; cons., lectr. computer literacy and software Abington (Pa.) Pub. Libr., 1983-84, Jenkintown (Pa.) Music Sch., 1984, Fudan U., Shanghai, People's Republic China, 1985, Abington Sch. Bd., 1989-91, invitational lectr., sr. tech. advisor UN Devel. Program Jao Tong U., Shanghai, 1988. Vol. aide Mercer County Geriatric Unit, Lawrenceville, N.J., 1986; bd. dirs. Rockledge (Pa.) Community Ctr., 1989; vol. aide Rydal Park (Pa.) Retirement Home, 1988—, Holy Redeemer Hosp., Meadowbrook, Pa., 1989—; tutor Abington Free Libr. Literacy Project, 1988; active headmaster's coun. Am. Boychoir, Princeton, 1987; active Abington Presbyterian Ch. Mem. Woodmere Art Mus. Phila., Temple U. CAS Alumni Assn., Nat. Coun. for Measurement in Edn., Am. Mgmt. Assn., Assn. for Systems Analysis, U. Pa. Faculty Club, Manorlu Swim Club (Dresher, Pa.). Home: 128 Blake Ave Philadelphia PA 19111-1209

BACON, JAMES EDMUND, banker; b. Mt. Vernon, N.Y., Feb. 27, 1931; s. John Anderson and Charlotte (Robb) B.; m. Caroline Sharp Sharfman, Nov. 4, 1989; children by previous marriage: Charlotte M., Rachel P., J. Nicholas. A.B., Harvard Coll., 1952, LL.B., 1958. Bar: D.C. 1959, N.Y. 1967. Assoc. Steadman, Collier & Shannon, Washington, 1958-61; atty.-adviser SEC, Washington, 1961-63; v.p. Am. Stock Exchange, N.Y.C., 1963-68; sr. v.p., dir. G.H. Walker & Co. and White, Weld and Co., N.Y.C., 1968-78; exec. v.p. U.S. Trust Corp., 1978-90; dir. U.S. Trust Corp., N.Y.C., 1986-90, Lone Star Industries, 1992—; con. U.S. Trust Corp., 1990—. Mem. banking and polit. com. U.S. C. of C., Washington, 1966-70; bd. dirs. N.Y. State Bankers Assn., N.Y.C., 1982-86; mem. N.Y. State Rep. Fin. Com., N.Y.C., 1981—; trustee The Day Sch., N.Y.C., 1982-88, Nuveen Select Tax-Free Income Portfolios, 1992; bd. dirs. Fedn. Protestant Welfare Agys., N.Y.C., 1989—, Prime Hospitality Corp., 1992—. Lt. (j.g.) USN, 1952-55. Mem. Downtown-Lower Manhatten Assn. (bd. dirs., treas. 1980-88), Racquet and Tennis Club, Met. Club (Washington).

BACON, JAMES JEFFREY, playwright, actor; b. Nyack, N.Y., Feb. 14, 1956; s. Robert Dunning and Jean (Billingsly) B. BA in Theatre and Film, U. Colo., 1978. Actor, stuntman The Wanderers Warner Bros., N.Y.C., 1978, actor Simon, 1979; editor Prentice-Hall, Inc., Englewood Cliffs, N.J., 1981-82; writer, dir. Spectrum Assocs., N.Y.C., 1984; tech. dir. Am. Stage Co., Teaneck, N.J., 1986-87; set designer Riverwest Theatre, N.Y.C., 1987; actor, stand-in for Paul Hogan Paramount, N.Y.C., 1987; actor, stage mgr. Tony and Tina's Wedding, N.Y.C., 1989-92; dramatist hist. dramas. Playwright (hist. dramas) Edward the Confessor, 1990, Warwick the Kingmaker, 1991, Treaty at Peronne, 1992; author (screenplay) Flat Out, 1986. Sr. mem., pilot Civil Air Patrol, Teterboro, N.J., 1990—. Mem. AFTRA, SAG, Dramatists Guild, Actors Equity Assn., Aircraft Owners and Pilots Assn.

BADALAMENTE, MARIE ANN, orthopaedics educator; b. Bronx, N.Y., July 17, 1949; d. John William and Elizabeth Ann (Castelluccio) B. BA, L.I. U., 1971, MS, 1973; PhD, Fordham U., 1977. Instr. of biology CUNY, Bronx, 1974-75; asst. prof. of biology C.W. Post Coll., L.I. U., Brookville, N.Y., 1975-78; asst. prof. of anatomy Sch. Medicine SUNY, Bklyn., 1978-79; asst. prof. of orthopaedics Sch. Medicine SUNY, Stony Brook, 1979-86, assoc. prof., 1986—. Contbr. over 35 articles to med. jours., including Proceedings of NAS; contbr. chpts. to books: Dupuytren's Disease, 1990, Operative Nerve Repair and Reconstruction, 1991. Grantee NIH, 1985-88, 88-91, 92-93, Orthopaedic Rsch. Found., 1982-84, 85-87, Easter Seals Found., 1981-85, Muscular Dystrophy Assn., 1979-81, FDA, 1991-92. Roman Catholic. Office: SUNY Sch Medicine Dept Orthopaedics Stony Brook NY 11794

BADALAMENTI, ANTHONY FRANCIS, mathematician; b. Bronx, N.Y., Feb. 2, 1943; s. Charles Salvator and Carmella-Maria (D'Ambrosio) B.; m. Karolina V. Kungl. Nov. 30, 1968 (div.); 1 child, Paul Anthony. BS, Manhattan Coll., 1964; MS, Stevens Inst. Tech., 1967; PhD, Poly. Inst. Bklyn., 1970. Mem. tech. staff Bell Telephone Labs., 1964-70; asst. prof. Fairleigh Dickinson U., 1970-72; mem. tech. staff Gen. Rsch. Corp., 1972-74; dir. revenue modeling and reporting Western Union Telegraph Co., 1974; rsch. scientist Rockland Rsch. Inst. (now Nathan Kline Inst. Psychiat. Rsch.), Orangeburg, N.Y., 1975—. Author publs. on systems, psychoanalysis and artificial intelligence. Italian Charities Am. scholar, Bklyn. Poly. Inst. scholar. Mem. Assn. Computing Machinery, Am. Math. Soc., Soc. Indsl. and Applied Math., Soc. Gen. Systems Rsch., N.Y. Acad. Scis., Am. Soc. Cybernetics, Soc. Psychoanalytic Psychotherapy, Bergen County Alumni Soc. Manhattan Coll. (v.p.). Home: 46 Crest St 46 Charles St Westwood NJ 07675-3144

BADALAMENTI, FRED LEOPOLDO, artist, educator; b. Long Island City, N.Y., June 25, 1935; s. Leopoldo and Concetta (Vitali) B.; m. Barbara J. Frankenfield, June 14, 1959; children: Katherine, Alexander, Frederick. Student, Pratt Inst., 1953-55, U. Alaska, 1957-58; BS, SUNY, New Paltz, 1961; MFA, Bklyn. Coll., 1967. Art tchr. Newburgh (N.Y.) Pub. Schs., 1960-63, Deer Park (N.Y.) High Sch., 1963-65; prof. art Bklyn. Coll., 1967—; vis. prof. art, lectr. SUNY, Stony Brook, 1977-78, 80, 81, 83; dep. chmn. for studio art Bklyn. Coll., 1990—, dep. chmn. for grad. art, 1972-89; dir. First St. Gallery, N.Y.C., 1978. One man shows include Suffolk Community Coll., 1971, First Street Gallery, 1973, 76, 80, 89, Nassau County Mus. of Fine Arts, 1987, St. Joseph's Coll., 1987; exhibited paintings and drawings of representational art in N.Y.C. and L.I., 1967—. With USAF, 1955-59. Bklyn. Coll. grad. fellow, 1965-67. Mem. Coll. Art Assn., AAUP. Home: 182 Lower Sheep Pasture Rd East Setauket NY 11733-1826 Office: Bklyn Coll Art Dept Bedford Ave # H Brooklyn NY 11222-3102

BADER, CAL JOSEPH, JR. See BAKER, CARL JOSEPH

BADER, HARRY FREDERICK, management consultant; b. Phila., Dec. 13, 1924; s. Henry Benjamin and Anna Dorothy (Hess) B.; m. Catherine Margaret Shibe, June 19, 1949; children: Curtis Michael, Holly Felice, Heather Fiona. BSChemE, Drexel U., 1951. Project engr. Internat. Playtex Corp., 1951-53; tech. mgr. Playtex (Ltd.) (Can.), 1953-55; dir. mfg. Playtex Ltd. (U.K.), 1955-62; chief mfg. engr. Internat. Playtex Corp., 1962-66; v.p. mfg. Seiberling Latex Products, Oklahoma City, 1966-80; dir. R & D, Ansell Internat., Melbourne, Australia, 1980-81; v.p., gen. mgr. Spanel Internat., Dover, Del., 1981-85; pres. Bader Cons. Inc., Dover, 1985—; Playtex rep. Brit. Inst. Mgmt., 1959-62; internat. cons. to condom and med. glove industry. Patentee in field. Founder mem. Greenock (Scotland) Jr. C. of C., pres. 1959-60. With USNR, 1942-46. Mem. Dover Supper Club, Friends of Old Dover. Episcopalian. Home and Office: 186 Carnoustie Rd Dover DE 19901

BADER, IZAAK WALTON, lawyer; b. N.Y.C., June 20, 1922; s. Maximillian Bader and Ida (Sussman) R.; m. Betty Sands Bader, Mar. 26, 1972. AB in Chemistry, NYU, 1942, JD, 1968. Bar: N.Y., D.C., U.S. Supreme Ct. Atty., FTC, Washington, 1948-50; asst. counsel N.Y. State Rent Com., N.Y.C., 1950-54; patent counsel Swingline Inc., 1954-72; sr. ptnr. Bader & Bader, White Plains, N.Y., 1972—; counsel Heart Disease Found., 1970-76, Ind. Investment Protective League, N.Y.C., 1972—; spl. counsel La. State Employees' Retirement System, Tchrs.' Retirement System of La., State Bd. Adminstrn. Fla., Lindner Fund, Inc. Mem. ABA, N.Y. State Bar Assn., Westchester County Bar Assn. Democrat. Home: 2980 Riverside Dr Coral Springs FL 33065-5518 Office: 65 Court St White Plains NY 10601-4205

BADERTSCHER, DAVID GLEN, law librarian, consultant; b. Morrow, Ohio, Jan. 31, 1935; s. Glen C. and Blanche (Cluff) B.; m. Betty Jo Shafer, June 25, 1965. BS, Ind. State U., 1957, MS, 1962; MS, Rosary Coll., 1967. Tchr. Rockville High Sch., Ind., 1957-59, Medinah Elem. Sch., Ind., 1961-63; libr. Elgin Acad., Ill., 1963-64; tchr. Beachwood High Sch., Ohio, 1964-65; libr. Chgo. Pub. Libr., 1965-66; circulation, asst. reference libr. U. Chgo. Law Sch., 1966-70; libr. Schiff Hardin Waite Dorschel & Britton, Chgo., 1970-73; exec. libr. Georgetown U. Law Ctr., Washington, 1973-78; dir. libr. Milbank, Tweed, Hadley & McCloy, N.Y.C, 1978-80; prin. law libr. N.Y. Supreme Ct., N.Y.C., 1980—; cons. Urban Research Corp., Chgo., 1970-73, Herner & Co., 1977—, R.R. Bowker & Co., 1981—; advisor Computer Law Svc., 1972-82, EIS, 1978—; adj. prof. Baruch Coll., 1982—; bd. dirs. N.Y. Met. Reference and Rsch. Libr. Agy., 1985—, chmn. bd. pers. com., 1989—. Contbr. articles to profl. jours. Served with AUS, 1959-61. Conv. grantee Am. Assn. Law Libraries, 1970. Mem. Medinah Tchrs. Assn. (pres. 1962-63), Am. Assn. Law Librs. (chmn. com. automation, sci. devel. 1970-72, chmn. state, ct. and county law librs. sect. 1989-90, adv. com. law libr. jour. 1989—), Chgo. Assn. Law Librs. (pres., conf. chmn. 1970-72), Am. Soc. Info. Sci. (editor SIG/Law Newsletter 1975-79), ABA (assoc.), Assoc. Info. Mgrs. Home: 46 Colony Ct New Providence NJ 07974-2332 Office: NY Supreme Ct 100 Centre St New York NY 10013-4308

BADIAN, ERNST, history educator; b. Vienna, Austria, Aug. 8, 1925; came to U.S., 1968; s. Joseph and Sally (Horinger) B.; m. Nathlie A. Wimsett, 1950; children: Hugh I., Rosemary J. B.A., U. N.Z., 1945, M.A., 1946; B.A., Oxford (Eng.) U., 1950, M.A., 1954, D.Phil., 1956; Lit.D., Victoria U., Wellington, N.Z., 1962. Jr. lectr. classics Victoria U., 1947-48; asst. lectr. classics and ancient history U. Sheffield, Eng., 1952-54; lectr. classics U. Durham, Eng., 1954-65; prof. ancient history U. Leeds, Eng., 1965-69; prof. classics and history State U. N.Y., Buffalo, 1969-71; prof. history Harvard, 1971-82, John Moors Cabot prof. history, 1982—; vis. prof. univs. Colo., Oreg., Wash., South Africa, Heidelberg, Tel-Aviv, Western Australia, UCLA; Sather prof. U. Calif., Berkeley, 1976; vis. mem. Inst. Advanced Study, Princeton, fall 1980, fall 1992, Nat. Humanities Ctr., fall 1988, Kommission für Alte Geschichte, Munich, May 1989. Author: Foreign Clientelae, 264-70 B.C., 1958 (Conington prize Oxford U.), Studies in Greek and Roman History, 1964, Roman Imperialism in the Late Republic, 1967, Publicans and Sinners, 1972, From Plataea to Potidaea: Studies in the History and Historiography of the Pentecontaetia, 1992; editor: Polybius, 1966, Ancient Society and Institutions, 1966, Sir Ronald Syme, Roman Papers vols. 1-2, 1979, Am. Jour. Ancient History, 1976—. Fellow Am. Council Learned Socs., 1972-73; Leverhulme fellow Eng., 1973; John Simon Guggenheim Meml. fellow, 1984; hon. fellow Univ. Coll., Oxford, England. Fellow Brit. Acad., Am. Acad. Arts and Scis., Am. Numismatic Soc.; hon. mem. Soc. Promotion Roman Studies; corr. mem. Austrian Acad. Scis., German Archeol. Inst.; fgn. mem. Finnish Acad. Scis.; mem. Am. Philol. Assn., Assn. Ancient Historians, Classical Assn. Can., U.K. Classical Assn., Soc. Promotion Hellenic Studies, Virgil Soc. Office: Robinson Hall Harvard Univ Cambridge MA 02138

BADLER, NORMAN IRA, computer and information science educator; b. L.A., May 3, 1948; s. Bernard and Lillian Lorraine Badler; m. Virginia Renke, June 14, 1968; children: Jeremy, David. BA in Creative Studies, U. Calif., Santa Barbara, 1970; MS in Computer Sci., U. Toronto, Ont., Can., 1971, PhD in Computer Sci., 1975. Lectr. U. Toronto, 1973-74; asst. prof. computer and info. sci. U. Pa., Phila., 1974-79, assoc. prof., 1979-86, prof., 1986—, Cecilia Fitler Moore prof., 1990—; cons. U.S. Army, Systems Exploration, AMP, Biomechanics Corp. Am.; mem., chmn. program coms. numerous confs. and workshops. Co-editor: Making Them Move, 1990; contbr. over 85 articles to profl. jours. Grantee NSF, 1975—, NASA, 1981—, U.S. Army, 1983—, Martin-Marietta Co., Lockheed, FMC, Deere & Co., Siemens, Moco, 1986—. Mem. IEEE Computer Soc., Assn. for Computing Machinery (vice chmn. spl. interest group on graphics 1979-81, mem. spl. interest group on artificial intelligence), Cognitive Sci. Soc., Am. Assn. for Artificial Intelligence, Phi Beta Kappa. Democrat. Jewish. Office: U Pa Computer & Info Sci Dept Philadelphia PA 19104-6389

BADMAN, JOHN, III, real estate developer, architect, construction executive; b. Kansas City, Mo., July 11, 1944; s. John II and Barbara (Smith) B.; m. Katherine Ballantine, May 12, 1984; children: Lindsay Cathryn, Barbara Smith, John IV. BA, Yale U., 1966, MArch, 1969, postgrad., 1969-70, M in Environmental Design, 1971. Registered architect, Conn.; real estate broker, Conn. Gen. mgr. S.J. Willy, Architects, New Haven, Conn., 1971-73; v.p. Schumacher & Forelle, Great Neck, N.Y., 1973-77, exec. v.p., 1986-87; dir. planning and devel. Dravo Engrs., N.Y.C., 1977-81; sr. v.p. Parsons, Brinckerhoff, Quade & Douglas, N.Y.C., 1981-86, also bd. dirs.; chmn., chief exec. officer Ballantine and Badman, Inc., Real Estate Developers, Greenwich, Conn., 1986—; sr. v.p. H.W. Lochner, Planners and Engrs., 1991—. Mem. Lacrosse all-Am. Team U.S. Intercollegiate Lacrosse Assn., 1966. Mem. AIA, Soc. Colonial Wars (steward 1986-89, coun. 1987—, marshall 1988-89, ofcl. nominating com. 1988-89, 90—, lt. gov. 1989—), Nat. Coun. Archtl. Registration Bds. (cert.), New Eng. Soc. N.Y., Round Hill Assn., Union League Club (N.Y.C.), Yale Club (N.Y.C.), Greenwich Country Club, Greenwich Polo Players Club, Adirondack League Club (Old Forge, N.Y.). Republican. Episcopalian. Home: 20 Mackenzie Gln Greenwich CT 06830-3421 Office: Ballantine & Badman Inc 3 Partridge Hollow Rd Greenwich CT 06831-2655

BADMINGTON, RICHARDS R., public relations counselor; b. Newport, N.H., Feb. 19, 1955; married. BA in Polit. Sci., U. N.H., 1977. Mktg. mgr. World Cup Sports, Inc., New City, N.Y., 1977-82; dir. mktg. German Ednl. TV Network, N.Y.C., 1982-83; v.p. mktg. N.Am. Soccer Camps Inc., Norwich, Conn., 1983-87; pres., chief exec. officer James Holechek Pub. Rels., Inc., Balt., 1987—. Mem. pub. rels. com. Greater Balt. Com., 1989—, Am. Heart Assn., Balt., 1991—; trustee Coun. on Econ. Edn. in Md. Mem. Pub. Rels. Soc. Am. (bd. dirs. Balt. chpt. 1989—), Baltimore County C. of C. (membership com. 1989—). Office: James Holechek Pub Rels Inc The Quadrangle Cross Keys # 347 Baltimore MD 21210

BADR, GAMAL MOURSI, consultant on laws of Arab countries; b. Helwan, Arab Republic of Egypt, Feb. 8, 1924; came to U.S., 1970; s. Ahmad Moursi and Aisha Morshida (Al-Alaily) B.; m. Fatima al-Zahraa Barakat, June 18, 1950; children: Hefni, Hussein. LLB, U. Alexandria, Arab Republic of Egypt, 1944, LLD summa cum laude, 1954; diploma in econs., U. Cairo, 1945, diploma in pvt. law, 1946. Asst. dist. atty. Mixed Cts. Egypt, Alexandria, 1945-49; from assoc. to ptnr. Vatimbella, Catzeflis, Garrana & Badr, Alexandria, 1949-63; legal adviser UN Congo Operation, Kinshasa, Zaire, 1963-64; justice Supreme Ct. Algeria, Algiers, 1965-69; from mem. to dep. dir. legal dept. UN Secretariat, N.Y.C., 1970-84; legal adviser Mission of Qatar to UN, N.Y.C., 1984—; permanent bur. mem. Pan-Arab Lawyers' Fedn., Cairo, 1959-61; adj. prof. law NYU, 1982—; lectr. The Hague Acad. Internat. Law, 1984. Author: Agency, 1980, State Immunity, 1984; gen. editor Commercial Law of the Middle East; contbr. articles to profl. jours. Mem. Internat. Law Assn. (London), Am. Soc. Internat. Law, Am. Arbitration Assn. (panel of arbitrators), Am. Fgn. Law Assn. (v.p. 1985-87, 89-92), Egyptian-Am. Assn. (pres. 1987-90), Princeton Club, Rotary (pres. Alexandria Club 1962-63). Muslim. Home: 18 Peter Lynas Ct Tenafly NJ 07670-1115 Office: Mission of Qatar to UN 747 3rd Ave New York NY 10017-2803

BADURA, CARL WERNER, data processing company executive; b. N.Y.C., Oct. 23, 1937; s. Carl Ottomar and Herta Helene (Goetze) B.; m. Christina Elizabeth Schrot, June 12, 1960; children: Carolyn, Carl H., Christopher, Curt. AAS in Elec. Engring., Westchester Community Coll., Valhalla, N.Y., 1963; student, NYU, 1963-64. Registered profl. engr., N.Y. Jr. elec. engr. Otis Elevator Co., N.Y.C., 1956-67; sr. programmer analyst Orange & Rockland Utilities, Spring Valley, N.Y., 1967-69; sr. systems engr. RCA Computer Div., N.Y.C., 1969-71; programming mgr. Nestle Co., Inc., White Plains, N.Y., 1971-78; data processing mgr. Columbus Line, Inc., N.Y.C., 1978-85; dir. info. svcs. Maryknoll (N.Y.) Fathers & Bros., 1985—. Spokes chmn. Jaycees, New City, N.Y., 1969; chmn. com. Boy Scouts Am., Congers, N.Y., 1975-77, scoutmaster, 1978-79; fin. sec. South Hudson Tres Dias, Peekskill, N.Y., 1988—. Mem. Am. Mgmt. Assn., Data Processing Mgmt. Assn. Home: 31 Pleasant Hill Rd Hopewell Junction NY 12533-7412 Office: Maryknoll Fathers & Bros 3D Fl Price Maryknoll NY 10545-9999

BADZIK, CAROLYN DONNA, accountant; b. Des Plaines, Ill., May 10, 1967; d. Donald Dominic Basile and Monica Joyce (Bobby) Hatfield; m. David Van Badzik, Dec. 31, 1988. BS in Acctg., San Diego State U., 1988. CPA, Pa. Staff acct. Deloitte & Touche, Pitts., 1989—. Mem. San Diego Zool. Soc., 1987; sponsor Sta. WQED Pub. TV, Pitts., 1991. Recipient Billy Mitchell award CAP, 1986. Mem. Am. Soc. Women Accts. (bd. dirs. Pitts. chpt. 1989-91), Pa. Inst. CPAs (candidate). Home: 16 Woodland Ln Gales Ferry CT 06335-1853 Office: Deloitte & Touche 2 Oliver Pla Pittsburgh PA 15222

BAECHEL, KENNETH EARL, communications executive; b. Canton, Ohio, Sept. 30, 1941; s. Charles William and Bessie Bernice (Bovey) B.; m. Ann Forrester Cook, July 8, 1967; children: Tara, Heath, Corey. BA, Webster U., 1965. Salesman MONY, Albany, N.Y., 1969-81; pres. Automated Communications, Inc./Community Alert Network, Schenectady, N.Y., 1981—. With Green Berets, U.S. Army, 1966-69. Recipient Nat. Quality award Nat. Assn. Life Underwriters; Named Outstanding Young Man, Schenectady (N.Y.) County Jaycees, 1985, Outstanding Vol. Schenectady County C. of C. Roman Catholic. Home: 315 Schermerhorn St Schenectady NY 12302-1147 Office: Automated Communications Inc 301 Nott St Schenectady NY 12305

BAENA, ROBERT BOB, interior designer; b. Bronx, N.Y., Aug. 24, 1930; s. Jacob and Luisa (Jaffe) B.; m. Rita R. Bejarano, July 15, 1951; children: Ellen R. Baena Youssef, Lisa R. Baena Horn, Andrea R. Baena Macdonald. Student, NYU, 1948-49, N.Y. Sch. Interior Design, 1952. V.p. Baena Decorators Inc., Bronx, 1948-68; pres. Baena Decorators Rockland Inc., Nanuet, N.Y., 1968-76, Robert B. Baena Inc., Spring Valley, N.Y., 1985—; sales mgr. Lexington Manor, Ethan Allen Gallery, Nanuet, 1977-85, 20th Century Draperies Inc., N.Y.C., 1986—. Mem. Am. Interior Design Soc. (assoc.), Rotary (editor bull. Nanuet 1970, pres. 1980-81, fellow 1986, v.p. Monsey, N.Y. chpt. 1989-90, pres. 1990-92). Democrat. Jewish. Home: 16 Southgate Dr Spring Valley NY 10977-2019 Office: 20th Century Draperies Inc 70 Wooster St New York NY 10012-4348

BAER, BARBARA SUE, psychologist; b. Staten Island, Mar. 28, 1958; d. Bernard Louis and Lillian Edith (Cohen) B.; m. Judah S. Shapiro, June 9, 1984; 1 child, Ariel Rebecca. PhD in Clin. Psychology, New Sch. for Social Rsch., 1987. Lic. psychologist, N.Y. Psychology extern Beth Israel Med. Ctr., N.Y.C., 1984-85, F.D.R. VA Hosp., Montrose, N.Y., 1985-86; postdoctoral fellow neuropsychology Beth Israel Med. Ctr., N.Y.C., 1986-87; assoc. psychologist Harlem Valley Valley Psychiat. Ctr., White Plains, N.Y., 1987—. Home: 1085 Warburton Ave Apt 717 Yonkers NY 10701-1012

BAER, ELIZABETH ROBERTS, academic administrator; b. Ithaca, N.Y., Mar. 4, 1946; d. James Herbert and Emmie Elizabeth (Herbermann) Roberts; m. Clinton D. Baer Jr., June 21, 1968; children: Hester Delacey, Nathaniel Roberts. BA summa cum laude, Manhattanville Coll., 1968; MA, NYU, 1970; PhD, Ind. U., 1981. Reading and study skills ctr. Dartmouth Coll., Hanover, N.H., 1977-81; asst. dean coll. Sweet Briar (Va.) Coll., 1981-85; provost, prof. English Washington Coll., Chestertown, Md., 1985-92; v.p. acad. affairs, profl. English Gustavus Adolphus Coll., St. Peter, Minn., 1992—; bd. dirs. Md. Humanities Coun., Balt., 1987-92, EDUCOM, Washington, 1991—. Reviewer Choice mag.; contbr. articles to profl. jours. Fellow Va. Found. Humanities, 1991, Christian A. Johnson Found., 1988, Mellon Found., 1982. Mem. MLA, Nat. Women's Studies Assn. (com. nat. steering 1978-79). Office: Gustavus Adolphus Coll Office of VP Acad Affairs Saint Peter MN 56082

BAER, GREGOR, lawyer; b. Pitts., Aug. 30, 1958; s. William Clarence and June Dorothy (Casey) B. Diploma, U. Vienna, Vienna, Austria, 1978; BA magna cum laude, MA, U. Pitts., 1980; MPhil 1st class hons., Oxford U., Eng., 1982; DPhil, Oxford U., 1986; JD, U. Va., 1986. Bar: N.Y. 1987, U.S. Dist. Ct. (so. and ea. dists.) N.Y. 1987, U.S. Ct. Appeals (2nd cir.) 1988, U.S. Ct. Appeals (1st cir.) 1989. Assoc. Davis Polk & Wardwell, N.Y.C., 1986—; vis. lectr. law Yale U., New Haven, 1989—. Author: The Right to Travel. Rotary Found. fellow, 1980, teaching fellow, U. Va., 1985, Oxford U., 1982. Mem. ABA, Henry Aldrich Soc. (Oxford, Eng.), Am. Friends of Christ Ch., Phi Beta Kappa. Episcopalian. Office: Davis Polk & Wardwell One Chase Manhattan Pla New York NY 10005

BAER, JON ALAN, political scientist; b. Southampton, N.Y., June 25, 1945; s. Kosty Joseph and Mary Olive (Klingler) B. BA, LIU, 1970; MA, SUNY, Albany, 1977, MA, 1978, postgrad., 1988. Entertainer, Sta. WLNG, Sag Harbor, N.Y., 1969-70, 74-75; research fellow, research asso. U.S. Adv. Commn. on Intergovtl. Relations, 1978-80; researcher N.Y. State Legis. Commn. on Expenditure Rev., 1979-81 lectr. polit. sci. Siena Coll., 1980; instr. polit. sci. Russell Sage Coll., 1981-82; research asso. SUNY, Albany, 1977—; cons. Office of Intergovtl. Relations, Suffolk County, N.Y., 1978-79. With U.S. Army, 1970-73. Decorated Army Commendation medal, N.Y. State Conspicuous Service Cross. Mem. Acad. Polit. Sci., Am. Polit. Sci. Assn., Am. Soc. Public Adminstrn., Center for Study of Presidency, Conf. Fedn. Studies, Nat. Mcpl. League, Neighborhood Orgn. Research Group, Northeastern Polit. Sci. Assn., Policy Studies Orgn., So. Polit. Sci. Assn., Midwest Polit. Sci. Assn. Episcopalian. Contbr. articles to profl. jours. Home: Franklin Ave PO Box 743 Sag Harbor NY 11963-0019 Office: SUNY Grad Sch Pub Affairs Albany NY 12222

BAER, MAX FRANK, consultant; b. Frankfurt, Germany, Nov. 10, 1912; came to U.S., 1921; s. Bernard Baer and Erna (Pollak) Hoelzel; m. Gertrude Smith, Feb. 14, 1967; children: Richard Rosenbaum, Randye Low. Student, U. Notre Dame, 1930-34, U. Ariz., 1934; LLB, JD, Creighton U., 1937; MA, Columbia U., 1942; EdD, George Washington U., 1947. Contract processor, typist Assoc. Investment Co., South Bend, Ind., 1931-34; acting exec. sec. AZA B'nai B'rith, Omaha, 1934-38; nat. dir. Vocat. Svc. B'nai Brith, Washington, 1938-54, internat. dir. Youth Orgn., 1948-77; cons. planning and rsch. Washington, 1977-91, sesquicentennial historian, 1991—. Author: Occupational Information, 1951, 3d edit., 1967, Dealing in Futures, 1983; editor: Careers in Retail Business Ownership, 1946, Playing Around With Words, 1990, Foundation Directory, 1991. Mem. fed. adv. coun. Bur. Employment Security, Washington, 1948-58, bd. mgrs. Adas Israel Congregation, Washington, 1954—. Recipient Bisno award Profl. Excellence J & C Spitzer, 1988; Max F. Baer Lodge named in his honor, Mukwonago, Wis., 1980, Baer Cultural Ctr. named in his honor, Ossifiya, Israel, 1975. Mem. APA, AACD, Acad. Cert. Social Workers (charter), Nat. Career Devel. Assn. (past pres.), Conf. Jewish Communal Svc., Phi Delta Kappa. Home: Apt 1123-E 4201 Cathedral Ave NW Washington DC 20016-4901 Office: 1640 Rhode Island Ave NW Washington DC 20036-3278

BAER, MICHAEL ALAN, political scientist, educator; b. Atlanta, Feb. 4, 1943; s. Kurt Arthur and Beulah (Mendelson) B.; m. Charlotte Glazer, Aug. 16, 1964; children: Daniel Noach, Naomi Aviva. B.A., Emory U., 1964; M.A., U. Oreg., 1966, Ph.D., 1968. Research asst. Center Advanced Study Ednl. Adminstrn., U. Oreg., 1964-68; mem. faculty U. Ky., Lexington, 1968-90, prof. polit. sci. and pub. adminstrn., 1980-90, chmn. dept. polit. sci., 1977-81, dean Coll. Arts and Scis., 1981-90; polit. analyst WAVE-TV, Louisville; prof. polit. sci. Northeastern U., Boston, 1990—, provost, sr. v.p. acad. affairs, 1990—. Co-author: Lobbying: Influence and Interaction in American State Legislatures, 1969; co-editor: Political Science in America, 1991; mem. editorial bd.: State and Local Govt. Rev, 1977-81; contbr. articles to profl. jours. Bd. dirs. Cen. Ky. Civil Liberties Union, 1973-77, Congregation Ohavay Zion, Lexington, 1976-78, Bluegrass chpt. NCCJ, 1980-81; bd. dirs. Cen. Ky. Jewish Assn., 1970-74, 79-84, pres., 1973-74; rec. sec. Bluegrass chpt. Ky. Assn. Gifted Edn., 1983-85; mem. Mayor's com. to establish Lexington Children's Mus., 1988-90, mem. bd. dirs., 1990; mem. coun. Inter Univ. Consortium for Polit. and Social Rsch. U. Mich., 1988—, chmn., 1990-92; bd. dirs. Coun. of Colls. of Arts and Scis., 1983-89, pres., 1988. Leverhulme fellow, 1974-75. Mem. Am. Polit. Sci. Assn., Midwest Polit. Sci. Assn. (exec. coun. 1980-83), Brit. Politics Group (exec. coun. 1978-80), So. Polit. Sci. Assn., Ky. Conf. Polit. Sci., Nat. Assn. Univ. and Land Grant Colls. (comm. on arts and scis. 1986-90, chmn. 1990). Home: 60 Burroughs St # 34 Jamaica Plain MA 02130-4019 Office: Northeastern U 111 Hayden Ave Lexington MA 02173-7942

BAERWALD, ERIC HARRIS, electrical engineer; b. Rome, N.Y., Aug. 13, 1964; s. Dean Lyle and Carole Dale (Harris) B. BSEE, U. Md., 1987; student, Armed Forces Staff Coll., 1991. Asst. elec. engr. IIT Rsch. Inst., Annapolis, Md., 1987-90, assoc. elec. engr., 1990—. Composer: Music to Mirror Each Day of Creation, 1992. Recipient Commitment to Excellence award IIT Rsch. Inst., 1990. Mem. Assn. Old Crows. Office: 185 Admiral Cochrane Dr Annapolis MD 21401

BAESCH, JOHN FRANCIS, railroad executive; b. Balt., Nov. 24, 1944; s. Rudolph William and Shirley Virginia (Crosby) B. AB, Loyola Coll., Balt., 1966. English tchr. So. High Sch., Balt., 1966-67; mgmt. trainee C&O/B&O Railroads, Balt., 1971, power coord., 1972-74; mgr. Chessie System Railroads, Balt., 1974-76; asst. dir. train ops. Amtrak, Washington, 1976-80, dir. train ops., 1980-82; transp. supt. Amtrak, Balt. and Phila., 1982-88; gen. supt. transp. Amtrak, Phila., 1988-90; asst. gen. supt. commuters Amtrak, Boston, 1990—. Capt. U.S. Army, 1967-71, Vietnam. Named to Hon. Order of Ky. Cols. Mem. Am. Assn. R.R. Supts. (dir.), World Affairs Coun. Boston, New Eng. R.R. Club, English Speaking Union U.S., Charitable Irish Soc. Boston. Democrat. Roman Catholic. Home: 1836 Columbia Rd # 2 Boston MA 02127-4342 Office: Amtrak Two South Sta Boston MA 02210

BÁEZ, ROBERTO A., sales account manager; b. N.Y.C., Jan. 25, 1962; s. Rafael A. and Matilde (González) B.; m. Helen Carol Bottari, Oct. 15, 1988. Student, NYU, 1980-82. Asst. equipment mgr. Healthco Internat., Maspeth, N.Y., 1980-83; sales rep. Lares Rsch., N.Y.C., 1983-84; equipment specialist Schein Dental Equipment Co., Great Neck, N.Y., 1984-87; account mgr. Xerox Corp., Woodcliff Lake, N.J., 1987—. Photographer Latin music industry, 1981-85. Roman Catholic. Office: Xerox Corp 300 Tice Blvd Woodcliff Lake NJ 07675

BAEZ, WILFRED JOHN, alcoholism clinic director; b. S.I., N.Y., Mar. 1, 1956; s. Wilfred John and Maureen Bernadette (Byrne) B.; m. Marcia Ann Cotton, Aug. 9, 1986; 1 child, Nicolas Dale Cotton-Baez. BA in Psychology, SUNY, Oswego, 1979; MA in Counseling Psychology, Calif. Inst. Integral Studies, 1981; PhD in Counseling Psycyhology, Columbia Pacific U., 1989. Nationally cert. alcoholism and addictions counselor II; N.Y. state credentialed alcoholism counselor. Psychology intern St. George Homes Residential Treatment Svcs., Berkeley, 1982-83, Southwest Mental Health Svcs., San Francisco, 1983-84; mental health counselor Bayview Hunters Point Found., San Francisco, 1984-85; dir clin svcs., dir. outpatient clinic, alcoholism counselor Alcoholism Coun. Tompkins County, Ithaca, N.Y., 1985—. Mem. Tompkins County Domestic Violence Coalition, Criminal Justice Adv. Bd. and Alternatives to Incarceration Bd. of Tompkins County Bd. of Reps., Tompkins County Child Protective Svcs. Planning Com., Tompkins County PINS Planning Com., 1989, Tompkins County Mental Health Svcs. Screening Com., Tompkins County Stop DWI Program Bd., 1985, Tompkins County Homeless Case Mgmt. Team, 1990. Mem. Am. Assn. Counseling and Devel., N.Y. State Fedn. Alcoholism Counselors. Home: 213 Willow Ave Ithaca NY 14850-3551 Office: Alcoholism Coun Tompkins 201 E Green St Ithaca NY 14850-5634

BAGDAN, GLORIA, interior designer; b. Bronx, N.Y., May 24, 1929; d. Max and Molly (Trufelman) Green; m. Kenneth Bagdan, Nov. 25, 1948 (dec. 1974); children: Meryl Bagdan Robins, Scott, Stacy. Student, CCNY, 1947-49, Inst. Interior Design, 1964, Wharton Sch., 1977. Founder, 1st pres. Bronx Mcpl. Hosp. Aux., 1955-60; interior designer Scarsdale, N.Y., 1964—; v.p., treas. Gold Medal Farms, Bronx, 1974-79; Active in fundraising Grasslands Hosp. Heart Assn.; cons. Mental Health Assn., 1967—; bd. dirs. 20 Sutton Pl. S., N.Y.C.; mem. Rep. Senatorial Inner Circle, Washington. Mem. Internat. Platform Assn., Mcpl. Art Soc. N.Y., Nat. Trust Hist. Preservation, U.S. Congl. Adv. Bd., English Speaking Union Club, Atrium Club, Internat. Club, Beaux Arts Club. Home: 20 Sutton Pl S New York NY 10022-4165

BAGG, THOMAS CAMPBELL, physicist; b. Phila., Oct. 28, 1917; s. Thoms Campbell and Anna Josephene (Vansant) B.; m. Elizabeth Miller, May 2, 1942; children: Patricia Bagg Cole, Carol Bagg Carpenter, Thomas Campbell III. BS in Engring., Physics, Lafayette Coll., Easton, Pa., 1939. Instrument maker dept. physics Lafayette Coll., 1935-39; lab. instr. dept. physiology U. Pa., Phila., 1939-41; jr. physicist DTM Carnegie Inst., Washington, 1941; physicist radio div. Nat. Bur. Standards, Washington, 1941-51, physicist radiometry, 1951-56; systems engr. computer div. Nat. Bur. Standards, Washington, Gaithersburg, Md., 1956—; cons. U.S. Patent Office, Washington, 1956-88, USN, Washington, 1956-85, Nat. Libr. Medica, Bethesda, Md., 1963—, NIH, Bethesda, 1960—. Contbr. articles to profl. jours. Recipient Bronze medal U.S. Dept. Commerce, 1987. Fellow Assn. for Info. and Image Mgmt. (Award of Merit), AAAS; mem. Soc. for Image Sci. and Tech. (bd. dirs. 1987—), Am. Phys. Soc., IEEE, Am. Soc. Info. Scientists. Republican. Episcopalian. Home: 9110 Northbranch Dr Bethesda MD 20817-1944 Office: Nat Inst Standards & Tech Rm A51 Technology Gaithersburg MD 20899

BAGLEY, BRIAN G., materials science educator, researcher; b. Racine, Wis., Nov. 20, 1934; s. Wesley John and Ethel (Rasmussen) B.; m. Dorothy Elizabeth Olson, Nov. 20, 1959; children: Brian John, James David, Kristin Marie. BS, U. Wis., 1958, MS, 1959; AM, Harvard U. , 1964, PhD, 1968. Metall. engr. U. Wis., Madison, 1959-60; mem. tech. staff Bell Telephone Labs., Inc., Murray Hill, N.J., 1967-83, Bell Communications Rsch. Inc., Red Bank, N.J., 1984-91; NEG endowed chair, dir. Eitel Inst., prof. physics U. Toledo, 1991—. Served to 1st lt. AUS, 1960-61. Xerox predoctoral fellow Harvard U., 1964-66, Robert J. Painter predoctoral fellow Harvard U., 1966-67. Mem. Am. Phys. Soc., Am. Vacuum Soc. (chpt. chmn. 1991), Materials Rsch. Soc. Home: 467 Ridge Rd Plainfield NJ 07060-5433 Office: U Toledo Dept Physics and Astronomy 2801 W Bancroft St Toledo OH 43606-3390

BAGLEY, EDYTHE SCOTT, theater arts educator; b. Marion, Ala., Dec. 13, 1924; d. Obie and Bernice (McMurry) Scott; m. Arthur Moten Bagley, June 5, 1954; 1 child, Arturo Scott. BEd, Ohio State U., 1949; MA in English, Columbia U., 1954; MFA in Theater Arts, Boston U., 1965. Instr. Elizabeth City (N.C.) State Coll., 1953-56; asst. prof. Albany (Ga.) State Coll., 1956-57, A&T U., Greensboro, N.C., 1957-58, Norfolk (Va.) State Coll., 1963-65; assoc. prof. theater Cheyney (Pa.) U., 1971—, also chair dept. theater arts; cons. in black theater Mich. State U., East Lansing, 1969-71. Dir. numerous coll. prodns., 1968-71. Spl. asst. to Coretta Scott King, Martin Luther King, Jr. Ctr. for Nonviolent Social Change, Atlanta. Mem. NAACP, Nat. Coun. Negro Women, Theater Assn. Pa., The Links Inc. (chair com. on arts 1972-80), Women's Internat. League for Peace and Freedom, The Pa. Martin Luther King Jr. Assn. for Nonviolence (bd. dirs.), The Martin Luther King Jr. Ctr. for Nonviolent Soc. Change (bd. dirs.). Home: 2 Derry Dr Cheyney PA 19319 Office: Cheyney U Cheyney PA 19319

BAGLIO, JOSEPH ANTHONY, chemist; b. N.Y.C., May 16, 1939; s. Salvatore A. and Theresa N. (Vilardi) B.; m. Helen S. Peters, Sept. 1, 1961; children: Frances Beeber, Christine. BS, St. John's U., 1958; PhD, Rutgers U., 1965. Chemist U.S. Atomic Energy Comm., New Brunswick, N.J., 1959-60, R.C.A. Labs., Princeton, N.J., 1960-61; teaching asst., grad. student Rutgers U., New Brunswick, 1961-65; prin. mem., tech. staff GTE Labs., Waltham, Mass., 1965—. Patentee in field of chemistry; contbr. over 30 articles to profl. jours. Dupont Teaching fellow, NSF fellow, NIH fellow. Mem. Am. Chem. Soc., Electro Chem. Soc., Materials Rsch. Soc., Sigma Xi (pres. 1984). Democrat. Roman Catholic. Home: 8 Forest Hill Dr Andover MA 01810-3243 Office: GTE Labs 40 Sylvan Rd Waltham MA 02154-1168

BAGLIO, VINCENT PAUL, aeronautical engineer; b. Patchogue, N.Y., Feb. 18, 1960; s. Lorenzo and Nancy (Morello) B.; m. Donna Marie Cappo, Sept. 8, 1985. BS, Princeton U., 1982; MS, Poly. U., Bklyn., 1986. Sr. engr. aircraft systems div. Grumman Aerospace Corp., Bethpage, N.Y., 1982—. Contbr. articles to profl. jours. Mem. alumni schs. com. Princeton (N.J.) U. Mem. AIAA (com. chmn. 1988-91), Soc. Automotive Engrs. (indsl. lectr. 1990-91), Internat. Coun. Aero. Scis. (program com. 1989—), Friends Princeton Football. Office: Grumman Aerospace Corp MS B21-35 Bethpage NY 11714

BAGNAL, CHARLES WILSON, JR., nuclear engineer; b. Florence, S.C., July 1, 1957; s. Charles W. and Patricia A. (Smith) B.; m. Linda L. Capaldi, June 10, 1978; children: Katherine L., John C., Jordan K. B.N.E., cert. in materials engring., Ga. Inst. Tech., 1980. Engr. in tng. Intelligence analyst CIA, Washington, 1975-78; engr. Ga. Power Co., Atlanta, 1978-79; rsch. asst. Ga. Inst. Tech., Atlanta, 1979-80; lead nuclear engr. Combustion Engring., Inc., Windsor, Conn., 1980-83; sr. cons. engr. SWUCO, Inc., Simsbury, Conn., 1983-87; asst. project mgr. advanced light water reactor design Asea Brown Boveri, Inc., Windsor, 1987—; guest lectr. WALKS Sci. Faculty Devel. program Loomis Chaffee Sch., 1992. Author numerous tech. papers and reports, 1981—; contbr. SWUCO Report, 1986-87, (newsletter) ANS Fuel Cycle & WM, 1987—. Chair bd. Christian edn. First Ch. in Windsor, 1983-84, chair ch. cabinet, 1984-85, sec. bd. deacons, 1985-88; del. Conn. conf. United Ch. of Christ, 1992—; life mem. Republican Nat. Com.; guest lectr. Nuclear Power course Thames Valley State Tech. Coll., 1990—; mem. project energy com. The Discovery Mus., 1992. Recipient Medal for Excellence in History, DAR, 1971, Scholarship medal Fairfax County Pub. Sch., 1975. Mem. NSPE, Am. Nuclear Soc., UN Assn. U.S.A., U.S. Coun. for Energy Awareness (participant citizen energy alert network 1989—, speaker Energy Am. program 1989—, tech. adviser Energy Am. program 1992—), Tau Beta Pi. Mem. United Ch. Christ. Home: 16 Priscilla Rd Windsor CT 06095-1944 Office: Asea Brown Boveri Inc 1000 Prospect Hill Rd Windsor CT 06095-1564

BAGSHAW, JOSEPH CHARLES, molecular biologist, educator; b. Niagara Falls, N.Y., Sept. 2, 1943; s. Joseph Stanley Pash and Nancy Jo (Pannabaker) Pash; m. Elizabeth Brevoort Potts, Nov. 27, 1971; children: Joseph Scott, Alan David. BA, Johns Hopkins U., 1965; PhD, U. Tenn., Oak Ridge, 1969. Research fellow Mass. Gen. Hosp., Boston, 1970-71; asst. prof. molecular biology Wayne State U., Detroit, 1971-77; assoc. prof. Wayne State U., 1977-84; prof., head dept. biology and biotechnology Worcester Poly. Inst., Mass., 1984—; dir. Worcester Consortium Ph.D. Program in Biomed. Sci., 1985—. Editor: (with others) Cell and Molecular Biology of Artemia Development, 1989. Predoctoral fellow NSF; research grantee NSF, NIH. Mem. Am. Soc. Biochemistry and Molecular Biology, Am. Soc. Cell Biology, AAAS. Office: Worcester Poly Inst Worcester MA 01609

BAHARY, WILLIAM SHAUL, chemist, researcher; b. Kermanshah, Iran, Jan. 20, 1936; came to U.S., 1951, naturalized, 1956; s. Shaul S. and Victoria (Menashi) B.; m. Susan C. Kurshan, Nov. 23, 1979. BA, Harvard U., 1957; MA, Columbia U., 1958, PhD, 1961. Sr. research chemist Tex.-U.S. Chem. Co., Parsippany, N.J., 1961-68; vis. asst. prof. Fairleigh Dickinson U., Teaneck, N.J., 1968-73; adj. asst. prof. Stevens Inst. Tech., Hoboken, N.J., 1973-79; supervising engr. Duracell, Inc., Tarrytown, N.Y., 1979-88; rsch. scientist, Unilever, Inc., Edgewater, N.J., 1989—; treas. Bahary & Co., Pearl River, N.Y., 1960—. Contbr. articles to profl. jours. Patentee in field. Mem. Am. Chem. Soc., AAAS, Hudson-Bergen Chem. Soc. (div. program dir. 1975-79). Club: Harvard (N.Y.). Home: 325 E 79th St New York NY 10021-0900

BAHLMAN, DAVID ARTHUR, cultural society administrator; b. Mishawaka, Ind., July 6, 1945; s. Henry Louis and Hanna (Haugen) B. BA, Ohio State U., 1967, MA, 1970; PhD, U. Pa., 1992. Exec. Lincoln Ctr., Inc., N.Y.C., 1981-83; assoc. dir. pub. rels. N.Y. Philharmonic, N.Y.C., 1983-85; exec. dir. Soc. of Archtl. Historians, Phila., 1985—. Mem. Mozart Soc. of Phila. (pres. 1981—), Phila. Historic Preservation Corp. (bd. dirs. 1989—), Charlotte Cushman Club (Phila.). Presbyterian. Home: PO Box 890 Valley Forge PA 19482-0890 Office: Soc Archtl Historians 1232 Pine St Philadelphia PA 19107-5944

BAHN, DAVID LOWELL, systems analyst; b. N.Y.C., July 24, 1963; s. Charles and Adele (Koolyk) B. BA in Computer Sci., Yeshiva U., 1985; MBA in Info. Systems, NYU, 1991. Instr. Courant Inst. Math. Sci., NYU, N.Y.C., 1981; computer specialist N.Y.C. Dept. for the Aging, 1987-89; proprietor, cons. AMPM Cons., N.Y.C., 1989-91; ops. systems analyst Health Mgmt. Systems, Inc., N.Y.C., 1991—; tech. computer support Merck & Co., Rahway, N.J., summer, 1990; cons. Lenox Hill Neighborhood Assn., N.Y.C., 1989—, also other non-profit orgns. Trustee Congregation Emunath Israel, N.Y.C., 1991—; del. candidate Wilder for Pres. Campaign, N.Y.C., 1992; campus chmn. Student Struggle for Soviet Jewry, 19981-82. NYU Stern Sch. Bus. scholar, N.Y.C., 1989, Samuel Belkin scholar Yeshiva U., N.Y.C., 1981-85. Mem. ASPA, N.Y. Computer Activists (sr. workshop leader 1988—). Jewish. Office: Health Mgmt Systems 401 Park Ave S New York NY 10016

BAHR, JAMES THEODORE, biophysical chemist; b. East Orange, N.J., Nov. 19, 1942; s. August Theodore and Naomi (Brittle) B.; m. Nora Horsey, Aug. 20, 1966; children: Andrea, Christina, Deborah. BS in Chemistry, MIT, 1964; PhD in Biophysics, U. Pa., 1971. Rsch. assoc. U. Ariz., Tucson, 1971-76; sr. rsch. biologist crop chems. Mobil Chem., Edison, N.J., 1976-79, group leader biol. testing crop chems, 1979-81; rsch. mgr. agrochem. div. Rhone-Poulenc Inc., Monmouth Junction, N.J., 1981-85; biorsch. mgr. agrl. chems. group FMC Corp., Princeton, N.J., 1985-90, discovery mgr., 1990—. Contbr. articles to profl. jours. and chpts. to books; patentee in field. Home: 68 Featherbed Ln Hopewell NJ 08525-1002 Office: FMC Corp Agrl Chems Group PO Box 8 Princeton NJ 08543-0008

BAHR, ROBERT LAWRENCE, ophthalmology educator; b. N.Y.C., May 12, 1945; s. Henry H. and Lore S. (Barth) B.; m. Susan J. Steinberg, June 28, 1970; children: Talia M., Danielle N., Jonathan A. BA, Williams Coll., 1967; MD, Harvard Med. Sch., 1971. Diplomate Am. Bd. Ophthalmology, Am. Bd. Med. Examiners. Intern Mt. Sinai Hosp., N.Y.C., 1971-72; resident in ophthalmology Yale U., New Haven, 1972-75, fellow in glaucoma rsch., 1972-74; asst. prof. Ophthalmology Yale U. Sch. Medicine, New Haven, 1975-78; ophthalmologist Ophthalmology Inc., Providence, 1976—; asst. clin. prof. Ophthalmology Brown Med. Sch., Providence, 1976—. Contbr. articles to profl. jours. Capt. USAR, 1972-78. Fellow Am. Acad. Ophthalmology; mem. Assn. Cataract and Refractive Surgery, Univ. Club, Aesculapian Club. Jewish. Home: 41 Cooke St Providence RI 02906 Office: Ophthalmology Inc 150 E Manning St Providence RI 02906

BAIER, KURT, philosophy educator; b. Vienna, Austria, Jan. 26, 1917; came to U.S., 1962; s. Emil Baier and Maria (Hunna) Csala; m. Annette Claire Stoop, Dec. 28, 1958. BA, U. Melbourne, Australia, 1945, MA, 1947; DPhil, Oxford (Eng.) U., 1952. Asst. lectr. philosophy U. Melbourne, 1945-47, lectr., 1947-49, 53-55, sr. lectr., 1955-56; found. prof. Canberra (Australia) U. Coll. (ANU), 1957-62; chmn. dept. philosophy U. Pitts., 1962-67, prof. philosophy, 1967-80, disting. svc. prof., 1980—. Author: The Moral Point of View, 1958. Fellow Am. Acad. Arts and Sci.; mem. Am. Philos. Assn. (pres. Ea. div. 1977, chmn. bd. govs. 1983-86). Office: U Pitts Dept Philosophy Pittsburgh PA 15260

BAILDON, JOHN DAVID, mathematics educator; b. Johnstown, Pa., Nov. 14, 1943; s. Vertney Robert and Helena May (Flickinger) B.; m. Rachel Price Winlock, June 29, 1968; children—Thomas Edward, Carolyn Price. B.S. in Math., Lafayette Coll., Easton, Pa., 1965; M.S. in Math., Rutgers U., 1967; Ph.D. in Math., SUNY-Binghamton, 1971. Instr. math. Pa. State U.-Dunmore, 1970-71, asst. prof., 1971-76, assoc. prof. 1976—; on sabbatical leave U. Okla., Norman, 1985. Contbr. articles to profl. publs. Vestryman St. Luke's Episcopal Ch., Scranton, Pa., 1974-79; coach Abington Youth Soccer League, Clarks Summit, Pa., 1980-84; edn. committeeman Ch. of Epiphany, Glenburn, Pa., 1981-84, vestryman, 1988—, sr. warden, 1990—; active Boy Scouts Am., 1984-89. Faculty grantee Pa. State U., 1975-77. Mem. Am. Math. Soc., Math. Assn. Am., Sigma Xi. Democrat. Avocations: camping; softball; soccer. Home: 410 Powell Ave Clarks Summit PA 18411-1810 Office: Pa State U 120 Ridge View Dr Dunmore PA 18512

BAILER, BONNIE LYNN, lawyer, professional fundraiser; b. N.Y.C., Oct. 11, 1946; d. Lloyd Harding and Marvelyne Amanda (Matthews) Bailer; 1 child, Miles Bailer Armstead. B.A., Queens Coll., 1968, M.S., 1975; J.D. Columbia U., 1992. Tchr. French, Intermediate Sch. 55, N.Y.C., 1968-75; acting chmn. fgn. lang. dept. N.Y.C. Public Sch. System, 1970-75; co-founder, v.p. Yellow Go-Rilla Prodns. Ltd., N.Y.C., 1975-78; nat. membership task force coordinator NAACP, N.Y.C., 1978-79, corp. devel. officer, 1979—; v.p. Gilbert Jones, Co., N.Y.C., 1979-86; dir. capital campaign UN Assn., 1986-88, fund-raising & ednl. cons. Bailer Assocs., N.Y.C., 1988-89; atty. Bettzedek Legal Svcs., 1992—; dir. Morningside Montessori Sch., N.Y.C., 1979-82; founder The Talkshop, fgn. lang. program for children, N.Y.C., 1982—; dir. Grinnell Housing Devel. Corp., 1984—. Adminstr. Manhattan Borough Pres. Campaign, 1977; press and info. cons. Annual Westside Community Conf., 1979-81; mem. NAACP. Fiske Stone scholar Columbia U., 1992. Mem. NAFE, NOW, Coun. Concerned Black Execs.

BAILER, WILLIAM GEORGE, environmental services executive, chemist; b. Phila., Dec. 5, 1953; s. Clifford J. Sr. and Elizabeth G. (Stoll) B. BS in Chemistry, Phila. Coll. Textiles Sci., 1979; postgrad., U. Pa., 1979-81; MS in Chemistry, St. Joseph's U., Phila., 1984. Asst. editor Inst. for Sci. Info., Phila., 1980-82; instr. in chemistry Ch. Farm Sch., Exton, Pa., 1982-85; tech. rep. Rollins Environ. Svcs., Wilmington, Del., 1985-87; pres., founder Progressive Disposal Group, Inc., West Chester, Pa., 1987—; chmn. bd. Progressive Disposal Group, Inc., 1989—. U. Pa. scholar, 1979-81. Mem. Am. Inst. Chem. Engrs., Pa. C. of C. Republican.

BAILEY, BETTY LOU, environmental engineer; b. Chgo., Apr. 25, 1929; d. Otterbein Andrew and Mable Mann (Young) B. BSME, U. Ill., 1950; M of Engring., Pa. State U., 1967. Registered profl. engr., Ohio, N.Y. Test engr. GE, various locations, 1950-51; design engr. GE-Jet Engine dept., Cin., 1951-60; engr. GE-Knolls Atomic Power Lab., Schenectady, N.Y., 1960-61; system engr. GE-Space Div., King of Prussia, Pa., 1961-69; sr. engr. GE-Gas Turbine Div., Schenectady, 1969-86; sr. environ. engr. GE-Power Plant Systems Dept., Schenectady, 1986—. Patentee in field. Conservation chair Schenectady (N.Y.) chpt., Adirondack Mountain Club, 1981—. Recipient Disting. Alumnus award mech. engring. dept. Univ. Ill., Urbana, 1988. Fellow Soc. Women Engrs. (counselor student sect. 1978—); mem. ASME, AIAA, NSPE, Am. Soc. for Engring. Edn., Air and Waste Mgmt. Assn., Tau Beta Pi. Methodist.

BAILEY, BRUCE EDWARD, marketing and communications company executive; b. Camp Kilmer, N.J., May 24, 1954; s. Lyndoll Edward and Edna Mae (Van Liew) B.; m. Barbara Ann Davison, Oct. 30, 1982. BA in Journalism, Glassboro (N.J.) State Coll., 1979. Reporter, editor InterCounty Newspaper Group, Turnersville, N.J., 1978-80; mng. editor CAM-GLO Newspaper Group, 1980-82; asst. editor Focus Mag./Bus. News, Inc., Phila., 1982-84; assoc. editor Focus Mag./Bus. News, Inc., 1984-87; communications mgr. Hansen Group/Hansen Properties, Horsham, Pa., 1987-90; asst. v.p. mktg. Hansen Group/Hansen Properties, 1988-90; owner, pres. Bailey Mktg./Communications, Wayne, Pa., 1990—. Office: Bailey Mktg/Communications 175 Strafford Ave Wayne PA 19087-3317

BAILEY, DENNIS RICHARD, dentist; b. Cleve., Apr. 13, 1945; s. Edward Richard and Jean Catherine (Roberts) B.; m. Donna Pizzo, Oct. 28, 1989; children: Melissa, Todd, Abbey, Mariel, Spencer. BA, Franklin Coll., 1968; DDS, Ind. U., Indpls., 1973. Lic. dentist, N.J., Pa. Systems engr. IBM Corp., Phila., 1968-69; dental resident Miami Valley Hosp., Dayton, Ohio, 1973-74; pvt. practice Sewell, N.J., 1974—; lectr. U.S. Dental Inst., Northbrook, Ill., 1982—; instr. U. Medicine and Dentistry N.J., Newark, 1988—. Contbr. articles to profl. jours. Fellow Acad. Gen. Dentistry, 1982, Acad. Dentistry Internat., 1987. Mem. ADA, Am. Acad. Pain Mgmt., Internat. Assn. Orthodontics, Acad. Gen. Dentistry. Office: S Jersey Family Dental Assn 438 Ganttown Rd B 2 Sewell NJ 08080

BAILEY, GLENN WALDEMAR, manufacturing company executive; b. Cleve., May 8, 1925; s. Harry W. and Elizabeth B.; m. Cornelia L. Tarrant, June 12, 1952. BS, U. Wis., 1946; MBA, Harvard U., 1951. Project engr. Thompson Ramo Wooldridge, Cleve., 1946-49; fin. staff Ford Motor Co., Dearborn, Mich., 1951-54; mgr. fin. analysis Curtiss Wright Corp., 1954-57; asst. to v.p., gen. mgr. Overseas div. Chrysler Corp., Detroit, 1957-60; group gen. mgr. ITT Corp., N.Y.C., 1960-67; chmn. bd., pres. Keene Corp., N.Y.C., 1967-81, 90—, Bairnco Corp., N.Y.C., 1981-90. Ensign USNR, 1943-46. Home: Ocean Reef Key Largo FL 33037 Office: Keene Corp 200 Park Ave New York NY 10166-0005

BAILEY, JOAN E., academic administrator; b. Wheeling, W.Va., May 16, 1942; d. John Edward Bailey and Eleanore Louise (Cooke) Galloway; m. Neville Chandler; children: Nevette, Joanelle. BA, Chatham Coll., 1964; MA, Yale U., 1966, MPh, 1967, PhD, 1971; labor studies cert., Cornell U., 1980. Assoc. prof. philosophy New Eng. Coll., Henniker, N.H., 1969-75; acting asst. dir. D.C. 37 Coll. of New Rochelle, N.Y., 1975-76, assoc. dir. D.C. 37 campus, 1976-83, campus dir., 1983-85, asst. v.p. acad. affairs, 1985-90, assoc. v.p. acad. affairs, 1990—. Mem. APA, AAAS, AAUP, No. New Eng. Philosophy (chairperson 1972-73), So. Poverty Law. Office: Coll of New Rochelle 29 Castle Pl New Rochelle NY 10805-2308

BAILEY, MICHAEL ROBERT, arts center director; b. Kansas City, Mo., Nov. 11, 1947; s. Milton H. and Jean Marie (DeGeorge) B.; m. Victoria Angelica Westover, June 30, 1984; 1 child, Nathan Westover. BFA, Kansas City Art Inst., 1969; MFA, Ind. U., 1974. Dir. placement and alumni rels. Kansas City Art Inst., 1974-77; dir. artist svcs. Mid-Am. Art Alliance, Kansas City, Mo., 1977-80; dir. career svcs. Md. Inst. Coll. Art, Balt., 1980-84; dep. dir. Md. State Arts Coun., Balt., 1984-90; exec. dir. Md. Hall for the Creative Arts, Annapolis, 1990—. Exhibition (one artist), Mickelson Gallery, Washington 1989, Meredith Gallery, Balt. 1986. With U.S. Army 1969-71 (Germany). Mem. Kansas City Artists Coalition (pres., dir., founding mem.) 1975-80. Office: Md Hall for Creative Arts PO Box 188 Annapolis MD 21401

BAILEY, NANCY JOYCE, educator; b. Detroit, May 9, 1942; d. Thomas Hill and Margaret (McGrath) Rainey; m. Carl John Bailey, June 12, 1963; 1 child, John. BA, Vanderbilt U., 1960; postgrad., U. Mex., 1957, U. Santa Clara, 1975, George Washington U., 1979-80. Cert. early childhood edn. tchr., early childhood specialist. Hostess Brentwood (Tenn.) Country Club, 1960; adminstrv. aide U.S. Senate, Washington, 1966; sec. U.S. Ho. of Reps., Washington, 1971-74; tchr. D.C. Pub. Schs., 1961—; bd. dirs. Cabvin Internat. Corp., 1985—; rep. Washington Tchr.'s Union, 1982—. Keyperson United Way campaign, Washington, 1974—; docent The White House, Exec. Office of the Pres., Washington, 1987—; founder David Lipscomb U., Nashville, 1988; vol. First Lady's Corr., The White House, Washington, 1990—; mem. Nat. Trust for Historic Preservation, 1990—. Recipient Internat. Cooperation award Am. Fgn. Study Program, Am. Study Program, 1984-86, Am. Student Ednl. Travel. Mem. Delta Group (mem. coun. 1989—). Home: 10729 Deborah Dr Potomac MD 20854-2714 Office: Miner Sch 601 15th St NE Washington DC 20002-4599

BAILEY, NORMAN ALISHAN, economist; b. Chgo., May 22, 1931; s. Percival and Yevnige (Bashian) B.; m. Lorraine Baillargeon, Sept. 1, 1962 (div. Feb. 1966); m. Suzin Robbins, July 8, 1966; children: Stacy, Anthony, Samara, Gabrielle. AB, Oberlin (Ohio) Coll., 1953; MA, Columbia U., 1955, PhD, 1962; LLD, Hanyang U., Seoul, Korea, 1983. Economist Mobil Oil Co., N.Y.C., 1960-62; prof. CUNY, Queens, 1962-83; pres. Bailey, Tondu, Warwick & Co., N.Y.C., 1962-75; spl. asst. to Pres. Reagan The White House, Washington, 1981-83; pvt. practice Washington, 1984—. Author 8 books; contbr. numerous articles to profl. jours. Cons. Rep. Campaign, N.Y., Washington, 1980, 84, 88. With U.S. Army, 1956-58. Named Knight of the Order of Our Lady of the Conception of Vila Vicosa, 1988. Mem. U. Club (Washington), Princeton Club of N.Y., Clube Micaelense (Ponta Delgada, Azores), Phi Beta Kappa. Office: Norman A Bailey Inc 1912 Sunderland Pl NW Washington DC 20036-1608

BAILEY, ROBERT JAY, jewelry retailer; b. Newburyport, Mass., Nov. 17, 1952; s. Daniel Simpson and Margaret (Hodge) B.; m. Denise Rita Lariviere, Jan. 22, 1973 (div. 1982); 1 child, Jay Robert; m. Adria Lee Garneau, Sept. 11, 1982. Student, Salem State Coll. Dept. mgr. J.M. Fields, Inc., Salem, N.H., 1973-75; sales rep. Cott Beverage Corp., New Haven, 1975-78; dept. mgr. Country Store, Newbury, Mass., 1978-81; prin. R.J. Bailey Co., Amesbury, Mass., 1981-83; gen. mgr. Gold Rush Jewelers, Georgetown, Mass., 1983-90; owner, pres. Karats Ltd., Methuen, Mass., 1991—. Methodist. Office: Karats Ltd 160 Haverhill St Methuen MA 01844

BAILLIEUL, JOHN BROUARD, applied mathematics and engineering educator; b. Boise, Idaho, May 13, 1945; s. Paul Brouard and Geneva (Gillam) B.; m. Patricia Pfeiffer; children: Emily, Charlotte, John Paul. BA, U. Mass., Amherst, 1967; M in Math., U. Waterloo, Waterloo, Can., 1969; MS, Harvard U., 1973, PhD in Applied Math., 1975. Asst. prof. math. Georgetown U., Washington, 1975-79; sr. mathematician Sci. Systems, Inc., Cambridge, Mass., 1979-83; Vinton Hayes vis. scientist Harvard U., Cambridge, 1983-85; prof. aerospace and mech. engring. Boston U., 1985—, prof. mfg. engring., 1988—, dir. div. engring. and applied sci., 1990—; cons. Sci. Systems, Inc., Cambridge, 1985-87, AMD Corp., Stratford, Conn., 1986, Computational Engring., Inc., Laurel, Md., 1988-89; vis. sr. scientist Lab. for Info. and Decision Systems, MIT, 1991. Assoc. editor IEEE Transactions on Automatic Control, 1984-85, 89—, IEEE Robotics and Automation Soc. newsletter, Bifurcation and Chaos in Applied Scis. and Engring.; editor-in-chief IEEE Transactions on Automatic Control, 1992—; contbr. articles to profl. jours. U.S. Dept. Energy grantee, 1983, USAF Office Sci. Rsch. grantee Boston U., 1985—, NSF grantee, 1988; frequent grantee for study nonlinear control theory and mechanics. Mem. Math. Assn. Am., Am. Math. Soc., IEEE (bd. govs. control systems soc. 1985, 89, editor in chief Trans. on Automatic Control 1992—). Home: 181 Common St Belmont MA 02178-2908 Office: Boston U Aero Mech Engring 110 Cummington St Boston MA 02215-2407

BAILY, ALFRED EWING, environmental engineer; b. Carmichaels, Pa., Jan. 20, 1925; s. Richard L. and Alta (Hebel) B.; student Waynesburg (Pa.) Coll., 1943, Bethany (W.Va.) Coll., 1943-44; B.S. in Physics, Duke U., 1945, B.S. in Civil Engring. magna cum laude, 1949; m. Hannah Jane Drake, Sept. 1, 1946; children: Judith Ann, Frank Henry, Louise Jane, Nancy Lee. With Chester Environ. Group (formerly Chester Engrs.), Coraopolis, Pa., 1949—, ptnr., 1965, dir. mcpl. svcs., 1974, dir., 1977—, chmn., 1990. Mem. Scott Twp. Planning Commn., 1963-64; elder Presbyn Ch. Served from ensign to lt., USNR, 1943-46, 52-53. Registered profl. engr., D.C., Del., Pa., W.Va., Ky., N.Y., Md., Va., Fla.; diplomate Am. Acad. Environ. Engrs.; certified Nat. Council Engring. Examiners. Fellow ASCE; mem. Nat. Soc. Profl. Engrs., Water Pollution Control Fedn., Am. Water Works Assn., Assn. Iron & Steel Engrs., Am. Iron and Steel Inst., Greater Pitts. C. of C. (dir.), Tau Beta Pi. Office: PO Box 15851 Pittsburgh PA 15244-0851

BAILY, JOHN THOMAS, auditor; b. Hanover, Pa., Feb. 17, 1944; s. Ralph Thomas and Florence Anna (Oplinger) B.; m. Donna Hornberger Baily, July 31, 1965; children: Jeffrey, Steven. BS cum laude, Albright Coll., 1965; MBA, U. Chgo., 1979. Mem. staff, ptnr. Coopers & Lybrand, Phila., 1965-76; ptnr. Coopers & Lybrand, Chgo., 1976-86; chmn. ins. industry Coopers & Lybrand, Hartford, Conn., 1986—; mem. Nat. Assn. Ins. Commrs. Emerging Issues Working Group, Kansas City, Mo. Mem. AICPA (mem. ins. cos. com. 1982—, chmn. 1989—), Ill. CPA Soc. (chmn. ins. cos. com.), Internat. Ins. Soc. (elector 1991—). Office: Coopers & Lybrand 280 Trumbull St Hartford CT 06103-3598

BAILYN, BERNARD, historian, educator; b. Hartford, Conn., Sept. 10, 1922; s. Charles Manuel and Esther (Schloss) B.; m. Lotte Lazarsfeld, June 18, 1952; children: Charles David, John Frederick. A.B., Williams Coll., 1945, Litt.D. (hon.), 1969; M.A., Harvard U., 1947, Ph.D., 1953; L.H.D. (hon.), Lawrence U., 1967, Bard Coll., 1968, Clark U., 1975, Yale U., 1976, Grinnell Coll., 1979, Trinity Coll., 1984, Manhattanvill Coll., 1991, Dartmouth Coll., 1991, U. Chgo., 1991; Litt.D., Rutgers U., 1976, Fordham U., 1976, Washington U., St. Louis, 1988. Faculty Harvard U., Cambridge, Mass., 1953—, prof. history, 1961-66, Winthrop prof. history, 1966-81, Adams Univ. prof., 1981—, James Duncan Phillips prof. early Am. history, 1991—, editor in chief John Harvard Library, 1962-70, dir. Charles Warren Ctr. for Studies in Am. History, 1983—; Colver lectr. Brown U., 1965; Phelps lectr. NYU, 1969; Trevelyan lectr. Cambridge U., 1971; Becker lectr. Cornell U., 1975; Walker-Ames lectr. U. Wash., 1983; Curti lectr. U. Wis., 1984; Lewin vis. prof. Washington U., St. Louis, 1985; Pitt prof. Am. history Cambridge U., 1986-87; Thompson lectr. Pomona Coll., 1991; Montgomery fellow Dartmouth Coll., 1991; mem. Inst. Advanced Study, Princeton U., 1980-81, now trustee. Author: New England Merchants in the 17th Century, 1955, (with Lotte Bailyn) Massachusetts Shipping, 1697-1714, A Statistical Study, 1959, Education in the Forming of American Society, 1960, Pamphlets of the American Revolution, 1750-1776, Vol. 1, 1965, The Ideological Origins of the American Revolution, 1967 (Pulitzer and Bancroft prizes 1968), The Origins of American Politics, 1968, The Ordeal of Thomas Hutchinson, 1974 (Nat. Book award 1975), The Peopling of British North America: An Introduction, 1986, Voyagers to the West, 1986 (Pulitzer Prize, Saloutos award Immigration History Soc., Triennial Book award Soc. of the Cin.), Faces of Revolution, 1990; co-author: The Great Republic, 1977; co-editor: The Intellectual Migration, Europe and America, 1930-1960, 1969, Law in American History, 1972, Perspectives in American History, 1967-77, 81-86, The Press and The American Revolution, 1980, Strangers Within the Realm, 1990. Served with AUS, 1943-46. Recipient Robert H. Lord award Emmanuel Coll., 1967. Fellow Christ's Coll. Cambridge U. (hon.), Brit. Acad. (corr.); mem. Am. Hist. Assn. (pres. 1981), Am. Acad. Arts and Scis., Nat. Acad. Edn., Am. Philos. Soc., Royal Hist. Soc., Mass. Hist. Soc., Mexican Acad. History and Geography. Home: 170 Clifton St Belmont MA 02178-2604 Office: Harvard U History Dept Cambridge MA 02138

BAILYN, LOTTE, psychology and management educator; b. Vienna, Austria, July 17, 1930; came to U.S., 1937; d. Paul Felix Lazarsfeld and Marie (Jahoda) Albu; m. Bernard Bailyn, June 18, 1952; children: Charles, John. BA in Math. with high honors, Swarthmore Coll., 1951; MA in Social Psychology, Radcliffe Coll.-Harvard U., 1953, PhD in Social Psychology, 1956. Rsch. assoc. Grad. Sch. Edn., Harvard U., Cambridge, Mass., 1956-57, rsch. assoc. dept. social rels., 1958-64, lectr., 1963-67; instr. dept. econs. and social sci. MIT, Cambridge, 1957-58, rsch. assoc. Sloan Sch. Mgmt., 1969-70, lectr., 1970-71, sr. lectr., 1971-72, assoc. prof. orgnl. psychology and mgmt., 1972-80, prof., 1980-91, T. Wilson prof. mgmt., 1991—; acad. visitor Imperial Coll. Sci., Tech. and Medicine, London, 1991; trustee Cambridge Savs. Bank; mem. adv. coun. Suffolk U. Mgmt. Sch., Boston, 1983-86; mem. sr. coun. Leadership Devel. Inst., Rutgers U., 1986-89; panel mem. NAS, NRC, Washington, 1988-90; mem. task force in career devel. and maintenance IEEE, Washington, 1982-90; vis. scholar Imperial Coll. Sci. and Tech., London, 1982, New Hall, Cambridge (Eng.) U., 1986-87; scholar-in-residence Rockefeller Found. Study and Conf. Ctr., Bellagio, Italy, 1983; vis. univ. fellow U. Auckland, N.Z., 1984. Author: Mass Media and Children, 1959, Living with Technology, 1980; co-author: Working with Careers, 1984; editor: (monograph) The Uses of Television, 1962; mem. editorial bd. Jour. Orgnl. Behavior, Human Resource Mgmt., Jour. Engring. and Tech. Mgmt.; contbr. articles to profl. jours., chpts. to books. Trustee Radcliffe Coll., 1970-77. Fellow APA, Am. Psychol. Soc. (charter); mem. Acad. Mgmt., Am. Sociol. Assn. Home: 170 Clifton St Belmont MA 02178-2604 Office: MIT Sloan Sch Mgmt 50 Memorial Dr Cambridge MA 02142-1347

BAIMAN, SYBIL, interior designer, retailer; b. Allentown, Pa., July 8, 1939; d. Joseph and Dora (Berkowitz) Snyderman; m. Barry Michael Baiman, Sept. 3, 1961; children: Paula, James Louis. AB, U. Pa., 1961. Editorial writer Va. Guidebook, Williamsburg, 1962-62; English tchr. Northampton (Pa.) High Sch., 1962-63; interior designer Sybil Baiman Interiors, Allentown and Haddonfield, N.J., 1965—; retailer Cosmetics, Etc., Allentown, 1985—. Pres. Jewish Fedn. Allentown, 1983-85, bd. mem., 1980—. Recipient George Feldman award Jewish Fedn. Allentown, 1979. Home: 2826 Sheffield Dr Emmaus PA 18049-1278

BAINBRIDGE, WILLIAM SIMS, sociologist, educator; b. Bridgeport, Conn., Oct. 12, 1940; s. William Wheeler and Barbara (Sims) B.; m. Erika Ohara, Nov. 6, 1986; children: William C., Lars L., E. Sims, Wilma Alice, Constance May. BA, Boston U., 1971; PhD, Harvard U., 1975. From asst. to assoc. prof. U. Wash., Seattle, 1975-82; assoc. prof. Harvard U., Cambridge, Mass., 1982-87; prof. Ill. State U., Normal, 1987-90; prof., chmn. dept. sociology and anthropology Towson (Md.) State U., 1990-92; sociology program dir. NSF, Washington, 1992—. Author: The Spaceflight Revolution, 1976, Satan's Power, 1978, Experiments in Psychology, 1986, Dimensions of Science Fiction, 1986, Sociology Laboratory, 1987, Survey Research, 1989, Goals in Space, 1991, Social Research Methods and Statistics, 1992, (with Rodney Stark) The Future of Religion, 1985 (Outstanding Book of Yr. Soc. for Sci. Study Religion), A Theory of Religion, 1987; contbr. articles to profl. jours. Mem. Am. Sociol. Assn. Office: Nat Sci Found 1800 G St NW Washington DC 20550

BAINTON, J(OHN) JOSEPH, lawyer; b. Long Branch, N.J., May 21, 1947; s. Robert L. and Elizabeth (Dowling) B.; l child, John Joseph Jr. BA, Kenyon Coll., 1969; JD, Rutgers U., Newark, 1973. Bar: N.Y. 1973. Assoc. Burke & Burke, N.Y.C., 1972-76; ptnr. Reboul, MacMurray, Hewitt, Maynard & Kristol, N.Y.C., 1976-89, Shea & Gould, N.Y.C., 1989-90, Whitman & Ransom, N.Y.C., 1991—. Contbr. articles to legal jours. Vol. mediator Mandatory Mediation Program So. Dist. N.Y. Mem. U.S. Trademark Assn. (editor 1976), Internat. Anticounterfeiting Coalition (bd. dirs. 1986—), Products Liability Adv. Coun., Nat. Inst. Trial Advocacy (faculty). Office: Whitman & Ransom 200 Park Ave New York NY 10166-0005

BAINUM, PETER MONTGOMERY, aerospace engineer; b. St. Petersburg, Fla., Feb. 4, 1938; s. Charles Joseph and Mildred Trincher (Salyer) B.; m. Carmen Cecilia Perez; 1 son, David P. B.S. in Aero. Engring, Tex. A&M U., 1959; S.M. in Aeros. and Astronautics, M.I.T., 1960; Ph.D. in Aerospace Engring, Cath. U. Am., 1967. Sr. engr. Martin Co., Orlando, Fla., 1960-62; staff engr. Fed. Systems div. IBM, Bethesda, Md., 1962-65; sr. staff engr., cons. Johns Hopkins U. Applied Physics Lab., 1965-69, 69-72; mem. faculty Howard U., Washington, 1969—, prof. aerospace engring., 1973-90, dir. grad. studies, 1974-84, Disting. prof. aerospace engring., 1990—; v.p. research, cons. WHF & Assos. Inc., Bethesda, Md., 1977-86; Summer faculty fellow NASA/Am. Soc. Engring. Edn., 1970-71. Contbr. articles to profl. jours. Recipient Teetor award Soc. Automotive Engrs., 1971; recipient

Howard U. award for outstanding research, 1981. Fellow AIAA, Brit. Interplanetary Soc., Am. Astron. Soc. (internat. v.p., Dirk Brouwer award 1989); mem. Internat. Acad. Astronautics. Home: 9804 Raleigh Tavern Ct Bethesda MD 20814-2129 Office: Howard Univ Dept Mech Engring Washington DC 20059

BAIR, JAMES FRIDOLIN, secondary school educator; b. Pitts., June 28, 1950; s. Homer Franklin Jr. and Leone (Baker) B.; m. Janet Machalowski, Oct. 3, 1981; children: Joanna L., Emily F. AB, Harvard U., 1972; MS, So. Conn. State U., 1987. Cert. secondary English tchr., Conn. Mng. Good News Book Shop, Norwich, Conn., 1979-84; high sch. tchr. Grace Heritage Christian Sch., New London, Conn., 1980-84, Christian Heritage Sch., Trumbull, Conn., 1985—; presenter in field. Editor newsletter Shroud of Turin Rsch. Project Update, 1979-81; contbr. articles, poems to profl. publs.; author computer program. Treas. Harvest Christian Ctr., Shelton, Conn., 1989—; sec. Full Gospel Businessmen's Fellowship, New London, 1978-85; pres., elder Faith Luth. Ch., Groton, Conn., 1979-83; chmn. The Lord's Inn, Norwich, 1980-82. Lt. (j.g.) USCG, 1972-76. Named Student and Tchr. Achievement and Recognition Tchr., GE, 1990; recipient Dept. Achievement cert. Nat. Coun. Tchrs. of English, 1987. Mem. Conf. on Christianity and Lit., Conn. Ornithol. Assn., Gideons (sec. 1990—). Office: Christian Heritage Sch 575 White Plains Rd Trumbull CT 06611-4898

BAIR, MYRNA LYNN, state senator; b. Huntington, W.Va., Oct. 26, 1940; d. Charles Thomas and Velma Elvera (Schoenlein) North; B.S. in Chemistry, U. Cin., 1962; Ph.D., U. Wis., 1968; m. Thomas Irvin Bair, Mar. 12, 1966; children—Thomas Irvin, Catherine Lynn. Asst. prof. chemistry Beaver Coll., Glenside, Pa., 1966-70; instr. chemistry U. Del., 1974-76, asst. prof. edn., 1977-79; asst. dir. pub. info. Del. Energy Office, Wilmington, 1978-79; mem. Del. Senate, 1981—; sr. mgmt. advisor Coll. Urban Affairs and PUb. Policy, dir. women's leadership tng. program, 1989—. Contbr. articles to sci. jours. Bd. dirs. Del. Lung Assn.; trustee Wesley Coll.; mem. Nat. Republican Com., Wilmington Rep. Women's Club. Recipient Freshman award Chem. Rubber Co., 1959; DuPont Co. Teaching award, 1963, Pres.'s award Jr. League, 1988; NSF fellow, 1964-66. Mem. AAUW, Phi Beta Kappa, Iota Sigma Pi, Alpha Lambda Delta. Methodist. Office: Del State Senate State Capitol Bldg Dover DE 19901

BAIR, WILLIAM ALOIS, engineer; b. Bklyn., Aug. 13, 1931; s. Henry Auchu and Anna Margaret (Zidar) B.; m. Patricia Anne Doyle, July 23, 1955; children: William A. Jr., Joseph M. Student, Pa. State U., 1949-51; BS in Engring., U.S. Naval Acad., 1955; BS in Civil Engring., Rensselaer Poly. Inst., 1958; MS in Nuclear Engring., U. Calif., 1966; grad. advanced mgmt. program, Wharton Sch., 1987. Registered profl. engr., N.Y., N.J., Pa., Conn., Md., Del., Va., S.C., Ga., D.C. Commd. ensign USN, 1955, advanced through grades to comdr., 1969; with USN Civil Engr. Corps, 1955-77; ret. USN, 1977; project mgr. Ebasco Svcs. Inc., Princeton, N.J., 1977-85; dir. program planning and devel. Ebasco Svcs. Inc., N.Y.C., 1985—; appointed mem. spl. 3 man NATO tech. com. to evaluate effectiveness of European Airfield Phys. Protection program to counter damage from attack by Warsaw Pact Nations. Author: Helium 3 Neutron Spectrometer, 1966; contbr. articles to profl. jours. Scoutmaster Boy Scouts Am., Rockville, Md., 1969-70; coun. mem. European br., CAsteau, Belgium, 1971-75. Decorated Legion of Merit, Bronze Star with V; Cross of Gallantry, Medal of Honor 1st class (Vietnam). Mem. ASCE, NSPE, Am. Nuclear Soc., Soc. Am. Mil. Engrs., Nat. Contract. Mgmt. Assn., Am. Legion. Republican. Roman Catholic. Home: 21 Lorrie Ln # 15 Trenton NJ 08648-5112 Office: Ebasco Svcs Inc 2 World Trade Ctr New York NY 10048-0203

BAIRD, DUGALD EUAN, oil field service company executive; b. Aberdeen, Scotland, Sept. 16, 1937; came to U.S., 1979; s. Dugald and Matilda Deans (Tennant) B.; m. Angelica Hartz, May 24, 1961; children—Camilla N., Maiken E. Student, Aberdeen U., Scotland, Trinity Coll., Cambridge; BA in Geophysics, Cambridge U., 1960. Joined Schlumberger, 1960, various field assignments in Europe, Asia, Mid. East, Africa, 1960-74; pers. mgr., v.p. ops. Schlumberger Tech. Svcs., Paris, 1974-79; exec. v.p. in charge of worldwide wireline ops. Schlumberger Ltd., N.Y.C., 1979-86, chmn. bd., pres., CEO, 1986—. Office: Schlumberger Ltd 277 Park Ave New York NY 10172

BAIRD, JAMES FRANK, lawyer; b. Hackensack, N.J., Apr. 15, 1937; s. John Sylvester Baird and Natalie Oakley (Hearne) Wells; m. Cynthia Jane Crosier, Nov. 21, 1964; children: James Frederick, Heather St. John. AB in Math. and Physics, Brown U., 1963; JD, Boston U., 1970. Atty. Bowditch, Gowetz and Lane, Worcester, Mass., 1970-72; pvt. practice West Brookfield, Mass., 1972—; town counsel Town of Barre, Mass., 1972—. Bd. dirs. Mary Lane Hosp., 1986—, sec. 1988—. Capt. USAF, 1959-66. Mem. Western Worcester Bar Assn. (pres. 1991—), Rotary (treas. 1986-87, dir. 1986-91, sec. 1987-88, v.p. 1988-89, pres. 1989-90). Office: 33 E Main St West Brookfield MA 01585

BAIRD, JAMES L., air conditioning company marketing executive; b. Chestnut Hill, Pa., Apr. 21, 1947; s. James William and Sara (Freas) B.; m. Debra Morris Baird, Nov. 16, 1986; 1 child, Brittany Nichole. BSEE, Pa. State U., 1969; MBA in Fin., U. Pa., 1978. Registered profl. engr., Pa. Mgr. constrn. Honeywell, Phila., 1969-76; mgr. energy systems group Williard, Inc., Phila., 1976-80; mgr. sales and mktg. Delaware Valley York, Phila., 1980-87; dir. mktg. for N.Am. York (Pa.) Internat. Controls Group, 1987—; instr. Pa. State U., Ogontz, 1981-85, Pa. Gov.'s Energy Commn., Phila., 1983-87. Contbr. articles to mag.; inventor super pak. With U.S. Army, 1969-72. Senatorial scholar Pa. State U., 1965-69. Mem. Assn. Energy Engrs. (instr. 1983-86, speaker 1985), U. Pa. Wharton Sch. Alumni Assn. (bd. dirs. 1971-87). Republican. Home: 2861 Exeter Dr N York PA 17403-9738 Office: York Internat Control Group 631 S Richland Ave York PA 17403-3478

BAIRD, JOHN ABSALOM, JR., college official; b. Honolulu, Sept. 13, 1918; s. John Absalom and Helen (Bates) B. m. Virginia Walton, Mar 8, 1941 (dec. 1983); children: Suzanne W. Baird Perot, Linda W., Barbara Baird Rogers; m. Clare A. Emmons, May 12, 1984. AB, Princeton U., 1940; postgrad., Johns Hopkins U., 1941. Asst. supt. Charles S. Walton Co., 1942-47, asst. sec. and dir., 1947-52, v.p., 1952-72; asst. pres. Ea. Bapt. Theol. Sem., Phila.; asst. pres. Ea. Coll., St. Davids, Pa., 1952-61, v.p., 1961-88, advisor to pres., 1988—. Author: A Leap of Faith, 1972, The Whole Gospel for the Whole World, 1975, All Things Are Thine, 1976, Profile of a Hero, 1977, The Shining Fire, 1979, Horn of Plenty, 1982, Great House, 1984, Promises to Keep, 1989; contbr. articles to profl. jours. Bd. corporators, bd. dirs. Covenant Life Ins. Co., Phila. Main Line dist. chmn. Valley Forge coun. Boy Scouts Am., 1952-54, dist. commr., 1954-56; vice chmn. Main Line br. YMCA Greater Phila., 1947-63; trustee, v.p. Pa. Lupus Found.; v.p. Pa. chpt. Lupus Found. Am.; trustee Vol. Svcs. for Blind, Phila., 1971-85; mem. adv. bd. Phila. Inglis House, Union League; chmn. bd. trustees Shipley Sch., Bryn Mawr, Pa., 1972-78; trustee 4th Bapt. Mission Found., 1976-80, Ludington Libr., Bryn Mawr, Ralston House, Phila.; v.p., bd. dir. Am. Sunday Sch. Union (Phila.) 1957-69; bd. dir. Watchman Examiner Corp. (N.Y.C.), 1958-70, Pa. United Theol. Sem. Found. (Pitts), Am. Ednl. Film and Video Ctr., St. Davids, Athenaeum, Phila. Recipient Freedom Founds. Honor medal, 1973. Mem. Am. Bapt. Pub. Rels. Assn., Am. Alumni Coun., Am. Coll. Pub. Rels. Assn., U.S. Naval Inst., U.S. Naval Found., Loyal Legion, Soc. of Cin. (pres. Del. 1972-75, sec. gen. 1977-83), Colonial Soc. Pa., Soc. Colonial Wars (gov. 1991), Order Fgn. Wars, S.R., Am. Assn. Sem. Staff Officers (pres. 1966-68), Pa. Acad. Fine Arts, Am. Rose Soc., Am. Philatelic Soc., English-Speaking Union, Hist. Soc. Pa., Nat. Hist. Soc., Geneal. Soc. Pa., Franklin Inn Club, Penn Club, Right Angle Club, Merion Cricket Club(Haverford, Pa.), Army-Navy Club (Washington). Republican. Baptist. Home: 108 Sunset Ln Haverford PA 19041-1714 Office: Ea Coll Saint Davids PA 19087

BAIRD, ROSEMARIE ANNETTE, pharmacist; b. Kingston, Jamaica, Oct. 30, 1956; came to U.S., 1981; d. Canute Egbert and Kathleen Gloria (Miles) B. BS cum laude, L.I. U., 1983, postgrad. in pharmacy and bus. adminstrn., 1984—. Registered pharmacist, N.Y., N.J. Grad. asst. Dean Undergrad. Bus. Sch. L.I. (N.Y.) U., 1983-85; pharmacist Nat. Pharmacy, Elmwood, N.J., 1985-86; pharmacist II Manhattan (N.Y.) Devel. Ctr., 1986-87, Kingsboro Psychiat. Ctr., Bklyn., 1987—; sr. assoc. pharmacist Kings County Hosp., Bklyn., 1986—. Mem. Am. Soc. Hosp. Pharmacists, N.Y. State Coun. Hosp. Pharmacists, Optima-Biology Hon. Soc., Caribbean-Am. C. of C., Rho Chi. Anglican. Home: 1200 E 53rd St Apt 6D Brooklyn NY 11234-2340

BAJIT, FERNANDO GAMBOA, surgeon; b. Penaranda, The Philippines, Apr. 13, 1941; came to U.S., 1964; s. Monico R. and Mercedes (Gamboa) B.; m. Winifreda Garcia, Aug. 14, 1965; children: Ronald, John, Robert. AA, U. Santo Tomas, Manila, 1958, MD, 1963. Diplomate Am. Bd. Surgery. Intern U. Santo Tomas, 1962-63; fellow V. Luna Gen. Hosp., Quezon City, The Philippines, 1963-64; intern Paterson (N.J.) Gen. Hosp., 1964-65; surgical resident Wyckoff Heights Hosp., Bklyn., 1965-70, emergency room svc., 1970-71, pvt. practice, 1972—; pvt. practice Marcy Ave Hosp., Bklyn., 1972—. Roman Catholic. Office: 529 Marcy Ave Brooklyn NY 11206

BAJPAI, SHYAM NARAYAN, electrical engineering educator; b. Kakor, India, Oct. 15, 1947; came to U.S., 1981; s. Chandrika Prasad and Ram (Beti) B.; m. Mira Devi, May 11, 1971; children: Vivek, Vipul. BS, Kanpur (India) U., 1967; MS, Agra (India) U., 1970; PhD, Indian Inst. Tech., Delhi, India, 1980. Asst. prof. Kanpur U., 1971-81; rsch. fellow Indian Inst. Tech., Delhi, 1977-80; sr. engr. Westinghouse R&D Ctr., Pitts., 1981-82; vis. assoc. prof. U. Tex., Arlington, 1983; asst. prof. SUNY, Stony Brook, 1983-91; electronics engr. Nat. Oceanic Atmosphere Adminstrn., Washington, 1991—. Reviewer rsch. jours; contbr. articles to profl. jours. Rsch. grant NSF, 1985-88; Rsch. fellowship U. Grants Commn., India, 1977-80; Bursary scholarship, Kanpur U., 1966-67, Merit scholarship U.P. Govt., 1961-66. Mem. IEEE (sr.), IEEE Microwave Theory and Techniques Soc. (mem. editorial bd.), IEEE Magentics Soc., Indian Assn. Physics Tchrs.. Hindu. Home: 44-92A Piedmont Dr Port Jefferson Sta NY 11776 Office: Nat Oceanic Atmosphere Adminstrn Advanced Systems Planning Divsn Nat Environ Satellite Data & Info Svc Washington DC 20233

BAKAITIS, VINCENT WILLIAM, JR., psychology educator; b. Washington, Pa., Feb. 4, 1941; s. Vincent William and Mary Josephine (Cario) B.; m. Nancy Thomas 1961 (div. 1966); m. Karen Crain (sep. 1990); 1 child, Celia. BA, Pa. State U., 1963; MA, New Sch. for Social Rsch., 1966. Researcher U. Chgo., Law Sch. Libr., 1963-64; social caseworker N.Y.C. Dept. Social Svc., 1964-67, social sci. supr., 1967-69; assoc. prof. behavioral sci. Dutchess Community Coll., Poughkeepsie, N.Y., 1969—; cons. N.Y. State Poison Ctr., Nyack, 1986—; rsch. assoc. Hudsonia/Bard Coll., 1989—, N.Y. State Mus. and Biol. Survey, Albany, 1990. Contbr. articles to profl. jours. Ednl. advisor, founder Mid-Hudson Mycol. Assn., Highland, N.Y., 1986—. Mem. N. Am. Mycol. Assn. Home: RR 4 Box 285 Pleasant Valley NY 12569-9436 Office: Dutchess Community Coll Pendell Rd Poughkeepsie NY 12601-1513

BAKAL, ABRAHAM ITSHAK, chemical engineer, food scientist; b. Baghdad, Iraq, July 5, 1936; came to U.S., 1968; s. Joseph and Naomi (Hacham) B.; m. Frida X. Shomer, Nov. 15, 1966; children: Gil J., Amir J. BSc in Chem. Engring., Technion Israel Inst. Tech., Haifa, Israel, 1962, MSc in Food and Biotech., 1965; PhD in Food Sci., Rutgers U., 1970. Tech. head Technion-Food Industry, Adv. Sta., Haifa, 1963-66; asst. prof. U. Sask., 1966-68; rsch. dir. Foster D. Snell subs. Booz Allen, Florham Park, N.J., 1969-73; tech. dir. CIEPE, San Felipe, Venezuela, 1973-75; prin. Foster D. Snell subs. Booz Allen, Florham Park, 1975-78; pres. ABIC Internat. Consultants, Inc., Fairfield, N.J., 1978—; bd. dirs. Legume, Inc., Pine Brook, N.J., Goosecross Cellars, Inc., Yountville, Calif., Calorie Control Coun., Atlanta. Author numerous sci. and profl. publs. in the areas of engring., food sci., product devel. and mgmt. With Israeli Army, 1954-56. Jewish. Office: ABIC Internat Cons 24 Spielman Rd Fairfield NJ 07004-3412

BAKALIAN, ALEXANDER EDWARD, public health engineer; b. Beirut, July 25, 1957; s. Edward Dikran and Verkin Bedros (Arpadjian) B. BCE, Am. U., Beirut, 1979; PhD in Environ. Engring., Johns Hopkins U., 1987; MBA, George Washington U., 1992. Project engr. Saulex Engrs. and Contractors, Alkhobar, Saudi Arabia, 1979-80; tech. specialist World Bank, Washington, 1986—. Contbr. articles to profl. jours. Bd. dirs. Miriam's Kitchen Feeding Program for Homeless, Washington, 1990—; vol. ARC, Balt. 1984-86. Mem. Armenian Network Am. (v.p. 1990-91), WorldAffairs Coun., Water Pollution Control Fedn., Am. WaterWorks Assn. Armenian Orthodox. Home: 10303 Montrose Ave Bethesda MD 20814-4151 Office: World Bank 1818 H St NW Washington DC 20433-0002

BAKALY, CHARLES GEORGE, JR., lawyer; b. Long Beach, Calif., Nov. 15, 1927; s. Charles G. Sr. and Doris (Carpenter) B.; m. Patricia Murphey, Oct. 25, 1952; children: Charles G. III, John W., Thomas B. A.B., Stanford U., 1949; J.D., U. S.C., 1952. Assoc. firm O'Melveny & Myers, 1956-63, ptnr., 1963—; mem. Pres.' Nat. Commn. on Employment Policy. Author: (with Joel M. Grossman) Modern Law of Employment Relationships, 1983, 3d edit. 1989; contbr. chpts. to books. Mem. 9th Circuit Judicial Conf. Lawyer Del., 1984-87, Indigent Defense panel, 1992—, adv. coun. chair Calif. Dispute Resolution adv. coun., 1987-88. Served to capt. JAG, U.S. Army, 1952-56. Fellow Am. Coll. Trial Lawyers; mem. ABA (chmn. sect. labor and employment law 1981-82), L.A. County Bar Assn. (trustee, chmn. labor law sect. 1976-77), NAM (labor adv. task force), U.S. C. of C. (labor rels. com.), Internat. Soc. Labor Law and Social Legis., Law Soc., Pres.'s Nat. Commn. for Employment Policy (commr. 1992—), Chancery Club, Valley Hunt Club (Pasadena, Calif.), Calif. Club (L.A.). Office: O'Melveny & Myers 400 S Hope St Los Angeles CA 90071

BAKER, BRUCE EDWARD, orthopedic surgeon, consultant; b. Oswego, N.Y., Mar. 22, 1937; s. Elbert J. and Reatha (Hartranft) B.; m. Patricia Therese Gormel, Aug. 19, 1961; children: Brett, Clayton, Sean, Reatha. BSME, Syracuse U., 1959; MD, SUNY-Syracuse, 1965. Intern State U. Iowa, Iowa City, 1965-66, asst. resident, 1966-67; resident orthopaedics SUNY-Upstate Med. Ctr., Syracuse, 1969-72, NIH orthopaedic rsch. fellow, 1972-73, asst. prof. orthopaedic surgery, 1973-79, assoc. prof., 1979-86, prof., 1986-89; dir. univ. sports medicine service div. dept. orthopaedic surgery 1980-89; team physician, dir. sports medicine athletic dept., Syracuse U., 1973—, orthopaedic cons. Student Health Ctr., 1973—; staff SUNY Hosp., Syracuse, 1973-89, Syracuse VA Hosp., 1973-89, A.C. Silverman Pub. Health Hosp., 1973-77, Crouse-Irving Meml. Hosp., 1973—; cons. in field. Contbr. numerous articles to profl. jours. Capt. USAF, 1967-69. Recipient AMA Physicians Recognition award, 1978, Bronze medal award Am. Roentgen Ray Soc., 1980, Gold medal award Sound Slide Prodn. Conditioning, 1977; Syracuse U. scholar, 1955; N.Y. State Regents scholar, 1955-59; USPHS grantee, 1973-74; Hendricks Research fund grantee, 1973-75; NIH grantee, 1974-76, 76-77. Fellow ACS, Am. Acad. Orthopaedic Surgeons; mem. AME, Med. Soc. State N.Y., Onondaga County Med. Soc., Orthopaedic Rsch. Soc., Am. Coll. Sports Medicine, Am. Orthopaedic Soc. for Sports Medicine, N.Y. Soc. Orthopaedic Surgeons, Royal Soc. Medicine, Internat. Arthroscopy Assn., Arthroscopy Assn. N.Am., Biolelec Repair and Growth Soc. Office: 475 Irving Ave Ste 108A Syracuse NY 13210-1756

BAKER, BURTON CARL, printer; b. Boston, May 22, 1941; s. Solomon and Florence (Berger) B. AA, Newton (Mass.) Jr. Coll., 1961. Printer Boston Globe, 1966—. Maj. Gen. U.S. Army, 1964-76, Vietnam. Democrat. Jewish. Home: 1455 Commonwealth Ave Brighton MA 02135-3616

BAKER, CARL JOSEPH (CAL JOSEPH BADER, JR.), broadcast executive; b. Phila., Aug. 13, 1950; s. Cal Joseph and Elizabeth (Jones) Bader; m. Carol Kelly, Mar. 24, 1973 (div. 1980); 1 child, Robert Joseph. Student, Northampton County Community, Bethlehem, Pa., 1970. Sales rep., prog. dir., news dir. Sta. WCRV-Radio, Washington, 1972-76; afternoon drive show host Sta. WNOW-Radio, York, Pa., 1977; afternoon show host Sta. WKAP-Radio, Allentown, Pa., 1983-84; sales rep./announcer Sta. WQQQ-Radio, Easton, Pa., 1984-85, Sta. WLEV-Radio, Easton, 1985-88; sales rep./reporter Cellular One Traffic Bur., Allentown, 1988-89; news dir. Sta. WODE AM-FM, Easton, 1989—; radio mktg. cons. Recipient N.Y. State Spot News Award, AP, 1973, Orson Wells award, Radio Advt. Bur., N.Y.C., 1988, Outstanding Contribution award, AP, Phila., 1990, 91. Republican. Roman Catholic. Home: PO Box 128 Easton PA 18044 Office: Sta WODE AM-FM PO Box 190 Easton PA 18044-0190

BAKER, CHARLES DAVID, JR., insurance executive; b. Abington, Pa., Aug. 27, 1951; s. Charles David and Irene (Loux) B.; m. Shirley Ann Taylor, Aug. 17, 1974; children: C. David III, William B. Student, Taylor U., 1970-72; BA in Polit. Sci., Ursinus Coll., 1974. Sales agt. Lapp & Alderfer Inc., Souderton, Pa., 1975-77; pres. C D Baker Ins. Inc., Dublin, Pa., 1978—; instr. Profl. Ins. Agts. Assn. of Pa., Md., Del., Mechanicsburg, Pa., 1989—; del. Erie (Pa.) Ins. Agts. Adv. Coun., 1991—. Author: The Fencerow Tails, 1989; contbg. author: Today's Best Poems, 1980, Lenin, A False Prophet, 1970. Bd. dirs. Pennridge Sch. Dist., Perkasie, Pa., 1980-81, Plumstead Christian Sch., Plumsteadville, Pa., 1991—; cons. Reaching Urban Neighborhoods, Telford, Pa., 1990—. Mem. Soc. Cert. Ins. Counsellors, Cert. Profl. Ins. Agts. Soc., Order of Eastern Star (pres. 1988). Office: C D Baker Ins Inc 404 Dublin Pike Dublin PA 18917-9709

BAKER, CHARLES ERNEST, stockbroker; b. Carthage, Mo., June 17, 1946; s. Ernest Roy Baker and Doris Elaine (Law) Bradshaw; m. Joanne Carolyn McCarthy, Sept. 30, 1990; 1 child, Amanda Jaclyn. BS in Math., Ill. State U., Normal, 1975. Lic. N.Y. Stock Exchange, Chgo. Bd. Trade. Sales engr. Honeywell, Peoria, Ill., 1972-76; registered rep. Loewi & Co., Milw., 1976-79; v.p. Kidder Peabody & Co., White Plains, N.Y., 1979-89; v.p. investments Dean, Witter, Reynolds, White Plains, 1989—; bd. dirs. Tri-State Motor Transit, Inc., TRISM Specilaized Carriers, Trism, Inc., mem. audit com., mem. compensation com. Mem. exec. com. March of Dimes, 1986—; pres. White Plains Guild, 1988—; mem. audit com. Camp Sloane, 1990, bd. dirs., 1991—. Recipient March of Dimes Disting. Vol. Leadership award 1988. Mem. Profl. Photographers of Am., Kiwanis, Shriners, Masons. Home: 150 Bedford Rd N Chappaqua NY 10514-2740 Office: Dean Witter Reynolds Inc 11 Martine Ave White Plains NY 10606-1934

BAKER, CORNELIA DRAVES, artist; b. Woodbury, N.J., Mar. 2, 1929; d. Carl Zeno and Cornelia (Powell) D.; m. Philip Douglas Baker, July 16, 1955; children: Brinton, Todd, Claudia, Samuel. Student, Ohio Wesleyan U., 1947-50, Goethe U., Frankfort, 1950-52. Travel dir. Am. Youth Hostels, Inc., N.Y.C., 1953-57; artist Cornelia Gallery, Kumamoto, Japan, 1990—, Jain Marunouchi Gallery, N.Y.C., 1991—, Bengent/MacRae Gallery, Nyckoff, N.J., 1992—; gallery dir. Presbyn. Ch., Franklin Lakes, N.J., 1989—. One woman shows include Ramapo Coll., 1986, Shimada Mus., Kumamoto, 1990, Sekaikan Gallery, Tokyo, 1990; represented in permanent collection Bergen Mus. Art and Sci., Paramus, N.J. Chair social problems com. Borough of Franklin Lakes Coun., 1973-76. Recipient Best of Show award Ringwood Manor Assn. of the Arts, 1987, Bergen Mus. Art and Sci., 1989, Emerti award for excellence N.J. Ctr. for Visual Arts, 1989; cet. excellence Internat. Art Competition, 1988. Mem. Nat. Assn. Women Artists (printmaking jury chmn. 1992—), Salute to Women in the Arts (pres. 1988-90). Republican. Presbyterian. Home: 293 Greenridge Rd Franklin Lakes NJ 07417-2011

BAKER, DANIEL NEIL, space plasma physicist; b. Postville, Iowa, Nov. 10, 1948; s. Joseph N. and Alvira H. (Amundson) B.; m. A. Victoria Vaughan, Aug. 14, 1971. BA, U. Iowa, 1969, MS, 1973, PhD, 1974. Research aide dept. physics U. Iowa, Iowa City, 1967-69, grad. research asst., 1970-74, postdoctoral research assoc., 1974-75; research fellow Calif. Inst. Tech., Pasadena, 1975-78; mem. staff Los Alamos (N.Mex.) Nat. Lab., 1978-81, group leader, 1981-87; chief Lab. for Extraterrestrial Physics NASA, Goddard Space Flight Ctr., Greenbelt, Md., 1987—; chmn. data systems users group NASA, Washington, 1982-90, tech. cons., 1985—, mem. space physics mgmt. and ops. com., adv. council Space Sci. and Applications, 1988—, grand tour cluster mission study scientist, 1991—; mem. com. solar and space physics NAS, Washington, 1983-86, com. data mgmt. and computation 1986-88; mem. panel on long-term observations Nat. Research Council, Washington, 1985-88, commn. D Sci. Com. on Solar-Terrestrial Physics, 1986—, U.S. coordinating com. Solar Terrestrial Energy Program, 1988—, U.S. STEP project scientist, 1990—, Geospace Environ. Modeling com. NSF, 1988-91; project scientist NASA small explorer program, prin. investigator NASA rocket program, numerous NASA ESA satellite missions in field. Assoc. editor Geophys. Research Letters, Washington, 1986-88; mem. space tech. rev. bd. Los Alamos Nat. Lab.; contbr. numerous articles to profl. jours. Mem. external adv. com. Boston U. Ctr. for Space Rsch., 1989—, sci. vis. com. U. Md. Inst. Phys. Sci. and Tech., 1990—. NSF research fellow U. Iowa, 1970-74; grantee Inst. Geophys. and Planetary Physics U. Calif., 1980-89. Mem. AAAS, Am. Geophys. Union (geomagnetism assessment panel 1987-88, sec. magnetospheric sect. 1988-90), Sigma Xi. Office: Code 690 NASA/Goddard Space Flight Ctr Greenbelt MD 20771

BAKER, DARRELL EDWARD, JR., lawyer; b. Pine Bluff, Ark., Mar. 4, 1955; s. Darrell Edward Sr. and Juanita (Nichols) B.; m. Deborah Whitt, Aug. 7, 1983; 1 child, Alexandra Whitt Baker. BA in Music, La. Tech. Coll., 1976; JD, U. Ark., 1981. Bar: Mass. 1987, U.S. Dist. Ct. Mass. 1988, U.S. Ct. Appeals (8th cir.) 1986, Ark. 1981, U.S. Dist. Ct. (we. dist.) Ark. 1984. Atty. Murphy and Carlisle, Fayetteville, Ark., 1981-83; dep. pub. defender Pub. Defender's Office, Fayetteville, 1982-86; assoc. Abraham-Hanna P.C., Boston, 1986-87, CNA Ins. Co., Boston, 1987-90, Morrison, Mahoney, and Miller, Boston, 1990—. Office: Morrison Mahoney and Miller 250 Summer St Boston MA 02210-1134

BAKER, DAVID ARTHUR, small business owner, manufacturer; b. Cranston, R.I., Jan. 5, 1941; s. Andrew Harris and Phyllis Evelyn (Partridge) B.; m. Anne Marie Perron, July 14, 1959; children: Susan Marie, Pamela Phyllis. Garment cutter Supreme Coat Co., Worcester, Mass., 1960-74; owner D.A. Baker Mfg. Co., Auburn, Mass., 1975—, Eagle's Nest Video Prodns., Auburn, 1985—. Producer (ednl. video) Popular Amazons, 1986, Macaws, 1987, Cockatoos, 1988, Parrot Keeping, 1989, and others. Treas. Boston Soc. Aviculture, 1983-85; co-founder, bd. dirs. Exotic Cage Bird Soc., 1986-88; mem. Plaza Club, Worcester, 1985-91. Recipient Outstanding Svc. award Boston Soc. Agr., 1984, Exotic Cage Bird Soc. New Eng., 1985, Cert. of merit Les Comité des Vins de France, 1982. Mem. Internat. Soc. Food and Wine, Rolls Royce Owners Club, Friends of Ballroom Dancing, Daimler and Lanchester Club, Club Maxine's. Republican. Home: Knight Cottage Bellevue Ave Newport RI 02840 Office: Eagles Nest PO Box 100 Auburn MA 01501-0100

BAKER, DAVID JOHNSON, criminal justice administrator; b. Danville, Pa., June 15, 1945; s. Gerald B. and Nola (Johnson) B.; m. Maryann, June 16, 1968. BA, Franklin & Marshall Coll., 1967. Parole officer Pa. Bd. Probation and Parole, Phila., 1967-72, parole supr., 1972-87; dist. dir. Pa. Bd. Probation and Parole, Williamsport, 1987—. Mem. Nat. Eagle Scout Assn. (Eagle scout 1959), Pa. Assn. Probation, Parole and Corrections, Fraternal Order Police, Am. Philatelic Soc., Internat. Soc. Japanese Philately. Office: Pa Bd Probation and Parole 450 Little League Blvd Williamsport PA 17701

BAKER, DEXTER FARRINGTON, manufacturing company executive; b. Worcester, Mass., Apr. 16, 1927; s. Leland Dyer and Edith (Quimby) B.; m. Dorothy Ellen Hess, June 23, 1951; children: Ellen L., Susan A., Leslie A., Carolyn J. B.S., Lehigh U., 1950, M.B.A., 1957. Sales engr. Air Products & Chems., Inc., Allentown, Pa., 1952-56, gen. sales mgr., 1956-57, mng. dir., 1957-64, chief exec. ops. in Europe, bd. dirs., 1964-67, exec. v.p., 1967-78, pres., 1978-86, 90-91, chmn., pres., 1990-91, chmn., chief exec. officer, 1986-92; bd. dirs. AMP, Inc.; mem., former chmn. investment policy com. U.S. Trade Rep.; mem. adv. bd. Iacocca Inst. Bd. assocs. Muhlenberg Coll.; trustee Lehigh U., Harry C. and Mary M. Trexler Found.; mem. Pa. Econ. Devel. Partnership Bd. Served with USNR, 1945-46; with U.S. Army, 1950-52. Mem. Am. Mgmt. Assn., Am. Inst. Chem. Engrs., Asa Packer Soc. Lehigh U., Nat. Assn. Mfrs. (chmn. bd., mem. exec. com.), Theta Chi. Presbyterian (elder). Office: Air Products and Chems Inc 7201 Hamilton Blvd Allentown PA 18195-9642

BAKER, DONALD JAMES, oceanographer, administrator; b. Long Beach, Calif., Mar. 23, 1937; s. Donald James and Lillian Mae (Pund) B.; m. Emily Lind Delman, Sept. 7, 1968. B.S., Stanford U., 1958; Ph.D., Cornell U., 1962. Postdoctoral fellow Grad. Sch. Oceanography, U. R.I., Kingston, 1962-63; NIH fellow in chem. biodynamics Lawrence Radiation Lab., U. Calif., Berkeley, 1963-64; research fellow, asst. prof., assoc. prof. phys. oceanography Harvard U., 1964-73; research prof. dept. oceanography, sr. oceanographer, applied physics lab. U. Wash., Seattle, 1973-77; sr. fellow Joint Inst. for Study Atmosphere and Ocean, 1977-86, prof. dept. oceanography, 1979-86, chmn. dept. oceanography, 1979-81; dean Coll. Ocean and Fishery

Scis., 1981-83; group leader deep-sea physics group Pacific Marine Environ. Lab., NOAA, Seattle, 1977-79; bd. govs. Joint Oceanographic Instns., Inc., 1979—, pres., 1983—; disting. vis. scientist Jet Propulsion Lab., Calif. Inst. Tech., 1982—; co-chmn. exec. com. Internat. So. Ocean Studies (NSF project), 1974-84; vice-chmn. joint panel, global weather experiment NAS, mem. ocean scis. bd., ocean scis. policy bd., ocean studies bd., 1987-91; mem. com. on atmospheric scis., 1978-81, mem. climate rsch. com., 1979-90; mem. space and earth sci. adv. com. NASA, 1982-86, mem. space sci. bd., 1984-87, chmn. com. on earth scis., 1984-87; mem. environ. panel Navy Rsch. Com., 1983-86, mem. NASA earth system scis. com., 1983-86; officer Joint Sci. Com. for World Climate Rsch. Program, 1987—; mem. U.S. nat. com. for internat. coun. sci. unions NAS, 1987-89, com. on global change rsch., 1987—, com. on environ. rsch., 1991—; mem. U.S. Sci. Steering Com. for World Ocean Circulation Experiment, 1985-90; chmn. NASA Ctr. Sci. Assessment Team, 1987-88; chmn. Internat. World Ocean Circulation Experiment Sci. Steering Group, 1988-92; mem. earth sci. and applications adv. com. NASA, 1989-90; chmn. tech. com. on ocean processes and climate Intergovtl. Oceanographic Commn., 1989—; bd. dirs. Coun. of Ocean Law, 1989—; mem. panel on megaprojects Pres.'s Coun. of Advisors on Sci. and Tech., 1991—; mem. NASA Earth Observing System Engring. Rev. Com., 1990-92; mem. com. on the future of the U.S. Space Program NASA, 1990-92; mem. adv. panel on climate and global change Nat. Oceanic and Atmospheric Adminstrn., 1989—; mem. V.P.'s Space Policy Adv. Bd., 1991—; mem. adv. panel Earth Observing System Data and Info. System., 1992—, adv. com. divsn. of polar programs, NSF, 1992—. Author: Planet Earth: The View from Space, 1990; mem. editorial bd. Oceanus Mag., 1992—; co-editor in chief: Dynamics of Atmospheres and Oceans Jour., 1975-79; contbr. sci. articles to profl. jours. Fellow AAAS, Explorers Club; mem. Am. Geophys. Union, Am. Meteorol. Soc. (coun. 1982-88), The Oceanography Soc. (pres. 1988-92), Marine Tech. Soc., Nat. Assn. State Univs. and Land Grant Colls. (bd. dirs. marine div. 1989—), Sigma Xi. Home: 4531 28th St NW Washington DC 20008-1035 Office: Joint Oceanographic Instns Inc 1755 Massachusetts Ave NW Washington DC 20036-2102

BAKER, EVAN, opera historian; b. L.A., Aug. 23, 1952; s. Louis Rockford and Marion (Ancel) B. BA, UCLA, 1974, MA, 1975; postgrad., NYU, 1992—. Asst. stage dir. Lucerne (Switzerland) City Theater, 1981-84, curator opera exhibits, 1982, 83, 84; curator exhibit Giuseppe Verdi Istituto de Studi Verdiani at Parma and City of Colorno, Italy, 1985; curator opera exhibit Teatro alla Scala, Milan, Italy, 1986; curator Operatic Beginnings exhibit Music Ctr. Opera Assn., L.A., 1986; curator Mozart exhibit N.Y. Pub. Libr. for the Performing Arts, N.Y.C., 1991; cons. Pierpont Morgan Libr., N.Y.C., 1990-91. Contbr. articles to profl. publs. Recipient NYU Dept. Performance Studies scholarship, 1987-88, Fulbright scholarship, Vienna, 1988-90. Home: 25-38 41st St Astoria NY 11103

BAKER, F. M., psychiatry educator; b. N.Y.C., Sept. 15, 1942. BA, Hunter Coll., 1964; MA, NYU, 1967; MD, U. Rochester, 1975; MPH, Johns Hopkins U., 1985. Diplomate Am. Bd. Psychiatry and Neurology. Intern Greenwich (Conn.) Hosp.Assn., 1975-76; resident in psychiatry Yale U. Sch. Medicine, New Haven, 1976-79, asst. prof. dept. psychiatry, 1979-84; liason psychiatrist Primary Care Ctr. Yale-New Haven Hosp., 1979-81, asst. dir. psychiat. cons. liason svc., dir. psychiat. emergency svc., 1979-82, liason psychiatrist geriatric assessment unit, 1981-84, med. dir. rape crisis team, 1981-82; cons. psychiatrist Gaylord Rehab. Hosp., Wallingford, Conn., 1979-82, Golden Manor Nursing Home, New Haven, 1980-81; assoc. ward chief Hill-West Haven div. Conn. Mental Health Ctr., 1982-83, ward chief 5th fl. in-patient div., 1983-84; med. staff fellow USPHS, NINCDS, NIH, 1984-87; assoc. prof. dept. psychiatry U. Tex. Health Sci. Ctr., San Antonio, 1987-90; chief geriatric psychiatry program Audie L. Murphy Meml. Vets. Hosp., 1987-90; assoc. prof. Inst. for Psychiatry and Human Behavior U. Md., Balt., 1990—; asst. prof. part-time dept. psychiatry Johns Hopkins U. Sch. Medicine, Balt., 1985-87; adj. researcher biometry and field studies br. Nat. Inst. Neurologic Disorders and Stroke NIH, Bethesda, 1987-89; vis. scientist dept. health scis. rsch. The Mayo Clinic, Rochester, Minn., 1987-90; vis. and cons. scientist mental disorders of the aging rsch. br. NIMH, Rockville, Md., 1989-92; cons. scientist geriatric div. Nat. Inst. Aging, NIH, Rockville, 1990-92. Author: (with others) Evaluation of the Consumer Health Training and Education Program, 1973, Manual of Psychiatric Peer Review, 2d edit., 1981, (with others), An Overview of Legal Issues in Geriatric Psychiatry, 1986, Dementing Illness in African American Populations, 1991; contbr. articles to profl. jours. Mem. psychogeriatric adv. bd. cen. office VA, Washington, 1990. Fellow AAAS, Am. Psychiat. Assn. (chmn. task force on forensic issues in geriatric psychiatry 1982-86, vice chmn. coun. on aging 1984-89, mem. com. on ethnic elders 1992—, mem. selection adv. com. for APA/NIMH fellowship 1988-91); mem. Am. Assn. for Geriatric Psychiatry (bd. mem. 1988-91), Black Psychiatrists Am. (rep. Nat. Conf. on Manpower and Recruitment 1980, ant. sec., asst. editor Bottom Line Newsletter 1980-82, assoc. editor 1982-84, editor 1987-90, nat. treas. 1984, 86, exec. com. 1987-89), Tex. Soc. Psychiat. Physicians, Nat. Coun. Negro Women, Boston Soc. for Gerontologic Psychiatry, Inc., Conn. Psychiat. Soc. (com. on women 1979-81, program com. 1980-81, ins. com. 1979-84), Am. Assn. for Geriatric Psychiatry (bd. dirs. 1987-90, chairperson com. ethic elders 1990, treas.-elect 1992—), Gerontol. Soc. Am., Internat. Psychogeriatric Assn., Psychiat. Physicians (chair sci. program ann. meeting 1989), Md. Psychiat. Soc. (geriatric psychiatry com. 1990—, editorial com. 1991—, continuing edn. com. 1991—).

BAKER, FRANCIS EDWARD, JR., electrical engineer; b. Balt., Nov. 11, 1944; s. Francis Edward and Theresa Marie (Heil) B.; m. Honora Patricia Lewis, June 11, 1966; children—Michael Edward, Jennifer Marie, Timothy Joseph. BSEE, Va. Poly. Inst. and State U., 1967, MSEE, 1969, PhDEE, 1971, diploma, U.S. Naval War Coll., 1988, MS in Mgmt. MIT, 1989. Registered profl. engr., Md. Instr., Va. Poly. Inst. and State U., 1970-71; elec. engr. David Taylor Naval Ship Research and Devel. Ctr., Annapolis, Md., 1971-78, sci. adv., 1978-80, supervisory elec. engr., 1980-83, head tech. intelligence and mil. effectiveness office, Bethesda, 1984-85; head surface warfare analysis, 1985-88, head combat systems engring. and assessment div. Naval Surface Warfare Ctr., Silver Spring, Md., 1989—; adj. asst. prof. mgmt. of tech. U. Md., College Park, 1991—; asst. dir. sci. and tech. Chief Naval Ops. Exec. Panel, Washington, 1983-84; vis. assoc. prof. physics U.S. Naval Acad., 1979-80; cons. Trident Engring. Assocs. Inc., Annapolis, 1978-89. Contbr. articles to tech. jours.; patentee el cell with integrated switch control, 1977. Scoutmaster, Balt. Area council Boy Scouts Am., 1982-87; mem. adv. bd. Anne Arundel Community Coll., 1976; v.p. Millersville (Md.) PTA, 1974-75. Mem. IEEE, Am. Soc. Naval Engrs., Sigma Xi, Tau Beta Pi, Phi Kappa Phi. Roman Catholic. Home: 1501 Kingsway Dr Gambrills MD 21054-2123 Office: Naval Surface Weapons Ctr White Oak Lab 10901 New Hampshire Ave Silver Spring MD 20903-5000

BAKER, FRANK, psychologist, educator; b. Dallas, Feb. 28, 1936; s. Dave and Estelle P. (Portnoy) B.; m. Adrienne Polland, Mar. 20, 1960; children: Steven Isaac, David Brian, Julie Suzanne. BA cum laude, Vanderbilt U., 1958; MA, Northwestern U., 1962, PhD, 1958. Lic. psychologist, Mass. Asst. prof. social psychology Lehigh U., Bethlehem, Pa., 1963-65; asst. prof. psychology and psychiatry Harvard U. Med. Sch., Boston, 1965-74, dir. orgnl. systems rsch. and evaluation sect., head program rsch. unit Lab. Community Psychiatry, 1969-74, vis. lectr. psychiatry, 1981-82; prof. psychology, psychiatry and preventive medicine, dir. div. community psychiatry SUNY Sch. Medicine, Buffalo, 1974-85; prof., chmn., dept. behavioral scis. and health edn. Johns Hopkins U. Sch. of Hygiene and Pub. Health, Balt., 1985-87, prof. health psychology dept. environ. health scis., 1987—; disting. vis. prof. sociology U. Mass., Boston, 1973-74. Editor: Work, Health and Productivity, 1991, Coordination of Alcohol, Drug Abuse and Mental Health Services, 1991. Fellow APA, Am. Orthopsychiat. Assn.; mem. APHA, AAAS. Home: 3029 St Paul St Baltimore MD 21218-3943 Office: Johns Hopkins Sch Hygiene & Pub Health 615 N Wolfe St Baltimore MD 21205-2103

BAKER, HERMAN, vitaminologist; b. N.Y.C., Jan. 22, 1926; s. Harry and Fannie Baker; m. Shirley Levitz, Nov. 15, 1952; children: Elliott Robert, Joel Martin. BS, CCNY, 1946; MS, Emory U., 1948; PhD, NYU, 1956. Cert. specialist human nutrition Am. Bd. Nutrition. Research asst. Columbia U., N.Y.C., 1949-50; research assoc. Mt. Sinai Hosp., N.Y.C., 1950-60; assoc. prof. medicine N.J. Med. Sch., Jersey City, 1960-70; prof. medicine and preventive medicine N.J. Med. Sch., Newark, 1970—. Contbr. over 240 articles on metabolic imbalances to profl. jours. Fellow Am. Coll. Nutrition; mem. Pan Am. Med. Assn. (pres. 1985— preventive medicine sect.), Am. Soc. Clin. Nutrition, Soc. for Exptl. Biology and Medicine, Sigma Xi. Home: 27 Wilk Rd Edison NJ 08837-2726 Office: NJ Med Sch Martland GB 159 65 Bergen St Newark NJ 07107

BAKER, J. A., pension plan design firm executive; b. N.Y.C., Dec. 12, 1944; s. Leonard Ernest and Miriam Violet (Roche) B. CLU; chartered fin. cons., fin. planning advisor. Cons. mgr. Met. Life Ins. Co., N.Y.C., 1964-79; supr. Physician's Planning Group, N.Y.C., 1979-80; chief exec. officer J A L B Enterprises, Garden City, N.Y., 1980—; CLU; Chartered Fin. Cons., Fin. Planning Advisor; fellow Life Underwriters Tng. Coun. Bd. dirs. Medic Alert, Nassau County, N.Y., 1985—. Mem. Nat. Assn. Life Underwriters (pres. Cortland chpt. 1974-75, v.p. pub. rels. Nassau County 1980-87, instr. Bklyn. 1987-90, Queens 1990-91), Am. Coun. Ind. Life Underwriters, Million Dollar Round Table (life). Home: Madison Sq Station PO Box 1200 New York NY 10159-1200 Office: J A L B Enterprises PO Box 2053 Garden City NY 11530-0218

BAKER, JAMES ADDISON, III, U.S. government official; b. Houston, Apr. 28, 1930; s. James A. and Bonner (Means) B.; m. Susan Garrett, Aug. 6, 1973; 8 children. B.A., Princeton U., 1952; LL.B., U. Tex., 1957. Bar: Tex. 1957. Assoc. Andrews Kurth Campbell & Jones, Houston, 1957-81; undersec. Dept. Commerce, Washington, 1975-76; deputy chmn. del. ops. Pres. Ford Com., Washington, 1976; campaign chmn. George Bush, 1979-80; sr. adviser Reagan-Bush Com., 1980-81; mem. Reagan Transition Team, Washington, 1980-81; chief of staff White House, Washington, 1981-85; sec. Dept. Treasury, 1985-88; campaign chmn. George Bush's Presdl. campaign, 1988; sec. Dept. of State, 1989-92; chief of staff, sr. counselor to Pres. The White House, Washington, 1992—. Trustee Woodrow Wilson Internat. Center for Scholars, Smithsonian Inst., 1977—. Served with USMC, 1952-54. Mem. ABA, Tex. Bar Assn., Houston Bar Assn., Am. Judicature Soc., Phi Delta Phi. Office: Chief of Staff 1600 Pennsylvania Ave NW Washington DC 20500*

BAKER, JOANNE EVELYN, retired government official; b. Crucible, Pa., Dec. 1, 1933; d. George Joseph and Anna Leona (Kagle) Cormack; m. Warren Clair Baker, July 7, 1956 (dec. May 1968); m. James Lewis Wilson, June 2, 1970; (div. Sept. 1984); former stepchildren: James Lloyd, John Thomas, Charles Edward, Debra Ruth, Jeff Lee Wilson. Cert. applied music, Waynesburg Coll., 1951. Various clerical positions, 1951-66; supr. USN, Washington, 1966-71; pres., treas. Little Round Top Farm, Inc., Gettysburg, Pa., 1971-86; logistician USN-U.S. Army, Gettysburg, Pa., 1974-81; insp. Office of Insp. Gen. 7th Signal Commd. U.S. Army, Ft. Ritchie, Md., 1981-84; chief supply and svcs. div. Fort Detrick, Frederick, Md., 1985-89, chief plans and resources mgmt. div., 1989-90, mgmt. cons., 1991—. Author: Reflections, 1974. Bd. dirs. Adams County Mental Health Assn., Gettysburg, 1982-87. Recipient Sustained Superior Achievement award Dept. Navy, 1975, Dept. of Army 1986; named Outstanding Woman of Yr. Ft. Detrick, 1986, recipient Comdr.'s award, 1990. Mem. Internat. Graphoanalysis Soc., Internat. Platform Assn., Adams County Amateur Radio Soc., World Inst. of Achievement (life). Roman Catholic. Home: 5605 Shookstown Rd Frederick MD 21702-2704

BAKER, JOHN COOPER, health benefits company executive; b. Princeton, N.J., Feb. 9, 1947; s. Richard Wheeler and Rachel Irvin (Cooper) B.; m. Dale Rose Raczkowski, Apr. 11, 1970 (div. Oct., 1983); m. Linda Alice Fennell, Dec. 3, 1983. BA, Rutgers U., 1969, MBA, 1981. Asst. v.p. First Nat. Bank, Princeton, N.J., 1974-84; v.p. Nassau Savs. & Loan Assn., Princeton, 1984-86; exec. v.p. Mercer Savs. Bank, Trenton, N.J., 1987-91; v.p. BeneCard Svcs. Inc., Trenton, 1991—; cons. tchr. Am. Inst. of Banking, Trenton, 1978-86, Inst. for Fin. Edn., Trenton, 1986—; bd. dirs. Mercer County N.J. Savs. League; owner Scotia Audio Prodns., 1990—. Producer radio programs Youth Speaks Up, Sta. WPST-RM, 1980—, The Scottish Digest Sta. WTMR-AM and Sta. WTTM-AM, 1990—; publisher (recs.) An Evening with Peter Morrison, 1990, 1990 Delco Scottish Games Pipes and Drums, 1990, Sounds of the 1990 Grandfather Mountain Highland Games, 1991, Carolyn Hannan-White Sands of Eriskay, 1991, Redbird Marching Band Live from New York, 1991, Peter Morrison From Glasgow to Hollywood, 1991, An Afternoon of Group Singing, 1991, Carl Peterson Sings Robert Burns, 1992, The Clansmen-Scotland My Home, 1992. Campaign chmn. United Way, Princeton, 1987-88; treas. Princeton Battlefield Area Preservation Soc., 1976—; chmn. Speaker's Bur. Com. for Employer Support of the Guard and Res., Lawrenceville, N.J., 1984—; pres. Princeton Pro-Musica, 1989-91, Youth Communications Inc., 1989—; trustee Anchor House for Runaways, 1988—; head sound engr. Trinity Episcopal Ch., 1988—. Capt. USNR. Recipient Naval Expeditionary Medal, USN, Washington, 1984. Mem. Fin. Insts. Mktg. Assn. N.J. Communications and Mktg. Assn., Naval Reserve Assn., Navy League, The Nassau Club, Brit. Officer's Club of Phila. Republican. Episcopalian. Home: 10D Shirley Ln Trenton NJ 08648-1403 Office: 118 W State St Trenton NJ 08608-1184

BAKER, JOHN DONALD, JR., federal agency administrator; b. Brewer, Maine, Jan. 20, 1938; s. John Donald and Helen Marie (Fallon) B.; m. Glenda M. Farrell, Nov. 18, 1962 (div. 1991); children: John Donald III, Daniella Helen Marie, Glenn Joseph. BA, U. Maine, 1960, MA, Georgetown U., 1971, PhD. Clin. psychologist Bangor (Maine) State Hosp., 1960-61; top secret control officer HQ Allied Forces Cen. Europe, Fontainbleau, France, 1963-66; exec. officer Asst. to the Chmn. JCS for Strategic Arms Negotiations, Washington, 1968-69; br. chief Viet Cong Infrastructure Br., U.S. Mil. Assistance Command, 1971-72; sr. strategic intelligence officer Def. Intelligence Agy., Washington, 1978-80; br. chief Command Control & Communications, Washington, 1982-85; sr. intelligence specialist HQ USAF, Washington, 1985-90; spl. asst. to dir. Air Force Intelligence Agy., Washington, 1990—; cons. Analytical Assessment Corp., Arlington, Va., 1980-81, Pacific Sierra Rsch. Corp., Arlington, 1981-82; prof. Soviet studies Def. Intelligence Sch., Washington, 1980. Contbr. articles to profl. jours. Lt. col. U.S. Army, 1960-80. Decorated Bronze Star, Joint Svc. Commendation medal, JCS Commendation, Def. Meritorious Svc. medal. Mem. Internat. Inst. for Strategic Studies, U.S. Strategic Inst., Am. Assn. for Advancement of Slavic Studies, U.S. Hypnosis Soc., Phi Alpha Theta. Republican. Roman Catholic. Home: 6338 Beryl Rd Alexandria VA 22312

BAKER, LAURENCE SPENCER, psychologist; b. N.Y.C., Aug. 12, 1925. BA, NYU, 1948, PhD, 1955. Lic. psychologist, N.Y. Psychologist child guidance dept. Mt. Vernon (N.Y.) Pub. Schs., 1950; psychologist Spl. Disabilities Clinic N.Y. Infirmary, 1951; psychologist Floral Park-Bellerose (N.Y.) Pub. Schs., 1951-52, Hewlett (N.Y.) Primary-Nursery Sch., 1952-53, Tappan Zee Mental Health Clinic, Tarrytown, N.Y., 1954-57; pvt. practice, 1955—; panel psychologist vocat. and edn. svcs. N.Y. State Dept. Edn., 1958—; psychologist Jennie Clarkson Home, Valhalla, N.Y., 1961-76; psychologist, exec. dir. Westchester Ctr. for Psychol. Edn., Inc., 1982-86; psychologist N.Y. State Commn. for Blind and Visually Handicapped, 1982—; cons. numerous orgns., including Westchester Assn. for Retarded Citizens, 1979—, Psychiat. Inst., Westchester County Med. Ctr., Valhalla, 1984—, Westchester County Probation Dept., 1989—; instr. New Rochelle (N.Y.) Adult Edn. Program, 1953-58, NYU Ctr. for Continuing Edn., White Plains, 1965-67; pres. TestFast Rsch. Svcs., Inc., 1982-86, TESTING Inc., White Plains, 1986—; assoc. dir. Psychol. Svcs. Inst., N.Y.C., 1951-58, Neuro-Cognitive Rehab. Svc., White Plains, 1990—; dir. Anxiety Disorders Westchester, White Plains; expert witness in criminal custody, compensation and other cases in state and county cts. Editor Westchester Psychologist, 1970-80; editor-in-chief N.Y. State Psychologist, 1983-89; cons. editor Keon Kang Digest, 1983-84; contbr. articles to profl. jours. Leader family living project Westchester Mental Health Assn., 1954-55; active Interagency Task Force on Suicide and Depression, White Plains, 1983—; speaker to community orgns. Recipient Founder's Day award NYU. Mem. APA, Am. Assn. for Med. Systems and Informatics (former mem. adv. bd. mental health systems specialty group), Westchester County Psychol. Assn. (past pres., rep. to N.Y. State Psychol. Assn., bd. dirs., 1st recipient Disting. Psychologist award), N.Y. State Psychol. Assn. (mem. coun. of reps.), Computer Based Assessment Assn. (founder, 1st pres.), Phi Delta Kappa. Office: 901 N Broadway Ste 4 White Plains NY 10603-2418

BAKER, MARK ALLEN, marketing executive, author; b. Binghamton, N.Y., Mar. 27, 1957; s. Ford William and Marilyn A. (Allen) B.; divorced; children: Aaron Anthony, Elizabeth Margaret, Rebecca Jeanne. BA, SUNY, Oswego, 1979. Computer operator Gen. Electric Corp., Liverpool, N.Y., 1980-81, tng. specialist, 1981-82; art dir. Genigraphics Corp., Liverpool, 1982-83, mgr. market research, 1983-85, exec. asst. to pres. and chief exec. officer, 1985-86, corp. bus. planner, 1986—; pvt. researcher and lobbyist to U.S. Senate, 1978—; corp. cons. Roger Sherman and Assocs., Liverpool, 1986—. Author: Baseball Autograph Handbook, I and II, 1990—, Team Baseballs; contbr. articles to profl. jours. Mem. Am. Mgmt. Assn. (pres. 1985—), Assn. Computer Mfrs. (pres. 1985—), Assn. Med. Illustrators (corp. rep., pres. 1986—), Am. Assn. Individual Investors (pres. 1987—), Siggraph (pres. 1985—). Home: PO Box 2492 4766 Stonedale Dr Liverpool NY 13089

BAKER, NORMAN LEE, editor; b. Reyno, Ark., July 24, 1926; s. Ottis King and Lora Faye (Weaver) B.; m. Lois C. Shanner, Jan. 1, 1960 (dec. 1985); children: Gary Kale, Mary Ellen Jones, Syntha, Suzanne, Margaret; m. Suzanne Thomas Brydges, Oct. 8, 1988. BS in Aero. Engring., Ind. Inst. Tech., 1956. Engr. missile devel. Pilotless Aircraft div. Boeing Co., Seattle, 1956-57; editor Missiles and Rockets mag. Am. Aviation Publs., Washington, 1957-59; pres., editor in chief Space Publs., Inc., Washington, 1959-86; editor in chief Def. Daily Phillips Pub., Inc., Washington and Potomac, Md., 1986—. Contbr. articles to profl. jours. With USNR, 1943-46, PTO; sgt. AUS, 1951-54, Korea. Decorated Combat Infantryman badge, others; recipient Order of Silver Slide Rule, Ind. Inst. Tech., 1960, Bausch & Lomb award, Best Exclusive Single News Story award Nat. Newsletter Assn., 1987, Space Pioneers award. Mem. AIAA (founder Ft. Wayne sect. Am. Rocket Soc. 1955), Soc. Profl. Journalists, White House Corrs. Assn., Pentagon Corrs., Senate and House Press Gallery, Nat. Space Club (life; founder, 3d v.p., 2d v.p., 1st v.p. 1963-64, pres., bd. govs., awards chmn., chmn., founder Astronautics Engr. award since 1959, Goddard meml. dinner), Nat. Press Club. Republican. Home: Summerset Delaplane VA 22025 Office: 1925 N Lynn St # 1000 Arlington VA 22209-1707

BAKER, PATRICIA ELLIS, education educator; b. Gaines, N.Y., Nov. 7, 1938; d. Charles Otis Ellis and Ruth (Winslow) Sprong; m. Roy J. Baker, Nov. 12, 1960 (div. 1979). BS in Edn., SUNY, Brockport, 1961, MS in Edn., 1966, cert. in ednl. adminstrn., 1981; EdD in Social Studies Edn., SUNY, Buffalo, 1975. Cert. tchr. N.Y. Tchr. Jamestown (N.Y.) Pub. Schs., 1961-62, Albion (N.Y.) Cen. Schs., 1962-69; instr., then asst. prof. SUNY, Brockport, 1969—. Contbr. articles to profl. publs. Chair Orleans County McGovern Com., 1971-72; del. Dem. Nat. Conv., 1972; committeeperson Monroe County Dem. Com., Town of Sweden Dem. Com., 1976—; pres. Oak Orchard Community Health Ctr., Brockport, 1979-81. Japan Found. fellow, 1991. Mem. Nat. Coun. Social Studies (vice chmn. awards com. 1991-92, chair 1992-93, Disting. Svc. award 1986), N.Y. State Coun. Social Studies (bd. dirs. 1975—, pres. 1990-91, Outstanding Svc. award 1986, Leadership award 1991), N.Y. State. Coun. Social Studies Supervisory Assn., Rochester Area Coun. Social Studies, Phi Delta Kappa. Office: Dept Edn/Human Devel SUNY Brockport NY 14420

BAKER, PETER HARRISON, lawyer; b. Elmira, N.Y., July 31, 1952; s. D. Robert and Gloria (Berman) B.; m. Catherine Chadwick, Sept. 25, 1983; children: Michael Harrison, Kelsey Aaron. BA in English Lit., Hiram Coll., 1975; JD, Pepperdine U., 1978. Bar: N.Y. 1978, Calif. 1978. Assoc. Brian C. Flynn, Bath, N.Y., 1978-80; founder, sr. ptnr. Peter H. Baker, Hammondsport, N.Y., 1980—; justice Barrington Justice Ct., 1978-81. Bd. dirs. Wine Country Tourism Assn., Hammondsport, 1985-88, Glen H. Curtis Mus., Hammondsport, 1986—. Mem. N.Y. State Bar Assn., Steuben County Bar Assn., Glenwood Club (assoc.). Jewish. Office: 51 Main St Box 398 Hammondsport NY 14840

BAKER, RICHARD ALBERT, JR., software engineer executive; b. Fitchburg, Mass., Apr. 17, 1959; s. Richard Albert and Margaret Terese (Geoghegan) B.; m. Leisa June Mingo, Sept. 21, 1985. BS, U. N.H., 1981; postgrad., U. Rochester, 1981, Harvard U., 1982-84. Software engr. Gen. Systems Group, Salem, N.H., 1981-84; software engring. mgr. Modicon, Inc., North Andover, Mass., 1984—. Contbr. book revs. to profl. jour. Co-leader First Bapt. Ch. Jr. High Youth Group, Wilmington, Mass., 1988-89. Mem. IEEE, IEEE Computer Soc., Assn. for Computing Machinery. Home: 288 Middle St West Newbury MA 01985-1610 Office: Modicon Inc 1 High St North Andover MA 01845-2699

BAKER, RICHARD BROWN, art collector; b. Providence, Nov. 5, 1912; s. Harvey Almy and Marion North (Brown) B. Student, Internat. Union, Geneva, 1932; BA, Yale U., 1935; BA, MA, Oxford U., 1943; DFA (hon.), R.I. Sch. Design, 1978. Reporter, edit. librarian Providence Jour., 1938-40; attache Am. Embassy Madrid, 1940; editorial asst. FCC, Washington, 1941; assoc. social sci. analyst Western European sect. div. spl. info. Library of Congress, Washington, 1941-43; rsch. analyst Western European sect. OSS, Rsch. and Analysis, Washington, London, Paris, 1943-45; rsch. analyst Dept. State, Washington, 1945-47; fgn. affairs officer CIA, Washington, 1947-48; nongovt. observer Internat. League Rights of Man UN, 1954-56; mem. mus. com. R.I. Sch. Design, 1966-75, mem. fine arts com. of mus., 1976—; mem. com. on art gallery Univ. Coun. Yale U., 1962-66, 71-76; mem. governing bd. Yale U. Art Gallery, 1974—, mem. exec. com., 1978—; mem. drawings com. Whitney Mus. Am. Art, 1976—. Collection of contemporary art has been basis for exhibits at R.I. Sch. Design Mus., Providence, 1959, 64, 73, 85, Drew U., Madison, N.J., 1960, 62, Walker Art Ctr., Mpls., 1961, Wellesley (Mass.) Coll., 1963, Yale, New Haven, 1963, 75, Larry Aldrich Museum, Ridgefield, Conn., 1965, Oakland U., Rochester, Mich., 1967, 74, 79, 91, U. South Fla., Tampa, 1967, 69, Selected Works World Art, Mexico City, 1968, U. Notre Dame, South Bend, Ind., 1969, San Francisco Mus. Art, 1973, U. Pa., Phila., 1973, Stamford (Conn.) Mus., 1978, Squibb Gallery, Princeton, N.J., 1979, Katonah (N.Y.) Gallery, 1980, San Diego Mus., 1985, Portland (Oreg.) Mus. Art, 1985; mem. N.Y.C. Art Commn., 1977-80 Author: The Year of the Buzz Bomb: A Journal of London, 1944, 1952; Stairways to Another Stage: Verse, 1952. Rhodes scholar Oxford U., 1935-38. Fellow Morgan Libr.; mem. Met. Mus. (life), Art Students League (life), Am. Fedn. Arts, Archives of Am. Art, Friends Am. Arts at Yale, Mus. Modern Art, Mus. Art R.I. Sch. Design, Whitney Circle, Yale Libr. Assn., Friend of Columbia Libraries, Phi Beta Kappa, Hope Club (Providence), Grolier Club, Century Club, Yale Club (N.Y.C.), Elizabethan Club (New Haven). Home: 1185 Park Ave New York NY 10128-1310

BAKER, RICHARD EARL, JR., podiatrist; b. Plymouth, Mass., June 12, 1960; s. Richard Earl and Therese Mary (Broullard) B. BA, Holy Cros Coll., 1982; postgrad., Bridgewater State Coll., 1982-85; D of Podiatric Medicine, Ohio Coll. Podiatric Medicine, 1989. Podiatric resident West Roxbury (Mass.) VA Med. Ctr., 1989-90, chief podiatric resident, 1990-91; chief podiatry Providence VA Med. Ctr., 1991—. Contbr. articles to profl. jours. Recipient KTE Pres.'s award, 1988. Mem. Am. Podiatric Med. Assn., Am. Coll. Podopediatrics, Am. Coll. Foot Orthopedics, Amn. Bd. Podiatric Orthopedics. Roman Catholic. Home: 736A Park Ave Cranston RI 02910-2115 Office: Providence VA Med Ctr 830 Chalkstone Ave Providence RI 02908-4799

BAKER, RICHARD JOINT, lawyer; b. Barre, Mass., June 4, 1931; s. Merton Orrin and Alice Eleanor (Blanchard) B.; m. Carol Hazel Schotte, Apr. 7, 1956; children: Laurie Ann Baker Bartholoma, Richard Joint Jr., Scott C. Baker. BBA, Clark U., 1954; JD, Boston U., 1959. Bar: Mass. 1959, U.S. Supreme Ct. 1969. Atty. State Mut. Life Assurance Co. of Am., Worcester, Mass., 1959-64, asst. counsel, 1964-69, assoc. counsel, 1969-70, asst. gen. counsel, 1970, 2d v.p., assoc. gen. counsel, 1970, v.p., assoc. gen. counsel, sec., 1973, v.p. govt. affairs, sec., 1981—; v.p. govt. affairs State Mut. subs. SMA Life Assurance Co. Vice chmn. planning coun., Clark U.; bd. dirs., community trustee United Way Greater Worcester, 1978-80. With U.S. Army, 1954-56. Mem. ABA, Assn. Life Ins. Counsel (legal sect.), Am. Coun. Life Ins. (chmn.), State Mut. Employees Polit Action Com. (treas.), State Mut. Fed. PAC (exec. com., chmn. fin. svcs. com., sec.), Life Ins. Assn. of Mass., Clark U. Alumni Assn. (past pres.), Worcester Econ. Club, Worcester Torch Club (pres., bd. dirs. 1977-78), Worcester Country Club. Home: 8 Townsend Cir West Boylston MA 01583-1027 Office: State Mut Life Assurance Co Am 440 Lincoln St Worcester MA 01653-0001

BAKER, ROBERT FRANCIS, publishing executive; b. Lyons, N.Y., Nov. 3, 1935; s. Harold Smith and Zenade Cecil (Gillespie) B.; m. Carol Lee Seaver, Nov. 18, 1961; children: Charles Robert, Elizabeth Marie, Matthew Thomas. BS, SUNY, Brockport, 1957; MS, Bowling Green State U., 1958; EdD, UCLA, 1961. Contractors' overseas rep. Peace Corps, Nigeria, 1961-64; assoc. dir. tng. for Africa Peace Corps, Washington, 1964-66; gen. mgr. ednl. systems div. Litton Industries, N.Y.C., 1966-67; pub. ednl. media Am. Book Co., N.Y.C., 1967-70; v.p. planning and bus. devel. edn. group Xerox Corp., Stamford, Conn., 1970-71; pres., chief exec. officer Ginn & Co., Lexington, Mass., 1971-89; from sr. v.p. fin. to pres., chief oper. officer Houghton Mifflin Co., Boston, 1989—. Mem. adv. bd. NAACP Legal Def. and Ednl. Fund, Inc., Hammond Mus.; mem. bd. visitors Grad. Sch. Edn., UCLA. Mem. Assn. Am. Pubs. Office: Houghton Mifflin Co One Beacon St Boston MA 02108*

BAKER, ROBERT JAY, medical academic dean, surgeon; b. Chgo., Feb. 17, 1927; s. Max and Rae Baker; m. Juanita Joan Anger, Apr. 20,1 958; children: Mark, Brian, Julie Ann. AB, Miami U., Oxford, Ohio, 1946; BS, MD, U. Ill., Chgo., 1950. Diplomate Am. Bd. Surgery. Intern Cook County Hosp., Chgo., 1950-51, resident in gen. surgery, 1953-58, assoc. chmn. dept. surgery, 1959-67, chmn. dept. surgery, 1967-69; prof. surgery U. Ill. Coll. Medicine, Chgo., 1967-88, chief gen. surgery, 1974-88; chmn. dept. surgery Med. Ctr. Del., Wilmington, 1988—; dean, bd. dirs. Nat. Ctr. Advanced Med. Edn., Chgo., 1974—. Editor: Mastery of Surgery, 1984, 2d edit., 1992; contbr. numerous articles to surg. publs. 1st lt. U.S. Army, 1951-53, Korea. Decorated Silver Star. Fellow ACS; mem. Am. Assn. for the Surgery of Trauma, Am. Gastroent. Assn., Am. Surg. Assn., Cen. Surg. Assn., Chgo. Surg. Soc., Collegium Internationale de Chirurgiae Digestivae, Ill. Surg. Soc., Shock Soc., Societe Internationale de Chirurgie, Soc. for Surgery of the Alimentary Tract, Soc. Univ. Surgeons, Western Surg. Assn. Office: Med Ctr of Del Dept Surgery 501 W 14th St PO Box 1668 Wilmington DE 19899

BAKER, ROGER WILLIAM WEATHERBURN, consumer product company executive; b. Dorking, Eng., July 7, 1944; came to U.S., 1978; s. William Cecil Weatherburn and Sybil Winifred Mary (Silverside-Jones) B.; m. Paula Weeks McDermott, Dec. 18, 1976. Degree, St. Edmund's Coll., Hertfordshire, Eng., 1961, English Sch. Paris, 1962. Reporter Fin. Times, London; press rep. Confedn. Brit. Industry, London; editor IBM (U.K.) Ltd., London, 1969; speechwriter, editor IBM European Hdqrs., Paris, 1975-79; with IBM Internat. Hdqrs. N.Y.C., 1979-81; with IBM Corp. Hdqrs., 1981-89; dir. comm. Am. Brands Inc., Old Greenwich, Conn., 1989—; bd. dirs. Audit Bur. Circulations, Chgo., 1987—. Co-dir. movie Here I Am, 1985 (Gold medal N.Y. Film Festival). Bd. dirs. Northwind Undersea Inst., 1983-86, Stamford Symphony Orch., 1992—; trustee Silvermine Guild and Arts Ctr., New Canaan, Conn., 1990—. Mem. Internat. Assn. Bus. Communicators (accredited). Roman Catholic. Office: Am Brands Inc 1700 E Putnam Ave Old Greenwich CT 06870-1300

BAKER, RONALD LEE, information system executive; b. Mattoon, Ill., Dec. 8, 1938; s. Grover and Marie (Pugh) B.; m. Elizabeth Mary Smith, Sept. 26, 1981. BS, U. Ill., 1961. Mgr. engring. design systems IBM, Poughkeepsie, N.Y., 1965-89; v.p. info. systems Conn. Mut. Life, Hartford, Conn., 1989—. Mem. Leadership of Greater Hartford, 1991. With U.S. Army, 1962-64. Home: 49 Buttonwood Hill Rd Avon CT 06001-3241 Office: Conn Mut Life 140 Garden St Hartford CT 06154-0001

BAKER, STANLEY BECKWITH, education educator; b. Mpls., Sept. 3, 1935; s. Stanley Forrest and Dorothy Ruth (Beckwith) B.; m. Barbara Ann Laufenburger, Aug. 17, 1957; children: Susan Elizabeth, David Allen. BA, Augsburg Coll., 1957; MA, U. Minn., 1963; PhD, SUNY, Buffalo, 1971. Lic. psychologist, Pa. Tchr. social studies Spring Valley (Wis.) High Sch., 1957-63; tchr. history Janesville (Wis.) High Sch., 1963-66, sch. counselor, 1964-67; sch. counselor Parker High Sch., Janesville, 1967-69; asst. prof. edn. Pa. State U., University Park, 1971-74, assoc. prof. edn., 1974-84, prof. edn., 1984—. Office: Pa State U 312 CEDAR Bldg University Park PA 16802

BAKER, STEVEN ROBERT, controller; b. York, Pa., Aug. 20, 1959; s. Kenneth Bartain Baker and Patricia Ann (Maze) Bean. BS in Fin., Pa. State U., 1983. Acctg. mgr. Fed. Bankruptcy Ct. Trustee, Greensboro, N.C., 1984-85; acct. Christopher J. Ingese, CPA, McLean, Va., 1985-87; fin. systems cons. Profl. Support Svcs., Inc., Fairfax, Va., 1987-88, cons., bd. dirs., 1990—; contr. USA Direct Inc., Manchester, Pa., 1988—. Home: 728 Madison Ave York PA 17404-3107 Office: USA Direct Inc 4075 N George Street Ext Manchester PA 17345-9639

BAKER, WALTER EDWARD, ergonomist, consultant; b. Tamworth, Great Britian, Dec. 23, 1928; came to U.S., 1955; BA, Oxford (England) U., 1952, MA, 1956; DPS, Pace U., 1977. Mgr. IBM, Purchase, N.Y., 1957-78; dir. health and safety 5, Purchase, N.Y., 1978-83, dir. human factors and ergonomics, 1983-88; pres. Ergonomic Environments, Inc., Hartsdale, N.Y., 1989—; adj. prof. Pace U., White Plains, N.Y., 1977—. Author: (with others) VDT's; Health and Safety, 1984, Practical Ergonomics, 1988, Human Factors Principles, 1989; contbr. articles to profl. jours. Mem. APA, Am. Physical Soc., Human Factors Soc. Office: Ergonomic Environments Inc 214 Dogwood Lane Hartsdale NY 10530

BAKER, WILLIAM OLIVER, research chemist; b. Chestertown, Md., July 15, 1915; s. Harold May and Helen (Stokes) B.; m. Frances Burrill, Nov. 15, 1941; 1 son, Joseph Burrill. BS, Washington Coll., 1935, ScD, 1957; PhD, Princeton U., 1938; ScD, Georgetown U., 1962, U. Pitts., 1963, Seton Hall U., 1965, U. Akron, 1968, U. Mich., 1970, St. Peter's Coll., 1972, Poly. Inst. N.Y., 1973, Trinity Coll., Dublin, Ireland, 1975, Northwestern U., 1976, U. Notre Dame, 1978, Tufts U., 1981, N.J. U. Medicine and Dentistry, 1981, Clark U., 1983, Fairleigh Dickinson U., 1983, Rockefeller U., 1990; DEng., Stevens Inst. Tech., 1962, N.J. Inst. Tech., 1978; LLD (hon.), U. Glasgow, 1965, U. Pa., 1974, Kean Coll., N.J., 1976, Lehigh U., 1980, Drew U., 1981, Monmouth Coll., 1973, Clarkson Coll. Tech., 1974. With AT&T Bell Labs., 1939-80, in charge polymer research and devel., 1948-51, asst. dir. chem. and metall. research, 1951-54, dir. research, phys. scis., 1954-55, v.p. research, 1955-73, pres., 1973-79, ohmn. bd., 1979-80; bd. dirs. Summit Trust Co., Gen. Am. Investors, Inc.; dir. Health Effects Inst., 1980—; vis. lectr. Northwestern U., Princeton U., Duke; Schmitt lectr. U. Notre Dame, 1968; Harrelson lectr. N.C. State U., 1971; Herbert Spencer lectr. U. Pa., 1974; Charles M. Schwab Meml. lectr. Am. Iron and Steel Inst., 1976; NIH lectr., 1958, Metall. Soc. Am. Inst. Mining Engrs./Am. Soc. Metals disting. lectr., 1976; Miles Conrad Meml. lectr. Nat. Fedn. Abstracting and Indexing Services, 1977; Wulff lectr. MIT, 1979; Mayo Found. lectr., 1980; Logue lectr., 1981; Whitehead lectr. U. Ga., 1985; Lazerow lectr. U. Pitts., 1984; Taylor lectr. Pa. State U., 1984; other lectureships; cons. Office Sci. and Tech., 1977-81; mem. Princeton Grad. Council, 1956-64; bd. visitors Tulane U., 1963-82; mem. commn. sociotech. systems NRC, 1974-78, also chmn. adv. bd. on mil. personnel supplies, 1964-78; mem. com. on phys. chemistry of div. chemistry and chem. tech., 1963-70; also steering com. Pres.'s Food and Nutrition Study Commn. Internat. Relations Nat. Acad. Scis.-NRC, 1975; mem. panel on phys. chemistry Office Naval Research, 1948-51; past mem. Pres.'s Sci. Adv. Com., 1957-60; nat. sci. bd. NSF, 1960-66; past chmn. Nat. Sci. Info. Council, 1959-61; mem. sci. adv. bd. Nat. Security Agy., 1959-76, cons., 1976—; cons. Dept. Def., 1958-71; cons. to spl. asst. pres. for sci. and tech., 1963-73; cons. Panel of Ops. Evaluation Group, USN, 1960-62; mem. N.J. Bd. Higher Edn., 1967—, exec. com., 1970—, vice chmn., 1970-72, 82-84; mem. liaison com. for sci. and tech. Library of Congress, 1963-73; mem. Pres.'s Fgn. Intelligence Adv. Bd., 1959-77, 81-90; chmn. diplomatic telecommunication systems policy bd. Dept. State, 1984—; chmn. Pres.'s Adv. Group Anticipated Advances in Sci. and Tech., 1975-76; vice chmn. Pres.'s Com. Sci. and Tech., 1976-77; bd. regents Nat. Library Medicine, 1969-73; bd. visitors Air Force Systems Command, 1962-73; mem. mgmt. adv. council Oak Ridge Nat. Lab., 1970-78; mem. Nat. Commn. on Libraries and Info. Scis., 1971-75, Commn. on Critical Choices for Ams., 1973-75, Nat. Cancer Adv. Bd., 1974-80, Nat. Commn. on Excellence in Edn., 1981-83, Nat. Commn. on Jobs and Small Bus., 1985-87, Nat. Commn. on Role and Future State Colls. and Univs., 1985-87; mem., vice chmn. Commn. on Sci. and Tech. N.J. 1985—; mem. Carnegie Forum on Edn. Sci. Tech. and The Economy, 1985—; co-chmn. nat. coun. on sci. and tech. edn. AAAS, 1985—; mem. panel adv. Inst. Materials Rsch., Nat. Bur. Standards, 1966-69; mem. Council Trends and Perspectives, U.S. C. of C., 1966-74; chmn. tech. panels adv. to Nat. Bur. Standards, Nat. Acad. Scis.-NRC, 1969-78; mem. Nat. Council Ednl. Research, 1973-75; mem. energy research and devel. adv. council Energy Policy Office, 1973-75; mem. Project Independence adv. com. Fed. Energy Adminstrn., 1974-75, Gov.'s Com. to Evaluate Capital Needs N.J., 1974-75; mem. governing bd. Nat. Enquiry into Scholarly Communication, 1975-79; adv. council N.J. Regional Med. Library, 1975—, Spl. Libr. Assn., 1985—, Fed. Emergency Mgmt. Adv. Bd., 1980—, Gas Rsch. Inst. Adv. Bd., 1978-85; mem. adv. bd. N.J. Sci./Tech. Center, 1980-86; mem. sci. adv. bd. Robert A. Welch Found., 1968—; vis. com. for chemistry Harvard, 1959-72; mem. council Marconi Fellowships, 1978—; vis. com., div. chemistry and chem. engring. Calif. Inst. Tech., 1969-72; vis. com. on scis. and math. Drew U., 1969—; assoc. in univ. seminar on tech. and social change Columbia, 1969-80; vis. com., dept. materials sci. and engring. MIT, 1973-76; bd. overseers Coll. Engring. and Applied Sci. U. Pa., 1975—; bd. dirs. Council on Library Resources, 1970—, Health Effects Inst., 1980—, Clin. Scholar Program Robert Wood Johnson Found., 1973-76, Third Century Corp., 1973-76, EDUCOM, 1985—; organizer labs. for numerous companies; originator nat. tech. means of satellite survey Nat. Security Orgn. Fed. Telecommunications System; co-sponsor Nat. Cancer Plan, Nat. Materials Program; co-founder Aerospace Corp., 1961, Health Effects Inst., 1980—, N.J. Commn. on Sci. and Tech., 1985—. Contbr.: High Polymers, 1945, Symposium on Basic Research, AAAS, 1959, Rheology, Vol. III, 1960, Technology and Social Change, 1964, Science: The Achievement and the Promise, 1968, Ann. Rev. Materials Sci, 1976, Advancing Materials Research, 1987, various other books.; mem. editorial adv. bd. Jour. Info. Sci; past mem. adv. editorial bd. Chem. and Engring. News; hon. editorial adv. bd. Carbon; contbr. numerous articles to tech. jours. Trustee Urban Studies, Inc., 1960-78, Aerospace Corp., 1961-76, Carnegie-Mellon U., 1967-87, now emeritus, Princeton, 1964-86, now emeritus, Fund N.J., 1974—, Harry Frank Guggenheim Found., 1976—, Gen. Motors Cancer Rsch. Found., 1978—, Charles Babbage Inst., 1978—, Newark Mus., 1979-89; trustee Rockefeller U., 1960—, chmn., 1980-90, chmn. emeritus, 1990—; trustee Andrew W. Mellon Found., 1965—, chmn., 1975-90, chmn. emeritus, 1990—. Named 1 of 10 top scientists in U.S. industry, 1954; recipient Perkin medal, 1963; Honor scroll Am. Inst. Chemist, 1962; award to execs. ASTM, 1967; Edgar Marburg award, 1967; Indsl. Research Inst. medal, 1970; Frederik Philips award IEEE, 1972; Indsl. Research Man of Year award, 1973; Procter prize Sigma Xi, 1973; James Madison medal Princeton U., 1975; Mellon Inst. award, 1975; Soc. Research Adminstrs. award for disting. contbns., 1976; von Hippel award Materials Research Soc., 1978; Fahrney medal Franklin Inst., 1977; N.J. Sci/Tech. medal, 1980; Harvard U. fellow, 1937-38; Procter fellow, 1938-39; recipient Jefferson medal N.J. Patent Law Assn., 1981; David Sarnoff prize AFCEA, 1981; Vannevar Bush prize Nat. Sci. Bd., 1981; Pres.'s Nat. Security medal, 1983; Baker medal Security Affairs Support Assn., 1984; co-recipient Nat. Medal Tech., 1985, Thomas Alva Edison Sci. medal State of N.J., 1987, Nat. Materials Advancement award Fedn. Materials Socs., 1987, Nat. Medal Sci., 1988. Fellow Am. Phys. Soc., Am. Inst. Chemists (Gold medal 1975), Franklin Inst., Am. Acad. Arts and Scis.; mem. Dirs. of Indsl. Research, Am. Chem. Soc. (past mem. com. nat. def., cons., past mem. com. chemistry and pub. affairs, Priestley medal 1966, Parsons award 1976, Willard Gibbs award 1978, Madison Marshall award 1980), Am. Philos. Soc., Nat. Acad. Scis. (council 1969-72, com. sci. and pub. policy 1966-69), Nat. Acad. Engring. (Bueche prize 1986), Inst. Medicine (council 1973-75), Indsl. Research Inst. (dir. 1960-63, medal 1970), Sigma Xi, Phi Lambda Upsilon, Omicron Delta Kappa. Clubs: Chemists of N.Y. (hon.), Cosmos, Princeton of Northwestern N.J. Office: AT&T Bell Labs 600 Mountain Ave New Providence NJ 07974-2010

BAKER, WILLIAM PARR, lawyer; b. Balt., Sept. 5, 1946; s. George William and Jane (Parr) B.; m. Christine Corbett, Oct. 23, 1982; children: William Corbett, Brendan Parr, Laura Elizabeth. B.A., St. Francis Coll., Loretto, Pa., 1968; J.D., U. Md., 1971. Bar: Md. 1971, U.S. Dist. Ct. Md. 1972, U.S. Tax Ct. 1978, U.S. Sup. Ct. 1980, U.S. Ct. Apls. (4th cir.) 1982. Law clk. Md. Ct. Apls., 1971-72; ptnr. Baker and Baker, P.A. and predecessors, Balt., 1972—. Vice pres. bd. dirs. Santa Claus Anonymous, 1973-76; bd. dirs. Balt. Assn. Retarded Citizens, 1981—. Mem. ABA, Md. Bar Assn., Bar Assn. Balt. City., Golfers Charitable Assn. (bd. dirs. 1989—). Roman Catholic. Club: Balt. Country. Office: 10 Charles Pla Ste 200 Baltimore MD 21201

BAKER KNOLL, CATHERINE, state treasurer; b. Pitts.; d. Nicholas James and Theresa Mary (May) Baker; m. Charles A. Knoll Sr. (dec.); children: Charles A. Jr., Mina B., Albert B., Kim Eric. BS in Edn., Duquesne U., 1952, MS in Edn., 1973. Dir. western Pa. region Safety Adminstrn. Dept. Transp., Pitts., 1971-79; exec. dir. community svc. Dept. of Adminstrn., Allegheny County, Pa., 1980-88; treas. Pa. Treasury Dept., Harrisburg, 1988—; owner, operator pvt. bus. firm, Pitts., 1952-70. Mem. Pa. Dem. State Com., Pa. Fedn. Dem. Women, YMCA Bd., Pitts., Harrisburg, Duquesne U. Alumni Bd., Mom's House, Zontas Inc. Bd. Mem. Nat. Assn. State Treas., Women Execs. in State Gov., Coun. State Gov. (exec. com. ea. region). Roman Catholic. Office: Treasury Dept Fin Bldg Harrisburg PA 17120*

BAKIS, CHARLES EMANUEL, engineering educator; b. Allentown, Pa., Dec. 9, 1959; s. Emanuel Charles and Helen (Kladias) B. BS, Lehigh U., 1981; MS, Va. Poly. Inst. and State U., 1984; PhD, Va. Tech. Inst., 1988. Staff engr. RCA Astro-Electronics, Princeton, N.J., 1981-82; rsch. asst. Va. Tech. Inst., Blacksburg, 1982-88; asst. prof. Pa. State U., University Park, 1988—. Recipient summer faculty fellowship NASA/Am. Soc. Engring. Edn., NASA Lewis Rsch. Ctr., 1990, 91. Mem. Am. Soc. for Testing and Materials, Am. Soc. Non-destructive Testing, Soc. for Exptl. Mechanics, Am. Soc. Mech. Engrs., Am. Ceramic Soc., Am. Soc. for Engring. Edn., Tau Beta Pi, Pi Tau Sigma, Sigma Xi. Home: 80832 Stratford Dr State College PA 16801-4360 Office: Pa State Univ 227 Hammond Bldg University Park PA 16802

BAKSHIAN, ARAM, JR., writer, broadcaster, political consultant; b. Washington, Mar. 11, 1944; s. Aram Sr. and Ruth (Yeatman) B. Speechwriter for chmn. Rep. Nat. Com., Washington, 1971-72; presdl. speechwriter The White House, Washington, 1972-76, dir. presdl. speechwriting, 1981-83; comm. mgr. Union Carbide, N.Y.C., 1977-78; columnist The Washington Times, 1983-85; v.p. exec. comm. Merrill Lynch, N.Y.C., 1985-86; cons./speechwriter Sec. Treasury Simon, Washington, 1976-77, Dir. U.S. Agy. Internat. Devel., Washington, 1988-90; ind. broadcaster, Washington, 1970—. Author: The Candidates, 1980, Servus Du, 1980, Winning the White House, 1984; co-author: The Future Under President Reagan, 1981; contbr. articles to Nat. Rev. Mag., Am. Spectator, others. Recipient Order of Merit, Nat. Capital Mil. Collectors, 1971, Col.'s Commn., Gov. La., 1970; fellow Harvard Inst. Politics, 1975. Mem. Nat. Press Club (Hard Work & Inspiration award 1989), Nat. Coun. on the Humanities, Cosmos Club, Washington Canoe Club. Presbyterian. Home and Office: 4211 48th Pl NW Washington DC 20016

BALABAN, ALEXANDER JOSEPH, linguist, translator; b. Newark, Nov. 15, 1958; m. Stanislawa Chrzan, Mar. 14, 1985 (dec. Nov. 1986); m. Barbara Szefler, May 6, 1988. BA with honors, Rutgers U., 1980; MS, U. Medicine and Dentistry N.J., 1982; diploma, Essex County Police Acad., 1983; scholar's diploma (hon.), Sch. Ukrainian Studies, 1976. Rsch. scientist U. Medicine and Dentistry N.J., Newark, 1980-82; med. underwriter Mut. Benefit Life, Newark, 1982; disability specialist dept. labor State of N.J., Newark, 1982—. Author numerous poems. Mem. Rep. Nat. Com., Washington, 1976—, Newark Aux. Police Dept., 1983—. Recipient Presdl. Bicentennial award Pres. Gerald Ford, 1976. Mem. Nat. Assn. Disability Examiners, Ukrainian Nat. Assn., Beta Beta Beta. Home: PO Box 682 Kenilworth NJ 07033 Office: State of NJ Dept Labor DDD PO Box 649 Newark NJ 07102-2902

BALANESI, CHRISTOPHER DOMENIC, insurance executive; b. San Mateo, Calif., May 9, 1950; s. Ralph Joseph and Geraldine (Johnson) B.; m. Donna Kay Hall, Oct. 21, 1972; children: Christopher D. II, Peter F., Alicia Mae. BA in Psychology, Calif. State U., Sacramento, 1977. Cert. safety profl. Trainee rep. Md. Casualty Co., Sacramento, 1977-79; sr. rep. Md. Casualty Co., Denver, 1980-82; dept. mgr. Md. Casualty Co., San Bruno, Calif., 1982-86; regional mgr. Md. Casualty Co., Sacramento, 1986-89; dir. home office Md. Casualty Co., Balt., 1990—; instr. Defensive Driving Ctrs. Nat. Safety Coun., Balt., 1991—, com. mem. market segmentation, Balt. Mem. Am. Soc. Safety Engrs. Democrat. Roman Catholic. Home: PO Box 1564K Glenville PA 17329-9998 Office: Md Casualty Co 3910 Keswick Rd Baltimore MD 21211-2255

BALAS, CHARLES, equipment and instrument development executive consultant; b. Jersey City, Sept. 20, 1945; s. Charles and Mary Josephene (Kolakowski) B.; m. Barbara Helen Walter, July 9, 1972; 1 child, Jane Victoria. BE with honors, Stevens Inst. Tech., 1967, MME, 1969; MBA, Fairleigh Dickinson U., 1980. Instr. engring. Stevens Inst. Tech., Hoboken, N.J., 1969-72; sr. program leader N.Am. Philips Corp., Briarcliff Manor, N.Y., 1972-77; program mgr. Exxon Corp., Florham Park, N.J., 1977-85; exec. v.p. C.A.S. Med. Systems, Branford, Conn., 1985-88; pres. Hudson Systems Inc., Madison, Conn., 1989—, also bd. dirs. Author: (with others) Advances in Cryogenic Engineering, 1978; patentee Archival Video Disk, Thermodynamic Apparatus; co-patentee Gas Fired Heat Pump. Mem. Rep. County Com., Hudson County, N.J., 1971, Morris County N.J., 1982-83; apptd. mem. planning bd., Twp. Denville, N.J., 1983. Mem. Sigma Xi (assoc.), Tau Beta Pi. Home: 45 Beekman Pl Madison CT 06443-2400

BALBIN, JULIUS, educator, poet, translator; b. Cracow, Poland, Jan. 12, 1917; came to U.S., 1951, naturalized, 1957; s. Fryderyk and Balbina (Meisler) Lôwy. MA, Jagiellonian U., 1939; PhD, U. Vienna, 1950; postgrad., Columbia U., N.Y.C., 1964-66. Translator Marks and Clerk, Patent Attys., N.Y.C., 1953-57; researcher, writer U.S. Joint Publs. Rsch. Svc., N.Y.C., 1957-59; asst. prof. French and Russian U.S. Merchant Marine Acad., Kings Point, N.Y., 1959-63; instr. French, German, Italian, Russian and Spanish Internat. Sch. of Lang., N.Y.C., 1965-67; assoc. prof. German, French, Spanish and English Essex County Coll., Newark, 1969-83. Author: Strangled Cries, 1982, The Bitch of Buchenwald, 1986, Imperio de l'koroj, 1989; contbr. articles and poems to scholarly and lit. publs. Survivor of four Nazi concentration camps. Recipient of numerous awards for original and translated poetry in Esperanto. Mem. Modern Lang. Assn., Am. Soc. Geolinguistics (pres.), Universala Esperanto Associo, Esperanto League for N.Am., N.Y. Esperanto Soc., Assn. of Esperanto Writers. Home: 945 W End Ave Apt 9A New York NY 10025-3566

BALCH, JEROLD HOWARD, safety engineer; b. Dunbar, W.Va., Jan. 27, 1943; s. Lester V. and Edna L. (Dotson) B.; m. Evelyn Connor, June 16, 1962 (div. July 1970); m. Margaret Campbell Conway, Nov. 21, 1970; children: Cheryl, Darren. BA, Kent State U., 1968. Cert. advanced safety certificate. Mgr. human resources and safety Corning Glass Works, Solon, Ohio, 1969-72; mgr. H.R. and safety Corning Glass Works, Bradford, Pa., 1972-73, Canton, N.Y., 1973-77; mgr. human resources and safety GTE, Central Falls, R.I., 1977-84; mgr. human resources G.T.E., Whippany, N.J., 1984-85; mgr. safety GTE, Danvers, Mass., 1985-88; mgr. human resources GTE, Manchester, N.H., 1988-89; mgr. safety GTE, Danvers, 1989—; pres. Balch House Assocs., Beverly, Mass., 1990—. Pres. RIGHA-Employee Assistance Program, Providence, 1983-84; vol. Mass. chpt. Multiple Sclerosis Soc., 1985—. With USAF, 1961-65. Mem. Masons. Office: GTE Sylvania 100 Endicott St Danvers MA 01923-3623

BALCH, JOHN W(AYNE), financial services executive; b. Cumberland, Md., June 6, 1947; s. John H. Balch and Betty E. (Linn) Metz; m. Mary Frances Corazza, May 23, 1980; children: Maria Elizabeth, Margaret Frances, Leo John. BS with distinction, U. Va., 1973; MS in Acctg., Georgetown U., 1976; postgrad. cert., U.S. Naval War Coll., 1980. CPA, cert. internal auditor. Various positions CIA, Washington, 1970-84; pres., chief exec. officer Interlaken Svcs. Group Ltd., Frederick, Md., 1985—; prof. acctg. Mt. St. Mary's Coll., Emmitsburg, Md., 1985—; chmn. Intergy. Internal Audit Auth., Frederick, 1987-90. Active in Repub. State Cen. Com. County of Frederick, Md.; asst. county chmn. George Bush for Pres. Campaign, 1988. Sgt. U.S. Army Spl. Forces, 1966-69, Vietnam. Congl. nominee to U.S. Mil. Acad., 1968. Mem. VFW (life mem.), AICPA, Md. Assn. CPA's, Inst. Internal Auditors, Assn. Former Intelligence Officers (life mem.), Elephant Club Frederick County, Am. Wine Soc. (pres. Frederick County chpt. 1988-90). Roman Catholic. Home: 7195 Meadowbrook Dr Frederick MD 21702-2552 Office: Interlaken Svcs Group Ltd 178 Thomas Johnson Dr Ste 200 Frederick MD 21702-4315

BALCH, WILLIAM, psychologist, educator; b. N.Y.C., Apr. 3, 1946; s. George and Frances (High) B.; m. Martha Arlene Giles, Dec. 27, 1969 (div. 1984); 1 child, Laura Alexis; m. Brenda Kay Martin, Feb. 1, 1992. BA, Haverford (Pa.) Coll., 1968; PhD, U. Minn., 1976. Teaching and rsch. asst. U. Minn., Mpls., 1971-76; instr. Davidson (N.C.) Coll., 1976-77; postdoctoral fellow U. Conn., Storrs, 1977-8; faculty mem. Pa. State U., Altoona, 1978—; mem. promotion and tenure coms. Pa. State U., Altoona, 1987—; chmn. behavior mgmt. com. Altoona Ctr., 1983-86. Contbr. articles to profl. jours. Trustee Humane Soc., Blair County, Pa., 1979-83. With U.S. Army, 1968-71. NIMH fellow, 1976. Mem. Am. Psychol. Soc. Office: Pa State U Altoona PA 16601

BALCHUNAS, GERARD ANDREW, graphic designer; b. Boston, July 24, 1955; s. Elizabeth (O'Leary) B.; m. Carol Lee Adkins. BA, Art Inst. Boston, 1975. Assoc. art dir. DCI Assocs., Boston, 1979-80; art dir. MWD, Inc., Providence, 1980-81; prin., graphic designer Adkins/Balchunas Design, Providence, 1981—; instr., R.I. Sch. Design, Providence, 1988—. Recipient Merit award N.Y. Art Dirs. Club, 1987, Creative Club of Boston, 1988, Boston Art Dirs. Club, 1987, Cert. of Design Excellence, Print Mag., 1986, Bronze award Nat. Calendar Assn., 1991. Office: Adkins/Balchunas Design 163 Exchange St Pawtucket RI 02860-2241

BALDACCHINO, JOSEPH FRANCIS, research institute administrator, publisher; b. Detroit, Mar. 17, 1948; s. Joseph and Sarah Elizabeth (McIntyre) B.; m. Ellen Torrey Prior, Apr. 7, 1973; children: John Granville, David Matthew, Rebecca Elizabeth, Elizabeth Anne. BS magna cum laude, Mount St. Mary's Coll., 1970; MA, The Cath. U. of Am., 1983. Editor Dorchester News, Cambridge, Md., 1971-72; assoc. editor Human Events, Washington, 1972—; pub. Humanitas, Washington, 1987—, editor, 1992—; pres. Nat. Humanities Inst., Washington, 1984—; mem. Main St. com. Rockford Inst. Editor: Educating for Virtue, 1988; author: Economics and the Moral Order, 1985, (with others) Irving Babbitt in Our Time, 1986; contbr. articles to profl. jours. Mem. Delta Epsilon Sigma, Pi Gamma Mu, Pi Sigma Alpha. Roman Catholic. Home: 12508 Killian Ln Bowie MD 20715 Office: Nat Humanities Inst 214 Massachusetts Ave NE Ste 470 Washington DC 20002

BALDACCI, ROBERT EUGENE, JR., real estate developer; b. Bangor, Maine, June 20, 1952; s. Robert Eugene and Rosemary (Karam) B.; m. Sept. 8, 1983 (div.); 1 child, Robert Eugene III; m. Kathleen Sue Brennan, Aug. 11, 1985; stepchildren: Sean, Darren, Shannon. BA, U. Maine, Orono, 1974, MPA, 1975. Researcher U. Maine, Orono, 1974-75; econ. developer Ea. Maine Devel. Corp., Bangor, 1976-80; devel. dir. City of Old Town, Maine, 1980-82; dir. devel. Fransway Realty, Bangor, 1982-83; pres. Baldacci Assocs., Bangor, 1984—; prin. Mariner Capital Group, Bangor, 1988—; bd. dirs. Bangor Ctr. Mgmt. Corp, Fin. Authority Maine, Augusta, chmn., 1983-85; vice chmn. Maine Guarantee Authority, Augusta, 1981-83; v.p. Maine Housing Enterprise, Portland, 1988—. Chmn. bd. regents Indsl. Devel. Coun. Maine, 1980-83; bd. dirs. Good Samaritan Agy., Bangor, 1982-83, Gov.'s Com. on Tax-exempt Bonds, 1985, Joint Standing Com. on Econ. Devel., 1987; mem. fin. com. Brennan for Gov., Portland, 1980, Mitchell for Senate, Portland, 1988; chmn. Gov.'s Inaugural Ball Com., Bangor, 1981. Named to polit. sci. honor soc. U. Main, Orono, 1975; recipient Family Project of Yr., Farmers Home Adminstrn., 1987. Mem. Maine Real Estate Devel. Assn. (bd. dirs. 1987—), Maine Housing Mgr.'s Assn., Manuscript Soc. Democrat. Roman Catholic. Home: 75 Boutelle Rd Bangor ME 04401-5842 Office: Baldacci Assocs 183 Harlow St Bangor ME 04401-4930

BALDRIDGE, HAROLD G., theatre director; b. Provost, Alta., Can., July 26, 1936; s. Burt Leland and Jean Louise (Ferris) B.; m. Mary Humphrey, Aug. 16, 1958; children: William, Elizabeth Ripley. BA in Drama, BEd, U. Alta., 1958. Cert. in Dramatic Arts. Instr., prodn. supr. Neighborhood Playhouse Sch. of the Theatre, N.Y.C., 1960-65; artistic dir. Woodstock Playhouse, Woodstock, N.Y., 1964-72, Theatre Calgary, Alta., 1972-79; dir. Neighborhood Playhouse Sch. of the Theatre, N.Y.C., 1981—. Office: Neighborhood Playhouse 340 E 54th St New York NY 10022-5099

BALDRIGE, LETITIA, writer, management training consultant; b. Miami Beach, Fla.; d. Howard Malcolm and Regina (Connell) B.; m. Robert Hollensteiner; children: Clare, Malcolm. BA, Vassar Coll., 1946; postgrad., U. Geneva, 1946-48; D.H.L. (hon.), Creighton U., 1979, Mt. St. Mary's Coll., 1980, Bryant Coll., 1987, Kenyon Coll., 1990. Personal-social sec. to amb. Am. Embassy, Paris, 1948-51; intelligence officer Washington, 1951-53; asst. to amb. Am. Embassy, Rome, 1953-56; dir. pub. rels. Tiffany & Co., 1956-60; social sec. The White House, 1961-63; pres. Letitia Baldrige Enterprises, Chgo., 1964-69; dir. consumer affairs Burlington Industries, 1969-71; pres. Letitia Baldrige Enterprises, Inc., N.Y.C. and Washington, 1972—; bd. dirs. Outlet Co., Fed. Home Loan Bank Atlanta, Hartmarx Corp. Author: Roman Candle, 1956, Tiffany Table Settings, 1958, Of Diamonds and Diplomats, 1968, Home, 1972, Juggling, 1976, Amy Vanderbilt's Complete Book of Etiquette, 1978, Amy Vanderbilt's Everyday Etiquette, 1979, Entertainers, 1981, Letitia Baldrige's Complete Guide to Executive Manners, 1985, Letitia Baldrige's Complete Guide to a Great Social Life, 1987, Complete Guide to the New Manners for the '90s, 1990; (novel) Public Affairs Private Relations, 1990; columnist Copley News Syndicate; contbr. to popular mags. Bd. dirs. Woodrow Wilson Found., Inst. Internat. Edn.; trustee Kenyon Coll., Gambier, Ohio; mem. adv. bd. Folger Shakespeare Libr., Washington, Mount Vernon Ladies Assn., Washington. Republican. Office: Letitia Baldrige Enterprises Inc PO Box 32287 Washington DC 20007-0587

BALDUCCI, STEPHEN WATTS, marketing and sales executive; b. Richmond, Va., Jan. 19, 1950; s. Giotto R. and Emily Jane (Snead) B.; m. Elaine Dawson, Mar. 1, 1980; 1 child, Natalie Lauren. BS in Bus. Adminstrn. and Mgmt., Va. Commonwealth U., 1977. Cert. sales exec. Sales rep., account mgr. Wright Brokerage Inc., Richmond, 1978-80; systems sales rep. Remco Bus. Systems, Inc., Washington, 1980-82; dist. sales mgr. Medline Industries, Inc., Northbrook, Ill., 1982-84; dir. physician mktg. MetPath, Inc., Washington, 1985—. Mem. Sales and Mktg. Execs. of Met. Washington, Sales and Mktg. Execs. Internat., Order Sons of Italy, Moose, Elks. Roman Catholic. Home: 4410 Vantage Ct Alexandria VA 22306-1238 Office: MetPath Inc 1550 E Gude Dr Rockville MD 20850

BALDWIN, CHARLES HENRY, financial services executive; b. New Haven, May 26, 1942; s. Charles Henry and Esther (Micknak) B.; m. Anne DeStefano, June 10, 1967; 1 child, Christopher N. MS with honors, Northeastern U., 1965; MBA, Amos Tuck Sch. Bus., 1967. CLU; chartered fin. cons. Ins. exec. Holiday Assocs., Boston, 1967-71; founder, ptnr. Baldwin & Clark Co., Boston, 1971—, Baldwin & Clarke Pension Cons., Inc., Bedford, N.H., 1981—, Baldwin & Clarke Adv. Svcs., Inc., Bedford, 1985—, Baldwin & Clarke Corp. Fin., Inc., Bedford, 1989—. Contbr. articles to profl. and recreational publs. Chairman Brentwood (N.H.) Planning Bd., 1970-71; dir., mem. exec., investment and fin. coms. Crotched Mountain Found. and Rehab. Ctr., Greenfield, N.H., 1980—; chmn. bd. trustees N.H. Retirement System, Concord, 1983—. 1st lt. U.S. Army, 1969. Mem. Assn. Advanced Life Underwriting, Am. Soc. CLUs and Chartered Fin. Cons., Million Dollar Round Table, Internat. Assn. Fin. Planners, Estate Planning Coun., Trout Unltd., BMW Car Club Am. (founder, officer 1969-73), Beta Gamma Sigma. Republican. Methodist. Office: Baldwin & Clarke Cos 116B S River Rd Bedford NH 03110-6734

BALDWIN, CHARLES WILLIAM, fund raising executive; b. Sharpsville, Ind., Mar. 1, 1915; s. James H. and Pearl Mabel (Fisher) B.; m. Marijean Harding, Sept. 1937 (div. 1942); children: Emily Lane, James William; m. Mary Jane Frisco, Nov. 23, 1943. AB, Ind. U., 1958; LLB, LaSalle Extension U., 1953; MEA, George Washington U., 1963. Registered profl. engr., Va. In various positions GM-Delco Products Div., 1965-85; dir. community devel. programs Adirondack Econ. Devel. Corp., Saranac Lake, N.Y., 1988—; sec. New Enterprise Devel. Programs, Inc., Saranac Lake, 1991—. Mem. Pendragon Theatre, Lake Placid Ctr. for Arts, Adirondack Ctr. for Arts, Visitors Interpretive Ctr. Inst., N.Y. Mem. Adirondack Mountain Club. Office: New Enterprise Devel Inc 30 Main St Saranac Lake NY 12983-1706

BALDWIN, DAVID ALLEN, political science educator; b. Indpls., July 28, 1936; s. James Howell and Pearl Mabel (Fisher) B.; m. Marilyn Claire Austin, Aug. 10, 1957 (div. Sept. 1990); children: Sarah, Rebecca, Emily; m. Helen Virginia Milner, May 24, 1991. AB, Ind. U., 1958; MA, Princeton U., 1961, PhD, 1965; MA (hon.), Dartmouth Coll., 1978. Asst. prof. govt. Dartmouth Coll., Hanover, N.H., 1965-70, assoc. prof. govt., 1970-75, John S. Dickey Prof., 1975-80, prof. govt., 1980-85; prof. polit. sci. Columbia U., N.Y.C., 1985-89, Ira Wallach Prof., 1989—; dir. Inst. of War and Peace Studies, Columbia U., 1987—. Author: Foreign Aid, 1966, Economic Statecraft, 1985 (Kammerer award 1986), Paradoxes of Power, 1989, Economic Development and Foreign Policy, 1966; editorial bd. Internat. Orgn., 1984—, Polit. Sci. quarterly, N.Y.C., 1989—, Jour. of Internat. Affairs, N.Y.C., 1988—. Mem. Coun. on Fgn. Rels., N.Y.C., 1986—. 1st lt. U.S. Army, 1962-63. Recipient Moffat Econs. prize Ind. U., Bloomington, 1958, fellowships German Marshall Fund, Washington, 1982-83, Brookings Instn., Washington, 1964-65, Danforth Found., St. Louis, 1958-64. Mem. Am. Polit. Sci. Assn. (recipient Kammerer award 1986), Internat. Polit. Sci. Assn., Internat. Studies Assn., British Internat. Studies Assn., Acad. Polit. Sci., Phi Beta Kappa. Home: 450 Riverside Dr New York NY 10027-6821 Office: Inst of War & Peace Studies Columbia University New York NY 10027

BALDWIN, DOROTHY LEILA, educator; b. Irvington, N.J., Feb. 28, 1948; d. Daniel Thomas and Lillian Frances (Wainright) B. BA, Kean Coll., Union, N.J., 1969, MA in Edn. and Humanities, 1971; EdD in Adminstrn. & Supervision, Seton Hall U., 1987, cert. reading specialist, 1979, cert. bus. adminstr., 1985. Tchr., reading coord. St. Paul Apostle Sch. Irvington, 1969-74; tchr. Summit (N.J.) Jr. High Sch., 1975-79; social studies coord. K-9, chmn. dept. 7-9 Summit Pub. schs., 1979-87; social studies supr. Livingston (N.J.) Pub. Schs., 1987; prin. Point Road Sch, Little Silver, N.J., 1987-89; dir. gifted edn. K-12 Clifton, N.J., 1989-90; prin. Sch. Two, Clifton, N.J., 1989-90, Deerfield Sch., Mountainside, 1990-92, Eisenhower Sch., Bridgewater-Raritan, N.J., 1992—; adj. prof. Montclair (N.J.) State Coll.; tchr. adult and community schs.; cons. in field; workshop coord. Author books; contbr. articles to profl. jours. PTA scholar, 1965. Mem. Nat. Assn. Elem. Sch. Prins., Nat. Coun. Social Studies Assn., Am. Assn. Sch. Adminstrs., ASCD, N.J. Assn. Elem. Sch. Prins., Somerset County Assn. Elem. Sch. Prins., Phi Delta Kappa, Kappa Delta Pi. Home: 737 River Rd Chatham NJ 07928-1136 Office: Eisenhower Sch Bridgewater NJ 08807

BALDWIN, IAN, JR., publisher, editor; b. N.Y.C., Dec. 18, 1938; s. Ian Sr. and Rose (Weld) B.; m. Sybil Kinnecutt, June 2, 1962 (div. 1976); children: Sarah, Benjamin; m. Margaret Preston, June 21, 1980; children: Angus, Rose. BA in English, Columbia U., 1962; MA in Psychology, Godard Coll., 1980. Coll. traveler Holt, Rinehart & Winston, Inc., N.Y.C., 1964-66, editor, 1966-69; publs. dir. Inst. for World Policy, N.Y.C., 1969-74; self employed cons. Environ. Defense Fund, N.Y.C., 1975-80, Nat. Audubon Soc., N.Y.C., 1980-83; pres. Chelsea Green Pub. Co., Post Mills, Vt., 1984—; trustee Buddhayana Found., Marion, Mass., 1974-82, E.F. Schumacher Soc., Great Barrington, Mass., 1978-84. Trustee Chelsea (Vt.) Pub. Library, 1990—; coord. Chelsea Recycling Vols., 1990—. Mem. Am. Booksellers Assn., Vt. Book. Pubs. Assn., Columbia Club. Democrat. Buddhist. Home: PO Box 283 Chelsea VT 05038-0283 Office: Chelsea Green Pub Co PO Box 130 Post Mills VT 05058-0130

BALDWIN, THOMAS JAMES, restaurant chain financial executive, accountant, educator; b. N.Y.C., May 31, 1955; s. Warren and Lillian Elizabeth (Oliveros) B.; m. Colleen Anne Dolan, Sept. 12, 1987. BBA in Acctg., Iona Coll., 1978, MBA in Fin. with honors, 1984. CPA, N.Y. Various sr. fin. mgmt. positions Gen. Foods Corp., N.Y.C. and Denver, 1976-85; v.p. strategic planning Citicorp-Citibank, N.Y.C., 1985-86; v.p. fin., chief fin. officer Le Peep Restaurants Inc., Denver and N.Y.C., 1986-89, Quantum Restaurant Group, Inc., N.Y.C., 1989—; bd. dirs. PJL Restaurant Corp., N.Y.C., Mortons of Chgo., Inc., ; adj. prof. Fordham U., 1985. Mem. AICPA, N.Y. Soc. CPAs, Ga. Soc. CPAs, Ill. Soc. CPAs, Am. Mgmt. Assn., Planning Forum, K.C. Republican. Roman Catholic. Office: Quantum Restaurant Group 97 Powerhouse Rd Ste 101 Roslyn Heights NY 11577-2046

BALDWIN, VELMA NEVILLE WILSON, personnel consultant; b. Meade, Kans., Aug. 31, 1918; d. Charles Chester and Anna Velma (Neville) Wilson; m. Claude David Baldwin, Jan. 31, 1942 (dec. Nov. 1976). AB, U. Kans., 1940. Placement working students U. Kans., 1940-41; with War Dept., Washington, 1942-45; rsch asst. Dr. A.C. Kinsey, Ind. U., 1946; with Carter Oil Co., Denver, 1948-50; with pers. Bur. Budget, Washington, 1951-55; asst. to dir. pers. Treasury Dept., 1955-59; pers. officer, dir. adminstrn. Office Mgmt. and Budget, 1959-79; cons. in field. Recipient Career Svc. award Nat. Civil Svc. League, 1975. Mem. Am. Soc. Pub. Adminstrn. (past exec. bd.), Soc. Pers. Adminstrn. (exec. bd.), Cosmos Club (Washington), Phi Beta Kappa. Home: 2234 49th St NW Washington DC 20007-1057

BALES, JOHN THOMPSON, sales executive; b. Dayton, Ohio, Apr. 13, 1941; s. Ferdinand F. and Reva L. Bales; m. Mary Alice Wilbrett, July 16, 1966; children: Thomas Michael, Melinda Rae. BS in Chemistry, Western Mich. U., 1964. With Hercules Inc., 1965-78; product supr. Hercules Inc., Wilmington, Del., 1970-73; asst. dist. mgr. Hercules Inc., Portland, Oreg., 1975-78, regional sales mgr., 1978-82; corp. accounts dir. Hercules Inc., Wilmington, 1984-87, sales dir., 1987-89, mktg. dir., 1989—; trustee Pulp & Paper Found., Kalamazoo, Mich., 1986—, pres., 1990—. Mem. Paper Industry Mgmt. Assn. (com. chmn. 1988), TAPPI. Lutheran. Office: Hercules Inc Hercules Pla Wilmington DE 19894

BALFE, HARRY, II, political science educator; b. N.Y.C., Apr. 27, 1922; s. Raymond Adams and Dorothy (MacDonald) B.; B.A., Trinity Coll., 1947; J.D., Cath. U., 1952; M.A., Am. U. Sch. Internat. Service, 1964; m. Judith Lee Huggins, May 8, 1965; children: Thomas James, Jennifer Linda. Advt. asst. to v.p. Macy's Dept. Store, 1946-47; intelligence research analyst Georgetown U. Research Project, Washington, 1953-57; tchr. history, econs. Montclair (N.J.) Acad., 1957-66, asst. prof. history Montclair State Coll., Upper Montclair, N.J., 1966-69, asst. prof. polit. sci., 1969-80, assoc. prof., 1980—; assoc. Danforth Found., 1970—. Chmn., Mayor's Com. UN Week, Montclair, 1966; mem. Charter Commn. Study Group, Montclair, 1963; N.J. election supr. NBC, 1970-73; Dem. candidate N.Y. State Assembly, N.Y.C., 1946; mem. Essex County Dem. Com., 1962-65, 68-78; mem. nat. bd. dirs. Am. Vets. Com., 1970-73; mem. bd. Nat. Consumers League, 1977-79; bd. dirs. Consumers League N.J., 1967—, Montclair Adult Sch., 1974-78, Montclair Bicentennial Com. to celebrate the U.S. Constn., 1987—. Served with USAF, 1943-46. Mem. UN Assn., Am. Polit. Sci. Assn., N.J. Polit. Sci. Assn. (exec. council 1978—), Am. Soc. Internat. Law, Supreme Ct. Hist. Soc. Common Cause, Pi Gamma Mu, Delta Kappa Epsilon. Unitarian. Home: 94 Mt Hebron Rd Montclair NJ 07043-1504 Office: Montclair State Coll Dept Polit Sci Upper Montclair NJ 07043

BALGA, JOHN THEODORE, JR., software development executive; b. Bridgeport, Conn., Oct. 4, 1958; s. John Theodore and Shirley (Segala) B.;m. Catherine Whitney Vollmer, Oct. 9, 1982; children: Christopher John, Miranda Paige. BS, U. Bridgeport, 1980, MS, 1982; MBA, U. New Haven, 1991. Software engr. GE, Bridgeport, 1980-83; sr. mem. ITT, Shelton, Conn., 1983-85; project mgr. United Techs., Stratford, Conn., 1985-89; mgr. software Pitney Bowes, Shelton, 1989—. Contbr. articles to profl. jours. Scoutmaster Boy Scouts Am., Stratford, 1990-91. Mem. Assn. for Computing Machinery (voting), IEEE. Office: Pitney Bowes 35 Waterview Ave Bridgeport CT 06608-2823

BALIN, NANCY ANNE, ophthalmologist; b. Phila., Oct. 5, 1954. BA cum laude, U. Vt., 1976; MD, U. Pa., 1980. Intern dept. internal medicine St. Joseph Hosp., Denver, 1980-81; resident dept. ophthalmology Albany (N.Y.) Med. Ctr., 1981-84; gen. ophthalmologist Community Health Plan, Latham, N.Y., 1984-85, Hampshire Eye & Ear Assn., Northampton, Mass., 1986—. Fellow Am. Acad. Ophthalmologists, Am. Coll. Surgeons; mem. AMA, Am. Kerato-Refractive Soc., Am. Acad. Cataract & Refractive Surgery, Mass. Soc. Eye Physicians & Surgeons, Mass. Med. Soc., Springfield Ophthalmologic Soc., Hampshire County Med. Soc. Office: Hampshire Eye & Ear Assocs 61 Locust St Northampton MA 01060

BALINSKY, BENJAMIN, retired psychology educator; b. N.Y.C., Oct. 26, 1913; s. Jacob and Jenny (Broder) B.; m. Ruth Goldberg, Oct. 10, 1937; children: Judith Knee, Frances Berger. BA, CUNY, 1935; MA, Columbia U., 1937; PhD, NYU, 1940. Lic. psychologist, N.Y.; diplomate in clin. psychology Am. Bd. Profl. Providers in Psychology. Intern, researcher Bellevue Hosp., N.Y.C., 1935-39; psychologist Nat. Youth Adminstrn., N.Y.C., 1939-42; cons. War Dept., N.Y.C., 1942-44; psychologist, counselor Vocat. Adv. Svc., N.Y.C., 1945-47; instr. to prof. psychology CCNY, 1947-69; prof. and chmn. psychology Baruch Coll., CUNY, 1969-79, prof. emeritus psychology, 1979—; chief cons.BFS Inc., 1960-89. Co-author: Counseling and Psychology, 1951, The Executive Interview, 1959; author booklets: The Selection Interview, 1962, Improving Personnel Selection Through Effective Interviewing, 1978. Lectr. Mental Hygiene Clinic, N.Y.C., 1989. Fellow AAAS, APA (Disting. Psychologist award 1990). Jewish.

BALINT, JOHN ALEXANDER, physician; b. Budapest, Hungary, Feb. 25, 1925; came to U.S., 1958; s. Michael M. and Alice (Szekely-Kovacs) B.; m. Jean M. Gibson, Jan. 15, 1949; children: Peter John, Jane Penelope. BA, Cambridge U., Eng., 1945, MBBChir, 1948; MRcP, Royal Coll. Physicians, London, 1952. House physician various London Hosps., 1949-53; registrar Cen. Middlesex Hosp., London, 1953-58; fellow in gastroenterology U. Cin., 1958-59; trainee in biochem. Johns Hopkins U., Balt., 1959-60; asst. prof. medicine U. Ala., Birmingham, 1960-63; assoc. prof., head div. of gastroenterology Albany (N.Y.) Med. Coll., 1963-68, prof., head div. of gastroenterology, 1968-81, prof., chair medicine, 1981-88, Beebe prof. of medicine, 1988—. Co-author several textbooks; contbr. 75 sci. papers and 80 abstracts to profl. publs. Squadron leader, Royal Air Force, 1950-52. Mem. Am. Physiological Soc., Am. Soc. Clin. Investigation, Am. Gastroent. Assn., British Soc. Gastroent. Office: Albany Med Ctr Dept Medicine Albany NY 12208

BALINT, PAUL RAYMOND, vocational school educator; b. McKeesport, Pa., Feb. 20, 1948; s. Paul Raymond and Susan Theresa (Chasko) B.; m. Leslie Ann Hartzer, June 10, 1967; 1 child, Lisa Anne Balint Novosel. Student, Community Coll. Allegheny Co., Monroeville and West Mifflin, Pa., 1984-91; BS in Vocat. Edn., U. Pitts., 1990. Machinist U.S.S. Homestead Wks., Homestead, Pa., 1966-83, machine shop apprentice instr., 1983-85; tech. instr. Forbes Rd. East Area Vocat. Tech. Sch., Monroeville, Pa., 1985—; resident resource person Indiana U., Monroeville, 1990—; mem. Students Assistance Program Core Team; instr. Community Coll. Allegheny County, 1985—. Coord. Stand By Me, Monroeville, 1990—. Mem. Am. Vocat. Assn., Vocat. Indsl. Clubs Am. (advisor 1989—, Appreciation award 1990). Democrat. Roman Catholic. Office: Forbes Rd E Area Vocat Sch 607 Beatty Rd Monroeville PA 15146-1550

BALKA, SIGMUND RONELL, lawyer; b. Phila., Aug. 1, 1935; s. I. Edwin and Jane (Chernicoff) B.; m. Elinor Bernstein, May 29, 1966. AB, Williams Coll., 1956; JD, Harvard U., 1959. Bar: Pa. and D.C. 1961, N.Y. 1969, U.S. Supreme Ct. 1966. Sr. atty. Lilco, Mineola, N.Y., 1969-70; v.p., gen. counsel Brown Boveri Corp., North Brunswick, N.J., 1970-75; asst. gen. counsel Power Authority State N.Y., N.Y.C., 1975-80; gen. counsel Krasdale Foods, Inc., N.Y.C., 1980—; bd. dirs. Am. Corp. Counsel Assn., Met. N.Y. chpt.; pres. Graphic Arts Coun. N.Y., 1980—. Chmn. Hunts Point Environ. Protection Coun., N.Y.C., 1980—; chmn. law com. N.Y.C. Community Bd. 6, Queens, 1980-88, chmn. econ. devel. com., 1988—; chmn. Soc. for a Better Bronx, 1985—; bd. dirs. Bronx Arts Coun., 1981—, Greater N.Y. Met. Food Coun., 1986—, Jewish Repertory Theatre, 1987—; chmn. Bronx Borough Pres.'s Adv. Com. on Resource Recovery, 1988-90. Mem. ABA (co-chmn. corp. law dept. pro bono project 1986-88, chmn. 1988-90), Ass. of Bar of City of N.Y., Fed. Bar Assn., Am. Corp. Counsel Inst. (bd. dirs. 1992—). Office: Krasdale Foods Inc 400 Food Center Dr Bronx NY 10474-7034

BALL, BENNETT LESTER, military officer; b. Tuscaloosa, Ala., Sept. 5, 1949; s. Oliver and Vera Mae (Hargrove) B.; m. Janta Sudta, Jan. 18, 1972; children: Weepargorn, Kanya Verna, Sarinya Leslie. Grad. high sch., Boston. Enlisted USAF, 1968, advanced through grades to master sgt., 1989; apprentice inventory mgmt. specialist 437 Svc. Squadron, Charleston, S.C., 1968-70; inventory mgmt. specialist 635 Supply Squadron, Utapao, Thailand, 1970-72; supply awp monitor 6280 Supply Squadron, Takhli, Thailand, 1972-74; non-commd. officer in charge 388 Supply Squadron, Korat, Thailand, 1977-82; wing verification monitor 380 Bomb Med. Wing, Plattsburgh, N.Y., 1976-77; with 43 Supply Squadron, Andersen, Guam, 1977-82, 83-85; unit material control liaison Detachment 4, 40th Tactical Group, Decimomanno, Italy, 1982-83; NCOIC bench stock 509 Supply Squadron, Pease, N.H., 1985-86, 87-88; NCOIC mgmt. system br. Detachment 4 4448th Mobility Support Squadron, Riyadh, Saudi Arabia, 1986-87; furnishing mgmt. supt. 509 Svc. Squadron, Pease, 1988-91; supt. furnishing mgmt. office Svcs. Squadron, Loring AFB, Limestone, Maine, 1991—. Mem. NAACP, VFW, Air Force Assn., Non-Commd. Officer Assn., Am. Legion. Home: 31 Forest Park Dr Rochester NH 03868-8704 Office: 42 Svc Squadron/SVD Loring AFB Limestone ME 04751-5000

BALL, GEORGE WILLIAM, computer science educator; b. Warren, Pa., Apr. 3, 1941; s. William Lincoln and Dorothy (Levey) B.; m. Sandra S. Shirk, June 6, 1963 (wid. Feb. 1975); 1 child, Christopher; m. Rita Mae Burns, Dec. 15, 1984; children: Derrick, Douglas, Jolene, Janice, Tobias, Thomas, Timothy. BS in Math., Union Coll., 1963; MS in Math., Syracuse U., 1965, PhD in Math., 1972; MS in Computer Sci., Rochester Inst. Tech., 1988. Grad. asst. Syracuse (N.Y.) U., 1963-68; math. educator Alfred (N.Y.) U., 1968-82; grad. asst. Rochester (N.Y.) Inst. Tech., 1982-83; assoc. prof. computer sci. Alfred U., 1983—. Treas. St. Peter's Meml. Ch., Dansville, N.Y., 1982—, Episcopal Triparish Ministry, Hornell, N.Y., 1984—. Mem. Assn. for Computing Machinery. Republican. Episcopalian. Home: 6929 County Line Rd Wayland NY 14572-9353 Office: Alfred U 26 N Main St Alfred NY 14802-1232

BALL, HOWARD LEE, editor; b. Haskell, N.J., July 3, 1929; s. Howard Lee and Harriet (Stephens) B.; m. Margaret Czinke, Oct. 31, 1955 (div. 1956); m. Diane Shwartz, July 27, 1957 (div. 1970); children: Diane, Guy, Patricia, Stephanie. BA, Western Mich. U., 1951. Newscaster Sta. WKMI, Kalamazoo, 1952-56; reporter Pompton Lakes (N.J.) Bulletin, 1956-58, Morning Call, Paterson, N.J., 1958-60; reporter Paterson News, 1960-64, suburban editor, 1964-67; news dir. Sta. WKER, Pompton Lakes, 1964-68; bur. chief Morning Call, Paterson, 1967-68; editor Suburban Trends, Butler, N.J., 1968—; cons. editor Suburban Newspapers N.J., Paramus, 1986-91; adjunct prof. Journalism, William Paterson Coll. N.J. Mem. Congl. Acad. Com., 8th Dist., N.J., 1970—, Spl. Adv. Com., Sen. Leanna Brown, 1988. M/Sgt. NG, 1947-56. Mem. Soc. Profl. Journalists, N.J. Press Assn. (Best Reporter award, 1970, 71), SAR, Descendants of Founders of N.J. Republican. Home: 130 Romain Ave Pompton Lakes NJ 07442-1229 Office: Suburban Trends 10 Park Pl Butler NJ 07405-1311

BALL, SUSAN, arts administrator, art historian; b. Altadena, Calif., May 25, 1947; d. Charles Russell and Catherine (Piller) B.; m. Edward Kaufman, Mar. 19, 1983; 1 child, Emily Catherine. BA, Scripps Coll., 1969; MA, U. Calif., Riverside, 1974; M of Philosophy, Yale U., 1976, PhD, 1978; postgrad., U. Chgo., 1983-85. Asst. prof. art history dept. U. Del., Newark, 1978-82; asst. treas. Chase Manhattan Bank, N.Y.C. and Chgo., 1982-85; dir. govt. affairs Art Inst. Chgo., 1985-86; exec. dir. Coll. Art Assn., N.Y.C., 1986—. Author: Ozenfant and Purism, 1982; contbr. articles to art catalogs. Mem. Nat. Humanities Alliance (bd. dirs. 1988—), Nat. Cultural Alliance (bd. dirs. 1989—), Am. Coun. Learned Socs. (exec. com. Conf. Adminstrv. Officers 1989—). Democrat. Office: Coll Art Assn 5th Fl 275 7th Ave New York NY 10001-6708

BALL, WILLIAM, microbiology educator, consultant; b. Phila., Mar. 3, 1921; s. Jacob Edward and Elsie (Greenberg) B.; m. Sylvia Braslow, Nov. 27, 1947; children: David Stuart, Lisa Robin. BSc in Biology, Phila. Coll. Pharmacy and Sci., 1943, MSc in Biology, 1948, ScD in Biology, 1950. Instr. biology Phila. Coll. Pharmacy and Sci., 1946-50, 65-66; microbiologist Med. Arts Lab., Jenkintown, Pa., 1950-51; parasitologist Albert Einstein Med. Ctrs., Phila., 1952-54; dir., owner Park Labs., Phila., 1954-70; tech. dir. Damon Med. Lab., Trevose, Pa., 1970-80; cons. William Ball, Sc.D., Inc., Erdenheim, Pa., 1980-82; adj. prof. biology Beaver Coll., Glenside, Pa., 1982—; cons. in microbiology and serology VA Hosp., Phila., 1966-80; cons. in infection control and parasitology. Co-editor: Infection Control in Health Care Facilities, 1977, Immunological and Serological Aspects of Clinical Parasitology, 1981, Free Living Amoebas in Human Infections, 1981. Coord. Erdenheim Town Watch, 1984—. Capt. U.S. Army, 1943-46, PTO. Recipient Legion of Honor, Chapel of Four Chaplains, 1973. Mem. Am. Soc. for Microbiology (co-chmn., mem. workshop com. and symposium com. Ea. Pa. br.), Am. Assn. Bioanalysts (cert. bioanalyst clin. lab. dir.), Am. Acad. Microbiology (registered). Jewish. Home: 411 Glenway Rd Philadelphia PA 19118-1019

BALL, WILLIAM AUSTIN, health facility director, researcher; b. L.A., Feb. 16, 1948; s. Joe Martin and Norma Lou (Schouweiler) B.; m. Rachel Yvette Jeanne Tullier, July 21, 1972. BA summa cum laude, Harvard Coll., 1970; student, Ecole Normale Supérieure, Paris, 1970-71; PhD, U. Mich., 1976; MD, U. Pa., 1983. Diplomate Am. Bd. Psychiatry. Asst. prof. psychology Swarthmore (Pa.) Coll., 1976-80; asst. prof. psychiatry U. Pa., Phila., 1988—; med. dir. inpatient psychiatry svc. Hosp. U. Pa., Phila., 1989—. Assoc. editor Jour. Genetic Psychology; contbr. articles to profl. jours. Recipient Rsch. Svc. award NIH, 1987, Earl Bond Teaching award 1991. Mem. Soc. for Neuroscience, Phi Beta Kappa. Office: Hosp U Pa Dept Psychiatry 3400 Spruce St Philadelphia PA 19104-4220

BALLADA, ANTONIO, chemical company executive; b. Milan, Feb. 8, 1944; came to U.S., 1988; s. Gino and Dusolina (Zozzoli) B.; m. Alberta Monticelli, June 17, 1972. Maturita classica, Liceo Classico Carducci, Milan, 1963; degree in indsl. chemistry, U. Di Stato Milan, 1968; postgrad., U. Bocconi, Milan, 1970-72. Planning and control mgr. Montedison SpA, Milan, 1969-80, bus. mgr., 1980-81, corp. strategist, 1982-88; gen. mgr. Retipolen SpA, Milan, 1981-82; v.p. functional chems. div. Himont Inc., Wilmington, Del., 1988—. Office: Himont Inc 2801 Centerville Rd Wilmington DE 19850

BALLANCE, JOHN B., professional society administrator; b. Four Oaks, N.C., May 28, 1941; s. Battle R. and Julia Irene (Rarigs) B.; m. Carol Sue Thurman, July 18, 1980; children: Heather, Rachel, Kelsey. BS in Metall. Engring., N.C. State U., 1965, MS in Metall. Engring., 1966. Rsch. metallurgist Rep. Steel Corp., Independence, Ohio, 1966-74; sr. metallurgist Brush Wellman Inc., Cleve., 1974-78; editor Jour. of Metals Metall. Soc. of AIME, Warrendale, Pa., 1978-83; exec. dir. Materials Rsch. Soc., Pitts., 1983—. Inventor bainitic steel, formable HSLA steel. Mem. Pine Twp. (Pa.) Planning Commn., 1988—, Pine Twp. Parks and Recreation Bd., 1990—, Pine Twp. Impact Fee Study Commn., 1991—; bd. trustees Unitarian Universalist Ch., Pitts., 1983-86. Mem. Am. Sokol Orgn., Am. Soc. Assn. Execs. Democrat. Office: Materials Rsch Soc 9800 Mcknight Rd Pittsburgh PA 15237-6005

BALLANTYNE, GARTH HADDEN, surgical educator, colon and rectal surgeon; b. Mineola, N.Y., June 4, 1951; s. Robert Heath and May (Hadden) B.; m. Helen Kilgrew, May 31, 1976; children: John, Mary, Elizabeth, James, Ann. Grad., Phillips Exeter Acad., 1969; AB magna cum laude, Harvard U., 1973; MD, Columbia U., 1977. Diplomate Am. Bd. Surgery, Am. Bd. Colon and Rectal Surgery. Intern Columbia Presbyn. Med. Ctr., 1977-78, surg. resident, 1978-79; surg. resident UCLA Med. Ctr., 1979-80, Northwestern Med. Ctr., Chgo., 1980-82; chief resident St. Luke's Hosp., 1982-83; fellow in colon and rectal surgery Mayo Clinic, 1983-84; assoc. prof. Yale U. Sch. Medicine, New Haven, 1989—, asst. prof. surgery, 1984-89. Pioneer of laparoscopic colon and rectal surgery; contbr. over 100 articles to med. jours. Fellow ACS, Am. Soc. Colon and Rectal Surgeons; mem. Soc. Univ. Surgeons, Assn. Acad. Surgeons, Assn. VA Surgeons, Soc. Am. Gastrointestinal Endoscopic Surgeons. Home: 1 Sunset Beach Rd Branford CT 06405-5046

BALLARD, IAN MATHESON, physician; b. Norristown, Pa., Jan. 13, 1937; s. Herbert Theodore Jr. and Margaret (Matheson) B.; m. Paula Ballard, Aug. 31, 1957 (div. 1982); children: Jennifer Ballard Hyde, Jill Ballard Hamilton, Ian Matheson Jr.; m. Helen Lyons Clothier, Apr. 16, 1982. AB, Lafayette Coll., 1958; MD, Temple U., 1962. Diplomate Am. Bd. Family Practice, Nat. Bd. Med. Examiners. Intern St. Luke's Hosp., Bethlehem, Pa., 1962-63, resident in internal medicine, 1965-66; pvt. practice Bethlehem, Pa., 1965-71; assoc. dir. Merck Sharpe & Dohme, West Point, Pa., 1971-73, Wyeth Lab., Phila., 1973-77; med. dir. Valleyforge Military Acad. & Jr.

Coll., Wayne, Pa., 1973—, Home Health Corp. Am., Bryn Mawr, Pa., 1976—; assoc. dir. Bryn Mawr Family Medicine, 1977-85; med. dir. Wayne Nursing & Rehab., 1983—; dir. Wyeth Ayerst Labs., Phila., 1985-89, sr. dir. clin. devel., 1989—; attending staff Bryn Mawr (Pa.) Hosp., 1972—. Contbr. articles to profl. jours. Pres. Radnor Twp. Bd. Health, Wayne, 1988. Comdr. USNR, 1963—. Fellow Am. Acad. Family Physicians, Am. Coll. Rheumatology; mem. Am. Soc. Internal Medicine, Am. Soc. Clin. Pharmacology and Therapeutics, St. Andrews Soc., Freemasonry. Episcopalian. Home: 529 County Line Rd Radnor PA 19087 Office: Wyeth Ayerst Labs PO Box 8299 Philadelphia PA 19101

BALLARD, ROBERT EUGENE, JR., engineering company executive; b. Pearisburg, Va., May 9, 1943; s. Robert Eugene and Rachel Helena (Collins) B.; m. Mary Martha Koether, Nov. 30, 1968; children: Emily Blair, Benjamin Jeffrey, Philip Christian, Sarah Suzanne. BSME, Va. Polytech. Inst., 1966; MBA in Fin., U. Pitts., 1975. Quality assurance engr. Westinghouse Electric, Pitts., 1968-73, sr. engr., 1973-78; project mgr. Gibbs & Hill, Inc., N.Y.C., 1979-84, dir. projects, 1984-88; dir. engrng. svcs. Nuclear Energy Svcs., Inc., Danbury, Conn., 1988-89; cons. Kuljian Corp., Phila., 1989-90, v.p. projects, 1990—. Lt. U.S. Army, 1966-68. Mem. ASME (pres. 1973-74), NSPE, U.S. Energy Awareness Assn., Pitts. Econs. Club. Republican. Episcopalian. Home: 291 Stonegate Dr Devon PA 19333-1858 Office: Kuljian Corp 3700 Sci Ctr Philadelphia PA 19104

BALLOU, GLEN MARTIN, public relations executive; b. Albany, N.Y., Dec. 31, 1935; s. Willard Rowse and Emily Penfield (Goodsell) B.; m. Beryl Helen Keith, Oct. 18, 1958 (div. 1980); children: Christine, Bonnie, David; m. Debra Jean Lawrence, Oct. 3, 1981; children: Nicole Faye, Scott Lawrence. BIE, GM Inst., 1958. Engr. Pratt & Whitney Aircraft Inc., East Hartford, Conn., 1958-69; mgr. AV/trade shows United Tech. Corp., Hartford, Conn., 1969-80; mgr. communication presentations Sikorsky Aircraft/UTC, Stratford, Conn., 1980—; owner, cons. Ballou Assocs., Guilford, Conn., 1980—. Author/editor: Handbook for Sound Engineers, 1986, 2d edit. 1991; contbr. articles to profl. jours. Bd. dirs. Southington YMCA, 1968-74. Mem. Audio Engrng. Soc. (chmn. 8th conv., bd. govs. 1982-83, Bd. Govs. award 1990), Soc. Motion Picture & TV Engrs., Duck Island Yacht Club (commodore 1991—). Republican. Baptist. Home: 1 Riverside Ct Guilford CT 06437-1949 Office: Sikorsky Aircraft 6900 Main St Stratford CT 06497-1361

BALLWEBER, HETTIE LOU, archaeologist; b. Pitts., Dec. 27, 1944; d. Nicholas George and Harriett Elizabeth (Tucker) Beresh; m. Walter David Boyce, Aug. 24, 1963 (div. 1984); children: Michael David, Steven Todd; m. William Arterberry Ballweber, Nov. 8, 1986. BA summa cum laude, Calif. U., Pa., 1985; M. Applied Anthropology, U. Md., 1987. Cons. archaeologist Monongahela, Pa., 1980-85; archaeologist archeology div. Md. Geol. Survey, Balt., 1985-86; dir. Md. New Directions, Balt., 1987; cons. Columbia, Md., 1987—; bd. dirs. Alternative Directions, Inc., Balt. Author: First People of Maryland, 1985; contbr. articles to profl. jours. State publicity chmn. Pa. Congress Parents and Tchrs., Harrisburg, Pa., 1981-84, regional v.p., 1984. With USN, 1979-87. Fellow Soc. Applied Anthropology; mem. Mon-Yough Archaeol. Soc. (pres. 1983-84), Westmoreland Archaeol. Soc. (v.p. 1982-83), Coun. Med. Archeology (pres. 1990-91), Wash. Assn. Profl. Anthropologists, Soc. Hist. Archaeology, Shriners, Order Eastern Star. Home and Office: 3212 Peddicoat Ct Woodstock MD 21163

BALMAGES, FRED IRA, music educator; b. Bklyn., May 1, 1948; s. Aaron and Irene (Gottlieb) B.; m. Marjorie Ann Lief, Mar. 18, 1970; 1 child, Brian. BMusEdn, Peabody Conservatory, Balt., 1969; postgrad., Morgan State Coll., Balt., 1980. Tchr. music Balt. County Bd. Edn., Towson, 1969—, repair technician, 1988—; repair technician Arundel Computers, Glen Burnie, Md., 1985—; pres. Ednl. Technologies Cons., Balt., 1989-91. Creator: Early Tunes for Children, 1991. Mem. Howard County Community Band, Ellicott City, Md., 1992, Balt. County Tchrs. Band, 1989—. Tri-Arts scholar Peabody Cons., 1969. Mem. NEA, Med. Music Educators Assn., Music Educators Nat. Conf., Tchrs. Assn. of Balt. County, Phi Mu Alpha. Office: Balt County Bd Edn 2410 Spring Lake Dr Timonium MD 21093

BALMORI, DIANA, landscape designer; b. Gijon, Spain, June 4, 1936; d. Clemente and Dorothy (Ling) Hernando-Balmori. Diploma in architecture, U. Tucuman, Argentina, 1960; BA in Urban History, UCLA, 1968, PhD, 1973. Asst. prof. SUNY, Oswego, 1974-78, assoc. prof., 1978-79; assoc. Cesar Pelli & Assocs., New Haven, 1977-81, prin. for landscape and urban design, 1981-90; prin. Balmori Assocs., New Haven, 1990—; vis. fellow Yale U., New Haven, 1983-84; lectr. Yale U. Sch. Forestry, 1990—; critic Yale U. Sch. Architecture, 1988—, Harvard Grad. Sch. Design, 1989. Author: Notable Family Networks in Latin America, 1984, (with others) Beatrix Farrand's American Landscapes--Her Gardens and Campuses, 1985. Grantee Ossabaw Found., 1980, N.Y. State Coun. Arts, 1987, Carolyn Found. grantee, 1990, Nat. Endowment for the Arts design advancement grantee, 1990, Nat. Endowment for the Humanities grantee, 1991; rsch. fellow NYU, 1982; recipient Pub. Space award Conn. chpts. AIA/Am. Soc. of Landscape Architects, 1990. Mem. Am. Hist. Assn., Am. Soc. Landscape Architects, Archtl. League of N.Y. (v.p. landscape), Catalog of Landscape Records (bd. dirs.), Garden History Soc., Latin Am. Studies Assn., Soc. Archtl. Historians (bd. dirs.) Urban Land Inst. Office: Balmori Assocs 279 Crown St New Haven CT 06511-6614

BALOGH, KAROLY, pathologist; b. Budapest, Hungary, Sept. 24, 1930; came to U.S., 1956; s. Karoly B. and Charlotte (Kaizler) B.; m. Judith Gyorgypaly, Jan. 22, 1955; children: Adam, Peter, Anna. MD, Semmelweis Med. U., Budapest, 1954. Rockefeller fellow Tulane U., New Orleans, 1957-58; USPHS trainee pathology Mass. Gen. Hosp., Boston, 1958-61, asst. pathologist, 1962-68; chief pathology Univ. Hosp., Boston, 1968-73; pathologist Mallory Inst. Pathology, Boston, 1973-75; chief of pathology Worcester (Mass.) City Hosp., 1975-77; pathologist New England Deaconess Hosp., Boston, 1977—; dir. anatomic pathology New England Bapt. Hosp., Boston, 1989—; assoc. prof. pathology Harvard U., Boston, 1977—; bd. dirs. Worldwide Hungarian Med. Acad. Recipient Semmelweis Meml. medal Semmelweis Med. U., 1978. Mem. Internat. Dendrological Rsch. Inst. (bd. dirs. 1990—), Hungarian Soc. Mass. (pres. 1989—). Office: New England Deaconess Hosp Dept Anatomic Pathology 185 Pilgrim Rd Boston MA 02215-5399

BALSER, PAUL FISHER, investment banker; b. N.Y.C., Feb. 12, 1942; s. Benjamin H. and Paula F. (Bassett) B.; grad. Lawrenceville Sch., 1960; BA, Yale U., 1964; GBS, N.Y.U.; m. Alexandra M. Balser; children: Paul Fisher II, Christopher C., Alessandra R. Loan officer Empire Trust Co., N.Y.C., 1964-66; v.p. Wertheim & Co., N.Y.C., 1966-77; mng. dir. Thomson McKinnon Securities, Inc., N.Y.C., 1977-82; mng. dir. J. Henry Schroder Corp., N.Y.C., 1982-86; ptnr. Centre Partners, Inc., N.Y.C., 1986—; dir. Kansas City So. Industries, Inc., Hale Found., Inc., Vintners Internat., Inc, Quarton Group, Rocky Mt. Fin., United Retail Group, Jungle Jim's Playland, Inc., Sci. Games, Inc. Trustee Hudson Guild. Mem. Assn. Corporate Growth, Yale Club, Ocean Reef Club, Club 29. Republican. Contbg. author: Handbook of Mergers, Acquisitions and Buyouts, 1981, The Role of Leveraged Buyout Sponsor, 1982. Home: 1365 York Ave New York NY 10021-4029 Office: Ctr Ptnrs Inc 1 Rockefeller Pla Ste 1025 New York NY 10020

BALSHI, JAMES D., vascular surgeon; b. Bethlehem, Pa., Aug. 18, 1955; s. Stephen Francis and Josephine Marie (Bartos) B; m. Jill Karen Poley, Jan. 30, 1982; children: Christopher John, Andrew Cyril. BS in Biology, St. Joseph's Coll., Phila., 1976; MD, Thomas Jefferson U., 1980. Diplomate Am. Bd. Surgery. Resident gen. surgery Hosp. of U. Pa., Phila., 1980-85, chief resident gen. surgery, 1985-86; Smithwick fellow vascular surgery Boston U. Med. Ctr., 1986-87; ptnr. Thoracic Assocs., Easton, Pa., 1987-88, Associated Vascular Surgeons, Bethlehem, 1988—; ptnr. Lehigh Valley Pacemaker Clinic, Easton, Pa., 1988—; pres. Med. Image Prodns., Bethlehem, 1988—. Contbr. articles on transplantation rsch. and vascular surg. techs. to profl. jours. Recipient Jobst award Jobst Corp., Toronto, Can., 1987. Fellow Am. Coll. Surgeons; mem. Am Med. Assn., Pa. Med. Soc., Northampton County Med. Soc. Bd., Delaware Valley Vascular Soc., Peripheral Vascular Surgery Soc., Am. Venous Forum. Office: Associated Vascular Surgeons 303 W Broad St Bethlehem PA 18018-5526

BALTAZAR, ROMULO FLORES, cardiologist; b. Naga, Camarines Sur, Philippines, Oct. 15, 1941; came to U.S., 1970; s.Melecio Perez and Socorro (Flores) B.; m. Ophelia Zarzuela, June 6, 1970; children: Maria Cristina, Romulo Jr. BA, U. Philippines, 1961, MD, 1966. Intern U. Philippines, Philippine Gen. Hosp., 1965-66; resident medicine Philippine Gen. Hosp., 1966-69, chief resident medicine, 1969-70; instr. medicine U. Philippines, 1969-70; resident medicine Sinai Hosp., Balt., 1970-71, resident cardiology, 1971-73, assoc. cardiology, 1975-87, dir. non-invasive cardiology, 1987—; resident pediatric cardiology Johns Hopkins Hosp., Balt., 1971-72; fellow cardiology Maimonides Med. Ctr., N.Y.C., 1973-75; instr. medicine Johns Hopkins U. Sch. Medicine, Balt., 1977-87, asst. prof. medicine, 1987—. Contbr. articles to med. jours. Fellow ACP, Am. Coll. Cardiology, Am. Coll. Chest Physicians. Roman Catholic. Office: Sinai Hosp Balt Div Cardiology Baltimore MD 21215

BALTER, FRANCES SUNSTEIN, civic worker; b. Pitts.; d. Elias and Gertrude (Kingsbacher) Sunstein. Student Sarah Lawrence Coll., 1939-41, New Sch. Social Rsch., 1941-43, Bennington Coll., 1941, 42; cert. Harvard Inst. Arts Adminstrn., 1973; m. James Stone Balter, May 15, 1948; children: Katherine (Mrs. Ross Anthony), Julia Frances, Constance (Mrs. Owen Cantor), Daniel Elias; m. Harry Philip Blum, Mar. 1, 1982. Adminstrv. asst., assoc. producer Ednl. Television Sta. WQED-TV, Pitts., 1963-67; producer, mng. dir. Freedom Readers, 1964-67; co-founder, incorporator, sec. bd. dirs. Pitts. Coun. for Arts, 1967-70; cultural cons. Mayor's Office, Dir. of Office of Cultural Affairs, Pitts., 1968; initiator Three Rivers Arts Festival 1960; co-dir. Ohio and Miss. River Valley Art Festival, 1961-62; mem. Pa. Coun. on Arts, 1972-78; co-founder Pioneer Crafts Coun. Mill Run Pa., 1972; exec. dir. Poetry On The Buses, 1974—; bd. dirs. Coun. for Arts MIT, 1985—, Palm Beach Festival, 1987-89. Named Woman of Yr. in Art Post-Gazette, 1969. Mem. Assoc. Councs. on Arts, Nat. Soc. Arts and Letters, Nat. League of Am. PEN Women (Pitts. chpt., assoc. 1990—). Home: 1021 Devonshire Rd Pittsburgh PA 15213-2913

BALTER, LESLIE MARVIN, educator; b. N.Y.C., Feb. 27, 1920; s. Harry and Rose B.; m. Frances Hughes; 1 son by previous marriage, Kenneth Robert (dec. 1979); 1 dau. Sheila Beth. BSEE, Columbia U., 1941; postgrad., Rutgers U.; MA, NYU, 1969. Civilian radio engr. Signal Corps Devel. Lab., Ft. Monmouth, N.J., 1941-45, in ETO, 1942; chief engr. Masters Crystal Co., quartz crystal prodn., 1945-46; founder Jersey City Tech. Inst., dir., 1947—, founded br. operation as Paterson (N.J.) Inst., 1956—; founder Sch. Bus. Machines, teaching IBM machines, Plaza Sch., Paramus, N.J., 1958—; cons. test engr. Consumers Rsch., Washington, N.J. Contbr. articles to Electronic Design Mag., Bus. Edn. World, Tech. Edn. News. Mem. N.J. Vocat. Edn. Master Plan Com. Communications chmn. Jersey City CD Coun., 1950-53; pres. Ferncroft Park Coop. Mem. IEEE (life), N.J. Assn. Pvt. Career Schs. (pres. 1971), N.J. Bus. Edn. Assn., Delta Pi Epsilon. Home: 41 Ferncroft Park Ramsey NJ 07446-2575 Office: Plaza Sch Bergen Mall Paramus NJ 07652-5001

BALTIMORE, DAVID, microbiologist, educator; b. N.Y.C., Mar. 7, 1938; s. Richard I. and Gertrude (Lipschitz) B.; m. Alice S. Huang, Oct. 5, 1968; 1 dau., Teak. BA with high honors in Chemistry, Swarthmore Coll., 1960; postgrad., MIT, 1960-61; PhD, Rockefeller U., 1964. Research assoc. Salk Inst. Biol. Studies, La Jolla, Calif., 1965-68; assoc. prof. microbiology MIT, Cambridge, 1968-72, prof. biology, from 1972, Am. Cancer Soc. prof. microbiology, 1973-83, dir. Whitehead Inst. Biomed. Rsch., 1982-90; pres. Rockefeller U., N.Y.C., 1990-91, now prof. Mem. editorial bd. Jour. Molecular Biology, 1971-73, Jour. Virology, 1969-90, Sci., 1986—, N. Eng. Jour. Medicine, 1990—. Bd. govs. Weizmann Inst. Sci., Israel; bd. dirs. Life Sci. Rsch. Found.; co-chmn. Commn. on a Nat. Strategy of AIDS; ad hoc program adv. com. on complex genome, NIH. Recipient Gustav Stern award in virology, 1970; Warren Triennial prize Mass. Gen. Hosp., 1971; Eli Lilly and Co. award in microbiology and immunology, 1971; U.S. Steel Found. award in molecular biology, 1974; Gairdner Found. ann. award, 1974; Nobel prize in physiology or medicine, 1975. Fellow AAAS, Am. Med. Writers Assn. (hon.); mem. Nat. Acad. Scis., Am. Acad. Arts and Scis., Inst. Medicine, Pontifical Acad. Scis., Royal Soc. (Eng.) (fgn.). Office: Rockefeller U 1230 York Ave New York NY 10021

BALUNAS, ROBERT JOHN, investment company executive; b. Poughkeepsie, N.J., Mar. 22, 1947; s. Leonard Charles and Dorothy Veronica (Opperman) B.; m. Cheryl Ann Gadonniex; children: Michael, Matthew, Robby. BA in Polit. Sci. cum laude, Marist Coll., 1972. Salesperson IBM Corp., N.Y.C., 1968-73; from dealer svc. mgr. to br. ops. mgr. Ziebart Internat. Corp., Troy, Mich., 1973-80; stockbroker Shearson Lehman Hutton, Newburgh, N.Y., 1980-83, E.F. Hutton, Poughkeepsie, 1983-87, Prudential-Bache Securities Inc., Poughkeepsie, 1987-90; v.p. investments Kopstein Van Alen & Co. Inc., Poughkeepsie, 1990—. Sgt. USMC, 1966-68. Democrat. Roman Catholic. Home: PO Box 483 Wappingers Falls NY 12590 Office: Kopstein Van Alen & Co Inc 321 Main Mall Poughkeepsie NY 12601

BAM, FOSTER, lawyer; b. Bridgeport, Conn., Jan. 11, 1927; s. Frederick and Alma (Foster) B.; m. Sallie A. Baldwin; children: Sylvia Carol, Sheila Catherine, Eric Foster. Grad., Loomis Sch., 1944; A.B., LL.B., Yale, 1950. Bar: N.Y. 1954, Conn. Mem. faculty acctg. Yale, 1952-53; with firm Spence & Hotchkiss, N.Y.C., 1954-55; asst. U.S. dist. atty. So. Dist. N.Y., 1955-58; ptnr. Kramer, Levin, Nessen, Kamin & Frankel (formerly Feldman, Kramer, Bam Nessen), N.Y.C., 1958-67; now ptnr. Cummings & Lockwood.; bd. dirs. Evergreen Fund, Evergreen Total Return Fund, Evergreen Valve Timing Fund, Evergreen Ltd. Market Fund, Symmetrix, Inc., Waste Disposal Equipment Acquisition Corp. Rehab. Hosp. Corp. Am. Trustee Bermuda Biol. Sta. for Rsch., Phoenix Sci. Ctr., chmn. Am. Mus. Fly Fishing, Bermuda Biol. Sta. for Rsch. Recipient Johny Foyle Meml. award, 1969. Mem. ABA, Conn. Bar Assn., Greenwich Bar Assn., N.Y. State Dist. Attys. Assn., Exptl. Aircraft Assn., Phi Beta Kappa. Home: 51 Londonderry Dr Greenwich CT 06830-3508 Office: Cummings & Lockwood 2 Greenwich Pla Greenwich CT 06836

BAMBACUS, JOHN NICHOLAS, political science educator; b. Washington, May 28, 1945; s. John P. and Theone K. B.; m. Karen Messina, Nov. 25, 1978; 1 child, Christopher J. AA in Humanities, Montgomery Jr. Coll., 1968; B.S. in Polit. Sci. Frostburg State Coll. (Md.), 1970; M.A. in Polit. Sci., W.Va. U., 1972. Dir. vets. affairs Frostburg State Coll., 1970-72, prof. polit. sci., 1972—, dir. Pub. Affairs Inst., 1974—; mem. Govt. Study Commn., Allegany County, Md., 1976-78; mem. Md. Senate, Annapolis, 1982-92; city councilman City of Frostburg, 1976-78; spl. asst. U.S. Senator Charles McC. Mathias Jr., Balt., 1979-81; bd. dirs. Frostburg Community Hosp., 1978—, Tri-County Council for Western Md., 1974—; commr. Human Resources Devel. Commn., 1974—; assoc. Frostburg State U. Found., 1982—. Served with USMC, 1964-67, Vietnam. Mem. VFW, Am. Legion, Vietnam Veterans Assn. Lodges: Rotary, Elks. Republican. Greek Orthodox. Home: PO Box 1 Frostburg MD 21532-0001 Office: Md State Senate Capitol Bldg Annapolis MD 21401

BAMBARA, ROBERT ANTHONY, biochemist, educator; b. Chgo., Jan. 3, 1949; s. Philip Henry and Phyllis (Zullo) B.; m. Bonnie Messersmith, Sept. 15, 1974; children: Rebecca Ann, Bradley Joel. BA, Northwestern U., 1970; PhD, Cornell U., 1974. Postdoctoral fellow Stanford U., 1975-76; asst. prof. U. Rochester, 1977-81, assoc. prof., 1981-89, prof. biochemistry, 1989—. Editorial bd. Jour. Biol. Chemistry, 1989—. Jane Coffin Childs Fund for Med. Rsch. fellow, 1975-77; Am. Cancer Soc. Faculty Rsch. awardee, 1979-83. Mem. Am. Soc. for Biochemistry and Molecular Biology. Office: Univ of Rochester 601 Elmwood Ave Rochester NY 14642-9999

BAMBERGER, FRED HANS, government official, lawyer, educator; b. Neustadt, Rheinpfalz, Germany, June 23, 1898; came to U.S. 1936; s. Adolf and Pauline (Goldenberg) B.; m. Mary Frances Hotchkiss, Oct. 10, 1942. LLM, JUD, U. Heidelberg, Germany, 1924; MA, Middlebury Coll., 1955. Bar: Germany, 1924, County Ct. Neustadt. Pvt. practice Germany, 1925-33; prodn. planner Am. Optical Co., Buffalo, N.Y., 1943-46; high sch. tchr. N.Y. Cen. Sch., Eden, 1946-48; prof., dept. head Ohio No. U., Ada, 1948-51; fgn. patent analyst U.S. Patent Office, Washington, 1951-70; freelance translator Washington, 1951-82. Contbr. articles to profl. jours. With Germany Navy, 1917-19; with U.S. Army, 1942-43. Mem. Am. Translators Assn., Soc. Fed. Linguists (v.p.), Gideons Internat. Democrat. Methodist. Home: 4450 S Park Ave Apt 1002 Bethesda MD 20815-3640

BAMBERGER, JULIA KATHRYN, social worker; b. Phila., Dec. 23, 1960; d. William Thomas and Julia Kathryn (O'Brien) B. BA in Social Work, Holy Family Coll., Phila., 1983. Cert. social worker. Recreational therapy asst., physical therapy asst. Ashton Hall Nursing Home, Phila., 1979-83; hairdresser asst. St. John Neumann Nursing Home, Phila., 1982-83; recreational therapy asst. Evangelical Manor, Phila., 1983; social worker The Consortium/Southwest Sr. Citizens Ctr., Phila., 1983-90; resource specialist Phila. Corp. for Aging, 1990—. Member, chairperson Alzheimer's Disease and Related Disorders Assn., Phila., 1983—; vol. Ashton Hall Nursing Home, Phila., 1983-89; V.I.P. blood donor ARC, 1978—; solicitor Cath. Charities Appeal, 1979—; me. Pro Life Coalition of Southeastern, Pa., 1986—; soprano singer guitar Mass. group Maternity Blessed Virgin Mary Roman Cath. Ch., Phila., 1977—, soprano singer Folk Mass Group, 1979—; vol. Perpetual Adoration Soc., Our Lady of Fatima Roman Cath. Ch., 1988—. Recipient cert. of appreciation Alzheimers Disease and Related Disorders Assn., 1985, 91, Outstanding Young Women of Am., 1985, 86, 88. Mem. Southeastern Pa. Assn. Sr. Ctr. Pers., Pa. Interagy. Coun. on Aging and Mental Health, Social Svc. Workers Assn. of Nursing Homes, Cath. Adult Singles Assn., Archbishop Ryan High Sch. for Girls Alumnae Assn. (corr. sec. 1985—), Holy Family Coll. Alumni Assn. (rec. sec. 1985-90, cert. appreciation 1984, 90), Assn. Ch. Musicians in Phila., Classic Thunderbird Club, Smoke Free Soc., Epsilon Nu Cath. Adult Club, Psi Chi. Democrat. Home: 2016 Tomlinson Rd Philadelphia PA 19116-3933 Office: Phila Corp for Aging 642 N Broad St Philadelphia PA 19130-3409

BAMFORD, THOMAS BENNETT, railroad executive; b. Neston, Eng., May 29, 1928; came to U.S., 1968; s. Alfred and Hannah Lilley (Swift) B.; m. Joyce Pauline Wignall, Oct. 1951 (div. 1964); 1 child, Nigel Thomas; m. Adelaide Veronica Ingham, Sept. 25, 1971. BE, U. Liverpool, Eng., 1951. Engr. Uganda Electricity Bd., Kampala, Uganda, 1951-53; field engr. British Insulated Callenders Constrn. Co., Kirkby, Eng., 1954-64; U.S. rep. British Insulated Callenders Constrn. Co., 1964-68; v.p. Electrack, Kirkby, 1968-73; sr. engr. Gibbs & Hill, Inc., N.Y.C., 1973-75; cons. Northport, Maine, 1975-85; pres. Traffic Svc., Inc., Northport, Maine, 1985-87; pres., treas. Aroostook Valley r.R., Presque Isle, Maine, 1987—; cons. in field. Mem. Gov.'s Rail Adv. Com., Augusta, Maine, 1983, State of Maine Mktg. Strategy Com. for Br. Line R.R., 1989. Mem. IEEE, Am. Railway Engrng. Assn. Home: RR 2 Box 210 Lincolnville ME 04849-9615

BAN, VLADIMIR SINISA, electronic industry executive; b. Bjelovar, Croatia, Sept. 7, 1941; s. Sinisa N. and Maja (Medur) B.; m. Edith Conyers Sayen, Oct. 2, 1976; children: Maya Alexandra, Sophie Louise. BS in Chem. Engrng., U. Zagreb, 1964; PhD in Solid State Sci., Pa. State U., 1969; postdoctoral studies, Imperial Coll., London, 1972. Mem. tech. staff RCA Labs., Princeton, N.J., 1969-78; group head, video disc RCA Labs., Princeton, 1978-84; founder, exec., v.p., tech. Epitaxx, Inc., Princeton, 1984—. Patentee in field; contbr. chpts. to books and articles to profl. jours. Recipient Sci. Rsch. grants NSF, NASA, Dept. of Defense, 1984-91. Mem. Am. Chem. Soc., Electrochem. Soc., Am. Assn. Crystal Growers, Materials Rsch. Soc., Alumni of Croatian Univ. (pres. Mid-Atlantic region). Office: Epitaxx Inc 3490 Route 1 Princeton NJ 08540

BANAS, CONRAD MARTIN, mechanical engineer, chief scientist; b. Warren, Mass., Nov. 27, 1927; s. Martin and Caroline (Krupska) B.; m. Erna Maier, Sept. 19, 1949 (div. Nov. 1970); children: Stephen, Richard, Susan, Patricia, Pamela; m. Gene Tomaiuolo Banas, July 19, 1974; children: Jonathan, Jeremy. BSME, Worcester Poly., 1953; MSME, U. Conn., 1957, MS in Physics, 1965. Registered profl. engr., Conn. Asst. rsch. engr. United Technologies Rsch. Ctr., East Hartford, Conn., 1953-57, rsch. engr., 1957-61, sr. rsch. engr., 1961-76, mgr. indsl. laser processing, 1976-90; chief scientist United Technologies Indsl. Lasers, South Windsor, Conn., 1990—; adj. asst. prof. U. Hartford, 1957-62; lectr. U. Conn., Storrs, 1963-67. Patentee in field; contbr. articles to profl. jours. Sgt. U.S. Army, 1945-48. Recipient Adams Lecture award Am. Welding Soc., 1988, Co. Excellence awards United Technologies, 1983, 87, 89. Mem. Am. Welding Soc., Am. Soc. Metals, Tau Beta Pi, Sigma Xi. Home: 56 Volpi Rd Bolton CT 06043

BANASZ, WALTER RONALD, management advisory services company executive; b. Camden, N.J., Nov. 18, 1943; s. Walter Stanley and Florence (Przybyszewski) B.; m. Theresa Marie Carullo, June 11, 1966; children: Gregory, Keith. BS in Acctg., Rider Coll., 1966. Programmer N.J. Treasury Dept., Trenton, 1966-68; system support rep. RCA, Cherry Hill, N.J., 1968-73, system mgr., 1973-76; mgr., cons. Coopers & Lybrand, Phila., 1976-83; dir. Coopers & Lybrand, Balt., 1983-87; ptnr. Laventhol & Horwath, Balt., 1987-89; pres. Banasz & Assocs., Glen Arm, Md., 1989—; mem. bus. adv. bd. Choppin State Coll., Balt., 1986—, Towson (Md.) State U., 1988—. Author: System Selection, 1980; contbr. articles to profl. jours. Mem., team leader Greater Balt. Com., 1986-89; pres. Baltimore County Police Found., 1989—. Mem. Inst. Mgmt. Cons. (founder, pres. Balt. 1987—), U.S. Power Squadron (editor newsletter and instr. Balt.), Tiger Club (Towson). Republican. Roman Catholic. Office: Banasz & Assocs 11128 Old Carriage Rd Glen Arm MD 21057-9416

BANCROFT, LEWIS CLINTON, research executive; b. Reading, Mass., Jan. 10, 1929; s. Clinton Lewis and Ruth Duthie (Beckford) B.; m. Shirley Irene Simonton, Feb. 2, 1962; children: Thomas, Jay; stepchildren: Donald, Fay, Frances Foster; m. Nancy Glover, June 6, 1951 (div. 1960); children: Stephen, Ellen, Betsey. BS in Engring., Princeton U., 1950, MS in Engring., 1952. Rsch. engr., area spvr. DuPont Co. Savannah River Plant, Aiken, S.C., 1952-60; rsch. spvr. to mgr. DuPont Engring. Physics Lab., Wilmington, Del., 1960-67; rsch. spvr. DuPont Photo Products Exploratory Rsch. Lab., Wilmington, Del., 1967-84; mgr. patents and contracts DuPont Photosystems and Electronic products, Wilmington, Del., 1984-85. Exec. Com. Alumni Coun. Princeton U., 1984-87; pres. Princeton Alumni Assn. Del., 1982-84. Sayre Fellow Princeton U., 1950-51, Eugene Higgins Fellow, 1950-51. Mem. Sigma Xi, Seapines Country Club, Wilmington Country Club, DuPont Country Club. Republican. Home: 12 Red Oak Rd Wilmington DE 19806-1248

BANCROFT, PAUL, III, investment company executive, venture capitalist; b. N.Y.C., Feb. 27, 1930; s. Paul and Rita (Manning) B. B.A., Yale U., 1951; postgrad. Georgetown Fgn. Svc. Inst., 1952; m. Monica M. Devine, Jan. 2, 1977; children by previous marriage: Bradford, Kimberly, Stephen, Gregory. Account exec. Merrill Lynch Pierce Fenner & Smith, N.Y.C., 1956-57; assoc. corp. fin. dept. F. Eberstadt & Co., N.Y.C., 1957-62; partner Draper, Gaither & Anderson, Palo Alto, Calif., 1962-67; with Bessemer Securities Corp., 1967-92; v.p. Venture Capital Investments, 1967-74, sr. v.p. securities investments, 1974-76, pres., chief exec. officer, dir., 1976-87; cons. Bessemer Securities Corp., 1988-92; ind. venture capitalist, N.Y.C., 1988—; bd. dirs. Measurex Corp., Litton Industries, Inc., Albany Internat. Corp., Scudder Devel. Fund, Scudder Equity Trust, Scudder Internat. Fund, Scudder Global Fund, Scudder New Asia Fund, Scudder New Europe Fund, Inc.; founder, past pres. and chmn. Nat. Venture Capital Assn. 1st lt. USAF, 1952-56. Clubs: River, Yale (N.Y.C.); Pacific Union, Bohemian (San Francisco). Home and Office: Cheston Ln Rte 2 Box 314 E Queenstown MD 21658

BANCROFT, ROBERT LEWIS, economics, educator, consultant; b. Barre, Vt., Sept. 29, 1947; s. Hartland and Phyllis (Whitney) B.; children: Sarah, Nathan, Ira. BA, U. Vt., 1974, MS, 1976; PhD, Purdue U., 1981. Owner dairy farm E. Montpelier, Vt., 1967-74; rsch. asst. U. Vt., Burlington, 1974-76, Purdue U., W. Lafayette, Ind., 1977-79; economist USDA, Washington, 1979-80, policy analyst, 1980-81; prof. agrl. econs. U. Vt., Burlington, 1981—; cons. economist, Westford, Vt., 1981—. Contbr. articles to profl. jours. Mem. E. Montpelier Planning Commn., 1969-73; founder, dir. Westford Ednl. Found., 1984-85; dir. Westford Sch. Bd., 1986-87; founder, dir. Vermonter's for Strong Families, E. Montpelier, 1989—. Purdue U. fellow, 1972-74, U. Vt., 1974-76. Mem. Nat. Assn. Forensic Economists, Am. Agrl. Econs. Assn., Northeastern Agrl. Econs. Coun. Home and Office: HC 64 Box 582A Westford VT 05494-7701

BANDERA, BOB, telecommunications executive; b. Queens, N.Y., Dec. 20, 1956. BEE, Poly. U., Bklyn., 1978. Communications specialist CBS-TV,

N.Y.C., 1980-84; pres. Telenetwork Inc., N.Y.C., 1984—. Mem. Ind. Computer Cons. Assn.

BANDES, DEAN, software engineer; b. N.Y.C., Jan. 16, 1944; s. Herbert Bandes and Joan (Korach) Downing; m. Arlene Doris Cohen, Aug. 18, 1968; children: Charles Mark, Anne Iva. MA, Brandeis U., 1973, PhD, 1974. Math. instr. Cambridge (Mass.) Jr. Coll., 1970-73; from instr. to asst. prof. U. Mass., Boston, 1973-76; rsch. assoc. Parke Math. Labs., Carlisle, Mass., 1976-79; software engr. LTX Corp., Westwood, Mass., 1979-88, Credence Systems Corp., Billerica, Mass., 1988—. Home: 225 Cypress St Newton MA 02159-2226 Office: Credence Systems Corp 900 Middlesex Turnpike Bldg # 8 Billerica MA 01821

BANDURSKI, BRUCE LORD, ecological and environmental scientist; b. Waterbury, Conn., June 28, 1940; s. Stanley Alexander Bandurski and Virginia Ann (VanRennselaer) Bandurski Hinckley; m. Ruth Anne Fuhrman Sudar, June 28, 1990; stepchildren: Adam Sudar, Karl Sudar. BS with honors, Mich. State U., 1962; postgrad., George Washington U., 1964-65, U.S. Dept. Agr. Grad. Sch., 1965-66. Park ranger Nat. Park Service, 1962-63; sci. reference analyst USPHS, Washington, 1963-65; intelligence ops. specialist U.S. Army, Washington, 1965-66; analyst planner U.S. Dept. Interior, Washington, 1966-74, coord., br. chief, 1974-84; on detail as ecologist, ecomgmt. advisor Internat. Joint Commn. U.S. and Can., Washington, 1983-85, ecomgmt. advisor, ecologist, 1985—; mem. faculty U.S. Dept. Agr. Grad. Sch., 1968—; guest lectr. No. Va. Community Coll., U. Wis., Bucknell U., Am. U., U. Pitts.; mem. subcom. Fed. Interagy. Com. on Edn., 1967—; watch dir., dep. and acting mission dir. U.S. Man-in-Sea program, St. John, V.I., 1970; chmn. Conservation Roundtable of Washington, 1970-71; chmn. com. on definitions, spl. com. on environ. protection U.S. nat. com. World Energy Conf., Washington, 1981—; initiator, dir. Binat. Workshop on Transboundary Monitoring, 1984; mem. exec. com. Great Lakes Sci. Adv. Bd., 1986-92; liaison Coun. Great Lakes Rsch. Mgrs.; mem. steering com. Great Lakes-St. Lawrence Ecosystem Model Framework; participant in ECE Seminar on Ecosystems Approaches to Water Management UN; mem. Lake Superior Biodiversity Project Adv. Com. Nat. Wildlife Fedn. Writer planning and recreation impact mgmt. series, 1967-73; author U.S. Bur. Land Mgmt. Environ. Mgmt. Procedures, 1976-84 (Achievement award 1978, 79, 84), Steering Group on Marine Environ. Monitoring, Commn. on Engring. and Tech. Studies, NRC, 1986-87, Complimentaries between holism and reductionism as they pertain to governance of human/environ. rels. MEM. AAAS, Ecol. Soc. Am. (charter Met. Washington chpt.), Internat. Assn. for Ecology, Am. Soc. Naturalists, The Wildlife Soc., Am. Soc. Mammalogists, Fed. Profl. Assn., Wash. Soc. Engrs., Outdoor Ethics Guild, Nature Conservancy, Maine Coast Heritage Trust, Island Inst., Earthwatch, Assn. Ecosystem Rsch. Ctrs., Alpha Zeta, Beta Beta Beta. Home: Bandura/Point of Maine/Starboard Bucks Harbor ME 04618

BANDY, GARY, artist; b. Pontiac, Mich., May 10, 1944; s. Gerald Leroy and Florence (Ogden) B.; m. Mary Lea Gibson, June 3, 1967. BA, Oakland U., 1965; MFA, Columbia U., 1968. One man show at Fawbush Gallery, 1990; exhibited in traveling group show, 1986. NEA artist fellow, 1983.

BANE, RICHARD COREY, health care executive; b. Salem, Mass., July 26, 1955; s. George Harold and Helen Frances (Simmons) B.; m. Tami Lee Greenberg, Aug. 26, 1984; children: Harrison Ross, Haley Joy. AB in Econs., Dartmouth Coll., 1977; MBA, Harvard U., 1981. Fin. analyst Morgan Stanley & Co., N.Y.C., 1977-79; mgmt. cons. Bain & Co., Boston, 1980-83; ptnr. Tamrock Ptnrs., Boston, 1983-86; prin., owner Bane Family Nursing Ctr., Lynn, Mass., 1987—. Pres. Project Cope Inc., Lynn, 1990-91, Success Inc., Swampscott, Mass., 1990-91; v.p. Salem State Coll. Found., Mass.; elected chmn. Bd. Selectmen, Swampscott, 1992. Mem. Jewish Fedn. North Shore (bd. dirs. 1987—, Nat. Young Leadership award 1990), Kernwood Country Club (bd. dirs. 1990—), Rotary. Office: Bane Family Nursing Ctrs 28 Essex St Lynn MA

BANEGAS, ESTEVAN BROWN, agricultural biotechnology executive; b. Hatch, N.Mex., May 10, 1941; s. Estevan Vera Banegas and Josephine (Brown) Crew; m. Amanda Martin, Sept. 5, 1970. BS, N.Mex. U., 1964; MBA, Wake Forest U., 1978. Sales mgr. agr. div. Ciba-Geigy Corp., San Juan, P.R., 1968-73; mktg. mgr. agr. div. Ciba-Geigy Corp., Greensboro, N.C., 1974-80; dir. corp. planning Ciba-Geigy Corp., Ardsley, N.Y., 1980-81; dir. product mgmt. agr. div. Ciba-Geigy Corp., Greensboro, 1981-83, dir. strategic planning agr. div., 1983-85; pres. joint venture Union Carbide Corp. & DNA Plant Tech. Agri-Diagnostics Assocs., Cinnaminson, N.J., 1985—, bd. dirs.; speaker mktg. biotech. products Agbio Conf., 1989; vis. faculty joint ventures and strategic partnering Internation Rsch. Inst., 1992. Bd. dirs. agrl. devel. bd. Ohio State U., Columbus, 1987—; bd. advisors U. Minn., St. Paul, 1985-88. Capt. USMC, 1964-67, Vietnam. Decorated Cross of Gallantry with silver star Govt. of South Vietnam, 1966. Mem. Am. Chem. Soc. (speaker mktg. strategies 1988), Am. Phytopathology Soc., Golf Course Supts. Am., Sedgefield Country Club, Rotary. Republican. Roman Catholic. Home: 3558 Old Onslow Rd Greensboro NC 27407-7826 Office: Agri Diagnostics Assocs 1 Executive Dr Moorestown NJ 08057

BANEVER, THOMAS CLARK, surgeon, educator; b. Bridgeport, Conn., Dec. 21, 1945; s. Marshall and Elizabeth (Clark) B.; m. Jennifer Burke, June 29, 1969; children: Gregory, Andrew, Seth, Sarah Kate, Abigail, Matthew, Emily. BA in Chemistry, Yale U., 1968; MD, Tufts U., 1972. Diplomate Am. Bd. Surgery. Pvt. practice Hartford (Conn.) Hosp., 1969—; asst. clin. prof. U. Conn. Med. Sch., Farmington, 1990—. Bd. dirs. Community Health Svcs., Hartford, 1972—. Fellow ACS; mem. AMA, Conn. State Med. Soc., Hartford County Med. Assn. (Community Svc. award 1992), Soc. Critical Care Medicine, Ea. Assn. Surg. Trauma, Physicians for Social Responsibility. Home: 31 Main St Farmington CT 06032 Office: Thomas Clark Banever MD 100 Retreat Ave Ste 808 Hartford CT 06106

BANEY, JOHN EDWARD, insurance company executive; b. Pitts., May 27, 1934; s. James V. and Mathilde M. (McGary) B.; m. Joan A. McGrath, June 14, 1958; children: Jay E., Diane L., Timothy J. B.A., U. Pa., 1957; grad. Advanced Mgmt. Program, Harvard U., 1980. With trust dept. First Pa. Bank & Trust, Phila., 1957-58, Remington Rand, Phila., 1958-62; brokerage cons. Conn. Gen. Life Ins. Co., Phila., 1962-68; brokerage mgr. Conn. Gen. Life Ins. Co., Detroit, 1968-72; dir. agys. Conn. Gen. Life Ins. Co., Hartford, 1972-73; v.p. brokerage div. Hartford, 1973-77, v.p. career agts. div., 1977-82; pres. bd. dirs. CG Equity Sales Co., Bloomfield, Conn., 1973, 82; sr. v.p. adminstrv. services Employee Benefits Group, 1982-83; pres. broker div. INA a CIGNA Co., Phila., 1983-85, pres. Internat. & Broker div., 1985-90; pres. J.E. Baney Holdings, Phila., 1990—; exec.-in-residence Baylor U., 1976; bd. dirs. Arbor Group, Boston; pres. Am. Excess Ins. Assn., 1987-88. Mem. port affairs com. Delaware Valley Council, Phila., 1960-68; mem. exec. com. Hartford Whalers hockey team, 1976-78; bd. dirs. Birmingham YMCA, Mich., 1970-71, Found. New Am. Music, 1982—; trustee Hartford Grad. Ctr., 1981-83; trustee, chmn. bd. mgrs. Moore Coll. Art, 1986—. Served with U.S. Army Res., 1958-64. Mem. Am. Coun. Life Ins., CLU Assn., Quechee Club, Union League, Phila. Country Club, Merion Cricket Club. Republican. Roman Catholic. Office: 220 Ivy Ln Haverford PA 19041

BANKER, THOMAS ANDREW, county official; b. Orange, N.J., July 3, 1950; s. Harry John and Patricia Claire (Vadnais) B.; m. Deborah Kim Rubin, Sept. 12, 1982; 1 child, Daniel Stephen. BS in Engring. Sci., Newark Coll. Egnring., 1972; MS in Communication, Rensselaer Poly. Inst., 1973. Cert. tree expert, N.J. Mgr. info. systems City of Newark, 1975-76, budget dir., 1976-78; asst. city adminstr. Newark Pub. Libr., 1979-87, adminstr., 1987-88; exec. dir. Essex County Improvement Authority, Fairfield, N.J., 1988—; adj. prof. Rutgers U., Newark, 1988—, Columbia U., N.Y.C., 1990—; cons. Twp. of Bloomfield, N.J., 1987-89, County of Essex, 1987-88, Newark Pre-Sch. Coun., 1989-90, Greater Newark C. of C., 1990-91; presenter and speaker in field. Trustee Pub. Employees Retirement System, Trenton, N.J., 1980; vice-chair N.J. Local Budget Limit Commn., Trenton, 1982; chair task force Newark Collaboration Group, 1990-91; chair NJIT Fin. Mgmt. Trustees. Named Editor of Yr., N.J. Collegiate Press Assn., 1972. Home: 118 Smull Ave West Caldwell NJ 07006 Office: Essex County Improvement Authority 125 Passaic Ave Fairfield NJ 07004

BANKS, ALBERT VICTOR, JR., municipal official; b. Harrisburg, Pa., Apr. 9, 1956; s. Albert Victor Sr. and Virginia Lee (Harris) B.; m. Judy Ann Williams, Jan. 22, 1984; children: Simóne Janae, Asha Victoria. AA in Psychology, Harrisburg Area Community Coll., 1976; BA in Urban Studies, Temple U., 1978; cert., Tufts U., 1986; MS, N.H. Coll., 1987. From intern to devel. planner Adv. Community Devel. Corp., Phila., 1976-80; housing program coordinator II Office Housing and Community Devel., Phila., 1980-83; dir. community devel. Livingston/Rosenwinkel, P.C. Architects & Planners, &, 1983-85; specialist econ. devel. Phila. Urban Coalition, 1985-87; program planning analyst II Phila. Housing Authority, 1987-91; dep. dir. community and econ. devel. dept. City of Harrisburg, 1991-92; cons. Phila. Comml. Devel. Corp., 1984-86, GMB, Assocs., Phila., 1987, PGM Assocs., 1987, Phila. Care, 1988, Keating Constrn. Co., 1989, Coleman Group, 1992, A.V. Banks; guest speaker Pa. State U. Author: (anthology) Voices, 1981. Vol. researcher Phila. Unemployment Project, 1979, bd. advisor Point Breeze Neighborhood Adv. Com. Phila., 1983; vol. instr. gen. equilvalency diploma program Temple U., Phila., 1985; pres. Edgmont Recreation Assn., 1992; mem. Nat. Trust for Hist. Preservation, 1983-87, World Affairs Coun., 1982-84; cons. YWCA, Germantown. Recipient Liberty Bell award Mayor of Phila., 1982. Mem. Am. Planning Assn. (sec. 1982-85, co-chmn. program com. 1985-88, sec. nat. com. 1985-88), Am. Soc. Notaries, Inst. for Coop. Housing (bd. dirs., com. chair 1986-88), Nat. Assn. Redevel. Officials (bd. dirs. 1981-83), Chapel of the Four Chaplains (hon.), African-Am. C. of C., Alpha Phi Alpha. Methodist. Home: 2323 Duke St Harrisburg PA 17111-1154

BANKS, ANNA DELCEINA, financial planner; b. Newark, Oct. 8, 1952; d. James William and Serena D. (Holland) B. BS, Rutgers U., 1975; grad., U.S. Postal Svcs. Mgmt. Acad., Potomac, Md., 1984; postgrad., NYU, 1988, 90—. Lic. life and health ins. agt., N.J., lic. securities series 6, N.Y., N.J. Clk. U.S. Postal Svc., Newark, 1974-78; acctg/ specialist N.Y. Postal Data Ctr., N.Y.C., 1978-83, mgr. women's program, 1983-85, acct., 1985-90; fin. planner PC Tax Prep. Assocs., Newark, 1985—; trainer various personal devel. seminars, 1980-85; workshop leader Basic Fin. Planning, 1990; instr. Am. Assn. Retired Persons, 1991—; instr., promoter Successful Money Mgmt. Seminars, Newark, 1991—; adj. prof. personal fin. Essex County Coll. Sch. Continuing and Community Edn., 1991—; instr. High Sch. Fin. Planning Program, Coll. for Fin. Planning, Denver, 1991—; bus. cons. Jr. Achievement No. N.J., Newark, 1992—. Fin. editor N.J. Perspectus News Mag., Newark, 1990—; contbr. articles to profl. jours. Lay minister Elmwood Presbyn. Ch., East Orange, N.J., 1992—. Mem. Nat. Assn. Tax Practitioners, Nat. Soc. Pub. Accts., Nat. Soc. Notaries, Nat. Tax Practitioners (charter bd. dirs., sec. N.J. chpt. 1987—), Nat. Assn. Negro Bus. and Profl. Bus. Women's Clubs (bd. dirs., treas. N.J. chpt. 1990—), Inst. Cert. Fin. Planners (cert.), Internat. Tng. in Communication Coun. I (pres. 1984-85, 1st place speech contest award 1985. Republican. Office: PC Tax Prep Assocs 78 Pine Grove Ter Newark NJ 07106-1909

BANKS, DAVID OWEN, public relations executive; b. Huntington Park, Calif., Dec. 9, 1940; s. Willard Louis and Winifred (Regan) B.; m. Lyneth Diane Soinski, Aug. 10, 1963; children: Matthew David, Michael Joseph, Joseph Stephen. BS, U. Dayton, 1964. Legis. asst. to Sen. Stephen M. Young U.S. Senate, Washington, 1965; exec. dir. Young Dem. Club of Am., Washington, 1966-67; dep. dir. pub. affairs Dem. Nat. Com., Washington, 1968-69; campaign aide to v.p. Hubert H. Humphrey Washington, 1968; sr. v.p. Daniel J. Edelman, Inc., Washington, 1969-80; v.p. Nat. Coal Assn., Washington, 1980-88; cons. Washington, 1988-89; mgr. spl. projects Am. Petroleum Inst., Washington, 1989—. Wports editor Fostoria Review-Times, 1960-62, Dayton (Ohio) Jour.-Herald, 1962-64. Fire commr. Fairfax County, Va., 1987-89, battalion fire chief, 1984—; fire chief Dunn Loring, Va., 1979—. Mem. Univ. Club (Washington).

BANKS, DELORES JOHNSON, human resources professional; b. Rochester, N.Y., Jan. 28, 1951; d. Frank and Mamie (Turner) Johnson; m. Philip Banks, Aug. 19, 1970; children: Tamara Delores, Natalie Mary, Kyle Philip. BA, St. John Fisher Coll., Rochester, 1973; grad. cert. in indsl. and labor rels., Cornell U., 1989; postgrad., Syracuse U., 1989—. Supr. underwriting Allstate Ins. Co., Rochester, 1977-82; mgr. human resource devel. Greater Rochester Cablevision, 1982—. Author, producer (tng. videos) The Eyptians, 1988, How To Connect Your VCR, 1989. Mem. alumni bd. St. John Fisher Coll., 1991; mem. bd. Higher Edn. Opportunity Program, 1990. Mem. ASTD. Episcopalian. Home: 271 Meadow Farm S North Chili NY 14514 Office: Greater Rochester Cablevision 71 Mount Hope Ave Rochester NY 14620-1090

BANKS, EPHRAIM, chemistry educator, consultant; b. Norfolk, Va., Apr. 21, 1918; s. Israel and Ada (Gezunsky) B.; m. Libby Kohl, Mar. 17, 1945 (dec. May 14, 1985); children: Thomas Israel, Jay Lewis. BS, CCNY, 1937; PhD, Poly. Inst. of Bklyn., 1949. Jr. metallurgist N.Y. Naval Shipyard, Bklyn., 1941-46; rsch. fellow Poly. Inst. of Bklyn., N.Y., 1946-49, rsch. assoc., 1949-50; instr. to prof. Poly. Inst. of Bklyn. (now Poly. U.), 1951-87, prof. emeritus, 1987—; cons. Westinghouse, GM, Mallinckrodt Chem., 1966—. Contbr. over 120 articles to profl. publs. including Jour. Am. Chem. Soc., Jour. Electrochem. Soc., Sci., Jour. Solid State Chemistry, Jour. Phys. Soc., Jour. Chem. Physics, and others. With USNR, 1944-46. Weizmann fellow, 1963-64; NSF Faculty fellow, 1971-72. Fellow AAAS, N.Y. Acad. Sci., Mineral. Soc. Am.; mem. Am. Chem. Soc. (mem. exec. com. inorganic div. 1959-62), Am. Phys. Soc., Electrochem. Soc. (assoc. editor jour. 1956-85), Am. Crystallography Assn. Office: Poly U 333 Jay St Brooklyn NY 11201-2990

BANKS, HENRY STEPHEN, systems software company executive; b. Chgo., Nov. 13, 1920; s. Joseph S. and Mary V. (Sparrow) B.; m. Marjorie June Martin, Feb. 19, 1955; children: Pamela Kae, Kimberly Karen. BS, Loyola U., Chgo., 1944; MBA, Northwestern U., 1953. Commd 2d lt. USAF, 1941, advanced through grades to lt. col., 1955; with Res., 1955-80; sr. account mgr. Recordak Bus. Products div. Eastman Kodak, Cedar Rapids, Iowa, 1955-60; mgr. regional br. govt. Itek Bus. Products, Bethesda, Md., 1960-67; dir. mktg. DASA Corp., Andover, Mass., 1967-68; dir. product devel. Dymo Bus. Systems, Bethesda, 1968-81; v.p. mktg. Automation Horizons, Inc., Beltsville, Md., 1982-83; dir. govt. mktg. InterSystems Corp., Bethesda, 1984-90; ret., 1990; mktg. cons. various cos.; owner HMB; lectr. mktg. Coe Coll.; lectr. math. Loyola U.; cons. in field. Elected vice comdr. Bethesda chpt. Mil. Order World Wars, 1991—. Mem. MUMPS Users Group. Republican. Roman Catholic. Clubs: Bethesda Naval Officers, Ft. Myer Officers. Home: 7211 Radnor Rd Bethesda MD 20817-6128

BANKS, RUSSELL, chemical company executive; b. N.Y.C., Aug. 2, 1919; s. Thomas and Fay (Cowen) B.; m. Janice Reed, June 19, 1949; 1 son, Gordon L. B.B.A., CCNY, 1936-40; J.D., N.Y. Law Sch., 1960. Bar: N.Y. 1961. Sr. acct. Selverne, Davis Co., N.Y.C., 1940-45; pvt. practice N.Y.C., 1945-61; exec. v.p. Met. Telecommunications Corp., Plainview, N.Y., 1961-62; pres., chief exec. officer Grow Group, Inc. (formerly Grow Chem. Corp.), N.Y.C., 1962—; also dir. Grow Group, Inc. (formerly Grow Chem. Corp.); dir. Bairnco Corp.; chmn. bd. dirs. GVC Venture Corp. Editor: Managing the Small Company. Recipient award of achievement Sch. of Bus. Alumni Soc. of CCNY, 1977; Winthrop-Sears medal Chem. Industry Assn., 1980. Mem. Nat. Paint and Coatings Assn. (past pres.), Am. Mgmt. Assn. (gen. mgmt. planning coun. 1966—, former trustee, exec. com.), N.Am. World Mgmt. Coun. (treas. bd. dirs.), Met. Club, Annabel's Club. Home: 1000 Park Ave New York NY 10028-0934 Office: Grow Group Inc 200 Park Ave New York NY 10166-0005

BANNAT, EDWARD GEORGE, metal processing executive; b. N.Y.C., June 3, 1947; s. Siegfried and Anne Marie (Klug) B.; m. Patti Jeanne Leitch, Nov. 7, 1970; children: Sarah Ann, Eric Edward. BS in Aerospace Engring. cum laude, U.S. Naval Acad., 1969; MS in Fin. Mgmt., Naval Postgrad. Sch., Monterey, Calif., 1974; MS in Taxation, Widener U., 1988. CPA, Pa.; cert. internal auditor, mgmt. acct. Commd. ensign USN, 1969, advanced through grades to lt., 1972, resigned, 1978; cost analyst Lukens Inc., Coatesville, Pa., 1978-80, fin. analyst, 1980-82, internal auditor, 1982-85, tax acct., 1985-88, sales and mktg. analyst, 1988-89, buyer, 1989—. Sec. New Holland (Pa.) Jaycees, 1980-82; fundraiser New Holland Pool Com., 1984. Am. Iron and Steel Inst. fellow, Washington, 1979-82. Mem. Inst. Mgmt. Accts., Inst. Internal Auditors, U.S. Naval Inst. Republican. Roman Catholic. Home: 220 Hill Rd New Holland PA 17557-9341 Office: Lukens Inc ARC Bldg Coatesville PA 19320

BANSAL, AMBRISH K., manufacturing company executive, consultant; b. Delhi, India, Oct. 19, 1947; came to U.S., 1970; s. Amrit Lal and Lilavati B.; m. Manju Gupta, Aug. 25, 1974; children: Parul, Shimul, Arjun. B in Tech., Indian Inst. of Tech., Kharagpur, 1970; MS, Ohio U., 1971; MBA, St. Bonaventure U., 1990. Cert. data processor. Systems analyst Univ. Hosps. of Cleve., 1971-73; programmer White Motors, Cleve., 1973-74; project mgr. Standard Oil of (Cleve.) Ohio, 1974-79; mgr. Price Waterhouse, Cleve., 1979-81, sr. mgr., 1981-83; project mgr. TRW, Cleve., 1983-85; dir. I.S., SKF MRC Bearings, Jamestown, N.Y., 1985-88, v.p. quality assurance, unit of SKF, 1988-91, v.p. bus. devel., unit of SKF, 1991—. Recipient Tech. Merit award Indian Govt., 1969. Mem. Am. Soc. for Quality Control. Home: 310 Weeks St Jamestown NY 14701-1770

BANTA, WILLIAM CLAUDE, biology educator; b. Long Beach, Calif., Nov. 13, 1941; s. Claude S. and Nedra K. (Baker) B.; m. Dawn Davis, Dec. 18, 1968 (div. 1974); m. Rochelle Barrios, May 28, 1975; children: Claude, Joshua, Jessica. BS in Zoology, U. Calif., Berkeley, 1963; PhD in Biology, U. So. Calif., 1969. Rsch. fellow Smithsonian Instn., Washington, 1969-70; mem. faculty, now prof. biology Am. U., Washington, 1970—; rsch. fellow U. Sydney, Australia, 1977; teaching fellow Bamfield (B.C., Can.) Lab., 1985; co-chair, panelist NAS, Washington, 1987—; cons. taxonomist Dames & Moore, Seattle, 1990—. Contbr. articles to profl. publs., chpts. to books. Grantee in field; recipient numerous awards. Democrat. Home: 3605 Stewart Dr Bethesda MD 20815-4732 Office: Am U Dept Biology Washington DC 20016

BANTEY, BILL, public relations executive; b. Québec City, Que., Can., Dec. 16, 1928; s. Louis and Maria (deLuce) B.; grad. high sch.; m. Judith Doonan, July 9, 1948; children—Daniel, Mark, Paul. Reporter, Que. Chronicle Telegraph, Québec City, 1944; police reporter Montreal Star, 1945-52; polit. writer, columnist Montreal Herald, 1952-56; feature writer, columnist Montreal Gazette, 1956-69; pres. Bill Bantey & Assos. Ltd., Montreal, 1968-—, Gagné, Bantey et Cie., Montreal, 1972-77; lectr. public relations Concordia U., Montreal, 1979-81; guest lectr. McGill U., Montreal, 1973-74, 82, 83, Carleton U., Ottawa, 1967. Recipient Golden Bell award Hotel Sales & Mktg. Assn. Internat., 1989. Mem. Canadian Public Relations Soc. (dir. 1975, fin. adminstrn. bd. 1975-76, awards of excellence 1975, 76, 78, 79, 80), City Hall Pub. Info. award Merit 1980, 82, Grand award 1981, 85), Am. Hotel Assn. (award of Excellence, 1979). Founding English editor City Montreal ofcl. mag. Montréal, 1964-69; editor M quar. rev. Montreal Mus. Fine Arts, 1970-76. Author guidebooks to Expo 67, Man and His World, Old Montreal; translator art book Pellan. Home: 3440 Beauséjour St, Saint Laurent, PQ Canada H4K 1W6 Office: 250 Youville Sq, 3d Floor, Montreal, PQ Canada H2Y 2B6

BANTRY, BRYAN, entrepreneur; b. Jacksonville, Fla., Oct. 12, 1956. Owner, operator dog-walking svc., 1969-73; photographer's agt. Patrick Demarchelier, 1973—; owner Bryan Bantry Hair-Makeup Agy., N.Y.C., 1973—; chmn., chief exec. officer Royal Atlantic Airways, N.Y.C., 1991—; cons. Targa Film Corp. Co-producer Broadway plays You Can't Take it With You, 1983, Aren't We All, 1985, off-Broadway plays Greater Tuna, 1982, Hey Ma...Kaye Ballard, 1984; creator TV pilot Man's Best Friend, 1983. Chmn. Batoto Yetu inner-city youth program, N.Y.C., 1992—. Mem. League of Am. Theatres and Producers, Creative Coalition.

BANYAS, JEFFREY BRIAN, otolaryngologist, educator; b. Washington, July 12, 1959; s. James Joseph and Martha Virginia (Cross) B.; m. Joann Matsko, Nov. 17, 1984; children: Jenna Marie, Julie Melinda. BS, Pa. State U., 1980; MD, Jefferson Med. Coll., 1982. Diplomate Am. Bd. Otolaryngology, Nat. Bd. Med. Examiners. Intern Western Pa. Hosp., 1982-83, resident in surgery, 1982-85; resident in otolaryngology SUNY, Buffalo, 1985-88; clin. asst. prof. Sch. Medicine SUNY, Buffalo, 1989, asst. prof., chief neuro-otology, 1990; neuro-otology fellow Echo Found., Birmingham, Ala., 1989-90; dir. otolaryngology-Erin County Med. Ctr.; dir. microsurgery lab. Sisters of Charity Hosp. Contbr. chpt. to book. Fellow Am. Acad. Otolaryngology; mem. AMA.

BANZETT, ROBERT BRUCE, physiologist; b. Englewood, N.J., Aug. 16, 1947; s. Howard and Edna Teresa Banzett. BS in Zoology, Pa. State U., 1969; PhD in Physiology, U. Calif., Davis, 1974. Postdoctoral fellow U. Calif., San Francisco, 1974-76; postdoctoral fellow Harvard Sch. Pub. Health, Boston, 1976-78, rsch. assoc., 1978-80, asst. prof., 1980-85, assoc. prof., 1985—. Contbr. articles to profl. jours. NIH rsch. grantee, 1985-93, 90-94. Mem. Am. Physiol. Soc. (editorial bd. 1989—). Office: Harvard Sch Pub Health 665 Huntington Ave Boston MA 02115-6021

BARABINO, WILLIAM ALBERT, science and technology researcher, inventor; b. Bay Shore, N.Y., Feb. 11, 1932; s. John Joseph and Anna Marie (Gates) B.; children: Susan Beth, William John. AS, SUNY, Farmingdale, 1952; student, St. Louis U., 1957; diploma, Alexander Hamilton Inst., N.Y.C., 1963. Dist. mgr. Piper Aircraft Corp., C.Am., 1960-62; application engr. Lab. for Electronics, Boston, 1962-63; mktg. mgr. spl. equipment div. Itek Corp., Waltham, Mass., 1963-65; bus. cons. North Reading, Mass., 1965-68; dir. Andover (Mass.) Inst. Bus., 1968-70; sci. and tech. researcher North Reading, 1970—; cons. CTS Corp., Proctor and Gamble, Scovill Corp., Am. Enviro. Products, Inc., Plessey Co., Ltd.; founder, chief exec. officer Brief Necessities, Agoura Hills,Calif., 1990. Patentee tire pressure alarm and warning systems, alarm systems for pneumatic tires, method and apparatus for monitoring tire pressure, brake wear warning system, fluid level and condition detection systems, disposal diaper with integral disposal system, single use disposal medical razor, treatment for causes of scalp diseases, liquid dispensing swab applicator, and others. Capt. USAF, 1952-59. Republican. Home and Office: 5 Westchester Dr North Reading MA 01864-1436

BARACH, BRUCE K., plastic surgeon; b. Albany, N.Y., Sept. 13, 1956; s. Jack A. and June (Tucker) B.; m. Irene Dana Bodnar, Aug. 18, 1984; children: Christopher M., Bryan E. AB, Dartmouth Coll., 1978; MD, SUNY, Syracuse, 1982. Diplomate Am. Bd. Plastic Surgery. Intern in surgery Hartford (Conn.) Hosp., 1982-83; resident in surgery Santa Barbara (Calif.) Cottage Hosp., 1983-85; resident in plastic surgery St. Francis Meml. Hosp., San Francisco, 1985-88; pvt. practice Schenectady, N.Y., 1988—. Mem. AMA, Am. Soc. of Plastic and Reconstructive Surgeons, N.Y. State Med. Soc., Schenectady County Med. Soc., Alpha Omega Alpha. Office: 1201 Nott St Ste 303 Schenectady NY 12308

BARACK, ROBIN SHEFFMAN, psychologist; b. St. John's, Nfld., Can., Jan. 20, 1946; d. Samuel B. and Alice (Serlin) Sheffman; m. Joseph P. Barack, June 14, 1966 (div. 1988); children: Shawn Beth, Ryan David. BA, U. Miami, 1966; MEd, U. Pitts., 1968, PhD, 1984. Lic. psychologist, cert. sch. psychologist, Pa. Tchr. Shaler Area Sch. Dist., Pitts., 1966-67, Allegheny County Intermediate U., Pitts., 1969; psychoednl. diagnostician Pitts. Child Guidance Ctr., 1969-81; sch. liaison, prin. Western Psychiat. Inst., Pitts., 1982-85, dir. psychoednl. assessment, 1985-86; clin. instr. dept. psychiatry U. Pitts., 1974—; pvt. practice Pitts., 1984—; consulting psychologist K.D. Tillotson Sch., Pitts., 1984-89, Temple Emanuel Nursery Sch., Mt. Lebanon, Pa., 1984—; bd. dirs. Chartiers Mental Health/Retardation, Bridgeville, Pa., 1985-90. Contbr. articles to profl. publs. Bd. dirs. Temple Emanuel of the Hills, Mt. Lebanon, 1984-89. Mem. Am. Psychol. Assn., Am. Orthopsychiat. Assn., Assn. Children with Learning Disabilities (adv. bd. 1980-91), Pa. Psychol. Assn., Pitts. Psychol. Assn. (edn. com. 1986—). Office: 401 Shady Ave Ste 107 Pittsburgh PA 15206-4409

BARANOWSKI, PAUL JOSEPH, nuclear instrumentation technician; b. Norwich, Conn., July 29, 1950; s. Joseph Baranowski Jr. and Margaret Olive (Croteau) Momut; m. S. Rose Bottom, Sept. 3, 1977; 1 child, Bettyann Cole. AS in Indsl. Electronics, Thames Valley State Coll., 1982. Cert. control technician Nat. Acad. Nuclear Tng. Welder Gen. Dynamics Elec. Boat, Groton, Conn., 1973-74; automotive technician Goodyear, Norwich, 1974-75, Mallon Chevrolet, Norwich, 1975-77; maintainence mechanic Wyre Wynd, Jewett City, Conn., 1977-79; engring. technician Victor Elec. Wire & Cable, Westerly, R.I., 1982-84; instrumentation and controls technician,

mech. tech. various nuclear facilities, 1984-90; instrumentation and controls technician Calvert Cliffs Nuclear Power Plant Balt. Gas & Elec. Co., Lusby, Md., 1990—. With USN, 1968-73. Mem. Am. Legion. Democrat. Home: PO Box 390 Solomons MD 20688-0390

BARASCH, MARIAN, mechanical engineer, educator; b. Braila, Romania, Jan. 21, 1948; came to U.S. 1974; s. Bendit and Rebeca (Ciobotaru) B.; m. Shari Gale Axelrod, June 5, 1979; children: Maxine Lynn, Brendan Jeffrey. Diplomate Engr., Bucharest Poly. Inst., 1970; MSME, U Houston, 1976; MS in Nuclear Engring., Rensselaer Poly. Inst., 1980. Energy engr. Energy Design Inst., Bucharest, 1970-73; rsch. asst. U. Houston, 1974-76, Rensselaer Poly. Inst., Troy, N.Y., 1976-79; sr. rsch. engr. Huyck Rsch. Centre, Rensselaer, N.Y., 1979-82; project engr. Mech. Tech., Inc., Latham, N.Y., 1982-85; cons. mech. engr. Watervliet Arsenal, Watervliet, N.Y., 1986-89; pres. Barasch Tech. Svcs., Inc., Albany, N.Y., 1987—; asst. prof. mech. engring. Hudson Valley Community Coll., Troy, N.Y., 1985—. Contbr. articles to profl. jours.; patentee in field. Mem. ASME, TAPPI, Vibration Inst., Can. Pulp and Paper Ind. Assn. Home: 109 Orlando Ave Albany NY 12203-2529 Office: Hudson Valley Community Col 80 Vandenburgh Ave Troy NY 12180-6025

BARASCH, SHIRLEY RUTH, musician, educator; b. Pitts., Jan. 13, 1933; d. Irving Arthur and Elizabeth (Karpilow) Schiffman; m. Ronald Henry Barasch, Aug. 15, 1954; children: Larry E., Karen B., Miriam S. BA, U. Pitts., 1954, MusM in Vocal Performance, B of Music Edn., 1969, postgrad., 1973, PhD, 1976. Cert. tchr., secondary edn., elem. and early childhood, music edn., Dalcroze Eurythmics, vocal pedagogy. Tchr. English, speech and drama J.T. Hutchinson Jr. High Sch., Lubbock, Tex., 1954-56; tchr. drama and music Ursuline Acad. and Hebrew Inst., Pitts., 1958-79; voice tchr. Ctrs. for Musically Talented, Bd. of Edn., Pitts., 1968-79; tchr. music and speech Point Pk. Acad., Point Pk. Coll., Pitts., 1969-72; asst. prof. edn. Point Pk. Coll., 1969-74, assoc. prof., dir. student teaching, 1974-80, prof. edn. and music, fine arts dir., 1981—, dir. music, 1981-86; cons. music Generations Together. Lyricist, author, composer (children's musicals) Button for Yarmulka, 1986, Emperor's Nightingale, 1986, Alice in Wonderland, 1987, Robin Hood, 1988, Wind in Willows, 1989, Legend of Sleepy Hollow, 1991; composer numerous songs and choral pieces; contbg. author tng. manual; contbr. poems, articles on ednl. theory and teaching music to publs. Bd. dirs. Pitts. Boys and Girls Choir, 1986—, Pitts. Concert. Soc., 1988—. Recipient award Warner TV Best Ednl. Children's Music Demo on Cable, 1984. Mem. ASCAP, Nat. Assn. Tchrs. of Singing (bd. dirs. 1989-91), Music Edn. Nat. Assn., Early Childhood Assn., Tuesday Mus., Children's Theatre Assn., Theater Alliance, Mu Phi Upsilon. Jewish. Office: Point Park Coll 201 Wood St Pittsburgh PA 15222

BARATTA, JOSEPH PRESTON, historian; b. Manhattan, Kans., June 24, 1943; s. Joseph John and Beatrice Wood (Preston) B.; m. Gay Diane Singer, June 16, 1968 (div. 1974). BA, St. John's Coll., 1969; MA, Boston U., 1977, PhD, 1982. Asst. prof. Boston U., 1982-83; UN rep. World Assn. for World Fedn., N.Y.C., 1985-88; exec. sec. Soc. for Study of Internationalism, Cambridge, Mass., 1988—; researcher Ctr. for UN Reform Edn., Washington, 1989-90. Author (monograph) Human Rights, 1990, Arbitration, 1989, Peacekeeping, 1989; compiler (bibliography) Strengthening the UN, 1987. Seminar leader World Federalist Assn., Cambridge, 1989. With USMC, 1962-65. Mem. Am. Hist. Assn. (Albert Beveridge grant 1984), Orgn. of Am. Historians, Soc. Historians of Am. Foreign Rels., Coun. on Peace Rsch. in History. Democrat. Roman Catholic. Home: 218 Thorndike St Apt 102 Cambridge MA 02141-1508 Office: Soc Study Internationalism PO Box 244 Cambridge MA 02238-0187

BARATZ, ROBERT SEARS, internist, dentist, researcher; b. New London, Conn., July 15, 1946; s. Wilbur Stanley and Frances B. (Sears) B.; m. Robin Sokoloff, July 20, 1975; children: Beth, Adam. AB in Biology cum laude, Boston U., 1969, MD, 1987; DDS, Northwestern U., Chgo., 1972; PhD in Anatomy and Cell Biology, Northwestern U., Evanston, Ill., 1975. Diplomate Am. Bd. Dental Examiners, N.E. Regional Bd. Dental Examiners, Am. Bd. Oral Medicine, Am. Bd. Med. Examiners. NIH postdoctoral fellow Northwestern U., Chgo., 1972-74, instr. anatomy, 1974-76; asst. prof. anatomy Sch. Medicine Boston U., 1976-85, dir. dept. anatomy Scanning Electron Microscope Lab., 1977-79; pvt. practice dentistry, Boston, 1979-81, 83-85; asst. prof. oral and maxillofacial surgery Boston U., 1977-86, asst. prof. nutritional scis., 1977-86; resident in internal medicine Carney Hosp.-Boston U., 1987-91, physician emergency dept., 1991—; asst. rsch. prof. oral pathology and oral medicine Tufts U. Sch. Dental Medicine, Boston, 1987—; physician, rsch. scientist dept. medicine and surgery VA Outpatient Clinic, Boston, 1988—; vis. prof. faculty medicine U. Kinshasa, Zaire, 1989; cons. U.S. Dept. State, AID, 1990—; cons. Polymedica Industries, Inc., 1990—, N.Y. State Edn. Dept, State Bd. for Dentistry, 1987—; ad hoc mem. oral biology I study sect. div. rsch. grants NIH, Bethesa, Md., 1991—; cons. in biomed. polymers Thermo Electron Corp., Waltham, Mass., 1982-83; cons. in oral medicine Mass. Rehab. Commn., 1986; numerous others. Mem. editorial bd. Jour. Biomaterials Applications, 1985—; mem. editorial rev. bd. Jour. Dental Edn., 1984-87; contbr. numerous articles and grants to sci. jours. Grantee NIH, 1974-79, 80-88, Boston U. Cancer Ctr., 1976-77, Hoffmann-LaRoche, Inc., 1977-79, Thermedics, Inc., 1983-87, VA, 1988-92. Mem. AAAS, AMA, ADA (spl. task force on dental amalgam 1991—), ACP, Internat. Assn. Dental Rsch., Am. Soc. for Cell Biology, Tissue Culture Assn., Soc. for Devel. Biology, Mass. Med. Soc., Am. Fedn. for Clin. Rsch., Am. Assn. Dental Schs., Am. Acad. Oral Medicine, Nat. Coun. Against Health Fraud, Am. Assn. for Dental Rsch. (pres. Boston chpt. 1989—). Home: 159 Bellevue St Newton MA 02158-1834 Office: Boston VA Outpatient Clinic 251 Causeway St Boston MA 02114

BARBA, FRANK PETER, insurance executive; b. N.Y.C., Nov. 7, 1932; s. Louis Frank and Ann (Giannantonio B.; m. Carolyn Straniero, Apr. 23, 1955; children: LuAnn Markowitz, Paula Soricelli. High sch. grad., N.Y.C.; grad., Mechanic's Inst. of N.Y., 1956, The Am. Coll., 1970. CLU. Pvt. practice builder N.Y.C., 1952-60; account exec. Met. Life Ins. Co., N.Y.C., 1960-66, sales mgr., 1966-75, dist. mgr., 1975-82; branch mgr. Met. Life Ins. Co., Larchmont, N.Y., 1982-91; instr. Life Underwriters Tng. Coun., Washington, 1971-75. Bd. dirs. Green Knolls, Green Vale Civic Assn., Eastchester, N.Y., 1973-76, '81-82; town bd. adv., 1973-82; minority hiring rep. Unidos, Inc., N.Y.C., 1972. With USMC, 1950-52. Mem. Nat. Assn. Life Underwriters (Nat. Mgmt. award 1975-82, Nat. Quality award 1961-66, Nat. Sales Achievment award 1961-66) N.Y. Life Underwriters Assn (bd. dirs. 1972-74, Westchester Life Underwriters ((bd. dirs. 1975-86, sec. 1984, v.p. 1985, chmn. sales congress, 1984-85, chmn. Life Insur. Week 1982-83). Roman Catholic. Home: 3 Shady Ln Scarsdale NY 10583-4923 Office: Met Life Ins Co PO Box 524 2365 Boston Post Rd Larchmont NY 10538

BARBAN, DORYS JOSEFINA, mathematics educator. BA in Maths. magna cum laude, Columbia U., 1976; MA, Hunter Coll., 1981; postgrad., CCNY, 1981-90. Adj. lectr. Johy Jay Coll. of Criminal Justice CUNY, N.Y.C., 1980-82; asst. prof. Montgomery Coll., Rockville, Md., 1982-85; instr. Christopher Newport Coll., Newport News, Va., 1985-87; asst. prof. Ramapo Coll. of N.J , Mahwah, 1987—. Mem. Ridgewood Schs. PTA, Ridgewood Schs. Curriculum 2000 Com. Mem. Am. Math. Assn. of Two Yr. Colls., MATHNET of N.J., ASCD, Nat. Coun. Tchrs. of Maths., Maths. Assn. Am. Home: 233 Bogert Ave Ridgewood NJ 07450-2701

BARBARINO, CRAIG MICHAEL, sports researcher; b. Port Jervis, N.Y., Dec. 11, 1962; s. George John and Rose (Calvario) B. AS in Bus., St. Johns U., Jamaica, N.Y., 1983, BA in Adminstrn., 1985. Pub. rels. asst. Baseball, Office of Commr., N.Y.C., 1985-88, researcher, 1988-92; pres. Keystone Sports, 1992—. rschr. game program Wold Series, 1990-92; rschr. game program All-Star Game, 1990-92, publs. and mags., 1989-92. Mem. Soc. Am. Baseball Rsch. Republican. Roman Catholic. Home and Office: RR 2 Box 610 Hawley PA 18428-9701

BARBARO, RONALD D., insurance company executive; b. 1931; married. Formerly pres. Can. ops. Scarborough, Ont.; with Prudential Ins. Co. Am., 1985—; pres. Prudential Ins. Co. Am., Newark, 1990—, also bd. dirs. Office: Prudential Ins Co Am Prudential Pla Newark NJ 07101 also: 751 Broad St Newark NJ 07102*

BARBEE, GEORGE E. L., financial services executive; b. Washington, Jan. 26, 1943; s. H. Randolph and Grace Lunt (Davenport) B.; m. Molly Morse Johnson, May 21, 1977; children—Gregory, John, Scott, Jefferson. AB, Brown U., 1965; MBA, U. Va., 1967. Fin. analyst W. R. Grace & Co., N.Y.C., 1968; product mgr. Wilkinson Sword Inc., Mountainside, N.J., 1968-70; mgr. new products Noxell Corp., Balt., 1970-74; sr. mktg. exec. Gillette Corp., Boston, 1974-79; co-founder, exec. dir. Consumer Fin. Inst., Newton, Mass., 1979-86; ptnr., exec. dir. personal fin. svcs. Price Waterhouse (merger with Consumer Fin. Inst.), Waltham, Mass., 1986-91, ptnr., exec. dir. client svcs. nat. office, N.Y.C., 1991—; dir. Victory Van Internat., Washington; weekly television columnist WBZ-TV, Boston, commentator fin. and bus. news NBC, CNN, PBS, ABC, CBS, 1981—. Author fin. articles. Mem. New Eng. Retirement Planners Council (pres.), Internat. Assn. Pre-Retirement Planners, Brown Alumni Assn., Va. Bus. Sch. Alumni Assn. (founding pres. New England chpt.), Leland Country Club, Chevy Chase Country Club, Scituate Harbor Yacht Club. Republican.

BARBEE, WILLIAM CLIFFORD, JR., finance educator; b. Washington, Feb. 1, 1944; s. William Clifford and Ruth Phyllis (Stone) B. BA with high honors, U. Md., 1965; MAT, U. Mass., 1966; PhD in Econs., Cath. U., 1974. Instr. bus. adminstrn. Montgomery Coll., Takoma Park, Md., 1967-71; mktg. analyst U.S. Steel, Pitts., 1973; asst. prof. econs. U. Md. Ea. Shore, Princess Anne, 1971-74; econ. analyst Fed. Res. Bank N.Y., N.Y.C., 1974, Morgan Guaranty, N.Y.C., 1974-75; assoc. prof. fin. and investments Howard U., Washington, 1975—; instr. fin., econs. USDA Grad. Sch. Internat. Programs Div., Washington, 1976-77; commentator Black Entertainment TV Network Arlington, Va., 1987; econ. cost benefit analyst Clean Capital City Com., Washington, 1987; expert witness in field; speaker in field. Contbr. to profl. publs. Carnegie-Mellon fellow Howard U., 1977. Mem. Phi Beta Kappa. Home: 6059 Tamar Dr Columbia MD 21045-4022 Office: Howard U Sch Bus 2600 6th St NW Washington DC 20059-0001

BARBER, EDMUND AMARAL, JR., retired engineer; b. East Providence, R.I., Oct. 20, 1916; s. Edmund Amaral and Clara Veronica (Amaral) B.; Sc.B., Brown U., 1938; postgrad. M.I.T., 1951, Syracuse U., 1955-57; m. Marion McKelvy Yost, Mar. 15, 1941; children—Marion Elizabeth Barber Goodrich, Jean Claire Barber Keehan. Designer, New Eng. Butt Co., Providence, 1936-38; with IBM, 1938-71, mgr. research, Endicott, N.Y., 1952-55, engring. mgr., Owego, N.Y., 1955-59, lab. adminstrn. mgr., Owego, 1959-64, spl. asst., Owego, 1964-66, avionics systems adminstrn. mgr., 1966-67, staff adminstrn. mgr., 1967-68, facility plans mgr., 1968-69, tech. staff mem., 1969-70, data mgr., 1970-71; ret., 1971; mem. Ithaca (N.Y.) chpt. Service Corps Ret. Execs., 1976—. Mem. Town of Owego Planning Bd., 1956-72. Pres. Tioga County Indsl. Devel. Corp., 1970-72, sec.-exec. dir., 1972, dir., 1967-72; adminstrv. dir. Tioga County Indsl. Devel. Agy., 1972; v.p. N.Y.-Penn Health Planning Council, 1969-72, dir., 1968-72; mem. exec. com., dir. N.Y.-Penn Health Mgmt. Corp., 1972; mem. exec. com. Tioga Gen. Hosp., Waverly, N.Y., 1962-72, dir., 1961-72, chmn. planning com., 1964-72; v.p. Owego Boys' Club, 1963-66, dir., 1962-66; pres. Christmas League, Owego, 1963-64, dir., 1961-70; bd. mgrs. Tompkins County Hosp., Ithaca, 1976, sec., 1976, chmn. planning com., 1976. Mem. ASME, Nat., N.Y. socs. profl. engrs., Sigma Xi, Tau Beta Pi. Republican. Roman Catholic. Clubs: Elks, Rotary (pres. Owego 1962-63, sec. 1965-66). Patentee in field of data processing machine, med. research equipment, music instrn. devices. Home: 42 Fairview Sq Ithaca NY 14850-4911 also: 2650 Pearce Dr Apt 311 Clearwater FL 34624-1133

BARBER, ILSA JOAN, accounting educator; b. N.Y.C., May 16, 1945; d. Emanuel Harry and Anne Grace (Hirsch) Demby; m. Rodney Hoy Bertrang, Jan. 19, 1964 (div. Jan. 1967). AB, CUNY, 1970, postgrad., 1990—. Jr. rsch. analsyt MPI, Inc., N.Y.C., 1970-71; media traffic control asst. Pro Clinica Inc., N.Y.C., 1980-81; with billing dept. Equity Advt., Inc., N.Y.C., 1984-85; cons. acctg. Friends of Israeli Def. Fund, N.Y.C., 1987-89, Inter-City Interior Svcs., N.Y.C., 1987-89; adj. lectr. Bronx Community Coll., N.Y.C., 1990; substitute instr. Baruch Coll., N.Y.C., 1991; adj. instr. Baruch Coll., Fordham U., N.Y.C., 1989, 91; v.p. Grad. Students Assembly, Baruch Coll., CUNY, 1987-88. Columnist Grad. Voice. Mem. Am. Acctg. Assn., Beta Alpha Psi. Democrat. Home: 1 Fordham Hill Oval Apt 3F Bronx NY 10468-8005 Office: Baruch Coll 46 E 26th St New York NY 10010-1703

BARBER, JAMES ALDEN, military officer; b. Poplar Bluff, Mo., May 6, 1934; s. James Alden and Ellamay (Morris) B.; m. Beverly June Kingsbury, June 12, 1955; children: Judith Lynn Barber Pratt, Steven Alden, Susan Elizabeth. BA in Econs., U. So. Calif., 1955; MA in Econs., Vanderbilt U., 1960; MA in Internat. Rels., Stanford U., 1964, PhD in Polit. Sci., 1965. Commd. ensign USN, 1955, advanced through grades to capt., 1975; commanding officer USS Hissem, 7th Fleet, Vietnam, 1966-68; Stephen B. Luce Prof. of Naval Strategy U.S. Naval War Coll., Newport, R.I., 1968-71; commanding officer USS Schofield, 7th Fleet, Vietnam, 1971-72; exec. asst. to under sec. of Navy Washington, 1975-76; commanding officer USS Horne, 7th Fleet, 1977-79; dep. dir. Politico-Mil. Affairs, Navy Dept., Washington, 1979-82; dep. dir., sr. fellow Strategic Concepts Devel. Ctr., Washington, 1982-84; exec. dir. U.S. Naval Inst., Annapolis, Md., 1984—. Author: Social Mobility and Voting Behaviour; co-author: Military and American Society; contbr. articles to encys. and profl. jours. Recipient Alfred Thayer Mahan award, U.S. Navy League, 1971; decorated Bronze Star with Combat "V", Def. Superior Svc. medal, Legion of Merit and others. Mem. Council on Fgn. Rels., U.S. Naval Inst., Internat. Inst. Strategic Studies, Interuniv. Seminar on Armed Forces and Soc., U.S. Nav. Acad. Found., N.Y. Yacht Club, Army and Navy Club. Democrat. Presbyterian. Office: US Naval Inst 118 Maryland Ave Annapolis MD 21402-5034

BARBER, KENNETH W., funeral director; b. Binghamton, N.Y., Nov. 18, 1952; s. Robert W. and Hawthorne (Corey) B.; m. Cynthia J. Cable, Sept. 20, 1975; children: Jocelyn C., Kyla D., Drew K. BSBA in Music, Lycoming Coll., Williamsport, Pa., 1974; grad. mortuary sci., Simmons Sch., Syracuse, N.Y., 1975. Pres. Barber Meml. Home, Inc., Johnson City, N.Y., 1975—; treas. Broome County Funeral Svc., Inc., Binghamton, N.Y., 1976—. Bd. dirs. Johnson City YMCA, 1986-89, Our Lady of Lourdes Hospice, Binghamton, 1978-81; chmn. United Health Svcs. Found., Johnson City, 1991—; mem. Wyoming Conf. Found. bd. United Meth. Ch., 1988—; mem. Broome County Coun. Chs., Binghamton, 1977—; bd. dirs. United Health Svcs., Inc., Diabetes Assn. of Southern Tier. Mem. Broome County Funeral Dirs. Assn. (pres. 1986-87), N.Y. State Funeral Dirs. Assn., Nat. Funeral Dirs. Assn., Trust 100, Internat. Order of Golden Rule, Rotary (bd. dirs. 1978-81). Republican. Methodist. Home: 708 Princeton Dr Vestal NY 13850-2936 Office: Barber Meml Home Inc 428 Main St Johnson City NY 13790-1995

BARBER, WILLIAM JOSEPH, educator, economist; b. Abilene, Kans., Jan. 13, 1925; s. Ward Seymour Henry and Esther (Roop) B.; m. Sheila Mary Marr, Apr. 16, 1955; children: Thomas, John, Charles. AB, Harvard U., 1949; BA, Oxford (Eng.) U., 1951, MA, 1955, DPhil, 1957; MA (hon.), Wesleyan U., Middletown, Conn., 1965. Asst. prof. Kans. State U., 1951-52; lectr. Balliol Coll., Oxford U., 1956; mem. faculty Wesleyan U., Middletown, Conn., 1957—; prof. econs. Wesleyan U., 1965—, Andrews prof. econs., 1972—, acting pres., 1988; vis. prof. econs. Yale U., 1982-84; Am. sec. Rhodes Scholarship Trust, 1970-80; bd. electors Eastman professorship Oxford U., 1970-81. Author: The Economy of British Central Africa, 1961, A History of Economic Thought, 1967, British Economic Thought and India 1600-1858, 1975, From New Era to New Deal, 1985; contbr. to Asian Drama: An Inquiry into the Poverty of Nations, 1968, Exhortation and Controls, 1975, Energy Policy in Perspective, 1980, Economists in Government, 1982; co-author, editor: Breaking the Academic Mold: Economists and American Higher Learning in the Nineteenth Century, 1988; editor: Perspectives on the History of Economic Thought, Vols. V-VI, 1991. Served with AUS, 1943-46, ETO. Decorated Order Brit. Empire; Rhodes scholar, 1949-51; Ford Found. Fgn. Area fellow Africa, 1955-56. Mem. Am. Econ. Assn., Royal Econ. Soc., Am. Assn. Rhodes Scholars, History of Econs. Soc. (pres. 1989-90), Phi Beta Kappa. Home: 306 Pine St Middletown CT 06457-3119

BARBERA, ANTHONY THOMAS, accountant, educator; b. Bklyn., Oct. 5, 1955; s. Thomas Anthony and Rachelle Regina (Crocitto) B. BS summa cum laude, St. John's U., Jamaica, N.Y., 1977, MBA, 1987. CPA, N.Y. Staff acct. Price Waterhouse, N.Y.C., 1977-80, sr. acct., 1980-83, audit mgr., 1983-84; grad. asst. St. John's U., Jamaica, N.Y., 1985-87, asst. prof., 1987—; mem. com. on fin. acctg. Savs. Banks Assn. N.Y. State, N.Y.C., 1983-84. Contbr. articles to profl. jours. Recipient William R. Donaldson award Catholic Accts. Guild, Diocese of Bklyn., 1977; N.Y. State Regents scholar, 1973-77; Robert E. Gilleece doctoral fellow CUNY Grad. Sch., 1989—; AICPA Doctoral fellow, 1989-92. Mem. AICPA, N.Y. State Soc. CPAs (profl. conduct com., recruitment com. CPA careers, cooperation com. with ednl. instns.), Am. Acctg. Assn., Securities Industry Assn., Decision Scis. Inst., Beta Alpha Psi, Beta Gamma Sigma, Omicron Delta Epsilon. Republican. Roman Catholic. Lodge: KC. Home: 32 Northcote Rd Westbury NY 11590-1504 Office: St Johns U Acctg Dept CBA Jamaica NY 11439

BARBERIS, DOROTHY WATKEYS, artist, educator; b. Newport News, Va., Sept. 20, 1918; d. Paul Fredrick and Ethel Rose (Mosher) Watkeys. Student, Syracuse U., 1936-37, 37-38. Designer Sherwin Bros., N.Y.C., 1938-39, Winborough Studio, N.Y.C., 1943-44; draftsman Johnson, Cushing & Neville, N.Y.C., 1944-45; owner, operator Barcedor Kennel, Pa., 1948-56. Pres. Desert Officer's Wives Club, Palm Springs, 1942; treas. Officer's Wives Club, Fort Lewis, Wash., 1947-50. Mem. Am. Artists Profl. League (bd. dirs. 1985-90, bd. dirs. N.J. chpt. 1983—), Nat. Assn. Women Artists, Nat. Arts Club, Salmagundi, North Shore Arts Assn., N.J. Watercolor Soc., Mid-West Watercolor Soc., S.W. Watercolor Soc., S.W. Watercolor Soc., N.E. Watercolor Soc., Catharine Lorillard Wolfe Art Club (dir. 1980-89, asst. treas. 1990, 2d v.p.), N.Y. Artists Equity, Artists Fellowship. Republican. Episcopalian. Home: 217 Lincoln Ave Elmwood Park NJ 07407-2822

BARBIERO, MICHAEL F., record producer, recording engineer; b. N.Y.C., June 25, 1949; s. Anthony and Lydia J. (Pappalardi) B.; m. Vivian Susan Hochstein, May 4, 1980; children: Raymond Douglas, Jessica Gabrielle, Alison Paige, Lauren Antoinette. BA, U. N.C., 1971. Rec. engr. Mediasound Studios, N.Y.C., 1971-72, 75-80; A&R, staff producer Paramount Records, N.Y.C., 1973-74; ind. engr., producer N.Y., N.J., 1980—; pres. Ring Bearer Music Ltd., N.Y.C., 1976—. Mem. ASCAP. Office: Advanced Alternative Media 121 W 27th St Ste 401 New York NY 10001-6207

BARBOZA, ANTHONY, photographer, artist; b. New Bedford, Mass., May 10, 1944; s. Anthony Canto and Lillian (Barros) B.; m. Laura Carrington, June 15, 1985; 1 child, Danica Chizu-Alita; children by previous marriage, Leticia, Laryssa. Grad. high sch., New Bedford. Lectr. Internat. Ctr. Photography, 1975, 83, Mass. State Coun. of Arts, 1982, Columbia Coll. Photography, Chgo., 1983, Oberlin (Ohio) Coll., 1984, Ohio U., Athens, 1986, Mus. Sch. Fine Arts, Boston, 1989, Lowell (Mass.) U., 1989, Rochester (N.Y.) Inst. Tech., 1991; freelance photographer for advt. campaigns including Clairol, Hanes, Coca-Cola, Pepsi-Cola, United Negro Coll. Fund., Burger King, Soft Sheen Products, Kodak, McDonalds, Anheiser Busch, AT&T, Coors, Universal Pictures, Spike Lee Prodns., numerous others; panelist, judge Mass. State Coun. of Arts, 1978, Nat. Endowment Arts, 1981. Solo exhbns. include Pensacola (Fla.) Art Mus., 1966, Jacksonville (Fla.) Art Mus., 1969, Light Impressions Gallery, Rochester, N.Y., 1973, Friends Gallery of N.Y., 1974, Studio Mus. Harlem, N.Y.C., 1982; group shows include Addison Gallery Am. Arts, Andover, Mass., 1971, Mus. Modern Art, N.Y.C., 1978, Photokina, Germany, 1982, 84, City of Munich, 1985, Washington Project for Arts, 1989; in permanent collections Mus. Modern Art, N.Y.C., Newark Art Mus., U. Ghana, U. Mex., others; contbr. to book Songs of My People, 1992. Grantee N.Y. State Coun. of Arts, 1974, 76, Nat. Endowment Arts, 1980. Home: 915 Gloucester St Westbury NY 11590 Studio: 853 Broadway Ste 1208 New Yorik NY 10003

BARCLAY, JUDITH SHAFFER, banker; b. Rummell, Pa., July 31, 1942; d. Charles Grant and Mary Naomi (Baumgardner) Shaffer; m. Harry Thomas Jr., Oct. 18, 1963; children: Sherry Dawn, Thomas James. AA, Valencia Community Coll., Orlando, Fla., 1982; BS, Ind. U. of Pa., 1984, MA, 1987. Salesperosn Nat. Bus. Builders, Orlando, Fla., 1980-82; substitute tchr. Blairsville (Pa.) Sch. Dist., 1985; adult edn. specialist Partnership With Industry, Indiana, Pa., 1985, dir., 1985-89; coord. mature market Nat. Bank of the Commonwealth, Indiana, 1989—; mature market dir., corp. officer First Commonwealth Fin. Corp., Indiana, 1990—. Core com. mem. We. Region Coalition for Mental Health Needs, Indiana, 1987—; task forse chmn. Human Svc. Coun., Indiana, 1986-87; com. mem. Coord. Svc. for the Handicapped, 1987. Mem. NAFE, Order Ea. Star. Republican. Southern Baptist. Home: RR 5 Box 558 Blairsville PA 15717-9680 Office: First Commonwealth Fin Corp PO Box 400 Indiana PA 15701-0400

BARCUS, FRANCIS EARLE, educator; b. Rossville, Ill., Feb. 1, 1927; s. Chauncey Hobart and Edna Rose (Smith) B.; m. Faith Nobuko Araki, Nov. 27, 1947; children: Julia, Gary, Mark. AB, U. Ill., 1952, MA, 1955, PhD, 1959. Rsch. asst. U. Ill., Urbana, 1956-59; prof. Boston U., 1959-89; rsch. cons. in field; cons. U.S. Dept. Agriculture, Washington, 1955-56; dir. communication rsch. ctr. Boston U., 1985-89; rsch. dir. Action for Children's TV, Newtonville, Mass., 1971-79. Author: Children's Television, 1980, Image of Life in TV, 1985; contbr. articles to profl. jours. Staff sgt. U.S. Army, 1946-47. Mem. Phi Kappa Phi. Democrat. Home: 23 Warwick Rd Brookline MA 02146

BARCUS, GILBERT MARTIN, medical products executive, educator; b. N.Y.C., Sept. 20, 1937; s. Leon A. and Dorothy (Brownstein) B.; m. Sondra Ettin, May 6, 1961; children: David A., Ruth A. Barcus Feinberg. BS, NYU, 1959; MBA, L.I. U., 1969. Stock broker Ernst & Co., N.Y.C., 1962-65; sales mgr. McNeil Labs., Ft. Washington, Pa., 1965-75; mktg. mgr. USA Devices Ltd., New Brunswick, N.J., 1976-77; dir. product mgmt. TENS div. Stimtech, Inc., Mpls., 1977-78; products dir. Critikon, Inc., Raritan, N.J., 1979-80; v.p. mktg. Electro Biology, Inc., Fairfield, N.J., 1980-82; dir. sales, mktg. Medtronic/Med. Data Systems, Ann Arbor, Mich., 1982-85; v.p. corp. devel. Am. Biomaterials Corp., Princeton, N.J., 1985-86, sr. v.p., 1986-88; pres. Sandar Assocs., North Brunswick, N.J., 1980—; gen. mgr. Creative Care Sytems, Maplewood, N.J., 1986-88; adj. prof. Middlesex Coll., Edison, N.J., 1986—; lectr. dept. bus. Brookdale C.C., Bus. Week Mktg. Seminars, 1988, UN Soviet Econs. Mission, 1992; bd. dirs. Life Scis., Inc., Lebanon, N.J., 1989-91; prof. bus. CUNY, S.I., 1990—. Contbr. articles to profl. jours. Chmn. Marlboro (N.J.) Fire Commn., 1970-76; dir. Small Bus. Devel. Ctr. Middlesex County, 1988-91. Fellow Assn. Advancement Med. Instrumentation, Internat. Assn. Study of Pain; mem. Ann Arbor C. of C. (legis. com.), NYU Alumni Assn. (dir. 1987-92), Travis Pointe Country Club, Princeton Club of N.Y., NYU Club, Forsgate Country Club (v.p. 1986-91), Pi Lambda Phi. Home and Office: 15 Wood Lake Ct North Brunswick NJ 08902-4836

BARCZAK, BERNARD GERARD, health care executive; b. Balt., Sept. 3, 1947; s. Benjamin Joseph and Leona Katherine (Gregorek) B.; m. Linda Ann Horecka, July 25, 1970; children: Andrew, Lisa. BS in Acctg., Loyola Coll., Balt., 1969. CPA, Md. Audit mgr. Arthur Andersen & Co., Balt., 1969-80; v.p. fin. Nat. Psychiat. Insts. Inc., Washington, 1980-82; pvt. practice CPA Balt., 1983-84; v.p., sec. United Psychiat. Group, Washington, 1985—; bd. dirs., treas. sec. Psychiat. Health Ctrs., Greater Kansas City, Inc., Kans., Altacare Corp., Columbia, Md., Ohio Psychiat. Insts., Inc., Dayton, Mesilla Valley Hosp., Inc., Las Cruces, N.Mex., Commonwealth Broadcasting Co., Inc., Stroudsburg, Pa., Western Psychiat. Inc., Wyo., Ind. Psychiat. Insts., Inc., Bloomington, Ea. Ohio Psychiat. Inst., Inc., Youngstown, Southea. Ohio Psychiat. Insts., Inc., St. Clairesville. With USAR, 1969-73. Mem. AICPA, Hosp. Fin. Mgmt. Assn. (advanced), BMW Car Club Am. Roman Catholic. Home: 13326 Springwood Ct Ellicott City MD 21042-1256 Office: United Psychiat Group 2001 L St NW Ste 200 Washington DC 20036-4910

BARE, THOMAS MICHAEL, biomedical research chemist; b. Lancaster, Pa., Nov. 24, 1942; s. John L. and Virginia M. (Boone) B.; m. Ann L. Loveless, July 8, 1967; children: Jennifer L., Kimberly A., Christine M. BS, Pa. State U., 1964; MS, MIT, 1967, PhD, 1969. Sr. rsch. chemist Lakeside Labs., Milw., 1968-75, Morton Chem. Co., Woodstock, Ill., 1975-76; prin. chemist ICI Ams., Inc., Wilmington, Del., 1976—. Contbr. articles to sci. jours; patentee on bioactive materials. Coord. gardening Gaudenzia House, West Chester, Pa., 1983, 84. Mem. Am. Chem. Soc., Internat. Soc. Hetero-

cyclic Chemistry, Sigma Xi. Office: ICI Ams Inc Medicinal Chemistry Dept Wilmington DE 19897

BAREIHS, DIETER ERICH, air force officer; b. Scranton, Pa., June 19, 1966; s. Erich Karl and Margrit Anna-Marie (Dengler) B. BS in Aero. Engring., USAF Acad., 1989. Cadet squadron commdr. USAF, 1988, commd. 2d lt., 1989, advanced through grades to 1st lt., 1991; pilot USAF, Alomogordo, N.Mex., 1990-91, Phoenix and Fairbanks, Alaska, 1991—. Mem. AIAA, Order of DeMolay (past master councilor 1982-83). Republican. Home: 1926 E Elm St Scranton PA 18505-3932

BARENTYNE, ROSS, musical director, vocal coach, accompanist; b. Denton, Tex., Nov. 30, 1939; s. Henry Ross and Josie (Lee) B. MusB, North Tex. State U., 1962; MusM, Mich. State U., 1967; postgrad., Fla. State U., 1969-74. Piano tchr. Houston, 1962-65; instr. music Ga. Coll., Milledgeville, 1967-69; adj. music faculty Fla. State U., Tallahassee, 1970-74; vocal coach N.Y.C., 1974—; mus. dir. LaGran Scena Opera, N.Y.C., 1984—; cons. Mus. Theatre Network, N.Y.C., 1980—; concert artist in U.S. and abroad. Contbr. to P.R. Culture in N.Y.C., Soc. de Culture de P.R. en Nueva York, 1980. Mem. Phi Mu Alpha Sinfonia, Pi Kappa Lambda. Democrat. Episcopalian. Home: 160 W 73rd St New York NY 10023-3012

BARETSKI, CHARLES ALLAN, political scientist, librarian, educator, historian; b. Mt. Carmel, Pa., Nov. 21, 1918; s. Charles Stanley and Mary Ann (Gorzelnik) B.; m. Gladys Edith von Nyitrai Yartin, Aug. 19, 1950 (dec. Oct. 1989). BA cum laude (scholar), Rutgers U., 1945; BSLS, Columbia, 1946, MSLS, 1951; Diploma, Inst. Bibliog. Orgn. of Knowledge U. Chgo., 1950; diplomas in archival adminstrn., Am. U., 1951, 55; MA in Polit. Sci., U. Notre Dame, 1957, PhD, 1958; MA in Govt. and Internat. Rels., NYU, 1965, PhD in Politics, 1969. From reference libr. to sr. libr. Newark Pub. Libr., 1938-54; rsch. intern Am. State Dept. Archives, Nat. Archives, 1951, br. libr. Van Buren br., 1954-56, br. dir., 1957-88, dir. fgn. lang. book collection, 1954-88; nat. archivist, historian Am. Coun. For Polish Culture, 1954-91; dir., chief lectr., rev. seminars on liberal arts courses and libr. sci., mem. staff groups for N.J. state civil svc. libr. exams., 1950-77; cons. doctoral candidates in grad. studies, 1957-58, Richmond Mcpl. Coun. election campaign, 1990; Richmond del. 4th & 5th Nat. Cath. Golden Age Assn. confs., 1990, 91; judge Richmond Mcpl. Spelling Bee in conjunction with Richmond Pub. Sch. System & Sr. Citizen Orgns., 1991; chief judge award com. Joseph Conrad Lit. Contest, 1968; mem. faculty Univ. Coll., Rutgers U., Newark, 1965-66; coord. Slavic-Am. hist. studies Sr. Citizens' Inst., Essex County Coll., Newark, 1977-78; dir. Baretski Tutorial Svc., 1935-68; founder, dir. Ethnic Rsch. Archives, 1971-91, dir. Rsch. Libr.; pres. Assn. Community Couns. Newark, 1969-88; pres. Ironbound (Newark) Community Coun., 1961-88; lectr., cons. Am. Ethnic Polit. History, 1968—; cons. Doctoral Candidates, U. Notre Dame, 1957-58, genealogical rsch., 1987—; mem. adv. coun. North Essex Ednl. Center, Essex County Coll., Belleville, N.J., 1973-88; treas., chmn. N.J. Coalition for Safe Communities, Anti-Crime N.J. State-wide Fedn., 1978-80. Author: Our Quarter Century: History of the American Council of Polish Cultural Clubs 1948-1973, 1973, Fond Memories of Ann Street School Neward, N.Y.: 1920's to 1950's, 1986, A Decade of Caring and Sharing: The History of Our Lady of Peace Chapter, Catholic Golden Age Association, Richmond, Virginia: 1981-91, 1991; co-author: The Polish University Club of New Jersey; A Concise History: 1928-88, 1988; author taped narrative The Legend of America's Santa Claus, 1987; author (radio play) The Life and Times of Samuel F.B. Morse: The Inventer of the Telegraph , 1936; editor: Higher Horizons Ednl. Program N.Y.C., 1961; editor and pub. Ironbound (N.J.) Counselor, Newark, 1965. Contbr. Lettersto-the-Editor columns in newspapers and periodicals including N.Y. Times, Newark Star-Ledger, Richmond News Leader, The Christian Science Monitor, Life mag., ALA Bull., articles to numerous profl. jours., also chpts. to books, compiler. Rsch. on contbns. Polish and other immigrants to Am. culture and history. Rep. Clean Govt. candidate for U.S. Congress, 10th Dist. N.J., 1962; N.J. chmn. Polish-Am. Citizens for Goldwater, 1964; N.J. liaison dir. Polish Am. Rep. Nat. Coun., 1971-88; rsch. dir., pub. rels. dir. Polish-Am. Rep. Club N.J. Vol., tutor Mt. Carmel, Pa. and Newark Elem. Schs., 1929-32, Newark Pub. High Schs., 1932-35; reporter Newark Sunday Ledger, 1935; mem. Va. Mus. Fine Arts, Richmond, The Poe Found., Inc.; founder, dir. Inst. Polish Culture, Seton Hall U., South Orange, N.J., 1953-54; rsch. historian of inst., 1953-88; nat. gen. sec. Am. Polish Civil War Centennial com., 1961-65; founder, dir., libr. Ctr. Advancement Slavic Studies, 1970-91; chmn. internat. com. 300th Ann. of Founding of Newark, 1965-66; founder, pres. Ind. Polish-Am. Voters of N.J., 1953-88; state del. Polish Hungarian World Fedn., 1977-83; founder, pres. Newark Pub. Libr. Employees Union Local 2298, Am. Fedn. State, County and Municipal Employees, AFL-CIO, 1971-77, del. internat. convs., 1974, 76, 78, 80, 82, trustee N.J. Pub. Employers Council 52, No. N.J. Pub. Employee Unions1978-84; mem. exec. bd. Newark Labor Coalition, 1972-77; bd. dirs. N.J. chpt. Confedn. Am. Ethnic Groups; organizer, cons. Newark Ironbound Sr. Citizen's Multi-Purpose Ctr. Satellite Libr., 1986-88; resource scholar N.J. Gov.'s Commn. on Eastern European and Captive Nation History, 1985-88; historian Newark Multi-Ethnic Coun., 1986-88; trustee Cath. Golden Age Sr. Citizens Club Richmond, 1990-91, historian and v.p., 1991—; v.p., program chmn. Soun. Sr. Citizens Orgn. Richmond, 1991—; commr. Richmond Mcpl. Commn. on Elderly, 1991—; judge 4th Ann. Mcpl. Intergenerational Spelling Bee, 1991; v.p., program chmn. Cosco Coun. 95 Federated Sr. Citizen Orgns. Richmond, 1991—. Rudgers U. Scholar, 1945; Edna Sanderson fellow, Columbia U., 1946, Newark Pub. Libr. Scholar, 1951; rsch. fellow U. Notre Dame, 1957; recipient Presdl. Leadership and Disting. Svc. award Am. Fedn. State, County and Mcpl. Employees, 1972, Founder's Day award N.Y. U., 1970, Svc. awards Newark Pub. Libr., 1972, 74, 76, 85, 88, Nat. Am. Heritage award J.F. Kennedy Library for Minorities, 1972, Outstanding State Labor Leader award N.J. Pub. Employees, AFL-CIO, 1978; Disting. Educator Am. award, 1979; New Internat. award Polish Govt. in exile, London, 30 years Profl. Svc. award Newark's Ironbound Community, 1984, Sixty Yr's Dedicated Vol. Turoring award, 1987; Named for the outstanding contbns. to the greater Newark community and devoted svcs. to the growth of the Newark Pub. Libr. system, 1988; elected Nat. Role Model for Am. Youth to Hall of Fame U.S. Acad. Achievement, Lexington, Ky., 1983, numerous others; decorated Knight's cross Polonia Restituta. Mem. Italian-Am. Cultural Assn. Va., Polish-Am. Unity League, Polish-Am. Hist. Assn. (asst. editor monthly Bull. 1959-61, nat. editor-in-chief 1961-65), Writers Soc. N.J. (exec. dir. 1947-56), Am. Polit. Sci. Assn., Am. Soc. Internat. Law, Am. Sociol. Assn., Soc. Historians Am. Fgn. Rels., Am. Hist. Assn., N.Y. Libr. Club, Polish-Hungarian World Fedn., Immigration History Soc., N.J., Middle States coun. social studies, Am. Coun. For Polish Culture, Newark Pub. Libr. Guild (founder, pres. 1970), Libr. Pub. Rels. Coun., ALA, N.J. Libr. Assn., Essex County Librs. Assn., Coll. Art Assn., Assn. Historians of Am. Art, Polish U. Club of N.J., Polish Arts Club Newark (pres. 1980-88, historian 1975-91). Roman Catholic. Home and Office: 2426 W Tremont Ct Richmond VA 23225-1956

BARIDON, PHILIP CLARKE, criminologist, policy analyst, consultant; b. Washington, Aug. 1, 1946; s. R. Clarke and Juanita (Ayers) B.; m. Beverly Ann Bruns, Feb. 3, 1990. B.A., Bucknell U., 1968; M.A., SUNY-Albany, 1971, Ph.D., 1975. Police officer Met. Police D.C., 1968-72; asst. prof. Am. U., Washington, 1972-74, mem. adj. faculty, 1974-76; rsch. assoc. Mid-Atlantic Research Inst., Bethesda, Md., 1974-75; prin. cons. P.R.C., McLean, Va. and San Francisco, 1975-78; chief program evaluation br., forensic programs St. Elizabeth's Hosp., Washington, 1978-84; sr. policy analyst criminal div. U.S. Dept. Justice, Washington, 1984—. Author: Addiction, Crime and Social Policy, 1976; contbr. articles to profl. jours. N.Y. State fellow, 1970-71; Ford Found. fellow, 1971-72; Nat. Inst. Justice grantee, 1980. Mem. Am. Soc. Criminology, Nat. Coun. Crime & Delinquency, Am. Acad. Polit. and Social Sci. Buddhist. Home: 4160 36th St S Arlington VA 22206-1806

BARIE, PHILIP STEVEN, surgeon, educator; b. Buffalo, Aug. 18, 1953; s. Kenneth George and Eleanor Lucille (Davis) B.; m. Elaine Catherine Dash, May 31, 1981; children: Catherine, Steven, Alexandra. AB cum laude, MD, Boston U., 1977. Diplomate and surgical critical care cert. Am. Bd. Surgery. Jr. resident in surgery N.Y. Hosp.-Cornell Med. Ctr., N.Y.C., 1977-79; fellow in surgery and physiology Albany (N.Y.) Med. Coll., 1979-81; sr. resident in surgery N.Y. Hosp.-Cornell Med. Ctr., 1981-83, adminstrv. chief resident surgery, 1983-84; asst. prof. surgery Cornell U. Med. Coll., N.Y.C., 1984-89, assoc. prof., 1989—; attending surgeon, dir. surg ICU, N.Y. Hosp., N.Y.C., 1984—; cons. in surgery Cath. Med. Ctr., N.Y.C., 1985—; chmn. inst. rev. bd. Med. Coll. Cornell U., N.Y.C., 1988—; cons. specialist, mem. med. control bd. Health Ins. Plan Greater N.Y., 1990—; cons. in critical care therapeutics U.S. Pharmacopeial Conv. Contbr. articles to profl. jours. Fellow ACS, Am. Coll. Critical Care Medicine; mem. N.Y. Acad. Medicine (sec. surg. sect. 1991-92), N.Y. Surg. Soc., Soc. Critical Care Medicine, Am. Assn. for Surgery of Trauma, Internat. Surg. Soc., Am. Physiol. Soc., N.Y. Acad. Scis., Surg. Infection Soc., Assn. for Acad. Surgery, Shock Soc., Ea. Assn. for Surgery of Trauma. Office: NY Hosp-Cornell Med Ctr Dept Surgery 525 E 68th St New York NY 10021-4873

BARIL, EARL FRANCIS, biochemist, educator, researcher; b. Claremont, N.H., Apr. 23, 1930; s. William Joseph and Agnes Georgiana (L'Hereuax) B.; m. Betty JoAnn Buckingham, June 19, 1965. BA, St. Anselm's Coll., 1959; MS in Biophysics, U. Houston, 1961; PhD in Biochemistry, U. Conn., 1966. Postdoctoral fellow U. Wis., Madison, 1966-69; asst. prof. in biochemistry Duke U., Durham, N.C., 1969-72, assoc. prof., 1972—; sr. scientist Worcester Found. for Exptl. Biology, Shrewsbury, Mass., 1972-86, prin. scientist, 1986—; prof. biochemistry and pharmacology U. Mass., Worcester, 1987—; Mem. editorial adv. bd., Molecular Pharmacology, 1978—; adv. com. NIH Physiol. Chemistry, Bethesda, Md., 1984-88; mem. adv. panel Idaho State Bd. Edn., Boise, 1988. Sgt., USMC, 1948-52, Korea. Nat. Cancer Inst. grantee, NIH, 1975; fellow NIH, 1961, NSF, 1960. Fellow Am. Inst. Chemists; mem. Am. Soc. Biochemists and Molecular Biologists, Biophys. Soc., The Protein Soc. (founder). Democrat. Home: 105 Wachusett St Rutland MA 01543-2011 Office: Worcester Found Exptl Biology 222 Maple Ave Shrewsbury MA 01545-2732

BARILE, MICHAEL FREDERICK, microbiologist, immunologist; b. Bound Brook, N.J., Jan. 9, 1924; s. Ferdinando and Santa (Tolomeo) B.; m. Grace Price, May 15, 1946; children: Michael F. II, Sondra Jean, Karin Jo, Deborah Ann. BS, U. Ga., 1949; MS, U. Mich., 1951, PhD, 1954. Rsch. asst. dept. bacteriology U. Mich., Ann Arbor, 1951-52, teaching fellow, 1952-53, instr. and rsch. assoc. depts. bacteriology and surgery, 1953-54; head venereal disease sect. U.S. Far East Med. Rsch. Unit 406 Med. Gen. Lab., Tokyo, 1954-58; rsch. microbiologist divsn. biologics standards NIH, Bethesda, Md., 1958-68, chief sect. on mycoplasma lab. bacterial products Bur. Biologics, 1968-72; dir. mycoplasma br. divsn. bacterial products Bur. Biologics FDA, Bethesda, 1972-74, dir. mycoplasma br. divsn. bacterial products office biologics rsch. and rev. Nat. Ctr. for Drugs and Biologics, 1974-85, chief lab. of mycoplasma, divsn. bacterial products office biologics, 1985-87; chief lab. of mycoplasma divsn. bacterial products, ctr. for biologics evaluation and rsch. FDA, Bethesda, Md., 1987—; pres. Internat. Orgn. for Mycoplasmology, 1980-82; mem. WHO/FAO expert bd. on Mycoplasma, 1974—; guest lectr. U. Md., Georgetown U. Med. Sch., Geo. Washington U. Med. Sch.; chmn. or convenor of over 30 sci. meetings nationally and over 20 internationally 1954—. Editor: (with others) The myocoplasmas, vols. I, II, III, 1979, vol. IV, 1985, vol. V, 1989; contbr. 185 articles to profl. jours. Recipient Fellowship Teaching award, U. Mich. 1952-53; third most cited of all microbiology and virology publications during period 1961-76. Mem. AAAS, Am. Acad. Microbiology, Am. Soc. for Microbiology, European J. Epidemiology, Soc. for Exptl. Biology and Medicine, Tissue Culture Assn., Internat. Orgn. for Mycoplamology (numerous offices including pres. 1980-82, treas. 1974-78, bd. dirs. 1974-84, Presdl. Citation award 1984), Sons of Italy (pres. 1986-88, Presdl. Citation award 1988), Sigma Xi, Phi Kappa Chi, Phi Eta Sigma, Phi Sigma. Home: 9716 Kensington Pky Kensington MD 20895-3519 Office: Dept Health & Human Svcs FDA Lab Mycoplasma Bldg 29 Rm 420 8800 Rockville Pike Bethesda MD 20892

BARIO, PATRICIA YAROCH, public relations executive; b. Kinde, Mich., Aug. 12, 1932; d. Edmund T. and Marie L. (Meagher) Yaroch; widowed; children: Gianfranco Edmundo and Marco Alessandro. BA in Journalism, Mich. State U., 1954. Reporter The Detroit Free Press, 1954-55; reporter, editor The Detroit News, 1955-61; dir. communications Senator Philip Hart, Washington, 1963-76; dep. press sec. Pres. Jimmy Carter, Washington, 1977-81; pres., owner Patricia Bario Assocs., Washington, 1981-83; v.p. Burson Marsteller, Washington, 1983-85; pres., owner Patricia Bario Assocs., Washington, 1985—. Recipient Writing award AP, 1952; named Outstanding Citizen Mich. State U., East Lansing, 1980; winner Silver Anvil Pub. Rels. Soc. Am., 1989. Mem. The Nat. Press Club. Democrat. Roman Catholic. Office: 512 11th St SE Washington DC 20003-2830

BARISH, JULIAN I., psychiatrist; b. Sault Ste Marie, Mich., Mar. 12, 1917; s. Max and Nancy Barish; m. Judith Sophian, June 7, 1941; children: Richard K., Patricia L. Speckert. AB, U. Mich., 1938, MD, 1941, MS, 1948; cert. in psychoanalysis, Columbia U., 1955. Diplomate Am. Bd. Psychiatry and Neurology. Intern Bridgeport Hosp., Bridgeport, Conn., 1941-42; resident psychiatry Neuropsychiat. Inst., U. Mich. Med. Ctr., Ann Arbor, 1946-48; fellow in psychiatry, instr. psychiatry N.Y. Hosp.-Cornell Med. Ctr., N.Y.C., 1948-56; pvt. practice psychiatry and psychoanalysis N.Y.C., Larchmont, N.Y., 1949—; candidate, preceptor, collaborating psychoanalyst Columbia U. Psychoanalytic Ctr., N.Y.C., 1949-57, 72-77; asst. prof. psychiatry Grad. Sch. Psychiatry, Downstate Med. Ctr., Bklyn., 1956-58; co-founder, co-dir. The Psychiat. Treatment Ctr., N.Y.C., 1961-68; chief adolescent svc. Four Winds Hosp., Katonah, N.Y., 1968-70; assoc. clin. prof. psychiatry Mt. Sinai Med. Ctr., N.Y.C., 1974—; mem. nat. bd. Soc. for Sci. Study of Sex, N.Y.C., 1978-80; councillor Westchester Psychiat. Soc., White Plains, N.Y., 1971-73; chmn. com. on adolescent care Nat. Assn. Pvt. Psychiat. Hosps., Washington, 1965-68. Contbr. articles to profl. jours. Panelist youth conf. Westchester Citizens Com., Nat. Coun. on Crime & Delinquency Jr. Leagues, Scarsdale, N.Y., 1967; del. White House Conf. on Youth, Estes Park, Colo., 1971; participant Spl. Action Office for Drug Abuse Prevention, Conf. on Youth Oriented Drug Programs, Washington, 1972; prin. speaker Riveredge Hosp. Conf. on Hosp. Treatment Adolescents, Forest Park, Ill., 1968. Major Med. Corps, U.S. Army, 1942-46, ETO. Fellow Am. Soc. Adolescent Psychiatry (life, pres. 1975-76), Am. Psychiat. Assn. (life, vice chmn. coun. on nat. affairs and social issues 1972-74); mem. AMA (life), Am. Psychoanalytic Assn. (life, cert.), Am. Acad. Psychoanalysis (life). Home and Office: 17 E 93rd St Apt A New York NY 10128

BARKER, HAROLD GRANT, surgeon; b. Salt Lake City, June 10, 1917; s. Frederick George and Jennetta (Stephens) B.; m. Kathleen Butler, July 29, 1949; children: Janet Stephens, Douglas Reid. A.B., U. Utah, 1939, postgrad., 1939-41; M.D., U. Pa., 1943. Diplomate Am. Bd. Surgery. Intern. Hosp. U. Pa., 1943-44, asst. resident in surgery, 1947-51, sr. resident in surgery, 1951-52, asst. attending surgeon, 1952-53; also asst. instr., research fellow U. Pa., 1946-51, instr., research fellow, 1951-52, assoc. in surgery, 1952-53; asst. prof. surgery Columbia U., 1953-57, assoc. prof., 1957-68, prof., 1968-82, prof. emeritus, 1982—; asst. attending surgeon Presbyn. Hosp., 1953-57, assoc. attending surgeon, 1957-69, attending surgeon, 1969-89, dir. med. affairs, 1974-82; pvt. practice, Phila., 1952-53, N.Y.C., 1953-88. Contbr. articles med. jours. Served from 1st lt. to capt., M.C. AUS, 1944-46, ETO. Fellow ACS; mem. Soc. U. Surgeons, N.Y. Surg. Soc., Am. Physiol. Soc., Soc. Exptl. Biology and Medicine, AMA, Halsted Soc., N.Y. State (chmn. surg. sect. 1961-62), N.Y. County med. socs., Am. Surg. Assn., N.Y. Gastroent. Assn., Société Internationale de Chirurgie, Soc. Surgery Alimentary Tract, Allen O. Whipple Surg. Soc., Am. Assn. History Medicine, Collegium Internationale Chirurgiae Digestivae. Republican. Presbyn. Clubs: Century Assn; Manursing Island (Rye, N.Y.); Am. Yacht. Home: 1 Forest Ave Rye NY 10580-4209

BARKER, RUTH ANNE, guidance counselor; b. Winchester, Mass., May 30, 1945; d. Walter Kittredge and Ruth Howland (Brown) Hutchinson; m. Christopher S. Lyon, Feb. 14, 1970 (div. 1978); children: Matthew Howland, Sarah Margaret; m. Robert Louis Barker, May 16, 1987. BA, Brown U., 1967; MEd, Lyndon State Coll., 1990; postgrad., Castleton (S.C.) State Coll., 1991—. Cert. in guidance and art K-12, Vt. Art tchr. The Bradley Sch., Providence, 1968-69; art and music tchr. Mt. Holly (Vt.) Elem. Sch., 1976-79; art tchr. Black River High Sch., Ludlow, Vt., 1977-78; art prof. Coll. St. Joseph, Rutland, Vt., 1979; art tchr. Wallingford (Vt.) Elem. Sch., 1984; interior designer Vt. Contract Furnishings, Rutland, 1978-81, Rutland House Ltd., 1981-89; dir. guidance Rochester (Vt.) Schs., 1989-90, West Rutland Schs., 1990—. Dir. publicity Chaffee Art Ctr., Rutland, 1987-89; chmn. Wallingford Dem. Party, 1982-85; county sec. Rutland County Dem. Party, 1985-86; chmn. Rutland Assn. Retarded Citizens, 1982-84; leader Community Sponsorship Team, Rutland Correctional Ctr., 1989-90; mem. Rutland Chorale, 1986-89, Ladies Night Out, 1989—. Mem. Am. Counseling Assn. (dist. rep.), Vt. Assn. Counseling and Devel., Crossroads Art Coun., Moonbrook Arts Union. Democrat. Episcopalian. Home: PO Box 102 Wallingford VT 05773-0102 Office: West Rutland High Sch 317 Main St West Rutland VT 05777

BARKER, WILLIAM HALL, JR., financial director; b. Harrisburg, Pa., Feb. 6, 1953; s. William H. and Goldie (Benkovic) B.; m. Denise Knisely, May 23, 1981; children: Matthew E., Christopher D. B in Fin. and Econs., Lehigh U., 1974; MBA, Shippensburg U., 1983. Assoc. nat. bank examiner Comptroller of the Currency, Washington, 1975-82; mgr. budget and reporting Commonwealth nat. Bank, Harrisburg, Pa., 1984-86; corp. fin. analyst Pa. Blue Shield, Camp Hill, Pa., 1986-88; dir. fin. acctg. Def. Activities Fed. Credit Union, Mechanicsburg, Pa., 1988—; treas. bd. Knisely's Agr. Ctr., Carlisle, Pa., 1990—. Mem. Internat. Assn. Accts. (dir. manuscripts 1991-92), Monimsith Issinrhyu Karate. Democrat. Roman Catholic. Home: 128 Lancaster Blvd Mechanicsburg PA 17055 Office: Def Activities Fed Credit Union 5275 E Trindle Rd Mechanicsburg PA 17055

BARKLEY, ERICH RUSSELL, mechanic, newspaper columnist; b. Punxsutawney, Pa., Sept. 10, 1948; s. Edwin Russell and Barbara Jane (Dixon) B.; m. Judith Marlene Wonderling, June 17, 1972 (div. 1983); children: Erin Joanne, Adam Patrick; m. Judy Ann Kendall, July 6, 1984. Student, Clarion State Coll., 1966-70. Mechanic Owens-Brockway Inc., Brookville, Pa., 1974—; columnist, reporter, photographer Brookville Newspapers, 1987—. Vol. YMCA, Brookville, 1982—. With U.S. Army, 1970. Mem. Pinecrest Country Club. Republican. Home: RR 3 Box 206A Brookville PA 15825-9803 Office: Brookville Newspaper Main St Brookville PA 15825-1642

BARKLEY, SCOTT GLENN, municipal official; b. Paterson, N.J., Jan. 26, 1960; s. Emma (Rembert) B.; m. Gina Mauritta Banks, June 11, 1985; children: David, Christa. BS in Biology, Winston-Salem State U., 1983. Loss control rep. Liberty Mut. Ins. Co., Phila., 1984-86, Cigna Ins. Co., Lemoyne, Pa., 1986-87; housing inspector City of Harrisburg, Pa., 1987-89, zoning adminstr., 1989—; founder, dir. Inner City Impact, Harrisburg, 1989—. Founder, pastor New Jerusalem Christian Ch., Harrisburg. 2d lt. U.S. Army, 1983-86. Home: 1513 Allison St Harrisburg PA 17104-3138

BARKMAN, JON ALBERT, lawyer; b. Somerset, Pa., Oct. 8, 1947; s. Blair Albert and Billie (Dietz) B.; m. Annette E. Shaulis, Dec. 1, 1983. BA, Washington and Jefferson U., 1969; JD, Duquesne U., 1975. Bar: Pa. 1975, U.S. Dist. Ct. (we. dist.) Pa. 1975, U.S. Supreme Ct. 1984, U.S. Ct. Appeals (3d cir.) 1989. Mem. claims dept. Liberty Mut. Ins. Co., Pitts., 1969-71; dist. justice Commonwealth of Pa., Somerset, 1973—; pvt. practice Somerset, 1975—; pres. Barkman Realty, Inc.; bd. dirs. First Nat. Bank, Garrett. Advisor Com. Against Sexual Assault, Somerset, Pa., 1984; Pa. del. for Nat. Spl. Ct. Judges Conv., Honolulu, 1989, Atlanta, 1991. Paul Harris fellow, 1989. Mem. ABA, Assn. Trial Lawyers Am., Pa. Trial Lawyers Assn., Somerset County Bar Assn. (pres. 1990—), Allegheny County Bar Assn., Elks, Moose, Rotary. Republican. Methodist. Home: 388 High St Somerset PA 15501-1301 Office: 118 N Center Ave Ste 2 Somerset PA 15501-2029

BARKOCY, ANDREW BERNARD, executive search firm executive; b. McAdoo, Pa., Feb. 22, 1932; s. John Michael and Margaret Ann (Kutchera) B.; m. Frances Rita Zaremba, May 19, 1956; children: Andrea, Allen, Gary. BS Commerce in Acctg., Rider Coll., 1963, postgrad., 1969-70. Cert. personnel cons. Acctg. mgr. McGraw Hill, Inc., N.Y.C., 1963-69; asst. contr. Transamerica DeLaval, Trenton, N.J., 1969-71; contr. glass div. Combustion Engring., Pennsauken, N.J., 1971-73; pres., owner Snelling & Snelling, Trenton, 1973-82, Princeton (N.J.) Exec. Search, 1982—; prin. Andrew B. Barkocy, Inc. Acctg. Svc., Princeton, 1963—; bd. dirs., v.p. Chambersburg Savs. and Loan, Trenton, 1976—. With USN, 1950-54, Korea. Mem. Inst. Mgmt. Accts. (pres. Trenton chpt. 1991—). Republican. Roman Catholic. Home: 49 Canal Run W Washington Crossing PA 18977 Office: Princeton Exec Search PO Box 7373 Princeton NJ 08543

BARKSDALE, CHARLES BEVERLY, lawyer; b. Huntington, W.Va., Sept. 14, 1963; s. John Beverly and Frances Irene (Jeter) B. BA in Philosophy, U. Richmond, Va., 1985; JD, U. Balt., 1988. Bar: Md. 1989, U.S. Dist. Ct. Md. 1990, D.C. 1991. Assoc. atty. Forman & Steinhardt, P.A., Glen Burnie, Md., 1989-90; asst. state's atty. Office of State's Atty. for Allegany County, Cumberland, Md., 1990-91; assoc. atty. Maher & Maher, Chartered, Laurel, Md., 1992—. Mem. ABA, Md. State Bar Assn., D.C. Bar Assn., Prince Georges County Bar Assn. Republican. Presbyterian. Home: 8725 Contee Rd Laurel MD 20708 Office: Maher & Maher Chartered 305 Compton Ave Laurel MD 20707

BARLIS, THOMAS K., podiatrist; b. N.Y.C., Nov. 17, 1959; s. Kostas and Marika (Gouvakis) B. BA in Biology, NYU, 1981; postgrad., Ill. Coll. Podiatric Medicine, 1981-83; DPM, N.Y. Coll. Podiatric Medicine, 1985. Diplomate Am. Bd. Podiatric Surgery. Attending podiatrist Beekman Downtown Hosp., N.Y.C., 1987—, St. Barnabas Hosp., Bronx, N.Y., 1987—, Astoria (N.Y.) Gen. Hosp., 1988—, French Ambulatory Ctr., N.Y.C., 1989—. Office: 27-47 Crescent St Astoria NY 11102 also: 133rd E 73rd St New York NY 10021

BARLOW, AUGUST RALPH, JR., minister; b. Sewickley, Pa., Oct. 9, 1934; s. August Ralph and Kathryn Viola (Adams) B.; m. Elizabeth Evone Anderson, Aug. 27, 1960; children: Paul Martin, Andrew Ralph, Ann Kathryn. BA, Haverford Coll., 1956; BD, Yale U., 1959, STM, 1964. Ordained to ministry Meth. Ch., 1959. Pastor Fox Chapel Meth. Ch., Pitts., 1959-60; pastor Butler St. Meth. Ch., Pitts., 1961-62, Lawrenceville Community Ch., Pitts., 1962-63; intern Cleve. Inner City Protestant Parish, 1960-61; teaching min. Beneficent Congl. Ch., Providence, 1964-70, pastor, 1970—; mem. bd. govs. Beneficent House; bd. dirs. Pastoral Counseling Ctr. Greater Providence, v.p., 1984-86; bd. dirs. Steere House, Providence, 1980-86, pres., 1983-86; bd. dirs. Home Health Svcs. of R.I., 1986—; chmn. ch. in soc. com., 1985-86; mem. R.I. Conf., United Ch. of Christ, 1964—, mem. com. on ministry, 1981-83; mem. urban dir. R.I. Council Chs., 1979-82. Contbr. articles to Christian Century, editorials, commentaries to Providence Jour.-Bull., Religious Broadcasting Sta. WEAN, 1964-87. Mem. adv. coun. Providence Pub. Libr., 1968-71; bd. dirs. Mouthpiece Coffee House, Providence, 1969-75, pres., 1974-75. Rsch. fellow Yale U. Div. Sch., 1979. Mem. Providence Intown Chs. Assn., Mins. Assn. R.I. Conf. United Ch. of Christ, Dodeka Symposium, Rotary (trustee Rotary Charities Found. 1977-82, Paul Harris fellow), Beneficent Order of Spike, Phi Beta Kappa. Democrat. Home: 95 Cole Ave Providence RI 02906-4629 Office: 300 Weybosset St Providence RI 02903

BARLOW, CARL MORTON, physician; b. N.Y.C., Dec. 8, 1925; s. David M. and Beatrice (Sarlin) B.; m. Shirley Lantner, Sept. 28, 1923 (dec. Apr. 1959); children: Richard Mark, Steven Joseph; m. June Williams, Oct. 9, 1935; 1 child, Carol Elizabeth. BA, NYU, 1946; DDS, Columbia U., 1950, MD, 1953. Diplomate Am. Bd. Plastic Surgery. Staff plastic surgery L.I. Jewish Hosp., Queens, 1963-71; chief div. plastic surgery Queens Hosp. Ctr., 1963-71; attending surgeon (sr.) Lenox Hill Hosp., N.Y.C., 1961-85; assoc. prof. micro-biology grad. div. Univ. City of N.Y., 1962-66; chmn. scientific program AMFA-Soc. Max Surgeons, Phila., 1968; chmn. med. econs. com. N.Y. Regional Soc. Plastic Surgery, N.Y.C., 1968-76; hon. surgeon Lenox Hill Hosp., N.Y.C., 1985—; guest lectr. William Alanson White Inst. Psychiatry, Psychoanalysis & Psychology, 1976-78; workshop dirl, instr. Am. Soc. Plastic Reconstruction Surgery. Contbr. articles to profl. jours. Capt. U.S. Army, 1955-57. Fellow ACS, N.Y. Acad. Medicine; mem. Am. Soc. Plastic and Reconstructive Surgery, Am. Soc. Maxillofacial Surgeons, N.Y. State Med. Soc., New York County Med. Soc., Explorers Club, Alpha Omega Alpha, Omicron Kappa Upsilon. Office: 799 Park Ave New York NY 10021-3275

BARLOW, CHARLES BEACH, investment advisor; b. Bridgeport, Conn., May 5, 1926; s. Herbert Woodward and Marian (Beach) B.; m. Jean Wellington, Aug. 25, 1973. BA, Yale U., 1950; MBA, Harvard U., 1952. Asst. treas Worcester (Mass.) County Trust Co., 1952-59; v.p., sr. trust officer Girard Bank, Phila., 1959-69; v.p., chief European rep. Girard Bank, London, 1969-73; sr. v.p. in charge internat. banking Colonial Bancorp, Waterbury, Conn., 1973-81; sr. cons. Noel Alexander Assocs., London,

1972—; v.p., sr. trust officer New Milford (Conn.) Savs. Bank, 1986-90; pres., dir. The C.M. Beach Co., New Milford, 1973—; pres., exec. dir. Taylor House Investment Mgmt., Inc., New Milford, 1982—. Pres. The Antiquarian and Landmarks Soc., Inc., Hartford, Conn., 1990—, trustee, 1984—, chmn. fin. com. 1984-90, mem. exec. com.; trustee New Milford Hosp., mem. bd. mgrs.; trustee, treas. New Milford Hosp. Found.; pres. The New Milford Hist. Soc., 1981-84, trustee, 1973-84, 1990—; pres. Weantinoge Heritage, Inc., 1984-90, dir., 1990—; trustee, treas., mem. fin. and long range planning com. The Eliot Pratt Edn. Ctr., New Milford; trustee New Milford Cemetery Assn., Higgins Armory Mus., Worcester, 1990—, others; mem. adv. bd. Goodspeed Opera House Found., East Haddam, Conn., 1989—. Mem. Fin. Analysts of Phila., The Union League of Phila., Merion Cricket Club (Haverford, Pa.), The Yale Club of N.Y.C., The Naval and Mil. Club (London), Harvard Bus. Sch. Club of London, The Lake Waramaug Country Club, Soc. of Mayflower Descendants, The Worcester Club. Republican. Congregationalist. Home: 34 Main St New Milford CT 06776 Office: Taylor House Investment 34-B Main St New Milford CT 06776

BARLOW, JOHN SUTTON, neurophysiologist; b. Raleigh, N.C., June 10, 1925; s. David Henry and Anne Mary (Sutton) B.; m. Sibylle E. Jahrreiss, Aug. 5, 1950; children: Thomas Walter, Robert Sutton, Lisa Katharine. BS, U. N.C., 1944, MS, 1948; MD, Harvard U., 1953. Diplomate Am. Bd. Cert. EEG. Clin. and rsch. fellow, asst. resident in neurology Mass. Gen. Hosp. and Harvard Med. Sch., Boston, 1953-57; rsch. assoc. in elec. engring. MIT, Cambridge, 1954-64, rsch. affiliate in elec. engring., 1964—; asst. neurology Mass. Gen. Hosp., Boston, 1957-61, neurophysiologist neurology svc., 1961—; rsch. assoc. neurology Harvard Med. Sch., Boston, 1961-69, prin. rsch. assoc., 1969-78, sr. rsch. assoc. neurology, 1979—; mem. neurology study sect. NIH, Bethesda, Md., 1966-70; mem. rev. panel on neurol. devices FDA, Washington, 1974-76. Cons. editor EEG Clin. Neurophysiology, 1970-86; translator/editor books from Russian, Czech, Chinese; contbr. articles and revs. to profl. jours. Lt. (j.g.) USN, 1944-46. Recipient Rsch. Career Devel. award NIH, 1962-71, Rsch. Grants, 1962-88, Fogarty Internat. fellow, 1979, Sr. Scientist award Alexander v. Humboldt Found., Göttingen, Germany, 1979, Sr. Scientist Exch. Nat. Acad. Scis., U.S.A./USSR Acad. Scis., Moscow, 1982, 83, 89. Mem. Internat. Brain Rsch. Orgn., Am. EEG Soc. (pres. 1975-76), Am. Neurol. Assn., Am. Acad. Neurology, Soc. Neurosci., Am. Geophys. Union, Ea. Assn. EEG (pres. 1971-72).

BARLOW, MICHAEL JOSEPH, furniture business owner, marketing consultant; b. Chester, Pa., Nov. 8, 1964; s. Joseph Henry and Kathleen Sarah (Bluzard) B. Owner, chief exec. officer, chief fin. officer Amishland Furniture, Aston, Pa., 1989—, Counter Culture, Aston, 1990—; mktg. cons. Barlow Cons. Svcs., Media, Pa. Mem. Boothwyn Presbyn. Ch. Softball (capt.), Clam Football Club (pres. 1989—). Office: Counter Culture 26 Penns Ct Aston PA 19014

BARNA, DOUGLAS PETER, collection agency executive; b. Passaic, N.J., Nov. 28, 1945; s. Peter Richard and Marie (Saltamachia) B.; m. Nancy M. Viverito, Oct. 1971 (div. Oct. 1974); m. Norma Rae Hudson, July 3, 1983; stepchidren: Sherry, Michael, Gail, Laura, Kelly, Kenneth. BS in Bus. Mgmt., Fairleigh Dickinson U., 1968. Product control and accounts receivable specialist IBM Corp., Franklin Lakes, N.J., 1964-72; credit mgr. Star Graphic Systems, Clifton, N.J., 1972-74; corp. credit mgr. The Harvey Group, Woodbury, N.Y., 1975; sales exec. Contract Equity Corp., Melville, N.Y., 1976, Media Coordinators Ltd., Levittown, N.Y., 1976-78; v.p. sales Valer Enterprises Inc., Bohemia, N.Y., 1978-84; pres. Douglas Equity Enterprises Ltd., Patchogue, N.Y., 1984—; owner Douglas Enterprises, Patchogue, 1985—; pres. Bulldog Devel. Inc., Patchogue, 1988-91. Mem. Comml. Law League Am., Comml. Agy. Sect., Greater Patchogue C. of C. (dir. 1987—), Kiwanis, Phi Gamma Pi (pres. 1967-68). Home: 51 Melrose Pky East Patchogue NY 11772-6231 Office: Nat Recovery Svcs 24 Railroad Ave Patchogue NY 11772-3518

BARNA, RICHARD ALLEN, lighting company executive, broadcasting executive; b. N.Y.C., Oct. 7, 1948; s. Raymond Alexander and Miriam (Friedman) B.; m. Eileen Maisel; children: Ross, Hayley. BA, Brown U., 1970; Owner-Pres. Mgmt. degree, Harvard U., 1985. Program dir. WHCN Concert Network, Inc., Hartford, Conn., 1970-71; pres. ProMedia, Inc., Northvale, N.J., 1971—; v.p. RAB Electric Mfg., Inc., Bronx, N.Y., 1976-78; pres. RAB Electric Mfg., Inc., Northvale, N.J., 1978—. Mem. curriculum com. Byram Hills Sch. Dist., Armonk, N.Y., 1986-91; v.p. Banksville Fire Dept., Bedford, N.Y., 1987—; trustee, treas. North Castle Pub. Libr., Armonk, 1991—. With U.S. Army, 1971-77. Office: RAB Electric Mfg 170 Ludlow Ave Northvale NJ 07647-2306

BARNATHAN, JACK MARTIN, chiropractor; b. Queens, N.Y., Aug. 19, 1959; s. Jack and Christa Bianca (Manschwedat) B. BBA, Adelphi U., 1981; D Chiropractic, N.Y. Chiropractic Coll., 1984. Community crisis counselor Reach of LongBeach, N.Y., 1981-84; chiropractic doctor Bethpage, N.Y., 1984—; dir. Coun. Chiropractic Care for Disabled; cons. Internat. Fedn. Bodybuilders, 1987—; adj. prof. N.Y Chiropractic Coll, 1992—. Recipient Presdl. Certificate of Merit, 1992. Mem. Internat. Chiropractors Assn. (chmn. Coun. on Fitness). Office: Barnathan Chiropractic 627 Hicksville Rd Bethpage NY 11714-3461

BARNES, CANDACE ECCLES, quality control professional; b. Quincy, Mass., Nov. 24, 1949; d. Alton and Pauline (Regnier) Eccles; m. Warren C. Barnes, Apr. 23, 1983; children: Kimberly Spaulding, Jeremy. BS in Biology, Rensselaer Poly. Inst., 1972. Rsch. asst. Albany (N.Y.) Med. Coll., 1972-73; chemist Beiersdorf, Inc., South Norwalk, Conn., 1979-81, quality control supr., 1981-86; quality control mgr. Inline Plastics, Corp., Milford, Conn., 1986—. Republican. Office: Inline Plastics Corp 40 Seemans Ln Milford CT 06460-4358

BARNES, CLIVE ALEXANDER, drama and dance critic; b. London, Eng., May 13, 1927; came to U.S., 1965; s. Arthur Lionel and Freda Marguerite (Garratt) B.; children from previous marriage to Patricia Amy Evelyn Winckley: Christopher John Clive, Joanna Rosemary Maya; m. Amy Pagnozzi, July 26, 1985. B.A., U. Oxford, Eng., 1951; LittD (hon.), Adelphi U., 1976, Albright Coll., 1982. Co-editor dance mag. Arabesque, 1950; asst. editor Dance and Dancers, 1950-58, assoc. editor, 1958-61, exec. editor, 1961-65; editor Dance and Dancers, N.Y.C., from 1965; writer music, dance, drama, films Daily Express, London, 1956-65; dance critic The Spectator, London, 1959-65, The Times, London, 1962-65, N.Y. Times, N.Y.C., 1965-67; drama and dance critic N.Y. Times, 1967-78; assoc. editor, drama and dance critic N.Y. Post, 1978—; N.Y. corr. The Evening Standard, London, 1988—; adj. prof. dept. journalism. NYU, 1968-75. Author: Ballet in Britain Since the War, 1953, Frederick Ashton and His Ballets, 1961, Nureyev, 1982; co-author: Ballet Here and Now, 1961, Dance Scene, U.S.A., 1967, Inside American Ballet Theatre, 1977; co-editor: Best American Plays, 6th, 7th, and 8th series. Served with RAF, 1946-48. Decorated comdr. Order Brit. Empire, 1975, knight Order of Dannebrog (Denmark), 1972. Mem. Critics Circle London (past sec., chmn. ballet sect.), N.Y. Drama Critics Circle (pres. 1973-75). Club: Century Assn. (N.Y.). Office: care NY Post 210 South St New York NY 10002*

BARNES, DAWN COOPER, performing arts educator; b. Nashville, Apr. 18, 1958; d. Henry Nehemiah and Izetta (Roberts) Cooper; m. Milton Nathaniel Barnes, Dec. 30, 1979; children: Nyema, Julien, Henry, Zwannah. BA in Theatre-French with distinction, U. Mich., 1978; MA in Theatre, CUNY, 1980; postgrad., U. Md., 1987—. Lectr. Fisk U., Nashville, 1980-83; adj. instr. Montclair (N.J.) State Coll., 1983-86, Seton Hall U., 1983-84; adj. asst. prof. County Coll. Morris, Randolph, N.J., 1986-87; instr. performing arts Howard Community Coll., Columbia, Md., 1990—; dir., choreographer Dawn Barnes Dancers, Nashville, 1980-83; dance panelist Tenn. Arts Commn., Nashville, 1982-83; instr. African dance Howard County Parks and Recreation Dept., Ellicott City, Md., 1991—. Author: (video) Origin of Afro-American Dance, 1983; choreographer Breaking Out, Black Entertainment TV, 1982. Actress Back Alley Players, Ann Arbor, 1976-78; mem. coun., chmn. faith devel. St. John United Meth./Presbyn. Ch., 1990—. Mem. Soc. for Cinema Studies. Democrat. Home: 7406 Weatherworn Way Columbia MD 21046-1480 Office: Howard Community Coll Little Patuxent Blvd Columbia MD 21044

BARNES, DUNCAN, magazine editor, writer; b. New Rochelle, N.Y., Nov. 15, 1935; s. Francis Duncan and Christine Sinclair (Lawther) B.; m. Anne E. Fiske, May 27, 1961; children—Lesley Thorp, Jason Coleman. B.A. in English, Dartmouth Coll., 1957. Staff writer St. Petersburg Times, Fla., 1958-61; staff writer Sports Illustrated, N.Y.C., 1961-68; dir. pub. relations, Winchester Group Olin Corp., N.Y.C., 1968-80; editorial dir. Winchester Press, N.Y.C., 1972-80; editor Field & Stream, N.Y.C., 1981—. Editor: History of Winchester Firearms, 1980, AKC's World of the Pure-Bred Dog, 1984; contbg. editor: The Random House Dictionary of the English Language, 1966. Mem. Outdoor Writers Assn. Am., Boone and Crockett Club. Office: Field & Stream 2 Park Ave New York NY 10016-5603

BARNES, JAMES ALFORD, chemist; b. Charlotte, N.C., Aug. 20, 1944; s. James Crowell and Margaret (Alford) B.; m. Helen Scroggens, June 11, 1966; children: Mary Alford, Curtis Crowell. BS in Chemistry, Davidson (N.C.) Coll., 1966; PhD in Inorganic Chemistry, U. N.C., 1971. Postdoctoral fellow U. Southampton, England, 1970-71; NIH postdoctoral fellow U.S.C., Columbia, 1971-72; asst. prof. Western Md. Coll., Westminster, 1972-73; assoc. prof. Austin Coll., Sherman, Tex., 1973-83; chemist Shell Devel. Corp., Houston, 1976; rsch. chemist Tex. Instruments, Sherman, 1980; chemist S.W. Rsch. Inst., San Antonio, 1981; rsch. chemist Naval Rsch. Lab., Washington, 1981-82, Naval Surface Warfare Ctr., Silver Spring, Md., 1982—; cons. on batteries and battery safety various govt. agys., 1984—. Contbr. articles to profl. jours. Active zoning bd. City of Sherman, 1974-81, recreation bd. City of College Park, Md., 1986—. Mem. Am. Chem. Soc., Royal Chem. Soc., AAAS, Electrochem. Soc. Home: 4611 Drexel Rd College Park MD 20740-3603 Office: Naval Surface Warfare Ctr Code R33 Silver Spring MD 20903

BARNES, JOHN JAY, securities trader; b. Schenectady, N.Y., May 28, 1957; s. James Chester and Rita Frances (Lolik) B.; m. Amanda May Eggleston, July 16, 1988. BA, Rochester (N.Y.) Inst. Tech., 1979. Mgr. Fenley Law Offices, Schenectady, 1980-84; stockbroker Baird, Patrick & Co., Inc., Delmar, N.Y., 1984—; fin. speaker Cunard Cruise Lines, Inc., N.Y.C., 1989. Republican. Methodist. Office: Baird Patrick & Co Inc 155 Delaware Ave Delmar NY 12054

BARNES, JOHN WADSWORTH, director, writer; b. Belford, N.J., Mar. 25, 1920; s. Edward Crosby and Dorothy M. (Leek) B.; m. Joan Waddell, Sept. 5, 1942 (div. Jan. 1952); m. Jeanne Leah Weinstein, June 6, 1953; children: Joshua Edward, Judith Ann, Ezra David. Diploma, Monmouth Jr. Coll., Long Branch, N.J., 1939; student, U. Chgo., 1939-42. Editor Trend, a literary mag., Chgo., 1941-42; writer, dir. Columbia Broadcasting System, Chgo., 1942-46; producer, freelance writer Chgo., 1946-50; writer radio office U. Chgo., 1942; writer, dir., producer Ency. Britannica Films, Wilmette, Ill., 1951-55, London, 1955-63, Rome, 1963-65; exec. producer N.Y. Film Unit, Ency. Britannica Ednl. Corp., N.Y.C., 1965-73; pres. John Barnes Prodns., N.Y.C., 1973—; bd. dirs. Nat. Shakespeare Co., N.Y.C.; Shakespeare adv. bd. Colonial Theatre, Westerly, R.I. Writer, dir., producer film The Baltimore Plan (Edinburgh Film Festival 1953), American Revolution (Boston Film Festival 1954), The Living City (Oscar nomination 1953), St. John's College (1st place NVPA 1963), Michelangelo (Am. Film Festival award 1966), The Spirit of the Renaissance (Golden Eagle award 1971); author: (book for musical) The Beautiful Dream of Ilya Ilich Oblomov, 1983; writer play Kidnapped, 1989, Kembies of the Garden, 1990, Huck and Jim, 1990, Alice James, 1991. Bd. of govs. St. Ann's Sch., Bklyn., 1970-73; pres. Bklyn. Heights Music Soc., Bklyn., 1985-88, pres. emeritus, 1988—. John Barnes week long showing of films Institutio Mexicano Norte Americano De Relaciones Culturales, 1966. Mem. Dramatists Guild. Democrat. Home: 144 Columbia Hts Brooklyn NY 11201-1631

BARNES, JUDITH ELAINE, medical administrator; b. Kingston, Jamaica, W.I., Feb. 18, 1954; d. Ivan Gladstone and Beryl Winifred (Palmer) B. BSc in Communications, St. Johns U., 1980; MS in Family Counseling, Iona Coll., 1991—. FCC lic. radio operator. Patient advisor Meml. Sloan Kettering Cancer Ctr., N.Y.C., 1986—; lectr. in field. Author: Poetry in Motion - Poetry in Bloom, 1986; author play: Single Life in New York, 1989; contbr. articles to profl. jours. Chmn. Wakefield Grace United Meth. Ch., Bronx, 1990—, youth coord., 1990—. Home: 545 S 6th Ave Mount Vernon NY 10550 Office: Meml Sloan Kettering Cancer 1275 York Ave New York NY 10021

BARNES, MICHAEL EDWARD, clinical psychologist; b. Wilson, N.C., Aug. 19, 1957; s. Frank W. and Elizabeth Barnes. BA, U. N.C., Chapel Hill, 1979; MS, Howard U., 1985, PhD, 1989. Cert. employee assistance profl.; nat. cert. counselor; lic. clin. psychologist. Rsch. cons. Lawrence Johnson & Assocs., Washington, 1979-81; EAP coord. Greater Southeast Community Hosp., Washington, 1985-88; psychol. counselor Howard U. Counseling Svc., Washington, 1981-88; EAP cons. Sheppard Pratt EAP for Washington Post, Inc., Washington, 1989—; dir. Howard U. Drug Edn. and Prevention Program, Washington, 1989—; pvt. practice specializing in psychol. evaluations, Washington; cons. clin. psychologist to Project SECTOR, Nida and Koba Assocs., 1992—. Adv. bd. P.G. County Pub. Schs. Drug Prevention Project, Landover, Md., 1990—; com. mem. UN Assn. Drug Demand Reduction Project, Washington, 1991—; steering com. Higher Edn. Leaders/Peers Network, 1990—. Recipient Disting. Svc. award D.C. Hosp. Assn., 1988, Outstanding Svc. award div. student affairs Howard U., 1988; scholar Men's Civic Club, 1975, 78, K.P. Grand Lodge, 1981, 82. Mem. AACD, APA, D.C. Assn. for Multicultural Counseling and Devel., Assn. Black Psychologists, Employee Assistance Program Assn., D.C. Assn. Counseling and Devel. Baptist. Home: 3324 Banneker Dr NE Washington DC 20018-1615 Office: Howard U Counseling Svc CB Powell Bldg 6th and Bryant Sts NW Washington DC 20059

BARNES, RONALD EDWIN, pharmacist; b. Sharon, Pa., Aug. 24, 1962; s. Lewis Edwin and Sarah (Heckman) B.; m. Cynthia Marie Kahrer, Apr. 4, 1987. BS in Pharmacy, Duquesne U., 1985. Staff pharmacist Eckerd Drugs, Meadville, Pa., 1985, Greenville (Pa.) Regional Hosp., 1986-87; sr. pharmacist Shenango Valley Med. Ctr., Farrell, Pa., 1985—; mem. pharmacy adv. com. Hosp. Coun. of Western Pa., Warrendale, 1990—; adj. prof. pharmacy Duquesne U., Pitts., 1989—, U. Pitts., 1989—. Mem. Pa. Soc. of Hosp. Pharmacists, Am. Soc. Hosp. Pharmacists, Am. Pharm. Assn., Western Pa. Soc. Hosp. Pharmacists. Democrat. Mem. United Ch. of Christ. Home: 3339 Cardinal Dr Sharpsville PA 16150-9236 Office: Shenango Valley Med Ctr 2200 Memorial Dr Farrell PA 16121-1398

BARNES, SAMUEL HENRY, political scientist, educator; b. Miss., Jan. 20, 1931; s. Eugene Ludlow and Christine (Thompson) B.; m. Annabelle Bivona, Nov. 30, 1954; children: Christopher F.E., Michael Andrew, Catherine Ann. BA, Tulane U., 1952, MA, 1954; PhD, Duke U., 1957; postgrad. (Fulbright scholar), Institut des Hautes Etudes Politiques, Paris, 1956-57. Instr. polit. sci. U. Mich., Ann Arbor, 1957-60, asst. prof. polit. sci., 1960-64, assoc. prof., 1964-68, prof., 1968-91, James Orin Murfin prof. polit. sci., 1982-85, acting chmn. dept. polit. sci., 1968-69, chmn. dept., 1977-82, research assoc. Survey Research Ctr., 1969-70, program dir. Ctr. for Polit. Studies, 1970-91; prof. Comparative European Politics, dir. Ctr.for German and European Studies Georgetown U., Washington, 1991—; Fulbright lectr. U. Florence, Italy, 1962-63, U. Rome, 1967-68; Ctr. Advanced Study in Behavioral Scis. fellow Stanford U., 1982-83, Hoover Instn. fellow Stanford U., 1989. Author: Party Democracy: Politics in an Italian Socialist Federation, 1967, Representation in Italy: Institutionalized Traditions and Electoral Choice, 1977, (with Max Kaase and others) Political Action: Mass Participation in Five Western Democracies, 1979, Politics and Culture, 1989, (with others) Continuities in Political Action, 1990; contbr. articles to profl. publs., book chpts. Trustee Duke U., 1989—. Served with USN, 1949-50. Mem. Am. Polit. Sci. Assn. (sec. 1972-74), Council Western European Studies (exec. com. 1971-72, steering com. 1975-78), Midwest Polit. Sci. Assn., Internat. Polit. Sci. Assn., Conf. Group for Italian Polit. Studies (v.p. 1975-77, pres. 1977-79). Club: Cosmos (Washington). Office: Georgetown U Sch Fgn Svc Washington DC 20057

BARNES, WALLACE, manufacturing executive; b. Bristol, Conn., Mar. 22, 1926; s. Harry Clarke and Lillian (Houbertz) B.; m. Audrey Kent, June 14, 1947 (div. Aug. 1962); children: Thomas Oliver, Jarre Ann; m. Mrs. Frederick B. Hollister, Jr. (div. Feb. 1973); 1 adopted son, Frederick Hollister; m. Joan C. Fierri, Mar. 3, 1973 (div. May 1985); m. Barbara Hackman Franklin, Nov. 29, 1986. BA, Williams Coll., 1949; LLB, Yale U., 1952; grad., Advanced Mgmt. Program, Harvard, 1973; LLB (hon.), U. Hartford, 1988. Bar: Conn. 1952. Assoc. firm Beach, Calder & Barnes (and predecessor), Bristol, 1952-55; partner Beach, Calder & Barnes (and predecessor), 1956-62; exec. v.p. Assoc. Spring Corp. (name changed to Barnes Group Inc.), 1962-64, pres., 1964-77, chmn., chief exec. officer, 1977-91, chmn. bd., 1991—; pres. Nutmeg Air Transport, Inc., 1949-55; asst. to treas. Northeast Airlines, Inc., Boston, 1951; dir., mem. exec. com. Aetna Life and Casualty Co.; incorporator, founding dir. Conn. Capitol Region Growth Coun., Inc.; dir. Conn. Innovations, Inc., Rogers Corp., Rohr, Inc., Loctite Corp., others. Pres. Bristol Community Chest, 1956; bd. dirs., mem. exec. com. Bristol Boys Club, pres., 1965-68; mem. bd. regents, U. Hartford, 1981-87, chmn., 1988—; trustee Bristol Girls' Club Assn.; bd. dirs. New Eng. Legal Found., 1986-90, New Eng. Council, 1980-83, Jr. Achievement N. Central Conn., 1980-90; Nominee for Congress, 1st Congl. Dist. Conn., 1954; town chmn., Bristol, 1953-55; mem. Conn. Senate from 5th Dist., 1958-62, from 8th Dist., 1966-70, minority leader, 1969; Bd. dirs. Community Coun. of Capital Region, 1975-77, Hartford Symphony Soc., 1971-78, Coun. on Employment and Fair Taxation, 1978-80, Bus. Coalition on Health, 1983-88, Conn. Pub. Expenditure Coun., 1979-85; trustee Am. Clock and Watch Mus., Bristol Regional Environ. Ctr.; bd. trustees New Eng. Air Mus.; corporator Inst. of Living, Hartford; bd. dirs. Conn. Econ. Devel. Corp. Served as aviation cadet USAAF, 1944-45. Recipient Disting. Svc. award Bristol Jaycees, Keystone award Boys Clubs Am., 1967, Humanitarian award Bristol Boys Club Assn., 1989, Hon. Alumnus award U. Hartford, 1985; Bartels fellow U. New Haven, 1992. Mem. ABA, Conn. Bar Assn., Am. Judicature Soc., Am. Arbitration Assn., Bristol Hist. Soc., Newcomen Soc., Conn. Bus. and Industry Assn. (past chmn., dir.), Am. Legion, Elks, Econ. Club, Yale Club, Williams Club, Hundred Club of Conn. Home: 1875 Perkins St Bristol CT 06010 Office: Barnes Group Inc 123 Main St Bristol CT 06011-0489

BARNES-FARRELL, JANET LORRAINE, psychologist; b. Toronto, Mar. 6, 1952; d. William George and Norma Marion (Telfer) Barnes; m. Robert Harry Farrell, May 28, 1979; children: Jessica, Caitlin. BS in Psychology, Rensselaer Poly. Inst., 1974, MS in Psychology, 1977; PhD in Psychology, Pa. State U., 1980. Asst. prof. Purdue U., West Lafayette, Ind., 1979-83, U. Hawaii, Honolulu, 1983-85; asst. prof. U. Conn., Storrs, 1985-92, assoc. prof., 1992—; v.p. Indsl./Orgn. Cons. of Hawaii, Kailua, 1984-85. Contbr. articles to profl. jours. Mem. Soc. for Indsl. and Orgnl. Psychology, APA, Am. Psychol. Soc., Eastern Psychol. Assn., Conn. Applied Psychologists Assn., Acad. of Mgmt. Office: U of Connecticut Psychology Dept U-20 Storrs CT 06269-1020

BAR-NESS, YEHESKEL, electrical engineer, educator; b. Baghdad, Iraq, Apr. 28, 1932; arrived in Israel, 1950; came to U.S., 1978; m. Varda Bar-Ness, Aug. 21, 1952; children: Yael, Yaron, Yegal. BEE, Technion U., Haifa, Israel, 1958, MEE, 1963; PhD, Brown U., 1969. Chief engr. Elscint Inc., Haifa, 1971-75; assoc. prof. Tel-Aviv U., 1973-78; vis. prof. U. Pa., Phila., 1979-81; prof. elec. engring. Drexel U., Phila., 1981-83; tech. staff mem. AT&T Bell Lab., Holmdel, N.J., 1983-85; disting. prof. elec. and computer engring. N.J. Inst. Tech., Newark, 1985—, dir. ctr. communication and signal processing rsch., 1985—. Recipient Kaplan Price award Gov. of Israel, 1974. Fellow IEEE; mem. Communication Soc. of IEEE (sec. communications systems engring. com. 1985-87, vice chmn., 1987-89, chmn. 1990—, editor IEEE transaction on communication). Home: 2 Etna Ct Marlboro NJ 07746-1307 Office: NJ Inst of Tech 323 Kings Blvd Newark NJ 07102

BARNETT, GENE AUSTIN, university educator; b. Wheaton, Mo., July 5, 1929; s. Orbon and Martha Elizabeth (Antle) B. AA, Southwest Bapt. Jr. Coll., 1950; BA, Okla. Bapt. U., 1952; MA, U. Okla., 1953; PhD, U. Wisc., 1961; MA, Fairleigh Dickinson U., 1990. Instr., asst. prof. Wayne State U., Detroit, 1961-67; asst. prof., assoc. prof., prof. ESL, modern and Irish drama Fairleigh Dickinson U., Teaneck, N.J., 1967—. Author: Denis Johnston, 1978, Lanford Wilson, 1987; contbr. articles to profl. journs. and books. With U.S. Army, 1953-55. Grantee Nat. Endowment for Humanities Inst. in Oriental Langs., NEH, Columbia U., 1987-89; U.S. Summer Fulbright fellow U.S. Gov., India, 1988. Democrat. Southern Baptist. Home: 780 Grange Rd Apt A Teaneck NJ 07666 Office: Fairleigh Dickinson U 840 River Rd Teaneck NJ 07666

BARNETT, GORDON JAMES, psychoanalyst; b. Upton, Maine, Mar. 13, 1921; s. James and Grace Darling (Bragg) B.; divorced; children: Gordon James Jr., James Bragdon, Jayson Wayne. BS, U. N.H., 1943; MA, Columbia U., 1945, PhD, 1950; diploma, William A. White Inst., 1961. Staff psychologist Salvation Army Guidance Bur., N.Y.C., 1945-48; clin. psychologist VA Hosp., N.Y.C., 1948-49, staff clin. psychologist neuropsychiat. unit, 1949-55, asst. chief clin. psychology, 1955-57; supr. psychotherapy postdoctoral program Gordon Derner Inst., Adelphi U., Garden City, N.Y., 1960—; pvt. practice, N.Y.C., 1955—. Contbr. articles to profl. jours. Fellow APA; mem. William A. White Psychoanalytic Soc., Adelphi U. Psychoanalytic Soc., SAR (assoc.), Order Founders and Patriots. Mem. Soc. of Friends. Home: 69 Washington Ave Garden City NY 11530-6237 Office: 903 Park Ave New York NY 10021-0338

BARNETT, MARK, aerospace engineer; b. Amityville, N.Y., Mar. 1, 1957; s. Benjamin and Dorothy (Capelson) B.; m. Deborah Joy Krieger, Mar. 29, 1987; 1 child, Laura Rebecca. BS, U. Cin., 1979, MS, 1981, PhD, 1984. Aerospace engring. trainee NASA Ames Rsch. Ctr., Moffett Field, Calif., 1977-78; sr. rsch. engr. United Techs. Rsch. Ctr., East Hartford, Conn., 1984—; adj. faculty mem. Hartford Grad. Ctr., 1988—. Contbr. articles to profl. jours. Mem. AIAA (treas. 1986-88), Sigma Xi. Office: United Techs Rsch Ctr Silver Ln MS 20 East Hartford CT 06108

BARNETT, RICHARD ALLAN, editor; b. Bklyn.; s. Charles Agnew and Sarah Shirley (Chasen) B.; m. Susan Ruth Cohen, Nov. 26, 1989. BA in Journalism, L.I. U., 1966. Asst. editor Outdoor Life Mag., N.Y.C., 1966-70; assoc. editor Mechanix Illustrated Mag., N.Y.C., 1970-80, Exec. Jeweler Mag., N.Y.C., 1980-82; writer 20/20 Mag., N.Y.C., 1982-84; copy editor Patient Care Mag., Montvale, N.J., 1990—; contbg. editor Eyecare Bus. Mag., Norwalk, Conn., 1985-92. Contbg. editor Complete Outdoors Ency., 1970; contbr. articles to profl. jours. Vol. Boys Club, Flushing, N.Y., 1982. Mem. West Englewood Residents Assn. Democrat. Jewish. Home and Office: 676 W Englewood Ave Teaneck NJ 07666-2212

BARNETT, VIVIAN ENDICOTT, curator; b. Putnam, Conn., July 8, 1944; d. George and Vivian (Wood) Endicott; m. Peter Herbert Barnett, July 1, 1967; children: Sarah, Alexander. A.B. magna cum laude, Vassar Coll., 1965; M.A., NYU, 1971; postgrad., CUNY, 1979-81. Research asst. Solomon R. Guggenheim Mus., N.Y.C., 1973-77, curatorial assoc., 1978-79, assoc. curator, 1980-81, rsch. curator, 1981-82, curator, 1982-91; dir. Roethel Benjamin Archive at Guggenheim Mus., N.Y.C., 1991—. Author: The Guggenheim Museum: Justin K. Thannhauser Collection, 1978, The Guggenheim Museum Collection 1900-1980, Kandinsky at the Guggenheim, 1983, 100 Works by Modern Masters from the Guggenheim Museum, 1984, Works by Robert Barry, Sol LeWitt, Robert Mangold, Richard Tuttle from the Collection of Dorothy and Herbert Vogel, 1987, Kandinsky and Sweden, 1989, Kandinsky in Major Collections in the West, 1989, Kandinsky Watercolours: Catalogue Raisonné, vol. I 1900-1921, 1992, Kleine Freuden, 1992; also articles; contbr. to Kandinsky in Paris: 1934-44, 1985. John Simon Guggenheim fellow, 1990. Mem. Am. Assn. Museums, Internat. Coun. Museums, Coll. Art Assn. Am. Office: Solomon R Guggenheim Mus 1071 5th Ave New York NY 10128-0173

BARNETT, WILLIAM JOHN, education educator; b. Rochester, N.Y., Aug. 30, 1921; s. James E. and Mary H. (Grant) Barnett; m. Susan Isable Edwards, Aug. 7, 1954; children: Ann Barnett Sorrento, Jean Barnett Mooney. BS, State Univ. Coll., Brockport, N.Y., 1947; MEd, U. Rochester, 1948; DEd, U. Buffalo, 1958. Cert. in teaching, sch. adminstrn. and supervision. Tchr. English East Rochester (N.Y.) Jr. High Sch., 1948-49; instr. State Univ. Coll., Oswego, 1949-50; from instr. to assoc. prof. State Univ. Coll., Buffalo, 1950-64, prof., 1964—; vis. prof. U. Siena, Italy, 1967-68, State Univ. Coll., Brockport, summer 1962; curriculum cons., Erie County, N.Y., 1966-67. Author: Freedom of Teachers, 1958; ednl. columnist Buffalo Courier Express, 1964—; contbr. articles to profl. jours. 1st It. U.S.

Army, 1943-46. Mem. NEA, ASCD, AAUP, United Univ. Profs. N.Y. State Univs., Am. Legion, Phi Delta Kappa, Sigma Tau Gamma. Presbyterian.

BARNEY, JOHN A., religious organization administrator; b. Rumney, N.H., Nov. 1, 1929; s. Earl Martin and Elva (Clough) B.; m. Jessie Bennett, Dec. 24, 1927; children: Paul Andrew, Janice Barney Syvertsen, Eunice Barney Paulson. BA, United Coll. Gordon & Barrington, Wenham, Mass., 1952. Ch. planter Africa Inland Mission, Napopo, Zaire, Africa, 1954-56; sch. activity dir. Africa Inland Mission, Rethy, Zaire, 1957-59; ch. planter Africa Inland Mission, Niangara, Zaire, 1960-61; constrn. engr. Africa Inland Mission, Kijabe, Kenya, Africa, 1961-72; dir. mobile film ministry Africa Inland Mission, Kijabe, 1973-77; dir. stewardship Africa Inland Mission, Pearl River, N.Y., 1978—; bd. dirs. Christian Stewardship Council, Daytona Beach, Fla., 1986—, Radio Sta. WIHS, Middletown, Conn., 1980-87. Deacon Calvary Ch., West Hartford, 1987—; alumni coun. Gordon Coll., Wenham, 1979-88. Home: 130 Clubhouse Rd Windsor CT 06095-2404

BARNHARD, SHERWOOD ARTHUR, printing company executive; b. Newark, Mar. 14, 1921; s. Charles L. and Blanche (Tarnow) B.; m. Esther Lasky, Feb. 21, 1946; children: Ronald Harris, Paul Ira. BS, Franklin & Marshall Coll., 1942. With Lasky Co., Millburn, N.J., 1946—, exec. v.p., 1956-61, pres., 1961—, chmn., 1986—; with N.J. Web and Sheetfed Color Lithographers; v.p. Daus. of Israel Geriatric Ctr., West Orange; N.J.; past trustee Temple Sharey Tefilo-Israel, South Orange, N.J.; bd. overseers NYU Ctr. Graphic Arts Mgmt. and Tech. Mem. Printing Industries N.J. (past pres.), Assn. Graphic Arts (past pres., past bd. dirs.), Met. Lithographers Assn. (past pres., mem. labor com.), Mktg. Communications Execs., Advt. Club N.Y., Crestmont Golf and Country Club (West Orange), Delaire Country Club (Delray, Fla.), Zeta Beta Tau.

BARNHART, RICHARD BROWN, university administrator; b. New Castle, Pa., Mar. 9, 1933; s. Lawrence Carl and Edith Copeland (Brown) B.; m. Mary Kathryn Neubauer, Sept. 3, 1955; children: David Brown, Jonathan Hall, Elizabeth Copeland. BA magna cum laude, Westminster Coll., 1955; MA, U. Pa., 1957; DA, Carnegie Mellon U., 1987. Instr. U. Pa., Phila., 1955-57; employee and community rels coord. Westinghouse Electric Corp., Cheswick, Pa., 1957-62; head spl. projects Carnegie Mellon U., Pitts., 1962-74, asst. pres., sec. bd. trustees, 1974-92; mem. faculty Community Coll. Allegheny County, Pitts., 1968-85, Pa. State U., New Kensington, 1958-68. Deacon, elder, clk. session Natrona Heights (Pa.) Presbyn. Ch., 1957—; dir. Greater Pitts. Conv. and Visitors Bur., Pitts., 1962-92; mem. bd. advisors Pitts. Pub. Theater, 1974-78; dir. Pitts. Coun. Internat. Visitors, 1984-89; pres. Community Libr. Allegheny Valley, Tarentum, Pa., 1975-76, bd. dirs., 1965-77. Honor fellow U. Pa., 1955-57; recipient Disting. Alumni Lectr. award Westminster Coll., New Wilmington, 1986. Mem. Assn. Governing Bds., Pitts. Coun. Higher Edn. (chmn. 1976-78, deputies com. 1987-88). Republican. Presbyterian. Home: 1232 Minnesota Ave Natrona Heights PA 15065-1030

BARNHILL, JOHN WARREN, psychiatrist, educator; b. Oklahoma City, Mar. 4, 1959; s. John Willis and Patricia Beth (Dale) B. AB magna cum laude, Duke U., 1981; MD, Baylor Coll. Medicine, 1985. Resident in pediatrics Baylor Coll. Medicine, Houston, 1985-86; resident in psychiatry The N.Y. Hosp.-Cornell Med. Ctr., N.Y.C., 1986-89, instr., 1989—; pvt. practice, staff psychiatrist Cornell Med. Ctr., 1989—; psychoanalytic candidate Ctr. for Psychoanalytic Tng. and Rsch. Columbia U., 1990—; student co-chmn. Baylor Med. Admissions Com., 1983-85; co-chmn. N.Y.C. Residents Com., 1987-89. Contbr. articles to med. jours. Interviewer Duke Undergrad. Admissions Com., Houston, 1981-86, N.Y.C., 1987—. Rock Sleyster scholar AMA, 1984-85. Mem. Am. Psychiat. Assn. (rep. exec. coun. 1987-89). Democrat. Office: Payne Whitney Clinic 525 E 68th St New York NY 10021-4873

BARNHOLDT, TERRY JOSEPH, lawyer, real estate negotiator; b. Charlotte, N.C., Nov. 30, 1954; s. Terry Joseph and Martha Frances (Cannon) B. BA, Duke U., 1977; JD, Wake Forest U., 1982. Bar: N.C. 1986. Assoc. Forsyth Legal Assocs., Winston-Salem, N.C., 1986; real estate negotiator JCP Realty, Inc., N.Y.C., 1986-89; asset mgr. N.Y. Life Ins. Co., N.Y.C., 1989=91; v.p., asset mgr. Citicorp Real Estate, Inc., N.Y.C. and Dallas, 1991—. Recipient Am. Jurisprudence award, 1982; William B. McMannis scholar, 1980-82. Mem. ABA, N.C. Bar Assn., Internat. Coun. Shopping Ctrs., Nat. Retail Mchts. Assn., N.Y. Real Estate Salesmen, Urban Land Inst., Washington Duke Club, Phi Delta Theta (pres. 1976). Republican. Home: 3701 Turtle Creek Blvd 5D Dallas TX 75219 Office: Citicorp Real Estate Inc 1400 Trammell Crow Ctr 2001 Ross Ave LB 114 Dallas TX 75201

BARNUM, WILLIAM DOUGLAS, communications company executive; b. Denton, Tex., July 28, 1946; s. Billie Douglas and Leticia Christina (Cox) B.; BSBA with distinction in Econs., Georgetown U., 1967; MBA, Fairleigh Dickinson U., 1985; m. Mary Ann Mook, Aug. 10, 1968. Acct., RCA Corp., Cherry Hill, N.J., 1967-68, Andros Island, Bahamas, 1968-70, budget and cost analyst, Cherry Hill, 1970, adminstr. telephone systems, 1970-73; mgr. project adminstrn. White Sands Radar Project, Holloman AFB, N.Mex., 1973-74; coord. profit ctr. acctg., N.Y.C , 1974-76, adminstr. globcom systems, N.Y.C., 1976-77, mgr. spl. project and accounts-payable, N.Y.C., 1978-79, mgr. fin., 1979-81, mgr. gateway ops., dir. field support svcs., 1982-88; sr. mgr. network svcs. MCI Internat., 1988—. Mem. Republican Presdl. Task Force. Mem. Am. Security Council, NRA (life), Knifemakers Guild (hon.) Am. Knife Throwers Alliance (hon.), Mensa, Delta Phi Epsilon, Delta Mu Delta. Presbyterian. Author: Kroodley Made Knife Catalog, 1977. Home: PO Box 893 Far Hills NJ 07931-0893 Office: MCI Internat 201 Centennial Ave Piscataway NJ 08854-3909

BARON, CAROLYN, editor, author, publishing executive; b. Detroit, Jan. 25, 1940; d. Gabriel and Viola Cohn; m. Richard W. Baron, Nov. 14, 1975. B.A. in Liberal Arts, U. Mich., 1961. Editor, editorial prodn. dir. Holt, Rinehart & Winston, N.Y.C., 1965-71; mng. editor E.P. Dutton Co., Inc., N.Y.C., 1971-74; exec. editor E.P. Dutton Co., Inc., 1974-75; adminstrv. editor Pocket Books, Simon & Schuster, N.Y.C., 1975-78; v.p., editor-in-chief Pocket Books, Simon & Schuster, 1978-79, Crown Pubs., N.Y.C., 1979-81; v.p., pub. Dell Pub. Co., N.Y.C., 1981-86, pres., pub., 1986—. Office: Dell Pub Co Inc 666 5th Ave New York NY 10103-0001

BARON, JUDSON RICHARD, aerospace educator; b. N.Y.C., July 28, 1924; s. Louis and Leah (Berzin) B.; m. Selma Francine Wasserman, Sept. 4, 1949; children—Jason Roberts, Jeffrey Scott. B.Aero. Engring., N.Y. U., 1947; S.M., Mass. Inst. Tech., 1948, Sc.D., 1956. Registered profl. engr., Mass. Stress analyst Chance Vought Aircraft Co., 1947; mem. research staff MIT, 1948-54, research asst., 1954-56, mem. faculty, 1957—, prof. aeros. and astronautics, 1957-89, prof. emeritus, sr. lectr., 1989—; cons. in field, 1957—. Mem. Air Force Sci. Adv. Bd., 1987-91. Served with AUS, 1943-46. Decorated Bronze Star; recipient Exceptional Civilian Svc. award. Dept. Air Force, 1991. Fellow AIAA (assoc. editor jour. 1990-92); mem. Sigma Xi, Tau Beta Pi. Home: 7 Gould Rd Lexington MA 02173-1003 Office: 77 Massachusetts Ave Cambridge MA 02139-4307

BARON, ROBERT ADELOR, lawyer; b. Evanston, Ill., Jan. 13, 1922; s. Delor F. and Helen C. (O'Keefe) B.; m. Mary F. Kwas, June 22, 1946; children: Robert J., Janet M. B.S., NYU, 1950; J.D., Seton Hall U., 1961. Bar: N.J. 1962, U.S. Dist. Ct. N.J. 1962, U.S. Supreme Ct. 1966. With surety dept. Aetna Casualty & Surety Co., N.Y., 1940-42, 46-50; mgr. surety dept. Employers Group Ins. Co., East Orange, N.J., 1950-55, Nat. Union Fire Ins. Co., East Orange, 1955-61; assoc. Rooney, Peduto & Sheehy, Esquires, Jersey City, 1961-62; pvt. practice law Englewood, N.J., 1962-85; ptnr. Baron & Baron, Englewood, 1985—; mcpl. prosecutor City of Bogota (N.J.), 1965-78, planning bd. atty., 1970-78, pub. defender, 1980-82, borough councilman 1982-87; judge mcpl. ct., 1987-90. Trustee Bergen County chpt. ARC, 1970-80; pres. Bogota Rep. Club, 1970-71. With USN, 1942-46; World War II; served to q.m. 1st class petty officer USN, 1950-52, Korea. Decorated 13 Battle Stars, commendation ribbon; recipient First Ann. Pro-Life award Archdiocese of Newark, 1989. Mem. ABA (vice chmn. gen. practice state orgn. com. 1973-76), N.J. Bar Assn. (chmn. gen. practice sect. 1973-76), Bergen County Bar Assn. (rep. to N.J. Bar Assn. gen. coun.), Comml. Law League, NYU Alumni Assn. Bergen County (pres. 1976-77, 79-80, trustee), Lawyers for Life (pres. 1985-87), Am. Legion, VFW, K.C., Trial Lawyers Assn. N.J. Roman Catholic. Office: 2 N Dean St Englewood NJ 07631-2807

BARONE, ANTHONY, anesthesiologist; b. N.Y.C., Aug. 18, 1938; s. Frank and Eleanor Rita (Ferraioli) B.; m. Maryann Joan Mieczkowski, May 18, 1963; children: Karen Lisa, John Christopher, Stephen Collins. AB, Columbia U., 1960; MD, N.Y. Med. Coll., 1964. Diplomate Am. Bd. Anesthesiology, Am. Acad. Pain Mgmt. Intern U.S. Naval Hosp., St. Alban's, N.Y.C., 1964-65, resident in anesthesiology, 1965-68; resident in anesthesiology Columbia Presbyn. Hosp., Albert Einstein Med. Ctr., N.Y.C., 1965-68; anesthesiologist Sacred Heart Hosp., Allentown, Pa., 1971—, also chmn. dept. anesthesiology, 1975-83, 87-90. Lt. commdr. USN, 1964-71, Vietnam. Fellow Am. Coll. Anesthesiologists. Roman Catholic. Office: Valley Anesthesia Inc 451 W Chew St Ste 406 Allentown PA 18102-3488

BARONE, ROSE MARIE PACE, writer, former educator; b. Buffalo, Apr. 26, 1920; d. Dominic and Jennie (Zagara) Pace; m. John Barone, Aug. 23, 1947. BA, U. Buffalo, 1943; MS, U. So. Cal., 1950; cert. advanced study, Fairfield (Conn.) U., 1963. Tchr. Angola (N.Y.) High Sch., 1943-46, Puente (Calif.) High Sch., 1946-47, Jefferson High Sch., Lafayette, Ind., 1947-50; dir. Warren Inst., Bridgeport, Conn., 1951-53; instr. U. Bridgeport, 1953-54; tchr. bus. subjects Bassick High Sch., Bridgeport, 1954-74, Harding High Sch., Bridgeport, 1974-80; instr. Fairfield U., Conn., 1969; freelance writer, 1980—; freelance writer, 1980—; chair State Poetry Festival, 1987. Founder Pet Rescue; chmn. community affairs com. Area Coun. Cath. Women, 1988-90, sec., 1990-91, chmn. family affairs com., 1991—; chmn. community affairs Ch. Women United, 1992—. Pace-Barone Minority scholar Fairfield U.; recipient Playwriting prize Conn. Federated Women's Clubs, 1955, 1st prize for poetry, 1985, Federated Women Conn. State Short Story award, 1987, 88, 90, Citizen award Bridgeport Dental Assn., 1982, State/Town Hero award, 1986; Auerbach Found. scholarship, 1956; also craft and flower awards, Fairfield U. 50th Anniversary medal and marble statuette. Mem. NEA, Am. Assn. Ret. People (v.p. 1987-88, pres. 1988-89, instr. 55 Alive, community affairs chair 1990—), Owl (sec. 1987-89, pres. 1989-90), AAUW (treas. 1957-58, named gift grant 1989cultural chair 1992—), Nat. League Am. Pen Women (Bridgeport historian 1966-84, state historian 1983—, treas. br. 1985-88, state pres. 1986-88, state lit. chair 1988—, br. membership chair 1990, Nat. Historian award 1976, 88), Fairfield Area Poets (founder, pres. 1990—), UN Assn. USA (pres. Bridgeport 1964-66, 68-70, v.p. 1988—, chmn. area UN Days 1960—, pres. Conn. 1971—, state chmn. UNICEF to 1984, area UNICEF Ctr.1984—, state historian 1984—), Conn. Bus. Tchrs., Bridgeport Edn. Assn. (sec. 1966-68), VFW (aux. 1989), Am. Legion (aux. contest chair 1989—), Fairfield Philatelic Soc. (sec. 1971-78, founder advisor Philatelic Jrs. 1972-80), Fairfield U. Women's Club (founder, pres. 1950, 74—, v.p. 1973-74), Southport Women's Club (garden dept. sec. 1981-85, chmn. 1985-87), Ch. Women United for Social Concerns, Pi Omega Pi. Home: 1283 Round Hill Rd Fairfield CT 06430-7329

BARONE, STEPHANIE LYNN, academic administrator, psychology researcher; b. Harrisburg, Pa., Aug. 15, 1965; d. Gary Andrew and Michaelene Ann (Verotsky) B. BS in Indsl. Psychology, Bus., Pa. State U., 1987, MS in Counselor Edn., Student Pers., 1990, postgrad., 1990—. Intern govt. svcs. Commonwealth of Pa., Harrisburg, 1986-88; coord. residence hall programs Pa. State U., University Park, 1988-90, asst. dir. office conduct standards, 1990—; counselor, trainer Oasis Counseling and Crisis Intervention Ctr., State College, Pa., 1984-86; co-instr. Pa. State U., University Park, 1987—; interviewer Dickinson Sch. Law, Carlisle, Mass., 1985—; lectr. Newman Ctr. Pa. State U., University Park. Mem. AACD, Pa. Assn. for Specialists in Group Work, Assn. for Specialists in Group Work, Assn. for Student Jud. Adminstrs., Sr. HAT Soc., Phi Beta Kappa, Chi Sigma Iota. Democrat. Roman Catholic.

BAROODY, MICHAEL NORMAN, JR., sales executive; b. Auburn, N.Y., Aug. 21, 1950; s. Michael Norman and Lucia (Petrosino) B.; m. Susan Rich; children: Alison Elizabeth, Laura Michelle. BS in Biology, SUNY, Brockport, 1980. Gen. mgr. Leanna, Inc., Rochester, N.Y., 1971-75; v.p., treas. Mr. Restaurant, Inc., Rochester, 1975-79; mktg. rep. Ortho Diagnostic Systems, Rochester, 1980-85; S.W. div. mgr. Ortho Diagnostic Systems, Raritan, N.J., 1985-87, Ea. region mgr., 1987-90, dir. sales, 1990—; dir. sales force automation Ortho Diagnostic Systems, Raritan, 1987-89. Mem. Am. Mgmt. Assn. Republican. Roman Catholic. Home: 2121 Jericho Dr Jamison PA 18929-1521

BAROZZI, ALVA COPLON, banking executive, portfolio manager; b. Buffalo, Sept. 6, 1937; d. David Hascal and Minnie Mildred (Greene) Coplon; m. Socrate Jean Barozzi, May 9, 1967 (dec. 1973). Student, Barnard Coll., 1955-57; BA, SUNY, Buffalo, 1960. Office mgr. Flintkote Co., N.Y.C., 1960-62; promotion dir. Neiman-Marcus, Dallas and Houston, 1962-67; treas., asst. sec. Ford, Powell & Carson, Inc., San Antonio, 1967-75; comptroller George M. Ewing Co., Phila., 1975-78; treas. Allen, Rogers & Co., Inc., Phila., 1978-82; v.p., chief compliance officer 1st Pa. Investments, Phila., 1982-89; adminstrv. officer, mgr. investment trading First Pa Bank N.A., Phila., 1989-91; investment officer, portfolio mgr. CoreStates Investment Advisers, Phila., 1991—. Mem. Am. Inst. Bankers, Fitler Sq. Improvement Assn., South St. West Civic Assn., Amnesty Internat. Democrat. Jewish. Office: CoreStates Investment Advis 1-3-86-13 Upper Mezz Ctr Sq W 16th and Market St Philadelphia PA 19102

BARR, DELORIS, computer programmer; b. Johnsonville, S.C., July 16, 1950; d. Luther Rufus and Mary Leona (Brown) B. Student, Del. Tech. Sch., 1991—. Keypuncher Bank of Del., Wilmington, 1970; keypuncher Delmarva Power & Light, Wilmington, 1970-82, computer operator, 1982-88, computer programmer, 1988—. Songwriter: (lyrics) He Came to Save, 1991, What an Amazing Child, 1991, In the Master's Plan, 1992, I'm Gonna Fly, 1992. Democrat. Baptist. Home: 3414 Broom Pl Apt H-7 Wilmington DE 19802

BARR, JAMES GEORGE, editor; b. Camden, N.J., July 11, 1951; s. James Joseph and Betty Ann (Blackner) B. AB in Physics, Rutgers U., 1973. Engring. applications programmer RCA Corp., Moorestown, N.J., 1973-74; customer svc. rep. RCA Corp., Cherry Hill, N.J., 1974-75, systems programmer, 1975-79, mgr. systems programming, 1979-85; project mgr. Gen. Electric Co., Moorestown, N.J., 1985-86; mgr. quality assurance Gen. Electric Co., Cherry Hill, 1986-89; dir. mktg. Seana Prodns., Cherry Hill, 1990-91; mng. editor Datapro Info. Svcs. Group, Delran, N.J., 1991—; systems devel. cons. Formation, Inc., Mt. Laurel, N.J., 1980; mgmt. cons. Genteel-Crosby Prodns., Spokane, Wash., 190. Contbr. articles to profl. jours. Foster parent Plan Internat., 1990; active Amnestry Internat. Mem. ACLU, Washington D.C. VM Users' Group. Democrat. Methodist. Home: 715 Kings Croft Cherry Hill NJ 08034-1108 Office: Datapro Info Svcs Group 600 Delran Pky Delran NJ 08075-1252

BARR, MICHAEL BLANTON, lawyer; b. Freeport, N.Y., July 24, 1948; s. Harry Kyle and Rosemary (Blanton) B.; m. Nancy Nickeson, Aug. 11, 1979; children: Nicholas Upton, Jessica Nickeson, Alice Primrose. B.S., Georgetown U., 1970; J.D., George Washington U., 1973. Bar: D.C. 1973. U.S. Dist. Ct. D.C. 1973, U.S. Ct. Appeals (D.C. cir.) 1974, U.S. Ct. Appeals (3d cir.) 1979, U.S. Ct. Appeals, (4th cir.) 1976, U.S. Ct. Appeals (6th cir.) 1981, U.S. Supreme Ct. 1980. Assoc. LeBoeuf, Lamb, Lieby & McRae, Washington, 1973-76, Hunton & Williams, Washington, 1976-80; ptnr. Hunton & Williams, Washington, 1980—, mng. ptnr. Washington office, mem. exec. com., 1985—. Contbr. articles to profl. jours. Bd. dirs. Am. Sch. of Tangier, Morocco, 1989—; trustee Fed. City Coun. Mem. ABA, Internat. Bar Assn., D.C. Bar Assn. Democrat. Club: City Tavern (Washington). Home: 7203 Exfair Rd Bethesda MD 20814-2353 Office: Hunton & Williams 2000 Pennsylvania Ave NW PO Box 19230 Washington DC 20036

BARR, MICHAEL CHARLES, securities company executive, lawyer; b. White Plains, N.Y., Nov. 2, 1947; s. Charles Yerger and Joan Tames (Biggar) B.; m. Helen June Rumsey, Mar. 17, 1973. BA, Rutgers U., 1969; JD, Columbia U., 1972, MBA, 1980. Bar: N.J. 1976, N.Y. 1978. Assoc. McCarter & English, Newark, 1976-77, Conboy, Hewitt, O'Brien & Boardman, N.Y.C., 1977-78, Kidder, Peabody & Co., Inc., N.Y.C., 1980-82; v.p. Mfrs. Hanover Trust Co., N.Y.C., 1982-90, A-L Assocs., N.Y.C., 1990-92; corp. sec. H. Rivkin & Co., Inc., N.Y.C., 1992—. Lt. USN, 1972-76. Recipient Loyal Son award Rutgers Alumni Assn., 1976. Mem. Far Hills Polo Cub, English-Speaking Union, Phi Beta Kappa. Office: H Rivkin & Co Inc Townhouse 5 2 South End Ave New York NY 10280

BARR, NANCY VERDE, culinary author, educator; b. Providence, Mar. 12, 1944; d. Charles C. and Katherine Wilhelmina (Higgins) V.; m. Philip Duane Barr, July 26, 1969; children: Philip Bradford, Andrew Gilmore. BA, U. R.I., 1967. Food cons. Good Morning America, ABC-TV, N.Y.C., 1981-87, ABC Hearts & "Look" TV, Boston, 1983; exec. chef Julia Child Prodns., Boston, 1980-88, Parade Mag. - Julia Child, Boston, 1980-85; tchr. culinary Sakonnet Vineyards, Boston U., Brown U. Learning Community; freelance cons. Author: We Called It Macaroni, 1991; contbr. articles to food mags. including Gourmet, Food and Wine, Bon Appetit, N.E. Living. Bd. dirs. R.I. Philharmonic Friends Soc., Providence, 1991—; food chmn. Internat. Inst., Providence, 1988, Providence Preservation Soc. Ball, 1991—. Mem. Internat. Assn. Culinary Profls., Am. Inst. Wine and Food, Agawam Hunt Club, Sakonnet Country Club, Boston Women's Culinary Guild, James Beard Found. Episcopalian. Home: 109 Williams St Providence RI 02906-1028

BARR, RICHARD ARTHUR, biology educator, researcher; b. Southport, N.Y., Mar. 12, 1925; s. Harold Arthur and Emma Marie (Ferguson) B.; m. Violet Marie Keens, Oct. 8, 1961; children: Robert Adrian, Elisa Marie. BS in Agrl., U. Vt., 1950, MS, 1955; PhD, Cornell U., 1963. Rose grower Elmira (N.Y.) Floral Products, 1950-55; rsch. asst. U. Vt., Burlington, 1953-56; rsch. asst. Cornell U., Ithaca, N.Y., 1958-61, teaching and rsch. asst., 1958-61, rsch. assoc., 1961-64, asst. prof., 1964-66; asst. prof. biology U. Mo., St. Louis, 1966-68; assoc. prof. Shippensburg (Pa.) State Coll., 1968-72; prof. Shippensburg U., 1972—. With USN, 1943-46. Republican. Presbyterian. Home: 55 Rich's Dr Shippensburg PA 17257-8619 Office: Shippensburg U Biology Dept Shippensburg PA 17257

BARR, ROGER MOORE, agricultural agent; b. Paterson, N.J., Sept. 25, 1934; s. Joseph and Doris Deborah (Blackshaw) B.; m. Beatrice Jeanette Moran, Sept. 30, 1955; children: Debroah Patricia, Janine Elizabeth, Roger Patton. BS, NYU, 1956; MBA, Fairleigh Dickinson U., 1961. Timestudy indsl. engr. Bendix Aviation Corp., Teterboro, N.J., 1956-59; engr. Ford Motor Co., Mahwah, N.J., 1959-62; programmer analyst System Devel. Corp., Paramus, N.J., 1962-66; systems programmer Western Union, Mahwah, 1966-67; county 4-H agent N.J. Coop. Extension Cook Coll. Rutgers U., New Brunswick, N.J., 1968—; cons. in field. Bd. edn. mem. No. Highland Regional High Sch., Allendale, N.J., 1974-77; pres. No. Highlander Band Parents Assn., Allendale, 1973-75. Recipient Disting. Svc. award Nat. Assn. Extension 4-H Agents, 1983, Communication award N.J. Assn. 4-H Agents, 1985, 87, 88. Mem. N.J. Assn. 4-H Agts. (v.p., pres. 1975-78), Nat. Assn. Extension 4-H Agts., Lions, Epsilon Sigma Phi. Home: 122 Hampshire Hill Rd Saddle River NJ 07458-1106 Office: Bergen County 4H Clubs 327 E Ridgewood Ave Paramus NJ 07652-4832

BARR, WILLIAM PELHAM, attorney general of United States; b. N.Y.C., May 23, 1950; s. Donald and Mary (Ahern) B.; m. Christine Moynihan, June 23, 1973; 3 children. AB, Columbia U., 1971, MA, 1973; JD, George Washington U., 1977. Bar: Va. 1977, D.C. 1978. Staff officer CIA, Washington, 1973-77; law clk. to presiding judge Cir. Ct., Washington, 1977-78; assoc. Shaw, Pittman, Potts & Trowbridge, Washington, 1978-82, 83-84, ptnr., 1985-89; dep. asst. dir. domestic policy staff The White House, Washington, 1982-83; asst. atty. gen. Office Legal Counsel, U.S. Dept. Justice, Washington, 1989-90, dep. atty. gen., 1990-91, atty. gen., 1991—. Mem. ABA, Va. State Bar Assn., D.C. Bar Assn., KC. Republican. Roman Catholic. Office: Dept Justice Office Atty Gen 10th Constitution Ave NE Washington DC 20530-0001

BARRACK, MARTIN KENNETH, communications executive; b. N.Y.C., Dec. 23, 1942; s. Max Barrack and Freda Barrack Ellman; m. Irene H. Barrack, Feb. 5, 1967. BA, Hunter Coll., 1967; MA, New Sch. for Social Rsch., 1969. Cert. amateur radio operator, FCC. Insp. U.S. Customs Svc., San Luis, Ariz., 1970-71; import specialist U.S. Customs Svc., L.A., 1971-74; communications specialist U.S. Customs Svc., Washington, 1974-85; communications specialist GSA, Washington, 1985-88, info. resources mgmt. policy analyst, 1988—; appearance on numerous radio and TV shows as expert on the art and sci. of communication. Author: How We Communicate: The Most Vital Skill, 1989. Mem. Love is Given Prayer Group. Mem. Telecommuting Adv. Coun., Mensa, Masons. Roman Catholic. Home: 6682 Old Blacksmith Dr Burke VA 22015-4137 Office: GSA KMP 18th and F Sts NW Washington DC 20405

BARRACLOUGH, CHARLES ARTHUR, endocrinologist, educator; b. Vineland, N.J., July 13, 1926; s. Charles A. and Martha (Romain) B.; m. Eleanor Pauline Kolakowski, June 28, 1952; children: Janet, Patricia. BS, St. Joseph's Coll., 1947; MS, Rutgers U., 1952, PHD, 1953. Asst. prof. UCLA, 1959-61; spl. rsch. fellow Cambridge (Eng.) U., 1961-62; assoc. prof. U. Md., Balt., 1962-65, prof. physiology, 1965—, dir. Ctr. Studies Reproduction, 1985—; reproduction biology study sec. NIH, Bethesda, 1967-69, 70-74. Contbr. over 125 articles to profl. jours., 25 chpts. to books. Recipient Rsch. award Soc. Study Reproduction, 1984, Carl Hartman award 1990. Fellow AAAS; mem. Endocrine Soc. (editorial bd. 1965-72), Soc. Neurosci., Soc. Exptl. Biology and Medicine (editorial bd. 1974-87), Am. Physiol. Soc. (editorial bd. 1979-83). Office: Sch Medicine U Md 655 W Baltimore St Baltimore MD 21201-1509

BARRANTE, JAMES RICHARD, chemistry educator, researcher; b. Torrington, Conn., Apr. 30, 1938; s. Joseph Carl and Josephine Margaret (Pilonero) B.; m. Marlene Gloria Buccos, May 1, 1965; children: Sharon, Stephen, Kimberly. BA, U. Conn., 1960; MA, Harvard U., 1962, PhD, 1964. Atomic Energy Commn. fellow Tufts U., Medford, Mass., 1963-64; sr. rsch. chemist Olin Corp., New Haven, Conn., 1964-66; asst. prof. So. Conn. State U., New Haven, 1966-69, assoc. prof., 1969-76, prof., 1976—; cons. MacDermid Corp., Waterbury, Conn., 1980-83. Author: Applied Math. Phys. Chemistry, 1972, Phys. Chemistry Life Science, 1974; contbr. articles to profl. jours. Cons. Mus. Modern Art, N.Y.C., 1986-88. Mem. Assn. Harvard Chemists. Office: So Conn State U 501 Crescent St New Haven CT 06515-1355

BARRÉ, CHARLES, business owner; b. N.Y.C., Aug. 19, 1950; s. Charles H. and Mildred Eleanor (Kranz) B.; m. Christina Ryan Christiansen, Mar. 12, 1968 (div. 1973); 1 child, Sean Charles; married, 1975 (div. 1991); 1 child, Desirae. AA in Bus. Mgmt., Suffolk Community Coll., 1976. Tractor trailer driver N.Y., N.J., Conn. Trucking Co., N.Y., La., Tex., Mo., Ariz., Wash., 1976-80; clerk, mgmt. SGC Corp., N.Y.C., 1980-82; night crew chief SGC Corp., 1982-87; owner, computer cons. CB Graphics, Selden, N.Y., 1986—. Author: (computer software) Lotto 17, 1988, Wordval, 1989. Avocation: photography. Office: CB Graphics 339 Middle Country Rd Selden NY 11784-2533

BARRE, ROBERT LAWRENCE, industrial development company executive; b. N.Y.C., Dec. 8, 1918; s. Harre Schwarz-Barre and Gertrude (Edleman) B.; m. Lois Aileen Smith, June 22, 1949 (dec. Jan. 1988). BS, Harvard U., 1946, BArch., 1949, MCP, 1950, MRP, MPA, PhD, 1951, 52, 53. Dir. rsch. Harvard Bur. Mcpl. Rsch., Cambridge, Mass., 1948-52; dir. planning Presdl. Task Force, Washington, 1952-58; chief social scientist to Adminstr. of Vet. Affairs, Washington, 1958-62; chief social scientist NASA, Washington, 1962-64; dir. Appalachian regional devel. program Litton Industries, 1964-65; pres. Cen. Econ. Devel. Orgn., Inc., Washington, 1965-70; exec. v.p. United Overseas Investment Co., Washington, 1971-79; pres., chmn. Am. Technology Corp., Washington, 1980—, Am. Dicalcium Phosphate Technology Corp., Washington, 1986—; indsl. devel. cons. to Pres. of Indonesia, 1967-68, to Mexican Govt., Mexico City, 1972, Yulsan Corp., Seoul, 1978; new cities cons. to Sec. of HUD, Washington, 1969-70. Contbg. author books in field. Advisor Mass. Community Orgn. Svc., Boston, 1951-52; chmn. Washington Colloquium on Sci. and Soc., Washington, 1964-66; vice-chmn. bd. govs. Nat. Grad. U. 1st lt. U.S. Army, 1942-46, PTO. Rsch. fellow Harvard U., 1950-51; recipient Presdl. Unit citation Exec. Office of Pres., Washington, 1955; Presdl. rep. European Study Group and White House Conf. on Aging, Washington, 1959-60. Mem. AAAS, AIAA, Harvard Grad. Soc., Washington Colloquium Sci. and Soc. (chmn. 1963-67), Harvard Club of Washington (activities com. 1990-91),

Washington Acad. of Sci. Democrat. Home: 1859 Redwood Ter NW Washington DC 20012-1022

BARRE, STEVEN CRAIG, lawyer; b. N.Y.C., Nov. 11, 1959; s. Gerald J. and Roslyn P. (Fink) B.; m. Rachel Brody, Aug. 21, 1983; 1 child, Andrea Gabrielle Brody Barre. BS, Cornell U., 1981; JD, Columbia U., 1984. Bar: N.Y. 1985. Assoc. Weil Gotshal & Manges, N.Y.C., 1984-88; asst. gen. counsel Hanson Industries, Iselin, N.J., 1988—. Book rev. editor Columbia Jour. of Environ. Law, 1983-84. Com. mem. Cornell U. Alumni Ambassadors, Ithaca, N.Y., 1981—. Harlan Fiske Stone scholar, 1984, Cornell Nat. scholar, 1977. Mem. ABA, N.Y. State Bar Assn.

BARRELL, BILL DOUGLAS, artist; b. London, Dec. 4, 1932; arrives in U.S., 1954; s. Stanley Joseph and Margret (Ablett) B.; m. Irene Baker, Mar. 24, 1959 (div. Aug. 1968); children: Joshua, Zacarias; m. Marilyn Faye Apt, June 11, 1976; children: Liza, Anna. Owner, dir. Sun Gallery, Provincetown, Mass., 1960-61; vis. guest artist La. State U., 1982—; advisor, curator Mus. Art for Art's Sake, N.Y.C., 1990—; dir. Orgn. Ind. Artists, 1976-78. One man show includes Sun Gallery, Provincetown, Mass., 1958, 59, East End Gallery, Provincetown, 1960, 61, 62, 64, Maple Gallery, N.Y.C., 1962, Castagno Gallery, N.Y.C., 1966, Pitt St. Salon, N.Y.C., 1966, 68, Dorsky Gallery, N.Y.C., 1969, Bank Sq. Gallery, Eastport, Maine, 1971, Winter Gallery, N.Y.C., 1976, Aaron Berman Gallery, N.Y.C., 1977, Bienville Gallery, New Orleans, 1977, 82, 87, Apollo Gallery, N.Y.C., 1979, Provincetown Group Gallery, 1979, Daedel Gallery, Balt., 1979, Blue Mountain Gallery, Blue Mountain Gallery, N.Y.C., 1981, Alain Belhaud Gallery, N.Y.C., 1982, Patricia Dow Gallery, N.Y.C., 1983, Jersey City Mus., 1983, Sonja Berryer Gallery, Brussels, 1984, Ingber Gallery, N.Y.C., 1985, 87, 88, David Brown Gallery, Provincetown, 1986, 87, Gallery Jupiter, Little Silver, N.J., 1987, 88, 89, 90, Schering-Plough Corp., Madison, N.J., 1987, others; group shows include Tomasula Gallery Union Coll., 1977, Lincoln Ctr., N.Y.C., 1978, U. N.D., 1981, Jersey City Mus., 1981, 86, 90, Newton (Mass.) Arts Ctr., 1986, Montclair (N.J.) Mus., 1987, Artworks, Trenton, N.J., 1989; represented in permanent collections including Housatonic Mus. Fine Art, Conn., Provincetown Mus., Jersey City Mus., Walker Art Inst., Mpls., Chrysler Mus., Norfolk, Va., Dayton (Ohio) Mus. Fine Art, Schering-Plough Corp., Columbia U., N.Y.C. Recipient Harry Devlin award N.J. State Coun. of Arts, 1983. Home: 71 Sussex St Jersey City NJ 07302-4525 Studio: 111 1st St Jersey City NJ 07302

BARRES, SAMUEL L(AWRENCE), psychologist, educator, consultant; b. Boston, Nov. 28, 1924; s. Isadore and Sarah Anne (Finkelstein) B.; m. Bernice Browndorf, Aug. 31, 1946; children: Rachel Barbara Barres Black, Joanne Barres Shaw, Rabbi Robert Alan. BS cum laude, Boston U., 1949, MA, 1951; postgrad., Mass. Inst. Tech., 1964-67. Lic. psychologist, Mass.; accredited pers. diplomate; sr. profl. in human resources. Pers. dir. Boston (Mass.) Lying-in Hosp., 1951-64; pers. cons. Boston (Mass.) Hosp. for Women, 1964-67; sr. assoc. Univ. Affiliates, Brighton, Mass., 1967-69; v.p. Edn. for Mgmt., Allston, Mass., 1969-70; dir. pers. and ednl. svcs. St. Vincent Hosp., Worcester, Mass., 1971-72; dir., pers. and edn. Faulkner Hosp., Boston, 1972-73; pvt. practice, psychology Newton, Mass., 1973—; adj. prof. Boston Univ., 1952-66, Northeastern Univ. Grad. Sch., Boston, 1964-66, Babson Coll. Grad. Div., Wellesley, Mass., 1969-71. Contbr. articles to profl. jours. Mem. resource group project on the handicapped in sci. AAAS, 1976—; chairperson employment com. Foun. for Sci. and the Handicapped, 1977-86; chairperson Psychologists with Disabilities, 1979-88; mem. adv. bd. Human Rights Commn., Newton; mem. Mayor's Com. on Environment of Handicapped, Newton; mem. social action com. Temple Region of Newton; vol. various nursing homes. With U.S. Army, 1943-46, ETO. Decorated Bronze Star, Purple Heart; Hayden scholar Boston U., 1942-43; named Outstanding Young Man, Boston Jaycees, 1959; MIT doctoral fellow, 1964-67. Mem. AAAS, APA, Am. Psychol. Soc., Am. Soc. Psychologists in Pvt. Practice, Consortium on Vets. Studies, Ea. Psychol. Assn., Fedn. Am. Scientists, Internat. Soc. Edn. in Health Scis., Mass. Psychol. Assn., New England Psychol. Assn., Soc. for Human Resource Mgmt., Soc. Indsl. and Orgnl. Psychology, Mass. Healthcare Human Resources Assn. (hon., pres. 1952-53, 58-60), DAV (life), Beta Gamma Sigma, Pi Gamma Mu. Democrat. Jewish. Home: 132 Sargent St Newton MA 02158-2345

BARRETT, BEATRICE HELENE, psychologist; b. Cin., Dec. 8, 1928; d. Oscar Slack and Helen (Kaiper) B.; m. Harold Sheffield Van Buren, Oct. 6, 1966 (div. Oct. 1985). BA, U. Ariz., 1950; MA, U. Ky., 1952; PhD, Purdue U., 1957. Lic. psychologist, Mass. Grad. tchg. asst. in psychology U. Ky., Lexington, 1950-52; psychology asst. Longview State Hosp., Cin., 1951, staff psychologist, 1952; staff psychologist Children's Outpatient and Cons. Svcs. Ind. U. Med. Ctr., Indpls., 1954-57, chief psychologist, 1957-59; instr. psychology Ind. U. Med. Sch., Indpls., 1956-60; rsch. assoc. dept. psychiatry Ind. U. Med. Ctr., Indpls., 1959-60; pvt. practice clin. psychology Indpls., 1957-60; research fellow in psychology Sch. of Medicine Harvard U., Boston, 1960-62; lectr. in spl. edn. Grad. Sch. Edn., Boston U., 1962-63; dir. psychol. rsch. Walter E. Fernald State Sch., Belmont, Mass., 1962-69; dir. behavior prosthesis lab. Walter E. Fernald State Sch., Belmont, 1963—; chief psychologist, 1969—; assoc. psychologist Enuice Kennedy Shriver Ctr. for Mental Retardation, Inc., Waltham, Mass., 1982—; instr. Mass. Psychol. Ctr., 1972; lectr. in spl. edn. Lesley Coll. Grad. Sch., 1974-76; adj. assoc. prof. Northeastern U., 1983—; psychology cons. Carter Meml. Hosp., Indpls., 1959-60; mem. exec. com. Boston Behavior Therapy Interest Group, 1973-74. Cons. editor, mem. adv. bds. various profl. jours.; contbr. numerous articles to profl. jours. Mem. Ind. Gov.'s Youth Coun., 1959-61; mem. spl. adv. com. on mental retardation Ind. Dept. Pub. Instrn., 1959-61; mem. task force Mass. Mental Retardation Planning Project, 1965-66; mem. adv. bd. Cambridge Ctr. for Behavioral Studies, 1981-87, trustee, 1987—, chair devel. com., 1987-89; mem. com. on dance edn. Spl. Commn. on Performing Arts, 1976-77; mem. art acquisition com. DeCordova Mus., 1978-80, mem. contemporary arts coun., 1985—; trustee Boston Repertory Ballet, 1977-79; trustee Boston Ballet Co., 1970-76, sec. bd., 1974-75, exec. com., 1974-76. Grantee Nat. Assn. for Retarded Citizens, 1963, NIHM, 1963-76. Fellow Am. Psychol. Assn., Mass. Psychol. Assn., Behavior Therapy and Rsch. Soc. (charter clin.); mem. Assn. for Mentally Ill Children (human rights com. 1979-81), Am. Acad. on Mental Retardation (v.p. 1969-74, at-large exec. com. 1975-77), Eastern Psychol. Assn., Assn. for Advancement of Behavior Therapy, Assn. Behavior Analysis (jour. adv. bd. 1983-87, chair task force on right to effective edn. 1986-91), Stage Harbor Yacht Club (Chatham, Mass., mem. race com. 1984-86). Home: RFD 7 Box 236A Winter St Lincoln MA 01773 Office: Walter E Fernald State Sch PO Box 9108 Belmont MA 02178-9108

BARRETT, CLARA HAYES, interior designer; b. Middleboro, Mass.; d. Francis Arlington and Margaret (McGee) Hayes; m. Peter Barrett, June 26, 1965; children: Peter Jr., Jonathan Hayes. Student, Lady Cliff Coll., Stonehill Coll.; BA, Stonehill Coll. Owner, prin. dsigner Clara Hayes Barrett Design, Hingham, Mass., 1972—. Mem. Am. Soc. Interior Designers. Roman Catholic. Home: 10 Martins Ln Hingham MA 02043-1020 Office: 300 Boylston St Boston MA 02116

BARRETT, ELIZABETH ANN MANHART, nursing educator, psychotherapist, consultant; b. Hume, Ill., July 11, 1934; d. Francis J. and Grace C. (Manhart) Fridy; children: Joseph B., Jeffrey F., Paula G. Brown, Pamela M. Shetler Carpino, Scott D. BS in Nursing summa cum laude, U. Evansville, 1970, MA, 1973, MS in Nursing, 1976; grad. Gestalt Assocs. for Psychotherapy, 1982; PhD in Nursing, NYU, 1983. Instr. nursing U. Evansville, Ind., 1970-73, asst. prof., 1973-76; staff nurse Welborn Bapt. Hosp., Evansville, 1975-76; staff nurse Bellevue Psychiat. Hosp., N.Y.C., 1976-79; clin. tchr. CUNY, 1977-82; asst. prof. Adelphi U., 1979-80; group practice Nurse Healers, 1979-82; pvt. practice psychotherapy, 1980—; nurse researcher Mt. Sinai Med. Ctr., N.Y.C., 1982-86, asst. dir. nursing, 1983-86; assoc. prof. Hunter Coll., N.Y.C., 1986-89, dir. grad. studies, 1989-92. Mem. com. Regional Health Planning Council, Evansville, 1974-77. Mem. Am. Nurses Assn. (cert. psychiat.-mental health, coun. nurse rschrs.), Nat. League Nursing, Ea. Nursing Rsch. Assn. (charter), Soc. ADavancement in Nursing, Soc. Rogerian Scholars (founder, 1st pres. 1988-90), NOW, Phi Kappa Phi, Sigma Theta Tau (Upsilon chpt. pres. 1986-88), Alpha Tau Delta, Sigma Xi. Home: 415 E 85th St Apt 9E New York NY 10028-6358 Office: Hunter Coll 425 E 25th St New York NY 10010-2590

BARRETT, EVELYN CAROL, educator; b. Ocean Springs, Miss., Feb. 6, 1928; d. Charles Edward and Irene Effie (Hopkins) Engbarth; diploma with honors Jr. Coll., Perkinston, Miss., 1945; B.S. in Commerce with high honors, Miss. So. Coll. (now U. So. Miss.), 1947; M.B.A. in Acctg., La. State U., 1950; also numerous continuing edn. courses, 1950-82; m. Arthur James Barrett, June 10, 1951; children: George Stanley, Ruth Anne, James Sidney, Carolyn Jean. Bookkeeper-sec. Non-Commn. Officers Club, Kessler AFB, Miss., summer 1947; asst., secretarial practice office and div. research, instr. in typing Coll. Commerce, La. State U., 1947-50; instr. Miss. So. Coll., summer 1950; clk.-stenographer dept. physics U. Ill., Urbana, 1951-52; instr. in shorthand Ill. Comml. Coll., 1951-52; tchr. Milford (N.H.) High Sch., 1957-58; tchr. bus. edn. Merrimack (N.H.) High Sch., 1958-90, head dept. bus. edn., 1971-81, ret., 1990; instr. auditing Rivier Coll., 1982; registered rep. R. Danais Investment Co., Manchester, N.H.; account exec. John, Edward & Co., Lebanon, N.H.; ind. beauty cons. Mary Kay Cosmetics, Merrimack; tutor in shorthand, acctg.; cons. acctg. systems. Grad. asst. La. State U., 1947-50. Active Girl Scouts U.S.A., including Cadette leader, 1959-63, sr. troop leader Swiftwater council, 1970-72, adult vol. trainer, 1964-66, troop program cons., 1963-64. Mem. N.H. Bus. Educators Assn. (v.p. 1964-65, pres. 1965-67, rep. to N.H. Vocat. Assn. 1986-87 (sec. 1967-68, treas. 1973-75, historian 1986-87), N.H. Supervisory Union 27 (sec.-treas. 1961-62), NEA, N.H. Edn. Assn., Merrimack Tchrs. Assn. (Disting. Educator award 1980, Excellence in Edn. award 1985, sec. 1984-85), New Eng. Bus. Educators Assn., Am. Vocat. Assn., N.H. Assn. Computer Edn. Statewide, Eastern Bus. Edn. Assn., Nat. Bus. Edn. Assn., AAUW, Delta Zeta, Phi Theta Kappa, Pi Omega Pi, Delta Pi Epsilon, Alpha Delta Kappa (historian N.E. region 1981-83, v.p. N.H. Alpha chpt. 1978-79, pres. N.H. Alpha chpt. 1979-82, N.H. State sgt.-at-arms 1982-84, N.H. State treas. 1984-88, State membership chmn. 1988-92, chpt. award of appreciation 1980), Delta Sigma Epsilon (chpt. corr. sec.). Roman Catholic. Clubs: Gen. Electric Women's, Manchester Coll. Women's, Our Lady of Mercy Ch. Guild.

BARRETT, JEREMIAH JOSEPH, federal government executive; b. N.Y.C., Dec. 13, 1941; s. Walter Patrick and Helen Marie (Condon) B. BA, Boston Coll., 1963; MEd, State Coll. at Boston, 1964. Dir. personnel Nat. Gallery of Art, Washington, 1968-79; agy. officer Office of Personnel Mgmt., Washington, 1979-82, asst. to dep. dir., 1982-86, dir. combined fed. campaign, 1986-92; deputy dir. adminstrn. group Office of Personnel Mgmt., 1992—. Lt. (j.g.) USN, 9164-68. Democrat. Roman Catholic. Home: 1514 R St NW Washington DC 20009-3818 Office: Office Personnel Mgmt 1900 E St NW Rm 5542 Washington DC 20415-0002

BARRETT, JOSEPH EDWARD, educational administrator; b. Chgo., June 17, 1937; s. Frank Fumio and Mary Louise (Nolan) Morikawa; m. Annyce Marita Adams, Feb. 10, 1958 (div. 1973); children: Robin Roxana, Reuben Edward; m. Judith Ann Grooters, May 27, 1974; 1 child, Casey Nolan. BEd, Chgo. Tchrs. Coll., 1963; MEd, U. Mo., St. Louis, 1970; Cert. Advanced Grad. Study, Va. Poly. Inst. and State U., 1992. Bus driver Chgo. Transit Authority, 1958-65; tchr. math. Yale Upper Grade Ctr., Chgo., 1963-65; sr. math. instr. Rodman Job Corps, New Bedford, Mass., 1965-68; program coord. Cen. Midwestern Regional Labs., St. Ann, Mo., 1968-70; dir. math. Quality Ednl. Devel., Brighton, Mass., 1970-72; assoc. dir. Project SPOKE, Norton, Mass., 1972-76; instructional devel. specialist Community Coll. of Phila., 1976—, dir. staff devel., 1989—; curriculum specialist Budd Co., Phila., 1986-87; curriculum prof. Thomas Jefferson U., Phila., 1988, Glassboro (N.J.) State Coll., 1991. Author: This Is for You, 1966; editor/author: Where Behavior Objectives Exist, 1973, Customized Job Training, 1987. Basketball coach Cath. Youth Orgn., Foxboro, Mass., 1972-74; baseball umpire Am. Legion, Foxboro, 1972-74; cubmaster Boy Scouts Am., Cherry Hill, N.J., 1984-86; polit. campaigner Pulliams Sch. Bd. Election Bid, Cherry Hill, 1991. Mem. NEA, Am. Ednl. Rsch. Assn. (nat. coun. bd. 1987-88), Nat. Coun. for Staff, Profl. and Orgnl. Devel., Phi Delta Kappa. Home: 505 Hastings Rd Cherry Hill NJ 08034-1320 Office: Community Coll of Phila 1700 Spring Gardens St Philadelphia PA 19130-3991

BARRETT, LAURENCE IRWIN, journalist; b. N.Y.C., Sept. 6, 1935; s. Harold and Ruth (Gaier) B.; m. Paulette Singer, Mar. 22. 1957 (div. 1982); children: Paul M., David A., Adam S.; m. Martha Priddy Patterson, July 24, 1988. BA, NYU, 1956; MS in Journalism, Columbia U., 1957. Polit. reporter and columnist N.Y. Herald Tribune, N.Y.C., 1958-62; Washington correspondent N.Y. Herald Tribune, Washington, 1962-65; assoc. editor Time Inc., N.Y.C., 1965-69; sr. editor Time Inc., 1970-75, N.Y. regional bur. chief, 1975-78, sr. White House correspondent, 1978-85, nat. polit. correspondent, 1986-91, 92—; Washington dep. bur. chief, 1989-91; panelist various TV and radio talk shows. Co-author: The Winning of the White House, 1988, 89; author: Gambling with History: Reagan in the White House, 1983, The Mayor of New York, 1965; contbr. articles to profl. jours. With U.S. Army, 1957. Mem. Nat. Press Club, Soc. of the Silurians. Jewish. Office: Time Washington Bur 1050 Connecticut Ave NW Washington DC 20036-5303

BARRETT, MATTHEW W., bank executive; b. County Meath, Ireland, Sept. 20, 1944; m. Irene Korsak; children: Tara, Kelly, Andrea, Jason. Grad. advanced mgmt. program, Harvard Bus. Sch. With Bank Montreal, 1962—, chief exec. officer, 1989-90, chmn. bd. dirs., 1989—; dir. Harris Bankcorp, Inc., Nesbitt, Thomson Corp. Limited; adv. com. U. Western Ont. Program. Dir. Montreal bd. Trade Heritage Found., Montreal Symphony Orch., faculty adminstrv. studies adv. coun. York U.; bd. dirs Ottawa chpt. Harvard Bus. Sch. Alumni; bd. trustee Toronto Hosp.; chmn. areawide campaign for United Way, Toronto, 1990; chmn. Capital Campaign Univ. Waterloo; dir. Regroupement Êconomie et Constitution, Coun. for Can. Unity; co-chair Royal Victoria Hosp.; dir., mem. policy com. Bus. Coun. Nat. Issues. Office: Bank Montreal, PO Box 1 First Canada Pl, Toronto, ON Canada M5X 1A1

BARRETT, THOMAS RAWSON, artist; b. N.Y.C., Feb. 17, 1927; s. Edward Anthony Barrett and Irene Lillian Blunt; m. Leni Mancuso, June 14, 1952; 1 child, Kedron Ryon. BA, Wesleyan U., Middletown, Conn., 1948; cert., Bklyn. Mus. Art Sch., 1950; MA, U. N.H., 1961. Math. tchr. St. Thomas Choir Sch., N.Y.C., 1951-52; English tchr. Rectory Sch., Pomfret, Conn., 1952-55; dir. studies Proctor Acad., Andover, N.H., 1955-60; English tchr. St. Paul's Sch., Concord, N.H., 1960-69, dir. art ctr., exhbn. dir., 1969-89; cons. New Eng. Found. for Arts, Boston, 1984-88. Author, editor exhbn. catalogs, 1970-81; author text: Understanding Sentences, 1967; contbr. art revs. to profl. publs. Bd. dirs. N.H. Art Assn., Manchester, 1970-76; pres. N.H. Visual Arts Coalition, Manchester, 1985-88; mem. Greater Concord (N.H.) Arts Coun., 1970-75. With USNR, 1944-46. Recipient Currier prize Currier Gallery of Art, 1965, City of Manchester award Currier Gallery of Art, 1972, award Yankee Mag., 1980. Mem. Am. Assn. Mus., Deer Isle Artist Assn., Union of Maine Visual Artists, Castine Men's Club. Home and Studio: PO Box 303 Madockawando Rd Castine ME 04421

BARRETT, WILLIAM JOEL, investment banker; b. Darien, Conn., Aug. 26, 1939; s. William J. and Virginia Barrett; BA, DePauw U., Greencastle, Ind., 1961; MBA, NYU, 1963; m. Sara Schrock, Sept. 1, 1962; children: William, Brian, Christopher, Peter. Investment analyst Met. Life Ins. Co., 1961-66; v.p. Gregory & Sons, investment bankers, 1966-69, G.A. Saxton, investment bankers, 1969-74; sr. v.p., Janney Montgomery Scott, Inc., N.Y.C., 1974—, also bd. dirs.; bd. dirs. ESI Industries, Inc., Shelter Components Corp., Fredericks Corp., TGC Industries, Inc., United Am. HealthCare Corp.; bd. trustees De Pauw U., Diocesan Investment Trust N.J. Republican. Episcopalian. Clubs: Navesink Country, Univ., India House, Bond of N.Y., Shrewsbury Sailing and Yacht, Sea Bright Lawn Tennis, Seabright Beach, Rumson Country.

BARRETT-KOBES, VIOLET ULINE, academic advisor; b. Chesterfield, Jamaica, Mar. 1, 1955; came to U.S., 1982; Tchr's. diploma in Elem. Edn., Mico Coll., 1969-73; cert. in Edn. in Counseling, U. of West Indies, 1980-81; BA in Spl. Edn., William Paterson, 1983-87, MEd, 1983-87; MSW, Rutgers U., 1991. N.J. Tchr. of Handicapped Pupil Personnel Svc. Social studies tchr. Guy's Hill Sch., Jamaica, West Indies, 1972-74; guidance counselor Bogwalk Sch., Jamaica, West Indies, 1974-81; student tchr. Hackensack (N.J.) Middle Sch., 1984-86; grad. intern career svcs. William Paterson Coll., Wayne, N.J., 1987-88, career planning asst., 1988; adjunct instr. Raritan Valley Community Coll., Somerville, N.J., 1989; acad. advisor Trenton (N.J.) State Coll., 1988—; vol. Trenton State Coll. Community Day, Planned Giving, Summer Reading group workshop, Welcome Week, CIRP Survey, Coll. Assessment Testing, Counselor Tng. Inst. Planning Office, N.J. Dept. Health Edn. and Employment Office. Named Dean's List. Mem. Acad. Advisement Assn., Trenton State Coll. Minority Exec. Coun., Trenton State Coll. Faculty Dame, Coun. for Exceptional Children, N.J. Placement Group, N.J. Ecnl. Opportunity Fund Program Assn. Home: 23-2B Bloomingdale Dr Hillsborough NJ 07601 Office: Trenton State Coll Trenton NJ 07771

BARRETT-MORAN, LINDA MARIE, psychologist, consultant; b. Reno, Mar. 28, 1947; d. Harry Robert and Irene Marie (McNamara) Barrett; m. Michael Wilder Moran, Oct. 20, 1979; children: Timothy Michael, Alicia Barrett. AB, San Diego State U., 1976, MS, 1980; PhD, U.S. Internat. U., 1983. Rsch. asst. Navy Pers. R & D Ctr., San Diego, 1976-78; instr. San Diego C.C. Dist., 1978-81; clin. intern Elmcrest Psychiat. Inst., Portland, Conn., 1981-82; staff clin. psychologist New Medico, Inc., Milford, Conn., 1983-84; clin. psychologist, dir. Assocs. Clin. Practice, Guilford, Conn., 1984—; cons. San Diego County Assn. for Retarded, 1978-80; docent Eating Disorders Clinic Yale U., New Haven, 1990—. Bd. dirs. Shoreline Unitarian Universalist Soc., Madison, Conn., 1986-89, A Better Chance of Madison, 1984—. Mem. APA, Conn. Psychol. Assn., Ea. Psychol. Assn. Congregationalist. Office: Assocs Clin Practice 450 Boston Post Rd Ste 207 Guilford CT 06437

BARRIE, JEFFREY EDWARD, marketing executive, consultant; b. Balt., Jan. 6, 1941; s. Seymour Theodore and Minna (Rankin) B.; m. Frances Evans, Dec. 29, 1963 (div. Sept. 1973); children: Marc Evans, Brian Evans; m. Maureen Linnea, Jan. 1, 1977. BA in Lit., The Citadel, 1963; MA in Soviet Studies, Fordham U., 1970. Advanced through ranks to lt. col. U.S. Army, 1968-83; project mgr. div. personal computer Satra Corp., Moscow, 1984-86; project mgr. Mosaic Rsch. U. Ariz., Tucson, 1987-88; dir. Kniga Printshop Joint Venture, Moscow, 1989-90; pres. Satra Aerospace, Moscow, 1990-91; pres. Barrie Assocs., Marblehead, Mass., Moscow, 1992—; cons. Satra Corp., N.Y.C., 1984-91, Apple Corp., Cupertino, Calif., 1985-87, PAC Aviation, Pompano Beach, 1987-91, Trace Worldwide, Torrance, Calif., 1991. Editor The Barrie Newsletter, 1989-91; contbr. articles to profl. jours. Nat. dir. Young Execs. Nat. Defense Transp. Assn., Washington, 1974. Mem. U.S. Parachuting Assn., Exptl. Aircraft Assn., Internat. Aerobatics Club. Home: 34 Russell St Marblehead MA 01945-3457

BARRINGER, J(OHN) PAUL, business executive, retired diplomat and career service executive; b. Stafford, Pa., Feb. 10, 1903; s. Daniel Moreau and Margaret (Bennett) B.; m. Dorothy Allen Pray; 4 children. BS, Princeton U., 1924. With Pa. Co. Banking and Trusts, 1925-35; specialist U.S. govt. securities Brown, Harriman & Co., Guaranty Trust Co., N.Y.C.; sr. ofcl., chief aviation div. Dept. State, Washington, 1946-48, dir. Office Transp. and Communications Policy, 1950-56; charge d'affairs Port-au-Prince, Haiti, 1956-58; charge d'affairs Am. Embassy, Tripoli, Libya, 1958-59, Benghazi-Beida, Libya, 1959-61; sr. fgn. service insp. with rank ambassador Washington, 1962-65; chmn. bd., mng. trustee Edn. Career Service, Inc., Princeton, N.J., 1965-75; chmn. bd. dirs. Barringer Crater Co., Princeton, 1975-92, 1992—; chmn. bd. dirs. Cass County Iron Co., 1975—; chmn. U.S. dels. to many Internat. Civil Aviation Orgns. Confs., 1947-55, Internat. Telecommunications Union, Rome, 1949-50, others. Author publs., lectrs. on govt. financing and mktg. securities, basic mil. tng., internat. civil aviation. Served as col. USAAF, 1941-46. Decorated Legion of Merit, Bronze Star (U.S.); Order Flying Cloud, Spl. Order Nun Hui, China. Mem. English Speaking Union (pres. Princeton br. 1965-75), U.S. Polo Assn. (past gov.). Republican. Episcopalian. Clubs: Army-Navy, Metropolitan (Washington); Racquet, Univ. Barge (Phila.); Princeton (N.Y.C.); Nassau (Princeton). Office: Barringer Crater Co 20 Nassau St # 672 Princeton NJ 08542-4509

BARRIOS, GEORGE G., colon rectal surgeon; b. Zamboanga, The Philippines, Apr. 24, 1943; came to U.S., 1973; s. Donaciano and Nemesia (Gatchalian) B.; m. Olga Cruz, Dec. 11, 1969; children: Kurt, Karl, Erik, Katrina. BA, Ateneo de Manila, Quezon City, The Philippines, 1963; MD, U. The Philippines, Manila, 1968. Diplomate Am. Bd. Surgeons. Resident in gen. surgery SUNY, Buffalo, 1975-78; resident in colon/rectal surgery, Buffalo Gen. Hosp., 1978-79; colon rectal surgeon Buffalo (N.Y.) Med. Group; clin. asst. prof. Dept. Surgery, SUNY, Buffalo. Fellow Am. Coll. Surgeons, Am. Soc. Colon and Rectal Surgeons. Office: Buffalo Med Group 50 High St Buffalo NY 14203

BARRON, CHARLES THOMAS, psychiatrist; b. Hattiesburg, Miss., May 2, 1950; s. Palmer H. and Eleanor Clarice (Sherman) B. BS, U. So. Miss., 1972; MD, U. Miss., 1976. Diplomate Am. Bd. Psychiatry and Neurology. Resident psychiatry St. Vincent's Hosp. and Med. Ctr. N.Y., N.Y.C., 1976-79; fellow inpatient psychiatry St. Vincent's Hosp. and Med. Ctr. N.Y., 1979-80; physician-in-charge psychiatry/substance abuse Beth Israel Med. Ctr., N.Y.C., 1980-84; physician-in-charge inpatient svcs. (psychiatry) Beth Israel Med. Ctr., 1984-88; instr. Mt. Sinai Sch. Medicine, N.Y.C., 1980-87; asst. clin. prof. psychiatry Mt. Sinai Sch. Medicine, 1987-88, 91—; assoc. dir. psychiatry Gouverneur Hosp., N.Y.C., 1988-90; clin. asst. prof. psychiatry NYU, 1989-90; dir. inpatient svcs. (psychiatry), assoc. dir. psychiatry Mt. Sinai Svcs., Elmhurst, N.Y., 1990—; author/presenter presentation World Psychiat. Assn., 1981; presenter Ottawa Child & Adolescent Conf., 1988. Mem. Am. Psychiat. Assn. (presenter 1990), Lower East Side Mental Health Consortium, Internat. AIDS Soc., Am. Orthopsychiat. Assn. Office: CIO-21 79-91 Broadway Elmhurst NY 11373

BARRON, FRANCES MARLENE, school system administrator; b. Balt., May 14, 1939; d. Alexander and Lillian Ray (Sklar) Bass; m. Joseph Lackey Barron (div.); children: Leslie Rachel Barron, Charles Jeffrey Barron, Joshua Simon Fetzer. AB in Psychology, Barnard Coll., 1959; MS in Early Childhood Edn., Wagner Coll., 1968; postgrad., NYU, 1986—. Cert. Montessori tchr.; cer. tchr. N-6, N.Y. Head of sch. S.I. Montessori Sch., 1965-79; lectr. Richmond Coll., S.I., 1971-74, Malcom King Community Coll., N.Y.C., 1970-84, NYU, N.Y.C., 1982—; head of sch. West Side Montessori Sch., N.Y.C., 1979—; cons. Ithaca (N.Y.) Sch. Dist., 1973-78, Montclair (N.J.) Pub. Sch. Dist., 1987-90, Lighthouse for the Blind, N.Y.C., 1977-80, Upsal Day Sch. for the Blind, Phila., 1977, others; speaker in field. Author: I Learn to Read and Write the Way I Learn to Talk: A Very First Book About Whole Language, 1990; contbr. numerous articles to profl. jours. Bd. dirs. Child Care, Inc., N.Y.C., 1986—. Recipient Leader in Ednl. Excellence award St. Albans Montessori, 1988. Mem. ASCD, Am. Montessori Soc. (bd. dirs., pres. 1987-89, treas. 1984-87, cons. 1974—), Ind. Schs. Admissions Assn. of Greater N.Y. (bd. dirs., treas. 1987—), Coalition of Ltd. Purchase of Svc. Schs./Agy. for Child Devel. (bd. dirs., co-chmn. 1988—), N.Am. Montessori Tchrs. Assn., Assn. for Childhood Edn. Internat., Coun. for Exceptional Children, Internat. Reading Assn., Nat. Assn. Early Childhood Tchr. Educators, Nat. Coun. Tchrs. English, Soc. for Rsch. in Child Devel. Home: 670 W End Ave Apt 9C New York NY 10025-7327 Office: West Side Montessori Sch 309 W 92nd St New York NY 10025-7213

BARRON, JAMES TURMAN, reporter; b. Washington, Dec. 25, 1954; s. James Pressley and Leirona Faith (Turman) B. AB cum laude, Princeton U., 1977. Copy person N.Y. Times, N.Y.C., 1977, rsch. asst., 1978-79, reporter, 1979—; broadcast corespondent Sta. WQXR-AM-FM, N.Y.C., 1987—. Mem. Princeton Club N.Y.C. Methodist. Office: NY Times 229 W 43d St New York NY 10036

BARRON, KENNETH GEORGE, cardiothoracic surgeon; b. Boston, Dec. 12, 1942; s. Alfred and Evelyn Sylvia (Druskin) B.; m. Karen Teruko Fujinaga, May 18, 1974; children: Tokimasa, Yoshimi, Henkie. AB, Harvard Coll., 1964; MD, Stanford U., 1969; MPM, Carnegie Mellon U., 1986. Diplomat Am. Bd. Surgery, Am. Bd. Thoracic Surgery. Cardiothoracic surgeon Pittsburgh Heart & Lung Inc., 1976—. Mem. Pitts. Thoracic Surg. Soc. (pres. 1991), Stanford Alumni Club (pres. 1989-91). Home: 822 Washington Rd Pittsburgh PA 15228-2007 Office: Pittsburgh Heart & Lung Inc 490 E North Ave Ste 210 Pittsburgh PA 15212-4740

BARRON, SUSAN, clinical psychologist; b. Chgo., May 13, 1940; d. Earl and Trixie (Chernoff) B.; m. Eugene Pratt, Jan. 18, 1975 (div. 1983). BBA, CCNY, 1960, MA, 1963; PhD, CUNY, 1973. Lic. psychologist. Intern psychologist Bellevue Psychiat. Hosp., N.Y.C., 1964-65, psychologist, 1966-67; teaching fellow CUNY, 1965-66; staff psychologist Lighthouse, N.Y.

Assn. for the Blind, N.Y.C., 1968-71, sr. clin. psychologist, 1971-74; dir. psychol. counseling svcs. Peninsula Ctr. for the Blind, Palo Alto, Calif., 1974-75; cons. psychologist N.Y. State Commn. for Blind and Visually Handicapped, N.Y.C., 1975-78, 86—; dir. psychol. svcs. Thoms Rehab. Hosp., Asheville, N.C., 1978-79; state coord. psychol. svcs. N.Y. State Office Vocat. Rehab., Albany, 1979-85; founder, dir. Family Support Program ICU N.Y. Infirmary-Beekman Downtown Hosp., N.Y.C., 1982-84; cons. clin. psychologist, behavioral scientist diabetes control and complications trial Nat. Inst. Health N.Y. Hosp.-Cornell U. Med. Ctr., 1987—; pvt. practice, 1987—; Mem. Nat. Human Svcs. Adv. Bd.-Retinitis Pigmentosa Found., Balt., 1975-82; cons. Del. State Commn. for Blind, 1975-78, Am. Found. Blind, 1974-82, Calif. Dept. Rehab., 1974-82, Hawaii State Svcs. Blind, 1974-82, Ariz. State Svcs. Blind, 1974-82, Nev. State Svcs. Blind, 1974-82; speaker Nat. Multiple Disabilities Conf., 1982, NAS, 1981; mem. adv. bd. doctoral psychology internship program Rusk Inst. of Rehab. Medicine, NYU Med. Ctr., 1979-84; behavioral scientist Diabetes Control and Complications Trial NIH-Cornell U. Med. Ctr., 1987—. Contbr. articles to profl. jours. Recipient Leadership award Alumni Assn. CCNY, 1960, 62, Rsch. award Retinal Dystrophy Soc., Australia, 1975. Fellow Am. Orthopsychiat. Assn.; mem. APA, AAAS, Calif. State Psychol. Assn., N.Y. Acad. Sci. Office: NY Hosp Cornell U Med Ctr 515 E 71st St # 5102 New York NY 10021-4895

BARROW, KAL, appraisal engineer; b. Bklyn., Dec. 6, 1933; s. Joseph Rogoff and Anna Rose (Barrow) Weiss; m. Grace Brandon, Mar. 17, 1963; children: Donna Lynn, Eric Jon. Student, NYU, 1957-58. Dir. engring. Consol. Appraisal Co., Inc., N.Y.C., 1963-76; owner Appraisal Engring. Svc., Middletown, N.J., 1976-78; sr. appraiser Internat. Appraisal Co., Paramus, N.J., 1978-81; pres. Barrow Appraisal Assocs., Montvale, N.J., 1981-84; mgr. machinery and equipment valuations Arthur Andersen & Co., N.Y.C., 1984—. Author: (with others) The Appraisal of Machinery & Equipment, 1988. With USN, 1952-56. Mem. Am. Soc. Appraisers (sr.), Am. Arbitration Assn. (panel mem. N.Y. chpt. 1987—). Office: Arthur Andersen & Co 1345 Ave Of The Americas New York NY 10105-0099

BARRY, DONALD MARTIN, management consultant; b. Chgo., Jan. 27, 1944; m. Carol Braham, June 15, 1968; children: Patrick, Stephen, Michael. BS in Psychology, Loyola U., Chgo., 1967; MA in Psychology, So. Ill. U., 1971, PhD in Psychology, 1975; MBA in Fin., Rutgers U., 1985. Instr., research coordinator adminstrn. of justice So. Ill. U., Carbondale, 1972-75, asst. prof., 1975-77; assoc. prof. criminal justice Rutgers U., Newark, 1977-84; assoc. Dr. H. Tschudin Assocs Inc., River Vale, N.J., 1984-90; pres. Satisfaction Measurements Inc., North Brunswick, N.J., 1990—; cons. Dept. Justice, Washington, 1978-85, States of N.Y., 1983-84, N.J., 1982-84, Ill., 1974-75. Editor, pub.: Customer Satisfaction Report; contbr. articles to profl. jours. Research grantee Adminstrv. Office Cts. N.J., 1983, Law Enforcement Commn. Ill, 1975, 1st Jud. Cir. Ill., 1974. Mem. Inst. Mgmt. Cons. (cert.; sec., bd. dirs. Princeton chpt.), Am. Psychol. Assn., Soc. for Consumer Psychology. Office: Satisfaction Measurements 1236 Carlisle Rd New Brunswick NJ 08902-1439

BARRY, HARRIET RITA See SEMEGRAM, HARRIET RITA

BARRY, MARILYN WHITE, educator; b. Weymouth, Mass., Sept. 12, 1936; d. Harland Russell and Alice Louise (Dwyer) White; m. Dennis Edward Barry, July 11, 1959; children—Dennis Edward, Christopher Gerard. BS in Edn. Bridgewater State Coll., 1958; Ed.M. in Spl. Edn., Boston U., 1969, Ed.D. in Spl. Edn., 1974. Tchr. Weymouth pub. schs. (Mass.), 1958-60; spl. edn. instr. Boston U., 1972-74; asst. prof. in spl. edn. Bridgewater State Coll., (Mass.), 1974-79, assoc. prof., 1979-83, prof., 1983—, chmn. spl. edn. dept., 1979-87, coordinator dept. grad. programs, 1979-87, adminstr. bilingual spl. edn. and continuing edn. tng. grant, 1983-86, dean grad. sch., 1987—. Co-author human service workers curriculum materials. Boston U. fellow, 1967-74; 3 Disting. Service awards, Bridgewater State Coll., 1980, 82, 85; Bilingual Spl. Edn. grantee, 1980, 83. Mem. Council Exceptional Children (Mass. chpt. founder, past pres.), Mass. Assn. Children With Learning Disabilities (past v.p.), Phi Delta Kappa, Pi Lambda Theta. Democrat. Roman Catholic. Home: 138 Bedford St Middleboro MA 02346-1026 Office: Bridgewater State Coll Grad Sch Conant Sci Bldg Bridgewater MA 02324

BARRY, MARK PHILIP, political scientist, consultant; b. N.Y.C., Oct. 31, 1952; s. Don and Margaret G. (Magdalany) B.; m. Kim Pickard, July 1, 1982; children: Jennifer K., Lani J., Joshua L., Benjamin Y. BA summa cum laude, Ariz. State U., 1987; MA in Nat. Security Studies, Georgetown U., 1988; postgrad., U. Va., 1990—. Exec. asst. to pres. News World Communications, N.Y.C., 1979-85, Internat. Security Coun., Washington, 1988-90; sr. rsch. assoc. Summit Coun. for World Peace, Washington, 1990—; cons. Fedn. for World Peace, 1990—, Assn. for the Unity of Latin Am., Washington, 1990—. Contbr. articles to profl. jours. City rep. United to Serve America, Charlottesville, 1990—. Davis fellow 1991, Gov.'s fellow, 1990, 91, DuPont fellow U. Va., 1991, Lassen fellow 1991. Mem. Acad. Polit. Sci., The Asia Soc., Golden Key. Home: 152 Harvest Dr Charlottesville VA 22903-4846 Office: Summit Coun for World Peace 818 Connecticut Ave NW Washington DC 20006-2702

BARRY, ROBERT LOUIS, diplomat; b. Pitts., Aug. 28, 1934; s. Louis T. and Margaret (O'Halloran) B.; m. Margaret Crim, Aug. 3, 1960; children: John, Peter, Ellen. BA summa cum laude, Dartmouth Coll., 1956; MA, Columbia U., 1962. Fgn. svc. officer U.S. Dept. State, Washington, 1962—, served as dept. dir. USSR, 1975-77, dir. UN Affairs, 1977-79, dep. asst. sec. State, 1979-81; U.S. amb. to Bulgaria U.S. Embassy, 1981-84; U.S. Rep. CDE, Stockholm, 1985-87; dep. dir. Voice of Am. USIA, 1987-89; spl. adviser to dep. sec. of state USIA, Sofia, 1989—. Lt. USN, 1957-60. Office: Dept of State Washington DC 20520

BARRY, THOMAS ANTHONY, academic official; b. Pitts., Feb. 8, 1918; s. Thomas William and Othelia (Gorius) B.; m. Ruth Edwards, Jan. 19, 1948; children: Theresa Ann, Anita Gail, Thomas Anthony, William Daniel, Mary Elizabeth. BS, Drexel U., 1972. Registered profl. engr., Pa. Commd. officer U.S. Corps of Engrs., 1941, advanced through grades to lt. col., 1963; bn. comdr. U.S. Corps of Engrs., Korea, 1952-55, Germany, 1957-60; mgr. maintenance and utilites, cons. engr. Drexel U., Phila., 1964—. Author engring. manuals, 1945-48. Mayor, Townsite, Riverdale, N.D., 1963. Decorated Bronze Star with oak leaf cluster, Purple Heart, 5 Battle Stars, 9 Overseas Combat ribbons. Mem. DAV (life), Alliance for Mentally Ill, Ret. Officers Assn., Assn. Energy Engrs., Mgrs. Inception Implementation of Plan Saving Energy, Smithsonian Instn., Woodrow Wilson Internat. Ctr. for Scholars, Navy Officers Club, Assn. West Point Grads., Audubon Soc. Republican. Roman Catholic. Home: 322 Riverview Ave Drexel Hill PA 19026-2225

BARRY, THOMAS M., banker; b. Bethesda, Md., Mar. 4, 1949; s. Clarence James and Helen (Kyak) B.; m. Susan C. Waltman, May 3, 1951; children: Karen Jennifer, Michael James. BA, U. Va., 1971; MBA, U. Chgo., 1976. V.p. Kidder, Peabody & Co., N.Y.C., 1976-86; mng. dir. First Boston Corp., N.Y.C., 1986—. Home: 256 Monterey Ave Pelham NY 10803-2310 Office: First Boston Corp 55 E 52d St 37th Fl New York NY 10055

BARRY, WILLIAM ANTHONY, priest, writer; b. Worcester, Mass., Nov. 22, 1930; s. William and Catherine (McKenna) B. AB, Boston Coll., 1956; STL, Fordham U., 1963; MA, Boston Coll., 1960; Fordham U.; PhD, U. Mich., 1968. Joined S.J., Roman Cath. Ch., 1950, ordained priest, 1962. Tchr. high sch. Fairfield (Conn.) Prep., 1956-58; lectr. U. Mich., Ann Arbor, 1968-69; from asst. to assoc. prof. Weston Sch. of Theology, Cambridge, Mass., 1969-78; rector Jesuit community Boston Coll., Chestnut Hill, Mass., 1988-91; vice provincial S.J. of New Eng., Boston, 1978-84, asst. novice dir., 1985-88, provincial, 1991—; dir. staff Ctr. for Religious Devel., Cambridge, 1971-78; trustee Boston Coll., Chestnut Hill, 1988-91, adj. assoc. prof., 1989-91. Co-author: Communication, Conflict, Marriage, 1974, The Parctice of Spiritual Direction, 1982, God and You, 1987, Seek My Face, 1989, Now Choose Life, 1990, Paying Attention to God, 1990, Finding God in All Things, 1991, Spiritual Direction and the Encounter with God, 1992; co-editor: A Hunger for God, 1991; contbr. numerous articles to profl. jours. Mem. Bread for the World, Washington, 1985—, Amnesty Internat., N.Y.C., 1988—. Mem. Phi Beta Kappa, Phi Kappa Phi. Democrat. Roman Catholic. Home and Office: Back Bay Annex PO Box 799 Boston MA 02117-0799

BARSALONA, FRANK SAMUEL, theatrical agent; b. S.I., N.Y., Mar. 31, 1938; s. Peter and Mary (Rotunno) B.; m. June Harris, Sept. 1, 1966; 1 dau., Nicole. BA, Wagner Coll., S.I., 1958; postgrad., Herbert Berghof Sch., N.Y.C., 1959-60. Agt. Gen. Artists Corp., N.Y.C., 1960-64; founder, since pres. Premier Talent Agy., N.Y.C., 1964—; co-founder, pres. Phila. Fury, 1977-80; lectr., moderator music industry; co-owner WKSS Radio, Hartford, Conn., WMYF/WERZ-FM, Exeter, N.H. Mem. bd. govs. T.J. Martell Leukemia Fund; bd. dirs. Rock & Roll Hall of Fame Mus. Recipient numerous awards Billboard Publs., cover subject spl. issue, 1984; named to Performance Mag. Hall of Fame, 1988. Mem. Mus. Am. Folk Art. (internat. adv. bd.). Office: Premier Talent Agy 3 E 54th St New York NY 10022-3108

BARSI, LOUIS MICHAEL, college dean, educational consultant; b. Port Reading, N.J., Aug. 26, 1941; s. Louis Joseph and Mary Alice B. BA, U. Okla., 1963; MA, Cen. Mich. U., 1966; MA in Edn., U. No. Iowa, 1971; EdS, U. Wis., Stout, 1978; D of Arts in Edn., George Mason U., 1991. Tchr. Searing Sch., N.Y.C., 1963-64, East Cath. High Sch., Detroit, 1964-65; dean of students Mount St. Clare Coll., Clinton, Iowa, 1969-76, chmn. social sci. div., 1975-76, athletic dir., 1970-76; coord. fin. aids U. Wis., Waukesha, 1977-80, adminstr. honors program, 1978-80; asst. campus dir., dean of student affairs Pa. State U., DuBois, 1980-87; rsch. asst. George Mason U., Fairfax, Va., 1987-88; assoc. acad. programs and dir. of the ctr. for ednl. opportunity and achievement Am. Assn. State Colls. and Univs., Washington, 1988-90, exec. asst. to the pres., 1990-91; dean students svcs. Del. Tech. and Community Coll., Terry Campus, Dover, 1991—; intern Office Ednl. Rsch. and Improvement U.S. Dept. of Edn., Washington, 1987-88, Coun. on Post-Secondary Accreditation, Washington, 1988; bd. dir. Ctr. for Ednl. Opportunity and Achievement; mem. rev. panel U.S. Dept. Edn.-Regional Tng. Workshop, 1989, rev. panel coun. advancement and support edn. 1988-91; group leader Student Pers. Conf., U. No. Iowa; speaker on student leadership tng. to various high schs., colls. and confs., 1987—. Co-developer of instnl., faculty, and student inventories of good practice in undergrad. edn.; contbr. articles to profl. jours. Bd. dirs. HANDS, Clinton, Iowa, 1970-71; mem. pers. com. Du Bois YMCA, 1982-84; bd. dirs., mem. budget and fin. com. DuBois United Way, 1983-87, chmn. long-range planning com., 1984-86, co-chmn. edn. div. 1985 campaign, sec., 1985-87, v.p. and chmn. campaign com., 1986, pres., 1987, campaign coord., 1990, 91; adv. Explorer Post, Boy Scouts Am., 1981-83, mem. exec. com. Bucktail coun., 1982-87, bd. dir. career svcs., 1984-87; mem. planning com. Tom Mix Festival, 1983-87, Higher Edn. Group Washington. Teaching asst. Cen. Mich. U., 1965-66; rsch. asst. U. No. Iowa, 1968-69, George Mason U.; assistantship U. Wis., Stout, 1976-77. Recipient Disting Svc. award for developing career awareness program Boy Scouts Am., 1985, Nat. Quality Dist. award Bucktail Coun., BSA, 1987. Mem. Am. Assn. State Colls. and Univs. (Spl. Achievement award 1990), Pa. Pers. and Guidance Assn., Am. Coll. Pers. Assn. (task force on consultation teams), Pa. Coll. Pers. Assn., Nat. Assn. Student Pers. Adminstrs., Eastern Assn. Coll. Deans, DuBois C. of C. (bd. dir. 1981-84, chmn. govtl. affairs com. 1981-83), Pa. State U. DuBois Campus Alumni Soc. (bd. dirs. 1980-87, bd. dirs. DuBois Ednl. Found. 1987-91), Greater Washington Soc. Assn. Execs. (vol. career counselor 1989-92), DuBois Area Hist. Soc. (co-founder), Rotary (bd. dir. 1982-87, v.p. 1983, pres.-elect 1984, pres. 1985-86), Phi Delta Kappa, Phi Alpha Theta. Home: 1300 S Farmview Dr Apt 33G Dover DE 19901-7718 Office: Del Tech and Community Coll Terry Campus 1832 N Dupont Pky Dover DE 19901-9832

BARSTOW, PAUL ROGERS, theatre studies educator; b. Madison, Wis., Oct. 22, 1925; s. Robbins Wolcott and Dorothy Millard (Rogers) B.; m. Eleanor Talcott Rubsam, June 20, 1953 (div. 1963); children: Victoria Talcott, Julia Robbins, Anthony Edward Chase. Student, Oxford U., Eng., 1945-46; BA magna cum laude, Williams Coll., 1948; MFA, Yale U., 1955; Dipl., Oomoto Sch. Trad. Japanese Art, Kyoto, 1984. Instr. English Williams, Williamstown, Mass., 1948-50; test developer Ednl. Testing Svc., Princeton, N.J., 1950-52; from lectr. to prof. theatre studies Wellesley (Mass.) Coll., 1955—; vis. prof. Thommasat U., Bangkok, Thailand, 1979; vis. lectr. U. Pitts., 1987; actor/dir. Ea. Slope Theatre, 1953, 54, 56, Harvard Summer Players, 1961-64, 75-77, Williamstown Theatre, 1965-66, Provincetown Playhouse, 1967-72, others; actor or dir. many community theatre prodns., film, TV, modeling, commls. Author: Images of Women on Stage, 1975. With U.S. Army, 1943-45; ETO. Danforth fellow. Mem. Actors Equity Assn., Screen Actors Guild, Am. Fedn. Radio and TV Artists, Assn. Asian Performance, Asia Soc., Japan Soc., Japan Soc. Boston, Phi Beta Kappa. Democrat. Shinto. Home: West Lodge 280 Central St Wellesley MA 02181 Office: Program in Theatre Studies Wellesley Coll Wellesley MA 02181

BARTCH, STEPHEN CARL, engineer; b. Columbia, Pa., Nov. 6, 1965; s. George F. and Janet E. (Hake) B. BS in Engring., Pa. State U., 1987. Asst. engr. ISC Def. Systems, Lancaster, Pa., 1986, Sensenich Propellers, Lancaster, 1987; engr. Machined Products, Lancaster, 1988-89, Main Street Software, Landisville, Pa., 1990-91, Quigley Motor Co., Inc., York, Pa., 1991—. Youth leader TEAMM Concept Youth Group, Lancaster, 1991. Profl. Engring. Soc. scholar, 1986. Mem. Soc. Automotive Engr. (assoc.). Republican. Office: 88 S Main St Manchester PA 17345

BARTEE, STEPHEN WILLIAM, accountant; b. Benkelman, Nebr., Aug. 17, 1950; m. Janet L. Bartee, Mar. 18, 1974; children: Jeremy, Ashley. Degree in acctg., U. Buffalo, 1981; student, Cornell U., 1984; M in Fin., N.Y. Inst. Fin., 1988. Cert. mgmt. acct. Acct., owner Phoenix Assocs., Buffalo, 1984—. Republican. Office: Phoenix Assocs 468 Amherst St Buffalo NY 14207-2844

BARTEK, KEVIN GEORGE, financial services manager; b. New London, Conn., Apr. 2, 1964; s. George John and Dorothy Helen (Kollar) B. Student, Christ the Saviour Sem., Johnstown, Pa., 1982-85; AA in Psychology, Sacred Heart U., Fairfield, Conn., 1987, BS in Mgmt., 1988; MPA, U. New Haven, 1992. Med. records technician Bridgeport (Conn.) Hosp., 1979-82, pharmacy technician, 1986-87, psychiat. technician, 1987-88, billing asst., 1988-90; accounts receivable supr., acctg. dept. St. Vincent Med. Ctr., Bridgeport, 1990—; advisor Med. Explorers. substitute tchr. Bridgeport Sch. System, 1987-89; probation intern Bridgeport Probation Dept., 1989. Active Big Bros./Big Sisters of Bridgeport, 1980-82; participant Easter Seals Telethon, Bridgeport, 1980, 82, Muscular Dystrophy Telethon, Milford, Conn., 1981; dir. choir St. John's Orthodox Ch., Stratford, Conn., 1988—, ordained reader; counselor Spl. Olympics, Trumbull, Conn., 1989. Recipients awards for vol. work. Fellow Am. Carpatho-Russian Youth (nat. auditor 1985, charter pres., v.p., 1988-90), Classroom for Young Ams. Carpatho-Russian Orthodox. Home: 39 Wayland Rd Milford CT 06460 Office: St Vincent Med Ctr 2800 Main St Bridgeport CT 06606

BARTELS, JOHN RIES, federal judge; b. Balt., Nov. 8, 1897; s. William Nicholas and Louise (Reuter) B.; m. Anne Bell Willson, May 3, 1930; children: John Ries, William Gilpin. A.B. cum laude, Johns Hopkins, 1920; LL.B., Harvard, 1923. Bar: N.Y. 1924. Since practiced in N.Y.C.; justice Supreme Ct. N.Y., 1950-51; mem. firm Bartels & Hartung, 1951-59; judge U.S. Dist. Ct., Bklyn., 1959-73, sr. judge, 1974—; mem. N.Y. Law Revision Commn., 1945-50, 52-57; spl. referee appellate div. N.Y. Supreme Ct.; excounsel fgn. debt readjustment Govt. Ecuador; former gen. counsel Gen. Acceptance Corp. (and subsidiaries), The Fyr-Fyter Co. (and subsidiaries), Brilhart Plastics Corp. Dir. Bklyn. Council for Social Planning, 1953-58; mem. Mayor's Com. on Puerto Rican Affairs, N.Y.C., 1955-57; Alumni trustee Johns Hopkins, 1953-54; former sec. bd. regents L.I. Coll. Hosp.; former chmn. lay adv. bd. Kings County Hosp. Center; bd. dirs. NCCJ, Brotherhood-in-Action, Bklyn. Boys Club. Named hon. citizen Md., 1958; recipient Johns Hopkins U. Distinguished Alumnus award, 1967. Fellow Am. Coll. Trial Lawyers; mem. Am., N.Y. State, Bklyn. bar assns., Assn. Bar City N.Y., N.Y. County Lawyers Assn., Fundacion Internacional Eloy Alfaro, Am. Law Inst., Fed. Bar Council, Am. Judicature Soc., Inst. Jud. Adminstrn., Squadron A Ex-Mems., Harvard Law Sch. Assn. N.Y.C. (v.p.), Omicron Delta Kappa, Delta Upsilon. Republican (past treas. exec. com. Kings County). Conglist. (trustee). Clubs: Harvard, Down Town Assn., Lawyers, Nat. Lawyers, Inc. (hon.). Office: US Dist Ct 225 Cadman Pla E Brooklyn NY 11201

BARTER, JUDITH ANN, museum director; b. Chgo., May 21, 1951; d. Frederick Joseph and Emily Mary (Bate) B. BA in Art History, Ind. U., 1973; MA in Art History, U. Ill., 1975; PhD in Cultural History, U. Mass., 1991. Curatorial asst. Krannert Art Mus., Univ. Ill., Urbana, 1974-75; asst. curator St. Louis (Mo.) Art Mus., 1975-78; curator of collections Mead Art Mus., Amherst (Mass.) Coll., 1978-86, assoc. dir., 1986—; vis. fellow Smithsonian Instn., summer 1992; Mass. state rep. Assn. Coll. and Univ. Mus. Author: Currents of Expansion, 1978, American Watercolors and Drawings, 1986, American Watercolors and Drawings at the Wadsworth Atheneum, 1988; mem. editorial bd.: Mass. Rev., Amherst, 1986-91; reviewer Choice Mag., Middletown, Conn., 1980—. trustee Williamstown (Mass.) Conservation Lab. Recipient travel fellowship NEH, Washington, 1989. Office: Amherst Coll Amherst MA 01002

BARTH, JOHN SIMMONS, writer, educator; b. Cambridge, Md., May 27, 1930; s. John Jacob and Georgia (Simmons) B.; m. Harriette Anne Strickland, Jan. 11, 1950; children: Christine Anne, John Strickland, Daniel Stephen; m. Shelly I. Rosenberg, Dec. 27, 1970. BA, Johns Hopkins U., 1951, MA, 1952. From instr. to assoc. prof. English Pa. State U., 1953-65; prof. English SUNY, Buffalo, 1965-73; prof. creative writing Johns Hopkins U., Balt., 1973-91, prof. emeritus creative writing, 1991—. Author: The Floating Opera, 1956, The End of the Road, 1958, The Sot-Weed Factor, 1960, Giles Goat-Boy, 1966, Lost in the Funhouse, 1968, Chimera, 1972 (recipient Nat. Book award in fiction 1973), Letters, 1979, Sabbatical: A Romance, 1982, The Friday Book, 1984, The Tidewater Tales: A Novel, 1987, The Last Voyage of Somebody the Sailor, 1991. Office: Writing Seminars Johns Hopkins U Baltimore MD 21218

BARTH, PETER, economics educator; b. Karlsruhe, Ger., Nov. 21, 1937; s. Lazarus and Olga (Bergmann) B.; m. Nancy J. Boor, Aug. 12, 1962; children: Sara E., Linda M., Steven L. AB, Columbia U., N.Y.C., 1958; PhD in Econs., U. Mich., 1965. Asst. prof. U. Chgo., 1968; assoc. prof. Ohio State U., Columbus, 1968-70; fellow Brookings Instn., Washington, 1970-71; exec. dir. Nat. Commn. on State Workmen's Compensation Laws, Washington, 1971-72; dir. Office of Rsch., Office of the Sec., U.S. Dept. Labor, Washington, 1972-73; head dept. econs. U. Conn., Storrs, 1973-78, 84-85, prof. econs., 1973—; cons. in field. Author: Worker's Compensation and Occupational Disease, 1981 (Kulp Prize 1981), Tragedy of Black Lung, 1987, Workers Compensation in Texas, 1988, Workers Compensation in Connecticut, 1987. Chmn. Blue Ribbon Commn. on Fair Wages, 1990-91. Brookings fellow, 1970-71; German Marshall Fund fellow, 1976-77; Nat. Distillers fellow, 1976; Swedish Inst. fellow, 1988. Jewish. Home: 76 Center Rd Tolland CT 06084-3102 Office: Dept Econs Univ of Conn U-63 Storrs CT 06269-1063

BARTH, ROGER, chemistry educator; b. N.Y.C., June 11, 1951; s. Max and Shirley (Levine) B.; m. Marcy Cohen Victor, Apr. 1, 1984; children: Naomi, David. BA cum laude, LaSalle Coll., 1973; MA, Johns Hopkins U., 1974, PhD, 1977. Rsch. chemist UOP, Inc., Des Plaines, Ill., 1977-79; postdoctoral fellow U. Del., Newark, 1980-82; instr., postdoctoral fellow Drexel U., Phila., 1982-84; asst. prof. chemistry West Chester (Pa.) U., 1985—. Contbr. articles to sci. publs. Mem. AAUP, Assn. Pa. State Coll. and Univ. Faculty (sec. 1991—), Am. Chem. Soc., Phila. Catalysis Club. Democrat. Jewish. Office: West Chester Univ Dept Chemistry West Chester PA 19383

BARTHA, RICHARD, microbiology educator; b. Budapest, Hungary, Nov. 14, 1934; came to U.S., 1962; s. Imre and Irene (Pfann) B.; m. Susi E. Fels, Dec. 29, 1966; children: Miriam, Doris. Student, Eötvös U., Budapest, 1953-56; PhD, U. Göttingen, Germany, 1961. Postdoctoral trainee U. Wash., Seattle, 1962-64; rsch. assoc. Rutgers U., New Brunswick, 1964-66, asst. prof., 1966-69, assoc. prof., 1969-73, prof., 1973-84, prof. II, 1984—. Author: Microbial Ecology, 1981, 2d rev. edit., 1986; mem. editorial bd. Applied & Environ. Microbiology, 1974-83, Soil Sci., 1978, Industrial Microbiology; contbr. articles to profl. jours. Mem. Am. Soc. for Microbiology (lectr. summer 1976), Am. Found. for Microbiology (lectr. 1977-78), Soil Microbiology (chmn. 1968-69), Applied Microbiology (chmn. 1979-81), Theobald Smith Soc. (pres. 1990-91). Office: Rutgers U Cook Coll Lipman Hall New Brunswick NJ 08903

BARTHOLOMAE, ERIC THOMPSON, management consultant; b. Summit, N.J., Oct. 6, 1961; s. Richard Carl and Charlotte (Kenney) B. BSE, Princeton (N.J.) U., 1982; MBA, Harvard U., 1987. Sales engr. Westinghouse Elevator Co., Boston, 1982-85; cons. The Boston Cons. Group, 1987-91; mgr. planning PepsiCo, Boston, 1992—.

BARTHOLOMEW, ALAN ALFRED, librarian, educator; b. Lancaster, Pa., June 10, 1953; s. Alfred Clinton and Joyce (Studenmund) B.; m. Mary Ellen Shope, June 21, 1975; children: Robert Alan, Daniel Nathan, Lydia Deniz. BA in History with honors, Ursinus Coll., 1975; MS, Drexel U., 1977; MA, Bryn Mawr Coll., 1985, PhD, 1989. Head libr. Tarsus (Turkey) Am. Sch., 1977-89; asst. prof. history Albertus Magnus Coll., New Haven, 1990—, dir. libr. svcs., 1990—; chairperson Greater New Haven Acad. Libr. Consortium, 1991—. Author: A History of Tarsus American School, 1988. Missionary United Ch. Bd. for World Ministries, 1977-78; mem. missions dept. Conn. Conf. United Ch. of Christ; chairperson Greater New Haven Acad. Libr. Consortium. Mem. ALA, Am. Hist. Assn., Am. Soc. of Ch. History, Conn. Libr. Assn., New England Libr. Assn. Democrat. Mem. United Ch. of Christ. Office: Albertus Magnus Coll Libr 700 Prospect St New Haven CT 06511-1189

BARTHOLOMEW, ANITA, freelance writer; b. Bay Shore, N.Y., Jan. 14, 1949; d. Guido and Elizabeth (Ornato) Del Giudice m. Frank J. Tomaino, Oct. 5, 1968 (div.); 1 child, Alexander G. Tomaino. Student, SUNY, Purchase, 1981-83, Sch. Visual Arts, N.Y.C., 1984. Copywriter Ventura Assocs., N.Y.C., 1982-83, Equity Advt., N.Y.C., 1983-84, Pace Advt., N.Y.C., 1984-85; prin. Anita Bartholomew Communications, Tarrytown, N.Y., 1985-91, 92—; dir. mktg. Chacma Inc., N.Y.C., 1991-92; freelance copywriter Donnelley Mktg., Holt, Rinehart/CBS Pub., SAS Airlines, The Luce Corp., Westchester Women's News, numerous others. Contbr. articles to profl. jours. Mem. Am. Soc. Psychical Rsch., Pub. Rels. Soc. Am., People for Ethical Treatment of Animals, Mensa.

BARTHOLOMEW, LINDA CURRY, electric utility executive; b. Punxsutawney, Pa., Apr. 23, 1948; m. Dean A. Bartholomew, July 27, 1974; children: Elise, Colin. BA in Math., Carnegie-Mellon U., 1970; MA, Lehigh U., 1976. Economist, sr. dir. pub. affairs Pa. Power and Light Co., Allentown, 1984-89, v.p. pub. affairs, 1989—; bd. dirs. U.S. Pub. Affairs Coun., Pa. Coun. Econ. Edn.; joint bd. dirs. Ben Franklin Tech. Ctr. and Mfg. Svc. Extension Ctr., Lehigh U. Mem. Pa. Chamber of Bus. and Industry (chmn. energy com. 1989-91). Presbyterian. Office: Pa Power and Light Co 2 N 9th St Allentown PA 18101-1139

BARTLETT, BRUCE REEVES, economist; b. Ann Arbor, Mich., Oct. 11, 1951; s. Frank and Marjorie (Stern) B. B.A., Rutgers U. 1973; M.A., Georgetown U., 1976. Spl. asst. to Congressman Jack F. Kemp, Washington, 1977-78; chief legis. asst. to U.S. Senator Roger Jepsen, Washington, 1979-80; dep. dir. Joint Econ. Com., U.S. Congress, Washington, 1981-83, exec. dir., 1983-84; v.p. Polyconomics, Inc., Morristown, N.J., 1984-85; sr. fellow Heritage Found., Washington, 1985-87; sr. policy analyst The White House, Washington, 1987-88; dep. asst. sec. for econ. policy Dept. Treasury, 1988—. Author: Coverup: The Politics of Pearl Harbor, 1941-46, 1978; Reaganomics: Supply Side Economics in Action, 1981; Co-editor: The Supply Side Solution, 1983. Contbr. articles to Washington Post, N.Y. Times, Wall Street Jour, numerous others. Served with USAF, 1973. Mem. Am. Econ. Assn. Republican. Home: 1606 Commonwealth Ave Alexandria VA 22301-1904 Office: Treasury Dept Rm 3445 Washington DC 20220

BARTLETT, BYRON ROBERT, consumer products company marketing executive; b. Phoenix, May 15, 1952; s. Gordon Arthur and Frances Rita (Bishop) B.; m. Sheila Gaye Rouse, June 14, 1975; children: Kara Michele, Kristen Marie, Kevin Michael, Katelyn Maura. BS, Purdue U., 1974. Brand asst. Procter & Gamble Co., Cin., 1974-75, asst. brand mgr., 1975-77; product dir. The Nestle Co., White Plains, N.Y., 1977-79, group product dir., 1979-82; group product dir. McNeil Consumer Products div. Johnson &

Johnson, Fort Washington, Pa., 1982-86; mktg. mgr. Binney & Smith div. Hallmark Cards Inc., Easton, Pa., 1986-88; dir. brand mgmt. SmithKline Beecham Consumer Brands, Pitts., 1988-92. Mem. Am. Mgmt. Assn. Republican. Lutheran. Home: 1889 Springmont Dr Pittsburgh PA 15241-2158 Office: SmithKline Beecham Consumer Brands PO Box 1479 Pittsburgh PA 15230-1479

BARTLETT, DEBRA MARIE, chiropractic physician; b. Washington, May 19, 1956; d. John Allen and Joan Marie (Henry) B. AA, Anne Arundel Community Coll., Arnold, Md., 1979; BS, Nat. Coll. Chiropractic, Lombard, Ill., 1983, DC, 1985. Owner Bartlett Chiropractic Health Svcs., Bowie, Md., 1986—; ltd. ptnr. Md. Diagnostic Imaging, Laurel, 1988—; cons. Cambridge Med. Cons., Brookline, Mass., 1991—; admission amb. Nat. Coll. Coll. Chiropractic, 1990. Author: (genealogy) Journal of Discovery, 1990. Mem. Am. Chiropractic Assn. (Health Awareness award 1988), Md. Chiropractic Assn. (chmn. ins. com. 1991—, legis. com., peer review com.), Found. for Chiropractic Edn. and Rsch., Nat. Coll. Devel. Club, Profl. Orgn. of Women (founder, pres.), Nat. Coll. Chiropractic (co-chair East coast chpt.), Assn. for the History of Chiropractic, Prince George's County Genealogy Soc. Republican. Roman Catholic. Office: Bartlett Chiropractic Health Svcs 2905 Mitchellville Rd # 104 Bowie MD 20716

BARTLETT, RICKY ALAN, military officer, electrical engineer; b. Lewisburg, Pa., Dec. 11, 1955; s. Henry H. Bartlett and Virginia E. (Day) Rovenolt. AAS, Community Coll. of Air Force, 1983; BSEE, No. Ariz. U., 1987. Entered USAF, 1973, advanced through grades to capt., 1992, ground navigation repairman 1964 Communications Group, 1974-78; ground navigation technician 1964 Communications Group USAF, Ramstein Air Base, Fed. Republic of Germany, 1978-82; ground navigation technician 2069 Communications Squadron USAF, Nellis AFB, Nev., 1982-83; with squadron tng. 2069 Communications Squadron, USAF, Nellis AFB, Nev., 1983-84; dep. program mgr. GMF SATCOM Hq. Electronics System Div., Hanscom AFB, Mass., 1988-92; program mgr. Hq. Electronics System div. USAF, Hanscom AFB, Mass., 1992—. Mem. IEEE, VFW, NRA, AFA, Am. Legion, Moose, Tau Beta Pi. Home: 111 Locust St # 89 Woburn MA 01801-3865 Office: USAF HQ ESD/TGT HA ESD/TCT Hanscom AFB Bedford MA 01731

BARTLEY, ROBERT LEROY, newspaper editor; b. Marshall, Minn., Oct. 12, 1937; s. Theodore French and Iva Mae (Radach) B.; m. Edith Jean Lillie, Dec. 29, 1960; children: Edith Elizabeth, Susan Lillie, Katherine French. BS, Iowa State U., 1959; MS, U. Wis., 1962; LLD, Macalester Coll., 1982, Babson Coll., 1987; LDH, Adelphi U., 1992. Reporter Grinnell (Iowa) Herald-Register, 1959-60; staff reporter Wall Street Jour., Chgo., 1962-63, Phila., 1963-64; editorial writer Wall Street Jour., N.Y.C., 1964-70, Washington, 1970-71; editor editorial page Wall Street Jour., N.Y.C., 1972-78; editor Wall Street Jour., 1979—, v.p., 1983—. Trustee Mayo Found. Served to 2d lt. USAR, 1960. Recipient Overseas Press Club citation, 1977, Gerald Loeb award, 1979, Pulitzer prize for editorial writing, 1980. Mem. Am. Soc. Newspaper Editors, Nat. Conf. Editorial Writers, Am. Polit. Sci. Assn., Council on Fgn. Relations, Heights Casino Club, Sigma Delta Chi. Office: Dow Jones & Co 200 Liberty St New York NY 10281-1003 also: Wall Street Jour 200 Liberty St New York NY 10281

BARTLEY, ROBERT PAUL, state official, consultant; b. Worcester, Mass., Oct. 17, 1926; s. Harry Eugene and Helen (Hamilton) B.; BS, U.S. Naval Acad., 1952; MBA, U.S. Air Force Inst. Tech., 1959; Cert. Energy Mgr.; m. Joan Anne Leahy, 1952; children: Robert, Brian, Maureen, Michael, Bridget, Timothy, Terrence, Patricia. Commd. 2d lt. U.S. Air Force, 1952, advanced through grades to capt., 1972, ret., 1972; mng. dir. Del. Soc. for Prevention of Cruelty to Animals, Newark, 1975; fiscal asst. Pres.'s Office, Del. Tech. and Community Coll., Dover, 1976-77; dir. Del. State Energy Conservation Plan, Office of Mgmt. and Budget and Planning, Dover, 1977-79; asst. dir. Del. Energy Office, Dover, 1979-81, acting dir., 1982, asst. dir. for energy div. facilities mgmt., 1982-91; prin. Cavalier Mgmt. Cons. Svcs., 1991—; instr. U. Dayton (Ohio), 1959; presenter 2d Mid-Atlantic Energy Conf. Chmn. com. on devel. and enforcement of energy savings in pub. schs., 1977-78; mem. citizens adv. group on regional transp., Kent County, Del., 1969; mem. tuition guidelines com. Holy Cross Sch., 1971-74. Decorated Air medal. Mem. Del. Assn. Pub. Adminstrn., Mcpl. Fin. Officers Assn., Del. Assn. Govt. Fin. Officers (treas. 1978-79, sec. 1982-83, exec. com. 1984), Nat. Assn. State Energy Ofcls., Assn. Energy Engrs., U.S. Dept. Energy Commn. Alternative Fin., Cavaliers of Del. Club, Blue and Gold Club. Roman Catholic. Contbr. articles to profl. jours. Office: 3706 Golfview Dr Newark DE 19702-1753

BARTLOW, THOMAS LOREN, mathematician, educator; b. Johnson City, N.Y., May 14, 1942; s. Keith Floyd and Martha Carolyn (Rowland) B.; m. Michele Lovett Wright, Dec. 27, 1971; children: Susannah, Laura, Amy. BS, SUNY, Albany, 1963; MA, SUNY, Buffalo, 1966, PhD, 1969. Teaching asst. SUNY, Buffalo, 1963-67; lectr. Temple U., Phila., 1967-68; instr. Villanova (Pa.) U., 1968-69, asst. prof., 1969—. Mem. Math. Assn. Am., Canadian Soc. for History and Philsophy of Math. Democrat. Methodist. Office: Villanova U Dept Math Sci Villanova PA 19085

BARTOK, FREDERICK FRANCIS, academic administrator; b. Johnstown, Pa., May 22, 1943; s. Francis Andrew and Margaret Elizabeth (Ritko) B.; m. Leslie Louise Andrews, Jan. 6, 1979; children: Rory Elizabeth, Keri Helene. BA, U. Pitts., 1965, D. Higher Edn. Adminstrn., 1980; MEd in Higher Edn. Adminstrn., Duquesne U., 1971. Br. mgr. Mellon Nat. Bank, Pitts., 1965-69; asst. prof. banking Boyce campus Community Coll. Allegheny County, Monroeville, Pa., 1969-75, asst. to exec. dean Boyce campus, 1975-77, asst. dean instrn., 1977-83; dean instrn. Community Coll. Allegheny County, Pitts., 1983-84, acting exec. dean, 1984-85, exec. dean, v.p., 1985—; bd. dirs. Greater Allegheny City Vocat. Edn., Pitts., 1985—. Contbr. articles to profl. jours. Bd. dirs. Renaissance City Winds, Pitts., 1989—, Hist. Soc. Western Pa., Pitts., 1989—; mem. World Affairs Coun. Sgt. U.S. Army, 1969-75. Mem. Am. Assn. Univ. Adminstrs., Nat. Coun. for Occupational Edn., Learning Resource Network Assn., Nat. Orgn. Staff and Profl. Devel., Mid. States Assn. (team 1974—, cons. 1988-90), New Eng. Assn. (team 1990—), North Allegheny C. of C. (bd. dirs. 1985—, Acadia award 1991), N.H. C. of C. (Merit award 1987). Democrat. Presbyterian. Home: 430B Trimont Ln Pittsburgh PA 15211-1251 Office: Community Coll Allegheny County 8701 Perry Hwy Pittsburgh PA 15237-5353

BARTOK, LESLIE ANDREWS, dean; b. Pitts., Dec. 4, 1951; d. Richard Cecil and Sarah Ann (Lardin) Andrews; m. Frederick Francis Bartok, Jan. 6, 1979. BA, Grove City (Pa.) Coll., 1973; MEd, U. Pitts., 1978, PhD, 1983. Adminstrv. sec. Community Coll. of Allegheny County, Pitts., 1973-76, asst. dir. continuing edn., 1976-79, dir. continuing edn., 1979-89; dean of continuing edn. Community Coll. of Allegheny County, West Mifflin, Pa., 1989—. Member adv. bd. McKeesport (Pa.) Area Vocat. Tech., 1989—; vol. Western Pa. Conservancy, Pitts., 1991—; chair adv. bd. Edco Park, Evans City, Pa., 1988-89; chair Women's Bus. Network East, Pitts., 1991—. Mem. Nat. Coun. Community Svcs. and Continuing Edn. (liaison Pa. chpt. 1989—), Pa. Deans and Dirs. of Continuing Edn. (pres. 1991—). Office: Community Coll Allegheny County 1750 Clairton Rd West Mifflin PA 15122-3097

BARTOL, ERNEST THOMAS, lawyer; b. Mineola, N.Y., Feb. 2, 1946; s. Frank Henry and Mary Ann (Kretlein) B.; m. Christine Ann Pillis; children: Jacqueline Marie, Aimee Elizabeth, Suzanne Melissa. BS in Acctg., Fordham U., 1967; JD, Villanova U., 1970. Bar: N.Y. 1971, U.S. Dist. Ct. (ea. and so. dists.) N.Y. 1973, U.S. Ct. Appeals (2d cir.) 1975, U.S. Supreme Ct. 1975. Staff acct. Pustorino, Puglisi, Behan & Co., N.Y.C., 1965-70; tax specialist Arthur Young & Co., Phila., 1970; acct. Arthur Andersen & Co., N.Y.C., 1970-71; assoc. Gehrig, Ritter, Coffey et al, Hempstead, N.Y., 1971-78; ptnr. Murphy and Bartol, Mineola, N.Y., 1978—; bd. dirs. numerous cos.; counsel to senator N.Y. State Senate, Garden City, 1985-90. Exec. leader Nassau County Rep. Com., Westbury, N.Y., 1978—, Osyter Bay Rep. Com., 1978—; sec., mem. parish coun. and spl. sch. com. St. Edward Roman Cath. Ch., Syosset, N.Y., 1978-80; mem. exec. com. United Cerebral Palsy Assn. Nassau County, 1978—, chmn. forget-me-not ball, 1987—; pres., founder Syosset Community Hosp. community adv. coun., 1987—. Mem. ABA, N.Y. State Bar Assn. (trusts and estates law com. 1983—, lectr. on estate topics), Nassau County Bar Assn. (estates and trusts law com. 1975—, profl. ethics com. 1980-86), Criminal Cts. Bar Assn., Nassau Lawyers Assn. L.I. (bd. dirs. 1977—), Cath. Lawyers Guild Diocese Rockville Centre, Chaminade High Sch. Alumni Assn. (class rep. 1971, class dir. 1971-72, 1st v.p. 1972-74, pres. 1974-76), Rotary (sec., treas, Syosset club 1980—), Alpha Kappa Psi. Roman Catholic. Office: 22 Jericho Tpke Mineola NY 11501-2937

BARTOLINI, BRUCE ANTHONY, real estate executive; b. Framingham, Mass., Mar. 4, 1950; s. Benjamen A. and Eleanor H. (Connery) B.; m. Elaine A. Dowd, Dec. 30, 1990; 1 child, Bethany Nicole. Student, Northeastern U., Boston, 1967-69, postgrad., 1986-88; BA in Biology, Framingham State Coll., 1971; postgrad., Keene State Coll., 1972. Sci. instr. Orford (N.H.) Acad., 1971-73; biology instr. J.P. Keefe Tech. Sch., Framingham, 1973—; pres. Bartolini Motor Sales, Inc., Medway, Mass., 1979—; trustee Milford Realty Devel., 1979—, Blackstone Realty, 1980, Bartolini Realty; securities investor A.G. Edwards & Sons; mem. Concord Auto Auction, 1979—. Contbr. articles to profl. jours. With USAR, 1984—. Decorated Army Achievement medal. Mem. NEA, Keefe Tech. Tchrs. Assn., Mass. Tchrs. Assn. Republican. Roman Catholic. Clubs: Southboro Rod and Gun (Mass.), Framingham Militia.

BARTOLINI, ROBERT ALFRED, electrical engineer, researcher; b. Waterbury, Conn., Apr. 4, 1942; s. Alfred N. and Maria D. (Cartoceti) B.; M. Janice M. Daly, June 13, 1964; children: Jill C., Ellen G., Robin M. BSEE, Villanova U., 1964; MSEE, Case Western Res. U., 1966; PhD, U. Pa., 1972. Rsch. scientist RCA Labs., Princeton, N.J., 1966-79, leader optical systems, 1979-83, head optoelectronic rsch., 1983-87; head laser diode rsch. David Sarnoff Rsch. Ctr., Princeton, 1987-89, dir. integrated cir., 1989—; chmn. elect. engring. dept. LaSalle U., 1982-90. Contbr. 35 articles to jours. in field; presenter 65 profl. presentations. Chmn. Sewer Oper. Com., West Windsor, N.J., 1974-82, assessment bd., 1984; vice chmn. Stony Brook Regional Sewerage Authority, Princeton, N.J., 1980—. Recipient 3 labs. achievement awards RCA Labs., 1970, 76, 80, Outstanding Paper award Soc. Internat. Display, 1979, Engring. Alumni award Villanova U., 1986, Sarnoff award RCA Corp., 1986. Fellow IEEE (Centennial medal 1984), Optical Soc. Am. (chmn. laser conf. 1987-91); mem. Sigma Xi (nat. lectr. 1983-84), Tau Beta Pi, Eta Kappa Nu. Office: David Sarnoff Rsch Ctr SRI Internat Princeton NJ 08540

BARTOLINO, JOHN BRUCE, clothing company executive, educator; b. Trenton, N.J., Mar. 31, 1944; s. John J. and Eleanor (Wylie) B.; m. Teresa Y. Aluise, July 2, 1966; children: Michael, Jodi, David, Jennifer. B Indsl. Engring., U. Dayton, 1966; MBA, Xavier U., Cin., 1969. Devel. engr. Inland div. GM, Dayton, Ohio, 1966-70; planning analyst Cities Svc. Co., N.Y.C., 1970-73; mng. planning TRW Crescent Wire, Trenton, 1973-76, mktg. mgr., 1976-78; asst. to pres. Keystone Lighting Co., Bristol, Pa., 1978-80; dir. adminstrn. Van Heusen Co., Piscataway, N.J., 1980-85; v.p. sales and mktg. ops. Van Heusen Co., N.Y.C., 1985-90; v.p. adminstrn. PVH Apparel Group, N.Y.C., 1990—; assoc. prof. Rider Coll., Lawrenceville, N.J., 1980—. Pres. Lawrence Jaycees, 1973; chmn. Lawrence Twp. Planning Bd., 1978—; v.p. N.J. Fedn. Planning Ofcls., 1979. Mem. Lawrence Italian Civic Assn. Roman Catholic. Home: 236 Glenn Ave Trenton NJ 08648-3744 Office: Van Heusen Co 1290 Ave of the Americas New York NY 10028

BARTOLOMEO, DANIEL ANTHONY, publishing operations executive, consultant; b. N.Y.C., Nov. 24, 1955; s. Dominic and Donata (Salvucci) B.; m. Patricia Mary DiMeola, Oct. 26, 1980; children: Daniel, Laura, Catherine. BA in Polit. Sci., St. John's U., Jamaica, N.Y., 1977; MBA in Mgmt., St. John's U., 1981. Dir. pub. ops. McGraw Hill, Inc., N.Y.C., 1981-99, 1981—; cons., prin. Bartolomeo & Assocs., Garden City, N.Y., 1989—. Mem. Mineola (N.Y.) Sch. Bd., 1986-89; coach Mineola Athletic Assn., 1989-91; chmn. pack 311 Boy Scouts Am., Williston Park, N.Y., 1990—. Mem. Assn. for Info. and Image Mgmt., Common-IBM Users Group, Nat. Trust-Hist. Preservation. Republican. Roman Catholic.

BARTON, BLAIR L., publishing company executive, real estate developer; b. Balt., Apr. 8, 1953; s. David Walker Jr. and Meta Margaret (Packard) B. AB, Middlebury Coll., 1975; MBA, Loyola Coll., Balt., 1978; small co. pres. cert., Stanford U., 1983. Sr. v.p. bus. devel. Barton Gillet Co., Balt., 1976-86; pres. Barton Dame Inc., Balt., 1986—; adj. prof. Johns Hopkins U., Balt., 1978. Pub: (books) Baltimore Surplus Property Guide, 1990, Best Bike Routes in Maryland, 1991, (book/directory) Maryland Production Guide, 1991 (Gov.'s citation 1992), (directory) Colorado Production Guide, 1990. Mem. Sparrows Point Club, Ctr. Club. Episcopalian. Office: Barton Dame Box 16388 Baltimore MD 21210

BARTON, EDWARD READ, educator; b. Kalamazoo, Mich., May 10, 1938; s. Clare A. and Caroline (Read) B. BS, Mich. State U., 1960; MPA, Cornell U., 1964, JD, 1964. Pres. Edward Read Barton P.C., Allegan, Mich., 1967-89; v.p. sales, treas. Diamond Tool Co., South Haven, Mich., 1989-90; exec. mgr. Consortium for Belizean Devel. Inc., Washington, 1990-92; adj. instr. Oakland Community Coll., 1990-92; adj. curator Changing Men Collection Spl. Collections, Mich. State U. Libr., 1990—; dir. West Mich. Men's Ctr., 1990—, pres., 1990-91. Mem. Allegan County Agrl. Assn. (life), Mich. Jaycees (area coord., life mem. senate 1990-91), FarmHouse (pres. Mich. assn. 1986-91, pres. Found. Coun. 1988-92). Home: 920 Miller Rd Plainwell MI 49080-1053

BARTON, JEAN MARIE, psychologist, educator; b. Pitts., Mar. 24, 1945; d. Joseph Paul and Jean Marie (Anderson) Adamchic; m. Robert L. Barton, Jr., Aug. 14, 1965; children: Robert Joseph, Katherine Anne. BS summa cum laude, U. Pitts., 1965; MEd, Boston U., 1969; CAGS, Cath. U. Am., 1985, PhD in Ednl. Psychology, 1988. Cert. sch. psychologist, Md., nationally certified sch. psychologist. Tchr./curriculum Wellesley (Mass.) pub. schs., 1965-69; lectr. U. R.I./R.I. Coll., Providence, 1969-72; curriculum specialist/tchr. St. Jane DeChantal Sch., Bethesda, Md., 1977-83; computer prog. dir. St. Jane DeChantal Sch., 1982-84; psychology assoc. Long Assocs., Bethesda, 1988—; psychol. cons. Gifted Unit, Montgomery County pub. schs., Rockville, Md., 1985—; sch. psychologist Archdiocese of Washington (Md.), 1987—; adj. mem. faculty Cath. U. Am., Washington, 1989—; mem. evaluation team Cath. Schs. Studies, 1987—; dir. Profl. Devel Inst., Cath. U. Am., 1985-86; mem. adv. com., chairperson identification com. Jacob Javits Grant, Montgomery County pub. schs., 1989—; cons. Chiavarini Assocs., Silver Spring, Md., 1992—; presenter nat. confs. Contbr. articles to profl. jours. U. Pitts. scholar, 1962-65. Mem. APA, ASCD, Nat. Assn. Sch. Psychologists, Am. Ednl. Rsch. Assn., Md. Sch. Psychologists Assn., Coun. Exceptional Children, Pi Lambda Theta. Home: 5008 Benton Ave Bethesda MD 20814-2804 Office: Cath U of America 216 O'Boyle Hall Washington DC 20064

BARTON, JERRY O'DONNELL, telecommunications executive; b. N.Y.C., Sept. 12, 1947; s. Wilford O'Donnell and Jean Dorethy (Lo Preste) B.; m. Sharon Davis (div. June 1977); children: Jennifer P., Samantha C., Gerard Jr.; m. Danielle Marie Acanfora, Oct. 28, 1980. AS in Electronics Tech., RCA Inst. Tech., 1969; student computer sci., S.I. Community Coll., 1975; postgrad. in bus., Wagner Coll., 1979. TV repair technician AAT Svc. Co., S.I., N.Y., 1964-66, Can Do TV Svc., S.I., 1966; air conditioning repairman AES Corp., S.I., 1966; communications technician AAT Electronics, S.I., 1966-77; v.p. engring. AAT Communications Corp., S.I., 1977-82, v.p., mgr., 1982—; speaker S.I. Community Coll., 1977-84; cons. Wall Street Telecommunications, N.Y.C., 1984—. Contbr. articles to communications mags.; designer voice patch for voice recorders for banks and brokers. Mem. Wall Street Telecommunications Assn., Sigma Epsilon Phi. Democrat. Home: 700 Victory Blvd Apt 18K Staten Island NY 10301 Office: AAT Communications Corp 1854 Hylan Blvd Staten Island NY 10305

BARTON, JOAN CHI-HUNG LO, sales executive; b. Nanking, Republic of China, Apr. 4, 1944; came to U.S., 1969; d. Shu Yen and Hua Yin (Chiang) Lo; m. Eugene W. Barton, July 31, 1976. BA, Coll. Chinese Culture, Taipei, Taiwan, 1969; MA, U. Ariz., 1971; AAS, Parsons Sch. Design, 1978. Freelance translator Lewis Bertrand Studio, N.Y.C., 1971-74, Med.-Pharm. Translation Svcs. Inc., N.Y.C., 1971-74; asst. to mgr. W. R. Grace, N.Y.C., 1974-77, Am. Home Products, N.Y.C., 1979-80; ptnr. Pacific Sunshine Co., N.Y.C., 1977-84; prop., mgr. Pacific Angel Sales Co., N.Y.C., 1984—. Author, illustrator children's books: The Talking Mushrooms, 1990, Naughty Nancy and Her Two Strange Chicken Friends, 1990; designer creative stuffed animals. Mem. Christian Edn. Com., 1990—. Mem. Packaging Inst. U.S.A. Episcopalian. Home: 4 Hudson Ter Fl 2D Dobbs Ferry NY 10522-2104

BARTON, JOHN FREDERICK, federal agency administrator, journalist; b. Saginaw, Mich., May 24, 1932; s. Glenn Earl Barton and Helen Ruth (Harkin) Leslie; m. Anne Louise Alderman, Nov. 29, 1975. Student, Kenyon Coll., 1950-51, Tulane U., 1956-57; BA, Mich. State U., 1959. Reporter UPI, Madison, Wis., 1959-61, Chgo. Tribune, 1961; mgr. for Pakistan UPI, Karachi, 1961-64; mgr. for South Asia UPI, New Delhi, India, 1964-66; night editor for Asia UPI, Tokyo, 1966-67; state dept., White House, congl. reporter UPI, Washington, 1967-84; acting editor, Asia Voice of Am., Washington, 1984-86; dep., European Wireless File U.S. Info. Agy., Washington, 1987—. Editor: European Wireless File. Vestryman St. Mark's Episcopal Ch., Washington, 1974-76. With USN, 1952-56. Mem. State Dept. Correspondents Assn. (pres. 1975), Nat. Press Bldg. Corp. (bd. dirs. 1978-84), Nat. Press Club (gov. 1978-84) (numerous merit awards), OverseasWriters Club, Overseas Press Club. Home: 5407 32nd St NW Washington DC 20015-1303 Office: US Info Agy 301 4th St SE Washington DC 20547-0001

BARTON, JOHN MURRAY, artist, consultant; b. N.Y.C., Feb. 8, 1921; s. Boris and Lena (Sirota) Silver; m. Irene Zevon, Dec. 15, 1945 (div. 1958); 1 child, Leonard Steven; m. Hilda, Jan. 21, 1966; 1 child, Erika Jane. Fine Art degree, Art Students League, 1936, 45; student, Tschachasov Sch. Creative Art, 1955. former pres. J.M.B. Pub. Ltd., N.Y.C., 1968-85, John Barton Assn., Inc., N.Y.C., 1967-85, Multiple Reproductions Inc., N.Y.C., 1968-85. One-man shows include Fantasy Gallery, Washington, Hudson Guild, N.Y., Highgate Gallery, N.J., Glassboro State Coll., N.J., Swain Art Gallery, N.J., Fromuth Gallery, Pa., J. Walter Thompson, N.Y.; represented in collections in Bklyn. Mus., Met. Mus., N.Y., Butler Mus., Ohio, Forth Worth Art Ctr., Tex., Haifa Mus. of Modern Art, Israel, N.Y. Pub. Libr., Newark Pub. Libr., Phila. Mus. Art, Phila., Yale U. Mus., New Haven, N.C. Coll., Durham, U. N.C., Greensboro, Libr. COng., Washington. Mem. Artists Equity Assn. Inc. Home: 45 Christopher St New York NY 10014-3533 Office: John M Barton 92 Grove St New York NY 10014-3548

BARTON, LEWIS, food manufacturing company executive; b. N.Y.C., Mar. 9, 1940; s. Louis and Mary (Mosca) Bologna; m. Barbara Joan Hummell, Sept. 6, 1964; children: Glenn Scott, Gregory Jon. Student, Adelphi U., 1957-59. Sales rep. Olivetti Corp., N.Y.C., 1962-64, W. Ralston Co., Chgo., 1964-65, Milprint Co., N.Y.C., 1965-66; pres., founder Sigma Quality Foods, Farmingdale, N.Y., 1966-88; v.p. bus. devel. Sugar Foods Corp., N.Y.C., 1988—. Patentee several package design constructions and methods. Lectr. Environ. Packaging Conf.,1992, Food Plastics Conf., 1992, GreenPak Expo, 1991, Reclaim Our City's Kids Conf., Very Spl. Arts. With USAF, 1961-62. Named to Pres. Coun. for Ednl. Distinction, Adelphi U. Mem. Nat. Single Svc. Food Assn. (charter, chmn. 1977-79, Svc. award 1982), Internat. Orgn. Packaging Profls., Soc. Plastics Engrs., Product Devel. and Mgmt. Assn. (bd. dirs.), Internat. Platform Assn., Dwight D. Eisenhower Soc. (founder), Columbus Citizen's Found., Actors Fund Am., Downtown Athletic Club, N.Y. Athletic Club. Home: 45 Sutton Pl S New York NY 10022-2444 Office: Sugar Foods Corp 21 W St New York NY 10006

BARTON, PAUL, chemical engineering educator; b. Heckscherville, Pa., July 9, 1936; s. Metro and Mary (Chaposky) B.; m. Rosemarie M. Ferenchick, Jan. 26, 1957; children: Marian M., Julia M., Charles M., Roseann, Peter P. BSChemE, Pa. State U., 1957, MSChemE, 1960, PhD in Chem. Engring., 1963. Registered profl. engr., Pa. Vis. scientist Argonne Nat. Lab., Idaho Falls, Idaho, 1971-72; sr. prin. engr. Air Products, Allentown, Pa., 1984-85; rsch. asst. Pa. State U., University Park, 1957-63, rsch. assoc., 1963-68, asst. prof. chem. engring., 1968—; cons. EPA, 1979, NIST, 1989-90 and other indsl. cos., 1966—. Author: (software) Distillation, 1989; contbr. articles to profl. jours. Mem. Am. Inst. Chem. Engrs., Am. Chem. Soc. Democrat. Roman Catholic. Home: 696 Buffalo Run Rd Bellefonte PA 16823-8862 Office: Pa State U 132B Fenske Lab University Park PA 16802-4400

BARTON, ROBERT L., JR., judge, educator; b. Ballston Spa, N.Y., June 19, 1943; s. Robert L. Sr. and Bertha (Di Pasquale) B.; m. Jean M. Adamchic, Aug. 14, 1965; children: Robert Joseph, Katherine Anne. BA, U. Pitts., 1965; JD, Boston Coll., 1969. Bar: Mass. 1969, R.I. 1970, D.C. 1972, U.S. Ct. Appeals (1st cir.) 1970, U.S. Ct. Appeals (D.C. cir.) 1973, U.S. Dist. Ct. R.I., 1971, U.S. Dist. Ct. D.C. 1973, U.S. Dist. Ct. Md. 1973. Law clk. U.S. Dist. Ct. R.I., Providence, 1969-70; staff atty. R.I. Legal Svcs., Providence, 1970-71; spl. asst. to solicitor U.S. Dept. Labor, Washington, 1971-72; assoc. Sherman, Dunn, Cohen & Leifer, Washington, 1972-75; trial atty. FTC, Washington, 1975-88; judge Pa. Office of Hearing & Appeals, Pitts., 1988-90, Office of Hearings, Washington, 1990—; trial instr. Nat. Inst. Trial Advocacy, Washington, 1982-86, U.S. Dept. Justice, Washington, 1986—. Chair com. Cath. League for Religious Rights, Milw., 1983-84, Maplewood Citizens Assn., Bethesda, Md., 1988. Mem. ABA, Am. Judges Assn., Fed. Bar Assn., Am. Judicature Assn., Fed. Adminstrn. Law Judges Assn. Roman Catholic. Office: Office of Hearings 400 7th Ste SW Ste 9228 Washington DC 20590

BARTOSZEK, JOSEPH EDWARD, marine products company executive; b. Chicopee, Mass., Feb. 27, 1952; s. Walter Joseph and Madonna Elizabeth (Haan) B.; m. Lila Diane Pizarro, Aug. 20, 1977. AS, Holyoke Community Coll., 1972; BS, Westfield State Coll., 1974; MS, No. Ariz. U., 1976. Animal health technician animal and plant health inspection svc., veterinary svcs. USDA, Waltham, Mass., 1977-79; chem. dir. Ultramotive Corp., Bethel, Vt., 1980-83, v.p. rsch. and devel., 1983-89, nat. mgr. marine products, 1987-89; pres. Tundico Inc., Tunbridge, Vt., 1987-91; environ. biologist spl. studies and surveillance unit Agy. Natural Resources, Montpelier, Vt., 1989-91; environmentalist Guernsey County Health Dept., Cambridge, Ohio, 1991—; cons. Scheindel Assocs., Randolph Center, Vt., 1984-89; sanitarian Guernsey County Health Dept., Cambridge, Ohio. Patentee pressurized barrier package in U.S. and fgn. countries. Sec. Tunbridge Planning Commn., 1987-88, chmn., 1988-91; sanitarian Guernsey County Health Dept., Cambridge, Ohio, 1991—. Mem. Chem. Spltys. Mfrs. Assn. (small bus. subcom. 1987-89). Unitarian. Office: Tundico Inc RR 1 Box 206 Tunbridge VT 05077 also: Guernsey County Health Dept 326 Highland Ave Cambridge OH 43725-9731

BARTUSIAK, MARCIA FRANCES, science writer; b. Chester, Pa., Jan. 30, 1950; d. Czeslaw A. and Wanda E. (Rogala) B.; m. Stephen A. Lowe, Sept. 10, 1988. BA in Communications, Am. U., Washington, 1971; MS in Physics, Old Dominion U., 1979. Reporter, anchorwoman Sta. WVEC-TV, Norfolk, Va., 1971-75; Univ. fellow Boston U., 1979-80; staff writer Discover mag., N.Y.C., 1980-82, contbg. editor, 1990—; freelance sci. writer Norfolk, 1982-89, Arlington, Mass., 1989—; book reviewer N.Y. Times Book Rev., 1986—; sci. writing award judge Am. Inst. Physics, N.Y.C., 1988-90. Author: Thursday's Universe, 1986 (named Notable Sci. Book 1987 N.Y. Times); contbr. over 100 articles to publs. including Omni, Popular Sci., Discover, Air and Space. Recipient Sci. Writing award Am. Inst. Physics, 1982, Astronomy Book of Yr. award Astron. Soc. Pacific, 1987. Mem. Nat. Assn. Sci. Writers, Authors Guild, Sigma Xi (assoc.).

BARTYNSKI, CYNTHIA LYNN, educational administrator, consultant; b. Allentown, Pa., May 21, 1958; d. Stanislaw Bartynski and Linda Gaye Davis. BS in Spl. Edn., Bloomsburg (Pa.) U., 1980; MEd, cert. reading specialist, Kutztown (Pa.) U., 1984; cert. elem. prin., Lehigh U., 1989, cert. secondary prin., 1990. Reading specialist Intermediate Unit 21, Schnecksville, Pa., 1980-87, coord. in-svc. program, 1987—. Mem. ASCD, Internat. Reading Assn., Pa. ASCD (sec. ea. region), Pa. Staff Devel. Coun., Phi Delta Kappa. Democrat. Lutheran. Office: Carbon Lehigh Intermediate 4750 Orchard Rd Unit 21 Schnecksville PA 18078-9301

BASA, ENIKÖ MOLNÁR, librarian; b. Huszt, Hungary, Sept. 7, 1939; came to the U.S., 1950; d. Julius Valentine and Terézia (Fejé)r) Molnár; m. Péter Basa, Oct. 19, 1966. BA, Trinity Coll., 1962; MA, U. N.C., 1965, PhD, 1972. Instr. U. Md., College Park, 1965-69; asst. prof. Dunbarton Coll., Washington, 1970-72; lectr. Am. U., Washington, 1972-75, Hood Coll., Frederick, Md., 1975-76; editor, libr. Libr. of Congress, Washington, 1977—. Author: Sandor Petöfi, 1980; translator: (play) Screenplay from

Örkény, 1983; editor: Twayne World Authors, 1974—; assoc. editor The Comparatist, 1976-82; jour. rev. editor: Hungarian Studies Newsletter, 1975-82; guest editor: Rev. Nat. Lits., 1992.; contbr. chpts. to books and articles and book revs. to profl. jours. Mem. MLA (Hungarian sect. chair 1980, 90), So. Comparative Lit. Assn. (founding, v.p. 1977-79, 89—, sec.-treas. 1985-89), Am. Hungarian Educators Assn. (pres. 1974-80, 88-92, exec. dir. 1980-88, 92—), Internat. Assn. Hungarian Studies, Libr. Congress Profl. Assn. (v.p. 1991). Home: 707 Snider Ln Silver Spring MD 20905 Office: Serial Record Libr Congress Washington DC 20540

BASBAS, MONTE GEORGE, judge; b. Manchester, N.H., May 6, 1921; s. George and Rose (Economou) B.; m. Audrey Ann Vagiates, Jan. 10, 1948; children: John Thomas, Monte George, Audrey Ann. AB, Dartmouth Coll., 1944; JD, Boston U., 1949. Bar: Mass. 1949, N.H. 1949, U.S. Supreme Ct. 1969. Justice Dist. Ct. Newton, Mass., 1971—, presiding justice, 1976—; Bar: Mass. 1949, N.H. 1949, U.S. Dist. Ct. Mass. 1950, U.S. Dist. Ct. N.H. 1951, U.S. Supreme Ct. 1969. mem. Dist. Ct. Dept. Stds. Com., 1973—, chmn., 1984—, others. Mayor City of Newton, 1966-71; mem. Prs.'s Adv. Bd., Bentley Coll., 1983—; bd. dirs. Newton Community Svc. Ctrs., Inc. Capt. USAAF, 1942-45; PTO. Decorated Air medal with clusters, D.F.C.; named Newton C. of C. Man of the Year, 1966; numerous citations. Mem. ABA, Mass. Bar Assn., Boston Bar Assn., Waltham Bar Assn., Watertown Bar Assn., Weston Bar Assn., Newton Bar Assn., Mass. City Clks. Assn. (past pres.), Mass. Mayors Assn. (past pres.), Am. Legion, Masons, Boston U. Nat. Alumni Council, Boston U. Sch. Law Alumni Assn., NAACP, Alpha Omega, Phi Delta Phi, Chi Phi, Knights of St. Andrew. Home: 25 Jeffrey Rd Wayland MA 01778-2505

BASCH, RICHARD VENNARD, photographer, producer, writer, director; b. Inpls., Jan. 22, 1945; s. Richard and Helen Louise (Vennard) B.; m. Meredith Baker, Feb. 12, 1966; 1 child, Nicholas; m. Vicki Sylvester, Aug. 15, 1977. Cert., U. Fine Arts, Perugia, Italy, 1965, London Film Sch., 1966; BA, Antioch Coll., 1968. Dir. filmmaker tng. Am. Film Inst., Washington, 1968-69; instr. film history R.I. Sch. Design, Providence, 1970-73; cons. in theatre Antioch Coll., Yellow Springs, Ohio, 1976-77; prin., photographer Richard Basch Studio, Washington, 1979—; dir. film programs Brown U., 1972-73; cons. Smithsonian Instn., Washington, 1979—. Author: Faces of Fairmont Heights, 1970. Mem. Am. Soc. Mag. Photographers. Episcopalian. Office: Richard Basch Studio 2627 Connecticut Ave NW Washington DC 20008-1522

BASCOM, ROBERT HOLDEN, accountant; b. Pitts., Feb. 11, 1940; s. Ralph Benjamin and Ethel Charlotte (MacRoberts) B.; m. Mary Ann Zaorski, July 3, 1982. Grad., Berkshire Bus. Coll., 1958. Lic. pub. acct. Staff acct. George P. Hunt, Pittsfield, Mass., 1958-65; pub. acct. Hunt, Bascom and Co., Pittsfield, Mass., 1965-74, pvt. practice, Pittsfield, Mass., 1974—. Treas. St. Stephen's Ch., Pittsfield, 1975-85, Pitts. Area C. of C., 1975-85, Christian Ctr., Pittsfield, 1968-77. With USCGR, 1961-69. Mem. Nat. Soc. Pub. Accts., Mass. Soc. CPA's, Mass. Assn. Pub. Accts., Kiwanis Club (Pittsfield chpt treas. 1988—, sec. 1983-91, lt. gov. 1979, pres. 1977). Episcopalian. Home: 74 Roberta Rd Pittsfield MA 01201 Office: Silber Kushi and Myers 105 South St Pittsfield MA 01201

BASCUÑANA, JOSÉ LUIS, mechanical engineer, economist; b. Paris, Feb. 10, 1927; s. Luís and Isabel (Merino) B.; came to U.S., 1958, naturalized, 1970; B.S., Cath. Inst. of Arts and Industries, Spain, 1947; M.S. in M.E., U. Rochester, 1961, Ph.D. (Broderson fellow (1964-67), 1968; M.A. in Econs., Eastern Mich. U., 1978; registered profl. engr.; m. Irene Farina, Mar. 11, 1957; children—Xavier, Alicia, William, Irene, Henry. Engine designer Center Automotive Tech. Studies, Madrid, 1947-56, head automotive sect., 1956-58; sr. project engr. Barreiros Diesel, S.A., Madrid, 1961-63; sr. research engr., emissions sect. Ford Motor Co., Dearborn, Mich., 1967-70; project mgr. div. emission control tech. EPA, Ann Arbor, Mich., 1970-77; sr. tech. adv. tech. assessment div., research and devel. Nat. Hwy. Traffic Safety Adminstrn., Dept. Transp., Washington, 1977—; cons. in field. Served with Spanish Air Force, 1947-8. Recipient Outstanding Performance award Nat. Hwy. Traffic Safety Adminstrn., 1979, 84, Superior Performance award, 1983. Mem. ASME, Soc. Automotive Engrs., Air Pollution Control Assn., Combustion Inst., Am. Econ. Assn., Nat. Soc. Profl. Engrs., Coordinating Research Council, Sigma Xi, Omicron Delta Epsilon. Roman Catholic. Contbr. articles to profl. jours. Home: 9104 Cranford Dr Rockville MD 20854-2227 Office: 400 7th St SW Washington DC 20590-0002

BASECH, ELINOR, actress, educator; b. Trenton, N.J., Mar. 5, 1927; d. David Samuel and Jenny (Randelman) Josephson; m. Sabert Basech, May 6, 1951; children: Claire, Neil, Maria. BA, Oberlin Coll., 1948. Actress Broadway and off-Broadway plays, TV prodns. N.Y.C., 1949-90, N.Y.C. Opera, 1990; tchr. acting, drama coach Elinor Basech Studio, N.Y.C., 1980—; tchr. acting The New Sch. for Social Rsch.; dir. documentary films. Appeared in: (Broadway play) Detective Story, 1949-50, (off-Broadway play) The Sea Gull, 1990, (opera) Street Scene, 1990; actress (recordings) The Diary of Anne Frank, Jane Eyre, Little Women, Beatrix Potter stories. Mem. AFTRA, SAG, Equity. Democrat. Jewish. Home: 516 Hommocks Rd Larchmont NY 10538-3912 Office: Elinor Basech Studio 529 W 42d St Ste 7D New York NY 10036

BASERGA, RENATO LUIGI, pathology educator; b. Meda, Milan, Italy, Apr. 11, 1925; came to U.S., 1949; s. Alessandro and Giuseppina (Annoni) B.; m. Jane Conrad, Dec. 23, 1954 (div. Sept. 1974); children: Susan Jane, Janice Rene; m. Beverly Lange, Oct. 12, 1974. MD, U. Milan, 1949. Diplomate Am. Bd. Pathology. Resident U. Milan, 1949-51; intern Columbus Hosp., Chgo., 1952-53; assoc. in oncology Chgo. Med. Sch., 1953-54; resident pathology St. Luke's Hosp., Chgo., 1955-58; instr. pathology Northwestern U., Chgo., 1958-60, asst. prof., 1960-64, assoc. prof., 1964-65; prof. Temple U., Phila., 1965-91, chmn. dept. pathology, 1980-91; prof. microbiology Thomas Jefferson U., Phila, 1991—; cons. Argonne (Ill.) Nat. Lab., 1959-65; sr. investigator Fels Rsch. Inst., Temple U., 1965—; Louis Gross Meml. lectr. NYU, 1974; Searle lectr. Brit. Soc. Cell Biology, 1976; Wellcome vis. prof., 1984. Author: Autoradiography Techniques and Applications, 1969, Multiplication and Division in Mammalian Cells, 1976, The Biology of Cell Reproduction, 1985; editor: The Cell Cycle and Cancer, 1971. Served with vol. forces, 1943-45, Italy. Recipient rsch. career devel. award USPHS, 1964-65, Samuel Noble Found. award, 1989, Rous-Whipple award, 1990, Fred Stewart award, 1990; Maria Antonietta Dellacare scholar, Milan, 1951; sr. rsch. fellow USPHS, 1958-60, Schiffer Meml. Lect. Internat. Cell Soc. award, 1992. Office: Jefferson Cancer Inst Bluemle Life Scis Bldg 233 S 10th St Fl 6 Philadelphia PA 19107-5566

BASFORD, ROBERT EUGENE, biochemistry educator, researcher; b. Montpelier, N.D., Aug. 21, 1923; s. Eugene M. and Bertha (Cudworth) B.; m. Carol Kaufman Phebus, Dec. 23, 1965; 1 child, Lee A. Phebus. B.S., U. Wash., 1951, Ph.D., 1954. Postdoctoral fellow U. Wis.-Madison, 1954-58; asst. prof. U. Pitts., 1958-63, assoc. prof., 1963-70, prof., 1970—; cons. Mine Safety Appliance Co., Pitts., 1966-69; mem. neurol. scis. study sect. NIH, Washington, 1977-80. Mem. Am. Soc. Biochemistry and Molecular Biology, Reticuloendothelial Soc., Am. Soc. Cell Biology, Oxygen Soc., Am. Thoracic Soc. Office: U Pitts Sch Medicine Dept Molecular Genetics & Biochem E1240 Biomed Sci Tower Pittsburgh PA 15261-2072

BASH, ROGER LEONARD, neuropsychologist, psychotherapist; b. Bklyn., Feb. 27, 1947; s. Jack M. and Jeannette (Braus) B.; m. Margo T. Yunik, June 14, 1987; 1 child, Jonathan M. BA in Anthropology, U. Ill., 1970; MA in Counselor Edn., Northeastern Ill. U., 1975; MSW in Adminstrn., Fla. State U., 1985, PhD in Counseling Psychology, 1987. Lic. psychologist, Fla., Pa., N.J., mental health counselor, Fla.; registered health svc. provider in psychology; cert. rehab. counselor. Rehabilitationist various positions, Ill. and Fla., 1975-87; doctoral intern Fla. State U. Student Counseling Ctr., Tallahassee, 1986-87; postdoctoral fellow in cognitive therapy Ctr. Cognitive Therapy, Phila., 1987-88; postdoctoral fellow in clin. neuropsychology Mediplex Rehab.-Camden, N.J., 1988-89; adj. clin. asst. prof. Widener U. Clin. Psychology, Phila., 1990-91; psychologist Bustleton Guidance Ctr., Phila., 1989-91; neuropsychologist New Medico Rehab. Ctr. of Phila., Lafayette Hill, 1989—; dir. neuropsychology Treasure Coast Rehab. Hosp., Vero Beach, Fla., 1991—; cons. First Rehab., Inc., Commerce, Ga., 1987, Fla. State U. Student Counseling Ctr., 1984-87, Goodwill Industries, Tallahassee, 1985, U. Miami Microcomputer Program, 1985, U. Pa. Dept. Psychiatry, 1991. Contbr. articles to profl. jours. Bd. dirs. Radio Reading Svc. for Blind, Miami, 1982, Broward County Employment Com. for Disabled Citizens, Ft. Lauderdale, Fla., 1981-82, Condominium Bd., Davie, Fla., 1980-81. Recipient fellowship Fla. State U. Coll. Edn., 1982-83. Mem. APA, Internat. Neuropsychological Soc., Soc. Exploration of Psychotherapy Integration. Office: Treasure Coast Rehab Hosp 1600 37th Ave Vero Beach FL 32960

BASHJAWISH, RAMZI, mechanical engineer; b. Jordan, Dec. 6, 1965; came to U.S., 1974; BS, N.Y. Inst. Tech., 1990. Asst. mech. engr. N.Y.C. Transit Authority, Bklyn., 1990—. Mem. ASME (assoc.), AIAA. Home: 1584 Heights Dr Yorktown Heights NY 10598 Office: NYC Transit Authority 1-25 12th St Brooklyn NY 11215

BASHKIN, LLOYD SCOTT, marketing and management consultant; b. Bridgeport, Conn., July 11, 1951; s. Jules Bernard and Luella (Kobre) B.; children: Marisa Elizabeth, Carly Michelle. BS in Fin., Syracuse U., 1973, MBA in Mktg. and Acctg., 1974; postgrad., Columbia U., 1975-78. Corp. staff mktg. cons. RCA, N.Y.C., 1974-77; mgr. entertainment, indsl. mktg. and nat. sales RCA, Cherry Hill, N.J., 1977-79; v.p. mktg. and sales CCA Electronics Corp. div. Singer Co., Cherry Hill, 1979-80; pres. Lloyd Scott & Co., Cherry Hill, 1980—, Sydex, Cherry Hill, 1987-88; adj. instr. Temple U. Grad. Sch., Phila., 1980-82; adj. prof. Drexel U. Grad. Sch., Phila., 1982—; speaker in field. Trustee, chmn. mktg. com. Food Bank South Jersey, 1985—; mem. Camden County Pvt. Industry Coun., 1989-90; mem. cabinet World Affairs Coun., 1989, Community Leaders Recognition Com., 1991—. Recipient Commendation award Gov. of N.J., 1981, SBA, 1983, Nat. Distbn. and Logistics Honorary award Delta Nu Alpha, 1973, Nat. Broadcasting Honorary award Alpha Epsilon Rho, 1979. Mem. Am. Mktg. Assn., C. of C. of So. N.J. (chmn. small bus. action com. 1982-85, strategic planning and mktg. com. 1985—, bd. dirs. 1984—, chmn. programming com. 1989-02), Greater Cherry Hill C. of C. (chmn. small bus. coun. 1982-83), Rotary (bd. dirs. Garden State club 1980-81). Office: Exec Mews 1930 Marlton Pike E Ste 102U Cherry Hill NJ 08003-2150

BASIL, AMY ELIZABETH, pediatric nurse practitioner; b. North Tonawanda, N.Y., July 15, 1962; d. Norman Robert and Mariwyn (Beiter) Tondrowski; m. Donald Martin Basil, June 6, 1987; children: Stephen John, Madeline Ann. ADN, Niagara County Community Coll., 1982; BSN, SUNY, Buffalo, 1984, MS, 1991. Cert. PNP. RN Erie County Med. Ctr., Buffalo, 1982-83, Children's Hosp. Buffalo, 1983-85, Dr. Norman Richard, Kenmore, N.Y., 1985-87; nursing instr. Niagara County Community Coll., Sanborn, N.Y., 1986-89; RN Children's Hosp. Buffalo, 1987; PNP Health Care Plan, Amherst, N.Y., 1991—. Author (booklet) Bicycle Helmet Safety, 1990. Mem. Nat. Assn. PNP. Home: 7113 Northview Dr Lockport NY 14094 Office: Health Care Plan 1185 Sweethome Rd Amherst NY 14226

BASILE, ANTOINE E., lawyer, economist, educator; b. Beirut, Nov. 24, 1938; came to U.S., 1985; s. Elie and Emma (Wetter) B. JD, St. Joseph U., Beirut, 1961, degree in econs., law, 1962; PhD in Econs. summa cum laude, Sorbonne U., Paris, 1969, SJD summa cum laude, 1986. Bar: Beirut 1967, Paris 1982. Adviser Cen. Bank and Bankers Assn., Beirut, 1965-86, Nomura Securities and Rsch. Inst., Tokyo, 1973-75; prof. St. Joseph U., Beirut, 1972-86; mng. ptnr. law firm Basile, Setrakian, Tyan, Paris and Beirut, 1976—; sr. cons. OECD, Paris, 1977—; vis. prof., adj. prof. U. Paris, 1985—; sr. interregional adviser UN Centre Transnational Corps., N.Y.C., 1986—; advisor to govts., internat. orgns., profl. bodies, rsch. instns.; mem. editorial bd. Mondes en Devel., Paris, 1972—; corr. Internat. Fin. Law Rev., London, 1980—; pres. arbitration tribunals ICC, AAA, Paris, 1982—. Author: Foreign Trade and Development, 1972, International Taxation, 1984; coauthor: Free Export Processing Zones, 1984, Lebanese Legal System, 1985, Privatization and Deregulation in Global Perspective, 1990, Debt Equity Conversions, 1990, Zones of Joint Entrepeneurship in CPE, 1991. Bd. dirs., Coun. Devel. and Reconstrn., Lebanon, 1977-83. With Lebanese armed forces, 1955-57. Fulbright scholar, Columbia U., 1985. Mem. ABA (assoc.), Paris Bar Assn., Beirut Bar Assn., Assn. PhDs in Law and Econs., Am. Fgn. Law Assn. (v.p.), Tiers Monde Assn., Internat. C. of C. (adviser, commr. 1984—), Internat. Rotary. Roman Catholic. Office: care Whitman and Ransom 522 5th Ave Fl 3 New York NY 10036-7695

BASILE, JOSEPH JOHN, JR., lawyer; b. South Weymouth, Mass., May 9, 1952; s. Joseph John and Donata Marie (Salvucci) B.; m. Amanda Marie Cherubino, June 12, 1976; children: Lisa, Amy Beth. AB, Stonehill Coll., 1974; JD, Harvard Law Sch., 1977. Bar: N.J. 1977, Mass. 1978, N.Y. 1981. Assoc. Lindabury, McCormick & Estabrook, Westfield, N.J., 1977-78, Bingham, Dana & Gould, Boston, 1978-79, Cravath, Swaine & Moore, N.Y.C., 1979-83; prof. law Western New Eng. Coll. Sch. Law, Springfield, Mass., 1983-88; sr. counsel United Techs. Corp., Hartford, Conn., 1988-90; asst. gen. counsel United Techs. Corp., Hartford, 1990; counsel, dir. contracts Internat. Aero Engines div. United Techs. Corp., Glastonbury, Conn., 1990—. Editor: State Limited Partnership Laws, 1987; contbr. various law rev. articles to profl. jours. Mem. Sch. Com., Wilbraham, Mass., 1990—, State Ethics Com., Mass., 1987-89, Planning Bd., Wilbraham, 1985-87; chmn. By Law Study Com., Wilbraham, 1986-87. Mem. ABA. Home: 12 Old Carriage Rd Wilbraham MA 01095-2415 Office: Internat Aero Engines 628 Hebron Ave Glastonbury CT 06033

BASILIO, ANTHONY JOSEPH, social services labor union administrator; b. Bklyn., Apr. 25, 1938; s. Joseph and Ann (Olshefski) B.; m. Mary Louise DeLucca, Aug. 26, 1967; children: Dianna Marie, Maryann Judith. BBA, St. John's U., 1959; MSW, Fordham U., 1966. Cert. social worker, N.Y., sch. social worker, N.Y. Caseworker N.Y.C. Dept. Social Svcs., 1961-65, unit supr., 1965-67, field instr., 1968-69, asst. adminstr. Office Staff Devel. and Tng., 1969-79; sr. case supr. N.Y.C. Dept. Income Maintenance, 1979-82; sr. svc. supr. N.Y.C. Dept. Gen. Svcs., 1982-85; trustee Social Svc. Employees Union Local 371, N.Y.C., 1982-85, sec.-treas., 1985—; trustee legal svcs. fund com., legal assistance com. Social Svc. Employees Union Local 371, N.Y.C., 1985—. Mem. exec. bd. social svcs. br. NAACP, N.Y.C., 1968-72. With U.S. Army, 1959-60. Recipient Fordham U. Sch. Social Svcs. Scholarship award N.Y. State Dept. Social Svcs., 1964-66. Mem. NASW, AFSCME (del. local 371 to dist. coun. 37), Acad. Cert. Social Workers, Social Svcs. Employee Union Local 371 (exec. com. mem.). Roman Catholic. Home: 2459 Gerritsen Ave Brooklyn NY 11229-5903 Office: Social Svc Employees Union Local 371 817 Broadway New York NY 10003-4709

BASINSKI, JOHN EDWARD, retail leasing specialist; b. Buffalo, Aug. 16, 1949; s. Edward Raymond and Marguerite Mary (Sweeney) B.; m. Alexandra Biddle, Mar. 13, 1971. BA, U. Pa., 1971. Owner Basinski Wood Studio, Phila., 1972-84; sales assoc. DePetris Realty Group, Phila., 1984-85; sr. leasing rep. Mark Devel. Co., Kingston, Pa., 1985-89; dir. leasing Zaremba Group Inc., Lakewood, Ohio, 1989-90; retail leasing specialist Strouse Greenberg and Co., Phila., 1991—; lectr. U. Pa. Grad. Sch. Fine Arts, Phila., 1975-81. Orgn. cons. Western Reserve Rowing Assn., Cleve., 1989-91; bd. dirs. Wyoming Valley Hist. Soc., Wilkes-Barre, Pa., 1988-89. Named finalist Daphine award Nat. Hardwood Inst., N.Y.C., 1981. Mem. Internat. Coun. Shopping Ctrs., Univ. Bridge Club (social chmn. 1977-84, Pres. Cup 1978). Office: Strouse Greenberg and Co 1626 Locust St Philadelphia PA 19103

BASIOTIS, PANAYOTIS PETER, economist, educator; b. Athens, Dec. 17, 1947; came to the U.S., 1967; s. Demetrius P. and Catherine D. (Spyropoulos) B.; m. Cheryl Ann Gernhardt, Dec. 22, 1970 (div. 1985); 1 child, Katie-Ann; m. Marsha Lee Anderson, Feb. 4, 1989; 1 child, Matthew. BA, U. Kans., 1973, MA, 1975; PhD, U. Mo., 1983. Asst. instr. U. Kans., Lawrence, 1975-78; instr. Westminster Coll., Fulton, Mo., 1978-80; rsch. assoc. U. Mo., Columbia, 1980-85; econ. Human Nutrition Info. Svc./USDA, Hyattsville, Md., 1985—; econ. Human Nutrition Info. Svc./USDA, Hyattsville, Md., 1985—; adj. asst. prof. dept. textiles and consumer econ. U. MD., College Park, 1988—. Contbr. articles to profl. jours. Mem. Am. Coun. Consumer Interest, Am. Econ. Assn., Am. Agriculture Econ. Assn., Econometric Soc. Greek Orthodox. Office: HNIS/USDA 10610 Rhode Island Ave # 304 Beltsville MD 20705-2511

BASKER, JAMES GLYNN, English educator; b. San Francisco, Aug. 28, 1952; s. James Wenzel and Anne Marlo (Glynn) B. BA, Harvard U., 1974; BA/MA, Cambridge U., Eng., 1976; DPhil, Oxford U., Eng., 1983. Lectr. and sr. tutor (asst. dean) Harvard U., Cambridge, Mass., 1982-84, asst. prof. and sr. tutor (asst. dean), 1984-87; assoc. prof. English Barnard Coll., N.Y.C., 1987—; dir. Enrichment at Oxford, summers 1985-89; dir., pres. Oxbridge Acad. Programs, N.Y.C., 1989—; co-pres. Stanford/Harvard Alumni Assn. Seminar in Oxford, 1990; cons. in field. Author: Tobias Smollett, Critic and Journalist, 1988 (Choice award 1989); contbr. articles to profl. jours. Exec. com. Am. Friends of Christ Ch., Oxford, 1983—. Rhodes scholar, 1976; MLA/Am. Antiquarian Soc. fellow, 1990; Clark Fund grantee, 1985-86. Mem. MLA, Am. Soc. for Eighteenth Century Studies, Brit. Soc. for Eighteenth Century Studies, The Johnsonians, Am. Assn. Rhodes Scholars. Office: Barnard Coll English Dept New York NY 10027-6598

BASKIN, BARBARA HOLLAND, education educator, researcher; b. Detroit, Aug. 27, 1929; d. Carl Floyd and Ruth Holland (Herman) Harriman; m. Alex Baskin, Aug. 15, 1954 (div. Nov. 1984); children: Julie S. Baskin Gamlin, Amy Shael Baskin. BA, Wayne State U., 1951, EdD, 1968; MA, U. Mich., 1957. Ednl. cons. Krell Software, Inc., Stony Brook, N.Y., 1982-83, dir. ednl. software devel., 1984-85; dir. program in spl. edn. and devel. disabilities SUNY, Stony Brook, 1981-85, assoc. prof. social sci. interdisciplinary program, 1981—; dir. cons. Bd. Cooperative Ednl. Svcs. Inst. for Gifted and Talented, Suffolk County, N.Y., 1981-83; dir. gifted youth program Saturday Sci. & More, Stony Brook, 1977-84. Co-author: Notes from a Different Drummer, Vol. 1, 1977 (ALA award 1977, Pres.'s Com. on the Employment of the Handicapped award 1978), Books for the Gifted Child, 1980 (Outstanding Reference Book of the Yr. ALA 1980), More Notes from a Different Drummer, Vol. 2, 1984; co-creator: (software) Plato's Cave, 1985 (Cert. of Honor 1986). Bd. govs. Canine Companions Internat., Farmingdale, N.Y., 1990; com. mem. N.Y. State Citizen's Task Force on Child Abuse and Neglect, Albany, N.Y., 1989-91; bd. mem. Suffolk County Coalition for Children and Families, Centereach, N.Y., 1989-91; co-chair campus chpt. NOW, 1989-91; v.p. Mother Child Home Program, 1981-91. Recipient Conversationin the Disciplines, N.Y. State, 1988; named Woman of the Yr. in Edn., Three Village Times, 1980; Whitney Carnegie grantee ALA, 1991. Mem. Univ. Assn., Coun. for Exceptional Children, Nat. Assn. for Gifted Children. Office: SUNY SS1 239 S SBS Bldg Stony Brook NY 11794-4333

BASS, ARTHUR, meteorologist; b. N.Y.C., Apr. 7, 1941; s. Samuel and Ray (Smolowitz) B.; m. Susan Lois Diamond, Sept. 11, 1966; children: Naomi A., Jennie S. AB, Columbia U., 1961; MS, Yale U., 1962; PhD, MIT, 1974. Staff scientist MITRE, Bedford, Mass., 1963-68, Am. Sci. & Engring., Cambridge, Mass., 1968-69, Flow Rsch., Cambridge, 1974-75; mgr. advanced tech. devel. ERT, Inc., Concord, Mass., 1975-85; prin. meteorologist TASC, Reading, Mass., 1985—. Mem. Am. Meteorol. Soc., Air and Waste Mgmt. Assn. Home: 119 Parker St Newton MA 02159-2545 Office: TASC 55 Walkers Brook Dr Reading MA 01867-3238

BASS, ELAINE TAMA, interior design company executive; b. Bklyn., Nov. 4, 1935; d. Harry and Lillian (Reiss) Meisnere; m. Marvin Arthur Bass, June 30, 1956; children: Saralyn, Pamela, David. BS, Cornell U., 1957. Owner Elaine Bass Interiors, Great Neck, N.Y., 1968—; admissions chmn. Interior Design Network, Roslyn, N.Y., 1990. Vice pres., dir. fundraising Am. Jewish Congress, 1980-82, 80-91; pres. governing coun. United Parent Tchr. Coun., Great Neck, 1968-72; bd. dirs., v.p. United Community Fund, 1970-72. Named Women of the Yr., Am. Jewish Congress, 1975. Mem. Am. Soc. Interior Designers, Coalition Against Domestic Violence (bd. dirs. 1990—), Great Neck Student Aid (bd. dirs. 1985-90). Democrat. Home & Office: 11 Rutland Rd Great Neck NY 11020-1805

BASSANO, C. LOUIS, state senator, fuel oil company executive; b. Newark, Oct. 29, 1942; s. Charles and Mildred (Tortoriello) B.; m. Joan DeFlores, May 25, 1984; children: Charles Louis II, Jennifer Ann, Kimberly Claire, Jeffrey Alan. Student, Bloomfield Coll., 1961-63. V.p. H & I Bassano Fuel Oil, Kenilworth, N.J.; mem. Gen. Assembly State of N.J., 1971-81, mem. State Senate, 1981—, asst. minority whip, 1987-88, minority whip, 1989, asst. senate minority leader, 1990—; mem. senate law, pub. safety & def. com., senate instns., health & welfare com.; chmn. legis. caucus on Israel. Chmn. Sammy Davis, Jr. Liver Inst.; mem. N.J. Monorail Legislation Commn., Senate Rep. Task Force on Liability Ins. Reform, Hazardous Waste Minimization Task Force, Law Enforcement Tng. Acad. Study Commn., Nat. Com. for Treatment of Intractable Pain; bd. dirs. Children's Specialized Hosp.; past chmn. fund drive Meml. Gen. Hosp.; past chmn. Union Township Epilepsy Fund; past co-chmn. Cancer Crusade. Recipient cert. of recognition Bd. Dirs. Home Health Agy. Assembly N.J./N.J. Home Care Coun., Outstanding Community Svc. award Cancer Care, Inc./Nat. Cancer Found., PTA Safety award State PTA, B'nai B'rith Youth Svc. award, Pub. Safety award N.J. Tire Dealers Assn., Good Govt. award Township of Union Gov. Body, Disting. Svc. award Jr. Achievement, certs. of appreciation Union County March of Dimes, LWV of Cranford; named Unicio Man of Yr. by Union chpt. Unico, Senator of Yr. by N.J. Builders Assn., Outstanding Rep. Legislator; honored by N.J. State Nurses Assn. Mem. Elks, K.C. Office: Senator 21st Dist (Union) 324 Chestnut St Union NJ 07083

BASSECHES, HARRIET ITKIN, psychoanalyst, clinical psychologist; b. N.Y.C., Oct. 9, 1936; d. Joseph A. and Minerva (Jonas) Itkin; m. Robert T. Basseches, July 6, 1958; children: K.B., Joshua T., Jessica. BA, Smith Coll., 1958; MA, George Washington U., 1972, PhD, 1979. Rsch. psychologist Lab. Psychology, NIMH, Washington, 1958-67; psychol. assessor Washington Dept. Human Resources, 1969-74; staff psychologist D.C. Inst. Mental Hygiene, Washington, 1976-81; pvt. practice psychoanalysis, Washington, 1990—, pvt. practice clin. psychology, 1980—; mem. adj. faculty George Mason psychology dept. U. D.C., 1983-85; faculty, mem. steering com. Dynamics Psychotherapy Program Washington Sch. Psychiatry, 1984—, mem. faculty supervision program, 1989—. Contbr. articles to profl. jours. Fellow Md. Psychol. Assn., D.C. Psychol. Assn.; mem. APA (co-chair prof. issues com., div. psychoanalysis, com. on newsletter), N.Y. Freudian Soc. (tng. and external affairs coms., co-chair D.C. sci. program com.), Washington Psychologists for Study Psychoanalysis (exec. bd. 1984-89, pres. 1989-90), Internat. Psychoanalytical Assn., D.C. Psychol. Assn. (chair psychologists well being com. 1991-92), Sigma Xi, Phi Beta Kappa. Office: 2301 Connecticut Ave NW Washington DC 20008-1730

BASSETT, ALTON HERMAN, health care company executive; b. Hartford, Conn., Nov. 27, 1930; s. Arthur and Martha B.; m. Joan Tolley, Jan. 7, 1956; children: Linda, Barbara. BA, Middlebury (Vt.) Coll., 1953. Plant chemist Am. Viscose Corp., Front Royal, Va., 1955-58; rsch. dir. Chicopee Inc., div. Johnson & Johnson, Milltown and Dayton, N.J., 1958-88, cons., 1988—. Patentee in field. Lt. USMC, 1953-55. Republican. Home: 73 Harriet Dr Princeton NJ 08540-3934 Office: Chicopee Rsch Rt 130 Box 940 Dayton NJ 08810-0940

BASSETT, CAROL HOFFER, educator; b. Scotland, S.D., Mar. 13, 1931; d. Joachim Francis and Clara Belle (Waggoner) Hoffer; m. Charles Walker Bassett, Sept. 15, 1956; children: David Francis, Elizabeth Alice. BA cum laude, U. S.D., 1953, MA, 1955. Tchr. math. Rock Rapids (Iowa) Regional High Sch., 1953-54; asst. instr. math. U. S.D., Vermillion, 1954-55; instr. math. Iowa State U., Ames, 1955-56, Kans. State U., Manhattan, 1956-58; tutor and sub. tchr. math. U. Kans., Lawrence High Sch., 1958-59; instr. math, asst. to chmn. U. Kans., Lawrence, 1959-64; instr. math. Colby Coll., Waterville, Maine, 1974-81, asst. prof. math., 1981—. Pres. Averill Sch. Parent/Tchr. Orgn., Waterville, Maine, 1972-73; coord. Colby Coll. Coop. Nursery Sch., Waterville, 1973-74; mem. affirmative action adv. com. Commn. Bd. Edn., Waterville, 1975-76, mem. ednl. devel. com., 1975-76. Mem. AAUP, Am. Math. Soc., Assn. for Women in Math., Math. Assn. Am., Nat. Coun. Tchrs. Math., Phi Beta Kappa (v.p. Colby Coll. chpt. 1983-84, pres. 1984-85, sec. 1985—), Chi Omega. Democrat. Roman Catholic. Home: 9 Martin Ave Waterville ME 04901-4625 Office: Colby Coll Dept Math Waterville ME 04901

BASSETT, CHARLES WALKER, English language educator; b. Aberdeen, S.D., July 7, 1932; s. Wilfred Walker and Angela (Jewett) B.; m. Carol

Hoffer, Sept. 15, 1956; children—David, Elizabeth. B.A., U. S.D., 1954, M.A., 1956; Ph.D., U. Kans., 1964. Asst. instr. English U. S.D., 1954-56; asst. instr. English U. Kans., 1958-64; instr. U. Pa., Phila., 1964-66, asst. prof., 1966-69; asst. prof. English Colby Coll., Waterville, Maine, 1969-74, assoc. prof., 1974-80, prof., 1980-83, Charles A. Dana prof. Am. studies and English, 1983—, dir. Am. studies, 1971-87, 89—, chmn. dept. English, 1987-89. Book rev. editor Am. Quar., 1983-91; assoc. editor: Ency. of Polit. Parties and Elections in the U.S., 1991; contbr. articles to profl. jours. S.L. Whitcomb fellow, 1961-62; U. Kans. fellow, 1962-63; U. Pa. faculty research grantee, 1966-68; Humanities and Mellon grantee, 1973-79. Mem. MLA (New Eng. rep. del. assembly), Maine Humanities Council, Am. Studies Assn. Democrat. Roman Catholic. Home: 9 Martin Ave Waterville ME 04901-4625 Office: Colby Coll Dept English Waterville ME 04901

BASSETT, GLENN ARTHUR, management educator, consultant; b. Ft. Collins, Colo., Dec. 19, 1930; s. Glenn Willard and Rosalie Alberta (Morrish) B.; m. M.E. Gregory, May 9, 1952 (div. Aug. 1977); children: Glenn Arthur Jr., Glenna Lynn; m. Olivette Irene Potts, Aug. 20, 1977; children: John Alfred, Olivette Irene. BA, U. Calif., Berkeley, 1954; PhD, Yale U., 1978. Pers. dir. Climax (Colo.) Molybdenum Co., 1960-62; cons. GE, Fairfield, Conn., 1962-79; prof. mgmt. U. Bridgeport, Conn., 1979—; cons. Orgn. Diagnostics Inc., Lyme, Conn., 1978—. Author: Practical Interviewing: A Handbook for Managers, 1965, Management Sytles in Transition, 1966, The New Face of Communication, 1968, Personnel Systems and Data Management, 1971, The Problem Employee Interview, 1975, Managerial Communication: How To Master It, 1976, Management Strategies for Today's Project Shop Economy, 1991; contbr. articles to profl. jours., chpts. to books. Chmn. bd. trustees Southport (Conn.) Congl. Ch., 1987-90. Mem. Acad. Mgmt., Soc. for Indsl. and Orgnl. Psychology, Prodn. and Ops. Mgmt. Soc., Rotary (bd. dirs. Bridgeport 1987-90). Home: 103 Shore Dr Rogers Lake W Lyme CT 06371 Office: U Bridgeport University Ave Bridgeport CT 06604-5739

BASSETT, LAWRENCE C, management consultant; b. N.Y.C., Dec. 11, 1931; s. David Isaac and Genia Esther Bassett; m. Charlotte Corinne Margolis, Jan. 24, 1960; children: Wendy Jill, Craig Henrid, Heidi Jill, Evan Henrid. BA, NYU, 1953, MBA, 1958. Pers. mgr. Republic Carloading & Distbg. Co., N.Y.C., 1956-61; dir. pers. Clay Adams Inc., N.Y.C., 1961-63; asst. dir. pers. Montefiore Hosp. and Med. Ctr., N.Y.C., 1963-65; dir. pers. Hosp. for Joint Diseases and Med. Ctr., N.Y.C., 1965-67; sr. cons. Orgn. Resources Counselors Inc., N.Y.C., 1967-76; pres. Applied Leadership Tech. Inc., Bloomfield, N.J., 1976-86, The Bassett Cons. Group Inc., Thornwood, N.Y., 1986—; adj. prof. NYU, 1978—, Fairleigh Dickenson U., Teaneck, N.J., 1964-86; instr. Helene Fuld Sch. for Registered Nurses, N.Y.C., 1966-67. Author: Achieving Excellence, 1986; contbr. articles to profl. jours. Pres., v.p. Mt. Pleasant Bd. Edn., Thornwood, N.Y., 1973-76, 81-87. With U.S. Army, 1953-55. Mem. Soc. Profl. Mgmt. Cons. (bd. dirs., v.p.), Inst. Mgmt. Cons. (cert. mgmt. cons.), Am. Soc. for Tng. and Devel., Am. Hosp. Assn., Am. Mgmt. Assn., Am. Arbitration Assn., Nat. Speakers Assn., Am. Seminar Leaders Assn. Lodge: Masons. Home and Office: 1 Ilana Ln Thornwood NY 10594-2001

BASSMAN, BRUCE D., pyrotechnic choreographer, designer; b. N.Y.C., Oct. 1, 1941; s. Jacob and Jean (Greensport) B. BS, Emerson Coll., 1964. Stage mgr., lighting designer Profl. Theatre, 1963—; fireworks display designer, cons. pvt. practice, 1978-85; rep., resident designer Garden State Fireworks Inc., Millington, N.J., 1985-91; event design cons. Celebrations Internat., Inc., N.Y.C., 1992—; sec., bd. dirs. Celebrations Internat. Inc., N.Y.C., 1980-91; judge ann. competition Pyrotechnics Guild Internat. Inc., 1986-91. Mem. Pyrotechnics Guild Internat. (judge annual competition 1986-92), Assn. Indians in Am. (life). Jewish.

BASSOW, WHITMAN, environmental executive, journalist; b. N.Y.C., Jan. 7, 1921; s. Max and Nellie (Galanter) B.; m. Margit Schendel, Apr. 16, 1956 (div. 1971); 1 child, Fern Elizabeth; m. Mary Elizabeth Clifford, May 13, 1979. Staff corr. UPI, N.Y.C., Moscow, 1954-58; corr. CBS News, N.Y.C., 1959-60; chief corr. Newsweek mag., Moscow, 1960-62; corr. Newsweek mag., Paris, 1963-66; writer, editor Ford Found., N.Y.C., 1969-71; sr. pub. affairs officer Environment Conf., UN, N.Y.C., 1971-73; pres., founder World Environment Ctr., N.Y.C., 1974-89; pres. Whitman Bassow & Assocs., Inc., N.Y.C., 1990—; bd. dirs. Environ. BanCorp, Inc., Southport, Conn., 1990—, Alliance for Internat. Environ. Studies, Inc., Hartford, Conn., 1991—. Author: The Moscow Correspondents, 1988 (Best bk. on Fgn. Affairs award 1989), contbg. editor Environ. Protection mag., 1990—; contbr. articles on internat. environ. affairs to profl. publs. With USAAF, 1942-45, ETO. Fulbright fellow, France, 1949. Mem. Coun. Fgn. Rels. (Edward R. Murrow Press fellow 1958), Overseas Press Club (gov. 1992—). Home: 112 Milford Rd Guilford CT 06437-1728 Office: 655 3d Ave New York NY 10017-5617

BAST, JAMES LOUIS, manufacturing company executive; b. Balt., Apr. 19, 1936; s. Louis and Evelyn Frances (Alling) B.; m. Mary Margaret Griffin, June 13, 1959; children: Andrew Griffin, James Mark, Cynthia Elizabeth. B.A., Columbia U., 1958, B.S.M.E., 1959; M.B.A., NYU, 1968. With Pitney Bowes Inc., Stamford, Conn., 1963-72, 73-90, chief fin. officer, 1976-82, v.p. fin., contr., 1976-77, sr. v.p. fin. and adminstrn., 1977-82; pres. Pitney Bowes Bus. Systems, Stamford, Conn., 1987-90; pres., chief exec. officer Dictaphone Corp. subs. Pitney Bowes Inc., Rye, N.Y., 1982-87; pres., chief exec. officer A. B. Dick Co., Chgo., 1990-92; dir. controller Bunker Ramo Corp., Trumbull, Conn., 1972-73. Served to lt. USN, 1959-63. Home: 1440 N Lake Shore Dr Chicago IL 60610-1679

BASTEDO, WAYNE WEBSTER, lawyer; b. Oceanside, N.Y., July 13, 1948; s. Walter Jr. and Barbara Catherine (Manning) B.; m. Bina Shantilal Mistry, Dec. 29, 1978. AB in Polit. Sci. cum laude, Princeton U., 1970; postgrad., NYU, 1977-78; JD, Hofstra U., 1978; LLM, NYU, 1988; postgrad., Fairleigh Dickinson U., 1988—. Bar: N.Y. 1980. Mgr. adminstrv. Law Jour. Seminars Press, N.Y.C., 1978-79; editor decisions and legal digests N.Y. Law Jour., N.Y.C., 1979-81; sole practice N.Y.C., 1981-82; atty. Western Union Corp., Upper Saddle River, N.J., 1983—; cons. litigation Exxon Corp., N.Y.C., 1982; cons. litigation Western Union Corp., Upper Saddle River, 1983, mem. corp. restructuring staff 1986-91. Author: A Comparative Study of Soviet and American World Order Models, 1978, Who Has the Edge on Justice? Computer Services Alter Fair Play, 1979; assoc. editor Hofstra U. Law Rev. 1976-77; editor (directory series) Outside Counsel: Inside Director, 1976-81; contbr. articles to profl. jours. Mem. policy com. Roosevelt Island (N.Y.) Residents Assn., 1981-82. Served to lt. USN, 1970-75, Vietnam. N.Y. State Regents scholar, 1966-70, USN Officer Tng. scholar, 1967-70. Mem. ABA, N.Y. County Lawyers Assn. Democrat. Methodist. Home: Riviera Towers 6040 Boulevard E Apt 26-D West New York NJ 07093 Office: Western Union Corp Office Gen Counsel 1 Lake St Saddle River NJ 07458-1813

BASTINELLI, ALEXANDER RICHARD, marketing executive; b. Phillipsburg, N.J., Aug. 9, 1950; s. Walter and Mary (Azzalina) B.; m. Cheryl Diane LaBarr, June 29, 1974; children: Adrienne Faye, Ashley Dawn, Alyson Lynne. BS, Bloomsburg U., 1972. With Copy World, Inc., Reading, Pa., 1973-90, v.p., ptnr., 1978-90; v.p., ptnr. Copy World of Susquehanna, Inc., Lancaster, Pa., 1986-90; pres. Copy World Balt., Inc., 1990—; bd. dirs. Copy World; mem. dealer coun. Savin Corp., Stanford, Conn., 1981. Mem. Rep. Task Force, Washington, 1984—; mem. English First, Springfield, Va., 1988—. Recipient Disting. Salesman award Sales and Mktg. Exec. Assn., 1974-76. Mem. Berks County C. of C., Y-R Club, Reciprocity Club. Roman Catholic. Home: 23 Eastport Ct Lutherville Timonium MD 21093 Office: Copy World Balt Inc 1708 Whitehead Rd Baltimore MD 21207-4021

BATALLA, PEDRO RAMON, management consultant, investment banker; b. Lerida, Spain, Aug. 14, 1950; came to U.S., 1984; s. Pedro Batalla and Isabel Casanovas; m. Silvia Ghersa, Apr. 18, 1986. BS, Escuela Ingenieros, San Sebastian, Spain, 1973; MBA, IESE, Barcelona, Spain, 1975. Registered profl. engr., Spain. Mktg. dir. Blasberg Iberica, Barcelona, 1975-78; cons. The MAC Group, Cambridge, Mass., 1978-82; v.p. The MAC Group, Washington, 1982-90, Italy, 1986-90; head Rome office The MAC Group, 1986-89; investment banker IFC, Washington, 1990—. Contbr. articles to profl. jours. Mem. Am. C. of C. in Italy, Rome, 1988. With Spanish Army, 1972-73. Mem. Turnaround Mgmt. Assn. Home: 5 Seline Ct Potomac MD 20854-2871 Office: IFC 1818 H St NW Washington DC 20433-0002

BATCH, MARY ARDEN, interior designer; b. Washington, Dec. 17, 1936; d. Charles Leo and Roberta Helena (Boswell) B. AA, Immaculata Jr. Coll., Washington, 1956. Lic. interior designer. Exec. sec. Matson Navigation Co., Washington, 1956-59; adminstrv. asst. A.L. Wheeer, Washington, 1960-73; conf. asst. to Gen. Counsel SBA, Washington, 1973-75; confidential asst. to solicitor U.S. Dept. of the Interior, Washington, 1975-77; owner Robechar Ltd., Bethesda, Md., 1977—; design cons. Brit. Govt., London and Washington, 1983—. Recipient Sr. Teresa Aloyse Outstanding Alumni award Immaculata Coll., 1970. Mem. Japan Internat. Christian Univ. Found., The Washington Club (bd. govs.), John Carroll Soc., John Beale Davidge Alliance U. Md., Immaculata Alumnae Assn. Republican. Roman Catholic. Office: Robechar Ltd PO Box 15158 Chevy Chase MD 20825

BATCHELOR, BETSEY ANN, artist, educator; b. Wilmington, Del., Dec. 12, 1952; d. Vance Roberts and Elizabeth Ann (Lemmon) B.; m. John W. Ferris, Oct. 23, 1989. BFA, Phila. Coll. Art, 1975; MFA, R.I. Sch. of Design, 1977. Asst. prof. Millersville (Pa.) U., 1983; artist in residence Munson-Williams Proctor Inst., Utica, N.Y., 1984-85; asst. prof. Swarthmore (Pa.) Coll., 1985-86, 89-90, Moore Coll. of Art, Phila., 1986-89, Beaver Coll., Glenside, Pa., 1990—. Group exhibitions at Woodmere Art Mus., Phila., 1990; one woman shows include Jessica Berwind Galley, 1989, 91, Swarthmore (Pa.) Coll., 1985, Matthews Hamilton Gallery, 1984; permanent collections at Cigna Corp., First National Bank of Chicago, Leif Johnson Collection, Jessica Berwind Collection. Recipient Artists fellowship R.I. State Coun. on the Arts, 1980, Pa. State Coun. on the Arts, 1984, Mac Dowell Colony, N.H., 1984.

BATCHO, ANDREW DAVID, chemist, researcher; b. Somerville, N.J., July 9, 1934; s. Andrew William Batcho and Madeline Dorothy (Pepe) Seigle; m. Lillian Elmira Loper, Jan. 24, 1970; 1 child, Andrea Elmira. BS, Rutgers U., 1955; PhD, U. Calif., Berkeley, 1959. Sr. chemist Am. Cyanamid Corp., Bound Brook, N.J., Am. Cyanamid Crop., New Castle, Pa., 1958-61; rsch. investigator Hoffmann-La Roche, Inc., Nutley, N.J., 1961—. Contbr. articles to profl. jours.; patentee 18 pharm. products. Mem. Am. Chem. Soc. Home: 19 White Oak Dr Caldwell NJ 07006-4123 Office: Hoffmann-La Roche Inc 340 Kingsland St Nutley NJ 07110

BATEMAN, CHRISTOPHER HALL, postal centers chain executive; b. Balt., July 27, 1958; s. Thomas Lee Bateman Jr. and Charlotte Miriam (Julier) Moore. BS in English, Towson State U., 1980. With Burger King, Balt., 1976-78, Hillendale Bowling Lanes, Towson, 1976-78; gen. mgr. Fair Lanes Pikesville, Md., 1978-83; sr. internal auditor Fair Lanes, Inc., Balt., 1983-87; pres., CEO Postman, Inc. T/A Postman Plus, Balt., 1989—; pres., chief exec. officer Bateman Plus, Inc. T/A Postman Plus Owings Mills, Md., 1987—, Postman Plus Couriers Inc., Balt., 1989—, Postman Plus, Inc., Balt., 1987—. Editor newsletter Postman Plus Network News. Actor Matthew Players. Recipient Red Ribbon award Royal Sch. of Ch. Music, 1969. Mem. Balt. County C. of C. (mem. exec. dialogue 1991—), Towson Bus. Assn., Parcel Shippers Assn., Assoc. Mail and Parcel Ctrs., Better Bus. Bur. of Balt., Matthews Players, Calvert Hall Coll. High Sch. Alumni Assn. (co-chmn. reunion com. 1981, 86, 91), Univ. Club. Democrat. Roman Catholic. Home: 1352 Walker Ave Baltimore MD 21239 Office: Postman Plus 1125 Cromwell Bridge Rd Baltimore MD 21204

BATEMAN, FRANK ELLIOT, interior designer; b. Brockton, Mass., Aug. 3, 1927; s. Leon Washburn and Hilda Juliana (Rantilla) B.; m. Barbara Lou Lindstrom, June 10, 1950 (div.); children: Pamela, Mark, Cynthia, Susan, Natalie; m. Judith Swan Littlefield, June 30, 1973; stepchildren: William, James. AB, Dartmouth Coll., 1948; MBA, Tuck U., 1949. Asst. buyer Abraham & Strauss, Bklyn., 1949-50; buyer Bateman's Dept. Store, Lexington, Mass., 1950-53, mgr. mdse., 1953-58, pres., gen. mgr., 1958-60, owner, gen. mgr., pres., 1962-66; field underwriter N.Y. Life Ins. Co., Waltham, Mass., 1960-61; asst. mgr. Jordan Marsh Co., Boston, 1961-62; owner, pres., designer Bateman's Home Decorating Ctr., Inc., Lexington, 1966-72; owner, designer Bateman's Interiors, Inc., Boxborough, Mass., 1972-89; owner, pres. In-Sol Inc., Boxborough, Mass., 1989-91, Fitzwilliam, N.H., 1991—. Patentee in field of thermal drapery system, thermally protective drapery constrn. for windows, sliding glass doors; inventor insulating fabric providing two reflectant air spaces. Served with USNR, 1945-47. Mem. Am. Soc. Interior Designers (chair membership com. New Eng. chpt. 1978-87, treas. 1983-85, Presdl. citation 1987), Soc. Cert. Kitchen Designers. Office: In-Sol Inc PO Box 594 Rockwood Pond Rd Fitzwilliam NH 03447

BATEMAN, MICHAEL JOHN, maintenance engineer; b. Oswego, N.Y., July 19, 1969. Student pub. schs., Oswego. Newspaper carrier Palladium Times, Oswego, 1979-82; grocery store clk. Price Chopper Co., Inc., Schenectady, 1986; head closer HNS Leasing, Syracuse, N.Y., 1989-90; maintenance engr. St. Mary's Ch./Sch., Oswego, 1990—. Author: (poems) Life, 1990 (Merit award 1990, 91), Alcoholic, 1990. Home: 155 Hamilton Homes Oswego NY 13126

BATES, BARBARA J. NEUNER, municipal official; b. Mt. Vernon, N.Y., Apr. 8, 1927; d. John Joseph William and Elsie May (Flint) Neuner; m. Herman Martin Bates, Jr., Mar. 25, 1950; children: Roberta Jean Bates Jamin, Herman Martin III, Jon Neuner. BA, Barnard Coll., 1947. Confidential clk. to supr. Town of Ossining, N.Y., 1960-63, receiver of taxes, 1971-90; pres. BNB Assocs., Briarcliff Manor, N.Y., 1963-83, Upper Nyack Realty Co., Inc., Briarcliff Manor, 1966-71. V.p. Ossining (N.Y.) Young Rep. Club, 1958; pres. Young Womens Rep. Club Westchester County (N.Y.), 1959-61; regional committeewoman N.Y. State Assn. Young Rep. Clubs, 1960-62; mem. Westchester County Rep. Com., 1963—; mem. Ossining Women's Rep. Club, 1960—, pres., 1984-85; mem. Westchester County Women's Rep. Club, 1957—. Mem. DAR, Jr. League Westchester-on-Hudson, N.Y. State Assn. Tax Receivers and Collectors, Receivers Taxes Assn. Westchester County (legis. liaison, v.p., pres. 1984-85), Hackley Sch. Mothers Assn. (pres. 1968), R.I. Hist. Soc., Ossining Hist. Soc., Ossining Bus. and Profl. Women's Club, Westchester County Hist. Soc., Briarcliff-Scarborough Hist. Soc. Congregationalist. Home: 78 Holbrook Ln Briarcliff Manor NY 10510-1122 also: 663 Reynolds Rd Chepachet RI 02814

BATES, DON, public relations and marketing executive; b. Boston, May 16, 1939; s. Clifford H. and Helen G. (McCormack) B.; m. Silvia Freschi, Dec. 31, 1984; 1 child, Francesca; 1 child from previous marriage, Kelly. BA summa cum laude, Northeastern U., 1965. Communications specialist Western Electric Co., N.Y.C., 1965-68; dir. public affairs Community Relations Conf. So. Calif., Los Angeles, 1968-69; publs. specialist McDonnell Douglas, L.A., 1969-70; dir. pub. relations Nat. Assn. Social Workers, Washington, 1970-73; dir. field ops. UN Assn., N.Y.C., 1973-74; exec. dir. Nat. Communications Council, N.Y.C., 1974-77; v.p. profl. devel. Pub. Relations Soc. Am., N.Y.C., 1977-79; v.p. communications Planned Parenthood Fedn. Am., N.Y.C., 1979-80; pres. Don Bates & Assocs., N.Y.C., 1980-83, The Bates Co., Inc., N.Y.C., 1983—; adj. prof. Columbia U. Sch. Social Work, 1977-78, New Sch. Social Rsch., 1978-91; instr. pub. rels. mgmt. program and profl. edn. seminars Bus. Mgmt. Programs, NYU; adminstr. Inst. Pub. Rels. Rsch. and Edn., 1981-90. Author: (with Anne L. New) Using Standards to Strengthen Public Relations, 1977, Communicating and Moneymaking, 1979; editor: New Technology and Public Relations , 1988, 91, The Public Relations Body of Knowledge, 1989, Public Relations and the Law, 1991; editor Channels Newsletter, 1974-80. Mem. pub. affairs com. Nat. Health Coun., 1975-77, nat. pub. rels. com. United Cerebral Palsy Assn., 1984-89, exec. coun. Nat. Soc. to Prevent Blindness, 1987-89; bd. dirs. Nat. Conf. Social Welfare, 1973-79, Quality of Life Found., 1975-77, Karen Horney Psychoanalytic Inst., 1976-79; trustee, sec. Inst. Pub. Rels. Rsch. and Edn., 1991—. Recipient newspaper fund award, 1963. Mem. Am. Soc. Assn. Execs., Pub. Rels. Soc. Am. (accredited), Am. Mktg. Assn., Northeastern U. Manhattan Alumni Club (pres. 1989—), Northeastern U. Nat. Coun., W.B. Yeats Soc. (bd. dirs. 1990—), James Joyce Soc. Armed Forces. Home: 150 E 18th St New York NY 10003-2444 Office: The Bates Co Inc 156 Fifth Ave New York NY 10010

BATES, JAMES EARL, college president; b. Ligonier, Pa., Aug. 10, 1923; s. Earl Barrington and Margaret (Kinsey) B.; m. Lauralou Courtney, Apr. 15, 1950; children: Susan Bates Jaren, Sara Bates Hudson, James Barrington, Willa Laurens. D.S.C., Temple U., 1946; D.P.M., Pa. Coll. Podiatric Medicine, 1970; Ed.D. (hon.), Franklin Pierce Coll., 1972. Practice podiatric medicine Phila., 1946-71; asso. prof. roentgenology Temple U., 1948-60; prof., pres. Pa. Coll. Podiatric Medicine, Phila., 1962—; cons. BHRD Region IX, HEW, San Francisco, 1973-74, Region V, Chgo., 1974-75; del. Nat. Commn. on Certifying Health Manpower; mem. health adv. com. HEW, 1972-73; adv. panel for podiatry Inst. Medicine, Nat. Acad. Scis., 1972-74; adv. council for comprehensive health planning Pa. Dept. Health, 1972-75, health manpower task force edn. com., 1976; mem. task force on health manpower distbn. Nat. Health Council, 1973, mem. com. on manpower, 1976-83; mem. Nat. Adv. Council on Health Professions Edn., 1983-87; cons. team So. Regional Ednl. Bd. Feasibility Study for So. Podiatry Sch., 1975-76; mem. Statewide Profl. Standards Rev. Council, 1976-82, Greater Phila. Com. for Med.-Pharm. Scis. Contbr. sci. articles to profl. jours. Trustee First United Meth. Ch. of Germantown, 1965-72, past chmn. fin. com.; v.p. bd. Germantown Businessmen's Assn., Disting. Service award, 1964; chmn. 277th and 278th Ann. Germantown Week, 1958-59; dep. service dir. Phila. CD Council, 1966-73; mem. Health Adv. Commn., Phila., 1976; past pres., bd. mgrs. Germantown YWCA; v.p. Phila. Boosters Assn.; trustee Univ. City Sci. Center, Phila. Served with M.C. AUS, World War II. Recipient citation Pa. Coll. Podiatric Medicine, 1970, citation Gov. Pa., 1973. Fellow Internat. Acad. Preventive Medicine (dir. 1973-78), Brit. Soc. Podiatric Medicine (hon. 1991—), Royal Soc. Health (Eng.), Am. Coll. Foot Roentgenologists (pres. 1958-59), Coll. Physicians Phila.; mem. Am. Podiatry Assn. (Merit award 1962, gen. chmn. Region Three Ann. Conv. 1975—), Pa. Podiatry Assn. (pres. 1959-60, Man of Yr. award 1961, Spl. citation 1973), Greater Phila. Podiatry Soc. (pres. 1955-56), Fedn. Assns. Schs. of Health Professions (pres. 1975-76), Am. Assn. Colls. Podiatric Medicine (pres. 1969-72), Pi Epsilon Delta, Pi Delta. Republican. Clubs: Greate Bay Country, Downtown, Union League. Office: Pa Coll Podiatric Medicine Race at 8th Sts Philadelphia PA 19107

BATES, PAMELA, data communications executive; b. New Rochelle, N.Y., May 4, 1953; d. Nicholas and Edna Theftecose. Student, N.Y. Inst. Tech., 1979-85. Data communications mgr. European Am. Bank, Uniondale, N.Y., 1979—; mem. telecommunications mgmt. adv. coun. Sch. Mgmt., N.Y. Inst. Tech., Westbury, 1988—. Mem. Nat. Systems Programmers Assn., L.I. Greenbelt Soc., Sierra Club. Office: European Am Bank EAB Plaza Uniondale NY 11555

BATES, RALPH SAMUEL, history educator; b. Oshkosh, Wis., June 19, 1906; s. Samuel and Alice (Burns) B.; m. Susie Mabell Thombs, Aug. 9, 1947; children—Thomas Samuel, James Ralph. AB, U. Rochester, 1927, AM, 1931; AM, Harvard U., 1930, PhD, 1938. Instr. history MIT, Cambridge, 1938-41, 46; instr. bibliography Brown U., Providence, 1946-47; prof. history Findlay Coll., Ohio, 1947-51; from instr. to prof. Bridgewater State Coll. (Mass.), 1952-76, prof. emeritus of history, 1976—. Author: Scientific Societies in the U.S., 1945; contbr. articles to profl. jours. Chmn., Bridgewater Hist. Commn. (Mass.), 1976-84. Served to 1st lt. U.S. Army, 1941-45. Mem. Mass. Archaeol. Soc. (pres. 1971-73, corr. sec., 1976-84, archivist, 1982—), Old Bridgewater (Mass.) Hist. Soc. (pres. 1957-76). Republican. Mem. United Ch. Christ. Home: 42 Leonard St Bridgewater MA 02324-2521

BATES, RICHARD DOANE, JR., chemistry educator, researcher; b. Elizabeth, N.J., July 24, 1944; s. Richard Doane and Sarah Newbold (Deacon) B.; m. Ruthann Iovanni, Mar. 13, 1971; children: Spencer Deacon, Dunlea Ristine. BA, Cornell U., 1966; MA, Columbia U., 1967, PhD, 1971. Asst. prof. chemistry Georgetown U., Washington, 1973-80, assoc. prof., 1980—. Contbr. articles to sci. jours. Vice pres. C.Z. Study Group, Schaumburg, Ill., 1980-86, pres., 1987—. 1st lt. U.S. Army, 1971-73. Predoctoral fellow NIH, 1967-70, Hammett travel fellow Columbia U., 1970. Mem. Am. Chem. Soc., Am. Phys. Soc., Royal Soc. Chemistry, Sigma Xi. Office: Georgetown U Dept Chemistry 606 Reiss Sci Bldg Washington DC 20057

BATHRICK, DAVID, foreign language educator, academic administrator; b. N.Y.C., Apr. 17, 1936; s. John Northrup and Margaret (Holmes) B.; m. Serafina Kent, July 1, 1960 (div. 1980); children: Jason, Brendan, Simon. BA, Dartmouth Coll., 1959; MA, U. Chgo., 1962, PhD, 1970. Instr. Lab. Sch. U. Chgo., 1961-67; asst. prof. St. Xavier Coll., Chgo., 1969-70; prof. U. Wis., Madison, 1970-87, Free U. of Berlin, 1982-83; prof. Cornell U., Ithaca, N.Y., 1987—, chmn. dept. German, 1991—; cons., reader in field; bd. dirs. Internat. Rsch. Exch. Bd., Princeton, N.J., 1986—. Author: Dialectic and the Early Brecht, 1976, Powers of Speech, 1992; author, editor: Modernity and the Text, 1989; editor, founder Jour. New German Critique, 1973—; contbr. articles to profl. jours. Internat. Rsch. Exch. Bd. fellow, 1982; Fulbright grantee, 1967-68. Mem. Am. Assn. German Tchrs., Am. Assn. Slavic Studies, Modern Lang. Assn., Internat. Brecht Soc. (v.p. 1980-81). Democrat. Home: 111 Stewart Ave Ithaca NY 14850-4513 Office: Cornell U Dept of German 183 Goldwin Smith Hall Ithaca NY 14853

BATISTA, KENNETH, educator; b. Pitts., Oct. 1, 1952. BFA, Columbus Coll. of Art & Design, 1975; MFA, Temple U., 1977. Inst. Kendall Coll. of Art & Design, Grand Rapids, Mich., 1977-78; asst. prof. Univ. Pitts., 1978-85, assoc. prof., 1985—; chair Univ. Pitts., 1987—. Pa. Coun. on the Arts fellow, Harrisburg, 1987; recipient Columbus Coll. of Art & Design Outstanding Alumni award, 1989. Mem. Nat. Assn. Schs. of Art & Design, Coll. Art Assn. Office: U Pitts Studio Arts Dept 104 Frick Fine Arts Pittsburgh PA 15260-7610

BATORSKI, JUDITH ANN, art association administrator; b. Eden, N.Y., Oct. 8, 1949; d. John Michael and Ethel (Owens) B.; m. Michael J. Rocco (div. Oct. 1980); 1 child, Flora. Student retail mgmt., Colo. Springs Coll. Bus., 1981; AS in Fine Arts, Suffolk Community Coll., 1983; BA, SUNY, Stonybrook, 1985, MA, 1987; postgrad., Columbia Coll. Chgo. Film Sch., 1985. Caretaker, asst. mgr. Farmer's Shared Home, Danbury, N.H., 1979-80; cert. educator Assn. for Childbirth at Home, Internat., L.A., 1980; accts. payable clk. Pikes Peak Community Coll., Colorado Springs, Colo., 1981-82; office mgr. Three Village Meals-on-Wheels, Stonybrook, 1984; grad. sec. art dept. SUNY, 1986-87, art gallery intern Fine Arts Ctr., 1987; dir. ops., dir. master classes and free concerts Islip Arts Coun., East Islip, N.Y., 1987-89; cons. N.Y. State Coun. on the Arts, N.Y.C., 1989—; participant Arts in Bus. Mgmt. seminar Citibank/ABC, N.Y.C., 1987, community leaders luncheon Fox Channel 5, N.Y.C., 1987; asst. to dir. Newsday's L.I. Summer Arts Festival '89 Community Affairs Dept., 1989, Suffolk County Motion Picture and TV Commn., Hauppauge, N.Y., 1988, 89, 90—, Summer Film Festival, 1988-90, cons. N.Y. State Coun. on Arts, 1989-90, cons., 1990-91; interior decorator Trans-Designs, 1992. Photographs included in Photography Forum's Coll. Photography Ann., 1985. Campaign dir. Food for Poland, Colorado Springs, 1982; organizer Granite State Alliance, Portsmouth, N.H., 1979, Safe 'n' Sound anti-nuclear campaign, Shoreham, N.Y., 1979; grad. rep. Sch. Continuing Edn. SUNY Stonybrook, judicial com. on acad. standing, SUNY Stonybrook, 1986-87; vol. Vietnam Vets. Theatre Ensemble, 1988, New Community Cinema, Huntington, N.Y., 1988; active exec. com. Dowling Coll. Spring Tribute Concert, Oakdale, N.Y., 1989; asst. to dir. Newsday Community Rels. Dept. L.I. Arts 89, 1989; founding mem. com. corr. L.I. Green Party, Brookhaven Twp., 1990—; participant Life in the Spirit seminar Cath. Charismatic Renewal, N.Y., 1992; tchr. Our Lady of Mt. Carmel Ch., N.Y., 1991—; active Pastoral Coun., 1992—. Mem. Internat. Platform Soc. (invited mem. 1989), Contemporary Hispanic Artists of L.I. (advisor to bd. dirs. Cen. Islip 1988-89). Roman Catholic. Home: # 2B 260-6 Waverly Ave Patchogue NY 11772

BATORY, STEPHEN STANLEY, marketing educator; b. Wilkes-Barre, Pa., Sept. 18, 1946; s. Stephen Frank and Helen Veronica (Kalafut) B.; m. Anne Marie Heineman, Feb. 1, 1969; children: Tairran Leigh, Stephen Stratford. BS, King's Coll., 1968; MBA, Old Dominion U., 1971; DBA, U. Md., 1981. Fin. loan adminstr. Export-Import Bank of U.S., Washington, 1971-72; adj. asst. prof. U. Md., College Park, 1973-80; assoc. prof. mktg. Bloomsburg (Pa.) U., 1981—; rsch. cons. Batory & Assocs., Dallas, Pa., 1986—. Contbr. articles to profl. jours.; reviewer acad. jours., 1989-91. Speaker Sml. Bus. Adminstrn., Wilkes-Barre, 1987—. Lt. USN, 1968-71, USNR, 1971—. Mem. Acad. Mktg. Sci., So. Mktg. Assn., S.W. Fedn. of Adminstrv. Sci., Sml. Bus. Inst. Dirs. Assn., U.S. Assn. Sml. Bus. En-

trepreneurs, Masons. Home: 22 Circle Dr Dallas PA 18612-9105 Office: Bloomsburg Univ Dept Mktg Bloomsburg PA 17815

BATT, RICHARD JAMES, geology educator; b. North Tonawanda, N.Y., Aug. 5, 1957; s. Melville J. and Gene A. (Stephey) B.; m. Suzanne E. Frusci, 1989; 1 child, Erika L. Batt. BA in Geology, SUNY, Buffalo, 1979; MS in Geology, U. Wyo., 1981; PhD in Geology, U. Colo., 1987; MS in Hydrogeology, Western Mich. U., 1989. Vis. asst. prof. Hope Coll., Holland, Mich., 1987-88; teaching faculty Western Mich. U., Kalamazoo, 1988-89; asst. prof. of geology Buffalo State Coll., 1989—; faculty advisor Buffalo State Coll. Geology Club, 1989—; guest speaker on paleontology, regional geology, and dinosaurs. Contbr. articles to profl. jours. Mem. Niagara River Action Com. for N.Y. Dept. of Environ. Conservation, 1990—. Mem. Geol. Soc. Am., Nat. Ground Water Assn., Nat. Wildlife Fedn., Am. Mus. Natural History, Buffalo Geol. Soc. (editor newsletter 1990—), Buffalo Assn. Profl. Geologists, Buffalo Zool. Soc., Buffalo Soc. Natural Scis. Office: Buffalo State Coll. Earth Scis Sci Edn Dept Buffalo NY 14222

BATT, RONALD ELMER, gynecologist; b. Buffalo, Sept. 24, 1933; s. Elmer Lawrence and Mary Catherine (Roll) B.; student Niagara U., 1951-54; M.D., U. Buffalo, 1958; m. Carol Mary Schaab, Dec. 28, 1957; children—Paula, Douglas, Thomas, Neil, Jennifer, John; m. 2d, Kathleen Over Cansdale, May 19, 1982; stepchildren—William, James, Suzanne, Timothy, John, Mark. Intern, Millard Fillmore Hosp., Buffalo, 1958-59; resident in obgyn SUNY, Buffalo, 1959-60, 62-66; research fellow Harvard U. Med. Sch., 1963-64; asst. in surgery Peter Bent Brigham Hosp., Boston, 1963-64; fellow in gynecologic surgery Mayo Clinic, 1965; practice medicine specializing in reproductive surgery, reproductive endocrinology, Buffalo, 1966—; clin. assoc. prof. gynecology SUNY Buffalo, co-founder Ctr. for Advanced Reproductive and Endometriosis Surgery, 1986. Served with M.C., USN, 1960-62. Fellow Royal Coll. Surgeons Can., Am. Coll. Obstetricians and Gynecologists, ACS; mem. Am. Fertility Soc., Soc. Reproductive Surgeons, Soc. Study Reproduction, Am. Assn. History Medicine, Internat. Soc. History Medicine, N.Am. Soc. for Pediatric and Adolescent Gynecology. Coauthor: The Chapel, 1979; Conservative Surgery for Endometriosis in the Infertile Couple, 1982; contbr. chpts. to books, articles to profl. jours. Office: 1000 Youngs Rd Buffalo NY 14221-2644

BATTAGLIA, JOSEPH PAUL, radio broadcast executive; b. Paterson, N.J., May 4, 1950; s. Paul and Connie (Migliarese) B.; m. P. LuAnn Lee. BS, Boston, 1972. Editor, pub. Alternatives Mag., Totowa, N.J., 1972-80; sales exec. Sta. WWDJ, Hackensack, N.J., 1974-82, gen. mgr., 1982—; sports editor Wayne (N.J.) Today, 1970, The Argus, West Milford, N.J., 1971; v.p. nat. sales and promotions Communicom Corp. Am., Hackensack, 1990. Author: A New Suit for Lazarus; columnist Contemporary Christian mag., 1978-81, 85-86. Bd. dirs. Walter Hoving Home, Garrison, N.Y., 1984—; trustee, bd. dirs. The King's Coll., Briarcliff Manor, N.Y., 1986—. Mem. Nat. Christian Radio Assn. (chmn. 1986—), Ea. Nat. Religious Broadcasters (bd. dirs. 1986—), Gospel Music Assn. (bd. dirs. 1980—, chmn. bd. 1991). Office: Sta WWDJ 167 Main St Hasbrouck Heights NJ 07604-2459

BATTAGLINI, FRANK PAUL, engineering company executive; b. Rochester, N.Y., May 31, 1944; s. Frank Paul and Elisa (Altobelli) B.; m. Helen Alexandra Grippo, Aug. 17, 1967 (div. Oct. 1985); children: Jennifer Jean, Melissa Ann, Frank Paul; m. Constance Jean Sparrer, Nov. 16, 1985. Grad. high sch., Fairport, N.Y.; student, Bradley U., Peoria, Ill., 1962-63. Account exec. TAD Tech. Service, Rochester, 1972-74; br. mgr. H.L. Yoh Co., Rochester, 1974-75, dist. mgr., 1975-83; div. mgr. CDI Corp., Rochester, 1983-86, v.p., N.E. div., 1986-87, sr. v.p., N.E. div., 1987—; corp. officer CDI Corp., Phila., 1986—. With USCG, 1966-72. Mem. Smithsonian Inst., Penfield Country Club, Safari Club Internat. Republican. Roman Catholic. Home: 4 Wenlock Rd Fairport NY 14450-3070 Office: CDI Corp NE Div 359 N Washington St Rochester NY 14625-2399

BATTAT, EMILE A., management executive; b. Mar. 17, 1938; s. Abe N. and Marguerite (Elias) B.; m. Vivian L. Masri, Apr. 12, 1964; children: Lisa, David. BS, MIT, 1959, MS, 1960; MBA, Harvard U., 1962. Mktg. analyst Standard Oil Co., N.Y.C. and N.J., 1962-65; mgr. corp. diversification Kaiser Aluminum, Oakland, Calif., 1965-69; v.p., dir. Kaiser Internat., Oakland, 1969-78; pres., chief exec. officer, dir. Minemet Inc., Stamford, Conn., 1978—; bd. dirs. Minemet Belgium, Alatenn Resources, Inc., Ala. Tenn. Pipeline Co., Coalco B.V., CTC-Minemet SA, CTC-Minemet Inc., Aleaciones No Ferrosas SA. Mem. Sigma Xi, Pi Tau Sigma, Tau Beta Pi. Office: Minemet Inc 6 Stamford Forum Stamford CT 06901-3202

BATTEN, WAYNE CARROLL, thermal engineer; b. Va. Beach, Va., Oct. 26, 1956; s. Dudley Wylie and Mary Phyllis (Reasor) B.; m. Kim Robin Fisher, Oct. 9, 1982; children: Laura Gaye, Jill Kristine. BSME, Old Dominion U., 1979; MSME, Ga. Inst. Tech., 1981. Analytical engr. Pratt & Whitney Aircraft Group, West Palm Beach, Fla., 1979; air conditioning engr. Am. Enka Co., Asheville, N.C., 1980; thermal analyst Westinghouse Electric Corp., Balt., 1981-84; thermal engr. Litton Systems, Inc., College Park, Md., 1984-89, GE Corp., East Windsor, N.J., 1989—. Mem. ASME, AIAA. Methodist. Home: 142 Sequoia Dr Newtown PA 18940-9240 Office: GE Astro Space Div PO Box 800 Princeton NJ 08543-0800

BATTERMAN, BORIS WILLIAM, physicist; b. N.Y.C., Aug. 25, 1930; children: Robert W., William E., Thomas A. Student, Cooper Union Coll., 1949-50, Technische Hochschule, Stuttgart, Germany; student (Fulbright scholar), 1953-54; S.B., Mass. Inst. Tech., 1952, Ph.D., 1956. Mem. tech. staff Bell Telephone Labs., Murray Hill, N.J., 1956-65; assoc. prof. Cornell U., 1965-67, prof. applied and engring. physics, 1967—, dir. Sch. Applied and Engring. Physics,, 1974-78, 1986—, dir. Synchrotron Radiation Lab. (CHESS),, 1978—, Walter S. Carpenter Jr. prof. engring., 1985—; cons. x-ray diffraction; mem. U.S.A. Nat. Com. Crystallography, Nat. Acad. Sci., 1969-72. Assoc. editor: Jour. Crystal Growth, 1964-74. Guggenheim fellow, 1971; Fulbright Hayes fellow, 1971; Alexander von Humboldt fellow, 1983. Fellow Am. Phys. Soc. Office: Cornell U Ithaca NY 14853

BATTIN, RICHARD HORACE, astronautical engineer; b. Atlantic City, Mar. 3, 1925; s. Horace Leslie and Martha Esther (Scheu) B.; m. Margery Katheryn Milne, Aug. 25, 1947; children: Thomas, Pamela, Jeffrey. BS, MIT, 1945, PhD, 1951. Instr. math. MIT, Cambridge, 1946-51, research mathematician Instrumentation Lab., 1951-56, adj. prof. aero. and astronautics, 1979—; sr. staff mem. Ops. Research Group, Arthur D. Little, Inc., Cambridge, 1956-58; tech. dir. Apollo Mission Devel.; assoc. dir. Instrumentation Lab., 1958-73; assoc. head NASA program dept. Charles Stark Draper Lab., Inc., 1973-87, mem. aerospace safety adv. panel, 1980-86. Author: (with J.H. Laning, Jr.) Random Processes in Automatic Control, 1956, Astronautical Guidance, 1964, An Introduction to the Mathematics and Methods of Astrodynamics, 1987; Mem. editorial com.: Celestial Mechanics, 1968-74. Pres. Project Impact, 1981-90; Mem. Lexington (Mass.) Town Meeting, 1956—; mem. Lexington Appropriations Com., 1958-64. Lt. (j.g.) Supply Corps USNR, 1945-46. Recipient Louis W. Hill Space Transp. award AIAA, 1972, Mechanics and Control of Flight award, AIAA, 1978; Superior Achievement award Inst. of Navigation, 1980; Teaching award dept. aeros. and astronautics M.I.T., 1981, Pendray Aerospace Lit. award, AIAA, 1987, von Karman Disting. Lectureship award in astronautics AIAA, 1989. Fellow AIAA (hon., assoc. editor jour. 1967-87, chmn. astrodynamics tech. com. 1978-80, dir. tech. 1979-82), Am. Astronautical Soc.; mem. Nat. Acad. Engring., Internat. Acad. Astronautics, Celestial Mechanics Inst., Sigma Xi, Hancock Men's Club (pres. 1974-76). Home: 15 Paul Revere Rd Lexington MA 02173-6632 Office: MIT 77 Massachusetts Ave Cambridge MA 02139-4307

BATTISTA, NICHOLAS RUDOLPH, bank executive; b. Bklyn., Aug. 23, 1951; s. Leonard and Jean (DiFilippi) B.; m. Ann Marie McNally, Aug. 17, 1974; children: Jocelyn Ann, Jill Nicole. BME, Pratt Inst., Bklyn., 1974; MBA, Fordham U., 1983. Registered profl. engr. N.Y. Mech. engr. Ebasco Svcs., Inc., N.Y.C., 1974-79, internat. mktg. rep., 1979-83, project fin. mgr., 1983-86; v.p. Swiss Bank Corp., N.Y.C., 1986-89, The CIT Group, N.Y.C., 1989—. Cons. Jr. Achievement, N.Y.C., 1991—. Republican. Office: The CIT Group 270 Park Ave 30th Fl New York NY 10017-2014

BATTJER, LAURA CATHERINE, computer consulting company executive; b. Jersey City, Jan. 6, 1951; d. William Joseph and Hannelora (Hicks) Bigley; m. Bruce Henry Battjer, Oct. 11, 1975; children: Christopher Bruce, Stephen Micheal. BA in Math. and Computer Sci., Douglass Coll., New Brunswick, N.J., 1973; MS in Engring. Mgmt., N.J. Inst. Tech., Newark, 1980. Engr. N.J. Bell Telephone, Clifton, 1973-76; data base mgr. N.J. Bell Telephone, Camden, 1976-78; computer cons., prin. Battjer and Assocs., Medford, N.J., 1983—; instr. Glassboro (N.J.) State Coll., 1986-88. Mem. Home and Sch. Assn., Medford, 1985—. Mem. Nat. Assn. Women Bus. Owners. Office: Battjer and Assocs One Lawrence Pl Ste 200 Medford NJ 08055

BATTON, KENNETH DUFF, federal agency administrator and consultant; b. Greenwood, S.C., May 30, 1942; s. Roy L. and Heppie Duff (Mayson) B.; BS, Mankato (Minn.) State U., 1970; m. Deborah Dean Solsaa, Feb. 14, 1965; children: James Stanislaus, Michele Dean; m. June L. Baker Anderson, July 22, 1989. EDP programmer operator Josten's, Inc., Owatonna, Minn., 1964-65; programmer, analyst, sr. analyst Mankato (Minn.) State U., 1965-70; EDP mgr. Associated Coll. Central Kans., 1971-72; EDP mgr. U. Va., Charlottesville, 1973-74; sr. mgr. U. Va. Med. Center, 1975-77; systems cons. Glen Raven Mills (N.C.), 1977; sr. assoc. PRC Data Services Co., McLean, Va., 1977-78; dep. project mgr. Computer Center, Exec. Office of Pres., Washington, 1978; project mgr. Alaska Fed. Data Processing Center, Anchorage, for PRC Govt. Info. Systems, McLean, Va., 1978-83, mgmt. analyst NASA Hdqrs., 1983-84, data base adminstr. NASA Sci. and Tech. Info. Ctr., 1984-85; prin. cons. govt. info. Systems Prince George's County, Md., 1985-86; principal cons. PRC/GIS NOAA GOES project, Washington, 1986-88; freelance cons., pub., researcher, 1988—; instr. computer sci. Associated Colls. of Cen. Kans., McPherson, 1971-72. Mem. Data Processing Mgmt. Assn. (chpt. pres. 1977). Republican.

BATTON, MONICA KIM, insurance company professional; b. Parkersburg, W.Va., July 3, 1956; d. William Ernest and Hope (Riddle) B.; 1 child, Jahda Hope. BA in Polit. Sci., W.Va. U., 1978; AA in Nursing, Wesley Coll., 1983; postgrad., Wilmington Coll., Georgetown, Del., 1988—. Res. librarian W.Va. U., Morgantown, 1978-79, tech. asst. II, 1979-80, tech. asst. I, 1980-81; nursing asst. Kent Gen. Hosp., Dover, Del., 1982-83, staff RN, 1983-86; rep. managed care Blue Cross & Blue Shield of Del., Dover, 1986-91; nurse cons. Aetna Life Ins. Co., Dover, 1991—. Chmn. pub. info. Am. Cancer Soc., Dover, 1985-86, chmn. pub. edn., 1986-87. Mem. NAFE, Gov.'s Coun. on Lifestyle and Fitness, Del. Assn. Utilization Mgmt. Profls.

BATTS, CONSTANCE BROOKS, psychiatric rehabilitation; b. Riverhead, N.Y., Sept. 9, 1954; d. Julius Barnett and Hattie Lee (Lancaster) Brooks; m. Gary Whitney Batts, May 16, 1987; 1 child, Dwaneti Aricqua. Diploma, Canarsie High Sch., Bklyn., 1972. Cert. remotivation therapy instr. II. Travel agt. Brentwood (N.Y.) Travel, 1974-75; food svc. worker Pilgrim Psychiatric Ctr., West Brentwood, N.Y., 1975, mental hygiene therapy aide, 1975-89, rehab. asst. I, 1989, rehab. asst. II, 1989-91, psychiatric rehab. team leader, 1991—; remotivation therapy cons. L.I. Devel. Ctr., Melville, N.Y., 1989, Bronx (N.Y.) Psychiat. Ctr., 1989. Exec. coun. mem. Wyandanch (N.Y.) PTA Coun., 1984; pres. Remotivators of L.I., West Brentwood, N.Y., 1986-87; pres. Bethel Day Care Parents Assn., Copiague, N.Y., 1981-82. Mem. Nat. Remotivation Therapy Orgn. (pres., past sec.). Home: 40 Belford Ave Bay Shore NY 11706 Office: Nat Remotivation Therapy Orgn Inc PO Box 361 Andover MA 01810

BATTY, GAYLE PRISCILLA, librarian; b. Marshalltown, Iowa, Aug. 7, 1936; d. Leroy and Gladys (James) Appelgate; m. Zia Araghi, June 18, 1961 (div. Sept. 1971); 1 child, Sarah; m. Charles David Batty, Dec. 12, 1974. Student, Park Coll., 1953-54, U. Iowa, Iowa City, 1959-61; BA, U. Colo., 1963; MLS, U. Md., 1969. Librarian, rsch. asst. Mountain States Employers' Coun., Denver, 1963-65; grad. asst. Sch. Library and Info. Svcs., Md., 1967-69; librarian, project dir. Herner & Co. Info. Cons., Washington, 1969-70; assoc. librarian Coll. Library and Info. Svcs., Md., 1970-72; law librarian KLGB&S Attorneys-at-Law, Beverly Hills, Calif., 1972-73; braille librarian Iowa Commn. for the Blind, 1973-74; librarian Iowa Dept. for the Blind (formerly Iowa Commn. for the Blind), Des Moines, 1988-89, librarian, supr., 1989-91; librarian McGill U. Redpath Library, Montreal, Que., 1975-76; v.p., info. sci. cons. CDB Enterprises, Inc., Md., 1977-87, 91—; info. sci. cons. Nat. Academy of Scis., Wash. 1980, P W Assocs., Coll. Park, 1977-79, Internat. Inst. Electricity, Cuernavaca, 1980-82, Food Mktg. Inst. Wash., 1983. Co-author: Reader in Research Methods for Librarianship, 1969, indexer, Directory of Training Consultants in Management, 1977, asst. editor, Ethnic Information Sources, 1979, indexer, Government Assistance Almanac, 1987. Democrat. Home: 11608 Gilsan St Silver Spring MD 20902-3123 Office: COB Enterprises Inc Silver Spring MD 20902

BAUER, BARBARA GAE, literary executive; b. Bklyn., Sept. 1, 1958; d. James Vincent and Gaetanina Antoinette (Palumbo) Mangano; m. Clinton Bonaventure Bauer; children: Guy, Lucy. BA, Hunter Coll., 1971; MA, St. John's U., N.Y.C., 1979, PhD, 1979. Pres., founder Barbara Bauer Lit. Agy., Matawan, N.J., 1979—. Democrat. Roman Catholic. Office: Barbara Bauer Lit Agy 179 Washington Ave Matawan NJ 07747-2944

BAUER, DANIEL GEORGE, communications company financial executive; b. Halifax, N.S., Can., Sept. 10, 1960; came to U.S., 1964.; s. Joseph John and Catherine Ann (Pickett) B. BBA, U. Toledo, 1982; MBA, Fordham U., 1988. In MIS/computer ops. Champion Spark Plug Co., Toledo, 1979-82; acctg. systems analyst Macmillan, Inc., N.Y.C., 1982-84; mgr. fin. planning CBS, Inc., N.Y.C., 1984-85; mgr. treasury dept.-credit leasing AT&T Co., Berkeley Heights, N.J., 1985-87, cash/fin., 1987-91, in corp. fin. and risk mgmt., 1991—. Vol. United Way Bergen County, N.J., 1984-85; active Ohio Hist. Soc., N.J. Hist. Soc., SBA. Recipient Small Bus Achievement award Kersher Elevator Co., 1982. Mem. Nat. Assn. Credit Mgmt. (chmn. fin. com. N.J. chpt. 1987-88), Nat. Corp. Cash Mgmt. Assn., Fin. Execs. Inst., Strategic Planning Inst., Am. Assn. Investment Mgmt. Rsch., Chatham Squash Club, Basking Ridge Country Club. Republican. Roman Catholic. Home: PO Box 753 Bedminster NJ 07921-0753 Office: AT&T 1 Oak Way Berkeley Heights NJ 07922-2727

BAUER, JOEL J., surgeon, educator; b. N.Y.C., Aug. 16, 1942; s. David W. and Toby B.; m. Judy Bauer, Dec. 3, 1967; children: Dana, Ross. BS, U. Vt., 1963; MD, NYU, 1967. Lic. physician, N.Y.; cert. Am. Bd. Surgery. Intern in surgery Mt. Sinai Hosp., N.Y.C., 1967-68, resident in surgery, 1968-72, chief resident in surgery, 1972-73, clin. asst. surgery, 1973-77, asst. attending surgeon, 1977-81, assoc. attending surgeon, 1981-88, attending surgeon, 1988—; instr. surgery to asst. clin. prof. to clin. prof. surgery Mt. Sinai Sch. Medicine, N.Y.C., 1972—; presenter in field. Contbr. articles to profl. jours. Fellow Am. Coll. Surgeons; mem. AMA, Assn. Acad. Surgery, Am. Coll. Gastroenterology, Am. Coll. Colon & Rectal Surgery, Soc. for Surgery fo teh Alimentary Tract, N.Y. Acad. Scis., N.Y. County Med. Soc., N.Y. Acad. Gastroenterology, N.Y. Soc. Colon & Rectal Surgeons, N.Y. Surg. Soc., N.Y. Acad. Medicine (sec. surg. sect. 1986-87, pres. surg. sect. 1987-88). Office: 25 E 69th St New York NY 10021-4925

BAUER, MARGARET SPEARLY, association executive; b. Bellefonte, Pa., Mar. 11, 1951; d. Ralph Frederick and Ella Mae (Gearhart) Spearly; m. James Richard Bauer; children: Abigail Elizabeth, Nathan Andrew. BS in Music Edn., Mansfield U., 1973; MA in Music History, Ind. U. of Pa., 1975; MLS, SUNY, Geneseo, 1979. Cert. assn. exec. Asst. libr. Bradford County Libr., Troy, Pa., 1976-79; libr. dir. Juniata County Libr., Mifflintown, Pa., 1979-83; cons. libr. State Libr. of Ohio, Columbus, 1983-84; exec. dir. Pa. Libr. Assn., Harrisburg, 1984—. Pres. of bd. Newport (Pa.) Pub. Libr., 1991; congl. advisor So. Pa. Dist., Ch. of the Brethren, New Oxford, 1990—. Recipient Cert. of Merit, Pa. Libr. Assn., 1991. Mem. ALA, Am. Soc. Assn. Execs., Pa. Soc. Assn. Execs. (bd. dirs. 1990—), Internat. Coun. Libr. Assn. Execs. (pres. 1989-90, treas. 1990—), Turbett Grange. Office: Pa Libr Assn 3107 N Front St Harrisburg PA 17110-1310

BAUER, MONICA ELIZABETH, political scientist, educator; b. Omaha, Nebr., Nov. 10, 1953; d. William F. and Leona T. (Liss) Teply; m. Neil F. Bauer, July 4, 1979; 1 child, Joanna. BA in History, Brown U., 1979; MDiv, Yale U., 1982; MA in Polit. Sci., U. Nebr., 1988, PhD in Polit. Sci., 1989. Vis. asst. prof. Williams Coll., Williamstown, Mass., 1989; asst. prof. Western New England Coll., Springfield, Mass., 1990—. Co-author: Financing the 1988 Elections, 1991. Vice chair Oxford (Mass.) Dem. Town Com., 1989—. With Nebr. Nat. Guard, 1976-79. Obermann fellow U. Iowa, 1991, Maud Hammond Fling fellow U. Nebr., 1987; recipient Ratcliffe-Hicks Debate prize Brown U., 1978. Mem. Am. Polit. Sci. Assn., Midwest Polit. Sci. Assn., New England Polit. Sci. Assn. Home: 3 Russell Ln Oxford MA 01540-2340 Office: Western New England Coll Springfield MA 01119

BAUER, NANCY ELAINE, marketing executive; b. Alexandria, Va., Sept. 4, 1953; d. Donald Robert and Geraldine (Pisko) B. BA, Glassboro State Coll., 1976, postgrad., 1977-78; postgrad., Rutgers U., 1979. Tchr. Gloucester Twp. Sch. Dist., Blackwood, N.J., 1976-80; group service mgr. Harrah's Holiday Inn Resort, Atlantic City, N.J., 1980-83; tour and travel dir. Resorts Internat. Hotel and Casino, Atlantic City, 1983-84, v.p. bus. devel., 1984-85, sr. v.p., 1987—; v.p. Trump's Castle Hotel and Casino, Atlantic City, 1985-87, Trump Taj Mahal, Atlantic City, 1990—; ednl. cons. Blackwood Ednl. Improvement Ctr., 1978-80; speaker Futures Unltd. at Camden County Coll., Blackwood, 1986-87. Author: (with others) Global Education, 1980; contbr. articles to profl. jours. Vol. learning disabled tchr., Runnemede, N.J., 1979. Grantee Fulbright Found./N.J. Dept. Edn. for "Project Kenya", 1979. Mem. Am. Mktg. Assn., Am. Mgmt. Assn., Am. Bus. Operators Assn., Promotion Mktg. Assn., Atlantic City C. of C. Home: 3071 Lenox Rd NE Apt 21 Atlanta GA 30324-2840 Office: Trump's Castle Huron and Brigantine Blvd Atlantic City NJ 08401

BAUER, NEIL STEPHEN, English educator; b. Cinn., July 2, 1943; s. Neil and Dorothea (Lynch) B.; m. Helen Margaret Pike, Oct. 5, 1974; children: Elizabeth, Anne. AB, Hamilton Coll., 1965; MA, Columbia U., 1966, PhD, 1971. Adminstrv. dir. British Am. Ednl. Found., N.Y.C., 1977-90; adjunct assoc. prof. English Manhattanville Coll., Purchase, N.Y., 1985—; exec. dir. Bristish Am. Endl. Found., N.Y.C., 1990—; dir. Harrow Sch. Found., Greenwich, Conn., 1989—. Author: William Wordsworth: A Reference Guide to British Criticism, 1793-1899, 1978; contbr. articles to profl. jours. Mem. Ojibway Club, Williams Club. Episcopalian. Office: British American Ednl Found 135 E 65th St New York NY 10021

BAUER, NORMAN JAMES, education educator; b. Milw., June 13, 1929; s. Hugo Andrew and Erna Theresa (Gocker) B.; m. Betty Jane Zwicky, Dec. 26, 1953; children: Michael James, Barbara Ann. BS, Wis. State Coll., 1953; MA, Northwestern U., 1956; EdD, Ind. U., 1964. Cert. elem., secondary tchr., Wis., sch. adminstr., Wis. Tchr. English, world history jr. and sr. high schs. Ripon, Wis., 1953; tchr. sci., math. Horace Mann Jr. High Sch., West Allis, Wis., 1954-57; instr. then asst. prof. Lab. Sch. Ea. Ill. U., Charleston, 1957-62; teaching assoc. Sch. Edn. Ind. U., Bloomington, 1962-64; dir. Lab. Sch. U. Wis., Oshkosh, 1964-67; prof., chmn. dept. curriculum and instrn. SUNY, Geneseo, 1967-71, prof. edn., 1971—, dir. video studies, 1985—; adj. prof. SUNY, Buffalo, 1974-77. Contbr. articles to profl. jours. V.p. program Rochester (N.Y.) chpt. Americans United for Separation Ch. and State, 1982—, mem. nat. adv. coun., 1985—; bd. dirs. Citizens for Religious Liberty and Pub. Edn., 1991—. Recipient Meritorious Svc. award United U. Profs., Albany, N.Y., 1983, Eric Steele Meml. award Americans United, 1988. Mem. Am. Humanist Assn., Am. Ednl. Studies Assn., John Dewey Soc., N.Y. State Found. Edn. Assn. (pres. 1989-91), Phi Lambda Chi (hon.), Phi Delta Kappa (Chpt. Leadership award 1988). Democrat. Home: 28 Westview Cres Geneseo NY 14454-1012 Office: SUNY Geneseo NY 14454

BAUER, RAYMOND GALE, sales professional; b. Merchantville, N.J., June 19, 1934; s. Robert Irwin and Florence Winifred (Guyer) B.; A.A., Monmouth Coll., West Long Branch, N.J., 1955; B.B.A., U. Miami, 1958; m. Jayne Whitehead, Feb. 15, 1955; 1 dau., Linda Joan. Div. mgr. R.J. Reynolds Tobacco Co., Winston-Salem, N.C., 1959-68; Middle Atlantic mgr. U.S. Envelope Co., Springfield, Mass., 1968-74; div. sales mgr. Eastern Tablet Corp., Albany, N.Y., 1974-75; owner Ray Bauer Assos., mfrs. reps., Haddonfield, N.J., 1975—. With USAFR, 1959-64; officer Air Force Aux. Mem. Friends of Haddonfield (N.J.) Library, Haddonfield Civic Assn., Smithsonian Assos., Monmouth Coll., U. Miami alumni assns., Nat. Philatelic Soc., Am. Security Council, Air Force Assn., Am. Conservative Union, Am. Mgmt. Assn., Internat. Platform Assn., Lambda Sigma Tau, Lambda Chi Alpha. Clubs: Republican (Haddonfield), U.S. Senatorial, Arrowhead Racquet, Iron Rock Swim and Country. Home and Office: 132 Maple Ave Haddonfield NJ 08033-1432

BAUER, RICHARD CARLTON, nuclear engineer; b. Batavia, N.Y., July 15, 1944; s. Willard Ronald and Ethel Ann (Roth) B.; B.S. in Chem. Engring. (Clarkson Trustee scholar), Clarkson Coll. Tech., 1966; M. in Engring., Cornell U., 1968; Ph.D. in Nuclear Sci., Engring. (Bettis Doctoral Program fellow), Carnegie-Mellon U., 1974; cert. in bus. mgmt. Am. Mgmt. Assn. Extension Inst., 1989; m. Madeline Joy Amreich, June 28, 1969; children—Jason Todd, Cheryl Robyn. Technician, Graham Mfg. Co., Batavia, N.Y., summer 1965; engr. Linde div. Union Carbide Corp., Tonawanda, N.Y., summer 1966; hot cell operator asst. Cornell U., Ithaca, N.Y., 1967; engr. Bettis Atomic Power Lab. div. Westinghouse Corp., West Mifflin, Pa., 1968-73, sr. engr., 1973-78, staff engr., 1978, mgr. AIW performance analysis, 1979-82, AIW/S5G performance analysis, 1982-86, mgr. centralized safety and plant analysis support, 1986—; employee tng. lectr. reactor safety, sec. lab. reactor ops. safety com. Chmn. Cornell Secondary Schs., Pitts.; chmn. P.E.I. Pitts. Regents fellow, 1962; AEC spl. fellow, 1967; registered profl. engr., Pa.; cert. fallout shelter analyst, multiprotection designer. Mem. Nat. Soc. Profl. Engrs., Pa. Soc. Profl. Engrs. (chmn. sustaining assocs. com., dir. chpt. 1981-83, 2d v.p. 1984, 1st v.p. 1985, chpt. pres. 1987, chpt. past pres. 1988, alt. state dir. 1989, state dir. 1990—, Mathcounts com. 1984, chpt. award for meritorious service 1984), Cornell Soc. Engrs. (regional v.p. 1970-83), Am. Nuclear Soc., Am. Mgmt. Assn., N.Y. Acad. Scis., Am. Inst. Chem. Engrs., Soc. Am. Mil. Engrs., Tau Beta Pi, Sigma Xi, Omega Chi Epsilon, Triangle Frat. Contbr. articles to sci. jours.

BAUER, ROBERT MICHAEL, orthopedic surgeon; b. Buffalo, May 2, 1953; s. Donald Francis and Gertrude Mary (Roarke) B.; m. Mary Jo Viragliano, Aug. 15, 1975; children: Robert, Michael, Jennifer. BA, Canisius Coll., Buffalo, 1975; MD, Wayne State U., 1981. Diplomate Am. Bd. Othopedic Surgery. Intern, resident Mt. Carmel Hosp., Detroit, 1981-86; pvt. practice Lockport, N.Y., 1986—; mem. staff Lockport Hosp., Neutone Hosp. Bd. dirs. Lockport (N.Y.) Hosp., 1990—. Fellow Am. Acad. Orthopedic Surgeons; mem AMA, N.Y. State Soc. Orthopedic Surgeons, N.Y. State Med. Soc., Niagara County Med. Soc. Roman Catholic. Office: 445 E Market St Lockport NY 14094-2598

BAUER, RUTH WARFIELD, elementary school educator; b. Bristol, Conn., Mar. 11, 1936; d. Charles Henry and Ruby (Martin) Warfield; m. June 22, 1958; children: Hans H. Bauer Jr., Paul M., Betsy. BA, Bates Coll., 1957; MS, Yeshiva U., 1958; cert. advanced study, Conn. Wesleyan U., 1978; PhD, U. Conn., 1988. Tchr. elem. and spl. edn. South Providence Elem. Sch., 1958-61; pvt. tutor, substitute tchr. Cheshire, Conn., 1961-68; dir. music 1st Congl. Ch., Cheshire, 1965-70, interim dir. music, 1979; tchr. elem. Chapman Sch., Cheshire, 1968-71, Highland Sch., Cheshire, 1971-81; tchr. elem. and English Dodd Jr. High Sch., Cheshire, 1981-91; edn. cons., 1991—; adj. prof. L.I. U., 1992—; mem. Town of Cheshire Mid. Sch. Com., 1987—; tchr., trainer Beginner Educator Support & Tng., Conn. State Dept. Edn., 1988—. Presenter Nat. Conv. Madeleine L'Engle, Washington, 1982; site visitor Blue Ribbon Schs. Program U.S. Dept. Edn., Washington, 1989—. Mem. NEA, Nat. Coun. Tchrs. of English, Conn. Edn. Assn., Edn. Assn. of Cheshire, Phi Delta Kappa, Delta Kappa Gamma (1st v.p.). Home and office: 1213 Avon Blvd Cheshire CT 06410-3607

BAUGH, CONSTANCE MARIE, clergy member, educator, consultant; b. McKeesport, Pa., July 22, 1949; d. Charles Edward Baugh and Mary Ellen (Englert) Harvey. BA, Pa. State U., 1971; MDiv, Union Theol. Sem., 1976; postgrad., Columbia U., 1982. Program specialist N.Y.C. Dept. of Corrections, 1973-77; asst. minister Central Presbyn. Ch., N.Y.C., 1977-86; founder, exec. dir. Citizen Advocates for Justice, Inc., Bklyn., 1978-86; founder, pastor The Ch. of Gethsemane, Bklyn., 1986—; cons. Nat. Presbyn. Criminal Justice Program, Louisville, 1990—, Interreligious Task Force on Criminal Justice, 1991—; adj. prof. Coll. New Rochelle (N.Y.), 1977-84; bd. dirs., pres. Citizen Advocates for Justice, Inc., 1986—; lectr. in field. Author: Women in Jail and Prison: A Training Manual for Volunteer Advocates, 1985; contbr. articles to profl. jours. Mem. Women in Criminal Justice, N.Y.C., 1981—. Recipient Humanitarian award Bklyn. Coun. of

Chs. Mem. Feminist Ethicists of the N.E. Democrat. Presbyterian. Office: The Church of Gethsemane 1012 8th Ave Brooklyn NY 11215-4312

BAUGHMAN, JAMES ALLAN, religious organization administrator; b. Savannah, Ga., July 29, 1951; s. James Allan and Pauline (Graff) B.; m. Mija Han, Jan. 8, 1980; children: Jimi Pauline, Nari Linette, Yuri Frances. BA in Physics, Benedictine Coll., 1973; MS in Physics, Kans. State U., 1975; MA in Polit. Sci., Drew U., 1985, PhD in Religion and Sociology, 1991. Instr. in physics Maur Hill High Sch., Atchison, Kans., 1973, Kans. Sch. for Blind, Kansas City, 1975, Drew U./Bros. Coll., Madison, N.J., 1979-84; instr. physics and chemistry Manhattan (Kans.) High Sch., 1974; GTA instr. in physics Kans. State U., Manhattan, 1973-75; instr. religious edn. Unification Theol. Sem., Barrytown, N.Y., 1973; exec. dir. Internat. Conf. on Unity of the Sci., N.Y.C., 1983—; pastor, religious instr. Unification Ch. Manhattan, N.Y.C., 1988—; pres. Unification Ch. Am., N.Y.C., 1989—; religious instr. Internat. Leadership Seminar, USSR, 1990—. Editor jour. Crysalis, 1980; assoc. editor Internat. Jour. on the Unity of the Scis., 1987—. Trustee Unification Theol. Sem., 1987—; mem. River Edge (N.J.) Bd. Elections, 1988-90. Mem. New Religious Ecumenical Assn., Profs. World Peace Acad., Assn. Am. Acad. Scis., Soc. for Sci. Study of Religion. Office: ICF/ICUS 4 W 43rd St New York NY 10036

BAUGHN, STEVEN PEYTON, internist; b. Selma, Ala., Sept. 8, 1947; s. Julius Henry and Neil (Simmons) B.; m. Rosemary Spall, July 27, 1986; children: Sara Tyler, Peyton Joseph, Justin Michael. Student, U. Ariz., 1965-67; BA, U. Tex., 1969; MD, Baylor Coll. Medicine, 1973. Resident internal medicine Montefiore Hosp. and Med. Ctr., Bronx, 1973-76; internist Hill Health Ctr., New Haven, 1976-77, Martin Luther King Health Ctr., Bronx, 1977-81, MAP Med. Assocs., Ltd., Phila., 1981-82; med. dir., v.p., internist CAMcare Health Corp., Camden, N.J., 1982—; instr. medicine Yale Sch. Medicine, 1976-77, Albert Einstein Coll. Medicine, Bronx, 1977-81, Hahnemann Med. Sch., Phila., 1981-82. Recipient Physicians Recognition award, AMA, 1989. Mem. Am. Coll. of Physician Execs., Med. Group Mgmt. Assn., Clin. Dirs. Network (sec.),. Democrat. Presbyterian. Home: 212 Fox Ln Wallingford PA 19086 Office: CAMcare Health Ctr 130 Mickle Blvd Camden NJ 08103

BAUM, HOWARD BARRY, physician; b. Passaic, N.J., Feb. 14, 1952; s. Samuel and Ethel (Stuhlbach) B.; m. Carolyn Frey, Sept. 7, 1986; 1 child, Eric. AB summa cum laude, Dartmouth Coll., 1973; MD, Cornell U. Med. Coll., 1977. Diplomate Am. Bd. Internal Medicine and Gastroenterology. Resident internal medicine Dartmouth-Hitchcock Med. Ctr., Hanover, N.H., 1977-80; fellow in gastroenterology The N.Y. Hosp., Cornell Med. Ctr., N.Y.C., 1980-82; ptnr. Passaic (N.J.) Med. Assocs., PA, 1982—; trustee Passaic (N.J.) Valley Prof. Standards Review Orgn., 1983-84, Passaic (N.J.) Beth Israel Hosp., 1987—; dept. chief gastroenterology, Passaic Beth Israel Hosp., Gen. Hosp. Ctr. at Passaic, 1990-91; governing body Region One Health Planning Consortium, N.J., 1991—. Co-founder Doctors Against Misusing Passaic's Environ. Resources, 1985; trustee Jewish Fedn. Greater Clifton, Passaic, 1987—; steering com. PASS Plan, Passaic County, 1988—; v.p. Assn. Jewish Fedns. N.J., 1990—. Recipient Arthur Palmer prize Cornell Med. Coll., 1977; named Disting. Health Profl. United Passaic Orgn., 1987. Mem. ACP, Passaic County Med. Soc. (v.p. 1991-92), N.J. Med. Soc., N.J. Gastroenterology Soc., Phi Beta Kappa. Office: Passaic Med Assocs 540 Broadway Passaic NJ 07055

BAUM, LAURA, educator; b. N.Y.C., Jan. 3, 1948; d. Morton and Selma (Wallman) Berdy Roblin; children: Alexander Klabin, Samantha Klabin; m. Jules Baum, June 16, 1990. BS with distinction, Boston U., 1969, EdM, 1974; . Cert. spl. edn. adminstrn., moderate spl. needs children elem. edn., instr. perceptually handicapped, Mass. Tchr. spl. edn. middle and high schs. Wellesley (Mass.) Pub. Schs., 1969—; chmn. spl. svcs. dept. Wellesley Middle Sch., 1974-77; instr., supr. Lesley Coll., Cambridge, Mass., 1980-84, supr. spl. edn. student tchrs., 1980-84, instr., 1988-89; mentor, Curry Coll., Milton, Mass., 1988; pvt. practice assessment, evaluation and diagnosis, Wellesley, 1969—. Bd. dirs. Wellesley Community Children's Ctr., 1979—; mem. children/youth com. Mass. Dept. Mental Health and Mental Retardation, 1979-81; chmn. mental retardation com. 1981-82, co-chmn. community edn. com. 1982-84, bd. dirs., 1981-84. Mem. AAUW (1st v.p. Wellesley chpt. 1978-79), NEA, Mass. Tchr.'s Assn., Wellesley Tchr.'s Assn. Home: 81 Maugus Ave Wellesley MA 02181-7614 Office: Wellesley Middle Sch 50 Kingsbury St Wellesley MA 02181-4833

BAUM, RALPH AUGUSTUS, electronics company executive; b. N.Y.C., Aug. 18, 1932; s. August and Lydia (Voight) B.; m. Lenore Alice Baum, Jan. 11, 1958 (dec. Aug. 1979); children: Lauren, Karen; m. Cecilia Ann Baum, Jan. 4, 1990. BBA, CUNY, 1963. Staff, dir. contract adminstr. Kollsman Instrument Corp., Syosset, N.Y., 1957-75; v.p. contract adminstr. ILC Data Device Corp, Bohemia, N.Y., 1975-91; v.p. svc. quality ILC Data Device Corp, Bohemia, 1991—; bd. dirs. L.I. Forum for Tech., 1988—. Sgt. U.S. Army, 1955-57. Mem. Nat. Contract Mgmt. Assn. (bd. dirs. 1983-88, cert. profl. contract mgr.), Am. Electronics Assn. (exec. coun. N.Y./Conn. chpts. 1991—), L.I. Skidaddlers. Lutheran. Office: ILC Data Device Corp 105 Wilbur Pl Bohemia NY 11716-2482

BAUM, RAYMOND NATHAN, lawyer; b. Pitts., Mar. 5, 1944; s. Ludwig and Margarete (Mueller) B.; m. Harriet Davidson, Aug. 23, 1968; children: Erica Beth, Kevin Michael. BS, U. Pitts., 1965, JD, 1968. Bar: 1969. Asst. prof. Point Pk. Coll., Pitts., 1968-70; atty. advisor HUD, Pitts., 1970-72; assoc. Baskin, Flaherty, Elliott & Mannino, P.C., Pitts., 1973-78, ptnr., 1978-90; ptnr. Rose, Schmidt, Hasley & Di Salle, Pitts., 1990—; gen. counsel ACTION-Housing, Inc., Pitts., 1978—; lectr. Pa. Bar Inst., Allegheny County Bar Assn. Mem. evaluation steering com. Magnet Sch., 1982-83, Citizens Com. on Excellence, 1983-84, hon. com. for accreditation Pitts. Pub. Mid. Schs., 1986-87; bd. dirs. Pitts. Coun. Pub. Edn., 1985—, pres. 1988-89; chmn. community involvement in schs. task force, 1989—; pres. Pitts Fund for Arts Edn., 1988-89; mem. Allegheny Conf. on Community Devel. Bus Forum on Edn.; bd. dirs. Citizens League of S. Western Pa.; mem. review com. VI United Way of Allegheny County, 1986-89. Mem. ABA (real property probate and trust sect., corp., banking and bus. law sect., individual rights and responsibilities sect.), Allegheny County Bar Assn. (bldg. com., comml. lease com., asst. treas. real property sect., chmn. legis. com.), Pa. Bar Assn. (real property probate and trust law sect., environ. law com.), Rivers Club. Office: Rose Schmidt Hasley & Di Salle PC 900 Oliver Pittsburgh PA 15222-2404

BAUM, RICHARD THEODORE, engineering executive; b. N.Y.C., Oct. 3, 1919. BA, Columbia U., 1940, BS, 1941, MS, 1948. Registered profl. engr., N.Y., D.C., and 20 other states, Nat. Bur. Engring. Registration. Engr. Electric Boat Co., Groton, Conn., 1941-43; with Jaros, Baum & Bolles, N.Y.C., 1946—, ptnr., 1958-86, ptnr. emeritus, cons. to firm, 1986—; mem. adv. coun., faculty of engring. and applied sci. Columbia U., N.Y.C., 1972—. 1st lt. USAAF, 1943-46. Egleston medalist Columbia U., 1985. Fellow ASME, ASHRAE, Am. Cons. Engrs. Coun.; mem. NAE (mech. engring. peer com. 1991—), NSPE, Nat. Soc. Energy Engrs., NRC (chmn. bldg. rsch. bd. 1987-91), Am. arbitration Assn. (panel arbitrators 1973—, bd. dirs. 1987-91), Coun. on Tall Bldgs. and Urban Habitat (vice chmn. N.Am. chpt., steering group 1991), Univ. Club N.Y.C. (steering group 1991). Office: Jaros Baum & Bolles 345 Park Ave New York NY 10154-0002

BAUMAN, BERNARD DANIEL, chemical company executive; b. Rochester, N.Y., June 15, 1946; s. Bernard J. and Florence (Fridd) B.; m. Ann Marie Bellotti, Oct. 1, 1983; children: Sarah, Brenden, Justin. BA in Chemistry, Ea. Nazarene Coll., Quincy, Mass., 1968; PhD in Chemistry, SUNY, Albany, 1973. Postdoctoral scholar Pa. State U., State College, 1973-74; sr. rsch. chemist Rohm and Haas Corp., Springhouse, Pa., 1974-76; sr. rsch. chemist Air Products & Chems. Inc., Allentown, Pa., 1976-79, sect. mgr., 1979-80, tech. mgr., 1980-85, mgr. tech. and comml. devel., 1985-88, venture mgr., 1988—. Recipient R&D 100 award for new product R&D mag., 1990. Mem. Soc. Plastics Engrs. (treas. Lehigh Valley sect. 1987—). Home: RR 2 Emmaus PA 18049-9802 Office: Air Products & Chems Inc 7201 Hamilton Blvd Allentown PA 18195-9642

BAUMAN, DALE ELTON, nutritional biochemistry educator; b. Detroit, Dec. 26, 1942; s. Elton Blaine and Waneta Mary (Taylor) B.; m. L. Marie Vinande, Aug. 28, 1965; children: Rebecca, Todd, Jeffrey. B.S., Mich. State U., 1964, M.S., 1968; Ph.D., U. Ill., 1969. Asst. prof., assoc. prof. U. Ill.-Urbana, 1969-78; vis. prof. Mich. State U., East Lansing, 1978; assoc. prof., then prof. Cornell U., Ithaca, N.Y., 1979—, Liberty Hyde Bailey prof., 1987; mem. U.S. Bd. Agr., U.S. Com. Biotech. Contbr. articles to profl. jours. Leader and scoutmaster Boy Scouts Am., Mich., N.Y., 1978-83. Recipient N.Y. Farmers award, 1982, Alexander von Humboldt award, 1985, USDA Superior Service award, 1986. Mem. Am. Dairy Sci. Assn. (Nat. Student award 1967, Nutrition Research award 1982, Biotech. award 1987), Am. Soc. Animal Sci. (Young Scientist award 1977), Am. Inst. Nutrition, Nat. Acad. Scis. Methodist. Home: 2 Eagleshead Rd Ithaca NY 14850-9659 Office: Cornell U 262 Morrison Ithaca NY 14853

BAUMAN, MARK LEE, podiatrist; b. Bronx, N.Y., Dec. 14, 1952; s. Jerrold Paul and Helen M. (Goldin) B.; m. Terri Ann Maurer, Aug. 31, 1974; children: Erica, Jaime. BS, CCNY, 1973; MS, C.W. Post Coll., 1974; D of Podiatric Medicine, Pa. Coll. Podiatric Medicine, 1978. Diplomate Am. Bd. Podiatric Surgery. Podiatry resident James G. Giuffre Med. Ctr., Phila., 1978-80; pres., podiatrist Mexford Leas Podiatry Assocs., Cherry Hill, N.J., 1980—; panel cons. Medig Rev. Svcs., Inc., Mt. Laurel, N.J., 1991—; med. opinion cons. to ins. cos., 1989—. Contbr. articles to profl. jours.; patentee in field. Pres. Men's Club Congregation Beth Jacob-Beth Israel, Merchantville, N.J., 1980-81; chmn. ritual com. Congregation Beth Tikvah, Marlton, N.J., 1989-92, v.p. ritual and adult edn., 1992. Fellow Am. Coll. Foot Surgeons; mem. Am. Podiatric Med. Assn. Democrat. Jewish. Office: Wexfordleas Podiatry Assocs 1949 E Marlton Pike # 7 Cherry Hill NJ 08003-2145

BAUMANN, DANIEL H., JR., sales executive business products; b. Summit, N.J., Jan. 3, 1969; s. Daniel H. and Jean (Bruce) B. Grad. high sch., Roselle, N.J. Pres. Time Recorder Assocs., Roselle Park, N.J., 1989—. Mem. Nat. Time Equipment Assn. (assoc.). Republican. Roman Catholic. Home: 304 Chestnut St Apt 3A Roselle Park NJ 07204-1955 Office: Time Recorder Assocs 9 W Grant Ave Roselle Park NJ 07204-1915

BAUMBACH, JONATHAN, creative writing academic director; b. N.Y.C., July 5, 1933; s. Harold and Ida Helen (Zackheim) B.; m. Georgia Brown, June 12, 1968 (div. May 1991); children: David, Nina, Noah, Nicholas. AB, Bklyn. Coll., 1955; MFA, Columbia U., 1956; PhD, Stanford U., 1961. Instr. Stanford (Calif.) U., 1958-60; asst. prof. Ohio State U., Columbus, 1961-64, NYU, N.Y.C., 1964-66; assoc. prof. Bklyn. Coll., CUNY, 1966-69, prof., 1969—, dir. MFA in creative writing, 1975—; vis. prof. U. Wash., Seattle, 1979-80, 85-86; bd. dirs. Tchrs. and Writers Collaborative, N.Y., 1971—. Author: The Landscape of Nightmare: Studies in the Contemporary American Novel, 1965, 66, Writers as Teachers/Teachers as Writers, 1970, (novels) A Man to Conjure With, 1965, 66, 68, What Comes Next, 1968, Reruns, 1974, 83, Babble, 1976, Chez Charlotte and Emily, 1979, My Father More or Less, 1982, Separate Hours, 1990, (story collections) Return of Service, 1979, The Life and Times of Major Fiction, 1987; co-editor: (with Arthur Edelstein) Moderns and Contemporaries, 1968, revised edit., 1977, (with P. Spielberg) Statements 2, 1979; editor: Statements: New Fiction, 1975. With U.S. Army, 1956-58. Creative Writing fellow NEA, 1968, Merrill Found., 1985; recipient Creative Writing award Guggenheim Found., 1980-81, O Henry prize Best Am. Short Stories Best of Tri Quarterly, Esquire mag. Mem. Nat. Soc. Film Critics (chmn. 1984-86), PEN. Democrat. Jewish. Office: Bklyn Coll Dept English Bedford Ave and Ave H Brooklyn NY 11226

BAUMEL, ABRAHAM, principal; b. Zloczow, Poland, Nov. 2, 1926; s. Harry and Molly (Spikulitzer) B.; m. Betty Fogel, Dec. 20, 1952; children: Judith Gail, Ellis Manuel, Sara Ann. BS, CCNY, 1948; MS, CUNY, 1959; MS in Physics, Manhattan Coll., 1969. Tchr. Morris High Sch., Bronx, N.Y., 1950-53, Jr. High Sch. 52, Bronx, 1953-57, Bronx High Sch. Sci., 1957-67; chmn. phys. sci. dept. Stuyvesant High Sch., N.Y.C., 1967-78; prin. New Dorp High Sch., S.I., N.Y., 1978-83, Stuyvesant High Sch., 1983—; adj. prof. physics Grad Sch. Edn./CCNY, 1966-70. Author: How to Improve Grades, 1964, Lab Manual Physics, 1977. Mem. Mayor's Commn. Sci. and Tech., N.Y.C., 1987. Sgt. AUS, 1945-46. Recipient Reliance award, 1992. Mem. AAAS, N.Y. Acad. Scis., N.Y.C. High Sch. Prins. Assn. (exec. bd. 1986), Nat. Assn. Secondary Sch. Prins., Nat. Geog. Soc., Phi Beta Kappa. Jewish. Office: Stuyvesant High Sch 345 E 15th St New York NY 10003-4098

BAUMEL, HERBERT, violinist, conductor; b. N.Y.C., Sept. 30, 1919; s. Leon and Fannie (Beckerman) B; m. Rachel Bail, Oct. 17, 1949 (div. Nov. 1970); children: Susan, Samuel, Mary Elizabeth (dec.); m. Joan Patricia French, July 11, 1971. Student, Mannes Sch. of Music, 1932-34; diploma, Curtis Inst. of Music, 1937-42; postgrad., Santa Cecilia, Accademia Chigiana, Rome and Siena, 1954-56. Violinist, concertmaster, conductor with orchs., chamber groups, Broadway shows, jazz ensembles, ballets, operas worldwide, 1939—; violinist/storyteller, 1970—; co-dir. Baumel Assocs., Yonkers, N.Y., 1984—; judge Fulbright Nat. Screening Com., 1965-67; guest artist Sponsors' Concerts of Dallas Chamber Music Soc., 1991, Internat. Piano Archives U. Md., College Park, Beveridge Webster Celebration Concert, 1991; lectr. Yonkers Pub. Libr., 1992, Greenburgh (N.Y.) Pub. Libr., 1992. Violinist Phila. Orch. with Ormandy, Toscanini, Walter, Monteux, Mitropoulos, Szell; first to play Samuel Barber's Violin Concerto with Curtis Symphony (Reiner), 1939 and Phila. Orch. (Ormandy); concert artist with: Stokowski, Stravinsky, Copland, Bernstein, Benny Goodman; concertmaster Phila. Opera, N.Y.C. Opera, N.Y.C. Ballet, Joe Bushkin Jazz Ensembles, (original Broadway musicals) New Girl in Town, Fiorello!, She Loves Me, Fiddler on the Roof, A Little Night Music, Rex, Dancin', also three Presdl. galas with Marilyn Monroe, Bill Cosby, Woody Allen, Jack Benny, Johnny Carson, Rudolph Nureyev, Margot Fonteyn; recs. with Heifetz, Horowitz, Rubinstein, Leonard Warren, Frank Sinatra, Edith Piaf, Tallulah Bankhead, many others; composer: Fiddlers Two, 1976, Caprice #48 1/2, 1978, Sentiment America, 1984, arranger 5 tunes from Fiddler on the Roof, 1971. Mem. adv. bd. Mark Brent Dolinsky Found., White Plains, N.Y., 1982—; played benefits for Westchester Assn. Retarded Citizens, 1982—, Coalition for the Homeless,Westchester County, N.Y., 1986—; guest artist Sponsor's Concerts of the Dallas Chamber Music Soc., 1991. Recipient Silver medal New York Music Week Assn., 1928, Gold medal New York Music Week Assn., 1929; 2-time Fulbright scholar to Rome, 1954-56; chosen for both Stokowski All-American Youth Orch. tours, S.Am., U.S., 1940, 41; chosen to organize, present and play concerts for U.S. Embassy and Cultural Offices throughout Italy with Anna Moffo, Ezio Flagello, Ivan Davis, Gimi Beni, and in honor of Queen Elisabeth of Belgium, 1954-56. Mem. Am. Fedn. Musicians, Curtis Inst. of Music Alumni Assn., Phila. Orch. Retirees and Friends. Democrat. Jewish. Home and Office: Baumel Assocs 86 Rosedale Rd Yonkers NY 10710-3033

BAUMEL, JOAN PATRICIA FRENCH, educator, author, lecturer; b. Winona, Minn., Mar. 12, 1930; d. William Oswald and Gertrude Marie (Fitzgerald) French; m. Herbert Baumel, July 11, 1971. Student, l'Ecole du Louvre, France, 1950-51; student with high honors, Institut de Phonetique, Sorbonne, 1950-51; student, Inste Phonétique, Sorbonne, Paris, 1950-51; BA magna cum laude, Douglass Coll., 1952; postgrad., U. Detroit, 1952-55, Case Western Reserve U., 1960, U. Akron, 1962, U. Notre Dame, 1963, Manhattanville Coll., 1971; MA in French, Rutgers U., 1965; PhD in Modern Langs., Fordham U., 1985. Tchr. French lang. and culture, elem., secondary, and coll. levels various schs. including Mother House of Religious of the Sacred Heart, Kenwood, Albany, N.Y., Ohio, Mich., 1955-66; tchr. French White Plains (N.Y.) Pub. High Sch., 1966-86; curricula creator Akron (Ohio) Pub. Schs.; co-dir. Baumel Assocs., Yonkers, N.Y., 1984—; dir. Women's Am. Ort, Scarsdale, N.Y., 1992; lectr. French lang. and culture Yonkers (N.Y.) Pub. Libr., 1992, Greenburgh (N.Y.) Pub. Libr., 1992, anti-Semitism CUNY Grad. Ctr., B'nai B'rith Internat. Mus., Washington, First Unitarian Soc., Westchester, N.Y., Rockland (N.Y.) Ctr. for Holocaust Studies, Unitarian Ch. of All Souls, N.Y.C., Temple Beth Israel, Port Washington, N.Y., Holocaust Resource Ctr. and Archives, Queensborough Community Coll., CUNY, 1991. Author: Paul Claudel and the Jews: A Study in Ambivalence, 1985; lectr. topics include French Anti-Semitism; The Gallic Road to the Concentration Camp; Klaus Barbie and the Children of Izieu; Americans in Paris: An Explosion of Genius in the 20s, numerous others. Mem. adv. bd. Mark Brent Dolinsky Meml. Found., Midchester Jewish Ctr., Yonkers, 1992, Cen. Queens YM & YWHA, N.Y.C., 1992. Recipient Woodrow Wilson fellowship, 1958-59. Mem. Am. Assn. Tchrs. French, Nat. Writers Union, White Plains (N.Y.) Tchrs. Assn., Am. Coun. Teaching Fgn. Langs., N.Y. State Assn. Fgn. Lang. Tchrs., French Inst./Alliance Fraciase, Alliance Francaise of Westchester, Phi Beta Kappa. Office: Baumel Assocs 86 Rosedale Rd Yonkers NY 10710-3033

BAUMGARTEN, REUBEN LAWRENCE, chemistry educator; b. N.Y.C., Nov. 19, 1934; s. Leon and Sonia (Jacobson) B.; m. Iris Marsha Lesson, Dec. 22, 1963; children: Lainie N., Steven C. BS cum laude, CCNY, 1956; MS, U. Mich., 1958, PhD, 1962. From instr. to assoc. prof. CUNY, Bronx, 1962-77, prof., 1977—; chmn. CUNY, 1978—. Author: Organic Chemistry: Brief Survey, 1977, Lab Exercises in Organic and Biological Chemistry, 1987. Mem. Am. Chem. Soc., Sigma Xi, Phi Lambda Upsilon. Jewish. Office: CUNY Lehman Coll Bedford Park Blvd W Bronx NY 10468-1539

BAUMRIN, JUDITH MARTI, psychologist; b. Longmont, Colo., Nov. 1, 1935; d. Fritz and Gertrude (Austin) Marti; m. Bernard Herbert Baumrin, Dec. 20, 1953; children: Seth Nathan, Rachel Austin. BA, Ohio State U., 1956; MA, Washington U., St. Louis, 1968, PhD, 1970; MA, Bank Street Coll., N.Y.C., 1979. Researcher sci. NYU, 1969-70; instr. Hunter Coll., 1970-72; asst. prof. CUNY, 1972-76; vis. asst. prof. U. Md., Balt., 1976-77; rsch. asst. Bank Street Coll., 1978-79; adj. asst. prof. Lehman Coll., 1980-81; asst. prof. doctoral faculty CUNY, 1988—; dir. Manhattan Ctr. for Learning, N.Y.C., 1979—; vol. faculty sch. medicine, Mt. Sinai, 1989; cons. Calhoun Sch., N.Y.C., 1986—. Contbr. articles to profl. jours. Mem. Am. Psychol. Assn. Orton Soc., Sigma Xi. Home: 590 W End Ave New York NY 10024-1722 Office: Manhattan Ctr for Learning 590 W End Ave New York NY 10024-1722

BAUMWELL, IVAN ADAM, ophthalmologist, educator; b. Flushing, N.Y., May 2, 1957. BS in Biochemistry, SUNY, Binghamton, 1978; MD, SUNY, Buffalo, 1982. Intern Millard Fillmore Hosp., 1982-83; intern ophthalmology SUNY, Buffalo, 1983-84; resident ophthalmology U. Mich., Ann Arbor, 1984-86; sr. med. staff Sewickley (Pa.) Valley Hosp., 1986—, Ohio Valley Gen. Hosp., McKees Rocks, Pa., 1986—; asst. clin. instr. dept. ophthalmology U. Pitts. Sch. Medicine, Montefiore U. Hosp., Pitts., 1987—. Mem. AMA, Am. Acad. Ophthalmology, Am. Soc. Cataract and Refractive Surgery, Contact Lens Assn. Ophthalmologists, Pa. Acad. Ophthalmology. Office: 527 Broad St Sewickley PA 15143 also: Med Office Bldg 27 Heckel Rd Ste 107 Mc Kees Rocks PA 15136

BAURS-KREY, DETLEV H. U., international management consultant; b. Berlin, July 13, 1943; U.S., permanent resident U.S., 1975; s. Reinhold W.H. and Ingeborg (Brauer) B-K.; B.B.A., U. Bonn, 1967; LL.M., U. Mainz, 1969; m. Kirsten Christine Geier, 1982. Mktg. trainee Pfizer, Inc., W.Ger., 1970; asst. to gen. mgr. H. Mack Nachf., W.Ger., 1971-74; mktg. mgr. Pfizer Internat., Inc., N.Y.C., 1974; v.p. Panta, Inc., internat. cons., N.Y.C., 1975-78; pres., chief exec. officer Euro-Am. Cons., Ltd., 1978—, also bd. dirs.; chmn., chief exec. officer Thermascan Inc. (Nasdaq) (formerly BCD Products, Inc.), N.Y.C., 1981—, also bd. dirs.; bd. dirs. Inter-Hermes Pharma, Inc., Miles USA, Inc.; minister plenipotentiary-at-large Republic of San Marino, 1985—; vis. prof. econs. and tech. transfer U. Francisco Marroquin, Guatemala, 1984; vice chmn. Internat. Symposium on AIDS, Republic of San Marino, 1988; mem. permanent sci. com. Annual San Marino Med. Confs., selection com. Annual San Marino Prize of Medicine. Mem. adv. bd. Am. Health Found., 1983, trustee, 1986; vice chmn., trustee Cultural Ctr., Village of Southampton, 1988. Decorated knight Order of St. Maria in Jerusalem, knight Sovereign Mil. Order of Malta, comdr. Order of St. Agatha, knight comdr. cross Order of Merit, Proclamation of the City of N.Y., 1988. Mem. German-Am. C. of C. (N.Y.), Am. C. of C. in Germany (Frankfurt), Fgn. Friends N.Y., Am. Council on Germany (N.Y.), N.Y. Fgn. Lawyers Assn., Metropolitan Club, Rockefeller Ctr. Club, Doubles Club (N.Y.C.), Lions (Wiesbaden, W.Ger.), Teutonic Order (knight comdr.), Sovereign Mil. Order of Malta. also: Euro-Am Cons Ltd Flying Point Rd Ste 200 Southampton NY 11968

BAUSCH, JAMES JOHN, foundation executive; b. New Brunswick, N.J., May 1, 1936; s. Charles John and Colette (Perdoni) B.; m. Janet Ellen Safer, May 22, 1970; children: Jennifer, David. Student, Fordham U., 1953-54; BS, St. Peter's Coll., 1955-58; postgrad., Emory U., 1958-61, Wharton Sch., U. Pa., 1977. Lectr. in social sci. Emory U., Ga. Inst. Tech., Atlanta, 1958-61; vol. U.S. Peace Corps, Bangladesh, 1961-63; chief U.S. Peace Corps South Asia div., Washington, 1965-69; dir. tng. Experiment in Internat. Living, Brattleboro, Vt., 1963-64; dir. edn. Coun. on Internat. Ednl. Exch., N.Y.C., 1964-65; program officer Ford Found., N.Y.C., 1969-71, 73-76; rep. Ford Found., Jakarta, Indonesia, 1971-73; v.p., sec. The Population Coun., N.Y.C., 1976-88; pres. Save the Children Fedn., Westport, Conn., 1988—; pres., dir. Mackay Ice Arena, Inc., Englewood, N.J., 1984—; trustee, mem. exec. com., chmn. fin. com., chmn. investment com., co-chmn. N.Y. Assocs. Experiment in Internat. Living, Brattleboro, Vt., 1980-88; trustee, sec.-treas. Internat. Child Health Found., Columbia, Md., 1985-87, chmn. bd. trustees, 1987—; pres., dir. Friends of Bangledesh, Wilmington, Del., 1986-92; mem. fin. com. Population Coun.; trustee Ctr. Pvt. Vol. Orgn./Univ. Collaboration, N.C., 1990—, Ind. Sector, Washington, 1991—. Mem. Bretton Woods Com., Washington, 1991—; chmn. UNICEF Action for Children, N.Y.C., 1986-89. Mem. AAAS, N.Y. Acad. Scis., Population Assn. Am., Am. Pub. health Assn., Nat. Coun. Internat. Health (mem. exec. com. 1991—), Carnegie Coun. on Ethics and Internat. Affairs. Democrat. Home: 706 Tulip Pl Westwood NJ 07675-6133 Office: Save The Children Fedn 54 Wilton Rd Westport CT 06880-3108

BAUSE, DAVID FRANCIS, printing company professional; b. Boyertown, Pa., Feb. 16, 1936; s. Daniel Eagle Sr. and Frances Margaret (Dieter) B.; m. Janice Elaine Croyle, Aug. 19, 1961; children: Erin Elaine Bause Landry, Amy F. Bause Bartra. BA in Communications, Am. U., 1957. Radio announcer Sta. WRAW, Reading, Pa., 1959-61; mdse. mgr. Bause Super Drug Stores, Boyertown, Pa., 1961-64; area dir. Dale Carnegie Courses, Phila., 1964-68; owner, operator Copy Fast Printing, Pottstown, Pa., 1968—; Instr. color photography Albright Coll., Reading, 1988; seminar presenter Nat. Assn. Quick Printers, Ill., 1985, N.J. Assn. Quick Printers, 1988. Author: Create Your Own Newsletter, 1985; editor Season, 1977— (Print award 1991); contbr. articles to profl. jours. Staff vol. Found. "I", Inc., 1989—. With U.S. Army, 1957-59. Scholar Am. U., 1956; recipient photog. awards Kodak, 1985, Individual Achievement award Freedoms Found., 1986. Mem. Internat. Jugglers Assn., Phila. Jugglers Club, Reading Jugglers Club (co-founder, coord.), Pottsgrove High Twelve Club (pres., sec. 1987-91), Pottstown Writer's Group (co-founder), Masons (25 Yr. award 1991), Omicron Delta Kappa. Republican. Lutheran. Home: 2156 Hill Camp Rd Pottstown PA 19464 Office: Copy Fast Printing 246 King St Pottstown PA 19464

BAUWIN, ROBERTA ELIZABETH, educational institution program administrator; b. Ashtabula, Ohio, Aug. 4, 1960; d. Robert Anthony and Marie Louise (Kastner) B. BA, Bluffton Coll., 1982; postgrad., Mont. State U., 1986-87; MA, No. Ariz. U., 1989. Human resources coord. TW Svcs., Yellowstone Nat. Park, Wyo., 1982-86; resident dir. Mont. State U., Bozeman, 1986-87; residence hall dir. No. Ariz. U., Flagstaff, 1987-89, Ohio State U., Columbus, 1989-90; asst. coord. student pers. SUNY, Binghamton, 1990—; consulting trainer Women's Ctr., Binghamton, 1990; cons. Corning (N.Y.) Community Coll., 1991, Lourdes Wellness Ctr., Binghamton, 1992; bd. dirs. Save Your Own Lives, Binghamton, 1992—. Co-author workbook in Breaking Co-Dependency series. Vol. YWCA, Binghamton, 1991-92, Mental Health Assn., Binghamton, 1992. Mem. Am. Coll. Pers. Assn. (directorate), Am. Assn. Counseling and Devel., Am. Mental Health Counseling Assn., Am. Multicultural Counseling Assn., Nat. Coun. Self-Esteem. Home: 7 Holland Ave Binghamton NY 13905 Office: SUNY Binghamton Residential Life Vestal Pkwy E Binghamton NY 13902

BAWDEN, HERBERT PERRY, JR., psychologist; b. Passaic, N.J., Apr. 27, 1943; s. Herbert P. and Agnes R. (Weglowski) B.; m. Donna Jean Hunter, Aug. 28, 1965; children: Jeffrey Allen, Jennifer Lynn, Stephanie Ann. BA in Psychology, Tusculum Coll., 1965; MS in Organizational Psychology, U. Tenn., 1969. Lic. psychologist, Pa.; diplomate Am. Bd. Vocat. Experts. Dir. spl. svcs. Personnel Rsch. Ctr., Phila., 1969-70; dir. ops. Wittreich Assocs., Inc., Phila., 1971; dir. spl. svcs. Personnel Rsch. Ctr., Phila., 1971-73; dir., sr. rsch. assoc., rsch. assoc., cons. Job Trials Rsch. Ctr., Phila., 1974-79; sect. rsch. specialist Colonial Penn Group, Phila., 1979-80;

rsch. assoc., cons. Pleasantville (N.Y.) Ednl. Supply Co., 1981-82; ptnr. Selection Systems Rsch., Southampton, Pa., 1979-83; mng. dir. Personnel Rsch. Ctr., Haverford, Pa., 1983-85; owner, pres. Personnel Rsch. Ctr., Horsham, Pa., 1985—; cons. Profl. Exam. Svc., N.Y.C., 1985—. Mem. Am. Psychol. Assn., Soc. Indsl. and Orgn. Psychology, Assn. Interest Measurement, Nat. Coun. Measurement in Edn., Eastern Psychol. Assn., Pa. Psychol. Assn. Home: 555 Buckstone Dr Southampton PA 18966-3617 Office: Personnel Rsch Ctr 316 Easton Rd Ste C Horsham PA 19044-2532

BAXTER, BRUCE OSBORNE, hotel executive; b. Washington, June 14, 1945; s. Charles Sayre and Ellie (Osborne) B.; m. Amanda Jane McKinney, Aug. 21, 1952. BA, Colgate U., Hamilton, N.Y., 1967. Pres. Bath Plantation, Ltd., Barbados, 1968-76; v.p. Resorts Mgmt., N.Y.C., 1976-82; pres. Flagship Hotels and Resorts Corp., N.Y.C., 1982—. Mem. West India Com., Caribbean Hotel Assn., N.Y. Hotel Execs. Club, Am. Soc. Travel Agts., Am. Assn. Travel Editors, S.R., St. Nicholas Soc., Windermere Island Club, Coral Beach and Tennis Club. Republican. Episcopalian. Home: 350 Old Oscaleta Rd South Salem NY 10590 Office: Flagship Hotels and Resorts 43 Kensico Dr Mount Kisco NY 10549

BAXTER, CATHERINE ELAINE, securities broker; b. N.Y.C., Jan. 2, 1964; d. Comer Cash and Betty Nan (Carpenter) B. BA, Duke U., 1986, MBA, 1987. Assoc. Morgan Stanley & Co., Inc., N.Y.C., 1987—; alumni coun. mem. Fuqua Sch. Bus., Durham, N.C.; alumni bd. dirs. Nightingale Bamford Sch., N.Y.C., mem. alumnae bd. Hockaday Sch., Dallas. Sec., bd. dirs. Vol. Svcs. for the Elderly of Yorkville, N.Y.C., 1991—; active Jr. League, N.Y.C., 1982—. Mem. NAFE, Am. Women's Econ. Devel. Assn. Republican. Presbyterian. Office: Morgan Stanley & Co Inc 1251 Avenue of the Americas New York NY 10021

BAXTER, ROBERT BANNING, insurance company administrator; b. Rochester, N.Y., Aug. 26, 1946; s. Robert Clarkson and Flora Corinne (Banning) B.; m. Sandra Anne Weber, Apr. 21, 1973; children: Matthew Hamilton, Darcy Colson, Jeffrey Ford. BA, U. Rochester, 1968. Chartered Property Casualty Underwriter; Cert. Ins. Counselor. Personal lines account underwriter Allstate Ins. Co., Rochester, 1973-77; asst. personal lines underwriting mgr. Reliance Ins. Co., Pitts., 1977-78; personal lines underwriting mgr. Reliance Ins. Co., Canandaigua, N.Y., 1978-79; regional personal lines underwriting mgr. Reliance Ins. Co., Cin., 1979-81, mktg. mgr., 1981-84; mktg. mgr. Hartford Ins. Group, Cleve., 1984-85; regional mktg. mgr. Nat. Grange Mut. Ins. Co., Syracuse, N.Y., 1985-88; asst. br. mgr., mktg. mgr. Gen. Accident Ins., Syracuse, 1988-90, br. mgr., 1990—; bd. dirs. GA Ins. Co. N.Y., Melville, PG Ins. Co. N.Y., Melville, Gen. Assurance Co., Melville. Capt. USAF, 1968-73, Thailand, also West Germany. Mem. Soc. Chartered Property Casualty Underwriters, Soc. Cert. Ins. Counselors, Ins. Mgrs. Coun. Syracuse (sec.-treas. 1992—), Ind. Ins. Agts. Assn. N.Y. (assoc.), Profl. Ins. Agts. N.Y. (assoc.), Honorable Order of Blue Goose Internat., Bellevue Country Club. Republican. Unitarian. Home: 5205 Winkworth Pky Syracuse NY 13215 Office: Gen Accident Ins 973 James St Syracuse NY 13203

BAXTER, VIOLET DIANE, artist; b. N.Y.C.; d. Meyer and Belle (Katz) B.; m. Martin J. Leff, Apr. 25, 1971; 1 child, Mara H. Leff. Cert., Cooper Union, 1960; student, Columbia U., 1961-62, Pratt Graphic Art Ctr., 1980-81. Solo show Aspects Gallery, N.Y.C., 1961, Brata Gallery, N.Y.C., 1962, Ruth Sherman Gallery, N.Y.C., 1963, Suffolk County Community Coll., Riverhead, N.Y., 1986, Cornerstone Gallery, Falls Village, Conn., 1990, Pleiades Gallery, N.Y.C., 85, 87, 89, 91; calligraphy mentor Pratt Inst., N.Y.C., 1974-75. Exhibited in group shows at Nat. Art Clubs, 1991, Heanah-Kent Gallery, 1991, Bowery Gallery, 1991, Cornerstone Gallery, 1991, Pen & Brush Club Invitational, 1991, Audubon Artists 49th Annual, 1991, Paper Mill Playhouse, 1991, Broome St. Gallery, 1990, Lever House, 1989, Nabisco Brands Gallery, 1988, Washington Irving Gallery, 1988, Sharon Creative Arts Foun. Gallery, 1987, Zenith Gallery, 1987, Nexus Found. for Today's Art, 1986, Monmouth Mus., 1985, Viewpoint Gallery, 1985. Recipient Highest Achievement in Art award The Cooper Union, 1960, award Dr.D. Rothschild Cornerstone Gallery, 1991, award Pastel Soc. Am., 1991. Mem. N.Y. Artists Equity Assn. (v.p. 1991, bd. dirs. 1988—), Am. Soc. Contemporary Artists. Home: 333 E 30th St Apt 18L New York NY 10016-6459 Studio: 41 Union Sq W New York NY 10003

BAXTER, WILLIAM G., counseling center director, counselor, mediator; b. Potsdam, N.Y., Aug. 26, 1952; m. Donna Marie Ionta, Oct. 27, 1973. BA, SUNY, Potsdam, 1978; MEd, St. Lawrence U., Canton, N.Y., 1986. Ordained to ministry Christian Ch., 1983. Dir., receiving home Morning Star Homes, Learnington, Ont., Can., 1979-81; caseworker Homes in Svc. Ministries, Rochester, N.Y., 1981-83; assoc. pastor Golden Heights Christian Ctr., Brockport, N.Y., 1983—; dir. Family Growth Counseling and Mediation Ctr., Brockport, N.Y., 1986—; bd. dirs. Homes in Svc. Ministries, Rochester, 1983-84, Golden Heights Christian Ctr., Brockport, 1986-88. Mem. AACD (assoc. mem., named Student of the Yr. 1985-86), Rochester Assn. Family Mediators.

BAYER, GEORGE HERBERT, weed scientist; b. N.Y., Dec. 7, 1924; s. George H. and Clara (Rebscher) B.; m. Helen T. McMullen, July 3, 1954. PhD, Cornell U., 1965. Herbicide devel. mgr. Agway Inc., Syracuse, N.Y., 1964-65, mgr. product devel., 1965-85; weed scientist, cons. Ithaca, N.Y., 1985—; courtesy prof. Cornell U., 1983-91. Contbr. articles to profl. jours. Fellow Weed Sci. Soc. Am. (treas. 1978-81); mem. Northeastern Weed Sci. Soc. (pres. 1970-71, Disting. mem. 1979), Pesticide Assn. N.Y. State (sec. 1989—), Coun. for Agrl. Sci. and Tech. (bd. dirs. 1992—). Home: 216 Forest Home Dr Ithaca NY 14850-2708 Office: 121 E Buffalo St Ithaca NY 14850-4222

BAYER, RAYMOND GEORGE, tribology consultant, physicist; b. N.Y.C., June 9, 1935; s. Adam George and Caroline (Hauck) B.; m. Barbara Ann Sartini, June 7, 1958; children: Joseph, Matthew, Mary, Karen. BS summa cum laude, St. John's U., 1956; MS, Brown U., 1959. Sr. engr. Internat. Bus. Machines, Endicott, N.Y., 1958-91; cons. tribology, 1992—; chmn. Wear of Materials Conf., 1988-89, proceedings editor, 1990—. Author: Analytical Design for Wear, 1966; contbr. articles to profl. jours. Fellow ASTM (chmn. wear and erosion 1988-89). Home: 4609 Marshall Dr W Vestal NY 13850-3929

BAYER, ROBERT CLARK, marine biology educator; b. N.Y.C., July 4, 1944; s. Byron Clarence and Marjorie (Rose) B.; m. Juanita Cobil, June 24, 1967; children: Meghan, Alison, Andrew. BS, U. Vt., 1966, MS, 1968; PhD, Mich. State U., 1972. Asst. prof. dept. animal and vet. sci. U. Maine, Orono, 1972-77, assoc. prof., 1977-83, prof., 1983—; vis. prof. Inst. Marine Biochemistry, Aberdeen, Scotland, 1979. Author: Lobsters Inside Out, 1989; contbr. more than 50 articles to profl. jours. Mem. Am. Inst. Nutrition, Nat. Shellfisheries Assn. Home: 99 Forest Ave Orono ME 04473-1417 Office: U Maine Dept Animal & Vet & Aquatic Sci Hitcher Hall Orono ME 04469

BAYLOR, MICHAEL JAY, bank officer; b. Danville, Pa., Jan. 18, 1961; s. Hurley Charles and Hilda Marie (Schmidt) B. BS in Acctg., Indiana U. Pa., 1983; MBA, Bloomsburg U., 1985. PortSS adminstr. Commonwealth Bank and Trust, Williamsport, Pa., 1986-87, credit analyst, 1987-89; loan rev. officer Commonwealth Bancshares Corp., Williamsport, 1989-91, Northeastern Bank Pa./PNC Fin. Corp., Scranton, Pa., 1991—. Vol. United Way, 1988-90. Mem. Robert Morris Assocs. (assoc.). Republican. Roman Catholic. Home: 2103 Applewood Acres Clarks Summit PA 18411 Office: Northeastern Bank 210 Penn Ave Scranton PA 18501

BAZERMAN, STEVEN HOWARD, lawyer; b. N.Y.C., Dec. 12, 1940; s. Solomon and Miriam (Kirschenberg) B.; m. Christina Ann Gray, Aug. 28, 1981 (div. June 1988). BS in Math., BS in Engring., U. Mich., 1962; JD, Georgetown U., 1966. Bar: D.C. 1967, N.Y. 1968, U.S. Dist. Ct. (so. dist.) N.Y. 1970, U.S. Dist. Ct. (ea. dist.) N.Y. 1973, U.S. Claims Ct. 1976, U.S. Ct. Appeals (2d cir.) 1978, U.S. Cts. Customs and Patents Appeals 1981-82, U.S. Ct. Appeals (fed. cir.) 1982. Assoc. Arthur, Dry & Kalish, N.Y.C., 1967-80, Offner & Kuhn, N.Y.C., 1980-83; ptnr., head litigation dept. Kuhn, Muller & Bazerman, N.Y.C., 1983-87; ptnr. Moore, Berson, Lifflander, Eisenberg & Mewhinney, N.Y.C., 1987-88; of counsel Lerner, David, Littenberg, Krumholz & Mentlik, Westfield, N.J., 1988, Sutton, Basseches, Magidoff & Amaral, N.Y.C., 1988-90, Graham, Campaign & McCarth. P.C., N.Y.C., 1990—; governing counsel Community Law Offices Legal Aid Soc., N.Y.C., 1974-83, treas., 1979-82. Vol. counsel community law offices Legal Aid Soc., N.Y.C., 1974-82, treas., 1979-82. Mem. Assn. of Bar of City of N.Y., Am. Intellectual Property Law Assn., N.Y. Patent, Trademark & Copyright Law Assn. Jewish. Home: 529 W 42d St New York NY 10036

BAZIGOS, MICHAEL NICHOLAS, academic administrator; b. Bklyn., July 14, 1957; s. Nicholas Michael and Mary (Panagakos) B.; m. Katerina Spilio, Nov. 1, 1987. BA in Psychology, Pace U., 1983; MA in Orgnl. Psychology, NYU, 1986; postgrad. in orgnl. psychology, Columbia U., 1990—. Project mgr. Pace Univ. Sch. of Edn., N.Y.C., 1986-88, grants dir., 1988-89, asst. dean, 1989—; pres. Bazigos and Assocs. Cons., N.Y.C., 1989—; trainer Mitchell and Assocs., Caldwell, N.J., 1983—; diversity trainer Anti-Defamation League, N.Y.C., 1990—; dir. Stay-in-Sch. Partnership Program, N.Y. State Edn. Dept., 1991—, I Have a Dream Partnership Program, The Guinzburg Found., 1991—. Pres. N.Y.C. Alopecia Areata Support Group, 1989—; trustee Boy Scouts Am. Recipient grants Student Literacy Corps, U.S. Edn. Dept., Washington, 1990-92, Liberty Partnerships Program, N.Y. State Edn. Dept., Albany, 1989—, Pioneer in Collaboration, Am. Assn. Higher Edn., Chgo., 1990, Tchr. Opportunity Corps, N.Y. State Edn. Dept., 1988-92, Stay-in-Sch. Partnerships, 1987-92, Dwight D. Eisenhower Title IIA, N.Y. State Edn. Dept., 1991-92, The Guinzburg Found., 1991-93. Mem. APA, Greek-Am. Behavioral Scis. Inst., N.Y. Met. Liberty Network, Am. Mensa, Phi Delta Kappa (rsch. rep. Pace chpt. 1989—), Psi Chi (chmn. adv. bd. 1990—, Nat. Svc. award 1990). Greek Orthodox. Office: Pace Univ Sch of Edn 1 Pace Plz New York NY 10038-1598

BAZZANO, EDIE See MILLERS, EDIE

BEACH, BERT BEVERLY, clergyman; b. Gland, Vaud, Switzerland, June 15, 1928; s. Walter Raymond and Gladys (Corley) B.; m. Eliane Marguerite Palange, Apr. 8, 1954; children: Danielle, Michele. BA, Pacific Union Coll., 1948; postgrad., Stanford U., 1948-49, 51; PhD, U. Paris, 1958; ThD, Christian Theol. Acad., 1986. Prin. West Liberty Union Intermediate Sch., Gridley, Calif., 1949-50, Italian Jr. Coll., Florence, Italy, 1952-58; chmn. history dept. Columbia Union Coll., Takoma Pk., Md., 1958-60; dir. edn. No. Europe-West Africa Div. of SDA, St. Albans, Eng., 1960-75, gen. sec., 1973-80; dir. pub. affairs Gen. Conf. of Seventh-day Adventists, Silver Spring, Md., 1980—; sec. gen. Internat. Religious Liberty Assn., Silver Spring, Md., 1980—; sec., bd. trustees Americans United for Separation for Ch. & State, Silver Spring, 1989—; sec. bd. dirs. Internat. Acad. for Freedom of Religion & Belief, Washington, 1987—; v.p. Internat. Commn. for Prevention of Alcoholism, Washington, 1980—; sec. Conf. of Secs. of Christian World Communions, Geneva, 1970—. Author: Vatican II: Bridging the Abyss, 1968, Ecumenism: Boon or Bane?, 1974, Bright Candle of Courage, 1988, Pattern for Progress, 1985; contbr. over 200 articles to profl. jours. and books. Recipient Citation, Senate of State of Md., 1984; named Paul Harris fellow Rotary Internat., 1984, Order of Bishop Hodura, Polish Nat. Cath. Ch., 1986, Order of St. Magdalene, Polish Orthodox Ch., 1987. Mem. Rotary Club of Silver Spring, Md., Cosmos Club, Nat. Press Club, Sons of Am. Revolution, Md. Soc. of Order of Founders and Patriots of Am. Seventh-day Adventist. Home: 14508 Cutstone Way Silver Spring MD 20905 Office: 12501 Old Columbia Pike Silver Spring MD 20904-6600

BEACH, MILO C., art museum director. Dir. Freer Gallery of Art, Washington, DC, 1988—. Author: The Imperial Image: Paintings for the Mughal Court, 1982; The Adventures of Rama, 1983; Early Mughal Painting, 1987;. Office: Freer Gallery Art Smithsonian Instn Washington DC 20560*

BEACH, MURRAY MACDONALD, investment banker; b. Wilmington, Del., Apr. 25, 1954; s. Thomas Coffing Jr. and Rose Mary (Randall) B.; m. M.K. Walkosh, Sept. 3, 1979 (div. July 1989); children: Maximillian, Hillary. AB in History, Harvard Coll., 1976; MBA, Amos Tuck-Dartmouth, Hanover, N.H., 1979. CPA. Acct. Alexander Grant & Co., Chgo., 1979-81; exec. v.p. Bus. Appraisals, Inc., Hanover, 1981-85; mng. dir. Ulin, Morton, Bradley & Welling, Inc., Boston, 1985-90; mng. dir. Advest, Inc., Boston, 1990-91, head of corp. fin., sr. v.p., 1991—. Office: Advest Inc 101 Federal St Boston MA 02110-1800

BEACH, ROBERT PRESTON, accountant, fraternal organization executive; b. Portland, Oreg., Jan. 29, 1916; s. Henry Edward and Olga Ruth (Lindblad) B.; m. Barbara Frances Harvey, July 12, 1941; 1 dau., Barbara Anne Beach Meek. BS, U. Calif., Berkeley, 1938; MBA, Harvard U., 1940. CPA, Mass. Acct. Coopers & Lybrand, Boston, 1940-42, 46-53; sec. corp. Brown & Sharpe Mfg. Co., Providence, 1953-55; bus. mgr. Metcalf & Eddy, Boston, 1956-60; prof. practice acctg. Boston, 1961—; corporator First Am. Bank for Savs., Boston, 1974-86; guest lectr. Boston U., 1966-67. Treas. Rep. Town Com., Natick, Mass., 1948-53; clk. First Congl. Ch. in Wellesley Hills (Mass.), 1967-72; mem. corp. New Eng. Bapt. Hosp. Health Care Corp. and New Eng. Bapt. Hosp. Corp., Boston, 1964—; trustee Leonard Morse Hosp., Natick, 1950-53. Lt. comdr. USN, 1942-46, PTO. Fellow Am. Inst. CPAs, Mass. Soc. CPAs (various coms.); mem. SAR (treas. Mass. chpt. 1975-77), Conf. Grand Secs. in N.Am. (sec.-treas. 1976-85, pres. 1985-86), Beta Alpha Psi, Harvard Club (Boston), Masons (editor publs. 1966-88, grand sec. 1968-88, 33d degree, D.S.M. and Henry Price medals 1963, 66, Philip C. Tucker medal 1983, past presiding officer many orgns., trustee Masonic Edn. and Charity Trust 1982-89). Home: 47 Black Oak Dr Hollis NH 03049-6400

BEACHLEY, ORVILLE THEODORE, JR., chemistry educator; b. East Orange, N.J., Nov. 8, 1937; s. Orville Theodore and Mabel (Williams) B.; m. Inez Southard Parker; children—Andrew Theodore, Jennifer Lynn. B.Sc., Franklin and Marshall Coll., 1959; Ph.D., Cornell U., 1963. NIH postdoctoral fellow U. Durham, Eng., 1963-64; acting asst. prof. Cornell U., Ithaca, N.Y., 1964-66; asst. prof. chemistry SUNY-Buffalo, 1966-69, assoc. prof., 1969-85, prof., 1985—. Contbr. articles to profl. jours. Recipient Chancellors award for excellence in teaching SUNY, 1975. Mem. Am. Chem. Soc., Royal Chem. Soc., Sigma Xi. Methodist. Avocations: fishing; boating. Office: Dept Chemistry SUNY Buffalo NY 14214

BEAKES, JOHN HERBERT, JR., consulting corporation executive; b. Balt., Feb. 24, 1943; s. John Herbert and Martha Caroline (Ailes) B.; m. Rosemary Brown, June 11, 1966; children: Susan Dawn, Sarah Elisabeth, John III. BS, U.S. Naval Acad., 1966; MS, Johns Hopkins U., 1977. Registered profl. engr., Md., Pa. With Gen. Physics Corp., Columbia, Md., 1974-88, sr. v.p., engring., ops., research, 1982-85, group v.p. engring. and technology, 1985-87; pres. subs. Gen. Tech. Svcs., Inc., 1984-87, group v.p. engring. and tech., 1987, exec. v.p., chief oper. officer, 1987-88; pres. subs. Power Mgmt. Assocs., Inc., 1986-88; exec. v.p., chief oper. officer RWD Tech., Columbia, 1988—. Elder, Christ Meml. Presbyn. Ch., Columbia, 1982-88. Served to lt. comdr. USN, 1966-74. Mem. ASME, Am. Soc. Mfg. Engrs., Am. Nuclear Soc. Republican. Home: 11699 Foxspur Ct Ellicott City MD 21042-1517 Office: RWD Tech 10480 Little Patuxent Pky Columbia MD 21044-3506

BEAL, DALLAS KNIGHT, university president; b. Ashtabula, Ohio, July 29, 1926; s. Ananias Porter and Clara (Blair) B.; m. Elizabeth Walton, June 9, 1951; children: Jeffrey T., Joan B. B.S., Ohio State U., 1950, M.A., 1951; Ed.D., Columbia U., 1958. Instr. edn. SUNY at New Paltz, 1951-52, Tchrs. Coll., Columbia U., 1952-54; dir. placement, lectr. edn. Queens Coll., CUNY, 1954-58; mem. adminstrn. State Univ. Coll. N.Y. at Fredonia, 1958-84, v.p. acad. affairs, 1969-70, acting pres., 1970-72, pres., 1972-84; pres. Conn. State U., New Britain, 1985—; acting exec. vice chancellor SUNY, 1984-85; Dir. Liberty Bank, Dunkirk, N.Y.; Adviser, editor N.Y. State Syllabus Reading and Lang. Arts, 1962-63; Mem. N.Y. Regents Task Force Evaluation N.Y.C. Pub. Schs., 1961-63; charter mem. adv. com. higher edn. N.Y. State Tchrs. Assn., 1966-67; com. on performance-based evaluation for certification N.Y. State Dept. Edn., 1968; chmn. com. on ednl. tech. Am. Assn. State Colls. and Univs.; mem. nursing edn. council, mem. telecommunications com. SUNY; chmn. Western N.Y. Consortium Public and Pvt. Colls. Author: (with Dr. H. Mitzel) Research Study of Campus Schools in American Colleges, 1966. Vice chmn. Community Devel. Com.; bd. dirs. Western N.Y. Ednl. TV Sta., Boorady Reading Ctr., Dunkirk, Brooks Meml. Hosp., Dunkirk; pres. United Fund, No. Chautauqua County, 1968-70; mem. adv. bd. Model Counties Assn., Chautauqua County, 1971-72; adviser Bd. Edn., Dunkirk, 1968—, Fredonia, 1966—; pres. Farmington (Conn.) Valley Music Found., 1987—; mem. planning com. ABC Task Force for State of Conn., 1990—. Recipient Music Advocate award Conn. Music Educators Assn., 1991. Mem. NEA, Southwestern N.Y. Assn. Instructional Improvement (founding pres.), Dunkirk C. of C. (bd. dirs.), Fredonia C. of C. (bd. dirs.), Greater Hartford C. of C., Lyric Arts Assn. (co-founder), Lake Shore Assn. for Arts (co-founder), Torch Club, Phi Delta Kappa, Kappa Delta Pi, Alpha Phi Omega. Office: Conn State U Office of Pres PO Box 2008 1615 Stanley St New Britain CT 06050

BEAL, DONNA LEE, association executive; b. Ticonderoga, N.Y., Aug. 22, 1952; d. Donald Lee and Beverley Ann (Burlow) McIntyre; m. Allan Grant Beal, July 15, 1972; children: Andrew, Alison. Assoc., Pierce Coll. for Women, 1972. Office mgr. Med.-Family Practice, Hamilton, N.Y., 1972-74, Gen. Dentistry, Westport, N.Y., 1978-84; sec. The Adirondack Coun., Elizabethtown, N.Y., 1984-85, adminstrv. asst., 1985-86, adminstr., 1986-89, acting co-dir., 1989, adminstr., membership dir., chief fin. officer, 1990—; treas. Environ. Fedn. N.Y., Albany, 1991—; vice chair Adirondack Centennial Com., Paul Smiths, N.Y., 1990—; project dir. Conf. Mng. Growth and Devel. in Unique, Natural Settings, Elizabethtown, 1990. Vice chmn. Essex County Sch. Bds. Assn., 1988; bd. dirs. Depot Theatre, Westport, 1988—, Champlain Health Concerns, Mineville, N.Y., 1980; mem. bd. edn. Westport Cen. Sch., 1984-88; mem. pastoral rels. com. Westport Federated Ch., 1990-91. Republican. Office: The Adirondack Coun PO Box D-2 Church St Elizabethtown NY 12932

BEAL, EDWARD WESCOTT, psychiatrist, educator; b. Pipestone, Minn., Aug. 12, 1940; s. Edward Herman and Wanita Viola (Beck) B.; m. Kathleen Mary Redpath, June 7, 1965; children: Alan Andrew, Amy Rebecca, Maryalice Kathleen. AB, Dartmouth Coll., 1962; MD, Hahnemann U., 1966. Diplomate Am. Bd. Psychiatry and Neurology. Intern Hahnemann Hosp., Phila., 1966-67; resident in adult psychiatry Menninger Found., Topeka, 1969-72, resident in child psychiatry, 1971-73; clin. assoc. prof. Georgetown U. Med. Sch., Washington, 1975—, dir., forensic psychiatry svcs., 1986-89; pvt. practice, Bethesda, Md., 1981—. Author: Adult Children of Divorce. Capt. M.C., U.S. Army, 1967-69. Fellow Am. Psychiat. Assn., Am. Orthopsychiat. Assn.; mem. Am. Family Therapy Asssn. (charter). Office: 4424 Montgomery Ave Ste 307 Bethesda MD 20814-4409

BEAL, SISTER MARY ARTHUR, dean, school psychologist; b. Camden, N.J., Apr. 26, 1922; d. John Thomas and Agnes (McVeigh) B. BA, Georgian Ct. Coll., 1955; MA, Fordham U., 1961, PhD, 1968. Joined Sisters of Mercy; cert. sch. psychologist, N.J. Primary grade tchr. Cathedral Grammar Sch., Trenton, N.J., 1942-50; jr. high tchr. Mt. St. Mary Acad., Plainfield, N.J., 1950-59; prin. Holy Cross Elem. Sch., Rumson, N.J., 1959-65; tchr. Georgian Ct. Coll., Lakewood, N.J., 1965-75; prof. Georgian Ct. Coll., Lakewood, 1975-84, dean of grad. sch., 1984—; psychologist Becoming a Person Program, Camden Diocese, N.J., 1980's, McAuley Sch. for Exceptional Children, Plainfield, 1970-80; speaker in field. Vol. psychologist Ocean County Mental Health Clinic, Toms River, N.J., 1973-76. Mem. NEA, Am. Assn. Colls. for Tchr. Edn., Assn. Tchr. Educators, N.J. Sch. Psychologist Assn., Mercy Higher Edn. Colloquium, Jean Piaget Soc. (charter). Roman Catholic. Home and Office: Georgian Ct Coll Grad Sch 900 Lakewood Ave Lakewood NJ 08701-2697

BEAL, ROBERT LAWRENCE, real estate executive; b. Boston, Sept. 10, 1941; s. Alexander Simpson and Leona M. (Rothstein) B. BS cum laude, Harvard U., 1963, MBA, 1965. Vice pres., ptnr. Beacon Cos., Boston, 1965-76; ptnr. The Beal Cos., Boston; exec. v.p. Beal and Co., Inc., Boston, 1976—; corporator, dir., mem. exec. com., lending com. Provident Instn. Savs., 1975-86, bd. dirs. U.K.-Am. Properties, bd. dirs. Ea. Realty Investment Corp., 1989—; chmn., bd. dirs. Mass. Indsl. Fin. Agy., 1976—; instr. real estate Northeastern U., 1969-75; mem. East Cambridge rezoning adv. com., 1989—; dir. treas. Artery Bus. Com., 1989—. Bd. dirs. Boston Zool. Soc., 1972-86, pres., 1980, chmn. 1981-84, hon. chmn., 1985; mem. vis. com. Sch. Mus. Fine Arts, Boston, 1974-76, 88-89; overseer Boys Club Boston, 1975—; mem. corp. Belmont Hill Sch.; trustee Beth Israel Hosp., 1981—, mem. bldg. and grounds com., 1976-82, 86-90; dir. Harvard Coll. Fund Coun., 1972-73, capital fund dr. Class '63, 1979-85, co-chmn. 25th reunion; exec. bd. Boston chpt. Am. Jewish Com., 1987—, mem. bd. govs., 1989-92; bd. dirs. Boston Mcpl. Rsch. Bur., 1978—, treas., 1988-89, 92, vice-chmn., 1990—; bd. dirs. Mass. Boston Housing Partnership, Inc., 1983—; trustee The Partnership, Inc., 1981-89, New Eng. Aquarium, 1987—; mem. adv. task force John F. Kennedy Libr., 1982; bd. overseers Mus. Fine Arts., Boston, 1988—; mem. vis. com. Harvard Div. Sch., 1989—, adv. com. Taubman Ctr., John F. Kennedy Sch. Govt., Harvard U., 1989—. Mem. Nat. Realty Com. (dir., past sec., mem. exec. com. 1974—, v.p., vice chmn.), Mass. Assn. Realtors (dir. 1979-81), Greater Boston Real Estate Bd. (bd. dir. 1970-72, 76-90, pres. 1978-79), Am. Soc. Real Estate Counselors, Bldg. Owners-Mgrs. Assn. Boston (dir. 1970-72), Ripon Soc. (co-founder, nat. treas. 1968-73, nat. governing bd. 1979-85), Nat. Assn. Real Estate Appraiser (cert.), Mass. Taxpayers Found. (dir. 1980-86), Inst. Property Taxation (affliate), Internat. Assn. Assessing Officers (primary subscribing mem. 1982—), Beacon Hill Civic Assn. (bd. dir. 1975-79), Bostonian Soc. (life), The Vault (coord. com. 1978—), Combined Jewish Philanthropies Greater Boston (vice chmn., exec. com.).. Republican. Jewish. Home: 21 Brimmer St Boston MA 02108-1001 Office: Beal and Co Inc 177 Milk St Boston MA 02109-3410

BEALE, DAVID A., lawyer, partner; b. N.Y.C., May 28, 1949; s. Martin and Roslyn Sybil (Perlin) B.; m Tina Iris Borger, Oct. 20, 1979; children: Janna, Joshua, Elana. BS, Cornell U., 1971; JD, Fordham U., 1974. Bar: N.Y. 1975, Fla. 1990; lic. real estate broker, N.Y. Ptnr. Albert & Beale, N.Y.C.; arbitrator Am. Arbitration Assn., N.Y.C. Pres. Park River Ind. Dems., N.Y.C.; com. mem. N.Y. County Dem. Com., N.Y.C.; v.p., trustee Temple Beth Abraham; v.p. Cornell Class of 1971, 1991-96. Mem. N.Y. State Bar Assn. (com. mem. media law, com. intellectual property law), The Fla. Bar Assn. (mem. media and comms. law com.). Office: Albert & Beale 750 3rd Ave New York NY 10017

BEALE, GEORGIA ROBISON, historian; b. Chgo., Mar. 14, 1905; d. Henry Barton and Dora Belle (Sledd) Robison; m. Howard Kennedy Beale, Jan. 2, 1942; children: Howard Kennedy, Henry Barton Robison, Thomas Wight. AB, U. Chgo., 1926, AM, 1928; PhD, Columbia U., 1938; student Sorbonne and Coll. de France, 1930-34. Reader in history U. Chgo., 1927-29; lectr. Barnard Coll., 1937-38; instr. Bklyn. Coll., 1937-39; asst. prof. Hollins (Va.) Coll., 1939-41, Wellesley Coll., 1941-42, Castleton (Vt.) State Coll., 1968-70; vis. asso. prof. U. Ky., Lexington, 1970-72; professorial lectr. George Washington U., 1983-84. Author: Revelliere-lépeaux, Citizen Director, 1938, 72, Academies to Institut, 1973, Bosc and the Exequatur, 1978; contbg. author Historical Dictionary of the French Revolution, 1985; also articles. Mem. Madison (Wis.) Civic Music Assn. and Madison Symphony Orch. League, 1958—; hon. trustee Culver-Stockton Coll., 1974—. Univ. fellow Columbia U., 1929-30. Mem. AAUW (European fellow 1930-31), Am., So. hist. assns., Soc. French Hist. Studies, Western Soc. French History (hon. mem. exec. council), Am., Brit. socs. 18th century studies, Phi Beta Kappa, Pi Lambda Theta, Phi Alpha Theta, Pi Kappa Delta. Clubs: Reid Hall (Paris); Brit. Univ. Women's (London). Address: The Ridge Orford NH 03777 also: 2816 Columbia Rd Madison WI 53705 also: 110 D St SE Washington DC 20003

BEALL, JOANNA MAY, painter; b. Chgo., Aug. 17, 1935; d. Lester Thomas and Dorothy Welles (Miller) B.; student Yale U. Sch. Fine Arts, 1953-57, Art Inst. Chgo., 1957; m. H.C. Westermann, Mar. 31, 1959. One-man shows include: Great Bldg. Crack-Up Gallery, N.Y.C., 1973, James Corcoran Gallery, Los Angeles, 1974, Gallery Rebecca Cooper, Washington, 1975; group shows: Allan Frumkin, Chgo., 1960, 61, Whitney Mus., N.Y.C., 1973, Art Inst. Chgo., 1976, Univ. Galleries, Los Angeles, 1979, Xavier Fourcade, N.Y.C., 1980, 85; vis. artist U. Colo., Boulder, 1979, 84. Mem. Artists Equity Assn., Visual Artists and Galleries Assn. Article The World of Joanna Beall (Melinda Wortz) appeared in Art Week mag., 1974. Home: PO Box 5028 Brookfield CT 06804-5028

BEAMES, PETER ANTHONY, insurance agent; b. Glens Falls, N.Y., Jan. 21, 1960; s. James Maurice and Alena Regina (Crescione) B.; m. Paula Frances Matte, May 19, 1990; 1 child, Peter Anthony Jr. BA, SUNY, Potsdam, 1983. Cert. ins. counselor. Sales agt. Jack Robinson Assn., South Glen Falls, N.Y., 1984-89, Community Ins., South Glen Falls, 1989—. Mem. Elks, Queensbury Kiwanis (pres. 1991, past sec., treas., v.p.). Roman Catholic. Home and Office: Community Ins 16 Marion Ave South Glen Falls NY 12803

BEAN, BENNETT, artist; b. Cin., Mar. 25, 1941; s. William Bennett and Abigail (Shepard) B.; m. Cathy Bao, Dec. 17, 1966; 1 child, William Bao. Student, Grinnell Coll., 1959-62; postgrad., U. Iowa, 1963, U. Wash., 1963; MFA, Claremont Grad. Sch., 1966. Asst. prof. art Wagner Coll., S.I., N.Y., 1966-79; trustee Am. Craft Enterprises, New Paltz, N.Y., 1982-85, Am. Craft Coun., N.Y.C., 1980-84; former chmn. bd. dirs. Peters Valley, Layton, N.J. One-man show Royal Marks Gallery, N.Y.C., 1969, Henri Gallery, Washington, 1969; exhibited in numerous groups show, including Whitney Mus. Am. Art, 1968-69, Newark Mus., 1968, 80, 89, 91, Am. Craft Mus. II, 1982, 86, N.J. State Mus., 19i4, Newport Art Mus., 1984, Hunter Mus., Chattanooga, 1990; represented in permanent collections Whitney Mus. Am. Art, Newark Mus., N.J. State Mus., St. Louis Mus. Art, Royal Ont. Mus., Ariz. State U., Grinnell Coll., Ark. Arts Ctr. Decorative Arts Mus., others. Recipient editorial award Met. Home mag., 1990; rsch. grantee Wagner Coll., 1968, 70, 77, 78; fellow N.J. Coun. on Arts, 1978, 88, Nat. Endowment for Arts, 1980. Tibetian Buddhist. Home and Studio: RD 3 Box 212 Blairstown NJ 07825

BEAR, LARRY ALAN, lawyer; b. Melrose, Mass., Feb. 28, 1928; s. Joseph E. and Pearl Florence B.; m. Rita Maldonado, Mar. 29, 1975; children: Peter, Jonathan, Steven. BA, Duke U., 1949; JD, Harvard U., 1953; LLM, (James Kent fellow), Columbia U., 1966. Bar: Mass., 1953, N.Y. 1967. Trial lawyer Bear & Bear, Boston, 1953-60; cons. legal medicine, prof. law P.R. Dept. Justice, U. P.R. Law Sch., Puerto Rico, 1960-65; legal counsel, then commr. addiction svcs. City of N.Y., 1967-70; dir. Nat. Action Com. Drug Edn. U. Rochester, N.Y., 1970-77; pvt. practice N.Y.C., 1970-82; pub. affairs radio broadcaster Sta. WABC, N.Y.C., 1970-82; U.S. legal counsel Master Enterprises of P.R., 1982-90; pres. Found. for a Drug Free Pa., 1991—; adj. prof. fin. grad. div. Stern Sch. Bus. NYU, 1986—; sr. rsch. assoc. New Era Philanthropy, 1987-91; vis. prof. legal medicine Rutgers U. Law Sch., 1969; mem. alcohol and drug com. Nat. Safety Coun., 1972-82; cons. in field; mem. Atty. Gen.'s Med./Legal Adv. Bd. on Drug Abuse, Pa., 1992—. Author: Law, Medicine, Science and Justice, 1964, The Glass House Revolution: Inner City War for Interdependence, 1990; contr. articles to profl. jours. Mem. adv. com. on pub. issues Advt. Coun., 1972—; mem.-at-large Nat. coun. Boy Scouts Am., 1972-85; chmn. Bd. Ethics, Twp. of Mahwah (N.J.), 1990-91; mem. alumni admissions adv. com. Duke U., 1987—. Mem. ABA, N.Y. State Bar Assn., Forensic Sci. Soc. Great Britain, Acad. Colombiana de Ciencias Medico-Forenses, Harvard Club (N.Y.C.). Home: 95 Tam Oshanter Dr Mahwah NJ 07430-1526 Office: Found for Drug Free Pa 105 N Front St Harrisburg PA 17101

BEARB, MICHAEL EDWIN, anesthesiologist; b. Beaumont, Tex., June 30, 1956; s. Edwin and Ella Lou (Broussard) B.; m. Joanne Ruth Patterson, Nov. 18, 1989; 1 child, Emily. BS in Psychology with highest honors, Lamar U., 1978; MD, U. Tex., Dallas, 1984. Diplomate Am. Bd. Anesthesiologists. Intern St. Paul Hosp., Dallas, 1984-85; resident in anesthesiology Parkland Meml. Hosp., Dallas, 1985-87; fellow in cardio-thoracic anesthesiology The Cleve. Clin. Found., Cleve., 1987-88; instr. in anesthesiology Georgetown U. Hosp., Washington, 1988-90, asst. prof. in anesthesiology, 1990—; chmn. resident selection com. Georgetown U. Hosp., 1990—, coord. cardiovascular lectr. series, 1990-91, attending intensivist cardiovascular ICU, 1989—. Contbg. author: Hemoglobinopathies and Anesthetic Care of the Trauma Patient, 1992. Palladian mem. Friends of Hist. Mt. Vernon, Alexandria. Fellow Am. Coll. Angiology; mem. AMA, Internat. Anesthesia Rsch. Soc., Soc. Critical Care Medicine, Soc. Cardiovascular Anesthesiologists, Anesthesia History Assn., Am. Soc. Anesthesiologists, Civil War Soc., Smithsonian Inst., Nat. Space Soc., Phi Kappa Phi. Home: 1162 North Pitt St Alexandria VA 22314 Office: Georgetown Univ Hosp Dept Anesthesia 3800 Reservoir Rd Washington DC 20057

BEARD, MICHAEL KENNETH, lobbyist; b. Huntington, W.Va., Jan. 22, 1941; s. Kenneth Arthur and Nora Romona (Nott) B.; m. Melinda Joan Meriam, Feb. 20, 1986; children: Charles Elliott, Avri Gabrielle. Student, Am. U., 1960-64, BA in Govt. and Pub. Adminstrn., 1965. Dir. Washington Study Programs, Washington, 1964-66; exec. dir. World Federalist Youth, Washington, 1967-70, Self Determination for D.C., Washington, 1970-71, Com. for Congl. Reform, Washington, 1971-72; congl. aide Congressman Walter E. Fauntroy, Washington, 1972-76; pres., chief exec. officer Coalition to Stop Gun Violence, Washington, 1976—; chmn. bd. dirs. Pax World Found., Washington; pres. Found. for Handgun Edn., Washington. Producer TV film Nat. Handgun Test, 1979; contbr. numerous articles on handgun control to mags. Named One of Outstanding Young Men of Am., Jaycees, 1971, One of Washington 500 Washington Dossier Mag., 1984; recipient Looking for Heroes award D.C. Pub. Schs. and Time Inc./Odyssey, Washington, 1987. Mem. UN Assn. (treas. Capitol area div. 1989—). Democrat. Methodist. Office: Coalition to Stop Gun Violence 100 Maryland Ave NE Washington DC 20002-5625

BEARD, ROBERT EARL, Russian and linguistics educator; b. Fayetteville, N.C., Feb. 26, 1938; s. LaVern and Kathleen (Bullard) B.; m. Helen Faye Jackson, June 11, 1960; children: Jeffrey, Owen. AB in English, U. N.C., 1959; MA in Russian, U. Mich., 1961, PhD in Slavic Linguistics, 1966. Lectr. U. Mich., Ann Arbor, 1964-65; asst. prof. Russian and linguistics Bucknell U., Lewisburg, Pa., 1965-72, assoc. prof., 1972-82, prof., 1982-89, Ruth Everett Sierzega prof., 1989—, dir. Russian studies, 1970—; rsch. prof. Cornell U., Ithaca, N.Y., 1983-84. Author: Indo-European Lexicon, 1981; co-author: Bibliography of Morphology, 1988. Fulbright fellow, 1963, 76. Mem. Am. Assn. Slavic and East European Langs., Linguistic Soc. Am., European Linguistics Soc., Am. Assn. for Advancement Slavic Studies. Office: Bucknell U. Lewisburg PA 17837

BEARDSLEY, BRUCE J., health facility administrator; b. Red Bank, N.J., Apr. 25, 1963; s. William Joseph and Marilyn L. (Goldfarb) B. BS, Lehigh U., 1985; MBA, Boston U., 1989. Forecaster Nat. Assn. Home Builders, Washington, 1985; real estate appraiser Epstein Real Estate Adv. Svc., Lynn, Mass., 1986, Clancy Appraisal, East Falmouth, Mass., 1986-87; spl. project mgr. Harborside Healthcare, Boston, 1988-89, asst. v.p., 1989-92, v.p. of planning, 1992—. Mem. Lehigh Club of Boston, Omicron Delta Kappa, Lambda Mu Sigma. Office: Harborside Healthcare 470 Atlantic Ave Boston MA 02210

BEARDSLEY, THEODORE S(TERLING), JR., association executive; b. East St. Louis, Ill., Aug. 26, 1930; s. Theodore Sterling and Margaret (Kienzle) B.; m. Lenora J. Fierke, May 26, 1955; children: Theodore Sterling III, Mark A., Mary Elizabeth. B.S., So. Ill. U., 1952; M.A. (Max Bryant fellow), Washington U., St. Louis, 1954; postgrad., U. Heidelberg, Germany, 1955-56; Ph.D., U. Pa., 1961; linguistic research, Inst. Caro y Cuervo, Bogota, Colombia, summer 1973. Asst. in English Lycee Wilson, Chaumont, France, 1952-53; mem. faculty Rider Coll., 1957-61, chmn. dept. modern lang., 1959-61; asst. prof. Spanish So. Ill. U., 1961-62, U. Wis., 1962-65; dir. Hispanic Soc. Am., N.Y.C., 1965—; adj. prof. NYU, 1967-69, 80, Adelphi U., 1966, 68, Columbia U., 1969; Fulbright lectr., Ecuador, 1974; guest lectr. U.Complutense, Madrid, 1990; chmn. Museums Council N.Y.C., 1972-73; spl. cons. Hispanic bibliography Library of Congress, fall 1973, N.J. State Dept. Edn., spring 1975, NEH, 1978—. Narrator Spanish lang. recorded tours, Nat. Gallery Art, Met. Mus., Mus. Natural Sci., Boston Sci. Mus., Smithsonian Instn.; continuing series on Caribbean popular music in U.S, WBGO-FM, 1979; Xavier Cugat, 1980, USA Latino, 1981, Enrique Madriguera, Spanish Nat. Radio, 1985. Author: Hispano-Classical Translations, 1482-1699, 1970, Tomas Navarro Tomas, A Tentative Bibliography, 1908-1970, 1971; also articles; Recordings include: Charla con Camilo José Cela, 1966, Visita a la Hispanic Society, 1969; narrator-author: 4 part series Hispanic Immigration to the United States (text pub. 1976), CBS-TV, 1972; Librettist: Ponce de Leon, 1973; mem. adv. bd.: Hispanic Rev., Studia humanitatis, Boletín de ANLE, Hispanic Sem. of Medieval Studies. Served with AUS, 1954-56. Decorated Orden de Mérito Civil, Spain ; Fulbright grantee, 1952-53; Jusserand traveling fellow, 1962; research grantee Am. Council Learned Socs., 1964; travel grantee, 1974; recipient Premio Bibliofilia Barcelona, Spain, 1973. Mem. ASCAP, Hispanic Soc. Am., Renaissance Soc. Am. (exec. coun., acting dir. 1981-82), Acad. Norteamericana Lengua Española, Internat. Inst. (Madrid), Internat. Linguistic Assn. (exec. coun.), Grolier Club, Century Assn., Sigma Delta Pi, Sigma Tau Gamma; corr. mem. Royal Spanish Acad., Real Acad. Bellas Artes San Carlos (Valencia), Acad. Guatemalteca de Lengua, Assn. Bibliofilos Barcelona, Fundacion Odón Betanzos (Rociana), Fundacion Santa Maria de la Rabida, Fundacion Universitaria Española (Madrid). Office: Hispanic Soc Am 613 W 155th St New York NY 10032-7501

BEARDSLEY, WILLIAM EDWARD, physician assistant; b. Hamden, Conn., May 23, 1950; s. William E. and Lois (Warner) B.; m. Linda S. Slazinik, June 16, 1974; children: Sara Marie, Nicholas Roth. AS, Charter Oak Coll., 1980; grad. physician asst., Bowman Gray Sch. Medicine, 1983. Cert. physician asst. Physician asst. procurement New Eng. Organ Bank, Boston, 1983-84; physician assn. orthopedics Dr. Joseph Abate, Melrose, Mass., 1984-86; physician asst. orthopedics/gen. surgery Harvard Community Health Plan, Medford, Cambridge, Mass., 1986-90; physician asst. emergency rm. Melrose-Wakefield Hosp., 1990-91; physician asst. orthopedics St. Elizabeth Hosp., Brighton, Mass., 1991—. Producer, writer A Life in the Day - The Melrose EMS System, 1990 (2d pl. award 1991). Chmn. Mayor's Cable TV Adv. Com., Melrose, 1990-91; co-chmn. Melrose Recycling Com., 1988-90; mem. Melrose C.A.R.E.S., 1990; sec. bd. dirs. MMTV-Melrose Public Access TV, 1991—. Fellow Am. Assn. Physician Assts., Mass. Assn. Physician Assts. (pres. 1988-89). Office: St Elizabeths Hosp 736 Cambridge St Brighton MA 02135-2997

BEARR, DAVID WILLIAM COMER, educational counselor, publications consultants; b. Richmond, Va., Jan. 16, 1945; s. Richard Joseph and Lilian Ann (Turner) B.; m. Dianne Zula Stewart, Aug. 16, 1968; children: Rachel Emma, David Stewart, Jonathan Shepherd. BS summa cum laude, U. Corpus Christi, 1967; MA, Washington U., St. Louis, 1968; cert. advance study, Johns Hopkins U., 1970; LittD (hon.), Blackstone Coll., 1992. Cert. profl. counselor, nat. cert. counselor. Counselor Brentwood (Mo.) High Sch., 1967-68; counselor Balt. County Pub. Schs., 1968-72, work study coord., 1972-76, counseling ctr. chmn., 1976—; evening couselor Catonsville (Md.) C.C., 1976-91; asst. to exec. dir. Carroll C.C., Westminster, Md., 1987-90; adj. faculty mem. Catonsville C.C., 1981-89; pub. cons., Carroll C.C, Westminster, 1991—. Author: Scholars for Blackstone, 1991; editor N.W. Passage edit. United Meth. Reporter; contbg. writer Counselor's Corner, 1988-89; contbr. articles to hist. jours. Bd. dirs. Strawbridge Shrine, Inc., New Windsor, Md., 1988—, George P. Adams Trust; active ARC Holocaust and War Victims Archival Project. Recipient Lay Leadership award United Meth. Ch., 1990. Mem. AACD, Balt. County Assn. Counseling and Devel. (past. bd. dirs.), United Teaching Profession, Blackstone Coll. Alumnae Assn. (bd. dirs. George P. Adams. Meml. Scholarship Trust Fund 1988—), Jamestowne Soc., Loyal Patrons Schwartz Tavern, Hist. Fincastle, Inc., Fluvanna Hist. Soc. Va. Democrat. United Methodist. Home: 313 Mary Ave Westminster MD 21157 Office: Counselors Office 10 Cockeys Mill Rd Reisterstown MD 21136

BEASLEY, MAURINE HOFFMAN, journalism educator, historian; b. Sedalia, Mo., Jan. 28, 1936; d. Dimmitt Heard and Maurine (Hieronymous) Hoffman; m. William C. McLaughlin, May 20, 1966 (div. 1969); m. Henry R. Beasley, Dec. 24, 1970; 1 child, Susan Sook. BJ, BA in History, U. Mo., 1958; MS in Journalism, Columbia U., 1963; PhD in Am. Civilization, George Washington U., 1974; Cert. in Brit. History, U. Edinburgh, Scotland, 1964. Edn. editor Kansas City (Mo.) Star, 1959-62; staff writer Washington Post, 1963-73; asst. prof. journalism U. Md., College Park, 1975-80, assoc. prof., 1980-86, prof. 1987—. Author: Eleanor Roosevelt and the Media: A Public Quest for Self-Fulfillment, 1987; (with others) Women in Media, 1977, The New Majority, 1988, Taking Their Place! Documentary History of Women and Journalism, 1992; editor: (with others) Voices of Change: Southern Pulitzer Winners, 1978, One Third of a Nation (hon. mention Washington Monthly Book Award 1982), 1981; editor: White House Press Conferences of Eleanor Roosevelt, 1983; mem. adv. bd. Am. Journalism, 1983—, Jour. of Mass Media Ethics, Mass Com. Rev.; contbr. articles to acad. jours. Violinist, Montgomery Coll. Symphony Orch., 1975—; pres., Little Falls Swimmings Club, Inc., 1988-89. Gannett Teaching Fellowships Program fellow, 1977; Pulitzer traveling fellow Columbia U., 1963; Eleanor Roosevelt studies grantee Eleanor Roosevelt Inst., 1979-80; named one of nation's outstanding tchrs. of writing and editing Modern Media Inst. and Am. Soc. Newspaper Editors, 1981. Mem. Assn. Edn. in Journalism and Mass Communications (exec. com. 1990-91, standing com. on profl. freedom and responsibility 1985, vice chair 1987-89, chair 1990-91, sec. history div. 1986-87, vice-head 1987-88, head 1988-89, pres. elect 1992), Am. Journalism Historians Assn. (pres.-elect 1988-89, pres. 1989-90, historian 1992), Am. News Women's Club (bd. govs. 1986-87), Women in Communications (bd. dirs. Washington chpt. 1985-87), Nat. Fedn. Press Women, Soc. Profl. Journalists (chair nat. hist. site com. 1986-87, bd. dirs. Washington chpt. 1988-90, pres. Washington chpt. 1990-91, dir. region 2 and mem. nat. bd. 1991-92), Phi Beta Kappa, Omicron Delta Kappa. Democrat. Unitarian. Home: 4920 Flint Dr Bethesda MD 20816-1746 Office: U Md Coll Journalism College Park MD 20742

BEASLEY, ROBERT SCOTT, aerospace company executive; b. Balt., Mar. 17, 1949; s. Robert F. and Marjorie (Scott) B.; m. Susan E. Gibson, Aug. l, 1978 (div. July 1987); l child, Robert W. BS in Bus., Lehigh U., 197l, MBA, 1972; JD, U. Md., 1976; MA Nat. Security Studies, Georgetown U., 1989; cert. in space ops. mgmt., U. Denver, 1990. Bar: Md. 1977; CPA, Md. Audit staff acct. Arthur Young & Co., Balt., 1972-73; pvt. practice Balt., 1973-78; with corp. fin. dept. Merc.-Safe Deposit & Trust, Balt., 1978-80, with asset mgmt. dept., 1980-8l; v.p. fin. Broventure Co., Balt., 198l-85, Astrotech Space Ops., LP, Silver Spring, Md., 1985-90; dir. strategic devel. Westinghouse Electronic Systems Group, 1990—. Mem. Radio Amateur Satellite Corp., Armed Forces Communications and Electronics Assn. Republican. Methodist. Home: 17911 Pond Rd Ashton MD 20861 Office: Westinghouse Electronic Systems Group Mail Stop 1201 PO Box 746 Baltimore MD 21203

BEASON, JAMES DOUGLAS, military officer, physicist, writer; b. Alexandria, La., Dec. 3, 1953; s. James Larry and Martha Grace (McCluney) B.; m. Cynthia Marie Olsen, Jan. 20, 1979; children: Amanda Grace, Tamara Jo. Student, La. Tech. U., 1972-73; BS in Physics and Math., U.S. Air Force Acad., 1977; MS in Physics, U. N.Mex., 1980, PhD in Physics, 1983. Commd. 2d lt. USAF, 1977, advanced through grades to lt. col., 1991; computational physicist USAF Weapons Lab. USAF, Kirtland AFB, N.Mex., 1977-79, sect. chief nuclear effects, 1979-80, chief plasma physics, 1986-88, chief advanced concepts, 1988-90, deputy dir. Advanced Weapons and Survivability Philips Lab., 1991; sr. policy analyst White House Office Sci. and Tech. Policy, Washington, 1991—; asst. prof. physics USAF Acad., Colorado Springs, Colo., 1983-86; rsch. advisor NRC; cons. Lawrence Livermore (Calif.) Nat. Lab., 1985—, Ames Rsch. Ctr., NASA, Sunnyvale, Calif., 1985; mem. Stafford Commn., Synthesis Group for Nat. Space Exploration Initiative. Author: Return to Honor, 1989, Assault on Alpha Base, 1990, Lifeline, 1990, Strike Eagle, 1991, The Trinity Paradox, 1991, Assemblers of Infinity, 1992. Bd. dirs. Albuquerque Bible Coll., 1987-88. Decorated Meritorious Svc. medal. Mem. Am. Phys. Soc., Sci. Fiction Writers Am., Air Force Assn., Air Force Acad. Assn. of Grads. Presbyterian. Office: White House Sci Office Washington DC 20500

BEASON, ROBERT CURTIS, biology educator; biology researcher; b. Ft. Scott, Kans., May 12, 1946; s. Eugene Mack and Lida Jane (Lawson) B.; divorced, Jan. 1988; 1 child, Zachery Adam Sloane. BA, Bethany Nazarene Coll., 1968; MS, Western Ill. U., 1970; PhD, Clemson U., 1976. Biology educator, SUNY, Geneseo, 1978—; cons. U.S. Park Svc., 1991, N.Y. State Dept. Environ. Conservation, Avon, 1983—, FAA, Riverside, Calif., 1977, NASA, Cape Canaveral, Fla., 1973-74. Contbr. chpt. to text, Biophys. Effects of Steady Magnetic Fields, Orientation and Navigation, Biologic Effects of Electric and Magnetic Fields, Orientation in Birds; contbr. articles to profl. jours. Served to E-4, USAF, 1970-74. Grantee U.S. Dept. Interior 1974-76, SUNY Rsch. Found. 1979, 86, NSF 1981, 86, 90, 91, Geneseo Found 1983—, NIH, 1988, Whitehall Found., 1991. Mem. AAAS, Am. Ornithologists Union (life), Animal Behavior Soc., Am. Soc. Naturalists, Internat. Soc. for Behavioral Ecology, Soc. for Neurosci. Avocations: backpacking, photography, flying. Achievements include discovery of neural basis for magnetic sensitivity in birds. Home: 23 Tuscarora Ave Geneseo NY 14454-9501 Office: SUNY Dept Biology Geneseo NY 14454

BEATIE, RUSSEL HARRISON, JR., lawyer; b. Lawrence, Kans., Jan. 20, 1938; s. Russel Harrison and Mary Louise (Zimmerman) B.; m. Julia Ferguson DuVall; children: Benjamin Wilson Parkhill, Amy Wilder. B.A. cum laude, Princeton U., 1959, LL.B. cum laude Columbia U., 1964. Bar: N.Y. 1964, U.S. Dist. Ct. (so. and ea. dists.) N.Y., U.S. Ct. Appeals (2d, 3d, 5th, 6th, 7th, 9th and 10th cirs.), U.S. Supreme Ct. Assoc. Dewey, Ballantine, Bushby, Palmer & Wood, N.Y.C., 1964-66, 68-72, Rogers & Wells, 1966-68; ptnr. Dewey Ballantine, 1972-83; pvt. practice, 1983-88; ptnr. Brown & Wood, 1989—. 1st lt., arty. U.S. Army, 1959-61. Mem. Assn. of Bar of City of N.Y. Republican. Clubs: Union, Univ., Leash, Verbank Hunting and Fishing. Author: Road to Manassas—The Growth of Union Command in the Eastern Theatre from the Fall of Fort Sumter to the First Battle of Bull Run, 1961. Office: 1 World Trade Ctr Ste 5700 New York NY 10048

BEATON, GREGORY THOMAS, chemical company executive; b. Boston, Aug. 13, 1956; s. Herbert J. and Janet M. (Gleason) B. BS in Chemistry, Tenn. Wesleyan Coll., 1978; MBA in Fin., U. Conn., Stamford, 1988. Patrolman City of Athens, Tenn., 1978-79; chemist Olin Corp., Tenn., La., 1979-86; distbn. mgr. Olin Corp., Stamford, Conn., 1986-88, sr. bus. evaluator, 1988-91, mgr. domestic funds, 1991—. Mem. allocations panel United Way, Stamford, 1991—. Mem. Treasury Mgmt. Assn., Fairfield County Treasury Mgmt. Assn., Sterling Farms Golf Club (treas. 1989—). Republican. Roman Catholic. Home: 71 Highland Rd Stamford CT 06902

BEATTIE, EDWARD JAMES, surgeon, educator; b. Phila., June 30, 1918; m. Nicole Mary; 1 son, Bruce Stewart. B.A., Princeton U., 1939; M.D., Harvard U., 1943. Diplomate Am. Bd. Surgery, Am. Bd. Thoracic Surgery (mem. bd. 1960-69, chmn. bd. 1967-69). Intern, surg. resident Peter Bent Brigham Hosp., Boston, 1942-46; Mosely traveling fellow (Harvard) to U. London, Eng., 1946-47; surg. fellow, Markle scholar George Washington U., 1947-52; chief thoracic surgery Presbyn. Hosp., 1952-54; chmn. dept. surgery Presbyn.-St. Luke's Hosp., 1954-65; cons. thoracic surgery Hines VA Hosp., Ill., 1953-65, Chgo. Tb San., 1954-65, Ill. Research and Edn. Hosp., 1956-65, Rockefeller U. Hosp., 1978—; prof. surgery U. Ill., 1955-65; prof. surgery Cornell U., 1965-83, emeritus, 1983—; prof. surgery, prof. oncology U. Miami, Fla., 1983-85; prof. surgery Mt. Sinai Sch. Medicine, N.Y.C., 1988—; chief thoracic surgery Meml. Hosp., N.Y.C., 1965-75, chmn. dept. surgery, 1966-78, chief med. officer, 1966-83, gen. dir., chief oper. officer, 1975-83; chief thoracic surgery, dir. Kriser Lung Cancer Ctr., dir. clin. cancer programs Beth Israel Med. Ctr., N.Y.C., 1985—. Mem. editorial bd. Jour. Thoracic and Cardiovascular Surgery, 1962-83, Pediatric Digest, 1962—, Cancer Clin. Trials, 1977-85, Internat. Advancs in Surg. Oncology, 1977. Fellow A.C.S.; mem. Am. Assn. Thoracic Surgery, Am. Surg. Assn., Soc. Vascular Surgery, AMA, Central, Western surg. assns., Internat. Soc. Surgery, Soc. Clin. Surgery, Am. Radium Soc., Soc. Thoracic Surgeons, Transplantation Soc., Am. Assn. Med. Colls., Pan Am. Med. Assn., Am. Cancer Soc., Am. Fedn. Clin. Research, Soc. Surg. Oncology. Republican. Office: Beth Israel Med Ctr 1st Ave New York NY 10009-7903

BEATTY, HENRY PERRIN, Canadian government official; b. Toronto, Ont., Can., June 1, 1950; s. George Ernest and Martha Letitia (Perrin) B.; m. Julia Florence Carroll Kenny; 2 children. Student, Upper Can. Coll.; BA, U. Western Ont., 1971. Mem. Ho. of Commons, Ottawa, Ont., Can., 1972—; min. of state for treasury bd. Ho. of Commons, Ottawa, 1979-84, min. nat. revenue, 1984-85; solicitor gen. of Can., 1985-86; min. nat. def. Can., 1986-89, min. nat. health and welfare, 1989-91; min. communications Ho. of Commons, Ottawa, Can., 1991—; spokesman on communications Progressive Conservative Caucus, 1980; chmn. Caucus Com. on Fed. Province Rels., 1983; Caucus spokesperson on Rev. Can., 1983; chmn. Progressive Conservative Caucus Task Force on Rev. Can., 1984; introduced a White Paper on Nat. Def., 1st in 16 yrs., 1987; chmn. for the Cabinet Com. on the Environ.; commn. Can. Unity and Constl. Negotiations. Office: Ho of Commons, Ottawa, ON Canada K1A 0A6 also: Ministry of Communications, Ottawa, ON Canada K1A 0A6

BEATTY, RICHARD PAUL, chemist; b. Amsterdam, N.Y., Oct. 6, 1953; s. Richard Stewart and Eleanor Helen (Tuman) B.; m. Kyoko Marukawa, Aug. 14, 1976. BS in Chemistry, SUNY, Albany, 1975; MS, PhD in Chemistry, Harvard U., 1982. Rsch. chemist DuPont Co., Orange, Tex., 1981-84; tech. supr. DuPont Co., La Place, La., 1984-88, sr. rsch. chemist, 1988-90; rsch. supr. DuPont Co., Wilmington, Del., 1990-91, sr. rsch. chemist, 1992—. Inventor in field; contbr. articles to profl. jours. Mem. Am. Chem. Soc. Office: DuPont Co Exptl Sta Chambers Works Wilmington DE 19880

BEATTY, WILBUR C., communications company purchasing executive; b. Sparta, N.J., Dec. 8, 1942; s. John Wesley and Bessie May (Sisco) B.; m. Frances Ann Giannone, June 26, 1965; 1 child, Lisa. BBA, Fairleigh-Dickinson U., 1976, MBA, 1982. Cert. purchasing mgr. Various adminstrv. positions Bell Telephone Labs., Murray Hill, N.J., 1961-78, fin. specialist, 1978-79, sr. contract buyer, 1980-83; supr. purchasing AT&T Tech., Short Hills, N.J., 1983-86; purchasing mgr. AT&T Techs., Short Hills, N.J., 1986—; cons. in field. Served with USAR, 1964-70. Mem. Nat. Assn. Purchasing Mgrs. (N.J. chpt.), Phi Omega Epsilon. Office: AT&T 101 John F Kennedy Pky Short Hills NJ 07078-2708

BEAUCHEMIN, JUDITH ANN, employment specialist; b. Rochester, N.Y., Mar. 14, 1939; d. Milton R. and Eunice L. (Consler) Swartzenberg; m. Joseph E. Beauchemin, Sept. 7, 1957; children: Josette Crane, Scott, Benjamin, Timothy, Tammy. Student, SUNY, Geneso, 1956-57. Unit mgr. Sarah Coventry, Inc., Newark, N.Y., 1968-72, pers. coord., 1972-84; employment specialist Clifton Springs (N.Y.) Hosp., 1984—; mem. adv. com. Blue Cross Blue Shield of Rochester Area, 1985-91; chair subcom. Job Svc. Employers Com. of Ont., Seneca, Wayne and Yates Counties, 1982-87, chairperson employer seminars, State Com. of Yr., 1989. Mem. student com. Coll. of Finger Lakes, Canandaigua, N.Y. Roman Catholic. Office: Clifton Springs Hosp Clifton Springs NY 14432

BEAUDOIN, CYNTHIA ANN, youth agency executive; b. Acushnet, Mass., July 31, 1940; d. Romeo and Agnes May (Donnelly) B. BS, Bridgewater State Coll., Mass., 1962; MS, Boston U., 1975. Prof. Lasell Jr. Coll., Auburndale, Mass., 1963-85; exec. dir. Camp Fire Boys and Girls Coun. Greater Boston/South Shore, Cambridge, Mass., 1985—; bd. dirs. Am. Camping Assn., Martinsville, Ind., 1988-92, treas., bd. dirs. New Eng. sect., Waltham, Mass., 1989—; treas., mem. exec. com. Child Care Careers Inst., Wheelock Coll., Boston, 1990—. Mem. Coll. Club Boston. Democrat. Office: Council for Greater Boston Camp Fire 380 Green St Cambridge MA 02139-3356

BEAUDOIN, PAUL E., composer, theorist, educator; b. Miami, Fla., Apr. 10, 1960. BM, U. Miami, 1983; MM with Acad. Distinction, New Eng. Conservatory of Music, Boston, 1987; PhD candidate, Brandeis U. Libr. New Eng. Conservatory, Boston, 1985-92; mem. music faculty Northeastern U., Boston, 1988—; chmn. young composers competition SCI/SESAC, 1989; lectr. in field. Composer: Stanzas, Aphorisms, A Ringing Bell, Etchings, Sandpoint Fragments. Mem. Soc. of Composers (co-chmn. New Eng. region 1988-90), Nat. Assn. Composers, Composers Forum, Boston Avant Garde Soc. Office: Music Dept Northeastern U 351 Ryder Hall Boston MA 02115

BEAUFORD, FRED, editor, educator; b. Neptune, N.J., Nov. 11, 1939; s. Robert Beauford and Louise (Morton) Scott; chidren: Danielle, Fred, Tama, Alexis. BS, NYU, 1971. Sr. lectr. U. So. Calif., L.A., 1977-81; editor, pub. Black Creation Mag., N.Y.C., 1969-73, Neworld Mag., L.A., 1974—; editor Crisis Mag., N.Y.C., 1985—; asst. prof. SUNY, Old Westbury, N.Y., 1990—. With U.S. Army, 1958-60, Germany. Home: 230 E 30th St New York NY 10016-8202 Office: Crisis Mag 260 E Fifth Ave 6th Fl New York NY 10061

BEAULIEU, JOSEPH ARMAND, interior designer; b. Webster, Maine, Sept. 15, 1934; s. Ludger and Yvonne (Poussard) B.; m. Beverly May Bonat,

June 3, 1960; children: Brian, Michele, Andre, Armand. Diploma, New Eng. Sch. Art, Boston, 1960. Designer Beacon Hill Furniture, Medford, Mass., 1961-64, Burke Furniture, Waltham, Mass., 1964-67; designer, owner Chestnut Hill Draperies, Newton, Mass., 1967—. With USCG, 1953-57. Mem. Boston Curtain and Drapery Club.

BEAUPAIN, ELAINE SHAPIRO, psychiatric social worker; b. Boston, Nov. 1, 1949; d. Abraham and Anna Marilyn (Gass) S.; m. Dean A. Beaupain, Feb. 14, 1987; 1 child, Andrew. BA, McGill U., Montreal, Que., 1971, MSW, 1974. Ind. clin. social worker, Mass.; cert. social worker, Maine; cert. social worker with pvt. practice lic., Maine. Psychiat. social worker Bangor (Maine) Mental Health Inst., 1974-75; outpatient therapist The Counseling Ctr., Bangor, 1975-76, The Counseling Ctr., Millinocket, Maine, 1979-86; asst. core group leader adolescent unit Jackson Brook Inst., Portland, Maine, 1986-87; area dir. Community Health and Counseling Svcs., 1981-86; pvt. practice social work, 1987—, psychotherapy with individuals, couples and families Millinocket and Bangor, 1987—. Mem. AAUW, Nat. Assn. Social Workers, Acad. Cert. Social Workers. Republican. Office: 122 Pine St Bangor ME 04401-5216

BEAUPRE, WALTER JOSEPH, speech-language pathologist/audiologist, educator; b. Franklin, N.H., Mar. 10, 1925; s. Joseph Walter and Daphne Arabelle (Young) B.; m. Kathryn Lesher Rafetto, May 24, 1960; 1 child, Laurier Walter. AB, Bates Coll., 1947; MA, Lehigh U., 1951; PhD, Columbia U., 1962. Cert. of clin. competence in speech-lang. pathology and audiology. Ast. prof. Moravian Coll., Bethlehem, Pa., 1948-59; instr. Columbia U., N.Y.C., 1959-62; prof. U. Nebr., Omaha, 1962-68, U. R.I., Kingston, 1968—; cons. R.I. div. Am. Cancer Soc., Providence, 1969-89; survey cons. Commn. on Accreditation of Rehab. Facilities, Tucson, 1970-90. Author: Gaining Cued Speech Proficiency, 1984; author standardized test; contbr. articles to profl. jours. Pres., Friends of R.B. Hale Libr., Wakefield, R.I., 1975-84, corr. sec., 1984-90. Recipient Cert. of Merit, Am. Cancer Soc., 1988. Mem. New Eng. Hist. Genealogic Soc., Nat. Cued Speech Assn. (rsch. com. 1989—, editor jour. 1984-86), R.I. Speech-Hearing Assn. (Disting. Svc. award 1991), Masons, Shriners, Scottish Rite. Republican. Mem. United Ch. of Christ. Home: 25 Segar Ct Wakefield RI 02879-5304 Office: U RI Dept Communicative Disorder Kingston RI 02881

BEAUREGARD, LUC, public relations executive; b. Montreal, Que., Can., Aug. 4, 1941; s. Francois and Gertrude (Lévesque) B.; m. Michelle Beauregard; children: Valérie, Stéphanie, Fracnois, Philippe. BA, Coll. Stanislas, Montreal. Reporter, parliamentary corr. in Ottawa, city editor Montreal (Que.) Daily La Presse, Can., 1961-68; press sec. Que. Ministry Edn., Quebec City, Que., 1968-69; founding ptnr. Beauregard, Landry, Nantel & Assocs. Pub. Rels. Cons., Montreal; pres., pub. Montreal-Matin Daily Newspaper, 1973-76; pres. Nat. Pub. Rels. Ltd., Montreal, 1976—; chmn. Amarc, City of Montreal Corp. managing Man and His World (formerly Expo '67), 1982-86. Sec. info. commn. Que. Liberal Party, 1978, 79, 80; chmn. Montreal Better Bus. Bur., 1983-84; dir. Nouvelle Compagnie Theatrale, St. Hubert BBQ, Que. Heart Found., 1983-85, active exec. com.; active Found. Montreal Mus. Contemporary Art, chmn., 1987-90; chmn. Found. Montreal Islam Sch. Coun., 1991—. Mem. N.Am. Pub. Rels. Coun. (chmn. 1985-86), Can. Pub. Rels. Coun. (pres. 1984-85, chmn. Cons. Inst. 1982-83), Club des Quinze. Office: Nat Public Relations, 770 Sherbrooke West Ste 1600, Montreal, PQ Canada H3A 1G1

BEAUSOLEIL, DORIS MAE, housing specialist, government agency official; b. Chelmsford, Mass., Jan. 9, 1932; d. Joseph Honorius and Beatrice Pearl (Smith) B.; student State Tchrs. Coll., Lowell, Mass., 1949-51; BA in Sociology and Psychology, Goddard Coll., Plainfield, Vt., 1954; MA in Human Relations, N.Y.U., 1957; postgrad. CUNY, N.Y.C., 1988—. With div. human rights N.Y. State, N.Y.C., 1960-69, housing dir., 1966-68; housing cons. Nat. Com. Against Discrimination in Housing, N.Y.C., 1969-70; housing cons. Edwin Gould Found., N.Y.C., 1970-71; human resources cons. interfaith housing strategy com., housing cons. Fedn. Prot. Welfare Agencies, Inc., N.Y.C., 1971-72; self-employed housing cons., 1972-74; equal opportunity compliance specialist Region II HUD, N.Y.C., 1975—, Fed. women's program coordinator, 1975-79; br. chief Title VI Sect. 109 Compliance div. fair housing and equal opportunity Region II, HUD, N.Y.C., 1979-84; founding mem. N.Y. State HUD Com.; adv. panel Housing Mag., 1979; cons., examiner N.Y. State Civil Service Commn., 1970—. Mem. Nat. Assn. Human Rights Workers (Outstanding Service award 1974), Citizens Housing and Planning Council, Federally Employed Women, Nat. Assn. Housing and Devel. Ofcls., Goddard Coll. Alumni Assn. (sec. 1988-90), Women's City Club N.Y., Rep. Bus. Women's Club (pres. 1985-88, bd. dirs. 1989-91). Republican. Unitarian. Home: 392 Central Park W New York NY 10025-5860 Office: 26 Federal Pla Rm 3532 New York NY 10278

BEAVEN, JOHN LEWIS, diplomat; b. Newport, Gwent, U.K., July 30, 1930; s. Charles and Doris Margaret (Lewis) B.; m. Jane Leigh Beeson, 1960 (div. 1975); children: Jacqueline Leigh, Christopher Nigel Gerard; m. Jean McComb Campbell, Sept. 10, 1975. Grad. high sch., Newport. Asst. trade commr. Brit. High Commn., Karachi, Pakistan, 1956-60; second sec. Brit. High Commn., Freetown, Sierra Leone, 1961-64; first sec. Brit. High Commn., Nicosia, Cyprus, 1964-66, Nairobi, Kenya, 1966-69; first sec. Fgn. Office, London, 1969-72; counsellor Brit. High Commn., Lagos, Nigeria, 1975-78; head of chancery Brit. Embassy, Jakarta, Indonesia, 1972-75; dep. consul gen. Brit. Consulate, N.Y.C., 1978-82; consul gen. Brit. Consulate, San Francisco, 1982-86; amb. Brit. Embassy, Khartoum, Sudan, 1986-90; U.S. rep. Save the Children Fund UK, 1990—. Pilot officer RAF, 1948-50. Comdr. Order of St. Michael and St. George, 1983, companion Royal Victorian Order, 1983. Mem. The Brook, Reform Club (London). Home: Scannell Rd Ghent NY 12075

BEAVEN, MARY H., educator; b. Evanston, Ill., Oct. 26, 1936; d. Charles F. and Sophia Marie (Flentye) Higginbotham; children: Mark W., Carey M. Student, Duke U., 1954-56; BS, Northwestern U., Evanston, Ill., 1959, MA, 1967, PhD, 1971. Tchr., English New Trier High Sch., Winnetka, Ill., 1957-58; tchr., English 2d lang. Waters Sch., Chgo., 1958-91; tchr., English Carleton Washburn Jr. High Sch., Winnetka, 1961-67; instr., creative arts, sch. music & sch. edn. Northwestern U., Evanston, 1968-69; asst. prof., dept. edn. Ind. U., South Bend, 1969-71; dir., assoc. prof. arts and humanities program, sch. edn. U. Mass., Amherst, 1971-73; assoc. prof., dept. elem. and secondary edn. Va. Commonwealth U., Richmond, 1977-78, dir. Inst. for Leadership Studies, 1978-83; prof. English Fairleigh Dickinson U., 1983-84, MBA program dir., 1983-86, prof. mgmt., 1987—; vis. scholar ctr. urban affairs and policy rsch. Northwestern U., Evanston, 1990-91. Author of poems; contbr. articles to profl. jours. Office: Fairleigh Dickinson U. 1000 River Rd Teaneck NJ 07666-1914

BEBELL, HARLAN, film distribution and production company executive; b. Danbury, Conn., Jan. 26, 1962; s. Norman Lars and Rochelle Harlan (Van Zandt) Bebell. BA, NYU, 1985; postgrad., Bryn Mawr Coll., 1985-87. V.p. Films for Educators, Inc./Films for TV, N.Y.C., 1987—; producer Paper Peter movie and TV series, 1990-91. Author: Dessert Recipes Children Love and Can Make, 1989. Nat. Endowment for Advancement of the Arts Presdl. scholar, 1980. Fellow The Netherland Club of N.Y. Republican. Episcopalian. Office: Films for Educators Inc 420 E 55th St Ste 6U New York NY 10022

BECCATELLI, THERESA CECILIA, educator; b. Norristown, Pa., Nov. 10, 1949; d. Joseph F. Jr. and Elsie M. (Caruso) Decker; m. John J. Beccatelli, June 27, 1987; 1 child, Anne Marie Foley. AA, Community Coll. Phila., 1969; BS, Ea. Ky. U., 1972; MEd, Temple U., 1975, EdD, 1986. Cert. tchr., Pa. Tchr. Sch. Dist. Phila., 1972-90; math. instr. Community Coll. Phila., 1979-82. Mem. Assn. for Supervision and Curriculum Devel., Assn. of Tchrs. of Math. Phila., Nat. Coun. Tchrs. Math., Kappa Delta Pi. Roman Catholic.

BECHERER, RICHARD JOHN, architectural educator; b. East St. Louis, Ill., Nov. 8, 1951; s. Adam Jacob and Agnes Evelyn (Baker) B.; m. Charlene Castellano, Aug. 13, 1982. Student Courtauld Inst., U. London, 1973; BA, BArch, Rice U., 1974; MA, Cornell U., 1977, PhD, 1981. Archtl. asst. Colin St. John Wilson and Ptnr., London, 1972-73; designer The Brooks Assn., Houston, 1973-74; grad. asst. Cornell U., Ithaca, N.Y., 1974-80, assoc. prof. architecture, 1981; assoc. prof. architecture Auburn (Ala.) U., 1980-82; asst. prof. architecture U. Va., Charlottesville, 1982-86; head grad. program architecture Carnegie Mellon U., Pitts., 1986-90; presenter seminars NEH, 1982, 88, 89, Am. Collegiate Schs. Architecture 1988—; lectr. various colls., univs. and nat. confs. Author: Science Plus Sentiment: César Daly's Formula for Modern Architecture, 1984, (mus. catalogue and display) Urban Theory and Transformation, 1976, (tourist guidebook) Canandaigua: A Walking Tour, 1977; contbr. articles to profl. jours.; prin. works include interiors Michael P. Keeley House, Belleville, Ill., 1978, Plandome, N.Y., 1990, Robert Becherer House, Stonybrook, N.Y., 1990; selected exhibitor Venice Biennale, Prato della Valle, Padua, 1985. Grad. fellow Cornell U., 1975-79, Eidlitz fellow, 1978, Soc. for Humanities and Mellon Found. fellow, 1984-85; fellow NEH, 1986; Travel to Collections grantee NEH, 1985; recipient Design Arts award Nat. Endowment Arts, 1989-90. Mem. AAUP, Soc. Archtl. Historians (session chmn. ann. meeting 1989), Coll. Art Assn., Rice U. Alumni Assn. Democrat. Roman Catholic. Home: 119 Race St Edgewood PA 15218 Office: Carnegie Mellon Univ Dept Architecture CFA 5000 Forbes Ave Pittsburgh PA 15213

BECHTEL, SARA ELIZABETH, clergywoman; b. Pottstown, Pa., July 11, 1954; d. Kenneth Franklin and Phyllis Jeanne (Griswold) B.; m. Stephen Frank Bueker, Oct. 1, 1989. BS in Secondary Edn., Math., West Chester State Coll., 1976; MDiv, Luth. Theol. Sem. at Phila., 1984. Ordained minister Luth. Ch., 1984. Math. tchr. Pottstown Sch. Dist., 1976-77; dir. Christian edn. Grace Luth. Ch., Pottstown, 1978-80; pastor Zion Luth. Ch., Balt., 1984-88; pastor-assoc. First Luth. Ch., Ellicott City, Md., 1988—; conf. rep. Del.-Md. Synod Evang. Luth. Ch. Am., 1987-88, 90—, mem. constn. and bylaws com., 1991, coun. liaison, mem. commn. for ch. in society, 1991, chmn. memls. com. for ann. conv., 1991. Bd. dirs. Nat. Luth. Home for the Aged, Rockville, Md. Democrat. Office: First Luth Ch 3604 Chatham Rd Ellicott City MD 21042-3920

BECHTLE, LOUIS CHARLES, federal judge; b. Phila., Dec. 14, 1927; s. Charles R. and Gladys (Kirchner) B.; m. Margaret Beck, Sept. 7, 1978; children: Barbara, Nancy, Amy; 1 stepchild, Samuel. B.S., Temple U., 1951, LL.B., 1954. Bar: Pa. 1954. Asst. U.S. atty. U.S. Dept. Justice, Phila., 1957-59, U.S. atty., 1969-72; pvt. practice law Jacoby & Maxmin, Phila., 1959-62; pvt. practice Wisler, Pearlstine, Talone, Gerber, Norristown, Pa., 1962-69; U.S. dist. judge U.S. Dist. Ct., Phila., 1972—; adj. faculty Temple U. Law Sch., Phila., 1974—, Villanova Law Sch., 1985-89. Served with U.S. Army, 1946-47. Mem. Montgomery County Bar Assn., Fed. Bar Assn. Republican. Presbyterian. Office: US Dist Ct US Courthouse Rm 17613 Independence Mall W Philadelphia PA 19106*

BECK, ANDREW JAMES, lawyer; b. Washington, Feb. 19, 1948; s. Leonard Norman and Frances (Greif) B.; m. Gretchen Ann Schroeder, Feb. 14, 1971; children: Carter, Lowell, Justin. BA, Carleton Coll., 1969; JD, Stanford U., 1972; MBA, Long Island U., 1975. Bar; Va. 1972, N.Y. 1973. Assoc. Casey, Lane & Mittendorf, N.Y.C., 1972-80, ptnr., 1980-82; managing ptnr. Haythe & Curley, N.Y.C., 1982—. Trustee Bklyn. Heights Synagogue, 1980-81; trustee Bklyn. Heights Montessori Sch., 1988—, treas., 1990—. Mem. ABA, Va. State Bar Assn., New York State Bar Assn., Assn. of Bar of City of N.Y. Home: 71 Willow St Apt 1 Brooklyn NY 11201-1618 Office: Haythe & Curley 237 Park Ave New York NY 10017

BECK, DOROTHY FAHS, social researcher; b. N.Y.C.; d. Charles Harvey and Sophia (Lyon) Fahs; m. Hubert Park Beck, Aug. 20, 1930 (dec. Jan. 1989); 1 child, Brenda E.F. AB, U. N.C., 1928; MA, U. Chgo., 1932; PhD (Gilder fellow), Columbia U., 1944, postdoctoral study, 1955-56. Am.-German Student Exch. fellow, Fed. Republic Germany, 1928-29. Dir. econ. rsch. ADA, 1929-32; social worker Emergency Relief Adminstrn. N.J., 1933-34, statistician, 1934-35; statistician U.S. Office Edn., 1935-36; assoc. social economist U.S. Cen. Statis. Bd., 1936-38; rsch. supr., author Am. Coll. Dentists, 1940-42; statistician Am. Heart Assn., 1947-53, Cornell U. Med. Coll., 1951-53; asst. prof. biostats. Am. U. Beirut, 1954: bd. dir. rsch. Family Svc. Am., N.Y.C., 1956-81, dir. study counselor attitudes and feelings, 1982-87, evaluation rsch. cons., 1982-87. Co-founder, Fahs-Beck Fund for Rsch. and Experimentation; donor-adviser The N.Y. Community Trust, 1986—. Fellow Am. Sociol. Assn.; mem. Acad. Cert. Social Workers, Am. Assn. Marriage and Family Therapy (affiliate), Nat. Coun. Family Rels., Groves Conf., Am. Statis. Assn., Nat. Assn. Social Workers, Soc. Study Social Problems, Am. Pub. Health Assn., Phi Beta Kappa. Unitarian-Universalist. Author: Patterns in Use of Family Agency Service, 1962, Marriage and the Family Under Challenge, 1976, New Treatment Modalities, 1978, Counselor Characteristics: How They Affect Outcomes, 1988; co-author: Costs of Dental Care Under Specific Clinical Conditions, 1943, Myocardial Infarction, 1954, Clients' Progress within Five Interviews, 1970, How to Conduct a Client Follow-Up Study, 1974, 2d enlarged edit., 1980, Progress on Family Problems, 1973. Home: Crosslands Apt 50 Kennett Square PA 19348

BECK, JEFFREY DENGLER, banking executive; b. Wilmington, Del., Apr. 2, 1948; s. Theodore S. and Alice (Palmer) B.; m. Elizabeth Jeannie Townsend, Nov. 29, 1969; children: Charles Andrew, David Hanby. BA, Ursinus Coll., 1970; MBA, U. Del., 1975. Cert. chartered fin. analyst, Del. Various positions Wilmington Trust Co., 1970-80; v.p. adminstrn., protfilio mgr., asset/liability planning Indsl. Valley Bank & Trust Co., Phila., 1980-85; v.p., portfolio mgr., asset/liability planning Fidelity Bank, Phila., 1985-86; sr. v.p., dir. funds mgmt., asset/liability planning Advanta/Colonial Nat. Bank USA, Wilmington, 1986—. Mem. Peoples Settlement Assn. Fed. Credit Union (adv. coun. 1990—). Republican. Episcopalian.

BECK, MANFRED HERMAN JOSEF, company executive; b. Tegernsee, West Germany, Feb. 18, 1943; came to U.S. 1979; s. Josef and Berta (Hilzensauer) B.; children: Sabine, Andreas. M.Econs., U. Munich, Ger. With Deutsche Babcock w. Wilcox AG, Oberhausen, W. Ger., 1970-74; mkt. research and advt. mgr. SKW Trostberg AG, Trostberg, W. Ger., 1976; gen. mgr. sales SKW Can., Inc., Montreal, Que., Can., 1976-79; exec. v.p. sales SKW Alloys Inc., Niagara Falls, N.Y., 1979-83; pres. SKW Metals and Alloys, Niagara Falls, 1983, Stollberg Inc., Niagara Falls, 1988—; bd. dirs. SKW East Asia, Tokyo, 1985—. With Ger. Air Force, 1962-64. Mem. Niagara Falls Country Club. Home: 766 S The Cir Lewiston NY 14092-2031

BECK, MARJORIE RUTH, communications company executive; b. Hartford, Conn., May 25, 1956; d. Louis A. and Etta (Pasternack) B. Grad. high sch., West Hartford, Conn., 1974; diploma, Conn. Stenographic Inst., 1976. Assoc. Howard Gustafson Reporting Svc., Middletown, Conn., 1976-77; owner Marjorie R. Beck Reporting Svc., Cromwell, 1977-79; adminstrv. asst. Entertainment and Sports Programming Network, Bristol, Conn., 1979-82; sales sec. Sta. WVIT-TV Viacom Internat., West Hartford, 1982-84; account exec. Sta. WTIC-TV Chase Communications, Hartford, 1984-86; sr. account exec. Sta. WHCT-TV Astroline Communications, Hartford, 1986-88; exec. v.p. Career Media Network, Farmington, Conn., 1988-89; pres., ind. radio and TV buyer MRB Media Svcs., Windsor, 1989—; exec. producer For Your Lesiure, TV program aired on various network affiliate stas. in targeted market areas. Exec. producer (TV program) For Your Leisure. Life mem. Jewish Childrens' Svc. Orgn., Jewish Assn. Community Living, Sigel Greater Hartford Community Hebrew Acad., Hebrew Home & Hosp., Am. Med. Ctr. at Denver. Mem. Women In Communications, Inc., New Eng. Broadcasting Assn., Advt. Club of Greater Hartford (bd. dirs.). Home and Office: 1179 Matianuck Ave Windsor CT 06095 Office: MRB Media Svcs 1179 Matianuck Ave Windsor CT 06095-3215

BECK, NANCY FLAHERTY, executive; b. Pitts.; d. John T. and Margaret Houlihan; m. Paul A. Beck, Aug. 10, 1990. BA, Carlow Coll., 1967; MEd, U. Pitts., 1969. Pres. Flaherty Assocs.; mktg. dir. History & Landmarks Fedn., Pitts.; comml. real estate sales Howard Hanna Real Estate, Pitts., 1980-82; dir. devel. Found. for Abraxas, Pitts., 1982-90; exec. dir. Extra Mile Edn. Found., Pitts., 1990—; bd. dirs. Leadership Pitts. Alumni Assn., 1990-91; leadership circle Family Hospice, Pitts., 1990—. Office: Extra Mile Edn Found 111 Blvd Of The Allies Pittsburgh PA 15222-1618

BECK, NORMAN WOOD, retired political science educator; b. Cottage Grove, Oreg., July 8, 1901; s. Lafayette Dillard Beck and Eugenie Fussell Steele; m. Evelyn Virginia Eastman Linn, Aug. 15, 1931; 1 child, Peter Lynwood. ABA, U. Chgo., 1923, PhD, 1941; postgrad., Columbia U., 1952-54. Acting asst. prof. U. Mo., Columbia, 1929-30; instr. Yale U., New Haven, Conn., 1931-32, Dartmouth Coll., Hanover, N.H., 1932-39, Hunter Coll., N.Y.C., 1939-43, 50-51, Bklyn. Coll., 1941-42, NYU, N.Y.C., 1941-42; vist. lectr. Smith U., Northampton, Mass., 1943-44; asst. prof. Wilson Coll., Chambersburg, Pa., 1944-47, Jersey City (N.J.) State Coll., 1947-57; prof. Jersey City State Coll., 1957-72, prof. emeritus, 1974—, chmn. polit. sci. dept., 1969-72; chmn. task force Jersey City State Coll., 1979-80, dir. practicum in practical politics, 1960-72. Author: Toward Understanding Power and Its Uses-Machiavelli, Jesus, I Thou, 1987; contbr. articles to profl. jours. Trustee Friends World Coll., Huntington, L.I., N.Y., 1971-74; com. chmn. Mendham (N.J.) Borough Dems., 1978-79; chmn. Mendham Borough Environ. Commn., 1978-82. Recipient Disting. Community Svc. award Mendham Borough, 1982; Polit. Sci. Dept. Honors fellow U. Chgo., 1926. Mem AAUP (chpt. pres. 1968-70), N.J. Polit. Sci. Assn. (exec. coun. 1972-78, Disting. Svc. award 1977), Phi Beta Kappa. Mem. Soc. of Friends. Home: 40 Morris Lake Rd Sparta NJ 07871-3616

BECK, ROBERT CHARLES, marketing company executive; b. Detroit, Dec. 27, 1951; s. Charles E. and Ruth Evelyn (Sintay) B. BA, NYU, 1975, MBA, 1991. Correspondent N.Y. Daily News, N.Y.C., 1972-75; proj. mgr. Norton Simon, Inc., N.Y.C., 1975-78; asst. account exec. Benton & Bowles, N.Y.C., 1978-79; sr. account exec. LKP Internat. Ltd., N.Y.C., 1980-82; dir. advt. and mktg. AMF, Inc., White Plains, N.Y., 1982-86; ptnr., pres. The Savant Group, N.Y.C., 1986—. Bd. dirs. Opera Ensemble of N.Y., N.Y.C., 1989—; mem. of session 1st Presbyn. Ch., N.Y.C., 1990—. Mem. Metropolitan Club (N.Y.C.). Republican. Home: 7 E 10th St New York NY 10003-5921 Office: The Savant Group 5 E 57th St # 18fl New York NY 10022-2515

BECK, ROBERT EDWARD, computer scientist; b. Denver, June 7, 1941; s. Arthur Walter and Caroline Adelheid (Petrie) B.; m. Barbara Ruth Pennell, Aug. 21, 1965; children: Philip Arthur, Christopher William, Jennifer Grove. BS in Math., Harvey Mudd Coll., Claremont, Calif., 1963; PhD in Math., U. Pa., 1969. Instr. Villanova (Pa.) U., 1966-69, asst. prof., 1969-74, assoc. prof., 1974-78, prof. computer sci., 1978—; visitor Computing Sci. Accreditation Bd., 1986—. Author: Elementary Linear Programming, 1980; editor: Computers in Nonassociative Rings and Algebras, 1978. Fulbright Exchange fellow, 1981-82. Mem. AAUP, ACM (computer sci. conf. steering com.), Am. Math. Soc., Sigma Xi. Office: Villanova U Dept Computing Sci Villanova PA 19085

BECK, WILLIAM AUSTIN, mathematician, educator; b. Lakewood, Ohio, Feb. 6, 1930; s. Clair Austin and Elizabeth Irene (Russell) B.; m. Dorothy Jane Wentworth, Mar. 31, 1951; children: David Austin, Norman Edward, Matthew Lewis. BS in Math., Case Inst. Tech., 1951; MS in Math., Purdue U., 1953, PhD, 1955. Grad. teaching asst. Purdue U., West Lafayette, Ind., 1951-53, grad. rsch. asst., 1953-55; asst. prof. math. Bucknell U., Lewisburg, Pa., 1955-58; from asst. to prof. math. Chatham Coll., Pitts., 1958—; lectr. in math. Ind. (Pa.) State U., 1960-65; Fulbright lectr. Al Hikma U., Baghdad, Iraq, 1965-66. Co-author: Elements of Mathematics-Physics, 1989. Treas. Advocates for Mentally Ill in Transition, Pitts., 1984—, Country Dance and Song Soc. Pitts., 1985—. Mem. Am. Math. Soc., Math. Assn. Am., AAUP, Pa. Coun. Tchrs. Math. Office: Chatham Coll Woodland Rd Pittsburgh PA 15232-2814

BECKEL, ROBERT GILLILAND, political analyst; b. N.Y.C., Nov. 15, 1948; s. Graham and Ellen (Gilliland) B. BS in Econs., Wagner Coll., 1970. Vol. Peace Corps, The Philippines, 1971-72; pvt. practice polit. cons. Washington, 1972-75; Washington dir. Nat. Com. for an Effective Congress, 1975-77; dep. asst. sec. state-congressional rels. U.S. State Dept., Washington, 1977-78; polit. cons. Bob Beckel & Assocs., Washington, 1980-82; campaign mgr. Mondale for Pres., Washington, 1983-84; ptnr. Nat. Strategies & Mktg. Group, Washington, 1985-89; chmn. BBA, Inc., Washington, 1989—; host TV program Off the Record, Fox TV, Washington, 1990-92; analyst TV program CBS This Morning, Washington; guest host TV programs Larry King Live, CNN, Washington, 1990—, Crossfire, CNN, Washington, 1990—; lectr. Sch. Pub. Affairs, U. Md., College Park, 1991. Contbr. articles to LA Times. Bd. dirs. City Lights, Washington, 1990-92. Democrat. Episcopal. Home: 3103 Hawthorne St NW Washington DC 20008-3540 Office: BBA Inc 1000 Potomac St NW # 301 Washington DC 20007-3501

BECKENSTEIN, JAY BARNET, musician, record producer, composer; b. N.Y.C., May 14, 1951; s. Leonard and Lorraine (Weinman) B.; m. Jennifer Anne Johnson, June 3, 1984; children: Claire Rossignol, Alexandra Rose. BFA, SUNY, Buffalo, 1973. Founder Spyro Gyra, Buffalo, 1975—; pres. Crosseyed Bear Prodns., Inc., Buffalo, 1976—, BearTracks Recording Studio, Inc., Suffern, N.Y., 1982—; clinician, endorsee Yamaha Mus. Instruments Corp., Grand Rapids, Mich., 1989—. Musician, producer, composer, leader numerous recordings. Recipient 3 Gold Record awards Recording Industry Assn. Am., 1979-81, Platinum Record award, 1987; named Jazz Artist of Yr., Billboard Mag., 1980, Jazz Group of Yr., Playboy Mag., 1990-91. Mem. Nat. Acad. Recording Arts and Scis. (Grammy nomination 1980, 82-85, 87, 90). Democrat. Jewish. Office: Crosseyed Bear Prodns Inc 278 Haverstraw Rd Suffern NY 10901

BECKER, BEVERLY JUNE, educator; b. Paterson, N.J., July 28, 1930; d. George Lawrence and Adelaide (Hulse) B. AB, Wellesley (Mass.) Coll., 1951; MEd, U. N.C., Greensboro, 1954; PhD, U. Oreg., Eugene, 1967. Instr. U. Nebr., Lincoln, 1954-56, Mt. Holyoke Coll., S. Hadley, Mass., 1956-59; prof. edn. Skidmore Coll., Saratoga Springs, N.Y., 1959—; vis. prof. U.S. Mil. Acad., 1984-85. Recipient Merit award, Ea. Assn. for Phys. Edn. of Coll. Women, 1977, Outstanding Civilian Svc. Medal, Dept. of the Army, 1985. Fellow Am. Coll. Sports Medicine; mem. Nat. Assn. for Phys. Edn. in Higher Edn. (pres. 1986-88, Past Pres.'s award 1991), Ea. Assn. for Phys. Edn. of Coll. Women (pres. 1974), AAHPERD. Office: Skidmore College North Broadway Saratoga Springs NY 12866

BECKER, BRIAN ELDEN, management educator; b. Springfield, Ill., Mar. 23, 1949; s. Elden Otis and Sara Jane (Fraley) B.; m. Mary Jan Walker, July 10, 1970; children: Emily, Ethan. Student, U. Ill., 1967-71; BA, Sangamon State U., 1971, MA, 1972; PhD, U. Wis., 1977. Rsch. scientist Inst. for Social Policy, Springfield, Ill., 1971-73; asst. prof. Sch. Mgmt. SUNY, Buffalo, 1977-83, assoc. prof. Sch. Mgmt., 1983-89, prof. Sch. Mgmt., 1989—. Co-author: The Impact of Collective Bargaining on Hospitals, 1979; contbr. articles to profl. jours. Mem. Indsl. Rels. Rsch. Assn., Am. Econ. Assn., Acad. Mgmt. Office: SUNYAB School Mgmt 268 Jacobs Mgmt Ctr Buffalo NY 14260

BECKER, BRUCE CLARE, clinical psychologist, neuropsychologist, administrator; b. Seattle, Dec. 9, 1929; s. Eugene J. and Hedwig (Gottschalk) B.; m. Margaret Carol Peddle, Nov. 26, 1955; children: Cheryl, Cecilia, Bruce Jr., Gregory, Kurt, Christopher, Lise. AB, St. Ambrose U., 1950; AM, St. Louis U., 1954; PhD, Loyola U., Chgo., 1962. Cert. clin. psychologist, clin. neuropsychologist Am. Bd. Profl. Psychology. Commd. ensign USN, 1954, advanced through grades to capt., 1975; clin. psychologist Tng. Ctr. USN, Great Lakes, Ill., 1975; dir. clin. psychology tng. USN, 1964-84; clin. psychologist U.S. Naval Hosp., Great Lakes, 1958-65; clin. neuropsychologist VA Hosp., Downey, Ill., 1965-68, chief of psychology svc., 1968-69; ret., USN, 1989; pres. Neuropsychology Assocs. Ltd., Bethesda, 1984—; ret. USN, 1989; cons. in neuropsychology U.S. Dept. State, Washington, 1975—, CIA, 1975—, Peace Corps, 1975—, U.S. Capitol Physician, 1988—. Cons. editor (jour.) The Clin. Neuropsychologist, 1988-90; contbr. chpts. to books and articles to profl. jours. Fellow APA; mem. Internat. Neuropsychol. Soc. Home and Office: 9508 Newbold Pl Bethesda MD 20817-2226

BECKER, CONNIE LYNN, accountant; b. Kansas City, Kans., June 20, 1968; d. Gerald Mathew and Bernita Marie (Gerstenkorn) B. BS, Villanova U., 1990. Staff acct. Ernst & Young, Phila., 1990—. Scholarship Nat. Soc. Pub. Accts., 1989, Arthur H. Carter scholarship Am. Acctg. Assn., 1989. Mem. Pa. Inst. CPA (scholarship 1989), Beta Gamma Sigma. Republican. Roman Catholic. Home: 4 W Athens Ave Apt I Ardmore PA 19003 Office: Ernst & Young 1800 John F Kennedy Blvd Philadelphia PA 19103-2925

BECKER, EDWARD ROY, federal judge; b. Phila., May 4, 1933; s. Herman A. and Jeannette (Levit) B.; m. Flora Lyman, Aug. 11, 1957; children: James Daniel (dec. 1969), Jonathan Robert, Susan Rose, Charles Lyman. B.A., U. Pa., 1954; LL.B., Yale U., 1957. Bar: Pa. 1957. Ptnr. Becker, Becker & Fryman, Phila., 1957-70; U.S. Dist. Judge, 1970-82; judge U.S. Ct. Appeals (3d cir.), 1982—; mem. Jud. Conf. Com. on Long Range Planning, 1990—; mem. Counsel Rep. City Com., Phila., 1965-70; mem. task force on implementation of new jud. article Joint State Govt. Commn., 1969; lectr. law U. Pa. Law Sch., 1978-83; mem. edn. adv. com. concerning Comprehensive Crime Control Act, Fed. Jud. Ctr., 1981-90, Fed. Jud. Ctr. Com. on Sentencing, Probation and Pretrial Svcs., 1985-90; bd. dirs. Fed. Jud. Ctr., 1991—. Bd. editors Manual for Complex Litigation, 1981-90. Trustee Magna Carta Found., Phila.; vis. com. U. Chgo. Law Sch., 1988-91. Mem. ABA (jud. rep. antitrust sect. 1983-86), Phila. Bar Assn., Am. Judicature Soc., Am. Law Inst. (adv. com. restatement conflict of laws 2d; ALI-ABA continuing edn. adv. com. on trial practice), Jud. Conf. U.S. (com. on adminstrn. probation system 1979-87, chmn. com. on criminal law and probation adminstrn. 1987-90), Phi Beta Kappa. Jewish. Home: 936 Herbert St Philadelphia PA 19124-2417 Office: US Ct Appeals 19613 US Courthouse 601 Market St Philadelphia PA 19106-1510*

BECKER, HERBERT S., information technology director; b. Rochester, N.Y., Dec. 4, 1931; m. Carol Ann Moody, Nov. 8, 1966; children: Scott MacPhie. BA with honors, Cornell U., 1954; MA, U. Chgo., 1956; postgrad., U. Ill., 1956-57. Instr. U. Ill., 1957-62; mgmt. intern, budget analyst, program analyst Dept. of the Navy, 1962-65; dir. mgmt. systems Post Office Dept., 1965; dir. program planning and evaluation Small Bus. Adminstrn., 1967-69; dir. adminstrn. and program analysis Econ. Devel. Adminstrn., 1969-80; dir. policy rsch. and info. MBDA, 1980-85; dir. automated systems office Libr. of Congress, Washington, Va., 1985-89, dir. info. tech. svcs., 1988—. Home: 2311 Connecticut Ave NW # 40 Washington DC 20008 Office: Libr Congress 1st and Independence SE Washington DC 20540

BECKER, HOWARD H., executive; b. Rochester, N.Y., June 20, 1940; s. Abe and Sylvia (Kaplan) B.; m. G. Sharon MacLaughlin, June 14, 1961 (div. 1982); children: Martin (dec.), Daniel, Scott. BS, Cornell U., 1962. Various positions Beckers Big Boy, Rochester, N.Y., 1954-68; v.p. B.W. Streeter Inc., McLean, Va., 1968-79, Reg Restaurants, Rochester, 1979-82; pres. Irby-Clark Corp., Holcomb, N.Y., 1982—; bd. dirs. N.Y. State Restaurant Assn., Rochester, 1979-81, pres. 1981-82. Mem. Loyal Order Moose, Cornell Hotel Assn. Republican. Jewish. Home: 80 Center Ln Holcomb NY 14469-9580 Office: Irby-Clark Corp Rts 5 & 20 Holcomb NY 14469

BECKER, LAWRENCE WILFRED, headmaster; b. Albany, N.Y., Nov. 16, 1941; s. Randall Damas and Hilda (Meuser) B.; m. Grace Marianne Zelinka, Aug. 23, 1969. BA, Amherst Coll., 1963; MA in Teaching, Harvard U., 1964. Math. instr. Hotchkiss Sch., Lakeville, Conn., 1964-86, dir. coll. counseling, 1969-80, dean admission and coll. counseling, 1980-82, dean faculty, 1982-86, asst. headmaster, 1983-86; headmaster Brooks Sch., North Andover, Mass., 1986—. Co-author: Relevant Mathematics/Algebra, 1970, Relevant Mathematics/Geometry, 1971, Relevant Mathematics/Advanced Algebra and Trigonometry, 1971. Trustee Brooks Sch., 1986—, Pike Sch., Andover, Mass., 1988—. Mem. Univ. Club, Lanam Club, North Andover Country Club. Home and Office: Brooks Sch 1160 Great Pond Rd North Andover MA 01845-1298

BECKER, MARY LOUISE, political scientist; b. St. Louis; d. W. R. and Evelyn (Thompson) Becker; divorced; children: James, John. BS, Washington U., St. Louis, 1949, MA, 1951; PhD, Radcliffe Coll., 1957; postgrad., U. Karachi (Pakistan), 1953-54. Intelligence rsch. analyst Dept. State, Washington, 1957-59; internat. rels. officer AID, Washington, 1959-64, community rels. officer, 1964-66, sci. rsch. officer, 1966-71, UN rels. officer, 1971-91; pres. Internat. Devel. Enterprises, Washington, 1992—; adviser U.S. dels. 19th, 21st, 23d, 24th, 26th, 28th, 30th, 32d, 34th Governing Coun. sessions UN Devel. Program; adv. U.S. del. 3d prep. com. meeting World Conf. UN Decade for Women; adviser U.S. dels. UNICEF exec. bd. sessions, 1987-91; lectr. internat. rels. civic orgns., student groups, 1954—; mem. U.S. Com. for UN Fund for Women. Author: Muhammed Iqbal, 1965; contbg. editor: Concise Ency. of Middle East, 1973; contbr. articles to govt. publs. Mem. adv. bd. chmn. internat. student placement Washington Citizenship Seminar, Nat. YMCA-YWCA, Washington, 1961-71. Blewett fellow Washington U., 1951, Resident fellow Radcliff Coll., 1952-56; Fulbright scholar U. Karachi, 1953-54. Mem. AAUW, Am. Polit. Sci. Assn., Soc. Internat. Devel., Assn. Asian Studies, Asia Soc., Middle East Inst., UN Assn. (bd. dirs. Nat. Capital area 1991—), South Asian Muslim Studies Assn. (v.p. 1992—), Mo. Soc. Washington (sec. 1959-60), Mortar Bd., Chimes, Internat. Club, Harvard Club (Washington), Alpha Lambda Delta, Beta Gamma Sigma, Eta Mu Phi, Pi Sigma Alpha. Presbyterian. Office: North Bldg Ste 700 601 Pennsylvania Ave NW Washington DC 20004

BECKER, MURRAY LEONARD, corporate financial consultant, consulting actuary; b. Phila., July 30, 1933; s. Simon and Bertha B. (Berlin) B.; m. Anita Goodman, Apr. 3, 1955; children: Mark, Lynn, Donna. BS in Econs., U. Pa., 1955. Actuary Mutual of N.Y., N.Y.C., 1955-70; v.p., cons. actuary Johnson & Higgins, N.Y.C., 1970-88; pres. Becker & Rooney, Inc., Teaneck, N.J., 1988—. Mem. actuarial adv. com. N.Y.C. Retirement System, 1990. Named Advisor of Yr., Pension World Magazine, 1986. Fellow Soc. of Actuaries; mem. Am. Acad. Actuaries, Actuarial Soc. N.Y. (pres. 1982-83). Home: 631 James Ln River Vale NJ 07675-6457 Office: Becker & Rooney Inc Glenpointe Centre E 300 Frank W Burr Blvd Teaneck NJ 07666-6703

BECKER, RALPH ELIHU, lawyer, diplomat; b. N.Y.C., Jan. 29, 1907; s. Max Joseph and Rose (Becker) B.; m. Ann Marie Watters; children: William Watters, Donald Lee, Pamela Rose, Ralph Elihu Jr. LL.B., St. John's U., 1928; L.L.D., St. Johns U., 1983; LL.D. (hon.), South Eastern U., Washington. Bar: N.Y. 1929, U.S. Supreme Ct. 1940, D.C. 1949. Practice in Washington, 1948-86; ret. ptnr. Breed, Abbott & Morgan, 1986; asst. counsel to U.S. Senate Subcom. Elections and Privileges, 1951; founding trustee John F. Kennedy Ctr. for Performing Arts, 1958-76, hon. trustee, 1980—; U.S. ambassador to Honduras, 1976-77; Disting. lectr. Strom Thurmond Inst. Clemson U., S.C.; assoc. mem. coun. NASA Task Force for Comml. Use Space. Author: Miracle on the Potomac: Kennedy Center from the Beginning, 1990, Hail to the Candidate: Presidential Campaigns from Banners to Broadcast, 1992, also numerous booklets, articles on constl. law, ins., space law, atomic energy. Chmn. cultural devel. com. Met. Washington Bd. of Trade, 1958, former bd. dirs., gen. counsel, 1964-71; dir. emeritus, bd. dirs., gen. counsel, sec. Albert Schweitzer Found., 1955; pres. bd. dirs. Voice Found., 1976—, Friends of LBJ Library; adv. com. L.B. Johnson Meml. Grove on the Park; founding dir., former gen. counsel Wolf Trap Found., 1964-76; mem. adv. com. Sec. Interior Wolf Trap Farm Park for Performing Arts; rep. of Pres. L.B. Johnson with rank spl. ambassador Independence Ceremonies, Swaziland, 1968; mem. Arctic Expdn. for polar bears Washington Zoo, 1962, Antarctic-South Pole Operation Deepfreeze, 1963; nat. chmn. Young Republicans, 1946-49; mem. Rep. Nat. Exec. Com., 1948-51, Pres.'s Inaugural Com., 1953, 57, 69, 73, 80, 83, Vice Pres. Rockefeller Inaugural Medal Com., Rep. Senatorial Inner Circle, fin. com. Rep. Eagle, Presdl. Task Force; charter mem. Nat. Rep. Congl. Com.; donor collection polit. Americana to Smithsonian Instn., Dartmouth Coll., St. Albans Sch., L.B.J. Library, U. Tex., Austin., Strom Thurmond Inst., Clemson U. (S.C.); founder, dir. Inter-Am. Music Festival; founding mem. Friends of the Nat. Zoo, 1958; mem. St. Albans Parish. Served to capt. JAGS, AUS, 1942-45 (ass't and acting judge advocate 30th Infantry Div.), ETO. Decorated Bronze Star medal U.S.; chevalier Legion of Honor; Croix de Guerre with palm France; Belgian Fourragere; Order Morazon 1st class Honduras; chevalier and officer So. Cross of Brazil; Knighthood of Order of Dannebrog, Denmark; Gt. Cross for Meritorious Services to Austrian Republic; Royal Order de Vasa Sweden; Netherlands Resistance Meml. Cross; Order Rising Sun Japan; Vets. of Battle of Bulge; recipient Smithsonian Instn. Benefactor medal, 1975; Antarctic Service medal; Mt. Becker Antarctic; honored with award by OAS, 1968, Man of Yrs. award Metropolitan (Wash.) Bd. Trade, 1989; N.Y. State Good Conduct medal. Fellow Corcoran Gallery Art, Aspen Inst. Humanistic Studies; mem. ABA (mem. major coms., del. Internat. Bar Assn. com. meeting Monte Carlo 1954, Oslo, 1956, chmn. Vienna post conv. ABA meeting London 1957), D.C. Bar Assn., N.Y. State Bar Assn., Westchester County Bar Assn., Internat. Bar Assn., Fed. Bar Assn. (nat. council), Am. Law Inst. (life mem.), 30th Inf. Div. Assn. (pres. 1958), U.S. Capitol Hist. Soc. (founding dir.), N.Y. State Soc. (pres. 1963-64), Hist. Soc. Washington, Arctic Polar Inst. (hon.), Smithsonian Assn. (nat. mem.), Supreme Ct. Hist. Soc. (founding dir., mem. exec. com., chmn. ann. meetings 1978, 79, 80), Am. Fedn. Musicians (hon.), James Smithson Soc. of Smithsonian Assocs. (life), Friends of the Folger Library, Friends of Nat. Zoo (founding), Ctr. For Study of Presidency, Dwight D. Eisenhower Soc. (hon. trustee), Nat. Wildflower Research Ctr., Dacor-Bacon House Found., Choral Arts Soc. (hon.), Coun. Am. Ambs., Am. Fgn. Service Officers Assn., Diplomatic and Consular Officers Ret., Capitol Hill Club, Masons (32 degree). Home: 4000 Massachusetts Ave NW Washington DC 20016-5105 Office: 1818 N St NW Ste 600 Washington DC 036-2479

BECKER, RAYMOND JOHN, JR., higher education administrator; b. Camden, N.J., Dec. 14, 1956; s. Raymond John and Janet Claire (Tiedeken) B. BS, Trenton State Coll., 1979; MA, Ball State U., 1982; EdD, Widener U., 1991. Fin. aid counselor Anderson (Ind.) U., 1980-81, dir. student activities, 1981-83; dir. student activities St. Joseph's U., Phila., 1983-85; dir. student activities Widener U., Chester, Pa., 1985-88, asst. dean student programs, 1988-91, assoc. dean student programs, 1991—, Widener Leadership Acad. program dir., 1989—. Group facilitator Action AIDS, Phila., 1985-88; bd. dirs. Chester East Side Ministries, 1989-91; bd. dirs. Community Housing Resource Bd. of Delaware County, 1990—, pres., 1991-92. Grantee Pew Charitable Trusts, Phila., 1989. Mem. Nat. Assn. Student Pers. Adminstrs., Am. Coll. Pers. Assn., Assn. Coll. Unions Internat., Assn. Vol. Adminstrn., Nat. Assn. Community Leadership. Democrat. Roman Catholic. Home: 810 E 16th St Chester PA 19013-5809 Office: Widener U Webb Hall Chester PA 19013

BECKER, ROBERT ALAN, entrepreneur; b. Rochester, N.Y., Nov. 28, 1931; s. Jacob Edward and Louise (Wittenberg) B.; m. Agnes Berberian. B Mech Engring., Poly. Inst. Bklyn., 1958. Various rsch. engring., mfg. and gen. mgmt. positions Eltra, Republic Aviation, Curtiss-Wright, 1949-69; pres., chief exec. officer Rabeck Inc., Upper Montclair, N.J., 1969—; guest lectr. productivity Columbia Grad. Sch. Bus., 1984-86. Contbr. articles to profl. jours. Witness N.J. Assembly and N.J. Gov.'s Health Care Commns., 1990; participant N.J. Assembly Health Care Summit, Princeton, 1991. With USAF, 1951-55, ETO. Mem. Columbia U. Seminar on Orgn. and Mgmt. (assoc.). Office: Rabeck Inc 639 Grove St Montclair NJ 07043-2016

BECKER, SEYMOUR, hazardous materials and wastes specialist; b. Bronx, N.Y., Feb. 14, 1924; m. Ruth Schmitt, Aug. 30, 1958. MS, U. Wis., 1949; PhD, Pacific Western U., 1981. Nationally cert. hazardous materials mgr. and hazardous control mgr. Radiation control insp. Suffolk County Dept. Health Svcs., Hauppauge, N.Y., 1960-81; tech. cons., 1981-83; hazardous materials and wastes cons. Environ. Svcs., Portland, Maine, 1983-85, Mercy Hosp., Portland, 1985—; del. to China, People to People, Spokane, Wash., 1987, Commonwealth of Ind. States (Russia, Ukraine), People to People, Spokane, Wash., 1992; advisor and cons. State of Maine Hosp. Assn., Augusta, 1988-90, Low Level Radioactive Wastes Authority, Augusta, 1989—, Dept. Environ. Protection, Augusta, 1989—. Contbr. articles to profl. jours. Cons. Emergency Mgmt. Agy., Windham, Maine, 1983—, Local Emergency Planning Com., Windham, 1989—. Fellow Am. Pub. Health Assn.; mem. Acad. Hazardous Materials Mgmt., Health Physics Soc., N.Y. Acad. Scis., Maine Pub. Health Assn. Home: 169 High St Apt 312 Portland ME 04101-2852 Office: Mercy Hosp 144 State St Portland ME 04101-3795

BECKER, STEVEN ALLEN, mechanical contracting company executive; b. Norwich, Conn.; married; 2 children. BS in Bus. Adminstrn., The Citadel, 1965. Pres. Kendland Co., Inc., Norwich, 1977—. Active Norwich Rep. Town Com., Rep. Senatorial Inner Cir., Rep. Nat. Com.; trustee Norwich Housing Authority. Mem. Associated Builders and Contractors (past bd. dirs.), Conn. Associated Gen. Contractors. Office: Kendland Co Inc 15 Wisconsin Ave Norwich CT 06360-1556

BECKER, SUSAN KAPLAN, consultant, educator; b. Newark, Jan. 4, 1948; d. Charles and Janet Kaplan; m. William Paul Becker, 1969 (div. 1977). BA in English cum laude, with distinction, U. Pa., 1968, MA, 1969, MBA in Fin., 1973, MBA, 1979. Instr. English Bryn Mawr (Pa.) Coll., 1972-74; assoc. editor U. Pa., Phila., 1975, asst. dir., lectr. urban studies, 1975-77; fin. analyst Phila. Nat. Bank, 1979-82; asst. v.p. Chem. Bank, N.Y.C., 1982-84; v.p. Bankers Trust Co., N.Y.C., 1984-85; prin. Becker Cons., N.Y.C., 1985—; clin. assoc. prof. mgmt. communication Stern Sch. Bus. N.Y.U., 1990—; cons./evaluator Pa. Humanities Council, Phila., 1977-78. Author: How to Develop Profitable Financial Products for the Institutional Marketplace, 1988; contbr. articles and revs. to profl. jours. Vol., N.Y. Cares, 1989—. U. Pa. fellow, 1968-72; E.I. DuPont de Nemours fellow, 1979, N.Y. Regents Coll. Teaching fellow, 1968-70. Mem. Assn. for Bus. Communication, Speech Communication Assn., Am. Mktg. Assn. (leadership coun. N.Y. chpt. 1988-91, EFFIE judge 1990—), Mcpl. Art Soc., Internat. Communication Assn. (reviewer tech. and communication div. 1991—). Democrat. Office: 155 E 29th St New York NY 10016-8173

BECKER, ULRICH J., physics educator, researcher; b. Dortmund, Germany, Dec. 17, 1938; came to U.S., 1968; s. Georg Ludwig and Auguste (Buehner) B.; m. Gerda Katharina Barthel, Apr. 29, 1966; children: Katharina, Peter, Robert. Grad., Leibniz Gymnasium, Dortmund, Germany, 1958; BS, Philipps U., Marburg, Germany, 1960; diplom, U. Hamburg, Germany, 1964; PhD, U. Hamburg, 1968, Dr.habil., 1976. Rsch. assoc. Deutsches Elektronen Synchrotron, Hamburg, 1964-68; rsch. assoc. MIT, Cambridge, 1968-70, asst. prof., 1970-73, assoc. prof., 1974-77, prof., 1978—; staff scientist CERN, European Orgn. for Rsch., Geneva, 1970-72, 86-88, mem. LEP physics com., 1986-89; vis. prof. ETH, Zürich, Switzerland, 1991-92; mem. rsch. coun. DESY, Hamburg, 1970-74. Originator Particle Chambers, permanent exhibit Smithsonian Instn., Washington, 1973-74. Mem. Am. Phys. Soc., AAS. Office: MIT 51 Vassar St Cambridge MA 02139-4308

BECKER, WILLIAM ADOLPH, insurance association executive; b. Kenosha, Wis., July 2, 1933; s. Adolph Gustav and Helen Marie (Rasmussen) B.; m. Mildred Lois Behr, Dec. 13, 1952; children: Verne W., Bradford S., Gregory T. BA, William and Mary Coll., 1957; diploma Cornell U., 1958. CLU. Mgr., Commodore Maury Hotel, Norfolk, Va., 1957-59; field underwriter Home Life Ins. Co. of N.Y., Norfolk, 1959-61; asst. to gen. agt. Union Mutual Life Ins. Co., Richmond, Va., 1961-65; supr. Aetna Life & Casualty, Richmond, 1965-70, mktg. dept. field dir., 1970-71, gen. agt., Utica, N.Y., 1971-74, Syracuse, N.Y., 1974-77; v.p. Life Underwriter Tng. Council, Washington, 1977-82, field exec., mgr. confs. and meetings, assoc. dir. mktg., 1982—; instr. C.L.U. diploma program, 1973-74, Life Underwriter Tng. Council, Richmond, 1964-68. Mem. Va. Health Ins. Council Hosp. Relations Com. Served with USN, 1950-54. Recipient Louis I. Dublin award for pub. service, 1976, 77. Mem. Utica Assn. Life Underwriters (pres. 1972-73), N.Y. Assn. Life Underwriters (regional v.p. 1977-78), Ins. Conf. Planners, Gen. Agts. and Mgrs. Assn., Richmond Assn. Life Underwriters, Internat. Platform Assn., Nat. Assn. Health Underwriters, Richmond Assn. Health Underwriters, Va. Assn. Health Underwriters, No. Piedmont Assn. Life Underwriters, Navy League. Republican. Contbg. editor LIMRA Mgrs. Mag., Dow Jones Irwin Pub. Co., Bests Convention Guide, 1988, Ins. Conf. Planners mag., 1989, 90, 91. Office: Life Underwriter Tng Coun 7625 Wisconsin Ave Bethesda MD 20814-3560

BECKERMAN, BARRY LEE, ophthalmologist; b. N.Y.C., Jan. 12, 1941; s. Bernard B. and Helen (Hyman) Beckerman-Colvin; m. Nancy Barbara Greyson, Oct. 9, 1965; children: Ellen Laurie, Sara Ann. BA, Cornell U., 1961; MD, NYU, 1965. Diplomate Am. Bd. Ophthalmology. Intern in surgery Tufts-New Eng. Med. Ctr., Boston, 1965-66; resident in ophthalmology NYU-Bellevue Med. Ctr., N.Y.C., 1968-71, fellow in med. retina, 1971-72; asst. clin. prof. Albert Einstein Coll. Medicine, N.Y.C., 1973—; adj. attending ophthalmologist No. Westchester Hosp. Ctr., Mt. Kisco, N.Y., 1973-76; assoc. attending ophthalmologist No. Westchester Hosp. Ctr., Mt. Kisco, 1976-80, attending ophthalmologist, 1980-81, chief of ophthalmology, 1981—; adj. attending ophthalmologist Montefiore Hosp., Mt. Kisco, 1978—; cons. McDonnell Douglas Astronautics, Universal Voltronics, Mt. Kisco. Co-author: Compendium of Ophthalmology, 1983; contbr. articles to Archives of Ophthalmology, Am. Jour. Ophthalmology, Survey of Ophthalmology, Jour. Pediatric Ophthalmology. Mem. sch. bd. nominating com., Bedford (N.Y.) Schs., 1991. Lt. comdr. U.S. Pub. Health Svc., 1966-68. Fellow Am. Acad. Ophthalmology, Westchester Acad. Medicine; mem. N.Y. Acad. Scis. Office: 344 Main St Mount Kisco NY 10549-3027

BECKERMAN, EDWIN PAUL, retired librarian; b. N.Y.C., Nov. 27, 1927; s. Morris and Elizabeth (Scheftel) B.; m. Jean R. Friedburg; children: James, Lee, Peter. Diploma, U. Mo., 1949, Columbia U., 1952. Jr. libr. N.Y. Pub. Libr., N.Y.C., 1952-58; br. libr. Leicester (Eng.) Pub. Libr., 1956-57; pub. libr. cons. N.Y. State Edn. Dept., Albany, N.Y., 1958-59; asst. dir. Yonkers (N.Y.) Pub. Libr., 1960-63; dir. Woodbridge (N.J.) Pub. Libr., 1964-91; mem. N.J. State Libr. Adv. Coun., Trenton, 1991—; mem. N.J. State Bd. Examiners, Trenton, 1968-83. Contbg. author: Library Accountability, 1991. Trustee Princeton (N.J.) Pub. Libr., 1991. Mem. ALA (coun. mem. 1975-77), N.J. Libr. Assn. (Libr. Svc. award 1987). Home: 27 Longview Dr Princeton NJ 08540-5636

BECKER-ROUKAS, HELANE RENÉE, securities analyst, financial executive; b. N.Y.C., May 7, 1957; m. Arnold and Ella Florence (Feldman) Becker; m. George Paul Roukas, Sept. 6, 1980; 1 child, Samuel Matthew Roukas. BA, Montclair State Coll., 1979; MBA in Fin., NYU, 1984. Options coordinator Donaldson Lufkin & Jenrette, N.Y.C., 1979-81; mktg. coordinator E.F. Hutton & Co., N.Y.C., 1981-82; securities analyst Prudential-Bache Securities, N.Y.C., 1982-86; v.p., analyst Drexel Burnham Lambert, N.Y.C., 1986-87; mng. dir., analyst Shearson Lehman Bros., Inc., N.Y.C., 1987—; speaker various airline industry confs. and panels. Columnist Corp. Travel Mag., 1990. Named to Instnl. Investor All-Am. Rsch. Team, 1985-91. Mem. Soc. Airline Analysts, Profl. Women in Bus., Wings Club. Club: Wings (N.Y.C.). Office: Shearson Lehman Bros Am Express Tower 200 Vesey St New York NY 10285-1400

BECKETT, EUGENE FRANCIS, engineer, consultant, business owner; b. Detroit, Nov. 27, 1929; s. Howard John and Luelle (Brown) B.; m. Esther May Doss, Sept. 3, 1950; children: Jeffrey, Kelly. BSCE, U. Cin., 1952; MS in Nuclear Engring., USAF Inst. Tech., 1959; JD, George Washington U., 1980. Registered profl. engr., Ohio. Commd. 2nd lt. U.S. Army, 1952, advanced through grades to capt., 1958, resigned, 1963, sr. project engr., 1963; sr. project engr. U.S. Atomic Energy Commn., N.Y.C., 1963-66, Bethesda, Md., 1972-74; engring. mgr. Westinghouse Electric Corp., Madison, Pa., 1966-72; project leader U.S. Dept. Energy, 1979-80; licensing mgr. Nuclear Projects, Inc., Rockville, Md., 1974-79, mgr. tech. svcs., 1980-87; sr. exec. cons. NUS Corp., Gaithersburg, Md., 1987; pres. Beckett Assocs., Inc., Rockville, 1987—. Contbr. articles to profl. jours. Decorated Bronze Star. Mem. ASCE.

BECKMAN, AILEEN KOHN, education educator; b. Phila., Mar. 4, 1933; d. Harry and Edith (Miller) Kohn; m. Donald Beckman, July 14, 1952; children: Howard, Richard (dec.), Bradley. BA, U. Pa., 1965, MS, 1970; PhD, U. London, 1983. Cert. reading supr., Pa. Tchr. Sch. Dist. Phila., 1966-70; reading specialist Mitchell Day Sch., Haverford, Pa., 1970-75, Haverford Pub. Schs., Havertown, Pa., 1975-79; asst. prof. edn. Chestnut Hill Coll., Phila., 1983-88, assoc. prof., 1989—, chmn. dept., 1991—. Author: Giggles and Guffaws, 1989. Pres. Main Line Reform Temple, Wynnewood, Pa., 1988-90. Grantee Teleflex Corp., 1989-91. Mem. Internat. Reading Assn. (elected bd. children's lit. spl. interest group 1992-95), Nat. Coun. Tchrs. English. Democrat. Home: 241 S 6th St # 1601 Philadelphia PA 19106 Office: Chestnut Hill Coll Germantown and Northwestern Aves Philadelphia PA 19118

BECKMAN, JUDITH KALB, financial counselor and planner, educator, writer; b. Bklyn., June 27, 1940; d. Harry and Frances (Cohen) Kalb; m. Richard Martin Beckman, Dec. 16, 1961; children: Barry Andrew, David Mark. BA, Hofstra U., 1962; MA, Adelphi U., 1984. Cert. fin. planner; registered investment adviser. English tchr. Long Beach High Sch., 1962-65; Promotion coordination pub. rels. Mandel Sch. for Med. Assts., Hempstead, N.Y., 1973-74; exec. dir. Nassau Easter Seals, Albertson, N.Y., 1974-76; dir. pub. info. Long Beach Meml. Hosp., Albertson, N.Y., 1976-77; account rep. First Investors, Hicksville, N.Y., 1977-78; sales asst., then account exec. Josephthal & Co. Inc., Great Neck, N.Y., 1978-81; v.p., cert. fin. planner Arthur Gould Inc., Great Neck, N.Y., 1981-88; pres. Fin. Solutions (affiliated with Seco West Ltd., Goldner Siegfried Assocs. Inc.), Westbury, N.Y., 1988—; adj. instr. Adelphi U., Garden City N.Y., 1981-83, Molloy Coll., Rockville Ctr., N.Y., 1982-84; lectr. SUNY-Farmingdale, 1984-85; creater, presenter seminars, workshops on fin., investing, 1981—. Fin. columnist The Women's Record, 1985—; writer quar. newspaper The Reporter, 1987. Coord. meat boycott, L.I., 1973; mentor SUNY Old Westbury, 1989—; co-founder, chair L.I. del. High Profile Men and Women, Colonie Hill, Hauppauque, N.Y., 1985; treas. L.I. Alzheimers Found., 1989—; apptd. to Nassau County Women's Adv. Coun. by County Exec., 1990. Recipient citation for leadership Town of Hempstead, N.Y., 1986, 89, L.I. Press Club award, 1987, 1st Place Bus. Reporting award L.I. Press Club, 1992, Mentor award Small Bus. Adminstrn., 1989, Fin. Svc. award Small Bus. Adminstrn., 1991, Advocate award L.I. Assn. Fin. Svcs., 1991, Woman of Distinction in Bus. award Women on the Job, 1989, Bus. Leadership citation Nassau County, N.Y., 1989, Supr. awrad Town of Hempstead, 1989. Mem. Nat. Assn. Women Bus. Owners L.I. (bd. dirs. 1987-89), Women's Econ. Developers of L.I. (bd. dirs. 1985-92), Internat. Assn. Fin. Planners, Inst. Cert. Fin. Planners, L.I. Ctr. Bus. and Profl. Women (pres. 1984-86, Pres.'s award 1992), Am. Soc. Women Accts., Nat. Assn. Life Underwriters. Republican. Jewish. Home: 2084 Beverly Way Merrick NY 11566-5418 Office: Fin Solutions Fin Planning Office 2084 Beverly Way Merrick NY 11566-5418 also: 400 Post Ave Ste 200 Westbury NY 11590

BECKMANN, JOHN WILLIAM, interior designer; b. Mt. Kisco, N.Y., Sept. 3, 1960; s. Norman Peter and Margret Rose (Gorog) B.; m. Antonia Polizzi. BFA in Environ. Design, Parsons Sch. of Design, 1982. Asst. D'Urso Design, Inc., N.Y.C., 1982; designer Shank Design Assocs., Inc., N.Y.C., 1984-87; project designer Lembo/Bohn Design Assocs., Inc., N.Y.C., 1988; freelance designer prodn. A. Michael Krieger Design, L.I. City, 1989; project designer Naomi Leff & Assocs., N.Y.C., 1990; freelance designer Met. Mus. of Art, N.Y.C., 1991—. Individual projects include Randolph Duke Boutique, N.Y.C., 1986, Polizzi Residence, N.Y.C., 1987-88, 300 Bloor St., Toronto, Can., 1990-91, Barbara Kramer Showroom, chinaware for Swid-Powell, 1992; exhbited in group shows at The Am. Crafts Mus., 1988, Nat. Arts Club, 1988, Design Gallery 91, 1991, Museo Alchimia, 1991, Fullscale, 1991, Entree Libre, 1992. Mem. Indsl. Design Soc. Am. Office: Axis Mundi Inc 361 W 36th St New York NY 10018-6408

BECKWITH, RODNEY FISK, management consulting firm executive; b. Passaic, N.J., Oct. 24, 1935; s. Raymond Fisk and Nancy Angel (Oberdorf) B. m. Elizabeth Ann Wedemann, July 23, 1960; children: Allison B. Melson, Kimberly Hall. BME with distinction, Cornell U., 1958; MBA with distinction, Harvard U., 1963. Plant engr. Western Electric Co., Kearny, N.J., 1960-61; sr. assoc. Cresap, McCormick and Paget, Inc., N.Y.C., 1963-68, prin., 1968-72; v.p. Cresap, McCormick and Paget, Inc., Melbourne, Australia, 1972-77; v.p., dir., exec. com. Cresap, McCormick and Paget, Inc., N.Y.C., 1977-83; v.p., dir. Fin. Instns. Svcs., 1983-84, v.p., dir. internat., 1984-90, v.p., chief adminstrv. officer, 1990—. Bd. dirs. Am. C. of C., Australia, 1975-77. With USN, 1958-60, lt. USNR, 1960-65. Mem. Inst. Mgmt. Cons. (founding), Harvard Club, Board Room (N.Y.C.), Australian Club (Melbourne), Wee Burn Country Club (Darien, Conn.), Delta Upsilon. Presbyterian. Home: 8 Nolen Ln Darien CT 06820-2720 Office: 245 Park Ave New York NY 10167-0002

BECOFSKY, ARTHUR LUKE, arts administrator, writer; b. N.Y.C., Sept. 17, 1950; s. Arthur and Frances (Oliva) B. BA in Polit. Sci., Duke U., 1972; MA in Polit. Sci., Columbia U., 1974. Adminstr. Cunningham Dance Found., N.Y.C., 1974-79, exec. dir., 1980—; world booking agt. Merce Cunningham Dance Co., N.Y.C., 1976—; cons. Found. for Extension and Devel. of Am. Profl. Theatre, N.Y.C., 1985; mem. dance panel Nat. Endowment for the Arts, 1983—. Guitarist with Rhys Chatham & The Din, 1981; composer: Secretarial Suite, 1980, Track, 1983, Get Real, Cassandra, 1985, Space Into Action, 1986; author: The Road Show Abroad, 1985, On Commissioning New Art, 1989, MMerce, 1991. Bd. dirs. Dancing for Life, 1987; U.S. Performing Arts subcom. CULCON for U.S.-Japan cultural

exch., 1989—. Mem. Dance/U.S.A. (treas., bd. dirs. 1983-87, 91—), Am. Arts Alliance (bd. dirs. 1983-87). Democrat. Home: 324 E 9th St # 8 New York NY 10003 Office: Cunningham Dance Found Inc 55 Bethune St New York NY 10014-2010

BECTON, HENRY PRENTISS, JR., broadcasting company executive; b. Englewood, N.J., Oct. 16, 1943; s. Henry Prentiss and Jean Sprague (Coggan) B.; m. Jean Campbell Redpath, Sept. 28, 1968; children: Sara Campbell, Wilson Prentiss, Elizabeth Campbell. BA magna cum laude, Yale U., 1965; JD cum laude, Harvard U., 1968. Tchr. Cambridge Sch., Weston, Mass., 1968-69; tel. producer WGBH Ednl. Found., Boston, 1970-73; program mgr. WGBH Ednl. Found., 1974-78, v.p., gen. mgr., 1978-84, pres., 1984—; bd. dirs. Becton, Dickinson & Co., Pub. Broadcasting Svc., Mass. Corp. for Ednl. Telecommunications; trustee Scudder Funds, Conn. Coll. Bd. dirs. Mass. Com. for Prevention of Child Abuse, 1979-81; trustee Boston Ballet, 1976-78, Met. Cultural Alliance, Boston, 1974-76, New. Eng. Aquarium, 1981—, Boston Mus. Sci., 1984—, Wang Ctr. for Performing Arts, 1985—; bd. overseers Boston Mus. Fine Arts, 1990—. Mem. Nat. Acad. Tel. Arts and Scis. (bd. dir. New Eng. chpt. 1980-84), Mass. Bar Assn., Somerset Club (Boston), Kollegewidgwok Yacht Club (Blue Hill, Maine), Blue Hill Country Club, Phi Beta Kappa. Office: Sta WGBH-TV 125 Western Ave Allston MA 02134-1098

BEDA, GAYE ELISE, fine arts artist; b. Warren, Ohio, Feb. 12, 1955; d. Alfred Carl and Eloise Dorothy (Sisley) B. BA, Coll. of Wooster, 1977; postgrad., N.Y. Sch. Visual Arts, 1981-82. Owner Beda Originals, N.Y.C., 1977—; mem. Ward-Nasse Gallery, N.Y.C., 1989—, Guild Hall, East Hampton, N.Y., 1990—. One-woman shows include U. League Gallery, Princeton, N.J., First N.Y. Bank for Bus., N.Y.C., 1992, LRG Enterprises, N.Y.C., 1986, Ward-Nasse Gallery, N.Y.C., 1989, 90, 91; exhibited in group shows at Hilton Hotel, 1986, Phoenix Gallery, N.Y.C., 1988, Lever House Gallery, N.Y.C., 1990, Cork Gallery, Lincoln Ctr., N.Y.C., numerous others; commd. murals Mesopotamia Courthouse, Ohio, 1973, Coll. Wooster, Ohio, 1976; represented in permanent collections at Brenau Coll., Gainesville, Ga. Recipient Junius Allen Meml. award, 1990, Elliot Liskin Meml. award, 1990, John R. McCathy award, 1989. Mem. Women In Arts (exec. bd. 1981—), Artists Equity (N.Y. chpt.), Artists' Fellowship Inc., Artists for a Better Image, Salmagundi Club (co-chair jr. scholarship program 1990). Republican. Home: 317 2d Ave # 16 New York NY 10003

BEDASKE, ANGELA MARGARET, marketing executive; b. Buffalo, Jan. 20, 1961; d. Chester Jay and Rose Mary (Carriero) B. BS in Fin., Canisius Coll., 1983. Proof machine operator Metroteller Systems, Inc., Buffalo, 1983-84, mgr. proofing dept., 1984-85, mgr. point of banking dept., 1985-86, asst. v.p. settlement ops. dept., 1986-91; mktg. officer Mac/Metroteller, Buffalo, 1991—. Active Ladies aux. Brant (N.Y.) Vol. Fire Co. #1, 1977—, Altar and Rosary Soc. Our Lady of Mt. Carmel Ch., Brant, 1977—, organist, choir dir., 1984—. Mem. Am. Inst. Banking, Nat. Assn. Female Execs. Republican. Home: 10083 Brant Angola Rd Angola NY 14006-9117 Office: Mac/Metroteller 237 Main St Ste 1200 Buffalo NY 14203-2788

BEDAW, BARRY LEWIS, environmental and safety consultant; b. Keene, N.H., Aug. 11, 1959; s. Barry Lewis and Margaret (Sullivan) B; child from previous marriage: Brandon Joseph; m. Joan Fitzgerald, Jan. 14, 1989; 1 child, Ryan Fitzgerald. BS in Occupational Safety, Keene (N.H.) Coll., 1988. Postal supr. U.S. Postal Svc., Keene, 1984-88; indsl. hygienist Cert. Engrng. & Testing, Providence, 1988-91; project mgr. Entek Environ. & Tech. Svc., Troy, N.Y., 1989—. Ski coach Mt. Assumption Inst., Plattsburgh, N.Y., 1979-82; asst. scoutmaster Boy Scouts Am., Keene, 1982. With USAF, 1978-82. Mem. Am. Soc. Safety Engrs. (environ. div.), Nat. Fire Protection Assn. (tech. com. on tank leakage and repair safeguards). Republican. Roman Catholic. Office: Entek Environ & Tech Svc 125 Defreest Dr Troy NY 12180-8361

BEDNASH, GERALDINE POLLY, executive; b. San Antonio, May 6, 1943; d. David Anthony and Bernice (Brewer) Parrott; m. Thomas Francis Bednash, June 24, 1967; children: Thomas F. Jr., Joseph Andrew. B of Nursing, Tex. Women's U., 1965; M of Nursing, Cath. U. Am., 1977; PhD, U. Md., 1989. Cert. nurse practitioner. Nurse Binghamton (N.Y.) Gen. Hosp., 1967-69; instr. Broome County Community Coll., Binghamton, 1967-71; asst. prof. No. Va. Community Coll., Annandale, 1977-78, George Mason U., Fairfax, Va., 1978-86; dir. govt. rels. Am. Assn. Coll. Nursing, Washington, 1986-89, exec. dir., 1989—; co-chmn. Nat. Com. Nursing Implementation Project, Washington, 1990-91; cons. in field. Contbr. articles to profl. jours. Polit. action chmn. Va. Nurses Assn., 1979-83; nurse clinician So Others Might Eat, Washington, 1981-83. Capt. U.S. Army, 1963-67. Primary Care fellow Robert Wood Johnson Found., U. Md., 1981-82, Nat. Rsch. Svc. fellow, Washington, 1983-87. Fellow Am. Acad. Nursing; mem. ANA, Sigma Theta Tau. Roman Catholic. Office: Am Assn Coll Nursing One Dupont Circle Ste 530 Washington DC 20036

BEDRIJ, OREST J., industrialist, scientist; b. Ukraine, May 24, 1933; arrived in U.S., 1949, naturalized, 1955; s. Eustachy and Olga (Banach) B.; m. Oksana Cymbalista, Nov. 10, 1956; children: Orest W., Roksana, Chrystyna Bedrij Stecyk. BSEE, Rochester Inst. Tech., 1956, MS in Humanities; PhD in Theoretical Physics, Columbia Pacific U., 1986. Various mgmt. positions IBM Corp., Poughkeepsie, N.Y. and Los Angeles, 1956-68; IBM tech. dir. Space Flight Facility Jet Propulsion Lab., Calif. Inst. Tech., 1962-63; pres., dir. Securities Council, Inc., 1965-83; founder, pres., dir. Profit Technology, Inc., 1983-89, Griffin Capital Mgmt. Corp., N.Y.C., 1989—; founder, dir. Advance Memory Systems Inc., now with G.E. Intersil, Inc., Sunnyvale, Calif., 1968, Xytex Corp. (merger with Calcomp Corp.), Boulder, Colo., 1970; exec. com., treas., dir. Ukrainian Studies Fund, Harvard U., 1959-72, adviser Ctr. for the Study of World Religions Harvard U., 1991—; trustee, treas. John E. Fetzer Found., 1987-89. Author: Yes It's Love: Your Life Can Be a Miracle, 1974, One, 1977, 2d rev. edit., 1978, The Proof, 1984, You, 1989; patentee in field; contbr. articles to profl. jours. With U.S. Army (Res.), 1954-60. Recipient Outstanding Contribution award IBM, 1967. Mem. AAAS, Royal Soc. Arts Mfr. and Commerce, N.Y. Acad. Arts and Scis., Inst. Noetic Scis., Found. Econ. Edn., World Trade Ctrs. Assn. Office: Griffin Captial Mgmt 200 Rector Pl Apt 41C New York NY 10280-1176

BEE, MARY RICE, marketing executive, consultant; b. Homer, N.Y., Aug. 11, 1933; d. John Moak and Isabella A. (Gilkerson) Rice; children: Heather Jo Bee Chestnut, Edward R. Jr. Student, Cortland (N.Y.) State Tchrs. Coll., 1951, 54, Russell Sage Coll., 1968. Co-founder, v.p. Bee Bus. Forms, Schenectady, 1964-68; sales mgr. Gideon Putnam Hotel, Saratoga Springs, N.Y., 1969-71; founder, pres. Madison North Mktg. Communications Agy. Ltd., Schenectady, 1971-82; exec. v.p. Wallace Armer Hardware, Schenectady, 1983-86; v.p., dir. mktg. and community relations Trust co Bank N.Y., 1988-91; mktg. and devel. adminstr. Capital Dist. Hospice, 1992—; bd. dirs. Flah's; mem. adj. faculty Union Coll., Schenectady; cons. mgmt. and mktg. Chmn. Schenectady Urban Cultural Park Com.; pres. Schenectady County Pvt. Industry council; mem. adv. council N.Y. State Regents Pvt. Industry Council, Proctor's Theatre, Schenectady; bd. dirs. Schenectady County chpt. ARC, Schenectady Symphony Orch., Family and Child Service Schenectady, Capital Dist. Hospice, Jr. Achievement Capital Dist. Bd., Cerebral Palsy, Schenectady; bd. trustees Charlton Sch. For Schs.; deacon 1st Dutch Reformed Ch., Schenectady; mem. exec. com. Capital Dist. Region Joint Tng. Ptnrship. Act; chmn. Schenectady County Tourism and Visitors Council; trustee Hospice Found. Schenectady, Hospice Oper. Bd., Schenectady. Recipient Crystal Prism award 2d dist. Am. Advertisers Fedn., 1975, Hans M. Rosendaal Hospice award, 1983. Mem. Northeastern Fedn. Profl. Communicators (Silver medal 1975), Schenectady County C. of C. (pres.). Democrat. Home: Snyder Rd Alplaus NY 12008 Office: 6 Union St Schenectady NY 12305

BEE, RONALD JOHN, security firm executive; b. Oakland, Calif., Feb. 22, 1955; s. Keith Willard and Virginia C. (Rakowski) B. BA in History, U. Calif., San Diego, 1978; postgrad., Johns Hopkins SAIS, Bologna, Italy, 1980-81. Fellow Princeton (N.J.) U., 1980; pub. info. asst. Internat. Atomic Energy Agy., Vienna, Austria, 1981; fgn. affairs analyst Libr. of Congress, Washington, 1982; spl. asst. for nat. security affairs Palomar Corp., Washington, 1982-87; cons. The Urban Inst., Washington, 1988-89, Nat. Security Archive, Washington, 1989-90; dir. rsch. and pubs. ACCESS: A Security Information Svc., Washington, 1990—. Co-author: Looking the Tiger in the Eye: Confronting the Nuclear Threat, 1988, The Land and People of Germany, 1992. Fellow Robert Bosch Found., Stuttgart, Germany, 1987-88, Christopher award, 1988. Mem. Am. Coun. on Germany, German Studies Assn., Washington Ind. Writers. Home: 816 Easley St # 1619 Silver Spring MD 20910-4549

BEEBE, GILBERT WHEELER, epidemiologist; b. Mahwah, N.J., Apr. 3, 1912; s. Edwin P. and Gertrude Mabel (Gilbert) B.; m. Ruth Lillian White, Dec. 29, 1933; children: Alfred, Beatrice, Brian, Christopher. AB, Dartmouth Coll., 1933; AM, Columbia U., 1938, PhD, 1942. Statistician Nat. Commn. Maternal Health, N.Y.C., 1934-41; rsch. assoc. Milbank Meml. Fund, N.Y.C., 1939-41, tech. staff, 1941-46; cons./hist. div. U.S. Army, Washington, 1946-50, cons./Hoover Commn., 1948; profl. assoc. NRC/NAS, Washington, 1946-58; dir. Med. Follow-up Agy., Washington, 1958-77; chief, dept. stats. Atomic Bomb Casualty Commn., Hiroshima, Japan, 1958-60, chief, dept. epidemiology and stats., 1966-68, 73-75; various to statistician Nat. Cancer Inst., Bethesda, Md., 1977—; chief scientist Radiation Effects Rsch. Found., Hiroshima, 1975. Author: Fertility and Contraception in Southern Appalachians, 1942, Battle Casualties, 1952, Follow-up Study of War Neurosis, 1956; editor: Peripheral Nerve Regeneration, 1957. Capt. U.S. Army, 1943-46. Recipient Lectureship/Cutter Lectr., Harvard Sch. of Pub. Health, Boston, 1979, Spl. Recognition award Pub. Health Svc., Washington, 1983, Dir.'s award NIH, Washington, 1985. Fellow Am. Pub. Health Assn. (Frost Lectr., N.Y.C. 1980), Am. Statis. Assn.; mem. Soc. for Epidmiol. Rsch., Radiation Rsch. Soc., Health Physics Soc., AAAS, Am. Epidemiology Soc.. Home: 7311 Stafford Rd Alexandria VA 22307-1808 Office: National Cancer Inst EPN 400 Bethesda MD 20892

BEEBE, WILSON HOLLISTER, JR., trade association executive; b. North Hornell, N.Y., June 18, 1954; s. Wilson Hollister B. and Polly (Carpenter) Bove; m. Anne Eileen Torre, Apr. 11, 1981; children: Sarah A., Laura T. BA, Fordham U., 1980. Asst. exec. dir. N.Y. State Funeral Dirs. Assn., N.Y.C., 1980-85; exec. dir. N.J. State Funeral Dirs. Assn., Sea Girt, 1985—. Author: OSHA Compliance in Funeral Service, 1990, Americans with Disability Act, 1991. With USN, 1972-76. Mem. Am. Soc. Assn. execs.

BEECHER, GEORGE, otolaryngologist; b. Barranquilla, Colombia, Sept. 26, 1940; came to U.S., 1946; s. Hugo and Margaret (Hahn) B.; m. Judith Ann Holt, Oct. 1, 1965; 1 child, James Hugo. Student, Tufts Coll., 1958-59; MD, Louvain (Belgium) U., 1965. Rotating intern Phila. Gen. Hosp., 1965-66; surg. resident St. Michael's Hosp., Newark, 1966-67, N.J. Coll. of Medicine, Newark, 1970-71; ENT resident NYU/Bellevue Hosp. Ctr., N.Y.C., 1971-74; physician ptnr. Summit (N.J.) Med. Group, 1974—; mem. Bd. of Health, New Providence, N.J., 1990—; clin. instr. NYU/Bellevue Med. Ctr., N.Y.C., 1975—; staff attending Overlook Hosp., Summit, 1974—. Mem. Crippled Children's Commn., N.J., 1974—. Capt. U.S. Army, 1968-70, Vietnam. Decorated Bronze Star. Mem. AMA, N.J. Med. Soc., Am. Bd. Otolaryngology, Lions. Republican. Jewish. Office: Summit Med Group 120 Summit Ave Summit NJ 07901

BEECHER, WILLIAM MANUEL, newspaper executive; b. Framingham, Mass., May 27, 1933; s. Samuel and Gertrude (Kradelman) B.; m. Eileen Brick, June 8, 1958; children: Debbie, Diane, Lori, Nancy. BA, Harvard U., 1955; MS, Columbia U., 1956. Reporter St. Louis Globe-Democrat, 1956-59; corr. Fairchild Pubs., Washington, 1959-60, Wall Street Jour., Washington, 1960-66, N.Y. Times, Washington, 1966-73; asst. sec. def. U.S. Dept. Def., Washington, 1973-75; corr. Boston Globe, 1975-87; Washington bur. chief Mpls. Star Tribune, 1987—. Author: Mayday Man, 1990; co-author: (newspaper study) U.S.-Soviet Relations, 1983 (Pulitzer prize 1983); bd. of editors Foreign Svc. Jour. 2d lt. U.S. Army, 1956. Recipient Weintal award Georgetown U., Washington, 1983, Excellence awards Overseas Press Club, N.Y.C., 1975, 79, 86. Mem. Internat. Inst. for Strategic Studies, State Dept. Corrs. Assn. (pres. 1982), Overseas Writers Assn. (pres. 1978-79), Aviation/Space Writers Assn. (pres. 1970-71), Coun. Fgn. Rels., Gridiron Club, Army and Navy CLub. Home: 7911 Robison Rd Bethesda MD 20817-6928 Office: Mpls Star Tribune 1627 I St NW Ste 800 Washington DC 20006-4014

BEER, JANUSZ ZYGMUNT, radiation and photo biologist, scientist; b. Warsaw, Poland, Apr. 18, 1930; came to U.S., 1978; s. Zygmunt Wlodzimierz and Maria (Zyskowska) B.; m. Zofia Stefania Olempska, May 5, 1960; children—Tomasz Michal, Kasia Barbara. M.S., Warsaw Poly. and U. Warsaw, 1952; Ph.D., U. Warsaw, 1964, D.Sc., 1976. From tech. asst. to asst. U. Warsaw, 1951-59; from sr. asst. to lab. head Inst. Nuclear Research, Warsaw, 1959-78; vis. scientist Bur. Radiol. Health FDA, Rockville, Md., 1978-84, branch chief Ctr. Devices and Radiol. Health, 1984-89, sr. scientist, 1989—; vis. scientist Chester Beatty Research Inst., London, 1962-63; reviewer NIH and EPA grant proposals and sci. papers for several profl. jours.; lectr. numerous nat. and internat. sci. meetings; cons. in field. Mem. adv. bd. Advances Radiation Biology, 1979-90; rsch. adviser Nat. Rsch. Coun.; resident Rsch. Associateship Program, 1988—, Oak Ridge Associated Univs./Food and Drug Adminstrn. Rsch. Program, 1990—. Contbr. articles to profl. jours.; patentee in field. Recipient several sci. awards Polish Biochem. Soc., Polish Assn. Radiation Research, Polish Council for Atomic Energy Devel.; Internat. Atomic Energy Agy. fellow, 1962; travel grants Internat. Assn. for Radiation Research, 1970, 74. Mem. Polish Assn. for Radiation Research (awards, hon. sec. 1968-74), U.K. Assn. for Radiation Research, European Soc. for Radiation Biology (mem. council 1976-84), Radiation Research Soc. U.S., Am. Soc. Photobiology, European Soc. Photobiology, Am. Conf. Govtl. Indsl. Hygienists, Polish Acad. Sci. (radiobiol. com. exec. sec. 1974-76), Union Polish Tchrs. (chpt. chmn. 1956-57), N.Y. Acad. Scis., Sigma Xi. Roman Catholic. Avocations: photography, mountain hiking. Home: 2 Lorre Ct Rockville MD 20852-4103 Office: FDA Ctr Devices Radiol Health HFZ-114 5600 Fishers Ln Rockville MD 20857

BEER, JONATHAN HILLEL, real estate broker, consultant; b. N.Y.C., Apr. 26, 1963; s. Murray Herbert and Mildred (Feder) B. BS, U. Vt., 1985; grad., Realtor Inst., 1988. Real estate broker, N.J., 1987. Commodity broker Clayton Brokerage, N.Y.C., 1985-86; real estate broker Re/Max Real Estate Assocs., Paramus, N.J., 1986—; chmn. Arbitration Com., Fairlawn, N.J., 1989—. Office: Re/Max Real Estate Assocs 40 E Midland Ave Paramus NJ 07652-2915

BEERS, CHARLOTTE L., advertising agency executive; b. Beaumont, Tex., July 26, 1935; d. Glen and Frances (Bolt) Rice; m. Donald C. Beers, 1971; 1 dau., Lisa. B.S. in Math. and Physics, Baylor U., Waco, Tex., 1958. Group product mgr. Uncle Ben's Inc., 1959-69; sr. v.p., dir. client services J. Walter Thompson, 1969-79; chief operating officer Tatham-Laird & Kudner, Chgo., from 1979, mng. ptnr., chmn. and chief exec officer; vice chmn. RSCG Group Roux Seguela, Cayzac & Goudard, France; chmn., c.e.o. Ogilvy & Mather Worldwide, N.Y.C.; dir. Federated Dept. Stores, Chgo. Public TV Channel 11. Named Nat. Advt. Woman of Yr. Am. Advt. Fedn., 1975. Mem. Am. Assn. Advt. Agencies (chmn. from 1987), Women's Advt. Club Chgo., Chgo. Network. Republican. Episcopalian. Office: Ogilvy & Mather Worldwide Worldwide Plz 309 W 49th St New York NY 10019*

BEERS, DAVID ROGERS, association director; b. Rochester, N.Y., Feb. 23, 1963; s. David Lynn and Carol Ann (Rogers) B.; m. Nancy Ann Bennett Beers, Apr. 26, 1986; 1 child, Carol Ann. BA, Colby Coll., 1985. Dir. annual giving Colby-Sawyer Coll., New London, N.H., 1990-91; dir. devel. Worcester (Mass.) Acad., 1991—. Office: Worcester Acad 81 Providence St Worcester MA 01604

BEERY, WILLIAM STOCKTILL, psychologist, clergyman; b. Bklyn., Nov. 27, 1947; s. Edwin Newman and Evelyn Vivian (Onken) B.; m. Margaret Augusta Broz, May 30, 1970; children: William, Gabriele; m. Ellen Agnes Sommers, Feb. 28, 1981; children: Matthew, Jonathan. AB, Colgate U., 1969; MDiv, Yale U., 1972; PhD, NYU, 1983. Ordained to ministry Episcopal Ch., 1972; lic. psychologist. Assoc. dir. V.I.P., Inc., Yonkers, N.Y., 1975-81; staff psychologist Sound Ctr., Rye, N.Y., 1981-82; exec. dir. Counseling and Testing Service, YMCA, N.Y.C., 1983-85; ptnr. Personnel Corp. Am., Norwalk, Conn., 1985-88; pres. Exec. Devel. Internat., Inc., 1988—; elected mem. Darien rep. town meeting; mem. Darien Bd. Ethics, chmn. pub. safety com.; adj. assoc. St. Luke's Parish, Darien, Conn., 1984—. Watson fellow Yale U., 1972-80. Fellow Am. Assn. Pastoral Counselors; mem. Am. Psychol. Assn., Am. Assn. Counseling and Devel., Met. N.Y. Assn. for Applied Psychology, Am. Soc. for Tng. and Devel., Norwalk Yacht Club (bd. govs.). Avocations: skiing, tennis, scuba, gardening, sailing. Home: 223 Old Kings Hwy S Darien CT 06820-5930

BEESMER, RONALD G., grocery chain executive; b. Kingston, N.Y., Mar. 31, 1958; s. George Henry and Jacqueline Rose (Singer) B.; m. Janet Marie Nichols, May 10, 1980; children: Eric Ronald, Alyson Elizabeth. Grad. high sch., Kingston, N.Y., 1976. Various managerial positions Grand Union Co., N.Y., 1977—; gen. mgr. Grand Union Co., Red Oaks Mill, N.Y., 1982-83, Hopewell Junction, N.Y., 1983-90, Highland, NY., 1990—. Named for Outstanding Performance in a Food Market, Progressive Grocer Mag., 1991.

BEESTMAN, DONNA M., human resources consulting executive; b. Waukesh, Wis., Apr. 14, 1943; d. Donald N. and Ardith (Ellis) McDowell; m. George B. Beestman, July 10, 1965; children: Joan, Scott. BA, Macalester Coll., 1965; MA, U. Wis., 1968. Cert. secondary tchr., Wis., Mo. Tchr. Madison (Wis.) Pub. Schs., 1965-67; grad. asst. U. Wis., Madison, 1967-68, admissions counselor Library Sch., 1968; reference librarian St. Louis County Library, 1969-71; high sch. librarian Parkway Sch. Dist., St. Louis, 1975-83; exec. dir. Conf. on Edn., St. Louis, 1983-86; tng. mgr. Maritz Motivation Co., St. Louis, 1986-89, tng. dir., 1989-90; v.p. Manchester, Inc., Wilmington, 1991—. Candidate Mo. State Legis., 1982; bd. dirs. Confluence St. Louis, 1986—, vice chmn., 1989—, vice chmn. task force, 1987-89; bd. dirs. KWMU Pub. Radio, St. Louis, 1987-89, mem. exec. com., 1989-90; bd. dirs. Jr. Achievement of Del., Inc., 1992—; active Leadership St. Louis, 1985—. Mem. Am. Soc. Tng. and Devel. Democrat. Presbyterian. Home: 309 Sharpley Rd Wilmington DE 19803-2441 Office: 1201 N Market St Wilmington DE 19801-1160

BEESTMAN, GEORGE BERNARD, chemist; b. Hammond, Wis., July 17, 1939; s. Herman Anton and Mary (TerBeest) B.; m. Donna Jane McDowell, July 9, 1965; children: Joan Ardith, Scott McDowell. BS in Agrl. Edn., River Falls State Coll., 1961; MS in Soil Sci., U. Wis., 1967, PhD in Soil Chemistry, 1969. Sr. rsch. chemist Monsanto, St. Louis, 1968-71, rsch. specialist, 1971-79, sr. rsch. specialist, 1978-89; dir. rsch. and devel. United Industries, St. Louis, 1989-90; sr. rsch. assoc. DuPont Agrl. Products, Wilmington, Del., 1990—. Contbr. articles to sci. jours.; patentee in field. Chmn. bd. United Way Agy. Outstanding Teaching fellow U. Wis.; recipient Disting. Svc. award Internat. Voluntary Svcs. Mem. ASTM (sec. main com. E35, pesticides 1989-91, editor spl. tech. publ. #968 1987, assoc. editor tech. publ. #980 1988, referee of manuscripts 1970—), Weed Sci. Soc. Am. (chmn. sect. on soil aspects 1975, referee of manuscripts 1970—), Am. Chem. Soc. (referee of manuscripts 1970—), Sigma Xi (pres. Monsanto chpt. 1974). Democrat. Presbyterian. Home: 309 Sharpley Rd Wilmington DE 19803-2441 Office: DuPont Agrl Products Exptl Sta 402/2112 Wilmington DE 19880-0402

BEG, M. RASHID, computer company executive; b. Allahabad, India, Oct. 15, 1949; arrived in Can., 1975, naturalized; came to U.S., 1981.; s. M. Hameedullah and Fathma (Imam) B.; m. Gillian Angela Chatterjee, July 19, 1976 (div. 1987) 1 child, Tehmina; m. Linda Susan Skerrett, May 14, 1988; 1 child, Jasmine Elisa. B Computer Sci., Concordia U., Montreal, Que., Can., 1980. Chief engr. display systems Matrox Electronic Systems, Montreal, 1978-80; engring. mgr. Datacube, Peabody, Mass., 1981; pres., chmn. Imaging Tech., Inc., Salem, N.H., 1982; chmn. Imaging Tech., Inc., Woburn, Mass., 1982—. Patentee, image processing system, programmable image transformation system. Mem. IEEE. Office: Imaging Tech Inc 55 Middlesex Turnpike Bedford MA 01730-1421

BEGG, VIRGINIA LOPEZ, historian, writer; b. Bklyn., Dec. 29, 1944; d. Felix Manuel and Regina Elizabeth (Powell) Lopez; m. Charles Frederic Begg II, Dec. 16, 1967; children: Eric Alexander, Ian Graham. BA cum laude, Trinity Coll., 1966; postgrad., Radcliffe Coll., 1986—. Pvt. practice landscape historian Andover, Mass., 1986—; writer, researcher Andover Hist. Soc., 1980—; landscape design critic Landscape Design Critics Coun., Wellesley, Mass., 1987—. Contbr. numerous articles to profl. jours. Bd. dirs. Four Seasons Garden Club, Andover, 1982-87. Woodrow Wilson Found. fellow, 1966. Mem. Soc. for Preservation New Eng. Antiquities, Mass. State Fedn. Garden Clubs (landscape design critic Wellesley, Mass. chpt. 1987—), Mass. Horticultural Soc., New Eng. Garden History Soc. (bd. dirs., chair 1990—), Andover Hist. Soc. (pub. rels. com.), Arnold Arboretum of Harvard U. Roman Catholic. Home and Office: 12 La Mancha Way Andover MA 01810

BEGGS, DAVID WALKER, dermatologist; b. East Orange, N.J., Apr. 21, 1929; s. Charles Wendell and Edith Elizabeth (Walker) B.; A.B., Centre Coll. of Ky., 1951; M.D., Jefferson Med. Sch., 1955; m. Evelyn Ann Stout, Aug. 21, 1953; children—Daniel L., Ann E. Intern, Muhlenburg Hosp., Plainfield, N.J., 1955-56; resident in dermatology Jefferson Med. Sch. Hosp., Phila., 1963-65, U. Pa. Med. Sch., Phila., 1965-66; indsl. physician Am. Cyanamid Co., Bound Brook, N.J., 1959-63; practice medicine specializing in dermatology, Red Bank, N.J., 1966—; assoc. dermatologist Riverview Hosp., Red Bank, 1966—, Monmouth Med. Center, Long Branch, N.J., 1966—. Clk. of vestry Ch. of Holy Communion, Fair Haven, N.J., 1967-71. Served with USNR, 1957-59. Ross V. Patterson fellow, 1964-65. Mem. N.J. Dermatol. Soc., Am. Acad. Dermatology, Monmouth County Med. Soc., N.J. Med. Soc., Hahnemann Med. Sch., Am. Physicians Art Assn. Republican. Episcopalian. Club: Early Am. Coppers. Home: 31 Heights Ter Fair Haven NJ 07704-3618 Office: 252 Broad St Red Bank NJ 07701-2012

BEGIN, ROGER NORMAND, state official; b. Woonsocket, R.I., Nov. 19, 1952; s. Paul A. and Rita H. (Beauchemin) B.; m. Diane F. Landry, 1976; children—Scott, David, Douglas, Stephanie. AS, R.I. Community Coll., 1974; B.S. in Bus. Adminstrn., Bryant Coll., 1976. Asst. v.p. Eastland (R.I.) Bank, 1976-84; gen. treas. State of R.I., Providence, 1984-89, lt. gov., 1989—; pres. R.I. State Senate; Mem. R.I. Ho. of Reps., 1972-84, dep. majority leader, 1976-80, chmn. Pub. Fin. Mgmt. Bd., 1986;. Mem. found. bd. Community Coll. R.I.; div. chmn., mem. campaign cabinet United Way Southeastern New Eng.; mem. Long Term Care Coord. Coun.; adv. bd. vice chmn. R.I. Coll. and U. Savs. Plan; adv. coun. chmn. R.I. Civil Def. Preparedness; chmn. Small Bus. Advocacy Coun.; mem. Commn. on Interste Cooperation; chmn. Task Force on Teenage Suicide Prevention, Am. Cancer Soc. Ball, 1991; mem. Commn. on Child Care, Dr. Martin Luther King Jr. Birthday Celebration Commn., Spl. Legis. Commn. to Study Guardianship of the Elderly, Spl. Senate Commn. on Edn., Leadership R.I., 1987—; trustee Bryant Coll., mem. hon. degree com., nominating com.; co-chmn. 21st Century Edn. Commn. Recipient Children's Friend award R.I. Youth Guidance Ctr., 1989, Legis. award of Appreciation Gov.'s Coun. on Mental Health, 1989, Leadership Recognition award R.I. Coun. Community Mental Health Ctrs., 1989; named Outstanding Young Man Woonsocket Jaycees, 1978. Mem. Kiwanis (pres. Woonsocket chpt. 1982-83, Citizen of the Yr. award 1981, edn. fund coord.). Democrat. Roman Catholic. Office: Office of Lt Gov State House Rm 317 Providence RI 02903

BEGLEY, EVELYN MARIA, sign language interpreter; b. N.Y.C., July 7, 1953; d. Peter Francis and Theresa Rose Begley. BA in English, L.I. Univ., 1977; MA in Spl. Edn. with Splty. in Deaf Edn., Columbia U., 1983. Cert. in transliteration, sign. lang. interpreter. Interpreter N.Y. Soc. for the Deaf, N.Y.C., 1975-83, 86—; tchr. deaf St. Francis De Sales Sch., Bklyn., 1983-86. Contbr. to book Insider's Baseball, 1983. Homeand Office: 625 E 14th St New York NY 10009-3220

BEHAR, DIANE SUSAN, marketing professional, consultant; b. N.Y.C., May 17, 1952; d. Solomon and Frieda Behar. Spanish language cert., La Universidad Internacional, 1969; BA, Cornell U., 1974; MBA, U. Pa., 1983. Legis. analyst Com. on the Budget U.S. Ho. of Reps., Washington, 1975-77, legis. asst. and speechwriter Office of Congressman Oberstar, 1977-81; account exec. Doyle Dane Advt., N.Y.C., 1983-85; dir. of pub. affairs and speechwriter Mayor's Office of Bus. Devel., N.Y.C., 1985-88; dir. of mktg. Mayor's Office of Bus. Devel., N.Y.C., 1988-91; sr. mktg. analyst Dep. Mayor's Office for Econ. Policy and Mktg., N.Y.C., 1991—; mktg. cons. Work Late/Eat Right Gourmet Food Delivery Svcs., N.Y.C., 1985-87; lectr. in field. Contbr. articles to profl. jours. Mem. coun., fundraiser Fresh Air Fund, 1987—; bd. dirs., fundraiser Pentacle Danceworks, 1984—, Children's Orch. Soc., 1990—. Morgenthau fellow, 1981-83, Dupont fellow, 1981-83, fellow Nat. Endowment for Arts, 1983. Mem. NATAS, NAFE, Am. Mgmt. Assn., Am. Mktg. Assn., Women Execs. in Pub. Rels., Global Bus. Assn.

N.Y., Musicians Soc. N.Y., Cornell Club. Home: 201 E 69th St New York NY 10021-5465 Office: NYC Office of Econ Policy & Mktg 110 William St New York NY 10038-2607

BEHLING, CHARLES FREDERICK, psychology educator; b. St. George, S.C., Sept. 8, 1940; s. John Henry and Floy (Owings) B.; m. Jennifer Crocker; children: John Charles, Andrew Crocker. BA, U. S.C., 1962, MA, 1964; MA, Vanderbilt U., 1966, PhD, 1969. Asst. dean of students U. S.C., Columbia, 1962-63; asst. state news editor The State Newspaper, Columbia, 1963-64; asst. prof. psychology Lake Forest (Ill.) Coll., 1968-74; assoc. prof. Lake Forest Coll., 1974-88, chmn. dept., 1977-84; pvt. practice psychotherapy Lake Bluff, Ill., 1970-88, Buffalo, 1988—; clin. assoc. prof. SUNY, Buffalo, 1988—; dir. of undergraduate studies, 1989—. Contbr. articles to profl. jours. Bd. dirs. Nat. Abortion Rights Action League, Planned Parenthood; mem. long-range planning com. Lake Bluff Bd. Edn. Named Outstanding Prof., Underground Guide to Colls., 1971, Outstanding Tchr., Lake Forest Coll., 1981, SUNY, Buffalo, 1991; NASA fellow. Mem. Am. Psychol. Assn., Soc. Psychol. Study of Social Issues, Assn. Humanistic Psychology, AAUP, Univ. S.C. Alumni Assn., Psi Chi, Sigma Delta Chi. Democrat. Home: 171 Chapin Pky Buffalo NY 14209-1040 Office: SUNY Dept Psychology Buffalo NY 14260

BEHM, MARK ANDREW, computer systems development technical consultant; b. San Francisco, June 7, 1954; s. Donnal George and Evelyn Marie (Box) B. BA, U. Calif., Santa Cruz, 1976; MusM, U. Ill., 1978. Lectr. music U. Ill., Urbana, 1981-82; editorial asst. Rockefeller U., N.Y.C., 1983-85; cons. AT&T Bell Labs., Liberty Corner, N.J., 1985-92, Bell Communications Rsch., Red Bank, N.J., 1992—; resident MacDowell Colony, Peterborough, N.H., 1983. Composer: Quite Winter, 1978, Echo, 1983, Continuing Cities, 1991; works performed at Am. Festival Microtonal Music, 1988. Grantee U. Ill., 1982. Democrat.

BEHM, MARK EDWARD, academic administrator; b. Balt., Apr. 21, 1945; s. Carl and Margaret Anderson (Weichman) B.; m. Linda Ann Walker, Oct. 9, 1976; children: Scott Anderson, Craig Redgwick. BS, U. Md., 1967; MBA, Loyola Coll., Balt., 1980. Co-owner Applied Light Tech. Co., Silver Spring, Md., 1968-69; product area adminstr. Singer Co., Link Div., Silver Spring, Md., 1969-73; asst. comptroller U. Md. Balt. County (UMBC), 1973-75, dir. fin. planning, 1976-85, dir. planning and budget, 1986-88, v.p. for adminstrv. affairs, 1988—, also mem. adv. bd. Tech. Enterprise Ctr.; founding mem., adv. bd. Triad Market Access Consortium, Phila., 1989—. Founding mem., bd. dirs. Grant-A-Wish Found., Balt., 1979-87; mem. Balt. County Govt. Econ. Devel. Commn. Mem. Assn. Univ. Related Rsch. Parks (host com. 1991), Ea. Assn. Coll. and Univ. Bus. Officers (host com. 1989, program com. 1990), MIT Enterprise Forum, Phi Kappa Phi. Home: 13809 Princess Anne Way Phoenix MD 21131-1521 Office: U Md Balt County Baltimore MD 21228

BEHNKE, MICHAEL CLARE, academic admissions director; b. Grand Rapids, Mich., May 15, 1943; s. Clarence W. and Norma (Sessink) B.; m. Mary Vanleer Hancort, May 30, 1966; children: Matthew, Margaret. BA, Amherst Coll., 1966; MA, U. Pa., 1971. Tchr. Northamdton (Mass.) Sch. for Girls, 1966-67; with Peace Corps U.S. Govt., Sierra Leone, 1967-69; assoc. deam of admissions and dean of freshmen Amherst (Mass.) Coll., 1971-76; dean of admission Tufts U., Medford, Mass., 1976-85; dir. of admission MIT, Cambridge, 1985—; trustee Coll. Bd., N.Y., 1989—; cons. Overseas Schs. Project, Washington, 1989—; scholarship selector United Techs. Corp., Hartford, Conn., 1986—, Cabot Corp., boston, 1986—. Contbr. articles to profl. jours. Bd. dirs. Winchester (Mass.) A.B.C., 1980-85, Winchester Music Sch., 1983-85. Democrat. Episcopalian. Office: MIT 77 Massachusetts Ave Rm 3108 Cambridge MA 02139-4307

BEHR, HEATHER ASHLEY, office manager; b. Chgo., Feb. 23, 1967; d. Richard Henry and Suzanne Irene (Caton) B. BA, Manhattanville Coll., 1989; student, Iona-Hagan sch., New Rochelle, N.Y., 1990—. Mgr., buyer Traprock Ste. Ltd., Scarsdale, N.Y., 1981-85; office mgr. Richard Henry Behr Architect, Armonk, N.Y., 1985—; sales person Julien Studley, Inc., New Paltz, N.Y., 1989—; officer Catskill Conservation Corp., Scarsdale, 1985—, Spencer Behr Leasing, 1989—. Democrat. Home: 1023 Post Rd Scarsdale NY 10583 Office: Richard Henry Behr Architect 169 King St Armonk NY 10504

BEHR, RAYMOND ANTHONY, psychiatrist; b. Johannesburg, South Africia, May 26, 1948; came to U.S., 1976; s. David Chone and Joan Roxanna (Lazarus) B.; m. Avril Pera Galasko; children: Gerald, Nadia, Warren. MD, U. Pretoria, South Africa, 1973. Diplomate Am. Bd. Psychiatry and Neurology (gen. psychiatry and child psychiatry). Intern H.F. Verwoerd Hosp., Pretoria, 1974-75; resident in psychiatry L.I. Jewish Med. Ctr., New Hyde Park, N.Y., 1976-78, fellow in child psychiatry, 1978-80; med. dir. project outreach L.I. Jewish Med. Ctr., New Hyde Park, 1980-81, psychiat. cons. child devel. clinic, 1985-87, dir. adolescent day hosp., 1987-88; coord. law and psychiatry program L.I. Jewish Med. Ctr., Schneider Childrens Hosp., New Hyde Park, 1988—; psychiat. cons. Peninsula Counselling Ctr., Woodmere, N.Y., 1981-85; pvt. practice Great Neck, N.Y., 1980—; asst. clin. prof. psychiatry Albert Einstein Sch. Medicine Yeshiva U. Mem. Am. Psychiat. Assn., Am. Acad. Child and Adolescent Psychiatry, Am. Acad. Psychiatry and the Law.

BEHR, RICHARD HENRY, architect, educator; b. Albert Lea, Minn., Apr. 23, 1942; s. Franklin Robert and Marilou (Clubb) B.; m. Suzanne Irene Caton, 1966; children: Heather, Mark, Spencer. BArch, U. Minn., 1965; MBA, NYU, 1978; postgrad., Cornell U., Columbia U., U. Ill. Pres. SMH Devel. Corp., Scarsdale, N.Y., 1978-81, Landmark Devel. Corp. Am., Greenwich, Conn., 1978-86; architect Perkins & Will, White Plains, N.Y., 1967-69; chief architect N.Y. State Urban Devel. Corp., N.Y.C., 1969-73, Skidmore, Owings, Merrill, N.Y.C., 1965-67, 73-76; prof. architecture Pratt Inst., Bklyn., 1972-76, Grad. Sch., Yale U., New Haven, 1976-88; ptnr. Maitland, Strauss, Behr, Greenwich, 1976-85; pres. Richard Henry Behr, Architect, P.C., Armonk, N.Y., 1985—; cons. Bolt Beraneck, Newman, Cambridge, Mass., 1967-69; pres. Catskill Conservation Corp. Author: Economics of Revitalization, 1977, Design for Living, 1977. Mem. archtl. bd. Town of Scarsdale, N.Y., 1980-82; coach football team Scarsdale, 1981-84. Mem. AIA, Conn. Soc. Architects, Nat. Trust Hist. Preservation, Acoustical Soc. Am., N.Y. Soc. Architects. Clubs: Yale; Mory's. Office: 169 King St Armonk NY 10504-1606

BEHRMAN, HAROLD RICHARD, endocrinologist, physiologist, educator; b. Sask., Can., Nov. 26, 1939; s. Henry Fred and Minnie Alice (Waslenko) B.; m. Carol Hope O'Rourke, Aug. 8, 1981; children: Tracy Lee, Terri Lynne, Russell Norman, Kevin Michael, Kathleen Hope. B.S., U. Man., (Can.), 1962, M.A., 1965; Ph.D., N.C. State U., 1967; M.S. (hon.), Yale U., 1982. Research fellow Harvard U. Med. Sch., Boston, 1967-71, asst. prof., 1971-72; dir. reproductive biology Merck Inst., Rahway, N.J., 1972-75; assoc. prof. gynecology and pharmacology Yale U., New Haven, 1975-81, prof. ob-gyn. and pharmacology, 1981—, dir. reproductive biology sect., 1975—; cons. NIH, 1978-83, 91—. cons. NIH, 1978-83, 91—, USDA, 1985, NSF, 1985, Med. Rsch. Coun. Can., 1990-91. Recipient Research award Lalor Found., 1971-72; Fulbright-Hays Disting. prof., 1978; MRC Can. fellow, 1967-70; recipient Alta. Heritage Vis. Prof. award, 1983. Mem. AAAS, Am. Physiol. Soc., Endocrine Soc., Soc. Study of Reprodn., Soc. Endocrinology, Can. Physiol. Soc. Home: 790 Green Hill Rd Madison CT 06443-2404 Office: Yale U Dept Ob-Gyn 1303A Yale Sta New Haven CT 06520

BEHUNIAK, PETER, JR., educator, consultant; b. Derby, Conn., Feb. 11, 1950; s. Peter and Stella (Spak) B.; m. Gail Ann Tomala, Mar. 8, 1986. BS with high honors, U. Conn., 1971, MA, 1973, PhD, 1981; postgrad., U. Mass., 1975-77. Cert. tchr., Conn. Tchr. Glastonbury (Conn.) Pub. Schs., 1971-78; research asst. U. Conn. Bur. Ednl. Research, Storrs, 1979-80; pres. Edn. Resource Assocs., Glastonbury, 1980-83; edn. cons. Conn. Dept. Edn., Hartford, 1983-89, coord. student assessment, 1989—, chief Bur. Evaluation and Student Assessment, 1991-92; lectr. U. Bridgeport, Conn., 1982-83, U. Conn., Storrs, 1980-85, Ea. Conn. State U., 1987-89; adj. faculty U. Hartford, 1990-91; dir. Conn. mastery test Conn. Dept. Edn., Hartford, 1986—; chief bur. evaluation and student assessment, Conn. Dept. Edn. Contbr. articles to profl. jours. Mem. evaluation com. Community Coun. of the Capitol Region, Hartford, 1984—; bd. dirs. Southeast Conn. Civil Liberties Union, Windham, 1977-80; bd. overseers Northeast Regional Labs.; pres. Edn. Adminstrs. Union, Conn. State Dept. Edn. Mem. Am. Ednl. Research Assn. (presenter), Nat. Council on Measurement in Edn. (presenter), Am. Evaluation Assn. (presenter), N.E. Ednl. Research Assn. (presenter, program reviewer 1983), Phi Delta Kappa. Office: Conn State Dept Edn PO Box 2219 Hartford CT 06145-2219

BEIL, MARSHALL HOWARD, lawyer; b. Bklyn., Jan. 4, 1946; s. Ralph Irwin and Frieda (Schwartz) B.; m. Dana D. Lichty, June 28, 1978 (div. 1985); children: Jessica, Sarah. BA, Swarthmore Coll., 1967; JD cum laude, Harvard U., 1971. Bar: N.Y. 1972, U.S. Supreme Ct. 1976 and various fed. dist. and cir. cts. Law clk. Fed. Dist., Ea. Dist. N.Y., N.Y.C., 1971-72; assoc. Paul, Weiss, Rifkind, Wharton & Garrison, N.Y.C., 1973-75; assoc. Karpatkin Pollet Perlmutter & Beil, N.Y.C., 1975-77, ptnr., 1978-85; of counsel Rembar & Curtis, N.Y.C., 1985-88; ptnr. Lefrak, Newman & Myerson, N.Y.C., 1989—; bd. dirs. Louis August Jonas Found., Inc. (treas. 1990—, chmn. fin. and investments com. 1985—). Author: Power for the People: Electricity and the Regulatory Agencies, in M. Green (ed.), The Monopoly Makers, Ralph Nader's Study Group Report on Regulation and Competition, 1973; co-author: The New York Not-for-Profit Organization Manual, 1978, numerous articles in profl. jours. Bd. dirs., INFORM, Inc., 1972-80. Mem. Assn. Bar City of N.Y., Fed. Bar Coun., Swarthmore Coll. Alumni Assn. (pres. 1981-83). Democrat. Jewish. Office: Lefrak Newman & Myerson 575 Madison Ave New York NY 10022-2511

BEINHOCKER, GILBERT DAVID, investment banker; b. Phila., July 7, 1932; s. Joseph A. and Florence (Shlifer) B.; BA, Pa. State U., 1954; MS, U. Pa., 1958; D.Eng., U. Detroit, 1968; m. Barbara Broadley, Dec. 17, 1960; children: Eric David, Elizabeth Broadley, Robert Marc. Engrng. dir. Epsco, Inc., 1958-61; pres. Syber Corp., Natick, Mass., 1961-64; div. mgr. Tech. Measurement Corp., 1964-65; dir. advanced planning Am. Optical Co., 1965-66; chmn. bd. Microdyne Instruments, Inc., Waltham, Mass., 1967-69; pres., chief exec. officer, dir. Mgmt. Scis., Inc., Cambridge, Mass., 1968—; dir. Nat. Info. Svcs. Inc., Cambridge; chief exec. officer, dir. Eurocom Inc., Cambridge, 1975—; dir. corp. finance Moors and Cabot, Boston, 1976-82; v.p., treas., dir. First New Eng. Corp. Fin., Inc., 1982—; pres. Excalibur Ventures, Inc.; chmn. bd. Paragon Plastics Inc.; bd. vice chmn., mem. exec. com. Regal Internat., bd. dirs.; sr. lectr. U. Detroit, 1967-68. Recipient Nat. Fight for Sight citation Nat. Council to Combat Blindness, 1963. Mem. AAAS, IEEE, Assn. Computing Machinery, Internat. Fedn. Med. Electronics and Biol. Engrng., Internat. Soc. Clin. Electroretinography, Assn. Research Ophthalmology, Am. Def. Preparedness Assn., Am. Mgmt. Assn., Instrument Soc. Am., Am. Assn. Med. Instrumentation, Pi Lambda Phi. Republican. Author: Theory and Operation of Stardac Computers, 1960, also articles. Patentee in field. Home: 36 Beatrice Cir Belmont MA 02178-2659 Office: Excalibur Ventures Inc 125 Summer St Ste 1800 Boston MA 02110-1627

BEISER, LEO, consulting physicist, researcher; b. N.Y.C., Sept. 18, 1924; s. Sigmund Nathan and Sarah (Weiner) B.; m. Edith Vegotsky, Aug. 31, 1946; children: Helene Ronni, Steve Scott. BEE, RCA Inst., 1948; BBA, Alexander Hamilton Inst., 1958; BS in Physics, Hofstra U., 1964, MS in Physics, 1966. Asst. chief engr. CBS-Columbia, Inc., N.Y.C., 1951-56; project mgr. Polarad Electronics Corp., N.Y.C., 1956-60; staff cons. Gen. Instrument Corp., Westbury, N.Y., 1960-61; staff rsch. specialist Autometric/Raytheon Corp., N.Y.C., 1961-63; dir., D. Gabor Labs. CBS Labs., Inc., Stamford, Conn., 1963-76; pres., rsch. dir. Leo Beiser Inc., Flushing, N.Y., 1976—; adj. prof. Polytechnic U., N.Y.C., 1986. Author: (chpt.) Laser Scanning Systems in Laser Applications, Vol. 2, 1974, (book) Holographic Scanning, 1988, (tutorial series) Laser Scanning Notebook, OE Reports; editor: Laser Scanning and Recording, Milestone Series, 1985; contbr. articles to profl. jours. With USAF, 1943-46. Recipient Indsl. Rsch. IR-100 award Apparatus in Smithsonian Instn., 1973. Fellow SPIE (gov. 1983-86, seminar leader 1975—, G.W. Goddard award 1991), Soc. for Info. Display (charter mem., chmn. 1966-69, regional dir. 1975-77, Recognition award 1978); mem. Optical Soc. Am., Soc. Motion Picture and TV Engrs. Office: Leo Beiser Inc 15177 28th Ave Flushing NY 11354-1548

BEISSWENGER, HARRY LOUIS, JR., computer company executive; b. Phila., Nov. 5, 1935; s. Harry Louis and Marcella (Kennedy) B.; m. Elva Elizabeth Mayer, Aug. 16, 1958; children: Harry Walter, Robert Louis, Elizabeth Ann. BS in Indsl. Engrng., Lafayette Coll., 1957; postgrad., Fairleigh Dickinson U., 1959. Sales engr. Aluminum Co. Am., N.Y.C., 1958-60; N.Y. dist. sales mgr. Hull Corp., 1961-65; asst. sales mgr. food, drug and chem. div. Hull Corp., Hatboro, Pa., 1966-69; founder, pres. Quorum Systems, a Control Data Co., Plymouth Meeting, Pa., 1970-88; mgmt. cons. various computer cos., real estate developer Quorum Systems, and other computer cos., Maple Glen, Pa., 1989—. Contbr. articles to profl. publs. 2d lt. U.S. Army, 1957-58. Mem. Huntington Valley Country Club (v.p.), Stone Harbor Country Club (Absecon, N.J.). Republican. Methodist.

BEJARANO, LUIS E(NRIQUE), developer, fundraising consultant; b. Bklyn., Aug. 9, 1917; s. Jose Miguel and Trinela (Lillo De) B.; m. Valerie Garrett, Jan. 1, 1944; children: Valerie Elena Bejarano Carter, Luis E. Jr., Joel A., Carlos R., Andrea Lisa Bejarano Cionchi, Deena Lyn. BA, Columbia U., 1938, MLS, 1940; LHD, London Inst. of Applied Research, 1973. Librarian preparations div. N.Y. Pub. Library, 1940-41; librarian Schenectady (N.Y.) Pub. Library, 1941-42; dir. library, dept. head, pub. relations officer U.S. Mcht. Marine Acad., Kings Point, N.Y., 1946-60; dir. devel. and pub. relations Hillside Hosp., Glen Oaks, N.Y., 1960-61; coordinator devel., v.p. Hofstra U., Hempstead, N.Y., 1961-76; pres. Luis E. Bejarano Assocs., Lynbrook, N.Y., 1976-81; from exec. dir. to dir. Fire Island Lighthouse Preservation Soc., Bay Shore, N.Y., 1982—; cons. Mano River Maritime Coll., Monrovia, Liberia, 1979; trustee Frank J. Becker Ednl. Found., 1984—, Emeritus Lynbrook Pub. Libr., 1979—; chmn. bd. trustees Nassau County Rsch. Libr., Garden City, N.Y., 1972-79; witness, expert testifier U.S. congl. com. Ho. of Reps., Washington, 1986. Contbr. articles to profl. jours. Mem. Nature Conservancy, Friends of Lynbrook Libr., 1980—, Friends of Malverne (N.Y.) Libr., 1982—; historian Village of Lynbrook, 1984-86; bd. dirs. L.I. Nautical Festival, 1979-81. Comdr. USN, 1942-46, capt. Res. ret. Recipient Cert. for Achievement in Hist. Preservation, State of N.Y., 1986, Sherwood award Soc. for Preservation of Antiquities, 1986, Commendation Resolutions, N.Y. State Legis., 1986, Stephen Sloan Commemorative Medallion, Lighthouse Relighting Commn., 1986. Mem. U.S. Lighthouse Soc., Res. Officers Assn., Kings Point Maritime Assn., U.S. Mcht. Marine Acad. Alumni Assn. (dir. Project Acta 1979-81, Maritime Achievement award 1987), Hofstra U. Club, Gray Wig Club (Hempstead), Univ. Club. Republican. Lutheran. Clubs: Hofstra U., Grey Wig (Hempstead). Home: 87 Grove St Lynbrook NY 11563-2125 Office: Fire Island Lighthouse Captree Island Babylon NY 11702

BEJIAN, DONNA VIRGINIA, rehabilitation specialist; b. Washington, May 25, 1951; d. Marshall Chapman and Phyllis Marie (Shaunessy) Pierce; m. Timothy Charles Bejian, June 12, 1971; 1 child, Matthew Christopher. BA, SUNY, Albany, 1980; MS, Syracuse U., 1990. Cert. rehab. counselor. Eligibility worker Miss. Dept. Pub. Welfare, Monticello, Miss., 1982-84; S.H.A.R.E. program dir. Rome (N.Y.) Family YMCA, 1985-90; community job specialist Resource Ctr. Ind. Living, Utica, N.Y., 1990-91; rehab. specialist Intracorp, Syracuse, N.Y., 1991—. Fundraiser YMCA, Rome, 1989-90, United Way, Rome, 1988-89. Recipient Cert. of Recognition, Cath. Charities, Utica, N.Y., 1985, award of merit Rainbow House, Rome, 1986. Mem. AACD, Am. Rehab. Counseling Assn., Nat. Rehab. Counseling Assn., Nat. Rehab. Assn., Nat. Assn. Rehab. Profls. with Pvt. Sector, Career Devel. Assn., Employment Counselors Assn., Nat. Alliance Mentally Ill. Baptist. Home: PO Box 847 Rome NY 13440-0847 Office: Intracorp 5794 Widewaters Pkwy Syracuse NY 13214

BEKEY, IVAN, systems engineer; b. Prague, Czechoslovakia, Nov. 21, 1931; came to U.S. 1945; s. Andrew and Elizabeth (Magyar) B.; m. Marlene Ann Woodbury, May 30, 1968; children: Lisa Ann, Suzanne Jeanine. BSEE, UCLA, 1954, MSEE, 1959. Sect. leader Douglas Aircraft Co., Santa Monica, Calif., 1954-56; sr. engr. RCA, L.A., 1956-59; sect. head Space Tech. Labs., L.A., 1959-61; dir. planning Aerospace Corp., L.A., 1961-73, group dir., 1973-78; dir. adv. programs NASA Hdqrs., Washington, 1978-87, spl. asst. exploration, 1989-90; dir. adv. programs Nat. Space Coun. - The White House, Washington, 1990-91; spl. asst. to dep. adminstr. NASA, Washington, 1992—; mem. Naval Studies Bd./Space, Washington, 1988—; pres. Bekey Designs, Inc., Annandale, Va., 1979—; ptnr. Mountain Venture Partnership, Monrovia, Calif., 1989-92. Editor: Space Stations and Space Platforms, 1987; contbr. articles to profl. jurs.; patentee in field. Bd. dirs. Community Orgn. Coun., Annandale, 1979, 82, 87. Recipient Exceptional Svc. medal NASA, 1983, Group Pub Svc. award, 1977, 86. Fellow AIAA, Washington Acad. Scis.; mem. Internat. Acad. Astronautics, Am. Astronautical Soc., Cosmos Club, Tau Beta Pi, Sigma Phi Delta. Republican. Home: 4624 Quarter Charge Dr Annandale VA 22003-4622

BELAFSKY, MARK LEWIS, otolaryngologist; b. Perth Amboy, N.J., June 8, 1939; s. Henry A. and Rose (Buckner) B.; m. Betty M. Forman, Dec. 25, 1962; children: Caryn, Peter. BA, U. Pa., 1960; MD, Chgo. Med. Sch., 1964. Diplomate Am. Bd. Otolaryngology. Intern Thomas Jefferson U., Phila., 1964-65, resident, 1967-71; pvt. practive Cherry Hill, N.J., 1971—; chmn. bd. dirs. Our Lady of Lourdes Hosp., Camden, N.J., Rancocas Valley Hosp., Willingboro, N.J. Chmn. bd. dirs. med. adv. coun. N.J. State Athletic Control Bd., 1987—. Capt. U.S. Army, 1965-67, Vietnam. Fellow ACS, Am. Acad. of Otolaryngology & Head & Neck Surgery, Am. Soc. Head & Neck Surgery, Am. Soc. of Facial, Plastic & Reconstructive Surgery, Phila. Coll. of Physicians. Office: 1910 E Rte 70 Cherry Hill NJ 08003

BELAK, MICHAEL JAMES, data processing executive; b. Cleve., Nov. 26, 1961; s. John James and Violet Mae (Yamek) B.; m. Eve Angela Hinds, June 15, 1985; 1 child, Michael James II. BS in Computer Engrng., Ohio State U., 1985; MBA in Info. Systems Mgmt., George Washington U., 1990. Application programmer office of registrar Ohio State U., Columbus, 1984-85; project leader database adminstrn. IBM, Gaithersburg, Md., 1985-88; cons. svcs. mgr. Gen. Electric, Rockville, Md., 1988-91; mgr. data adminstrn. PHH Corp., Hunt Valley, Md., 1991—. Contbr. articles to profl. jours. Mem. Internat. DB2 Users Group (conf. com. 1990—), Washington Case Users Group (exec. com. 1991—), Assn. for Computing Machinery (profl. devel. com. 1989-91). Republican. Home: 4475 Rolling Meadows Ellicott City MD 21043 Office: PHH Corp Mail Code JA 11333 McCormick Rd Hunt Valley MD 21031

BEL BRUNO, JOSEPH JAMES, chemistry educator; b. Passaic, N.J., June 30, 1952; s. Joseph and Carmella (Nicastro) Bel B.; m. Kathleen B. Cassidy, Aug. 10, 1980; children: Joseph Hugh, Elizabeth Kelly. BS, Seton Hall U., 1974; PhD, Rutgers U., 1980. Rsch. asst. chemistry Princeton (N.J.) U., 1980-82; asst. prof. chemistry Dartmouth Coll., hanover, N.H., 1982-88; assoc. prof. chemistry Dartmouth Coll., Hanover, N.H., 1988—. Contbr. over 40 articles to profl. jours. Bd. dirs. Cradle and Crayon Child Devel. Ctr., Hanover, 1991—. Alexander von Humboldt Found. fellow, 1988. Mem. Am. Chem. Soc., Am. Phys. Soc., Sigma Xi. Office: Dartmouth Coll Steele Hall Hanover NH 03755

BELFORTE, DAVID ARTHUR, company president; b. Framingham, Mass., Oct. 25, 1932; s. Arthur David and Jean Louise (Purcell) B.; m. Virginia Elizabeth Crowley, Aug. 2, 1958; 1 child, Steven, David. BS, Northeastern U., 1963, MS, 1970. Staff scientist Raytheon Co., Waltham, Mass., 1951-65; v.p. Thomson Gen. Corp., Lynn, Mass., 1965-70; dir. mktg. Am. Optical Corp., Southbridge, Mass., 1970-73; mgr. Ferranti Elec. Inc., Sturbridge, 1973-76; dir. mktg. Avco Everett Metal Working Lasers, Somerville, Mass., 1976-81; pres. Belforte Assocs., Sturbridge, 1982—. Editor: Industrial Laser Handbook, 1986-92; editor Indsl. Laser Rev., 1986-92. Fellow Laser Inst. Am. (Pres.'s award 1988); mem. Soc. Mfg. Engrs. Office: Belforte Assocs PO Box 245 Sturbridge MA 01566-0245

BELICA, MARINA ELENA, music company executive; b. Cold Spring, N.Y., Dec. 11, 1959; d. Paul and Mary (Karas) B. Student, Aspen Sch. Music, 1978; BA in Music magna cum laude, Yale U., 1981. Musical dir. archival rec. project Cole Porter Music and Lit. Trust, New Haven, 1981-82; prodn. coord. Ciani/Musica, Inc., N.Y.C., 1982-83, exec. dir., 1983-85, v.p., 1985-89; assoc. Depth of Field Mgmt., N.Y.C., 1989—; panelist Women In Music, N.Y.C., 1986; judge CLIO awards, 1985. Mem. SAG, AFTRA, NARAS, Yale Club. Office: Depth of Field Mgmt 1501 Broadway Ste 1506 New York NY 10036-5503

BELL, BRITTIAN DUDLEY, III, publishing executive; b. Houston, Oct. 27, 1942; s. Britt Jr. and Geraldine (Jones) B.; m. Jennifer Moyer, Dec. 20, 1981; children: Ana Bess Moyer Bell, Niall Reed Moyer Bell. BBA, U. Houston, 1967. Mng. editor Dial Press, N.Y.C., 1975-79; sales mgr. Farrar, Straus and Giroux, N.Y.C., 1979-84; account exec. Princeton (N.J.) Univ. Press, 1990—; pub. Moyer Bell Ltd., Mt. Kisco, N.Y., 1984—; pres. Small Press mag., Mt. Kisco, 1991. Office: Moyer Bell Ltd Colonial Hill Mount Kisco NY 10549

BELL, BYRON, architect; b. N.Y.C., June 15, 1935; s. James Byron and Virginia (Dame) B.; m. Joyce Denebrink, May 1, 1966 (div. 1970); m. Susan Thompson Koelle, May 6, 1972. BA, Princeton U., 1957; MArch, Columbia U., 1962. Registered architect N.Y. With James Byron Bell Assocs., N.Y.C., 1964-65, Walker O. Cain Assocs., N.Y.C., 1965-67; owner James Byron Bell Assocs., Architects, N.Y.C., 1967-78; ptnr. Cain, Farrell & Bell, N.Y.C., 1978-86, Farrell, Bell & Lennard, N.Y.C., 1986—; design critic various univs., archtl. juries. Archtl. works include Columbia U.'s Rare Book and Manuscript Libr., The Grolier Club, St. James Ch., pvt. residences; contbr. articles to profl. jours.; editor 57 Varieties mag. Mem. Blue Hill Troupe, N.Y.C., pres., 1966, bd. dirs. (6 terms); v.p. Clarion Music Soc., N.Y.C., 1985—. Lt. USN, 1957-60. Kinne Fellows fellow, 1962. Mem. AIA, Am. Arbitration Assn. (arbitrator), Nat. Inst. for Archtl. Edn. (former chair, former treas.), Amateur Comedy Club, World Craft Found. (sec., Bd. dirs. 1986—), The Century Assn., The Grolier Club, Augustus-Saint Gaudens Meml. (trustee 1992—), Onteora Club. Episcopalian. Home: 136 W 15th St New York NY 10011-6702 Office: Farrell Bell & Lennard 123 W 3d New York NY 10012

BELL, CAROLYN SHAW, economist, educator; b. Framingham, Mass., June 21, 1920; d. Clarence Edward and Grace (Wellington) Shaw; m. Nelson S. Bell, Aug. 26, 1953; 1 dau. by previous marriage, Tova Maria. AB magna cum laude, Mt. Holyoke Coll., 1941; PhD, London (Eng.) Sch. Econs., 1949; LHD (hon.), Babson Coll., 1983, Denison U., 1988, North Adams State Coll., 1991. Economist OPA, 1941-45; rsch. economist London Sch. Econs., 1946-47, Social Sci. Rsch. Coun., Harvard, 1950-53; mem. faculty Wellesley Coll., 1950-89, prof. econs., 1962-89, chmn. dept., 1962-65, 79-82, Katharine Coman prof. econs., 1970-89, Katharine Coman prof. econs. emerita, 1989—; cons. Lexington, Mass., 1989—; pub. mem. Fed. Adv. Coun. on Unemployment Ins., 1974-77, chmn., 1975-77; bd. econ. advisors Pub. Interest Econ. Ctr.; bd. overseers Amos Tuck Grad. Sch. Bus. Adminstrn., Dartmouth, 1973-79; mem. econs. policy coun. UN Assn., 1976-85, trustee, 1981-90; trustee Joint Coun. Econ. Edn., 1975-83, Tchrs. Ins. and Annuity Assn., 1977-85; mem. NRC Com. for Behavioral and Social Scis., 1977-83; bd. dirs. Red Acre Farm Hearing Dog Ctr., 1989-91. Author: Consumer Choice in the U.S. Economy, 1967, The Economics of the Ghetto, 1970; coauthor: (with W.W. Cochrane) Economics of Consumption, 1956; co-author: Coping in A Troubled Society, 1974; contbr. articles to profl. jours; radio and TV commentator; mem. bd. editors: Challenge, Jour. Edcons. Edn., Jour. Econ. Issues. Mem. Hearing Dog Adv. Coun., 1990—. Mem. AAUP (pres. Wellesley chpt. 1965-66), AAUW (Shirley Farr fellow 1961-62), ACLU, Assn. for Advancement Socio-Econs., Manhattan Inst. (adv. bd.), Am. Econs. Assn. (chmn. com. on status of women in econs. profession 1972-74, mem. exec. com. 1975-77), Assn. Evolutionary Econs. (bd. dirs. 1973-75), Ea. Econs. Assn. (exec. bd. 1983-85), Phi Beta Kappa (pres. Eta of Mass. chpt. 1978-80), Delta Soc. Home and Office: 1010 Waltham St # 8F Lexington MA 02173-8044

BELL, CLARENCE DESHONG, lawyer, state senator; b. Upland, Pa., Feb. 4, 1914; s. Samuel Robert and Belle (Hanna) B.; m. Mary James, Nov. 24, 1939; children: Clarence, Mary D. AB, Swarthmore Coll., 1935; JD, Harvard U., 1938; grad., U.S. Army Command and Gen. Staff Coll., 1942; advanced course, U.S. Army Field Arty. Sch., 1945. Bar: Pa. 1939. Pvt. practice law Delaware County, Pa., 1939—; mem. Pa. Ho. of Reps., 1954-60; mem. Pa. Senate, 1960—, chmn. joint legis. budget and fin. commn., chmn. consumer protection and profl. licensure com., vice-chmn. appropriations com. With U.S. Army, 1935-74; to brig. gen. Army N.G., 1964-74; to maj. gen. Pa. N.G., 1974—. Named Labor's Man of Yr. Delaware County chpt.

AFL-CIO, 1980; recipient awards and citations from Pa. Gold State Mothers, Jewish War Vets., VFW, Res. Officers Assn., Mil. Govt. Assn., B'nai B'rith, KC, Polish-Am. Citizens Club, SSS, N.G. Assn. Pa., Am. Legion, various others; decorated U.S. Legion of Merit, U.S. Army Commendation medal (2), Pa. Disting. Svc. medal (2), others. Mem. ABA, Pa. Bar Assn., Fraternal Order of Police (hon.), Teamsters (hon.), Transport Workers Union (hon.), Mil. Govt. Assn. (past nat. pres.), Res. Officers Assn. (past state pres.), Mil. Order World Wars, N.G. Assn., Exch. Club (past state pres.), Masons. Republican. Office: Pa State Senate State Capitol Harrisburg PA 17120-0030 also: 280 N Providence Rd Media PA 19063

BELL, DIANE ROBIN, educator, writer; b. Melbourne, Victoria, Australia, June 11, 1943; d. Allan Thomas and Florence Edna Haig; m. Allan James, Oct. 9, 1967 (div. 1972); children: Genevieve, Morgan. BA with honors, Monash U., Clayton, Victoria, 1975; PhD, Australian Nat. U., 1980. Primary sch. tchr. Edn. Dept., Victoria, NSW, 1962-66; sr. anthropologist Aboriginal Sacred Sites Authority, Darwin, N.T., Northern Territory, 1981; cons. anthropologist Bell and Assocs., Canberra, A.C.T., Australian Capital Territory, 1980-88; prof. Australian Studies Deakin U., Geelong, Victoria, 1986-88; Henry R. Luce prof. religion, econ. devel. & social justice Coll. Holy Cross, Worcester, Mass., 1989—; cons. Cen. Land Coun. Alice Springs, No. Territory, 1978-88, Australian Law Reform Commn. Sydney, NSW, 1980-86, Aboriginal Land Commr., Darwin, No. Territory, 1978-83, Aboriginal Legal Aid Svcs., Alice Springs, Darwin, 1978-84; broadcaster Australian Broadcasting Commn., Melbourne, Australia, 1990—. Author: Law: The Old and the New, 1980, Daughters of the Dreaming, 1983, Generations, 1987 (Landmark Bicentennial Vol. award 1988); editor: Religion in Aboriginal Australia, 1984; mem. editorial bd. Women's Studies Internat. Forum, 1990—, Aboriginal History, 1980—. Trustee Hampshire Coll., Amherst, Mass., 1991—. Named High Achiever, Zonta, 1988; Charles Stong fellow Charles Strong Trust, 1980, John Curtin fellow Australian Nat. U., 1988, grad. scholar, 1976-80. Fellow Australian Anthropol. Soc.; mem. Am. Anthropol. Assn., Am. Acad. Religion, Lyceum Club. Office: Coll of the Holy Cross Worcester MA 01610

BELL, FRANCES LOUISE, medical technologist; b. Milton, Pa., Apr. 28, 1926; d. George Earl and Kathryn Robbins (Fairchild) Reichard; m. Edwin Lewis Bell II, Dec. 27, 1950; children: Ernest Michael, Stephen Thomas, Eric Leslie. BS in Biology cum laude, Bucknell U., 1948; MT, Geisinger Meml. Hosp., 1949. Registered med. technologist. Med. technologist Burlington County Hosp., Mt. Holly, N.J., 1949-50, Robert Packer Hosp., Sayre, Pa., 1950, Carle Hosp./Clinic, Urbana, Ill., 1951-52, St. Joseph Hosp., Reading, Pa., 1972-83. Vol. Crime Watch, City Hall, Reading, 1985-90, Am. Heart Assn., Reading, 1956—, March of Dimes, Reading, 1956-72, Am. Cancer Soc., Reading, 1956-71, Multiple Sclerosis, Reading, 1956-72, Reading Musical Found., 1985-90, Hist. Soc. Berks County; corr. sec. women's aux., 1986-90; fin. sec. women's aux. Albright Coll., 1988—; hospitality co-chmn. women's com. Reading Symphony Orch., 1985-90, co-editor yearbook women's com., 1990-92, editor yearbook women's com., 1992—; chmn. hospitality Reading-Berks Pub. Librs., 1988-91; mem. Friends Reading Mus., Berks County Conservancy. Mem. Woman's Club of Reading (treas. 1986-88, fin. sec. 1991—), AAUW (assoc. editor bull. 1961-63, cultural interests rep. 1967-68), United Meth. Women, Phi Beta Kappa. Republican. Methodist. Home: 1454 Oak Ln Reading PA 19604-1865

BELL, FRANK JOSEPH, III, architect; b. Paterson, N.J., Sept. 30, 1955; s. Frank Joseph and Evelyn Dorothy (Nemeth) B.; m. Greta Eichlin, Sept. 13, 1987; children: Marjorie Blair, Caroline Frances. Student, U. Miami, Coral Gables, Fla., 1976-78; BArch, N.J. Inst. Tech., 1981. Registered architect, N.J., N.Y., Pa.; cert. profl. planner, N.J. Staff architect Houghton-Quarty-Warr, Architects, 1981-86; prin. Frank Joseph Bell, Architect, Newton, Pittstown, N.J., 1986—; appointed county architect County of Hunterdon, 1990. Secretary, chmn. bd. dirs. Highlands Workshop/Easter Seal Soc., Franklin, N.J., 1981—; chmn. bldg. and grounds com. St. Joseph's Ch., Newton, 1984—. Mem. AIA, N.J. Soc. Architects. Office: 43 Trinity St Newton NJ 07860-1823

BELL, IRVING, newspaper columnist, publisher, author; b. Malden, Mass., June 22, 1912; s. Otis Irving and Garda Marie (Anderson) B.; m. Phyllis E. Hatch, Sept. 5, 1942; 1 child, Carlton Frederick. Student, U. Wis., 1930-34. Editor, pub. Tunesmith, Buffalo, 1939-42; state editor Daily Monitor-Patriot, Concord, N.H., 1945-62; owner Bell Audio-Visuals, 1948—; editor Concord News, weekly, 1962-7l; owner, mgr. Three R's Bookshop, Springfield, Vt., 1972-78, April Hill Pubs., Springfield, 1979—, Abatis Books, Springfield, 1980-88; columnist (under pseudonym Mike Twine) Springfield Reporter, 1973—; editor Bell Chimes, Springfield, 1980—; exec. dir. Clan Bell, Springfield, 1980—. Author: They Knew Franklin Pierce, 1980, Christmas in Old New England, 1981; pub., editor quar. Franklin Pierce Times, 1992—. Fell Soc. of Antiquaries of Scotland; mem. New Eng. Hist. Geneal. Soc., N.H. Hist. Soc., Calvin Coolidge Meml. Found., Clan Bell Descs. (founder). Republican. Congregationalist. Office: PO Box 451 Springfield VT 05156

BELL, JACK P., marketing professional, biochemist; b. San Francisco, Jan. 24, 1940; s. John M. and Jean E. (Perkins) B.; m. Sherry S. Smith, Aug. 14, 1965; children: Elizabeth, Christina. BS in Chemistry cum laude, U. Wash., 1962; PhD in Organic Chemistry, U. Wis., 1967. Postdoctoral fellow, staff researcher in cancer rsch. Stanford Rsch. Inst., Menlo Park, Calif., 1967-69; project mgr., Syntex Rsch. Ctr. Syntex Pharms., Palo Alto, Calif., 1969-78; tech. sales rep., liquid chromatography Walters Assocs., N.J., 1978-80; regional sales mgmt. Applied Analytical Industries, N.E., 1980-81; product line mgr. Varian Instruments, Walnut Creek, Calif., 1981-89; field marketing devel., Western region Suprex Corp., Pitts., 1990-91; bioseparations field mktg. Beckman Instruments, 1992—; instr. DeAnza Coll., Cupertino, Calif., 1977; advisor Stanford Affiliates, Stanford, Calif., 1976-78; cons. Jr. Achievement, San Francisco, 1984. Author: 30 sci. publs. on cancer rsch. and separation scis., 1968-78, a review of commercially available instruments, 1984; speaker 23 seminars on Genetic Engring. and Chromatography, 1974-90; developer customer, sales tng. courses on analytical techniques, 1976-90. Vestryman Episcopal Ch., N.J., 1980. Recipient Dow Chem. scholarship U. Wash., 1961. Mem. Am. Chem. Soc., Alpha Chi Sigma, Sigma Xi, Phi Lambda Upsilon, Alpha Epsilon Delta, Phi Beta Kappa. Home: 2950 Windtree Ct Lafayette CA 94549-4824

BELL, JAMES KEITH, entertainment company executive; b. Cin., Mar. 12, 1955; s. Clinton Collins and Betty Mae (Winkle) B.; m. Kathryn Ann O'Rourke, Nov. 28, 1982; 1 child, Samantha Morgan. BA in Polit. Sci., York U., Toronto, Ont., Can., 1977. Rep. Can. Life, Stamford, Conn., 1978; cons. Chodos Assoc., Stamford, 1978-79; sr. customer svc. rep. Ga. Pacific, Stamford, 1979-81; sales promotion mgr. Internat. Playtex, Stamford, 1981-84; dir. Simplicity, N.Y.C., 1984-87; dir. mktg. and licensing The Muppets, N.Y.C., 1987-90, Rabbit Ears Prodns., Westport, Conn., 1991—; cons. Direct Connect Internat., Ridgewood, N.J., 1991—, Dick Levy UniWorld/Levy, N.Y.C., 1991—. Recipient numerous awards. Mem. Licensing Industry Merchandisers Assn. (prins. adv. com. Norwalk, Conn. chpt.), Am. Film Inst. Home: 16 Muriel St Norwalk CT 06851-3019

BELL, JAMES MILTON, psychiatrist; b. Portsmouth, Va., Nov. 5, 1921; s. Charles Edward and Lucy (Barnes) B. Student, Va. State Coll., 1939-40; BS, N.C. Cen. U. (formerly N.C. Coll.), 1943; MD, Meharry Med. Coll., 1947. Diplomate in psychiatry and child psychiatry Am. Bd. Psychiatry and Neurology (examiner 1980—), Pan. Am. Med. Assn. (coun. psychiatry sect.); cert. N.Y. State Dept. Mental Hygiene. Harlem Hosp. N.Y.C., 1947-48; asst. physician to clin. dir. Lakin (W.Va.) State Hosp., N.Y.C., 1948-51; fellow gen. psychiatry Menninger Sch. Psychiatry-Menninger Found., Topeka, 1953-56, tng. child psychiatry, 1957-58; resident Winter VA Hosp., Topeka, 1953-56; asst. sect. chief childrens unit Topeka State Hosp., 1956-58; clin. teaching staff Menninger Sch. Psychiatry, 1956-58; clin. dir., psychiatrist Berkshire Farm Ctr. and Svcs. for Youth, Canaan, N.Y., 1959-86, sr. child and adolescent psychiatrist, 1986—; clin. asst. to clin. prof. psychiatry Albany Med. Coll., Union U., 1959—, mem. admission com., 1972-79; psychiatrist-in-charge Albany Home for Children, N.Y., 1959-77; staff psychiatrist Parsons Child and Family Ctr., 1977—; asst. dispensary to dispensary psychiatrist Albany Med. Ctr. Clinic, 1960; trainee cons. Albany Child Guidance Ctr. Psychiat. Svc., Inc., 1961. cons. Keller U.S. Army Hosp., U.S. Mil. Acad., West Point, N.Y. Contbr. numerous articles to profl. jours. Cons. Astor Home for Children, Rhinebeck, N.Y., 1965; instrnl. staff Frederick Amman Meml. Inst. Delinquency and Crime, St. Lawrence U., 1965-70; cons. adolescence N.Y. State Div. Youth, 1966-76, mem. med. rev. bd., 1974-76; mem. Child Abuse Adv. Coun., Albany; bd. dirs., mem. com. on proposed policy N.Y. Spaulding for Children, v.p., 1988-89; bd. dirs., exec. com. Guold Farm, Barrington, Mass. Capt. M.C., AUS, 1951-53; col. USAR, 1955-85, ret., 1985. Decorated Army Commendation medal, Meritorious Svc. medal, others; named Disting. Alumnus, Meharry Med. Coll., 1980. Fellow AAAS (life), Am. Psychiat. Assn. (life, chmn. coun. nat. affairs 1973-75, past vice-chmn.), Am. Acad. of Child and Adolescent Psychiatry (life, chmn. com. psychiat. facilities for children and adolescence 1973-75), Am. Orthopsychiat. Assn. (life, past dir.), Am. Soc. Adolescent Psychiatry, N.Y. Acad. Scis., Am. Coll. Psychiatrists (past mem. Stanley Dean award com.), Am. Psychopathol. Assn.; mem. AMA, NAACP (life), Am. Acad. Polit. and Social Sci., Am. Soc. Addiction Medicine, Black Psychiatrists Am., Group for Advancement of Psychiatry (com. on child psychiatry), Inst. Religion and Health (charter), Council for Exceptional Children, Nat. Assn. Tng. Schs. and Juvenile Agys., Assn. N.Y. Educators of Emotionally Disturbed, Nat., N.Y. State, Columbia Country med. assns., Child Care Workers (bd. dirs. N.Y.), Assn. Psychiat. Treatment of Offenders, N.Y. State Soc. Med. Rsch., N.Y. Capitol Dist. Coun. Child Psychiatry (pres. 1974), Am. Legion, Rotary, Alpha Omega Alpha. Home: Hudsonview Old Post Rd N Croton-on-Hudson NY 10520 Office: Berkshire Farm Ctr & Svcs for Youth Canaan NY 12029

BELL, J(AMES) MILTON, religious society official; b. Orillia, Ont., Can., Nov. 12, 1925; s. Harold James and Margaret Olive (Deck) B.; m. Ellen Virginia Gibb, Nov. 14, 1953. BA, Queens U., 1946; BD, Queens Theol. Sem., 1950; ThM, Princeton Theol. Sem., 1951; STD, Temple U., 1955. Asst. pastor St. Paul Presbyn. Ch., Phila., 1950-52; pastor Christ-West Hope Presbyn. Ch., Phila., 1952-60; sr. pastor Cen. Brick Presbyn. Ch., East Orange, N.J., 1960-70; dir. planned giving Am. Bible Soc., N.Y.C., 1970—; vis. evangelist Ranchmens' Camp Meetings, Tex., 1967-68, N.Mex., 1967-68; pvt. charitable trust cons. numerous charitable, religous and ednl. instns., 1974—; pvt. fiduciary, trust adminstr., 1969—; specialist creation in pubs., developing charitable gift annuities, charitable remainder trusts and charitable bequests; planning giving lectr. Internat. Fund Raising Workshop, Amsterdam, the Netherlands, 1991, European Fund Raisers' Meeting, 1992. Author: The Churchman's Almanac, 1959, The Minister As Investor, 1961. Mem. Presbytery of Newark. Republican. Home: 160 Sunset Ave Verona NJ 07044-2316 Office: Am Bible Soc 1865 Broadway New York NY 10023-7503

BELL, JAMES TYLER, biology researcher; b. Washington, Nov. 26, 1960; s. Leslie Bradford Bell, Jr. and Mary Catherine (Fox) Drury; m. Jane Frances Kostenko, June 17, 1989. BS, St. Mary's Coll. of Md., 1985; MS, U. Md., 1990. Grad. rsch. asst. Chesapeake Biol. Lab, U. Md., Solomons, 1985-87, faculty rsch. asst., 1990—; lab. scientist Benedict (Md.) Estuarine Rsch. Lab., 1988-90. Mem. Archaeol. Soc. Md. (So. Md. chpt.). Democrat. Roman Catholic. Office: U Md Chesapeake Biol Lab PO Box 38 Solomons MD 20688-0038

BELL, JEANNE LOWER, music director, conductor; b. Phila., June 23, 1934; d. George Grafley and Emily Elizabeth (Hallauer) Lower; m. Guy C. Bell, Jr., Dec. 26, 1959; children: George Walton, Cynthia Joyce, Gordon Hallauer, Douglas Lower. BS in Elem. Edn. and Music, Bucknell U., 1956; M. Violin, West Chester U., 1988. The Ardensingers, Arden, Wilmington, Del.; Tchr. Wayne (Pa.) Elem. Sch., 1956-57, West Chester Elem. Sch., 1957-58; music tchr. Springfield (Pa.) Pub. Schs., 1959-61; tchr. Marple-Newtown (Pa.) Sr. High Sch., tchr. music, 1977-85; concertmaster and orch. coord. The Ardensingers, Arden, Wilmington, Del., 1991—; co-music dir. Gilbert & Sullivan Soc. of Chester County, West Chester, 1987—; founder, music dir., conductor Rose Tree Pops Orch., Inc., Media, Pa., 1985—; violinist Reading (Pa.) Symphony, 1988—; concertmaster Rose Valley Chorus and Orch., Springfield, 1971-91, music. dir., 1981-84; ski instr. Buck Ridge Ski Club; lectr. in elem. schs.; music dir. children's concerts with orch.; solo performances violin concerts, 1956—; dir. youth auditions Lansdowne Symphony Orch., 1971—. Writer, dir. musicals; choir dir., ch. concerts; guest performer Phila. area. Active in past Boy Scouts Am., Girl Scouts U.S. Mem. NAFE, NAACP, AAUW (Award for Leadership 1956), PEO, Mu Phi Epsilon, Kappa Delta Epsilon. Republican. Presbyterian. Home and Office: 844 Crestview Dr Springfield PA 19064

BELL, JOSEPH CHARLES, lawyer; b. Louisville, Nov. 11, 1940; s. Robert Franklin and Nell (Trenkle) B.; m. Ruth Greenspan, July 7, 1968; children: Samuel Robert, Johanna Rebecca. BA summa cum laude, U. Colo., 1962; AM in Econs., Harvard U., 1965; postgrad., U. Calif., Berkeley, 1966-67; LLB, Yale U., 1968. Bar: Mass. 1968, D.C. 1977. Economist Office of Tax Analysis, U.S. Treasury Dept., Washington, summer 1965, 66; teaching asst. econs. Harvard U., Cambridge, Mass., 1968-69; legal advisor Cabinet Task Force on Oil Import Control, Washington, 1969-70; atty. advisor antitrust div. U.S. Dept. of Justice, Washington, 1970-72; asst. prof. Law Sch. and Inst. Policy Studies Duke U., Durham, N.C., 1972-74; asst. gen. counsel for internat. and spl. programs Fed. Energy Adminstrn., Washington, 1974-77; assoc. Hogan & Hartson, Washington, 1977-78, ptnr., 1979—; resident ptnr. Hogan & Hartson, Warsaw, Poland, 1991—; mem. nat. adv. bd. Ctr. for Nat. Policy, Washington, 1985—; gen. counsel Citizens' Energy Corp., Cambridge, Mass., 1979-88; spl. counsel Ministry of Fin., Republic of Poland, Warsaw, 1989-91; founder, dir. Project on Econ. Reform in Ukraine, 1990—; advisor Supreme Soviet and Ministry of Privatization, Ukraine, Kiev, 1 991—. Author, editor: Petroleum Regulation Handbook, 1980; editor Calif. Law Rev., 1966-67; editor Yale Law Jour., 1965, 67-68; contbr. articles to profl. jours. Mem. ABA (adminstrv., corp. and internat. sects.), Am. Econ. Assn. Office: Hogan & Hartson 555 13th St NW Washington DC 20004-1109 also: Hogan & Hartson, Marszalkowska 6/6, 00-590 Warsaw Poland

BELL, LARRY JOHN, fine arts educator; b. Niagara Falls, N.Y., Aug. 20, 1940; s. Lawrence Charles and Irene Beatrice (Lapointe) B. BS, State U. Coll. Buffalo, 1964, MS, 1969; grantee, N.Y. Inst. for the Arts, 1986. Art edn. K-6 tchr. Niagara Falls (N.Y.) Bd. Edn., 1964-68; art edn. tchr. Lasalle Jr. High, Niagara Falls, N.Y., 1968-71; sabbatical award Rsch. and One Man Exhbn., Washington, 1975-76; art instr. Lasalle Sr. High, Niagara Falls, N.Y., 1971-82; art instr. Niagara Falls (N.Y.) High, 1983—, chmn. fine arts, 1985—; head tchr. Curriculum Devel., Niagara Falls, 1986-89, 89—; pres. Buffalo Soc. Artists, 1977, 83, 87; chmn. fine arts Niagara Falls (N.Y.) High Sch., 1985—; exec. coun. Buffalo Soc. Artists, 1972-74, 1978-84, 1986-89, 1990-91; ad hoc com. Albright-Knox Art Gallery, Buffalo, 1977-78. One-man show includes Millicent Chatel Gallery, Washington, 1976; contbr. articles to profl. jours. Bd. dirs. Allentown Village Soc., Buffalo, 1979-80; co-dir. Gallery West Art Gallery, Buffalo, 1968-73; gallery adv. Clarey-Miner Gallery, Buffalo, 1985-91; life mem. Western N.U. Inst. for Arts in Edn., Buffalo, 1986—. Recipient Silver Medal award, 82nd Nat. Buffalo Soc. Artists Exhbn., 1977; Bronze Medal award, 92nd nat. Buffalo Soc. Artists Exhbn., 1987; Adam, Meldrum and Anderson award Albright-Know Art Gallery, Buffalo, 1990. Mem. Buffalo Soc. Artists, N.Y. State United Tchrs., Burchfield Art Ctr., State U. Coll. Buffalo, N.Y. State Art Tchrs. Assn., Western N.Y. Coun. of Arts, Sigma Tau Rho Frat. Democrat. Roman Catholic. Home: 58 Claremont Ave Buffalo NY 14222-1146 Office: Niagara Falls High Pine Ave and Portage Niagara Falls NY 14301

BELL, PATRICIA MONDELLO, academic director; b. Chelsea, Mass., Nov. 29, 1956; d. Frank Norman and Mary Beatrice (Cassidy) Mondello; m. Michael Joseph Bell, May 22, 1963; 1 child, Jennifer Lauren. BS in Earth Sci., U. Mass., Boston, 1989. Securities trader Fidelity Brokerage Svcs., Boston, 1981-87; asst. dir. Univ. Mass., Boston, 1989—. Episcopalian. Home: 121 Turnpike Rd Chelmsford MA 01824-3555 Office: Univ Mass Boston Harbor Campus Morrissey Bld Boston MA 02125

BELL, RAYMOND JOSEPH, manufacturing executive, engineer; b. Paterson, N.J., July 23, 1949; s. Raymond Joseph Sr. and Mildred Elizabeth (Staiber) B.; m. Nancy Elizabeth Lee, Apr. 22, 1972; children: Aaron, Jocelyn, Colleen, Nathaniel. BA in Chemistry, SUNY, Buffalo, 1971, MS, 1976. Cert. in prodn. and inventory mgmt. R&D engr. Hewlett-Packard Co., Palo Alto, Calif., 1976-83; owner Morris & Lee, Inc., Buffalo, 1983—. Treas., PTO, City Honors Sch., Buffalo, 1989—; chmn. troop 5, Boy Scouts Am., Buffalo, 1990—. Mem. Am. Prodn. and Inventory Control Soc. Office: Morris and Lee Inc 95 Botsford Pl Buffalo NY 14216

BELL, RICHARD TRENT, physician; b. Balt., Mar. 14, 1946; s. Vernon Adam Veith and Clara Beatrice (Scull) B.; m. Karen Louise Taylor, Aug. 23, 1969; children: Kristin, Allison, Lauren. BA with honors, Lehigh U., 1968; MD, Jefferson Med. Coll., 1972. Diplomate Am. Bd. Internal Medicine. Resident internal medicine Lankenau Hosp., Phila., 1972-75; fellow pulmonary diseases Einstein Med. Ctr., Phila., 1977-79; ptnr. Pulmonary Med. Assocs., West Reading, Pa., 1979—. Contbr. articles to profl. jours. Chmn. chpt. ARC of Berks County, Reading, Pa., 1989-91; dir. Am. Lung Assn. Pa., Harrisburg. Maj. USAF, 1975-77. Fellow ACP, Am. Coll. Chest Physicians; mem. AMA (alternate Pa. del. 1991—), Pa. Soc. for Pulmonary Disease (pres. 1991—), Berks County Med. Soc. (pres. 1988, chmn. bd. 1989—), Pa. Med. Soc., Am. Thoraic Soc. Office: Pulmonary Med Assocs 301 S 7th Ave West Reading PA 19611

BELL, ROBERT ARNOLD, sales and promotions executive; b. Springfield, Mass., Oct. 12, 1950; s. Irwin and Vivian (Rulnick) B.; m. Brandi Merryl Kane; 1 child, Jolie Eve. Student, Babson Coll., 1968-72. V.p. Standard Svcs., Springfield, 1972-74; exec. v.p. Marden-Kane, Inc., N.Y.C., 1974-87, pres., 1987—. Treas. new leadership div. North Shore U. Hosp., Manhasset, N.Y., 1985—, assoc. trustee. Mem. Promotion Mktg. Assn. Am. (chmn. membership com. N.Y.C. 1984—, sec. 1986, vice chmn. 1988, chmn. 1989, outstanding com. chmn. award 1985). Club: Fresh Meadow Country (Great Neck, N.Y.) Lodge: Friars. Office: Marden-Kane Inc 410 Lakeville Rd New Hyde Park NY 11042-1101

BELL, ROBERT COLLINS, lawyer; b. St. Joseph, Mo., Sept. 19, 1912; s. Robert Cook and Mamie Burke (Collins) B.; m. Mary-Katherine Morris, Mar. 22, 1941; children—Robert III, Marianne. Student Carleton Coll., 1929-32; A.B., U. Minn., 1933; J.D., Harvard U., 1936. Bar: Minn. 1936, Conn. 1942, D.C. 1949, N.Y. 1953. Assoc. Fowler, Youngquist, Furber, Taney and Johnson, Mpls., 1936-37; atty. U.S. Wage and Hour Div.-Minn., N.D., S.D., Mont., 1939-40; chief tax amortization sect. War Prodn. Bd., 1940-42; assoc. Cummings and Lockwood, Stamford, Conn., 1942-52; ptnr. Smith Mathews, Bell and Solomon, N.Y.C., 1952-62; practice, New Canaan, Conn., 1962—; pros. atty., New Canaan, 1948-50. Mem. War Dept. Bd. Contract Appeals, Office of Under Sec. of War, 1944-45. Mem. ABA, Conn. Bar Assn., Internat. Bar Assn. Democrat. Congregationalist. Clubs: Harvard (N.Y.C.); Tokeneke (Darien, Conn.); Masons. Obtained judgments totalling over 25 million dollars on behalf of the Pottawatomi, Miami and Chippewa Indian Tribes in U.S. Ct. Claims and U.S. Indian Claims Commn. Home and Office: 528 Main St New Canaan CT 06840-5998

BELL, ROBERT LAWRENCE, publisher; b. Everett, Mass., Feb. 21, 1919; s. Joseph S. and Mary Elizabeth (Kiernan) B.; m. Rose Edith Hogan, June 2, 1942; children: Marlene, Robert L. Jr., Stephen, Christine. BS with honors, Bowdoin Coll., 1942. Salesman Hallmark Greeting Cards, Boston, 1946-50; football scout Harvard Coll., 1947-50; sales trainer Rust Craft Greeting Cards, Boston, 1950-55; sales mgr. and v.p. Allied Pubs., Portland, Oreg., 1956-60; pres. Reliance Corp., Boston, 1960-68; pres., pub. Crescendo Pub. Co., Boston, 1968-80; pub. Bell Pubs. Co., Melrose, Mass., 1980—; pres. Advance Corp., Melrose, 1962-91. Patentee digital timer, copyholder. Hon. trustee Bridgton Acad., North Bridgton, Maine, 1976—; head fundraising Sapphire Shores Assn., Sarasota, Fla., 1990-91. Lt. USN, 1942-46, PTO. Mem. ASCAP, Small Pubs. Assn. (pres. 1976-78), Union Boat Club, Meadows Country Club, Bowdoin Club (pres.), UN Club. Home: 427 S Shore Dr Sarasota FL 34234-3748 Office: 669 Main St Melrose MA 02176-3138

BELL, WILLIAM ALEXANDER, association management company executive; b. N.Y.C., Sept. 26, 1941; s. William A. and Dorothy (Nutt) B.; m. Marilyn Saxby, Nov. 30, 1963 (div. Nov. 1986); children: Gwendolyn, Forrest. BA, Yale U., 1963. Cert. assn. exec. Legis. asst. to Rep. Peter Kyros, U.S. Ho. of Reps., 1969-74; legis. asst. Maine Senate, 1974-77; exec. dir. Maine Poultry Fedn., 1977-85; pres. William Bell Assocs. Inc., Augusta, Maine, 1985—; sec. Agrl. Coun. Maine, Augusta, 1990—; exec. dir. New England Grain & Feed Coun., Augusta, 1981—; sec., treas. New England Brown Egg Coun., Augusta, 1981—. Asst. editor: The Maine Catalog, 1973. Mem. agrl. adv. com. U. Maine, 1990—; pres. Cen. Maine Soccer Ofcls. Assn., 1988-90. Mem. Am. Soc. Assn. Execs., New Eng. Intercollegiate Soccer Ofcls. Assn. Home: Town House Rd Whitefield ME 04353 Office: 77 Water St Hallowell ME 04347-1457

BELL, WILLIAM ROBERT, hematologist, internist, educator, scientist; b. Greece, N.Y., Oct. 14, 1943; s. William Robert and Dorothy (Efing) B.; m. May 14, 1966; children: William R. III, George H., Elizabeth E. BS, U. Notre Dame, 1957; MS, George Washington U., 1961, PhD, 1962; MD, Harvard U., 1964. Intern Johns Hopkins U. Sch. Medicine, Balt., 1964-65, resident, 1967-68, chief resident, 1969-70, asst. prof. medicine, 1970, prof. medicine, radiology, nuclear medicine, 1978—; rsch. assoc. NIH, Bethesda, Md., 1965-67; fellow U. London-Hammersmith Hosp., 1967-68; resident in medicine Peter Bent Brigham Hosp., Boston, 1968-69; cons. NIH, 1978—, Walter Reed Army Hosp., USN, Washington, Bethesda, 1978—. Contbr. articles to profl. jours.; patentee in field. Fellow ACP; mem. Am. Soc. Hematology, Am. Soc. Clin. Investigation, Phi Beta Kappa, Alpha Omega Alpha. Jewish. Home: 601 N Broadway Baltimore MD 21205-2101 Office: Johns Hopkins U Dept Medicine Blalock 1002 600 N Wolfe St Baltimore MD 21205-2104

BELLACOSA, JOSEPH W., state judge; b. Bklyn., Sept. 1, 1937; s. Frank and Antoinette Bellacosa; m. Mary Bellacosa; children: Michael, Peter, Barbara. JD, St. John's U., 1961. Law sec. N.Y. Cts. Appellate Div., 1963-70; prof. law, asst. dean St. John's U., 1970-75; chief clk., counsel N.Y. Ct. Appeals, 1975-83; judge N.Y. Ct. Claims, 1985-87; apptd. chief adminstr. of cts. State of N.Y., 1985; apptd. judge Ct. Appeals, 1987. Co-author: Criminal Procedure Law of the State of New York, 1974-85. Mem. ABA (vice chair accreditation com.), Am. Law Inst. Office: NYS Ct of Appeals 20 Eagle St Albany NY 12207

BELL-ALSTON, CLARENCE MARTIN, small business owner; b. N.Y.C., Nov. 7, 1955; s. Charles Alston and Anna Bell. Student, U. D.C., 1981-83, 85-88, Borough of Manhattan Community Coll., 1983-85. From teller to supr. Chase Manhattan Bank, N.Y.C., 1973-81; asst. mgr. Nat. Bank of Washington, 1981-90; pres. ACB Enterprises, Inc., Washington, 1990—. Inventor N-The Know, Perfect Match. Office: ACB Enterprises Inc PO Box 3374 Washington DC 20010-0374

BELLANGER, SERGE RENÉ, banker; b. Vimoutiers, France, Apr. 30, 1933; s. René Albert and Raymonde Maria (Renard) B. MBA, Paris Bus. Sch., 1957. With Citibank, 1966-73, mem. Paris br., 1966-69; world corp. rels. officer for Europe Citibank, N.Y.C., 1969-73, asst. v.p., 1969-71, v.p., 1972-73; sr. v.p., gen. mgr. Compagnie Financière de CIC et de l'Union Européenne, N.Y.C., 1973-79; exec. v.p., gen. mgr. Crédit Industriel et Comml., N.Y.C., 1979—; U.S. gen. rep. CIC Group, N.Y.C., 1973-88; prof. banking French Banking Inst., 1961-64; mem. adv. com. French House, Columbia U., 1976—, Ctr. for Study of French Civilization & Culture, NYU, 1988—; dir. Am. Ctr. in Paris, 1985—, N.Y. Forum on Internat. Bus., 1988—; mem. U.S. Com. Fgn. Trade Advisors for France, 1979-83, v.p. U.S. com., 1984-85, exec. v.p., 1985—, bd. dirs. nat. com., 1990—; chmn. internat. banking course New Sch. Social Rsch., N.Y.C., 1981-83. With French Air Force, 1958-60. Decorated Algeria Commemorative medal Chevalier Legion of Honor, Officer Nat. Order of Merit. Mem. French-Am. C. of C. (councillor 1973-74, exec. com. 1974-80, v.p. 1980-82, exec. v.p. 1982-83, nat. pres. 1983—, pres. N.Y. chpt. 1983—), European-Am. C. of C. (pres., chief exec. officer, 1990—), Assn. French C. of C. and Industry Abroad (v.p. 1991—), French Overseas Assn., Inst. Fgn. Bankers (trustee 1975-77, v.p. 1977-79, chmn. legis. and regulatory com. 1977-79, chmn. 1979-80), Lyonnaise de Banque (bd. dirs. 1986-89), Assn. for the Promotion of French Sci. Industry and Tech. (pres. 1986-91), Banque de l'Union Européenne (bd. dirs. 1989-90), Food and Wines from France (SOPEXA) (bd. dirs. 1983—), N.Y. Futures Exchange (dir. 1980-87, chmn. fgn. exchange steering com. 1981-82), N.Y. Cotton Exchange (bd. dirs. fin. instrument exchange div. 1985—), N.Y. C. of C. (internat. bus. initiative 1991—), N.Y.C. Partnership, Bank Adminstrn. Inst. (editorial bd. World of Banking

Mag. 1981-87, columnist Bankers Mag. 1986—), Bd. Rm. Club, River Club, Automobile Club France. Home: 860 UN Plz Apt 23/24C New York NY 10017 Office: 520 Madison Ave New York NY 10022-4213

BELLEMARE, DAVID JOHN, architectural designer; b. Waterbury, Conn., Dec. 25, 1960; s. John Arthur and Lucille (Cianciolo) B. Student, Boston Archtl. Ctr., 1984—. Drafter Monacelli Assocs., Inc., Cambridge, Mass., 1985; designer, drafter The Architects Group, Boston, 1986—. Served with USMC, 1980-84. Mem. Boston Soc. Architects. Home: 134 Oldham Ave Waterbury CT 06705-3035 Office: The Architects Group 451 D St Boston MA 02210-1950

BELLER, MARTIN LEONARD, retired orthopaedic surgeon; b. N.Y.C., Apr. 30, 1924; s. Abraham Jacob and Ida (Fishkin) B.; m. Wilma Gertrude Kjelgaard, June 29, 1947; children: Alan Lewis, Beatrice Ann Beller Foreman, Peter James. A.B. with honors, Columbia U., 1944, M.D., 1946. Diplomate: Am. Bd. Orthopaedic Surgery. Intern Mt. Sinai Hosp., N.Y.C., 1946-47; resident in orthopaedic surgery Hosp. Joint Diseases, N.Y.C., 1949-52; practice medicine specializing in orthopaedic surgery Phila., 1952-87; asst. prof. orthopaedic surgery U. Pa. Sch. Medicine, Phila., 1967-72; assoc. prof. U. Pa. Sch. Medicine, 1972-80, clin. prof., 1980-87; attending orthopaedic surgeon Hosp. U. Pa., 1963-87; assoc. attending orthopaedic surgeon Albert Einstein Med. Center, Phila., 1960-70; chmn. dept. orthopaedic surgery Albert Einstein Med. Center (Daroff div.), 1970-79. Author: (with I. Stein and R. O. Stein) Living Bone in Health and Disease, 1955, (with I. Stein) Clinical Densitometry of Bone, 1970. Served from 1st lt. to capt., M.C. AUS, 1947-49. Am. Orthopaedic Assn. exchange fellow Gt. Britain, 1963. Fellow ACS, Am. Acad. Orthopaedic Surgeons (bd. councilors 1978-81, Pa. rep. commn. on trauma 1984-87), Internat. Soc. Orthopaedic Surgery and Traumatology; mem. Am. Orthopaedic Assn., Pa. Orthopaedic Soc. (pres. 1975-77), ACS (chmn. Pa. com. on trauma 1978-82), Orthopaedic Research Soc., Am. Coll. Rheumatology, N.Y. Acad. Sci., Phila. Coll. Physicians, Phi Beta Kappa, Alpha Omega Alpha, Phi Delta Epsilon (nat. pres. 1975-76, chmn. bd. trustees 1984-85, assoc. exec. sec. 1991—). Republican. Episcopalian (vestryman 1966-70, 71-87, 90—, sr. warden 1985-87). Club: Union League of Phila. Home: RR 1 Box 256 B Gaines PA 16921-9768

BELLERMANN, PETER ROBERT WILHELM, foundation executive; b. Friemar, Thuringia, Germany, Nov. 26, 1939; came to U.S., 1960; s. Walter Paul Oskar and Lucie Elsbeth (Reindanz) B.; m. Ayer Bellermann, June 8, 1963 (div. 1980); children: Mark, Wendy, James; m. Pamela Maniet, Aug. 8, 1987. BA, U. Minn., 1962; MPA, Princeton U., 1964. Asst. v.p. Citibank, N.Y.C., 1964-70; sr. polit. advanceman Presdl. Campaign for Sen. Edmund Muskie, Washington, 1970-72; gen. mgr. Performing Arts Found. L.I., Hungtington, N.Y., 1973-75; dep. dir. Vol. Cons. Group, N.Y.C., 1975-86; pres. Nat. Neurofibromatosis Found., N.Y.C., 1986—; Pres. Maniet Bellermann Found., Bayville, N.Y., 1988—, Bellermann & Co., Bayville, 1986—; chmn. Appeals Panel N.Y. State Coun. on the Arts, N.Y.C., 1972-92. Assoc. editor, columnist Lavine Newspaper Group, Chippewa Falls, Wis., 1982-88. Named Hon. Citizen, Tacoma Park, Md., 1958; recipient Nat. Woodrow Wilson Found. Fellowship, Princeton, N.J., 1962. Mem. Am. Soc. Human Genetics, Princeton Club. Home: 29 Jefferson Ave Bayville NY 11709-1329 Office: Nat Neurofibromatosis Found 141 5th Ave Ste 7S New York NY 10010-7105

BELLIN, MILTON ROCKWELL, artist; b. New Haven, Conn., June 6, 1913. BFA, Yale U., 1936. Cert. asst. prin., N.Y. Artist-in-residence Cen. Conn. State U., New Britain, 1937-40; illustrator-designer Houghton Mifflin Pub. Co., Boston, 1936-41; chief confidential designer Gould Aeronaut. Corp., Deep River, Conn., 1941-42; tech. designer Johnson, Cushing & Nevell, N.Y.C., 1942-46; art dir. Cinefects, Inc., N.Y.C., 1946-54, Republic Aviation Corp., Farmingdale, N.Y., 1954-66; asst. prin. High Sch. of Art and Design, N.Y.C., 1966-78; pres. Bellin Studio, N.Y.C., 1978-91; owner studio N.Y.C., Norwich, Conn., 1936—; art dir. Warner Bros. Cinerama, N.Y.C., 1955-56, Thunderbolt-P47 Pilots Assn., Farmingdale, 1964—; art coord. Air France, N.Y.C., Paris, 1975-76. One man show includes New Britain (Conn.) Mus. Am. Art, 1958; painter (mural) Fairfield and Stamford, Conn., 1936-37, Cen. Conn. State U., 1984, Nathan Hale-Slater Meml. Mus., Norwich, Conn., 1984, Farm Fire-Slater Meml. Mus., Norwich, 1991. Photographer Murray Hill Community Com., N.Y.C., 1986-88. Recipient First prize Springfield (Mass.) Art Mus., 1937, Graphic award Mus. Modern Art, N.Y.C., 1940, Sage Allen award Wadsworth Atheneum, Hartford, Conn., 1952, First prize Ridgewood Art Inst., 1986, Harrisburg (Pa.) Art Assn., 1989, Kans. Soc. Pastel Soc. award, 1991; finalist Am. Art Mag., 1986. Mem. Conn. Watercolor Soc. (hon. life.), Pastel Soc. Am. (bd. dirs. 1981-86), Am. Artist Profl. League, Met. Mus. Art, Audubon Artists, Allied Artists. Home: 303 E 37th St New York NY 10016-3226

BELLINGER, HAROLD, civil rights program director, legal assistant; b. N.Y.C., Mar. 28, 1951; s. Lionel Harcourt and Naomi Alice (Lynch) Jordan; m. Deborah Llenas-Bellinger, Jan. 5, 1964 (separated Aug. 1991). AAS, SUNY, Farmingdale, 1972; BS in Social Work, Rochester (N.Y.) Inst. Tech., 1974; M of Pub. and Internat. Affairs, U. Pitts., 1975; grad. lawyers asst. program, Adelphi U., 1989. Sr. assoc. N.Y. State Legis. Commn. on Expenditure Rev., Albany, 1976-79; legis. budget analyst fin. com. N.Y. State Senate, Albany, 1979-81; bus. affairs and contract compliance mgr. N.Y. State Dept. Correctional Svc., Albany, 1981-82, asst. dir. mktg. and sales, correctional industries, 1982-84; asst. dir., AVE project coord. Econ. Opportunity Commn. Nassau County, Hempstead, N.Y., 1984-85; dir. affirmative action SUNY, Farmingdale, 1985-89; asst. to pres. for affirmative action Nassau C.C., Garden City, N.Y., 1989—. Kellogg fellow League for Innovation in Comm. Colls., 1991-92, fellow W.K. Kellogg Found., City of Rochester, 1973-74; recipient Dist. Alumni award SUNY, 1989. Mem. 100 Black Men Nassau/Suffolk Counties (project coord. 1989—, econ. devel. com. 1992—, community rels. coord. 1992—). Home: 1191 Little East Neck Rd North Babylon NY 11704 Office: Nassau C C 1 Education Dr Garden City NY 11530-6793

BELLINGER, JOHN BELLINGER, JR., federal official; b. N.Y.C., May 21, 1926; s. John Bellinger and Margaret (Thomson) B.; m. Anne Taliafero Tynes, Dec. 19, 1953; 1 child, John Bellinger, III. BS, U.S. Mil. Acad., 1948; MA, Georgetown U., 1962, PhD, 1975; grad., U.S. Army War Coll., 1969. Commd. U.S. Army, 1948; advanced through grades to col., chief of strategy div. Joint Chiefs of Staff, 1978; sr. adviser Kien Giang Province Republic of Vietnam, 1966-67; cmmdr. 1st bn. 37th Armor Ansbach, Fed. Republic Germany, 1967-68; chief, plans div. U.S. Army Vietnam Republic of Vietnam, 1971-72; dep. to army planner Washington, 1973-76, chief strategy div. joint chiefs of staff, 1976-77; ret., 1978; study dir., sr. staff mem. Pres.'s Def. Reorgn. Studies, Washington, 1978-79; dir. def. guidance and program planning Under Sec. Def. (policy), Washington, 1981-89; policy planner Under Sec. Def. (policy), 1989-92. Author: Decision Making in Arms Control, 1975; contbr. articles to profl. jours.; lectr. in field. Chmn. budget and fin. com., vestryman St. Peter's Episc. Ch., 1981-84, chmn. ushers, 1986—. Decorated Def. Superior Svc. medal, Legion of Merit with oak leaf cluster, Air medal with oak leaf cluster, Bronze Star, Cross of Gallantry (Republic of Vietnam), Combat Infantry Badge, Def. Superior Svc. medal. Mem. Nat. Polit. Sci. Honor Soc., Cum Laude Soc., U.S. Squash Racquets Assn. (ranked 19th in Men's 60 plus singles 1990), Army Navy Country Club (tennis com. 1973-79, bd. govs. 1975-78). Home: 4001 N Ridgeview Rd Arlington VA 22207-4615 Office: Undersec Def (policy) The Pentagon Washington DC 20301-2200

BELLIZZI, JOHN J., law enforcement administrator, educator, pharmacist; b. N.Y.C., July 26, 1919; s. Francis X. and Carmela (Bruno) B.; m. Celeste Morga, Sept. 1, 1942; children: John J. Jr., Robert F. PhG, St. John's U., N.Y.C., 1939; LLB, Albany Law Sch., 1960; JD, Union U., 1968; LLD, St. John's U., 1981. Pharmacist St. Luke's Hosp., N.Y.C., 1939-44; police officer N.Y.C. Police Dept., 1944-53; narcotics agt. N.Y. Bur. Narcotics Enforcement, N.Y.C., 1953-59; dir. N.Y. Bur. Narcotics Enforcement, Albany, 1959-81; exec. dir. N.Y. State Drug Abuse Commn., Albany, 1981-84, Internat. Narcotics Enforcement Assn., Albany, 1984—; prof. pharmacy law St. John's U., N.Y.C., 1962-76; lectr. in field. Contbr. articles to profl. jours. Recipient Papal medal Vatican, 1965. Mem. Internat. Narcotics Enforcement Officers Assn. (pres. 1960-62, Anslinger medal 1979, chmn. law enforcement com. Paramount Pictures, 1972-75, Svc. award 1975), Ft. Orange Club, Albany Country Club, Univ. Club (Albany), Phi Alpha Delta, Phi Sigma Chi (pres. 1939), Sigma Chi (fellow). Office: Internat Narcotics Enforcement Officers Assn 112 State St Albany NY 12207-2005

BELLO, GERALD ANTHONY, language educator; b. New Britain, Conn., Oct. 17, 1947; s. Generoso and Edith (Melito) B. BA, Tufts U., 1970; MA, U. Pa., 1971, PhD, 1979. Lectr. Hahnemann U., Phila., 1976-77, sr. instr., 1977-80, asst. prof., 1980-87, assoc. prof., 1987—. Editor, founder Humanities Mag. Handprints, 1988—; composer, author music and lyrics broadcast Radio Free Europe and Voice of Am., 1989-90; author: (poems) Affront, More Than I Can Say, 1989-92. Sec.-treas. The Am. Raoul Wallenberg Com., Inc., 1989-91; bd. dirs. Phila. Flag Day Assn., 1991—, Southeastern Pa. Arthritis Found., Phila., 1989—. U. Pa. fellow, Phila., 1971-73; recipient Disting. Faculty award Hahnemann U., 1988, Golden Poet award World of Poetry, Sacramednto, 1991. Mem. AAUP, N.E. MLA, ASCAP, Samuel Beckett Soc. Am., Edgar Allan Poe Soc. Balt., Alpha Eta. Home: 4617 Pine St 4617 Pine St Apt G-305 Philadelphia PA 19143-1833 Office: Hahnemann U Broad and Vine Mail Stop 503 Philadelphia PA 19102-1192

BELLONI, FRANCIS LOUIS, physiologist; b. N.Y.C., Jan. 23, 1949; s. Francis Peter and Frances Marie (Asaro) B.; m. Susan Marie Kelly, May 1, 1971; children: Benjamin Francis. BS in Biology cum laude, Providence Coll., 1970; PhD in Physiology, U. Mich., 1975. Grad. teaching asst. U. Mich., Ann Arbor, 1971-75, postdoctoral fellow, 1975-78; rsch. asst. prof. U. Va., Charlottesville, 1979-81; asst. prof. N.Y. Med. Coll., Valhalla, 1981-86, assoc. prof., 1986—. Editorial cons., contbr. articles and rsch. reports to numerous profl. jours. Dir. Cortlandt Am. Little League, Cortlandt Manor, N.Y., 1985-92; mem. long-range planning com. Lakeland Cen. Sch. Dist., 1990-92; mem. adv. bd. Town of Cortlandt Parks & Recreation, 1991—. Mem. Am. Physiological Soc. (edn. com. 1990—), Fedn. Am. Socs. for Exptl. Biology, Am. Heart Assn. (coun. on circulation 1987—). Roman Catholic. Office: NY Med Coll Dept Physiology Basic Scis Bldg Valhalla NY 10595

BELLOWS, JEAN FARLEY, clinical psychologist; b. Cleve., Mar. 14, 1940; d. John Wesley Farley and Renee (Blunt) Teas; m. A. Robert Bellows, May 30, 1964; children: Matthew, Kristen, Nathaniel. BS, Wheelock Coll., 1962; MEd, Tufts U., 1978; Psych.D., Mass. Sch. Profl. Psychology, 1991. Cert. tchr., Mass. Tchr. Hingham (Mass.) Pub. Schs., 1962-64, Boston Assn. Retarded Children, 1962-63, USAF Schs., Tripoli, Libya, 1964-65, Oil Co. Sch., Tripoli, 1965-66; child devel. specialist, clinician Pre-Sch. Unit, Cambridge, Mass., 1976-82; pvt. practice psychotherapy Boston-North Shore Assocs., Salem, Mass., 1984-90; clin. psychologist trauma ctr. Mass. Gen. Hosp., 1991—; cons. child devel. programs, clinician Lynn (Mass.) Community Health Ctr., 1986-88; cons., clinician Mass. Mental Health Trauma Ctr., Boston, 1988-91. Bd. dirs. Topsfield (Mass.) br., A Better Chance, 1979-84; cons., mem. adv. bd., Glen Urquhart Sch., Beverly, Mass., 1985—. Mem. Am. Psychol. Assn., Soc. Traumatic Stress Studies, Internat. Soc. Study of MP and Dissociative Disorders. Democrat. Office: Boxford Psych Assocs 17 Elm St Boxford MA 01921-2399

BELL-THOMSON, JOHN, cardiothoracic surgeon, educator; b. Buenos Aires, May 25, 1947; s. Harry and Betty Bell-Thomson; m. Barbara Hunt; children: Sean, Lauren, Patricia, Melissa. BA, LaSalle Coll., Buenos Aires, 1964; MD, U. Buenos Aires, 1971. Diplomate Am. Bd. Thoracic Surgery. Resident surgery Lenox Hill Hosp., N.Y.C., 1972-77; fellow cardiothoracic surgery New Eng. Deaconess Hosp., Boston, 1977-79; clin. fellow surgery Harvard U., 1979; staff surgeon Brookdale Hosp., Bklyn., 1979-82, L.I. Coll. Hosp., Bklyn., 1979-82, Bklyn. Jewish Hosp., 1979-82, Maimonides Med. Ctr., 1979-82, L.I. Jewish Med. Ctr., New Hyde Park, N.Y., 1982-87; chmn. cardiothoracic surgery Albert Einstein Med. Ctr., Phila., 1987-91; chief med. officer Franklin Sq. Hosp., 1992—; clin. assoc. prof. surgery Temple U. Sch. Medicine, Phila., 1990—. Editor: Chest; author, producer med. film Use of the Operating Room Microscope in Coronary Bypass Surgery; contbr. articles to profl. jours. Mem. ACS, AMA, Am. Heart Assn., Soc. Thoracic Surgeons, Pa. Med. Soc., Phila. County Med. Soc., Piping Rock Club, Beaver Dam Winter Sports Club. Home: 170 King Rd Chalfont PA 18914 Office: 201 Old York Rd 201 N 8th St Philadelphia PA 19106

BELSER, JAMES BURKEY, graphic designer, illustrator; b. Columbia, S.C., July 8, 1947; s. Townsend Mikell Belser and Margaret (Burkey) Polk; m. Donna Helene Greenfield; 1 child, Mikell Anna. BA, Davidson Coll., 1969. Circulation mgr. Avant Garde mag., N.Y.C., 1971; pres. Burkey Belser, Inc., Washington, 1975-85, Greenfield/Belser, Ltd., Washington, 1985—. Contbr. articles to various mags. Recipient Graphis, 1985-91, N.Y. Art Dirs. Club, 1987-89, Print Reg. Anns., 1985-89, Soc. Publ. Designers Best Redesign award 1987, Communication Arts, 1989-91, Am. Trademarks, 1988-90, Soc. Illustrators, 1988, Am. Corp. Identity, 1988-90. Mem. Art. Dirs. Met. Washington (pres. 1988-90; Gold Medal 1985), Am. Inst. Graphic Art, Graphic Artists Guild. Office: Greenfield Belser Ltd 1818 N St NW Ste 110 Washington DC 20036-2406

BELSON, JAMES ANTHONY, judge; b. Milw., Sept. 23, 1931; s. Walter W. and Margaret (Taugher) B.; m. Rosemary P. Greenslade, Jan. 11, 1958; children: Anthony James, Marie Taylor, Elizabeth Ann, Stephen Griffin. AB cum laude, Georgetown U., 1953, JD, 1956, LLM, 1962. Bar: D.C. 1956, Md. 1962. Law clk. U.S. Ct. Appeals (D.C. cir.), 1956-57; assoc. Hogan & Hartson, Washington, 1960-67, ptnr., 1967-68; trial judge D.C. Superior Ct., 1968-81, presiding judge civil div., 1978-81; assoc. judge D.C. Ct. Appeals, Washington, 1981-91, sr. judge, 1991—; faculty mem. Nat. Jud. Coll., 1973-80; bd. dirs. Coun. for Ct. Excellence, 1982—; bencher Am. Inn of Ct. VI, 1983—. Bd. editors Georgetown Law Jour., 1955-56. With JAGC, U.S. Army, 1957-60. Mem. ABA, Bar Assn. of D.C. (bd. dirs. 1966-67, chmn. jr. bar 1965-66), Fed. Bar Assn., Am. Judicature Soc. (bd. dirs. 1980-85), World Peace Through Law Ctr., Am. Bar Found., John Carroll Soc. (bd. govs. 1978-85, 1st v.p. 1989-91), Soverign Mil. Order of Malta Fed. Assn. (pres. 1991—). Home: 2220 46th St NW Washington DC 20007-1054 Office: D C Ct Appeals 6th Fl 500 Indiana Ave NW Washington DC 20001

BELT, ROBERT HOWARD, JR., insurance company executive; b. St. Louis, Jan. 3, 1951; s. Robert Howard and Janet Gardner (Hausman) B.; m. Denise Leslie Weiler, Aug. 13, 1988. BA, U. Va., 1975. Claims rep. Reliance Ins. Co., Washington, 1975-77; claims supr. Reliance Ins. Co., Columbia, Md., 1977-79; claims mgr. Reliance Ins. Co., Birmingham, Ala., 1979-81; from claims examiner to property claims mgr. Reliance Ins. Co., Phila., 1981-88, asst. v.p., 1988—; chmn., adv. com. Nat. Forum for Property Loss Profls., Phila., 1990-91; adv. com. claims Pa./Del. FAIR Plan, Phila., 1986—. Mem. Property Claims Svcs., Loss. Exec. Assn. Republican. Office: Reliance Insurance Co 4 Penn Ctr Pla Philadelphia PA 19103

BELTZ, JOHN DAVID, physiology educator; b. Watertown, Wis., June 5, 1961; s. Bertram Daniel and Leila Jane (Arneson) B.; m. Kelly Rae Schuman. BS, U. Wis., LaCrosse, 1984; MA, Ball State U., 1987. Fitness dir. Madison Ave. Health Club, Ft. Atkinson, Wis., 1984-85; rsch. asst. Ball State Human Performance Lab., Muncie, Ind., 1985-87, U. Tex. Human Performance Lab., Austin, 1987-89; assoc. prof. anatomy, physiology and exercise physiology N.H. Tech. Coll., Manchester, 1989—; rsch. asst. Tufts Sch. Vet. Medicine, Grafton, N.H., 1991—; lectr. in physiology Boston U., 1992—; speaker Pan Am. Sports Medicine, 1989. NIH tng. grantee Tufts U. Home: 502 Barnard Hill Rd Weare NH 03281-5102 Office: NH Tech Coll 1066 Front St Manchester NH 03102-8518

BELTZNER, GAIL ANN, educator; b. Palmerton, Pa., July 20, 1950; d. Conon Nelson and Lorraine Ann (Carey) Beltzner. BS in Music Edn. summa cum laude, West Chester State U., 1972; postgrad., Kean State Coll., 1972, Temple U., 1972, Westminster Choir Coll., 1972, Lehigh U., 1972. Tchr. music Drexel Hill Jr. High Sch., 1972-73; music specialist Allentown (Pa.) Sch. Dist., 1973—; tchr. Corps Sch. and Community Developmental Lab., 1978-80, Corps Community Resource Festival, 1979-81, Corps Cultural Fair, 1980, 81. Mem. aux. Allentown Art Mus., aux. Allentown Hosp.; mem. womans com. Allentown Symphony; bd. dirs. Allentown Area Ecumenical Food Bank. Decorated dame comdr. Ordre Souverain et Militaire de la Milice du St. Sepulcre; recipient cert. of appreciation Lehigh Valley Sertoma Club; Excellence in the Classroom grantee Rider-Pool Found., 1988, 91-92; mem. Nat. Women's Hall of Fame. Mem. AAUW, NAFE, Internat. Platform Assn., Allentown Edn. Assn., Music Educators Nat. Conf., Pa. Music Educators Assn., Am. Orff-Schulwerk Assn., Soc. Gen. Music, Am. Assn. Music Therapy, Internat. Soc. Music Edn., ASCD, Choristers Guild, Lenni Lenape Hist. Soc., Allentown Symphony Assn., Allentown 2d Civilian Police Acad., Nat. Sch. Orch. Assn., Lehigh County Hist. Soc., Confederation of Chivalry (life mem. of merit, grand coun. 1988), Maison Internationale Des Intellectuels Akademie, Order of the White Cross Internat. (apptd. dist. comdr. for Pa./U.S.A dist., nobless of humanity), Kappa Delta Pi, Phi Delta Kappa, Alpha Lambda. Republican. Lutheran. Home: PO Box 4427 Allentown PA 18105-4427

BELZ, CARL IRVIN, museum director; b. Camden, N.J., Sept. 13, 1937; s. Irvin Carl and Ella Herta (Engler) B.; m. Joan Elizabeth, (div. 1968); children: Melissa Elizabeth, Gretchen Meagan; m. Barbara Ann Vetter, Sept. 3, 1946; children: Portia Engler, Emily Bradford. BA, Princeton U., 1959, MFA, 1962, PhD, 1963. Asst. prof. U. Mass., Amherst, 1963-65; asst. prof., dir. art gallery Mills Coll., Oakland, Calif., 1965-68; asst. prof. Brandeis U., Waltham, Mass., 1968-74, dir. Rose Art Mus., prof. art, 1974—; cons. Paine-Webber Group, Inc., N.Y.C. , Boston, 1984-87; mng. dir. Herbert W. Plimpton Found., Waltham, 1983—. Curator, author: (exhbn. and catalog essays) Frank Stella, 1979, Mel Ramos, 1980, Helen Frankenthaler, 1981, William Beckman, 1984, Gregory Gillespie, 1984, Charles Garabedian, 1983, Katherine Porter, 1985, Stephen Antonakos, 1986, Jake Berthot, 1988. Mem. Am. Assn. Museums. Democrat. Home: 79 Ridge Rd Newton MA 02168-2137 Office: Brandeis U Rose Art Mus 415 South St Waltham MA 02154-2700

BEM, EUGENE S., management consultant; b. Morgantown, W.Va., Oct. 1, 1966; s. Stanley Joseph and Louise (Sharbough) B. BS in Indsl. Engring., W.Va. U., 1988. Quality engr. Pa. Dept. Transp., Indiana, Pa., 1985-87, NV Ryan Homes Inc., Pitts., 1988; rsch. assoc. Symmetrix, Inc., Ipswich, Mass., 1988-89; assoc. Symmetrix, Inc., Burlington, Mass., 1989; prin. Symmetrix, Inc., Lexington, Mass., 1989—. Mem. Amnesty Internat., Boston, 1988-91. Recipient Prof. Robert D. Fowler Design award W.Va. U., 1988. Office: Symmetrix Inc 1 Cranberry Hill Lexington MA 02173

BEMAK, FRED PAUL, psychology educator; b. Boston, Oct. 23, 1948; s. Walter I. and Ruth B. (Ruskin) B.; m. Adi Bemak (div. 1988); children: Amber, Lani. BA, Boston U., 1970; MEd, U. Mass., 1971, EdD, 1975. With Upward Bound Program, Amherst, Mass., 1970-75, dir., 1974-75; dir. Mass. Region I Adolescent Treatment Program, Northampton, 1977-79; clin. dir. tng. consortium U. Mass. Med. Sch., Worcester, 1980-82; assoc. dir. psychology dept. New Eng. Grad. Sch. Antioch U., Keene, N.H., 1982-86; asst. prof. U. Wis., Oshkosh, 1986-88, assoc. prof., coord. community human svcs. grad. program, 1989; dir. Human Svcs. Consortium U. Wis. System, 1988-89; asst. dir. div. edn., coord. grad. programs in counseling and human svcs. Johns Hopkins U., Balt., 1989—; cons. in field; vis. psychologist APA, 1982; vis. scholar Antioch U., 1984. Contbr. articles to profl. publs. Kellogg Found. fellow, 1989-90, World Rehab. Fund fellow, 1982; grantee El Salvador Nat. Assn. Psychologists-U.S. Embassy, 1990, Ptnrs. of Ams., 1984—, rsch. grantee U.S. Dept. HHS, 1989-90, rsch. grantee NIMH, 1991. Fellow Am. Orthopsychiat. Assn.; mem. AACD, Am. Psychol. Assn., Internat. Coun. Psychologists, Ptnrs. of Ams. (chair health com. 1990—, bd. dirs. 1982—). Office: Johns Hopkins U Div Edn 105 Whitehead Hall Baltimore MD 21218

BEMAN, LYNN SUSAN, museum administrator; b. Buffalo, Dec. 23, 1942; d. Roger C. and Mary Louise (Gibbons) Zimmerman; m. Donald K. Beman, Dec. 14, 1963; children: Christopher A., Tracy K. Student, Goucher Coll., 1960-62; BA in Art History, Briarcliff Coll., 1975. Dir. Trisdonn Gallery, Ltd., Nyack, N.Y., 1978-85; curator, co-dir. Beman Galleries, Inc., Nyack, 1986-89; exec. dir. Hudson River Maritime Mus., Kingston, N.Y., 1990—; guest curator Edward Hopper Landmark Found., Nyack, 1984, Hist. Soc. Rockland City, New City, N.Y., 1986, Bergen Mus. of Art and Sci., Paramus, N.J., 1989. Author: 19th Century Painters and Paintings of Rockland County, N.Y., 1984, Julian O. Davidson (1853-94): American Marine Artist, 1986 (L.H.C. award of Excellence 1987). Named Disting. Historian, Tappantown Hist. Soc., Tappan, N.Y., 1986. Mem. Am. Assn. Appraisers, Am. Assn. Mus., Mid-Atlantic Assn. Mus. Office: Hudson River Maritime Mus One Rondout Landing Kingston NY 12401

BEMIS, HAL LAWALL, engineering and business executive; b. Palm Beach, Fla., Jan. 30, 1912; s. Henry E. and Elise (Lawall) B.; m. Isabel Mead, June 27, 1942 (div.); children: Elise, Carolyn, Claudia; m. Jeanne Chatham, June 5, 1982. B.S., MIT, 1935. With Campbell Soup Co., 1935-53; mgr., asst. to pres., v.p., dir. Campbell Soup Co., Ltd., 1946-53; organizer, pres. Mariner Corp., 1954—; v.p. Hosp. Food Mgmt., Inc., 1954-57; sec., treas. Bell Key Corp., 1955—; v.p. Coral Motel Corp., 1963—; pres. Jennings Machine Corp., 1957—; cons. Coopers & Lybrand, 1973—; dir., mem. exec. and audit coms. Publicker Industries; chmn., dir. Phila. Reins. Corp.; dir. Ott, Hertner, Ott & Assos., Colonial Savs. Bank. Past pres. Commn. Twp. Lower Merion, Pa.; bd. dirs., chmn. Spring Garden Coll.; exec. bd. Com. of 70; chmn. bd. Am. Cancer Soc.; bd. dirs. Delaware Valley area Nat. Council on Alcoholism; adv. bd. Salvation Army; past trustee Haverford Sch.; dir. Phila. Port Corp., West Phila. Corp., Phila. Indsl. Devel. Corp.; trustee United Fund, Young Men's Inst.; pres., trustee Greater Phila. Found.; bd. dirs. Am. Diabetes Assn., M.I.T. Devel. Found., Broad St. So. Com.; mem. corp. bd. Goodwill Industries, Garrett-Williamson Found., chmn. Spring Garden Coll. Served 1st lt. to lt. col. AUS, 1942-45. Decorated Legion of Merit with oak leaf cluster, Bronze Star medal; Croix de Guerre (France). Mem. Greater Phila. C. of C. (past chmn. bd., past pres.), SAR, S.R., Pa. Soc., Newcomen Soc., Mil. Order World Wars, Mil. Order Fgn. Wars, Am. Legion (past comdr.), Tau Beta Pi, Delta Psi. Clubs: Union League (pres.), Racquet, Rittenhouse, Penn, Philadelphia; St. Anthony (N.Y.C.), Merion Golf (Ardmore, Pa.); Merion Cricket (dir.) (Haverford, Pa.); Bachelor's Barge, IV Street, Pine Valley Golf, Sunday Breakfast, Right Angle, Toronto Golf, Royal Canadian Yacht, Brit. Officers. Home: 101 Cheswold Ln Haverford PA 19041-1801 Office: 410 Lancaster Ave Haverford PA 19041-1329

BENACERRAF, BARUJ, pathologist, educator; b. Caracas, Venezuela, Oct. 29, 1920; came to U.S., 1939, naturalized, 1943; s. Abraham and Henriette (Lasry) B.; m. Annette Dreyfus, Mar. 24, 1943; 1 child, Beryl. B es L, Lycee Janson, 1940; BS, Columbia U., 1942; MD, Med. Sch. Va., 1945; MA, Harvard U., 1970; MD (hon.), U. Geneva, 1980; DSc (hon.), NYU, 1981, Va. Commonwealth U., 1981, Yeshiva U., 1982, U. Aix-Marseille, 1982, Columbia U., 1985, Adelphi U., 1988, Weizmann Inst., 1989. Intern Queens Gen. Hosp., N.Y.C., 1945-46; rsch. fellow dept. microbiology Med. Sch. Columbia U., 1948-50; charge de recherches Centre Nat. de Recherche Scientique Hosp. Broussais, Paris, 1950-56; asst. prof. pathology Sch. Medicine NYU, 1956-58, assoc. prof. Sch. Medicine, 1958-60, prof. Sch. Medicine, 1960-68; chief immunology Nat. Inst. Allergy and Infectious Diseases NIH, Bethesda, Md., 1968-70; Fabyan prof. comparative pathology, chmn. dept. Med. Sch. Harvard U., 1970-91; ret. Med. Sch., Harvard U., Cambridge, Mass., 1991; pres., chief exec. officer Dana-Farber Cancer Inst., 1980-91; pres., chief exec. officer Dana-Farber Inc., 1990; mem. immunology study sect. NIH; pres. Fedn. Am. Socs. Exptl. Biology, 1974-75; chmn. sci. adv. com. Centre d'Immunologie de Marseille. Trustee, mem. sci. adv. bd. Trudeau Found.; mem. sci. adv. com. Children's Hosp. Boston; bd. govs. Weizmann Inst. Medicine; mem. award com. GM Cancer Rsch. Found., also chmn. selection com. Sloan prize, 1980. Capt. M.C. AUS, 1946-48. Recipient T. Duckett Jones Meml. award Helen Hay Whitney Found., 1976, Rabbi Shai Shacknai lectr. and prize Hebrew U. Jerusalem, 1974, Waterford award, 1980, Nobel prize, 1980, Corr. Emerite de l'Institut de la Sante et de la Recherche Scientifique, Nat. Medal of Sci., 1991. Fellow Am. Acad. Arts and Scis.; mem. NAS, Nat. Inst. Medicine, Am. Assn. Immunologists (pres. 1973-74), Brit. Assn. Immunology, French Soc. Biol. Chemistry, Internat. Union Immunology Socs. (pres. 1980-83). Home: 111 Perkins St Jamaica Plain MA 02130-4313 Office: Dana-Farber Cancer Inst 44 Binney St Boston MA 02115-6084

BENARESH, EHSANOLLAH, anesthesiologist; b. Kashan, Iran, Apr. 22, 1934; came to U.S., 1958; s. Leon and Cecile (Shaker) B.; m. Marcelle A. Gold, July 9, 1964; children: Lamont, Jennifer. BS, Alborz Coll., Teheran, Iran, 1951; MD, Teheran U., 1957. Diplomate, Am. Bd. Anesthesiology. Intern Beth David Hosp., N.Y.C., 1958-59; resident in anesthesia Bellevue Hosp., N.Y.C., 1959-61; chief resident in anesthesia Jewish Hosp. Bklyn., 1961-62; fellow in anesthesia, rsch. assoc. Flower-Fifth Ave. and Met. Hosp.

Ctr., N.Y.C., 1962-65; rsch. assoc. in anesthesiology Hosp. for Joint Diseases, Bronx, N.Y., 1965-66; anesthesiologist, med. dir. Hurley Ave. Surgicenter, Kingston, N.Y., 1966-88; anesthesiologist Columbia-Green Med. Ctr., Hudson, N.Y., 1990-91; cons. anesthesiologist Benedictine Hosp., Kingston; anesthesiologist N.Y. Downtown Cornell Med. Ctr., N.Y.C., 1991—. Fellow Am. Coll. Anesthesiology; mem. Am. Soc. Anesthesiologists, N.Y. State Soc. Anesthesiologists, Med. Soc. State N.Y., Ulster County Med. Soc., Internat. Anesthesia Rsch. Soc. Home and Office: 3 Arapaho Ct Suffern NY 10901

BEN-ASHER, DANIEL LAWRENCE, legislative researcher, writer; b. Newark, Apr. 15, 1946; s. Jerry and Florence (Tasoff) B.; m. Michele Lauren Cohn, July 16, 1978; children: Sarah, Joshua. AB, Rutgers Coll., 1968; MA, U. Minn., 1970. Plant pers. adminstr. Tanatex Chem. Co. div. Sybron Corp., Lyndhurst, N.J., 1970-71; rsch. asst. Office Legis. Svcs. N.J. State Legislature, Trenton, 1971-76, rsch. assoc., 1976-87, sr. rsch. assoc., 1987—; staff N.J. Assembly Labor Com., 1974-81, Assembly Commerce and Industry Com., 1981-82, Alcoholic Beverage Control Study Commn., 1986-88, Assembly Drug and Alcohol Abuse Policy Com., 1990-91; mem. politics and govt. judges panel "The Best in America" spl. edit. U.S. News and World Report, 1990. Mem. Ewing Twp. (N.J.) Rent Control Bd., 1976-77; fin. coordinator Lawrence Twp. (N.J.) Hist. Preservation Adv. Com., 1985—. Home: 11 Bennington Dr Lawrenceville NJ 08648-1536 Office: NJ Office Legis Svcs Legis Office Bldg CN 068 Trenton NJ 08625-0068

BENBROOK, CHARLES MALLARD, executive consulting company; b. L.A., Nov. 26, 1949; s. Samuel Benbrook and Barbara Arons; m. Donna Mae Benbrook, July 23, 1974; children: Stephen, Rachel, Michael. BS, Harvard U., 1971; MS, U. Wis., 1979, PhD, 1980. Policy analyst President's Coun. on Eviron. Qualty, Washington, 1980-81; staff dir. subcom. on dept. ops., rsch. and fgn. agr. U.S. Ho. of Reps., Washington, 1981-83; exec. dir. Bd. on Agriculture, Nat. Acad. Scis., Washington, 1984-90; pres., prin. Benbrook Consulting Svcs., Washington, 1991—. Home and Office: Benbrook Consulting Svcs 24222 Whites Ferry Rd Dickerson MD 20842-9206

BENCIVENGO, ELAINE PALUSCI, psychologist; b. Camden, N.J., May 13, 1942; d. Victor Palusci and Adeline (Olvieri) Farr; m. Mark R. Bencievngo, June 5, 1976. BA, Rutgers U., 1964; MA, New Sch. for Social Rsch., 1969, postgrad., 1969-71. Lic. psychologist, Pa. Health program analyst City of Philadelphia, Pa., 1971-72; sr. analyst City of Philadelphia, 1972-74; dir. Cen. Med. Intake, 1974-77; exec. dir. Joseph J. Peters Inst., 1977-88; pvt. practice, 1988—; project coord. Univ. N.H., Durham, 1988-89; cons. U.S. Dept. Health and Human Svcs., Washington, 1984-85. Contbr. chpts. to books and articles to profl. jours. Mem. Am. Psychol. Assn. (assoc.), Ea. Psychol. Assn., Pa. Psychol. Assn., Internat. Soc. for the Study of Multiple Personality Assn. Office: 1601 Walnut St Fl 1516 Philadelphia PA 19102-2915

BENCSÂTH, KATALIN A(GNES), mathematics and computer sciences educator; b. Szeged, Hungary; came to U.S., 1973; d. Aladâr and Ilona (Hajôs) B.; m. Mihaly Mezei, July 2, 1970. Diploma, Eötvös U., Budapest, Hungary, 1968; MA, Queens Coll., 1975; PhD, CUNY, 1983. Cert. mathematician. Systems analyst Közti Inst. Architecture, Budapest, 1968-69; ops. researcher INFELOR Systems Engring. Inst., Budapest, 1969-72; assoc. prof. Manhattan Coll., Riverdale, N.Y., 1981—, chmn. coun. for faculty affairs, 1987-88; adj. instr. Hunter Coll., N.Y.C., 1976-81; guest lectr. Fairfield (Conn.) U., 1986, 92, Santa Clara (Calif.) U., 1991; coord. in IBM computer literacy project Manhattan Coll., 1986-88; invited participant Internat. Group Theory Confs., 1984—; mem. faculty resources network program, univ. assoc. NYU, 1986—; scholar in residence Courant Inst., fall 1989. Contbr. articles to profl. jours. and books. Mem. Am. Math. Soc., Math. Assn. Am., N.Y. Acad. Scis., Sigma Xi.

BEN DANIEL, DAVID JACOB, entrepreneurship educator, consultant; b. Phila., Nov. 10, 1931; s. Daniel and Rosella (Soffian) Berkowitz; m. Judith Milgram, June 3, 1957 (div. Nov. 1976); children: Matthew, Elisabeth. BA with honors, U. Pa., 1952, MS in Physics, 1953; PhD in Engring., MIT, 1960. Physicist GE, Schenectady, N.Y., 1961-67, mgr. advanced programs R & D Ctr., 1967-70, mgr. tech. ventures ops., 1970-76; area mgr. advanced energy Exxon Corp., Florham Park, N.J., 1976-79; group v.p. Exxon Enterprises Co., Florham Park, 1979-81; sr. v.p. Am. R & D, Boston, 1981-83; exec. v.p. Genesis Venture Capital, Boston, 1983-84; Berens prof. entrepreneurship Johnson Grad. Sch. Mgmt., Cornell U., Ithaca, N.Y., 1984—; cons. Venture Capital Partnerships, 1984-89. Contbr. articles to profl. jours. Chmn. Citizens for Keating, Schenectady, 1966, Human Rights Commn., Schenectady, 1970-73; trustee Union Am. Hebrew Congregations, N.Y.C., 1972-80. Lt. USN, 1953-56. Recipient Disting. Svc. award Jaycees of Am., 1968; vis. fellow Harvard Bus. Sch., 1970. Mem. Harvard Club (N.Y.C.), Cornell Club (N.Y.C.), Sigma Xi. Republican. Jewish. Home: 111 Kelvin Pl Ithaca NY 14850-2319 Office: Cornell U Johnson Grad Sch Mgmt Ithaca NY 14853

BENDELAC, ROGER EMILE, investment executive, financial consultant; b. Oct. 5, 1956; s. David and Marie (Fedida) B. Diplome, Institut D'Etudes Politiques, Paris, France, 1978; MBA, Columbia U., 1980. Lic. securities and commodities registered rep. Acct. exec. Oppenheimer & Co., Inc., N.Y.C., 1980-83, v.p. retail sales dept., 1983-84, sr. v.p. retail sales dept., 1984-85; sr. v.p. internat. br. Shearson Lehman Hutton, Inc., N.Y.C., 1985-87; pres., chief exec. officer REB Futures, Inc., N.Y.C., 1987-90; investment exec. Westminster Securities Corp., N.Y.C., 1988—; pres., chief exec. officer Generis Capital Corp., N.Y.C., 1990-91; mng. dir. Genersis Assocs., Inc., N.Y.C., 1991—. Editor bus. rev. Columbia U., 1979. Mem. N.Y. Acad. Scis. (elected mem.), Columbia Bus. Sch. Club, The Downtown Athletic Club. Office: Genersis Assocs Inc 1202 Lexington Ave Ste 174 New York NY 10028-1425

BENDER, ADAM NORMAN, physician, educator; b. N.Y.C., June 29, 1942; s. Morris B. and Sara S. (Spirtes) B.; m. Dec. 26, 1966 (div. 1978); 1 child, Melissa Amy; m. Paula Elbirt, Mar. 9, 1981; children: David Joseph Samuel, Shira Tamar. AB in Zoology, Columbia Coll., 1964, MD, 1968. Diplomate, cert. in neurology Am. Bd. Psychiatry and Neurology; cert. Nat. Bd. Med. Examiners, 1969; lic. physician and surgeon, N.Y. Intern Columbia Univ., Harlem Hosp. Ctr., N.Y.C., 1968-69, resident internal medicine, 1969-70; resident neurology Columbia Univ., Neurol. Inst. N.Y., N.Y.C., 1970-73; clin. assoc., med. neurology br. NIH, Bethesda, Md., 1973-75; staff physician neurology Bronx (N.Y.) VA Hosp., 1975-89; dir., Neuromuscular Clinic Mt. Sinai Med. Ctr., N.Y.C., 1975—; asst. prof. neurology Mt. Sinai Sch. Medicine, N.Y.C., 1975-80, assoc. prof. neurology, 1980-89, assoc. clin. prof. neurology, 1989—; examiner Am. Bd. Psychiatry and Neurology, 1970—; v.p. Muscular Dystrophy Assn., 1979-80, corp. mem., 1980—; med. adv. bd. Myasthenia Gravis Found., Greater N.Y. chpt., 1975—, nat., 1982—; sci. adv. bd. Nat. ALS Found., 1979—; assoc. attending neurologist Mt. Sinai Med. Ctr., N.Y.C., 1980—; attending neurologist Doctors Hosp., N.Y.C., 1989—, Lenox Hill Hosp., N.Y.C., 1989—. Contbr. articles to profl. jours. Trustee Congregation Kehilath Jeshurun, N.Y.C., 1985—; vol. Hatzoloh Ambulance Corps., N.Y.C., 1989—. Sr. asst. surgeon USPHS, 1973-75, USPHSR, 1975—. Fellow N.Y. Acad. Medicine; mem. AMA, Am. Bd. Psychiatry and Neurology (self assessment steering sub com. and task force 1991—), Am. Acad. Neurology, Am. Assn. Neuropathologists (assoc.), Am. Neurol. Assn., Assn. for Rsch. in Nervous and Mental Diseases, Histochemical Soc., Med. Soc. County of N.Y., N.Y. Soc. Electron Microscopists, N.Y. Acad. Scis., Soc. Neurosciences, Undersea Med. Soc. Jewish. Office: 1150 Park Ave New York NY 10128-1244

BENDER, GARY WILLIAM, school administrator; b. West Chester, Pa., Aug. 24, 1948; s. William Levi and Mary Alice (Mendenhall) B.; m. Nancy Lee Fisher, 1991. AA, Mercer County Coll., 1968; BS, Trenton State Coll., 1971; MA, Rider Coll., 1975; postgrad., Rutgers U., 1986. Cert. elem. tchr., school administrator, N.J. Pub. health worker N.J. Dept. Environ. Protection, Trenton, 1968-70; tchr. Hamilton Twp. Sch. System, Hamilton Square, N.J., 1970-80, asst. coordinator environ. edn., 1974-80, elem. sch. prin., 1980—. Author: (with others) Environmental Education Today for a Better Earth Tomorrow, 1976, A Guide for Parents/Guardians of Preschool Children and Beyond, 1983. Trustee Crosswicks Creek Watershed Assn., North Crosswicks, N.J., 1984—; v.p. Kisthardt Sch. PTA, Trenton, 1974-75. Named Conservation Tchr. of Yr. Mercer County Soil Conservation Dist., 1979; recipient Disting. Service citation Keep Am. Beautiful Inc., 1977. Mem. Hamilton Twp. Adminstrs./Suprs. Assn. (pres. 1984-86), N.J. Prins./Suprs. Assn. for Supervision and Curriculum Devel., N.J. Congress Parents and Tchrs. (life), Cranbury Golf Club, Kappa Sigma Kappa. Democrat. Methodist. Home: 22 Crosswicks Ellisdale Rd Allentown NJ 08501-1201 Office: Mercerville Sch 60 Regina Ave Trenton NJ 08619-2299

BENDER, MICHAEL A., geneticist; b. N.Y.C., July 25, 1929; s. Clifford Arthur and Margaret (Rigg) B.; m. Belinda Susan Gilmer, June 1979; children: Michèle, Leslie, Sabina, William. BS, U. Wash., 1952; PhD, Johns Hopkins U., 1956. Postdoctoral fellow Johns Hopkins U., Balt., 1956-58, vis. prof. radiology, 1973-75; group leader Oak Ridge (Tenn.) Nat. Lab., 1958-69; assoc. prof. Vanderbilt U., Nashville, 1969-73; sr. scientist Brookhaven Nat. Lab., Upton, N.Y., 1975—; mem. Nat. Commn. on Radiation Protection, Bethesda, Md., 1987—; mem. editorial bd. Mutation Rsch., Radiation Protection Dosimetry. Contbr. articles to profl. publs. Fellow AAAS; mem. Radiation Rsch. Soc., Am. Soc. for Cell Biology, Am. Soc. Pathobiology, Environ. Mutagen Soc. (counselor 1980-83). Home: Valentine Rd # 666 Shoreham NY 11786-1240 Office: Brookhaven Nat Lab Med Dept 30 Bell Ave Upton NY 11973-9999

BENDICH, ADRIANNE, clinical nutritionist, nutritional immunologist; b. N.Y.C., Aug. 4, 1944; d. Joseph and Lillian (Nashorn) B.; m. David Kafkewitz, May 7, 1984; children: Jorden Schiff, Debra Schiff. MS, Iowa State U., 1966; PhD, Rutgers U., Newark, 1981. Sr. scientist Hoffmann-La Roche Inc., Nutley, N.J., 1981-88, sr. clin. rsch. coord., 1988—. Co-author: Vitamin intake and Health, 1990; editor: Antioxidant Nutrients and Immune Functions, 1990, Micronutrients and Immune Functions, 1990, Jour. Nutritional Immunology, 1990—; co-editor Micronutrients in Health and Disease Prevention, 1991; mem. editorial bd. Jour. Nutrition, 1989—. Mem. Am. Inst. Nutrition, Am. Assn. Immunologists (del. Fed. Am. Socs. exptl. biology, life sci. rsch. office 1989—), N.Y. Acad. Scis. (conf. com. 1989—). Home: 178 Stone St Maywood NJ 07607-1251 Office: Hoffmann-La Roche Inc 340 Kingsland St Nutley NJ 07110-1199

BENDIXEN, WARREN E., architect; b. Bklyn., Oct. 25, 1930; s. Jacob E. and Dorothy Harriet (Monaghan) B.; m. Carol Ann Anderson, Dec. 20, 1953; children: Lisa, Erik, Karl, David. BArch, Pratt Inst., 1954, MArch, 1958. Registered architect, N.J., N.Y., Pa., Mass., Conn., Del. Ga., Md. Archtl. designer Briggs & Wood, N.Y.C., 1957-59; assoc. architect Paul Wood & Assocs., N.Y.C., 1959-61; ptnr. Becker, Bendixen, Murphy & Ridgefield, Newark, 1961-85; ptnr., sr. v.p. RBA Group, Morristown, N.J., 1985—. Chmn. Constrn. Bd. Appeals, Morris County, N.J., 1977-91; pres. Montville (N.J.) Bd. Edn., 1970; v.p. Montville Libr. Bd., 1980; mem. Morris 2000, Morris County, 1989—. With U.S. Army, 1954-56. Mem. AIA, Newark Suburban Soc. Architects (pres. 1970). Republican. Presbyterian. Office: RBA Group 1 Evergreen Pl Morristown NJ 07960-4086

BENECKI, ANITA, college administrator; b. Erie, Pa., Dec. 4, 1934; d. John and Dorothy (Zielinski) B. BS, Medaille Coll., Buffalo, 1965; MA, NYU, 1970. Joined Sisters of St. Felix, Roman Cath. Ch., 1952. Elem. edn. tchr. Diocese of Buffalo, 1954-60, Diocese of Syracuse, N.Y., 1960-61; secondary edn. tchr. Villa Maria Acad., Buffalo, 1961-62, Diocese of Buffalo, 1962-69; instr. Villa Maria Coll. of Buffalo, Cheektowaga, N.Y., 1969-71, registrar, 1973-74, dir. institutional rsch., 1986—; sec. Clergy Pers. Bd., Buffalo, 1974-86; bus. coord. Diocese of Buffalo, 1972-73. Editor jour. Bus. Edn. Rev., 1970-71; editor in-house publ. Environ. Scanning, 1986-91. Chair Felician Sisters Centennial in Am., Buffalo Province, 1973; treas. Sisters Assembly Diocese of Buffalo, 1975-77; co-chair Provincial Assembly Bd., Buffalo Province, 1989-91. Systems and Tech. Corp. travel grantee, 1986. Mem. Cath. Bus. Edn. Assn. (bus. mgr. 1967-70, nat. exec. bd. 1967-71), Assn. for Institutional Rsch., North East Assn. for Institutional Rsch., Delta Pi Epsilon. Democrat. Roman Catholic. Office: Villa Maria Coll of Buffalo 240 Pine Ridge Rd Buffalo NY 14225-3999

BENEDETTO, LORRAINE ANN, computer science professional; b. Newark, Oct. 17, 1949; d. Frank and Hilda May (Holt) Vanna; m. William Robert Benedetto, Sept. 12, 1970; children: Annemarie Lyn, William Francis. BA, Newark State Coll., 1972. Secondary tchr. St. Casimir's Sch., Newark, 1972-73; substitute tchr. various schs., N.J., 1975-86; mgr. Burger King, Hazlet, N.J., 1979-81; computer operator Miller-Wohl Corp., Secaucus, N.J., 1981-83, supr. computer ops., 1983-84, mgr. computer ops., 1984-86; tech. support computer ops. Petrie Stores Corp., Secaucus, 1986—. organizer Local Neighborhood Improvement, Union Beach, N.J., 1977-80. Mem. NAFE. Democrat. Roman Catholic. Home: 144 Arlington Blvd North Arlington NJ 07031-5733

BENEJAM, GUSTAVO RICARDO, food products executive; b. Havana, Cuba, July 30, 1955; s. Miguel Gustavo and Mercedes Benejam; m. Nilma V. de Benejam, Dec. 1, 1979; children: Gustavo Alberto, Alberto Ignacio. BSIE, U. P.R., Mayaguez, 1978; MBA, Ind. U., 1981. Cons. Citibank, San Juan, P.R., 1979; brand mgr. Procter & Gamble, San Juan, P.R., 1981-83; mktg. mgr. Gen. Foods P.R., San Juan, 1983-84; gen. mgr. Porta Pack Cor. (Subs. of Gen. Foods), San Juan, 1984-85, KGF P.R., San Juan, 1985-89, Kraft/O. Mayer Venezuela, Caracas, 1990—; gen. mgr. Mex. and v.p. North Latin Am. Philip Morris Internat., Mex. and N.Y., 1990-91; v.p. Latin Am. Food Philip Morris Internat., N.Y., 1991—; cons. design Internat. Mktg. seminar for Citibank L.A., 1985; tchr. design Communications Coll., 1986. Communications dir. United Way, San Juan, 1988-89. Mem. Am. Mktg. Assn. (v.p. San Juan chpt. 1986-87). Home: 41 Longledge Dr Rye Brook NY 10573 Office: Philip Morris Internat 250 N Street Fl RA4N White Plains NY 10601

BENENSON, CLAIRE BERGER, investment and financial planning educator; b. N.Y.C.; d. Nathan H. and Alice E. (Zeisler) B.; m. Lawrence A. Benenson; children: Harold, Gary. BA, Wellesley Coll.; postgrad. N.Y. Inst. Fin., New Sch. Social Rsch., 1965-69. Security analyst Merrill Lynch, N.Y.C., 1940-43; rsch. assoc. Conn. Coll., 1943-45; lectr. NYU Mgmt. Inst., N.Y.C., 1960-68; lectr. New Sch. for Social Rsch., N.Y.C., 1963-86, dir. ann. conf. Wall St. and Economy, 1967-87, dir. ann. conf. Futures and Options, 1979-86, chmn. dept. investment and fin. planning, 1974-86; cons. fin. confs., N.Y.C., 1987—; mem. adv. bd. The First Women's Bank, N.Y.C., 1984-86; bd. dirs. Drexel Burnham Fund, DBL Cash Fund, DBL Tax Free Cash Fund, Drexel Series Trust, N.Y.C., 1970-89, Burnham Fund, Zweig Cash Fund, Zweig Tax Free Fund, Zweig Series Trust, N.Y.C., 1989—; trustee Simms Global Fund, 1987-89; pres. Money Marketeers, NYU, N.Y.C., 1979-80. Contbg. editor Exec. Jeweler, 1981-83; creator, moderator NBC-TV series, Wall St. for Everyone, 1967-68. Mem. bd. overseers Parsons Sch. of Design, N.Y.C., 1974—, br. librs. and annual fund com. and coun. conservaters N.Y. Pub. Libr., 1990—; mem. bus. leadership coun. Wellesley Coll., 1991— Named Disting. Alumna Wellesley Coll., 1968, Durant Scholar, Wellesley Coll.; Alt. fellow in econs. Columbia U., 1938-39. Mem. Fin. Women's Assn. (bd. dirs., chair dirs. resource adv. com., co-chair program com. 1988-89), Nat. Assn. Bus. Econs., Women's Econ. Roundtable, Econ. Club N.Y., N.Y. Assn. Bus. Economists, Money Marketeers NYU, Durant Soc. Wellesley Coll., Women's Bond Club, Harmonie Club (mem. forum com.), Phi Beta Kappa. Jewish.

BENFIELD, DAVID WILLIAM, philosophy educator; b. Des Moines, Jan. 12, 1941; s. Walter Edwin and Frances Louise (Brantley) B.; m. Kathleen Harris, June 22, 1980; 1 child, John David Bradshaw. BA cum laude, St. John's Coll., 1962; MA, Brown U., 1966, PhD, 1972. Instr. SUNY, Stony Brook, 1967-72, asst. prof., 1972-73; asst. prof. philosophy and religion Montclair State Coll., Upper Montclair, N.J., 1973-76, assoc. prof., 1976-91, chmn. conf. on methods in philosophy and the scis., 1983-84, chmn. acad. computing com., 1987-88; full prof., 1991—. Contbr. articles to profl. jours. Mem. Am. Philos. Assn., L.I. Philos. Soc. (pres. 1970-73), Soc. for Philosophy and Pub. Affairs (chmn. N.Y. group 1979-80), Leibniz Soc., Hume Soc., So. Soc. for Philosophy and Psychology, Phi Beta Kappa. Office: Montclair State Coll Dept Philosophy & Religion Upper Montclair NJ 07043

BENGE, JAMES EDWARD, safety engineer; b. Wilmington, Del., Oct. 14, 1952; s. John Howard and Alice Marie (McMeekin) B.; m. Joanne Sykes, Oct. 25, 1975; children: Jordan, Jessica. BS, Lehigh U., 1974. Asst. supr. Hercules Inc., Hattiesburg, Miss., 1974-79; safety supr. Hercules Inc., Brunswick, Ga., 1979-84; div. mgr. Hercules Inc., Wilmington, 1984—. Mem. Am. Soc. Safety Engrs., Del. Safety Engrs. Office: Hercules Inc Hercules Pla Wilmington DE 19894

BENGELS, BARBARA NATALIE, English educator, writer; b. Bklyn., July 21, 1943; d. Louis and Toby (Weinstein) Steinman; m. Dennis A. Bengels, Aug. 23, 1965; children: Elizabeth, Emily, Jessica, Melinda. BA, Hofstra U., 1965; MA, Hunter Coll., 1969; postgrad., CUNY, 1965-69, U. Kans., 1978—. From instr. to adj. assoc. prof. Hofstra U., Hempstead, N.Y., 1968—. Contbr. feature and ednl. articles to newspapers, including N.Y. Times, Newsday. Com. on gifted and talented PTA, Garden City, N.Y., 1982—, com. for arts in edn., 1976-81. NDEA fellow, 1965-69. Mem. Sci. Fiction Rsch. Assn. Office: Hofstra U English Dept Hempstead Tpke Hempstead NY 11550

BENGLIS, LYNDA, artist, sculptor; b. Lake Charles, La., Oct. 25, 1941; d. Michael A. and Leah Margaret (Blackwelder) B. B.F.A., Sophie Newcomb Coll., 1964. Asst. prof. sculpture U. Rochester, 1970-72; vis. artist Yale-Norfolk, summer 1972; prof. Hunter Coll., 1972-73; vis. artist Calif. Inst. Arts, 1974, 76, Kent State U., 1977, Skowhegan Sch. Painting Sculpture, 1979; vis. prof. Princeton, 1975; asst. prof. Hunter Coll., 1980, prof., 1981; prof. U. Ariz., Tucson, 1981, Sch. Visual Arts fine arts workshop, 1985-90; Avery prof. Bard Coll., 1987; master artist Atlanta Ctr. Arts, New Symerna, Fla., 1989. One-woman shows include U. R.I., 1969, Paula Cooper Gallery, N.Y.C., 1970-71, 74-78, 80, 82, 84, 87, 90, Hayden Gallery, Cambridge, Mass., 1971, Kans. State U., 1971, Fuller-Gross Gallery, 1972-74, 77, 79, 82, 86, 88-89, Portland Center Visual Arts, 1972, The Clocktower, N.Y.C., 1972, The Tex. Gallery, Houston, 1974-75, 77, 79-81, 84, 89, Margo Leavin Gallery, Los Angeles, 1977, 80, 83, 85, 87, 89, Dart Gallery, Chgo., 1979, 81-83, 85, Richard Gray Gallery, Chgo., 1990, Tilden Foley, New Orleans, 1989, Real Art Ways, New Haven, 1979, Ga. State U., Atlanta, 1979, Galerie Albert Baronian, Belgium, 1979, 81; one-person retrospective shows include U. South Fla., Tampa, 1980, Lowe Art Mus., Miami, 1980, Atlanta Ctr. Arts, New Symerna, Fla., 1989, David Heath Gallery, Atlanta, 1980, 85, Chatham Coll., Pitts., 1980, Susanne Hilberry Gallery, Birmingham, Mich., 1980, 83, 85, U. Ariz., 1981, Tilton-Foley Gallery, New Orleans, 1984, 86, 89, Landfall East, N.Y.C., 1987, Cumberland Art Gallery, Nashville, 1988, High Mus. Art, Atlanta, 1991, others; group shows include Bykert Gallery, N.Y.C., 1969, Detroit Inst. Arts, 1969, Milw. Art Ctr., 1971, Walker Art Ctr., Mpls., 1971, 81, Balt. Mus. Art, 1975, Mus. Contemporary Art, Chgo., 1977, 80, Stedelijk Mus., Amsterdam, 1978, Mus. Modern Art, N.Y.C., 1979, 86-87, Palazzo Reale, Milan Italy, 1979, Guggenheim Mus., N.Y.C., 1979, 87, Contemporary Arts Mus., Houston, 1980, San Diego Mus. Art, 1980, Whitney Mus., N.Y.C., 1981; Between the Geometry and the Gesture, N.Am. Sculpture 1965-75 by minister of culture Valesquez Palace, Madrid, 1986, Wadsworth Atheneum, Hartford, 1987, Albright Knox Art Gallery, Buffalo, 1987, The New Sculpture, 1965-67: Between Geometry and the Gesture, Whitney Mus., 1990, others; numerous other one and two-person and group exhbns. nationally and internat.; represented in permanent collections Mus. Modern Art, N.Y.C., Guggenheim Mus., Whitney Mus., Walker Art Ctr.; Olympic Com. artist, 1983, High Mus. Art, Atlanta, Balt. Mus. Art, Canberra , Nat. Gallery Australia, Mus. Fine Arts, Houston, New Orleans Mus. Art, Phila. Mus. Art, Burroughs-Wellcome Corp., Research Triangle Park, N.C., Hokkaido Mus. Modern Art, Sapporo, Japan, "American Sculptors", N.Y., L.A., Kamakura Gallery, Tokyo, Suzanne Hillberry Gallery Group Show, 1990, Nat. Mus. Am. Art, Washington; works are subject of hundreds of mag. and jour. articles and books. Recipient Australian Art Coun. award 1976, Distinction award Nat. Coun. Art Adminstr., 1989; Yale-Norfolk scholar, 1963, Max Beckman scholar, 1965; Guggenheim fellow, 1975, Avery fellow, Bard Coll., 1987; Artpark grantee, 1976, Nat. Endowment for Arts grantee, 1979, 90. Address: 222 Bowery New York NY 10012

BENI, JOHN JOSEPH, publisher; b. Mt. Kisco, N.Y., Feb. 26, 1932; s. John and Carmela (Vasta) B.; m. Joan Raymaster, Oct. 17, 1957; children: Bruce, Brian, Holly, Craig. BA, Yale U., 1955. With advt. sales Am. Weekly, Hearst Advt. Service, 1955-62, Farm Jour. Co., 1962-64; advt. sales Redbook Mag., N.Y.C., 1964, then mgr. advt. v.p. advt., v.p., pub., 1978; pres., chief oper. officer Gruner & Jahr USA div. Parents' Mag. Enterprises, N.Y.C., 1978—, dir. parent co. Gruner & Jahr div., 1980-85, pres., chief oper. officer, 1985-88; pres., chief oper. officer McCalls mag., N.Y. Times Co., N.Y.C., 1988—; chmn., pub. Info. Bur., 1987—; pres. Working Woman McCall's Group. Trustee Hackley Sch. Mem. Mag. Pubs. Assn. (bd. dirs. 1981— , chmn. mktg. com.), Yale Alumni Assn., Yale Club N.Y.C. Episcopalian. Home: PO Box 7232 Ardsley On Hudson NY 10503-0232 Office: McCall's Mag 110 5th Ave New York NY 10011-5601*

BENJAMIN, GILBERT LEON, career counselor; b. Bklyn., Dec. 28, 1936; s. Carl and Esther (Tuvim) B.; m. Joan Warshaw, Apr. 15, 1962; children: Marc, Daniel. BA, Bklyn. Coll., 1958; MS, Columbia U., 1960; cert. advanced study, NYU, 1969. Nat. cert. career counselor, lic. career counselor, N.J.; nat. cert. counselor. Employment interviewer, vocat. counselor Hotel Placement office/Youth Placement Svc., N.Y.C., 1960-63; sr. counselor B'nai B'rith Career Counseling Svc., N.Y.C., 1963-68; asst. prof., dir. career devel. and placement Coll. S.I., N.Y., 1968—; pres. N.Y. Sate Career Devel. Assoc., N.Y.C., 1990-92. Vice-pres. Pied Piper Playhouse Nursery Sch., Englishtown, N.J., 1974—, Iron Ore Realty Co., Englishtown, 1974—. Mem. ACA, N.Y. State Assn. Counseling and Devl. (strategic planning com. 1990—), N.J. Assn. Counseling and Devel. Assn., Met. N.Y. Coll. Placement Officers Assn. (dir. continuing edn. 1990—), Nat. Career Devel. Assn., N.Y. Career Devel. Assn., N.J. Career Devel. Assn., Middle Atlantic Career Counseling Assn. Jewish. Home: 7 Mccue Rd Morganville NJ 07751-1642 Office: College Staten Island 715 Ocean Ter Staten Island NY 10301-4547

BENKO, DONALD JAMES, aerospace systems engineer; b. Cleve., Aug. 14, 1954; s. Thomas James and Margaret (Janov) B.; m. Nancy Christine Elden, June 23, 1984. BS in Aerospace Engring., U. Cin., 1977; MBA, U. Houston, 1983. Assoc. engr. Vought Corp., Dallas, 1974-79; lead engr. LTV Aerospace and Def. Co., Dallas, 1979-86; sr. engr. Grumman Corp., Bethpage, N.Y., 1986-87, RCA Astro-Space Div., Princeton, N.J., 1987-89; systems engr. GE Aerospace, Princeton, 1989—; pres. Benko Enterprises, Inc., Princeton, 1990—; v.p. Clevco Products, Inc., Parma, Ohio, 1972—. Contbr. articles to profl. jours.; patentee in field. Mem. SAE, AIAA. Roman Catholic. Home: 15 Hanover Ct Princeton NJ 08540-7066

BENNACK, FRANK ANTHONY, JR., publishing company executive; b. San Antonio, Feb. 12, 1933; s. Frank Anthony and Lula W. (Connally) B.; m. Luella M. Smith, Sept. 1, 1951; children: Shelley, Laura, Diane, Cynthia, Julie. Student, U. Md., 1954-56, St. Mary's U., 1956-58. Advt. account exec. San Antonio Light, 1950-53, 56-58, adv. mgr., 1961-65, asst. pub., 1965-67, pub., 1967-74; gen. mgr. newspapers Hearst Corp., N.Y.C., 1974-76, exec. v.p., chief oper. officer, 1975-78, pres., chief exec. officer, 1978—; chmn. Mus. of Broadcasting, N.Y.C., 1991—; dir. Mfrs. Hanover Trust Co., N.Y.C, Am. Home Products Corp. Chmn. bd. San Antonio Symphony, 1973-74; Trustee Our Lady of Lake Coll.; hon. trustee Witte Meml. Mus.; bd. govs. N.Y. Hosp., N.Y.C. Served with AUS, 1954-56. Mem. Tex. Daily Newspaper Assn. (pres. 1973—), Am. Newspaper Pubs. Assn. (dir.), Greater San Antonio C. of C. (pres. 1971—). Club: Rotarian (pres. 1974-75). Office: The Mus of TV and Radio 1 E 53rd St New York NY 10022-4201 also: The Hearst Corp 959 8th Ave New York NY 10019*

BENNER, CAROL ANN, state official; b. El Paso, Tex., Dec. 31, 1948; d. John Arthur and Mary Louise (Monroe) B. BA, Towson State Coll., 1971; ScM in Hygiene, Johns Hopkins U., 1981. Dir. clin. lab Shock Trauma Ctr., U. Md., Balt., 1972-80; dir. quality assurance U. Md. Hosp., Balt., 1980-82, dir. profl. affairs, 1982-85; dep. dir. hosps. and ambulatory care Md. Dept. Health and Mental Hygiene, Balt., 1986-89, dir. licensing and cert., 1989—; guest lectr. numerous colls., trade assns. and profl. orgns., 1976—. Contbr. numerous articles to profl. jours.; author computer programs. Vol. People's Free Med. Clinic, Balt., 1971-78; trustee Md. Zool. Soc., 1984-88. Mem. Nat. Assn. Quality Assurance, Am. Soc. for Healthcare Risk Mgrs., Nat. Assn. Med. Staff Scientists, Balt. Community Assn. Democrat. Roman Catholic. Home: PO Box 13470 Baltimore MD 21203-3470 Office: Md Dept Health 201 W Preston St Baltimore MD 21201-2323

BENNETT, BETTY T., university dean, writer; children: Peter, Matthew. B.A., Bklyn. Coll., 1962; M.A., NYU, 1963, Ph.D., 1970. Adj. asst. prof. dept. English and comparative lit. SUNY-Stony Brook, 1970-75, asst. chmn. comparative lit., 1971-72, asst. to dean Grad. Sch., 1970-79, adj. assoc. prof., 1975-79; assoc. prof. English and humanities Pratt Inst., Bklyn., 1979-81, prof., 1981—, dean Sch. Liberal Arts and Scis., 1979—; now dean Coll. Arts and Scis. The Am. U., Washington; Danforth Found. fellowship reader, 1978-79; edn. liaison officer N.Y. State, 1977-80; co-dir. NEH Inst., 1989-90; bd. dirs. Keats-Shelley Assn. Am. Inc. Author: British War Poetry in the Age of Romanticism: 1793-1815, 1976, The Evidence of the Imagination, 1978, The Letters of Mary Wollstonecraft Shelley, Vol. I, 1980, The Letters of Mary Wollstonecraft Shelley, Vol. II, 1983, The Letters of Mary Wollstonecraft Shelley, Vol. III, 1988; co-editor: (with Dr. Charles Robinson) The Mary Shelley Reader, 1990; A Gentleman and a Scholar (Mary Diana Dods), 1991; book review editor Keats-Shelley Journal. NEH fellow, 1974-75; Henry E. Huntington Library fellow, 1976; Am. Coun. Learned Socs. fellow, 1977-78; Am. Philos. Soc. grantee, 1979-80, NEH grantee, 1984-90. Mem. MLA, Bklyn. Coll. Alumni Assn., Byron Assn., Keats-Shelley Assn., NYU Alumni Assn., Phi Beta Kappa. Home: 4269 Embassy Park Dr NW Washington DC 20016-3605 Office: American Univ College of Arts and Sciences 4400 Massachusetts Ave NW Washington DC 20016-8001

BENNETT, BRIAN TIMOTHY, chemical company safety professional; b. Newark, Apr. 22, 1962; s. Gerald Edward and Barbara Gail (D'Ascensio) B.; m. Sharon McCann, July 4, 1986; 1 child, Brian Timothy Jr. B. in Chem. Engring. Tech, U. Dayton, 1984. Firefighter, emergency med. technician Huber Heights Fire Dept., Huber Heights, Ohio, 1982-84; plant chemist Apache Bldg. Products Co., Linden, N.J., 1985; process engr. Codi Semiconductor, Inc., Linden, N.J., 1985; safety engr. Hercules, Inc., Parlin, 1985-87; mgr. safety and tng. Akzo Chems. Inc., Edison, 1987-89; corp. safety mgr. Akzo Chems. Inc., 1989—; lectr. varous community orgns. concerning safety and health. Lt. Edison Vol. Fire Dept., 1986-89; instr. ARC, New Brunswick, N.J., 1983—, capt. disaster action team, Iselin Vol. Fire Dept., 1990—, deputy chief Woodbridge Township Hazmat, 1990—. Mem. Am. Soc. Safety Engrs. (com. chmn. 1986—), Indsl. Fire Chiefs N.J., Nat. fire Protection Assn., Soc. Mfg. Engrs., Raritan Valley Hazardous Materials Adv. Coun., N.J. State Indsl. Safety Com., Middlesex-Somerset County Safety Com., Edison Twp. Hazardous Materials Planning Com., Socma Nat. Com. for Occupational Safety and Health, Union-Middlesex County Hazardous Materials Com. Adv. Coun., KC. Roman Catholic. Home: 58 Atlantic St Metuchen NJ 08840-2939 Office: Akzo Chems Inc Meadow Rd Edison NJ 08817-5523

BENNETT, CAROL ELISE, reporter, actress; b. New Orleans, Dec. 27, 1938; d. Gerald Clifford Graham and Edna Doris (Toennies) Kerr; m. Ralph Decker Bennett Jr., Feb. 27, 1966; children: Ralph Decker III, Katherine Elise. BA, U. B.C., Vancouver, Can., 1960; BLS, McGill U., Montreal, Que., Can., 1962. Libr. various locations, 1962-76; reporter TV/radio Washington-Ala. News Report, Washington, 1981—. Actress appearances include (stage) Girl in My Soup, 1978, (movie) Kennedy, 1983, (film) Prime Risk, 1984; host (weekly TV show) Modern Maturity, 1986-88. Vol. reader Recording for the Blind, Washington, 1985—. Mem. SAG, AFTRA, Actor's Equity, Soc. Profl. Journalists. Home: 115 Southwood Ave Silver Spring MD 20901-1918

BENNETT, EDWARD HENRY, reinsurance executive; b. Glens Falls, N.Y., July 22, 1917; s. Harry and Elizabeth Chandler (Clark) B.; m. Louise Faris, Aug. 3, 1946; children: Faris Elizabeth Ramseur, Anne Louise Petronis. AB, Princeton U., 1940. With Guy Carpenter & Co., Inc., N.Y.C., 1940-51; asst. v.p. Guy Carpenter & Co., Inc., 1951-54, v.p., dir., 1954-76, vice chmn., chief adminstrv. officer, 1976-82; dir. Taisho Marine & Fire Ins. Co. of Am., N.Y.C., 1987—; bd. dirs. Bartlett Carry Club, Inc., Tupper Lake, N.Y., 1988—. Maj. USAAF, 1942-46, lt. col. USAFR. Decorated Legion of Merit. Mem. SAR, Res. Officers Assn., Am. Def. Preparedness Assn., Princeton Club of N.Y., City Midday, Drug and Chem. Club of N.Y., Nassau Club of Princeton. Republican. Episcopalian. Address: RR 4 Heerdt Farm Lane Pound Ridge NY 10576

BENNETT, EDWARD VIRDELL, JR., surgeon; b. Nashville, July 17, 1947; s. Edward Virdell and Florence Elaine (Nelson) B.; m. Mari Lora Preacher, Jan. 27, 1968; children: Elizabeth, Christina, Melanie. BA in Biology, Fisk U., 1969; MD cum laude, Ohio State U., 1973. Fellow in surgery Johns Hopkins U., Balt., 1973-75; intern, then resident Johns Hopkins Hosp., Balt., 1973-75; resident in surgery and cardiothoracic surgery Albany Med. Ctr. Hosp., N.Y., 1975-80, instr. in surgery, 1976-80; asst. prof. surgery Health Ctr., U. Tex.-San Antonio, 1980-83; practice medicine specializing in cardiothoracic surgery, Sayre, Pa., 1983-91; chief cardiac surgery Guthrie Clin. Ltd., Sayre, 1990-91; mem. staff Robert Packer Hosp., Sayre, 1983-91; mem. Guthrie Clinic, Ltd., Sayre, 1983-91; cardiac surgeon Albany Cardiothoracic Surgeons, P.C., 1991—; mem. staff Albany Med. Ctr. Hosp., 1991—, St. Peters Hosp., Albany, 1991—; clin. asst. prof. surgery Albany Med. Coll., 1991—. Contbr. articles to med. jours. Producer med. motion picture. Fellow Am. Coll. Chest Physicians, Am. Coll. Cardiology, ACS; mem. Soc. Thoracic Surgeons, Internat. Soc. for Heart Transplantation, Sigma Xi, Alpha Omega Alpha, Omega Psi Phi. Republican. Episcopalian. Avocations: sailing; scuba diving; skiing. Office: Albany Cardiothoracic Surgeons 317 S Manning Blvd Ste 210 Albany NY 12208

BENNETT, GEORGETTE, communications and planning consultant; b. Budapest, Hungary, Nov. 12, 1946; d. Ignatz Beitscher and Sidonie (Horvath) Beitscher Bennett; m. Warren J. Sandler, June 9, 1968 (div. 1972); m. Marc Herman Tanenbaum, June 6, 1982. BA in Sociology, Vassar Coll., 1967; PhD in Sociology, NYU, 1972; postgrad., Am. Inst. Banking, 1988, Omega Comml. Lending, 1989, Stonier Grad. Sch. Banking, 1992. Asst. prof. sociology CUNY, 1970-77; dep. asst. dir. adminstrn. of justice Office Mgmt. & Budget, N.Y.C., 1977-78; network corr. NBC-TV News, N.Y.C., 1978-80; owner, pres. Bennett Assocs., N.Y.C., 1980-87, 92—; v.p., mktg. dir. 1st N.Y. Bank for Bus. (formerly 1st Women's Bank), N.Y.C., 1987, 1st v.p., chief mktg. officer, 1987-88, sr. v.p. div. exec. domestic and internat. pvt. banking, chief mktg. officer, 1988-92; owner Bennett Assocs., N.Y.C., 1992—; host PBS-TV program Why In The World; network corr. NBC news; commentator, host, guest, cons., writer, local and nat. syndicated TV and radio programs; exec. v.p. Camad Media Prodns., N.Y.C., 1970; cons. in field. Author: Unlocking America, 2 vols., 1981, A Safe Place to Live, 1982, Crimewarps: The Future of Crime in America, 1987; co-author: Women in Policing, 1975, Law Enforcement and Criminal Justice, An Introduction, 1979; contbr. articles to profl., popular and scholarly publs. Mem. Women's Advocacy Com., N.Y.C., 1971-74; active People for the Am. Way, N.Y.c., 1986—; bd. dirs. Creative Arts Rehab. Ctr., N.Y.C., 1983-88, cons., 1989—; bd. dirs., treas., chmn. fin. com. Am. Jewish World Svc., N.Y.C., 1987—. Mem. NOW, ACLU, Am. Sociol. Assn., Am. Soc. Criminology, Am. Soc. Pub. Adminstrn. (exec. bd. sect. criminal justice adminstrn. 1976-79, chmn. com. rsch., survey program evaluation 1976-78, convener nat. conf. 1976, award for outstanding nat. contbn.), Am. Women in Radio and TV (chmn. banquet com. 1985, cert. appreciation 1985, Founders Day award NYU 1972), Acad. Criminal Justice Scis., Women's Econ. Round Table, Ea. Sociol. Soc. (session chmn. ann. meetings 1973). Office: Bennett Assocs 100 Park Ave Ste 1700 New York NY 10017

BENNETT, JAMES FRANKLIN, advertising executive; b. Pitts., Apr. 21, 1955; s. Harry Franklin and Marcia Ann (McDowell) B.; m. Cynthia Ann Kuchta, Aug. 18, 1960; 1 child, Leanne Elizabeth. BFA in Communications, Edinboro U., 1978. Gen. laborer U.S. Steel Corp., Braddock, Pa., 1973-78; advt. mgr. Gen. Nutrition Corp., Pitts., 1978-81; account exec. Robert A. Aaley Advts., Pitts., 1981-83; advt. mgr. Flexion, Inc., Pitts., 1983—; teaching asst. Dale Carnegie Sales Course, Pitts., 1986—; publicist pub. rels. campaign Plant Engring., (award) 1990, Food Processing (award) 1990; creative dir. mag. advt. Modern Materials Handling (award) 1989. Recipient Capitol award Nat. Leadership Coun., Washington, 1991. Mem. Bus. Profl. Advertiser's Assn., Edinboro Alumni Assn. Republican. Roman Catholic. Office: Flexion Inc 510 Vista Park Dr Pittsburgh PA 15205-1281

BENNETT, JAMES MARVIN, consulting company executive; b. St. Louis, June 28, 1939; s. Marvin L. and Florence Antonette (Rumph) B.; m. Barbara Virginia Rostron, July 2, 1965; children: J. Justin, Bradley Alexander. BS, Washington U., St. Louis, 1963, PhD in Botany, 1968. Prof. biology NYU, 1968-70; Ford Found. lectr. New Sch. Social Rsch., 1968-70; dir. environ. affairs Joseph Schlitz Brewing Co., Milw., 1970-75, dir. environ. and indsl. affairs, 1975-78, dir. govt. relations, 1978-82; exec. v.p., gen. mgr. Consultancy Internat., N.Y.C., 1984-86; pres., CEO Bennett & Assocs. (name now Bennett Environ. Mgmt., Inc.), Inc., N.Y.C., 1982—; cons. A.T. Kearney, Inc., N.Y., 1986—; NSF fellow, 1965-68; Mem. N.Y. Acad. Scis., AAAS. Office: Bennett Environ Mgmt Inc PO Box 1425 Ridgewood NJ 07451-1425

BENNETT, JOHN EDWARD, marketing professional; b. Charleston, S.C., Oct. 7, 1954; s. Floyd Edward and Patty Ann (Frakes) B.; m. Elizabeth M. Frank, May 10, 1980. BS in Math., Rensselaer Poly. Inst., 1975, MS in Computer Sci., 1976; MBA, Clark U., 1984. Mem. tech. staff Bell Telephone Labs., Naperville, Ill., 1976-78; sr. software engr. Digital Equipment Corp., Maynard, Mass., 1978-80, prin. SW engr., 1980-82, product mgr., 1982-84, sr. product mgr., 1984-86, mktg. cons., 1986-89, sci. mktg. mgr., 1989—. Mem. Pi Mu Epsilon. Home: 49 Rublee St Arlington MA 02174-5736 Office: Digital Equipment Corp Sci Mktg 4 Results Way Marlborough MA 01752-3070

BENNETT, JOHN L., electrical engineer; b. Peking, China, Jan. 25, 1920; came to U.S., 1920; s. Benjamin F. and Elvira (Wallis) B.; m. Harriet Siegmund, Feb. 14, 1948; children: William, Robert, David. BEE, Johns Hopkins U.; postgrad., McCoy Coll. Elec. engr. Black & Decker, 1946-53, elec. engring. supr., 1953-55, rsch. mgr., 1955-60, devel. mgr., 1960-65, applied rsch. and internat. engring. mgr., 1964-66, lab. mgr., 1966-69, tech. liaison mgr., 1969-71, safety assurance mgr., 1971-86, ret., 1986; lectr. in field. Capt. U.S. Army, 1942-46, ETO. Mem. IEEE, Standards Engrs. Soc., Tau Beta Pi. Lutheran. Home: 627 Coventry Rd Baltimore MD 21204-7824

BENNETT, JOSHUA HENRY, physician; b. Amityville, N.Y., July 1, 1952; s. Joshua Henry Jr. and Alice Helen (Oswald) B.; m. Patricia Anne Bernier, Sept. 9, 1984; 1 child, Amanda. BS in Premedicine, Pa. State U., 1974; MD, Johns Hopkins U., 1978. Resident family practice Naval Regional Med. Ctr., Jacksonville, Fla., 1978-81; staff physician family practice Newport (R.I.) Naval Hosp., 1981-84; staff physician Newport Hosp., 1984-85, Charlton Meml. Hosp., Fall River, Mass., 1985-88; faculty physician Harrisburg (Pa.) Hosp., 1988, med. dir., 1988-92, dir. edn., 1992—; mem. med. bd. Planned Parenthood, Harrisburg, 1989—. Lt. comdr. USN, 1978-84. Fellow Am. Acad. Family Physicians. Office: Harrisburg Hosp Family Practice Residency 205 S Front St Harrisburg PA 17105

BENNETT, MICHAEL STEVEN, pastor; b. Seattle, Jan. 22, 1961; s. Raymond Charles and Dorothy Elizabeth (Skonnord) B.; m. Susan Marshall Frost, Aug. 24, 1985; 1 child, Elizabeth Marshall Frost Bennett. BA cum laude, U. Wash., 1983; MDiv, Yale U., 1986. Ordained to ministry United Ch. of Christ, 1986. Pastor Ch. of Christ, Congl., Granby, Mass., 1986-90, Ellington (Conn.) Congl. Ch., 1990—; dean ch. camp United Ch. of Christ, Cummington, Mass., 1988-90; at-large mem. exec. com. Hampshire Assn., 1988-90. Bd. dirs. Coun. on Aging, Grandy, 1986-90. Mem. Phi Beta Kappa, Omicron Delta Epsilon. Home: 17 Middle St Ellington CT 06029-3615 Office: Ellington Congl Ch 72 Main St Ellington CT 06029-3315

BENNETT, ROBERT LEROY, computer software development company executive, lawyer; b. Salt Lake City, May 16, 1937; s. Edward L. and Helen (Hofheins) B.; m. Linda Lou Anderson, Aug. 25, 1961; children: Keri Lynn, Troy, Nicole, Jessica, Candice, Chelsea. BA, Brigham Young U., 1962; JD, UCLA, 1965. Bar: Calif. 1966, U.S. Supreme Ct. 1969. Atty., advisor CIA, Washington, 1965-70; exec. v.p., chief operating officer Mead Data Central, Inc., Washington and N.Y.C., 1970-81; assoc. Heidrick and Struggles, Inc., N.Y.C., 1982-83; pres., chief exec. officer Mirror Systems, Inc., Cambridge, Mass., 1983—; bd. dirs. Mirror Systems, Inc., Cambridge, Nationar, N.Y.C., Raytech Corp., Trumbull, Conn. Mem. ABA, Mass. Computer Software Coun. Mormon. Office: Mirror Systems Inc 2067 Massachusetts Ave Cambridge MA 02140

BENNETT, STEPHEN A., newspaper editor; b. Fairfax, Okla., Mar. 20, 1938; s. Cedric Alden Bennett and Mabel Star (Darden) Ball; divorced; children: Patrick A., Meredith W.; m. Shaunna M. Bennett, Nov. 22, 1975; 1 child, Rachel D. BA, Oka. State U., 1961. Reporter The Balt. Sun, 1962-68; editor The Carroll County Times, Westminster, Md., 1968-73; editor, owner Publick Occurences, Newmarket, N.H., 1973-74; editor The Irregular, Conway, N.H., 1977-1981, Mt. Washington Valley News, Conway, N.H., 1977-81, North Shore Sunday, Danvers, Mass., 1982, Manchester (N.H.) Jour., 1983-85, N.H. Profiles, Concord, 1985; reporter The Boston Globe, Manchester, 1986-89; mng. editor The Post Star, Glens Falls, N.Y., 1989—. With U.S. Army, 1956, USNG 1956-59. Office: The Post Star Lawrence and Cooper Sts Glens Falls NY 12801

BENNEY, DOUGLAS MABLEY, marketing executive, consultant; b. Cold Spring Harbor, N.Y., Aug. 7, 1922; s. William Mabley and Wilhelmina (Walters) B.; m. Eugenia Sammis, Sept. 30, 1944 (div. Jan. 1980); children: William Douglas, Barbara Gates, Robert Scott; m. Barbara Mueller, July 8, 1983; stepchildren: Gregory Carmichael, Andrew Carmichael. Navy air cadet, U. N.C.-Chapel Hill, 1943, Cornell U., 1943; student in engring., Purdue U., 1939-41; AB, Colgate U., 1946-49; postgrad., Columbia U., 1951-52. With Curtis Publs., Phila., 1950-63; editor, assoc. pub. Jack & Jill, 1960-63; mktg. mgr. edn. div. Doubleday & Co., N.Y.C., 1963-67; advt. and sales mgr. Hearst Book div., N.Y.C., 1967-68; v.p. creative svcs. Nat. Liberty Corp., Valley Forge, Pa., 1968-72; v.p. mktg. Gerber Life Ins. Co., N.Y.C., Pa., 1972-75; sr. mktg. officer Internat. Group Plans, Washington, Pa., 1975-78; v.p. mktg. Maxon Adminstrs., Inc., Washington, Pa., 1978-89; pres. A&B Advt., Inc., Temple Hills, Md., 1989—. Patentee newspaper inserts, self-mailers. Lt. (j.g.) AC, USN, 1943-46; PTO. Recipient award Artists Guild Del. Valley, 1969, Direct Mail Mktg. Assn., 1965, Myasthenia Gravis Found., 1985. Mem. Direct Mktg. Assn. Washington, Direct Mktg. Creative Guild, Greater Washington Soc. Assn. Execs., Mt. Vernon Country Club (Alexandria, Va.).

BENNICE, ANGELO PHILIP, county official, consultant; b. Brocton, N.Y., Aug. 13, 1931; s. Dominec and Anna (Greco) B.; m. Rosemary Terese Michalak, Jan. 17, 1953; children: Gretchen, Gregory, Benjamin. BS in Chemistry, SUNY, Fredonia, 1973; postgrad., Niagara U., Syracuse U., Pa. State U. Supt. Dunkirk (N.Y.) Water Pollution Control Facility, 1958-78; dir. South and Cen. Chautauqua Lake Sewer Dists., Celoron, N.Y., 1978—; chmn. adv. bd. Ohio River Valley Sanitation Commn., Cin., 1984; former mem. N.Y. State Commr.'s Task Force on Water Resources; former mem. N.Y. State Operators Award Com.; bd. dirs. Adams Art Gallery, Dunkirk. Editor newsletter County Mgrs. Assn., 1989. Chmn. Continuing Edn. Coun., 1977, Dunkirk CSC, 1988; councilman-at-large City of Dunkirk, 1990—; mem. Chautauqua County Emergency Planning Commn.; mem. coll. coun. SUNY, Fredonia, 1977-91; mem. parish coun. Holy Trinity Roman Cath. Ch.; mem. troop coun. Boy Scouts Am., Dunkirk; co-chmn. United Way, Dunkirk; mem., foreman Pioneer Hook and Ladder Co.; chmn. Dunkirk City Safety Co.; numerous others. With USN, 1952-56, Korea. Recipient Presdl. award of honor Dunkirk-Fredonia Jaycees, 1967, Jacyee of Yr. award, 1968; Honored Chemistry Alumnus award SUNY, 1980. Mem. Am. Chem. Soc., Water Pollution Control Fedn., Am. Pub. Works Assn., N.Y. Water Pollution Control Assn. (bd. dirs. Western sect. 1975, exec. bd.), Chautauqua Regional Profl. Wastewater Operators Assn., Dunkirk-Exempt Fireman's Assn. (life), Moose. Democrat. Office: South and Cen Chautauqua Lake Sewer Dists PO Box 458 Celoron NY 14720-0458

BENNS, ROBIN ANISE, human resources professional; b. Phila., July 28, 1958; d. Norris Elton and Amaza (Manley) B. Cert. in Equal Employment Opportunity studies, Cornell U., 1990; BS in Human Devel., Howard U., 1992. Adminstrv. asst. Rohm and Haas Co., Phila., 1984-86, adminstrv. asst tng. and devel., 1986-88, EEO specialist, 1988—; co. rep., vice chmn. communications com. Chem. Industry for Minorities in Engring., Wilmington, Del., 1989. Mentor, role model Phila. Futures, 1990—. Mem. Orgn. Devel. Network, Soc. for Human Resourc Mgmt. Office: Rohm & Haas Co Ind Mall W Philadelphia PA 19105

BENOIT, RICHARD ARMAND, police chief, lawyer; b. New Bedford, Mass., Jan. 29, 1942; s. Oliver Maurice and Delina Marie (Barie) B.; m. Elizabeth Joan Nobrega, Nov. 17, 1962; children: Karen Marie Carvalho, Richard Michael. AS, Bristol Community Coll., Fall River, Mass., 1972; BS, Salve Regina U., 1975, MS, 1979; JD, So. New Eng. Sch. Law, New Bedford, 1989. Bar: Mass. 1990. Police officer New Bedford Police Dept., 1967-71, sgt., 1971-75, lt., 1975-82, capt., 1982-86, chief of police, 1986—; pvt. practice law New Bedford, 1990—; dir., instr. New Bedford Police Acad., 1975-85. Mem. Mayor's Task Force on Drug Free Community, New Bedford, Neighborhood Crime Watch, New Bedford, YMCA, New Bedford. With U.S. Army, 1959-62. Mem. ABA, Mass. Bar Assn., Boston Bar Assn., Mass. Chiefs of Police Assn., Internat. Assn. Chiefs of Police. Home: 209 Maywood St New Bedford MA 02745 Office: New Bedford Police Dept 25 Spring St New Bedford MA 02742

BENOWITZ, ROBERT BARRY, lawyer, consultant; b. Perth Amboy, N.J., Jan. 8, 1934; s. Max and Fannie (Lipack) B.; m. Nancy Ellen Lipschutz, June 30, 1963; children: Adam David, Abbey Lynne. BSEE, Lehigh U., 1955; JD, Temple U., 1975. Bar: Pa., 1975. Engr. various elec. cos., N.J., N.Y., Calif. and Pa., 1955-71; pres., safety cons. RMS Assocs., Plymouth Meeting, Pa., 1971—; pvt. practice law Norristown, Pa., 1975—. Chmn., mem. Plymouth Twp. Planning Agy., 1979-89; former chmn. Plymouth Twp. Comprehensive Plan Com., 1989-90, candidate for coun., 1987; active Ad Hoc Solid Waste Adv. Com., 1986; alt. mem. Plymouth Twp. Zoning Bd., 1991—. With U.S. Army, 1958. Mem. Internat. Assn. Arson Investigation, Am. Soc. Safety Engrs., Assn. Advancement Med. Instrn., Pa. Bar Assn., Montgomery County Bar Assn., Forensic Profl. Soc. (pres. 1986-88). Home: 109 Shasta Rd Plymouth Meeting PA 19462 Office: 526 Swede St Norristown PA 19401

BENRUBI, BONNI, art dealer; b. N.Y.C., June 5, 1953; d. Harry and Salle Benrubi; m. Dennis H. Powers, Sept. 20, 1987; 1 child, Samuel Tyler Powers. BFA in Art History, Boston U., 1975. Asst. dir. Blum Helman Gallery, N.Y.C., 1975-77; dir. Daniel Wolf Gallery, N.Y.C., 1977-87; pres. Benrubi Fine Art Photographs, N.Y.C., 1987—. Mem. Assn. Internat. Photography Art Dealers. Democrat. Jewish. Office: Benrubi Fine Art Photographs 150 E 74th St New York NY 10021-3528

BENSON, BARBARA ELLEN, state agency administrator; b. Rockford, Ill., June 5, 1943; d. Olander Anton and Eleanor Margaret (Lydon) B. BA, Beloit Coll., 1965; MA, Ind. U., 1969, PhD, 1976. Editor Eleutherian Mills-Hagley Found., Wilmington, Del., 1973-80; dir. libr. Hist. Soc. Del., Wilmington, 1980-90, exec. dir., 1990—. Author: Logs and Lumber, 1989, (with Michael Biggs) Wilmington: the City and Beyond, 1990; contbr. articles to jours., chpts. to books. Vice chair Del. Humanities Forum, 1987-92, chair, 1992—; bd. dirs. Sister Cities, Wilmington, 1985-89 (ofcl. visitor to Kalmar, Swede, 1985), State Records Commn. Del., 1987—, Gov.'s Tourism Adv. Bd., Del., 1987—. Mem. Orgn. Am. Historians, Am. Assn. State and Local History (state awards chmn. 1987—), Mid Atlantic Regional Archivists (bd. dirs. 1983-87). Office: Hist Soc Del 505 N Market St Wilmington DE 19801-3091

BENSON, CHARLES EVERETT, microbiology educator; b. Dayton, Ohio, Dec. 15, 1937; s. Charles Prue Jr. and Virginia Elizabeth (Zindorf) B.; m. Gail Elizabeth Smith, June 5, 1960; children: Deborah Elizabeth, Charles Nathaniel. AB, Franklin Coll., 1960; MS, Miami U., Oxford, Ohio, 1963; PhD, Wake Forest U., 1969; MS (hon.), U. Pa., 1985. Tchr. Dayton Pub. Schs., 1960-61; rsch. asst. Miami Valley Hosp., Dayton, 1963-65; asst. prof. U. Pa. Sch. Allied Med. Professions, Phila., 1975-80; assoc. prof. U. Pa. Sch. Vet. Medicine, Phila., 1980-88, prof., 1988—; chmn. dept. clin. studies U. Pa. Sch. Vet. Medicine, Kennett Square, Pa., 1989—. Author/co-author rsch. papers in field. Pres. Haddonfield (N.J.) Rep. Party, 1982-85, pres. Haddonfield Friends of the Libr., 1986-90; chmn. Haddonfield United Meth. Ch. Nursery Sch. Com., 1980-88; scout master Cub Scouts, Boy Scouts Am., Haddonfield, 1985-89. Scholar U. Pa. Sch. Medicine, 1972-75. Mem. Am. Soc. for Microbiology (fellowship 1969), Soc. for Gen. Microbiology, AAAS, N.Y. Acad. Sci., U.S. Animal Health Assn., Am. Assn. of Vet. Lab. Diagnosticians, Lions Club, Sigma Chi Alpha. Home: 123 Hawthorne Ave Haddonfield NJ 08033 Office: Univ Pa Sch Vet Medicine 382 W Street Rd Kennett Square PA 19348

BENSON, PRISCILLA JENKINS, astronomy educator; b. Newton, Mass., May 6, 1940; d. Benjamin Gilbert and Rebecca (Martin) Jenkins; m. John K. Benson Jr., June 23, 1962; children: Karen Benson Lachance, John K. III. BA, Smith Coll., 1962; SM, MIT, 1979; PhD, Mass. Inst. Tech., 1983. Math, sci. tchr. Tahanto Regional High Sch., Boylston, Mass., 1962-63; actuarial asst. Paul Revere Life Ins. Co., Worcester, Mass., 1963-64; from instr. to assoc. prof. Wellesley (Mass.) Coll., 1972—; mem. coun. on Undergrad. Rsch., 1987—, physics/astronomy editor newsletter. Contbr. articles to Astrophys. Jour., Astronomical Jour. Dudly Obs. grantee, Albany, N.Y., 1984, Research Corp. grantee, 1984-86, NSF grantee, Washington, 1986—. Mem. Am. Astron. Soc. (rsch. grantee 1983), Am. Assn. Variable Star Observers (editorial bd., councilor, chair CCD com.), Internat. Amateur-Profl. Photographic Photometry, Sigma Xi (v.p. local chpt. 1985-86, 89-90, pres. 1986-87, 90—), Phi Beta Kappa. Office: Wellesley Coll Whitin Obs Wellesley MA 02181

BENSON, RAYMOND ELLIS, academic exchange program administrator; b. N.Y.C., Nov. 2, 1924; s. Morris and Vera (Peskin) B.; m. Shirley Margaret Sherman, Aug. 31, 1956; children: Carolyn Margaret, Michael Raymond, Nicholas Vance. BA, U. Wis., 1950, MA, 1954. Soviet internal affairs editor The Current Digest of the Soviet Press, N.Y.C., 1955-56; asst. editor Problems of Communism, Washington, 1956-57; Yugoslav desk officer USIA Rsch. Svc., Washington, 1957-58; fgn. svc. officer USIA, Washington, 1958-87; dir. The Am. Collegiate Consortium, Middlebury, Vt., 1987—; dir. Ctr. for Russian Eurasian Studies Middlebury (Vt.) Coll., 1988—; dir. Middlebury Ctr. for Russian and Soviet Studies. dir. Middlebury Ctr. for Russian, Eurasian and East European Studies. Sgt. U.S. Army, 1946-48. Recipient Edward R. Murrow award Tufts U., 1986. Mem. Am. Assn. for Advancement of Slavic Studies. Democrat. Jewish. Home: RR 4 Box 50 Middlebury VT 05753-8602 Office: Am Collegiate Consortium Middlebury Coll Middlebury VT 05753

BENSON, ROBERT CLINTON, JR., investment banker; b. Lynn, Mass., Dec. 8, 1946; s. Robert Clinton and Lillian M. (MacArthur) B.; m. Jo-Ann Murphy, Aug. 26, 1977 (div. Dec. 1989); children: Jarrod Grayson, Marissa Ashley. BS, Suffolk U., 1970; MA, Boston U., 1979; MBA, N.H. Coll., 1982. Lic. real estate broker, N.H.; lic. pvt. pilot; justice of the peace. Planner City of Lynn, Mass., 1972-73, asst. supt. parks, 1973-74, spl. asst. to mayor, 1974-75; dep. exec. dir. Dept. Community Devel., Mass., 1975-78; dir. econ. devel. City of Portsmouth, N.H., 1978-80; founder Benson & Co. Mgmt. Cons., N.H., 1980-84, Robert C. Benson, Inc., Investment Bankers, N.H., 1984-90, Benson Assocs., Fin. Cons. (merger Olmstead MacArthur & Co. Inc. Investment Bankers), North Hampton, N.H., 1990-91; pres. Olmstead MacArthur & Co., Investment Bankers, North Hampton, N.H., 1991—; mng. ptnr. OMC Devel. Group, North Hampton, 1991—; bd. dirs. Sesame Tape Systems, Inc., Beacon Health HMO; adj. faculty Golden Gate U. Editor Cruiser-Destroyerman Mag., 1971; contbr. articles to profl. publs.; research on labor market in Portsmouth, 1978-80; drafter model environ. statutes Mass. Legislature, 1968. Bd. dirs. Portsmouth Community Health Services, 1980-82; chmn. Swampscott (Mass.) Conservation Commn., 1967-70; mem. Swampscott Town Charter Commn., 1968-69. Served with USNR, 1970-72. Mem. Am. Indsl. Devel. Coun., Inc., Am. Planning Assn., Northeastern Indsl. Devel. Assn., Portsmouth C. of C. (bd. dirs.), Greenleaf Athletic Club. Episcopalian. Office: Olmstead MacArthur & Co 110 Lafayette Rd North Hampton NH 03862-2409

BENSON, ROBERT FREDERICK, space physicist; b. Mpls., Mar. 16, 1935; s. Carl Sidney and Esther I. (Johnson) B.; m. Marilyn Jean Evers, July 26, 1958; children: Maia Jean, Susan Gayle, Gregory Frederick. BS, U. Minn., 1956, MS, 1959; PhD, U. Alaska, 1963. Asst. Internat. Geophys. yr. scientist Arctic Ins. N.Am., 1956-58; geophysicist Geophs. Inst., U. Alaska, Fairbanks, 1959-63; asst. prof. astronomy U. Minn., Mpls., 1963-64; resident rsch. assoc. Goddard Space Flight Ctr. NAS/NRC, Greenbelt, Md., 1964-65; space physicist NASA/Goddard Space Flight Ctr., Greenbelt, 1965—. Contbr. articles to profl. jours. Mem. Am. Geophys. Union, Internat. Union Radio Sci. (chmn. U.S. Nat. Com./ URSI Commn. H waves in plasmas 1982-85, chmn. Commn. H. 1990-93), Antarctican Soc., Am. Polar Soc.

Democrat. Lutheran. Home: 10 Shanandale Ct Silver Spring MD 20904-1625 Office: NASA/Goddard Space Flight Ctr Code 692 Greenbelt MD 20771

BENSON, WILLIAM EDWARD (BARNES), geologist; b. West Haven, Conn., May 15, 1919; s. John Edward and Lura Purdy (Barnes) B.; m. Mary Freda Hill, July 11, 1944; children—Sharon (Mrs. J.G. Rachel), Lynn (Mrs. J.D. Walker), William Edward. B.A., Yale, 1940, M.S., 1942, Ph.D., 1952. Geologist Conn. Geol. and Natural History Survey, 1940-42; geologist U.S. Geol. Survey, 1942-54, br. chief, 1953-54; exec. sec. div. earth sci. Nat. Acad. Scis./NRC, 1954-55; chief geologist Manidon Mining Inc., N.D., 1955-56; program dir., sect. head NSF, 1956-75, chief scientist earth sci. div., 1975-79; sci. advisory to Office of Pres., Washington, 1976-77; pvt. cons., 1980—; vis. prof. U. Hawaii, 1980; sr. staff assoc. NAS, 1980—. Contbr., editor profl. jours. Served with USNR, 1944-45. Yale fellow, 1940-42. Fellow Geol. Soc. Am., Am. Geophys. Union, AAAS (sec. sect. E 1969-73, chmn. sect. E 1974-75); mem. Geol. Soc. Washington (v.p. 1958), Pick and Hammer Soc. (chmn. 1970-73), Phi Beta Kappa, Sigma Xi. Home: 7531 Parish Ln Falls Church VA 22042-3521

BENSON, WILLIE MCWHORTER, federal agency administrator; b. Birmingham, Ala., Nov. 1, 1949; s. Charles and Vinie Elizabeth (Jackson) B. BA, Knoxville Coll., 1972. Benefit authorizer Social Security Adminstrn., Birmingham, 1973-76, inquiry specialist, 1976-77, claims authorizer, 1978-87, systems specialist, 1988—. Staff sgr. USAR, 1973-86. Mem. BLEWS (editor newsletter 1992), Alpha Phi Alpha (editor newsletter 1988, Eugene K. Jones award 1990, Journalistic Achievement award 1990, named Brother of Yr. 1991). Baptist. Home: 301G Sun Shine Pl Baltimore MD 21228-1715 Office: Social Security Adminstrn 6401 Security Blvd Baltimore MD 21235

BENTINCK-SMITH, WILLIAM, former university administrator; b. Boston, Jan. 22, 1914; s. William Frederick and Marion (Jordan) Bentinck-S.; m. Phebe Keyes, June 26, 1937; children: Michael, Judy, Nancy, Peter. A.B., Harvard U., 1937; M.S., Columbia U., 1938. Reporter Boston Globe, 1938-40; mng. editor Harvard Alumni Bull., 1940-46, editor, 1946-54, editorial adv. com., 1954-76; asst. to pres. Harvard, 1954-71, assoc., 1971-84; editor Harvard Today, 1957-69, editorial chmn., 1969-72, adv. com., 1971-75; hon. curator type specimens and letter design Harvard Coll. Library. Author: The Harvard Book, 1953, rev., 1982, Building A Great Library, The Coolidge Years At Harvard, 1976, Lives of Harvard Scholars, 1986, History of Harvard Named Chairs, 1991. Dir. Cambridge Trust Co.; Sec. Harvard Class of 1937. Served to lt. comdr. USNR, 1942-45. Decorated Bronze Star; recipient Harvard medal, 1987. Mem. Am. Antiquarian Soc., Mass. Hist. Soc., Colonial Soc. Mass., Phi Beta Kappa (hon.). Home: 62 Peabody St PO Box 979 Groton MA 01450 Office: 219 Western Ave Allston MA 02134-1040

BENTIVEGNA, PETER IGNATIUS, architectural company executive; b. N.Y.C., Dec. 2, 1941; s. Peter and Catherine Bentivegna; m. Louise Catherine Foulkrod, Aug. 20, 1989. BArch, Pratt Inst., 1963. Registered architect, D.C., Ky., Mass., N.C., N.J., N.Y., Pa., Tex., W.Va. V.p. Am. Medicorp Inc., Bala Cynwyd, Pa., 1975-78; exec. v.p. Medifac, Inc., Jenkintown, Pa., 1978-83; mng. ptnr. Bentivegna, Lindsay Maron Merlino Archictes., Bala Cynwyd, 1983—; pres. BLM Group, Bala Cynwyd, 1983—. Contbr. articles to profl. jours. Lt. U.S. Army, 1964-66. Mem. AIA (com. on architecture for health), Pa. Soc. Architects, Constrn. Specifications Inst., Nat. Fire Protection Assn. Office: BLM Group 161 Rockhill Rd Bala Cynwyd PA 19004-2048

BENTIVEGNA, SANTO WILLIAM, clinical psychologist; b. Rochester, N.Y., Nov. 1, 1955; s. Carmello and Josephine (Miceli) B.; m. Nancy Ann Panzarella, May 26, 1979; children: David, Laura, Roseann. BA, St. John Fisher Coll., Rochester, 1977; MA, U. New Haven, 1979, Calif. Sch. Profl. Psychology, 1981; PhD, Calif. Sch. Profl. Psychology, 1983. Lic. psychologist, N.Y.; diplomate Am. Bd. Adminstrv. Psychology. Intern in psychology Fresno (Calif.) Family Ct. Counseling Ctr., 1979-80, Sch. for Neurologically Handicapped, Fresno, 1980-82, Convalescent Hosp. for Children, Rochester, 1982-83; ct. psychologist Agy. for Children and Youth, Wellsboro, Pa., 1983-84; assoc. psychologist Rochester Psychiat. Ctr., 1984-86; pvt. practice Rochester, 1985—; chief psychologist Continuing Devel. Svcs., Rochester, 1986—. Contbr. articles to profl. jours. Scout leader Boy Scouts Am., Rochester, 1990—; baseball coach local Little League Orgn., Rochester. Recipient Disting. Citizens award Monroe County Dist. Atty.'s Office, Rochester, 1991. Mem. Am. Psychol. Assn., Genesee Valley Psychol. Assn., Rochester Area Clin. Psychologists. Office: 1654 Monroe Ave Rochester NY 14618-1417

BENTLAGE, DEBRA S., marketing executive; b. Carthage, Mo., Sept. 30, 1957; d. Kenneth Darvin and Lala May (Kinser) B. Student, U. Tex., 1972-74; BFA, S.W. Mo. State U., 1978. Asst. to advt.-communications mgr. Welcome Wagon Internat., Memphis, 1975-76; news reporter, ABC local corresp. Sta. KWTO-AM-FM, Springfield, Mo., 1978-79; copywriter, then program dir. Maritz Inc., St. Louis, 1979-82, creative supr., 1982-84, sr. creative supr., 1984-85; account supr. Daniel J. Edelman, Inc., St. Louis, 1985-86; dir. communications Hermann Mktg., St. Louis, 1986-87; sr. creative dir. Adworks Inc., St. Louis, 1987; account mgr. Maritz Inc., N.Y.C., 1987—; clients include Philip Morris U.S.A., N.Y. Telephone, MasterCard Internat., Avon Products, Citibank; script cons., writer, film producer in field, 1977-86. Exhibited photographs in group shows at St. Louis Art Mus., 1976, Nelson Art Gallery, 1976; represented in permanent collections U. Mo., St. Louis. Recipient hon. mention Nikon Response and Recognition Competition, 1976, Flair award Advt. Fedn. St. Louis, 1984, Emmy award for Outstanding Achievement in the Sales/Promotion Mktg. for Philip Morris U.S.A., NATAS, 1989, Spl. Team award N.Y. Telephone Co., 1990. Office: Maritz Inc 100 Park Ave New York NY 10017-5516

BENTLEY, ANNETTE CAMNETAR, researcher, educator, counselor, nutritionist; b. New Orleans, May 6, 1939; d. Paul Edward and Annette (Berdou) Camneter; m. James Ray Bentley, Feb. 17, 1979. BA in Psychology, Rutgers U., 1991. Dir. Whoo Sprue Celiac Group, West Orange, N.J., 1983-88; program asst. pathology residency program U. Medicine and Dentistry N.J., Newark, 1985-90; dir. Am. Celiac Soc. Dietary Support Coalition, West Orange, N.J., 1988—; adminstr., sec. Mental Health Ctr., Newark, 1990-91; founder, news editor Whoo Sprue Celiac Group, West Orange, N.J., 1983-87, Am. Celiac Soc., West Orange, N.J., 1988—. Author, editor: Whoo's Report, 1983; contbr. articles to Jour. Gen. Psychology. Rep. Gov. Commn., La., 1973-79. Recipient Svc. award St. Barnabas Med. Ctr. Our Lady of Lourdes, West Orange, N.J., 1983-87, 89, Outstanding Svc. award Rutgers U., Newark, 1991. Mem. Psi Chi. Roman Catholic. Home and Office: American Celiac Society Dietary Suppt Coalition 58 Musano Ct West Orange NJ 07052-4103

BENTLEY, HELEN DELICH (MRS. WILLIAM ROY BENTLEY), congresswoman; b. Ruth, Nev.; d. Michael and Mary (Kovich) Delich; m. William Roy Bentley, June 7, 1959. Student, U. Nev., 1941-42, George Washington U., 1943; BJ, U. Mo., 1944; LLD (hon.), U. Md., 1970, U. Alaska, 1973, U. Mich., 1974; LHD (hon.), Bryant Coll., 1971, U. Portland, 1972, L.I. U., 1976, Goucher Coll., 1979, Villa Julie Coll., Maine Maritime Acad., 1991. Reporter Ely (Nev.) Record, 1940-42; polit. campaign mgr. for late Senator James G. Scrugham, White Pine County, Nev., 1942; bur. mgr. UP, Fort Wayne, Ind., 1944-45; reporter Balt. Sun, 1945-53, maritime editor, 1953-69; chmn. FMC, Washington, 1969-75, Am. Bicentennial Fleet, Inc., 1973-76; pres. Internat. Resources & Devel. Corp., Washington, 1976-85, HDB Internat., Inc., 1977-85; pub. relations adviser Am. Assn. Port Authorities, 1958-62, 64-67; mem. 99th— Congresses from 2d Md. dist., 1985—. TV and film producer world trade and maritime shows, 1950-64; Editor: Ports of Americas, 1961. Board dirs., mem. coun. Ch. Home and Hosp.; bd. dirs. United Seamen's Svc., Oceanic Ednl. Found.; mem. coun. Md. Hist. Soc., Villa Julie Coll., Stevenson, Md., Montessori Soc. Cen. Md., Slavic-Am. Nat. Assn.; bd. visitors U.S. Naval Acad.; Rep. nominee for Ho. of Reps., 2d dist. Md., 1980, 82, 84, 86, 88; Md. nat. committeewoman, 1988; chmn. Md. campaign Bush for U.S. Pres., 1988. Recipient numerous honors including awards from AFL-CIO Maritime Port Council Greater N.Y., 1965, Ironworkers and Shipbuilders Council AFL-CIO, 1966, AOTOS award United Seamen's Service, 1971, Man of Yr. award N.Y. Freight Forwarders and Brokers Assn., 1972, Robert L. Hague Post award Am. Legion, 1973, Robert M. Thompson award Navy League U.S., 1973, Jerry Land medal Soc. Naval Architects and Marine Engrs., 1974, George Washington Honor medal Valley Forge Freedoms Found., 1971, 76, Salute To Congress award Propeller Club of U.S., 1987, Freedom award Alliance Metalworking Industries, 1987, Maritime Industry Salute to Congress award, 1987, Dr. John H. Griffin award KC, 1988, Minute Man award Reserve Officers Assn., 1988, Free State award of Excellence AMVETS Dept. Md., 1989, Sr. John H. Griffin award KC, 1988, Minute Man award Res. Officers Assn., 1988, AMVETS award Dept. Md., 1989, Free State award of Excellence, 1989 award for Leadership as a Mem. of Peace Through Strength caucus Am. Security Coun., 1986, 90, Disting. Citizen of Yr. award Balt. coun. Boy Scouts Am., 1989, Medal of St. Andrew Greek Orthodox Archdiocese North & South Am. 1990; named GOP Woman of Year, 1972, Ethnic Woman of Yr., Republican Nat. Heritage Council, 1985; 1st non-Briton to address and be honored by U.K. Chamber Shipping, 1973; only woman to trek Northwest Passage on S.S. Manhattan, 1969. Greek Orthodox. Office: PO Box 10619 Baltimore MD 21285-0619

BENTLEY, MARGARET ESPLIN, anthropologist, educator; b. Chgo., June 22, 1947; m. William Bentley, Dec. 1975 (div. Oct. 1990); children: Anne, Andrew. BA, Mich. State U., 1976; MA, U. Conn., 1983, PhD, 1987. Rsch. assoc. Johns Hopkins U. Sch. Pub. Health, Balt., 1985-87, asst. prof., 1987-89, 90—, acting dir. div. human nutrition, 1989-90. Contbr. chpts. to books, articles to profl. jours. Pew Faculty scholar in nutrition Internat. Food Policy Rsch. Inst., 1991-92; rsch. grantee Ford Found., 1990—. Mem. Am. Inst. Nutrition. Democrat. Home: 104 Yorkleigh Rd Baltimore MD 21204-7511 Office: Johns Hopkins U 615 N Wolfe St Baltimore MD 21205-2103

BENTLEY, RICHARD NORCROSS, regional planner, consultant; b. Chgo., Mar. 17, 1937; s. Richard and Phoebe Wrenn (Norcross) B.; m. Carolyn Stiglic, Sept. 10, 1977; children: Nicholas Northrup, Julia Wrenn. BA, Yale U., 1959; Cert. in Real Estate, NYU, 1973; MFA, Norwich U., 1992. Cert. real estate, Mass. Chief project mgr. Mass. Dept. Community Affairs, Boston, 1978-83; chief planner Mayor's Office Housing, Boston, 1983-86; planning dir. Boston Housing Authority, 1986-87; sr. planning mgr. Pioneer Valley Planning Commn., West Springfield, Mass., 1987-88; instr. Internat. City Mgmt. Assn., Washington, 1982—; tchr. creative writing U. Mass., 1992—. Editor Peregrine Mag., 1991—; contbr. articles to profl. jours. Bd. dirs. Hanover Housing Authority, 1980-82. Served with U.S. Army, 1960-62. Mem. Nat. Assn. Housing and Redevelopment Officals, Am. Planning Assn. Club: Yale (Boston), Harvard (Boston), Huron Mountain. Home: 24 N Prospect St Amherst MA 01002-2014

BENTLEY, WILLIAM ROSS, forestry educator; b. Oakland, Calif., Jan. 29, 1938; s. Jay R. and Olive (Manson) B.; m. Margaret Esplin, Dec. 27, 1975 (div.); children: Michael, Anne, Andrew; m. Ann Wilhelm, Dec. 1, 1990. BS, U. Calif., Berkeley, 1960, PhD, 1965; M Forestry, U. Mich., 1961. Asst. prof. Iowa State U., Ames, 1963-66; assoc. prof. U. Wis., Madison, 1966-69; assoc. prof. U. Mich., Ann Arbor, 1969-74, prof., 1974-76; prof. U. Conn., Storrs, 1980-84; mgr. forest rsch. Crown Zellerbach Corp., Wilsonville, Oreg., 1976-80; program officer Ford Found., India, 1983-85; dir. Winrock Internat., Morrilton, Ark., 1985—; lectr., sr. assoc. Sch. Forestry Yale U., New Haven, Conn., 1990—; cons. George Banzhaf & Co., Milw., 1968-69, U.S. Dept. Justice, 1981-85; dir. Tropical Resources Inst., 1990-91, Weyerhaeuser Ctr. on Forest Mgmt. and Policy, New Haven, 1991—. Author: Management of Agroforestry Research, 1990, In the Long Run, 1991; editor: Agroforestry In South Asia, 1991. Bd. dirs. Nitrogen Fixing Tree Assn., Maui, Hawaii, 1992—; chair bd. dirs. Childrens Community Ctr., Storrs, Conn., 1980-83. Fellow Schoen-Rene, 1960-61, Bullard, 1975-76, Fulbright, 1991-92. Mem. Internat. Soc. Tropical Foresters, Soc. Am. Foresters (chair internat. forestry 1986-90). Democrat. Home: 83 Day St Granby CT 06035-2901 Office: Yale U Sch Forestry & Environ Studies 205 Prospect St New Haven CT 06511-2189

BENTON, EDWARD HENRY, lawyer; b. Norwalk, Conn., Dec. 1, 1950; s. Edward Failing and Margaret Theresa (Sabo) B. BA, Yale U., 1974; JD, Vanderbilt U., 1981. Bar: N.Y. 1982. Pres. POS Corp., New Haven, 1974-76; asst. account exec. Benton & Bowles Inc., N.Y.C., 1976-78; assoc. Simpson Thacher & Bartlett, N.Y.C., 1981-85, Skadden, Arps, Slate, Meagher & Flom, N.Y.C., 1985-86, Cadwalader, Wickersham & Taft, N.Y.C., 1987; chmn. bd. dirs. Video Cave, Inc., Hudson, N.Y., Benton Enterprises, Inc., Malden Bridge, N.Y., 1988—. Mem. Vanderbilt U. Law Rev., 1980-81. Patrick Wilson scholar, 1978-81. Mem. Yale Club (N.Y.C.), Royal Hong Kong Yacht, Capital Dist. Aikikai. Episcopalian. Home and Office: Richmond Rd Malden Bridge NY 12115

BENTON, MARY JOSEPHINE, writer, clergyman; b. Lubbock, Tex., Oct. 13, 1925; d. Albert Charles and Hilah Olena (Atwood) Griffin; divorced; children: Roy Albert, David Elvin. BA, Union Coll., Lincoln, Nebr., 1947; MA, U. Denver, 1962, PhD, 1968; postgrad., Wesley Theol. Sem., Washington, 1978-82. Ordained local elder Brotherhood Seventh-day Adventist Ch., 1973. Instr. speech Union Coll., 1947-48; tchr. English and speech Mile High Acad., Denver, 1960-63; asst. prof. speech Columbia Union Coll., Takoma Park, Md., 1963-73, assoc. dir. adult evening program, 1985-87, dir., 1987-88, prof. communication, 1988-90; assoc. pastor Sligo Seventh-day Adventist Ch., Takoma Park, 1973-79; pastor Rockville (Md.) Seventh-day Adventist Ch., 1979-82; assoc. prof. humanities Montgomery Jr. Coll., Germantown, Md., 1982-85; writer, Smithsburg, Md., 1990—; pres. Rockville Ministerium, 1981-82. Author: Called by God: Stories of Seventh-day Adventist Women Ministers, 1990. Named Alumna of Yr., Southwestern Adventist Coll., Keene, Tex., 1979. Home and Office: 11727 Crystal Falls Dr Smithsburg MD 21783-9730

BENTON, NICHOLAS, theater producer; b. Boston, Oct. 18, 1926; s. Jay Rogers and Frances (Hill) B.; m. Kate Lenthal Bigelow, June 5, 1954; children: Frances Hill, Kate, Emily Weld, Louisa Barclay. Grad., Phillips Exeter Acad., 1945; AB, Harvard U., 1951. Promotion writer Life mag., N.Y.C., 1951-55, Fortune mag., N.Y.C., 1955-56; staff writer Time Mag., N.Y.C., 1956-57; advt. promotion mgr. Archtl. Forum, N.Y.C., 1957-64; gen. promotion mgr. Time-Life Books, Alexandria, Va., 1965-68, dir. pub. rels., 1968-83, v.p., 1977-83; lectr. pub. procedures course Radcliffe Coll., 1976-82; producing dir. Am. Kaleidoscope Theatre, 1983-85; mem. Nat. Book Awards Com., 1971; co-chmn. Nat. Book Awards Week Com., 1975-79; vice chmn. Am. Book Awards, 1981-82. Author: A Benton Heritage, 1964; co-producer musical Salad Days, 1958, The Golden Age, 1984, The Perfect Party, 1986, Love Letters, 1989, The Heart's a Wonder, 1990. Pres. East 69th St. Assn., 1963-64; 1st v.p. Soc. Meml. Sloan-Kettering Cancer Ctr., 1963-64, asst. treas., 1964-66, treas., 1967-68; mem. exec. com. Friends of the Theatre Collection, Mus. of City of N.Y., 1983-86, exec. com. 1984-87. With AUS, 1945-46. Mem. Pubs. Publicity Assn. (pres. 1970-71), New Eng. Historic Geneal. Soc. (trustee 1979-82, corr. sec. 1982-88, v.p. 1988—), N.Y. Geneal. and Biog. Soc., Assn. Am. Pubs. (freedom to read com. 1974-78, internat. freedom to pub. com. 1979-82), Soc. of Colonial Wars, Harvard Club (bd. mgrs. N.Y.C. chpt. 1971-73), Bourne Cove Yacht Club (commodore Wareham, Mass. chpt. 1988-91). Home and Office: 129 E 82d St New York NY 10028

BENZE, JAMES GAUSS, JR., education educator; b. Ashtabula, Ohio, May 1, 1952; s. James Gauss Sr. and Mary Catherine (Foster) B.; m. Pamela Halco, Jan. 3, 1976; 1 child, James Andrew. BA, Miami U., Oxford, Ohio, 1974; MA, Purdue U., 1975, PhD, 1980. Asst. prof. Merrimack Coll., North Andover, Mass., 1981-85; asst. prof. Washington and Jefferson Coll., Washington, Pa., 1985-88, assoc. prof., 1988—; cons. United Way, Washington, 1989—. Author: Presidential Power and Management Techniques, 1987. Vice-chmn. Bethel Park (Pa.) Bd. of Parks and Leisure Svcs., 1987—; coord. Woodrow Wilson Fellowship Found., N.Y.C. Mem. Pa. Polit. Sci. Assn.

BENZIN, MICHAEL ERIC, fund raiser; b. Hampton, Va., Apr. 14, 1964; s. Eric Louis and Elizabeth S. (Bennett) B. BA in Communications, Canisius Coll., 1986. Community dir. March of Dimes, Buffalo, 1987-89, Am. Heart Assn., Buffalo, 1989; cons. pvt. practice, Buffalo, 1989-90; devel. assoc. Heritage Ctr., Buffalo, 1990-91; corp. and found. dir. Buffalo Philharm. Orch, 1991-92; asst. dir. ann. giving Univ. at Buffalo Found., 1992—. Bd. dirs. A Taste of Buffalo, 1990-94; vol. Multiple Sclerosis Soc., 1990—. Named Vol. of Yr., Multiple Sclerosis Soc., Buffalo, 1990. Mem. Nat. Soc. Fund Raising Execs., Compeer West (Student Vol. of Yr. 1986), N.Y. Jaycees (V.P. of Quarter region 8 1991), Buffalo Jr. C. of C. (v.p. 1990-92). Lutheran. Home: 266 Elmwood Ste 159 Buffalo NY 14222 Office: Univ at Buffalo Found PO Box 590 Buffalo NY 14231

BENZING, CYNTHIA DELL, economics educator; b. Upper Darby, Pa., Oct. 23, 1951; d. Martin Paul and Alyce (Chapman) Dell; m. William Thomas Benzing, Oct. 21, 1972; children: William, Daniel, Edward. BS in Psychology, Pa. State U., 1972; MBA, Drexel U., 1977, PhD in Bus., 1987. Asst. controller Parade Publs., Inc., Phila., 1972-76; teaching asst. Drexel U., Phila., 1976-77; acctg. instr. St. Joseph's U., Phila., 1977-80; teaching fellow Drexel U., Phila., 1983-87; assoc. prof. West Chester (Pa.) U., 1987—. Editor-in-chief Pa. Econ. Rev., 1991—; contbr. articles to profl. jours. Instr. Thresholds Vols. in Prison, Delaware County, Pa., 1989; foster parent Children and Youth Svcs., Delaware County, 1986-88, 90-92. Mem. Pa. Econ. Assn. (bd. dirs. 1989-91, treas. 1991-93), So. Econ. Assn., Ea. Econ. Assn., Atlantic Econ. Assn., Fin. Mgmt. Assn. Home: 246 Lewis Rd Media PA 19064-2129 Office: West Chester U Dept Econs West Chester PA 19383

BEQUETTE, B. WAYNE, chemical engineer, educator; b. Fayetteville, Ark., July 13, 1957; s. William Hal and Virginia Ayleen (Cammack) B. BS, U. Ark., 1980; PhD, U. Tex., 1986. Process engr. Am. Petrofina, Port Arthur, Tex., 1980-82; postdoctoral rsch. assoc. U. Tex., 1986-87; vis. lectr. U. Calif., Davis, 1987-88; asst. prof. Rensselaer Poly. Inst., Troy, N.Y., 1988—; fin. chmn. Am. Control Conf., Boston, 1989-91. Contbr. articles to profl. jours. NSF grantee, 1989-91, 90-92. Mem. AAUP, Am. Inst. Chem. Engrs. Office: Rensselaer Poly Inst Dept Chem Engring Troy NY 12180-3590

BERA, REGINA HELEN, nursing administrator; b. Bayonne, N.J., July 1, 1938; d. Charles John Hagan and Helen Theresa (Regan) Hewitt; m. Walter Stanley Bera, May 3, 1957; children: Catherine, Jeanette, Ronald, Stacie, Colleen, Melanie. AS in Nursing, NYU, 1983; cert. in gerontology, Kean Coll., 1990. From lic. practical nurse to RN Bayonne (N.J.) Hosp., 1976-87; dir. nursing svcs., asst. dir. Sr. Health Ctr., Bayonne (N.J.) Hosp., 1987—. Mem. Nat. Gerontology, Acad. Honor and Profl. Soc. Sigma Phi Omega, Marine Corps. League Aux. Democrat. Roman Catholic. Office: Sr Health Ctr Bayonne Hosp 115 W 42nd St Bayonne NJ 07002-2035

BERAN, DENIS CARL, publisher; b. Detroit, Apr. 14, 1935; s. Carl Earl and Jessica Mary (Bogue) B.; B.A. in Econs., U. Mich., 1958; postgrad. in mktg. mgmt. Harvard Bus. Sch., 1976; Internat. Strategies Program, Columbia U., 1984; m. Virginia Martha Knox, Feb. 20, 1960; children—Michael Knox, Elizabeth Virginia. With McGraw-Hill Pubs. Co., N.Y.C., 1962—, advt. sales trainee, 1962, dist. mgr. nucleonics, 1962-65, dist. mgr. Business Week, 1965-70, sales devel. mgr., 1970-72, mktg. dir., 1972-76, asst. pub., 1979, internat. pub. dir., 1980-85, v.p. Europe McGraw-Hill, 1976-79; v.p. advt. Gannett Internat., 1986-87, v.p. mktg., 1988-89. Chmn., New Canaan Am. Cancer Soc., 1973-75; dir. So. Fairfield County Am. Cancer Soc., 1972-76, 80—, 1st. v.p., 1975-76. Served to 1st lt USMC, 1958-61. Mem. Internat. Periodical Pubs. Assn. (exec. com.), Mag. Pubs. Assn., Internat. Advt. Assn. (Global Media Commn.), Aircraft Owners and Pilots Assn. (v.p. 1990—). Republican. Roman Catholic. Clubs: New Canaan Country; Racquet & Tennis (N.Y.C.). Home: 103 W 2nd St Frederick MD 21701-5328 Office: 421 Aviation Way Frederick MD 21701-4798

BERARDI, RONALD STEPHEN, pathologist, educator; b. Rochester, Pa., Jan. 12, 1943; s. Desiderio John and Florence (Salvaggio) B.; m. Diane Lenore Wytaske, June 17, 1967; children: Lenore Christine, James Ronald, Anne-Marie. BS in Chemstry, U. Pitts., 1963; MD, Loyola U., Chgo., 1967. Diplomate Am. Bd. Pathology. Intern Presbyn.-St. Lukes Hosp., Chgo., 1967-68, resident in pathology, 1968-69; resident in pathology Malcolm Grow USAF Med. Ctr., Washington, 1969-71, New Eng. Deaconess Hosp., Boston, 1971-72, U. Pitts. Health Ctr. Hosp., 1972-73; Sarah Mellon Scaife fellow in immunopathology U. Pitts., 1973-74; assoc. pathologist Latrobe (Pa.) Area Hosp., 1974-80, chief pathologist, dir. labs., 1980—; co-dir. labs. Henry Clay Frick Community Hosp. Latrobe Area Hosp., Mt. Pleasant, Pa., 1974-80; assoc. instr. U. Ill., Chgo., 1967-69; teaching fellow U. Pitts., 1972-74, teaching faculty, 1974-76; instr. Thomas Jefferson Coll. Medicine, Phila., 1977—; med. dir. Sch. Med. Tech. Ind. U. Pa., 1980—; lab. insp. Coll. Am. Pathology, Chgo., 1980—; chmn. infection control com., tissue transfusion com., cancer registry, cost containment com. Latrobe Area Hosp., 1980—. Contbr. articles to profl. jours. Mem. Nat. Adv. Bd. Am. Security Council, Boston, 1985; mem. Rep. Presdl. Task Force, Washington, 1985-88; mem. Rep. Nat. Com., Washington, 1985. Senatorial scholar, 1961-63; mem. Rep. Senatorial Inner Circle, U.S. Senatorial Bus. Adv. Bd., 1988, state advisor to U.S. Congl. Adv. Bd.; U.S. Congressional Adv. Bd. (state advisor). Fellow Am. Soc. Clin. Pathologists, Coll. Am. Pathologists, U.S.-Can. Acad. Pathology Inc., Internat. Biographical Assn.; mem. Am. Assn. Blood Banks, AMA (Physicians Recognition award 1985), Am. Chem. Soc., N.Y. Acad. Scis., Internat. Platform Assn., Am. Biographical Inst. (disting. leadership award), Am. Inst. Chemists, Am. Med. Writers Assn., Westmoreland County Med. Soc. (editor bulletin), Pitts. Cancer Inst. (affiliate), Latrobe Country Club, Univ. Club, U.S. Senatorial Club, Phi Eta Sigma, Alpha Epsilon Delta. Roman Catholic. Home: 811 Spring St Latrobe PA 15650-2025 Office: Latrobe Area Hosp 2D W Ave Latrobe PA 15650

BERCHER, THOMAS EUGENE OWEN, city manager; b. Palestine, Tex., Sept. 20, 1944; s. Josey Weindel and Lurene (Owen) B.; m. Frances Lee, July 28, 1973; children: Thomas, Steven, Brian. BA, U. Ark., 1973, MPA, 1978. Grants adminstr. Dept. Pollution Control, Little Rock, 1976-78; dir. ops. City of Bentonville, Ark., 1978-79; village mgr. City of Holly, Mich., 1979-85; city adminstr. City of Hartford, Wis., 1985-86; town mgr. City of East Hampton, Mass., 1986-88, City of Burrillville, R.I., 1989—; bd. dirs. R.I. Interlocal Ins. Assocs., Providence; adj. lectr. U. Mich., Flint, 1984-85. Contbr. essays to jours. Del. Dem. State Conv., Ark., 1972; bd. dirs. East Hampton Scholarship Found., 1987. With USAF and USN, 1963-69. Mem. Internat. City Mgmt. Assn., Am. Soc. Pub. Adminstrn. (chpt. bd. dirs. 1978, 87), R.I. City Mgrs. Assn., Lions (chpt. bd. dirs. 1991). Roman Catholic. Office: Town of Burrillville 105 Harrisville Main St Harrisville RI 02830-1499

BERCHUCK, IVY SCHIFF, educator; b. N.Y.C., July 20, 1933; d. Joseph Nathan and Jeannette (Meyerson) Graber; m. Lawrence Robert Schiff (dec. July 1979); children: Robin, Matthew, Claudia, Jennifer; m. Irving Berchuck, June 26, 1983. BA, Queens Coll., 1969, cert. in adminstrn. and supervision, 1988; MA in Edn., St. John's U., 1976. Tchr. N.Y.C. Bd. Edn., 1969-85, gifted and talented resource tchr., 1985-89; workshop staff trainer gifted edn. Dist. 28 Sch. Bd., N.Y.C., 1985-89, trainer critical thinking skills, 1989—, coord. gifted and talented programs, 1989—. Mem. ednl. adv. bd. Mus. N.Y.C., 1988—. Mem. Assn. for Supervision and Curriculum Devel., Phi Delta Kappa. Home: 99-57 74th Ave Forest Hills NY 11375

BERD, MORRIS, artist; b. Phila., Mar. 12, 1914; s. Benjiman and Ida (Solatsky) B.; m. DeEtta Nelson, Oct. 12, 1943; children: Jared, Caleb. Diploma, Phila. Coll. Art, 1936; studied and painted, U. Stranieri de Perugia, Europe, Mex., North Africa, 1956. Prof. Phila. Coll. of Art, 1936-86. Represented by Ross-Constantin Gallery, N.Y.C.; represented in many pvt. and pub. collections. Recipient mural award Gimbel Bros., 1952. Mem. Phila. Artists Equity (pres. 1955-56). Home and Studio: 350 Howarth Rd Media PA 19063

BERDNIK, CARL OLIVER, middle school principal; b. Pitts., Nov. 7, 1940; m. Martha Alice Srsic, Apr. 23, 1966; children: Carla Agnes, Christopher Matthew, Victoria Lynn. BS in Edn., Slippery Rock U., 1962, MEd, 1967; MEd, U. Pitts., 1969. Tchr. Conroy Jr. High Sch., Pitts., 1962-67; tchr. Columbus Middle Sch., Pitts., 1967-69, coord. of instrn., 1969-70; vice-prin. Schenley High Sch., Pitts., 1970-72; prin. Arsenal Middle Sch., Pitts., 1972-82, Sterrett Classical Acad., Pitts., 1982—; sch. dist. scheduling specialist and staff devel. specialist Pitts. Pub. Schs., 1990—; cons. in field. Author: Procedures for Scheduling the Elementary School, 1991. GE Econs. fellow, 1963; NDEA history fellow, 1967. Mem. Pitts. Adminstrs. Assn., Pa. Sch. Bds. Assn., Pa. Middle Sch. Assn., K.C. Home: 116 Waldorf St

Pittsburgh PA 15214-1924 Office: Sterrett Classical Acad 7100 Reynolds St Pittsburgh PA 15208-2927

BEREDJICK, NICKY, management consultant; b. Sofia, Bulgaria, Oct. 6, 1929; m. Esther Arditi, May 29, 1960; 1 child, Jack. MSc in Chemistry, Syracuse U., 1954, PhD, 1957. Researcher McGill U., Can., 1957; various positions Union Carbide Co., Standard Oil Co. (Ind.), Amoco Chems. Co., 1957-64; with UN Indsl. Devel. Orn. (UNIDO), Vienna, Austria, 1964-72; dep. dir. UN Relief Ops. (UNROB), Bangladesh, 1972-75; chief of adminstrn. and aid ops. UN Emergency Ops., 1974-75, officer-in-charge, 1975-77; dir. UN Administrv. Mgmt. Svc., 1977-81; dir. pers. adminstrn. UN, 1981-83; from dir. programme support div. to dep. UN under-sec. gen. UN Dept. Tech. Coop. for Devel. (DTCD), 1983-90; pres. Assoc. Internat. Cons. (AIC), Hollis, N.Y., 1990—. Contbr. articles to profl. jours. Mem. N.Y. Acad. Scis., Am. Chem. Soc., Chem. Soc. (U.K.). Home and Office: Associated Internat Cons 19406 87th Rd Jamaica NY 11423-1402

BERENATO, ANTHONY FRANCIS, financial executive; b. Phila., Dec. 3, 1922; s. Frank A. and Eleanor A. (Siderio) B.; m. Dena Marie Marchione, Sept. 5, 1946; children—Anthony F., Mark Anthony. B.S. in Econs., Villanova U., 1949; postgrad., Am. U., Biarritz, France, 1945-46; student-philosophy and art appreciation, Barnes Found., 1966-68. C.P.A., Pa. Ptnr. Steinberg, Spiegel & Berenato, Springfield, Pa., 1956-91; pres. Roger Fin. Corp., Phila., 1961-63, Sure Loan Corp., Phila., 1961-65, Cobbs Fla. Cupboard Inc., Bala Cynwyd, Pa., 1965-67, Phila. Arena Corp., 1961-65; chmn. Crescent Iron Works, Phila., 1974-86; chmn., chief exec. officer Custom Art Metals, Inc., Barrington, N.J., 1967-89, pres., chief exec. officer, 1991—; founder, chmn. Crescent Cab Co., Phila.; funder, chmn., pres., chief exec. officer Custom Art Metals P.R. Inc., 1987-90. Trustee Anthony F. and Dena Marie Berenato Charitable Trust. Served with U.S. Army, 1942-46, ETO, active Res. 1946-49. Fellow Am. Inst. Mgmt., Navy League of U.S. (life member), Pa. Soc., Am. Inst. CPA's, Pa. Inst. CPA's, U.S. Naval Inst. (life), Am. Sec. Council. Republican. Roman Catholic. Clubs: Bala Golf (treas. 1974-76); Rio Mar Country (P.R.); Sands Country, Rolling Green Golf, Hamilton. Home: 411 Schollar Ln Media PA 19064-1719

BERENATO, MARK ANTHONY, lawyer, steel company executive; b. Lansdowne, Pa., Feb. 24, 1958; s. Anthony Francis and Dena Marie (Marchione) B.; m. Linnie Louise Swineford, Sept. 9, 1989. Diploma, Episcopal Acad., 1976; BS in Acctg., Villanova U., 1980; JD, Am. U., 1983; postgrad., Temple U., 1984. Bar: Pa. 1984, U.S. Dist. Ct. (ea. dist.) Pa. 1987. Tax lawyer Deloitte, Haskins & Sells, N.Y.C., 1984-85; pvt. practice law Mark A. Berenato & Assocs., Phila., 1985-91; counsel Custom Art Metals, Inc., Barrington, N.J., 1989—; pres. Cumberland Devel. Corp., Voorhees, N.J., 1989—; sec., gen. counsel Sterling Metal Fabricators, Inc., Barrington, N.J., 1990—. Mem. ABA, Pa. Bar Assn., Phila. Bar Assn., Rolling Green Golf Club, Vesper Club, Phi Alpha Delta. Republican. Roman Catholic. Home: 344 Danbury Ln Glen Mills PA 19342-2039 Office: 181 E Gloucester Pike Barrington NJ 08007-1331

BERENSON, ROBERT LEONARD, advertising agency executive; b. Chgo., Nov. 14, 1939; s. James Morton and Harriet Ruth (Fisher) B.; m. Elizabeth Segal, Sept. 9, 1962; 1 dau., Cindy Elizabeth. B.A., Syracuse U., 1961; M.S.J., Northwestern U., 1962. Mgmt. trainee Grey Advt., Inc., N.Y.C., 1964-67; v.p., account supr. Grey Advt., Inc., 1967-70, v.p., mgmt. supr., 1970-71, sr. v.p., mgmt. rep., 1971-77, exec. v.p., 1977-82, exec. v.p. adminstrn. and account mgmt., 1982—; guest lectr. mktg. U. Conn., Syracuse U., Northwestern U., St. John's U., 1974-88; bd. govs. 4A's Ea. region coun. Agy. Mgmt. Com.; bd. dirs. Burgundy Wine Co. Chmn. bd. dirs. Better Business Bur.; bd. dirs. 4As. 1st lt. U.S. Army, 1962-64. Jewish. Home: 7 Farmers Rd Great Neck NY 11024-1125 Office: Grey Advt Inc 777 3d Ave New York NY 10017

BERES, KENNETH DAVID, pastor, educator; b. Torrington, Conn., Mar. 12, 1931; s. Gus Geza and Ruth Alice (Geer) B.; m. Eftychia (Effie) Zika, June 21, 1961; 1 child, Kenneth Philotheos. BA in Behavioural Scis., Hartford U., 1960; M of Div., Hartford Sem. Found., 1970; PhD cum laude, Trinity Theol. Sem., 1979; BS in Nutripathy, 1988. Ordained to ministry Congl. Ch., 1970. Missionary social worker Thrace/Macedonia, Greece, 1965-67; student pastor Colebrook (Conn.) Congl. Ch, 1967-68; pastor, tchr. Mohegan Congl. Ch., Uncasville, Conn., 1969-70, Montville Ctr. Congl. Ch., Oakdale, Conn., 1968-78, Goshen Congl. Ch., 1968-78; squadron chaplain USAF CAP, Moodus, Conn., 1977-79; advanced through grades to chaplain maj. USAF CAP, 1980; squadron chaplain USAF CAP, Alton, Ill., 1979-84, dep. wing chaplain, 1982-84; chaplain So. Ill. Group 19 unit USAF CAP, Scott AFB, Ill., 1981-84; advanced through grades to chaplain lt. col. USAF CAP, 1991; pastor, tchr. Alton First Congl. Ch., 1983-84; interim pastor Darlington (Ind.) Christian Congl. Ch., 1984; prof. Greek, librarian Muncie (Ind.) Bible Coll., 1984-85; pres. Kenefil Assocs., Uxbridge, Mass., 1980—; sqdn. chpl. USAF CAP, Southbridge, Mass., 1985-86; cmdr. Webster Composite Sqdr., 1985-87; pastor, tchr. Holland (Mass.) Congl. Ch., 1985—; owner, cons. Health Hut, Webster, 1986—; chief exec. officer Nutripathic Health Orgn., 1990—; pres. High Mountain Health Ctr., 1991—; mem. Conn. Fellowship C.C.C., 1974-78, chmn. religious edn. com., 1976-77, moderator, 1977-78, Northeast region 1978-79, Midwest, 1982-83. Author: Shroud, 1979; ghost editor: Love Never Fails, 1st edit., 1979, 2d edit., 1988. Mem. Civil Air Patrol, Conn. Wing, Ill. Wing, Mass. Wing. Served with USN, 1951-55. Mem. Nat. Assn. Congl. Christian Chs., Conservative Congl. Christian Conf., Nat. Assn. Profl. Cons. Home and Office: 932 Aldrich St Uxbridge MA 01569-2112

BERESFORD, DOUGLAS LINCOLN, lawyer; b. Washington, June 1, 1956; s. Spencer Moxon and Ann (Lincoln) B.; m. Lori Anne Mainous, Sep. 22, 1990. AB cum laude, Harvard U., 1978; JD, Georgetown U., 1982. Bar: D.C. 1982, U.S. Ct. Appeals (D.C. cir.) 1984, U.S. Supreme Ct. 1986. Assoc. Morgan, Lewis & Bockius, Washington, 1982-83; assoc. Newman & Holtzinger, P.C., Washington, 1983-89, ptnr., 1989—. Office: Newman & Holtzinger PC 1615 L St NW Washington DC 20036-5610

BERESFORD-HILL, PAUL VINCENT, international educator; b. Dublin, Ireland, May 15, 1949; came to U.S., 1974, naturalized, 1978; s. Francis John and Alexandra (de La Poer Beresford) H.; m. Kathryn Elizabeth Ernyei, Apr. 11, 1976; children: Christopher Tristram, Timothy Alexander. Cert. in Edn., BEd, Oxford (Eng.) U., 1971; MA, New Sch., 1979; MSc Oxford (Eng.) U., 1991. Gov., Milton Keynes' Coll. Edn. (U.K.), 1969-71; curriculum coord. Buckinghamshire Edn. Authority, Milton Keynes, Eng., 1971-74; lectr. Bletchley (Eng.) Coll. of Further Edn., 1972-74; founder, headmaster Anglo-Am. Internat. Sch., N.Y.C., 1974-90; rsch. assoc. Ctr. for Comparative Studies Edn. Oxford U., 1991—; project officer TEMPUS Programme for Ednl. Leadership in Eastern Europe, 1991-92; pres. Wesminster Internat. Placement Group, N.Y.C.; pres. bd. dirs. Am. Home Study Inst., 1981-88; dir. Wolsey Hall Oxford, N.Am. Ltd., 1981-88; mem. grad. faculty New Sch. Social Rsch., 1979; pres. GAP Activity Project Inc., 1985—; chmn. Mountbatten Internship Program, 1985—. Mem. edn. com. Brit. Council Chs., 1970-74; bd. dirs. Internat. Baccalaureate N.Am. Inc., 1979-89, Riverside Shakespeare Co., N.Y.C., 1984-87, Malignant Hyperthermia Assn. U.S., 1984—; vice chmn. Prew Sch. Bd. Trustees, Sarasota, 1987-90, Internat. Sch. Found., London, 1984-89; chmn. bd. dirs. Am. Friends of Shaftesbury Homes and Arethusa, 1987—; founder English Speaking Union U.S. Nat. Shakespeare Recitation Competition; founder, chmn. N.Y.C. Coalition Concerned Students; officer Most Venerable Order St. John of Jerusalem. Fellow Royal Anthrop. Inst. (U.K.), Coll. Preceptors, Inst. Dirs. London; mem. Royal Soc. Lit., Guild Ind. Schs. (bd. dirs. 1985-89), European Council Internat. Schs., Oxford Union Soc., English-Speaking Union, St. George's Soc., Brit.-Am. C. of C., Most Excellent Order of the Brit. Empire, Brit. Schs. and Univs. Club N.Y. (dir.). Roman Catholic. Clubs: Metropolitan (N.Y.C.); Carlton (London). Home: 21 Sprain Rd Hartsdale NY 10530-3016 Office: 211 E 51st St # 12A New York NY 10024 also: Oxford U Dept Ednl Studies, 15 Norham Gardens, Oxford OX2 7PY, England

BERESIN, EUGENE VICTOR, psychiatrist; b. Phila., Jan. 26, 1950; s. Victor Eugene and Marcella Grace (Suskind) B.; m. Mary Michaela Moran, Sept. 6, 1981; children: Jade Moran, Caitlin Rebecca, Glennon Alexa, Zachary Ivan. BA, Princeton U., 1971; MA, U. Pa., 1974, MD, 1977. Diplomate Am. Bd. Psychiatry and Neurology. Intern in pediatrics Yale New Haven Hosp., 1977-78; resident in psychiatry Mass. Gen. Hosp., Boston, 1978-80; resident in child psychiatry Children's Hosp. Med. Ctr., Boston, 1980-82; dir. gen. residency tng. dept. psychiatry Mass. Gen. Hosp., Boston, 1990—; assoc. dir. continuing edn. Dept. Psychiatry Mass. Gen. Hosp., Boston, 1982—, dir. child psychiatry residency tng., 1984—, pvt. practice of psychiatry, 1982—. Contbr. numerous articles to profl. jours. Recipient Kenneth Appel Award in Psychiatry U. Pa. Med. Sch., 1977, Lowenberg Award in Pediatrics U. Pa., 1977, Dunlop Award in Psychiat. Research Mass. Gen. Hosp., 1980. Mem. Am. Assn. Dirs. Psychiat. Residency Tng., Am. Acad. Child & Adolescent Psychiatry, Am. Psychiat. Assn. Home: 80 School St Acton MA 01720-3626 Office: Mass Gen Hosp Dept Psychiatry Bulfinch 3 Boston MA 02114

BERESTON, EUGENE SYDNEY, dermatologist; b. Balt., Feb. 21, 1914; s. Arthur and Sarah Bertha (Hillman) B.; m. Marion Ableman, Jan. 15, 1942 (dec. May 1975); children: Linda Bereston Katz, David, Michael; m. Bertha G. Kaufman, June 7, 1980; stepchildren: Felix Kaufman, Bruce Kaufman. A.B., Johns Hopkins U., 1933; M.D., U. Md., 1937; M.Sc., U. Pa., 1945, D.Sc., 1955. Diplomate Am. Bd. Dermatology. Intern Meml. Hosp., Johnstown, Pa., 1937-38, Mercy Hosp., Balt., 1938-39; resident in dermatology U. Pa., Phila., 1939-40, Montefiore Hosp., N.Y.C., 1940-41; practice medicine specializing in dermatology Balt., 1946—; faculty U. Md., 1946—, prof. medicine in dermatology, 1972—; instr. dermatology Johns Hopkins U., 1946-60; chief dermatology Mercy Hosp., 1968—; part-time chief dermatology VA Hosp., Washington, 1977-83; cons. dermatology VA Hosp. Balt., 1951-76, Spring Grove State Hosp., 1952-82. Bd. dirs., chmn. Religious Sch., Temple Oheb Shalom, 1960-72, trustee, 1977-80. Served to maj. M.C. AUS, 1941-46, PTO. Recipient research grant U.S. Army, 1951-57, award Ner Israel Rabbinical Coll., 1970. Fellow ACP, Am. Acad. Dermatology, Royal Soc. Health (Eng.); mem. AMA, Am. Legion (comdr. 1971-73), Dermatology Found., Md. Dermatol. Soc., Royal Soc. Medicine (affiliate mem.), Md. Med. Soc., Balt. City Med. Soc. Clubs: Civitan (bd. dirs. Balt. chpt. 1964-78), Johns Hopkins, Suburban. Home: 7 Slade Ave Apt 221 Baltimore MD 21208-5227 Office: 22 E Eager St Baltimore MD 21202-2536

BEREZDIVIN, ROBERT, electronics and systems executive; b. Havana, Cuba, July 18, 1945; came to U.S., 1960.; s. Morris and Sara (Scheiner) B.; m. Yibis M. Buenaver; children: Bryan, Janice. BS, U. Fla., 1965, MS, 1966; PhD, U. Calif., Berkeley, 1972. Latin Am. fellow Tufts U., 1972-73; asst. prof. Cen. U. Venezuela, Caracas, 1973-75; rsch. fellow U. Cin., 1974-75; mem. tech. staff Inco, Inc., McLean, Va., 1975-77; scientist Sci. Applications Internat. Corp., McLean, 1977-78; staff to v.p./gen. mgr. E-Systems Ctr. for Advanced Planning & Analysis, McLean, Va., 1978-82; mgr. Advanced Systems, Amecom Div. Litton Systems, College Park, Md., 1982-90, dir. Advanced Systems, Amecom Div., 1990—; adj. prof. George Mason U., 1980-82, U. Md., 1984—. Speaker in field; contbr. articles profl. jours. Coach Neighborhood Athletic Assn., Great Falls, Va., 1982—. Ford Fdn. Fellow, 1965. Mem. Inst. Elec. and Electronic Engrs., Am. Inst. Physics, Assn. Old Crows, Sigma Xi, Great Falls Swim and Tennis Club. Jewish. Home: 1123 Trotting Horse Ln Great Falls VA 22066-2012 Office: Litton Amecom 5115 Calvert Rd College Park MD 20740-3898

BEREZIN, MARTIN ARTHUR, retired psychiatrist; b. Wrentham, Mass., Sept. 14, 1912; s. Samuel and Fannie (Fliegleman) B.; m. Evelyn Polan, Jan. 14, 1942; children: Jane, Robert, Charles. BS, Boston U., 1934, MD, 1937. Diplomate Am. Bd. Psychiatry and Neurology. Intern Mars Meml. Hosp., Boston, 1937-39; resident Medfield State Hosp., Harding, Mass., 1939-40; prof. med. sch. Harvard U., Boston, 1947-79, prof. emeritus, 1979—; staff physician Beth Israel Hosp., Boston, 1947-87, McLean Hosp., Belmont, Mass., 1951-87; ret., 1987; tng. analyst Boston Pscyhoanalytic Soc., 1965-80. Editor: Geriatric Psychiatry, 1965; contbr. articles to profl. jours. Col. U.S. Army, 1940-46. Fellow Am. Pscyhiat. Assn. (Weinberg award 1987); mem. Am. Psychoanalytic Assn., Phi Beta Kappa. Home: 241 Perkins St # 105C Jamaica Plain MA 02130-4002

BERG, HOWARD C., biology educator; b. Iowa City, Iowa, Mar. 16, 1934; s. Clarence P. and Esther M. (Carlson) B.; m. Mary E. Guyer, Dec. 19, 1964; children—Henry G., Alexander H., Elena C. B.S. in Chemistry, Calif. Inst. Tech., Pasadena, 1956; A.M. in Physics, Harvard U., 1960, Ph.D. in Chem. Physics, 1964. Jr. fellow Harvard Soc. Fellows, Cambridge, Mass., 1963-66; asst. prof. dept. biology Harvard U., Cambridge, 1966-69, assoc. prof. dept. biochemistry and molecular biology, 1969-70, prof. dept. cellular and developmental biology, 1986—; assoc. prof. to prof. dept. molecular, cellular and developmental biology U. Colo., Boulder, 1970-79; prof. div. biology Calif. Inst. Tech., Pasadena, 1979-86; mem. Rowland Inst. Sci., Cambridge, 1986—. Author: Random Walks in Biology, 1983; contbr. articles to profl. jours. Fulbright fellow, 1956-57; NSF Sci. Faculty Devel. awardee, 1978-79; recipient Biol. Physics prize, Am. Phys. Soc., 1984. Mem. Am. Phys. Soc., Biophys. Soc., Am. Soc. Microbiology, Am. Soc. Biol. Chemists, AAAS, N.Y. Acad. Sci., Nat. Acad. Sci., Am. Acad. Arts and Sci. Office: Harvard Bio Labs 16 Divinity Ave Cambridge MA 02138-2097 Office: Rowland Inst Sci 100 Cambridge Pky Cambridge MA 02142-1297

BERG, IVAR ELIS, JR., social science educator; b. Bklyn., Jan. 3, 1929; s. Ivar Elis and Hjordis (Holmgren) B.; m. Calli J. Smallwood, Feb. 16, 1991; 1 child, Geoffrey Sverre. AB, Colgate U., 1954; postgrad., U. Oslo, Norway, 1954-55; PhD, Harvard U., 1959; MA (hon.), U. Pa., 1979. Asst. prof. to prof. sociology Columbia U., N.Y.C., 1959-75; dean faculties Columbia U., 1969-71; prof. sociology Vanderbilt U., Nashville, 1975-79; Justin Potter prof. bus. Vanderbilt U., 1983-84; prof. and chmn. dept. sociology U. Pa., Phila., 1979-83, prof. sociology/dean of coll., 1984-89, dean social sci., 1989—; cons. Chancellor of Higher Edn., Trenton, N.J., 1982-89, Pres.'s Commn. on Crime, Washington, 1966-67; chmn. coll. svcs. Coll. Bd., N.Y.C., 1989—. Author: Great Training Robbery, 1970, Managers and Work Reform, 1978, Work and Industry, 1987; contbr. articles to profl. jours. Conciliator Ad Hoc Com. on Pub. Edn., Hastings-on-Hudson, N.Y., 1967-69. Maj. USMC, 1946-65; ATO. Guggenheim fellow, 1973-74, Rockefeller fellow, 1975-76, Woodrow Wilson fellow, 1954-55. Fellow AAAS, N.Y. Acad. Sci., Internat. Acad. Mgmt.; mem. Am. Sociol. Assn. (coun. mem. 1989-91), Ea. Sociol. Soc. (v.p. 1991), Harvard Club (N.Y.C.), Pres.'s Club of Colgate U., Phi Beta Kappa. Presbyterian. Home: 2501 Christian St # 405 Philadelphia PA 19146-2322 Office: U Pa 113 McNeil Bldg Philadelphia PA 19104

BERG, JEAN HORTON LUTZ, writer; b. Clairton, Pa., May 30, 1913; d. Harry Heber and Daisy Belle (Horton) Lutz; m. John Joseph Berg, July 2, 1938; children: Jean Berg Eselgroth, Julie Berg Mulvey, John Joel. B.S. in Edn, U. Pa., 1935, A.M. in Latin, 1937. Tchr. creative writing Wayne, Pa., 1968—; speaker in field of creative writing. Author 50 books for children and young people, 1950—, articles, stories, poems for young people, articles for adults. Former mem. Health and Welfare Bd., Phila.; former chmn. Main Line Parents Council. Recipient U. Pa. Alumni award of merit, 1969, Follett award for beginning-to-read book, 1961, Disting. Alumni award Friends' Cen. Sch., 1978, medallion City of Phila.; named Disting. Dau. of Pa., 1990. Mem. ASCAP, LWV (Disting. Dau. of Pa. award 1990), Authors Guild, Authors League, Nat. League Am. Pen Women, Phila. Childrens Reading Round Table. Home: 207 Walnut Ave Wayne PA 19087-3422

BERG, JOHN CONRAD, political science educator; b. Louisville, Nov. 19, 1943; s. William G. and Mary E. (DeBardeleben) B.; m. Emily S. Perkins, Nov. 29, 1969; children: Andrew C., Thomas W., Katherine M. BA in English, U. Wis., 1964; PhD in Polit. Sci., Harvard U., 1975. Instr. govt. Suffolk U., Boston, 1974-75, asst. prof. govt., 1975-80, assoc. prof. govt., 1980-85, prof. govt., 1985—; acting chair dept. govt. Suffolk U., 1989; mem. liaison adv. bd. The Washington Ctr.; chair spl. projects com. Boston-Cambridge Ministry in Higher Edn.; bd., chair edn. com. John Coleman Wright, Jr. Meml. Scholarship. Contbr. articles to profl. jours. Grantee Everett McKinley Dirksen Congl. Leadership Rsch. ctr., 1988-89. Mem. AAUP, New Eng. Polit. Sci. Assn. (John Donovan award), N.Y. State Polit. Sci. Assn. (award 1989), Am. Polit. Sci. Assn., Am. Soc. Pub. Adminstrn., Nat. Soc. Internships and Experiential Edn. (chair New Eng. regional conf. planning com. 1986, mem., chair faculty spl. interest group 1985-88), Caucus for a New Polit. Sci. (treas., newsletter editor). Home: 22 Rockwell St Dorchester MA 02124-4410 Office: Suffolk U Dept Govt Boston MA 02108-2770

BERG, SAUL R., obstetrician, gynecologist, educator; b. Pitts., Apr. 11, 1940; s. Harry S. and Betty H. Berg; m. Rhonda S. Cohen, June 2, 1963; children: Rebecca I., David J., Suzy H. BA, Washington and Jefferson Coll., 1961; MD, W.Va. U., 1965. Diplomate Am. Bd. Ob-Gyn. Intern Allegheny Gen. Hosp., Pitts., 1965-66; resident U. Pitts., 1966-70; pvt. practice, Pitts., 1972—; clin. asst. prof. Magee Women's Hosp., U. Pitts., 1972—; prof. U. Pitts., 1972—. Maj. USMC, 1970-72. Mem. AMA, Pa. Med. Soc., Allegheny County Med. Soc., Pitts. Ob-Gyn Soc. Office: 532 S Aiken Ave Pittsburgh PA 15232-1521

BERGEN, ROBERT LUDLUM, JR., materials scientist; b. Islip, N.Y., Oct. 29, 1929; s. Robert Ludlum and Alice (D'Oench) B.; m. Grace-Elizabeth Field, June 11, 1951; children: Beryl F., Alice D'Oench, Robert Ludlum III, Jennifer U. AB cum laude, Williams Coll., 1951; MS, Cornell U., 1953, PhD, 1955. Various tech. assignments Uniroyal Chem. div. Uniroyal, Inc., Naugatuck, Conn., 1955-68; mgr. plastics and fibers rsch. corp. R&D Uniroyal, Inc., Wayne, N.J., 1969-72; various mgmt. assignments Uniroyal Chem. div. Uniroyal, Inc., Naugatuck, 1972-75; mgr. elastomers R & D Uniroyal, Inc., Wayne, N.J.; group mgr. chems. and polymers R & D Uniroyal Chem. div. Uniroyal, Inc., Naugatuck, 1975-79; dir. corp. R & D Uniroyal, Inc., Middlebury, Conn., 1979-81, dir., rsch., devel. and engring., Engineered Products Group, 1981-84; dir. corp. engring. Uniroyal, Inc., Middlebury, 1985; adj. prof. math. U. New Haven, 1986—; cons. Bethany, Conn., 1986—; mem. adv. bd. Inst. Materials Sci., U. Conn., 1979—; adj. prof. chemistry U. New Haven, 1964-69; chmn. Soc. Plastic Engrs., Engring. Properties, 1970-71. Author: Testing of Polymers-Stress Relaxation Tests, 1966, various publs., 1954-68. Pres. Bethany Conservation Trust, 1979-82; moderator New Haven Assn. of United Ch. of Christ, 1991—. Fellow AAAS; mem. Am. Chem. Soc., Sigma Xi. Home and Office: 79 Lebanon Rd Bethany CT 06524-3033

BERGER, ANITA HAZEL, psychotherapist, adult educator; b. N.Y.C., Mar. 27, 1930; d. Harry William and Sadye (Lauzar) Fink; m. Ramon Francis Berger, May 6, 1951; children: Elizabeth Harrie, Gideon Samuel. BA cum laude, Bklyn. Coll., 1951; MSW, U. Pa., 1953; postgrad., Columbia U., NYU. Diplomate Am. Bd. Examiners in Clin. Social Work; cert. ind. social worker, R.I.; lic. ind. social worker, Mass.; cert. social worker, N.Y. Psychotherapist Jewish Community Svcs. L.I., N.Y.C., 1953-57; psychotherapist, field work instr. Jewish Family Svc., N.Y.C., 1957-60; supr. lower Manhattan social svc. dept., dir. student unit N.Y.C. Housing Authority, 1972-74; asst. prof. SUNY Grad. Sch. Social Work, Buffalo, 1974-75; psychotherapist Ch. Mission of Hope Family Svc., Erie County Mental Health Svcs., Buffalo, 1975-77; pvt. practice Providence, 1978—; instr. Brown Learning Community Brown U., 1988—. Coord. Community Ctr. Art Show, N.Y.C., 1964-71; rep. community planning bd. 2 Congressman Koch's, N.Y.C., 1968-71; mem. adv. com. to bd. dirs. Mental Health Clinic, Buffalo, 1976-77; bd. dirs., chmn. tng. and edn. com., trainer Vols. in Action, Providence, 1979-85; mem. R.I. adv. com. U.S. Commn. on Civil Rights, 1981-85; rep. R.I. Coalition Against Bigotry, 1982-85; mem. allocations and budget com. United Way Southeastern New Eng., Providence, 1981-84; mem. R.I. Gov.'s Adv. Commn. on Women, 1982-85. Recipient Woman of Yr. award Providence Bus. and Profl. Women's Orgn., 1984. Fellow N.Y. State Soc. Clin. Social Work Psychotherapists; mem. Nat. Assn. Social Workers, R.I. Group Psychotherapy Assn. (pres. 1988-89), Alpha Kappa Delta. Jewish. Office: 155 Laurel Ave Providence RI 02906

BERGER, BEATRICE RUTH, healthcare professional; b. N.Y.C., Apr. 26, 1927; d. Isaac and Ida (Katz) Braunstein Laufer; m. Sam Berger; children: Eric E., Roy D. BA summa cum laude, SUNY, New Paltz, 1972; MS in Counseling, So. Conn. State U., 1992; Cert. of Completion, Barbizon Sch. Acting, 1982, N.Y. Sch. Interior Design. Cert. therapeutic recreation dir.; activity dir. cert. Tchr. English Onteora Cen. Sch., Boiceville, N.Y., 1972-74; interior decorate Beatrice Berger Interiors, Trumbull, Conn., 1976-80; tchr. acting Barbizon Sch. Acting, Stamford, Conn., 1980-84; therapeutic recreation dir. Jewish Home for the Elderly Adult Daycare, Fairfield, Conn., 1985-90, St. Vincent's/Barnett Adult Med. Day Program, Bridgeport, Conn., 1987-90, Jewish Home for the Elderly, Fairfield, Conn., 1990—; conductor art appreciation and dancercise classes Jewish Community Ctr., Bridgeport, 1976-84; dancer Confetti Dancers, 1976-80, Joe Vilane Dance Co., 1976-80. Contbr. articles to newspapers and profl. jours.; one woman art exhibits Conn., 1976-84. Mem. cultural affairs com. Jewish Community Ctr., 1975-78. Mem. AACD, Nat. Assn. Activity Profls., Conn. Assn. Therapeutic Recreation Dirs., Am. Fedn. TV and Radio Artists, Conn. Assn. for Counseling and Devel., Assn. for Adult Devel. and Aging, Kappa Delta Pi. Home: 5211 Madison Ave Trumbull CT 06611

BERGER, BONNIE G., sport psychologist, educator; b. Champaign, Ill., May 20, 1941; d. Bernard G. and Mildred W. Berger; 1 son, Stephen Casher. BS, Wittenberg U., 1962; MA, Columbia U., 1965, EdD, 1972. Tchr., George Rogers Clark Jr. High Sch., Springfield, Ohio, 1962-64; supr. phys. edn. Agnes Russell Elem. Sch., N.Y.C., 1964-65; asst. prof. SUNY, Geneseo, 1965-66; asst. prof. Dalhousie U., Halifax, N.S., Can., 1969-71; asst. prof. Bklyn. Coll., 1971-77, assoc. prof., 1978-81, prof., 1982—, dir. Sport Psychology Lab., master degree program in psychosocial aspects of physical activity; cons. sport psychology. Fellow Assn. for the Advancement of Applied Sport Psychology (exec. bd.), Am. Acad. Phys. Edn.; mem. Am. Psychol. Assn., AAHPERD, Internat. Soc. Sports Psychology, N.Am. Soc. Psychology Sport and Phys. Activity, Can. Soc. Psychomotor Learning and Sport Psychology. Author: Free Weights for Women, 1984; contbr. articles to profl. jours., chpts. to books. Home: 20 Waterside Plz New York NY 10010-2612 Office: Bklyn Coll Roosevelt Hall Dept Phys Edn Brooklyn NY 11210

BERGER, BRUCE WARREN, physician, urologist; b. Auburn, N.Y., Sept. 25, 1942; s. Samuel E. and Sally (Schenberg) B.; m. Toni M. LeRoy, Aug. 27, 1966; children: Jill, David. BA, Cornell U., 1964; MD, Upstate Med. Ctr., 1968. Diplomate Am. Bd. of Urology, Nat. Bd. of Med. Examiners. Surg. intern Hosp. U. of Pa., Phila., 1968-69; surgery resident NYU Hosp.-Bellevue (N.Y.) Med. Ctr., 1969-70; resident in urology Johns Hopkins Hosp., Balt., 1972-76; urologist Cohen, Berger, Epstein & Jaskulsky, P.A., Balt., 1976—; assoc. prof. clin. surgery urology U. Md., Balt., 1976—; attending, pres. med. staff Sinai Hosp., 1989-90, bd. dirs.; cons. Loch Raven Vets Hosp.; assoc. attending Balt. County Gen. Hosp., Greater Balt. Med. Ctr., Union Meml. Hosp. Maj. USAR, 1970-72, Vietnam. Mem. AMA, Balt. Med. Soc., Am. Assn. Clin. Urologists, Md. Urologist Assn., Am. Urologist Assn., The Associated Jewish Community Fedn. (chmn. physicians div. 1991—), Alpha Omega Alpha. Office: Cohen Berger Epstein et al 2411 W Belvedere Ave Ste 305 Baltimore MD 21215-5213

BERGER, CHARLES MARTIN, food company executive; b. Wilkes-Barre, Pa., May 2, 1936; s. Edward and Sadie (Zwass) B.; m. Jane Elrod Purdy, June 5, 1960; children: Cary John Aaron, Elizabeth Anne, Valerie Ann. A.B., Princeton U., 1958; M.B.A., Harvard U., 1960. Mktg. mgmt. Procter and Gamble Co., Cin., 1960-64; with H.J. Heinz Co., 1964—; gen. mgr. mktg. U.S.A. div. H.J. Heinz Co., Pitts., 1964-69, dir. corp. planning world hdqrs., 1969-70; mktg. dir. Heinz-London, 1970-72; mng. dir. Plasmon Diet Alim., Spa, Milan, Italy subs. H. J. Heinz Co., 1972-78; pres., chief exec. officer, chmn. Weight Watchers Internat. Inc. subs. H. J. Heinz Co., Jericho, N.Y., 1978—; lectr. Cannregie-Mellon Grad. Sch. Indsl. Adminstrn., 1968-69. Chmn. bd. dirs. Am. Sch. of Milan, 1975-78; bd. dirs. Am. C. of C. in Italy, 1976-78, Buckley Country Day Sch., Manhasset, N.Y., 1983—. Served with U.S. Army, 1960-61. Mem. World Bus. Council. Republican. Jewish. Clubs: Princeton (N.Y.); Concordia (Pitts.); North Shore Country Club (Glen Head, N.Y.). Office: Weight Watchers Internat 500 N Broadway Jericho NY 11753-2111

BERGER, EDWARD BENJAMIN, biofeedback therapist; b. Washington, Sept. 13, 1956; s. Meyer and Dorothy (Platt) B. BS in Psychology, U. Md., 1978, MA in Biomed. Health, 1981. Cert. biofeedback therapist, profl. counselor, stress mgmt. educator, pain mgmt. specialist. Biofeedback therapist Inst. for Behavioral Rsch., Silver Spring, Md., 1978-80, Behavioral Medicine Ctr., No. Va. Psychiat. Group, Fairfax, 1981-90; dir. biofeedback svcs. Behavioral and Phys. Medicine Assocs., Rockville, Md., 1991—. Mem. AACD, Assn. Applied Psychophysiology and Biofeedback, Am. Acad. Pain Mgmt., Am. Pain Soc., Biofeedback Soc. Washington, Md. and Va.

BERGER, EDWARD PAUL, mathematician; b. Passaic, N.J., Mar. 1, 1937; s. Samuel and Tybie (Nordy) B.; m. Linda Baker, Aug. 2, 1959; children: Glenn S., Daniel M. BS, Duke U., 1958, MA, 1959. Instr. maths. U. Nev., Las Vegas, Nev., 1959-60; asst. prof. maths. USN Acad., Annapolis, Md., 1960-64; instr. statistics Kans. State U., Manhattan, 1965-67; stock broker Merrill Lynch, Boston, 1967-75, White Weld & Co., Boston, 1975-78; fin. reporter Sta. WBZ-TV, Boston, 1979-80; prin. Ed Berger & Co., Boston, 1981—; fin. reporter Sta. WEEI, Boston, 1974-79, Sta. WHDH, Boston, 1981-87; bd. dirs. Harbor Adv. Corp., Portsmouth, N.H., Gloucester (Mass.) Stage Co., 1990—. Author, pub. newsletters Boston Five, 1981-88, Numerica Savings, 1982-83, Salem Five, 1983-86, Bank of Newport, 1983-87. Mem. Mass. Bay Transp. Authority Adv. Bd., Boston, 1975-86; trustee Econ. Edn. Coun. Mass., 1980-84. Grad. fellow Duke U., 1959; grantee NSF, 1962, Ford Found., 1978. Mem. Mass. Bar Assn., Duke Club Boston (pres. 1981-83), Duke U. Alumni Bd. (exec. com. 1986-91), Manchester Yacht Club (fin. com. 1978—), Bundy Squash Club (treas. 1980—), U. Club Boston, Sigma Xi, Pi Mu Epsilon. Jewish. Home: 914 Hale St Beverly Farms MA 01915 Office: Ed Berger & Co 40 Court St Boston MA 02108

BERGER, ELLEN TESSMAN, psychologist; b. Berlin, Feb. 3, 1922; came to U.S., 1938; d. Arthur and Regina (Schainthal) Philipsborn; m. Jack Robert Tessman, June 20, 1951 (div. 1961); m. Arthur Victor Berger, Dec. 8, 1967. BA, U. Calif., Berkeley, 1944; PhD, Pa. State U., 1955. Lic. psychologist, Mass. Pre-doctoral intern U. Calif. Psychiat. Inst., San Francisco, 1947-48; postdoctoral intern Judge Baker Child Ctr., Boston, 1956-57, staff psychologist, 1957—; instr. Med. Sch. Harvard U., Boston, 1969—; NIMH postdoctoral rsch. fellow Sch. of Edn. Harvard U. Sch. of Edn., Boston, 1970-71. Contbr. articles to profl. jours. Fellow Mass. Psychol. Assn.; mem. APA, N.Y. Acad. Sci., Sigma Xi. Home: 9 Sparks St Cambridge MA 02138-4711 Office: Judge Baker Childrens Ctr 295 Longwood Ave Boston MA 02115-5794

BERGER, E(VAN) ROY, medical oncologist and hematologist; b. Bklyn., Aug. 2, 1944; s. Theodore Trietsch and Ida (Elion) B.; m. Joan Carol Askins, Mar. 21, 1971; children: Allison Lara, Jessica Karen. BS in Chemistry, Bucknell U., 1966; MD, SUNY, Bklyn., 1970. Diplomate Am. Bd. Internal Medicine, sub-bds. med. oncology and hematology. Intern, resident in medicine Roosevelt Hosp.-Columbia Coll. Phys. and Surg., N.Y.C., 1970-73, fellow in hematology, 1973-74; fellow in med. oncology Meml. Sloan-Kettering Cancer Ctr., N.Y.C., 1974-75; pvt. practice North Shore Hematology-Oncology Assocs. P.C., Port Jefferson/Smithtown, N.Y., 1975—; chmn. tumor bd. Community Hosp. of Western Suffolk, Smithtown, 1977—, St. John's Episcopal Hosp., Smithtown, 1977—; mem. Prostate Cancer Edn. Coun., N.Y.C., 1989—; chmn. Prostate Cancer Oncology Group, Grand Rapids, Mich., 1990—. Contbr. articles to profl. jours. Mem. AMA, Am. Soc. Hematology, Am. Soc. Clin. Oncology, Suffolk County Med. Soc. Office: North Shore Hematology-Oncology 11 Medical Dr Port Jefferson NY 11767

BERGER, FRANK STANLEY, consultant; b. N.Y.C., 1936; s. Ernest A. and Anna (Weiss) B.; m. Judith Kugel, 1966; children: Evan, Stacey. B.A., Queens Coll., 1958; M.B.A., NYU, 1960; postgrad., N.Y. Law Sch., 1961, IBM Edn. Center, 1960. Supr. dept. mktg. and fin. analysis Lever Bros., 1959-61; v.p. fin. and adminstrn. Pacific Enterprises, 1961-62; mem. corp. mktg. staff Joseph E. Seagram & Sons, Inc., 1962-63; mktg. asst. to mgr. cen. div. Calvert Distillers, 1964, asst. mgr. Fla. region, 1965, mgr. N.J. region, 1966-67, asst. mgr. ea. div., 1967-68, mgr. so. div., 1969-70; v.p., gen. sales mgr. Frankfort Distillers, 1970-71, exec. v.p. mktg. and fin., 1972-73; pres. Gen. Wine & Spirits Co., N.Y.C., 1973-76, Seagram Distillers Co., 1976-77; pres., chief exec. officer House of Seagram, 1978-79; dir. Joseph E. Seagram & Sons, Inc., 1974-79; chmn. bd. Quadrillon Investments Inc., 1980-86, Viceroy Imports, Inc., 1981-86; chmn. Hazel Bishop Cosmetics, Paramus, N.J., 1981-87; dir. Majestic PLC, 1988; chmn. Gunneson Group Internat., Inc., 1988—. Trustee N.Y. Hall of Sci.; chmn. N.Y. Lunch-o-Ree Boy Scouts Am., United Jewish Appeal, Gaucho Basketball Assn., Cystic Fibrosis Soc.; exec. com. wine and spirits div. Anti-Defamation League, Pro-Am. tennis sponsor Cerebral Palsy; bd. dirs. Bronfman Found. With AUS, 1958. Mem. AIM, Am. Mgmt. Assn., Am. Mktg. Assn, N.Y. C. of C., Young Pres.' Orgn., Quality and Productivity Mgmt. Assn. Clubs: Advt. of N.Y, N.Y. Sales Execs.

BERGER, HAROLD, lawyer, engineer; b. Archbald, Pa., June 10, 1925; s. Jonas and Anna (Raker) B.; m. Renee Margareten, Aug. 26, 1951; children: Jill Ellen, Jonathan David. B.S. in Elec. Engring. U. Pa., 1948, J.D., 1951. Bar: Pa. 1951. Since practiced in Phila.; judge Ct. of Common Pleas, Phila. County, 1971-72; chmn., moderator Internat. Aerospace Meetings Princeton (N.J.) U., 1965-66; chmn. Western Hemisphere Internat. Law Conf., San Jose, Costa Rica, 1967; chmn. internat. Confs. on Aerospace and Internat. Law, Coll. William and Mary; permanent mem. Jud. Conf. 3d Circuit Ct. of Appeals; mem. County Bd. Law Examiners, Phila. County, 1961-71; chmn. World Conf. Internat. Law and Aerospace, Caracas, Venezuela, Internat. Conf. on Environ. and Internat. Law, U. Pa., 1974, Internat. Confs. on Global Interdependence, Princeton U., 1975, 79; mem. Pa. State Conf. Trial Judges, 1972-80, Nat. Conf. State Trial Judges, 1972—; chmn. Pa. Com. for Independent Judiciary, 1973—; adv. coun. Biddle Law Libr., U. Pa., 1991—. Mem. editorial advisory bd.: Jour. of Space Law, U. Miss. Sch. of Law, 1973—; Contbr. articles to profl. jours. Mem. We the People 200 Com. for Constn. Bicentennial; mem. adv. com. Biddle Law Libr., U. Pa., 1991—. Served with Signal Corps AUS, 1946-48. Recipient Alumnus of Year award Thomas McKean Law Club, U. Pa. Law Sch., 1965, Gen. Electric Co. Space award, 1966, Nat. Disting. Achievement award Tau Epsilon Rho, 1972, Spl. Pa. Jud. Conf. award, 1981. Mem. Inter-Am. Bar Assn. (past chmn. aerospace law com.), Fed. Bar Assn. (chmn. class action and complex litigation com. 3rd cir. 1990—, past nat. chmn. com. on aerospace law, pres. Phila. chpt. 1983-84, mem. nat. exec. coun., past nat. chmn. fed. jud. com., Presdl. award 1970, Nat. Distinguished Service award 1978, nat. com. 1987 bicentennial of U.S. Constn.), ABA (Spl. Presdl. Program medal 1975, past chmn. aerospace law com., mem. state and fed. ct. com., nat. conf. of state trial judges), Phila. Bar Assn. (past chmn. jud. liaison com. 1975, chmn. internat. law com. 1977), Assn. U.S. Mems. Internat. Inst. Space Law Internat. Astronautical Fedn. (former bd. dirs.), Internat. Acad. Astronautics Paris. Office: 1622 Locust St Philadelphia PA 19103-6365

BERGER, HARVEY ROBERT, psychologist; b. Quincy, Mass., Nov. 3, 1927; s. Joel Joseph and Helen Esther (Stone) B.; m. Thelma Lee Cohen, July 11, 1954. BA, Tufts U., 1949, MA, 1950; PhD, U. Mo., 1953. Diplomate Am. Bd. Examiners Profl. Psychology. Psychologist Marblehead (Mass.) Pub. Schs., 1953-79; dir. psychol. svcs. federally assisted programs Salem (Mass.) Pub. Schs., 1967-76; cons. Revere (Mass.) Pub. Schs., 1979-90; nat. svc. officer Jewish War Vets. U.S.A., 1984—; assoc. prof. Salem State Coll., 1963; clin. dir. North Shore Psychol. Counseling and Testing Ctr., 1963-75; pres. Paul Revere Savs. & Loan Assn., 1971-76, William Dawes Realty Corp.; with U.S. Dept. Commerce, 1983-84. Mem. Nat. Commn. on Safety Edn., 1952-54; capt., Mass. comdt. U.S. Naval Cadet Program, 1966-86; col. Gov.'s staff Ky. N.G.; pres. Area Bd. on Mental Health and Retardation, 1975-78; vice chmn. Greater Lynn (Mass.) Coun. for Children, Mass. Office for Children, 1977-78; mem. governance bd. Greater Lynn Community Mental Health Ctr., 1977-90; auditor Rep. City Com., Lynn, 1970-75; pres. Mass. Am. Legion Coll., 1964-66; pres. NEA Mut. Fund; mem. congl. adv. bd. Am. Security Coun.; chmn. bd. NEA Income Fund; trustee Ida C. Romanow Fund, Jewish Community Rels. Coun. of Greater Boston; pres. Congregation Chevra Tehillim; diplomat World Jewish Congress. With U.S. Army, 1945-47. Sch. Alcohol Studies fellow Yale U., 1957, John F. Kennedy Libr. fellow. Fellow Am. Assn. Mental Retardation, Am. Orthopsychiat. Assn., Royal Soc. Health, NEA (life, Disting. Svc. award), VFW (life), DAV (life), Am. Women in Torah (life, patron and benefactor), Am. Psychol. Assn., Soc. for Personality and Social Psychology, Nat. Assn. Sch. Psychologists (life), Nat. Assn. Sch. Counselors, Mass. Schoolmasters Club (life), Am. Psychology-Law Soc., Soc. for Advancement Social Psychology, Soc. for Psychol. Study Social Issues, Am. Security Coun. Found. (congl. adv. bd.), Soc. Behaviorists, Religious Zionists Am. (life), Mass. Bar Assn., Am. Legion (life), Mil. Order Purple Heart (life), Navy League (life), U.S. Naval Inst. (life), Nat. Soc. Profs. (life), Am. Assn. Higher Edn. (life), Jewish War Vets. (life, nat. svc. officer 1984—, Disting. Svc. award), Tufts Jumbo Club, Nat. Eagle Scout Assn., Masons (32 deg.), Shriners (fire brigade chaplain), Legion of Honor, Order Eastern Star, Order of the Amaranth (auditor), Phi Beta Kappa, Phi Delta Kappa. Home: 31 Tudor St Lynn MA 01902-4617 Office: John F Kennedy Fed Bldg Boston MA 02203 also: 380 Westminster Mall Providence RI 02903

BERGER, HOWARD STEPHEN, psychiatrist; b. N.Y.C., Apr. 18, 1941; s. Morris Marvin and Lillian (Richel) B.; m. Frances Erica Rosen; children: Daniel, Jeffrey. BA, Amherst Coll., 1962; MD, U. Rochester, 1966. Med. intern U. Pitts., 1966-67; surgeon USPHS, 1967-69; resident in psychiatry Sch. Medicine Boston U., 1969-72; assoc. dir. psychiatry inpatient svc. Boston City Hosp., 1972-73; asst. attending psychiatrist McLean Hosp., Belmont, Mass., 1973-75; chief of psychiatry The Meml. Hosp., Worcester, Mass., 1975-82; assoc. prof. psychiatry Med. Sch. U. Mass., Worcester, 1979—; clin. instr. in psychiatry Med. Sch. Harvard U., Boston, 1973—; chairperson psychiat. div. The Med. Ctr. of Cen. Mass./Meml., Worcester, 1982-91; pvt. practice Worcester, 1991—; bd. dirs. Cen. Mass. Health Systems Agy., 1986-88; mem. bd. corporators Worcester Fights Back, 1990—. Mem. Temple Emanuel, Worcester. Fellow Am. Psychiat. Assn.; mem. Mass. Psychiat. Soc., Mass. Med. Soc., Am. Acad. Psychiatrists in Alcoholism and Addictions. Home: 65 Kinnicutt Rd Worcester MA 01602-1548 Office: 25 Burncoat St Worcester MA 01605-2903

BERGER, MELVYN STUART, mathematics professor; b. Bklyn., Aug. 23, 1939; s. Abraham and Hilda (Heller) B.; (divorced); 1 child, Emily Miriam; m. Diane Helen Kaiser, Dec. 25, 1977; 1 child, Elisabeth JoAnna. BA, U. Toronto, Can., 1961; MA, Yale U., 1963, PhD, 1964. From asst. to assoc. prof. U. Minn., Mpls., 1964-69; from assoc. to full prof. Grad. Sch. of Sci. Yeshiva U., N.Y.C., 1969-78; prof. U. Mass., Amherst, 1978—; dir. Ctr. for Applied Math., U. Mass., Amherst, 1980-91. Author: book, monograph Perspectives in Nonlinearity, 1968, monograph Nonlinearity & Functional Analysis, 1977, Mathematics of Nonlinear Phenomena, 1990; editor: Maxwell Sesquicentennial, 1984; contbr. 100 articles to profl. jours. NSF Rsch. grantee, 1964-91; recipient Innovative Tech. Rsch. award NSF, 1983. Mem. Am. Math. Soc. Jewish. Home: 345 Elm St Northampton MA 01060-2829 Office: U Mass Dept Math Amherst MA 01003

BERGER, MIRIAM ROSKIN, creative arts therapy director, educator, therapist; b. N.Y.C., Dec. 9, 1934; d. Israel and Florence (Frankel) Roskin; m. Meir Berger, July 16, 1967 (div. June 1981); children: Jonathan Israel. Student, Barnard Coll., 1952-53; BA, Bard Coll., 1956; postgrad., CCNY, 1956-58, NYU, 1981—. Alumni dir. Bard Coll., Annandale-on-Hudson, N.Y., 1958-59; dance therapist Manhattan Psychiatric Ctr., N.Y.C., 1959-60; performer, educator Jean Erdman Theater of Dance, N.Y.C., 1959-62; dir. adult program Hebrew Arts Sch., N.Y.C., 1964-68; faculty Dance Notation Bur., N.Y.C., 1974-75, 77; asst. prof. dance therapy program NYU, 1975—, acting dir. dance therapy program, 1991; dir. creative arts therapies Bronx Psychiatric Ctr., N.Y.C., 1970-90; leader internat. workshops on arts therapy, Gt. Britain, France, Sweden, Brazil, Italy, Yugoslavia, and Holland. Producer off-Broadway The Coach with the Six Insides, 1962-63; author, producer Non-Verbal Group Process, 1978; co-editor Am. Jour. Dance Therapy, 1991; led dance therapy session Senate Hearing on Aging, 1992; contbr. articles to profl. jours. Bd. dirs. Theater Open Eye, 1978-82, v.p. bd. trustees, 1982-89, pres., 1989—. Recipient NYU scholarship, 1981, Best Paper award Med Art World congress on Arts and Medicine, 1992. Mem. Am. Dance Therapy Assn. (founder, bd. dirs. 1967-76, v.p. 1974-76, credential com. 1976, 82, keynote speaker nat. conf. 1991), Acad. Registered Dance Therapists, Am. Orthopsychiat. Assn. Home: 2 Horizon Rd Fort Lee NJ 07024-6525 Office: NYU 35 W 4th St New York NY 10012-1120

BERGER, OSCAR, artist; b. Presov, Eperjes, Czechoslovakia, May 12, 1901; came to U.S., 1928, naturalized, 1955; s. Henry and Regina (Berger) B.; m. Ann Arany I. Varga, Feb. 9, 1937. Art study, in Europe. Cartoonist world celebrities drawn from life; sketched meetings at League of Nations, Geneva, 1925, House of Commons, London, 1935-45, San Francisco Conf. of UN for N.Y. Times and Daily Telegraph, London, 1945, UN confs., 1945-89, UN gen. assemblies, 1946-90; work represented in permanent collections Library of Congress, Nat. Portrait Gallery, Met. Mus., also pvt. collections and museums.; author: Tip and Top, 1933, A La Carte, 1948, Aesop's Foibles, 1949, Famous Faces, 1950, My Victims, 1952, I Love You, 1960, The Presidents, 1968; contbr. to Am., European publs.; portrait subjects include: Winston Churchill, Eleanor Roosevelt, Queen Elizabeth II, Prince Philip of Eng., Bernard Shaw, H.G. Wells, Robert Frost, King Paul I of Greece, Gen. de Gaulle, King Baudouin, King Feisal, Emperor Haile Selassie, Gorbachev, Gromyko, Premier Kruschev, Premier Indira Gandhi, Pope Pius XII, Pope Paul VI, Anna Pavlova, Toscanini, Prof. Einstein, Jacqueline Kennedy Onassis, Pres. Pompidou, Alexei Kosygin, Molotov, Brezhnev, Chancellor Brandt, Gen. Carlos P. Romulo, Premier Golda Meir, Pres. Tito, Anwar Sadat, last 12 U.S. presidents, from Calvin Coolidge to George Bush (all portraits drawn from life). Club: Nat. Press (Washington). Address: Berkeley House 120 Central Park South New York NY 10019

BERGER, ROBERT CANAVAN, religious studies educator; b. N.Y.C., June 4, 1951; s. Milton Robert and Eleanor Florence (Canavan) B. BS, Manhattan Coll., 1973; MS in Edn., Monmouth Coll., 1978; MDiv, Princeton U., 1988; D Ministry, Drew U., 1990. Tchr. Christian Bros. Acad., Albany, N.Y., 1973-75, Lincroft, N.J., 1976-85; asst. prof. religious studies Manhattan Coll., Bronx, N.Y., 1988—. Roman Catholic. Home: 4415 Post Rd Bronx NY 10471-3499 Office: Manhattan Coll Bronx NY 10471

BERGERON, BRUCE JOSEPH (IKE BERGERON), business educator; b. Keene, N.H., Jan. 20, 1953; s. Marshall Lucien and Janet Irene (Russell) B.; m. Maureen Patricia Miller, Nov. 24, 1978; children: Joseph Anthony, Colleen Anne. BSBA, Northeastern U., 1976; vocat. teaching cert., Keene State Coll., 1979; MBA, Plymouth State Coll., 1989. Cert. bus. tchr.; cert. vocat. bus. tchr. Acctg. clk. Kingsbury Machine Tool Corp., Keene, N.H., 1973, 74, Stride Rite Corp., Boston, 1975; athletic trainer Keene High Sch., 1976-79, tchr. assoc., 1977-78; vocat. bus. tchr. Southeastern Vt. Career Edn. Ctr., Brattleboro, 1979—; bus. instr. Community Coll. Vt., Brattleboro, 1980—; founder banking and fin. svcs. program, 1st student run br. bank Community Coll. Vt., Brattleboro; chmn. supervisory com. Windham County Vt. Edn. Assn. Credit Union, Putney, 1980—. Auditor Wingham S.E. Edn. Assn., Brattleboro, 1984—; advisor Brattleboro chpt. Future Bus. Leaders Am., 1980—; mem. state adv. com. Mentor Program U. Vt., Burlington, 1985—; treas. Brattleboro Boys Youth Basketball Program, 1990—; coach Brattleboro Little League, 1990—; mem. elem. com. on space problems Brattleboro Town Sch. Bd., 1988-90. Daute Competitive grantee Vt. Dept. Edn., 1990. Mem. NEA, Am. Vocat. Assn. (region 1 Vocat. Program award of Yr. 1991), Nat. Bus. Tchrs. Assn., Vt. Vocat. Assn. (ctr. rep., 100 percent membership awards 1986-91, Vt. Vocat. Tchr. of Yr. 1991), New Eng. Bus. Tchrs. Assn., Vt. Bus. Tchrs. Assn., Vt. Edn. Assn. Roman Catholic. Office: Southeastern Vt Career Edn Ctr Fairgroung Rd Brattleboro VT 05301

BERGERON, LIN PAUL, credit union executive; b. Rochester, N.H., Nov. 16, 1948; s. Lucien Etienne and Catherine Estelle (Johnson) B.; m. Deborah Kathleen Flynn, Jan. 8, 1977; children: Joshua Michael, Brian Lin. BS, U. N.H., 1976. Advanced advisor in ins. V.p. Bergeron Ins., Rochester, 1977-86, Holy Rosary Credit Union, Rochester, 1986—. Dir. Friends of U. N.H. Hockey, Durham, 1989—, Rochester Youth Hockey, 1991—. With USN, 1968-72. Mem. Ind. Agts. N.H. (coms. 1979-85), N.H. Credit Union League (coms. 1989—), Rotary (pres. Rochester 1987-88). Democrat. Office: Holy Rosary Credit Union 50 Brock St Rochester NH 03867-4404

BERGERON, YVETTE TUCKER, bookkeeping service owner; b. Atlanta, Mar. 11, 1944; d. Clinton James and Rita E. (Demby) Tucker; m. Jack P. Bergeron Sr., June 24, 1961; children: Jack P. Jr., Susan Vandine, Michael W., Denise Brogan. Student, Pa. State U., 1971-72, Bucks County Community Coll., 1980-87. Operator Mighty Bite Computer Ctr., Phila., 1981; owner Bergeron Bookkeeping Svcs., Lansdale, Pa., 1983—; on-call cons. Consolidated Concepts, Inc., Kimberton, Pa., 1988-92. Leader, neighborhood chmn. Gir Scouts U.S.A., Allentown, Pa., 1971-75; vol. musician, author newsletter Pa. State Nursing Home, Allentown, 1974-76. Mem. DAR, Am. Assn. Profl. Bookkeepers, United Daus. of Confederacy. Home and Office: Bergeron Bookkeeping Svc 2041 Hollis Rd Lansdale PA 19423

BERGESEN, CHRISTOPHER ECHOLS, data base developer; b. Rangoon, Burma, Dec. 25, 1952. BS, George Washington U., 1976, MS, 1980. V.p. Utility Data Inst., Inc., Washington, 1981—. Contbr. articles to profl. jours. Office: Utility Data Inst Inc 1700 K St NW Ste 400 Washington DC 20006-3817

BERGETHON, PETER ROALD, medical educator; b. Providence, Nov. 3, 1955; s. Kaare Roald and Katherine (Lind) B.; m. Elcinda Lou McCrone, May 7, 1983; 1 child, Kristin Elizabeth. BA, Williams Coll., 1977; MD, Jefferson Med. Coll., 1983. Diplomate Am. Bd. Internal Medicine. Rsch. instr. in biochemistry Sch. of Medicine, Boston U., 1986-89, rsch. asst. prof. biochemistry, 1990—, teaching fellow in neurology, 1991—. Co-author: Biophysical Chemistry: Molecules to Membranes, 1990; co-contbr. articles to profl. jours. NIH grantee, 1986; recipient Whitaker Found. Health Sci. award, 1988. Mem. AAAS, Am. Chem. Soc., Am. Acad. Neurology (jr.), Electrochem. Soc., Inc. Office: Boston City Hosp Neurol Unit 818 Harrison Ave Roxbury MA 02118-2999

BERGEVINE, GEORGE JOHN, educational agency administrator; b. Attleboro, Mass., Sept. 1, 1948; s. George C. and Muriel A. (Bora) B.; m. Nancy J. Melton, Aug. 18, 1972; children: Cory A., Kyle M. BA, Hope Coll., 1970; MEd, U. Vt., 1975. Tchr. Attleboro (Mass.) Sch. System, 1970-73; grad. asst. U. Vt., Burlington, 1973-75, mem. adj. faculty, 1975-80; cons. tchr. Rutland S.W. Supts. Union, Poultney, 1975-80, dir. spl. edn., 1978-80; dir. spl. edn. Manchester (N.H.) Schs., 1980-86; exec. dir. Regional Svcs. and Edn. Ctr., Milford, N.H., 1986—; instr. Coll. of St. Joseph, Rutland, Vt., 1978-80; cons. Claremont (N.H.) Schs., 1978; mem. profl. standards bd. N.H. Dept. Edn., 1992—. Vice chmn. long-range planning com. Candia (N.H.) Sch. Dist., 1988, chmn. facilities com., 1989, mem. sch. bd., 1991-94. U. Vt. fellow, 1973-75. Mem. ASCD, Coun. Exceptional Children, N.H. Spl. Edn. Adminstrs. (treas. 1987-89, pres. 1989-91). Office: Regional Spl Edn Consortium 6 Medlyn St Milford NH 03055-4907

BERGEY, GREGORY KENT, neurology educator, neuroscientist; b. Bryn Mawr, Pa., Nov. 9, 1949; s. Robert Harr and Kathryn (Schmidt) B.; m. Stefanie Friday Antonakos, Aug. 27, 1972; children: Alyssa Noelle, Alexander Christian. AB, Princeton U., 1971; MD, U. Pa., 1975. Diplomate Am. Bd. Psychiatry and Neurology, diplomate internal medicine. Intern internal medicine Yale U., New Haven, 1975-76, resident internal medicine, 1975-77; fellow neurophysiology Lab. Devel. Neurobiology Nat. Inst. Child Health and Human Devel., NIH, Bethesda, Md., 1977-79, 82; resident neurology Johns Hopkins, Balt., 1979-83; assoc. prof. U. Md. Sch. Medicine, Balt., 1989—; dir. Md. Epilepsy Ctr. Md. Epilepsy Ctr., Balt., 1988—. Contbr. articles to med. jours. Bd. dirs. Epilepsy Assn. Md., Balt., 1984—, pres.-elect, 1991—. Lt. comdr. USPHS, 1977-79, 81-82. Mem. Soc. for Neurosci., Am. Acad. Neurology, Am. Epilepsy Soc. Office: 5310 Tilbury Way Baltimore MD 21212-3541 Office: U Md Sch Medicine Dept Neurology 22 S Greene St Baltimore MD 21201-1544

BERGLEITNER, GEORGE CHARLES, JR., investment banker; b. Bklyn., July 16, 1935; s. George Charles and Marie (Preitz) B.; m. Betty Van Buren, Oct. 29, 1966; children—George Charles III, Michael John, Stephen William. B.B.A., St. Francis Coll., Bklyn., 1959; M.B.A., Coll. City N.Y., 1961; Ph.D. in Bus. Adminstrn. (hon.), Colo. State Christian Coll. Dir. instl. sales A.T. Brod & Co., N.Y.C., 1965-66; dir. instl. sales Weis, Voisin & Cannon, Inc., N.Y.C., 1966-67, C.B. Richard, Ellis & Co., N.Y.C., 1967-68; pres. Stamford (N.Y.) Fin. Co., also bd. dirs.; pres. M.J. Manchester & Co., Fashion & Time, Inc., B.J.B. Graphics, Inc., First Coinvestors, Inc., Smart Fit Foundations, Inc., Jay Co., Computer Holdings Corp., Ltd., Delhi Mfg. Corp.; pres. Delhi Chems., Inc., Walton; chmn. bd. dirs. Delhi Industries, Delhi Mfg., Inc., Delhi Internat., Inc., Luxemborg; bd. dirs. Alpha Capital Corp., Am. Energy Mgmt. Corp., Stamford Fin., Electronic Tax Ctrs., Inc., Leonia Enterprises, L.I. Venture Capital Group, L.I.V.G.; sponsor N.Y. Venture Group. Chmn. Franciscan Fathers Devel. Program, 1967-71; mem. President's Council, Franciscan Spirit award, 1959—; pres. South Kortright Central Sch.; chmn. No. Catskills Econ. Devel. Council.; Regent St Francis Coll.; bd. dirs. Econ. Devel. Council Delaware County, Printing Trade Sch., Community Hosp., Stamford, N.Y., Western Catskills Community Revitalization Council, Inc. Served with U.S. Army, 1952-55. Paul Harris fellow Rotary Internat.; recipient St. Francis Coll. Alumni Fund award, 1965, Del. County Youth award, 1991, John F. Kennedy Meml. award, 1972, Internat. award for Svc. to Investment Commn., 1972, Youth Bur. award, 1991; named Stamford Citizen of Yr., 1992. Mem. Conn. Venture Capital Assn., Venture Assn. N.J. (bd. dirs.), Security Traders Assn. N.Y., Nat. Security Traders Assn., Assn. Investment Bankers, Otsego-Delaware Bd. Realtors (P.A.F. chmn.), Stamford C. of C. (pres. 1991-92), Am. Legion, Am. Inst. Mgmt., Cath. War Vets., Honor Legion N.Y.C. Police Dept., CCNY Alumni Assn. Republican. Home: Red Rock Rd Stamford NY 12167 Office: Stamford Fin Bldg Stamford NY 12167

BERGLUND, ALICE MAE, neuroanatomist, translation company executive; b. Medford, Mass., Jan. 19, 1943; d. Allan D. and Mary E. (Turner) Russell; m. Robert A. Keeley, Sept. 7, 1966 (div. 1974); 1 child, Elise C.; m. Arthur E. Berglund, Mar. 25, 1975; 1 child, Joan M. BA, U. Mass., 1964; postgrad., U. Calif., Berkeley, 1964-66; ALM, Harvard U., 1985, PhD, 1990. Sci. libr., translator NRC, Inc., Cambridge, Mass., 1967-70; transl. mgr. Etymon Assn., Medford, Mass., 1970-73; dir. Internat. Transl. Co., Boxford, Mass., 1973-91; pres. InTransCo., Inc., Lynnfield, Mass., 1991—; teaching fellow Harvard U. Med. Sch., Boston, 1983-86, rsch. fellow, 1986-90; postdoctoral fellow MIT, Cambridge, 1990—; rsch. assoc. Eaton-Peabody Lab., Mass. Eye and Ear Infirmary MIT, Boston, 1990—. Contbr. articles to profl. jours. Mem. Am. Transl. Assn., N.Y. Acad. Sci., Soc. for Neurosci. Home: PO Box 239 Lynnfield MA 01940-0239 Office: Eaton Peabody Lab MEEI 243 Charles St Boston MA 02114-3004

BERGMAN, DAVID LEWIS, English educator; b. Fitchburg, Mass., Mar. 13, 1950; s. Stanley S. and Rita (Fergenson) B. AB, Kenyon Coll., 1972; MA, Johns Hopkins U., 1974, PhD, 1977. Prof. English Towson (Md.) State U., 1978—. Author: Cracking the Code, 1985 (Elliston prize), Gaiety Transfigured, 1991; editor: Reported Sightings: John Ashbery's Art Chronicles, 1989. Mem. MLA, Phi Beta Kappa. Home: 3024 N Calvert St Apt 5C Baltimore MD 21218-3921 Office: Towson State Univ Dept English Towson MD 21204

BERGMAN, GARRETT EDWARD, pharmaceutical company executive; b. San Luis Obispo, Calif., Aug. 31, 1946; s. Sydney and Anna (Shapiro) B.; m. Marilyn Harriet Malamud, Dec. 25, 1967; children: Ben Haim, Aviva Rachael. BS, Pa. State U., 1967; MD, Jefferson Med. Sch., 1969; MBA, Temple U., 1990. Asst. prof., assoc. prof., prof. Med. Coll. Pa., Phila., 1975-88, med. co-dir. humanities program, 1978-88; assoc. dir. clin. rsch. Rorer Central Rsch. div. Rorer Group Inc., Ft. Washington, Pa., 1988-89; dir. med. and sci. affairs Armour Pharm. Co. div. Rhône-Poulenc Rorer Inc., Collegeville, Pa., 1989—; clin. prof. Med. Coll. Pa., Phila., 1988—; chief com. in childhood cancer Am. Cancer Soc., Phila. divsn., 1985-90, bd. dirs., 1990-92; pres. med. staff Med. Coll. Pa., Phila., 1987-88. Contbr. articles to profl. jours., chpts. to books. Bd. dirs. Parents Anonymous Pa., 1982-89, Fanconi Anemia Rsch. Found., 1988—. Maj. U.S. Army, 1971-73. Recipient Lindback Disting. Teaching award Christina R. and Mary F. Lindback Found., 1987. Fellow AAP, Am. Acad. Pediatrics, Am. Soc. Hemotology, Am. Soc. Pediatric Hemotology; mem. Alpha Omega Alpha. Democrat. Jewish. Home: 9 Shirley Rd Narberth PA 19072-2015 Office: Armour Pharm Co 500 Arcola Rd # 1200 Collegeville PA 19426-3907

BERGMAN, KLAUS, utility executive, lawyer; b. Nurnberg, Fed. Republic Germany, May 24, 1931; came to U.S., 1936; s. Ludwig and Else (Wertheimer) B.; m. Barbara E. Redman, Jan. 30, 1954; children: Nicole V.F., Cathryn L. AB, Columbia U., 1953, LLB, 1955. Bar: N.Y. Assoc. Mudge Rose Guthrie & Alexander, N.Y.C., 1959-65; asst. gen. counsel Am. Electric Power Service Corp., N.Y.C., 1965-71; v.p. Allegheny Power System, Inc., N.Y.C., 1971-82, exec. v.p., 1982-85, pres., chief exec. officer, dir., 1985—; chief exec. officer, dir. various subs.; bd. dir. Ohio Valley Electric Co., Piketon Ohio. Lt. (j.g.) USCGR, 1956-59.

BERGMAN, MARK STEVEN, lawyer; b. Washington, June 27, 1956; s. Paul M. and Arlene (Stern) B.; m. Kainan Cramer, Jan. 6, 1990. BA, Bowdoin Coll., 1978; MA, U. Va., 1979; JD with honors, Am. U., 1982.

Bar: N.Y. 1983, DC 1991. Assoc. Paul, Weiss, Rifkind, Wharton & Garrison, N.Y.C., 1982-90, ptnr., 1991—, resident U.S. ptnr. in Paris, 1992—. Contbr. articles to profl. jours. Mem. ABA, Am. Soc. Internat. Law, Assn. of Bar of City of N.Y. Office: Paul Weiss Rifkind Wharton & Garrison 1285 Ave Of The Americas New York NY 10019-6028

BERGMAN, NAOMI MIRON, data processing consultant; b. Birmingham, Ala., Sept. 11, 1963; d. Robert James and Diane Beth (Goldblatt) Miron. Student in econs. and statistics, U. Rochester, 1985. Sr. staff mem. Arthur Andersen & Co., Stamford, Conn., 1985-87; cons. data processing Advance Publs. Systems Group, Newark, 1987-90, Vision Cable Communications, Paramus, N.J., 1990—. Tutor Literacy Vols. Am., Hackensack, N.J.; mem. steering com. Vol. Ventures, Hackensack. Mem. Cabledata Users' Group, Nat. Cable TV Assn. Office: Vision Cable Communications 15 E Midland Ave Fl 3D Paramus NJ 07652-2926

BERGMAN, RICHARD ISAAC, consulting company executive; b. Bklyn., Jan. 18, 1934; s. Joseph and Clara (Menchel) B.; m. Judith Hyman, June 24, 1956 (div. 1974); children: Deborah Jill, Susan Bergman Hackett; m. Victoria Smalley, June 9, 1987. S.B., MIT, 1955, S.M., 1956. Devel. engr. Exxon Research, Linden, N.J., 1956-60; mem. adj. faculty N.J. Inst. Tech., Newark, 1957-58; dir. engring. Princeton Chem. Research (N.J.), 1960-67; exec. v.p. Systemedics, Inc., Princeton, 1967-80; pres. Savant Assocs., Inc., Princeton, 1980—; exec. dir. White House Task Force on Workplace Safety and Health, Washington, 1977-78; pres. Project Masters, Inc., Princeton, 1980—; mem. vis. com. med. dept. MIT, Cambridge, Mass., 1973-83, 86-88; Whitaker Coll., 1979-85, dir. Response Analysis Corp., Princeton, 1970-77. Contbr. articles to profl. jours.; patentee in field. Mem. Am. Inst. Chem. Engrs. (past chmn. N.J. sect.), Am. Chem. Soc., AAAS, Am. Pub. Health Assn., N.Y. Acad. Sci., Sigma Xi. Home: 134 Leabrook Ln Princeton NJ 08540-3622 Office: Savant Assocs Inc PO Box 329 Princeton NJ 08542-0329

BERGMAN, ROBERT PAUL, museum administrator, art historian, educator, lecturer; b. Bayonne, N.J., May 17, 1945; s. Abe and Ethel (Leitner) B.; m. Marcelle Posnak, June 30, 1971, 1 child, Maggie. B.A., Rutgers U., 1966; M.F.A., Princeton U., 1969, Ph.D., 1972. Asst prof. history of art U. Rochester, N.Y., 1971-72; asst. prof. history of art Princeton U., N.J., 1972-76; assoc. prof. Harvard U., Cambridge, 1976-81; adj. prof. Johns Hopkins U., Balt., 1981—; dir. Walters Art Gallery, Balt., 1981—; vis. instr. Lincoln U., fall 1968. Author: The Salerno Ivories, 1980; cons. editor: Art Bull.; contbr. articles and revs. in art field. Vol. various mayoral and gubernatorial coms., Balt.; fundraiser for various causes. Guggenheim fellow; Dumbarton Oaks fellow; Fulbright fellow; Henry Rutgers scholar. Fellow Am. Acad. in Rome; mem. AAUP, Assn. Art Mus. Dirs. (trustee, pres.), Coll. Art Assn., Internat. Ctr. of Medieval Art (bd. dirs.), Soc. Archtl. Historians, Medieval Acad. Am., Am. Arts Alliance (bd. dirs., treas.), Phi Beta Kappa. Office: Walters Art Gallery 600 N Charles St Baltimore MD 21201-5185

BERGMANN, ARTHUR M., writer, investor, former county official, former newspaperman; b. N.Y., Nov. 24, 1927; s. Augustus H. Bergmann; m. Marilyn Elaine Hyde; children by previous marriage: Susan M., Joel M., Kathy G., Jonathan M. BS in Polit. Sci. and Pub. Adminstrn., Empire State Coll., SUNY, Old Westbury, 1974; M in Pub. and Gen. Adminstrn., L.I.U., 1979. With N.Y. Herald Tribune, 1945-63; asst. news editor Riverhead News, 1949-50; Suffolk County (N.Y.) corr. for N.Y.C. newspapers, 1949-63; news editor Moriches (N.Y.) Tribune, 1950-51; mem. staff Newsday, 1951-71, Suffolk County polit. editor, columnist, 1965-71; chief dep. Suffolk County Exec., Hauppauge, N.Y., 1972-79. Chmn., Suffolk Criminal Justice Coordinating Coun., 1975-79, Arson Action Com.-Suffolk Arson Task Force, 1978-79; mem. Juvenile Justice Task Force, 1975-77, MTA Permanent Citizens Adv. Com., 1978-79; adv. coun. N.Y. State Crime Victims Compensation Bd., 1978-79; trustee Suffolk Acad. Medicine, 1976. With USAAF, 1946-47. Recipient Disting. Svc. award United Jewish Appeal, 1976; Pub. Adminstrn. award C. W. Post Coll., 1977; Disting. Svc. plaque L.I. Assn. Commerce & Industry, 1977; Exemplary Svc. award Empire State Coll., SUNY, 1981; nominated for Pulitzer prize (2). Mem. Acad. Polit. Sci., Soc. Silurians, Am. Legion, Moriches Yacht Club (past commodore, Center Moriches, N.Y.), Palm Beach Yacht Club (Fla.), Pi Alpha Alpha. Address: Waterview Tower Ste 1906 400 N Flagler Dr West Palm Beach FL 33401

BERGMANN, DONALD GERALD, pharmaceutical company executive; b. N.Y.C., Aug. 13, 1949; s. Edgar Frank and Dorothy Bertha (Kurtz) B.; m. Kathy Jeanne Dumont, Sept. 4, 1976; children: Karen Ann, Kim Jeanne. BS, Mich. State U., 1972; PhD, Ohio State U., 1978. Researcher UCLA, 1978-81; project leader Burroughs-Wellcome Co., Kansas City, Kans., 1981-83; scientist Genentech, Inc., South San Francisco, Calif., 1983, ops. mgr., 1983-87; sr. project mgr. Genentech, Inc., South San Francisco, 1987-88; dir. biopharmaceutical mfg. SmithKline Beecham Pharms., Phila., 1988-91, group dir. biopharm. mfg. and quality assurance, 1991—. Contbr. articles to profl. jours. and publs. Fellow Nat. Cancer Inst., 1978-80; grantee Nat. Cancer Inst., Am. Cancer Soc. Mem. Internat. Soc. Pharm Engring. (lectr.), Pharm. Mfrs. Assn. (lectr.). Home: 784 Tree Ln West Chester PA 19380-2000 Office: SmithKline Beecham Pharms PO Box 1539 King Of Prussia PA 19406

BERGQUIST, ARNOLD EVERETT, accountant; b. Jamestown, N.Y., July 10, 1935; s. Nils Gottfried and Irene Lucy (Swanson) B.; m. Marilyn Ruth Cook, Aug. 17, 1957: children: Michael J., Anne Mary, John Eric. BS in Acctg., Gannon U., 1958. CPA, Pa., N.Y. From staff acct. to sr. acct. Root, Spitznas & Smiley, CPAs, Erie, Pa., 1960-65; ptnr. Brown Schwab Bergquist & Co., CPAs, Erie, 1966—. Active Erie Conf. on Community Devel., 1975—; mem. adv. coun. Gannon U., Erie, 1988—; corporator St. Vincent Health Ctr., Erie, 1991—; chair fin. com. Erie Corps Salvation Army, 1970—; treas. Millcreek Community Hosp., Erie, 1981-87, bd. trustees, 1975-87. 1st lt. U.S. Army, 1958-60. Recipient Disting. Alumni award Gannon U., 1990. Mem. AICPA, Pa. Inst. CPAs (pres. Erie chpt. 1981-82), Nat. Assn. Accts. (bd. dirs.), Aviation Country Club, Kahkwa Club Erie, Erie-Maennerchor Club. Republican. Roman Catholic. Office: Brown Schwab Bergquist & Co 3800 W 12th St Erie PA 16505-3352

BERGQUIST, JAMES MANNING, history educator; b. Council Bluffs, Iowa, Feb. 1, 1934; s. Reuben Neil and Irene Mary (Norton) B.; m. Joan Marie Solon, May 17, 1969; children: John Norton, Charles James. BA, U. Notre Dame, 1955; MA in History, Northwestern U., 1956, PhD in History, 1966. Instr. history Coe Coll., Cedar Rapids, Iowa, 1961-63; instr. history Villanova (Pa.) U., 1963-66, asst. prof., 1966-69, assoc. prof., 1969-86, prof., 1986—. Contbr. articles on Am. social history and immigration to profl. jours., chpts. to books. Trustee Balch Inst. for Ethnic Studies, Phila., 1988—. With M.I., U.S. Army, 1956-58,. Fellow NEH, summers 1967, 77, 80. Mem. AAUP (pres. Pa. div. 1988-90), Am. Hist. Assn., Orgn. Am. Historians, Am. Studies Assn., Immigration History Soc., Am. Assn. for State and Local History, Ethnic Studies Assn. Phila. (pres. 1980-82). Democrat. Roman Catholic. Home: 217 Devon Blvd Devon PA 19333-1616 Office: Villanova U History Dept Villanova PA 19085

BERGREEN, LAURENCE ROGER, writer; b. N.Y.C., Feb. 4, 1950; s. Morris Harvey and Adele (Gabel) B.; m. Elizabeth Freeman, June 1, 1975; children: Nicholas, Sara. BA, Harvard U., 1972. Corres. Newsweek Internat., 1973-74; asst. editor The New Leader, N.Y.C., 1974; asst. to pres. Mus. of Broadcasting, N.Y.C., 1977-80; faculty New Sch. for Social Rsch., N.Y.C., 1980-81. Author: As Thousands Cheer: The Life of Irving Berlin, 1990, James Agee: A Life, 1984, Look Now, Pay Later: The Rise of Network Broadcasting, 1980 (1st prize Ralph J. Gleason Music Book award, 1990, ASCAP-Deems Taylor award, 1991). Recipient First Fiction award Ingram Merrill Found., 1986. Mem. PEN Am. Ctr., Authors Guild of Am., Harvard Club of N.Y. Office: 40 E 94th St Apt 5E New York NY 10128

BERGSON, HENRY PAUL, association executive; b. Boston, Dec. 22, 1942; s. Harry Jr. and Elizabeth (Paul) B.; m. Jacqueline Hope Wilson, June 11, 1966; children: Susan Elizabeth, Abigail Anne. BS, U. N.H., 1966. Various mgmt. positions Fed. Signal, Blue Island, Ill., 1970-78; dir. mktg. Tork, Mt. Vernon, N.Y., 1978-83; v.p. ops. G.C.S. Svc., Chappaqua, N.Y., 1983-85; exec. v.p. Nat. Elec. Mfrs. Reps. Assn., Armonk, N.Y., 1985—, also bd. dirs.; bd. dirs. Elec. Industry Joint Coun.; fire commr. Katonah Fire Dist., 1992—. Contbr. articles to profl. jours. Elder 1st Presbyn. Ch. of Katonah, N.Y., 1991—; chief Katonah (N.Y.) Vol. Fire Dept., 1980-84, v.p., pres. 1984-90, bd. dirs. 1990—; mem. Bedford Transp. Com., 1984-86. Capt. U.S. Army, 1967-70. Decorated Bronze Star with two oak leaf clusters, Air medal with three oak leaf clusters, Purple Heart, Army Commendation medal, Vietnam Medal of Honor. Mem. Nat. Elec. Mfrs. Assn., Nat. Assn. Elec. Distributors. Republican. Home: PO Box 182 Katonah NY 10536-0182 Office: NEMRA 200 Business Park Dr Armonk NY 10504-1700

BERGSTEIN, STANLEY FRANCIS, horse racing executive; b. Pottsville, Pa., June 19, 1924; s. Milton Isidore and Esther Miriam (Rosenzweig) B.; m. June Carol Hanna, June 4, 1950; children: Alfred M., Lisa R. BS, Northwestern U., 1947. Writer James S. Kearns Assoc., Chgo., 1947-50, CBS TV, Chgo., 1956-57; racing sec. Sportsman's Pk., Chgo., 1957-60; exec. dir. Harness Racing Inst., Chgo., 1961-68; exec. v.p. Harness Tracks Am., Morristown, N.J., 1961—; pres. Am. Horse Publs., Lexington, Ky., 1969-70; trustee Hall of Fame of Trotter, Goshen, N.Y., 1980—. Editor Hoof Beats Mag., Columbus, Ohio, 1968-75; columnist Harness Horse Mag., Harrisburg, Pa., 1979-90, Times: in Harness Mag., 1990—. Named Horseman of Yr. Horseman and Fair World Mag., Lexington, 1972; recipient Proximity award U.S. Harness Writers, Goshen, 1978, Writers Hall of Fame award, 1986, Hall of Fame of Trotter award Trotting Horse Mus., Goshen, 1987, Internat. award Racing Commrs., 1990, Amtote Internat. award, 1992. Mem. U.S. Trotting Assn. (v.p. publicity 1968-75). Office: Harness Tracks Am 35 Airport Rd Morristown NJ 07960-4642

BERGSTROM, ALBION ANDREW, army officer, federal official; b. Salem, Mass., Sept. 2, 1947; s. Eric Hjalmar and Helen Lawrence (Andrew) B. BA in Polit. Sci., Colo. State U., 1969; MA in Pers. Mgmt., Cen. Mich. U., 1978; grad. Command and Gen. Staff Coll., U.S. Army, 1982; postgrad., Harvard U., 1989-90. Commd. 2d lt. U.S. Army, 1969, advanced through grades to col., 1991; platoon leader, aide de camp, Vietnam, 1970-71; co. comdr., Ft. Hood, Tex., 1974-75; bn. exec. officer, Erlangen, Fed. Repubic Germany, 1980-81, assignment officer, 1983-85, bn. comdr. 1-35 Armor Bn., 1986-88; cols'. assignment officer Pers. Command, Alexandria, Va., 1988-89; chief, officer div. DCS pers., The Pentagon, Washington, 1990—. Program chmn. Pinewood Forest Assn., Lake Ridge, Va., 1982-84; del. N.H. Rep. convs., 1966, 68. Decorated Bronze Star, Purple Heart, Bronze medal, Order of St. George; Nat. Security fellow John F. Kennedy Sch. Govt., Harvard U., 1989-90. Mem. VFW, Armor Assn., Assn. U.S. Army, 1st Cavalry Div. Assn., Masons, Shriners, Phi Sigma Delta, Zeta Beta Tau. Congregationalist. Avocations: photography, cross-country skiing. Home: 12700 Knightsbridge Dr Lakeridge VA 22192-5158

BERGSTROM, JOAN MARGOSIAN, education educator; b. Boston, July 20, 1940; d. Sally (Chooljian) Walden; m. Gary Leonard Bergstrom, Sept. 3, 1966; 1 child, Craig. BS in Edn., Tufts U., 1962; MS in Ednl. Psychology, U. Mich., 1963; PhD in Edn., U. Mass., 1972; postgrad., Northwestern U., 1979. Tchr. lab sch. U. Mich., Ann Arbor, 1962-63; instr. U. R.I., Kingston, 1963-64; asst. prof. Cornell U., Ithaca, N.Y., 1964-66; prof. grad. sch. Wheelock Coll., Boston, 1972—, coord. grad. program in Singapore, 1991; pres. The Activities Club Inc., 1988. Author: School's Out--Help Your Child Have a Fund and Fabulous Summer, 1986, School's Out--Now What? Help Your Child Have a Fabulous Summer!, 1988, School's Out--Now What? Choices For Your Child's Time--Afternoons, Weekends, Vacations, 1984, 2d edit., 1990, School's Out! It's Summer, 1992 (with C. Bergstrom) All the Best Contests for Kids, 1988, 3d edit., 1992 (Parents' Choice award in Doing and Learning 1990), (with R. Margosian) Teaching Young Children: Basic Concepts and Resources, 1976, (with L. Joy) Going to Work? Choosing Care for Infants and Toddlers, 1981, (with R. Margosian, F. Olson) Enhancement of Growth and Learning in Early Childhood, 1976, (with J. Gold) Checking Out Child Care: A Parent Guide, 1975, transl. Spanish, 1976, transl. Chinese, 1977, Swedish Day Nurseries: Focus on Programs for Infants and Toddlers, 1974, (with G. Morgan) Issues in the Design of a Delivery System for Preventative Services to Children and Their Families, 1975; contbr. chpts. to books, articles to jours. Bd. dirs. Prospect Hill Parents' and Children's Ctr., 1983—; overseer Boys and Girls Club, 1985—. Recipient Disting. Svc. citation Tufts Alumni Assn., 1976; named Outstanding Young Woman in Mass., State of Mass., 1971. Mem. Activities Club (pres. 1987—). Home: 303 Marsh St Belmont MA 02178-1714

BERGSTROM, WILLIAM HUGO, physician, educator, researcher; b. Bay City, Mich., Jan. 1, 1921; s. Victor William and Jessie Broadfoot (Masterton) B.; m. Charlotte Stuart, June 19, 1944; children: William, John, Mary Linn, David. BA, Amherst Coll., 1942; MD, U. Rochester, 1945. Prof. pediatrics SUNY Health Sci. Ctr., Syracuse, 1952-77, prof. emeritus pediatrics, 1977—. Author textbook chpts.; contbr. articles to profl. jours. Maj. USAF, 1955-57. Markle Found. scholar, 1954. Mem. Am. Pediatric Soc. Office: SUNY Health Sci Ctr Dept of Pediatrics 750 E Adams St Syracuse NY 13210-2306

BERIGAN, RORY ANN, apparel manufacturing company executive; b. Omaha, Mar. 31, 1954; d. George Thomas Berigan and Dorothy Jeanne (Robert) Jackson. BA summa cum laude, Creighton U., 1979, MS, 1983. Spl. projects coord. Father Flanagan's Boys' Home, Nebr., 1985; assoc. devel. officer, 1986; dir. mktg. McDonald's Corp., Omaha, 1986-87; account mgr. Fox/Ektra Photofinishing, Omaha, 1987; regional coord. Ektra Photofinishing, Orlando, Fla., 1987-88; nat. account mgr. Ektra/Qualex Inc., Durham, N.C., 1988-90; nat. account sales mgr. footware div. Reebok Internat. Ltd., Stoughton, Mass., 1990—. Algur H. Meadows fellow So. Meth. U., 1979. Mem. Photog. Mktg. Assn., NAFE, Nat. Assn. Children with Learning Disabilities, Am. Speech and Hearing Assn. (cert.). Republican. Roman Catholic. Office: Reebok Internat Ltd Corp Hdqrs Stoughton MA 02072

BERINSTEIN, WILLIAM PAUL, business executive; b. Elmira, N.Y., Dec. 25, 1935; s. Benjamin M. and Ann (Newhouse) B.; m. Phyllis Altman, Aug. 22, 1964; children: Benjamin M., Dorothy C. BA, U. Mich., 1957. Pres. Polk Properties, Inc., Syracuse, N.Y., 1960-89; prin. HLB Assocs. Investments, Syracuse, 1973—, ANB Assocs. Investments, Syracuse, 1964—; pres. Cortland Cinema Corp., Syracuse, 1967—, Cornell Theatres, Inc., Syracuse, 1973—; owner Euclid Enterprises, Syracuse, 1973—; bd. dirs. Frigo Design, Inc., Syracuse, Advanced DC Motors, Inc., Syracuse, ACI, Inc., Syracuse. Trustee Temple Soc. of Concord, Syracuse, 1968-74, 1992—. Named to Hall of Fame, Syracuse Men's Bowling Assn., 1990. Mem. Onondaga County Bowling Coun. (sec. 1985—), N.Y. State Bowling Proprs. Assn. (bd. dirs. 1958-65), Bowling Proprs. Assn. Am. (bd. dirs. 1958-64). Jewish. Home: 4820 Candy Ln Manlius NY 13104-1604 Office: 1067 W Genesee St Syracuse NY 13204-2244

BERK, MINDY LYNN, controller; b. N.Y.C., Nov. 27, 1965; d. Sidney D. and Judith G. (Krieger) B. BBA in Acctg., Am. U., 1987. CPA, N.Y. Sr. acct. Ernst & Young, N.Y.C., 1987-90; asst. contr. Harry Winston, Inc., N.Y.C., 1990—. Mem. AICPA, N.Y. State Soc. CPAs. Office: Harry Winston Inc 718 5th Ave New York NY 10019-4195

BERK, PEGGY FAITH, public and financial relations consultant; b. N.Y.C., Feb. 3, 1951; d. Stanley and Naomi Elaine (Herskowitz) B.; divorced; 1 child, Mason Ben-Yair. Student, NYU, 1968-71, New Sch. for Social Rsch., 1971-73. News editor Herald Newspapers, N.Y.C., 1972-73; mktg. liaison U.S. Dept. Commerce, Tel Aviv, Israel, 1973; mgr. fgn. currency dept. Bank Le'umi BM, Arad, Israel, 1974-75; exec. v.p. Peter Small & Assocs., N.Y.C., 1978-81; prin., pres. Strategic Communications, N.Y.C., 1981—; cons. sr. v.p. The Rowland Co., N.Y.C., 1984-85; prin., pres. BFP Internat. Inc., N.Y.C., 1987—; cons. Coun. on Fin. Aid to Edn., N.Y., 1979-81, Global Link, Tokyo, 1986—, Vols. for Israel, 1991—, nat. bd. dirs., 1992—; bd. dirs. New Networking Aquisition Corp., Hartford, Conn., 1988-90. Contbr. numerous news articles. Bd. dirs. Child Net, Inc., Mass., 1987—; steering com. Am. Mus. Fin. History, 1989—. Mem. Citiwomen, Women's Am. ORT, U.S. Amateur Snowboard Assn. Office: Strategic Communications 276 5th Ave New York NY 10001-4509

BERKE, STEVEN LEIGH, oral surgeon; b. Balt., Oct. 1, 1954; s. Harvey Robert and Marie Ellene (Harris) B.; m. Nola Ann Wolf, June 20, 1987; 1 child, Megan. BA in Biology, Bucknell U., 1976; DMD, U. Pa., 1980. Diplomate Am. Bd. of Oral and Maxillofacial Surgery. Intern Cook County Hosp., Chgo., 1982-83; resident Woodhull Med. Ctr., Bklyn., 1983-85; chief resident Woodhull Med. Ctr./Interfaith Med. Ctr., Bklyn., 1985-86; teaching fellow NYU Coll. Dentistry, 1985-86; practice dentistry specializing in oral and maxillofacial surgery Norwich, Conn., 1986—; mem. med. staff W.W. Backus Hosp. Served with USPHS, 1980-82. Fellow Am. Assn. Oral and Maxillofacial Surgeons, Am. Coll. Oral and Maxillofacial Surgeons, Am. Dental Soc. Anesthesiology; mem. ADA, Internat. Coll. Oral Implantology, Conn. Soc. Oral and Maxillofacial Surgeons, Rotary Internat. Republican. Home: 130 New London Tpke Norwich CT 06360-2624

BERKELHAMMER, GERALD, chemical company executive; b. Newark, Feb. 3, 1931; s. Max and Cecelia (Schein) B.; m. Sheila Rosenson, June 20, 1954; children: Jill Barbara, Frederick Andrew, Paul David. AB, Brown U., 1952; PhD, U. Wash., 1957. Research chemist Am. Cyanamid Co., Stamford, Conn., 1957-60; group leader Am. Cyanamid Co., Pearl River, N.Y., 1960-61; group leader Am. Cyanamid Co., Princeton, N.J., 1961-70, mgr. organic synthesis Agrl. Research div., 1970-85, dir. chem. discovery Agrl. Research div., 1985-91; exec. dir. chem. discovery agrl. rsch. div. Am. Cyanamid Co., Princeton, 1991—. Patentee 41 antiparasitic and insecticidal inventions. Mem. Bd. Edn. Ewing Township, N.J., 1966-68. Mem. AAAS, Am. Chem. Soc., Sigma Xi, Phi Lambda Upsilon. Club: Brown U. (sec. 1964-66, v.p. 1967-68, pres. 1968-69). Home: 147 Laurel Rd Princeton NJ 08543-0400 Office: Am Cyanamid Co PO Box 400 Princeton NJ 08543-0400

BERKELL, DIANNE E., special education educator; b. Newark, Mar. 12, 1948. BS, Boston U., 1970, EdM, 1971; PhD, Hofstra U., Hempstead, N.Y., 1981. Tchr. Adams Sch., N.Y.C., 1970-72; tchr. Half Hollow Hills Sch. Dist., Dix Hills, N.Y., 1972-75, LD Specialist, 1975-76; program coord. tchr. training Northport Schs., Northport, N.Y., 1978-80; adminstr. Suffolk Child Devel. Ctr., Smithtown, N.Y., 1978-80; prof. C.W. Post Campus Long Island U., Brookville, N.Y., 1981—; dir. of rsch. The Nassau Ctr. for the Developmentally Disabled, Woodbury, N.Y., 1983—. Editor: Transition From School to Work, 1990, Autism, 1992, NERA Researcher newsletter, 1985-87. Recipient Personnel Preparation, Project READDY, U.S. Dept. of Edn., Washington. Mem. N.Y. State Coun. for Exceptional Children (pres., mental retardation div. bd. dirs.), Northeastern Ednl. Rsch. Assn. Office: C W Post Campus LIU Brookville NY 11548

BERKEY, CATHERINE SUSAN, biostatistician; b. Dayton, Ohio, Jan. 23, 1951; d. Harry Elmer and Loveda J. (Allen) Grooms; m. Dennis Dale Berkey, Aug. 24, 1974; children: Cristin, Aaron, Jessica. BA, Miami U., 1973; MA, Boston U., 1975; DSc, Harvard U., 1980. Rsch. assoc. Sch. Pub. Health, Harvard U., Boston, 1980-82, postgrad. fellow Med. Sch., 1982-84, asst. prof. Sch. Dental Medicine, 1984—, lectr. tech. assessment group, 1991—. Contbr. articles to Biometrics, Statistics in Medicine, Annals of Human Biology, Am. Jour. Epidemiology, Community Dentistry & Oral Epidemiology; contbr. chpt. to book. Agy. for Health Care Policy and Rsch. grantee, 1987-90. Mem. Am. Statis. Assn., Am. Math. Soc., Mass. Pub. Health Assn., Am. Pub. Health Assn., Biometric Soc. Office: Harvard U HSDM 188 Longwood Ave Boston MA 02115-5888

BERKEY, DENNIS D., mathematics educator; b. Wooster, Ohio, May 27, 1947; s. William Brice and Mary Louise (Schrock) B.; m. Catherine Grooms, Aug. 24, 1974; children: Cristin, Aaron, Jessica. BA, Muskingum Coll., New Concord, Ohio, 1969; MA, Miami U., Oxford, Ohio, 1971; PhD, U. Cin., 1974. Lectr. U. Cin., 1972-73; instr. Miami U., Oxford, Ohio, 1973-74; asst. prof. math. Boston U., 1974-79, assoc. prof. math., 1979—, dean grad. sch., 1987—, dean liberal arts, 1987—, provost, 1987-91. Author: Calculus: 2d edit., 1983, 88, 3d edit., 1992, Applied Calculus, 2nd edit., 1986, 90, Calculus for Management, 2d edit., 1986, 90. Recipient Metcalf Award for Excellence in Teaching, Boston U., 1978. Mem. Am. Math. Soc., Math. Assn. Am., Soc. for Indsl. and Applied Math. Home: 30 Nobscot Rd Weston MA 02193-1147 Office: Boston U Rm CLA 106 Boston MA 02215

BERKICH, DONALD RODNEY, emergency rescue executive; b. Harrisburg, Pa., Aug. 20, 1946; s. Peter and Carrie Phyllis (MacLeod) B.; m. Jean Elizabeth Hill, Apr. 14, 1973; children: Todd, Amy. AA in Acctg., Harrisburg (Pa.) Area, Community Coll., 1968; BSBA, W.Va. U., 1974. Staff acct. Gen. Waterworks M&S Co., Harrisburg, 1970-74, regional acctg. mgr., 1974-82, dist. acct., 1982-85; div. acct. Empire Kosher Poultry, Inc., Mifflintown, Pa., 1985-87; asst. controller Food Svc. Specialists Co., Mechanicsburg, Pa., 1987; exec. dir. River Rescue of Harrisburg, Inc., 1987—. Mem. steering com. Harrisburg Area healthcare Coalition, 1990—, Capital Area Healthcare Coalition. Mem. Ambulance Assn. of Pa. (treas., bd. dirs. 1988—), Am. Ambulance Assn., Capital Region C. of C. (mem. govt. affairs com. 1989—, benefits subcom., 1989—), Elks, Rotary. Home: 501 Linden St Mechanicsburg PA 17055-2827 Office: River Rescue of Harrisburg 1119 South Cameron St PO Box 2908 Harrisburg PA 17105

BERKLEY, BURTON, judge; b. Chgo., May 10, 1934; s. Ralph Albert and Frieda (Fleischman) Berkowitz; m. Carol Grace Goldberg, Dec. 22, 1955; children: David Saul (dec.), Florence Melissa Berkley-Yokie. AB, Harvard U., 1955, JD, 1958. Bar: Ill. 1958, U.S. Supreme Ct. 1962, N.Y. 1969, D.C. 1978. Asst. atty. gen. Ill. Atty. Gen.'s Office, Chgo., 1958-59; asst. U.S. atty. Dept. of Justice, Chgo., 1959-61; appellate trial atty. Tax Div. Dept. of Justice, Washington, 1961-67; dep. tax counsel GE, N.Y.C., 1967-70; legal advisor NIH HEW, Washington, 1971-72, dep. gen. counsel, 1972-77; spl. counsel to assoc. commr. Office of Hearings and Appeals Social Security Adminstrn., Arlington, Va., 1977-80, dep. chmn. appeals coun. Office of Hearings and Appeals, 1980-88; adminstrv. law judge Office of Hearings and Appeals Social Security Adminstrn., Washington, 1988—. Co-editor: Ethical Issues in Human Genetics, 1973. Mem. ABA, D.C. Bar Assn., Harvard Club (bd. dirs.). Office: Social Security Adminstrn Office Hearings and Appeals 820 1st St NE Ste 950 Washington DC 20002

BERKMAN, JAMES ISRAEL, pathologist laboratory director; b. Cambridge, Mass., Nov. 14, 1913; s. Joseph and Anna (Wallace) B.; m. Harriet N. Noyer, Dec. 6, 1942 (dec.); children: Anthony Steven, Amy Beth. AB, Harvard Coll., 1935; MA, Harvard Grad. Sch., 1936; MD, N.Y. U., 1940. Diplomate Am. Bd. Pathology. From asst. to attending pathologist Montefiore Med. Ctr., N.Y.C., 1948-85; clinical asst. dean SUNY Coll. Med., Bklyn., 1971-80; from chmn. dept. labs. to chmn. emeritus dept. labs. Long Island Jewish Med. Ctr., New Hyde Park, N.Y., 1953—; prof. pathology SUNY, Stony Brook, N.Y., 1971-89; lab. dir. Nat. Health Labs., Plainview, N.Y., 1982-90, N.Y.C., 1985—; profl. lectr. SUNY Coll. Med., 1959—; cons. dept. labs. Queens Hosp. Ctr., N.Y.C., 1986—; cons. pathologist Cath. Med. Ctr., N.Y.C., 1978-86 (honorary pathologist 1986—); cons. pathologist Jewish Geriatric Ctr., N.Y.C., 1975-80. Contbr. numerous articles to profl. jours. Lt. Col. US Army, 1942-45. Recipient Max Ellenberg award N.Y. Diabetec Assn., 1991. Fellow Am. Assn. Pathologists, Am. Soc. Clinical Pathologists, Internat. Acad. Pathology; mem. Harvey Soc., N.Y. Acad. Med. Jewish. Home: 70 E 10th St New York NY 10003-5102 Office: National Health Lab 1015 Madison Ave New York NY 10021-0261

BERKON, MARTIN, artist; b. Bklyn., Jan. 30, 1932; s. Samuel F. and Sara (Hodes) B.; m. Eileen Phyllis Eichel, July 10, 1960. Student, Pratt Inst., 1952; BA, Bklyn. Coll., 1954; MA, NYU, 1959. mem. adj. faculty Fairleigh Dickinson U., 1966, Nassau Community Coll., 1966-67; lectr. City Coll., CUNY, 1968-69; guest lectr. Middlebury Coll., 1977, Nassau Community Coll., 1982.; interviewed Long Island Art Scene, 1986. One man shows Smolin Gallery, N.Y.C., 1962, 20th Century West Gallery, N.Y.C., 1967, Soho Center for Visual Artists, N.Y.C., 1974, Genesis Galleries, N.Y.C., 1978, Adelphi U., Garden City, N.Y., 1983; exhibited in group shows Bklyn. Mus., 1958, Silvermine (Conn.) Guild Artists, 1963, Ohio U. Gallery, 1964, Ball State U., 1965, Wesleyan Coll. at Ga., 1965, Butler Inst. Am. Art, 1965, 67, 69, Aldrich Mus. Contemporary Art, Ridgefield, Conn., 1974, 75, 82, New Britain (Conn.) Mus., 1974, Am. Fedn. Arts traveling show, 1975-77, Meadowbrook Art Gallery Oakland U., Rochester, Mich., and Flint (Mich.) Inst. Art, 1975-76, Firehouse Gallery, Garden City, 1982, Barbara Walter Gallery, N.Y.C., 1982, Spaceport USA, Kennedy Space Ctr., 1985, 87, NASA collection traveling exhbn., Visions of Flight, 1988—; represented in permanent collection Aldrich Mus. Contemporary Art, Texaco Inc., White Plains, N.Y., Pepsico Inc., Somers, N.Y., commd. NASA, 1984, 87, NASA Gallery of Art, Kennedy Space Ctr., Ctr. for Arts, Vero Beach, Fla. Home: 51-25 Van Kleek St Elmhurst NY 11373

BERKOW, IRA HARVEY, author, journalist; b. Chgo., Jan. 7, 1940; s. Harold Grosswald and Shirley (Halperin) B.; m. Dolores Case, Apr. 18, 1978. BA, Miami U., Oxford, Ohio, 1963; MS in Journalism, Northwestern

U., 1964. Reporter Mpls. Tribune, 1965-67; sports columnist, sports editor Newspaper Enterprise Assn., N.Y.C., 1967-76, N.Y. Times, N.Y.C., 1981—. Author: (Oscar Robertson) Golden Year, 1971, (with Walt Frazier) Rockin' Steady, 1974 (Am. Libr. Assn. Best Books of Yr. 1975), Beyond the Dream, 1975, Maxwell Street, 1977, The DuSable Panthers, 1978, (with Rod Carew) Carew, 1979, Red: The Biography of Red Smith, 1986, The Man Who Robbed the Pierre, 1987, Pitchers Do Get Lonely and Other Sports Stories, 1988; editor: Hank Greenberg: The Story of My Life, 1989, (with Jackie Mason) How to Talk Jewish, 1991; writer TV documentary Champions of American Sport, 1983. Recipient Page One award Newspaper Guild, Mpls., 1966, Scipps-Howard Feature award N.Y.C., 1969, N.Y. Pub. Libr. commendation, 1978, AP Sports Editors award, 1982, Disting. Achievement medal Miami U., 1988; nominee ACE awards, 1983, Edgar award, 1988; finalist Pulitzer prize for commentary, 1988. Mem. Baseball Writers Assn. Am., Authors Guild, PEN, Mystery Writers Am. Office: NY Times 229 W 43d St New York NY 10036

BERKOWITZ, A. MENACHEM, accountant; b. Bklyn., Mar. 31, 1962; s. Joseph and Grace (Newman) B.; m. Heidi Z. Gendelman, Mar. 5, 1984; children: Rachael, Esti, Adina. BS magna cum laude, Touro Coll., 1985. CPA, N.Y. Staff acct. Schwartz and Co., N.Y.C., 1983, Joseph Berkowitz, CPA, Bklyn., 1984-88; ptnr. JMB Assocs., Bklyn., 1989—. Cons. Kahal Tefilo Lemoshe, Bklyn., 1991. Office: JMB Assocs 1749-49th St Brooklyn NY 11204

BERKOWITZ, BARRY ALAN, pharmaceutical company executive; b. Brookline, Mass., Dec. 29, 1942; s. Frank and Frances (Richman) B.; m. Barbara, Aug. 4, 1963; children: Lauren, Brian. BS in Pharmacy, Northeastern U., 1964; PhD, U. Calif., San Francisco, 1968. Assoc. dir., pharmacology Smith Kline and Frank, Phila., 1979-83, dir. pharmacology, 1980-83, v.p., 1983-88; chief exec. officer, pres. Magainin Sci., Plymouth Meeting, Pa., 1988-91; chmn. of bd. Magainin Sci., Plymouth Meeting, Pa., 1991—, 1991; adj. prof. Cornell U. Med. Coll., N.Y.C., 1985—; asst. and assoc. mem. Roche Inst. Molecular Biology, 1971-79. Contbr. scientific articles to profl. jours. Postdoctoral fellow Roche Inst. Molecular Biology, Nutley, N.J., 1968-71. Mem. Am. Soc. Pharmacology and Expiremental Therapeutics (chmn. nominating com. 1990-91).

BERKOWITZ, BERNARD JOSEPH, lawyer; b. Newark, Jan. 23, 1945; s. Sigmund and Gertrude (Zimmer) B.; m. Barbara Jean Haddock, Nov. 25, 1970; children: Brian, Gail, Mark. BA, Rutgers U., 1967; JD, Suffolk U., 1970. Assoc. Lewis B. Rothbart, Whippany, N.J., 1971-73, Yanowsky & Rosen, Boonton, N.J., 1973-76, Pressler & Pressler, Pine Brook, N.J., 1976-77; pvt. practice Parsippany, 1977—; ptnr. Berkowitz & Decker, Parsippany, N.J., 1982-87; mcpl. ct. judge Rockaway Boro, 1988—, Netcong Boro, 1991—, Parsippany-Troy Hills Twp., 1983-87; planning bd. atty. Parsippany Planning Bd., 1982-83. Mem. Suffolk U. Law Rev., 1969-70. Mem. Parsippany-Troy Hills Twp. Bd. Adjustment, 1978-82, Parsippany-Troy Hills Twp. Bd. Edn., 1988; bd. dirs. March of Dimes, 1979; v.p. Parsippany-Troy Hills Twp. Little League, 1987-90. Mem. N.J. State Bar Assn., Morris County Bar Assn., Parsippany Area C. of C. (v.p. 1989—), Parsippany Jaycees (pres. 1979-80). Republican. Jewish. Home: 19 Ashwood Pl Parsippany NJ 07054-2261

BERKOWITZ, DAVID ANDREW, healthcare planning company executive, consultant; b. Bklyn., Mar. 21, 1952; s. Charles and Anne (Rovinsky) B.; m. Amy S. Silverman, June 15, 1975; children: Aaron, Leah, Daniel. BS in Biomed. Engring., Rensselaer Poly. Inst., 1974, M Engring. in Biomed. Engring., 1975. Project engr. Automatech Industries, Bridgeport, Conn., 1975-77; pres. Biotech Enterprises, Bridgeport, 1975-77; project engr. ECRI (Emergency Care Rsch. Inst.), Plymouth Meeting, Pa., 1977-79, sr. project engr., 1979-81, cons., 1981-84, sr. cons., 1984-86, v.p. cons. svcs., 1986—; internat. lectr. on tech. mgmt.; expert witness in field; presenter in field; lectr. Bridgeport Engring. Inst., 1975-77. Contbr. articles to sci. jours. Mem. ASME, ASTM (chmn. subcom. on EMS ground vehicles), Assn. for Advancement Med. Instrumentation (subcom. on hemodialysis systems standards renal disease and detoxification com.). Office: ECRI 5200 Butler Pike Plymouth Meeting PA 19462-1241

BERKOWITZ, KENNETH PAUL, public affairs executive; b. N.Y.C., July 7, 1942; s. Max and Flo Berkowitz; married, 1966; children: Mindy, Lori, Gregg. BA, Hunter Coll., 1964; JD, Bklyn. Law Sch., 1967; LLM in Trade Relation, NYU, 1969. Bar: N.Y. 1967, N.J. 1974. Atty., advisor Fed. Trade Commn., N.Y.C., 1967-69; with Hoffmann-LaRoche, Inc., Nutley, N.J., 1970—, v.p., 1974—. Treas., v.p., dir spl. advisor Pharm. Advt. Counsel, N.Y.C., 1973—; bd. trustees via pres. Emanuel Cancer Found., Cranford, N.J., 1987—; trustee Lautenberg Inst. for Cancer Tumorology, N.Y.C., 1988—; bd. dirs. Pub. Affairs Coun., Washington, 1988—, United Way, Essex, New Hudson, N.J., 1989. Recipient Pres.'s award Pharm. Advt. Counsel, 1970's. Mem. ABA, N.J. Bar Assn. (founder, pres. food, drug, cosmetic law sect. 1970's), Pub. Relations Soc. Am. Office: Hoffmann La Roche Inc 340 Kingsland St Nutley NJ 07110-1199

BERKOWITZ, PHILIP JOSEPH, lawyer; b. Bronx, N.Y., Nov. 25, 1965; s. William and Rita F. (Grossman) B. AB, Columbia U., 1988, JD, 1988. Bar: N.Y. 1989. Assoc. Paul, Weiss, Rifkind, Wharton & Garrison, N.Y.C., 1988-92; staff atty. Enforcement Div. Securities and Exch. Commn., Washington, 1992—. Home: Apt 130 1255 N Hampshire Ave NW Washington DC 20036 Office: Securities and Exch Commn 450 5th St NW Washington DC 20549

BERKOWITZ, TERRY, artist, fine arts educator; b. Bklyn.; s. Alfred David and Ruth Anna (Weisberg) B. Cert., Sch. of Visual Arts, 1971; MFA, Sch. of the Art Inst. of Chgo., 1973. Asst. prof. Montclair (N.J.) State Coll., 1982-88; asst. prof. Baruch Coll. CUNY, N.Y.C., 1988-89, assoc. prof. Baruch Coll., 1990—. One-woman shows include P.S.I., Long Island City, 1978, Joseloff Gallery, Hartford (Conn.) Art Sch., 1982, Contemporary Arts Mus., Houston, 1990, Whitney Mus. Am. Art, N.Y.C., 1992; group exhbns. include The Alternative Mus., N.Y.C., 1990, Constrn. in Progress/Lodz, Poland, 1990, Circulo de Bellas Artes, Madrid, 1991. Creative Arts in Pub. Svc. fellow NEA, 1974-75, MacDowell Colony fellow, 1989; Jerome Found. grantee, 1990.

BERKSON, JACOB BENJAMIN, lawyer, writer, conservationist; b. Washington County, Md., Dec. 6, 1925; s. Meyer and Ida Evelyn (Berman) B.; m. Ann Goldstein, June 25, 1955 (div.); children: Daniel Jeremy, Susan Kay, James Meyer. BA, U. Va., 1947, LLB, 1949, JD, 1970; grad., Fed. Exec. Inst., Charlottesville, Va., 1972. Bar: Md. 1949, Va. 1949, U.S. Supreme Ct. 1965, Calif. 1975. Sole practice Hagerstown, Md., 1949-52, 54-65; ptnr. McCauley, Cooey, Berkson & Wright, Hagerstown, 1964-70; dep. gen. counsel U.S. GSA, Washington, 1970-76; pvt. practice law Hagerstown, 1976—; instr. Law Hagerstown Bus. Coll., 1986; trial magistrate, Hagerstown and Washington County, Md., 1951-52; mem. Legis. Coun. Md., 1955-58; del. Md. Legislature, 1955-58; trial magistrate, Hagerstown, 1958-59. Recipient commendation for svc. to U.S. Naval Acad. and pub. interest Chief of Naval Personnel, 1956. Lt. USNR, 1944-46, 52-54. Author: Shingahi Saburo and Short Stories, 1978; contbr. address to Congrl. Record. Scoutmaster local coun. Boy Scouts Am.; organizer, dir. County Youth Conservation Corps; active Big Bros.; bd. dirs. Doub's Woods County Park, Devil's Backbone County Park; assisted in establishment of C&O Canal Nat. Histo. Park, 1954-70; camp sponsor YMCA; adv. Model Youth Legis.; pres. PTA; chmn. Washington County Park Commn., 1961-66. Mem. ABA, Calif. Bar Assn., Va. Bar Assn., Md. Assn. County Civil Attys. (pres., award for svcs. as pres. 1966), Washington County Bar Assn. (pres.), Am. Legion, Hagerstown Club, Lions (pres.). Republican. Jewish. Office: 1419 Potomac Ave Hagerstown MD 21740

BERLAGE, GAI INGHAM, sociologist, educator; b. Washington, Feb. 9, 1943; d. Paul Bowen and Grace (Artz) Ingham; m. Jan Coxe Berlage, Aug. 7, 1965; children: Jan Ingham, Cari Coxe. BA, Smith Coll., 1965; MA, So. Meth. U., 1968; PhD, NYU, 1979. Tchr. math. Piner Jr. High Sch., Sherman, Tex., 1968-69; asst. prof. sociology Iona Coll., New Rochelle, N.Y., 1971-83, assoc. prof., 1983-88, chmn. dept., 1981-90, prof., 1988—; coord. urban studies program, 1984-90; treas. The North Am. Soc. for Sociology of Sports, 1992—. Author: Experience with Sociology: Social Issues in American Society, 1983, Understanding Social Issues: Sociological Fact Finding, 1987, 2d edit., 1990, 3d edit., 1992; editorial bd. Jour. Sport and Social Issues; contbr. articles to profl. jours. Commr. Wilton Commn. on Aging and Social Svcs., 1980-88, chmn., 1982-88; co-chmn. Wilton Task Force on Youth Coun., 1988; chmn. Wilton Task Force Com. for Outreach Program, 1981-82, Wilton Task Force on Day Care, 1983-88; mem. Wilton Task Force for Pub. Health Nursing Assn., 1981-82, Wilton Sport Coun., 1985-88; bd. dirs. Wilton Meals on Wheels, 1983-88; fellow N.Am. Faculty Network of Northeastern Univs. Ctr. for Study of Sport in Soc. Recipient Best Profl. Paper award Third Annual Cooperstown Symposium on Baseball and the Am. Culture. Mem. Am. Sociol. Assn., N.Y. State Sociol. Assn., N.Am. Soc. Sociology of Sport, Inst. Sport and Social Analysis, Internat. Com. Sociology of Sport, Wilton Assn. Gifted Edn. (pres. 1980-81), Internat. Soc. of Sport Psychology, N.Am. Soc. for Sport History Soc. for Am. Baseball Rsch. Office: Iona Coll Dept Sociology New Rochelle NY 10801

BERLEANT-SCHILLER, RIVA, anthropology educator; b. Buffalo, N.Y., Nov. 19, 1935; d. Rudolph Schiller and Sarah (Bookbinder) Lavenda; m. Arnold Berleant, Aug. 1, 1957; children: Jared Daniel, Andrea Berleant Ravitch, Anne Nicole. BA, U. Buffalo, 1956; MLS, L.I. U., 1967; PhD, SUNY, Stony Brook, 1974. Libr. Nassau County Mus. Natural History, Glen Cove, N.Y., 1967-69; lectr. Queensborough Coll., CUNY, Bayside, N.Y., 1974-78; post-doctoral fellow Columbia U., N.Y.C., 1979-80; asst. prof. L.I. U., Greenvale, N.Y., 1978-79; asst. prof. U. Conn., Torrington, 1980-84, assoc. prof., 1985-91, prof., 1992—. Author: Montserrat: A Critical Bibliography, 1991; co-author: A Directory of Business and Financial Services, 1984; co-editor: The Keeping of Animals, 1983; contbr. numerous articles to profl. jours. Freedom writer Amnesty Internat., 1986—; mem. Women's Internat. League for Peace and Freedom, 1959—, Anti-Slavery Internat., London, 1985—. Doctoral traineeship SUNY, 1969-72; dissertation fellow Woodrow Wilson Nat. Fellowship Found., 1972-73; post-doctoral fellow Social Sci. Rsch. Coun., 1979-80; summer fellow Newberry Libr., 1988. Fellow Am. Anthropol. Assn.; mem. Soc. for Feminist Anthropology, Caribbean Studies Assn., Soc. for Caribbean Studies, Assn. Am. Geographers (rsch. grantee 1983), Assn. for the Study for Common Property, Coun. Latin Americanist Geographers. Home: 18 Stonebridge Ln Goshen CT 06756-1107 Office: U Conn Dept Anthropology Torrington CT 06790

BERLET, NANCY WEIR, cultural organization administrator; b. Niskayuna, N.Y., June 8, 1949; d. John Declan and Phyllis Marie (Colls) Weir; m. Bruce Edward Berlet, Apr. 19, 1975; 1 child, Brooke Elizabeth Grace. BA in Elem. Edn., St. Joseph Coll., 1971. Tchr. Corpus Christi Schs., Wethersfield, Conn., 1971-75; sportswriter (1st woman sportswriter hired) The Hartford Courant, Hartford, Conn., 1974-79; cons. Moses Assocs., West Hartford, Conn., 1986-87; freelance writer Glastonbury, Conn., 1980—; exec. dir. Historical Soc. of Glastonbury, 1987—. Author: Historical Soc. of Glastonbury Newsletter, 1987—. Bd. dirs. Jr. League of Hartford, 1988-89, editor newsletter, 1984-86; mem. rep. Greater Hartford Assn. Historic Houses and Mus., Hartford, 1987—, v.p., 1989-91, pres. 1991—; mem. steering com. Glastonbury's Tercentenary Celebration, 1987—; mem. awards com., Conn. League of Hist. Socs., 1991—. Home: 202 Carriage Dr Glastonbury CT 06033-3232 Office: Hist Soc Glastonbury PO Box 46 Glastonbury CT 06033-0046

BERLIN, ALAN DANIEL, lawyer, international legal consultant, real estate executive; b. Bklyn., Oct. 20, 1939; s. Joseph Jacob and Rose (Smith) B.; m. Renee Wellinger, Dec. 22, 1962; children—Nicole Suzanne, Allison Leigh. B.B.A., CCNY, 1960; LL.B., NYU, 1963, LL.M., 1968. Bar: N.Y. 1963. Assoc. Aranow, Brodsky, Bohlinger, Einhorn & Dann, N.Y.C., 1965-68; asst. counsel Gen. Electric Co., N.Y.C., 1968-70; tax counsel Norton Simon Inc., N.Y.C., 1970-77; asst. prof. Pace U. Grad. Sch. Bus., 1977-85; pres. Belco Petroleum Corp., N.Y.C., 1977-88, The Crown Group, White Plains, N.Y., 1988—; spl. cons. to UN Dept. Tech. Cooperation for Devel., 1989—, UN Ctr. for Transnat. Corps., 1990—. Author monographs on fed. income tax. Bd. dirs. Mental Health Assn., Westchester. With U.S. Army, 1963-65. Mem. ABA, Internat. Bar Assn., N.Y. State Bar Assn., Assn. of Bar of City of N.Y., Inter-Am. Bar Assn., Internat. Petroleum Negotiators. Lodge: Masons. Office: 2 Gannett Dr White Plains NY 10604-3404

BERLIN, CHARLES, librarian; b. Boston, Mar. 17, 1936; s. Joseph and Etta (Fox) B.; m. Judith Louise Armet, Mar. 21, 1965; children: Anne D., Jonathan M. B of Jewish Edn., Hebrew Coll., Brookline, Mass., 1956, M Hebrew Lit., 1959; MLS, Simmons Coll., Boston, 1964; AB, Harvard U., 1958, PhD, 1963. Lectr. modern Hebrew Harvard U., Cambridge, Mass., 1962-65; Lee M. Friedman bibliographer in Judaica, head Judaica div. Harvard Coll. Libr., Cambridge, Mass., 1962—, head area studies dept., 1990—; cons. U. Fla., U. Tex., Emory U.; dir. Lucius N. Littauer Found., N.Y.C., 1983—; trustee Hebrew Coll., Brookline, 1962—. Editor: Index to Festchriften in Jewish Studies, 1971, Studies in Jewish Bibliography, History and Literature, 1971, Judaica Librarianship: Facing the Future, 1989. Mem. Assn. for Jewish Studies (treas. 1969-72, exec. sec. 1972—), Assn. Jewish Librs. (pres. 1968-69). Office: Judaica div Harvard Coll Li Widener M Cambridge MA 02138

BERLIN, CHESTON MILTON, JR., pediatrician, educator; b. Pitts., Mar. 28, 1936; s. Cheston Milton and Gladys Irene (Vance) B.; m. Anne Risher, July 9, 1960; children: Jean Vance, Douglas Cheston, Alexander Lindsay, Gordon Johnston. BA, Haverford (Pa.) Coll., 1958; MD, Harvard U., 1962. Intern Boston Children's Hosp., 1962-63, resident in pediatrics, 1965-67; asst. prof. pediatrics U. Ala. Sch. Medicine, Birmingham, 1967-68, George Washington U. Sch. Medicine, Washington, 1968-71; assoc. prof. pediatrics Pa. State U. Coll. Medicine, Hershey, 1971-75, prof. pediatrics and pharmacology, 1975-86, univ. prof. pediatrics, prof. pharmacology, 1986—; pediatric panel mem. U.S. Pharmacopeia, Rockville, Md., 1970-75, 80—. Contbr. articles to profl. jours. Sr. asst. surgeon USPHS, 1963-65. Markle Found. scholar, 1969, 74; recipient Cheston M. Berlin Alumni Svc. award Pa. State U. Coll. Medicine, 1987. Mem. Am. Acad. Pediatrics, Am. Soc. Experimental Pharmacology and Therapeutics, Am. Soc. Clin. Pharmacology and Therapeutics, Am. Pediatric Soc., Phi Beta Kappa, Alpha Omega Alpha, Alpha Epsilon Delta. Episcopalian. Office: MS Hershey Med Ctr Dept Pediatrics PO Box 850 Hershey PA 17033-0850

BERLIN, MEREDITH RISE, editor; b. Bronxville, N.Y., Nov. 22, 1955; d. Marvin and Seena (Goldsmith) Brown; m. Jordan Stuart Berlin, Aug. 13, 1988; children: Gregory Samuel, Lauren Julia. BS, Emerson Coll., 1976. With circulation-subscription World Bus. Weekly, N.Y.C., 1978-79; feature editor Soap Opera Digest, N.Y.C., 1979-82, editor-in-chief, 1982-91; editor-at-large, 1991—, Soap Opera Digest, N.Y.C.; exec. producer Soap Opera Awards NBC-TV, L.A., 1988-91; commenttor WCBS-TV Noon News, 1987—; commentator NBC's House Party; producer, journalist Afternoon TV Show, 1982. Recipient 3 Emmy nominations, 1988, 89; named N.Y. Alumni of Yr. Emerson Coll. Mem. NOW, AFTRA, Am. Soc. Mag. Editors, Overseas Press Club. Office: Soap Opera Digest 45 W 25th St New York NY 10010-2003

BERLINER, PATRICIA MARY, psychologist; b. Bklyn., Mar. 14, 1946; d. Monroe and Rose (Schmidt) B. BA, St. Joseph Coll., Bklyn., 1966; MA, NYU, 1974, PhD, 1990. Joined Sisters of St. Joseph, 1966. Tchr. parochial schs., Bklyn., Queens, L.I., 1968-73; counselor Bishop Kearney High Sch., Bklyn., 1973-79; dir. religious edn. Our Lady of Guadalupe Parish, Bklyn., 1979-82; counselor Office Counseling Svcs., NYU, 1982-84; psychotherapist Mich. State U., E. Lansing, 1984-85; dir. counseling svc. St. John's Hosp., Elmhurst, N.Y., 1985-89; psychotherapist, clin. coord. New Hope Guild Ctr., Howard Beach, N.Y., 1989—; co-founder/dir. Women for a New World, 1980—; pvt. practice, 1991—; cons. Marriage Tribunal, Rockville Centre, N.Y., 1991—. Contbr. articles to profl. jours. NYU grad. assistantship, 1982-84. Mem. APA, N.Y. State Psychol. Assn., Psychologists Interested in Religious Issues. Roman Catholic. Home: 111-20 115th St Jamaica NY 11420-1115 Office: New Hope Guild Center 151-20 88th St Jamaica NY 11414-2034 also: 101-18 104th St Ozone Park NY 11416

BERLINER, RUTH SHIRLEY, real estate company executive; b. N.Y.C., June 20, 1928; d. Irving William and Florence (Tomback) Blum; m. Arthur Ivan Berliner, Sept. 23, 1948; children: Daniel Scott, Michael Robert, Eric Lance. BA, Empire State Coll., Westbury, N.Y., 1974; diploma, Wilsey Sch. Interior Design, Hempstead, N.Y., 1975; MBA, Adelphi U., 1980. Lic. real estate broker, N.Y. Sec. to dir. librs. NYU, N.Y.C., 1948-50; sec. Paragon Mut. Syndicates Inc., N.Y.C., 1958-72; v.p. Paragon Mut. Investors Svcs., N.Y.C., 1972-78; pres. Ruth S. Berliner, Inc., N.Y.C., 1978—; pres. Irmed Corp., 1983-92; cons. E. 59th St. Assocs., N.Y.C., 1962-70, Amrep Corp., N.Y.C., 1968-75, FKBA Assocs., N.Y.C., 1974-78; mem. stores com. Real Estate Bd. N.Y., 1984-92. Vice pres. NYU Dental Sch. Parents Assn., 1974-76; bd. dirs. Hadassah, Hewlett, N.Y., 1978-87; advisor Citizens for Charter Change, N.Y.C., 1987—. Mem. Nat. Assn. Realtors, Real Estate Bd. N.Y. (stores com. 1984-92), Town Club, Inwood Club (N.Y.). Office: 450 7th Ave Rm 1604 New York NY 10001

BERLINER, WILLIAM MICHAEL, business educator; b. Aug. 24, 1923; s. Samuel L. and Anna (Josephine) B.; m. Bertha A. Hagedorn, Apr. 27, 1946. B.S., N.Y. U., 1949, M.B.A., 1953, Ph.D., 1956. With Continental Casualty Co., 1941-42 45-46; retail div. mgr. B.F. Goodrich Co., 1949-50; asst. purchasing agt. Cutler-Hammer, Inc., 1950-51; mem. faculty NYU, N.Y.C., 1951—, prof. mgmt. and orgnl. behavior, chmn. dept. mgmt., 1965-74; dir., cons. ECCO Services, Inc., 1958—; cons. Mfrs. Hanover Trust Co., 1956-90; edn. adviser Am. Inst. Banking sect. Am. Bankers Assn., 1962—; Ford Found. cons. exec. program, N.Y.C. and Met. Area, 1961-65; mem. policy com. Regents Coll. Univ. of State of N.Y. Kellogg Found.; cons. exec. program Boys Clubs Am., 1962-67; faculty Stonier Grad. Sch. Banking, 1970—, Bank Personnel Grad. Sch., Am. Bankers Assn., 1980—; ednl. cons. Bank Adminstrn. Inst., 1976-81, Grad. Sch. Banking, U. Wis., 1982-88, N.Y. State Bankers Assn., 1977—; policy and adv. com. Non-collegiate sponsored instrn. program, Univ. State of N.Y., 1983-90, policy com. mem. Regents Coll. degrees, 1970-90. Author: (with F.A. DePhillips and J.J. Cribbin) Management of Training Programs, 1960, (with W.J. McLarney (dec.) Management Practice and Training, Cases and Principles, 1974, Managerial and Supervisory Practice, 1979. Served to 1st lt. USAAF, 1942-45. Decorated D.F.C., Air medal with 6 oak leaf clusters, Purple Heart; Ford Found. grantee, 1960. Mem. Acad. Mgmt., Soc. for Human Resources Mgmt. (sr. profl. human resources), Am. Mgmt. Assn., Am. Mktg. Assn., Beta Gamma Sigma, Alpha Kappa Psi. Home: 27 Perkins Rd Greenwich CT 06830-3510 Office: NYU Grad Sch Bus Adminstrn 100 Trinity Pl New York NY 10006-1524

BERLS, ROBERT EDWIN, JR., association administrator, past air force officer; b. Bklyn., Nov. 11, 1939; s. Robert Edwin and Sarah Marian (Springmeyer) B.; m. Tatiana Grivsky, May 30, 1969; children: Natalia Grivsky, Gregory Grivsky. BA, Colgate U., 1961; MA, Harvard U., 1963; PhD, Georgetown U., 1972. Commd. 2d lt. USAF, 1963, advanced in grades to col., 1983; asst. prof. Russian, chmn. dept. USAF Acad., Colorado Springs, Colo., 1965-66; polit. and mil. analyst Hdqrs. Intelligence USAF, Washington, 1974-77; del. SALT II Joint Chiefs Staff, Washington and Geneva, 1979-81; chief Soviet intelligence Hdqrs Intelligence USAF, Washington, 1979-81; prof. Nat. War Coll., Washington, 1981-85, 88-89; advanced through grades to col. USAF, 1984; air attache Am. Embassy, Moscow, 1985-88; ret. USAF, 1989; dep. dir. Am. Com. on U.S.-Soviet Rels., Washington, 1989—; lectr. in field. Author: Soviet Aerospace Handbook, 1978; editor jour. New Outlook, 1989—; contbr. articles to profl. jours. Mem. AAASS, Internat. Inst. for Strateegic Studies. Russian Orthodox. Home: 4607 Country Ln Annandale VA 22003-4523 Office: Am Com US Soviet Rels 109 11th St SE Washington DC 20003-3997

BERLYNE, GEOFFREY MERTON, nephrologist, researcher; b. Manchester, Eng., May 11, 1931; came to U.S., 1976, naturalized, 1981; s. Charles Solomon and Miriam Hannah (Rosenthal) B.; m. Ruth Selbourne, June 7, 1969; children: Jonathan, Benjamin, Suzannah. MBChB with honors, Manchester U., 1954, MD, 1966. Lectr. U. Manchester, 1961-62, sr. lectr., 1964-68, reader, 1969-70; prof. medicine and life scis. Negev (Israel) U., 1970-79; prof. medicine SUNY, Bklyn., 1976—; chief nephrology sect. Brooklyn VA Med. Center, 1976—. Author courses sci. topics, including renal diseases, 1966, electrolytes and body fluids, 1981; editor: Nephron; contbr. articles to profl. jours. Pres. area synagogue, 1982-90. Fellow Am. Coll. Nutrition; mem. Japanese Nephrology Soc. (named Disting Nephrologist 1979), Assn. Physicians Gt. Britain, Am. Fedn. Clin. Rsch. Jewish (chmn. 1970-74, pres. synagogue 1982-90). Office: Bklyn VA Hosp 800 Poly Pl Renal Sect III 800 Poly Pl Brooklyn NY 11209

BERMAN, ARTHUR JEROME, gastroenterologist; b. N.Y.C., May 3, 1928; s. Henry and Frances (Sapir-Cohen) B.; m. Carol Michaelson, Oct. 25, 1959; children: Douglas, Judith, Susanne. BS, NYU, 1948, MD, 1951. Diplomate Am. Bd. Internal Medicine, Am. Bd. Internal Medicine-Gastroenterology, Nat. Bd. Med. Examiners. Intern Kings County Hosp., Bklyn., 1951-52; asst. resident Montefiore Hosp., Bronx, N.Y., 1952-53; asst. resident in pathology Montefiore Hosp., Bronx, 1955-56; asst. resident medicine Montefiore Hosp., 1956, 57-58; gastroenterology resident U.S. VA Hosp., N.Y.C., 1958-59; Fulbright fellow infectious diseases U. Tokyo, 1957; assoc. attending div. gastroenterology Dept. Medicine Montefiore Hosp., 1959—; dir. dept. medicine, chief sect. gastroenterology Lawrence Hosp., Bronxville, N.Y., 1963—; asst. clin. prof. medicine Albert Einstein Coll. Contbr. articles to profl. jours., chpt. to book. Fulbright scholar, 1957. Fellow Am. Coll. Physicians, Am. Coll. Gastroenterology; mem. AMA, Med. Soc. State of N.Y., Westchester County Med. Soc., Am. Gastroenterol. Assn., N.Y. Acad. Gastroenterology, N.Y. Soc. Gastrointestinal Endoscopy, Am. Soc. Gastrointestinal Endoscopy. Home: 10 Deerhill Rd Scarsdale NY 10583-1048 Office: 1180 Midland Ave Bronxville NY 10708-6419

BERMAN, BARRY LOUIS, physicist; b. Chgo., Mar. 8, 1936. BA, Harvard U., 1957; MS, U. Ill., 1959, PhD, 1963. Researcher in nuclear physics U. Ill., Champaign, 1961-63; physicist E Div., Lawrence Livermore Nat. Lab., U. Calif., 1963-85; lectr. U. Calif., Davis, 1969-85; vis. assoc. prof. Yale U., New Haven, 1969-70; vis. prof. U. Toronto, Ont., Can., 1970, 75, U. Frankfurt, 1974, U São Paulo, 1977; Sir Thomas Lyle fellow U. Melbourne, Australia, 1978, MIT, 1982; prof. Dept. Physics, The George Washington U., Washington, 1985—; guest scientist Centre d'Etudes Nucleaires de Saclay, 1980-81, Lawrence Berkeley Lab., 1986, Los Alamos (N.Mex.) Nat. Lab., 1985, 88-89, 91; chmn., editor Internat. Conf. on Photonuclear Reactions and Applications, 1973, Internat. Symposium on Three-Body Force in Three-Nucleon System, 1986; organizer Joint George Washington U.-NSF Colloquia and others, 1985-90. Contbr. 200 publs. to profl. jours. Recipient citations Pres. of U. Calif., 1979, 80, citations Sci. Adv. Com. on Lawrence Livermore Nat. Lab., 1977, 80, Disting. Faculty award George Washington U., 1988, award for exptl. verification of channeling radiation Cath. U. Am., 1990; grantee Dept. Energy, Div. Basic Energy Scis., 1977-83, Div. Nuclear Physics, 1978-85, 86—, George Washington U. Com. on Rsch., 1985-86, NSF, 1973, 86. Fellow Am. Phys. Soc. (program com. of div. nuclear physics 1972-73, fellowship com. 1986-88, chmn. 1987-88). Office: George Washington U Washington DC 20052

BERMAN, CAROL MAY, animal behavior researcher; b. San Francisco, Apr. 11, 1949; d. Horace Aaron and Florence (Levine) B.; m. Edward Cooper, Jan. 2, 1983; 1 child, Samuel Berman-Cooper. BA, Brandeis U., 1971; PhD, U. Cambridge, 1979. Psychologist EPA, Rockville, Md., 1971-72; rsch. psychologist FDA, Rockville, 1972-73; vis. scientist Caribbean Primate Rsch. Ctr., Punta Santiago, P.R., 1973-75; animal behavior cons. New Scientist Mag., London, 1977-78; vis. scholar U. Cambridge, U.K., 1985-86; collaborating scientist U. P.R. Sch. Medicine, Rio Piedras, 1988—; asst. prof. SUNY, Buffalo, 1979-85; assoc. prof. SUNY, 1985-92; full prof. SUNY, Buffalo, 1992—; mem. policy com. of faculty of social scis. SUNY, 1989—, mem. computer com. dept. anthropology, 1989, other coms.; co-dir. grad. group in evolutionary biology and ecology SUNY, Buffalo, 1990—; mem. rev. com. for Ctr. for Behavioral and Social Aspects of Health, 1990; mem. sci. coun. Buffalo Zoo, 1980—; cons. in field. Reviewer jours.; contbr. numerous articles to profl. jours. Harry Frank Guggenheim Found. rsch. grantee, 1990-91; NIMH grantee, 1984-87; NIH rsch. travel grantee, 1988; NSF fellow, 1978-79; NIMH fellow, 1975-77; grantee Wenner Gren Found. for Anthrop. Rsch., 1974-75, Sigma Xi, 1974, Explorers Club, 1974, others. Mem. AAAS, Primate Soc. Gt. Britain, Internat. Primatol. Soc., Assn. for Study of Animal Behavior, Cambridge U. Phil. Soc., Animal Behavior Soc., Am. Assn. Phys. Anthropologists, Am. Primatol. Soc., N.Y. Acad. Scis., Internat. Soc. for Human Ethology, Phi Beta Kappa. Office: Dept Anthropology SUNY 380 MFAC Buffalo NY 14261

BERMAN, GARY SCOTT, construction executive, consultant; b. N.Y.C., Jan. 18, 1956; s. Edward Francis and Estelle (Pfeferblum) B.; m. Susan Lynn

Andrus, Oct. 24, 1978; children: Joshua Alexander, Stacey Michelle. BS, Fla. Inst. Tech., 1978; postgrad., Rice U., 1978-82, Va. Poly. Inst. and State U., Fairfax, 1988-89. Registered profl. engr. Assoc. engr. Brown & Root, Inc., Houston, 1978-80; sr. engr. Fluor Engrs., Inc., Houston, 1980-81; mgr. projects Consafe Inc., Houston, 1981-86; gen. mgr. Wexco Internat., L.A., 1986-87; asst. to pres. Parsons Brinckerhoff Constrn. Svcs., Inc., Herndon, Va., 1987-90; asst. v.p. O'Brien-Kreitzberg & Assocs., Inc., N.Y.C., 1990—; pres., founder Sand Dollar Engrng., Houston, 1978-86; faculty Small and Disadvantaged Bus. Alliance, N.Y.C., 1990. Asst. den leader Boy Scouts Am., Setauket, N.Y., 1991. Mem. Constrn. Mgmt. Assn. Am. (disting. svc. award 1990), Am. Arbitration Assn.; assoc. mem. ABA. Office: OBrien Kreitzberg Assoc Inc 1515 Broadway 35th Fl New York NY 10036

BERMAN, JEFFREY L., secondary school educator, artist; b. Bklyn., May 19, 1943; s. Max and Lotte (Pasternack) B. BS, Bklyn. Coll., 1966, MS, 1969. Cert. tchr. health edn., N.Y. Tchr. Alexander Hamilton High Sch., Bklyn., 1966-92, F.K. Lane High Sch., Bklyn., 1981—; instr. judo, private practice, Bklyn., 1965-70, karate, 1988-90; photographer Bud Johnson Assocs., N.Y.C., 1979-81. Artist: exhibited in one-man shows and Port Authority Show. Vol. YMCA judo instr., N.Y.C., 1968; tchr. drug rehab. spark program N.Y.C. Bd. Edn., 1978-80; self defense trainer vol. aux. police, Queens, N.Y., 1988; curator rotating art shows Zeckendorf Towers, N.Y.C., 1991-92. Recipient N.Y. State Regents' scholarship Bklyn. Coll., 1962-66, Art Student's League scholarship, N.Y.C., 1980, Work scholarship, 1988-92; N.Y. State Judo champion, N.Y. Judo Assn., 1965, Northeast U.S. Judo Champion, 1966, N.Y. State Sr. Karate Champion, 1985. Mem. N.Y. State Health and Phys. Edn. Assn., am. Artist Profl. League, Oil Pastel Assn. Internat., N.Y.C. Art Tchrs. Assn., N.Y. Artist Interaction, Marshall Chess Club, Orgn. of Ind. Artists, Alliance of Queens Artists. Home: 1 Irving Pl Apt 3-8E New York NY 10003-9701

BERMAN, MARLENE OSCAR, neuropsychologist, educator; b. Phila., Nov. 21, 1939; d. Paul Oscar and Evelyn (Hess) Oscar; m. Michael Brack Berman, June 23, 1963 (div. Feb. 1980); 1 son, Jesse Michael. BA, U.Pa., 1961; MA, Bryn Mawr Coll., 1964; PhD, U. Conn., 1968; postgrad., Harvard U., 1968-70. Research assoc. Boston VA Med. Ctr., 1970-72, clin. investigator, 1973-76, research psychologist, 1976—; assoc. prof. neurology Boston U. Sch. Medicine, 1975-82, prof. neurology and psychiatry, 1982—, dir. Neuropsychology Lab., dept. psychiatry, 1981—; mem. Com. for Protection Human Participants in Rsch., 1979-82, chmn., 1983-85; affiliate prof. psychology Clark U., Worcester, Mass., 1975—; mem. biomed. rsch. initial rev. group Nat. Inst. Alcohol Abuse and Alcoholism, 1987-91, chmn. 1990-91. Contbr. articles to profl. jours. Coordinator Newton Community Schs. (Mass.), 1978-80. Recipient rsch. scientist devel. award Nat. Inst. Neurol. and Communicative Disorders and Stroke, 1976-81, Nat. Inst. Alcohol Abuse and Alcoholism, 1981-86, clin. investigator award VA, 1973-76; grantee USPHS and HHS, 1964—; Fulbright sr. scholar, 1991. Fellow Mass. Psychol. Assn., Am. Psychol. Assn. (sec.-treas. 1981-83) ; mem. Acad. Aphasia, Soc. Neurosci., Internat. Neuropsychol. Soc., Psychonomic Soc., Huntington's Disease Soc. Am., Internat. Council Psychologists, N.Y. Acad. Scis., Eastern Psychol. Assn. Democrat. Jewish. Office: Boston U Lab Neuropsych Dept Psychiatry M-9 80 E Concord St Roxbury MA 02118-2394

BERMAN, PAUL, theater educator; b. N.Y.C., June 10, 1937; s. Harry and Mae (Minsky) B.; m. Joy Swernoff, Nov. 25, 1954; children: Claudia, Elizabeth. BA, CUNY, MA. Chair theatre dept. Towson State U., Balt., 1970-80; prof. theatre Temple U., Phila., 1981-85, SUNY, Purchase, 1981-86; chair theatre dept. Barnard Coll., Columbia U., N.Y.C., 1986—; dir. theatrical prodns. Ctr. Stage, Wilmer Theatre, Guggenheim Mus., Barter Theatre, others. Home: 4415 Norwood Rd Baltimore MD 21218-1121 Office: Barnard Coll Columbia U 3009 Broadway New York NY 10027-6598

BERMAN, PETER ALAN, health economics and public health educator; b. N.Y.C., May 20, 1951; s. Kenneth William and Ellen Miriam (Taussig) B.; m. Jenny M. Ruducha, Oct. 30, 1987; children: David Max, Ethan Edward, Nina Ellen. BA, Oberlin Coll., 1973; MSC, Cornell U., 1979, PhD, 1984. From program assoc. to project officer UNICEF, Jakarta, Indonesia, 1973-77; asst. prof. Johns Hopkin U., Balt., 1984-91; program officer Ford Found., New Delhi, 1987-91; lecturer Harvard U., 1991—; cons. UNICEF, Indonesia, 1982-83, Asian Devel. Bank, Philippines, 1985-86, Ford Found., India, 1986, World Bank, Washington, 1991. Author numerous academic articles. Fulbright-Hays disertation grantee U.S. Dept. of Edn., 1981-83; disertation grantee Ford Found., 1981-83. Mem. APHA, Am. Economics Assn., Nat. Coun. Internat. Health, Internat. Union Sci. Study of Population. Office: Harvard Sch of Public Hlth 665 Huntington Ave Boston MA 02115-6021

BERMAN, PETER HENRY, physician educator; b. Vienna, Austria, Dec. 29, 1931; came to U.S., 1940; s. Paul and Alice (Kalman) B.; m. Lynne Moskowitz, Dec. 17, 1961; children: John K., Elizabeth, Michael C. BA, NYU, 1952, MD, 1957; MA (hon.), U. Pa., Phila., 1970. Asst. prof. medicine NYU, N.Y.C., 1965-69; assoc. prof. neurology U. Pa., 1969-80, prof. neurology, 1980—; dir. div. neurology Childrens Hosp. Phila., 1969—. Mem. editorial bd. jours. Pediatrics, 1989—, Pediatric Neurology, 1985-91; contbr. chpts. to books and articles to profl. jours. Mem. Child Neurology Soc. (pres. 1991—), Profls. of Child Neurology (pres. 1987--89). Democrat. Office: Childrens Hosp Phils Div Neurology Philadelphia PA 19104

BERMAN, VIVIAN, artist, printmaker; b. N.Y.C., Aug. 28, 1928; d. Joseph and Lena (Sunshine) Mutchnick; m. Samuel Berman, June 21, 1951; children: Mark, David, Jonas, Michael. BFA, Cooper Union, N.Y.C., 1960. Book jacket designer N.Y.C., 1948-51, Boston, 1951-65; instr. De Cordova Mus. Sch., Lincoln, Mass., 1981—. One woman shows include Cary Meml. Libr., Lexington, Mass., 1981, 84, 86, 88, Winifisky Gallery, Salem (Mass.) Coll., 1989, George Sherman Union Gallery, Boston U., 1991; exhibited in group shows at Boston Visual Arts Union, Bklyn. Mus., Libr. of Congress, Pa. Acad. Art, Seattle Mus., Boston Inst. of Contemporary Art; pvt. collections include Hopkins Art Ctr., Dartmouth Coll., Wiggin Collection, Boston Pub. Libr., IBM, Bedford, N.H., Drexel-Burnham, N.Y.C. Pres. Five Fields Community Orgn., Lexington, Mass., 1989. MacDowell Colony fellow, 1981. Mem. Boston Printmakers (bd. dirs., pres. 1971-76), Lexington Coun. for the Arts (coun. mem. 1989—). Home: 11 Barberry Rd Lexington MA 02173-8034

BERMANT, OSER IRVIN, computer systems executive, consultant, educator, mediator; b. N.Y.C., Apr. 4, 1927; s. Ralph and Julia (Billauer) B.; m. Lili Maringer, May 28, 1950; children: Charles Mark, Julie Rae. B in Mech. Engrng., CUNY, 1949; MS, Am. U., 1982. Human resource devel. Swivelier Corp., N.Y.C., 1949-51; sr. planner, mgr. industry mktg., customer engrng. IBM, N.Y.C. and Brussels, 1951-87; pvt. practice cons. Potomac, Md., 1987-90; dir. The Concordia Systems Group, Potomac, 1990—; v.p., bd. dirs. Ctr. for Dispute Resolution, Washington, 1986-90; adj. prof. dept. pub. adminstrn. Am. U., 1991—. Contbr. numerous articles to profl. jours. President The Hilltop Civic Assn., Potomac, 1982-84; bd. dirs. Scotland Community Devel. Corp., Potomac, 1987—. With USN, 1945-46. Recipient Svc. award Scotland Community Devel. Leadership Group, 1991. Mem. Soc. Profls. in Dispute Resolution (pres.-elect Washington chpt. 1991—), Am. U./Nat. Tng. Labs. Assn. (pres. 1987-89). Home: 11029 Seven Hill Ln Rockville MD 20854-3245 Office: The Concordia Systems Group 11029 Seven Hill Ln Rockville MD 20854-3245

BERMAS, NEAL F., management consultant; b. N.Y.C., Oct. 10, 1950; s. Stephen and Mildred (Hershenhart) B. BS, U. Miami, 1973; PhD, Brandeis U., 1980. Nat. dir. health care planning and productivity svcs. Arthur Young & Co., L.A., 1982-85; mng. ptnr. Bermas Assocs., L.A., 1985-90; dir. mgmt. cons. Coopers & Lybrand, N.Y.C., 1990—; adj. faculty NYU, 1990—, UCLA, 1989—, U. So. Calif., L.A., 1985-87; advisor White House Conf. on Productivity, 1985. Contbr. numerous articles to profl. jours. Founding bd. mem. The Wellness Community: A Cancer/Health Ctr., L.A., 1985-90. Grantee NIMH, 1975-77; rsch. fellow VA, 1978-80. Mem. APA, APHA, N.Y. Acad. Scis., Nat. Assn. Sr. Living Industries (bd. dirs.), Nat. Multi-Housing Coun. (bd. dirs. sr. housing com.). Office: Coopers & Lybrand 1301 Ave Of The Americas New York NY 10019-6022

BERMINGHAM, DEBRA PANDELL, artist; b. Northampton, Mass., Sept. 18, 1953; d. N. William and Sylvia Mae (Bates) Pandell; m. Eldredge Langstaff Berm,ingham, Oct. 27, 1973 (div. 1982); m. Kim Thomas Engle, May 26, 1984. BFA, Cornell U., 1976; MFA, U. Wash., 1979. Lectr. painting and drawing Ithaca (N.Y.) Coll., 1983-91. Solo exhbns. include Midtown Payson Galleries, N.Y.C., 1991, Augustus Sain-Gaudens Meml., Cornish, N.H., 1992; exhibited in group shows at Sherry French Gallery, N.Y.C., 1990, World's Fair U.S. Pavilion, Seville, Spain, 1991-92, Am. Acad. and Inst. of Arts and Letters, N.Y.C., 1992. Nat. Endowment for Arts fellow 1985, 87; recipient Kauffmann Fund, Am.-Scandinavian Found., 1991.

BERMINGHAM, JOHN ANTHONY, electronics company executive; b. Chgo., Aug. 29, 1944; s. John L. and Josephine (Logan) B.; m. Marie Ann Jennino, May 3, 1981; children: John Anthony Jr., William James, Michael Robert, Robert Joseph, Lindsay Catherine. BA in Bus. Adminstrn., St. Leo Coll., 1967; postgrad., Harvard U., 1987. Regional sales mgr. Shure, Inc., Evanston, Ill., 1971-73, Panasonic, Des Plaines, Ill., 1973-76; nat. sales and merchandise mgr. Sharp Electronics Corp., Paramus, N.J., 1976-80; dir. mktg. Fuji Photo Film, N.Y.C., 1980-82; v.p. sales and mktg. Sony Magnetic Products Group, Park Ridge, N.J., 1982-87; sr. v.p. sales and mktg. Sony Magnetic Product Group, Park Ridge, 1987-89, pres., 1989-91; exec. v.p. Sony Corp. Am., Park Ridge, 1991—; mem. mktg. bd. Lotus Devel. Corp., Cambridge, Mass., 1990—. With U.S. Army, 1968-71. Mem. Internat. Tape Assn. (bd. dirs. 1991—), Nat. Assn. Record Merchandisers. Republican. Episcopalian. Home: 6 Round Hill Rd Kinnelon NJ 07405 Office: Sony Corp Am Sony Dr Park Ridge NJ 07656-8001

BERMUDEZ, JORGE ALBERTO, bank executive; b. Gibara, Oriente, Cuba, Apr. 29, 1951; came to U.S., 1961; s. Diomedes R. and Melba (Santos) B.; m. Denise M. Pressley, Nov. 8, 1974; children: Jorge II, Andres, Elena, Antonio. BS, Tex. A&M U., 1973, MA, 1975. Teaching asst. Tex. A&M U., College Station, 1973-75; intern Fed. Intermediate Credit Bank, Houston, 1974; exec. trainee Citibank, N.Am., N.Y.C., 1975, v.p., 1981-88, head credit policy Latin Am., 1988—; bd. dirs. Fomento Economico Mexicano S.Am., Monterrey, Mex., 1988—, United Bank Trinidad, Port of Spain, 1985-86. bd. dirs., treas. Norfield Children's Ctr., Weston, Conn., 1989—; coun. mem. St. Francis of Assisi, Weston, 1991—. Republican. Roman Catholic. Home: 30 Kettle Creek Rd Weston CT 06883 Office: Citibank NA 399 Park Ave New York NY 10043

BERN, MURRAY MORRIS, hematologist, oncologist; b. Montgomery, Ala., Feb. 26, 1944; s. Hymie and Ruth Edith (Schaeffer) B.; m. Nancy Frazee, Nov. 23, 1967; 1 child, Alan. BA, Vanderbilt U., 1966; MD, Tulane U., 1970. Diplomate Am. Bd. Internal Medicine, Am. Bd. Hematology, Am. Bd. Oncology. Intern, then resident New Eng. Deaconess Hosp., Boston, from 1970; resident in medicine Boston City Hosp.; fellow Ctr. for Blood Rsch., Boston; sr. staff, sect. chief hematology New Eng. Deaconess Hosp., Boston, 1975-86; dir. hematology, lab. dir. Cancer Ctr. Boston, 1986—; prin., founder, Cancer Ctr. Boston, 1986—; asst. prof. medicine Harvard U., 1980-87, asst. clin. prof. medicine, 1987—. Author, editor: Urinary Track Bleeding, 1985, Hematologic Disorders in Maternal and Fetal Medicine, 1990. Bd. med. advisors Am. Cancer Soc. Mass., 1976-80. Fellow Am. Coll. Physicians; mem. Am. Soc. Hematology, Am. Soc. Clin. Oncology. Office: Cancer Ctr Boston 125 Parker Hill Rd Boston MA 02120

BERNARD, BESS MARY, interior designer; b. Bklyn.; d. Hyman and Fannie Bernard. Formerly, with Melanie Kahane Assoc.; pres. Bernard Design Internat., Ltd., N.Y.C., 1960—; internat. cons. in field. Prin. works include dining room for kindergarten children Marymount Sch., boutique for East Park Cultural Ctr., various projects for Waldorf Astoria hotel, apt. for pres. of Mitsubishi, numerous corp., hosp. and internat. projects. Chmn. Bklyn. Jewish Hosp. Recipient various vol. awards Bklyn. Jewish Hosp., United Hosp. Fund. Office: Waldorf Astoria 301 Park Ave New York NY 10022

BERNARD, JAMES ROBERT, natural resources executive; b. Santa Monica, Calif., May 27, 1952; s. Richard Frank Bernard and Dorothy Margaret (Greiner) Bernard Miller; m. Tatiana Brailovsky, Sept. 11, 1982; 1 child, Gregory Brouillet. BA in Environ. Studies, Polit. Sci., and Cultural Anthropology, U. Calif., Santa Barbara, 1981; MS in Resource Policy, Econs., and Mgmt., U. Mich., 1983. Legis. analyst, rschr. Great Lakes Commn., Ann Arbor, Mich., 1982-84, natural resources mgt. specialist, 1985; environ. issues coord. Ecology Ctr. Ann Arbor, 1984-85; asst. dir. Mich. Great Lakes and Water Resources Planning Commn., Lansing, 1986-87; dir. Maine Land and Water Resources Coun., Augusta, 1987-89; coord. Land For Maine's Future Bd., Augusta, 1987—; dir. natural resources policy divsn. Maine State Planning Office, Augusta, 1987—; cons. grant writing Ecology Ctr. Ann Arbor, 1984, conf. coord., 1984-85. Contbr. articles to profl. jours. Mem. Maine Exec. Inst. (pres. 1988—). Office: Maine State Planning Office 184 State St State House Sta 38 Augusta ME 04333

BERNARD, JUDD BENJAMIN, mechanical engineering educator, researcher; b. N.Y.C., Oct. 6, 1962; s. Kenneth and Elaine B. BS in Mech. Engrng. summa cum laude, CCNY, 1985; MS in Mech. Engrng., MIT, 1987; PhD, Columbia U., 1990. Adj. prof. L.I. U., N.Y.C., 1988-90; asst. prof. Manhattan Coll., N.Y.C., 1990—; adj. prof. Poly. U., N.Y.C., 1989. Scholar MIT, Cambridge, 1985. Mem. Am. Soc. of Mech. Engrs., Am. Soc. Engrs. Edn., Tau Beta Pi, Pi Tau Sigma. Home: 765 Riverside Dr New York NY 10032-7337 Office: Manhattan Coll Manhattan College Pky Bronx NY 10471-3913

BERNARD, RONALD ALLAN, computer performance analyst; b. Dover, N.H., Sept. 28, 1953; s. Robert Ronald and Joyce (Bodwell) B.; children: Laura Jean, Jessica Diane. BS, U. Vt., 1975. Characterization engr. IBM, Essex Junction, Vt., 1979-83; diffusion engrng. group leader IBM, 1983-85, evaporation engrng. group leader, 1985-87, VM performance analyst, 1987-89, performance group leader, 1989—; task force mem. IBM NE region Info. and Telecommunications Support Svcs. Consolidation, Endicott, N.Y., 1988-89; speaker VM Internal Tech. Exchange, 1988, SHARE, 1988-89, Latin Am. Guide Group, 1989. Bd. dirs. Royal Parke Assn., 1986—, v.p. 1987-91. Mem. Racquet Edge Club (Essex, Vt.), Amnesty Internat. (writer 1988—). Roman Catholic. Home: 1F 86 Pinecrest Dr Essex Junction VT 05452

BERNARDO, RAYMOND FRANCIS, realty company executive; b. Providence, Apr. 22, 1917; s. Eugene Gregory and Sarah Cecilia (Conway) B.; m. Alcia Elizabeth McIntyre (dec.); 1 child, Bradford Craig. BS, Providence Coll., 1939. Navy auditor Bur. Yards and Docks Navy Dept., Washington, 1941-45; contract negotiator Winston Bros. Co., Mpls., 1945-47; pres., chief exec. officer Providence Granite Co., Inc., 1947-80, Rockport Quarries Co., Inc., Providence, 1947-80, Moose-A-Bec Quarries Co., Inc., Providence, 1947-80, Westerly Quarries Co., Inc., Providence, 1947-80, E.R.H. Realty Co., Inc., Providence, 1947-80, Gateway Constrn. Co., Inc., Providence, 1947-80, K.G.R. Realty Co., Narragansett, R.I., 1970—; bd. dirs. 1st Fin. Corp., Providence, 1st Bank and Trust Co., Providence. Mem. adv. coun. Small Bus. Adminstrn., Providence, 1963, S. County Tourism Coun., Wakefield, R.I., 1988. Mem. Narragansett C. of C. (bd. dirs. 1977), R.I. Police Chiefs' Assn. Republican. Roman Catholic. Office: KGR Realty Co Great Island Rd Narragansett RI 02882-5603

BERNARDONE, JEFFREY JOHN, podiatrist; b. Southbridge, Mass., Feb. 10, 1958; s. John Paul Jr. and Lina (Bonadies) B.; m. Janet Rae Bolea, June 3, 1990; 1 child, Jeffrey Michael. BA, Assumption Coll., Worcester, Mass., 1980; D Podiatric Medicine, N.Y. Coll. Podiatric Medicine, 1984. Preceptorship N.Y. Coll. Podiatric Medicine, 1986; pvt. practice Quincy, Mass., 1986—; cons. to various hosps.; podiatrist Boston Marathon. Mem. Am. Podiatric Med. Assn., Mass. Podiatric Med. Assn., Am. Diabetes Assn. Office: 1157 Hancock St Quincy MA 02169-4329

BERNASEK, STEVEN LYNN, chemist; b. Holton, Kans., Dec. 14, 1949; s. Frank Eugene and Marie Helen (Stueve) B.; m. Sandra Lynn Taylor, June 5, 1971; children: Lisa Marie, Eric Dean. BS magna cum laude, Kans. State U., 1971; PhD, U. Calif., Berkeley, 1975. Asst. prof. Princeton (N.J.) U., 1975-81, assoc. prof., 1981-86, prof. chemistry, 1986—; Contbr. over 80 articles to profl. jours. Editor: (with others) Advanced Surface Processes for Optoelectronics, 1988, Reactivity of Solids, 1989. Exxon fellow in solid state chemistry Am. Chem. Soc. Div. Inorganic Chemistry, 1981, Alexander von Humboldt fellow Alexander von Humboldt Found., Jülich, Fed. Republic Germany, 1985-86. Mem. Am. Chem. Soc., Am. Phys. Soc. Republican. Roman Catholic. Home: 6 Brendan Pl Lawrenceville NJ 08648 Office: Princeton U Dept of Chemistry Princeton NJ 08544

BERNATOWICZ, FELIX JAN BRZOZOWSKI, mechanical engineer, consultant; b. Warsaw, Poland, Sept. 12, 1920; came to U.S., 1956; s. Jan and Leokadia (Malinowska) Brzozowski-Bernatowicz; m. June 26, 1948 (div. 1973); 1 child, Monica D. Fulton. Dipl. Ing., Swiss Fed. Inst. of Tech., Zurich, 1946; MSME, U. Conn., 1962. Asst. to the dir. Inst. of Exptl. Physics U. Bern, Switzerland, 1946-49; tech. officer New South Wales U. Tech., Sydney, Australia, 1950-56; R & D engr. Armzen Co., Waterbury, Conn., 1956-58, Bristol Co., Naugatuck, Conn., 1958-66; analytical engr. Colt Chandler Evans Control Systems Div., West Hartford, Conn., 1966-68; sr. engr. Gen. Dynamics Electric Boat Div., Groton, Conn., 1969-90, ret., 1990; pvt. practice cons. New London, Conn., 1990—. Vol. Rep. Party, New London, 1972, 80. Cpl. French Army, 1940, ETO. Mem. AAAS, IEEE, ASME, Am. Assn. for Artificial Intelligence, Am. Def. Preparedness Assn., N.Y. Acad. Scis., Polish Inst. Arts and Scis. of Am., Inc., U.S. Naval Inst. Roman Catholic. Home: 91 Crown Knoll Ct Ste # 124 Groton CT 06430

BERNBACH, JOHN LINCOLN, advertising executive; b. 1944; s. William Bernbach. Grad. polit. sci., Georgetown U. Trainee account mgmt., then v.p. account services Gilbert Advt., 1966-72; with DDB Needham Worldwide, Inc. (formerly Doyle Dane Bernbach), Paris, 1972-79, London, 1979-84; pres., chief exec. officer internat. div. DDB Needham Worldwide, Inc. (formerly Doyle Dane Bernbach), N.Y.C., 1984-86, pres., 1986—. Office: DDB Needham Worldwide Inc 437 Madison Ave New York NY 10022-7001

BERNDT, ERNST RUDOLF, economist, educator; b. Crespo, Entre Rios, Argentina, Apr. 13, 1946; came to U.S., 1949; s. Markus William and Charlotte Marie (Zimmermann) B.; m. Martha Ann Mirly, June 10, 1967 (div. 1982); children: Jeffrey, Nathan; m. Catherine Joan Morrison, Jan. 4, 1985. BA with honors, Valparaiso U., 1968; MS., U. Wis., 1971, PhD, 1972; PhD (hon.), Uppsala U., 1991. Staff economist Exec. Office of the Pres. U.S. Govt., Washington, 1971-72; asst. prof. U. (Vancouver) B.C., Can., 1973-78, assoc. prof., 1978-80; prof. applied econs. MIT, Cambridge, Mass., 1980—; rsch. assoc. Nat. Bur. Econ. Rsch., Cambridge, 1980—; acad. affiliate Analysis Group, Inc., Belmont, Mass., 1985—. Contbr. profl. articles. Most cited economist under age 40 in 1985. Mem. Am. Econ. Assn., Econometric Soc., Conf. Rsch. in Income and Wealth. Independent. Lutheran. Office: MIT 50 Memorial Dr ES2 452 Cambridge MA 02139

BERNE, PATRICIA HIGGINS, psychologist, writer; b. Indpls., Feb. 21, 1934; d. Edward Robert and Esther Josephine (Maschino) Higgins; m. John Henry Berne, June 19, 1957 (div. May 1979); children: Suzanne, Eve, Serena. Student, Am. U., 1970-72, George Washington U., 1974; MA, Goddard Coll., 1975; PhD, Union Inst., Cin., 1978. Lic. clin. psychologist, Washington. Counselor Campus Ministry Georgetown U., 1978-80; dir. Counseling Ctr. Trinity Coll., Washington, 1979-81; pvt. practice Washington, 1981—; co-dir. Inner Devel. Assocs., Washington, 1990—, adj. prof., 1981—; adj. faculty at several colls. and univs., 1978—; lectr. at confs. internationally, 1980—; cons. Lightworks, Arlington, Va., 1990—, Holy Trinity Ch., Washington, 1990—, DMA, Salem, Mass., 1984-89. Co-author: Prayerways, 1980, Building Self-Esteem in Children, 1981, Dreams and Spiritual Growth, 1984, Kything, 1988, Dream Symbol Work, 1991. Mem. APA, Washington Ind. Svcs. for Ednl. Resources, Assn. for Transpersonal Psychology, Inst. for Noetic Sci., D.C. Psychol. Assn. Roman Catholic. Office: Inner Devel Assocs 5201 Macarthur Ter NW Washington DC 20016-2617

BERNER, DAVID PAUL, marketing firm executive, consultant; b. Rochester, N.Y., June 20, 1949; s. Marvin R. and Jean F. (McVeal) B.; m. Susan L. Cartwright, Aug. 7, 1976; children: Jeremy, Jillian. BS in Edn., U. Tenn., 1972. Cert. tchr., N.Y. Adminstr. Town of Huntington, N.Y., 1974-75; city mgr. Inc. Village of Patchoque, N.Y., 1975-83; account exec. Dean Witter Reynolds, N.Y.C., 1983-84; dep. commr. Town of Brookhaven, Medford, N.Y., 1984-90; sr. v.p. Ashner Assocs., Medford, 1990—; chief exec. officer Royal Prestige-Atlantic, Hauppauge, N.Y., 1991—; mem. adv. bd. dir continuing edn. Patchoque-Medford Sch. Dist., Patchoque, 1978—, Coop. Ednl. Svcs., Bellport, N.Y., 1986—. Editor Annual Report Inc. Village of Patchoque, 1975-82. Vol. sch. dist. Patchoque, 1975—; program chmn., Brookhaven Town Rep. Com., 1982—; pres. Great South Bay Rep. Club, 1986-88. Named to All-County and All-State Track and Skiing Teams, N.Y. State Athletic Bd., 1966, '67. Home: 137 Oak St Medford NY 11763-4033

BERNER, RICHARD BRIAN, economist; b. N.Y.C., May 3, 1946; s. Robert Charles and Hilda Rose (Schwall) B.; m. Bonnie Kay Back, July 12, 1980; children: Matthew John, Laura Anne. BA, Harvard U., 1968; PhD, U. Pa., 1976. Economist Bd. Govs. FRS, Washington, 1972-80; economist, dir. Wharton Econ. Forecasting Assocs., Washington, 1980-82; economist, v.p. Morgan Guaranty Trust Co., N.Y.C., 1982-85; economist, dir. Salomon Bros. Inc., N.Y.C., 1985—; vis. lectr. Japanese Minstry Fin., Tokyo, 1980—. Editor, contbr. Comments on Credit, 1986—; contbr. numerous articles to scholarly jours. Mem. Am. Econ. Assn., Nat. Assn. Bus. Economists. Office: Salomon Bros Inc 7 World Trade Ctr New York NY 10048-1102

BERNEY, ELIZABETH GOTTLIEB, organizational psychologist; b. New Haven, Conn., May 6, 1957; d. Mischa and Charlotte (Fishman) Schwartz; m. Michael Gottlieb Berney, May 2, 1988; 1 child, Sara Rebecca Gottlieb Berney. BA with distinction, Yale U., 1979; MA, U. Md., 1983, PhD, 1985. Asst. prof. George Mason U., Fairfax, Va., 1985-88; cons., prin. Berney Assocs., Silver Spring, Md., 1988—; adj. faculty George Mason U., 1988—, Georgetown U., Washington, 1988—, dir. orgnl. devel. program, 1989—; instr. Am. Mgmt. Assn., N.Y.C., 1991; conf. chair 3d Annual IO-OB Student Conf., College Park, Md., 1982-83. Contbr. articles to profl. jours. Active Ams. for Dem. Action, Washington, 1985—. Mem. Am. Psychol. Assn., Orgn. Devel. Network. Home and Office: 1960 Flowering Tree Ter Silver Spring MD 20902-5817

BERNFELD, WILLIAM STEVEN, accountant; b. Port Chester, N.Y., Sept. 22, 1950; s. Arnold Arthur and Sonya (Azorsky) B.; m. Catherine Ellen Lindhurst, June 28, 1974; children: Rebecca Lynn, Jennifer Lynn, Adam Steven. BS in Mgmt., Rensselaer Poly. Inst., 1972; MBA, SUNY, Albany, 1974; MS in Acctg., Pace U., 1986. CPA, N.Y. Commd. 2d lt. U.S. Army, 1972, advanced through grades to capt., 1984; staff acct. Ernst & Whinney, White Plains, N.Y., 1986-87; lectr. acctg. Pace U., Pleasantville, N.Y., 1987—; pvt. practice Port Chester, 1987—. Mem. affordable housing bd. Town of Yorktown, 1988-90; mem. supt. fin. adv. com. Yorktown Ctrl. Sch. Dist., 1986-88; den leader pack 126 Boy Scouts Am., 1990—; coach Yorktown Youth Soccer Club, 1989—. Lt. col. USAR, 1984-91. Mem. Res. Officers Assn. (life), N.Y. State Soc. CPAs, Nat. Assn. Pub. Accts., Nat. Soc. Tax Profls., Nat. Assn. Tax Preparers, Nat. Eagle Scout Assn. (life). Republican. Jewish. Office: 125 N Main St Ste 501 Port Chester NY 10573-4225

BERNFIELD, MERTON RONALD, pediatrician, educator; b. Chgo., Apr. 9, 1938; s. Harry B. and Adeline A. (Fischer) B.; m. Audrey A. Rivkin, Aug. 30, 1959; children: Susan, James, Mark. BS, U. Ill., 1957, MS, 1961; MD, U. Ill., Chgo., 1961. Intern U. Ill. Research Hosps., Chgo., 1961-62; asst. resident in pediatrics N.Y. Hosp.-Cornell U. Med. Center, N.Y.C., 1962-63; research assoc. NIH, Bethesda, Md., 1963-65; research investigator Nat. Inst. Child Health and Human Devel., U. Calif., San Diego, 1965-66; chief resident in pediatrics Stanford U. Med. Center, 1967; asst. prof. pediatrics Stanford U., 1967-70, assoc. prof., 1970-75, prof., 1975-89, Josephine Knotts Knowles prof. human biology, 1977-89, dir. med. scientist MD-PhD tng. program, 1974-77, chmn. program in human biology, 1977-80, dir. fellowship program in membrane pathobiology, 1975-85, dir. fellowship program in developmental and neonatal biology, 1982-89; dir. cystic fibrosis rsch. devel. program, 1987-89; Clement A. Smith prof. pediatrics, prof. anatomy and cellular biology Harvard U Med. Sch., 1989—; chief div. newborn medicine Children's Hosp., Boston; chmn. dept. newborn medicine Brigham and

Women's Hosp., Boston, Beth Israel Hosp., Boston; mem. research com. Cystic Fibrosis Found., 1972-76; mem. developmental biology panel NSF, 1976-77; mem. physiol. chemistry research com. Am. Heart Assn., 1979-83; mem. craniofacial anomalies evaluation panel Nat. Inst. Dental Research, 1980-81; mem. health adv. com. Calif. Medfly Eradication Project, 1981-82; mem. sci. adv. bd. Collagen Corp., 1981-90; chmn. Neonatal Biology Group, 1984—; chmn. Ciba Symposium, Basement Membranes and Cell Movement, 1984; chmn. Gordon Rsch. Conf. on Basement Membranes, 1986; cons. in field. Contbr. articles to profl. jours.; mem. editorial bd. Archives Biochemistry and Biophysics, 1972-79, Cell Differentiation and Devel., 1980-90, Jour. Craniofacial Genetics and Devel. Biology, 1980-83; assoc. editor Developmental Biology, 1981—; mem. editorial bd. Jour. Biol. Chemistry, 1987—, Am. Jour. Respiratory Cell and Molecular Biology, 1988—, Cell Regulation/Molecular Biology of the Cell, 1989—; exec. editor MATRIX, 1989—; sect. editor Current Opinion in Cell Biology, 1988—. Mem. working group Organ Systems Program Nat. Cancer Inst., 1986-89, selection com. Pediatric Scientist Tng. Program, Assn. Med. Sch. Pediatric Dept. Chairmen, 1987-91, Middle Grades Life Sci. Adv. Bd. Carnegie Corp., N.Y., 1988—, Maternal and Child Health Rsch. Com. Nat. Inst. Child Health and Human Devel., 1988—, working group on Early Life and Adolescent Health Policy, Harvard U., 1989—. With USPHS, 1963-66. Guggenheim fellow, 1972-73; Josiah Macy scholar, 1980-81; recipient Merit award Nat. Inst. Child Health and Human Devel., 1988. Mem. Am. Pediatrics Soc. (Centennial Symposium lectr. 1988), Am. Acad. Pediatrics, Am. Soc. for Biochemistry and Molecular Biology, Am. Soc. Cell Biology (chmn. pub. policy com., treas.), Internat. Soc. for Devel. Biology, Perinatal Research Soc., Soc. Devel. Biology (pres. 1991), Soc. Pediatric Research, Teratology Soc., Western Soc. Pediatric Research (Ross award 1973). Home: 25 Brimmer St Boston MA 02108-1001 Office: Harvard Med Sch Joint Program in Neonatology Boston MA 02115

BERNHANG, ARTHUR M., orthopaedic surgeon, sculptor; b. N.Y.C., June 21, 1934; s. Clare (Kessler) B.; m. Judy Lynne Pertz, Dec. 3, 1961. AB, U. Rochester, 1955; MD, Chgo Med. Sch., 1959. Diplomate Am. Bd. Orthopaedic Surgery. Intern Hosp. for Joint Diseases, N.Y.C., 1959-60, resident, 1960-64; pvt. practice Huntington, N.Y.; attending orthopaedist Huntington Hosp., 1970—; vis. prof. U. Papua New Guinea, 1986, Orthopaedics Overseas, Indonesia, 1989. Works shown at one man shows and exhbns. Lt. comdr. USNR, 1966-68. Fellow Royal Soc. Arts, Internat. Arthroscopy Assn., Internat. Soc. Orthopaedics and Tramatology, Am. Orthopaedic Soc. for Sports Medicine; mem. Explorers Club. Office: 124 Main St Huntington NY 11743-6922

BERNHARD, JEFFREY DAVID, dermatologist, educator; b. Buffalo, Oct. 31, 1951. AB, Harvard Coll., 1973; MD, Harvard Med. Sch., 1978. Diplomate Am. Bd. Dermatology. Chief resident dermatology Harvard Med. Sch., Boston, 1982—; fellow photomedicine Mass. Gen. Hosp., 1983; faculty U. Mass. Med. Sch., Worcester, 1983-86, dir. dermatology, assoc. prof., 1986—, assoc. dean for admissions, 1986-92, prof., 1992—. Mem. editorial bd. Yearbook of Dermatology, Jour. of the Am. Acad. of Dermatology, Internat. Jour. Dermatology. Fellow Am. Acad. Dermatology; mem. Soc. for Investigative Dermatology, Royal Soc. Medicine, Sir James Saunders Soc., Aesculapian Club of Boston, Assn. Profs. Dermatology, New Eng. Dermatol. Soc. (pres. 1990-91). Office: U Mass Med Ctr 55 Lake Ave N Worcester MA 01655-0001

BERNHARD JACKSON, GABRIELE JOHANNA, English literature educator; b. Berlin, Nov. 17, 1934; came to U.S., 1939; d. Ernest George Bernhard and Ruth Friederike (Friedlander) Engel; m. Thomas Herbert Jackson, Dec. 16, 1961; children: Olivia Kate, Emily Anne. BA, Bard Coll., 1955; postgrad., Oxford U., 1955-56; MA, Yale U., 1958, PhD, 1961. Instr. English Yale U., New Haven, 1961-63; asst. prof. English Wellesley (Mass.) Coll., 1963-68; assoc. prof. English Temple U., Phila., 1968-70, prof., 1970—, interim dean Grad. Sch., 1977-80; vis. assoc. prof., prof. U. Pa., Phila., 1968, summers 1970, 81, 82, 85, 87, 90; vis. prof. Bryn Mawr (Pa.) Coll., 1990; rsch. fellow Am. Coun. Learned Socs., Eng., 1971-72; dir. summer seminar for coll. tchrs. NEH, Temple U., 1985; mem. affirmative action program grad. students HEW, Temple U. Grad. Sch., 1978-80. Author: Vision and Judgment in Ben Jonson's Drama, 1968, Ben Jonson's Every Man in His Humor, 1969; editorial bd. Assays; contbr. articles to profl. jours., chpts. to books. Recipient Fulbright Scholarship, U.S. Govt., Eng., 1955-56. Mem. Renaissance Soc. Am., Shakespeare Assn. Am., N.E. Modern Lang. Assn. Office: Temple U Dept English Philadelphia PA 19122

BERNHARDT, ARTHUR DIETER, building industry executive and consultant; b. Dresden, Germany, Nov. 19, 1937; came to U.S., 1966; s. Rudolf B. and Charlotte (Apitz) B. Dipl. Ing., U. Tech., Munich, Fed. Republic Germany, 1965; postgrad., U. So. Calif., 1966-67; M. City Planning, MIT, 1969. Various positions constrn. cos., 1955-68; dir. Program in Industrialization of Housing Sector, MIT, Cambridge, Mass., 1969-76; pres. Program in Industrialization of Housing Sector, Cambridge, 1977-89; chief exec. officer, dir. Program in Industrialization of Housing Sector, Inc., Cambridge and N.Y.C., 1989—; internat. building industry cons., Cambridge, Mass., and N.Y.C., 1973—; asst. prof. MIT, 1970-76. Author books; contbr. articles to profl. jours. Mem. exec. com. Mass. Gov.'s Adv. Com. on Manufactured Housing, 1974-75; NRC del. 8th Gen. Assembly Internat. Council Bldg. Research, 1974. Fed. Republic Germany fellow, 1965, 66, 67, 68; MIT fellow, 1968, 69; MIT grantee, 1970; Fed. Republic Germany grantee, 1965; Alfred P. Sloan Found. grantee, 1970; Dept. Commerce grantee, 1972; HUD grantee, 1972, 74. Mem. Internat. Council Bldg. Research, Am. Acad. Polit. and Social Sci., Am. Planning Assn., Deutscher Hochschulverband, Am. Judicature Soc. (assoc.). Office: Rockefeller Ctr Box 9 New York NY 10185

BERNHEIMER, ALAN WEYL, microbiologist; b. Phila., Dec. 9, 1913; s. Eugene Seligman and Helen (Weyl) B.; m. Harriet Poller, MAr. 29, 1942; 1 child, Alan Jr. BS, Temple U., 1935, MA, 1937; PhD, U. Pa., 1942. Biology asst. Temple U., Phila., 1935-37; instr. bacteriology Pa. State Coll. Optometry, Phila., 1937-39; instr. bacteriology N.Y. U. Coll. Medicine, N.Y.C., 1941-45, asst. prof., 1945-52; assoc. prof. N.Y. U. Sch. Medicine, N.Y.C., 1952-58, prof., 1958-84, chmn. basic sci., 1969-74, prof. emeritus, 1984—; cons. in field; trustee Cold Springs Harbor Lab., 1963-68; mem. micro tng. com. NIH, 1960-62. Author: Reflectographs, 1965, Perspectives in Toxinology, 1977; editor: Mechanisms in Bacterial Toxinology, 1976. Fellow AAAS, N.Y. Acad. Sci.; mem. Am. Soc. Microbiology, Am. Acad. Microbiology, Am. Microscopical Soc., Mineralogical Soc. Am., Am. Assn. Immunologists. Home: 51 5th Ave New York NY 10003 Office: NYU Med Sch 550 1st Ave New York NY 10016

BERNIER, WILFRED ALCIDE, engineer; b. Amesbury, Mass., Feb. 1, 1943; s. Wilfred A. and Marguerite M. (Thibault) B.; m. Paula Theresa Rogers, Aug. 8, 1970; children: Kevin Wilfred, Bethann Rogers. ASME, Lowell Tech. Inst., 1974; BSME, U. Lowell, 1978. Cert. mfg. engr. Assoc. design engr. Western Electric Co. Inc., North Andover, Mass., 1968-75; electro/mech. engr. Alco Elec. Product Inc., North Andover, Mass., 1976-78; mech. engr. Field Machine and Tool Co., Wilmington, Mass., 1978; tool design engr. Northeast Tool Co., Haverhill, Mass., 1978-79; mfg. engr. Adams Russell Co., Amesbury, Mass., 1979-85; surface mount tech. process engr. AT&T, North Andover, 1985—; chmn. surface mount repair com. AT&T, North Andover, 1989-92. With USN, 1964-68, res., 1976—. Mem. Soc. Mfg. Engrs. Roman Catholic. Home: 21 Cutting Dr Newburyport MA 01950 Office: AT&T 1600 Osgood St North Andover MA 01845

BERNOSKY, HERMAN GEORGE, retail gasoline dealer; b. Minersville, Pa., Aug. 16, 1921; s. Peter and Mary Bernosky; student Rider Coll., Trenton, N.J., 1947-48. With Bernosky's Exxon Sta., Llewellyn, Pa., 1940-42, 46-90, owner, operator, 1949-90. Treas. Minersville Area Bicentennial, 1976. Served with AUS, 1942-46; ETO. Decorated Bronze Star (3). Mem. Internat. Platform Assn., Am. Legion. Democrat. Roman Catholic. Club: Minersville Lions (past pres., dir. 1957—). Home: 622 Lytle St Minersville PA 17954-1813 Office: PO Box 170 Llewellyn PA 17944

BERNS, PETER VERNON, attorney; b. Newark, Sept. 22, 1956; s. Robert S. and Roslyn (Weinbaum) B.; m. Melissa Robin Zieve, Sept. 10, 1989; c1 child, Eli L. Berns-Zieve. BA, U. Pa., 1978; JD, Harvard U., 1981; LLM, Georgetown U., 1983. Bar: Washington 1981, Md. 1983. Staff attorney, grad. fellow Inst. for Pub. Representation, Washington, 1981-83; asst. atty. gen. consumer protection div. Office of Atty. Gen., Balt., 1983-88, deputy chief consumer protection div., 1988-92; exec. dir. Md. Assn. Nonprofit Orgns., 1992—. Contbr. articles to profl. jours. V.p. Md. Food Com., Balt., 1989—; sec. ACLU, Md., 1978. Mem. Washington Bar. Assn. Home: 6305 Clearspring Rd Baltimore MD 21212 Office: Md Assn Nonprofit Orgns 22 Light St Baltimore MD 21202

BERNSTEIN, ALVIN STANLEY, psychophysiology and behavior science educator; b. Bklyn., Nov. 2, 1929; s. Joseph and Clara (Schwartz) B.; m. Elly Rattner, Sept. 1, 1968; 1 child, Peter S. BA, NYU, 1950; postgrad., Columbia U., 1950-51, U. Mass., 1952; PhD, U. Buffalo, 1958. Ward psychologist, rsch. ward adminstr. VA Hosp., Montrose, N.Y., 1958-66; asst. prof. Med. Sch. Cornell U., N.Y.C., 1965-66; from asst. to assoc. prof. Coll. of Medicine SUNY, Bklyn., 1966—, asst. prof. clin. behavior Grad. SCh., 1970—, assoc. prof. neurol. and behavior sci. Coll. of Medicine, 1975—; sr. rsch. scientist Kings County Med. Ctr., Bklyn., 1970—; dir. psychophysiology schizophrenia rsch. unit Creedmoor State-N.Y. Psychiat. Inst., Queens; vis. prof. dept. psychology U. York, Eng., 1976; mem. rsch. rev. com. NIMH, 1979-81, mem. spl. rev. coms., 1985, 88, cons. panel on nat. plan for schizophrenia rsch., 1987, NSF, 1988; cons. Nat. Sci. and Engring. Rsch. Coun., Can., 1982. Assoc. editor Psychophysiology Jour., 1986—; contbr. numerous articles to profl. jours. Fellow NIMH, 1960-68, grantee, 1969-72, 75, 76-89. Fellow Internat. Orgn. for Psychophysiology; mem. Soc. for Psychophysiology Rsch. (bd. dirs. 1989—, chmn. by-laws com. 1990—).

BERNSTEIN, BERNARD ALEXANDER, physician, educator; b. Fulton, N.Y., Feb. 24, 1938; s. Alex and Florence (Esterson) B.; m. Carolyn Harriet, May 12, 1963; children: Marc Jordan, Cheryl Denise. AB, Cornell U., 1959; MD, SUNY, N.Y.C., 1963. Acting chmn., prof. family practice SUNY Upstate Med. Ctr., Syracuse, 1974; clin. prof. medicine SUNY Health Scis. Ctr., Syracuse, 1986—; pres., treas. Nephrology and Internal Medicine Specialists, PC, Syracuse, 1980—. Lt. comdr. USNR, 1967-69. Jewish. Home: 5219 Winterton Dr Fayetteville NY 13066 Office: NIMS 2215 E Genesee St Syracuse NY 13210

BERNSTEIN, CHARLES, poet, writer; b. N.Y.C., Apr. 4, 1950; s. Herman and Sherry (Kegel) B.; m. Susan Bee Laufer, Aug. 17, 1977; children: Emma Bee, Felix Laufer. AB, Harvard U., 1972. David Gray prof. poetry and letters SUNY, Buffalo, 1990—; presenter of poetry readings, lectrs. worldwide. Author numerous poetry books including Resistance, 1983, The Sophist, 1987, Veil, 1987, Rough Trades, 1990; author: Content's Dream: Essays, 1975-84, 1986, L=A=N=G=U=A=G=E, 1984, A Poetics, 1992, others; contbr. poems, essays to numerous mags., anthologies. Fellow Nat. Endowment for Arts Creative Writing, 1980, John Simon Guggenheim Meml., 1985, U. Auckland Found., 1986, N.Y. Found. for Arts, 1990. Office: SUNY Dept English 306 Clemens Hall Buffalo NY 14260

BERNSTEIN, HARVEY MICHAEL, research foundation executive, engineer; b. Newark, N.J., Dec. 3, 1945; s. Bernard and Jennie (Gerber) B.; m. Millicent Sue Jacobson Kirk, Aug. 19, 1967 (div. Mar. 1979); children—Evan, David; m. Karen Pallotta, June 21, 1980; children: Jeffrey, Eric. B.S. in Civil Engring., Newark Coll. Engring., 1967; M.S. in Engring., Princeton U., 1968; M.B.A., Loyola Coll., Balt., 1978. Jr. engr. Goodkind and O'Dea, Consulting Engr., Montclair, N.J., 1966-67; engr. Bell Helicopter Co., Ft. Worth, 1968-71; naval architect Naval Ship Engring. Ctr., Hyattsville, Md., 1971-73; program mgr. Booz-Allen Applied Research, Bethesda, Md., 1973-74; v.p., Hittman Assocs./Hittman Corp., Columbia, Md., 1974-79, also corp. dir.; v.p. Applied Mgmt. Scis., Silver Spring, Md., 1979-89; pres., bd. dirs. Civil Engring. Rsch. Found., Washington, 1989—; mem. task force Nat. Gas Survey Conservation Com. Adv. Task Force on Efficiency in the Use of Gas for Fed. Power Commn., 1976-77; panel mem. Gas Research Workshop to Develop Research and Devel. Plans in Field of Energy Conservation Techs., Chgo., 1981; mem. working group U.S./USSR Agreement on Housing and other Constrn., 1985-89; mem. Transp. Rsch. Bd., 1992—; mem. nat. team Ctr. for Analysis and Dissemination of Demostrated Energy Techs., Internat. Energy Agy; presenter in field. Mem. editorial adv. bd. Constrn. Bus. Rev., 1990—; mem. publs. bd. Pub. Rds. mag., 1992—; contbr. articles in field to profl. jours. Chmn. bd. dirs. U. Md. Dance Theater, College Park, 1981-85; mem. civil and environ. engring. adv. com. to bd. trustees N.J. Inst. Tech., 1991—. Recipient award Am. Concrete Inst., 1967, Navy Outstanding Rating award, 1972; NDEA fellow, 1967-68. Mem. ASCE (mng. dir. 1989—), Nat. Coun. for Civil Engring. Rsch. (secretariat 1990—), Am. Gas Assn., ASME, Am. Mgmt. Assn., ASHRAE, Am. Mktg. Assn., Am. Pub. Works Assn., Am. Cons. Engrs. Coun. (program adv. com. Rsch. Found. 1990—), Tau Beta Pi, Chi Epsilon (former pres., v.p. local chpt.), Tau Epsilon Phi. Office: Civil Engring Rsch Found Ste 600 1015 15th St NW Washington DC 20005-2605

BERNSTEIN, HERBERT JOSEPH, physicist, consultant, educator; b. Washington, Apr. 21, 1943; s. Harry S. and Edith Bernstein; m. Mary Marcia Mayers, Apr. 4, 1971; children: Carolyn Joy, Laila Jael. BA, Columbia U., 1963; MS, U. Calif., San Diego, 1965, PhD, 1967; postgrad., Inst. for Advanced Study, Princeton, N.J., 1967-69. Rsch. physicist Cambridge (Mass.) Electron Accelerator, 1969-70; prof. physics Hampshire Coll., Amherst, Mass., 1971—, dir. sci. policy program, 1972-73; vis. scientist MIT, Cambridge, 1981—, Brookhaven Nat. Lab., Upton, N.Y., 1968; guest scientist Stanford (Calif.) Linear Accelerator Ctr. 1974; vis. asst. prof. physics U. Leuven, Louvain, Belgium, 1970-71; asst. prof. physics Southeastern Mass. U., North Dartmouth, Mass., 1969-70; cons. Gov. Am. Samoa, Pago Pago, 1971; dir. Inst. for Sci. and Interdisciplinary Studies, Amherst, 1991—; tech. dir. Vols. in Tech. Assistance, Washington, 1977-78; sci. tech. cons. World Bank, 1976-79. Co-author: New Ways of Knowing, 1987; contbr. articles to profl. jours. Active Havurat Ha-Emek Tzedaka Collective, Amherst, Mass., 1979—. Kellogg Found. fellow, 1985-88, NSF fellow, 1965-67; recipient Procter prize Sigma Xi, 1984. Fellow Inst. for Advanced Studies in Humanities; mem. Am. Phys. Soc., Assn. Mems. Inst. for Advanced Study (trustee, nominating chair 1986—). Jewish. Office: Inst for Sci & Interdisciplinary Studies Hampshire Coll Amherst MA 01002

BERNSTEIN, ILEANE JANIS, photographer; b. Mar. 25, 1956; d. Jack M. and Myra (Cohen) B. Student, U. Hartford, 1975; Fine Arts degree, Lasell Coll., 1977. One-woman shows at Nat. Mus. Women in the Arts, Washington, 1990-91, Bernhardt Collection at Touchstone Galleries; exhibited in group shows at Ward-Nasse Gallery Soho, N.Y.C., 1990, Wetherholt Galleries, Washington, 1991, The Funding Ctr., Old Town Alexandraia, 1991, Am. Soc. Archtl. Landscape, Washington, 1991-92; represented in permanent collections at Ellis Island Mus., N.Y.C., Nat. Mus. Women in Arts, Washington. Home: 75 Bank St New York NY 10014

BERNSTEIN, IRVING, international organization executive; b. N.Y.C., Aug. 9, 1921; s. Jacob and Ethel (Potasewitz) B.; m. Judith Muniz, Jan. 2, 1952; children: Robert, Joseph. B Social Sci., CCNY, 1942; MA, Columbia U. Tchrs. Coll., 1946; DHL (hon.), Yeshiva U., 1987. Secondary sch. tchr. N.Y.C. Public Sch. System, 1946; social worker N.Y.C. Dept. Welfare, 1947; field rep. midwest region United Jewish Appeal, 1948-50, West Coast regional dir., 1950-62, nat. asst. exec. vice chmn., 1962-68, nat. exec. vice chmn., 1969-84; founder Inst. for Fund-Raising Jewish Agy., Jerusalem, mem. bd. govs., 1984-88; 1st chmn. meml. mus. com. Pres.'s Coun. on Holocaust, 1980-86; bd. dirs. United Israel Appeal, Am. Jewish Joint Distbn. Com., Inst. on Am. Jewish Israeli Rels. of Am. Jewish Com.; vis. prof. Brandies U.; chmn. bd. advisors Hornstein Program for grad. studies in Jewish communal svcs. Brandeis U., 1980-84; mem. Internat. Ctr. for Univ. Teaching of Jewish Civilization in Jerusalem; chmn. Inst. Contemporary Jewry of Hebrew U. Contbr. articles to profl. jours. Mem. Com. for Econ. Growth of Israel; bd. dirs. Childrens Med. Ctr. Israel Hewbrew U., Techhnion U., Jersulam Coll. of Tech., Internat. Ctr. Film Prodn., Jersulam. With USAF, 1942-45. Recipient First Disting. Svc. award Assn. for Jewish Community Organizational Profls., 1986; Milender fellow Brandeis U., 1980. Mem. Nat. Soc. Fundraising Execs. Club: Lambs. Home: 1 Stoneleigh Rd Scarsdale NY 10583-4708

BERNSTEIN, JERALD JACK, neuroscience and physiology educator; b. Bklyn., Mar. 30, 1934; m. Frances Ann Pitlick, 1986. BS, Hunter Coll., Bronx, N.Y., 1955; MS, U. Mich., 1957, PhD, 1959. Prof. neurosci. U. Fla. Sch. Medicine, 1965-80, prof. ophthalmology, 1967-80; chief lab. cen. nervous system ing. regen VA Med. Ctr., Washington, 1980—; prof. neurol. surgery and physiology George Washington U. Sch. Medicine, Washington, 1980—, dir. lab exptl. neurol. surgery. Grantee NIH, 1965—; USPHS fellow Lab. Neroanat. 1959-65; recipient Elaine Snider award for Cancer Rsch., 1992. Mem. Soc. for Neurosci., Am. Assn. Pathologists, Neurotrauma Soc., Am. Soc. Neurochemistry, Internat. Devel. Neurosci., Internat. Soc. Neurochemistry, Internat. Brain Rsch. Orgn. Office: VA Med Ctr (151Q) 50 Irving St NW Washington DC 20422-0002

BERNSTEIN, LAWRENCE, computer software executive; b. N.Y.C., Jan. 20, 1940; s. Max Bernstein and Lillian (Schwartz) Shelly; m. Christine Marie Yuhas, Sept. 26, 1975; children: Michael, Leon, David. BEE, Renssalaer Poly. Inst., 1961; MEE, NYU, 1963. From engr. to exec. dir. Bell Labs, Middletown, N.J., 1961-88; exec. dir. Bell Labs, Summit, N.J., 1987-90; v.p. ops. system ATT Network Systems, Middletown, N.J., 1990—; bd. dirs. Resumix, Santa Clara, Calif. Patentee in field. Charter mem. Common Cause. Recipient Cert. for Patriotic Civilian Svc. U.S. Army, 1973. Fellow IEEE; mem. Assn. Computing Machinery, Tau Beta Pi, Eta Kappa Nu. Office: AT&T Network Systems 480 Red Hill Rd Middletown NJ 07748-3072

BERNSTEIN, RICHARD MARK, trust company executive; b. Balt., Mar. 10, 1957; s. Malcolm Erwin and Loraine Agatha (Panek) B.; m. Carol Louise Dreyer, Oct. 30, 1983; children: Katherine, Gregory. BA with honors, Johns Hopkins U., 1979, MA, 1983. Asst. buyer Balt. Gas & Electric Co., 1979-81, assoc. engr., 1983; investment rep. Alex. Brown & Sons, Inc., Balt., 1983-85; v.p. Merc.-Safe Deposit & Trust Co., Balt., 1985—; bd. dirs. Human Equations, Inc., Balt.; ptnr. Arbormasters, Inc., Randallstown, Md., 1981—. Mem. Pikesville (Md.) Community Growth Corp., 1988. Johns Hopkins U. fellow, 1981-83. Mem. Inst. Chartered Fin. Analysts, Balt. Security Analysts Soc. (pres. 1990-91), Sudbrook Club (pres. Pikesville chpt. 1988). Office: Merc-Safe Deposit & Trust 2 Hopkins Pl Baltimore MD 21201

BERNSTEIN, STEPHEN MICHAEL, lawyer, real estate developer; b. Bklyn., Feb. 10, 1941; s. Murray P. and Harriet L. (Rosenberg) B.; m. Lois Blitzer Kleinerman, July 15, 1984; 1 stepchild, Matthew. B.A., Bklyn. Coll., 1962; LL.B., Columbia U., 1965. Bar: N.Y. 1965. Atty. HUD, N.Y.C., 1966-69; asst. counsel N.Y. State Urban Devel. Corp., N.Y.C., 1969-72, assoc. dir. housing devel., 1972-75; practice law, N.Y.C., 1975—; real estate developer, N.Y.C., 1975—; vis. prof. real estate fin. Pratt Inst., 1985. Bd. dirs. Am. Cancer Soc., N.Y.C., 1980-86; bd. dirs. Florence Court Corp., Bklyn., 1982—, pres., 1982—. Mem. Nat. Housing Conf., Citizens Housing and Planning Council, N.Y. State Bar Assn. Club: City N.Y. Avocations: baseball, history. Home: 187 Hicks St Brooklyn NY 11201-2373 Office: 10 E 40th St New York NY 10016-0200

BERNSTEIN, STEVEN MICHAEL, fundraising executive; b. N.Y.C., July 25, 1953; s. Lawrence Jay and Lorraine (Katz) B.; m. Debbie Sue Cohen, June 21, 1975; children: Andrew Michael, Allison Kate. BA, York Coll., 1975. Gordon fellow Brandeis U., Waltham, Mass., 1976; dir. Coun. for Nat. Policy Planning, N.Y.C., 1977-78; devel. assoc. Human Resources Ctr., Albertson, N.Y., 1978-81; dir. devel. Am. Lung Assn., East Meadow, N.Y., 1981-83, Vis. Nurse Svc. of N.Y., N.Y.C., 1983-87; v.p. devel. The Community Hosp. at Glen Cove, N.Y., 1987-91; exec. dir. New Rochelle (N.Y.) Hosp. Med. Ctr. Found., 1991—; ptnr. Image Assocs., Old Bethpage, N.Y., 1985—. Contbr. articles to profl. jours. Mem. Nat. Soc. Fundraising Execs., Assn. Health Care Philanthropy. Jewish. Home: 44 Voorhis Dr Old Bethpage NY 11804 Office: New Rochelle Med Ctr Found 16 Guion Pl New Rochelle NY 11802

BEROZA, MORTON, chemist; b. New Haven, Mar. 7, 1917; s. Jacob and Tina (Chatzek) B.; m. Hannah Hurwitz, June 29, 1946; children: Robert J., Rosalyn J. BS, George Washington U., 1943; MS, Georgetown U., 1946, PhD, 1950. Sci. aide FDA, Washington, 1939-43; chemist, chem. engr. Naval Ordnance Lab., White Oak, Md., 1946-48; rsch. chemist, chief organic chems. synthesis lab. USDA, Beltsville, Md., 1948-74; sci. coord. Assn. of Official Analytical Chemists, Washington, 1975-81; cons. to many cos., 1975-88; cons. Booz Allen & Hamilton, Bethesda, Md., 1990—; adj. prof. Am. U., Washington, 1965-75. Adv. bd. mem. Jour. Agr. Food Chem., Jour. Chromatoqr. Sci., Environ. Anal. Chem., Rev. Anal. Chem., Jour. Chem. Ecology, Jour. Assn. Ofcl. Anal. Chem., Toxicol. and Environ. Chem. Rev.; editor: Chemicals Controlling Insect Behavior, 1970, Pest Management With Insect Sex Attractants, 1976; co-editor: Insect Suppression with Controlled Release Pheromone Systems, 1982, Insect Pheromone Technology: Chemistry and Applications, 1982, Insect Juvenile Hormones, Chemistry and Action, 1972. With USN, 1943-46. Recipient Internat. Award for Rsch. in Pesticide Chemistry, Am. Chem. Soc., 1977, Gold Medal Award for Outstanding Achievement in Environ. Chemistry, Synthetic Organic Chem. Mfrs. Assn., 1973, Harvey W. Wiley Award in Analytical Chemistry, Assn. of Official Analytical Chemists, 1970, Award in Chromatography & Electrophoresis, Am. Chem. Soc., 1969, Hillebrand prize Chem. Soc. of Washington, 1963. Home: 821 Malta Ln Silver Spring MD 20901-1134

BERR, STEPHEN FREDERICK, education; b. Bklyn., May 24, 1936; s. Barnett and Rose Helen (Mirkin) B.; m. Barbara Adele Solomon, Jan. 17, 1965; children: Laura Ellen Berr Brundage, Jonathan Daniel, Rebecca Miriam Steinberg. BS, Bklyn. Coll., 1957; MEd, Temple U., 1969. Tchr. Lafayette High Sch., Bklyn., 1958-59, Wingate High Sch., Bklyn., 1959-60, Pacific High Sch., San Leandro, Calif., 1960-61; investigator Dun & Bradstreet, San Francisco, 1961-62; tchr. Midwood High Sch., Bklyn., 1962-66, Plymouth Whitemarsh High Sch., Plymouth Meeting, Pa., 1966-68; ednl. researcher Bucks County Bd. Edn., Doylestown, Pa., 1968-69; tchr., planetarium dir. Colonia Sch. Dist., Plymouth Meeting, 1969—; project star tchr. Harvard Ctr. for Astrophysics, Cambridge, Mass., 1987-89, asst. Project SPICA, 1989-91. Contbr. articles to profl. jours. Bd. trustees Congregation of Ami, Lafayette Hill, Pa., 1985-90. With U.S. Army, 1957-58. Recipient award for excellence in edn. Whitemarsh Women's Club, 1986; named semi-finalist Pa. Tchr. of Yr., 1989, Tchr. of Yr. Montgomery County Ret. Tchrs., 1991. Fellow Nat. Sci. Tchrs. Assn.; mem. Mid-Atlantic Planetarium Soc., Delaware Valley Amateur Astronomers, Delaware Valley Apple Users Group (pres. 1988-91), Optical Soc. Am. Home: 2910 Sheffield Dr Norristown PA 19401-2228 Office: Colonial Middle Sch 716 Belvoir Rd Norristown PA 19401-2577

BERREBY, DAVID, journalist; b. Versailles, France, May 19, 1958; mother Am. citizen; s. Jean-Jacques Berreby and Ruth (Ryan) Hawkins; m. Gail Appleson, May 29, 1988. BA in English Lit., Yale U., 1981. Intern reporter Phila. Bull., 1978; reporter Providence Jour., 1979-80; staff writer The Nat. Law Jour., N.Y.C., 1981-83, nat. editor, 1983-84; assoc. editor The Scis., N.Y.C., 1984-85; editor CUNY, 1985-87; freelance journalist N.Y.C., 1987—; theater critic N.Y. Law Jour., 1982—. Contbr. theater revs., articles to newspapers and gen. interest publs. Mem. AAAS, Am. Theater Critics Assn., Nat. Book Critics Circle, Outer Critics Circle. Home and Office: 366 12th St Apt 4 Brooklyn NY 11215-5002

BERRESFORD, SUSAN VAIL, philanthropic foundation executive; b. N.Y.C., Jan. 8, 1943; d. Richard Case and Katherine Vail (Marsters) Berresford Hurd; m. David F. Stein (div.); 1 son, Jeremy Vail Stein. Student, Vassar Coll., 1961-63; B.A. cum laude in Am. History, Radcliffe Coll., 1965. Vol. UN Vol. Services, N.Y.C., summer 1962; sec. to Theodore H. White, summer 1964; program officer Neighborhood Youth Corps, N.Y.C., 1965-67; program specialist Manpower Career Devel. Agy., N.Y.C., 1967; human resources adminstrn. specialist Manpower Career Devel. Agy., 1968; freelance cons., writer Europe and U.S., 1968-70; program officer nat. affairs div. Ford Found., N.Y.C., 1970-80; program officer in charge Ford Found., 1980-81, v.p., 1981—. Home: 36 E 10th St New York NY 10003-6219 Office: Ford Found 320 E 43d St New York NY 10017

BERRETTONE, ROBERT J., marketing professional; b. Rochester, N.Y., Feb. 8, 1948; s. Michael and Yolanda B.; m. Sandra Anne Berrettone, July, 1987; 1 child, Elisa. BA in Psychology, U. Rochester, 1974, MBA. Pres. Scarber Mailer, Rochester, 1972-76; pres. Icon Direct, Rochester, 1976-90, chmn., 1991—; bd. dirs. Mktg. Communications, Rochester, 1977-84. Codir. Childrens Youth Assn., Rochester, 1982-87. With USNG, 1972-73. Best direct mktg. piece of show, best sales promotion direct mktg. Bus. Profl. Advertisers, Rochester, 1978; winner 3rd place best direct mktg. piece

in Sat. Evening Post, 1973. Mem. Upstate Direct Mktg. Assn. of N.Y. Roman Catholic. Office: Icon Direct 224 Edgerton St Rochester NY 14607-3317

BERREY, BEDFORD HUDSON, JR., orthopedic surgeon; b. Harlingen, Tex., Nov. 12, 1950; m. Rosalind Therese Mack Berrey, Apr. 5, 1975; children: Alison Elizabeth, Jillian Elise. BS, U.S. Mil. Acad., 1972; MD, U. Tex., Galveston, 1977. Diplomate Nat. Bd. Med. Examiners, Am. Bd. Orthopedic Surgery. Orthopedic resident Tripler Army Med. Ctr., Honolulu, 1977-81; fellow orthopedic oncology Mass. Gen. Hosp./Harvard Med. Sch., Boston, 1984-85; chief orthopaedic oncology Walter Reed Army Med. Ctr., Washington, 1985-87, chief orthopaedic surgery, 1987—; orthopedic cons. Office of Surgeon Gen., U.S. Army. Col. AUS, 1972—. Decorated Bronze Star medal, Army Commendation medal, Meritorious Svc. medal, Army Achievement medal. Fellow ACS, Acad. Orthopaedic Soc., Am. Acad. Orthopaedic Surgeons; mem. Musculoskeletal Tumor Soc., Orthopaedic Rsch. Soc., So. Med. Assn., So. Orthopaedic Assn., West Point Med. Assn. (v.p. 1988-89), Soc. Mil. Orthopaedic Surgeons (pres. 1987-88), Residents Coun. Tripler Army Med. Ctr. (pres. 1980-81), Med. Assn. Panama Canal Area (sec.-treas. 1984-85), Army Navy Club. Republican. Office: Walter Reed Army Med Ctr Chief Orthopaedic Surgery Washington DC 20307-5001

BERRINGER, GARY REVERE, nursing educator; b. Indiana, Pa., Jan. 16, 1952; s. Ivan Revere and Lois Nadine (McCoy) B.; m. Charlotte Ann Yoder, June 9, 1979; 1 child, Elizabeth Ann. BS in Biology, Indiana U. Pa., 1973, BSN, 1978; MSN in Perinatal Nursing, U. Pa., 1981. Cert. neonatal nurse practitioner, clinician, profl. nurse. Staff nurse Hahnemann Hosp., Phila., 1978-81; MCH clin. specialist Maple Ave. Hosp., DuBois, Pa., 1981-82; perinatal clin. nurse specialist St. Vincent Hosp., Erie, Pa., 1982-86; asst. prof. perinatal nursing Gannon U., Erie, 1986—, coord. computer assisted instrn. lab. Coll. Health Scis., 1991—; cons. Greater Erie Community Action Com., 1983. Chmn. profl. adv. com. March of Dimes, Erie, 1983; active Erie Philharm. Chorus, 1985, First Assembly of God Sanctuary Choir, Erie, 1982—. Ednl. Material grantee March of Dimes, Faculty Devel. grantee Gannon U., 1991. Mem. Nat. Assn. Neonatal Nurses, Nat. League Nursing, Pa. Perinatal Assn., Nurses Assn. Am. Coll. Ob-Gyn. (item writer 1990—). Republican. Home: 1726 W 40th St Erie PA 16509-1138 Office: Gannon U 2551 W 8th St Erie PA 16505-4494

BERRY, ALAN LINDSAY, architect; b. Greensboro, N.C., Apr. 16, 1954; s. Rudolf and Jean (Lindsay) B.; m. Kathy Ann Ramos, July 29, 1978; children: Nicole Lindsay, Sonya Sullivan. B in Creative Writing, Roger Williams Coll., 1976; BFA, RISD, 1980, BArch, 1981. Registered architect, R.I. Apprentice architect Belluschi/Daskalaskis Architects, Boston, 1980; project architect Mark Ramaeker Architects, Sarasota, Fla., 1981-82, Long Staats & Simpson, Newport, R.I., 1983-85; dir. archtl. design The Sakonnet Group, Portsmouth, R.I., 1985-89; architect in pvt. practice Newport, 1989—; guest lectr. Roger Williams Coll. Ctr. for Historic Preservation, Bristol, R.I., 1991; guest speaker Bristol Hist. Soc., Bristol, 1991. Bd. dirs. Friends of Linden Pl., Bristol, 1990—; bd. trustees 1st Congl. Ch., Bristol, 1991—; sec. Bristol Hist. Dist. Commn., 1991—. Mem. AIA (nat. del. 1987), R.I. AIA, Nat. Trust for Hist. Preservation, Rotary Club of Newport (bd. dirs. 1990—, dir. Internat. Svc. 1991—, chmn. Youth Exchange Com. 1990—). Home: 11 Ruth Ave Bristol RI 02809 Office: 20 Bellevue Ave Newport RI 02840

BERRY, BRIAN SHEPHERD, materials scientist; b. Manchester, Eng., Feb. 27, 1929; came to U.S., 1954; s. William and Mabel Selena (Shepherd) B.; m. Maureen Sheila-Marie Keen, Apr. 19, 1952; children: Alison Caroline, Christopher John. BSc with 1st class honors, U. Manchester, Eng., 1949, MSc, 1951, PhD, 1954. Asst. lectr. U. Manchester, 1951-54; rsch. asst. Yale U., New Haven, 1954-56; investigator Fulmer Rsch. Inst., Stoke Poges, Eng., 1956-58; mem. rsch. staff IBM Rsch. Div., Yorktown Heights, N.Y., 1958-91, ret., 1991—. Co-author: Anelastic Relaxation in Crystalline Solids, 1972; contbr. articles to profl. jours., encys., chpts. to books; patentee in field. Pres. Metal Sci. Club N.Y., N.Y.C., 1970. Fellow Am. Phys. Soc.; mem. Materials Rsch. Soc., Minerals, Metals and Materials Soc.

BERRY, ROBERT JOHN, architect; b. Concord, Mass., Nov. 10, 1947; s. John Harmon and Ruth Johanna (Berlied) B.; m. Helen Chapa, May 30, 1971; children: Amanda Kirsten, Heather Marie. A in Archtl. Engring., Wentworth Inst. Tech., 1967; BArch, U. Ariz., 1971. Registered architect, Mass. Asst. prof. Wentworth Inst. Tech., Boston, 1974-81, 90—; prin. Robert J. Berry, Architect, Boxborough, Mass., 1981—. Mem. Am. Soc. Archtl. Perspectivists (exhibitor 1986). Home and Office: 171 Summer Rd Boxboro MA 01719-2001

BERRY, THOMAS HARRISON, financial services company officer; b. Phila., Apr. 26, 1944; s. Harrison Morton and Dorothy Mae (Thornburg) B.; m. Mary Anne Davidson, Dec. 22, 1966; children: Mark Harrington, Adam Thomas. BA, Washington Coll., Chestertown, Md., 1966. Human resources generalist Colonial Penn Group, Phila., 1970-74, mgr. compensation, 1974-77, dir. human resources, 1977-83, v.p. orgn. devel., 1983-86, v.p. quality, 1986-90; dir. quality mgmt. The Vanguard Group, Wayne, Pa., 1990—; examiner Malcolm Baldrige nat. quality award Nat. Inst. Standards and Tech., U.S. Dept. Commerce, 1991-92; speaker on total quality mgmt.; cons. in field. Author: Managing the Total Quality Transformation, 1991; also articles. 1st lt. USMC, 1966-70, Vietnam. Mem. Assn. Internal Mgmt. Cons. (publs. dir. 1988-92, v.p. 1992—), Am. Soc. Quality Control, Assn. Quality and Participation, Phila. Area Coun. for Excellence, Barnegat Light Yacht Club (commodore 1982, trustee 1983—). Home: 577 Winston Way Berwyn PA 19312-1147 Office: The Vanguard Group 1300 Morris Dr Wayne PA 19087

BERS, ABRAHAM, electrical engineering educator; b. Cernauti, Bukovina, Romania, May 28, 1930; came to U.S., 1949; s. Isaias and Berta (Lechter) B.; m. Anita Alden Burrage, June 17, 1966; children: Rachel, Joshua. BS, U. Calif. with highest honors, Berkeley, 1953; SM, MIT, 1955, ScD, 1959. Rsch. asst. Rsch. Lab. Electronics MIT, Cambridge, Mass., 1953-58, instr. dept. elec. engring. and computer sci., 1958-59, asst. prof., 1959-63, assoc. prof., 1963-71, prof., 1971—; vis. prof. U. Paris-Orsay, France, 1981—; dir. Inst. Advanced Physics Studies, La Jolla, Calif., 1990—. Co-author: Waves in Anisotropic Plasmas, 1963; contbr. articles to profl. jours., chps. to books. Faculty Exch. fellow Ford Found., Tech. U. Berlin, 1966, fellow J.S. Guggenheim Meml. Found., U. Paris, 1968-69. Fellow Am. Phys. Soc. (chmn. div. plasma physics 1991); mem. AAAS, St. Botolph Club Boston, Univ. Fusion Assn. (pres. 1988-89).

BERSOFF, DONALD NEIL, lawyer, psychologist; b. N.Y.C., Mar. 1, 1939; s. Irving and Mina (Cohen) B.; children by previous marriage: Benjamin, David; m. Deborah Leavy, Oct. 16, 1988; 1 child, Judith. BS, N.Y. U., 1958; MA, NYU, 1960, PhD, 1965; student, U. Va. Law Sch., 1973-74; JD, Yale U., 1976. Bar: Md. 1976, D.C. 1984, Pa. 1990. Asst. prof. Ohio State U.; assoc. prof. U. Ga., U. Md. Sch. Law; ptnr. Ennis, Friedman & Bersoff, Washington, 1982-88, Jenner & Block, Washington, 1988-89; coord. joint J.D. and Ph.D. program in law and psychology U. Md. Sch. Law and Johns Hopkins U. Dept. Psychology., 1976-82; dir. law and psychology program Hahnemann U. Grad. Sch., Villanova Law Sch., Phila. and Villanova, Pa., 1990—. Author: Learning to Teach: A Decision-Making System, 1976. Served with USAF, 1965-68. N.Y. State Regents coll. teaching fellow. Mem. ABA, Am. Psychology-Law Soc. (pres. 1980-81), APA (coun. of reps. 1991—). Home: 780 College Ave Haverford PA 19041-1205 Office: Villanova Law Sch Villanova PA 19085

BERSTEIN, IRVING AARON, biotechnology and medical technology executive; b. Providence, Oct. 11, 1926; s. Robert Louis and Laura (Sperber) B.; m. Suzanne D'Amico, Apr. 16, 1972; children: Jonathan, Robert Laurance. ScB, Brown U., 1946; PhD, Cornell U., 1951. Pres., tech. dir. Controls for Radiation, Inc., Cambridge, Mass., 1957-68; dir. med. div., v.p. AGA Corp., Secaucus, N.J., 1969-71; asst. dir. rsch. program devel. div. health sci. and tech. Harvard U.-MIT, 1972-86; chmn. bd. Hygeia Scis. Inc., 1980-87, pres., 1985-87, sr. sci. advisor, 1988-90; chmn. bd. Endogen, Inc., Boston, 1990—; pres. Berstein Tech. Corp., 1980—; cons. for Med. & Biotechnology Investment, Corp. Devel., 1971—. Francis Wayland scholar; Cornell U. fellow. Mem. World Bus. Council, Forty-Niners, Harvard Club Boston, Brown Club Boston, Cornell Club Boston, Sigma Xi. Home and Office: 451 D St Boston MA 02210-1950

BERTELE, WILLIAM, environmental engineer; b. Phila., Aug. 7, 1935; s. William J. and Viola H. (DeFant) B.; children: William Bradford, Theodore, Amanda. BS in Commerce and Engring., Drexel U., 1963. Registered profl. engr., N.J., 1980. Field engr. Sam P. Wallace Co., Santurce, P.R., 1960-65; ptnr. Engineered Products Co., Santurce, 1965-68; sr. application engr. Am. Air Filter, Louisville, 1969-78; v.p. engring. Recon Systems Inc., Raritan, N.J., 1978-92; pvt. practice New Hope, Pa., 1992—. With USAR, 1960-65. Mem. CAP (dep. comdr. 1985-90, comdr. 1991, commendation 1984). Home and Office: 163 N Sugan Rd New Hope PA 18938

BERTELL, MARY KATHERINE, retired art educator, executive secretary; b. Buffalo, July 13, 1925; d. Paul George and Helen Josephine (Twohey) B. BS in Edn., SUNY, Buffalo, 1946, postgrad., 1947-65. Tchr. art grades 1-12 Skaneateles, N.Y., 1946-48; tchr. art grades 9-12 Buffalo, 1949-82; exec. sec. Ministry of Concern for Pub. Health, Buffalo, 1988—. Roman Catholic. Office: Ministry of Concern for Pub Health 5495 Main St Ste 147 Buffalo NY 14221

BERTENSHAW, WILLIAM HOWARD, III, radio and television producer; b. N.Y.C., Nov. 28, 1930; s. William Howard Jr. and Grace Annette (Miller) B.; m. Betty J. Underriner, July 7, 1956 (dec. Nov. 1975); children: Jane Ann, Judith Ann, Jo Ann; m. Bobbi C. Slachofsky, Dec. 16, 1984. BA in Communications, Ohio Wesleyan U., 1950. Asst. mktg. editor Bus. Week mag., N.Y.C., 1953-55; radio-TV dir. Hardy Burt Assocs., N.Y.C., 1955-57; radio-TV producer Empire Broadcasting Corp., N.Y.C., 1957-60, Nat. Episcopal Ch., N.Y.C., 1960-70; producer MBS, N.Y.C., 1970-75; dir. communications Council of Chs. City of N.Y., 1975-84; exec. producer, chief exec. officer Radio & TV Roundup Prodns., N.Y.C., 1984—; producer TKR Cable TV, N.Y.C., 1987—; guest lectr. So. Meth. U., Dallas, 1972, Seton Hall U., South Orange, N.J., 1974, Pace U., N.Y.C., 1980, Syracuse (N.Y.) U., 1982; vice chmn. dept. communications N.J. Coun. Chs., 1986—; host People Working for People, Sta. WOR-TV, N.Y.C., 1988; programmer Cable TV Newtork of N.J., 1985—; producer The Jersey Cape TV series, 1990—. Host Inner-Dimension Community Concerns, Union Eyes and Perspective on the News Sta. WOR Radio, N.Y., 1970—. Pres. Rep. Club, West Cape May, N.J., 1986-87; vice chmn. communications N.J. Coun. Chs., 1986-89; committeman Cape May County N.J. Rep. Orgn., 1987-90, Essex Coun. N.J. Rep. Orgn., 1960-85. Sgt. U.S. Army, 1951-53. Recipient Gabriel award Washington Conf., 1966-67, Radio Programming award Ohio State U., 1969, Columbus Film Festival award Ohio Coun. Chs., 1970, Radio-TV award N.J. Coun. Chs., 1983, Cape award Cable TV Network N.J., 1987. Mem. AFTRA, Nat. Lima Bean Assn. (founder), Alpha Sigma Rho. Episcopalian. Club: Suburban Sports Car (N.J.) (v.p., co-founder 1956-61). Home: 426 Sunset Blvd Cape May NJ 08204-4138

BERTH, DONALD FRANK, university official; b. Ludlow, Mass., Mar. 2, 1935; s. Frank and Wilma (Duffus) B. BSChemE, Worcester Poly. Inst., 1957, MSChemE, 1959; postgrad. in history and social scis., Cornell U., 1959-65. Instr. chemistry and physics, dir. admissions Corning (N.Y.) Community Coll., N.Y., 1960-62; adminstrv. asst., asst. dean and assoc. dean engring. Cornell U., Ithaca, N.Y., 1962-83, dir. engring. coop. program, 1975-80; v.p. univ. rels. (devel., pub. rels.) Worcester (Mass.) Poly. Inst., 1983—; engring., ednl. and devel. cons. colls. and univs. Founding editor Engring.: Cornell Quar., 1965-71; contbr. numerous articles to profl. jours. Trustee Rockwell Found., Denver, 1965-80, Worcester Hist. Mus., chmn. trustee nominating com., 1985—; active Met. Mus. Art, N.Y.C., Mus. Fine Arts, Boston, Mus. Fine Arts, Springfield, Mass., Worcester Art Mus., Smithsonian Instn.; trustee, mem. devel. com. New Eng. Sci. Ctr., 1992—. NSF fellow, 1962. Mem. AAAS, Am. Soc. for Engring. Edn. (editorial bd. 1985-90), Soc. for History Tech., Coun. for Advancement and Support Edn. (grand award for univ. mag. 1966, 69), Nature Conservancy, Vt. Inst. Natural Scis., Cornell Lab. Ornithology, Mass. Audubon Soc., Trustees of Reservations, Country Club Ithaca, Quechee Club Vt., Tatnuck Country Club, Worcester Econ. Club, Cornell Club N.Y., Sigma Xi, Phi Delta Kappa. Office: Worcester Poly Inst 100 Institute Rd Worcester MA 01609-2276

BERTHIAUME, WAYNE HENRY, electrical engineer; b. Worcester, Mass., Aug. 3, 1955; s. Henry Louis and Lorraine Anne (Beland) B.; m. Mary Louise Metivier, Aug. 21, 1976. AS in Elec. Engring. cum laude, Worcester Jr. Coll., 1982; BEE cum laude, Cen. New Eng. Coll., Worcester, 1987. Draftsman Henry L. Berthiaume Design Svcs., Northboro, Mass., 1969-71; TV repair technician Color Visual Tech., Northboro, 1971-72; technician Data Gen. Corp., Southboro, Mass., 1972-76, lead technician, 1974-76, final acceptance technician, 1976-77, lead technician, 1977, engr., 1977-83, sr. engr., 1983—. Marshal Boston Five Classic Golf Tournament, Danvers, Mass., Digital Sr. Golf Classic, Sudbury, Mass. Mem. NRA (life). Roman Catholic. Home: 129 Wheeler Rd Princeton MA 01541-1917 Office: Data Gen Corp Rte 9 Southboro MA 01772

BERTONAZZI, LOUIS PETER, state senator; b. Milford, Mass., Oct. 9, 1933; s. Peter John and Concetta (Rossi) B.; B.A., Tufts U., 1955; M.A., Suffolk U., 1960; m. Barbara Szymanski, June 7, 1957; children—Gregg, Lisa, David. Guidance dir. Medway (Mass.) High Sch., 1961-65; 1st dep. commr. Mass. Dept. Youth Services, 1966-69; mem. Mass. Ho. of Reps., 1969-78, Mass. State Senate, 1979—; asst. adj. prof. Boston U. Sch. Medicine. Mem. adv. bd. Office of Children, Internat. Yr. of Child, 1979; mem. nat. consumer rep. W.K. Kellogg Found., 1978—; mem. Mass. Citizens Com. on Tort Law Reform, 1980-81; mem. com. on human resources Eastern Regional Conf. Council State Govts., 1981—; mem. adv. com. Mass. Cancer Registry; chmn. subcom. Joint Legis./Exec. Commn. on Hosp. Reimbursement Systems; mem. Gov.'s/MBA Com. on Alcoholic Client. Served with U.S. Army, 1956-58. Mem. Nat. Conf. State Legislatures (fiscal affairs and oversight com.). Democrat. Roman Catholic. Office: Mass State Senate State Capitol Boston MA 02133

BERTOT, TED F., radio executive; b. N.Y.C., Mar. 8, 1945; s. Teodoro and Ruth Drew (Sherer) B.; Diane Sweet, Aug. 20, 1966 (div. 1979); children: Dinees June, Ted Herbert, Jaeseena Grace; m. Michele Ann Rufle, Sept. 1, 1984; 1 child, Joshua Andrew Aaron. Student, Wheaton Coll., 1963-65, SUNY, Canandaigua, 1991—. Program & news dir. WRUN AM/FM Radio, Utica, Rome, N.Y., 1971-73; writer, producer WMBO-WRLX Radio, Auburn, N.Y., 1973-79; program coord. Cayuga County Action Program, Auburn, 1980-81; ops. mgr. WSFW FM/AM Radio, Seneca Falls, N.Y., 1982-84; program dir. WACK Radio, Newark, N.Y., 1984-86; human svc. specialist Cath. Diocese of Rochester, Geneva, N.Y., 1986-88; ops. mgr. WACK-WNNR Radio, Newark-Sodus, N.Y., 1988—. Vol. Palmyra (N.Y.)-Macedon Food Pantry, 1988-90. Mem. Finger Lakes Office of Social Ministry (bd. dirs. 1982-86, pres. 1985-86), Diocese of Rochester Social Ministry (bd. dirs. 1983-86), KC Coun. 7424. Democrat. Roman Catholic. Home: 4058 Ny Route 31 Palmyra NY 14522 Office: WACK-WNNR Radio 187 Vienna Rd # 1420 Newark NY 14513-9124

BERTRAND, CHARLES A., cardiologist; b. N.Y.C., Mar. 6, 1925; s. Charles Arthur and Catharine M. (McKenna) B.; m. Maria Bertrand, Dec. 18, 1971. BS, Fordham U., 1944; MD, SUNY, 1948. Diplomate Am. Bd. Internal Medicine. Intern Bellevue Hosp., N.Y.C.; fellow in Cardiology The Johns Hopkins Hosp., Balt.; dir. Cardiology St. Agnes Hosp., White Plains, N.Y.; mem. Cardiology staff Westchester County Med. Ctr., Valhalla, N.Y.; dir. Cardiology Lawrence Hosp., Bronxville, N.Y.; dir. Cardio-Pulmonary dept. Roosevelt Hosp., N.Y.C., 1956-68; pres., chief med. staff St. Agnes Hosp., White Plains, 1964-68, Lawrence Hosp., Bronxville, 1984-88; cons. cardiologist Roosevelt Hosp., N.Y.C., No. Westchester Hosp., Mt. Kisco, N.Y., Peekskill (N.Y.) Hosp., Burke Found., White Plains, N.Y., Polyclinic Hosp., N.Y.C., Dobbs Ferry (N.Y.) Hosp., Phelps Meml. Hosp., Tarrytown, N.Y., Putnam Community Hosp., Carmel, N.Y., United Hospital, Port Chester, N.Y., IBM, 1968—, Gen. Foods, 1973—. Reviewer Am. Jour. of Cardiology, Jour. Am. Med. Assn.; contbr. articles to profl. jours. Active Pub. Health Commn., N.Y.C. Fellow ACP, Am. Coll. Cardiology; mem. AMA, Am. Heart Assn., Am. Trudeau Assn., N.Y. Acad. Sci., N.Y. Clin. Soc., Johns Hopkins Med. and Surg. Assn., Westchester Acad. of Medicine, Westchester County Med. Soc., N.Y. Heart Assn., Westchester Heart Assn., Am. Coll. of Physician Execs. Roman Catholic. Office: 311 North St White Plains NY 10605

BERTSCH, JAMES ALLEN, marketing executive; b. Rochester, N.Y., Nov. 30, 1947; s. Albert Herman and Elsa (Belke) B.; m. Beverly June Voorhies, Aug. 30, 1969 (div. June 1975); m. Sandra Lee Jardine, Aug. 9, 1975; children: Stephanie, Jillian. BA, St. John Fisher Coll., 1970; MS, Rochester Inst. Tech., 1979. Chemistry supr. Genesee Hosp., Rochester, 1971-77, lab. adminstr., 1978-82; bus. analyst Eastman Kodak Co., Rochester, 1982-84, mktg. dir., 1984-86, dir. product devel., 1986-88, dir. mktg., 1988—; adj. faculty Rochester Inst. Tech., 1979-83. Mem. Am. Chem. Soc., Am. Assn. for Clin. Chemistry. Home: 70 Phaeton Dr Penfield NY 14526-1218 Office: Eastman Kodak Co 343 State St Rochester NY 14652-3512

BERZOK, ROBERT MARTIN, communications executive; b. Bklyn., Oct. 28, 1944; s. Benjamin and Dorothy (Schoenbrun) B.; m. Deirdre Channing, Jan. 30, 1966 (div. 1980); 1 child, Matthew; m. Sharon Comey, Sept. 12, 1982 (dec.). BA, NYU, 1966, MPA, 1974. Reporter, tabulator Reuters News Agy., N.Y.C., 1961-66; mgr. employee publs. Uniroyal, Inc., Middlebury, Conn., 1969-84; mgr. info. and internal communications IBM Corp., N.Y., N.J., 1974-81; dir. corp. communications Union Carbide Corp., Danbury, Conn., 1981—. With U.S. Army, 1966-69. Fellow Internat. Assn. Bus. Communicators (chmn. exec. bd. 1986-87); mem. Coun. Communications Mgmt., Pub. Rels. Soc. Am., Arthur Page Soc., Issues Mgmt. Assn. (bd. dirs. 1988—). Jewish. Home: 53 Mill Rd Stamford CT 06903-1629 Office: Union Carbide Corp 38C Grove St Ridgefield CT 06877-4657

BESS, HAROLD LEON, physician, surgeon; b. Atlantic City, Oct. 25, 1924; s. Edward and Lillian (Rubenstein) B.; m. Elaine Sabott, Aug. 22, 1948; children: Alan, Ronald, Barbara. AB magna cum laude, Rutgers U., 1950; DO, U. Calif., Irvine, 1954. Cert. in gen. practice. Intern Mass. Osteo. Hosp., Boston, 1954-55; resident Bristol (Pa.) Gen. Hosp., 1955-57; chmn. dept. gen. practice Del. Valley Hosp., Bristol, 1968-74, chmn. utilization com., chief of staff, dir. med. edn., 1971-74, pres. bd. dirs., 1976-77, pres. bd. dirs. Exit Drug Treatment Ctr., 1976-78; med. dir. H.L. Bess Neuromuscular Pain Clin., Levittown, Pa., 1985-92; lectr. on thermography with attention to neck and low back injuries. Contbr. articles to profl. jours. With USNR, 1943-46. Decorated 3 bronze stars. Fellow Acad. Psychosomatic Medicine (cert.); mem. AAAS, Am. Acad. Thermology (cert.), Royal Soc. Medicine, Internat. Assn. for Study of Pain, Am. Pain Soc., Am. Assn. Orthopaedic Medicine, Am. Coll. Neuropsychiatry, Internat. Soc. Comprehensive Medicine, Am. Osteo. Assn., Am. Coll. of Gen. Practice in Osteo. Medicine and Surgery (cert.), Acad. of Neuro-Muscular Thermography (cert.), Am. Osteo. Acad. of Sports Medicine, Internat. Rehab. Medicine Assn., Am. Coll. Medicine, Can. Pain Soc., People to People Pain Mgmt. to Soviet Union, Intractable Pain Soc. of Gt. Britain and No. Ireland, Internat. Soc. Gen. Semantics, Inst. Gen. Semantics, Internat. Soc. Transactional Psychiatry, Bucks County Osteo. Soc. (sec.-treas. 1959-62), Masons, Phi Sigma Gamma. Address: 2 Red Rose Dr Levittown PA 19056 *Died Feb. 1992.*

BESS, JAMES LAWRENCE, academic administration educator; b. N.Y.C., Oct. 11, 1934; s. John Morris and Ina (Palton) B.; m. Nancy Moore, May 1, 1971; children: Isaac, Ivan. AB, Cornell U., 1956; MBA, Harvard U., 1960; AM, NYU, 1965; PhD, U. Calif., Berkeley, 1971. Asst. to exec. v.p. Harper & Row, N.Y.C., 1960-63; program assoc. NYU, 1963-65; asst. to pres. Cornell U., Ithaca, N.Y., 1965-67; dir. instl. rsch. SUNY, Stony Brook, 1971-76; assoc. prof. Tchr.'s Coll. Columbia U., N.Y.C., 1976-80; prof. NYU, 1980—; vis. scholar Nat. Inst. for Ednl. Rsch. of Japan, vis. rsch. fellow Nat. Inst. for Rsch. Advancement in Japan, 1986-87; dir. Program in Higher Edn., NYU, 1982-86; cons. NSF, William Paterson Coll., Morris County Coll., Bridgeport U., N.Y. Inst. Tech.; chair editorial bd. Jour. Higher Edn., editorial bd. Internat. Jour. of Ednl. Adminstrn; consulting editor ASHE-ERIC Higher Edn. Rsch. Report Series; mem. editorial bd. Assn. Study Higher Edn. Readers. Author: Collegiality and Bureaucracy in the Modern University, 1988, University Organization: A Matrix Analysis of the Academic Professions, 1982; editor: Foundations of American Higher Education, 1991, College and University Organization: Insights from the Behavioral Sciences, 1984, New Directions for Teaching and Learning: Motivating Professors to Teach Effectively, 1982, Academic Work: Doing It Well/Doing It Better, 1980; also articles, book chpts., monographs and book revs. 1st lt. U.S. Army, 1958-60. Fulbright scholar to Japan, 1986-87; grantee Tokyo Club, 1989-90, Xicom Corp., Inc., 1986, Exxon Edn. Found., 1984, U.S. Office Edn., 1973-75. Mem. Am. Ednl. Rsch. Assn., Assn. for Study of Higher Edn., Acad. of Mgmt., Am. Assn. Higher Edn., Internat. Assn. Conflict Mgmt. Office: NYU/Dept Adminstrn Leadership & Tech 300 E Bldg Washington Sq New York NY 10003

BESSENYEY, FRANCIS B., banker; b. Budapest, Hungary, May 5, 1925; came to U.S. 1946; s. Baron Georges B. and Gisele (Bene) B.; m. Eva Barcza, Dec. 19, 1924; children: Margit, Ilona, Kristina. Licence en Droit, U. Lausanne, Switzerland, 1946. Clk. to office mgr. A. Kremer & Co., Inc., N.Y.C., 1947-53; fgn. exchange trader J. Henry Schroder Bank, N.Y.C., 1953-58; sr. v.p. Europe J. Henry Schroder Bank, 1958-84; pres. MTB Banking Corp., 1984-90. Bd. dirs. Am. Found. Hungarian Lit. and Edn., N.Y.C., 1970—. Comdr. Order Infante Dom Henrique, Republic of Portugal, 1985, Grand Officer Pro Merito Melitensi, Mil. Order of Malta. Mem. Am. Portuguese Soc. (pres., bd. dirs.), Hungarian Knights of Malta (pres. 1983-90), Forex U.S.A. (hon.), India House. Roman Catholic.

BESSERMAN, ELLEN RAE, playwright, poet; b. Bklyn., Sept. 26, 1958; d. Sol and Adele (Sluzak) B. Student, Bklyn. Coll., 1976-77, 81-83. tchr. South Shore Adult Edn., Bklyn., 1984, 92. Playwright: (dramatic, comic plays) Closet Play, After the Party, From This Day Forward; author numerous poems. Active Pro-choice, ERA, Dem. campaign for pres., N.Y.C., 1984. Mem. Dramatists Guild (assoc.).

BESSEY, JEFFREY L., psychologist; b. Lafayette, Ind., Sept. 24, 1957. BA, Kalamazoo Coll., 1979; MA, U. Mich., 1981; PhD, U. Mo., 1986. Lic. psychologist, N.J. Dir. psychology svcs. Wellspring Ctr. for Human Devel., Maple Shade, N.J., 1986—; staff psychologist Pain Ctr. Loures Med. Ctr., Camden, N.J., 1987—; cons. psychologist Bancroft Sch., Mullica Hill, N.J., 1986—; lectr. on self-esteem, stress mgmt., anxiety., 1987—. Contbr. articles to profl. jours. Mem. Am. Psychol. Assn., N.J. Psychol. Assn., Am. Assocs. Mental Retardation, Am. Pain Soc., Internat. Assn. for Study of Pain. Home: 138 N Drexel St Woodbury NJ 08096-1581

BEST, EDGAR EVERETT, rehabilitation services consultant; b. Elrama, Pa., Mar. 21, 1904; s. Edward Everett and Ella Jane (Wray) B.; BS, California (Pa.) U., 1940; m. Pauline Phillips, Sept. 4, 1943; 1 child, Ellen Rae Best Anderson. With Carnegie Illinois Steel Corp., Clairton, Pa., 1925-40, insp. steel quality, 1934-40; tchr. vocat. machine shop and indsl. arts Prince George's County Pub. Schs., Upper Marlboro, Md., 1940-42; with VA, 1945-69; nat. chief manual arts therapy and ednl. therapy, acting chief corrective therapy, spl. asst. to dir. physcial medicine and rehab. service center. office, Washington, 1961-69; cons., exec. dir. Rehab. Cons. Svc., Beltsville, Md., 1970—. Maj. USAAF, 1942-45. Recipient Meritorious Svc. award Tri-Organizational Rehab. Conf., 1970. Mem. Registry Med. Rehab. Therapists, Specialists. Am. Assn. Rehab. Therapy (life, Wise Owl award 1969), Am. Assn. Ret. Persons, Epsilon Pi Tau (Hon. citation 1964, Corrective Therapy award Mid-Atlantic chpt. 1968), Ret. Officers Assn., Internat. Platform Assn., Rotary, Masons, Shriners, Craftsmen of U.S. (life mem.), Freestate Sq. Club, Beltsville Young-at-Heart Club (past pres.). Methodist. Contbr. articles to profl. publs. Home and Office: 4112 Kenny St Beltsville MD 20705-2732

BEST, FRANKLIN LUTHER, JR., lawyer; b. Lock Haven, Pa., Dec. 14, 1945; s. Franklin L. and Hazel M. (Yearick) B.; m. Kimberly R., May 1, 1982. BA, Yale U., 1967; JD, U. Pa., 1970. Bar: Pa. 1970. Assoc. MacCoy, Evans & Lewis, Phila., 1970-74; asst. counsel Penn Mut. Life Ins. Co., Phila., 1974-77, asst. gen. counsel, 1978-84, assoc. gen. counsel, 1985—; counsel, asst. sec. Penn Ins. and Annuity Co., Phila., 1983—; lectr. Pa. Bar Inst. Author: Pennsylvania Insurance Law, 1991; contbr. articles to profl. jours. Bd. dirs. Ctr. City South Neighborhood Assn., 1979-80, pres., 1978-79; mem. Com. of Seventy, 1978-84; sec. Washington Sq. Assn., 1977-87; mem. 30th

Ward Rep. Exec. Com., 1972-84, West Pikeland Twp. Open Spaces Com., 1987—. Mem. ABA, Phila. Bar Assn., Internat. Claim Assn. (exec. com. 1979-81, 85-88), Yale Club of Phila. Presbyterian. Office: Penn Mut Life Ins Co Independence Sq Philadelphia PA 19172

BEST, ROBERT A., foundation administrator; b. Long Beach, N.Y., Aug. 23, 1937; s. George Robert and Josephine (La Spina) B. BS in Econs., Villanova U., 1959; MA in Econs., Cath. U., 1962. Internat. economist U.S. Treasury, Washington, 1962-64; sr. economist Internat. Econ. Policy Assn., Washington, 1964-66; chief economist U.S. Senate Fin. Com., Washington, 1966-78; exec. v.p. Am. Export League, Washington, 1978-82; pres. Allen-Best Assn., Washington, 1983-88, Pacific Trade & Investment Corp., 1988-89, Pvt. Sector Initiatives Found., Washington, 1989—; pres. Best Assocs., Washington, 1983—; cons. World Bank, Washington, 1989-91. Vol. Tenley Study Ctr., Washington, Gift of Peace, Washington, 1990. Office: PSI Inc 816 Connecticut Ave NW Washington DC 20006

BEST, SHARON LOUISE PECKHAM, college administrator; b. Elmira, N.Y., Aug. 4, 1940; d. Paul Arthur and Beatrice L. (Hunter) Peckham; m. Willard C. Best, Sept. 3, 1961; children: Meryl Elizabeth, Kevin Hunter. BA cum laude, William Smith Coll., 1977. Acting dir. alumnae relations William Smith Coll., Geneva, N.Y., 1976-77; assoc. dir. devel. Hobart & William Smith Colls., Geneva, 1977, dir. devel., 1978-81, exec. dir. devel., 1981-87, v.p. for devel., 1988—; cons. Nazareth Coll., Rochester, N.Y., 1985. Active Ontario County (N.Y.) rep. com., 1968-78, Geneva Hist. Soc., 1975-80; active Geneva Concerts, Inc., 1965—, bd. dirs. 1974-82, pres., 1976-78. Recipient Case award capital fundraising USX Found., 1988. Mem. Council for Advancement and Support Edn. (bd. trustees Mid-Atlantic Dist. II 1987—, Gold Medal-Decade Improvement in Fund Raising 1987), Nat. Soc. Fund Raising Execs., League of Women Voters, Phi Beta Kappa, Phi Sigma Iota. Presbyterian. Club: Geneva Country. Home: 859 S Main St Geneva NY 14456-3205 Office: Hobart & William Smith Colls Geneva NY 14456-3397

BEST, THIRZA LOUISE, retired educator; b. Leesport, Pa., June 26, 1934; d. Crawford James and Juliette Ida (Havy) B. Student, East Stroudsburg U., 1952-54; BS in Edn., Kutztown U., 1957; MEd, Pa. State U., 1963. Tchr. social studies 7th grade Wilson Sch. Dist., West Lawn, Pa., 1957-58; tchr. 4th grade Holy Guardian Angels Sch., Laureldale, Pa., 1958-59; tchr. geography Northeast Jr. High Sch., Reading, 1959-60; tchr. English, geography, ancient and U.S. history, health Northwest Jr. High Sch., Reading, 1960-88, ret., 1988; with H&R Block; asst. softball coach Alvernia Coll., 1991; coach girl's track, volleyball, co-ed bowling and sch. Broadway shows, 1960-88, advisor sch. paper and yearbook, 1963-65. Bus. mgr., producer Green Hills Theatre, 1958-59, prof. equity; past mem. bd. Camp Fire Girls, Reading; active Reading Community Players, Genius Theater; mem. Ontelaunee Aux. to St. Joseph Hosp. Mme. NEA, Pa. Edn. Assn., Reading Edn. Assn., Woman's Club of Leesport (treas.), Lambda (treas.). Home: 12 Huntzinger Rd Wernersville PA 19565-9711

BEST, WILLIAM ANDREW, III, financial executive; b. Madrid, May 6, 1961; came to U.S., 1970; s. William Andrew and Marion (Wendt) B. BA, Williams Coll., Williamstown, Mass., 1983; MBA, U. Pa., 1989. Fixed income rsch. The First Boston Corp., N.Y.C., 1982; fin. analyst Lehman Bros., N.Y.C., 1983-85; assoc. risk capital Arral & Ptnrs. (Asia) Ltd., Hong Kong, 1986-87; summer intern Internat. Fin. Corp., Washington, 1988; asst. to ptnr. Brown Bros. Harriman & Co., N.Y.C., 1989-90; portfolio mgr., global fixed income Brown Bros Harriman & Co., N.Y.C., 1990—. Contbr. travel articles to profl. jours. Wharton Govt. and Bus. fellow, Dr. Alfred G. Buehler Meml. fellow The Wharton Sch., Phila., 1988. Office: Brown Bros Harriman & Co 59 Wall St New York NY 10005-2818

BETANCOURT, MARY ALIECE, school system administrator; b. Tulsa, Oct. 24, 1938; d. Ross L. and Allie L. (Epperson) Standefer; m. Philip P. Betancourt, June 20, 1959; children: John Gregory, Michael William. BS in Edn., S.W. Mo. State U., 1959; MEd, U. Mo., 1967. Tchr. Waynesville (Mo.) Bd. Edn., 1959-60; tchr., curriculum coord. Riverview Gardens (Mo.) Bd. Edn., 1960-68; tchr. Pennsauken (N.J.) Bd. Edn., 1968-71; supr. Moorestown (N.J.) Bd. Edn., 1972—; cataloguer Pseira Excavations, Crete, Greece, 1985—. Mem. Rep. Orgn., Moorestown, 1985—; advisor ABC's, Moorestown, 1989—; bd. dirs. N.J. Forensic League, 1988. Mem. Assn. for Secondary Curriculum Devel., Prins. and Suprs. Assn., Nat. Coun. Tchr.'s of English, Nat. Forensic League, Moorestown Adminstrs. Assn. Methodist. Office: Moorestown High Sch Bridgeboro Rd Moorestown NJ 08057-1412

BETH, ERIC WALTER, physicist; b. Vienna, Austria, June 7, 1912; came to U.S., 1937; Student, U. Vienna, 1930-31, 33-35, Phd, 1934; student, U. Gottingen, Germany, 1931-32, U. Munich, 1932-33. Asst. in physics U. Vienna, 1936-37; rsch. fellow U. Calif., 1937-38, asst. in physics, 1938; asst. in physics Reed Coll., 1939-40; vis. instr. physics, math. Mills Coll., Calif., 1940-41; spl. cons. in physics Cambridge (Mass.) Rsch. Lab., 1946-53; mem. sci. staff Melpar, Inc., Alexandria, Va., 1953-54; physicist Union Switch and Signal div. Westinghoue Air Brake Co., Swissvale, Pa., 1954-62; asst. prof. physics SUNY, Buffalo, 1962-82, asst. prof. emeritus, 1982—. Contbr. articles to profl. jours. With U.S. Army, PTO. U. Calif. scholar, 1937-38. Mem. Am. Phys. Soc., N.Y. Acad. Scis., Sigma Xi. Office: SUNY Dept Physics/Astronomy 239 Fronczak Hall Buffalo NY 14260

BETHANY, ADELINE CARAVELLI, music educator, academic administrator; b. Phila., Oct. 27, 1935; d. Vito and Mary Theresa (Tori) Caravelli; m. Gordon Wallace Bethany, May 17, 1958; children: Karen Marie, Robert Gordon, Paul Michael. MusB, Phila. Mus. Acad., 1957; MusM, West Chester (Pa.) U., 1974; EdD, Nova U., 1985. Choral dir. Del. County Community Coll., Media, Pa., 1975—; instr. Neuman Coll., Aston, Pa., 1976-80; prof., chairperson fine arts dept. Cabrini Coll., Radnor, Pa., 1979—; founder, dir., condr. DCCC-Cabrini Singers, Media and Radnor, Pa., 1982—. Named to Legion of Honor, Chapel of Four Chaplains, 1980; nominated Hazlett award, 1982; recipient Christian R. and Mary F. Lindback Disting. award Cabrini Coll., 1991. Mem. Music Educators Nat. Conf., Coll. Music Soc., Pa. Music Educators Assn. (exec. bd. 1985—), Am. Choral Dirs. Assn., Assn. Performing Arts Presenters. Roman Catholic.

BETHEA, CHARLES, real estate analyst, consultant; b. Phila., July 14, 1933; s. Sampson Benjamin Washington and Mary Elizabeth (Melvin) B.; m. Carmen Romero, Oct. 31, 1971; 1 child, Angela Regan. BBA, U. Pa., 1975; student, Temple U., 1977-79. Lic. real estate broker, Pa. Engrng. aide I City of Phila., 1953-56, engring aide II, 1956-65, real estate asst. I, 1965-70, real estate asst. II, 1970-81; real estate rep. McDonald's Corp., Cherry Hill, N.J., 1981-83; asst. mgr. real estate Consol Rail Corp., Phila., 1983-86; corp. analyst-real estate Shared Med. Systems Corp., Malvern, Pa., 1986-88; pvt. practice cons. Phila., 1981—. Author booklet How to Avoid Foreclosure, 1984. Mem. adv. bd. Lee Cultural Ctr., Phila., 1969; real estate advisor Adv. Community Devel. Corp., 1973; real estate sites and selection com. Sch. Dist. Phila., 1970-81; exec. com. New Path Montessori Sch., Phila., 1983; real estate cons. Phila. Bd. Dirs. of City Trusts, 1965-81; spl. counsel to Phila. city solicitor for negotiating econ. terms of City-Pa. Railroad agreements, 1972-76; mem. Morris Arboretum. Recipient Commonwealth of Pa. scholarship, 1973-75. Mem. Wharton Club of Phila., Faculty Club of U. Pa., U. Pa. Real Estate Soc. Democrat. Baptist. Home: 325 Winding Way Glenside PA 19038-2114

BETHEL, HELEN CORDERO, psychotherapist; b. N.Y.C., Apr. 10, 1935; d. Joseph and Mary (Colon) Cordero; m. Eddie Mack Bethel, Nov. 6, 1965; children: Darryl, Daniel, Janet. BA, U. P.R., San Juan, 1973; MEd, U. Lowell, Mass., 1977; PhD, U. Mass., 1990. Tchr. ESL Lawrence (Mass.) High Sch., 1974-79; bilingual sch. psychologist Chelsea (Mass.) Sch. System, 1979-82; psychology intern Greater Framingham (Mass.) Mental Health Ctr., 1985-86; psychologist Mass. Dept. of Corrections, Framingham, 1986-88; pvt. practice psychotherapist Derry, N.H., 1988-90; clin. psychotherapist Concord (N.H.) Psychol. Assocs., 1990—; cons. Social Justice for Women, Boston, 1987, Womens Health & Learning Ctr., Boston, 1987. Member adv. com. State of N.H., 1982—; chairperson Coun. for Civil Rights of N.H., Derry, 1978-80, U.S. Commn. on Civil Rights, 1989-90; trustee Monsignor Philip J. Kenny Scholarship Bd., Concord, 1988—; bd. dirs. YMCA, Manchester, N.H., 1978-81. Recipient Disting. Svc. award UN, 1979. Mem. ASCD, Nat. Hispanic Psychol. Assn., Internat. Soc. for Study of Multiple Personality and Dissociation, Assn. Christian Therapists, Mass. Sch. Psychologists. Democrat. Roman Catholic. Home: 2 Elaine St Derry NH 03038-5264 Office: Concord Psychol Assoc 6 Loudon Rd Concord NH 03301-5321

BETHJE, ROBERT, general surgeon, retired; b. Braunschweig, Fed. Republic of Germany, Nov. 15, 1922; came to U.S., 1923; s. Robert Paul and Elisabeth Augusta (Lieder) B.; m. Maria Vatral, June 11, 1955; children: Susan Leslie, Robert Eric, Alan Randolph. BS, CUNY, 1945; MD, N.Y. Med. Coll., 1949. Diplomate Nat. Bd., 1950, Am. Bd. Surgery, 1958. Asst. treas. Broome County Med. Soc., Binghamton, N.Y., 1964, v.p., 1965, pres., 1966; pres. med. staff Ideal Hosp., Endicott, N.Y., 1973-76, chief of surgery, 1971-77; chief of surgery Wilson Meml. Hosp., Johnson City, N.Y., 1979-80. Bd. dirs. Broome-Tioga Assn. for Retarded Children, Binghamton, 1983—. Capt. U.S. Army Med. Corps, 1951-53. Fellow Am. Coll. Surgeons; mem. Rotary (Endicott v.p. 1980-81, dir. 1981-84, pres. 1985-86). Home: 4 Ivanhoe Rd Binghamton NY 13903-1424

BETHKE, WILLIAM MILFORD, investment management executive; b. White Plains, N.Y., Apr. 13, 1947; s. Robert Harder and Patricia (Davis) B.; m. Susan Martha Schroeder, Aug. 21, 1973; children: Corinne Barbara, Brian Davis. BA, Middlebury Coll., 1969; MBA, Stanford U., 1971. Analyst F.S. Smithers & Co., Inc., N.Y.C., 1971-73; asst. v.p. Paine, Webber, Jackson & Curtis, Inc., N.Y.C., 1973-74; sr. analyst Prudential Ins. Co. of Am., Newark, 1974-75, gen. mgr., 1975-79, v.p., 1979-86; sr. v.p. Prudential Ins. Co., Newark, 1986—; pres., chief exec. officer Prudential Affiliated Investors, Newark, 1986-92; pres. Prudential Asset Mgmt. Co., Newark, 1989-92, Capital Markets Group, Newark, 1992—; dir. Investor Responsibility Rsch. Ctr., Washington, 1979—, Prudential Asia Investments, Inc., 1986—. Contbr. articles to profl. jours. Mem. Mountain Lakes Club, Park Lakes Club. Home: 151 Lake Dr Mountain Lakes NJ 07046 Office: Prudential Capital Markets Group Newark NJ 07101

BETHLEN, FRANCIS RHEDEY, business and economics educator; b. Budapest, Hungary, July 2, 1925; came to U.S., 1952; s. Paul and Gabriella (Serenyi) B.; m. Ilona R. Szentimrey, Oct. 7, 1948; children: Anna Maria, Mihaly Antal. BS, Polytechnic U., Budapest, 1947; MS, Cornell U., 1956; PhD, Purdue U., 1962. Teaching asst. dept. agrl. econs. Purdue U., Lafayette, Ind., 1959-61; assoc. prof. econs. SUNY, Plattsburgh, 1961-63, prof., chmn. dept. econs., 1963-69, prof. bus. and econs., 1971-78, prof. mktg., 1981—; sr. vis. Fulbright prof. dept. econs. Rosario U., Cordoba, Argentina, 1969-70; vis. sr. prof. econs. and mktg. U. Nicaragua, Managua, 1978-79, UN Mgmt. Inst., Arusha, Tanzania, 1979; vis. lectr. Rosario, Argentina, 1987, Budapest, 1989, 90, Moscow, 1990, 91; exec. tng. specialist, Hungary, 1989, 90, 91, 92; market extensionist Grange League Fedn., Batavia, N.Y., 1955-59; grad. rsch. asst. Cornell U., Ithaca, N.Y., 1953-56; livestock market specialist Est. San Antonio, Olavarria, Argentina, 1949-52; milling products specialist Aranka Flour Mills, Bicske, Hungary, 1945-49. Contbr. articles to profl. jours. Fulbright scholar, 1969, 70, 78. Mem. Am. Mktg. Assn., Rakoczi Found. (bd. dirs. 1984—), Global Energy Soc., Internat. Econs. Soc., Latin Am. Project Evaluators, Kiwanis, Knight of Malta. Home: 18 Wells St Plattsburgh NY 12901-2713 Office: SUNY Redcay Bldg Beekman St Plattsburgh NY 12901-2701

BETIT, BRENT EUGENE, college administrator, fiction writer; b. Bennington, Vt., May 28, 1957; s. Roy Eugene and Antoinette Teresa (Stone) B.; m. Julie Ellen Bostwick, Mar. 23, 1985; children: Matthew Bryant, Nicholas Christian. BA in English Lit. magna cum laude, Dartmouth Coll., 1979. Staff editor Family Jour., Dummerston, Vt., 1980-81; project mgr. Griswold Constrn., Inc., Shelburne, Mass., 1981-84; owner dB Constrn., Inc., Shelburne, 1985; facilities mgr. Landmark Coll., Putney, Vt., 1986—; instr. Landmark Coll., Putney, 1991. Author: (short fiction) Eye of the Storm, 1991; contbr. articles to profl. jours. Lindsay spl. scholar Dartmouth Coll., 1976-79, Rufus Choate scholar, 1977-79. Home: River Rd Putney VT 05346 Office: Landmark Coll River Rd Putney VT 05346

BETONI, THEODORE ANTHONY, JR., reinsurance management company executive; b. Phila., Aug. 3, 1951; s. Theodore Anthony Sr. and Concetta Eleanor (Zuccheli) B.; divorced; 1 child, Michelle Lyn; m. Anne Marie Cavaliere, Mar. 17, 1984; 1 child, Laura Anne. BS, Pa. State U., 1973. Account analyst Travelers Ins., Phila., 1973-75; casualty underwriter Interstate Nat., Phila., 1975-76; sr. casualty underwriter Comml. Union, Phila., 1976-78; casualty underwriter Am. Re-Ins., Phila., 1978-80; casualty mgr. Transatlantic Re, Phila., 1980-81, Commodore Re Mgmt., Haddonfield, N.J., 1981-82; pres., chmn. Motors Re Mgmt., Burlington, N.J., 1982-90; exec. v.p. MIC Re Mgmt., Mt. Laurel, N.J., 1990—; chmn. Motors Re Mgmt., Burlington, N.J., 1982-90. Mem. baseball USA, Trenton, N.J., 1991, USA Olympics 1992, 1990. Mem. Mensa, Pa. State Alumni Assn., Delta Tau Kappa. Office: MIC Re Corp 6000 Midlantic Dr Laurel Corp Ctr PO Box 5041 Mount Laurel NJ 08054

BETSCHART, JEAN ELIZABETH, nursing educator; b. Pitts., Nov. 25, 1948; d. Albert John and Elizabeth Mary (Lockard) Eisenbeis; m. James Martin Betschart; children: Julie, Kelly, Jeff. BSN, U. Pitts., 1970, M in Nursing, 1980. RN, Pa. Staff nurse ICU recovery rm. Children's Hosp., Pitts., 1970-72, diabetes educator, 1980-91, diabetes program coord., 1991—; adj. instr. nursing care of children U. Pitts. Parent-Child Nursing Grad. Program, 1985—; presenter at Internat. Diabetes Fedn. ADA meeting, Washington, 1991, 2nd N.Am. Symposium on Diabetes Edn., Las Vegas, 1990. Author: It's Time to Learn About Diabetes: A Progressive Learning Workbook for Children 8-10, 1991 (with L. Siminerio), Children with Diabetes, 1986 (with S. Puczynski) Foundation for the Future: Understanding of the Child with Diabetes in the Classroom, 1989-90, 1991; series editor Diabetes Self-Management; contbr. articles to The Diabetes Educator, Diabetes Forecast. Mem. Am. Assn. Diabetes Educators (pres. 1991-92), Am. Assn. Diabetes Educators Edn. and Rsch. Found. (trustee 1988-91), Am. Diabetes Assn. (editorial bd. 1988-90, mem. com. on profl. practice 1990-92, mem. edn. program review panel 1991-93), Assn. Care of Children's Health, Sigma Theta Tau. Office: Childrens Hosp Pitts 3705 5th Ave Pittsburgh PA 15213

BETTELHEIM, FREDERICK ABRAHAM, chemistry educator; b. Gyor, Hungary, June 3, 1923; came to U.S., 1951; s. Anton and Elizabeth (Gyarfas) B.; m. Vera Deutsch, May 12, 1989; 1 child, Adriel A. BS, Cornell U., 1953; MS, U. Calif.-Davis, 1954, PhD, 1956. Lab. technician Agr. Expt. Sta., Rehovoth, Israel, 1946-51; rsch. instr. U. Mass., Amherst, 1956-57; asst. prof. chemistry Adelphi U., Garden City, N.Y., 1957-60, assoc. prof., 1960-63, prof., 1963—, chmn. dept. chemistry, 1985-91; Fulbright prof. Weizmann Inst., Rehovoth, 1984; vis. prof. U. Uppsala, Sweden, Technion, Israel, Weizman Inst., U. Fla., Nat. Eye Inst., NIH, Bethesda, Md. Author: Experimental Physical Chemistry, 1971; Introduction to General Organic and Biochemistry, 1984, 3d edit., 1991, Introdution to Organic and Biochemistry, 1990; editor Exptl. Eye Research, 1984-91; contbr. articles to profl. jours. Served with Israeli Def. Army, 1947-50. Recipient Disting. Teaching award Adelphi U., 1974. grantee NIH, NSF, Cystic Fibrosis Fund, Office Naval Research, 1956—; Mem. Am. Chem. Soc., Am. Soc. Biol. Chemists, Internat. Soc. Eye Research (treas. 1984-89), Assn. Research in Vision and Ophthalmology. Jewish. Avocations: tennis, racquetball, squash, piano playing, bridge. Office: Dept Chemistry Adelphi Univ Garden City NY 11530

BETTENCOURT, ALFRED RICHARD, JR., state executive director; b. Fall River, Mass., May 20, 1950; s. Alfred Richard and Margaret Olga (Enders) B.; children: Alfred R. Bettencourt III, Lynn Ann Bettencourt. AA in Liberal Arts, R.I. Jr. Coll., 1970; BA in Social Sci., R.I. Coll., 1972; MPA, U. R.I., 1978. Cert. secondary tchr., R.I. Tchr. St. Mary's Sch., Pawtucket, R.I., 1972-73, Jesus Saviour Sch., Newport, R.I., 1974-79, Newport Pub. Sch., 1979-81; farmer Bettencourt Farms, Warren, R.I., 1959; tax preparer H&R Block, Johnston, R.I., 1991-92, tax instr., 1991-92; state exec. dir. Agrl. Stabil Conservation Svc. USDA, Warwick, R.I., 1981—; chmn. Food and Agriculture Coun., Warwick, 1983—; sec. R.I. Agriculture in the Classroom, Warwick, 1984—. Author: Living is Hazardous to Health, 1992. Sec. Warren Rep. Town Com., Warren, 1972-78; del. R.I. Rep. State Cen. Coun., Providence, 1974-81; town moderator Warren Town Govt., 1981-82; mem. Save the Bay, Providence, 1991—. Roman Catholic. Home: 9 Spring St Riverside RI 02915 Office: USDA ASCS 60 Quaker Ln Rm 40 Warwick RI 02886

BETTS, RICHARD KEVIN, political science educator; b. Easton, Pa., Aug. 15, 1947; s. John Rickards and Cecelia Agnes (Fitzpatrick) B.; m. Adela Maria Bolet, July 25, 1987; children: Elena, Michael, Diego. BA, Harvard U., 1969, MA, 1971, PhD, 1975. Lectr. in government Harvard U., Cambridge, Mass., 1975-76; vis. prof. Harvard U., Cambridge, 1985-88; rsch. assoc. Brookings Instn., Washington, 1976-81, sr. fellow, 1981-90; prof. polit. sci. Columbia U., N.Y.C., 1990—; mem. staff Senate Select Com. on Intelligence, Washington, 1975-76, NSC, Washington, 1977; adj. prof. Johns Hopkins U., Washington, 1978-85, 88-90; cons. CIA, 1980-91; occasional lectr. Nat. War Coll., Fgn. Svc. Inst., U.S. Mil. Acad. Author: Soldiers, Statesmen and Cold War Crises, 1977 (Lasswell award 1979), Surprise Attack, 1982, Nuclear Blackmail and Nuclear Balance, 1987; co-author: The Irony of Vietnam, 1979 (Woodrow Wilson award 1980). Mem. foreign policy staff Mondale Presidential Campaign, Washington, 1984; mem. Assn. for Retarded Citizens, Bergen County, N.J., 1990—. Recipient Sumner prize Harvard U., 1976, Article award Nat. Intelligence Study Ctr., Washington, 1979, '81. Mem. Coun. on Fgn. Rels, Am. Polit. Sci. Assn., Internat. Studies Assn., Soc. for Historians of Am. Fgn. Rels., Consortium for Study of Intelligence. Democrat. Home: 1199 The Strand Teaneck NJ 07666-2020 Office: Columbia U Inst War & Peace Studies 420 W 118th St New York NY 10027-7213

BETTS, WILLIAM WILSON, JR., English educator; b. Clearfield, Pa., July 25, 1926; s. William Wilson Betts and Bernyce Nineveh (Anderson) Dufton; m. Jane Buckley Jackson, June 29, 1951; children: Michael Jackson, Thomas Anderson. AB, Dickinson Coll., 1949; AM, Pa. State U., 1950, PhD, 1954; postgrad., U. Minn., 1950. Tchr. Greenwood (Del.) Consol. Sch., 1950-52; instr. Ohio U., Athens, 1954-55; prof. Indiana U. of Pa., 1955—; radio sports broadcaster Sta. WDAD, Indiana, 1969-89; assoc. dean Grad. Sch., Indiana U. of Pa., 1967-71; field corr. Defenders of Wildlife, Washington, 1978-89. Author: Lincoln and the Poets, 1965, A Docketful of Wry, 1970, 71; contbr. articles to profl. jours. Deputy waterways patrolman Pa. Fish Commn., Indiana County, Pa., 1967-77; bd. dirs. Ken Sink chpt. Trout Unltd., Indiana, 1965-76, Indiana County Parks & Recreation Commn., 1967-77, Indiana County YMCA, 1968-77. With USNR, 1944-46, PTO. Recipient Disting. Scholarship award Indiana U. of Pa., 1971, Commonwealth of Pa. Lay Honor award Pa. Recreation & Parks Soc., 1975, Disting. Faculty award Pa. State Colls. and Univ., 1977. Mem. Phi Kappa Phi. Republican. Methodist. Home: RD# 6 Box 73 Indiana PA 15701

BEUBE, FRANK EDWARD, periodontist, educator; b. Kingston, Ont., Can., July 1, 1904; came to the U.S., 1930; naturalized, 1937; s. Gabriel and Fannie Bessie (Florence) B. L.D.S., D.D.S., U. Toronto, 1930. Diplomate Am. Bd. Periodontology; m. Edith Schweitzer, Oct. 5, 1930; children: Eric, Stephen. Clin. asst. div. periodontology Sch. Dental and Oral Surgery, Columbia, 1930-37, instr., 1937-41, asst. prof., 1941-46, assoc. prof., 1946-53, head div., 1948-68, clin. prof. dentistry, 1953-84, clin. prof. emeritus, 1984—, emeritus prof.-spl. lectr., 1984—; head dept. periodontology Presbyn. Hosp., N.Y.C., 1941-70; lectr. dept. periodontology, Dental Sch. N.Y. U., 1973—; found. mem. Hebrew U. Recipient William J. Gies award, 1979, Disting. Alumnus award Columbia U. Periodontal Alumni Assn., 1984, Isidore Herschfeld award, 1990. Fellow AAAS, Am. Coll. Dentists, Am. Acad. Periodontology (councilman 1962, chmn. edn. com. 1963, chmn. com. on coms. 1964, pres. 1964-65, chmn. exec. council 1965-66, Pres. award 1988); mem. ADA (chmn. periodontia sect. 1964-65), Western Soc. Periodontology (hon.), Acad. Oral Pathology, So. Acad. Periodontology (hon.), Internat. Assn. Dental Rsch., First Dist. Dental Soc. (past pres. pathodontia sect.), Sigma Xi. Author: Periodontology: Diagnosis and Treatment, 1953; Prevention of Periodontal Diseases, 1956; Gingivectomy in the treatment of Periodontal Diseases, 1957; Disadvantages of Surgical Techniques, 1960; contbr. chpts. to books, articles to dental jours. Rsch. in study of healing of cementum and bone, periodontal diseases and their treatment. Home: 701 Pelham Rd New Rochelle NY 10805 Office: 933 5th Ave New York NY 10021-2603

BEUTH, PHILIP ROY, television executive; b. N.Y.C., May 20, 1932; s. Philip John and Margaret (Long) Morrill; m. Elizabeth C. Yost, Sept. 5, 1953 (div. May 1989); children: Philip S., Robert A., Jane M.; m. Mary S. Grace, Feb. 21, 1991. BA in Econs., Union Coll., Schenectady, N.Y., 1954; MS in TV Prodn., Syracuse U., 1955; LHD (hon.), Medaille Coll., 1991. Film editor Sta. WROW-TV Capital Cities, Albany, N.Y., 1955; pub. affairs dir. Sta. WTEN CBS, Albany, 1956, producer, dir., promotion mgr., sales mgr. Sta. WTEN-TV, 1958-64; gen. sales mgr. Sta. WSAZ-TV NBC, Huntington, W.Va., 1964, v.p., gen. mgr. Sta. WSAZ-TV, 1969; v.p., gen. mgr. Sta. KFSN-TV CBS, Fresno, Calif., 1971; v.p., gen. mgr. Sta. WKBW-TV ABC, Buffalo, 1975, pres. Sta. WKBW-TV, 1976; sr. v.p. Capital Cities/ABC (merger Capital Cities and ABC), N.Y.C., 1986, pres. early morning, late night entertainment, 1990; bd. govs. ABC, 1970-84; bd. dirs. CBS Affiliate, 1971-74. Trustee Childrens Hosp., Buffalo, 1980-86; bd. dirs. U.S. com. UNICEF, N.Y.C., 1988—. Named Man of Yr., Fresno Advt. Assn., 1972, 73, Vol. of Yr., Buffalo Charities, 1984, Citizen of Yr., Buffalo Evening News, 1986; recipient Fellows medal Hilbert Coll., 1979, Citizenship Honor award Variety Club Internat., 1982. Office: Capital Cities Good Morning Am 147 Columbus Ave New York NY 10023-6201

BEUTNER, ERNST HERMAN, microbiology educator; b. Berlin, Germany, Aug. 27, 1923; came to U.S., 1923; s. Reinhard and Hermine (Aye) B.; children: Eric, Karen, Jean. BA, Pa. State U., 1947; PhD, U. Pa., 1951. Cert. Am. Bd. Med. Microbiology, Am. Bd. Med. Lab. Immunology, Am. Bd. Bioanalysis. Rsch. supr. Sias Labs. at Brook Hosp., Brookline, Mass., 1951-55; rsch. assoc. Harvard Sch. of Dental Medicine, Boston, 1955-56; prof. microbiology SUNY at Buffalo, 1956—. Mem. editorial bd. Internat. Jour. of Dermatology Autoimmunity. Fellow Coll. of Physicians of Pa.; mem. AAAS, Am. Soc. Microbiologists, Histochem. Soc., Boston Bug Club, Tissue Culture Assn., Am. Assn. Immunologists, N.Y. Acad. Scis., Soc. for Exptl. Biology and Medicine, Brit. Immunology Soc., London Immunology Club, Acad. Microbiology of ASM, Am. Acad. Dermatology, Japanese Soc. for Investigative Dermatology. Office: SUNY at Buffalo Dept of Microbiology Buffalo NY 14214

BEVERLEY, CORDIA LUVONNE, internist; b. Jamaica, W.I., Oct. 19, 1950; d. Hurdley Aston and Joyce Ruby (Baker) B.; B.A., Hunter Coll., 1971; M.D., N.Y. U., 1975. Diplomate Am. Bd. Gastroenterology, Am. Bd. Internal Medicine. Intern, Columbia U., Harlem Hosp. Center, N.Y.C., 1975-76, resident in medicine, 1976-78; clin. fellow div. gastroenterology N.Y. Hosp./Cornell U. Med. Coll., N.Y.C., 1979-82; asst. physician Rockefeller U. Hosp., N.Y.C., 1978-81. Nat. Inst. Alcohol Abuse and Alcoholism postdoctoral fellow, 1980-82. Mem. Am. Soc. Internal Medicine, Women's Med. Assn. N.Y.C. Office: 1150 Park Ave New York NY 10128-1244

BEVILACQUA, ANTHONY JOSEPH CARDINAL, cardinal; b. Bklyn., June 17, 1923; s. Louis and Maria (Codella) B. Student, Cathedral Coll., Bklyn., 1941-43, Sem. of Immaculate Conception, Huntington, N.Y., 1943-49; JCD, Gregorian U., Rome, Italy, 1956; MA in Polit. Sci, Columbia U., 1962; JD, St. John's U. Sch. Law, 1975. Ordained priest Roman Cath. Ch., 1949; ordained bishop, 1980. Bar: N.Y. 1976, Pa. 1988, U.S. Dist. Ct. (we. dist.) Pa. 1984, U.S. Dist. Ct. (ea. dist.) Pa. 1988, U.S. Supreme Ct., 1989. Asst. pastor Sacred Heart, St. Stephen's Ch., St. Mary's Ch., 1949-50; prof. history Cathedral Prep. Sem., Bklyn., 1950-53; prof. canon law Sem. of Immaculate Conception, Huntington, N.Y., 1968-80; adj. prof. law St. John's U. Sch. Law, Queens, N.Y., 1976-80; successively asst. chancellor, vice-chancellor, chancellor Diocese of Bklyn., 1965-83, dir. Cath. migration and refugee office, 1971-83, ordained aux. bishop, 1980; bishop Diocese of Pitts., 1983-88; archbishop Archdiocese of Phila., 1988—; elevated to cardinal Coll. of Cardinals, 1991; chmn. com. on canonical affairs Nat. Conf. Cath. Bishops, 1991—, com. on migration and tourism, 1980-86; mem. com. pro-life activities, 1989—; mem. com. migration, 1989—; mem. Pontifical Congregation for Causes of Saints, 1991—; mem. Pontifical Coun. "Cor Unum", 1991—. Contbr. articles to profl. jours. Bd. dirs. Mercy Home for Children; chmn. Nat. Coalition for Haitian Refugees. Mem. Canon Law Soc. Am., ABA, Pa. Bar Assn., Fellowship of Am. Cath. Scholars. Office: Archdiocese Phila 222 N 17th St Philadelphia PA 19103-1299

BEX, MARY ANN THERESA, guidance counselor; b. Jersey City, Apr. 20, 1947; d. Domenick George and Anna Mary (Lentine) Staffa; m. Frederick James Bex, June 24, 1972; children: Susan Meredith, Katherine Mary, Amanda Laura. BA, Montclair (N.J.) State Coll., 1969; MA, U. Conn., 1975. Cert. counselor K-12, N.J., Pa, 9-12, Conn. Spanish tchr. Saddle Brook (N.J.) High Sch., 1969-72, Bennett Jr. High Sch., Manchester, Conn., 1972-77, Lansdowne-Aldan Jr./Sr. High Sch., Lansdowne, Pa., 1977-78; substitute tchr., counselor Marple Newtown Sch. Dist., Newtown Square, Pa., 1979-88; guidance counselor Radnor (Pa.) High Sch., 1988-89, Cedarbrook Middle Sch., Wyncote, Pa., 1990—; v.p. A Better Chance, Inc. Radnor, 1989—. Mem. AAUW (treas. 1980-85), Am. Assn. Counseling and Devel., Am. Sch. Counselor Assn., Assn. for Specialists in Group Work, Sigma Delta Pi, Pi Lambda Theta. Office: Cedarbrook Middle Sch 300 Longfellow Rd Wyncote PA 19095-2999

BEY, GWENDOLYN KONIGSBERG, legal administrator; b. N.Y.C., Feb. 1, 1954; d. Hyman Joseph and Anna (Dorf) Konigsberg; m. Amir H. Bey, Sept. 24, 1989. Student, Bergen Community Coll., 1972-74, Am. Mgmt. Assn. Extension Inst., N.Y. Personnel mgr. Pitney, Hardin, Kipp & Szuch, Morristown, N.J., 1983-84, McCarter & English, Newark, 1984-85; legal adminstr. Porzio, Bromberg & Newman, Morristown, 1985-88, Kreindler & Relkin, P.C., N.Y.C., 1988—; 2nd v.p. N.J. Assn. Legal Adminstrs., 1986-87, sec., 1987-88. Mem. ABA (econs. of law practice sect.), Am. Mgmt. Assn., N.Y. Assn. Legal Adminstrs. (program planning com. 1991-92), Nat. Assn. Legal Adminstrs. Jewish. Home: 252 Wierimus Rd Hillsdale NJ 07642

BEYER, KLAUS DIETRICH, industrial chemist; b. Berlin, Jan. 23, 1937; came to U.S., 1966; s. Eduard and Waltraud L. (Eggers) G.; m. Linda M. Hunt, Aug. 2, 1968; children: Sylvia J., Julia N. BS, U. Bonn, 1959, MS, 1964, PhD, 1966. Postdoctoral fellow Ohio State U., Columbus, 1966-68; staff chemist gen. tech. div. IBM, Hopewell Junction, N.Y., 1968-73, adv. chemist, 1973-86, sr. chemist, 1986—. Contbr. numerous articles to profl. jours.; patentee in field. Mem. Am. Chem. Soc. (chmn. Mid-Hudson sect. 1973), Electrochem. Soc., Poughkeepsie Tennis Club, Rotary (bd. dirs. Poughkeepsie 1983-86). Home: 4 Kingwood Ln Poughkeepsie NY 12601-5451 Office: IBM Gen Tech Div Rte 52 Box H Hopewell Junction NY 12533

BEYER, ROBERT THOMAS, physicist, educator; b. Harrisburg, Pa., Jan. 27, 1920; s. James M. and Mary (Gibney) B.; m. Ellen Fletcher, Feb. 14, 1944; children: Catherine E., Margaret A., Richard J., Mary L. AB, Hofstra U., 1942; PhD, Cornell U., 1945; MA (hon.), Brown U., 1957; DSc (hon.), Hofstra U., 1985. Teaching asst. Cornell U., 1942-45; instr. physics Brown U., 1945-47, asst. prof., 1947- 51, asso. prof., 1951-58, prof., 1958-84, Hazard prof., 1984-85, Hazard prof. emeritus, 1985—, adj. prof., 1986-91, exec. officer dept. physics, 1966-68, 81-85, chmn. dept., 1968-74; vis. prof. Technische Hochschule, Stuttgart, Germany, 1961-62, U. Birmingham, Eng., 1971, U. Tex., Austin, 1977, Pa. State U., 1982, 85, 86; cons., chmn. Am. Inst. Physics transls. adv. bd., 1957-77, chmn. transls. edn. bd., 1980—; cons. on underwater sound Raytheon, 1962-72; cons. Office of Naval Research, 1974-75. Editor: Soviet Physics JETP transls. jour, 1955-57, Soviet Physics Acoustics transl. jour, 1974—, Soviet Astronomy trans. jour., 1985-89, Soviet Physics, Low Temperature Physics, 1985—; translated (from German): Practical Analysis (F. A. Willers), 1948, Mathematical Foundations of Quantum Mechanics (Johann von Neumann), 1955; translated (from Russian): Acoustics of a Moving Inhomogeneous Medium (D.I. Bkokhintsev and D. Mintzer), 1952, Molecular Scattering of Light (I.L. Fabelinskii), 1968, Theoretical Foundations of Nonlinear Acoustics (O.V. Rudenko and S.I. Soluyan), 1977, Waves in Layered Media (L.M. Brekhovskikh), 2d edit, 1979, Nonlinear Theory of Sound Beams (N.C. Bakhvalov, Ya. M. Zhileikin and E.A. Zabolotskaya), 1987, (B.K. Novikov, O.V. Rudenko and V.I. Timoshenko) Nonlinear Underwater Acoustics, 1987; author: (with A.O. Williams, Jr.) College Physics, 1957, (with Stephen V. Letcher) Physical Ultrasonics, 1969, Nonlinear Acoustics, 1974; editor: transl. from Chinese Acta Physica Sinica, 1966-68. Fellow Fund for Advancement Edn., 1953-54. Fellow Am. Phys. Soc., Acoustical Soc. Am. (pres. 1968-69, treas. 1974—, acting editor Jour. 1985, gold medal 1984), Internat. Commn. Acoustics (chmn. 1978-84), IEEE, AAAS. Home: 132 Cushman Ave East Providence RI 02914-1955 Office: Brown U Dept Physics Box 1843 Providence RI 02912

BEYER, SUZANNE, advertising agency executive; b. N.Y.C., Dec. 28, 1928; d. Harry and Jennie Hillman; student Nassau Community Coll., 1963-65; grad. Conservatory of Musical Art, N.Y.C., 1947; m. Isadore Beyer, Oct. 19, 1947; children—Pamela Claire, Hillary Jay. Singer, tchr. piano, N.Y.C., 1947-66; asst. to v.p. media dir. Robert E. Wilson, Advt., N.Y.C., 1967-72; media planner, media buyer Frank J. Corbett div. BBDO Internat., N.Y.C., 1972-77; media planner, media buyer Lavey/Wolff/Swift div. BBDO Advt., N.Y.C., 1977-80, sr. media planner, 1980-83, media supr., 1983—; soprano Opera Assn. Nassau, 1976—; soprano United Choral Soc., Woodmere, L.I., 1970—, Armand Sodero Chorale, Baldwin, L.I., 1980-86, Rockville Centre Choral Soc, 1986—. Mem. Pharm. Advt. Council, L.I. Advt. Club, Healthcare Bus. Women's Assn. Home: 66 Fonda Rd Rockville Centre NY 11570-2751 Office: 488 Madison Ave New York NY 10022-5702

BEYER, WAYNE CARTWRIGHT, lawyer; b. Bklyn., Feb. 21, 1946; s. Gerhard Robert and Barbara Janeway (Fein) B. AB, Dartmouth Coll., 1967; MAT, Harvard U., 1970; Jd, Georgetown U., 1977. Bar: N.H. 1978, U.S. Dist. Ct. N.H. 1978, U.S. Tax Ct. 1986, U.S. Ct. Appeals (1st cir.) 1979, U.S. Supreme Ct. 1986. Mem. staff U.S. Ho. of Reps., Washington, 1973-75; assoc. atty. McLane, Graf, Raulerson, P.A., Manchester, N.H., 1977-83; chief of staff GSA, Washington, 1983-84, dep. gen. counsel, 1984-86; dir., mem., stockholder Cleveland, Waters & Bass, P.A., Concord, N.H., 1986—. Contbr. articles to profl. jours. N.H. counsel, co-chmn. Lawyers for George Bush for pres., Washington, 1988. Mem. ABA, N.H. Bar Assn., Assn. Trial Lawyers Am., N.H. Trial Lawyers Assn., Federalist Soc., Lions, Phi Delta Phi. Home: 1316 Alton Woods Dr Concord NH 03301-7864 Office: Cleveland Waters & Bass PA 125 N State St Concord NH 03301-6430

BEYMAN, JONATHAN ERIC, securities company executive; b. Newark, Dec. 31, 1955; s. Bernard B. and Miriam (Simon) B.; m. Susan Elizabeth Bleckman, Aug. 23, 1981; children: Michael, Daniel. BS, U. Ct., 1976; MBA, Cornell U., 1981. CPA, Conn. Sr. acct. Arthur Young and Co., N.Y.C., 1976-79; asst. v.p. Chem. Bank, N.Y.C., 1981-84; sr. cons. Am. Mgmt. Systems, N.Y.C., 1985; v.p. Citibank North Am. Investment Bank, N.Y.C., 1985-86; v.p. Lehman Bros., N.Y.C., 1986-88, sr. v.p., 1988-91, mng. dir., 1991—; bd. dirs. Participants Trust Co., N.Y.C., 1991—. Mem. AICPA, Pub. Securities Assn. (ops. com. 1986-89). Democrat. Jewish. Home: 1 Singing Woods Ct Norwalk CT 06850 Office: Lehman Bros 8th Fl 200 Vesey St New York NY 10285-0001

BEZURSIK, EDWARD ANTHONY, JR., marketing professional; b. Hartford, Conn., Aug. 20, 1951; s. Edward Anthony Sr. and Alberta Dorothy (Czarnecki) B.; m. Domna Lynn Candido, July 19, 1975. MusB, U. Conn., 1975; MA, Queens Coll., 1977; postgrad., Columbia U., 1977-81, NYU, 1990—. Salesman Ostrovsky Piano Co., N.Y.C., 1981-84; dir. instl. sales Steinway & Sons, N.Y.C., 1984—; adj. lectr. Queens Coll., Flushing, N.Y., 1975-77, Columbia U., N.Y.C., 1978-81. Composer of chamber music, orch. music. V.p. Flushing Meadow Track Club, 1976-79; bd. dirs. Newport Coop. Apts., Flushing, 1982-83. Mem. Nat. Piano Found. (2d v.p. 1987—). Office: 109 W 57th St New York NY 10019-2268

BHARGAVA, ANJU PAGE, banker; b. New Delhi, July 4, 1956; came to U.S., 1978; d. Mohan Krishan and Sarla Bhargava; divorced; 1 child, Anisha. BSc, Stella Maris Coll., Madras, India, 1976; MBA, Rutgers U., Newark, 1980. Strategic planner Chase Manhattan Bank, N.A., N.Y.C., 1980-82, asst. treas., program mgr., 1982-83; mgmt. cons. Nat. Westminster Bank USA, N.Y.C., 1983-86, loan officer devel. program, 1986-88, asst. v.p., trans./relationship mgr., trustee, 1988—. Founder Asian Indians in Livingston (N.J.), 1984; rep. White House Briefings for Asian and Pacific Women, 1984, dir. pub. rels., 1985—; bd. dirs. Fedn. Indian Assns., N.Y.C., 1988, 89; advisor Livingston Twp. Com., 1989; advisor Livingston Bd. Edn., 1991; exec. com. Livingston Edn. Found.; appointee Livingston Twp. Coun. Adv. Comn., 1991. Mem. AAUW (treas. 1992—), Nat. Assn. Banking Women, Asian Indian Women in Am. (dir. pub. rels. 1984—). Hindu. Home: 53 Trocha Ave Livingston NJ 07039-2313

BHAT, RAMACHANDRA K., biochemistry educator; b. Kerala, India, Sept. 22, 1941; came to U.S., 1966; s. K. Krishna and Haimavathi B.; m. Susheela, July 8, 1972; 1 child, Haimavathi. BSc, Mysore U., 1961; MS, Ohio State, 1969; MSc, Banaras Hindu U., 1964; PhD, Rutgers U., 1974. Postdoctoral fellow U. So. Calif., L.A., 1974-76; rsch. assoc. U. Md. Balt. County, Balt., 1976-78, Johns Hopkins U., Balt., 1978-85; asst. prof. Lincoln U., Lincoln University, Pa., 1986—. Rsch. grantee EPA, 1987, NIH, 1988. Mem. Am. Chem. Soc., AAAS, N.Y. Acad. Scis., Am. Assn. for Cancer Rsch., Soc. of Sigma Xi. Hindu. Office: Lincoln U Lincoln University PA 19352

BHATNAGAR, GOPAL MOHAN, health scientist; b. Lucknow, India, July 15, 1937; came to U.S., 1963; s. Jahmohan Lal and Gopi Devi Bhatnagar. BSc, Lucknow U., 1955, MSc, 1957, PhD, 1961. Sr. rsch. fellow Nat. Chem. Lab., Poona, India, 1961-63; rsch. scientist Commonwealth Sci. and Indsl. Rsch. Orgn., Melbourne, Victoria, Australia, 1965-69; staff scientist Boston Biomed. Rsch. Inst., 1969-73; prin. assoc. Med. Sch. Harvard U., Boston, 1974-77; assoc. prof. Sch. of Medicine Johns Hopkins U., Balt., 1977-88; chemist FDA, Rockville, Md., 1988-91; sci. rev. adminstr. NIH, Bethesda, Md., 1991—. NIH grantee, 1976-86. Mem. Am. Soc. Biochemistry and Molecular Biology. Office: NIH/Nat Inst Child Health & Human Devel Div Sci Rev Exec Plz N Rm 520 Bethesda MD 20892

BHATTACHARYA-CHATTERJEE, MALAYA, cancer research scientist; b. Cooch-Behar, India, Jan. 16, 1946; came to U.S., 1969; d. Nalini Nath and Kanak Prova (Chakravorty) Bhattacharya; m. Sunil Kumar Chatterjee, Oct. 25, 1972; children: Indranil, Sumana. BS, Presidency Coll., Calcutta, 1963; MS, Calcutta U. Coll. Sci., 1965, PhD, 1969. Postdoctoral fellow Roswell Park Cancer Inst., Buffalo, N.Y., 1969-71, cancer rsch. scientist III, 1971-79, cancer rsch. scientist IV, 1979—; asst. rsch. prof. exptl. pathology Grad. Study div. Roswell Park, 1990—; asst. rsch. prof. ob-gyn. SUNY, Buffalo, 1989—; cons. NIH Study Sect., 1991—. Contbr. chpts. to books, articles to profl. jours. Grantee NIH, 1976-79, NSF, 1980-81, Am. Cancer Soc., 1983-86, Nat. Cancer Inst., 1989—. Mem. Am. Assn. for Cancer Rsch., Fedn. Am. Socs. for Exptl. Biology. Office: Roswell Park Cancer Inst Elm and Carlton Sts Buffalo NY 14263

BHOWMIK, PRASANTA CHITTA, weed scientist; b. Bayenda, West Bengal, India, Oct. 1, 1943; came to U.S., 1978; m. Beverley D. Tom, Feb. 23, 1974; children: Kiran, Monica, David. BSc in Agr. with honors, U. Kalyani, W. Bengal, 1964; MSc in Agronomy, Indian Agrl. Rsch. Inst., 1966; MS in Weed Physiology, U. Guelph, Ont., Can., 1970; PhD Weed Sci., U. Wis., 1981. Grad. rsch. asst. Indian Agrl. Rsch. Inst., New Delhi, 1965-67; grad. rsch. asst. U. Guelph, Ont., Can., 1967-70, sr. rsch. technician, 1970-78; grad. rsch. asst. U. Wis., Madison, 1978-81; asst. prof. weed sci. U. Mass., Amherst, 1981-87, assoc. prof., 1987—. Contbr. numerous articles to profl. jours., chpts. to books. Grantee, USDA, 1982-88, U. Mass., 1982, Mass. Dept. Food and Agr., 1986, 87, 88, 89, Mass. Turf and Lawn Grass Coun., 1990, Monsanto Agrl. Co., 1991, NRC of Can., 1967-70, Wis. Alumni Rsch. Found. fellow, 1978-81, others. Mem. Northeastern Weed Sci. Soc. (pres. 1991—), Weed Sci. Soc. Am., Internat. Weed Sci. Soc., Am. Soc. Agronomy, Internat. Turfgrass Soc., Am. Soc. for Hort. Sci., Coun. for Agrl. Sci. and Tech., Sigma Xi. Home: 17 Pomeroy Ct Amherst MA 01002-2901 Office: Stockbridge Hall U Mass Dept Plant & Soil Scis Amherst MA 01003

BIAETT, DODDRIDGE HEWITT, III, lawyer; b. Aurora, Ill., Nov. 20, 1942; s. Doddridge Hewitt and Ruthanne (Migely) B.; m. Jean Iden, Apr. 13, 1969; children: Elizabeth Iden, Doddridge Hewitt, Maryanne Migely. BS, Hampden-Sydney Coll., 1965; LLB, U. Va., 1968. Bar: Va. 1968. Atty., Govt. Employees Ins. Co., Washington, 1970-73, sr. counsel, 1973-76; atty., Crum & Forster Corp., Morristown, N.J., 1976-79, v.p., counsel, 1979-87, asst. gen. counsel, 1987, corp. sec., 1992—; vice chmn. adminstrn. coun. Mendham United Meth. Ch., 1992—. Comdr. USNR, 1968—, Vietnam. Mem. ABA, N.J. Assn. Corp. Counsel. Republican. Office: 211 Mt Airy Rd Basking Ridge NJ 07920

BIAGETTI, RICHARD VICTOR, electrochemical engineer; b. Woonsocket, R.I., Jan. 13, 1940; s. Alvaro and Lauretta (Sylvester) B.; m. Lorraine S. Jutras, July 11, 1965; children: Anthony Richard, Melissa Anne. BS in Chemistry, Providence Coll., 1960, MS in Chemistry, 1962; PhD in Chemistry, U. N.H., 1966. Mem. staff AT&T Bell Labs., Murray Hill, N.J., 1965-72, supr., 1972-92; dir. rsch. and devel. Yuasa-Exide, Inc., Laureldale, Pa., 1992—. Patentee in field; contbr. articles to profl. jours. Dir. children's activities North Plainfield Jaycees, 1970-74 (Named Jaycee of the Yr. 1972). Providence Plantation Bank scholar, 1956. Mem. IEEE, Electrochem. Soc., Nat. Geographic Soc., Sigma Chi. Roman Catholic. Office: Yuasa-Exide Inc Montrose and Vine Sts Laureldale PA 19605-2010

BIALY, LINDA LEE, hospital official; b. Webster, Mass., Sept. 19, 1947; d. Leon O. and Rita F. (Collette) Bonnette; m. John E. Bialy, Apr. 15, 1967; children: Beth C., Dawn M. Student, Nichols Coll., 1984-85. Data procesing mgr. Hubbard Regional Hosp., Webster, 1971-85, patients accounts mgr., 1986-87; patients accounts mgr. Harrington Meml. Hosp., Southbridge, Mass., 1987—. Town meeting rep. Town of Webster, 1989-92. Mem. NAFE, Am. Guild Patient Account Mgrs., Mass. Assn. Patient Account Mgmt. (bd. dirs. 1985-92, audit chmn. 1985, legis. chmn. 1986, membership chmn. 1987-90, spl. projects 1991-92). Democrat. Roman Catholic. Home: 50 Boyden Street Ext Webster MA 01570-2813 Office: Harrington Meml Hosp 100 South St Southbridge MA 01550

BIANCONI, GREGORY FREDERICK, family practitioner; b. Meriden, Conn., July 24, 1952; s. Natale P. and Constance (Siino) B.; m. Deborah Sisson-Bianconi, June 9, 1979; children: Matthew, Anna, Joseph. ScB, Brown U., 1974, MD, 1977. Diplomate Am. Bd. Family Practice. Resident Meml. Hosp., Pawtucket, R.I., 1977-80; staff physician Nat. Health Svc. Corps, Parsons, Tenn., 1980-83; pvt. practice Lisbon, Maine, 1983—; adj. instr. Family Practice Residency, U. Tenn., Jackson, 1980-83, Family Practice Residency, Central Maine Med. Ctr., Lewiston, 1983—. Adv. bd. Town of Lisbon, Maine, 1987—; bd. dirs. First Universalist Ch., Auburn, Maine, 1989-92. Fellow Am. Acad. Family Physicians. Unitarian-Universalist. Home: RR 1 Box 372 Lisbon Falls ME 04252-9706 Office: Lisbon Family Practice Two Rivers Med Ctr Lisbon Center ME 04251

BIBBS, KAROL LEE, publishing executive; b. Boston, Dec. 16, 1935; d. John Harold and Katherine (Kerrigan) Kavanagh; m. Frank Carroll Bibbs, Sept. 7, 1972 (dec. 1982). Student, U. Edinburgh, Scotland, 1955-56; AB, Wells Coll., Aurora, N.Y., 1957. Sec. to sr. v.p. Houghton Mifflin Co., Boston, 1962-71, asst. to sr. v.p., 1971-85, nat. exhibits mgr., 1985-89, assoc. dir. sch. advt., 1989—; mem. corp. contbns. com. Houghton Mifflin Co., 1983-86, chmn. grievance com., 1985—. Trustee Community Arts Ctr., Cambridge, Mass., 1982-85; active Rep. ward 2 com., Cambridge, 1982-87. Mem. Internat. Exhibitors Assn., Boston Athenaeum (life mem.). Roman Catholic. Home: 100 Memorial Dr Cambridge MA 02142-1314 Office: Houghton Mifflin Co 1 Beacon St Boston MA 02108-3106

BICKEL, JOHN FREDERICK, consulting engineer; b. Cleona, Pa., Feb. 25, 1928; s. Frederick Phillip and Margaret Catherine (Miller) B.; m. Dorothy Marie Saunders, Oct. 23, 1954; children: Richard George, Jane Dorothy. BS in Engring., Drexel U., 1962, MS in Engring. Mgmt., 1968. Registered profl. engr., Pa., Del., N.J.; profl. planner, N.J. Engr. Fischer & Porter Co., Warminster, Pa., 1956-66; chief engr. W.F. Keegan & Co., Haverford, Pa., 1966-73; cons. engr. JBPE Cons. Engrs., Hatboro, Pa., 1973-88, J & B Design Engring., Hatboro, 1988—; dir. Drexel U. Coll. Engring. Alumni Assn., Phila., 1991—. Dir. Upper Moreland Swim Club, Hatboro, 1969—. Pfc. U.S. Army, 1950-51. Mem. Inst. Transp. Engrs., Cons. Coun. ITE, Expert Witness Coun. ITE, Nat. Soc. Profl. Engrs. Home: 3700 Meyer Ln Hatboro PA 19040-3720 Office: J & B Design Engring 126 S York Rd Hatboro PA 19040-3327

BICKFORD, CHRISTOPHER PENNY, association executive; b. Bklyn., Feb. 27, 1943; s. Addison Duncan and Carol Anita (Penny) B.; B.A., Union Coll., 1964; M.A., Harvard U., 1965; Ph.D., U. Conn., 1971; m. Roberta Robbins, Sept. 18, 1965. Librarian, Conn. Hist. Soc., Hartford, 1975-79, asst. dir., 1979-80, dir., 1980—. Woodrow Wilson fellow, 1964-65. Mem. Soc. Am. Archivists, Am. Assn. State and Local History, Am. Assn. Mus., New Eng. Mus. Assn. Author: The Connecticut Historial Society: A Short Illustrated History, 1825-1975, 1975; Farmington in Connecticut, 1983. Office: Conn Hist Soc 1 Elizabeth St Hartford CT 06105-2292

BICKFORD, GAIL HOLMGREN, publishing executive; b. N.Y.C., Feb. 14, 1930; d. R. John and Emilie Mary Antonia Doyle (Pope) Holmgren; m. Arthur Fillmore Bickford, Dec. 16, 1951 (div. Jan. 1980); children: Geoffrey, Alison. BA, Wellesley (Mass.) Coll., 1951; MA, U. Pa., 1956, PhD, 1972. Asst. instr. U. Pa., Phila., 1953-58; prof. Cape Cod Community Coll., Hyannis, Mass., 1965-68; owner, operator Freedom (N.H.) Press Assocs., 1979—; lectr. to Freedom, Ossipee (N.H.) and Brownfield (Maine) Hist. Socs., 1991. Author: Here Is Freedom, 1975, Freedom Crossroads, 1989; editor: Reminiscences of the French War, 1988, Tales of Effingham, 1988; columnist Carroll County Ind., 1988-89, 91—; designer, layout artist, and typesetter The Good News, Conway, N.H.; contbr. articles to various mags. Member com. Dennis (Mass.) Sch., 1968-76; trustee Freedom Pub. Libr., 1985-91; sec. Old Home Week Assn., 1988—; rec. sec. Freedom Conservation Commn., 1987-89; sec. Friends of the Libr., 1991—; exec. bd., chmn. pubs. com., Freedom Hist. Soc., 1991—, writer, editor Quicksilver Times, 1992—. Mem. Freedom Hist. Soc. (exec. bd. 1991—, editor, writer newsletter 1992—). Democrat. Office: Freedom Press Assocs PO Box 88 Freedom NH 03836-0088

BICKFORD, JAMES GORDON, banker; b. Huntingdon, Que., Can., 1928; s. Harold Gordon and Jean Forbes (Stark) B.; m. Jetta Goodger-Hill, Aug. 6, 1951. Exec. v.p. Office of Chmn., pres., chief exec. officer Canadian Imperial Bank of Commerce, Toronto, ret.; bd. dirs. Morgan Trust Co. Can., Toronto, Gt. Lakes Re Mgmt. Corp. N.Y. Mem. Royal Can. Mil. Inst. (Toronto), City Club (London), Overseas Bankers Club (London), Nat. Club (Toronto). Presbyterian. Office: Can Imperial Bank Commerce, Commerce Ct, Toronto, ON Canada M5L 1A2

BICKNELL, NEIL CLEMENT, investment company executive; b. Burlington, Vt., Aug. 27, 1942; s. Keith Clement and Gertrude May (Gilpen) B.; m. Judy Ann Fuller, Dec. 30, 1971; children: Charles Bristol, Katharine May. AB, Amherst Coll., 1964; MBA, Columbia U., 1966. Adv. fin. analyst IBM-Americas/Far East, Mt. Pleasant, N.Y., 1969-74; v.p., dir. corp. planning and devel. PaineWebber, Inc., N.Y.C., 1974-80; v.p., mgr. fin. analysis and planning Goldman, Sachs & Co., N.Y.C., 1980-87; pres. Bicknell Adv. Svcs., Scarsdale, N.Y., 1987—; chmn. Wall St. Planning Group, N.Y.C., 1979-81. Trustee Village Scarsdale, 1991—; chmn. The Procedure Com., Scarsdale, 1990-91; active The Citizens Com., Scarsdale, 1985-88; bd. dirs. The Town Club, Scarsdale, 1988-91. Lt. (j.g.) USN, 1966-69. Mem. Nat. Assn. Bank Servicers, Software Pub. Assn. Presbyterian. Home: 91 Garden Rd Scarsdale NY 10583 Office: Bicknell Advisory Svcs Inc 495 Central Park Ave # 205 Scarsdale NY 10583

BICOFSKY, DAVID MARC, public relations executive; b. N.Y.C., Mar. 11, 1947; s. Samuel and Dorothy (Krinsky) B.; m. Catherine Ah Nue Wang, Aug. 30, 1984; children: Robyn Joy, Amanda Lior. AB in Polit. Sci., Hunter Coll., 1969. Reporter, sports writer Herald Statesman, Yonkers, N.Y., 1966-68; copy, layout editor The Record, Hackensack, N.J., 1968-70; editor N.Y. Tel., N.Y.C., 1970-73; pub. rels. supr. AT&T, N.Y.C., 1973-76; dist. staff mgr. pub. rels. N.Y. Tel., 1976-83, div. mgr. pub. rels., 1983-85, dir. editorial svcs., 1985—; lectr. pub. rels. Mem. cable TV adv. bd. Twp. of Teaneck, N.J; trustee Temple Emeth, Teaneck. Fellow Pub. Rels. Soc. Am. (accredited, pres. N.Y.chpt. 1990); mem. Internat. Pub. Rels. Assn., Sigma Delta Chi, Tau Epsilon Phi. Office: NY Tel Co 1095 Ave Of The Americas New York NY 10036-6702

BIDDLE, ARTHUR WILLIAM, English educator; b. Bronxville, N.Y., Feb. 12, 1936; s. Arthur William and Cecilia Dorothy (Vedovato) B.; m. Evelyn Yavinski, Feb. 10, 1962 (div. 1985); children: Carter William, Ellen Irene. BA, U. Conn., 1961; MA, Trinity Coll., 1967; PhD, Mich. State U., 1970. Instr. Cen. Mich. U., Mt. Pleasant, 1966-68; teaching fellow Mich. State U., East Lansing, 1968-70; prof. English, U. Vt., Burlington, 1970—. Author: Writer to Writer, 1985; co-editor: Literature of Vermont, 1973; gen. editor: (series 4 books) Writer's Guide, 1987; co-author/editor: Reading, Writing & Study of Literature, 1989, Community of Voices, 1992, Angles of Vision, 1992. Sgt. 1st class U.S. Army, 1955-58. Mem. Nat. Coun. Tchrs. English, Conf. on Coll. Composition and Communication, Ctr. for Rsch. on Vt., Internat. Thomas Merton Soc. Office: U Vt Dept English Burlington VT 05405

BIDDLE, DANIEL R., reporter. Grad., U. Mich. With Cleve. Plain Dealer, 1976-79; reporter Phila. Inquirer, from 1979, asst. city editor, 1991-92, editor N.J. bur., 1992—. Co-recipient Pulitzer prize for investigative reporting, 1987. Office: Phila Inquirer 53 Haddonfield Rd Ste 300 Cherry Hill NJ 08002*

BIDDLE, FLORA MILLER, art museum administrator. Chmn. Whitney Mus. Am. Art, N.Y.C. Office: Whitney Museum Am Art 945 Madison Ave New York NY 10021-2705

BIDEN, JOSEPH ROBINETTE, JR., senator; b. Scranton, Pa., Nov. 20, 1942; m. Jill Tracy Jacobs, June 17, 1977; children: Ashley Blazer, Joseph Robinette, Robert Hunter. A.B., U. Del.; J.D., Syracuse U. Bar: Del. 1968. Practice law Wilmington, 1968-72; U.S. senator from Del., 1972—; chmn. judiciary com., mem. foreign relations com.; mem. New Castle (Del.) County Council, 1970-72. Democrat. Office: Senate Bldg 221 Russell Senate Bldg Washington DC 20510*

BIDWELL, KAREN RUBINO, psychotherapist; b. Providence, Aug. 26, 1957; d. Michael Joseph and Rose Marie (Ranieri) Rubino; m. David T. Bidwell, Oct. 3, 1981; children: Kathryn Celeste, Emily Jayne. BA, Assumption Coll., 1979; cert. counselor alcohol & drug abuse, U. R.I., 1981; MS, Cen. Conn. State U., 1989. Psychol. technician Butler Hosp., Providence, 1979-81; social club dir. Genesis Ctr., Manchester, Conn., 1985-89; psychotherapist North Cen. Conn. Mental Health System, Enfield, 1989-90, Pastoral Counseling Ctr. of Manchester, Conn., 1989—. Mem. AACD, Am. Rehab. Counselors Assn. Home: 31 Love Ln Manchester CT 06040-2626 Office: Pastoral Counseling Ctr 945 Main St Ste 305 Manchester CT 06040-6064

BIDWELL, ROBERT ERNEST, inventor; b. Bklyn., Jan. 15, 1926; s. Ernest Martin and Helen (Hamilton) B.; degree in Archtl. Design, Pratt Inst., 1953; m. Patricia Murphy, July 1, 1950; children: Robert Bruce, Kerry Martin, Jane, James Patrick. Designer, Harrison & Abramovitz, Rockefeller Center, N.Y.C., 1955-58; pres. Robert Bidwell Assos., Farmingdale, N.Y., 1958-68; gen. mgr., dir. design Bioresearch, Inc., Farmingdale, 1968-80; founder, chmn. bd. Bidwell Vineyards and Winery, Cutchogue, N.Y. Served with AUS, 1944-46. Mem. Soc. Plastic Engrs. (sr.), Am. Soc. Metals, Assn. Advancement Med. Instrumentation, Def. Preparedness Assn., Bidwell Family Assn., U.S. Naval Inst., SAR, L.I. Grape Growers Assn. (com. on new by-laws), Rep. Senatorial Inner Circle (Washington). Republican. Mem. Christian Ch. Inventor, holder 103 patents. Home: 27 Montrose Pl Melville NY 11747-3403 Office: Bidwell Vineyard Rte 48 Cutchogue NY 11935

BIEBER, MARK ALLAN, nutrition scientist, researcher; b. Cleve., Sept. 16, 1946; s. Lester and Ethel R. (Rubin) B. BS in Chemistry, U. Pitts., 1968; PhD in Biochemistry, Mich. State U., 1973. Cert. Am. Chem. Soc. Predoctoral trainee NIH, 1968-73; postdoctoral trainee NIH, Bethesda, Md., 1975-77; fell in pediatrics and human nutrition Columbia U. Coll. Physicans and Surgeons, N.Y.C., 1973-77; sr. nutritionist Best Foods, Union, N.J., 1977-79, prin. nutritionist, 1979-83, nutrition rsch. assoc., 1983—; $D, $D; mem. steering com. N.J. Nutrition Coun., 1978-82; com. mem. Internat. Life Sci. Inst., Washington, 1986—. Contbr. articles to sci. jours. Chmn. bd. Congregation Beth Simchat Torah, 1987-88. Fellow Mataheson Found., 1973-74. Fellow Am. Heart Assn. (food criteria com. 1991-92), Am. Coll. Nutrition; mem. Am. Oil Chemists Soc. (pres. N.E. region 1987-88, merit award 1989), Am. Inst. Nutrition, N.Y. Inst. Food Technologists (com.

chmn. 1988-90), Soc. for Nutrition Edn. Democrat. Office: Best Foods 1120 Commerce Ave Union NJ 07083-5088

BIEGER, ELAINE MINDICH, educational administrator; b. N.Y.C., Aug. 25, 1932; d. Anne (Bergman) Abraham Mindich; m. Joseph Bieger, Apr. 6, 1952; children: Lisa Sue Sternbach, Edward Sternbach, Gary Seth Bieger. BS in Edn., CCNY, 1953; MS in Edn., CUNY, 1969, PD in Supervision, 1972; PhD, Fordham U., 1979. Tchr. N.Y.C., 1953-65; tchr.-in-charge Reading and Diagnostic Ctr., N.Y.C., 1965-75, staff developer, 1975-85, asst. prin., 1985—; adj. prof. L.I. U., Dobbs Ferry, N.Y., 1984—, Fairleigh Dickinson U., Teaneck, N.J., 1979-84, 89-90; reading cons. Oceana Edn. Corp., Dobbs Ferry, 1979-87. Author 7 books on reading comprehension; contbg. author Instructivision-Video Workshop, 1990—; author test and tng. program Bieger Test of Visual Discrimination, 1982; contbr. articles to profl. publs. Mem. ASCD, Coun. Suprs. and Adminstrs., Internat. Reading Assn., Manhattan Reading Coun. (bd. dirs. 1980-81), Bronx Reading Coun. (bd. dirs. 1990—), Phi Delta Kappa.

BIEKER, RICHARD FRANCIS, economics educator, consultant, program director; b. St. Anthony, Ind., July 2, 1944; s. Oscar Edward and Viola Eva (Lubbers) B.; m. Kathleen Ann Keusch, June 10, 1967; 1 child, Daniel Michael. BA with honors, Murray (Ky.) State U., 1965; PhD, U. Ky., 1970. Tchr. St. Ferdinand (Ind.) High Sch., 1966; rsch. assoc. U. Ky., Lexington, 1969-70; asst. prof. U. Del., Newark, 1970-72; assoc. prof. Del. State Coll., Dover, 1972-75, prof., 1975—, dir. MBA program, 1985—; pvt. practice econ. and fin. cons., Dover, 1972—. Contbr. numerous articles to profl. jours. NDEA fellow, 1966-69, UCLA fellow, 1989. Mem. Am. Econ. Assn., Assn. for Fin. Planning and Counseling Edn., Am. Agrl. Econs. Assn., N.E. Resource Econs. Assn., Inst. Cert. Fin. Planners, Delta Mu Delta, Alpha Chi. Roman Catholic. Home: 482 S Old Mill Rd Dover DE 19901-6202

BIEL, HOWARD STEVEN, real estate developer; b. Cleve., June 16, 1947; s. Sol Irwin and Sara Esther (Stein) B.; m. Rene A., June 8, 1972; children: Matthew Graham, Spencer Elliott, Stuart Isaac. BA in Geography, Miami U., 1969; MA in Geography, Ohio State U., 1971, PhD in Geography, 1976. Teaching assoc. Ohio State U., Columbus, 1970-73; asst. prof., dir. urban and environ. studies program Case Western Res. U., Cleve., 1974-77, U. Vt., Burlington, 1977-78; adj. prof. geography Middlebury (Vt.) Coll., 1977-78; dir. east coast ops. Ilium Assocs., Inc., Seattle, 1978-79; sr. v.p. The Edward J. Debartolo Corp., Youngstown, Ohio, 1979-86; exec. v.p. Western Devel. Corp., Washington, 1986-91; pres. Palisades Realty & Devel. Corp., Bethesda, Md., 1991—; assoc. dir. Cleve. Area Survey, 1975-77; cons. in field, 1973-79. Contbr. various articles to profl. jours. Mem. Washington Hebrew Congregation, 1990-92. Recipient Univ. fellowship Miami U., 1968-69, Ohio State U., 1969-73, Outstanding Prof. award Case Western Res. U., 1975. Mem. Internat. Coun. of Shopping Ctrs., Assn. of Am. Geographers, Urban Land Inst. Democrat. Jewish. Home: 5427 Falmouth Rd Bethesda MD 20816 Office: Palisades Realty & Devel 6931 Arlington Rd #501 Bethesda MD 20814

BIELLO, STEPHEN JOSEPH, III, business executive; b. Burlington, Vt., Nov. 6, 1940; s. Stephen Joseph and Marie (Pidgeon) B.; m. Beatrice A. Morris, July 1, 1963; children: Lisa Ann, Stephany Marie. BSEE, Southneastern Mass. U., 1962; MSEM, Northeaster U., 1979. Registered profl. engr., Mass.; cert. quality auditor. With Raytheon Co., 1968—; system engr. Raytheon Co., Bedford, Mass., sr. engr.; P.A. mgr. Raytheon Co., Bedford, support engring. mgr.; mgr. MSD support dept. Raytheon Svc. Co., Burlington, Mass.; mgr. tech. svc. ops. Raytheon Svc. Co., Burlington, mgr. facilities and adminstrn., mgr. of quality. Mem. Soc. of Logistics Engrs. (sr., Cert. Appreciation 1991), Am. Soc. Quality Control. Office: Raytheon Svc Co 2 Wayside Rd Burlington MA 01803

BIELORY, ABRAHAM MELVIN, lawyer, financial executive; b. Modena, Italy, Sept. 20, 1946; came to U.S., 1948; s. Motel and Basia (Spielberg) B.; m. Beverly B. Berkowitz, Jan. 26, 1969; children: Jennifer Rebecca, Debra Elizabeth, David Ethan. BS, N.J. Inst. Tech., 1968; JD, U. Denver, 1973. Bar: N.J. 1974, U.S. Dist. Ct. N.J. 1974, U.S. Supreme Ct. 1979. Field engr. Control Data Corp., Mpls., 1968-69; assoc. Paschon & Feurey, Toms River, N.J., 1973-77, ptnr., 1978; ptnr. VanSicle & Bielory, Toms River, 1978-88, Babcock, Hennes & Bielory, P.C., Bricktown and Toms River, N.J., 1989—; owner ABEV Fin. Svc., Toms River, 1976—. V.p. Lakewood Hebrew Day Sch., N.J., 1975-82, pres., 1982-86; trustee Hillel High Sch., Deal, N.J., 1983—; v.p. Congregation Sons of Israel, Lakewood, 1984-86, pres. 1986-88. Sgt. USAF, 1969-73. Fellow ABA; mem. Assn. Trial Lawyers Am., N.J. State Bar Assn., Trial Atty. N.J., Ocean County Bd. Realtors, Women's Coun. of Realtors (assoc.), Ocean County Bar Assn. (chmn. ins. com. 1975), Hudson County Bar Assn. (sr. citizen com. 1984), Internat. Lawyers Assn., Jewish War Vets. Republican. Home: 1422 14th St Lakewood NJ 08701-1504

BIELUCH, PHILIP JAMES, actuary; b. Hartford, Conn., Mar. 1, 1955; s. William Charles and Nellie (Sidor) B.; m. Gayle Denise Ashley, Feb. 16, 1985; 1 child, Christopher Henry. BS in computer, Trinity Coll., 1976. Chartered life underwriter; chartered fin. cons. Actuarial assoc. Covenant Life Ins., Hartford, 1973-77; asst. v.p. Huggins & Co., Hartford, 1977-79; v.p. Sorensen & Assocs., Hartford, 1979-80; assoc. actuary Security-Conn., Avon, 1980-81; pres. Delta Actuaries, Inc., Hartford, 1982-85; cons. Tillinghast, A Towers Perrin Co., Hartford, 1985—, prin., 1986—; corporator St. Francis Hosp. Bd. dirs. N.W. Cath. High Sch., 1991—. Fellow Soc. Actuaries (chmn. com. on annuities, mem. experience studies com., vice chmn. exam. com.); mem. Am. Acad. Actuaries, Am. Soc. CLUs, Conf. Consulting Acturaries, Club of Hartford (pres.), U. Club Hartford (bd. dirs. 1985-88). Republican. Roman Catholic. Home: 3 Glenmore Dr Farmington CT 06032-1430 Office: Tillinghast a Towers Perrin 175 Powder Forest Rd Weatogue CT 06089-9658

BIELY, DEBRA MARIE, military officer; b. Columbus, Ohio, June 8, 1957; d. Joseph Richard and Mary Narcissus (Quin) Szulewski; m. Robert Lee Biely, July 31, 1977; children: Kevin Lee, Kelsey Lynn, Kerry Logan. BS, Ohio State U., 1979. Commd. 2d lt. USMC, 1979, advanced through grades to major; bn. adjutant 3d recruit tng. bn. USMC, Parris Island, S.C., 1980-82; asst. div. personnel officer 2d Marine div. USMC, Camp Lejeune, N.C., 1982-84, regimental adjutant 10th Marines, 1984-85; group adjutant 3d Force Serv SPT group USMC, Okinawa, Japan, 1986-88; squadron exec. officer hdqrs. squadron MCAS USMC, Futenma, Japan, 1988-89; div. adminstrv. officer human resources div. USMC, Washington, 1989-90, sect. mgr./adminstrv. officer requirements and programs div. HQMC, 1990-92, analyst Office Program Appraisal Sec. Navy, 1992—. Instr. Presdl. Classroom, Washington, 1991. Decorated Navy Commendation, Achievement medal. Mem. Women Officers Profl. Assn. (ex officio, bd. dirs.), Woodlake Country Club. Office: Office of Sec Navy (OPA) Navy Dept Washington DC 20350-1400

BIEMER, LINDA HILL, university administrator, social studies educator, author, consultant; b. Cortland, N.Y., May 24, 1942; d. Horace Edward and Jane Magoris (King) Hill; m. Mark Charles Briggs, Sept. 8, 1962 (div. Dec. 1968); 1 child, Chance; m. Robert Biemer, May 22, 1970. AB, Elmira Coll., 1963; MS, SUNY, Cortland, 1967; PhD, Syracuse U., 1979. Cert. high sch. tchr., N.Y. Tchr. social studies Cortland City Schs., 1963-68; instr. history SUNY, Cortland, 1968-72; lectr., instr. SUNY, Binghamton, 1972-79, asst. prof., 1979-85, assoc. prof., dir., 1986-88, acting dean sch. edn. human devel., 1988-90, dean, prof., 1990—; cons. N.Y. State Edn. Dept., Albany, 1974—, various sch. dists., 1980—. Author: Women and Property in Colonial New York, 1983, New York: Our Communities, 1983, New York and Its Western Hemisphere Neighbors, 1988; co-author: Teaching Social Studies in Middle and Senior High Schools, 1990; contbr. articles to profl. jours. Bd. dirs. LWV, Cortland, 1972-79, YWCA, 1984-88; Dem. committeewoman, 1975-90. Named Outstanding Young Educator, N.Y. State Jaycees, 1968, Outstanding Social Studies Educator, N.Y. State State Council for Social Studies, 1985-86; Women Historian fellow Syracuse U., 1974-75. Mem. AAUW (chair women's issues com. 1985-88), N.Y. Assn. Colls. of Tchr. Edn. (bd. dirs. 1990—), Nat. Coun. Social Studies (bd. dirs. 1985-90), N.Y. State Tchr. Edn. (bd. dirs. 1985-90), Nat. Coun. Accreditation Tchr. Edn. (bd. dirs. 1986—), Social Sci. End. Consortium (bd. dirs. 1989-92, pres. 1990-91). Office: SUNY Sch Edn and Human Devel Binghamton NY 13902-6000

BIENENSTOCK, GEORGE, advertising and marketing agency executive; b. N.Y.C., Mar. 3, 1945; s. Arnold and Jeannette (Fuld) B.; m. Rose LaPlaca, Feb. 6, 1972; children: Esther, David. BS in Mktg., Rutgers U., 1971. Sales mgr. Ace Sci. Supply Co., East Brunswick, N.J., 1967-81; br. mgr. Sargent-Welch Sci., Springfield, N.J., 1981-85; v.p. sales Sargent-Welch Sci., Skokie, Ill., 1985-86; corp. sales mgr. Continental Water Systems, Broadview, Ill., 1986-88; pres. Beehive Mktg. Group, Murray Hill, N.J., 1988—. Committeeman, Boy Scouts Am., Lake Forest, Ill., 1987-88. With U.S. Army N.G., 1965-71. Office: Beehive Mktg Group 125 Roland Rd New Providence NJ 07974-2774

BIENKOWSKI, SIGMUND JOHN, information systems technology executive; b. Bklyn., May 20, 1941; s. Sigmund Sr. and Stella (Voytus) B.; m. Rose Marie Ognibene; children: Christine Marie, Catherine Renee, Diana Lee, Michael Sigmund. BS in Math., St. Peter's Coll., Jersey City, 1964; MS in Mgmt. Engring., L.I. U., 1970; MBA in Fin., Lehigh U., 1985. Computer systems analyst Sperry Systems Mgmt. Div., Syosset, N.Y., 1967-69; sr. advanced systems planner Grumman Data Systems Corp., Bethpage, N.Y., 1969-73; data processing prodn. supr. George B. Buck Cons. Actuaries, Inc., N.Y.C., 1973-76; performance measurement specialist Doubleday and Co., Inc., Garden City, N.Y., 1976-79; project mgr. AT&T, Morristown, N.J., 1979-89; sr. cons. SHL Systemhouse, Inc., Balt., 1990; products mgr. Concurrent Engring. Rsch. Ctr., W.Va. U., Morgantown, 1990—. Capt. signal corps. U.S. Army, 1964-67. Mem. Am. Mgmt. Assn., Data Processing Mgmt. Assn., Res. Officers Assn. Home: 11 Devon Dr Easton PA 18042

BIERKAN, DEAN ANDREW, lawyer; b. New Britian, Conn., Mar. 18, 1945; s. John ANdrew and Virginia (Parson) B.; m. Amber Lee Fairfield, Mar. 23, 1974; children: Aren, Chelsea. BA, Colgate U., 1967; JD, Georgetown U., 1973. Bar: Mass. 1974. Atty. Am. Optical Corp., Southbridge, Mass., 1973-76; atty. H.J. Heinz Co., Pitts., 1976-80, sr. atty., 1980-91, gen. atty., 1991—. With U.S. Army, 1969-71, Vietnam. Mem. Am. Bar Assn., Mass. Bar Assn., U.S. Trademark Assn. Office: HJ Heinz 1062 Progress St Pittsburgh PA 15212

BIERNACKI, HALINA T., civic worker. BS in Mgmt., Calif. Coast U., 1987, postgrad., 1987—. guest speaker Villa Maria Coll. Buffalo, N.Y., 1986, Adam Mickiewicz Dramatic Circle and Libr., Buffalo, 1989. Mem. Nat. Mus. of Women in Arts, Washington, Albright Knox Gallery, Buffalo, Polish Arts Club, Buffalo, Kosciuszko Found.; vol. tax counseling for elderly. With USAFR, 1981. Decorated comdrs. cross and cross with star Order of Polonia Restituta, dame Lofsensic Ursinius Order; recipient Certs. of Appreciation and Spl. Recognition, Dept. of Treasury, IRS. Mem. NAFE, Buffalo IBM PC User's Group, Inc. (bd. dirs., treas. 1990), Better Bus. Bur. of Western N.Y. (mediator, arbitrator dispute resolution ctr. 1987), Am. Biog. Inst. (bd. govs.).

BIERNAT, LILLIAN M. NAHUMENUK, interior designer; b. Phila., Apr. 27, 1931; d. Peter and Anna (Wolonick) Nahumenuk; m. Joseph Anthony Biernat, July 22, 1951; children: Joseph A., Daria Ann, Karen Marie, Mark Allen, Brent Hilary. Student, N.Y. Sch. Interior Design, 1955. Receptionist, sec. Mayer, Magaziner & Brunswick, Phila., 1950-53; owner Town House Interiors, Columbia, Conn., also Newton Square, Pa., 1956—, Lillian Biernat Interiors, Columbia and Avon, Conn.; bd. dirs. Conn. à la Carte Cook Book. Mem. fund raising com. Girl Scouts U.S., 1968; mem. exec. bd. Conn. Opera Guild, Hartford Ballet; pres. Friends of Hartford Ballet. Mem. Women's Club, Garden Club (Newtown Square), Villagers Women's Club (Columbia), Garden Club of Avon (pres.). Address: 30 Hurdle Fence Dr Avon CT 06001

BIESEL, DAVID BARRIE, publishing executive; b. Chgo., Sept. 12, 1931; s. William James Trimble and Aileen Louise (Jacquith) B.; m. Donna Louise Scoggan, May 25, 1958 (div. 1975); children: Deborah Louise Biesel Brugger, William Warren; m. Diane Jane Stevens, Sept. 25, 1982. Student, U. Md., 1950-53. Supr. editorial dept. Fed. Electric Corp., Paramus, N.J., 1958-62; mgr. editorial dept. Am. Inst.Physics, N.Y.C., 1962-69; ref. book editor R. R. Bowker Co., N.Y.C., 1969-73; sr. editor Macmillan Pub. Co., N.Y.C., 1973-82, Elsevier Sci. Pubs., N.Y.C., 1983-84; v.p., editor-in-chief R. R. Bowker Co., N.Y.C., 1984-85; v.p., editorial dir. M. E. Sharpe, Armonk, N.Y., 1986-88; pres. St. Johann Press, Haworth, N.J., 1988—. Author: Can You Name That Team; contbr. articles to profl. jours. Warden All Saints Episcopal Ch., Bergenfield, N.J., 1985-88, vestryman, 1982-85. With USMC, 1953-57. Mem. ALA, Assn. Ednl. Communications and Tech., Soc. Am. Baseball Rsch., Profl. Football Rsch. Assn. Home and Office: 315 Schraalenburgh Rd Haworth NJ 07641-1200

BIGBY, MICHAEL ELLIOTT, dermatologist; b. Glen Cove, N.Y., Feb. 13, 1949; s. Laura Odessa Bigby; m. Judyann Rollins, Sept. 4, 1971; children: Kenan Ali, Naima Alexis. BA, Princeton U., 1971; MD, Harvard U., 1975. Intern, resident in medicine Mass. Gen. Hosp., Boston, 1975-78; instr. medicine U. Wash., Seattle, 1978-81, asst. clin. prof., 1981; dermatology resident Harvard Med. Sch., Boston, 1982-85, rsch. assoc., 1985-88, asst. prof. dermatology, 1991—; assoc. dermatologist Beth Israel Hosp., Boston, 1985—; asst. immunology Mass. Gen. Hosp., Boston, 1988-91; mem. adv. bd. dermatology sect. U.S. Pharm., Washington, 1985—. Editor: Manual of Clinical Problems in Dermatology, 1992; book rev. editor Archives of Dermatology, 1985—. V.p. Lupus Found. Am., Newton, Mass., 1991, pres., 1992. Lt. USPHS, 1978-81. Mem. Soc. Investigative Dermatology, Am. Assn. Immunologists, Sigma Xi, Phi Beta Kappa. Office: Cutraneous Biology Rsch Ctr 149 13th St Charlestown MA 02129-2060

BIGELEISEN, JACOB, chemist, educator; b. Paterson, N.J., May 2, 1919; s. Harry and Ida (Slomowitz) B.; m. Grace Alice Simon, Oct. 21, 1945; children: David M., Ira S., Paul E. A.B., NYU, 1939; M.S., Wash. State U., 1941; Ph.D., U. Calif., Berkeley, 1943. Rsch. scientist Manhattan Dist., Columbia, 1943-45; rsch. assoc. Ohio State U., Columbus, 1945-46; fellow Enrico Fermi Inst., U. Chgo., 1946-48; sr. chemist Brookhaven Nat. Lab., Upton, N.Y., 1948-68; prof. chemistry U. Rochester, N.Y., 1968-78; chmn. dept. U. Rochester, 1970-75; Tracy H. Harris prof. U. Rochester (Coll. Arts and Scis.), 1973-78; v.p. research, dean grad. studies SUNY, Stony Brook, 1978-80; Leading prof. chemistry SUNY, 1978-89, Disting. prof., 1989, Disting. prof. emeritus, 1989—; vis. prof. Cornell U., 1953; NSF sr. fellow, vis. prof. Eidgen Techn. Hochschule, Switzerland, 1962-63; chmn. Assembly Math. and Phys. Scis., NRC-Nat. Acad. Scis., 1976-80. Mem. editorial bd. Jour. Phys. Chemistry, Jour. Chem. Physics. Trustee Sayville Jewish Center, 1954-68. Recipient Nuclear award Am. Chem. Soc., 1958, Gilbert N. Lewis lectr., 1963, E.O. Lawrence award, 1964, Disting. Alumnus award Wash. State U., 1983; John Simon Guggenheim fellow, 1974-75. Fellow Am. Phys. Soc., Am. Chem. Soc., AAAS, Am. Acad. Arts and Sci.; mem. Nat. Acad. Scis. (councilor 1982-85), Phi Beta Kappa, Sigma Xi, Phi Lambda Upsilon. Home: PO Box 217 Saint James NY 11780-0217

BIGELOW, EUGENE THAYER, JR., media company executive; b. Boston, Oct. 22, 1941; s. Eugene Thayer and Natalie (Corcoran) B.; m. Ann Rogerson, Aug. 17, 1968; 1 child, Katharine. A.B., Trinity Coll., Hartford, Conn., 1965; M.B.A., U. Va., 1967. Exec. v.p. Manhattan Cable TV, N.Y.C., 1975-76, pres., 1976-80; sr. v.p. Time-Life Films, N.Y.C., 1980-81; pres. Time-Life Video, N.Y.C., 1981-82; v.p., treas. Time Inc., N.Y.C., 1982-84, chief fin. officer, 1984-87; pres. Am. TV & Communications Svc. Co., 1988, Home Box Office, N.Y.C., 1988-91, Time Warner Cable Programming, Stamford, Conn., 1991—; bd. dirs. Crane Co., N.Y.C., BET Holdings, Inc., Medusa Corp. Served with USMCR, 1960-66. Home: 1112 Park Ave New York NY 10128-1235 Office: 300 First Stamford Pl Stamford CT 06902

BIGGAR, JAMES MCCREA, food and hospitality company executive; b. Cleve., Dec. 5, 1928; s. Hamilton Fisk and Ruth Carolyn (McCrea) B.; m. Margery Dean Stouffer, Dec. 29, 1950; children: Elizabeth, James, William, David. B.S. in Mech. Engring. and Engring. Adminstrn., Case Inst. Tech., 1950. With Reliance Electric Co., Cleve., 1950-60, mgr. alternating current products, 1955-60; dir. mktg. frozen foods div. Stouffer Corp., Cleve., 1960-63, v.p., 1963-66, gen. mgr., 1966-67, pres., 1967-72; pres., chmn. bd., dir. Stouffer Corp., Solon, Ohio, from 1972; chmn., chief exec. officer Nestle Enterprises, Inc., Solon, Ohio, 1983—, also dir.; pres., chmn., dir. Nestle Holdings Inc. (subs. Nestle S.A., Verey, Switzerland), Wilmington, Del., 1985—; bd. dirs. Nat. City Corp. of Cleve., Sherwin-Williams Co., Cleve. Pres. Orange Local Sch. Bd., Pepper Pike, Ohio, 1967-68; v.p. Vocat. Guidances Svcs., Cleve., 1970-76; trustee Cleve. Clinic Found., Univ. Schs.; bd. overseers Exec. Coun. Fgn. Diplomats. Mem. Am. Frozen Food Inst. (past chmn., dir.), Grocery Mfrs. Am., Phi Kappa Psi, Theta Tau, Beta Gamma Sigma. Presbyterian. Clubs: Cleve. Country, Clevelander, Pepper Pike Country, Rolling Rock. *

BIGGERS, EMORY MELVIN, programmer; b. Washington, June 12, 1951; adopted s. Earl and Agnes (Morgan) Edwards. Student, Howard U., 1973. Statis. asst. U.S. Internat. Trade Commn., WAshington, 1973-79; programmer Computer Data Systems, Inc., Rockville, Md., 1979, U.S. Dept. Commerce, Washington, 1979-80; programmer-analyst Planning Research Corp., McLean, Va., 1980-87; cons. EDP Temps, Inc., Vienna, Va., 1987-88; sr. systems analyst Gen. Analytics Corp., McLean, 1988-89; programmer analyst Planning Rsch. Corp., McLean, 1989—. Contbr. poems to anthologies. Recipient Golden Poet award World of Poetry, 1987. Episcopalian. Home: 1110 Fidler Ln Apt 823 Silver Spring MD 20910-3452

BIGGS, EDMUND LOGAN, college administrator; b. Mattoon, Ill., Dec. 17, 1938; s. Lloyd William and Florence Violet (Fairbanks) B.; 1 child, Lloyd John. BS in Acctg., Kansas State U., 1965; MBA in Mgmt., U. New Haven, 1983; PhD, SUNY, Buffalo, 1991. Computer specialist Union Nat. Bank, Manhattan, Kans., 1963-65, mgmt. trainee, 1965-66; nuclear logistics officer USN, Kirtland AFB, N. Mex., 1967-68, computer programming officer, 1968-69; data automation officer Tan Son Knut, Vietnam, 1969-70; computer systems analyst Stuttgart, Fed. Republic Germany, 1970-72; supply officer USS Sellers, 1973-74; procurement officer def. gen. supply ctr. Richmond, Va., 1974-76; asst. supply/material officer, support force Antarctica, 1976-78; planning and adminstrv. officer, aviation supply officer China Lake, Calif., 1978-79; comptr., commanding officer regional acctg. and disbursing ctr. Subase, New London, Conn., 1980-82; liaison officer def. logistics agy for maj. def. systems Syracuse, N.Y., 1982-83; instr. bus. Erie Community Coll., Buffalo, 1983-86, dept. head banking, ins., real estate, 1986—; adminstr. Structurally Unemployed Retng. Program, Buffalo, 1985—. Presbyn. deacon. Mem. VFW, Am. Legion, Optimist Internat., Lions. Republican. Office: Erie Community Coll 121 Ellicott St Buffalo NY 14203-2601

BIGLEY, WILLIAM JOSEPH, JR., control engineer; b. Union City, N.J., May 8, 1924; s. William Joseph and Mary May (Quigley) B.; B.M.E., Rensselaer Polytech. Inst., 1950; M.S. in Elec. Engring., N.J. Inst. Tech., 1962, M.S. in Computer Sci., 1973; Ed.D., Fairleigh Dickinson U., 1984; m. Hannelore Hicks, June 24, 1950; children—Laura C., William Joseph IV, Susan J. Project engr. Tube Reducing Corp., Wallington, N.J., 1953-58, Flight Support, Inc., Metuchen, N.J., 1958-59, Airborne Accessories, Inc., Hillside, N.J., 1959-61; prin. staff engr. in control engring. Lockheed Electronics Co. div. Lockheed Aircraft, Inc., Plainfield, N.J., 1961-90; pres. Systems Engring. Corp. N.J. Inst. Tech., Newark, 1990—; prof. engring. control systems, George Washington U., 1989—; prof. cons. engr. Automatic Control Systems, 1958—. Named Engr.-Scientist of Yr., Lockheed Electronics Co., Inc., 1980, recipient Robert E. Gross award for tech. excellence, 1980; Achievement Honor Roll award N.J. Inst. Tech. Alumni Assn., 1982; registered profl. engr., N.Y., N.J., Calif. Mem. Nat. Soc. Profl. Engrs., IEEE, ASME, NRA, Tau Beta Pi (eminent engr. 1986). Contbr. articles to profl. jours. Office: Systems Engring Corp Enterprise Devel Ctr 240 Dr King Blvd Newark NJ 07102

BIGMAN, ANTON W., lawyer; b. Braddock, Pa., Apr. 6, 1929. AB cum laude, U. Pitts., 1951; LLB, Harvard U., 1954. Bar: Pa. 1955, U.S. Supreme Ct. 1965. Pvt. practice Pitts., 1955—; solicitor Braddock Sch. Dist., 1956-71, No. Braddock Sch. Dist., 1957-69; No. Braddock Sch. Bldg. Authority, 1960-69, Gen. Braddock Area Sch. Dist., 1971-72, 1980-81. Chmn. Braddock Borough Parking Authority, 1958-59; v.p. Beth Hamedrash Hagadol-Beth Jacob Congregation, Pitts., 1986—. Mem. ABA, Pa. Bar Assn., Allegheny County Bar Assn., Assn. Trial Lawyers Am., B'nai Brith, Harvard-Yale-Princeton Club (Pitts.). Home: 15H Chatham Towers # S Pittsburgh PA 15219-3430 Office: 210 Fort Pitt Commons Pittsburgh PA 15219

BIHOVSKY, RON HANS, medicinal chemist; b. Ithaca, N.Y., Nov. 9, 1948; s. Martin R. and Esther B. (Neustatter) Bates; m. Anita J. Weisberger, July 4, 1985; children: Eric, Michael. BS, SUNY, Stony Brook, 1970; PhD, U. Calif., Berkeley, 1977; postgrad., U. Wis., 1980. Chemist USDA, Beltsville, Md., 1971-72; asst. prof. SUNY, Stony Brook, 1980-87; scientist, medicinal chemist Berlex Labs., Cedar Knolls, N.J., 1987-92; sr. scientist Cephalon, Inc., West Chester, Pa., 1992—. Contbr. articles to profl. jours. Mem. Am. Chem. Soc., Am. Peptide Soc. Office: Cephalon Inc 145 Brandywine Pkwy West Chester PA 19380-4245

BIKALES, NORBERT M., chemist, science administrator; b. Berlin, Jan. 7, 1929; came to U.S., 1946; s. Salomon and Bertha (Bander) B.; m. Gerda V. Bierzonski, Apr. 28, 1951; children: Marguerite Sarlin, Edward A. BS in Chemistry, CCNY, 1951; MS in Chemistry, Polytech. U., 1956; PhD in Chemistry, Poly. U., 1961. Rsch. chemist Am. Cyanamid Co., Stamford, Conn., 1951-62; tech. dir. Gaylord Assocs., Newark, 1962-65; pres. N.M. Bikales & Co., Cons., Livingston, N.J., 1965-76; prof. chemistry, dir. continuing edn. in scis. Rutgers U., New Brunswick and Newark, N.J., 1973-79; dir. polymers program NSF, Washington, 1976—. Editor Encyclopedia of Polymer Science and Technology, 1962-77; mem. editorial bd. Encyclopedia of Polymer Science and Engineering, 1982-90; contbr. articles to profl. jours., chpts. to books. Pres., Friends of Livingston (N.J.) Libr., 1968-72, Livingston Symphony Orch., 1970-76; judge Internat. Tech. Film '89 Festival, Pardubice, Czechoslovakia, 1989. Recipient award Twp. of Livingston, 1976, Great Medal City of Paris, 1985, Disting. Alumnus award Poly. U., Bklyn., 1986, Disting. Lectr. award Soc. Polymer Sci., Tokyo, 1986. Fellow AAAS, Am. Phys. Soc., N.Y. Acad. Sci.; mem. Am. Chem. Soc. (councilor 1987-89, chmn. polymer div. 1983), Internat. Union Pure and Applied Chemistry (titular mem., sec. 1979-87), Soc. Plastics Engrs. (sr., bd. dirs. 1979-82), Polish Chem. Soc. (hon.). Office: NSF 1800 G St NW Washington DC 20550-0002

BIKEL, THEODORE, actor, singer; b. Vienna, Austria, May 2, 1924; came to U.S., 1954, naturalized, 1961; s. Josef and Miriam (Riegler) B.; m. Rita Weinberg, 1967. Student, U. London; grad., Royal Acad. Art, London, 1948; DFA (hon.), U. Hertford, 1992. Apprentice with Habimah Theatre, Tel Aviv, 1942-44, a founder, Tel Aviv Chamber Theatre, 1944-46; theatrical prodns. include A Streetcar Named Desire, London, 1950, The Love of Four Colonels, London, 1950-52, Tonight in Samarkand, N.Y.C., 1954, The Lark, N.Y.C., 1955-56, Rope Dancers, N.Y.C., 1957-58, Sound of Music, N.Y.C., 1959-61, Fiddler on the Roof, various cities, 1968-72, 74, 77, 79, 80, 82-83, 85, 87-92, The Rothschilds (nat. co.), 1972, Jacques Brel is Alive and Well and Living in Paris, various cities, 1974-75, The Good Doctor, various cities, 1975, Zorba, various cities, 1976, 78, Inspector Gen., N.Y.C., 1978, Threepenny Opera, Mpls., 1983, My Fair Lady, Phoenix, 1988-89, She Loves Me, various cities, 1989-90; opera prodns. include La Gazza Ladra, Phila., 1990, Abduction from the Seraglio, Cleve., 1992; motion pictures include African Queen, 1951; The Little Kidnappers, 1951, The Enemy Below, 1957, I Want to Live, 1958, The Defiant Ones, 1958 (Academy award nomination), Blue Angel, 1959, My Fair Lady, 1964, Sands of the Kalahari, 1965, The Russians are Coming, 1966, Sweet November, 1967, My Side of the Mountain, 1969, Darker Than Amber, 1970, The Little Ark, 1971, See You in the Morning, 1989, Shattered, 1991; also numerous TV appearances, 1954—; star: TV prodns. The Eternal Light, 1958, Look Up and Live, 1958-60; host-editor: TV prodn. Directions 61, 1961; weekly radio program At Home with Theodore Bikel, 1958-63; concert folk singer, 1955—, rec. artist for, Elektra and Reprise; Author: Folksongs and Footnotes, 1960. Mem. Nat. Coun. for Arts, 1977-82; founder Arts chpt. Am. Jewish Congress, 1961-63, nat. v.p., 1963-70, chmn. governing coun., 1970-80, sr. v.p., 1980—; del. Dem. Nat. Conv., 1968. Mem. AFTRA, SAG, Acad. TV Arts and Scis. (gov. 1961-65), Actors Equity Assn. (councillor 1961-64, 1st v.p. 1964-73, pres. 1973-82, pres. emeritus 1982—), Internat. Fedn. Actors (v.p. 1981-91), Associated Actors and Artists of Am. (pres. 1989—), Acad. Motion Picture Arts and Scis., Am. Fedn. Musicians. Address: Associated Actors & Artists of Am 165 W 46th St New York NY 10036

BIKERMAN, MICHAEL, geologist, educator; b. Berlin; s. Jacob Joseph and Valentine (Leivand) B.; m. Viola Adler, June 2, 1956; children: Jennifer, David, Tania. BS in Chemistry, Queens Coll., 1954; BS in Geology, N.Mex. IMT, 1956; MS in Geology, U. Ariz., 1962, PhD in Geology, 1965. Assayer Cinnabar Mine, Idaho, 1957; instr. Boise (Idaho) Jr. Coll., 1958-60; rsch. asst. U. Ariz., Tucson, 1960-65; asst. prof. Wichita (Kans.) State U., 1965-67; asst. prof. U. Pitts., 1967-71, assoc. prof., 1971—; rsch. assoc. Carnegie Mus., Pitts., 1979—. Co-author: Isotopic Ages of Post-Paleocene Igneous Rocks Within and Bordering the Clifton 1 x 2 Degree Quadrangle/Arizona-New Mexico, 1987. Fellow Geol. Soc. of Am.; mem. AAAS, Geochem. Soc. Office: Univ Pitts 321 OEH Pittsburgh PA 15260

BIKLEN, DOUGLAS, special education educator; b. Sept. 8, 1945; s. Paul Frederick and Anne (Chenoweth) B.; m. Sari Knopp, Nov. 28, 1970; children: Noah Knopp Biklen, Molly Knopp Biklen. BA in History, Bowdoin Coll., 1967; MRP in Planning, Syracuse U., 1973, PhD in Social Sci., 1973. Rsch. asst. Syracuse U., 1969-72, advocacy dir., asst. prof. spl. edn. and rehab., 1973-77, assoc. dir. of the Ctr. on Human Policy, 1975-77, assoc. prof. coord. grad. program in mental retardation, 1977-82, prof. coord. grad. program in mental retardation, 1982-83, dir. ctr. on human policy, 1976-83, prof. spl. edn., dir. div. spl. edn. and rehab., 1983-92, prof., 1983—; guest lectr. Commonwealth Schs. Commn., Australia, 1986, McGill U./G. Allan Roeher Inst., 1985-88, Melbourne U., Australia, Ministry of Edn., Melbourne, 1989; vis. scholar Calif. State Coll., 1987; acad. mem. Canadian Centre for Habilitation Edn. and Rsch. U., Waterloo, Ont., Can., 1990—; mem. internat. review panel Office of Intellectual Disability Svcs., Melbourne, 1990; adv. com., peer review panel Internat. Exchange of Experts and Info. in Rehab., World Rehab. Fund, 1990 and others. Contbr. chpts. to books and articles to profl. jours. Bd. dirs. Onondaga Neighborhood Legal Svcs., 1977-79. Mem. ACLU, AAAS, AAUP, Assn. for Persons with Severe Handicaps (chair exec. com. 1986-88, 91-92, v.p. TASH 1988-89), Assn. for Retarded Citizens, Am. Ednl. Rsch. Assn., Coun. for Exceptional Children (assoc. editor 1976-82), Am. Assn. on Mental Retardation, Am. Orthopsychiat. Assn. Home: 106 Circle Rd Syracuse NY 13210-3046 Office: Syracue U Div Spl Edn/Rehab 805 S Crouse Ave Syracuse NY 13244-0001

BILBOW, JAMES ROBERT, police officer; b. Phila., Feb. 2, 1923; s. James Michael and Jane Marie (Barrett) B.; Asso. Aero. Engring., Pa. Inst. Tech., 1954-56; m. Blanche Colley, Sept. 1, 1951. Technologist survival equipment U.S. Naval Air Engring. Center, Phila., 1951-75, program mgr. life support equipment, 1975-86; dep. chief police Delaware County Park Police Dept., Media, Pa., 1977-86, now officer in charge tactical unit. Pres., Delaware County Police Officers Legal Rights Fund, 1975—; nat. adv. bd. Am. Police Hall of Fame, 1975-79. Mem. bd. Hero Scholarship Fund Delaware County, 1976—, chmn. Hero Scholarship Day. Served with USMCR, 1942-83; ETO, PTO, Korea; lt. col. Res. (ret.). Recipient Freedoms Found. awards, 1977-78; Legion of Honor, Chapel of Four Chaplains; cert. sr. engring. technician instr. police firearms and profl. law enforcement skills. Mem. Internat. Police Chiefs Assn., Internat. Assn. Law Enforcement Firearms Instrs., U.S. Assn. Firearms Instrs. and Coaches, Am. Law Enforcement Officers Assn. (Good Samaritan award 1975, Commendation awards 1974, 76, Honor award 1976, nat, v.p. publs. 1977), Fraternal Order Police (dir. Delaware County Lodge 27, 1977—), Internat. Acad. Criminology, Nat. Police Officers Assn. (certificates of commendation 1975, 76), Police Marksman Assn., Nat. Assn. Chiefs of Police, Pa. Chiefs of Police Assn., Southeastern Police Chiefs Assn. Home: 628 N Lemon St Media PA 19063-2318 Office: Delaware County Park Police Courthouse Media PA 19063

BILDNER, JAMES LEBSON, food company executive; b. Orange, N.J., Jan. 26, 1954; s. Allen Irwin and Joan (Lebson) B.; m. Nancy J. Weimer, Sept. 27, 1981; children: Peter Grant, Elizabeth Lyndsey. AB, Dartmouth Coll., 1975; JD, Case Western Res. U., 1979. Bar: Mass., 1983. Legis. asst. U.S. Senate, Washington, 1977; mgmt. trainee Kings Supermarket, Inc., West Caldwell, N.J., 1980-81; sr. cons. Touche Ross & Co., Boston, 1981-82; v.p. Store 24, Inc., Waltham, Mass., 1982-83; pres. T. Bildner & Sons, Brookline, Mass., 1983—. Bd. dirs. Boston Ctr. for Adult Edn., 1987—, Manchester (Mass.) Community Ctr., 1988—; alt. mem. bd. appeals Town of Manchester, 1989—. Mem. ABA, Mass. Bar Assn., Young Pres.' Orgn., Bus. Assocs. Club, Dartmouth Club of Ea. Mass., Ea. Yacht Club, Univ. Club of Boston. Office: 1309 Beacon St Brookline MA 02146-5252

BILFINGER, THOMAS VICTOR, surgeon, educator; b. Ridgewood, N.J., May 4, 1952; s. Victor Wilhelm and Heidi Erika (Muser) B.; m. Celia Betty Dameron; children: Elizabeth, Christine. MD, U. Zurich, Switzerland, 1978, ScD, 1979. Intern U. Chgo., 1980-81, rsch. fellow, 1981-82; resident in surgery U. Tex. Med. Br., Galveston, 1982-86, resident in cardiovascular surgery, 1986-88, instr. in surgery, 1988-89; asst. prof. surgery SUNY, Stony Brook, 1989-92, assoc. prof. surgery, 1992—; bd. dirs. cardiovascular intensive care unit SUNY, Stony Brook. Co-author: Evaluation of the Cardiac Surgical Candidate, 1992; contbr. articles to profl. jours. Recipient Rsch. grant U. Chgo., 1981, Rsch. grant Eli Lilly, 1989, Rsch. grant NIH, 1991. Fellow Am. Coll. Cardiology, Am. Coll. Chest Physicians, ACS (assoc.); mem. AMA, Assn. for Acad. Surgery, Soc. Critical Care Medicine, Societe Suisse de Chirurgie Thoracique et Cardiovasculaire. Office: SUNY Health Sci Ctr T19 R 080 Stony Brook NY 11794

BILICH, MARION YELLIN, psychologist, writer; b. Bklyn., Feb. 14, 1949; d. Bernard Perry Yellin and Sylvia (Spector) Reveman; m. Charles Allen Bilich, Aug. 23, 1970; 1 child, Karin. BA, New Coll. of Hofstra U., 1970; MS, Columbia U., 1975; PhD, Fielding Inst., Santa Barbara, Calif., 1989. Cert. in psychology, social work. Tchr. Brookline (Mass.) Pub. Schs., 1971-72; researcher Ctr. for the Study of Anorexia and Bulimia, N.Y.C., 1984-89; psychotherapist in pvt. practice Hewlett, N.Y., 1977—; speaker at nat. confs. Author: Weight Loss From the Inside Out: Help for the Compulsive Eater, 1983; contbr. articles on eating disorders to profl. jours. Mem. Am. Psychol. Assn., N.Y. Acad. Scis.

BILLHARZ, CONSTANCE ELLEN CLARK, speech educator, educational diagnostician; b. Golden City, Mo., July 29, 1921; d. Harley B. and Flossie J. (Mitchell) Clark; m. Roger William Billharz, Jan. 12, 1946; 1 child, Roger Clark. BA, Pace U., 1971; MA, NYU, 1975; MPS, Manhattanville Coll., 1978. Cert. tchr., N.Y. Mem. N.Y. Opera Co., N.Y.C., 1943-46; speech pathologist St. Joseph's Mental Health Clinic, Peekskill, N.Y., 1978-79; speech and lang. pathologist Rye (N.Y.) City Sch. Dist., 1980-82; speech therapist, spl. edn. tchr. Hartsdale Sch., Elmsford, N.Y., 1985-90; adj. prof. speech Westchester Community Coll., Valhalla, N.Y., 1991—; ednl. diagnostician, North Tarrytown, N.Y., 1979—. Mem. New Opera Co., N.Y.C., 1943-46. Mem. Am. Speech, Lang. and Hearing Assn. (cert. clin. competence), N.Y. State Speech, Lang. and Hearing Assn., Westchester Speech, Lang. and Hearing Assn., Westchester Assn. for Children with Learning Disabilities, Am. Arbibtration Assn. Republican. Home and Office: 467 Munroe Ave Tarrytown NY 10591-1610

BILLINGS, FRANKLIN SWIFT, JR., federal judge; b. Woodstock, Vt., June 5, 1922; s. Franklin S. and Gertrude (Curtis) B.; m. Pauline Gillingham, Oct. 13, 1951; children: Franklin, III, Jireh Swift, Elizabeth, Ann. S.B., Harvard U., 1943; postgrad., Yale U. law Sch., 1945; J.D., U. Va., 1947. Bar: Vt. 1948, U.S. Supreme Ct., 1958. With dept. electronics Gen. Electric Co., Schenectady, N.Y., 1943; bldg. dept. Vt. Marble Co., Proctor, 1945-46; pvt. practice law Woodstock, 1948-52; mem. firm Billings & Sherburne, Woodstock, 1952-66; asst. sec. Vt. Senate, 1949-55, sec., 1957-59; sec. civil and mil. affairs State of Vt., 1959-61; exec. clk. to gov., 1955-57; judge Hartford Mcpl. Ct., 1955-63; mem. Vt. Ho. of Reps., 1961-66, chmn. jud. com., 1961, speaker of ho., 1963-66; judge Vt. Superior Ct., 1966-75; assoc. justice U.S. Supreme Ct. Vt., Montpelier, 1975-83, chief justice, 1983-84; judge U.S. Dist. Ct. Vt., 1984—, chief judge, 1988-92. Bd. dirs. Norman Williams Library, Woodstock, 1950—, active, Town of Woodstock, 1948-72. Served as warrant officer 1st class attached Brit. Army, 1944-45. Decorated Purple Heart; Brit. Empire medal. Mem. Vt. Bar Assn., Delta Theta Phi. Office: US Dist Ct PO Box 218 Rutland VT 05702-0218

BILLINGS, RICHARD WHITTEN, association executive; b. Bar Harbor, Maine, Jan. 5, 1924; s. John Theodore and Evelyn (Ritchie) B.; m. Norma Julia Taraldsen, Apr. 19, 1947; children: Cynthia, Marilyn, John, Amy. BA, Colby Coll., 1948; MEd, Springfield Coll., 1951. Program exec. YMCA, Watertown, N.Y., 1948-50; youth work exec. YMCA, Schenectady, N.Y., 1951-56; dist. dir. YMCA, Hudson Valley, N.Y., 1956-60; exec. dir. Assn. Island, YMCA, Henderson Harbor, N.Y., 1960-67; exec. dir. ea. region FCA, Canton, Conn., 1967-70; exec. dir. Assn. Island REcreat. Corp., Henderson Harbor, 1970-74; bur. dir. Maine Land Use Regulation Commn., Augusta, 1974-76; ins. agt. John Hancock Mut. Life Ins., Augusta, 1976-86; exec. dir. Maine Assn. Life Underwriters, Augusta, 1987—. Fellow Life Underwriters Tng. Coun.; mem. Chartered Life Underwriers, Chartered Fin. cons., VFW, Golden Key Soc., Am. Soc. Assn. Execs., Alumni Coun. Colby Coll. Republican. Congregational. Home: RR 7 Box 1940 Augusta ME 04330-9807 Office: Maine Assn Life Underwriter 432 Western Ave # B Augusta ME 04330-6046

BILLINGTON, JAMES HADLEY, historian, librarian; b. Bryn Mawr, Pa., June 1, 1929; s. Nelson and Jane (Coolbaugh) B.; m. Marjorie Anne Brennan, June 22, 1957; children: Susan Billington Harper, Anne Billington Fischer, James Hadley, Thomas Keator. BA, Princeton U., 1950; PhD, Oxford (Eng.) U., 1953; LittD (hon.), Lafayette Coll., 1981, U. Pitts., 1988; LHD (hon.), LeMoyne Coll., 1982; LittD (hon.), Williams Coll., 1991; LHD (hon.), Rhode Island Coll., 1982, Cath. U. Am., 1983, NYU, 1987, Furman U., 1986, Va. Theol. Sem., 1990; HHD (hon.), Ball State U., 1988; D Pub. Svc. (hon.), George Washington U., 1990. Instr. history Harvard U., Cambridge, Mass., 1957-58, fellow Russian Research Ctr., 1958-59, asst. prof. history, 1958-61; assoc. prof. history Princeton (N.J.) U., 1962-64, prof., 1964-73; dir. Woodrow Wilson Internat. Ctr. for Scholars, Washington, 1973-87; librarian of Congress Libr. of Congress, Washington, 1987—; chmn. Bd. Fgn. Scholarships (Fulbright, Hays), 1971-73, mem. 1973-76; vice-chmn. Atlantic Council's Working Group on the Successor Generation, 1982-86; trustee St. Alban's Sch., 1979-82; dir. Am. Assn. for the Advancement of Slavic studies, 1968-71; spl. cons. to Chase Manhattan Bank on East-West matters, 1971-73; guest commentator for CBS on Nixon-Brezhnev summit meetings, 1972, 73; vis. research prof. to Inst. History of Acad. Scis. of USSR in Moscow, 1966-67, U. Helsinki, 1960-61, École des Hautes Études en Sciences Sociales, Paris, 1985, 88; vis. lectr. to various universities in Europe and Asia; scholar-in-residence, Aspen Inst. for Humanistic Studies, 1974, 75, 77; disting. visitor, Japan Found. 1976. Author: Mikhailovsky and Russian Populism, 1958, The Icon and the Axe: An Interpretive History of Russian Culture, 1966, The Arts of Russia, 1970, Fire in the Minds of Men: Origins of the Revolutionary Faith, 1980, Russia Transformed: Breakthrough to Hope, 1992; contbr. to books and jours.; mem. adv. bd. Foreign Affairs, Theology Today, 1974-84; script writer and host of Humanities Film Forum, 1973. Trustee John F. Kennedy Ctr. for the Performing Arts, Nat. Bldg. Mus., Woodrow Wilson Internat. Ctr. for Scholars, Am. Folklife Ctr.; bd. regents Nat. Libr. Medicine. 1st lt. U.S. Army, 1953-56. McCosh Faculty fellow Princeton U., Guggenheim fellow, 1960-61; Rhodes scholar, 1950-53; Fulbright rsch. professorship U. Helsinki, 1960-61; decorated Comdr. of Order of Arts and Letters of France; recipient Gwanghwa medal Republic of Korea. Mem. Assn. Am. Oxonians (bd. dirs.), Am. Philos. Soc., Am. Acad. Arts and Scis., Coun. of Fgn. Rels., Century Club, Phi Beta Kappa. Clubs: Cosmos (Washington), Century (N.Y.C.). Office: Libr of Congress Washington DC 20540

BILLS, GERALD FREMONT, research mycologist; b. Norfolk, Va., June 4, 1955; s. Gerald Eugene and Betty Caroline (Pickering) B.; m. Maria Eugenia Herrero-Zabaleta, Jan. 19, 1990. BS in Agr. cum laude, W.Va. U., 1978, MS in Plant Pathology, 1980; PhD in Botany, Va. Poly. Inst. and State U., 1985. Grad. rsch. asst. dept. plant pathology and bacteriology W.Va. U., Morgantown, 1978-80; grad. teaching asst. dept. biology Va. Poly. Inst. and State U., Blacksburg, 1980-85; rsch. affiliate botanist Systematic Botany and Mycology Lab. USDA Agrl. Rsch. Svc., Beltsville, Md., 1985-87; asst. prof. dept. botany U. Wyo., Laramie, 1987-88; sr. rsch. microbiologist Merck Rsch. Labs., Rahway, N.J., 1988-92, rsch. fellow, 1992—; foreman multiflora rose extermination program W.Va. Dept. Agr., Clarksburg, summer 1980; vis. scientist Commonwealth Mycol. Inst., U.K., 1986; vis. scientist Merck Sharp & Dohme de España, 1989; instr. field mycology SUNY, Cortland, 1987; referee Mycologia, Can. Jour. Botany, Mycotaxon; presenter at profl. meetings, 1980—; rsch. fellow Buffalo Mus. Sci., 1988. Co-author: Fungi on Plants and Plant Products in the United States, 1989; contbr. articles on fungal systematics, ecology or natural products to sci. jours.; co-patentee on prodn. and use of novel fungal metabolites as therapeutic agts. G.S. Burlingham fellow N.Y. Bot. Garden, Bronx, 1984. Mem. Mycol. Soc. Am. (program com. ann. meetings 1989—), Brit. Mycol. Soc., Am. Phytopath. Soc., Soc. Indsl. Microbiology. Office: Merck Rsch Labs PO Box 2000 Rahway NJ 07065-0900

BILLS, MITCHELL EDWARD, design educator; b. Auburn, N.Y., Dec. 23, 1950; s. Fitch and Jeanette (Maywalt) B.; m. Rebecca Staples, Sept. 18, 1971. BA in English, Pa. State U., 1972; MFA in Visual Design, Temple U., 1984. Editorial cons. McCann Assocs., Inc., Phila., 1975-80; art coord. TVSM, Inc., Hatboro, Pa., 1980-82; type lab. tech. asst. Tyler Sch. of Art, Elkins Park, Pa., 1983-84; design assoc. Home Viewer Publs., Phila., 1985-88; asst. prof. design S.D. State Univ., Brookings, 1988-90; prin. assoc. Studio 605, Brookings, 1988-90; asst. prof. design So. Conn. State Univ., New Haven, 1990—; freelance designer various, 1979—; lectr., design Beaver Coll., Glenside,Pa., 1983; design cons. S.D. Pub. TV, Brookings, 1988-90, Media Arts Ctr., New Haven, Conn., 1990—. Artist: (videotape) Reading the Whirlwind, 1989, idiolect. JAM, 1991; author, designer: (book) Zero Through One, 1984. Media Prodn. grantee Intermedia Arts, Mpls., 1989, Exptl. TV Ctr., Owego, N.Y., 1990, 92. Mem. Media Arts Ctr. of Arts Coun. of Greater New Haven, Coll. Art Assn., Yale MAC Users' Group. Office: So Conn State Univ Art 501 Crescent St New Haven CT 06515-1355

BILOTTA, PETER FRANCIS, computer operations manager; b. Easton, Pa., Aug. 5, 1960; s. Frank and Julia Anita (Spinozzi) B. BS, Rider Coll., 1982; M in Engring., Lehigh U., 1987. Cert. internal auditor. Internal auditor County of Northampton, Easton, 1983; corp. auditor Amstar Corp., N.Y.C., 1983-85; ops. mgr. Am. Computer Repair, Inc., Allentown, Pa., 1987—; mem. adv. bd. Lincoln Tech. Inst., Allentown, 1990—. Mem. scholarship com. Northampton County Am. Legion Baseball League, 1989—. Recipient Cert. of Recognition, Northampton County Am. Legion Baseball League, 1988, 90. Mem. Inst. Indsl. Engrs., Inst. Internal Auditors, Am. Mensa, Ltd., Lehigh Wheelman Assn. (bd. dirs. 1990-91, racing div. bd. dirs., pres. 1991—). Republican. Roman Catholic. Home: 208 Folk St Easton PA 18042-6215 Office: Am Computer Repair Inc 6330 Farm Bureau Rd Allentown PA 18106-9223

BILOTTI, RICHARD, newspaper publisher; b. Harrison, N.J., Nov. 13, 1942; s. Carmine and Janina (Czaikowski) B.; m. Katherine Hatton, May 24, 1980. Student, Rutgers U., Newark, N.J., 1960-61, Goddard Coll., 1968-71. Reporter The Star Ledger, Newark, 1960-66; editor U.S. Army, Fairbanks, Alaska, 1966-68; writer The Newark News, 1968-72, AP, Cleve. and Columbus, Ohio, 1972-75; Sunday mag. editor The Cleve. Plain-Dealer, 1975-79; pub., pres., editor The Gloucester County Times, Woodbury, N.J., 1979-84; pub., pres. The Times of Trenton (N.J.), 1984—; bd. dirs. N.J. Press Assn., Trenton, 1980—. Pres. Pride-in-Trenton, 1984-86; 1st v.p. Greater Trenton Urban League, 1985; chmn. bd. Trenton Symphony Orch., 1986—, pres. 1989—. Served with U.S. Army, 1966-68. Mem. Am. Soc. Newspaper Editors, Am. Newspaper Publishers Assn., Mercer County C. of C. (bd. dirs. 1984—, pres. 1989-91). Clubs: Trenton, Trenton Country, Hopewell Valley Golf. Office: Times 500 Perry St PO Box 847 Trenton NJ 08605

BILTZ, RALPH EDWARD, environmental and safety administrator; b. Balt., July 13, 1944; s. Edward Michael and Ester Barbara (Black) B.; m. Kathleen Elizabeth O'Leary, Jan. 26, 1968; children: Candace Barbara, Amy Elizabeth. Cert. mech. engring., Anne Arundel Community Coll.; cert. occupational safety and health, Catonville Community Coll., 1992. Machine operator Koppers Co., Balt., 1965-73; indsl. engr. Koppers Co., Harmans, Md., 1974-75, foreman, 1975-82; union rep. Internat. Assn. Machinists, Balt., 1973-74; quality control circle facilitator Koppers Co./Kop-Flex, Inc., Harmans, 1982-89; environ. and safety adminstr. Kop-Flex, Inc., Harmans, 1989—; adv. bd. Dundalk (Md.) Community Coll., 1986-87, Labor Employment Achievement Program AFL/CIO/Md. Dept. Edn., Balt., 1989—. Pres. Green Haven Improvement Assn., Pasadena, Md., 1985, v.p., 1986, chmn., bd. govs., 1987. Named Supr. of Yr., U. Md., 1989. Mem. Internat. Assn. of Quality Circles (recording sec.), Nat. Fire Protection Assn., Nat. Safety Coun., Local Emergency Planning Com. Home: 678 207th St Pasadena MD 21122-1422 Office: Kop-Flex Inc Harmans Rd Harmans MD 21077-1500

BINDER, AMY FINN, public relations company executive; b. N.Y.C., June 13, 1955; d. David and Laura (Zeisler) Finn; m. Ralph Edward Binder, Aug. 15, 1976; children: Ethan Max, Adam Finn, Rebecca Eve. BA with honors, Brown U., 1977. Freelance photographer N.Y.C., 1977-78; account exec. Newton & Nicolazza, Boston, 1978-79, Agnew, Carter, McCarthy, Boston, 1979-80; dir. pub. relations City of New Rochelle, N.Y., 1980-82; dir. urban communications Ruder-Finn, N.Y.C., 1982-85, v.p., 1985-86, exec. v.p., 1986-87, pres., 1987—. Photographer: Museum without Walls, 1975, The Spirit of Man: Sculpture of Kaare Nygaard, 1975, Knife Life and Bronzes, 1977, St. Louis: Sculpture City, 1988, The Triumph of the American Spirit: Johnstown, Pennsylvania, 1989. Mem. Internat. Ctr. of Photography (mem. pres. coun.), Pres. Assn. of Am. Mgmt. Assn. Democrat. Jewish.

BINDER, DAVID FRANKLIN, lawyer, author; b. Beaver Falls, Pa., Aug. 1, 1935; s. Walter Carl and Jessie Maivis (Bliss) B.; m. Deana Jacqueline Pines, Dec. 25, 1971; children: April, Bret. BA, Geneva Coll., 1956; JD, Harvard U., 1959. Bar: Pa. 1960, U.S. Ct. Appeals (3rd cir.) 1963, U.S. Supreme Ct. 1967. Law clk. to chief justice Pa. Supreme Ct., 1959-61; counsel Fidelity Mut. Life Ins. Co., Phila., 1964-66; ptnr. Bennett, Bricklin & Saltzburg, Phila., 1967-68; mem. Richter, Syken, Ross, and Binder, Phila., 1969-72, Raynes, McCarty, Binder, Ross and Mundy, Phila., 1972—; mem. faculty Pa. Coll. Judiciary; judge pro tempore Phila. Common Pleas Ct., 1991, 92; lectr., course planner Pa. Bar Inst. Author: Hearsay Handbook, 1975, ann. supplements, 2nd edit., 1983, 3rd edit., 1991. Recipient Disting. Alumnus award Geneva Coll., 1981. Mem. ABA, Pa. Bar Assn., Phila. Bar Assn., Assn. Trial Lawyers Am. (lectr.), Pa. Trial Lawyers Assn., Harvard Law Sch. Assn., Am. Bd. Trial Advs., Am. Coll. Trial Lawyers, Union League. Office: Raynes McCarty Binder Ross & Mundy 1845 Walnut St Ste 2000 Philadelphia PA 19103-4767

BINDER, ELAINE KOTELL, foundation administrator; b. Boston, Oct. 12, 1938; d. Maxwell and Florence (Blumsack) Kotell; m. Richard A. Binder, Aug. 28, 1960; children: Mark Stephen, Jonathan Stuart. AB, Radcliffe Coll., 1960; MA, U. Md., 1975. Tchr. City of Medford, Mass., 1960-62; project dir. Wider Opportunities for Women, Washington, 1971-75, Women's Equity Action League Fund, Washington, 1976-78; mng. ptnr. Binder, Elster, Mendelson, Wheeler, Bethesda, Md., 1978-80; adminstrn. dir. AAUW, Washington, 1980-85; exec. dir. B'nai B'rith Women, Washington, 1985—; cons. Bethesda, 1975-76. Co-author: Careers for Peers, 1973; contbr. articles to profl. jours. Trustee Temple Shalom, Silver Spring, Md., 1974-76; pres., v.p. Montgomery County Commn. for Women, Rockville, Md., 1978-80; commr. Anti-Defamation League, N.Y., 1985—. Fellow Am. Soc. Assn. Execs. (bd. dirs. 1990—), Greater Washington Soc. of Assn. Execs. (com chair 1989—). Democrat. Jewish. Office: Bnai Brith Women 1828 L St NW Ste 250 Washington DC 20036

BINDER, MICHAEL ALAN, urologist; b. Bklyn., Sept. 17, 1955; s. Lee Stevens and Sylvia (Klempner) B.; m. Amy Dee Feder, May 30, 1982; children: Mara, Aaron, Anna. BA, Clark U., 1977; MD, SUNY, 1982. Resident surgery SUNY-Downstate, Bklyn., 1982-84, resident urology, 1984-87; pvt. practice urology Media, Pa., 1987-88, Oil City, Pa., 1988—; chmn. div. urology N.W. Med. Ctr., Oil City, 1990—; affiliate Cleve. Clinic Coop. Mem. AMA, Am. Urol. Assn., Pa. Med. Soc., Pitts. Urol. Assn., Venango County Med. Soc., Del. County Med. Soc. (alt. del. 1987-88), Am. Assn. Clin. Urologists. Republican. Jewish. Office: 180-A E Bissell Ave Oil City PA 16301

BINDER, ROBERT HENRI, association executive; b. N.Y.C., Aug. 19, 1932; s. Ernest Robert and Lily (Simmons) B.; m. Mallory Roedy, Dec. 27, 1981 (div. 1991); children: Ainslie, Hilary, Meredith. BA, Princeton (N.J.) U., 1953; JD, Harvard U., 1958. Bar: D.C., N.Y. Atty. Kirlin Campbell & Keating, Washington, 1966-69; asst. sec. policy U.S. Dept. Transp., Washington, 1969-77; prin. Booz Allen & Hamilton, Bethesda, Md., 1978-80; pres. Transp. Assn. Am., Washington, 1981-83; pvt. practice law Washington, 1984-88; membership mgr. U.S. C. of C., Washington, 1989—. With U.S. Army, 1954-56. Mem. Met. Club, Congl. Country Club, Internat. Club, Princeton Club.

BINDERMAN, MELVIN DAVID, health and medical management company excutive; b. Phila., June 14, 1940; s. John Abraham and Sophye (Schwartz) B.; m. Rochelle Keyser, Aug. 26, 1962; children: Warren Saul, Pamela Beth. BS in Chem. Engring., Drexel U., 1962; MS in Chem. Engring., Lehigh U., 1964; MS in Bus. Adminstrn., Ind. U., Fort Wayne, 1986. Registered profl. engr., Pa. Process engr. Day & Zimmermann, Inc., Phila., 1964-69; project engr. Campbell Soup Co., Camden, N.J., 1969-79; prin. project engr. Central Soya Co., Inc., Ft. Wayne, 1979-87; exec. v.p. Internat. Pain Resources, Inc., Rockville, Md., 1987—; pres. Potomac Valley Med. Supply, Inc., 1991—. Patentee in field. Mem. Am. Inst. Chem. Engrs. Jewish. Home: 19031 Steeple Pl Germantown MD 20874 Office: Potomac Valley Med Supply Inc PO Box 2514 Germantown MD 20886-2514

BINDSEIL, LEE ANTON, III, bank executive; b. Balt., Oct. 7, 1938; s. Lee Anton and Anne Marie (Bartoch) B. BS in BA, U. Balt., 1969; Cert. Banking, Stonier Grad. Sch. Banking, New Brunswick, N.J., 1974. Cert. data processor. Programmer, analyst New Amsterdam Casualty Co., Balt., 1960-64; sr. systems analyst Suburban Trust Co., Hyattsville, Md., 1964-69; v.p. and cashier Am. Nat. Bank of Md., Silver Spring, 1969-76; pres. Mid-Atlantic Clearing House, Linthicum Hts., Md., 1976—. With USAR, 1960-66. Mem. Nat. Automated Clearing House Assn. (bd. dirs. 1990—), Mid-Atlantic Treasury Mgmt. Assn. Republican. Methodist. Home: 6213 Woodland Rd Linthicum Heights MD 21090-2336 Office: Mid-Atlantic Clearing House 201 Benton Ave Apt 200 Linthicum Heights MD 21090-2522

BINER, MARGARET LAVIN, communications company executive; b. Worcester, Mass., May 1, 1952; d. Walter Douglas and Ellen M. (Gilligan) Lavin; m. Stanley Biner, Sept. 4, 1983; children: Walter Joseph, Adam Tobias. B.A., Assumption Coll., 1974; M.B.A., Clark U., 1976, postgrad., 1976-77. Asst. mgr. New Eng. Tel. and Tel., Boston, 1978-80; sr. rate analyst Am. Electric Power, Columbus, Ohio, 1980-81; mkt. supr. GTE Satellite Co., Stamford, Conn., 1981-83; dist. mgr. AT&T Communications, Basking Ridge, N.J., 1983—. Solicitor AT&T Polit. Action Com., Basking Ridge, 1985; ritual com. Temple Emanu-El, Westfield, N.J., 1982. Mem. Am. Statis. Assn., Nat. Assn. Bus. Economists, Am. Mktg. Assn. (v.p. programs for N.J. 1985-86). Jewish. Office: AT&T Communications 295 N Maple Ave Basking Ridge NJ 07920-1025

BING, OSCAR HAROLD LEE, research chief of staff; b. N.Y.C., July 13, 1935; s. Herbert Maurice and Karolina Grete (Tuchmann) B.; m. Barbara Kay Nelson, May 13, 1976; children: David Charles, Michael Herbert, Benjamin Lee, William Nelson. BS, Washington & Lee U., 1956; MD, U. Md., 1961. Diplomate Am. Bd. Internal Medicine and Cardiovascular Disease. Intern Boston City Hosp., 1961-62; capt. med. corp. U.S. Med. Corp, Edgewood, Md., 1962-64; resident in medicine Georgetown U. Hosp., Washington, 1964-66; cardiology fellow New Eng. Med. ctr. Hosps., Boston, 1966-69; cardiologist Boston City Hosp., 1969-74, Beth Israel Hosp., Boston, 1974-81; assoc. chief of staff R & D Boston VA Med. Ctr., 1981—; instr. medicine Tufts U. Sch. Medicine, Boston, 1969-72, prof., 1981—; asst. prof. medicine Harvard Med. Sch., Boston, 1974-78, assoc. prof., 1978-81. Contbr. over 94 book chpts. and articles to profl. jours. Recipient Rsch. Career Devel. award NIH, 1975-80. Mem. Am. Heart Assn., Internat. Soc. Heart Rsch., Am. Physiologic Soc. (assoc.). Office: Boston VA Med Ctr 150 S Huntington Ave Jamaica Plain MA 02130-4820

BINGHAM, JUNE, author, playwright; b. White Plains, N.Y., June 20, 1919; d. Max J.H. and Mabel (Limburg) Rossbach; m. Jonathan B. Bingham, Sept. 20, 1939 (dec. July 1986); children: Sherry B. Downes, Micki B. Esselstyn, Timothy, Claudia B. Khalsa; m. Robert B. Birge, Mar. 28, 1987; 1 stepchild, Robert R. Student, Vassar Coll., 1936-38; BA, Barnard Coll., 1940. Writer, editor U.S. Treasury, Washington, 1943-45; editorial asst. Washington Post, 1945-46; writer Tarrytown (N.Y.) Daily News, 1946. Author: Do Cows have Neuroses?, Do Babies Have Worries?, Do Teenagers

have Wisdom?, Courage to Change: An Introduction to Life and Thought of Reinhold Niebuhr, 1961, paperback, 1992, U Thant: The Search for Peace, 1970, (play) Triangles, 1986, You and the I.C.UJ., 1990, (with others) The Inside Story: Psychiatry and Everyday Life, 1953, The Pursuit of Health, 1985; contbr. articles to nat. mags., newspapers and profl. jours. Bd. dirs. Barnard Coll., 1970-76, African-Am. Inst., N.Y.C., 1973-90, Riverdale Mental Health Assn., 1983—, Woodrow Wilson Found., Princeton, N.J., 1959-64, 83-89, Lehman Coll. Found., 1983-90, Ittleson Ctr. for Childhood Rsch., 1958-90; mem. Presbyn. Hosp. Aux., N.Y.C.; founder T.L.C. Named Alumna of the Yr., Rosemary Hall, 1976. Mem. Authors Guild (nominating com. 1987-90), Dramatists Guild, PEN, Cosmopolitan Club. Democrat. Home: 5000 Independence Ave Bronx NY 10471-2898

BINGHAM, RUSSELL NEVINS, physician; b. New London, Conn., Nov. 4, 1944; s. Mitchell Bingham and Norris (Nevins) Fowler; m. Diana Jeanne Pottinger, May 3, 1969; children: Joshua, Simon. BSc, McGill Coll., Montreal, Can., 1967, MD, 1971. Diplomate Am. Bd. Family Practice and Emergency Medicine. Intern Swedish Hosp. Med. Ctr., Seattle, 1971-72; gen. med. officer USCG, Savannah, Ga., 1972-74, USPHS, N.Y.C., 1974-75, USCG Acad., New London, 1975-78; emergency rm. physician Westerly (R.I.) Hosp., 1978—. Mem. Am. Coll. Emergency Physicians. Home: 8 Mill Pond Ln Old Lyme CT 06371 Office: Westerly Hosp Wells St Westerly RI 06300

BINNS, CAROL ANN, cash flow executive, consultant; b. Fairfield, Calif., Sept. 25, 1955; d. Bobby Roy and Patsy Lee (Sherwood) Smith; m. Eugene Mikolajczyk June 29, 1974 (div. Dec. 1981); m. James Walter Binns, June 30, 1990. BSBA summa cum laude, Shippensburg U., 1979. Cost acct. Westinghouse Electric, Pitts., 1979-81, internal auditor, 1981; internal auditor Timex Corp., Waterbury, Conn., 1981-83, mgr., internal audit, 1983-84, mgr., WW cash. mgmt., 1984-87, U.S. controller, 1987-89; treas. Pratt & Whitney Machine Tool Co., West Hartford, Conn., 1989-90; pres. Cash Performance, Inc., Cheshire, Conn., 1990—. Publisher Cash Performance Report, 1991. Mem. Cheshire (Conn.) C. of C., 1991, Waterbury (Conn.) C. of C., 1991. Mem. Entrepreneurial Women's Network, Nat. Corp. Cash Mgmt. Assn., NAFE. Home and Office: Cash Performance Inc 615 Broad Swamp Rd Cheshire CT 06410-2918

BINNS, JAMES W., watch manufacturing company executive; b. Los Angeles, July 16, 1946; s. John H. and Elizabeth R. (Sturtevant) B.; m. Lynn L. Binns, Nov. 2, 1979; children: Jeffrey, Gregory, Russell; m. 2d, Carol A. Binns, June 20, 1990. BS, UCLA, 1967, MS, 1969; MBA, U. So. Calif., 1973. Engring. sr. Lockheed Aircraft, Los Angeles, 1968-73; dir. fin. planning Rockwell Internat., Pitts., 1973-78; treas. Timex Group Ltd., Middlebury, Conn., 1978-80, chief fin. officer, 1980-83, pres., chief operating officer, 1983-85, chief exec. officer, 1985—; prof. bus. Orange Coast U., Santa Ana, Calif., 1975-76. Chmn. corp. campaigns United Way Greater Waterbury, Conn., 1979-80; bd. dirs. Conn. Bus. and Industry Assn. Mem. Beta Gamma Sigma. Republican. Methodist. Office: Timex Group Ltd Park Rd Middlebury CT 06762-1817*

BIONDO, BRADLEY EDWARD, computer consultant; b. Albany, N.Y., Sept. 20, 1953; s. Nunzio Edward and Verna Mae (Minnie) B.; m. Deborah Ann Flynn, Aug. 28, 1976; children: Kristi Elizabeth, Courtney Ann. AS, Rochester Inst. Tech., 1973, BS in Math., 1975; MS in Computer Sci., Rensselaer Poly. Inst., 1979. Computer programmer, systems programmer, ops. mgr. State Bank Albany, United Bank N.Y., 1975-77; programmer, analyst, programming supr. Blue Cross-Blue Shield Northeastern N.Y., Albany, 1977-83, Mgmt. Data Communications Corp., Albany, 1977-83; analyst, programmer, database adminstr., mgr. database adminstrn. GE Co., Schenectady, 1983-88; computer cons. ICOSA Cons. Svcs., Inc., Albany, 1988-89; owner, mgr., computer cons., shareware distbr. Future Enterprises, Slingerlands, N.Y., 1989—; guest speaker user meetings DBMS, Inc., Montreal, Que., Can., N.Y.C., Boston, 1986-87. Mem. Bethlehem C. of C. Home and Office: 18 Mohawk Trail Slingerlands NY 12159-9434

BIRCH, DAVID WILLIAM, business manager; b. Crawfordsville, Ind., Oct. 28, 1913; s. Charles Evan and Edna (Vest) B.; m. Elizabeth Marie Casto, Oct. 5, 1946; children: Anthony David, Michael Allen, William Hayes. Student, Trinity Coll., Hartford, Conn., 1956-58; MBA, SUNY, Buffalo, 1966. Engr. Delco-Remy div. Gen. Motors, Anderson, Ind., 1931-51; supt. New Britain (Conn.) Machine Co., 1951-57; plant mgr. Fasteners, Inc., Boston, 1957-60, Curtis Screw Co., Buffalo, 1960-63; ops. mgr. Delevan Elects., East Aurora, N.Y., 1963-66; pres. Essex Recon Corp., Lancaster, N.Y., 1966-78; cons. Anthony, Hayes & Allen, Inc., East Aurora, 1978-80; program chmn. Medaille Coll., Buffalo, 1980-83, bus. mgr., 1983—; bd. dirs. Strickler Road Housing Devel., Clarence, N.Y. Mem. N.Y. State Orgn. Bursars & Bus. Adminstrs. (bd. dir. 1988-90). Methodist. Home: 212 Hillcrest Rd East Aurora NY 14052-1316 Office: Medaille Coll 18 Agassiz Cir Buffalo NY 14214-2695

BIRCH, DOUGLAS MALCOLM, reporter, educator; b. Pasadena, Calif.; s. Malcolm Francis and Yvonne Elizabeth (Pettite) B.; m. Jane Tobin, Jan. 25, 1975; 1 child, Alison Tobin. BA, Columbia U., 1974, M in Journalism, 1982. Reporter The Evening Sun, Balt., 1983-87; reporter The Balt. Sun, 1987—, Washington corr., 1987-88, Annapolis State House corr., 1988-91, sci. writer, 1991—; adj. prof. writing and media Loyola Coll. Md., Balt., 1992. Recipient award Md.-D.C.-Del. Press Assn., 1991. Congregationalist. Home: 50 Dunkirk Rd Baltimore MD 21212 Office: Balt Sun 501 N Calvert St Baltimore MD 21202

BIRCH, GRACE MORGAN, library administrator, educator; b. N.Y.C., June 3, 1925; d. Milton Melville and Adeline Ellsdale (Springer) Morgan; m. Kenneth Francis Birch, Oct. 26, 1947; children: Shari R., Timothy F. B.A., U. Bridgeport, 1963; M.L.S., Pratt Inst., 1968. With Bridgeport Pub. Library, Conn., 1949-66; asst. town librarian Fairfield Pub. Library, Conn., 1966-69; dir. Trumbull Library System, Conn., 1969—; lectr. Housatonic Community Coll., Bridgeport, 1970—; lectr. self-motivation, 1989—. Judge, Barnum Festival Soc. Bridgeport, 1971-73; mem. Trumbull Multi-Arts Com., Trumbul Prevention Coun. Mem. ALA, New Eng. Library Assn., Conn. Library Assn. (pres. 1972), Southwestern Conn. Library Council (pres. 1975-77), Fairfield Library Adminstrs. Group (pres. 1976-77). Democrat. Episcopalian. Avocations: sketching, dancing, traveling. Home: 175 Brooklawn Ave Bridgeport CT 06604-2011 Office: The Trumbull Libr 33 Quality St Trumbull CT 06611-3189

BIRCH, GREGORY MARK, podiatrist; b. N.Y.C., Mar. 31, 1952; s. Merwin David and Gloria Renee (Levine) B.; m. Shari Flisler, Sept. 1, 1984. BS in Chemistry, Wagner Coll., S.I., N.Y., 1975; D of Podiatric Medicine, N.Y. Coll. Podiatric Medicine, 1979. Pvt. practice Bklyn., 1979—; mem. cons. staff S.I. U. Hosp. Mem. Am. Assn. Hosp. Podiatrists, Acad. Ambulatory Foot Surgery, Am. Podiatry Circulatory Soc., Am. Podiatric Med. Assn., Am. Soc. Podiatric Legal Medicine. Home: 120B Dinsmore St Staten Island NY 10314-3837 Office: 6724 Bay Pky Brooklyn NY 11204-4734

BIRCH, WILLIAM DUNHAM, JR., asset manager; b. Orange, N.J., Dec. 16, 1940; s. William Dunham and Helen (Ross) B.; m. Tina-Maria Muccino, Feb. 22, 1969; children: Marco, Marina. BA, Princeton U., 1964; MBA, Columbia U., 1966. Instl. sales Halsey Stuart & Co., Phila., 1968-70, F.S. Smithers & Co., N.Y.C., 1970-71, Loeb Rhoades & Co., N.Y.C., 1971-72; mng. dir. Morgan Stanley & Co., N.Y.C., 1972-91, Geometry Asset Mgmt., N.Y.C., 1992—; bd. dirs. Classical Keyboard Instruments, N.Y.C., 1010 5th Ave. Corp., N.Y.C., Prime Asset Mgmt., N.Y.C., Investarit, AG, Zurich, Retirement Advisors Am., Dallas. Mem. Siwanoy Country Club (Bronxville, N.Y.), Union Club (N.Y.C.), N.Y. Athletic Club. Republican. Presbyterian. Home: 1010 5th Ave New York NY 10028-0130 Office: Geometry Asset Mgmt Co 1270 Ave of the Americas New York NY 10020

BIRCHFIELD, JOHN KERMIT, JR., lawyer; b. Roanoke, Va., Jan. 8, 1940; s. John Kermit and Christine (Luke) B.; m. Glenys Garnell, Nov. 14, 1964; 1 child, Guthrie Kathryn. B.S. in Econs., Roanoke Coll., 1968; J.D., U. Va., 1971. Bar: N.Y., 1972, U.S. Dist Ct. (so. dist.) N.Y., 1972, U.S. Ct. Appeals (2d cir.), 1972. Assoc. Shearman & Sterling, N.Y.C., 1971-81; ptnr. Holtzmann, Wise & Shepard, N.Y.C., 1981-83; sr. v.p. legal and govtl. affairs, gen. counsel Ga. Pacific Corp., Atlanta, 1983-88; mng. dir. Century Ptnrs., Atlanta, Darien, Conn., 1988—; sr. v.p., gen. counsel, corp. sec. M/A-COM, Boston, 1990—; bd. dirs. Intermountain Gas Industries, 1988—; chmn. bd. dirs. Chas. P. Young Co., 1989—. Author: How to Borrow on the Eurodollar Market, 1981, The Multinational Joint venture, 1981. Chmn. adv. bd. Park Pride, 1986-90; bd. dirs. Atlanta Preservation Ctr., 1986-89; bd. dirs., exec. com. Atlanta Ballet, 1984-88, chmn., 1987-88, vice chmn., 1986-87; bd. dirs. Atlanta Music Festival Assn., 1984-90, Friends Piedmont Hosp., 1985-90; bd. dirs., exec. com., treas. Assn. Am.-Indian Affairs, 1983-86; bd. dirs. High Mus. Art, 1986-91, exec. com., 1988-89; bd. visitors Emory U., 1985-88, bd. dirs. Emory U. Mus. Art and Archaeology, 1988-92; trustee Roanoke Coll., 1988—, Chatham Hall. Mem. ABA, Atlanta Bar Assn., Assn. of Bar of City of N.Y., N.Y. State Bar Assn., Am. Law Inst., Am. Arbitration Assn. (bd. dirs.), Racquet and Tennis Club, India House Club, Piedmont Driving Club, Carlton Club of London, Farmington Country Club, Roanoke Country Club, Annisquam Yacht Club, Union Boat Club.

BIRD, EUGENE HALL, foreign affairs corporation executive; b. Spokane, Wash., Mar. 17, 1925; s. James Arthur and Ebba (Swanson) B.; m. Jerine Newhouse, Oct. 15, 1948; children: Christina, Kai, Nancy, Shelly. BS in Journalism, U. Oreg., 1948, MA in History, 1951. Fgn. svc. officer, 1952-67; econ. officer U.S. Fgn. Svc., Bombay, 1967-70; econ. counselor U.S. Fgn. Svc., New Delhi, India, 1970-72; econ. and polit. counselor U.S. Fgn. Svc., Jidda, Saudi Arabia, 1972-75; trade rep. N.W. Regional Trade, Portland, 1976-78; v.p. Getsco, Riyadh, Saudi Arabia, 1978-82; pres. Tie West Corp., Washington, 1981-91, Softgraf Corp., Washington, 1983-89, Fgn. Affairs Assistance Corp., Washington, 1990—. Pres. Rainbow Child Devel. Ctr., Washington, 1989—. Lt. USN, 1943-47. Democrat. Episcopalian. Home: 3133 Connecticut Ave NW Washington DC 20008-5147 Office: Fgn Affairs Assistance Corp 3133 Connecticut Ave NW Washington DC 20008-5147

BIRD, HARRY H., state health commissioner, physician; b. Melrose, Mass., Apr. 7, 1933; s. Harry H. and Edna (Ayscough) B.; m. Carolyn Danforth Stone, June 15, 1957; children: Suzanne, Steven. AB, Harvard U., 1954; MD, Tufts U., 1958. Prof. clin. anesthesiology Dartmouth Coll., Hanover, N.H., 1964-90; pres. Hitchcock Clinic Dartmouth Med. Ctr., Hanover, 1983-90; commr. health, human svcs. State of N.H., 1990—; pres. Am. Bd. Anesthesiology, 1985. Selectman Town of Hanover, 1982; trustee Univ. System of N.H., 1989—. Comdr. USN, 1957-64. Recipient Josiah Bartlett award N.H. Med. Soc., 1991. Mem. Am. Soc. Anesthesiologists (pres. 1988). Office: Health & Human Svc Dept 6 Hazen Dr Concord NH 03301

BIRD, JUANITA DELORES (DELORES BIRD CARPENTER), English educator; b. Chattanooga, Dec. 6, 1942; d. Basil Ivan and Hazel Leona (Hawkins) B.; m. Joe Keith Carpenter, Dec. 27, 1959 (div. 1987); 1 child, Frederic Keith. Student, U. Miss., 1963; BA summa cum laude, Boston U., 1967; MA, U. Hartford, 1973; PhD, U. Mass., 1978. Cert. secondary sch. tchr., Mass. 7th and 8th grade tchr. Shrewsbury (Mass.) Jr. High Sch., 1967-70; prof. Cape Cod Community Coll., West Barnstable, Mass., 1977—. Editor: The Life of Lidian Jackson Emerson, 1980, paperback edit., 1992, The Selected Letters of Lidian Jackson Emerson, 1987; author: The Early Days of Cape Cod Community College, 1989, (with others) Studies in American Renaissance, 1980. Mem. Emily Dickinson Soc., Emerson Soc., Thoreau Lyceum, Phi Beta Kappa. Democrat. Home: 89 S Sandwich Rd Mashpee MA 02649-2222 Office: Cape Cod Community Coll Rt 132 West Barnstable MA 02668

BIRD, L. RAYMOND, investor; b. Plainfield, N.J., Jan. 22, 1914; s. Lewis Raymond and Bessie (MacCallum) B.; student N.Y. U., 1946-47; m. May Ethel Siercks, June 5, 1949. With shipping dept. Horn & Hardart Co., 1936-46, control auditor, 1946-49, gen. supt. in commissary, 1949-51; asst. to treas. fin. and legal Lockheed Electronics Co. (formerly Stavid Engring., Inc.), 1951-55, treas., 1955-60; pres., dir. State Bank of Plainfield (N.J.), 1960-62; investor, 1962—; treas. Route Twenty Two Corp. Plainfield area committeeman Young Life Campaign, Inc.; pres. Plainfield Camp of Gideons, 1956—; mem. exec. com., treas. Christian Bus. Men's Com. of Cen. Jersey, 1956—; bd. dirs. Child Evangelism Fellowship N.J.; bd. dirs. Sudan Interior Mission; chmn. bd. trustees, chmn. exec. com., chmn. fin. and investments com. Barrington Coll.; trustee Evangelistic Com. Newark and Vicinity. Served from pvt. to 1st lt. 6th Armored Div., AUS, 1941-45. Mem. Am. Mgmt. Assn., Internat. Christian Leadership, Plainfield Area C. of C. Baptist (deacon). Home and Office: 625 Robert Fulton Hwy Quarryville PA 17566-9608

BIRD, LARRY JOE, professional basketball player; b. French Lick, Ind., Dec. 7, 1956; s. Joe and Georgia B; m. Dinah Mattingly Oct. 1, 1989. Student, Ind. U., 1974, Northwood Inst., West Baden, Ind., 1974; BS, Ind. State U., 1979. Player Boston Celtics, 1979-92, spl. asst. to exec. v.p., 1992—; mem. U.S. Olympic Basketball Team, 1992. Author: (with Bob Ryan) Drive, 1989. Mem. U.S. Gold Medal team World Univ. Games, Sophia, Bulgaria, 1977, Nat. Basketball Assn. championship team, 1981, 84, 86, Nat. Basketball Assn. All-Star Team, 1980-92; named Collegiate Player of Yr. AP, UPI and Nat. Assn. Coaches, 1978-79; Rookie of Yr. Nat. Basketball Assn., 1980; Most Valuable Player Nat. Basketball Assn. All-Star Game, 1982, Nat. Basketball Assn., 1984-86, Nat. Basketball Assn. Playoffs, 1984, 86. Office: care Boston Celtics North Station Boston MA 02114*

BIRD, MARGARET HELENA, social insurance operations supervisor; b. N.Y.C., May 31, 1954; d. Ashton Joseph and Mildred (Hebert) B.; m. Fred Torres, June 29, 1981; 1 child, Vanessa H. BA magna cum laude, CUNY, N.Y.C., 1976. Ops. supr. Social Security Adminstrn., Yonkers, N.Y., 1977—; real estate broker Nat. Assn. Bd. Realtors, White Plains, N.Y., 1987—. Recipient Downer Meml. scholarship, CUNY, 1974. Mem. Phi Beta Kappa. Democrat. Roman Catholic. Home: 6629 Broadway Bronx NY 10471-2032

BIRD, PHYLIS SHUTTLEWORTH, association executive, small business owner; b. Atlanta, May 20, 1941; d. Philip James and Melba Ann (Brooks) Shuttleworth; m. Kermit Molyneux, May 28, 1969. BA, Tift Coll., 1966; MA in Edn., Va. Poly. Inst., 1988. Cert. assn. exec., 1988. Appearance counselor United Airlines, Washington, 1968-70; receptionist Melpar/E-Systems, Falls Church, Va., 1980-82; sec. Am. Gas Assn., Arlington, Va., 1982-84; program mgr. Am. Bankers Assn., Washington, 1984-86; account exec. Drohan Mgmt. Group, Arlington, 1986-88; owner Creative Image, Annandale, Va., 1989—; exec. dir. Am. Coun. State Savs. Suprs., Washington, 1990—. Com. chair Salvation Army Homeless Shelter Adv. Coun., Bailey's Crossroads, 1990—. Named Outstanding Young Women of Am., Ga., 1968.

BIRD, THOMAS EDWARD, educator; b. Rome, N.Y., Mar. 28, 1935; s. Harry J. and Paula W. (Boyce) B.; m. Mary Lynne Miller, Aug. 23, 1958; children: Matthew David, Lisa Bronwen. AB magna cum laude, Syracuse U., 1956; postgrad., Harvard U., 1958-59; MA, Middlebury Coll., 1960; postgrad., Princeton U., 1965. Lectr., assoc. prof. Slavic langs. and lit. Queens Coll., CUNY, Flushing, 1965—; bd. dirs. Pax Romana, Benyumin Shekhter Found., Cymdeithas Madoc. Author: Patriarch Maximos IV, 1964; editor: Aspects of Religion in the Soviet Union, 1971, The Hard Life of Jura Odcesty, 1980, The 1863 Uprising in Byelorussia, 1980; mem. editorial bd. Diakonia, Nationalities Papers, Polish Rev., Zapisy. Recipient George Arents Library award. Fellow Soc. for Values in Higher Edn.; mem. AAUP, MLA, Columbia U. Faculty Seminars, Byelorussian Inst. Arts and Scis., Polish Inst. Arts and Scis., Ukrainian Acad. Arts and Scis., Hon. Soc. of Cymmrodorion, Dobro Slovo, Phi Beta Kappa (pres. chpt. 1978-81), Phi Kappa Alpha. Club: Princeton. Office: Queens Coll Kiely Hall 65-30 Kissena Blvd Flushing NY 11367

BIRDWHISTELL, ANNE DAVISON, education educator; b. Evanston, Ill., Mar. 3, 1944; d. John Murdoch and Carol (Crawford) Davison; m. Ray Lee Birdwhistell, Mar. 11, 1976. Student, Columbia U., 1965; BA summa cum laude, U. Pa., 1966; MA, Stanford U., 1968, PhD, 1974. Lectr. U. Pa., Phila., 1974-75; from asst. prof. to prof. Stockton State Coll., Pomona, N.J., 1979—; adj. instr. Stockton State Coll., Pomona, spring, 1979; article and book reviewer, 1988—; co-chair Neo-Confucian Seminar, Columbia U., 1991—. Author: Transition to Neo-Confucianism, 1989; contbr. articles to profl. jours. Benjamin Franklin nat. scholar U. Pa., 1962-66; NDEA fellow Stanford U., 1966-69, Nat. Def. Fgn. Lang. fellow Columbia U., 1965, disting. faculty fellow Stockton Found., 1989, 92. Mem. Am. Philos. Assn., Soc. for Comparative and Asian Philos. (bd. dirs. 1991—), Am. Hist. Assn., Assn. for Asian Studies, Soc. for the Study Chinese Religion, Am. Assn. for Chinese Studies, Phi Beta Kappa. Democrat. Office: Stockton State Coll Jimmie Leeds Rd Pomona NJ 08240-9998

BIREN, DAVID ROBERT, outplacement executive; b. Detroit, Sept. 21, 1937; s. Robert I. and Helen Marjorie (Hilborn) B.; m. Pamela Oakes Hill, Feb. 10, 1979; children: David, Margot, Laura, Gregory, James, Cheryl, Diana. BS in Indsl. Rels., U. N.C., 1959; MBA, U. Mich., 1968; MA in Counseling Psychology, Immaculata Coll., 1987. Supr. labor rels. Ford Motor Co., Dearborn, Mich., 1963-66; corp. dir. orgn. rsch. Scott Paper Co., Phila., 1967-79; assoc. prof. mgmt. West Chester U. of Pa., 1980-82; prin. Beginnings, West Chester, Pa., 1983-89; v.p., dir. profl. svcs. Right Assocs., Phila., 1990—. Author: An Examination of Alternative Management Systems: A Quality of Work Life Project, 1973. Adv. bd. RSVP, West Chester, Pa., 1985—. Lt. USN, 1959-62. Mem. AACD, Nat. Career Devel. Assn., Pa. Counseling Assn., Pa. Career Devel. Assn. Office: Right Associates Penn Ctr Pla Ste 610 Philadelphia PA 19102

BIRENBAUM, DAVID ELIAS, lawyer; b. Waterbury, Conn., Nov. 30, 1937. AB cum laude, Brown U., 1959; JD, Harvard U., 1962. Bar: Conn. 1962, D.C. 1963. Law clk. U.S. Dist. Ct. Conn., Hartford, 1962-63; asst. gen. counsel Nat. Adv. Commn. on Civil Disorders, 1967-68; resident ptnr. Fried, Frank, Harris, Shriver & Jacobson, London, 1970-73; ptnr. Fried, Frank, Harris, Shriver & Jacobson, Washington, 1973—; chmn. subcom. Extraterritorial Provisions of Restatement of Fgn. Law, 1984; mem. program com. Ctr. for Nat. Policy; instr. internat. trade law U. Pa. Law Sch., 1989-90; adj. prof. internat. law Georgetown Law Ctr., 1991. Co-author: Business Ventures in Eastern Europe and the Soviet Union: The Emerging Legal Framework for Foreign Investments, 2 vols., 1991; contbr. articles to profl. jours. Coord. domestic policy issues Humphrey for Pres., 1968; issues dir., gen. counsel Shriver for Pres. com., 1975-76; mem. Montgomery County, Md. Dem. Cen. Com., 1975-76; gen. counsel, bd. dirs. Handgun Control Inc.; with Ctr. for Prevention of Handgun Violence. Mem. ABA (co-chmn. ad hoc task force extraterritorial application of U.S. law internat. law sect. 1984), U.S. C. of C. (internat. svc. industry com.), Am. Law Inst., Phi Beta Kappa. Home: 2804 34th Pl NW Washington DC 20007-1405 Office: Fried Frank Harris Shriver & Jacobson Ste 800 1001 Pennsylvania Ave NW Washington DC 20004-2505

BIRKENHEAD, THOMAS BRUCE, theatrical producer and manager, educator; b. N.Y.C., Dec. 19, 1931; s. Thomas A. and Florence (Morison) B.; m. Susan Leslie Arkin, Dec. 3, 1954 (div. 1983); children: Peter Lawrence, David Andrew, Richard James, Alison Jane. BA, Bklyn. Coll., 1954, MA, 1958; PhD, New Sch. Social Rsch., 1963. Lectr. econs. Bklyn. Coll. CUNY, 1957-60, instr. Bklyn. Coll., 1960-65, asst. prof. Bklyn. Coll., 1965-69, assoc. prof. Bklyn. Coll., 1969-71, prof. econs. Bklyn. Coll., 1972-80, prof. emeritus Bklyn. Coll., 1975—; dean Sch. Social Scis., 1972-75; bus. mgr. Theatre II of Glen Cove, N.Y., 1970-74; sec.-treas. Highly Enterprises; bd. dirs. Broadway Today, Broadway Arts. Co. Co-mgr. Do Black Patent Leather Shoes Really Reflect Up?, Present Laughter, Master Harold and the Boys, Children of a Lesser God, Ain't Misbehavin, Brighton Beach Memoirs, Biloxi Blues, Broadway Bound, Barbara Cook in Concert, Run For Your Wife, Rumors, Lost in Yonkers, Jake's Women; gen. mgr. Cape Cod Melody Tent, Hyannis, Mass., 1969-71, Twyla Tharp on Broadway, 1980, 81, Joe Egg, 1985, Social Security, 1986, Long Days Journey Into Night, London and Tel Aviv, 1986, Ain't Misbehavin, N.Y.C., 1988-89, Japan, 1990, Fresh Air Taxi, 1990. Mem. ednl. bd. advisors Broadway Arts Co. Theatre for Young Audiences. Mem. Am. Econs. Assn., Am. Def. Preparedness Assn., NRA, Rolls Royce Owners Club, Rover P4 Drivers Guild, Groucho Club (london), U.S. Naval Inst., Amnesty Internat., So. Poverty Law Ctr. Home: 353 W 44th St Apt 1A New York NY 10036-5416 Office: 410 W 53d St Apt 129 New York NY 10019-5629

BIRKETT, JAMES DAVIS, management consultant; b. Norwalk, Conn., Sept. 30, 1936; s. John George and Doris (Walker) B.; m. Sarah Page Burley, Dec. 17, 1960; children: Benjamin Thaddeus, John Hill, Lucy Belinda. BA, Bowdoin Coll., 1958; MS, Yale U., 1960, PhD, 1963. Sr. cons. Arthur D. Little, Inc., Cambridge, Mass., 1962-88; propr. West Neck Strategies, Nobleboro, Maine, 1988—. Mem. editorial bd. Desalination, 1985—. Chmn. Nobleboro Comprehensive Planning Com., 1990—; mem. Lincoln (Mass.) Town Planning Bd., 1979-85; bd. dirs. Christmas Cove Improvement Assn., 1982-86; commodore Christmas Cove Fleet, 1986-88; trustee Lincoln Acad., Newcastle, Maine, 1991—. Mem. Internat. Desalination Assn. (bd. dirs., treas. 1981—, pres. 1985-87), Nat. Water Supply Improvement Assn. (bd. dirs. 1980-85). Home: PO Box 412 Nobleboro ME 04555-0412 Office: West Neck Strategies PO Box 193 Nobleboro ME 04555-0193

BIRMAN, RONNIE RATHKOPF, educator; b. N.Y.C., Dec. 24, 1947; d. Julius and May (Levy) Rathkopf; m. Michael Simon Birman, Oct. 16, 1983 (div. 1990). BS in Edn., CCNY, 1969; MA in Sociology, MS in Social Rsch., CUNY, 1977, MS in Sci. Edn., 1990, cert. in adminstrn. and supervision, 1992. Cert. tchr., N.Y. Elem. sch. tchr. P.S. 316, Bklyn., 1969-84, elem. sch. sci. tchr., 1984-91; bldg. sci. mentor, 1991-92; freelance curriculum writer N.Y.C., 1989—; staff intern, coord. tchr. workshops Impact II Grants, N.Y.C., 1991—; curriculum disseminator, facilitator workshops Impact II Office, Bklyn. Coll., several sch. dists. in N.Y., 1990—; grant writer for PIP, Bklyn. Coll., 1992; mem. Whole Lang. Inst. for Ctrl. Bd. at Dist. 8, 1992. Author oral communications curriculum "Can We Talk?"; writer for CIMS Sci. and Learning-Link Curriculum. Active parent workshops in communication/experimentation in sci. P.S. 316, Dist. 17, Bklyn., 1991-92. Recipient Impact II grant, 1991. Mem. United Fedn. Tchrs., Elem. Sch. Sci. Assn., N.Y. State Adminstrn. and Supervision Assn., Assn. Computer Educators, N.Y. State Marine Edn. Assn., Kappa Delta Pi. Home: 32 Gramercy Park S New York NY 10003-1707 Office: PS 316 750 Classon Ave Brooklyn NY 11238-4685

BIRNBAUM, HERMANN, chemistry consultant; b. Gera, Thuringia, Germany, Apr. 30, 1905; came to U.S., 1935; s. Juda and Rosa (Wiesenthal) B.; m. Minnie Wise, Jan. 30, 1944; 1 child, Mark Joel. PhD, U. Leipzig, Germany, 1932. Rsch. asst. Carnegie Inst. Tech., Pitts., 1935-36; instr. Duquesne U., Pitts., 1936-37; tech. dir. Hachmeister Inc. (subs. H.J. Heinz Co. 1961), Pitts., 1937-61, v.p., 1961-70; chemistry cons., U.S. and Germany, 1970—. Contbr. articles to profl. jours.; patentee in field. Mem. Am. Chem. Soc., Oil Chemists Soc., Am. Assn. Cereal Chemists, Inst. Food Tech. Jewish. Home and Office: 5701 Munhall Rd Pittsburgh PA 15217-2060

BIRNBAUM, IRWIN MORTON, lawyer; b. Bklyn., July 15, 1935; s. Sol N. and Rose (Cohen) B.; m. Arlene R. Burrows, June 8, 1957; children: Bruce J., Leslie R. Birnbaum Ventura, Amy G. Birnbaum Heath. BS in Acctg., Bklyn. Coll., 1956; JD, NYU, 1961. Bar: N.Y. 1962. Budget officer Montefiore Med. Ctr., Bronx, N.Y., 1962-70, v.p., chief fin. officer, 1970-86; counsel Proskauer Rose Goetz & Mendelsohn, N.Y.C., 1986-89, ptnr., 1989—; bd. dir. N.Y. Regional Transplant Program, N.Y.C.; trustee Maimonides Med. Ctr., Bklyn., 1988—. Editor: Health Care Law Treatise, 1990. Active special com. Health Care Systems. Mem. Assn. of Bar of City of N.Y. (sec. com. on medicine and law 1989-90), Am. Acad. Hosp. Attys. (spl. com. on health care systems). Office: Proskauer Rose Goetz & Mendelsohn 1585 Broadway New York NY 10036-8200

BIRNBERG, JACK, financial executive; b. June 15, 1937; s. Max and Yetta (Halpern) B.; m. Louise Rothstein, June 7, 1959; children: Michael, Steven, John, Jeffrey. BS, Fairleigh Dickinson U., 1959. Acct. firm Scholtz, Simon & Miller, 1960-61; controller, officer Scott, Harvey Co., Inc., 1962-63; pres. M.A. Allan & Co., Inc., Clifton, N.J., 1963-71, dir., 1963-71; chmn. bd. Edios, Inc., 1969-77, Jack Birnberg & Assocs. Inc., pres. NE Regional Assn. Small Bus. Investment Corp.; Clifton, 1970—, Internat. Equities, Ltd., Clifton, 1970-71; chmn. bd., dir. Tappan-Zee Capital Corp., 1973—; exec. com. NE region; chmn. bd. BB Energy Corp., Waldorf Auto Leasing Corp., Waldorf Group, Inc.; dir., chmn. exec. com. Ferdon Equipment Corp.; dir. Tolchin Instruments, N.Y.C., 1970-71, Kraftware Corp., N.Y.C., 1969-71, San Sebastian Gold Mines, 1969-71, Color Canvas, Inc., N.Y.C., 1969-72, Cytoarchectronics, N.Y.C., 1970-72, Tech.-Am. Resources Corp., Paterson, N.J., 1970-71, Joy Footwear Corp., 1974-78, Authenticolor, Inc., 1976—, Williston Oil Co., 1979-81, Ultra Dynamics Corp., Santa Monica, Calif.,

1976-79, Studio Color, 1976-82; mem. Midwest Stock Exchange, 1968-76, Phila.-Balt.-Washington Stock Exchange, 1966-72. Pres., Passaic County Children's Shelter, 1967-68; bd. dirs. Boys Club, Paterson, N.J., 1970-75; chmn. met. div. United Jewish Appeal, 1970; dir. greater Paterson (N.J.) YW-YMHA, 1970-75; bd. dirs. Birnberg Found., 1969—, Barnert Hosp., 1971—; bd. dirs., v.p. Daus. Miriam Home for Aged, 1971—; bd. dirs. Employee Retirement Benefit Assn., 1975—, Barnert Temple, 1976—; chmn. Expo 200 Barnert Temple, 1976—; trustee for various corps., U.S. Bankruptcy Ct. Mem. N.E. Regional Assn. Small Bus. Investment Corps. (pres. 1985-86), Nat. Assn. Small Bus. Investment Corps. (bd. govs. 1985—). Jewish. Clubs: B'nai B'rith (trustee Greater Clifton chpt. 1962-64); Preakness Hills (N.J.) Country; Inverarry Country (Fla.). Home: 409 Carriage Ln Wyckoff NJ 07481-2306 Office: 201 Lower Notch Rd Little Falls NJ 07424-1841

BIRNHAK, SANDRA JEAN, film company executive; b. L.A., Apr. 27, 1945; d. Charles William and Edna Mae (Cante) Reynolds; m. Bruce I. Birnhak, Feb. 4, 1964 (div. 1970); 1 child, Scott Alan; m. David R. Ames, Dec. 22, 1984. Degree in Advanced Film Studies, MIT, 1981-82, Am. Film Inst., 1983. Pres., dir. Subtle-T, Inc., Boston, 1974-77; dir. mktg. RKO Gen. Broadcasting, Boston, 1978-80; vis. lectr. pub. relations Boston Coll., 1980-81; line producer, auditor Cannon Films Internat., N.Y.C., 1983; exec. v.p., chief fin. officer Hartwest, Inc., N.Y.C., 1983-85; chmn., chief exec. officer Showcase Prodns. Internat., N.Y.C., 1985—; bd. dir. Women's Perspective Prodns., Boston, 1981; cons. in field. Producer, dir. Corporate Women, 1980, Balloons, 1981, Father, Son and Holy Coach, 1990; assoc. producer Mr. North, 1987; exec. producer Curse of the Starving Class; producer Flight of the Swallow, Through You; producer Forsaking All Others. Vol. Kennedy Meml. Hosp. for Children, Boston, 1980, St. Vincent's Hosp., N.Y.C. Recipient Nat. Disting. Service award March of Dimes, Boston, 1980, Govs. award, Boston, 1979. Mem. NOW, N.Y. Third Decade Coun. Women in Film, Ind. Filmakers Assn., Nat. Assn. Broadcasters, Am. Fedn. TV and Radio Artists. Democrat. Unitarian. Home: 145 W 55d St Apt 7-D New York NY 10019

BIRNIE, RICHARD WILLIAMS, graduate studies dean; b. Boston, Dec. 8, 1944; s. Walter Hart and Mary (Kidder) B.; m. Pieter Van Dyk, Oct. 7, 1973; children: Katherine, Peter, Elisabeth. AB, Dartmouth Coll., 1968, MA, 1971; MS, Harvard U., 1972, PhD, 1975. Instr. geology Dartmouth Coll., Hanover, N.H., 1975, asst. prof., 1975-81, assoc. prof., 1981-87, prof., 1987—, dean grad. studies, 1990—; cons. in field. Contbr. articles to profl. jours. With U.S. Army, 1968-70. Mem. Mineral. Soc. Am., Am. Soc. Photogrammetry and Remote Sensing. Office: Dartmouth Coll Dept Earth Scis Hanover NH 03755

BIROL, ANDREW JOHN, sales and marketing executive; b. N.Y.C., Mar. 8, 1959; s. M.F. and Jacqueline (MacMillan) B. BSBA summa cum laude, Boston U., 1981; M Mgmt., Northwestern U., 1985. Mktg. analyst Union Camp Corp., Wayne, N.J., 1981-83, mgr. new product planning, 1983-84; assoc. MAC Group, Cambridge, Mass., 1985-86; mgr. new bus. devel. Plymouth Rubber Co., Canton, Mass., 1986-87; assoc. product mgr. Bank of Boston, 1987-89; retail market mgr. New Eng. Bus. Svc., Groton, Mass., 1989-91, mgr. nat. accounts, 1991-92; sr. account exec. Creative Profl. Svcs., Woburn, Mass., 1992—; dir. Boston U. Sch. Mgmt., 1986—. Bd. dir. Boston chpt. Am. Youth Hostel, 1990—; bd. dirs. Stoneham Skiddadlers Ski Club, Conway, N.H., 1987—, pres., 1992—. Mem. No. N.J. Alumni Club (v.p. 1982-83), Downtown Alumni Club (v.p., sec. 1987—), Beta Gamma Sigma. Home: 577 Great Elm Way Village Of Nagog Woods MA 01718-1005

BIRON, CHRISTINE ANNE, medical science educator, researcher; b. Woonsocket, R.I., Aug. 8, 1951; d. R. Bernard and Theresa Priscilla (Sauvageau) B. BS, U. Mass., 1973; PhD, U. N.C., 1980. Rsch. technician U. Mass., Amherst, 1973-75; grad. researcher U. N.C., Chapel Hill, 1975-80; postdoctoral fellow Scripps Clinic and Rsch., La Jolla, Calif., 1980; fellow U. Mass. Med. Sch., Worcester, 1981-82, instr., 1983, asst. prof., 1984-87; vis. scientist Karolinska Inst., Stockholm, 1984; asst. prof. Brown U., Providence, R.I., 1988-90, assoc. prof., 1990—; mem. AIDS and related rsch. study sect. 3 NIH, 1991—. Assoc. editor Jour. Immunology, 1990—; contbr. articles, revs. to sci. jours. Leukemia Soc. Am. fellow, 1981, Spl. fellow, 1983, scholar, 1987; grantee NIH, 1985—. Mem. Am. Assn. Immunologists (co-chmn. symposium 1990), AAAS, Sigma Xi. Office: Brown U Biomed Ctr Box G-B618 Providence RI 02912

BIRSH, ARTHUR THOMAS, publisher; b. Englewood, N.J., Oct. 6, 1932; s. Abraham S. and Mary (Levinsohn) B.; m. Judith Rosenberg, June 29, 1955 (div. 1982); children: Andrew, Philip, Joanne; m. Joan Alleman, 1983. Grad., Lawrenceville N.J. Sch., 1950; B.A., Yale, 1954. Engaged in sales Western Pub. Co., Poughkeepsie, N.Y., 1956-58; founder Cross Road Press, Hyde Park, N.Y., 1958; pres. Cross Road Press, 1958-60; with Playbill mag., N.Y.C., 1961—; publisher Playbill mag., 1965—; exec. v.p. Am. Theatre Press, Inc., 1961-68, pres., 1974—; group v.p. Metromedia, Inc., 1968-73. Served with AUS, 1954-56. Home: PO Box 273 Villas NJ 08251-0273 Office: Playbill 52 Vanderbilt Ave New York NY 10017-3808

BIRSTEIN, SEYMOUR JOSEPH, aerospace company executive; b. N.Y.C., May 1, 1927; s. Harry D. and Golde (Lenoff) B.; divorced; 1 child, Diane. BA in Chemistry, NYU, 1947; MS in Phys. Chemistry, Mont. State U., 1948; postgrad., Bklyn. Poly. Inst., 1949-50, Cornell U., 1953. Rsch. chemist Airco, Murray Hill, N.J., 1949-50; br. chief Air Force Cambridge Rsch. Labs., Bedford, Mass., 1951-76; pres. SJB Assoc., Inc., Marlborough, Mass., 1977—. Contbr. articles to profl. jours.; patentee in field. Fellow Am. Inst. Chemists; mem. Am. Chem. Soc., Am. Meteorol. Soc., Sigma Xi. Home and Office: 24 Pippen Rd Marlborough MA 01752-1419

BIRTWISTLE, MARGARET ANNE, admissions director; b. Phila., Apr. 5, 1948; d. Edward William and Anna Elizabeth (McAnulty) B. BA in English, Chestnut Hill Coll., 1979; MS in Ednl. Adminstrn. and Supervision, Fordham U., 1981. Tchr. Most Holy Redeemer, Westville Grove, N.J., 1968-72, St. Peter, Point Pleasant Beach, N.J., 1972-77; prin. St. Ambrose, Old Bridge, N.J., 1977-83; admission dir. Chestnut Hill Coll., Phila., 1983—. Mem. Pa. Assn. Cath. Coll. Admission Officers (sec. 1989—). Democrat. Roman Catholic. Home and Office: Chestnut Hill Coll 9601 Germantown Ave Philadelphia PA 19118-2695

BIRX, H. JAMES, anthropology and philosophy educator, lecturer, author; b. Canandaigua, N.Y., June 1, 1941; s. Harry Charles and Jane Ann (Cermak) B. BS in Natural Scis., SUNY Coll., Geneseo, 1963, MS in Biology, 1964; MA in Anthropology, SUNY, Buffalo, 1966, PhD in Philosophy with distinction, 1971; postdoctorate in German studies, Canisius Coll., 1974-77, 80. Instr. SUNY, Buffalo, 1964-71; prof. anthropology Canisius Coll., Buffalo, 1968—, chmn. anthropology/sociology dept., 1980—; instr. Consortium Western N.Y., Attica, 1979-85; vis. prof. Freie U., Berlin, 1977, Brock U., St. Catharines, Ont., Can., 1983-84, McMaster U., Hamilton, Ont., Can., 1984, Shippensburg (Pa.) U., 1989-90, SUNY Coll., Geneseo, 1990, Humboldt U., Berlin, 1990, Friedrich Schiller U., Jena, Germany, 1990, U. Utah, Salt Lake City, 1991, U. Hawaii at Manoa, Honolulu, 1991, U. North Tex., Denton, 1992; researcher geobiology Galapagos Islands, 1973, 81, Rarotonga/Aitutaki, Cook Islands, 1992, paleoanthropology Harvard U. and Nat. Mus. of Kenya, 1985; adj. prof. Inst. Inquiry Coll. Humanism SUNY, Buffalo, 1990—; pub. speaker on Aristotle, Bruno, Darwin, Haeckel, Wagner, Nietzsche, Teilhard, Marvin Farber and various topics in evolutionary thought; internat. symposium speaker Pierre Teilhard de Chardin, Arcosanti, Ariz., 1981, Marvin Farber, SUNY, Buffalo, 1982, Charles Darwin, SUNY, Buffalo, 1982, On Wisdom, Brock Philosophy Soc., St. Catharines, Ont., Can., 1984, Ont. Archaeologists Abroad, Toronto, 1988, Evolution Vs. Creationism, Inst. Inquiry Coll. Humanism, 1991, Postmodernism, Soc. Humanist Philosophers, Brock U., 1991, Paul Kurtz and Promethean Love, Soc. Humanist Philosophers, Brock. U., 1992; Canisius Coll. symposium chair New Frontiers Social Scis., 1981, Darwin and Evolution: A Centennial Tribute, 1982; Lilian Fairchild lectr. Buffalo Mus. Sci., 1982; chair Wagner in Retrospect: A Centennial Reappraisal, U. Ill., Chgo., 1983, Defending the Enlightenment, Coalition for Secular Humanism and Freethought, Toronto, 1992; speaker Goethe Inst., Toronto, Ont., Can., 1984, Hilbert Coll., Hamburg, N.Y., 1987, Katholische Akademie Schwerte, Dortmund, Germany, 1988, Inst. Applied Philosophy, Ft. Lauderdale, Fla., 1991, 92; lectr. NSF seminar Roswell Park Meml. Inst., Buffalo, 1990; keynote speaker Ernst Haeckel Haus, Friedrich Schiller U., 1990; speaker Charter Day, invited vis. scholar North Lake Coll., Irving, Tex., 1992. Author: Theories of Evolution, 1984 (CHOICE award outstanding book in history of sci. 1984-85), Physical Anthropology, 1985, Science and Nature, 1986, Human Evolution, 1988, Interpreting Evolution: Darwin and Teilhard de Chardin, 1991, Craniometry of the Orchid Site Ossuary, 1991, Charles Darwin, 1992, Emerging Humankind, 1992, Apes, Monkeys, and Prosimians, 1992; author (introduction) Ernst Haeckel's The Riddle of the Universe, 1992, (introduction) Julian Huxley's Evolutionary Humanism, 1992; editorial assoc. Proteus, Free Inquiry; reviewer sci. books Libr. Jour., 1991—; contbr. more than 100 revs., articles and features to profl. jours. and encys. Grantee NSF, 1964-66, Ont. Heritage Found., 1988; recipient Citation The Libr. Congress, 1985, Bene Merenti award Canisius Coll., 1989, Citations of Merit Inst. for Anthropology/Charité and Interdisciplinary Inst. for Sci. Philosophy and Human Existence, Humboldt U. Berlin, 1990, Inst. for History of Medicine, Natural Scis., and Tech., Friedrich Schiller U., 1990. Mem. AAUP, Inst. Applied Philosophy, Soc. Humanist Philosophers, John Dewey Soc., Assn. Process Philosophy Edn., Nat. Ctr. Sci. Edn., N.Y. Coun. Evolution Edn., Western N.Y. Skeptics, N.Y. Acad. Scis., N.E. Anthrop. Assn. (keynote address 1986), L.S.B. Leakey Found., Am. Humanist Assn., Am. Culture Assn., N.Am. Nietzsche Soc., Washington Evolutionary Systems Soc., Internat. Assn. Campus Law Enforcement Adminstrs., Sigma Xi (sec. Buffalo chpt. 1984-85, keynote speaker 1986), Phi Delta Kappa. Democrat. Home: 189-7 Palmdale Dr Buffalo NY 1421-4026 Office: Canisius Coll Dept Anthropology/Sociology 2001 Main St Buffalo NY 14208-1098

BISBEE, GERALD ELFTMAN, JR., investment company executive; b. Waterloo, Iowa, July 12, 1942; s. Gerald Elftman Bisbee and Maxine Cole Prather; m. Linda Elaine Ude, Aug. 22, 1970; children: Gerald Elftman III, Katherine Elizabeth. BA, North Cen. Coll., Naperville, Ill., 1967; MBA, U. Pa., 1972; PhD, Yale U., 1975. Adminstr. Med. Ctr. Northwestern U., Chgo., 1968-70; asst. prof. Yale U., New Haven, 1974-78, assoc. dir. health svcs., 1975-78; pres. Hosp. Rsch. and Ednl. Trust, Chgo., 1978-84; v.p., shareholder Kidder, Peabody & Co., N.Y.C., 1984-87; chmn., chief exec. officer Sequel Corp., New Canaan, Conn., 1987-89, Apache Med. Systems, Inc., Washington, 1989—; adj. prof. Northwestern U., Kellogg Sch. of Mgmt., Evanston, Ill., 1979-83; mem. visiting com. Harvard U. Health Svcs., Boston, 1986—, exec. adv. com. Weatherhead Sch. of Mgmt. Health Systems Program, Case Western Res. U., Cleve., 1984-86; bd. dirs. Cerner Corp., Yamaichi Funds, Inc., Geriatrics and Med. Ctrs., Inc. Author: (book) Multihospital Systems: Policy Issues for the Future, 1981, co-author: Managing the Finances of Health Institutions, 1980, Financing of Health Care, 1979, Musculo-skeletal Disorders: Their Frequency of Occurrence and Their Impact on the Population of the United States, 1978. Mem. adv. com. Waveney Care Ctr., New Canaan, 1987. Grantee USPHS, Washington, 1972-75. Mem. Yale Club (N.Y.). Office: Apache Med Systems 1901 Pennsylvania Ave NW Washington DC 20006-3405

BISBING, STEVEN B., mental health law consultant, psychologist; b. Carlisle, Pa., May 12, 1956; s. Raymond H. and Patricia A. (Bricker) B.; m. Janet A. Vecchia, Sept. 12, 1987; children: Daniel Vecchia, Zoe Vecchia. AB in Human Rels., High Point Coll., 1978; MS in Clin. Psychology, U. Cen. Fla., 1986; PsyD, Fla. Inst. Tech., 1986; JD, Antioch Sch. of Law, Washington, 1986. Lic. psychologist, Md. Psychotherapist pvt. practice Bethesda, Md., 1986-89, 90—; sr. damages analyst Med-Psych Corp., Gaithersburg, Md., 1987—; mental health law cons. Mental Health Consultation Analysis, Inc., Takoma Park, Md., 1987—. Co-author: Sexual Exploitation by Health Providers, 1987, Forensic Psychiatry and Psychology, 1988, Law and Mental Health: DC, 1991, (with others) Competency and Capacity, 1991. Mem. APA, Am. Acad. Forensic Sci., Am. Coll. Legal Medicine (Pres. award 1988-90), Md. Psychol. Assn.

BISCAYE, PIERRE EGINTON, oceanographer; b. N.Y.C., Nov. 24, 1935; s. George Eugene and Ruth (Eginton) B.; m. Nedaleine Ruth Bell, Aug. 23, 1958; children: Timothy G., David E., Sara R., Rachel E. BS, Wheaton (Ill.) Coll., 1957; PhD, Yale U., 1964. Scientist Jersey Prodn. Rsch. Co., Tulsa, Okla., 1964-65, Isotopes, Inc., Westwood, N.J., 1965-67; sr. rsch. scientist Lamont-Doherty Geol. Observatory Columbia U., Palisades, N.Y., 1967—. Contbr. 60 articles to profl. jours. 1st lt. U.S. Army, 1957-59. Fellow Geol. Soc. Am.; mem. Am. Geophys. Union, AAAS. Office: Lamont Doherty Geol Observa Columbia Univ Palisades NY 10964

BISCHOFF, MARILYN BRETT, social worker; b. Mt. Vernon, N.Y., Apr. 16, 1930; d. Arthur Cushman and Mary Kathryn (Clark) Brett; m. Walter A. Bischoff, Mar. 25, 1961; children: Holly, Robert. BA magna cum laude, CCNY, 1959; MSW, Columbia U., 1961; D in Social Work, Boston Coll., 1985. Diplomate Clin. Social Work. Clin. social worker Providence Child Guidance Clinic, 1961-65, 69-73; pvt. practice clin. social worker Providence, 1965—; instr. Providence Coll., 1988-89; speaker in field. Active Attleboro (Mass.) Area Mental Health Assn., 1975—. Columba Univ. fellow, N.Y.C., 1959-60; Nat. Inst. Mental Health fellow, 1960-61. Mem. NASW (sec./treas. S.E. Mass. chpt. 1967-68, mem. speaker's bur. R.I. chpt. 1987), Acad. Cert. Social Workers, R.I. Group Psychotherapy Soc. (membership com. 1985—), Am. Group Psychotherapy Assn., Northeastern Soc. Group Psychotherapy, Columbia U. Alumni Assn., Phi Beta Kappa. Club: Attleboro Ski. Home: 10 Norfolk Row Attleboro MA 02703-1629 Office: 154 Waterman St Providence RI 02906-3116

BISH, DONNA LOUISE, special education educator, counselor, consultant; b. Franklin, Pa., May 11, 1949; d. Donald Burnett and Ruth Helen (Kiskadden) Blair; divorced; children: Donald William, Stefani Lyn. BS in Spl. Edn., Clarion State Coll., 1971, MS in Spl. Edn., 1984; postgrad., U. Pitts., 1986-87, Indiana U. of Pa., 1989-90; Cert. Secondary Sch. Prin., Edinboro U., 1991-92. Cert. spl. edn. tchr.; secondary guidance counselor; coop. edn. coord., Pa.; cert. secondary sch. prin. Pa. Spl. edn. tchr. Redbank Valley Sch. Dist., New Bethlehem, Pa., 1971-72, Armstrong Sch. Dist., Ford City, Pa., 1972-80; spl. edn. cons. Ind. Univ. of Pa., 1986-89, various areas, 1987-90; spl. needs coor. Riverview Intermediate Unit, Shippenville, Pa., 1982-91; instr. in spl. edn. sch. psychology dept. Edinboro U. of Pa., 1991—; adj. faculty mem. Ind. Univ. of Pa., 1986-89; exhibit chairperson Pa. Assn. of Vocat. Edn. Spl. Needs, Ind., Pa., 1987-89. Contbr. articles to profl. pubs. Flutist Franklin Pa. Silver Coronet Band, 1991—. Mem. AACD, Am. Sch. Counselors Assn., Am. Assn. Tchr. Educators, Pa. Sch. Counselors Assn., Pa. Assn. Colls. and Tchr. Educators, Phi Delta Kappa. Office: Spl Edn/Sch Psychology Dept 138B Butterfield Hall Edinboro PA 16412

BISHOP, ANDRE, producer, director; b. N.Y.C., Nov. 9, 1948; s. Andre V. and Felice H. (Francis) Smelianinoff. Attended, Harvard Coll. Producer, at Playwright's Horizon, N.Y.C. (plays): Table Settings, Coming Attractions, March of the Falsettos, The Dining Room, The Transfiguration of Benno Blimpie, Sister Mary Ignatius Explains It All For You, Geniuses, Isn't It Romantic, Sunday in the Park with George; worked with New York Shakespeare Restival and Am. Place Theatre, N.Y.C.; cons. CAPS Playwrighting Program; tchr. NYU, Hunter Coll.; former artistic dir. Playwrights Horizon, from 1978; now artistic dir. Lincoln Ctr. Theatre, N.Y.C., 1992—. Office: Lincoln Ctr Theatre 150 W 65th St New York NY 10023-6903*

BISHOP, ETHEL MAE See GULLETTE, ETHEL MAE BISHOP

BISHOP, GEORGE REGINALD, JR., foreign language educator; b. Altoona, Pa., Jan. 17, 1922; s. George Reginald and Charlotta (Miller) B.; m. Alice Elgin, Aug. 9, 1952; children: Anne, Charlotta, Alice Anderson. AB with highest honors, Princeton U., 1946, MA, 1948, PhD, 1952. Commd. 2d lt. U.S. Army, 1944, advanced through grades to lt. col., 1958; ret. U.S. Army, ETO, 1962; teaching asst. Princeton (N.J.) U., 1950-51; instr., asst. prof. Rutgers Coll., New Brunswick, N.J., 1952-60, assoc. prof., 1960-65, prof., 1965-75, Disting. Prof., 1975—, asst. to assoc. dean, 1960-68, dean of instrn., 1968-72, 74-80, acting dean, 1972-74, prof. of French, 1974—; chmn. faculty coun. Rutgers U., 1989-90; mem. State of N.J. Coun. on Coll. Outcomes, Trenton, 1990-91. Editor: (books) Readings in the European Renaissance, 1955, Culture in Language Learning, 1960, Culture in Language Learning: Supplementary Report, 1960; contbr. articles to profl. jours. Recipient faculty grant Ford Found., N.Y.C., 1954-55, teaching grant State of N.J., Trenton, 1984-86. Mem. Modern Lang. Assn., AAUP, Am. Tchrs. French, Am. Coun. Teaching Fgn. Langs., Northeast Conf. on Teaching Fgn. Langs. (chmn. 1965-66, bd. dirs. 1958-67), Phi Beta Kappa. Republican. Episcopalian. Home: 166 Wilson Rd Princeton NJ 08540-2604 Office: Dept French/Rutgers Univ New Brunswick NJ 08903

BISHOP, HOWARD STUART, management consultant; b. Pawtucket, R.I., May 27, 1938; s. Howard Stuart and Eloise (Dowell) B.; m. Marilyn Ruth Davies, Apr. 7, 1957 (div. Feb. 1974); children: Sherie, Wendy, Kristen, David. BS in Acctg., Bryant Coll., 1957; MBA, U. Hartford, 1966. CPA, Conn. Sr. acct. Deloitte, Haskins & Sells, New Haven, Conn., 1959-62; mktg. mgr. Stanley Works, New Britain, Conn., 1962-67; dir. mktg. Berol Corp., Danbury, Conn., 1967-70; gen. mgr. Victor Systems & Equipment, Marietta, Ohio, 1970-72; v.p. sales and distribution Magic Marker Corp., Cherry Hill, N.J., 1972-74; dir. mktg. Sperry Corp. (Unisys), Blue Bell, Pa., 1974-78; pres. BOPCO Mgmt. Cons., Huntingdon Valley, Pa., 1978—; pres. MGB Bus. Svcs. Co., Lansdale, Pa., 1984—. Author: Framework Made Easier, 1985, Master Guide to Field Sales Management Tactics and Techniques, 1987, Model Sales Scripts, 1988; contbr. articles to numerous mags.; feature columnist North Penn Chamber, 1986-89. Pres. R.I. Congregational Conf., Providence, 1953-54, editor, 1954-56; internat. dir. YMCA, Boston, 1963-66; treas., bd. mem. Yale U. Campus Ministry, New Haven, Conn., 1960-67; bldg. com. chmn. St. John's Meth. Ch., Ivyland, Pa., 1967-70. With U.S. Army, 1957-59. Named Pa. Speak-up Champion, U.S. Jaycees, 1969. Mem. AICPA, Pa. Inst. CPAs, Am. Mktg. Assn., Nat. Office Products Assn. (convention co-chmn. 1972, com. mem. 1972-76, young execs. forum 1968-78). Republican. Office: 817 Birch Ct Ste 100 Bensalem PA 19020

BISHOP, JAMES FRANCIS, executive search consulting company executive; b. Chgo., Mar. 14, 1937; s. Francis Joseph and Margaret Rose (Nagle) B.; m. Shirley Ann McNulty, Oct. 13, 1962; children: Michael Francis, Noreen Maura, James Francis Jr. BA, Marquette U., 1961, MA, 1965. Spl. agt. Office of Naval Intelligence, Chgo., 1962-65; sr. assoc. Burke & O'Brien Assoc., Inc., N.Y.C., 1965-67, v.p., 1967-74, sr. v.p., 1974-78, pres., 1978-83; pres. Burke, O'Brien & Bishop Assoc., Inc., Princeton, N.J., 1983—. Trustee George St. Playhouse, 1988—, trustee St. Francis Med. Ctr., Trenton, N.J., 1989—, chmn. bd., 1991—; councilman Piscataway, 1968-71. With USMC, 1954-57. Mem. Marquette U. Alumni Assn. (v.p. 1985-87, pres. 87-88). Republican. Roman Catholic. Clubs: Union League (Chgo.); Marquette (N.Y.C.), Forsgate Country. Home: 33 Richard Ct Princeton NJ 08540-3802 Office: Burke O'Brien & Bishop Assocs 1000 Herrontown Rd Princeton NJ 08540

BISHOP, JEMMA WON-JA, training executive, consultant; b. Wando, Chonnam, Korea, Apr. 15, 1944; came to U.S., 1973; d. Ch'ong-T'ae and Hyon-Sim (Kim) Chong; m. Donald Michael Bishop, July 25, 1973; children: Jerome, John Patrick, Edward. BS, Seoul Nat. U., Suwon, Korea, 1966; student, Ohio State U., 1973-74; MIS cert., U. So. Calif., 1985. Nutritionist Daegun Brennan Catholic Sem., Kwang Ju, Korea, 1966-68; dir. food service Sogang Jesuit U., Seoul, Korea, 1970-71; asst. USAF, Kwang Ju, 1971-73; city and county ct. and social svcs. interpreter Colorado Springs, Colo., 1975-79; interpreter/consultant Hong Kong, Fairfax, Va., 1979-84; dir. bicultural family programs U.S. Army, Taegu, Korea, 1985-86; dir. program for advanced English studies Am. Inst. in Taiwan, Taipei, 1987-91. Leader, Chonnam Province, 1972; advisor, Korean Catholic Assn. of Colo., 1975-79, chpt. chmn. Deerfield Acad. Parents Assn., 1984-87. Recipient Meritorious Honor award Am. Inst. in Taiwan, 1989, 91. Mem. Royal Asiatic Soc. Roman Catholic. Home: 10215 Marshall Pond Rd Burke VA 22015

BISHOP, RAND, educator; b. Lansing, Mich., Feb. 3, 1933; s. David Rand and Myra Lu (Deacon) B.; 1 child, Andrew Nelson. BA, U. Mich., 1954, MA, 1961; cert., Fgn. Svc. Inst., 1964; PhD, Mich. State U., 1970. Cultural affairs officer USIA, Lomé, Togo, 1964-66, acting pub. affairs officer, 1965-66; asst. prof. Calif. State U., Sacramento, 1966-69, Mich. State U., East Lansing, 1970-71; prof. SUNY, Oswego, 1971—; scholar-in-residence Fulbright program USIA, Washington, 1983-84; Fulbright prof. U. Nat. du Gabon, Libreville, 1974-75; vis. prof. McGill U., Montreal, Que., Can., 1974, U. Fla., Gainesville, 1979. Author: African Literature, African Critics: The Forming of Critical Standards, 1947-66, 88; contbr. articles to profl. jours., poems to lit. mags. Fellow NEH, UCLA, 1978. Office: SUNY Dept English Oswego NY 13126

BISHOP, THOMAS WALTER, educator; b. Vienna, Austria, Feb. 21, 1929; came to U.S., 1940, naturalized, 1944; s. Martin M. and Katherine (Abeles) B.; m. Muriel Hausman, June 30, 1950 (div. 1967); children: Jeffrey Bishop (dec.), Katherine; m. Helen Gary, Dec. 15, 1967. AB, NYU, 1950; AM, U. Md., 1951; postgrad., U. Paris, 1950-51; PhD, U. Calif., Berkeley, 1957. Asst. in French U. Calif., Berkeley, 1951-55; instr. NYU, 1956-59, asst. prof., 1959-61, assoc. prof., 1961-64, prof., 1964—, Florence Gould prof. French lit., 1975—, dir. La Maison Française, 1959-64, chmn. dept. French, 1966—; chmn. Ctr. for French Civilization and Culture, 1978—; vis. prof. Ecole des Hautes en Scis. Sociales, Paris, 1980, 87; cons. NEH, 1980—. Author: Pirandello and the French Theater, 1960, rev. edit., 1970, L'Avant-Garde Théâtrale: French Theater Since 1950, 1970, rev. edit., 1975, Huis Clos de Jean-Paul Sartre, 1975, Beckett, 1976, 2d edit. 1985, Le Passeur d'Océan, 1989; French TV program on U.S., 1980. Trustee French Inst.-Alliance Française N.Y., 1971—, Lycée Francais, N.Y.C., 1989—; bd. dirs. French-Am. Found., 1976-86. Decorated chevalier Légion d'Honneur, commandeur Ordre Nat. du Mérite, officer Ordre des Arts et Lettres, officer Palmes Académiques; recipient Obie award, 1979; Fulbright fellow, 1965. Fellow N.Y. Inst. Humanities, Soc. Fellows NYU; mem. MLA, PEN, Beckett Soc. (pres. 1986-88). Home: 56 Washington Mews New York NY 10003-6608 Office: NYU 19 University Pl New York NY 10003-4501

BISHOP, WILLIAM PAUL, insurance company executive; b. Denver, Aug. 15, 1956; s. Robert Paul and Elaine (Payne) B.; m. Cheryl Cowan, June 28, 1980; 1 child, William P. BSBA, U. Denver, 1978, MBA, 1991. CLU, chartered fin. cons. Am. Coll. Rep. group Union Mutual Cos., Denver, 1978-80, State Mutual Cos., Denver, 1980-82; group mgr. dist. State Mutual Cos., Dallas, 1982-86, asst. v.p. regional sales, 1986-87; v.p. regional sales State Mutual Cos., Denver and Dallas, 1987-90; v.p. group life and health sales State Mut. Cos., Worcester, Mass., 1990—. Mem. Am. CLU Soc., SE Denver Exchange (pres. 1982), Kiwanis, Los Charros Club. Republican. Roman Catholic. Office: State Mut Cos 440 Lincoln St # 57D Worcester MA 01653-0001

BISINEERU, JAYADEV REVANNA, food technologist; b. Bangalore, Karnataka, India, May 15, 1952; s. Revanna and Jayamma (Kalyana) B.; m. Tammie Mae Rowan, Mar. 16, 1978; children: Yogesh, Sharmila, Sangeetha. B of Fisheries Sci., U. Agrl. Scis., Bangalore, 1976. Quality assurance asst. mgr. Con-Agra Poultry Co., El Dorado, Ark., 1978-84; quality assurance mgr. Mavar Shrimp Loyster Co., Biloxi, Miss., 1984-88, Heinz Pet Products, Biloxi, 1988-89; quality assurance supr. Alpo Pet Foods, Allentown, Pa., 1989-90, food technologist, 1990—. Tata Endowment Scholarship J.N. Tata Found., 1976. Mem. Inst. of Food Tech. Hindu. Home: 5591 Wedge Ln Wescosville PA 18106-9663

BISKIN, BRUCE HOWARD, psychometrician; b. Bronx, N.Y., Nov. 21, 1950; s. George and Theresa (Bolinsky) B.; m. Barbara R. Gronsky, Feb. 14, 1982; 1 child, Lee Jordan Gronsky Biskin. BBA cum laude, Baruch Coll., 1972; MA, U. Minn., 1975; PhD, U. Md., 1982. Cons. psychol. and behavioral assessment Univ. Md., Univ. Coll., College Park, 1979-88; rsch. assoc. Am. Psychol. Assn., Washington, 1979-81, cons. psychol. svcs. rev., 1981-82; researcher Johnson O'Connor Rsch. Found., Chgo., 1983; test and measurement specialist N.Y.C. (N.Y.) Bd. Edn., 1984-85; psychometrician AICPA, N.Y.C., 1985-88, sr. psychometrician, 1988—; project mgr. Practice Analysis of CPAs in Pub. Acctg., AICPA, N.Y.C., 1988-91. Editorial bd. mem.: Advances in Accounting, 1986—, Measurement & Evaluation in Counseling and Development, 1986—; mem. adv. bd.: Professional Education Research Quarterly, 1991—; contbr. articles to profl. jours. Mem. AACD, APA, Am. Ednl. Rsch. Assn., Nat. Coun. on Measurement in Edn., Am. Psychol. Soc., Audubon Soc., Nature Conservancy, Psi Chi (pres. Baruch Coll. chpt. 1971-72). Office: AICPA 1211 Ave Of The Americas New York NY 10036-8775

BISSELL, JOHN W., federal judge; b. Exeter, N.H., June 7, 1940; s. H. Hamilton and Sarah W. B.; m. Caroline M.; July 15, 1967; children—Megan L., Katharine W. A.B., Princeton U., 1962; LL.B., U. Va., 1965. Law clk. U.S. Dist. Ct., N.J., 1965-66; assoc. Pitney, Hardin & Kipp, Morristown, N.J., 1966-69, ptnr., 1972-78; asst. U.S. atty. N.J., 1969-71; judge Essex County, N.J., 1978-81, N.J. Superior Ct., 1981-82, U.S. Dist. Ct. N.J., Trenton and Newark, 1983—. Office: US Dist Ct US PO & Courthouse PO Box 419 Nutley NJ 07110-0499*

BISSON, LINDA GALE STEVENS, public utilities executive; b. Tex., Sept. 1, 1946; 1 child, Teresa Adrienne. BA in History, U. N.H., 1972; MBA, Simmons Coll., Boston, 1980. Cert. utility regulation studies, Mass., Mich. Law sch. admissions dir. Franklin Pierce Law Ctr., Concord, N.H., 1978-79; v.p., co-founder BCI Geonetics, Inc., Santa Barbara, Calif., 1981-87; commr. Pub. Utilities Commn., Concord, N.H., 1987—; adj. faculty bus. Daniel Webster Coll., Nashua, N.H., 1986-91; vice-chmn. Def. Adv. Com. on Women in the Svcs., D.C.; del. 1st Japan-Am. Grassroots Summit; with NARUC; chmn. Com. on Water, subcom. on Conservation. Trustee New Eng. Coll., fin. com.; bd. dirs., chmn. Def. Issues Task Force, WESG; trustee The Nature Conservancy, N.H.; incorporator N.H. Charitable Fund; adv. bd. mem. MIT Energy Lab., NH DRED Econ. Adv. Group; pub. coun. mem. Am. Water Works Assn. Rsch. Found.; admissions coun. mem. Simmons Coll. GSM; active numerous nat. and local regulatory agys. RJR Nabisco Fellow Harvard U. Kennedy Sch. Govt.; recipient Rappaport Achievement award Simmons Coll., 1990. Mem. Univ. N.H. Alumni Assn. (nat. pres., bd. dirs.), Rotary Internat., Army and Navy Club, Bald Peak Colony Club, Ida Lewis Yacht Club. Office: Pub Utilities Commn 8 Old Suncook Rd Concord NH 03301-7320

BITNER, JOHN WILLIAM, banker; b. Jersey Shore, Pa., July 6, 1948; s. John W. and Gertrude Elizabeth (Brownlee) B.; m. Jennifer M. Berringer, Sept. 4, 1976 (div. 1979). BS in Econs., Lebanon Valley Coll., Annville, Pa., 1970; MBA, Boston Coll., Chestnut Hill, Mass., 1983. V.p. Commonwealth Bank, Williamsport, Pa., 1970-78, Neworld Bank, Boston, 1978-81; fixed income mgr. Digital Equipment Co., Maynard, Mass., 1981-84; sr. v.p. Ea. Bank, Salem, Mass., 1984—. Author: Successful Asset/Liability Management, 1992; contbr. articles to profl. jours. Mem. adv. bd. Lebanon Valley Coll., Annville, Pa., 1986—; past pres. Boys and Girls Club Greater Salem. Mem. Fin. Analysts Fedn., Boston Security Analysts Soc., North Shore C. of C. (econ. devel. com.), Rotary (bd. dirs. Salem).

BITTINGER, DOUGLAS EDWARD, executive; b. Meyersdale, Pa., July 7, 1966; s. Robert Earl and In Sok Bittinger. Student, Northern Md. U., 1983, Garrett Community Coll., McHenry, Md., 1984, Frostburg State U., 1984. V.p. BBCI, Cumberland, Md., 1983—. Mem. Nat. Assn. Home Builders. Republican. Home: 190 Grant St Grantsville MD 21536 Office: BBCI Inc 152A Christie Rd Cumberland MD 21502

BITTLEMAN, DOLORES DEMBUS, public relations official; b. N.Y.C.; d. Samuel and Molly (Schindler) Dembus; m. Arnold I. Bittleman, June 8, 1958 (dec. Apr. 1985); children: David B., Sarah. BS cum laude, Columbia U., 1958, M Pub. Svc., 1988. Tchr. Union Coll., Schenectady, 1969-74; pres. Cambridge (N.Y.) Textiles, Restorations, 1974-86; state lobbyist Am. Assn. Ret. Persons, Washington, 1986-90; dir. sch. affairs Am. Montessori Soc., N.Y.C., 1990—. One woman show include Silvermine (Conn.) Coll. of Art, 1974, Bennington (Vt.) Coll., 1979, and others; group exhibitions at U.S. Info. Svc. (Europe), 1960, Mus. of Modern Art, N.Y.C., 1969; represented in permanent collections Mus. Modern Art, N.Y.C., Yale U., New Haven. Fund raiser Met. Rep. Club, N.Y.C.; bd. dirs. Block Assn., N.Y.; mem. N.Y.C. Street Tree Consortium, Am. Tree Farm System. Fulbright grantee, Paris. Jewish. Home: PO Box 54 Cambridge NY 12816-0054

BITTNER, RICHARD RUSSELL, sales executive; b. Summit, N.J., Dec. 15, 1950; s. Walter Wallace and Jean (Himmelberger) B.; m. Elizabeth Meyer Filosa (div. June 1987); m. Vera Cvikevich, May 21, 1989. Student, Davidson Coll., 1969-70; cert., U. de Friburg, Switzerland, 1974, U. di Perugia, Italy, 1977; BA, Columbia U., 1984. Acct. mgr. Pvt. Satellite Network Inc., N.Y.C., 1984-86; acct. exec. Videostar Connections Inc., N.Y.C., 1987-90; dir. sales The Kenwood Group, N.Y.C., 1990—. Office: The Kenwood Group 222 E 44th St New York NY 10017-4334

BITTNER, RONALD JOSEPH, computer systems analyst; b. Schenectady, N.Y., July 30, 1954; s. Richard Joseph and Catherine (Stepnowski) B.; m. Elayne Louise Simpson, May 14, 1983; 1 child, Krysten Elayne. AS in Chemistry, Orange County Community Coll., Middletown, N.Y., 1978; BA in Bus. Mgmt., Herbert Lehman Coll., Bronx, N.Y., 1983. Internal cons. Internat. Paper Co., Tuxedo, N.Y., 1978-87; systems analyst McGraw-Hill News, N.Y.C., 1987-89; sr. systems analyst Orange County Info. Svcs., Goshen, N.Y., 1989-91, Columbia Tristar Home Video, N.Y.C., 1991—; cons. in magic Shawnee Playhourse, Poconos, Pa., 1985. Contbr. articles to newspapers and mags., 1980-88. Mem. Variety Clubs Internat., Soc. Am. Magicians (pres. 1985-87), Internat. Brotherhood of Magicians. Home: RR 2 Box 173B Wallkill NY 12589-9802

BITZER, JEFFREY T., lawyer; b. York, Pa., July 7, 1952; s. Roy T. and Thelma L. (Keeney) B.; m. Joan Louise Fink, May 29, 1982; children: Zachary T., Allison Witherow. BS, U. Md., 1974; JD, Dickinson Sch. Law, 1982. Bar: U.S. Supreme Ct. 1990, U.S. Dist. Ct. (fed. dist.) 1982, Pa. 1982. Radio reporter WNOW/WQXA Radio, York, Pa., 1971-74; reporter, producer WHP TV, Harrisburg, Pa., 1974-81; prof. Shippensburg (Pa.) U., 1981—; lawyer Law Office Jeffrey T. Bitzer, York, 1982—; editorial bd. Pa. Bar Assn., Harrisburg, 1989—; juvenile master Ct. Common Pl., York, 1988—; bd. dirs. Pa. Radio Theater, Harrisburg, 1986—. Producer (TV series) Legal Brief, 1984-88; columnist Advocacy, 1986—; host (TV series) Newsmakers, 1983-85. Bd. dirs. Common Cause Pa., Harrisburg, 1989-90. Named Outstanding Young Man Am., 1987. Mem. Soc. Profl. Journalists Cen. Pa. (pres. 1975), Hist. York Inc. (bd. dirs. 1986-90). Democrat. Episcopalian. Home: 566 Gravel Hill Rd Mount Wolf PA 17347-9710 Office: Law Office Jeffrey T Bitzer One West Market St York PA 17401

BIXLER, HERBERT EDWARDS, transportation executive; b. New London, Conn., June 10, 1911; s. James Wilson and Mabel (Seelye) B.; m. Agnes Rodgers, June 26, 1937 (dec. Feb. 5, 1986); children: Sidney Rodgers, Agnes Seelye Bixler Kurtz, Elizabeth James; m. Judith Emery Millican, June 7, 1987. AB, Amherst Coll., 1932; MS in Transp., Yale U., 1933. Car agt. N.Y. Cen. System, 1934-36; transp. inspector New Haven R.R., 1936-37, supr., 1937-41, supt. freight transp., 1941-45, transp. asst., 1945-48; gen. supt. transp. New Haven R.R., N.Y.C., 1948-49, N.Y.C. R.R., 1949-50, Boston & Maine R.R., Boston and Maine, 1950-55; asst. to pres. Northeast Airlines, 1955-56; pvt. practise cons. Northeast Airlines, Jaffrey, N.H., 1962—; assoc. Systems Analysis and Rsch. Corp., 1962-64, v.p., 1964-70; transp. cons. Jaffrey, N.H., 1971—. Author: Railroads-Their Rise and Fall, 1982. Mem. Mass. Legis. Com. to Investigate MBTA. Home and Office: 13 S Hill Rd PO Box 371 Jaffrey NH 03452-0371

BIXLER, JOHN MOURER, lawyer; b. Washington, Oct. 14, 1927; s. John S. and Elsie (Mourer) B.; m. Miriam Calhoun, Aug. 16, 1952; children: Allyson Sue Switzer, Stephen J., Mary Lynn Frye. BS, U. Pa., 1949; LLB, Harvard U., 1954. Bar: D.C. 1954, Md. 1960, U.S. Dist. Ct., CPA. Staff mem. Charles S. Rockey & Co. CPAs, Phila., 1949-51; assoc. Miller & Chevalier, Washington, 1954-61; mem. Miller & Chevalier, Chartered, Washington, 1962—; lectr. NYU Inst. Fed. Taxation. Mem. editorial bd. Estate Planning Mag. Trustee D.C. Legal Aid Soc., Washington, 1975—, U. Pa., Phila., 1975-80, Concord-St. Andrew's United Meth. Ch., Bethesda, Md., 1981—, Meth. Home of D.C., 1982—; bd. dirs., pres. Miller and Chevalier Charitable Found., Washington, 1969—. Recipient Joseph Wharton award Wharton Sch. Club of Washington, 1982. Fellow Am. Bar Found.; mem. The Met. Club of City of Washington, Lawyers Club, The Barristers, Am. Coll. Trust and Estate Counsel (regent 1987—, D.C. state chmn. 1983-87), Am. Coll. Tax Counsel, Confrerie des Chevaliers du Tastevin (sec., treas. sous-commanderie de Washington). Republican. Methodist. Home: 5304 Moorland Ln Bethesda MD 20814-1334 Office: Miller & Chevalier Charterd 655 15th St NW Ste 900 Washington DC 20005-5701

BIZAR, IRVING, lawyer; b. N.Y.C., June 30, 1932; s. Samuel Bizar and Julia Weinberg; m. Beverly J. Goldstein, Sept. 1, 1960 (div. June 1982); children: Steven E., Carolyn S.; m. Eileen Joy Schwartz, June 30, 1985. BA in Acctg., CUNY, 1953; JD cum laude, Bklyn. Law Sch., 1956. Bar: N.Y. 1957, U.S. Ct. Appeals (2d cir.) 1958, U.S. Ct. Appeals (5th cir.) 1974, U.S. Supreme Ct. 1977, U.S. Ct. Appeals (11th cir.) 1985, U.S. Ct. Appeals (4th cir.) 1986. Assoc. Pomerantz, Levy & Haudek, N.Y.C., 1957-62, Cravath, Swaine & Moore, N.Y.C., 1962-63, Demov & Morris, N.Y.C., 1963-68; ptnr. Demov, Morris, Levin & Shein, N.Y.C., 1968-77, Pincus, Ohrenstein, Bizar & D'Alessandro, N.Y.C., 1978-83, Bizar D'Alessandro Shustak & Martin, 1985-90, Bizar, Martin & Schneider, N.Y.C., 1990—. Dem. dist. leader 84th Assembly Dist., N.Y.C., 1966-68. Mem. Assn. of Bar of City of N.Y., N.Y. State Bar Assn. (fed. judiciary com. litigation comml. sect.). Office: Bizar Martin & Schneider 485 Madison Ave New York NY 10022-5803

BIZZOCO, DANIEL JOSEPH, real estate appraiser and consultant; b. N.Y.C., May 8, 1953; s. Andrew Frank and Stella Theresa (Graziano) B.; m. Linda Morlano, children: Gina Marie, Michelle Lynn. BS, Manhattan Coll., 1975. Staff appraiser North Side Savings Bank, Bronx, N.Y., 1975-77; sr. appraiser Bklyn. Savings Bank, 1977-80; asst. v.p. Chase Manhattan Bank, N.Y.C., 1980-83; sr. analyst Integrated Resources, Inc., N.Y.C., 1983-85; sr. appraiser Albert Appraisal Co., Inc., Croton, N.Y., 1985-87; sr. v.p. Weitzman Group, Inc., N.Y.C., 1987—. Recipient MAI award Appraisal Inst., 1988. Mem. Appraisal Inst. (MAI award 1988), Young Mortgage Bankers Assn., Rho Epsilon (past pres.). Republican. Roman Catholic. Office: Weitzman Group Inc 355 Lexington Ave New York NY 10017-2023

BJERKE, HAROLD WILLIAM, association executive; b. N.Y., July 16, 1940; s. Harold William and Margaret (Whitty) B.; m. Maureen Elaina, Apr. 29, 1975. BS, Ithaca Coll., 1963; MS, Adelphi U., 1971. Cert. internat. and USA gymnastics ofcl. Pres. Nat. Gymnastics Judges Assn., Bay Shore, N.Y., 1987—, tech. dir. east region, 1984-87; bd. dirs. U.S. Gymnastics Fedn.; internat. gymnastics ofcl. 1991 World Championships, Indpls., 1991 Pre-Olympic Meet, Barcelona, 1990 World Cup, Brussels, 1990 Goodwill Games, Seattle, Pan Am. Games, 1987, Am. Cups, 1980-92, 1983 World Championships, Budapest, Hungary; gymnastics ofcl. NCAA, USA Nat. Championships, USA Olympic Team Trials, USA World Team Trials. Editor Nat. Gymnastics Judges Assn. Newsletter, 1987—. Bd. mem., 1st v.p. O'Conee Assn., Bay Shore, 1990—. Named Judge of Yr., Nat. Gymnastics Judges Assn., 1977, 85; inducted Ea. Gymnastics Hall of Fame, 1991. Mem. Southward Ho Country Club. Republican. Roman Catholic. Home: 44 Lawrence Ln Bay Shore NY 11706-8626

BJORO, EDWIN FRANCIS, JR., nuclear engineer; b. Chgo., Nov. 14, 1928; s. Edvin Francis and Florence Laverne (Francis) B.; m. Barbara Anne Hanrahan, Aug. 2, 1952; 1 child, Michael Edwin. BA, Columbia U., 1950; B in Aero. Engring., NYU, 1957. Asst. dept. mgr. Titan III program United Tech. Corp., Sunnyvale, Calif., 1963-64; mem. tech. staff Rsch. Analysis Corp., McLean, Va., 1964-65; program mgr. Vitro Labs., Silver Spring, Md., 1965-69; mgr. reliability skylab program Martin Marietta, Washington, 1969-74, tech. dir., cons., 1974-76; with U.S. Dept. of Energy, Washington, 1976—, acting dir. nuclear energy quality assurance, 1990—. Contbr. articles to profl. jours. cons., data rev. bd., reliability audit com., artificial heart program Nat. Heart, Lung, and Blood Inst., NIH, Washington, 1987-92. 1st lt. USAF, 1951-55. Mem. Am. Soc. Quality Control, Tau Beta Pi. Home: 4206 Pebble Branch Rd Ellicott City MD 21042 Office: US Dept of Energy Washington DC 20585

BLACK, CATHLEEN PRUNTY, newspaper executive; b. Chgo., Apr. 26, 1944; d. James Hamilton and Margaret (Harrington) B. BA, Trinity Coll., 1966. Advt. sales rep. Holiday mag., N.Y.C., 1966-69, Travel & Leisure mag., N.Y.C., 1969-70, New York mag., 1970-72; advt. dir. Ms. mag., 1972-75, assoc. pub., 1975-77; assoc. pub. New York mag., 1977-79, pub., 1979-83; pres. USA Today, 1983, pub., 1984-91; exec. v.p. mktg. Gannett Co., Inc., from 1985, also bd. dirs.; pres., c.e.o. Newspaper Assn. Am., Reston, Va., 1991—; pres., c.e.o. Am. Newspapers Pubs. Assn., 1991—; bd. dirs. Coca Cola Co. Home: 2915 Woodland Dr NW Washington DC 20008-3542 Office: Newspaper Assn Am 11600 Sunrise Valley Dr Reston VA 22091*

BLACK, DEVEN KEITH, restaurant manager; b. N.Y.C., Oct. 2, 1953; s. Arthur Black and Vivian (Cohen) Black Powell; m. Jill Elizabeth Rovitzky, May 29, 1983. Student, SUNY, Saratoga Springs, 1991—. News dir. Sta. WCOD-FM, Hyannis, Mass., 1973-77; asst. mgr. Martell's, N.Y.C., 1981-83; gen. mgr. North Star Pub, N.Y.C., 1983—. Mem. editorial bd. Top Shelf Mag., 1991—; contbr. articles to mags. Mem. N.Y. Restaurant Assn., Nat. Restaurant Assn., Friends of the Nyacks. Office: North Star Pub 93 South St New York NY 10038

BLACK, JOSEPH THOMAS, JR., transportation executive; b. Phila., Apr. 22, 1967; s. Joseph Thomas and Elizabeth Doris (Heavern) B. BA magna cum laude, Villanova U., 1989; postgrad., U. Pa. R.r. ticket sales mgr. Southeastern Pa. Transp. Authority, Phila., 1988-91, r.r. sta. ops. mgr., 1991—. Author musical compilations: December Girl, 1990 (AFA award 1990), Roses in the Rain, 1991, Council "Works in Progress", 1989. Recipient Hon. medal Mil. Order of Loyal Legion U.S., 1986; Nat. Merit scholar, 1985-89, City of Phila. scholar, 1985-89. Republican. Roman Catholic. Home: 3612 Weightman St Philadelphia PA 19129-1621

BLACK, LINDSAY MACLEOD, plant virologist; b. Edinburgh, Scotland, Apr. 20, 1907; came to U.S. 1930; s. Lindsay James Black and Anne MacLeod; m. Helen Meta Wilhelm, Apr. 11, 1936; children: Lindsay Wilhelm, Douglas Robert, Anne Ethel. BSA, U. B.C., 1929; PhD, Cornell U., 1936. Instr. U. B.C., 1929-30; asst. Cornell U., 1930-36; nat. rsch. coun. fellow Rockefeller Inst., 1936-37; from asst. to assoc. Rockefeller Inst. for Med. Rsch., N.Y.C., 1937-46; curator Bklyn. Botanic Garden, N.Y.C., 1946-52; prof. U. Ill., 1952-75; prof. virology Plant Biology Dept. U. Ill., 1952-75; editor Virology, 1955-64. Recipient Ruth Allen award Am. Phytopathological Soc., 1978.; numerous grants from Am. Cancer Soc., Nat. Insts. of Health, NSF., 1946-75. Home: 550 Stratford Ln Ridge NY 11961-2038

BLACK, PAGE MORTON, civic worker; b. Chgo.; d. Alexander and Rose Morton; m. William Black, Mar. 27, 1962. Student, Chgo. Mus. Coll. Singer, pianist, Pierre Hotel, N.Y.C., Warwick Hotel, One Fifth Ave. Sherry Netherland Hotel; singer radio show and comml. Chock Full o' Nuts Corp.; rec. artist Atlantic Records, Rohit Internat. Records Corp.; co-founder Page and William Black Post-Grad. Sch. Medicine, Mt. Sinai Med. Sch., 1965—; chmn., mem. exec. bd. Parkinsons' Disease Found., Columbia U. Med. Ctr. (mem. adv. coun.); mem. nat. vis. coun. Columbia U. Health Scis. Faculties; hon. chmn. Chock Full O' Nuts Corp., 1983-90; founding mem. ASPCA. Recipient Ann. award Parkinsons' Disease Found., 1987. Home: Premium Pt New Rochelle NY 10801

BLACK, PERCY, psychology educator; b. Montreal, Que., Can., Jan. 6, 1922; s. Ovido and Rose (Vasilevsky) B.; m. Virginia Arne, June 21, 1951; children—Deborah, David, Elizabeth, Jonathan. B.S., Sir George Williams Coll., Montreal, 1944; M.Sc., McGill U., 1946; Ph.D., Harvard U., 1953. Instr. in Social Scis. U. Ky., 1948-49; rsch. assoc. in Child Psychology U. Minn., 1949-50; rsch. asst. in Race Rels. U. Chgo., 1950-51; Asst. prof. psychology U. N.B., Fredericton, 1951-53; vis. scholar Univ. Coll., London, 1953-54; dir. research Social Attitude Survey, Yonkers, N.Y., 1955-67; prof. emeritus in Psychology Pace U., Pleasantville, N.Y., 1967—; Contbg. author: Societies Around the World, 2 vols., 1953; author: The Mystique of Modern Monarchy, 1953; contbr. articles to profl. jours. Fellow AAAS; mem. Am. Psychol. Assn., N.Y. Acad. Scis. Lodge: B'nai B'rith. Home: 29 Cross Hill Ave Yonkers NY 10703-1422 Office: Pace U Pleasantville NY 10570

BLACK, SYDNEY DOREE, manufacturing engineer, consultant; b. Newcastle-on-Ty, Jesmond, England, Aug. 17, 1915; came to U.S., 1921; s. William and Janetta (Goodman) B.; m. Harriet Louise Cohen, Oct. 7, 1945; 1 child, Barbara Ellen. BEE, Washington U., St. Louis, Mo., 1938; MS in Engring. Physics, Ill. Inst. Tech., Chgo., 1941; DSc in Applied Engring., U. Cin., 1946. Registered profl. engr., Ohio, Mass. Dept. head vehicle engring. Gen. Precision, Inc., Systs Div., Little Falls, N.J., 1962-65; sr. staff mem. Riverside Research Inst., N.Y.C., 1965-77; applied math. Grumman Data Systems, Bethpage, N.Y., 1977-78; assoc. prof. U.S. Mcht. Marine Acad., Kings Point L.I., N.Y., 1978-80; project engring. Norden Systems (United Tech. Corp.), Bridgeport, Conn., 1980-81; supr. support engring. Digital Equipment Corp., Bridgeport, Conn., 1981-83; EMI-engr. Digital Equipment Corp., Salem, N.H., 1983-84, prin. mech. engr., 1984-87, mfg. plant staff tech. cons., 1987--; adj. prof. mech. engring. CCNY, 1972-78, also various Colls. and Univs. midwest and east; cons. to Def. Adv. Research Projects Agy. propulsion and laser weaponry, Washington, 1965-77; pres. S. Black & Assocs. Contbg. author to numerous profl. jours.; author of book in aeromachines; estab. theory of ferromagnetic fluids, 1940, conducted first wind tunnel experiments on supersonic aeroelasticity, 1947. Comdr. U.S. Mcht. Marines, 1978-80. Fellow AIAA (assoc.), Sigma Xi; mem. Soc. Mfg. Engrs. (sr.), Pi Mu Epsilon. Home: PO Box 721 Derry NH 03038-0721 Office: Digital Equipment Corp 7 Northeastern Blvd Salem NH 03079-1983

BLACK, THEODORE HALSEY, manufacturing company executive; b. Jersey City, Oct. 22, 1928; s. Theodore Charles and Mary (Carroll) B.; m. Marilyn Rigsby, 1979; children: Deborah, Theodore Jr., Susan, Zelda, Carol, Brian. BSEE, U.S. Naval Acad., Annapolis, 1953; Advanced Mgt. Program, Harvard U., 1974. Salesman, sales mgr. Ingersoll-Rand Co., N.Y.C., 1957-67, gen. mgr. turbo products div., 1967-72, v.p., 1972-87; pres., chief oper. officer Ingersoll-Rand Co., Woodcliff Lake, N.J., 1988, chmn., pres., chief exec. officer, 1988—; pres., chief exec. officer Dresser-Rand Co., Corning, N.Y., 1987-88; pres., chief exec. officer Dresser-Rand Co., Corning, N.Y., 1987-88; bd. dirs. Gen. Pub. Utilities, Parsippany, N.J., CPC Internat., Englewood Cliffs, N.J., Zeigler Coal Holdings Co., St. Louis. Trustee Bus. Coun. for UN, Boys and Girls Clubs Am. Capt. USMC, 1946-49, 53-59. Recipient Naval Aviator award USN, Corpus Christi, Tex., 1955. Mem. Machinery and Allied Products Industry Assn. (exec. com.). Roman Catholic. Office: Ingersoll-Rand Co 200 Chestnut Ridge Rd Westwood NJ 07675-7700

BLACK, WALTER EVAN, JR., federal judge; b. Balt., July 7, 1926; s. Walter Evan and Margaret Luttrell (Rice) B.; m. Catharine Schall Foster, June 30, 1951; children: Walter Evan III, Charles Foster, James Rider. A.B. magna cum laude, Harvard U., 1947, LL.B., 1949. Bar: Md. 1949. Assoc. Hinkley & Singley, Balt., 1949-53; ptnr. Hinkley & Singley, 1957-67; asst. U.S. atty. Dist. Md., Balt., 1953-55; U.S. atty. Dist. Md., 1956-57; ptnr. Clapp, Somerville, Black & Honemann, Balt., 1968-82; U.S. dist. judge Dist. Md., Balt., 1982—, chief judge, 1991—; Sec.-treas. Parkwood Cemetery Co., Balt., 1967-82; also dir.; sec. So. Mech. Inc., Balt., 1971-82; also dir.; pres. Charles T. Brandt Inc., Balt., 1972-82; also dir. Chmn. Bd. Municipal and Zoning Appeals, Balt., 1963-67; mem. Jail Bd., Balt., 1971-73, Atty. Grievance Commn., 1978-82, Rev. Bd., 1975-78, chmn., 1975-76; mem. Gov.'s Commn. to Revise Annotated Code, 1975-82. Alt. Md. del. Republican Nat. Conv., 1960; chmn. Rep. City Com., Balt., 1962-66; Md. del. Rep. Nat. Conv., 1964; Bd. dirs. Balt. Urban League, 1963-69, 76-82; bd. dirs. Union Meml. Hosp., Hosp. for Consumptives of Md. Mem. Bar Assn. Balt. City, ABA, Md. Bar Assn., Rule Day Club, Lawyers' Round Table. Baptist. Office: US Dist Ct 101 W Lombard St Baltimore MD 21201-2626

BLACKBURN, GEORGE LINCOLN, surgical educator, nutritionist; b. McPherson, Kans., Feb. 12, 1936; children: David, Amy Matthew; m. Susan E. Kelly; 1 child, Valeria. AB, U. Kans., Lawrence, 1958; MD, U. Kans., Kansas City, 1965; PhD, MIT, 1973. Diplomate Am. Bd. Surgery, Am. Bd. Nutrition. Assoc. surgeon New Eng. Deaconess Hosp., Boston, 1972-75, active staff surgeon, 1974-75, chief Nutrition and Metabolism Lab., 1973—, dir. nutrition support svc., 1973—, dir. clin. devel. Deaconess Health Mgmt. Ctr., 1991—; assoc. prof. surgery Harvard U. Med. Sch., Boston. Author: Amino Acids: Metabolism and Medical Applications, 1983; contbg. author: New Horizons—Multiple Organ Failure, 1989; editor: Management of Obesity by Severe Caloric Restriction, 1985, Nutritional Medicine: A Case Management Approach, 1989; also articles. Lt. USNR, 1958-61. Fellow ACS, Am. Fedn. for Clin. Rsch.; mem. AMA, APHA, Mass. Med. Soc., Am. Cancer Soc., Am. Coll. Nutrition, Soc. for Critical Care Medicine. Office: New Eng Deaconess Hosp 194 Pilgrim Rd Boston MA 02215-5317

BLACKBURN, ULRIC, mayor; b. Chicoutimi, Que., Can., Oct. 19, 1926; s. Jean-Baptiste and Diana (Perron) B.; m. Georgette Girard, July 14, 1951; children—Bruno, Richard, Martine, Suzanne. Student pub. schs. Chicoutimi. Controller, Important Food House, Chicoutimi, 1949-69; co-owner, L.B. Electrque Inc., Chicoutimi, 1964-82; mayor City of Chicoutimi, 1981—. First v.p. Saguenay-Lake St. John Sch. Bd. Assn., 1966-69; pres. Chicoutimi Sch. Bd., 1966-81, Chicoutimi Met. Party, Chicoutimi, 1981—; dir. Can.'s Winter Games, Saguenay-Lake St. John, 1982; pres. Diocesan Catholic Young Workers, 1948—; pres. Econ. Devel. Corp. Chicoutimi; v.p. Quebec Union of Municipalities, 1988—; mem. Chicoutimi C. of C.; vice prefect of Municipalite Regionale de Comte. Mem. Regional Coun. of Concertation and Devel., Knights of Columbus. Office: 201 rue Racine est, Chicoutimi, PQ Canada G7H 5B8

BLACKHAM, ANN ROSEMARY (MRS. J. W. BLACKHAM), realtor; b. N.Y.C., June 16, 1927; d. Frederick Alfred and Letitia L. (Stolfe) DeCain; m. James W. Blackham Jr., Aug. 18, 1951; children: Ann C., James W. III. AB, Ohio Dominican Coll., 1949; postgrad., Ohio State U., 1950. Mgr. br. store Filene & Sons, Winchester, 1950-52; broker Porter Co. Real Estate, Winchester, 1961-66; sales mgr. James T. Trefrey, Inc., Winchester, 1966-68; pres., founder Ann Blackham & Co. Inc., Realtors, Winchester, Mass., 1969—. Mem. bd. econ. advisors to Gov., 1969-74; participant White House Conf. on Internat. Cooperation, 1965; mem. Presdl. Task Force on Women's Rights and Responsibilities, 1969; mem. exec. coun. Mass. Civil Def., 1965-69; chmn. Gov.'s Commn. on Status of Women, 1971-75; regional dir. Interstate Assn. Commn. on Status of Women, 1971-74; mem. Gov. Task Force on Mass. Economy, 1972; mem. Gov.'s Jud. Selection Com., 1972, Mass. Emergency Fin. Bd., 1974-75; mem. bd. registration Real Estate Brokers & Salesman Commonwealth of Mass., 1991—; corporator, trustee Charlestown Savs. Bank, 1974-84; corporator Winchester Hosp., 1983—; mem. Winchester 350th Anniversary Commn.; mem. design rev. commn. Town of Winchester; bd. dirs. Phoenix Found., Bay State Health Care, Mass. Taxpayers Found., Speech and Hearing Found., Baystate Health Mgmt.; mem. regional selection panel White House Fellows, 1973-74; mem. com. on women in svc. U.S. Dept. Def., 1977-80; 2d v.p. Doric Dames, 1971-74, bd. dirs., 1974—; dep. chmn. Mass. Rep. State Com., 1965-66; sec. Mass. Rep. State Conv., 1970, del., 1960, 62, 64, 66, 70, 72, 74, 78, 90; state vice chmn. Mass. Rep. Fin. Com., 1970; alt. del.-at-large Rep. Nat. Conv., 1968, 72, del., 1984; pres. Scholarship Found., 1976-78, Mass. Fedn. Women's Clubs. Recipient Pub. Svc. award Commonwealth of Mass., 1978, Merit award Rep. Party, 1969, Pub. Affairs award Mass. Fedn. Women's Clubs, 1975; named Civic Leader of Yr., Mass. Broadcasters, 1962. Mem. Greater Boston Real Estate Bd. (bd. dirs.), Mass. Assn. Real Estate Bds. (bd. dirs.), Nat. Assn. Real Estate Bd. (women's coun.). Brokers Inst., Coun. Realtors (pres. 1983-84), Winchester C. of C. (bd. dirs.), Greater Boston C. of C., Nat. Assn. Women Bus. Owners, ENKA Soc., Capitol Hill Club, Ponte Vedra Club, Winchester Boat Club, Winchester Country Club, Wychemere Harbor Club, Womens City Boston Club, Winton Club (sec., bd. dir.). Home: 60 Swan Rd Winchester MA 01890-3747 Office: Ann Blackham & Co Inc 9 Thompson St Winchester MA 01890-2999

BLACKLOW, NEIL RICHARD, physician educator, virologist researcher; b. Cambridge, Mass., Feb. 26, 1938; s. Leo Alfred and Clara Edna (Cumenes) B.; m. Margery Lois Brown, June 2, 1963; children: Jon Andrew, Peter Douglas. BA magna cum laude, Harvard U., 1959; MD, Columbia U., 1963. Intern Beth Israel Hosp., Boston, 1963-64, resident in medicine, 1964-65; rsch. assoc. Nat. Inst. Allergy and Infectious Diseases, Bethesda, Md., 1965-68, sr. scientist, 1969-71; fellow in infectious diseases Mass. Gen. Hosp. and Harvard Med. Sch., Boston, 1968-69; from asst. prof. to assoc. prof. medicine Boston U. Sch. Medicine, 1971-76; prof. medicine, molecular genetics and microbiology U. Mass. Med. Sch., Worcester, 1976-90, dir. div. infectious diseases, 1976-90, Richard M. Haidack Disting. prof. medicine, 1990—, chmn. dept., 1990—; lectr. dept. medicine Harvard Med. Sch., Boston, 1983—. Contbr. articles to profl. jours. Served to lt. comdr. USPHS, 1965-68. NIH grantee, 1971—; Med. Found. Boston fellow, 1972-74. Fellow ACP, Infectious Diseases Soc. Am.; mem. Am. Soc. Clin. Investigation, Am. Assn. Immunologists, Am. Epidemiol. Soc., Am. Soc. Microbiology, Assn. of Profs. of Medicine. Office: U Mass Med Sch 55 Lake Ave N Worcester MA 01655-0001

BLACKMAN, JOAN, management consultant; b. N.Y.C., May 25, 1948; d. Samuel William and Clara (Gershunoff) B.; m. Edward J. Weaving Jr.; 1 child, Michael. BA, Case Western Res. U., 1968. Analyst Gruden Appel Rsch., N.Y.C., 1968-69; project dir. BBDO Advt., N.Y.C., 1969-70; mgr. mktg. rsch. Nabisco Inc., N.Y.C. and Parsippany, N.J., 1975-82; product mgr. Nabisco Brands Inc., Parsippany, 1975-82; v.p. mktg. Equitable Life Assurance, Pension Fin. Mgmt. Group, Secaucus, N.J., 1982-87; cons. Joan Blackman & Assocs., Ridgewood, N.J., 1987—; instr. Counseling Women, Inc., N.Y.C., 1977-82. Rep. Fort Lee (N.J.) Tenants Coun., 1979-81. Mem. AACD, ASTD, Fin. Woman's Assn. Home and Office: Joan Blackman & Assocs 715 N Monroe St Ridgewood NJ 07450

BLACKMAN, MURRAY IVAN, lawyer; b. Phila., Feb. 4, 1945; s. Isadore Edward and Mary (Rinis) B.; children: Loren Heather, Mara Ann. BS cum laude, Temple U., 1967; JD magna cum laude, U. Pa., 1970. Bar: Pa. 1970, U.S. Dist. Ct. (ea. dist.) Pa. 1970, U.S. Ct. Appeals (3d cir.) 1970. Assoc. Kleinbard, Bell & Brecker, Phila., 1970-74, ptnr., 1974-86, mng. ptnr., 1986—. Editor U. Pa. Law Rev. Mem. ABA, Pa. Bar Assn., Phila. Bar Assn., Thanatopsis Soc., U. Pa. Alumni Club, Order of Coif, Beta Alpha Psi, Beta Gamma Sigma (pres.). Office: Kleinbard Bell & Brecker 1900 Market St Ste 700 Philadelphia PA 19103-3573

BLACKMAN, SAMUEL WILLIAM, retired research chemist; b. N.Y.C., Aug. 25, 1913; s. Jacob and Ethel (Rose) B.; m. Clara Gershunoff, Nov. 19, 1939; children: Susan Betty, Elinor Ann, Joan Sara. AB, Cornell U., 1935; MS, NYU, 1937; PhD, Polytechnic U., Bklyn., 1960. Analytical chemist Premo Pharm. Labs., N.Y.C., 1935-41; rsch. chemist Hoffman LaRoche, Nutley, N.J., 1941-44, Burroughs Wellcome, Tuckahoe, N.Y., 1944-70; patent cons. Onyx Chem. Co., Jersey City, 1971-89; prof. organic chemistry Yeshiva U., N.Y.C., 1960-79. Mem. Am. Chem. Soc. Home: 1349 Lexington Ave New York NY 10128-1511

BLACKMUN, HARRY ANDREW, U.S. Supreme Court justice; b. Nashville, Ill., Nov. 12, 1908; s. Corwin Manning and Theo H. (Reuter) B.; m. Dorothy E. Clark, June 21, 1941; children: Nancy Clark, Sally Ann, Susan Manning. B.A. summa cum laude in Math, Harvard U., 1929, LL.B., 1932; numerous hon. degrees. Bar: Minn. 1932. Law clk. to judge U.S. Ct. Appeals (8th cir.), St. Paul, 1932-33; assoc. Dorsey, Colman, Barker, Scott & Barber, Mpls., 1934-38, jr. ptnr., 1939-42, gen. ptnr., 1943-50; instr. St. Paul Coll. Law, 1935-41, U. Minn. Law Sch., 1945-47; resident counsel Mayo Clinic, Mayo Assn., Rochester, Minn., 1950-59; mem. sect. adminstrn. Mayo Clinic, 1950-59; judge 8th Cir. U.S. Ct. of Appeals, 1959-70; assoc. justice U.S. Supreme Ct., 1970—; chmn. faculty Salzburg Seminar in Am. Studies, July 1977, mem. faculty, July 1989; mem. bd. dirs. Mayo Assn. Rochester, 1953-60; mem. adv. com. in jud. activities Jud Conf., 1969-79; co-moderator seminar on justice and soc. Aspen (Colo.) Inst., 1979-92, seminar on constl. justice and soc., Aspen Inst. Italia, Rome, 1986; vis. instr. Constl. Law La. State U. Law Sch., Summer Session at Aix-en-Provence, France, 1986, 92; participant seminar on the role of cts. in Soc. Hebrew U., 1986; vis. instr. in constln. law Tulane U. summer session, Berlin, 1992. Contbr. articles to legal, med. jours. Bd. dirs., mem. exec. com. Rochester Meth. Hosp., 1954-70; trustee Hamline Univ., St. Paul, 1964-70, William Mitchell Coll. Law, St. Paul, 1959-74; jud. mem. Nat. Hist. Publs. and Records Commn., 1975-82, 86—; participant Franco-Am. Colloquium on Human Rights, Paris, 1979. Mem. ABA, Minn. Bar Assn., Olmsted County Bar Assn., 32 Jud. Dist. Bar Assn., Phi Beta Kappa. Office: US Supreme Ct 1 1st St NE Washington DC 20543

BLACKSMITH, WILLIAM AUGUST, IV, counselor; b. Harrisburg, Pa., Nov. 25, 1963; s. William August III and Linda Diane (Hall) B. BE, Ind. U. of Pa., 1986, MEd, 1987. Cert. secondary tchr., counselor, Pa. Sci. tchr. Susquenita Sch. Dist., Duncannon, Pa., 1987-88; grad. student Ind. U. Pa., Indiana, 1988-89; sch. counselor Northwestern Lehigh Sch. Dist., New Tripoli, Pa., 1989-90, Clearfield (Pa.) Area Sch. Dist., 1990-91, Cen. Cambria (Pa.) Sch. Dist., Edensburg, Pa., 1991—. Editor: (newsletter) Counselor Edn. Newsletter, 1986-87. Mem. AACD, Am. Sch. Counselors Assn., Pa. State Edn. Assn. Presbyterian. Home: 129 E High St Apr 1-R Ebensburg PA 15931 Office: Cen Cambria Mid Sch 205 W Highland Ave Ebensburg PA 15931

BLACKSON, BENJAMIN F(RANKLIN), clinical social worker; b. Newark, Del., Nov. 4, 1933; s. Benjamin Franklin and Lulu Etta (Taylor) B.; m. Sirletta Fordelma Belcher, Feb. 28, 1957 (dec. Aug. 1990); children: Benita, Barbara. BS, Trenton State Coll., 1972; MSW, MBA, Rutgers U., 1975; MSW advanced cert., U. Pa., 1980; D of Human Service, The Fielding Inst., DHS, 1988. Bd. cert. diplomate in clin. social work; cert. social work. Commd. USAF, 1952, advanced through grades to maj., 1975, air traffic contr., 1952-59, multi engine pilot, 1957-65, 75-85; ret. USAFR, 1985; mem. Blackson Enterprises, Bordentown, N.J., 1969-81; CEO B.E. Inc., Bordentown, 1975—; cons. USAFR. vice-chmn. Bordentown Recreation Com., 1973. Fellow Am. Orthopsychiat. Assn.; mem. Acad. Cert. Clin. Social Worker, Nat. Assn. Social Workers (clin. chmn. N.J. 1978-80), Nat. Fedn. Socs. for Clin. Social Work, Am. Assn. Sex Edn. Counselors and Therapists. Home and Office: 200 Mary St Bordentown NJ 08505-1816

BLACKSTONE, PATRICIA CLARK, bank officer, psychotherapist; b. Louisville, June 30, 1952; d. Robert Phillips and Jeanne Orr (Rice) Clark; m. Patrick H. Thorpe, June 8, 1974 (div. March 1981); m. William M. Blackstone II, Nov. 2, 1985. BA, Indiana U., 1974; MEd, U. North Tex., 1990. Mgr. Citizens Fidelity Bank & Trust Co., Louisville, 1974-77; pers. mgr. Am. Gen. Corp., Houston, 1977-81; asst. v.p. human resources MCorp (name now BANK ONE), Dallas, 1983-87, 90; v.p. adminstrn. Tex.-PCS Industries, Inc., Dallas, 1987-89; mgr. employment and tng. First Nat. Bank Pa., Erie, Pa., 1990-92; mgr. employee rels. Bank One, Akron, Ohio, 1992—; cons. First Am. Bankshares, Washington, 1987, Interstate Battery Co. Am., Dallas, 1987, Guaranty Fed. Savs. Bank, Dallas, 1989, BANK ONE, Tex., 1990, Lake Erie Presbytery, Erie, Pa.; cert. instr. Main Event Mgmt. Corp., Sacramento, 1977-81. Co-author: (with William M. Blackstone II) (workshop) Preparing for Christian Marriage, 1987. Ruling elder edn. Preston Hollow Presbyn. Ch., Dallas, 1987-90, First Presbyn. Ch. of the Covenant, Erie, Pa., 1992—; mem. Dallas Mus. Art, 1985-87, The 500, Inc., Dallas, 1986, First Presbyn. Ch. Covenant, 1990—. Fellow Life Mgmt. Inst.; mem. Soc. Human Resources Mgmt. (designated Sr. Profl. in Human Resources 1990), Am. Soc. Tng. and Devel. (bd. dirs. Erie Tri-State chpt.), Am. Inst. Banking (bd. dirs. Erie/Crawford chpt.), Am. Assn. Counseling and Devel. Democrat. Presbyterian. Office: Bank One Akron NA 50 S Main St Akron OH 44301-1280

BLACKSTONE, PAUL CARROLL, chemical engineer; b. Perham, Maine, May 31, 1930; s. Carroll Fayette and Glenna Blanche (Estey) B. Student, U. Maine, 1947-49; BSChemE, U. R.I., 1955. Staff chem. engr. Cranston (R.I.) Print Works, 1955-61; process engr. Lever Bros. Co., Edgewater, N.J., 1961-69, sr. devel. engr., 1969-76, prin. devel. project engr., 1976-81; AEGIS tech. change coord., sr. mem. engring. staff RCA/GE Aerospace, Moorestown, N.J., 1981—. Inventor, experimenter with detergents; contbr. articles to profl. jours. Chmn. Non-Partisan Citizens' Com., Seekonk, Mass., 1955-58. Mem. Elfun Soc. Home: 214 Park Ave Collingswood NJ 08108

BLACKWELL, JAMES MADISON, IV, publishing consultant; b. N.Y.C., Feb. 5, 1931; s. James Madison and Betsy Rich (Talbot) b.; m. Amanda Cushman, July 11, 1957 (div. Apr. 15, 1960); m. Anne Hardwick Stires, Apr. 6, 1963; children: Stephen, Hillary, Carolyn. AB, Harvard U., 1952. Asst. prodn. mgr. Street & Smith Publs., Inc., N.Y.C., 1954-59; asst. bus. mgr. Conde Nast Publs., Inc., N.Y.C., 1959-63; prodn. mgr. Newsweek, Inc., N.Y.C., 1963-66, editorial ops. dir., 1966-72, sr. editor, 1972-85; pub. cons. Blackwell Cons., Ridgefield, Conn., 1985—. Mem. sch. bd., Ridgefield, Conn., 1973-77. Sgt. U.S. Army, 1952-54. Mem. Assn. Publ. Prodn. Mgrs. (pres. 1962-63), Graphic Communications Assn. (mem. exec. com. 1986-88), Rsch. and Engring. Coun. Graphic Arts (mem. exec. com. 1987-89), Tech. Assn. Graphic Arts, Harvard Club, Silver Spring Country Club. Home and Office: 20 Old South Salem Rd Ridgefield CT 06877-4827

BLACKWELL, LUCIEN E., congressman. Former longshoreman and city union local pres.; former chmn. Phila. Gas Commn.; former state rep.; former city councilman Phila.; mem. 102nd Congress from 2nd dist. Pa., 1991—. With U.S. Army. Office: 1725 Longworth Washington DC 20515-3802*

BLACKWOOD, WILLIAM JONATHAN, marketing executive; b. Little Rock, Apr. 8, 1953; s. William Harold and Bonnie Esther (Harrod) B. BA, Ark. Tech. U., 1979. Mktg. coord. Wittenberg, Delony & Davidson, Little Rock, 1980-82; mgr. account svcs. CRS Sirrine, Inc., Houston, 1982-86; mgr. tech. communications Western Stress, Inc., Houston, 1986; dir. mktg. Helpern Architects, N.Y.C., 1986-88; sr. assoc., dir. corp. communications Ryan Gibson Bauer Kornblath, P.A., N.Y.C., 1988-91; regional mktg. dir. Perkins & Will Architects, N.Y.C., 1991—. Mem. Soc. Mktg. Profl. Svcs. (bd. dirs. Houston chpt. 1982-85, N.Y.C. chpt. 1989-91, mem. long range planning com. 1988, 1st place award for ann. report 1985), Adminstrv. Mgmt. Soc. (pres. N.Y.C. chpt. 1987-88). Democrat. Presbyterian. Home: 208 W 23d St Apt 716 New York NY 10011-2306 Office: Perkins & Will 1 Park Ave New York NY 10016-5802

BLAESE, R(OBERT) MICHAEL, biomedical researcher, physician; b. Mpls., Feb. 16, 1939; s. Robert Marion and Eva Ruth Blaese; m. Julianne Eleanor Johnson, june 23, 1962; children: Elise, Kristianne. BS, Gustavus Adolphus, 1961; MD, U. Minn., 1964. Cert. Am. Bd. Allergy and Immunology. Intern internal medicine Parkland Meml. Hosp., Dallas, 1964-65; resident pediatrics U. Minn. Hosps., Mpls., 1965-66; clin. assoc. metabolism br. Nat. Cancer Inst., NIH, Bethesda, Md., 1966-68, sr. investigator metabolism br., 1968—, chief cellular immunology sect. metabolism br., 1973—, dep. chief metabolism br., 1985—; mem. sci. adv. bvd. Genetic Therapy, Inc., Gaithersburg, Md., 1985-88. Assoc. editor Jour. Immunology, 1972-78; author over 250 sci. rsch. reports, chpts. to books, etc., 1964—. Sr. surgeon USPHS, 1966-68. Recipient Mead Johnson award for rsch. in pediatrics Am. Acad. Pediatrics, 1980, USPHS Superior Svc. award, 1985, Maxwell Finland award Infectious Disease Soc., 1991. Fellow AAAS; mem. Soc. for Pediatric Rsch., Am. Soc. for Clin. Investigation, Am. Assn. Immunologists, Am. Fedn. for Clin. Rsch. Office: NIH Bldg 10 Rm 6B05 Bethesda MD 20892

BLAI, BERTHA, ceramics educator, artist; b. Balt., May 24, 1915; d. Abraham and Mollie Rosenberg; m. Boris Blai (dec. 1985); children: Anita, Ruth. BFA, Temple U., 1965. Instr., ceramics Ocean County (N.J.) Coll., 1968-69; instr., head ceramics dept. DuCret Sch. Art, North Plainfield, N.J., 1969-74; artist-in-residence, ceramics Glassboro (N.J.) State Coll., 1972-75; instr., ceramics Blai Master Workshop, Melrose Park, Pa., 1976-85, Logan Square East, Phila., 1985-91; head ceramics dept., instr., ceramics counselor Camp Scatico, Elizaville, N.Y., 1989—; studied with Rudy Staffel, Raymond Gallucci, Toshicko Takieusi, Karen Karnes, others. Exhibited in group shows at Phila. Civic Ctr., 1970, Paley Libr. Temple U., 1971, Widener Coll., Chester, Pa., 1972, others. Mem. Pa. Guild Crafts (hon. mem.), Long Beach Island Found. Arts & Scis. (hon. mem.). Home and office: 1500 Locust St Apt 313P Philadelphia PA 19102-4328

BLAINE, FREDERICK MATTHEW, artist, educator; b. Balt., May 24, 1947; s. George William and Pauline Elizabeth (Carroll) B.; m. Dona Watson Foulk, Jan. 26, 1968; 1 child, Michael William. BA, U. Miss., 1970; postgrad., Towson U. Lic. tchr. secondary art. Owner, operator Broad Creek Pottery, Laurel, Del., 1972-88; asst. prof. art Salisbury (Md.) State U., 1983, guest lectr., 1984-88; tchr. aft Seaford (Del.) High Sch., 1970—; chmn. art dept. Seaford Sch. Dist., 1986—; conductor workshops Md., Del., 1988—. Trustee Rehoboth (Del.) Art League, 1988—; councilman Town of Laurel, Del., 1975-83, commr. of police, 1977-83, mem. urban devel. commn., 1981-82, mem. pub. works commn., 1975-77. Mem. Internat. Soc. Copier Artists, Del. Art Educators Assn. Home: 908 West St Laurel DE 19956-1932

BLAIR, B(ALLARD) GLENN, podiatrist; b. Providence, Dec. 18, 1957; s. Ballard Glenn and C. Mafalda (Angelone) B.; m. Emily E. Tirpaeck, June 25, 1982; children: Hillary Candice, Madeline Evelyn. BS in Microbiology, U. R.I., 1980; D of Podiatric Medicine, Coll. Podiatric Medicine & Surgery, 1986. Diplomate Am. Bd. Podiatry Examiners. Podiatric surg. resident West Haven (Conn.) Veterans Hosp., 1986-88; pvt. practice Shelton, Conn., 1988—, Bridgeport, Conn., 1992—; clin. asst. instr. U. Osteopathic Medicine, Coll. Podiatric Medicine & Surgery, Des Moines, Iowa, 1986—. Mem. Am. Coll. Foot Surgeons (eligible), Am. Bd. Podiatric Surgery (eligible). Republican. Roman Catholic. Office: 513 Howe Ave Shelton CT 06484-3157 also: 4920 Main St Bridgeport CT 06606

BLAIR, CHARLES LEE, physician; b. Stamford, Conn., May 1, 1954; s. Charles Francis Jr. and Mae E. (Gallmoyer) B.; m. Ellen Jill Weiss; children: Eric Charles, Melanie Alison. BA, U. Vt., 1976; MD, U. Conn., 1981. Diplomate Am. Bd. Psychiatry and Neurology. Resident in psychiatry U. Conn. Sch. Medicine, Farmington, 1981-85; John C. Leonard fellow Hartford (Conn.) Hosp., 1985-86, dir. psychiat. edn., 1988-90; pvt. practice Hartford, 1985—; mem. psychiatry residency tng. com. U. Conn. Sch. Medicine, Farmington, 1983-84, 88-90. Rock Sleyster Meml. scholar AMA, 1980-81. Mem. APA, Conn. Psychiat. Soc., Hartford County Med. Assn., Hartford Psychiat. Soc. (treas. 1991-92), Phi Beta Kappa. Home: 11 Foxcroft Rd West Hartford CT 06119-1150 Office: 100 Retreat Ave Ste 612 Hartford CT 06106-2587

BLAIR, DAVID WILLIAM, mechanical engineer; b. Santa Barbara, Calif., Oct. 5, 1929; s. David Sutherland and Norah Mildred (Higgins) B.; m. Rosemary Constance Miles, Jan. 30, 1954; children: Karen E., Barbara A., M. Maria, Amanda M., David B. O., Rachel P. BS, Oreg. State U., 1952; MS, Columbia U., 1954, PhD, 1961. From asst. to instr. mech. engring. Columbia U., N.Y.C., 1952-58; rsch. assoc. Princeton (N.J.) U., 1958-61; rsch. scientist AeroChem Rsch. Labs., Princeton, 1961-62; postdoctoral fellow Royal Norwegian Coun. Indsl. and Engring. Rsch., Kjeller, Norway, 1962-63; assoc. prof. Polytechnic Inst. Bklyn., 1962-69; engring. assoc. Corp. Rsch. Labs. Exxon Rsch. and Engring. Co., Linden, N.J., 1969-83; pres. Princeton Sci. Enterprises, Inc., 1985—. Contbr. articles to Handbook of the Engring. Scis., AIAA Jour., Jour. Quantitative Spectroscopy and Radiative Transfer, Environ. Sci. and Tech.; patentee for multi-stage process for combusting fuels containing fixed-nitrogen chemical species, efficient high temperature radiant furnace. Mem. Princeton Township Com., 1975-82, Princeton Joint Commn. on Civil Rights, 1975-87. Mem. Am. Inst. Chem. Engrs., Am. Phys. Soc., Combustion Inst., Sigma Xi, Tau Beta Pi, Sigma Tau, Phi Kappa Phi, Pi Mu Epsilon, Pi Tau Sigma. Democrat. Home and Office: Princeton Sci Enterprises Inc 1108 Kingston Rd Princeton NJ 08540-4132

BLAIR, LESTER WINSTON, physician, medical educator; b. Bronx, N.Y., Dec. 17, 1949; s. Lester Winston and Verna (Witter) B. BA, Columbia Coll, 1970, MD, 1974. Asst. prof. clin. medicine Coll. Physicians and Surgeons Columbia U., N.Y.C., 1979-83; clin. asst. prof. medicine Sch. Medicine NYU, N.Y.C., 1983—; dir. pulmonary and crit. care medicine N.Y. Downtown Hosp., N.Y.C., 1986—; pres. PVN Med. Diagnostics, N.Y.C., 1989—; sec. DMA Med. Group, N.Y.C., 1989—. Fellow ACP, Am. Coll. Chest Physicians. Office: 170 William St New York NY 10038-2612

BLAIR, PATRICIA WOHLGEMUTH, economics writer; b. N.Y.C., Nov. 30, 1929; m. James P. Blair, Aug. 13, 1964; children: David A., Matthew W. BA with honors, Wellesley Coll., 1950; MA, Haverford Coll., 1952. Officer U.S. Agy. Internat. Devel., New Delhi, 1953-55, 63-64; editor Carnegie Endowment for Internat. Peace, N.Y.C., 1956-63, Devel. Digest, Nat. Planning Assn., Washington, 1965-68; staff assoc. Commn. on Internat. Devel., World Bank, Washington, 1969-70; ind. cons., writer, editor, 1970—. Editor: Health Needs of the World's Poor Women, 1980; contbr. articles to profl. publs. Mem. adv. com. Unitarian-Universalist Holdeen India Fund, Washington, 1984—; bd. dirs. Equity Policy Ctr., Washington, 1980-85. Mem. Soc. Internat. Devel. (internat. governing coun. 1975-79), Assn. Women in Devel., Asia Soc., World Affairs Coun. Home and Office: 1411 30th St NW Washington DC 20007-3141

BLAIR, SIDNEY ROBERT, petroleum company executive; b. Port of Spain, Trinidad, Aug. 13, 1929; s. Sidney Martin and Janet (Gentleman) B.; m. Lois Wedderburn, June 13, 1953; children: Megan, James, Robert, Martin, Charlotte. BS, Queens U., 1951. Field engr., mgr. constrn. of gas and oil pipe lines and refineries, 1951-58; dir. gas ops. and purchasing Alta. (Can.) and So. Gas Co. Ltd. and affiliates, 1959-69; exec. v.p. The Alta. Gas Trunk Line Co. Ltd., 1969-70, pres., chief exec. officer, from 1970; former pres., chmn. bd. dirs. Husky Oil Ltd. subs. Calgary; chmn., chief exec. officer, dir. Nova Corp. Alta., Calgary, 1988-91, hon. dir., chmn. emeritus, 1991—. Office: Nova Corp Alta, 801 7th Ave SW, Calgary, AB Canada T2P 2N6

BLAIR-LARSEN, SUSAN MARGARET, educator; b. Plainfield, N.J., May 28, 1950; d. Adam Craig and Edith Elizabeth (Wessel) Blair; m. Bruce Osborn Larsen, July 15, 1989. BS, Castleton (Vt.) State Coll., 1972; MS, U. Scranton, Pa., 1974; EdD, U. Pa., 1984. Tchr. Palisades Sch. Dist., Kintnersville, Pa., 1973-75; reading specialist Lakewood (N.J.) Sch. Dist., 1975-84; prof. U. Minn., Morris, 1984-85, Rutgers U., Newark, 1985-88, Trenton (N.J.) State Coll., 1988—; evaluator Literacy Vols. of Am., Toms River, N.J. Editor: Higher Education and Reading Instruction, 1988. Mem. Mantoloking and Bay Head (N.J.) Women's Rep. Club. Mem. N.J. Assn. Tchr. Educators (exec. bd. 1989-90, v.p. 1990-92), N.J. Reading Assn. (bd. dirs. 1988-91), Internat. Reading Assn., Ocean County Coun. Reading, Ea. Ednl. Rsch. Assn., Phi Delta Kappa (Ten Yr. award 1990), Pi Lambda Theta. Roman Catholic.

BLAIS, PIERRE, Canadian government minister; b. Berthier-sur-Mer, Que., Can., Dec. 30, 1948; s. Edmond and Marguerite (Mercier) B.; m. Chantal Fournier, June 4, 1972; children: Marie-Hélène, Pierre-François, David, Julie. Grad., Laval U. Dir. recreation City of Montmagny, Can., 1974-76; sec.-treas. Le Havre de Berthier-sur-mer, 1978-83; pres. Caisse Populaire, Berthier-sur-mer, 1978-84; mem. Ho. of Commons, Can., 1984—, parliamentary sec. to minister of agr., 1984, parliamentary sec. to dep. prime minister, 1986, minister of agr., 1987—, solicitor gen. of Can., 1989-90, min. consumer and corp. affairs, 1990—. Progressive Conservative. Roman Catholic. Office: House of Commons, Parliament Bldgs, Ottawa, ON Canada K1A 0A6

BLAISDELL, ERNEST ATWELL, mathematics educator; b. Brewer, Maine, Jan. 10, 1940; s. E. Atwell Blaisdell and Thelma (Turner) Fitz; m. Judith A. St. Lawrence, June 20, 1959; children: Lee Ann, Mark A. BA, U. Maine, Orono, 1962, MA, 1964; PhD, Temple U., 1979. Instr. math. Clarkson Coll. Tech., Potsdam, N.Y., 1964-68; asst. prof. math. Elizabethtown (Pa.) Coll., 1968-70, assoc. prof. math., 1970-80, prof. math., 1980—; cons. in field. Author: Minitab Supplement for Statistics, 1988, 90, Statistics in Practice, 1992; contbr. papers to profl. publs. Recipient John F. Steinman award Elizabethtown Coll., 1980. Mem. AAUP (treas. 1986—), Am. Statis. Assn., Math. Assn. Am., Sigma Xi, Phi Kappa Phi, Pi Mu Epsilon. Home: 606 Aspen Ln Lebanon PA 17042-9001 Office: Elizabethtown Coll Elizabethtown PA 17022

BLAKE, CARL, marketing executive; b. Hot Springs, Ark., June 19, 1935; s. Carlton LeRoy and Elfie Mae (Bacon) B.; m. Irene Elvin, Feb. 14, 1982. BS, Tex. Christina U., 1957; B of Fgn. Trade, Am. Grad. Sch. Internat. Mgmt., 1967; MBA, Fairleigh Dickinson U., 1982. Mgr. Plasta-Flex div. C.L. Blake & Assocs., Ft. Worth, 1958-66; mktg. mgr. Philip Morris Internat., Caracas, Venezuela and Buenos Aires, 1967-71; dir. internat. mktg. Joseph Dixon Crucible Co., Jersey City, 1973-83; mgr. worldwide mktg. Capital Controls Co., Colmar, Pa., 1986-89, internat. mktg. cons., 1990—; adj. prof. internat. mktg. Montclair (N.J.) State Coll., 1983. Contbr. articles on mktg. to various publs. Organizer, Tarrant County Rep. Party, Ft. Worth, 1960-62, precinct chmn., 1961-62, asst. County chmn., 1962. Mem. Assn. Polit. Risk Analysts, TAPPI, Instrument Soc. Am., Am. Mgmt. Assn., Coun. Internat. Bus. Risk Mgmt. Home: 150 Shoen Rd Exton PA 19341-2100

BLAKE, JAMES JOSEPH, English educator; b. N.Y.C., Apr. 29, 1939; s. Patrick Joseph and Mary (Blake) B. BA, Manhattan Coll., 1962; MA, NYU, 1964, PhD, 1979. Asst. prof. Nassau Community Coll., Garden City, N.Y., 1965-71, assoc. prof., 1972-83, prof., 1984—; instr. Gaelic Soc. of N.Y., 1978-80; adj. assoc. prof. John Jay Coll., CUNY, 1980-81, Queens Coll., CUNY, 1982; adj. prof. Coll. Arts and Sci., NYU, 1988—, Grad. Sch. NYU, 1991—; broadcaster Sta. WFUV-FM, Fordham U., 1978—. Editor-in-chief Éire-Ireland: Jour. of Irish Studies, St. Paul, Minn., 1986-89; contbr. articles to profl. jours. Pres. Gaelic Soc. of N.Y., 1979-80; exec. com. Columbia U. Seminar on Irish Studies, N.Y.C., 1981—. Fulbright fellow Trinity Coll., Ireland, 1969-71, Mellon fellow Grad. Ctr., CUNY, 1987; NEH grantee U. Rochester, 1989; faculty rsch. scholar SUNY, 1990—. Mem. MLA (chair discussion group for the two-yr. coll., exec. com. 1986-90, celtic studies dir. ann. Internat. Bibliography 1978—, rep. to del. assembly parliamentary body 1981-83, 87-89), Am. Conf. for Irish Studies (sec. sub-com. on Irish lang.). Home: 230 E 15th St Apt 9P New York NY 10003-3946 Office: English Dept NYU 19 University Pl New York NY 10003-4501

BLAKE, JEANNETTE BELISLE, psychotherapist; b. Manchester, N.H., Aug. 1, 1920; d. Emile Henry and Mathilda Cecelia (Martin) Belisle; m. Roland Oscar Royer, Sept. 6, 1937 (div. 1948); 1 child, Dorothy Marie Royer Lyman; m. Albert Willard Blake Sr., Aug. 11, 1979. Cons. Al Blake Advt. Cons., Manchester, N.H., 1959-68; pvt. practice Manchester, 1968—; founder, dir. N.H. Metaphys. Establishment, Manchester, 1976—; presenter workshops in field. Recipient medal N.H. Metaphysicians, 1978; cert. Greater Manchester Mental Health Ctr., 1985, 86. Mem. AACD, N.H. Assn. for Counseling and Devel., N.H. Assn. of Family Counselors, Am. Assn. of Mental Health Counselors (N.H. br.), Therapeutic Touch Healing (Manchester and Nashau chpts.), Soc. for Psychic Rsch. of N.H. and Mass. (adv. bd.), Assn. for Psychical Rsch. of Fla. Roman Catholic. Home and Office: 131 Russell St Manchester NH 03104-3769

BLAKE, JEFFREY MICHAEL, photography educator, artist; b. Akron, Ohio, Oct. 25, 1954; s. Harold D. and Patricia (Smith) B. BA in Philosophy, U. Akron, 1978; MFA, Temple U., 1981. Instr. photography St. Joseph's Univ., Phila., 1982—, photographer, Univ. Press, 1987—; adj. faculty Stockton State Coll., Pomona, N.J., 1982, Bucks County Community Coll., Newtown, Pa., 1982-87; instr. photography Moore Coll. of Art, Phila., 1985-86. Represented in permanent collections at The Mus. of Modern Art, N.Y.C., The Met. Mus. Art, N.Y.C., The Phila. (Pa.) Mus. Art, Allentown (Pa.) Art Mus., The Univ. Okla. Mus. Art, Norman, Erie (Pa.) Art Mus., Haverford (Pa.) Coll. Collection; one person shows Janvier Gallery, Univ. Del., Newark, 1988, The Photography Gallery, Sacramento, 1989, The Pitts. (Pa.) Filmmakers Gallery, 1991, others; various group exhibitions. Named Guggenheim fellow Guggenheim Found., N.Y.C., 1991. Mem. Coll. Art Assn., Phi Sigma Tau. Office: St Josephs Univ 5600 City Ave Philadelphia PA 19131-1376

BLAKE, ROBERT FREDERICK, media relations and broadcast executive; b. N.Y.C., Oct. 20, 1915; s. Joseph Everett and Vivian (Parker) B. Student, pub. and pvt. schs., N.Y.C. Motion picture editor The New Yorker Mag., N.Y.C., 1937-39; continuity editor WOR, N.Y.C., 1939-41; dir. publicity WOR/WWOR-TV, N.Y.C., 1945-50; owned station div. NBC, N.Y.C., 1951-53; dir. press info. CBS TV Network, Hollywood, Calif., 1954-60; dir. pub. info. Group W (Westinghouse Broadcasting Co.), N.Y.C., 1960-74; dir. pub. relations WPIX, Inc., N.Y.C., 1974-80; dir. press info. CBS Cable Div., N.Y.C., 1980-83; pres. pub. relations/TV prodn. Robert Blake Enterprises, Inc., Bridgehampton, N.Y., 1983—; cons. Primetime Entertainment Inc., N.Y.C., 1984—. Contbr. articles to Stars and Stripes, and Yank Mag. Served with USAF, 1941-45, ETO. Decorated Bronze Star. Mem. NATAS (founding mem. N.Y. chpt., 1956), media rels. cons. 1988—, Overseas Press Club. Home: Brick Kiln Rd Bridgehampton NY 11932-9999 Office: 111 W 57th St Ste 1020 New York NY 10019-2271

BLAKELEY, HELEN BEATTY, real estate executive; b. Miami Beach, Fla., Aug. 31, 1954; d. John Francis and Jacquelyn (Coogan) Beatty; m. Bradford Williams Blakeley, June 17, 1979 (div. 1990). BA magna cum laude, Boston Coll., 1976. Sr. buyer Mark, Fore & Strike, Del Ray Beach, Fla., 1976-78; dir. mktg. Co-Mark Devel., Boston, 1979-81; pres. Investre Corp., Boston, 1981-83; v.p. The Mayhood Co., McLean, Va., 1983-91; pres. Blakeley & Assoc., Washington, 1991—. Election staff Sharon Pratt Dixon Mayor, Washington, 1990. Mem. Washington Sales and Mktg. coun. (com. mem. 1984-92), Comml. Real Estate Women (CREW). Home: 4609 MacArthur Blvd NW Washington DC 20007

BLAKELY, JAMES RUSSELL, publishing company executive, financial editor; b. Princeton, Ind., Mar. 21, 1935; s. Russell Harold and Mildred Mae (Newman) B.; B.A., U. Ill., 1957, postgrad. in law, 1957-58; children—Karen Holmes, Thomas Howard. Reporter, Champaign (Ill.) News-Gazette, 1964-65; feature writer Sunday mag. Chgo. American, 1965-67; consumer affairs editor Rochester (N.Y.) Democrat and Chronicle, 1967-72; asst. editor Consumer Reports Mag., Mt. Vernon, N.Y., 1972-74; mng. editor Gold & Silver Newsletter, New Rochelle, N.Y., 1974-76; editor/pub. Silver & Gold Report, Newtown, Conn., 1976-80, assoc. editor, 1985-88 ; editor/pub. Blakely's Commodity Rev., 1983-85; editor Gold Stocks Adv., Bethel, Conn., 1986-88; editor/pub. Gold Investment Review, Newtown, 1988—; pres., treas., bd. dir. Precious Metals Report, Inc., Newtown, 1976-80, Gold Coin Jewelry Corp., Newtown, 1979-80, Silver & Gold Money Mgmt. Corp., Newtown, 1978-80; pres., treas., bd. dir. James Blakely Investments, Inc., Sandy Hook, 1980—; chmn. dir., pres. Gold Investment Rev., Inc., Sandy Hook, 1988—. With AUS, 1958-59. Mem. Soc. Profl. Journalists, Internat. Precious Metals Inst., Com. for Monetary Reform and Edn., Phi Alpha Theta, Theta Delta Chi. Club: Nat. Press. Office: PO Drawer A Sandy Hook CT 06482

BLAKE-MACINTOSH, MONICA BERNADETTE, artist; b. Phila., Sept. 27, 1957; d. Lawrence John and Alice Elizabeth (Spering) Blake; m. Williami Leslie MacIntosh, Oct. 9, 1982. Student, Pa. State U., 1976; AS, Art Inst. Phila., 1979. Artist Quicksilver Printing Svcs., Bryn Mawr, Pa., 1979-84; art dir. BPM Enterprises Inc., Merion Station, Pa., 1984-91; artist, designer To Coin A Phrase, Bridgeport, Pa., 1991. Designer: Type Catalog, 1983 (Neographic award 1983). Republican. Roman Catholic. Home: 40 N Brookside Rd Media PA 19064-2503

BLAKESLEE, GEORGE EDWARD, education educator; b. Delaware, Ohio, Sept. 29, 1948; s. George Edward and Jean Carolyn (Humphreys) B.;m. Carolyn Lavonne Adams, Aug. 21, 1970; children: Marsha Lynn, Carrie Elizabeth, Allison Judith. BS in Edn., Miami U., Oxford, Ohio, 1970; MEd, Boston U., 1972, EdD, 1984. Sci. tchr. Weston (Mass.) High Sch., 1970-86; sci. chmn. Weston Middle and High Schs., 1979-86; assoc. prof. ednl. tech. Grad. Sch. Lesley Coll., Cambridge, Mass., 1986—; cons. Sturbridge (Mass.) Schs., 1986-87, Software Arts, Newton, Mass., 1984-85. Coauthor: Integrating Telecommunications Into Education, 1990. Scholarship Framingham (Mass.) Amateur Radio Assn., 1979-89. NSF grantee, 1988—. Mem. Nat. Biology Tchrs. Assn., Mass. Computer Using Educators, Nat. Geog. Soc., Am. Radio Relay League, Apple Programmers and Developers Assn. Office: Lesley Coll 29 Everett St Cambridge MA 02138-2790

BLAKLEY, BENJAMIN SPENCER, III, lawyer; b. DuBois, Pa., Sept. 1, 1952; s. Benjamin Spencer Jr. and Mary Jane (Campney) B.; m. Kathleen M. Ellermeyer, Oct. 20, 1989; children: Benjamin Spencer IV, Kevin Charles. BA, Grove City Coll., 1974; JD, Duquesne U., 1977. Bar: Pa. 1977. Ptnr. Blakley & Jones, DuBois, 1977—; pub. defender Clearfield (Pa.) County, 1977-84; instr. Pa. State U., DuBois, 1979-85. Mem. adv. bd. Salvation Army Pa. Corp., DuBois, 1978—, chmn., 1988-91; mem. DuBois Area Youth Aid Panel, 1984-87; mem. Citizens for Effective Govt., DuBois, 1985—; mem. DuBois Ednl. Found., 1990—; trustee DuBois Vol. Fire Dept., 1986-87, treas., 1987-90; bd. dirs. DuBois Sr. and Commun. Ctr., 1992—. Mem. Pa. Bar Assn., Clearfield County Bar Assn. Democrat. Methodist. Office: Blakley & Jones PO Box 6 90 Beaver Dr Du Bois PA 15801

BLANC, PETER (WILLIAM PETERS BLANC), sculptor, painter; b. N.Y.C., June 29, 1912; s. Edward H. and Martha Elliott (King) B. B.A., Harvard U.; LL.B., St. Johns U.; postgrad., Corcoran Sch. Art.; M.A., Am. U. Instr. Am. U., Washington, 1950-53. One-man shows include Passedoit Gallery, 1951, 53, 58, Albert Landry Galleries, N.Y., 1960, La Galeria Escondida, Taos, 1955, Hudson River Mus., 1961, 65, Associated Artists Gallery, Washington, 1962, Amel Gallery, N.Y.C., 1964, Ft. Worth Art Mus., 1966, Thomson Gallery, N.Y.C., 1969, Benson Gallery, Bridgehampton, N.Y., 1969, Southampton Coll., 1971, Avanti Galleries, N.Y.C., 1974, Elaine Benson Gallery, Bridgehampton, 1979, Goat Alley Gallery, Sag Harbor, N.Y., 1984, 86, 91, Benton Gallery, Southampton, N.Y., 1988; group shows include Whitney Mus. Am. Art, 1952, City Art Mus., St. Louis, 1951, Washington Water Color Club, 1949, 51, 52, Riverside Mus., 1950, 54, 58, 64, New Sch. for Social Research, 1956, Springfield Mus. Art, 1952, Nat. Collection Fine Art, Washington, 1953, Balt. Mus. Art, 1953, Bklyn. Mus., 1955, Fogg Mus. Art, 1959, NYU, 1960, St. Paul Gallery, 1961, Internat. Gallery N.Y., 1961, Fort Worth Art Mus., 1963, Assoc. Art Gallery, Washington, 1961, Hudson River Mus., 1965, Parrish Art Mus., Southampton, N.Y., 1965, Benson Gallery, Bridgehampton, N.Y., 1966-67, 77, Daniels Gallery, N.Y.C., 1965, East Hampton Guild Hall, N.Y.C., 1966-67, 73, Southampton (N.Y.) Coll., 1967-72, Iona Coll., N.Y., 1968, Mercy Coll., N.Y., 1970, Ashawagh Hall, Springs, N.Y., 1971-77, 80, 82-87, 89, 91, Artists Equity Assn., N.Y.C., 1975, N.Y. Artists-Union Carbide Gallery, N.Y.C., 1975, 77, Art Guild, N.Y.C., 1976, Abe Rattner Ctr. for Arts, Sag Harbor, N.Y., 1979, Guild Hall Mus., East Hampton, 1980, 86, 87, 89, Rattner Meml. Studio, Sag Harbor, 1980, Jacob K. Javits Fed. Bldg., N.Y.C., 1983, Old Jail Art Ctr., Albany, Tex., Lever House, N.Y.C., 1985, Goat Alley Gallery, Sag Harbor, 1983-91, Gallery Art 54, N.Y.C., 1986, Taos Arts Festival, N. Mex., 1986, Benton Gallery, Southampton, N.Y., 1987-90, Westbeth Galleries, N.Y.C., 1988-91. Lt. U.S. Army, 1944-46. Recipient awards Corcoran Gallery Art, 1949, awards Soc. Washington Artists, 1951, 53, awards Washington Water Color Club, 1949, 52. Mem. Spiral Group, N.Y. Artists Equity Assn. (dir. 1963-70), Artists Guild Washington (pres. 1951-53), Soc. Washington Artists, Proto-V Group, Am. Soc. Contemporary Artists. Home (winter): 161 W 75th St New York NY 10023 Home (summer): Jermain Ave and Palmer Terr Sag Harbor NY 11963

BLANCATO, ROBERT BENEDICT, university administrator; b. Bronxville, N.Y., Mar. 30, 1951; s. Louis Sebastian and Nancy (Benedict) B.; m. Janice Marie Blancato, July 20, 1985. BA in Govt., Georgetown U., 1973; MPA, Am. U., 1985. Legis. asst., adminstrv. asst. Congressman Mario Biaggi, Washington, 1972-88; staff dir. subcom. on human svcs. U.S. House Aging Com., Washington, 1977-89; adminstr. 19th Congl. Dist. N.Y., Washington, 1988-89; exec.dir. Italian Am. Heritage Ctr., Cath. U., Washington, 1989—; dir. insts. and pub. policy Nat. Italian Am. Found., Washington, 1989—; adj. faculty New Sch. for Social Rsch., N.Y.C., 1983—, Hunter Coll., Brookdale Ctr. on Aging, N.Y.C., 1990—. Pres. bd. dirs. Nat. Meals on Wheels Found., 1990—. Mem. Nat. Coun. on Aging, Am. Soc. on Aging, Nat. Com. for Provention of Elder Abuse (1st v.p. 1990—), Order of Sons of Italy. Roman Catholic. Home: 138 N Jackson St Arlington VA 22201-1244 Office: Italian Am Heritage Ctr 3901 Harewood Rd NE Washington DC 20064-0001

BLANCHARD, ELWOOD P., JR., chemical company executive. Chmn. bd. Du Pont Can., E.I. du Pont de Nemours & Co., Wilmington, Del. Office: E I Du Pont de Nemours & Co 1007 N Market St Wilmington DE 19898-0001

BLANCHARD, HARRY RUSSELL, JR., temperament therapist; b. Williamsport, Pa., Sept. 4, 1950; s. Harry Russell and Charlene (Solt) B.; m. Dawn Schon, July 1, 1970; children: Harry, Samuel, Joycelyn, Abby. BS, Lock Haven U., 1971; MDiv, Ea. Bapt. Theol. Sem., Phila., 1977, D of Ministry, 1990; PhD, Emmanuel Bapt. U., Shelby, N.C., 1991. Lic. temperament therapist; lic. pastoral counselor. Elem. tchr. Selinsgrove (Pa.) Area Sch. Dist., 1971-72; parish min. Cen. Pa. Conf. of United Meth. Ch., Harrisburg, 1973-91; temperament therapist New Life Counseling Ctr., Harrisburg, 1991—; trustee Pa. Alcohol Edn. Found., Harrisburg, 1988, Pa. Coun. Alcohol Problems, Harrisburg, 1988; pres. Loyalsock Twp. Ministerium, Williamsport, 1990-91; short-term mission vol. United Meth. Ch., Harrisburg, 1980-91; chmn. sect. on vols. in mission Cen. Pa. Conf. United Meth. Ch., 1989-91; tour leader to Israel, 1985-90; chmn. social concerns United Chs. of Lycoming County, Williamsport, 1985. Author: A Manual for Leaders of Overseas Short-Term Volunteer Work Camps of the Central Pennsylvania Conference of the United Methodist Church, 1990. Elder United Meth. Ch.; sec. Human Rels. Com., Lycoming County, 1985—; treas., chaplain Windsor (Pa.) Vol. Fire Co., 1980—; pres. West Br. Commodore Computer User's Group, Williamsport, 1988, Internat. Student Coordinating Assn. of Lycoming County, 1990-91; bd. dirs. Planned Parenthood of Cen. Pa., York, 1979. Mem. Masons. Republican. Office: New Life Counseling Ctr 209 Calder St Harrisburg PA 17102-2625

BLANCHARD, JAYNE M., writer, commentator; b. Balt., Dec. 4, 1957; d. Richard Earl and Viola Marie (Villmar) B. BA in English cum laude, Coll. Notre Dame, Balt., 1979. Advt. copywriter Hottman-Edwards Advt., Balt., 1979-80; writer, editor Chesapeake Pub., Lexington Park, Md., 1980-84; writer, movie critic Jour. Newspapers, Springfied, Va., 1984-91; writer The Washington Post, 1991—, The Washington Times, 1991—, The Washingtonian Mag., 1991—; commentator Sta. WETA-TV, PBS, Washington, 1990—, Sta. WETA-FM, Washington, 1990—; freelance writer AP, UPI, Gannett News Svc., Newsday, L.A. Times, others, 1984—; lectr. Women in Comm., Washington, 1992, various schs., civic and women's groups, 1984—. Author: (screenplays) Feeding the Monster, Nick of Time, Disturbing the Peace; editor: Daddy's Girl, 1991. Recipient 1st place Words and Pictures award Va. Press, 1988, 1st place Feature Writing award, 1989-90, 91, Hon. Mention award Art Dirs. Club Met. Washington, 1984.

BLANCHARD, JOSEPH PROCTER, financial company executive; b. Boston, Mar. 30, 1945; s. John Adams and Mary Wurrell (Procter) B.; m. Akiko Hasegawa, Mar. 15, 1975; children: Sara Yoko, Christopher Hasegawa, Andrew Koji. AB, Harvard U., 1967. V.p. Chase Manhattan Bank, N.Y.C., 1971-83, Nat. Westminster Bank U.S.A., N.Y.C., 1983-85; ptnr. LPC Assocs., N.Y.C., 1985-87; v.p. Mitchell Hutchins Instnl. Investors, N.Y.C., 1987-91; sr. v.p. Barclay Capital Mgmt., N.Y.C., 1991—. Vol. U.S. Peace Corps, Peru, 1967-68; pres. United Community Chest, Port Washington, N.Y., 1988-90; bd. dirs. Nassau County ARC, Mineola, N.Y., 1978, Residents for a More Beautiful Port Washington, 1986—, Landmark on Main Street, 1991—. Mem. Nat. Futures Assn. (registered), Harvard-Radcliffe Club L.I. Home: 54 Locust Ave Port Washington NY 11050-2712

BLANCHARD, NORMAN HARRIS, pharmaceutical executive; b. Pittsfield, Mass., Aug. 21, 1930; s. Norman Harris and Edna May (Perkins) B.; m. Margaret Eugenie Rahm, Apr. 10, 1954; children: Norman James, Michèle Blanchard Langstaff. BS in Geology, Tufts U., 1953; BS in Internat. Trade, Am. Grad. Sch. Internat. Mgmt., 1959. Geologist U.S. Geol. Survey, Harrisburg, Pa., 1957-58; internat. mgmt. trainee Upjohn Internat. Ops., Kalamazoo, 1959-60; adminstrv. dir. Sprout Waldron of France, Paris, 1961-66; european dir. Salsbury Labs., Charles City, Iowa, 1967-71; european dir. Smith Kline Animal Health, Phila., 1972-74, internat. dir., 1975-76, internat. v.p., 1977-81, pres., 1982-89; corp. v.p. Smith Kline Beckman Corp., Phila., 1983-89, pres., 1989—; chmn. Animal Health Inst., Alexandria, Va., 1988-89; mem. president's council Am. Grad. Sch. Internat. Mgmt., Phoenix, 1985-89. Chmn. Jr. Achievement of Del. Valley, Newtown Sq., Pa., 1986, 87; trustee Internat. House, Phila., 1984, 85. With CIC, U.S. Army, 1953-56. Republican. Home: 553 Tanglewood Ln Devon PA 19333-1025 Office: Smith Kline Beecham Corp 1600 Paoli Pike West Chester PA 19380-6005

BLANCHARD, RONALD JOSEPH, food service executive; b. Camden, N.Y., June 27, 1946; s. Earl Roland and Margaret Virginia (Platt) B. AS in Hotel and Restaurant Tech., SUNY, Canton, 1968; BA in Human Svcs., U. Mass., Boston, 1990. Gen. mgr. restaurant Howard Johnson Co., Miami, Fla., 1968-83, gen. mgr. hotel, 1983; mgr. tng. and devel. Marriott Family Restaurants, Quincy, Mass., 1984-87; mgr. sr. tng. and devel. Ground Round, Inc., Braintree, Mass., 1987—. Bd. dirs. Worcester Sq. Area Neighborhood Assn., Boston, 1988—, pres. 1992—; block leader East Brookline St. Neighborhood, Boston, 1988—; mem. Boston Redevel. Authority Working Group for Master Plan, Boston, 1991. Mem. ASTD, Zeta Alpha Phi. Democrat. Roman Catholic. Home: 102 E Brookline St # 1 Boston MA 02118-2325 Office: Ground Round Inc 35 Braintree Hill Park Braintree MA 02184-8703

BLANCHFORD, JEFF AULD, commodities executive; b. Rahway, N.J., Aug. 23, 1939; s. Henry Elmslie and Lois (Acker) B.; m. June Cheng, Nov. 17, 1966; children: Phoebe and Christy (twins), Luke. BA in Philosophy, Kenyon Coll., 1962; postgrad., U. N.D., 1964, Chula Lung Kow U., Bangkok, Thailand, 1974. Sr. ops. specialist Air Am. Inc., Thailand and Laos, 1967-73; chief exec. officer Creasia House Ltd., Bangkok, 1971-75; freelance internat. trade cons., author and lectr. Tokyo, 1975-77; commodity trader Merrill Lynch, Manhasset, N.Y., 1977-78; commodity cons. Shearson Lehman Bros., Garden City, N.Y., 1978-87; v.p. commodities Paine Webber Inc., Melville, N.Y., 1987—. Contbr. articles on S.E. Asian geopolitics to profl. jours. Mem. Thai C. of C., Bangkok, 1974. 1st lt. USAF, 1962-66, Vietnam and CBI. Decorated Bronze Star, Legion of Merit. Office: Paine Webber Inc 225 Broadhollow Rd Melville NY 11747

BLANDINO, RAMON ARTURO, psychologist, consultant, researcher; b. Santo Domingo, Dominican Republic, Oct. 22, 1956; came to U.S., 1990; s. Ramon Arturo Blandino and Yolanda Gomez; m. Esther Wong, 1980 (div. 1984); 1 child, Solange; m. Aida Ripley, Sept. 21, 1986; children: Ramon, Enrique, Aidat, George. BA in Clin. Psychology, U. Autonoma Santo Domingo, 1987, MA in Community Psychology, 1990. Lic. psychologist, Dominican Republic. Assoc. producer Radio HIN and TV (Rahintel), Dominican Republic, 1974-76; editor Pubs. Decada/Genesis, Dominican Republic, 1976-78; v.p. Promuca, Dominican Republic, 1978-85, Audiolab, Dominican Republic, 1983-88, Musicor/CBS, Dominican Republic, 1985-89; cons. Programa Control ETS and SIDA (Procets), Dominican Republic, 1988-90; vis. researcher, intern in psychology Bellevue Hosp., NYU, 1990—; cons. A.V. Blandino Ltd., Dominican Republic, 1989—; chief psychol. intern NYU-Roberto Clemente Family Guidance Ctr.; vis. researcher N.Y.C. Health & Hosp. Corp./Inst. for Family & Community Care; program dir. Health Industry Resources Enterprises, Inc., 1992. Mem. task force on learning Assn. Scouts Dominicanos, Dominican Republic, 1983. Mem. APA, AAAS, N.Y. Acad. Sci., Internat. Coun. Psychologists, Assn. Dominicana Psicologos (Dominican Republic) (bd. dirs.), N.Y. State Psychol. Assn., Assn. of Hispanic Mental Health Profl.

BLANEY, HARRY CLAY, III, international affairs consultant; b. N.Y.C., Mar. 21, 1938; s. Harry Clay and Mae A. (Planagan) B.; m. Julia A. Moore. BA, Allegheny Coll., 1959; postgrad., Sch. Advanced Internat. Study, 1959-60, Yale U., 1960-64, London Sch. Econs., 1964-65; MA, Yale U., 1961. Fgn. svc. officer U.S. Dept. State, Washington, 1965-87; diplomat U.S. Mission to European Communities U.S. Dept. State, Brussels, 1966-68; spl. asst. White House staff U.S. Dept. State, Washington, 1969-72, fellow Woodrow Wilson Internat. Ctr., 1972-73, mem. policy planning staff, 1973-79; counselor for econs. affairs U.S. mission to NATO U.S. Dept. State, Brussels, 1979-81; vis. fellow Coun. on Fgn. Rels. U.S. Dept. State, N.Y.C., 1982-83; dir. Office Asian Refugee Assistance U.S. Dept. State, Washington, 1983-85, sr. adviser Bur. Intelligence and Rsch., 1986-87; pvt. practice cons. on internat. affairs Washington, 1989—. Author: Golbal Challenges: A World at Risk, 1979; editor: The Future of Conventional Arms Central in Europe, 1988; contbr. articles, columns to mags. and newspapers. Rusk fellow Inst. for Study of Diplomacy, Georgetown U., 1985-86, sr. rsch. fellow Ctr. for Study of Fgn. Affairs, 1987-89; recipient Gold citation Allegheny Coll., 1989. Internat. Inst. Strategic Studies, Internat. Studies Assn., Am. Fgn. Svc. Assn., Arms Control Assn., Yale Club. N.Y. Office: PO Box 5545 Washington DC 20016-1145

BLANK, HOWARD STEVEN, physician, educator; b. Bklyn., Feb. 24, 1948; s. Carl and Bertha (Greenberg) B.; m. Jessica Beth Spielman, June 15, 1969; children: Evan Scott, Daniel Jason. BS, Bklyn. Coll., 1968; MD, Mt. Sinai Sch. Medicine, 1972. Diplomate Am. Bd. Internal Medicine, Am. Bd. Internal Medicine-Rheumatology. Intern internal medicine Mt. Sinai Hosp., 1972-73, resident, 1973-75, chief med. resident, 1975-76; physician Good Samaritan Hosp., Suffern, N.Y., 1977—, Nyack (N.Y.) Hosp., 1977—; rehab. physician Helen Hayes Hosp., West Haverstraw, N.Y., 1977-91; fellow rheumatology Mt. Sinai Hosp., N.Y.C., 1975-77; instr. Columbia Presbyn. Med. Ctr., N.Y.C., 1991—; pvt. practice Suffern, 1977—; pres. med. staff Helen Hayes Hosp., 1981-83; co-chmn. pharmacy com. Good Samaritan Hosp., 1987—; chief, div. rheumatology Good Samaritan Hosp., 1989—. Fellow Am. Coll. Rheumatology; mem. Rockland County Med. Soc., N.Y. State Med. Soc., Alpha Omega Alpha. Jewish. Office: 222 Route 59 Suffern NY 10901-5204

BLANK, JONATHAN WILLIAM, anesthesiologist; b. Bloomington, Ind., May 17, 1960; s. Gordon Coleman and Joan Lee (Bevirt) B.; m. Lane Hoffman, Aug. 8, 1987. BA, Johns Hopkins U., 1981; MD, Cornell U., 1985. Diplomate Am. Bd. Med. Examiners, Am. Bd. Anesthesiology. Surg. intern U. N.C. Hosps., Chapel Hill, 1985-86; resident in orthopedic surgery N.C. Meml. Hosp., Chapel Hill, 1986-87, resident in anesthesiology, 1987-90; asst. prof. dept. anesthesiology Uniformed Svcs. U. of the Health Scis., Bethesda, Md., 1990—. Maj. M.C., USAF. Cornell U. scholar, 1981-82, Johns Hopkins U. scholar, 1977. Mem. AMA, N.C. Med. Soc., Am. Soc. Anesthesiologists, Am. Soc. Regional Anesthesia, Internat. Anesthesia Rsch. Soc. Home: 5500 Burling Ct Bethesda MD 20817-6309

BLANK, MARTIN, physiology educator, consultant, editor; b. N.Y.C., Feb. 28, 1933; s. Leon and Rebecca (Quart) B.; m. Marion Sue Hersch, July 3, 1955; children: Donna, Jonathan, Ari. BS, CUNY, 1954; PhD, Columbia U., 1957, Cambridge U., 1959. Postdoctoral fellow in colloid sci. Cambridge (England) U., 1957-59; instr., asst. prof. Columbia U., N.Y.C., 1959-68; liaison scientist Office of Naval Rsch., London, 1974-75; biophysicist Office of Naval Rsch., Arlington, Va., 1984-85; assoc. prof. physiology Columbia U., N.Y.C., 1968--; rsch. chemist Unilever Rsch. Labs., England, Netherlands, summer 1964, 67, 69; vis. prof. Hebrew U., Jerusalem, 1970; vis. lectr. Monash U., Melbourne, Australia, 1982; cons. Office of Naval Rsch., Electric Power Rsch. Inst.; organizer of internat. scientific meetings, schs. Editor of 8 scientific books on biology and chemistry; contbr. over 150 articles to scholarly and profl. jours. NIH Rsch. fellow, 1957-59; rsch. grantee NIH, NSF, DOI, DOD, EPRI; recipient Rsch. Career Devel. award NIH, 1960-70, IWAO Yasuda award Bioelec. Repair and Growth Soc., 1990. Mem. Bioelectrochemical Soc. (pres. 1988--), Electrochemical Soc. (div. chmn. 1983-85), Internat. Sch. Biophysics, Italy (co-dir. bioelectrochemistry 1981--), Bioelectromagnetics Soc. (bd. dirs. 1989--). Office: Columbia Univ Dept of Physiology 630 W 168th St New York NY 10032-3702

BLANK, RAYMOND MICHAEL, management executive, author; b. Balt., Mar. 27, 1933; s. Benjamin and Bessie (Schreiber) B.; divorced; children: Paul Jeffrey, Jamie Allison, Adam Douglas, Peter Joshua. BA, U. Md., 1955; JD, U. Md., Balt., 1958. Founder No. Acceptance Corp. Credit Corp., Balt., 1958-68; cons. U.S. Agy. for Internat. Devel., Washington, 1965-70; adminstrv. v.p. Korvettes Dept. Store, N.Y.C., 1969-74; dir. Spartan Industries, N.Y.C., 1974-76, Arlen Properties, N.Y.C., 1976-78; prin. R.M. Blank Assocs. Rsch., Balt., 1978—; pres. Balt. Bullets, 1970-74; bd. dirs. Better Bus. Bur., N.Y.C., 1975-76. Author: Playing the Game: A Psychopolitical Strategy for Your Career, 1980. Bd. dirs. Ctr. Stage, Balt., 1976-80; cons. Gov.'s Commn. to Restructure Edn. in Md., Balt., 1989-70. Recipient Mktg. award Seklemian Com., 1966; named hon. permanent cons. to U.S. Agy. for Internat. Devel., 1970. Mem. Ctr. Club, Princeton Club (charter, N.Y.). Office: R M Blank Assocs Rsch 1219 S Charles St Baltimore MD 21230-4238

BLANK, STEVEN PAUL, publishing executive; b. N.Y.C., Nov. 12, 1952; s. Benjamin Blank and Mary (Rubner) Applemon; m. Holly Lynn, Mar. 3d, 1990; 1 child, Joshua. BS, Boston U., 1974. Reporter, editor The Daily Record, Morristown, N.Y., 1976-79; reporter The Post Std., Syracuse, N.Y., 1979-83, The Kansas City (Mo.) Star, 1983-86; mktg. dir. SaveMart Inc., Bronx, N.Y., 1986-89; pub. Queens (N.Y.) Pub. Corp., 1989—. Home: 16-70 Bell Blvd Flushing NY 11361 Office: Queens Pub Corp 214-11 41st Ave Flushing NY 11361

BLANK, THOMAS RANNELS, public relations executive; b. Lancaster, Pa., June 20, 1952; s. Thomas Metzger and Harriet Wolfe (Rannels) B.; m. Joyce Ann Haschert, May 21, 977; children: Thomas H., Michael H. BA in English and Speech, Wake Forest U., Winston-Salem, N.C., 1974. Press sec. U.S. Rep. Robert S. Walker, Washington, 1977, adminstrv. asst., 1979-81; spl. asst. pub. affairs U.S. Dept. Transp., Washington, 1981-83, acting dir. pub. affairs, 1983; assoc. dir. pub. affairs U.S. AID, Washington, 1983, asst. adminstr. external affairs, 1986-88; v.p. external affairs Rollins Environ. Svcs., Wilmington, Del., 1983-86; sr. v.p. Hager Sharp Inc., Washington, 1989—. Cert. referee No. Va. Swimming League, Fairfax, 1989—, referee U.S. Soccer Fedn.; dir. Community Family Life Svcs. Mem. Univ. Club. Republican. Lutheran. Office: Hager Sharp Inc 1090 Vermont Ave NW 3d Fl Washington DC 20005

BLANKE, RICHARD DONALD, history educator; b. Pasadena, Calif., July 8, 1940; s. Donald and Elma (Jones) B.; m. Ann Weldon, Jan. 2, 1977; children: Friedrich, Roman, Marie, Claire. BA, Calif. State U., Northridge, 1963; MA, U. Calif., Berkeley, 1970, PhD, 1970. Asst. prof. dept. history U. Maine, Orono, 1969-74, assoc. prof. dept. history, 1974-82, prof. dept. history, 1982—. Author: Prussian Poland in the German Empire, 1981, The German Minority in Interwar Poland, 1992; co-author: National Minorities in Eastern Europe, 1985. With U.S. Army, 1957-60. Fulbright fellow, Germany, 1966, 68, 84; sabbatical grantee Am. Cou. Learned Socs., Germany, 1984, travel grantee Internat. Rsch. and Exchs. Bd., Poland, 1989. Mem. Am. Assn. Advancement Slavic Studies, Am. Hist. Assn., German Studies Assn. Republican. Home: 144 Essex St # 1 Bangor ME 04401-5345 Office: Univ Maine Dept History Orono ME 04469

BLANKENHORN, DAVID GEORGE, III, foundation administrator; b. Baumholder, Germany, May 25, 1955; s. David George Jr. and Diane (Weaver) B.; m. Raina Alexandra Sacks, Sept. 13, 1986; 1 child, Raymond David. BA magna cum laude, Harvard U., 1977; MA with high honors, Warwick U., Coventry, Eng., 1978. Community organizer Citizen Action, several cities, Mass., Va., 1978-84; founder, pres. Institute for American Values, N.Y.C., 1985—. Editor: (book) Rebuilding the Nest, 1990. Democrat. Presbyterian. Office: Inst for Am Values 1841 Broadway Ste 211 New York NY 10023

BLANKLEY, WALTER ELWOOD, manufacturing company executive; b. Phila., Sept. 23, 1935; s. George William and Martha Emily (McCord) B.; m. Rosemary Deniken, Aug. 16, 1958; children: Stephen Michael, Laura Ann. BSME, Princeton U., 1957. Mgr. planning Ametek Hunter Spring, Hatfield, Pa., 1965-66, gen. mgr., 1966-69; asst. to pres. Ametek, Inc., San Francisco, 1969-71; v.p. Ametek, Inc., Watsonville, Calif., 1971-78, group v.p., 1978-82, sr. v.p., 1982-90; pres., chief exec. officer Ametek, Inc., Paoli, Pa., 1990—; dir. Kinark Corp., Tulsa, 1988-90. Mem. ASME (adv. bd. 1991—), Aluminum Extruders Coun. (pres. 1974-76, bd. dirs. 1971-78), World Affairs Coun. (bd. dirs. 1992—). Office: Ametek Inc Station Sq Paoli PA 19301-1307

BLANPIED, WILLIAM ANTOINE, science policy analyst; b. Rochester, N.Y., May 11, 1933; s. Charles Wesley and Maria Angela (Fanelli) B.; m. Sara Frances Pattershall, July 18, 1959 (div. Jan. 1972); 1 child, Eric Wesley; m. Nancy Ann Nawor, Jan. 27, 1973 (div. Jan. 1986); children: Wendy Marie, Jessica Lynn. BS, Yale U., 1955; PhD in Physics, Princeton (N.J.) U., 1959. Rsch. assoc. Nat. Sychrotron Lab., Frascati, Italy, 1959-60; instr. to asst. prof. Dept. Physics, Yale U., 1960-66; assoc. prof. Dept. Physics, Case Western Res. U., 1966-69, 71-72; staff assoc. U.S. Nat. Sci. Found. Liaison Staff, New Delhi, 1969-71; sr. rsch. fellow Dept. Physics, Harvard U., 1972-74; head, div. of pub. sector programs AAAS, 1974-76; program dir., ethics and values in sci. and tech. program NSF, 1976-79, head office of spl. projects, 1979-84, sr. internat. analyst, 1984-87, 89—; vis. scholar Grad. Sch. of Internat. Rels. and Pacific Studies, U. Calif., San Diego.. Editorial adv. bd. Chem. and Engrng. News, Sci., Tech. and Human Values; author: Physics: Its Structure and Evolution, 1969, Modern Physics: An Introduction to its Mathematical Language, 1970, Science and its Public: The Changing Relationship, 1976; contbr. numerous articles to profl. jours. Postdoctoral fellowship NSF, 1959-60; Jr. Faculty fellowship Yale U., 1964-65; recipient U.S. Govt. Intergovernmental Exchange award, 1987-89. Mem. Am. Phys. Soc. (chair internat. physics group 1992-94). Episcopalian. Home: 1530 Key Blvd Apt 812 Arlington VA 22209-1500 Office: NSF 1800 G St NW Washington DC 20550-0002

BLANTON, LAWTON WALTER, retired academic dean; b. Perry, Fla., Oct. 25, 1914; s. Lawton Walter and Minnie Florelle (Truesdale) B.; BS, U. Fla., 1936, MS, 1941; postgrad. U. Chgo., 1949, Columbia, 1951-53. Rsch. assoc. U. Fla., Gainesville, 1941-42, asst. prof. math., 1942-53; asst. dean students Coll. City N.Y., 1955-57; dir. admissions Montclair Coll., Upper Montclair, N.J., 1957-61, dean students, 1961-80, ret., 1980. Lawton W. Blanton Hall named in his honor Montclair State Coll., 1982. Mem. Am. Assn. Higher Edn., Nat. Assn. Student Pers. Adminstrs., Am., N.J. pers. and guidance assns., N.Y. Schoolmasters, Eastern Assn. Coll. Deans and Advisers of Students, N.J. State Coll. Chief Student Affairs Officers (pres.

1977-78), Nat. Collegiate Honors Council, Am. Hort. Soc., Am. Hemerocallis Soc., Am. Plant Life Soc., Am. Rhododendron Soc. Home: 1 Oak Cres Little Falls NJ 07424-2414

BLASCOVICH, JAMES JOSEPH, psychologist, researcher; b. Chgo., Nov. 8, 1946; s. Albert Lawrence and Jennie Loretta (Cocozza) B.; m. Susan Lorraine Botsford, Sept. 5, 1970 (div. 1979); 1 child, Elizabeth Marie; m. Brenda Nelle Major, June 26, 1982; children: Meridith Major-Blascovich, Gregory Major-Blascovich. BS, Loyola U., 1968; PhD, U. Nev., 1972. Asst. prof. U. Nev., Reno, 1972-73; asst. prof. Marquette U., Milw., 1973-77, assoc. prof., 1977-81; assoc. prof. SUNY, Buffalo, 1981—, dir. Ctr. for Study of Behavior & Social Aspects of Health, 1987—; pres. Advanced Automation Concepts, Inc., Buffalo, 1982-87; cons. in field; mem. panel NSF, 1990—; vis. scholar U. Calif., Santa Barbara, 1992. Contbr. over 50 articles to profl. jours. Mem. rsch. govt. coun. N.Y. State chpt. Am. Lung Assn., Albany, 1989-91; mem. Buffalo Ambs., 1989—. Staff sgt. USAF N.G., 1969-75. NSF grantee, 1990—. Fellow APA, Am. Psychol. Soc.; mem. Soc. for Exptl. Social Psychology, Soc. for Personality and Social Psychology (sec.-treas. 1988-91, exec. officer 1992—), Sigma Xi. Office: SUNY Park Hall Dept Psychology Buffalo NY 14260

BLASE, WILLIAM THOMAS, corporate communications executive; b. Hartford, Conn., Aug. 30, 1949; s. John Joseph and Grace Shirley (Thomas) B.; m. Linda Mary Blanchfield, Jan. 8, 1972; children: Sara Elizabeth, Megan Anne. BA, Cen. Conn. State U., 1973; postgrad., Western New Eng. Law Sch., 1975-77; MBA, Maryville U., 1992. Reporter The Hartford Times, 1976-77; editor, columnist The Bristol (Conn.) Press, 1977-78; news editor United Press Internat., Hartford, 1978-79; dir. communications Hamilton Standard div. United Tech. Corp., Windsor Locks, Conn., 1979-81; dir. communications United Tech. Corp., Bldg. Systems Co., Farmington, Conn., 1981-82; mgr. news svcs. United Tech. corp., Hartford, 1982-83, mgr. corp. contbns., 1983-84; dir. communications United Tech. Communications Co., St. Louis, 1984-85; sr. v.p. communications Hellmuth, Obata & Kassabaum, Inc., St. Louis, 1985-89; v.p. corp. communications Scudder, Stevens & Clark, Inc., N.Y.C., 1989-92; pres. W.T. Blase & Assoc., Trumbull, Conn., 1992—; guest lectr. at various colls. and univs. Contbr. articles to profl. jours. Drill sgt. USAR, 1969-75. Recipient Marconi award St. Louis Advt. Club, 1985, Excellence in Journalism awards Soc. Profl. Journalist Conn. chpt., 1978, Laurel awards Conn. Art Dirs., 1981. Mem. Internat. Assn. Bus. Communicators (bd. dirs., chmn. mktg. coun. 1988—, bd. govs. N.Y. chpt. 1989-90, Bronze Quill award 1987, Silver Quill award 1988), Bus. Profl. Advt. Assn. (editorial bd. advisor 1981), Pub. Rels. Soc. Am., Soc. Profl. Journalists, Fin. Communications Soc. (bd. dirs. 1992—).

BLASEK, WILLIAM EDWARD, III, sales executive; b. Peoria, Ill., Sept. 13, 1952; s. William Edward and Othelia Roseta (Doll) B.; children by previous marriage: William Edward IV, Michael Joseph; m. Jill Laurie Domosh, Feb. 25, 1984; 1 child, Melissa Beth. BA, Bradley U., 1974. Sales mgr. Isaac Walker Co., Peoria, 1975-80; nat. sales mgr. Nora Flooring, Madison, Ind., 1980-88; v.p. sales Freudenberg Bldg. Systems Inc., Lawrence, Mass., 1988—. Rep. precinct committeeman, Peoria, 1974. Mem. Constrn. Specifications Inst., Am. Soc. Interior Designers, Am. Standards and Testing Methods, Nat. Assn. of Floor Covering Distbrs. Home: 43 Sunview St Derry NH 03038 Office: 94 Glen Ave Methuen MA 01844-4812

BLASIER, COLE, political scientist; b. Jackson, Mich., Mar. 16, 1925; s. Stewart Parnell and Helen (Cole) B.; m. Martha Hiett, Sept. 20, 1947; children: Peter Cole, Martha Hamilton. AB, U. Ill., 1947; postgrad., U. Mex., 1947; AM, Columbia U., 1950, cert. Russian Inst., 1950, PhD in Polit. Sci., 1955. Career fgn. svc. officer U.S. Dept. State, Belgrade, Yugoslavia, 1951-54, Bonn, Federal Republic of Germany, 1954-56, Washington, 1957-60, Moscow, 1958; exec. asst. to pres., sec. bd. trustees Colgate U., Hamilton, N.Y., 1961-63; prof. polit. sci. U. Pitts., 1964-88; chief hispanic div. Libr. Congress, Washington, 1988—; dir. ctr. Latin Am. studies U. Pitts., 1964-74; adv. bd. Handbook Latin Am. Studies, 1972-88; exchange scholar Polish Inst. Internat. Affairs, Warsaw, Poland, 1975, Inst. Latin Am., Moscow, 1979; U.S. chmn. U.S./USSR Exchange in Latin Am. Studies, 1980-86. Author: The Hovering Giant, U.S. Responses to Revolutionary Change in Latin America, 1976, rev. 1985, The Giant's Rival, the USSR and Latin Am., 1976, rev. 1987, Cuba in the World, 1979; editor: U. Pitts. Press Latin Am. Series, 1968-91. Pres. UN Assn. Pitts., 1985. Lt. (j.g.) USNR, 1943-46. Fellow Rotary, 1947-48, Fulbright, Buenos Aires, Argentina, 1986, Heinz Endowment, 1988; Rockefeller Found. grantee, 1963-64. Mem. Lat. Am. Studies Assn. (pres. 1986-87), Am. Polit. Sci. Assn., Pitts. Golf Club. Home: 5904 Mt Eagle Dr # 1414 Alexandria VA 22303-2543

BLASIOTTI, ROBERT VINCENT, accountant, consultant; b. Phila., Nov. 15, 1949; s. Vincent Mario Blasiotti and Hilda (Romani) Greer; m. Katheryn Phyllis Ombres, Dec. 15, 1973 (div. Apr. 1982); m. Gilda Maria Cipriani, June 17, 1988; children: Melissa, Gabriella, Robert Jr. BS, Pa. State U., 1971, MBA, 1973. CPA, Pa. Jr. acct. Goldenberg, Rosenthal & Co., Phila., 1971-73, sr. acct., 1973-75; mgr. acctg. Gross & Co., Jenkintown, Pa., 1975-77; owner Blasiotti & Co., West Chester, Pa., 1977—; CPA, advisor Big Bros. Chester County, West Chester, 1985—; cons. Presdl. Adv. Coun., 1984. Mem. Big Bros.-Big Sisters Chester County, 1978—; trustee Rep. Presdl. Task Force, 1982—. Capt. U.S. Army, 1973-81. Mem. C. of C., Jaycees (chmn. 1980-84), Italian Social Club, KC, Lions (treas. 1980-81). Roman Catholic. Office: Blasiotti & Co 933 S High St West Chester PA 19382-5489

BLASLAND, WARREN VINCENT, JR., consulting engineer; b. N.Y.C., Jan. 16, 1945; s. Warren Vincent and Mary Clare (McCarthy) B.; m. Normajean Stagnitta; children: Warren, David Alan, Brian Joseph, Ashley Linsey. BCE, Manhattan Coll., 1966; MSSE, Syracuse U., 1971. Project engr. Havens & Emerson, Cons. Engrs., N.Y.C., 1966; project engr. O'Brien & Gere Engrs., Inc., Syracuse, N.Y., 1966-71, mng. engr., 1971-77, v.p., 1977-81, sr. v.p., 1981-83, dir., 1980-83; pres. Blasland & Bouck, 1983—; lectr. Syracuse U. Engring. Grad. Sch., 1976, Princeton U. Grad. Sch., 1983, Clarkson Sch. Engring., 1984. Mem. N.Y. State Soc. Profl. Engrs. (pres. 1975-76, dir. 1976-78), Am. Pub. Works Assn. (dir. 1978—), Am. Water Works Assn., N.Y. Water Pollution Control Fedn., Internat. City Mgrs. Assn. Home: 6903 Shalimar Way Fayetteville NY 13066-9793 Office: 6723 Towpath Rd Syracuse NY 13214

BLASS, BILL (WILLIAM RALPH BLASS), designer apparel, home furnishings; b. Ft. Wayne, Ind., June 22, 1922; s. Ralph Aldrich and Ethyl (Keyser) B. D.F.A. (hon.), R.I. Sch. Design, 1977; L.H.D. (hon.), Ind. U., 1984. Asst. designer for David Crystal, 1950-51, Anna Miller & Co., 1951-59; designer Maurice Rentner, Ltd. (now Bill Blass Ltd.), 1959—, v.p., 1963-70; pres. Bill Blass Ltd., 1970—. Trustee N.Y. Pub. Library, 1986—. Served with AUS, World War II. Recipient Coty award Am. Fashion Critics, 1961, 63, 70, 1st Men's Coty award Am. Fashion Critics, 1968, 71, 82, 83, Hall of Fame award Am. Fashion Critics, 1970, spl. citation Am. Fashion Critics, 1971, 82, 83, Cartier Santos award, Lord & Taylor's Creative Design award, Indpls. Art Commn. award., Chgo. Gold Coast Fashion award, 1965; recipient Cotton Council award, 1965, "Millie" Fashion award Boston Academie, 1969, Neiman-Marcus award, 1969, Print Council award, 1971, Martha award, 1974, Great Am. Designers award I. Magnin, 1974, Am. Fashion awards, 1975, First Annual Ayres Look award, 1978, Man Style award Gentleman's Quarterly mag., 1979, Cutty Sark Hall of Fame award, 1979, New York award Citizens Com. N.Y., 1984, Am. Lifetime Achievement award Council Fashion Designers, 1986. Mem. Council Fashion Designers Am. (v.p.). Office: Bill Blass Ltd 550 7th Ave New York NY 10018-3203

BLASS, WALTER PAUL, consultant, management educator; b. Dinslaken, Germany, Mar. 31, 1930; came to U.S., 1941, naturalized, 1947; s. Richard B. and Malvi (Rosenblatt) B.; m. Janice L. Minott, Apr. 2, 1954; children: Kathryn, Christopher, Gregory. B.A., Swarthmore Coll., 1951; postgrad. Princeton U., 1951-52; M.A., Columbia U., 1953. Asst. Laos and Cambodia desk officer ICA, Washington, 1957-58; gen. mgr. R.B. Blass Co., Deal, N.J., 1958-61; economist AT&T, N.Y.C., 1961-66; country dir. Peace Corps, Afghanistan, 1966-68; asst. v.p. revenue requirement studies N.Y. Telephone Co., N.Y.C., 1968-70, dir. corp. planning, 1970-82; dir. strategic planning AT&T, N.Y.C., 1982-85 (ret.); pres., Strategic Plans, Unltd., Warren, N.J., 1985—. Exec. Fellow-in-Residence Martino Grad. Sch. Bus. Adminstrn., Fordham U., N.Y.C., 1986-90; cons. McKinsey & Co., Telecommunications Authority Ireland, McDonnell Douglas, Heller Fin., Inc.; lectr. in field; vis. prof. U. Grenoble, France, 1988. Trustee Guilford Coll., 1975—. Lt., j.g., USNR, 1953-56. Woodrow Wilson Found. sr. fellow, 1974—. Mem. N.Y. Acad. Scis., Soc. Values in Higher Edn. (dir. 1983-86), Am. Econ. Assn., Nat. Assn. Bus. Economists, N.Am. Soc. Corp. Planning (dir. 1972), Royal Econ. Soc., Princeton Club. Co-author: The Strategic Planning Handbook, 1982, Handbook of Stratgic Planning, 1986. Home and Office: 6 Casale Dr Warren NJ 07059-6703

BLATT, ETHEL SHAMES, human services director; b. Phila., Oct. 30, 1931; d. Solomon and Fannie (Robin) Shames; m. Sidney Jules Blatt, Feb. 1, 1951; children: Susan, Judith, David. BA, So. Conn. State U., New Haven, 1976. Rsch. asst. Yale U., Devel. Office, New Haven, Conn., 1977-78, asst. dir., 1978-82; dir. Goodwill Industries, Bridgeport, Conn., 1982-83; devel. dir. Jewish Home for Aged, New Haven, Conn., 1984-91, Soc. to Advance the Retarded and Handicapped, Inc., Norwalk, Conn., 1992—. Author: Continuity and Change in Art, 1984. Treas. of Sisterhood, Congregation Miskan Israel, Hamden, Conn., 1970. Mem. Planned Giving Group of Conn. Office: Soc to Advance Retarded and Handicapped Inc 182 Wolfpit Ave Norwalk CT 06851

BLATT, S. LESLIE, physics educator, dean; b. Phila., June 10, 1935; s. Israel and Celia (Wiener) B.; m. Susanne R. Schwarz, Mar. 22, 1959; children: J. Daniel, Jeremy, Elliott. AB in Physics, Princeton U., 1957; MS in Physics, Stanford U., 1959, PhD in Physics, 1965. Teaching asst., rsch. asst. Stanford U., Palo Alto, Calif., 1957-64; rsch. asst. Brookhaven Nat. Lab., Upton, N.Y., 1958; rsch. assoc. Ohio State U., Columbus, 1964-66; vis. rsch. physicist SUNY, Stony Brook, 1968; vis. rsch. scientist Centre de Recherches Nucleaires, Strasbourg, France, 1972-73; asst. prof. The Ohio State U., Columbus, 1966-69, assoc. prof., 1969-75, prof. physics, 1975-87, chmn. physics dept., 1980-86; dean grad. studies & rsch., prof. physics Clark U., Worcester, Mass., 1987—; cons. Am. Sci. & Engring. Corp., Cambridge, Mass., 1969-71. Contbr. over 62 articles to profl. jours. and 73 presentations to profl. meetings. Recipient Rsch. grant NSF, 1967-87, Teaching grants NSF, 1991. Mem. AAUP (pres. 1975-76), Am. Phys. Soc., Assn. Grad. Schs. of the AAU, Coun. Grad. Schs., Soc. Rsch. Adminstrs. Home: 6 Knollwood Dr Worcester MA 01609-1204 Office: Clark U 950 Main St Worcester MA 01610-1473

BLATTMANN, MARGOT CONRAD, marketing and sales executive; b. Princeton, N.J.; d. Walter and Eleanor Blattmann. BA in History, Trinity Coll., Hartford, Conn., 1983. Monbusho English fellow Japanese Govt. Ministry of Edn., Nagano, Japan, 1983-85; sales coord. Tokio Marine & Fire Ins. Co. Inc., N.Y.C., 1986-88; internat. and nat. sales and mktg. mgr. Fujisankei Communications Internat. Inc., N.Y.C., 1988—. Office: FCI 150 E 52 St New York NY 10022

BLATZ, LINDA JEANNE, marketing professional; b. N.Y.C., Dec. 8, 1950; d. William Edmund and Jeanne Grace (Hyman) B. BS, U. Md., 1972. Mgr. sales Milliken & Co., N.Y.C., 1972-81; retail market mgr. Greenwood Mills Mktg. Co., N.Y.C., 1981-89; dist. mgr. Steelcase Inc., N.Y.C., 1989—. Contbr. articles to profl. jours. Mem. N.Y.C. Ballet Guild, PEO; mem. jr. com. N.Y.C. Ballet; tng. mgr., v.p. membership N.Y. Jr. League (Outstanding Vol. award 1991-92). Recipient Outstanding Vol. of the Yr. award N.Y. Jr. League, 1992. Mem. Nat. Assn. Uniform Mfrs. and Distbrs., U. Md. Alumni Assn., Am. Woman's Econ. Devel. Corp., East River Rowing Club, Alpha Gamma Delta. Congregationalist. Club: Sandbar Beach (membership bd.). Home: 2 Tudor City Pl New York NY 10017-6800 Office: 510 5th Ave New York NY 10036-7507

BLAUFOX, MORTON DONALD, physician, educator; b. N.Y.C., July 19, 1934; s. Emanuel and Elizabeth (Rosenblum) B.; m. Paulette Goldberg, Dec. 20, 1958; children: Laurie Beth, Ellen Ruth, Andrew David. Student, Harvard U., 1952-55; M.D., SUNY, 1959; Ph.D., U. Minn., 1964. Diplomate Am. Bd. Internal Medicine, Am. Bd. Nuclear Medicine (bd. dirs. 1985—). Intern Jewish Hosp. of Bklyn., N.Y.C., 1959-60; fellow in medicine Mayo Found. Med. Edn. and Research, Rochester, Minn., 1960-64; advanced research fellow Am. Heart Assn., 1964-66; research fellow in medicine Harvard Med. Sch., Boston, 1964-66; asst. in medicine and radiology Peter Bent Brigham Hosp., Boston, 1964-66; asst. prof. radiology, also assoc. in medicine Albert Einstein Coll. Medicine, Bronx, N.Y., 1966-71; dir. sect. nuclear medicine Albert Einstein Coll. Medicine, 1966—, dir. unified dept., 1976—, chmn. unified dept., 1983—, assoc. dir. clin. research center, 1968-72, assoc. prof. radiology, 1971-76, prof. radiology, 1976—, assoc. prof. medicine, 1972-78, prof. medicine, 1978—; asst. attending physician Bronx Mcpl. Hosp. Center, 1966-71, assoc. attending, 1972, attending physician, 1972—; dir. div. nuclear medicine Montefiore Med. Center, 1976—, chmn. dept. nuclear medicine, 1983—; cons. kidney disease control program USPHS, 1967-72; mem. adminstrv. coun. nuclear medicine VA, 1970-73; mem. panel on radiopharms. U.S. Pharmacopeia, 1970-85; mem. hypertension adv. com. N.Y.C. Dept. Health, 1975-76; treas. exec. com. Am. Bd. Nuclear Medicine, 1987-89, chmn., 1990; mem. clin. trials rev. com. Nat. Heart, Lung and Blood Inst., 1988—; mem. subcom. on none pharmacologic therapy of Joint Nat. Com. on Detection Evaluation and Treatment of High Blood Pressure, 1991—. Editor: (with others) Seminars in Nuclear Medicine, 1970—, Evaluation of Renal Function and Disease with Radionuclides, 1972, 2d edit., 1989, Procs. Internat. Symposium, 1971, 75, 86, 90, PDR for Nuclear Medicine and Radiology, 1972-80, Unilateral Renal Function Studies, 1978 (with others) Secondary Hypertension: Current Diagnosis and Management, 1981, (with others) Non-Pharmacologic Therapy of Hypertension, 1986, (with others) Newer Diagnostic Methods in Nephrology and Urology, 1986; mem. editorial bd. Radionuclides in Nephrology, 1980, editor; mem. editorial bd. Jour. Nuclear Medicine, 1973-81, Nephron, Uroradiology, 1978—, Jour. Nuclear Medicine and Allied Sci., 1982—, Nuclear Medicine Communications, 1979—, Renal Failure, 1986-90, Am. Jour. Hypertension, 1987—; assoc. editor: Barnet's Pediatrics; contbr. The Merck Manual, 14th, 15th and 16th edits., 1982-91; contbr. articles to profl. jours. Recipient Edward Nobel Found. award, Albert Lasker pub. health service award, 1980. Fellow ACP, Am. Coll. Nuclear Physicians, Coun. on High Blood Pressure Rsch., N.Y. Acad. Medicine (libr. com. 1986—); mem. Am. Heart Assn., AMA, Am. Physiol. Soc., Am. Fedn. Clin. Rsch., Am. Soc. Hypertension (membership com.), Soc. Nuclear Medicine (pres. Greater N.Y. chpt. 1976-77, chmn. acad. coun. 1976-77, exec. and sci. coms., chmn. publ. com. 1979-82, trustee, Berson-Yalew award 1989), Ind. Soc. Nuclear Medicine (Sarabhai Oration 1989—), Internat. Soc. Nephrology, Internat. Hypertension Soc., Coun. on High Blood Pressure Rsch. (med. adv. bd.), N.Y. Med. Soc., N.Y. Nephrology Soc., Med. Collectors Assn. (pres. 1983—), Swiss Soc. Nuclear Medicine (hon., corr.), Sigma Xi. Home: 101 Drake-smith Ln Rye NY 10580 Office: Eastchester Rd & Morris Park Ave Bronx NY 10461

BLAUFUSS, DAVID RONALD, optician; b. Buffalo, Jan. 28, 1941; s. Fred and Francis (Michalski) B.; m. Joan Theresa Wojciechowski, Aug. 4, 1962; children: Paul, Mary, Donna. AAS, Erie Community Coll., Williamsville, N.Y., 1960. Optician Dick O'Connor Optical, Cheektowaga, N.Y., 1960-65; optician Beckes Optical, Hamburg, N.Y., 1965-72, Dr. Ed Mehl OD, East Aurora, N.Y., 1972-80; owner Main-Transit Optical, Williamsville, N.Y., 1980—. Bd. dirs. Buffalo Eye Bank, 1986—, N.Y. State Speech and Hearing Clinic, Spencer, N.Y., 1989—, Niagra Frontier Radio Reading Svc. (chmn., recipient Eleanor Roosevelt community svc. award, 1990), Cheektowaga, 1987—. Fellow Nat. Acad. Opticianry; mem. Lions (recipient internat. president's leadership award 1989). Republican. Roman Catholic. Home: 515 Meadow Dr West Seneca NY 14224 Office: Main-Transit Optical 8226 Main St Williamsville NY 14221

BLAUSTEIN, MORDECAI P., medical educator; b. N.Y.C., Oct. 19, 1935; s. Norman and Gertrude (Hellman) B.; m. Ellen Baron, June 21, 1959; children: Laura M., Marc B. BA in Zoology, Cornell U., 1957; MD, Washington U., St. Louis, 1962; postgrad., Cambridge (Eng.) U., 1966-68. Assoc. prof. physiology and biophysics Washington U. Sch. Medicine, 1968-75; prof. physiology and biophysics Washington U. Sch. of Medicine, 1975-80; NATO sr. fellow Phamacology Inst., Bern, Switzerland, 1971; guest scientist Marine Biol. Assn., Plymouth, Eng., 1973; prof., chmn. dept. physiology U. Md., Balt., 1979—, prof. medicine, 1983—; dir., chmn. exec. bd. Hypertension Ctr., U. Md., Balt., 1985—; mem. study sect. NIH, Bethesda, Md., 1982-84; mem. rsch. com. Am. Heart Assn., Dallas, 1984-89. Commr. Md. Commn. on High Blood Pressure and Related Cardiovascular Risk Factors, Balt., 1986—. Lt. USN, 1963-66. Recipient Cardiovascular award Robert J. & Claire Pasarow Found., 1990. Fellow AAAS; mem. Am. Physiol. Soc. (coun. 1992—), Soc. Gen. Physiology (coun.), Physiol. Soc., Soc. for Neurosci., Biophys. Soc. Office: U Md Sch Medicine Dept Physiology 655 W Baltimore St Baltimore MD 21201-1509

BLAVAT, JERRY (GERALD JOSEPH BLAVAT), radio and television personality, actor; b. Phila., July 3, 1940; s. Louis Blavat and Lucille (Capuano) Gunnella; children: Kathy, Geraldine, Stacy, Deserie. Grad. high sch., Phila. Dancer Bandstand TV show, Phila., 1953-55; record promoter Cameo/Parkway Records, Phila., 1956-59; road mgr., mgr. various rock and roll groups including Danny and the Juniors, also Don Rickles, 1957-59; night club performer, live radio show host various clubs, radio stas., Phila., 1959-62; disc jockey radio stas. including Stas. WCAU, WFIL, WCAM, WPGR, Phila., Delaware Valley, 1962—; program dir. Sta. WPGR-AM, Phila., Delaware Valley, 1989—; owner night club Memories, Margate, N.J., 1970—; mem. nominating com. Rock & Roll Hall of Fame, Phila., 1988—. TV appearances include The Monkees, Mod Squad, Joey Bishop Show, Tonight Show, Mike Douglas Show, Pat Boone Show, Merv Griffin Show; movie appearances include Baby, It's You, 1983, Desperately Seeking Susan, 1985, Cookie, 1989; producer, host TV shows Discophonic Scene, 1965-66, Jerry Blavat Show, 1966-70, On the Air with the Geator, 1991—; producer over 27 record albums of collections/anthologies; rec. artist 5 pop singles. Bd. dirs., performer Hero Scholarship Fund, Phila., 1963-70; bd. dirs. Police Athletic League, Phila., 1966-70. Inductee Rock & Roll Hall of Fame, 1986. Mem. AFTRA, SAG, Am. Guild Variety Artists, Nat. Music Found. (adv. bd. 1989—). Roman Catholic. Office: Celebrity Showcase PO Box 25010 Philadelphia PA 19147

BLAYTON-TAYLOR, BETTY, artist, arts administrator; b. Newport News, Va., July 10, 1937; d. James Blain and Alleyne (Houser) B. BFA, Syracuse U., 1959; postgrad., Arts Students League, N.Y.C., Bklyn. Mus. Sch. Exec. dir. Children's Art Carnival, N.Y.C., 1968—, pres. bd., 1984—; bd. dirs. Printmaking Workshop, N.Y.C. Author: Making Thoughts Become, 1978; one woman show include Women Students Gallery, Brown U., 1986, Bedford Stuyvesant Gallery, N.Y., 1987, three woman show include Isabel Neal Gallery, Chgo., 1990. Recipient Empire State Woman of Yr. award Gov. of N.Y., 1984, Black Women in Arts award Gov. of N.Y., 1988. Mem. Assn. Supervision and Curriculum Devel., Art and Bus. Coun. (bd. dirs.), United Fedn. Tchrs. Home: 2001 Creston Ave Bronx NY 10453-4246 Office: Children's Art Carnival 62 Hamilton Ter New York NY 10031-6403

BLAZAK, PAIGE GAYLE, psychotherapist, school counselor; b. Rochester, N.Y., Feb. 16, 1947; d. Morry and Diane (Jacobs) Storm; m. Robert S. Blazak, Apr. 22, 1967; children: Robin, Eric. BSW, Keuka Coll., Keuka Park, N.Y., 1978; MS, SUNY, Brockport, 1988. Cert. sch. counselor, credentialed alcohol counselor. Realtor Sail Realty, Canandaigua, N.Y., 1975-89; weight counselor Nutri-Systems, Rochester, N.Y., 1986-87; dir. Cultured Concepts, Canandaigua, 1982-90; chem. dependency counselor Park Ridge Chem. Dependency, Canadaigua, 1987-89; sch. counselor Geneva (N.Y.) Middle Sch., 1989—; psychotherapist in pvt. practice Canandaigua, 1989—; cons. Cultural Concepts, Canandaigua, 1982-90; dir. Geneva Middle Sch. Theater Group, 1989—. Coord. Am. Cancer Soc., 1975. Breakfast Club grantee geneva Sch. Dist., 1990-91, GMS Theatre Group grantee, 1990—; Creative Works grantee Canandaigua Nat. Bank, 1985. Mem. Am. Assn. Counseling and Devel., N.Y. State Assn. Counseling & Devel., N.Y. State Tchrs. Assn. Home: 3694 W Lake Rd Canandaigua NY 14424-2449 Office: Geneva Middle Sch 63 Pulteney St Geneva NY 14456-2388

BLAZEK, WAYNE JOSEPH, quality assurance engineer, nuclear utility engineer; b. Masontown, Pa., Mar. 21, 1950; s. Joseph Edward and Helen (Kurella) B.; m. Rebecca Cayce, Aug. 23, 1975; 1 child, John Franklin. AS in Welding Tech., Fayette Tech. Sch., 1969; AS in Mech. Design, Fayette Inst. Commerce and Tech., 1971; cert. in indsl. mgmt., Emporia State U., 1979. Sr. draftsman, then mech. inspector Bechtel Power Corp., Gaithersburg, Md., 1971-74; sr. nuclear designer Ebasco Services Inc., Norcross, Ga., 1974-75; welding engr. Kaiser Engrs. Inc., Moscow, Ohio, 1975-77; quality control welding coordinator, then quality control tng. coordinator Daniel Internat., Strawn, Kans., 1977-80; auditor quality assurance, vendor rep. Houston Light and Power Co., 1980-81; quality assurance engr. Perini Corp., Framingham, Mass., 1981-83; lead quality assurance engr. Pub. Service Electric & Gas Co., Hancock Bridge, N.J., 1983-85, sr. staff engr. quality assurance procurement, 1985-90; sr. staff engr. quality assurance procurement Pub. Svc. Electric & Gas Co., Hancock Bridge, N.J., 1990—. Mem. Am. Welding Soc., Am. Soc. Quality Control, Jaycees, NRA, Ducks Unltd. Republican. Roman Catholic. Home: 49 Adams St Swedesboro NJ 08085-1569 Office: Pub Svc Electric & Gas Co PO Box 236 Hancocks Bridge NJ 08038-0236

BLAZIN, MICHAEL JOSEPH, banking executive; b. Lancashire, England, Nov. 22, 1955; came to U.S., 1957; s. Atlee Raymond and Felice Mary (Pado) B. BS, U.S. Naval Acad., 1977; MBA, Harvard U., 1985. Cert. cash mgr., naval nuclear engr. Distbn. mgr. Procter & Gamble Mfg. Co., Balt., 1985-86; lockbox mgr. Equitable Bank, N.A., Balt., 1986-88, MNC Fin., Balt., 1988—. Lt. USN, 1977-83. Mem. Bank Adminstrn. Inst., Treasury Mgmt. Assn., Naval Inst., Harvard Club Md., Harvard Bus. Sch. Club Md. Republican. Roman Catholic. Home: 731 Farnham Pl Bel Air MD 21014-6835 Office: MNC Fin Inc 225 N Calvert St MS 011804 Baltimore MD 21202

BLAZINA, VAY JOHN, neurologist; b. Seattle, Feb. 23, 1941; s. Vay Theodore and Jean (Robinson) B.; m. Christine Victoria Blazina, Dec. 3, 1966; children: Jennifer Ann, David Robert. BA in History, U. Wash., 1963; MD, George Washington U., 1967. Diplomate Am. Bd. Qualiftcational EEG, Am. Bd. Electrodiagnosis, Am. Bd. Neurology. Intern in gen. medicine Mt. Sinai Hosp. Svcs./Elmhurst (N.Y.) Hosp., 1967-68; fellow in neurology Mayo Clinic, Rochester, N.Y., 1970-73; instr. in neurology Columbia U. Neurol. Inst., N.Y.C., 1973-74; asst. chief neurology dept., chief electroencephalography Washington Hosp. Ctr., 1974-77; chief neurophysiology dept. The Neurology Ctr., Washington & Chevy Chase, Md., 1974—; assoc. prof. Med. Sch., George Washington U., Washington, 1976-88, 88—; adj. prof. neurology George Washington U., Washington, 1989—. Mem. Am. Acad. Neurology, Am. Epilepsy Soc., Am. Electroencephalography Soc., Am. Acad. Electrodiagnostic. Office: The Neurology Ctr 5454 Wisconsin Ave # 1750 Chevy Chase MD 20815

BLEAM, LAURA JANE, nursing educator, pediatrics nurse; b. New Britain, Pa., Mar. 27; d. Andrew Y. Jr. and Edna (Tagert) Michie; m. Brian L. Bleam, Apr. 8, 1978; 1 child, Jennifer Lynn. BSN, Alderson-Broaddus Coll., Philippi, W.Va., 1963; MA, Villanova (Pa.) U., 1971; MSN, Gwynedd-Mercy Coll., Gwynedd Valley, Pa., 1985; postgrad., Villanova U., 1991. RN, W.Va., N.J., Pa.; cert. pediatrics nurse, elem. counselor, Pa. Instr. nursing Grand View Hosp. Sch. Nursing, Sellersville, Pa., 1963-67, Gwynedd-Mercy Coll., 1967-69; assoc. prof. pediatric nursing Montgomery County Community Coll., Blue Bell, Pa., 1971—. Contbr. articles to newspapers. Bd. dirs. Ea. Pa. Eastern Star Home, 1987—, chmn., 1992-93; past bd. dirs. Bucks County Am. Lung Assn. Mem. Nat. League for Nursing, Pa. League for Nursing, Alderson-Broaddus Nursing Alumni Assn., Gwynedd-Mercy Coll. Nursing Honor Soc., Order of Eastern Star (chmn. eastern Pa. home bd. 1991-92), Sigma Theta Tau.

BLECHARCZYK, STEPHANIE RUSSELL ADAMS, education educator, consultant; b. Englewood, N.J., Dec. 29, 1935; d. Stephen and Ruth Isabel (Chase) Adams; m. Stephen Stanley Blecharczyk, Apr. 13, 1957 (div. Aug. 1974); children: Jeffrey David, Jennifer Ruthd. BS, U. R.I., 1957, MS, 1961; PhD, U. Conn., 1979. Rsch. assoc. Charles Pfizer Co., Groton, Conn., 1957-58; tchr. home econs. Groton Sch. Dept., 1958-59; rsch. assoc. U. R.I., Kingston, 1959-61, instr., 1961-73; instr. U. Conn., Storrs, 1973-75; lectr. edn. Keene (N.H.) State Coll., 1975-79, asst. prof., 1979-85, assoc. prof., 1985—; project dir., cons. N.H. Dept. Edn., Concord, 1975—; cons., editor Maine Dept. Cultural and Ednl. Svcs., Augusta, 1990—. Author: Investigating Human Development, 1990, rev. edit., 1991; contbr. articles to profl.

jours., chpt. to book. Mem. Keene Gateway Civic Assn., 1988—. Recipient medal for excellence in econ. edn. Freedoms Found., 1985, 86; Edn. Professions Devel. Act fellow U. Conn., 1975. Mem. Am. Vocat. Assn. (policy and planning bd. guidance div. 1980-88, program chmn. interest sect. 1980-88), Am. Ednl. Rsch. Assn., New Eng. Ednl. Rsch. Orgn. (v.p., chmn. ann. program 1983-84, pres. 1983-85). Republican. Home: 15 Appleton St Keene NH 03431-4620 Office: Keene State Coll 229 Main St Keene NH 03431-4101

BLECK, MAX EMIL, aircraft company executive; b. Buffalo, Apr. 11, 1927; s. Max W. and Dora (Loos) B.; m. Gloria H. Robinson, Apr. 18, 1949; children: Mark E., Cynthia Joanne, Sandra Louise. BS in Mech. Engring., Rensselaer Poly. Inst., 1949; postgrad., U. Buffalo, 1950-51. Design engr. Stanley Aviation Corp., Denver, 1950-55, project engr., 1955-57, chief engr., 1957-59, v.p. engring., 1959-62; chief engr. Mil. and Twin div. Cessna Aircraft Co., Wichita, Kans., 1962-66, gen. mgr., 1966-68, v.p., gen. mgr., 1968-72, group v.p., 1972-75; sr. v.p. ops. Piper Aircraft Co., Lockhaven, Pa., 1975-76, exec. v.p., 1976-78, pres., chief operating officer, 1978, pres., chief exec. officer, 1979-85; exec. v.p., chief operating officer Gates Learjet Corp., Wichita, 1985-87; pres. Cessna Aircraft Co., Wichita, 1987; pres., chief exec. officer Beech Aircraft Corp., Wichita, 1987-92; pres. Raytheon Co., Lexington, Mass., 1992—, also bd. dirs. Office: Raytheon Co 141 Spring St Lexington MA 02173*

BLEIMANN, ALEXANDER A., editor; b. N.Y.C., Jan. 28, 1918; s. Eugene and Elizabeth (Melega) Bleiman; m. Jeanne Vincenza Rispoli, Nov. 5, 1942; children: Eugene Richard, George Allen, Kenneth Marc. Student, U. S.C., 1942; BS, Columbia U., 1953; postgrad., Wagner Coll., 1953. Owner, v.p. Chem. Mfg. Co., N.Y.C., 1945-81; editor-in-chief Am. Lodge Rsch., Free & Accepted Masons Publs., N.Y.C., 1985—. Author: George Washington in New York, 1989. Pres. Temple Emanu-el, S.I., N.Y., 1971; trustee, v.p. Chancellor Robert R. Livingston Masons Libr. & Mus., 1986—; candidate for N.Y. State Senate, 1952. Staff sgt. Chem. Warfare Svc., 1939-45, PTO. Fellow Masons (past master Richmond lodge 1967, dist. dept. grand master 1968), Masonic War Vets. (past comdr. 1971), Shriners (past pres. S.I. club 1969), Vets. of 7th Regiment (life); mem. DAV, Rotary Club S.I. Home: 2427 Presidential Way West Palm Beach FL 33401-1343

BLENKO, WALTER JOHN, JR., lawyer; b. Pitts., June 15, 1926; s. Walter J. and Ardis Leah (Jones) B.; m. Joy Kinneman, Apr. 9, 1949; children: John W., Andrew W. BS, Carnegie-Mellon U., 1950; JD, U. Pitts., 1953. Bar: Pa. 1954. Pvt. practice law Pitts., 1954—; ptnr. Eckert, Seamans, Cherin & Mellott, Pitts., 1984—; mem. adv. bd. Carnegie-Mellon U. dept. mech. engring., 1992—. Active Churchill Vol. Fire Co., 1970-82; charter and hon. mem. Wilkinsburg Emergency Med. Svce.; sec. Hampton Twp. Zoning Hearing Bd., 1991—. With U.S. Army, 1944-46, ETO. Decorated Bronze Star. Fellow Am. Coll. Trial Lawyers; mem. ABA, ASME, Pa. Bar Assn., Allegheny County Bar Assn., Am. Patent Law Assn., Patent Law Assn. Pitts. (pres. 1977-78), Assn. of Bar of City of N.Y., Engrs. Soc. Western Pa., Internat. Patent and Trademark Assn., Duquesne Club, Univ. Club, Rolls-Royce Owners Club (bd. dirs. 1982-84, v.p. publs. 1984-87, treas. 1987-89). Home: 4073 Middle Rd Allison Park PA 15101-1207 Office: Eckert Seamans Cherin & Mellott 600 Grant St Pittsburgh PA 15219-2701

BLESSING, GERALD VINCENT, physicist; b. Cin., July 7, 1942; s. Vincent Joseph and Elizabeth Marie (Bucher) B.; m. Mary Louise Paulson, Sept. 23, 1967; children: C. Denise, Dawn Blessing. BS, Xavier U., 1964; MS, Coll. William and Mary, 1966; PhD, Cath. U. Am., 1973. Instr. physics Randolph-Macon Coll., Ashland, Va., 1966-68; rsch. physicist Naval Surface Warfare Ctr., Silver Spring, Md., 1973-80; group leader ultrasonic stas. Nat. Inst. Standards and Tech., Gaithersburg, Md., 1980—. Patentee ultrasonics. Pres. Local Civic Assn., Frederick, Md., 1983—. Named among Indsl. Rsch. 100 R&D Indsl. Mag., Des Plaines, Ill., 1987. Mem. IEEE (vice chair 1987—), ASTM, Am. Phys. Soc., Am. Soc. Nondestructive Testing, Sigma Xi. Home: 5017 Camelback Ln Frederick MD 21702-6901 Office: Nat Inst Standards and Tech Gaithersburg MD 20899

BLESSING, SCOTT FRANCIS, marketing executive; b. Reading, Pa., Dec. 17, 1957; s. Theodore Robert and Mary Catherine (Brailer) B. BSBA, Shippensburg U., 1979; postgrad. in mktg., St. Joseph's U., Phila., 1987—. Dir. nat. mktg. and promotions Dolfin Corp., Shillington, Pa., 1979-82, asst. v.p. sales, 1982-84; mdse. mgr. VF Corp., Wyomissing, Pa., 1985-88, dir. mktg., 1988—. Volunteer Big Bros./Big Sisters Berks County, Reading, 1981—, v.p., 1983-85; bd. dirs. youth svcs. YMCA of Reading and Berks County, 1990—. Recipient Outstanding Svc. to Children award Big Bros.-Big Sisters Berks County, 1980-88. Mem. Reciprocity Club (Reading) Splash Club (pres. 1989—), Sigma Tau Gamma. Republican. Roman Catholic. Home: 143 Valley Greene Cir Wyomissing PA 19610

BLEVINS, ANNE HELEN, microbiologist; b. Kankakee, Ill.; d. George and Mary Anne (Hoffman) B.; R.N., Wausau Meml. Hosp. Sch. Nursing, 1927; student Columbia U., 1929-36, Marquette U., 1941, N.Y. U., postgrad. Med. Sch., Columbia U., 1936. Research asso. Post Grad. Hosp., Columbia U., N.Y.C., 1940-47; chief bacteriologist Univ. Hosp., N.Y.U. Bellevue Med. Center, 1948-53; chief supervising bacteriologist Meml. Hosp., Meml. Sloan-Kettering Cancer Center, N.Y.C., 1953-68, asst. to dir., 1968-85; cons. hosp. epidemiology, 1985—. Fellow Am. Acad. Microbiology; mem. Am. Soc. Microbiology (hon. mem. southeastern br., recipient life achievement award N.Y.C. br., 1987, Elizabeth O. King award in clin. microbiology, 1970) Am. Pub. Health Assn. (life), N.Y. Acad. Scis. (life). Club: Soroptimist International of New York. Home: 501 W 123d St New York NY 10027 Office: Memorial Hosp 1275 York Ave New York NY 10021

BLEVISS, ALAN DAVID, actor; b. Edmonton, Alta., Can., Aug. 6, 1941; s. Joseph Harold and Leena (Motkovich) B.; m. Frances Anne Silverberg, May 28, 1968 (div. 1983); 1 child, Lisa Aviva; m. Susan Barbara Lipkin, Mar. 12, 1983; children: Sarah Jenny, Joshua Eli. Student, Nat. Theatre Sch. Can., Montreal, 1963-66; BA, U. Alta., Edmonton, 1967; diploma edn., U. Toronto, Can., 1968. Pres. Pine Apple Sounds Prodns. Inc., N.Y.C., 1976-90, Alan Bleviss, Ltd., Toronto, 1973—; gen. ptnr. Pine Apple Sounds, Ltd., Short Hills, N.J., 1985—; gov. bd. Nat. Theatre Sch. Can., Montreal, 1989—. Narrator (film) Finland: A Fire in Your Heart, 1990 (Telly award 1991); announcer (comml.) Julie, 1990 (Internat. Film and TV award 1990). Bd. dirs. Brotherhood B'nai Jeshrun, Short Hills, 1990—. Mem. SAG, Actors Equity, Am. Fedn. Radio Artists (dir. local bd. 1989—), Alliance of Can. TV and Radio Artists (pres. Toronto chpt. 1972-75, dir. local bd. 1971-76), Friars Club. Democrat. Jewish. Office: Pine Apple Sounds Ltd PO Box 504 Short Hills NJ 07078

BLEYMAN, LEA KANNER, biology educator, genetics researcher; b. Halle, Germany, Nov. 9, 1936; came to U.S., 1946; d. Salomon David and Amalia Kanner; 1 child, Anne. BA magna cum laude, Brandeis U., 1958; MA, Columbia U., 1961; PhD, Ind. U., 1966. Rsch. assoc. U. Ill., Urbana, 1964-69, U. N.C., Chapel Hill, 1970-72; assoc. prof. biology Baruch Coll., CUNY, 1973-78, prof., 1979—, chmn. dept. natural scis., 1981-83. Co-author: (lab. manual) General Biology, 1982; asst. editor Protozoological Actualities, 1979; mem. editorial bd. Jour. Protozoology, 1985-92; contbr. articles to profl. jours. Bd. dirs. Aux. Enterprises Corp., N.Y.C., 1983—, CUNY Women's Rsch. and Devel. Fund, 1986—, 305 E 24th Street Corp., N.Y.C., 1989—. Grad. fellow USPHS, 1961-64, rsch. fellow Sigma Xi, 1974, Max Planck Inst., Berlin, 1974, Chancellors faculty fellow CUNY, 1985-86; scholar Baruch Coll., 1987. Mem. AAAS, Am. Assn. Women in Sci., Am. Genetics Assn., Am. Soc. Cell Biology, Genetics Soc. Am., Soc. Protozoologists (exec. com. 1981-86, sec. 1991—), N.Y. Acad. Scis. Office: Baruch Coll CUNY 17 Lexington Ave New York NY 10010-5526

BLICHER, ADOLPH, consulting engineer; b. Warsaw, Poland, Oct. 13, 1907; came to U.S., 1946; s. Joseph and Pauline (Rasolt) B.; m. Anna Blicher, 1934 (dec. 1991); 1 child, A. Peter Blicher. BSEE, U. Tolouse, France, 1928; MSEE, Ecole Superieure d'Electricte, Paris, 1933; DSc, Tech. U., Warsaw, 1938. Dir. engring. Polish Broadcasting Co., Warsaw, 1944-46; sr. physicist Radio-Receptor Co., Bklyn., 1951-55; mgr. advanced semiconductor device and device physics dept. RCA Corp., 1955-74; cons. engr., scientific writer North Plainfield, N.J., 1974—. Author: Thyristor Physics, 1976, Field-Effect and Bipolar Transistor Physics, 1981, (with others) Ency. of Sci. and Technology, 1986; contbr. articles to profl. jours.; patentee in field. Mem. IEEE (life sr. mem.).

BLICK, AMBLER MONTQUIRE, construction company executive; b. Balt., Feb. 1, 1947; s. Ambler Montquire Blick and Jeanne Harriat (Cox) Bohanan; m. Cindy L. Cullen, May 26, 1984; children: Gregory, Paul, Megan, Lauran. AA, Community Coll. Balt., 1971; BA, U. Md., 1972, cert. acctg., 1986. Exec. v.p. NLP Enterprises, Inc., Owings Mills, Md., 1972—. Active Rep. Nat. Com., Washington, 1988—, PTA, Balt., 1988—, Mus. Natural History. With USN, 1966-70. Decorated Cert. of Merit. Fellow Smithsonian Instn.; mem. Balt. County C. of C., Am. Legion, Masons, Scottish Rite, Shriners. Episcopalian. Home: 902 Bond Ave Reisterstown MD 21136-1812 Office: NLP Enterprises Inc PO Box 349 Owings Mills MD 21117-0349

BLISS, CAROL LOUISE, guidance counselor; b. Butler, Pa., Dec. 10, 1949; d. Harold Frank and Eleanor Louise (George) Scott; m. Larry Keith Bliss, Sept. 1, 1973; children: Casey Keith, Corey Quinn. BS in Sci., Pa. State U., 1971, MEd in Human Devel. and Family Studies, 1974; cert. in secondary guidance, Westminster Coll., New Wilmington, Pa., 1991. Bus. mgr. H. F. Scott Engring., Rimersburg, Pa., 1973-91; guidance counselor Abraxas I High Sch., Marienville, Pa., 1991—. Mem. AACD, Am. Sch. Counselors Assn. Home: PO Box 141 Rimersburg PA 16248

BLISSERT, JULIE HARRISON, public relations administrator; b. Cottage Grove, Oreg., Mar. 23, 1954; d. Wilfred James and Marjorie Frances (Stennick) Harrison; m. Albert Duryea Blissert, June 25, 1977. Student, U. Sussex, Eng., 1974-75; AB summa cum laude, Occidental Coll., 1976; cert., Radcliffe Coll., 1976. Editorial asst. Simon & Schuster Pocket Books, N.Y.C., 1976-77; prodn. asst. U. Okla. Press, Norman, 1977-79; copy editor Post-Standard, Syracuse, N.Y., 1979-80; reporter Syracuse Newspapers Oswego (N.Y.) Bur., 1980-83; asst. dir. pub. affairs SUNY, Oswego, 1983-84, dir. pub. affairs, 1984—; freelance editor U. Okla. Press, Norman, 1978-79, Health Awareness Publs., East Syracuse, N.Y., 1979-87, Syracuse U. Press, 1982-83. Mem. Women in Communications, Inc., Nat. Issues Forum of Oswego (steering com. 1983—, convenor 1984, 85), Greater Oswego C. of C. (mem. com. 1986—, com. chair 1990—), SUNY Coun. Univ. Affairs and Devel., Oswego County Press Club, Phi Beta Kappa. Office: SUNY 210 Culkin Hall Oswego NY 13126-3500

BLITZ, DANIEL, electrical engineer; b. N.Y.C., Feb. 8, 1920; s. Samuel and Amelia (Hirsch) B.; m. Peggy Schulder, Aug. 5, 1963. BS, MIT, 1940. Research engr. Radio Corp. of Am., Camden and Princeton, N.J., 1940-47, Raytheon Mfg. Corp., Waltham, Mass., 1947-51; co-founder Sanders Assocs., Inc., Waltham, 1951; research engr. Sanders Assocs., Inc., Waltham and Nashua, 1951-87; corp. engr. Sanders Assocs., Inc., Nashua, N.H., 1974-80; engring. fellow Sanders Assocs., Inc., 1980-87, cons., 1987-88; vis. scholar Ctr. for Electromagnetics Rsch. Northeastern U., Boston, 1992—; mem. expedition to study and film Bushmen of Africa's Kalahari Desert, Harvard U. Peabody Mus., 1955; cons. in field. Patentee in field (50). Chmn. Spl. Com. on Radar Altimeters, Radio Tech. Commn. for Aeronautics, 1979-82; mem. Spl. Com. on Loran-C Receivers, Radio Tech. Commn. for Marine Services., 1978-79. Mem. IEEE (life), AAAS. Home and Office: 242 Beacon St Boston MA 02116-1232

BLITZER, ANDREW, otolaryngologist, educator; b. Pitts., Apr. 25, 1946; s. Martin Hollander and Lyrene Iris (Lave) B.; m. Patricia Volk, Dec. 21, 1969; children: Peter Morgen, Polly Volk. BA, Adelphi U., 1967; DDS, Columbia U., 1970; MD, Mt. Sinai Sch. Medicine, 1973. Diplomate Am. Bd. Otolaryngology. Resident in gen. surgery Beth Israel Hosp., N.Y.C., 1973-74; resident in otolaryngology Mt. Sinai Hosp., N.Y.C., 1974-77; asst. prof. otolaryngology Coll. Phys. & Surg., Columbia U., N.Y.C., 1977-82, assoc. prof. otolaryngology and oral surgery, 1982-84, prof. clin. otolaryngology and oral surgery, 1984—, vice chmn. dept. otolaryngology, 1983—, acting chmn., dir., 1991—; dir. div. head and neck surgery Columbia-Presbyn. Med. Ctr., N.Y.C., 1980—, acting chmn. dept. otolaryngology, dir. otolaryngology svc., Columbia-Presbyn. Med. Ctr., 1991—, dir. residency edn., 1978—; lectr. dept. otolaryngology Mt. Sinai Sch. Medicine, N.Y.C., 1977—. Co-Author several books; assoc. editor: Oncology Times, Controversies in Otolaryngology; mem. editorial rev. bd. The Laryngoscope, Otolaryngology-Head and Neck Surgery, Jour. Otolaryngology; contbr. chpts. to books, articles to profl. jours. Recipient award for excellence Am. Assn. Orthodontists, 1970, Tchr.-Investigator award Nat. Inst. Neurol. Communicative Disorders and Strokes, 1978-83. Fellow ACS, N.Y. Acad. Medicine, Am. Soc. Head and Neck Surgery, Am. Acad. Facial Plastic and Reconstructive Surgery, Am. Laryngol. Assn., Am. Larynol., Rhinol. and Otol. Soc., Am. Acad. Otolaryngology-Head and Neck Surgery (honor award), Am. Broncho-esophagological Assn. Home: 1136 5th Ave New York NY 10128-0122 Office: Columbia U Coll Physicians & Surgeons Dept Otolaryngology 630 W 168th St New York NY 10032-3702

BLITZER, DAVID MAYERS, economist; b. N.Y.C., Nov. 1, 1948; s. Edward H.R. and Nancy (Mayers) B.; m. Judi Rappoport, June 8, 1973; children: Mark Rappoport, Julie Rappoport. B.S., Cornell U., 1970; M.A., George Washington U., 1973; Ph.D., Columbia U., 1978. Energy economist Nat. Commn. on Materials Policy, Washington, 1972-73; cons., 1973-77; sr. econ. analyst Nat. Econ. Research Assocs., Inc., N.Y.C., 1977-80; corp. economist McGraw-Hill, Inc., N.Y.C., 1980-82; chief economist Standard & Poors Corp., N.Y.C., 1982-86, v.p., chief economist, 1986—. Served to lt. (j.g.) USPHS, 1970-72. Mem. Am. Econ. Assn., Econometric Soc. Club: Downtown Athletic (N.Y.C.). Avocation: sailing. Office: Standard & Poors Corp 25 Broadway New York NY 10004-1010

BLIVEN, BRUCE, JR., writer; b. L.A., Jan. 31, 1916; s. Bruce and Rose (Emery) B.; m. Naomi Horowitz, May 26, 1950; 1 child, Frederic Bruce. AB, Harvard U., 1937. Reporter Manchester (Eng.) Guardian, 1936, corr., 1940-42; editorial asst. New Republic mag., 1937-38; editorial writer N.Y. Post, 1939-42; contbr. New Yorker (other nat. mags.), 1946—; tchr. Writers Conf. Ind. U., 1955, 66. Author: The Wonderful Writing Machine, 1954, Battle for Manhattan, 1956, Under the Guns, 1972, Book Traveller, 1975, Volunteers, One and All, 1976, The Finishing Touch, 1978, New York: A Bicentennial History, 1981; juveniles The Story of D-Day, 1956, The American Revolution, 1958, From Pearl Harbor to Okinawa, 1960, From Casablanca To Berlin, 1965, (with Naomi Bliven) New York: The Story of the World's Most Exciting City, 1969. Pvt. to capt. F.A. AUS, 1942-45. Decorated Bronze Star with oak leaf cluster. Mem. Authors Guild, P.E.N., Soc. Am. Historians, Century Assn. Office: care The New Yorker 20 W 43d St New York NY 10036

BLIZZARD, RICHARD TYRONE, health care executive; b. Balt., Oct. 10, 1947; s. Donald Ralph and Virginia Adell (Zepp) B.; m. Amanda Carlaine, Sept. 21, 1968; children: Meghan Michelle, Bindi Kai. BS, La. State U., 1969, MS, 1971; DBA, U. Colo., 1976. Lectr. New South Wales Inst. of Tech., Sydney, Australia, 1973-76; assoc. prof. Susquehanna Univ., Selinsgrove, Pa., 1976-81; market analyst United Health Svcs., Johnson City, N.Y., 1981-85; asst. v.p. community health svc. United Health Svcs., Binghamton, N.Y., 1985-86; v.p. corp. devel. United Health Svcs., Binghamton, 1986-90, corp. devel. officer, 1990—; cons. Australian Dept. of Def., Sydney, 1974, N.S.W. Inst. of Export, Sydney, 1974-76, Indsl. Design Coun., Sydney, 1975-76, Hood Light and Guise Ad Agy., Harrisburg, Pa., 1977-81; lectr. SUNY-Binghamton, 1984—; speaker Nat. Health Care Mktg. Symposiums, 1987, 88, 89. Editorial reviewer Jour. Mktg. Edn., 1983—; contbr. articles to profl. jours. Bd. dirs. Endicott (N.Y.) Sr. Housing; vice chmn. Broome-Tioga Sch. and Bus., Binghamton. Mem. Sales and Mktg. Execs. of So. Tier (bd. dirs. 1984-89, pres. 1987-88), Endicott (N.Y.) Sertoma (found. rep. 1986-88, treas. 1987-88, sec. 1988-89, pres. 1989-90, chmn. bd. 1990-91), Union Aquatic Club (pres. 1982-83). Republican. Methodist. Office: United Health Svcs 20-42 Mitchell Ave Binghamton NY 13903

BLOCH, ALAN, technical consultant; b. N.Y.C., Nov. 28, 1915; s. Alexander and Blanche Bloch; divorced; children: Alison, Christoper. BA cum laude, Swarthmore Coll., 1938; MA, Oberlin Coll., 1939; postgrad., Iowa State U., 1940-41. Asst. pres. Lear Avia, Piqua, Ohio, 1939-40; engr. Eclipse Pioneer, Hasbrouch Heights, N.J., 1946; lab. head Arma Corp., Bklyn., 1947-49; co-owner Audio Instrument Co., N.Y.C., 1950-54; with Gen. Precision, 1955-65; engr. Gyrodyne, St. James, N.Y., 1965-69; ind. cons. Port Washington, N.Y.C., 1970—. Author short story; contbr. articles to profl. jours.; patentee in field. Flight lt. Royal Can. Air Force, 1941-45. Grantee Ford Found., 1975. Mem. AAAS, N.Y. Acad. Sci., Am. Phys. Soc., Audio Engring. Soc., Assn. for Computing Machinery, Fedn. Am. Scientists, Mensa, Sigma Xi. Democrat. Home and Office: 333 E 30th St 14-J New York NY 10016

BLOCH, ALAN NEIL, federal judge; b. Pitts., Apr. 12, 1932; s. Gustave James and Molly Dorothy B.; m. Elaine Claire Amdur, Aug. 24, 1957; children: Rebecca Lee, Carolyn Jean, Evan Amdur. B.S. in Econs, U. Pa., 1953; J.D., U. Pitts., 1958. Bar: Pa. 1959. Indsl. engr. U.S. Steel Corp., 1953; practice law Pitts., 1959-79; U.S. judge Western Dist. Pa., Pitts., 1979—; mem. Jud. Conf. U.S. Com. on Ct. Security, 1987—; chmn. joint task force on death penalty representation Supreme Ct. Pa.-Ct. Appeals; past mem. Rule 11 task force Ct. Appeals (3d cir.). Contbr. articles to legal publs. Vice chmn. Stadium Authority Pitts., 1970-80; bd. dirs. St. John's Gen. Hosp., Pitts., 1975-80. Served with AUS, 1953-55. Mem. Am. Bar Assn., Acad. Trial Lawyers Allegheny County. Jewish. Club: River. Office: US Dist Ct US PO & Courthouse 7th & Grant Sts Rm 11 Pittsburgh PA 15219*

BLOCH, ERIC, biochemistry educator; b. Munich, Apr. 4, 1928; came to U.S., 1939; s. Alexander and Hilda (Loeb) B.; m. Pnina Pauline Gruenberg, July 30, 1961; children: Talia, Alexandra. BS, CCNY, 1948; MA, U. Tex., 1950, PhD, 1953. Staff scientist Worcester Found. for Exptl. Biology, Shrewsbury, Mass., 1952-57, Children's Cancer Rsch. Found., Boston, 1957-58; assoc. Harvard Med. Sch., Boston, 1957-58; asst. prof. Albert Einstein Coll. of Medicine, Bronx, N.Y., 1958-65, assoc. prof., 1965-76, prof. biochemistry and obstetrics, 1976—; mem. study NIH, Washington, 1978-82. Contbr. articles to Jour. Biol. Chemistry, Endocrinology, Vitamins & Hormones, others. Sci. fair judge N.Y. Acad. Scis., N.Y.C., 1987—. Fellow AAAS.; mem. Endocrine Soc., Soc. Study of Reproduction, Soc. for Biol. Chemistry, Soc. for Gynecol. Investigation, Sigma Xi, Phi Lambda Upsilon. Office: Albert Einstein Coll Med 1300 Morris Park Ave Bronx NY 10461-1924

BLOCH, JULIA CHANG, government official; b. Chefoo, Peoples Republic of China, Mar. 2, 1942; came to U.S., 1951, naturalized, 1962; d. Fu-yun and Eva (Yeh) Chang; m. Stuart Marshall Bloch, Dec. 21, 1968. BA, U. Calif., Berkeley, 1964; MA, Harvard U., 1967, postgrad. in mgmt., 1987; DHL (hon.), Northeastern U., Boston, 1986. Vol. Peace Corps, Sabah, Malaysia, 1964-66, tng. officer East Asia and Pacific region, Washington, 1967-68, evaluation officer, 1968-70; mem. minority staff U.S. Senate Select Com. on Nutrition and Human Needs, Washington, 1971-76, chief minority counsel, 1976-77; dep. dir. Office of African Affairs, U.S. Internat. Communications Agy., Washington, 1977-80; fellow Inst. Politics, Harvard U., Cambridge, Mass., 1980-81; asst. adminstr. Bur. for Food for Peace and Voluntary Assistance, AID, Washington, 1981-87, asst. adminstr. Bur. for Asia and Near East, 1987-88; assoc. U.S.-Japan Rels. Program, Ctr. for Internat. Affairs, Harvard U., Cambridge, Mass., 1988-89; ambassador to Kingdom of Nepal, 1989—; U.S. Senate rep. World Conf. on Internat. Women's Yr., Mex., 1975; advisor U.S. Del. to Food and Agr. Orgn. Conf., Rome, 1975; rep. Am. Council Young Polit. Leaders, Peoples Republic China, 1977; charter mem. Sr. Exec. Service, 1979; head U.S. del. Biennial Session World Food Programme, Rome, 1981-86, Devel. Assistance Com. Meeting on Non-Govtl. Orgns., Paris, 1985, Intergovtl. Group on Indonesia, The Hague, The Netherlands, 1987, World Bank Consultative Group Meeting, Paris, 1987, mem. exec. women in govt., 1988—, mem. coun. fgn. rels., 1991—; mem. com. to visit art mus., 1989—; mem. U.S. Nat. Com. for Pacific Econ. Cooperation, 1984—; mem. adv. bd. Women's Campaign Fund, 1976-78; exec. bd. mem. Internat. Ctr. for Research on Women, 1974-81; bd. dirs. Minority Legis. Edn. Program, 1976-78; pres. Nat. Peace Corps counsel, 1988-89; mem. presdl. adv. coun. Peace Corps, 1988-89. Author: A U.S.-Japan Aid Alliance, 1991; co-author: Chinese Home Cooking, 1986. Mem. exec. bd. Internat. Ctr. for Research on Women, 1974-81; mem. adv. bd. Women's Campaign Fund, 1976-78, Nat. Women's Polit. Caucus, 1978-84, Nat. Presdl. Debate Forum, 1987-92; mem. nat. adv. council Experiment in Internat. Living, 1981—; bd. dirs. Minority Legis. Edn. Program, 1976-78. Recipient Hubert Humphrey award for internat. service, 1979, Humanitarian Service award AID, 1987, Leader for Peace award Peace Corps, 1987, Asian Am. Leadership award, 1989; named Outstanding Woman of Color, Nat. Inst. for Women of Color, 1982, Woman of Distinction, Nat. Conf. for Coll. Women Student Leaders and Women of Achievement, 1987, Woman of Yr. Orgn. Chinese Am. Women, 1987, Disting. Pub. Svc. award Nat. Assn. Profl. Asian Pacific Am. Women, 1989; Ford Found. Study fellow for internat. devel. Harvard U., 1966, Paul Harris award Rotary, 1992. Mem. Exec. Women in Govt., Orgn. Chinese Am. Women (founder, chair 1977—, bd. dirs., Woman of Yr. 1987), Asia Soc. (pres. coun. 1989), Prytannean Honor Soc., Mortar Bd. Republican. Avocations: ceramics, gourmet cooking, collecting art. Office: Am Embassy Kathamandu Dept State Washington DC 20521

BLOCH, PETER, historian, writer; b. Frankfurt-Main, Fed. Republic Germany, Oct. 19, 1921; came to U.S., 1949; s. Arthur and Else (Israel) B. Student, U. Brussels, 1939-40, U. Geneva, 1943-45. Corres. European publs., radio stas., 1949—; U.S. del. League of Belgian and Allied Patriots, Brussels, 1949-70; founder, pres. Assn. for Puerto Rican-Hispanic Culture, Inc., N.Y.C., 1965—; U.S. del. Acad. Soc. Arts-Scis.-Letters of France, Paris, 1976—; chmn. of bd. Internat. Immigrants Found., Inc., N.Y.C., 1989—. Author: La-Le-Lo-Lai Puerto Rican Music, 1973, Painting and Sculpture of the Puerto Ricans, 1978, James Israel 1848-1936, 1983, De Van Eyck a Chagall-Once Grandes Pintores, 1987; culture editor mag. Canales, 1976—; author numerous essays and articles, 3 plays. Recipient Key to the City, Mayor of San Juan, P.R., 1964; named to Hon. Order of Isabel la Católica, 1969. Mem. Assn. Hispanic Critics of N.Y. (pres. ethics commn.). Home: 83 Park Ter W New York NY 10034

BLOCK, BARRY HERBERT, podiatrist, lawyer, educator, magazine editor; b. Scranton, Pa., Jan. 7, 1949; s. Jerome and Cherie (Gold) B.; m. Hermine Sudiker, Apr. 3, 1976; children: Steven, Julie, Michael. BA, Hunter Coll., 1971; DPM, N.Y. Coll. Podiatric Medicine, 1976; JD cum laude, N.Y. Law Sch., 1991. Diplomate Am. Bd. Podiatric Pub Health. Gen. editor Jour. Am. Podiatric Med. Assn., Bethesda, Md., 1979-81; editor-in-chief Podiatry Mgmt., Upper Darby, Pa., 1982—; asst. prof. N.Y. Coll. Podiatric Medicine, 1989—; chief podiatry staff Cardinal Cooke Med. Ctr., N.Y.C., 1990—. Author: Foot Talk, 1984, Complications in Foot Surgery, 1984, Podiatric Marketing and Practice Management, 1988. Fellow Am. Assn. Hosp. Podiatrists; mem. Am. Podiatric Med. Assn., ABA, Am. Soc. Authors and Journalists, Am. Coll. Foot Surgeons (assoc.). Jewish. Office: PO Box 50 New York NY 10044-0201

BLOCK, FRANCINE ELLEN, educational consultant; b. Barre, Vt., Apr. 10, 1947; d. Joseph and Anna (Moisoff) Rome; m. Alan Joseph Block, July 27, 1969; children: Justin Andrew, Darren Stuart. BS, U. Vt., 1969, MAT, 1972. Tchr. Burlington High (Vt.) Sch., 1969-72; dir. career and coll. resource ctr. Westborough (Mass.) High Sch., 1979-84; ednl. cons., chief exec. officer Am. Coll. Admissions Cons., Richboro, Pa., 1984—; alumni admissions rep. U. Vt., Burlington, 1978—. Regional officer Assn. Jr. League Internat., N.Y.C., 1987-88; bd. dirs., officer Jr. League, Worcester, Mass., 1980-86, Princeton, N.J., 1989-90; chmn. allocations United Way Bucks County, 1990—. Mem. AACD, AAUW (bd. dirs. 1989—), Am. Sch. Counselors Assn., Am. Bus. Women's Assn., Nat. Assn. Coll. Admissions Counselors, Nat. Assn. Fgn. Student Affairs, New Eng. Assn. Coll. Admissions Counselors, Pa. Assn. Coll. Admissions Counselors, N.Y. Assn. Coll. Admissions Counselors, N.J. Assn. Coll. Admissions Counselors, Bucks County C. of C. (mem. com.), Hadassah Internat. (bd. dirs. Newtown chpt. 1990—, v.p. Hosp. Guild chpt. 1990—, supt sch. adv. panel, 1991—). Office: Am Coll Admissions Cons PO Box 701 Richboro PA 18954

BLOCK, GARY BROOKS, counselor; b. Phila., May 2, 1964; s. Naomi Carol Brooks. BS, LaSalle U., Phila., 1986; MS in Edn., U. Pa., 1988. Lic. in sec. and elem. sch. counseling. Sch. counselor CORA Svcs. (Counseling or Referral Assistance), Inc., Phla., 1987-90, New Hope-Solebury (Pa.) Sch. Dist., 1990—. Home: 608 Oakfield Ln Philadelphia PA 19115-1107 Office: New Hope-Solebury Sch Dist 180 W Bridge St New Hope PA 18938-1498

BLOCK, HERBERT LAWRENCE (HERBLOCK), editorial cartoonist; b. Chgo., Oct. 13, 1909; s. David Julian and Tessie (Lupe) B. Student, Lake Forest (Ill.) Coll., 1927-29, LLD (hon.), 1957; LittD (hon.), Rutgers U.,

1963; LHD, Williams Coll., 1969, Haverford Coll., 1977, U. Md., 1977; LHD (hon.), Colby Coll., 1986; student, Art Inst. Chgo. (part time classes). Editorial cartoonist: Chgo. Daily News, 1929-33, NEA Service, 1933-43, U.S. Army, 1943-45; editorial cartoonist: The Washington Post, 1946—; author: The Herblock Book, 1952, Herblock's Here and Now, 1955, Herblock's Special for Today, 1958, Straight Herblock, 1964, The Herblock Gallery, 1968, Herblock's State of the Union, 1972, Herblock Special Report, 1974, Herblock On All Fronts, 1980, Herblock Through the Looking Glass, 1984, Herblock At Large, 1987; designer U.S. postage stamp commemorating 175th anniv. of Bill of Rights, 1966. Recipient Pulitzer prize, 1942, 54, 79; Am. Newspaper Guild award, 1948; Heywood Broun award, 1950; Sigma Delta Chi Nat. Editorial Awards, 1949, 50, 52, 57; Sidney Hillman award (for book), 1953; Reuben Award Nat. Cartoonists Soc., 1957; Lauterbach award for civil liberties, 1959; Florina Lasker award N.Y. Civil Liberties Union, 1960; Disting. Service Journalism award U. Mo., 1961; Golden Key award, 1963; Capital Press Club award, 1963; Bill of Rights award, 1966; Nat. Headliners award, 1976; Power of Printing award, 1977; Nat. Press Club 4th Estate award, 1977; award for human relations NEA, 1979; Overseas Press Club Citation, 1979; ACLU award for def. Bill of Rights, 1981; World Hunger Media Award, 1984; People for the Am. Way First Amendment award, 1985; Elijah Parish Lovejoy award for freedom of the press, 1986; Hubert H. Humphrey Civil Rights award Leadership Conf. on Civil Rights, 1987; Franklin Roosevelt Freedom medal F.D.Roosevelt Four Freedoms Found., 1987; World Humor award Workshop Libr. on World Humor, 1988; Overseas Press Club award, 1988; Outstanding Consumer Media Svc. award Consumer Fedn. Am., 1989, Good Guy award Nat. Woman's Polit. Caucus, 1989, Exceptional Merit Media award, 1990, Global Media award Population Inst., 1990, Maggie award Planned Parenthood Fedn. Am., 1991. Fellow Am. Acad. Arts and Scis., Sigma Delta Chi; mem. Phi Beta Kappa (hon.). Office: Washington Post 1150 15th St NW Washington DC 20071-0002*

BLOCK, JOHN ROBINSON, newspaper publisher; b. Toledo, Oct. 1, 1954; s. Paul Jr. and Marjorie Jane (McNab) B. BA, Yale U., 1977. Reporter AP, Miami, Fla., 1977-78, N.Y.C., 1978-80; Washington corr. The Toledo Blade, 1980-82; European corr. The Toledo Blade, London, 1982—; Sunday editor The Toledo Blade, 1983-85, asst. mng. editor, 1985-87, exec. editor, 1987-89; co-pub., editor-in-chief The Blade, Toledo, 1989—; co-pub. Pitts. Post-Gazette, 1989—; v.p., bd. dirs. P.G. Pub. Co., Pitts., Monterey (Calif.) Peninsula Herald Co.; bd. dirs. Blade Communications, Inc., Toledo. Chmn. City Mgr.'s Hist. Preservation Com., Toledo, 1983-85. Mem. Am. Soc. Newspaper Editors, Soc. Profl. Journalists. Clubs: Yale (N.Y.C.); Belmont Country (Perrysburg, Ohio). Home: 5502 N Citation Rd Toledo OH 43615-2158 Office: Blade Communications Inc 541 N Superior St Toledo OH 43660-0001

BLOCK, RICHARD RAPHAEL, lawyer, arbitrator; b. Phila., Nov. 9, 1938; s. Harry and Ida (Brandes) B.; m. Joanne Kramer, July 1, 1943 (div. Jan. 1973); 1 child, Jeffrey. AB, Dickinson Coll., 1959; LLB cum laude, U. Pa., 1962. Bar: Pa. 1963, N.J. 1980, D.C. 1982. Assoc. Folz & Bard, Phila., 1963-64; ptnr. Melzer & Schiffrin, Phila., 1964-75, Beitch & Block, Phila., 1975-90; dir. community rels. Dist. Atty. of Phila., 1991—; chmn. hearing com Disciplinary Bd. Supreme Ct. Pa., 1982-90. Contbg. author: Handbook of Pennsylvania Courts, 1970, Divorce Mediation, 1985, Prenuptial Agreements, 1989, Encyclopedia on Matrimonial Practice, 1991; assoc. editor U. Pa. Law Rev.; contbr. articles to profl. jours. Vice pres. Am. Jewish Congress, Phila., 1975; campaign mgr. Elect Joan Specter to City Coun., Phila., 1978, 82, 86. Mem. Pa. Bar Assn. (arbitrator Inter-Atty. Dispute Resolution 1987—, speaker 1988) Am. Arbitration Assn., Phila. Coll. Judiciary (lectr. 1984). Republican.

BLOCK, WILLIAM, newspaper publisher; b. N.Y.C., Sept. 20, 1915; s. Paul and Dina (Wallach) B.; m. Maxine Horton, Mar. 23, 1944; children: William, Karen Block Ayars, Barbara Block Burney, Donald. A.B., Yale U., 1936. With circulation, other depts. Toledo Blade, 1937-39, asst. to gen. mgr., 1939-41; co-pub. Pitts. Post-Gazette and Toledo Blade, 1941-87, pub., 1987—; chmn. bd. Blade Communications, Inc. Bd. dirs. Pitts. Communications Found., Pitts. Symphony Soc., Pitts. Ctr. for the Arts, Gateway to Music Inc.; trustee Am. Assembly; sponsor Allegheny Conf. on Community Devel. Served to capt. AUS, 1941-46; served in mil. govt. in 1945-46, Korea. Mem. Internat. Press Inst., Am. Soc. Newspaper Editors., Soc. Profl. Journalists, Am. Newspaper Pubs. Assn., Hist. Soc. Western Pa. (bd. dirs.).

BLOCK, WILLIAM KENNETH, lawyer; b. N.Y.C., Oct. 23, 1950; s. Louis and Catherine Veronica (Kerr) B. BA, Colgate U., 1973; JD, Union U., Albany, N.Y., 1976. Bar: N.Y. 1977. Gen. counsel N.Y.C. Tax Commn., 1978-81; asst. commn. fin. N.Y.C. Dept. Fin., 1981-84, dep. commr. fin., 1984-89; assoc. Schwartz, Weiss, Steckler & Hoffman, P.C., N.Y.C., 1989-91; prin. William K. Block, Atty.-at-Law, N.Y.C., 1992—; adj. lectr. real estate NYU, 1992—. Contbr. articles on real property tax law and procedure to profl. jours. Mem. Internat. Assn. Assessing Officers (presdl. citation 1986, McCareen award 1988, chmn. met. jurisdiction coun. 1987-88), ABA, N.Y. State Assessor's Assn., N.Y. State Bar Assn., N.Y. County Bar Assn. (com. on City of N.Y., real property com.), Real Estate Rev. Bar Assn., Assn. of Bar City N.Y. (com. on lectures and continuing edn.). Democrat. Roman Catholic. Home: 360 E 57th St Apt 24A New York NY 10022-2906 Office: 360 E 57th St New York NY 10022-2906

BLODGETT, TODD ALAN, marketing professional, consultant; b. Iowa City, Sept. 10, 1960; s. Gary Burl and Sandy Jean (Hodgson) B. BA in Journalism. Fin. dir. Senator Roger W. Jepsen Re-election Com., Des Moines, 1983-84; staff asst. Reagan-Bush Inaugural Com., Inc., Washington, 1984-85; copywriter Stephen Winchell & Assocs., Inc., Rosslyn, Va., 1985; editorial asst. White House Staff (news summary), Washington, 1985-86; acct. exec. J.L. Whitehead & Assoc., Washington, 1986-87; domestic policy advisor Bush-Quayle '88 Com., Washington, 1987-88; sr. policy advisor analyst Rep. Nat. Com., Washington, 1989-90; mktg. cons. Washington, 1991—; pub. rels. cons. Penny Wise Office Products, Washington, 1991—; campaign advisor"Blodgett for Iowa Legislature" campaign, Mason City, Iowa, 1991-92. Contbr. editor "American Conservative", 1991—; contbr. political editorials to popular mags. Bd. dirs. "The University Reporter" newspaper, Washington, 1991—; mem. The Conservative Network, Washington, 1985—, (contbr. mem.) Rep. Cen. Com. of Iowa, Des Moines, 1983, (sustaining mem.) Lincoln Club of Iowa, Des Moines, 1988—, Chevy Chase Presbyn. Ch., Washington, 1990—. Mem. NRA (life), Ducks Unltd., Reagan Appointees Alumni Assn. (Reagan mem.), Kennedy-Warren Residents Assn. (pres. 1989-92), U.S. C. of C., Watergate Health Club, Sigma Alpha Epsilon. Presbyterian. Home: 3133 Connecticut Ave NW Washington DC 20008-5147 Office: The University Reporter 1155 15th St NW Ste #810 Washington DC 20005

BLOEDE, MERLE HUIE, civic worker; b. Brady, Tex., May 4, 1921; d. Hulon William and Anna (Lohn) Huie; student San Angelo Bus. Coll., 1944; m. Victor G. Bloede III, Mar. 11, 1945; children—Dee Anna Smith (Mrs. Jerry Willis), Victor G. IV, Susan Lohn Quaid. Asst supr. Office Censorship, San Antonio, 1942-43, Patroness North Shore Hosp., Manhasset, N.Y., 1954-56, 67-68; vol. Waldorf Sch. Scholarship Fund, Garden City, N.Y., 1957; asst. treas., exec. bd., mem. art com. Meml. Sloan-Kettering Cancer Ctr. Soc., N.Y.C., chmn. pub. relations com., 1982-83 Mem. North Shore So. Soc. (pres. 1963-65). Republican. Mem. Community Reformed Ch. Clubs: Sands Point (N.Y.) Golf, Flower Hill Garden (chmn. community service com. 1967), Delray Dunes (Fla.) Golf and Country. Home: 4923 King Palm Cir Boynton Beach FL 33436-5902 also: 19 Duke of Gloucester Manhasset NY 11030 also: Cow Creek Ranch Lohn TX 76852

BLOEMBERGEN, NICOLAAS, physicist, educator; b. Dordrecht, The Netherlands, Mar. 11, 1920; came to U.S., 1952, naturalized, 1958; s. Auke and Sophia M. (Quint) B.; m. Huberta D. Brink, June 26, 1950; children: Antonia, Brink, Juliana. BA, Utrecht U., 1941, MA, 1943; PhD, Leiden U., 1948; MA (hon.), Harvard U., 1951; D of Sci. (hon.), Laval U., 1987, U. Conn., 1988, U. Hartford, 1991. Teaching asst. Utrecht U., 1942-45; research fellow Leiden U., 1948; mem. Soc. Fellows Harvard U., 1949-51, assoc. prof., 1951-57, Gordon McKay prof. applied physics, 1957—, Rumford prof. physics, 1974, Gerhard Gade univ. prof., 1980, prof. emeritus, 1990; vis. prof. U. Paris, 1957, U. Calif., 1965, Collège de France, Paris, 1980; Lorentz guest prof. U. Leiden, 1973; Raman vis. prof. Bangalore, India, 1979; Fairchild Disting. scholar Calif. Inst. Tech., 1984; von Humboldt Sr. Scientist, Munic, Fed. Republic Germany.; hon. prof. Fudan U., Shanghai, People's Republic of China. Author: Nuclear Magnetic Relaxation, 1948, Nonlinear Optics, 1965; also articles in profl. jours. Recipient Buckley prize for solid state physics Am. Phys. Soc., 1958, Dirac medal U. New South Wales (Australia), 1983, Stuart Ballantine medal Franklin Inst., 1961, Half Moon trophy Netherlands Club N.Y., 1972, Nat. medal of Sci., 1975, Lorentz medal Royal Dutch Acad., 1978, Frederic Ives medal Optical Soc. Am., 1979; von Humboldt sr. scientist award Munich, 1980, von Humboldt medal, 1989, Nobel prize in Physics, 1981; Guggenheim fellow, 1957. Fellow Am. Phys. Soc., Am. Acad. Arts and Scis., IEEE (Morris Liebmann award 1959, Medal of Honor 1983, Indian Acad. Scis.(hon.); mem. Optical Soc. Am. (hon.), Nat., Royal Dutch acads. scis., Nat. Acad. Engring., Am. Philos. Soc., Deutsche Akademie der Naturforscher Leopoldina, Koninklyke Nederlandse Akademie von Wetenschappen (corr.), Paris Acad. Scis. (fgn. assoc.). Office: Harvard U Div Applied Scis Pierce Hall Cambridge MA 02138

BLOES, RICHARD KENNETH, video artist; b. Waterloo, Iowa, Sept. 8, 1951; s. Kenneth N. and Helan (Nuebel) B.; m. Caitilin P. Driscoll, July 29, 1989; 1 child, Ryan. BFA, U. Iowa, 1973, MFA, 1977. Audio visual tech. Whitney Mus., N.Y.C., 1979—; adj. prof. Coll. of S.I., 1990. One-man shows include exhibitions at Inst. for Art and Urban Resources, 1984, New Mus. Contemporary Art, 1984, Port Washington Pub. Libr., 1977, Am. Mus. of Moving Image, 1989, Donnell Media Ctr., 1990, Feature Gallery, 1990, East End Art Ctr., 1990; exhibited in group shows including Ann Arbor Film Festival, 1976, Film Forum, 1976, The Kitchen Ctr. for Video, 1977, Anthology Film Archives, 1980, 81, Sixth Tokyo Video Festival, 1983, New Orleans World's Fair, 1984, The Kitchen, 1985. Recipient Media Bur. Finishing Funds grant, 1983, Jerome Found. grant, 1983, Fellowship, The MacDowell Colony, 1983, N.Y. Found. for the Arts grant, 1985, NEA New Genres fellowship, 1987, NYSCA Media Prodn. grant, 1988, 90.

BLOKSBERG, FRAN ELLEN, social services administrator; b. Balt., Nov. 15, 1957; d. Leonard Martin and Lois Jean (Bamberger) B. BA, Cornell U., 1979; MBA, Stanford U., 1983. Parent trainer Lincoln Hill Day Sch., Foxboro, Mass., 1979-81; bus. mgr. Harvard Sch., North Hollywood, Calif., 1983-85; fin. dir. Sisters of Mercy, Burlingame, Calif., 1985-88; v.p. Hanson Group, Los Altos, Calif., 1988; dir. fin. and devel. Family and Children's Svc. of Albany, N.Y., 1990—. Bd. dirs. Pocket Opera, San Francisco, 1987-88. Mem. Nat. Soc. Fundraising Execs. Office: Family & Children's Svc 12 S Lake Ave Albany NY 12203-1196

BLOM, JOHANNES, oncologist/hematologist; b. Amsterdam, The Netherlands, Sept. 11, 1928; s. Johannes and Jannetje Blom; m. Bohen Ferrari, June 22, 1960; children: Hans, James, Robert. MD, U. Utrecht, The Netherlands, 1957. Intern Cen. Dispensary and Emergency Hosp., Washington, 1957-58; resident Washington Hosp. Ctr., 1958-61; internist Group Health Assn., Washington, 1961; fellow Walter Reed Army Med. Ctr., Washington, 1961-64, chief oncology sect., 1964-79; chief med. oncology Divine Providence Hosp., Williamsport, Pa., 1979—; prin. investigator Cancer and Acute Leukemia, Group B., Washington, 1962-79; clin. assoc. prof. Georgetown U. Med. Ctr., Washington, 1977-80. Author: Guide to Therapeutic Oncology, 1979. Recipient Jonathan Wainwright award Moses Taylor Hosp., Scranton, Pa., 1988. Fellow ACP; mem. Am. Soc. Clin. Oncology, Am. Soc. Hematology. Office: Cancer Treatment Assocs PC 1100 Grampian Blvd Williamsport PA 17701

BLOM, RICHARD FREDERICK, small business owner; b. Louisville, June 10, 1932; s. Edward Charles Blom and Edna Alice (Bopp) Reiner; m. Eleanor Gertrude Seifried, Oct. 15, 1955; children: Margaret Ellen, Lisa Mae. Grad. high sch., Dunkirk, N.Y. Mgr. Captiol Radio Communications, York, Pa., 1959-69; owner York Answering Service, 1965-69; pres. York Mail Service Inc., 1969—. Served with USN, 1951-56, Korea. Mem. Mail Advt. Assn., Am. Legion (comdr. 1965-67), VFW (dep. comdr. 1960-62). Republican. Episcopalian. Lodges: Kiwanis, Moose. Home: 1771 Hilltop Dr York PA 17402-1440

BLOMGREN, RONALD WALTER, business executive; b. Chgo., May 18, 1934; s. Carroll L. and Geraldine (Traver) B.; m. Jorja Lembke, Jan. 5, 1947; children: Lisa Blomgren Moseley, Ronald Walter, Jr., Justin Chasen. Student, N.C. State U., 1956. Salesman Dixie Yarns, Chattanooga, 1956-57; exec. Milliken & Co., N.Y.C., 1957-77; group v.p. Texfi Industries, N.Y.C., 1977-79; v.p. Werner Mgmt., N.Y.C., 1979-81; exec. v.p. Jesse Jeans & Kim, N.Y.C., 1981-83; with Office of Chmn. J.P. Stevens & Co., N.Y.C.; dir. retail E. I. DuPont de Nemours & Co., 1989—; mng. dir. "The Principles" mgmt. and cons. film prodn., spl. event mktg., advt. and promotion. Trustee Mus. Theater Workshop, N.Y.C., 1988—; elder local Presbyn. Ch. Republican.

BLONSKY, STEPHEN LAWRENCE, nephrologist; b. Elizabeth, N.J., May 9, 1955; s. Milford and Miriam (Landerman) B.; m. Susan Huza, Apr. 8, 1984; children: Daniel, Rebecca, Sarah. BS, Union Coll., 1977; MD, U. of the East, Manila, 1981. Diplomate Am. Bd. Internal Medicine, Am. Bd. Nephrology. Resident Interfaith Med. Ctr., Bklyn., 1981-84, chief resident, 1984; fellow R.I. Hosp., Providence, 1984-86; physician Royce C. Lin MD. Svc. Corp., Greenbay, Wis., 1986-89, Nephrology Assocs., Watertown, N.Y., 1989—. Contbr. articles to profl. jours. Bd. dirs. Congregation Degel Israel, Watertown, 1991—. Fellow Am. Coll. Physicians; mem. AMA, Internat. Soc. Nephrology, Am. Soc. Nephrology. Office: Nephrology Assocs Watertown 218 Stone St Watertown NY 13601

BLOOD, ANTOINETTE MARIE, university administrator, consultant; b. Niles, Mich., Dec. 8, 1941; d. Benedict Eugene and Frances Rita (Roti) Bilotti; m. Gerald Wayne Blood, May 4, 1968; children: Rebecca, Jeremy. BA in Polit. Sci., U. Mich., 1963; postgrad., George Washington U., 1964-65. Cert. in principles of pub. utilities mgmt. Polit. officer U.S. Fgn. Svc., Washington and abroad, 1963-68; editor, writer various firms and colls., including Yale U., 1968-81; Congl. aide Congressman from Conn., 1981-83; asst. to pres. Svc. Nat. Corp., East Haven, Conn., 1983-85; exec. aide to chmn. Conn. Dept. Pub. Utility Control, New Britain, 1985-88; dir. pub. rels. U. New Haven, 1988—; pub. rels. chair Network Inc. of Conn., New Haven, 1980-85; exec. bd., pub. rels. chair Cornerstone, Inc., New Haven, 1982-85. Assoc. editor Yale Alumni Mag., 1977-78; contbr. articles to newspapers and mags. Chmn. commn. Hamden (Conn.) Mental Health Svc., 1989—, Hamden Econ. devel. Commn., 1985-86, Conn. Dental Commn., Hartford, 1987—; mem. Task Force on Quality Edn., Hamden, chair subcom. on schs. and the community, 1992—; founder mem. Hamden Arts Coun.; mem. sec. Hamden Dem. Town Com., 1984-90. Recipient Cert. for Appreciation for Svc. to State Gov. of Conn., 1986, Plaque in Recognition of Svc. to Town of Hamden, 1986. Mem. NAFE, Conn. Women in Higher Edn., Greater New Haven C. of C. (govt. affairs com. 1989—), High Lane Club. Roman Catholic. Office: U New Haven 300 Orange Ave West Haven CT 06516-1999

BLOOM, ALFRED HOWARD, college president; b. N.Y.C., Feb. 27, 1946; s. Alfred H. and Martha (Berrol) B.; m. Margaret Hennigan, Aug. 22, 1971. BA, Princeton U., 1967; PhD, Harvard U., 1974. Asst., assoc. prof. Swarthmore (Pa.) Coll., 1974-86, assoc. provost, 1985-86, pres., 1991—; dean of faculty, v.p. acad. affairs Pitzer Coll., Claremont, Calif., 1986-90, exec. v.p., 1990-91; pres. Swarthmore (Pa.) Coll., 1991—. Author: The Linguistic Shaping of Thought, 1981; contbr. articles to profl. jours. Fulbright-Hayes fellow, 1968, Rsch. grantee SSRC, 1978, 81, NEH, 1975, 86. Mem. Assn. for Asian Studies. Office: Swarthmore Coll Office of Pres 500 College Ave Swarthmore PA 19081-1397

BLOOM, D. A., venture capitalist; b. Phila., Jan. 19, 1958; s. Louis and Theresa (Severino) M. AB, Colgate U., 1979; MS and Engring., Moore Sch. of Engring., 1983; MBA, U. Pa., 1986. Sr. analyst Smith Kline Beckman R&D, Phila., 1980-85; sales/trading assoc. Salomon Bros., N.Y.C., London, 1985-86; assoc. Edison Vent Fund, Princeton, N.J., 1987-90; founder, pres. Innovative Consulting Enterprises, Flourtown, Pa., 1990—; founder, bd. dirs. Black Diamond Software, Inc., Ridgefield, Conn.; bd. dirs. Centerfield Collectibles, Inc., Ambler, Pa. Named All Star Goalkeeper, United Soccer League, Phila., 1983-88. Mem. Montco Men's Sr. Baseball League (asst. commr. 1990—), Roslyn (Pa.) Soccer Club (coach 1991—). Home and Office: 6314 Arlingham Rd Flourtown PA 19031

BLOOM, DAVID EDWARD, consultant; b. Hammond, Ind., June 23, 1938; s. Robert Reilly and Marguerite Sylvia (Wise) B.; m. Joan Emma Hefty, Oct. 29, 1971; children: Terri, Dione, Debra, Dara, David Jr. B.G.E., U. Nebr., 1960; MA, George Washington U., 1964. Advisor compensation/labor rels. Esso Libya/Humble Oil, Libya/Tex., 1964-71; employee relations mgr. Esso Math & Systems, Inc., Florham Park, N.J., 1971-73, Bayway Refinery-Exxon USA, Linden, N.J., 1973-77; mgr. manpower resources Esso Inter-Am., Coral Gables, Fla., 1977-81; mgr. compensation Exxon Co. USA, Houston, 1981-83; employee relations mgr. Exxon Enterprises, N.Y.C., 1983-86; sr. advisor human resources Exxon Corp., N.Y.C., 1986-88; pres. David Edward Assocs., Weston, Conn., 1989—; cons. Jr. Achievement N.Y., N.Y.C., 1988, Parker & Bonnell, Inc., Westport, Conn., 1989, Sears Roebuck & Co., Chgo., 1989, Exxon, N.Y.C., 1989. Author: The Acquisition Handbook, 1987, A Human Resources Environmental Scan, 1989. Trustee Bayway Opportunity Sch., Baytown, Tex., 1967-68, Rahway (N.J.) Rahway Gen. Hosp., 1974-76. 1st lt. U.S. Army. Mem. Am. Mgmt. Assn., Human Resources Inst., Human Resources Planning Soc. Republican. Home and Office: David Edward Assocs 66 White Birch Rd Weston CT 06883-3025

BLOOM, MARGO JUDITH, museum director; b. N.Y.C., Feb. 25, 1953; d. Joel N. and Paula (Yackira) B.; m. Mark A. Seal, June 19, 1983. BA, Hampshire Coll., Amherst, Mass., 1976; MA, Columbia U., N.Y.C., 1981. Program specialist Jewish Assn. for Cll. Youth, N.Y.C., 1977-79; coord., pub. programs The Jewish Mus., N.Y.C., 1979-83; exec. dir. Creative Alternatives of New York, N.Y.C., 1983-87; dir. Nat. Jewish Archives of Broadcasting, Jewish Mus., N.Y.C., 1987-89, Nat. Mus. Am. Jewish History, Phila., 1989—; mem. adv. bd. Ctr. for Am. Jewish History, Phila., 1991—. Bd. dirs. Greater Phila. Cultural Alliance, 1992—. Democrat. Jewish. Office: Nat Museum American Jewish 55 N 5th St Philadelphia PA 19106-2121

BLOOM, MARTHA LOUISE, artist, educator; b. Paterson, N.J., Aug. 5, 1951; d. Jack Clark and Jeanne Elizabeth (Brown) B. Student, Green Mountain Coll., 1970-71; cert. in fine arts, Art Students League, 1974. Tchr. Lindgren Nursery Sch., Closter, N.J., 1972-78, Woodstock (N.Y.) Elem. Sch., 1974; tchr. etching and monotype Cooper-Hewitt Mus., N.Y.C., 1980, 81; children's coord. Alexander Calder Exhbn., Cooper-Hewitt Mus., N.Y.C., 1989-90; tchr. painting Teaneck (N.J.) High Sch., 1986; tchr. outreach programs N.Y.C., 1986—; children's instr. Art Students League, N.Y.C., 1986—; tchr. Silvermine Sch. of Art, Conn., 1992—. One woman show includes Art Student's League, 1977; exhibited in group shows at Pioneer-Moss, N.Y.C., 1973, Audubon Soc./Nat. Acad. Galleries, N.Y.C., 1974, Nat. Arts Club, 1974, 90, Woodstock Artists Assn., N.Y.C., 1974, 75, Pratt Graphics Miniature Competition, N.Y.C., 1975, 79, Internat. Minature Show, Korea, 1980, Marilyn Pearl Gallery, 1980, Am. State of the Arts Gallery Exch., N.Y.C., 1979-86, Associated Am. Artists, N.Y.C., 1980-86, Sylvan Cole Gallery, N.Y.C., 1986—, Midtown-Payson Gallery, N.Y.C., 1990; Met. Mus., N.Y., 1991. Tchr. Creative Child Inc., N.Y.C., 1990-91; creator Exhibition Gallery, Union Settlement, N.Y.C., 1991; mural commn. mem. Union Settlement, N.Y.C., 1992. Mem. Art Students League (life), Artist Equity Assn., Westport Art Ctr., ARtists Alliance N.Y.C., Nat. Arts Club (lectr. children's art com. 1990). Office: Art Students League 215 W 57th St New York NY 10019

BLOOM, MAX ROBERT, economics educator, consultant; b. N.Y.C., Dec. 4, 1916; s. Borice and Dora (Rosenbloom) B.; m. Pearl Brook, May 25, 1941; children: Diane, Amy Bloom Connolly. BS, CCNY, 1939; cert., New Sch. for Social Rsch., 1940; PhD, Am. U., 1959. Prof. Sch. of Mgmt. Syracuse (N.Y.) U., 1956-83, prof. emeritus Sch. of Mgmt., 1983—; asst. prof. Sch. of Bus. Adminstrn. U. Calif., Berkeley, 1955-56; Fulbright prof. Israel Inst. Tech., Haifa, 1960-61; vis. prof. N.Y. State Coll. of Human Ecology, Cornell U., Ithaca, N.Y., 1976; cons. Joint Legis. Com. on Housing and Urban Devel., Albany, N.Y., 1969-73, Senate Select Com. on Housing and Urban Devel., 1973-75, Master Plan Nicosia, Cyprus, 1982, others; mem. adv. bd. Study Inst. in Urban Planning and Devel. Hebrew U., Jerusalem; speaker in field. Contbr. numerous articles to profl. jours. Bd. dirs. Syracuse Friends of Chamber Music, 1975-90; coord. Citizens Adv. Coun. Rehab. Downtown Bus. Areas, 1963-65. 1st lt. AUS, 1943-45, CBI. Mem. Am. Econ. Assn., Am. Real Estate and Urban Econs. Assn. (bd. dirs. 1968), Regional Sci. Assn. (chmn. panel of 21st European Cong. 1981), Soc. Govt. Economists, Beta Gamma Sigma. Home: 319 Hillsboro Pky Syracuse NY 13214-2026 Office: Syracuse U Sch Mgmt Fin Dept 900 S Crouse Ave Syracuse NY 13244-2130

BLOOM, PAUL, pediatrician; b. N.Y.C., Jan. 29, 1944; s. Marvin Lawrence and Rhoda (Kurz) B.; m. Rae Ellen Schmall, Aug. 30, 1967; children: Rebecca, Aaron. AB, Amherst Coll., 1966; MD, Albert Einstein Coll. Medicine, Bronx, 1970. Diplomate Am. Bd. Pediatrics. Pediatric resident Albert Einstein Coll. Medicine/Lincoln Hosp., Bronx, 1970-73, instr. pediatrics, 1973-75, asst. prof. pediatrics, 1975; pvt. practice, Haverstraw, N.Y., 1975—; attending physician Nyack Hosp., 1975—; profl. adv. bd. Dominican Sisters Home Health Agy., Ossining, 1977—. Democrat. Jewish. Office: 85 New Main St Haverstraw NY 10927-1599

BLOOM, RUTH ELSA, educational administrator; b. Phila., Jan. 13, 1954; d. George and Signe Elizabeth (Andersen) Kulp; m. David Allen Bloom, Oct. 4, 1975; children: Amy Elizabeth, Lisa Catherine. BS, Millersville U., 1975; MEd, Kutztown U., 1983; elem. prin. cert., Lehigh U., 1987. Cert. elem. prin., elem. tchr., special edn. Elem. tchr. Brandywine Heights Area Sch. Dist., Topton, Pa., 1975-88, elem. adminstrv. asst., 1987-88, elem. prin., 1988—; coord., dir. Chpt. 1 Fed. Program, Topton, 1987—, Pa. State Testing Program, Topton, 1987-89. Trustee Brandywine Libr., Topton, 1989—; mem. elem. edn. adv. com. Kutztown U.; coord. Pa. Framework II, Brandywine Heights. Recipient Ednl. Tech. Grant, 1986. Mem. NAESP, Pa. Assn. Elem. Sch. Prins., Assn. Fed. Program Coords., Berks County Reading Alliance, Phi Delta Kappa. Office: Brandywine Heights Sch Dist Weis St Topton PA 19562-1218

BLOOM, SAMUEL MICHAEL, otolaryngologist; b. Portland, Maine, Dec. 27, 1908; s. Max Laib and Bessie Devorah (Baum) B.; m. Zita S. Greene, June 17, 1945; children: Lloyd Jay, Betty Ann. BS cum laude, NYU, 1932, MD, 1935. Diplomate Am. Bd. Otolaryngology. Intern Mt. Sinai Hosp., N.Y.C., 1935-36; resident medicine and surgery Chesapeake & Ohio Hosp., Clifton Forge, Va., 1936-37; resident otolaryngology Mt. Sinai Hosp., N.Y.C., 1937-39, clin. asst., 1946-50, adj. attending, 1950-60; assoc. attending, 1960-72; cons. Mt. Sinai Hosp., N.Y.C., 1973-77; ret., 1977; staff ENT VA Med. Ctr., N.Y.C., 1980-90; assoc. clin. prof. Mt. Sinai Sch. Medicine, N.Y.C., 1965-77, assoc. clin. prof. emeritus, 1977—. Nat. comdr. Am. Defenders of Bataan and Corregidor, McKees Rocks, Pa., 1958-59; dept. surgeon Jewish War Vets. U.S.A., 1984-87. Maj. M.C., U.S. Army, 1941-46, PTO. Decorated Bronze Star. Fellow ACCS, Am. Acad. Otolaryngology, Head and Neck Surgery, Am. Acad. Facial Plastic and Reconstructive Surgery (treas. 1969-74, guest of honor 1985), Am. Laryngologic, Rhinologic and Otologic Soc., N.Y. Acad. Medicine; mem. AMA, Med. Soc. State of N.Y., New York County Med. Soc., Alpha Omega Alpha. Jewish. Home: 150 E 77th St Apt 4E New York NY 10021-1927 Office: 115 E 61st St New York NY 10021-8172

BLOOMER, HAROLD FRANKLIN, JR., lawyer; b. N.Y.C., Nov. 4, 1933; s. Harold Franklin and Allene (Cress) B.; m. Mary Jane Lloyd, July 16, 1955 (div. June 1976); children: Sarah Allene, Margaret Gail, Leslie Lloyd; m. Freya Donald, Nov. 30, 1985; children: Katharine Roma, Alice Donald. AB, Amherst Coll., 1956; LLB, Columbia U., 1967. Bar: Conn. 1967, N.Y. 1968, U.S. Dist. Ct. Conn. 1968, U.S. Dist. Ct. (so. and ea. dists.) N.Y. 1974, U.S. Ct. Appeals (2d cir.) 1974. Assoc. Debevoise, Plimpton, Lyons & Gates, N.Y.C., 1967-77; counsel Burlington, Underwood & Lord, Jeddah, Saudi Arabia, 1977-78; chief internat. counsel Saudi Rsch. & Devel. Corp., London, 1978-80; counsel Morgan, Lewis & Bockius, London and N.Y.C., 1980-81, ptnr., 1981—; adj. prof. law Pepperdine U. Sch. Law, London, 1985. Mem. Rep. Town Meeting, Greenwich, Conn., 1964-74, 92—, chmn. pub. works com. and dist. delegation; mem. Rep. Town Com., Greenwich, 1973-74; trustee San. Products Trust, Riverside, Conn., 1965-74. Lt. (j.g.) USNR, 1957-60. Named Kent scholar Columbia U., 1965-66,

Stone scholar Columbia U., 1966-67. Mem. ABA, Am. Arbitrators Assn. (panel of arbitrators 1990—), Assn. of Bar of City of N.Y., Riverside Yacht Club. Republican. Episcopalian. Office: Morgan Lewis & Bockius 101 Park Ave New York NY 10178-0002

BLOOMER, JAMES LAWRENCE, chemist, educator; b. Knoxville, Tenn., Jan. 6, 1939; s. Fred Samuel and Bessie (Walker) B.; m. Iris Linda Barnett, Aug. 28, 1968 (div. 1978). BS, U. Tenn., 1959, MS, 1961; PhD, U. London, 1964; diploma, Imperial Coll., London, 1964. Asst. prof. Temple U., Phila., 1965-70, assoc. prof., 1970—. Contbr. articles to profl. jours.; patentee in field. Office: Temple U Dept Chemistry 13th and Norris Sts Philadelphia PA 19122

BLOOM-FESHBACH, JONATHAN STEPHEN, clinical psychologist; b. New Haven, Jan. 7, 1950; s. Seymour and Norma (Deitch) Feshbach; m. Sally Jan Bloom, Aug. 29, 1976; children: Alison, Kimberly. BA, U. Oreg., 1974; MS, Yale U., MPhil, PhD, 1980. Lic. clin. psychologist, D.C. Staff writer Yale Bush Ctr. CHild Devel. and Social Policy, New Haven, 1979-80; sci. fellow U.S. Senate Com. Labor and Human Resources, Washington, 1980-81; coord. rsch. and evaluation Counseling and Psychiat. Svc./Georgetown U., Washington, 1981-84; cons., pvt. practice psychotherapy Washington, 1982—; asst. clin. prof. dept. psychiatry, child health and devel. George Washington Sch. Medicine, Washington, 1981—; mem. faculty Wash. Sch. Psychiatry, 1992—. Co-editor: Psychology of Separation and Loss, 1987; contbr. articles to profl. jours., chpts. to books. Mem. Am. Psychol. Assn., Soc. Rsch. in Child Devel., Am. Orthopsychiat. Assn., Internat. Coun. Psychologists, D.C. Psychol. Assn., Washington Psychologists for Study of Psychoanalysis. Home: 2919 Garfield St NW Washington DC 20008-3504 Office: 1301 20th St NW Ste 608 Washington DC 20036

BLOOM-FESHBACH, SALLY, psychologist; b. Balt., Feb. 11, 1953; d. Jordan and Carol (Wallerstein) Bloom; m. Jonathan Bloom-Feshbach, Aug. 29, 1976; children: Alison, Kimberly. A.B., Brown U., 1975; M.S., Yale U., 1977, M.Phil., 1979, Ph.D., 1980. Lic. psychologist, Washington. Research cons. Nat. Acad. Scis.-NRC Com. on Child Devel., Washington, 1980-83; staff psychologist Am. U. Ctr. for Psychol. and Learning Services, Washington, 1980-84, dir. of postgrad. tng., 1982-84; psychotherapist in ind. practice, Washington, 1982—; asst. clin. prof. dept. of psychiatry and behavioral sci. George Washington U., Washington, 1985—. Contbr. articles to profl. jours., chpts. to profl. books. Co-editor Psychology of Separation and Loss, 1987. Yale U. fellow, 1975-77, NIMH fellow, 1977-80; travel grantee NATO, Am. Psychol. Assn., 1981, 82; research grantee, Sigma Xi, 1978. Mem. Phi Beta Kappa, Sigma Xi. Clubs: Brown U., Yale U. Home: 2919 Garfield St NW Washington DC 20008-3504 Office: 1301 20th St NW Apt 608 Washington DC 20036-6016

BLOOMFIELD, ARTHUR IRVING, economics educator; b. Montreal, Que., Can., Oct. 2, 1914; came to U.S., 1936; s. Samuel and Hanna Mai (Brown) B.; m. Dorothy E. Reese, Jan. 18, 1987. B.A., McGill U., 1935, M.A., 1936; Ph.D., U. Chgo., 1942; M.A. (hon.), U. Pa., 1971; Doctorate in Econs. (hon.), Han Yang U., Seoul, Republic of Korea, 1987. Economist Fed. Res. Bank N.Y., 1942-53, sr. economist, officer, 1953-58; prof. econs. U. Pa., Phila., 1958-85, prof. emeritus, 1985—; vis. prof. Johns Hopkins U., 1961, Princeton U., 1963, CCNY, 1965, U. Melbourne, 1972; cons. Fgn. Econ. Adminstrn., UN Korean Reconstrn. Agy., U.S. State Dept., Ford Found. Author: Capital Imports and U.S. Balance of Payments, 1950, Banking Reform in South Korea, 1951, Monetary Policy under the International Gold Standard, 1880-1914, 1959. Social Sci. Research Council fellow, 1939-40; Rockefeller fellow, 1957-58; Ford Found. faculty fellow, 1962-63. Mem. Am. Econs. Assn., AAUP, Cosmos Club. Home: 2362 King Pl NW Washington DC 20007-1029

BLOOMFIELD, MICHAEL IVAN, marital therapist; b. Bklyn., Oct. 4, 1950; s. Warren and Rosalie (Tisch) B.; m. Kathleen Maura Hickey, Aug. 27, 1983; children: Luke, Aila. BS, Cornell U., 1972; MEd, Antioch U., Cambridge, Mass., 1982; EdD, U. Mass., 1992. Lic. social worker, marriage and family therapist, mental health counselor. Clin. fellow North Charles Inst. for the Addictions, Harvard U., Cambridge, 1983-84; clin. supr. Maple Valley Sch., Wendell, Mass., 1985-86; marriage counselor The Relationship Ctr., Amherst, Mass., 1987—; instr. U. Mass., Amherst, 1988—; lectr. in field. Justice of the Peace Commonwealth of Mass., 1986—. Mem. AACD, Internat. Assn. of Marriage and Family Counselors, Mass. Assn. for Counseling and Devel., Soc. of Psychologist in Addictive Behaviors. Home: PO Box 284 Wendell Rd Shutesbury MA 01072-0284

BLOOMGARDEN, GARY MICHAEL, neurosurgeon; b. N.Y.C., Apr. 12, 1954; s. Leonard J. and Annette B.; m. Jennifer Anne Frenzilli, Mar. 16, 1957; children: Jessica Ellen, Kara Elizabeth. BA summa cum laude, SUNY, Buffalo, 1976; MD, NYU, 1980. Surg. intern Parkland Meml. Hosp., Dallas, 1980-81; resident in neurosurgery Yale-New Haven Hosp., 1981-86, attending neurosurgeon, 1986—; attending neurosurgeon Hosp. of St. Raphael, New Haven, 1986—, Milford (Conn.) Hosp., 1986—; clin. instr. in surgery Yale U. Sch. of Medicine, 1987—. Diplomate Am. Bd. Neurosurgery. Alternate del. Rep. Town Com., Woodbridge, Conn., 1990-91. Fellow Am. Coll. Surgeons, Internat. Coll. Surgeons; mem. AMA, Am. Assn. Neurologic Surgeons, Congress of Neurologic Surgeons, Conn. State Med. Soc., Conn. State Neurol. Soc. Republican. Jewish. Office: Neurosurgical Assocs 60 Temple St New Haven CT 06510

BLOOMGARDEN, KATHY FINN, public relations executive; b. N.Y.C., June 9, 1949; d. David and Laura (Zeisler) Finn; m. Zachary Bloomgarden; children: Rachel, Keith, Matthew. BA, Brown U., 1970; MA, Columbia U., PhD. Pres. Rsch. & Forecasts, N.Y.C., Ruder Finn, N.Y.C., 1988—. Bd. dirs. N.Y. Arthritis Found. Mem. Pub. Rels. Soc. Am., Nat. Investor Rels. Inst., Women's Forum, Pharm. Advt. Coun., Swedish-Am. C. of C., CARE (bd. dirs.). Jewish. Home: 1084 North Ave New Rochelle NY 10804-3618 Office: Ruder Finn 301 E 57th St New York NY 10022-2905

BLOUCH, WILLIAM EDWARD, educator; b. Lebanon, Pa., July 19, 1951; s. George Henry Blouch and Mary Ann (Heckendorn) Reifsnyder; m. Virginia Ann Ebersole, Jan. 15, 1971; children: William Edward Jr., Jennifer Lynn. BSBA, Shippensburg (Pa.) U., 1973, MBA, 1974; D of Bus. Adminstrn., Kent (Ohio) State U., 1987. Staff acct. Arthur Andersen & Co., Balt., 1974-75; asst. prof. acctg. Shippensburg U., 1975-84; assoc. prof. Loyola Coll. of Md., Balt., 1984—; chmn. dept. acctg. Loyola Coll. in Md., Balt., 1989—. Author: (with others) Quality Management Handbook, 1988; contbr. articles to profl. jours. Mem. Am. Acctg. Assn., Inst. of Mgmt. Accts., Beta Alpha Psi, Beta Gamma Sigma. Home: 820 Twilight Dr York PA 17402-9240 Office: Loyola Coll in Md 4501 N Charles St Baltimore MD 21210-2601

BLOUGH, FREEMAN, JR., construction executive; b. Johnstown, Pa., Aug. 13, 1946; s. Freeman William and Mary Rahchel (Gindlesperger) B.; m. Mary Ann Caplinger; children: Brian Keith, Beth Ann. Grad. high sch., Davidsville, Pa. Apprentice Holsopple (Pa.) Electric Co., 1964-68; journeyman Shank Electric, Willow Street, Pa., 1968-69; foreman Jaden Electric, Lititz, Pa., 1969-72; contract mgr. Jaden Electric, Lititz, 1975-80; mgr. Jaden Svc. Co., Lititz, 1972-75; v.p. The Farfield Co., Lititz, 1980—. Bus. mgr. Warwick Community Ambulance, Lititz, 1978-82. Mem. Assoc. Builders and Contractors (com. chmn. 1976-80), Lancaster County Elec. Contractors Assn. (pres. 1975-76), Am. Bus. Club (pres. 1980-81), Masons. Republican. Brethren. Home: 151 Warwick Rd Lititz PA 17543-9103

BLOUGH, RICHARD JOHN, human resources executive; b. Highland Park, Mich., Jan. 20, 1947; s. John Earl and Catherine (Donlin) B.; m. Maureen Ann Kosmyna, Jan. 27, 1989. BS in Indsl. Mgmt., Lawrence Tech. U., 1975; MBA in Human Resources, Wayne State U., 1977, JD in Labor Law, 1982. Bar: Mich. 1982. Machinery designer, purchasing agt. LaSalle Machine Tool, Inc., Warren, Mich., 1970-76; systems analyst Greyhound Corp., Detroit, 1976-77; from labor rels. rep. to mgr. employee rels. Ford Motor Co., Inc., Mich., 1977-89; dir. human resources Outokumpu Am. Brass, Inc., Buffalo, 1989—; lectr. in field. Loaned exec. Washtenaw United Way, Ann Arbor, 1986, allocations panel, 1986-89, campaign com., 1988. With U.S. Army, 1967-70. Mem. ABA, Indsl. Rels. Rsch. Assn., Soc. Human Resources Mgmt., Mich. Bar Assn., Lambda Iota Tau (life), Sigma Iota Epsilon (life). Office: Outokumpu Am Brass PO Box 981 Buffalo NY 14240-0981

BLOUSE, BEN U., entrepreneur; b. York, Pa., Jan. 18, 1950; s. Glenwood Pershing and Rachel Elizabeth (Hench) B.; m. Sallyanne Richards Blouse, May 10, 1985; children: Ashley Richards, Brittany Richards. Student, Mercersburg (Pa.) Acad., 1967, Yampa Valley Coll., 1967-68, Wyndam Coll., 1968-72. Singer, guitarist Rock Band, U.S., 1965-78; mason contractor Curtis M. Hoffman, Inc., Dallastown, Pa., 1976-92; owner Britley Ltd., Red Lion, Pa., 1992—. Author popular songs; inventor water resistant radio. Vol. Spl. Olympics, York, Pa., 1989-91, Handicapped Riding, York, 1989—. Mem. Pa. Horse Breeder Assn., York County Farmland Trust, York County Builders Assn. Republican. Lutheran. Home: Box 400 RD # 5 Red Lion PA 17356

BLOZNALIS, PETER JAMES, mechanical engineer; b. Hartford, Conn., Aug. 31, 1963; m. Pamela Lyn Alix, June 18, 1988. BS in Engring., Brown U., 1985; MSME, Worcester Poly. Inst., 1990. Mech. engr. Electric Boat, Groton, Conn., 1985-87; rsch. asst. Worcester (Mass.) Poly. Inst., 1988-90; mech. engr. Canberra Industries, Meriden, Conn., 1990—. Recipient grad. student rsch. fellowship NASA, 1988-90. Mem. ASME, AIAA.

BLUCHER, LILLIAN H., portfolio manager; b. Shanghai, China, Mar. 8, 1933; came to U.S., 1941; d. Leon Albert and Nelly (Arditti) Jaffe; m. Richard Alan Blucher, June 9, 1957; 1 child, Edward Charles. BA summa cum laude, Hunter Coll., 1954; MBA, NYU, 1957. Chartered fin. analyst. V.p. sr. industry specialist Merrill Lynch, N.Y.C., 1957-70; pntr. Mersereau, Meek & Blucher, Washington, 1971-78; sr. v.p. capital mgmt. Folger Nolan Fleming Douglas, Washington, 1978-86; mng. dir. investments Howard Hughes Med. Inst., Bethesda, Md., 1986—. Author: (with others) Investments and Security Analysis, 1960; contbr. articles to profl. jours. Mem. fiscal affairs adv. com. Howard County (Md.) Coun., 1970; bd. dirs. Harper's Choice Village, Howard County, 1978-83. Mem. Washington Soc. Investment Analysts (v.p. 1987-88, pres. 1988-89, bd. dirs.). Office: Howard Hughes Med Inst 6701 Rockledge Dr Bethesda MD 20817-1813

BLUESTEIN, CLAIRE, chemist; b. Phila., May 3, 1926; d. Louis Allen and Bessie (Millstein) Kraiman; m. Bernard R. Bluestein, June 22, 1947; children: Rhona C., Sherrie Lee, Hazel M., Carol J. AB, U. Pa., 1947; MS, U. Ill., 1949, PhD, 1950. Postdoctoral fellow Purdue U., West Lafayette, Ind., 1951-52; chemistry instr. Pa. State U., 1958-59; sr. rsch. chemist Witco Chem. Corp., Petrolia, Pa., 1959-62; dept. mgr. Witco Chem. Corp., Oakland, N.J., 1962-75; founder, owner Captan Assocs., Inc., Brick, N.J., 1976—; co-founder, v.p. Epolin Inc., Newark, 1984-92. Pubr., editor: Reactive Cure Systems, 1980—, mo. newsletter, Cureletter, 1984—; contbr. articles to profl. jours., chpts. to books; patentee in field. Bd. dirs. Harmon Cove Condo Assn., Secaucus, N.J., 1984-87. Rubber Res. fellow, U. Ill., 1949-50. Mem. Radtech N. Am. Internat., Radtech Europe, SAMPE, Soc. Mfg. Engrs., Am. Chem. Soc. (N.J. councilor 1982-85), Phi Beta Kappa. Office: Captan Assocs Inc PO Box 504 Brick NJ 08724

BLUHM, HEINZ, educator; b. Halle, Germany, Nov. 23, 1907; came to U.S., 1925, naturalized, 1931; s. Fritz and Luise (Henke) B.; m. Helen McClure Berry, Aug. 15, 1938; children—Peter, Louise, Margaret, Christopher. B.A., Northwestern Coll., Watertown, Wis., 1928; M.A., U. Wis., 1929, Ph.D., 1932; postgrad., Yale, 1930-31, M.A. (hon.), 1950. Instr. German U. Wis., 1931-37; instr. German Yale U., 1937-39, asst. prof., 1939-44, asso. prof., 1944-50, prof., 1950-67, Leavenworth prof. German lang. and lit., 1957-67, chmn. dept. Germanic lang., 1954-63; prof. Germanic studies Boston Coll., 1967—, dir. Germanic studies, 1967-68, chmn. dept., 1968-76; vis. prof. German U. Minn., 1938, 61, Dartmouth, 1964, U. Calif.-Berkeley, 1968; adj. prof. Boston Theol. Inst., 1976—. Author: Martin Luther, Creative Translator, 1965, Luther Translator of Paul, 1984; contbr. to: Luther for an Ecumenical Age, 1967; Editor: Letters and Diaries of the Goethe Family, 7 vols, 1961-79, Newberry Library, Essays in Language and Literature, 1965, Luther's Essays on Christian Culture and Education, 1968, Das Erlebnis und die Interpretation, 1973; Luther translator of Paul: Studies in Romans and Galatians, 1984, Studies in Luther, 1987; contbr. articles on Luther and German lit. to profl. periodicals. Decorated Grand Cross of Order of Merit (Fed. Republic W. Germany).; Fellow Pierson Coll., Yale U.; Guggenheim fellow, 1957; Newberry fellow, 1958-60, 80, 87-92; sr. fellow, 1967; Huntington Libr. fellow, 1973; Folger Shakespeare Libr. fellow, 1974; Am. Coun. Learned Socs. fellow, 1975, 78; Herzog August Bibliothek fellow, 1979. Mem. MLA, Renaissance Soc. Am. Club: Elizabethan (Yale U.). Office: 354 Carney Hall Boston Coll Chestnut Hill MA 02167

BLUHM, NATHAN MARK, diplomat, administrative officer; b. St. Paul, Minn., July 23, 1954; s. Gerhardt Richard and Mildred Norma (Schroeder); m. Christina Mulford, May 29, 1990. BA with distinction, Valparaiso U., 1975; M in Internat. Mgmt. with honors, Am. Grad. Sch., Glendale, Ariz., 1984. Statistician State of Montana, Helena, 1975-77; sales rep. Mountain Bell Telephone, Helena, 1978-83; consumer cons. Calif. Pub. Utilties Co., L.A., 1985-86; diplomat U.S. Dept. State, Washington, 1986—; adminstrv. coord. White House Advance Team Presidential Visit to Bonn, Fed. Republic Germany, 1989. Composer: Jubilee in Germany, 1990. Mem. Nat. Right to Life Com., Washington, 1986—, Rep. Presidential Task Force, 1990; chmn. Combined Fed. Campaign United Way, Munich, Fed. Republic of Germany, 1988, '89, Malabo, Equatorial Guinea, 1990. Office: Dept State Am Embassy Malabo Washington DC 20521-2320

BLUM, BRUCE IVAN, computer science researcher; b. N.Y.C., Apr. 17, 1931; s. Manick H. and Shirley (Feinstein) B.; m. Harriet Roth, Aug. 22, 1954; children: Jody M., Marcy B. Del Grosso. BS, Rutgers U., 1951; MA in History, Columbia U., 1955; MA in Math., U. Md., 1964. Instr. Fairleigh Dickenson U., Teaneck, N.J., 1955-60; mathematician Applied Physics Lab./Johns Hopkins U., Laurel, Md., 1962-67, prin. staff, 1974—; v.p. Wolf Rsch. and Devel., Riverdale, Md., 1967-73; assoc. prof. Sch. of Medicine Johns Hopkins U., Laurel, Md., 1976—; dir. Clin. Info. Systems Div., Johns Hopkins Sch. of Medicine, 1976-83. Author: Clinical Information Systems, 1986, Tedium and the Software Process, 1990, Software Engineering: A Holistic View, 1992; series editor: Computers and Medicine, 1984-88; assoc. editor Jour. Systems and Software, 1989—. With U.S. Army, 1952-54. Fellow Am. Coll. Med. Info.; mem. Assn. Computing Machinery, IEEE Computer Soc., Am. Assn. Artificial Intelligence, AAAS. Jewish. Home: 5605 Vantage Point Rd Columbia MD 21044-2621 Office: Applied Physics Lab Johns Hopkins Rd Laurel MD 20723-6099

BLUM, CAROL KATHLYN, language professional, educator; b. St. Louis; d. Francis and Frances (Brazier) O'Brien; m. Martin Blum, July 5, 1968 (div. 1990); children: Asher, Agnes; m. Lauren Vedder Ackerman, Nov. 19, 1990. BA, Washington U., 1956; PhD, Columbia U., 1966. Instr. to prof. of French SUNY, Stonybrook, 1961—. Author: Diderot: Virtue of a Philosopher, 1974, Rousseau and the Republic of Virtue: The Language of Politics in the French Revolution, 1986, Anne's Head, 1982; book reviewer/editor: Eighteenth-Century Studies, 1989-92. Recipient NEA award, 1974; John Guggenheim Found. fellow, 1974. Mem. Modern Lang. Assn. (exec. com. eighteenth century French lit. 1989-94). Home: 8 Chickadee Way East Setauket NY 11733-3013 Office: SUNY at Stony Brook Stony Brook NY 11794-3359

BLUM, HOWARD ROBERT, writer; b. N.Y.C., July 11, 1951; s. Harold K. and Gertrude (Gross) B. BA, Stanford U., 1973, MA, 1974. Reporter N.Y. Times, N.Y.C., 1980-86; staff writer Village Voice, N.Y.C., 1975-79; bd. dirs. Low Country Ledger, Beaufort, S.C. Author: Wanted!, The Search for Nazis in America, 1979, Wishful Thinking, 1985, I Pledge Allegiance, 1987, Out There, 1990; assoc. producer film mini-series. Home and Office: 40 5th Ave New York NY 10011-8843

BLUM, JAY HERMAN, fabric manufacturing company executive; b. N.Y.C., Dec. 31, 1965; s. Robert Bruce and Leslie (Rogers) B. BA, Trinity Coll., 1988; MS, U. Hartford, 1989. Acct. Coopers & Lybrand, Hartford, Conn., 1988-90; mgr. aircraft div. Craftex Mills, Inc., Blue Bell, Pa., 1990—. Rep. United Way Phila., 1991—. Mem. Union League of Phila. Office: Craftex Mills Inc 450 Sentry Pkwy E Blue Bell PA 19422

BLUM, JOHN ROBERT HALSEY, state commissioner of agriculture; b. Bklyn., July 21, 1929; s. Robert Edward and Ethel (Halsey) B.; m. Susanne Delatour, June 9, 1950 (dec.); children: Anne Brengle, John R.H. Jr., Sara Hadden, Jane Burdett, Robin Wiseman, Alice Pollard, Suzette; m. Jeanne C. Thompson, Jan. 2, 1971. BA, Yale U., 1951; LLB, Harvard U., 1956. Bar: N.Y. 1957. Assoc. Milbank, Tweed, Hope & Hadley, N.Y.C., 1956-63, David Rockefeller, N.Y.C., 1963-69; chmn. Kings LaFayette Bank, Bklyn., 1969-72; pres. Security Mortgage Investors, Bklyn., 1972-76; ptnr. Richards, O'Neil & Allegaert, N.Y.C., 1976-86; pvt. practice Millerton, N.Y., 1986-92; commr. of agr. State of Conn., Hartford, 1992—; bd. dirs. Vista Mutual Funds, N.Y.C., Greenwood Cemetery Assn., Bklyn. Bd. dirs. The Dreyfus Found., N.Y.C., 1987; active Sharon (Conn.) Hosp. Fin. & Investment Com. Episcopalian. Home: Sharon Rd Lakeville CT 06039 Office: State Office Bldg Hartford CT 06106

BLUM, MELVIN, chemical company executive, researcher; b. N.Y.C., Jan. 8, 1936; s. Paul Henry and Dora (Schneiderman) B.; m. Paula Linda Weiss, July 11, 1969; 1 child, Lara Joyce. BS, Columbia U., 1957, MA, 1959, PhD, 1964; PhD, U. Pitts., 1964. Sales mgr. Nuclear Corp. Am., Burbank, Calif., 1960-62; pres. Atomergin Chemetals Corp., Farmingdale, N.Y., 1963—, Burlington Sci. Corp., Farmingdale, 1974—; v.p. Am. Roland Chem. Co., S.I., N.Y., 1984—. Author: Handbook of Rare Elements, Encyclopedia of Chemical Technology, Strategic Metal Investments, (mag.) DMSO Reporter. Capt. USAFR, 1959-65. Mem. Am. Chem. Soc., Am. Soc. Metals, Am. Nuclear Soc., Am. Inst. Physics. Home: 1385 Lyon Pl Wantagh NY 11793-2919 Office: Atomergic Chemetals Corp 222 Sherwood Ave Farmingdale NY 11735-1718

BLUM, RONALD JOSEPH, sales executive; b. Phila., May 21, 1948; s. Albert Augustas and Elsie (Lewis) B.; m. Rita Harrison, Sept. 15, 1978; children: Kaye, Bradley. BS in Commerce, Ga. Tech. U., 1971. Corp. tng. Acme Markets, Phila., 1973-82; dist. sales mgr. A.R.A. Svcs., Cherry Hill, N.J., 1982-84, Am. Suzuki, Brea, Calif., 1984-90; sales mgr. Exec. Apparel, Phila., 1990—; tng. cons. AMA, Phila., 1984-90. Chmn. B'nai B'rith, Phila., 1975-84. Republican. Home: 2143 Sunrise Way Jamison PA 18929-1348

BLUM, ROSALIND F., psychologist; b. N.Y.C., Mar. 30, 1910; d. Charles B. and Jennie (Prince) B.; m. Saul T. Schulman, Oct. 16, 1934 (dec. 1959); children: Susan Linda Schulman, Donald Michael Schulman. BS, Columbia U., 1940, MA, 1943. Diplomate Am. Bd. Profl. Psychology. Exec. sec. guidance lab. Tchrs. Coll. Columbia U., N.Y.C., 1934-41, instr. reading, spl. edn. and tests Tchrs. Coll., 1943-55; dir. Psychol. Testing Ctr., N.Y.C., 1941—. Trustee Congregation Rodeph Sholom, N.Y.C., 1968-76, chmn. nursery sch. and day sch., 1958-76. Mem. APA, N.Y. Psychol. Assn., N.Y.C. Soc. Clin. Psychologists. Jewish. Home and Office: 40 W 86th St New York NY 10024-3605

BLUMBERG, BARBARA SALMANSON (MRS. ARNOLD G. BLUMBERG), housing consultant, retired state housing official; b. Bklyn., Oct. 2, 1927; d. Sam and Mollie (Greenberg) Salmanson; m. Arnold G. Blumberg, June 19, 1949 (dec. June 1989); children: Florence Ellen Schwartz, Martin Jay, Emily Anne. BA, De Pauw U., 1948; postgrad., New Sch. for Social Rsch., N.Y.C. Mem. pub. rels. dept. Nate Fein & Co., N.Y.C., 1948-51; freelance pub. rels. cons., 1960—; councilwoman North Hempstead, N.Y., 1975-82; adviser to energy com. N.Y. State Assembly, N.Y.C., 1982-84; dir. spl. needs housing Div. Housing and Community Renewal, State of N.Y., 1984-89; ret.; bd. visitors Pilgrim State Hosp. Pres. UN Assn. Great Neck, N.Y., 1967-69, chmn. China Study Workshop, 1966-67; pres. Shalom chpt. Hadassah, 1955-57; exec. v.p. Lakeville P.T.A., Great Neck, 1963-65; exec. v.p. Great Neck S. Jr. High Sch., 1965-66; co-chmn. Great Neck UNICEF, 1968-70, mem. speakers bur., 1971—; v.p. Herricks Community Life Ctr., 1976-77, B'nai B'rith, Lake Success, N.Y.; coord., 6th Congl. Dist., N.Y. McGovern for Pres.; bd. dirs. New Dem. Coalition of Nassau, Am. Jewish Congress, Am. Jewish Com., Day Care Coun. of Nassau County, Citizen's Sch. Com., Great Neck; mem. Reform Dem. Assn. Great Neck; mem. platform com. Nassau Dem. Com.; mem. adv. com. to speaker N.Y. State Assembly; mem. resource coun., housing devel. co. Community Advocates; bd. visitors Pilgrim State Hosp. Recipient award Anti-Defamation League, New Hyde Park, N.Y., 1975, Alumni award DePauw U., 1977, Hadassah New Life award, 1980. Mem. N.Y. Alumni Club DePauw U. (trustee), North Shore Archeol. Assn. (chmn. study group), Women in Communication, Internat. Platform Assn., L.I. Women's Network (co-convenor), Interfaith Nutrition Network (bd. dirs.), Community Advocates (bd. dirs.), Mental Health Assn. of Nassau County (bd. dirs.), Alpha Lambda Delta. Home: 12 Birch Hill Rd Great Neck NY 11020-1309

BLUMBERG, BARUCH SAMUEL, academic administrator; b. N.Y.C., July 28, 1925; s. Meyer and Ida (Simonoff) B.; m. Jean Liebesman, Apr. 4, 1954; children: Anne, George, Jane, Noah. BS, Union Coll., Schenectady, 1946; MD, Columbia U., 1951; PhD, Oxford (Eng.) U., 1957; 20 hon. doctoral degrees. Intern, then resident Columbia div. Bellevue Hosp., N.Y.C., 1951-53; fellow in medicine Columbia-Presbyn. Med. Ctr., N.Y.C., 1953-55; chief geog. medicine and genetics sect. NIH, Bethesda, Md., 1957-64; assoc. dir. clin. rsch. Fox Chase Cancer Ctr., Phila., 1964-86, v.p. population oncology, 1984-89, disting. scientist, 1989—; master Balliol Coll., Oxford U., 1989—; prof. medicine and anthropology U. Pa.; George Eastman vis. prof. Balliol Coll., Oxford U., 1983-84; Raman vis. prof. Indian Inst. Scis., Bangalore, 1986; Ashland vis. prof. U. Ky., Lexington, 1986, 87; sr. advisor to pres. Fox Chase Cancer Ctr., 1989—. Contbr. articles to profl. jours. Served to ensign USNR, 1943-46. Recipient Albion O. Berstein, M.D. award Med. Soc. State of N.Y., 1969, Grand Sci. award Phi Lambda Kappa, 1972, Ann. award Eastern Pa. br. Am. Soc. Microbiology, 1972, Passano award Williams & Wilkens Co., 1974, Modern Medicine Disting. Achievement award, 1975, Internat. award Gairdner Found., 1975, Karl Landsteiner Meml. award Am. Assn. Blood Banks, 1975, Nobel prize in physiology or medicine, 1976, Scopus award Am. Friends of Hebrew U., 1977, Strittmatter award Philadelphia County Med. Soc., 1980, Disting. Service award Pa. Med. Soc., 1982, Zubrow award Pa. Hosp., 1986, Achievement award Sammy Davis Jr. Nat. Liver Inst., 1987, John P. McGovern award Am. Med. Writers Assn., 1988, Gov.'s Award in the Scis. Commonwealth of Pa., 1989, John Blundell award Brit. Blood Transfusion Soc., 1989, Gold Medal award Can. Liver Found. and Can. Assn. Study of Liver, 1990. Fellow ACP, Royal Coll. Physicians; mem. NAS, Assn. Am. Physicians, Am. Soc. Clin. Investigation, Am. Soc. Human Genetics, Am. Assn. Phys. Anthropologists, John Morgan Soc., Chesapeake and Ohio Canal Soc., United Oxford and Cambridge Explorers Club N.Y., Athenaeum. Office: Fox Chase Cancer Ctr 7701 Burholme Ave Philadelphia PA 19111-2497

BLUMBERG, JOEL MYRON, cardiologist; b. N.Y.C., Oct. 17, 1940; s. Howard Godfrey and Lily Ruth (Goldberg) B.; B.A., DePauw U., 1962; M.D., N.Y. U., 1966; m. Judith Ellen Green, Aug. 23, 1964; children—Amy, Hillary, Michelle. Intern, N.Y. U.-Bellevue Med. Center, N.Y.C., 1966-67, resident in internal medicine, 1969-71; fellow in cardiology Cornell U.-N.Y. Hosp., 1971-73; pvt. practice internal medicine and cardiology, Greenwich, Conn., 1973—; attending staff Greenwich Hosp., 1973—, coronary care cons., 1973—; physician to out-patients N.Y. Hosp., 1973-77; clin. instr. Cornell U. Med. Coll., 1971-77; clin. asst. prof. Yale Sch. Medicine, 1975—; lectr. in preventive cardiology to civic groups. Trustee, Temple Sholom, Greenwich, Conn. Diplomate Am. Bd. Internal Medicine. Fellow A.C.P., Am. Coll. Cardiology, Am. Coll. Chest Physicians, Am. Heart Assn. (council on clin. cardiology); mem. Am. Soc. Internal Medicine, N.Y. Heart Assn., Greenwich, Fairfield County, Conn. State med. socs. Club: B'nai B'rith (Stamford, Conn.). Contbr. articles to profl. jours. Home: 59 Old Stone Bridge Rd Cos Cob CT 06807-1511 Office: 2 1/2 Dearfeild Dr Greenwich CT 06830-5348

BLUMBERG, JUNE BETH, artist; b. Abington, Pa., May 14, 1959; d. Frederick Blumberg and Elin (Brunswick) Binder. A of Gen. Studies, Montgomery Community Coll., 1985; BFA, Moore Coll. of Art, Phila., 1991. Stats. clk. Crime Prevention Assn., Phila., 1980-81; workshop tchr. Jefferson Hosp. Evening Program, Phila., 1986-87; art asst. Mildred Greenberg, Phila., 1988-89; vis. artist Moore Coll. of Art & Design, Phila., 1990; admission rep. Franklin Inst., Phila., 1990-92; rsch. scientist, artist Phila., 1979—. Contbr. rsch. to profl. jours. Tutor Homeless Shelter, 1986. Recipient scholarship, 1983-85, Spl. Merit award Pen and Brush Club, 1990.

Mem. NAFE, World Affairs Coun., Pastel Soc. of West Coast, Oil Pastel Assn. Democrat.

BLUMBERG, LAWRENCE, orthopedic surgeon; b. Westchester, Pa., May 26, 1947; s. Howard and Sylvia Ruth (Richards) B.; m. Joan S. Laytin, June 15, 1971 (dec. 1989); children: Eric, Michael; m. Sharon M. Blumberger, Apr. 26, 1992. BA, Western Md. Coll., 1967; MD, U. Md., 1971; MBA, Loyola Coll., Balt., 1983. Intern U. Md. Hosp., 1971-72, resident, 1972-75; pres., chief exec. officer Cohen & Blumberg, M.D., P.A., Balt., 1975—. Trustee Western Md. Coll., Westminster, 1990—; adv. bd. Nat. Aquarium Balt., 1990—. Capt. USARMC, 1971-83. Mem. U. Md. Surg. Soc., Balt. County Med. Soc., Am. Coll. Sports Medicine, Undersea and Hyperbaric Med. Soc., Med Chi, Alpha Sigma Nu. Office: Cohen & Blumberg MD PA Ste 310 9101 Franklin Square Dr Baltimore MD 21237-3988

BLUMBERG, LEROY NORMAN, physicist; b. Atlantic City, N.J., June 22, 1929; s. Abraham and Elizabeth (Cohen) B.; m. Sydel Barkin, Mar. 2, 1957; children: Manya Helman, Deborah, Julia. BS, MIT, 1951; MA, Columbia U., 1955, PhD, 1962. Physicist Los Alamos (N.Mex.) Nat. Lab., 1955-60, Oak Ridge (Tenn.) Nat. Lab., 1962-65; rsch. fellow Harvard U., Cambridge (Mass.) Electron Accelerator, 1965-66; physicist alternating gradient synchrotron Brookhaven Nat. Lab., Upton, N.Y., 1966-78, sr. physicist Nat. Synchrotron Light Source, 1978—; vis. prof. Nat. Lab. High Energy Physics, Tsukuba, Ibaraki, Japan, 1975-76; vis. scholar Stanford (Calif.) U., Stanford Synchrotron Radiation Lab., 1982-83; vis. physicist div. high energy physics U.S. Dept. Energy, Germantown, Md., 1985-88. Contbr. articles to Phys. Rev., Physics Rev. Letters, Nuclear Physics, Nuclear Instrumentsand Methods, IEEE Proc. Nuclear Sci. Fulbright fellow Technische Hogeschool, Delft, The Netherlands, 1951. Fellow Am. Phys. Soc. Home: 21 Landing Ln Prt Jefferson NY 11777-1106 Office: Brookhaven Nat Lab NSLS Bldg 725 25 Brookhaven Ave Upton NY 11973

BLUMBERG, PETER STEVEN, manufacturing company executive; b. Bklyn., Feb. 18, 1944; s. Howard G. and Lily G. (Goldberg) B.; m. Judith E. Pauly, Apr. 22, 1967; children: Anne Pauly, Matthew Edward, Heather Rebecca, Emily Jessica. BS, U. Va., 1967 Salesman Coll. House, Inc., Westbury, N.Y., 1967-71, sales mgr., 1971-76, gen. mgr., 1977-78; sec.-treas. Sch. Tchrs. Supply Corp., Westbury, N.Y., 1979—, also pres. Coll. House, Inc., 1979—; dir. WUVA, Inc., Charlottesville, Va. Active, Nat. Right-to-Work Legal Def. Found., United Jewish Appeal-Operation Exodus, Leukemia Soc. Am., Coalition to Stop Gun Violence, Handgun Control, Inc., Simon Wiesenthal Ctr. Holocaust Studies, Ams. Against Union Control of Govt., Jewish Chautauqua Soc.; charter supporter U.S. Holocaust Meml. Coun. Mem. Nat. Assn. Coll. Stores, Imprinted Sportswear Assn., Nat. Cath. Edn. Assn., Screen Printing Assn. Internat. Jewish. Clubs: N.Y. Road Runners, Hurrycanes Running. Home: 55 Hummingbird Dr Roslyn NY 11576-2534 Office: 601 Cantiague Rd Westbury NY 11590-1708

BLUME, CLINTON WILLIS, JR., private investment executive; b. N.Y.C., July 8, 1932; s. Clinton Willis and Winifred (Grey) B.; m. Joan Torrance Hadly, June 25, 1955 (div. 1975); children: Clinton Willis III, Alison Preble, William Fairhurst. BA, Colgate U., Hamilton, N.Y., 1956. Pres. Blume & Sons, Inc., N.Y.C., 1986—. Lt. USMC, 1951-53. Mem. Real Estate Bd. N.Y. (Lawrence award 1984), Young Men's Real Estate Assn. (chmn. 1965). Republican. Episcopalian. Office: Blume & Sons Inc 67 Irving Pl New York NY 10003-2202

BLUME, LAWRENCE DAYTON, lawyer; b. Kansas City, Mo., July 7, 1948; s. Dayton G. and Meredith L. (Bruns) B.; m. Marilyn L. Moore, Sept. 6, 1975. BA, U. Ariz., 1970; JD, U. Mo., 1974. Bar: Mo. 1974, U.S. Dist. Ct. (we. dist.) Mo. 1974, U.S. Supreme Ct. 1978, U.S. Tax Ct. 1980, U.S. Ct. Internat. Trade 1981, U.S. Ct. Customs and Patent Appeals 1982, D.C. 1989. Ptnr. Swanson, Midgley, Gangwere, Clarke & Kitchin, Kansas City, 1973-80; prin. Miller & Blume, P.C., Kansas City, 1980-89; ptnr. Graham & James, Washington, 1989—; instr. Kansas City Sch. Dist., 1974-76; lectr. Nat. Assn. Fgn. Trade Zones, Washington, 1981—; lectr. U.S. SBA, Kansas City, 1983—, Am. Assn. Exporters and Importers, N.Y.C., 1984—, various colls., univs. and trade groups, 1980—; chmn. Ad Hoc Com. on Internat. Trade, Kansas City, 1983-89; prin. instr. Seminar on Internat. Bus. Transactions and Litigation Techniques, Monte Carlo, 1984; dir. Internat. Trade Club, Kansas City. Mem. Friends of Art, Kansas City, 1978-90, United Cerebral Palsy Assn., Kansas City, 1981-83; bd. dirs. Kansas City Philharm. Orch., 1981-83, Am. Royal Assn., Kansas City, 1984-90; sponsor Cystic Fibrosis Assn., Kansas City, 1980-81; pres. Lakas, Kansas City, 1981-82. Recipient Regional Advocacy award Coll. Trial Lawyers, 1974. Mem. ABA (adv. bd. disability law project 1981-82), Kansas City Bar Assn. (chmn. law sch. com. 1975-80, co-chmn. speakers bur. 1980-83), Inter-Am. Bar Assn. (sr.), Internat. Trade Bar Assn., Am. Assn. Exporters and Importers, Lawyers Assn. Kansas City, Order of Barristers. Democrat. Office: Graham & James Ste 700 2000 M St NW Washington DC 20036-3313

BLUME, PETER FREDERICK, museum director; b. Syracuse, N.Y., June 5, 1946; s. Edward Frederick and Charlotte (Murray) B.; m. Karolyn Waller Vreeland, Oct. 4, 1980; 1 child, Susanna. BFA, Syracuse U., 1967, post-grad., 1972-73; postgrad., Attingham Summer Sch., Eng., 1976, Mus. Mgmt. Inst., Berkeley, Calif., 1986. Curator Allentown (Pa.) Art Mus., 1974-84, dir., 1984—; mem. museums panel Pa. Council on Arts, Harrisburg, 1983-87. Author exhbn. catalogs. Mem. Hist. Archtl. Rev. Bd., Allentown, 1978-83; acquisitions com. Hist. Bethlehem (Pa.) Inc., 1982—; mem. Old Allentown Preservation Assn., 1977—. Served with U.S. Army, 1967-73. Rockefeller Found. fellow Met. Mus. Art, N.Y.C., 1973-74. Mem. Assn. Art. Mus. Dirs., Am. Assn. Mus., Mid-Atlantic Mus. Conf. Lodge: Rotary. Home: 420 N 8th St Allentown PA 18102-2816 Office: Allentown Art Mus PO Box 388 Allentown PA 18105-0388

BLUMENSTOCK, MARVIN WALTER, forestry educator; b. Topeka, Kans., May 22, 1932; s. John William and Helen F. (Schwerin) B.; m. Helen Lambert Grant; children: Laura, Lee, Patricia. BS, Rutgers U., 1955; MFA, Yale U., 1957; MBA, U. Maine, 1978. Forester Rayonier Inc., Fernandina Beach, Fla., 1957-62; paper specialist Hudson Pulp and Paper, Palatka, Fla., 1962-64; logger J.M. Huber Corp., Old Town, Maine, 1964-74; mgr. Walpole Woodworkers, Chester, Maine, 1974-76; forestry specialist Univ. of Maine Cooperative Extension, Orono, 1976; bd. dirs. New England Forestry Found., Boston, Maine Forest and Logging Mus., Bradley. Assoc. producer: (TV progs.) Yankee Woodlot, 1982, Great American Woodlot, 1987, Woodcock Woodlands, 1988, Wetlands, 1989. Recipient awards U.S. Dept. Agr., 1988, Soc. Am. Foresters, 1987; co-recipient award for Forest Industry Edn., Northern Logger mag., 1987. Home: PO Box 262 Stillwater ME 04489-0262 Office: U Maine Coll of Forest Resources Orono ME 04469

BLUMENTHAL, BRUCE, psychologist; b. Phila., June 11, 1952; s. Albert and Annette (Fink) B.; m. Eileen Saundra Lokyitch, June 9, 1974; children: Kim H., Alana J. BA in Psychology, Temple U., 1974; MS in Clin. Psychology, Hahnemann Med. Coll., 1976. Lic. psychologist, Pa. Rehab. counselor Gloucester County Jail, Woodbury, N.J., 1976-77; clin. coord. outpatient satellite Eagleville Hosp., Abington, Pa., 1977-81; sr. psychologist outreach drug and alcohol program Thomas Jefferson Univ. Hosp., Phila., 1981-86; psychotherapist Family and Community Svcs., Burlington, N.J., 1986—; staff clin. psychologist Trenton (N.J.) State Prison, 1986-87; sr. clin. psychologist N.J. Dept. Corrections, Trenton, 1987—; acting dir. psychol. svcs. N.J. Dept. Corrections, 1991—; group psychotherapist Alcoholism/Addictions Program, Burlington, N.J., 1991—; lectr. dept. psychiatry and human behavior Jefferson Med. Coll., Phila., 1986; advisor on post-traumatic stress disorder N.J. Dept. Mil. and Vets. Affairs, 1991—. Mem. Am. Psychol. Assn. (assoc.), Psychologists in Pub. Svc., Psi Chi (life). Democrat. Office: NJ Dept Corrections Stuyvesant Ave & Whittlesey Rd Trenton NJ 08625

BLUMENTHAL, GERALD PAUL, educator; b. Everett, Mass., May 17, 1945; s. Max and Sarah (Rutstein) B.; m. Adrienne Chaskes, July 5, 1969; children: Jason (dec.), Dara, Derek, Rachel-Leah, Seth (dec.). BA, State Coll. Boston, 1967, MEd, 1968. Cert. tchr., adminstr., supt., Mass. Tchr. Boston Pub. Schs., 1968-74, math. specialist, 1974-76, media specialist, 1968-88, reading specialist, 1976—. Bd. dirs., Seth Pediatric Hospice, Brockton, Mass., 1988-89, Pride of Brockton Cemetery Lodge, Stoughton, Mass., 1988-89. Mem. Boston Tchrs. Union (bldg. rep. 1975-89), Am. Fedn. Tchrs., Mass. Fedn. Tchrs., Temple Beth Emunah Brotherhood. Democrat. Home: 82 Candy Ln Brockton MA 02401-2810

BLUMENTHAL, RICHARD, state attorney general. BA, Harvard Coll.; JD, Yale U. Former rep. State of Conn., from 1985, atty. gen., 1991—. Office: Atty Gen Office 55 Elm St Hartford CT 06106-1773*

BLUMSTEIN, RENEE, research and statistical consultant; b. Bklyn., Apr. 1, 1957; d. Robert and Rosalie (Burak) B. BA, Queens Coll., N.Y., 1978; MA, Columbia U., 1980, MEd, 1982, MPhil, 1984, PhD, 1986. Rsch. psychologist CCNY, 1980-85; rsch. cons. AT&T, N.Y.C., 1986; rsch. analyst Citibank, N.Y.C., 1986-87, rsch. and statis. cons., 1987—; rsch. and statis. cons. Informed Decision Svcs., Englewood, N.J., 19876; adj. prof. rsch. methods CUNY, 1990—. Scholar Columbia U., 1981. Mem. Am. Psychol. Assn., Am. Soc. Tng. and Devel., Metro. Home and Office: Informed Decision Svcs Ste 5 51 W Hudson Ave Englewood NJ 07631-1700 also: 160-52 89th St Queens NY 11414

BLUMSTEIN, RITA BLATTBERG, chemistry educator; b. Krakow, Poland, Jan. 11, 1937; came to U.S. 1960; d. Leiser and Anna (Schreiber) Blattberg; m. Alexandre Blumstein, Dec. 6, 1959; children: Sylvie, Tanya. BSc, U. Paris, 1959; PhD, U. Del., 1965. From asst. to assoc. prof. U. Lowell, Mass., 1975-80; prof. chemistry U. Mass., Lowell, 1981—; vis. prof. Nuclear Rsch. Ctr., Grenoble, France, 1980. Contbr. over 100 articles to profl. jours. Recipient numerous rsch. grants NSF, NATO, Army Rsch. Office, others. Mem. Am. Chem. Soc. Office: U Mass Dept Chemistry 1 University Ave Lowell MA 01854

BLUMSTEIN, SUSAN BENDER, fundraiser; b. Phila., Dec. 20, 1943; d. Israel Boris and Lillian (Zebooker) B.; m. Allan Blumstein, Oct. 3, 1967; children: Eve, Zachary. BA, U. Pa., 1965. Exec. v.p. Am. Friends Israel Philharmonic Orch., N.Y.C., 1981-89; asst. v.p. devel. Jewish Theol. Sem., N.Y.C., 1989—; cons. Nat. Found. Jewish Culture, N.Y.C., 1989, Israel Bonds, N.Y.C., 1990. Chair U.S.A. Women's Lecture Series, N.Y., 1990-92. Home: 941 Park Ave New York NY 10028-0318 Office: Jewish Theol Sem 3080 Broadway New York NY 10027-4650

BLUTSTEIN, HARVEY M., financial planner; b. N.Y.C., June 17, 1927; s. Charles and Ethel (Zive) B.; m. Fanny Morgenstern, Nov. 26, 1950; children: Jeffrey Alan, Marcy Joy. BS, NYU, 1950; MS in Fin. Svcs., Am. Coll., 1981; Exec. Devel. Program, Dartmouth Coll. Grad. Sch. Bus., 1979. CLU, registered SEC investment advisor, chartered fin. cons. Agt., Conn. Mut. Life, N.Y.C., 1954—, agy. supr., 1957-63, asst. gen. agt., 1963-68, gen. agt., 1968-80, agt. in pvt. practice, 1980—. Asst. dep. camp chief Boy Scouts Am., 1967-69. Served with U.S. Army, 1945-47, ETO. Recipient Nat. Mgmt. award, 1973-80. Mem. N.E. Mgmt. Forum (pres. 1978-79), Nat. Assn. Life Underwriters (dir. 1975-77), N.Y. Estate Planning Coun. (pres. 1986-87), N.Y. Life Mgrs. Assn. (pres. 1975-76), Am. Soc. CLUs (v.p. N.Y. chpt. 1983-84), Internat. Assn. Fin. Planners, Internat. Assn. Registered Fin. Planners, Registry Fin. Planning Practitioners. Jewish. Home: 164 Church St New Rochelle NY 10805-3254 Office: Blutstein Assocs Ltd 280 N Central Ave Hartsdale NY 10530-1835

BLY, CHARLES ALBERT, nuclear engineer, research scientist; b. Winchester, Va., Jan. 11, 1952; s. Theodore and Nancy Irma (Fisher) B.; m. April Marie Monnen, July 24, 1976. BS in Nuclear Engring., U. Va., 1978, MS in Nuclear Engring., 1983. Nuclear reactor operator Nuclear Reactor Facility of the U. Va., Charlottesville, 1977-80, sr. reactor operator, 1980-83, rsch. engr., 1981-83; nuclear engr. Comml. Nuclear Fuel div. Westinghouse Electric, Pitts., 1983-92, Beaver Valley Power Sta. Duquesne Light Co., Shippingport, Pa., 1992—. Inventor fusion and hybrid fission/fusion fuel rod; discoverer neutrino-driven nucleon fission chain reactions; contbr. numerous articles to profl. jours. Candidate Shenandoah County (Va.) Bd. of Supervisor, 1975; mem. Ad Hoc Com. to Prevent Extension of I-66 Hwy. Through George Washington Nat. Forest, Strasburg, Va., 1979, Ad Hoc Com. to Preserve the Pitts. Aviary, 1991. Mem. ASME, IEEE, ASTM, AAAS, Am. Nuclear Soc., Am. Phys. Soc., ASM Internat., Assn. Energy Engrs, The Engring. Soc., Profl. Engr's. Soc., Fedn. Am. Scitnists, Engr's. Soc. Western Pa. Democrat. Lutheran. Home: 908 William Penn Ct Pittsburgh PA 15221 Office: Duquesne Light Co Beaver Valley Power Sta PO Box 4 Mail Drop SBX Shippingport PA 15077

BLY, JAMES CHARLES, JR., financial services executive; b. Kane, Pa., Jan. 24, 1952; s. James Charles Bly and Dorothy Rose Hau Smith; m. Laurie Ann Ramadon, June 6, 1987; children: Alana W., Bridget R., James C. III. BA, St. Bonaventure U., 1973. CLU. Mgmt. trainee Conn. Gen. Life, Washington, 1974-76; rep. CIGNA Fin. Svcs., McLean, Va., 1976-79; mng. exec. Integrated Resources Equity Corp., N.Y.C., 1980-83; pres. Source Capital, Ltd., Pitts., 1983—; adv. bd. John J. Kirlin, Inc., Rockville, Md., 1980—, Equico Securities, Inc., N.Y.C., 1991; dir. Orr Felt Co., Piqua, Ohio. Author: Business Preservation Trusts, 1991. Mem. Rep. Nat. Com., Nat. Rep. Congl. Com. Mem. Am. Soc. CLUs and ChFCs, Nat. Assn. Life Underwriters, Estate Planning Coun. (Pitts.), Y Group, Centurion Club, Edgeworth Club. Home: Blackburn Rd Sewickley PA 15143 Office: Source Capital Ltd 4 Gateway Ctr #1700 Pittsburgh PA 15222

BLY, SHARON VERNICE, human resource professional; b. N.Y.C., Dec. 5, 1963; d. Clarence Allen and Beulah (Adger) Williams; m. Steven Eric Bly, Sept. 23, 1989. BS, L.I. U., 1985; human resource mgmt. diploma, NYU, 1992. Asset control analyst Dean Witter Reynolds, N.Y.C., 1985-88; human resource analyst Barclays Interpayment, N.Y.C., 1988—. Telephone vol. United Negro Coll. Fund Telethon, N.Y.C., 1988-90. Mem. NAFE. Office: Barclays Interpayment 75 Wall St New York NY 10265

BLYN, GEORGE, economics educator; b. N.Y.C., May 2, 1919; s. Philip and Rose (Faiby) B.; m. Charlotte Lilly; children: Stefany, Roslyn, Corliann. BA, U. Pa., 1951, MA, 1953, PhD, 1961. Chmn. econs. dept. Rutgers U., Camden, N.J., 1962-71, 77-79, 83-89; prof. emeritus Rutgers U., Camden, 1989—. Contbg. author: Contributions to Asian Studies, 1979, Population Geography, 1970; author: Agricultural Trends in India, 1966. Sgt. U.S. Army, 1943-46, ETO. Named Sr. Faculty Rsch. Fellow, Am. Inst. Indian Studies, 1965-66, 1979; recipient George Harrison Fellowship, U. Pa., 1952-53. Mem. Am. Econs. Assn., Assn. Am. Geographers, Assn. Indian Econ. Studies, Del. Valley Geographers Assn. (exec. com. 1970-89), Econs. of N.J. (v.p. 1986-89). Home: 511 Winding Way Merion Station PA 19066-1118 Office: Rutgers U Dept Econs Camden NJ 08102

BLYN, STEFANY, artist; b. Phila., Feb. 8, 1953; d. George and Charlotte Anne (Lilly) B. Cert. in Painting, Pa. Acad. Fine Arts, Phila., 1974; BA summa cum laude, Rutgers U., 1975; MFA, Columbia U., 1978. Instr. Va. Commonwealth U., Richmond, 1979-82; lectr., Princeton (N.J.) U., 1985; adj. instr. Middlesex County Coll., Edison, N.J., 1988—; artist mem. 1708 East Main Gallery, Richmond, 1979-82, Ward-Nasse Gallery; artist studio resident Cité Internationale des Arts, Paris, 1983; studio artist, P.S.1, The Inst. for Art and Urban Resources, Queens, N.Y., 1978-79. One-person shows include Parker-Bratton Gallery, N.Y.C., 1987; two-person exhbn., A.I.R. Gallery, N.Y.C., 1987; other exhbns. include The Greater Midwest Internat., Bronx Mus. of the Arts Satellite Gallery, 1991, Art Ctr. Gallery, Cen. Mo. State U., Warrensburg, 1991, The Greensboro Artists' League 21st Annual Travelling Competition 1991, Ward-Nasse Gallery, N.Y.C., Greensboro (N.C.) Cultural Ctr., 10th Anniversary Exhbn., 1708 East Main Gallery, 1989, A Decade of Visual Arts at Princeton U., 1985. Recipient Toppan Prize for Drawing, Pa. Acad. Fine Arts, 1974, Undiscoverd Artists award, Jewish Community Ctr., Richmond, 1979, Faculty Grant-in-Aid, Va. Commonwealth U., Richmond, 1980, Purchase Acquistion, Best Products, Inc., Eatontown, N.J., 1981. Mem. Artists Equity, Orgn. Ind. Artists, Coll. Art Assn., Women's Caucus for Art (newsletter ed. 1984); fellow Fellowship of Pa. Acad. Fine Arts. Home: 69 Tiemann Pl Apt 64 New York NY 10027-3356

BLYTH, MYRNA GREENSTEIN, publishing director, editor, author; b. N.Y.C., Mar. 22, 1939; d. Benjamin and Betty (Austin) Greenstein; m. Jeffrey Blyth, Nov. 25, 1962; children: Jonathan, Graham. B.A., Bennington (Vt.) Coll., 1960. Sr. editor Datebook mag., N.Y.C., 1960-62, Ingenue mag., N.Y.C., 1963-68; book editor Family Health mag., 1968-71; book and fiction editor, then assoc. editor Family Circle mag., N.Y.C., 1972-78; exec. editor Family Circle mag., 1978-81; editor-in-chief Ladies' Home Jour., 1981—, pub. dir., 1987—; freelance writer, contbr. mags. Author: (novels) Cousin Suzanne, 1975, For Better and For Worse, 1978; contbr. articles to New Yorker mag., New York mag., Redbook mag., Cosmopolitan mag., Reader's Digest. Bd. dirs. Child Care Action Campaign, N.Y.C., 1989—. Mem. Am. Soc. Mag. Editors (exec. com. 1989—), N.Y. Women in Communications, Inc., Women's Media Group, Authors League, Overseas Press Club (bd. govs.). Office: Ladies' Home Jour 100 Park Ave New York NY 10017-5516

BOARDMAN, HAROLD FREDERICK, JR., lawyer, corporate executive; b. Darby, Pa., Nov. 23, 1939; s. Harold Frederick and Juanita (Sorzano) B.; m. Martha Eltie, May 23, 1987; children: Kimberly, Leslie. BS, Trinity Coll., Hartford, Conn., 1961; JD with honors, George Washington U., 1964; grad. advanced mgmt. program, Duke U., 1988. Bar: D.C. 1964, Hawaii 1971, N.J. 1974, U.S. Dist. Ct. D.C. 1964, U.S. Ct. Appeals (D.C. cir.) 1965, U.S. Ct. Mil. Appeals 1964, U.S. Supreme Ct. 1974. Gen. atty. Fed. Home Loan Bank Bd., Washington, 1964-65; atty. Hoffmann-LaRoche, Inc., Nutley, N.J., 1965-66; with Hoffmann-LaRoche, Inc., Nutley, 1973—, sec., 1979—, assoc. gen. counsel, 1981-88, asst. v.p., 1983-88, v.p., gen. counsel, bd. dirs. exec. com., 1988—, fiduciary rev. com.; corp. counsel faculty Seton Hall U. Cabinet mem. United Way Passaic Valley, N.J., 1991. Capt. JAGC, USAF, 1966-73. Mem. ABA, N.J. Bar Assn., Hawaii Bar Assn., D.C. Bar Assn., N.J. Corp. Counsel Assn., Am. Corp. Counsel Assn., Pharm. Mfrs. Assn. (exec. com. law sect. 1988—), Orange Lawn Tennis Club. Republican. Episcopalian. Avocations: golf, tennis, fishing. Home: 19 Holly Ln Essex Fells NJ 07021-1208 Office: Hoffmann-La Roche Inc 340 Kingsland St Nutley NJ 07110

BOARDMAN, JAMES PAUL, science administrator; b. Columbus, Ohio, Sept. 21, 1947; s. James Swaim Boardman and Jean (Paul) Davis; m. Elizabeth (div. Apr. 1974); 1 child, James; m. Joyce Moore, Oct. 17, 1981; children: Brian, Brandon. AAS, Clark Coll., 1976, Ft. Steilacoom Coll., 1978; BS, Ohio State U., 1985. Cert. lab. animal technologist. Asst. teratologist Adria Labs., Columbus, 1980-85; facility supr. Battelle Meml. Inst., Columbus, 1985-89; ops. mgr. Jackson Lab., Bar Harbor, Maine, 1989—. Contbr. articles to profl. jours. Chmn. adv. bd. animal prodn. and mgmt. program Columbus Pub. Schs. Capt. U.S. Army, 1967-71, Vietnam. Mem. Am. Assn. for Lab. Animal Sci. (chmn. com. on lab. animal technicians 1989, animal technician cert. bd. 1990), Lab. Animal Mgmt. Assn., Teratology Soc. Office: Jackson Lab 600 Main St Bar Harbor ME 04609-1500

BOARDMAN, MICHAEL NEIL, lawyer; b. N.Y.C., Jan. 7, 1942; s. Martin Vincent and Hannah (Greisman) B.; m. Constance Hallie Kramer, Aug. 28, 1966; children: Adam Lawrence, Amy Suzanne. AB, Syracuse U., 1964; JD, Seton Hall U., 1967. Bar: N.J. 1968, U.S. Dist. Ct. N.J. 1968, U.S. Supreme Ct. 1971. Assoc. Liebowitz, Krafte & Liebowitz, Englewood, N.J., 1968-69; ptnr. Boardman & Epstein, Saddle Brook, N.J., 1969-75; pvt. practice Saddle Brook and Ridgewood, N.J., 1975—; designated counsel State of N.J. Office of Pub. Defender, 1970-77; mem. skills tng. course faculty Inst. Continuing Legal Edn., Newark, 1976—; vice-chmn. Bergen County dist. fee arbitration com. Supreme Ct. N.J., 1987-88, chmn. 1988-89, mem. Bergen County dist. ethics com., 1991.; lectr. Inst. Continuing Legal Edn., Newark, 1979—. Dem. committeeman County of Bergen, N.J., 1974-76; mem. Citizens Com. to Study Declining Enrollment, Glen Rock, N.J., 1975-77; panelist Matrimonial Early Settlement Program, Bergen County, 1978—; mem. Glen Rock Jewish Ctr., Soc. of the Valley Hosp., Ridgewood, N.J.; mem. profl. adv. bd. Nat. Hypoglycemia Assn., Inc., 1985—. Mem. ABA, N.J. State Bar Assn., Bergen County Bar Assn., Am. Judicature Soc., NOW, Adoptive Parents Orgn. Bergen County Club. Home: 48 Glen Blvd Glen Rock NJ 07452-1626 Office: 4 Franklin Ave Ridgewood NJ 07450-3202

BOARMAN, GERALD JUDE, distribution executive, religious organization administrator; b. Indpls., July 12, 1940; s. John Eldon and Agnes (Dugan) B.; m. Susan Marie Schmalz; children: Gerald II, Jeffrey, Michael, Daniel. Student, Purdue U., 1959, Butler U., 1960, W.Va. State U., 1964. Br. mgr. Dynamic Distbrs., Indpls., 1959-62; paper sales rep. Proctor & Gamble, St. Albans, W.Va., 1963-65; instr. soap salesman Proctor & Gamble, Camp Hill, Pa., 1965-66; equipment salesman Breuer Electric Mfg. Co., Camp Hill, 1967-69; v.p. Janitor Supply House, Inc., Harrisburg, Pa., 1969-80; sec. Servo Systems, Inc., Harrisburg, 1977-80; chmn. bd. dirs., founder Bortek Industries, Inc., Mechanicsburg, Pa., 1980—; chmn. bd., founder Multi-Media Ministries, Inc., Mechanicsburg, 1980—; pres., founder World Christian Monetary Fund, Mechanicsburg, 1987—; chmn. bd. Task Masters, Inc., Mechanicsburg, 1981-87; mem. pres.'s coun. advisors Regent U., Virginia Beach, 1987—. Chmn. adv. bd. Bible Rsch. Ministries, Inc., Nashville, 1990—; dep. dir. gen. Internat. Biog. Ctr., Cambridge, Eng.; mem. rsch. bd. advisors Am. Biog. Inst., 1989; speaker Nat. Edn. Ctr. Thompson Inst., Harrisburg, 1984; city fin. mgr. Ams. for Robertson, Washington, 1987; vol. disaster assistance team ARC. Mem. Internat. Sanitary Supply Assn., Internat. Platform Assn. Republican. Home: 478 Woodcrest Dr Mechanicsburg PA 17055-6810 Office: Bortek Industries Inc 4713 Old Gettysburg Rd Mechanicsburg PA 17055-4326

BOAS, KATHLEEN LAWRENCE, social worker, administrator, educator; b. Grandview, N.Y., July 13, 1925; d. Gilbert Fenno and Elsie Katherine (Grout) Lawrence; m. Charles William Boas, Jan. 26, 1954 (div. Dec. 1979); children: Charles Lawrence, Laura Catherine, Mary Constance, Elizabeth Ann. BA, Pa. State U., 1947; MSW, U. Md., 1975. Lic. social worker, Pa. Part-time geriatric case worker Luth. Social Svcs., East, York, Pa., 1965-68; bus. mgr., corp. treas. Circus Kirk, East Berlin, Pa., 1966-71; instr., prof. York Coll. Pa., 1980-87; adminstr. York County Area Agy. Aging, 1975-87; pvt. practice social work, York and Harrisburg, Pa., 1977—; asst. to bishop Lower Susquehanna Synod, Harrisburg, 1988-89; social worker Options Program, Sunbury, Pa., 1989-90; part-time adminstr. Harrisburg Civic Opera Assn., 1990-92; part-time facilitator Cumberland Sheltered Housing, Carlisle, Pa., 1990—; part-time resource assoc. Temple U., Harrisburg, 1991-92. Cons. Theos Program, Linglestown, Pa., 1990—; counselor teen contraceptive counseling program Harrisburg Hosp., 1989—. Mem. NASW, Am. Assn. Ret. Persons (asst. state rep. 1992—), Torch Club (bd. dirs. 1991—). Lutheran. Home and Office: 6104 Linglestown Rd Harrisburg PA 17112-1209

BOAS, NORMAN FRANCIS, consulting physician; b. N.Y.C., Aug. 4, 1922; s. Ernst Philip and Helen Boas; m. Doris Whitehead, Mar. 14, 1945; children: Deborah Howarth, Stephen, Barbara Johnson. Student, U. Wis., 1939-42; MD, Harvard U., 1945. Intern, then resident Michael Reese Hosp., Chgo., 1945-47; fellow Mt. Sinai Hosp., N.Y.C., 1947-51; investigator NIH, Bethesda, Md., 1951-55; sr. attending physician Norwalk (Conn.) Hosp., 1955-76; cons. Lawrence & Meml. Hosps., New London, Conn., 1976-85, ret., 1985; pres. Conn. chpt. Arthritis Found., Hartford; asst. clin. prof. Yale U. Sch. of Medicine, New Haven, 1975-80. Co-author books. Sr. surgeon USPHS, 1951-91. Fellow Manuscript Soc. (v.p. 1989-91); mem. Stonington Hist. Soc. Home and Office: 6 Brandon Ln Mystic CT 06355-3103

BOATENG, JOSHUA YAW, podiatrist; b. Techiman, Brong Ahafo, Ghana, Sept. 18, 1947; came to U.S., 1974; s. Isaiah Nuroh-B. and Grace (Donkor) B.; m. Mary Sanders, May 2, 1977; 1 child, Joshua Kwadwo. BS in Biology, St. Joseph's U., 1980; D in Podiatric Medicine, Ohio Coll. Podiatry, 1985. Diplomate Am. Bd. Podiatric Medicine. Owner, dir. Mt. Airy Foot Clinic, Phila., 1989—; mem. staff John F. Kennedy Meml. Hosp., Phila., Kensington Hosp., Phila., Neuman Med. Ctr., Phila. Mem. Am. Podiatric Med. Assn., Am. Acad. Podiatric Sports Medicine (assoc.), Am. Podiatric Circulatory Soc., Pa. Podiatric Med. Assn., Ohio Coll. Podiatric Med. Alumni Assn. Office: Mt Airy Foot Clinic 1400 E Mt Pleasant Ave Philadelphia PA 19150-2004

BOATWRIGHT-MCEVOY, MARGARET ROBERTA, data communications course and curriculum development consultant; b. Boston, June 29, 1950; d. Robertson Grady and Elizabeth Margaret (Deyo) Boatwright; m. Joseph Paul McEvoy, Jr., June 25, 1971 (div. 1981). BS in Edn., Worcester State Coll., 1982. Cons. pvt. practice, Worcester, Mass., 1983-85; instr., technologist Data Gen. Corp., Westboro, Mass., 1985-87, Tech. Concepts, Inc., Sudbury, Mass., 1987-88; prin., cons. MBM Assocs., Worcester, 1988—; guest instr. Worcester State Coll. Master's Program, 1987, '88. Del. Mass. Dem. COnv., 1982-86; bd. dirs. Daybreak Inc., Worcesterm 1983-86,

Mass. Girl Scout Coun., Worcester, 1987-89; steering com. Cen. Mass. United Way, Worcester, 1985-87; vol Art Mus., 1982—; vol., docent Worcester County Hort. Soc., 1989—; fund-raising efforts for other charitable orgns. Mem. ASTD, Worcester County Hort. Soc. Roman Catholic. Home: 81 Park Ave Apt 4 Worcester MA 01605-3925

BOBINSKI, GEORGE SYLVAN, librarian, educator; b. Cleve., Oct. 24, 1929; s. Sylvan and Eugenia (Sarbiewski) B.; m. Mary Lillian Form, Feb. 20, 1953; children-George Sylvan, Mary Anne. BA, Case Western Res. U., 1951, MS in Libr. Sci., 1952; MA, U. Mich., 1961, PhD, 1966. Rsch. asst. Bus Info. Bur., Cleve. Pub. Libr., 1954-55; asst. dir. Royal Oak (Mich.) Pub. Libr., 1955-59; dir. librs. State U. Coll. at Cortland, N.Y., 1960-67; prof., asst. dean Sch. Libr. Sci. U. Ky., 1967-70; prof., dean Sch. Info. & Libr. Studies SUNY, Buffalo, 1970—; Fulbright-Hays lectr. in libr. sci. U. Warsaw, Poland, 1977; trustee Western N.Y. Libr. Rsch. Coun., 1971-87, pres., 1972, 82. Author: A Brief History of the Libraries of Western Reserve University, 1826-1952, 1955, Carnegie Libraries, Their History and Impact on American Public Library Development, 1969, Dictionary of American Library Biography, 1978, also articles. Mem. N.Y. Gov.'s Commn. on Librs., 1990—. With AUS, 1952-54. Mem. ALA (mem. pub. com., mem. coun.), N.Y. Libr. Assn., Assn. Am. Libr. Schs. (chmn. coun. of deans 1985-86). Home: 69 Little Robin Rd Buffalo NY 14228-1125 Office: SUNY Buffalo Sch Info and Libr Studies Baldy Hall Buffalo NY 14260

BOBROW, HENRY BERNARD, lawyer; b. N.Y.C., Mar. 31, 1924; s. Jacob and Sayde (Smollen) B.; m. Phyllis-Fein, July 6, 1952; children: Joanne Schoelkopf, Richard S. BA, Johns Hopkins U., 1947; JD, Cornell U., 1952; LLM, N.Y.U. Law Sch., 1956. Bar: N.Y. 1952, U.S. Dist. Ct. (so. and ea. dists.) N.Y. 1954. Assoc. to ptnr. Carroad & Carroad, N.Y.C., 1953-58; ptnr. Bobrow, Handman & Katz, N.Y.C., 1958-69, Cutler & Cutler, N.Y.C., 1968-72, Candee, Solomon, Bobrow, Burton, Davidowitz & Distler, N.Y.C., 1972-75, Bobrow, Greenapple, Skolnik & Shakarchy (and predecessors), N.Y.C., 1975—; pres. U.S. Patent Model Found., Washington, 1985-90; mem. Real Estate Bd. N.Y.C., 1987-91. Mem. Bd. Appeals, Scarsdale, N.Y., 1988-91; trustee Jewish Child Care Assn., N.Y.C., 1958—. Cpl. AUS, 1943-45, ETO. Named Outstanding Alumnus, Johns Hopkins U., 1978. Mem. ABA, Assn. of the Bar of the City of N.Y., N.Y. County Lawyers Assn., Johns Hopkins Club (pres. 1966-68), Cornell Club of N.Y., B'nai B'rith (pres. 1964-66). Republican. Hebrew. Office: Bobrow Greenapple et al 630 3d Ave New York NY 10017-6705

BOBROW, LAURA JUDITH, storyteller; b. Mt. Vernon, N.Y., Dec. 25, 1928; d. Isidor and Nettie (Levine) B. BS in Edn., Tufts U., 1949; postgrad., SUNY, Purchase, 1984-91. Author, performer: Sing With Me, Laurie Bee, 1967, reissued, 1991, Grimm Tales Retold, 1991; contbr. poetry to children's mags. Mem. ASCAP, Soc. Children's Book Writers, Women's Nat. Book Assn., Nat. Assn. for the Preservation and Perpetuation of Storytelling, Conn. Storytelling Ctr., Storytelling Ctr., Inc. (bd. dirs.), Storytellers ANON, Rye Storytellers' Guild (co-dir.), Westchester Storytelling Guild. Home: 380 Summit Ave Mount Vernon NY 10552-2206

BOBULINSKI, GREGORY ALEXANDER, musician, composer, educator; b. Bklyn., Dec. 1, 1950; s. Alexander Michael and Suzie Caroline (Labant) B. Student, Ohio State U., 1968-70; MusB, North Tex. State U., 1974. Cert. music educator, Tex. Trumpet performer Red Garland Quintet, Dallas, 1970-72; performer, recording artist, clinician Clark Terry Orch., 1973-82; recording artist Ford Found, Woodstock, N.Y., 1975; performer, recording artist Chris Woods Ensemble, 1973-85; composer Breuckelen Brass Quintet, Bklyn., 1983; guest radio host WNYG/AM Radio, Babylon, N.Y., 1986; trumpet performer Internat. Art of Jazz, Inc., Islip, N.Y., 1984-90; leader, composer, performer Greg Bobulinski's Energy Field, Manhattan, N.Y., 1984—; clinician, educator Louis Armstrong Mid. Sch., East Elmhurst, N.Y., 1992; guest artist Louis Armstrong House, Corona, N.Y., 1991; guest clinician Half Hollow Hills Sch. Dist., Dix Hills, N.Y., 1984-85; guest performer JVC Festival, Manhattan, 1989; composer, conductor Artist's Mass for the Laity, St. Peter's Ch., Manhattan, 1993; entertainer Found. for the Blind, Manhattan, 1991. Video artist: Profile of a Trumpet Virtuoso Meet the Composer, 1987-88; composer: Songs for the American Indian, 1981-83; author: War or the World of Light, 1990; recording artist: Odyssey, 1992. Recipient Jazz Musician's Honor award City of Stockholm, 1977, Ensemble Leader Commn., Queens (N.Y.) Borough Libr., 1986-87, Trumpet Recogniton award Thomas Wicker Assocs., Manhattan, 1989, Compostion Grant, Nat. Endowment for Arts, 1978, Performance Grant, 1980-81. Assoc. Jazz Composers Orch. Am.

BOCARSLY, ANDREW BRUCE, chemistry educator; b. L.A., Apr. 23, 1954; s. Sidney I. and Zivian Z. (Zeitlin) B.; m. Patricia Ann Fitzgerald, Aug. 21, 1977; children: Miriam, Naomi. BS, UCLA, 1976; PhD, MIT, 1980. Asst. prof. chemistry Princeton (N.J.) U., 1980-87, assoc. prof., 1987—. Contbr. articles to profl. jours. Grantee DuPont, 1980, Dreyfus Found., 1980; A.P. Sloan Found. fellow, 1986-88. Mem. Am. Chem. Soc. (Solid State award 1984), Electrochem. Soc. Office: Princeton U Dept Chemistry Princeton NJ 08544

BOCCHIMUZZO, VINCENT LOUIS, marketing consultant; b. N.Y.C., July 17, 1952; s. Silvio and Gertrude (Berardi) B. Student, Fordham U., 1970-74. Stockbroker FIC Corp., N.Y.C., 1975-78, VAS Securities, N.Y.C., 1978-82, First Eastern Securities, N.Y.C., 1982-88; exec. dir. Univest Techs. Ltd., N.Y.C., 1982—; stockbroker Continental Brokers, N.Y.C., 1989—; arbitrator Nat. Future Assn., N.Y.C., 1988-89; bd. dirs. Ex-Cel Resources; mem. adv. bd. Mktg. Cons. & Rsch., 1978—, Entertainment Devel. Corp., 1987—. Home: 2118 Tomlinson Ave Bronx NY 10461-1202

BOCCONE, ANDREW ALBERT, chemical company executive; b. Bklyn., Dec. 24, 1945; s. Charles Andrew and Florence (Basile) B.; m. Janet Marie Nucci, Aug. 23, 1969. BA in Chemistry, Hofstra U., 1968; MBA, Seton Hall U., 1971. Sales engr. Am. Cyanamid, Wayne, N.J., 1968-74; cons. Kline & Co., Fairfield, N.J., 1974-77, project mgr., 1977-80, dir., 1980-84, v.p., 1984-86, exec. v.p., 1986-90, pres., 1990—; bd. dirs. Findtech, Fairfield. Mem. Comml. Devel. Assn., Chem. Mgmt. and Resources Assn., Synthetic Organic Chem. Mfrs. Assn., Societe Chemie Industrielle, Planning Forum. Office: Kline & Company Inc 165 Passaic Ave Fairfield NJ 07004

BOCHNER, MARTIN BARRY, executive; b. Newark, N.J., Jan. 22, 1934; s. Allan and Viola (Gelber) B.; m. Phyllis Slone, Nov. 22, 1959; children: Joy Elisa, Howard Seth. BS, Lehigh U., 1955; MA, Princeton U., 1957, PhD, 1962. Devel. chemist Am. Cyanamid Co., Boundbrook, N.J., 1959-63; chief chemist Am. Cyanamid Co., Willow Island, W.Va., 1963-68; v.p., tech. dir. Atlantic Inds., Nutley, N.J., 1968-91; v.p. Fabricolor Inc., Paterson, N.J., 1991—; adj. prof. County Coll. Morris, Randolph, N.J., 1977-87. Contbr. articles to profl. jours. Pres. Wilson Sch. PTA, West Caldwell, N.J., 1971-72, Congregation Asudath Israel, Caldwell, 1975-77, N.J. Region Unit Syn Am., Linden, N.J.; bd. dirs. United Syn Am., N.Y.C. 1st lt. U.S. Army, 1959. Mem. Am. Chem. Soc., Environ. and Toxicological Assn. of Dye and Pigment Mfrs. (chmn. U.S. operating com.), AATCC (Colour Index edit. bd.), Sigma Xi. Office: Fabricolor Inc 24 1/2 Van Houten St Paterson NJ 07509

BOCHNOWSKI, JEAN ELISE, public relations executive; b. Gary, Ind., Aug. 30, 1962; d. John Francis and Ruth (Frazee) B. BS, Boston U., 1984; postgrad., Wilmington Coll., Dover, Del., 1990—. Communications coord. The Medical Found., Boston, 1984-86; dir. mktg. communications Kent Gen. Hosp., Dover, 1986—; adj. faculty Wesley Coll., Dover, 1988—. Bd. dirs. Am. Cancer Soc. of Kent County, Dover, 1989-90. Mem. Women in Communications (sec. 1984-86, Founder's award 1984), Peninsula Press Club (sec. 1987-88), Soc. for Health Care Mktg. and Pub. Rels. Democrat. Office: Kent Gen Hosp 640 S State St Dover DE 19901-3503

BOCK, CHARLES WALTER, physicist, educator; b. Phila., Jan. 19, 1945; s. Eugene August and Katherine (Hascher) B.; m. Lorraine Carolyn Robinson, Aug. 17, 1968; children: Cindy Lorraine, Carolyn Suzanne. BS, Drexel U., 1968, MS, 1970, PhD, 1972. Teaching asst. Drexel U., Phila., 1969-72; from instr. to assoc. prof. Phila. Coll. Textiles and Sci., 1972-89, prof., 1989—; bd. dirs. Am. Rsch. Inst., Upper Darby, Pa., 1986—; mem. dept. sci. Phila. Coll. Textiles and Sci., 1972—. Contbr. articles to profl. jours. Mem. Am. Phys. Soc. Office: Phila Coll Textiles and Sci Henry Ave and Schoolhouse Ln Philadelphia PA 19144

BOCKELMAN, CHARLES KINCAID, physics educator; b. San Francisco, Nov. 29, 1922; s. Bernhardt Jacob and Ruth Gladys (Kincaid) B.; m. Elizabeth Button, June 15, 1950 (div. July 1, 1978); 1 child, Faith; m. Christina DiGiusto, Feb. 16, 1991. PhB, U. Wis., 1947, PhD, 1951; MA, Yale U., 1965. Rsch. assoc. MIT, Cambridge, 1951-55; prof. physics Yale U., New Haven, 1955—. Sgt. USAF, 1942-46. Fellow Inst. Theoretical Physics, 1958, Guggenheim, 1971; vis. fellow Nat. U. Mexico, 1964. Fellow Am. Phys. Soc. Home: 22 Mt Nebo Rd Newtown CT 06470-2434 Office: Yale U A W Wright Nuclear Lab New Haven CT 06511

BOCKIAN, JAMES BERNARD, computer systems executive; b. Jersey City, Sept. 16, 1936; s. Abraham and Evelyn (Skner) B.; m. Donna M. Hastings; children: Vivian Shifra, Adrian Adena, Lillian Tova. BA, Columbia U., 1953; MPA, U. Mich., 1955; MA, Yale U., 1957. Vice-consul, 3d sec. Embassy Dept. State, Washington, 1957-61; sr. systems analyst J.C. Penney Co., N.Y.C., 1961-67; mgr. systems svcs., head dept. systems projects McDonnell Douglas Automation Co., East Orange, N.J., 1967-76; prin. JBBA, Inc. (formerly James B. Bockian & Assocs., Inc.), Morristown, N.J., 1976—; v.p. MIS Thomas Cook, Inc., 1980-83, exec. cons. to Thomas Cook Group; lectr. in field. Author: Management Manual for Systems Development Projects, 1979, Project Management for Systems Development, 1981, AT&T User Guide to Information Systems Development, 1980; contbr. treatises and articles to profl. publs. Mem. Internat. Assn. Cybernetics, Assn. Computing Machinery, Data Processing Mgmt. Assn., Am. Mgmt. Assn., Systems and Procedures Assn., Yale Club (N.Y.C.). Home: 26 Farmhouse Ln Morristown NJ 07960-3019 Office: JBBA Inc Olde Forge E Ste 26-5B Morristown NJ 07960-3019

BODEK, ARIE, physics educator; b. Tel-Aviv, May 11, 1947; s. Moshe and Lea (Braunfeld) B.; m. Yaffa Tatiana Harper, 1972 (div. 1990); children: Haim Yigal, Esther Hana, Aviva Yael; m. Priscilla Stanton Auchincloss, June 16, 1991; 1 child, Avi Shalom Auchincloss. BS, MIT, 1968, PhD, 1972. Rsch. assoc. MIT, Cambridge, Mass.; Millikan rsch. fellow Calif. Inst. Tech., Pasadena; asst. prof. U. Rochester (N.Y.), 1977—, assoc. prof.; sci. fellow Japanese Soc. for Promotion of Sci., Tsukuba, Japan, 1980—; prof. physics U. Rochester, 1987—; physicist Dept. of Energy, Washington, 1990-91. U.S. editor: Zeitschrift für Physike Saridesand Fields, 1992—. Sloan fellow, 1979-81. Fellow Am. Phys. Soc. Office: U Rochester Physics Dept Rochester NY 14627

BODEN, WILLIAM DAVID, real estate corporation executive; b. Jersey City, N.J., Jan. 24, 1941; s. John David and Alice G. (Bauer) B.; m. Dana Diane Spencer, Sept. 9, 1962; chldren: David, Katherine, Richard. BS in Indsl. Mgmt., Purdue U., 1963, MS in Indsl. Relations, 1965. Dir. personnel Comml. Solvents Corp., Terre Haute, Ind., 1964-73; dir. indsl. relations Potomac Electric Power Co., Washington, 1973-77; v.p. employee relations Carling Nat. Breweries, Inc., Balt., 1977-79; v.p. personnel adminstrv. services. The Rouse Co., Columbia, Md., 1979—. Contbr. articles, book reviews to profl. jours. Rep. precinct committeeman, Vigo County, 1972-73; chmn. Mid Md. Pvt. Industry Coun., Balt., 1987—; chmn. Md. Assn. of Pvt. Industry Couns., 1990—; chmn. Literacy Works Mgmt. Team state of Md.; bd. dirs. Ctr. Svc. Corp Ethics and Pub. Policy (Md.); mem. Md. Gov.'s Edn. and Tng. Coun.; chmn., nat. bd. dirs. Inroads Inc. Recipient Dist. Citizen award Howard County Exec., 1985. Mem. Am. Soc. Personnel Adminstrn., Am. Compensation Assn., ASTD, Soc. Human Resource Mgmt. Episcopalian. Home: 226 Melanchton Ave Lutherville Timonium MD 21093-5320 Office: The Rouse Co 10275 Little Patuxent Pky Columbia MD 21044-3414

BODENSIECK, RAYMOND ALAN, psychologist; b. Newburgh, N.Y., Mar. 18, 1959; s. Charles Phillip Jr. and Rosemary (Kehr) B.; m. Karen Michelle Kapsalis, Aug. 20, 1983; children: Alexander Vandris, Stephanie Kehr. BS, SUNY, Oneonta, 1981; D in Psychology, Chgo. Sch. Profl. Psychology, 1989. Lic. psychologist, N.Y. Asst. psychologist Astor Home for Children, Beacon, N.Y., 1987-90; psychologist Montgomery County Mental Health, Amsterdam, N.Y., 1990—. Mem. APA. Office: Montgomery County Mental Health Clinic Guy Park Ave Amsterdam NY 12010-4117

BODMAN, SAMUEL WRIGHT, III, specialty chemicals and materials company executive; b. Chgo., Nov. 26, 1938; s. Samuel W. Jr. and Lina (Lindsay) B.; children: Elizabeth L., Andrew M., Sarah H. BSChemE, Cornell U., 1961; ScD, MIT, 1964. Tech. dir. Am. Rsch. and Devel., Boston, 1964-70; prof. and lectr. MIT, Cambridge, Mass., 1964-70; v.p. Fidelity Venture Assn., Boston, 1970-74; pres. Fidelity Venture Assocs., 1974-77; chmn. Fidelity Venture Assn., 1977; pres. Fidelity Mgmt. & Rsch. Co., Boston, 1976-86; pres., chief oper. officer FMR Corp., 1982-86; exec. v.p., dir. Fidelity Group Mut. Funds, 1980-86; pres., chief operating officer Cabot Corp., Boston, Mass., 1987-88; chmn., chief exec. officer Cabot Corp., Waltham, Mass., 1988—; bd. dirs. Cabot Corp., Bank of Boston Corp., Boston, Westvaco, Inc., N.Y., Am. Oil and Gas Corp., Cabot Oil & Gas Corp. Trustee, mem. exec. com. MIT, Cambridge, Mass.; trustee MITRE Corp., Bedford, Mass., Isabella Stewart Gardner Mus., Boston, New Eng. Aquarium, Boston. Episcopalian. Home: 24 Chestnut St Boston MA 02108-3602 Office: Cabot Corp 75 State St Boston MA 02109-1806

BODNAR, RICHARD, psychology educator; b. N.Y.C., Feb. 21, 1946; s. Julius J. and Irene A. (Monette) B.; m. Carol B. Greenman, July 4, 1981; children: Benjamin, Nicholas. BA, Manhattan Coll., 1967; MA, CCNY, 1973; PhD, CUNY, 1976. Postdoctoral fellow N.Y. State Psychiat. Inst., N.Y.C., 1976-78, rsch. scientist, 1978-79; asst. prof. Queens Coll., CUNY, N.Y.C., 1979-82, assoc. prof., 1982-85, prof., 1986—; adj. prof. pharmacology Mt. Sinai Sch. Medicine, N.Y.C., 1991—. Contbr. sci. articles and abstracts to profl. jours. Capt. USAF, 1967-71, Vietnam. Pub. Health Svc. grantee Nat. Inst. Drug Abuse, Queens Coll., CUNY, 1989-92. Mem. Soc. for Neurosci., Am. Psychol. Soc. (charter), AAAS. Office: CUNY Queens Coll Dept Psychology Flushing NY 11367

BODNER, SEYMOUR S., mechanical engineer; b. Newark, Sept. 26, 1927; s. Isadore and Alice (Silpe) B.; m. Rita R. Horowitz, Sept. 3, 1951; children: Marc, Russel, Faye. BSME, N.J. Inst. Technology, 1948, MS in Mgmt. Engring., 1954. Lic. profl. engr. Plant engr./sales engr. Am. Abrasive Metals Co., Irvington, N.J., 1948-53; methods engr. Internat. Projector Corp., Bloomfield, N.J., 1953-54; project engr./process engr. Manhattan Rubber Div./Raybestos Corp., Passaic, N.J., 1954-56; project engr. Kaysam Corp. of Am., Paterson, N.J., 1956-57; chief engr. Wilpet Tool & Mfg. Co., Kearny, N.J., 1957-61; plant mgr. Garmold Div./Container Corp. of Am., Totawa, N.J., 1961-62, Pyro Plastics, Union, N.J., 1962-68; v.p. and works mgr. Perry Plastics Div./Blasius Industries, Erie, Pa., 1968-71; cons. engr., pvt. practice Livingston, N.J., 1971—; instr. plastics technology New Coll. of Engring. Contbr. articles to profl. jours. With U.S. Army, 1951. Mem. Soc. Profl. Engrs., Soc. Plastics Engrs. (edn. chmn. Newark sect. 1965-68), Am. Soc. Safety Engrs., Soc. Mfg. Engrs. Home and Office: 27 Shadowlawn Dr Livingston NJ 07039-3215

BOE, NILS ANDREAS, federal judge; b. Baltic, S.D., Sept. 10, 1913; s. Nils and Sissel C. (Finseth) B. AB, U. Wis., 1935, LLB, 1937; LLD (hon.), Huron Coll., Augustana Coll., S.D., 1986. Bar: Wis. 1937, S.D. 1938, U.S. Supreme Ct. 1944, D.C. 1970. Practice in Sioux Falls, S.D., 1938-65; lt. gov. S.D., 1963-65; gov., 1965-67, 67-69; dir. Office of Intergovtl. Relations, Exec. Office of Pres., Washington, 1969-71; judge U.S. Ct. Internat. Trade, 1971—, chief judge, 1971-77, sr. judge, 1984—; Mem. S.D. Ho. of Reps., 1951-59, speaker, 1955, 57. Served with USN, 1942-46. Mem. Phi Alpha Delta. Republican. Lutheran. Club: Elks. Home: 504 S Duluth Ave Sioux Falls SD 57104-4327 Office: US Ct Internat Trade 1 Fed Plz New York NY 10007

BOEDECKER, ANNE LOUISE, psychologist, business owner; b. Poughkeepsie, N.Y., Jan. 20, 1951; d. Ray F. and Elizabeth (Hutchinson) B.; m. Terrence P. Kimper, Aug. 19, 1979; 1 child, Wendy. Student, Dartmouth Coll., 1971-72; BA, Vassar Coll., 1973; MS, Pa. State U., 1975, PhD, 1978. Lic. psychologist, N.H. Adj. prof. Pa. State U., College Park, 1977-78; intern U. Tex. Counseling Ctr., Austin, 1978-80; staff psychologist Cen. N.H. Community Mental Health Svcs., 1980-81; prof. Grad. Sch. Antioch Coll., Keene, N.H., 1981-83; counselor, cons. Rundlett Jr. High Sch., Concord, N.H., 1983-85; adj. prof. New Eng. Coll., Henniker, N.H., 1985-86, Notre Dame Coll., Manchester, N.H., 1986-87; pvt. practice Concord, 1981—; exec. dir. Wellspring Ctr. for Human Devel., Concord, 1987—; mem. adv. coun. counseling program Notre Dame, Manchester, 1985-88; cons. Rape & Domestic Violence Crisis Ctr., Concord, 1986-88; mem. psychiatry dept. Concord Hosp., 1989—. Editor: Women Therapists Resource Directory, 1986; chmn. publs. com. NHPO, editor Networker, 1990—; contbr. articles to profl. jours. Founder, sec. Coalition Against Sexual Exploitation, Concord, 1987-89; mem. Bow (N.H.) PTA, 1989—. Rufus Choate scholar Dartmouth Coll., 1972. Fellow N.H. Psychol. Assn. (chair women and minorities com. 1986-89, editor Networker 1991—, sec. 1992—); mem. APA. Home: 4 One Stack Dr Bow NH 03304-4707 Office: Wellspring Ctr Human Devel 38 Warren St Concord NH 03301-4053

BOEHLERT, SHERWOOD LOUIS, congressman; b. Utica, N.Y., Sept. 28, 1936; s. Sherwood John and Elizabeth Monica (Champoux) B.; divorced; children: Mark C. Brooks, Tracy Boehlert Suk, Leslie; m. Marianne Willey Phillips, July 10, 1976; 1 stepchild, Laura Brooke Phillips. B.S. in Pub. Relation, Utica Coll., Syracuse U., 1961. Mgr. pub. relations Wyandotte Chems. Corp., Mich., 1961-64; chief of staff Rep. Alexander Pirnie, Washington, 1964-73, Rep. Donald J. Mitchell, 1973-79; exec. Oneida County, 1979-82; mem. 98th-101st Congresses from 25th N.Y. Dist., 1983—; del. North Atlantic Assembly; mem. N.E.-Midwest Congl. Coalition. Author: Telling the Congressman's Story The Voice of Government, 1968. Bd. dirs. Utica Coll. Found. Served with U.S. Army, 1956-58. Republican. Lodge: Rotary. Office: Ho of Reps House Office Bldg 1127 Longworth Washington DC 20515 also: Alexander Pirnie Fed Bldg Rm 200 10 Broad St Utica NY 13501-1233

BOEHM, C. NORMAN, JR., project management consultant; b. Dover, N.J., Feb. 12, 1928; s. C. Norman Boehm Sr. and Erna Elsa (Sehm) Mitchell; children: Erik Norman, Kara Lucia Molenhouse, Kurt Stephen; m. Aleksandra Ziolkowska, June 8, 1990; 1 child, Thomas J. BS in Chem. Engring., U. N.D., 1950. Process engr. Arabian Am. Oil Co., Ras Tanura, Saudi Arabia, 1954-56; sr. process engr. Arabian Am. Oil Co., N.Y.C., 1956-59; sr. facilities engr. Arabian Am. Oil Co., Dhahran, Saudi Arabia, 1959-72; contracts engr. Exxon Rsch. & Engring. Co., Florham Park, N.J., 1972-76; sr. contracts engr. Shell U.K. Exploration & Prodn., London, 1976-80; contracts coord. Esso Exploration & Prodn., Stavanger, Norway, 1980-84; project engr. H.L. Yoh Co. (DuPont), Wilmington, Del., 1985-91; prin. assoc. Pathfinder Inc., Cherry Hill, N.J., 1991—. With USN, 1946-47. Mem. Masons, Shriners. Republican. Home: 13 Servan Ct Wilmington DE 19805-2995 Office: Pathfinder Inc 11 Allison Dr Cherry Hill NJ 08003-2309

BOEHM, GEORGE AUGUST WESTALL, science writer, mathematical consultant; b. N.Y.C., Aug. 3, 1922; s. Henry and Minnie (Westall) B.; m. Alexandria Sarno, Apr. 1, 1944; children: August W., Margaret S., Barbara A., Juliana M., Henry N. BS, Columbia U., 1942. Sci. editor Newsweek, N.Y.C., 1949-54, Sci. Am., N.Y.C., 1955-56, Fortune, N.Y.C., 1956-66; freelance sci. writer and editor N.Y.C., 1966—. Author: The New World of Math, 1959. Mem. Am. Math. Soc., Nat. Assn. Sci. Writers. Home: 330 E 79th St New York NY 10021-0966

BOERMEESTER, DONALD ALAN, accountant; b. Woburn, Mass., Aug. 24, 1967; s. Donald Alan and Marsha Jean (Murray) B.; m. Paula Anne Contrado, July 14, 1991. BS in Accountancy, Bentley Coll., Waltham, Mass., 1989; postgrad., Boston Coll., 1991—. Jr. acct. Eastman Kodak Co., EPPS, Billerica, Mass., 1986-87, cost acct., 1987-89; sr. inventory acct. The Gillette Co., Braun Inc., Lynnfield, Mass., 1989-92, fin. analyst, 1992—. Mem. Am. Mgmt. Assn., Inst. Mgmt. Accts., Grad. Mgmt. Assn. of Boston Coll. Home: 25 Glen Ave Burlington MA 01803 Office: Braun Inc 66 Broadway Rt 1 Lynnfield MA 01940

BOESCH, FRANCIS THEODORE, electrical engineer, educator; b. N.Y.C., Sept. 28, 1936; s. Victor and Margaret (Wright) B. B.S., Poly. Inst. N.Y., 1957, M.S., 1960, Ph.D., 1963. Instr., then asst. prof. elec. engring. Poly. Inst. N.Y., 1957-63; mem. mil. research staff Bell Telephone Labs., 1963-68, mem. research staff, 1969-79; McKay prof. elec. engring. and computer sci. U. Calif., Berkeley, 1968-69; prof. pure and applied math. and Charles Batchelor prof. elec. engring. and computer sci., head dept. Stevens Inst. Tech., Hoboken, N.J., 1979-88, dean of faculty, 1988—. Author: Large-Scale Networks, 1976; editor-in-chief: Networks, 1970-81; editor: Graph Theory, 1978-81; contbr. articles to profl. jours. Vice pres. Fair Haven (N.J.) Little League, 1974; scoutmaster Fair Haven council Boy Scouts Am., 1973-78, dist. commnr. Monmouth council, 1978-80. Fellow IEEE, N.Y. Acad. Scis.; mem. Assn. Computing Machinery, Am. Math. Soc., Sigma Xi, Eta Kappa Nu. Home: 1 9th St Hoboken NJ 07030-5052 Office: Stevens Inst Tech Castle Point Sta Hoboken NJ 07030-5907

BOESHE, BARBARA LOUISE, real estate executive; b. Phila.; d. Raymond Gerard and Gilda (Nicotera) Lepone; children: Diedrich R., Alison Dru, Tyson Phillip. BS, Temple U., 1963. Lic. real estate broker, N.J. Sales person Sofroney Real Estate, Sea Isle City, N.J., 1978-88; broker, ptnr. Hoey Real Estate, Sea Isle City, 1988—; ptnr., developer Boeshe-Federico, Sea Isle City, 1986—. Vice chmn. bd. adjustment, Sea Isle City, 1982-86, active Mayor's Adv. Com., 1985-86, Parking Authority, 1984-85; committeewoman Rep. County Com., Sea Isle City, 1982-85, 89-90, alt. Rep. city leader, 1991-92, 1992—; v.p. Cape May County Planning Bd., 1992—. Mem. Sea Isle City C. of C. (bd. dirs., sec. 1986-89, treas. 1989-90, v.p. 1991-92, pres. 1992—), Greater Wildwood/Cape May County Bd. Realtors (million dollar award 1982-85, 2-1/2 million dollar award 1986-89). Roman Catholic. Home: 9 68th St Sea Isle City NJ 08243-1305 Office: Hoey Real Estate 4105 Landis Ave Sea Isle City NJ 08243-1920

BOGARD, TERRY LEE, medical researcher; b. Bicknell, Ind., Aug. 8, 1936; s. Bryce Clinton and Doris June (Highsmith) B.; m. Phyllis Jeanette White, Aug. 16, 1962; children: Denise Annette, Brian Andrew, Suzanne Marie. BSc, Ohio State U., 1958; PhD, UCLA, 1963. Postdoctoral fellow Eidgen. Tech. Hochschule, Zürich, 1962-64, Brandeis U., Waltham, Mass., 1964-65; sr. rsch. chemist Lederle Labs. subs. Am. Cyanamid Co., Pearl River, N.Y., 1965-70, mgr. pharm. devel. Lederle Internat. subs., 1971-81; mgr. clin. supplies Lederle Labs. subs. Am. Cyanamid Co., Pearl River, 1981-85, mgr. clin. supplies Lederle Internat., 1983-85, mgr. project mgmt. support med. rsch. div., 1985-87, mgr. internat. regulator affairs, 1987-89, mgr. rsch. info., 1989—. Bd. dirs. Nanuet (N.Y.) Pub. Libr., 1970—. Mem. Am. Chem. Soc., Royal Soc. Chemistry, Pharm. Mfrs.' Assn. (info. mgmt. subsect.). Democrat. Home: 102 W Prospect St Nanuet NY 10954-2633 Office: Med Rsch care Lederle Labs 54/237 N Middletown Rd Pearl River NY 10965-2650

BOGARDUS, E. HAL, manufacturing technologist; b. N.Y.C., Feb. 20, 1931; s. Egbert Hal and Margaret (Kluepfel) B.; m. Jean Claeys, Sept. 10, 1953; children: Karen, Lisa, Eric. BS, U. Tex., 1955, MS, 1957; PhD, Pa. State U., 1964. Rsch. assoc. Cornell U., Ithaca, N.Y., 1964-66; mem. tech. staff Tex. Instruments, Dallas, 1966-68; engr. IBM, Hopewell Juction, N.Y., 1968-73; rsch. engr. IBM, Yorktown Heights, N.Y., 1973-80; mem. hdqrs. staff IBM, Harrison, N.Y., 1980-83; mgr. IBM, Tucson, 1983-85; program mgr. of future mfg. tech. IBM, Hopewell Junction, N.Y., 1985—. Contbr. articles to profl. jours.; inventor mfg. semiconductor device, ink jet. Mem. IEEE, Am. Phys. Soc., Sigma Xi. Home: 1222 Elmwood Ave # 2N Evanston IL 60202-1271

BOGART, BRENDAN JAMES, financial consultant; b. N.Y.C., Sept. 17, 1967; s. Richard Bogart and Anne Murphy. BA in Philosphy, Polit. Sci., Fordham U., 1992. Registered fin. cons. Fin. cons. Shearson Lehman Bros., N.Y.C., 1989—; cons., seminar leader, lectr. in field, 1990—. Dem. committeeman, N.Y.C., 1988—; active athletic league Cath. Youth Orgn. , 1974—.

BOGART, KENNETH PAUL, mathematics educator, consultant; b. Cin., Oct. 6, 1943; s. Raymond L. and Ruth Pauline (Bauer) B.; m. Ruth Tucker, July 16, 1966; children—Pamela, Thomas. B.S., Marietta Coll., Ohio, 1965; Ph.D., Calif. Inst. Tech., 1968. Asst. prof. math. Dartmouth Coll., Hanover, N.H., 1968-74, assoc. prof., 1974-79, prof. math. and computer sci., 1979—,

chair math. and computer sci., 1989—. Author: (textbooks) Functions of Algebra and Trigonometry, 1977, Introductory Combinatorics, 1983, 89, Discrete Mathematics, 1988, The Dilworth Theorems, 1990; contbr. articles to profl. jours. Mem. Am. Math. Soc., Math. Assn. Am., Soc. for Indsl. and Applied Math, Phi Beta Kappa. Office: Dartmouth Coll Dept of Math and Computer Sci Hanover NH 03755

BOGER, KENNETH SNEAD, lawyer; b. Concord, N.C., Sept. 8, 1946; s. Charles E. Jr. and Mary (Snead) Boger; m. Robin Zaverl, Oct. 10, 1969; children: Adam S., Hallie S., Fiona G. AB, Duke U., 1968; MBA, U. Chgo., 1973; JD, Boston Coll., 1976. Bar: Mass. 1977. Assoc. Warner & Stackpole, Boston, 1976-82, ptnr., 1983—. 1st lt. inf. U.S. Army, 1968-71, Vietnam. Home: 200 Church St Newton MA 02158 Office: Warner & Stackpole 75 State St Boston MA 02109

BOGGAN, BRIDGITT FREDIA, poet, general and special education educator; b. Memphis, Mar. 23, 1960; d. John Edgar and Kay Roslyn (Clark) B.; m. Guy Tracey Dunn, May 5, 1983 (div. June 1989). BA in Psychology, Spelman Coll., 1982. Telecom. rep. Coordinated Planning Assocs., Atlanta, 1981; word processor, sales rep. Positive Image Resumes, Plainfield, N.J., 1983-84; program dir. South Second St. Youth Ctr., Plainfield, 1984; tchr. Plainfield Bd. Edn., 1984—; coord. Time Out project Mid. Coll. High Sch., Cranford, N.J., 1989. Author numerous poems. Active World Citizen Assembly. Recipient The Golden Poet award The World of Poetry, 1987, 88, Award of Merit cert., 1989 Poet of Merit award, The Am. Poetry Assn., Editor's Choice award Nat. Libr. Poetry, 1990. Mem. Am. Black Book Writers Assn., Internat. Soc. Poets.

BOGGESS, JOHN J., librarian; b. Murray, Ky., Aug. 13, 1928; s. Herman H. and Minne (Workman) B.; m. Jennylind Craig, Aug. 1, 1959. BS, Murray (Ky.) State U., 1958. Engring. clk. Peter Dewit & Sons Co., Portsmouth, Ohio, 1953-54; bookmobile librarian Decatur (Ill.) Pub. Libr., 1958-59; ref. librarian Atlanta Pub. Libr., 1960-61; spl. librarian U.S. Navy, Bethesda, Md., 1962-66, NASA/Goddard Space Flight Ctr., Greenbelt, Md., 1966—. Author: Bibliography of Hospital Administration, 1962. With U.S. Army, 1948-53. Democrat. Methodist. Home: 4205 Glenrose St Kensington MD 20895 Office: NASA/Goddard Space Flight Code 252 Bldg 21 Greenbelt MD 20771

BOGGS, DUANE GARY, automotive company executive; b. Salisbury, Md., Aug. 16, 1945; s. Wayne Harold and Mary Elizabeth (Marvel) B.; m. Brenda Lee Oliphant, Aug. 26, 1966; children: Lisa Michelle, Jennifer Lynne. Student, U. N.C., 1967. Sales rep. N.Y. Life Ins. Co., Wilmington, Del., 1969-70; v.p., bd. dirs. Oliphant Inc., Salisbury, Md., 1970—; ptnr. Boggs & Oliphant, Salisbury, 1973—; bd. dirs. Oliphant Leasing Corp., Salisbury; chmn. Md. Automobile Dealers Benefits Trust, Balt., 1983-86. Mem. Wicomico County Personnel Bd., Salisbury, 1987—; chmn. bd. dirs. Wor-Wic Community Coll., Salisbury, 1989—. Sgt. U.S. Army, 1966-69, Vietnam. Mem. Nat. Vehicle Leasing Assn., Salisbury C. of C. (pres. 1985), Lions. Republican. Baptist. Office: Oliphant Inc Bateman St PO Box 1838 Salisbury MD 21802-1838

BOGGS, WADE ANTHONY, professional baseball player; b. Omaha, June 15, 1958; m. Deborah Bertercelli; children: Meagann, Brett. Baseball player Boston Red Sox, 1982—. Mem. Am. League All-Star Team, 1985-87. Office: Boston Red Sox 24 Yawkey Way Boston MA 02215-3409*

BOGGS, WILLIAM MORRIS, physician; b. Kissimmee, Fla., June 21, 1952; s. Winston Morris and Margaret Joella (Daniels) B.; children by previous marriage: William Morris, Kristen Claire; m. Rosella Doreen Smith, Sept. 20, 1980; children: Gabriella Marie, Geoffrey Smithson Canedo, Jackson Daniel McAlister. BS with high honors, U. Fla., 1979, MD, 1982; MBA with honors, Loyola Coll., Balt., 1991. Assoc. med. dir. Pfizer Inc., N.Y.C., 1987-88; chief med. officer Pharmakinetics Inc., Balt., 1988-89; med. dir. Nova Pharm. Corp., Balt., 1988-91; sr. dir. clin. devel. ARC, Rockville, Md., 1991—. Mem. Balt. Coun. Fgn. Affairs, 1991—. Mem. ACP, Mensa, Phi Beta Kappa, Alpha Sigma Nu, Omicron Delta Kappa, Beta Gamma Sigma. Office: ARC 15601 Crabbs Branch Way Rockville MD 20855

BOGLE, WILLIAM YATES, IV, financial analyst; b. Evanston, Ill., Aug. 9, 1957; s. William Yates III and Florence Rollins (Andrew) B.; m. Gail Carol Awad, Sept. 8, 1990. BA, Bates Coll., 1979; MBA, Babson Coll., 1985. Announcer St. WERI, Westerly, R.I., 1979-81, Sta. WECM, Claremont, N.H., 1981-83, Sta. Waaf, Worcester, Mass., 1984-88, Sta. WBOS, Boston, 1989; sr. assoc. New Eng. Pension Cons., Boston, 1986—. Home: 31 Concord Sq # 2 Roxbury MA 02118-3101 Office: New Eng Pension Cons 253 Summer St Boston MA 02210-1114

BOGORAD, LAWRENCE, biologist; b. Tashkent, U.S.S.R., Aug. 29, 1921; came to U.S., 1922; s. Boris and Florence (Bernard) B.; m. Rosalyn G. Sagen, June 29, 1943; children—Leonard Paul, Kiki M. Lee. B.S., U. Chgo., 1942, Ph.D., 1949. Instr. botany U. Chgo., 1948-51, asst. prof. dept. botany, 1953-57, assoc. prof., 1957-61, prof., 1961-67; prof. biology Harvard U., Cambridge, Mass., 1967—; chmn. dept. biology Harvard U., 1974-76; dir. Maria Moors Cabot Found. Harvard U., Cambridge, Mass., 1976-87; Maria Moors Cabot prof. biology Harvard U., 1980—; vis. investigator Rockefeller Inst., N.Y.C., 1951-53; mem. com. on sci. and public policy Nat. Acad. Scis., 1977-81; mem. Assembly of Life Scis., NRC; mem. joint council on food and agrl. scis. Dept. Agr., 1978-82. Assoc. editor Bot. Gazette, 1958; mem. editorial com. Ann. Rev. Plant Physiology, 1963-67, Ann. Rev. Cell Biology, 1984-88; mem. editorial bd. Plant Physiology, 1965-66, Biochimica Biophysica Acta, 1967-69, Jour. Cell Biology, 1967-70, Jour. Applied and Molecular Genetics, 1981-85, Plant Molecular Biology, 1981-85, Plant Cell Reports, 1981-85; editor, chmn. editorial bd. Proc. Nat. Acad. Scis., 1991—. Served with AUS, 1943-46. Merck fellow, 1951-53; Fulbright fellow, 1960; recipient Career Research award NIH, 1963. Fellow Am. Acad. Arts and Scis.; mem. NAS (chmn. botany sect. 1974-77, mem. coun. 1989-92, editor proc., chmn. editorial bd. 1991—), AAAS (bd. dirs. 1982-86, pres. 1986-87, chmn. bd. 1987), Am. Philos. Soc., Am. Soc. Biol. Chemistry, Am. Soc. Cell Biology, Am. Soc. Plant Physiologists (pres. 1968-69, Stephen Hales award 1982), Royal Danish Acad. Scis. and Letters (fgn.), Soc. Developmental Biology (pres. 1984). Office: Harvard U Dept of Biology 16 Divinity Ave Cambridge MA 02138-2097

BOGOSIAN, ERIC, actor; b. Boston, Apr. 24, 1953. Student, U. Chgo., 1971-73; BA, Oberlin Coll., 1976. Author, star Off-Broadway prodns. Men Inside, N.Y. Shakespeare Festival, N.Y.C., 1982, Funhouse, N.Y. Shakespeare Festival, N.Y.C., 1983, Actor's Playhouse, N.Y.C., 1983, Drinking in America, Am. Place, N.Y.C., 1986, Talk Radio, N.Y. Shakespeare Festival, N.Y.C., 1987, Sex, Drugs, Rock & Roll Orpheum Show Theatre, N.Y.C. 1990; appearances in several TV shows and movies, including Caine Mutiny Court Martial, Drinking in America (Cinemax spl.), Talk Radio, 1988, Sex, Drugs, Rock & Roll, 1991; author: Drinking in America, 1987, Talk Radio, 1988, Sex, Drugs, Rock & Roll, 1991. Recipient Obie, 1986, 90, Drama Critics Circle award; grantee Nat. Endowment for Arts, Berlin Film Fest Silver Bear award, 1988. Mem. SAG, AFTRA, Writer's Guild, Actor's Equity.

BOGUMILL, MICHAEL THOMAS, federal agency executive; b. Owen, Wis., Dec. 20, 1938; s. Edward Leonard and Clara Emma (Pierce) B. BS, U. Wis., Eau Claire, 1961; MA in Teaching, U. N.C., 1970. Cert. tchr. Wis., Calif., specialized law enforcement officer Calif. Tchr. Auburndale (Wis.) Pub. Sch., 1961-63, Neillsville (Wis.) Pub. Sch., 1963-69, Hilmar (Calif.) Unified Sch. Dist., 1969-70; food and drug inspector Bur. Food and Drugs, Berkeley, Calif., 1971-73; food and drug supervising inspector Bur. Food and Drugs, Los Angeles, 1973-78; food and drug program coordinator Bur. Food and Drugs, Sacramento, 1978-88; compliance officer U.S. Consumer Product Safety Commn., L.A., 1989-91, Bethesda, Md., 1991—. Contbr. articles to profl. jours. Mem. Am. Assn. Ret. Persons. Recipient Cert. Appreciation U.S. Consumer Product Safety Commn., 1982, 87. Mem. The Cousteau Soc., The Nature Conservancy, Assn. Food and Drug Ofcls., Nat. Coun. Against Health Fraud, Sacramento Bowling Assn. (bd. dirs. 1984-89), River City Bowlers (sec., treas. 1983-88), Nat. Audubon Soc., Chesapeake Bay Found., Nat. Pks. and Conservation Assn., Wilderness Soc., Conservation Internat., Nat. Wildlife Found., Smithsonian Assocs., Nat. Apple Works Users Group, Kiwania (pres. Neillsville 1968-69). Democrat. Roman Catholic. Home: 12403 Braxfield Ct Apt 5 Rockville MD 20852-2030 Office: US Consumer Product Safety Commn 5401 Westbard Ave Rm 222B Washington DC 20207-0002

BOHANAN, DAVID JOHN, management consultant; b. Utica, N.Y., Dec. 13, 1946; s. Clifton Ralph and Florence Susan (Dunham) B.; m. Judith Ann Petrocci, July 31, 1977; children: Luke, Jacob. BFA in Ceramics and Painting, Alfred U., 1968; BS in Commerce, U. Md., 1979; MBA in Mgmt., Boston U., 1981. Pub. R&R in the Med Mediterranean Pubs. Srl., Vicenza, Italy, 1974-81; pvt. practice fin. cons. Jersey City, 1981-86; bus. cons. S&B Practice Mgmt. Assocs., Greenbrook, N.J., 1986—; fin. planner Fin. Found., Inc., Greenbrook, N.J., 1986—; rep. Nathan & Lewis Securities, Inc., N.Y.C., 1982—. Capt. field arty., U.S. Army, 1968-74, Vietnam. Decorated Bronze Star with oak leaf cluster. Mem. Inst. Cert. Fin. Planners (cert.). Republican. Home: 198A Saw Mill Rd Lebanon NJ 08833 Office: S&B Practice Mgmt Assocs 314 Rt 22 Green Brook NJ 08812

BOHLEN, JEANNE LOUISE, librarian; b. Kansas City, Mo., July 30, 1938; d. Roger Morton and Louise (Fischer) Alexander; m. Donald Adam James Bohlen, Aug. 27, 1960 (div. Aug. 1972); children: Stephen Adam, Christopher Alexander. BA, Oberlin Coll., 1960; MLS, Rutgers U., 1962. Librarian long range planning and analysis staff system div. System div. Bendix Cor., Ann Arbor, Mich., 1962-63; books editor U. Microfilms, Inc., Ann Arbor, 1963-65; dir. Trails Regional Library, Warrensburg, Mo., 1965-67; reference supr. Kansas City (Mo.) Pub. Library, 1972-77; founding dir. The Found. Ctr., Cleve., 1977-85; assoc. dir. Ind. Sector, Cleve., 1985-87; v.p. membership Ind. Sector, Washington, 1987-89; dir. Jeannette Rankin Library program U.S. Inst. of Peace, Washington, 1989—; panelist NEH Challenge Grant Program, Washington, 1980, 84, 85; vis. asst. prof. Kent (Ohio) State U. Sch. Libr. Sci., 1980-84; del. fed. pre-White House Conf. on Librs. and Info. Svcs., 1990. Contbr. (book) Source Book Profiles, 1980; contbr. articles to profl. jours.; speaker in field. Mem. adv. council Shaker Heights (Ohio) Youth Ctr., 1983-84, Women's Found., Cleve., 1984-85; bd. dirs. Ohio coun. Fund Raising Execs., 1983-85. Fellow Inst. Ednl. Leadership, Washington, 1982-83. Mem. ALA (exec. com. fund raising and resource fund devel. sect., libr. adminstrn. and mgmt. div. 1989-91, chair spl. activities com. 1987-88), Spl. Librs. Assn. (adv. coun. Cleve. chpt. 1978-84, bd. dirs. 1981-84, pres. 1982-83, adv. coun. Washington chpt. 1987-88, circulation mgr. social sci. div. 1985, chair social sci. div. 1989-90, recording sec. Washington chpt. 1990—, chair tellers com. 1990-91, mem. 1993 ann. conf. com. 1991-93), Women and Philanthropy, D.C. Libr. Assn. Office: US Inst of Peace 1550 M St NW Ste 700 Washington DC 20005-1708

BOHLEN, WALTER FRANKLIN, oceanography educator; b. June 21, 1938; s. Walter Herman and Mary (McHale) B.; m. Elisabeth Pope, Oct. 14, 1967; children: Christopher, Megan, Anne, Susan. BSEE, U. Notre Dame, 1960; PhD, MIT, 1969. Prof. oceanography U. Conn., Groton, 1969—. Contbr. articles to profl. jours. Lt. (j.g.) USNR, 1960-62. Home: 1 Scott Ln Mystic CT 06355-2313 Office: U Conn Avery Point Groton CT 06340

BOHLIN, R. PAUL, lawyer; b. Bayonne, N.J., Feb. 10, 1936; s. Ragnar T. and Juliette (McCarthy) B.; m. Deirdre McCabe, Feb. 23, 1964; children: Sheila K., Karen L. AB, Manhattan Coll., 1957; LLB, NYU, 1960; MBA, U. Pa., 1961. Bar: U.S. Dist. Ct. (so. dist.) N.Y., 1968, U.S. Tax Ct., 1965, N.Y., 1968. Asst. mgr. law dept. Merrill Lynch and Co., N.Y.C., 1963-71; asst. gen. counsel, asst. corp. sec., sr. v.p. Dean Witter Reynolds, N.Y.C., 1971-83; dir. Dean Witter Internat., Inc., N.Y.C., 1976-83; sec., dir. Dean Witter P.R., Inc., San Juan, 1980-83; sr. v.p. Dean Witter Reynolds, Inc., N.Y.C., 1983—; pvt. practice N.Y.C., 1983—; pres. Colo. Nebrash Mountain Resort Corp., N.Y.C., 1976—; cons. Quadrex Securities, Inc., N.Y.C., 1986—; bd. arbitrators N.Y. Stock Exchange, Nat. Assn. Securities Dealers Inc. Author: Broker-Dealer Compliance, 1980. Mem. Rep. Congrl. Com., 1980—, Rep. Nat. Com., 1981—. Served with USMC, 1961-65. Mem. ABA, Assn. Trial Lawyers Am., N.Y. Law Inst., Am. Arbitration Assn. (bd. arbitrators). Roman Catholic. Home and Office: Wagon Wheel Ranch PO Box 2 40 Park Ave Burns CO 80426

BOHLKE, GARY LEE, lawyer, playwright; b. Yakima, Wash., Mar. 9, 1941; s. Francis Douglas and Laura Mae (Bianchi) B. B.A., U. Wash., 1963; J.D., Am. U., 1966; LL.M., U. London, 1967; diploma London Inst. of World Affairs, 1967. Bar: D.C. 1967. Assoc. firm Mason, Fenwick & Lawrence, Washington, 1967-70; atty.-advisor U.S. C.E., Washington, 1972-74; asst. solicitor environ. law U.S. Dept. Interior, Washington, 1974-83, asst. solicitor for environ. and realty, 1983-86, sr. atty. environ. protection, 1986-88; assoc. gen. counsel litigation and enforcement Farm Credit Adminstrn., 1988-90; of counsel Ackerson & Feldman Chartered, 1991—. Author: (plays) Echoes, 1988, The Crime Tetraology consisting of Double Cross, 1982, Obsession, 1984, Judgment, 1985, Act of Justice, 1987; (novel) Forever a Stranger, 1990; (screenplay) Double Cross, 1992. Vice chmn. com. on environ. and transp. Washington, Adv. Neighborhood Commn. 4C, 1980-88. Recipient outstanding service award Office of Solicitor, Dept. Interior, 1979, 80, 81, 83, 84, 85, 86, Farm Credit Adminstrn., 1989, Spl. Achievement award 1981, 86. Mem. D.C. Bar Assn. (chmn. environ. law com. 1977-78, ABA del. 1978-79). Lutheran. Home: 1716 Eutaw Pl Baltimore MD 21217-3730 Office: Ackerson & Feldman Chartered 901 15th St NW Ste 1250 Washington DC 20005-2327

BOHNEN, BLYTHE, artist; b. Evanston, Ill., 1940. BA in Art, Smith Coll., 1962; BFA, Boston U., 1967; MFA in Painting, Hunter Coll., 1972. artist-in-residence Nat. Endowment for Arts, Douglass Coll., New Brunswick, N.J., 1976. Works included in (books) Art of the Seventies, 1980, Great Drawings of All Times, 1981; contbr. articles and revs. to profl. jours.; one-woman shows at Wadsworth Atheneum, Hartford, Conn., 1975, Internat. Cultural Ctr., Antwerp, Belgium, 1978, Light Gallery, N.Y.C., 1984, Galerie Mukai, Tokyo, 1984; exhibited in group shows at State Mus., Ghent, Belgium, 1976, Chgo. Art Inst., 1977, Documenta, Kassel, Germany, 1977, Mus. Modern Art, N.Y.C., 1977, 91; represented in permanent collections at Mus. Modern Art, Met. Mus. Art, N.Y.C., others. Nat. Endowment Arts fellow, 1978. Studio: 205 Mulberry St New York NY 10012

BOHORQUEZ, FERNANDO AUGUSTO, surgeon; b. Bogota, Colombia, July 17, 1945; came to U.S., 1972; s. Saul and Graciela (Mahecha) B.; m. Olga Martinez, June 21, 1969; children: Fernando Jr., Alex, Mauricio, Michael. MD, U. Colombia, Bogota, 1970. Diplomate Am. Bd. Surgery. Intern Montfort Hosp., Villavicencio, Colombia, 1970-71; mem. staff St. Rafael Hosp., Ibague, Colombia, 1971-72; intern Community Hosp., Roanoke, Va., 1972-73; resident in gen. surgery St. Joseph Hosp., Towson, Md., 1973-78; mem. staff Provident Hosp., Balt., 1978-80; pvt. practice Balt., 1980—; chmn. nutritional support com. St. Joseph Hosp., Towson, 1986—. Mem. ACS, Balt. County Med. Assn. (bd. dirs. 1990-91), Am. Soc. Parenteral and Enteral Nutrition, U.S.A. Colombian Med. Assn. Office: 7505 Osler Dr #503 Towson MD 21204

BOICE, CRAIG KENDALL, management consultant; b. Portland, Oreg., June 25, 1952; s. Charles A. and Audrey (Larson) B.; m. Jacinta E. Remedios, Nov. 21, 1979. BA summa cum laude, Beloit Coll., 1973; MA, Yale U., 1974, M.Phil., 1976, M in Pub. and Pvt. Mgmt., 1979. Instr. fellow philosophy Yale U., New Haven, 1978-79; economist Overseas Pvt. Investment Corp., Washington, 1978; sr. cons. Coopers and Lybrand, Washington and London, 1979-81; v.p. ops. Internat. Licensing Network, N.Y.C., 1981-82; pres., chmn., chief exec. officer Boice Dunham Group, N.Y.C., 1983—; adj. asst. prof. NYU, 1984—. Cons. Lake Placid Olympic Organizing Com., (N.Y.), 1979, New Haven Homesteading Program, 1979. Mem. Info. Industry Assn., Computer and Automated Systems Assn., Soc. Mfg. Engrs., Corp. Growth Assn., Soc. Photog. Scientists and Engrs., Planning Forum., World Future Soc., Internat. Platform Assn. Democrat. Office: Boice Dunham Group 437 Madison Ave New York NY 10022-7001

BOICE, JOHN KYLE, diplomat, electrical engineer; b. Dallas, Mar. 22, 1961; s. Elwood Lee and Mary Edna (Telford) B.; m. Dianne Elizabeth Brandt, Sept. 3, 1963; children: Hollis Danielle, Julian Christopher. BS in Engring. Sci., Baylor U., Waco, Tex., 1983. Design engr. Datapoint Corp., Austin, Tex., 1983-86; systems engr. Zenith Data Systems, St. Joseph, Mich., 1986-87; engring. mgr. Zenith Data Systems, Vienna, Va., 1987-90; joined fgn. svc. Dept. State, Washington, 1990; vice-consul Haiti, 1991. Tchr. No. Va. Lit. Coun., Fairfax, 1988-90. Mem. IEEE. Office: Consulate Am Embassy Port-au-Prince Washington DC 20521-3400

BOISE, AUDREY LORRAINE, educator; b. Hackensack, N.J., Feb. 12, 1933; d. Paul George and Lillian Rose (Goedecker) B. BA, Wellesley (Mass.) Coll., 1955; MA, Fairleigh Dickinson U., 1977. Cert. tchr. K-8, learning disabilities, supervision. Tchr. Township of Berkeley Heights (N.J.), 1958-67; learning cons. Borough of New Providence (N.J.), 1978-82, 1986—, Scotch Plains/Fanwood (N.J.), 1984-86; instr. Fairleigh Dickinson U., Madison, N.J., 1983, 1975-76; several other short-term teaching positions; supr. student tchrs., 1975-78; lectr. on fgn. countries and U.S. History, N.J., 1967—; travel agt. (part-time) 1972—. Mem. Republican Nat. Com., Washington, U.S. Senatorial Club, Washington, Republican Presidential Task Force, Washington, N.J. State Republican Com., Trenton, N.J., Nat. Fedn. of Republican Women, Washington. Mem. Nat. Edn. Assn., N.J. Assn. of Learning Cons., Assn. for Children with Learning Disabilities, N.J. Edn. Assn., Internat. Platform Assn., Coll. Club of Summit, Fortnightly, Hist. Soc. of Summit. Methodist. Office: Dept of Spl Svcs New Providence Bd of Edn 340 Center Ave New Providence NJ 07974

BOISSEAU, JERRY PHILIP, financial services company executive; b. Plattsburgh, N.Y., June 5, 1939; s. Augustine Arthur and Genevieve Francis (Poland) B.; m. Linda Gael Cummings Aug. 18, 1961; children: Gregory Philip, Lisa Michele. B of Gen. Studies, U. Nebr., 1970; MEd in Adminstrn., Fitchburg State Coll., 1978; MBA, Western New Eng. Coll., 1981. Cert. fin. planner; lic. registered prin.; registered investment advisor. Enlisted U.S. Army, 1961, commd. 2d lt., 1963, advanced through grades to lt. col., 1979, ret., 1981; account exec. Prudential-Bache Securities, Springfield, Mass., 1981-87; pres. Arlington Beach Co., Seaside Park, N.J., 1987-91, resigned, 1991; lectr. Ocean County Coll., 1991—; owner, mgr. Amherst Fin. Svcs., Toms River, N.J., 1987—; instr., lectr. U. Mass., Amherst, 1982-87, Greenfield (Mass.) Community Coll., 1983-86. Pres. parish coun. St. Catharines of Siena Ch., Seaside Park; mem. adj. faculty Coll. for Fin. Planning, 1991—; mem. Seaside Park Rep. Club. Mem. Inst. Cert. Fin. Planners, Internat. Assn. Fin. Planners (pres. Cen. N.J. chpt. 1991—), Toms River C. of C., Toms River Country Club, Rotary (pres. Amherst chpt. 1986-87), KC (4th degree), Seaside Pk. Yacht Club, Better Bus. Bureau. Roman Catholic. Home: PO Box 591 Seaside Park NJ 08752 Office: PO Box 1959 Toms River NJ 08753

BOISSELLE, ALLAN ALBERT, composer, guitarist, fireman; b. Holyoke, Mass., Dec. 6, 1947; s. Albert Joseph and Laura (Cousineau) B.; m. Shirley Ann Higgens, 1952 (div. Mar. 1992); children: Belinda, Michelle, Michael. Grad., Westfield State U., 1975. Composer (guitar solo) Sonatina, 1986, Tema Differcias, 1989, I-8 Practical Studies, 1989, Tone Poem, 1988, Solo Concerto, 1989, Opus, Vols. I and II, others; composer coll. level curriculum and recital work, 1990. Cpl. USMC, 1967-71, Vietnam. Home and Office: Box 331 Rfd 2 Holland MA 01521

BOIT, CHRISTIAN ULRICH, physicist; b. Hamburg, Germany, Nov. 6, 1952; came to U.S. 1990; s. Hermann and Charlotte (Paschelke) B. Physics Dipl., Tech. U. Berlin, 1981, PhD, 1987. Staff engr. Siemens AG, Munich, 1986-90; asst. tech. mgr. IBM/Siemens, East Fishkill, N.Y., 1990—; physics tchr. Tech. U. Berlin, 1977-80, semiconductor device physics tchr., 1981-86. Contbr. articles to profl. jours. Mem. IEEE. Office: IBM Siemens 64 M Project Rt 51 Hopewell Junction NY 12533

BOJARCZUK, DAVID CHARLES, controller, auditor; b. Portland, Maine, June 5, 1956; s. Edward and Thelma Helen (Forrest) B.; m. Linda Helen Baker, Nov. 27, 1982; 1 child, Erika Paige. BS in Accountancy with honors, Bentley Coll., 1981. CPA, Mass. Staff acct. Joseph B. Cohan & Assocs., Worcester, Mass., 1981-82, Peck Assocs., P.C., Wellesley, Mass., 1982-84, Kenneth Elgart & Co. CPAs, Brookline, Mass., 1984-85, P.F. Bruno & Co. CPAs, Boston, 1985-86; asst. contr. Medford (Mass.) Savs. Bank, 1986-89, contr., 1990—; part-time instr. acctg. and fin. New Eng. Banking Inst., Boston, 1989—. cons. applied econs. program Jr. Acievement, Medford High Sch., 1989—; mem. north area coun. ARC Massachusetts Bay, Peabody, Mass., 1990—, mem. fin. com. Recipient Recognition award Jr. Achievement, 1990. Mem. Mass. Assn. Savs. Bank Auditors and Contrs. (officer 1990—). Republican. Jewish. Home: 290 Grove St Apt 9 Newton MA 02166-2227 Office: Medford Savs Bank 29 High St Medford MA 02155-3885

BOJE, DAVID LEONARD, aerospace engineer; b. Buffalo, Nov. 23, 1965; s. Norman L. and Carol Anne (Bell) B.; m. Joan M. Roll, Feb. 21, 1987; children: Jonathan Nicholas, Kelly Catherine. AAS in Engr. Sci., Erie Community Coll., Buffalo, 1986; BS in Aerospace Engring., SUNY, Buffalo, 1989. Systems design engr. Keller Tech. Corp., Buffalo, 1989-91; application engr. Parametric Tech. Corp., Waltham, Mass., 1991—; cons., Buffalo, 1991—. Soccer coach North Tonawanda (N.Y.) Athletic Assn., 1983-87. Mem. AIAA. Home: 5829 Cameron Dr Lockport NY 14094-6638 Office: Parametric Tech Corp 5820 Main St Ste 602 Buffalo NY 14221-5734

BOK, JOAN TOLAND, utility executive; b. Grand Rapids, Mich., Dec. 31, 1929; d. Don Prentiss Weaver and Mary Emily (Anderson) T.; m. John Fairfield Bok, July 15, 1955; children: Alexander Toland, Geoffrey Robbins. A.B., Radcliffe Coll., 1951; J.D., Harvard U., 1955. Bar: Mass. 1955. Assoc. Ropes & Gray, Boston, 1955-61; pvt. practice Boston, 1961-68; atty. New Eng. Electric System, Westborough, Mass., 1968-73; asst. to pres. New Eng. Electric System, 1973-77, v.p., sec., 1977-79, vice chmn., dir., 1979-84, chmn., 1984—, pres., chief exec. officer, 1988-89; bd. dirs., vice chmn. New Eng. Power Co.; bd. dirs. Mass. Electric Co., Narragansett Electric Co., Avery Dennison Corp., Fed. Res. Bank of Boston, Monsanto Co., John Hancock Mut. Life Ins. Co. Bd. dirs. Com. for Econ. Devel.; trustee Library of Boston Athenaeum, MGH Inst. Health Professions; former pres. Harvard Bd. Overseers; councillor Am. Antiquarian Soc.; mem. of the corp. Mass. Gen. Hosp.; trustee Urban Inst., Worcester Found. for Exptl. Biology. Fellow Am. Bar Found.; mem. ABA, Boston Bar Assn., Woods Hole Oceanographic Instn., Phi Beta Kappa. Unitarian. Home: 53 Pinckney St Boston MA 02114-4506 Office: New England Electric System 25 Research Dr Westborough MA 01582-0001

BOKAT, STEPHEN ARTHUR, lawyer; b. Washington, July 30, 1946; s. George and Golda (Shurack) B.; m. Karen Gilbert, June 17, 1972; children: Christina Elise, Rebecca Suzanne. BA, Adams State Coll., 1968; JD, George Washington U., 1972. Bar: D.C. 1973, U.S. Dist. Ct. D.C. 1974, U.S. Ct. Appeals (D.C., 7th and 9th cirs.) 1976, U.S. Supreme Ct. 1976, U.S. Ct. Appeals (8th cir.) 1977, U.S. Ct. Appeals (4th cir.) 1979, U.S. Ct. Appeals (5th cir.) 1980, U.S. Ct. Appeals (3d cir.) 1985. Atty., advisor NLRB, Washington, 1972-74, Occupational Safety and Health Rev. Commn., Washington, 1974-76; appellate atty. solicitors office U.S. Dept. of Labor, Washington, 1976-77; sr. labor counsel Nat. Chamber Lit Ctr., Washington, 1977-82; v.p., gen. counsel U.S. C. of C., Washington, 1983—; exec. v.p. Nat. Chamber Litigation Ctr., 1990—. Co-editor in chief: Occupational Safety and Health Law, 1988. V.p. Nat. Chamber Litigation Ctr., Washington, 1985-90, exec. v.p., 1990—. Mem. ABA (co-chmn. occupational safety and health com. 1983-86), Am. Corp. Counsel Assn. (bd. dirs. 1983—, treas. 1987-88, vice chmn. 1988-89, chmn. 1989-90). Office: US C of C 1615 H St NW Washington DC 20062-0002

BOKSER, LEWIS, newspaper publisher; b. Phila., Mar. 23, 1904; s. David and Yetta B.; student U. Pa., 1930-31, Temple U., 1972, Villanova U., 1972-73; m. Sara A. Lipschutz, Feb. 11, 1931 (dec. June 1985). Mgr., announcer Sta. WNAT, Phila., 1922-28; paving contractor, Phila., 1924-54; pub. Phila. Beacon, 1943-50, Phila. Civil Service Sentinel, 1945-50; sec.-treas. Lewis Bokser Inc., Phila., 1957—. Alt. del. Republican Nat. Conv., 1952; nat. bd. dirs. Yeshiva U., N.Y.C., 1950-60; co-founder Einstein Coll. Medicine, N.Y.C., 1950; treas. Contractors Assn. Eastern Pa., 1956-57. Mem. Am. Arbitration Assn., Am. Public Works Assn. Jewish. Clubs: Fourth Estate Sq., Centurions (co-founder 1946), Masons (master lodge 1945). Editor Am. sect. Jewish Travel Guide; contbr. hist., humanitarian articles to newspapers. Home: 5108 N 10th St Philadelphia PA 19141-4008 Office: 2829 N Broad St Philadelphia PA 19132-2728

BOLAND, GERALD LEE, health facility financial executive; b. Harrisburg, Pa., Apr. 2, 1946; s. Vincent Harry and Alice Jane (Geiste) B.; 1 child, Peter Alexander. BS, Lebanon Valley Coll., 1968. Acctg. trainee Armstrong Cork Co., Millville, N.J., 1968; payroll supr., plant ops. acct., 1969-70; sr. fin. acct. Lancaster (Pa.) Gen. Hosp., 1970-71, mgr. gen. acctg., 1972; corp. acctg. mgr. HMW Industries, Inc., Lancaster, 1972; corp. controller Fleck-Marshall Co. subs. Gable Industries, Lancaster, 1973-74, sec.-treas., 1974-75; contr. Dominion Psychiat. Treatment Ctr., Falls Church, Va., 1975-76; contr., dir. fin. Miller & Byrne, Inc., Rockville, Md., 1976-79; v.p. internal auditing Medlantic Healthcare Group, 1979-88; v.p. ops. Kapner, Wolfberg & Assocs., Van Nuys, Calif., 1988-89; acct. mgr. Providence Hosp., 1989—. Mem. Am. Acctg. Assn., Nat. Assn. Accts., Hosp. Fin. Mgmt. Assn., Eastern Fin. Assn., Am. Hosp. Assn., Am. Mgmt. Assn., Fin. Mgmt. Assn., Inst. Internal Auditors. Home: 13021 Silver Maple Ct Bowie MD 20715

BOLAND, JOHN THOMAS, educational administrator; b. N.Y.C., Sept. 5, 1944; s. Joseph Michael and Dorothy (Hamm) B.; m. Cherly Elizabeth Heckendorn, Nov. 26, 1966; children: John, Stacy, Kelly. BS, Fordham U., 1966; MBA, U. Conn., 1967; postgrad., U. Ky., 1988. Registrar, bus. mgr. Southeastern br. U. Conn., Avery Point, 1967-71; dean adminstrn. Quinebaug Valley Community Coll., Danielson, Conn., 1971—; acting pres. Quinebaug Valley Community Coll., Danielson, 1979-80, 85-86. Pres. Killingly-Bklyn. Cultural Devel. Fedn., Danielson, 1977-78, Killingly Right to Read Com. Task Force, Danielson, 1979-80, Griffin Youth Hockey Assn., Danielson, 1983-84; chair Northeastern Conn. Sexual Assault Ctr., Willimatic, 1983-85. Mem. Eastern Assn. of Col. and Univ. Bus. Officers (chair 1989-91), Coun. of Adminstrv. Deans (chair 1991—). Roman Catholic. Office: Quinebaug Valley Community Coll 742 Upper Maple St Danielson CT 06239-1440

BOLAND, MATTHEW FREDERICK, music educator, composer; b. Chelsea, N.Y., Apr. 10, 1962; s. Austin Mead and Jane (Jacek) B.; m. Louise Daniele Faro, Sept. 29, 1991. MusB cum laude, Berklee Coll. Music, 1984. Cert. electronic technician. Electronic technician Lexicon Inc., Waltham, Mass., 1988-91; self-employed music educator, composer Brighton, Mass., 1991—; music educator The Paul Monte Music Studio, Wellesley, Mass., 1991—, Am. Sch. Music, Peabody, Mass., 1991—; producer, orchestrator Children's Music Workshop, Weston, 1991-92; collaborator Carolyn Legg-local Boston lyricist, Medford, Mass., 1990-92; performing sideman Ellen Bennet Group, Boston, 1991; recording engr. Martin Sexton-local Boston musician, 1990. Composer: (music for video) Quasar, 1992, Don't Look Back, Rough Touch (instrumental), 1992, various music 1988-92; producer, orchestrator (children's music edn. tape) Music Magic with Cheryl, 1991-92. Contbr., mem. Green Peace U.S.A. Inc., local Mass. chpt., 1991-92; contbr. Mass. Coalition for Cleaning Up Hazardous Waste, Boston, 1991. Mem. Parker Adams Group, Nat. Acad. of Songwriters. Home and Office: 669 Washington St # 1 Brighton MA 02135

BOLAND, PATRICIA ANN, museum director; b. Rochester, N.Y., Aug. 24, 1935; d. James Patrick and Florence Elva (Miller) Neary; m. Gerald Patrick Boland, June 30, 1956 (wid. June 1989); children: Patrick, Matthew, Daniel, Timothy, Sheila, Catherine. Student, Nazareth Coll., Rochester, N.Y., 1952-54. Tchr. St. Michael's Sch., Rochester, 1954-56, St. Peter and Paul Sch., Rochester, 1956-57; edn. dir. Ontario County Hist. Soc., Canandaigua, N.Y., 1972-81; city coun. mem. City of Canandaigua, 1975-79, mayor, 1979-85; owner Gourmet Deli, Canandaigua, 1983-84; dir. Granger Homestead Soc., Canandaigua, 1989—; bd. dirs. Canandaigua Nat. Bank. Contbr. articles to profl. jours. Mem. Canandaigua Dem. Com., 1975—, Ontario County Dem. Com., 1975—; elected to Ontario County Bd. Suprs., 1991-93; bd. dirs. Bristol Valley Playhouse, Naples, N.Y., 1980-87, Neighbor-to-Neighbor, Canandaigua, 1985—. Recipient William Mitchell award Canandaigua C. of C., 1989, Main St. award N.Y. State, HUD award, 1984. Office: Granger Homestead Soc 295 N Main St Canandaigua NY 14424-1289

BOLANOWSKI, STANLEY JOHN, JR., educator; b. Utica, N.Y., Feb. 22, 1950; s. Stanley John Sr. and Stella Agnes (Kieler) B.; m. Pauline Dimitry, Mar. 5, 1983; children: Paul Smith, Dena Smith. AAAS, SUNY, Morrisville, 1970; BA in Psychology, Syracuse U., 1973, BSEE, 1974, PhD in Sensory Sci., 1981. Postdoctoral fellow U. Rochester (N.Y.) Med. Ctr., 1980-82, asst. prof., 1982-88; assoc. prof. neurosci. Syracuse U., 1988—, affiliate assoc. prof. bioengring., 1988—; lectr. Colgate U., Hamilton, N.Y., 1991—; adj. asst. prof. Syracuse U., 1984-88, U. Rochester Med. Sch., 1988—; cons. Hamilton Coll., Clinton, 1987—, Bausch & Lomb, Rochester, 1991—. Editor: Ratio Scaling of PSychological Magnitudes, 1991; contbr. articles to profl. jours. Rsch. grant Nat. Eye Inst., U. Rochester Med. Sch., 1982-85, NIH, Rochester Med. Sch., 1984-85, NIH, Syracuse U., 1987-91. Mem. AAAS, Acoustical Soc. Am., Assn. Rsch. in Vision and Ophthalmology, Internat. Brain Rsch. Orgn., N.Y. Acad. Sci., Soc. for Neurosci., Psychonomics Soc. Home: 2582 Clover St Rochester NY 14618 Office: Syracuse U Inst for Sensory Rsch Merrill Ln Syracuse NY 13244

BOLDUC, BRUCE JOSEPH, financial planner, chemical company executive; b. Yonkers, N.Y., July 26, 1958; s. Raymond Daniel and Anne (Chedrick) B.; m. Maureen Ivers, May 25, 1985; 1 child, Kaitlyn Anne. BSChemE, Manhattan Coll., 1980, MSChemE, 1983; MBA, NYU, 1988. Economic analyst Texaco Inc., White Plains, N.Y., 1980-85; staff cons. Chem Systems Inc., Tarrytown, N.Y., 1985-89; mgr. fin. and planning Airco Carbon Dioxide, Murray Hill, N.J., 1989—. Home: 147 John St Ridgewood NJ 07450 Office: Airco Carbon Dioxide 575 Mountain Ave Murray Hill NJ 07974

BOLDUC, J. P., specialty chemicals company executive; b. 1939. BA, St. Cloud State U. Asst. sec. U.S. Dept. Agr., Washington, until 1977; v.p. Booz, Allen & Hamilton, N.Y.C., 1977-83; sr. v.p. W.R. Grace & Co., N.Y.C., 1983-86, exec. v.p., chief fin. officer, vice chmn., 1986-90; pres., chief operating officer W.R. Grace & Co., 1990—; bd. dirs. Marshall & Ilsley Corp., Grace Energy Corp., Sundstrand. COO for Pres. Reagan's Pvt. Sector Survey on Cost Control in the Fed. Govt., 1982-84. Recipient Disting. Alumni award St. Cloud State U., 1983, Person of Yr. award Inst. of Internal Auditors, 1985. Office: W R Grace & Co One Town Center Rd Boca Raton FL 33486-1010

BOLEBRUCH, JEFFREY JOHN, sales representative; b. Gloversville, N.Y., Jan. 13, 1963; s. John George and Peggy Ann (Spawn) B.; m. Abagail Trainor, July 16, 1988. BS in Geography (Environ. Sci.), U.S. Mil. Acad., 1985. Commd. 2d lt. U.S. Army, 1985, advanced through grades to capt., 1989; served with 1st Cavalry Div., 4th Bn., 5th Air Defense Arty. U.S. Army, Ft. Hood, Tex., 1985-90; tech. sales rep. Blasch Precision Ceramics, Schenectady, N.Y., 1990—. Mem. Am. Inst. Chem. Engrs., Am. Ceramic Soc. Republican. Home: 217 Hillview Rd Gloversville NY 12078 Office: Blasch Precision Ceramics 99 Cordell Rd Schenectady NY 12304

BOLLE, JAMES DOUGAN, conductor, composer; b. Evanston, Ill., July 26, 1931; s. Theodore Bernhard Henry and Dorothy Elizabeth (Dougan) B.; m. Jocelyn Hale Faulkner, Mar. 21, 1953; children: Christopher Philip, Edward Nathaniel, Susanna Thayer. Student, Harvard U., 1949-51; BA, Antioch Coll., 1957; MusM, Northwestern U., 1968; LHD (hon.), Franklin Pierce Coll., 1983. Asst. dir. North Shore Community Music Ctr., Winnetka, Ill., 1959-61; dir. Chgo. Community Music Found., Living Music Concert Series, 1961-68; music dir. South Suburban Symphony Orch., Park Forest, Ill., 1963-68, Monadnock Music Festival, Peterborough, N.H., 1966—, N.H. Symphony Orch., Manchester, N.H., 1974—; instr. U. Sask. (Can.), Saskatoon, 1959-61, Keene (N.H.) State Coll., 1969-73. Composer: (for piano) Dream Pieces, (for violin and bass) Through a Looking Glass Darkly, Eight Pieces for Violin and Oboe. With U.S. Army, 1955-57. Recipient award for disting. svc. to Hungarian music Artisjus, 1987. Home: Main St Francestown NH 03043 Office: Monadnock Music Festival PO Box 255 Peterborough NH 03458-0255

BOLSTRIDGE, JUNE C., environmental engineering executive, consultant; b. Syracuse, N.Y.. BS in Botany and Chemistry, SUNY, Syracuse, 1980; MS in Environ. Engring., U. Wash., 1982. Rsch. assoc. U. Wash., Seattle, 1980-82; environ. engr. Martin Marietta Environ. Systems, Columbia, Md., 1983-85, mgr. info. systems tech., 1985-86; dir. environ. tech. and info. systems Rsch. and Data Systems Corp., Greenbelt, Md., 1986-87; sr. environ. engr. ICF Kaiser Engrs., Fairfax, Va., 1987-89; project mgr. ICF Inc., Fairfax, 1989-90; pres. Gaia Corp., Silver Spring, Md., 1990—; tech. advisor Thompson Pub. Group (Right to Know Manual), Washington, 1990—; course leader and trainer govt. insts., Washington, 1989—. Author: EPCRA Data on Chemical Releases, Inventories and Emergency Planning. , 1992; contbr. articles to profl. jours. Mem. ASCE, Am. Chem. Soc., Air and Waste Mgmt. Assn., Soc. Mfg. Engrs., Assn. for Finishing Processes (bd. advisors 1992—), Soc. for Computer Simulation. Office: GAIA Corp 8401 Colesville Rd Ste # 342A Silver Spring MD 20910

BOLT, MICHAEL GERALD, metallurgist; b. Sharon, Pa., Mar. 3, 1953; s. Thomas Bennett and Mary Jane (Lyons) B.; m. Roberta Ann Taylor, Oct. 14, 1972; 1 child, Jennifer Lynn Bolt. BA, Mansfield U., 1975; MS in Student Personnel, Slippery Rock U., 1991. Sci. tchr. Cranford (N.J.) Sch. Dist., 1975-76; metallurgical lab. tech. Wheatland (Pa.) Tube Co., 1976—. Treas. Mercer Crawford County Rails to Trails. Recipient Citizenship award Mercer (Pa.) County Govt., 1974. Mem. Am. Assn. Counseling and Devel., Western Pa. Conservancy, Shenago Conservancy, Rails to Trails. Democrat. Roman Catholic. Home: RD2 Box 252 Patricia Dr W Transfer PA 16154-9305 Office: Wheatland Tube Co Council Ave Wheatland PA 16161

BOLTER, EUGENE PAUL, investment counselor; b. Bklyn., Aug. 17, 1932; s. Eugene and Hedwig (Mahr) B.; m. Mary Jane Ullrich, Nov. 26, 1977; 1 child, Margaret Beaumont. BS in Commerce and Fin., Bucknell U., 1954; postgrad., NYU, 1961-64. Asst. to pres. Wedemann & Godknecht, Inc., N.Y.C., 1956-58; with First Boston Corp., N.Y.C., 1958-79; sr. v.p. Edgewood Mgmt. Co., N.Y.C., 1979-84, Prescott Asset Mgmt., N.Y.C., 1984—. Served to 1st lt. U.S. Army, 1954-56. Mem. N.Y. Soc. Security Analysts. Clubs: Rolling Rock; Cherry Valley; De Bruce. Home: 90 4th St Garden City NY 11530-4408 Office: Prescott Asset Mgmt 1 World Trade Ctr New York NY 10048-0202

BOLTON, JULIA GOODEN, hospital administrator; b. Wilmington, Del., Nov. 11, 1940; d. Merrill Harvey and Mary Rose (Amoroso) Gooden; m. Roger Edwin Bolton, June 27, 1964; children: Christopher Andrew, Jonathan Hughes. RN with honors, Johns Hopkins Hosp., Balt., 1961; BSN with honors, Case Western Res. U., Cleve., 1964; postgrad., Boston U., 1964-65; MS with honors, Russell Sage Coll., 1986. Lic. nurse, Vt. Staff nurse operating rm., clin. instr. Johns Hopkins Hosp., Balt., 1961-62; instr. practical nursing, acting coord. med. programs Charles H. McCann Vocat. Sch., North Adams, Mass., 1966, clin. instr. manpower devel. tng. act program, 1968, clin. instr. med., surg. and pediatric nursing, 1972-73; staff orientation and tour program for children North Adams Regional Hosp., 1973-74; health edn. cons. Williamstown (Mass.) Pub. Schs., 1978-81, Pine Cobble Sch., 1978-81; clin. cons. patient care stds. project North Adams Regional Hosp., 1985-86; dir. staff edn. and quality assurance Southwestern Vt. Med. Ctr., Bennington, 1986-87, asst. v.p. nursing, 1988, v.p. nursing, 1988—, interim pres., 1991; mem. client adv. com. Seiler's Corp., 1992. Adv. com. Putnam Meml. Sch. Practical Nursing, 1989—; profl. adv. com. Bennington Home Health Agy., 1988; alt. del. Diocesan Conv. No. Berkshire Deanery, Episcopal Ch., 1987; dir. Vt. div., Bennington County unit, Am. Cancer Soc., 1986-88; mem. Williamstown Betterment Study Com., 1985; adv. com. to plan for declining enrollments Mt. Greylock Reg. High Sch., 1985; bd. dirs. exec. com. Vt. Nursing Initiative Implementation Grant, Pew Charitable Trust Grant, 1992; vestry St. John's Episcopal Ch., Williamstown, 1992—; active many other civic and charitable orgns. in past. Recipient Hannah Karp award as outstanding student, Russell Sage Coll., 1985, traineeship, 1983-85, others. Mem. Am. Orgn. Nurse Execs., Nat. Forum Women Health Care Leaders, Nat. League for Nursing, Vt. Orgn. Nurse Execs., Rotary, Phi Kappa Phi, Sigma Theta Tau.

BOLTON, KENNETH ALBERT, corporate professional; b. Mar. 6, 1941; s. Albert and Myrtle (Nelting) B.; m. Maryanne Lavelle; 1 child, Katharine. BS in Indsl. Engring., Pa. State U., 1978. Registered profl. engr., Calif. With GE, Allentown, Pa., 1961-63; system mgr. GE, Phila., 1963-72; mgr. MCS Mgmt. Internat., Washington, 1972-80, Coopers & Lybrand, Phila., 1980-82; dir. cons. Worden & Risberg, Phila., 1982-83; v.p. mktg. Laminated, Inc., Hatfield, Pa., 1983-86; pres. Mgmt. Internat., Phila., 1986-90, Wm. P. Bolton, Inc., Phila., 1990—; bd. dirs. Ent., Internat., Phila., 1978—. Contbr. articles to profl. jours. Advisor Jr. Achievement, Media, Pa., 1970; mem. adv. bd. Salvation Army. Mem. NSPE, am. Arbitration Assn. (panel of arbitrators), Phila. C. of C. (bd. dirs. 1975, lobbyist small bus. coun. 1978), Union League Phila., St. George's Club Bermuda. Republican. Home: 5900 Atlantic Ave Ventnor City NJ 08406 Office: Mgmt Internat The Kenilworth Ste 706 Philadelphia PA 19144-9969

BOLTON, RONALD MCLEAN, cartographer, computer specialist; b. Washington, June 26, 1933; s. Richard Antony and Lucille (Lyman) B.; m. Gail Weatherhead, June 30, 1961 (div. Oct. 1987); children: Martha M., Ronald M. Jr., Christopher M. BS, D.C. Tchrs. Coll., 1963. Math. technician USN Weapons Lab., Dahlgren, Va., 1959-61; cartographer, computer specialist Navy Oceanographic Office, Suitland, Md., 1963-72, Def. Mapping Agy., Suitland, 1972-74, Nat. Oceanic and Atmospheric Adminstrn., Rockville, Md., 1974—. Contbr. articles to profl. jours. Recipient Silver medal Dept. Commerce, 1981. Mem. Inst. Navigation, N.Am. Cartographic Info. Soc. (bd. dirs., chief exec. officer 1986—), Soc. Automotive Engring. (astronautics div.). Democrat. Episcopalian. Home: 201 Wilder Ave Colonial Beach VA 22443 Office: NOAA/NOS/ACB 6010 Executive Blvd Rockville MD 20852

BOLVIN, JOHN ORVARD, academic administrator; b. Pitts., Apr. 11, 1929; s. Orvard and Clara (Michaels) B.; m. Marjorie Cameron Mitchell, Dec. 6, 1952; children: Joan Margaret, Nancy Jean. BA, Coll. Wooster, 1952; MEd, U. Pitts., 1955, EdD, 1958. Tchr., coach North Allegheny Sch., Pitts., 1954-59; prin. Beaver (Pa.) Area Schs., 1959-64; asst. dir. Learning Rsch.-Devel. Ctr., Pitts., 1964-66; lectr. U. Pitts., 1957-64, asst. prof., 1964-66, assoc. prof., 1966-70, prof., 1970—, assoc. dir. Learning Rsch.-Devel. Ctr., 1970-74, assoc. dean Sch. Edn., 1974-83, dean Coll. Gen. Studies, 1983—; cons. Korean Edn. Devel. Inst., 1974-79, Inst. U. Tech., Venezuela, 1977-82; lectr. U. London, 1976-84; vis. scholar U. Malawi, Africa, 1983, 85, 87; faculty rep. NCAA U. Pitts., 1977—. Author: (with others) To Improve Learning: An Evaluation of Instructional Technology, 1971, Developmental Efforts in Individualized Learning, 1971, Individualized Instruction and Learning, 1974, Encyclopedia of Educational Research, 1982, International Encyclopedia of Education Reseach Studies, 1984; contbr. articles to profl. jours. Bd. dirs. Camdes Corp., Pitts., Tng. Wheels Nursery Sch., Manchester, Pa., Western Pa. Advanced Tech. Ctr.; pres. bd. trustees Bidwell Music, Edn. and Recreation Ctr. Recipient Disting. Alumnus award Sch. Edn. U. Pitts., 1984, Gus award Staff Assn. U. Pitts., 1985. Mem. Am. Edn. Rsch. Assn., Pa. Edn. Rsch. Assn., Kappa Delta Pi, Phi Delta Kappa. Office: U Pitts 5th Avenue Blvd Pittsburgh PA 15260-0001

BOLYAI, STEPHEN, college executive, controller; b. Budapest, Hungary, Dec. 22, 1951; s. Oscar and Violet (Tartar) B.; m. Annette Lia, Sept. 15, 1973; children: Melani, Christopher, Kayla. BA, Northeastern U., Boston, 1973; MBA, Fairleigh Dickinson U., 1982. Installment loan mgmt. trainee BMC Durfee Trust Co., Fall River, Mass., 1973-76; credit mgr. Westinghouse Corp., Boston, 1976-78; from asst. bursar to asst. bus. mgr. Fairleigh Dickinson U., Teaneck, N.J., 1978-83; from bus. mgr. to dir. adminstrn. svcs. Fairleigh Dickinson U., Rutherford, N.J., 1983-86; bus. mgr. U. Medicine & Dentistry of N.J., Newark, 1986-88; from asst. v.p. for bus. to assoc. v.p./cont. William Paterson Coll., Wayne, N.J., 1988—. Trustee 1st Congl. Ch., Park Ridge, N.J., 1989—. Mem. Nat. Assn. Coll. & Univ. Bus. Officers, Univ. Risk Mgmt. & Ins. Assn., N.J. Bus. Officers Coun. (treas. 1989—). Office: William Paterson Coll 300 Pompton Rd Wayne NJ 07470-2103

BONACCI, CARLA, architect; b. Buffalo, Dec. 13, 1959; d. John Carl and Annette Marie (Masella) B.; m. Robert Edmund McNamara. BS in Architecture, Pa. State U., 1981, BArch, 1982. Lic. architect. Jr. architect, assoc. architect, asst. architect, architect Port Authority of N.Y. and N.J., N.Y.C., 1982-92; sr. architect, project dir. Bonacci-McNamara Architects, Westfield, N.J., 1992—. Mem. AIA (chmn. women in architecture com. 1990, regional liaison/state chmn. women in architecture com. 1992). Roman Catholic. Office: Bonacci-McNamara Architects 425 Baker Ave Westfield NJ 07090

BONACORSI, GREGORY JAMES, mechanical engineer; b. Lawrence, Mass., Dec. 16, 1955; s. Dominic and Elaine Mary (Maloney) B.; m. Jody Michele St. Germain, Aug. 16, 1980 (div.); children: Jaime Michele, Jacquelyn Arlyne. BSME, U. N.H., 1978; MSME, Northeastern U., 1984. Registered profl. engr., Mass., N.H. Self-employed carpenter, Salem, N.H., 1972-78; with engring. devel. program Aircraft Engine Bus. Group, Gen. Electric Co., Lynn, Mass., 1978-80, evaluation engr., 1981-89; program mgr. Gen. Electric Co., Lynn, Mass., 1989—; ind. bldg. cons., Methuen, Mass., 1983—. Bd. dirs. Colonial Village Condo Assn., Methuen, 1986-88. Recipient Sanford A. Moss award, 1987, Managerial award Gen. Electric Co., 1987. Republican. Roman Catholic. Home: 7 Dana Rd Salem NH 03079-3481

BONANNO, JACQUELINE, counselor, therapist; b. Reading, Pa., Oct. 29, 1944; d. Jere H. and Isabel (McDonnell) Babb; m. William S. Bonanno, June 18, 1966; children: Susan, Brian, Christine. AD, St. Joseph Hosp., Reading, Pa., 1965; BA, Caldwell (N.J.) Coll., 1985; MA, Montclair State Coll., 1990; postgrad in family therapy, N.J. Family Therapy Inst., 1991—. RN, N.J.; cert. alcoholism counselor. Nurse Fair Oaks Hosp., Summit, N.J., 1980-86; nurse, health educator Roselle (N.J.) Sch. Dist., 1986-87; counselor Outpatient Recovery, F.O.H., Summit, 1987—; educator Inst. of Transition and Devel., Bedminster, N.J., 1991. Contbr. articles to profl. jours. Program monitor N.J. Task Force on Women and Alcohol, 1989—; mem. Mayor's Task Force on Drugs and Alcohol, Madison, 1987-89, Morris County Adv. Bd. for Substance Abuse, Morristown, 1985-86. Mem. N.J. Assn. Women Therapists, Am. Assn. Counseling and Devel. Office: Outpatient Recovery Ctr 2 Broad St Summit NJ 07901-4013

BONANNO, ROBERT DONALD, automotive executive; b. N.Y.C., Jan. 6, 1927; s. Salvatore and Bernadetta (Scheps) B.; m. Margaret Elizabeth Armstrong, Aug. 10, 1950; children: Lorraine, Robert J., Keith. Grad. high sch., Lodi, N.J. Pres. Goodyear Motors, Inc., Lodi, 1948—; assoc. mgr. Real Estate Holdings, Lodi, 1948—. Mem. Tide Orgn.; dir. Lodi Boys and Girls Club, 1990-91. Seaman 1st class USN, 1944-46. Mem. Lodi C. of C. (dir. 1988-91). Office: Goodyear Motors Inc 86 State Rt 46 E Lodi NJ 07644-3698

BONAZINGA, MARIE THERESE, manufacturing company executive; b. Bklyn., May 10, 1948; d. Bartholomew and Ann (Palermo) B. AA, Gloria K. Bus. Sch., 1967, U. Louisville, 1975. Adminstrv. asst. Gallard-Schlesinger Chem. Mfg. Corp., Carle Place, N.Y., 1967-75; v.p. Accurate Chem. & Scientific Corp., Westbury, N.Y., 1975—; pres. Accurate Surg. & Scientific Instruments Corp., Westbury, 1979—, Leeches USA Ltd., Westbury, 1986—. Recipient Boli award L.I. Advt. Club, 1981. Mem. Nat. Assn. Women Bus. Owners, Roslyn Heights Civic Assn. Office: Accurate Surg & Sci Instruments 300 Shames Dr Westbury NY 11590-1725

BONAZZO, ANTHONY HENRY, II, computer company executive; b. Bridgeport, Conn., Aug. 13, 1957; s. Robert Enrico Sr. and Lena (DeVellis) B. BA, U. Bridgeport, 1979; MD, Ross U., 1984. Gen. mgr. Northeastern Software, Shelton, Conn., 1984-86; pres. Bright Ideas Computer, Guilford, Conn., 1986-87; dir. ops. MAC Warehouse, Norwalk, Conn., 1987-88; bus. devel. mgr. Micro Warehouse, Norwalk, 1988; dir. retail sales div. Micro Age Computers, Norwalk, 1988—; mktg. cons. AHB Cons., Shelton, 1988—. Home: 27 Meeting House Ln Shelton CT 06484-2869 Office: Micro Age Computer 701 Main Ave Norwalk CT 06851-1127

BOND, A(MANDA) ODESSA, educator; b. Phila., Dec. 4, 1942; d. Noah and Elizabeth (Watlington) B. BA, Morgan State U., Balt., 1965; MA, Villanova U., 1979; postgrad., U. Pa., 1986—. Cert. tchr. Pa. Tchr. Bd. Edn., Phila., 1969—; pres. Watlington O Bond Ednl. Corp., Wilmington, Del., 1979—. Author: The Double Tragedy, 1970; contbr. articles to newspapers, mags. and profl. jours. Active Rep. Presdl. Task Force, 1982—, World Affairs Council, 1976—, Goodwill Industries, life mem., 1981; mem. Jr. League, Native Am. Ch., 1990. Mem. AAUW. Club: Peale.

BOND, GEORGE CLEMENT, anthropologist, educator; b. Knoxville, Tenn., Nov. 16, 1936; s. J. Max and Ruth Elizabeth (Clement) B.; m. Alison Murray, Sept. 21, 1940; children: Matthew, Rebecca, Jonathan, Sarah. BA, Boston U., 1959; MA, London Sch. Econs., 1962, PhD, 1968. Lectr. U. East Anglia, Norwich, Eng., 1966-68; asst. prof. Columbia U., N.Y.C., 1968-74, assoc. prof. Tchrs. Coll., 1974-80, prof., 1980—, dir. Inst. African Studies, 1989—. Author: Politics of Change in a Zambia Community, 1976; editor: African Christianity, 1979, Social Stratification and Education, 1981; contbr. articles to scholarly publs. Home: 229 Larch Ave Teaneck NJ 07666-2345 Office: Columbia U Tchrs Coll New York NY 10027

BOND, JOHN WALTER, historian; b. Orlando, Ky., May 17, 1933; s. John Y. and Mary A. (McCracken) B.; m. Betty P. Cloyd, Aug. 17, 1957; children: Beverly, Tammy, Jonna. BA in History, Berea Coll., 1956; MA in History, Ind. U., 1959; postgrad., Am. U., 1967-68. Historian Petersburg (Va.) Nat. Mil. Park, 1959-60, Pea Ridge (Ark.) Nat. Mil. Park, 1960-62; rsch. historian Jefferson Nat. Expansion Meml., St. Louis, 1962-63; historian Home of Franklin D. Roosevelt Vanderbilt Mansion, Hyde Park, N.Y., 1963-66; rsch. historian Nat. Park Svc., Washington, 1966-69; historian Statue of Liberty, Ellis Island Fed. Hall Theodore Roosevelt, N.Y.C., 1969-72; regional historian Mid-Atlantic Region U.S. Nat. Park Svc., Phila., 1972-77, chief history, archeology, architecture, 1977-79, assoc. regional dir., 1979-86, chief, park historic pres., 1986—. Author: Home of Andrew Johnson, 1967, Augustus Saint-Gaudens: The Man and His Art, 1968, ASPET (Home of Saint-Gaudens), 1969, East Saint Louis, Illinois, 1969; contbr. articles to profl. jours. Chmn. bd. dirs. Bethel Bapt. Ch., Cherry Hill, N.J., 1983-84, bd. deacons, 1979-85, 89-92, pres. Berean Class, 1976-79, 92—. With U.S. Army, 1953-55. Mem. Nat. Parks and Recreation Assn., Pi Gamma Mu, Pi Alpha Theta. Republican. Home: 309 Old Orchard Rd Cherry Hill NJ 08003 Office: Mid-Atlantic Region 143 South 3d St Philadelphia PA 19106

BOND, NELSON LEIGHTON, JR., health care executive; b. Glen Ridge, N.J., Apr. 17, 1935; s. Nelson Leighton and Dorothy Louise (Minsch) Hudson B.; m. Susan Priscilla McDonald, June 7, 1958 (div. May 1981); children: Sally Louise, Nelson Leighton III, Trevor Paul, Elizabeth Prescott, Susan Bond Kearney; m. Gwendolen Nash Gorman, July 24, 1982. BA, Lehigh U., 1957; MBA, Harvard U., 1966. Dist. mgr. McGraw Hill, Inc., N.Y.C., 1957-64; assoc. McKinsey and Co., Inc., N.Y.C., 1966-68; fin. analyst Drexel Harriman Ripley, Inc., N.Y.C., 1968-69; instl. salesman Faulkner Dawkins and Sullivan, N.Y.C., 1969-70; v.p. Alex Brown and Sons, Balt., 1970-77; pres., dir. Blood Pressure Testing, Inc., Reisterstown, Md., 1977—; pres. Consumer Micrographics, Inc., Balt., 1980-83; pres. Medscreen, Inc., Balt., 1987-89, also bd. dirs.; mng. dir. Offutt Securities, Inc., 1987—, Bond & Assocs., Reisterstown, Md., 1991—; chmn., pres., chief exec. officer, bd. dirs. XL Corp., Reisterstown, Power Source, Inc., Reisterstown, The Green Spring Group, Inc., Reisterstown. Pres. Parents' Club St. Paul's Sch., Brooklandville, Md., 1978-79. 1st lt. USAR, 1958-60. Foote, Cone and Belding fellow Harvard U., 1965. Republican. Episcopalian. Office: Bond & Assocs PO Box 1053 Reisterstown MD 21136-7053

BOND, RANDALL CLAY, lead engineer; b. Tulsa, Aug. 26, 1953; s. Clay Boyd Bond and Mildred Gaylnn (Christian) Davidson; m. Regina Obutelewicz, Jan. 1975 (div. July 1980); 1 child, Katheryne Marie; m. Kimberll Ann Dingman, Sept. 28, 1984; children: Jamie, Amanda, Andrew. AA, La. Tech. Inst., 1978; AAS, USAF Community Coll., 1980; AS, Salem Community Coll., 1987; BS, Thomas A. Edison Coll., 1989. Cert. mech. and welding insp. With quality control div. Tom Co. Equipment Co., Loganville, Ga., 1979-80; quality engr. Avondale (La.) Shipyards, 1980-81; lead auditor Nuclear Installation Svc., Taft, La., 1981-82; sr. quality engr. Nuclear Installation Svc., Lakeland, Fla., 1983-84; quality engr. ITT-Grinnell, Oswego, N.Y., 1982-83; quality cons. Mich. Quality Systems, Midland, 1983-84; lead engr. Pub. Svc. Electric and Gas, Hancocks Bridge, N.J., 1985—. Vol., March of Dimes, Salem County, N.J., 1988, 89, 9, 92, mem. corp. steering com., 1992; youth advisor Our Merciful Savior Ch., Carney's Point, N.J., 1989-92; radiol. officer Emergency Mgmt. Office, Salem County, 1985-86; sect. chmn. United Way, Salem 1988-90; craftsman Tree of Autumn State Fair, 1987; cook barbecue sauce State Fair, 1990; mem. dist. com. So. N.J. coun. Boy Scouts Am., 1991—. With USAF, 1972-79. Mem. Am. Soc. Quality Control (vice chmn. 1990-91, various awrds), PSE and G Speakers Bur (adv. com. 1991—,. Silver Club award 1991, Gold Club award 1992),

Tall Cedars of Lebanon, Masons (sr. master of ceremonies 1986-87), Toastmasters Internat. Episcopalian. Office: Pub Svc Electric & Gas PO Box 236 Hancocks Bridge NJ 08038-0236

BOND, REBECCA ROSE, financial executive; b. Jacksonville, Fla., Sept. 14, 1957; d. James Oliver and Patricia Grace (Hornbrook) B. BA, Mt. Holyoke Coll., 1979. Asst. field dir. ER America, Washington, 1979-82; program coord. Dem. Nat. Com., Washington, 1982; phone bank coord. Harriett Woods U.S. Senate, Kansas City, Mo., 1982; rsch. dir. Com. for Study of Am. Electorate, Washington, 1983-84; field dir. No. Calif. Mondale-Ferraro Pres. Campaign, Sacramento, Calif., 1984; program dir. Nat. Women's Edn. Fund, Washington, 1985-86; dir. devel. and fin. Nat. Inst. Citizen Edn. and the Law, Washington, 1986—. Democrat. Office: Nat Inst Citizen Edn & Law 711 G St SE Washington DC 20003-2861

BOND, THOMAS JEFFERSON, JR., federal agency administrator; b. Chattanooga, Tenn., Aug. 27, 1936; s. Thomas Jefferson and Clara Emmalynne (Chisam) B.; m. Wilma W. McCrary, Mar. 14, 1959; children: Thomas Jefferson III, Julia Anne Bond Kelly. BS in Edn., Tenn. Tech. U., 1958; MA in Biology, Vanderbilt U., 1959; postgrad., U. Louisville, Am. U., Antioch Sch. Law. Biology instr. U. Tenn., Chattanooga, 1959-60, 61-63, U. Louisville, 1963-64; various positions U.S. Dept. Interior, Washington, 1964—; supervisory fish and wildlife biologist U.S. Dept. Interior, 1974-77, 78-81, staff asst. sec. land and water resources, 1977-78, trust services officer ea. area bur. Indian affairs, 1981—; pres. Chisam Meml. Trust. Mem. subcom. for comml. redevel., Town of Vienna, Va., 1983. Lt. U.S. Army, 1960-64. Congl. fellow, 1988-89, Exchange fellow, 1989. Mem. NRA, SAR (various offices D.C. Soc. 1980—, nat. chmn. govt. rels. 1989-91, nat. chmn. congress planning 1991—), Mensa, Westerners Club (publs. com. 1981—), Soc. War 1812, Continental Soc. Sons Indian Wars (historian gen. 1991, dept. lt. gov. gen. 1991—), Sons Am. Colonists (archivist gen. 1988-91, lt. gov. gen. 1991—), Colonial Order Acorn, SCV, Sons Union Vets (assoc.), Mil. Order Loyal Legion (companion), 1st Families Ga., Nat. Order of Blue and Gray, Heredity Order Loyalists and Patriots, Sovereign Mil. Order Temple Jerusalem (chevalier). Home: PO Box 1301 Vienna VA 22183-1301

BONDUR, JOHN MAURICE, executive recruiter; b. Newburgh, N.Y., Dec. 24, 1943; s. John Thomas and Othelia Fayetta (O'Bryan) B.; m. Katherine Anne Leach, July 29, 1967; children: Brooke Noel, Jessica Courtney. BS, Sam Houston State U., 1966; postgrad., U. Tex., 1966-67; MEd, U. Houston, 1970. Cert. secondary tchr., Tex. With human resources dept. Conoco, Inc., Houston, Denver, Stamford, Conn., 1967-74; mgr. pers. svcs. Schlumberger Well Svcs., Houston, 1974-76; asst. v.p. human resources Tex. Commerce Bancshares, Houston, 1976-78; dir. pers. Helmerich & Payne, Inc., Tulsa, 1977-78; dir. compensation and benefits Internat. Playtex, Inc., Stamford, 1978-80; v.p. human resources Kennecott Corp., Stamford, 1980-82; ptnr. Alexander Proudfoot Co., West Palm Beach, Fla., 1982-88; pres. Kasser Distillers Products, Phila., 1988-89; ptnr. Ward Howell Internat., N.Y.C. and Stamford, Conn., 1990—. Contbr. articles to profl. jours. Bd. mem. Operation SER, Denver, 1970-71, Black Coll. Consortium, Tex., 1974-76, Harris County Community Action Assn., Houston, 1974-76, Camp Fire, Inc., Danbury, Conn., 1983-84, Redevel. Commn., Danbury, 1985-86. With USMCR, 1961-67. Democrat. Home: 79 Middle River Rd Danbury CT 06811-4351 Office: Ward Howell Internat Inc One Landmark Sq Ste 1810 Stanford CT 06901-0001

BONDY, MICHAEL FRANK, electrical engineer, consultant; b. Vienna, Austria, Dec. 6, 1923; came to U.S., 1940; m. Enid Pincus, Sept. 15, 1950; children: Peter, Mark, Alan. BEE, George Washington U., 1943; MSEE, U. Buffalo, 1961. Registered profl. engr. Rsch. assoc. George Washington U., Washington, 1943-45; jr. engr. Raytheon, Waltham, Mass., 1946-49; assoc. engr. Glenn L. Martin Co., Balt., 1950-54; systems engr. Bell Aircraft, Buffalo, N.Y., 1955-58; engring. mgr. RCA, Camden, N.J., 1958-66; v.p. Butler & Smith Inc., Norwood, N.J., 1966-70; cons. engr. Michael Bondy Assocs., Haworth, N.J., 1970—. Patentee in field, 1944. Sgt. U.S. Army, 1945-46. Mem. IEEE (sr.), Sigma Xi. Home: 145 Surbeck Pl Haworth NJ 07641-1205

BONEE, JOHN LEON, III, lawyer; b. Hartford, Conn., Dec. 16, 1947; s. John Leon, Jr. and M. Elaine (Sheridan) B. BA, Trinity Coll., Hartford, 1970; JD, Suffolk U., Boston, 1974; postgrad., Hague Acad. Internat. Law, The Netherlands, 1975. Bar: Conn. 1974, U.S. Dist. Ct. Conn. 1974; U.S. Ct. Appeals (2d cir.) 1975, U.S. Supreme Ct. 1979. Assoc. Kenyon, Bonee & Greenspan, Hartford, 1974-78, ptnr., 1979—; mem. ct. legis. task force on juvenile justice system State of Conn., 1990—. Contbr. articles to profl. jours. Mem. bd. edn. Town West Hartford, 1981-83, corp. counsel, 1983, mem. community planning adv. com., 1984, mem. town coun., 1985-89; bd. dirs. World Affairs Coun., Hartford, 1980-91. Mem. ABA (gen. practice and internat. law sects.), Conn. Bar Assn. (editor at large jour. 1978-84, probate and family law sects.), Hartford County Bar Assn. (bd. dirs. 1991—, treas. 1992—), co-chair bench/bar com.). Office: Kenyon Bonee & Greenspan 1 State St Hartford CT 06103-3102

BONFIELD, EDWARD HARVEY, marketing educator, consultant; b. Birmingham, Ala., Apr. 28, 1938; s. Louis and Gertrude (Kessler) B.; m. Phyllis Ann Kline, May 16, 1975; children: Brett Jason, Jeffrey Kline, Robin Michelle. BS, U. Ala., 1962, MS, 1963; PhD, U. Ill., 1972. Rsch. analyst Market Facts, Inc., Chgo., 1963-64, assoc. study dir., 1964-66; lectr. U. Ala., Tuscaloosa, 1970-72, asst. prof. mktg. and behavioral sci., 1972-76; assoc. prof. Temple U., Phila., 1976-84; dir. PhD in bus. Temple U., 1981-84; prof. Rider Coll., Lawrenceville, N.J., 1984—; cons. Old York Rd Temple Beta-Am, Abington, Pa., 1988, Mercer County C. of C., Trenton, N.J., 1989-91, N.J. Dept. Motor Vehicles, Trenton, 1990-91, Implementation Rsch. Assocs., Abington, 1991—. Contbr. articles to profl. jours. Nominee Abington-Rockledge Dem. Com., Abington, 1979; bd. dirs. Old York Rd. Temple Beth-Am, 1982-87. Mem. Am. Mktg. Assn. (chpt. treas. 1969-70), Assn. for Consumer Rsch. Jewish. Office: Rider Coll 2083 Lawrenceville Rd Trenton NJ 08648-3099

BONFIELD, PHYLLIS KLINE, public relations executive; b. San Antonio, Apr. 14, 1942; d. Sidney and Beatrice (Gans) Kline; m. Edward H. Bonfield, May 16, 1965; children: Brett, Jeffrey, Robin. BJ, U. Tex., 1964. Asst. editor Ill. Natural Hist. Survey, Urbana, 1967-69; tech. editor U. Ala., Tuscaloosa, 1970-71; dir. mem. svcs. Adminstrv. Mgmt. Soc., Willow Grove, Pa., 1978-86; dir. pub. rels. Am. Soc. CLU and Chartered Fin. Cons., Bryn Mawr, Pa., 1986-89, asst. v.p. pub. rels., 1989—. Contbr.: Handbook of Wage and Salary Administration, 2d edit., 1984 (Wiliam Winter award 1984); contbr. articles to profl. jours. Mem. Abington (Pa.) Sch. Dist. Gifted Adv. Bd., 1986-90; mem. Internat. Children's Festival, U. Pa., Phila., 1987-89; pres. Glenside (Pa.) Elem. Sch. PTA, 1980-81; sch. rep. Parent-Tchr. Adv. Coun., Abington, 1981-82. Recipient Addy award Phila. Club Advt. Women, 1987, 91. Mem. Pub. Rels. Soc. Am. (Pepperpot award 1987), Am. Soc. Assn. Execs. Democrat. Jewish. Home: 2030 Woodland Rd Abington PA 19001-3628 Office: Am Soc CLU and Chartered Fin Cons 270 S Bryn Mawr Ave Bryn Mawr PA 19010-2105

BONFIGLIO, ROBERT ANTHONY, college administrator; b. Bklyn., July 23, 1954; s. Joseph and Juliette (Sora) B.; m. Catherine Richard, June 26, 1981; children: Anne Elizabeth, William Joseph. BA, Stonehill Coll., 1976; MA, Columbia U., 1978, M. Philosophy, 1989, EdD, 1990. Asst. dir. student life LaSalle U., Phila., 1978-81; dir. student activities Coll of New Rochelle (N.Y.), 1981-83, dir. student life, 1983-87, asst. v.p. for student svcs., 1987-88; dean of students Cabrini Coll., Radnor, Pa., 1988-91, v.p. for student affairs, 1991—. Contbr. article and book revs. to profl. jours. Mem. Nat. Assn. Student Pers. Amdinstrs. Roman Catholic.

BONHAG, THOMAS EDWARD, insurance company executive, financial consultant, financial planner; b. Bronxville, N.Y., Jan. 19, 1952; s. Herman Arthur and Anne Elizabeth (Sage) B.; m. Noreen Patricia Early, Apr. 24, 1976 (div. Dec. 1981); m. Cornelia Hackett Lyons, Oct. 8, 1983. BS, Fordham U., 1973; MBA, St. John's U., 1979; postgrad., Am. Coll., 1979-84. CLU; cert. fin. planner, chartered fin. cons. Field sales rep. Colgate-Palmolive Co., N.Y.C., 1973-74; employee relations officer The Chase Manhattan Bank, N.Y.C., 1974-78; agt., dist. mgr. The Equitable Life Assurance Soc., N.Y.C., 1979-83; v.p. northeastern region mktg. The Equitable Life Assurance Soc., Edison, N.J., 1984-90; sr. v.p. Kornreich Life Assocs., Inc., N.Y.C., 1990—; fin. cons. Am. Geriatrics Soc., N.Y.C., 1983-86. Mem. Hoboken (N.J.) Environ. Com., 1983—; mayoral appointee citizens' budget adv. com. Twp. of Cranford, N.J., 1991; mem. Cranford Bd. Edn., 1991—; pres. Cranford Bd. Edn., 1992—. Mem. Am. Soc. CLUs, Nat. Assn. Life Underwriters, Inst. Cert. Fin. Planners, Assn. for MBA Execs. Republican. Roman Catholic. Home: 706 Orange Ave Cranford NJ 07016-2052

BONIME, WALTER RAYMOND, psychiatrist, psychoanalyst, educator; b. Monteville, Conn., July 12, 1909; s. Ellis and Rebecca (Strongin) B.; m. Mary McGovern, Dec. 7, 1940 (div. 1953); children: Karen, Stephen; m. Florence Cummings, Sept. 5, 1953; stepchildren: Frank Cummings, Norma Lovins; children: Karen, Stephen. BA, U. Wis., 1933; MD, Columbia U., 1938. Intern Sinai Hosp., Balt., 1938-39; resident Cen. Islip State Hosp., L.I., N.Y., 1939-41; pvt. practice, N.Y.C., 1941—; clin. prof. psychiatry N.Y. Med. Coll., Valhalla, 1947—; tng. analyst Dept. Psychiatry, Inst. of Psychoanalysis of N.Y. Med. Coll. Author: (with Florence Bonime) The Clinical Use of Dreams, 1962; author: Collaborative Psychoanalysis, 1989. Passed asst. surgeon USPHS, 1943-46. Fellow Am. Psychiat. Assn., Am. Acad. Psychoanalysis (charter, editorial bd. jour. 1973—); mem. Soc. Med. Psychoanalysts (pres. 1963-64). Home and Office: 37 Washington Sq W New York NY 10011-9181

BONIME-BLANC, ANDREA, lawyer; b. Kassel, Hessen, Fed. Republic of Germany, Oct. 1, 1957; d. Lawrence Hubert and Ruth L. (Reimann) Bonime; m. Roger Blanc, Apr. 19, 1985. BA in Polit. Sci., Bernard Baruch Coll., 1979; MA in Polit. Sci., Columbia U., 1980, M in Philosophy, Polit. Sci., 1982, JD, PhD in Polit. Sci., 1985. Bar: N.Y. 1987. Polit. risk analyst, cons. Bankers Trust Co., N.Y.C., 1981-84; teaching asst. Columbia U., N.Y.C., 1982-85, rsch. assoc. inst. internat. change, 1986-89; assoc. Cleary, Gottlieb, Steen & Hamilton, N.Y.C., 1985-90; sr. assoc. Porter & Travers, N.Y.C., 1990—. Author: Spain's Transition to Democracy, 1987; editor: Columbia Jour. Transnational Law, 1983-85; contbr. numerous articles to profl. jours. Herbert H. Lehman Social Sci. fellow Columbia U., 1979-82; Pres.'s fellow Columbia U., 1980-82. Mem. ABA, N.Y. County Lawyers, Assn. of Bar of City of N.Y. (com. internat. arms control and security affairs), Coun. on Fgn. Rels., The Spanish Inst., Am. Assn. for Internat. Commn. Jurists (sec., del. to Budapest 1990, bd. dirs. 1991—). Democrat. Office: Porter & Travers 120 W 45th St New York NY 10036-4003

BONITSIS, THEOLOGOS HOMER, finance educator, economic-financial consultant; b. Bklyn., June 3, 1953; s. Socrates Demetrios and Mary Anastasia (Haritakis) B. AA with honors, NYC Community Coll., Bklyn., 1975; BA magna cum laude, CUNY, 1976, MA, 1981, PhD, 1984. Asst. traffic mgr. S.F. Pellas & Co., Inc., N.Y.C., 1973-74, asst. commodities trader, 1976; adj. lectr. econs. and fin. Bernard M. Baruch Coll., CUNY, 1978-81, instr. Hunter Coll., 1981-82; assoc. prof. fin. Grad. Sch. Mgmt. Rutgers U., Newark, 1984-90; assoc. prof. fin. Sch. Indsl. Mgmt. N.J. Inst. Tech., Newark, 1990—; asst. prof. fin. Rutgers U., Newark, 1988-90, assoc. prof. fin. Grad. Sch. Mgmt.,, 1990—; pres. THB Fin. Cons., 1989—; cons. on equity account churning case, 1989, forensic econ., 1990—. Contbr. articles to profl. jours., chpt. to book. Mem. Am. Econ. Assn., Am. Fin. Assn., Fin. Mgmt. Assn., Internat. Trade and Fin. Assn., Internat. Soc. Statis. Sci. in Econs. (assoc. editor 1991—), Nat. Assn. Forensic Economists, New Eng. Bus. Adminstrn. Assn. (bd. reviewers fin. area Bus. Jour. 1991—), Decision Scis. Inst., Ea. Econ. Assn., Hellenic U. Club N.Y. (treas. 1985-86, pres. 1988-89). Greek Orthodox. Home: 7304 6th Ave Brooklyn NY 11209-2608 Office: N J Inst Tech Sch Indsl Mgmt Newark NJ 07102

BONKOVSKY, HERBERT LLOYD, physician, educator; b. Cleve., Dec. 29, 1941; s. Otto Rudolph and Hanna (Ludwig) B.; m. Marilyn Louise Cahoon, June 3, 1967; children: Laura, Sarah, Erik. AB, Earlham Coll., 1963; MD, Case Western Res. U., 1967. Diplomate Am. Bd. Internat. Medicine, Am. Bd. Gastroenterology, Nat. Bd. Med. Examiners. Intern Duke U. Med. Ctr., 1967-68; rsch. fellow, chief resident Dartmouth Med. Sch., Hanover, N.H., 1971-73, asst. prof., then assoc. prof., 1974-83; prof. Dartmouth Med. Sch., Hanover, 1983-85; rsch., clin. fellow Yale U. Sch. Medicine, New Haven, 1973-74; dir. digestive disease and liver rsch. lab. VA Med. Ctr., White River Junction, Vt., 1976-85; prof. medicine and biochem., dir. liver study unit Emory U., Atlanta, 1985-90; dir. hemochromatosis unit, dir. porphyria unit Emory U., 1985-90; dir. digestive disease lab. Emory Clinic, 1988-90; dir. div. digestive disease and nutrition, prof. medicine biochemistryand molecular biology U. Mass. Med. Ctr., 1990—. Author, editor ednl. materials, articles, papers, book chpts. Mem. adminstrv. bd. Oak Grove Meth. Ch., Decatur, Ga., 1989-90; trustee, chmn. bd. dirs. Norwich (Vt.) Congl. Ch., Norwich, 1975-78, moderator, 1978-85, deacon, 1978-79; mem. Harvard Pro-Musica, 1990—. Lt. comdr. USPHS, 1969—. Earlham merit scholar, 1959-63, Binz Meml. scholar, 1963-67. Fellow ACP, Am. Coll. Gastroenterology, Alpha Omega Alpha; mem. Am. Fedn. Clin. Rsch., Am. Soc. Clin. Investigation, Am. Gastroenterol. Assn., Iron Overload Diseases Assn. (sci. adv. bd.), Am. Porphyria Found. (chair profl. edn. com.), Am. Assn. for Study Liver Diseases (editorial bd., nominating com.), AMA, Am. Soc. Biochemistry and Molecular Biology, Internat. Assn. Study Liver. Office: U Mass Med Ctr Worcester MA 01655

BONNER, BARBARA, museum director; b. Danbury, Conn., Feb. 10, 1948; d. Kenneth Bonner and Helen (Howard) Lane; children: Alexandra Anne Socarides, Charles William Socarides, Jr. MFA, Columbia U., N.Y.C., 1989; MA, CUNY, 1973; BA, Wells Coll., Aurora, N.Y., 1969. Researcher Spencer Samuels and Co., Ltd., N.Y.C., 1973-74, 78-79; dir. Cathedral of St. John the Divine Mus., N.Y.C., 1980-82; pres. Bonner & Co., N.Y.C., 1983-86; curator, devel. specialist Asia Soc., N.Y.C., 1989-90; deputy dir. Mus. N.Y.C., N.Y.C., 1990=92; sr. v.p. for the arts Ronald LaRose & Assocs., N.Y.C., 1992—. Mem. Cosmopolitan Club N.Y., Eric Watson Dance Found. (trustee), Women in Fin. Devel. (bd. dirs.). Office: 27 E 95th St New York NY 10128

BONNER, CRAIG ALAN, accountant; b. Meshoppen, Pa., Mar. 7, 1956; s. Alvin Leland and Ruth Ann (Dixon) B. Student electronic engring., De Vry Tech. Inst., Woodbridge, N.J., 1974-75; AA in Bus. Adminstrn., Acctg., Keystone Jr. Coll., La Plume, Pa., 1984; BA in Bus. Adminstrn., Acctg., Millersville U., 1986; postgrad., Lancaster Bible Coll., 1990-91. Acct. Don White, CPA, Elizabethtown, Pa., 1986; temp. acct. Computer Adv. Group, Lancaster, Pa., 1986-87; staff acct. The SICO Co., Mount Joy, Pa., 1987—. Full tuition scholarship De Vry Tech. Inst., Woodbridge, 1974, Jr. Women's Club scholarship, 1974. Mem. Nat. Assn. Accts. Baptist. Home: 130 E Main St Mount Joy PA 17552-1514

BONNER, DANIEL PATRICK, microbiologist, researcher; b. Bayonne, N.J., Oct. 9, 1945; s. Michael Francis and Agnes Margaret (Heeney) B.; m. Marianne Bernadette Walsh, June 3, 1972; children: Timothy, Mary Kate. BS, Fairleigh Dickinson U., 1967; MS, Rutgers U., 1969, PhD, 1972. Postdoctoral fellow Rutgers U., New Brunswick, N.J., 1972-76, asst. rsch. prof., 1977-78; rsch. investigator Squibb Inst. Med. Rsch., Princeton, N.J., 1978-79, sr. rsch. investigator, 1979-81, group leader, 1981-82, sect. head, 1982-83, asst. dept. dir., 1982-89; exec. dir. microbiology Bristol-Myers Squibb Co., Wallingford, Conn., 1989—. With U.S. Army, 1969-71. Fellow Am. Soc. Microbiology (div. chmn. 1989); mem. AAAS, Theobald Smith Soc., N.Y. Acad. Scis., Japan Antibiotics Rsch. Assn., Sigma Xi. Office: Bristol Myers Squibb Co Microbiology 104 5 Research Pky Wallingford CT 06492-1929

BONNER, MONICA ROSSI, oil company executive; b. Hazleton, Pa., June 1, 1946; d. Thomas Vincent and Assunta (Rossi) B. Student, Pa. State U., 1963-68. V.p. Basic Petroleum Internat. Ltd., Nassau, The Bahamas, 1971—; bd. dirs. Basic Holdings Ltd., Nassau, 1989—. Republican. Home: 105 E 63d St New York NY 10021-7327 Office: Basic Petroleum Internat, East Bay, Nassau The Bahamas

BONNIWELL, KATHERINE, magazine executive. Grad., Vassar Coll., 1969, Stanford U. With Morgan Guaranty Trust Co., 1969—; corp. analyst, then asst. circulation dir. Time, Inc., 1976-78; circulation dir. Money mag., 1978-80; v.p. Time-Life Films, 1980-81; v.p., dir. mktg. and communications Sotheby Park Bernet, 1981—; pub. LIFE, N.Y.C., from 1988; now pres. mags. LIFE; gen. mgr. People mag. Office: Life Mag Time & Life Bldg New York NY 10020*

BONNOT, BERNARD ROBERT, priest, telecommunications executive; b. Canton, Ohio, Mar. 6, 1941; s. Bernard Robert and Mary Elizabeth (Mang) B. S.T.L., Gregorian U., Rome, 1968; PhD, U. Chgo., 1976. Ordained priest Roman Cath. Ch., 1967. Assoc. pastor Immaculate Conception Ch., Youngstown, Ohio, 1968-71; asst. supt. schs. Diocese of Youngstown, 1971-73, dir. adult spiritual growth, 1976-80, dir. communications, 1980-87; pres., chief exec. officer CTNA Telecommunications Inc., Youngstown, 1987-90; dir. community rels. VISN Interfaith Satellite Network, N.Y.C., 1990—; pastor St. Stephen of Hungary, Youngstown, 1981-87. Author: Pope John XXIII, 1979; exec. producer CTNA Teleconfs., telecourses, 1987-90. Lt. col. USANG, 1977—. Recipient Basselin scholarship Cath. U. of Am., 1961-64, Ford fellowship U. Chgo., 1973-76. Mem. Unda-U.S.A. (1st v.p., Pres.'s award 1989), Cath. Theol. Soc. Am., Cath. Bibl. Assn., Canon Law Soc. Am., UN Assn. USA. Office: VISN Interfaith Satellite Network 74 Trinity Pl # 915 New York NY 10006-2003

BONOMO, JOSEPH RALPH, naval officer; b. N.Y.C., Mar. 20, 1951; s. Ralph J. and Anita R. (Curiale) B.; m. Janet M. Storace, Apr. 6, 1991. BBA, Iona Coll., 1973; MPA, SUNY, Albany, 1975; student, USN Officer Candicate Sch., Newport, R.I., 1976, Navy Supply Corps Sch., Athens, Ga., 1976, USN Submarine Sch., Groton, Conn., 1977; MS, Naval Postgrad. Sch., 1985. Data adminstr. Welfare Research Inc., Albany, N.Y., 1975-76; advanced through grades to commdr. USN; supply officer USS Henry Clay (Blue Crew) USS Henry Clay Blue Crew, Charleston, S.C., 1977-79; supply officer Fighter Squadron 101, Oceana, Va., 1979-81; aviation support officer USS Constellation, San Diego, 1981-83; info. systems officer Comdr. Naval Air Force, U.S. Atlantic Fleet, Norfolk, Va., 1985-88, USS Saratoga, 1988-90; COMNAVSUPSYSCOM COMNAVSUPSYSCOM, Washington, 1990—. Vol. WHRO Pub. TV, Norfolk, 1987-88; mem. Smithsonian Assocs., Washington, 1984-92; mem. Planetary Soc., Pasadena, Calif., 1983-92, Nat. Geog. Soc., Washington, 1986-92. Mem. Supply Corps Sch. Alumni Assn., Hampton Roads Supply Corps Assn., Iona Coll. Alumni Assn., SUNY-Albany Alumni Assn., U.S. Naval Inst., Delta Lambda Kappa. Roman Catholic. Office: COMNAVSUPSYSCOM (SUP-4123A) Washington DC 20376-5000

BONSAL, DUDLEY BALDWIN, federal judge; b. Bedford, N.Y., Oct. 6, 1906; s. Stephen and Henrietta Fairfax (Morris) B.; m. Lois Abbott Worrall, May 16, 1931 (dec. Aug. 1981); children: Lois (Mrs. Frederic B. Osler, Jr.), Stephen.; m. Lucia Turner Faithfull, Mar. 5, 1983. A.B., Dartmouth Coll., 1927; LL.B., Harvard, 1930. Bar: N.Y. bar 1932. Asso. firm Curtis, Mallet-Prevost, Colt & Mosle, N.Y.C., 1930-38; mem. firm Curtis, Mallet-Prevost, Colt & Mosle, 1938-42, 45-61; U.S. dist. judge So. dist. N.Y., 1961—; judge Temporary Emergency Ct. Appeals of U.S., 1977-87; chief counsel Office Inter-Am. Affairs, Washington, 1942-45; mem. U.S. del. Inter-Am. Conf. on Problems of War and Peace, Mexico City, 1945; legal adviser Fgn. Bondholders Protective Council, Conf. on German Debts, London, 1951, 52; mem. Internat. Commn. of Jurists, Geneva, Switzerland, 1953-73; chmn. spl. com. on fed. loyalty-security program Assn. Bar City N.Y., 1955-57; mem. com. on criminal justice act Jud. Conf. of U.S., 1964-79, chmn., 1974-79. Trustee Inst. Internat. Edn., 1948-64, Sterling and Francine Clark Art Inst., Williamstown, Mass., 1960-73, William Nelson Cromwell Found., Practising Law Inst., 1969-85. Fellow Am. Bar Found. (dir. 1967-75); mem. Am., N.Y. bar assns., Assn. Bar City N.Y. (pres. 1958-60), N.Y.C. Council on Fgn. Relations. Club: Century Assn. (N.Y.C.). Home: St Mary's Church Rd Bedford NY 10506 Office: US Courthouse Foley Sq New York NY 10007-1501*

BONTZ, MARUITA CAROLYN, association administrator; b. Carrollton, Ill., June 20, 1930; d. George and Ollie Mae (Bell) Henkel; m. Robert D. Bontz, Jan. 21, 1950; children: Joseph E., George R. Student U. Md., 1965-68, Catonsville Community Coll., 1968-70. Pres. Ind. Truckers and Drivers Assn., Balt., 1982—; expert witness U.S. Senate, U.S. Ho. Reps., Md. Gen. Assembly, U.S. DOT, ICC, others. Mem. Gov.'s Task Force Motor Carrier Safety and Uniformity, Balt., 1986—, Mayor's Task Force on Truck Safety, 1990—, Md. Safety Coun. Comml. Vehicle Safety Com., 1988—; v.p. Md. Hwy. Users Fedn., 1988—; mem. Comml. Vehicle Safety Alliance. Recipient numerous safety awards and citations from orgns. Home and Office: 1109 Plover Dr Baltimore MD 21227

BONUCCELLI, CHARLES LOUIS, accountant, consultant, executive; b. Washington, Nov. 28, 1955; s. Hugo Anthony and Priscilla Ann (Bill) B.; m. Mary Ellen Thomas, May 19, 1984. BA in Econs. and Acctg., Catholic U., 1977; MA in Acctg., 1979. CPA, Md. Contract acct. Catholic U., Washington, 1977-78; sr. auditor Defense Contract Audit Agy., Washington, 1978-82; corp. controller, chief fin. officer Info. Systems & Networks Corp., Chevy Chase, Md., 1982-83; corp. controller Aurora Assocs., Washington, 1983-84; instr. in cost acctg. U. Md., College Park, Md., 1985; chief exec. officer Bonucelli & Co., P.C., Lanham, Md., 1984-85; sr. mgr. Price Waterhouse, Bethesda, Md., 1985—; cons. GE, IBM, Corning Inc., UTC, others, 1985—; speaker Md. Assn. CPAs, 1988-89, Nat. Contract Mgmt. Assn., West Palm Beach, Fla., 1990. Contbr. articles to profl. jours. Bd. dirs. East Balt. Resources, Balt., 1988—; vol. cons. A.E. Hosper Found., Columbia, Md., 1989-90. Mem. ABA (assoc.), AICPA, Md. Assn. CPA's, Inst. for Internal Auditors, Nat. Contract Mgmt. Assn., KC. Roman Catholic. Office: Price Waterhouse 6500 Rock Spring Dr Bethesda MD 20817-1105

BOODHOOSINGH, YASMIN SHANTA, secondary school educator; b. Washington, May 6, 1950; d. Lazina Ali BoodhooSingh. BS in Spl. Edn., U. Md., 1972; MS in Spl. Edn., Coppin State Coll., Balt., 1974; postgrad., Loyola Coll., Balt., 1974—. Tchr. Balt. City Pub. Schs., 1973, Catonsville Middle Sch., 1973-75, Lansdowne High Sch., 1975-86; with WEBCO, 1987-88; field counselor Balt. County Occupational Tng. Adminstrn., 1989; tchr. social studies and English Ea. Voc-Tech High Sch., 1986—, spl. edn. tchr.-in-charge, 1983-84, spl. edn. dept. chmn., 1984-86; Conductor workshops in field; lectr. in field. Contbg. writer Essex Times, 1986-89, Teacher-to-Teacher, 1986-89. Mem. NEA, Am. Vocat. Assn., Coun. Exceptional Children, Md. Tchrs. Assn., Md. Vocat. Assn., Tchrs. Assn. of Baltimore County. Home: 6025 Hanover Rd Hanover MD 21076-1037

BOOHER, ALICE ANN, lawyer; b. Indpls., Oct. 6, 1941; d. Norman Rogers and Olga (Bonke) B. BA in Polit. Sci., Butler U., 1963; LLB, Ind. U., 1966, JD, 1967. Bar: Ind. 1966, U.S. Dist. Ct. (so. dist.) Ind. 1966, U.S. Tax Ct. 1970, U.S. Ct. Customs and Patent Appeals 1969, U.S. Ct. Mil. Appeals 1969, U.S. Ct. Appeals (D.C. cir.) 1969, U.S. Supreme Ct. 1969; cert. tchr., Ind. Rsch. asst., law clk. Supreme and Appellate Cts. Ind., Indpls., 1966; legal intern, atty., staff legal advisor Dept. State, Washington, 1966-69; staff legal adviser Bd. Vets. Appeals, Washington, 1969-78, sr. atty., 1978—, counsel, 1991—; former counselor D.C. Penal Facilities and Shelters. Author: The Nuclear Test Ban Treaty and the Third Party Non-Nuclear States, also children's books; contbr. articles to various publs., chpts. to Whiteman Digest of International Law; exhibited crafts, needlepoint in juried artisan fairs. Bd. dirs. numerous community groups, including D.C. Women's Commn. for Crime Prevention, 1980-81; pres., legal adviser VA employees Assn. Recipient various awards; named Ky. Col., 1988. Mem. ABA, DAV Aux., VFW Aux., LWV, Women's Bar Assn. D.C., D.C. Sexual Assault Coalition (chmn. legal com.), Butler U. Alumni Assn., Nat. Mus. Women in Arts, Bus. and Profl. Women (pres. D.C. 1980-81, nat. UN fellow 1974, nat. bd. dirs. 1980-82, 87—, Woman of Yr. award D.C. 1975, Marquerite Rawalt award D.C. 1986), USO, Women Officers Profl. Assn., Navy League U.S.A., Am. Legion Aux., Vietnam Vets. Am., Task Force on Women of the Mil. and Women Vets (chmn. 1986-90), Salute to Am. Women Mil. POWs.

BOOK, SAMUEL HOWARD, economist, consultant; b. Scranton, Pa., May 21, 1940; s. George Book and Adele (Spitalnick) Baldinger; m. Nancy S. Wald, July 12, 1981. BS, Wilkes Coll., 1962; PhD, Columbia U., 1970. Asst. prof. York Y., Toronto, Ont., Can., 1970-75; pres. Miller-Book & Co., Ltd., Toronto, 1976-79; rsch. dir. Nat. Rsch. Group, L.A., 1980-84; pres. Malarkey-Taylor Rsch., Washington, 1985—; cons. Ont. Arts Coun., Toronto, 1974-76, City of L.A., 1988—, N.Y. Times Co., N.Y.C., 1989—; bd. dirs., exec. com. Malarkey-Taylor Assocs., Washington, 1987—. Contbr. articles to profl. jours. U. Md. fellow, 1970. Mem. Cable TV Adminstrn. & Mktg. Soc., Am. Econs. Assn., Am. Mktg. Assn., Nature Conservancy,

Jewish Orgns. Democrat. Office: Malarkey Taylor Assocs 1130 Connecticut Ave NW Washington DC 20036-3904

BOOKE, HENRY EDWARD, scientific director; b. Bklyn., Jan. 14, 1932; m. Norma Jean Wilcox, June 12, 1959; 1 child, Charles E. BS, Cornell U., 1959; MS, Mich. State U., 1962; PhD, U. Mich., 1967. Biol. aide N.Y. State Conservation Dept., Watertown, N.Y., 1954; instr. Yale U., New Haven, Conn., 1968-69; asst. prof. Boston U., 1969-72; asst. unit leader U.S. Fish and Wildlife Svc., Stevens Point, Wis., 1973-80; unit leader U. Mass., Amherst, 1980-88; scientific dir. Conte Anadromous Fish Ctr., Turners Falls, Mass., 1988—. Author: (papers) Anadromous Fish, 1980-91 (Gulf Conservation award 1982). Bd. dirs. Shea Theatre, Turners Falls, Mass., 1990—, All Souls Ch., Greenfield, Mass., 1991. With U.S. Army, 1954-57, Fed. Republic Germany. Mem. Am. Fisheries Soc., AAAS, Am. Soc. Zoologists. Office: US Fish and Wildlife Svc 1 Migratory Way Turners Falls MA 01376-1000

BOOKER, ALVIN EUGENE, publishing executive; b. Phila., Jan. 17, 1928; s. Samuel Bear and Yetta (Stein) B.; B.A., Temple U.; m. Janice Leah Lekoff, Dec. 16, 1951; children—Ellis Carl, Susan Barbara. Social worker YMHA, 1950-51; pres. Shopper Publs., Inc., 1952—; bus. cons. trustee, Oak Lane Day Sch.; pub. Svc. Dealer's Newsletter. Home: 2 Crescent Rd Wyncote PA 19095 Office: 1400 Easton Rd Roslyn PA 19001

BOOKHARDT, FRED BARRINGER, JR., architect; b. New Orleans, May 14, 1934; s. Fred B. and Leticia (Chevez) B. BArch, Tulane U., 1959; postgrad., U. Pa., 1960-61. Designer Freret and Wolf, Architects, 1959-60, Kenneth Ripnen, Architect, 1961-63, Francis X. Gina, Architects, 1963-64, Smith, Smith, Haines, Lundberg and Waehler, N.Y.C., 1965; ptnr., v.p. William F. Pedersen & Assocs., N.Y.C. and New Haven, 1965-77; prin. Fred B. Bookhardt, Architect, N.Y.C., 1977—; pres. 28 E. 4th St. Housing Corp.; cons. Engring. Cons. Group, Cairo, Heliopolis and Alexandria, Egypt, 1983—, Egyptian Govt. 1977-78. Contbg. editor Uptown mag., New Orleans Archtl. works include: Superior Cts. Bldg., New Haven, 1974, Hall Minerals and Gems of Am. Mus. Natural History, 1976, Fed. Office Bldg., New Haven, 1978, Restaurant Claire, Key West, Fla., 1978, Woodmere Kingdom of Minerals, 1980, exec. offices So. Container Corp., Hauppauge, N.Y., 1981, Mus. shop Am. Mus. Natural History, N.Y.C., 1982, renovation of pub. spaces lower level, 1984, employees' cafeteria, 1984, Children's Reception Ctr., 1986, Sadowsky residence, Northport, N.Y., 1987, Kaufman residence, N.Y.C., 1987, Grossman residence, Montauk, N.Y., 1983, St. Barts, W.I., 1990, Zweibel residences, N.Y.C., 1983, Ft. Lauderdale, Fla., 1984, exec. offices Bon Temps Employment Agy., N.Y.C., 1984, Dieckmann residence, Manhasset, N.Y., 1985, master plan Am. Mus. Natural History, N.Y.C., 1989, space analysis The Trotting Horse Mus., Goshen, N.Y., 1989, addition and renovation, 1990, De Roy residence, N.Y.C., 1991. With U.S. Army, 1954-56. Recipient Lumen award Illuminating Engrs. Soc., 1977. Mem. AIA, N.Y. State Assn. Architects, Architects Coun. N.Y.C., N.Y. Soc. Architects, Am. Assn. Mus., N.E. Mus. Conf., Nat. Cert. Archtl. Rev. Bd. (cert.). Home and Office: 28 E 4th St New York NY 10003-7004

BOOKHART, SAMUEL WINGARD, JR., chemical company executive; b. Kingstree, S.C., Sept. 30, 1931; s. Samuel Wingard Sr. and Martha Gertrude (O'Bryan) B.; m. Betty Jane Davis, Apr., 1, 1961; children: Samuel Wingard III, Davis Boyd, Carolyn O'Bryan. BS, Clemson U., 1953. With DuPont Fibers, 1959—; mgr. benchmarking DuPont Fibers, Wilmington, Del., 1987—; presenter profl. confs. Contbr. articles to profl. jours. 1st lt. Chem. Corps., U.S. Army, 1954-56. Mem. Am. Productivity and Quality Ctrs. (design coordinating team, steering com. Internat. Benchmarking Clearinghouse 1991), Am. Soc. Quality Control, Strategic Planning Inst. (steering com. coun. for benchmarking 1990—), Soc. Competitive Intelligence Profls. Presbyterian. Home: 3 Fox Run Dr Chadds Ford PA 19317 Office: DuPont Co PO Box 80721 Wilmington DE 19880-0721

BOONE, KURT BRADLEY, marketing professional; b. Bklyn., Sept. 24, 1959; s. Elliott William and Thelma Lenora (Strother) B. AA, L.A. City Coll., 1984; postgrad., Calif. State U., 1984-86, U. So. Calif., 1985; postgrad, NYU Sch. Continuing Edn., 1991. Mailrm. clk. United Artist/MGM Corp., N.Y.C., 1978; floor porter R.H. Macy Inc., N.Y.C., 1980; indoor messenger D'Arcy, Massius, Benton & Bowles Inc., N.Y.C., 1980-81; microfilmer Mfr. Hanvoer Trust Co., N.Y.C., 1981; store mgr. Radio Shack-Tandy Corp., Costa Mesa, Calif., 1986-87; account rep. Met. Life Ins., Maspeth, N.Y., 1989-90; mktg. rep. John Hancock Fin. Svcs., Garden City, N.Y., 1990—; internat. runner. Movie extra in Malcolm X. V.p. NAACP Youth Coun., Jamaica, N.Y., 1981; mem. So. Queens Park Assn., Jamaica, 1981; pres. 210th St. Youth Block Assn., Cambria Heights, 1976; youth advisor Laurelton (N.Y.)/Springfield Gardens C. of C., 1990. With USN, 1982. Recipient Award of Participation, Nat. Youth Sports Program, 1975, Cert. of Appreciation, U.S. Olympic Com., L.A., 1984. Mem. Black Filmmakers Found., Met. Athletic Congress, N.Y. Road Runners Club. Democrat. Baptist. Home: 11410 210th St Jamaica NY 11411-1012

BOOSER, EARL RICHARD, chemical engineer; b. Harrisburg, Pa., Jan. 7, 1922; s. Charles Edgar and Etta (Paul) B.; m. Katherine Elizabeth Swavely; children: Judith Ann Gallo, Joan Elizabeth Ropel. BSChemE, Penn State U., 1942, MSChemE, 1944, PhDChemE, 1948. Registered profl. engr., N.Y. Rsch. asst. Penn State U., University Pk., Pa., 1943-48; unit mgr. bearing and lubrication devel. GE, Lynn, Mass., 1948-55, Schenectady, N.Y., 1955-86; cons. engr. self-employed Scotia, N.Y., 1987—. Co-author: Bearing Design and Application, 1956; editor: Handbook of Lubrication, Vol. 1, 1983, Vol. 2, 1984; contbr. over 80 articles to profl. jours. Gov. bd. East Glenville Community Ch., Scotia, 1970-92. Fellow Soc. Tribologists and Lubrication Engrs. (nat. pres. 1957, Svc. Award 1984, Nat. award 1992); mem. Am. Chem. Soc., ASME. Home: 65 Stephens Ln Scotia NY 12302

BOOT, JOHN C. G., economics educator; b. Semarang, Java, Indonesia, June 10, 1936; came to U.S. 1965; s. Frederik Rutger and Maria (den Tex) B.; m. A.M. Hinke Tuinman, May 22, 1965; children—Maren Caroline, Mark Frederik Abe. Ph.D., Netherlands Sch. Econs., Rotterdam, 1964. Prof. econs. and stats. SUNY-Buffalo, 1965—. Author: Quadratic Programming, 1964, others. Home: 177 Beard Ave Buffalo NY 14214-1729 Office: SUNY Amherst Campus Buffalo NY 14260

BOOTH, ANNA BELLE, accountant; b. Homesville, Ohio, Jan. 15, 1912; d. John Wilson and M. Pearl (Toomey) B.; m. Guy DiAmbrosio, Apr. 29, 1930; 1 child, Guy Booth. BA, Taylor Coll., 1930. Office mgr. in charge of mfg. Jacobs Tailored Clothes, Inc., Phila., 1931-41; acct., corp. cashier Lehigh Coal and Navigation Co., Phila., 1941-55; acct. Bishop & Hedberg, Phila., 1955-57; acct., office mgr. The Camax Co., Phila., 1957-60; office mgr., cashier New Eng. Mutual Life Ins. Co., Phila., 1960-67; acct. Wall & Ochs, Inc., Phila., 1967-71; comptr. Bisler Packaging Div./Pet, Inc., Phila., 1971-82; ret. Mem. Am. Soc. Women Accts. (Phila. pres. 1956-58, dir. 1952-54, 62-64, 73-75), LWV (Phila.). Home: 2122 Sansom St Philadelphia PA 19103-4429

BOOTH, BONNIE NELSON, compensation benefits consultant; b. Lynn, Mass., Aug. 28, 1942; d. Vincent Carl and Merchelle Romaine (Eastman) Nelson. Student, Mary Washington Coll., 1960-61, Columbia U., 1965, Carnegie-Mellon U., 1962, 78-80; EdM in Adminstrn., Planning and Social Policy, Harvard U., 1979. Exec. sec. Kenyon and Eckhardt, Inc., N.Y.C., 1964-65; exec. sec., asst. to assoc. dir. Am. Press. Inst., Columbia U., N.Y.C., 1965; prin. sec. to chief housing sect. UN Hdqrs., N.Y.C., N.Y.C., 1965-68; adminstrv. asst. sec. UN Mission, Magadiscio, Somalia, 1968, Tripoli, Libya, 1968-69; research asst. Stockholm Sch. Econs., 1970; adminstrv. sec. to dep. dir. UN Conf. Trade and Devel./GATT, Geneva, 1970; adminstrv. asst. Harvard U., 1970-74, personnel officer dept. psychology and social relations, 1974-75; adminstrv. asst. Dravo Corp., Pitts., 1975-76; assoc. dir. admissions Chatham Coll., Pitts., 1976-77, acting dir. admissions, 1977-78; mgmt. devel. trainer and adminstr. Westinghouse Credit Corp., Pitts., 1981-86, human resources adminstr., 1986-89, human resources cons., 1989-91, pension cons., 1991—. Dem. committeewoman 7th Ward, Pitts., 1980—, vice chmn., 1990—; del. Shadyside Action Coalition, 1988—, sec., 1991-92, pres., 1992—. Recipient Hon. diploma for outstanding performance Internat. Seminar on Rural Housing and Community Facilities, Venezuelan Govt., 1967, Outstanding Quality Circle Facilitator award Westinghouse Electric Corp., 1985. Mem. ASTD, Internat. Assn. Quality Cirs. (pres. Pitts. chpt. 1985-90), Am. Soc. Exec. Women, Rotary. Episcopalian. Home: 5825 5th Ave Pittsburgh PA 15232-2749 Office: Westinghouse Electric Corp Gateway 3d Fl 11 Stanwix St Pittsburgh PA 15222

BOOTH, LILA, communications consultant; b. Phila., May 21, 1930; d. Nathan and Elizabeth (Coff) Wolfman; m. Newlin Booth, Mar. 21, 1976; children: Robert Rosenbaum, David Rosenbaum, Beth Rosenbaum, Barbara, Robert, Priya Abbate, Carolin Murphy. BS in Edn., U. Pa., 1951. Cert. masters equivalency, Pa.; cert. secondary edn. techr.: social studies, English, Pa. Educator Cheltenham Schs., Wynote, Pa., 1954-55; instr. U. Pa., Phila., 1962-63; educator of the gifted Sch. Dist. of Cheltenham Twp., Wynote, 1968-85; educator, co-founder Free Enterprise Fellowhips, Fort Washington, Pa., 1979-89; communication skills cons. LBC-II, Blue Bell, Pa., 1985—; adj. prof. Beaver Coll. Glenside, Pa. 1976-77; cons. Inroads, Phila., 1980—, Nat. Assn. Women's Bus. Owners, Phila., 1986—; dir. Women's Way, Phila., 1989—; mem. adv. com. Free Enterprise Fellowships, 1989—; instr. Inst. of Exec. Edn., Wharton Sch., U. Pa., Phila., 1989—. Speaker Inc. Mag. seminars for entrepreneurs, Boston, 1989, New Orleans, 1991. Named Women in Bus. Advocate of the Year Small Bus. Adminstrn., 1991. Mem. Forum of Exec. Women. Office: LBC-II PO Box 144 Blue Bell PA 19422-0144

BOOTH, MALCOLM AARON, town official; b. Ogdensburg, N.Y., Apr. 22, 1936; s. Emmett H. and Pauline A. (Rice) B. BA, St. Lawrence U., 1956; MA, SUNY, Oneonta, 1965. Reporter, editor Times Herald-Record, Middletown, N.Y., 1961-66; dir. Orange County Community of Museums, Goshen, N.Y., 1966-77; coord., bus. mgr. Neversink Valley Area Mus., Cuddebackville, N.Y., 1973-83; instr. Ulster County Community Coll., Stone Ridge, N.Y., 1980-83; budget officer Town of Goshen, 1984—; sec.-treas. BTK Assocs., Inc., Goshen, N.Y., 1990—. Author: Short History of Orange County, N.Y., 1975. Mem. Goshen Rep. Com., 1973—, vice chmn., 1991—. Mem. N.Y. State Archaeol. Assn. (cert. of merit 1992), Neversink Valley Area Mus., N.Y. Parks and Conservation Assn. Home: PO Box 527 Goshen NY 10924-0527 Office: Town of Goshen 41 Webster Ave Goshen NY 10924-1520

BOOTH, MARGARET A(NN), communications company executive; b. N.Y.C., Dec. 25, 1946; d. Herbert and Alice (Traum) B.; m. Marvin E. Schechter, Jan. 22, 1984. BS, U. Wis., 1968. Editorial asst. Bantam Books, N.Y.C., 1968-70; publicity asst. Ruder & Finn Inc., N.Y.C., 1970-71, dir. radio and TV, 1971-76, v.p., 1974-76; pres. Pub. Interest Pub. Rels., N.Y.C., 1976—, M. Booth & Assocs., Inc., N.Y.C., 1983—. Author: Promoting Issues and Ideas, 1987; contbr. articles to profl. jours. Bd. dirs. Ctr. for Population Options, N.Y.C., 1986—, Citizens Union Found., 1989. Recipient YWCA Salute to Women Achievers, City of N.Y., 1985. Mem. Women in Communications (Matrix award for Pub. Rels. 1987), Pub. Rels. Soc. of AM., Women Execs. Pub. Rels. Office: M Booth & Assocs Inc 470 Park Ave S # 10N New York NY 10016-6819

BOPP, MARY ANN, educator; b. Hudson, N.Y., Jan. 18, 1955; d. Angelo. G. Barca and Constance Mary Anna (Gradowski) MacGiffert; m. Christopher Harold Bopp, Oct. 8, 1988; stepchildren: Bryan, Gary. BBA in Acctg., Siena Coll., 1977; MBA, Rensselaer Poly. Inst., 1983. Cert. mgmt. acct., 1991. Auditor N.Y. State Dept. Audit and Control, Albany, 1977; various fin. positions IBM Corp., Poughkeepsie, N.Y., 1978-84, fin. planning and analysis mgr., 1984-87, adv. bus. planner, 1987-88; program mgr. IBM Corp., Briarcliff Manor, N.Y., 1988—; real estate agt. Chris Bopp Real Estate, Beacon, N.Y., 1991—; adj. instr. Mercy Coll., Dobbs Ferry, N.Y., 1986, Dutchess C.C., Poughkeepsie, 1987-90, Pace U., Pleasantville, N.Y., 1989—; mem. acctg. adv. coun. Dutchess C.C., 1987—. Mem. Inst. Mgmt. Accts. Home: 10 Orbit Ln Hopewell Junction NY 12533-6706

BOQUET, YVES ANDRÉ, history and geography educator; b. Montluçon, Allier, France, Jan. 7, 1956; came to U.S., 1981; s. Guy Maurice and Simone Marie (Daubigny) B; m. Carol Jean Wolfe, Nov. 9, 1988. M in Geography, Université Paris X, Nanterre, France, 1978, Agregation de Geographie, 1979; cert. of chinese studies, Université Paris III, 1981. Geograhy prof. Lycée Fernand Lèger, Sarcelles, France, 1979-80, Lycée Marie Curie, Versailles, France, 1980-81; geography prof. French Internat. Sch., Washington, 1981. Co-author: (with others) Geographie Terminales, 1989; contbr. articles to profl. jours. Mem. Assn. Am. Geographers, Assn. de Geographes Français. Office: French Internat Sch 9600 Forest Rd Bethesda MD 20814-1792

BORAN, RAYANNE MARIE, office manager, consultant; b. Havertown, Pa., Sept. 24, 1968; d. Raymond Richard and Anna Marie (Ruff) Buchianico; m. Thomas James Boran III, Dec. 31, 1988; children: Elizabeth Jeannette, Thomas James IV. Paralegal, PJA Sch., Upper Darby, Pa., 1988; student, Delaware County Community Coll., Media, Pa., 1991—. Sales asst. Met. Life Ins., Drexel Hill, Pa., 1986-87; mgr. legal dept. GAMUT, Inc., Drexel Hill, 1987-88; mgr., firm. adminstr. Preston, Barrett & Co., Havertown, Pa., 1988—; owner Rayanne M. Boran-Paralegal and Adminstrv. Svcs., Upper Darby, Pa., 1991—. Treas. South Stonehurst Civic Assn., Upper Darby, 1990. Mem. NAFE. Roman Catholic. Home: 7198 Ruskin Ln Upper Darby PA 19082

BORCHARD, CRAIG LEE, writer, public relations consultant; b. Sioux City, Iowa, May 7, 1962; s. Howard Lee and Carol Maude (Lowry) B. BA, Buena Vista Coll., 1984; MA, U. No. Iowa, 1986. Account exec. Beswick Communications, Pitts., 1986-90; sr. writer Allegheny Gen. Hosp., Pitts., 1990—; cons. pub. rels. Pitts. AIDS Task Force, 1989—. Author, editor, project coord. Pitts. AIDS Task Force Annual Report, 1989-92 (several awards 1990). Active Big Bros./Big Sisters of Greater Pitts. With U.S. Army NG, 1983-89. Mem. Pub. Rels. Soc. Am., Internat. Assn. Bus. Communicators. Home: 129 Norman D Coraopolis PA 15108 Office: Allegheny Gen Hosp 320 E North Ave Pittsburgh PA 15212-4772

BORCHARDT, ANNE, publishing executive; b. Newark; d. Harry Bolton and Shirley Slatin; m. Georges Borchardt, May 26, 1959; 1 child, Valerie. BA, NYU, 1956; MA, Columbia U., 1957-58. V.p. Georges Borchardt Inc., N.Y.C., 1959—. Translator: The Accident, 1963, Monsieur Andemas, 1965, 10:30 On a Summer Night, 1965, The Golem, 1983.

BORDEN, SANDRA MCCLISTER, day care center administrator, dancer; b. Trenton, Oct. 18, 1946; d. Harry Arthur and Ruth West McClister; m. Robert Stetson Borden, Mar. 23, 1968; children: Robert Freeman, Randolph McClister, David Buckley, Christian Delano. BA, Eastern Nazarene Coll., Quincy, Mass., 1968; MA, Nova U., 1986. Tchr. kindergarten Doves Nest Day Care Ctr., Rockland, Mass., 1979-84, owner, adminstr., 1979—; owner, adminstr. Dove's Nest Day Care Ctr., Weymouth, Mass., 1980-82, Abington, Mass., 1980-83; owner, editor Barter & Trade Jour., Rockland, 1980-83; owner Dove's Nest Family Day Care System, Rockland, 1984—; co-owner Carriage House Day Care Ctr., Brockton, Mass., 1986-92, Commonwealth Child Care Cons., 1987—, Bevell Assocs., Stoughton, Mass., 1987-90, Beginning Roots Day Care Ctr., Stoughton, 1987—; pres. Ednl. Videos of New Eng., 1990—; owner Angels Consignment Shop, Rockland, Mass.; ptnr. Tender Loving Child Care Inc., 1988-89; dancer Foggs Dancers, Boston, 1980—; dir. Country Dance Soc., Boston, 1982—, v.p., 1986—, dancer, 1984-85, pres., 1988; co-founder, dancer Rapscallion Rapper Sword Team, 1985—. Foster mother for Helping Hands monkey, Boston U. Sch. Medicine; bd. dirs. LWV, Rockland, 1972-73. Mem. Nat. Assn. Young Children, Royal Scottish Dance Soc., Country Dance Soc., Rose Galliard N.W. Clog Team, 1989—), NAFE, Assn. for Childhood Edn. Internat., Women Aglow Club (sec., bd. dirs.), New Eng. Folk Festival Assn. Boston. Baptist. Home: 1040 Plymouth St Abington MA 02351-2617

BORDEN, SPENCER, IV, medical director; b. Boston, Jan. 26, 1941; s. Richard and Elizabeth (McGinley) B.; m. Dorothy B. Borden, June 23, 1963 (div. 1980); children: Jennifer L., Richard II, Rebecca B.; m. Elizabeth L. Clemens, June 6, 1981; children: Sarah Clemens Borden, Andrew Clemens Borden. AB, Harvard U., 1963; B Med. Sci., Dartmouth Coll., 1966; MD, Harvard Med. Coll., 1968; MBA, U. Pa., Phila., 1986. Diplomate Am. Bd. Med. Mgmt., Am. bd. Radiology, Nat. Bd. Med. Examiners; cert. med. mgr. and quality assurance mgr. Intern in pediatrics Children's Hosp., Boston, 1968-69, fellowship, 1972-73; radiologist-in-chief Children's Hosp., Phila., 1978-88; resident in radiology Mass. Gen. Hosp., Boston, 1969-72, dir. pediatrics radiology, 1975-78; med. dir. Aetna Life Ins. Co., Hartford, Conn., 1988-89, Mediqual Systems, Westboro, Mass., 1989—. Asst. dir. United Way Aetna Life-EBD div., Middletown, Conn., 1988-89. Maj. USAF, 1973-75. Fellow ACP Execs., Am. Acad. Pediatrics, Am. Coll. Med. Quality, Am. Coll. Radiology. Home: 278 Hunters Ridge Rd Concord MA 01742-4718 Office: Mediqual Systems Inc 1900 W Park Dr Westborough MA 01581-3919

BORDES, ADRIENNE, painter, educator; b. N.Y.C.; d. Jean Baptiste and Adrienne (Baycere) B. BA, NYU, 1957; postgrad., Hunter Coll., 1969-71. Adj. instr. art edn. dept. Pratt Inst., Bklyn., 1969; adj. instr. fine arts dept. Coll. Mount St. Vincent, Riverdale, N.Y., 1977-78, Adelphi U., Garden City, N.Y., 1977-80, Fordham U., Rose Hill Campus, Bronx, N.Y., 1978-80; adj. asst. prof. edn. dept. Fiedel Sch. C.W. Post Coll., 1967-80; adj. instr. fine arts dept. Hunter Coll., N.Y.C., 1978-80; asst. prof. interior design dept. Fashion Inst. Tech., N.Y.C., 1980—; lectr. Fine Arts Mus. of L.I., 1982, SUNY at Old Westbury, 1979, Adlephi U., 1978, N.J. State Tchrs. Coll., 1968; vis. artist SUNY at Old Westbury, 1979, Wilkes Coll., 1978. Exhibited in group shows at Federal Hall, 1982, A. Wallace Gallery, SUNY, 1979, Katherine Markel Fine Arts, 1978, Image Gallery, 1977, Univ. inf Wis., 1972, Bklyn. Mus., 1968-69, Capricorn Gallery, 1967, Loeb Ctr., NYU, 1968; one-person shows include Timothy Blackburne Gallery, 1978, Coyningham Gallery, Wilkes Coll., 1978, Millay Colony, 1975, Capricorn Gallery, 1968, 67, Instituto de Estudios Norteamericanos, Barcelona, Spain, 1960. Recipient Fine Arts Painting grant N.Y. State Coun. of Arts. Mem. Interior Design Educators Coun. Office: Fashion Inst Tech Interior Design Dept 227 W 27th St New York NY 10001-5902

BORECKI, KENNETH M(ICHAEL), bank executive; b. Rockville Centre, N.Y., June 29, 1955; s. Theodore and Florence (Kay) B. BS in Fin., CW Post L.I. U., 1976, MS in Acctg., 1978. CPA, N.Y. Mem. audit staff Kenneth Leventhal & Co., N.Y.C., 1978-82; asst. v.p. E.F. Hutton & Co., N.Y.C., 1982-84, v.p., 1985-88; v.p. Shearson Lehman Hutton, N.Y.C., 1988-89; v.p., dir. owned real estate Dime Savs. Bank of N.Y., Uniondale, 1989—; treas. Hutton Real Estate Services, Inc., Garden City, 1986-88; pres. Hutton Real Estate Equity Ptnrs. Inc., 1988. Mem. AICPA, N.Y. Soc. CPAs, Soc. Real Property Adminstrs. Ukranian Catholic. Office: Dime Savs Bank NY Asset Recovery Div EAB Plz 11th Fl East Tower Uniondale NY 11556

BOREL, RICHARD WILSON, communications executive, consultant; b. Columbus, Ohio, June 10, 1943; s. Richard Alfred and Margaret (Wilson) B.; m. Kathy Teaford, July 17, 1965; 1 child, Meredith Lynn. BS in Mktg., Ohio State U., 1964; MBA in Fin., U. Pa., 1966. Mgr. sales and svcs. budgets TWA, N.Y.C., 1966-69; mgr. planning and devel. John Blair & Co., N.Y.C., 1969-76; v.p., sta. mgr. Sta. WHOH Corp., Boston, 1976-84; sr. v.p., chief oper. officer Ea. Exclusives, Inc., Boston, 1984-85; pres., chief oper. officer Borel & Co., Dover, Mass., 1985-86, Metro Net, Inc., Boston and Vt., 1986-89; exec. v.p., chief operating officer Target Prodns., Inc., Boston, 1989—. Author: (with others) Broadcast and Cable Management, 1986. Mem. New Eng. Broadcasting Assn. (pres. 1977-78), Wharton Club (bd. dirs. 1988—), Beta Gamma Sigma. Republican. Episcopalian. Home: 6 Circle Dr Dover MA 02030-2106

BORELLA, LUIS ENRIQUE, pharmacologist, research scientist; b. Buenos Aires, Sept. 29, 1930; s. Luis and Carmen (Genaula) B.; m. Jean Anne Willday, Dec. 17, 1967; children: Amanda Anne, Amelia Carmen. BS in Pharmacy, U. Buenos Aires, 1954, MS in Pharmacy, 1956; MS in Biochemistry, U. Conn., 1962, PhD in Pharmacology, 1964. Pharmacist Buenos Aires, 1954-59; teaching asst. U. Conn., Storrs, 1960-62, rsch. asst., 1962-64; rsch. fellow U. Toronto, Ontario, Can., 1964-65; sr. rsch. assoc. Ayerst Labs., Montreal, Quebec, Can., 1965-84; prin. scientist Wyeth-Ayerst Rsch., Princeton, N.J., 1984—. Author: Experimental Ulcer, 1975; patentee in field; contbr. over 40 articles to profl. jours. Recipient Anna Bradbury Springer Fellowship award U. Toronto, 1964. Mem. AAAS, Montreal Physiol. Soc., Sigma Xi, Phila. Physiol. Soc., Canadian Pharmacological Soc. Home: 42 Slayback Dr Princeton Junction NJ 08550-1912 Office: Wyeth Ayerst Rsch Princeton NJ 08540

BORENFREUND, ELLEN, research scientist, educator; b. Leipzig, Fed. Republic Germany, Mar. 15, 1922; came to U.S., 1938; BS, Hunter Coll., 1946; MS, NYU, 1948, PhD, 1957. Rsch. asst. Coll. Physicians and Surgeons, N.Y.C., 1948-57; rsch. assoc. Sloan Kettering Inst., N.Y.C., 1957-61, assoc., 1961-65, assoc. mem., 1965-87, asst. prof., 1961-68, assoc. prof., 1968-87; adj. assoc. prof. Rockefeller U., N.Y.C., 1981-88, adj. faculty, 1988—. Contbr. articles to profl. jours. Recipient Rsch. Career Devel. award NIH, 1963-66; named one of Outstanding Women in Sci. Assn. of Women in Sci.,1 983; named to Hunter Coll. Hall of Fame, 1981. Jewish. Office: Rockefeller U 1230 York Ave New York NY 10021-6341

BORENSTEIN, MILTON CONRAD, lawyer, manufacturing company executive; b. Boston, Oct. 21, 1914; s. Isadore Sidney and Eva Beatrice B.; m. Anne Shapiro, June 20, 1937; children: Roberta, Jeffrey. AB cum laude, Boston Coll., 1935; JD, Harvard U., 1938. Bar: Mass. 1938, U.S. Dist. Ct. 1939, U.S. Ct. Appeals 1944, U.S. Supreme Ct. 1944. Pvt. practice law Boston, 1938—; officer, dir. Sweetheart Paper Products Co., Inc., Chelsea, Mass., 1944-61; pres. Sweetheart Paper Products Co., Inc., Chelsea, 1961-83, chmn. bd., 1984; with Sweetheart Plastics, Inc., Wilmington, Mass., 1958—; v.p. Sweetheart Plastics, Inc., Wilmington, 1958-84, also dir.; v.p. Md. Cup Corp., Owings Mills, 1960-77, exec. v.p., treas., 1977-84, also dir. Bd. dirs. Am. Assocs. Hebrew U., 1968—; trustee Boston Coll., 1979-87, assoc. trustee, 1987—, chmn. estate planning coun., 1981-83, mem. coun. exec. com., 1984—; trustee Combined Jewish Philanthropies, Boston, 1969—, N.E. Sinai Hosp., Stoughton, Mass., 1974—, Ben-Gurion U., 1975-85, 87—; bd. overseers Jewish Theol. Sem. Am., 1971—; mem. pres.'s coun. Sarah Lawrence Coll., 1970-79; pres. Congregation Kehillath Israel, Brookline, Mass., 1977-79, hon. pres., 1979—; mem. pres.'s coun. Brandeis U., 1979-81, fellow, 1981—; v.p. Assoc. Synagogues of Mass., 1980-81; bd. dirs., nat. governing coun. Am. Jewish Congress, 1984—; exec. com. New Eng. region Anti-Defamation League, 1980—; assoc. chmn. scholarship com. Harvard Law Sch., 1964-66, mem. spl. gifts com., 1990, mem. Langdell com., 1991, 92, Boston regional campaign com., 1992. Recipient Community Svc. award Jewish Theol. Sem. Am., 1970; recipient Bald Eagle Outstanding Alumnus award Boston Coll., 1991. Fellow Mass. Bar Found.; mem. ABA, Mass. Bar Assn., Boston Bar Assn. (mem. bicentennial com. 1986-87). Home: 273 Eliot St Chestnut Hill MA 02167-1445 Office: Concorde Assocs Ste 2912 1 Devonshire Pl Boston MA 02109

BORENSZTEIN, EDUARDO ROBERTO, economist; b. Buenos Aires, Argentina, Feb. 14, 1954; came to U.S. 1980; s. Daniel Saul and Chana (Izbicki) B.; m. Liliana Noemi Letzen, Jan. 27, 1977; children: Alejandra G., Nicolas G. Lic., U. Buenos Aires, 1976; PhD in Econs., MIT, 1986. Economist Central Bank, Buenos Aires, 1976-78, FIEL, Buenos Aires, 1979-80; economist in rsch. dept. IMF, Washington, 1984—; referee of submitted papers Jour. Internat. Econs., 1988, Jour. Internat. Money and Fin., 1989, Jour. Devel. Econs., 1989, 90, Am. Econ. Rev., 1990, World Bank Econ. Rev., 1990. Contbr. articles to profl. jours. Recipient Exxon Fellowship, Econs. Dept., MIT, Cambridge, Mass., 1984. Mem. Am. Econ. Assn. Jewish. Home: 6306 Marywood Rd Bethesda MD 20817-2310 Office: Internat Monetary Fund 700 19th St NW Rm 9548 Washington DC 20431-0002

BORER, EDWARD TURNER, investment banker; b. Phila., Nov. 30, 1938; s. Robert Chamberlin and Helen Elizabeth (Clawges) B.; B.S., U. Pa., 1960; m. Amy Hamilton Ryerson, Aug. 8, 1959; children—Edward Turner, Catherine Hamilton, Elizabeth Taft. Rep., Hopper Soliday & Co., Inc., Phila., 1960-67, v.p. research, 1967-73, sec., 1971-85, sr. v.p., 1973-82, exec. v.p., 1982-84, pres., 1984-88, also bd. dirs.; dir. Manchester Gas Co. (N.H.), 1965-88, pres., 1970, chmn. bd., chmn. exec. com., 1970-82; chmn. bd. EnergyNorth, Inc., 1982—; pres., dir. Phila. Corp. for Fin. Investment (and subs.), 1989—; dir., sec. Disaster Control, Inc., 1981-83, Omni Oil & Gas Mgmt. Co., 1981-84; dir. Hopper Soliday Corp., 1988-89; founder, treas., sec., dir. Creative Information Systems, Inc., Chadds Ford, Pa., 1967-77; v.p. Sovereign Investors, 1980-86 ; arbitrator N.Y. Stock Exch., 1992—, Phila. Stock Exch., 1992—; bd. dirs. Energy North Natural Gas, Inc., Energy North Propane, Inc. (formerly Rent-A-Space of New Eng., Inc.). Chmn. West Met. Area-Wide Com., Regional Med. Program, 1969-70; pres, bd. dirs. Phila. Corp. for Fin. Investment, Phila. Corp. for Investment Svcs.,

Phila. Corp. for Investment Mgmt., 1989—. Pres. Swarthmore Home and Sch. Assn., 1973; bd. dirs. Freedom Valley council Girl Scouts U.S.A., 1974-75, also chmn. finance com.; bd. dirs., chmn. fin. com. Planned Parenthood Southeastern Pa., 1980-85, dir. 1988-90; treas., 1986-87 trustee George W. South Meml. Ch. of the Adv., Phila., 1978-88; dir. Nat. Kidney Found. Del. Valley, 1990—, treas., mem. exec. com., 1990—. Served to 1st lt., Q.M.C., AUS, 1961-62. Chartered fin. analyst. Mem. Fin. Analysts Fedn., Phila. Securities Assn. (dir. 1979-83, v.p. 1980-81, pres. 1981-82), Nat. Assn. Securities Dealers (arbitrator 1982—, chmn. dist. 11 and bus. conduct com. 1986), Fin. Analysts Phila. (treas. 1976-77), N.Y. Soc. Security Analysts, Am. Arbitration Assn. (arbitrator 1988—), N.Y. Stock Exch. (arbitrator 1992—), Phila. Stock Exch. (arbitrator 1992—), Delta Upsilon. Episcopalian (vestryman 1970-73, 74-77, 85-88). Club: Union League (Phila.). Home: 125 Guernsey Rd Swarthmore PA 19081-1210 also: Box 643 Saint John VI 00831 Office: 2303 Fidelity Bldg Broad & Walnut Sts Philadelphia PA 19109

BORER, JEFFREY STEPHEN, cardiologist; b. Deland, Fla., Feb. 22, 1945; s. Lee Norton and Rita Doris (Feldt) B.; m. Brondi Beth Topchik, Sept. 16, 1978; children: Justine Isolde, Jon Andrew. BA in Govt., Harvard U., 1965; MD, Cornell U., 1969. Diplomate Am. Bd. Internal Medicine, Am. Bd. Cardiovascular Disease. Intern, then resident in medicine Mass. Gen. Hosp., Boston, 1969-71; clin. fellow in medicine Harvard U. Sch. Medicine, Boston, 1969-71; clin. assoc. in cardiology Nat. Heart, Lung and Blood Inst., NIH, Bethesda, Md., 1971-74, chief resident physician, 1973-74, sr. investigator, cardiology br., 1975-79; sr. Fulbright-Hays scholar, Glorney-Raisbeck fellow med. scis Guy's Hosp., U. London, 1974-75; assoc. prof. medicine Cornell U. Med. Coll., N.Y.C., 1979-82, prof., 1982—, Gladys and Roland Harriman prof. cardiovascular medicine, 1983—; prof. cardiovascular med. in radiology Cornell Univ. Med. Coll., N.Y.C., 1990—; chmn. cardiac and renal adv. com., U.S. FDA, Washington, 1981-82, 83-87, cons., 1989—; mem. life scis. adv. com. NASA, Washington, 1984-88, mem. aero. med. adv. com., 1988—. Contbr. more than 200 articles on cardiovascular disease to med. jours. Trustee N.Y.C. Historic Properties Fund, 1984-90; mem. steering com. Assocs. of the Jewish Bd. of Family and Children Svcs., 1989-91; pres. Am. Friends of Israel Nat. Heart to Heart Assn., 1991—. Sr. surgeon USPHS, 1971-79. Recipient Investigator's award prize European Cardiol. Soc., 1978, spl. award for contbns. to cardiology, Assn. Thoracic and Cardiovascular Surgeons of India, 1985, William A. Johnston award, Internat. Soc. Heart Rsch., 1986, spl. citation Israel Nat. Heart to Heart Assn., 1992; travelling fellow Am. Physicians Fellowship, 1981. Fellow ACP, Am. Soc. Clin. Investigation, Am. Coll. Cardiology (governing coun. N.Y. chpt. 1991-92), Am. Heart Assn. (coun. clin. cardiology and circulation, established investigator 1979-84), Am. Coll. Chest Physicians (chmn. cardiology forum 1985-86, exec. com. clin. cardiology sect. 1991—), N.Y. Cardiol. Soc. (pres. 1990-91), Argentine Heart Assn. (hon.); mem. Soc. Nuclear Medicine (trustee cardiovascular coun. 1991—), Harvard Club N.Y.C., Am. Friends of Israel Heart to Heart Assn. (pres. 1990—). Office: NY Hosp 525 E 68th St New York NY 10021-4873

BORETZ, NAOMI MESSINGER, artist, educator; b. Bklyn., June 9, 1935; d. Joseph and Sarah (Lesser) Messinger; m. Benjamin A. Boretz, Sept. 1, 1954; 1 child, Avron Albert. BA, Bklyn. Coll., 1957; MFA, CUNY, 1971; MA, Rutgers U., 1976; postgrad., Art Students League N.Y. Assoc. prof. fine arts, dir. arts program Wilson Coll., Chambersburg, Pa., 1985—. Exhbns. include Westminster Arts Coun. Arts Ctr., London, 1971, Carnegie-Mellon Art Gallery, Pitts., 1989, Hudson River Mus., N.Y.C., 1975, others; represented in pub. collections Met. Mus. Art, N.Y.C., Solomon R. Guggenheim Mus., N.Y.C., Brit. Mus., London, Nat. Mus. Am. Art, Washington, Yale U. Art Gallery, others; contbr. articles, book revs. to arts publs. Artist-fellow Va. Ctr. Creative Arts, 1973, 86, Ossabaw Found., 1975, Tyrone Guthrie Arts Ctr., Ireland, 1987, Writers-Artists Guild Can., 1988; grantee N.J. State Coun. on Arts, 1985-86. Home: 15 Southern Way Princeton NJ 08540-5318 Office: Wilson Coll Chambersburg PA 17201

BOREY, NADINE MARIE, sales executive; b. Southbridge, Mass., Oct. 9, 1966; d. Wilfred Jules and M. Constance (McGann) B.; 1 child, M. Jarrod. Assoc., Nichols Coll., 1988. Claims typist Commerce Ins. Co., Webster, Mass., 1986-87; customer svc. rep. Dennis A. McCurdy Ins. Agy., Sturbridge, Mass., 1987-88; front desk clk., asst. to mgr. Fitness Express, Charlton, Mass., 1988-89; support staff mem. sales adminstrn. Coherent Gen. Inc., Sturbridge, 1989—. Mem. LASER Assn. (editor employee newsletter, mem. adv. coun.). Roman Catholic. Home: 24 Plimpton St Southbridge MA 01550-1242 Office: Coherent Gen Inc 1 Picker Rd Sturbridge MA 01566-1298

BORGER, HENRY ADOLPH, mechanical engineer; b. Washington, Feb. 9, 1933; s. H. Adolph and Mary Genevieve (Van Ryswick) B.; m. Martha Ann Goad, May 29, 1962; children: Karen, Kathryn, Christina, Stephen, James. BSME, Cath. U. Am., 1956. Mfg. engr. Westinghouse Elec. Corp., Balt., 1960-62; exec. sec. Fed. Constrn. Coun. Nat. Acad. Scis., Washington, 1962—; mem. constrn. ind. coord. com. Am. Nat. Metric Coun., Washington, 1975-78. Project coord./editor adv. reports to fed. govt. Vice pres. South Laurel Recreation Coun., Laurel, Md., 1985—. 1st lt. USAF, 1957-60. Recipient Fed. Design Achievement award Nat. Endowment for the Arts, 1988, Chairman's award Constrn. Rsch. Coun., 1976. Mem. ASHRAE (chpt. pres. 1979-80), ASME, ASCE (editorial bd. 1986—). Republican. Roman Catholic. Office: Nat Acad Scis 2101 Constitution Ave NW Washington DC 20418-0001

BORGMAN, ERIC BRUNO, filmmaker; b. Chelsea, Mass., June 23, 1970; s. George Allan and Janet Claire (Ferroli) B. Student, Emerson Coll., 1988-92. Actor Warner Bros., Spenser for Hire, Lexington, Mass., 1986, April Morning, Can., 1987, Against the Law, Boston, 1990, PBS, The Road from Runnymede, Concord, Mass., 1990, Wind, Newport, R.I., 1991, Primary Motives, Boston, 1991, Paramount Pictures, School Ties, Concord, 1991; employee Nat. Amusements, Dedham, Mass., 1989—. Mem. AFTRA, SAG, 10th Regiment of Foot, Sons of the Desert, New Eng. Hist. Geneal. Soc., Doctor Who Appreciation Soc., Nat. Honor Soc. (treas. 1987-88). Home and Office: 158 Burgess Ave Westwood MA 02090-3010

BORGMAN, GEORGE ALLAN, journalist; b. St. Louis, Jan. 22, 1928; s. Herman Francis and Martha Vivien (Wecker) B.; m. Ann Nettarose Graber, July 29, 1949 (div. Oct. 1953); 1 child, Andrea Vivien Schnarr; m. Janet Claire Ferroli, Feb. 27, 1957; children: Carole Elaine (dec.), Paul Allan, Eric Bruno. Student, U. Mo., 1945-46, 48; MusB in History and Lit., St. Louis Inst. Music, 1952; MusM in Musicology, Ind. U., Bloomington, 1953. Musician, dance bands various locations, 1948-50; music educator various sch. systems in Colo. and Nev., 1953-57; freelance asst. cinematographer N.Y.C., 1957-58; spl. agt. mil. intelligence U.S. Army, various locations, 1958-79; film editor, TV cameraman Sta. KOMU-TV, Columbia, Mo., 1958; investigator Wackenhut Corp., Boston, 1980-81; personnel security specialist U.S. Army, Alexandria, Va., 1981-85; sportswriter Suburban World (newspapers), Needham, Mass., 1988—; freelance jazz writer, 1988—; New England corr. and jazz writer T-J Today, 1991—; New England corr. and jazz writer Mississippi Rag, 1992—, record and book reviewer, 1992—. Musician Met. Wind Symphony, Boston, 1981, Fairfax (Va.) City Band, 1982-83, Canton (Mass.) Mcpl. Band/Am. Legion Band, 1981-82; assoc. mem. Westwood (Mass.) Rep. Com., 1988-89. With U.S. Army, 1946-48, 58-79. Mem. Am. Legion, DAV. Republican.

BORGSTEDT, HAROLD HEINRICH, pharmacologist, toxicologist; b. Hamburg, Germany, Apr. 21, 1929; came to U.S., 1956, naturalized, 1962; s. Gustav Johannes and Anni (Wulf) B.; M.D., U. Hamburg, 1956; m. Agneta D. von Rehren, Apr. 3, 1957; children—Eric von R., Astrid Anne. Intern, Rochester (N.Y.) Gen. Hosp., 1956-57; fellow in pharmacology and anatomy U. Rochester, 1957-59, instr. pharmacology, 1959-63, sr. instr., 1963-65, research sr. instr. anesthesiology, 1963-65, asst. prof. pharmacology, research asst. prof. anesthesiology, 1965-83; v.p. medicine and toxicology Health Designs, Inc., Rochester, N.Y., 1983-91; v.p. toxicology Compudrug USA, Inc., Rochester, N.Y., 1991-92, Compudrug Chemistry Budapest, 1991—; pres. Compudrug N.A., Inc., Rochester, N.Y., 1992—; vis. staff U. Surrey, Guildford, Eng. Mem. AAAS, N.Y. Acad. Scis., Am. Soc. Pharmacology and Exptl. Therapeutics, Soc. Toxicology, Internat. Narcotic Enforcement Officers' Assn., Leica Photog. Hist. Soc., Photog. Hist. Soc. (pres. 1986-88), Leica Historica (Germany), Am. Chem. Soc., European Soc. of Toxicology (Eurotox), Sigma Xi. Unitarian. Contbr. to sci. jours., books. Home: PO Box 38 Henrietta NY 14467-0038 Office: Compudrug NA Inc PO Box 23196 Rochester NY 14692-3196

BORIE, JOHN STEWART, environmental project development executive; b. Sewickley, Pa., July 8, 1956; s. David Boyd and Mary Washington (Stewart) B.; m. Greta Zuckerkandel, May 13, 1979; 1 child, John Stewart Jr. BA, U. Pa., 1978, MBA, 1986. Account exec. Dun & Bradstreet, Phila., 1979-81; assoc. ENI Corp., Phila., 1981-82; account exec. Merrill, Lynch, Pierce, Fenner & Smith, Phila., 1982-84; cons. Indsl. Valley Bank and Trust, Phila., 1985; founder, v.p. Phila. Recycling Ptnrship., 1986-87; pres. Nat. Recycling Devel. Corp., Phila., 1987-89; chief exec. officer ENTX, Inc., Phila., 1989—; registered rep. Windmill Group, Inc., Armonk, N.Y., 1991—; cons. Internat. Telecommunications Systems, White Plains, N.Y., 1990—, C.E. Boyd & Assocs., Inc., Riverside, Calif., 1991—. Mem. St. Anthony Hall, Racquet Club (Phila.). Home: 580 Lake Ave Greenwich CT 06830-3853 Office: 500 Lake Ave Greenwich CT 06830-3852

BORIS, BESSIE, artist; b. Johnstown, Pa., June 6, 1917; d. Hyman and Sadie Boris; 1 child, Rachel. Student, Pratt Inst., 1934, Art Students League, 1938-41. One woman shows include Cober Gallery, N.Y.C., 1960, 61, 63, 65, 68, Babcock Gallery, 1970, Image Gallery, Stockbridge, Mass., 1970, 76, 80, 83, 86, Touchstone Gallery, N.Y.C., 1976, Zone, Springfield, Mass., 1986, Berkshire Mus., Pittsfield, Mass., 1987, Katharine Rich Perlow Gallery, N.Y.C., 1990. Group exhibits include Va. Mus. Fine Arts, 1945, Norfolk (Va.) Mus. Fine Arts, 1947, Butler Inst. Am. Art, 1945, Corcoran Gallery Art, Washington, 1949, Bertha Schaefer Gallery, N.Y.C., 1948, Denver Art Mus., 1949, William Rockhill Nelson Gallery Art, 1949, Inst. Contemporary Art, Boston, 1951, Cober Gallery, 1960, others; collections include Norfolk Mus., U. Mass., Montclair (N.J.) Mus., Newark Mus., Berkshire Mus., Pittsfield, Mass., Denver Mus., Smith Coll. Mus., Northampton, Mass., many others. Home: 485 Devon Rd Lee MA 01238

BORISSOFF, ERAST, trade association executive; b. Munich, Sept. 15, 1946; came to U.S., 1951; s. Nicholas and Militza (Shekmatoff) B.; m. Kathryn Ann Schnabel, Sept. 30, 1972; 1 child, Alexandra. BS in Fgn. Svc., Georgetown U., 1968; M in Internat. Comml. Representation, Am. U., 1970, postgrad., 1972. Researcher Curber Assocs., Inc., Washington, 1970; mgmt. analyst U.S. Dept. Commerce, Washington, 1970, mgmt. intern, 1971-73, coal export staff, 1982-85; v.p. WJS, Inc., Washington, 1973-77; ptnr. S&S Mgmt. Cons., Washington, 1977-78; head Washington office Unit Rig & Equipment Co., Washington, 1978-81; mktg. mgr. Unit Rig & Equipment Co., Tulsa, 1981-82; with market devel. St. Lawrence Seaway Devel. Corp., Washington, 1985-87; exec. dir. Am. Coal Ash Assn., Washington, 1987—; bd. dirs. Pitts. Coal Conf. Bd. Capt. USAR, 1970-76. Mem. Am. Chief Exec. Coun., Am. Soc. of Assn. Execs., Constrn. Industry Materials and Svcs. Suppliers Coalition (chmn. 1990), Am. Road Builders (vice chmn. airports coun. 1990—). Office: Am Coal Ash Assn 6th Fl 1913 I St NW Washington DC 20006-2106

BORITT, GÁBOR SZAPPANOS, history educator; b. Budapest, Hungary, Jan. 26, 1940; came to U.S., 1957, naturalized, 1963; s. Paul Szappanos Boritt and Rosa Theresia Schwartz; m. Elizabeth Lincoln Norseen, 1968; children: Norse, Jake, Daniel. BA, Yankton Coll., S.D., 1962; MA, U. S.D., 1963; PhD, Boston U., 1967. Asst. prof. Boston U., 1967-68; lectr. U. Md. Far East, 1968-70; asst. prof. Mt. Wachussetts Community Coll., 1972-73, Memphis State U., 1975-76, 77-81; vis. prof. U. Mich., Ann Arbor, 1973-74, Washington U., St. Louis, 1974-75; vis. fellow Harvard U., Cambridge, Mass., 1976-77, Darwin Coll., Cambridge, Inst. U.S. Studies, U. of London, 1987; assoc. prof. Gettysburg Coll., Pa., 1981—, Robert C. Fluhrer prof. Civil War Studies, 1986, founder, dir. Civil War Inst., 1983—; dir. Lincoln 175 nat. conf. Lincoln scholars, Gettysburg, 1984, Lincoln Image exhibit, 1984-85, Confederate Image exhibit, 1987-89, Gettysburg Address 125 exhibit, 1988; Fortenbaugh Lecture Series; chmn. bd. Lincoln Prize, 1990—. Author: Lincoln and the Economics of the American Dream, 1978 (award of merit 1979), Abraham Lincoln: War Opponent and War President, 1987; co-author The Lincoln Image, 1984, Changing the Lincoln Image, 1985; The Confederate Image, 1987; co-author, editor: The Historians' Lincoln: Pseudohistory, Psychohistory, and History, 1988, Historian's Lincoln: Rebuttals, 1988, Lincoln: The War President, 1992; editor: Why the Confederacy Lost, 1992; contbr. articles to N.Y. Times, Christian Sci. Monitor, profl. jours. Social Sci. Research Council fellow, 1976-77; NEH grantee, 1984; Am. Philos. Soc. grantee, 1973, 86; Newberry Library grantee, 1975; recipient Henry E. Huntington Library and Art Gallery Research award, 1971, award Pa. Humanities Council, 1984, 87. Mem. Am. Hist. Assn., Orgn. Am. Historians, Phi Alpha Theta (Hammond prize 1965). Avocation: farming. Home: Farm The Ford Plank Rd Gettysburg PA 17325 Office: Gettysburg Coll Civil War Inst Gettysburg PA 17325

BORK, ROBERT HERON, lawyer, former federal judge; b. Pitts., Mar. 1, 1927; s. Harry Philip and Elizabeth (Kunkle) B.; m. Claire Davidson, June 15, 1952 (dec. 1980); children: Robert Heron, Charles E., Ellen E.; m. Mary Ellen Pohl, Oct. 30, 1982. BA, U. Chgo., 1948, JD, 1953; LLD (hon.), Creighton U., 1975, Notre Dame Law Sch., 1982; LHD, Wilkes-Barre Coll., 1976; JD (hon.), Brlyn. Law Sch., 1984; ThD, DeSales Sch. Theology, 1990; LLD honoris causa, Adelphi U., 1990. Bar: Ill. 1953, D.C. 1977. Assoc., then ptnr. Kirkland, Ellis, Hodson, Chaffetz & Masters, Chgo., 1955-62; assoc. prof. Yale Law Sch., 1962-65, prof. law, 1965-75, on leave, 1973-75, Chancellor Kent prof. law, 1977-79, Alexander M. Bickel prof. pub. law, 1979-81; ptnr. Kirkland & Ellis, Washington, 1981-82; judge U.S. Ct. Appeals for D.C. Cir., 1982-88, resigned, 1988; resident scholar Am. Enterprise Inst. for Pub. Policy Rsch., Washington, 1977, adj. scholar, 1977-82, John M. Olin scholar in legal studies, 1988—; mem. Presdl. Task Force on Antitrust, 1968; cons. Cabinet Com. on Edn., 1972; trustee Woodrow Wilson Internat. Ctr. for Scholars, 1973-78; nominated for position assoc. justice U.S. Supreme Ct., 1987, confirmation denied by U.S. Senate. Author: The Antitrust Paradox: A Policy at War with Itself, 1978, The Tempting of America: The Political Seduction of the Law, 1990. Mem. bd. govs. Smith Richardson Found., 1988; mem. legal adv. bd. Nat. Legal Ctr for the Pub. Interest, 1988; bd. dirs. Inst. for Ednl. Affairs, 1988; apptd. Permanent Com. for the Oliver Wendell Holmes Devise, 1989. With USMCR, 1945-46, 50-52. Recipient Francis Boyer award Am. Enterprise Inst., 1984. Fellow AAAS; mem. Federalist Soc. (devel. bd. law and pub. policy studies 1988).

BORKOWSKY, WILLIAM, pediatrician, educator; b. Germany, Mar. 6, 1947; s. David Borkowsky; m. Joan Kaiser, Nov. 23, 1969; children: Heather, Shane, Ariel. BS, CCNY, 1968; MD, NYU, 1972. Diplomate Am. Bd. Pediatrics. Intern NYU Med. Ctr.; resident Bellevue Hosp. Ctr., 1972-75; asst. prof. NYU Med. Ctr., N.Y.C., 1977-84, assoc. prof., 1984—, dir. pediatric infectious disease, 1985—; prin. investigator Nat. Inst. Allergy Infectious Diseases, Nat. Inst Child Health and Human Devel.-NIH, 1987—; dir. pediatric AIDS clinic trial group NYU, 1987—. Contbr. articles to profl. publs. Mem. Assn. Allergy and Immunology, Infectious Disease Soc. Am., Soc. for Pediatric Rsch., Am. Fedn. Clin. Rsch., Pediatric Infectious Disease Soc., Am. Soc. Microbiology, Harvey Soc., Alpha Omega Alpha. Office: NYU Med Ctr Bellevue Hosp Med Ctr 550 1st Ave New York NY 10016-6402

BORLE, ANDRÉ BERNARD, physiologist; b. La Chaux-de-Fonds, Switzerland, May 27, 1930; came to U.S., 1956, naturalized, 1969; s. Andre Leon and Fernande Alice (Rubeli-Courvoisier) B.; m. Beverly Ann George, Dec. 17, 1966; children—Caroline Juliette, Christian Dominique. M.D., U. Geneva, Switzerland, 1955. Ship surgeon Johnson Line, Stockholm, 1956; intern Mt. Auburn Hosp., Cambridge, Mass., 1956-57; research fellow in biochemistry Harvard U., Boston, 1957-59; asst. in medicine Peter Bent Brigham Hosp., Boston, 1957-59; resident in medicine Clinique Therapeutique Universitaire Hosp. Cantonal, Geneva, Switzerland, 1959-61; instr. dept. radiation biology and biophysics U. Rochester, 1961-63; asst. prof. physiology U. Pitts., 1963-70, asso. prof., 1970-75, prof., 1975—; cons. research program Atomic Energy Project, U. Rochester, 1969; program-project con. Div. Research Grants NIH Arthritis and Metabolic Diseases, 1971, 72; research program atomic energy project U. Rochester, 1972; mem. Arthritis and Metabolic Diseases Program Project Com., 1973-77; vis. prof. Med. Faculty U. Geneva, 1976. Contbr. articles to profl. jours. Bd. dirs. Association Pour La Creation D'une Fondation Pour Recherches Medicales, Geneva, 1967-72. Recipient Lederle Med. Faculty award, 1964-67, Prix Andre Lichtwitz Republique Francaise, 1970. Mem. Endocrine Soc., Am. Physiol. Soc., Biophys. Soc., Assn. Des Medecins Assts. (pres. Geneva sect. 1960-61). Home: 900 Delafield Rd Pittsburgh PA 15215-1908

BORMAN, TERRY REED, army officer; b. Irvington, Nebr., June 16, 1949; s. Wallace Lynn and Lorraine A. (Polenz) B.; m. Rebecca Lynn Gloor, Aug. 13, 1971; children: Erik Reed, Katherine Lynn. BS, U. Nebr., 1971, MA, 1972; MA, U. Ala., 1982, PhD, 1984. Commd. 2d lt. U.S. Army, 1971, advanced through grades to lt. col., 1990; ADP officer 3d inf. div. U.S. Army, Fed. Republic of Germany, 1975-78; asst. prof. mil. sci. U. Ala. U.S. Army, Tuscaloosa, 1979-83; systems engr. U.S. Army, Ft. Belvoir, Va., 1983-86; directorate for Operational Plans and Interoperability, Joint Chiefs of Staff, J-7 Pentagon, Washington, 1987-90; dir. U.S. Army Artificial Intelligence Ctr./Pentagon, Washington, 1990-91, chief info. tech. officer, 1991—; asst. prof. U. So. Calif., Washington, 1984—, U. Md., College Park, 1985—. Republican. Roman Catholic. Home: 7604 Chancellor Way Springfield VA 22153-2343

BORNAND, RUTH CHALOUX, antique music box specialist; b. N.Y.C., Oct. 13, 1901; d. Frank and Ruby (Forsyth) Chaloux; m. Adrian V. Bornand (dec.); children: Hilaire Bornand Coy, Elise Bornand Wegener. Student, Woods Bus. Coll., 1920-21. Proprietor Bornand Music Box Co., Pelham, N.Y., 1945—. Organizer Handicapped Children's Group, N.Y.C., 1950-51; mem. ladies guild Ch. of the Redeemer, Pelham, 1947-48. Mem. Musical Box Soc. Internat. (co-founder 1949, corresponding sec., trustee 1978, historian 1959, museum com. 1980—), Order Eastern Star. Republican. Home and Office: Bornand Music Box Co 139 4th Ave Pelham NY 10803-1409

BORNET, STEPHEN FOLWELL, public relations and marketing executive; b. Miami Beach, Fla., Nov. 22, 1947; s. Vaughn Davis and Mary Elizabeth (Winchester) B.; m. Ellen Jean Gribben, June 28, 1980; 1 child, Stephen F. Jr. BA, U. Oreg., 1971; MA, So. Oreg. State Coll., 1972. Account exec. Grey Advt., N.Y.C., 1972; editor pub. relations Abex Corp., N.Y.C., 1973-76; mgr. mktg. communications and spl. sect. editor N.Y. Daily News, N.Y.C., 1976-80; specialist media rels. Texaco Inc., White Plains, N.Y., 1980-84; mgr. media rels. Orange & Rockland Utilities, Pearl River, N.Y., 1985; mgr., editor NYNEX Corp., White Plains, 1985-86; dir. pub. rels. NYNEX Bus. Info. Systems, White Plains, 1986-87, NYNEX Systems Mktg., N.Y.C., 1987-88; staff dir. product devel. NYNEX Svc. Co., White Plains, 1989-90; staff dir. catalogs and communications NYNEX/TRG, N.Y.C., 1990—. Contbr. numerous articles to profl. jours. Re-election campaigner, photographer N.Y. State Sen. Roy M. Goodman, 1980-83;sailing instr. N.Y. Sailing Sch., Network for Learning and Learning Annex, 1979-82. Comdr. USNR, 1967—, Vietnam. Recipient Nat. Def. Svc. medal, 1968, Vietnam Svc. medal, 1968, Expeditionary medal Armed Forces, 1969, Freedom's Found. Honor medal, 1969, Achievement medal U.S. Navy, 1988; named Eagle Scout, Boy Scouts Am. Mem. Pub. Rels. Soc. Am., Internat. Assn. Bus. Communicators (accreditation, v.p. 1972-76, Photo Excellence award 1975, George Washington Freedom's Found. Honor medal 1969), Stuyvesant Yacht Club (commodore 1986-88), N.Y. Athletic Club. Republican. Home: 1874 Pelham Pkwy S 5-P Bronx NY 10461 Office: NYNEX/TRG 441 9th Ave New York NY 10001-1617

BORNMANN, CARL M(ALCOLM), lawyer; b. Somerville, N.J., Aug. 13, 1936; s. John Carl Bornmann and Dorothy Louise (Balliet) Capparelli; m. Billie Wollen, Aug. 24, 1985; children: Carl, Gregory, Melissa. BS, Ohio U., 1958; JD with distinction, Ind. U., 1961; MALS, Columbia U., 1989. Bar: Ind. 1961, N.Y. 1962, U.S. Dist. Ct. (so. and ea. dists.) N.Y. 1962, U.S. Ct. Appeals (2d cir.) 1962, U.S. Supreme Ct. 1965. Assoc. Cahill, Gordon, Reindel & Ohl, N.Y.C., 1961-69; ptnr. Cahill, Gordon & Reindel, N.Y.C., 1970—. Mem. legal del. to USSR, citizen ambassador program People to People Internat., 1990. Mem. ABA (bus. law sect.), N.Y. State Bar Assn., Japan Soc. of N.Y.C., Order of Coif. Home: 7 Lewiston Ct Briarcliff Manor NY 10510-2536

BORNSCHEUER, GEORGE CHARLES, new business development consultant; b. N.Y.C., Feb. 24, 1922; s. Charles F. and Susane Bornscheuer; m. Doris A. Woods, Feb. 3, 1945; children: Doris J., Susan A. BCE cum laude, Poly. Inst. N.Y., 1955. Designer M.W. Kellogg Co., N.Y.C., 1946-48; asst. chief engr. Fellheimer & Wagner, N.Y.C., 1948-57; chief engr. Maiman Assocs., N.Y.C., 1957-58; v.p. Burns and Roe, Washington, 1965-84; dir. sales Dravo, Gibb & Hill, Washington, 1984-86; owner, bus. cons. George C. Bornscheuer Assocs., Washington, 1986—. Pres. Swan Point (Md.) Civic Assn., 1989—. With USNR, 1942-45. Mem. Am. Nuclear Soc., NSPE, Am. Mgmt. Assn., Soc. Am. Mil. Engrs., Washington Soc. Engrs., Bethesda Country Club, Internat. Club Washington, Swan Point Yacht and Country Club, Sigma Xi, Tau Beta Pi, Chi Epsilon. Home and Office: George C Bornscheuer Assocs 204 Locust Ct Issue MD 20645-9779

BORNSTEIN, ARNOLD FREDRICK, railroad advertising executive; b. Camden, N.J., Feb. 4, 1953; s. David and Thea (Berney) B.; m. Bonnie Jean Leak, June 22, 1986. BA in Communications, Glassboro State Coll., 1977. Dir. mktg. communications Consol. Rail Corp., Phila. Mem. Assn. R.R. Advt. and Mktg. Office: Consol Rail Corp 6 Penn Plz Philadelphia PA 19103

BORNSTEIN, LINDA UPHAM, company official, educational administrator; b. Boston, June 27, 1952; d. Horace Emerald and Betty Hope(Lawrence) Upham; m. Peter Hartwell Bornstein, Aug. 7, 1976; children: Alison Lawrence, Christopher Alexander. BA, U. Mass., Boston, 1977. Research asst. U. Mass., 1975-77; sec. Prog. of Applied Sci., Coll. William and Mary, Williamsburg, Va., 1978-80; lectr. Weight Watchers of N.H., Nashua, 1983-89; bookkeeper Bergeron, Hanson & Bornstein, Berlin, N.H., 1987—; ednl. advocate Parent Info. Ctr., Concord, N.H., 1985—; surrogate parent State of N.H., Dept. Edn., Concord, 1986—; learning resource coordinator Sch. for Lifelong Learning, Berlin, N.H., 1988—. Incorporator No. N.H. Found., 1986—; bd. dirs. Androscoggin Valley Hosp., Berlin, 1986-88; auditor Milan Meth. Ch., 1986—; chmn. Androscoggin Valley Hosp. Gov. Golf Tournament, 1989—; mem. adv. com. to Sch. Bd., Berlin, 1988—; mem. adv. bd. Salvation Army, 1990—. Mem. AAUW, Androscoggin Valley Hosp. Aux. (pres. 1986-88). Republican. Methodist. Office: Bergeron Hanson & Bornstein 110 Pleasant St Berlin NH 03570-2086

BORNSTEIN, ROBERT JOSEPH, hospital administrator; b. Rockaway Beach, N.Y., Nov. 11, 1937; s. Joseph I. and Marjorie (Hogan) B.; m. Ingrid F.; 1 child, Debra E. BA, Adelphi U., 1959; MPA, NYU, 1972; PhD, Columbia Pacific U., 1980; postgrad. in law, Touro Coll., 1987. Assoc. dir. Goldwater Meml. Hosp., Roosevelt Island, N.Y., 1970-73; adminstr. Massapequa Gen. Hosp., Seaford, N.Y., 1973-74, Lydia E. Hall Hosp., Freeport, N.Y., 1974-76, Cen. Gen. Hosp., Plainview, N.Y., 1977—; preceptor hosp. adminstrn. program U. Buffalo and Ithaca Coll., C.W. Post Coll., SUNY, Stony Brook, NYU, Hofstra U., 1979—; prof., preceptor St. Joseph's Coll., Patchogue, N.Y., 1978-83. Contbr. articles to profl. jours. Chmn. bd. Am. Cancer Soc., 1979—; mem. Community Planning Bd., Queens, N.Y., 1973-76; vice chmn. Comprehensive Health Planning Agy., 1974-76; bd. mgrs. Blue Ridge Condominiums/Coventry Home Owners Assn., 1977-85; mediator Community Mediation Ctr., 1982—; cons. Ret. Police Assn. of N.Y. With U.S. Army, 1959-65. Recipient Outstanding Community Svc. award United Fund, 1968. Fellow Am. Acad. Med. Adminstrs., N.Y. Acad. Scis., Am. Coll. Health Care Execs.; mem. Assn. Mental Health Adminstrs., Am. Hosp. Assn., N.Y. State Pub. Health Assn., Mensa. Office: 888 Old Country Rd Plainview NY 11803-4978

BORNSTEIN, STEVEN M., broadcast executive; b. Fair Lawn, N.J., Apr. 20, 1952; m. Sharon Bornstein; children: Cori, Alanna, Carly. BS, U. Wis., 1974. Mgr. program coordination ESPN, Inc., Bristol, Conn., 1980-81, dir. program planning and qcauisitions, 1981, dir. programming, 1981-83, v.p. programming, 1983-85, sr. v.p. programming and prdn., 1985-88, exec. v.p. programming and prodn., 1988-90, pres., CEO, 1990—, also bd. dirs. Mem. Nat. Acad. Cable Programming (bd. govs.), European Sports Network (dir. Lafayette Beveer bd.), Cable TV Advt. Bur. Office: ESPN Inc 1 Espn Plz Bristol CT 06010-7454

BORO, STEPHEN ANDREW, college program director; b. N.Y.C., June 14, 1966; s. Michael Joel and Miriam (Eckstein) B.; m. Alisa Pomerantz, June 17, 1990. Student, Hebrew U., Israel, 1983-84; BA, SUNY, Albany,

1987; postgrad., Baruch Coll., San Diego State U. Waterfront dir. Hartman YM-YWHA, Far Rockaway, N.Y., 1987; asst. to registrar Jewish Theol. Sem., N.Y.C., 1987-89, asst. to dir. fin. aid, 1989-90, asst. dir. student fin. aid, 1990—. Field worker United Synagogue Youth, 1985-87. Mem. N.Y. State Fin. Aid Adminstrs. Assn. (spl. award 1988), Am. Assn. Coll. Registrars and Admissions Officers, Tau Epsilon Phi. Home: 7812 Winflight Ct San Diego CA 92119

BORO, WILLIAM JEFFREY, chiropractor; b. Annapolis, Md., Sept. 11, 1948; s. Alex L. and Ruth (Weinstein) B.; m. Helen C. Villanueva, Nov. 10, 1985; children: Sam, Deborah. BA, Brandeis U., 1970; MAT, Wesleyan U., 1971; D of Chiropracty, Logan Chiropractic Coll., 1983. Rsch. asst. The Population Coun., N.Y.C., 1971-72; tchr. N.Y.C. (N.Y.) Bd. Edn., 1972-76, New South Wales Bd. Edn., Sydney, Australia, 1976-78; chiropractor Chiropractic Ctr. of Annapolis, Md., 1983—; pres. Entrepreneur's Exchange, Annapolis, 1989—; chmn. bd. The Annapolis (Md.) Holistic Health Ctr., 1990—. Editor: Cranial Adjusting Compendium, 1983. Mem. Nat. Safety Coun., N.Y. Acad. Scis., Internat. Oceanographic Found., Nat. Wildlife Assn. Office: Chiropractic Ctr Annapolis 49 Old Solomons Island Rd Annapolis MD 21401-3820

BOROSON, FLORENCE, university ombudsperson; b. N.Y.C., May 27, 1927; d. Irving and Lillian (Markowitz) Rothman; m. Louis Nathan Boroson, June 22, 1958; children: Martin Andrew, Barbara Lee. BA, Bklyn. Coll., 1948. Cert. social sci. rsch. technician. Ins. broker, ptnr. Bros. Ins. Brokerage Co., N.Y.C., 1954-62; asst. to dir. libs. SUNY, Stony Brook, 1974-78, asst. dean Coll. Arts and Scis., 1978-90, campus community advocate (univ. ombudsperson), 1990—. Mem. Univ. and Coll. Ombudsmen Assn., NOW. Home: 26 Parsons Dr Stony Brook NY 11790-2615 Office: SUNY Rm 115 Humanities Stony Brook NY 11794-5336

BOROWIEC, STANLEY PAUL, chemical company executive; b. Bklyn., Feb. 2, 1955; s. Paul and Ann Theresa (Arcndarczyk) B.; m. Ann Dully, Sept. 26, 1987. BS in Chem. Engring., Columbia U., 1976, MS in Chem. Engring., 1977; MBA, Harvard U., 1985. Engr. Exxon Chem., Florham Park, N.J., 1977-80; process engr. Esso Chemie BV, Rotterdam, The Netherlands, 1980-82; sr. engr. Exxon Chem., Florham Park, 1982-83; planning mgr. Airco Indsl. Gases, Murray Hill, N.J., 1985-86; mgr. fin. Airco PSA, Murray Hill, 1986-88; dir. fin. Airco Carbon Dioxide, Murray Hill, 1988-92; dir. mktg. svcs. Airco Bulk Gases, New Providence, N.J., 1992—. Bus. mgr. N.Y. Ridgemen Drum & Bugle Corps, Bklyn., 1976-78; mem. Poles Organized to Minister to Our Citizens, Bklyn., 1979-80. Mem. ACS, Am. Inst. Chem. Engrs. Roman Catholic. Home: 642 Forest Ave Westfield NJ 07090-4321 Office: Airco Gases 575 Mountain Ave New Providence NJ 07974-2002

BOROWITZ, IRVING JULIUS, chemistry educator, researcher; b. Bklyn., May 15, 1930; s. Simon Meyer and Sonia Shifra (Pollack) B.; m. Grace Burchman, Nov. 26, 1959; children: Susan Debra, Lisa Noami. BS cum laude, CCNY, 1951; MA, Ind. U., 1952; PhD, Columbia U., 1956; postgrad., Yale U., 1957-58. Instr. chemistry CCNY, 1960-62; asst. prof. Lehigh U., Bethlehem, Pa., 1962-65, assoc. prof., 1965-66; rsch. assoc. Allied Chem. Corp., Morristown, N.J., 1978-80; assoc. prof., prof. Yeshiva U. Belfer Grad. Sch., N.Y.C., 1966-78, vis. prof., prof., 1981—; prof. Columbia U., N.Y.C., summers 1980—; hon. rsch. scientist Ramapo Coll. N.J., Mahwah, 1978—; acad. guest Swiss Fed. Inst. Tech., Zurich, summer 1972. Contbr. over 50 articles on organophosphorus chem. synthesis and ionophores to sci. jours., chpt. to book. Active Temple Emeth, Teaneck, N.J. Rsch. grantee NSF, NIH, Air Force Office Sci. Rsch., Am. Chem. Soc., N.Y.C. Health Rsch. Coun., Sigma Xi, 1962-78. Mem. AAUP, Am. Chem. Soc. (econ. status com. 1973-74, bd. dirs.-at-large N.Y. chpt. 1991, continuing edn. com. 1983—, bd. dirs. Hudson-Bergen chpt. 1980, 84, 86-90), N.Y. Acad. Scis., Phi Beta Kappa, Sigma Xi. Democrat. Home: 912 E Lawn Dr Teaneck NJ 07666-6607 Office: Yeshiva U-Yeshiva Coll 500 W 185th St New York NY 10033-3201

BOROWITZ, SIDNEY, retired physics educator; b. N.Y.C., June 12, 1918; s. Morris and Rose (Cohen) B.; m. Ruth Aaron Meyer, June 20, 1943; children: Michael, Elizabeth. BS, CCNY, 1937; MS, NYU, 1941, PhD, 1948. Instr. NYU, N.Y.C., 1946-48, asst. prof., 1950-55, assoc. prof., 1955-59, prof. physics, 1959-84, prof. emeritus, 1984—, dean, 1969-71, chancellor, 1971-77; instr. Harvard U., Cambridge, Mass., 1948-50; chief exec. officer Cistron Biotech., Pine Brook, N.J., 1981-84; chmn. bd. dirs. Aesculapius Internat. Medicine, N.Y.C., 1987-90, Inst. for Sch. of the Future, N.Y.C., 1987—; cons. NYU, 1987—; exec. dir. N.Y. Acad. Scis., N.Y.C., 1977-81. Author: Fundamentals of Quantum Mechanics, 1967; co-author: Essentials of Physics, 1966, A Contemporary View of Elementary Physics, 1968. Home: 70 E 10th St New York NY 10003-5102 Office: NYU Washington Sq N New York NY 10003-6635

BOROWSKA, ZOFIA KURYLO, biochemist, biophysicist, educator; b. Lublin, Poland, May 13, 1928; came to U.S., 1961; d. Jozef and Ludwika (Gdulewicz) Kurylo; m. Edward Borowski, Sept. 14, 1952 (div. 1966); m. Edward Rzucidlo, Sept. 4, 1977 (dec. 1990). BA, Sch. of Music, Lublin, 1945; BS in Chem. Engring., Polite U., Gdansk, Poland, 1950; DSc in Biochemistry, Polite U., 1958; MS in Chemistry, U. Gdansk, Poland, 1950. Asst. prof. Inst. Marine and Tropical Medicine, Gdansk, 1958-61; guest investigator Inst. Microbiology Rutgers U., New Brunswick, N.J., 1961; rsch. assoc McArdle Inst., Madison, Wis., 1961; rsch. assoc Rockefeller U., N.Y.C., 1962-1967, asst. prof., 1967-72, assoc. prof., 1972-82, sr. rsch. asst., 1982-88, adj. faculty, 1988—; dir. adv. com. Alfred Jurzykowski Found., N.Y.C., 1971-78. Contbr. articles to sci. publs. Mem. Am. Soc. Biol. Chemists, Polish-Am. Inst. of Arts and Scis. (bd. dirs. 1966-72). Office: Rockefeller U 1230 York Ave New York NY 10021-6341

BOROWSKY, RICHARD LEWIS, biology educator; b. N.Y.C., Oct. 21, 1943; s. Nathan and Miriam Edith (Pector) B.; m. Betty Marian Edelstein, June 3, 1965; children: Stewart, Benjamin. BA, Queens Coll., 1964; MPh, Yale U., 1967, PhD, 1969. Asst. prof. NYU, N.Y.C., 1970-76, assoc. prof., 1976—. Co-author: Genetics of Fishes; contbr. articles to profl. jours.; U.S. patents for variable optical density contact lens sunglasses. NSF grantee, 1974-78. Office: NYU Washington Sq N New York NY 10003-6635

BORRELL, PAUL NICHOLAS, sales executive; b. Hoboken, N.J., Apr. 17, 1949; s. Samuel Vincent and Dorothy Diane (Watt) B.; m. Linda Marie DiAnthony, Dec. 6, 1975; children: Vanessa Marie, Jessica Lin. AB in Econs., Muhlenberg Coll., 1971. Enforcement officer Pa. Liquor Control Bd., Pitts., 1971-73; sales rep. PVO Internat., St. Louis, 1973-80, Meer Corp., North Bergen, N.J., 1980-85, Fallek Chem., Ft. Lee, N.J., 1985-86; mgr. regional sales Takeda USA, Inc., Orangeburg, N.Y., 1986—. Parish confirmation tchr. Roman Cath. Ch. Mem. N.J. Pharm. Discussion Group, Sales Assocs. Am. Chem. Industry. Democrat. Roman Catholic. Home: 16 Perera Ave Wayne NJ 07470-4330 Office: Takeda USA 8 Corporate Dr Orangeburg NY 10962-2614

BORRELLI, NICHOLAS FRANCIS, physicist; b. Phila., Nov. 30, 1936; s. Rocco Nicholas and Sara (Bitto) B.; m. Nancy Joan Arnold, Sept. 10, 1960 (dec. 1986); children: Barbara, Stephen, Matthew; m. Kaye Newbury, Apr. 22, 1989. B.S., Villanova U., 1958; M.S., U. Rochester, 1960, Ph.D., 1963. With Corning, Inc., N.Y., 1962—; spl. lectr. in math. Elmira Coll., N.Y., 1970—, Corning Community Coll., 1976—. Contbr. articles to profl. jours. Patentee in field. Recipient Disting. Alumni award U. Rochester, 1985, rsch. fellow, 1992. Mem. Am. Chem. Soc. (Sullivan award 1990), Soc. Phto-optical Instrumentation Engrs., Sigma Xi. Home: 935 W Water St Elmira NY 14905-2316 Office: Corning Glass Works Rsch and Devel Lab Sullivan Pk Corning NY 14831

BORRUS, AMY S., correspondent; b. New Brunswick, N.J., Nov. 7, 1956; d. Jack and Adele R. (Margolis) B.; m. Richard M. Miller, June 16, 1991. BA in English and History, U. Pa., 1978; MSc in Econs., London Sch. of Econs., 1983. Fin. reporter Commodity News Svc. Inc. (Knight-Ridder), N.Y.C., 1979-80; corr. Bus. Week, Phila., 1981; freelance corr. Bus. Week, Boston, 1981-82, London, 1983-86, Tokyo, 1986-90, Washington, 1990—. Office: Bus Week 1120 Vermont Ave NW # 1200 Washington DC 20005-3533

BORRUS, JACK, lawyer; b. N.Y.C., Aug. 8, 1928; s. David Samuel and Mary (Kessler) B.; m. Adele R. Margolis, Sept. 6, 1953; children: Amy Sue. Janet Lee, David Neil. BS cum laude, Columbia U., 1950, JD, 1953; LLM in Fed. Taxation, NYU, 1954. Bar: N.Y. 1954, N.J. 1956, U.S. Tax Ct. 1969, U.S. Supreme Ct. 1978. Law clk. to Judge Edward Gaulkin Newark, 1956-57; assoc. Toolan, Haney and Romond, Perth Amboy, N.J., 1957-59; sole practice New Brunswick, N.J., 1959-62; sr. ptnr. Borrus & Goldin (name later changed to Borrus, Goldin & Foley), New Brunswick, 1962-65, '65—, 1965-85; asst. prosecutor Middlesex County, N.J., 1965-67; sr. ptnr., pres. Borrus, Goldin, Foley, Vignuolo, Hyman & Stahl, P.C., North Brunswick, N.J., 1985—; of counsel North Brunswick Bd. Edn., 1969-87, Middlesex County, Bd. Edn. and Tech. High Schs., E. Brunswick, 1973—, Middlesex County Ednl. Svc. Commn., 1979—, Matuchen (N.J.) Bd. Edn., 1979-88, Highland Pk. (N.J.) Bd. Edn., 1981-89, Milltown Bd. Edn., Branchburg Bd. Edn., 1986-91, gen. counsel Ins. Brokers Assn., N.J., 1979-83, spl. counsel to Franklin Twp., 1965-67, to Gen. Assembly of N.J., 1975-77; N.J. Corp. Law Rev. Commn., 1979-90; co-chmn. 1979-80, and others. Served with U.S. Army, 1954-56. Mem. ABA, N.J. Bar Assn. (panel mem. corp. law sect. 1985, judicial and prosecutor's appointments com. 1985-91), Middlesex County Bar Assn. (trustee 1963), Trial Lawyers Assn. N.J., MIddlesex County Trial Lawyers Assn. (trustee 1966), N. J. Sch. Bd. Attys. Assn., High Point Tennis Club, Harvey Cedars, N.J., (pres. 1972-79). Club: High Point Tennis (Harvey Cedars, N.J.) (pres. 1972-79). Home: 41 Constitution Hl Princeton NJ 08540-6739 Office: Borrus Goldin Foley Vignuolo Hyman & Stahl PC 2875 US 1 North Brunswick NJ 08902

BORSKI, ROBERT ANTHONY, congressman; b. Phila., Oct. 20, 1948; s. Robert Anthony and Rita (Savage) B.; children: Jill Michele, Dorothy Lynn, Jennifer Marie, Robert A. III. B.A., U. Balt., 1971. Floor mgr. Raymond James & Assoc., Phila., 1971-77; mem. Pa. Ho. of Reps., 1977-82, 98th-101st Congresses from Pa., 1983—. Democrat. Roman Catholic. Office: Cannon House Office Bldg Rm 407 Washington DC 20515

BORTOLAN, PETER ROGER, legal administrator; b. New Haven, Nov. 26, 1937; s. Napoleon Caesar and Josephine Louise (Seretny) B.; m. Ruth Anne Hallowell, Dec. 29, 1962; children: Cynthia Marie, Eleanor Nancy, Andrea Ruth. BS, Providence Coll., 1960; MBA, U. Conn., 1963. Various acctg. and data processing mgmt. positions Conn., 1962-72; sec., treas. O'Neal & Prelle, Hartford, Conn., 1972-80; adminstr. Schatz & Schatz, Ribicoff & Kotkin, Hartford, 1980-88; exec. dir. Bacon Wilson, P.C., Springfield, Mass., 1988—. Mem. Dem. Town Com., South Windsor, Conn., 1982-83; chmn. South Windsor Econ. Devel. Commn., 1983-88. 1st lt. USAF, 1962-65. Mem. ABA, Assn. Legal Adminstrs. (charter mem. Nutmeg Chpt.). Roman Catholic. Office: Bacon Wilson PC 95 State St Springfield MA 01103-2005

BORTS, GEORGE HERBERT, economist, educator; b. N.Y.C., Aug. 29, 1927; s. Elias Alexander and Etta (Silberg) B.; m. Muriel Levenson, Dec. 26, 1948; children: David, Richard, Robert. AB, Columbia U., 1947; AM, U. Chgo., 1949, PhD, 1953; AM (hon.), Brown U., 1957. Prof. econs. Brown U., Providence, 1960—. Mng. editor Am. Econ. Rev., Nashville, 1968-80, World Bus. Adv., Providence, 1990-91; co-author: Economic Growth in a Free Market, 1964. Mem. Am. Econ. Assn., Econometric Soc., Phi Beta Kappa. Home: 220 Slater Ave Providence RI 02906-3440 Office: Brown U 64 Waterman St Providence RI 02912-0001

BORTZ, DONALD RICHARD, education educator; b. Bethlehem, Pa., Mar. 24, 1935; s. Elmer Eugene and Alvina Marion (Pursell) B.; m. Dolores Barbara Polack, Dec. 31, 1955; children: Curt Lee, Kevin Eugene. BA, Moravian Coll., 1957; MEd, Lehigh U., 1960, EdD, 1969. Cert. elem., secondary tchr., Pa.; cert. prin., supt., Pa. Tchr. Bethlehem Area Sch. Dist., 1958-62; prin. Nazareth (Pa.) Area Sch. Sch., 1962-66; prof. East Stroudsburg (Pa.) U., 1966-76, dir., cons. Ednl. Devel. Ctr., 1976-87, prof., dir. Ctr. for Sch. Svcs., 1987—; cons., Nazareth, Pa., 1987—. Pres. adminstrv. bd. Fritz Meml. Ch., Bethlehem, 1965—. Recipient Merit Svc. award Pa. Higher Edn., 1979; named Young Man of Yr. Nazareth Jaycees, 1964. Mem. ASCD, Assn. for Profs. of State Colls. and Univs. Faculty (social chairperson 1985—). Methodist. Home: 95 El Reno Ave Nazareth PA 18064-1706 Office: East Stroudsburg U Dept Edn East Stroudsburg PA 18301

BORUN, VICTOR MAREK, finance educator; b. Warsaw, Poland, Apr. 8, 1943; came to U.S., 1970; s. Jozef and Helena (Miecznik) B.; m. Nelly Kramaric, Dec. 17, 1977; 1 child, Eric. MS, Cen. Sch. Planning and Stats., Warsaw, 1967; MPh, NYU, 1979, PhD in Bus., 1984. Cert. coll. tchr., Warsaw. Advisor Planning Com. Coun. and Mins., Warsaw, 1967-70; acctg. supr. Belgian Line, N.Y.C., 1972-74; teaching and rsch. asst. NYU, N.Y.C., 1974-78; fin. analyst Nat. Econ. Rsch. Assn., N.Y.C., 1978-80; assoc. prof. fin. Fordham U. Grad. Sch. Bus. Adminstrn., N.Y.C., 1980—, area chmn., 1985—; cons. Swiss Bank Corp., N.Y.C., 1986-89, Mfrs. Hanover Trust, N.Y.C., 1987—, NatWest U.S.A., N.Y.C., 1988—, Merrill Lynch, N.Y.C., 1976-77; advisor Ministry Ownership Changes, Warsaw, 1990—. Contbr. articles to profl. jours. Evaluator State N.Y. Bd. Regents, Albany, 1988—; adv. bd. Polish Nat. Fund, N.Y.C., 1990—. Fellow NYU, 1974-79. Mem. Am. Fin. Assn., Am. Stat. Assn. Fin. Mgmt. Assn., Beta Gamma Sigma. Roman Catholic. Office: Fordham U Grad Sch Bus 113 W 60th St New York NY 10023-7404

BORWICK, RICHARD, management consultant; b. Elmira, N.Y., Aug. 15, 1908; s. Abram and Phyllis (Gould) B.; m. Lillian Fine, June 22, 1938; 1 child: Anthony Stephen. AB in Classics and Philosophy with honors, Harvard U., 1929. Reporter Brockton Mass. Enterprise, 1928-30; researcher current history N.Y. Times, N.Y.C., 1932; analyst Fairchild Publs., N.Y.C., 1933; sales promotion Quality Group Mags., N.Y.C., 1933; fin. reporter Washington (D.C.) Herald, Washington Times Herald, 1934-42; pub. exec. Phila. Record, 1943; co-founder Newmyer Assocs. Inc., Washington, 1944—, v.p., 1959-83; cons. in oil industry, ins., electric mfg., telephone communications, industries., 1983—. Speech writer, policy adviser Presdl. Candidates Sen. Estes Kefauver, Washington, 1952, Sen. Henry Jackson, Washington, 1960-82. Mem. Nat. Press Club, Harvard Grad. Soc. (chmn. 1983-85). Clubs: International (Washington); Harvard (N.Y.C.). Home: 3301 O St NW Washington DC 20007-2814 Office: Newmyer Assocs 1220 L St NW Washington DC 20005-4018

BORYS, THEODOR JAMES, state agency data administrator; b. Buffalo, N.Y., June 17, 1954; s. Svyatoslav and Lorenza Natalie (Bertolino) B.; m. Melissa Joy Ares, June 12, 1976; children: Tasha Rose, Leda Marie. BA in Math., SUNY, Albany, 1976, MS in Computer Sci., 1977. Computer programmer N.Y. State Dept. of Tax & Fin., Albany, 1976; programmer/analyst SUNY, Albany, 1976-78; data base adminstr. N.Y. State Dept. Mental Hygiene, Albany, 1978-81; software engr. Gen. Elec., Schenectady, N.Y., 1981; dir. tech. svcs. N.Y. State Office Mental Health, Albany, 1981-82, dir. systems devel., 1982-84, data adminstr., 1984—; lectr. SUNY, Albany, 1978—. Mem. Assn for Computing Machinery, IDMS User Assn. (guest speaker 1989 annual conf., N.Y.C., Seattle, 1990). Republican. Home: 125 Poplar Dr Delmar NY 12054-2224 Office: State Office Mental Health 44 Holland Ave Albany NY 12229-0001

BOSACK, THEODORE NICHOLAS, psychology educator; b. Wilkes-Barre, Pa., Dec. 19, 1940; s. John and Tillie (Krasnavage) B.; m. Sharon Ann O'Donnell, Aug. 1, 1965 (dec. Feb. 1985); children: Sean, Seth; m. Jeanne Marie Schwager, Aug. 11, 1990. AB, Brown U., 1962, SCM, 1965, PhD, 1967; MsC, U. Conn., 1962-63. Prof. psychology Providence Coll., 1967—, chmn. dept., 1982—; mem. Providence Coll. Corp., 1990—. Mem. AAUP (pres. Providence Coll. chpt. 1991-92), APA, Am. Psychol. Soc., New Eng. Psychol. Assn., Ea. Psychol. Assn., Coun. Undergrad. Psychology Programs (chmn. 1989-90, 92-93, steering com. 1987—), Sigma Xi (assoc.). Office: Providence Coll Dept of Psychology Providence RI 02918

BOSCO, ANTHONY GERARD, bishop; b. New Castle, Pa., Aug. 1, 1927; s. Joseph M. and Theresa (Pezone) B. BA, St. Vincent Sem., Latrobe, Pa.; juris canonici licentiatus, Lateran U., Rome; LLD (hon.), Duquesne U., 1971; LHD (hon.), St.Vincent Coll., 1988. Ordained priest Roman Cath. Ch., 1952. Asst. chancellor Diocese of Pitts., 1955-65, vice chancellor, 1965-67, chancellor, 1967-85, aux. bishop, 1970-87; bishop Diocese of Greensburg, Pa., 1987—; chmn. Communications Found., 1984—, U.S. Cath. Conf. Communications Com., 1990—; hon. chmn., bd. trustees Seton Hill Coll., Greensburg, 1987—; ex officio mem., chmn. bd. regents St. Vincent Sem., Latrobe, Pa., 1987—. Recipient Leonardo Da Vinci award for Religion Order of Italian Sons and Daughter, 1970; named Pitts.'s Man of Yr. in Religion Pitts. Jaycees, 1975. Mem. Nat. Conf. of Catholic Bishops (communications com. 1985-88, 90), Christian Assocs. of Southwest Pa., Christian Housing Inc. (sec.-treas.).

BOSCO, PHILIP MICHAEL, actor; b. Jersey City, Sept. 26, 1930; s. Philip Lupo and Margaret Raymond (Thek) B.; m. Nancy Ann Dunkle, Jan. 2, 1957; children: Diane, Philip, Christopher, Jennifer, Lisa, Celia, John. B.A. in drama, Catholic U. Am., 1957. Roles include Brian O'Bannion in Auntie Mame, City Ctr., N.Y.C., 1958; Angelo in Measure for Measure, Belvedere Lake Amphitheatre, N.Y.C., 1960; Heracles in The Rape of the Belt, 1960; Will Danaher in Donnybrook, 1961; Hawkshaw in The Ticket-of-Leave Man, 1961; King Henry in Henry IV Part 1, Shakespeare Festival, Stratford, Conn., 1962; Kent in King Lear; Rufio in Antony and Cleopatra; Pistol in Henry V; Aegeon in Comedy of Errors, 1963; Benedick in Much Ado About Nothing; Claudius in Hamlet, 1964; title role in Coriolanus, 1965; Lovewit in The Alchemist, Lincoln Ctr. Repertory Theatre, 1966; Jack in The East Wind, 1967; appeared in Galileo, 1967, Saint Joan, 1968, Amphytrion in 3 Zones, Tiger at the Gates, 1968, Cyrano de Bergerac, 1968, Camino Real, 1970, Operation Sidewinder, 1970, The Playboy of the Western World, 1971, An Enemy of the People, 1971, Antigone, 1971, Mary Stuart, 1971, Narrow Road to the Deep North, 1972, Twelfth Night, 1972, The Crucible, 1972, Enemies, 1972, The Plough and the Stars, 1973, The Merchant of Venice, 1973, A Streetcar Named Desire, 1973, Mrs. Warren's Profession, 1976, Man and Superman, 1978, Whose Life Is It Anyway?, 1979, A Month in the Country, 1979, Major Barbara, 1980, Inadmissable Evidence, 1981, Hedda Gabler, 1982, Ah! Wilderness, 1983, Misalliance, 1983, Come Back, Little Sheba, 1984, Eminent Domain, 1984, Caine Mutiny, 1984, Be Happy For Me, Masterclass, 1986, You Never Can Tell, 1986, A Man for All Seasons, 1986, The Devil's Disciple, 1988, (on Broadway) Lend Me A Tenor, 1989 (Antoinette Perry award, 1989), The Miser, 1990, Breaking Legs, 1991; films including Requiem for a Heavyweight, A Lovely Way to Die, The Pope of Greenwich Village, Walls of Glass, Heaven Help Us, The Money Pit, Children of a Lesser God, 1986, Suspect, 1987, Three Men and a Baby, 1987, The Luckiest Man in the World, 1988, Working Girl, 1988, Dream Team, 1988, Blue Steel, Quick Change, FX-2, 1990, True Colors, 1990, Straight Talk, 1991; TV Shows including The Prisoner of Zenda, The Nurses, O'Brien, Hawk, The Net Play of the Month; TV spl. for PBS Grandpa and the Globetrotters, 1987, Echoes in the Darkness, Internal Affairs, 1988, Murder in Black and White, 1989, Return of Eliot Ness, 1991. Served with U.S. Army, 1951-54. Recipient Critic's Circle award N.Y. Drama Critics, 1960-61; recipient Clarence Derwent award, 1966-67, Tony award nominations, 1961, 84, 87, OBIE award, 1987, Emmy award, 1988, Tony award, Drama Desk award, Outer Critic's Circle award all for best leading actor, 1988-89. Mem. Actor's Equity Assn., Screen Actor's Guild, AFTRA. Roman Catholic. Office: Select Artists 337 W 43d St New York NY 10036

BOSCOE, CLAUDIA FRANCES, office machine company executive; b. Chgo., Aug. 3, 1948; d. Leland Orville and Marie (Swakow) Stromquist; m. John J. Boscoe, Apr. 17, 1983. Paralegal cert., Pa. State U., 1992. Cert. flight attendant. Sec. The Selz Orgn., Chgo., 1966-68; flight attendant Republic Air Lines, Mpls., 1969-84; pres. Concepts Unltd., Inc., Chester Heights, Pa., 1988—. Co-chairperson Libr. Fundraising Campaign, Concord Twp., 1987-88; chairperson Dedication Com. Twp. and Libr. Bldgs., Concord Twp., 1989; bd. dirs. Fox Valley Community Assn., Glen Mills, Pa., 1985-86, pres., 1987; bd. dirs. Delaware County S.P.C.A., 1991—; minority insp. Dem. Party Delaware County, Concord Twp., 1989—. Mem. 2d Edit. Cub (pres. 1988-89), Welcome Wagon Club (pres. 1986-87). Roman Catholic.

BOSCOE, RICHARD WILLIAM, veterinarian; b. Phila., Dec. 19, 1950; s. William Frank and Joanne (McKinley) B. BS, Pa. State U., 1972; VMD, U. Pa., 1976. Lic. veterinarian, Pa. Vet. med. officer Animal and Plant Health Inspection Svc., USDA, Lafayette Hill, Pa., 1976-91; rsch. assoc. Fla. State Collection Arthropods. Mem. Nat. Assn. Fed. Veterinarians, Lepidopterists Soc., Lepidoptera Rsch. Found., So. Lepidopterists Soc., Assn. for Tropical Lepidoptera, Xerces Soc., Nature Conservancy. Home and Office: 150 Ridge Pike Apt 101A Lafayette Hill PA 19444-1906

BOSE, PRADIP, computer science researcher, consultant, educator; b. Calcutta, India, Aug. 26, 1955; came to U.S., 1977; s. Harsha Narayan and Reba (Guha) B.; m. Sharmila Ghosh, Dec. 14, 1983 (dec. April 1989); 1 child, Ranjini; m. Sharmila Chakravarty, March 9, 1991. B of Tech. in Electronics and Elec. Communication Engring. with honors, Indian Inst. of Tech., Kharagpur, 1977; MS in Elec. and Computer Engring., U. Ill., 1981, PhD in Elec. and Computer Engring., 1983. Teaching asst. dept. of elec. engring. U. Ill., 1977-79, rsch. asst. coordinated sch. lab., 1979-83; rsch. staff mem. IBM Thomas J. Watson Rsch. Ctr., Yorktown Heights, N.Y., 1983—; adj. assoc. prof. Queens Coll. CUNY, N.Y.C., 1991—, dept. of computer sci. NYU, 1991; pres./chief tech. cons. Bosetek Computer Rsch., Inc., Yorktown Heights, 1992—. Author: Programming Languages and Data Structures, 1992; contbr. tech. papers to jours. and confs. Recipient Govt. of India Nat. scholarship, 1972, Nat. Sci. Talent Search scholarship, Govt. of India, 1972, IIT Silver medal Indian Inst. of Tech., 1977. Mem. IEEE. Home: 50 Page Ct Yorktown Heights NY 10598 Office: IBM Thomas Watson Rsch Ctr Yorktown Heights NY 10598

BOSHKOV, STEFAN ROBERT, lawyer; b. White Plains, N.Y., Nov. 3, 1949; s. Stefan H. and Bianca Gloria (Amaducci) B.; m. Barbara Louise Jetton, Aug. 8, 1975; children: Stefan Alexander, Anna Caroline. BA, Columbia U., 1971, JD, 1975; LLM in Tax, NYU, 1981. Bar: N.Y. 1976. Assoc. Debevoise & Plimpton, N.Y.C., 1976-78, Olwine Connelly Chase O'Donnell & Weyher, N.Y.C., 1978-81; from. assoc. to ptnr. Reavis & McGrath, N.Y.C., 1981-87; ptnr. Anderson Kill Olick & Oshinsky, P.C., N.Y.C., 1987—; panelist tax seminar Inst. for Internat. Rsch., N.Y.C., 1991. Contbr. articles to profl. jours. Mem. ABA, N.Y. State Bar Assn. Home: 473 W End Ave # 2B New York NY 10024 Office: Anderson Kill Olick & Oshinsky 666 3d Ave New York NY 10017

BOSKELLO, DENNIS JON, educator; b. Greenwich, Conn., June 10, 1953; s. Anthony Joseph and Irene Florence (Chiappetta) B.; m. Margo Lynn Godlewski, Dec. 18, 1976; 1 child, David Jon. BS in Elem. Edn., Western Conn. State U., 1975; MA in Edn. Media, Fairfield (Conn.) U., 1980, cert. of advanced study in adminstrn. and supervision, 1987. Cert. supervision and adminstrn., elem. and secondary tchr, mentor tchr., Conn. Tchr. Fairfield (Conn.) Pub. Schs., 1975—, coord. bldg. computer edn., 1987—; mem. steering com. project SMARTNET, 1990—; tchr. assessor, mentor and cooperating tchr. State of Conn., 1990—; mem. project LEAD adminstrv. aspirant program, 1991-92. Mem. Barnum Festival com., Bridgeport, 1975, 82, Spirit of Discovery com., Discovery Mus., Bridgeport, 1992; v.p. Calvin United Brotherhood, Fairfield, 1982-86, 88-90, sec., 1988; bldg. coord. 350th anniversary celebration for Stratfield Sch.; bd. dirs. nursery sch. 1st Presbyn. Ch., Fairfield. Grantee GE, 1984, 85. Mem. NEA, Conn. Edn. Assn. (dist. and bldg. profl. devel. com. 1989—), Fairfield Edn. Assn. (chmn. fin. com. 1981-85, exec. bd. 1981-85), Dist. Computer Edn. Com. Office: Fairfield Pub Schs Stillson Rd Fairfield CT 06430-3212

BOSSERT, EDYTHE HOY, educator; b. Jacksonville, Pa., July 18, 1908; d. George Nevin and Minnie Elizabeth (Swope) Hoy; m. Willard Max Bossert, Oct. 24, 1931; children: Jane B., Thomas H., W. Max, Susan B., Bethany A. Student, Lock Haven U., 1926-30, 60. Tchr. Greensburg (Pa.) Sch. Dist., 1928-33; tchr., supr. pub. sch. art Keystone Cen. Sch. Dist., Lock Haven, 1958-68; exhibiting mem. Nat. assn. Women Artists, N.Y.C., 1945—, North Shore Art Assn., Glouster, Mass., Bucknell U. One woman shows include Millbrook Art Gallery, Mill Hall, Pa., Ross Libr., Lock Haven U., others. Charter mem. Millbrook Playhouse Bd., Mill Hall, 1966—; mem. adv. bd. Clinton-Lycoming Mental Health/Mental Retardation Bd., Williamsport, Pa., 1974—; mem., sec. Ross Libr., Lock Haven, 1958—; trustee, past pres. Laurelton State Ctr., Pa. Mem. Pa. State Edn. Assn., Rep. Women (pres. Bald Eagle chpt. 1968—), Beta Sigma Phi (internat. hon. mem.). Republican. Presbyterian. Home: RD Box 36 Beech Creek PA 16822

BOSSIDY, LAWRENCE ARTHUR, industrial manufacturing executive; b. Pittsfield, Mass., Mar. 5, 1935; m. Nancy, 1956; children: Lynn, Larry, Paul, Pam, Nancy, Mary Jane, Lucy, Michael, Kathleen. BA in Econs., Colgate U. With GE, 1957-91; chief exec. officer Allied-Signal Inc., Morristown, N.J., 1991—, chmn., 1992—; now chmn. GE Capital Corp.; chief exec. officer Allied-Signal Inc., Morristown, N.J., 1991—; chmn. Allied-Signal Inc., 1992—; vice chmn., dir. GE Investment Corp., GE Indsl. and Power systems, GE Lighting, GE Motors, GE Elec. Distbn. and Control, GE Can. Inc., GE Communications and Svcs., Ladd Petroleum Corp., GE Fin. Svcs. Inc., Employers Reinsurance Corp., Kidder Peabody. Mem. adv. com. on Trade policy and negotiations, 1987, chmn. Europe '92 Task Force. Mem. Elfun. Roman Catholic. Office: Allied Signal Inc 101 Columbia Rd Morristown NJ 07960-4658

BOSTER, CONSTANZA HELENA G., marketing and product development executive; b. San Salvador, Apr. 18, 1944; came to U.S. 1959; d. Raul and Alice (Interiano) Gamero; m. Davis E. Boster, May 25, 1978 (div. 1985); 1 child, Valerie Anne. BA cum laude, Dunbarton Coll., Washington, 1964. Owner Co. Centro Americana Corp., Guatemala, 1969-78; mgr. Traulsen & Co., Inc., College Point, N.Y., 1983, v.p., 1985-89; exec. v.p. Traulsen & Co., Inc., College Park, 1989—. Mem. NAFE, Nat. Restaurants Assn., Am. Mgmt. Assn., Round Table Women in the Food Svc. Industry, James Beard Found., Network Exec. Women in Hospitality, Inc. Republican. Roman Catholic. Office: Traulsen & Co Inc 11402 15th Ave College Point NY 11356-1430

BOSTIN, MARVIN JAY, hospital and health services consultant; b. Toronto, Ont., Can., July 3, 1933; s. Samuel and Rose (Mandel) B.; came to U.S., 1956; BS, U. Toronto, 1955; MS in Hosp. Adminstrn., Columbia U., 1958; PhD in Pub. Adminstrn. (Gottlieb Meml. scholar), N.Y.U., 1972; 1 child, Shepard Craig. Pharmacist, New Mount Sinai Hosp., Toronto, 1953-56; asst. adminstr. L.I. Jewish Hosp., New Hyde Park, N.Y., 1958-62; assoc. dir. Mt. Sinai Med. Ctr., Miami Beach, Fla., 1962-65; exec. v.p. E.D. Rosenfeld Assos. Inc., hosp. and health svcs. cons. White Plains, N.Y., 1965-78; pres. M. Bostin Assos., Inc., Elmsford, N.Y., 1979—; guest scholar Brookings Instn., Washington, 1965; lectr. Sch. of Pub. Health and Adminstrv. Medicine, Columbia U., N.Y.C., 1965-78, Grad. Sch. of Pub. Adminstrn., N.Y.C., 1967; lectr. Grad. Sch. of Architecture and Planning, Columbia U., N.Y.C., 1975-78; cons. to Bur. of Hearings and Appeals, Social Security Adminstrn., HEW, 1967-68, task force on guidelines for constrn. and equipment hosp. and med. facilities USPHS, DHHS, 1987; spl. cons. to Office of Equal Health Opportunity, Office of Surgeon Gen., USPHS, 1966-67. Mem. Dade County (Fla.) Welfare Planning Coun., Miami, 1962-65; bd. dirs. South Fla. Hosp. Coun., Miami, 1963-65. Fellow Royal Soc. Health (London), Am. Pub. Health Assn., Am. Assn. Healthcare Consultants (chmn. monograph series com. 1970-71, exec. com. 1972-75, profl. standards com. 1974-76), mem. Am. Hosp. Assn., Forum for Health Care Planning (dir. 1982-91, treas. 1988-89, sec. 1989-90), Am. Coll. Healthcare Execs., AIA (mem. com. on architecture for health 1974—), Can. Coll. Health Svc. Execs. (fgn. affiliate), Internat. Hosp. Fedn., Can. Pharm. Assn. Address: 45 Knollwood Rd Elmsford NY 10523

BOSTOCK, ROY JACKSON, advertising agency executive; b. Glen Ridge, N.J., Sept. 25, 1940; s. James Franklin Bostock and Jane (Ritter) Bostock Addis; m. Merilee Huser, 1962; children—Victoria, Matthew, Kate. A.B., Duke U., 1962; M.B.A., Harvard U., 1964. Asst. account exec. Benton & Bowles, N.Y.C., 1964-66, account exec., 1966-68, account supr., v.p., 1968-70, sr. v.p., from 1970, group exec., 1976-81, exec. v.p., gen. mgr., 1981-84; pres. Benton & Bowles, Inc., N.Y.C., 1984-85; pres. D'Arcy Masius Benton & Bowles, Inc., N.Y.C., 1985-88, pres., chief operating officer, 1988-89, pres., chief exec. officer, from 1989, now chmn., chief exec. officer. Mem. Am. Assn. Advt. Agys., Phi Beta Kappa. Republican. Presbyterian. Clubs: Apawamis (Rye, N.Y.); Manursing Island (Rye) (pres. 1983-85); Racquet & Tennis (N.Y.C.). Home: S Manursing Island Rye NY 10580 Office: D'Arcy Masius Benton & Bowles 1675 Broadway New York NY 10019-5820*

BOSTON, EDWARD WILLIAM, paramedic; b. Clymer, Pa., Oct. 11, 1949; s.Francis A. and Anna Elizabeth (Esposito) B.; m. Bernadette E. McDonald, June 18, 1976; children: Stacy-Lynn, Eric. Student, Indiana U. of Pa., 1987, 88, 90. With Dave Walker Auto, Punxsutawney, Pa.; correction officer Jefferson County Jail, Brookville, Pa.; paramedic II Punxsutawney Area Ambulance, 1965—; CPR instr. ARC, Am. Heart Assn., 1965—; EMT paramedic instr. Emergency Mgmt., Harrisburg Community Coll., 1986—. Treas., trustee Cen. Fire Co. Mem. Gold Wing Rd. Riders Assn., Bus. Men's Assn. of Punxsutawney, Slovak Club, Moose, Eagles, Masons. Democrat. Roman Catholic.

BOSWELL, GARY TAGGART, electronics company executive; b. Ft. Worth, Dec. 24, 1937; s. David W. and Marjory (Taggart) B.; B.A., Tex. Christian U., 1958, M.S., 1965; postgrad. San Diego State Coll., 1960-61; m. Margaret Ruth Yelvington, Sept. 8, 1957; children—Michael David, Margaret McQuiston, Susannah Ruth. Scientist U.S. Govt., White Sands (N.M.) Missile Range, 1958-59; research engr. Gen. Dynamics, San Diego, 1959-60; programmer Bell Helicopter, Hurst, Tex., 1960-63; sect. head Collins Radio Co., Dallas, 1963-68; mgr. software devel. Tex. Instruments, Inc., Austin, 1968-72; mgr. ASC (Advanced Sci. Computer) Mktg., 1973-75, mgr. ASC div., 1975-76, mgr. computer systems, 1976-80, mgr. global positioning systems, 1980-81, mgr. TI engrng. systems, 1981-83, v.p. equipment group, mgr. intelligent systems div., 1983-86, pres. Aydin Monitor Systems, Ft. Washington, Pa., 1987-88, Aydin Computer and Monitor, Horsham, Pa., 1988—. Mem. Am. Nat. Fortran Standards Com., 1970-74. Mem. Assn. Computing Machinery, Snipe Class Internat. Racing Assn. Club: White Rock Sailing. Designer several Fortran Compliers. Winner Western Hemisphere Snipe championship, 1970, also other maj. regattas. Home: 1130 Welsh Rd Ambler PA 19002-2225 Office: Aydin Computer & Monitor 700 Dresher Rd Horsham PA 19044-2280

BOSWELL, MARY ROSE, performing arts center director; b. Richmond, Va.; d. Ralph Emmett and Elizabeth Rose (Stambaugh) Fall; m. Thomas Greenwood Boswell, May 29, 1976. AB, Coll. William & Mary, 1976; MA, SUNY, Cooperstown, 1979. Curator Assn. for Preservation of Va. Antiquities, Richmond, 1972-78; exhibition curator N.H. Hist. Soc., Concord, 1979-83; curator, acting dir. Shaker Village, Inc., Canterbury, N.H., 1983-87; dir. Belknap Mill Soc., Laconia, N.H., 1987—; cons. City of Richmond, 1976, N.H. Constitution Bicentennial Com., Concord, 1983, Canterbury Hist. Soc., 1984-86, Gov. Wentworth Home, Portsmouth, N.H., 1986. Co-author: New Hampshire in the 1930s: The Great Depression & The New Deal, 1983, The Earth Shall Blossom, 1991; editor: Seasoned with Grace, 1987; editor, author: (newsletter) Discovery, 1974-78. Mem. Laconia Downtown Assn., 1989—, N.H. Travel Coun., Concord, 1991; mem. com. Gov.'s Coun. on Volunteerism, Lakes Region, N.H., 1991; bd. dirs. Greater Laconia-Weirs Beach C. of C., 1990—. Recipient Grant award Early Am. Industries Assn., 1986, Excellence in Mgmt. award Corp. Fund of the N.H. Charitable Fund, 1988, 89, 91. Mem. Am. Assn. Mus., N.H. Hist. Soc. (com. mem. 1987—), New Eng. Mus. Assn. (com. mem. 1979—), Inst. Mus. Svcs. (cons. 1990), Internat. Coun. Mus., Am. Assn. for State and Local History (cons. 1991). Office: The Belknap Mill Soc The Mill Plz Laconia NH 03246

BOTHWELL, ALFRED LESTER MEADOR, immunobiology educator; b. Springfield, Mo., Apr. 29, 1949; s. Wilber Clarence and Marcella Pearl (Lester) B.; m. Sallye Beth Fink, Dec. 29, 1974 (div. June 1983); children: Sara Gurley, Laura Elizabeth; m. Glenna Shirleen Roeder, Mar. 30, 1985. AB, Washington U., 1971; MPhil, Yale U., 1974, PhD, 1975. Postdoctoral fellow Cold Spring Harbor (N.Y.) Lab., 1975-76, MIT, Cambridge, Mass., 1976-82; asst. prof. pathology dept. Med. Sch. Yale U., New Haven, 1982-88; assoc. prof. immunobiology dept. Med. Sch. Yale Med. Sch., New Haven, 1988—. Author: (with Yancopoulos and Alt) Methods for Cloning and Analysis of Eukaryotic Genes, 1990; contbr. articles to profl. publs. Mem. Am. Soc. Microbiology, Am. Assn. Immunologists. Democrat. Office: Yale Med Sch Immunobiology Dept 310 Cedar St New Haven CT 06510-3218

BOTHWELL, ROBERT OTTO, association executive; b. Cin., Sept. 17, 1937; s. Harry Unversagt and Elsie (Dunkmann) B.; m. Jill Louise Schrote, June 12, 1959 (div. 1973); children: Thomas Otto, Maria Ann; m. Sharon Kay Benjamin, Aug. 7, 1982. BA, Ohio State U., 1959; MA, Ind. U., 1964. Mgmt. intern NASA, Washington, 1964-65, asst. to dir. tech. utilization div., 1965-66; field rep. mid-Atlantic region OEO, Washington, 1967-68, program officer, acting dep. dir. rsch. and demonstration div. Community Action Program, 1968-69; field rep. Ctr. for Study of Pub. Policy, Cambridge, Mass., 1970; dir. sch. fin. reform project Nat. Urban Coalition, Washington, 1971-76; assoc. dir. vet. edn. project U.S. Conf. Mayors/Nat. League Cities, Washington, 1971-73; exec. dir. Nat. Com. Responsive Philanthropy, Washington, 1976—; founding bd. dirs. Am. Sch. Fin. Assn., Gainesville, Fla., 1976-77; health charities reform project adv. com. Ctr. for Sci. in Pub. Interest, Washington, 1981-83; mem. adv. com. Combined Health Appeal of Nat. Capital Area, 1982-84; mem. Form 990 adv. com. IRS, 1984-86; mem. pvt. sector adv. group Nat. Assn. Attys. Gen., Washington, 1984-86; mem. lobby steering group for Ind. Sector, Washington, 1987-90, govt. rels. com., 1992—. Contbr. articles to profl. jours. Lt. (j.g.) USN, 1959-62. Democrat. Home: 406 Highland Pl Alexandria VA 22301-2712 Office: Nat Com Responsive Philanthropy Ste 620 2001 S St NW Washington DC 20009-1125

BOTSFORD, KEITH, publisher, writer, educator; b. Brussels, Belgium, Mar. 29, 1928; s. Willard Hudson and Carolina (Rangoni-Machiavelli) B.; m. Ann Winchester, Dec. 19, 1949 (div. 1968); children: Aubrey, Clarissa, Giannandrea, Josue, Flora; m. S.E. Weekes; children: Matthew, Polly; m. Nathalie Fabre-Gilly, Feb. 4, 1984; children: Thomas, Xenia (dec.). AB, Yale U. of Iowa, 1949, AM, 1950. Reporter France-Amerique, N.Y.C., 1945; instr. Yale, New Haven, Conn., 1950-51; translator Human Rels. Area Files, Conn., 1951-53; asst. prof. Bard Coll., Annandale-on-Hudson, N.Y., 1954-56; lectr. New Sch. Social Rsch., N.Y.C., 1955-56; various teaching and producer positions, corr. The Sunday Times, The Independent, London, 1987—; asst. to rector U. P.R., 1958-61; dir. Nat. Translation Ctr. U. Tex., 1966-71; corr. Sunday Times, London, 1973-84; pub., editor-in-chief Bostonia Mag., 1989—; prof. jour. Boston U., 1988—. Author: The Master Race, 1955, The Eighth-Best-Dressed Man in the World, 1957, Benvenuto, 1961, The March-Man, 1964, Dominguin, 1972, Driving Ambition, 1981, Keke, 1985, Cockpits, 1988, (as I.I. Magdalen) The Search for Anderson, 1982, Ana P, 1985; editor Yale Poetry Rev., Poetry New York, The Noble Savage, Delos, Grand Prix Internat.; contbr. articles to N.Y. Times Mag., others. With mil., 1947, Fed. Rep. Germany. Recipient City of Ravenna Translation prize, N.Y. PEN Translation medal, Grants Ford Found. award, Rockefeller Found. award, Moody Found. award. Democrat. Home: 120 Cushing Ave Dorchester MA 02125-2033 Office: Boston U Boston MA 02215 also: 10 Lenox St Brookline MA 02146

BOTT, PATRICIA ALLEN, artist; b. Old Lyme, Conn., Mar. 17, 1911; d. George Brainard and Lucretia Allen (Phinney) Burr; m. George Martin Bott. Student, Rollins Coll., 1942-48; studies with Malcolm Fraser, 1923-42, studies with George Burr, 1915-30. Dir. Burr Gallery, N.Y.C., 1960-68; sec., mem. gallery staff Salmagundi Club, N.Y.C., 1969-72; sales mgr. G and Cen. Galleries, N.Y.C., 1972-79; rep. A.M. Adler Fine Arts Inc., N.Y.C., 1979-86. One-woman shows in Nairobi, Kenya, 1968, Burr Gallery, N.Y.C.; exhibited in numerous group shows. Tour guide Bronx Zoo, N.Y.C., 1978. Mem. Nat. Assn. Women Artists, Am. Artists Profl. League, Soc. Animal Artists (founder, sec. 1960—, writer/editor newsletter), Art Students League (life), Burr Artists (pres. 1984-92), Salmagundi Club. Home: 151 Carroll St Bronx NY 10464-1430

BOTTA, LOUIS HENRY, military officer; b. Santiago, Cuba, Sept. 7, 1953; came to the U.S., 1967; s. Guillermo A. and Mirta D. (Reyes) B. BA, St. Michaels Coll., Winooski Park, Vt., 1975; postgrad., Webster Coll., St. Louis, 1978, Air U., 1978, Sch. Advanced Studies, Caracas, Venezuela, 1989. Lic. comml. pilot. Commd. 2d lt. USAF, 1976, advanced through grades to lt. col., 1992; sect. comdr. 375 supply squadron USAF, Scott AFB, Ill., 1976-78; sect. comdr. 603 mil. airlift support squadron USAF, Kadena Air Base, Japan, 1978-79, exec. officer and chief adminstrn. 18 tactical fighter wing, 1979-80; student undergrad. pilot tng. 54 flying tng. squadron USAF, Reese AFB, Tex., 1981-82; asst. chief combat plans hdqrs. 374 tactical airlift wing USAF, Clark Air Base, Philippines, 1982-85; chief combat plans, instr. pilot 317 tactical airlift wing USAF, Pope AFB, N.C., 1986-87; exch. officer command and gen. staff coll. USAF, Caracas, 1988-89; politico-mil. affairs officer directorate of plans USAF, Washington, 1989—. Decorated Meritorious and Commendation medals. Mem. Air Force Assn. (life), Order of Daedalians (life), Interam. Def. Bd. Republican. Roman Catholic. Home: 2301 S Jefferson Davis Hwy Arlington VA 22202

BOTTIGLIA, FRANK ROBERT, bank executive; b. S.I., Jan. 12, 1946; s. Hugo and Rose (Renzi) B.; m. Madalyn Theresa Castelucci, June 1, 1974; children: Christine Anne, Catherine Rose, Elizabeth Mary, Laura Michele. BBA, CCNY, 1968; MBA, Baruch Coll., 1976. Adv. profl. cert. pub. acctg. Fin. analyst corp. human resources Chase Manhattan Bank, N.Y.C., 1971-73, mgr. fin. controls corp. human resources, 1974-75, mgr. fin. and adminstrn. corp. human resources, 1976-77, sr. fin. mgmt. officer real estate fin., 1978-83, v.p., contr. U.S. regional comml. sector, 1984-89, v.p., budge dir. N.Am. sector, 1990—. Bd. mgr. Town and Country Villas Home Owners Assn., S.I., 1991. Sgt. U.S. Army, 1968-70. Roman Catholic. Home: 42A Country Drive E Staten Island NY 10314 Office: Chase Manhattan Bank 1 Chase Manhattan Plz New York NY 10081

BOTTO, ANTONY ALAN, producer; b. Sunbury, Pa., Dec. 31, 1938; s. Attilio and Evadna (Brosius) B. BBA, Ursinus Coll., 1967; Student, U. Pa., Phila., 1972-73, Drexel U., 1973. Engr. Ralbar Prodns., Pottstown, Pa., 1960-64; producer, dir. Vantage/Semaphore Records, Princeton, N.J., 1964-70; exec. producer Vantage/Semaphore Records, 1970-80; producer Worldnet U.S. Info. Agy., Washington, 1981-86; producer, dir. USIA Fgn. Press Ctr., Washington, 1986—. Producer record album Here Comes the American Freedom Train; sound producer movie Inside/Out; developer DynaGrove recording system, Panorama 235 wide screen motion picture projection system. Bd. dirs. Nat. Choir Sch., 1980-88; trustee The Gow Sch., South Wales, N.Y., 1978—. Mem. Record Industry Assn. Am., Nat. Acad. Recording Arts and Scis., Ursinus Coll. Alumni Assn. (exec. bd. 1967-70), Masons (32 degree). Republican. Mem. Soc. of Friends. Home: PO Box 22304 Alexandria VA 22304-9230 Office: USIA Nat Press Bldg Fgn Press Ctr Ste 860 Washington DC 20045

BOTTY, KENNETH JOHN, editor, newspaper executive; b. Aug. 10, 1927; s. John and Norma (Solary) B.; m. Eileen Barnett, Oct. 25, 1953 (div. May 1991); children: John Taylor, Carol Jayne; m. Carolyn J. Foisy, Dec. 31, 1991. B.J., U. Mo., 1949. V.p., editor in chief Telegram & Gazette, Worcester, Mass., 1956-90; ret., 1990; v.p. Millbury Savs. Bank, Mass., 1964—. Author: (mag. feature) Outdoors and Nature, 1956—. Served with USN, 1944-46. Mem. New Eng. A.P. News Execs. Assn. (pres. 1977-78), Am. Soc. Newspaper Editors, Outdoor Writers Assn. Am., New Eng. Outdoor Writers Assn. (past pres.), Soc. Profl. Journalists, Mass. Thoroughbred Breeders Assn. (bd. dirs. 1984-88). Home: 49 South Rd Holden MA 01520-1002

BOTWINICK, MOSHE LEV, communications educator; b. Phila., Apr. 24, 1953; s. Israel Eli and Dorothy (Shestack) B.; m. Tova Moldovan, Oct. 28, 1990. BA with honors, Bklyn. Coll., 1975; MA, U. Pa., 1978; postgrad., NYU, 1989. Exec. dir. Communications for the Humanities, N.Y.C., 1979-90; v.p. Comet Internat., 1991—; prof. communications Coll. Mt. St. Vincent, Riverdale, N.Y., 1982—; cons. Jewish Edn. Svcs., N.A., N.Y.C., 1982-85, Children's TV Workshop, N.Y.C., 1983-91; editorial bd. ETC Jour. Gen. Semantics, 1982-86. Produced radio series People's University, 1985, films including Mothers, 1984, Echoes of a Nightmare, 1984. NSF grantee, 1984. Mem. AAUP, Alpha Kappa Delta. Home: 204 W 78th St New York NY 10024-6614 Office: CTW One Lincoln Plz New York NY 10023

BOUBLIK, MILOSLAV, molecular biologist, electron microscopist; b. C. Ardov, Czechoslovakia, Apr. 13, 1927; came to U.S., 1971; s. Joseph and Ruzena (Markova) B.; m. Magda Voctova, July 16, 1959; children: Martin, Michael. MS, Tech. U., Prague, Czechoslovakia, 1952; PhD, Czechoslovak Acad. Scis., Prague, 1965. Registered profl. engr. Rsch. fellow Inst. of Tech., Prague, 1954-60; rsch. fellow Czechoslovak Acad. of Scis., Prague, 1960-64, sr. rsch. fellow, 1964-68; vis. scientist Portsmouth (Eng.) Polytech. Inst., 1968-71, asst. mem., 1971-77; assoc. mem. Roche Inst. Molecular Biology, Nutley, N.J., 1977-86, full mem., 1986—. Contbr. over 100 articles to profl. jours. European Molecular Biology Orgn. fellow, 1968-70. Mem. AAAS, Am. Soc. Biol. Chemists, N.Y. Acad. Scis., Electron Microscopy Soc. Am. Office: Roche Inst Molecular Biology Kingsland St Nutley NJ 07110

BOUCHARD, STEPHEN ALFRED, lawyer; b. Austin, Tex., Jan. 3, 1958; s. Harry A. and Ruby Irene (Condra) B. BBA with highest honors, U. Tex., 1979, JD with honors, 1982. Bar: D.C. 1982. Securities analyst Tex. State Securities Bd., Austin, Tex., 1978-82; assoc. Fulbright & Jaworski, Washington, 1982-85; assoc. Fleischman and Walsh, Washington, 1985-87, ptnr., 1987—. Deacon First Bapt. Ch., Washington, 1983-86, mem. bd. Christian edn., 1986-89, mem. staff selection com., 1989-92, chmn. nominating com., 1990—; mem. religious liberty coun. Bapt. Joint com. on Pub. Affairs. Mem. ABA, Phi Kappa Phi, Phi Delta Phi, Beta Alpha Psi. Republican. Baptist. Office: Fleischman and Walsh 1400 16th St NW Ste 600 Washington DC 20036-2225

BOUCHER, DAVID H., state agency administrator, accountant; b. Hartford, Conn., Dec. 28, 1954; m. BonnieE. Stimpson, May 7, 1983; children: David A., Diane E. AS in Acctg., Greater Hartford Community Coll., 1987; BSBA, Ea. Conn. State U., 1990. Adminstr. unclaimed property div. State of Conn. Treasury Dept., Hartford, 1987—. Mem. Bd. of Tax Rev., Town of Ellington. Mem. Nat. Assn. Unclaimed Property Adminstrs. (rep. Conn. chpt. 1987—), Corp. Transfer Assn. (assoc.), Unclaimed Property Clearinghouse (exec. com. Boston chpt. 1987—), Soc. Govtl. Accts., Am. Legion, SAR. Office: State of Conn Dept Treasury 55 Elm St Hartford CT 06106-1773

BOUCHER, HENRY JOSEPH (BUD BOUCHER), management consultant; b. Waterbury, Conn., Sept. 1, 1947; s. Henry J. Sr. and Mary K. (Lawlor) B.; m. Toni Iannuzzi, Aug. 8, 1970; children: Jean Paul, Marie, Christopher. BS, St. Michael's Coll., Burlington, Vt., 1969; M.Econs., S.D. State U., Brookings, 1972. Cert. mgmt. cons. Auditor Main, Hurdman, Kansas City, Mo., 1973-75; sr. cons. Touche Ross & Co., Kansas City, 1975-80; ptnr. Touche Ross & Co., Stamford, Conn., 1983-88; v.p. ops. Forrest T. Jones Co., Kansas City, 1980-83; chmn., sr. ptnr. Martin Boucher & Assoc., Norwalk, Conn., 1988-89; pres., co-founder M/B Systems, Inc., Norwalk, 1988—; chmn. Exec. Enterprise Ins. Industry Seminars, N.Y.C., 1987-90; nat. ins. ptnr. in charge of metro N.Y. ins. practice Coopers & Lybrand, CPAs, N.Y.C., 1989—; bd. dirs. Tin Plate Internat., Inc. Author: Workbook on the Insurance Regulatory Information System, 1989; (with others) Living Within Our Means, 1988. Commr. YMCA/Ernie Mele Baseball League, Kansas City, 1973-78; bd. dirs. United Way, 1980-83, Pvt. Commn. on Conn. Pub. Expediture Coun., Hartford, 1987-89; mem. Rep. Town Com., 1991—. Capt. USAF, 1969-72. Mem. Inst. Mgmt. Cons. (chmn. membership devel. 1984-89), Rotary (pres. 1990-91), Optimist (pres. 1974-78), Rolling Hills Country Club. Home: 5 Wicks End Ln Wilton CT 06897-2633 Office: Coopers and Lybrand 1301 Ave Of The Americas New York NY 10019-6022

BOUCHER, JOHN HENRI, medical technologist, real estate agent; b. Buffalo, Dec. 28, 1956; s. Jean Henri and Helen (Fenato) B. AAS in Med. Tech., Alfred (N.Y.) State Coll., 1976; BS in Bus, SUNY, Buffalo, 1988. Cert. med. lab. technologist Am. Soc. Clin. Pathologists; cert. clin. lab. technologists HHS. Tech. sales rep. Baxter Healthcare Corp., West Sacramento, Calif., 1988-90; sales mgr. USA Jobseekers Directory, Hamburgh, N.Y., 1990; sales assoc. M.J. Peterson Real Estate, Buffalo, 1990-91, Grandview Devel. Group Inc., Buffalo, 1991—; sr. med. technician Children's Hosp. Buffalo, 1978-88, med. technologist, 1990—. Mem. Willow Ridge Civic Assn., Amherst, N.Y., 1982—; mem. games com. World U., Buffalo, 1991. Sarah Helen Kish Meml. scholar SUNY, 1985-86. Mem. Grant Amherst Bus. assn., NRA (life), U. Buffalo Alumni Assn., U. Buffalo Sch. Mgmt. Alumni Assn., Buffalo Athletic Club, Alpha Sigma Lambda, Beta Gamma Sigma. Home: 378 Kaymar Dr Amherst NY 14228

BOUCHER, TANIA KUNSKY, artist, sculptor; d. Ivan Ivanovich and Anna (Marozova) Kunsky; m. William H. Boucher, Sept. 18, 1948; children: William H. Jr., Joshua C., Pamela B. Sharpe. BS, CCNY; MS, U. Pa.; BA, U. Del. Dir. Aeolian Palace Gallery, Pocopson, Pa., 1974-82; editor Aeolian Palace Press, Pocopson, 1977—; 1964; instr. Westtown Friends Sch., Pa., 1964-69; art tchr. West Chester (Pa.) Adult Night Sch., 1970-72. Solo exhbns. include Westtown Friends Sch., 1971, Univ. Del., 1973, Station Gallery, Wilmington, 1989-92; group shows include Carspecken Scott Gallery, Wilmington, 1974, Woodmere Art Mus., Chestnut Hill, Pa., 1980, Balt. Mus. Loan Libr., 1989, Aeolian Palace, Hotel Dupont Gallery, 1991, U. Del. Women's Exhibit, 1992; author: Bostelle: Seated Self, 1980; editor: Hob House, 1983; contbr. articles to newspapers. Home: PO Box 188 Mendenhall PA 19357-0188 Studio: Aeolian Palace PO Box 8 Pocopson PA 19366

BOUCHER, THOMAS OWEN, engineering educator, researcher; b. Providence, June 25, 1942; s. Joseph William and Anne Marie (Byrne) B.; m. Unn Gunnerus Jermstad, Mar. 30, 1974. BSEE, U. R.I., 1964; MBA, Northwestern U., 1970; PhD in Indsl. Engrng., Columbia U., 1978. Sr. project engr. Continental Can Co., Chgo., 1967-69; sr. staff cons. ABEX Corp., N.Y.C., 1970-72; asst. prof. Cornell U., Ithaca, N.Y., 1978-81; asst. prof. Rutgers U., New Brunswick, N.J., 1981-87, assoc. prof., 1987—. Dept. editor IIE Transactions, 1987-91; area editor Engrng. Economist, 1989—; assoc. editor Jour. Productivity Analysis, 1989-92; co-author: Analysis & Control of Production Systems, 1985; contbr. articles to Internat. Jour. Prodn. Rsch., Advanced Mfg. Engrng. 1st lt. U.S. Army, 1965-67, Vietnam. Grantee Def. Logistics Agy. Mem. Am. Soc. for Engrng. Edn. (chmn. engrng. econ. div. 1986-87), N.Y. Acad. Scis., Inst. Indsl. Engrs. (sr.), Soc. Mfg. Engrs. (sr.), Sigma Xi. Roman Catholic. Home: 65 Douglas Rd Glen Ridge NJ 07028-1227 Office: Rutgers U Coll of Engrng PO Box 909 Piscataway NJ 08855-0909

BOUDREAU, A. ALLAN, historian, author; b. Albany, N.Y., Aug. 1, 1936; s. Alexander and Lillian (Allan) B.; children: Kirstin Rosamund, Andrew Allan. BS, 1958; MBA, 1964; MS, 1972; PhD, 1973. Adminstrv. asst. N.Y. State Dept. Edn., 1958-59; adminstrv. officer N.Y. State Libr., 1959-62; asst. dir. NYU Librs., 1962-73; sr. rsch. assoc. NYU, 1973-74; sec. Libr. Trustees Found., 1973-88; dir. libr. and mus. Grand Lodge Masons N.Y., 1974-91; asst. dir. N.Y. State AARP, 1992—; pub. acct. N.Y. State, 1961—; cons. librs., mus., rsch. orgns., mfrs., architects, state and local govtl. units; lectr. colls. and profl. groups. Author: The Library and Scholarly Research, 1964, The Research Resources at Washington Square, 1831-1970, 1972, 200 Years of Freemasonry in New York, 1981, George Washington in New York, 1988, George Washington and N.Y.C., 1989; contbr. articles to profl. jours. N.Y. State Exempt vol. fireman; trustee Allan Found., 1970—; trustee Livingston Library, 1983-86. With AUS, 1953-55. Recipient Founder's Day award NYU, 1973. Mem. ALA (life), AARP, N.Y. Libr. Assn., N.Y. State Assn. Libr. Bds. (bd. dirs. 1973-88), Am. Legion. Club: N.Y. Athletic, Collectors. Lodge: Masons. Home: 1 Washington Square Village New York NY 10012-1611

BOUGERE, C. ANTHONY, insurance company executive; b. N.Y.C., Jan. 18, 1945; s. Mac R. and Grace C. (Kelly) B.; m. Elizabeth Cockburn Wargo, July 11, 1970; children: Jason, Kelly. BA, Trinity Coll., 1967; MBA, Columbia U., 1972. Account mgr. Compton Advt., N.Y.C., 1972-74; mktg. mgr. Heublein Inc., Farmington, Conn., 1974-78, mktg. dir., 1978-81, v.p. mktg., 1981-87, v.p. Western hemisphere, 1987-90; asst. v.p. Aetna, Rock Hill, Conn., 1990-91; customer team leader Aetna, Middletown, Conn., 1991—; mem. adv. bd. Trinity Coll. Alumni Assn., 1970—; mem. mktg. bd. advisors U. Conn. Bus. Sch., 1988—. 1st lt. U.S. Army, 1967-70. Republican. Office: Aetna Health Plans MCCA 151 Farmington Ave Hartford CT 06156

BOUGHER, AUBREY NELSON, pastor, headmaster; b. Easton, Pa., Oct. 17, 1943; s. Aubrey Roscoe and Gertrude Mae (Rice) B.; m. Mary Ann Horvath, Aug. 14, 1965; children: Ann Elizabeth, Philip Martin. BA, Muhlenberg Coll., 1965; BD, Lutheran Theol. Sem., 1968, postgrad., 1975-80. Ordained to ministry Luth Ch., 1968. Pastor Christ Luth. Ch., Mahanoy City, Pa., 1968-72, Grace Luth. Ch., Allentown, Pa., 1972-81; asst. to pastor St. Peter's Luth. Ch., Greenport, N.Y., 1981; asst. to adminstr. San Simeon by the Sound Home, Greenport, N.Y., 1981; pastor Christ Luth. Ch., Rosedale, N.Y., 1981—; headmaster Christ Luth. Sch., Inc., Rosedale, N.Y., 1981—; chmn. Synod Communication Com., 1974-77; mem. Synod

Worship Com., 1979-87; pres. S.E. Queens Luth. Cluster, 1983-87; guest presenter Ad Fontes Conf., 1991; dean S.E. Queens Conf., 1991-92. Author: History, Grace, 1981, Christ, 1988; mem. editorial bd. Bride of Christ, 1980—; contbr. articles to profl. jours. Mem. Coalition of Concerned Clergy, N.Y.C., 1990—; chaplain Rosedale Civic Assn., 1983—, Good Shepherd Home, Allentown, 1972-80. Mem. Luth. High Sch. Assn. N.Y.C. (del. mem. 1982—), Ptnrs. in Reconciliation (co-founder, mem. 1979-82). Republican. Office: Christ Luth Ch 24801 Francis Lewis Blvd Jamaica NY 11422-2236

BOUGHTON, ROSS BYRON, composer, television producer; b. Northampton, Mass., Aug. 6, 1960; s. Walter Leroy and Georgia Dagmar (Aune) B. Student, Roger Williams Coll., 1978-80, Berklee Sch. Music, 1980-82. Touring musician, 1985-88; filmmaker Cable TV, N.Y.C., 1988—; freelance composer, arranger N.Y.C., 1988—. Composer, author mus. works. Activist Save the Bandshell, Cen. Park, N.Y.C., 1992. Recipient Excellence in Music award Madrigal Soc. We. Mass., 1983, Promoting Chamber Music award Chamber Orch. Greenfield Mass., 1984. Mem. ASCAP. Republican. Episcopalian. Home: 48 W 68th St 8F New York NY 10023

BOUGIE, JACQUES, metal processing executive; b. Montreal, Que., Can., 1947. BBA, Ecole des Hautes Etudes Commerciales; JD, U. Montreal. With Alcan Smelters and Chems. Ltd., Montreal, 1979-81; dir. devel. Aluminium Co. of Can., Manitoba, Que., 1981; pres., chief oper. officer Aluminium Co. of Can., 1982—; pres. Alcan Enterprises div. Aluminium Co. of Can., 1988; pres., chief oper. officer Alcan Aluminium Ltd., 1989—, also bd. dirs.; bd. dirs. Bell Can., BCE Mobile Communications, Inc., Royal Bank of Can., Conf. Bd. of Can. Office: Alcan Aluminium Ltd, 1188 Sherbrooke St W, Montreal, PQ Canada H3A 3G2

BOUHET, JACQUES EMILE, banker; b. La Souterraine, Creuse, France, June 22, 1942; s. Roger and Raymonde (Deluchat) B.; m. Katharina Paslat, Oct. 30, 1968; children: Alexandra, Frederic, Emilie. Student, Ecole Poly, Paris, 1962-65. With Societe Generale, Paris, 1965-68; asst. v.p. Sogen Internat., N.Y.C., 1969-71; asst. mgr. Societe Generale, N.Y.C., 1971-72; v.p. E.A.B. & Trust, N.Y.C., 1972-77; dep. gen. mgr. Societe Generale, London, 1977-80; gen. mgr. Societe Generale, Hong Kong, 1980-84; dir. dept. in charge Asian sector Societe Generale, Paris, 1984-88; gen. mgr. Societe Generale U.S.A., 1988—. Home: 1115 5th Ave New York NY 10128-0100 Office: Societe Generale 50 Rockefeller Plz New York NY 10020-1605

BOULDEN, ANNE MARION, hospitality executive; b. Abington, Pa., July 8, 1961; d. David Marion and Joan (Schick) B. BS, U. Del., 1983. Cons. M.A. Boulden Assoc., King of Prussia, Pa., 1983-86; account exec. Spirit of Washington (Cruise Line), 1987-88, dir. of sales and mktg., 1988-89; gen. mgr. Spirit of Phila. (Cruise Line), 1989-90, Spirit of N.Y. (Cruise Line), 1990—. Vol. Jr. League Phila., 1989-90. Mem. N.Y. Conv. and Vis. Bur., C. of C., Lower Manhattan Mktg. Assn. Office: Spirit of New York 99 Wall St Rm 500 New York NY 10005-4386

BOULOUKOS, DON P., broadcast company executive. Grad., De Paul U., 1972. Pres., owned radio stas. Group I Capitol Cities/ABC Radio Network, N.Y.C. Office: ABC Radio Network 77 W 66th St New York NY 10023*

BOULTBEE, JOHN ARTHUR, publishing executive; b. Toronto, Ont., Can., July 4, 1943; s. Thomas Edward and Helene Marion (Pattison) B.; m. Eleanor Rose Moore, Nov. 02, 1968 (div. 1985); children: Paul Kieth, Leslie Elizabeth; m. Sharon Ann Whitby, Dec. 29, 1985; 1 child, Michael James Edward. B in Commerce, U. Toronto, 1967, CA, 1970. CPA, Ont. Mgr. Coopers & Lybrand, Toronto, Ont., Can., 1973-78, ptnr., 1978-85, ptnr. in charge of tax group, 1985-86; v.p. Hollinger Inc., Toronto, 1986—; pub. Saturday Night Mag., Toronto, 1988-89; pres. Saturday Night Mag. Inc., Toronto, 1989—; bd. dirs. Hollinger Inc., Toronto, 1987—; bd. dirs. Hollinger, Inc., Toronto, Argus Corp. Ltd., Toronto, Gordon Investment Corp., Toronto, Consolidated Enfield Corp., Toronto, Key Pubs., Inc., Toronto. Editor, contbr. Can. Tax Jour., 1980-86. Mem. Can. Inst. Chartered Accts., Boulevard Club. Office: Hollinger Inc, 10 Toronto St, Toronto, ON Canada M5C 2B7

BOUNDY, DAVID ERIC, patent lawyer, computer engineer; b. Puyallup, Wash., July 14, 1957; s. Bruce K. and Henriette E. (Fikse) B. BS cum laude, Hope Coll., 1980; MS, U. Mich., 1983; postgrad., MIT, 1984-90. Sr. software engr. Pixel Computer, Woburn, Mass., 1983-85; engr. Apollo Computer/Hewlett Packard, Chelmsford, Mass., 1986-92; lectr. Merrimack Coll., North Andover, Mass., 1987-90; patent agt. Fish & Richardson, Boston, 1992—. Author: A Taxonomy of Programmers, 1991. Condr. Ars Canticorum, Renaissance Choir, Cambridge, Mass., 1988-90. Mem. Assn. for Computing Machinery, IEEE Computer Soc. Home: PO Box 10 Nutting Lake MA 01865 Office: Fish & Richardson 225 Franklin St Boston MA 02110

BOURASSA, ROBERT, premier of Quebec, lawyer, economist; b. July 14, 1933; s. Aubert and Adrienne (Courville); m. Andrée Simard; children: François, Michelle. BA, Coll. Jean-de-Brébeuf, Montréal, Que., Can., 1953; LLB, U. Montréal, 1956; MA in Econs. and Polit. Sci., Oxford (Eng.) U., 1959; MA in Internat. Taxation and Corp. Law, Harvard U., 1960; PhD (hon.), U. Tel Aviv, 1987. Taxation advisor Dept. Nat. Revenue, 1960-63; prof. econs. and taxation U. Ottawa, Ont., Can., 1961-63; sec., rsch. dir. Bélanger Commn., 1963-65; spl. advisor econ. and fin. Fed. Dept. of Fin.; prof. pub. fin. U. Montréal and Laval U., 1966-69; Premier Province of Que., 1970-76, 85—; vis. prof. Inst. Européen Adminstrn., 1976, U. So. Calif., L.A., 1981, Yale U., New Haven, Conn., 1982; prof. ctr. advanced internat. studies John Hopkins U., 1978. Author: Bourassa/Québec!, 1970, La Baie James, 1973, Les Années Bourassa: l'intégrale des entretiens Bourbassa-St-Pierre, 1977, Deux fois la Baie James, 1981, Power from the North, L'Energie du Nord: la force du Québec, Le Défi technologique, 1985. Re-elected leader of Que. Liberal Party, 1983; 20th recipient Order of Merit of Grads. of U. Montréal. Office: Office Premier, 885 Grande Allee Est, Quebec, PQ Canada G1A 1A2

BOURNE, MALCOLM CORNELIUS, food scientist; b. Moonta, Australia, May 18, 1926; came to U.S., 1958; s. Herbert Cornelius and Winifred (Collins) B.; m. Elizabeth Hillson Schumacher, Sept. 30, 1953; children: Gwendolyn, Jonathan, Lincoln, Virginia, Andrew. BSc in Chemistry, U. Adelaide, Australia, 1948; MS in Food Sci., U. Calif., Davis, 1961, PhD in Agrl. Chemistry, 1962. Chief chemist Brookers Australia Ltd., Adelaide, 1948-58; rsch. asst. U. Calif., Davis, 1958-62; prof. food sci. Cornell U., Geneva, N.Y., 1962—. Author: Food Texture and Viscosity, 1982; contbr. articles to profl. jours. Fellow Inst. Food Technologists, Inst. Food Sci. and Tech.; mem. Am. Chem. Soc., Royal Australian Chem. Inst., Philippine Assn. Food Technologists (hon. life), Phi Kappa Phi. Seventh Day Adventist. Office: Cornell U NY State Agrl Experiment Sta Geneva NY 14456

BOURNE, MARY BONNIE MURRAY (MRS. SAUL HAMILTON BOURNE), music publishing company executive; b. Salix, Iowa, Sept. 13, 1903; d. Thomas William and Kathryn (McDermott) Murray; student Morningside Normal Coll., 1922-23; student Am. Banking Inst., N.Y.C.; m. Saul Hamilton Bourne, Apr. 12, 1928; 1 dau., Mary Elizabeth. Appeared with George White Scandals, Ramblers, Cocoanuts, Ziegfield Follies, 1925-28; owner, mgr. Bourne Co., N.Y.C., 1960—. Mem. social work recruiting com. United Hosp. Fund. Trustee S.H. Bourne Found., Coll. New Rochelle; trustee N.Y. Infirmary, 1945—, chmn. social service youth bd., 1947—, bd. visitors Sch. Music, Catholic U. Am., Washington. Recipient Abe Olman Pub. award. Mem. A.S.C.A.P. (dir., pubs. adv. com.). Home: 14 E 75th St New York NY 10021-2657 Office: 5 W 37th St New York NY 10018-6222

BOURQUE, MICHAEL H., interior designer; b. Leominster, Mass., Aug. 8, 1948; s. Raymond H. and Rachel (Mercier) B.; m. Susan Bowden, Jan. 29, 1972; children: Nathan, David. BA, American U., Washington, 1970. Sr. project mgr. G.H.K. Assocs., Inc., Boston and N.Y.C., 1972-79; sr. vice pres., prin. Earl R. Flansburgh & Assocs., Boston, 1979—; mem. adv. bd. Boston Design Ctr., 1985-87; nat. pres. Inst. Bus. Designers, 1987-89, mem. Coll. of Fellows, 1989; trustee Who's Who in Interior Design. Mem. adv. bd. Profl. Office Design mag., 1989; mem. adv. bd. Interiors Mag., 1991. Mem. curriculum adv. bd. Boston Archtl. Ctr., 1989. Mem. AIA, Bldg. Owners and Mgrs. Assn., Internat. Facility Mgmt. Assn., Nat. Legis. Coalition for Interior Design (founding mem.), Design Mgmt. Inst., Inst. Bus. Designers, Boston C. of C. Roman Catholic. Home: 404 Canton Ave Milton MA 02186-3337 Office: Earl R Flansburgh & Assocs 77 N Washington St Boston MA 02114-1908

BOUSCAREN, ANTHONY TRAWICK, political science educator; b. Winchester, Mass., July 7, 1920; s. Louis Henri Gustave and Ethel Byrd (Trawick) B.; m. Barbara McNulty, Jan. 20, 1944 (dec. 1969); children: Anthony Gustave, Michael Frederic, Joseph Gustave; m. Sylvia Swan, May 29, 1971. AB, Yale U., 1943; MA, U. Calif., Berkeley, 1948, PhD, 1951. Asst. prof. polit. sci. U. San Francisco, 1946-51; assoc. prof. polit. sci. Marquette U., Milw., 1953-57; prof. polit. affairs Nat. War Coll., Washington, 1957-59; prof. polit. sci. Le Moyne Coll., Syracuse, N.Y., 1959-87, prof. emeritus, 1987—; lectr. Inst. Comparative Govts., Georgetown U., 1972-79; dir. Internat. Rels. Inst., Westminster Coll., 1965-68; bd. dirs. America's Future, New Rochelle, U.S. Coun. World Freedom, Phoenix, Univ. Profs. Acad. Order, Washington; mem. nat. adv. bd. internat. ednl. programs Dept. Edn., Washington, 1985-88. Author of 24 books including Soviet Foreign Policy, 1962, Left of Liberal, 1972, All Quiet on the Eastern Front, 1977, Enduring the Soviets, 1987; contbr. over 200 articles to profl. jours. Chmn. Upstate N.Y. Com. for Goldwater, 1964, Nixon, 1968, Sen. Buckley, 1972, Reagan, 1984. Maj. USMCR, 1943-45, PTO. Decorated Disting. Flying Cross; recipient Schevchenko award U.S. Ukrainian Found., 1966, Freedoms Found. award, 1953, 58, Christopher award, 1953. Mem. Yale Club of N.Y.C., Century Club, Cazenovia Club, Onondaga Golf and Country Club, Tequesta Country Club. Republican. Roman Catholic. Home: PO Box 279 Fayetteville NY 13066-0279

BOUTWELL, WAYNE ALLISON, farmer cooperatives executive; b. Newton, Miss., Jan. 27, 1944; s. Kenneth and Elizabeth (Wilson) B.; m. Connie Loletta Weems, June 5, 1965; children: Mark, Connie. BS, Miss. State U., 1966, MS, 1968; PhD, Va. Poly. Inst. and State U., 1972. Agrl. economist econ. rsch. svc. USDA, Washington, 1970-72, program leader commodity econs. div., 1972-77, outlook coord. Adminstr.'s Office, 1978-79; agrl. specialist to Senator Thad Cochran, U.S. Senate, Washington, 1979-83; pres., chief exec. officer Nat. Coun. Farmer Coops., Washington, 1983—. Bd. dirs. Vols. Overseas Coop. Assistance, Washington, 1983—, Overseas Coop. Devel. Com., Washington, 1983—; trustee Grad. Inst. Coop. Leadership, Columbia, Mo., 1983—. Named Man of Yr. in Svc. to Agr., Progressive Farmer mag., 1987. Office: Nat Coun Farmer Coops 50 F St NW Washington DC 20001-1530

BOUVIER, JANE ALPERT, advertising manager, public relations executive; b. N.Y.C., Aug. 7, 1945; d. Milton Alpert and Kathryn Hayman; div.; children: J.C., Liz, Margot, William. Publicity agt. Micky Alper Agency, N.Y.C., 1962-64; personal mgr. pvt. practice, N.Y.C., 1964-70; advt. mgr. The Groton (Mass.) Herald, 1988—; exec. dir., publicity chmn. Groton Ctr. for the Arts, Groton Performing Arts Coun. Coord. September Fest Groton Phone Book, Groton Ctr. for the Arts, 1989—; mem. Vestry Trinity Chapel, Shirley, Mass., 1990—; personnel bd. Town of Groton, 1991—. Mem. ASCAP. Republican. Episcopalian. Home: PO Box 105 Groton MA 01450-0105 Office: Groton Herald Main St Groton MA 01450-1868

BOUVIER, JANET LAUBACH, educator; b. Benton, Pa., Nov. 27, 1930; d. Jonathan Paul and Ethel Irene (Bray) L.; m. Roland Joseph Bouvier, Sept. 29, 1930; children: Ann, Caroline, Susan. BA, Wilson Coll., 1952; MS in Edn., Temple U., 1973, EdD, 1988. Legal correspondent Pa. Bur. Motor Vehicles, Harrisburg, Pa., 1952-53; tchr. Columbus High Sch., Columbus, Ga., 1954-55; English tchr. Mechanicsburg (Pa.) Area Sch. Dist., 1967—; instr. of "Women in Politics" More Women Candidates, Harrisburg, 1986. Mem. Mechanicsburg Edn. Assn. (v.p. 1988—), Phi Delta Kappa, Omicron Tau Theta. Republican. Home: 307 W Green St Camp Hill PA 17011-6522

BOVA, JEFFREY STEPHEN, musician, keyboards; b. D.C., June 22, 1953; s. John William and Doris June (Howe) B. Student, Berklee Coll. Music, 1971-72, Manhattan Sch. Music, 1972-75. Artist Vanguard Records, N.Y.C., 1975-78; freelance musician, composer N.Y.C., 1978-89; artist Warner Bros. Records, Burbank, Calif., 1988-90; musician, composer Island Music, United Kingdom, 1990—; musician, composer Lou Garisto Prodns., N.Y.C., 1981-83; keyboards Herbie Hancock, composers asst., 1987-88; programmer, asst. Ryuichi Sakamoto, Tokyo, 1988-89; composer, arranger Cyndi Lauper, N.Y.C., 1987-89; musician, composer Distance, Burbank, Calif., 1988-90; producer Toshinobu Kubota, Kobojah, 1991. Keyboards for records including Riptide, 1986 (Platinum 1987), The Bridge, 1987 (Platinum 1988), True Colors, 1987 (Platinum 1988), Eat 'em and Smile, 1987 (Platinum 1988), Instinct, 1988, Neo-Geo, 1988, Foreign Affair, 1989, Journeyman, 1990 (Double Platinum 1990), Under the One Sky, 1990, Stranger in this Town, 1991, Adam Ant, 1991, Akiko yano, Love Life, 1991, Womack and Womack, 1992, Michael McDonald, 1992, Jenni Muldaur, 1992; composer, arranger (film soundtrack) Colors, 1989, The Handmaids Tale 1989, Pretty Woman, 1990. Mem. ASCAP.

BOVAIRD, BRENDAN PETER, lawyer; b. N.Y.C., Mar. 9, 1948; s. John Francis and Margaret Mary (Endrizzi) B.; m. Carolyn Warren Boyle, Dec. 18, 1971; children: Anne Warren, Sarah Grant. B.A., Fordham U., 1970; J.D., U. Va., 1973. Bar: N.Y. 1974, D.C. 1980, Pa. 1983, U.S. Dist. Ct. (so. and ea. dists.) N.Y. 1974, U.S. Ct. Appeals (2d cir.) 1974. Atty., Dewey, Ballantine, Bushby, Palmer & Wood, N.Y.C., 1973-82; asst. gen. counsel Campbell Soup Co., Camden, N.J., 1982-90; sr. v.p., gen. counsel, sec. Orion Pictures Corp., N.Y.C., 1990-91; counsel, Wyeth-Ayerst Internat. Inc., 1992—; bd. dirs. Motion Picture Export Assn. Am., Inc. Mem. Motion Picture Assn. Am. (legal com. 1990-91), ABA (com. on corp. counsel, litigation sect., antitrust law sect.), Assn. Bar City N.Y., Phi Delta Phi. Office: Wyeth-Ayerst Internat Inc PO Box 8616 Philadelphia PA 19101

BOVBJERG, DANA H., psychoneuroimmunologist, consultant; b. St. Louis, May 3, 1951; s. Richard V. and Dianna B. BA in Philosophy, Carleton Coll., 1973; BS in Psychology, U. Iowa, 1977; MA in Neuroscience, U. Rochester, 1983, PhD in Neuroscience, 1983. Instr. dept. medicine Cornell U. Med. Coll., N.Y.C., 1984-86, asst. prof., 1986—; asst. attending Meml. Sloan-Kettering Cancer Ctr., N.Y.C., 1989—. Author: The Joy of Cheesecake, 1980. Recipient Jr. Faculty award Am. Cancer Soc., 1990. Mem. Am. Assn. Immunologists, Am. Psychosomatic Soc., Soc. Behavioral Medicine, N.Y. Acad. Scis. Office: Meml Sloan Kettering Cancer Ctr 1275 York Ave Box 457 New York NY 10021

BOVE, ALFRED ANTHONY, medical educator; b. Phila., Apr. 28, 1938; s. Alfred Anthony and Adeline Amelia (DeRose) B.; m. Sandra Ann Seltzer, June 25, 1966; children: Jacqueline, Christopher, Andrew. BSEE, Drexel U., 1962; MD, Temple U., 1966, PhD, 1970. Diplomate Am. Bd. Internal Medicine, Am. Bd. Cardiology. Med. intern Temple U. Hosp., Phila., 1966-67, med. resident, 1969-70, postdoctoral fellow, 1967-69, asst. prof. medicine, 1973-81, prof. medicine, 1986—; postdoctoral fellow Mayo Clinic, Rochester, Minn., 1970-71; prof. medicine Mayo Clinic, Rochester, 1981-86; chief of cardiology Temple U. Med. Sch., 1986—; team internist Phila. 76ers Basketball Team, Phila., 1987—. Co-author: Diving Medicine, 1990, Exercise Medicine, 1982; editor: (med. column) Skin Diver mag., 1981—; contbr. articles to profl. jours. Capt. USNR, 1971-73, 91. Recipient Established Investigator award Am. Heart Assn., 1975. Fellow ACP, Am. Coll. Cardiology (state gov. 1989-92); mem. Am. Physiologic Soc., IEEE, Undersea and Hyperbaric Med. Soc. (pres. 1983, Craig Hoffman award 1988, Stover-Link award 1974). Roman Catholic. Office: Temple Univ Hosp Cardiology Sect Philadelphia PA 19140

BOVÉ, CAROL MASTRANGELO, French educator, researcher; b. Phila., Mar. 26, 1949; d. Domenic and Theresa (Centofanti) M.; m. Paul A. Bové, Aug. 16, 1970; 1 child, Laura. BA, U. Pa., 1970; PhD, SUNY, Binghampton, 1979. Asst. prof. French Va. Tech., Blacksburg, Va., 1980-84; assoc. prof. Westminster Coll., New Wilmington, Pa., 1984—. Translator: Writing and Fantasy in Proust (Serge Doubrousky) 1986. Office: Westminster Coll New Wilmington PA 16172

BOVE, ROSEANN, financial planner; b. Celina, Ohio, Sept. 26, 1942; d. Arlie and Mary Amanda (Wilson) Bixler; m. Joseph J. Bove, June 4, 1966 (div. Dec. 1982); children: Steven, Kevin. Student, Miami U., Oxford, Ohio, 1960-62. Cert. fin. planner; CLU. Field underwriter N.Y. Life Ins. Co., Cherry Hill, N.J., 1977-81; owner Bove & Assocs., Medford, N.J., 1981-88; ptnr. The Breton Co., Medford, 1988—. Contbr. articles to profl. publs. Mem. Am. Soc. CLU, Greater Phila. Estate Planning Coun., Nat. Assn. Personal Fin. Advisors, Inst. Cert. Fin. Planners. Democrat. Office: The Breton Co 105 Atsion Rd Medford NJ 08055

BOVES, JOAQUIN LORENZO, marketing consultant; b. Camaguey, Cuba, Apr. 30, 1949; came to U.S., 1962; s. Joaquin Boves and Esperanza Gomez-Varona. BA, U. Miami, Coral Gables, Fla., 1972, BBA, 1974, MBA, 1975. Marine biologist Nat. Marine Fisheries Svc., Miami, Fla., 1972-74; export mktg. mgr. Aquachem Co., Inc., Coral Gables, 1976-78; cons. Charles McKay & Assocs., Coral Gables, 1979-80; sr. mktg. analyst Ryder Systems, Inc., Miami, 1981-82; cons. D'Arcy MacManus & Massius, Coral Gables, Fla., 1983-84, Citibank/Citicorp Internat., N.Y.C., 1984-86; cons. Santiago, Chile, 1984-86, N.Y.C., 1987—. Cons. Radio Marti, Miami, 1982. Fellow Am. Mktg. Assn. Republican. Roman Catholic. Office: PO Box 5261 New York NY 10150-5261

BOVIK, HARRY Q., computer scientist, consultant; b. Pitts., Apr. 1, 1943. BA, Carnegie-Mellon U., 1965, PhD, 1969; DSc (hon.), Universitaet Unter-Oberflunken, Main, Germany, 1979. Project scientist Millenium Falcon Engrng. Co., Mars, Pa., 1972-75; staff scientist Foundry and Software Co., Ambridge, Pa., 1976-77; White House fellow U.S. Govt., Washington, 1978; mem. tech. staff Socio-Pathways Software, Inc., Ambridge, 1983-84; sr. computer scientist Carnegie-Mellon U., Pitts., 1979—; sci. cons. Weekly World News, 1986—. Author: Theory of Hyper Driven Devices, 1976, The Happy Hacker, 1983; patentee in field. Recipient D.S. Green award Royal Aero. Soc., London, 1975; Disting. Achievement award D'Abro Phys. Soc., 1982; NIMH grantee, 1983. Mem. Assn. Computing Machinery (editorial bd. 1983-84), Delta Epsilon Iota. Office: Carnegie Mellon U SCS 5000 ForbesAve Pittsburgh PA 15213-3890

BOVO, MARY JANE, obstetrician-gynecologist, laser surgeon; b. New Castle, Pa., June 15, 1946; d. James Louis and Betty Jane (Klingensmith) B.; m. William Bingham Kay (div. 1979); 1 child, Christine Anne Kay. BS cum laude, Youngstown State U., 1978; MD, Pa. State U., 1982. Diplomate Nat. Bd. Med. Examiners, Am. Bd. Ob-gyn. Intern Hosp. of the U. of Pa., Phila., 1982-83, resident ob-gyn., 1983-85, chief resident ob-gyn., 1985-86; pvt. practice medicine Parsippany, N.J., 1986, N.Y.C., 1988—; asst. clin. instr. ob-gyn. U. Pa. Med. Sch., Phila., 1982-86; pvt. practice medicine specializing in ob-gyn. S.H.E. Med. Assocs., P.C., Hartford, Conn., 1987-88; mem. staff Morristown (N.J.) Meml. Hosp., 1986-87, Mount Sinai Hosp., Hartford, 1987-88, St. Luke's-Roosevelt Hosp., Manhattan, 1987-89, St. Vincent's Hosp. and Med. Ctr., Manhattan, 1989—, Doctor's Hosp., Manhattan, 1990—, Beth Israel Med. Ctr., Manhattan, 1992—. Contbr. articles to profl. jours. Campaign worker Pitts. Dems., 1960-75; mem. Hartford Women's Network, 1987-88; mem. Rep. Senatorial Inner Cir., 1992—. Fellow ACOG, AAUW; mem. Am. Med. Women's Assn., N.J. Med. Soc., N.Y. Gynecol. Soc., Omicron Lambda. Office: 11A E 74th St New York NY 10021-2622

BOWDEN, GORDON TOWNLEY, telecommunications industry executive, retired; b. Huron, S.D., May 15, 1915; s. Aberdeen Orlando and Katharine Kennan (Marsh) B.; m. Mary Ellen Burkholder, Sept., 1941 (div. 1961); children: Gordon Burkholder, Katharine Marsh; m. Mary Virginia Brown, Sept. 17, 1961. AB magna cum laude, Harvard Coll., 1937; PhD, Harvard U., 1943. Tutor sociology Harvard U., Cambridge, Mass., 1939-40; instr. bus. adminstrn. Harvard Bus. Sch., Boston, 1940-44; pers. counselor Western Electric Co., Kearny, N.J., 1944-46; rsch. staff in pers. and labor rels. Pacific Telephone Co., L.A., 1946-48, traffic mgr., 1948-52; from staf asst. pers. to dir. urban affairs and ednl. rels. AT&T, 1952-71, dir. ednl. rels., 1972-80, retired, 1980; cons. Found. Industrie-Universite, Brussels, 1980-85; mem. Coun. on Grad. Sch. Arts and Sci., Harvard U., 1980-85, mem. vis. com. for Sch. Edn., Harvard Bd. Overseers, 1962-68; adv. coun. on univ. seminars program Columbia U., 1983—, chmn., 1985—; mem. adv. bd. on continuing edn. in bus. Com. for Econ. Devel., 1964-67; mem. coun. on devel. edn. and mgmt. tng. Nat. Indsl. Conf. Bd., 1957-68, chmn., 1964-67; mem. staff edn. task force Coun. of Chief State Sch. Officers, 1975-77. Contbr. articles to profl. jours. Mem. Nat. Com. on Youth, 1976-82. Fellow Rockefeller Found., 1940-42. Mem. Harvard Club (N.Y.). Home: 300 E 33d St New York NY 10016

BOWE, CAROL ANN, publisher; b. Evanston, Ill., June 21, 1953; d. Ray A. and Rose Marie (Montalto) Ginocchio; m. James J. Bowe, Sept. 16, 1978; children: Brooke Marie, Laura Ann. BA in Econs., Barat Coll., 1974; MA in Econs., L.I. U., 1986. Compliance investigator Chgo. Bd. of Trade, 1974-77; compliance mgr. Commodity Exch. Inc., N.Y.C., 1977-79, v.p., 1979-80; pvt. practice commodities cons. N.Y.C., 1980-88; author, pres. Ednl. Adventures, N.Y.C., 1990—. Author: Educational Adventures, 1990. Home: 283 Palisade Ave Dobbs Ferry NY 10522-3513 Office: Ednl Adventures PO Box 647 Dobbs Ferry NY 10522-0647

BOWE, PETER ARMISTEAD, manufacturing executive; b. Balt., Apr. 13, 1956; s. Richard Eugene and Virginia Welbourn (Cooley) B.; m. Claudia DeSantis, May 31, 1980; children: Alexander Armistead, Clara Kathleen MacBain. BA with high honors, Yale U., 1978; MBA with distinction, Harvard U., 1982. Banker J. P. Morgan Co., N.Y.C., 1978-80; sec., treas. Ellicott Machine Corp., Balt., 1982-85, gen. mgr. dredge div., 1985-87, pres. dredge div., 1987—, also bd. dirs.; bd. dirs. IHC Holland N.V., Sliedrecht, Holland. Contbr. articles to profl. jours. Mem. Walters Art Gallery Coun., Balt., 1988—; agt. alumni fund Yale U., New Haven, 1978—; pres. Harvard Bus. Sch. Club of Md., 1983-85. Recipient Pres.'s "E" award for exports, 1986, Venture award Greater Balt. Com., 1989; co. named Co. of Yr., Balt. Bus. Jour., 1989. Mem. Young Pres.' Orgn. (sec. Balt. chpt. 1991—), Balt. Coun. on Fgn. Affairs (bd. dirs.), World Trade Ctr. Inst. (bd. dirs.). Office: Ellicott Machine Corp 1611 Bush St Baltimore MD 21230-2093

BOWE, RICHARD EUGENE, machine company executive; b. Van Wert, Ohio, Aug. 27, 1921; s. Hugh Horatio and Clara Magdalene (Heiby) B.; m. Virginia Welbourn Cooley, May 17, 1947; children—Richard Welbourn, Michael Ames, Peter Armistead. Student, U. Mich., 1939-40; B.S., U.S. Naval Acad., 1943; M.B.A., Harvard U., 1949. Salesman Buck Glass Co., Balt., 1949-54; with Ellicott Machine Corp., Balt., 1954—; chmn. bd., pres. Ellicott Machine Corp., 1965—; adv. dir. Arkwright, Boston.; bd. dirs. First Md. Bancorp., Balt.; adv. dir. Liberty Mutual Ins., Boston, 1965-89, Arkwright-Boston Ins., Malvern, Pa., 1964—. Trustee Gilman Sch., 1970-78, Balt. Mus. Art, 1979-85. Lt. comdr. USN, 1940-47. Decorated Silver Star, Bronze Star, Gold Star. Mem. Army Navy Club, Army Navy Country Club, Am. Bur. Shipping, Duquesne Club. Republican. Office: Ellicott Machine Corp 1611 Bush St Baltimore MD 21230-2093

BOWEN, CHARLES REVELLE, data processing company executive; b. Chgo., Dec. 8, 1926; s. Neely and Marguerite (Van Dervoort) B.; m. Margaret Ann Huck, Aug. 27, 1955; children: Julie Ann, Charles Neely, Sarah Margaret. BA summa cum laude, Yale U., 1948. With Prudential Ins. Co., Newark, 1949-53; program mgr. Am. Gas Assn., N.Y.C., 1953-58; adminstrv. asst. IBM Corp., N.Y.C., 1958-61, mgr. ednl. support, 1961-66; dir. edn. program IBM Corp., Armonk, N.Y., 1966-75, dir. plans and program adminstrn., 1975—; sec. Navy Bd. Edn. and Tng., 1978-81; bd. dirs. Ednl. Testing Svc., Princeton, N.J., 1981-84; mem. NSF Commn. on Equal Opportunity in Sci. and Engring.; mem. Nat. Action Coun. for Minorities in Engring. Chmn. Nat. Com. for Support of Pub. Schs., Washington, 1970-73. Lt. (j.g.), USN, 1948-49. Mem. Am. Assn. Higher Edn., Phi Beta Kappa. Republican. Episcopalian. Office: IBM Corp Old Orchard Rd Armonk NY 10504

BOWEN, DAVID HYWEL MICHAEL, scientific society administrator; b. Gorseinon, Wales, July 1, 1939; s. Philip Jackson and Beryl Monica (Williams) B.; m. Joy Cecilia Spartin, June 17, 1967; children: Jennifer Sian, James Philip. BS, U. Birmingham, 1960, PhD, 1963. Rsch. engr. E.I. Du Pont de Nemours, Inc., Wilmington, Del., 1963-67; asst. editor Am. Chem. Soc., Washington, 1967-69, mng. editor, 1969-72, head journals, 1972-75, dir. books and jours., 1975-88, dir. membership, 1988—. Author, editor: Economics of Scientific Journals, 1982. Pres. St. David's Welsh-Am. Soc. Washington, 1971-73, v.p., 1986. Mem. AAAS, Am. Inst. Chem. Engrs.,

Am. Chem. Soc., U. Club (Washington), Md. Ornithol. Soc. (v.p. Montgomery County chpt. 1975). Democrat. Episcopalian. Home: 8609 Ewing Dr Bethesda MD 20817 Office: Am Chem Soc 1155 16th St NW Washington DC 20036

BOWEN, JAMES HAROLD, JR. (HAL BOWEN, JR.), chiropractor; b. Belmar, N.J., Dec. 5, 1948; s. James Harold and Janet Marjorie (Haberstick) B.; m. Elaine Stone Bowen, Mar. 27, 1976; children: Adam Truett Bowen, Rebecca Lynn Bowen, Shannon Leigh Bowen. AB, Lafayette Coll., 1970; D of Chiropractic summa cum laude, Sherman Coll. of Chiropractic, 1981. Dr. of Chiropractic, Del., Pa., Mich., Ga., S.C. Diplomate Nat. Bd. Chiropractic Examiners, Boulder, Colo., 1980—; trustee Pa. Coll. Straight Chiropractic, Phila., 1987—; founding mem. World Chiropractic Alliance, Phoenix, 1988; regent Sherman Coll. Straight Chiropractic, Spartanburg, S.C., 1983—; pres. Del. Chiropractic Soc., 1991—; mem. Assn. for Rsch. Chiropractic Scis., Levittown, Pa., 1982—, Fedn. Chiropractic Edn. & Rsch., Washington, 1989—; treas. Del. Chiropractic Soc., Rehoboth Beach, Del., 1984-91. Contbr. articles to profl. jours. Recipient ADIO award, ADIO Seminars, Chandler, Phoenix, Ariz., 1991. Baptist. Office: Bowen Family Chiropractic Ctr 26 Midway Shopping Ctr Rehoboth Beach DE 19971-9735

BOWEN, JOHN JOSEPH, educational administrator; b. Utica, N.Y., Feb. 20, 1952; s. Robert Charles and Irene M. (Bowen) B.; m. Bernadette Rossi, June 21, 1986; 1 child, Garret. AS, Culinary Inst. Am., 1973; BS in Food Svc. Mgmt., Johnson and Wales U., 1977; M Mgmt., Am. Mgmt. Assocs., 1981; diploma, Soc. Culinaire Philanthropique. Notary Pub., R.I. Dir. food svc. and tng. Internat. Food Rsch. and Edn. ctr., North Easton, Mass., 1973-74; instr. gourmet cooking Brockton (Mass.) High Sch., 1973-76; exec. v.p. Johnson and Wales U., Providence, 1974—; exc. bd. Aquinas Coll., Newton, Mass. Bd. dirs. budget panel rev. com. Diocese of Providence. Recipient Antonin Careme medal Chef's Assn. Pacific Coast. Mem. Conseiller de la Toque des Etats-Unis, Leadership R.I., Confrerie de la Chaine des Rotisseurs, Chevaliers du Tastevin, Order Golden Toque, Phi Delta Kappa. Roman Catholic. Office: Johnson and Wales U 8 Abbott Park Pl Providence RI 02903-3703

BOWEN, PAUL RHYS, sculptor; b. Colwyn Bay, Wales, G.B., July 12, 1951; s. Stewart Powell and Betty Thelma (Grice) B.; m. Anita Elise Waddell, Sept. 4, 1979; 1 child, Pamela Megan. Diploma in art and design, Newport Coll. Art, Wales, G.B., 1972; MFA, Md. Inst., 1974. mem. exhbn. com. Provincetown Art Assn. & Mus., 1988-90, mem. collection com., 1990; mem. artists adv. bd. Truro Ctr. for the Arts, 1990. Represented in pvt. collections Solomon R. Guggenheim Mus., N.Y., Assn. of the Mus. of Contemporary Art, Ghent, Belgium, Welsh Arts Coun., Cardiff, Wales, G.B., Provincetown (Mass.) Art Assn. and Mus., The Swiss Bank Collection, N.Y., Prudential Ins. Collection, The Progressive Corp. Hoffberger fellow Md. Inst., 1972-74, Hudson D. Walker fellow Fine Arts Work Ctr., 1977-79, Mass. Artists Found. fellow, 1981; Pollock-Krasner Found. grantee, 1987. Home: PO Box 301 Provincetown MA 02657-0301

BOWEN, ROBERT WILLIAM, association executive; b. Wynnewood, Pa., Mar. 24, 1960; s. Thales Jr. and Sally Louise (Hale) B. BSBA, Drexel U., 1983. Program host Sta. WKDU-FM, Phila., 1980-83; announcer Sta. WZZD-AM, Phila., 1981-82; asst. to pres. Dash Communications, Inc., Phila., 1982; publicity and promotion mgr. Nat. Religious Broadcasters, Parsippany, N.J., 1983-85; program host Sta. WXMC-AM, Parsippany, Troy Hills, N.J., 1984-85; conv. coord. Nat. Religious Broadcasters, Morristown, N.J., 1985-87, dir. mem. svcs., 1987—. Contbg. editor: Religious Broadcasting mag. Charter mem. Rep. Presidential Task Force (trustee, 1991—). Mem. Gospel Music Assn., Am. Soc. Assn. Execs., Fellowship Contemporary Christian Ministries, Nature Conservancy (life), Zool. Soc. Phila., Com. for an Affordable N.J. (adv. bd. 1991—), Nat. Trust For Hist. Preservation, Western Reserve Hist. Soc., Nat. Rep. Com. Republican. Office: Nat Religious Broadcasters 299 Webro Rd Parsippany NJ 07054-2800

BOWEN, RONALD SCOTT, air force officer; b. Huntington, W.Va., Feb. 16, 1943; s. Garland Buffington and Alice Ruth (Humphries) B.; m. Sally Ann Lieblein, Feb. 27, 1965; children: Sally Lynn, Steven Scott, Alisa Marie. BS in Metallurgy, Case Inst. Tech., 1964; MBA, U. So. Calif., 1971; postgrad., Air U., 1969, 75, U. Houston, 1986. Commd. 2d lt. USAF, 1964, advanced through grades to col., 1986; staff intelligence officer USAF, Andrews AFB, Md., 1971-74; exec. officer requirements devel. and acquisition, Pentagon USAF, Washington, 1974-75, Congl. activities officer, Pentagon, 1975-78; spl. asst. to comdr. Air Force Systems Command USAF, Andrews AFB, 1979-82; dir. cost analysis electronic systems div. USAF, Hanscom AFB, Mass., 1982-85, dep. dir. MILSTAR terminals system program office, 1985-86; comptr., dep. info. systems ballistic missile office USAF, Norton AFB, Calif., 1986-89; dir. cost USAF, Andrews AFB, 1989-90; comdr. Air Force Cost Analysis Agy. USAF, 1990—. Decorated Legion of Merit, Meritorious Svc. medal with 4 oak leaf clusters, Air Force Commendation medal with 1 oak leaf cluster. Mem. Am. Soc. Mil. Comptrollers (pres. Nations Gateway chpt. 1988-89), Mil. Ops. Rsch. Soc., Soc. Cost Estimating and Analysis, Beta Gamma Sigma. Home: 9815 Indian Queen Point Rd Fort Washington MD 20744 Office: SAF/FMC Pentagon Rm 4D159 Washington DC 20330

BOWER, DAVID HARRISON, dentist; b. Lafayette Hill, Pa., Jan. 18, 1947; s. Herbert Harrison and Helen Victoria (Swope) B.; m. Patrice Ann Campbell, July 31, 1984 (div. Mar. 1986). AB in English Lit., Syracuse U., 1968; DMD, U. Pa., 1973. High sch. tchr. Green Bank Pvt. Sch., Glenmoor, Pa., 1968-69; dental intern, resident Einstein No. Div., Phila., 1973; dentist Dr. Morris Saltz, Chester, Pa., 1975-77, Colonial Sch. System, Plymouth Meeting, Pa., 1975-78, Vis. Nurse Assn., Ambler, Pa., 1976-78; pvt. practice Lafayette Hill, Pa., 1976—. Contbr. articles to local newspapers. Pres. Whitemarsh Twp. Bus. Assn., Lafayette Hill, 1986-88, 90-91. 2d lt. USPHS, 1973-75. Bus. award Whitemarsh Twp. Bus. Assn., Lafayette Hill, 1988. Mem. ADA, Acad. Gen. Dentistry, King Prussia Study Club. Republican. Methodist. Home and Office: 3000 Joshua Rd Lafayette Hill PA 19444-2003

BOWER, HAROLD EUGENE, JR., seminary administrator; b. Williamsport, Pa., July 27, 1955; s. Harold Eugene Sr. and Rosanna Mae (Wright) B.; m. Cheryl Mae Green, May 7, 1977; children: Heather, Melynda, Kristen, Andrew. BA, Lycoming Coll., 1981; MDiv, Pitts. Theol. Sem., 1985. Asst. trust officer No. Cen. Bank, Williamsport, 1981-82; acct. Richard King Mellon Found., Pitts., 1984-85; bus. mgr. Fredonia (N.Y.) Coll. Found., 1985-89; fiscal affairs officer City of Dunkirk (N.Y.), 1986-89; v.p. New Brunswick (N.J.) Sem., 1989—; con. Blackbaud Microsystems, Charleston, S.C., 1990—. With USN, 1973-75. Mem. Phi Kappa Phi. Republican. Baptist. Office: New Brunswick Sem 17 Seminary Pl New Brunswick NJ 08901-1196

BOWER, JOSEPH LYON, business administration educator, academic dean; b. N.Y.C., Sept. 21, 1938; s. Morris L. and Florence (Turitz) B.; m. Nancy Milender, Feb. 16, 1958; children: Jonathan, Deborah. AB, Harvard U., 1959, MBA, 1961, D Bus. Adminstrn., 1963. Asst. prof. Grad. Sch. Bus. Adminstrn. Harvard U., Boston, 1963-68, assoc. prof. Grad. Sch. Bus. Adminstrn., 1968-71, Donald K. David prof. bus. adminstrn. Grad. Sch. Bus. Adminstrn., 1972—, sr. assoc. dean for external rels. Grad. Sch. Bus. Adminstrn., 1986-89, chmn. doctoral programs, dir. of rsch. Grad. Sch. Bus. Adminstrn., 1989—; faculty mem. John F. Kennedy Sch. Govt. Harvard U., Cambridge, Mass., 1969—; bd. dirs. Arrow Automotive Industries, Framingham, Mass., Brown Group Inc., St. Louis, Sonesta Internat. Corp., Boston, ML-Lee Acquisition Fund, L.P., Boston. Author: Managing Resouce Allocation Process, 1971 (McKinsey Found. award 1971), Two Faces of Management, 1983, When Markets Quake, 1986; co-author: Public Management: Text and Cases, 1978, Business Policy: Text and Cases, 6th edit., 1986. Trustee Lincoln (Mass.) Found., 1968—, New Eng. Conservatory Music, Boston, 1984—, DeCordova and Dana Mus. and Pk., Lincoln, 1987—. Mem. Am. Econ. Assn., Coun. Fgn. Rels., St. Botolph Club (Boston), Harvard Club (N.Y.C.). Office: Harvard U Grad Sch Bus Adminstrn Morgan 141 Boston MA 02163

BOWER, WILLIAM RICHARD, mathematics educator, swimming coach; b. Jamestown, N.Y., Mar. 22, 1955; s. Charles Richard Bower and Betty (Cottrell) Culligan; m. Deborah J. Crawford, May 21, 1977 (div. June 1989); children: Ashley, William, Matthew, Sarah. BA, Tulane U., 1977; MS, Loyola U., New Orleans, 1987. Tchr., coach Kiski Sch., Saltsburg, Pa., 1977-86, 90—, St. Martin's, New Orleans, 1986-88, Tuloso-Midway, Corpus Christi, Tex., 1988-90. Sponsor Young Reps., New Orleans, 1988. Named Coach Yr. Greater New Orleans High Sch. Swimming League, 1987, 88, Whataburger, Tex., 1990. Home and Office: 1888 Brett Ln Saltsburg PA 15681-8951

BOWERS, GRAYSON HUNTER, building parts manufacturing company executive; b. Frederick, Md., Nov. 18, 1897; s. Grayson Eichelberger and Chrisse Byrd Dell (Firestone) B.; ed. Gettysburg Coll., 1919; m. Isabel Houck, June 6, 1921 (dec. Dec. 1961); children: Grayson Hunter, Charles R., Alice Josephine Bowers Butler; m. 2d, Frances L. Crilly, June 20, 1964. Vice pres. William D. Bowers Lumber Co. and pres. allied corps., Frederick, 1919—; pres. Fidelity Bldg. & Loan Assn., 1961-80; Mt. Olivet Cemetery Co.; sr. v.p., dir. Fredericktown Bank & Trust Co., 1931-79; dir., officer Lumbermens Merchandising Corp., Wayne, Pa., 1945-70. Alderman, City of Frederick, 1928-34; pres. Bd. Election Suprs., 1934-38, Frederick City Planning Commn., 1943-70; trustee Hood Coll., 1950-74; mem. adv. council Md. Hosp. Constrn., 1968-71. Served to 1st lt. U.S. Army, 1919. Club: Masons. Mem. Frederick County Hist. Soc. (pres. 1965-67, 70-72). Home: 1st Fl 101 Council St Frederick MD 21701 Office: William D Bowers Lumber Co 10620 Woodsboro Rd Woodsboro MD 21798-8215

BOWERS, JAMES THOMAS, communications company executive; b. Wilmington, Del., Oct. 6, 1958; s. George Henry and Dorothy Marie (Figenshu) B.; m. Rebecca Ann Neary, July 8, 1989; 1 child, James Thomas Jr. BBA, U. Notre Dame, 1980. Account exec. Diamond State Telephone, Wilmington, 1980-86; sales instr. Bell Atlantic, Phila., 1986-87; telemktg. mgr. Bell of Pa., Bala Cynwyd, 1987-88; adminstrv. mgr. Bell of Pa., Malvern, 1988—. Engaged encounter vol.; fundraiser Archmere Acad. Mem. Notre Dame Club Del. Roman Catholic.,. Home: 5 Richards Dr Wilmington DE 19810-3902 Office: 50 E Swedesford Rd Malvern PA 19355-1484

BOWERS, PATRICIA ELEANOR FRITZ, economist; b. N.Y.C., Mar. 21, 1928; d. Eduard and Eleanor (Ring) Fritz. Student scholar, Goucher Coll., 1946-48; B.A., Cornell U., 1950; M.A., NYU, 1953, Ph.D., 1965. Statis. asst. Fed. Res. Bank N.Y., N.Y.C., 1950-53; lectr. Upsala Coll., East Orange, N.J., 1953-59; researcher Fortune mag., N.Y.C., 1959-60; teaching fellow NYU, N.Y.C., 1960-62, instr., 1962-64; mem. faculty Bklyn. Coll., 1964—, prof. econs., 1974—. Author: Private Choice and Public Welfare, 1974. Sec. Friends of the Johnson Mus., Cornell U., 1989—. Mem. Am. Econ. Assn., Econometric Soc., N.Y. Acad. Scis., Fgn. Policy Assn., Women's Econ. Round Table, Met. Econ. Assn. (sec. 1963-68, pres. 1974-75), Am. Statis. Assn. (univs. chmn. ann. forecasting confs. 1970-71, 71-72), Cornell Club N.Y., Kappa Alpha Theta. Home: 145 E 16th St New York NY 10003-3405 Office: CUNY Bklyn Coll Dept Econs Brooklyn NY 11210

BOWERS, PATRICIA NEWSOME, communications executive; b. Baton Rouge, June 21, 1944; d. Carl Allen and Sue Mayre (Powell) Newsome; m. Robert Lloyd Bowers Jr., Aug. 19, 1967 (div. Nov. 1979); children: Paige Ivy, Katherine Elizabeth. BJ, La. State U., 1967. Sr. writer, editor Litton Industries, Pascagoula, Miss., 1978-80; sr. presentations supr. Martin Marietta Aerospace, Orlando, Fla., 1980-81; mgr. presentations Martin Marietta Aerospace, Balt., 1981-85, mgr. pub. rels., 1985-90; dir. pub. rels. and corp. comm. Contraves USA, Pitts., 1990-92; sr. mgr. sector communications Harris Electronic Systems sector Harris Corp., Melbourne, Fla., 1992—. Coach Parkville Recreation Council, Balt., 1985-87; bd. dirs. Salvation Army, Human Resources Devel. Agy. Balt. County; adv. bd. Nat. Aquarium in Balt. Mem. Pub. Rels. Soc. Am. (bd. dirs. Chesapeake conf. 1987, Silver Anvil Judge, 1991, 92), Navy League (bd. dirs. Balt. council 1986-87), Balt. County C. of C. (leadership program 1986-87), Pitts. Press Club. Republican. Episcopalian. Office: Harris Corp PO Box 37 (MS: 2-1713) Melbourne FL 32902-9739

BOWERS, PETER GEORGE, chemistry educator, researcher; b. Eastbourne, Sussex, Eng., May 14, 1937; came to U.S., 1967; s. George William and Carrie (Moore) B. BA, U. Cambridge, Eng., 1961; PhD, U. B.C., 1964. NATO rsch. fellow Sheffield (Eng.) U., 1964-66; prof. chemistry Simmons Coll., Boston, 1968—; vis. prof. Boston U., 1967-68, U. B.C. (Can.), 1974-75, U. Oreg., Eugene, 1982, 89. Contbr. numerous articles to profl. jours. With RAF, 1956-58. Mem. Am. Chem. Soc., Sigma Xi. Office: Simmons Coll 300 Fenway Boston MA 02115-5898

BOWERS, PHILLIP FREDERICK, astronomer; b. Huntington, Ind., Dec. 14, 1947; s. Frederick Wallace and Frances Maxine (Everett) B. BS in Astrophysics, Ind. U., 1969; PhD in Astronomy, U. Md., 1977. Rsch. assoc. Nat. Radio Astronomy Obs., Charlottesville, Va., 1977-80, U. Md., College Park, 1980-82; rsch. astronomer SFA, Inc. and Naval Rsch. Lab., Washington, 1983—. Contbr. articles to profl. jours. E.O. Hulburt fellow Naval Ksch. Lab., 1980-82. Mem. Am. Astron. Soc., Internat. Astron. Union. Office: SFA Inc 1401 Mccormick Dr Landover MD 20785-5322

BOWERS, THOMAS GLENN, clinical psychologist; b. Lincoln, Nebr., Nov. 3, 1950; s. Glenn Forrest and Shirley Belle (Parker) B. BS, U. Wash., Seattle, 1975; MA, U. B.C., Vancouver, 1979; PhD, Va. Poly. State U., 1984. Lic. psychologist, Pa. Staff psychologist New River Valley Mental Helath Svcs., Radford, Va., 1984-86; dir. N.W. Counseling Ctr., Dyersburg, Tenn., 1986-87, Family Devel. Svcs. Pa. State U., Harrisburg, Pa., 1988—; asst. prof. Pa. State U., Middletown, 1987—. Contbr. articles to profl. jours. Mem. Am. Psychol. Assn., Pa. Psychol. Assn., Ea. Psychol. Assn. Office: Pa State U Family Devel Svcs Middletown PA 17057 also: Pa State U Harrisburg PA 17110

BOWLER, MARIANNE BIANCA, judge; b. Boston, Feb. 15, 1947; d. Richard A. and Ann C. (Daly) B. BA, Regis Coll., 1967; JD cum laude, Suffolk U., 1976. Bar: Mass. 1978. Rsch. asst. Harvard Med. Sch., Boston, 1967-69; med. editor Mass. Dept. of Pub. Health, Boston, 1969-76; law clk. Mass. Superior Ct., Boston, 1976-77, dep. chief law clk., 1977-78; asst. dist. atty. Middlesex Dist. Atty.'s Office, Cambridge, Mass., 1978; asst. U.S. atty. U.S. Dept. of Justice, Boston, 1978-90, exec. asst. U.S. atty., 1988-89, sr. litigation counsel, 1989-90; U.S. magistrate judge U.S. Dist. Ct. Mass., Boston, 1990—; chmn. bd. trustees New Eng. Bapt. Hosp., Boston, 1990—. Mng. editor: This Week in Public Health, 1969-75. Mem. Jr. League Boston, Suffolk Law Sch. Alumni Assn. (pres. 1979-80), Vincent Club. Democrat. Roman Catholic. Home: Brookline MA 02146 Office: US Dist Ct 908 McCormack Post Office Boston MA 02109

BOWLES, ALAN DEREK, security consultant, investigator; b. London, Eng., Oct. 4, 1960; came to U.S., 1981; s. Derek George and Yvonne (Wielder) B.; m. Diane Tomlinson, May 17, 1981 (div. Dec. 1988) 1 child, Chas. Alan; m. Julie Lee Koehler, Feb. 4, 1989; 1 child, Chelsea Lee. Cert. Protection Profl., 1990. Mgr. Burns Internat. Security, Mpls., Dallas & Bethesda, Md., 1981-86, Pinkerton Detective Agy., N.Y.C., 1986-88, Nat. Guardian, N.Y.C., 1988-89; cons., v.p. sales Servicelink, Inc., N.Y.C., 1989—; co-owner New Age Inc., 1990—, Tranquility, Inc., 1991—; cons. Dean Witter Reynolds, Drexel Burnham Lambert, Citicorp., Merrill Lynch, Mobil Oil Corp., Bowery Savs. Bank. Author: Security Procedures for Security Officers, 1988; co-editor: Voices. Security mgr. Burns Internat. for Rep. Nat. Com., Dallas, 1984. Mem. Am. Soc. Indsl. Security. Office: Servicelink Inc 595 Madison Ave New York NY 10022-1907

BOWLES, GEORGE MCMILLAN, philosophy educator; b. Waterloo, Iowa, May 13, 1944; s. George Worth and Georgiana (McMillan) B.; m. Elizabeth Roberts Cheyney, Aug. 12, 1981. BA, U. Denver, 1966; PhD, Stanford U., 1970. Asst. prof. Morningside Coll., Sioux City, Iowa, 1970-71; assoc. prof. Augustana Coll., Sioux City, 1971-81; adj. assoc. prof. George Washington U., Washington, 1984—. Co-author: Logic For Writers, 1987; contbr. articles to profl. jours. Recipient Fellowship, Woodrow Wilson Found., 1966-67. Mem. Am. Philos. Assn., Assn. for Informal Logic and Critical Thinking, Phi Beta Kappa. Home: 4466 Arlington Blvd Arlington VA 22204-1340 Office: George Washington U Philosophy Dept Washington DC 20052

BOWLES, PATRICIA MARY, educator; b. Reading, Pa., Jan. 15, 1950; d. Charles Worthington Doane and Mary Augusta (Kershner) B. BS, Kutztown (Pa.) U., 1971; MEd, Temple U., 1987. Cert. elem. tchr. and elem. prin., Pa. Tchr. visually impaired Reading (Pa.) Sch. Dist., 1972-75, adminstrv. intern, 1986-87; tchr. visually impaired Berks County Intermediate Unit, Reading, 1975—. Account exec. United Way, Berks County, 1988—; bd. dirs. Leadership Berks, Reading, 1988—, Nat. Coun. on Alcoholism, Berks County, 1988—; pres. Leadership Berks Alumni Assn., Reading, 1987, bd. dirs., 1987—. Eleanor Long Tchr. of the Yr., Pa. Div. Visually Impaired, 1984. Mem. Assn. for Edn. and Rehab. Visually Impaired, Assn. for Supervision and Curriculum Devel., Flying Dutchmen Ski Club (trip dir. Reading chpt. 1975-76), Phi Delta Kappa, Delta Kappa Gamma. Republican. Lutheran. Home: 5 Eagle Ct Reading PA 19605 Office: Berks County Intermediate Unit 1111 Commons Blvd Reading PA 19605

BOWLEY, DONOVAN AIDAN ROBIN, ecologist; b. Waltham, Pa., May 20, 1945; s. Robert Prescott and Jane Iris (Aldro) B. BA in Biology, Ea. Nazarene Coll., 1967; MA in Biology, Boston U., 1970, PhD in Biology, 1978. Libr. asst. Mus. of Comparative Zoology Harvard U., Cambridge, Mass., 1967-68; asst. horticulturalist Ea. Nazarene Coll., Quincy, Mass., 1972-74; assoc. ecologist Helden Engring. Assocs., Inc., Boston, New Bedford, Mass., 1974-77; asst. survey analyst Mass. Dept. Environ. Quality Engring., Boston, 1978; assoc. planner New Eng. Water Pollution Control Commn., Boston, 1978-85; regional planner IV Div. Water Supply Mass. Dept. Environ. Protection, Boston, 1985-91, environ. analyst VI, 1991—; adj. faculty Antioch Coll., Boston, 1974; instr. in sci. Boston U., 1975-77. Contbr. articles to profl. jours. Provincial of New Eng. Province, Brotherhood of St. Gregory, White Plains, N.Y., 1988—; trustee Iona Cornerstone Found., Falmouth, Mass., 1991—; clk. of vestry Parish of the Messiah, 1991—. Mem. Assn. Groundwater Scientists and Engrs., N.Y. Acad. Sci., New Eng. Bot. Club (curator nonvascular plants 1975-86), New Eng. Hist. Geneal. Soc., Waltham Triad Lodge Masons, Scottish Rite Bodies Valley of Boston. Episcopalian. Home: 1500 Worcester Rd 1500 Worcester Rd #332E Framingham MA 01701-8953 Office: Mass Dept Environ Protect One Winston St One Winter St Boston MA 02108

BOWLING, JAMES CHANDLER, food products company consultant; b. Covington, Ky., Mar. 29, 1928; s. Van Dorn and Mary Bell (Johnson) B.; m. Ann Jones, Oct. 20, 1951; children: Belinda, Nancy, James Jr., Stephanie. B.S., U. Louisville, 1951; LL.D. (hon.), Murray U., 1976, U. Ky., 1981. With Philip Morris, Inc., N.Y.C., 1948-86, various positions from campus rep. to v.p. sales and corp. relations; then exec. v.p., group v.p., dir. marketing, asst. to chmn. bd., sr. v.p., dir., now cons.; dir. Miller Brewing Co., until 1986, Seven Up Co.; bd. dirs., mem. exec. com. Tobacco Inst., Washington., until 1984; sr. adv. bd. Burson-Marsteller, 1986—; advisor USIA; bd. dirs. Cherokee Farms, Union Trust, Darien, Conn., Centurion, Inc., Centurion Stables, Inc.; chmn. bd. Pub. Rels. News; chmn. Bowling Investments, Inc. Author: How To Improve Your Personal Relations, 1959. Mem. nat. coun. Boy Scouts Am., 1961—; trustee Boy Scout Mus.; justice of peace, Rowayton, Conn., 1960-68; vice chmn. Clean World Internat.; chmn. Pub. Affairs Coun., Washington; bd. overseers U. Louisville; bd. dirs., past pres.and chmn. Keep Am. Beautiful; bd. dirs. Nat. Automatic Merchandising Assn., Ky. Ind. Coll. Found., Nat. Tennis Found. Hall of Fame, Sanders Brown Found., Ky. Ctr. Aging, Country Music Hall Fame, 1956, U. Ky. Devel. Coun.; trustee, vice chmn. Berea Coll., Midway Coll. Recipient Kolodny award as outstanding young exec. in tobacco industry, 1963; named U.S. Young Businessman of Year St. John's U., 1967, Outstanding Alumnus U. Louisville, 1970, 86, 90, Kentuckian of Year, 1977; elected to Tobacco Industry Hall of Fame, 1976. Mem. Nat. Assn. Tobacco Distbg. (bd. dirs. exec. mgmt. div.), Pub. Rels. Soc. Am., Sales Execs. Club N.Y., The Kentuckians (past pres.), Laymen's Nat. Bible Assn. (v.p., bd. dirs.), World Press Inst., Lambda Chi Alpha (found. v.p., pres.). Episcopalian. Clubs: Wee Burn Country, Union League, John's Island. Home: 400 Ocean Rd #170 John's Island Vero Beach FL 32963 Home (summer): 13 Tokeneke Tr Darien CT 06820 Office: 230 Park Ave S New York NY 10003-1513

BOWLUS, DALE RICHARD, environmental scientist, educator, consultant; b. Fremont, Ohio, Mar. 31, 1948; s. Dale Roscoe and Margaret Ann (Richard) B.; m. Vicki Marlene Sexton, Dec. 20, 1986; children: Kameron Michele, Lyndsey Nichole, Meganne Oneile. BS, Bowling Green State U., 1970; MS, Morgan State U., 1975. Registered hazardous substances and environ. profl., cert. hazardous materials mgr. Sci. instr. Harford County Bd. Edn., Bel Air, Md., 1970-79, county sci. resource tchr., 1976-78; environ. scientist U.S. Army Environ. Hygiene Agy., Aberdeen Proving Ground, Md., 1977—, Army hazardous materials spill response team, 1981-90; v.p. Enteco, Inc., Bel Air, 1981-84, A&B Cons., Havre De Grace, Md., 1984-88. Author over 100 waste mgmt. reports, tech. papers and guides; contbr. articles to Municipal and Solid Waste;. Mem. exec. bd. Susquehannock Environ. Ctr., Bel Air, 1987-91, v.p., 1988-91; scholarship adv. bd. United Meth. Ch., Bel Air, 1990—; mem. adv. bd. Harford Community Coll., Bel Air, 1990—. Recipient Exceptional Performance award U.S. Dept. Def., 1983, 86, 89, 90, Unsung Hero award Susquehannock Environ. Ctr., 1990, Govt. Salute to Excellence award Gov's. Office State Md., 1990, Outstanding Hazardous Waste Mgmt. Support awards Dept. U.S. Army, Air Force NG Bur., 1985, Mass. NG, 1987, U.S. Army, 1987. Mem. ASTM (F-20 subcom. recording sec. 1984-87, v.p. 1987-89), Nat. Environ. Health Assn., Nat. Environ. Tgn. Assn., Bowling Green State U. Alumni Assn., Soc. Risk Analysis. Republican. Methodist. Home: 3717 Berkley Rd Darlington MD 21034-1209 Office: US Army Environ Hygiene Agy HSHB-ME-SR Aberdeen Proving Ground MD 21010-5422

BOWMAN, GEORGE LEO, artist; b. Newburyport, Mass., Dec. 25, 1935; s. George Leo and Dorothy Maude (Fosse) B.; div. BS in Edn., Tufts U., 1960; diploma in fine arts, Boston Sch. Mus. Fine Arts, 1960. Freelance illustrator childrens publs. N.Y.C., 1960; designer Ginn & Co. Pub., Boston, 1960-62, D.C. Heath Pub. Co., Boston, 1962-64; art instr. Boston Sch. Mus. Fine Arts, 1964-69; designer, illustrator Analytical Systems Engring. Corp., Burlington, Mass., 1980—; fine arts painter-artist Rockport and Westford, Mass., 1960—. Recipient New Eng. Book Designers award, 1963-64, Copley Soc. Painting award, 1970, Nat. Casein Show Painting, N.Y.C., 1972. Mem. Rockport Art Assn. (John Cooley Painting award 1980, Louis Bankoff Painting award 1981, Aldro Hibbard Painting award 1982). Episcopalian. Home: 3 Old Homestead Rd Westford MA 01886-2403

BOWMAN, PEYTON GRAHAM, III, lawyer; b. Richmond, Va., Feb. 3, 1929; s. Peyton Graham and Elinor Coleman (Hargrave) B.; m. Suzanne Wilkes Nagel, April. 28, 1973; children: Lindsay Spencer, Peyton Graham IV. BA, U. Va., 1952, LLB, 1953. Bar: Va. 1952, D.C. 1958, Fed. Energy, 1958. Assoc. Reid & Priest, Washington, 1957-72, ptnr., 1972—. Served to capt. U.S. Army, 1953-60. Mem. ABA. Republican. Presbyterian. Clubs: Metropolitan (Washington), Chevy Chase (Washington). Home: 4940 Hillbrook Ln NW Washington DC 20016-3208 Office: Reid & Priest Market Sq 701 Pennsylvania Ave NW Washington DC 20004-2608

BOWNE, DALE RUSSELL, religion educator, minister; b. Ohio, Aug. 19, 1934; s. Francis Thomas and Dorothy (Duer) B.; m. Anne Channing Parr, Aug. 24, 1956; children: Susannah, Elisabeth. BA, Washington & Jefferson Coll., Washington, Pa., 1956, DD, 1981; MDiv, Pitts. Theol. Sem., 1959; ThD, Union Theol. Sem., N.Y.C., 1963. From asst. prof. to assoc. prof. Grove City (Pa.) Coll., 1963-71, prof. & chair dept. religion & philosophy, 1971—; alumni coun. Pitts. Theol. Sem., 1989—. Author: Paradigims & Principal Parts, 1989, How to Choose a Bible, 1979, Harbison Heritage, 1989, Greek Practice, 1990. Mem. Soc. Biblical Lit., The Cleric (past pres.). Presbyterian. Home: 156 Edgewood Ave Grove City PA 16127-1657 Office: Grove City Coll PO Box 2623 Grove City PA 16127-5128

BOWSHER, CHARLES ARTHUR, government official; b. Elkhart, Ind., May 30, 1931; s. Matthew A. and Ella M. (West) B.; m. Mary C. Mahoney, Dec. 14, 1963; children: Kathryn M., Stephen C. BS, U. Ill., 1953; MBA, U. Chgo., 1956; DSc in Bus. Adminstrn. (hon.), Bryant Coll., 1984. C.P.A., Ill. Ptnr. Arthur Andersen & Co., Chgo., 1956-67, Washington, 1971-81; asst. sec. of Navy for fin. mgmt. Dept. Def., Washington, 1967-71; comptroller gen. U.S., 1981—; mem. nominating com. Acctg. Hall Fame, adv. com. Fin. Acctg. Standards Bd., adv. coun. Govt. Acctg. Standards Bd., 1981. Mem. adv. council dept. sociology Princeton U.; mem. vis. com. Miami U. Sch. Bus., Conf. Bd.; hon. bd. Ctr. Excellence Govt.; adv. com. office for govtl. acctg. rsch. and edn. U. Ill. Coll. Bus. Adminstrn.; mem. bus. adv. coun. U.

Ill.; pub. sector com. Internat. Fedn. of Accts.; adv. council Office of Tech. Assessment; bd. of overseers Wharton Sch., U. Pa.; mem. vis. com. Sch. Bus., U. So. Calif.; mem. Adv. Bd. Huntsman Ctr. for Global Competition and Leadership Wharton Sch.; mem. editorial bd. Acctg. Horizons; mem. bd. advisors A Presdl. Classroom for Young Ams.; mem. selection com. Roger W. Jones Award for Exec. Leadership. Served with U.S. Army, 1953-55. Recipient Distinguished Pub. Service award U.S. Navy, 1969, Distinguished Pub. Service award Dept. Def., 1971. Mem. AICPA, Nat. Acad. Pub. Adminstrn., Am. Mgmt. Assn. (gen. mgmt. council, bd. trustee), Nat. Assn. Govt. Accts., Beta Alpha Psi (adv. forum). Clubs: Burning Tree (Washington). Home: 4503 Boxwood Rd Bethesda MD 20816-1815 Office: GAO 441 G St NW Rm 7000 Washington DC 20548-0002

BOX, VERNON GEORGE S., organic chemist, educator, researcher; b. Montego Bay, Jamaica, June 20, 1946; s. Lester and Julia Mae (Blake) B.; m. Lynda Lynette Box, July 3, 1976; children: Samantha Nalini, Ananda Shaula. BSc, U. West Indies, Kingston, Jamaica, 1967, PhD, 1971. From asst. lectr. to sr. lectr. U. West Indies, 1969-82; scientist Schering-Plough Corp., Bloomfield, N.J., 1982-84; assoc. prof. CCNY, 1984-91, prof., 1992—. Author: (molecular graphics computer program) STR3D1, 1989; contbr. articles to profl. jours. Fellow Am. Inst. Chemists, Am. Chem. Soc., Inter-Am. Photochem. Soc., N.Y. Acad. Scis. (chmn. 1990-91, asst. chmn. 1989-90), Masons. Home: 4 Wakefield Dr Edison NJ 08820-1654 Office: CCNY Dept Chemistry Convent Ave at 138th St New York NY 15031

BOXENHORN, BURTON, aerospace engineer; b. N.Y.C., Apr. 22, 1928; s. Max Boxenhorn and Rose Zvebel; m. Marianne Fedder, Jan. 7, 1962; children; David, Elizabeth. BSME, Clarkson U., 1952; MSME, Carnegie-Mellon, 1956; MSEE, N.Y. U., 1960. Registered profl. engr., Mass. Engr., dept. rsch. United Aircraft, East Hartford, Conn., 1952-54; engr. Hamilton-Standard, Windsor Locks, Conn., 1956-57; instr., dept. mech. engring. N.Y. U., 1957-60; staff engr. MIT Instrn. Lab., Cambridge, Mass., 1962-64; engr. Philco, Willow Grove, Pa., 1965-66; staff engr. C.S. Draper Lab., Cambridge, 1966—. Contbr. articles to profl. jours. Rep. Brookline (Mass.) Town Meeting. Mem. AIAA, IEEE.

BOXER, STANLEY ROBERT, painter, sculptor; b. N.Y.C., June 26, 1926; s. Max and Ida (Gordon) B.; m. Joyce Weinstein, Nov. 28, 1952. Student, Bklyn. Coll., Art Students League, 1946-49. Vis. Artists' Program lectr. Harvard U., 1984. Artist suite of etchings: vol. aquatint etchings Ringofdustinbloom, 1984, Monotypes, 1985-88, monotypes and prints, 1989-91; one-man exhbns. include Andre Emmerich Gallery, Zurich, Switzerland, 1975-91, 78, N.Y.C., 1975-91, Galerie Wentzel, Cologne, Fed. Republic Germany, 1975, 78, 80, 82, 83, 85, 87-88, 1990, Tibor de Nagy Gallery, N.Y.C., 1971-75, 80, 82, 87, Hokin Gallery, Bay Harbor Island, Fla., 1981, 90-91, Chgo., 1982, 84, 86, 88, Palm Beach, Fla., 1978, 81, 82, 85, 88, Galerie von Braunbehrens, Munich, Fed. Republic Germany, 1982, Am. House, Berlin, 1982, Gallery One, Toronto, Ont., Can., 1980-85, 86, 88, 90-91, Downstairs Gallery, Edmonton, Alta., Can., 1981, 83, Frances Aronson Gallery, Atlanta, 1983-88, Salander/O'Reily Gallery, N.Y.C., 1983, Ivory Kimpton Gallery, San Francisco, 1983, 85, 86, Ruth Bachofner Gallery, Los Angeles, 1986, 87, 89, Pa. Acad. Fine Arts, Phila., 1976, Dorsky Gallery, N.Y.C., 1991, Laca Gallery, L.A., 1991, Ruth Bochofner Gallery, L.A., 1992, Lewison Gallery, Boston, 1992, Posner Gallery, Milw., 1990, Rose Art Mus., Brandeis U., Waltham, Mass., 1992, Elka London Gallery, Montreal, Can., 1990; sculpture, Boston Mus., 1977, Allrich Gallery, San Francisco, 1979, 81, Galerie Regard, Paris, 1979, 81, Meredith Long & Co., Houston, 1979-81, 83-91, Thomas Segal Gallery, Boston, 1980-82, 84, Richard Gray Gallery, Chgo., 1980, Woltjen/Udell Gallery, Edmonton, Alta., Can., 1984 and Vancouver, B.C., 1986, Art Mus. Santa Cruz county, 1987, Smith Anderson Gallery, Palo Alto, Calif., 1987, 90, Graystone Gallery, San Francisco, 1987, 90, Mixografia Workshop Gallery, L.A., 1987, Harvard U., Cambridge, Mass., 1988, Assoc. Am. Artists, N.Y.C., 1988, 90, Lafayette Coll., Williams Ctr. for Arts, Easton, Pa., 1988, Posner Gallery, Milw., 1990, Elca London Gallery, Montreal, Can., 1990, Galerie Wentzel, Cologne, Fed. Republic of Germany, 1990, Meredith Long & Co., Houston, 1990-91, Laca Gallery, L.A., 1991; retrospectives: (paintings), Boston Mus. Fine Arts, 1977, drawings, Mint Mus. Art, 1978, Rose Art Mus., Waltham, Mass., 1992, numerous group exhbns.; represented in permanent collections, Guggenheim Mus., N.Y.C., Whitney Mus., N.Y.C., Boston Mus. Fine Arts, Houston Mus. Fine Arts, Mus. Modern Art, N.Y.C., Corcoran Gallery Art, Washington, Albright-Knox Mus., Buffalo, Mint Mus. Art, Charlotte, N.C., Edmonton (Alta., Can.) Art Gallery Mus., others, also numerous pvt. collections; designer, builder sculptural set for, Erick Howkins Dance Co., 1972. Served with USN, World War II. Guggenheim fellow, 1975, Visual Artists fellow Nat. Endowment for Arts, 1989.

BOY, STEPHEN FRANCIS, psychologist, health care consultant; b. Brighton, Mass., July 8, 1952; s. Joseph Paul and Helen Claire (Sacco) B.; m. Theresa Katherine Newkirk, Aug. 19, 1978; children: Natalie, Stephen. BA, U. Notre Dame, 1974; MEd, U. N.H., 1979; PhD, Boston Coll., 1986. Lic. psychologist, Mass.; cert. psychologist, N.H. Dir. svcs. Elder Svcs. of Merrimack Valley, Lawrence, Mass., 1974-79; dir. elderly svcs. North Essex Mental Health Ctr., Haverhill, Mass., 1979-81; pvt. practice, 1981—; psychologist Ctr. for Counseling, Haverhill, 1986-91; dir. Riverside Couneling Assocs., Haverhill, 1991—; cons. psychologist Whittier Rehab. Hosp., Haverhill, 1989—, Hale Mcpl. Hosp., Haverhill, 1989—, Glynn Meml. Nursing Home-Alzheimer's unit, Haverhill, 1989—; dir. Riverside Counseling Assocs., Haverhill, 1991—; instr. psychology No. Essex Community Coll., Haverhill, 1990—. Producer, host (video) Loss of the Will to Live, 1989; guest expert (video) Grief & the Older Adult, 1989. Mem., expert Legis. Subcom. on Elderly Mental Health, Boston, 1990; mem. Mass. Dem. Com., Boston, 1989—; mem. Alzheimer's Task Force/Partnership, Lawrence, 1989—. Mem. APA, Mass. Psychol. Assn. (legis. com.), Nat. Register Health Care Providers. Roman Catholic. Home: 11 Arlington St Newburyport MA 01950-3807 Office: Riverside Counseling Assocs 10-12 Phoenix Row Haverhill MA 01832

BOYCE, MEREDITH ANN, school counselor; b. N.Y.C., Oct. 26, 1946; d. Myron and Lorraine Dorothea (Nierenberg) B.; 1 child, Jonathan Randolph Boyce. BS in Elem. Edn., NYU, 1971, MA in Ednl. Psychology, 1974, cert. in advanced studies in counseling, 1990. Real estate mgr., rental agt. N.Y.C., 1980-82, Cable Estates, N.Y.C., 1982-83; real estate mgmt. cons. Parilo Holding Corp., N.Y.C., 1983-87; tchr. Bd. of Edn. J.H.S. 60, N.Y.C., 1987-91; sch. counselor Bd. Edn. City Wide Svcs. Manhattan Occupational Tng. Ctr., N.Y.C., 1991—. Counselor, vol. Help Line Telephone Svcs., N.Y.C., 1991—; chair community affairs Village Ind. Dems., N.Y.C., 1980-85. Mem. AACD, N.Y. State Assn. of Counseling and Devel. Home: 95 Christopher St New York NY 10014-4238 Office: Manhattan Occupl Tng Ctr 250 W Houston St New York NY 10014-4880

BOYCE, PETER BRADFORD, astronomer, professional association executive; b. N.Y.C., Nov. 30, 1936; s. Burke and Mabel (Zoeckler) B.; m. Mary Elizabeth Saffell, Nov. 6, 1976; children: Kevin Robert, Colin MacDonald. AB, Harvard U., 1958; MS, U. Mich., 1962, PhD, 1963. Staff astronomer Lowell Obs., Flagstaff, Ariz., 1963-73; program dir. NSF, Washington, 1973-79; sci. cons. to Congressman Morris K. Udall, Congl. fellow Washington, 1977-78; exec. officer Am. Astron. Soc., Washington, 1979—. Contbr. articles to profl. jours. Dept. Commerce Sci. and Tech. fellow, 1977-78. Mem. AAAS, Am. Astron. Soc., Optical Soc. Am., Am. Phys. Soc., Am. Inst. Physics (bd. dirs. 1979-92, mem. exec. com. 1980-82, 85-92), Internat. Astron. Union, Sigma Xi. Home: 5700 Sherier Pl NW Washington DC 20016-5320 Office: Am Astron Soc 2000 Florida Ave NW Ste 300 Washington DC 20009-1231

BOYD, GORDON MCARTHUR, environmental public affairs consultant; b. Bryn Mawr, Pa., Feb. 24, 1946; s. Alfred Gordon and Etheldreda Helene (McArthur) B.; m. Sharon Walker, Oct. 8, 1971; children: Louise Petersen, James Walker. BA, Hamilton Coll., 1970. Reporter Schenectady (N.Y.) Gazette, 1967-68, 70-72, Utica (N.Y.) Daily Press, 1968-70; owner Saratoga Traders, Inc., Saratoga Springs, N.Y., 1972-74; dep. dir. adminstrn. and ops. N.Y. State Assembly, Albany, 1975-78, coord. planning and devel., 1979-84; exec. dir. N.Y. State Legis. Commn. on Solid Waste Mgmt., Albany, 1984-87; pres. Schillinger, Salerni & Boyd, Inc./Taconic Resources, Inc., Albany, 1988—; v.p. Environ. Data Systems, Inc., Albany, 1990—. Exec. producer (ednl. video) Mountain in the City, 1986 (Hon. Mention, 2 Gold awards, Silver award); contbr. articles to profl. jours. Mem. Empire State Coll. Coun., Saratoga Springs, 1989—; bd. dirs. Home of the Good Shepherd, Saratoga Springs, 1992—. Mem. N.Y. State Solid Waste Mgmt. Bd., N.Y. State Bus. Coun. (environ. com. Albany chpt. 1988—), N.Y. C. of C. (chmn. environ. com. N.Y.C. chpt. 1990—). Democrat. Episcopalian. Office: Schillinger Salerni Boyd Inc/Taconic Resources Inc 15 Elk St Albany NY 12207

BOYD, JOHN HOWARD, corporate location consultant; b. Trenton, N.J., Mar. 13, 1950; m. Nov. 17, 1973; 2 children. AB, Rutgers Coll., 1972; postgrad., Rutgers Grad. Sch., 1972-73. Location analyst div. mgmt. cons. Dun & Bradstreet, N.Y.C., 1973-75; pres. The Boyd Co., Inc., Princeton, N.J., 1975—; cons. U.S. and overseas corps. on facilities location. Henry Rutgers scholar, 1971-72, Bevier fellow, 1973. Office: The Boyd Co Inc 301 N Harrison St Princeton NJ 08540-3512

BOYD, LARRY CHESTER, military officer; b. Newberry, S.C., Nov. 6, 1958; s. Andrew Larkin Sr. and Anna Lee (McMorris) B.; m. Paula Annette Harris, Aug. 19, 1989; 1 child, Larry Jr. BA in Polit. Sci. cum laude, S.C. State Coll., 1980; MSA in Adminstrn., Cen. Mich. U., 1990. Commd. 2d lt. U.S. Army, 1980, advanced to capt., 1984; adminstrv. officer 800th Materiel Mgmt. Ctr. U.S. Army, Nelligan, Fed. Rep. Germany, 1980-82; asst. sec. gen. staff, protocol officer Hdqrs. VII Corps U.S. Army, Stuttgart, Fed. Rep. Germany, 1982-83; chief reenlistment Hdrs. and Hdrs. Co. U.S. Army Garrison U.S. Army, Ft. Polk, La., 1984; comdr. 5th Adj. Gen. Replacement Detachment, Ft. Polk, La., 1984-85; chief, officer records 5th Adj. Gen. Co. U.S. Army, Ft. Polk, La., 1985, chief, pers. records 5th Pers. Svc. Co., 1985, chief, Co. Spt. Div., 1986, chief, G-1/Adj. Gen. Plans and Ops. Hdrs. and Hdqrs. Co. 5th Inf. Div., 1986; advisor Readiness Group Dix First U.S. Army, Ft. Dix, N.J., 1987-88; tng. mgmt. officer, asst. ops. officer U.S. Army, Ft. Dix, N.J., 1988-89, chief adminstrn. logistics assistance div., 1989—. Intern State of S.C. Task Force on Structure of State and Local Govt., 1980; mem. Bush River Bapt. Ch., Newberry, S.C., 1973—; mem. Tabernacle Bapt. Ch., Burlington, N.J. Decorated Army Commendation medal with oak leaf clusters, Meritorious medal with oak leaf cluster, Meritorious Svc. medal with oak leaf cluster, Nat. Def. Svc. medal, Allen W. Reese Meml. scholar; named of Outstanding Men of Am., U.S. Jaycees, 1984, 86, 87, 88, 89. Mem. Assn. U.S. Army, Pi Gamma Mu, Omega Psi Phi (vice basileus 1978-79, basileus 1979-80, dean of edn. 1981-82, 85-86, area coord. 1982-83, keeper of records and seal 1984-86, asst. keeper of records and seal 1990-92, Omega Man of Yr. 1985, 86, 91.). Home: 8 Robin Rd Mount Holly NJ 08060-3397 Office: 8 Robin Rd Mount Holly NJ 08060

BOYD, LINDA SMITH, analytical engineer; b. Dayton, Ohio, May 31, 1961; d. Ambrose E. and Helen K. Smith; m. Charles W. Boyd. BSME, U. R.I., 1983; MSME, Rensselaer Poly. Inst., 1990. Sr. engr. Hamilton Standard div. United Techs. Corp., Windsor Locks, Conn., 1983—; mem. SAE-AC-9C Subcom. for Aircraft Icing. Mem. AIAA (presenter joint propulsion conf. 1987, aerospace scis. meeting 1991), ASME (assoc. presenter, speaker gear tech. conf., Wallingford, Conn. chpt. 1989), Tau Beta Pi. Home: 38 Hemlock Rd Granby CT 06035-2616 Office: Hamilton Standard div UTC 1 Hamilton Rd Windsor Locks CT 06096-1000

BOYD, MILDRED WERNET, nurse, educator; b. Framingham, Mass., July 1, 1947; d. William B. and Ceslava R. (Pieloch) Wernet; m. Kenneth R. Boyd, Feb. 22, 1970; children: Christopher, Timothy. BSN, U. Md., 1969; MSN, Boston U., 1974; MS, Cen. Mich. U., 1992. Ind. cons. Ayer, Mass.; mental health cons. Spouse Abuse Resource Ctr., Bel Air, Md., Harford Home Health, Bel Air; assoc. prof. Essex Community Coll., Balt.; participant Nat. Inst. Leadership Devel., 1992. Author: Springhouse Notes, Medical-Surgical Nursing, 2d edit., 1992. Pres. adv. bd. Dept. Social Svcs., Harford County, Md. Named Outstanding Vol., ARC. Mem. Am. Assn. Women in Community and Jr. Colls., Nat. League Nursing, Sigma Theta Tau, Alpha Eta. Home: 908 E Broadway Bel Air MD 21014-3345

BOYD, ROBERT THOMPSON, minister, ministry educator; b. Charlotte, N.C., Dec. 8, 1914; s. Robert Thompson and Frances (Little) B.; m. Peggy Tuffy, Jan. 15, 1942. BA in Bibl. Edn., Washington Bible Coll., 1958; MDiv., Antietam Bible Sem., 1988, D. Ministry, 1989; DD (hon.), Indian Orthodox Ch., Madras, India, 1954. Ordained to ministry Bapt. Ch., 1942. Pastor Colerain Bapt. Ch., Kirkwood, Pa., 1941-44, Denbigh Bapt. Ch., Newport News, Va., 1944-56, Conklin (N.Y.) Ctr. Bapt. Ch., 1956-60; tchr. Bible conf. Evang. Bible Ministries, U.S., Can., 1961—; summer sch. prof. Antietam Bible Sem., Hagerstown, Md.; lectr. bibl. archaeology; spl. rep. World Radio Missionary Fellowship, Sta. HCJB, Quito, Ecuador; former program coord. Sandy Cove Bible Conf. of North East Md., former head cassette ministry. Author: A Pictorial Guide to Biblical Archaeology, 1969, Boyd's Bible Handbook, 1983, Scientific Facts in the Bible, 1983; contbg. editor Archaeology and Bibl. Rsch. Active in radio and TV ministry Sta. WNBF-TV, Binghamton, N.Y.; radio broadcaster over Sta. HCJB, Quito, Sta. KCRM, Pusan, Republic Korea, Sta. HOXO, Panama City, Panama. Named Alumnus of Yr., Washington Bible Coll., 1978; recipient Alumnus Award in Communications, Phila. Coll. Bible, 1989. Republican. Home: 1712 Academy St Scranton PA 18504-2309 Office: Evang Bible Ministries 1712 Academy St Scranton PA 18504-2309

BOYD, ROBERT WILLIAM, physics educator; b. Buffalo, Mar. 8, 1948; s. Robert Paul and Erma Lorraine (Seitz) B.; m. Katherine Ellen Conway, De. 18, 1971; children: Jessica, John, Brendan. BS in Physics, MIT, 1969; PhD in Physics, U. Calif., Berkeley, 1977. Asst. prof. U. Rochester (N.Y.), 1977-82, assoc. prof., 1982-87, prof., 1987—. Author: Radiometry..., 1983, Nonlinear Optics, 1992, Contemporary Nonlinear Optics, 1992; editor: Optical Instabilities, 1986. Fellow Optical Soc. Am., 1989. Mem. Am. Phys. Soc. Office: U Rochester Inst of Optics Rochester NY 14627

BOYD, V(IRGINIA) ANN LEWIS, biology educator; b. Shreveport, La., Nov. 15, 1944; d. Fletcher Willard and Bess Juanita (Sherman) Lewis; m. James P. Boyd, June 4, 1965 (div. 1973); children: Kathryn Ann, David Gregory. BS, Northwestern State U., Natchitoches, La., 1965, MS, 1968; PhD, La. State U., 1971. Postdoctoral fellow Baylor Coll. Medicine, Houston, 1971-73; rsch. scientist Frederick (Md.) Cancer Rsch. Ctr., 1973-82; assoc. prof. of biology Hood Coll., Frederick, 1982-88, prof., chair biology dept., 1988—; cons. Frederick Cancer Rsch. Ctr., 1982—; fellowship panelist AAUW, Washington, 1988-92, chmn. fellowship panel, 1992-94; designer, tchr. grad. and undergrad. courses in virology, molecular genetics, bioethics; citizen amb. for biotech. People to People Internat., China, 1988, USSR, 1991. Contbr. articles to sci. jours., chpts. to books. Bd. dirs. Girl Scouts U.S.A., Frederick, 1979-82, Advs. for Homeless, Frederick, 1989-92; vestry officer Episcopal Ch., Frederick, 1980—. Grantee NCI, 1983-86, NSF, 1986-88. Mem. Am. Soc. Virology, Am. Soc. for Microbiology, N.Y. Acad. Scis., AAUW (fellowship panelist 1988-91, chmn. Am. fellowship panel 1992-94), Sigma Xi, Phi Kappa Phi, also others. Office: Hood Coll Rosemont Ave Frederick MD 21701-8524

BOYER, EDWIN LYMAN, industrial psychologist; b. Ashland, Maine, June 6, 1939; s. Edmund and Lottie (Boyce) B. BS, Lesley Coll., 1984; MEd, Cambridge Coll., 1985; MA, Goddard Coll., 1989; PhD, Union Inst., 1991. Fin. mgr. Children's Hosp., Boston, 1963—. Mem. Isabella Stewart Gardner Mus.; vol. St. John of God Hosp., Brighton, Mass.; advocate animal protection rights. Mem. AACD, Nat. Guild Hypnotists, Nat. Assn. Alcoholism and Drug Abuse Counselors, Nat. Employment Counselors Assn., Am. Mental Health Counselors Assn., Mass. Mental Health Counselors Assn., Mass. Assn. Alcoholism Counselors, Inc., Am. Legion, WGBH Pub. Broadcasting Channel. Home: 14 Susan Dr Billerica MA 01821-4441 Office: Children's Hosp 300 Longwood Ave Boston MA 02115-5737

BOYER, GREGORY MARTIN, composer; b. Upper Darby, Pa., Feb. 14, 1954; s. Claude Clemens and Fae Thornton (Ang) B.; m. Rebekah Feldman, Aug. 13, 1988; 1 child, Samuel Clemens. Assocs., Brandywine Coll., 1973; postgrad., Temple U., 1974-77. Lectr. Downingtown, Pa., 1973-75; from bandleader to songwriter John Cadillac Band, Phila., Chgo., N.Y.C., 1976-91; songwriter Bklyn., 1992—; performer Hosp. Audiences, Inc., N.Y.C., 1987-89; model numerous mags., 1982-88. Bandleader Walkin By Myself, 1978, Quiet Whiskey, 1978; composer more than 100 titles; inventor Wireless Microphone Holder, 1991. Home: 178 8th St Brooklyn NY 11215

BOYER, ROBERT ALLAN, business executive; b. Detroit, Mar. 2, 1934; s. Robert Allan and Elizabeth (Szabo) B.; children: Jennifer, Stephen, Lorna. MBA, Cornell U., 1959. Exec. asst. to pres. Merck & Co., Inc., Rahway, N.J., 1962-68; dir. fin. TWA Corp., N.Y.C., 1969-72; nat. dir. fin. Coopers & Lybrand, N.Y.C., 1972-79; dir. adminstrn. Sullivan & Cromwell, N.Y.C., 1979-; chmn., founder Legal Execs. Group, Law Firm Tech. Group, 1979. Mem. congl. support com.; mem. Pres.'s Club Rep. Party, 1990. Mem. ABA, Assn. Legal Adminstrs. (exec. com. 1986-87), Aircraft Owners and Pilots Assn., Yorktown Bicentennial Com. (bd. dirs., sec.), Echo Lake Country Club (Westfield, N.J.), Cornell Club (N.Y.), Cornell Club (N.J.). Republican. Presbyterian. Club: Echo Lake Country (Westfield, N.J.). Office: Sullivan & Cromwell 125 Broad St New York NY 10004-2400

BOYER, TIMOTHY HOWARD, physics reseacher and educator; b. N.Y.C., Mar. 20, 1941; s. Carl Benjamin and Marjorie Duncan (Nice) B.; m. Marilyn Elise Abel, May 28, 1977; children: Laurette Christine, Michael Christopher. BA, Yale U., 1962; MA, Harvard U., 1963, PhD, 1968. Postdoctoral fellow U. Md., College Park, 1968-70; asst. prof. physics CCNY, 1970-73, assoc. prof., 1974-79, prof., 1980—. Contbr. articles to profl. jours. Mem. AAAS, Am. Phys. Soc., Sigma Xi. Office: CCNY Convent Ave at 138th St New York NY 10031

BOYES, FRED HOWARD, marketing research professional; b. Pulaski, Va., Apr. 16, 1933; s. Fred and Justine (Boyes) Vaden; m. Sandra Elizabeth Papay, Sept. 6, 1958; children: Alexandra, Gregory. BA in Math. cum laude, Ohio State U., 1957; MS in Psychology, U. Wis., 1960. Rsch. psychologist Gen. Motors Corp., Warren, Mich., 1960-62; rsch. account exec. firm Campbell-Ewald, Detroit, 1962-64, mgr. advt. evaluation, 1964-66; staff cons. Marketing Strategy, Inc., Detroit, 1966-67, v.p., 1967-68; consumer rsch. mgr. May Dept. Stores Co., St. Louis, 1968-70; v.p., assoc. dir. rsch. Kenyon & Eckhardt Advt., N.Y.C., 1970-72; v.p. Data Devel. Corp., N.Y.C., 1973-75; exec. v.p. R.H. Bruskin Assocs., New Brunswick, N.J., 1975-79; pres., owner Focus on Groups, Ltd., Huntington, N.Y., 1979—. Mem. Am. Mktg. Assn., Huntington Yacht Club, Phi Beta Kappa.

BOYKIN, FRANCES LEWIS, retired social worker; b. Boston; d. Joel Randolph and Frances Virginia (Kenney) Lewis; m. Herbert Charles Boykin Jr., Dec. 23, 1951 (div. 1958). BS, Simmons Coll., 1945, MS, 1946. Cert. social worker, N.Y. Caseworker Family Service of Orange County, Maplewood, N.J., 1946-47; child welfare worker Riverdale Children's Assn., N.Y.C., 1946-51; supr., casework coordinator Assoc. Day Care Services of Greater Boston, 1952-53; caseworker, advancing to sr. caseworker Salvation Army-Family Service, N.Y.C., 1955-74; psychiat. researcher, 1957-62; student supr. NYU Sch. Edn., 1969-74, field supr. student unit, 1976-79; field supr. for student unit Salvation Army Corps and Community Ctrs., N.Y.C., 1974-79, adv. orgn. mem. Salvation Army N.Y. State, 1979-86 (meritorious service award); adj. asst. prof. NYU Sch. Social Work, 1977-79. Bd. dirs. Assn. Bronx Community Orgns., 1964-73, v.p., 1968-69, treas., 1970-73; bd. dirs. N.Y.C. region NCCJ, 1976-85, mem. exec. com., 1977-85; mem. Bronx adv. com. Urban League, 1966-69; pres. corp. body 12th Ch. Christ Scientist, N.Y.C., 1988; active mother ch. 1st Ch. Christ Scientist, Boston. Recipient Service plaque for 30 yrs. with Salvation Army N.Y.C., 1986. Mem. Nat. Assn. Social Workers, Acad. Cert. Social Workers, Internat. Conf. Social Work (del. 1964-84). Home: 2235 5th Ave New York NY 10037-2114

BOYLAN, STANLEY LOUIS, academic dean, consultant; b. Bronx, N.Y., Sept. 21, 1941; s. Morris and Ruth (Geller) B.; m. Esther Nevenansky, Jan. 2, 1968; children: Joseph, Avigail, Isaac N., Yocheved, Elisheva, Adina. BA, Yeshiva Coll., 1963; MS in Maths., NYU, 1965, PhD in Maths., 1969. Ordained Rabbi, Yeshiva Univ., 1971. Asst. prof. Rutgers Univ., Newark, 1968-76; assoc. prof. Touro Coll., N.Y.C., 1976-82, asst. dean acad. affairs, 1977-78, assoc. dean acad. affairs, 1978-81, prof. math., dean faculties, 1982—; ednl. dir. Camp Tagola, Sackett Lake, N.Y.; cons. N.J. Dept. Higher Edn., Trenton. Contbr. chpt. to book and articles to profl. jours. Guest lectr. various synagogues, Bklyn., 1977—. Recipient scholarship Woodrow Wilson Found., 1964, fellowship NSF, 1964-67, Sloan Found., 1968-69. Mem. Am. Math. Soc., Rabbinical Coun. Am. Home: 1625 E 23d St Brooklyn NY 11229-1518 Office: Touro Coll 844 Ave Of The Americas New York NY 10001-4103

BOYLAN, WILLIAM ALVIN, lawyer; b. Marshalltown, Iowa, Sept. 18, 1924; s. Glen D. and Dorothy I. (Gibson) B.; m. Nancy Dickson, Aug. 5, 1950; children: Ross, Laura. Student, U. Iowa, 1943-44; BA, Drake U., 1947; LLB, Harvard U., 1950. Bar: Ill. 1950, N.Y. 1952. Practiced in N.Y.C., 1952—; mem. Gould & Wilkie, N.Y.C., 1987—. Contbr. articles to profl. jours. Served with USAAF, 1943-46. Mem. ABA, N.Y. State Bar Assn., Assn. of Bar of City of N.Y., Fed. Bar Council, Phi Beta Kappa, Sigma Alpha Epsilon. Episcopalian. Clubs: Harvard, The Down Town Assn. Home: 108 E 82d St New York NY 10028 Office: Gould & Wilkie 34th Fl 1 Wall St New York NY 10005

BOYLE, BARBARA MERLE PRINCELAU, retired intelligence officer; b. Oakland, Calif., Sept. 21, 1923; d. Paul and Mary Emilie (Rueger) Princelau; m. John Joseph Boyle, Oct. 21, 1950 (dec.). AB, U. Calif., Berkeley, 1948. Intelligence officer CIA, Langley, Va., 1954-82. Bd. dirs. The Thrift Shop, Washington, 1988-92; mem. Women's Bd. Columbia Hosp. for Women Med. Ctr., Washington, 1986—, mem. exec. com., 1989-91; mem. The Washington Antiques Shows com., 1989-92. Recipient Cert. of Distinction CIA, 1982. Mem. Cen. Intelligence Retiree Assn., Assn. Former Intelligence Officers, Sulgrave Club, U. Calif. Berkeley Alumni Club of Washington (rec. sec. 1976-77, v.p. 1984-86), Sigma Kappa (v.p. No. Va. alumnae 1992—). Episcopalian. Home: 5101 River Rd Bethesda MD 20816-1512

BOYLE, FRANCIS JOSEPH, federal judge; b. 1927; m. M. Delores Roderick; children: Deborah, Carole, Christopher, Mathew, Susan, Patrick, Katherine. Postgrad., Providence Coll., 1949; JD, Boston Coll., 1952. Bar: bar 1952. Assoc. Cornelius C. Moore, 1953-61; ptnr. Moore, Virgadamo, Boyle & Lynch, 1961-77; judge U.S. Dist. Ct. for R.I., Providence, 1977-82, chief judge, 1982—. With USN, 1945-46. Mem. Am. Bar Assn., Fed. Bar. Assn., R.I. Bar Assn., Newport County Bar Assn. Office: US Dist Ct 314 Fed Bldg & US Courthouse Providence RI 02903*

BOYLE, JAMES JOSEPH, higher education administrator, researcher; b. Wilkes-Barre, Pa., July 5, 1951; s. Joseph A. and Rita G. (McDermott) B.; m. Patricia Weigel, Oct. 8, 1977; children: James T., Margaret M., Brendan J. BA in Arts & Scis., Boston Coll., 1973; MPA, Penn State U., State College, 1980; PhD, Syracuse U., N.Y., 1990. Dir., mem. and funds Boston Red Cross, Boston, 1973-76; vol. coord. Office for Aging, RSUP, Wilkes-Barre, Pa., 1976-80; dir. coll. rels. Keystone Jr. Coll., LaPlume, Pa., 1980-84; assoc. v.p. SUNY at Binghamton, Binghamton, N.Y., 1984-91; cons. Exxon Edn. Found., Dallas, 1989. Grantee Lilly Endowment, Inc., Indpls., 1990; recipient CASE/Grezenbach award for philanthropy rsch., 1992. Mem. Coun. for Advancement and Support of Edn. Home: HC 79 Box 35 Glen Aubrey NY 13777-9706 Office: Binghamton Found PO Box 6005 Binghamton NY 13902-6005

BOYLE, KEVIN JOHN, economics educator, consultant; b. Montgomery, Ala., Sept. 15, 1955; s. John Farley and Elaine Ruth (Keaney) B.; m. Nancy Jean Becraft, June 12, 1983. BA in Econs., U. Maine, 1978; MS in Econs., Oreg. State U., 1981; PhD in Econs., U. Wis., 1985. Rsch. asst. Oreg. State U., Corvallis, 1979-80; economist U.S. Forest Svc., Corvallis, 1981; rsch. asst. U. Wis., Madison, 1982-85, rsch. assoc., 1985-86; asst. prof. econs. U. Maine, Orono, 1986-91, assoc. prof., 1991—; vis. assoc. prof. econs. N.C. State U., 1992—; resource economist HBRS, Madison, 1985-86; pres. regional project benefits and costs in natural resource planning USDA, 1988-89. Mem. editorial bd. Jour. Environ. Econs. and Mgmt., 1989-92; contbr. articles to profl. jours. Recipient Cert. of mertit USDA 1981; Maine Legis.-U.S. Fish and Wildlife Svc. grantee 1988-92, U.S. Forest Svc. grantee 1989—, Maine Dept. Marine Resources grantee 1989-91, Oakd Ridge Nat. Labs. grantee 1989-90, Exxon, USA, 1989-92, Maine Dept. Inland Fisheries and Wildlife grantee 1990-91, Bangor Hydro-Electric Co. grantee 1991-92. Mem. Am. Econ. Assn., Am. Agrl. Econs. Assn., Assn. Environ. and Resource Economists, Northeastern Agrl. and Resource Econs. Assn., Western Region Sci. Assn. Home: 322 Main Rd S Hampden ME 04444-1103 Office: U Maine Econs Dept Winslow Hall Orono ME 04469

BOYLE, PYOTR J., mathematician; b. Callicoon, N.Y., Jan. 2, 1951; s. Peter Edward and Eva (Mantwilov) B. BA, SUNY, Oneonta, 1983; MA, NYU, 1985; PhD, Columbia U., 1989. Rsch. fellow Columbia U., N.Y.C., 1986-87, assoc. prof., 1988-90; sr. editor R.R Bowker Co., N.Y.C., 1987-90; sr. rsch. scientist Courant Inst. Math., NYU, N.Y.C., 1991—; cons. R.R. Bowker Co., New Providence, N.J., 1991; cons., analyst Yamaha Mus. Instruments-USA, N.Y.C., 1989-91. Contbr. articles to profl. jours. Lorna Found. for Sci. grantee, 1987. Fellow AAAS; Mem. ACLU, Amnesty Internat., Transp. Alternatives, Am. Mus. Natural History, Nat. Acad. Sci., Am. Math. Soc., Mensa. Democrat. Roman Catholic. Home: PO Box 66 New York NY 10113-0066

BOYLE, RENÉE KENT, cultural organization executive, translator, editor; b. Cairo, July 4, 1926; came to U.S., 1946; d. Maurice Colin and Victoria Smith; m. John E. Whiteford Boyle, Feb. 2, 1950; children: Vanessa Whiteford Wayne, Christopher, Andrea Heller, Mara Holloway. Diploma, St. Clare's Coll., Heliopolis, Egypt, 1944; postgrad., Rice U., 1947-48, Santa Monica Coll., 1950-51. Dep. dir. Am. Friends of Mid. East, Tehran, Iran, 1959-62, Les Amis Americains du Maghreb, Tunis, Tunisia, 1962-64; v.p. Fgn. Services Research Inst., Washington, 1964—; v.p. Whiteford Internat. Enterprise, Villars sur Ollon, Switzerland, 1967-74; pres. Wheat/Forders Press. Editor: Primers for the Age of Inner Space series, Beyond the Present Prospect, 1978, The Indra Web, 1982, Graffiti on the Wall of Time, 1982, Of the Same Root: Heaven, Earth & I, 1989. Mem. Dem. Nat. Com., Washington, 1982—. Mem. Acad. Ind. Scholars (exec. dir.), Ams. for Dem. Action, People for Ethical Treatment of Animals, Sierra Club. Unitarian. Avocation: cordon bleu cooking. Home: 2718 Unicorn Ln NW Washington DC 20015-2234 Office: Fgn Svcs Rsch Inst PO Box 6317 Washington DC 20015-0317

BOYLE, ROBERT DANIEL, business educator; b. Havre de Grace, Md., June 27, 1965; s. Vincent Michael Sr. and Margaret Kathleen (Helton) B. BS, U. Md., 1987; MBA, Loyola Coll., Balt., 1989, MS in Fin., 1990. CPA, cert. mgmt. acct. Pres. Sunquest of Md., Inc., Aberdeen, Md., 1985-88; adj. prof. Loyola Coll., Balt., 1989—; rsch. fellow David D. Lattanze Ctr., Balt., 1989—; prin. Sandlot Strategists, Balt., 1990—; cons., speaker in field. Contbr. articles to profl. publs. David D. Lattanze Ctr. fellow, 1989—. Mem. AICPA, Am. Prodn. and Inventory Control Soc., Inst. Mgmt. Accts., Am. Mensa, Ltd., Phi Theta Kappa, Alpha Sigma Lambda, Phi Kappa Phi, Alpha Sigma Nu, Beta Gamma Sigma. Home: 3419 Walnut Rd Aberdeen MD 21001-1034

BOYLE, WILLIAM LEO, JR., educational consultant, former college president; b. Utica, N.Y., July 23, 1933; s. William Leo and Gladys (Kuney) B. A.B., Colgate U., 1955; postgrad., Cornell U. Law Sch., 1960-61; M.A., Columbia U., 1964, Profl. Diploma in Ednl. Adminstrn., 1967, Ed.D., 1969; LL.D. (hon.), Hawthorne Coll., 1979; postdoctoral, Harvard U., 1979-81; L.H.D. (hon.), Mercy Coll., 1983; LittD (hon.), Curry Coll., 1992. Participant advanced mgmt. program, recruiter, ednl. adviser Procter & Gamble Co., Cin., 1958-60; legis. aide edn. com. N.Y. State Senate, Albany, 1961-62; account exec., ednl. cons. Batten, Barton, Durstine & Osborn, N.Y.C., 1962-64; asst. dir. devel., presdl. asst. Wesleyan U., Middletown, Conn., 1964-65; program cons. Council for Fin. Aid to Edn., N.Y.C., 1965-70, asst. v.p., 1970-72, v.p., 1972-75; pres. Keuka Coll., Keuka Park, N.Y., 1975-78; pres. Curry Coll., Milton, Mass., 1978-92, pres. emeritus, 1992—, also trustee and lectr. polit. sci.; pvt. practice in ednl. cons. to colls. and univs. Utica, 1992—. Author: The National Corporate Educational Support Movement, 1954-1966, 1969. Contbr. articles to ednl. and profl. jours. Vice chmn. nat. bus. and industry com. Colgate U., Hamilton, N.Y., 1974—, mem. nat. coun., 1975—, ann. fund exec. com., 1975—; ednl. cons. to Pres. Ford Com., Washington, 1976; bd. dirs. Slocum-Dickson Found., Utica, 1991—; mem. leadership com. Utica Found., 1992—; established Boyle Scholarship at Colgate U., 1985, Boyle Fund, Utica Found., 1991. Capt. USAF, 1955-58. Recipient Comdr.'s Citation USAF. Mem. various ednl. and profl. orgns., Columbia Univ. Club (N.Y.C.) Ft. Schuyler Club (Utica), Sadequada Golf Club (Utica). Home: 12 Rose Pl Utica NY 13502

BOYLSTON, BENJAMIN CALVIN, steel company executive; b. Spartanburg, S.C., Dec. 19, 1932; s. Howard Bridges and Lucile (Peace) B.; m. Eleanor Addison, Mar. 30, 1933; children: Nancy Eleanor, Susanna Daphne. AB, Duke U., 1954; MA, U. Chgo., 1955; cert. program for mgmt. devel., Harvard U., 1972. Mgmt. trainee Bethlehem Steel Corp., Johnstown, Pa., 1955-57; labor rels. rep. Bethlehem (Pa.) Steel Corp., 1957-64, sr. labor rep., 1964-66, mgr. pers., 1966-70, mgr. pers. mgmt. devel., 1970-74, asst. v.p. indsl. rels., 1974-84, gen. mgr. human resources, 1984-86, v.p. human resources, 1986—; bd. dirs. Capital Blue Cross, Harrisburg, Pa., 1982—, St. Luke's Hosp., Bethlehem, 1988—; corp. mem. Pa. Blue Shield, Camp Hill, Pa., 1983—; chmn. Lehigh Valley Bus. Conf. on Health, Behtlehem, 1989-92, bd. dirs., 1986—. Co-author: Teamwork-Joint Labor-Management Programs in America, 1986. President, bd. dirs. Kemerer Mus., Bethlehem, 1987-91; bd. dirs. ARC, Bethlehem, 1982-88, New Bethany Ministries, Bethlehem, 1985—; appointed mem. by gov. pers. com. Pa. Little Hoover Commn., Harrisburg, 1969-71; mem. Vision 2000 com. Hosp. Assn. Pa., 1990-92; mem. edn. com. Hosp. Trustee Assn., 1992—. Mem. Internat. Platform Assn., Am. Iron and Steel Inst. (chmn. employee rels. com. 1989-91), Nat. Assn. Mfrs., ERISA Industry Com. (bd. dirs. 1990—), Human Resources Planning Soc., Univ. Club N.Y.C., Saucon Valley Country Club. Republican. Presbyterian. Office: Bethlehem Steel Corp 701 E 3d St Bethlehem PA 18016-7500

BOYTIM, JAMES ALVIN, psychology educator; b. Tyrone, Pa., May 19, 1937; s. George Jr. and Nellie (Merritts) B.; m. Joan Lois Frey, Aug. 4, 1961. BS, Ind. U. of Pa., 1959, MEd, 1966; MS in Edn., Temple U., 1965; EdD, Ind. U., 1971. Lic. psychologist; nat. cert. counselor; cert. clin. mental health counselor, sch. counselor, gerontol. counselor. Tchr., math. Carlisle (Pa.) Area Sch. Dist., 1959-70, sch. counselor, 1970-75, counseling psychologist, 1975-80; asst. prof. psychology and edn. Dickinson Coll., Carlisle, 1980-85, asst. prof. psychology, 1985—; pvt. practice counseling psychology, Carlisle, 1971—; cons. Piezo Crystal Co., Carlisle, 1980—. Contbr. articles to profl. jours. Mem. adv. bd. Program for Edn., Enrichment and Recreation, Carlisle, 1982—; bd. dirs. Meals on Wheels, Carlisle, 1982-85, Carlisle Day Care Ctr., 1981-83; trustee Bosler Free Libr., Carlisle, 1979-81. With U.S. Army, 1960. Recipient Ganoe award for Inspirational Teaching, Dickinson Coll., 1985-86. Fellow Pa. Psychol. Assn.; mem. ACA, APA, Pa. Assn. for Specialists in Group Work (pres. 1986-87, Outstanding Svc. award 1989), Pa. Counseling Assn. (Outstanding Counselor award 1985), Pa. Assn. for Adult Devel. and Aging (charter pres. 1989-90), Pa. Mental Health Counselors Assn. (pres. 1982-83, Leadership award 1984), Kiwanis (Legion of Honor award Carlisle club 1990). Republican. Methodist. Home: 160 Glendale St Carlisle PA 17013-2703 Office: Dickinson Coll Dept Psychology PO Box 1773 Carlisle PA 17013-2896

BOYTIM, THOMAS EDWARD, periodontist; b. Homestead, Pa., Aug. 15, 1948; s. Edward Francis and Irene (Thomas) B; m. Beverly Ann Weir, Aug. 21, 1971 (div. 1987); children: David Joshua, Justin Weir. BS, U.S. Mil. Acad., 1970; DMD, Univ. Pa., 1979; splty. cert., Univ. Fla., 1989. Cert. Dental Spl. Periodontics. Battery commdr. U.S. Army, Bitburg, Germany, 1971-74; battalion adjutant 759 M.P. Battalion, Ft. Dix, N.J., 1974-75; gen. dentist USAF Dental Clinic, McGuire AFB, N.J., 1979-83; base dental surgeon USAF Dental Clinic, Izmir, Turkey, 1983-84; gen. dentist USAF Dental Clinic, McGuire AFB, N.J., 1984-85; asst. base dental surgeon USAF Hosp, Incirlik, Turkey, 1985-87; periodontist USAF Dental Clinic, Bolling AFB, D.C., 1989—; tchr. Bolling AFB, 1989—; gen. practice for residents, 1989—. Lt. Col. USAF 1979-89. Recipient: Leadership Award, Sr. Student Perio Award, Acad. of Gold Foil Operators Award, Univ. Pa. 1979. Mem. ADA, Am. Acad. Periodontology, Acad. Gen. Dentistry. Democrat. Episcopalian. Home: 6208 Jane Ct Temple Hills MD 20748-6022 Office: Det MGMC Bolling AFB DC 20332

BOYUM, JOY GOULD, English educator; b. N.Y.C., Dec. 8, 1934; d. David and Beatrice (Levine) Gould; m. Asmund Boyum, Sept. 5, 1960; children: David Anders, Ingrid Anne. BA, Barnard Coll., 1955; MA, NYU, 1957, PhD, 1962. From instr. to assoc. prof. NYU, N.Y.C., 1960-72, prof., 1972—; film critic Wall St. Jour., N.Y.C., 1971-83, Glamour Mag., N.Y.C., 1981-89, Nat. Pub. Radio, N.Y.C., 1979-85. Author: Double Exposure: Fiction into Film, 1985; (with others) Film as Film: Critical Approaches to Film Art, 1970. Contbr. articles to profl. jours. Mem. N.Y. Film Critics Circle (chmn. 1976), Nat. Soc. Film Critics, Nat. Soc. Tchrs. English, MLA, Soc. Cinema Studies. Home: 45 Remsen St Brooklyn NY 11201-4112 Office: NYU Dept Communication Arts 239 Greene St Ste 735 New York NY 10003-6601

BOZICH, ROBERT, engineering executive; b. Greensburg, Pa., Dec. 15, 1942; s. George and Mildred (Karanovich) B.; m. Linda Lou Bates, Oct. 30, 1965; children: Robert G., Janna L., Richard J. BS in Meteorology, Pa. State U., 1964; MS in Meteorology, Naval Post Grad. Sch., Monterey, Calif., 1972. Commd. ensign USN, 1964, advanced through grades to comdr., 1976, ret., 1985; sr. engr. Hamilton Standards/United Technologies, Farmington, Conn., 1985-87; program mgr. Bendix Flight Systems/Allied Signal Inc., Teterboro, N.J., 1987—. Chmn. Little League Challenger Div., Vernon, N.J., 1990—; vol. spl. olympics. Mem. AIAA, Soc. for Info. Display, Assn. of Naval Aviation, Nat. Geog. Soc. Home: 8 Hemlock Dr Sussex NJ 07461 Office: Bendix Allied Signal Inc Rt 46 M/S 1-45A Teterboro NJ 07608

BOZZELLI, JOSEPH W., chemistry educator; b. Sept. 16, 1942. BS in Chemistry, Math., Marietta Coll., 1964; MS in Chemistry, U. Dayton, 1968; PhD in Phys. Chemistry, Princeton U., 1973; postgrad., U. Pitts., 1973-75. Chemistry specialist Monsanto Rsch. Corp., Miamisburg, Ohio, 1964-67; analyst U. Dayton Rsch. Inst., 1968; analyst chemistry and space sci. projects U. Pitts., 1973-75; project leader Computer Sci. Corp./NASA, Wallops Island, Va., 1975; disting. prof. dept. chem. engring. and chemistry N.J. Inst. Tech., Newark, 1975—; rsch. peer rev. panel US EPA. Contbr. articles to profl. jours., publs. in field. Recipient Joseph Hyman award for Excellence in Teaching, Am. Chem. Soc., H. Perlis award for Rsch., numerous grants in field. Roman Catholic. Office: NJ Inst Tech Dept Chem Engring/Chemistry University Heights NJ 07104

BRACCINI, LISA ANN, pharmacist; b. Wilkes Barre, Pa., Feb. 6, 1963; d. Frank Joseph and JoAnn (Dente) B. BS, Phila. Coll. Pharmacy, 1986; postgrad., Pa. State U., 1987-90; MBA, Lebanon Valley Coll., 1992. Registered pharmacist, Pa. Resident Milton S. Hershey Med. Ctr., Pa. State U., Hershey, Pa., 1986-87; staff pharmacist Milton S. Hershey Med. Ctr., Pa. State U., Hershey, 1987, coord. ancillary svcs., 1988-92; supr. outpatient pharmacy svcs. Pa. State U. Hosp., Hershey, 1992—. Mem. Am. Soc. Hosp. Pharmacists, Pa. Soc. Hosp. Pharmacists, Kappa Epsilon (nat. bylaws chmn. 1987-89, v.p. province program 1989-91, 91—, Madelline Holland McDonnell award 1985, 86, Sr. of Yr. award 1986, Unicorn award nat. convention 1991). Republican. Roman Catholic. Home: 950 Innsbruck Dr Hummelstown PA 17036-9749 Office: Pa State U Hosp PO Box 850 Hershey PA 17033-0850

BRACEY, COOKIE FRANCES LEE, minister; b. Phila., Mar. 14, 1945; d. John Daniels and Evelyn (Jarvis) Bracey. B in Social Work, Temple U., 1983; MDiv, Wesley Theol. Sem., 1990. Administrv. asst. United Meth. Ch., Phila., 1963-86, parish community devel., 1984-86; local pastor United Meth. Ch., Catonsville, Ellicott City, Md., 1986-90; chaplain Meth. Hosp., Phila., 1990—; pastor St. Luke Snyder Ave United Meth. Ch., Phila., 1990-92, St. Matthews United Meth. Ch., Trevose, Pa., 1992—; Missionary, Brazil, 1988, Costa Rica, 1989, Dominican Republic, 1992; pastor St. Matthews United Meth. Ch., Trevose, Pa., 1992. Mem. Multi-Cultural Task Force, Phila. 1980, Victims & Crime Task Force, Phila. Ministers Law Enforcement Support Unit, Phila. Community Assistance Network. Recipient Outstanding Clergywoman award Nat. Assn. Clergywomen, 1990, Peace & Justice award Ch. Women United, 1992, Ministry award Harry Hosier United Meth. Ch., 1992. Mem. Temple Univ. Soc. Adminstrn. Alumni Assn., Asian Am. Youth Assn., Nat. Fellowship Local. Democrat. Home: 337 Christian St Apt 3 Philadelphia PA 19147

BRACKEN, LOUIS EVERETT, sales executive, health services administrator, consultant; b. Altoona, Pa., July 1, 1947; s. Everett William and Antonnette Virginia (DeFalco) B.; m. Virginia Elizabeth Frezza, Sept. 17, 1966; children: William Joseph, Jennifer Lynn. BS, U. Md., 1970. Sales trainee DeVilbiss Co., Somerset, Pa., 1970; dist. sales rep. DeVilbiss Co., 1970-71, dist. sales mgr., 1971-75, regional sales mgr., 1976-82; pres. Health Care Equipment Mktg. Assocs., Inc., Scituate, Mass., 1982—; v.p. Associated Home Health Care Svcs., Inc., Everett, Mass., 1988—; co-founder Home Strategic Planning, Inc., Boston, 1981-83, Mass. Rehab. Svcs., Inc., Randolph, Mass., 1981, Health Care Distbn. Svcs., Inc., Hanover, Mass., 1984, Associated Home Health Svcs., Inc., Everett, 1985, Health Care Billing Systems, Inc., Hanover, 1985, Continuing Med. Corp. Inc., Providence, 1987, Nat. Homecare Purchasing Network, Boca Raton, Fla., 1990, Health Care Equipment Leasing Ltd., Boca Raton, 1991. Dir. U.S. Jr. Chamber of Congress in Scituate, Scituate, Mass., 1978-81; head coach Pop Warner in Scituate, 1978. Grantee U. Md., 1965-70. Mem. Boys Club (Altoona, Pa., pres.). Republican. Roman Catholic. Home: 200 SW 8th Ave Boca Raton FL 33486-4659 Office: No Health Care Equipment Mktg Assocs Inc PO Box 398 North Scituate MA 02060 also: So Health Care Equip Mktg Assoc Inc PO Box 579 Boca Raton FL 33429

BRACKEN, NANCY JEAN, health care administrator; b. Jamestown, N.Y., Oct. 5, 1944; d. James P. and Vivian E. (Moore) Knowles; m. John S. Bracken, June 23, 1969. AA, Jamestown Community Coll., 1964; AB in English, SUNY, Fredonia, 1966; MPA, SUNY, Brockport, 1986. Permanent teaching cert. Tchr., English Brockton (N.Y.) Cen. Sch., 1966-67; tchr. spl. edn. Falconer (N.Y.) Cen. Sch., 1967-68; tchr. Warsaw (N.Y.) Cen. Sch., 1968-82; exec. dir. Art Coun. for Wyoming County, Perry, N.Y., 1982-84, Letchworth Area Primary Care Ctr., Castile, N.Y., 1983-86, Oak Orchard Community Health Ctr., Brockport, 1986—; adj. faculty SUNY, Brockport, 1989—. Vol. March of Dimes, Brockport, 1989-90; pres. bd. dirs. Orleans County Arts Coun., Albion, N.Y., 1991. Mem. APHA, Am. Soc. Pub. Adminstrs., Nat. Rural Health Assn., Community Health Care Assn. N.Y. State. Home: 8107 W Canal Rd Brockport NY 14420-2103 Office: Oak Orchard Community Health Ctr 80 West Ave Brockport NY 14420-1309

BRACKMAN, SELMA, business executive; b. Bronx, N.Y., Oct. 25, 1922; d. Julius Gedalia and Anna (Jacobs) Rabinowitz; m. Arthur Brackman, Oct. 13, 1946 (dec. 1982); children: Rebecca, Deborah, Susanna, Jessica. BA, Hofstra Coll., 1945. Researcher, mgr., sec.-treas. Freelance Photographers Guild, N.Y.C., 1955—, also chmn. bd., also chmn. emeritus; researcher, mgr., v.p. Alpha Photo Assocs., N.Y.C., 1969-87. Asst. editor: (newspaper) MAN, 1966, (newsletters) Propaganda, 1940, Propaganda Analysis, 1940. Exec. dir. War and Peace Found., N.Y.C., 1982—, publisher War and Peace Digest newsletter; del., trustee World Constitution and Parliament Assn., Colo., 1969—; vol. UN, N.Y.C., 1985—; activist Nat. Intervenors, Washington, 1979. Home: 20 E 9th St New York NY 10003 Office: Freelance Photographers 32 Union Sq New York NY 10003

BRADBERRY, RICHARD PAUL, library director; b. Florala, Ala., Dec. 6, 1951; s. Sam and Nettie Ruth (Hightower) B. BS, Ala. State U., 1973; MS in Libr. Sci., Atlanta U., 1974; PhD, U. Mich., 1988. Humanities libr. Auburn (Ala.) U., 1974-76; libr. dir. Langston (Okla.) U., 1976-83, Lake Erie Coll., Painesville, Ohio, 1983-84, U. Conn., West Hartford, 1984-89, Del. State Coll., Dover, 1989—; evaluator Mid. States Ccom. on Higher Edn., Phila., 1991—. Contbr. articles to profl. publs. Tutor Literacy Vols. of Hartford, Conn., 1985, tutor record adminstr., 1986-89, bd. dirs., 1989. Recipient Doctoral Student award State Regents for Higher Edn., Oklahoma City, 1980-82; grantee Dept. Higher Edn., Hartford, 1987; Edn. Profls. fellow Atlanta U., 1973, Title II-B fellow U. Mich., 1980. Mem. ALA, Assn. Libr.-Info. Sci. Edn., Assn. Coll.-Rsch. Librs., 1890 Land-Grant Libr. Dir.'s Assn. (treas. 1989—). Home: 1300 S Farmview Dr # 31H Dover DE 19901-3374 Office: Jason Libr Del State Coll 1200 N Dupont Hwy Dover DE 19901-2202

BRADDOCK, RICHARD S., banker; b. Oklahoma City, Nov. 30, 1941; s. Robert L. and Mary Alice (Krueger) B.; m. Susan Schulte, Feb. 14, 1978; 1 child, Christina; children by previous marriage: Jennifer, Richard, Derek. B.A., Dartmouth Coll., 1963; M.B.A., Harvard Bus. Sch., 1965. Mem. mktg. staff General Foods, White Plains, N.Y., 1965-73; mem. staff Citicorp, N.Y.C., 1973—, sector exec. in charge of worldwide consumer fin. svcs., info. bus., investor rels., corp. pub. affairs, customer affairs, corp. advt., 1985-90, also bd. dirs.; pres. Citibank/Citicorp, N.Y.C., 1990—; bd. dirs. Eastman Kodak. Bd. dirs. Cancer Rsch. Inst., N.Y.C., Lincoln Ctr., N.Y.C. Partnership; mem. Coun. on Fgn Rels. Mem. N.Y. C. of C. (bd. dirs.). Office: Citicorp 399 Park Ave New York NY 10043-0001

BRADE, COLLEEN ANNE SWIERCZNSKI, development professional; b. Albion, N.Y., July 28, 1964; d. Stanley Theodore and Mary Geraldine (Palmer) Swierczski; m. Ricky Lee Brade, Oct. 12, 1991. BS in Mktg., Canisius Coll., 1986; postgrad., St. Bonaventure U., 1990—. Mktg. asst. Office Automation, Inc., Williamsville, N.Y., 1986-87; asst. dir. devel. rsch. St. Bonaventure (N.Y.) U., 1987-88, dir. devel. rsch., 1988—; mem. devel. com. N.Y. State Spl. Olympics, Albany, 1992—. Mem. Am. Prospect Rsch. Assn. (v.p., sec. Upstate N.Y. chpt. 1990-91, program dir. 1992—). Democrat. Roman Catholic. Home: 324 N 3d St Olean NY 14760 Office: St Bonaventure U Saint Bonaventure NY 14778

BRADFORD, BARBARA TAYLOR, author, journalist, novelist; b. Leeds, Eng.; came to U.S., 1964; d. Winston and Freda (Walker) Taylor; m. Robert Bradford, Dec. 24, 1963. Student pvt. schs., Eng.; LittD (hon.), Leeds U., 1990. Women's editor Yorkshire (Eng.) Evening Post, 1951-53, reporter, 1949-51; editor Woman's Own, 1953-54; columnist London Evening News, 1955-57; exec. editor London Am., 1959-62; editor Nat. Design Center Mag., 1965-69; syndicated columnist Newsday Spls., L.I., 1968-70; nat. syndicated columnist Chgo. Tribune-N.Y. (News Syndicate), N.Y.C., 1970-75, Los Angeles Times Syndicate, 1975-81. Author: Complete Ency. Homemaking Ideas, 1968, A Garland of Children's Verse, 1968, How to be the Perfect Wife, 1969, Easy Steps to Successful Decorating, 1971, Decorating Ideas for Casual Living, 1977, How to Solve Your Decorating Problems, 1976, Making Space Grow, 1979, Luxury Designs for Apartment Living, 1981; (novels) A Woman of Substance, 1979, Voice of the Heart, 1983, Hold the Dream, 1985, screen adaptation, 1986, Act of Will, 1986, To Be the Best, 1988, The Women in His Life, 1990, Remember, 1991. Recipient Dorothy Dawe award Am. Furniture Mart, 1970, 71, Matrix award N.Y. Women in Communications, 1985. Mem. Authors Guild, Nat. Soc. Interior Designers (Distinguished Editorial award 1969, Nat. Press award 1971), Authors Guild Am. (coun. mem. 1989—), Am. Soc. Interior Designers. Office: 450 Park Ave New York NY 10022-2605

BRADLEE, BENJAMIN CROWNINSHIELD, executive editor; b. Boston, Aug. 26, 1921; s. Frederick J. and Josephine (deGersdorff) B.; m. Jean Saltonstall, Aug. 8, 1942; 1 son, Benjamin Crowninshield; m. Antoinette Pinchot, July 6, 1956; children: Dominic, Marina; m. Sally Quinn, Oct. 20, 1978; 1 son, Josiah Quinn Crowninshield. A.B., Harvard U., 1943. Reporter N.H. Sunday News, Manchester, 1946- 48, Washington Post, 1948-51; press attachè embassy Paris, France, 1951-53; European corr. Newsweek mag., Paris, 1953-57; reporter Washington bur. Newsweek mag., 1957-61, sr. editor, chief bur., 1961-65; mng. editor Washington Post, 1965-68, v.p., exec. editor, 1968-91, v.p., dir., 1991—. Author: That Special Grace, 1964, Conversations with Kennedy, 1975. Served to lt. USNR, 1942-45. Home: 3014 N St NW Washington DC 20007-3404 Office: care Washington Post 1150 15th St NW Washington DC 20071-0002

BRADLEY, AMELIA JANE, lawyer; b. Columbia, S.C., Apr. 18, 1947; d. Hugh Wilson and Amelia Jane (Wylie) B.; m. Richard Bancroft Hovey, Apr. 1, 1977. BA, U. Va., 1968; MA, George Washington U., 1971. Bar: Va. 1976, D.C. 1985. Budget and mgmt. analyst NLRB, Washington, 1968-71, 72; clk. Cohen and Vitt, PC, Alexandria, Va., 1972-76; assoc. Cohen, Vitt & Annand, PC, Alexandria, 1976-80; White House fellow USDA, Washington, 1980-81; White House fellow Office U.S. Trade Rep., Exec. Office of Pres., Washington, 1981, asst. gen. counsel, 1981-82, assoc. gen. counsel, 1982-84; prin. dep. gen. counsel Office U.S. Trade Rep., Exec Office of Pres., Washington, 1989-92;, 1990—; asst. U.S. trade rep. for dispute resolution Office U.S. Trade Rep., Exec. Office of Pres., Washington, 1991—; legal advisor to U.S. GATT del. Office U.S. Trade Rep., Exec. Office of Pres., Geneva, 1984-87; counsel to U.S. Del. GATT Ministerial Conf., Punta del Este, Uruguay, 1986; chief negotiator U.S. GATT Uruguay Round Dispute Settlement Negotiating Group, 1986-87, 89—; chmn. Interagy. Sect. 301 Com., Washington, 1988-92; vis. rsch. assoc. Fletcher Sch. Law and Diplomacy, Tufts U., Medford, Mass., 1987-88; vis. researcher Harvard U. Law Sch., Cambridge, Mass., 1988. Mem., chmn. Alexandria Human Rights Commn., 1975-80; pres., trustee Alexandria Law Libr., 1978-80; founding mem. Lawyer Referral Svc., Alexandria, 1978. NEH fellow, 1978. Mem. ABA, Am. Soc. Internat. Law, Va. State Bar (mem., chmn. com. on legal edn. and admission to bar 1977-84), D.C. Bar (chmn. internat. trade com. 1989-90). Episcopalian. Office: Office US Trade Rep 600 17th St NW Washington DC 20506-0001

BRADLEY, BILL, senator; b. Crystal City, Mo., July 28, 1943; s. Warren W. and Susan (Crowe) B.; m. Ernestine Schlant, Jan. 14, 1974; 1 dau., Theresa Anne. BA, Princeton U., 1965; MA, Oxford (Eng.) U., 1968. Player N.Y. Knickerbockers Profl. Basketball Team, 1967-77; U.S. senator from N.J., 1979—; mem. fin., energy coms., spl. com. on aging, select com. on intelligence; mem. Nat. Adv. Coun. on Rights of the Child; mem. Nat. Commn. to Prevent Infant Mortality. Author: Life on the Run, 1976, The Fair Tax, 1984. Served with USAFR, 1967-78. Rhodes scholar, 1965-67. Democrat. Office: US Senate 731 Hart Senate Bldg Washington DC 20510

BRADLEY, E. MICHAEL, lawyer; b. N.Y.C., Apr. 13, 1939; s. Otis Treat Bradley and Marian Booth (Alling) Ward; m. Judith Allen Thompson, June 29, 1962; children: Jennifer Treat, Michael Thompson, Thomas Alcott, Samuel Allen. BA, Yale U., 1961; LLB, U. Va., 1964. Bar: N.Y., 1965. Assoc. Davis, Polk & Wardwell, N.Y.C., 1964-72; assoc. Brown & Wood, N.Y.C., 1972-73, ptnr., 1974—; lectr. Practicing Law Inst., N.Y.C., 1970-79, 86, Am. Law Inst.-ABA, Phila., 1977-78; arbitrator Am. Arbitration Assn., N.Y.C., 1975—. Contbg. editor: The Use of Experts in Corporate Litigation, 1978, Securites Law Techniques, 1985. Bd. dirs. Bennett Coll. Found., N.Y.C., 1984—; trustee Salisbury (Conn.) Sch., 1987—. Mem. ABA, N.Y. State Bar Assn., Fed. Bar Assn., Assn. of Bar of City of N.Y., River Club, Union Club, Coral Beach Club, The Downtown Assn., Quogue Field Club, Shinnecock Yacht Club, Nat. Golf Links of Am., L.I. Wyandanch Club. Republican. Presbyterian. Home: 125 E 72d St New York NY 10021 Office: Brown & Wood 1 World Trade Ctr New York NY 10048-0202

BRADLEY, EDWARD WILLIAM, sports foundation executive; b. Milltown, N.J., Aug. 12, 1927; s. William Ernest and Hilda (Schwendeman) B.; m. Eleanor A Massing, Apr. 12, 1952; children: Scott Richard, Gail Sharon Bradley Klewsaat, Lisa June Bradley Robertson. BE, Panzer Coll., 1950. Dir. athletics, supr. phys. edn. and health Milltown Pub. Schs., 1951-69; owner, pres. The Exec. Health Club, East Brunswick, N.J., 1965-84; chmn., chief exec. officer N.J. Fitness and Sports Found., Milltown, 1984—; writer Middlesex County Govt., North Brunswick, N.J., 1985—; dir. activities Playboy Club Resort Hotel at Great Gorge, 1972. Apptd. chmn. chief exec. officer Gov.'s Coun. on Phys. Fitness and Sports, 1983—; chmn., chief exec. officer Middlesex County Coun. on Physical Fitness and Sports (div. Pres.'s Coun. on Physical Fitness), 1992—, N.J. Youth Fitness Coalition; chmn. N.J. Torch Relay Com., 1984; dist. coord., cons. Nat. Assn. Disabled Athletes; founder, chmn. Gov.'s Blue Ribbon Panel on Fitness and Sports, N.J. Healthy Am. Fitness Leaders Award Program; mem. State of N.J. Blue Ribbon Com. for Baseball in N.J.; dir. Phys. Fitness and Sports for U.S. Job Corp., Edison, N.J.; mem. Mission Possible task force NEA-AAHPERD; supt. recreation Borough of Milltown, 1951-64; active Pres.'s Coun. on Phys. Fitness and Sports, 1964—; cons. Pres. Kennedy, Johnson, Carter, Nixon, Ford, Reagan, Bush, master cons., adv. Pres's. coun. the White House, 1988. With USN, 1945-46, ATO. Recipient U.S. Outstanding Phys. Leadership award Pres.'s Coun. on Phys. Fitness and Sports and U.S. Jaycees, 1962, U.S. Healthy Am. Fitness Leaders award Pres.'s Coun., U.S. Jaycees and Allstate, 1985, Svc. in Phys. Fitness and Sports award Montclair State Coll., 1988, Phys. Edn. award for Excellence Pancer Coll., Svc. Award Ea. Dist. AAHPERD, N.J. Award for People to Watch, 1984, Jerseyan of Week award Newark Star Ledger, 1988, Honor Fellow award N.J. Assn. Health, Phys. Edn. and Recreation, 1964, Young Man or Yr. award Milltown Jaycees, 1962; honored guest Pres. Nixon, 1975, Pres. Reagan, 1987, Richard Nixon Libr., 1990, Pres. Bush-The White House, 1991, 92. Mem. Outstanding Phys. Fitness Leadership Congress, U.S. Jaycees, Nat. Fitness Leadership Assn., Internat. Assn. Approved Basketball Officials, Am. Legion, N.J. Youth Fitness Coalition, Pres.'s Club, Court Club. Home: 225

Highland Dr Milltown NJ 08850-1142 Office: NJ Fitness and Sports Found CN 487 Milltown NJ 08850

BRADLEY, GEORGE E., JR., sales manager; b. Somerville, N.J., May 1, 1957; s. George E. and Carmella (D'Ovidio) B.; m. Laura Clair Messemer, Nov. 2, 1979; children: Kyle George, Ryan James. BA, William Paterson Coll., Wayne, N.J., 1983; postgrad., Rutgers U. Sales rep. Eco Lab., Edison, N.J., 1984-86, Pariser Ind., Wayne, N.J., 1986-87, Miele Appliances, Somerset, N.J., 1987-90; mkt. devel. mgr. Micle Appliances, Somerset, N.J., 1990-91, dist. sales mgr. Ea. Atlantic region, 1991—. Mem. Nat. Kitchen and Bath Assn., Vacuum Dealers Trade Assn., Internat. Foods & Fragrances, Nat. Hotel Motel Assn., K.C. Roman Catholic. Home: 45 Hickory Ct Jamesburg NJ 08831-2507 Office: Miele Appliances Inc 22D Worlds Fair Dr Somerset NJ 08873-1346

BRADLEY, ROGER WILLIAM, lawyer; b. N.Y.C., Sept. 25, 1944; s. Joseph Wilson and Alyce (Halferty)úB.; m. Ann Marie Cummings, Aug. 27, 1977; children: Daniel, Brendan. BA, Colgate U., 1966; JD (magna cum laude), Syracuse U., 1969. Bar: N.Y. 1970, U.S. Ct. Appeals (2d cir.) 1975, U.S. Dist. Ct. (no. dist.) N.Y. 1974, U.S. Dist. Ct. (so. dist.) N.Y. 1975, U.S. Dist. Ct. (we. dist.) N.Y. 1979. Law asst. Appellate div. 3d jud. dept. N.Y. Supreme Ct., Binghamton, N.Y., 1969-71; spl. asst. atty. gen. State of N.Y., Albany, 1971-73; ptnr. Melvin & Melvin, Syracuse, N.Y., 1973—. Mem. Am. Arbitration Assn. (panel of arbitrators 1980—, mediator 1990), ABA (forum of constrn. industry 1989—, litigation sect. 1989—, tort and ins. practice sect.), N.Y. Sate Bar Assn. (fed. comml. litigation sect., com. on constrn. 1989—), Onondaga County Bar Assn., Internat. Platform Assn. Republican. Roman Catholic. Office: Melvin & Melvin 220 S Warren St Syracuse NY 13202-1613

BRADLEY, SAMUEL MCKNIGHT, marketing executive; b. Upland, Pa., Mar. 25, 1956; s. Samuel McKnight and Patricia Ann (Reilly) B.; m. Anne Brady Shew, Nov. 3, 1984. BA cum laude, West Chester (Pa.) U., 1978; MBA, Drexel U., Phila., 1981. Grad. teaching asst. Drexel U., Phila., 1980-81; product specialist AMP, Inc., Valley Forge, Pa., 1981-82, inside sales rep., 1982-84, field sales engr., 1984-85, tng. specialist, 1985-86, asst. product mgr., 1986-87, product mgr., 1987—; author seminar on fiber tech., 1990. Mem. Am. Radio Relay League, Pi Gamma Mu. Office: AMP Inc 450 W Swedesford Rd Berwyn PA 19312-1164

BRADLEY, WANDA LOUISE, librarian; b. Havre de Grace, Md., June 6, 1953; d. William Smith and Josephine Viola (Miller) B. BA, U. Md., 1975; MSLS, Atlanta U., 1976; postgrad., Cath. U.; MPA (scholar), U. Balt., 1986. Libr. Harford County Pub. Libr., Bel Air, Md., 1976, Harford County Bd. Edn., Bel Air, Md., 1977-81, Nat. Grad. U., Arlington, Va., 1982, Md. State Dept. Edn., Balt., 1982-83, U.S. Dept. Labor, Washington, 1984, Balt. Gas and Electric Co., 1984-85, Morgan State U., Balt., 1985, Coppin State Coll., Balt., 1985-86, Montgomery County Pub. Sch. System, Rockville, Md., 1985-86, Community Coll., Balt., 1987-88; grant adminstr. Howard County Pub. Libr., 1988; libr., media specialist Balt. City Pub. Sch. System, 1992—; acad. advisor George Mason U., Fairfax, Va., 1981-82. Dept. Edn. fellow, 1983-84; U. Balt. Merit scholar, 1984, Atlanta U. scholar, 1976, U. Md. scholar, 1992; Howard County Pub. Libr. grantee, 1988. Mem. ALA, ASIS, Md. Libr. Assn., Spl. Librs. Assn., Med. Libr. Assn. Methodist. Office: Balt City Pub Sch System Lombard Sch 1601 E Lombard St Baltimore MD 21231

BRADSHAW, J(OHN) ROBERT, office furnishings executive; b. Washington, July 11, 1954; s. J. Douglas and Alcena (White) B.; m. Anne Burns, Mar. 4, 1983; children: Meghan A., J. Patrick. BA, Lynchburg Coll., 1976; MA, Cen. Mich. U., 1982. V.p. Prince Georges Realty, Inc., Riverdale, Md., 1976-82; asst. comptr. Frenchmen's Reef Resort, St. Thomas, V.I., 1982-84; sales mgr. Stern's, Inc., Washington, 1984-90; v.p., owner Md. Office Interiors, Inc., Balt., 1990—. Dir. Lynchburg (Va.) Coll. Alumni Assn., 1977-78, class chmn., 1977-89, 89-90; dir. Kings Retreat Homeowners Assn., Davidsonville, Md., 1987-90. Mem. Internat. Facilty Mgmt. Assn., Inst. Bus. Designers. Republican. Roman Catholic. Office: Md Office Interiors 1405 G St NW Washington DC 20005

BRADSHAW, RICHARD EUGENE, international science and technologies analyst; b. Rocky Mount, N.C., Jan. 15, 1950; s. Harvey Edmond and Grace Darling (Cowley) B.; m. Pamela Anne Lacey, June 3, 1989. BA in Polit. Sci., U. N.C., 1974; MA in Internat. Rels., East Carolina U., 1977; postgrad., U. S.C., 1977-78. Fgn. svc. officer U.S. Dept. of State, Washington, Paris, 1978-82; dir. rsch. North Am. Telecommunications Assn., Washington, 1982-83; R&D policy cons. Washington Nichibei Consultants, Washington, 1983-87; asst. prof. George Mason U., Fairfax, Va., 1987—; sr. policy analyst NSF, Washington, 1988-92; pres. Trans Atlantic Techs., Washington, 1992—. Office: Trans Atlantic Techs 1701 21st St NW Washington DC 20009

BRADY, EAMONN FEENEY, financial planner; b. Bronx, N.Y., Aug. 5, 1964; s. Edward Graven and Agnes Elizabeth (Feeney) B. AB, Dartmouth Coll., 1985, MBA, 1987. CLU. Fixed income specialist McLaughlin, Piven, Vogel, N.Y.C., 1987-89; v.p. fixed income Tripp and Co., N.Y.C., 1989-90; brokerage supr. Cowan Fin. Group, N.Y.C., 1990-91; ptnr. Sands Bros., N.Y.C., 1991—; proprietor O'Neill's Irish Castle, Poughkeepsie, N.Y., 1991—. Campaign staff mem. Bush Campaign, N.Y.C., 1988, 92; charter mem. Rep. Presdl. Task Force, 1990—; founder Ronald Reagan Rep. Ctr., Washington, 1991. Mem. Nat. Restaurant Assn., Nat. Lic. Beverage Assn., Irish Northern Aid, Dartmouth Club of N.Y.C. Roman Catholic. Home: 120 E 83d St New York NY 10028 Office: 101 Park Ave New York NY 10178

BRADY, GENE FRANKLYN, business educator, consultant, researcher; b. Honolulu, Nov. 20, 1932; s. Harvey Franklin and Susie Maude (Jordan) B.; m. Maria Strasser, Apr. 3, 1953 (div. July 1977); children: Cynthia, Loretta, Mark; m. Mari Ann Laurel Zarrello, Sept. 24, 1977; children: Jennifer, Gene Franklyn. BS in Commerce, U. Va., 1958; MBA, Wayne State U., 1965; PhD in Bus., U. Oreg., 1971. Budget acct. Am. Viscose Corp., Front Royal, Va., 1958-59; assoc. prof. mgmt. U. New Haven, West Haven, Conn., 1976-82; prof. mgmt. U. Bridgeport, Conn., 1982—; vis. fellow Yale U., New Haven, 1978. Author: Management by Involvement, 1989; co-author: Executive Succession, 1984; contbr. articles to profl. jours. Lt. col. USAF, 1952-76. Mem. Acad. Mgmt., Eastern Acad. Mgmt., So. Mgmt. Assn. Home: 22 Windsor Rd E North Haven CT 06473-3017 Office: U Bridgeport Mandeville Hall Bridgeport CT 06601

BRADY, KENT MASON, international marketing administrator; b. San Diego, Feb. 15, 1941; s. Merle Brady and Barbara (Hilliard) B.; m. Eunice Ann Coville, Mar. 21, 1964; children: Shireen, Michele, Kristen. BA, Calif. State U., San Francisco, 1964. Vol. Peace Corps, Liberia, 1964-66; asst. dir. Care Inc., New Delhi, India, 1966-71, Islamabid, Pakistan, 1972-73; mng. dir. Peavey Assn. Ltd., Hong Kong, 1973-75; dir. U.S. Feed Grains Coun., Tokyo, 1975-82; dir. internat. mktg. Nat. Renderers Assn. (now Smith Bucklin and Assocs.), Washington, 1989—; mem. Citizens Forum, Washington, 1991—. Mem. U.S. Agrl. Export Devel. Coun. Home: 10 Cape Anne Ct Gaithersburg MD 20879

BRADY, LAWRENCE PETER, lawyer; b. Jersey City, July 26, 1940; s. Lawrence Peter and Evelyn (Mauro) B.; div; children: Deegan, Tara, Kerry, James; m. Mary Helen Reynolds, Mar. 28, 1984. BS in Acctg., St. Peters Coll., 1961; JD, Seton Hall U., 1964; LLM, Bklyn. Law Sch., 1966. Bar: N.J. 1964, N.Y. 1991, U.S. Dist. Ct. N.J. 1964, U.S. Supreme Ct. 1969, U.S. Ct. Appeals (3rd cir.) 1972; cert. civil trial atty. State of N.J. 1982; cert. Nat. Bd. Trial Advocacy 1989. Asst. prosecutor Hudson County, Jersey City, 1964-70; prosecutor Town of Kearny, N.J., 1971-74; sr. ptnr. Doyle & Brady, Kearny, 1974—; dir. and founding incorporator Growth Bank, New Vernon, N.J. Mem. N.J. State Bar Assn., Hudson County Bar Assn., West Hudson Bar Assn. (sec. 1980, treas. 1981, v.p. 1982, pres. 1983), Assn. Trial Lawyers Am., Nat. Bd. Trial Advocacy (cert.), Am. Trial Lawyers N.J. (bd. govs.), Roxiticus Golf Club (Mendham, N.J.), Sandalfoot Country Club (Boca Raton, Fla.), Ocean Reef Club (Key Largo, Fla.). Roman Catholic. Home: PO Box 127 Anthony Wayne Rd New Vernon NJ 07976-0127 Office: Doyle & Brady 377 Kearny Ave Kearny NJ 07032-2601

BRADY, NICHOLAS FREDERICK, secretary of treasury; b. N.Y.C., Apr. 11, 1930; s. James C. and Eliot (Chace) B.; m. Katherine Douglas, Sept. 5, 1952; children: Nicholas Frederick, Christopher D., Anthony N., Katherine C. B.A., Yale U., 1952; M.B.A., Harvard U., 1954. With Dillon Read & Co. Inc., N.Y.C., 1954-82, former chmn., chief exec. officer, from 1982; former dir., chmn. exec. com. Purolator Courier Corp. Inc., Basking Ridge, N.J., from 1983; appointee to U.S. Senate from N.J. to fill unexpired term of Harrison Williams, 1982, resigned, Dec. 1982; secretary Dept. of the Treasury, Washington, 1988—; dir. Bessemer Securities Corp., Doubleday & Co., Ga. Internat. Corp., Wolverne World Wide Inc., ASA Ltd., Media Gen. Inc., NCR Corp. Trustee assoc. Boys' Club Newark.; Reagan appointee MX missile devel. options panel, Central Am. Study Commn., 1983. Clubs: Bond (N.Y.C.), Lunch (N.Y.C.) (bd. govs.), Links (N.Y.C.). Office: Treasury Dept 15th & Pennsylvania Aves NW Washington DC 20220*

BRADY, ROBERT FREDERICK, JR., chemist; b. Washington, July 20, 1942; s. Robert Frederick Sr. and Mary Catherine (Spillan) B.; m. Sharon Anne Callison Aug. 12, 1965; children: Sheila Mary Speth, Robert Michael, Patrick Christopher. BS in Chemistry, U. Va., 1964, PhD, 1967. Rsch. chemist organic chemistry group U.S. Nat. Bur. Standards, Washington, 1967-72; rsch. chemist U.S. Customs Svc., Washington, 1972-75; chief paints and adhesives sect. U.S. Gen. Svcs. Adminstrn., Washington, 1975-82; head coatings sect. U.S. Naval Rsch. Lab., Washington, 1982—; vis. scientist Def. Materials Rsch. Lab., Melbourne, Victoria, Australia, 1990-91. Mem. editorial bd., tech. editor Jour. Coatings Tech., Phila., Jour. Protective Coatings and Linings, Pitts., 1986-90; contbr. articles to chem. jours.; patentee in field. Pres. Washington Paint Tech. Group, 1979-80, Chem. Soc. Washington, 1982, U. Va. Chemists, 1991-92. Fellow Royal Soc. Chemistry (London), Washington Acad. Scis.; mem. Am. Chem. Soc. (chmn. admissions com. 1985-88), Fedn. Socs. for Coatings Tech. Roman Catholic. Home: 706 Hope Ln Gaithersburg MD 20878-1883 Office: US Naval Rsch Lab Code 6120 Washington DC 20375

BRADY, TERESA PATRICIA, educator, lawyer; b. Phila., June 20, 1956; d. John Joseph and Concetta (Leone) B. BA, Holy Family Coll., 1978; MBA, La Salle U., 1984; JD, Temple U., 1989. Bar: Pa. 1989, U.S. Dist. Ct. (ea. dist.) Pa. 1990. Asst. prof. Holy Family Coll., Phila., 1984—; atty. Law Offices of Paul Beckert, Bensalem, Pa., 1989—; mem. adv. bd. Swenson Sch., Phila., 1991—. Author: Instructor's manual and text book for George Spiro's Legal Environment of Business. Mem. PA. Bar Assn., Phila. Bar Assn., Labor Law Employment Sect. Phila. Bar Assn. Home: 4414 Pearson Ave Philadelphia PA 19114-3719 Office: Holy Family Coll Grant & Frankford Aves Philadelphia PA 19114

BRADY, THOMAS CARL, lawyer; b. Malone, N.Y., Sept. 5, 1947; s. Francis Robert and Rosamond Ethel (South) B.; m. Joan Marie Murray, Dec. 4, 1971; children: Erin Marie, Ryan Thomas, Trevor Michael. BA, Niagara U., 1969; JD, SUNY, Buffalo, 1972. Bar: N.Y. 1973, U.S. Dist. Ct. (we. dist.) N.Y. 1973, Fla. 1981. City ct. judge City of Salamanca, N.Y., 1973; atty. County of Cattaraugus, Little Valley, N.Y., 1973-76; ptnr. Eldredge, Brady, Peters & Brooks, Salamanca and Ellicottville, N.Y., 1976-82; sr. ptnr. Brady, Brooks & Smith, Salamanca and Ellicottville, 1982—. Capt. USAR, 1969-76. Mem. ABA, Assn. Trial Lawyers Am., N.Y. State Trial Lawyers Assn., N.Y. STate Bar Assn., Cattaraugus County Bar Assn. (pres. 1984), Kiwanis (pres. Salamanca club 1983-84). Republican. Roman Catholic. Home: PO Box 195 Great Valley NY 14741-0204 Office: Brady Brooks & Smith 41 Main St Salamanca NY 14779-2092

BRADY-AMOON, PEGGY, educational administrator-counselor; b. N.Y.C., Aug. 4, 1956. BA, SUNY, Oswego, 1978; MS, L.I. U., 1988. Admissions and fin. aid counselor St. Thomas Aquinas Coll., Sparkill, N.Y., 1980-84, asst. dir. admissions and fin. aid, 1984-85, dir. higher edn. opportunity program, 1985—. Co-leader Girl Scouts Am., 1991. Mem. AACD, Higher Edn. Opportunity Program Profl. Orgn., N.Y. State Assn. Counseling and Devel., N.Y. State Fin. Aid Adminstrs. Assn., Sigma Delta Pi. Office: St Thomas Aquinas Coll Rt 340 Sparkill NY 10976

BRAESTRUP, PETER, editor; b. N.Y.C., June 8, 1929; s. Carl Bjorn and Elsebet (Kampmann) B.; m. Angelica Hollins (div. 1985); children: Angelica, Elizabeth Kate, Carl Peter; m. Sandra Cornelia Newing, 1989. BA, Yale U., 1951. Contbg. editor Time Mag., N.Y.C., 1953-55; corr. Time Mag., Chgo., 1955-57; reporter N.Y. Herald Tribune, N.Y.C., 1957-59, N.Y. Times, Washington, 1960-62; corr. N.Y. Times, Algiers, 1962-65, Paris, 1965, Bangkok, Saigon, 1966-68; bur. chief Washington Post, Saigon, 1968-69; nat. staff writer Washington Post, 1969-73; founding editor Wilson Quar., Washington, 1975-89; sr. editor, dir. communications Libr. of Congress, Washington, 1989—. Author: Big Story, 1977 (Sigma Delta Chi award 1978), (with others) Battle Lines, 1985; editor: Vietnam as History, 1984; contbr. articles to profl. jours. Mem. Yale Alumni Publs. Bd., 1975-88, Yale U. Coun., 1984—, 20th Century Fund Task Force on Mil. Media Rels., 1984-85; chmn. Media Studies Project, Washington, 1987—. 1st lt. USMC, 1951-53, Korea. Nieman fellow Harvard U., 1960, Woodrow Wilson Internat. Ctr. for Scholars fellow, 1973-75. Mem. Cosmos Club (Washington). Office: Libr Congress LM 608 Washington DC 20540

BRAFF, HOWARD, brokerage house executive, financial analyst; b. Bklyn., July 18, 1952; s. Emanuel and Rose (Schlamberg) B.; m. Cindi Louise Sansone, Mar. 25, 1975; 1 child, Shana. BA in Math. and Psychology summa cum laude, Hofstra U., 1974, MBA in Fin., 1984. Fin. mgr. Save On Oil, Inc., Merrick, N.Y., 1974-83; acct. exec., portfolio mgr., high-tech. and health care ind. analyst Laidlaw, Adams & Peck, Inc., Westbury, N.Y., 1983-86; ind. investment adv. Merrick, 1977-83; account exec., portfolio mgr. high tech and health care industry analyst Investors Ctr. Inc., Farmingdale, N.Y., 1986-87; health care industry analyst, portfolio mgr. Strasbourger Pearson Tulcin Wolff Inc., N.Y.C., 1987-88; br. mgr. Olde Discount Corp., Hicksville, N.Y., 1988-91; pres., chmn., chief exec. officer Save on Discount Stockbrokers Corp., Bellmore, N.Y., 1991—. Mem. Phi Beta Kappa. Home: 4 Mews Ct Holtsville NY 11742-1900 Office: Save On Discount Stockbrokers Corp 1499 Bellmore Ave Bellmore NY 11710

BRAGAW, GEORGE DRIVER, financial consultant; b. Bethesda, Md., Nov. 29, 1957; s. George D. Bragaw Jr. and Mary Elizabeth (Lux) Patton. BS, Shepherd Coll., 1979; MA in Govt. and Politics, U. Md., 1984. Account exec. Jefferson Fin., Washington, 1984-85; fin. cons. Wheat First Securities, Washington, 1986—; instr. Frederick (Md.) Community Coll., 1991; radio talk show host Sta. WPGC-AM, Greenbelt, Md., 1991-92; mcpl. bond coord. Wheat First, 1991-92. Pres. Shepherd Coll. Alumni Assn., Shepherdstown, W.Va., 1990-92. Democrat. Roman Catholic. Office: Wheat First Securities 2300 M St NW Washington DC 20037

BRAGDON, ALLEN DAVENPORT, publishing executive; b. Cleve., Oct. 21, 1930; s. Clifford Richardson and Joanna (Davenport) B.; children: Allen Clifford, Sara Bragdon Ray. BA, Read Coll., Portland, Oreg., 1952; postgrad., Howard U., 1952-53. Mgmt. trainee Doubleday and Co., N.Y.C., 1957-58; advt. and sales promotion mgr., trade dept. Doubleday and Co., 1958-59; dir. advt. and sales promotion The Macmillan Co., 1959-62; v.p., gen. mgr. book div. The Am. Heritage Pub. Co., 1962-67; pres., pub., editor-in-chief Plenary Publs. Internat., Inc., Amsterdam, The Netherlands, 1972-74; pub., packager Products, 1974-76; founding editor Games Mag., N.Y.C., 1977; editor-in-chief book div. Hearst Corp., N.Y.C., 1978-81; pres. Allen D. Bragdon Pubs., Inc., N.Y.C., 1976—; pub. cons. Columbia Broadcasting System, Inc., N.Y.C., CBS News, N.Y.C., The Hamlyn Group Ltd., London, Am. Bicentennial Co., Inc., N.Y.C., Simplified Travel, Inc., London, The Royal Mint of Gt. Britain, London, 1967-72. Author: Playspace Puzzles, 1974-79, The Gingerbread Book, A Country Treasury, Can You Pass These Tests, The Book of Tests, Ingenious Inventions, American Pastimes, 18 vols., 1980-90, others. Lt. comdr. USN, 1954-57. Mem. The Corinthians, Hobby Industry Am. Office: Allen D Bragdon Pubs Inc New Venture Dr South Dennis MA 02660-3432

BRAGDON, BRUCE RICHARD, dentist; b. Anchorage, Mar. 12, 1948; s. Richard Alton and Thelma (Basler) B.; m. Irene Bouchard, June 21, 1969; children: Todd, Tara. BS, Bowdoin Coll., 1970; DMD, U. Pa., 1974. Resident in gen. dentistry Boston City Hosp., 1974-75; pvt. practice Durham, N.H., 1975—; asst. vis. prof. Boston City Hosp., 1976—. Active Planning Bd. Town of Durham, 1978-84, charter com., 1986-87, town councilor, 1987-91. Mem. ADA, S.E. N.H. Dental Soc. Office: 10 Mathes Ter Durham NH 03824-2321

BRAGOLE, ROBERT ANTHONY, adhesives company executive; b. Somerville, Mass., Oct. 17, 1936; s. Louis John and Emily Maria (Terenzio) B.; m. Jean Doris Beaulieu, June 17, 1962; children: Linda Ann, Lisa Ann, Robert Anthony II, Michele Ann, John Louis. AB, Boston U., 1958; MS, Northeastern U., 1960; PhD, Yale U., 1965. Rsch. scientist Upjohn, North Haven, Conn., 1965-66; sr. rsch. chemist Bostik div. USM Corp., Middleton, Mass., 1966-68, sr. staff chemist, 1968-70, mgr. applied rsch., 1970-72, mgr. liquid adhesive div., 1972-74, mgr. solid adhesive div., 1975-76; dir. Cen. Rsch. Lab., Bostik div. EM Hart, MiddletoN, 1976-78, lab. mgr., 1978-85; dir. R & D, Upaco Adhesives div. Worthen Industries, Nashua, N.H., 1985-87, v.p. R & D, 1987—. Contbr. articles to profl. jours.; patentee on treatment of polyolefins. Named to Coll. Disting. Alumnae, Boston U., 1974. Mem. Am. Chem. Soc., Soc. Automotive Engrs., Soc. Mfg. Engrs., Adhesive and Sealant Coun. (rep.). Roman Catholic. Home: 5 Innis Dr Danvers MA 01923-1620

BRAHA, THOMAS I., business executive; b. Austin, Tex., Sept. 3, 1947; s. Jacob and Valentine (Capone) B.; m. Nancy Elizabeth Rowe, Mar. 31, 1973; children—Nancy Elizabeth, Jeanne Valentine, Travis Ian. B.S.M.E., U. Tex., 1969; M.B.A., Temple U., 1971; postgrad., N.Y. U., 1971-73. Engr. Davis Electronics, Inc., Austin, 1967, Whirlpool Corp., Evansville, Ind., 1968; project engr. ITE Imperial Corp., Phila., 1969-71; sr. supply analyst Mobil Oil Corp., N.Y.C., 1971-74; pres. Western Hemisphere Bulk Oil (U.S.A.), Inc., N.Y.C., 1974-75; pres., chief exec. officer Braha Oil Inc., Braha Oil Ltd., Braha Oil B.V., Braha Estates, Inc., Braha Farms, Braha Profit and Pension Trusts. Mem. ASME, Am. Mgmt. Assn., Am. Petroleum Inst., Inst. Petroleum (U.K.), Nat. Petroleum Refining Assn. Office: Braha Holding Co PO Box 787 Bryn Mawr PA 19010-0787

BRAININ, FREDERICK, poet, technical translator; b. Vienna, Austria, Aug. 22, 1913; came to U.S., 1938, naturalized, 1943; Matura degree Realschule, Vienna, 1931; M.S., CCNY, 1955 . Fed. examiner for German, U.S. Office Wartime Censorship, Port of N.Y., 1944-45; patent abstractor Sci. Digest, Chgo., 1950; tech. writer Kollsman Instrument Corp., N.Y.C., 1960's; tech. translator U.S. Joint Publs. Research Service, Washington area, 1963-69; fgn. tech. indexer AIAA, N.Y.C., 1970-73; editor U.S. Navy manuals for Grumman Aerospace Corp., L.I., 1974-77; free-lance electronic and computer patent translator for various patent attys., N.Y.C., 1977—. With Mil. Police Corps, U.S. Army, 1943-44. Recipient cert. of merit U.S. Office Sci. Censorship, 1945. Mem. Am. Literary Translators Assn., Internat. PEN (London chpt.). Author: Die Eherne Lyra, 1934, German-lang. version World Satellite Almanac, CommTek, 1985, (poetry collection) The Seventh Vienna, 1990; contbr. poems to various publs. including anthology, War Poems of the United Nations. Office: Rm 180-M 137-47 45th Ave Flushing NY 11355

BRAITHWAITE, JOHN MICHAEL, title examiner; b. Bridgewater, Mass., Nov. 11, 1958; s. John James and Helen Wanda (Wolski) B. BA in History, Cath. U. Am., 1980. Law clk. Murphy, Lamere and Murphy, P.C., Braintree, Mass., 1982; exec. asst. Energy Ptnrs., Inc., Boston, 1983; title examiner Edward Rainen, P.C., Boston, 1983-85, Golden and Cenower, P.C., Boston, 1985-86; chief title examiner Scheier, Scheier, Graham and Harsip, Acton, Mass., 1986-90; prin. John M. Braithwaite and Assocs., Chelmsford, Mass., 1990—, Jobra, Inc., 1986—. Mem. Mass. Ballot Law Commn., Boston, 1991; treas. Sullivan for State Senate Campaign, Lowell, Mass., 1990—, Lowell Rep. City Com., 1988—; dist. mgr. Citizens for Ltd. Taxation, Boston, 1990—. Mem. Mass. Assn. Title Examiners (pres. 1988-89), Mass. Conveyancers Assn. Roman Catholic. Home: 128 Warren St Lowell MA 01857 Office: Ste 253 1268 Main St Tewksbury MA 01876

BRAKE, JOHN RONALD, agricultural economics educator; b. Stanton, Mich., Jan. 22, 1932; s. D. Hale and Marjorie Naomi (Valentine) B.; m. Betty Jane Neitzel, Sept. 21, 1952; children—Susan Rene, Catherine Joanne, Jan Michelle, Elisa Marie. B.S., Mich. State U., 1955, M.S., 1956; Ph.D., N.C. State U., 1959. Asst. prof. Mich. State U., East Lansing, 1959-63, assoc. prof., 1963-69, prof., 1969-80; W.I. Myers prof. agrl. fin. Cornell U., Ithaca, N.Y., 1981—; contr. Office Tech. Assessment, Washington, 1985; spl. advisor to chief exec. officer Farm Credit Adminstrn., Washington, 1989-90. Mem. Am. Agr. Econ. Assn. (found. bd. 1989-92). Author Farm and Personal Finance, 1968. Editor Agrl. Fin. Rev., 1983—. Home: 11 Stormy View Rd Ithaca NY 14850-9774 Office: Cornell U 157 Warren Hall Ithaca NY 14853

BRAKELEY, GEORGE ARCHIBALD, JR., fund raising counsel; b. Washington, Apr. 18, 1916; s. George Archibald and Lillian (Fay) B.; m. Roxana Byerly; children: George Archibald III, Deborah Fay Buri, Joan Keller. BA, U. Pa., 1938. V.p., dir. John Price Jones Co., Inc. (fund-raising counsel), N.Y.C.; pres., treas. John Price Jones Co. (Can.), Ltd., 1950-52, G.A. Brakeley & Co., Ltd., 1952-61; chmn., chief operating officer G.A. Brakeley & Co., Inc., L.A., 1956-69; chmn., chief exec. officer Brakeley, John Price Jones, Inc., 1972-83, chmn., 1983-87, sr. cons., 1987—. Author: Tested Ways to Successful Fund Raising. Trustee Ctr. Study for Presidency, Internat. Coun. to Coordinate Cancer Rsch. Capt. C.E., AUS, WW II. Mem. Mayflower Soc., Anglers Club (N.Y.C.), Montreal Racket Club (hon.), Wee Burn Golf Club (Darien, Conn.), Met. Club (Washington), Royal Poinciana Golf Club (Naples, Fla.). Episcopalian. Home: 185 South Ave # 26 New Canaan CT 06840-5729 Office: 2777 Summer St Stamford CT 06905-4310

BRALEY, RUSSELL NORTON, retired journalist, author; b. Seattle, Nov. 10, 1921; s. Edward Russell and Gladys Bernita (Norton) B.; m. Madeleine Elizabet Karacsony, Mar. 25, 1953. BA, U. Wash., 1944; French cert., Sorbonne U., Paris, 1950. Reporter The Oakland (Calif.) Post-Enquirer, 1947-49, The Stars and Stripes, Darmstadt, Fed. Republic of Germany, 1951-52; mng. editor Overseas Weekly, Frankfurt, Fed. Republic of Germany, 1952-55; Germany corr. The N.Y. Daily News, 1955-75, UN corr., 1975-82; news editor Voice of Am., Washington, 1984-86; dep. fgn. editor The Washington Times, 1986-87; freelance writer. Author: Bad News: The Foreign Policy of the New York Times, 1984; contbr. articles to profl. jours. Lt. (j.g.) USNR, 1944-46.

BRAMAN, GRENVILLE C., JR., cosmetics executive; b. Buenos Aires, Nov. 1, 1946; came to U.S., 1946.; s. Grenville C. and Frances (Becker) B.; m. Suzanne Grimes, Dec. 27, 1969. BA, Williams Coll., 1969. Mktg. planner Avon Products, N.Y.C., 1969-73, mktg. mgr. internat., 1973-78, 1987—, mktg. dir. Latin Am., 1978-80, mktg. dir. U.S., 1981-82, mktg. dir. Brazil (overseas), 1983-87; implemented CDSS for global mktg. Republican. Home: 430 Mill Hill Ter Southport CT 06490-1232

BRAMFITT, BRUCE LIVINGSTON, research metallurgist; b. Troy, N.Y., Feb. 4, 1938; s. Thomas and Ruth (Livingston) B.; m. Joan Flora Sunukjian, June 30, 1963; children: Christopher Livingston, David Livingston. B-SMetE, U. Mo., 1960, MSMetE, 1962, PhDMetE, 1966, Profl.MetE (hon.), 1989. Metall. trainee Allegheny-Ludlum, Watervliet, N.Y., 1957; metallurgist Watervliet (N.Y.) Arsenal, 1959-64; instr. U. Mo., Rolla, 1960-66; rsch. engr. Bethlehem (Pa.) Steel, 1966-79, rsch. supr., 1979-84, sr. scientist, 1984-87, rsch. fellow, 1987—. Editor: Fundamentals of Dual Phase Steels, 1981, Metallurgy of Continuous-Annealed Sheet Steel, 1982, MiCon 86, 1988; patentee in field; contbr. papers to profl. jours. Scout master Boy Scouts Am., Bethlehem, Pa., 1981-83. Recipient Joseph Vilella award ASTM, 1974. Fellow Am. Soc. for Metals Internat. (chpt. chmn. 1989-90, Bradley Stoughton award 1991); mem. AIME (The Metall. Soc. com. chmn. 1983-85, The Iron & Steel Soc. com. chmn. 1990—, Michael Tenenbaum award 1987, C. D. Moore award 1977, 79), Internat. Metallographic Soc., Saucon Valley Country Club, Sigma Xi, Alpha Sigma Mu, Sigma Gamma Epsilon. Home: 1647 Pleasant Dr Bethlehem PA 18015-9246 Office: Bethlehem Steel Corp Homer Rsch Labs Bethlehem PA 18016

BRAMWELL, HENRY, federal judge; b. Bklyn., Sept. 3, 1919; s. Henry Hall and Florence Elva (MacDonald) B.; m. Ishbel W. Brown, Jan. 29, 1966. LL.B., Bklyn. Law Sch., 1948, LL.D. (hon.), 1979. Bar: N.Y. bar 1948. Asst. U.S. atty. Bklyn., 1953-61; asso. counsel N.Y. State Rent Commn., 1961-63; judge Civil Ct., N.Y.C., Bklyn., 1966, 69—; asst. ad-

minstrv. judge Kings County, Bklyn., 1974—; judge U.S. Dist. Ct., Bklyn., 1975—; U.S. Sr. Dist. judge, 1987—; Mem. Community Mayors N.Y. State; trustee Bklyn. Law Sch., 1978—. Served with AUS, 1941-45. Mem. ABA, N.Y. State Bar Assn., Bklyn. Bar Assn. (trustee 1968-74), Nat. Bar Assn. (life), Am. Judicature Assn., Fed. Judges Assn. (founding). Home: 101 Clark St Brooklyn NY 11201-2746 Office: US Dist Ct 225 Cadman Plz E Brooklyn NY 11201-1818

BRANCA, FRANK JOSEPH, police officer; b. Norwalk, Conn., Dec. 4, 1948; s. Joseph and Angela Ann (Grallo) B.; m. Judy Ann Perry, July 10, 1975; children: Meredith Lynn, Kristin Jane, Ashley Marie. BS in Criminal Justice, Iona Coll., 1983. Police officer Greenwich Police Dept., Greenwich, Conn., 1970-77, youth officer, 1977-78, detective, 1978-87, sgt., 1987-90, lt., 1990—; pres. Fairfield County (Conn.) Police Tng. Officers Assn., 1990-92. Coord. United Way of Greenwich (Conn.), 1989-90. With USNG, 1970-76. Named Police Officer of the Year, Greenwich (Conn.) Lions Club, 1983; recipient Ofcl. Citation, State of Conn. Gen. Assembly, 1983. Mem. Silver Shield Assn. (pres. 1977-78), Greenwich Old Timers Athletic Assn. (dir. 1990—), Hon. Order of Ky. Cols. Republican. Office: Greenwich Police Dept 11 Bruce Pl Greenwich CT 06830

BRANCH, DAVID W., publishing executive, sales consultant; b. N.Y.C., Jan. 25, 1965; s. James Elliot and Doris (Parrotte) B.; m. Cornelia Klenk, Aug. 17, 1991. A in Hotel and Restaurant Mgmt., Johnson and Wales, Providence, 1985. Mgr. N.J. sales Sta. WPAT, Clifton, N.J., 1987-89; prin. Rothstein, Bluestein Advt., Englewood, N.J., 1989-90; mgr. mid-Atlantic sales Personal Computing Mag., Totowa, N.J., 1990; mgr. regional sales New Media Mag., Clifton, 1990-92; pub., owner PSRS Mag., Suffern, N.Y., 1992—. Author, producer: (ballad) Dream Girl, 1990, (song) My Ex, 1990. Republican. Presbyterian. Office: PSRS Mag Ste 115 78 Lafayette Ave Suffern NY 10901

BRANCH, M. KENYA, student scheduling coordinator; b. Phila., Jan. 10, 1957; s. John Floyd and thelma (Griffin) B.; children: Tamyra, Jelani. Circulation clk. Phila. Tribune, 1971-72; dir. extrnal communications Ujima Record Co., Phila., 1979-85; student scheduling specialist Sch. Dist. Phila., 1976-88, coord. student scheduling, 1988—; pres. MKB Prodns., Phila., 1988—. Writer, producer: (history album) I Didn't Know That, 1981; co-author: (book of essays) About You, 1982; writer, co-producer: (TV drama) Dumped On, 1992. Sr. tutor Ctr. for Literacy, Phila., 1980-81. Mem. Internat. Assn. Motion Picture and TV Producers, Am. Film Inst., Black Filmmakers Found., Phi Eta Sigma. Home: 152 W Coulter St Philadelphia PA 19144-3407

BRANCO, JAMES JOSEPH, finance company executive; b. Santa Maria, Azores, Portugal, Mar. 14, 1951; came to U.S., 1954; s. Leroy and Michele (Desroches) B.; m. Wendy Thompson, July, 12, 1972 (div. July 1982); children: James II, Natalie. BA, Brandywine Coll., 1973. Chief exec. officer Profl. Fin. Mgrs., Inc., Spring Lake, N.J., 1974—; ptnr. Atlantic Drilling Co., Sea Girt, 1982—; pres. Profl. Condo Conversions, Belmar, N.J., 1977—; v.p. N.J. Mortgage Co., Lakewood, 1980-87, also bd. dirs., Sea Girt. Chmn. cub scouts Boy Scouts Am., Se Girt, 1982. Mem. Nat. Assn. Life Underwriters (Agt. Yr. award Del. Valley 1977, Broker Yr. award 1978, 87, 88), Internat. Peoples Orgn. (pres. 1983-86), Phi Epsilon. Republican. Roman Catholic. Office: Profl Fin Mgrs Inc PO Box 67 Spring Lake NJ 07762-0067

BRANCONE, LOUIS MARIA, retired chemist; b. N.Y.C., Nov. 13, 1915; s. Giuseppe and Anna (Depascale) B.; m. Edna Mina Mueller, June 15, 1946; children: Ann Susan, Kathy Laurel, Laurie Lynn. BA, NYU, 1936, MS, 1940. Microchemist GAF, Linden, N.J., 1941, Lederle Labs. div. Am. Cyanamid Co., Pearl River, N.Y., 1941-82; analytical chemist Am. Home Products, Jersey City, 1941; retired, 1982. Author 2 books, numerous papers in microchemistry and analytical chemistry; patentee in field. Mem. Am. Chem. Soc., Am. Microchem. Soc. (mem. various coms. 1961-65, chmn. com. 1965-66), Eastern Analytical Symposium (gen. chmn. 1973). Roman Catholic. Home: 370 Wierimus Rd Hillsdale NJ 07642-1146

BRAND, DANIEL, transportation planner; b. N.Y.C., June 6, 1937; s. E. Millen and Pauline (Leader) B.; m. Erika Marquardt, Dec. 22, 1962 (div. 1984); children: Anika, Taika, Tilo, Joshua; m. Winifred Dornhofer, July 22, 1990. BSCE, MIT, 1958, MS, 1961. Group dir. Traffic Rsch. Corp., Boston, 1963-67; ptnr. Peat, Marwick, Mitchell, Boston, 1967-69; lectr. MIT, Cambridge, Mass., 1969-70; assoc. prof. Harvard U., Cambridge, 1970-75; undersecretary Mass. Dept. Transp., Boston, 1975-77; prog. v.p. Charles River Assocs., Boston, 1977—; chmn. Transp. Rsch. Bd. Com. on Intelligent Vehicle Hwy. Systems/NAS, 1988—; dir. High Speed Rail and Maglev Travel Demand Forecasting, Tex., Fla., Washington, Balt., Las Vegas, Nev.; presenter in field. Editorial adv. bd. Transp. Jour., 1979—; book reviewer Choice/ALA, 1972—; author tech. reports in field; editor: Dual Mode Transportation, 1976, Urban Travel Demand Forecasting, 1973, Urban Transportation Innovation, 1975, others; contbr. articles to profl. jours., books in field. Mem. ASCE, Inst. Transp. Engrs., Transp. Rsch. Forum, Advanced Transit Assn., Regional Sci. Assn., Tau Beta Pi, Chi Epsilon, Sigma Xi. Office: Charles River Assocs 200 Clarendon St Boston MA 02116-5021

BRAND, MICHAEL DEAN, non-profit executive; b. Kintnersville, Pa., Feb. 13, 1961; s. Arthur August and Lucienne June (Simmons) B. BA in Polit. Sci., Mont. State U., 1985. Field organizer Mont. Pub. Interest Rsch. Group, Bozeman, Mont., 1982-86; alliance organizer Alliance of Community-Based Orgns., Apopka, Fla., 1986-88; communications mgr. Vis. Health Svc., Quakertown, N.J., 1988-91; organizing cons. PRIDE, Revere, Pa., 1988; fundraising cons., pub. rels. cons. Pubr., editor: Taking Care newsletter, 1990—. Organizer Jesse Jackson campaign, Cen. Fla., 1988; counselor Teen Inst. of the Garden Stae, N.J., 1991—; adv. bd. Anderson House, Flemington, N.J., 1991—. Recipient Community Svc. award Walt Disney World, 1987. Democrat. Presbyterian. Home and Office: PO Box 315 Quakertown NJ 08868-0315

BRANDENBERGER, ROBERT HANS, physicist, educator; b. Bern, Switzerland, Mar. 15, 1954; came to U.S., 1978; s. Hans and Roberta (Hanson) B. Diploma in Physics, Fed. Poly. Sch., Zurich, 1978; MA, Harvard U., 1979, PhD, 1983. Rsch. assoc. U. Calif., Santa Barbara, 1983-85, Cambridge (Eng.) U., 1985-87; asst. prof. physics Brown U., Providence, 1987-91, assoc. prof. physics, 1991—. Recipient Outstanding Jr. Investigator award U.S. Dept. Energy; Alfred P. Sloan Found. fellow, 1988-92. Office: Dept Physics Brown U Providence RI 02912

BRANDLAND, CARYN MARIE, podiatrist; b. St. Peter, Minn., Jan. 15, 1961; d. Curtis William Brandland and Norma Ilene (Johnson) Talbert. BA in Chemistry, Western md. Coll., 1983; D Podiatric Medicine, N.Y. Coll. Podiatric Medicine, 1987. Resident podiatric surgery and medicine Beekman Downtown Hosp., N.Y.C., 1987-88; pvt. practice N.Y.C., 1988—; instr. CPR, ARC, N.Y.C., 1987—. Mem. Am. Podiatric Med. Assn., Am. Acad. Podiatric Sports Medicine, Am. Podiatric Women's Assn., Crohn's and Colitis Found. Lutheran. Home: 207 E 27th St Apt 2C New York NY 10016-9131 Office: 62 W 14th St New York NY 10011-7503

BRANDON, LIANE, filmmaker, educator; d. Philip and Nita (Poster) B. Student, St. Lawrence U., U. Edinburgh, Scotland; exchange student, U. Moscow; A.B., Boston U., M.Ed. Ski instr. Mt. Tremblant, Que., Can.; actress Children's Theatre, Cambridge, Mass.; film project dir. English dept. Quincy pub. schs., Mass.; prof. film prodn. and media studies Sch. Edn. U. Mass., Amherst, 1973—; co-founder, mem. New Day Films, 1971—; media cons. N.Y. State Dept. Edn., 1968, Mass. Dept. Edn., 1970-74; film cons. Mass. Gov.'s Commn. on Status of Women, 1974; cons. Mass. Artists Found., 1975, 82; judge Regional Student Acad. Awards, 1991, Emmy Awards, 1992; trustee Theaterworks, 1981-83; bd. dirs. Boston Film-Video Found., 1983-87, Civil Liberties Union Mass., 1988—; guest lectr. various confs. on edn. and film, colls. and art schs. in U.S. Exhibited film, Mus. Modern Art, Whitney Mus. Am. Art, Chgo. Art Inst., Nat. Film Theatre, London, Internat. Women's Film Festival, Paris, John F. Kennedy Ctr. Performing Arts, Washington; dir., producer: (films) Anything You Want to Be, 1971 (Blue Ribbon, Am. Film Festival award), Betty Tells Her Story, 1972 (Internat. Festival of Women's Films award 1974), Once Upon a Choice, 1980 (Silver medal Houston Internat. Film Festival), How to Prevent A Nuclear War, 1987 (Blue Ribbon award Am. Film Festival 1988). Recipient Creative Artist award AAUW, 1975, Disting. Alumni award Boston U., 1985; Careth Found. grantee, 1988, Funding Exchange grantee, 1989, Mass. Found. for Humanities and Pub. Policy grantee, 1975, Film Fund grantee, 1985. Mem. New Eng. Screen Edn. Assn. (v.p. 1972-83), Assn. Ind. Video and Filmmakers. Office: U Mass Sch Edn Furcolo Hall Amherst MA 01003

BRANDRUP, DOUGLAS WARREN, lawyer; b. Mitchel, S.D., July 11, 1940; s. Clair L. and Ruth M. (Wolverton) B.; m. Patricia R. Tuck, Dec. 20, 1986; children: Kendra, Monika, Peter. AB in Econs., Middlebury Coll., 1963; JD, Boston U., 1966. Bar: N.Y. 1969, U.S. Dist. Ct. (so. dist.) N.Y. 1970, U.S. Ct. Appeals (2d cir.) 1970. Assoc. Donovan, Leisure, Newton & Irvine, N.Y.C., 1968-72; ptnr. Griggs, Baldwin & Baldwin, N.Y.C., 1972—, sr. ptnr., 1980—; bd. dirs. Equity Oil Co., A.T. Info. Products Inc., The Co. Store., Inc., Ardshiel, Inc. Mem. Govs. Security Adv. Com., State of N.J., 1975-90. Capt. U.S. Army, 1966-68. Mem. ABA, N.Y. County Bar Assn., N.Y. State Bar Assn., Dancers Club (N.Y.C.), Met. Club (pres.), Club de Mar (Palma, Majorca Spain). Republican. Episcopalian. Office: Griggs Baldwin & Baldwin Ste 201 127 E 59th St New York NY 10022

BRANDT, GRACE BORGENICHT, art dealer; b. N.Y.C., Jan. 25, 1915; d. Samuel Lazarus and Jeanette (Salny) Lubell; m. J. Borgenicht, Jan. 20, 1938; children: Jan Schwartz, Berta Kerr, Lois Borgenicht; m. Warren Brandt, Dec. 27, 1960. MA, Columbia U., 1937. Dir., owner Grace Borgenicht Gallery, Inc., N.Y.C., 1951—; adviser Tupperware Art Found. Scholarship, Bus. Meets the ArtYoung Pres.'s Orgn. One-woman shows include Laurel Gallery, N.Y.C., 1947, 48, 50, Philbrooks Mus., Tulsa, 1948, Everhart Mus., Scranton, Pa., 1948; exhibited in group shows at Nat. Assn. Women Artists, 1948, 49, L'Association Nationale des Femmes Artistes Americaines, 1949, Internat. Watercolor Exhbn., 1949, 53, 55, 59, Contemporary Am. Painting, 1951, N.Y. Soc. Women Artists, 1953, Whitney Mus. ann. exhbn., 1954, Aquarelles Contemporaines aux Etats-Unis, France, 1954, Martha Jackson Gallery, N.Y.C., 1955; represented in permanent collections Philbrook Mus., Everhart Mus. Mem. Nat. Assn. Women Artists (first prize watercolor 1949), Art Dealers Assn. Am., N.Y. Soc. Women Artists, N.Y.C. Artists Club. Office: Grace Borgenicht Gallery 724 5th Ave New York NY 10019-4106

BRANDT, JOHN HENRY, physician; b. Cleve., July 30, 1940; s. Harold Paul and Dorothy Helen (Kern) B.; m. Jon Ellison, July 30, 1963 (div. 1971); children: Sylvia Ann, Laura Ann; m. Marilyn Ruth Brandt, July 25, 1980. BA, Yale U., 1962; postgrad., Cambridge (Eng.) U., 1962-64; MD, Harvard U., 1970. Asst. to dir. Harvard Ctr. for Community Health, Boston, 1968-69; clin. fellow Med. Sch. Harvard U., Boston, 1970-73, instr. in psychiatry Med. Sch., 1973-74, 74—; resident psychiatrist McLean Hosp., Belmont, Mass., 1970-73, dir. Waverley House, 1973-74, attending psychiatrist, 1974-90; attending psychiatrist Mass. Mental Health Ctr., 1991—; staff psychiatrist med. dept. MIT, Cambridge, 1979—. Mem. archives com. Trinity Ch., Boston, 1988—. Mem. AAAS, Am. Psychiat. Assn., Mass. Med. Soc., N.Y. Acad. Medicine, N.Y. Acad. Scis., Boston Athenaeum, Yale Club of Boston, (sec. 1988-90, dir. 1990—), Harvard Club of Boston (chmn. House com. 1989-91, v.p. 1991—), Harvard Musical Assn. (dir. 1990—), St. Botolph Club, Union Club, Harvard Club N.Y.C., Cosmos Club, Yale Elizabethan Club, Yale Mory's Assn., Phi Beta Kappa. Republican. Episcopalian. Home: PO Box 530 Lincoln MA 01773-0005 Office: MIT Med Dept 77 Massachusetts Ave Cambridge MA 02139-4307

BRANDT, MARY KATHLEEN, fund raising executive; b. Rochester, N.Y., Aug. 3, 1946; d. Neill Matteson and Dorothy Elizabeth (Engelmann) B. BA, Annhurst Coll., S. Woodstock, Conn., 1968; MA, Clark U., Worcester, Mass., 1970. Assoc. editor Econ. Geogrpahy, Clark U., Worcester, 1969-73; dir. alumni affairs Clark U., Worcester, 1973-75; dir. alumni rels. Brandeis U., Waltham, Mass., 1975-78; assoc. dir. devel. Joslin Diabetes Dtr., Boston, 1979-80, dir. corp. and found. rels., 1980-82; sr. assoc. Ruotolo Assocs., Englewood, N.J., 1983-85; dir. devel. Hurricane Island Outward Bound Sch., Rockland, Maine, 1985-86; dir. devel. and membership Old Sturbridge Village, Sturbridge, Mass., 1987—; cons. in field. Bd. dirs. Health Awareness Svcs. Cen. Mass., 1987—, pres., 1991—; bd. dirs. South Cen. Mass. Am. Cancer Soc., 1992—. Mem. Am. Mus. Assn. (devel. and membership com.), New Eng. Mus. Assn., New Eng. Devel. Rsch. Assn., Planned Giving Group New England. Office: One Old Sturbridge Village Rd Sturbridge MA 01566-1138

BRANDT, RONALD MARVIN, pharmaceutical executive; b. Grinnell, Iowa, Apr. 28, 1946; s. Marvin George and Leslie Lucille (Robinson) B.; m. Suzanne Lynn Meeker, Aug. 31, 1968 (div.); children: Steven Ronald, Megan Suzanne; m. Teri Lynn Waffle, June 13, 1987. BS in Indsl. Engring., Iowa State U., 1969; postgrad., Ill. Inst. Tech., 1971-74. Coop. trainee Deere & Co., Ottumwa, Iowa, 1965-68; indsl. engr. Collins Radio Co. div. Rockwell Internat., Cedar Rapids, Iowa, 1969, Western Electric Co. div. AT&T, Cicero, Ill., 1970-71; systems analyst Western Electric Co. div. AT&T, Warrenville, Ill., 1972-75, Abbott Labs., North Chicago, Ill., 1975-77; sr. inventory analyst Abbott Labs., N. Chgo., Ill., 1978; materials and export mgr./mid. east Abbott Labs., Athens, Greece, 1978-81; area mgr. middle east Norwich (N.Y.) Eaton, 1981-86; mktg. mgr. Norwich Eaton Pharmaceuticals, Inc. div. Procter & Gamble, 1987-88, mgr. coverage and reimbursements, 1988—. Mem. Conservative Caucus. Mem. Am. Pharm. Assn., Am. Mgmt. Assn., Nat. Assn. Retail Druggists, Nat. Coun. for Prescription Drug Programs, Nat. Pharm. Coun., Rep. Nat. Com., Colgate U. Seven Oaks Golf Club. Methodist. Home: 40 Brookview Dr Hamilton NY 13346

BRANDT, WERNER W., federal agency official; b. N.Y.C., Aug. 29, 1938; s. Werner and Marie (Mittmeyer) B.; m. V. Martha Valuch, June 29, 1963; children: K. Alyssa, Nicholas C. BA, Hamilton Coll., 1960. Fgn. svc. officer Dept. State, Washington, 1962-72; exec. asst. to the speaker U.S. Ho. Reps., Washington, 1972-92, sgt. at arms, 1992—. Home: 4006 N Taylor St Arlington VA 22207-4657 Office: US Ho Reps US Capital Bldg-H204 Washington DC 20515

BRANDT-SARIF, THEODORE SONIAN, pharmaceutical company executive; b. Johannesburg, South Africa, Jan. 24, 1959; s. Sydney Benjamin and Alicia Lea (Weinstein) B.-S.; m. Deborah Ann Pollock, May 27, 1990. BS, U. Witwatersrand, Johannesburg, 1979, MD, 1982; MBA, U. Pa., 1986. Cons. Kaiser Permanente, Portland, Oreg.; med. resident Coronation Hosp., Johannesburg; bus. intern, asst. dir. med. svcs. Bristol-Myers Squibb Pharm. Co., Evansville, Ind.; dir. clin. ops. clin. projects div. Parexel Internat. Corp., Waltham, Mass., 1990—. Mem. Am. Acad. Med. Dirs. Home: 118 Winchester St # 1 Brookline MA 02146-2763

BRANDWEIN, DANIEL SCOTT, podiatrist; b. Union, N.J., Dec. 3, 1964; s. Lewis Jay and Alice Carol (Reitman) B. BS in Biology, U. Pitts., 1986; D of Podiatric Medicine, U. Osteo. Med. and Health Sci., 1990. Pvt. practice Kenilworth, N.J., 1991—. Office: 20 N 20th St Kenilworth NJ 07033-1614

BRANIN, FRANCIS SUNFIELD, JR., investment company executive; b. Plainfield, N.J., Feb. 13, 1947; s. Francis Sunfield and Edna Juanita (Warren) B.; m. Marcia Anne Herz, Sept. 30, 1972 (div. July 1981); 1 child, Hallee Elizabeth; m. Cordelia Penn Wilcox, May 26, 1984; 1 child, Francis Sunfield III. BA, U. Pa., 1969; MBA, NYU, 1980. Security analyst Harris Upham & Co., N.Y.C., 1969-72; investment officer J&W Seligman & Co., N.Y.C., 1972-77; ptnr. Brundage, Story & Rose, N.Y.C., 1977—; trustee Brundage Story & Rose Investment Trust, N.Y.C., 1990—; bd. dirs. Glen Raven Mills, Inc., Burlington, N.C. Trustee St. George's Sch., treas., 1990—. 2d lt. USAR, 1970-71. Mem. Seabright Beach Club (gov. 1988—), Union Club, Rumson Country Club, Downtown Athletic Club. Office: Brundage Story & Rose One Broadway New York NY 10004

BRANIN, LORA B., health care executive, search consultant; b. Abington, Pa., Jan. 12, 1941; d. Paul Benton and Lora (Leadbetter) B.; m. Peter Harrington Wilson, Oct. 10, 1960 (div. Apr. 1974); children: Kimberly Wilson Christie, Kristen Wilson Creighton, Heather Wilson. BA, U. Del., 1964; MS, Villanova U., 1983. Dir. chem. dependency program Community Life Svcs., Media, Pa., 1983-85; exec. dir. ARC, So. Chester County Med. Ctr., West Grove, Pa., 1985-87; account mgr. Garofolo, Curtiss & Co., Ardmore, Pa., 1987-89, v.p., 1989-91; ptnr. Garofolo, Curtiss, Lambert & MacLean, Ardmore, Pa., 1991—; liaison Ohio Hosp. Assn., Columbus, 1989—. Mem. Wistar Inst., Phila., 1983—. Mem. Nat. Assn. Physician Recruiters, Assn. Exec. Search Cons. Office: Garofolo Curtiss Lambert & MacLean 326 W Lancaster Ave Ardmore PA 19003-1228

BRANMAN, MARTIN JEFFREY, investment banker; b. N.Y.C., Sept. 12, 1955; s. Sol and Anita G. (Berlinsky) B. BA, U. Calif., Berkeley, 1976; MBA, Carnegie Mellon U., 1980. Case leader Boston Cons. Group, Chgo., 1980-84; v.p. May Dept. Stores Co., St. Louis, 1984-85, First Boston Corp., N.Y.C., 1985-89; mng. dir. Financo, Inc., N.Y.C., 1989—. Office: Financo Inc 3d Fl 535 Madison Ave New York NY 10022-4212

BRANN, EVA TONI HELENE, educator; b. Berlin, Jan. 21, 1929; came to U.S., 1942; d. Edgar and Paula (Sklarz) B. BA, Bklyn. Coll., 1950; MA, Yale U., 1951, PhD, 1956. Instr. archaeology Stanford (Calif.) U., 1956-57; tutor St. John's Coll., Annapolis, Md., 1957—, dean, 1990; mem. Inst. for Advanced Study, 1958; mem. U.S Adv. Commn. for Internat. Edn., 1975-77; vis. prof. Whitman Coll., Walla Walla, Wash., 1978-79; honors prof. U. Del., Newark, 1984-86. Author: Protoattic Pottery from the Athenian Agora, 1962, Paradoxes of Education in a Republic, 1979, The World of the Imagination, 1991; translator: Greek Mathematics and the Origin of Algebra, 1968. Mem. state adv. com. U.S. Commn. on Civil Rights, Md., 1988—. Woodrow Wilson Ctr. fellow, 1976; NEH grantee, 1987. Mem. Phi Beta Kappa. Democrat. Jewish. Office: St John's Coll PO Box 2800 Annapolis MD 21404-2800

BRANNIGAN, MICHAEL CHRISTOPHER, philosophy educator; b. Fukuoka, Kyushu, Japan, July 13, 1948; came to U.S., 1952; s. Thomas Harry and Mary Misae (Kimura) B.; m. Carin Brooke Wilhelm, Oct. 15, 1988. PhB in Philosophy, U. Leuven, Belgium, 1972, MA in Religious Studies, 1973, PhL in Philosophy with great distinction, 1974, PhD in Philosophy with great distinction, 1982. Instr. philosophy and religion Mercy Coll., Dobbs Ferry, N.Y., 1981-84, asst. prof., 1984-87, assoc. prof., 1987-89; ethics com. mem. Phelps Meml. Hosp., North Tarrytown, N.Y., 1984-89, hospice vol., 1983-89; assoc. prof. philosophy dept. LaRoche Coll., Pitts., 1989-92, prof., 1992—; cons. Phelps Meml. Hosp., 1984-89, St. Margaret Meml. Hosp., 1992—; vis. assoc. Ctr. for Med. Ethics, U. Pitts.; adv. Inst. for Advanced Philosophic Rsch., Boulder, Colo., 1985—. Author: Everywhere & Nowhere, 1988, Dialogue: The First Step in Philosophy, 1990; contbr. articles to profl. jours. Grantee NEH, Fordham U., 1986. Mem. AAUP, Assn. for Asian Studies, Am. Philos. Assn., Soc. for Asian and Comparative Study, Found. for Thanatology, Inst. for Advanced Philos. Rsch. (advisor), Park Ridge Ctr. Health Faith and Ethics, European Soc. for Philosophy of Medicine and Health Care. Office: LaRoche Coll 9000 Babcock Blvd Pittsburgh PA 15237-5898

BRANT, WILLIAM MORTON, management educator; b. Elmira, N.Y., Nov. 21, 1937; s. Glen and Marjorie (Sykes) B.; m. Catharine S. Polocz, Feb. 11, 1972; children: Steven, William Jr. BA, U. Fla., 1959, MA, 1962; MBA, U. Pitts., 1964, PhD, 1968. Chartered fin. cons., CLU. Mgmt. cons. Consolidated Rsch. Assn., Washington, 1962-70; dir. mgmt. devel. So. Railway Co., Washington, 1968-70; dir. orgn. devel. Phila. Quartz Co., Valley Forge, Pa., 1970-73; prof. Trenton (N.J.) State Coll., 1973-80; dir. edn. Adminstrv. Mgmt. Soc., Willow Grove, Pa., 1980-82; assoc. prof. Am. Coll., Bryn Mawr, Pa., 1982-90; prof. Rider Coll., Lawrenceville, N.J., 1990—; pres. William M. Brant Assn., Malton, N.J., 1976—; bd. dirs. Delta Mgmt. Systems, Willow Grove, 1980—. Author: MBO for Non Profit Organizations, 1988, Human Resource Management, 1991. Recipient Silver Beaver award Boy Scouts AM., Camden County, N.J., 1984. Mem. AAUP, Am. Psychol. Assn., Am. Soc. CLU and ChFC, Acad. Mgmt., Human Resource Planning Soc. Home: 61 Apple Way Marlton NJ 08053-1248 Office: Rider Coll 2083 Lawrenceville Rd Trenton NJ 08648-3099

BRANTLEY, BRUCE BARTON, executive agronomist; b. Queens, N.Y., Dec. 31, 1933; s. Frank Alfred and Inez (Sanelli) B.; m. Eva E. (Monai) Brantley, Dec. 31, 1947 (div. Aug. 1982); children: Vivianna E. Albert, Robert Bruce, Richard Scot. BS, Rutgers U., 1954, postgrad., 1959-62; postgrad., U. Cin., 1968-71, Ohio State U., 1975, 76. Fertilizer salesperson Armour Agri Chem. Co., Chicago Heights, Ill., 1962-67; horticulture distributing sales mgr. Illiana Chem. Co., Fowler, Ind., 1967-68; mineral absorbents specialist-agronomist Wyandotte (Mich.) Chems. Corp., 1968-73; owner, exec. agronomist Environ. Svcs. Co., Cin., 1970-78; rsch. dir., gen. mgr. Environ. Products Co., Cin., 1973-74; horticulture instr. Ohio Joint Vocat. Sch. System, Cin., Amela, Ohio, 1974-76; mgmt. cons. George S. May Co., Des Plaines, Ill., 1980-86; landscape-turf horticulture instr. Community Coll. of Allegheny County-West Branch, Pitts., 1988-91; exec. agronomist Rohoza Turf Profls., Sewickley, Pa., 1991—; mineral absorbents cons. Wyandotte Chems. Corp., 1968-73; turf cons. Environ. Svcs. Co., 1970-84, King Bee ATC, Pitts., 1984—. Inventor ideal-drain system, co-inventor Ideal-green design, Divot-Pak. Activities dir. North Pitts. Opera Guild, 1991—; mem. Republican Nat. Com., Washington, 1981-82, Nat. Geog., Halt, Sierra Club, Smithsonian, Washington; PTA pres. Woodlawn-Greenhills (Ohio) Elem. Sch., 1973; mem. Am. Assn. Retired People, Pitts. Symphony Soc., Pitts. Opera Guild-North (activities chmn.). Mem. Internat. Graphoanalysis Soc., ASTM (com. sports facilities), Pa. Turfgrass Coun., Am. Soc. Agronomy, Soil Sci. Soc. Am. Republican. Roman Catholic. Home: 205 Newton Square Dr Coraopolis PA 15108 Office: Rohoza Turf Profls 2250 Big Sewickley Creek Rd Sewickley PA 15143

BRASSARD, ROGER PAUL, physician; b. Ashland, N.H., Feb. 21, 1913; s. Edgar and Isabel (Savage) B.; m. Vivian Leonora Flanders, Apr. 12, 1950; children: Ann Louise, Deborah, Mary Jane. BS, U. N.H., 1935, MS, 1936; MD, Albany (N.Y.) Med. Coll., 1940. Intern Waterbury (Conn.) Hosp., 1940-41, resident, 1941-42; pvt. practice Laconia, N.H., 1946—. Maj. M.C., U.S. Army, 1942-46. Mem. Am. Acad. Family Practice, Am. Bd. Family Practitioners, N.H. Acad. Family Practice (Family Practitioner of the Yr. 1984). Republican. Roman Catholic. Home: 328 Union Ave Laconia NH 03246-2812 Office: 354 Main St Laconia NH 03246-3794

BRATHWAITE, MELLISSA ANNETTE, radio announcer, producer; b. Bklyn., Aug. 2, 1961; d. Erskine and Virginia (Higgins) B. BBA, Howard U., 1985, postgrad., 1991—. Mgmt. asst. Sta. WHMM-TV, 1980-82; mgmt. asst., assoc. producer Sta. WHUR, Washington, 1982-85; mgmt. asst. Sta. WHMM-TV, 1980-82, Sta. WBLS/WLIB, N.Y.C., 1983, Sta. NBC/WKYS, Washington, 1985; announcer, engr. Sta. WOL, Washington, 1985; mktg. rep. Diaspora Records, Washington, 1985-86; music dir., announcer, engr. Sta. WYCB, Washington, 1985-87; promotions rep. A&M/Word Records, Washington, 1986-87; producer, announcer, engr. Sta. WOL, 1987—; asst. community affairs dir. Sta. WHUR-FM, Washington, 1990—; bd. engr. Sta. WAVA-Radio, 1992—; radio monitor Video Monitoring Services, Washington, 1986. Author, publisher: Sunshine: A Collection of Poetry, 1985. Counselor Cath. Charities, Washington, 1986; counselor/recruiter Nat. Council on Negro Women, Washington, 1986; adv. bd. mem. SPECTRUM: Cobra Assocs., 1984; coord. Just Say No To Drugs program YMCA, vol. Big Sister Growin'Up program, intergeneration program; vocal minister, eucharistic minister St. Augustine Gospel Choir; mem. N.Y. Mission Soc., Black Women in Ministry, 1991-92; aerobic instr. Roman Catholic.

BRATTER, THOMAS EDWARD, psychologist, educator; b. N.Y.C., May 18, 1939; s. Edward Maurice and Marjorie (Polikoff) B.; BA, Columbia Coll., 1961, MA, 1963, EdM, 1969; Columbia U., EdD, 1974; m. Carole Ann Jaffe, Aug. 25, 1963; children: Edward Philip, Barbara Ilyse. Youth resources dir. Village Scarsdale (N.Y.), 1970-72; dir. City Island Methadone Clinic, Bronx, N.Y., 1972-74; instr. dept. health edn. Tchrs. Coll., Columbia U., N.Y.C., 1969-81; pres., founder John Dewey Acad., Gt. Barrington, Mass., 1984—; prof. Union Inst., Ohio, 1975-81; pvt. practice psychotherapy, 1970-84; cons. Dept. Probation City N.Y., 1973-77, Pan Am Commodities Corp., 1975-78, N. Castle Police Dept., 1978-88; adolescent group psychotherapy cons. Pelham (N.Y.) Guidance Council, 1973-79. Bd. dirs. Odyssey Inst., N.Y.C., 1975-77, Nat. Health Inst., Inc., 1974-76, Nat. Ind. Pvt. Schs. Assn., 1988-91; trustee Daytop Village, Inc., N.Y.C., 1972-84, Forest Inst. Profl. Psychology, Des Plaines, Ill., 1981-84, Gabelli Equity Trust (NYSE), N.Y.C., 1986—, Dewey Acad., 1991; chmn. bd. dirs. John Dewey Found., 1991; troop master Boy Scouts Am., Scarsdale; varsity bas-

ketball coach Sarah Lawrence Coll., 1977-78. Served with NG, 1960-61. Mem. Am. Group Psychotherapy, Am. Psychol. Assn., Am. Assn. Marriage and Family Therapy, Kappa Delta Pi, Phi Delta Kappa. Author: (with A. Bassin and R.L. Rachin) Reality Therapy Reader, 1976; (with R. and N. Kolodny) How to Survive Your Adolescent's Adolescence, 1984, (with G. Forrest) Alcoholism and Substance Abuse: Strategies for Clinical Intervention, 1985, (with N. and R. Kolodny) Smart Choices, 1986; also over 125 articles on adolescent substance abuse and alcoholism treatment, individual and group psychotherapy and edn.; assoc. editor Jour. Drug Issues, 1970-78; mem. editorial bd. Jour. Corrective and Social Psychiatry, 1974-78, Addiction Therapist, 1975-78, Jour. Specialists in Group Work, 1975-78, Jour. of Mental Health Counseling Assn., 1979-82, Jour. Reality Therapy, 1980-85, Jour. Counseling and Devel., 1983-88, Jour. of Humanistic Education, 1989—. Home: 53 Logan Rd Salisbury CT 06068-1513

BRATTIN, JOEL JAMES, English and humanities educator; b. Lansing, Mich., July 30, 1956; s. John Bowlby and Alice Jane (Knight) B.; m. Elizabeth Hope Westie, July 26, 1980; children: Kate Emma, John James. AB with highest distinction, U. Mich., 1978; PhD, Stanford U., 1985. Asst. prof. English Mo. So. State Coll., 1986-90, Worcester (Mass.) Poly. Inst., 1990—. Author: Our Mutual Friend: An Annotated Bibliography, 1984; textual editor: On Heroes, Hero-Worship and the Heroic in History, 1992; contbr. articles on Dickens, Austen, Thackeray and Gissing to scholarly publs. Whiting Found. fellow, 1985; rsch. fellow Am. Coun. Learned Socs., 1987-88. Mem. MLA, N.E. MLA, Soc. Textual Scholarship, Dickens Soc. (sec.-treas. 1992—), Dickens Fellowship,. Phi Beta Kappa. Office: Dept Humanities Worcester Poly Inst Worcester MA 01609-2280

BRAUER, BARBARA ANN, psychologist; b. Evanston, Ill., Oct. 18, 1937; d. John August and Elsie Lillian (Carlson) Brauer; m. Reynold Michael Sachs, June 16, 1962 (div. 1979); 1 child, Caryn Pilar Sachs; m. Allen Edwin Sussman, Apr. 19, 1984. BA, Oberlin (Ohio) Coll., 1959; MA, Columbia U., N.Y.C., 1962; PhD, NYU, 1979. Lic. psychologist, D.C. Rsch. asst. N.Y. State Psychiatric Inst., N.Y.C., 1960-62; staff psychologist St. Elizabeths Hosp., Washington, 1968-80; rsch. scientist/prof. Gallaudet U., Washington, 1980—; pres. B.A. Brauer Assocs., PhD., P.A., Greenbelt, Md., 1982—. Contbr. articles to profl. jours.; producer psychol. tests in ASL translation. Chmn. State of Md. Adv. Com. on Hearing Impaired Persons, 1981-91. Fellow Am. Orthopsychiatric Assn.; mem. Am. Psychol. Assn., Am. Deafness and Rehab. Assn. (bd. dirs. 1985-91), Nat. Assn. of the Deaf. Democrat. Lutheran. Home: 7105 Megan Ln Greenbelt MD 20770-3015 Office: Gallaudet U 800 Florida Ave NE Washington DC 20002-3660

BRAUN, ALAN JOSEPH, manufacturer's representative; b. Bronx, N.Y., July 8, 1953; s. Ralph C. and Blanche (Garsson) Brown; m. Janice Craig, Aug. 1977 (div. Mar. 1982); m. Mary Sporer, Sept. 1982 (div.); m. Patrice Arthur, Oct. 18, 1986. BS in Music Edn., CUNY, 1975; MA in Spl. Edn., Columbia U., 1976. Cert. tchr. music K-12, spl. edn. K-12, N.Y., N.J. Dir. spl. edn. N.Y.C. Dept. Recreation, 1972-77; music tchr. Dyker Heights Jr. High Sch., Bay Ridge, Bklyn., 1975; spl. edn. tchrs. aide Archie F. Hays Sch., Rockleigh, N.J., 1971-77; spl. edn. tchr. Coastal Learning Ctr., Morganville, N.J., 1977, Columbia Sch., Berkeley Heights, N.J., 1977-78; regional acct. mgr. Am. Greetings Corp., Cleve., 1978-88; regional sales mgr. Maui Gold, Honolulu, Hawaii, 1988-90; mfrs. rep. Meteor Skelly, Inc., Larchmont, N.Y., 1989-90; prin. Carney Braun, Inc., Fairport, N.Y., 1990—; vocalist, tech. dir., Bronx Opera Co., 1966-75; vocalist, asst. dir., N.Y. City Chorus and Concert Choir, 1969-78. Senator Lehman Coll. Campus Assn. for Student Activities, 1971-75; vol. Ind. Living for the Handicapped, Bklyn., 1973-75; mem. Harbour Lane Assn. (pres. 1986-91). Democrat. Jewish. Home: Bristol Harbour Village 12 Harbour Ln Canandaigua NY 14424-8959 Office: Carney Braun Inc 4 Sandpiper Hl Fairport NY 14450-9366

BRAUN, CRAIG ALLEN, producer; b. Chgo., June 1, 1939; s. Joseph Aloysius and Blanche Lamont (Rice) B.; m. Madeleine O'Leary, Oct. 28, 1961 (div. 1966); 1 child, Timothy; m. Elizabeth Lyle Whiteman, Oct. 4, 1986; children: Nicholas, Christopher. Student, U. Ill., 1958-59; BBA in Mktg., DePaul U., 1963. Pres., creative dir. Craig Braun Inc. Advt., various cities, 1968-75; ind. producer N.Y.C., L.A., 1975-79; mktg. dir. Cartier Internat. USA, N.Y.C., 1979-81; pres. Fisher/Braun Communications, N.Y.C., 1981-83; pres., chief exec. officer FBC Prodns., Inc., N.Y.C., 1983-88; account exec. Ivy Hill Corp. (Div. Time Warner Inc.), N.Y.C., 1989—. With USNR, 1958-64. Recipient Gold medal N.Y. Art Dirs. Club, 1972, Best of Show medal L.A. Art Dirs. Club, 1973, Grammy award Nat. Assn. Recording Arts and Scis., 1973, Broadcast Journalism award DuPont/Columbia U., 1984. Republican. Roman Catholic. Home: 5 Berkeley Hl Westport CT 06880-1611 Office: Ivy Hill Corp 375 Hudson New York NY 10014 also: PO Box 366 New York NY 10022

BRAUN, MARTIN, mathematics educator; b. N.Y.C., July 26, 1941; s. Aaron and Jean (Brickman) B.; m. Zelda Lee Badner, Aug. 22, 1971; children: Adeena, Nasanayl, Shulamit, Nachum. BA, Yeshiva U., 1963; MS, NYU, 1965, PhD, 1968. Asst. prof. Brown U., Providence, 1968-75; asst. prof. Queens Coll., CUNY, Flushing, 1975-79, assoc. prof., 1979-85, prof., 1985—. Author: Differential Equations, 1975; editor: Modules in Applied Mathematics, 1979; editor Internat. Jour. Math. Modelling, 1980—. Recipient rsch. grant NSF, Washington, 1972. Mem. Math. Assn. Am. Home: 13846 76th Ave Flushing NY 11367-2820 Office: Queens Coll Dept Math 65-30 Kissena Blvd Flushing NY 11367

BRAUNLICH, HELMUT KARL, composition educator; b. Brünn, Moravia, Czechoslovakia, May 19, 1929; came to U.S., 1951; s. Kurt and Irma (Schmidt) B.; m. Inga Britta Elgcrona, July 10, 1960 (div. Mar. 1974); 1 child, Karl; m. Patricia Deeney, June 25, 1974; children: Kurt, Martin. Diploma Mozarteum, Salzburg, 1949; MusB, Cath. U., 1957, MusM, 1958, PhD, 1965. 1st violinist Innsbruck (Austria) Symphony, 1950-51, Indpls. Symphony, 1952-54; prof. violin Cath. U., Washington, 1960, head composition, 1989—; violinist, composer, dir. pers. Contemporary Music Forum, Washington, 1976—. Composer chamber music, orch. music, music for solo instruments, vocal music, 1951—. Staff sgt. USAF, 1954-58. Recipient Sudentendeutscher Kulturpreis State of Bavaria, 1989. Home: 5901 Sonoma Rd Bethesda MD 20817-3450 Office: Cath U Washington DC 20064

BRAUNSTEIN, MARK MATHEW, curator, nature photographer; b. N.Y.C., Aug. 6, 1951; s. Benjamin and Clare (Pitalon) B. BA, SUNY Binghamton, 1974; MS, Pratt Inst., Bklyn., 1978. Editor Rosenthal Arts Slides, Chgo., 1978-80; asst. editor Art Index, N.Y.C., 1980-83; head of slides and photog. R.I. Sch. Design, Providence, 1983-87; art slide curator Conn. Coll., New London, 1987—. Author: Radical Vegetarianism, 1981, Sprout Garden, 1992; co-editor Slide Buyer's Guide, 1986; asst. editor Art Index, 1981-83; contbr. articles to profl. jours. Faculty Devel. grantee R.I. Sch. Design, Providence, 1984-85. Buddhist. Home: PO Box 456 Quaker Hill CT 06375-0456 Office: Conn Coll PO Box 5458 New London CT 06320

BRAVARD, ROBERT STATON, library director; b. Dayton, Ohio, Nov. 2, 1935; s. Elmer Staton and Martha Helen (Schneider) B.; m. Cynthia Ann Buttolph, Aug. 16, 1958; children: Jonathan Staton, Christopher Mark, Thomas Andrew. AB, Wilmington Coll., 1957; MS in Libr. Studies, Syracuse U., 1959. Asst. libr. Findlay (Ohio) Coll., 1959-60, head libr., 1960-63; tech. svcs. libr. Lock Haven (Pa.) U., 1963-70, dir. libr. svcs., 1970—; cons. Choice, Middletown, Conn. 1964—; chair State System of Higher Edn. Libr. Coun., 1976-78, 82-84; adv. bd. Popular Culture Libr. Bowling Green State U., 1987—. Co-autor: Samuel R. Delany, A Primary and Secondary Bibliography, 1980; editor mag. Lock Haven Internat. Rev., 1987—; mem. editorial bd. The Acquisitions Libr., 1987—. Pres. Cen. Pa. Health Systems Agy., Lewisburg, 1982-83, Friends of Ross Libr., Lock Haven, 1983-85; councilman Lock Haven City, 1992—. Mem. Phi Beta Delta, Phi Kappa Phi, Beta Phi Mu. Democrat. Office: Lock Haven U Stevenson Libr Lock Haven PA 17745

BRAVERMAN, LOUISE MARCIA, architect; b. N.Y.C., Nov. 23, 1948; d. Don S. and Madlyn (Barotz) B.; m. Steven Z. Glickel, July 1, 1984; 1 child, Jennifer Liberty. BA, U. Mich., 1970; MArch, Yale U., 1977. Registered architect, N.Y. Ptnr., architect Austin Braverman Patterson, Architects, N.Y.C. and Southport, Conn., 1982-90; pres. Louise Braverman, Architect, N.Y.C., 1990—; guest design critic Yale U., Columbia U., U. Pa., Cooper Union U., Syracuse U., Bryn Mawr Coll., Ohio State U.; speaker Poets House, N.Y.C., 1992. V.p. bd. dirs. Diller Quaile Sch. Music. Mem. Am. Inst. Architects, Archtl. League, Assn. Real Estate Women, Nat. Women's Mus. (charter). Club: Yale (N.Y.C.).

BRAVO, ANTHONY JOHN, radiologist; b. Schenectady, N.Y., Oct. 3, 1938; s. Dominick and Teresa (Cerniglia) B.; m. Beverly Ann Olympia, June 22, 1963; children: Stephen, Anthony, Michelle. BS, Holy Cross U., Worcester, Mass., 1960; MD, Yale U., 1964. Intern SUNY, Syracuse, 1964-65; NIH fellow diag. radiology Yale U., New Haven, Conn., 1965-68; cardiologist-radiologist NIH, Bethesda, Md., 1968-70; radiologist BPT Hosp., Trumbull, Conn., 1970-79; chmn. dept. radiology BPT Hosp., 1979—; bd. dirs. Fairfield First Bank & Trust, Fairfield, Conn. Contbr. articles to profl. jours. Commr. Fairfield Town Planning & Zoning Commn., 1972-76. Lt. comdr. USPHS, 1968-70. Fellow Am. Coll. Radiology, Conn. State Radiology Soc., Conn. State Med. Soc., AMA. Home: 160 Red Oak Rd Fairfield CT 06430-1815 Office: BPT Radiology 15 Corporate Dr Trumbull CT 06611-1351

BRAWERMAN, GEORGE, biochemist, researcher; b. Poland, June 12, 1927; came to U.S., 1949; s. Mozko and Bella (Piow) B.; m. Ruth Huppert, Nov. 23, 1953; children: Carole Miriam, Jane Lisette. BS in Chemistry, Brussels U., 1949; PhD in Biochemistry, Columbia U., 1953. Rsch. assoc. Columbia U., N.Y.C., 1956-60, asst. prof. biochemistry, 1960-61; asst. prof. Yale U., New Haven, Conn., 1961-65, assoc. prof., 1965-70; prof. Tufts U., Boston, 1970—; vis. prof. Coll. de France, Paris, 1990. Contbr. articles, revs. and book chpts. to profl. publs. With U.S. Army, 1953-55. Recipient Rsch. Career Devel. award, NIH, 1963-67; Fogarty Internat. Rsch. fellow, NIH, Rehovot, Israel, 1977; grantee NIH, NSF, 1961-91. Mem. AAAS. Home: 29 Jeffrey Rd Wayland MA 01778-2505 Office: Tufts U Sch Medicine 136 Harrison Ave Boston MA 02111-1800

BRAWN, LINDA CURTIS, state legislator; b. Rockland, Maine, June 16, 1947; d. Charles Samuel and Alice (Jenkins) Curtis; m. William Preston Brawn, Aug. 19, 1969; children: Charles, Michael. A in Liberal Studies, U. Maine, Augusta, 1978; BS in Edn., U. Maine, Orono, 1981. Tchr. Mother Goose Nursery Sch., Camden, Maine, 1973-82; kindergarten tchr. Rockland, Maine, 1983-85; mem. Maine State Senate, Augusta, 1986—. Author: Festival Memories, 1987. Mem. Camden Conservation com., 1984—; bd. dirs., chmn. pub. issues Am. Cancer Soc., 1986—; chmn. Knox County Rep. Com., 1985-86. Mem. Maine Fedn. Women's Clubs (pres. elect), Order Eastern Star. Baptist. Home: PO Box 1346 Camden ME 04843-1346 Office: Maine State Senate PO Box 1346 Augusta ME 04330-3001

BRAXTON, KARRYE YVONNE, management consultant; b. Williamsburg, Va., Aug. 14, 1960; d. Arthur Henry and Edna Yvonne (Reid) B. BA in Econs., Harvard U., 1982; MBA in Fin., U. Pa., 1986; postgrad., Johns Hopkins U., Washington, 1986-87. Mgmt. assoc. Sovran Bank, Richmond, Va., 1983-84; intern Trans Africa, Washington, 1984; summer assoc. Chem. Bank, N.Y.C., 1985; fin. acctg. intern U.S. Overseas Pvt. Investment Corp., Washington, 1986; summer intern World Bank/IFC, Washington, 1986; cons. Booz-Allen & Hamilton, Inc., Bethesda, Md., 1987-89; sr. cons. Deloitte & Touche, Washington, 1989-91, Consulting Internat., Ghana, 1991, Deloitte & Touche Consulting Internat., Washington, 1992, Madentch Consulting Inc., Washington, 1992—; cons. Job American Mgmt., Newport News, Va., 1989—. Camp counselor/workshop coord. Initiatives Summer Camp, Leesburg, Va., 1991. Katherine Tuck scholar Student Aid Found. Mich., 1978-82; Nat. Achievement scholar, 1978-82; Detroit scholar Harvard Club of Ea. Mich., 1978. Mem. NAFE, Nat. Black MBA Assn., Harvard Club of Washington. Democrat.

BRAY, GORDON LOUIS, pediatrics educator; b. Bronx, N.Y., Sept. 29, 1953. BA summa cum laude, CUNY, 1975; MD, Yeshiva U., 1979. Diplomate Nat. Bd. Med. Examiners. Intern in pediatrics Children's Hosp. of Northern Calif., Oakland, 1979-80, resident in pediatrics, 1980-82; clin. fellow div. pediatric hematology/oncology Children's Orthopedic Hosp. and Med. Ctr., Seattle, 1982-83, jr. rsch. fellow div. hematology/oncology, 1983-84; sr. rsch. fellow div. hematology depts. pediatrics/medicine U. Wash., Seattle, 1984-85; asst. prof. dept. pediatrics George Washington U. Sch. Medicine, Washington, 1985-91, assoc. prof. dept. pediatrics, 1991—; attending physician dept. hematology/oncology Children's Nat. Med. Ctr., Washington, 1985—; regional liaison Nat. Resources and Consultation Ctr. for AIDS and HIV Infection, Nat. Hemophilia Found., 1987-88; regional project dir. HHS Region III Network of Federally Funded Hemophilia Treatment Ctrs.; cons. div. blood diseases and resources, Nat. Heart, Lung and Blood Inst., NIH, 1990—. Contbr. articles to profl. jours. Judith Graham Pool fellow Nat. Hemophilia Found., 1984, Poncin Fund fellow Seafirst Corp., 1984; NIH grantee, 1987—, Baxter Internat. grantee, 1990—. Fellow Am. Acad. Pediatrics; mem. Am. Soc. Hematology, N.Y. Acad. Scis., World Fedn. Hemophilia, Internat. Soc. on Thrombosis and Haemostasis, Phi Beta Kappa. Home: 1715 Swann St # 5 Washington DC 20009 Office: Childrens Nat Med Ctr Div Hematology/Oncology 111 Michigan Ave NW Washington DC 20010

BRAY, GRADY P., psychologist; b. Macon, Ga., Nov. 23, 1944; s. Sue Helen (Shiver) Brown; m. Marjorie Elizabeth Walker, Aug. 24, 1963; children: April, Scott. BA, David Lipscomb Coll., 1966; MEd, U. Ga., 1972, PhD, 1974. Diplomate Am. Bd. Sexology. Sci. tchr. Houston County Schs., Warner Robins, Ga., 1966-67; pyrotechnic chemist Maxon Electronics, Macon, Ga., 1967-68; sci. tchr. Bibb County Schs., Macon, 1968-70, spl. counselor, 1970-72; counseling psychologist U. Ga. Testing & Evaluation Ctr., Athens, Ga., 1973-74; dir. psychology dept., clin. psychologist Warm Springs (Ga.) Hosp., 1974-76; rsch. div. dir. Ga. Warm Springs Rehab. Ctr., 1976-77; asst. prof. rehab. medicine U. Rochester (N.Y.) Sch. Medicine, 1977-84; pres. Human Potentials, Rochester, 1984-91; pres., CEO Bray Associates, 1991—; cons., adj. faculty Fed. Emergency Mgmt. Agy., Emmitsburg, Md., 1984—; adj. faculty Nat. Fire Acad., Emmitsburg, 1989—. Co-author: Emergency Services Stress, 1990; author: A Stroke Family Guide, 1984; mem. editorial bd. Rehabilitation in the Aging, 1984; contbr. articles to profl. jours. EMT vol. N.Y. State; fire psychologist Henriett Vol. Fire Dept., Rochester, 1989—. Mem. APA. Home: 131 E Lake Rd Penn Yan NY 14527-9566 Office: Bray Assocs Rochester NY 14618

BRAY, LAURACK DOYLE, lawyer; b. New Orleans, Nov. 13, 1949; s. Laudrack Doyle Bray and Helen (Howard) Davis. AA, L.A. City Coll., 1969; BA, Long Beach State U., 1972, MS, 1977, MPA, 1981; JD, Howard U., 1984. Bar: Pa. 1986, D.C. 1986, U.S. Ct. Appeals (D.C. and fed. cirs.) 1987, U.S. Dist. Ct. D.C. 1987, U.S. Supreme Ct. 1992. Community rsch. worker Crenshaw Consortium, L.A., 1977-79; adminstrv. intern City of Lawndale, Calif., 1981; legis. intern U.S. Congress, Washington, 1982; law clk. FDIC, Washington, 1983-84; pvt. practice, Washington, 1987—; mem. moot ct. team Howard U., Washington. Contbr. articles to law jours. Recipient Am. Jurisprudence award, 1982, Best Brief award ABA, 1984. Mem. D.C. Bar Assn., Pi Alpha Alpha, Phi Kappa Phi. Democrat. Home and Office: 624 17th St NE Washington DC 20002-4682

BRAY, MELVYN KENNETH, banking administrator; b. Belleville, N.J., Feb. 15, 1946; s. Donald Theodore and Romanie (van steenberghe) B.; m. Virginia Margaret Brenner, June 17, 1967; children: Christopher Edward, Sherri Ann. Student, Rutgers U., Newark, 1966-67, 71-73; grad., Nat. Sch. Fin. and Mgmt., Fairfield, Conn., 1986. Check filing clk. Bank of Nutley, N.J., 1965; mgmt. trainee 1st Nat. State Bank N.J., Newark, 1969-71, loan rev. asst., 1971, sr. exec. asst., 1972; asst. ops. officer 1st State Bank of Ocean County, Toms River, N.J., 1972-73, br. mgr., 1974; asst. br. mgr. Hudson City Savs. Bank, Brick, N.J., 1974; asst. sec., mgr. Hudson City Savs. Bank, Westfield, N.J., 1974-83; v.p., regional mgr. Hudson City Savs. Bank, Toms River, N.J., 1983—; tchr. Am. Inst. Banking, Toms River, 1973-82; exec. sec. N.J. State Safe Deposit Assn. Inc., Whiting, 1984—. Pub.: Digest of Opinions Relating to Safe Deposit Practice, 1992. Co-founder, treas. Sight and Handicapped Found. Ocean County, Inc., Whiting, 1976—. With USN, 1967-69, Viet Nam. Named Man of Yr., Toms River Jaycees, 1978. Mem. Am. Inst. Banking, Toms River Lions Club (past zone chmn.). Episcopalian. Home: 1921 Delaware Ave Whiting NJ 08759-2719 Office: Hudson City Savs Bank 577 Lakehurst Rd Toms River NJ 08755-8045

BRAYSON, ALBERT ALOYSIUS, II, educational association administrator; b. Port Jefferson, N.Y., June 28, 1953; s. Albert Aloysius and Julie Elizabeth (Krantz) B.; m. Barbara Norris Skretch, June 18, 1977; children: Albert III, Caroline Elizabeth. BA, Elmira (N.Y.) Coll., 1975; MS in Edn., Adelphi U., 1979. Tchr. Lake Grove (N.Y.) Sch., 1975-77, asst. headmaster, 1977-79, exec. dir., 1979—; pres. Lake Grove Sch. and Treatment Ctrs., Durham, Conn., 1985—; cons. Valleyhead Sch., Lenox, Mass., 1985—; grant reviewer U.S. Govt., 1985-87; pres. BABSCorp., Sayville, N.Y., 1984—; sec. Safeway, Inc., Simsbury, Conn., 1989—; ptnr. Second Realty, Durham, Conn., 1985, Housatonic Everfloat Shelton, Conn., 1987. Treas. Lake Grove Village Ind. Party, 1980; co-chmn. com. to re-elect Sen. LaValle, 1990; co-chmn. fin. com. Rep. A Conn. Party, 1991. Mem. Nat. Assn. Pvt. Schs. for Exceptional Children, Coun. for Exceptional Children, Orgn. to Assure Svcs. to Exceptional Students, Mental Health Assn of N.Y. (bd. dirs. 1990, exec. com. 1991), Lions (pres. 1986), Stony Brook Yacht Club, Hartford Club. Republican. Office: Lake Grove Experience PO Box 1306 921 Hawkins Ave Lake Grove NY 11755

BRAYTON, TAMMY ANN, political organization worker; b. Tampa, Fla., Mar. 9, 1962; d. William Nash and Alice Ann (Shepard) B. Student, U. Surrey, Guildford, England, 1983-84; BS, Mich. State U., 1984, MusM, 1985. Devel. systems coord. Hartford (Conn.) Symphony, 1989-90; exec. sec. Oboe Internat., Inc., N.Y.C., 1990—; dep. exec. dir. Nat. Com. on Am. Fgn. Policy, N.Y.C., 1991-92. Mem. Internat. Double Reed Soc., Am. Fedn. Musicians, Alpha Delta Kappa (Internat. Edn. grantee 1983.). Office: PO Box 1335 New York NY 10023

BRAZAITIS, PETER JOHN, zoological park administrator; b. N.Y.C., Aug. 13, 1936; s. Peter John and Jeanette (Corino) B.; m. Winifred Yolla, 1959 (div. 1981); children: Wendy, Bonnie; m. Myrna E. Watanabe, Jan. 1984; 1 child, Peter John. BS, SUNY, N.Y.C., 1985. Wild animal keeper N.Y. Zool. Park, N.Y.C., 1954-67, sr. animal keeper, 1967-70; supt. reptiles Cen. Park Zoo, N.Y. Zool. Park, N.Y.C., 1970-88; curator of animals Cen. Park Zoo/N.Y. Zool. Soc., N.Y.C., 1990—; forensic examiner U.S. Fish and Wildlife Svc., Washington and N.Y., 1973—, N.Y. State Dept. Environ. and Conservation, N.Y.C., 1973—; rsch. investigator UN Environ. Program/Conv. on Internat. Trade in Endangered Species Wild Fauna and Flora, Switzerland, 1986—, World Wildlife Fund, Washington, 1989—. Contbr. articles to profl. jours. Sgt. U.S. Army, 1955-57. Grantee UN, World Wildlife Fund, Explorers Club, U.S. Fish and Wildlife Svc., N.Y. Zool. Soc. Mem. Am. Acad. Forensic Scis., Am. Chem. Soc., Soc. for the Study of Amphibians and Reptiles. Office: NY Zool Soc/Cen Park Zoo 830 5th Ave New York NY 10021-7095

BRAZEAL, EARL HENRY, JR., electrical engineer; b. Springfield, Vt., Aug. 24, 1939; s. Earl Henry and Nellie Mary (Krasofski) B.; m. Jennifer Pease Clark, Nov. 24, 1962 (div. 1980); children: Tracy, Suzanne, Jeremy; m. Beverly May Green, Apr. 24, 1982; 1 stepchild, Dulcie. Cert., Ward Tech. Inst., Hartford, Conn., 1959; BSEE, U. Conn., 1964, MSEE, 1966. Engr. electronics United Technologies, East Hartford, Conn., 1965-69; sr. engr. Scan-Optics, East Hartford, 1969-76, mgr. electronic engring., 1976-78; sr. engr. electronics Mediscan/SKI, South Windsor, Conn., 1978-81; mgr. surface receiver devel. program Teleco Oilfield Svcs., Meriden, Conn., 1981-82; adv. engr. electronics Scan-Optics, East Hartford, Conn., 1982-85, mgr. imaging electronics, 1985-90, mgr. electronic imaging and hardware support, 1990—; instr. Sch. Engring., U. Conn., Storrs, 1974-80. Inventor various systems, 1970—. Mem. stewardship com. United Ch. of Christ, 2d Congl., Coventry, Conn., 1983-86, 89—, treas. deacon's, 1984, 85. Mem. IEEE (first prize N.E. sect. 1964), Sigma Xi, Eta Kappa Nu. Democrat. Home: 134 Ash Brook Dr Coventry CT 06238-1401 Office: Scan-Optics Inc 22 Prestige Park Cir East Hartford CT 06108-1917

BREADING, ROBERT PICKET, architect; b. Uniontown, Pa., July 16, 1933; s. Ralph Mitchel and Emma Jane (Picket) B.; m. Joyce Ann McDonald, May 22, 1965 (div. June 1982). B of Archt., Pa. State U., 1956; M of Atcht., MIT, 1957. Project architect H2L2 Architects & Planners, Phila., 1960-65, ptnr., 1965-90, sr. ptnr., 1990—. Patentee carpet edge strip. Bd. dirs. Choral Arts Soc. Phila. 1st lt. U.S. Army, 1957-60. Mem. AIA, Carpenters Co. Phila., Soc. Sons St. George, Racquet Club Phila. Office: H2L2 Architects & Planners 714 Market St Philadelphia PA 19106-2312

BREAKSTONE, ARNOLD, professional organization executive; b. N.Y.C., Oct. 4, 1933; s. Sidney Breakstone and Minnie Avrut; m. Pearl Katz, May 26, 1956 (div. Mar. 1991); children: Karen Marci, Steven Marc; m. Cory Paige Zaidins, May 26, 1991. BA, CCNY, 1955. Pers. mgr. United Mchts. & Mfrs., N.Y.C., 1959-66, Revlon, Inc., N.Y.C., 1966-69; dir. of pers. Philip Morris, Inc., N.Y.C., 1969-77, Burlington Industries, N.Y.C., 1977-78, Honeywell Corp., N.Y.C., 1978-79; v.p. human resources Blessings Corp., Piscataway, N.J., 1980-83; dir. of pers. ASCE, N.Y.C., 1986—; adj. assoc. prof. NYU, 1966-86; mgmt. cons. Breakstone Assocs., Spring Valley, N.Y., 1978-80. Mem. compensation com. Nat. Soc. to Prevent Blindness, N.Y.C., 1973-76. Mem. ASTD, N.Y. Pers. Mgmt. Assn., Soc. Human Resources Mgmt., Dir.'s Forum (chair 1989-90). Home: 1299 Palmer Ave Larchmont NY 10538

BREARLEY, CANDICE, fashion designer; b. Trenton, N.J., Jan. 2, 1944; d. Joseph William and Lillian (Mieler) Szalay; m. Purvis Brearley, Sept. 2, 1965. BFA, Mus. Sch., Phila., 1965, MFA, 1968; BFA, Parsons Sch. Design, 1975, New Sch. Social Rsch., 1975. Freelance portrait artist Trenton, 1965-72; asst. designer Malcolm Starr, N.Y.C., 1974-75; designer Originala, N.Y.C., 1975-77, Vignette, N.Y.C., 1977-78; pres., designer Candice Brearley, Inc., Trenton, 1978—; pres. Wickford Corp. of N.J., Trenton, 1986—; bd. dirs. Beta Con Corp., Lawrenceville, N.J. One-woman shows Nat. State Bank, N.J., 1971; exhibited in group show at N.J. State Mus., Trenton, 1970. Recipient award Lane Bryant Design Competition, 1974. Fellow Phila. Mus. Art, Met. Mus. Art, Princeton U. Mus., N.J. State Mus. Roman Catholic. Office: Candice Brearley Inc 128 Buckingham Ave Trenton NJ 08618-3314

BREAULT, THEODORE EDWARD, lawyer; b. N.Y.C., Mar. 7, 1938; m. Gretchen S. Clements, Dec. 10, 1966; children: Victoria Ann, Theodore Edmund, Heidi Sherwin, Edmund Clements. BS, Manhattan Coll., 1960; JD, Cath. U. Am., 1963. Bar: D.C. 1964, Va. 1964, Pa. 1970, U.S. Ct. Appeals (D.C. cir.) 1964, (4th cir.) 1969, U.S. Supreme Ct. 1967. Assoc. Seltzer & Suskind, Washington, 1964-69, Egler & Reinstadtler, Pitts., 1969-77; pvt. practice Fairfax, Va., 1967-69, Pitts., 1977—; lectr. Cath. U. Am. Sch. Nursing, Robert Morris Coll.; mem. Pa. Workmen's Compensation Sect.; spl. master Allegheny County Ct. of Common Pleas. Pres. Sewickley (Pa.) Symphony Orch., 1974-75. Fellow Pa. Bar Found. (life); mem. Pa. Bar Assn. (civil litigation sect.), Va. State Bar Assn., D.C. Bar Assn., Allegheny County Bar Assn. (health law sect., workmen's compensation sect.), Am. Soc. Law and Medicine, Pa. Def. Inst., Am. Arbitration Assn. (arbitrator accident claims), Am. Coll. Legal Medicine (assoc. in law). Home: 108 Claridge Dr Coraopolis PA 15108-3204 Office: 3800 Gulf Tower 707 Grant St Pittsburgh PA 15219

BREAUX, ANNA MARIE, psychologist; b. Pitts., July 29, 1958; d. Osvaldo and Rose Marie (Caloger) Fontecchio; m. Edwin Henry Breaux Jr., July 26, 1980; children: Edwin Henry III, Rosanna Patrice. BA magna cum laude, U. Pa., 1980; MS, U. Pitts., 1983, PhD, 1987; cert. in sch. psychology, Duquesne U., 1990. Cert. sch. psychologist, Pa. Clin. fellow psychology Guidance Ctr. Children's Hosp., Boston, 1984-85; staff psychologist Children's Hosp. Pitts., 1985-90; sr. clinician Western Psychiat. and Inst., Pitts., 1990-92; guest speaker Cystic Fibrosis, St. Louis, 1988, PAEYC, 1988, 89, 91, 92. Contbr. articles to profl. jours. Mem. APA, Greater Pitts. Psychol. Assn., Soc. Pediatric Psychology, Pitts. Assn. for Edn. of Young Children, Nat. Assn. for Edn. Young Children. Office: 4284 Rt 8 Ste 301 Allison Park PA 15101

BREAZEALE, ROBERT DAVID, chemist; b. Ames, Iowa, Aug. 30, 1935; s. Delbert F. and Ruth (Lacey) B.; m. Almut Frerichs, Dec. 5, 1964; children: Steven, Daniel. BS, S. Dak. State U., 1957; PhD in Organic Chemistry, U. Wash., 1964. Chemist Sinclair Oil Rsch., Harvey, Ill., 1957-59; rsch. chemist E. I. duPont de Nemours, Wilmington, Del., 1964-69; rsch. supr. E. I. duPont de Nemours, Wilmington and Phila., 1969—. Patentee in field. Mem. Am. Chem. Soc. Home: 1306 Newcomb Rd Wilmington DE

19803-5108 Office: DuPont Marshall Lab 3500 Grays Ferry Ave Philadelphia PA 19146-3229

BRECHER, BERND, management consultant; b. Germany, Oct. 2, 1932; came to U.S. 1940; s. Jacob and Betty (Lewinsohn) B.; m. Helen Edith Casel, Feb. 1, 1959; children: Jacalyn Naomi, Alison Fay, Daniel Evan. BA, Columbia U., 1954, MS in Journalism, 1955. Dir. devel., pub. rels. and alumni affairs Coll. Physicians and Surgeons, Sch. Dentistry, Columbia U., N.Y.C., 1954-57; campaing dir., supr. John Price Jones Co., Inc., N.Y.C., 1958-67; v.p. Hamilton Coll. and Kirkland Coll., Clinton, N.Y., 1967-69; exec. v.p. John Price Jones Internat., Inc., N.Y.C., 1969-71; sr. v.p. Brakeley, John Price Jones, Inc., N.Y.C., 1971-73; pres. Bernd Brecher & Assocs., Inc., N.Y.C. and Scarsdale, 1973—, Instl. Advancement Programs, Inc., Tuckahoe, N.Y., 1979—; cons., strategic planner to not-for-profit instns. Pres. Bd. Edn., Greenburgh, N.Y., 1977-78, Woodlands Scholarship Fund, Hartsdale, N.Y., 1965-66, Soc. of Columbia Graduates, 1980-85; mem. exec. com. Columbia Journalism Sch. Alumni, 1981-89. With U.S. Army, 1957-58. Recipient Alumni Medal for Svc., Columbia U., 1983, Pres.'s Cup, 1980, Two Lion awards, 1979, 80. Mem. Coun. for Advancment and Support of Edn. (Quarter Century Svc. award 1981), Nat. Soc. Fund Raising Execs. (v.p. N.Y. chpt. 1987-89), Am. Assn. Community and Jr. Colls., Am. Hosp. Assn., Am. Assn. Mus., Princeton Univ. Club, Univ. Club of Chgo. Home: 99 Harvard Dr Hartsdale NY 10530 Office: Instl Advancement Programs Inc 65 Main St Tuckahoe NY 10707-2908

BRECHER, EPHRAIM FRED, consultant; b. Bklyn., Nov. 22, 1931; s. Morris Abraham and Mary (Wiener) B.; m. Sandra Louise Footer, Aug. 7, 1955 (div. Dec. 1990); children: Leslie, Deanne, Neil, Andrew. BS, MIT, 1953. Registered profl. engr., Pa., N.J., Md., Del., Ky., N.C., Fla., Conn., N.Y., W.Va. Jr. engr. Dorfman-Bloom, Inc., Phila., 1955-59; staff engr. David Bloom, Inc., Phila., 1959-64, assoc., 1964-71; v.p., sr. engr. Caltech & Assocs., Phila., 1971-72; chief structural engr. GBQC, Phila., 1972-74, assoc., chief structural engr., 1974-76, prin., chief structural engr., 1976-90; pres. Brecher Assocs., Phila., 1990—; cons., expert witness to legal and ins. communities, 1971—. Com. mem. for triennial rewrite PCI Design Handbook, 1991. Ednl. counselor MIT Admissions Office, Phila., 1984—. 1st lt. USAF, 1953-55. Fellow ASCE, Am. Concrete Inst. (local chpt. pres. 1981-82); mem. Carpenters Co. of the City and County of Phila. (mng. chair 1989, jr. warden 1990, middle warden 1991, sr. warden 1992), Franklin Inst. Com. for Sci. and Arts. Democrat. Jewish. Office: Brecher Assocs 2300 Walnut St Philadelphia PA 19103-5552

BRECHER, KENNETH, astrophysicist; b. N.Y.C., Dec. 7, 1943; s. Irving and Edythe (Grossman) B.; m. Aviva Schwartz, Aug. 18, 1965; children: Karen, Daniel. B.S., MIT, 1964, Ph.D., 1969. Research physicist U. Calif., San Diego, 1969-72; asst. prof. physics MIT, Cambridge, 1972-77; assoc. prof. MIT, 1977-79; assoc. prof. astronomy and physics Boston U., 1979-81, prof., 1981—, dir. Sci. and Math. Edn. Ctr., 1990—. Author, editor: (with G. Setti) High Energy Astrophysics and Its Relation to Elementary Particle Physics, 1974, (with M. Feirtag) Astronomy of the Ancients, 1979; contbr. numerous articles to profl. jours. Mem. Mass. Cultural Coun., 1989-91. Guggenheim fellow, 1979-80; W.K. Kellogg fellow, 1985-88; NRC sr. research assoc., 1983-84. Fellow Am. Phys. Soc. (chmn. astrophysics div. 1990-91); mem. Am. Aston. Soc., Internat. Astron. Union, Sigma Xi. Home: 35 Madison St Belmont MA 02178-3535 Office: Boston U Dept Astronomy 725 Commonwealth Ave Boston MA 02215-1401

BRECK, SYLVIA THORINGTON, historical researcher; b. Roxbury, Vt., Aug. 1, 1922; d. James Wallace and Lucia Madeleine (Sowles) Thorington; m. Richard Winslow Breck Jr., July 7, 1943; children: Mary Young, David Stoddard Greenough. Student, Union Meml. Hosp., Balt., 1940-41; real estate lic., Mister Lister Sch., Duxbury, Mass., 1971. Clk., supr. Camp Holabird Supply Base, Balt., 1941-43; statis. typist Office of Strategic Svcs., Washington, 1944; researcher U.S. Bur. Ships, Washington, 1945; ad placer Humphrey's Advt. Agy., Boston, 1946-47; sec., bookkeeper Better Packaging, Inc., Boston, 1948; pvt. sec. Cornelius Wood, Andover, Mass., 1959-62; sec. Dean of Students Phillips Acad., Andover, Mass., 1964-69; sales, listing John D. Walsh Real Estate, Pembroke, Mass., 1972-74. Contbr. articles to profl. jours.; writer, editor: Eddy Homesteader, 1988—, Eddy Family Bulletin, 1985—; author, editor: Eddyville-Middleboro, Mass., 1961-87. Legis. chmn. LWV, Andover, Mass., 1958-59; v.p. Navy League of U.S.-New England, Andover, 1960-62; invited artisan Duxbury (Mass.) Art Assn., 1988; hist. lectr. Middleboro (Mass.) Founders Day Celebrations, 1990-91; leader Girls Scouts Am., Andover, 1957-62, Medfield, Mass., 1954-56; pres. PTA, Andover, 1962-64; active Girl Scouts Am. 50th Anniversary, Duxbury, 1992. Mem. Eddyville Homestead Assn., Inc. (pres. 1990—, exec. sec. 1987—), Eddy Family Assn., Inc. (pres. 1980-87, exec. sec. 1987—), Duxbury Art Assn. Republican. Home: Box 354 570 Washington St Duxbury MA 02331

BREDENBERG, CARL E., surgeon; b. San Maeo, Calif., Mar. 18, 1940; s. Carl E. and Emma J. (Jeager) B.; m. Patricia Ann Vreeland; children: Carl E. III, Linnea J. Student, Princeton U., 1957-59; AB, Johns Hopkins U., 1962, MD, 1964. Diplomate Am. Bd. Surgery, Am. Bd. Thoracic Surgery; cert. special qualifications vascular surgery, added qualifications critical care; lic. physician Md., N.Y., Maine. Resident in surgery Johns Hopkins Hosp., Balt., 1964-72; asst. prof. dept. surgery SUNY, Syracuse, 1972-76, assoc. prof., 1976-80, prof. surgery, 1980-90, surgeon-in-charge vascular surgery svc., 1978-90, vice chmn., 1984-88, interim chmn., 1988-90; chief sect. of thoracic surgery Syracuse VA Med. Ctr., 1973-90; surgeon-in-chief Maine Med. Ctr., Portland, 1990—; prof surgery U. Vt.; staff U. Hosp. SUNY, Syracuse, 1972-90, VA Hosp., Syracuse, 1972-90, Crouse-Irving Meml. Hosp., Syracuse, 1972-90, Maine Med. Ctr., Portland, 1990—; courtesy staff Mercy Hosp., Portland, 1990—. Contbr. numerous articles to profl. jours. Bd. dirs. Syracuse Rowing Assn., 1975-76; mem. vestry St. David's Episcopal Ch., 1979-82, chmn. fin. com. 1979-83, ch. sch. instr., 1981-90. Capt. U.S. Army, 1965-67. Mem. AMA, Soc. for Vascular Surgery, Am. Assn. for Thoracic Surgery, Soc. U. Surgeons, Cen. Surg. Assn., New Eng. Surg. Soc., Am. Physiol. Soc., N.Y. Acad. Sci., Internat. Soc. for Cardiovascular Surgery, New Eng. Soc. for Vascular Surgery, Ea. Vascular Soc. (exec. coun. 1987-91), ACS, Ea. Assn. for Surgery of Trauma, Soc. of Critical Care Medicine, Societe International de Chirugie, Assn. of Acad. Surgery, Upstate N.Y. Vascular Soc. (pres. 1989-90), Maine Vascular Soc. (sec.-treas. 1991—), many others. Office: Maine Med Ctr Surg Assocs 229 Vaughan St Portland ME 04102

BREDIN, J(OHN) BRUCE, real estate executive; b. Wilmington, Del., June 1, 1914; s. Robert and Margaret (Starrett) B.; m. Octavia M. duPont, Aug. 4, 1945; children: Stephanie du P. B. Speakman, Margaretta Starrett Bredin Brokaw, Jonathan Bruce, Alletta Bredin-Bell, Laura L. Bredin Hussey, Antonia Bredin Massie. Student, Coll. William and Mary, 1932-34, LLD (hon.), 1986; student, U. Pa., 1938-40; LHD (hon.), U. Del., 1991; HHD (hon.), 1991. Civilian employee U.S. Govt., 1934-38; with E.I. du Pont de Nemours & Co., 1939-45, 49-52, Texaco, 1945-46; pres. Bredin Realty Co., 1950-81; participant in Smithsonian expdns. to Africa and West Indies; mem. spl. fine arts com. Dept. State; chmn. Fund for the Diplomatic Reception Rms. Found., Dept. State, Endowment of Diplomatic Reception Rms. mem. trustee adv. com. Longwood Gardens Inc.; mem. devel. com. Woods Hole Oceanographic Inst.; pres. Bredin Found.; founding chmn. Henry Francis Du Pont Collectors Circle; emeritus bd. dirs. Med. Center of Del.; trustee Unidel Found.; trustee, vice chmn. Henry Francis du Pont Winterthur Mus.; trustee Endowment Assn. Coll. William and Mary; hon. trustee Foxcroft Sch. (life, trustee), U. Del.; bd. dirs. U. Del. Library Assocs.; pres. Bartol Research Inst. U. Del.; mem. fin. com. Christ Ch., Christiana Hundred; lifetime trustee & dir. Med. Ctr. Del. Hosp. Found.; corp. mem. Nantucket Cottage Hosp. Fellow Smithsonian Instn. (hon.); mem. Del. Acad. Medicine (dir.), Hist. Soc. Del. (trustee), Am. Competitive Enterprise System (hon. life dir.) Confrerie des Chevaliers du Tastevin. Clubs: Vicmead Hunt, Greenville Country, Wilmington, Wilmington Country; Corinthian Yacht (Phila.); Everglades, Soc. of Four Arts (Palm Beach, Fla.); Gulf Stream Bath and Tennis, Gulf Stream Golf (Delray Beach, Fla.); Nantucket Yacht, Sankaty Head Golf (Nantucket); Met. (Washington). Home: PO Box 3598 Wilmington DE 19807-0598 Office: 5724 Montchanin Bldg PO Box 87 Wilmington DE 19899-0087

BREED, DAVID SCRANTON, automotive executive; b. Chgo., Sept. 13, 1938; s. J. Ernest and Genevieve (Shephard) B.; m. Ria E. Trienekens, Sept. 5, 1976; children: Ryan, Christian, Genevieve. BA in Physics, Carlton Coll., 1961; SB Mech. Engring., MIT, 1961, SM in Engring., MIT, 1961, SM Indsl. Mgmt., 1962; PhD Mech Engr., Columbia U., 1972. V.p. Breed Corp., Lincoln Park, N.J., 1965-86; pres. Breed Automotive Corp., Boonton, N.J., 1987-88, Automotive Technologies Internat., Denville, N.J., 1988—. Contbr. numerous articles to profl. mags. on automotive safety; patentee in field. Recipient H.H. Bliss award Ralph Nader, consumer advocate, 1991. Home: 270 Hillcrest Rd Boonton NJ 07005 Office: Automotive Technols Internat PO Box 1028 Denville NJ 07834-0628

BREEDEN, RICHARD C., federal agency administrator; b. 1949; married; 3 children. BS, Stanford U., 1972; JD, Harvard U., 1975. Law tchr., 1975-76; atty. N.Y.C., 1976-81; exec. asst. to under sec. Dept. of Labor, 1981-82; former exec. dir. White House Regulatory Task Force; former counsel Vice pres. George Bush; former ptnr. Baker & Botts, Houston, 1985-89; now chmn. SEC, Washington. Contbr. articles to profl. jours. Office: SEC Office of the Chmn 450 5th St NW Washington DC 20549-0001*

BREEDING, DAVID C., manufacturing executive, educator; b. Knoxville, Tenn., Dec. 28, 1952; s. Clarence H. and Edith (Sharp) B. BS in Environ. Health, George Washington U., 1974; Ms in Environ. Health, East Tenn. State U., 1979; MBA, Vanderbilt U., 1988. Head athletic trainer dept. athletics East Tenn. State U., Johnson City, Tenn., 1970-74; owner Faquier Home Svc., Warrenton, Va., 1975-77; chief exec. officer, gen. mgr., purchasing agt. Urban Rsch. Group, Inc., 1980; owner, mgr. residential apt. complex Morristown, Tenn., 1980-83; environ. engring. advisor Am. Mus. Sci. and Energy, Oak Ridge, Tenn., 1987-89; farmer Speedwell, Tenn., 1964—; asst. prof., dir. environ. health tech. program Walters State Community Coll., Morristown, 1978-87; asst. prof. environ. health scis. Western Carolina U., Cullowhee, N.C., 1987-89; dir. bur. edn., tng. and tech. assistance, indsl. hygienist N.C. Dept. Labor, Raleigh, 1989-91; corp. indsl. hygienist Champion Internat. Corp., Stamford, Conn., 1991—; adj. faculty prof. environ. and occupational health scis. U. N.C. at Western Carolina U. Sch. Nursing and Health Scis., 1989. Contbr. numerous articles to profl. jours. Named one of Outstanding Young Men of Yr., 1987, 88, 89. Mem. Am. Acad. Sanitarians, Am. Soc. Safety Engrs., Nat. Assn. Scholars, Nat. Environ. Tng. Assn., Am. Indsl. Hygiene Assn., N.C. Pub. Health Assn., So. Health Assn. (chmn. continuing edn. com. 1988-89, governing coun. 1988-89), Western N.C. Pub. Health Assn., Tenn. Pub. Health Assn., Tenn. Water Quality Mgmt. Assn. (editor jour. 1987), Am. Pub. Health Assn., Nat. Environ. Health Assn. (chmn. com. on household hazardous waste 1988-89, environ. mgmt. sect. 1989), Tenn. Environ. Health Assn. (sec., treas. 1986-87). Home: 42 Berkley Rd Fairfield CT 06430-4418 Office: Champion Internat Corp One Champion Plz Stamford CT 06921

BREEN, FAITH FEI-MEI LEE, economist, management consultant; b. Burbank, Calif., Feb. 3, 1951; d. John Quong and Eleanor S.G. (Choy) Lee; m. George Edward Breen, Jr., Nov. 30, 1974; children: Erika Lee, George Edward III. BA, U. Md., 1972; MA, U. Pitts., 1975; PhD, U. Md., 1990. Asst. dir. Ctr. for Health Policy Rsch., Am. Enterprise Inst. Pub. Policy, Washington, 1975-77; economist U.S. Dept. Labor, Bur. Internat. Labor Affairs, Washington, 1978; Nat. Gov.'s Assn., Ctr. Pub. Policy Rsch., Washington, 1978-79; expert cons., economist Pres.'s Adv. Com. Women, Washington, 1979-81; polit. econ. cons. Nat. Assn. State and Territorial Solid Waste Mgmt. Ofcls., Washington, 1981-82; expert cons., economist to dep. under sec. mgmt. U.S. Dept. Edn., Washington, 1980-83; adj. faculty dept. econs. Central Mich. U., Washington, 1978—; assoc. prof. Sch. Bus. and dept. econs., Largo, Md., 1985—; pres. Systems Resources Mgmt., Inc., 1983—; lectr. in field. Contbr. articles to profl. jours.; exec. producer TV program: Saccharin and the Public Interest, 1978. past pres. Inner Wheel of College Park, 1986-87, chmn., bd. dirs. Orgn. Chinese Am. Women, 1990, del. Women-to-Women Exchange program, 1987; chair fin. com. University Park Rep. Women's Club, 1985; controller Nat. Rep. Com.'s Nat. Rep. Heritage Group Council, 1985—. Recipient Nat. Def. Lang. fellow, 1973-75; cert. of appreciation Sec. U.S. Dept. Edn., 1983; Fulbright-Hays Seminar Abroad, 1986. Mem. Am. Econ. Assn., Fulbright Alumni Assn., Ashton Swim Club. Roman Catholic. Avocations: tennis, swimming, bridge. Home: 2021 Avoca Ln Silver Spring MD 20905-3973 Office: Systems Resource Mgmt Inc Ste 300 1155 Connecticut Ave NW Washington DC 20036

BREEN, MICHAEL, product manager; b. N.Y.C., Nov. 5, 1961; s. Edward Joseph and Leslie Frances (Dapper) B. BA, U. Notre Dame, 1983; MBA, U. S.C., 1985. Systems coord J.P. Stevens & Co., Inc., Greer, S.C., 1985-86; planning coord. J.P. Stevens & Co., Inc., Clemson, S.C., 1986-87; customer svc. coord. J.P. Stevens & Co., Inc., Greenville, S.C., 1987-88; asst. bus. mgr. J.P. Stevens & Co., Inc., N.Y.C., 1989-90; product mgr. Revman Industries, Inc., 1990—. Coach Greenville (S.C.) Ch. League Basketball, 1987-89, Northwood Little League, Taylors, S.C., 1988-89; big brother Big Brothers Big Sisters, Greenville, 1989. Named Big Brother of Yr., Greenville Big Brothers Big Sisters, 1989. Mem. Am. Mgmt. Assn., Am. Soc. Prodn. & Inventory Control. Republican. Roman Catholic. Home: 51 College Ave Tarrytown NY 10591-2710

BREHM, HENRY, entertainment and sports company executive; b. Tachikawa, Japan, Nov. 1, 1953; came to U.S., 1953; s. Harold Lincoln and Ella (Plavin) B.; m. Deborah Setzer, Apr. 12, 1980; children: Jonathan, Ryan, Matthew, Jennifer. BA in Edn., Am. U., 1975. Tchr. Applewilde Sch., Fitchburg, Mass., 1975-77, Bryant Woods, Columbia, Md., 1977-78; program dir. NFL Players Assn., Washington, 1977-80; asst. dir. Walden Resources, Silver Spring, Md., 1980-81; exec. dir. Washington Area Tennis Patrons Found., 1981-82; sr. v.p. Pro Serv Inc, Washington, 1982-89; pres. Network Internat., Phila., 1989—. Mem. Am. Mktg. Assn., Am. Mgmt. Assn., Pres. Assn. Office: Network Internat 701 Market St Ste 4400 Philadelphia PA 19106-1585

BREHM, JOHN JOSEPH, physicist, physics educator; b. Memphis, Dec. 6, 1934; s. John J. and Mattie (Thornell) B.; m. Mary Ellen Kempers, Nov. 26, 1959; children: John, Robert, Richard, Jennifer. BS, U. Md., 1956, PhD, 1963; MS, Cornell U., 1959. Physicist U.S. Naval Ordnance Lab., Silver Spring, Md., 1958-62; NSF postdoctoral fellow Princeton (N.J.) U., 1962-63; asst. prof. Northwestern U., Evanston, Ill., 1963-66, assoc. prof., 1966-67; assoc. prof. U. Mass., Amherst, 1967-71, prof., 1971—; undergrad. program dir. Dept. of Physics, U. Mass., Amherst, 1988-92. Co-author: Intro to the Structure of Matter, 1989; contbr. articles on theoretical physics to profl. jours. Mem. Am. Phys. Soc. Home: 8 Kingman Rd Amherst MA 01002-1585 Office: U Mass Dept of Physics LGR Tower C Amherst MA 01003

BREITBARTH, GARY GLEN, architect; b. Akron, Iowa, Aug. 10, 1950; s. Glen August and Elinore Kathleen (Harms) B.; m. Barbara Ann Martinick, Feb. 21; children: Matthew Gary, Kathryn Ann. Student, Cerritos Jr. Coll., 1968-70; BArch, Calif. Polytech. U., 1974. Registered architect, Calif., Pa.; cert. Nat. Coun. Archtl. Registration Bds. Project mgr. Neil Stanton Palmer, Rolling Hills Estate, Calif., 1974-78; assoc. architect Acad. Design Concepts, Inc., Rolling Hills Estate, 1978-82; proj. arch. Musil Perkowitz Ruth Inc., Long Beach, Calif., 1983-84; project architect Rhett Hamilton Jones Assocs., Berwyn, Pa., 1984-86; prin. architect Gary Breitbarth Assoc., Audubon, Pa., 1986—. Recipient Achievement award Bank Am., Norwlk, Califl, 1968. Mem. Soc. Am. Registered Architects. Republican. Home and Office: 2844 Ringneck Rd Norristown PA 19403-1813

BREITENECKER, RUDIGER, pathologist; b. Vienna, Austria, 1929; came to U.S., 1954, naturalized, 1969; s. Leopold and Irma B.; m. Robin Jacques, 1963; children: Rudiger, Richard C., Roland. M.D., U. Vienna, 1954. Intern E.W. Sparrow Hosp., Lansing, Mich., 1955-56; resident in pathology Clevel. Met. Gen. Hosp., 1957-59; mem. teaching staff Western Res. U., 1958-59, Duke U., 1960-61; asst. med. examiner State of Md., Balt., 1962-67; asst. prof. forensic pathology U. Md., 1962—; prof. justice adminstrn. U. Louisville, 1978—; lectr. Johns Hopkins Sch. Medicine, 1979-84; pathologist Greater Balt. Med. Ctr., 1967—, assoc. dir. pathology lab., 1970—; cons. legal medicine to fed. govt. Contbr. research publs. on forensic pathology. Fellow Am. Soc. Clin. Pathologists; mem. AMA, Am. Acad. Forensic Sci., Nat. Assn. Med. Examiners, Coll. Am. Pathologists, Am. Med. Soc., Md. Soc. Pathologists (pres. 1988, 89). Office: Greater Balt Med Ctr Baltimore MD 21204

BREITNER, GERARD T., financial planner; b. Bklyn., Aug. 14, 1947; s. William and Ruth (Funk) B.; m. Joann Milack, Feb. 28, 1969; children: Lauren, Elizabeth. BA, St. John's U., Jamaica, N.Y., 1970; cert. CLU, Am. Coll., 1980, cert. in chartered fin. cons., 1983, MS in Fin. Svcs., 1983—. CLU. Mgr. MONY Fin., N.Y.C., 1978-82; pres. Excomp, N.Y.C., 1982—. Mem. Assn. for Advanced Life Underwriting, Internat. Assn. Fin. Planners, Registry Fin. Planning Practitioner, Million Dollar Round Table, Estate Planning Coun. N.Y. Repubican. Roman Catholic. Office: Excomp Inc 120 W 45th St New York NY 10036-4003

BRELIS, DEAN CONSTANTINE, reporter, correspondent, author; b. Newport, R.I., Apr. 1, 1924; s. Christopher and Mary (Phillips) B.; m. Nancy Burns, Nov. 11, 1949, (div. June 1967); children: Doron, Jane, Tia, Matthew; m. Mary Anne Weaver, Apr. 21, 1971. BA, Harvard U., 1949. Fgn. correspondent Time, N.Y.C., 1949-55, 74—, NBC, N.Y.C., 1961-70, CBS, N.Y.C., 1971-73. Author: Mission, 1957, Shalom, 1959, My New Found Land, 1960. Capt. OSS, 1943-45. Decorated Bronze Star, Combat Infantry Badge; Nieman fellow, Harvard U., 1958. Mem. Harvard Club of N.Y.C., Signet Soc. Home: Main Street Milbridge ME 04658

BRELIS, MATTHEW DEAN BURNS, journalist; b. Boston, Aug. 30, 1957; s. C. Dean Brelis and Nancy Emerson (Burns) Jay; m. Mary Morgan Baker, Sept. 10, 1988; 1 child, Mary Margaret. AB, Vassar Coll., 1980. Reporter trainee/clk. The Washington Star, 1980-81; reporter The Pitts. Press, 1981-89, Boston Globe, 1989—. Recipient Pulitzer Prize, Columbia U., 1987, Keystone award Pa. Newspaper Pubs. Assn., 1987, Roy Howard award Scripps-Howard, 1987. Club: Pitts. Vassar (chmn. admissions com. 1985-88), Mt. Auburn. Office: Boston Globe Globe Newspaper Co 135 Morrissey Blvd Dorchester MA 02125-3338*

BREMENKAMP, VICTOR DALE, retired science-research administrator, consultant; b. Colby, Kans., Oct. 13, 1935; s. George Michael and Anna Rictrude (Spielman) B. (div.); children: Lynda Lou, Eric George. BS, Calif. State Poly. U., Pomona, 1962; postgrad., Oreg. State U., 1962-63. Rsch. engr. Jet Propulsion Lab., Pasadena, Calif., 1962-65; rsch. officer ACDA, Washington, 1965-66; U.S. sec. COSPAR Nat. Acad. Scis., Washington, 1966-68; asst. to pres., asst. sec. Assoc. Univs., Inc., Washington, 1991—, cons. sci. mgmt., 1991—; cons. NASA, Washington, 1968-70, Lunar Sci. Inst., Houston, 1970-73, Super Collider Project, Berkeley, Calif., 1983-88; coord. U.S./USSR Solar Energy Project, NSF, Washington, 1974-79. Pres. Hollin Hall Civic Assn., Alexandria, Va., 1970-74. Office: Assoc Univs Inc 1717 Massachusetts Ave NW Washington DC 20036-2001

BREMER, FRANCES WINFIELD, non-profit agency director; b. St. Paul, May 25, 1942; d. William Hood and Alice (Turner) Winfield; m. L. Paul Bremer III, June 11, 1966; children: L. Paul IV, Leila Ames. BA, Conn. Coll., 1964. Cert. tch. English to fgn. speakers. Tchr. Am. Sch., Kabul, Afghanistan, 1966-68, Limbe Convent Sch., Malawi, Africa, 1968-70; founder, pres. Washington Area Refugee Com., 1974-76; dir. Fgn. Student Svc. Coun., Washington, 1976—; docent Folger Shakespeare Libr., Washington, 1971-73; play therapist Childrens Hosp., Washington, 1980-83; organizer Frances Bremer Prize for the Best Essay on Am. Lit., The Hague, Netherlands, 1985. Co-author: Coping With His Success, 1984, Niet Zeuren, 1987. Mem. Nat. Assn. Fgn. Student Affairs. Republican. Episcopalian. Office: Fgn Student Svc Coun 2337 18th St NW Washington DC 20009-1814

BREMER, L. PAUL, III, diplomat; b. Hartford, Conn., Sept. 30, 1941; s. L. Paul and Nina (Struthers) B.; m. Frances Winfield, June 11, 1966; children: Paul, Leila. B.A., Yale U., 1963; cert. d'etudes poliques, Inst. d'etudes Politiques, Paris, 1964; M.B.A., Harvard U., 1966. Exec. asst. to sec. of state Dept. State, Washington, 1974-76; dep. chief of mission Am. embassy, Oslo, Norway, 1976-79; dep. exec. sec. Dept. State, Washington, 1979-81, exec. sec., spl. asst. to sec. of state, 1981-83; amb. Am. Embassy, The Hague, The Netherlands, 1983-86; amb.-at-large for counter-terrorism U.S. Govt., 1986-89; mng. dir. Kissinger Assocs., 1989—. Recipient Superior Honor award Dept. State, 1974, Presdl. Merit Pay award, 1983. Mem. Internat. Inst. Strategic Studies, Coun. on Fgn. Rels. (bd. dirs.), UN Assn., Netherlands-Am. Found., U.S. Ski Team, Execs. Club Chgo. Republican. Episcopalian.

BREMER, MARLENE SCHUBERT, artist, art appraiser; b. Coburg, Bavaria, Germany; came to U.S., 1957; d. Hans Kurt and Eleonore Maria Teresia (Nuernberger) Schubert; m. Herman Carl Bremer, July 19, 1958; children: Stephen, Peter, Cornelia. BA, Fairleigh Dickinson U., 1979; MA, William Paterson Coll., 1981; cert. in fine arts appraisal, NYU, 1989. Tchr. sculpture Ridgewood (N.J.) Community Sch., 1984-85; instr. art history Bergen Community Coll., Paramus, N.J., 1985-87; asst. art appraiser Van Cline & Davenport, Franklin Lakes, N.J., 1989; art appraiser Athena Art Svcs., N.Y.C., 1989—; pres., fine arts cons., appraiser M.S. Bremer, Inc., Englewood, N.J., 1990—. One-woman shows include Burgundy Cafe-Gallery, N.Y.C., 1985, J.K. Javits Fed. Bldg., N.Y.C., 1985, Galerie Vereinigte Coburger Sparkassen, Coburg, Germany, 1986, John Harms Intermission Gallery, Englewood, 1989; exhibited in group shows at Cork Gallery, Lincoln Ctr., N.Y.C., 1984, Ben Shahn Galleries, N.J., 1989, 91, St. Peters at City Corp, N.Y.C., 1991, N.Y. Acad. of Sci., N.Y.C., 1991, Carlos Williams Ctr. for the Arts, Rutherford, N.J., 1991, Paterson (N.J.) Mus., 1991, others. Recipient awards Fedn. Women Clubs, 1974-76, Bicentennial Arts and Craft Show, 1976, Inst. Audio Visuel, Paris, 1982. Mem. Nat. Assn. Women Artists (nominating com. 1989), Artists Equity, Salute to Women in Arts, Watercolor Affiliates, Painting Affiliates, Friends Ben Shahn Gallery. Home: 440 Egan Pl Englewood NJ 07631-3110

BRENDLER, WALTER CLARK, health facility administrator, nurse; b. Yonkers, N.Y., Dec. 20, 1949; s. Walter and Geraldine (Ferguson) B.; m. Mary Ann Fennell, Mar. 17, 1973 (div. Mar. 1992); 1 child, Mary Elizabeth. Diploma, Westchester Sch. Nursing, 1972; BS in Health Care Adminstrn. with distinction, Iona Coll., 1981; MPA in Health Care Adminstrn. with distinction, Pace U., 1985. RN, N.Y. Staff nurse emergency dept. Westchester County Med. Ctr., Valhalla, N.Y., 1972-78, asst. nursing care coord., 1978-82, nursing care coord., 1982-84, area adminstr., program adminstr., 1984-91, program coord., 1991—; inter-veinus therapist Phelps Meml. Hosp.; charge nurse emergency dept. St. Josephs Hosp.; nurse Jeffrey A. Weisberg M.D., P.C.; adj. asst. prof. health care dept., adminstrv. intern supr. Iona Coll.; mem. Westchester County Emergency Operating Ctr. for Natural and Man-Made Disasters; critical care nurse Westchester County's Fed. Disaster Mgmt. Assistance Team. Mem. Emergency Dept. Nurses Assn. Roman Catholic. Home: 25 Maurice Ave Ossinging NY 10562-5204 Office: Westchester County Med Ctr Eastview Hall Ste 103 Valhalla NY 10595-1689

BRENEMAN, DAVID WORTHY, educator; b. Albuquerque, Oct. 24, 1940; s. Clement Daniel and Muriel Ruth B.; m. Judith Dodge, June 10, 1962; children: Erica, Carleton. BA, U. Colo., 1963; PhD, U. Calif.-Berkeley, 1970. Asst. prof. econs. Amherst Coll., 1970-72; staff dir. Nat. Acad. Sci., 1972-75; sr. fellow Brookings Instn., 1975-83; pres. Kalamazoo Coll., 1983-89; professorial lectr. econs. George Washington U., 1979-82; vis. fellow The Brookings Instn., 1989-91; vis. prof. Harvard U., 1990—; cons. NAS, 1991—. Author: Public Policy and Private Higher Education, 1978, Financing Community Colleges, 1981, Academic Labor Markets and Careers, 1988; exec. editor: Change Mag., 1980-84. Trustee Woodrow Wilson Nat. Fellowship Found., 1980-90, W.E. Upjohn Inst., 1983-90; bd. dirs. Am. Coun. on Edn., 1985-89 . Woodrow Wilson fellow, 1963; Danforth fellow, 1963; NDEA fellow, 1967; recipient Buchanan prize U. Calif.-Berkeley, 1970. Mem. Am. Econ. Assn., Am. Assn Higher Edn. (bd. dirs 1982-85), Univ. Club, Phi Beta Kappa. Democrat. Home: 24 Coolidge Ave Cambridge MA 02138 Office: Harvard U Monroe C Gutman Libr Appian Way Cambridge MA 02138

BRENNAN, CHARLES KEVIN, chemical consultant; b. Phila., Nov. 4, 1949; s. Kenneth Arvil and Helen Constance (Luczak) B.; m. Kathleen Ann Jarkiewicz, Oct. 23, 1976; 1 child, Drew Alden. BS, Alliance Coll., Cambridge Springs, Pa., 1971; postgrad., Temple U., 1971-72, Edinboro (Pa.) State Coll., 1974-75; MBA, Fla. Atlantic U., 1979. Chemist Pennwalt Corp., King of Prussia, Pa., 1972-73; tech. salesman Pennwalt Corp., Phila., 1973-74; mktg. specialist Nalco Chem. Co., Chgo., 1974-75; tech. salesman Nalco Chem. Co., Oak Brook, Ill., 1975-77; cons. C.H. Kline & Co., Fairfield, N.J., 1980-82, project mgr., 1982-86; bus. mgr. Kline & Co., Fairfield, 1986-89;

v.p. Phillip Townsend Assocs., Mt. Olive, N.J., 1989-91; pres. Brennan Rsch. Group, Verona, N.J., 1991—. Mem. Chem. Mgmt. and Resources Assn., Golden Triangle East, KC, Sigma Tau Gamma. Republican. Roman Catholic. Home: 101 Morningside Rd Verona NJ 07044-1028 Office: PO Box 43 Verona NJ 07044-0043

BRENNAN, GEORGE GERARD, pediatrician; b. N.Y.C., Nov. 6, 1931; s. George and Bertha (Bradley) Brennan; m. Joan Worfolk, Oct. 31, 1959; children: Jeanne, Gerry, Robert, James, Thomas. AB, Fordham U., 1953; MD, Loyola U., Chgo., 1957. Intern Jersey City Med. Ctr., 1957-58; pediatric resident St. Vincent's Med. Ctr., N.Y.C., 1958-60; pediatrician Old Bridge-Sayneville Med. Group, P.A., 1960—. Fellow Am. Acad. Pediatrics; mem. N.J. State Med. Soc., Middlesex County Med. Soc. Republican. Roman Catholic. Office: Old Bridge-Sayneville Med Group PA 26 Throckmorton Ln Old Bridge NJ 08857

BRENNAN, GLEN, psychologist, neuropharmacology researcher; b. Dayton, Ohio, Sept. 28, 1929; s. Harold McAdoo and Alwilda (Holsapple) Brennan; m. Joan Schwarz, Sept. 17, 1960; children: Nina, Alyssa. BA, Columbia U., 1951; PhD, NYU, 1959. Registered psychologist, N.Y. Rsch. assoc. Nathan Kline Rsch. Inst., Orangeburg, N.Y., 1958-60; ward psychologist F.D. Roosvelt VA Hosp., Montrose, N.Y., 1960-62; rsch. assoc. primate lab. Queens Coll., Flushing, N.Y., 1963-65; staff psychologist Stony Lodge Hosp., Ossining, N.Y., 1966-85; psychologist, pvt. practice Croton On Hudson, N.Y., 1966—; rsch. scientist Rockefeller U., N.Y.C., 1987-90. Contbr. articles to profl. jours., sci. papers to confs., meetings. Mem. AAAS, Soc. for Neurosci., Internat. Brain Rsch. Orgn., Inst. Noetic Scis. Home and Office: PO Box 160 Croton On Hudson NY 10520-0160

BRENNAN, JOSEPH THOMAS, auto parts distribution company executive; b. Shamokin, Pa., Mar. 30, 1931; s. Edward William and Julia E. (Wychulis) B.; m. Margaret C. Brennan, Sept. 1953; children: Margaret Kathleen, Robert Joseph, Matthew Edward. BS in Econs., U. Pa., Phila., 1951. Commd. 2d lt. USAF, 1952, advanced through grades to lt. col., 1969; fighter pilot, flight commdr. various bases, 1958-66; chief Tactical Air Control Ctr., Osan Air Base, Korea, 1969-70; with exec. office, Dover, Del., 1966-69; exec. officer Loring, Maine, 1970-72, ret., 1972; sr. v.p. Quaker City Motor Parts, Middletown, Del., 1972—. Recipient Meritorious Achievement award DAV, 1975. Home: RR 4 Dover DE 19901-9804

BRENNAN, MICHAEL EDWARD, freelance writer; b. Golden Valley, Minn., July 31, 1962. BA, St. Mary's Coll., 1984; MA, Ner Israel Rabbicinal Coll., 1991. Freelance writer Mpls., Boston, Portsmouth, N.H., 1984—; cons. Citizens for Interpretive Dance, Eden Prairie, Minn. Author: Fluffy Gets a Garden, 1991; actor (play) Catch That Cat; co-editor Entomology and You, 1991-92. Recipient Golden Scimitar, Knights of Malta, 1989. Mem. Moose (vice chair fundraising com. 1990-91).

BRENNAN, NOEL-ANNE GERSON, anthropology educator, writer; b. N.Y.C., Apr. 12, 1948; d. Noel Bertram Gerson and Nancy (Hasenwinkle) Hendriks; m. James Beach Brennan, July 27, 1968; 1 child, Anne Wendy. B.A. in Anthropology, Brown U., 1970; M.A. in Sociology and Anthropology, U. R.I., 1982. Writer and researcher, 1973-78, 80—; teaching asst. anthropology U. R.I., Kingston, 1978-80; ptnr. Ocean Wind Electric Co., Peace Dale, R.I., 1980-86; mem. women's studies adv. bd. U. R.I., 1980—, women's ctr. governing bd., 1981-83; instr. anthropology YWCA of R.I., Saunderstown, 1983; instr. sociology U. R.I., 1985—, adj. asst. prof. women's studies, 1986—. Author: The Goodspeed Opera House, 1974, Winter Reckoning, 1986. Contbr. poetry anthology Nine Apples, 1979 (poetry competition winner Northeast Jour. 11986). Contbr. articles and poems to various profl. jours. and mags. Sponsor, Ctr. Environ. Edn., 1981—. Mem. Internat. Snow Leopard Trust, World Wildlife Fund. Mem. Nat. Women's Anthropology Caucus, New England Women's Studies Assn., Sociologists for Women in Soc., Nature Conservancy, Planetary Soc., R.I. Animal Rescue League. Home: 231 Curtis Corner Rd Wakefield RI 02879-2129

BRENNAN, NORMA JEAN, professional society publications director; b. Helena, Mont., Apr. 16, 1939; d. Harland Sanford Herrin and Elizabeth (Wardlaw) Brumfield; m. Anthony E. Brennan, Dec. 4, 1964 (div. Mar. 1986); children: Christopher E., Kimberly A. BA, U. Pacific, 1960. Editorial asst. Am. Rocket Soc., N.Y.C., 1961-62, asst. mng. editor, 1962-65; mng. editor AIAA, N.Y.C., 1978-80; publs. dir. AIAA, N.Y.C., Washington, 1980—. Mem. Young Republicans, Stockton, Calif., 1958-60; vol. Mt. Sinai Hosp., N.Y.C., 1962-64. Mem. Soc. for Scholarly Pub., Coun. Biology Editors, Assn. Am. Pubs., European Assn. Sci. Editors, Coun. Engring. and Sci. Soc. Execs., Wash. Women's Info. Network, AIAA (sr., Space Shuttle Flag award). Home: 11551 Links Dr Reston VA 22090-4820 Office: AIAA 370 Lenfant Promenade SW Washington DC 20024-2518

BRENNAN, PATRICK THOMAS, meteorology company executive; b. Fabius, N.Y., Jan. 29, 1952; s. Thomas William and Mary Patricia (Herlihy) B. BA in Meteorology, SUNY, Oswego, 1974; MS, SUNY, Stony Brook, 1978. Cert. cons. meteorologist. Meteorologist Smith-Singer Meteorologist, Amityville, N.Y., 1974-76; meteorologist Meteorol. Evaluation Services, Amityville, 1977-81, v.p., 1981-86, pres., 1987—. Contbr. articles to profl. jours. Mem. AAAS, Am. Nuclear Soc., Am. Meteorol. Soc., Wind Engring. Research Council, N.Y. Acad. Sci. Republican. Roman Catholic. Club: Clocks Blvd. Yacht. Home: 201 Trouville Rd Copiague NY 11726-3018 Office: Meteorol Evaluation Svcs Co Inc 165 Broadway Amityville NY 11701-2703

BRENNAN, TERRENCE MICHAEL, publisher; b. Phila., Jan. 6, 1947; s. Bernard J. and Ruth (Cantwell) B.; m. Andrea C. Loscalzo; children: Michael, Patrick, Meghan, Matthew. BA in Secondary Edn., Pa. State U., 1968. Sports editor Today's Spirit, Hatboro, Pa., 1970-75; Sunday sports editor The Bull., Phila., 1975-82; asst. sports editor The Daily Times, Primos, Pa., 1982-85; editor The Mercury, Pottstown, Pa., 1985-88; pub., pres. The Telegraph, Alton, Ill., 1988-89; exec. editor Ingersoll Publs., Princeton, N.J., 1989-90; editor, pub. The Record, Troy, N.Y., 1990-91, pub., 1991—. Found. mem. Samaritan Hosp., Troy, 1991—; bd. dirs. Troy Area YMCA, 1991—; trustee LaSalle Inst., Troy, 1991—. Recipient Sports Writing award Keystone Press Assn., 1985, Editorial Writing award, 1987. Mem. Rensselaer County C. of C. (bd. dirs. Troy chpt. 1990—). Office: The Record 501 Broadway Troy NY 12181

BRENNAN, THOMAS JOHN, city official, consultant, educator; b. Bklyn., Mar. 23, 1923; s. Thomas Joseph and Violet Emma (Jurgens) B.; m. Margaret Karen Jensen, Sept. 18, 1948; children: Debra Gail, Mark Kevin, Laurie Kathleen. A.B., Wittenberg Coll., 1949; M.G.A., Fels Inst. of Local and State Govt., Wharton Grad. Sch., 1950. Dep. sec. for adminstrn. Dept. Welfare, Commonwealth Pa., Harrisburg, 1957-59, dep. sec. for state properties Pa. Dept. Property and Supplies, 1959-64; exec. officer Del. Dept. Mental Health, Dover, 1965-67; v.p. Exec. Mgmt. Svc., Arlington, Va., 1967-76; exec. dir. Gov.'s Justice Commn. and Pa. Commn. on Juvenile Delinquency, 1976-79; dir. water utility City of New Brunswick, N.J., 1983-91; chief labor negotiator City of New Brunswick, N.J., 1988-91; pers. mgr., 1988-91, exec. officer police dept., 1989-91; pub. mgmt. cons., 1991—; adj. instr. U. Del., 1965-67; adj. assoc. prof. Rider Coll., Lawrenceville, N.J., 1983-84, 84-85; hearing officer N.J. Dept. Civil Svc., Trenton, 1976—, cons. exam. constrn., 1985; cons. to staff com. UN, 1982-84; cons. various municipalities and agys.; presenter papers to profl. orgns. Bd. dirs. Bucks County Opera, Pa., 1975-80, Bucks County Play House, New Hope, Pa., 1970s; active mem. Bucks County Hist. Soc., Doylestown, Pa., 1983—; elected mem. alumni coun. Wittenberg U., 1989—; mem. Merrill's Maurauders, World War II. Decorated Silver Star, Bronze Star with 2 oak leaf clusters, Combat Infantry badge; recipient various plaques; Fels scholar U. Pa., 1948. Mem. Internat. Personnel Mgmt. Assn., Am. Pub. Works Assn. (dist. rep. Eastern Pa. bldg. and grounds com.), Am. Water Works Assn., Internat. Chiefs of Police Assn., Nat. Conf. State Justice Planning Adminstrn. (regional chmn., mem. exec. com.), Criminal Justice Tng. Inst. (chmn. planning com. 1978, 79). Club: Huntington Valley Hunt (Bucks County) (bd. dirs. 1975-80), Wharton Alumni (Phila.), U. Pa. Faculty. Lodge: Fraternal Order of Police. Avocations: fox hunting, pleasure riding. Home: 327 Pineville Rd Newtown PA 18940-3111 Office: PO Box 21 Pineville PA 18946-0021

BRENNAN, TIMOTHY JOHN, public policy educator; b. Washington, Dec. 26, 1952; s. Thomas Leo and Vivian (Anderson) B.; m. Sarah Margaret Pritchard, Aug. 20, 1977. BA, U. Md., 1973; MA, U. Wis., 1975, U. Wis., 1976; PhD, U. Wis., 1978. Economist Antitrust div. U.S. Dept. of Justice, Washington, 1978-86, cons. Antitrust div., 1986—; assoc. prof. George Washington U., Washington, 1986-89; assoc. prof. policy sci. U. Md., Balt., 1990—; lectr. U.S. Telecommunications Tng. Inst., Washington, 1989—, Annenberg Program in Communication Policy, Washington, 1989—. Contbg. author: Magill's Survey of Social Science: Economics, 1991, Social Norms and Economic Institutions, 1991, Price Caps and Incentive Regulation in Telecommunications, 1991, After the Break-Up: Assessing the New Post-AT&T Divestiture Era, 1991, Competition and the Regulation of Utilities, 1990, Manual on the Economics of Antitrust Law, 1988, Economic Analysis and Antitrust Law, 1988; contbr. articles to profl. jours. WARF grad. fellow, 1974-78. Mem. ABA, Am. Econ. Assn., Am. Philos. Assn., Broadcast Edn. Assn., History Econs. Soc., Assn. Social Econs., Washington Area Music Assn. Office: Policy Scis Grad Program U Md Baltimore MD 21228-5398

BRENNAN, W. NEIL, financial executive; b. Phila., Aug. 7, 1962; s. William J. and Mary Francis (Hughes) B.; m. Justine M. Hojnowski, July 15, 1989. BA in English, Villanova (Pa.) U., 1985. Supr. UPS, Phila., 1982; hub coord. UPS, Willow Grove, Pa., 1983-85; project mgr. DDD Co., Landover, Md., 1986; quality assurance asst. Nuclear Quality Assurance Phila. Elect. Co., 1986-88; tech. asst. Phila. Elec. Co., Wayne, Pa., 1989-90; analyst Corp. and Pub. Affairs Phila. Elec. Co., Phila., 1990, sr. analsyt, 1991—. Developer (software) DSM Abstracts, 1990. Republican. Office: Phila Elect Co 2301 Market St # 131S Philadelphia PA 19103-1380

BRENNAN, WILLIAM JOHN, manufacturing executive; b. Westerly, R.I., Dec. 6, 1940; s. Arthur Leo and Nancy Lee (Terranova) B.; m. Jacqueline Frances Larkin, Oct. 10, 1959; children: Melinda Louise, William John Jr., Dawn Marie, Alison Elizabeth. BS, Bryant Coll., 1969. With AMF, Inc., Conn., 1973-85; v.p. Hosokawa USA, N.Y.; mng. dir. Srague H.K., 1986-87; sr. v.p. Hosokawa Micron Internat., N.Y.C., 1987—. Mem. Yokohama (Japan) Country Club. Republican. Roman Catholic. Home: 32 Woonsocket Ave Shelton CT 06484-5537 Office: Hosokawa Micron Internat 780 3d Ave New York NY 10017-2024

BRENNAN, WILLIAM JOHN, JR., food service executive; b. Westerly, R.I., July 16, 1961; s. William John and Jacqueline Francis (Larkin) B.; m. Delanie Brown, Feb. 6, 1989; 1 child, William John III. BSBA, U. Denver, 1983. Restaurant mgr. Red Lobster Inns of Am., Falls Church, Va., 1985-87; food svc. mgr. Seiler Corp., Madison, N.J., 1987, McDonough, Md., 1987-88; asst. dir. Seiler Corp., Washington, 1988-89; asst. dir. food svc. Seiler Corp., Fairfield, Conn., 1989-90; dir. food svc. Seiler Corp., Fairfield, 1990—. Home: 32 Woonsocket Ave Shelton CT 06484-5537 Office: Seiler Corp N Benson Rd Fairfield CT 06430

BRENNAN, WILLIAM JOSEPH, JR., former U.S. Supreme Court justice; b. Newark, Apr. 25, 1906; s. William J. and Agnes (McDermott) B.; m. Marjorie Leonard, May 5, 1928 (dec.); children—William Joseph, Hugh Leonard, Nancy; m. Mary Fowler, Mar. 9, 1983. B.S., U. Pa., 1928; LL.B., Harvard, 1931, LL.D. (hon.), 1968; LL.D. (hon.), U. Pa., 1957, Wesleyan U., 1957, St. Johns U., 1957, Rutgers U., 1958, Jewish Theol. Sem. Am., 1964, George Washington U., 1965, U. Notre Dame, 1968, Yale U., 1987, Ohio State U., 1987, Glasgow U., 1989; LLD (hon.), Univ. Coll. Dublin in N.Am., 1990; LLB (hon.), Princeton U., 1986, Columbia U., 1986, Brandeis U., 1986, N.Y. Law Sch., 1986, John Marshall Law Sch., 1986; D Jud. Sci. (hon.), Suffolk U., 1956; DCL (hon.), NYU, 1957, Colgate U., 1957; LittD, U. Miami, 1991. Bar: N.J. bar 1931. Practiced Newark, 1931-49; mem. firm Pitney, Hardin, Ward & Brennan; superior ct. judge, 1949-50, appellate div. judge, 1950-52; justice Supreme Ct. N.J., 1952-56; assoc. justice U.S. Supreme Ct., 1956-90. Served to col. with gen. staff corps AUS, World War II. Decorated Legion of Merit. Office: US Supreme Ct DC Washington DC 20543

BRENNAN, WILLIAM PHILIP, contractor; b. Plattsburgh, N.Y., Feb. 17, 1936; s. William James and Marguerite (Langey) B.; m. Barbara Ellen Kurz, Sept. 6, 1958; children: Michael Patrick, Marcia Elizabeth, Sandra Leigh, Lynn Marie. AB, U. Miami, Coral Gables, Fla., 1961; banking cert., Rutgers U., 1973; mortgage banking cert., Northwestern U., 1988. Br. office asst. Nat. Comml. Bank, Plattsburg, N.Y., 1961-62; collections supr. Key Bank, N.A., Albany, N.Y., 1963-64, consumer credit mgr., 1965-67, asst. cashier and credit mgr., 1968-71, asst. v.p., 1972-74, v.p., 1975-80, sr. v.p., 1981-82; exec. v.p. Key Mortgage Funding, Inc., Albany, 1983-90; pres. Questor Corp., Albany, N.Y., 1991—; instr. Sch. Labor and Indsl. Rels., Cornell U., Albany, 1969-76. Director Plattsburgh Soap Box Derby, 1967, Capital City Housing Devel. Fund Co., 1989-91; pres. Cliff Haven Home Owners Assn., Plattsburgh, 1971; scoutmaster Clifton Park (N.Y.) Saratoga coun. Boy Scouts Am., 1974-76, exec. bd. govs., Clinton coun., 1983-85; active Albany County Civic Ctr. adv. com., 1985, City of Albany Neighborhood, Revitalization and Housing Com., 1985-91; commr. City of Albany Tricentennial Commn., 1985-86. With USAF, 1954-57. Mem. Investment Soc. Northeaster N.Y., Am. Inst. Banking (instr. 1966-72, chmn. local chpt. 1969-72), Albany C. of C. (chmn. legis. com. 1980-81, 1st v.p., bd. dirs. 1982), Albany Area Bldrs. Assn. (assoc., remodelers coun.), Nat. Assn. Home Bldrs. and Its Remodelers Coun. Democrat. Roman Catholic. Home: 6 Forest Dr Country Knolls Ballston Lake NY 12019

BRENNEMAN, CHRISTINE DEE, interior designer; b. York, Pa., Feb. 22, 1960; d. Frederick George and Deanna Lorraine (Barnhart) B. Swatcher/designer Eisenhart Wallcoverings, Hanover, Pa., 1981-83; designer computer graphics York (Pa.) Wall Coverings, Inc., 1983—. Office: York Wallcoverings Inc 750 Linden Ave York PA 17404-3373

BRENNER, ALAN IRA, rheumatologist; b. Providence, Aug. 24, 1942; s. Louis Raymond and Jean (Poritsky) B.; m. Beverly Farber, Aug. 29, 1965 (div. 1983); m. Lynn Katoff, Jan. 8, 1984; children: Jessica, Adam, Richard, Cara. BA in Biology, Brown U., 1964; MD, U. Cin., 1968. Diplomate Am. Bd. Internal Medicine, Am. Bd. Rheumatology. Intern Northwestern U., Chgo., 1968-69; resident in medicine New Eng. Med. Ctr., Boston, 1969-70; fellow in rheumatology Boston U., 1972-74; pres. Rheumatol. Svcs., Framingham, Mass., 1974—; cons. immunology Metro West Med. Ctr., Framingham, 1978—; cons. rheumatology Milford Hosp., 1980—; cons. Lupus Found., Wellesley, Mass., 1991—. Bd. dirs. Marlboro Cultural Affairs, 1988—. Maj. USAF, 1970-72. Fellow Am. Coll. Rheumatology; mem. AMA, New Eng. Rheumatism Soc., N.Y. Acad. Sci., Am. Acad. Sci., Am. Soc. Internal Medicine. Jewish. Office: Rheumatol Svcs 475 Franklin St Framingham MA 01701

BRENNER, AMY REBECCA, podiatrist; b. N.Y.C., Dec. 31, 1958; d. Frank and Betty (Gitelman) B.; m. Peter Louis Klinge Jr., June 28, 1985. BS, Ithaca Coll., 1980; MA, Columbia U., 1982; D of Podiatric Medicine, N.Y. Coll. Podiatric Medicine, 1988. Cert. athletic trainer; health edn. instr., N.Y. State. Fellow Rusk Inst. Rehab. Medicine, N.Y.C., 1978; podiatrist, athletic trainer Athletic Events, N.Y., 1976—; physiology intern Chase Manhattan Cardiovascular Fitness Lab., N.Y.C., 1981; asst. athletic trainer Barnard Coll., N.Y.C., 1980-81; surg. resident Liberty Med. Ctr., Inc., Balt., 1989; staff podiatrist Bronx Cross County Med. Group, P.C., Bronx, Yonkers, N.Y., 1990—; pvt. practice podiatry N.Y.C. and Westchester County, 1990—; test site adminstrs. com. Nat. Athletic Trainers Assn. Bd. Certification, Greenville, N.C., 1990—. Contbr. articles to profl. jours including Jour. Am. Podiatric Med. Assn. V.p. Bd. Dirs. Vernon Woods Apts., Inc., Mount Vernon, N.Y., 1990—; lectr. Am. Podiatric Med. Assn. Region VIII Meeting, Bethesda, Md., 1989, Liberty Med. Ctr., Inc., Balt., 1989. Mem. Am. Podiatric Med. Assn., Nat. Athletic Trainers Assn., Am. Coll. Sports Medicine, Am. Assn. for Women Podiatrists, Am. Alliance Health, Phys. Edn., Recreation and Dance. Home: 154 Pearsall Dr Apt 4E Mount Vernon NY 10552-3905

BRENNER, MARSHALL LEIB, lawyer; b. N.Y.C., Aug. 8, 1933; s. Samuel and Ruth (Novak) B.; m. Gwen A. Krakower, Aug. 9, 1959; children: Scott David, Louri Ann, Robin Lynn. BA, St Lawrence U., Canton, N.Y., 1955; JD, Bklyn. Law Sch., 1959. Bar: N.Y. 1960, U.S. Dist. Ct. (no. and ea. dists.) N.Y. 1960, U.S. Ct. Claims 1964, U.S. Supreme Ct. 1964, U.S. Dist. Ct. (so. dist.) N.Y. 1969. Assoc. Spitz & Levine, Poughkeepsie, N.Y., 1960-62; sr. ptnr. Brenner, Gordon & Lane, Poughkeepsie, 1977—; chief appeals sect. Dutchess County Pub. Defenders Office, Poughkeepsie, 1966-78; tchr. law Marks Realtors/Appraisors, Poughkeepsie and Fishkill, N.Y., 1968-72, Robert-Mark Realtors, Hopewell Junction, N.Y., 1979—; lectr. Dutchess County Realty Bd. for Sales/Broker Lic. Applicants, 1985—. Contbr. articles to profl. jours. Pres., bd. dirs. Sloper-Willen Community Ambulance, Wappingers Falls, N.Y., 1966-79; bd. dirs. Poughkeepsie Jewish Community Ctr., 1980-82, Dutchess County Assn. for Sr. Citizens, Dutchess County Youth Bd., Anderson Sch., Staatsburg, N.Y. Capt. U.S. Army, 1956-63. Mem. N.Y. State Bar Assn., Dutchess County Bar Assn., N.Y. State Trial Lawyers Assn. Republican. Jewish. Clubs: Harding (Poughkeepsie) (pres. 1968-69); County Players (Wappingers Falls) (bd. dirs. 1963-74). Lodges: Masons, Rotary (pres. 1973-74, 78-79, Govs. Trophy 1978). Home: 30 Robin Rd Poughkeepsie NY 12601-5654 Office: Brenner Gordon & Lane 247 Church St Poughkepsie NY 12601-4137

BRENNER, THEODOR EDUARD, academic administrator; b. Zurich, Switzerland, May 9, 1942; came to U.S., 1962; s. Eduard and Wally Frieda (Thiele) B.; m. Vivienne Frances Shaw, June 11, 1966 (div.); children: Benedikt Eduard, Tristan Mark. Diploma, Kantonale Handelsschule, Zurich, 1962; LHD (hon.), Pace U., 1986. Dir. summer programs Am. Sch. Switzerland, Montagnola, 1963-65; dir. Inst. for European Studies Fleming Coll., Lugano, Switzerland, 1967-69; adminstrv. dean Franklin Coll., Lugano, 1970-78, pres., 1979—. Contbr. articles to profl. jours. Apptd. rep. Consiglio Comunale, Novaggio, Switzerland, 1976-80; mem. Am. Swiss Assn., Inc., N.Y.C., 1985—. Mem. Assn. Internat. Colls. and Univs. (v.p. 1984-87, 1991—), Swiss-Am. C. of C. (Ticino chpt. bd. dirs. 1987—), Middle States Assn. Colls. and Schs. (evaluator), Coll. Bd., Coun. Advancement and Support of Edn., Nat. Assn. Fgn. Student Advisors, Lions (charter), Canottieri Club (Lugano). Republican.

BRENNER, WILLIAM BOWER, company executive; b. Newburgh, N.Y., Feb. 16, 1944; s. Lee Don and Henrietta (Maxwell) B.; m. Leslie Pesetzky, Jan. 22, 1981 (div. 1987); 1 child, Benjamin Adam. BS, Ball State U., 1972; MS, SUNY, New Paltz, 1989. Tchr. Newburgh (N.Y.) Bd. Edn., 1986-89; dist. sales mgr. Hudson Valley News, Newburgh, 1990-91; pres. Pitch In Orgn., Newburgh, 1987—. Author: Thinking is Hard, 1989; inventor Buddy Seat, 1990; author environ. program: American Families Making a Difference (Environ. Award Hall of Fame), 1991. Bd. dirs. Newburgh Hts. Assocs., Inc., 1988—, City of Newburgh Planning Bd., 1991—; mem. Dem. Com., Newburgh, 1990—. With U.S. Army, 1965-67. Recipient Mayor's Proclamation, City of Newburgh, 1990. Episcopalian. Home: 43 L-1 Hawthorne Gardens Newburgh NY 12550

BRENT, CAROLYN MAAS, retired educator; b. N.Y.C., Dec. 6, 1925; d. Michael and Clara (Mendelson) Maas; div.; children: Meg Susan, Mark Lawrence, Donna Ruth. BA, Ind. U., 1949; MA, Columbia U., 1950. Cert. tchr., N.Y. Tchr. English Ossining (N.Y.) Sch. System, 1965-91, ret., 1991—. Mem. Nat. Coun. Tchrs. English, Am. Fedn. Tchrs., N.Y. State United Tchrs., Westchester County Tchrs. English, NOW, LWV, NAACP, Upward Bound, Ossining Tchrs. Assn., Health and Tennis Club, Shattemuk Yacht Club, Order Eastern Star, Phi Delta Kappa. Democrat. Jewish. Home: 1459 Providence Blvd Deltona FL 32725

BRENT, CHRISTOPHER JOSEPH, health facility administrator; b. York, Pa., Apr. 5, 1952; s. Joseph Francis and Esther Virginia (Bridy) B.; m. Donna Palmisano, Aug. 14, 1976. BS in Psychology, U. Scranton, 1974. Dir. devel. Community Renewal Team, Hartford, Conn., 1989-90, Charter Oak Terrace-Rice Heights Health Ctr., Hartford, 1990—; cons. Conn. Assn. for Community Action, Hartford, 1988-90, Data Inst., East Hartford, Conn., 1984-85. Exhibited in juried show at Pump House Gallery, Hartford, 1990. Mem. Nat. Soc. Fund Raising Execs. (scholar 1990). Roman Catholic. Office: Charter Oak Terrace-Rice Heights 81 Overlooe Terr Hartford CT 06106

BRENT, HAL PRESTON, sales executive; b. Jackson, Miss., Dec. 30, 1955; s. Mildred (Newman) Brent. BBA, U. Miss., 1978; student, Naval Jet Pilot Sch., 1981. Sales rep. Control Data, Avon, Conn., 1984-87, sales mgr., 1987-89, v.p. sales, 1989—. Capt. USMC, 1978-84, Korea and CBI. Home: 97 Foxton Ct Beacon Falls CT 06403 Office: Control Data 150 Fisher Dr Avon CT 06403

BRENTON, VIRGINIA MARY, industrial hygienist; b. Trenton, N.J., Nov. 10, 1961; d. Charles James and Virginia M. (Robison) B. AA, Keene (N.H.) State Coll., 1982, AA in Alcohol Studies, 1983, BS in Occupational Safety, 1983; MS in Indsl. Hygiene, Temple U., 1990. Safety intern IBM Corp., Princeton, N.J., 1982; pub. health rep. trainee N.J. Dept. Health, Trenton, 1984-85, pub. health rep. III, 1985-86, pub health rep. II, 1986-87, program specialist III, 1987-88, program specialist II, 1988-90, rsch. scientist II, 1990—. Contbr. articles to profl. jours. Mem. Am. Soc. Safety Engrs., Am. Conf. Govtl. Indsl. Hygienists, Ancient Order Hibernians. Democrat. Roman Catholic. Home: 107 Mcadoo Ave Trenton NJ 08619-1753 Office: NJ Dept Health CN360 Rm 701 Trenton NJ 08625

BREON, PAUL DOUTY, retired educational administrator; b. Coburn, Pa., Nov. 29, 1915; s. Myles Wayne and Sabina Amanda (Douty) B.; m. Roberta Amelia Smith, May 6, 1939; children: Nancy Marie, Judith Rae. BS, Lock Haven U., 1937; MEd, Pa. State U., 1951. Cert. secondary English, social studies, health, phys. edn. tchr., prin., Pa., supt. of schs. Visitor Pa. Dept. Welfare, Harrisburg, 1937-41; tchr., coach Centre Hall (Pa.)-Potter High Sch., 1941-53; prin. Millersburg (Pa.) Jr.-Sr. High Sch., 1953-55, Kittanning (Pa.) Sr. High Sch., 1955-60; prin. Greensburg (Pa.) Salem High Sch., 1960-66, asst. supt., 1966-74, spl. asst., 1974-75; supt. North East (Pa.) Sch. Dist., 1975-79; ret., 1979; chmn. Mid. States sect. evaluation of secondary schs. and colls., Phila., 1966-84; pres. Pa. Assn. Secondary Sch. Prins., 1967-68; speaker on Pa. Dutch Pres.'s of U.S., 1960—; speaker on local history and govt. waste, 1990—. Contbr. articles to profl. publs. Bd. dirs. Dept. State, Harrisburg, 1986-91; pres. Penns Valley Sch. Bd., Spring Mills, Pa., 1984-85. With USN, 1944. Recipient Proclamation, City of Greensburg, 1975. Mem. Pa. State U. Alumni Sec. (bd. dirs. Coll. of Edn. sect. 1986—), Lock Haven U. Alumni (sec. bd. dirs. 1982-92), Centre County Assn. Sch. Retirees (pres. 1985-89, Svc. award 1990), Miles Twp. Alumni Assn. (pres. 1982-83), AARP (vol. tax aide 1987-92, Cert.), Lions (pres. Kittanning chpt. 1959-60, pres. Centre Hall 1952-53, 50 Yrs. Svc. award 1992). Republican. Methodist. Home: 126 Grandview Rd Centre Hall PA 16828

BRESANI, FEDERICO FERNANDO, business executive; b. Lima, Peru, Apr. 27, 1945; came to U.S., 1964; s. Federico L. and Beatriz (Ferrer) B.; m. Patricia Anne Grannis, Aug. 26, 1972; children: Christina Anne, Vianna Clarissa. BS in Elect. Engring., Milw. Sch. of Engring., 1970; MBA, Fairleigh Dickinson U., 1980. Engr. Cerro Corp., Lima, Peru, 1973-76; supr. Cerro Corp./CMP, N.Y.C., 1976-77, mgr., 1978, purchasing mgr., 1979-80; product mgr. Schumag, Inc., Norwood, N.J., 1980-82, v.p., 1982; sales, mktg. mgr. EVG, N.Y.C., 1983-85, v.p., 1986-92, pres., 1992—. Mem. Wire Assn. Internat., Wire Reinforcement Inst., Concrete Reinforcement Steel Inst., Omicron Delta Epsilon. Home: 77 Chuckanutt Dr Oakland NJ 07436-3728 Office: EVG 220 E 42d St New York NY 10017

BRESCIA, FRANK JOSEPH, medical oncologist, educator; b. Yonkers, N.Y., Feb. 24, 1942; s. Alfred Louis and Marie (Colucci) B.; m. Alicia Heine, June 29, 1985; children: Andria, Frank, Michaelann, Monica. BS, Fordham U., 1963, MA in Philosophy, 1988; MD, N.J. Coll. Medicine, Newark, 1968. Diplomate Am. Bd. Internal Medicine, Am. Bd. Med. Oncology. Intern Cornell Med. Coll. programs North Shore Univ. Hosp., 1968-70; fellow in oncology Meml. Sloan-Kettering Cancer Ctr., N.Y.C., 1972-74; pvt. practice Millburn, N.J., 1974-80; med. dir. Calvary Hosp., Bronx, N.Y., 1980—; asst. clin. prof. N.Y. Med. Coll., Valhalla, N.Y., 1981—; preceptor Kennedy Ctr. for Bioethics, Washington, 1986—. Contbr. articles on clin. ethics and philosophy of care to med. jours. Maj. M.C., U.S. Army, 1970-72, Vietnam. Mem. Am. Soc. Clin. Oncology. Roman Catholic. Office: Calvary Hosp 1740 Eastchester Rd Bronx NY 10461

BRESCIA, MARY ELIZABETH, nurse outpatient medical/surgical; b. Bronx, N.Y., Jan. 7, 1955; d. Bertram John and Emma Elizabeth (Bond)

Ross; m. Michael Joseph Brescia, Apr. 10, 1976. AAS, Orange County Community Coll., Middletown, N.Y., 1980; postgrad., SUNY, New Paltz. Adminstrv. asst. Mid-Hudson Psychiat. Ctr., New Hampton, N.Y., 1973—; RN Horton Meml. Hosp., Middletown, 1980-88, First Care of Middletown, 1988—. Republican. Roman Catholic. Home: RR 2 Box 193 New Hampton NY 10958-9763

BRESCIA, MICHAEL JOSEPH, physician; b. N.Y.C., Jan. 11, 1933; s. Louis Kingsley and Olympia (Cimorelli) B.; m. Monica Ann Clinton, Dec. 3, 1936; children: Michael, Mark, Andrea, Monica, Christopher, Marisa. BS, Fordham U., 1954; MD, Georgetown U., 1958. Intern Nassau County Hosp., L.I., N.Y., 1958-59; resident Bronx VA Hosp., N.Y.C., 1959-62, attending physician, 1962-77, asst. dir. renal svc., 1962-68; attending physician Our Lady of Mercy Hosp., N.Y.C., 1962-66; attending physician Calvary Hosp., N.Y.C., 1962—, coord. med. program, 1988—; chief renal svc. St. Joseph's Hosp., Yonkers, N.Y., 1963-70, cons. nephrology, 1970—; cons. nephrology N.Y.C. Dept. Health, 1971-74; clin. asst. prof. medicine N.Y. Med. Coll., Valhalla, 1979—. contbr. articles to profl. jours.; co-inventor Brescia-Cimino fistula hemodialysis method. Recipient Dialysis Pioneering award Fed. Govt., 1968, Good Samaritan award Nat. Cath. Devel. Coun., 1981, Il Leone San Marco award Italian Heritage Com. for Medicine, 1991. Mem. AMA, Am. Soc. Nephrology, Internat. Soc. Nephrology, N.Y. State Soc. Nephrology, Am. Soc. Artificial Internal Organs. Roman Catholic. Home: 1814 Dogwood Dr Yorktown Heights NY 10598 Office: Calvary Hosp 1740 Eastchester Rd Bronx NY 10461-2392

BRESLER, SIDNEY ALAN, corporate executive; b. Aug. 12, 1923; s. Henry and Pola (Lobsenz) B. BChemE, CUNY, 1943; MChemE, Polytechnic Inst., N.Y.C., 1956; MBA, Columbia U., 1960. Project mgr., chmn. computer com. Chem. Constrn. Corp., N.Y.C., 1946-64; pres. Bresler and Assocs., Inc., N.Y.C., 1966—. Patentee in field; contbr. articles to profl. jours. Fellow Am. Inst. Chem. Engrs. Office: Bresler & Assocs Inc PO Box 931 New York NY 10023-0931

BRESLIN, DONALD JOSEPH, internist; b. Toronto, Ont., Can., Mar. 16, 1929; s. R.H. Breslin and S.T. Breslin Dobkins; m. Evalynne Louise Wood, Jan. 30, 1954; children: Lisa, Mark, Paul. BA, Yale U., 1946; postgrad. Columbia U., 1947; BS, McGill U., 1950, MD, 1954 . Diplomate Am. Bd. Internal Medicine. Intern Cleve. Met. Gen. Hosp., 1954-55, resident in internal medicine, 1955-57; fellow in internal medicine Mayo Clinic, Rochester, Minn., 1957-60, 1st asst. internal medicine, 1960-61; pvt. practice internal medicine, Canton Ohio, 1961-66; mem. med. sch. faculty Case Western, 1962-66; mem. staff dept. internal medicine Lahey Clinic, Boston, 1966—, mng. editor Clinic Bull., 1975-83, head sect. vascular medicine, 1976-90, sr. cons. vascular medicine, 1990—; clin. instr. internal medicine Harvard Med. Sch., 1977-78, asst. clin. prof. medicine, 1979—. Active med. div. Northeastern sect. United Fund, 1968-70, chmn., 1970-71. Research fellow Royal Postgrad. Med. Sch., U. London, 1973-74. Editor: Vascular Disease in Elderly for Cardiology Clinics, 1991. Fellow ACP, Soc. for Vascular Medicine and Biology; mem. AMA, Mass. Med. Soc., Mass. Soc. Internal Medicine, Am. Heart Assn. (sci. councils clin. cardiology, hypertension), Am. Soc. Echocardiography, Mayo Alumni Assn., Yale Alumni Assn., Yale Alumni Greater N.Y., Yale Class of '46 Assn. Sr. editor Renovascular Hypertension (Williams and Wilkins), 1982; guest editor Cardiol. Clinics N.Am., 1991; contbr. articles on systemic hypertension and its med. and surg. aspects, idiopathic hypotension and vascular disease to profl. jours. Office: Lahey Clinic Found 41 Mall Rd Burlington MA 01805-0002

BRESLIN, JIMMY, newspaperman, author; b. Jamaica, N.Y., Oct. 17, 1929; s. James Earl and Frances (Curtin) B.; m. Rosemary Dattolico, Dec. 26, 1954 (dec. June 1981); children: James and Kevin (twins), Rosemary, Patrick, Kelly, Christopher,; m. Ronnie Myers Eldridge, Sept. 12, 1982; stepchildren: Daniel, Emily, Lucy Eldridge. Student, L.I. U., 1947-50. Syndicated columnist N.Y. Herald-Tribune, Paris Tribune, N.Y. Daily News, Newsday, L.I., N.Y. Commentator Sta. WNBC-TV; host: (TV series) Jimmy Breslin's People, 1986; author: Can't Anybody Here Play This Game?, 1963, The Gang That Couldn't Shoot Straight, 1969, World Without End, Amen, 1973, How The Good Guys Finally Won, 1975, (with others) Forty-Four Caliber, 1978, Forsaking All Others, 1982, The World According to Breslin, 1984, Table Money, 1986, He Got Hungry and Forgot His Manners, 1988, Damon Runyon, 1991; drama: The Queen of the Leaky-Roof Circuit, 1988. N.Y.C. Candidate for pres. City Council, N.Y.C., 1969; del. Democratic Nat. Conv., 1972, 76. Recipient award for nat. reporting Sigma Delta Chi, 1964, Meyer Berger award for local reporting, 1964, N.Y. Reporters Assn. award reporting, 1964, Pulitzer Prize for commentary, 1986, George K. Polk award, 1986. Mem. Screen Actors Guild, AFTRA, Writers Guild Am. Office: NY Newsday 2 Park Ave New York NY 10016-5603

BRESLIN, MICHAEL JOSEPH, III, social services administrator, educator; b. Fountain Springs, Pa., Feb. 5, 1949; s. Michael Joseph Jr. and Barbara Ellin (Mellet) B. BS in Sociology, U. Scranton, 1971; MS in Adminstrn., Shippensburg (Pa.) U., 1984. Tchr. aide Selinsgrove (Pa.) Ctr., 1968, 69, 70; caseworker Northumberland County Children and Youth Agy., Sunbury, Pa., 1971-73; juvenile probation officer Northumberland County Juvenile Ct., 1973-74, supr., 1974-75, dir., 1976-87; dir. human svcs. Northumberland County Human Svcs., 1987—; adminstr. Northumberland County Mental Health and Mental Retardation Program, 1984-87; mem. adj. faculty Susquehanna U., Selinsgrove, 1989—; cons. Tng. & Mgmt. Systems, Gibsonia, Pa., 1983-85; mem. Youth Svcs. Tng. Ctr., 1986—. Mem. adv. bd. White Deer Run Treatment Ctr., Allenwood, Pa., 1975-77; advisor Explorer Pres. Assn., Netami dist. Boy Scouts Am., 1980-81, tng. coord. Explorer program, 1982-86, scouting coord. Explorer Post 2312, 1986—; coord. high sch. youth program St. Michael's Ch., Sunbury, 1981-87, pres. parish coun., 1989—; vice chmn. SSS, Sunbury, 1982-89; chmn. Sunbury Govt. Study Commn., 1989—; bd. dirs. Hemlock coun. Girl Scouts U.S.A., 1990—. Named Chief Probation Officer of Yr., Juvenile Ct. Judges Commn., Harrisburg, Pa., 1985; recipient Liberty Bell award Northumberland County Bar Assn., 1986, Meritorious Svc. award Pa. Foster Parents, 1988, affiliate award Pa. Assn. County Commrs., 1990. Mem. Nat. Juvenile Ct. Svcs. Assn. (regional rep. 1989—), Nat. Coun. Juvenile and Family Ct. Judges (awards com.), Nat. Juvenile Detention Assn., Nat. Juvenile Ct. Svcs. Assn., Mental Health and Mental Retardation Program Adminstrs. Assn., Mental Health and Mental Retardation Adminstrs. Assn. Pa. (chmn. 1989—). Democrat. Home: 516 N 7th St Sunbury PA 17801-1718 Office: Northumberland County Human Svcs 370 Market St Sunbury PA 17801-3409

BRESSI-STOPPE, ELIZABETH RITA, educational administrator; b. Bklyn., Aug. 8, 1946; d. Saverio Bressi and Rosina (Teti) Del Vecchio; m. Arthur Joseph Stoppe, Dec. 3, 1983. AS, Gwynedd-Mercy Coll., 1966. Exec. asst. to pres., affirmative action officer Phila. Coll. Pharmacy and Sci., Phila., 1981—; bd. dirs. Prime, Inc., Phila., 1986—, West Phila. Partnership, 1991—. Co-author: Minorities on Campus: Independent Institutions in Partnership, 1991. Mem. Nat. Assn. Women in Edn., Am. Assn. Affirmative Action, Presdl. Assists in Higher Edn. Office: PCPS 600 S 43d St Philadelphia PA 19104

BRESSLER, BERNARD, lawyer; b. N.Y.C., Jan. 2, 1928; s. Morris and Masha (Roitman) B.; m. Teresa Stern, June 25, 1950; children: Lisa, Jeanette. B.A., Rutgers U., 1949; LL.B. summa cum laude, Harvard U., 1952. Bar: N.Y. 1953, N.J. 1977. Atty. firm Greenman, Shea, Sandomire & Zimet, N.Y.C., 1952-60; ptnr. Bressler, Amery & Rothenberg, N.Y.C., 1960—, Bressler, Amery & Ross, Morristown, N.J., 1981—; sec., dir. Plenum Pub. Corp., Tad's Enterprises, Inc., Sonomed Tech., Inc., Gradco Systems Inc.; sec. Conf. Ctr. Devel. Corp. Author: (with others) Tax Annotations Nichols Ency. Forms, 1954-59; Editor: (with B. Meislin) New York Lawyers Manual, 1954, Harvard Law Rev., vol. 65. Campaign dir. Summit (N.J.) United Jewish Appeal, 1957-60; chmn. Summit Democrat Club, 1957; trustee Summit Civic Found., 1958-65; chmn. Summit Area United Negro Coll. Fund, 1979—. Served with USNR, 1945-46. Jewish (v.p. temple). Club: Lotos (N.Y.C.). Home: 101 Kent Place Blvd Summit NJ 07901-4703 Office: 90 Broad St New York NY 10004-2205

BRESSLER, MARTIN SCHMEISSER, marketing educator, consultant; b. Marlboro, Mass., Aug. 24, 1951; s. Abner Wilson Bressler and Barbara Phyllis (Martlin) Howard; m. Linda Ann LaPlante, Aug. 26, 1972; children: Martin S. Jr., Mark E. BA, Worcester State Coll., 1980; MBA, Anna Maria Coll., 1983; advanced cert., Suffolk U., 1985. Div. mgr. Sears, Roebuck & Co., Auburn, Mass., 1971-85; assoc. prof. mktg., dir. Small Bus. Inst., Thomas Coll., Waterville, Maine, 1986—; adj. instr. Quinsigamond Community Coll., Worcester, Mass., 1984-86, Nichols Coll., Dudley, Mass., 1984-86, Bryant Coll., Smithfield, R.I., 1985-86; tng. cons. Mgmt. and Supervisory Tech. Inst., Worcester, 1985-86; mem. adv. bd. Dushkin Pub., Guilford, Conn., 1991; bus. counselor Active Corps Execs., Augusta, Maine, 1988—. Contbr. articles to profl. publs. Active Rep. Town Com., Sidney, Maine, 1990-91. Recipient Small Bus. Inst. Dist. awards 1988, 89, 91; named Maine Small Bus. Advocate of Yr. Gov.'s Adv. Coun. on Small Bus., 1991. Mem. Am. Mktg. Assn., Am. Mgmt. Assn., Assn. Mgmt., New Eng. Bus. and Econs. Assn., Small Bus. Inst. Dirs. Assn. (v.p. region I), Masons. Episcopalian. Home: Quaker Rd Oakland ME 04963 Office: Thomas Coll West River Rd Waterville ME 04901

BREST, JOEL IRA, economist; b. Brockton, Mass., Nov. 9, 1938; s. Irving I. and Phyllis F. (Robbins) B.; m. Wendy W. Friedman, June 12, 1960; children: Diana, Daniel, Richard. AB, Brown U., 1960, PhD, 1965. Rsch. economist Fed. Res. Bank, N.Y.C., 1964-67; econometrician IBM, Armonk, N.Y., 1967-69, mgr. econs., 1967-84, dir. econs., 1984-90, chief economist, dir. econs., 1990—; adj. prof. NYU, N.Y.C., 1966-67; mem. Roundtable, Harvard Indsl. Economists, Cambridge, Mass., 1985—. Author econometric software EPLAN, 1972. Treas. Roxbury Community Assn., Stamford, Conn., 1970-76. Mem. Nat. Assn. Bus. Economists. Office: IBM Old Orchard Rd Armonk NY 10504-1709

BRESTICKER, STANLEY, anesthesiologist, consultant; b. Hoboken, N.J., May 2, 1926; s. Hyman and Fannie (Faber) B.; m. Eileen Georgette Kandracs, Oct. 19, 1958; children: David, Michael, Julianne. BSc, Seton Hall U., 1949; MA, NYU, 1950; B in Med. Sci., U. Geneva, 1952, MD, 1956. Diplomate Am. Bd. Anethesiology. Intern St. Mary Hosp., Hoboken, 1956-57; resident in anesthesiology Bellevue Med. Ctr., N.Y.C., 1958-60; asst. chmn. anesthesiology dept. Middlesex Gen. Hosp., New Brunswick, N.J., 1960-72; chmn. anesthesiology dept. Robert Wood Johnson U. Hosp., New Brunswick, 1972-84; med. dir. Middlesex Same Day Surgery Ctr., East Brunswick, N.J., 1984-90; asst. clin. prof. anesthesiology Robert Wood Johnson Med. Sch., New Brunswick, 1978—; Facility surveyor AAAHC, Skokie, Ill., 1991; anesthesia cons., N.J., 1990—. Recipient lifetime membership Am. Heart Assn., 1979. Mem. Acad. of Medicine of N.J. (pres. 1990—), N.J. Assn. for Ambulatory Surgery Ctrs. (pres. 1990—), N.J. State Soc. of Anesthesiologists (past pres.), N.J. Assn. of Med. Speciality Studies (past pres.), Somerset County Heart Assn. (past pres.), Am. Soc. Anesthesiologists (bd. dirs. 1990—), Soc. Ambulatory Anesthesia (bd. dirs. 1982—). Home: 1465 Easton Ave Somerset NJ 08873-1397 Office: Robert Wood Johnson Univ Hosp 1 Robert Wood Johnson Pl New Brunswick NJ 08901-1928

BRETON, JOSEPH RAYMOND, acoustical engineer; b. Hartford, Conn., Nov. 14, 1931; s. Joseph Armand and Celestine (Poirier) B.; m. Elizabeth Breen, July 1, 1961; children: Thomas, Peter, Andrew, Mary Beth, Ann Elise, Matthew. MS, U. R.I., 1975, PhD, 1977; AM, Harvard U., 1958; MA, Boston Coll., 1957. RC RCA, Burlington, Mass., 1959-61; FSO Dept. of State, Washington, 1961-63; engr. Gen. Dynamics, San Diego, 1963-65, TRW, Redondo Beach, Calif., 1965-67, USN, New London, Conn., 1967-82, Gen. Instrument Corp., Westwood, Mass., 1982-88; pres. B.R. Enterprises, Norwood, Conn., 1988—. Patentee in field. Bd. trustees, v.p. Medfield (Mass.) State Hosp., 1989, bd. dirs. Mass. Alliance for Mentally Ill, Boston, 1990. Mem. IEEE (sr.). Roman Catholic. Office: BR Enterprises PO Box 71 Norwood MA 02062-0071

BRETSCHNEIDER, BARRY EASTBURN, lawyer; b. Phila., Sept. 17, 1947; s. Gordon Henry Bromley and Mary Jane (Hughes) B.; m. Kathryn Ann King, June 12, 1971 (div. Dec. 1977); m. Keiko Kochiyama, Feb. 1, 1981; children: Carol Emi, Karen Misa. AB, Princeton (N.J.) U., 1968; JD, U. Iowa, 1971; LLM, George Washington U., 1974. Bar: Iowa 1971, D.C. 1975, Tex. 1976. Atty., advisor Naval Air Systems Command, Washington, 1971-73; trial counsel Office Gen. Counsel U.S. Dept. of Navy, Washington, 1973-74; tech. advisor U.S. Ct. Customs & Patent Appeals, Washington, 1974-76; assoc. Arnold, White & Durkee, Houston, 1976-78, Keil & Witherspoon, Washington, 1978-80; mem. Wegner & Bretschneider, P.C., Washington, 1980-90; ptnr. Fish & Richardson, 1990—. Mem. ABA, Am. Intellectual Property Law Assn. Home: 5822 Bent Twig Rd Mc Lean VA 22101-1808 Office: Fish & Richardson 601 13th St NW Washington DC 20005-3807

BRETZFELDER, ROBERT BENJAMIN, photographer, economist; b. New Haven, Apr. 29, 1929; s. Karl Benjamin and Amelia (Kafka) B.; m. Deborah May Hirsh, Dec. 24, 1955; children: Karl, Marc. BA, Goddard Coll., 1952; MS, Syracuse (N.Y.) U., 1955; postgrad., New Sch. for Social Rsch., 1954-55. Economist Libr. of Congress, Washington, 1955-56, Office of Bus. Econs., Washington, 1960-63, U.S. Dept. of Labor, Washington, 1964-68, Fed. Res. Bd., Washington, 1968-70, Bur. Econ. Analysis, Washington, 1970-86; prin. D&R Bretzfelder, Washington, 1988—. Contbr. numerous articles to profl. jours. Mem. Art Club of Davis (W.Va. chpt.). Home: 2748 Woodley Pl NW Washington DC 20008-1517

BREUER, HANS-PETER, English and comparative literature educator; b. Cologne, Germany, Jan. 5, 1939; naturalized U.S. citizen, 1957; s. Peter Breuer and Theresia (Siemes) Callicott; m. Angela Mary Lett, Dec. 19, 1970; children: Nicola Theresa Amaris, Alexander Michael Johannes. BA cum laude, Ind. U., 1961; MA, Stanford U., 1966, PhD, 1971. Teaching asst. Stanford (Calif.) U., 1965-67; lectr. Notre Dame Coll., Belmont, Calif., 1968; asst. prof. U. Calif., Riverside, 1968-71; asst. prof. English and comparative lit. U. Del., Newark, 1971-77, assoc. prof., 1977-87, prof., 1987—. Violinist in orchs. and ensembles, 1956—. Lectr. libr. program Del. Humanities Forum, Newark, 1988—. With U.S. Army, 1961-63. Faculty grantee U. Del., 1972, 76, 80, 82, 86, grantee NEH, 1975. Mem. MLA, Am. Comparative Lit. Assn., Soc. for Sci. and Lit., Am. Fedn. Musicians, Nat. Assn. Scholars, Phi Beta Kappa. Roman Catholic. Office: U Del English Dept Newark DE 19716

BREVE, FRANKLIN STEPHEN, pharmacist; b. Phila., Jan. 25, 1955; s. Albert Francis and Lillian Marie (Di Biase) B.; m. Linda Ruth Maedel, Mar. 16, 1985; children: Christina Lynn, Rebecca Anne, Allison Marie. BA in Psychology, Temple U., 1977, BS in Pharmacy, 1981. Registered Pharmacist. Oncology pharmacist Thomas Jefferson U., Phila., 1981-86, nuclear pharmacist, 1986-87; oncology pharmacist Rancocas Valley Hosp., Willingboro, N.J., 1987-88; night phramacy coord. West Jersey Hosp., Camden, N.J., 1988—; cons. in field; pres. Pharma Tech, Inc., Laurel Springs, N.J., 1992—; instr. in field. Mem. Am. Soc. Hosp. Pharmacists, Pa. Soc. Hosp. Pharmacists, N.J. Soc. Hosp. Pharmacists, N.Y. Acad. Scis., Am. Soc. Cons. Pharmacists, N.J. Pharm. Assn. Republican. Roman Catholic. Home: 45 Lincoln Dr Laurel Springs NJ 08021-2850 Office: West Jersey Health System Mt Ephriam and Atlantic Aves Camden NJ 08104

BREW, GEORGE WILLIAM, real estate broker and appraiser; b. Washington, May 13, 1947; s. Bernard M. and Margaret (Miceli) B.; m. Shelesa L. Allison, Apr. 4, 1970; children: M'lesa, George. BS, U. Md., 1986. Cert. real estate appraiser. Real estate agt. Wozin Realty, Ashton, Md., 1983-85, Cosmopolitan Realty, Rockville, Md., 1985-86; assoc. real estate broker Robert H. Kent Co., Rockville, 1986-89; real estate broker and appraiser George W. Brew, Rockville, 1989—; cons., pres. ALGEO, Rockville, 1986—. Trustee Woods Acad., Bethesda, Md., 1984-87; mem. alumni rels. com. U. Md. Univ. Coll. Mem. Nat. Assn. Real Estate Appraisers. Republican. Roman Catholic.

BREWER, BOYD CLARENCE, JR., program director; b. Johnstown, Pa., Nov. 11, 1936; s. Boyd Clarence and Katherine (Langer) B.; m. Sharon Louise Callihan, June 6, 1961; children: David Boyd, Nancy Christine, Shauna Colleen. BS in Edn., Penn State U., 1960, MEd in Counseling, 1964. Tchr., counselor Williamsburg (Pa.) Area Sch. Dist., 1960-66; counselor adminstr. Ridgway (Pa.) Area Sch. Dist., 1966-72; counselor Butler (Pa.) County Community Coll., 1972-91, dir. enrollment mgmt., 1991—. Bd. dirs. South Butler County Sch. Dist., Saxonburg, Pa., 1979-87, pres., 1983-87; bd. dirs. Butler Area Vocat. Tech. Sch., 1980-87, treas., 1984-87. 1st lt. USAR, 1960-68. Recipient Silver Beaver award Boy Scouts of Am., 1985, Pres.'s award Lions Club, 1975. Mem. ACA, Nat. Coun. on Student Devel., Pa. Assn. Student Fin. Aid Adminstrs. Republican. Methodist. Office: Butler Community Coll College Dr/Oak Hills Box 1203 Butler PA 16003-1203

BREWER, DAVID MADISON, lawyer; b. Bordeaux, Gironde, France, July 8, 1953; s. Herbert L. and Paulyne B. (Ver Benec) B.; m. Andrea M. Bordiga, May 20, 1978; children: James David Madison, Caroline Elizabeth, Geoffrey Andrew. AB summa cum laude, Yale U., 1975, JD, 1978. Bar: N.Y. 1979. Assoc. atty. Cravath Swaine & Moore, N.Y.C., 1978-84; assoc. gen. tax counsel Union Pacific Corp., N.Y.C. and Bethlehem, Pa., 1984-89; pres. Madison Co., Inc., N.Y.C., 1990—. Editor Yale Law Jour., 1977-78. Policy asst. Office of the Campaign Mgr., Bush-Quayle campaign, 1988; bd. dirs. Yale U. Law Sch. Fund, 1989—, Yale Alumni Fund, 1989—; spl. gifts chmn. Yale U. Class of 1975 and Law Sch. Class of 1978, 1985—; nat. vice chmn. Smithsonian Friends of First Ladies, 1989-92. Mem. N.Y. Bar Assn., Phi Beta Kappa. Republican. Episcopalian. Clubs: Yale (N.Y.C.); Mory's (New Haven, Conn.). Office: 666 5th Ave Ste 3700 New York NY 10103-0001

BREWER, JOHN NOLAN, III, secondary educator, real estate investor; b. Memphis, Apr. 7, 1954; s. John N. Jr. and Betty (Cockrill) B.; m. Jeannine Rochelle Green, Sept. 24, 1987. BS in Bus. and Fin., Mt. St. Marys Coll., 1977; MS in Adminstrn. and Mgmt., Hood Coll., 1984. Mktg., retailing, automotive tchr. Bethesda (Md.)-Chevy Chase High Sch., 1979—. Treas. Frederick (Md.) Heights Community Assn., 1988. Home: PO Box 451 Clear Spring MD 21722 Office: Bethesda-Chevy Chase High Sch 4301 East-West Hwy Bethesda MD 20814

BREWER, LEROY EARL, physicist; b. Hagerstown, Md., June 1, 1936; s. LeRoy Earl and Odessa Marie (Green) B.; m. Sue Strother Yancey, Dec. 29, 1956; children: Jennifer Olivia. BS, U. Fla., 1960; MS, U. Tenn., 1965; PhD, U. Brussels, 1975. Research physicist ARO, Inc., Tullahoma, Tenn., 1960-66; staff physicist GE, Valley Forge, Pa., 1966-69; sr. physicist ARO, Inc., Tullahoma, 1969-81; mgr., exec. scientist Calspan Corp., Tullahoma, 1981-85; sr. infrared phenomenologist GE, Valley Forge, 1985—; adj. faculty mem. Motlow Community Coll., Tullahoma, 1976-80. Contbr. articles to profl. jours. Mem. Charlestown Civic Assn., Chester County, Pa., 1986—. Fellow AIAA (assoc.), mem. Am. Physical Soc., Sigma Pi Sigma, Sigma Xi. Republican. Methodist. Home: 317D Howell Rd Malvern PA 19355-9660 Office: GE PO Box 8555 Philadelphia PA 19101-8555

BREWER, TIMOTHY FRANCIS, III, cardiologist; b. Hartford, Conn., Oct. 30, 1931; s. Timothy F. Jr. and Catherine Marie (Sullivan) B.; m. Norma Rae Flicker, June 14, 1954 (div. 1980); children: Raymond, Donna, Timothy, Kevin, William; m. Barbara Grace Bagdasarian, May 28, 1983. BA, Yale Coll., 1953; MD, N.Y. Med. Coll., 1957. Diplomate Am. Bd. Internal Medicine Cardiovascular Diseases. Intern St. Francis Hosp., Hartford, 1957-58; resident in internal medicine VA Ctr., L.A., 1958-60; spl. fellow in cardiovascular diseases Cleve. (Ohio) Clinic, 1960-62; pvt. practice St. Francis Hosp., Hartford, 1962-64; assoc. dir. clin. rsch. Pfizer Inc., Groton, Conn., 1964-71; dir. Clin. Pharmacology Miles Lab., West Haven, Conn., 1971-74; pvt. practice Middlesex Hosp., Middletown, Conn., 1974—; pres. med. staff Middlesex Hosp., Middlesex, 1981-83, chief, sec. cardiology, 1988—. Fellow ACP, Am. Coll. Cardiologists, Am. Coll. Chest Physicians, Coun. of Clin. Cardiology; mem. AMA (pres. South Cen. Conn. chpt. 1982, bd. dirs. 1980), Am. Heart Assn. (Conn. affiliate). Office: Middlesex Cardiology Assocs 520 Saybrook Rd Middletown CT 06457

BREWSTER-WALKER, SANDRA JOANN, publishing executive, genealogist, historian, consultant; b. Copiaque, N.Y., June 16, 1942; d. Willis Hodges and F. Wilda (Scurlock) Brewster; m. Stuart M. Walker (div. 1984); children: Jeffrey, Carlton, Cassandra. Cert., Island Drafting Sch., 1965; BA, Dowling Coll., 1972; MA, SUNY, New Paltz, 1978. Acting asst. dir. Urban Ctr., Vassar Coll., Poughkeepsie, N.Y., 1972-74; tchr. Middletown Jr. High Sch., N.Y., 1974-78; elec. mfg. engr. Perkin-Elmer Corp., Norwalk, Conn., 1978-84; pub., editor Ram's Horn Pub. Co., Stamford, Conn., 1983-84; software mgr. Pergamon Press, Inc., Elmsford, N.Y., 1985-86; pres., owner The Brewster Group, Inc., Stamford, 1986—. Pub., editor Conneticut Update, 1984; editor: Augustus M. Hodges Project, 1978-86, Fairfield County Black Biograph. Index Project, 1980—; contbr. to Westchester Women mag., 1985. Mem. Town of Walkill Bicentennial Com., 1976, Bicentennial Com., Middletown Pub. Schs., 1976; mem. Circleville Pub. Sch. PTA, 1975-77, v.p., 1977-78; instr. genealogy Greater Orange YMCA, Middletown, N.Y., 1975, 77, mem. planning bd., 1976; vice chmn. to corp. campaign advisor United Negro Coll. Fund, Lower Fairfield, Conn., 1980-81; mem. John Anderson for Pres. Com., 1980; exec. dir. Conn. Legis. Black Caucus, Hartford, 1981-82; aide to State Senator J.C. Daniels, 1981-82; founder, bd. dir. Bridgeport Black History Project, 1982-83; adv. com. Conn. Democrats, 1984; inaugural com. Mayor Serrani, Stamford, 1984-85; coord. Lower Fairfield County Mondale/Ferraro Campaign, 1984; state coord. Conn. Com. to Elect Jesse Jackson Pres., 1984; Stamford coord., 1988—; mem. Conn. chpt. Coalition of 100 Black Women, 1980-81, Nat. Project Vote, 1984, adv. com. black women's exhibit L.I. and Bklyn. Hist. Soc.; vol. Alberta Jagoes for Mayor campaign, Milford, Conn., 1982, Christine M. Niedermeier for Congress Com., 1984; mem. steering com. Margaret Morton for Congress, 1987; candidate state rep. 145th dist., 1988. Named Woman of Month, Conn. Women's Mag., 1983, Working Woman of Month, Essence mag., 1983. Mem. NAFE, NOW, Coalition of 100 Black Women (Lower Fairfield chpt. 1986, 89-90), Nat. Abortion Rights Action League, Rainbow Coalition (computer cons.), National Club. Home and Office: 1450 Washington Blvd # 902 Stamford CT 06902-2451

BREZIANU, ANDREI PETRE, author; b. Bucharest, Romania, Nov. 14, 1934; came to U.S., 1985; s. Barbu and Adina (Assan) B.; m. Alexandra Târziu, June 11, 1973. BD, R.C. Theol. Inst., Iasi, Romania, 1959; MA, U. Bucharest, 1969, PhD, 1981; MA, U. Cambridge, England, 1985. English editor Secolul 20 World Lit. Jour., Bucharest, 1970-85; rsch. assoc. Cath. U. Am., Washington; editor Voice of Am., Washington, 1986-91; chief editor Romanian Svc., Washington, 1988-91; chief Romanian svc. Voice of Am., Washington, 1991—; lectr. in lit. U. Bucharest, 1970-78, Cath. U. Am., 1990-91; cons. Ctr. for Applied Linguistics, Washington, 1985-88. Author: Odysseus and the Atlantic, 1977 (Romanian Writers Union award 1978), Translations, 1982, The Roman's Castle, 1981, Down to the Shore, 1979. Fellow Salzburg Seminar in Am. Studies, 1973, Commoner Churchill Coll., Cambridge, 1985; Great Britain/East Europe Ctr. grantee, London, 1978. Mem. Romanian Writers Union. Roman Catholic. Home: Apt 319 700 7th St SW Washington DC 20024-2479 Office: Voice of Am 330 Independence Ave SE Washington DC 20547-0001

BRIAN, DOUGLAS RICHARD, investment banker; b. Englewood, N.J., Oct. 4, 1945; s. Harold and Ruth (Richardson) B.; m. Frances Fitzgerald; children: Georgia, Wendy. BBA, Northeastern U., Boston, 1971; MBA, Babson Coll., Wellsely, Mass., 1973. Investment officer John Hancock Life, Boston, 1973-80; treas. John Hancock Leasing, Boston, 1980-83, dir. syndication, 1983-85; v.p. mktg. Ind. Fin., Waltham, Mass., 1985-87; v.p. mktg., chief fin. officer Nord Fin., Waltham, Mass., 1987-91; prnr. Aberlyn Capital Mgmt. Co. Inc., Waltham, 1991—. Home: 21 E Main St Hopkinton MA 01748-1236 Office: Aberlyn Capital Mgmt Co Inc Ste 1100 1000 Winter St Waltham MA 02154

BRICKACH, ALICE ALEXANDRA, consultant, retired counselor; b. Pawtucket, R.I., Sept. 1, 1924; d. Alexander and Dominika (Wasilewich) B. Diploma, Bryant Coll., 1943; BSBA, U. R.I., 1973; diploma, Carl Jung Inst., Zurich, Switzerland, 1975; MA in Edn., U. R.I., 1977; diploma, Pontifical U., Salamanca, Spain, 1983. Cert. profl. sec., 1965, counselor of alcohol troubled people and other drug users, 1985, cert. TV prodn. Colony Communications, 1991. Exec. sec. Cumberland Engring. Co., Inc., South Attleboro, Mass., 1946-69; adminstrv. sec. Brown U., Providence, 1970-73; v.p. Robert Jackson & Co., Inc., Boston, 1973-75; dept. sec. dept. pediatrics Women and Infant's Hosp., Providence, 1975-77; clk./typist U.S. Property and Fiscal Office, Providence, 1985-86. Author: Trip to Rome, 1981; editor, typist The Providence Visitor, 1980—; guest columnist The Sun Chronilcle, Attleboro, Mass., 1985—. Citizens Adv. Bd. mem. R.I. Solid Waste Mgmt. Corp., Providence, 1988—; charter mem. Citizens Against Govt. Waste; mem. Washington Nat. Cathedral; clk. Bd. Canvassers, Pawtucket, 1985—.

Recipient Gold Medal award Bryant Coll., 1943, Sec. of Week award Nat. Secs. Assn., 1959, Pawtucket Blackstone Valley C. of C., 1959, Toys for Tots award USMCR, 1968, Jerusalem Pilgrim Attestation award Terry Kollek, Mayor of Jerusalem, 1969, Transworld Radio award, 1980. Mem. N.Y. Acad. Scis., Bibl. Archaeology Soc., Ecumenical Assn. John XXIII (sec. U.S. chpt. 1977—), U. R.I. Alumni Assn., Bryant Coll. Alumni Assn. Episcopalian. Home: 265 Evergreen St # 9 Pawtucket RI 02861-2834

BRICKHOUSE, TODD CRAIG, architectural designer; b. Queens, N.Y., Dec. 30, 1952; s. Vinston Vernon and Leone (Samuels) B.; m. Frances Celina D'Angelo, Mar. 18, 1979; 1 child, Mackenzie Nova. Student, Hofstra U., 1971-72; cert. dental technician, N.Y. Sch. Mech. Dentist, 1975. Prosthetic techician Dorsch Prosthetics, N.Y.C., 1975-79; prosthetic technician Sunrise Surg. and Orthopedics, Smithtown, N.Y., 1979-82; mktg. sales rep. Hygeia Med. Supply Co., Carle Place, N.Y., 1982—; v.p. Hygeia Design Assocs., Carle Place, 1983—, Creative Products, Inc., Carle Place, 1984—; pres. Brickhouse Design Group, Ltd., Massapequa Park, N.Y., 1990—; cons. on vocat. edn. svcs. for indivudual disabled Office Vocat. Rehab., Nassau and N.Y.c., 1983—; cons. Nassau County (N.Y.) Recreational Parks, 1984—, Crime Victims Bd., N.Y.C., 1986—. Utility patentee in field. Vol. Internat. Games for the Disabled, Eisenhower Park, N.Y., 1984, Mitchell Field, N.Y., 1991; organizer tech. showcase Nassau County Recreation Pks., Hofstra U., 1990, 91. Recipient award Internat. Games for the Disabled, 1984; recipient citation County Exec., Nassau County, N.Y., 1990. Mem. AIAA, Space Studies Inst., Rehab. Engrs. Soc. N.Am. (cert. rehab. engr., cons. 1986—), Profl. Rehab. Assn., Brooks Archery Range. Home and Office: 8 Joan Ln Massapequa Park NY 11762-1417 Office: Hygeia Design Assocs 555 Westbury Ave Carle Place NY 11514-1757

BRIDE, JOHN WILLIAM, communications executive, entrepreneur; b. Boston, Sept. 12, 1937; s. William T. and Elsie Francis (Duffy) B.; m. Marjorie McHenry, May 13, 1966 (div. 1984); children: John Hambleton, Christopher McHenry; m. Mary Eileen Kiniry, Feb. 15, 1985. BA in Econs., Norwich U., 1960; LLB, U. Maine, 1964; Owner/Pres. Mgmt. degree, Harvard Bus. Sch., 1980. Staff atty. FCC, Washington, 1964-66; account exec. Sta. KDKA-TV, Pitts., 1966-70; pres. Bride Broadcasting, Inc., Portland, Maine, 1970-86, Chandler Broadcasting, Inc., Portland, Maine, 1970-86, Greater Portland Radio, Inc., Portland, Maine, 1972-86, B-T Satellite, Portland, Maine, 1980—, Triangle Properties, Portland, Maine, 1980-85, Bride Communications, Inc., Portland, Maine, 1980—, Portland Broadcast, Inc., Portland, Maine, 1987—; trustee John W. Duffy Trusts, Boston, 1978—; mem. com. fgn. rels., Portland, 1976—; mem. adv. com. Back Cove Improvement Project, Portland, 1984—; mem. adv. bd. Lifeline U. So. Maine, Portland, 1983—; chair communications adv. bd. Norwich U., 1988—; pres. Bride Charitable Found., Portland, 1978—; instr. Jr. Achievement, Portland, 1980; treas., bd. dirs. ABC Talkradio Affiliates, N.Y.C., 1983—. Served with U.S. Army, 1960-61. Mem. Maine Bar Assn. Harvard Bus. Club (v.p. 1984—), Pitts. Golf Club. Democrat. Episcopalian. Home: 83 West St Portland ME 04102-3415 Office: Bride Communications Inc 2320 Congress St Portland ME 04102-1908

BRIDE, THOMAS PATRICK, physician, anesthesiologist, pediatrician; b. Newark, Aug. 6, 1948; s. James Denis and Mary Katherine (McDade) B.; m. Linda Ann Aungst, June 8, 1974; children: Juleen, Patricia. BA, Franklin and Marshall Coll., 1970; DO, Phila. Coll. Osteo. Medicine, 1974. Diplomate Am. Bd. Pediatrics, Am. Bd. Anesthesiology. Resident in pediatrics Polyclinic Med. Ctr., Harrisburg, Pa., 1974-77; attending pediatrician Ephrata (Pa.) Community Hosp., 1977-78, Meml. Hosp., York, Pa., 1978-83; resident in anesthesiology U. Md., Balt., 1983-85; attending anesthesiologist Community Gen. Hosp. and Day Surgery Ctr., Reading, Pa., 1985-86, York Hosp. and Apple Hill Surgicenter, 1986—; chief pediatric anesthesiology York Hosp., 1988—; clin. asst. prof. pediatrics Phila. Coll. Osteo. Medicine, 1978-83; clin. adj. prof. pediatrics Coll. Osteo. Medicine and Surgery, Des Moines, 1978-83. Bd. dirs. Children's Home of York, 1980-84, South Ctrl. Pa. Cystic Fibrosis Found., Harrisburg, 1981-84. Fellow Am. Acad. Pediatrics; mem. AMA, Am. Soc. Anesthesiologists, Pa. Med. Soc., York County Med. Soc. (pres. 1982, v.p. 1983), Internat. Anesthesia Rsch. Soc., Soc. Pediatric Anesthesia. Home: 329 Kirkham Dr York PA 17402 Office: Anesthesia Assoc York Pa Inc 110 Pine Grove Commons York PA 17403

BRIDEAU, LEO PAUL, hospital administrator; b. Leominster, Mass., Mar. 1, 1947; s. Alfred Joseph and Marie Yvonne (Poulin) B.; m. Kathleen Margaret Quinlan, Oct. 5, 1968; children: Alexander, Elizabeth, Neil, Katherine, William. BS, Georgetown U., 1968; MHA, Med. Coll. of Va., 1980. Counselor vets. benefits VA, Togus, Maine, 1971-73; asst. dist. coord. VA, Richmond, Va., 1975-80; mgmt. analyst VA Med. Ctr., Togus, 1973-75; dep. dir. patient care services Strong Meml. Hosp., Rochester, N.Y., 1980-84; acting exec. dir. Strong Meml. Hosp., Rochester, 1984, dir. hosp. ops., 1984-89, exec. dir., 1990—; bd. dirs. Premier Hosps. Alliance, Inc.; preceptor dept. health svcs. Va. Commonwealth U., Richmond, 1985—; preceptor Washington U. Sch. Medicine, St. Louis; instr. health svcs. U. Rochester, 1985—. Author: chpt. Cost Containment in a University Hosp., 1987. Chmn. adv. bd. Lifeline, Rochester, 1982-85; bd. dirs. Monroe County Medicap Inc., Rochester, 1984-87, Finger Lakes Health Systems Agy., Rochester, 1985-92; bd. dirs. Rochester Regional Joint Ventures Corp., 1985—, chmn., 1987-89, bd. dirs. Rochester Area Health Maintenance Orgn., Inc., 1985-88. Mem. Am. Coll. Healthcare Execs., Am. Hosp. Assn., Hosp. Assn. N.Y. State (chair govt. rels. com. 1985-89), trustee 1989—, chair strategic planning com. 1991—), Rochester Regional Hosp. Assn. (bd. dirs. 1985—, chmn. 1987-89, Assn. Univ. Programs in Health Adminstrn., Pi Sigma Alpha. Office: Strong Meml Hosp 601 Elmwood Ave # 612 Rochester NY 14642-9999

BRIDGE, CARL JAMES, psychiatrist; b. South Milwaukee, Wis., Feb. 14, 1922; s. Arthur and Anne Susan (Kuhls) B.; m. Ann Margaret Kilbourn, Feb. 17, 1951; children: Barbara Bridge Bassingthwaite, Kathryn Jane Bridge DeVine, Mary Elizabeth Bridge Lavine, John Kilbourn, Robert James. BS, U. Wis., 1947, MD, 1950. Diplomate Am. Bd. Psychiatry and Neurology. Intern Burbank Hosp., Fitchburg, Mass., 1951-52; pvt. practice gen. medicine Beresford, S.D., 1951-55; fellow in anatomy U. S.D., Vermillion, 1954-55; rsch. fellow Harvard U. Med. Sch. and Mass. Gen. Hosp., Boston, 1956-57; resident in gen. psychiatry Worcester (Mass.) State Hosp., 1960-63; psychiatrist and neurologist Keene (N.H.) Clin., 1963-87; clin. dir. Gardner (Mass.) State Hosp., 1963-64; forensic psychiatrist Probate Ct., Concord, N.H., 1982—. Author: Alcoholism and Driving, 1973; contbr. articles profl. jours. Capt. U.S. Army, 1958-59. Mem. Am. Psychiat. Assn., N.H. Psychiat. Soc., Monadnock Rails, New England Hist. Genealogic Soc., Masons. Episcopalian. Home and Office: 620 West St Keene NH 03431-2142

BRIDGES, DAVID M., manufacturing executive; b. Lima, Ohio, June 29, 1954. BS, Bowling Green State U., 1976. Cert. purchasing mgr. Sr. buyer Raytheon Co., Bedford, Mass., 1977-81; purchasing supr. Adage, Inc., Billerica, Mass., 1981-86; materials mgr. Azonix Corp., Burlington, Mass., 1986-87, dir. of mfg., 1987—. mem. budget com. Town of Plaistow, N.H., 1982-87. Mem. Purchasing Mgmt. Assn. of Boston. Home: 4 Laperle Ave Plaistow NH 03865-3126 Office: Azonix Corp 25 Adams St Burlington MA 01803-4915

BRIDGES, JEFFREY OTIS, flooring company executive; b. Hartford, Conn., Mar. 31, 1958; s. Edward Francis and Harriet Ellen (Carlton) B.; m. Eileen Kathy Zielinski, June 4, 1988. AB in Econs., Bowdoin Coll., 1980; MBA, Dartmouth Coll., 1982. Participant leadership devel. program Congoleum Corp., Portsmouth, N.H., 1982; mgr. new products Congoleum Corp., Kearny, N.J., 1982-83, mgr. bus. devel., 1983-85, dir. planning, 1986-89; gen. mgr. Congoleum Corp., Lawrenceville, N.J., 1989, asst. to chief exec. officer, 1989-90; corp. dir. quality Congoleum Corp., Trenton, N.J., 1990—; co-chmn. Customer Driven Quality Conf., Internat. Quality and Productivity Ctr., Chgo., 1991. Contbr. articles to mags. Co-chmn. United Way, Trenton, 1990. Tuck scholar Dartmouth Coll., 1981. Mem. Am. Mgmt. Assn., Am. Soc. for Quality Control, Phi Beta Kappa. Office: Congoleum Corp 861 Sloan Ave Trenton NJ 08619-2198

BRIDGES, JULIAN CURTIS, sociologist educator, department head; b. Miami, Apr. 3, 1931; s. Clyde Clifton and Bessie Myrtle (Williams) B.; m. Charlotte Annelle Martin, Aug. 24, 1954; children: Rebecca Ann, Deborah Lea Gil, Esther Marelyn Shedd. AB, U. Fla., 1952; BD, ThD, Southwestern Bapt. Theol. Sem., Ft. Worth, 1956, 61; MA, U. Fla., 1968, PhD, 1973. Cert. family life educator, marriage and family therapist. Pastor So. Bapt. Conv., Dallas, Rhome, Tex., 1953-59; rep. in Mexico Fgn. Mission Bd., Mexico City, 1959-73; prof., dept. head sociology Hardin-Simmons U., Abilene, Tex., 1973—; cons. William Jewel Coll., Liberty, Mo., 1984; prof. sociology and ethics Bapt. Theol. Sem., Madrid, Spain, 1981, Arusha, Tanzania, 1987, Hong Kong Bapt. Coll., 1991. Editor, sr. author: Sociology: A Pragmatic Approach, 1986; author: Expansion Evangelica en Mexico, 1973, Into Aztec Land, 1968; contbr. articles to profl. jours. and encys. Mem. city coun. City of Abilene, 1982-85, mayor pro-tempore, 1984-85, human rels. com., 1988—; chair election com. Atty. Gen., State of Tex., Taylor County, 1984; pres. bd. Harmony Family Svcs., Abilene, 1992—; v.p., bd. dirs. Mental health Mental Retardation, Abilene, 1985-88. Recipient Faculty Rsch. award Hardin-Simmons U., 1985, Lily Found. Teaching fellow, Southwestern Bapt. Theol. Sem., Ft. Worth, 1957-58; named Nat. Def. Edn. Act Title VI fellow U. Fla., 1969-70. Mem. Tex. Coun. on Family Rels. (pres. 1983-84), Southwestern Sociol. Assn. (clin.), Am. Assn. Marriage & Family Therapists. Baptist. Home: 1526 N Pioneer Dr Abilene TX 79603 Office: Box 1302 HSU Sta Abilene TX 79698

BRIDGES, LEON, architect; b. Los Angeles, Aug. 18, 1932; s. James A. Bridges and Agnes (Johnson) Goodall; m. Eloise Avonne Jones, Sept. 21, 1960; children: Venessa, Elise, Leon Jr., Elliott. Student, East Los Angeles Coll., 1950, Los Angeles City Coll., 1951; BArch, U. Wash., 1959, postgrad. urban design, 1959; MBA, Loyola U., Balt., 1984. Registered architect, Wash., Md., Fla., D.C., Mass., Pa., Va., N.J. Architect various firms, Seattle, 1957-63; pvt. practice architecture Seattle, 1963-65; architect, planner Bridges/Burke, Seattle, 1966-72, Balt., 1970-72; prin. The Leon Bridges Co., Balt., 1972-87, Sheladia/Bridges, Balt., 1987-89; pres. TLBC Inc., Balt., 1989—; vis. prof. So. U., Baton Rouge, 1970, Hampton Inst., Va., 1971, 73, 75, Prairie View A&M U., Tex., 1972; assoc. prof. Morgan State U., Balt., 1985—; panelist Mental Health Ctr. NIMH, NIH, 1969-70; bd. advisors Sch. Architecture U. of Tenn., Knoxville, 1981—. Prin. works include Adminstrn. Bldg. Coppin State Coll. (award Am. Assn. Sch. Adminstrs.), Balt. Pa. Station Renovation/Restoration (awards Washington AIA chpt., 1982, Nat. Orgn. Minority Architects 1983, Balt. chpt. AIA, 1985, others), Lexington Market Subway Sta. (award Nat. Orgn. Minority Architects 1985), Ft. McHenry Tunnel East Ventilation Bldg. and Ops. Control Bldg. (Grand Conceptor award Am. Cons. Engrs. 1986). Participant Black Exec. Exchange Program, 1970-73, Wash. State Council Higher Edn., 1970-72, Tuskegee Inst. Community Architecture Design Charette, Ala., 1971; mem. Ctr. for Met. Planning and Research Johns Hopkins U., 1972—, exec. com., 1974-83; mem. City of Balt. Archl. and Engring. Awards Commn., 1978-88, Md. State Arts Coun., 1980-83, White House Conf. Small Bus., 1980, del. Md.; mem. exec. com. Planned Parenthood/World Population, nat. bd. dirs., 1968-74; mem. commn. on architecture Episcopal Diocese Md., 1985-88; bd. dirs. Planned Parenthood Md., 1969-74; v.p. Met. YMCA, Balt., 1972-75, 1st v.p., 79-80; pres. African-Am. Devel. Corp., 1979-80; chmn. urban devel. commn. Morgan State U., 1981-84; bd. trustees Community Chest Balt., 1972-75; bd. govs. Luth. Hosp., 1980—; bd. visitors Md. Sch. for Deaf, 1981-85; bd. dirs. Roland Park Pl., 1981-83, Md. Minority Contractors Assn., Inc., 1981-84; bd. mem. NAACP Act So Bad, 1982—, chair, 1990—. Recipient Recognition award King County Planning Commn., 1966-69, Victor Frenkil Achievement award Balt. Jaycees, 1973, Nat. Endowment for Arts award, 1975, Neighborhood Design Ctr. awards, 1976, Black Pages award, 1981, Founder's award Conf. Minority Transp., 1984; named Man of Yr., Nat. Assn. Negro Bus. and Profl. Women's Clubs, Inc., 1978. Fellow AIA (nat. task force on profl. responsibility 1969-71, nat. scholarship com., Ford scholarship program com. 1970-76, chmn. 1977-79, fed. agencies com. 1974-76, jury on inst. honors 1974, chmn. commn. on community services 1976, bd. dirs. 1976, 84-86, v.p. Balt. chpt. 1979-80, dir. middle atlantic region 1984-86, design commn. 1984, commr. housing com. 1984, nat. bd. dirs. found. 1985-86, assoc. treas. 1985-86, nat. v.p. 1987, Seattle chpt. Home of Yr. award 1973, Nat. Citation for Design Excellence, 1971, Outstanding Merit award 1981, Design Excellence award 1985, outstanding civil engineering, 1988); mem. Am. Soc. Civil Engrs. (S.W. corridor project-Green Street Station, Masonry Inst. Md. award of Excellence 1988), Nat. Orgn. Minority Architects (bd. dirs. 1974-76, sec. 1978, v.p., pres. 1979-80, historian-parliamentarian 1984, Design Excellence award 1983, 85), Md. State Soc. Architects (bd. dirs. 1975), Nat. Urban League, Nat. Council Architecture Rev. Bds. (cert.). Office: TLBC Inc 805 E Fayette St Baltimore MD 21202-4726

BRIEF, HENRY, association executive; b. Bklyn., Feb. 18, 1924; s. Jacob and Clara (Tennenbaum) B.; m. Rosalie Menchin, Apr. 16, 1950; children: Andrew S., Judith M. BBA, CCNY, 1948. Features writer Overseas News Agy., N.Y., 1948-50; news editor, announcer Sta. WEOK, Poughkeepsie, N.Y., 1950-52; editor radio-TV dept. Home Furnishings Daily, N.Y., 1952-60; exec. dir. Rec. Industry Assn. Am., N.Y.C., 1960-79; exec. v.p. ITA, N.Y.C., 1979—. Staff sgt. USAF, 1943-45, ETO. Office: ITA 505 8th Ave Fl 12A New York NY 10018-6505

BRIEGS, DAVID MICHAEL, financial consultant; b. Perth Amboy, N.J., Mar. 29, 1965; s. Fred Arthur and Patricia Jean (Rechnitzer) B. BS in Bus. Econs., Rutgers U., 1989. Cert. fin. mgr. Dist. mgr. N.B.I. Food Svcs., Inc., Plainfield, N.J., 1986-88; account exec. Internat. Trading Group, Somerset, N.J., 1988-89; fin. cons. Merrill Lynch, Iselin, N.J., 1989—. Author newsletter Dave's Money Talk, 1991-92. Mem. U.S. Parachute Assn. Presbyterian. Office: Merrill Lynch 120 Wood Ave S Iselin NJ 08830

BRIENZA, ANTHONY JOHN, pharmaceutical specialist, researcher; b. Bklyn., Mar. 10, 1945; s. Pasquale Joseph and Filomenia Elvera (DeRosa) B.; m. Lillian Victoria Ciago, Apr. 5, 1970; children: Christopher J., Victor J. BS, Fordham U., 1966; MS, NYU, 1968; MPA, SUNY, Albany, 1969. Cert. pub. adminstr., cert. med. rep.; lic. N.Y.C. Bd. Edn.-high sch. Senate staff adminstr. N.Y. State Legis., Albany, 1967-69, cons., Senate com. on cities, 1969-72; clin. researcher for cardiovasculars Pfizer Pharmaceuticals, N.Y.C., 1972—. Bd. govs. Com. for South Shore Hospice, Bklyn., 1987—; county committeeman Bay Ridge Dem. Club, Bklyn., 1990—. N.Y. State Senate intern Ford Found. Grant, N.Y.C., 1966. Mem. Am. Soc. Pub. Adminstrs., N.Y.C. Soc. Hosp. Pharmacists (bd. govs. 1980-85), Phi Beta Kappa. Office: Pfizer Pharm 230 Brighton Rd Clifton NJ 07012-1414

BRIERE, RONALD ARMAND, psychologist; b. Fall River, Mass., Feb. 14, 1952; s. Armand and Doris (Longchamps) B. BA in Psychology, Southeastern Mass. U., 1973; MA in Counseling, Assumption Coll., 1976. Lic. social worker, Mass., lic. rehab. counselor, Mass. Adolescent counselor St. Vincent's Home, Fall River, 1970-76; vocat. evaluator Opportunity Ctr., New Bedford, Mass., 1976-79; psychologist Mass. Dept. Mental Retardation, Fall River, 1979—. Mem. APA (assoc.), Mass. Psychol. Assn. Home: 792 Old County Rd Westport MA 02790-1105 Office: Mass Dept Mental Retardation Fall River MA 02723

BRIESS, ROGER CHARLES, brewing and food industry executive; b. Paris, Feb. 11, 1937; s. Eric and Vera (Maltenfort) B.; m. Monica Gerst, Dec. 10, 1964; children: Colin, Craig. BS in Econs. and BSBA, Lycoming Coll., 1960; MS in Food Scis., V.L.B. Free Univ., West Berlin, 1961; cert. advanced brewing studies, U.S. Brewers Acad., 1963. Asst. brewmaster Elbschloss Brauerei, Hamburg, Fed. Republic Germany, 1961-62; trader commodities Interbrau Gesellschaft Mit Begrenzte Haftpflicht, Hamburg, 1962; mgr. project Kosmos GMBH, Hamburg, 1962; cons. malting Chilton (Wis.) Malting Co., 1964; mgr. export Cereal Products Corp., N.Y.C., 1965-66; mgr. export sales Am. Briess Corp., N.Y.C., 1967-70, exec. v.p., 1971—; chief exec. officer Briess Industries, Inc., N.Y.C., 1972—; sr. v.p. S.O.S. Children's Villages, Inc.; cons. Brewing Systems Inc., St. Petersburg, Fla., 1986-92. Sr. v.p. SOS Children's Villages (USA) Inc., N.Y.C., 1976—; children's religious tchr. Unitarian Ch. of All Souls, N.Y.C., 1987. Mem. Master Brewers Assn. Am. (fgn. liaison com. 1976—, Speaker of Merit award 1986), Inst. Food Technologists, Inst. for Brewing Studies (bd. advisors 1992—), Am. Soc. Brewing Chemists, Am. Assn. Cereal Chemists, Deutscher Brauer U. Maelzerbund, Internat. Club (Hamburg, v.p. 1962-63). Office: Briess Malting Co 250 W 57th St Ste 1020 New York NY 10107-0134 also: Briess Industries Inc 29 S Columbia St Chilton WI 53014

BRIGANTI, STEPHEN ANTHONY, foundation administrator, consultant; b. N.Y.C., Dec. 18, 1941; s. Benjamin and Celeste (Massa) B. BA, Butler U., 1964, LLB (hon.), 1991. Tchr. Met. Sch. Dist. Perry Twp., Indpls., 1964-69; unit dir. United Way of Greater N.Y., N.Y.C., 1969-70, div. dir., 1970-74, v.p., 1974-76; group v.p. United Way of Tri-State, Inc., N.Y.C., 1977-80, group v.p., campaign dir., 1982-84; dir. of ops. Statue of Liberty-Ellis Island Found., N.Y.C., 1984-86, exec. v.p., 1984-86, pres., chief operating officer, 1987—; cons. N.Y. Internat. Festival of the Arts, N.Y.C., 1987, U.S. Holocaust Meml. Coun. Trust, Washington, 1989-91, Peace Corps Partnership in Teaching English, Phila., 1990—; spl. adv. dir. Dr. Armand Hammer, Stop Cancer Inc., L.A., 1988-90. Bd. trustees Butler U., 1992—. Named Person of the Week, ABC-TV World News Tonight, 1990. Home: 25 E End Ave New York NY 10028-7052 Office: Statue of Liberty Ellis Island Found 52 Vanderbilt Ave New York NY 10017-3808

BRIGGIE, CLIFFORD RANDALL, mental health administrator, consultant; b. Hartford, Conn., Aug. 26, 1952; s. Francis Richard and Helen Mary (Kaminskas) B.; m. Margaret Ellen Wilson, Jan. 3, 1981; children: Andrew Wilson Briggie, Alexis Margaret Briggie. BA, U. Conn., Storrs, 1974; MSW, U. Conn., West Hartford, 1979; D in Psychology, Heed U., Hollywood, Fla., 1983; MBA, U. New Haven, Conn., 1991. Clin. Social Worker. Program dir., diagnostic unit Elmcrest Psychiat. Inst., Portland, Conn., 1974-79; asst. clin. dir., treatment unit Altobello Psychiat. Hosp., Meriden, Conn., 1979-82; clin., crisis svc., dir. social work training Hartford Hosp., Hartford, Conn., 1982-86; dir., social work and continuing care Meriden-Wallingford Hosp., Meriden, Conn., 1986-87; adminstr., dept. of psychiat. Hosp. St. Raphael, New Haven, Conn., 1987—; clin. faculty U. Conn., Storrs, Conn., 1988—, Columbia U., N.Y.C., 1991—; mem. human rights com., bd. dirs. Marrakech, Inc., New Haven, Conn., 1988—; mem. Boston Ctr., A.K. Rice Inst., 1991—, Alban Inst., 1991—. Contbr. articles to profl. jours. Mem. Assn. Psychiat. Clin. of Conn. (past treas., v.p., pres.). Office: Hosp of St Raphael 1450 Chapel St New Haven CT 06511-4405

BRIGGS, DONALD KNOWLES, hematologist, researcher; b. Northampton, Eng., Apr. 10, 1924; came to U.S., 1953; s. James Parker and Esther Mary (Reid) B.; m. June Nasseau, July 19, 1958; children: Lincoln Wiliam, Claudia Louise. BA, Cambridge U., Eng., 1946, MA, 1948; MB BChir, Cambridge U., 1947; MD, NYU, 1955. Registrar London U. King's Coll. Hosp., 1949-50; sr. resident Am. Hosp., Paris, 1951-53; prin. investigator USPHS, 1955-56; chief sect. hematology, dir. spl. hematology lab. Lenox Hill Hosp., N.Y.C., 1967-78; asst. prof. clin. medicine NYU, N.Y.C., 1956—; cons. physician James Lenox House, N.Y., 1988—. Author: Abnormalities of Leukocytes, 1963. Capt. Royal Army Med. Corps, 1947-49. Fellow ACP, Royal Soc. Medicine; mem. Listerian Soc. (life), St. George's Soc. (life), Union Club. Episcopalian. Home and Office: 170 E 79th St New York NY 10021

BRIGGS, JOHN PHILIP, English educator, writer; b. Detroit, Jan. 8, 1945; s. John Philip and Muriel Ann (Moyer) B.; m. Barbara Joan Anna Myhrberg, June 16, 1968. BA in Letters, Wesleyan U., Middletown, Conn., 1968; MA in English, NYU, 1972; PhD in Aesthetics and Psychology, Union Inst., Cin., 1981. Reporter Tarrytown (N.Y.) Daily News, 1962-63; reporter Hartford (Conn.) Courant, 1965-68, copy editor, 1978-79; mng. editor The Acad., N.Y.C., 1970-76, N.Y. Quar., N.Y.C., 1972-77; mem. humanities faculty New Sch. for Social Rsch., N.Y.C., 1973-87; adj. mem. English faculty Mercy Coll., Dobbs Ferry, N.Y., 1974-87; assoc. prof. Western Conn. State U., Danbury, 1987—; freelance sci. writer, 1981—. Co-author: Looking Glass Universe, 1984, Turbulent Mirror, 1989, Metaphor: The Logic of Poetry, 1990; author: Fire in the Crucible, 1988, Fractals: The Patterns of Chaos, 1992. Selectman Town of Granville, Mass., 1987—. Mem. AAUP (rsch. award 1988), Investigative Reporters and Editors. Home: Barnard Rd Granville MA 01034-9513 Office: Western Conn State U English Dept White St Danbury CT 06810-6639

BRIGGS, REGINALD PETER, geologist; b. Port Chester, N.Y., Mar. 12, 1929; s. Reginald Joseph and Marion Lois (Kendig) B.; m. Henrietta Ferris, Sept. 15, 1956; children: Wendy Ferris, Mark Kendig, James Mandeville. BA, Wesleyan U., 1951; postgrad., Drexel U., W. Va. U., U. Pitts. Registered profl. geologist, Del. Geologist U.S. Geol. Survey, Lexington, Ky., 1953-55; geologist U.S. Geol. Survey, San Juan, P.R., 1955-64, project chief, 1964-70; project dir. U.S. Geol. Survey, Pitts., 1971-76; pres., chief geologist Geomega, Inc., Pitts., 1976—; chmn. 45th Field Conf. of Pa. Geologists, 1980; lectr. in field. Author or co-author numerous geologic maps and reports of P.R., Pa.; contbr. articles to profl. jours. Prime mover Pa. Hist. & Mus. Commn. Hist. Marker-Coal Mining, Pitts., 1985, Climax Locomotives, Corry, Pa., 1987. With C.E., U.S. Army, 1951-53. Fellow Geol. Soc. Am.; mem. Assn. Engring. Geologists, Am. Geophys. Union, Am. Inst. Profl. Geologists (Pa. sect. pres. 1975), Pa. Coun. Profl. Geologists (dir. 1991-92), No. Appalachian Geol. Soc., Geol. Soc. Washington (corres. mem.); hon. mem. Geol. Soc. of P.R., Pitts. Geol. Soc. (dir. 1972-77, 83-87, 90-92, W.S. Skinner award 1990). Republican. Home: 101 Algonquin Rd Pittsburgh PA 15241-1509

BRIGGS, ROBERT MERVYN, plastic and reconstructive surgeon; b. Rochester, N.Y., Jan. 12, 1939; s. Robert Mervyn and Gertrude Edna (Broadwell) B.; m. Christine Martha Horgen, Oct. 17, 1964; children: Kari H., Heide A., Amy E. AB, Princeton U., 1960; MD, Yale U., 1964. Diplomate Am. Bd. of Surgery, Am. Bd. of Plastic and Reconstructive Surgery. Intern surgery U. Rochester-Strong Meml. Hosp., 1964-65; resident gen. surgery, plastic surgery Stanford U., Palo Alto, Calif., 1965-70; attending physician, reconstructive surgeon St. Barnabas Med. Ctr., Livingston, N.J., 1972—; pvt. practice Livingston, 1972—; chmn. dept. plastic surgery St. Barnabas Med. Ctr., Livingston, 1990—; clin. asst. prof. surgery Rutgers-Robert Wood Johnson Med. Sch., Piscataway, N.J., 1975—. Contbr. chpts. to books, articles to profl. jours. Mem. Roseland (N.J.) Recreation Com., 1984-87; bd. mem., v.p. West Essex Bd. of Edn., North Caldwell, N.J., 1987—; bd. dirs. Emmanuel Cancer Found., 1983-87. Decorated Bronze Star. Fellow Am. Coll. Surgeons; mem. Am. Soc. Plastic and Reconstructive Surgery (com. mem.), Am. Assn. Plastic and Reconstructive Surgery, N.Y. Regional Soc. Plastic and Reconstructive Surgery (pres., v.p., treas. 1973—), N.J. Regional Soc. Plastic and Reconstructive Surgery (pres. 1985-86), Med. Soc. N.J. (chmn. plastic sect.), Essex County Med. Soc. (mem. com.), Kiwanis (pres. and officer 1980-88). Office: 349 E Northfield Rd Livingston NJ 07039

BRIGGS, SHERRY WELCH, small business owner, writer; b. Hartford, Conn., July 25, 1945; d. Nicholas Anthony and Betty (Slocombe) W.; m. David Lawrence Briggs, July 31, 1976; children: Benjamin Welch, Jennie Susan. AA, Hartford Coll., 1965; BFA, Lake Erie Coll., 1967; D. Dental Medicine, Boston U., 1978. Prin. Sherricats, Co., Boston Area, 1962—, Jewelry-To Go!, Boston Area, 1990—; freelance writer, 1980—. Author: Seppuku, 1990; author short stories. Home-stay parent Showa Women's Inst., Boston Branch, Boston, Tokyo, 1987, Sunday sch. tchr., Needham (Mass.) Congl. Ch., 1989—, storyteller, 1989—. Mem. Greater Boston Sci. Fiction Writer's Group. Home and Office: 12 Hampton Ave Needham MA 02194-2615

BRIGGS, TOM, copyright administrator, librettist, director; b. Janesville, Wis., Aug. 17, 1952; s. Theodore Frank and Charlotte Jean (McCaskey) B. Student Herbert Burghof Studio, U. Wis.; student, N.Y.C. Am. Conservancy Theatre, San Francisco. Artistic dir. St. Bart's Playhouse, N.Y.C., 1983-86; dir. Rodgers & Hammerstein Theatre Libr., N.Y.C., 1986—; guest artist in residence Nat. Theatre Inst. at O'Neill Theatre Ctr., Conn., 1978, 79; guest faculty in residence Union Coll., Schenectady, N.Y., 1979, 80; composer, lyricist Nat. Theatre Workshop of the Handicapped, N.Y.C., 1979-81. Casting dir., dir.-producer Joshua Logan, N.Y.C., 1982; actor, singer, dancer for theatres, indsls., recording studios, TV, 1964-76; dir., choreographer theatres throughout U.S.A., 1971—; co-author: (with Louis Mattiol) Rodgers and Hammerstein's State Fair, Close to You: The Sounds of Bacharach and David, Me and Mickey. Mem. Dramatists Guild Am. Office: Rodgers & Hammerstein Theatre Libr 1633 Broadway Ste 3801 New York NY 10019-6746

BRIGGS, VERNON MASON, JR., economics educator; b. Washington, June 29, 1937; s. Vernon Mason and Anne Maria (Cox) B.; m. Martijna Antonia Aarts, Dec. 29, 1971; children: Vernon Mason III, Kees Kanen. B.S., U. Md., 1959; M.A., Mich. State U., 1960, Ph.D., 1965. Asst. instr. econs. Mich. State U., 1960-64; asst. prof. U. Tex., Austin, 1964-68;

asso. prof. U. Tex., 1968-74, prof. econs., 1974-78; prof. indsl. and labor relations Cornell U., Ithaca, N.Y., 1978—; research dir. Com. on Adminstrn. Tng. Programs, HEW, 1967-68; mem. Nat. Council Employment Policy, 1977-87, chmn., 1985-87; bd. dirs. Corp. Public and Pvt. Ventures, 1978-83, Ctr. for Immigration Studies, 1987—. Author: (with Ray Marshall) The Negro and Apprenticeship, 1967, The Chicano and Rural Poverty, 1973, (with Walter Fogel and Fred Schmidt) The Chicano Worker, 1977, (with John Adams, Brian Rungeling and Lewis Smith) Employment, Income and Welfare in the Rural South, 1977, (with Ray Marshall and Allan King) Labor Economics: Wages Employment and Trade Unionism, 1980, rev., 1984, (with Felician Foltman) Apprenticeship Research: Emerging Findings and Future Trends, 1981, Immigration Policy and the American Labor Force, 1984, (with Marta Tienda) Immigration Issues and Policies, 1985, The Internationalization of the U.S. Economy, 1986, (with Leon Bouvier) The Population and Labor Force Future of New York, 1988, (with Ray Marshall) Labor Economics: Theory, Institutions and Public Policy, 1989. Recipient Jean Holloway Teaching Excellence award, 1974. Mem. Phi Sigma Kappa, Delta Sigma Pi, Omicron Delta Kappa, Omicron Delta Epsilon. Home: 332 Winthrop Dr Ithaca NY 14850-1751

BRIGHAM-GRETTE, JULIE, geology educator; b. Albion, Mich., Jan. 11, 1955; d. Jesse William Jr. and Betty Ann (Hossfield) Brigham; m. Roger Olaf Grette, Sept. 24, 1983; 1 child, Karl Olaf. BA magna cum laude, Albion Coll., 1977; MS, U. Colo., Boulder, 1980, PhD, 1985. Postdoctoral fellow dept. geology U. Bergen, Norway, 1983-84, U. Alta./Geol. Survey of Can., Edmonton, 1985-87; asst. prof. dept. geology and geography U. Mass., Amherst, 1987—; vis. prof. Alaska Quaternary Ctr., Fairbanks, 1990. Contbr. articles on glacial and sea level history of Arctic N.Am. to numerous sci. jours. Grantee NSF, 1987-89, 90-93, 91-94. Mem. Geol. Soc. Am. (div. panel 1988-90, sec. 1990—, Harold T. Sterns fellow 1981, Mackin award 1981), Am. Quaternary Assn. (sec. 1990—), Can. Quaternary Assn., Assn. Women Geoscientists (Outstanding Women Geoscientist 1981), Internat. Glaciology Soc., Am. Geophys. Union, Arctic Inst. N.Am. Democrat. Methodist. Office: Univ Mass Dept Geology and Geography Amherst MA 01003

BRIGHT, THOMAS RHODES, shoe company retail executive; b. Boston, Mar. 13, 1952; s. Arthur Aaron and Evelyn Miller (Fay) B.; m. Kathleen Gould Friedman, June 9, 1973; children: Arthur Aaron, Elizabeth Benson. BA, Yale U., 1973. Speechwriter U.S. Sen. Charles H. Percy, Washington, 1973-74; reporter/editor Torrington (Conn.) Register, 1974-75; press sec. U.S. Rep. William S. Cohen, Washington, 1975-79; v.p. Hitchcock Shoes, Inc., Hingham, Mass., 1979—.

BRIGHTMAN, RICHARD WARREN, data processing executive; b. Newark, Sept. 25, 1948; s. Robert Lloyd and Marion Boyd (Altreuter) B.; m. Aimee Teresa Ruzicka, Oct. 9, 1987. BS in Computer Sci., Rutgers U., 1975; MS in Mgmt., Stevens Inst. Tech., 1981. Programmer trainee Nabisco Inc., East Hanover, N.J., 1975-76, programmer, 1976-81; systems programmer Nabisco Brands Inc., Parsippany, N.J., 1981-83, project leader, 1983-85; project mgr. Nabisco Brands Inc., East Hanover, 1985-87; sr. project mgr. Nabisco Foods Co., Parsippany, 1987-89; dir. info. systems RJR Nabisco Inc., N.Y.C., 1989—. With USN, 1969-73. Office: RJR Nabisco Inc 1301 Ave of the Americas New York NY 10019

BRILL, ALAN EDWARD, computer, telecommunications security consultant; b. N.Y.C., Feb. 7, 1947; s. William and Pearl (Solomon) B.; m. Linda Pisetzner, Aug. 17, 1974; 1 child, Rachel. BA, NYU, 1966, MBA, 1968. Tech. assoc. NASA Manned Spacecraft Ctr., Houston, 1967; sr. systems analyst Chase Manhattan Bank, N.Y.C., 1970-73; sr. mgr. Ernst and Whinney, N.Y.C., 1973-80; dir. profl. svcs. Yourdon Inc., N.Y.C., 1980-83; dir. ISIS bur. N.Y.C. Dept. Investigation, 1983-88; mng. dir. Kroll Assocs. Inc., N.Y.C., 1988—; adj. instr. U.S. Secret Svc., Washington, 1988-90, Fed. Law Enforcement Tng. Ctr., Brunswick, Ga., 1985-90. Author: The Right to Financial Provacy, 1976, Building Controls Into Space, 1981; editor: Techniques of M.I.S. Management, 1983; contbr. articles to profl. jours. Mem. N.Y.C. Community Planning Bd., S.I., 1982-84. Maj. U.S. Army, 1968-89. NSF Summer Rsch. grantee, 1960-61. Mem. High Tech. Crime Investigators Assn. Office: Kroll Assocs 900 Third Ave New York NY 10022

BRILL, EDGAR LEWIS, administrator; b. Filmore, N.Y., Apr. 2, 1951; s. edgar Lewis and Ethelmae (Dawson) B.; m. agnes Maloney, July 28, 1979; 1 child, Sarah Agnes. BS in Chemistry, Wilkes U., Wilkes-Barre, Pa.; 1977. Cert. quality auditor, internal Malcolm Baldrige examiner. Quality control tech. Air Products & Chems., Tamaqua, Pa., 1980—. lectro Freeland Roman Cath. Ch., 1990—. Mem. Am. Chem. Soc., Am. Soc. Quality Control. Republican. Home: 901 Birkbeck St Freeland PA 18224-1505 Office: Air Products & Chems RR 1 Box 351 Tamaqua PA 18252-9475

BRILL, MARTIN ROBERT, marketing executive; b. Pitts., Aug. 9, 1951; s. William Leonard and Dorothy Jean (Pretter) B.; m. Deborah Aliya Borsuk, Jan. 18, 1987; children: Tamar, Daniel. BSFS, Georgetown U., 1973; MA, Sch. of Oriental & African Stu, London, 1974. Info. officer Del. of Comm. of European Communities, Washington, 1978-81; v.p. First Nat. Bank of Chgo., 1981-87; mng. dir. MNC Internat. Bank, Balt., 1987-90; internat. sales dir. B. Green & Co., Balt., 1990-91; dir. export sales Lankford Sysco Food Svcs., Inc., Pocomoke City, Md., 1991—; lectr. in field. Home: 370 Michelle Way Baltimore MD 21208-1744

BRILL, WILLIAM FRANKLIN, chemist, consultant; b. Utica, N.Y., Feb. 16, 1923; s. Michael and Bella (Godfrey) B.; m. Yvonne Claeys, Dec. 15, 1952; children: Naomi, Matthew, Joseph. BS, U. Conn., 1944, MS, 1948, PhD, 1950. Instr. U. Conn., Storrs, 1950; rsch. assoc. U. Calif., L.A., 1950-52; sr. chemist Olin-Mathieson, New Haven, 1952-55; group leader Petro-Tex, Princeton, N.J., 1955-60, rsch. assoc., 1960-66; dir. chem. rsch. Princeton Chem. Rsch., 1966-69; sr. scientist Halcon R&D, Montvale, N.J., 1969-86; Dana fellow Drew U., Madison, N.J., 1986-90, ret., 1990; pvt. practice cons., Skillman, N.J., 1986—. Author: (with others) Condensation Monomers, 1972, Selective Oxygenations, 1986; patentee in field; contbr. articles to profl. jours. With USN, 1944-46, CBI. Princeton U. fellow, 1986-87, 91—. Mem. Am. Chem. Soc., Catalysis Soc. of N.Y., Phi Lambda Upsilon, Sigma Xi. Home and Office: 914 Rt # 518 Skillman NY 08558

BRILL, YVONNE CLAEYS, engineer, consultant; b. St. Norbert, Manitoba, Canada, Dec. 30, 1924; d. August and Julienne (Carette) Claeys; m. William Franklin Brill, Dec. 15, 1951; children: Naomi, Matthew, Joseph. BS, U. Manitoba, Canada, 1945; MS, U. So. Calif., 1951. Mathematician Douglas Aircraft, Santa Monica, Calif., 1945-46; research analyst Rand Corp., Santa Monica, 1946-49; group leader Marquardt Corp., Van Nuys, Calif., 1949-52; staff engr. UTC Research, East Hartford, Conn., 1952-55; project engr. Wright Aeronautical, Wood Ridge, N.J., 1955-58; mgr. propulsion systems RCA AstroElectronics, Princeton, N.J., 1966-81, staff engr., 1983-86; mgr. solid rocket motor NASA Hdqrs., Washington, 1981-83; with space engring segment Internat. Maritime Satellite Orgn., London, 1986-91; cons. Brill Assocs., Skillman, N.J., 1991—; mem. USAF Sci. Adv. Bd., Washington, 1982-83, Nat. Acad. Engring. Internat. Affairs Adv. Com., 1991-94. Contbr. articles to sci. jours.; patentee in field. Bd. dirs. Princeton YWCA, 1981-82. Recipient Engr. of Yr. award Cen. Jersey Engring. Councils, 1979, Diamond Superwoman award Harpers Bazaar/DeBeers Corp., 1980, Marvin C. Demlar award AIAA, 1983. Fellow AIAA and Soc. Women Engrs. (dir. student affairs 1979-80, 83-84, treas. 1980-81, Engring. Achievement award 1986); mem. Internat. Astronautical Acad. (academician, edn. com. 1983-85), U.S. Nat. Acad. Engring. (elected 1987), Sigma Xi, Tau Beta Pi. Republican. Home and Office: 914 Rt 518 Skillman NJ 08558-2616

BRILLIANT, BARBARA, television host, producer, consultant; b. Montreal, Que., Can., Sept. 24, 1935; d. Saul and Esther (Saltzman) Lecker; m. Erwin Brilliant, June 29, 1958; children: Bradley, Todd, Michelle. Student, McGill Tchrs. Coll., 1953, McGill Conservatory of Music; AA, Sir George Williams U., Montreal, 1955; BA in Psychology summa cum laude, Boston Coll., 1975. Tchr. Protestant Sch. Bd., Montreal, 1953-58, dir. drama sch., 1957-58; artist-in-residence City of Boston, 1978-83; TV host, producer Sta. WBZ-TV, Boston, 1979-90; freelance news producer AARP News Network, 1989—; freelance writer, composer, lyricist; columnist "Dear Barbara", advice for people 40 plus; advisor Radcliffe Coll., Cambridge, Mass., 1985—. Actress Montreal area, 1957-58, Boston area, 1985—; artistic dir. City of Boston, 1985—; vocalist, mus. dir. Two on the Aisle, Newton, Mass., 1985—; speaker in field; contbg. writer Vitality Mag., Boston Woman Mag., N.H. Senior Times, among others; composer songs (with Charles Segal) You're Not Alone, Time to Care, Talk to Me, many others; columnist: "Tell It to Barbara" in the Jewish Advocate, 1992—. Advisor Cultural Affairs Commn., Newton, Mass., 1980-82, Nat. Com. to Study and Resolve Problems of Older Ams., Boston, 1984—; mem. adv. bd. Radcliffe Coll. Women; spokesperson Alzheimers Disease and Related Disorders Assn., Boston, 1985—; mem. White House Conf. on Aging, Washington, 1981; mem. Time Capsule Harvard Schlessinger Library, Cambridge, Mass., 1980. Recipient Cert. of Recognition City of Boston, 1979, Media award Am. Assn. Retired Persons, 1980, Lifestyle Achievement award WW Group Internat., Boston, 1987, Sandoz Gerentol. Found. awards, 1989, 91; Nat. Press Found., fellow, Washington, 1987; named to Hon. Order Ky. Cols., 1987, One of Boston's 100 Most Interesting Women, Boston Woman Mag., 1988, Gov. Michael Dukakais proclamation service in media to elderly, 1989; Mayor Raymond Flynn declared Barbara Brilliant Day, Sept. 24, 1989; Awareness of Aging tree planted in her honor Newton City Hall. Mem. Screen Actors Guild, Am. Fedn. TV and Radio Artists. Office: Brilliant Communications PO Box 310 Newton MA 02161-0004

BRINE, MARK VINCENT, musician, entertainer; b. Cambridge, Mass., Nov. 28, 1948; s. Francis Joseph and Catherine Ramona (Kirby) Byrne; m. Mary Jane Sherman, May 12, 1968 (div. Sept. 1979); children: Michelle Elizabeth (dec.), Jenipher Michelle; m. Karen Lynette Kriss, Dec. 8, 1982; 1 child, Keeve Kristian. Grad. high sch., Cambridge. Artist, writer Door Knob Records, Nashville, 1977-80, Roxy Records, Nashville, 1982, Tom Pomposello Prodn., N.Y.C., 1986-87; pvt. practice artist, writer Balt., 1987—; pub. asst. Gene Kennedy Enterprises, Nashville, 1977-80. Author: The Carol: The True Folk Legend of Jack Frost, 1992; songwriter numerous songs, 1977—. Recipient 1st place Nat. Talent Contest Jimmie Rodgers Festival, Meridian, Miss, 1979. Mem. Broadcast Music Inc., Am. Fedn. Musicians. Home and Office: 1341 Taylor Ave Baltimore MD 21234

BRINES, SEYMOUR, psychotherapist, research consultant, educator; b. N.Y.C., July 9, 1927; s. Benjamin S. and Rose (Symbol) B. AB, Cornell U., 1951; postgrad., U. Ill., 1952-53; MA in Psychology, NYU, 1979. Nat. cert. sch. psychologist. Rsch. asst. Inst. Communications Rsch., 1952-53; rsch. analyst NBC, N.Y.C., 1955-57; study dir. McCann-Erickson Inc., N.Y.C., 1958-62; rsch. dir. Forell, Thomas Assocs., N.Y.C., 1962-68; pres. Brines Assocs., N.Y.C., 1968—; summer rsch. fellow N.Y. State Office Mental Health, 1976; cons. N.Y.C. Bd. Edn., 1991—; staff psychotherapist St. Vincent's Svcs. Outpatient Clinic, 1986-91; lectr. psychology Bloomfield (N.J.) Coll., 1987; vis. asst. prof. Pratt Inst., Bklyn., 1988-89; adj. lectr. Kingsborough Community Coll., CUNY, 1989—; cons. N.Y. State Office Mental Health, 1981, Readership Rsch. Co., Tuckahoe, N.Y., 1973-76; dir. market rsch. Hayden Pub. Co., Rochelle Park, N.J., 1973. With USNR, 1945-46. N.Y. tuition scholar Cornell U., 1948-51. Mem. Am. Psychol. Assn., Am. Mental Health Counselors Assn., Ea. Evaluation Soc., Cornell U. Alumni Assn., Cornell Club (N.Y.). Home: 2930 W 5th St Brooklyn NY 11224-3963

BRINEY, LESTER STAFFORD, computer company executive; b. Akron, Ohio, Mar. 13, 1944; s. Gerald Stafford and Helen Margaret (Hardesty) B.; m. Winifred Stroup, Jan. 5, 1974. BSEE, U. Calif., Berkeley, 1966. Exec. asst. IBM, White Plains, N.Y., 1967-82; v.p. engring. Internat. Digital Electronics, Elmsford, N.Y., 1982-85; dir. Prodigy Svcs. Co., White Plains, 1985—. Inventor automotive diagnostics. With U.S. Army, 1968-70. Mem. IEEE. Republican. Methodist. Home: 37 Ferncliff Rd Cos Cob CT 06807-1206 Office: Prodigy Svcs Co 445 Hamilton Ave White Plains NY 10601-1814

BRINK, ARTHUR M., hospital administrator; b. Madison, Wis., Sept. 20, 1943; s. Arthur M. and Shirlee (Quinn) B.; children: Damon J., Justin K.; m. Katharin R. Brink; children: SEan K. Riehl, Caroline M. Riehl, Katie K. Riehl. BS in Edn., U. Vt., 1966, MAT in History, 1969. Cert. fin. planner. Alumni dir. U. Vt., Burlington, 1966-77, dir. ann. fund, 1977-78; dir. devel. U. Vt. and Med. Ctr. Hosp., Burlington, 1978-83; v.p. Vt. Health Found., Burlington, 1983—; bd. dirs. Franklin Lamoille Bank, Burlington; chmn. dist 1 Council for Advancement and Support Higher Edn., New Eng., 1982-83; chmn. Assn. Am. Med. Colls./Group on Pub. Affairs, Washington, 1986-87. Contbr. articles to profl. jours. Pres. Burlington Boys Club, 1986-88; bd. dirs. United Way, Burlington. Served to capt. U.S. Army, 1969-71, Vietnam. Decorated Bronze Star with Oak Leaf cluster, Air Medal with Oak Leaf cluster. Fellow Nat. Assn. Hosp. Devel.; mem. Rotary (pres. 1985-86). Home: 20 Hagen Dr Essex Junction VT 05452-3365 Office: Vt Health Found 219 Briggs Burlington VT 05401-5310

BRINKER, EDWARD JESSE, human resources specialist; b. Greensburg, Pa., Dec. 4, 1950; s. Edward Jesse and Dorthy Mae (Armstrong) B.; m. Sandra Barbara Nelson, July 2, 1968; 1 child, Cassandra Edlynn. AS in Bus., Westmoreland Community Coll., 1977; BS in Fin. and Indsl. Rels., St. Vincent Coll., Latrobe, Pa., 1977; MA in Indsl. Rels., St. Francis Coll., Pitts., 1982. Indsl. rels. asst. Mackintosh Hemphill div. GFW, Pitts., 1977-78; plant pers. mgr. Jeannette (Pa.) Glass Corp., 1978-83; mgr. pers. svcs. Anchor Glass Container Corp., Connelsville, pa., 1983-84; mgr. human resources Newcomer Products Inc., Latrobe, 1984—; pres. E.J. Brinker Assocs., Greensburg, 1987—; adj. instr. Westmoreland County Community Coll., Youngwood, Pa., 1987—. With USN, 1969-72. Mem. Pitts. Pers. Assn., Human Resources Soc., Cemented Carbide Products Assn. (human rels. com. 1984—), Latrobe Pers. Assn. (chmn. 1988-89), Westmoreland County Mfrs. Assn. (chmn. 1987-88). Presbyterian. Office: Newcomer Products Inc Rt 982 N Latrobe PA 15650

BRINKER, THOMAS MICHAEL, finance executive; b. Phila., Sept. 8, 1933; s. William Joseph and Elizabeth C. (Feeley) B.; m. Doris Marie Carlin, Oct. 11, 1958; children—Thomas Michael, James E., Joseph F., Diane M. Student, St. Joseph's U., U. Pa.; MS in Fin. Svcs., Am. Coll., 1980; DBA, Heed U., 1990; BA in Orgnl. Mgmt., Ea. Coll., 1991. Registered investment advisor. With Ice Capades, 1951-52, 56; with Casa Carioca, Garmisch, Fed. Rep. Germany, 1954-56; profl. ice skating tchr. and mfrs. rep. Ridley Park, Pa., 1956-60; agt., div. mgr. Prudential Ins. Co., Phila., 1960-65; gen. agt. Mut. Trust Life Ins. Co., 1965-70; pres., founder Fringe Benefits Inc., Havertown, Pa., 1970—, Fin. Foresight Ltd., Havertown, Pa., 1983—; adj. prof. Pa. State U., 1984—, St. Joseph's U., 1985—. Host. weekly radio show: Financial Forum, Sta. WWDB-FM, 1982-90, Sta. WCZN-AM, 1990-91; author: Hi, I'm Tom Brinker, You're on WWDB, 1987; columnist: Financially Yours, 1983—; ghostwriter: Nat. Assn. Life Underwriters' Fin. Fitness campaign, 1985; contbr., author, conductor of seminars on fin. planning; contbr. articles to profl. jours. Pres., Delaware County Estate Planning Council, 1979-80, Pipeline Inc., Springfield, Pa., 1970-71; dir. nat. council Invest-in-Am., 1986. Served with US Army, 1954-56. Recipient Nat. Quality awards Nat. Assn. Life Underwriters, 1966—, Nat. Sales Achievement awards, 1970—. Mem. CLU (chartered fin. cons.), Delaware County Life Underwriters (pres. 1975-76, 82-83), Am. Coll. Life Underwriters, Nat. Assn. Life Underwriters, Internat. Platform Assn., Internat. Assn. Fin. Planners (registered planning practitioner, v.p. Delaware Valley chpt. 1986-88, pres. 1989—, chmn. 1990—), Million Dollar Round Table (life, ct. of table 1988-92, Top of the Table award 1991), Twenty Five MIllion Dollar Internat. Forum, Lake Naomi Club (v.p., bd. govs. 1982, pres. 1986), Manor Club, K.C. Roman Catholic. Home: 115 Locust Ave Media PA 19064-1619 Office: 1 N Ormand Ave Upper Darby PA 19083

BRINKERHOFF, PETER JOHN, manufacturing company executive; b. Hackensack, N.J., Aug. 1, 1945; s. James Walter II and Janet Stole (Mohair) B.; m. Jeannine Teresa Heneault, Aug. 2, 1969; children: Jodie, Peter, Jill. BA in Polit. Sci., Georgetown U., 1967; MBA in Fin., Am. U., 1972. Investment mgr. Am. Security & Trust Co., Washington, 1969-72; ops. exec. ITT, N.Y.C., 1972-75; mgr. corp. devel. Chgo. Pneumatic Tool Co., N.Y.C., 1975-76; v.p. mktg., exec. v.p., pres. Jacobs Mfg. Cos. subs. Chgo. Pneumatic Tool Co., Bloomfield, Conn., 1976-85; founder, chmn., chief exec. officer Polestar Group, Inc., West Simsbury, Conn., 1985—; also bd. dirs.; pres. chief exec. officer, bd. dirs. J.H. Williams Indsl. Products Inc., Columbus, Ga., 1987—; bd. dirs. Am. Supply & Machinery Mfg., Cleve., Merrill Lynch Interfunding, Inc. N.Y.C., advisor; interim chief operating officer Shape, Inc., Biddeford, Maine, 1988; interim chief exec. officer Cannon Ball Industries, Inc., Harvard, Ill., 1989; pres., chief exec. officer Aqua Fab Industries, Inc., East Greenwich, R.I., 1990—; chmn. bd., chief exec. officer Gt. Hill Ins. Co., Ltd., 1991—. Bd. dirs. Conn. Bus. Coalition on Health, Hartford, 1984-85; grad., mem. Hartford Leadership Coun., 1982-83. Lt. USNR, 1967-69. Mem. Am. Supply and Machinery Mfrs. Assn. (bd. dirs. 1983-85, 89—), Nat. Spa and Pool Inst. (mfrs. coun. 1991—), Hand Tool Inst. Inc., Hartford Club (Conn.), Worl Affairs Coun., Western Hwy. Inst., Hartford County Mfrs. Assn. (bd. dirs. 1983-85). Roman Catholic. Office: Polestar Group Inc 20 N Canton Rd West Simsbury CT 06092-2000

BRINKLEY, DAVID, news commentator; b. Wilmington, N.C., July 10, 1920; s. William Graham and Mary (West) B.; m. Ann Fischer, Oct. 11, 1946; children: Alan, Joel, John; m. Susan Adolph, June 10, 1972; 1 child, Alexis. Reporter Wilmington (N.C.) Star-News, 1938-41; reporter, bur. mgr. United Press Assns., various So. cities, 1941-43; news writer, broadcaster radio and TV NBC, Washington, 1943—; Washington corr. NBC, 1951-81; anchorman ABC This Week, 1981—. Recipient duPont award, Peabody award, Sch. Bell award, other journalism awards. Office: ABC News 1717 Desales St NW Washington DC 20036-4407

BRINKMAN, CARL ALEXANDER, neurosurgeon; b. Resht, Iran, June 17, 1932; (parents Am. citizens); s. Harry and Adrianna (Van Lopik) B.; m. Diane Butler, June 12, 1957; children: Sharon, Valerie. AB cum laude, Bowdoin Coll., 1953; MD, Yale U., 1957. Intern U. Mich., Ann Arbor, 1957-58, resident, 1958-63; cons. neurosurgeon Bath (Maine) Meml. Hosp., 1958—, Franklin County Meml. Hosp., Farmington, Maine, 1958—, No. Cumberland Meml. Hosp., Bridgton, Maine, 1959—, Webber Hosp., Biddeford, Maine, 1960; dir. dept. neurosurgery Maine Med. Ctr., Portland; attending Mercy Hosp., Portland; treas. Maine Magnetic Imaging, Portland; pres. So. Maine Neurosug. Assoc.; sr. clin. instr. U. Vt. Diplomate Am. Bd. Neurol. Surgery. Contbr. articles to profl. publs.; speaker symposium, 1965. Mem. ACS, Maine, New Eng. neurosurg. socs., AMA. Republican. Congregationalist. Club: Maine Charitable Mechanic Assn. Library. Office: 932 Congress St Portland ME 04102-3032

BRINKMAN, HENK-JAN, economist; b. Hellendoorn, The Netherlands, May 19, 1961; came to U.S., 1987; s. Teunis and Wilhelmina (Van Oorspronk) B.; m. Marcy K. Krever, Aug. 29, 1991; 1 child, Mick Brinkman Krever. BA in Econs., U. Groningen, The Netherlands, 1984, MA in Econs. cum laude, 1987; PhDC in Econs. with honors, New Sch. for Social Rsch., 1989. Assoc. econ. officer UN, N.Y.C., 1989—. Contbr. articles to profl. jours. Mem. bd. faculty of econs. U. Groningen, 1982-83. Prize fellow New Sch. Social Rsch., 1987-90. Office: UN New York NY 10017

BRINKMAN, WILLIAM FRANK, physicist, research executive; b. Washington, Mo., July 20, 1938; s. William F. Sr. and Mildred A. (Bocklege) B.; m. B. Carol, Aug. 27, 1960; children: David, Curtis. BS, U. Mo., 1960, PhD, 1965. Postdoctoral fellow Oxford U., 1966; mem. staff Bell Labs., Murray Hill, N.J., 1966-72, dept. head, 1972-74, dir., 1974-84; v.p. research Sandia Nat. Lab., Albuquerque, 1984-87; exec. dir. physics research AT&T Bell Labs., Murray Hill, N.J., 1987—. Contbr. numerous articles on theoretical physics to sci. jours. Fellow Am. Phys. Soc., AAAS; mem. Nat. Acad. Sci. (chmn. 8-vol. report Physics Through the 1990's). Home: 45 Jeffrey Ct Basking Ridge NJ 07920-1967 Office: AT&T Bell Labs 600 Mountain Ave New Providence NJ 07974-2010

BRINLEY, TIMOTHY DELANE, small business owner; b. Escondido, Calif., July 15, 1954; s. Herbert DeLane and Virginia Ann (Heman) B.; m. Rebecca Lynn Kramar, Apr. 6, 1980; children: Andrew David, Anna Elizabeth, Michael Alexander, Marcus DeLane. BA in Bible, Am. Bible Coll., West Monroe, La., 1981; M.Missions, Abilene Christian U., 1983. Missions evangelist Chs. of Christ, Escondido, Calif., 1974-76, Turkey, 1976-78, Abilene, 1978-82, Athens, Greece, 1983-84, Thessalonica, Greece, 1985-88, Boston, 1988-90; sml. bus. owner Classic Connections Internat., Boston, 1990—; pub. speaker seminars; travel lectr. motivational series. Republican. Office: Classic Connections PO Box 4066 Peabody MA 01961-4066

BRINSTER, BARRY, public relations company executive. Exec. v.p., dir. Ketchum Pub. Rels. Ketchum Communications, Inc., Phila. Office: Ketchum Pub Rels 1717 Arch St 33d Fl Philadelphia PA 19103 also: 1133 Ave of the Americas New York NY 10036*

BRIODY, LAURENCE PATRICK, software company executive; b. N.Y.C., July 27, 1936; s. Thomas M. and Mae (Allen) B.; children: John, Mary, Kevin, Joseph, Patricia, Laurence Jr., Daniel. BA, Villanova U., 1957; postgrad., St. Johns U., 1959-60. Methods analyst Met. Life Ins. Co., N.Y.C., 1958-61; various mgmt. positions IBM Corp., N.Y., N.J., 1962-81; industry mgr. utilities IBM Corp., White Plains, N.Y., 1981-89; v.p. Stagg Systems, Phoenix, 1990; prin. Briody Assocs., Newtown, Conn., 1989—; trombonist Park Ave. Ragtime and Blues Soc. Contbr. articles to profl. jours. Team leader Aristotle/2000, Danbury, Conn., 1992; exec. dir. Pony Colt League, Ridgefield, Conn., 1975. With USMC, 1957-61. Mem. Toastmasters (pres. 1968). Republican. Roman Catholic. Home: 41 Flat Swamp Rd Newtown CT 06470 Office: Briody Assocs PO Box 27 Newtown CT 06478

BRION, JOHN MARTIN, writer; b. N.Y.C., Dec. 27, 1922; s. Lester E. and Lucille (Demarest) B.; children: John Jr., William R. Indsl. adminstrn., Yale U., 1942; MBA, Pace U., 1972. V.p. ops. Peter A. Frasse and Co., Inc., N.Y.C., 1948-58; gen. sales mgr. Eastern Rolling Mills, Inc., N.Y.C., 1958-61; mgr. sales and gen. adminstrn. Engineered Products Group, Crane Co., N.Y.C., 1962-64; v.p. Day and Zimmerman Consulting Svcs., Phila., 1967-71; mgr. corp. mktg. and devel. Johns-Manville Corp., N.Y.C., 1971-73; writer N.Y.C. Author: Decisions, Organization Planning, and Marketing Concept, 1965, Marketing Through the Distribution Channel, 1966, Corporate Marketing Planning, 1967, Organizational Leadership of HR, (3 vols.), 1989. Home and Office: 17A 420 E 79th St New York NY 10021

BRISSENDEN, PRISCILLA ARTHUR (SALLY BRISSENDEN), retired psychotherapist; b. Wollaston, Mass., Mar. 3, 1925; d. William Glen and Elsie Catherine (Thompson) Arthur; m. Arik Brissenden, Sept. 5, 1954; children: Mark, Kira, Noel. BA, Smith Coll., 1946, M of Social Svc., 1954; Cert. in Gerontology, Hunter Coll., 1986. Pers. asst. Peter Bent Brigham Hosp., Boston, 1946-48; adminstrv. asst. Fletcher Sch. Law and Diplomacy, Tufts U., Medford, Mass., 1948-50; secretarial asst. Am. Embassy, Paris, 1950-52; caseworker Family Svcs. Cin., 1954-56; staff therapist Geraldine Pederson-Krag Clinic, Huntington, N.Y., 1968-89; pvt. practice psychotherapy, 1970-91, ret., 1991; student supr., field adv. Adelphi U. Sch. Social Work. Fellow Clin. Social Work Psychotherapists; mem. Nat. Assn. Social Workers, Acad. Cert. Social Workers, Smith Coll. Alumni Assn. (past chpt. pres.). Home: RR 1 Box 206 Union SC 29379-9134

BRISTOL, BETTY JANE, government official, nurse; b. St. Petersburg, Fla., June 9, 1946; d. Robert William and Mary Jane (Davidson) Hess; m. Matt Combes Cavendish Bristol III, May 30, 1967; children: Matt C.C. Bristol IV, Allison Willis Bristol. BS in Nursing, Baylor U., 1968; MS in Nursing, Cath. U., 1978. RN, Tex., Md. Staff nurse Chickasawba Hosp., Blytheville, Ark., 1968-70, dir. edn., 1970-71; nurse cons. Med. Assistance Unit, San Antonio, 1975-76; sch. nurse Dept. Def., Fed. Republic Germany, Eng., 1978-83; dir. nursing Meridian Nursing Ctr., LaPlata, Md., 1984-85; staff nurse Hosp. Home Care, VA, Washington, 1986-88; research asst. VA Med. Ctr., Washington, 1986-88; edn. specialist VA, Washington, 1988-90, budget analyst, 1990—; participant women's exec. leadership program Office of Pers. Mgmt., 1989; adj. instr. Auburn U., Montgomery, Ala., 1983-84; substitute tchr. Anne Arundel Pub. Schs., Annapolis, Md., 1985-86; instr. CPR, 1987—. Contbg. author: Technological Foundation in Nursing, 1989. Chmn. Sch. Adv. Bd., RAF Upper Heyford, Eng., 1981-82, mem. Health Care Adv. Bd., 1981-83; co-chmn. St. Jude's Bike-a-thon, Churchton, Md., 1985; dir. Sunday Sch. Mt. Vernon Bapt. Ch., Arlington, Va., 1990. Mem. Am. Nurses Assn., Officers Wives Club (welfare chair 1982-83), League for Nursing (bd. dirs. Washington chpt.), Sigma Theta Tau. Republican. Baptist. Office: VA 810 Vermont Ave Washington DC 20420-0002

BRISTOL, RAYMOND CURTIS, psychiatrist, psychoanalyst, educator; b. Brawley, Calif., Dec. 18, 1932; s. Raymond Cecil and Amy (Ross) B.; m. Marie Drissel, June 2, 1979. BA, Stanford U., 1958; MD, U. So. Calif., 1962; cert. social psychiatry, Washington Sch. Psychiatry, 1970. Med. intern Univ. Hosp., Ann Arbor, Mich., 1962-63; postgrad. fellow N.Y. Hosp.-Cornell U., New York, 1963-64, Yale U., New Haven, 1964-65; postgrad. fellow Austen Riggs Ctr., Stockbridge, Mass., 1965-68, supr. psychiatry, 1968-69; psychiat. cons. Peace Corps, Brazil, 1969; chief psychiatrist Peace Corps, Washington, 1969-71; asst. prof. Georgetown U., Washington, 1975-88, assoc. prof., 1989—, co-dir. postgrad. edn., 1990—; mem. faculty Balt.-Washington Inst. Psychoanalysis, Laurel, Md., 1982—, Washington Sch. Psychiatry, 1990—; acting med. dir. Peace Corps, Washington, 1971, chief psychiatrist, Washington, 1969-71; chmn. Forum Psychiatry, Psychoanalysis and the Humanities Georgetown U.; faculty, co-chmn. Nat. Conf. on Romantic and Love, 1990—. Fellow Am. Psychiat. Assn. (chmn. task force on conflict resolution 1990—), Washington Psychiat. Soc., Internat. Psychoanalytical Assn., Am. Psychoanalytic Assn.; mem. Balt.-Washington Psychoanalytic Soc., So. Med. Assn., Am. Assn. Pvt. Practice Psychiatrists (founding), Wis. Psychoanalytic Soc. (corr.). Episcopalian. Office: 1325 18th St NW Washington DC 20036-6515

BRISTOL, ROBERT FRANCIS, landscape architect, educator; b. Glen Falls, N.Y., Sept. 20, 1940; s. Russell Charles and Leona Grace (Pattee) Barot; m. Donna E. Wardlaw, July 14, 1970; children: Leslie-Jo Athanasiou, R. Baird Hiser. B of Landscape Architecture, Syracuse U., 1963, M of Landscape Architecture, 1966; MBA, R.P.I., Troy, N.Y., 1979. Faculty mem. state univ. coll. environ. sci. and forestry Sch. Landscape Architecture, Syracuse (N.Y.) U., 1963-66; landscape architect Currier, Anderson & Geda, Hartford, Conn., 1966-68; pres. The Saratoga Assocs., Saratoga Springs, N.Y., 1968—; adj. prof. Sch. Architecture and Sch. Mgmt. Rensselear Poly. Inst.; dir., v.p. for program Landscape Architecture Found., Washington. Contbr. numerous articles to profl. jours. Mem. Am. Soc. Landscape Architects (exec. com.), Am. Planners Assn. Office: The Saratoga Assocs 443 Broadway Saratoga Springs NY 12866-2203

BRISTOW, MATTHEW M., manufacturing executive; b. Fall River, Mass., Sept. 23, 1945; s. John C. and Stasia (Serwatka) B.; m. Janet E. Severi, Nov. 30, 1968; children—Elizabeth K., Amanda J. B.S., U. Hartford, 1967. Sr. auditor Ernst & Whinney, Hartford, Conn., 1967-70; internal auditor Stanley Works, New Britain, Conn., 1970-72, mgr. acctg. Stanley-Vidmar Div., Allentown, Pa., 1972-76, contr., 1976-81, asst. corp. contr. Stanley Works, New Britain, 1981-82, corp. contr., 1982-83, v.p., contr., 1983-90, v.p. productivity, 1990—. Mem. Fin. Execs. Inst. (chpt. pres. 1979-80), Nat. Assn. Accts.

BRISTOW, WILLIAM HARVEY, JR., psychiatrist; b. Harrisburg, Pa.; s. William H. and Rosa Leah (St. Clair) B.; m. Lillian H. Heise; children: Jill Virgina, Lisa Ann, William H. III. AB, Harvard U., 1949; MD, NYU, 1953. Diplomate, Am. Bd. Psychiatry and Neurology. Intern 4th Med. div. Bellevue Hosp., N.Y.C., 1953-54, resident 4th Med. div., 1954-55; resident N.Y. VA Hosp. Dept. Psychiatry, N.Y.C., 1957-60; VA fellow Bellevue Psychiat. Hosp., N.Y.C., 1959-60; pvt. practice Ridgewood, N.J., 1960—; chmn. dept. psychiatry Bergen Pin County Hosp., Paramus, N.J., 1961; former chmn. dept. psychiatry Wayne Gen. Hosp.; former vice chmn. dept. psychiatry Valley Hosp.; clin. dir. Ramapo Ridge Psychiat. Hosp. Fellow Am. Psychiat. Assn. (life); mem. AMA, Bergen County Med. Soc., Med. Soc. N.J., N.J. Psychiat. Assn. Congregationalist. Office: 10 Wilsey Sq Ridgewood NJ 07450-3729

BRITT, JACQUELYN G., planning specialist, image consultant; b. Washington, Aug. 25; d. Joe Samuel and Mary Ann (Holloway) B. Student, U. D.C., 1991—. Film technician Martin Luther King Jr. Pub. Libr., Washington, 1969-78; data monitor Biometric Rsch. Inst., Washington, 1978-81; tchr. Children Pre-Sch., Washington, 1981-82; data Coord. Fed. Home Loan Bank Bd., Washington, 1982-83; legal clk. Howrey & Simon Anti Trust Law Firm, Washington, 1983-85; data base analyst Dist. Govt. Cancer Registry, Washington, 1985-89; planning specialist Fed. Emergency Mgmt. Agy., Washington, 1989—. Leader Girl Scouts of Am., Washington, 1985-87. Recipient Recognition of Zealous and Meritorious Svc. award Mt. Airy Bapt. Ch. Youth Tng. Com., Washington, 1985, Outstanding and Dedicated Svc. award Mt. Airy Bapt. Ch. Bd. Christian Edn., Washington, 1985. Mem. NAACP, NAFE, Nat. Coun. Negro Women (asst. corr. sec. Washington sect. 1985, award 1990-91, 2d v.p. 1991-92), Assn. Tchr. Educators, Spl. Needs Com. (trainer 1989—), Sr. Usher Bd. #2, Get Acquainted Club (v.p. 1988—). Baptist.

BRITT, MAISHA DORRAH, protective services official; b. S.C.; d. Charles Joseph Britt and Versena (Kennedy) Dorrah; m. W. Benjamin Williams, Dec. 14, 1963 (div. June 1976); children: Terri Rochelle, Trina Michelle. AS, BS, Phila Coll. Textiles and Sci.; MA, Antioch U., Phila., 1986. Cert. in Electronic Surveillance. Physician's asst. Dr. Leonard B. Segal, Phila., 1973-76; police officer Phila. Police Dept., 1976-79; sgt. county detective Phila. Dist. Atty's Office, 1979-90; spl. agt. Bur. Consumer Protection Office of Atty. Gen., Phila., 1990-91; orgn. devel. cons., v.p. Applied Resource Mgmt., Inc., 1991—; founder, dir. Creative Awareness Workshop, Phila., 1978—. Sec. bd. Horizon House, Phila., 1988—; vol. Women Against Abuse, Phila., 1983—, youth adv. New Gethsemane Bapt. Ch., Phila., 1978—; mem. bd. trustees Ctr. for Literacy, 1990—, vice chmn. Recipient award of Appreciation Dobbins High Sch. Alumni Assn., 1991, Woman of Yr. citation Pa. Fedn. Bus. and Profl. Women's Clubs Inc. Mem. Am. Soc. for Indsl. Security, County Detectives Assn. Pa. (exec. bd. 1990—), Fraternal Order of Police, Internat. Police Assn., Internat. Assn. Women Police, Nat. Women's Hall of Fame, Nat. Assn. Chiefs of Police, Bus. and Profl. Women's Club, Internat. Platform Assn. Democrat.

BRITTAIN, ROSS, radio personality; b. Chgo., May 31, 1951; s. Arthur Martin and Jeanne (Riemenschneider) Smith; m. Rasa Kaye Bobelis, Feb. 20, 1982. BS in Applied Psychology, Ga. Tech. U., 1974. Morning and afternoon disk jockey, program dir. Sta. WIIN Radio, Atlanta, 1974-76; talk show host Sta. TV 36, Atlanta, 1976-77; afternoon disk jockey Sta. WSSA Radio, Atlanta, 1976-77; corr. Cable News Network, Atlanta, 1980-81; morning disk jockey Sta. Z93 Radio div. 1st Media Corp., Atlanta, 1978-81, Sta. WABC Radio div. ABC Broadcasting, N.Y.C., 1981-83, Sta. Z100 Radio div. Malrite Broadcasting, N.Y.C., 1983-85, 87—, Sta. WEGX Radio div. Malrite Broadcasting, Phila., 1985-87. Host many radio shows, including National Lampoon True Facts, L.A., 1987-90, Trivia Quiz, N.Y.C., 1984-86; columnist: O'Liners, 1980-85, ABC Show Prep Service, 1988—; writer, producer: Rockin' America, 1984-86. Celebrity co-chmn. N.J. Coun. for Spina Bifida, 1989—. Named Major Market Air Personality Billboard Mag., 1988. Mem. Christian Ch. Office: Sta WHTZ PO Box 7100 New York NY 10150-7100

BRITTO, RONALD, economics educator; b. Karachi, Pakistan, Apr. 19, 1937; came to U.S., 1960; s. Charles Francis and Elvira (Pereira) Britto Desouza; m. Zenaida Borja Pacumio, Aug. 20, 1975; 1 child, Ruth. BA, St. Patrick's Coll., Karachi, 1956; diploma in econs., U. Heidelberg, Fed. Republic Germany, 1960; PhD, Brown U., 1966. Asst. prof. Tufts U., Medford, Mass., 1963-68, UCLA, 1968-74; assoc. prof. econs. SUNY, Binghamton, 1974-83, prof., 1983—. Contbr. articles to profl. jours. Mem. Am. Econ. Assn. Office: SUNY Dept Econs Binghamton NY 13903

BRITTON, JOANNE HESS, newspaper executive; b. Syracuse, N.Y.; d. Bernard J. and Mary L. (Jost) Hess; m. William C. Britton; children: Scott Dennis, Mary Dennis Swanson, (step-daughter) Barbara, (step-son) Christopher. BA in Journalism and Spanish, Syracuse U., 1957; postgrad. extension program., U. Wis. Feature writer The Syracuse Newspapers, 1968-77, lifestyle editor, 1977-81, dir. community rels., 1981-85, dir. ednl. svcs., 1985—. Mem. bd. dirs. Syracuse Girls Club, 1987-88. Recipient Community Svc. award, Syracuse, award Cen. N.Y. chpt. Am. Cancer Soc., N.Y.C. Heart Assn., Literacy award, Oswego Reading Coun., 1988. Mem. Am. Newspapers Pubs. Assn. (coord. Newspapers in Edn. Weeks, 1988—), Internat. Reading Coun., N.Y. State Reading Coun., (literacy award 1989), Women in Communications (past pres.), Onondage County Libr. Assn., Literacy Vols. of Am., Laubach Literacy Coun., N.Y.C. Literary Vols. Office: The Syracuse Newspapers PO Box 4915 Syracuse NY 13221-4915

BRITTON, JOHN EDGAR, lawyer; b. Erie, Pa., June 4, 1921; s. Ray W. and Freda (Berlin) B.; married, June 17, 1950; children: Judith B. Bonanno, John W. AB, Bucknell U., 1942; JD, Harvard U., 1948. Ptnr. MacDonald, Illig, Jones & Britton, Erie, Pa., 1948—; pres. Erie Bottling Corp., 1953-88, Tannetics, Inc., 1969-83; bd. dirs. Eriez Mfg. Co., McInnes Steel Co., Efco, Inc., The Britton Family Found., pres. 1988—. Pres. Hamot Health Systems, Inc., Erie, 1969, trustee 1970-80; founder, dir. Greater Erie Charity Golf Classic, 1970—. 1st lt. USAF, 1942-45. Fellow Am. Coll. Trial Lawyers; mem. Erie County Bar Assn. (Chancellor of the bar 1991), Kahkwa Club (pres. 1968), Fiddlesticks Country Club. Republican. Lutheran.

BRITTON-RILEY, DEBORAH ALEXIS, health program analyst; b. N.Y.C., Oct. 28, 1953; d. Theodore Daniel and Verdelle Dorothy (Pickett) Britton; m. Michael Anthony Riley; 1 child, Marc Anthony. BA in Social Scis., SUNY, Stony Brook, 1978, MS in Healthcare Mgmt., 1981. Rsch. analyst U. Hosp., Stony Brook, 1981-83; adminstr. Planned Parenthood, Huntington, N.Y., 1983-85; sr. health planner Health Systems Agy. of N.Y., 1985-87; regional health analyst Nassau-Suffolk Health Systems Agy., Plainview, N.Y., 1987-88, sr. health program analyst, 1988—. Pres. Parents Community Adv. Bd., Teaneck, N.J., 1985; bd. dirs. Planned Parenthood, Suffolk County, N.Y., 1987-89, North Brookhaven Health Coun., Coram, N.Y., 1988; chmn. edn. com. NAACP, 1990; v.p. PTA. Recipient Rockefeller fellowship, Rockefeller Found., N.Y., 1978-81. Mem. NAACP (chair edn. com., 1990). Republican. Episcopalian. Home: 35 Country Club Dr # B Coram NY 11727-3426 Office: Suffolk County Dept Health 225 Rabro Dr Hauppauge NY 11788-4290

BRITZ, DIANE EDWARD, investment company executive; b. York, Pa., June 15, 1952; d. Everett Frank and Billie Jacqueline (Sherrill) B.; m. Marcello Lotti, Sept. 9, 1978 (dec. Apr. 1990); children: Ariane Elizabeth, Samantha Alexis. BA, Duke U., 1974; MBA, Columbia U., 1982. Asst. mgr. Columbia Artists, N.Y.C., 1974-76; gen. mgr. Eastern Music Festival, Greensboro, N.C., 1977-78; v.p. Britz Cobin, N.Y.C., 1979-82; pres. Pan Oceanic Mgmt., Inc., N.Y.C., 1983-90, chmn., 1990—, 1990—, also bd. dirs.; pres. Pan Oceanic Advisors, Ltd., N.Y.C., 1988—, also bd. dirs; chmn. bd. Pan Oceanic Mgmt., N.Y.C., 1990—; bd. dirs. Qualitech, Inc., 1990-91. Bd. advisors Turtle Bay Music Sch.; bd. dirs. The 1148 Corp. Mem. Fin. Women's Assn. (bd. dirs.), Caramoor Garden Guild (bd. dirs.), Columbia Bus. Sch. Club of N.Y. (reunion chmn.), Doubles Club. Mem. Soc. of Friends.

BRNA, SUSAN EILEEN, musician; b. Atlantic City, N.J., Sept. 29, 1956; d. Robert Calvin and Vincenzina Marie (Briguglio) B. Diploma in profl. music, Berklee Coll. Music, Boston, 1985. Free-lance musician, guitarist, songwriter, 1975—; musician, guitarist, songwriter First Impression, N.J., 1990—. Composer song "Love Won't Pass Me By". Faculty scholar Atlantic Community Coll., 1979-80, Berklee Coll. Music, 1984-85.

BROADBENT, J. STREETT, engineering executive; b. Balt., Nov. 15, 1942; s. Walter Scott and Mabel Naomi (House) B.; m. Barbara Bea Petschke, Aug. 14, 1965; children: Kenneth Streett, Sandra Lynn. AB in Physics, Western Md. Coll., Westminster, 1964; postgrad., Johns Hopkins U., 1969-75. Applied research engr. Black & Decker, Towson, Md., 1964-67; instrumentation engr. Black & Decker, 1967-68, test supr., test mgr., 1969-76; resident engring. mgr. Black & Decker, Hampstead, Md., 1976-79; engring. mgr. Black & Decker, 1979-84; real estate sales rep. Towson, Md., 1972-76; engring. mgr. Black & Decker, Towson, 1985—. Advancement chmn. Boy Scouts Am., Reisterstown, Md., 1985-87; chmn. Md. Young Woman of the Yr., 1983—; treas., 1979-83; treas. Greenbrier Improvement Assn., 1967-69, pres., 1969-70; mem. adv. bd. Essex Community Coll., 1988-89; fund raising com. Western Md. Coll., 1968-72; com. Reisterstown Revializtion, 1976-77. With U.S. Army N.G., 1964-70. Mem. Instrumentation Soc. Am. (sr.), Am. Soc. for Metals, NSPE, Computer and Automated Systems Assn., U.S. Power Squadrons (Dunalk instr. 1990-91), Bull/Bear Invesment Club (treas. 1985-91). Home: 3 Meadowmist Ct Reisterstown MD 21136-1318 Office: Black & Decker Corp 701 E Joppa Rd Baltimore MD 21204-5502

BROADHURST, MARTIN GILBERT, physicist; b. Washington, Apr. 28, 1932; s. Gilbert Samuel and Estelle (Martin) B.; m. Virginia Ruth Viemeister, June 5, 1955 (div.); children: David Martin, Steven Gilbert; m. Helen Ann Phillips. AA in Sci., Montgomery Coll., 1952; BA in Physics, Western Md. Coll., 1955; MS in Physics, Pa. State U., 1957, PhD in Physics, 1959. Rsch. assoc. Pa. State U., State College, 1959-60; rsch. physicist Nat. Bur. Standards, Washington, 1960-67; sect. chief Nat. Bur. Standards, Gaithersburg, Md., 1967-80, dep. div. chief, 1980-83, asst. div. chief, 1983-88; cons. Broadhurst Cons., Washington Grove, Md., 1988—. Contbr. articles to profl. jours. Fellow Am. Phys. Soc., Washington Acad. Scis.; mem. Am. Chem. Soc., IEEE, Joint Bd. Sci. & Engring. Edn. Republican. Unitarian. Home: 116 Ridge Rd # 163 Washington Grove MD 20880-0163 Office: Nat Inst Stds & Tech Gaithersburg MD 20899

BROADUS, JAMES MATTHEW, research center administrator; b. Mobile, Ala., Feb. 24, 1947; m. Victoria Anne Gordon; children: Matthew Lee, Victoria Rose, Joseph Gordon. BA, Oberlin Coll., 1969; MA, Yale U., 1972, M.Phil., 1974, PhD, 1976. Economist U.S. Dept. Justice, Washington, 1975-79; vis. asst. prof. econs. U. Ky., Lexington, 1979-81; rsch. fellow Marine Policy Ctr., Woods Hole (Mass.) Oceangraphic Instn., 1981-82; policy assoc. Marine Policy Ctr., 1982-84, social scientist, 1984—, dir., 1986—; mem. marine bd. NRC, Washington, 1989—, Panel on the Law Ocean Uses, N.Y.C., 1988—; bd. govs. Bigelow Lab., W. Boothbay Harbor, Maine, 1983-89; vis. assoc. prof. sci. and soc. Wesleyan U., 1986; adj. prof. marine policy U. Del., 1990—; adv. com. U.S.-Japan Nat. Resources Agreement, 1991—; mem. UN Group of Experts on Sci. Aspects of Marine Pollution (GESAMP), 1986-89; mem. UN Regional Working Groups on Implications of Climatic Change, 1989-91. Editorial bd. Jour. Aquatic Conservation; editorial advisor Oceanus; assoc. editor Jour. Coastal Rsch. Grad. fellow Yale U., 1971-75. Mem. Am. Econ. Assn., Assn. Environ. Resource Economists, Marine Tech. Soc., AAAS, Nat. Man and the Biosphere Program, Marine & Coastal Ecosystems Directorate (chmn.). Office: Woods Hole Oceanographic Inst Woods Hole MA 02543

BROADWELL, RICHARD DOW, neurocytologist, neuropathologist, researcher, educator; b. Oak Park, Ill., Nov. 4, 1945; s. Robert and Dorothy Jane (Dow) B. BA, Knox Coll., 1967; MS, U. Wis., Madison, 1971, D Phil, 1974. Staff fellow in neurocytology/neuropathology Nat. Inst. Neurol. and Communicable Diseases and Stroke, NIH, Bethesda, Md., 1974-80; full prof. pathology and neurol. surgery, head Lab. Exptl. Neuropathology and Labs. Neuro-Oncology and Cerebrovascular Studies (Neurol. Surgery), Brain Transplantation, U. Md. Sch. Medicine, 1980—; dir. molecular and cellular neurobiology program NSF, Washington, 1987-89; coord. Decade of the Brain, Vets. Rsch. Adminstrn., Washington, 1991-92; cons. in field. Contbr. numerous articles, chpts. on brain and neurocytology to profl. publs.; mem. editorial bd. Jour. Neurocytology, Jour. Histochemistry and Cytochemistry, Exptl. Neurol., Rstorative Neurology and Neurosci. Recipient Rsch. award NSF, 1966-67; Japanese Soc. for Promotion of Sci. fellow, 1980-81; NIH Nat. Inst. Neurol. and Communicable Diseases and Stroke grantee, 1982—. Mem. Neurosci. Soc., Am. Soc. Cell Biology, Histochem. Soc., Chesapeake Electron Microscopy Soc. Republican. Presbyterian. Home: 10939 Brewer House Rd Rockville MD 20852-3456 Office: U Md Div Neurol Surgery 10 S Pine St Baltimore MD 21201-1192

BROCATO, ANDREW, JR., public affairs coordinator; b. Buffalo, Jan. 22, 1965; s. Andrew Charles Brocato and Nancy Ann (Dolan) McNutt; m. Rosetta Christina Farruggia, May 26, 1990. BS in Media Communications, Medaille Coll., 1987. Account exec. William Collins Assocs., Buffalo, 1987-89; cons., spl. events coord. Sta. WKBW-TV, Buffalo, 1989-90; pub. affairs coord. Buffalo Zool. Gardens, 1990—. Mem. Tourism Mktg. Com., Buffalo, 1990-92, Cultural Consortium, Buffalo, 1990-92, Young Profls. Bd. of the Zoo, Buffalo, 1990-92; parliamentarian Medaille Coll. Alumni Bd., Buffalo, 1989-91, sec., 1991-92. Mem. Pub. Rels. Assn. Western N.Y. (treas. 1990-91, v.p. 1991—, sec. communications steering com.). Democrat. Roman Catholic. Home: 33 Caroline Ln Depew NY 14043-1905 Office: Buffalo Zool Gardens Delaware Park Buffalo NY 14214-1999

BROCHU, CLAUDE RENAUD, professional sports team executive; b. Quebec City, Quebec, Can.; m. Michelle Dénommée. BA, U. Ottawa, Ont., Can., 1966; MBA, McMaster U., Hamilton, Ont., 1971. Worked in cosmetics industry, 1971-76; exec. v.p. mktg. Joseph E. Seagram & Sons, Ltd., Montreal, Can., 1976-86; pres., operating officer Montreal Expos, 1986—, pres., gen. ptnr. Capt. Can. armed forces. Office: Montreal Expos, PO Box 500 Sta M, Montreal, PQ Canada H1V 3P2

BROCK, CHARLES LAWRENCE, lawyer, business executive; b. Ottumwa, Iowa, Mar. 7, 1943; s. Charles Harlan and Betty Arlene (Ream) B.; m. Mary Jane Hipp, June 17, 1978; children: William Walker, Susanna Lawrence. BA with highest distinction, Northwestern U., 1964; JD, Harvard U., 1967; postgrad. (Rotary Found. fellow), U. Delhi (India) and India Law Inst., 1967-68; grad., Advanced Mgmt. Program, Harvard Bus. Sch., 1979. Bar: N.Y. 1968. Asso. firm Sullivan & Cromwell, N.Y.C., 1969-74; v.p., corp. sec., gen. counsel Scholastic Mags., Inc. (now Scholastic, Inc.), N.Y.C., 1974-80; interim chief fin. and chief ops. officer Scholastic Mags., Inc., 1975-76, pub. internat. div., 1976-80; pres. Scholastic Tab Publs. Ltd., Can., 1976-80, Ashton-Scholastic Pty. Ltd., Australia, 1976-80, Ashton-Scholastic Ltd., N.Z., 1976-80; chmn. Scholastic Publs. Ltd., U.K., 1976-80; sr. v.p., mgmt. dir. Compton Communications, 1980-82; mgr. subsidiaries Compton Advertising, 1980-82; counsel Drinker, Biddle & Reath, N.Y.C., Phila., Washington, 1982-84; ptnr. Carter, Ledyard & Milburn, 1984—; bd. dirs., chmn. audit coms. B&H Bulk Carriers Ltd., B&H Ocean Carriers Ltd., B&H Maritime Carriers Ltd., Harvard Alumni Assn., bd. dirs. 1990— (two terms), chmn., grad. schs. Relations Comm. 1992—; Harvard Coll. Bd. Overseers Comm. on University Resources, 1992—; coun. Harvard Law Sch. Assn., 1983-85, sec., 1988-90, treas., 1990—, mem. exec. com., 1986—, chmn. membership com., 1987—, internat. com., 1991—; vis. com. Coll. Arts and Scis., Northwestern U., 1989—, Campaign for Gt. Tchrs. Com., 1989-90; John Evans Club, Northwestern U. 1989—; guild hall trustee, mem. exec. comm. chmn. nominating committee, 1986-90, chmn. bd., 1990-92, Acad. of the Arts 1990—, trustee, treas. Family Dynamics, 1981-88. Anniversary gift chmn. Harvard Law Sch. Fund, 1967-68, vice chmn., 1975-77; trustee Harvard Law Sch. Assn. N.Y.C., 1982-85, chmn. placement com., 1983-86, v.p.,1985-86, originator, chmn. summer reception, 1982; mem. Harvard Bus. Club of N.Y., v.p. 1984-86, chmn. Harvard Community Ptnrs., 1984-86; co-chmn. Ann. Giving, St. Barnard's Sch., 1989—; deacon Brick Presbyn. Ch., N.Y.C., 1973-76. Mem. Am. Bar Assn., N.Y. State Bar Assn., N.Y. County Lawyers Assn., Assn. Bar City N.Y., Assn. Am. Pubs., Guild Hall (trustee, exec. com., chmn. nominating com. 1986-90, chmn. bd. 1990-92), Harvard Alumni Assn. (bd. dirs. 1990—, chmn. grad. schs. rels. com. 1992), Acad. of Arts (chmn. bd. 1990—), Phi Beta Kappa, Kappa Sigma. Clubs: Union (N.Y.C.), N.Y. Yacht (N.Y.C.), Down Town (N.Y.C.); Piping Rock (Locust Valley, N.Y.); Maidstone (East Hampton, N.Y.). Home: 765 Park Ave New York NY 10021-4254 Office: Carter Ledyard & Milburn 2 Wall St New York NY 10005-2001

BROCK, WILLIAM ALTON, pediatric urologist; b. Bklyn., Mar. 29, 1946; s. Charles Henry and Mary (Campisi) B.; m. Patricia Pfirman, June 16, 1968 (div. 1983); m. Patricia Skelton, Dec. 8, 1983. BS, Fordham U., 1967; MD, Emory U., 1971. Diplomate Am. Bd. Urology. Intern surgery N.Y. Hosp., N.Y.C., 1971-72, resident surgery, 1972-73; resident urology U. Calif., San Diego, 1975-79; fellow pediatric urology U. Liverpool, Eng., 1979; chmn. dept. pediatric urology Children's Hosp., San Diego, 1984-85; prof. urology Albert Einstein Coll. Medicine, Bronx, N.Y., 1989—; ptnr. Pediatric Urologic Assocs., San Diego, 1979-85; chief pediatric urology L.I. Jewish Med. Ctr., New Hyde Park, N.Y., 1985—; assoc. prof. urology U. Calif., San Diego, 1980-85, SUNY, Stony Brook, 1985-89; sci. advisor Nat. Kidney Found., San Diego, 1981-85; chmn. quality assurance dept. urology L.I. Jewish Med. Ctr., New Hyde Park, N.Y., 1989-92; vis. prof. Wake Forest Sch. Medicine, Winston-Salem, N.C., 1988. Reviewer Jour. Urology, 1990-92; author med. textbooks; contbr. articles to profl. jours. Maj. USAF, 1973-75. Fellow ACS, Am. Acad. Pediatrics, N.Y. Acad. Medicine; mem. AMA, Soc. Pediatric Urology, Am. Urologic Assn., Pediatrics Soc. Dominican Republic (hon.). Roman Catholic. Office: Schneider Childrens Hosp New Hyde Park NY 11042

BROCKENBROUGH, ROGER LEWIS, engineering company executive, consultant; b. Buena Vista, Va., July 31, 1934; s. Bernard Jeremiah and Lucy Myrtle (Orr) B.; m. Nancy Ann Thibodeau, Oct. 5, 1957; children: John Roger, Allan Edward, Elaine Marian, Roger Thomas. BSCE, Va. Poly. Inst. and State U., 1954, MS in Structural Engring., 1956. Registered profl. engr., Pa. Engr. trainee Newport News (Va.) Shipbuilding and Dry Dock Co., 1954; engr. Pitts. (Pa.) Des Moines Steel Co., 1957-61; sr. rsch. cons. U.S. Steel Group, USX Corp., Pitts., 1961-91; pres. R.L. Brockenbrough & Assocs., Inc., Pitts., 1989—; chmn. com. on specifications for steel design Am. Inst. Steel Constrn., Chgo., 1985-91. Author: (computer program) STEEL-PIPE, 1990; patentee in field; contbr. chpts. to books and articles to profl. jours. 1st lt. U.S. Army, 1956-57. Fellow ASCE (com. on composite constrn.); mem. ASTM (subcom. chair 1980—), Am. Assn. State Hwy. Ofcls. (liaison com.), Am. Iron and Steel Inst. (chmn. com. on specifications for cold-formed steel 1990—), Nat. Corrugated Steel Pipe Assn. Home and Office: 17 Carleton Dr Pittsburgh PA 15243

BROCKINGTON, HORACE, gallery director, consultant, curator; b. N.Y.C., Apr. 30, 1954; s. Horace and Mattie (Kennedy) B. BA, Columbia U., 1975, postgrad., 1977; postgrad., Brown U., 1979—. Curatorial intern Whitney Mus. of Am. Art, N.Y.C., 1975; gallery asst. Just Above Midtown Gallery, 1974-78; curatorial dir. Roosevelt Art Gallery, Hempstead, N.Y., 1978-80; dir., co-founder Art Across the Park, N.Y.C., 1980-85; prof. Kean Coll., Union, N.J., 1981-82, 84-85; prof. art history Brown U., 1982; curator Inst. for Contemporary Art, N.Y.C., 1982; curatorial dir. Horace Brockington Gallery, N.Y.C., 1985—; tchr. fine arts CCNY/CUNY, summer 1970; asst. to curator of exhibitions Studio Mus. in Harlem, N.Y.C., 1972-73, guest lectr., 1975, guest curator, 1979, Franklin Furnace, N.Y., 1979, 83, Brown U./Afro-Am. Studies Dept., Providence, 1980, 81, Real Art Ways, Hartford, Conn., 1982, Alternative Mus., N.Y., 1982, N.Y. Art Parade, 1983, Sculpture Ctr., N.Y., 1984, Tyler Sch. Art Temple U., Phila., 1988, Montage Found., Cambridge, Mass., 1990—, others; intern primitive art dept. Balt. Mus. Art, 1973; art cons. edn. program Northside Ctr. for Child Devel., N.Y., 1974; guest curator, cons. Met. Mus. Art, N.Y., 1974; co-curator Whitney Mus. of Am. Art, N.Y., 1975; spl. lectr. in Am. art history Dalton Sch., N.Y., 1976; asst. to account exec. Ruder and Finn Inc., N.Y., 1976-77; asst. to coord. Video/Media Resource Ctr. Columbia U., N.Y.C., 1977; cons. V.A.R.A.C., N.Y., 1978, Nippon Mus./Ruder and Finn., N.Y., 1978, Chester (Pa.) Mus., 1987, Just Above Midtown, N.Y., 1978, guest lectr., 1979; artists studio visits coord. Lafayette Club, N.Y., 1981, Stanford Club, N.Y., 1980-82, 84; curatorial dir. Projects in Art and Architecture, N.Y., 1989-91, Archit, N.Y., 1986—; active numerous other career related activities. Workshop asst. Children's Art Carnival/Mus. of Modern Art, N.Y., 1973-74; panelist com. for small instns. NEA, N.Y., 1972; contbn. advisor Pvt. Donor Art to Small Instns., N.Y.C., 1981. Ralph Bunche fellow U.S. Assn. UN, 1973, Rubinstein fellow Whitney Mus., 1975, Brown U. fellow, 1979-82; Nat. Merit scholar, 1970-71, Martin scholar Columbia U., 1973. Mem. Am. Mgmt. Assn., BTC Book Club (v.p.). Office: Horace Brockington Gallery PO Box 1880 New York NY 10025-1558

BROCKS, ERIC RANDY, ophthalmologist, surgeon; b. N.Y.C., Apr. 24, 1946; s. William Benjamin and Muriel (Welk) B.; m. Irene Loretta Kraut, Dec. 19, 1970; children: Jason Matthew, Daniel Charles. BA with high honors, U. Rochester, 1968, MD, 1972. Diplomate Am. Bd. Ophthalmology, Nat. Bd. Med. Examiners. Intern medicine NYU Sch. Medicine, N.Y.C., 1973, resident, chief resident ophthalmology, 1973-76; chief resident ophthalmology Bellevue Hosp., NYU Hosp., Manhattan VA Hosp., N.Y.C., 1975-76; attending physician St. Francis Hosp., Beacon, N.Y., 1976-89; asst./assoc. attending physician Vassar Bros. Hosp., Poughkeepsie, N.Y., 1976-80, attending physician, 1980—; clin. asst. ophthalmology Tisch (NYU) Hosp., N.Y.C., 1976—; clin. asst. attending physician Bellevue Hosp. Ctr., N.Y.C., 1976—; eye physician and surgeon Hudson Valley Eye Surgeons, P.C., Fishkill, N.Y., 1976—; cons. ophthalmology Julia Butterfield Hosp., Cold Spring, N.Y., 1981—, West Point (N.Y.) Mil. Acad., Keller Army Hosp., 1989—; chief surgery St. Francis Hosp., beacon, 1988-89, dir. ophthalmology sect., 1981-88, chief of staff, 1979-81; dir. dept. ophthalmology Vassar Bros. Hosp., 1992—; clin. asst. prof. ophthalmology NYU Sch. Medicine, N.Y.C., 1983—, course dir. ophthalmology elective, 1976-91; so. N.Y. coord. Nat. Eye Care Project, San Francisco, 1985—. Contbr. articles to profl. jours. Vol. admissions network U. Rochester, 1986—. Fellow ACS, Am. Acad. Ophthalmology (media

coord. N.Y. state Nat. Eye Care projects 1978—, pub. info. coun. 1985—); mem. AMA, Am. Acad. Cataract and Refractive Surgery, Med. Soc. State N.Y. (ho. of dels. 1984-89, govt. affairs subcom. 1987), Dutchess County Med. Soc. (exec. com. 1982—, chmn. legis. liaison com. 1990—, pres. 1990-91), Boca West Club. Office: Hudson Valley Eye Surgeons So Dutchess Profl Park 335 Rt 52 Fishkill NY 12524

BRODER, DAVID SALZER, reporter; b. Chicago Heights, Ill., Sept. 11, 1929; s. Albert I. and Nina M. (Salzer) B.; m. Ann Creighton Collar, June 8, 1951; children: George, Joshua, Matthew, Michael. BA, U. Chgo., 1947, MA, 1951; LittD, Denison U., 1975; LLD (hon.), Wabash Coll., 1977, Kenyon Coll., 1980, Cleve. State U., 1981, Wittenberg Coll., 1982, Yale U., 1984, Ind. U., 1985, Kalamazoo Coll., 1988, Rider Coll., 1989, Dartmouth Coll., 1990, Colby Coll., 1990, Lawrence U., 1991. Reporter Pantagraph, Bloomington, Ill., 1953-55, Congressional Quar., Washington, 1955-60, Washington Star, 1960-65, N.Y. Times, Washington bur., 1965-66; reporter Washington Post, 1966-75, assoc. editor, 1975—; syndicated columnist. Author: (with Stephen Hess) The Republican Establishment, 1967, The Party's Over: The Failure of Politics in America, 1972, Changing of the Guard: Power and Leadership in America, 1980, Behind The Front Page: A Candid Look At How the News Is Made, 1987; contbr. articles on public affairs to mags. and books. Former mem. U. Chgo. Alumni cabinet. Served with AUS, 1951-53. Recipient Pulitzer prize in journalism, 1973, Common Wealth award, Elijah Parrish Lovejoy award, 1990; fellow Inst. Politics, John F. Kennedy Sch. of Govt., Harvard U., 1969-70; Poynter fellow Yale and Ind. univs., 1973. Fellow Inst. Policy Scis. and Pub. Affairs of Duke, Am. Acad. Arts and Scis., Sigma Delta Chi; mem. Am. Polit. Sci. Assn. (adv. bd. Congrl. Fellows Program 1964—, Carey McWilliams award 1983), Am. Soc. Pub. Adminstrn., Nat. Press Club (4th Estate award 1988), Gridiron Club. Home: 4024 27th St N Arlington VA 22207-5207 Office: Washington Post 1150 15th St NW Washington DC 20071-0002

BRODER, DOUGLAS FISHER, lawyer; b. Cleve., Sept. 30, 1948; s. Harry M. and Peggy (Fisher) B.; m. Rebecca Northey, Jan. 24, 1976; 1 child, Julia N. BA, Vassar Coll., 1970; JD cum laude, Boston U., 1977. Bar: N.Y. 1978, U.S. Dist. Ct. (so. and ea. dists.) N.Y. 1978, U.S. Ct. Appeals (2d cir.) 1983, U.S. Ct. Appeals (6th cir.) 1986, U.S. Ct. Appeals (4th cir.) 1987, U.S. Dist. Ct. (ea. dist.) Mich. 1987. Assoc. Lord, Day & Lord, N.Y.C., 1977-86; ptnr. Coudert Bros., N.Y.C., 1986—. Contbr. articles to profl. publs. Mem. Assn. of Bar of City of N.Y., Internat. Bar Assn. Home: 300 Central Park W New York NY 10024-1513 Office: Coudert Bros 200 Park Ave New York NY 10166-0005

BRODERICK, GREGORY PHILIP, university educator, consultant; b. Boston, July 24, 1952; s. Edward Philip and Alice Broderick; m. Deanna Tear; children: Jennifer, Alex-Andrea. BS in Civil Engring., Northeastern U., 1975, MS in Civil Engring., 1978; PhD, U. Tex., 1987. Lectr. Northeastern U., Boston, 1978-82; asst. prof. U. New Haven, 1987-90, assoc. prof., 1990—; cons. Dames & Moore, N.J., 1986, Woodside Offshore Petroleum PTy Ltd, Australia,1987, T.W. Lambe Inc., Boston, 1979-82, Casio & Bechir Inc., North Haven, Conn.,. Recipient Yale Univ./Mellon fellowship, Yale Univ., New Haven, 1988-89. Mem. ASCE, Conn. Soc. Civil Engrs. (newsletter editor 1990-92, pres. award 1991), Am. Soc. of Testing Materials, Am. Soc. of Engring. Educators, Internat. Soc. of Soil Mechanics and Found. Engrs. Home: 616 Nortontown Rd Guilford CT 06437 Office: U of New Haven 300 Orange Ave West Haven CT 06516-1999

BRODERICK, VINCENT LYONS, federal judge; b. N.Y.C., Apr. 26, 1920; s. Joseph A. and Mary Rose (Lyons) B.; m. Sally Brine, Apr. 15, 1950; children: Kathleen, Vincent, Mary, Ellen, Joan, Justin. A.B., Princeton U., 1941; LL.B., Harvard U., 1948. Bar: N.Y. 1948. Assoc. Hatch, Root and Barrett, N.Y.C., 1948-54; dep. commr. charge legal matters N.Y.C. Police Dept., 1954-56; gen. counsel Nat. Assn. Investment Cos., N.Y.C., 1956-61; chief asst. U.S. atty. U.S. Dist. Ct. (so. dist.), N.Y., 1961-62, 62-65, U.S. atty., 1962; judge U.S. Dist. Ct. (so. dist.) N.Y., N.Y.C., 1976—; police commr. N.Y.C., 1965-66; mem. firm Phillips, Nizer, Benjamin, Krim & Ballon, 1966-71, Forsyth, Decker, Murray & Broderick, 1971-76; chmn. com. on criminal law Jud. Conf. U.S. Office: US Dist Ct 101 E Post Rd White Plains NY 10601-5086

BRODEUR, JOHN HOMER, corporate executive; b. Worcester, Mass., Dec. 6, 1935; s. Edward Alfred and Albani (Rocheleau) B.; m. Jean Filoramo, June 20, 1961 (div. 1966); 1 child, Russell P.; m. Celine Marie Delaney, June 27, 1970; children: Ann M., Marc A., Julienne A. BS in Acctg., Rutgers U., 1965. Jr. acct. Hackeling, Oberkirch, Corbin & Co., N.Y.C., 1959-62; gen. acctg. mgr. Art Metal, Inc., Avanel, N.J., 1962-63; asst. treas. Bowen Engring., Inc., Somerville, N.J., 1963-74; cons. Raritan, N.J., 1974-77; contr. Keenan Binders, Inc., Middlesex, N.J., 1977-80; sec.-treas. Cooper Alloy Corp., Hillside, N.J., 1980—; cons. Printmaking Coun. N.J., North Branch, 1978-80. Pres. Jaycees, Bridgewater, N.J., 1971. With U.S. Army, 1956-58. Mem. Nat. Assn. Accts., Contrs. Coun., Planning Coun. Republican. Roman Catholic. Office: Cooper Alloy Corp Bloy St and Ramsay Ave Hillside NJ 07205

BRODEUR, PAUL ADRIAN, journalist; b. Boston, May 16, 1931; s. Paul A. Brodeur and Sarah Marjorie (Smith) Totten; divorced; children: Stephen Baird, Adrienne Willets. BA in English, Harvard U., 1953. Lectr. Sch. Journalism, Columbia U., N.Y.C., 1969-80; staff writer New Yorker mag., N.Y.C., 1958—. Author: The Sick Fox, 1963, The Stunt Man,, 1970, Downstream, 1972, Asbestos and Enzymes, 1972, Expendable Americans, 1974, The Zapping of America, 1977, Outrageous Misconduct, 1985, Restitution, 1985, Currents of Death, 1989; contbr. articles on environ. hazards to The New Yorker, 1965—. With Counterintelligence Corps, U.S. Army, 1953-56. Recipient Journalism prize Sidney Hillman Found., 1973, Nat. Mag. award Columbia U., 1973, Sci. award AAAS, 1976; named to Global 500 Honor Roll, UN Environment Programme, 1989; fellow Guggenheim Found., 1976-77, Alicia Patterson Found., 1978. Office: The New Yorker 20 W 43d St New York NY 10036

BRODHEAD, DAVID CRAWMER, lawyer; b. Madison, Wis., Sept. 16, 1934; s. Richard Jacob and Irma (Crawmer) B.; m. Nancie Christensen, Aug. 17, 1963; children: Compton, Peter, Christoffer. B.S., U. Wis., 1956, LL.B., 1959. Bar: N.Y. 1960, Wis. 1959, D.C. 1979. Assoc. firm Paul, Weiss, Rifkind, Wharton & Garrison, N.Y.C., 1959-68, ptnr., 1969—; dir. Centennial Industries, Inc., N.Y.C. Editor-in-chief: Wis. Law Rev, 1958-59. Trustee Collegiate Sch., N.Y.C., 1978-85; vestryman Christ and St. Stephen's Episcopal Ch., 1972-82. Mem. N.Y. State Bar, Assn. of Bar of City of N.Y., Wis. Bar. Assn., D.C. Bar Assn., ABA, Westside C. of C. of City of N.Y. (dir. 1970-83), Order of Coif, Delta Theta Phi. Clubs: Washington (Conn.); Holland Soc. of N.Y.

BRODHURST, ALBERT EDWARD, business executive, lawyer; b. St. Petersburg, Fla., Sept. 26, 1934; s. George Henry and Olive Agnes (Padget) B. BS in Civil Engring., Tri-State Coll., 1960; LLB, John Marshall Law Sch., 1965; BS in Logistics Engring., Army-Navy Sch., Washington, 1969. Bar: Ill. 1966. Cadastrial surveyor U.S. Coast and Geodetic Survey, Menlo Park, Calif., 1956-59; design engr. Boeing Corp., New Orleans, 1965-67; pres. The Brodhurst Corp., 1974—. Alderman Chgo., 1963. Served to commdr. U.S. Army, 1952-89. Mem. ABA, Am. Preparedness Assn., Soc. Logistics Engrs. Democrat. Roman Catholic. Lodge: Elks. Home and Office: The Brodhurst Corp Rt 140 Box 183 Owings Mills MD 21117

BRODIE, JONATHAN MICHAEL, investment manager; b. Cape Town, Republic South Africa, Sept. 17, 1955; came to U.S., 1982; s. Neville Brodie and Selma (Gordon) Sussman; m. Fay-Ann Brodie, Mar. 14, 1982; children: Nicola, Kerry. BBus Sci in Mktg., U. Cape Town, 1979, BA Hons in Econs., 1979; MBA, Stanford U., 1984. Investment analyst, v.p. Allan Gray Internat., Cape Town, San Francisco, Md., 1980-85; teaching asst. Stanford (Calif.) U., 1983-84; v.p., investment analyst, portfolio mgr. T. Rowe Price Assocs., Balt., 1985-88; founder, portfolio mgr. JMB Assocs., Bethesda, 1986—. Author: (with others) Economics of Health Care, 1980; contbr. articles to Businessmans Law. Bd. dirs. Ben Gurion Club, Rockville, Md., 1989—. Weiner scholar U. Cape Town 1979, Washkansky scholar 1979. Fedn. Wash., Inst. Cert. Fin. Analysts, Washington Soc. Investment Analysts, Ben Burion Club, Omicron Delta Epsilon.

BRODSKY, ALLEN, radiological and health physicist, consultant; b. Balt., Nov. 5, 1928; s. Nathan Michael and Gertrude Devera (Silberman) B.; m. Paula Fishman, June 17, 1951 (div. 1983); children: Richard, Karen, Jay; m. Phyllis Levin, Mar. 16, 1984. BS in Engring., Johns Hopkins U., 1949, MA in Physics, 1960; ScD, U. Pitts., 1966. Diplomate Am. Bd. Health Physics, Am. Bd. Indsl. Hygiene, Am. Bd. Radiology. Radiol. physics fellow Oak Ridge (Tenn.) Nat. Lab., 1950; head health physics unit U.S. Naval Rsch. Lab., Washington, 1950-52; physicist region 2 FCDA, Olney, Md., 1956-57; health physicist AEC, Washington, 1957-61; assoc. prof., rsch. assoc. Grad. Sch. Pub. Health U. Pitts., 1961-71; radiation physicist Mercy Hosp., Pitts., 1971-75; sr. health physicist U.S. Nuclear Regulatory Commn., Washington, 1975-86; prin. Allen B. Cons., Inc., Berlin, Md., 1986—; cons. CD, NAS, Washington, 1975; adj. prof. sch. pharmacy Duquesne U., Pitts., 1971-75; radiation sci. fellowship bd. Oak Ridge Associated Univs., 1967-70. Author, editor: Radiation Measurement and Protection, Vol. I, 1979, Vol. II, 1982; contbr. regulatory guides, book chpts., articles in field. Pres. Western Pa. Profs. for Peace in Mid. East, Pitts., 1970-71; witness on radiation effects U.S. Ho. of Reps., Washington, 1978, witness on radiation studies U.S. Senate, Washington, 1978-81, expert witness U.S. Dept. Justice, Washington, 1983-84. Lt. C.E., U.S. Army, 1952-54. Named W.H. Langham lectr., U. Ky., 1979, Failla Meml. lectr., Radiol. and Med. Physics Soc., Health Physics Soc. N.Y., N.Y.C., 1987; recipient Leadership and Sci. Contbns. cert. Conf. on Bioassay, Environ., and Analytical Radiochemistry, 1986. Mem. APHA, Am. Nuclear Soc., Am. Assn. Physicists in Medicine, Am. Indsl. Hygiene Assn., Am. Statis. Assn., Health Physics Soc. (chmn. standards com. 1959-61, 67-70, bd. dirs. 1967-70, pres. Western Pa. chpt. 1967-68, Western. Pa. chpt. disting. svc. award 1966, pres. Balt.-Washington chpt. 1982-83, sec.-treas. govt. sect. 1988-92, nat. founder's award 1986, Fellow award 1992). Home and Office: 2765 Ocean Pines Berlin MD 21811-9127

BRODSKY, ARTHUR JAMES, lawyer; b. N.Y.C., Aug. 29, 1946; s. Samuel William and Ruth Lila (Stolzer) B.; m. Karen S. Dworkin; 1 child, Alexandra. AB with honors, Franklin & Marshall Coll., 1967; JD, NYU, 1972. Bar: N.Y. 1972, U.S. Dist. Ct. (ea. dist.) N.Y. 1975, U.S. Ct. Appeals (2d cir.)1975. Atty. Dime Savs. Bank, N.Y.C., 1972-75; counsel Am. Ins. Assn., N.Y.C., 1975-82, corp. sec., counsel, 1982—; dir. trusts Am. Ins. Assn., Washington, 1990—; sec. Am. Ins. Services Group, Inc., N.Y.C., 1984—; sec., treas. Ctr. for Office Tech.Washington, 1984—. Editor: Survey of State Laws on Lobbying and PACs, 1986. Mem. ABA (labor law, tort and ins. practice sects.), Am. Ins. Assn. (dir. trust adminstrn. 1990—). Democrat. Home: 8205 Bondage Dr Gaithersburg MD 20882-1103 Office: Am Ins Assn 1130 Connecticut Ave NW Washington DC 20036-3904

BRODSKY, FRANK, investment executive; b. Phila., June 10, 1933; s. Max and Gertrude (Kauffman) B.; m. Elayne K. Green, Dec. 1, 1957; children: Charles, Nancy, Julie. Student, Pierce Bus. Coll., Phila., 1951-53, St. Joseph Coll., Phila., 1956-57. Vice pres. Robinson & Co., Phila., 1956-70; sr. v.p. investments Drexel Burnham Lambert, Phila., 1970-89, Prudential Securities, Phila., 1989—. Pres. Adelphi lodge B'nai B'rith, Phila., 1963-64, Golden Slipper Club and Charities, Phila., 1975-76, Jewish Nat. Fund Phila., 1982-83; co-chmn. Soviet Jewry Coun. Phila., 1987-88; trustee Fedn. Jewish Agys. Phila. Cpl. U.S. Army, 1953-55, Korea, Japan. Named Man of Yr. Adelphi lodge B'nai B'rith, 1957, recipient Youth Svcs. award, 1978; recipient Gold Medallion Golden Slipper Club and Charities, 1984; honoree investment div. Fedn. Jewish Agys., Phila., 1986. Mem. Phila. Securities Assn., Passover League Phila. (bd. dirs.), Am. Friends of Ben Gurion (bd. dirs.), B'nai B'rith (charter mem. fin. svcs. unit). Republican. Home: 106 McClenaghan Mill Rd Wyppewood PA 19096 Office: Prudential Securities 20 S 17th St 20th Fl Philadelphia PA 19103

BRODSKY, IRVING, retired social service organization administrator; b. N.Y.C., July 6, 1915; s. Abraham and Lena (Levine) B.; m. Jeanne Elizabeth Blum, May 13, 1918; children: Ellen, Robert. BA, Bklyn. Coll., 1938; cert. in social work, Columbia U., 1940. Exec. dir. Jewish Assn. for Neighborhood Ctrs., N.Y.C., 1946-57; exec. v.p. Associated YM-YWHA's of Greater N.Y., N.Y.C., 1957-81, vice chmn. bd. trustees, 1981, ret.; adj. prof. Columbia U. Sch. Social Work, N.Y.C., 1984-90; chmn. community adv. bd. Columbia U. Brookdale Inst. on Aging and Adult Human Devel., N.Y.C., 1984-90. Co-author: Adventure in Mental Health, 1946; contbr. articles to profl. jours. Assoc. chmn. Bd. Assoc. Camps-Vacation Ctrs. for Elderly, N.Y.C., 1985—; trustee, cons. Price Inst. for Entrepreneurial Studies; chmn. Roze Z. Goldstein awards com. United Jewish Appeal-N.Y. Fedn. Jewish Philanthropies; past trustee Florence G. Heller-JWB Rsch. Ctr., former chmn. program adv. com.; past trustee, mem. exec. com. Nat. Jewish Welfare Bd.; past chmn. tech. adv. com. on group work N.Y.C. Youth Bd.; chmn. com. on pub. recreation Community Coun. Greater N.Y. Cpl. U.S. Army, 1945-46. Recipient Florence Heller award Nat. Jewish Welfare Bd., 1970, Naomi and Howard Lehman Meml. award N.Y. Fedn. Jewish Philanthropies, 1978. Fellow Am. Assn. for Social Psychiatry, Internat. Assn. for Social Psychiatry; mem. Nat. Assn. Social Workers (cert.), Nat. Assn. Jewish Ctr. Workers. Home: 30 Lake Rd Rye NY 10580-1020

BRODSKY, JOSEPH ALEXANDROVICH, poet, educator; b. Leningrad, USSR, May 24, 1940; expelled from Russia, came to U.S., 1972; s. Alexander I. and Maria (Volpert) B.; 1 child, Andrei. Student, Russian secondary schs., until 1956; D.Litt. (hon.), Yale U., 1978, Dartmouth Coll., U. Keele, Amherst Coll., Uppsala U., U. Rochester, Williams Coll., Colchester U. At fifteen, began writing poetry; former milling machine operator, hospital morgue worker, metalworker, laborer on a geological expedition, stoker, translator, spent eighteen months on Soviet state farm doing hard labor; after emigration to U.S., served as poet-in-residence U. Mich., Ann Arbor, 1972-73, 74-79; former tchr. poetry and lit. Columbia Univ., NYU; tchr. Queens Coll., Smith Coll., Cambridge Univ.; Andrew W. Mellon prof. lit., Russian Mount Holyoke Coll., South Hadley, Mass., 1986—; poet laureate of U.S., 1991. Works include poetry and essays in Russian and English, Selected Poems, 1973, A Part of Speech, 1980, Uranian, 1988, Marbles, 1989, (essays) Less Than One, 1981 (Nat. Book Critics Circle award); contbr. numerous articles to profl. jours. N.Y. Inst. Humanities fellow NYU; Grantee John D. and Catherine T. MacArthur Found., 1981; recipient Nobel prize for Lit., 1987. Jewish. Office: Dept Russian Mt Holyoke Coll South Hadley MA 01075 Office: care Farrar Straus Giroux 19 Union Sq W New York NY 10003-3304*

BRODY, AARON LEO, food and packaging consultant; b. Boston, Aug. 23, 1930; s. Nathan and Lillian (Gorman) B. m. Carolyn Goldstein, Apr. 11, 1953; children: Stephen, Glen, Robyn. BS, MIT, 1951, PhD, 1957; MBA, Northeastern U., 1970. Head food rsch. labs. Whirlpool Co., St. Joseph, Mich., 1957-61; packaging and product devel. mgr. Mars, Inc., Hackettstown, N.J., 1961-66; packaging coord. Arthur D. Little, Inc., Cambridge, Mass., 1967-73; new ventures mgr. Mead Packaging, Atlanta, 1973-81; mgr. mktg. devel. Container Corp. Am., Oaks, Pa., 1981-85; v.p. strategic studies Schotland Bus. Rsch. Inc., Princeton, N.J., 1985-91; mng. dir. Rubbright/Brody, Inc., Devon, Pa., 1991—; course dir. Mich. State U., East Lansing, 1959-61; instr. Emory U., 1979, St. Joseph's U., Phila., 1990—; adj. assoc. prof. dept. food sci. U. Del., Newark, 1983-86; adj. prof. Spring Garden Coll., Phila., 1990. Contbr. articles to profl. jours.; author books; patentee in field. Mem. optimal program for edn. DeKalb County (Ga.), 1975, sec., 1975; mem. food svc. adv. com. USN, 1958-62; active Kerry for Congress campaign, 1972, Levitas for Congress campaign, 1974; mem. legis. subcom. on spl. edn. State of Ga., 1974; mem. Nat. Def. Exec. Res., 1978-88; mem. pres.'s coun. Spring Garden Coll., Phila., 1984-89. Served with AUS, 1952-54. William Underwood fellow, 1955-56; recipient Willis H. Carrier award ASHRAE, 1960, Indsl. Achievement award Inst. Food Technologists, 1972, Braverman Meml. award Israel Inst. Tech., 1976, Outstanding Alumnus award Northeastern U., 1982; named Packaging Man of Yr. Nat. Inst. Packaging, Handling and Logistic Engrs. Fellow AAAS, Packaging Inst.; mem. Inst. Food Technologists (Riester-Davis Food Packaging Achievement award 1988), Packaging Inst. (v.p. 1973-79), Soc. Packaging Profls., Inst. Packaging Profls., League Internat. Food Edn., Planning Execs. Inst., N.Y. Acad. Scis., Product Devel. and Mgmt. Assn., Sigma Xi., M.I.T. Club (pres. 1977-79, exec. com., v.p. ednl. coun., Phila. Sailing Club, Toastmasters. Home and Office: 733 Clovelly Ln Devon PA 19333-1808

BRODY, EUGENE B., psychiatrist, educator; b. Columbia, Mo., June 17, 1921; s. Samuel and Sophie B.; m. Marian Holen, Sept. 23, 1944; children: Julie Anne Brody d'Autremont, James Clarke, John Holen. AB, MA, U. Mo., 1941, DSc (hon.), 1991; MD, Harvard, 1944; grad., N.Y. Psychoanalytic Inst., 1957. Resident Yale Med. Sch., 1944-46, 48-49, from instr. to assoc. prof., 1949-57; prof. psychiatry U. Md. Sch. Medicine, Balt., 1957-76; chmn. dept., also dir. Inst. Psychiatry and Human Behavior, 1959-76, prof. psychiatry and human behavior, 1976-87, prof. emeritus, 1987—; sr. assoc. sch. of hygiene and pub. health Johns Hopkins U., 1986—; vis. prof. U. Brazil, 1968, U. W.I., Kingston, Jamaica, 1972, 73, James Cook U., No. Queensland, Australia, 1992; fellow Center for Advanced Studies in Behavioral Scis., Stanford, 1975-76, U. Otago (N.Z.), 1981, Inst. for Advanced Studies, Tel Aviv U., 1986; mem. adv. bd. Inst. Social Psychiatry, U. San Marcos, 1968-70; mem. nat. profl. adv. bd. psychiatry, psychology and neurology service VA, 1963-67; cons. WHO (Pan Am. Health Orgn. and Geneva, Switzerland), 1965—; program dir. Interam. Mental Health Studies Program, 1967-69; mem. exec. bd. World Fedn. Mental Health, 1969—, adminstrv. mem., 1972-74, mem.-at-large, 1979—, pres., 1981-83, sec. gen., 1983—; mem. epidemiol. studies rev. com. NIMH, 1975-79, cons. clin. infant devel. program, 1979-81, hosp. rev. com., 1979—, AIDS grant rev. com. 1987—; mem. internat. adv. bd. Peruvian Nat. Inst. Mental Health, 1984—, mem. editorial bd. jour., 1985—; mem. adv. coun. Hogg Found., 1986-89; mem. sci. com. Internat. Social Sci. Council, 1989, exec. com. 1989-91; cons. UNESCO, 1986—. Author: The Lost Ones, Social Forces and Mental Illness in Rio de Janeiro, 1973, Sex, Contraception and Motherhood in Jamaica, 1981, Psychoanalytic Knowledge, 1990; editor: (with F.C. Redlich) Psychotherapy with Schizophrenics, 1952, (with R. Monroe and G. Klee) Psychiatric Epidemiology and Mental Health Planning, 1967, Minority Group Adolescents in the United States, 1968, Behavior in New Environments, 1970; cons. editor Jour. Nervous and Mental Disease, 1959-67, editor in chief, 1967—; adv. editor: Tice Med. Ency., 1967-80, Harper & Row Med. Ency., 1980-86; mem. editorial bd. Psychiatry Digest, 1967-71, Mental Hygiene, 1968-70, Social Psychiatry, 1970-81, Internat. Jour. Psychosomatic Obstetrics and Gynecology, 1984-92, Population and Environment, 1987-92; contbr. numerous articles to profl. jours. Chmn. adv. bd. Balt. chpt. Internat. Students Council, ARC, 1964-67; bd. dirs. Md. Partners of Alliance for Progress, 1965-66, Nat. Assn. Mental Health, 1964-66, mem. profl. adv. bd., 1967-71; mem. adv. bd. Inst. for Victims of Trauma, 1988—. Served to capt. M.C. AUS, 1946-48. Fellow Am. Psychiat. Assn. (life; chmn. com. transcultural psychiatry 1966-68, rep. interam. council 1965-71, trustee 1968-71, chmn. task force family planning 1973-75), Am. Coll. Psychiatrists (charter), Am. Coll. Psychoanalysts (charter); mem. Assn. Behavioral Sci. and Med. Edn. (pres. 1981), Am. (life), Internat. psychoanalytic assns., Internat. Coll. Pediatrics (senate 1978-86), Internat. Assn. Psychosomatic Ob-Gyn (exec. bd. 1977-86), Peruvian Psychiat. Assn. (hon.), Peruvian Assn. Psychiatry, Neurology and Neurosurgery (hon.). Club: Cosmos (Washington), West River Sailing Assn., 14 W. Hamilton St. Club (Balt.). Home: 70 Olmstead Green Ct Baltimore MD 21210-1508 Office: Sheppard & Enoch Pratt Hosp PO Box 6815 Baltimore MD 21285-6815

BRODY, HAROLD DAVID, engineering educator; b. Boston, Apr. 13, 1939; s. Abraham and Gertrude (Weiner) B.; m. Katharine Tatem, Aug. 20, 1966; children: Michael Seth, Shayna Lynn. SB in Metallurgy, MIT, 1960, SM in Metallurgy, 1961, ScD, 1965. Rsch. metallurgist MIT, Cambridge, 1965-66; sr. rsch. metallurgist Monsanto Rsch. Corp., Everett, Mass., 1965-66; asst. to assoc. prof. materials engring. Univ. Pitts., Pa., 1966-68, 68-74; prof. materials engring. Univ. Pitts., 1974-91, chmn. metallurgical and materials engring., 1971-79; dir. casting industries sci. and engring. inst. U. Pitts., 1984-91; prof. metallurgy Univ. Conn., Storrs, 1991—, dean of engring., 1991—; vis. prof. MIT, Cambridge, 1987—; cons. SLM Assocs., Storrs, 1987—; bd. dirs. Stardyne Inc., Johnstown, Pa. Co-editor: Modeling of Casting and Welding Processes, 1981; contbr. articles to profl. jours. Key prof. Foundry Ednl. Found. Mem. Am. Foundrymen's Soc., Am. Inst. Metallurgical Engrs., ASM Internat., Materials Rsch. Soc., Sigma Xi, Alpha Sigma Mu (pres. 1991-92). Office: U Conn 191 Auditorium Rd Storrs Mansfield CT 06269-3237

BRODY, MARCIA BERNICE AUERBACH, office manager, mathematics educator; b. Phila., Dec. 6, 1937; d. Isadore Pincus and Ruth Kapelow Auerbach; m. Franklin L. Brody, Feb. 14, 1959; children: Robert Egan, Susan Karen, Michael Jay, Marla Ava. BA, U. Pa., 1959, MS, 1962. Tchr. high sch. math. Phila. Bd. Edn., 1959-65; mgr. physician's office, asst. F. L. Brody, DO, PC, Phila., 1969—. Mem. sch. bd. Cheltenaam Adult Sch., Wyncote, Pa., 1975-76. Phila. Bd. Edn. scholar, 1955-59, NSF scholar, 1959-62. Republican. Jewish. Office: F L Brody DO PC 8501 Williams Ave Philadelphia PA 19150-1912

BRODY, STUART MARTIN, analytical chemist; b. Bklyn., June 25, 1936; s. Michael and Celia (Kreps) B.; m. Helene Levine, Feb. 8, 1958; children: Russell, Elyse. BSc in Chemistry, Queens Coll., 1958. Jr. chemist CIBA Pharm. Co., Summit, N.J., 1958-66, lab. supr., 1967-68; sr. scientist I CIBA-GEIGY Corp., Summit, 1969-80, sr. scientist II, 1981-83, sr. rsch. scientist, 1984-85, asst. mgr., 1985-91, mgr., 1992—. Contbr. articles to profl. jours. Fellow Am. Inst. Chemists; mem. N.Y. Acad. Scis., Am. Soc. Mass Spectrometry, Assn. Ofcl. Analytical Chemists, Am. Chem. Soc. (div. analytical chemistry). Jewish. Home: 8 Timberlane Dr Colonia NJ 07067-2932 Office: CIBA-GEIGY Corp 556 Morris Ave Summit NJ 07901-1398

BRODZINSKI, FREDERICK RONALD, college administrator, management consultant; b. Phila., Aug. 27, 1948; s. Alfred L. and Jean (Cyzio) B.; m. Lynda D. Kenney, Apr. 15, 1971 (div. 1991); children: Byron, Bridget. AB, St. Joseph's Coll., 1970; MS, Ind. U., 1972; MA, Columbia U., 1978, EdD, 1991. Asst. head counselor Indiana U. Pa., Phila., 1971-72; dir. housing Iona Coll., New Rochelle, N.Y., 1972-75; assoc. dean of students St. Mary's Coll. Md., St. Mary's City, 1975-77; coord. student activities, adminstrv. cons. Tchrs. Coll., Columbia U., N.Y.C., 1977-79, acting dir. admissions, 1979-80; dean of students Ramapo Coll. N.J., Mahwah, 1980-85; asst. dir. Inst. Transp. Systems CUNY, 1985-88, assoc. dir., 1988—; assoc. prof. John Jay Coll., N.Y.C., 1988—; ind. cons. in higher edn., 1976—; rsch. assoc. CCNY, N.Y.C., 1991—. Author: Futures Research, 1979; editor: College Athletes, 1984; editorial bd. Jour. ACPA/NASPA, 1980-86. Mem. Am. Coll. Pers. Assn. (commn. chmn. 1982-84, Disting. Svc. award 1984), Soc. Wine Educators, Phi Delta Kappa. Republican. Roman Catholic. Home: 5622 Delafield Ave Bronx NY 10471 Office: Inst Transp Systems City Coll Y220 New York NY 10031

BROENIMAN, CLIFFORD SCOTT, classical philology educator; b. Oconomowoc, Wis., July 19, 1960; s. Chistlieb Frederick and Betty Broeniman; m. Elizabeth Broeniman, Aug. 5, 1989. BA in Classics, U. Wis., 1983; MA in Classics, U. Ill., 1986, PhD in Classical Philology, 1989. Instr. classics Westminster Coll., Fulton, Mo., 1988-89; asst. prof. classics St. John Fisher Coll., Rochester, N.Y., 1989—, adj. prof. history. Author: (translations) Renaissance Polish Law, 1990; contbr. articles to profl. jours. Mem. Am. Philol. Assn., N.Y. Coll. English Assn., Atlantic States Classical Assn., Ohio Classical Assn., Classical Assn. of Atlantic States. Office: St John Fisher Coll 3690 East Ave Fairport NY 14450-1491

BROFMAN, LANCE MARK, portfolio manager, mutual fund executive; b. N.Y.C., Nov. 24, 1949; s. Jerome Harold Brofman and Vivian (Lefkowitz) Kaufman; m. Ellen Barbara Laskowitz, Aug. 12, 1973; 1 child, Michael. BS in Nuclear Engring., NYU, 1971, MBA in Fin., 1973, PhD in Econs., 1977. Research assoc. Am. Stock Exchange, N.Y.C., 1971-74; economist White Weld & Co., N.Y.C., 1974-78; v.p. A. Gary Shilling & Co., N.Y.C., 1978-80; pres., founder, chief portfolio strategist N.Y. Muni Fund, N.Y.C., 1980—; bd. dirs. Liberty Petroleum Co., N.Y.C.; trustee Cryonic Asset Trust, N.Y.C., 1989—. Edwin Posner Meml. fellow Am. Stock Exchange/NYU Grad. Bus. Sch., 1971. Democra. Jewish. Home: Apt 30E 60 E 8th St New York NY 10003-6527 Office: NY Muni Fund Inc 90 Washington St New York NY 10006-2214

BROGAN, JAMES, insurance and investments financial consultant; b. N.Y.C., Sept. 28, 1941; s. James F. and Anne Brogan; (div.); children: James, Michael, David. BA in History, Columbia U., 1963; postgrad., Harvard U., 1978. CLU. 2d v.p. mktg. Guardian Life, N.Y.C., 1963-80; gen. agt. Monarch Life, N.Y.C., 1980-82; v.p. mktg. New Eng. Life, Boston, 1982-91; assoc. mktg. dept. Baystate Fin., Boston, 1991—. Author: Disability Planning for Business, 1976. Mem. Am. Assn. Life Underwriters, Boston Life Underwriters Assn. Home: 63 Atlantic Ave Boston MA 02110 Office: Baystate Fin 100 N Washington St Boston MA 02114

BROKAW, THOMAS JOHN, journalist; b. Webster, S.D., Feb. 6, 1940; s. Anthony Orville and Eugenia (Conley) B.; m. Meredith Lynn Auld, Aug. 17, 1962; children—Jennifer Jean, Andrea Brooks, Sarah Auld. BA in Polit. Sci, U. S.D., 1962, hon. degree; hon. degree, Washington U., St. Louis, Syracuse U., Hofstra U., Boston Coll., Emerson Coll., Simpson Coll. Morning news editor Sta. KMTV, Omaha, 1962-65; 11:00 news editor, anchorman Sta. WSB-TV, Atlanta, 1965-66; reporter, corr., anchorman Sta. KNBC-TV, Los Angeles, 1966-73; White House corr. NBC, Washington, 1973-76; anchorman Sat. Night News, N.Y.C., 1973-76; host Today show, N.Y.C., 1976-82; anchorman NBC Nightly News, 1982—; corr. Exposé NBC, 1991—; corr. NBC coverage U.S. Presdl. elections, 1976, 80, anchor, 1984, 88; mem. adv. com. Reporters Com. for Freedom of Press, Gannett Journalism Ctr., Columbia U. Corr. numerous NBC News specials, including To Be A Teacher, 1987, Wall Street: Money Greed and Power, 1987, A Conversation with Mikhail S. Gorbachev (Alfred I. DuPont award), 1987, Home Street Home, 1988. Trustee Norton Simon Mus. Art, Pasadena, Calif., U. S.D. Found.; adviser Asia Soc. Mem. AFTRA (dir. 1968-72), Sigma Delta Chi. Office: NBC News 30 Rockefeller Pla New York NY 10112

BROMBERG, MURRAY H., podiatrist; b. Bklyn., Oct. 30, 1924; s. Benjamin and Beckie B.; m. Marcia Gilbert (dec. 1985); 1 child, Daniel Seth Bromberg; m. Helen Pechanick, Dec. 23, 1990; stepchildren: Mark Leinkram, Sharon Leinkram. DSC, Chgo. Coll. Chiropody, 1951; DPM, Pa. Coll. Podiatric Medicine, 1970. Diplomate Am. Bd. Podiatric Orthopedics. Dir. Childrens Clinic Foot Clinics of Chgo., 1951-52; pvt. practice Bloomfield, N.J., 1952—. Contbr. articles to profl. jours. Dist. commr. Boy Scouts Am., Chgo., 1947-52, Bloomfield, 1952-62, asst. scoutmaster, Bklyn., 1946-56; joint meml. com. mem. Twp. of Bloomfield; bd. dirs. Duncan YMCA, Chgo., 1949-52. With USN/USMC, 1943-46. Recipient Brachman Orthopedic award Chgo. Coll. Podiatric Medicine, 1951. Fellow Am. Coll. Foot Orthopedists (pres. 1960-61); mem. Am. Acad. Podiatry Adminstrn. (assoc.), Am. Podiatry Assn. (podopediatrics com. 1968-70, Stickel award for rsch. 1958), Am. Assn. of Colls. of Podiatric Medicine (reviewer 1968-70), N.J. Podiatry Soc. (ea. div. chmn. sci. com. 1962), Jewish War Vets. of U.S. (comdr. North Essex Post 142). Home: 111 Martin Ave Clifton NJ 07012 Office: 315 Broad St Bloomfield NJ 07003-2745

BROMLEY, MARILYN MODLIN, librarian; b. Cleve., Mar. 14, 1951; d. Robert A. and Helen F. (Hicks) Modlin; m. Haworth P. Bromley, Nov. 7, 1987. BA magna cum laude, Randolph-Macon Woman's Coll., 1973; MSLS, Cath. U. Am., 1978. Librarian ICF Inc., Washington, 1978-83, Bur. Nat. Affairs Inc., Washington, 1983—. Editor: Direct-Line Distances: U.S. Edition, 1986, Direct-Line Distances: International Edition, 1986, BNA's Directory of State Courts, Judges and Clerks, 1986. Mem. Spl. Librs. Assn. (treas. Washington chpt. 1984-87, bd. dirs. 1988-90, v.p., pres.-elect 1991-92, pres. 1992-93), Phi Beta Kappa, Bet Phi Mu. Episcopalian. Office: Bur Nat Affairs Inc 1231 25th St NW Washington DC 20037-1157

BRONER, MATHEW, artist, educator; b. Detroit, Jan. 26, 1924; s. Abraham and Ida Broner. Student Detroit Soc. Arts and Crafts, 1942, Wayne State U., 1943-45; B.F.A., Cranbrook Acad. Art, 1948, M.F.A., 1949. Adj. instr. painting and drawing Lawrence Inst. Tech., Detroit, 1948-49; instr. design and drawing Syracuse (N.Y.) U., 1949-51; adj. instr. painting and lectr. art C.W. Post Coll. of L.I. U., N.Y., 1967-68, also summer 1968; mem. faculty art dept. Manhattanville Coll., Purchase, N.Y., 1967—, assoc. prof., 1974-81, prof., 1981—, chmn. dept., 1974-76, 80-82, 86-88; painter, printmaker; one-man shows of paintings include: Cranbrook Art Acad., Mich., 1949, Contemporary Art Gallery, Chgo., 1949, Manhattanville Coll., 1968, 72, 78, 90, Chuck Levitan Gallery, N.Y.C., 1980; numerous group shows, 1945—, latest being Manhattanville Coll., 1967-91, 393 Gallery, N.Y.C., 1977, Inst. for Art and Urban Resources, N.Y.C., 1979, Internat. Art Fair, Bologna, Italy, 1978, Landmark Gallery, N.Y.C., 1978-80, A.I.R. Gallery, N.Y.C., 1984, Broome St. Gallery, N.Y.C., 1991; represented in permanent collections: Ill. State Mus., Springfield, Cranbrook Mus., Manhattanville Coll., also pvt. collections. Recipient First Prize award Northwest Terr. Exhbn., 1948, 1st Prize in Painting award Cranbrook Acad. Art, 1947, 48, 49; MacDowell fellow, 1979. Mem. AAUP. Studio: 66 Greene St New York NY 10012 Office: Manhattanville Coll Dept Art Purchase NY 10577

BRONFMAN, EDGAR M., religious organization executive. Pres. World Jewish Congress, N.Y.C. Office: World Jewish Congress 501 Madison Ave 17th Fl New York NY 10022-5602*

BRONFMAN, PETER FREDERICK, independent investor; b. Montreal, Que., Can., Oct. 2, 1929; s. Allan and Lucy (Bilsky) B.; m. Diane Feldman; m. Theodora Reitsma (div.); children—Linda, Bruce, Brenda; m. Lynda Hamilton. Student, Lawrenceville Sch., 1948; B.A., Yale U., 1952. Chmn. Edper Enterprises Ltd., Toronto.

BRONKESH, ANNETTE CYLIA, public relations executive; b. Vineland, N.J., Dec. 18, 1956; d. Manasha and Miriam (Kutlan) B.; m. Steven Silver Schwartz, Aug. 18, 1985; children: Sarah, Emily. BA, NYU, 1979. Sr. editor Instnl. Investor, N.Y.C., 1979; chief editor McGraw-Hill, N.Y.C., 1980-85; dir. Am. Stock Exchange, N.Y.C., 1985-87; v.p. pub. rels. Nikko Securities, N.Y.C., 1987-90; pres. Bronkesh Assocs., Passaic, N.J., 1990—. Mem. Securities Industry Assn. (pub. rels. roundtable), Phi Beta Kappa. Home and Office: Bronkesh Assocs 417 Terhune Ave Passaic NJ 07055-2448

BRONLEY, GLENN I., psychologist; b. N.Y.C., Feb. 17, 1953; s. Frank and Bertha (Hyman) B.; m. Sarah Medak, Dec. 24,1976; children: Jonathan, Matthew. BA, CUNY, Queens, 1976; MS, U. Utah, 1979, PhD, 1981. Assoc. psychologist Harlem Valley Psychiatric Ctr., Carmel, N.Y., 1981-83; chief psychologist Fishkill (N.Y.) Cons. Group, 1982-1986; clin. coord. Harlem Valley Psychiatric Ctr., Peekskill, N.Y., 1983—; pvt. practice Peekskill, N.Y., 1983—. Fellow Am. Orthropsychiatric Assn., mem. APA, Am. Assn. Marriage and Family Therapy, Phi Beta Kappa, Phi Kappa Phi. Office: 2117 Crompond Rd Cortlandt Manor NY 10566-4363

BRONNER, ETHAN SAMUEL, news correspondent; b. N.Y.C., Nov. 26, 1954; s. Felix and Leah (Horowitz) B.; m. Naomi Kehati, June 27, 1985; children: Eli Kehati Bronner, Gabriel Kehati Bronner. BA in Letters, Wesleyan U., 1976; MS in Journalism, Columbia U., 1980. Corrs. Reuters, Madrid, 1981-82, Brussels, 1982-83; sr. corrs. Reuters, Jerusalem, 1983-85; legal affairs reporter The Boston Globe, Boston, 1986-89; corrs. Supreme Ct. The Boston Globe, Washington, 1989-91; bur. chief Mid. East The Boston Globe, Jerusalem, 1991—. Author: Battle for Justice, 1989 (selected One of 25 Outstanding Books, N.Y. Pub. Libr., 1989, Washingtonian award 1989, ABA Silver Gavel 1990). Office: The Boston Globe, 37 Hillel St PO Box 53 Beit Agron, Jerusalem Israel

BRONNER, FELIX, physiologist, biophysicist, educator, painter; b. Vienna, Austria, Nov. 7, 1921; came to U.S., 1937, naturalized, 1943; s. Maurice and Lotte (Vogler) B.; m. Leah Horowitz, Oct. 12, 1947; children: Deborah Rachel, Ethan Samuel. BS, U. Calif. at Berkeley and Davis, 1941; PhD (Quaker Oats fellow 1950-52), MIT, 1952; student, Kans. State Coll., 1938, U. Minn., 1943, U. Va., 1946. Rsch. assoc. MIT, 1952-54; Helen Hay Whitney fellow, Arthritis and Rheumatism fellow Rockefeller Inst. Med. Rsch., N.Y.C., 1954-56, asst., 1956; dir. lab. mineral metabolism Hosp. for Spl. Surgery, N.Y.C., 1957-63; asst. prof. Cornell U. Med. Coll., 1961-63; assoc. prof. physiology U. Louisville Sch. Medicine, 1963-69; prof. oral biology U. Conn., 1969-86, prof. nutrition scis., 1976-89, prof. biostructure and function, 1986-89, prof. emeritus, 1989—; vis. scientist Weizman Inst., Israel, 1965, 76, Varon vis. prof., 1988; vis. scientist Pasteur Inst., Paris, 1977; vis. scientist U. Cape Town Med. Sch., 1984, 88, MRC Disting. vis. scientist, 1991; guest scientist INSERM, Paris, 1972, Lyon, France, 1988; cons. USPHS, 1965-68, 70-71, U.S. Dept. Agr., 1978-79; vis. prof. Tel Aviv U. Sch. Medicine, Israel, 1976. Editor: Intracellular Calcium Regulation, (with A. Kleinzeller) Current Topics in Membranes and Transport, (with C.L. Comar) Mineral Metabolism: An Advanced Treatise, (with J. Coburn) Disorders of Mineral Metabolism, (with M. Peterlik) Calcium and Phosphate Transport Across Biomembranes, Epithelial Calcium and Phosphate Transport: Molecular and Cellular Aspects, Cellular Calcium and Phosphate Transport in Health and Disease, Molecular and Cellular Regulation of Calcium and Phosphate Metabolism, Extra- and Intracellular Calcium and Phosphate Regulation: From Basic Research to Clinical Medicine, (with D. Pansu) Calcium Transport and Intracellular Calcium Homeostasis, (with R.V. Worrell) A Basic Science Primer in Orthopaedics; mem. editorial bd. Am. Jour. Clin. Nutrition, 1968-76, Am. Jour. Physiol. (Modeling Forum), 1985—, Jour. Nutrition, 1986-90, 91—; contbr. numerous articles to profl. jours; paintings exhibited in 3 one-man shows, numerous juried shows. Pres. Bur. Jewish Edn., Louisville, 1968-69. Served with AUS, 1942-46. Recipient André Lichwitz prize, 1974, prizes for paintings. Fellow AAAS; mem. Am. Physiol. Soc., Biophys. Soc., Harvey Soc., Soc. Exptl. Biology and Medicine, Am. Inst. Nutrition, Orthopedic Research Soc., Am. Fedn. Clin. Research, N.Y. Acad. Scis., Am. Soc. Clin. Nutrition, Am. Soc. Bone and Mineral Research. Home: 33 Ferncliff Dr West Hartford CT 06117 Office: U Conn Health Ctr Dept BioStructure and Function Farmington CT 06030

BRONNER, MICHAEL B., educator; b. Morgan Hill, Calif., Sept. 29, 1936; s. Wallace B. and Julia T. (Lytle) B.; m. Bridget N. O'Connor, Jan. 7, 1989; 1 child, Linda E. BA, San Jose State U., 1958, MA, 1962; PhD, NYU, 1973. Pvt. pilot's lic.; cert. of systems profls. Bus. tchr. and dept. chemn. East Side Union High Sch., San Jose, 1958-68; sponsoring editor McGraw Hill Book Co., N.Y.C., 1968-70; from instr. to prof. and dir. bus. edn. program NYU, 1970—; dir. NYU P.R. Residence Ctr., San Juan, 1989—; cons. N.Y.C. Bd. Edn., Calif. Bankers Assn., various schs. and bus. Author teaching kit: The How and Why of Banking, 1961; contbr. over 50 articles to profl. jours. With U.S. Army, 1959-65. Mem. Office Systems Rsch. Assn. (pres. 1990-91), Nat. Assn. for Bus. Tchr. Edn. (rsch. coord. 1981-83, 89-91), N.Y. Bus. Tchrs. Assn. (exec. bd.), Calif. Bus. Edn. Assn., Bus. Edn. Assn. N.Y.C. Office: NYU 239 Greene St Bldg 300 New York NY 10003-6601

BRONSON, RANDOLPH CLIFTON, financial services executive; b. L.I., N.Y., May 30, 1944; s. Randolph and Lillian (Wiebold) B.; m. Monique Markwalder, July 3, 1971 (div.); 1 child, Nathalie; m. May H. Wong, Sept. 30, 1983. AA in Chem. Engring., Nassau Coll., L.I., 1965; BBA, Pace U., 1968; MBA, Iona Coll., New Rochelle, N.Y., 1972. Research/devel. chem. engr. Union Carbide Corp., Tarrytown, N.Y., 1965-68; mgr. Byrnes & Baker CPA's, N.Y.C., 1968-73; controller Litton Med. Systems, Inc., N.Y.C., 1973-78; asst. chief fin. officer Butler Aviation Internat., Inc., Montvale, N.J., 1978-82; chief fin. officer, dir. fin. and adminstrn. A.H.E., Inc., Jersey City, 1982-86; corp. comptroller/treas. V.C.A. Teletronics, Inc., Leonia, N.J., 1986-89; v.p. fin., gen. mgr. Bearsville (N.Y.) Group Cos., 1989—. Mem. Am. Mgmt. Assn., Internat. Teleprodn. Soc., Motion Picture and TV Credit Group, Am. Nat. Def. Preparedness Assn. Republican. Roman Catholic. Home: 40 Decker Dr Washingtonville NY 10992-1313

BRONSTEIN, ALVIN J., lawyer; b. Bklyn., June 8, 1928. LLD, N.Y. Law Sch., 1951, LLD (hon.), 1990. Bar: N.Y. 1952, Miss. 1967, La. 1971, U.S. Ct. Appeals (D.C., 1st, 2d, 3d, 4th, 5th, 9th, 10th and 11th cirs.), U.S. Supreme Ct. 1961. Ptnr. Bronstein & Bronstein, Bklyn., 1952-63; pvt. practice Elizabethtown, N.Y., 1963-64; chief staff counsel Lawyers Constl. Def. Com., Jackson, Miss., 1964-68; fellow Inst. Politics, Kennedy Sch. Govt. Harvard U., Cambridge, Mass., 1968-69, assoc. dir. Inst. Politics, Kennedy Sch. Govt., 1969-71; ptnr. Elie, Bronstein, Strickler & Dennis, New Orleans, 1971-72; exec. dir. Nat. Prison Project, Nat. Jail Project ACLU Found., Washington, 1972—; cons., trial counsel CORE, NAACP, NAACP Legal Def. Fund, SCLC, SNCC, Miss. Freedom Dem. Party, Black Panther Party, Nat. Inst. for Edn. in Law and Poverty, and others; guest lectr. various law schs., 1964—; cons. various state corrections depts., 1972—; adj. prof. Am. U. Law Sch., 1973; expert witness in various prison litigations, 1978—; appointed mem. Fed. Jud. Ctr. Adv. Com. on Experimentation in the Law, 1978-81. Contbg. author: The Evolution of Criminal Justice, 1978, Prisoners' Rights Sourcebook, Vol. II, 1980, Confinement in Maximum Custody, 1980, Sage Criminal Justice Annual, Vol. 14, 1980, Readings in the Justice Model, 1980, Our Endangered Rights, 1984, Prisoners and the Courts: The American Experience, 1985; author: (with Rudovsky and Koren) The Rights of Prisoners, 1988; author, editor: Representing Prisoners, 1981; editor: Prisoners' Self-Help Litigation Manual, 1977; contbr. articles to profl. jours. MacArthur Found. fellow, 1989; named one of the 100 most influential lawyers in Am., Nat. Law Jour., 1985, 88, 91; recipient Roscoe Pound award Nat. Coun. on Crime and Delinquency, 1981, Karl Menninger award Fortune Soc., 1982, Pa. Prison Soc. award, 1991. Office: Nat Prison Project ACLU Found 1875 Connecticut Ave NW Washington DC 20009

BRONSTEIN, MELVIN, ophthalmic surgeon; b. Yonkers, N.Y., Apr. 9, 1924; s. Harry and Betty (Mandel) B.; m. Gloria Liebman, May 20, 1956; children: Charles, Glen, Adam, Wendy. AB, Columbia U., 1948, MA, 1949; MD, N.Y. Med. Coll., 1953. Diplomate Am. Bd. Ophthalmology. Intern N.Y. Med. Coll., 1953-54; resident in ophthalmology Montefiore Hosp., Bronx, N.Y., 1954-56, assoc. surgeon, 1970—; pvt. practice medicine specializng in ophthalmic surgery, Yonkers, 1960—; chief of staff, attending ophthalmic surgeon, dir. ophthalmology dept. St. John's Riverside Hosp., Yonkers, 1970—; attending in ophthalmic surgery Bronx Mcpl. Hosp. Ctr., Westchester Med. Ctr.; assoc. clin. prof. ophthalmology Albert Einstein Coll. Medicine, 1976—, N.Y. Med. Coll., Valhalla, 1970—; cons. in field. Bd. dirs. Family Svc. Soc., 1970-73; pres. Yonkers Cancer Soc., 1976-78. Contbr. articles to profl. publs. With Ordnance Dept., U.S. Army, 1942-46. Decorated Bronze Star with cluster. Fellow Am. Acad. Ophthalmology (Honor award), ACS (counselor 1974-82), Internat. Coll. Surgeons, N.Y. Acad. Medicine; mem. AMA, AAAS, Assn. Rsch. in Vision and Ophthalmology, Internat. Coll. Eye Surgeons, Intraocular Lens Implant Soc., N.Y. Acad. Scis., N.Y. State Ophthal. Soc. (bd. dirs. 1986—), Yonkers Acad. Medicine (pres. 1971-72), Nat. Soc. Prevention of Blindness, Westchester Acad. Medicine (pres. eye sect. 1982-86), Vitreous Soc., N.Y. State Ophthalmol. Soc. (bd. dirs. 1986—), Phi Delta Epsilon. Office: 984 N Broadway Yonkers NY 10701-1308

BRONZAFT, ARLINE L., psychology educator; b. N.Y.C., Mar. 26, 1936; d. Morris and Ida Cohen; m. Bertram Bronzaft, Oct. 7, 1956; children: Robin, Susan. BA, Hunter Coll., 1956; MA, Columbia U., 1958, PhD, 1966. Lectr. Hunter Coll., N.Y.C., 1958-65; instr. Finch Coll., N.Y.C., 1965-67; prof. psychology Lehman Coll., N.Y.C., 1967—; cons. N.Y. Transit Authority, N.Y.C., 1977-85. Contbr. chpts. to books, articles to profl. jours. and popular mags. Bd. dirs. N.Y. C. Coun. on the Environment, 1985—; bd. dirs., v.p. Hebrew Immigrant Aid Soc., N.Y.C., 1988—; active in Democratic politics. Recipient Cert. of Appreciation, U.S. EPA Region 2, 1976, Outstanding Woman of Bklyn. Cert. from Bklyn. NOW, 1974, Service to Bronx Cert., Bronx NOW, 1988. Mem. Am. Psychol. Assn. Office: Lehman Coll Bronx NY 10468

BROOKER, GERARD T., secondary education educator, social services developer; b. Danbury, Conn., Feb. 24, 1936; s. Geroge Brooker and Rita Dougherty; m. Sheila F. Moore; children: Kevin, David, Suzanne, Jessica, Jay. BA, Iona Coll., 1958; MS, St. John's U., N.Y.C., 1962, MA, 1976, PhD, 1977, EdD, 1978. Tchr English various schs., 1958-70; curriculum coord. Staples High Sch., Westport, Conn., 1967-68, headmaster, 1971-72, chair English dept., 1973—; chair English dept. Kings Park High Sch., L.I., N.Y., 1970-72. Contbr. articles, poetry to profl. publs. Advisor Youth Ending Hunger in Conn., Westport, 1979—; chmn. Cambodian Refugee com., Newtown, Conn., 1981; active Social Concerns com., Diocese of Bridgeport, Conn., 1982-83; chmn., co-founder Young Playwrights Festival of Conn., Westport, 1984—. Recipient Govs. Youth award State of Conn., 1980, 83, 87, 91, award Voluntary Action Com. of Fairfield County, 1990, award Dr. Falk Found., 1988, award Nat. Sch. Bds. Assn., 1988. Mem. NEA, Conn. Edn. Assn. (Mahatma Gandhi Peace award 1987, Jefferson award 1992), Westport Edn. Assn., Assn. Supervision and Curriculum Devel., Educators for Prevention of Nuclear War. Office: Staples High Sch 70 North Ave Westport CT 06880-2799

BROOKER, WALTER ERIC, college administrator, consultant; b. Pittsfield, Mass., Dec. 2, 1916; s. Edward Ernest and Lillian Adele (Robair) B.; m. Barbara Ann Carrick, Nov. 22, 1938; children—Eric Edward, David Krickel. A.B., Middlebury Coll., 1937, Ed.D. (hon.), 1982. Claims adjustor Liberty Mut. Ins., Boston, 1937-40, salesman, 1940-42; advt. rep. Curtis Pub., Phila., 1946-56; v.p. Middlebury Coll., Vt., 1956-81, emeritus v.p., 1981-86; pres. Middlebury Nat. Corp., 1986—; cons. C.A. Johnson Endeavor Found., N.Y.C., 1981—; sr. cons. Snelling, Kolb & Kuhnle, Inc., Burlington, Vt., 1982—; chmn. bd. dirs. Nat. Bank of Middlebury. Contbr. articles to profl. publs. Trustee, Porter Med. Ctr., Middlebury, 1981—, Sheldon Mus., Middlebury, 1965—; bd. dirs. United Way of Addison County, Middlebury, 1980—. Served to lt. (s.g.) USN, 1942-46, PTO. Republican. Congregationalist. Avocations: English water colors, golf. Home: PO Box 584 Middlebury VT 05753-0584 Office: Middlebury East 2A Middlebury VT 05753

BROOKS, CLYDE SPEER, chemist, consultant; b. Pitts.; s. Clyde and Marie (Thompson) B.; m. Ruth Bolton, Aug. 8, 1946 (dec. July 1987); children: Suzanne, Philip. BS in Chemistry, Duke U., 1940; postgrad., Carnegie Tech., 1946-49. Rsch. assoc. to jr. fellow Mellon Inst. Indsl. Rsch., Pitts., 1941-49; project leader Shell Devel. Co., Houston, 1949-61; sr. rsch. scientist United Technologies Rsch. Ctr., East Hartford, Conn., 1961-81; pres. Recycle Metals, Glastonbury, Conn., 1981—; chair com. and task force on tech. assistance and recycling Conn. Hazardous Waste Mgmt. Svc., Hartford, 1983-87. Author: Metal Recovery from Industrial Waste, 1991; patentee in field. Chmn., trustee subchpt. Conn. Nature Conservancy, Glastonbury, 1965-91; chmn. Conn. chpt. Sierra Club, Glastonbury, 1981-91; treas. Kongscut Trust, Glastonbury, 1981-91; dir. Conn. Forest and Park Assn., Glastonbury, 1984-91; program com. Conn. Audubon, Glastonbury, 1987-91; pres. Great Meadows Conservation Trust, Glastonbury, 1989-91. 1st lt. USN, 1944-46, lt. comdr. USNR, 1946-69. Fellow Am. Inst. Chemists; mem. Am. Chem. Soc. (councilor S.E. Tex. chpt., archivist), Metals Soc., New Eng. Catalysis Soc., Sigma Xi, Phi Eta Sigma, Pi Mu Epsilon. Home and Office: Recycle Metals 41 Baldwin Ln Glastonbury CT 06033-3845

BROOKS, HARVEY, dentist; b. Newark, Mar. 15, 1931; s. Meyer and Fannie Brooks; m. Toby Englart, Dec. 16, 1956 (div. 1974); children: Joel, Judy; m. Marcia Hammer, Apr. 6, 1975. BA, Rutgers U., 1953; DDS, Temple U., 1957. Pvt. practice Hillside, N.J., 1957—; mem. dental staff Elizabeth Gen. Med. Ctr., 1983—; co-chmn. Hillside (N.J.) Health Fair, 1970-71, dental chmn. oral cancer screening, 1972—. Capt. U.S. Army, 1957-59. Fellow Acad. Gen. Dentistry; mem. Union County Dental soc. (pres. 1988-89), N.J. Dental Assn., ADA. Jewish. Office: 1156 Liberty Ave Hillside NJ 07205-2103

BROOKS, HENRY WILSON, construction management educator; b. Burlington, Vt., Apr. 1, 1949; s. James H. and Christine J. (Slack) B.; m. Carol J. Gitzendanner, June 28, 1969; children: Andrew J., Clinton W. BS in Constrn. Mgmt., Utica (N.Y.) Coll., 1971. Field engr. JGA Constrn. Corp., Syracuse, N.Y., 1971-74; mgmt. engr. Town of Salina Hwy. Dept., Liverpool, N.Y., 1975-76; mgr. systems design Lamson Corp., Syracuse, 1977-87; instr. constrn. mgmt. Utica (N.Y.) Coll., 1988—. Fire commr. New Woodstock (N.Y.) Fire Dist., 1986—. Mem. Associated Schs. Constrn.

BROOKS, HERBERT PAUL, hockey coach; b. St. Paul, Aug. 5, 1937; s. Herbert David and Pauline E. (Johnson) B.; m. Patricia Diane Brooks, Sept. 27, 1965; children: Daniel, Kelly. BA, U. Minn., 1962. Coach U. Minn., Mpls., 1972-79, U.S. Olympic Team, 1979-80, N.Y. Rangers, N.Y.C., 1981-85, St. Cloud (Minn.) State U., 1986-87, Minn. North Stars, Mpls., 1987-88, N.J. Devils, 1992—; salesman Jostens, Mpls., 1985-86. Home: 5423 Carlson Rd Saint Paul MN 55126-1216 Office: NJ Devils Meadowlands Arena PO Box 504 East Rutherford NJ 07073*

BROOKS, HOWARD ZACHARY, financial administrator; b. N.Y.C., Mar. 26, 1956; s. Martin and Cecile (Siskind) B.; m. Carol Teitelbaum, June 25, 1978; children: Scott Gregory, Erica Lauren. BA, St. John's U., Jamaica, N.Y., 1978. Supr. client svcs. Law Offices Hayt, Hayt & Landau, Great Neck, N.Y., 1975-80; sr. methods analyst Natwest U.S.A., Melville, N.Y., 1980-82; asst. v.p. adminstrn. regional mgmt. Western Hemisphere Bank Hapoalim, N.Y.C., 1982-87, bank secrecy compliance officer, 1987-89; adminstr. Grubman, Indursky, Schindler, Goldstein & Flax, P.C., N.Y.C., 1989-90; dir. spl. projects Sony Music U.S., N.Y.C., 1990-92; dir. ops. and MIS Sony Electronic Pub., N.Y.C., 1992—. Mem. Am. Inst. Indsl. Engrs. (sr.), Internat. Brotherhood Magicians, Lambda Epsilon Chi Alumni Assn. (chpt. treas. 1980). Jewish. Home: 23 Riesling Ct Commack NY 11725-1735

BROOKS, JOHN EDWARD, college president; b. Boston, July 13, 1923; s. John Edward and Mildred (McCoy) B. B.S. in Physics, Coll. Holy Cross, 1949; postgrad. in geophysics, Pa. State U., 1949-50; M.A. in Philosophy, Boston Coll., 1954, M.S. in Geophysics, 1959; S.T.D. in Dogmatic Theology, Gregorian U., Rome, Italy, 1963; H.H.D. (hon.), St. Ambrose Coll., 1976; D.Sc. (hon.), Worcester Poly. Inst., 1980; D Humanities, Assumption Coll., 1990. Joined Soc. of Jesus, 1950; ordained priest Roman Catholic Ch., 1959; instr. mathematics and physics Coll. of Holy Cross, Worcester, Mass., 1954-56; instr. theology Coll. of Holy Cross, 1963-64, asst. prof., 1964-67, asso. prof. religious studies, 1967—, chmn. dept. theology, 1964-69, v.p., dean coll., 1968-70, pres., trustee, 1970—, sec. com. ednl. policy, 1968-70, chmn., 1970—; Participant bibl. and archeol. consortium Jewish Inst. on Religion, Hebrew Union Coll., 1968; inst. academic deans Am. Council Edn., St. Louis U., 1968; trustee St. Peter's Coll., Jersey City, 1969-75, Canisius Coll., Buffalo, 1974-80, Spring Hill Coll., 1981—; mem. Mass. Postsecondary Edn. Commn., Mass. 1202 Commn., 1974-77; mem. exec. com. New Eng. Colls. Fund, 1974, 78; mem. Mass. Pub./Pvt. Forum; bd. dirs. Worcester Consortium for Higher Edn., chmn., 1976-77; mem. Worcester Downtown Devel. Corp., Mass. Biotech. Research Inst., 1985—; bd. visitors Air U., 1978—; bd. dirs. Worcester Mcpl. Research Bur., Inc., 1985—. Community trustee United Way Cen. Mass.; consortium dir. Social Svcs. Corp., Worcester; bd. dirs. Worcester Mechanics Hall Assn.; mem. commn. govtl. rels. Am. Coun. on Edn., 1989—. With U.S. Army, 1942-46. Mem. Assn. Jesuit Colls. and Univs. (bd. dirs. 1970—), Assn. Ind. Colls. and Univs. in Mass. (v.p. 1972-73, chmn. coms., exec. com.), New Eng. Assn. Schs. and Colls. (sec.-treas. 1985—), Econ. Club (Worcester, pres. 1977-78, exec. com. 1978—), Delta Epsilon Sigma, Alpha Sigms Nu. Office: Coll of Holy Cross Fenwick Hall Worcester MA 01610

BROOKS, LEWIS ALEXANDER, psychologist; b. Jersey City, Mar. 13, 1931; s. Joel Nathaniel and Louise (Tucker) B.; m. Lucille Hatchett, June 15, 1970 (div. 1983); m. Anna Erzsebet Toth, May 20, 1984. BA in English, Empire State Coll., 1979; MS in Edn., SUNY, New Paltz, 1983; MA in Psychology, CUNY, 1986, PhD in Psychology, 1992. Cert. spl. edn. tchr., N.Y. Residential aide Crystal Run Village, Fallsburg, N.Y., 1976-83, tchr., 1983-86, psychologist, 1986—; instr. in psychology Orange County Community Coll., Middleton, N.Y., 1991—; lectr. Janus Pannonius Egyetem, Pecs, Hungary, 1988; adj. instr. in psychology Marist Coll., Poughkeepsie, N.Y., 1990—. Mem. APA, Ea. Psychol. Assn., Soc. for Rsch. in Child Devel., Jean Piaget Soc., Coun. for Exceptional Children, N.Y. Acad. Scis., N.E. Ednl. Rsch. Assn. (presenter 1988-91, bd. dirs. 1990—), Sullivan County Assn. for Retarded Citizens, Assn. for Study Afro-Am. Life and History (pres. 1989), Nat. Rainbow Coalition. Democrat. Roman Catholic. Home: 3 Lincoln Pl Liberty NY 12754-1731 Office: Crystal Run Village Box AA Fallsburg NY 12733 also: Orange County Community Coll 115 South St SW 210 Middletown NY 10940

BROOKS, MAGGIE (MARGARET DARDEN), journalist, newscaster; b. Rochester, N.Y., Mar. 16, 1955; d. Eugene C. and Shirley J. (Kennedy) Gribbroek; m. Charles R. Darden, Aug. 5, 1983; children: Julia LeMay, Jensen Faye. Student, Cath. U. Am., 1974; BS, Ithaca Coll., 1977. Newscaster, reporter Sta. WTKO-AM, Ithaca, N.Y., 1975-77, Sta. WHAM-AM-FM, Rochester, 1977-80; newscaster, anchor Sta. WHEC-TV/Viacom Internat., Rochester, 1980—; news. dir. N.E. Satellite Entertainment Network, Rochester, 1991—. Author: Grandma Lives in My Room, 1991. Bd. dirs. Muscular Dystrophy Assn. Rochester, 1988—, Highland Hosp., Rochester, 1989—, Jr. League Rochester, 1991—; cons. Jr. Achievement, Rochester, 1990—. Named Communicator of Yr. Rochester Inst. Tech., 1990; recipient N.Y. State Broadcasters award N.Y. State Broadcasters Assn., 1980. Mem. AFTRA (sec. 1986-87). Office: Sta WHEC-TV 191 East Ave Rochester NY 14604

BROOKS, MARK HUNTER, network systems engineer, consultant; b. Pinehurst, N.C., Mar. 14, 1960; s. Brady Hunter and Mary Ann Brooks; m. Selina Malherbe, June 30, 1984. BS in Textile Mgmt., N.C. State U., 1982; MBA in Info. Systems, NYU, 1992. Asst. dir. R & D Reliance Cons. Group, N.Y.C., 1982-86; network planning analyst Sterling Drug Inc., N.Y.C., 1986-90; sr. systems engr. Chase Manhattan Bank, N.A., N.Y.C.,

1990-91; sr. LAN specialist TIAA-CREF, N.Y.C., 1991—; mem.-at-large bd. dirs. N. Am. region NetWare Users Internat., 1991, v.p., pres.-elect, 1992; founder, pres. N.Y. LAN Assn., Inc., N.Y.C., 1990-91; adv. bd. NETWORLD, 1992—. Chmn. fin. com. Metro. Bapt. Ch., N.Y.C., 1986-88, trustee, 1988-90, vice chmn. bd. trustees, 1990. Democrat. Baptist.

BROOKS, MARTIN, publishing company exective; b. N.Y.C., Aug. 26, 1950; s. Kenneth and Ruth (Schubert) B.; m. Stacey Savage, May 30, 1973 (div. 1980); 1 child, Kerin. BFA, NYU, 1973. Sr. prodn. engr. Cinema Sound, N.Y., 1971-78; chief rec. engr. G&T Harris, N.Y., 1978; mgr. rec. ops. CBS Pub., N.Y.C., 1978-81, mgr. audio visual devel., 1981-83, mgr. software devel., 1983-84, dir. software devel., 1984-86; exec. editor, electronic publ. Bowker Electronic Pub., N.Y.C., 1986-90; v.p. Bowker Electronic Pub., New Providence, N.J., 1991—; bd. dirs. Optical Pub. Assn. Designer, editor: (cd-rom) Books in Print Plus, 1986, Books in Print with Book Reviews Plus, 1987, Variety's Video Directory Plus, 1986, Enviro Energyline Abstracts Plus, 1991, Library Reference Plus, 1992, Children's Reference Plus, 1992; designer, producer: (software) Class II, 1984, Adventures in Science Series, 1985; engr., producer: (radio program) Crawdaddy Rock Review, 1978. Mem. Audio Engring. Soc., Soc. Motion Picture and TV Engrs. Home: 112-20 72d Dr Forest Hills NY 11375-5661 Office: Bowker Electronic Pub 121 Chanlon Rd New Providence NJ 07974-1544

BROOKS, MARVIN ALAN, chemist, researcher; b. Trenton, N.J., Jan. 28, 1945; s. Hyman and Miriam (Lipschutz) B.; m. Susan Pristoop, June 16, 1968; children: Paul, Cheryl. BS, Lafayette Coll., 1966; PhD, U. Md., 1971. Chemist Hoffmann-LaRoche, Nutley, N.J., 1971-85, Merck Sharp & Dohme Rsch. Labs., West Point, Pa., 1985—. Author monographs on pharm. analysis. Mem. Am. Chem. Soc., Am. Assn. Pharm. Scientists. Office: Merck Sharp & Dohme Rsch Labs Dept Pharm Rsch West Point PA 19486

BROOKS, MICHAEL LEE, neuroradiologist; b. Phila., Dec. 3, 1955; s. Robert Charles and Judith Bell (Segal) B. BA in Biology, U. Pa., 1977; MD, Hahnemann U., 1981. Bd. cert. in diagnostic radiology; med. lic., Pa., Mass. Resident radiology Mercy Cath. Med. Ctr., Darby, Pa., 1982-84; chief radiology resident Mercy Cath. Med. Ctr., Darby, 1984-85; neuroradiology fellow Brigham and Women's Hosp./Harvard Med. Sch., Boston, 1985-87; neuroradiologist Brigham and Women's Hosp., Boston, 1987-88; cons. neuroradiology Dana Farber Cancer Ctr., 1987-88; instr. radiology med. sch. Harvard U., Boston, 1987-88; assoc. dir. Grad. Hosp. Imaging Ctr., Phila., 1988—; sr. neuroradiologist The Grad. Hosp., Phila., 1989—; vis. faculty Community Coll. Phila., 1988-90; adj. clin. faculty Phila. Coll. Podiatric Medicine, 1988-91; neuroradiologist Temporomandibular Joint disease and facial pain program Sch. of Dental Medicine U. Pa., Phila., 1988—; co-investigator NIH, 1987-88; clin. asst. prof. diagnostic imaging Sch. of Medicine Temple U., Phila., 1989; clin. asst. prof. oral surgery and pharmacology U. Pa. Sch. Dental Medicine, Phila., 1990; co-founder Imaging Rsch. Found. of Grad. Hosp., 1989; mem. sci. adv. com. Phila. Field Initiating Group for HIV Trials; mem. neuroradiology sect. Com. to Establish a Registry for Althzeimer's Disease; cons. in neuroradiology Phila. Office of Med. Examiner, 1992—; instr. in med. imaging Jefferson U. Coll. Allied Health, Phila., 1991—. Contbr. multiple papers in profl. jours.; co-author multiple abstracts presented at profl. meetings. Fellow Phila. Coll. Physicians; mem. AMA, Radiol. Soc. N.Am., Am. Soc. Neuroradiology (sr.), Soc. for Magnetic Resonance Imaging, Am. Roentgen Ray Soc., Phila. Neuroradiology Soc., Ea. Neuroradiology Soc., Pa. Med. Soc., Phila. County Med. Soc., Internat. Soc. for Minimal Intervention in Spine Surgery. Republican. Home: 781 S 2d St Philadelphia PA 19147 Office: Grad Hosp Imaging Ctr 1840 South St 3d Fl Philadelphia PA 19146-1419

BROOKS, PETER STUYVESANT, real estate consultant; b. Newburgh, N.Y., June 23, 1942; s. Frank A. Brooks and Anne Corbin (Armstrong) Rice; m. Frances A. Camera, June 30, 1990. Instr. Duchess Community Coll., Poughkeepsie, N.Y., 1966-67, Mt. St. Mary Coll., Newburgh, 1969-70, Southampton (N.Y.) Coll., 1970-72; real estate broker Newburgh, 1972-77; from asst. sec. to sr. v.p. Chem. Bank, N.Y.C., 1977-91; ptnr. Austrian Roth & Ptnrs., N.Y.C., 1992—; treas. N.Y.C. chpt. Appraisal Inst., 1989, sec., 1990, 1st v.p., 1991, pres. 1992. Bd. dirs. Grand Cen. Partnership, N.Y.C., 1988—, Citizens Crime Commn., N.Y.C., 1989—. With U.S. Army, 1967-68. Mem. Am. Soc. Real Estate Counselors, Appraisal Inst. Home: 435 Martling Ave Tarrytown NY 10591-4714 Office: Austrian Roth & Ptnrs 488 Madison Ave New York NY 10022

BROOKS, ROGER CHARLES, educational administrator; b. Mpls., Apr. 14, 1947; s. Chester L. and Ebba (Johnson) B.; m. Carol Durgy, Aug. 24, 1973; children: Evan, Cameron. AA, George Mason U., 1967; BA, U. Va., 1970; MEd, Antioch U. New Eng., 1974, 85; EdD, Nova U., 1988. Tchr. Millville Sch., Concord, N.H., 1974-76, head tchr., 1976-78, prin., 1978-80; prin. Garrison Sch., Concord, 1978-87, Beaver Meadow Sch., Concord, 1987—; bd. dirs. ICM, Inc., N.Y.C. Author: Green Feet, 1977, Teaching Poetry in the Schools, 1980, No Stars, Improvisational Theatre in the Classroom, 1982, A Teacher's Guide to Classroom Architecture, 1984. Chmn. N.H. Coun. on Arts, 1983-87; bd. dirs. Arts 1000, Concord, 1988—; chmn. budget com., bd. govs. United Way, Concord, 1989—. Recipient Award for Cablecasting Excellence award, 1980, award Action for Children's TV, 1981, Excellence in Arts Edn. award Alliance for Arts Edn., 1982. Mem. Nat. Elem. Prins. Assn., N.H. Elem. Prins. Assn., Assn. for Supervision and Curriculum Devel. Home: 11 Auburn St Concord NH 03301 Office: Beaver Meadow Sch 40 Sewalls Falls Rd Concord NH 03301-4649

BROOKS-GUNN, JEANNE, psychologist; b. Bethesda, Md., Dec. 9, 1946; d. Richard D. and Mary J. (Wood) Brooks; BA, Conn. Coll., 1969; EdM, Harvard U., 1970; PhD in Human Learning and Devel., U. Pa., 1975; m. Robert W. Gunn, 1970. Assoc. dir. Inst. for Study of Exceptional Children, Ednl. Testing Svc., Princeton, N.J., 1977-82; sr. rsch. scientist, dir. adolescent study program Ednl. Testing Svc. and St. Luke's-Roosevelt Hosp. Ctr., 1983—; rsch. scientist The Pediatric Svc. St. Luke's Roosevelt Med. Ctr., N.Y.C., 1977-85; asst. prof. pediatric psychology Coll. Physicians and Surgeons, Columbia U., N.Y.C., 1978-83; Virginia and Leonard Marx prof. in child devel. Tchrs. Coll., Columbia U., 1991, dir. Adolescent Study Program, 1991, dir. Ctr. for Study of Children and Families Tchrs. Coll., 1992—; adj. assoc. prof. pediatrics U. Pa., 1985-91; vis. scholar Russell Sage Found., 1989-90. Trustee N.J. Neuropsychiat. Inst., 1979-85; pres. Soc. Rsch. in Adolescence. Grantee NSF, Commonwealth Fund, NIH, Ford Found., Robert Wood Johnson Found., W.T. Grant Found. Fellow Am. Psychol. Assn., Am. Psychol. Soc.; mem. AAAS, Ea. Psychol. Assn., Am. Edn. Research Assn., Soc. for Research in Child Devel., N.Y. Acad. Scis., N.J. Counsel on Prevention Mental Retardation, NAS Coms. (preventing AIDS, defining poverty, child abuse). Author: (with W. Matthews) He and She: How Children Develop Their Sex-Role Identity, 1979, (with M. Lewis) Social Cognition and the Acquisition of Self, 1979, (with A. Petersen) Girls at Puberty, 1983, (with G. Baruch) Women in Midlife, 1984, (with A. Petersen and D. Eichorn) The Study of Maturational Timing Effects in Adolescence, 1985, (with F. Furstenburg) Adolescent Mothers in Later Life, 1987, (with A.C. Petersen) The Emergence of Depression and Depressive Symptoms During Adolescence, 1987, (with A. Petersen) Emergence of Depression in Adolescence, 1990, (with R. Lerner and A.C. Petersen) The Encyclopedia of Adolescence, 1991, (with L. Chase-Lansdale) Escape from Poverty, 1992 ; contbr. numerous articles on child devel. and social psychology to profl. jours. Office: Ednl Testing Svc Princeton NJ 08541

BROOTEN, GARY, public relations executive; b. St. Paul, Aug. 11, 1938; s. Alfred LeFroy and Barbara Louise (Drost) B.; m. Dorothy Herhal, July 27, 1963; children: Lisa Booth, Lars Alfred. BA, Harvard U., 1960. Reporter St. Paul Dispatch-Pioneer Press, 1961-62; sci. writer Phila. Inquirer, 1962-66; sci. writer, editor Phila. Evening Bull., 1966-72; dir. pub. affairs Region III U.S. EPA, Phila., 1972-75; exec. dir. Mental Health Assn. Pa., Phila., 1975-78; dir. editorial svcs. Phila. Nat. Corp., 1978-83; dir. corp. pub. rels. Core-States Fine. Corp. (formerly Phila. Nat. Corp.), 1983—, v.p., 1985—; editor, owner Del. Valley Agenda, Phila., 1979-82; owner Glen Mills (Pa.) Communications, 1987—. Contbr. articles to profl. publs. Pres. Phila. Civic Ballet Co., 1988-90; bd. dirs. Pa. Environ. Coun., Phila., 1978-81, PALINET (Libr. Svc. Orgn.), Phila., 1981-83; mem. communications com. United Way of Southeastern Pa. With USAR, 1960-61. Mem. Pub. Rels. Soc. Am. (nat. del. Phila. chpt. 1985—, Pepperpot award 1989), World Affairs Coun. Phila., Nat. Assn. Sci. Writers, Pa. Bankers Assn. (pub. rels. com.), Harvard Club (Phila.), Antique Auto Club Am. (sr. master judge). Home: 1517 Gradyville Rd Glen Mills PA 19342-1915 Office: CoreState Fin Corp PO Box 7558 Philadelphia PA 19101-7558

BROSKY, JOHN G., judge; b. Scott Twp., Pa., Aug. 4, 1920; m. Rose F. Brosky, June 24, 1950; children: John C., Carol Ann, David J. BA, U. Pitts., 1942, LLB, 1949, JD, 1968. Bar: Pa. 1950. Asst. county solicitor, Allegheny County, Pa., 1951-56; judge County Ct. Allegheny County, 1956-61; adminstrv. judge family div. Common Pleas Ct. Allegheny County, 1961-80; judge Superior Ct. Pa., 1980—; mem. faculty Pa. Coll. Judiciary. Chmn. Operation Patrick Henry, Boy Scouts Am.; pres. Scott Twp. Sch. Bd., 1946-56; 1st pres. Chartiers Valley Joint Sch. Dist., Allegheny County, Pa.; pres. Greater Pitts. Guild for Blind. Served with U.S. Army, 1942-46; maj. gen. (ret.) USAF-Pa. Air N.G. Recipient Disting. Jud. Service award Pa., Mason Juvenile Ct. Inst., Man of Yr. award in law Pitts. Jr. C. of C., 1960, Humanitarian award New Light Men's Club, 1960, Loyalty Day award VFW, 1960, Four Chaplains award, 1965; Man of Yr. award Cath. War Vets., 1960, 62; Service award Alliance Coll.; Disting. Citation, Mil. Order World Wars; Humanitarian award Variety Club, 1974; Jimmy Doolittle fellow award Aerospace Edn. Found., 1975; Pa. Meritorious Service medal Pa. N.G., 1976; State Humanitarian award Domestic Relations Assn. Pa., 1978; Man of Yr. award Am. Legion, 1978; Pa. Disting. Service medal; Disting. Service award Pa. N.G. Assn., 1980; Exceptional Service award USAF, 1982; General Ira Eaker fellow, 1981; Brotherhood of Man award Fraternal Socs. of Greater Pitts., 1987; Community Service award Chartiers Valley Commn. on Human Relations, 1988, George Washington Honor medal Freedoms Found., 1990; named Pitts. Polonian of Yr., 1988, Man of Yr. Am. Biog. Inst., 1990; recipient St. Thomas More award Allegheny County Bar Assn., 1989, Man of Yr. award Kosciuszko Found., 1991. Mem. Am. Judicature Soc., ABA, Pa. Bar Assn. (co-chmn. professionalism com. 1987-88), Assn. Trial Lawyers Am., Inst. Jud. Adminstrn., Inc., Internat. Platform Assn., Air Force Assn. (nat. dir., nat. pres., chmn. bd., presidential citation 1974, 80, 81), Am. Acad. Matrimonial Lawyers, N.G. Assn. of Pa. (pres.), Pa. Conf. State Trial Judges (past pres.), Pa. Joint Family Law Council. Clubs: Press, Variety, Aero (past pres.) (Pitts.). Office: 2703 Grant Bldg Pittsburgh PA 15219

BROSNAN, CAROL RAPHAEL SARAH, arts administrator, musician; b. Paterson, N.J., July 19, 1931; d. Basil Roger Warnock and Mary Ellen Carroll (McDonald) B. Student, George Washington U., Washington, 1956-61, U. Va., 1975, U. Oxford (Eng.), 1975; B.A. in History, George Washington U., 1981, postgrad., 1983-87; studied with Iris Brussels and Helen Yakobson, 1983-87. Adminstrv. clk. Dept. of Army, Def., Pentagon, Office of asst. chief of staff intelligence, Washington, 1955-58; clk. fgn. sci. info. program NSF, Washington, 1958-60, adminstrv. clk., 1960-65, adminstrv. fellowship clk. grad. fellowship program, 1965-72; spl. asst. to sr. dep. chmn. Nat. Endowment for Arts, Washington, 1972—; music tchr. piano, Paterson, N.J., 1945-53; piano recitalist U.S., Heidelberg, W. Ger. Served with WAC, 1953-55. Recipient Young People's Concerts award, 1945. Hon. fellow Harry S. Truman Libr. Inst. Nat. and Internat. Affairs, 1975. Fellow Intercontinental Biog. Assn.; mem. Am. Assn. for Advancement Slavic Studies, Am. Hist. Assn., Am. Philol. Assn., Acad. Polit. Sci. (contbg.), Am. Classical League, Friends of Bodleian Libr. (Oxford U.), Luther Rice Soc. of George Washington U. (life), Phi Alpha Theta. Home: 7523 Mcwhorter Pl Apt 303 Annandale VA 22003-5266 Office: Nat Endowment for Arts 1100 Pennsylvania Ave NW Washington DC 20506-0005

BROSS, ALBERT LOUIS, JR., artist; b. Newark, June 29, 1921; s. Albert L. and Ann Rita (Sinkovits) B.; m. Barbara Ann Tries, Apr. 12, 1946; children: Albert L. III, Eric A. Student, Art Students League N.Y., N.Y.C., 1939-42, 46-49. Lectr. Talens & Son (Holland), Union, N.J., 1965-70, Langnickle Inc., N.Y.C., 1968-72; art instr. Art Ctr. of the Oranges, East Orange, N.J., 1962-67, Cranford (N.J.) Art Assn., 1960-62, Summit (N.J.) Art Assn., 1965-72, YWCA Adult Sch., Summit, 1950-72. Staff sgt. U.S. Army, 1942-46, PTO. Recipient Lt. Melvin Brewer award Hudson Valley Art Assn., 1977, Philip Shumaker award Hudson Valley Art Assn., 1991, Oil award Interant. Miniature Art Exhbn., 1985-86, Seascape award, 1986, Landscape award, 1991. Mem. Art Students League N.Y. (life), Hudson Valley Art Assn., Miniature Art Soc. N.J., Associated Artists N.J., Chaffee Art Ctr. Republican. Home: PO Box 282 New Vernon NJ 07976-0282

BROSS, JOHN JOSEPH, business executive, management consultant; b. Troy, N.Y., Sept. 16, 1939; s. John Joseph and Dorothy Rose (Rodgers) B.; m. Barbara Ann Kramer (div. 1982); children: John J. III, Kevin M., Michael W.; m. Barbara Anne Bean, Oct. 13, 1990. Grad. high sch., Albany, N.Y. Owner, operator Bross Texaco Svc., Albany, 1965-70; technician Metroland Motors, Albany, 1970-73; dir. svc. Back Bay Motors, Boston, 1973-78; dir. fixed ops. Colony Motors, Edgartown, Mass., 1978-79; mgr. svc. Braymans, Attleboro, Mass., 1979-80, Midway Auto Ctr., Framingham, Mass., 1980-81; pres. Jack Bross Assocs., Groveland, Mass., 1981-83; gen. mgr. Merrimack Valley Datsun, Haverill, Mass., 1982-83; sr. cons. Dealer Mgmt. Assn., Exeter, N.H., 1983-88; founder Achiever Group, Georgetown, Mass., 1989—; exec. dir. Mass. Inst. of Neuro-Linguistic Programming, 1990—. With USMC, 1961-64. Mem. Soc. Automotive Engrs., Haverhill C. of C., Neuro Linguistic Programing Practitioners. Home and Office: PO Box 264 198 Jewett St Georgetown MA 01833

BROTHERS, BARRY, painter, muralist, graphic designer; b. Bklyn., Jan. 18, 1955; s. James and Blanche (Wagner) B. BS in Photography/Art, Bklyn. Coll., 1977, MFA in Painting, 1980. Advt./graphic artist various cos., N.Y.C., 1974—; owner graphic design, advt. and fine arts studio Two-B Art Studios, N.Y.C., 1974—. Executed murals ABC, 1985-86, Capital Cities/ABC, 1989, various pvt. residences, N.Y.C.; exhibited in group and one-man shows including Mus. Nat. Arts Found., N.Y.C., 1989, Henry Hicks Gallery, 1986, Bklyn. Mus., 1985, Mus. Borrough Bklyn., 1983, 84, 87, Adelphi U. Art Gallery, 1982, Milw. Ctr. Photography, 1978, Bklyn. Coll. Fine Arts Gallery, 1976, 77, Herbert F. Johnson Mus. Art and numerous others; represented in permanent collections including Herbert F. Johnson Mus. Art, Bklyn. Coll.; photographer, illustrator various mags. and publs. including The N.Y. Art Rev., Gran Bazaar Mag., Art Product News Mag., Print Mag., Fortune Mag.; contbr. articles to profl. jour. Recipient DESI 9 award, 1986, award merit Soc. Publ. Design XVII, 1982, cert. distinction Creativity 11, 1981, hon. mention award NYU, 1980, award Mus. Nat. Arts Found., 1989, Charles G. Shaw Meml. award in painting, 1979, Landscape Painting Competition Artist Mag., 1987. Home and Office: 1922 E 18th St Brooklyn NY 11229-3410

BROTMAN, STANLEY SEYMOUR, federal judge; b. Vineland, N.J., July 27, 1924; s. Herman Nathaniel and Fanny (Melletz) B.; m. Suzanne M. Simon, Sept. 9, 1951; children: Richard A., Alison B. B.A., Yale U., 1947; LL.B., Harvard U., 1950. Bar: N.J. 1950, D.C. 1951. Pvt. practice law Vineland, 1952-57; ptnr. Shapiro, Brotman, Eisenstat & Capizola, Vineland, 1957-75; judge U.S. Dist. Ct. N.J., Camden, 1975—; acting chief judge Dist. Ct. of V.I., 1989—; mem. N.J. Bd. Bar Examiners, 1970-74. Chmn. editorial bd. N.J. State Bar Jour, 1969-74; contbr. articles to profl. jours. Trustee Newcomb Hosp., Vineland, 1953-68. With U.S. Army, 1943-45, 51-52. Fellow Am. Bar Found., Jud. Conf. U.S. (space and facilities com. 1988—); mem. ABA (ho. of dels. 1975-80, state del. 83—), Nat. Conf. Fed. Trial Judges (exec. com. 1984-87, chmn.-elect 1986-87, chmn. 1987-88, chmn. standing com. jud. selection, tenure & compensation 1988—), Am. Judicature Soc., Fed. Bar Assn., N.J. State Bar Assn. (pres. 1974-75), Cumberland County Bar Assn. (pres. 1969-70), Assn. of Fed. Bar of State of N.J., Harvard U. Law Sch. Assn. N.J. (pres. 1974-75), Yale U. Alumni Assn., Harvard Law Sch. Assn. N.J., Am. Legion, Jewish War Vets., Yale Club, B'nai B'rith, Masons, Shriners. Office: US Dist Ct 230 US Courthouse 4th & Market Sts Box 1029 Camden NJ 08101

BROUGHAM, ROBERT POWERS, marketing executive; b. Joliet, Ill., Dec. 4, 1943; s. Erwin Roy and Viola Ann (Powers) B.; m. Linda Rae Garrett, Sept. 1, 1972; children: Matthew Garrett, Robert Jacob. BS, U. Wis., 1966; MBA, Roosevelt U., 1984. Dist. sales mgr. Corning (N.Y.) Glass Works, 1970-76; sr. product mgr. GCA Corp., Bedford, Mass., 1976-80, Miles Labs., Elkhart, Ind., 1980-82; dir. bus. planning and devel. Warner Lambert, Morris Plains, N.J., 1982-85; gen. mgr. Delsi Intruments, Fairfield, N.J., 1985-87; group bus. mgr. Schott Am., Yonkers, N.Y., 1988—; pres. Strategic Bus. Alternatives, Randolph, N.J., 1984—; sales broker Schlott Realtors, Morristown, N.J., 1987—. Mem. Rep. Nat. Com., Washington, 1987, Shongum Lake Assn., Randolph, 1986—. Capt. USMC, 1966-69, Vietnam. Mem. Am. Mktg. Assn., Am. Chem. Soc., Soc. Plastic Engrs., Disabled Am. Vets., Beta Theta Pi. Presbyterian. Home: 18 Red Barn Ln Randolph NJ 07869-3816 Office: Schott Am 3 Odell Plz Yonkers NY 10701-1405

BROUGHTON, BRADFORD BROWNE, English language and communications educator; b. Allentown, Pa., Feb. 6, 1926; s. Harold Earle and Margaret Stevens (Browne) B.; m. June Margaret Barnum, Oct. 7, 1950; children: Megan, Thaddeus. BA, Allegheny Coll., 1947; MA, U. Pa., 1949, PhD, 1961. Instr. Utica (N.Y.) Coll., 1949-50; instr. Clarkson U., Potsdam, N.Y., 1955-57, asst. prof., 1957-61, assoc. prof., 1961-66, prof., 1966—, chmn. dept. humanities, 1973-81, prof. tech. communications, 1981—; vis. prof. Trinity Coll., Dublin, 1970-71, 82-83, 86-87. Author: Legends of Richard Coeur de Lion, 1966, The Romance of Richard the Lion-Hearted and Other English Metrical Romances, 1966, Twenty-Seven to One, 1970, Dragons are Here to Stay, 1979, Sir Gawain: From Scoundrel to Hero, 1980, Dictionary of Medieval Knighthood and Chivalry, vol. I, 1986, vol. II, 1988. With USN, 1944-46, 50-52, PTO, Korea. Mem. MLA (N.E. sect.), Internat. Arthurian Soc., Société Rencesvals, Coll. English Assn., New Chaucer Soc. Republican. Episcopalian. Home: 4 Leroy St Potsdam NY 13676-1739 Office: Clarkson U Potsdam NY 13699-5760

BROUGHTON, JOHN MARCUS, psychology educator; b. Sutton, Surrey, Eng., Apr. 5, 1947; came to U.S., 1968; s. Ralph Leonard and Doris Edith (Willis) B. BA, MA, Cambridge U., Eng., 1968; PhD, Harvard U., 1975. Lic. psychologist, N.Y. Asst. prof. psychology Wayne State U., Detroit, 1974-76; asst. to assoc. prof. psychology and edn. Columbia U. Tchrs. Coll., N.Y.C., 1976—; visiting assoc. prof. edn. U. Rochester Grad. Sch. Edn., N.Y.C., 1986. Editor: The Cognitive Developmental Psychology of James Mark Baldwin, 1982, Critical Theories of Psychological Development, 1987; co-editor: New Ideas in Psychology Jour., 1982-91, PsychCritique: Internat. Jour. Critical Psychology & Psychoanalysis, 1985-87. Recipient Passingham prize Cambridge U., 1968; Choate fellow Harvard U., 1968-70; Rockefeller fellow Wesleyan U., 1987. Mem. Internat. Soc. Theoretical Psychology, Psychologists for Peace. Office: Tchrs Coll 525 W 120th St New York NY 10027-6625

BROUGHTON, T. ALAN, English language educator; b. Bryn Mawr, Pa., June 9, 1936; s. T. Robert S. and Annie Leigh (Hobson) B.; m. Laurel Ginter; children: Shannon Leigh Broughton-Smith, Camm, T. Nathaniel. Student, Harvard U., 1954-57, Juilliard Sch. Music, 1957-59; BA with honors, Swarthmore Coll., 1962; MA, U. Wash., 1964. Instr. U. Wash., Seattle, 1962-64, Sweet Briar (Va.) Coll., 1964-66; mem. faculty dept. English, U. Vt., Burlington, 1966—, prof. English, 1974—; reader, lectr. USIA, Republic of Korea, Thailand, Singapore, The Philippines, 1982, Egypt, 1984, 88, Italy, 1992, also univs., colls., schs. and communities in Ala., Ark., Maine, N.H., N.Y., Okla., Pa., Va., Vt. Author: (fiction) A Family Gathering, 1977, 79, The Man on the Moon, 1979, Winter Journey, 1980, 81, The Horsemaster, 1981, Hob's Daughter, 1984, The Jesse Tree, 1988, (Poetry) In the Face of Descent, 1975, Far from Home, 1979, Dreams before Sleep, 1988, Preparing To Be Happy, 1988; contbr. poems and stories to numerous quars., jours. and mags., also anthologies. Recipient poetry award Yankee Ann., 1971, 73, 75, 92, Emily Balch award Va. Quar. Rev., 1974, Borestone award, 1972, 73, 74, 5th ann. Angoff award The Lit. Rev., 1986, Prize Stories award The O. Henry Awards, 1991; NEA fellow, 1976-77, Guggenheim fellow, 1982-83; PEN grantee, 1981, 86, 87. Mem. Phi Beta Kappa. Home: 124 Spruce St Burlington VT 05401-4522 Office: U Vt English Dept 315 Old Mill Burlington VT 05405

BROUILETTE, YVES, insurance company executive; b. Ste.-Geneviére de Batiscan, Que., Can., May 2, 1951; s. Wallace and Mariette (Jacob) B.; m. Dominique Savard, Dec. 30, 1972; children: Benoit, Luc, Catherine. BS in Actuarial Sci., Laval U., Que., 1972; grad. advanced mgmt. program, Harvard U. Rsch. asst. Gauvin study com. on automobile ins. Govt. of Que., 1972-74; actuary Commerce Group Ins. Co., St.-Hyacinthe, Que., 1974-84, v.p., 1978-84, exec. v.p. personal lines, 1984-90, pres., chief exec. officer, 1990—; pres., chief exec. officer Commassur Inc., 1990—; bd. dirs. Underwriters Adjustment Bur. Ltd.; mem. Que. com. IBC. Fellow Can. inst. Actuaries, Casualty Actuarial Soc. N.Y.; mem. Internat. Assn. Actuaries, St.-Denis Club. Office: Le Groupe Commerce Co, 2450 Girouard St W, Saint Hyacinthe, PQ Canada J2S 3B3

BROUMAS, JOHN GEORGE, retired banker, retired theatre owner; b. Youngstown, Ohio, Oct. 12, 1917; s. George Elias Broumas and Evelyn Vaveris; m. Ruth Darr, Sept. 20, 1944; children: Carole Ann, Sue Ann. Chem. warfare officer, Officer Candidate Sch., Edgewood Arsenal, Md., 1944; mem. class 1954 (hon.), West Point (N.Y.) Mil. Acad., 1975. Gen. mgr. Roth Theatres, Washington, 1946-54; chmn., pres. Broumas Showcase Theatres, Washington, 1954-83; dir. McLean and Madison Bank Va., 1975-91, chmn. of bd., 1983-91; chmn. of bd., pres. Madison Nat. Bank Va., 1986-91; chmn. bd. dirs. Grey Eagle, Ltd. Import and Export, McLean; lectr. motion pictures and film making Georgetown U., 1972-78; chmn. exec. com. Madison Nat. Bank Va., 1987-91; dir. James Madison Ltd., Washington, 1987-90; dir. Potomac Fin. Group, 1991—. Trustee Leukemia Soc. Am., 1988, Edn. and Tng. Found. Ptnrs. Am. Vocat. Edn., 1991—; dir. USO, 1956-80, Found. Religious Action, 1965-76, Washington chpt. Coll. Football Hall of Fame, 1989 (appreciation award 1989); adv. coun., chm. D.C. area Will Rogers Hosp., 1968-78; exec. com. East Coast div. Child Help U.S.A., 1989; vol. Am. Cancer Soc., Kidney Found., United Way, Salvation Army, Boy Scouts Am., others. Maj. U.S. Army, 1941-46. Recipient Presdl. Disting. Svc. medal Cath. U., 1989, Ahepa Achievement of Excellence award, 1981, Gold Reel award 50 Yrs. Motion Picture Industry, 1978, Outstanding Svc. award, 1978, Gold medal, 1978, Fairfax County, Va. Sch. Patrol Appreciation award, 1977, Good Guy award Motion Picture Industry, 1974, Humanitarian award Local Area Motion Picture Industry, 1972, Muscular Dystrophy Appreciation award Jerry Lewis Telethon, 1972, and others; named to Order of St. Andrew, Greek Orthodox Ch., 1987. Mem. Res. Officers Assn. (life), Variety Club Internat. (Variety medal 1985, Life Liner award 1985, Humanitarian award 1965-66, 78-79). Republican. Home: 5505 Grove St Chevy Chase MD 20815

BROUN, ELIZABETH, art historian, museum administrator; b. Kansas City, Mo., Dec. 15, 1946; d. Augustine Hughes and Roberta Catherine (Hayden) Gibson; m. Ronald Broun, June 5, 1968; 1 dau., Katherine. B.A., U. Kans., 1968, Ph.D., 1976; cert. advanced study, U. Bordeaux, France, 1967. Curator prints and drawings Spencer Mus. Art, Lawrence, Kans., 1976-83; asst. prof. U. Kans., Lawrence, 1978-83; asst. dir. chief curator Nat. Mus. Am. Art, Washington, 1983-88; acting dir., 1988-89; dir. Nat. Mus. Am. Art, Washington, 1989—. Author: exhbn. catalogues Prints of Zorn, 1979, Prints and Drawings of Pat Steir, 1983, Patrick Ireland; Drawings 1965-85, 1986, Albert Pinkham Ryder, 1989; co-author: Benton's Bentons, 1980, Engravings of Marcantonio Raimondi, 1981. Woodrow Wilson fellow, 1968-69; Ford. Found. fellow, 1970-72. Mem. Phi Beta Kappa. Office: Nat Mus Am Art 8th & G Sts NW Washington DC 20560

BROUSE, DEBORAH ELIZABETH, education and outreach director; b. Buffalo, Oct. 3, 1950; d. Richard William Jr. and Mary (Brewer) B.; m. George Osborn Bergantz, June 7, 1969 (div. 1973); m. Elliott Jan Gilberg, Apr. 11, 1980; children: Stephen Brouse Gilberg, Sarah Brouse Gilberg. BA in Music magna cum laude, Brown U., 1972; MA in Planning and Adminstrn., Antioch U., 1981. Health worker Feminist Women's Health Ctr., Santa Ana, Calif., 1974; program dir. Teen Help, Inc., Fountain Valley, Calif., 1974-75; program coord. Diogenes Youth Svcs., Davis, Calif., 1975-76, program dir., 1976-78; tng. and tech. assistance specialist Ctr. for Community Change, Washington, 1978-84; dir. edn. and outreach Zero Population Growth Inc., Washington, 1985—; tng. and tec. assisance specialist Environ. Support Ctr., Washington, 1991; bd. dirs. Nat. Assn. for Sci., Tech. and Soc., University Park, Pa., 1987-89. Mem. Alliance for Environ. Edn. (exec. com. 1987-89, bd. dirs. 1985-89). Democrat. Home: 5527 Nevada Ave NW Washington DC 20015-1768 Office: Zero Population Growth Inc 1400 16th St NW # 320 Washington DC 20036-2290

BROWDER, EVA TISLOWITZ, university administrator; b. Vienna, Austria, June 27, 1929; d. Erna (Klein) Tislowitz; m. Felix Earl Browder, Oct. 5,

1949; children: Thomas Earl, William Felix. BS, MIT, 1951; postgrad., Boston U., 1951-53; MEd, Harvard U., 1962. Tchr. Hillhouse High Sch., New Haven, 1956-57, Hamden (Conn.) Hall Country Day Sch., 1959-61; rsch. asst. sch. math. study group Yale U., New Haven, 1958-59; tech. editor Ency. Brit., Chgo., 1967-70; tech. editor Astrophys. Jour., U. Chgo., 1970-72, adminstr. dept. computer sci., 1982-87; adminstr. Lab. for Cancer Rsch. dept. chem. biology and pharmacognosy Rutgers U., New Brunswick, N.J., 1987-90, adminstr. dept. molecular biology, 1990—; alumni sec. for student recruitment MIT, Chgo., 1972-78; asst. dir. NSF Summer Inst. for Talented High Sch. Students, Chgo., 1979. Fellow NSF, U. Calif., Berkeley, 1959, Harvard U., 1961-62. Mem. Nat. Coun. Univ. Rsch. Adminstrs.

BROWDER, FELIX EARL, mathematician, educator; b. Moscow, July 31, 1927; s. Earl and Raissa (Berkmann) B.; m. Eva Tislowitz, Oct. 5, 1949; children: Thomas, William. SB, MIT, 1946; PhD, Princeton U., 1948; MA (hon.), Yale U., 1962; D (hon.), U. Paris, 1990. C.L.E. Moore instr. math. MIT, 1948-51, vis. assoc. prof., 1961-62, vis. prof., 1977-78; instr. Boston U., 1951-53; asst. prof. Brandeis U., 1955-56; from asst. prof. to prof. Yale U., 1956-63; prof. math. U. Chgo., 1963-72, Louis Block prof. math., 1972-82, Max Mason disting. svc. prof., 1982-87, chmn. dept., 1972-77, 80-85; v.p. rsch. Rutgers, The State U. N.J., 1986-91; univ. prof. Rutgers U., New Brunswick, 1986—; vis. mem. Inst. Advanced Study, Princeton (N.J.) U., 1953-54, 63-64, vis. prof., 1968; vis. prof. Inst. Pure and Applied Math., Rio de Janiero, 1960, U. Paris, 1973, 75, 78, 81, 83, 85; sr. rsch. fellow U. Sussex, Eng., 1970, 76; Fairchild disting. visitor Calif. Inst. Tech., Pasadena, 1975-76. Contbr. theorems to books, including Nonlinear Problems, 1966, Functional Analysis and Related Fields, 1970, Nonlinear Operators and Nonlinear Equations of Evolution in Banach Spaces, 1976, Nonlinear Functional Analysis and Its Applications, 1986. With AUS, 1953-55. Guggenheim fellow, 1953-54, 66-67, Sloan Found. fellow, 1959-63, NSF sr. postdoctoral fellow, 1957-58. Fellow Am. Acad. Arts and Scis.; mem. AAAS (chmn. sect A 1982-83), Nat. Acad. Scis (coun. 1992—), Am. Math. Soc. (editor bull. 1959-68, 78-83, mem. coun. 1959-72, 78-83, mng. editor 1964-68, 80, mem. exec. com. coun. 1979-80), Math. Assn. Am., Sigma Xi (pres. chpt. 1985-86).

BROWDER, LESLEY HUGHES, III, marketing professional; b. Concord, Mass., July 1, 1962; s. Lesley Hughes Jr. and Marilyn (Taylor) B. BSBA, Lehigh U., 1984, MBA, 1990. Sales rep. 3-D Sports, York, Pa., 1984-85, gen. mgr., 1985-88; fin. analyst Susquehanna Broadcasting, York, 1988-90; credit analyst CoreStates Bank, Phila., 1990-91; mktg. mgr. H.L. Miller & Son, Schuykill Haven, Pa., 1991—. Trustee 1st Presbyn. Ch., Reading, Pa., 1990-91. Republican. Home: 135 Medinah Dr Reading PA 19607

BROWER, DAVID CHARLES, transportation executive; b. Glens Falls, N.Y., Oct. 3, 1945; s. Charles William and Doris Mae (Hubbell) B.; m. Eloise Mary O'Neil, Sept. 11, 1965 (div. 1986); children: Benjamin, Daniel; m. Jeanne M. Douglass, July 23, 1988. BBA, U. Vt., 1970. Indsl. engr. IBM Corp., Burlington, Vt., 1970-71; mktg. rep. IBM Corp., Albany, N.Y., 1971-77; sr. sales rep. Digital Equipment Corp., Syracuse, N.Y., 1977-79; corp. adminstrn. cons. Digital Equipment Corp., Maynard, Mass., 1979-83; ops. cons. Digital Equipment Corp., Marlborough, Mass., 1983-85, dist. ops. mgr., 1985-88, product ops. mgr., 1988-90; pres. Marlboro Transp., Marlborough, 1991—. Mem. Rotary. Office: Marlboro Transp 455 Elm St Marlborough MA 01752

BROWN, AARON CARL, management consultant; b. Seattle, Nov. 27, 1956; s. Arthur Charles and Margaret (Martell) B.; m. Deborah Ann Pastor, Mar. 21, 1987. SB, Harvard U., 1978; MBA, U. Chgo., 1982. Cons. Am. Mgmt. Systems, Rosslyn, Va., 1978-80; dir. Prudential Ins., Newark, 1982-83; mgmt. cons. N.Y.C., 1983—. Democrat. Jewish. Home: 839 W End Ave New York NY 10025-5350 Office: PO Box 1671 New York NY 10025-1560

BROWN, ALAN ANTHONY, marketing executive; b. Winthrop, Mass., Feb. 6, 1936; s. Joseph Raymond and Harriet (Taylor) B.; m. Margret Egan, Aug. 8, 1961 (div. Feb. 1971); 1 child, Alan Jr.; m. Virginia A. Preno, Apr. 12, 1975; children: Linda, Diane, Michael, Sandra. BBA, Suffolk U., 1981, MBA, 1984. Test methods engr. RCA, Burlington, Mass., 1964-68; field svc. engr. BLH Electronics, Waltham, Mass., 1968; sales engr. AVCO Corp., Wilmington, Mass., 1968-71; sales rep. ITT Tech. Inst., Chelsea, Mass., 1971-75; dist. mgr. Continental Resources, Bedford, Mass., 1975-78; area mgr. Philips Test & Measurement, Woburn, Mass., 1978-81; distributor sales mgr. Hayes InstSer Inc., Billerica, Mass., 1981-85; sr. sales engr. Eaton Corp., Beverly, Mass., 1985-86; v.p. mktg. Hayes Inst Ser Inc., Billerica, Mass., 1986—; del. Nat. Conf. of Standards Lab., Boulder, Colo., 1985—. Campaign worker Richard Deminto, Winthrop, 1988. Recipient Acad. Achievement award Sch. of Mgmt., 1983. Mem. Assn. MBAs, IEEE, Winthrop Lodge of Elks, VFW Post #6712,, Delta Mu Delta. Home: 57 Central St Winthrop MA 02152-1633 Office: Hayes Instrument Svc Inc 530 Boston Rd Billerica MA 01821-3712

BROWN, ALBERT THADDEUS, state agency administrator; b. Malden, Mass., July 9, 1941; s. Albert Thaddeus and Barbara Cornelia (Grady) B.; divorced; children: Albert Jason, Tara Marie L. Bhay, Delaney Erica. BS, So. Conn. State Coll., New Haven, 1964, MS, 1970; EdD, Syracuse U., 1980. Vocat. guidance counselor Southbury (Conn.) Tng. Sch., 1969-70, dept. head, 1970-76; assoc. dir. Boston Project, 1976-78; asst. supt. Hogan Regional Ctr., Danvers, Mass., 1978-81; asst. dir. Woodhaven Ctr., Temple U., Phila., 1981-84; asst. regional adminstr. Div. Devel. Disabilities, State of N.J., Camden, 1984—; asst. fellow Ctr. on Human Policy, Syracuse, N.Y., 1974-76; cons. Rochester Sch. for Hearing Impaired, 1976. Author: (rsch. manual) Assessment of Special Service Needs, 1977; author, chairperson: Regional Resource Guide So. Region Resource Guide, 1988; contbr. articles to profl. jours. Regional rep. N.J. Prevention Coalition, Trenton, 1989—; div. rep. Human Svcs. Adv. Coalition, Camden, 1987—; adminstrv. cons. Boston Pub. Sch. System, 1978-91; vol. New Haven Boys Club, 1964, Light House, Syracuse, 1974-76, N.J. Speakers Bur., Trenton, 1987. Mem. Am. Assn. for Mental Retardation, Coun. for Exceptional Children, Assn. for Persons with Severe Disabilities, Disability Rights Advocacy Group. Office: Div Devel Disabilities Ste 17 101 Haddon Ave Camden NJ 08103-1485

BROWN, ALICE DALTON, artist; b. Danville, Pa., Apr. 17, 1939; d. Robert Hatcher and Elizabeth (Pond) Dalton; m. Eric Russell Brown, Aug. 20, 1960; children: Curtis, Colin, Eric. Student, Cornell U., 1958-59; BA, Oberlin Coll., 1962. Exhibited in one-person shows at Fischbach Gallery, N.Y.C., 1985, 87, 89, 91, William Sawyer Gallery, San Francisco Coll., 1988; exhibited in group shows at McNay Mus., San Antonio, 1981, 89, 90; in permanent collections at Maier Mus. Art, Va., Am. Express, N.Y.C., AT&T, N.Y.C., Gen. Electric Co., N.Y.C., Bank of N.Y., Southwestern Bell, St. Louis. Office: 262 Mott St Apt 307 New York NY 10012-3481

BROWN, ALLEN LEON, JR., computer scientist, educator; b. Washington, Nov. 8, 1946; s. Allen Leon and Martha Ada (Drake) B.; m. Susan Jane Foster, Sept. 4, 1969 (div. Oct. 1972); m. Karen Laree Taylor, Jan. 1, 1986. SB, MIT, 1967, PhD, 1975. *. Rsch. assoc. Columbia U., N.Y.C., 1968-69, MIT, Cambridge, 1969-72; mem. rsch. staff T. J. Watson Rsch. Ctr. IBM, Yorktown Heights, N.Y., 1975-79; section mgr. Office Systems div. Xerox, Palo Alto, 1979-84; computer scientist R&D div. GE, Schenectady, N.Y., 1984-88; prin. scientist Webster Rsch. Ctr. Xerox, Webster, N.Y., 1988—; prof. computer and info. sci. Syracuse (N.Y.) U., 1989—. Contbr. articles to profl. jours. Rsch. grantee Def. Advanced Rsch. Projects Agy., 1985. Mem. Soc. Indsl. and Applied Math. Home: 80 Wilshire Rd Rochester NY 14618-1219 Office: Xerox Webster Rsch Ctr 800 Phillips Rd # 2829E Webster NY 14580-9791

BROWN, ARTHUR EDWARD, JR., state government administrator; b. Trenton, N.J., Oct. 24, 1951; s. Arthur Edward and Mary Verna (DeVaney) B. BA in English and Psychology, Rider Coll., Lawrenceville, N.J., 1973, MA in Adminstrn., 1976. Cert. pub. mgr. Exec. asst. to supt. Tng. Sch. for Boys, Skillman, N.J., 1970-73; mgmt. devel. specialist N.J. Dept. Instns. and Agys., Trenton, 1973-75; examiner, dept. civil svc. N.J. Dept. Civil Svc., Trenton, 1975-76; dep. dir. human resource devel. N.J. Dept. Human Svcs., Trenton, 1976-91; adminstr. client and inst. tng. N.J. Human Resource Devel. Inst., Princeton, 1991-92, dep. dir., 1992—; adj. prof. Trenton State Coll., 1978—; v.p. Arthur Brown Assocs., Ewing, N.J., 1977—; mgmt. cons. UN Indsl. Devel. Orgn., Vienna, 1985-88, Baruch Coll., CUNY, 1980-83. Bd. dirs. Trenton chpt. ARC, 1969; treas. Trenton chpt. UNA/USA, 1985-88; mem. Diocese of Trenton Synod, 1990-91. Mem. Am. Soc. for Tng. and Devel., Cert. Pub. Mgrs. Assn., Nat. Assn. Pastoral Musicians. Roman Catholic. Home: 31 Woodmont Dr Trenton NJ 08648-2118 Office: Human Resource Devel Inst Dept Pers 600 College Rd E Princeton NJ 08540-6698

BROWN, BARBARA JEAN, economist; b. N.Y.C., May 3, 1936; d. Michael and Ann (Rosen) Bandes; m. Jerome P. Brown, Aug. 27, 1961; children: Anthony, Timothy. BA, Oberlin (Ohio) Coll., 1956; PhD, CUNY, 1979. Assoc. prof. econs. Pace U., Pleasantville, N.Y., 1988—. Contbr. articles to profl. jours. Mem. Am. Econ. Assn., N.Y. Women Economists. Office: Econs Dept Pace U 861 Bedford Rd Pleasantville NY 10570-2799

BROWN, BETTY MARIE, government agency administrator; b. Siler City, N.C., June 11, 1952; d. Ardentries and Emma (Peoples) Mason; m. Tommy E. Brown, Aug. 8, 1968 (dec.); 1 child, Christopher T.; m. Roger L. Cook, June 10, 1973 (dec. Feb. 1981); 1 child, Felicia M. AAS, Phila. Community Coll., 1981; BS, Drexel U., 1986. Cert. early childhood edn. tchr., Pa. Mgr. Mr. Gourmet Deli, Phila., 1977-80; pres. Parents, Friends and Vols. Community Svc. Orgn., Phila., 1983—; tchr. Phila. Sch. Dist., 1988-89; remittance perfection clk. IRS, Phila., 1989—; tchr. Mid City YWCA, Phila., 1983-88. Sec. support community outreach project Dept. Human Svcs., Phila., 1990-91. Recipient Community Svc. award Dept. Human Svc., 1988. Baptist. Home: 4603 Greene St Philadelphia PA 19144-6024 Office: Parents Friends & Vols 2111 W Tioga St Philadelphia PA 19140-3922

BROWN, BRUCE MAITLAND, bank executive; b. Bryn Mawr, Pa., Sept. 2, 1947; s. Charles Stuart and Margaret (Houston) B.; m. Elaine Eldredge, Sept. 3, 1983. BA, Lawrence U., 1969; MA, U. Ky., 1973. Program analyst FDA, Rockville, Md., 1973-75; exec. secretariat FDA, Rockville, 1975-78, spl. asst., 1978-82, dep. dir., press ofc., 1982-86; v.p. communications Council for Responsible Nutrition, Washington, 1986-87; v.p. for charitable trusts CoreStates Trust and Investment Group, 1987—; meteorologist Sta. WCAU-Radio, Phila., 1965; reporter Sta. WLFM-Radio, Appleton, Wis., 1965-69; aide U.S. Sen. Hugh Scott, Washington, 1969; pub. relations contractor Fellowship of Reconciliation, Nyack, N.Y., 1982; writer speeches FDA Commrs., 1979-82. Co-pres., bd. dirs. Brooke Valley Conservancy Assn., 1988—; officer Paint Br. Farms Civic Assn., Colesville, Md., 1978-83; founder, trustee HBE Found.; mem. non-profit MBA adv. coun. Ea. Coll., 1990—; bd. dirs. Bermuda Artworks Found. With U.S. Army, 1969-71. Mem. Nat. Trust for Hist. Preservation, Union League of Phila., Delaware Valley Grantmakers (founding bd. dirs., v.p. 1989-91), The Assemblies, Skytop Club. Episcopalian. Office: WW Smith Charitable Trust Ste 200 101 Bryn Mawr Ave Bryn Mawr PA 19010-3167

BROWN, CARY DOUGLAS, surgeon; b. Balt., Mar. 13, 1946; s. Paul Lucian and Eleanor June (Naugle) B.; m. Linda Kay Roberts, Aug. 8, 1970 (div. 1977); m. Christine M. Nelka, May 1, 1978; 1 child, Phillip. BS, Capital U., 1968; Md, U. Md., Balt., 1972. Diplomate Am. Bd. Surgery. Chief surg. svcs. USAF Hosp., Patrick AFB, Cocoa Beach, Fla., 1977-84, USAF Hosp., Elmendorf AFB, Anchorage, 1984-89; emergency rm. physician Mercy Med. Ctr., Balt., 1989-90; surgeon Montgomery Med. Group, Rockville, Md., 1990—. Contbr. articles to profl. jours. Col. USAF, 1986-89. Fellow Am. Coll. Surgeons; mem. Soc. Air Force Clin. Surgeons, Undersea Med. and Hyperbaric Soc., Md. Med. and Chiurgical Faculty, Montgomery County Med. Soc. Office: Ste 102 15225 Shady Grove Rd Rockville MD 20850

BROWN, CHARLES SAMUEL, music educator; b. Marianna, Ark., Sept. 26, 1940; s. Carey Brown and Narcisse (Angel) Richards. Student, Morehouse Coll., 1963-66; MusB, U. Mich., 1974, MusM, 1975, postgrad., 1975-77. Asst. prof. music Lincoln U. Mo., Jefferson City, 1977-80; adj. prof. music Borough of Manhattan Community Coll., N.Y.C., 1980-81; tchr. music N.Y.C. Bd. Edn., 1986—; artist, faculty Berkshire Choral Inst., Sheffield, Mass., 1983-85; mus. dir. The Open Eye Inst., N.Y.C., 1991-92. Composer: The Barrier, 1974, A Song Without Words, 1977, Calvary, 1972, 5 Spiritual Settings for Chorus, 1991. With U.S. Army, 1966-69, Vietnam. Mem. Music Educators Nat. Conf., Am. Guild Mus. Artists, Music Educators Assn. N.Y.C., Pi Kappa Lambda.

BROWN, CHARLES THEODORE, retired clergyman; b. West Stockbridge, Mass., Nov. 21, 1912; s. Willie Comstalk and Edith Ann (Janes) B.; m. Mary Flanders, Aug. 31, 1942; children: Sharon Elaine, Kendall Harold, Deborah Ann Brown Betit. BS, Bowdoin Coll., 1940; BD, Bangor Theol. Seminary, 1946. Asst. pastor Aroostook Larger Parish, Portage, Maine, 1936-37; pastor Woolwich (Maine) Union for Christian Svcs., 1937-41, Monmouth (Maine) United Ch., 1941-43, Elm St. Congrl. Ch., Bucksport, Maine, 1946-53, 57-79, 1st Ch. Congrl., Stockbridge, Mass., 1953-57; ret. pastor Sandy Point (Maine) Congrl. Ch., 1983—. Columnist: Bucksport Free Press, 1956—; contbr. articles to newspapers. Pres. Bucksport Hist. Soc., Inc., 1954-91. Capt., chaplain USAAF, 1943-46. Named Disting. Alumnus Alumni Assn. Bangor Theol. Seminary, 1969. Mem. Maine Audubon Soc., Nat. Audubon Soc., various environ. groups. Republican. Home: RR 1 Box 1203 Stockton Springs ME 04981-9755

BROWN, CLINTON EGBERT, architect; b. Niagara Falls, N.Y., July 18, 1953; Clinton Salt and Jane Kirkpatrick (Egbert) B.; m. Alma O'Connell, Aug. 20, 1988; children: Clinton Stewart, Peter Hearth. B degree, Franklin & Marshall Coll., 1975; MArch, U. Va., 1980. Registered architect, N.Y. Intern Inst. for Archtl. and Urban Studies, N.Y.C., 1976-77; architect Cannon, Buffalo, N.Y., 1980-81, Bazemore Architects, Niagara Falls, 1983-86, Buffalo Urban Renewal Agy., 1983-86, Snyder Corp., Buffalo, 1986-88; pres. Clinton Brown Co. Architecture, PC, Buffalo, 1988—; instr. SUNY, Buffalo, 1983-88. Founder Buffalo Spirit of the City Conf., 1983; vestryman Trinity Episcopal Ch., Buffalo, 1988-91; trustee Community Music Sch., Buffalo, 1985-90; dir. Sacred Sites Restoration Corp., Buffalo, 1990—; mem. Leadership Buffalo, 1991. Mem. AIA (pres. Buffalo chpt. 1982). Episcopalian. Home: Clinton Brown Co Architecture PC 25 E Huron St Buffalo NY 14203-1691

BROWN, DALE SUSAN, government administrator, writer; b. N.Y.C., May 27, 1954; d. Bertram S. and Beatrice Joy (Gilman) B. B.A., Antioch Coll., 1976. Research asst. Am. Occupational Therapy Assn., Rockville, Md., 1976-79; writer Pres.' Com. on Employment of People with Disabilities, Washington, 1979-82, program mgr., 1982—; dir. new products devel. team Ams. with Disabilities Act, 1991—; cons. in field; gen. assembly speaker nat. conv. Gen. Fedn. Women's Clubs, 1981; mem. Rehab. Svcs. Adminstrn. Task Force on Learning Disabilities, 1981-83. Author: Steps to Independence for People with Learning Disabilities, 1980; writer film: They Could Have Saved Their Homes, 1982; editorial bd. Perceptions, 1981-83. Pres. Assn. Learning Disabled Adults, Washington, 1979-80; bd. dirs. Closer Look Nat. Info. Ctr., Washington, 1980-83, Am. Coalition of Citizens with Disabilities, 1985-86; chair 5th ann. conf. on Info. Tech. for User With Disabilities, 1989; spl. asst. for people with disabilites Federally Employed Women, 1991—; mem. congrl. task force Rights and Empowerment of Ams. with Disabilities, 1988-90; mem. editorial bd. Learning Disabilites Focus, 1988-90; cons. editor Learning Disabilites Rsch. and Practice, 1990—; co-editor Learning Disabilities and Employment; author: Pathways to Employment for People with Learning Disabilities, 1991.blue ribbon panel on Nat. Telecommunications Access for People with Disabilities, 1989—. Found. for Children with Learning Disabilities grantee, 1982; recipient Margaret Byrd Rawson award, 1989, Personal Achievement award, 1989, Individual Achievement award Nat. Coun. on Communication Disorders, 1991, Spl. Achievement award Pres.'s Com. on Employment of People with Disabilities, 1991, Gold Screen award Nat. Assn. Govt. Communicators, 1991. Mem. Nat. Network of Learning Disabled Adults (founder, pres. 1980-81, rep. Inter-agy. com. on computer support handicapped employess 1988—), Nat. Assn. Govt. Communicators (Blue Pencil award 1986, rep. inter-agy. com. on handicapped employees 1989—, Learning Disabilities Assn. (bd. dirs. 1986—), ALA. Democrat. Jewish. Office: Pres' Com on Employment People with Disabilities 1331 F St NW Washington DC 20004

BROWN, EDWARD JAMES, utility executive; b. Ft. Wayne, Ind., Sept. 30, 1937; s. William Theodore and Jane Elizabeth (Dix) B.; m. Margaret Bessey, June 17, 1989; 1 child, Edward James Jr. BA, Yale U., 1959; MA, Fordham U., 1962. Chartered fin. analyst. Fin. writer E.F. Hutton & Co., N.Y.C., 1970-71; economist N.Y. Power Authority, N.Y.C., 1971-74, prin. economist, 1974-80, mgr., customer svcs., 1980-83, mgr. spl. projects, 1983-86, dir. strategic planning, 1986—; mem. mgmt. com. Iroquois Gas Transmission System, 1989—. Pres. Park Ave. Meth. Trust, N.Y.C., 1981—; pres. Friends of the Shakers, Inc., Sabbathday Lake, Maine, 1982-84, dir., 1980—; trustee John St. Meth. Episc. Trust Soc., N.Y.C., 1982—; mem. investment com. Meth. Home, Riverdale, N.Y., 1983—; dir. Yorkville Emergency Alliance, N.Y.C., 1982-88; internat. adv. coun. Mus. of Am. Folk Art, N.Y.C., 1988—. Mem. N.Y. Soc. Security Analysts, Assn. Investment Mgmt. and Rsch. Home: 500 E 85th St New York NY 10028-7407 Office: NY Power Authority 1633 Broadway New York NY 10019-6708

BROWN, ETHEL ELDRIDGE, guidance counselor; b. Asheville, N.C., Sept. 25, 1928; d. Louis William and Marjorie Elizabeth (Gaylord) Thompson; m. Vasco P. Eldridge, Jan. 1, 1958 (div.); children: Louis P., Earle G.; m. Shirley O'Donnell Brown, Apr. 12, 1980. BS in Biol. Scis., N.C. A & T U., 1943; MA in Adminstrn., George Washington U., 1968; postgrad., Coastal U., 1980-81. Lic. guidance counselor. Info. specialist U.S. Labor Dept., Washington, 1944-46; verifier U.S. Treasury Dept., Washington, 1946-48; stats. analyst Housing Urban Devel., Washington, 1948-54; asst. to chief psychology Walter Reed Inst. of Rsch., Washington, 1954-58; chmn. guidance dept. D.C. Pub. Schs., Washington, 1958-81; court mediator D.C. Superior Ct., Washington, 1983-91; counselor cons. D.C. Dept. Corrections, Lorton, Va., 1990; pres. D.C. Assn. for Counseling and Devel., Washington, 1982-83, D.C. Sch. Counselor Assn., Washington, 1972-73; class coord. N.C. A&T State Univ., Greensboro, 1985-90. Editor: (newsletter) The Touch, 1989. Pres., organizer No. Michigan Park Civic Assn., Washington, 1956-80; mem. D.C. Assn. for Rapid Transit, D.C., Md., Va., 1966; v.p. D.C. Fedn. Civic Assns., Washington, 1980-81; com. mem. D.C. Rep. Com., Washington, 1989—. Named Most Outstanding Citizen, D.C. Fedn. Civic Assns., Washington, 1983. Mem. Nat. Assn. Fashion & Accessory Designers (exec. sec. 1989—), D.C. Assn. for Adult Devel. and Aging (pres. 1991-92), Top Ladies of Distinction (Potomac treas. 1991—, organizer), Top Ladies of Distinction (nat. chmn. 1991—, com. mem.), Alpha Wives of D.C. (pres. 1990-92), Capitol Hill Kiwanis Club (2d v.p. 1991-92, pres. elect 1992—). Home: PO Box 4526 Washington DC 20017-0526

BROWN, FLORENCE STEWART, religious organization administrator; b. Ballston Spa, N.Y., Dec. 15, 1929; d. Alexander Austin and Emma Marian (Connoly) Stewart; m. Malcolm D. Brown, Dec. 28, 1954; children: Douglas, Timothy. BA, Hope Coll., 1952; MA, U. Pa., 1953. Tchr. Willow Grove (Pa.) Christian Sch., 1953-55, Berne (N.Y.) Westerlo Sch., 1957-59, Council Rock Sch., Newtown Sq., Pa., 1960-61, Chester (Pa.) Christian Acad., 1963-70; orgn. adminstr. Schenectady (N.Y.) Christian Sch., 1975-78; freelance writer Burnt Hills, N.Y., 1979-82; bus. mgr. Peniel Bible Conf., Lake Luzerne, N.Y., 1983-84; adminstrv. coord. Evangel. and ecumenical Women's Caucus, Hadley, N.Y., 1987—; coord. Evangel. Women's Caucus, Burnt Hills, 1982, 83. Contbr. articles to ednl. publs.. Inspector local elections, Ballston, 1980-85; mem. Alcohol and Drug Prevention Task Force, Burnt Hills, 1982, 83; bd. trustees Spa Christian Sch., Saratoga, N.Y., 1984-86; lobbyist NOW, Okla. and Fla.; ch. elder. Home and Office: Evangel Ecumencial Woman Caucus RD 1 Ave of Pines Hadley NY 12835

BROWN, FORBES TAYLOR, mechanical engineer, educator; b. Newton, Mass., Oct. 12, 1934; s. Kenneth G. and Hazel (Frost) B.; m. Marjorie L. Howe, June 5, 1963; children: David, Gordon, Scott. SB, MIT, 1958, SM, 1958, diploma in mech. engring., 1959, ScD, 1962. Instr. MIT, Cambridge, 1958-62, asst. prof., 1962-66, assoc. prof., 1966-70; prof. Lehigh Univ., Bethlehem, Pa., 1970—; mem. exec. com. Fluids Engring. div. ASME, 1970-75; bd. govs. Nat. Conf. on Fluid Power, Chgo., 1981-91. Assoc. editor: Jour. Fluids Engring., 1973-74; contbr. articles to profl. jours. Recipient several rsch. grants. Mem. Pi Tau Sigma, Tau Beta Pi, Sigma Xi. Home: 1715 Sunderland Dr Bethlehem PA 18015-9369 Office: Lehigh U Packard Lab # 19 Bethlehem PA 18015

BROWN, FREDERICK HAROLD, insurance company executive; b. Troy, N.Y., Apr. 21, 1927; s. Harold Lamphere and Maida Adelaide (Wooden) B.; m. Mary Lee Lamar, Aug. 12, 1950; children: Deborah Elaine Wright, Frederick Harold. BS in Mech. Engring., Bucknell U., 1949. Registered profl. engr., Wis., Pa. With CIGNA and Subs., Phila., 1949-73, asst. v.p., 1970-71, v.p., 1971-73; founder, pres., chief exec. officer Jersey/Internat. Group, Cherry Hill, N.J., 1973-84; pres., chief exec. officer Admiral Ins. Co. subs. W.R. Berkeley Corp., Greenwich, Conn., 1979-84; sr. v.p. W.R. Berkley Corp., Greenwich, 1984-87; chmn. bd., pres., chief exec. officer Investors Ins. Holding Corp. and all subs., 1987-89, chmn., 1989—; chmn., pres., treas. Brown/Wright Risk Cons. Inc., Ocean City, N.J.; chmn., pres., treas. Brown/Wright Risk Cons., Inc., Ocean City, N.J.; bd. dirs. Alliance Holding Corp. and subs., Cherry Hill, N.J. Contbr. articles to profl. jours. Mem. Phila. Fire Prevention Com., 1958-68; exec. treas. Camden County (N.J.) Rep. Orgn., 1968-73; clk. bd. chosen freeholders of Camden County, 1969-73; active United Way, Boy Scouts Am. With USNR, 1944-46. Named Citizen of Yr., INA, 1970, Honoree of Yr. N.J. Surplus Lines Assn., 1983. Mem. Soc. Fire Protection Engrs., Nat. Fire Protection Assn., Conf. Spl. Risk Underwriters, U.S. Jaycees (hon. life, Outstanding State V.P. 1961, Outstanding Nat. Dir. 1962), Nat. Assn. Ind. Insurers (surplus lines com.), Nat. Assn. Profl. Surplus Lines Officers (bd. dirs. 1980-86), Nat. Assn. Ins. Commrs. (surplus lines adv. com.), N.J. Surplus Lines Assn. (Honoree of Yr. 1983), Tavistock Country Club, Rodney Square Club, Kiwanis Haddonfield. Home: PO Box 1136 Ocean City NJ 08226-7136

BROWN, GERALDINE, nurse, freelance writer; b. Clemson, S.C., Nov. 1, 1945; d. Isaac and Gladys (Patterson) B. AS in Nursing, U. D.C., Washington, 1973; real estate cert., Long and Foster Inst., College Park, Md., 1984; cert. in TV broadcasting, Columbia Sch., Bailey's Crossroads, Va., 1987; BS in Nursing, Bowie State U., 1989, MA in Communications, 1991; postgrad., Howard U., 1991—. RN, D.C., FCC Third Class License. Supr. staff nurse Walter Reed Hosp., Washington, 1970-76; supr. clin. nurse Dept. Human Svcs., Washington, 1976-78, community health nurse, 1978-84; nursing instr. Phillips Bus. Sch., Alexandria, Va., 1984-85; pvt. nurse Washington, 1973—; dir. pub. affairs Bible Way Chs. Worldwide, Inc., Washington, 1978—; society columnist As It Happens, Charlotte (N.C.) Post, 1964-66; society editor Washington Cafe. Soc. mag., 1971; contbr. feature stories Capital Spotlight newspaper, 1978—. Asst. organizer DC Mayor's United Nations Day, 1980; vol. Met. Boys and Girls Clubs, Washington, 1980—; vol. Nursing Instr., The Washington Saturday Coll., 1982-84; Co. ARC, 1973—, Big Sisters of the Washington Met. Area, 1988—. Recipient certs. of excellence Govt. of D.C., 1978-84; cert. of appreciation Mayor of D.C., 1980, meritorious pub. svc. award, 1980; svc. trophy Washington Saturday Coll., 1984. Mem. Am. Nurses Assn., Nat. Coun. Negro Women, Smithsonian Inst. (assoc.), NAACP, Washington Urban League, Chi Eta Phi. Democrat. Apostolic.

BROWN, GLENN ARTHUR, dental association administrator, consultant; b. Ft. Knox, Jan. 27, 1953. AB, Harvard U., 1975; MBA, U. Pa., 1980, DMD, 1982. Dental dir. About Your Smile, Phila., 1983—. Bd. dirs. Luth. Child and Family Svc., 1990—, Greater Phila. Health Action, 1990—. Mem. New ERA Dental Soc., Nat. Dental Assn., Nat. Black MBA Assocs. (life), Soc. Dentistry for Children, Harvard Club Phila. (bd. dirs.). Office: About Your Smile 6772 Market St Upper Darby PA 19082-2432

BROWN, G(LENN) WILLIAM, JR., lawyer, investment banker; b. Waynesville, N.C., June 9, 1955; s. Glenn William Sr. and Evelyn Myralyn (Davis) B.; m. Amy Margaret Moss, Apr. 14, 1984; childrne: Elizabeth Quinn, Lauren Alexandra. BS in Biology and Polit. Sci., MIT, 1977; JD, Duke U., 1980. Bar: N.Y. 1981. Assoc. Donovan Leisure Newton & Irvine, N.Y.C., 1980-84; assoc. Sidley & Austin, N.Y.C., 1984-87, ptnr., 1988-89; v.p. currency and commodities div. Goldman, Sachs & Co., N.Y.C., 1989—. Editorial bd. Duke Law Jour. Mem. ABA (sect. internat. law, com. internat. fin., comml. transactions, and pvt. internat. law 1988—), N.Y. State Bar Assn., Am. Fin. Assn., Am. Assn. Agrl. Econs. Democrat. Mem. Dutch Reform Ch. Home: 171 State St Brooklyn NY 11201-5609 Office: Goldman Sachs & Co 85 Broad St 5th Fl New York NY 10004

BROWN, GORDON E., surgeon, consultant; b. Highland Park, Mich., Mar. 4, 1931; s. Cecil E. and Margaret Glenn (Thurston) B.; m. Christina Cordell Krauss, Feb. 1, 1990. AB, Kenyon Coll., 1953; MD, Columbia U.,

1957; postgrad., Pa. State U., 1989—. Pvt. practice gen. surgery Bishop, Calif., 1971-82; gen. surgeon Whitaker Corp., 1982-84, Locum Tenens, 1984-86, Lancaster (Pa.) Cardiothoracic Surgeons, 1986-88; cons. Blue Shield of Pa., Camp Hill, 1988—; quality assurance coord. dept. surgery Lancaster Gen. Hosp., 1991—. Capt. USAF, 1959-62. Home and Office: 623 N Lime St Lancaster PA 17602

BROWN, HELEN GURLEY, writer, editor; b. Green Forest, Ark., Feb. 18, 1922; d. Ira M. and Cleo (Sisco) Gurley; m. David Brown, Sept. 25, 1959. Student, Tex. State Coll. for Women, 1939-41, Woodbury Coll., 1942; LLD (hon.), Woodbury U., 1987. Exec. sec. Music Corp. Am., 1942-45, William Morris Agy., 1945-47; copywriter Foote, Cone & Belding (advt. agy.), Los Angeles, 1948-58; advt. writer, account exec. Kenyon & Eckhardt (advt. agy.), Hollywood, Calif., 1958-62; editor-in-chief Cosmopolitan mag., 1965—; editorial dir. Cosmopolitan internat. edits., 1972—. Author: Sex and the Single Girl, 1962, Sex and the Office, 1965, Outrageous Opinions, 1967, Helen Gurley Brown's Single Girl's Cook Book, 1969, Sex and the New Single Girl, 1970. Named 1 of 25 most influential women in U.S., World Almanac, 1976-81; recipient Francis Holmes Achievement award for outstanding work in advt., 1956-59, Disting. Achievement award U. So. Calif. Sch. Journalism, 1971, Spl. award for editorial leadership Am. Newspaper Woman's Club, Washington, 1972, Disting. Achievement award in Journalism Stanford U., 1977, Matrix award in mag. category, N.Y. Women in Communications, 1985; Helen Gurley Brown Rsch. Professorship established in her name Northwestern U. Medill Sch. Journalism, 1986; inducted into Pubs.' Hall of Fame, 1987. Mem. Authors League Am., Am. Soc. Mag. Editors, AFTRA, Eta Upsilon Gamma. Office: Cosmopolitan The Hearst Corp 224 W 57th St New York NY 10019-3203

BROWN, I. STEPHEN, periodontist; b. Oceanside, N.Y., Apr. 17, 1940; s. Bernard D. and Selma (Weidhorn) B.; m. Pauline Sablove, June 27, 1965; children: Jason Samuel, Samantha Jill. Student, Western Res. U., 1958-61; DDS, Temple U., 1965; Cert. of Proficiency Periodontics, U. Pa., 1969, Cert. of Proficiency Adult Orthodontics, 1970; Cert. of Proficiency Anesthesia, Med. Coll. of Pa., 1975. Diplomate Am. Bd. Periodontics; cert. profl. sci. instr. Rsch. teaching fellow periodontics U. Pa., 1969-70, assoc. periodontics, 1970-74; dir. periodontics Med. Coll. of Pa., 1972-78; asst. prof. periodontics U. Pa., 1974-82; clin. asst. prof. periodontics Med. Coll. of Pa., 1974—; clin. assoc. prof. periodontics U. Pa. Sch. of Dental Medicine, 1980—; attending staff dept. dental medicine The Grad. Hosp., Phila., 1982—; guest lectr. in field at various colls. and univs.; attending in periodontics Albert Einstein Med. Ctr., founding mem., surg. dir. dental implant team. Contbr. articles to profl. jours. and books. Recipient C.V. Mosby Scholarship award Temple U. Sch. of Dentistry, 1965, Gen. Rsch. grant U. Pa., 1970. Fellow Am. Coll. Dentists; mem. ADA, Pa. Dental Assn., Phila. County Dental Soc., Am. Acad. Periodontology (bd. dirs. 1982-86), Pa. Soc. Periodontology, Phila. Soc. Periodontology (pres. 1977-78), N.Am. Soc. Periodontics (pres. 1991), Acad. Osseointegration, Am. Acad. Oral Medicine, Am. Soc. Preventive Dentistry, Pa. Soc. Periodontology (pres. 1976-77), Del. Valley Acad. Osseointegration (pres. elect 1992), Ea. Dental Soc. (pres. 1976-77), Phila. Dental Study Club, So. Dist. Dental Soc., Internat. Assn. Dental Rsch., Soc. for Advancement of Anaesthesia in Dentistry, Dental Clinic Club Phila., Acad. Gen. Dentistry, Am. Assn. Dental Schs., Alumni Assn. Temple U. Sch. Dentistry (bd. dirs.). Home: 284 Saint James Pl Philadelphia PA 19106 Office: I Stephen Brown DDS Ste 300 220 S 16th St Philadelphia PA 19102

BROWN, JAMES NELSON, JR., accountant; b. Bronx, N.Y., Apr. 17, 1929; s. James Nelson and Agnes Mary (Cummins) B.; m. Lila Barbara Watt, Dec. 12, 1950; children: Constance Ellen Brown Buttacavole, Nelson Arthur, Richard John. BSBA, Drake U., 1956. CPA; cert. internal auditor, fraud examiner. Sr. acct. Arthur Andersen & Co., N.Y.C., 1956-61; asst. v.p., dir. internal auditing Salomon Inc., N.Y.C., 1961-86, asst. v.p., dir. projects mgmt. dept., 1986-91; asst. v.p. environ. litigation dept. Salomon Inc., 1991—. Com. chmn. Cub Scouts, 1973-75; troop com. chmn. Boy Scouts Am., Carteret, N.J., 1976-77, 88-90, com. mem., 1978-87. Sgt. AUS, 1947-52. Mem. AICPA, Am. Mgmt. Assn., N.J. Soc. CPAs, Nat. Assn. Cert. Fraud Examiners, Inst. Internal Auditors, Am. Legion, Elks. Republican. Roman Catholic. Home: 47 Pinho Ave Carteret NJ 07008-1235 Office: 7 World Trade Ctr New York NY 10048-1102

BROWN, JAMES TONER (JIM BROWN), librarian; b. Burlington, Vt., Jan. 30, 1949; s. Howard Francis and Mary Alice (Haynes) B.; m. Patricia Anne Miller, May 6, 1972. BA, U. Conn., 1972; MLS, Columbia U., 1977. Cataloger Ferguson Libr., Stamford, Conn., 1978-86, sr. cataloger, 1987—. Author, compiler: (index) Fishing Reel Patents of U.S., 1838-1940, 1985; author, cataloger (mus. catalog) A Treasury of Reels, 1990; contbr. numerous articles to profl. jours. Mem. Am. Mus. Fly Fishing (hist. cons.), Catskill Fly Fishing Ctr. (bd. dirs., hist. cons.), Fedn. of Fly Fishers, Theodore Gordon Fly Fishers, Housatonic Fly Fisherman's Assn., Trout Unltd., Nat. Fishing Lure Collectors Club. Home: 97 Franklin St Stamford CT 06901-1309

BROWN, JAMES-KEITH, investment banker, college development director; b. Pinehurst, N.C., Aug. 15, 1962; s. James Clifton and Mary Etta (Williams) B. BA in Psychology with honors, U. N.C., 1984. Rsch. fellow FPG/Robert Wood Johnson Found., Chapel Hill, N.C., 1984-85; asst. v.p., sr. assoc. J.P. Morgan Inc., N.Y.C., 1985-90; regional devel. dir. Dartmouth Coll., Bear Stearns, N.Y.C., 1991—; cons. art to artists Carol Chapman, Joel Nakamura, San Francisco, L.A., 1990—; mem., cons. Non Profit Coordinating Com., N.Y.C., 1990—; mem. com. chair F and CR group Ivy/MIT/Stanford, Providence, 1990—. Bd. dirs. Campus Y, U. N.C., Chapel Hill, 1989—; bd. dirs. Stephen Petronio Dance Co., 1988—, chmn., 1988—; mem. Arts and Bus. Coun., N.Y.C., 1987—, Vol. Cons. Group, N.Y.C., 1987—, N.Y. Cares, N.Y.C., 1990—; tutor Internat. Ctr. of N.Y.C., 1986-87; founder Lincoln Ctr. Theater Assocs., 1988—, chmn., 1988—; founder Drama League of N.Y.C. Assocs., 1987-91, chmn., 1989-90. Recipient Gov. James R. Hunt Outstanding Svc. award N.C. State Govt., 1984; rsch. fellow FPG/Robert Wood Johnson Found., 1984-85. Mem. N.C. Soc. of N.Y.C., Yale Club, Univ. Club (N.Y.C.), Dartmouth Outing Club. Office: Dartmouth Coll c/o Bear Stearns 245 Park Ave 38th Fl New York NY 10167

BROWN, JANET R., psychologist, eductor; b. Cleve., Oct. 8, 1933; d. Sylvester and Ruth (Feigenbaum) B. AB, Flora Stone Mather Coll., Cleve., 1955; MA, Case Western Res. U., Cleve., 1961, PhD, 1967. Tchr. Solebury Sch., New Hope, Pa., 1955-57, Maple Hts. (Ohio) High Sch., 1957-59, Cleveland Hts. (Ohio) High Sch., 1959-65; adj. prof. Case Western Res. U., Cleve., 1965-66; prof. ednl. psychology Queens Coll., CUNY, Flushing, N.Y., 1966-91; psychol. cons. Hastings-on-Hudson, N.Y., 1970—; cons. Rockland Community Coll., Suffern, N.Y., 1974—. Contbr. articles to profl. jours. Mem. AAUP, Am. Psychol. Assn., Am. Ednl. Rsch. Assn.

BROWN, JAY MARSHALL, educator; b. Bklyn., July 26, 1933; s. Sidney and Bertha (Swirsky) B.; m. Merle Thelma Kaminsky, Nov. 4, 1956; children: Sidney Matthew, Ellen Beth Factor. BS in Journalism, NYU, 1955, MA in Am. Civilization, 1960; postgrad., Yeshiva U., 1958-60, U. Conn., West Hartford, 1968-70; 6th yr. profl. diploma, So. Conn. State Coll., 1977. Pub. relations dir, asst. credit mgr. Colonial Sand & Stone Co., N.Y.C., 1955-60; employment counselor N.Y.C. Dept. Welfare, 1960-63; attendance tchr. Bd. Edn., N.Y.C., 1963-65; youth dir. Jewish Community Ctr., Rochester, N.Y., 1965-67; exec. dir. Conn. Valley Regional B'nai B'rith Youth, New Haven, 1967-70; resource tchr. Sheridan Middle Sch., Bd. Edn., New Haven, 1970-72; learning ctr. tchr. Bd. Edn., New Haven, 1972-74; social studies tchr. Troup Middle Sch., Bd. Edn., New Haven, 1974-80; history tchr. Hillhouse High Sch., Bd. Edn., New Haven, 1980—; U.S. history tchr. New Eng. Acad. for Jewish Studies, New Haven, 1984-85; audio-visual and media specialist Quinnipiac Coll., Hamden, Conn., 1983-84; v.p. Reliable Transp. Co., 1992—. Contbr. articles to profl. jour.; editor BBYO Bd. dirs. newsletter, Bklyn., 1961-62; columnist The Luna Spark, Bklyn., 1961-63. Chmn. clear sch. mission com. Hillhouse High Sch., 1984, mem. effective sch. steering com., 1984, mem. sch. planning and mgmt. team, 1988-91, coord. teenagers adv. prog., 1989-91, mem. faculty senate, 1991—; bd. dirs. Citizen Television, Inc., 1991—; mem. faculty senate Hillhouse High Sch., 1991—; pres. Brotherhood of Mishkan Israel, 1976-78, 83-84, 88-89, asst. treas. Congregation, 1983-84, budget chmn., 1987-88, chmn. house and property com., 1979-84, trustee, 1978-84, 86-92, libr. and archivist, 1981-84; past chmn. Hamden Community Devel. Action Planning Com. on Youth Svcs.; past sec. Hamden Anti-Drug Task Force; mem. Hamden Dem. Town Com., 1974-76; corr. sec. Jewish Hist. Soc., New Haven, 1980-81. Recipient Man of Yr. award of merit Congregation Mishkan Israel's Brotherhood, 1978; named Outstanding Profl. in Human Svcs., 1974-75. Mem. Phi Delta Kappa. Democrat. Jewish. Home: 130 Centerbrook Rd Hamden CT 06518-3402

BROWN, JEFFREY, physician, lawyer; b. N.Y.C., June 20, 1946; s. Harry and Annette Brown; m. Ronni Susan Schuman, June 6, 1971; children: Ross Harris, Jordan Adam, Jeremy Barrett. BA, U. Rochester, 1967; MPH, U. Calif., Berkeley, 1971; MD, Stanford U., 1973; JD, Yale U., 1976. Bar: Conn. 1984; diplomate Am. Bd. Psychiarty. Resident in psychiatry Yale Med. Sch., New Haven, 1974-77; med. dir. Psychiatric and Counseling Assocs., Stamford, Conn., 1977-78; pvt. practice psychiatry, cons. Stamford, 1979-80; of counsel Bello, Lapire & Casone,, Stamford, 1984-88; chief exec. officer Quality Health Internat., Santa Monica, Calif., 1985-87; mng. dir. Brown & Greenfield, Short Hills, N.J., 1989—; chief exec. officer Risk/Benefit Mgmt. Co., Milburn, N.J., 1990—; CEO Hosp. Planning and Rescue Co., Florham Park, N.J., 1992—. Co-author: Approaching the Bench, 1978; contbr. articles to profl. jours. Co-pres. Intervale Homewoners Assn., Stamford, 1984. Alway and Alumni scholar Stanford U., 1973. Fellow Am. Orthospychiat. Assn.; mem. Am. Coll. Forensic Psychiatry, Assn. Trial Lawyers Am., Am. Pub. Health Assn., Phi Beta Kappa. Home and Office: 212 Old Short Hills Rd Short Hills NJ 07078-2122

BROWN, JEROME MILES, academic administrator; b. Denver, Sept. 5, 1941; s. Kenneth William and Margaret Crista (Miles) B.; m. Judith Ann Rasmussen, Oct. 28, 1978; children: Erik David Moore, Alec Travis Moore, Hillary Conley Moore, Chistopher Benson Brown, Amy Allison Brown. AB, Hamilton Coll., 1963; MS, SUNY, Albany, 1977. Mem. faculty SUNY, Geneseo, 1966-73; mem. faculty Mohawk Valley Community Coll., Utica, N.Y., 1973-81, exec. asst. to v.p. for instrn., 1981-88, dean human resources, 1988—. Bd. dirs. United Way, Utica, 1992—; pres. New Sch. Utica Bd. dirs., 1977, Neighborhood Ctr. Bd. Dirs., Utica, 1985; mem. Mayor's Sr. Citizen Adv. Bd., Utica, 1988; warden Grace Ch., Utica, 1989. Episcopalian. Home: 8143 Phillips Rd Rome NY 13440 Office: Mohawk Valley Community Coll 1101 Sherman Dr Utica NY 13501-5308

BROWN, JOHN CARTER, art museum directior emeritus; b. Providence, Oct. 8, 1934; s. John Nicholas and Ann Kinsolving B.; m. Pamela Braga, 1976 (div. 1991); children: John Carter IV, Elissa Lucinda Brown Rionda. AB summa cum laude, Harvard U., 1956, MBA, 1958; postgrad., Munich (Germany) U., 1958; studied with, Bernard Berenson, Florence, Italy, 1958; mus. tng. course, Ecole du Louvre, Paris, 1958-59, The Netherlands Inst. Art History, 1960; MA, Inst. Fine Arts, N.Y. U., 1961; LLD (hon.), Brown U., 1970; LHD (hon.), Mt. St. Mary's Coll., 1974, Georgetown U., 1975, George Washington U., 1978; DFA (hon.), Roger Williams Coll., 1978, Coll. William and Mary, 1984, R.I. Sch. Design, 1984, Phila. Coll. Arts, 1987, Marquette U., 1988; DPS (hon.), Bowling Green Coll., 1979; DHL (hon.), Mount Vernon Coll., 1987, U. Md., 1990. Asst. to dir. Nat. Gallery Art, Washington, 1961-63, asst. dir., 1964-68, dep. dir., 1968-69, dir., 1989-92, dir. emeritus, 1992—; chmn. U.S. Commn. of Fine Arts; bd. govs. John Carter Brown Libr., Brown U.; mem. Pa. Ave. Devel. Corp., Fed. Coun. on Arts and Humanities, Internat. Com. for History of Art, Com. for Preservation of White House. Author-dir.: film The American Vision, 1965. Trustee NYU Inst. Fine Arts, John F. Kennedy Ctr. for the Performing Arts, Am. Acad. in Rome, Nat. Geog. Soc., Storm King Art Ctr., Henry Francis Du Pont Winterthur Mus., World Monuments Fund., Am. Fedn. Arts., John Nicholas Brown Ctr. for Study Am. Civilization; treas. White House Hist. Assn. Decorated comdr. Ordre des Arts et des Lettres (France); knight Légion d'Honneur (France); comdr. Order Republic of Egypt; comdr. Order of Orange-Nassau (The Netherlands); commendatore Order of Merit of Italian Republic; knight Order of St. Olav (Norway); knight comdr. Order of Isabel la Católica (Spain), Order of Prince Henry the Navigator (Portugal), 1992; Austrian Cross of Honor for Arts and Letters; comdr. Royal Order of Polar Star (Sweden); recipient Gold medal of honor Nat. Arts Soc., 1972, Disting. Grotonian award Groton (Mass.) Sch., 1986, Gold medal Nat. Inst. Social Scis., 1987, Nat. Medal of Arts U.S., 1991; named Washingtonian of Yr. Washingtonian mag., 1977. Fellow Royal Acad. Arts (hon.); mem. AIA (hon.), N.Y. Yacht Club, Century Club (N.Y.C.), Knickerbocker Club (N.Y.C.), Phi Beta Kappa. Episcopalian. Office: Nat Gallery Art 1201 Pennsylvania Ave NW Washington DC 20044

BROWN, JOHN EDWARD, textile company executive; b. N.Y.C., Feb. 13, 1936; s. John Edward and Anne Marie (Douglas) B.; m. Barbara Ann Reiss, May 21, 1960; children: Kathleen, Michael, Douglas, Kevin. BA, Hofstra U., 1959. Salesman Riegle Textile, N.Y.C., 1960-64; mgr. merchandising Greenwood Mills, N.Y.C., 1964-72; v.p. M. Lowenstien, N.Y.C., 1972-76, Texfi Industries, N.Y.C., 1976-80; mgr. sales Burlington Industries, N.Y.C., 1980-82; exec. v.p. Brucol Industries, N.Y.C., 1982-83; v.p. Channel Textile Co., N.Y.C., 1983-86, Lida Mfg. Co., N.Y.C., 1986-88; v.p. mktg. and sales Ren Rob Fabrics, N.Y.C., 1988-89; pres. Copensport, N.Y.C., 1989—, J.T.J. Repair, Amityville, N.Y., 1976-89; exec. v.p. mktg. and sales Cameron, Ind. Bd. dirs. St. Joseph's Cath. Youth Orgn., Kings Park, N.Y., 1974-85. Named Hofstra U. assoc., 1969-70. Mem. Am. Arbitration Assn. Democrat. Home: 44 Woodfield Ave Northport NY 11768-2441 also: Copensport Industries 350 Fifth Ave New York NY 10018

BROWN, JOHN LACKEY, comparative literature educator, diplomat; b. Ilion, N.Y., Apr. 29, 1914; s. Leslie Beecher and Katherine Anne (Lackey) B.; m. Simonne Yvette L'Evesque, Aug. 25, 1941; children: Michel-Simon, John-Halit. AB, Hamilton Coll., 1935; postgrad., Ecole des Chartes, Paris, 1937-38; PhD, Cath. U. Am., 1939; Doctorate (hon.), U. Guanajuato, Mexico, 1967. Instr. Cath. U., Washington, 1939-41; asst. chief fgn. publs. OWI, N.Y.C., 1942-43; corr. Sunday edit. N.Y. Times, Paris, 1945-47; European editor Houghton-Mifflin Co., Paris, 1945-47, Boston, 1947-48; dir. info. div. Marshall Plan Econ. Coop. Adminstrn., 1948-50; cultural attaché U.S. Embassy, Paris, 1950-54, Brussels, 1954-58, Rome, 1958-62; counselor for cultural affairs U.S. Embassy, Mexico City, 1964-68; fellow Ctr. of Advanced Studies Wesleyan U., Middletown, Conn., 1962-63; prof. comparative lit. grad. sch. Cath. U., Washington, 1968-79, 87—; dir. Am. Bicentennial Exposition, Paris, Warsaw, 1975; sr. Fulbright prof. Am. Fulbright Assn., Lisbon, Portugal, 1979; lectr. Fgn. Svc. Inst., U.S. Dept. State, 1985-89, Instituto Mexican-Norteamericano de Relaciones Culturales, others; Brown vis. prof. U. of the South, 1987. Author: The Methodus of Jean Bodin, 1939, Panorama de La Littérature contemporaine aux Etas-Unis, 1954 (le Grand Prix de la Critique), Discovering Belgium, 1957, Hemingway, 1961, Il Gigantesco teatro: Saggi europei e americani, 1963, Diálogos trasatlánticos, 1966, Valery Larbaud, 1981, (poetry) Signs, 1956, Weights and Measures, 1958, Antoher Language, 1961, Numina, 1969, Tributes, 1980, Shards, 1982, Celebrations, 1990; translator; contbr. numerous articles to profl. jours. Chmn. Fulbright Commn., Brussels, 1954-58, Rome, 1958-62; panelist Congress on World Affairs, U. Colo., 1980-90. Mem. MLA, Am. Comparative Lit. Assn., Fgn. Svc. Assn., Internat. Assn. Critics (v.p. 1975—), Ea. Comparative Lit. Assn. (mem. exec. com.), Am. Lit. Translators Assn., Chevaliers du Tastevin, Le Grand Ordre Des Côteaux, Found. Univ. (Brussels), Cercle Internallié (Paris), Univ. Club (Mexico City), Cosmos Club (Washington). Home: 3024 Tilden St NW Washington DC 20008-3020 Office: Cath U Am Michigan Ave NE Washington DC 20064

BROWN, JOSEPH SAMUEL, government official; b. N.Y.C., Dec. 3, 1943; s. Austin Samuel and Ruby (Reid) B.; m. Beverly Mallory, May 18, 1968 (div. 1988); children: Jamal Hassan, Kareem Saladin, Paul Emmanuel. BS, Elizabeth City State U., 1966; MS, N.C. Cen. U., 1967. Prin. N.Y.C. Bd. Edn. Harlem High Sch., 1975-77; adminstrv. staff analyst N.Y.C. Dept. of Gen. Svcs., 1977-79; dir. N.Y.C. Dept. of Econ. Devel. Minority Bus. Devel. Office, 1979-85; mng. dir. Darryl E. Greene & Assocs., N.Y.C., 1985-88; dir. Monroe County Dept. Affirmative Action/Human Rels., Rochester, N.Y., 1988-92. Active Baden St. Ctr. Adv. Bd., Rochester, 1988—, Montgomery Neighborhood Bd. Dirs., Rochester, 1988—, ACLU Genesee Valley chpt. Bd. Dirs., 1988-91; chair Bias Related Violence subcom., Minority Enterprise Devel. Com.; mem. N.Y. State Human Rights Regional Adv. Coun., 1988—, East Ho. Bd. Dirs. Personnel Com., 1988—, New Life Fellowship; chmn. Bldg. Fund Com., Polit. Action Com.; founding mem. African-Am. Leadership Devel. Program, with mentors program Urban League of Rochester. Recipient Cert. of Recognition Nat. Alliance of Businessman, 1972-73, Citizenship award N.Y. State Assembly, 1971, Cert. of Appreciation, Jr. Achievement; named Outstanding Young Men in Am. U.S. Jaycees, 1979. Mem. Omega Psi Phi. Home: 385 Columbia Ave Rochester NY 14611-3637 Office: Dir Dept Affirmative Action 39 W Main St Ste 205 Rochester NY 14614-1408

BROWN, JUDITH ARNER, management development consultant; b. N.Y.C., Dec. 15, 1947; d. Milton and Hope (Coe) Arner; m. Alfred Wallace Brown Jr., Aug. 8, 1976; 1 child, Zachary Zoeth. BA, Bard Coll., 1968. Dir. alumni relations Bard Coll., Annandale, N.Y., 1972-76; dir. devel. Hood Coll., Frederick, Md., 1976-79; devel. officer Children's Meml. Hosp., Chgo., 1979-80; v.p. devel. Barat Coll., Lake Forest, Ill., 1980-81; dir. devel. Sch. Social Work Columbia U., N.Y.C., 1981-84; v.p. devel. Phelps Meml. Hosp., North Tarrytown, N.Y., 1984-89; pres. CauseWorth, South Salem, N.Y., 1989—. Homeand Office: Route 1 Stewart Rd South Salem NY 10590

BROWN, KATHARINE EISENHART, artist; b. Princeton, N.J., Mar. 21, 1921; d. Luther P. and Katharine S. (Schmidt) Eisenhart; m. W. Danforth Compton, June 13, 1942 (dec.); children: John, Christina; m. 2d, Robert P. Brown, Apr. 3, 1959. BA, Vassar Coll., 1942; MS in Journalism, Columbia U., 1944; spl. studies in sculpture, Corcoran Gallery, Washington, 1944; pottery workshop, Boston Mus. Sch., Washington, 1944. founder, dir. Martin St. Collage Dance Group, Cambridge, performance Greensboro, Vt., 1989, South Shore Art Ctr., Colasset, Mass., 1990. Exhbns. include Main Gallery Boston City Hall, 1978, Copley Art Assn., Boston, 1980, Clark Gallery, Lincoln, Mass., Cambridge (Mass.) Art Assn., 1981, Currier Art Gallery, Manchester, N.H., 1981, Hyatt Art Gallery, Cambridge, 1983, Simmons Coll., Boston, 1986, various art assns.; one person shows include Cambridge Art Assn., 1976, 87, Episcopal Theol. Sch. Library, Cambridge, 1973, 78, 88, Hilles Library of Radcliffe Coll., 1975, 82, 85, Johnson (Vt.) State Coll., 1977, Vassar Coll., 1977, Harvard Law Sch. Libr., 1978, World Affairs Council, Boston, 1981, Marion (Mass.) Art Ctr., 1983, Atrium Gallery, WGBH, Boston, 1988, South Shore Art Ctr.; exhibited in group shows at Concord (Mass.) Art Assn., 1984, Copley Soc. Fed. Reserve, Boston, 1985, Cambridge Art Assn., 1985, Am. Stage Festival, N.H., 1986, Obsidian Gallery, Tucson, Ariz., 1986, Simmons Coll., Boston, 1986; many pvt. collections including Boston Globe, Bank Am., First Nat. Bank of Boston, Hearthstone Ins. Co. of Mass., Charleston Savings Bank, others in Mich., Ariz., N.Mex. Recipient 1st prize Cambridge Art Assn., 1986, Quincy Coop. Bank award South Shore Art Center, 1977, hon. mention Sudbury Art Assn., 1979, hon. mention Concord Art Assn., 1979, juror's choice award, 1980, juror's award Cambridge Art Assn., 1981; Best of Show, medal of honor Concord Art Assn., 1983, Crumbacher Award, Concord, 1984, others. Mem. Boston Visual Artists Union, Cambridge Art Assn., Copley Soc. Boston, Mass. (Best in Show, 1986), Concord Art Assn., Sharon Art Center, N.H. Art Assn., Phi Beta Kappa. Democrat. Episcopalian. Home: 16 Avon St Cambridge MA 02138-1508

BROWN, KEIRN CLARKE, JR., military officer; b. Port Jefferson, N.Y., Jan. 19, 1947; s. Keirn Clarke and Jane (Schuhl) B.; m. Joan Tower Bowie, June 27, 1981; children: Lee Randolph, Pamela Maenner, Keirn Clarke III. BS, U.S. Mil. Acad., 1969; postgrad., Mainz U., Germany, 1977-79; MA, Middlebury Coll., 1979; grad., Coll. Naval Command and Staff, 1982, Army War Coll., 1987. councillor Atlantic Coun. U.S.; lectr. Nat. Defense U. Commd. 2d lt. U.S. Army, 1969, advanced through grades to col., 1990; infantry platoon leader, 82d Airborne Div. U.S. Army, Ft. Bragg, N.C., 1969-70; infantry co. comdr., 101st Airborne Div. U.S. Army, Vietnam, 1970-71; instr. U.S. Army Ranger Sch. U.S. Army, Ft. Benning, Ga., 1971-74; co. comdr. Berlin Brigade U.S. Army, 1974-77; asst. prof. fgn. langs. U.S. Mil. Acad., West Point, N.Y., 1979-81; staff officer 3d div. and VII corps U.S. Army, Fed. Republic Germany, 1982-84; comdr. 4th battalion, 502d Infantry U.S. Army, Berlin, 1984-86; asst. exec. to vice chief of staff U.S. Army Pentagon, Washington, 1987-89; spl. asst. to chief of staff U.S. Army, Washington, 1989-90; asst. to Supreme Allied Comdr., Europe U.S. Army, 1990-92; fellow Ctr. for Internat. Affairs Harvard U., Cambridge, Mass., 1992—; councillor Atlantic Coun. U.S.; lectr. Nat. Def. U. Decorated Legion of Merit, Soldier's medal, Bronze Star, Air medal. Mem. Assn. U.S. Army. Episcopalian. Club: Army and Navy (Washington). Home: 9624 Shipwright Dr Burke VA 22015-4436 Office: Ctr for Internat Affairs Harvard U 179 Cambridge St Cambridge MA 02138

BROWN, KEVIN MICHAEL, treasurer; b. Morristown, N.J., June 15, 1948; s. Michael Xavier and Jean Margaret (McCormack) B.; m. Patricia Lynn Macce, Nov. 16, 1975; children: Meredith Lynn, Michael Kevin. BS in Bus. Mgmt., Monmouth Coll., 1971. Sales mgr. ISD Inc., Union, N.J., 1971-76; dir. profit share plan, trustee Brown Dist. Corp., Fairfield, N.J., 1981—; mng. ptnr. Brown Gypsum Co., Fairfield, 1985—, 55 Laura Equities, Morristown, 1987—; sec, treas. Brown Distbg. Corp., Fairfield, 1976—, bd. dirs. Active Peck Sch. PTA, Morristown, Assumption Sch. PTA, Assumption Parish, Morristown, Blackberry Hills Property Owners Assn., Morristown. Mem. Ceiling and Interior Systems Contractor Assn., Drywall and Interior Systems Contractor Assn., Bldg. Contractors Assn. N.J., Porsche Club, Spring Brook Country Club. Roman Catholic. Office: Brown Distbg Corp 18 Commerce Rd Fairfield NJ 07004-1603

BROWN, L. ALEX, consultant; b. Akron, Ohio, July 15, 1952; s. Ralph Seaton and Mary Catherine (Guinther) B.; m. Clarke Harbison Jordan, May 26, 1990; children: Corinna Jordan, Sarah Jordan. BA, Bennington (Vt.) Coll., 1974; postgrad., NYU, 1975-76. Asst. editor House Beautiful Mag., N.Y.C., 1974-75; pubs. dir. Bennington Coll., 1976-78; mfg. dir. Hemmings Pub., Bennington, 1978-83; assoc. pub. Small Boat Jour., Bennington, 1983-84; cons. Printmark, Montpelier, Vt., 1984—; seminar leader Mag. Pubs. Assn., N.Y.C., 1987—, Mag. Week, Natick, Mass., 1989—. Author: In Print, 1989; contbr. articles to profl. pubs. Office: Printmark 28 Elm St Montpelier VT 05602-2814

BROWN, LAWRENCE CLIFTON, JR., foundation administrator; b. Wakefield, Mass., July 9, 1950; s. Lawrence Clifton and Marguerite Anne (MacLellan) B.; m. Rosemary Dixon, Aug. 21, 1976. BA, Boston Coll., 1972; JD, Suffolk U., 1979. Bar: Mass. 1979. Dir. planning and devel. 735, Inc., Melrose, Mass., 1972-73; regional supr. Mass. Office for Children, Toppsfield, 1973-75; exec. dir. Youth and Family Resources Inc., Melrose, 1975-78; pres. Wave, Inc., Washington, 1978—; bd. dirs. Jobs for the Future, Boston, Nat. Youth Employment Coalition, N.Y.C., Nat. Ctr. for Appropriate Tech., Washington. Mem. ABA, Mass. Bar Assn. Office: Wave Inc 501 School St SW Ste 600 Washington DC 20024-2754

BROWN, LAWRENCE S., JR., physician; b. Bklyn., Dec. 4, 1949; s. Lawrence S. and Mae Rose (Harris) B.; married. BA, Bklyn. Coll., 1976; MD, NYU, 1979; MPH, Columbia U., 1979. Lic. physician, Calif., N.Y. Intern Harlem Hosp. Med. Ctr., N.Y.C., 1979-80, resident, 1980-82, chief resident, 1982-83; staff physician Addiction Rsch. and Treatment Corp., Bklyn., 1981-82, sr. med. coord., 1982-85, v.p. resch. and med. affairs Urban Resources Inst., 1986-88, sr. v.p. rsch. and med. affairs, 1988—; instr. clin. medicine Coll. Physicians and Surgeons Columbia U., N.Y.C., 1986-91; asst. clin. prof. medicine Coll. Physicians and Surgeons Columbia U., N.Y.C., 1991—; asst. attendint physician hosps. Columbia U., N.Y.C., 1986-90; vis. clin. fellow Columbia U., 1979-82, adj. prof., lectr. div. health adminstrn. and health policy, 1988—; mem. various com. NIH, 1986—. Pres. Greater Brownsville Athletic Coun., 1983—. With U.S. Army, 1970-72, Vietnam. Decorated Bronze Star.; recipient Dr. Ralston R. Fillmore, Jr. award, 1976, Achievers award Alpha Upsilon chpt. Omega Psi Phi Fraternity, Inc., 1988; Sheldon E. Kalis Meml. scholar, 1967, N.Y. State Regents War Svc. scholar, 1973. Fellow N.Y. Acad. Scis.; mem. AAAS, APHA, Pub. Health Assn. N.Y.C. (bd. dirs. 1989—), Am. Soc. Addiction Medicine, Am. Soc. Internal Medicine, Am. Diabetes Assn. (profl. sect., N.Y. affiliate), Am. Coll. Physicians, Manhattan Cen. Med. Soc., Med. Soc. State N.Y.,. Office: Addiction Rsch & Treatment Corp 22 Chapel St Brooklyn NY 11201-1903

BROWN, LEANNA, state senator; b. Providence, 1935; d. Harold and Esther Young; m. W. Stanley Brown; children: William, Stephen. BA with honors, Smith Coll., 1956. Mem. profl. staff Ednl. Testing Svc., Princeton, N.J., 1956-60, Chatham Borough, 1969-72; mem. Morris County Bd. Chosen Freeholders, 1972-81, bd. dirs., 1976; bd. dirs. Chatham Trust Co., 1982-92;

pres. N.J. Assn. Counties, 1978; chmn. N.E. N.J. Transp. Coordinating Com., 1979-80; mem. N.J. Assembly, 1980-83, N.J. Senate, 1984—; mem. Casino Revenue Fund Study Commn., 1984-86, Madiosn YMCA Capitol Campaign Com., 1986—, chmn., Primary Gifts com., 1987—; trustee Ctr. for Nonprofit Coprs, 1985—; mem. Gov.'s Commn. on Internat. Trade, 1986—; vice chmn. Congressman Dean Gallo's Small Bus. Export Opportunity Task Force, 1987—; mem. exec. com., chair internat. trade com. Nat. Adv. Coun., U.S. Small Bus. Adminstrv., 1990—; cable TV host Upbeat N.J. Cable TV program host, Upbeat N.J. Vice chair Nat. Rep. Platform Com., 1992; co-chair N.J. Bush/Quayle Campaign, 1988; campaign coord. State Rep. Majority, 1991; trustee Morris Mus. Arts and Sci., 1975—, Arts Coun. Morris Area, 1973—; del. White Ho. Conf. on Librs. and Info. Svcs., 1991—; devel. coun. N.J. Sci. and Tech. Ctr., Liberty State Park, 1986—; mem. bd. visitors Drew U. Mem. N.J. Assn. Elected Women (pres. 1982, 83). Home: 7 Dellwood Ave Chatham NJ 07928-1701 Office: Cory Commons 123 Columbia Tpke Florham Park NJ 07932-2116 Other: NJ State Senate State Capitol Trenton NJ 08625

BROWN, LEE PATRICK, police commissioner, educator; b. Wewoka, Okla., Oct. 4, 1937; s. Andrew and Zelma (Edwards) B.; m. Yvonne Carolyn Streets, July 14, 1958; children: Patrick, Torri, Robyn, Jenna. BA, Fresno State U., 1960; MA, San Jose State U., 1964; MS, U. Calif., 1968, D in Criminoloy, 1970; D of Pub. Affairs (hon.), Fla. Internat. U., 1982; LLD (hon.), John Jay Coll., 1985; HHD (hon.), Portland State U., 1990. Officer San Jose (Calif.) Police Dept., 1960-68; prof. Portland (Oreg.) State U., 1968-72; assoc. dir. Urban Affairs Inst. Howard Inst., Washington, 1972-75; sheriff Sheriff's Dept., Mulnomah County, Oreg., 1975-76; dir. Dept. Justice Services, Mulnomah County, 1976-78; commr. Dept. Pub. Safety, Atlanta, 1978-82; chief of police Houston Police Dept., 1982-90; police commr. N.Y.C., 1990-92; adj. prof. U. Houston, U. Tex. Health Sci. Ctr., Houston, Tex. So. U., Houston; cons. U.S. Dept. Justice, Washington, Police Found., Washington, various state and local govts., Houston; chmn. Nat. Minority Adv. Council on Criminal Justice; mem. Nat. Adv. Commn. on Criminal Justice Standards and Goals, Washington, Nat. Commn. on Higher Edn. for Police, Washington, Commn. on Accreditation for Law Enforcement Agencies, Washington. Co-author: Attitudes of Black Police Officers, 1976, Police and Society, 1981; editor: Neighborhood Team Policing, 1976, Violent Crime, 1981; author of numerous articles and book chpts. Bd. dirs. Boy Scouts Am., United Way, Urban League, Blue Bonnet Bowl, "Just Say No", Peoples Workshop for Visual and Performing Arts, Houston, 1987—, Nat. Black Child Devel. Inst., Washington, 1987—, Nat. Alliance Against Violence, N.Y., 1986—, Sheltering Arms, Houston, 1985—; task forcemem. Nat. Ctr. for Missing and Exploited Children, Washington, 1986—; adv. bd. Nat. Inst. Against Prejudice and Violence, Balt., 1987—; mem. Police Activities League, Houston, 1987—; mem. adv. policy bd. Nat. Incident Based Reporting System, 1988—. Recipient Peace and Justice award Martin Luther King Jr., 1981, Nat. Law Enforcement award Nat. Black Police Assn., 1982, Disting. Alumnus award Fresno State U., 1983, Police Leadership award, Police Exec. Research Forum, 1987, Liberty Bell award Houston Young Lawyers Assn., 1987, August Vollmer award Am. Soc. Criminology, 1988; named Mgr. of Yr., Nat. Mgmt. Assn., Practitioner of Yr., Nat. Assn. of Blacks Criminal Justice, 1984, Communicator of Yr. Washington News Service, 1986; rsch. fellow Harvard U., 1988. Mem. Internat. Assn. Chiefs of Police (immediate past pres.), Nat. Orgn. of Black Law Enforcement Execs. (v.p. 1985, Robert Lamb Jr. Humanitarian award 1987), Police Exec. Research Forum, Internat. Narcotic Enforcement Officers Assn., Nat. Forum for Black Pub. Adminstrs., N.Y. Police Chiefs Assn., Tex. Police Assn., Tex. Criminal Justice Task Force, Nat. Police Athletic League, Mich. State U. (adv. council nat. neighborhood foot patrol ctr.), Nat. Research Council (com. on research on law enforcement and the adminstrn. of justice, com. on status of Black Ams.), Harvard U. (com. exec. session on community policing), Nat. Council on Crime and Delinquency (bd. dirs.), Nat. Acad. Pub. Adminstrn. (Nat. Pub. Svc. award 1988), Am. Soc. Pub. Adminstrn. (Nat. Pub. Svc. award 1988), Am. Leadership Forum, Forum Club of Houston (bd. dirs. 1987—), Calif. Alumni Club of Tex., Houston Bus. and Profl. Men's Club, Alpha Phi Alpha, Sigma Pi Phi. Democrat. Office: Tex So U Coll Arts and Scis 3100 Cleburne Houston TX 77004

BROWN, LESLIE ANN, biologist; b. Tucumcari, N.Mex., Nov. 28, 1961; d. David Elmer and Charlotte Suzanne (Six) B. BA in Biology, Kans. State U., 1983. Ward attendant Oak Park Vet. Clinic, Lenexa, Kans., 1978-79; undergrad. lab. tech. Div. Biology, Kans. State U., Manhattan, 1981-83; receptionist Service Merchandise, Houston, 1985; sales rep. LKB Instruments, Houston, 1986-87; sr. tech. specialist Pharmacia LKB Biotech., Piscataway, N.J., 1987-89, assoc. mgr. electrophoresis tech. svc., 1990, mgr. area tech. support, 1990-91; tech. mgr. svc. and support Pharmacia LKB Biotech, Piscataway, N.J., 1992—. Com. chmn. Fone Crisis Ctr., Manhattan, Kans., 1981-83; mem. Vol.-Sci.-by-Mail program, 1990—. Vanderbilt fellow, 1983-85; named one of Outstanding Young Women of Am., 1984, 87, 88. Republican. Presbyterian.

BROWN, MARIAN ELSA, association administrator; b. Beirut, Oct. 8, 1962; d. Gordon Stewart and Olivia Margaret (Collins) B. BA, Duke U., 1984. Adminstrv. asst. Very Spl. Arts, Washington, 1985; adminstrv. asst. Found. for Hospice and Homecare, Washington, 1986-87, program dir., 1987-88, assoc. dir., 1988—; assoc. dir. Caring Inst., Washington, 1990—, sec., bd. dirs., 1991-92. Dir. spl. projects Ptnrs. in Edn., Washington, 1988—; vol. Make-a-Wish Found., Washington, 1986—. Office: Caring Inst 519 C St NE Washington DC 20002

BROWN, MARSHA ANN STOKES, lyricist, composer; b. Bryn Mawr, Pa., Apr. 17, 1952; d. Ophalina and Edith (Miller) Stokes; m. Norman Brown, 1970 (div. 1980); children: Anthony, Norman, Bryan, Joseph. Diploma med. asst., McCarrie Sch. Health and Tech., 1976; diploma in acctg., Community Coll. Phila., 1988; MA, 1992. Psychiat. aide Phila. State Hosp.; now, freelance writer and lyricist Phila. :yricist Nashville Music Co.; composer Prayer Records) Prayer to God, 1986; author of poems, 1981-91. Mem. Franciscan Mission Assocs. Recipient Iliad Lit. award 1990, Parent Teaching award, 1979; Named to World of Poetry Hall of Fame, 1990. Mem. AMA, RMT, ABI, BMI (N.Y. br.), Am. Bible Soc. Address: 2209 Edgley St Philadelphia PA 19121

BROWN, MARTIN DAVID, hospital administration professional; b. Lockport, N.Y., July 27, 1956; s. Richard Starr and Eunice Ann (Gritzmacher) B.; m. Diane Blazejeski, July 2, 1976; children: Paul Martin, Marilyn Christine. BS in Pharmacy, Albany Coll. Pharmacy, 1979; MS in Computer Sci., Union Coll., 1989. Registered pharmacist, N.Y. Staff pharmacist St. Clare's Hosp., Schenectady, N.Y., 1980-87; chief pharmacist Nathan Littauer Hosp., Gloversville, N.Y., 1987-90, dir. info. svcs., 1990—; pharmacy cons. Johnstown (N.Y.) Hosp., 1987, Fulton County Infirmary, Gloversville, 1988. Mem. Am. Soc. Hosp. Pharmacists, Northeastern N.Y. Soc. Hosp. Pharmacists. Roman Catholic. Office: Nathan Littauer Hosp 99 E State St Gloversville NY 12078-1203

BROWN, MARTIN HOWARD, physician; b. Bklyn., Feb. 21, 1953; s. Alan Aaron and Clarice (Steinberg) B.; m. Rebecca Jeanne Sarley; children: Meghan E., Elliott A. BS with honors, George Washington U., 1974, MD, 1978. Chief med. resident George Washington U. Hosp., Washington, 1981-82; staff physician Emergency Medicine Assocs., Bethesda, Md., 1982-83; asst. prof. medicine George Washington U. Med. Ctr., 1983—; aeromed. dir. Worldcare Travel Assistance Assn., Washington, 1985-88; vice chmn. dept. emergency medicine Nat. Hosp., Arlington, Va., 1985-87, chmn. dept., 1987-91; asst. prof. medicine Georgetown U. Hosp., Washington, 1988—; med. dir. USASSIST, Washington, 1988—; chmn. dept. emergency medicine Washington Adventist Hosp., 1991—; trauma ctr. site reviewer State of Va.; mem. adv. com. Emergency Med. Svcs. Curriculum, No. Va. Community Coll., 1990—; cons. in field. Trustee Nat. Hosp. Bd. Trustees, 1987—; mem. adv. com. emergency med. svcs. Arlington County Bd., 1987—, chmn. adv. com., 1991. Fellow Am. Coll. Emergency Physicians, Am. Coll. Physician Execs., Alpha Omega Alpha. Jewish. Home: 3245 Cleveland Ave NW Washington DC 20008-3450 Office: Emergency Medicine Assocs 6701 Rockledge Dr Bethesda MD 20817-1813

BROWN, MICHAEL MARSHALL, public relations executive; b. Burlington, Vt., Apr. 26, 1955; s. Richard Everett and Judith (Marshall) B.; m. Jaclin Peper, June 27, 1982; 1 child, Shane Marshall; children: Shane Marshall, Cody Peper. BA, St. Michael's Coll., 1977. News reporter Burlington (Vt.) Free Press, 1977; news reporter, photographer Plattsburgh (N.Y.) Press., 1978-80; sports editor Oneonta (N.Y.) Daily Star, 1980-82; owner, publisher, editor The Sporting Eye, Oneonta, 1982-84; sports writer Plattsburgh (N.Y.) Press., 1984-87; pub. rels. specialist The Olympic Authority, Lake Placid, N.Y., 1987-89; pub. rels. dir. Clinton Community Coll., Plattsburgh, 1989-90; exec. asst. for coll. affairs Dutchess Community Coll., Poughkeepsie, N.Y., 1990—; outdoor columnist Poughkeepsie (N.Y.) Jour., 1990—; mem. SUNY Govtl. Affairs Coun., 1990—, SUNY Coun. for Univ. Affairs, 1990—. Writer DeBrett's Directory-Europe-American Tourism Opportunities, 1988. V.p. Profl. Communicators of the Hudson Valley, Poughkeepsie. Mem. Nat. Coun. for Mktg. and Pub. Rels. (regional bd. dirs.), N.Y. State Outdoor Writer's Assn. Republican. Home: 9 Tina Dr Highland NY 12528-2424 Office: Dutchess Community College 53 Pendell Rd Poughkeepsie NY 12601-1595

BROWN, NORMAN, materials science educator, researcher; b. Lynn, Mass., Feb. 7, 1921; s. David and Ruth Thelma (Franklin) B.; m. Doris June Gordon (dec. Aug. 1969); children: Fredric, Hollis, Norman, Jonathan, Edmund; m. Miriam Elizabeth Jones, Oct. 24, 1970. BS, MIT, 1942; MS, Stanford U., 1950; PhD, U. Calif., Berkeley, 1952. Metallurgist Naval Torpedo Sta., Newport, R.I., 1942-43; asst. prof. U. Pa., Phila., 1952-55, assoc. prof., 1955-61, prof., 1961—; cons. numerous labs. Contbr. 150 articles to profl. jours. Pres. Grange Estate, Haverford, Pa., 1971-76. Lt. U.S. Army, 1943-48. Guggenheim fellow, 1958-59, Spl. fellow, NIH, 1966-67. Fellow Am. Phys. Soc.; mem. Am. Soc. Metals. Mem. Soc. of Friends. Home: 727 Panmure Rd Haverford PA 19041-1217 Office: U Pa Dept Materials Sci Philadelphia PA 19104

BROWN, NORMAN HOWARD, chief executive officer; b. Patchogue, N.Y., Aug. 5, 1929; s. Bertram G. and Elizabeth C. (Swezey) B.; m. Freda D. Goldman, Sept. 27, 1959; children: Amy Susan, Burton Jay, Toby Ellen. Student, Armed Forces Info. Sch., 1951, U. Calif., 1953; BS, Columbia U., 1959. Tech. writer Eaton Corp., Deer Park, N.Y., 1960-67; advt. & pub. rels. mgr. Pall Corp., Glen Cove, N.Y., 1967-69; acct. exec. Robert S. Taplinger Assoc., N.Y.C., 1969-71; acct. supr. Irving L. Straus Assocs., N.Y.C., 1971-73; pres. Norman Brown & Assocs., Providence, 1973—. Author: The Trace Your Own Roots Workbook, 1978; co-author: Get Rich Investment Guide, 1985. Sgt. USAF, 1951-53, Korea. Home and Office: 50 Blackstone Blvd Providence RI 02906-5444

BROWN, PAMELA JOY CLARK, business educator; b. Breaux Bridge, La., Feb. 10, 1954; d. Glenwood and Myrtle (Conrad) Clark; m. Frederick Jeffrey Brown, Aug. 28, 1982; 1 child, Kimberly. BA, Rollins Coll., 1976; MS, Clemson U., 1978; PhD, Stanford U., 1984. Tech. staff mem. Hughes Aircraft Co., Canoga Park, Calif., 1978-81; researcher Naval Postgrad. Sch., Monterey, Calif., 1982; visiting lectr. U. Manchester Inst. Sci. & Technology, Manchester, England, 1987-88; cons. ICI Corp. Mgmt. Svcs., Northwich, England, 1987-89; asst. prof. U. Del., Newark, 1983-90, assoc. prof., 1990—. Contbr. articles to profl. jours. Rsch. fellow Smithsonian Inst., 1977; Rsch. grantee U. Del., 1984, 90, Dupont Bus. grantee, 1986, NSF grantee, 1991. Mem. The Inst. Mgmt. Sci., Econometric Soc., Am. Econs. Assn. Home: 112 Great Circle Rd Newark DE 19711-2334 Office: U Del Dept Bus Adminstrn Newark DE 19716

BROWN, PAMELA WEDD, artist; b. Cauderan, Gironde, France, Nov. 21, 1928; came to U.S., 1953; d. William Basil and Nora Marsh (van Nostrand) Wedd; m. Charles Freeman Brown, Nov. 29, 1952; children: Penelope Susan, Nicholas Wedd. Student, Ecole des Beaux Arts, Paris, 1947-48, Academie Julian, Paris, 1946-51. Free lance fashion illustrator Paris, 1947-48; dir. arts and crafts YWCA, Toronto, Ont., Can., 1951; dir. Washington Womens Arts Ctr., 1987-88, Washington Printmakers Gallery, 1990-91; co-pres. Studio Gallery, 1992—; artist in residence The Art Barn, Washington, 1986. Designer book plate Nat. Mus. Women in Arts Libr., 1985; represented in permanent collections Libr. of Congress, NIH, Nat. Mus. History, Nat. Mus. Women in Arts. Precinct capt. Bd. of Elections and Ethics, Washington, 1970-80. Recipient First Prize Drawing, Academie Julian, Paris, 1947, Purchase award The Jr. League, Newport News, Va., 1971, Equal awards The Art League, Alexandria, Va., 1980, 82, 85, 88. Mem. Studio Gallery D.C., The Art League, Artists' Equity, Washington Project for th Arts. Home: 3500 Macomb St NW Washington DC 20016-3162

BROWN, PATRICIA ANNE, administrative assistant; b. N.Y.C., Nov. 17, 1962; d. James Joseph and Mary Ellen (McKeon) B. BA, Fordham U., 1984. Acct. adminstr. Scudder, Stevens & Clark, N.Y.C., 1984-86; compliance analyst Goldman, Sachs & Co., N.Y.C., 1986-89; dir. investor programs KCS & A Pub. Rels., N.Y.C., 1989-90; account exec. St. Vincent, Milone & O'Sullivan Advt. & Pub. Rels., N.Y.C., 1990-91; adminstrv. asst. corp. fin. Morgan Stanley, N.Y.C., 1991—. Home: Apt 8C 181 E 73d St New York NY 10021 Office: Morgan Stanley 1251 Ave of the Americas New York NY 10020

BROWN, PATRICIA COCHRAN, artist, educator; b. Pitts., Nov. 16, 1955; d. Paul Edmund and Patricia Wilson (Cochran) B. BS, Purdue U., 1979; MS, East Tenn. State U., 1983. State park naturalist State of Ind., Indpls., 1975; botanist Carnegie Mus. Natural HIstory, Pitts., 1977-79; instr. chemistry East Tenn. State U., Johnson City, 1981-83; instr. biology U. Pitts., 1984-87; instr. art South Arts, Bethel Park, Pa., 1987-89; botany artist Bayberry Studio, Upper St. Clair, Pa., 1987—; instr. art Lincoln Community Ctr., West Lafayette, Ind., 1974; v.p. Boyce Road Gardeners Corp., 1991. Exhibited in group shows Pitts. Soc. Artists, 1987, Am. Artists Profl. League, N.Y.C., 1987 Salmagundi Club, N.Y.C., 1987. Winner Pa. Dept. Transp. graphics design contest for signs to designate wildflower areas along state roads, 1989. Mem. Soc. Econ. Botany, Ft. Pitt Soc. DAR, Nat. Soc. DAR (chmn. Am. heritage and conversation Pitts. chpt. 1989—), Am. Rabbit Breeders Assn., Beta Beta Beta. Republican. Episcopalian. Home and Office: Bayberry Studio 1531 Redfern Dr Pittsburgh PA 15241-2936

BROWN, PATRICIA IRENE, lawyer, retired law librarian; b. Boston; d. Joseph Raymond and Harriet A. (Taylor) B. BA, Suffolk U., 1955, JD, 1965, MBA, 1970; MTS, Gordon Conwell Theol. Sem., 1977. Bar: Mass. 1965. Library asst. Suffolk U., Boston, 1951-60, asst. librarian, 1960-65, asst. law librarian, 1965-85, assoc. law libr., 1985-92. Dir. Referral/Resource Ctr., Union Congl. Ch., Winthrop, Mass. First Woman inducted into Nat. Baseball Hall of Fame, Cooperstown, N.Y., 1988, All- Am. Girls Profl. Baseball League, 1950-51. Mem. Mass. Bar Assn., Boston Bar Assn., Assn. Am. Law Libraries, Am. Congl. Assn. (bd. dirs. 1982—).

BROWN, PAUL LEE, public relations professional; b. Marshalltown, Iowa, Aug. 27, 1938; s. Gilbert Crosby and Maxine Mathilda (Eige) B.; m. Nancy Sue Strunce, Sept. 3, 1960; children: Judith Kay Brown Schmidt, Laura Jean. BA, Simpson Coll., 1960; MS, Columbia U., 1962. City editor Oelwein (Iowa) Daily Register, 1960; edn. editor Nonpareil, Council Bluffs, Iowa, 1960-61; editor, then sr. editor U. Mich., Ann Arbor, 1963-75, asst. dir. univ. publs., 1975-83, mgr. publs., 1983-84, coord. spl. projects, devel. and mktg., 1984-87; dir. pub. rels. U. Scranton, Pa., 1987—; dir. pub. rels. Scranton Assn., Inc., 1990. Founding mem. Shelter Assn. Ann Arbor, 1982; sr. warden St. Luke's Episcopal Ch., Scranton, 1988—; v.p. Robert Dale Chorale, Scranton, 1988-91; bd. dirs. Lucan Ctr. for Arts, Scranton, 1989—. Mem. Coun. Advancement and Support of Edn. Democrat. Home: 751 N Main Ave Scranton PA 18504-1514 Office: U Scranton Scranton PA 18510-4615

BROWN, PAUL WOODROW, surgeon; b. N.Y.C., Dec. 28, 1919; s. La Verne C. and Mayme Catherine (DeClarke) B.; m. Patricia Ann Burris, May 24, 1986. BS, U. Mich., 1942, MD, 1950. Diplomate Am. Bd. Orthopaedic Surgery. Commd. pvt. U.S. Army, 1942, advanced through grades to col., ret., 1969; intern, resident Letterman Army Hosp., San Francisco, 1950-51, 51-54; resident Shriner's Hosp. for Crippled Children, San Francisco, 1954-55; prof. surgery U. Colo., Denver, 1969-72, U. Miami, Fla., 1972-74; chief surgery St. Vincent's Med. Ctr., Bridgeport, Conn., 1974-82; clin. prof. orthopaedic surgery Sch. Medicine, Yale U., New Haven, 1985—, clin. prof. plastic and reconstructive surgery, 1986—; pvt. practice surgeon Conn. Hand Surgery Ctr., Bridgeport, 1978—; fellowship hand surgery Walter Reed Army Hosp., Washington, 1962-63. Contbr. articles to profl. publs., chpts. to books. Home: 3071 North St Fairfield CT 06430-1627 Office: Conn Hand Surgery Ctr 3101 Main St Bridgeport CT 06606-4258

BROWN, PEGGY (MARGARET C. BROWN), fundraising executive; b. Balt., Feb. 26, 1936; d. Alfred Grant and Ruth Thomas (Grant) Clarke; m. Arthur Leslie Peter Brown, Feb. 16, 1957; children: Arthur Leslie Peter Jr., Susan Clarke Brown, Alexandra Grant Brown. Student, Vassar Coll., 1954-56. Fundraiser for family planning, edn., and mental health, 1963—; fundraiser Nature Conservancy, Chapel Hill, N.C., 1983-90; nat. dir. devel. The Nature Conservancy, Arlington, Va., 1989-90; dir. devle. and mktg. Nat. Fish & Wildlife Found., Washington, 1990-92; v.p., sr. fundraising counselor Capital Consortium, Inc., Raleigh, N.C., 1992—. Trustee N.C. Natural Heritage Found., Raleigh, 1991—. Mem. Nat. Soc. Fundraising Execs. (chpt. dir. 1980-82), Leadership Greater Washington. Home: 304 Estes Dr Chapel Hill NC 27514-3415 Office: Capital Consortium Inc 2700 Wycliff Rd Raleigh NC 27602

BROWN, PETER DAVID GILSON, German educator; b. Alton, Ill., Oct. 18, 1943; s. Weir Messick and Vivian Virginia (Bauer) B.; m. Elaine Greenblatt, Sept. 10, 1969 (div. Aug. 1970); 1 child, Stephanie; m. Susan Roberta Jensen, Sept. 11, 1970 (div. Mar. 1992); 1 child, Andrew J.B. BA summa cum laude, Columbia Coll., 1964; MA, Columbia U., 1965, PhD, 1971. Instr. of German Columbia U., N.Y.C., 1967-71, Barnard Coll., N.Y.C., 1969-71; asst. prof. German SUNY, New Paltz, 1971-74, assoc. prof. German, 1974-86, prof. German, 1986—; dir. SUNY Acad. Summer Program, Hamburg/Stade, Fed. Republic Germany, 1974—; mem. editorial adv. bd. Peter Lang Pub., N.Y.C., 1986—. Author: Oskar Panizza: His Life and Works, 1983; editor: (book series 50 vols.) Studies in Modern German Literature, 1985—; contbr. articles to profl. jours. Chmn. Mid-Hudson Nuclear Opponents, New Paltz, N.Y., 1974-80; legis. coord. Safe Energy Coalition of N.Y. State, Albany, 1974-75; bd. dirs. Environ. Planning Lobby, Albany, 1976-77, Hudson River Sloop Clearwater, Poughkeepsie, N.Y., 1981-83. Recipient Advanced German Studies Prize German Consulate, 1963, Experienced Faculty Travel award NYS/UUP, 1987; Woodrow Wilson fellowship Woodrow Wilson Found., 1964; Tech. Assistance Study grant U.S. Dept. Energy, 1980. Mem. Am. Assn. of Tchrs. of German, Modern Lang. Assn. of Am. Office: SUNY Dept Fgn Langs 414 Faculty Tower New Paltz NY 12561

BROWN, PETER OGDEN, trust company executive; b. Ithaca, N.Y., Aug. 20, 1940; s. Frederick Shiras and Helen (Ogden) Brown; m. Nancy Tredwell Sunderland, Aug. 25, 1962; children: Jeffrey Scott, Douglas Henderson, Lori MacArthur. BA cum laude, Amherst Coll., 1962; LLB, Duke U., 1965. Assoc. Harter, Secrest & Emery, Rochester, N.Y., 1965-73, ptnr., 1973-80; sr. v.p., mgr. personal banking and trust group Chase Lincoln First Bank N.A., Rochester, 1981-90; exec. v.p., chief operating officer The Glenmede Trust Co., Phila., 1990—. Co-author: How to Live and Die with New York Probate, 1975, Proceedings of the 25th Univ. of Miami Institute on Estate Planning, 1991; contbr. articles to profl. jours. Overseer U. Mus. of the U. Pa., Phila., 1991—; trustee Colgate Rochester Div. Sch., 1987—;mem. The Acad. of Music com., Phila.; mem. endowment com. Phila. Mus. Art, 1990—; chancellor Episcopal Diocese of Rochester, 1979-90; hon. dir. Meml. Art Gallery of U. Rochester, 1990—, pres. and chmn. 1980-84. Mem. Am. Bankers Assn. (exec. com. trust div., chmn. personal svc. com. 1989—), N.Y. State Bar Assn. (chmn. com. on taxation of trusts and estates 1988-89), The Fla. Bar, Pa. Bar Assn., Genessee Valley Club (treas. 1987-89), Union League of Phila., Trust Mgmt. Assn. Republican. Episcopalian. Office: The Glenmede Trust Co 229 S 18th St Philadelphia PA 19103-6144

BROWN, PETER STONE, music critic; b. Phila., July 10, 1951; s. Joseph Henry and Jessie (Stone) B. Grad. high sch., Millburn, N.J. Disc jockey, announcer Sta. WXPN-FM, Phila., 1977-81; music critic The Welcomat/After Dark, Phila., 1983—, East Coast Rocker, Montclair, N.J., 1987-89, Big Shout Mag., Wilmington, Del., 1990—; faculty mem. Phila. Music Found. Seminar IV, 1990. Office: The Welcomat 1816 Ludlow St Philadelphia PA 19103

BROWN, PHILIP HENRY, psychiatric social worker; b. N.Y.C., May 18, 1952; s. Max B. and Sylvia (Lippman) B.; m. Doreen O. Muller, Aug. 1, 1976; children: Caitlin, Matthew. BA, U. Conn., 1974, MSW, 1978. Bd. cer. diplomate in clin. social work. Mem. VISTA Conn. Dept. Corrections, Hartford, 1974-76; psychiat. social worker div. psychiatry Waterbury Hosp., Waterbury, Conn., 1978-85, Winchester Pub. Schs., Winsted, Conn., 1980-83; coord. emergency svc. Day Kimball Hosp., Putnam, Conn., 1985-87; pvt. practice psychiat. social work Plainfield, Conn., 1985-89; pvt. practice Canterbury, Conn., 1989—; cons. New Milford (Conn.) Hospice, 1985-86; instr. psychology and sociology U. Conn., Torrington, Waterbury, Groton, Conn., 1981—, Northwestern Conn. Community Coll, Winsted, 1982-85. Instr. Conn. Emergency Med. Svcs., Hartford, 1981—; bd. dirs. Ea. Conn. Mental Health Bd., Norwich, Conn., 1986. mem. Acad. Cert. Social Workers, Nat. Assn. Assn. Social Workers (Conn. bd. dirs. 1982-86), Washington Red Cross (bd. dirs. 1985). Home: 30 Major Dr Plainfield CT 06374-1720 Office: Canterbury Profl Bldg PO Box 266 39 S Canterbury Rd Canterbury CT 06331

BROWN, RICHARD LAURENCE, broadcast executive; b. N.Y.C., Jan. 10, 1962; s. Theodor and Vivian Susan (Kamins) B.; m. Elizabeth Ann Gaughan, Oct. 31, 1987. Student, Syracuse U., 1984. Assoc. studio producer Sta. ABC-TV, N.Y.C., 1980; broadcaster Sta. WNDR/WNTQ Radio, Syracuse, N.Y., 1982-84; producer, prodn. dir. Sta. WBZ, Group W Radio Boston, 1984-85; broadcast account exec. Sta. WAVA Radio, Washington, 1985-86, Sta. CBS Radio, Boston, 1986-87, Sta. WBCN Radio, Infinity Broadcasting, Boston, 1987-89; Sta. WLNE-TV Sta. WLNE-TV, Providence, 1989-92; broadcast account exec. Sta. WTTG/Fox TV, Washington, 1992—. Recipient Outstanding Ednl. Communications award Regents Adv. Council, 1978, 79, Outstanding Pub. Service award N.Y. State Assembly, 1979. Office: Sta WTTG/Fox TV 5151 Wisconsin Ave NW Washington DC 21044

BROWN, RICHARD LAVERNE, educational association executive; b. Hutchinson, Kans., Dec. 13, 1943; s. John Lewis and Ina Fay (Turner) B.; m. Diane Marie Petersen, June 25, 1966; children: Jodi Lynn, Richard Lewis, Stefanie Anne. BS, Okla. State U., 1965. Math. tchr. Wakita (Okla.) Bd. Edn., 1965-66; math./computer tchr. Sayreville Bd. Edn., Parlin, N.J., 1966-91; assoc. dir. rsch. N.J. Edn. Assn., Trenton, 1991—; SAT tchr. Huntington Learning Ctr., 1990-91; computer tchr. Ocean County Coll., Toms River, 1990-91. Mem. local edn. agy. data collection and rev. com. Dept. Edn., State of N.J. Fellow NEA, Middlesex County Edn. Assn., N.J. Edn. Assn.; mem. Sayreville Edn. Assn. (v.p. 1988-90), Masons. Office: NJ Edn Assn 180 W State St Trenton NJ 08608-1104

BROWN, ROBERT CECIL, lawyer; b. Portland, Oreg., Dec. 29, 1928; s. Cecil Doak and Louise Elizabeth (Leaming) B.; m. Virginia Lea Egge, Feb. 6, 1954 (div. May 1972); children: Jay M., Randall C., Kevin B.; m. Karen Virginia Baer, June 12, 1972. BA, Reed Coll., 1951; JD, U. So. Calif., 1959. Bar: U.S. Patent Office, 1954, Calif. 1959, U.S. Dist. Ct. (so. dist.) Calif. 1959, U.S. Ct. Customs & Patent Appeals 1959, U.S. Supreme Ct. 1963, N.Y. 1969, U.S. Ct. Appeals (2d cir.) 1969, U.S. Ct. Appeals (Fed. cir.) 1982, Conn. 1989. Examiner U.S. Patent Office, Washington, 1951-53; patent counsel Aerojet Gen. Corp., Azusa, Calif., 1953-62, asst. v.p., 1962-65; v.p., sec. Aerojet Delft Corp., Melville, N.Y., 1965-68; patent atty. Union Carbide Corp., N.Y.C., 1969-78, group patent counsel, 1978-86; mng. patent counsel Union Carbide Corp., Danbury, Conn., 1986—. 1st lt. U.S. Army, 1947-53, Korea. Mem. ABA, Am. Intellectual Property Law Assn., Calif. Bar, N.Y. Bar, Conn. Bar. Office: Union Carbide Chems Corp 39 Old Ridgebury Rd Danbury CT 06817-0001

BROWN, ROBERT EDWARD, finance executive; b. Annapolis, Md., Dec. 28, 1949; s. Charles Wesley and Opal Demarest (Washington) B.; m. Lydia Patricia Romano, Aug. 5, 1972. BS in Math., Lynchburg Coll., 1972; BSBA, U. Md., 1990. CPA, Md. Contr. Shields Assocs., Inc., Hanover, Md., 1972-81; v.p. fin. Adrian L. Merton, Inc., Capitol Heights, Md., 1981—. Mem. AICPA, Inst. for Mgmt. Accts., Md. Assn. CPAs. Republican. Home: 1915 Chaparrall Ct Crownsville MD 21032-2318 Office: Adrian L Merton Inc 9011 E Hampton Dr Capital Heights MD 20743-3800

BROWN, ROBERT HAINES, orthopedic surgeon; b. Atlantic City, N.J., June 9, 1938; s. J. Carlisle and Mary Elizabeth (Rosenberger) B.; m. Beverly Rennild Anderson, June 13, 1964; children: Joanne Elizabeth, Kristin Lee. BS, Northwestern U., 1960; MD, Temple U., 1964. Bd. cert. Am. Bd. Orthopedic Surgery. Pvt. practice orthopedic surgery Cherry Hill, N.J., 1972—. Capt. USAF, 1965-67. Office: 1210 Brace Rd Cherry Hill NJ 08034

BROWN, ROBERT MOTT, III, investment banker; b. Washington, Feb. 21, 1947; s. Robert Mott Jr. and Helen Priscilla (Johnson) B.; m. Yvonne "Bonnie" Lynn Palmer, June 30, 1973; children: Jessica Lee, Robert Mott IV. BA in Econs., Carnegie-Mellon U., 1969; MBA, U. Mich., 1971. Spl. asst. to exec. dir. Mich. State Housing Devel. Authority, Lansing, 1970-73; chief fin. officer Va. Housing Devel. Authority, Richmond, 1973-77; mng. dir. Lehman Bros., N.Y.C., 1978—; cons. U.S. Dept. Housing & Urban Devel., Washington, 1973; dir. and chmn. Corp. com. Friends of Vielles Maisons Francaises, N.Y.C., 1988—. Bd. dirs. Jamestown-Yorktown Ednl. Trust, 1989—; vestry St. Luke's Episcopal Ch., Darien, Conn., 1987-89; mem. fin. com. John Glenn U.S. presdl. campaign, Washington, 1984; mem. adv. bd. Dem. Leadership Coun., Washington, 1986—. Mem. Pub. Securities Assn. (exec. com. 1990—), Contrerie de Chevaliers du Tastevin, Wee Burn C. of C. Home: 86 Ridge Acres Rd Darien CT 06820-2616 Office: Lehman Bros World Fin Ctr 20th Fl New York NY 10028

BROWN, RONALD JAMES, clinical psychologist, educator; b. Kalamazoo, July 28, 1953; s. James Dean and Marilyn Ethel (Elwood) B.; m. Janet Kay Bayleran, Aug. 30, 1975; 1 child, Madeleine Bayleran-Brown. BA in Psychology, U. Mich., 1975; PhD in Clin. Psychology, McGill U., 1984. Lic. clin. psychologist, Maine. Staff psychologist, adj. faculty U. Conn. Health Ctr., Farmington, 1985-86; staff psychologist Bangor (Maine) Mental Health Inst., 1986-89, dir. psychology, 1989—; adj. faculty/lectr. dept. psychology U. Maine, Orono, 1990—; mem. mgmt. team Bangor Mental Health Inst., 1989—. Mem. Am. Psychol. Assn., Bangor Area Psychol. Soc. Home: 112 Franklin St # C3 Bangor ME 04401 Office: Bangor Mental Health Inst PO Box 926 Bangor ME 04402

BROWN, RONALD OSBORNE, telecommunications and office information systems consultant; b. Winchester, Mass., Apr. 9, 1941; s. Herbert Walcott and Madeleine Louise (Osborne) B.; m. Annette L. Brown; children: Melinda E., Jeffrey J. BS with distinction, U. Maine, 1963; MS, Tufts U., 1965; PhD, Queens U., Kingston, Ont., 1972. Mem. tech. staff RCA Corp., Burlington, Mass., 1965-66; rsch. assoc. Queen's U., Kingston, Ont., 1966-71; mem. sci. staff BNR, Ottawa, Ont., 1971-72; sr. systems engr. GTE Corp., Needham, Mass., 1973-83; mgr. Coopers & Lybrand, Boston, 1983-87, nat. dir, 1987-88; pvt. practice cons. Melrose, Mass., 1988-91; pres. R.O. Brown Cons., Melrose, 1991—; program coord. Northeastern U., Boston, 1976—; cons. Bell Can., 1968-71; program chmn. Networking Mgmt. Inst.; lectr. U. Wis., 1990—. Contbg. editor Networking Mgmt. Mag.; contbr. articles to profl. jours. Mem. IEEE, Assn. Profl. Engrs. Ont., Tau Beta Pi, Phi Kappa Phi, Eta Kappa Nu. Home: Quaker Ridge Rd PO Box 470 South Casco ME 04077-0470 Office: 23 Baxter St Melrose MA 02176-3639

BROWN, S.M. HENRY, JR., electric utility company executive; b. Bluefield, W.Va., Nov. 27, 1938; s. S.M. and Katherine (Heisler) B.; m. Linda Jean Humphries, Aug. 23, 1963; children: David Christopher, Michael Scott, Robert Andrew. BSCE, Va. Mil. Inst., 1960. Archtl. cons. Gen. Stone and Materials Corp., Roanoke (Va.) and Atlanta, 1963-67; gen. mgr. Constrn. Chems., Inc., Chgo., 1967-69; asst. to pres. Gen. Stone and Materials Corp., Roanoke, 1969-70; dir. corp. devel. Riverton Corp., Front Royal, Va., 1970-72; exec. v.p. N.C. Aggregates Assn., Raleigh, 1971-77; dir. legis. affairs N.C. Citizens Bus. and Industry Assn., Raleigh, 1977-79; dir. congl. affairs Carolina Power and Light Co., Raleigh, 1979-86, mgr. pub. affairs dept., 1986-89; v.p. govtl. affairs Entergy Corp., 1989—; bd. dirs. Pub. Affairs Council, Washington; chmn. nuclear power legis. com. Edison Electric Inst., Washington, 1983-85, fed. affairs com. 1985-87. Mem. exec. bd. Occoneechee Council Boy Scouts Am., Raleigh, 1986-89; chmn. bd. Montessori Sch., Raleigh, 1974-75. Capt. U.S. Army, 1960-62. Mem. NAM (chmn. nat. pub. affairs com. Washington 1987-89), Am. League Lobbyists. Democrat. Episcopalian. Club: Raleigh Racquet (pres. 1977-78). Lodge: Kiwanis (bd. dirs. Raleigh club 1978-79). Home: 15555 Smithfield Pl Centreville VA 22020-4902 Office: Entergy Corp Ste 275 1776 I St NW Washington DC 20006

BROWN, STEPHEN ANDREW, exhibition designer, industrial designer; b. Norwood, Mass., Feb. 9, 1955; s. Andrew James and Evelyn (Merrifield) B.; m. Paula Pitman; children: Jeremy, Eliza. BFA, Mass. Coll. Art, Boston, 1982. Exhbn. planner Needham (Mass.) Hist. Soc., 1978-79; model maker F.W. Dixon Co., Woburn, Mass., 1981-82, Jerry M. Johnson Assocs., Boston, 1982-83; exhbn. planner Joseph Wetzel Assocs., Boston, 1983—; instr. exhbn. design Mass. Coll. Art, 1986-88. Researcher, illustrator: I Am. Nehoiden, 1980; designer toy Rocking Dolphins, 1991; exhibited in group show at DeCordova Mus., Lincoln, Mass., 1991. Recipient Excellence in Optics Use award Optical Soc. Am., 1989, Best in Exhbn. Design award Print Publs., 1990. Mem. Am. Craft Soc., Am. Assn. Museums, Am. Assn. Zool. Parks and Aquariums. Home: 110 Lakeview Ave Waltham MA 02154 Office: Joseph A Wetzel & Assocs 77 N Washington St Boston MA 02114

BROWN, STEPHEN LANDESMAN, investment company executive; b. N.Y.C., July 13, 1938; s. Paul Landesman and Sadie (Collins) B.; m. Barbara Jane Spitz, Aug. 22, 1964; children: Spencer, Andrew, Christina. AB, Brown U., 1961; LLB, NYU, 1965. V.p. Goodkind and Co., N.Y.C., 1966-72; gen. ptnr. Monness Williams and Co., N.Y.C., 1975-78; v.p. Rosenkranz and Co., N.Y.C., 1979-82; chmn. S.L Brown & Co., Inc., N.Y.C., 1983—, The Franklin Holding Corp., N.Y.C., 1986—; bd. dirs. Copley Fin. Svcs. Corp.; adviser Copley Fund. Trustee The Peddie Sch., Hightstown, N.J. Mem. Assn. Corp. Growth, Doubles, Metropolis Country Club, City Athletic Club. Office: S L Brown & Co Inc 767 5th Ave New York NY 10153-0002

BROWN, STEPHEN MICHAEL, college dean; b. New Bedford, Mass., Sept. 11, 1950; s. Walter H. and Hilda M. (DaCosta) B.; m. Kathleen A. Vincent, Aug. 2, 1974; children: Jonathan Vincent, Jared Vincent. BA, U. Mass., North Dartmouth, 1972; MA, U. R.I., 1976; EdD, Boston U., 1981. Instr. Daniel Webster Jr. Coll., Lakenheath, Eng., 1973; staff assoc. Southeastern Mass. U., North Dartmouth, 1975-77; program dir. No. Essex Community Coll., Haverhill, Mass., 1977-78, dir. skills ctr., 1978-83; asst. dean Lesley Coll., Cambridge, Mass., 1983-86, dean, 1987—. Mem. ASTD (bd. dirs. Mass. chpt. 1990—), Soc. for Human Resource Mgmt. Office: Lesley Coll Sch Mgmt 29 Everett St Cambridge MA 02138-2790

BROWN, STEVEN FORD, writer, editor, publisher; b. Florence, Ala., 1952; s. Ford Malcolm and Gloria (Peters) B. Student, U. Houston, 1983-88; BA in English, U. Ala., 1988. Editor, pub. Ford-Brown & Co., Pubs., Houston and Boston, 1975—; Latin Am. editor The Literary Olympics, San Diego, 1991-92; editor Am. Poets Profile Series, Houston and Boston, 1982—. Editor: Contemporary Literature in Birmingham, 1983; co-translator: Astonishing World: Selected Poems of Angel Gonzalez, 1993. Recipient Silver Bowl for Lit., Birmingham Festival of Arts, 1982; pub. grantee NEA, 1979, 83, 88, Tex. Comm. on the Arts, 1988. Mem. Am. Lit. Translators Assn. Office: Ford-Brown & Co Pubs PO Box 2764 Boston MA 02208-2764

BROWN, THEODORE D., computer scientist, researcher; b. Bklyn., Apr. 25, 1944; s. William Brown and Alice Kormen; m. Linda Charne, June 19, 1966; children: Elicia, Nina. BME, CCNY, 1966; MS, NYU, 1968, PhD, 1971. Ops. rsch. Chem. Bank, N.Y.C., 1969-71; asst. prof. computer sci. Queens Coll., Flushing, N.Y., 1971-81, assoc. prof., 1981-91, chmn. computer sci. dept., 1988—, prof., 1991—; vis. assoc. prof. Einstein Coll. of Medicine, Bronx, N.Y., 1981. Contbr. 29 articles to profl. jours. Recipient ILI award NSF, 1987. Mem. Am. Stat. Assn., Assn. Computer Machinery, Operations Rsch. Soc. Office: Queens Coll Dept Computer Sci Flushing NY 11367

BROWN, THOMAS GLENN, college administrator; b. Portsmouth, Va., Aug. 10, 1948; s. Harold Clifford and Mary Alice (Rorie) B.; m. Civita Ann Caruso, Jan. 6, 1979; children: Amy Elizabeth Brown, Megan Glenn Brown. BA, U. Va., Charlottesville, 1970; MA, Hollins Coll., Roanoke, Va., 1972; PhD, U. Maine, Orono, 1975. Asst. prof. Utica Coll. Syracuse U., Utica, N.Y., 1975-79, assoc. prof., 1979-84, prof. psychology, 1984—, chmn. div. behavioral studies, 1983-88, dean, 1988—, v.p., 1990—. Contbr. articles to profl. jours. Recipient research grants, Nat. Inst. Mental Health. Mem. Eastern Psychological Assn., Ft. Schuyler Club, Ctr. Casaurian Studies, Utica Zoological Soc., Psi Chi, Pi Kappa Phi. Methodist. Home: 318 Graffenburg Rd New Hartford NY 13413 Office: Syracuse U Utica Coll 1600 Burrstone Rd Utica NY 13502-4857

BROWN, THOMAS H., academic administrator; b. Phila., Dec. 27, 1941; s. Alfred E. and Eleanor Phyllis (Shivers) B.; m. Tressa A. Brown, Jan. 22, 1985; children: Kelli, Jessica, Timothy, Maura, Ryan. BA, U. Md., 1963; MA, NYU, 1965, PhD, 1979. Prof. U.S. and Latin Am. History Cumberland County Coll., Vineland, N.J., 1967-72, chair dept. Social and Behavioral Sci., 1972-79, chair. div. Liberal Studies, 1979-81, dean, instr., 1981-84; v.p., instr. Mohawk Valley Community Coll., Utica, N.Y., 1984-90; pres. Union County Coll., Cranford, N.J., 1990—; rep. N.Y. State Nat. Coun. Instrnl. Adminstrs., 1987-90. Author (book) George Sewall Boutwell: Human Rights Advocate, 1989. Chmn. Cumberland County Cultural & Heritage Commn., Bridgeton, N.J., 1972-76; bd. trustees Cumberland County Hist. Soc., Bridgeton, N.J., 1976-84; chair Higher Edn.-Utica United Way, Utica, 1988-90. Named Prof. of Yr., Cumberland County Coll., 1969. Mem. Acad. Officers Assn. N.Y. and N.J., Nat. Coun. Community Svcs. and Continuing Edn., Oneida County Hist. Soc., Utica. Home: 1121 Evergreen Ave Plainfield NJ 07060-2630 Office: Union County Coll 1033 Springfield Ave Cranford NJ 07016-1598

BROWN, THOMAS HUNTINGTON, neuroscientist; b. N.Y.C., June 13, 1945; s. Thomas Huntington and Elvira R. (Crandall) B.; m. Patricia Ann Carson, Aug. 10, 1968. BA in Molecular Biology, Calif. State U.-San Jose, 1972; MA in Psychology, 1972; PhD in Neurosci., Stanford U., 1977. Postdoctoral fellow Stanford U., Calif., 1977-79; asst. rsch. scientist Beckman Rsch. Inst., Duarte, Calif., 1979-82, assoc. rsch.scientist, 1982-86, rsch. scientist, 1986-88; prof. dept. psychology Yale U., New Haven, 1988—, mem. joint appt. dept. cellular molecular physiology Yale U., 1992—, dir. Ctr. for Theoretical and Applied Neurosci., 1992—; adviser NIH, NIMH study sects., 1982-83, 89. Mem. editorial bd. Behavioral Neurosci. Jour., 1983-89, Network: Computation in Neural Systems, 1990—, Hippocampus, 1990—; contbr. articles to sci. jours., 1976—. Recipient Epilepsy Found. Am. award, 1980, McKnight Found. Scholar's award, 1981; McKnight Found. Career Devel. award, 1984; Muscular Dystrophy Found. fellow, 1977, NIH fellow, 1978; grantee in field, 1980—. Mem. AAAS, Am. Psychol. Soc., Soc. Neurosci., Internat. Neurol. Network Soc. Office: Yale U Dept Psychology PO Box 11A New Haven CT 06520-7447

BROWN, TIMOTHY SHAWN, association executive; b. Hazleton, Pa., Nov. 3, 1961; s. Hugh Thomas and Amy (Maslo) B.; m. Sheri Lynn Eshleman, June 3, 1989. BA in Journalism, Pa. State U., 1983; MA in English, George Mason U., 1990. News dir. WAZL/WVCD Radio, Hazleton, 1983-84; pub. rels. asst. EIG (Equity Investment Group), McLean, Va., 1984-85; mgr. pub. info. Water Pollution Control Fedn., Alexandria, Va., 1985-89; mgr. pub. rels. ASCE, Washington, 1989—. Editor: Public Information Manual, 1986; contbr. articles to profl. jours. Pa. State U. scholar, 1983. Mem. Am. Soc. Assn. Execs., Pub. Rels. Soc. Am., Coun. of Engring. and Sci. Soc. Execs. Office: ASCE 1015 15th St NW Ste 600 Washington DC 20005-2605

BROWN, TIMOTHY STUART, mergers and acquisitions consultant; b. Springfield, Ohio, Sept. 6, 1949; s. Vernie Leonard and Laura Jean (Pierson) B.; m. Debra Sharon Miller, May 9, 1981 (div. Jan. 24, 1984). BS, U.S. Merchant Marine Acad., 1971; MS, Penn State U., 1976. Registered profl. engr., Pa. Third engr. D.D.G. Hansa Lines, Bremen, West Germany, 1971-72; chief engr. Milchem, Morgan City, La., 1972-73; supervising inspector Hartford Steam Boiler Ins. Co., Phila., 1974-75; product mgr. Flexitallic Gasket Co., Camden, N.J., 1975-77; pres. Thermal Con-Serv Corp., Houston, 1977-85; mgmt. cons. George S. May Internat., Chgo., 1985-86; gen. mgr. R.J. Rhodes Transit Inc., Freedom, Pa., 1986-90; pres. T. Stuart Brown & Assoc., Inc., Sewickley, Pa., 1990—. patentee in field. Ltjg. USNR, 1971-75. Mem. Benevolent & Paternal Order of Elks, Frat. Order of Eagles. Office: Kasten Group Inc Ste 801A 1108 Ohio River Blvd Sewickley PA 15143

BROWN, TINA, magazine editor; b. Maidenhead, Eng., Nov. 21, 1953; d. George Hambley and Bettina Iris Mary (Kohr) B.; m. Harold Evans, Aug. 20, 1981; children: George Frederick, Isabel Harriet. M.A., Oxford U. Columnist Punch Mag., London, 1978; editor in chief Tatler Mag., London, 1979-83, Vanity Fair Mag., N.Y.C., 1984-92; editor New Yorker Mag., N.Y.C., 1992—. Author: (play) Under the Bamboo Tree, 1973 (Sunday Times Drama award), (play) Happy Yellow, 1977, (book) Loose Talk, 1979, (book) Life As A Party, 1983. Named Most Promising Female Journalist, recipient Kathrine Pakenham prize Sunday London Times, 1973; named Young Journalist of Yr., 1978, Mag. Editor of Yr. Advt. Age mag., 1988. Office: The New Yorker 20 W 43rd St New York NY 10036*

BROWN, WEIR MESSICK, international economist; b. Brighton, Ill., Jan. 27, 1914; s. Spencer Gilson and Nellie Rebecca (Messick) B.; m. Vivian Virginia Bauer, Apr. 24, 1942 (dec. Dec. 1981); children: Suzan L. Meves, Peter D.G. Brown; m. Maxine Glad Stewart, June 4, 1983. AB in Econs., Oberlin Coll., 1936; AM in Econs., Brown U., 1938, PhD in Econs., 1941. Various economist positions, 1938-48; with U.S. Dept. of the Treasury, Washington, 1948; fin. adviser U.S. Marshall Plan mission to the Netherlands The Hague, the Netherlands, 1949-51; chief European div. U.S. Dept. of the Treasury, Washington, 1951-52; fin. attache, Treasury rep. Am. Embassy, Bonn, Fed. Republic Germany, 1952-60; from dep. chief to acting chief U.S. mission Orgn. for Econ. Cooperation and Devel., Paris, 1961-74; fed. exec. fellow The Brookings Inst., Washington, 1974-75; inspector gen. for internat. fin. U.S. Dept. of the Treasury, Washington, 1975-80; pvt. practice econ. cons. Washington, 1981—; guest scholar The Brookings Inst., Washington, 1985-91; cons. Atlantic Coun. U.S., Washington, 1977-83, U.S. Dept. State, Washington, 1986; vis. prof. econs. dept. U. Ill., Urbana, 1975. Author: Keeping the Central Bank Central, 1987, Bank Lending to Business Borrowers, 1992; contbr. articles to econ. jours., 1948-80; mem. of panel, published reports Atlantic Coun., 1979-83. Mem. steering com. Friends of Music at Smithsonian, Washington, 1982—; mem. bd. Friday Morning Music Club, Washington, 1984-88. Lt. (j.g.) USNR, 1943-46. Mem. Am. Econ. Assn., Nat. Economists Club, Cosmos Club. Democrat. Home: 4100 Cathedral Ave NW # 702 Washington DC 20016-3584

BROWN, WILLIAM LEWIS, financial executive; b. East Mecca, Ohio, Jan. 25, 1926; s. Emerson Wheeler and Helen Grace (Lewis) B.; m. Joy Anne Sagle, June 24, 1950 (div. 1975); children: Marla, Cynthia, Valerie, Eric; m. Carolyn Ann Neuberg, Aug. 1, 1975; stepchildren: Cynthia, Brian, Sharon; 1 child, Nancy. BA in Sociology, Ohio State U., 1950, cert. in nursing home adminstrn., 1975; cert. in nursing home adminstrn., Garrett Theol. Sem., 1975, BDiv, 1953, MDiv, 1962. Sr. minister Delason Meth. Ch., Youngstown, Ohio, 1953-60; with Wesley Meml. Meth. Ch., Youngstown, 1953-60; sr. minister Lisbon (Ohio) United Meth. Ch., 1960-63; sr. minister First United Meth. Ch., Norwalk, Ohio, 1963-67, North Canton, Ohio, 1967-74; asst. chief exec. officer Copeland Oaks Retirement Community, Sebring, Ohio, 1974-77; chief exec. officer Wesley United Meth. Ch., Meadville, Pa., 1977—; chair Eagle com. United Meth. Nat. Orgn., Dayton, Ohio, 1986-91. Chair Meml. Day com. Meadville City, 1985-89, vice chair bi-centennial com., 1987-88. Staff sgt. USAF, 1944-46, CBI. Named Man of the Yr., Lisbon C. of C., 1966, Adminstr. of the Yr., United Meth. Ch., 1989. Fellow Am. Coll. Health Care Adminstrs.; mem. Pa. Assn. Non-Profit Homes (treas. 1988—), Kiwanis (pres. Meadville chpt. 1984-85), Shriners (pres. Meadville chpt. 1987-88). Republican. Home: 1309 Sarah Dr Meadville PA 16335-8413 Office: Meth Community 31 Park Ave Meadville PA 16335-9430

BROWNE, CHARLIE, communications executive; b. N.Y.C., Jan. 18, 1948; s. Charles Butler Browne and Maxine (Marshall) Odenwald; m. Eileen Ruth Semelka, Jan. 30, 1971; children: Shannon Eileen, Charles Butler IV. BA, Valparaiso U., 1970. Copywriter J.C. Penney Co., N.Y.C., 1971-72; head copywriter Elliott Hirsch Advt., White Plains, N.Y., 1972-75; direct mail dir. Am. Consumer, Westport, Conn., 1975-80; pres. Charlie Browne Communications, Newtown, Conn., 1980—; cons. Political Cons. of Fairfield County, Newtown, Conn., 1978—. active mem. Newtown Dem. Town Com., Conn., 1978—; justice of the peace State of Conn., 1985—. Democrat. Lutheran. Office: Charlie Browne Communications 9 Hawthorne Hill Rd Newtown CT 06470-1404

BROWNE, DONALD VICTOR, journalist; b. Passaic, N.J., May 16, 1943; s. Donald James and Roseanna (Hopp) B.; m. Maria Junquera, May 9, 1981; children: Christopher Barret, Ryan Alexander. BS in Mktg., Fairleigh Dickinson U., 1971. Traffic expediter CBS News, N.Y.C., 1967-70, producer, 1970-71, reporter, assignment editor, 1971-75; producer, dep. bur. chief CBS News, Atlanta, 1975-79; bur. chief, Fla., Latin Am. NBC News, Miami, Fla., 1979-88, bur. chief, Latin Am., S.E. U.S., 1988-89; exec. news dir. NBC News, N.Y.C., 1989-90, exec. v.p., 1990—. With USCG, 1967-73.

BROWNE, HOWARD STORM, orthopaedic surgeon; b. Ponca City, Okla., July 1, 1925; s. Howard STorm and Margaret May (Melvin) B.; m. Doris Mae Cox, Nov. 26, 1949; children: Stephen W., Catharine, Elizabeth, Alastair. Student, U. Okla., 1942-44; MB, Northwestern U., Chgo., 1948; MD, Northwestern U., 1949. Diplomate Am. Bd. Orthopaedic Surgery. Pvt. practice Newport, R.I., 1967-78; course dir. Harvard Orthopaedic Residency Program Faculty, Boston, 1979—; cons. orthopedic surgery RI Group Health/Harvard Community Health Plan, Providence, 1981-92; med. expert Social Security Hearings & Appeals, Providence, 1987—. Author: The Newport Hospital: A History, 1974; editor: So Few the Brave, 1976; editor Mil. Collector and Historian Jour., 1977-85; reviewer Jour. Bone and Joint Surgery, 1980—; contbr. articles to profl. jours. Bd. dirs., chmn. pubs. com. Newport Hist. Soc., 1985—; trustee Long Wharf Assn., Newport, 1985—; cons. Seaport '76, 1976—; sec. Newport & Old Colony R.R., Newport, 1980—. Capt. USN, 1943-67. Recipient Alan Weaver Hazleton award Mil. Order St. Lazarus of Jerusalem. Fellow Am. Acad. Orthopaedic Surgeons, Med. Soc. London; mem. R.I. Orthopaedic Soc. (pres. 1976-78), Venerable Order of St. John of Jerusalem in the Brit. Realm, The Newport Reading Rm. (gov. 1979-82), The Savile Club (London), The Naval Club (London), N.Y. Yacht Club, Nat. Tennis Club (Newport). Episcopalian. Home and Office: 24 Kay St Newport RI 02840-2792

BROWNE, JEFFREY FRANCIS, lawyer; b. Clare, South Australia, Australia, Mar. 1, 1944; came to U.S., 1975; s. Patrick Joseph and Irene Kathleen (Cormack) B.; m. Deborah Mary Christine West, Aug. 28, 1971; children: Veronique Namur Irene, Jeffrey James, Nicholas Patrick, Sophie Christina, Amy Elizabeth. LLB, Adelaide U., South Australia, 1966; LLM, Sydney U., Australia, 1968, Harvard U., 1976. Bar: South Australia 1969, Australian Capital Territory 1973, N.Y. 1978, Victoria 1982, New South Wales 1983, Western Australia 1983. Assoc. High Ct. Australia, Canberra, Australian Capital Territory, 1967-68; diplomat Dept. Fgn. Affairs, Canberra, 1969; 2d sec. Australian High Commn., London and Malaysia, 1970-71; acting high commr. Australian High Commn., Ghana, 1972; counsel nuclear tests case Internat. Ct. Justice, 1973-74; assoc. Sullivan & Cromwell, N.Y.C., 1976-81, ptnr., 1983—; gen. counsel Alcoa of Australia, Melbourne, 1981-82; bd. dirs. Compinvest Pty. Ltd. Mem. Law Inst. Victoria, Australian Mining and Petroleum Law Assn., Law Coun. Australia (chmn. fin. and securities subcom., internat. trade and bus. law com.), Inst. Dirs. of Australia, Internat. Bar Assn. (sect. on energy and natural resources), Am. C. of C. in Australia (bd. dirs.), Am. Soc. Internat. Law, N.Y. Yacht Club, Australia Club (Melbourne). Office: Sullivan & Cromwell 125 Broad St New York NY 10004-2400 also: 140 William St, Melbourne Victoria 3000, Australia

BROWNELL, HIRAM HENRY, psychology educator; b. Northampton, Mass., Oct. 13, 1952; s. William Henry and Nancy (Bowker) B. BA, Sanford U., 1974; MA, Johns Hopkins U., 1976, PhD, 1978. Asst. prof. psychologoy U. So. Calif., L.A., 1978-80; rsch. psychologist dept. vets. affairs VA Med. Ctr., Boston, 1980—; asst. prof. neurology Boston U. Sch. Medicine, 1983-87, adj. asst. prof., 1987—; asst. prof. psychology Boston Coll., Chestnut Hill, 1987-91, assoc. prof. psychology, 1991—. Editorial bd. Brain and Language, 1987—; editor: Discourse Ability and Brain Damage, 1990; contbr. articles to profl. jours. Rsch. grantee VA, NIH, Div. Stroke and Trauma, 1991—. Mem. APA, Acad. Aphasia, Internat. Neuropsychol. Soc. Office: Boston Coll Dept Psychology Chestnut Hill MA 02167

BROWNELL, KELLY DAVID, psychologist, educator; b. Evansville, Ind., Oct. 31, 1951; s. Arnold Buffum and Margaret Elizabeth (Egly) B.; m. Mary Jo Gabriele, Aug. 20, 1977; children: Matthew Joseph, Kevin David, Kristy Elizabeth. BA, Purdue U., 1973; PhD, Rutgers U., 1977. Lic. clin. psychologist, Pa. Postdoctoral fellow Brown U., Providence, 1977; asst. prof. U. Pa., Phila., 1977-82, assoc. prof., 1982-87, prof., 1987-90; prof. psychology Yale U., New Haven, Conn., 1991—; prof. epidemiology and pub. health Yale U., New Haven, co-dir. Yale Ctr. for Eating and Weight Disorders. Author: Handbook of Behavioral Medicine, 1988, Handbook of Eating Disorders, 1986, Eating Disorders in Athletes, 1991; contbr. more than 100 articles to profl. jours. Recipient Cattell award N.Y. Acad. Scis., 1978, Choice award ALA, 1989. Fellow Am. Psychol. Assn. (pres. div. health psychology 1989-90), Soc. Behavioral Medicine (pres. 1988-89), Acad. Behavioral Medicine Rsch.; mem. Assn. for Advancement Behavior Therapy (pres. 1988-89). Office: Yale U Dept Psychology PO Box 11A New Haven CT 06520-7447

BROWN-GRIFFIN, SHELLEY ELIZABETH, kindergarten educator; b. Phillipsburg, N.J., July 3, 1949; d. Roland Russling and Elizabeth Annette (Roby) Brown; m. Ron William Griffin, Sept. 27, 1986; 1 child, Brent William. AA, Centennary Coll., 1969; BS in Edn., Millersville U., 1971; MA in Student Pers. Svcs., Glassboro State Coll., 1987. Cert. elem. educator, student pers. svcs., substance awareness coord. Counselor St. Francis Counseling Svc., Long Beach Island, N.J., 1986-88; kindergarten tchr. Stafford Twp. Schs., Manahawkin, N.J., 1971-92; guidance counselor McKinley Ave Sch., Manahawk, 1992—. Named Tchr. of Yr., Stafford Twp. Bd. Edn., Manahawkin, 1990-91. Mem. AACD, Assn. Sch. Counselors, N.J. Edn. Assn., N.J. Sch. Counselors Assn., Assn. Student Assistance Profls. N.J., Stafford Twp. Mcpl. Alliance. Home: 80 Pine St Tuckerton NJ 08087-9758

BROWNING, COLIN ARROTT, bank executive; b. Jersey City, June 24, 1935; s. Colin John Herbert and Ellenor May (Coughlin) B.; m. Ellen Miriam McNeill, July 18, 1964; children: Colin Robertson, Paul William. BA, Cornell U., 1957; MBA, NYU, 1964. Trust adminstr. Chase Manhattan Bank, N.Y.C., 1960-64; v.p. Midlantic Bank, Newark, 1964-70; v.p. IBJ Schroder Bank and Trust Co., N.Y.C., 1970-71, sr. trust officer, 1971-72, sr. v.p., 1972-77, exec. v.p., mem. exec. com., 1977—; chmn., pres. IBJ Schroder Internat. Bank and Trust Co., Miami, 1985—. Trustee Upper N.J. Chpt. Multiple Sclerosis Soc., Newark, 1965-72, pres. 1969-70; trustee N.J. Shakespeare Festival, 1988—. Served with intelligence corps U.S. Army, 1959-60. Mem. Corp. Fiduciaries Assn., Am. Lepidopterists Soc., Am. Orchid Soc., Xerces Soc., Pi Kappa Alpha, Beta Theta.

BROWNLEE, PAULA PIMLOTT, association president; b. London, June 23, 1934; came to U.S., 1959; d. John Richard and Alice A. (Ajamian) Pimlott; m. Thomas H. Brownlee, Feb. 10, 1961; children: Kenneth Gainsford, Elizabeth Ann, Clare Louise. B.A. with honors, Somerville Coll., Oxford (Eng.) U., 1957; D.Phil. in Organic Chemistry, Oxford (Eng.) U., 1959; Postdoctoral fellow, U. Rochester, N.Y., 1959-61. Research chemist Am. Cyanamid Co., Stamford, Conn., 1961-62; lectr. U. Bridgeport, Conn., 1968-70; from asst. to assoc. prof. chemistry Rutgers U., N.J., 1970-76, assoc. dean, then acting dean Douglass Coll., 1972-76; dean faculty, prof. chemistry Union Coll., Schenectady, N.Y., 1976-81; pres., prof. chemistry Hollins (Va.) Coll., 1981-90; pres. Assn. Am. Colls., Washington, 1990—. Author articles, lab. manual. Bd. dirs. C&P Telephone Co. Va.; vice chair Ednl. Testing Svc., U. Rochester Nat. Humanities Ctr., Assn. Religion in Intellectual Life. Mem. Am. Chem. Soc., Royal Chm. Soc. London, Soc. Values in Higher Edn., Cosmos Club, Sigma Xi. Episcopalian. Office: Assn Am Colls 1818 R St NW Washington DC 20009-1692

BROWNLOW, DONALD GREY, educator; b. Germantown, Pa., Jan. 17, 1923; s. John Charles Victor and Ruth (Hutchinson) B.; m. Sandra Barbara Dobbs, July 16, 1987; children: Kendall Hutchinson, Pamela Cooke, Douglas Grey, Priscilla Dobbs. Student U. Zürich, 1946-47; BA, U. Pa.,

1948, MA, 1949. Rsch. libr. Presbyn. Hist. Soc., Phila., 1949-50; master Am. history and internat. rels. Haverford (Pa.) Sch., 1951—; dir. Haverford Tours, 1956-75, 81—; mem. faculty grad. div. Pa. State U., 1966—; cons. Imperial War Mus., London. Chmn. Planning Bd. West Nantmeal Twp., 1964-71; mem. Emergency Com. Chinese Refugees, 1962, Com. of One Million; chmn. Zoning Hearing Bd., Warwick Twp., 1976-84; bd. dirs. Gt. Valley Assn., 1959-62; mem. planning bd. Ctr. Teaching Ams., Immaculata Coll., 1961-69; eagle scout Boy Scouts Am., 1939, quartermaster sea scout, 1943. Served to maj. AUS, 1942-64. Recipient Valley Forge Freedoms Found. medal, 1962; Suez medal from gov. Suez, UAR, 1966; named Citizen of Honor of Utah Beach, Mayor of Sainte-Marie-du-Mont, France, 1975. Mem. Am. Hist. Assn., Paoli Meml. Assn., Germantown Hist. Soc., Chester County Hist. Soc., Smithsonian Assos., Geneal. Soc. Pa., Pa. Soc., Am. Mus. Natural History, Res. Officers Assn., Soc. Am. Magicians., Nat. Audubon Soc., Nat. Trust for Hist. Preservation, Zool. Soc. Phila., Am. Legion. Republican. Episcopalian. Author: Documentary History of the Paoli Massacre, 1952; Documentary History of the Battle of Germantown, 1955; the Battle of Brandywine, 1957; The Accused: The Ordeal of Rear Admiral Husband E. Kimmel, USN, 1968; Panzer Baron: The Military Exploits of General Hasso von Manteuffel, 1975; Checkmate at Ruweisat: Auchinleck's Finest Hour, 1977; Hell Was My Home, 1983; author, producer Haverford School Faces the Cold War, Vol. 1, 1962, Vol. 2, 1963. Home: RD 1 Box 161 Redding Furnace Rd Elverson PA 19520 Office: Haverford Sch Haverford PA 19041

BROWNSTEIN, HOWARD, otolaryngologist; b. N.Y.C., June 25, 1933; s. Sol and Irene (Karp) B.; married, May 21, 1978; children: Stacey, Justin. BS, Columbia U., 1956; MD, St. Andrews U., 1961. Diplomate Am. Bd. Otolaryngology. Intern Meadowbrook Hosp., East Meadow, N.Y., 1961-62; resident N.Y. Eye and Ear Infirmary, N.Y.C., 1963-66; pvt. practice Bklyn., 1966—; chief otolaryngology Hempstead Gen. Hosp., 1986—; assoc. chief otolaryngology Luth. Med. Ctr., Bklyn., 1988—. Fellow ACS, Am. Acad. Facial Plastic and Reconstructive Surgery, Am. Acad. Otolaryngology; mem. Kings County Soc. Otolaryngology (pres. 1975-77). Office: 9602 4th Ave Brooklyn NY 11209-7851

BROWNSTEIN, VIVIAN CARMEL, economist, journalist; b. Oakland, Calif., Sept. 4, 1930; d. Alexander Moses and Miriam (Shapiro) Rosenson; m. Edward J. Brownstein, June 25, 1967; children: Alison Jane, Katherine Samantha. BA, George Washington U., 1952. Staff economist Bd. Govs. FRS, Washington, 1953-59, Com. for Econ. Devel., N.Y.C., 1959-60; assoc. economist Fortune Mag., N.Y.C., 1960-68, 76-88, writer, 1976—, sr. economist, bd. editors, 1989-91, chief economist, bd. editors, 1991—. Mem. Am. Econ. Assn., Nat. Assn. Bus. Economists, N.Y. Assn. Bus. Economists, Downtown Economists (v.p. 1991-92). Office: Fortune Mag 1271 Ave of Americas Rm 1569 New York NY 10020

BROWNSTONE, HUGH MICHAEL, banker; b. N.Y.C., Feb. 18, 1957; s. Paul Lotan and Enid Barbara (Klein) B.; m. Laura Jane Kaplon, June 2, 1985; 1 child, Sydney Victoria. BA in Psychology, Cornell U., 1979; MBA in Fin., U. Pa., 1981. Sr. bus. analyst Am. Mgmt. Systems, N.Y.C., 1981-83, 84-85, prin., 1985-86; owner H.M. Brownstone Cons., N.Y.C., 1983-85; v.p., software devel. Barclays Bank, PLC, N.Y.C., 1986-88, v.p. and mgr., MIS Group, 1988-89, v.p. and mgr., corp. banking systems and ops., 1989-90, v.p. and mgr. banking tech. unit, 1989-91, v.p. strategic planning, 1991; sr. v.p. and dir. info. tech. strategy, investment banking Barclays Bank, PLC, 1992—; mem. Conf. Bd. Internat. Coun. on Mgmt. Innovation and Tech. Mem. The Mus. of Modern Art, N.Y.C. Recipient award for Innovative Microcomputer Application in Major Corp., Nat. Inst. Mgmt. Rsch., 1987. Mem. Assn. Computing Machinery. Office: Barclays Bank PLC 75 Wall St New York NY 10265-0002

BROWN-WEST, ORIKAYE GOGO, engineering executive, academic administrator; b. Buguma, Rivers, Nigeria, Aug. 24, 1945; came to U.S., 1977; s. Gogo Elliott and Finta (Johnson) Brown-West; m. Anne Prudence Medinus, Apr. 19, 1980; children: Diepriye, Isoboye, Abiye, Otonye, Boma, Obele, Nonye. MS, N.Y. Poly. U., 1978, 79; PhD, U. Conn., 1983. Field engr. Shell, B.P., Port-Harcourt, Nigeria, 1973-75, asst. head dept. civil planning, 1975-76; spl. rsch. fellow Office of Sci. and Tech. UN, N.Y.C., 1978-79; assoc. prof. Tuskegee (Ala.) U., 1984-88; v.p. Oriann Interests, Inc., Salisbury, Md., 1986—; dir. capital planning U. Md., Princess Anne, 1988-91; asst. v.p. facilities planning and mgmt. Bridgewater (Mass.) State Coll., Bridgewater, Mass., 1992—; dir. Archtl. Title III Tuskegee U., 1984-88; tech. advisor Minority Bus. Devel. Ctr., Montgomery, Ala., 1985-87; cons. FAA, Montgomery, 1986. Contbr. articles to profl. jours. Booster Ala. State Troopers Assn., Montgomery, 1985-87; treas. St. Bedes Sch. PTA, Montgomery, 1987-88. Mem. ASCE, Am. Inst. Constructors, Nat. Soc. Profl. Engrs., N.Y. Acad. Scis., Constrn. Surveyors Inst. Great Britain, Inst. Transp. Engrs., Sigma Xi, Sigma Lambda Chi. Home: 812 Upland Dr Salisbury MD 21801-7468 Office: Bridgewater State Coll Bridgewater MA 02325

BROWNWOOD, DAVID OWEN, lawyer; b. L.A., May 24, 1935; s. Robert Scott Osgood and Ruth Elizabeth (Bellamy) B.; m. Sigrid Carlson, Mar. 3, 1956 (div. 1972); children: Jeffrey Owen, Kirsten, Scott David, Daniel Stuart; m. Susan Sloane Jannicky, July 4, 1975; 1 child, Mary Ruth Bellamy; stepchildren: Bradbury, Stephanie Ellington. AB with distinction, Stanford U., 1956; LLB magna cum laude, Harvard U., 1964. Bar: Calif. 1965, N.Y. 1969. Assoc. McCuthen, Doyle, Brown & Emersen, San Francisco, 1964-66; lectr. law U. Khartoum, Sudan, 1966-67, Kenya Inst. Adminstrn., Lower Kabete, 1967-68; assoc. Cravath, Swaine & Moore, N.Y.C., 1968-72, ptnr., 1973—; treas. N.Y. Law Inst., 1978-83, chmn. exec. com., 1983-88, pres., 1988—. Mem. editorial bd. Harvard U. Law Rev., 1963-64. Dir. Literacy Assistance Ctr., N.Y.C., 1983—, co-chmn., 1987—; trustee Greenwich (Conn.) Country Day Sch., 1985—, v.p., 1986-88, pres., 1988—; trustee Harvard U. Law Sch. Assn. of N.Y.C., 1974-77; co-chmn. Harvard U. Law Sch. 25th Reunion Gift, 1988-89; nat. chair Harvard U. Law Sch. Fund, 1991—, N.Y. regional com. campaign for Harvard Law Sch., 1991—; com. on univ. resources Harvard U., 1991—; keystone regional vice chair centennial campaign Stanford U., 1986-92. 1st lt. USAF, 1956-61, capt. USAF Res., Mass. Air N.G., 1961-66. Fellow Am. Bar Found., N.Y. State Bar Found.; mem. ABA, N.Y. State Bar Assn., Assn. of Bar of City of N.Y., Stanford Assocs., Field Club (Greenwich), Sankaty Head Club (Nantucket), Siasconset Casino Assn. (Nantucket), Harvard Club (N.Y.C.), Chi Psi. Home: 296 Old Church Rd Greenwich CT 06830-4823 also: 39 Baxter Rd Siasconset MA 02564 Office: Cravath Swaine & Moore 825 8th Ave New York NY 10019-7416

BROZEK, JOSEF, psychology educator, scientist; b. Melnik, Bohemia, Aug. 14, 1913; came to U.S., 1939, naturalized, 1945; s. Josef Francis and Filomena (Sourek) B.; m. Eunice Magnuson, Mar. 23, 1945; children: Josef, Margaret, Peter. Ph.D., Charles U., Prague, Czechoslovakia, 1937. Asst. dept. philosophy Charles U., 1936-37; psychotechnologist Bata Shoe Co., Zlin, Czechoslovakia, 1937-39; jr. psychologist lab. physiol. hygiene Sch. Pub. Health, U. Minn., 1941-43, assoc. scientist, 1943-44, asst. prof., 1944-49, assoc. prof., 1949-56, prof., 1956-59; prof. psychology, chmn. dept. Lehigh U., Bethlehem, Pa., 1959-63, research prof., 1963-79, adj. prof. psychology, 1982-84; resident coordinator UN Univ. World Hunger Program, M.I.T., 1980-81; vis. prof. U. Passau, Fed. Republic of Germany, 1986, 87; bd. dirs. Archives of the History Am. Psychology U. Akron, 1971—; dir. Summer Inst. Hist. Psychology, U. N.H., 1968, Lehigh U., 1971; adviser nutrition WHO, 1964-68, 73; mem. U.S. Malnutrition Panel, U.S.-Japan Coop. Med. Sci. Program, 1973-78; mem. com. on nutrition, brain devel and behavior Food and Nutrition Bd., NRC, 1974-79, chmn., 1980. Author: Soviet Studies on Nutrition and Higher Nervous Activity, 1962, Malnutrition and Human Behavior, 1985; co-author: The Biology of Human Starvation, 1950, J.E. Purkyně and Psychology, 1987; editor, contbr.: Symposium on Nutrition and Behavior, 1957, Body Measurements and Human Nutrition, 1956, Performance Capacity A Symposium, 1961, Techniques for Measuring Body Composition, 1961, Body Composition, 1963, Human Body Composition, 1965, The Biology of Human Variation, 1966, Physical Growth and Body Composition, 1970, Origins of Psychometry, 1970, Psychology in the USSR, 1972, R.I. Watson's Selected Papers on the History of Psychology, 1977, Behavioral Effects of Energy and Protein Deficits, 1979, Historiography of Modern Psychology, 1980, Explorations in the History of Psychology in the United States, 1983, Malnutrition and Behavior: Critical Assessment of Key Issues, 1984, G.T. Fechner and Psychology, 1988; collaborator: The Influence of European Thought on the Development of American Psychology: The First Decades, 1988; adv. editor: Slavic lits. Contemporary Psychology, 1960-79; mem. editorial bd. Jour. of History of Behavioral Scis, 1976—, Revista de Historia de la Psicología, 1980-90, Storia e Critica della Psicologia, 1980-84, Archiv für Psychologie, 1980-91, Storia della Psycologia, 1989—, Archivo Latino-americano de la Psicologia y Ciencias Afines, 1989—. Sr. Fulbright rsch. fellow U. Würzburg, Fed. Republic Germany, 1979-80, Inst. for Psychology exch. fellow Czechoslovak Acad. Scis., 1973, 85, 90, 92. Mem. AAAS, Am. Psychol. Assn., Am. Psychol. Soc., History of Sci. Soc., Pavlovian Soc., Deutsche Gesellschaft für Psychologie, Internat. Soc. for the History Behavirol and Social Scis., European Soc. for the History Behavioral and Social Scis., Sigma Xi. Home: 265 E Market St Bethlehem PA 18018-6231

BRUBAKER, JAMES EDWARD, engineer; b. Chgo., Feb. 24, 1935; s. Samuel James and Mary Louise (Alward) B.; m. Phyllis Ann Evans, Aug. 18, 1956; children: David, Richard, Lisa, Mark. BS in Gen. Engring., U. Ill., 1956. Instr. engring. U. Ill., 1956-57; mgr. mechanism devel., advanced reactor control devel. Westinghouse Elec. Corp., Pitts., 1959-75, prin. engr. Clinch River Breeder Reactor Project, 1975-83, with MX Missile Project, 1984-85, with West Valley Nuclear Demonstration, 1985-87; with mechinery tech. divsn. NAVSEA Weapons Systems, Pitts., 1987—; chmn. Mechanism Design Com., Pitts., 1965; cons. USN, USAF and DOE. Patentee in field; editor Mechanism Design Manual and Mil. Specification for Naval Reactors. Mem. Pleasant Hills Athletic Assn. (pres. 1976-77), Lions (pres. 1984-85), Phi Kappa Tau. Republican. Home: 372 Cavan Dr Pittsburgh PA 15236-4341 Office: Westinghouse MTD Pittsburgh PA 15236

BRUBAKER, MICHAEL WILLIAM, agronomist, consultant; b. Lancaster, Pa., Nov. 24, 1957; s. William Levi and Mary Alice (Swiegort) B.; m. Cindy Jo Asprił; children: Alyson, Christopher, Ryan. Student, W.Va. U., 1981. Pres. Brubaker Agronomic Cons. Svc. Inc., Lititz, Pa., 1978—, Nutrient Resource Mgmt. Inc, 1987—, Turf Mgmt. Assocs., 1986—. Editor BACS Farms Newsletter. Supervisor Warwick Twp., Lititz, 1988; vice chmn. Lancaster Co. Assn. Twp. Supervisors. Named Outstanding Community Leader, Lititz Jaycees, 1991; Communicator of Yr., 1991. Mem. Keystone Farm Credit ACA (bd. dirs. Shoemakersville, Pa. chpt. 1989—), Lancaster C. of C. (chmn. agr. com. 1991—). Republican. Lutheran.

BRUCE, (MARY) CHARLOTTE, producer, performer, playwright, musician, singer; b. Atlanta, May 7, 1921; d. Harris Josephus and Nell Idolyn (Menkee) B.; m. John King Roosa Jr., Oct. 31, 1947; children: Janet Marijka, Robert Bruce, John King III. Student, Bergen Community Coll., Paramus, N.J. Tchr. Tenafly (N.J.) Adult Edn., 1985—; pres. Deirdre Prodns., Inc., Englewood, N.J., 1989—. Author: T'Nod, The Fat Frog, 1984, The Fairy Clan, 1984, Clarence, The Bug You Could Hug, 1991; (opera-drama) The Eagle Among Ravens, 1990; co-producer Barn Dinner Theatre, 1966. With USO, 1945-46. Mem. Actors Equity (life), Dramatists Guild, Bruce Internat., Family of Bruce Soc. in Am. Democrat. Home and Office: 143 Tenafly Rd Apt 3F Englewood NJ 07631-2252

BRUCE, JOHN FOSTER, lawyer; b. Washington, Aug. 19, 1940; s. John Gregory and Zilpha (Foster) B. BA, George Washington U., 1962; LLB, U. Va., 1965; LLM, George Washington U., 1966. Bar: D.C. 1966, U.S. Ct. Internat. Trade 1982, U.S. Ct. Mil Appeals 1970, U.S. Ct. Appeals (D.C. cir.) 1966, U.S. Ct. Appeals (fed. cir.) 1986, U.S. Supreme Ct. 1968. Teaching fellow George Washington U. Sch. Law, Washington, 1965-66; law clk. to judge U.S. Ct. Appeals (D.C. cir.), Washington, 1966-67; ptnr. Howrey & Simon, Washington, 1968—. Contbr. articles to ABA Antitrust Jour., 1968-74, ABA Bus. Lawyer, 1983. Mem. ABA (antitrust, internat. law, litigation and bus. law sects.), D.C. Bar Assn., Met. Club, Army and Navy Club. Mem. Christian Ch. (Disciples of Christ). Office: Howrey & Simon 1730 Pennsylvania Ave NW Washington DC 20006-4706

BRUCE, KERRY WILLIAM, physical education educator, sales associate; b. York, Pa., June 20, 1948; s. William Lloyd and Kathryn (Myers) B.; m. Marian Theresa Mancini, June 21, 1969. BS in Health and Phys. Edn., Lock Haven (Pa.) State Coll., 1970. Tchr. elem. Pasadena (Md.) Elem. Sch., 1970—; part-time pool mgr. Village Sq. Apts., Glen Burnie, Md., 1971-74; part-time gymnastics coach Tumbleweeds Gymnastics, Glen Burnie, 1974-77; part-time security squad leader Merriweather Post Pavilion, Columbia, Md., 1977-80; part-time asst. mgr. Record & Tape Collector, Pasadena, 1980-86; part-time sales clk. Best Products, Glen Burnie, 1988—; asst. wrestling coach Andover Sr. High Sch., Linthicum, Md., 1972-74; head gymnastic coach N.E. Sr. High Sch., Pasadena, 1975, Chesapeake Sr. High Sch., Pasadena, 1987—, asst. track coach, 1977-78. Recipient Citation, Gov. of Md., 1991. Mem. Md. Congress of Parents and Tchrs. (life). Democrat. Lutheran. Home: 6506 Pampano Dr Glen Burnie MD 21061-1421 Office: Pasadena Elem Sch 105 Spruce Ave Pasadena MD 21122-4399

BRUCE, MARTIN MARC, psychologist, publisher; b. N.Y.C., Mar. 28, 1923; s. David Isaac and Sarah Miriam (Rosen) B.; m. Betty Krassner, Aug. 16, 1942; children: Laurance David, Barbara Ann Elish. BSS, CCNY, 1946; MA, Columbia U., 1947; PhD, NYU, 1952. Psychologist, instr. Dept. Correction, N.Y.C., 1946; rsch. psychologist Office of Adj. Gen. War Dept., N.Y.C., 1946-47; chief psychologist Pers. Inst., N.Y.C., 1947-50; pub. Martin M. Bruce, PhD, Publishers, Larchmont, N.Y., 1949—; pvt. practice N.Y.C., New Rochelle, Larchmont N.Y., 1949-91; psychologist Dunlap & Assocs., Inc., Stamford, Conn., 1950-58; psychologist, v.p. Clark Channel, Inc., Stamford, 1958. Author, editor numerous psychol. tests; editor 4 books; contbr. articles to profl. jours. County Dem. committeeman, N.Y.C., 1953. With USAAF, 1942-46. Fellow APA (treas. conv. 1955); mem. Ea. Psychol. Assn. (treas. 1956-62, bd. dirs. 1956-62), Am. Guidance and Pers. Assn., N.Y. State Psychol. Assn., N.Y. Clin. Psychol. Assn., Soc. Projective Techniques. Home: 50 Larchwood Rd PO Box 248 Larchmont NY 10538 Office: Martin M Bruce PhD Pubs PO Box 248 50 Larchwood Rd Larchmont NY 10538

BRUCE, NEAL DOUGLAS, metal products executive; b. Kansas City, Kans., Mar. 16, 1969; s. Ralph Gordon and Suzanne (Cordil) B. BS, Boston Coll., 1991. V.p. Internation Bus. and Investment Corp., Boston, 1991—. Mem. Christian Ch. Office: Internation Bus and Investment Corp 9 Commonwealth Ct Ste 10 Boston MA 02135

BRUCE, ROBERT VANCE, historian, educator; b. Malden, Mass., Dec. 19, 1923; s. Robert Gilbert and Bernice Irene (May) B. Student, MIT, 1941-43; BS, U. N.H., 1945; MA, Boston U., 1947, PhD, 1953. Instr. U. Bridgeport, Conn., 1947-48; master Lawrence Acad., Groton, Mass., 1948-51; research asst. to Benjamin P. Thomas, Washington, 1953-54; mem. faculty Boston U., 1955—, assoc. prof. history, 1960-66, prof., 1966-84, prof. emeritus, 1984—; vis. prof. U. Wis., Madison, 1962-63. Author: Lincoln and the Tools of War, 3d edit., 1989, 1877: Year of Violence, 3d edit, 1989., Bell: Alexander Graham Bell and the Conquest of Solitude, 2d edit. 1990, Japanese edit., 1991, Lincoln and the Riddle of Death, 1982, The Launching of Modern American Science, 2nd edit., 1988, (Pulitzer Prize, 1988); contbr. articles to profl. jours. Served with AUS, 1943-46. Guggenheim fellow, 1957-58; Henry E. Huntington fellow, 1966; recipient Pulitzer Prize in history, 1988. Fellow AAAS, Soc. Am. Historians; mem. Orgn. Am. Historians (life mem.), AAAS, Lincoln Group of Boston (pres. 1969-74), Phi Beta Kappa. Democrat. Home: 28 Evans Rd Madbury NH 03820

BRUCK, CONNIE JANE, reporter; b. Newark, May 22, 1946; d. Carl and Edith Mora (Bornstein) B.; m. Ben Schlossberg, Dec. 8, 1970 (div. 1978); 1 child, Ari. Student, Wellesley Coll., 1964-66; BA, Barnard Coll., 1968; MS, Columbia U. Sch. Journalism, 1969. Reporter Am. Lawyer Mag., N.Y.C., 1979-89; staff writer New Yorker mag., 1989—. Author: The Predators' Ball, 1988. Recipient Nat. Mag. award for Reporting, 1990.

BRUCKENSTEIN, STANLEY, chemistry educator; b. Bklyn., Nov. 1, 1927; s. Morris and Rose (Kaltoon) B.; m. Pearl Yavel, Sept. 3, 1950; children: Barbara Bruckenstein Kanter, David Avrom, Lisa Sarah Bruckenstein Cole. BS, Poly. Inst. Bklyn., 1950; PhD, U. Minn., 1954. Instr. U. Minn., Mpls., 1954-55, asst. to assoc. prof., 1955-63, chief div. analytical chemistry, 1962-68, prof., 1963-68; prof. SUNY, Buffalo, 1968—, A. Conger Goodyear Prof. dept. chemistry, 1972—, chmn. dept. chemistry, 1974-83; program dir. analytical chemistry NSF, Washington, 1985-86; cons. Argonne (Ill.) Nat. Lab., 1964-75, Los Alamos (N.Mex.) Nat. Lab., 1983-89. Contbr. articles to profl. jours. Grantee NSF, USAF Office Sci. Rsch., Office Naval Rsch. Fellow N.Y. Acad. Scis.; mem. AAAS, Am. Chem. Soc. (Schoellkopf medal Western N.Y. sect. 1987), Electrochem. Soc. Am., Soc. for Electroanalytical Chemistry (C.N. Reilley award 1991). Office: SUNY Dept of Chemistry Buffalo NY 14260

BRUCKNER, K. JEFFREY, management consultant; b. N.Y.C., June 21, 1955; s. Karl Theodore and Suzanne (Berry) B.; m. Willa Cohen, May 18, 1986; children: Joshua Stephen, Zachary Glen. BA, Harvard U., 1977. Analyst Coll. Obs. Harvard U., Cambridge, Mass., 1977-78, Comml. Union Leasing Corp., N.Y.C., 1978-79; mgr. Canavest, Inc., Dedham, Mass., 1979-82; dir. Meml. Sloan-Kettering, N.Y.C., 1982-87; mgr. Schering-Plough Corp., Madison, N.J., 1987-89; mng. dir. The DMW Group, Stamford, Conn., 1989—. Office: The DMW Group Inc 1 Canterbury Green Stamford CT 06901

BRUDNER, HELEN GROSS, social sciences educator; b. N.Y.C.; d. Nathan and Mae (Grichtman) Gross; m. Harvey Jerome Brudner, Dec. 18, 1963; children: Mae Ann, Terry Joseph, Jay Scott. B.S., NYU, 1959, M.A., 1960, Ph.D., 1973. Tchr. N.Y.C. Bd. Edn., 1959-60; instr. Pratt Inst., Bklyn., 1959-61; asst. prof. history N.Y. Inst. Tech., N.Y.C., 1961-63, dir. guidance, 1962-63; assoc. prof. Fairleigh Dickinson U., Rutherford, N.J., 1963-73, prof. history and polit. sci., 1974—, dir. Honors Coll., 1972—, chmn. dept. social sci., 1980—, pres. univ. senate, 1975-78, asst. provost, 1983—, dean, 1984; v.p. HJB Enterprises, Highland Park, N.J., 1970—; vice chmn. bd. dirs. WLC Inc., Highland Park, 1990—; cons. auto ednl. systems, 1971—; participant bd. trustees F.D.U. Contbr. articles to profl. jours. on constl. law, transfer of tech., futurism. Active NSF Women in Politics project, 1981, NEH and Woodrow Wilson Found. Consortium project Women in Am. History, Princeton, N.J., 1980, Consortium on Global Interdependence, Princeton, 1984; bd. dirs. Options Speakers Bur.; mem. Mcpl. Alliance, Highland Park; chmn. bd. dirs. Fairleigh Dickinson U. Fed. Credit Union. Recipient Woman of Yr. award Am. Businesswomen's Assn., 1980. Mem. Am. Judicature Soc., Am. Hist. Soc., Acad. Polit. Sci., Phi Alpha Theta. Office: Fairleigh Dickinson U Dept History and Polit Sci Teaneck NJ 07666 also: HJB Enterprises Inc 812 Abbott St Highland Park NJ 08904-2909

BRUENN, HOWARD GERALD, physician; b. Youngtown, Ohio, June 6, 1905; s. Alexander H. and Fanny (Bergstein) B.; m. Dorothy Conner, June 10, 1937; children: Stephen, Nancy Bruenn Clement, James. A.B., Columbia U., 1925, M.S., 1934, D.M.S., 1934; M.D., Johns Hopkins U., 1929. Diplomate: Am. Bd. Internal Medicine, Am. Bd. Cardiovascular Disease. Intern Boston City Hosp., 1929-31; asst. resident Presbyn. Hosp., N.Y.C., 1932-34; chief med. resident Presbyn. Hosp., 1934-35, attending physician, 1961—; chief cardiology Bethesda Naval Med. Center and 3d Naval Dist., 1942-46; chief Vanderbilt Cardiac Clinic, N.Y.C., 1946-70; asso. attending physician Vanderbilt Cardiac Clinic, 1946-61; clin. prof. medicine Columbia U., N.Y.C., 1962-70; cons. in medicine Columbia Med. Center, 1970—; physician to Pres. F. Roosevelt, 1944-45. Contbr. articles on cardiology to profl. jours. Served to comdr. USNR, 1942-46. Markle fellow medicine, 1935-37. Fellow Am. Heart Assn., Am. Med. Assn., Coun. of Clin. Cardiology; mem. AMA, Soc. Med. Cons. to Armed Svcs., N.Y. County Med. Soc., N.Y. Acad. Medicine, N.Y. Acad. Sci., Harvey Soc. Home: 5355 Henry Hudson Pky Apt 8F Bronx NY 10471-2837

BRUGGER, DAVID JOHN, association executive; b. Bethlehem, Pa., Feb. 5, 1943; s. Vincent Francis and Frances Stephanie (Miller) B.; m. Joanne Kay Strouf, Oct. 26, 1973. BA in Journalism, Duquesne U., 1965; MS in Theater, CUNY, 1968; postgrad., Drake U., 1973-74, Harvard U., 1980. Exec. producer KDIN-TV, Des Moines, 1968-70; prodn., ops. mgr. Iowa Pub. Broadcasting Network, Des Moines, 1970-71; network ops. mgr. Iowa Pub. Broadcasting Network, 1971-73, dir. adminstrn., 1973-77; gen. mgr. WUFT-TV-FM, Gainesville, Fla., 1977-81; dir. Broadcast Svc. Corp. for Pub. Broadcasting, Washington, 1981-83; v.p. Telecomm Corp. for Pub. Broadcasting, Washington, 1983-87; sr. v.p. Corp. Pub. for Broadcasting, Washington, 1987; pres., bd. dirs. Assn. Am.'s Pub. TV Stas., Washington, 1988—; cons. Fla. Postsecondary Edn. Planning Commn., Tallahassee, 1990, Va. Dept. Info. Technology, Richmond, 1989, Republic of China, Taipei, Taiwan, 1983, cons., lectr. Fundacion Angel Ramos, Hato Rey, P.R., 1990. Producer TV program Interracial Dating and Marriage, 1967 (N.E.T. award 1968), exec. producer TV program The Bicycle, 1968 (Ohio State award 1968). Bklyn. Coll. TV Ctr. scholar, 1965; recipient Disting. Svc. award Eastern Pub. Radio Network, 1984; named Outstanding Sr. in Journalism, Duquesne U., 1965; named to Nat. Hall of Fame, Boys and Girls Clubs Am., 1992. Mem. Nat. Boys Club Alumni Assn. (award 1988), Am. Soc. Assn. Execs. (Excellence in Govt. Rels. award 1992), Greater Washington Soc. Assn. Execs., Soc. Profl. Journalists, USIA Pvt. Sector Ctr. Roman Catholic.

BRUGGINK, ERIC G., judge; b. Kalidjati, Indonesia, Sept. 11, 1949; naturalized citizen U.S., 1961; m. Melinda Harris; children: John, David. BA in Sociology cum laude, Auburn U., 1971, MA in Speech, 1972; JD, U. Ala., 1975. Bar: Ala., D.C. Law clk. to chief judge U.S. Dist. Ct. (no. dist.) Ala., 1975-76; assoc. Hardwick, Hause & Segrest, Dothan, Ala., 1976-77; asst. dir. Ala. Law Inst., 1977-79; assoc. Steiner, Crum & Baker, Montgomery, Ala., 1979-82; dir. Office of Appeals Counsel Merit Systems Protection Bd., 1982-86; judge U.S. Ct. Claims, Washington, 1986—. Office: US Claims Ct 717 Madison Pl NW Washington DC 20005-1011*

BRUN, LESLIE ADOLPHE, investment advisor; b. Port-Au-Prince, Haiti, Aug. 3, 1952; s. Louis Adolphe and Josette (Valme) B.; m. Somi Bae, May 13, 1979 (div. Sept. 1983); m. Marcia Saar Kennedy, Jan. 7, 1984; 1 child, Michael. BS, SUNY, Buffalo, 1974. Asst. v.p. Chem. Bank, N.Y.C., 1977-82; v.p. Lloyds Internat. Corp., N.Y.C., 1982-85, E. F. Hutton & Co., Inc., N.Y.C., 1985-88; mng. dir. First Fidelity Bancorporation, Investment Banking Group, Phila., 1988-90; mgr. gen. ptnr., chief exec. officer Hamilton Ln. Advisors, Phila., 1990—. Trustee Pa. Ballet, Phila., 1990; dir. Greater Phila. (Pa.) Urban Affairs Coalition, 1990; dir., exec. com. Phila. (Pa.) Coun. Boy Scouts Am., 1990. Mem. White Manor Country Club. Republican. Home: 150 Jennifer Ln Bala Cynwyd PA 19004-2222 Office: Hamilton Ln Advisors 1411 Walnut St Ste 200 Philadelphia PA 19102

BRUNALE, VITO JOHN, aerospace engineer; b. Mt. Vernon, N.Y., July 2, 1925; s. Donato and Antoinette (Wool) B.; m. Joan Florence Montuori, Apr. 23, 1949; 1 child, Stephen. AAS, Stewart Aero. Inst., 1948; BSAE, Tri-State U., 1958; MSME, U. Bridgeport, 1966; DSc, Nev. Inst. Tech., 1973; PhD (hon.), Internat. U., Spain, 1987; DSc, Pacific Western U., 1984. Rsch. engr. Norden Labs., White Plains, N.Y., 1948-55; instr. Tri-State U., Angola, Ind., 1955-58; engring. cons. Norden Div. United Aircraft, Norwalk, Conn., 1958-67; chief engring. cons. Singer-Kearfott Corp., Pleasantville, N.Y., 1967-73; chief engr. Diagnostic/Retrieval Systems, Mt. Vernon, N.Y., 1973-76; tech. problem mgr. Fairchild Republic Co., Farmingdale, N.Y., 1977-87; sr. tech. expert Sikorsky Aircraft, 1987—; cons. in field; engring. tutor to coll. students; v.p. Lithoway, Inc., 1969-73; lectr. in field; tech. guest speaker numerous tech. soc. meetings.; participant engring. exchange program, USSR, People's Republic China. Contbr. articles to profl. jours. including Product Engring., Aviation Week, Environ. Scis. Participant U.S.A. Citizen Amb. Program. Served with USAAF, 1943-45. Decorated Purple Heart (3), Air medals, D.F.C. Tri-State U. teaching fellow, 1955-58; NSF grantee; recipient Aircraft Design award, 1948, Inst. Aero. Sci. Lecture award, 1948, Norden Rsch. award, 1963, Cost Reduction award, 1965, Singer Engring. award, 1970, 72, Fairchild outstanding achievement award, Fairchild award of excellence, 1984, Am. Biographical Inst. and Research Assn. Outstanding Performance award, 1985, Aircraft Recognition award, 1986, citation N.Y. State Assembly, 1988, Conspicuous Service Cross N.Y. State, 1988, Prisoner of War medal, 1988, others. Mem. AIAA, U.S. Naval Inst., Air Force Assn., Am. Ordnance Assn., Inst. Environ. Sci., Nat. Space Inst., K.C., VFW, DAV, Newman Club, Internat. Students Assn., Internat. Platform Assn., World Inst. of Achievement. Roman Catholic. Home: 459 Bronxville Rd Bronxville NY 10708-1102 Office: Main St Bridgeport CT 06604-5706

BRUNDA, MICHAEL JOHN, immunologist; b. Passaic, N.J., Dec. 16, 1950; s. John and Helena (Gawronsky) B.; m. Patricia Katherine Ann Mongini, July 28, 1979; children: Nicole, John. AB, U. Rochester, 1971; PhD, Stanford U., 1975. Postdoctoral fellow Nat. Jewish Hosp. & Rsch. Ctr., Denver, 1975-78; immunologist Nat. Cancer Inst., Bethesda, Md., 1978-81; sr. scientist Hoffmann-LaRoche Inc., Nutley, N.J., 1982-86, rsch. investigator, 1986-91, rsch. leader, 1991—. Contbr. more than 50 articles to profl. jours. Mem. AAAS, Soc. for Leukocite Biology, Am. Assn. Immunologists, Am. Assn. for Cancer Rsch. Office: Hoffmann-LaRoche Inc 340 Kingsland St Nutley NJ 07110-1199

BRUNDAGE, GERTRUDE BARNES, pediatrician; b. Neptune, N.J., May 13, 1941; d. John Holt and Mary Downey (Chatham) B. BS in Chemistry, Marietta Coll., 1964; MD, Jefferson Med. Coll., 1971. Diplomate Am. Bd. Pediatrics. Chemist Lederle Labs., Pearl River, N.Y., 1964-67; intern pediatrics Harrisburg (Pa.) Polyclinic Hosp., 1971-72; resident pediatrics Wilmington (Del.) Med. cTr., 1972-74; pediatrician Orange, N.J., 1974—; chief dept. pediatrics Hosp. Ctr. at Orange, 1990—. Mem. AMA, N.J. Med. Women's Assn., Am. Med. Women's Assn., Essex County Med. Soc., Med. Soc. N.J., Alpha Gamma Delta, 1st Presbyn. Ch. (elder, trustee 1982-87, 89-92). Republican. Presbyterian. Home: 18 Farrington St West Caldwell NJ 07006-7716 Office: Gertrude B Brundage MD 572 Park Ave East Orange NJ 07017-1998

BRUNDIN, JAN ROYAL, computer marketing executive; b. St. Paul, June 5, 1938; s. Milton Eric and LuVerne (Johnson) B.; m. Kathleen Marie Howard, July 4, 1964; children: Lea Marie, Keith Eric. Student, U. Minn., 1956, 61; BS in Math., U. Alaska, 1960; postgrad., U. Hawaii, 1965. V.p. product strategy Sperry Computers, Blue Bell, Pa., 1961-87; v.p. program mgmt. Multiflow Computer, Branford, Conn., 1987-88; dir. connectivity Ashton-Tate, Torrance, Calif., 1988-89; v.p. corp. mktg. Unisys, Blue Bell, 1989—; founder Corp. of Open Systems, 1985-87. Mem. Internat. Shooter Devel. Fund. Home: 1009 Saw Mill Way Lansdale PA 19446-4675 Office: Unisys PO Box 500 Blue Bell PA 19424-0001

BRUNELLE, MICHAEL JOSEPH, engineer; b. Lowell, Mass., Jan. 21, 1965; s. Donald Harold and Diane Marie (Martineau) B. BSEE, U. Lowell, 1987, MSEE, 1990. SW engr. Interleaf, Inc., Wilmington, Mass., 1988-90, Aries Tech., Inc., Lowell, 1990—. Republican. Home: 1 Appaloosa Ave Pelham NH 03076

BRUNER, WILLIAM GWATHMEY, III, lawyer; b. Gadsden, Ala., Nov. 29, 1951; s. William G. and Nicolette A. (Diprima) B.; m. Eloisa Fernandez, Aug. 7, 1976; children: Nicolette, Virginia, William, Weston. BSE, U. Mich., 1973; JD, U. Va., 1976. Bar: Ind., Pa. Assoc. Bingham, Summers, Indpls., 1976-78; corp. counsel Scott Paper Co., Phila., 1978-86; group counsel Emhart Corp., Farmington, Conn., 1986-89; corp. counsel Black & Decker, Towson, Md., 1989—. Mem. ABA (EEO com. labor and employment law sect., litigation sect.). Republican. Roman Catholic. Office: Black & Decker Corp 701 E Joppa Rd Baltimore MD 21204-5502

BRUNGRABER, ROBERT J., civil engineer, educator; b. Birmingham, Mich., Dec. 20, 1929; s. Louis Rudolph and Beatrice Emogene (Crawford) B.; B.S. in Civil Engring. (Regents Alumni scholar), U. Mich., 1951; M.S. (John McMullen scholar), Cornell U., 1956; postgrad. U. Pitts., 1957-58; Ph.D. (Ford Found. fellow), Carnegie Inst. Tech., 1963; m. Ruth Ann Rupp, June 13, 1951; children—Robert Lyman, Margaret Ruth. Field engr. Porter-Urquhart-Skidmore, Owings & Merrill, cons. engrs., Casablanca, Morocco, 1951-53; instr. Cornell U., Ithaca, N.Y., 1953-56; research engr. Alcoa Research Labs., New Kensington, Pa., 1956-60; asst. prof. civil engring. Princeton, 1962-66; assoc. prof. civil engring. Union Coll., Schenectady, 1966-68; prof. civil engring. Bucknell U., Lewisburg, Pa., 1968—, Presdl. prof., 1979-92, prof. emeritus, 1992—; founder, pres. Slip-Test, 1976; structural cons. Borough Hall, Princeton, N.J., 1966; Intergovtl. Personnel Act appointee Nat. Bur. Standards, 1974-75; structural cons. English Engring., Williamsport, Pa., 1970—, Sprout-Waldron, Muncy, Pa., 1973—; dir., treas., mem. nat. exec. com. Nat. Inst. Bldg. Scis., 1976-81. Patentee (3) in field. AAAS Congl. fellow, 1975-76. Mem. ASCE (chmn. com. lightweight alloys of metals structural div. 1969-73), Moles, Sigma Xi, Tau Beta Pi, Chi Epsilon, Phi Kappa Phi, Phi Gamma Delta. Clubs: Nassau, Cosmos. Extensive research in structural applications of aluminum, particularly welded applications, pile foundations, and slip resistance of walkway surfaces; supr. design and constrn. of Stephen J. Potter Meml. Lab., Union Coll., 1967, structural test facility at Bucknell U., 1985; designer original system for reinforcing obsolete steel truss bridges; inventor NBS-Brungraber device for measuring the slip-resistance walkway surfaces. Contbr. articles on civil engring. to profl. publs. Office: Dana Engineering Bldg Lewisburg PA 17837

BRUNI, STEPHEN THOMAS, art museum director; b. Phila., Feb. 3, 1949; s. Eugene Thomas and Frances Isabel (McMorran) B.; m. Barbara Natalie Plunket, May 13, 1949; children: Christopher Stephen, Katherine Elizabeth. BA, George Washington U., 1971. Curatorial asst. Del. Art Mus., Wilmington, 1972-74, program asst., 1974-77, adminstrv. asst., 1977-79, mgr. support svcs., 1979-82, asst. dir. adminstrn., 1982-84, dep. dir. adminstrn., 1984-85, acting dir. adminstrn., 1985-86, exec. dir., 1986—; mem. arts selection com. Del. State Arts Coun., 1985-86, State Div. Librs., 1984-86; mem. Gov.'s Arts Adv. Com., 1983-85. Mem. bd. Literacy Vols. Am. (affiliate Wilmington Libr.). Mem. Am. Assn. Mus., Assn. Art Mus. Dirs., Bd. Greater Wilmington Conv. and Visitors Bur. Lodge: Rotary. Office: Del Art Mus 2301 Kentmere Pky Wilmington DE 19806-2096

BRUNING, DONALD FRANCIS, curator; b. Boulder, Colo., Dec. 18, 1942; s. Francis and Ilse (Behrman) B.; m. Barbara Lee, Aug. 23, 1969; children: Heather, Cynthia, April. BA, Colo. U., 1966, MA, 1967, PhD, 1974. Curatorial trainee N.Y. Zool. Soc., Bronx, 1967-69, asst. curator, 1969-71, assoc. curator, 1971-74, curator, 1974-86, curator, chmn. dept. ornithology, 1986—; cons. U.S. Fish and Wildlife Svcs.; bd. dirs. Am. Pheasant and Waterfowl Soc.; founding dir. Rsch. and Conservation Found. Papua, New Guinea; dir. AAZPA, 1984-87, legis. com. chmn., 1979-84, conservation and mgmt. com. chmn., 1984-90; chmn. IUCN/ICBP Parrot Specialist Group, 1987-91. Mem. Am. Ornithologist Union, Wilson Ornithologist Soc. (life), Am. Zoo Assn. (com. chmn. 1980-90). Lutheran. Office: NY Zool Soc Bronx NY

BRUNNER, RALPH WILLIAM, public relations executive; b. Schenectady, Apr. 28, 1964; s. Otto Gustave and Marygene (Montanye) B. BS in Pub. Rels. and Journalism, Syracuse U., 1985; MBA, Boston U., 1988. Pub. rels. rep. GE, Albany, N.Y., 1984; reporter Oneida (N.Y.) Daily Dispatch, 1985; pub. rels. rep. John Hancock Fin. Svcs., Boston, 1985-89, dir. corp. pub. rels., 1989-91, dir. pub. rels., 1991—. Contbr. numerous articles to mags. and newspapers. Fundraiser, walker Project Bread, Boston, 1987—; chmn. pub. rels. com. United Ways Ea. New Eng., Boston, 1988. Recipient Outstanding Mag. Writer award Reader's Digest, 1985; scholar Assn. Profl. Communicators, 1982, Gannett Newspapers, 1985. Mem. Pub. Rels. Soc. Am., Life Ins. Assn. Mass. (pub. info. com. 1988—), Korean Inst., Publicity Club New Eng. (Bell Ringer award 1991), Beta Gamma Sigma. Office: John Hancock Fin Svcs 54th Fl 200 Clarendon St Boston MA 02116-5021

BRUNO, DAVID ALFONSE, educator, translator; b. Waterbury, Conn., Mar. 3, 1950; s. James V. and Marie E. (Scalzo) B. Cert. advanced meritorious studies European study program, Cen. Coll. Iowa, 1971-72; BA, St. Leo Coll., 1973; postgrad. U. Conn., 1974-77, 91, Fairfield U., 1978-80; MEd, U. Hartford, 1979; cert. Internat. Migrant and Bilingual Tng. Inst., SUNY, 1983. Cert. in C.P.R., Am. Heart Assn. Designer, implementer new program dept. edn. City of Waterbury, 1974-75, tchr., lang.-devel. specialist bilingual edn. and migrant edn. programs, tutorial svcs. specialist, 1975—, tchr., curriculum cons. adult and community edn. programs, part-time, 1974-80; tchr., curriculum cons. Conn. Dept. Edn., summers 1976-79. Dist. moderator Registrar of Voters, Waterbury; mem. Waterbury Town Com., 1988—; mem. New Haven, Conn. Tchrs. Ctr.; study in sign language Am. Sch. for Deaf, 1980, 86; mem. Internat. Fund for Animal Welfare. Prodn. asst., extra (film) Stanley & Iris, 1988; contbr. to lit. mags.; translator various publs. Mem. ASCD, MLA, NEA (alt. ann. rep. assembly 1985, 86), Linguistic Soc. Am., Internat. Soc. for Gen. Semanitcs, Conn. Edn. Assn. (chmn. migrant edn. com. 1980-81, Inst. Profl. Devel., Leadership cert. 1983, del. rep. assembly 1981-89), Conn. Assn. for Bilingual Bicultural Edn. (treas. 1979-83, bd. dirs. 1983-88, conf. co-planner 1982-86), Conn. Coun. Lang. Tchrs., Conn. Assn. for Pub. Adult Edn., No. Calif. Translators Assn., Am. Translators Assn. (panel moderator internat. conf. 1979), Am. Lit. Translators Assn., Am. Coun. Tchrs. Fgn. Langs., Conn. Tchrs. English to Speakers of Other Langs. (bd. dirs. 1986-90), Internat. Tchrs. English to Speakers of Other Langs. (conf. com. 1987-89), Nat. Coun. Tchrs. English, Nat. Humane Edn. Soc., Am. Assn. Tchrs. Spanish and Portuguese, Nat. Assn. for Bilingual Edn., East Park Community Assn. (pres. 1987—), Greater Waterbury Club (homecoming and reunion com. 1987), KC (grand knight 1972-73) (St. Leo, Fla.). Roman Catholic. Home and Office: Bracewood Rd Waterbury CT 06706-2409

BRUNO, GRACE ANGELIA, accountant, educator; b. St. Louis, Oct. 11, 1935; d. John E. and Rose (Goodwin) B. BA, Notre Dame Coll., 1966; MEd, So. Ill. U., 1972; MAS, Johns Hopkins U., 1983; PhD, Walden U., 1985. CPA, Mo., Md., N.J. Tchr. Sisters of Notre Dame, St. Louis, 1962-80; pres. Bruno-Potter, Inc., Avon By The Sea, N.J., 1981—; asst. treas., instr. acctg. Coll. of Notre Dame of Md., Balt., 1978-79, treas., 1979-80; asst. prof. acctg. Georgian Ct. Coll., Lakewood, N.J., 1985-91; fin. advisor James Harry Potter gold medal award, N.Y.C., 1980—. Elected to Internat. Platform Assn., 1987. Mem. AICPA, N.J. Assn. Women Bus. Owners, N.J. Soc. CPA's, St. Louis Bus. Educators (treas. 1972-73). Democrat. Roman Catholic. Home and Office: 419 3d Ave Avon By The Sea NJ 07717-1244

BRUNO, RICHARD LOUIS, psychophysiologist, educator; b. Englewood, N.J., Nov. 19, 1954; s. Louis Sebastian and Linda (Ross) B.; m. Nancy M. Frick, May 28, 1983. BA, Springfield, 1977; PhD, Yeshiva U., 1981. Clin. rsch. scientist dept. clin. psychopharmacology N.Y. State Psychiat. Inst., N.Y.C., 1978-81; fellow Columbia U., N.Y.C., 1981-84, clin. rsch. coord., asst. prof. Coll. Physicians & Surgeons, 1984-88; dir. post-polio svc., clin. psychophysiologist Kessler Inst. Rehab., East Orange, N.J., 1988—; pres. Harvest Ctr., Hackensack, N.J., 1987—; cons. VA, Bklyn., 1982-85, Social Security Adminstrn., Balt., 1986; organizer, chmn. Internat. Post-Polio Task Force, 1984—; asst. prof. U. Medicine and Dentistry N.J.-N.J. Med. Sch., 1989—. Contbr. articles to profl. jours.; editor jour. Orthopedics, 1985, 91. Adviser labor and human resources com. U.S. Senate, 1985. Grantee J.M. Found., 1982, Joel Leff Found., 1983-84, George Ohl Found., 1990, 91, 92. Mem. Am. Congress Rehab. Medicine, Assn. for Advancement of Psychophysiology and Biofeedback. Office: Kessler Inst for Rehab 240 Central Ave East Orange NJ 07018-3460

BRUNOW, GORDON PETER, lawyer, consultant; b. Alliance, Neb., Mar. 17, 1926; s. Frederick and Edna Ethel (Bussell) B.; m. Grace Dorothy Balzer (div. July, 1977)Elizabeth Jean Sullivan, Apr. 25, 1979; children: Cynthia Marie Brunow Ferraro, Glenn Keith. BS in Physics, NYU, 1955, JD, 1982. Dir. mgmt. info. systems Winchester Arms, New Haven, 1963-70; cons. Cheshire, Conn., 1970-72; dir. mgmt. info. systems P&W Machine Tool, West Hartford, Conn., 1972-73; regional dir. GSA, N.Y.C., 1973-78; cons. Sayville, N.Y., 1978-83; atty. sole practice Mattituck, N.Y., 1983—; arbitrator A.A.A., N.Y.C., 1983—, N.Y. State Cts., Mattituck, 1983—. Contbr. articles to profl. jours. Chmn. Town Blood Program, Southold, N.Y., 1983-90, Town Landfill Program, Woodbridge, Conn., 1965-70; pro bono legal svc. County of Suffolk, Hauppauge, N.Y., 1983—. Served with AUS, 1942-46, PTO. N.Y. State Regent scholar, 1952-56, J. Ben Snow Law scholar NYLS, 1979-82. Mem. ABA, N.Y. State Bar Assn. (mem. com.), Conn. Bar Assn., Suffolk County Bar Assn. (mem. com.), Soc. for Advancement Mgmt. (committeman), Data Processing Mgmt. Assn., SAR. Home and Office: Box 89P RR 2 Mattituck NY 11952

BRUNS, PAUL, food products executive; b. Manchester, Eng., Apr. 17, 1946; s. Walter Hanley and Alice Bruns; m. Janice A. Felczak, Nov. 22, 1969; children: John D., Thomas J. BS in Agr., U. Vt., 1968, MS in An. Phys. and Dairy Chemistry, 1970; PhD in Food Sci., Cornell U., 1974. Coord. tech. regulations T.J. Lipton, Inc., Englewood Cliffs, N.J., 1974-75, mgr. tech. regulations, 1975-77; mgr. tech. regulations Standard Brands, Inc., Stamford, Conn., 1977-80; dir. regulatory and consumer affairs Standard Brands, Inc., Wilton, Conn., 1980-84; dir. tech. regulatory affairs Nabisco Brands, Inc., East Hanover, N.J., 1985—; pres. Cornell Food Sci. Adv. Coun., Ithaca, N.Y., 1990—; chmn. Grocery Mfrs. Am. environ. task force, Washington, 1988—, mem. exec. tech. com., 1988—. Contbr. articles to profl. jours. Com. mem. Boy Scouts Am. Troop 36, Long Valley, N.J., 1987—. Mem. Am. Assn. Cereal Chemists (treas., bd. dirs. 1985—), Inst. Food Technologists, N.Y. Acad. Scis., N.Y. Inst. Food Technologists. Office: Nabisco Brands Inc 200 Deforest Ave East Hanover NJ 07936-1944

BRUSH, ANDREW FRANCIS, accountant; b. Syracuse, N.Y., Aug. 13, 1950; s. Joseph Robert and Irene Louise (Andrews) B.; m. Teresa Marie Karakas, July 1, 1972; children: Robert, Catherine. BS in Acctg., Syracuse U., 1972, MS in Acctg., 1977. Cost acct. Rockwell Internat., Syracuse, 1973-76, supr. cost and budgets, 1976-77, mgr. fin. planning and costs, 1977-79; plant controller Wilson Sporting Goods, Cortland, N.Y., 1979-83; plant acct. Rubbermaid-Cortland Inc., Cortland, N.Y., 1983—. Mem. Inst. Mgmt. Accts. Office: Rubbermaid-Corland Inc 106 Central Ave Cortland NY 13045-2755

BRUSILOW, SAUL, pediatrics educator; b. Bklyn., June 7, 1927; s. Samuel Michael and Marie (Arenson) B.; m. Sallie Evans (dec.); children: William, Susan, Alexander (dec.). A.B., Princeton U., 1950; M.D., Yale U., 1954. Diplomate: Am. Bd. Pediatrics, Am. Bd. Pediatric Nephrology. Intern, asst. resident Grace-New Haven Hosp., 1954-56; asst. resident Johns Hopkins U., Balt., 1956-57, research fellow, 1957-59, instr., 1959-60, asst. prof., 1960-64, assoc. prof., 1964-74, prof., 1974—. Contbr. articles on pediatrics to profl. jours.; patentee in field; author: Inborn Errors of Metabolism. Served with USNR, 1945-46. Grantee NIH, 1959—. Mem. Soc. Pediatric Research, Am. Fedn. Clin. Research, Am. Physiol. Soc., Am. Pediatric Soc. Democrat. Jewish. Home: 4804 Keswick Rd Baltimore MD 21210-2325 Office: Johns Hopkins U Sch Medicine 600 N Wolfe St Baltimore MD 21205-2104

BRUSKI, FRED JOHN, automotive executive; b. Stevens Point, Wis., May 11, 1929; s. Joseph and Helen (Cadman) B.; m. Anna M. Zehner, May 21, 1955; children: Stephen, Paul, Mary, Patricia, John. Cost acct. Oliver Corp., South Bend, Ind., 1950-52; treas. Bendix Home Appliance, South Bend, 1952-53; treas. staff Avco Corp., Cin., 1953-54; acct. Chevrolet Motor Div., Flint, Mich., 1954-60; staff auditor Gen. Motors Corp., Detroit, 1960-68; div. auditor Harrison Radiator Div., Gen. Motors, Lockport, N.Y., 1968-72; dir. acctg. Harrison Radiator Div., Gen. Motors, Lockport, 1972-79, asst. compt., 1979—. Treas. Comprehensive Health Planning Agy., Buffalo, N.Y., 1970-75, Health Systems Agy. Western N.Y., Buffalo, 1975-85; bd. mem. Profl. Med. Conduct of N.Y., Albany, N.Y., 1975-84, Lockport Meml. Hosp., 1988—; v.p. fin. Boy Scouts Am., Lewiston Trail, 1980—. With USN, 1946-50. Recipient Silver Beaver award, Boys Scouts Am., Lockport, 1978; named Man of Yr., G-9 Mgmt. Club, Lockport, 1979. Am. Legion, Lockport, KC, Lockport. Republican. Roman Catholic. Home: 7095 Fieldcrest Dr Lockport NY 14094-1611

BRUST, SUSAN MELINDA, telecommunications executive; b. N.Y.C., Sept. 27, 1951; d. Stanley Milton and Preva Joan (Simons) B.; m. William S. Boorstein; children: Jon Bradley, Leigh Rachel. BA in Geology, Hunter Coll., 1973; postgrad., Bernard Baruch Coll., 1988—, Tel Aviv U., 1971, U. Colo., 1973. Sales rep. Burroughs Corp., N.Y.C., 1976-81; pvt. network specialist Tymnet, Inc., N.Y.C., 1981-85; regional sales mgr. Dama Telecommunications, N.Y.C., 1985-87; account exec. Network Equipment Tech., N.Y.C., 1987—; ind. telecommunications cons. Brust & Assocs., N.Y.C., 1983—. Exec. bd. mem. Jewish Guild for the Blind, N.Y.C., 1975; assoc. Spl. Olympics, N.Y.C., 1984—. Mem. Nat. Tay-Sachs Found., NAFE, Assn. Women in Computing, Empire Wo/Men in Telecommunications. Democrat. Home: 21 Dante St Larchmont NY 10538-1608 Office: Network Equipment Tech 33 Whitehall St New York NY 10004-2112

BRUSTEIN, ABRAM ISAAC, insurance agent; b. Bridgeport, Conn., Jan. 14, 1946; s. Louis and Flora (Forman) B.; m. Barbara Bederick Rudman, July 3, 1969; children: Asher Jeremey, Darrah Bethany, Garrett Michael. BA, U. Conn., 1968; MS in Mgmt., Am. Coll., 1985. CLU, chartered fin. cons. Agt. N.Y. Life Ins. Co., Stamford, Conn., 1968-70, sales mgr., 1970-75; gen. mgr. N.Y. Life Ins. Co., Amherst, N.Y., 1975-79, Bala Cynwyd, Pa., 1979-87; gen. agt. Penn Mut. Life Ins. Co., Phila., 1987—; mem. rev. panel Am. Coll., Bryn Mawr, Pa., 1984—, focus group mem. Masters Degree com., 1986; lectr. local univs., 1985—. Served with USAR, 1969-75. Mem. Gen. Agts. and Mgrs. Assn. (pres. 1986-87, Nat. Mgmt. award 1978-91), Am. Soc. CLUs and Chartered Fin. Cons., Phila. Assn. Life Underwriters (pres. 1988-89), Penn Mutual Agy. Assn. (pres. 1990-91). Jewish. Club: Germantown Cricket (Phila.). Home: 730 Schlosser Rd Harleysville PA 19438-2616

BRUSTEIN, MARTIN, financial consultant; b. N.Y.C., Feb. 4, 1924; s. Max and Blanche (Haft) B.; m. Guenne Rabin (div. 1975); children: Jamie Abrams, Richard; m. Millicent Stein Cooper, May 29, 1976. Student, Swarthmore Coll., 1942-43; BS in Bus., Lehigh U., 1947. Lic. life ins., N.Y.; registered rep. N.Y. Stock Exchange. Sales mgr. S. Brustein Inc., N.Y.C., 1947-49; pres. Walter Marshall Spinning Corp., Thornton, R.I., 1949-69, Glenn Brustein Yarn Corp., N.Y.C., 1969-73; sec.-treas. Glenn of Am. Spinning Corp., Thornton, 1969-73, Jaymee Industries Inc., N.Y.C., 1971-74; pres. M. Brustein Textile Corp., N.Y.C., 1974-81; account exec. Philips Appel & Walden, N.Y.C., 1981-88; fin. cons. Robert Thomas Securities, N.Y.C., 1988—. Chmn. yarn div. United Jewish Appeal, N.Y.C., 1965. Comdg. officer USN, 1942-46. Mem. Am. Arbitration Assn., Nuveen Adv. Coun. (charter), Century Club Oppenheimer Mgmt. Corp., Fresh Meadow Country Club, Shelter Rock Tennis Club (Manhasset, N.Y.), Westhampton Sport and Tennis Club, Sigma Alpha Mu. Home: 206 Melbourne Rd Great Neck NY 11021-4913 also: Club Ln Remsenburg NY 11960 Office: Robert Thomas Securities 434 6th Ave New York NY 10011-8411

BRUSTOWICZ, ROBERT MARJAN, anesthesiologist, hospital administrator, educator; b. N.Y.C., Nov. 3, 1951; s. Stanislaw H. and Wanda F. (Seglow) B.; m. Barbara K. Soborski, May 21, 1983; children: Alexander, Katherine. BA summa cum laude, Adelphi U., 1973; MD, Baylor Coll. Medicine, 1976. Diplomate Am. Bd. Anesthesiology, Am. Bd. Quality Assurance and Utilization Review Physicians. Intern/resident Baylor Affiliated Hosps., Houston, 1977, Columbia-Presbyn. Med. Ctr., N.Y.C., 1977-79; instr. anesthesia Harvard Med. Sch., Boston, 1981-88, asst. prof. anesthesia, 1988—; med. dir. dept. risk and utilization mgmt. Children's Hosp., Boston, 1990—; med. dir. recovery rm. Children's Hosp., Boston, 1981—; cons. Project Hope, Am. Children's Hosp., Krakow, Poland, 1989-91. Assisted (cons.) editorial bds. Anesthesia and Analgesia, 1987-88, Quality Rev. Bull., 1990; lectr., presenter in field. Recipient award Am. Inst. Chemists, 1972. Mem. AMA, Am. Soc. Anesthesiologists, Internat. Anesthesia Rsch. Soc., Mass. Soc. Anesthesiologists, Mass. Med. Soc., Norfolk Dist. Med. Soc., Anesthesia Patient Safety Founds., Soc. for Pediatric Anesthesia, Am. Coll. Utilization Review Physicians, Alpha Epsilon Delta, Delta Tau Alpha, Flambeau. Office: Childrens Hosp Anesthesia Found 300 Longwood Ave Boston MA 02115

BRUZS, BORIS OLGERD, management consultant; b. Riga, Latvia, July 11, 1933; s. Boris and Zelia (Neumanis) B.; m. Anne Quoniam de Schompre, Feb. 10, 1988. Lic. es Sc., La Sorbonne, Paris; BA, Bowdoin Coll., Maine; MPC, U. Strasbourg, France. Tech. svc. mgr. Union Carbide Internat., Geneva, Switzerland, 1959-62; gen. mgr. Profile Steel Co., Detroit, 1962-64; cons. Booz, Allen & Hamilton, Zurich, 1964-66; ptnr. Booz, Allen & Hamilton, Dusseldorf, 1966-69; mng. ptnr. Booz, Allen & Hamilton, Paris, 1969-79; pres. internat. affairs Booz, Allen & Hamilton, N.Y.C., 1979—. Mem. Inst. Mgmt. Cons., Polo Club. Home: 641 5th Ave New York NY 10022-5908 Office: Booz Allen & Hamilton 101 Park Ave New York NY 10178-0002

BRYAN, BILLIE MARIE (MRS. JAMES A. MACKEY), biologist; b. Norfolk, Va., Dec. 30, 1932; d. William B. and Marie (Fortescue) Bryan; B.A. in Biology, U. Richmond, 1954; M.Ed., Am. U., 1966; m. James A. Mackey. Bacteriologist, Arlington County Health Dept., Arlington, Va., 1954-58; med. bacteriologist Walter Reed Army Inst. Research, Walter Reed Army Med. Center, Washington, 1959-62; tchr. Fairfax (Va.) High Sch., 1962-66; biologist NIH, Washington, 1966—. Mem. Am. Pub. Health Assn., Am. Soc. Info. Sci., Am. Med. Writers Assn., DAR. Contbr. articles to profl. jours. Home: 201 Quaint Acres Dr Silver Spring MD 20904-2715 Office: NIH-NIDDK Westwood Bldg Rm 3A04 Bethesda MD 20892

BRYAN, KATHERINE BYRAM, health care executive; d. John Charles and Jane Ballew (Price) Byram; 1 child by previous marriage, George Gurley III; m. John Shelby Bryan, Mar. 12, 1982; children: Austin, Jack. BA, U. Mo., 1969, PhD in Counseling Psychology, 1979. With Corp. Health Examiners, N.Y.C., 1978—, v.p. mktg., 1980-84. Author articles in field. Jr. bd. dirs. Nelson Gallery, Kansas City, Mo., 1973-76; bd. dirs. Family Dynamics, N.Y., 1987-92. Mem. Am. Psychol. Assn., Biofeedback Soc. Am. Clubs: Maidstone (East Hampton, N.Y.); River (N.Y.C.). Home: 136 E 71st St New York NY 10021-5011

BRYANT, BONNIE LEE, psychotherapist, counselor educator; b. Washington, Apr. 30, 1953; d. Robert William and Betty Lou (Whitney) B.; m. Keith Victor Bird, Nov. 13, 1972. BA in Social Scis., Am. U., 1974; MA in Counseling Psychology, Bowie State U., 1984, post-masters cert. Adlerian therapy, 1987; PhD in Counseling Psychology, Temple U., 1991. High sch. tchr. Montgomery County Pub. Schs. & Elizabeth Seton Cath. Sch., Rockville, Bladensburg, Md., 1980-84; addictions counselor, Drug Intervention Counseling Action Prince Georges County Health Dept., College Park, Md., 1984-86; psychology intern Counseling Ctr., George Washington Univ., Washington, 1988-89; clin. dir. Drug Abuse Treatment Program Charles County Health Dept., La Plata, Md., 1987-90; instr., Office of Edn. & Tng. in Addiction Svcs. Md. State Dept. Health and Mental Hygiene, Balt., 1989-90; instr. grad. sch. Bowie (Md.) State Univ., 1990—; coord. alcohol and other drug edn. Am. Coll. Health Assn., Rockville, Md., 1990-91; clin. mental health counselor Potomac Ctr., Inc., Alexandria, Va., 1991—; clin. supr. City of Rockville (Md.) Youth and Family Svcs., 1991-92, City of Alexandria Substance Abuse Residential Svcs., 1992—; bd. dirs. D.C. Counselor Cert. Bd., Alcohol and Other Drugs of Addiction, Washington, 1991-92. Contbr. poetry and articles to jours. Vol. counselor, counselor supr. Prince Georges County Hotline, Riverdale, Md., 1983-85. Recipient Russell Conwell fellowship Temple Univ., Phila., 1985, 86, grad. rsch. award N.Am. Soc. for Adlerian Psychology, Chgo., 1990. Mem. AACD, APA, Md. Psychol. Assn., Md. Assn. for Counseling and Devel., Am. Mental Health Counselors Assn., Md. Mental Health Counselors Assn. Democrat. Episcopalian. Office: PO Box 1564 Temple Hills MD 20757-1564

BRYANT, DAVID STUART, library director, artist, educator; b. Bklyn., Jan. 31, 1948; s. Stuart Graham and Ethel (Hooban) B.; m. Janet Susan Fondiler, Jan. 3, 1971; children: Kiva, Sarah. AB, Rutgers U., Newark, 1971; MLS, Rutgers U., New Brunswick, N.J., 1972. Prin. libr. Passaic (N.J.) Pub. Libr., 1972-81; dir. Patten Free Libr., Bath, Maine, 1981-83, Belleville (N.J.) Pub. Libr., 1983—; mem. adj. faculty Montclair State Coll., Upper Montclair, N.J., 1983—. Author: Finding Information the Library Way, 1987; contbr. articles to libr. jours.; exhibited in group show Leslie Levy Gallery, Scottsdale, Ariz., 1989; archtl. models represented by galleries, Ariz., N.Y., Ga. Chmn. Belleville 150th Anniversary Com., 1989; bd. dirs. Family Svc. Bur., Newark, 1989—. Mem. ALA, N.J. Libr. Assn., Calif. Libr. Assn., Soc. Comml. Archaeology, Belleville C. of C. (v.p. 1988—), Rotary (bd. dirs. Belleville 1983—). Home: 47 Coolidge Rd Maplewood NJ 07040-1419 Office: Belleville Pub Libr 221 Washington Ave Belleville NJ 07109-2923

BRYANT, EDWARD CURTIS, educational association executive; b. Albany, N.Y., Oct. 23, 1925; s. Wilbur Curtis and Hilda Elizabeth (Lauritzen) B.; m. Mary Lou Ellis, Dec. 1, 1972; children: Ellen Bryant Aulson, Curt, Kim Bryant Watson, Daron Jacobs, Carrie Burns. BS, Boston U., 1950, MS, 1951, Cert. Advanced Grad. Specialization, 1953; EdD, U. Palm Beach, 1970; HHD (hon.), Sussex (Eng.) Coll. Tech., 1970. Nat. cert. counselor and career counselor. Tchr., coach Weston (Mass.) Pub. Schs., 1951-52, Melrose (Mass.) Pub. Schs., 1952-53; counselor Boston U., 1953-58, sailing coach, asst. dean men, 1958-62; dir. guidance Masconomet Regional High Sch., Boxford, Mass., 1962-66, Rockport (Mass.) Pub. Schs., 1969-82; pres. Bryant-McIntosh Jr. Coll., Lawrence, Mass., 1966-69; edn. specialist USN, Boston, 1982-88; exec. dir. Mass. Sch. Counselors Assn., Ipswich, 1988—; admissions counselor USCG Acad., U.S. Naval Acad.; mem. Nat. Def. Exec. Res., Washington, 1988—; chmn. admissions com. bd. fellows Norwich U., Northfield, Vt., 1983—. Monthly columnist Ed's Views. Chmn. Winthrop

(Mass.) Sch. Bd., 1956-62; mem. Masconomet Sch. Bd., 1967-71; pres. Parents Assn. Norwich U., 1979-82, New Eng. Safe Boating Coun., 1982—; mem. Navy Recruiting Dist. Assistance Coun, 1977—. Capt. USCG, USN, 1943-46, PTO. Recipient tchr.'s medal Freedoms Found., 1962, Educator's medal, 1981; commendation VA, 1973, USCG, 1982, Achievement medal USCG, 1982, Brotherhood citation NCCJ, 1962, leadership award Navy Recruiting Dist. Assistance Coun., 1988. Mem. New Eng. Conf. Counseling and Devel. (bd. dirs. 1983—), Mass. Coll. Pers. Assn. (Leadership award 1986), Mass. Sch. Counselors Assn. (Leadership award 1988), North Shore Guidance Dirs. (pres. 1966, Hall of Fame award 1985), Res. Officers Assn. (life, pres. 1974-75, Leadership award 1975), USCG Aux. (flotilla comdr. Mass. 1984, recruiting award 1990), Navy League (bd. dirs. Mass. Bay Coun., pres., 1983-84, cert. of merit 1986), Am. Legion (post comdr. Boxford 1988), Rotary (pres. Ipswich 1990-91), VFW (life). Republican. Home and Office: 132 Topsfield Rd Ipswich MA 01938-1650

BRYANT, HOWARD SEWALL, chemical engineer; b. Kansas City, Mo., May 26, 1928; s. Howard Sewall and Thelma (Reel) B.; m. Jane Elizabeth Steuernagel, Dec. 2, 1972; children: Mary, Edward. BSChemE, Ga. Inst. Tech., 1950; SMChemE, MIT, 1952, SCDChemE, 1956. Devel. engr. Union Carbide Corp., Oak Ridge, Tenn., 1952-54; group leader, chem. engr. Courtaulds, Mobile, Ala., 1956-61; supr. process devel. Mobil Chem. Co., Beaumont, Tex., 1961-65; mgr. process engring. Mobil Chem. Co., N.Y.C., 1965-68; mgr. cen. rsch. Mobil Chem. Co., Edison, N.J., 1968-71; sr. cons. engr. Mobil Rsch. and Devel. Corp., Princeton, N.J., 1971-74; corp. v.p. engring. Witco Corp., Woodcliff Lake, N.J., 1974—. Contbr. articles to profl. publs.; patentee in field. Sgt. U.S. Army, 1946-48. Mem. Am. Inst. Chem. Engrs. (mem. exec. bd. engring. and constrn. contracting div. 1990—). Office: Witco Corp 155 Tice Blvd Woodcliff Lake NJ 07675-7664

BRYANT, JAMES MONTGOMERY, museum director; b. Dallas, July 27, 1954; s. John Rutherford and Adeline Janet (Montgomery) B.; m. Judith Ann Lawrence, Nov. 20, 1988. BA with hons. in biology, Austin Coll., Sherman, Tex., 1976; MAT in sci., U. Tex., Richardson, 1979; postgrad., So. Meth. U., 1989, George Washington U., 1980. Sci./history tchr. The Selwyn Sch., Denton, Tex., 1976-78; mus. technician Nat. Mus. of Natural History, Washington, 1980-81; with retail sales dept. S.W. Gallery, Dallas, 1981-82; sci. tchr. Dallas Acad., 1982-87; adj. sci. instr. Brookhaven Community Coll., Farmers Branch, Tex., 1988-89; cons. Sojourn - Sci. Edn., Dallas, 1987-89; grad. fellow geosci. So. Meth. U., Dallas, 1989-90; dir. edn. Va. Mus. Natural History, Martinsville, Va., 1990; dir. Pember Mus. Natural History, Granville, N.Y., 1990—. Contbr. to non-fiction columns, The Virginia Explorer, 1990—, The Fossil Record, 1986—; contbr. articles to profl. jours. So. Meth. U. grad. fellow, 1989; Woodrow Wilson Nat. fellow, 1976; recipient English award, Brown U. Alumni Assn., 1972. Mem. Am. Assn. Mus., Dallas Paleontol. Soc. (prog. chmn. 1987-89), Smithsonian Inst., Woodrow Wilson Ctr. Assocs., Costeau Soc. Office: The Pember Mus Natural History 33 W Main St Granville NY 12832

BRYANT, WILLARD F., JR., university official; b. Balt., Feb. 28, 1960; s. Willard F. Sr. and Victoria S. (Switalski) B.; m. Renee Ann Elliott, Oct. 23, 1982; 1 child, Jeffrey Scott. AA, Essex Community Coll., Balt., 1980; BS, Towson State U., 1986. Civil draftsman Rummel, Klepper & Kahl, Balt., 1977; store mgr., bookkeeper Endicott Johnson, Endicott, N.Y., 1978-84; account mgr. The News Am., Balt., 1984-86; contr. Johns Hopkins Inn, Balt., 1986-88; fin. mgr. Welch Med. Libr., Johns Hopkins U., Balt., 1988—. Republican. Roman Catholic. Home: 213 S East Ave Baltimore MD 21224 Office: Johns Hopkins U Welch Med Libr 1900 E Monument St Baltimore MD 21205

BRYANT, WILLIAM B., federal judge; b. Wetumpka, Ala., Sept. 18, 1911; s. Benson and Alberta B.; m. Astaire A. Gonzalez, Aug. 25, 1934; children: Astaire, William B. A.B., Howard U., 1932, LL.B., 1936. Asst. U.S. atty. for D.C., 1951-54; partner firm Houston, Bryant & Gardner, 1954-65; U.S. sr. dist. Judge for D.C., 1965—; prof. law Howard U. Sch. Law, 1965—; Sec. D.C. Bd. Edn. Served with AUS, 1943-47. Mem. ABA. Office: US Dist Ct US Courthouse 3d & Constitution Ave NW Washington DC 20001

BRYER, JACKSON ROBERT, English educator; b. N.Y.C., Sept. 11, 1937; s. Joseph Jerome and Muriel Irma (Jackson) B.; m. Deborah Churchill Chase, Aug. 27, 1960 (div. 1969); children: Kathryn Chase, Jeffrey Russell, Elizabeth Jackson; m. Mary Claire Hartig, Apr. 27, 1988; 1 child, Margaret Anne Hartig Bryer. BA, Amherst Coll., 1959; MA, Columbia U., 1960; PhD, U. Wis., 1965. Asst. prof. English U. Md., College Park, 1965-68, assoc. prof., 1968-72, prof., 1972—. Author: The Critical Reputation of F. Scott Fitzgerald: A Bibliographical Study, 1967, Checklist of Eugene O'Neill, 1971, Louis Auchincloss and His Critics, 1977, William Styron: A Reference Guide, 1978, The Critical Reputation of F. Scott Fitzgerald: A Bibliographical Study--Supplement One through 1981, 1984, (with S.F. Morse and J.N. Riddel) Wallace Stevens Checklist and Bibliography of Stevens Criticism, 1963, (with R.A. Rees) A Checklist of Emerson Criticism: 1951-61, 1964, (with R.J. Davis, M.J. Friedman, and P.C. Hoy) Samuel Beckett: Calepins de Bibliographie, No. 2, 1971, (with E. Harding) Hamlin Garland and the Critics: An Annotated Bibliography, 1973, (with A.M. Shapiro and K. Field) Carson McCullers: A Descriptive Listing and Annotated Bibliography of Criticism, 1980; editor: Fifteen Modern American Authors: A Survey of Research and Criticism, 1969, Sixteen Modern American Authors: A Survey of Research and Criticism, 1973, 74, Vol. 2, 1990, F. Scott Fitzgerald: The Critical Reception, 1978, The Short Stories of F. Scott Fitzgerald: New Approaches in Criticism, 1982, Conversations with Lillian Hellman, 1986, (with J. Kuehl) Dear Scott/Dear Max: The Fitzgerald-Perkins Correspondence, 1971, The Theatre We Worked For: The Letters of Eugene O'Neill to Kenneth Macgowan, 1982, (with T. Bogard) Selected Letters of Eugene O'Neill, 1988, Conversations with Thornton Wilder, 1992; co-editor, book reviewer, contbr. to numerous books. Bd. dirs. New Playwrights Theatre, Washington, 1976-88, PEN-Faulkner Found., Washington, 1990—. Travel grantee Am. Philos. Soc., 1965, gen. rsch. bd. summer grantee U. Md., 1965, 67, 73-76; summer grantee NEH, 1979, grantee, 1985-86; fellow U. Md. Rsch. Ctr. for Arts and Humanities, 1991. Mem. MLA, South Atlantic MLA, New Eng. MLA (exec. coun. 1986-89), F. Scott Fitzgerald Soc. (pres. 1990—), Eugene O'Neill Soc. (v.p. 1989—). Democrat. Home: 4205 Glenridge St Kensington MD 20895-3712 Office: U Md Dept English College Park MD 20742

BRYNER, PEGGY CULBERTSON, school counselor; b. Chambrsburg, Pa., Oct. 14, 1943; d. Ellis Ross and Pearl Irene (Pilgrim) C.; m. John William Bryner, Apr. 14, 1973; 1 child, Timothy John. BA, Messiah Coll., Grantham, Pa., 1970; MEd, Temple U., 1972, EdD, 1988. Counselor Fulton Elementary Sch., Phila., 1972-85; counselor physically handicapped students Widener Meml. Sch., Phila., 1985—; support group trainer Cleft Lip and Palate Support Group of Phila., Cooper Med. Ctr., Children's Hosp. of Phila., 1976—. Contbr. articles to profl. jours. Adv. coun. Phila. Soc. for Svcs. to Children, 1990—; v.p. Nat. Cleft Palate Assn., Pitts., exec. bd., 1988-91. Recipient Award of Achievement, Sch. Dist. of Phila., 1986. Mem. ACA, Assn. for Care of Children's Health, Am. Sch. Counselors Assn., Counseling Assn. Phila. (pres. 1992-93), Pa. Counseling Assn., Montgomery County Counseling Assn., Pa. Sch. Counselors Assn. Office: Widener Meml Sch Broad St & Olney Ave Philadelphia PA 19141

BRYSON-ISRAEL, DORIS LORRAINE, academic administrator; b. Elizabeth, N.J., Sept. 19, 1938; d. John Wallace Kay and Frances Elizabeth (Crater) Helfrecht; m. William Elwood Bryson, Nov. 7, 1955 (div. 1982); children—Debra, William Jr., Frances; m. 2d, William Douglas Israel, July 30, 1982. A.A. summa cum laude, Anne Arundel Community Coll., 1969; B.A., U. Md.-Balt., 1972; M.Ed., Johns Hopkins U., 1974; postgrad., U. Md., 1985—. Teaching asst. U. Md., Balt., 1972-74; research assoc. DISCOVER, Westminster, Md., 1974-77; asst. dir. acad. advising and career devel. Anne Arundel Community Coll., Arnold, Md., 1977—, coordinator community service career planning, 1980—, facilitator math. anxiety program, 1983-85; cons. Severn Career Assessment Service, Annapolis, 1987; reporter Md. Gazette newspaper, Annapolis, 1965-69. Troop service dir. Central Md. Girl Scouts U.S., 1965-69. Cooperative Edn. grantee, 1986-88. Mem. Am. Assn. Counseling and Devel., Am. Coll. Counselor Assn., Nat. Bd. Cert. Counselors (cert. career counselor), Nat. Career Devel. Assn., Phi Theta Kappa. Republican. Club: Ulmstead. Office: Anne Arundel Community Coll Arnold MD 21012

BRYT, ALBERT, psychiatrist; b. Marburg, Germany, Mar. 8, 1913; came to U.S., 1944; s. David Naftula and Rajzla (Malc) B.; m. Meta Sebag, June 17, 1935 (div. 1943); m. Natalie Lewy, April 19, 1957; children: Marguerite Maude, Allison Bartley. BS, Oberrealschule, Butzbach, Germany, 1932; PCN in Natural Sciences, Ecole de Plein Exercise, Tours, France, 1934; MD, U. de la Sorbonne, Paris, 1939; cert. in psychoanalysis, William Alanson White Inst., N.Y.C., 1950. Diplomate Am. Bd. Psychiatry and Neurology. Pvt. practice Tunisia, 1941-44; Fellow, intern, resident, jr. psychiatrist Bellevue Hosp., N.Y.C., 1945-47; pvt. practice N.Y.C., 1947--; psychiatrist in charge Adolescent Girls Ward Bellevue Hosp., 1949; chief Adolescent Outpatient Univ. Hosp., N.Y.C., 1951-57; supr., clin. dir. Northside Ctr. Child Devel., N.Y.C., 1957-60; psychiatrist in charge Adolescent Outpatient Bellevue Hosp., 1964-70; resident tng. Adolescent Psychiatry NYU-Bellevue Med Ctr., 1970-72; cons. psychiatrist Human Resource Adminstrn. City of N.Y., 1978-89; team psychiatrist Project Assist Manhattan Children's Psychiat. Ctr., N.Y.C., 1989; mem. attending staff Univ. Hosp., N.Y.C., 1950; vis. neuro-psychiatrist Bellevue Hosp. Ctr., 1950; mem. exec. com., dir. of curriculum William Alanson White Inst., 1960, 62, 64-67, 69-71; cons. Luth. Community Svcs., 1954—; cons. The Salvation Army Social Svcs. for Children, 1975-90; cons. Dept. Mental Health, State of N.Y. Co-author: Facial Disfigurement and Plastic Surgery, 1953; contbr. to other books, scientific jours. With French Army Med. Corps, 1940. Named team psychiatrist USPH Rsch. Grant, NYU-Bellevue, 1948-51. Fellow Am. Psychiat. Assn. (life), N.Y. Soc. for Adolescent Psychiatry; mem. N.Y. Coun. on Child Psychiatry, William Alanson White Psychoanalytic Soc. (treas. 1954-56, com. on ethics 1989). Democrat. Jewish. Home: 130 E 75th St New York NY 10021-3277 Office: 4 E 89th St New York NY 10128-0636

BRZEZINSKI, ZBIGNIEW, political science educator, author; b. Warsaw, Poland, Mar. 28, 1928; came to U.S., 1953, naturalized, 1958; s. Tadeusz and Leonia (Roman) B.; m. Emilie Ann Benes, June 11, 1955; children: Ian, Mark, Mika. B.A. with 1st class honors in Econs. and Polit. Sci., McGill U., 1949, M.A. in Polit. Sci., 1950; Ph.D., Harvard U., 1953. Inst. govt. and research fellow Russian Research Center, Harvard U., 1953-56; asst. prof. govt., research assoc. Russian Research Center and Center Internat. Affairs, Harvard U., 1956-60; assoc. prof. public law and govt. Columbia U., 1960-62, prof., 1981-89; dir. Rsch. Inst. Internat. Change, 1962-77; mem. faculty Russian Inst., 1960-77; dir. Trilateral Commn., 1973-76; asst. to pres. U.S. for nat security affairs, 1977-81; ofcl. Nat. Security Coun., 1977-81; counselor Ctr. Strategic and Internat. Studies, 1981—; prof. Nitze Sch. Advanced Internat. Studies, Johns Hopkins U., 1989—; mem. policy planning coun. U.S. Dept. State, 1966-68, Pres.'s Fgn. Intelligence Adv. Bd., 1987-91; mem. Joint Com. Contemporary China, Social Sci. Rsch. Coun., 1961-62; guest lectr. numerous pvt. and govt. instns. 1953—, participant internat. confs., 1955—. Author: The Permanent Purge-Politics in Soviet Totalitarianism, 1956, The Soviet Bloc—Unity and Conflict, 1960, Ideology and Power in Soviet Politics, 1962, Alternative to Partition, 1965, Between Two Ages, 1970, The Fragile Blossom, 1971, Power and Principle, 1983, Game Plan, 1986, The Grand Failure: The Birth and Death of Communism in the Twentieth Century, 1989; co-author: Totalitarian Dictatorship and Autocracy, 1957, Political Power: USA/USSR, 1964 (German edit. 1966), also numerous articles.; editor, co-author, contbr.: Political Controls in the Soviet Army, 1954; Editor, co-author, contbr.: Africa and the Communist World, 1963, Dilemmas Of Change In Soviet Politics, 1969, Dilemmi Internationazionali In Un-epoca. Teconetronica, 1969; columnist: Newsweek, 1970-72. Mem. hon. steering com. Young Citizens for Johnson, 1964. Guggenheim fellow, 1960, Ford Found. fellow, 1970. Fellow AAAS; mem. Coun. Fgn. Relations. Club: Internat. (Washington). Office: Ctr Strategic & Internat Studies 1800 K St NW Washington DC 20006-2202

BUBARIS, GUS JOHN, real estate analyst; b. N.Y.C., Feb. 3, 1952; s. Gus and Athena (Chandris) B. BA, C.W. Post Coll., L.I. U., 1974; MA, SUNY, Binghamton, 1976. Real estate dir. OPM Leasing Services, inc., N.Y.C., 1976-80; real estate mgr. Bell System, East Orange, N.J., 1980-86; asst. treas. Chase Manhattan Bank, N.Y.C., 1986-89; account officer Fed. Deposit Ins. Corp., N.Y.C., 1989—; bd. dirs. Bubaris Enterprises, Astoria, N.Y. Bd. dirs. Elytis Chair Fund Rutgers U. Mem. Nat. Assn. Corp. Real Estate Execs., Hellenic Univ. Club (treas. 1986-87, computer cons. 1984—) (N.Y.C.), Hellenic Am. C. of C. Republican. Greek Orthodox. Home: 206-1 Salem Ct Princeton NJ 08540 Office: Fed Deposit Ins Corp 1100 Cornwall Rd Monmouth Junction NJ 08852-2410

BUBBA, JOSEPH L., account executive, state senator; b. Easton, Pa., Feb. 28, 1938; s. Mary Sadie (Belloni) B.; m. Patricia Ann LeLena, Apr. 18, 1964; children: Joseph, Lisa Ann. BS, Seton Hall U., 1966. Account exec. N.J. Bell Co., Clifton, 1978—; mem. N.J. Senate, 1981—. Mem. bd. edn. Twp. of Wayne, N.J., 1971-75; freeholder County of Passaic, Paterson, N.J., 1975-78, party chmn., 1980; v.p. youth Our Lady of Valley Roman Cath. Ch., Wayne, 1960; pres., dir. UNICO, Wayne, 1971; dir. fund drive Am. Cancer Fund, 1978-81; basketball coach Cath. Youth Orgn., 1969. With USN, 1959-61. Named Legislator of Yr. Bldg. Assn. Met. N.J., 1983. Republican. Home: 19 Williamsburg Ct Wayne NJ 07470-2939 Office: W Park Plz 1117 Rt 46 Clifton NJ 07013 Other: NJ State Senate State Capitol Trenton NJ 08625

BUCCHERE, VICTOR SAL, real estate investment company executive; b. Bklyn., Sept. 2, 1956; s. Vito Louis and Rosaria Sadie (Fraschilla) B.; m. Annie Marie Pugliese, May 26, 1979; children: Anthony, Thomas. BBA, Pace U., 1979. Cert. rev. appraiser. V.p. Jabro Automotive Products, Bklyn., 1974-76; fin. analyst Centennial Industries, N.Y.C., 1976-77; mgr. benefit plans investments J C Penney, N.Y.C., 1977-86; v.p. TCW Realty Advisors, Boston, 1986—. Cubmaster Rochester Cubscouts, 1988. Roman Catholic. Home: 1029 Walnut Plain Rd Rochester MA 02770-2104 Office: TCW Realty Advisors 30 Rowes Wharf Boston MA 02110-3326

BUCCHERI, ANTHONY THOMAS, computer executive; b. Bklyn., Sept. 26, 1953; s. Thomas and Mary Buccheri. BS, N.Y. Inst. Tech., 1975. Dir. ADP, Jersey City, 1976-89; v.p. J.P. Morgan, N.Y.C., 1989—. Mem. KC. Republican. Roman Catholic. Office: JP Morgan 60 Wall St New York NY 10005-2807

BUCH, DAVID LESLIE, psychiatrist; b. Bklyn., May 31, 1952; s. Herbert and Jeanette (Dunst) B.; m. Fran Carol Thomas, June 12, 1978; stepchildren: Laurance, Donna, Andrea. BA, Bklyn. Coll., 1973; MD, Vanderbilt U., 1977. Diplomate Am. Bd. Psychiatry and Neurology, Am. Bd. Quality Assurance Utilization Rev. Physicians. Intern U. Calif., San Diego, 1977-78; resident East Carolina U., Greenville, 1981-84; psychiatrist Penn Found., Sellersville, Pa., 1984-88; asst. prof. clin. mental health scis. Hehnemann U., Phila., 1988-91; chief adult inpatient psychiatric svcs. Hahnemann U. Hosp., Phila., 1988—; asst. prof. mental health sci. Hehnemann U., Phila., 1991-92, clin. asst. prof., 1992—; assoc. dir. geriatric psychiatry Inst. Pa. Hosp., 1992—. Bd. dirs. Lupus Assn. Del. Valley, 1985-86. Mem. AMA, Am. Psychiat. Assn., Am. Soc. Addiction Medicine, Phi Beta Kappa. Democrat. Episcopalian. Home: 306 Wyncote Rd Jenkintown PA 19046-3121 Office: Hahnemann U MS 350 Broad and Vine Philadelphia PA 19102

BUCHA, EDWARD RICHARD, fund raising executive; b. Pitts., Aug. 29, 1954; s. Edward Joseph and Mary Elizabeth (Kolivosky) B.; m. Christine Marie Bolton. BA in Journalism, Duquesne U., 1976; MA in Journalism, Point Park Coll., 1984. Staff writer Greenville (Pa.) Record-Argus, 1976-77; pub. rels writer Dudreck, DePaul, Ficco & Morgan, Inc., Pitts., 1977-78; pub. rels. account exec. David Westhead Co., Inc., Pitts., 1978-79; pub. rels. assoc., assoc. dir. Ketchum, Inc. Fund-Raising Counsel, Pitts., 1980-81; dir. univ. rels., New Kensington campus Pa. State U., 1981-84; assoc. dir. ann. and planned giving Indiana U. of Pa., 1984-86; dir. ann. giving Slippery Rock (Pa.) U., 1986-90; exec. dir. univ. advancement, exec. dir. Slippery Rock Found. Inc., 1990—. Bd. dirs. Easter SEal Soc. Butler County, 1986-90, Slippery Rock Heritage Assn., 1988-89, Slippery Rock Town-Gown Orgn., 1989. Mem. Coun. Advancement and Support Edn., Nat. Soc. Fund Raising Execs., Coll. and Univ. Pub. Rels. Assn. Pa., Assn. Tech. Communicators, Butler County C. of C. (pub. rels. com. 1986-90). Democrat. Roman Catholic. Home: RR 2 Box 1484C Volant PA 16156-9802 Office: Slippery Rock U 100 Old Main Slippery Rock PA 16057

BUCHAKJIAN, SERGE DIKRAN, aerospace company executive; b. Beirut, Lebanon, Aug. 12, 1954; came to U.S. 1975; s. Dikran and Laurice (Imad) B. BBA, Haigazian Coll., Beirut, 1975; MBA, Northeastern U., Boston, 1977. Internat. trademark researcher Thomson & Thomson, Boston, 1976-78; asst. to the pres., dir. exports H.H. Scott Inc., Woburn, Mass., 1978-81; mktg. mgr. Lear Siegler Inc., Port Chester, N.Y., 1981-83; dir. mktg. Lear Siegler Inc., Stamford, Conn., 1983-85, Smiths Ind., Stamford, Conn., 1985—; pres. SDI Investments, Ossining, N.Y., 1988—. Mem. Tech. Transfer Inst., U.S. Arab C. of C., Am. Mgmt. Assn., Northeastern Univ. Alumni Assn., Assn. MBA Execs., Manhattan Club. Home: 8 London Ct Teaneck NJ 07666

BUCHAN, RONALD FORBES, physician; b. Concord, N.H., Sept. 24, 1915; s. Robert and Mary Jean (Forbes) B.; m. Maureen O'Regan, June 17, 1940; children: Robert Bruce, Joan Dallas (Mrs. Fleming), Ian Forbes Morgan. A.B., U. N.H., 1936; M.D., C.M., McGill U., 1942; postgrad., Princeton U., 1958. Diplomate Nat. Bd. Med. Examiners, Am. Bd. Preventive Medicine. Reporter Concord Daily Monitor, 1936; asst. exec. sec. Unemployment Compensation Commn., N.H. Dept. Labor, 1937; sanitarian City of Concord and Eastern Health Dist. N.H., 1938; chief, med. unit Bur. Indsl. Hygiene, Conn. Dept. Health, 1943-46; dir. Hartford Small Plant Indsl. Med. Svcs., 1946; clin. dir., asst. prof. indsl. medicine Yale U. Inst. Occupational Medicine and Hygiene, 1946-48; assoc. clin. prof. indsl. medicine N.Y.U. Bellevue Post Grad. Med. Sch., 1948-57; assoc. med. dir. Prudential Ins. Co. Am., 1948-49, dir. employee health, 1949-57; med. dir., v.p. med. svcs. Prudential Ins. Co. Am., Boston, 1957-74, cons. occupational medicine, environ. medicine, toxicology, 1974—; chief med. dir., v.p. Mediscreen, 1974-87; propr. Portsmouth (N.H.) Athenaeum; assoc. clin. prof. preventive medicine Tufts U. Sch. Medicine, 1958-74; vis. lectr. numerous med. schs., 1948-89. Narrator (audio hist. tour) The Freedom Trail, Boston, (audio visual hist. survey) Shipbuilding on the Kennebec-Maine Maritime Mus.; author: Industrial Toxicology; contbr. Oxford Medicine, Current Therapy, Occupational Medicine, Encyclopedia-Medico-Chirurgicale (Paris); also numerous articles to profl. and lit. jours. Chmn. rsch. adv. com. Brattleboro (Vt.) Retreat, 1960-70; mem. sci. adv. bd. Office Chief Staff USAF, chmn. life scis. human factors facilities, 1960-65, protocol rank, lt. gen.; cons. R.I. Group Health Assn., 1973-75, Harvard Community Health Plan, 1972-75; bd. dirs. Met. Boston chpt. ARC, 1971-73, chmn. com. on safety, 1972-74; founding mem. Challenger Space Ctr., 1987; trustee Miles Meml. Hosp., Damariscotta, Maine, 1988-91. Sr. asst. surg., USPHS, 1943-46; surgeon-lt. York (Maine) Militia-Gov.'s Footguard, 1971—. Recipient Honor award Wisdom Soc., 1970. Fellow Am. Coll. Occupational and Env. Medicine (past pres.), Am. Coll. Preventive Medicine (chmn. com. on clin. procedures 1972-74), Am. Coll. Occupational Med. (past pres.), Acad. Medicine N.J. (past pres.); mem. AAAS, Am. Indsl. Hygiene Assn., Am. Acad. Ins. Medicine, AMA (assoc. editor Archives environmental Health), Assn. Internationale Pour La Medicine Du Travail (permanent commn. 1965-74), Mass. Med. Soc., Ramazzini Soc., Academie Europeene des Arts, Sciences et des Lettres, Am. Assn. Sr. Physicians, N.Y. Acad. Scis., Nat. Trust Historic Preservation, Soc. for Preservation of New Eng. Antiquities, John Buchan Soc. (Edinburgh), Soc. for Protection of N.H. Forests, North Country Authors and Scientists League (past pres.), Newcomen Soc. N.Am., St. Andrew's Soc. of Maine, Clan Buchan U.S.A., Clan Forbes U.S.A., U. N.H. Alumni Assn. (gen. awards com. 1987-90, sec. U. N.H. class of '36, 1981—), McGill U. Alumni Assn., Friends of Bowdoin Coll. Home: Hill Winds Millay Hill RR 3 Box 8400 Union ME 04862-9500

BUCHANAN, ELLERY RIVES, executive; b. Albany, N.Y., Sept. 5, 1950; s. Oliver Henry and Alicia Henning (Johnson) B.; m. Dorothy Elizabeth Diehl (div. 1977); 1 child, Erin; m. Paulette Bernice Gomes; children: Ryan, Derek. BS, Gettysburg Coll., 1972; MS, U. Pa., 1973. CPA, Conn., Mass. Audit mgr. Price Waterhouse & Co., Stamford, Conn., 1973-77; sr. fin. mgr. Polaroid Corp., Cambridge, Mass., 1977-80; controller GCA Corp., Andover, Mass., 1980-85; v.p. sales/svc. GCA Corp., 1985—. Mem. AICPA, Mass. Soc. CPAs, Wharton Club (Boston). Republican. Lutheran. Home: 120 Carlton Ln North Andover MA 01845 Office: GCA Corp 7 Shattuck Rd Andover MA 01810-2496

BUCHANAN, LISA CYR, rehabilitation nurse consultant; b. Bangor, Maine; d. Eddie Albert and R. Eleanor (Grinnell) Cyr; m. Malcolm Vail Buchanan, Apr. 29, 1990. BS in Nursing, U. Maine, Portland, 1980; MS summa cum laude, Boston U., 1987. Staff and charge nurse acute rehab. unit Ea. Maine Med. Ctr., Bangor, 1980-81; community health nurse Bangor Dist. Nursing Assn., Inc., 1982-87, quality assurance coord., 1987-88, mgr. skilled svcs., 1988—; rehab. nurse cons. Lisa B. Cyr and Assocs., Charleston, Maine, 1989—; chmn. profl. adv. com. Bangor Dist. Nursing Assn., Inc., 1989—; editorial bd. Maine Geriatric Tng. Program, Augusta, 1989-91; chmn. clin. dirs. com. Homecare Alliance of Maine, Augusta, 1990-91. Contbg. author: Rehabilitation Nursing: Concepts and Practice, 3d edit., 1993; contbr. articles to state and local newspapers. Mem. ANA (cert. community health nurse, mem. inst. constituent mems. on nursing practice 1991-93), Assn. Rehab. Nurses (cert., presenter at nat. confs., continuing edn. rev. panel 1988-92), Maine State Nurses' Assn. (continuing edn. com. on nursing practice 1989—, chmn. 1990-93), Maine Nursing Honor Soc., Sigma Theta Tau. Republican. Home: RR 1 Box 1620 Charleston ME 04422-9750 Office: Bangor Dist Nursing Assn 268 State St Bangor ME 04401-5490

BUCHANAN, LOVELL, entertainer; b. Ephrata, Pa., Mar. 22, 1949; s. Virginia (Eidemiller) Windham; m. Marie Veronica Sheetz. BS cum laude, Millersville (Pa.) U., 1977. Cert. tchr., Pa. Machinist Alcoa Corp., Lancaster, Pa., 1973-74; tchr. Manheim Twp. Sch. Dist., Lancaster, 1978-81, Downingtown (Pa.) Sch. Dist., 1982-83; tech. trainer Hamilton Tech. Co., Lancaster, 1984-88;, 1988-91. Creator Dimmer the Million Dollar Robot, Prof Funfoolery character, Uncle Chuckles, the Clown (permanent collection Clown Hall of Fame, Delevan, Wis.); sculptor: It's Magic, 1978 (permanent collection Magician's Hall of Fame, Hollywood, Calif.). With USN, 1968-72, Vietnam. Decorated Gallantry Cross. Mem. Internat. Brotherhood Magicians, Soc. Am. Magicians, Internat. Platform Assn., Internat. Jugglers Assn., Puppeteers of Am., World Clown Assn., Humane League (Appreciation award, 1985), VFW, Epsilon Pi Tau. Republican. Home: 2726 Chapel Rd Lancaster PA 17603-5917

BUCHANAN, NEIL HAROLD, economics educator; b. Hartford, Conn., Apr. 20, 1959; s. Calvin Hazlett and Doris Edna (Reitz) B. BA, Vassar Coll., 1981; MA, Harvard U., 1991. Teaching fellow in econs. Harvard U., Cambridge, Mass., 1982-84, 85-90, instr. in econs., summer sch., 1984, 86-88; instr. in econs., summer sch. U. Calif., Berkeley, 1989; instr. in econs. Wellesley (Mass.) Coll., 1990-91; asst. prof. econs. Goucher Coll., Balt., 1991—; vis. instr. econs. U. Utah, Salt Lake City, 1984; debate adviser Harvard Speech and Parliamentary Debate Soc., Cambridge, 1981-90, nat. parliamentary debate champion, 1983. Recipient grad. fellowship NSF, 1981-83, Outstanding Instr. award Dept. Econs., Harvard U., 1987, 89. Mem. Phi Beta Kappa. Office: Goucher Coll Dept Econs and Mgmt Baltimore MD 21204

BUCHANAN, PATRICK JOSEPH, journalist; b. Washington, Nov. 2, 1938; s. William Baldwin and Catherine E. (Crum) B.; m. Shelley Ann Scarney, May 8, 1971. A.B. in English cum laude, Georgetown U., 1961; M.S. in Journalism, Columbia U., 1962. Editorial writer St. Louis Globe Democrat, 1962-64, asst. editorial editor, 1964-66; exec. asst. to Richard M. Nixon, 1966-69; spl. asst. to Pres. Nixon, 1969-73; cons. to Presidents Nixon and Ford, 1973-74; syndicated columnist N.Y. Times Spl. Features, 1975-78, Chgo. Tribune-N.Y. News Syndicate, 1978-85, Tribune Media Svcs., 1987—; commentator NBC Radio Network, 1978-82; asst. to Pres., dir. communications White House, Washington, 1985-87; co-host Buchanan-Braden Show, Sta. WRC, 1978-83, Crossfire, TV show Cable New Network, 1982-85, 87—; panelist The McLaughlin Group, NBC/PBS, 1982-85, 88—; moderator Capital Gang TV show Cable News Network, 1988—. Author: The New Majority, 1973, Conservative Votes, Liberal Victories, 1975, Right from the Beginning, 1988. Mem. President's Commn. White House Fellowships, 1969-73; v.p. Am. Council of Young Polit. Leaders, 1974-75, 76-79. Named Knight of Malta, 1987. Republican. Roman Catholic. Office: 1017 Savile Ln Mc Lean VA 22101-1830

BUCHANAN, PETER MCEACHIN, educational association executive; b. Bridgeport, Conn., Nov. 4, 1935; s. Beaufort Eliot and Helen (Coffin) B.; m. Jane Larkin Howard, Feb. 20, 1960; children: Kathleen, Susan, Elizabeth, Jane. BA, Cornell U., 1957; MBA, Columbia U., 1962, EdD, 1977.

Product mgr. toilet article div. Colgate Palmolive Co., N.Y.C., 1962-67; asst. gen. mgr. Colgate Palmolive Internat., Venezuela, 1967-69; dir. devel. for continuing edn. Sch. Bus. Columbia U., N.Y.C., 1969-71, asst. dean, dir. devel. and alumni affairs Sch. Bus., 1971-73, dir. univ. devel. and alumni rels., 1973-77, v.p. univ. devel. and alumni rels., 1982-90; v.p. for resources Wellesley (Mass.) Coll., 1977-80, v.p. for planning and resources, 1980-82; v.p., chief oper. officer Columbia Presbyn. Med. Ctr. Fund, N.Y.C., 1987-89; pres. Coun. for Advancement and Support Edn., Washington, 1991—. Trustee Dana Hall Sch., Wellesley, 1979-83, corporator, 1983-85; trustee Episcopal Div. Sch., Cambridge,Mass., 1980-82. Mem. Larchmont Yacht Club, Cornell Club, Chi Psi. Office: Coun Advancement & Support 11 Dupont Cir NW Washington DC 20036-1207

BUCHER, NANCY LESLIE RUTHERFURD, cell and molecular biology educator, researcher; b. Balt., May 4, 1913; d. John Howard and Lula E. (Langrall) B. AB, Bryn Mawr (Pa.) Coll., 1935; MD, Johns Hopkins U., 1943. Intern., fellow in medicine Univ. Hosp./Boston U., 1943-45; from fellow to asst. prof. medicine Med. Sch., Harvard U., Boston, 1945-72, assoc. prof. med. (oncology), 1972-79, assoc. prof. surgery (oncology), 1979-83; rsch prof. pathology Mass. Gen. Hosp., Boston, 1972-79, biologist, 1979-83; rsch. prof. pathology Boston U., 1983—. Contbr. numerous articles to profl. jours. Grantee Nat. Cancer Inst., Am. Cancer Soc., Damon Runyon Fund, and others. Fellow AAAS, Am. Acad. Arts and Scis., N.Y. Acad. Scis.; mem. Am. Assn. Cancer Rsch., Am. assn. Study of Liver Diseases, Am. Physiol. Soc., Am. Soc. Biochemistry and Molecular Biology, Am. Soc. Cell Biology (sec. 1973-78), Tissue Culture Assn., Internat. Soc. Study of the Liver. Office: Boston U Dept Pathology Sch of Medicine 80 E Concord Boston MA 02118

BUCHER, RICHARD DAVID, sociology educator; b. New Haven, Apr. 13, 1949; s. Charles Augustus and Jacqueline (Dubois) B.; m. Patricia Lawrence, July 28, 1973; children: James, Kathryn, Suzette. BA in Sociology, Colgate U., 1971; MA in Sociology, NYU, 1974; PhD in Sociology, Howard U., 1983. Instr. sociology Rock Valley Coll., Rockford, Ill., 1972-73; prof. sociology Balt. City Community Coll., 1974—; dir. Inst. Intercultural Understanding New Community Coll. Balt., 1991—, coord. sociology, 1982-89. Co-author: Recreation for Today's Society, 1974, 2d edit., 1984. Chair Carroll County Community Rels. Commn. Westminster, Md., 1990-91; chair pers. parish rels. com. Wesley-Freedom Ch., Eldersburg, Md., 1982-84. Grantee Fund for Improvement Post-Secondary Edn., Washington, 1989-90. Mem. Am. Sociol. Assn., Soc. Disability Studies, So. Sociol. Soc. Democrat. Methodist. Home: 2538 Vance Dr Mount Airy MD 21771-8814 Office: Balt City Community Coll 2901 Liberty Heights Ave Baltimore MD 21215-7893

BUCHHOLZ, WILLIAM JAMES, communications specialist, educator; b. Ladysmith, Wis., July 17, 1945; s. James Fossegard and Hazel Winnefred (Crandell) B.; m. Dorothy Ann Kostka, June 17, 1967; children: Christopher, Jeffrey. BA, U. Wis., Eau Claire, 1967; MA, Ohio U., 1968; PhD, U. Ill., 1976. Grad. asst. U. Ill., Urbana, 1972-76; asst. prof. English, bus. communication Bentley Coll., Waltham, Mass., 1976-83; assoc. prof. Bentley Coll., Waltham, 1983-91; prof. Bentley Coll., Waltham, Mass., 1991—; dir. undergrad./grad. bus. communication programs Bentley Coll., Waltham, 1988—; cons., 1978—; mgr. pubs. Scholastech Inc., Cambridge, Mass., 1983-90. Editor, author: Communication Training and Consulting in Business, Industry and Government, 1983; co-editor, contbr.: The Challenge of Change, Managing Communications and Building Corporate Image in the 1990s, 1989, Global Communications: Applying Resources Strategically, 1990; co-editor: New Corporate Relationships, 1991; contbr. articles to profl. jours. With USN, 1968-72. Grantee FIPSE, 1986, 87; fellow NDEA-IV, 1967-68, inst. fellow Bentley Coll., 1991-92. Mem. Assn. for Bus. Communications, Soc. Tech. Communications, Assn. for Profl. Writing Cons., Phi Sigma Epsilon. Roman Catholic. Home: 69 School St Lexington MA 02173-7429 Office: Bentley Coll Grad Ctr 175 Forest St Waltham MA 02154-4705

BUCHIN, JEAN, psychologist; b. N.Y.C., Aug. 15, 1920; d. Mac and Celia Jacobs; BA, CUNY, 1941; MA, Tchrs. Coll. Columbia U., 1948; PhD, NYU, 1965; m. May 18, 1941; children: Peter J., John D. Tchr., N.Y.C. Pub. Schs., 1946-59, part time 1959-62; counselor, asst. prof. CUNY, 1962—; Mem. Nat Bd. Cert. Counselors, Nat. Bd. of Cert. Career Counselors; asst. prof. coord. Which Way With Women program Baruch Coll., 1980-82; vis. asst. prof. N.Y.U., 1969-72; cons. N.Y.C. Tchrs. Consortium, 1981-85; mgmt. tng. cons. Met. Life Ins. Co., N.Y.C., 1985—; cons. assessment programs N.Y.C. Div. of Pers.; cons. N.J. Human Resources Div.; lectr., leader workshops 53d St. Y, NYU, Queens Coll., A.W.E.D. Author: Singular Parent, 1982, Noah's Ark Minus One, 1989. Washington Sq. Coll. fellow, 1961-62. Mem. AAUP, Am. Psychol. Assn. (pres. Tri State chpt. Div. 35, 1977—), Am. Assn. Counseling and Devel., Met. N.Y. Assn. for Applied Psychology, Bus. and Profl. Women, Muttontown Golf and Country Club.

BUCHIN, STANLEY IRA, management consultant; b. N.Y.C., Sept. 7, 1931; s. K. and Bertha (Handman) B.; m. Jacqueline Thurber Chase, Sept. 14, 1957; children: Linda C., David L., Gordon T. SB, MIT, 1952; MBA, Harvard U., 1956, DBA, 1962. Asst. to treas. Bay State Abrasives, 1956-58; rsch. asst. Harvard Bus. Sch., 1958-59, rsch. assoc., 1959-60, instr., 1960-61, lectr., 1961-62, asst. prof., 1962-66, assoc. prof., 1966-69; pres. Applied Decision Systems, Wellesley, Mass., 1969-78; v.p. Temple, Barker & Sloane, Inc., Lexington, Mass., 1975-80, sr. v.p., 1980-90; sr. cons. Arthur D. Little, 1991—, Intrico, 1991—; vis. lectr. Templeton Coll. Oxford U., 1991—; bd. dirs. Geller & Co., Diamond Machining Tech. Trustee Mass. Sch. Profl. Psychology. Served in Chem. Corps, U.S. Army, 1952-54. IBM fellow, 1962-63; George F. Baker scholar, 1956. Mem. Am. Mktg. Assn., Inst. Mgmt. Sci., Fin. Mgmt. Assn., Harvard Club Boston, Tau Beta Pi. Republican. Congregationalist. Home and Office: 65 E India Row Boston MA 02110

BUCHNER, ARETA, educator; b. Buffalo, Mar. 23, 1951; d. Walter and Daria (Polowyj) Wojtowych; m. Raymond Dennis Buchner, Jan. 14, 1983. BA, SUNY, Buffalo, 1973, MEd, 1977. Tchr. grade 5-8 St. Nicholas Ukrainian Cath. Sch., Buffalo, 1973-74; tchr. grade 7-8 Immaculate Heart of Mary Childrens' Home Sch., Buffalo, 1974-79; lectr. adults GED sci. Ednl. Opportunity Ctr., Buffalo, 1979—; sci. fair judge grades 5-8 SS Peter and Paul Sch., Buffalo, 1983-85. Speaker SUNY, Buffalo, 1983—; vol. Linde Union Carbide 10K Run, Tonawanda, N.Y., 1989-90, N.Y. State Spl. Olympics, SUNY, Buffalo, 1988; presenter, demonstrator, lectr. Clarence (N.Y.) Sr. Ctr., 1984-86. Mem. Buffalo Geol. Soc., Niagara Frontics Sci. Suprs. Assn. (treas.), N.Y. Coll. Learning Skills Assn., United Univ. Professions, Sci. Tchrs. Assn. N.Y. State, Phi Delta Kappa. Ukrainian. Office: Ednl Opportunity Ctr 465 Washington St Buffalo NY 14203-1707

BUCHSBAUM, GERSHON, bioengineer, educator; b. Tel-Aviv, July 24, 1949; came to the U.S., 1979; m. Maya Y. Hecht, June 8, 1976; 3 children. BEE, Tel-Aviv U., 1974, MEE, 1975, PhD, 1978; MA (hon.), U. Pa., 1986. Asst. prof. bioengring. U. Pa., Phila., 1979-85, assoc. prof. bioengring., 1985—. Contbr. articles to profl. jours. Named Presdl. Young Investigator NSF, 1984. Office: U Pa Dept Bioengring 220 S 33d St Philadelphia PA 19104-6315

BUCHWALD, ART, columnist, writer; b. Mt. Vernon, N.Y., Oct. 20, 1925; s. Joseph and Helen (Kleinberger) B.; m. Ann McGarry, Oct. 11, 1952; 3 children. Student, U. So. Calif., 1945-48. Syndicated columnist, 550 newspapers throughout world; columnist Los Angeles Times Syndicate. Author: Paris After Dark, 1950, Art Buchwald's Paris, 1954, The Brave Coward, 1957, A Gift From the Boys, 1959, More Caviar, 1958, Un Cadeau Pour Le Patron (Prix de la Bonne Humeur 1958), Don't Forget to Write, 1960, Art Buchwald's Secret List to Paris, 1963, How Much Is That in Dollars?, 1961, Is It Safe to Drink the Water?, 1962, I Chose Capitol Punishment, 1963, And Then I Told the President, 1965, Son of the Great Society, 1966, Have I Ever Lied To You, 1968, The Establishment Is Alive and Well in Washington, 1969, Counting Sheep, 1970, Getting High in Government Circles, 1971, I Never Danced at the White House, 1973, The Bollo Caper, 1974, I Am Not a Crook, 1974, Irving's Delight, 1975, Washington is Leaking, 1976, Down the Seine and Up the Potomac, 1977, The Buchwald Stops Here, 1978, Laid Back in Washington, 1981, While Reagan Slept, 1983, You CAN Fool All of The People All The Time, 1985, I Think I Don't Remember, 1987, Whose Rose Garden Is It Anyway?, 1989, Lighten Up, George, 1991. Served as sgt. USMCR, 1942-45. Recipient Pulitzer prize for outstanding commentary, 1982. Mem. Am. Acad. and Inst. Arts and Letters, Am. Acad. Humor Columnists. Office: 2000 Pennsylvania Ave NW Washington DC 20006-1812

BUCK, DONALD TIRRELL, finance educator; b. Manchester, N.H., Nov. 17, 1931; s. Harry Forrest and Gladys (Tirrell) B.; m. Marion Gilmour, Aug. 2, 1969; children: Marianne Elizabeth, Elizabeth Allison Tirrell. BS, U. N.H., 1955, MA, 1961. Analyst New England Mut. Life Ins. Co., Boston, 1957-59; instr. fin. Wharton Sch. Bus., U. Pa., Phila., 1961-65; asst. prof. So. Conn. State Coll., New Haven, 1965-74; assoc. prof. So. Conn. State U., New Haven, 1975-80, prof., 1981—; mem. faculty senate, 1968-76, chmn. coll.-wide promotion and tenure com., 1975-76, chmn. dept. acctg. fin., 1984-85; pub. mem. investment adv. coun. Treas. State of Conn., Hartford, 1983—. Contbr. articles to profl. publs. Mem. adv. coun. Bd. Higher Edn. State of Conn., 1983-85; participant econ. workshop hearings legis. fin. com. Gen. Assembly, Conn., 1978-83. With U.S. Army, 1955-57. Mem. AAUP (pres. So. Conn. State U. chpt. 1981-83), SAR, Am. Econ. Assn. Mem. Congregational Ch. Home: Old Town St Hadlyme CT 06439-9999 Office: So Conn State U 501 Crescent St New Haven CT 06515-1355

BUCK, JAMES E., financial exchange executive. Sr. v.p., sec. N.Y. Stock Exch., N.Y.C. Office: NY Stock Exch 11 Wall St New York NY 10005*

BUCK, JANE LOUISE, psychology educator; b. Reading, Pa., Mar. 10, 1933; d. C. Robert and Viola Louise (Berger) B.; m. Leo Laskaris, Oct. 7, 1954 (div. Aug. 1978); 1 child, Julie. BA, U. Del., 1953, MA, 1959, MEd, 1966, PhD, 1971. Instr. U. Del., Newark, 1964-66; rsch. assoc. Rsch. for Better Schs., Phila., 1967-68; asst. prof. Del. State Coll., Dover, 1969-73, assoc. prof., 1973-77, prof. psychology, 1977—; cons. in stats. E.I. duPont de Nemours, Wilmington, Del., 1985—; vis. prof. Ctr. for Sci. and Culture, U. Del., 1986. Author: Specifying the Risk, 1985; contbr. articles to profl. jours. Speaker, evaluator Del. Humanities Forum, 1980-88; pres. Del. Gerontol. Soc., Newark, 1987-88. Mem. AAUP (mem. coun. 1987-90, pres. Del. State Coll. chpt. 1976-80, chief negotiator 1982—, mem. com. on historically Black colls. and univs. and status of minorities in the profession 1988-90, interim sec. Del. conf. 1991-92), APA, Am. Psychol. Soc., Am. Statis. Assn., Danforth Assocs., Kappa Delta Pi, Psi Chi, Alpha Phi Omega. Office: Del State Coll Psych Dept Du Pont Pky Dover DE 19901

BUCK, ROBERT TREAT, JR., museum director, educator; b. Fall River, Mass., Feb. 16, 1939; s. Robert Treat and Hazel (Sayward) B.; m. Nicole Challamel, July 2, 1966; children: Thomas, Philip. BA, Williams Coll., 1961; student, Mus. Tng. Program Met. Mus. Art, 1963-64; MA, NYU, 1965. Lectr., researcher Toledo Mus. Art, 1964-65; asst. curator, instr. art and archaeology Washington U., St. Louis, 1965-67; dir. art gallery Washington U., 1968-70; asst. dir. Albright-Knox Art Gallery, Buffalo, 1970-73, dir., 1973-83; dir. Bklyn. Mus., 1983—; adj. prof. dept. art SUNY at Buffalo, 1972-73; adj. prof. dept. art SUNY at Buffalo, 1972-73; mem. N.Y. Coun. for Humanities, 1976-82, art adv. panel IRS, 1978-82; bd. rep. Pratt Inst. Arts, 1984—, Hirshhorn, 1987—, Am. Fedn. Arts, 1987—, Internat. Coun. Mus., Modern, 1987—. Author: Sam Francis: Paintings, 1947-1972, 1972, Diebenkorn: The Ocean Park Paintings, 1976, Sonia Delaunay: A Retrospective, 1980, Ferdinand Leger Retrospective, 1982. Mem. Assn. Art Mus. Dirs. (trustee, sec., treas., 2d v.p.). Office: Bklyn Mus 200 Eastern Pky Brooklyn NY 11238

BUCK, ROSWELL SEYMOUR, retired banker; b. Buffalo, Aug. 22, 1904; s. George Sturges and Louise (Hussey) B.; m. Sally Smith, Aug. 19, 1939; children: Catherine Buck Damon, Winthrop Lawrence. BS, Yale U., 1926. V.p. Hill Mortgage Corp., Buffalo, 1935-69; pres. 1st Fed. S&L, Hamburg, N.Y., 1969-74; pres. Dominion Mortgage & Realty Trust, Buffalo, 1974-79, ret., 1979. Past pres. Mid Day Club, Buffalo, PTA Buffalo State Coll.; past v.p. Greater Buffalo Bd. Realtors. Capt. U.S. Army, 1942-45. Mem. Buffalo Club, Buffalo Canoe Club (past treas. and fleet capt.), Mid Day Club (pres.), Buffalo Yacht Club. Republican. Presbyterian. Home: PO Box 1150 Buffalo NY 14205-1150

BUCKALEW, ROBERT JOSEPH, psychologist, consultant; b. Eustis, Fla., Mar. 24, 1924; s. Alfred Henry and Jessie Olive (Bowron) B.; m. Flora Jean Kissinger, Aug. 16, 1959; children: Flora C., Faye R. BS, West Chester (Pa.) U., 1948; MEd, Temple U., 1949, EdD, 1962. Lic. psychologist, Pa. Group living tchr. N.J. Reformatory for Boys, Bordentown, 1948-49; social studies tchr., high sch. guidance counselor Milford (Del.) Spl. Sch. Dist., 1949-52, elem. guidance counselor, reading clinic, 1952-53; psychologist Del. Colony for the Feebleminded, Stockley, Del., 1953; guidance counselor, sr. high sch. tchr. sci., social studies Lord Balt. Cons. Schs., Millville, Del., 1953-55; spl. edn. tchr. Delhaas Sch. System, Bristol, Pa., 1955-57; asst. county supr. spl. edn. Carbon County Sch. Bd., Jim Thorpe, Pa., 1957-62; dir. rsch. and curriculum Kutztown (Pa.) U., 1962-70, prof., 1962-89; cons., pres. Assn. of Pa. State Colls. and Univ. Ret. Faculties, Inc., 1990—. Treas. Tarsus Manor, Inc., Fleetwood, Pa., 1989-91. Maj. USAF, 1943-45. Decorated Air Medal with 2 oak leaf clusters. Mem. NEA, Am. Psychol. Assn., Pa. Psychol. Assn. (Outstanding Psychologist 1978), Berks County Psychol. Assn. (pres. 1978-79), Berks County Res. Officers Assn. (pres. 1980-83), SAR (pres. 1983-85, Silver Citizenship medal 1991), A. Legion, Phi Delta Kappa. Republican. Home: 113 N Richmond St Fleetwood PA 19522-1304

BUCKLA, JOHN DAVID, medical equipment manufacturing company executive; b. Olyphant, Pa., Sept. 6, 1953; s. John and Irene Ann (Straka) B.; m. Lynn Marie Howard, May 27, 1978; children: Christine, Adrienne. BS in Acctg., LeMoyne Coll., 1975; MBA, Syracuse U., 1985. CPA, N.Y. Staff acct. Coopers & Lybrana, N.Y.C., 1975-79; staff acct. Price Waterhouse, 1979, sr. acct., 1979-80; asst. contr. Columbian Rope Co., Auburn, N.Y., 1980-81; div. contr. machinery div. Nat. Standard Co., Rome, N.Y., 1981-82; corp. acctg. mgr. P&C Foods, Syracuse, N.Y., 1982-85; asst. contr. Diagnostic Med. Instruments Inc., Syracuse, 1985-88; v.p., prin. T.A. Holmes, Syracuse, 1988-89; v.p. fin. Prodn. Products Co., Manlius, N.Y., 1989-91; chief fin. officer, treas. Diagnostic Med. Instruments Inc., Syracuse, 1991—. Home: 204 Mallard Dr Camillus NY 13031-2016

BUCKLEY, EDWARD JOSEPH, retired academic dean; b. Belleville, Ont., Can., Aug. 28, 1920; s. William John and Mary Jane (Conlin) B. B.A., U. Ottawa (Ont.), 1952, M.A., 1958. Teaching master, Ont. Coll. Edn., Toronto. Treas., Famous Players Can. Corp., Belleville, 1940-60; dir. Fed. Govt. Adult Tng. Program, Belleville, 1960-70; dir. tech. div. Loyalist Coll. Applied Arts and Tech., Belleville, 1970-75, dean continuing edn., 1976-85. Author: History of St. Michael's Parish, 1829-1979, 1983. Mem., chmn. Belleville Separate Sch. Bd., 1943-60; mem. Belleville Retarded Children Authority, 1952-59; mem., chmn. bd. dirs. Belleville Dept. Health, 1949-56. Decorated Knight Equestrian Order Holy Sepulchre, Knight Sovereign M.I. Order Maltn. Liberal. Roman Catholic. Lodge: K.C. (state dep. Ont. 1978-80, dir. New Haven 1983-90). Home: 153 Dundas St W, Belleville, ON Canada K8P 1A7

BUCKLEY, GAIL GEARY, health administrator; b. Providence, Jan. 18, 1951; d. Thomas Francis and Marianne (Stauble) Geary; m. Glenn William Buckley, Feb. 5, 1972 (div. Aug. 1988); children: Eric W., Aaron W. BA, U. R.I., 1972; MS in Health Adminstrn., U. Colo., 1983. Admintrv. asst. Yale-New Haven Hosp., 1973-78, Rose Med. Ctr., Denver, 1978-81; staff analyst Colo. Dept. Health, Denver, 1982; mgr. utilization Blue Cross/Blue Shield Co., Cheyenne, Wyo., 1984-85; health services coordinator ConnectiCare, Inc., Hartford, Conn., 1985-86; data adminstr. ConnectiCare, Inc., Hartford, 1986-87, sysrems coordinator, 1987-88, mgr. mgmt. info. systems, 1988-91; dir. MIS CliniCare Inc., Rockford, Ill., 1992—.

BUCKLEY, JAMES LANE, federal judge; b. N.Y.C., Mar. 9, 1923; s. William Frank and Aloise Josephine (Steiner) B.; m. Ann Frances Cooley, May 22, 1953; children: Peter P., James F. W., Priscilla L., William F., David L., Andrew T. BA, Yale U., 1943, LLB, 1949. Bar: Conn. 1950, D.C. 1953. Asso. Wiggin & Dana, New Haven, 1949-53, Reasoner & Davis, Washington, 1953-57; v.p. Catawba Corp., N.Y.C., 1956-70; mem. U.S. Senate from N.Y. State, 1971-77; mem., bd. dirs. Donaldson, Lufkin & Jenrette, N.Y.C., 1977-78, cons., 1978-80; undersec. for security assistance U.S. Dept. State, Washington, 1981-82; pres. Radio Free Europe/Radio Liberty, Munich, 1982-85; cir. judge U.S. Ct. Appeals for D.C. Cir., 1985—; co-chmn. U.S. del. to UN Conf. on Environ., Nairobi, 1982; chmn. U.S. del. UN Conf. on Population, Mexico City, 1984. Author: If Men Were Angels, 1975. Rep. candidate for U.S. Senate, Conn., 1980. Lt. (j.g.) USNR, 1943-46. Office: US Ct Appeals 3d & Constitution Ave NW Washington DC 20001

BUCKLEY, JOSEPH WALTER, television producer; b. Pittston, Pa., Oct. 3, 1955; s. Walter John and Mary Louise Elizabeth (Moran) B. BA, Wilkes U., Wilkes-Barre, Pa., 1977; postgrad., Pa. State U., 1979-80. Editor What's Happening!, Morrisville, Pa., 1977-79; tchr. English Morrisville Pub. Schs., 1977-79; editor The Liberal Arts Rev., University Park, Pa., 1980; tchr. English Pittston (Pa.) Area Schs., 1980-81; adj. prof. Wilkes U., Wilkes-Barre, 1983-84; exec. news producer WDAU-TV, Scranton, Pa., 1985-86; communications instr. Marywood Coll., Scranton, 1990—; producer 6:00 news WYOU TV, Scranton, 1981—. Writer TV documentary: Little League: 50 Years of Dreams, 1990; contbr. articles to profl. jours. Bd. dirs. Wyoming Valley AIDS Coun., Wilkes-Barre, 1991—. Mem. N.E. Pa. News Media Assn., Soc. Profl. Journalists. Office: WYOU-TV 415 Lackawanna Ave Scranton PA 18503-2013

BUCKLEY, MICHAEL FRANCIS, lawyer; b. Saranac Lake, N.Y., Nov. 1, 1943; s. Francis Edward and Marjorie (Mooney) B.; m. Mary Thornton, June 26, 1965; children: Sean, Kathleen. BA, Dartmouth Coll., 1965; JD, Cornell U., 1968. Bar: N.Y. 1969, Fla. 1982, U.S. Dist. Ct. (we. dist.) N.Y. 1970. Assoc. Harter, Secrest & Emery, Rochester, N.Y., 1968-75, ptnr., 1976—. Contbg. author: Estate Planning and Probate in New York, 1985; co-editor: Administration of New York Estates, 1990. Bd. dirs. Highland Hosp. Found., Rochester, 1981—, pres., 1984-87; bd. dirs. Highland Hosp., 1987—, pres., 1992—. Fellow Am. Coll. Trusts and Estates Counsel; mem. ABA, N.Y. State Bar Assn. (exec. com. trusts and estates law sect. 1988-92), Monroe County Bar Assn. (chmn. trusts and estates sect. 1984-85, banking liaison com. 1985-86), Fla. Bar Assn., Estate Planing Coun. Rochester, Internat. Assn. Fin. Planners, Dartmouth Club (Rochester). Roman Catholic. Home: 571 Thomas Ave Rochester NY 14617-1432 Office: Harter Secrest & Emery 700 Midtown Tower Rochester NY 14604-2002

BUCKLEY, ROBERT JOHN, academic research administrator; b. N.Y.C., Jan. 12, 1949; s. John Patrick and Mary Elizabeth (Carroll) B.; m. Lillian Perez, Apr. 28, 1973. BA, Fordham U., 1970; MBA, NYU, 1976. Asst. dir. devel. Hunter Coll. CUNY, 1970-72, asst. to dean programs in edn., 1972-77, dir. office research adminstrn., 1977—; chair coun. grants officers CUNY, 1984-86, 88—. Mem. Nat. Council Univ. Research Adminstrs., Soc. Research Adminstrs., Soc. Univ. Patent Adminstrs. Office: CUNY Hunter Coll 695 Park Ave New York NY 10021-5085

BUCKLEY, ROBERT PAUL, aerospace company executive; b. Portsmouth, N.H., Aug. 18, 1947; s. Paul John and Margaret Mary (Bennett) B.; m. Evelyn L. Levesque, Jan. 12, 1985; children: Mark Robert, Maeghan Margaret, Caitlin Evelyn. AB with honors, Providence Coll., 1969; MBA with honors, Harvard Bus. Sch., 1975. Bus. analyst Lockheed, Sunnyvale, Calif., 1975-76, asst. to v.p., 1976-77; bus. devel. mgr. Textron Def. Systems (name formerly Avco), Wilmington, Mass., 1977-78, mgr. bus. planning, 1978-80, bus. line controller, 1980-82, dir. bus. devel., 1982-83, deputy, tactical systems, 1983-85, dir. research & devel. programs, 1985-89, asst. to pres., 1989-90, v.p., 1990—. Contbr. articles to profl. jours. Mem. local Rep. election campaign staffs, Providence, 1969, N.H. 1980, 1984. Served to capt. U.S. Army, 1969-73, Vietnam. Decorated two Bronze Stars, 16 Air medals. Mem. Am. Mgmt. Assn., Am. Defense Preparedness, USAF Assn. Republican. Roman Catholic. Office: Textron Def Systems 201 Lowell St Wilmington MA 01887-2969

BUCKMORE, ALVAH CLARENCE, JR., ballistician, computer scientist; b. Lewiston, Maine, Sept. 11, 1944; s. Alvah Clarence and Mary (Begin) B. Student, Holyoke Community Coll., Nat. Radio Inst., Famous Writers Sch., U. Mass. Cert. firearms instr.; lic. amateur radio operator. Chief exec. officer, chief scientist Buckmore Enterprises, Westfield, Mass., 1974—; developer math./engring. software database for microcomputer Calculated Solutions (formerly SC Applied Tech. Inc.), Columbia, S.C.; pioneer in amateur radio satellite communications, ballistics devel.; made over 38 major discoveries in ballistics, 1975—; mgmt. cons. firearms industry; instr. Mass. Mil. NCO Acad., 1976; mem. Mass. State Rifle and Pistol Team, 1976. Contbr. Collier's Ency., articles to profl. jours. Mem. Mass. Rep. Party; Rep. Presdl. Task Force; Mass. Rep. Senate Com. With U.S. Army, 1974, prisoner of war, Vietnam; with Mass. Army N.G., 1975-78. Recipient Internat. Recognition award, 1979; NSF fellow, 1978—. Mem. AAAS, IEEE Computer Soc., Am. Def. Preparedness Assn., NRA, DAV (life), Vietnam Vets. Am. (vets. coun. for liberty chpt. 219), Assn. for Computer Tng. and Support, Math. Assn. Am. Address: 18 Tannery Rd Westfield MA 01085-4822

BUCKNELL, ANITA, direct marketing executive, entrepreneur; b. N.Y.C., May 7, 1934; d. William Harlan and Anita Reed (Rathbun) B. BA, Mt. Holyoke Coll., 1957; MA, R.I. Coll., 1973. Technician Rockefeller U., N.Y.C., 1957-58; chemist, technician Columbia Presbyn., N.Y.C., 1958-62; tchr. N.Y. Pub. Schs., Bklyn, 1965-69, St. Xavier High Sch., Providence, 1974-76; substitute tchr. high sch. 5 community schs., Newport County, 1977-80; nurses aide Grand Islander, Portsmouth, R.I., 1982-83; owner Bucknell Enterprises, Little Compton, R.I., 1983-85, Compton Mktg., Little Compton, 1985—. Republican. Congregationalist. Home and Office: 77 Meeting House Ln Little Compton RI 02837-1212

BUCKWALTER, RONALD LAWRENCE, district court judge; b. Lancaster, Pa., Dec. 11, 1936; s. Noah Denlinger and Carolyn Marie (Lawrence) B.; m. Dollie May Fitting, May 9, 1963; children: Stephen Matthew, Wendy Susan. AB, Franklin and Marshall Coll., 1958; JD, Coll. William and Mary, 1962. Prin. Ronald L. Buckwalter, Esquire, Lancaster, 1963-71; ptnr. Shirk, Reist and Buckwalter, Lancaster, 1971-80; dist. atty. Lancaster County, Lancaster, 1978-80; judge 2nd Jud. Dist. Commonwealth Pa., 1980-90, U.S. Dist. Ct., Phila., 1990—. Sec. City Lancaster Authority, 1970; bd. dirs. Am. Cancer Soc., Lancaster, 1982, Boy Scouts Am., Lancaster, 1984, YMCA, Lancaster, 1990. 1st lt. U.S. Army NG, 1962-68. Mem. Am. Judicature, Fed. Bar Assn., Fed. Judges Assn., Pa. Bar Assn., Lancaster Bar Assn. (pres. 1988), Phi Sigma Alpha. Office: US Dist Ct 601 Market St Philadelphia PA 19106

BUCOVE, ARNOLD DAVID, psychiatrist; b. Toronto, Ont., Can., Sept. 22, 1934. BA, Columbia U., 1956; MD, NYU, 1961. Diplomate Am. Bd. Psychiatry and Neurology. Pvt. practice psychiatry Pleasant Valley, N.Y., 1967—; attending staff Craig House, Beacon, N.Y., 1977—; asst. dir. Dutchess County Mental Health Clinic, Poughkeepsie, N.Y., 1967-68; cons. psychiatrist Greer Children's Community, Millbrook, 1967-77; courtesy staff Sharon (Conn.) Hosp., 1967-90. Contbr. articles to profl. jours. Bd. dirs. Town of Washing Civic Assn., Millbrook, 1986—, Millbrook Music Assy., 1986—; mem. vestry Grace Ch., Millbrook, 1972-75, vestry St. Peter's Ch., Millbrook, 1989-92. Capt. USAF, 1965-67. Fellow Am. Psychiatric Assn. (pres. Mid-Hudson 1977-79); mem. N.Y. State Med. Soc., Millbrook Hunt (bd. govs. 1968-71), Millbrook Golf and Tennis Club, Mashomack Fish & Gam Preserve. Office: PO Box 593 Pleasant Valley NY 12569-0593

BUDD, BERNADETTE SMITH, newspaper executive, public relations consultant; b. N.Y.C., Feb. 23, 1948; d. Stanley Allen and Toby (Percak) Smith; children: Amanda Rose, Karen Wendy, Paige Elizabeth, Kelly Lyn Budd Tinsley; m. Thomas Witbeck Budd, July 4, 1988. B.A. in History and English, Bucknell U., 1964; M.A. in Liberal Studies, SUNY-Stony Brook, 1971; Ed.M., Columbia U., 1982. Tchr. history N.Y., 1964-69; innovator presch. programs, Shoreham, N.Y., 1975-79; editor, pub. Community Jour., Wading River, N.Y., 1978—, advt. mgr., 1978—; editor Shoreham-Wading River Newsletter, 1978-88; profl. breeder, shower A.K.C. golden retriever dogs; cons., workshop leader, 1979—; owner CJ Typesetting and Printing. Editor: C. of C. Directory, Shoreham, 1983, 84; contbr. articles N.Y. Times, Reader's Digest, Psychology Today Mag. Advisor Teen Recreation Adv. Com., Shoreham-Wading River, 1979-82; mem. Nuclear Emergency Evacuation Com., 1979-82; pres. PTA, Wading River, 1980-83; v.p. Spl. Edn. PTA,

Wading River, 1979-80; active Com. Gifted and Talented Children, Wading River, 1979-80, Occupational Edn. Commn., 1979-80; mem. Suffolk County Human Rights Commn. Recipient Disting. Service award Am. Cancer Soc., 1982-83; award of merit N.Y. State Pub. Relations Assn., 1982-83; award of honor Nat. Sch. Pub. Relations Assn., 1981. Mem. Wading River C. of C. (bd. dirs. 1979-80), Suffolk County Bus. and Profl. Women's Assn., Women's Equal Rights Congress, East End Women's Network, N.Y.C. Press Assn., Rocky Point C. of C. (bd. dirs.), Soc. Profl. Journalists, Sigma Delta Chi, Kappa Kappa Gamma. Roman Catholic. Club: L.I. Press. Home: PO Box 619 Wading River NY 11792-0619 Office: Community Jour PO Box 619 Wading River NY 11792-0619

BUDD, EDWARD HEY, insurance company executive; b. Zanesville, Ohio, Apr. 30, 1933; s. Curtis Eugene and Mary (Hey) B.; m. Mary Goodrich, Aug. 24, 1957; children: Elizabeth, David, Susan. BS in Physics, Tufts U., 1955. With The Travelers Corp., Hartford, Conn., 1955—, v.p., then sr. v.p., 1967-76, pres., chief operating officer, 1976-82, chief exec. officer, 1981—, chmn. bd., 1982—, also dir., pres., 1985-90; bd. dirs. Delta Air Lines, GTE Corp., The Inst. of Living. Chmn. bus. com. Nat. Ctr. State Cts.; chmn. pub. awareness com. Conn. Bus. for Edn. Coalition. Mem. Bus. Roundtable, Am. Acad. Actuaries, The Bus. Coun., Am. Ins. Assn. (bd. dirs.), Am. Coun. Life Ins. (bd. dirs.), Health Ins. Assn. Am. (bd. dirs.). Episcopalian. Office: Travelers Corp 1 Tower Sq Hartford CT 06183-0001

BUDD, PATRICIA JEAN, counselor; b. Phillipsburg, N.J., May 6, 1947; d. Joseph Lewis and Josephine (Lesko) B. BS, Bloomsburg U., 1969; MEd, Lehigh U., 1974, PhD, 1991. Secondary English tchr. Phillipsburg High Sch., 1969-73; secondary sch. counselor Whitehall (Pa.) High Sch., 1974—; psychotherapist Alliance for Creative Devel., Allentown, Pa., 1987—; workshop presenter Pa. State Counselors Conv., Hershey, 1986, Pa. State Assn. Student Couns., Allentown, 1986, 88, NEA N.E. Regional Leadership Conf., Portland, Maine, 1988; mem. allied health staff/dept. psychiatry Quakertown (Pa.) Community Hosp., 1987-91. Guest speaker Whitehall Exch. Club, 1986. Mem. Am. Assn. Counseling and Devel., NEA, Am. Psychol. Assn., Pa. Sch. Counselors Assn., Chi Sigma Iota (pres. Alpha Tau chpt. 1988-90, William W. Purkey Profl. Devel. award 1992). Office: Whitehall High Sch 3800 Mechanicsville Rd Whitehall PA 18052-3348

BUDD, RICHARD WADE, communications scientist, educator, lecturer, consultant, university dean; b. Henderson, Md., Aug. 24, 1934; s. Bryan William and Dorothea Marie (Fouvy) B.; m. Beverly Ann Knight, Aug. 28, 1955; children: Kimberly, Richard Wade, Janna. B.A., Bowling Green U., 1956; M.A., U. Iowa, 1962, Ph.D., 1964. Reporter, staff writer Dayton (Ohio) Daily News, 1956-57; research assoc., instr., asst. prof., dir. inst. communication studies U. Iowa, Iowa City, 1960-71; prof., disting. prof., assoc. dean (Rutgers Coll.); chmn. dept. human communication Rutgers U., New Brunswick, N.J., 1971-80, dir. Sch. Communication Studies, 1980-83; dean. Sch. Communication, Info. and Library Studies Rutgers U., 1983—; chmn. bd. Newstatements Communications Cons., 1973-80; cons. in field. Author: Introduction to Content Analysis, 1964, Content Analysis of Communication, 1967, Approaches to Human Communication, 1972, Human Communication Handbook Simulations and Games, 1975, Mass Communication: Dialogue and Alternatives, 1976, Interdisciplinary Approaches to Communication, 1979, Beyond Media, 1988; assoc. editor Human Communication Research, 1974-83, Communication Quar, 1975-83; mem. editorial bd. Jour. Communication, 1976-82, Communication Yearbook, 1977-86, Mass Communications Yearbook, 1979—. Mem. Community Arts Council East Brunswick, 1973-80; exec. council East Brunswick Youth Baseball Program, 1974; active Boy Scouts Am.; deacon Diocese of N.J. Served to lt. USNR, 1957-60. Mem. Internat. Communication Assn. (pres. 1976-77), AAAS, Speech Communication Assn., Am. Assn. Public Opinion Research, Assn. Edn. in Journalism., ALA, Assn. Library Info. Edn. Episcopalian. Home: 3 Pilgrim Run East Brunswick NJ 08816-3237 Office: Rutgers U Sch Communication Info & Libr Studies 4 Huntington St New Brunswick NJ 08901-1071

BUDELIS, JOSEPH JOHN, data processing executive; b. Balt., Dec. 1, 1943; s. Joseph John and Louise Gertrude (Noeth) B.; m. Valerie Susan Sands, Jan. 15, 1983; 1 child, Kristina Dawn. BS in Mechanics, Johns Hopkins U., 1964, BEE, 1964; MS in Engring., Harvard U., 1965, PhD, 1970. Ops. research analyst electronics command U.S. Army, Eatontown, N.J., 1972-74; simulation specialist Applied Data Research, Inc., Princeton, N.J., 1974-76; assoc. mgmt. scis. cons. Mobil Corp., Princeton, 1976-81, facilities mgr. corp. computer ctr., 1981-84, mgr. computer ctr. support services, 1984-86, hardware/facilities planner, 1986, assoc. tech. cons., 1986-87, facilities mgr. computer ctr., 1987-90; mgr. facilities and configuration support, 1991—; pres., chief pilot Rainbow Air, Inc., Princeton, 1986—, bd. dirs. Bd. dirs. Princeton Horizon Condo Assn., 1984—. Home: 14 Southern Way Princeton NJ 08540-5319 Office: PO Box 1033 Princeton NJ 08543

BUDICK, CYNTHIA CHERNER, clinical psychologist, psychoanalyst; b. N.Y.C., Sept. 27, 1942; d. Sid and Julia (Breitman) Cherner; m. Burton Budick, Aug. 9, 1964; children: Ariella, Seth. AB, Barnard Coll., N.Y.C., 1963; MS, CCNY, 1971; PhD, U. R.I., 1985; Postdoctoral Cert. in Psychoanalysis, Adelphi U. Psychotherapist Nat. Inst. for Psychotherapies, N.Y.C., 1982-85; staff clin. psychologist Brookdale Hosp. Med. Ctr., Bklyn., 1986-88; pvt. practice psychotherapy N.Y.C., 1986—; adj. asst. prof. psychology NYU, 1990—. Mem. Am. Psychol. Assn., N.Y. Soc. Clin. Psychologists, Adelphi Soc. for Psychoanalysis and Psychotherapy. Home and Office: 156 W 86th St New York NY 10024-4002

BUDNICK, ERNEST JOSEPH, broadcast executive; b. N.Y.C., July 3, 1948; s. Louis and Caroline (Probert) B.; m. Susan Swingle, Sept. 8, 1984. Cert. Data Processing, Comml. Programming Unltd., N.Y.C., 1968; grad., Dale Carnegie Inst., 1988; cert. in pub. rels., NYU, 1991. IBM computer operator Seamen's Bank for Savs., 1966-68; programmer/analyst W.T. Grant and Co., 1969-73; owner Underground Records, N.Y.C., 1970; systems analyst Ins. Svcs., N.Y.C., 1973-77; pres., owner Bernard Friedman Video Prodns., N.Y.C., 1973-85, Nat. Digital Diagnostics, N.Y.C., 1973-75; systems analyst Mfrs. Hanover, N.Y.C., 1977-80; mgr. corp. video/media Salomon Bros., Inc., N.Y.C., 1980—. Composer, singer, engr. (single) Keep on Playing, 1980. Conservator N.Y. Pub. Libr., 1990—; mem. Am. Mus. of Moving Image, 1990—. Fellow Mus. of Broadcasting; mem. Am. Film Inst. (mem. coun. 1984—), Pub. Rels. Soc. Am., Internat. Assn. Bus. Communicators, Nat. Assn. TV Arts and Scis., Am. Mgmt. Assn., Toastmasters. Home: 10 W 15th St Ste 313 New York NY 10011-6829 Office: Salomon Bros Inc 7 World Trade Ctr New York NY 10048-1102

BUDY, SONIA LIM, medical technologist; b. Guinobatan, Albay, The Philippines, Oct. 11, 1937; came to U.S., 1960; d. Andres Rabelas Lim and Adelina Oblicacion Navarro; m. Amado B. Budy, Dec. 28, 1958. BS in Pharmacy, U. Santo Tomas, Manila, 1954. Chief pharmacist Metro Drug Corp, Legaspi City, Philippines, 1955-60; intern Sch. Med. Tech., St. Mary's Hosp., Waterbury, Conn., 1960-61, rotating med. technologist dept. labs., 1961-69, supr. blood bank, 1969—, clin. assoc. instr., 1981—; clin. assoc. clin. med. tech. program U. Conn. Sch. Allied Health Profesions, 1981—. Mem. Am. Soc. Clin. Pathologists. Republican. Roman Catholic. Home: Visitation Plz 100 Jefferson Sq Waterbury CT 06702

BUDZEIKA, GEORGE, economist; b. Vilnius, Lithuania, May 19, 1921; M.A., U. Innsbruck (Austria), 1946, Ph.D., 1947, N.Y. U., 1970. Came to U.S., 1949, naturalized, 1955. Economist, Am. Inst. Econ. Research, Great Barrington, Mass., 1950-54; instr. econs. Manhattan Coll., N.Y.C., 1954-57; economist Fed. Res. Bank N.Y., N.Y.C., 1957—; faculty Baruch Coll. of City U. N.Y., N.Y.C., 1958—, adj. asso. prof. econs., 1970—. Mem. Am. Econ. Assn., Am. Fin. Assn. Contbr. articles to profl. jours. Home: 34 1/2 Van Corlear Pl New York NY 10463 Office: 33 Liberty St New York NY 10045

BUECHNER, THOMAS SCHARMAN, painter, retired glass manufacturing company executive, museum director; b. Sept. 25, 1926; s. Thomas Scharman and Anne Evans (Lines) B.; m. Mary C. Hawkins, Sept. 15, 1949; children: Barbara Lines, Thomas Scharman, Matthew. Student, Princeton U., 1945, Ecole des Beaux Arts, Fontainebleau, 1946, U. Paris, 1947, Arts Studenst League, N.Y.C., 1946, 48, Institut voor Pictologie, Amsterdam, 1947. Designer Compañia de Fomento, San Juan, P.R., 1946; asst. display mgr. Met. Mus. Art, N.Y.C., 1949-51, tchr., 1949-51; dir. Corning Mus. Glass, N.Y., 1951-60, 75-80, pres., 1971-87; v.p., dir. cultural affairs Corning Glass Works, 1985-87, ret., 1987, cons., 1987—; faculty art sch. Bild-Werk, Fravenau, Fed. Republic Germany, 1988—; head dept. art Corning Community Coll., 1958-60; bd. dir. Bklyn. Mus.; chmn. Corning Glass Works Found., 1971-87; v.p. Steuben Glass, Corning, 1971-73, pres., 1973-82, chmn., 1982-85. Author: Glass Vessels in Dutch Painting of the 17th Century, 1952, Life and Work of Frederick Carder, 1952, Guide to the Collections of the Corning Museum of Glass, 1955, Guide to the Collections of Brooklyn Museum, 1967, Norman Rockwell, Artist Illustrator, 1970, Arts of David Levine, 1979, Ogden Pleissner, 1984; portrait and landscape painter; one-man shows: Adler Gallery, N.Y.C., 1982, 84, Arnot Art Mus., 1985, Heller Gallery, N.Y.C., 1989, Gallery M, Lindau, Germany, 1989, Gallery Nakama, Tokyo, 1990, O.K. Harris Gallery, N.Y.C.; represented in permanent collections Met. Mus. Art., Nat. Mus. Am. Art, Smithsonian Inst., Bklyn. Mus., Lincoln Ctr., Herbert F. Johnson Mus. Cornell U., Musee Des Arts Decoratif, Lausanne, Switzerland, Renwick Mus., Smithsonian, Washington, Corning Mus. Of Glass, Corning, N.Y. Trustee Tiffany Found., Pilchuck Sch., Corning Mus. Glass, Corning Glass Works Found., Rockwell Mus, Chemung County Performing Arts; pres. Rockwell Mus., 1982-87, trustee 1987—. Recipient Forsythia award Bklyn. Bot. Garden, 1971, Gari Melchers medal Am. Artist fellows, 1971. Mem. Bklyn. Inst. Arts and Sci. (trustee 1971-72, pres. 1971-72), Nat. Collection Fine Arts. (commr. 1972-91). Episcopalian. Clubs: Century Assn. Studio: 11 North Rd Corning NY 14830

BUEHLMEIER, HARRY SCOTT See GORDON, SCOTT

BUENAVENTURA, MILAGROS PAEZ, psychiatrist; b. Munoz, Nueva Ecija, Philippines, Oct. 28, 1943; came to U.S., 1974; s. Lupo P. and Pilar (Paez) B.; children: Robert, Melani. AA, U. Santo Tomas, Manila, 1962, MD, 1967. Clinic physician Dr. Jose R. Reyes Meml. Hosp., Manila, 1968-71, resident in neurology and psychiatry, 1971-74; resident dept. psychiatry Milton S. Hershey Med. Ctr., Hershey, Pa., 1975-78; staff psychiat. Holy Spirit Hosp., Camp Hill, Pa., 1978-82, Harrisburg (Pa.) State Hosp., 1982—; cons. Dauphin County Counseling Ctr., Harrisburg, 1984—; mem. courtesy staff Harrisburg Hosp., 1987; psychiat. cons. Helen Stevens Ctr., Carlisle, Pa. Mem. Am. Psychiat. Assn., Pa. Med. Soc., Pa. Psychiat. Soc., Cen. Pa. Psychiat. Soc. Republican. Roman Catholic.

BUENZLY, ROBERT CHARLES, safety engineer; b. Phillipsburg, N.J., Jan. 31, 1943; s. Albert Vincent and Florence (O'Brien) B.; m. Janie Ellen Bergenback, June 10, 1972; 1 child, Shaun Marshall. BA in Liberal Arts, Thomas A. Edison Coll., 1977; cert. in safety mgmt., Allentown Coll. St. Francis de Sales, 1991. Project coord. Middlesex Engrs., East Brunswick, N.J., 1975-76; rsch. and devel. technician Kohinoor Rapidograph Inc., Bloomsbury, N.J., 1976-79; chassis engr. Mack Trucks, Allentown, Pa., 1979-90; security profl. Bethlehem (Pa.) Steel, 1990—; with Air Products, Allentown. Contbr. articles to hobby mags. With U.S. Army, 1964-66. Mem. Am. Soc. Safety Engrs., Am. Indsl. Hygiene Assn., Phillipsburg Rail Historians. Home: 1408 N 21st St Allentown PA 18104-2504

BUERGER, CHARLES ALTER, publisher; b. Pitts., Oct. 23, 1938; s. David B. Buerger and Geraldine (Alter) Jacobson; m. Brona Stein (dec. 1967); m. Ronnie Lynn Uslan, Sept. 1968; children: Jodi A., Andy A., Kevin A., Danielle A., Lauren A. BS in Printing Mgmt., Carnegie-Mellon U., 1960. Prodn. mgr. Achrovure, Inc., Englewood, N.J., 1962-67; v.p. mfg. Wespak, Englewood, 1967-72; pub. Balt. Jewish Times, 1972—, Detroit Jewish News, 1984—, Atlanta Jewish Times, 1989—; v.p. Typog. Shop Blue Sky Advt., 1983—; bd. dirs. Jewish Telegraphic Agy., N.Y.C. Pres. Glen Rock and Ridgewood, N.J. United Fund, 1971; chmn. media div. Associated Jewish Charities, Balt., 1987-88, bd. dirs. 1980-84, 88; bd. dirs. Balt. Jewish Coun., 1978-82, Balt. Hebrew U., 1988, Meals on Wheels, 1988-92, Am. Jewish Com., 1992. Named Man of Yr., Pikesville C. of C., 1988. Mem. Llama Club Md., Jewish Press Club (v.p. 1982-83), Suburban Club Balt., Ctr. Club. Office: Balt Jewish Times 2104 N Charles St Baltimore MD 21218-5795

BUERGER, DAVID BERNARD, lawyer; b. Phila., Dec. 1, 1909; s. Charles B. and Ada (Fischel) B.; m. Anne M. Fortun, June 30, 1946; children: David C., Charles A. AB, U. Pitts., 1928, AM, 1929; LLB, Columbia U., 1932, JD, 1969. Bar: Pa. 1932, U.S. Supreme Ct. Since practiced in Pitts.; mem., sr. ptnr. Buchanan, Ingersoll, Rodewald, Kyle & Buerger (and predecessors), 1932-83; sole practice, 1983—, litigation in 48 states; lectr. taxation and corp. law Com. Continuing Legal Edn., Am. Law Inst., 1951—; pres., dir. Fourteen Bell Corp., Jersey City Investment Co.; bd. dirs. Don Irwin, Inc., O. Hommel Co., Munroe, Inc., Gestion Milway; sec. Elmhurst Co.; sec., bd. dirs. Vantage Broadcasting Co., Heritage Hills Realty, Energy Prodn. Co., Energy Pipeline Co., Energy Sales Co., Major Gathering, Inc., Pitts Stage Inc., Munroe Enterprises, Inc., Power Assoc., Inc.; gen. counsel, trustee Davis and Elkins Coll.; gen. counselMagee Womens Hosp., Hunt Found., Roy A. Hunt Found., Allegheny Acad.; trustee Helen Clay Frick Found. Editor Columbia Law Rev, 1930-32. Pres. Hampton Civic Assn., 1956-57. Fellow Am. Bar Found.; mem. ABA, Am. Law Inst. (life), Am. Arbitration Assn., Am. Judicature Soc., Wildwood Golf Club (hon.), Sigma Alpha Mu, Omicron Delta Kappa, Delta Sigma Rho. Home: 3000 Mccully Rd Allison Park PA 15101-1330 Office: Rm 2983 600 Grant St Pittsburgh PA 15219-2887

BUERK, DONALD GENE, medical educator; b. St. Louis, Jan. 28, 1946; s. Charles Albert and Virginia (Kirkpatrick) B.; m. Steffie Greif, July 7, 1968; children: Jesse Nathaniel, Daniel Joshua. BS, Case Western Res. U., 1969, MS, 1976; PhD, Northwestern U., 1980. Biomed. engr. St. Vincent Charity Hosp., Cleve., 1969-75; rsch. asst. Case Western res. U., Cleve., 1976; rsch. fellow Evanston Hosp., Northwestern U., 1980-82; prof. La. Tech. U., Ruston, La., 1982-87; rsch. prof. Drexel U., Phila., 1987-90, Sch. Medicine, Dept. Ophthalmology, U. Pa., Phila., 1990—; vis. scientist Cath. U., Nijmegen, The Netherlands, 1988; vis. prof. Johns Hopkins U., Balt., 1986—. Contbr. over 40 articles to profl. jours. Recipient Travel award Internat. Soc. on Oxygen Transport, U.K., 1978, Outstanding Researcher award La. Tech. U., Ruston, 1984, New Investigator award NIH, 1986, Vis. Scientist award Dutch Govt., 1988, Individual Investigator award NSF, 1990. Mem. IEEE, Am. Heart Assn., Am. Physiol. Soc., Assn. for Rsch. in Vision and Ophthalmology, Biomed. Engring. Soc., Microcirculatory Soc., Sigma Xi. Office: U Pa IFEM-1 John Morgan Bldg Philadelphia PA 19104-6068

BUERMANN, PETER BRUCE, educational administrator, psychologist; b. Mineola, N.Y., July 3, 1938; s. Ralph and Marjorie Elizabeth (Peters) B.; m. Dorothy Richardson, June 15, 1963; children: Jennifer Beth, Amy Marie, Andrea Lee. BS in Edn., Upsala Coll., E. Orange, N.J., 1959; EdM, Rutgers U., 1961, EdS, 1969; EdD, Temple U., 1984. Tchr. Atlantic Highlands (N.J.) High Sch., 1959-60, Clinton Place Jr. High Sch., Newark, 1961-62; psychologist South River (N.J.) Schs., 1963-64; dir. spl. svcs. Ewing Twp. Schs., Trenton, N.J., 1964-78; exec. dir. Project Child Infant & Presch. Program, Trenton, N.J., 1973—; dir. student personnel svcs. Mercer County Spl. Svcs., Trenton, N.J., 1978—. Fellow Acad. for Cerebral Palsy and Devel. Medicine, Am. Orthopsychiatric Assn.; mem. Am. Psychol. Assn., Soc. for Pediatric Psychology, Assn. for Child Psychology and Psychiatry. Home: 19 S Chancellor St Newtown PA 18940-2107 Office: Project Child 1050 Old Trenton Rd Trenton NJ 08690-1230

BUETTNER, MICHAEL LEWIS, healthcare manufacturing executive; b. East St. Louis, Ill., July 24, 1957; s. Lewis Edwin and Ethel Mae (Gummersheimer) B.; m. Dawn Elaine Strand, Aug. 16, 1980. BS in Acctg., U. Ill., 1983. CPA, Ill. Acct. Carboline Co., St. Louis, 1981-83; sr. analyst planner Moog Automotive Inc., St. Louis, 1983-85; mgr. acquisition analysis Bausch & Lomb Inc., Rochester, N.Y., 1985-87, project mgr. fin., 1987, dir. corp. bus. devel., 1987-89, v.p. new ventures, 1990—. With USNR, 1975-77. Mem. AICPA, Nat. Assn. Accts., Am. Acctg. Assn., Licensing Exec. Soc., Tech. Transfer Soc., Product Devel. and Mgmt. Assn., U. Ill. Alumni Club, Rochester (founder 1987, dir., v.p. 1987—).

BUFFINGTON, JODY LYNN, advertising executive; b. Clarksburg, W.Va., Oct. 5, 1959; d. Ulysses Pershing and Helen Lee (Bryant) B. BA, U. Richmond, 1981; MA, U. Md., 1988. Reporter/intern Clarksburg Telegram, 1977-81; communications specialist Litton Industries Amecom, College Park, Md., 1981-84; communication specialist Prince George's Gen. Hosp., 1984-85; dir. community rels. Springhill Lake Apts., Greenbelt, Md., 1985-86; pub. rels. rep. Blue Cross/Blue Shield, Balt., 1986-87, mgr. employee communications, 1987-88, mgr. pub. affairs, 1988-89, dir. corp. advt., 1989—; adj. prof. Loyola Coll. of Md., Balt., 1989—. Pub. rels. cons. Mutual Housing Authority, United Way of Cen. Md., Balt. Mem. Pub. Rels. Soc. Am. (bd. dirs. Md. chpt. 1990—). Office: Blue Cross Blue Shield Md 10455 Mill Run Cir Owings Mills MD 21117-5559 Home: 8118 Derby Ln Owings Mills MD 21117-5219

BUFFINTON, KEITH WILLIAM, mechanical engineer; b. Ridgewood, N.J., Jan. 11, 1957; s. Lester William and Jean Elizabeth (Hinton) B.; m. Christine Elise Miller, Sept. 17, 1988. BSME, Tufts U., 1979; MSME, Stanford U., 1981, PhD, 1985. Engr. Structures Rsch. Dept./Boeing, Seattle, 1980; rsch. asst. Applied Mechanics Div./Stanford (Calif.) U., 1981-82, teaching asst., 1980-83, acting instr., 1983; rsch. assoc. Swiss Fed. Inst. Technology, Zurich, Switzerland, 1984-87; asst. prof. Mech. Engring. Dept., Bucknell U., Lewisburg, Pa., 1987—; cons. Bucher-Guyer AG, Niederwenigen, Switzerland, 1986. Contbr. articles to Jour. Applied Mechanics, Internat. Jour. Solids and Structures, Jour. Mech. Design. Mem. ASME, AIAA, Tau Beta Pi. Republican. Home: RR 1 Box 248 Lewisburg PA 17837-9536 Office: Bucknell U Mech Engring Dept Lewisburg PA 17837

BUFFUM, CHARLES WALBRIDGE, JR., business writer, public relations consultant; b. Washington, Dec. 11, 1939; s. Charles Walbridge and Katherine (Swartwout) B.; m. Elizabeth Veihmeyer, Sept. 2, 1961 (div. 1976); children: Stephen W., Kathleen C. BS in Journalism, U. Md., 1962. Pub. info. specialist FPC, Washington, 1962-65; reporter Standard Times, New Bedford, Mass., 1965-67; reporter, mem. editorial bd. Akron (Ohio) Beacon Jour., 1967-78; writer, cons. Charles Buffum Assocs., N.Y.C., 1978—; cons. Poly. U., Bklyn., 1984—, Am. Kennel Club, N.Y.C., 1986—, Bus. Roundtable, N.Y.C., 1987—. With USMC, 1960-61. Co-recipient Pulitzer prize for local news, 1971, Silver Anvil award, Pub. Rels. Soc. Am., 1979. Democrat. Home and Office: 425 Park Ave S New York NY 10016-8016

BUGBEE, ALAN CAMPBELL, JR., psychology educator; b. Allentown, Pa., Sept. 28, 1950; s. Alan Campbell and Patricia Pierce (Towle) B.; m. Pamela Jane Briney, Aug. 1, 1981. BA summa cum laude, U. Vt., 1973; MA in Edn., George Washington U., 1976, MPA, 1977; PhD, U. Pitts., 1983. Rehab. counselor Div. Vocat. Rehab., St. Louis, 1978-79; instr. in anesthesiology Sch. Medicine U. Pitts., 1983; quality and measurement specialist Data Gen. Corp., Woodstock, Conn., 1984-86; asst. prof. psychology Am. Coll., Bryn Mawr, Pa., 1986-91, assoc. prof., 1991—, dir. examination rsch., 1986-88, dir. ednl. systems, 1988—; cons. Banyan Systems Inc., Westboro, Mass., 1990—; psychometrist Columbia (Mo.) Pub. Schs., 1979-80; trainee NIMH, Washington, 1974-76. Contbr. articles, reports to profl. publs., chpt. to book. Judge Delaware Valley Sci. Fair, Phila., 1990, medals judge, 1991. Mem. Am. Ednl. Rsch. Assn., Nat. Coun. on Measurement in Edn., Boulder Soc. Democrat. Congregationalist. Office: Am Coll 270 S Bryn Mawr Ave Bryn Mawr PA 19010-2105

BUGENHAGEN, THOMAS GORDON, mathematician; b. Derby, N.Y., Dec. 16, 1932; s. Albert Henry and Edith (Teresa) B.; m. Katherine Leeth, May 25, 1956; children: Karl, Jeff, John. BA, Maryville Coll., 1956; MA, U. Tenn., 1959. Math. instr. Maryville (Tenn) Coll., 1957-58, U. Tenn., Knoxville, 1958-59; assoc. staff mathematician Johns Hopkins U., Applied Physics Lab., Laurel, Md., 1959-62; sr. staff mathematician Johns Hopkins U., Applied Physics Lab., Laurel, 1962-80, prin. staff mathematician, 1980-91, group supr., 1981—. Pres. PTA Rockinghorse Elem. Sch., Rockville, Md., 1969. Seaman USN, 1951-55. Recipient Math prize Maryville Coll., 1955, Rist prize for Best Paper Presented Mil. Ops. Rsch. Soc., 1976. Fellow AAAS; mem. Mil. Ops. Rsch. Soc., Ops. Rsch. Soc. Am. Democrat. Unitarian. Office: Johns Hopkins U Applied Physics Lab Johns Hopkins Rd Laurel MD 20723-6099

BUGGLIN, CAROL STEPHANIE, clinical psychologist, psychotherapist; b. Rockville Ctr., N.Y., Dec. 20, 1958; d. George Raymond and Helen Ann (Glavin) B.; m. Mark Steven Borer, Aug. 1, 1987; children: Eric Daniel Bugglin-Borer, Brett Joseph Bugglin-Borer. BA, SUNY, Binghamton, 1981; MA, U. Conn., 1986, PhD, 1987. Lic. psychologist, Md., Del. Child psychologist Upper Shore Mental Health Ctr., Chestertown, Md., 1987-89; child and family psychologist Tressler Ctrs. Del., Dover, 1987-90, Psychiat. Assess for Cen. Del., Dover, 1990—; coord. Profls. Educating for and Advocating for Children, Dover, 1989—; radio talk show guest. Contbr. articles to profl. jours. Mem. APA, Del. Psychol. Assn., Phi Beta Kappa. Roman Catholic. Office: Psychiat Access Ctrl Del 846 Walker Rd Ste 32-2 Dover DE 19901-2756

BUGOSH, JOHN, chemical company executive; b. Cleve., July 1, 1924; s. Andrew and Mary Veronica (Forgach) B.; m. Nancy Ann Perron, May 31, 1952; children: Nancy Jane, Pamela Marie, John Andrew. BS, Heidelberg Coll., Tiffin, Ohio, 1945; Dipl., Escuela Interam. De Verano, Saltillo, Mexico, 1948; MS, Case Western Res. U., 1947, PhD, 1949. Physics instr. Western Res. U., Cleve., 1950-51; rsch. assoc. E.I. DuPont de Nemours & Co., Inc., Wilmington, Del., 1949-63, devel. supr., 1963-66, planning specialist, 1966-70, mgr. environ. venture, 1970-78, mgr. distbr. programs, 1978-89; pres., chief exec. officer Trakon, Inc., West Chester, Pa., 1989—; pres., chief exec. officer Trakon, Inc., West Chester, Pa., 1989—. Contbr. over 25 articles to profl. jours.; author or co-author of 31 patents in colloidal alumina/silica/zirconia. Named Man of the Yr. Nat. Assn. Chem. Distbrs., 1979. Mem. Am. Chem. Soc. (Best Tech. paper of the Yr. 1961), Scientific Rsch. Soc. Am., Plantation Golf and Country Club, Radley Run Country Club, Dupont Country Club, Sigma Xi, Lambda Chi Alpha, Delta Phi Alpha.

BUHITE, THOMAS JESSE, SR., employee benefits consultant, broker; b. Balt., Aug. 26, 1946; s. Jesse Paul and Bernice June (Dixon) B.; m. Janet Lynn Fields, oct. 6, 1968; children: Thomas Jesse Jr., John Michael. BS, U. Md., 1977; postgrad., Loyola Coll. Md., 1981-83, Potomac Sch. Law, Washington, 1980-82. Lic. life, health, property and casualty ins. advisor, Md.; lic. life, health, property and casualty ins. broker-agt. Claims mgr. Hardester Corp., Balt., 1975-76; claims mgr./asst. to gen. counsel Johns Hopkins Hosp., Balt., 1977-81; dir. risk mgmt. Johns Hopkins U., Balt., 1981-86; asst. v.p. Med. Mut. Liability Ins. of Md., Balt., 1986-87; sr. v.p. Coastal Group, Inc./Century Am. Ins. Co., Durham, N.C., 1987-88; pres., chief exec. officer Risk Mgmt., Inc., Columbia, Md., 1988-90, Health Claims Adminstrs., Inc., Columbia, Md., 1988-90; pres., chief exec. officer, chmn. bd. dirs. Health Benefits Adminstrs. Inc., Forest Hill, Md., 1990—; bd. dirs. Genesis Ltd., Hamilton, Bermuda, 1981-86, chmn. bd. ops. com., sr. claims officer; bd. dirs. Risk Mgmt., Inc.; faculty adminstrv. tng. program Johns Hopkins U., Balt., 1981-86, guest lectr. exec. small bus. program, 1989—. Co-author: Employer's Workers' Compensation Handbook, 1981, The Physician's Guide to the Worker's Compensation System, 1982; contbr. articles to profl. jours. Chmn. bd. trustees Jarrettsville United Meth. Ch., 1989-90; coord., organizer Tiger Cub Scouts, Madonna, Md., 1988-89; com. chmn. Cub Scouts, Jarrettsville, 1989-90, asst. cub master, 1990-91, cub master, 1992-93. Mem. Am. Soc. Healthcare Risk Mgmt. of Am. Hosp. Assn., Practising Law Inst., Risk and Ins. Mgmt. Soc. (chpt. pres. 1989-90), Md. Self-Insurers & Employers Compensation Assn. (treas. 1981-82), Sparrows Point Country Club, Balt. Yacht Club, Masons. Democrat. Methodist. Home: 4160 Norrisville Rd White Hall MD 21161-9309 Office: Health Benefits Adminstrs Inc PO Box 179 109 E Jarrettsville Rd Forest Hill MD 21050-0179

BUHL, DAVID, astronomer; b. Newark, Nov. 20, 1936; s. Paul Julius and Dorothy Jane (Smith) B.; m. Pauline Sandra Ittner, July 7, 1962 (div. Dec. 1989); 1 child, Erica Louise; m. Nancy Marin, July 13, 1990; 1 child, Danielle Marie. BS, MIT, 1960, MS, 1960; PhD, U. Calif., Berkeley, 1967. Scientist Nat. Radio Astronomy Obs., Charlottesville, Va., 1967-74; scientist, astronomer NASA Goddard Space Flight Ctr., Greenbelt, Md., 1974—. Contbr. over 100 articles to profl. jours. Student counselor MIT Alumni Orgn., 1971-84. Mem. IEEE, Am. Astron. Soc., IAU, Astron. Soc. Pacific, DRADA-Johns Hopkins. Office: NASA Goddard Space Flight Ctr Code 693 Greenbelt MD 20771

BUHLER, JAMES WARREN, accountant; b. Bronx, N.Y., Nov. 27, 1959; s. Warren H. and Norma (Felker) B.; m. Patricia Meredith; children: Jennifer, Matthew. AS, Orange County Community Coll., Middletown, N.Y., 1980; BS in Acctg., SUNY, Oswego, 1982; MBA, Pace U., 1986. Cert. Mgmt. Acct. Acctg. mgr. Wehran Engring. Co., Middletown, 1983-85; sr. acct. 3M-MNI, Stamford, Conn., 1985-88; contr. Gen Svc. Corp., Newark, Del., 1988—. Fellow Nat. Assn. Accts. Office: Gen Svc Corp 206 Hansen Ct Newark DE 19713-1150

BUHLER, PATRICIA MARLENE, business consultant, educator; b. Chestertown, Md., Dec. 22, 1953; d. William Cooper and Betty Jean (Newsome) Meredith; m. James Warren Buhler; children: Jennifer Lynn, Matthew James. BA in Pol. Sci., U. Del., 1975; AA in BA, Coll. San Mateo, 1981; MBA in Mgmt., Pace U., 1986. Store mgr. N.E. region The Gap Stores, Inc., 1976-79; mgr. cash audit The Gap Stores, Inc., San Bruno, Calif., 1979-80; supr. cash mgmt. Robert A. McNeil Corp., San Mateo, Calif., 1981-82, mgr. real estate acctg., 1982, mgr. accounts receivable, 1982-83; grad. asst. Pace U., White Plains, N.Y., 1985-86; owner Buhler Bus. Cons., Newark, Del., 1989—; adj. asst. prof. Goldey-Beacon Coll., Wilmington, Del., 1989—, mem. adv. bd. for bus. adminstrn., 1991—, mem. bd. advisors, 1989—. Contbr. numerous articles to profl. jours. Mem. DAV Aux. (editor newspaper 1989—, guest speaker dist. # 4 1991). Home: 8 Rossiter Cir Newark DE 19702-2845 Office: Goldey-Beacon Coll 4701 Limestone Rd Wilmington DE 19808-1927

BUIST, RICHARDSON, corporate executive, retired banker; b. Bklyn., Aug. 8, 1921; s. George Lamb and Adelaide (Richardson) B.; m. Jean Mackerley, Oct. 2, 1948; children: Peter Richardson, Jean Morford Buist Earle, Mary Elizabeth Buist Leuth. Student, Yale U. Advt. copywriter Ecloss Co., Sparta, N.J., 1946-48; advt. mgr. Sussex County Ind., Newton, N.J., 1948-50, Dover (N.J.) Advance, 1950-53; bus. mgr. N.J. Herald, Inc., Newton, 1953-70, dir., v.p., 1958-70, pub., 1967-70; dir. N.J. Press Assn., 1966-70; asst. sec., asst. treas. Morford Conservation Co., Hamburg, 1965-72, pres., 1986—; trust officer Midlantic Nat. Bank/Sussex & Mchts., Newton, 1971-88, Midlantic Nat. Bank, Edison, N.J., 1972-86, cons., 86-90. Pres. Sussex County chpt. Am. Cancer Soc., 1956-58, Sussex County Music Found., 1959-61; mem. Morris-Sussex Area Health Facilities Planning Coun., 1965-68; v.p. Sussex County Coun. Arts, 1971-73; chmn. pub. rels. Morris-Sussex Area Council Boy Scouts Am., 1986-88; trustee Sussex County Music Found., 1955-75; v.p., chmn. fin. devel. com. Newton Meml. Hosp., 1966-68, bd. govs. 1962-88, pres. bd. govs., 1968-71, chmn., 1971-73; founding incorporator, trustee NW Jersey Health Care, 1971-76; trustee, mem. exec. com. regional health planning council Health Systems Agy., 1976-82, 1984-87, v.p., 1978-79; trustee United Way of Sussex County, 1984-90, spl. gifts chmn., 1984-88, mem. allocations com. 1990—; dir. North Jersey Health Care Corp., 1988—, asst. treas., 1991—; dir. Prime Care, Inc., 1989—, chmn. bd. trustees, 1989-92. Mem. N.J. Vet. Med. Soc. Aux. (del. 1979-82, 88-91, 2d v.p. 1990-91), Am. Vet. Med. Soc. Aux. (nat. chmn. legis. com. 1986-88, long range planning com. 1990—, chmn. 1992), Morristown (N.J.) Club, Rotary (pres. 1967-68, Paul Harris Fellow 1988). Home: 68 Sand Pond Rd Hamburg NJ 07419

BUKOWSKI, JULIA VICTORIA, electrical engineering educator; b. Phila., Jan. 24, 1953; d. Thomas Joseph and Julia Anna (Kot) B. BSEE, U. Pa., 1974; DIC, Imperial Coll., London, 1976; PhD, U. Pa., 1979. Asst. prof. systems engring. U. Pa., Phila., 1979-85; assoc. prof. elec. engring. Villanova (Pa.) U., 1985—; Fulbright sr. Am. lectr. and vis. assoc. prof. Technion, Haifa, Israel, 1992—. Contbr. articles to profl. jours. Recipient Silver medal, Royal Soc. Arts, London, 1974, A. Atwater Kent prize, Moore Sch. Elec. Engring., 1974. Mem. IEEE (sr. mem., Outstanding Yougn Engrs. award 1984), Soc. for Women Engrs. (sr. mem.), Am. Soc. Engring. Edn. (Outstanding Young Tchr. 1981), AAUW (Dissertation fellow 1978-79). Office: Villanova U Dept Elec Engring Villanova PA 19085

BUKSBAUM, DAVID EUGENE, television executive, journalist; b. N.Y.C., Mar. 1, 1935; s. Lewis and Claire (Weldon) B.; m. Susan Ravitch, July 10, 1966; 1 child, Jennifer. Student, U. Miami, 1953-56. Prodn. mgr. CBS News, N.Y.C., 1956-60, assoc. producer, 1960-62, producer, 1962-66, dep. dir. spl. events and prodn., 1972-79, sr. producer evening news, 1979-81, v.p. ops. and news coverage, 1981-89; sr. producer Pub. Broadcast Lab., N.Y.C., 1966-68, ABC News, N.Y.C., 1968-72; pres. Imtec Global Inc., N.Y.C., 1989—; cons. Drug Enforcement Adminstrn., Alexandria, Va., 1990-91. Producer TV documentary Legacy of the Thrasher, 1963 (award USN 1964); sr. producer Sadat, 1981 (Emmy award 1981), In Celebration of the U.S., 1976 (Peabody award 1977); exec. producer election yrs., 1976-88. Recipient gold medal Christopher Soc., 1969. Office: Imtec Global Inc 1095 Park Ave New York NY 10128-1154

BULKIN, MICHAEL HERBERT, management consultant; b. N.Y.C., July 26, 1938; s. Bernard and Sylvia (Gelman) B.; m. Rosemary Elizabeth Morris, May 5, 1967; children: Mark Gregory, Joseph Michael. BS in Engring. Sci., Pratt Inst., 1960; postgrad., Brown U., 1961; M in Indsl. Adminstrn., Yale U., 1963. Ops. analyst Hughes Aircraft Co., El Segundo, Calif., 1963-65; assoc. McKinsey & Co., N.Y.C., 1965-70, prin., 1970-76; dir., 1976—; dir., mgr. McKinsey & Co., Chgo., 1976-81, N.Y.C., 1981—; trustee Com. on Econ. Devel., N.Y.C., 1987—; mem. adv. coun. Yale U. Sch. Orgn. & Mgmt., New Haven, Conn., 1986—. Mem. Bus. Com. for the Arts, N.Y.C., 1986—. Mem. Country Club of Darien, Bd. Room (bd. govs. 1989—), Tau Beta Pi, Sigma Xi. Office: McKinsey & Co 55 E 52d St New York NY 10022

BULKLEY, GREGORY BARTLETT, surgeon, educator, director of surgical research; b. Spokane, Wash., Apr. 28, 1943; s. George J. and Patricia (Bartlett) B.; m. Bernardine P. Healy, Aug. 13, 1967 (div. Aug. 1982); 1 child, Bartlett Anne. BA, Princeton (N.J.) U., 1965; MD, Harvard U., 1970. Diplomate Am. Bd. Med. Examiners, Am. Bd. Surgery. Intern in surgery Johns Hopkins U., Balt., 1977; rsch. fellow Nat. Cancer Inst., 1972-74; resident in surgery Johns Hopkins U. Hosp., Balt., 1974-78; asst. chief of svc. dept. surgery Johns Hopkins U., Balt., 1977-78; instr. Sch. of Medicine, Johns Hopkins U., Balt., 1978-79, assoc. prof., 1979-82, dir. rsch. and surgery, 1985—, prof., 1988—, Mark M. Ravitch prof., endowed chair, 1989—; mem. staff Sch. Hygiene and Pub. Health Johns Hopkins U., Balt., 1991—; mem. staff Johns Hopkins Hosp., Balt., 1977—; vis. prof. in field; cons. in field; chmn. GMA II study sect. NIH, Bethesda, Md., 1990-91; reviewer Jour. Sci., New Eng. Jour. Medicine, Am. Jour. Physiology, Jour. Clin. Investigation, and others; dean's lectr. Johns Hopkins U. Sch. Medicine, 1988. Editor, author: Measurement of Blood Flow, 1980, Splanchnic Ischemia and Multiple Organ Failure, 1990; mem. editorial bd. Jour. Gastroenterology, Jour. Surgery, Jour. Free Radical Biology and Medicine; contbr. articles to profl. jours. Lt. comdr. USPHS, 1972-74. NIH grantee, 1983—; recipient Shipley award Southern Surg. Assn., 1987. Fellow ACS; mem. Am. Physiol. Soc., Am. Surg. Assn., Am. Gastroenterol. Assn., Halsted Soc., So. Surg. Assn., Cosmos Club, Sigma Xi, Alpha Omega Alpha. Office: Johns Hopkins U Sch of Medicine 600 N Wolfe St # 685 Baltimore MD 21205-2104

BULL, FRAN, artist; b. Orange, N.J., Sept. 22, 1938; d. Samuel Sidell and Myra (Nelson) Grossman; m. Richard Niles Bull (div. 1969); 1 child, Katherine June. BA, Bennington, 1960; MA, NYU, 1980. Set designer The Shoe Co., Caldwell, N.J., 1990—; mask maker Theatrekore, N.Y.C., 1990—; exhibiting artist Morgan Gallery, Kansas City, Mo., 1976—, Louis K. Meisel Gallery, 1976-86; vis. artist Towson (Md.) State U., 1986-87. Artist (drawings) Mordant Rhymes for Modern Times (design award Am. Inst. Graphic Arts). Home: PO Box 442 Appletree Ln Alpine NJ 07620 Studio: 250 Herbert Ave Closter NJ 07624

BULLARD, JENNIE KNEPP, school system administrator; b. Indiana, Pa., Nov. 30, 1936; d. George Gus and Inez Marie (Busani) Sackandy; m. Ray Elva Bullard, Jr. BS in Edn., Pa. State U., 1966, MEd, 1972; PhD, U. Pitts., 1982; MA, Indiana U. Pa., 1984; JD, Duquesne U., 1990. Bar: Pa. 1991. Tchr. Penns Valley Area Schs., Spring Mills, Pa., 1966-69, Centre County Pub. Schs., State College, Pa., 1969-71; adminstr. Mental Health/Mental Retardation, State College, 1973-76; edn. adminstr. I.U. # 10, Phillipsburg, Pa., 1969-73, Pitts. Bd. Edn., 1976—; pvt. practice, atty. Torrance, Pa., 1991—; arbitrator Pa. Bur. of Mediation, 1991. Mem. ABA, Pa. Bar Assn., Westmoreland Bar Assn. (assoc.), Allegheny County Bar Assn. (assoc.).

BULLARD, JOHN KILBURN, mayor; b. New Bedford, Mass., Aug. 21, 1947; s. John Crapo and Katharine (Kilburn) B.; m. Anne Dunbar, June 27, 1981; children: Elizabeth, Anthony, Matthew. BA magna cum laude, Harvard U., 1969; MArch, M in City Planning, MIT, 1974. Agt. Waterfront Hist. Area League (WHALE), New Bedford, 1974-85; mayor City of New Bedford, 1986-92; dir. fisheries representation New Bedford (Mass.) Seafood Co-op, 1992—; bd. dirs. Mass. Mcpl. Assn., 1986-92; chmn. urban econ. policy com. U.S. Conf. of Mayors, 1988-92. Photographer 3 covers for Sail mag., 1970-71. Recipient Honor Award Nat. Trust for Hist. Preservation, 1981, Preservation award Mass. Hist. Commn., 1983, Design award Mass. Gov. Michael Dukakis, 1987. Democrat. Unitarian. Home: 19 Irving St New Bedford MA 02740-3426 Office: Coop-Wha-f New Bedford MA 02740-6113

BULLIS, JOHN DOUGLAS, academic administrator; b. Herkimer, N.Y., Dec. 3, 1948; s. Douglas Eugene and Joyce (Carroll) B.; m. Barbara Jo Morse, July 5, 1969 (div. Nov. 1988); 1 child, Amy Jo. AA, Herkimer County Community Coll. 1973; BA, SUNY, Cortland, 1975; MS, SUNY, Oneonta, 1980. Counselor, asst. dir. Alpha House Treatment Ctrs., Trumansburg, N.Y., 1975-78; dir., Alpha House Inc. Alpha House Treatment Ctrs., Trumansburg, 1978-80; asst. to the pres. Herkimer (N.Y.) County Community Coll., 1980-91, dir. coll. rels., 1991—. Editor: (tng. catalog) American Cancer Society Volunteer Development, 1990; author: Legendary Guided Trips, 1991. Bd. mem. Am. Cancer Soc.-N.Y. State Div., Syracuse, N.Y., 1987-91; com. chair N.Y. State Coalition on Smoking or Health, Albany, N.Y., 1989-91; commr. Herkimer (N.Y.) County Conditional Release Commn., 1989-91; chair Herkimer (N.Y.) County Bicentennial Bike Ride, 1990-91. With USNA 1967-71. Fellow Cen. N.Y. Poets Soc. (pres. 1980-86); mem. State Univ. Coun. on Univ. Affairs and Devel., N.Y. State Outdoor Guides Assn. (v.p. 1988-90). Republican. Presbyterian. Office: Herkimer County Community Reservoir Rd Herkimer NY 13350-1545

BULLOCK, R(ONALD) MORRIS, research chemist; b. Greensboro, N.C., Apr. 18, 1957; s. Claude George and Doris (Morris) B.; m. Cindy Blenke, Aug. 20, 1983; 1 child, Claude George, III. BS, U. N.C., 1979; PhD, U. Wis., 1984. Postdoctoral rsch. assoc. Colo. State U., 1984-85; chemist Brookhaven Nat. Lab., Upton, N.Y., 1985—. Contbr. numerous articles to profl. jours.; patentee Hydrogenation Using Hydrides and Acid., 1990. Mem. Am. Chem. Soc. Office: Brookhaven Nat Lab Dept of Chemistry Upton NY 11973

BULLOUGH, VERN L., historian, nurse, sexologist, researcher; b. Salt Lake City, July 24, 1928; s. D. Vernon Bullough and Augusta Rueckert; m. Bonnie, Aug. 2, 1947; children: David, James, Steven, Susan, Michael. BSN, Calif. State U., Long Beach, 1981; BS, U. Utah, 1951; MA, U. Chgo., 1951, PhD, 1954. Dean, faculty of nat. and social scis. SUNY, Buffalo, Disting. Prof. Contbr. articles to profl. jours.; author of over 30 books. With U.S. Army Security Agy., 1946-48. Named Outstanding Prof. Calif. State U. system, Disting. Prof., SUNY. Fellow Am. Acad. Nursing, Soc. Scientific Study Sex (past pres.).

BULMAN, WILLIAM PATRICK, data processing executive; b. Corona, N.Y., Jan. 11, 1925; s. William T. and Bridget A. (Gibbons) B.; m. Jane G. Jones, June 30, 1952. BS, U. Upper N.Y., 1947; BBA, Syracuse (N.Y.) U., 1949, MBA, 1977. In systems/programming Mohawk Airlines, Utica, N.Y., 1951-55; data processing mgr. Gold Medal Packing, Utica, 1956-59, West End Brewing, Utica, 1960-73; coord. on-line data processing systems Sperry-Univac, Utica, 1973-76, data processing mgr., 1976-77; programmer/analyst MDS, Herkimer, N.Y., 1977-86; sr. programmer, analyst, Momentum Techs., Herkimer, N.Y., 1986-89; ret., 1989; cons. Bilb-Tech, 1989—. With USN, 1941-46. Mem. Data Processing Mgmt. Assn. (v.p., treas.), Assn. Systems Mgmt. Address: 35 Ashwood Ave Whitesboro NY 13492

BULYK, JOHN-CONRAD (SPIDER J. C. BULYK), organizational transformation consultant; b. N.Y.C., June 11, 1949; s. John and Cathryn (Romanyshyn) B.; m. Stephanie Mary Musso, July 15, 1972; children: Jamin Delaney, Taralyn Zanot. BChE, NYU, 1971, postgrad., 1972-73, 76-81; postgrad., U. New Haven, 1991. Cert. mgmt. cons. With Francis Thompson Inc., N.Y.C., 1972; chief operating officer BEA Assocs., Inc., N.Y.C., 1972-80; mng. dir. Orgnl. Resources Group, Inc., N.Y.C., 1978-88, Pierce Bulyk & Co., Inc., N.Y.C., 1985-86; v.p. corp. devel. Ulbrich Stainless Steels & Spl. Metals, Inc., North Haven, Conn., 1988—; mng. dir. Met. Bus. Network, N.Y.C., 1983-88, N.J. Network, Newark, 1986-88; pres. The 3/4 Morgan Group, Ltd., N.Y.C., 1981. Editor The Morganeer newsletter, 1982; author short stories in Rough Rider, 1986, poetry; contbr. articles to profl. jours. Home: 31 Field Brook Rd Madison CT 06443-2468 Office: 57 Dodge Ave North Haven CT 06473-1191

BUMCROT, ROBERT JUDSON, mathematics educator; b. Kansas City, Mo., Nov. 24, 1936; s. Byron H. and Elsie M. (Oney) B.; m. Dolores Kale, Aug. 20, 1960 (div. Dec. 1974); children: Christopher B., David A.; m. Francesca Turchiano, Aug. 27, 1975. BS, U. Chgo., 1959, MS, 1960; PhD, U. Mo., 1962. Asst. prof. Ohio State U., Columbus, 1962-66, 67-68; lectr. U. Sussex, Eng., 1966-67; assoc. prof. Hofstra U., Hempstead, N.Y., 1968-72; prof. Hofstra U., Hempstead, 1972—. Author: Projective Geometry, 1968, Matrix Methods, 1976, Finite Mathematics, 1978, Discrete Mathematics, 1988. Mem. Am. Math. Soc., Math. Assn. Am. (gov. N.Y. sec. 1988-90). Lutheran. Home: 120 E 90th St New York NY 10128-1546 Office: Hofstra U Dept Math Hempstead NY 11550

BUNCE, DONALD GEORGE, SR., accountant; b. Niagara Falls, N.Y., July 22, 1938; s. Herbert Aaron and Margaret (Hickox) B.; m. Clara M. Wilcox, May 11, 1958 (div. Feb. 1969); children: Don Jr., BunniLynn, Terry H., Ramar L., Robin L.; m. Mary Ann Wieder, Apr. 24, 1987. AAS, SUNY, 1958; MBA, U. Calif., Santa Barbara, 1963. Sales clk. Sears Roebuck, Utica, N.Y., 1956-58; promotion mgr. Dunlap Co., San Padro, Calif., 1958-65; with customer rels. Moore Bus. Forms, Quakertown, Pa., 1965-72; registered rep. Met. Ins., Easton, Pa., 1972-82; acct. Tax Busters, Riegelsville, Pa., 1972—. Boro Councilman, Trumbauersville, 1963; sch. dir. Palisade Sch. Dist., Kintnersville, 1982-86. With USCG, 1958. Home and Office: 820 Easta Rd Riegelsville PA 18077

BUNDI, RENEE, art director, graphic designer; b. Elmont, N.Y., Apr. 20, 1962; d. Anthony Joseph and Marion Rose (Graziano) B. Student, St. John's U., 1980-84. Creative dir. Coastal Communications, N.Y.C., 1985-86; art and prodn. coord. Cahner's Pub. Co./Datamation mag., N.Y.C., 1986-87; sr. prodn. editor CMP Publs./Var Bus. Computer Systems News, Manhasset, N.Y., 1987-89; asst. art dir. CMP Publs./Var Bus. Computer Systems News, 1989-91; assoc. art dir. Varbus. CMP Publs., 1991—. Recipient Print Design award Print mag., 1988, 91, The Ozzie Design award Mag. Design and Prodn., 1988, 89, 90, 91. Mem. Graphic Artist Guild, Soc. Publ. Designers (Excellence in Design award 1987, 88, 91), Atex User's Group, MacIntosh User's Group. Roman Catholic.

BUNDY, JUDITH COX, executive recruiter; b. High Point, N.C., July 29, 1941; d. Henry Clay Jr. and Ann Crichton (Watkins) Cox; m. Thomas Freeborn Bundy Jr., Dec. 18, 1965 (div. 1985); children: Carter Alden, Graham Lewis. BA, U. Nebr., 1963. Intelligence officer CIA, Washington, 1963-65, 65-66; coord. Shearman & Sterling, N.Y.C., 1983-85; assoc. Ingram, Inc., N.Y.C., 1985-88, Norman Broadbent Internat., N.Y.C., 1988—. Host family for UN, 1977-81. Mem. Jr. League, Nat. Soc. Colonial Dames, Onteora Club. Republican. Episcopalian. Home: 94 Pecksland Rd Greenwich CT 06831-3649 Office: Norman Broadbent Internat 200 Park Ave New York NY 10166-0005

BUNDY, MARY LOTHROP, social worker; b. Boston, Apr. 9, 1925; d. Francis B. and Eleanor (Abbott) Lothrop; m. McGeorge Bundy, June 10, 1950; children: Stephen M., Andrew L., William L., James A. AB magna cum laude, Radcliffe Coll., 1946; MSW, Hunter Coll., 1980. Assoc. dir. admissions Radcliffe Coll., Cambridge, Mass., 1949-50; clin. social worker Jewish Bd. of Family and Children's Svcs., Bklyn., 1980-84; pvt. practice N.Y.C., 1984—; vice-chmn. and trustee Radcliffe Coll., Cambridge, 1962-80, acting v.p., 1978-79; overseer Harvard U., Cambridge, 1971-77; bd. dirs. Corning (N.Y.) Inc., 1973—; trustee and chair Edward W. Hazen Found., N.Y.C., 1985—; bd. dirs. Found. for Child Devel., N.Y.C., 1985—. Trustee Metropolitan Museum of Art, N.Y.C., 1968-78. Mem. Nat. Assn. Social Workers, Assn. Cert. Social Workers, Forum for Women Dirs., Phi Beta Kappa. Office: 246 E 83d St New York NY 10028-2894

BUNIN, JEFFREY HOWARD, manufacturing company executive; b. N.Y.C., July 15, 1948; s. Herbert Bunin and Ruth (Eisenberg) Lefkowitz. BS in Engring., CUNY, 1971; MBA, Rutgers U., 1976. Engr. Airco Carbon Graphite, Niagrara Falls, N.Y., 1971-72, Airco Indsl. Gases, Murray Hill, N.J., 1972-76; fin. analyst Great A&P Tea Co., Montvale, N.J., 1976-78; sr. fin. analyst MRI Div., Am. Can, Clark, N.J., 1978-80; dir. planning Matheson Gas Products Inc., Secaucus, N.J., 1980—. Mem. Alumni Assn. Rutgers U. (trustee Alumni Assn. Sch. Bus. Mgmt. 1986—), Masons. Home: 159 Franklin St Bloomfield NJ 07003-4978 Office: Matheson Gas Products 30 Seaview Dr Secaucus NJ 07094-1882

BUNK, GEORGE MARK, civil engineer, consultant; b. Beverly, Mass., June 23, 1952; s. George and Katherine (Montoni) B. BS in Civil Engring., Northeastern U., Boston, 1975; MS in Civil Engring., U. Wyoming, 1976. Civil engr. Hittmann Assocs., Columbia, Md., 1979-80; sr. engr. Morrison-Knudsen Engrs., Norwalk, Conn., 1980-83, dir. water resources, 1987-89; constrn. mgr. Morrison-Knudsen Engrs., Little Falls, N.Y., 1983-87; project mgr. Stetson-Harza, Utica, N.Y., 1989-91, program mgr., 1991-92; pvt. cons. Stetson-Harza, Little Falls, N.Y., 1992—. Commr. Bd. Edn., Little Falls Sch. Dist. Mem. ASCE, Constrn. Specifications Inst., Am. Water Resource Assn., Water Pollution Control Fedn., Am. Concrete Inst., Soc. Am. Mil. Engrs., Am. Correctional Assn., Rotary (group study exch. to Thailand 1983), Patria e Lavoro Soc. Home: 19 Arthur St Little Falls NY 13365 Office: 19 Arthur St Little Falls NY 13365 : PO Box 308 Little Falls NY 13365-0308

BUNKER, SAMUEL EMMET, international development consultant; b. Yonkers, N.Y., June 8, 1927; s. Ellsworth and Harriett Allen (Butler) B.; m. Margery Laub, Oct. 21, 1950; children: Stephen, Jennifer, James. BA, Yale U., 1950; MA, Harvard U., 1970. Farmer Vt., 1950-59; ins. adjuster Fla., 1960-62; asst. rep. Ford Found., New Delhi, India, 1963-68; program advisor Ford Found., N.Y.C., 1969-72; assoc. rep. Ford Found., Beirut, Lebanon, 1972-73; dep. regional rep. Ford Found., Cairo, Egypt, 1974-77; dep. head Middle East and Africa Ford Found., N.Y.C., 1977-78; adminstr. internat. programs div. Nat. Rural Electric Coop. Assn., Washington, 1978-90; internat. devel. cons. Vice chmn. CARE, N.Y.C., 1979—; treas. CARE Internat., Brussels, 1986—; chmn. Coop. Housing Found., Washington, 1981—; pres. Philippine Am. Found., Washington, 1990—. Sgt. U.S. Army, 1945-46. Named to Coop. Hall of Fame, Coop. Devel. Found., Washington, 1992. Mem. Nat. Coop. Bus. Assn., Cosmos Club, Elks. Home: Rte 2 Box 182 RR 2 Box 948 Putney VT 05346 Office: Nat Rural Elec Coop Assn 1800 Massachusetts Ave NW Washington DC 20036

BUNN, GEORGE H., financial company executive; b. Phila., Mar. 22, 1945; s. Harold T. and Marie A. (Drake) B.; m. Constance M. Fahey, June 3, 1967; children: Raymond, John, Timothy, Patrick, Brian, Catherine, Kristin, Allison. Student, LaSalle U., Phila., 1965-69, Am. Inst. Banking, Phila., 1963-66. Cert. cash mgr. Check processing specialist First Pa. Bank, Phila., 1963-66, mgr. domestic collections, 1966-71, mgr. employee svcs., 1971-73, asst. div. head acctg. svcs., 1973-78, asst. div. head trust ops., 1978-80, sr. product mgr., 1980-81, v.p., div. dir. cash mgmt., 1981-90; v.p., mgr. corp. payment products CoreStates Fin. Corp., Phila., 1990—. Fin. com. Roman Cath. High Sch., Phila., Holy Family Ch., Phila. Mem. Nat. Corp. Cash Mgmt. Assn., Rd. to Ednl. Achievement Through Choice. Democrat. Roman Catholic. Home: 537 Leverington Ave Philadelphia PA 19128-2635 Office: CoreStates Fin Corp FC 1-7-9-20 Box 7618 Philadelphia PA 19101-7618

BUNN, TOM CADE, airline pilot; b. Raleigh, N.C., June 1, 1936; s. Thomas C. and Lois (Tunnell) B.; m. Priscilla Andersen (div. 1987); children: Theresa, Lauren, Cynthia, Griffin, Kari, Ashley, William. BA, Wake Forest U., 1958; MSW, Fordham U., 1992. Pilot Pan Am, 1965-86, United Airlines, 1986—; founder Soar Inc., Westport, Conn., 1983—. Capt. USAF, 1958-65. Office: Soar Inc PO Box 747 Westport CT 06881-0747

BUNSHAFT, ROBERT, marketing executive, consultant; b. Boston, Oct. 19, 1947; s. Robert and Doris (Witkin) B.; m. Alexandra Arendt, July 18, 1981. BA, U. N.C., 1970; MBA, Boston Coll., 1984. Area coord. World Plan Exec. Coun., L.A., 1974-78; v.p. ops. United Overton Corp., Newton, Mass., 1978-80; exec. v.p. mktg. Boston Paper Mail Order, Newton, 1980-86, E & B Giftware, Mt. Vernon, N.Y., 1986-88; v.p. new products T. J. Litle & Co., Salem, N.H., 1988—; chmn. Am. Fedn. Sci. of Creative Intelligence Cambridge, Mass. chpt., 1981-85. Mem. Direct Mktg. Assn. (speaker 1981—).

BUNTING, JOHN PEARCE, stock exchange executive; b. Toronto, Ont., Can., Sept. 6, 1929; s. Alfred and Harriet (Lee) B.; m. Stephanie Keeley, Sept. 26, 1977; children: Mark Alfred, Elsa Brend, Harriet Elizabeth, Alexandra Keeley. BComm, McGill U., 1952. With McLeod, Young Weir & Co., Ltd., Toronto, 1952-55; with Alfred Bunting & Co., Ltd., Toronto, after 1955; pres. Alfred Bunting & Co., Ltd., 1967-77; mem. Toronto Stock Exchange, 1962-77, bd. govs., 1968-74, vice-chmn., 1972-73, chmn., 1973-74, mem., 1962-77, pres., chief exec. officer, 1977—; dir. Can. Gen.-Tower Ltd.; mem. bd. Trade Met. Toronto. Bd. govs. Appleby Coll., from 1968, bd. dirs. St. John's Convalescent Hosp., Toronto, from 1968, pres. 1983-84; pres. Fed. Internat. des Bourses de Valeurs, 1983-84; pres. Lakeland Conservation Assn., 1983-84. Mem. Kappa Alpha. Anglican. Clubs: Ticker (Toronto) (pres. 1976-77), Univ. (Toronto) (pres. 1979-80), Toronto Golf (Toronto); Granite, Osler Bluff Ski. *

BUNUAN, JOSEFINA SANTIAGO, early childhood education educator, graduate program coordinator; b. Cabanatuan, Nueva Ecija, The Philippines, Sept. 11, 1935; came to U.S., 1963; d. Jose Villanueva and Ignacia (Santiago) B. AB in Psychology, U. Philippines, 1958; diploma, Melbourne (Australia) Coll. of Early Childhood Edn.; MEd in Psychometrics, Boston U., 1965, EdD in Psychometrics, 1969; postgrad. in devel. psychology, Harvard U., 1985-86. Instr. U. Philippines, Quezon City, 1960-62; grad. asst. Boston Coll., 1963-64; elem. sch. tchr. St. ColumbKille's Sch., Brighton, Mass., 1964-65; resident counselor Boston U., 1965-67; prof. edn. Worcester (Mass.) State Coll., 1969—, grad. coord., 1985—; mem. adv. bd. Worcester State Coll. Child Ctr., 1975—, dir. Piaget Inst., 1980; ednl. cons. Filipino Assn. of Greater Boston, 1986-90; presenter, speaker 20th World Congress Orgn. for Early Childhood Edn. No. Ariz. U., Flagstaff, 1992. Contbr. articles to profl. jours. Cons. Benigno Aquino Found., Chestnuthill, Mass., 1986-88. Recipient UN scholarship Melbourne Dept. Edn., 1959-61, Colombo Plan scholarship, 1959-61; fellow U. Philippines, 1965-69. Mem. Nat. Assn. Early Childhood Tchr. Educators, Nat. Assn. for Edn. Young Children, Orgn. Mondiale pour l'Edn. Prescolaire, Mass. Assn. Early Childhood Edn., Mass. State Coll. Assn., Early Childhood Ednl. Exch., Phi Delta Kappa. Democrat. Roman Catholic. Office: Worcester State Coll 486 Chandler St Worcester MA 01602-2597

BUONANNI, BRIAN FRANCIS, health care facility administrator, consultant; b. Pawtucket, R.I., Sept. 2, 1945; s. James and Roselle B.; m. Lynne Buonanni (div. 1982); children: Donna, Karen, Jamie; m. Diane Manenty, Feb. 23, 1985. BA, Providence Coll., 1967; EdM, Boston Coll., 1968; M in Health Adminstrn., St. Louis U., 1973. Lic. nursing home adminstr., N.J. Rehab. counselor, tchr. R.I. Assn. for Blind, Providence, 1968-71; adminstrv. resident Carney Hosp., Boston, 1972; asst. adminstr. Alton (Ill.) Meml. Hosp., 1973-77, Gnaden Huetten Meml. Hosp., Lehighton, Pa., 1977-80; v.p. ops. Burdette Tomlin Hosp., Cape May Ct. House, N.J., 1980-85; chief oper. officer St. Elizabeth's Hosp., Elizabeth, N.J., 1985—, exec. v.p., 1989—; pres. Health Care Practice Mgmt., Jenkinstown, Pa., 1984—; chmn., mem. adv. bd. Shifa, McFaul & Lyons, Morristown, N.J., 1987—; mem. rev. com. N.J. Health Council, Trenton, 1987—. Fellow Am. Coll. Healthcare Execs.; mem. NAACP, Nat. Assn. Purchasing Agts., Rotary (pres.). Home: 12 Coldevin Rd Clark NJ 07066-1237 Office: St Elizabeth Hosp 225 Williamson St Elizabeth NJ 07202-3625

BUONCORE, RICHARD JAMES, financial executive; b. Queens, N.Y., Sept. 3, 1956; s. John Charles and Carmella Buoncore; m. Lorraine Marie Lackner, Aug. 1, 1988; children: Jessica Marie, Richard Charles, Christopher John. BS, Fordham U., 1978. CPA, N.Y. Auditor Peat Marwick Mitchell, N.Y.C., 1978-85; investment banker Lehman Bros., N.Y.C., 1985-91; chief fin. officer, prin. Spears Benzak Salomon & Farrell, N.Y.C., 1991—. Mem. AICPAs, N.Y. State Soc. CPAs. Republican. Roman Catholic. Home: 21 Holt Ct Glen Rock NJ 07452 Office: Spears Benzak Salomon & Farrell 45 Rockefeller Plz New York NY 10111

BUONOCORE, RICHARD ANTONIO, corporate executive; b. Jersey City, N.J., May 12, 1946; s. Antonio T. and Mary M. (Scala) B.; m. Patricia M. Orefice, June 8, 1968; children: Jennifer, Jason. BA, Rutgers Coll., 1968; JD, St. John's Law Sch., 1973. Detachment comdr. Def. Investigative Agy., Queens, N.Y., 1969-73; dir. ct. referral unit Office of the Inspector Gen., N.Y.C., 1973-74; dir. corp. security SCM Corp., N.Y.C., 1974-79; sr. v.p. adminstrn./asst. sec. Colonial Penn Group, Phila., 1979-89; v.p. adminstrn. Maxwell Macmillan, N.Y.C., 1989—; cons. The Scoreboard, Inc., Cherry Hill, N.J., 1989—, Bala Engrs., Inc., Wynnewood, Pa., 1989. Pres. trustees Woodcrest Community Assn., Cherry Hill, 1985-86. Capt. USAF, 1969-72. Mem. N.Y. State Bar Assn., Cert. Protection Profls., Am. Soc. Indsl. Security, Indsl. Devel. Rsch. Coun., Nat. Assn. Real Estate Execs. Home: 36 Providence Dr Princeton Junction NJ 08550-2153 Office: Maxwell MacMillan 866-3d Ave New York NY 10022

BURANDT, GARY EDWARD, advertising agency executive; b. Kansas City, Mo., Apr. 13, 1943; s. Herman Edward and Reka Lovice (Harrison) B.; m. Harriet Frances "Freddye" Krumrey, Aug. 12, 1966; children: Heather Lynn, Greta Anne. BJ, U. Mo., 1966. Advt. mgr. GE, Pittsfield, Mass., 1972-74; account supr. Marsteller Inc., Chgo., 1974-76; v.p., mgmt. supr. D'Arcy McManus & Masius, Chgo., 1976-77; sr. v.p. group dir. Marsteller Inc., Chgo., 1977-80; sr. v.p., gen. mgr. Marsteller, Brussels, 1981-84; exec. v.p., mktg. dir. Marsteller Europe, Brussels, 1984-85; exec. v.p., ops. mgr. Havas Conseil Marsteller, Paris, 1985-86; sr. v.p. group dir. Y & R Inc., N.Y.C., 1986-88; chief exec. officer Young & Rubicam/Sovero, Moscow, 1989-90; pres. and chief exec. officer HDM Worldwide, N.Y.C., 1990-92; pres., chief exec. officer Dentsu, Young & Rubicam Partnerships, N.Y.C., 1991—. With USN, 1968-71. Office: Dentsu Young & Rubicam Partnerships 810 7th Ave New York NY 10019-5818

BURBEA, JACOB N., mathematics educator; b. Livorno, Italy, Dec. 13, 1942; came to U.S., 1974; s. Amos Clemente and Dvora (Jonas) B.; m. Claire M. Moss; children: John, Michelle. BS, Hebrew U., Jerusalem, 1966; MS, Weizmann Inst., Rehovoth, Israel, 1968; PhD, Stanford (Calif.) U., 1971. Rsch. assoc. Stanford U., 1970-71; lectr. Tel Aviv (Israel) U., 1971-74; vis. prof. Pa. State U., University Park, 1974-76; prof. U. Pitts., 1976—; vis. prof. U. Pisa, Italy, 1972-73; vis. scholar Swedish Acads. Sci.-Inst., Mittag Leffler Djursholm, Sweden, 1981-82, 91, IBM T.J. Watson Rsch. Ctr., Yorktown Heights, N.Y., 1982-83, Korea Inst. of Tech., Taejon, 1987, U. Barcelona, Spain, 1988-89, 91, U. Provence, Marseilles, France, 1989-90; sr. scientist IBM Corp., Yorktown, 1982-83, Westinghouse Corp., Pitts., 1985-86, PPG Industries, Pitts., 1986—. Author: Banach & Hilbert Spaces, 1986; contbr. articles in areas of math. analysis, applied math., stats. and fluid mechanics to profl. jours. U.S. Army grantee, 1973, NSF grantee, 1976, 78, French Acad. Sci. grantee, 1984. Fellow Rend Circle Mat. Palermo; mem. Am. Math. Soc., London Math. Soc. Home: 409 S Dallas Ave Pittsburgh PA 15208-2818 Office: U Pitts Dept Math Pittsburgh PA 15260

BURCH, JOHN WALTER, mining equipment company executive; b. Balt., July 14, 1925; s. Louis Claude and Constance (Boucher) B. m. Robin Neely Sinkler, Apr. 19, 1952; children—John C., Robert L., Charles C., Anne N. BS in Commerce, U. Va., 1951; postgrad., U.S. Coast Guard Acad., 1951. With Procter & Gamble Co., Phila., 1953-65, sales mgr., 1960-65; v.p. Warner Co., Phila., 1965-73; chmn. bd., chief exec. officer S.S. Keely Co., Phila., 1973-75; pres., chmn. bd., chief exec. officer Burch Materials Co., Inc., Wayne, Pa., 1975—; dir. Eagle's Eye, Inc., Wayne. Bd. dirs. Nat. Multiple Sclerosis Soc., 1970-81, v.p., mem. exec. com., 1974-77; bd. dirs. Pa. Sports Hall of Fame, 1974—, v.p., mem. exec. com., 1974-79; chmn. Am. Legion Tennis Tournaments for State of Pa., 1975-82; mem. U.S. Congl. Adv. Bd., 1982—; bd. dirs. Eagle's Eye Lacrosse Club, 1982—. With USN, 1943-46, USCG, 1951-53. Named All-Am. in lacrosse, 1949. Mem. Am. Mgmt. Assn., Soc. Advancement of Mgmt., Internat. Platform Assn., Merion Cricket Club, Merion Golf Club. Republican. Roman Catholic. Home: 412 Conestoga Rd Wayne PA 19087-4812 Office: Burch Materials Co Inc 685 Kromer Ave Berwyn PA 19312-1317

BURCH, ROBERT STUART, marketing executive; b. Balt., June 3, 1959; s. Francis Boucher and Mary Patricia (Howe) B.; m. Kimberly Goetze, May 19, 1989; 1 child, Spencer. BA, U. Del., 1981; MBA, Harvard U., 1991. Mktg. rep. IBM, Balt., 1982-84, account mktg. rep., 1985-87; adv. cons. IBM, Washington, 1988-89, bus. sector mgr., 1991—. Mem. Balt. Country Club. Office: IBM 1301 K St NW Washington DC 20005

BURCHELL, ALBERT ROBERT, surgeon; b. N.Y.C., Dec. 26, 1932; s. Nicholas Anthony and Florence (Doscher) B.; m. Barbara Jean Conway, Dec. 26, 1956; children: Theresa, Karen, Patricia, Susan, Maureen, Richard, Margaret, Donna, Amy, Kathleen. BA, Fordham U., 1954; MD, Cornell U., 1958. Intern, resident surgery St. Vincent's Hosp., N.Y.C., 1958-63, attending surgeon, 1963—; surg. rsch. fellow NIH, N.Y.C., 1963-65; instr. clin. surgery NYU Sch. Medicine, N.Y.C., 1962-70, asst. prof., 1970-81; assoc. prof. surgery N.Y. Med. Coll., Valhalla, N.Y., 1980—; mem. exec. com. med. staff St. Vincent's Hosp., N.Y.C., 1980-90; co-investigator NIH, Health Rsch. Coun., City N.Y., N.Y. Heart Assn., NIH, 1960-80; prin. investigator John A. Hartford Found., Inc., Irene Heinz and John Laporte Given Found., Irwin Strasburger Found., N.Y.C., 1966-73. Contbr. articles to profl. jours., chpts. to books. Trustee St. Vincent's Hosp., N.Y.C., 1985-89, mem. exec. com., 1988-89. Recipient Surg. Rsch. award Internat. Coll. Surgeons, 1962, Horace Aryes Surg. Rsch. award N.Y. State div. Internat. Coll. Surgeons, 1963. Fellow ACS; mem. Assn. Surg. Edn., N.Y. Surg. Soc., N.Y. Cancer Soc., N.Y. Soc. Cardiovascular Surgery, Surg. Soc. N.Y. Med. Coll., Internat. Soc. Chirurgie. Home: 120 Stacey Ct River Vale NJ 07675 Office: 2 Fifth Ave New York NY 10011

BURCHENAL, JOAN RILEY, science teacher; b. N.Y.C., Dec. 11, 1925; d. Wells Littlefield and Bertha Barclay (Fahys) Riley; m. Joseph Holland Berchenal, Mar. 20, 1948; children: Elizabeth Payne, Joan Littlefield, Barbara Fahys, Caleb Wells, David Holland, Joseph Emory Barclay. BA, Vassar Coll., 1946; MAT, Yale U., 1971; MA, Fairfield U., 1981. Sci. tchr. New Canaan (Conn.) Country Sch., 1968-69, Low Heywood Sch., Stamford, Conn., 1968-69, The Thomas Sch., Rowayton, Conn., 1972-73; sci. tchr. Darien Bd. Edn., Conn., 1973-91, ret. Bd. dirs., chmn. standards com. A Better Chance, Darien, 1985—; bd. dirs. Darien Nature Ctr., 1979-91, Adirondack Trail Improvement Soc., 1975—, Darien Audubon Soc., 1978-86, Darien LWV, 1951-63; panel on grants for tchr. enhancement program NSF, 1987, 92; hon. chmn. Darien Sci. Fair, 1986; steering com. Holly Pond Saltmarsh Conservation Com., 1968-71; mem. acad. courses com. Darien Community Assn., 1964-71, chmn., 1971; trustee Garrison Forest Sch., 1959-62; bd. dirs. Alumnae & Alumni Vassar Coll. Recipient Presdl. award for excellence in sci. teaching Nat. Sci. Tchrs. Assn., NSF, Washington, 1985. Mem. AAAS, Nat. Assn. Biology Tchrs., Nat. Sci. Tchrs. Assn., Assn. Presdl. Awardees in Sci. Teaching (nominating com. 1987—), Cosmopolitan Club, Ausable Club, Noroton Yacht Club, Phi Beta Kappa. Republican. Presbyterian. Home: Juniper Rd Darien CT 06820-5707

BURCHFIEL, BURRELL CLARK, geology educator; b. Stockton, Calif., Mar. 21, 1934; s. Beryl Edward and Agnes (Clark) B.; m. Leigh H. Royden; children: Brian Edward, Brook Evans, Benjamin Clark. B.S., Stanford U., 1957, M.S., 1958; Ph.D., Yale U., 1961. Prof. geology Rice U., 1961-76; Prof. geology M.I.T., 1977-84, Schlumberger prof. geology, 1984—. Served with U.S. Army, 1958-59. Fellow Geol. Soc. Am., Am. Acad. Arts and Scis., Nat. Acad. Scis., Am. Geophys. Union, European Union Geoscis. (hon. fgn.); mem. Geol. Soc. Australia, Am. Assn. Petroleum Geologists. Home: 9 Robinson Pk Winchester MA 01890-3717 Office: 54-1010 MIT Cambridge MA 02139

BURCHILL, JOHN BRABAZON, machine tool executive; b. Dublin, Ireland, Nov. 6, 1938; came to U.S., 1957; s. Herbert and Hilda (Brabazon) B.; m. Ismay E. Hood, July 22, 1961; children: Jennifer, Michael. BSME, Princeton U., 1961. Asst. pers. mgr. The Singer Mfg. Co. Ltd., Clydebauh, Scotland, 1961-66; product sales mgr. The Singer Co., Findern, N.J., 1966-70; mgmt. indsl. prodn. div. The Singer Co., Elizabeth, N.J., 1970-71; mgmt. tech. sales Union Spl. Corp., Chgo., 1971-74; asst. gen. mgr. Egan Machinery Co., Somerville, N.J., 1974-79; sales mgr. Allen Stevens, Somerset, N.J., 1979-80, Hoglund Corp., Berkely Hts., N.J., 1980-86; v.p. Eisenberg & Co., N.Y.C., 1986-90; mgr. sales & mktg. AMI, North Branch, N.J., 1990—. Fellow Schs. & U. Club N.Y. Office: AMI PO Box 5049 Somerville NJ 08876-1301

BURD, ROBERT MEYER, hematologist, educator; b. N.Y.C., Aug. 25, 1937; s. David and Anne (Popkin) B.; m. Alice Stoller, May 30, 1964; children: Russell J., Stephen J. AB, Columbia U., 1959, MD, 1963. Diplomate Am. Bd. Internal Medicine, Am. Bd. Hematology and Oncology. Intern Albert Einstein Med. Sch., N.Y.C., 1963-64, resident in internal medicine, 1964-66; hematology fellow Montefiore Hosp., N.Y.C., 1966-67; pvt. practice medicine, specializing in hematology and oncology, Fairfield, Conn., 1969—; assoc. prof. medicine Yale U., New Haven, 1975; assoc. clin. prof. of medicine, 1975—; chief of hematology/oncology St. Vincent's Med. Ctr., 1980—, chmn. oncology practice com.; attending physician Yale Hosp., New Haven; mem. staff Park City, Yale-New Haven hosps., Bridgeport Hosp. Editorial bd. Conn. Medicine, 1974-78; med. cons. U.S. News and World Report, 1990; dir. oncology fellowship Yale-St. Vincent, 1991-92. Active Leukemia Soc. Am., Hemophilia Found.; chmn. profl. edn. com. Am. Cancer Soc., 1982. Fellow ACP; mem. AMA, Am. Soc. Hematology, Am. Soc. Internal Medicine, Am. Soc. Clin. Oncology, N.Y. Acad. of Scis., Soc. Columbia Grads., Columbia U. Alumni Fedn. Coun., Columbia U. Alumni Club (pres. Fairfield County 1983-85, editor newsletter 1982—). Office: 1305 Post Rd Fairfield CT 06430-6016

BURDESHAW, WILLIAM BROOKSBANK, engineering executive; b. East Orange, N.J., Nov. 20, 1930; s. Thomas Anderson and Margaret (Villecco) B.; m. Monica Dorr, Sept. 27, 1957; children: Leath, Thomas, Anne, Alison. BS, U.S. Mil. Acad., 1953; MSEE, Ga. Inst. of Tech., 1961. Commd. 2d lt. U.S. Army, 1953, advanced through grades to brig. gen., 1975, ret., 1979; pres. Burdeshaw Assocs., Ltd., 1979—; cons. Defense Sci. Bd., 1985-87. Engring. mgmt. cons. co. named by INC. mag. as 121st of 500 fastest growing pvt. cos., 1985. Mem. Kenwood Golf and Country Club (Bethesda), The George Town Club (Washington), Cripple Creek Club (Bethany Beach, Del.). Republican. Episcopalian. Office: Burdeshaw Assoc Ltd 4701 Sangamore Rd Bethesda MD 20816-2508

BURDICK, DAVID CHARLES, psychology educator; b. Ridgewood, N.J., Aug. 30, 1954; s. Charles Harold and Joyce (Griffith) B. BA in Environ. Studies & Psychology, Alfred U., 1977; MA in Psychology, U. Notre Dame, 1980, PhD in Psychology, 1983. Rsch. assoc. GERAS Ctr., Univ. Notre Dame, Ind., 1980-83; rsch. faculty GERAS Ctr., Univ. Notre Dame, 1983-84; asst. prof. Stockton State Coll., Pomona, N.J., 1984-88; assoc. prof. Stockton State Coll., Pomona, 1988—, coord. gerontology program, 1984—; mem. standards com. Assn. for Gerontology in Higher Edn., Washington, 1985-90. Contbr. articles to profl. jours. Trustee Caring House Projects, Pleasantville, N.J., 1987-91, sec., 1988-91; trustee Southshore Found., Linwood, N.J., 1989—, v.p., 1991—. Mem. Am. Soc. on Aging, Gerontol. Soc. N.J. (trustee 1990—, pres. 1992—), Gerontol. Soc. of Am., Northeastern Gerontol. Soc. Office: Stockton State Coll Pomona NJ 08240

BURDICK, WILLIAM MACDONALD, biomedical engineer; b. Providence, R.I., Apr. 24, 1952; s. Franklin Pierce and Lola Alice (Cook) B. BS, Ind. U. Pa., 1975; M of Engring., Tex. A&M U., 1981; postgrad., U. Tex., 1982-86. Engring. analyst FDA, Winchester, Mass., 1988-90; reviewer neurological devices FDA, Rockville, Md., 1990—. Inventor in field; contbr. articles to profl. jours. With USAF, 1976-78. Mem. Biomed. Engring. Soc., Amnesty Internat., World Wildlife Fund, Nature Conservancy, Greenpeace. Congregationalist. Office: HHS/PHS/FDA/ODE/NEDB 1390 Piccard Dr Rockville MD 20850

BURENGA, KENNETH L., publishing executive; b. Somerville, N.J., May 30, 1944; s. Nicholas Jr. and Louanna (Chamberlin) B.; m. Jean Case, Oct. 29, 1964; children: Kean L., Diene M. BS, Rider Coll., 1970. Budget acct. Dow Jones & Co., South Brunswick, N.J., 1966-67, asst. mgr. data processing control, 1968-69, staff asst. for systems devel., 1970-71, mgr. systems devel. and control, 1972-76, circulation mktg. mgr., 1977-78, circulation sales dir., 1979-80, v.p. circulation, circulation dir., 1980-86; chief fin. officer and adminstrv. officer Dow Jones & Co., N.Y.C., 1986-88, exec. v.p., gen. mgr., 1989-91; pres., chief oper. officer Dow Jones & Co., Inc., 1991—, also bd. dirs.; gen. mgr. Wall Street Jour., 1989—; bd. dirs. Ottaway Newspapers, Inc. Bd. dirs. Better Bus. Bur., N.Y., 1987. Staff sgt. USAR. Office: Dow Jones & Co Inc 200 Liberty St New York NY 10281-1003

BURG, FRED MURRAY, communications professional; b. N.Y.C., Sept. 22, 1951; s. Sandy and Blanche (Berger) B.; children: Elyssa, Scott. BS in Math., Poly. Inst. Bklyn., 1972, MS in Ops. Research, 1973. Guest lectr. Poly. Inst. Bklyn., 1975; mem. tech. staff AT&T Bell Labs., Holmdel, N.J., 1973-83, AT&T Info. Systems, Lincroft, N.J., 1983-84; mem. tech. staff AT&T Bell Labs., Holmdel, 1984-86, supr., 1986—; vice chmn., chmn. task group X3S3.7 Am. Nat. Standards Inst., 1986—; vice chmn., chmn. workshop on lower layers Nat. Inst. Standards and Tech., Open Systems Environment Implementors Workshop, Gaithersburg, Md., 1988; spl. rapporteur study group VII, ITT Consultative Com., Geneva, 1989—, editor V.42 error-correcting modems study group XVII, 1988-90; editor Internat. Orgn. for Standardization, Internat. Electrotech. Commn., Geneva; chmn. 802-Interworking IEEE, 1985-89. Editor, author 3 ISO internat. standards, 1983-89, 1 CCITT recommendation, 1988; guest editor IEEE Network Jour., 1991; contbr. articles to profl. jours. Office: AT&T Bell Labs 4K-335 Crawfords Corner Rd Holmdel NJ 07733-3030

BURG, STEVEN L., political science educator; b. N.Y.C., Mar. 28, 1950; s. Frank and Sarah (Edelman) B.; m. Judith Anne Roswick, June 18, 1972; children: Sarah Samantha, David Graham. BA, SUNY, Stony Brook, 1970; MA, Hunter Coll., 1973; PhD, U. Chgo., 1980. Lectr. Brandeis U., Waltham, Mass., 1979-80, asst. prof., 1980-86, assoc. prof., 1986—, dean Coll. Arts and Scis., 1990-92. Author: Conflict and Cohesion in Socialist Yugoslavia, 1973, Introduction to Comparative Politics, 1991; contbr. articles to profl. jours. Rsch. grantee, Nat. Coun. Soviet and Ea. European Rsch., 1988; Rsch. fellow Harvard U., 1984, Whiting Found., 1985, Exch. fellow Am. Coun. Learned Socs., 1983. Office: Dept Politics Brandeis U Waltham MA 02254

BURGART, HERBERT JOSEPH, education consultant; b. St. Marys, Pa., Apr. 27, 1932; s. Herbert Edmond and Bertha Elizabeth (Franzen) B.; divorced; children: Herbert Andrew, Nicolas Walter, Sarah Marie, Rachel Helene, Joshua William. BA, Calif. State U., Long Beach, 1954; MEd, Pa. State U., 1957, EdD, 1961. Cert. art tchr., supr., K-12. Prof., chmn. La. State U., Baton Rouge, 1958-60, Pa. State U., University Park, 1960-61, U. South Fla., Tampa, 1961-62, U. Ga., Athens, 1962-65, Peabody Coll., Nashville, 1965-66; dean, prof. Va. Commonwealth U., Richmond, 1966-76; pres., chief exec. officer Moore Coll. Art, Phila., 1976-81, Ringling Sch. of Design, Sarasota, Fla., 1980-84; cons. edn. Port Allegany, Pa., 1984—; dir. Port Allegany Sch. Dist., 1991—. Author: Creative Art: The Child and The School. Councilman Port Allegany Borough Coun., 1991; chmn. area chpt. ARC, 1990—. Sgt. U.S. Army, 1954-62. Republican. Home: 206 Chestnut St Port Allegany PA 16743

BURGE, F. WELDON, writer, researcher; b. Wilmington, Del., Feb. 14, 1956; s. G. Clark and (Duhadaway) D.; m. Cynthia J. Decker, June 16, 1990; 1 child, Eric; 1 stepson, Christopher O'Neill. BA in English, Bob Jones U., 1978. Proofreader Internat. Computaprint Corp., Newport, Del., 1979-90; prodn. editor, writer Ind. Sch. Mgmt., Wilmington, 1990—. Author: Grow the Best Root Crops, 1991; contbr. articles to profl. jours. Den leader Boy Scouts Am., Newark, 1991-92. Office: Ind Sch Mgmt 1316 N Union St Wilmington DE 19806

BURGER, GARY C., cultural center executive; b. Greenville, S.C., Nov. 6, 1943; s. Robert L. and Edith (Gray) B.; m. Pamela Bucklin, Sept. 12, 1964; children: Semantha Vail, Amanda Gray. BA, William's Coll., 1965, MA in Art History, 1976. Regional mktg. asst. Time, Inc., N.Y.C., 1965-69; asst. product mgr. Reader's Digest, Pleasantville, N.Y., 1969-70; v.p., owner Reed Worthley Advt., Burlington, Vt., 1970-73; assoc. dir. Mass. Coun. on the Arts and Humanities, Boston, 1976-78; dir. The Berkshire Mus., Pittsfield, Mass., 1979-89, Williamstown (Mass.) Regional Art Conservation Lab., 1989—; mem. vis. com. Williams Coll. Mus. Art, Williamstown, 1989—; treas. Nat. Inst. Conservation, Washington, 1990—; chmn. Assn. Regional Conservation Ctrs., 1990—. Author: (catalog) 100 American Drawings From J.D. Hatch Collection, 1976. Pres. New England Mus. Assn., Charlestown, Mass., 1987-89. Gary C. Burger Gallery named in his honor Berkshire Mus., 1989. Mem. Nat. Inst. Conservation (treas. 1990—), Assn. Regional Conservation Ctrs. (chmn. 1990—). Office: Williamstown Regional Art Conservation Lab 225 South St Williamstown MA 01267

BURGER, RICHARD MELTON, research biochemist; b. N.Y.C., Mar. 23, 1941; s. Sidney Joseph and Regina (Biederman) B.; m. Linda Kalver, 1969 (div. 1971); m. Deborah Mellis, Feb. 6, 1977; children: Claudia, Abigail. Student, Brandeis U., 1958-60, 65-68; BA, Adelphi Coll., 1962; postgrad., Harvard U., 1964-65; PhD, Princeton U., 1969. Postdoctoral fellow in virology U. Calif., Berkeley, 1968-71; asst. prof. biology Mid. East Tech. U., Ankora, Turkey, 1971-72; assoc. Sloan-Kettering Inst. for Cancer Rsch., N.Y.C., 1972-77; asst. prof. biochemistry Grad. Sch. Med. Sci. Cornell U., N.Y.C., 1973-77; from assoc. to prin. assoc. Albert Einstein Coll. Medicine, Bronx, 1977-86; assoc. Pub. Health Rsch. Inst., N.Y.C., 1986—; adj. assoc. prof. biology H.H. Lehman Coll. CUNY, Bronx, 1980-81; adj. assoc. prof. pharmacology NYU Med. Ctr., 1986—; adj. prof. chemistry and biology Coll. Arts and Scis. NYU, 1991—. Contbr. articles to profl. jours. Rsch. grantee Nat. Cancer Inst., 1976, Am. Cancer Soc., 1988, NATO Sci. Affairs Div., 1987; Stohlman Meml. scholar Leukemia Soc. Am., 1987, spl. fellow and scholar, 1981, 83. Mem. Am. Chem. Soc., Am. Soc. Biochemistry and Molecular Biologists. Office: Pub Health Rsch Inst 455 1st Ave New York NY 10016-0109

BURGER, SUZANNE LESLIE, psychologist; b. N.Y.C., Aug. 15, 1960; d. Walter Maurice and Ruth Hannah (Mayer) B.; m. David B. Wagner, May 29, 1988. BA, Yale U., 1982; PsyD, Yeshiva U., 1988. Lic. clin. psychologist Conn., Ohio. Psychology intern Yale U., New Haven, 1987-88, postdoctoral fellow, 1988-90, asst. prof. psychology, 1990-91; clin. supr. Yale U., 1988-91. Recipient David Rapaport award Clin. Psychology Student Assn. N.Y., 1987. Mem. Am. Psychol. Assn., Conn. Soc. Psychoanalytic Psychologists, Conn. Psychol. Assn. Home: 3 Sertz Ln Cos Cob CT 06807

BURGER, WARREN EARL, former chief justice of U.S. Supreme Court, academic administrator; b. St. Paul, Sept. 17, 1907; s. Charles Joseph and Katharine (Schnittger) B.; m. Elvera Stromberg, Nov. 8, 1933; children: Wade Allan, Margaret Mary Elizabeth. Student, U. Minn., 1925-27; LL.B. magna cum laude, St. Paul Coll. Law (now Mitchell Coll. Law), 1931; LL.D. (hon.), William Mitchell Coll. Law, Macalester Coll., U. Minn., NYU, Columbia U., U. Pa., N.Y. Coll. Law, Georgetown U., Am. U., Coll. William and Mary, Mercer U., Yeshiva U., Howard U., Ripon Coll., Washington Coll., Brigham Young U., George Washington U., W.Va. U., Pace U.; H.H.D. (hon.), other colls. and univs. Bar: Minn. 1931. Mem. firm Boyeson, Otis, Brill & Faricy (and successor firm Faricy, Burger, Moore & Costello), St. Paul, 1931, ptnr., 1933-53; asst. atty. gen., civil litigation div. U.S. Dept. Justice, 1953-56; judge U.S. Ct. Appeals D.C., 1956-69; Chief Justice U.S. Supreme Ct., 1969-87; now chancellor Coll. William and Mary, Williamsburg, Va.; adj. prof. Mitchell Coll. Law, 1931-46; chmn. Jud. Conf. of U.S., 1969—; chmn. Fed. Judicial Ctr. by tradition; hon. chmn. Inst. Jud. Adminstrn.; chmn. Commn. on Bicentennial of U.S. Constitution, 1985—. Chancellor emeritus Smithsonian Instn.; trustee emeritus Mitchell Coll. Law, Macalester Coll., St. Paul, Mayo Found., Rochester, Minn.; trustee Nat. Geog. Soc.; hon. chmn. Nat. Jud. Coll. U. Nev., Nat. Ctr. for State Cts., Williamsburg; hon. chmn. Supreme Ct. Hist. Soc.; trustee and chmn. Nat. Gallery of Art, 1969-86; pres. emeritus Bentham Club, London, 1971-72. Hon. Bencher Middle Temple, London and Kings Inn, Dublin; recipient Thomas Jefferson award U. Va., John Marshall award Coll. William and Mary, James Madison award Princeton U. *

BURGER, WERNER CARL, fine arts educator; b. Pforzheim, Baden, Germany, Dec. 27, 1925; arrived in U.S., 1926; s. Carl Frederick and Helen Rosalie (Schzaefle) B. BA, NYU, 1950, MA, 1951; postgrad., Columbia U., 1958, Rutgers U., 1963. Dir. fine arts dept. Westfield (N.J.) Sr. High Sch., 1951-56, West Morris Regional High Sch., Chester, N.J., 1956-60; prof. fine arts Kean Coll. N.J., Union, 1961—; cons. N.J. State Coun. of Arts, Trenton, 1975, 88. One man shows include Kean Coll., 1961, 90, Seton Hall U., Soth Orange, N.J., 1970, Signature Gallery, Far Hills, N.J., 1983, AT&T, Bernardsville, N.J., 1983, Schering Plough, Kenilworth, N.J., 1985, N.J. State Mus., Trenton, 1987, Morris Mus., Morris Plains, N.J., 1989, Jersey City State Coll., 1989, Church Door Gallery, Califon, N.J., 1989, Morris Mus., Morristown, N.J., 1990; retrospective at Schering Plough Corp. Gallery, Madison, N.J., 1991; exhibited in group shows Cork Gallery, Lincoln Ctr., N.Y.C., 1986, N.J. Watercolor Soc. Ann., 1988, Hunterdon Hospice, 1988-89, others. Trustee Hunterdon Art Ctr., Clinton, N.J., 1975-79, Federated Art Assn. N.J., Westfield, 1980-86. Carl Burger scholarship for arts named in his honor, 1991; recipient Grumbacher Outstanding Contbn. to Arts award Federated Art Assn. N.J. Mem. N.J. Water Color Soc. (2d prize 1990), Assoc. Artists N.J. (pres. 1981-84), Audubon Artists N.J., Phi Delta Kappa. Home: RR 1 Box 322 Califon NJ 07830-9605 Office: Kean Coll NJ Morris Ave Union NJ 07083-7117

BURGESS, DAVID, lawyer, government official; b. Detroit, Nov. 30, 1948; s. Roger Edward and Claire Theresa (Sullivan) B.; m. Rebecca Culbertson Stuart, 1985 (dec. Dec. 1988). BS in Fgn. Svc., Georgetown U., 1970, MS in Fgn. Svc., 1978, JD, 1978. Bar: D.C. 1978, U.S. Dist. Ct. D.C. 1979, U.S. Ct. Appeals (D.C. cir.) 1979, U.S. Ct. Appeals (fed. cir.) 1988, U.S. Ct. Internat. Trade 1988. Rsch. asst. Georgetown U. Sch. Bus. Adminstrn., Washington, 1975, asst. to dean, 1975-76; rsch. asso., prof. Acad. in the Pub. Svc., Washington, 1976-79; asst. editor Securities Regulation Law Report, Washington; legal editor Internat. Trade Reporter Bur. Nat. Affairs, Washington, 1978-79; atty. Cadwalader, Wickersham & Taft, Washington, 1979-81; mng. editor Bur. Nat. Affairs, Washington, 1981-82; dir. U.S. Peace Corps, Niamey, Niger, 1982-84, Rabat, Morocco, 1984-85; dir. policy planning, mgmt. Peace Corps, Washington, 1985-87; dir. Bur. Human Rights and Humanitarian Affairs U.S. Dept. State, Washington, 1987—; speaker workshops Minority Legis. Edn. Program, Ind. Assn. Cities and Towns, Georgetown U. Continuing Edn. Program, Communications Workers Am., Colo. State U., U. Wis. Alumni rep. Internat. Sch. Bangkok, 1972-74. Author: Financing Local Government, 1977, 2d edit., 1978, Preparation of the Local Budget, 2 vols., 1976, 2d edit., 1978, Local Government Accounting Fundamentals, 2d edit., 1977, Understanding Federal Assistance Programs, 2d edit., 1978, The POW/MIA Issue: Perspectives on the National League of Families, 1978; contbr. articles to pubs. With USAF, 1970-74. Mem. D.C. Bar Assn., Washington Internat. Trade Assn., Am. Acad. Arts and Scis., Washington Fgn. Law Soc., Federalist Soc., Rep. Nat. Lawyers Assn., Georgetown U. Alumni Assn. (bd. govs. 1975—, class rep. 1971-91), Nat. Press Club, Pres.'s Club, Fed. City Club. Roman Catholic. Home: 3115 1st Pl N Arlington VA 22201-1037 Office: Dept State Bur Human Rights and Humanitarian Affairs 2201 C St NW Washington DC 20520-9997

BURGESS, FREDERICK MANLEY, retired marketing and economics educator; b. Phila., Nov. 7, 1908; s. William Marsden Burgess and Edna Louise (Manley) Foster; m. Alice Trundy, Dec. 8, 1938 (div. 1940); m. Barbee Gale Lawson, Jan. 18, 1941; children: Eric Lawson, Geoffrey Marsden. BS, Haverford Coll., 1928; postgrad., Columbia U., 1931-35, 37-38, Am. U., 1945-46, U. Pa., 1949-52; MBA, Ind. U., 1949. Reporter New Rochelle (N.Y.) News, 1928-29; pub. mgr. Lay Co., Inc., N.Y.C., 1929-30; merchandising specialist DuPont Co., N.Y.C., 1930-37; asst. advt. mgr. Am. Cynamid and Chem. Corp., N.Y.C., 1937-38; mgr. sales promotion Columbia Mills, Inc., 1938-40; instr. Ind. U., 1946-49; sales mgr. Sta. WTTS, Bloomington, Ind., 1949; lectr. in mktg. U. Pa., 1949-51; pub. info. mgr. Office of Price Stabilization, Phila., 1951-53; assoc. dean, dir. admissions Univ. Coll.; assoc. prof. mktg. and econs. Villanova (Pa.) U., 1953-85.

Author: An Outline of Current Trademark Law, 1949. Publicity dir. Phila. Fire Prevention Week Program, 1953, dir. fire prevention programs, 1955-78; vice chmn. citizens com. Phila. Fire Dept., 1986, chmn. pub. rels. com., 1987; bd. dirs. Marple Newtown Sch. Dist., 1968-73, v.p. bd. Marple Newtown Adult Sch., 1974-86. With AUS, 1940-46. Mem. Am. Econ. Assn., Assn. for Continuing Higher Edn. (merit award 1976), Beta Gamma Sigma, Quarterly Club Villanova U. Ret. Faculty (pres. 1989—). Republican. Episcopalian. Home: 11 Marwood Dr Broomall PA 19008-1419

BURGH, RICHARD W., philosophy educator; b. N.Y.C., Mar. 7, 1945; s. George M. and Helen (Tanklefsky) B.; m. Janice Jaffe, June 7, 1980; 1 child, Jessica. BA, Rider Coll., 1968; MA, U. Wis., 1971, PhD, 1975. Asst. prof. Rider Coll., Lawrenceville, N.J., 1975-81; assoc. prof. Rider Coll., 1981-87, prof., 1987—; pre-law program dir. Rider Coll., 1987—. Contbr. articles to profl. pubs. Pres. Men's Club, Temple B'Nai Or, 1991—. NEH fellowship, 1981; Rider Coll. Summer fellowship, 1983-91. Office: Rider Coll 2083 Lawrenceville Rd Trenton NJ 08648-3099

BURGMAN, DIERDRE ANN, lawyer; b. Logansport, Ind., Mar. 25, 1948; d. Ferdinand William Jr. and Doreen Yvonne (Walsh) B. BA, Valparaiso U., 1970, JD, 1979; LLM, Yale U., 1985. Bar: Ind. 1979, U.S. Dist. Ct. (so. dist.) Ind. 1979, N.Y. 1982, U.S. Dist. Ct. (so. dist.) N.Y. 1982, U.S. Ct. Appeals (7th cir.) 1982, U.S. Ct. Appeals (D.C. and 2d cirs.) 1984, U.S. Supreme Ct. 1985, D.C. 1988, U.S. Dist. Ct. (ea. dist.) N.Y. 1992. Law clk. to chief judge Ind. Ct. Appeals, Indpls., 1979-80; prof. law Valparaiso (Ind.) U., 1980-81; assoc. Dewey, Ballantine, Bushby, Palmer & Wood, N.Y.C., 1981-84, Cahill Gordon & Reindel, N.Y.C., 1985—. Note editor Valparaiso U. law rev., 1978-79; contbr. articles to law jours. Mem. bd. visitors Valparaiso U. Sch. Law, 1986—, chmn., 1989—. Ind. Bar Found. scholar, 1978. Mem. ABA (trial evidence com. 1983-86, profl. liability com. 1986-89, ins. coverage litigation com. 1990—), Assn. Bar City N.Y. (com. profl. responsibility 1988-91, com. profl. and jud. ethics 1991—), N.Y. County Lawyers Assn. (asst. com. Supreme Ct. 1987—, exec. vice chmn. 1990, chmn. 1990—, bd. dirs. 1991—, exec. com. bd. dirs. 1992—, Outstanding Svc. award 1988, Chmn.'s award 1990), N.Y. State Bar Assn., Law and Humanities Inst., Fed. Bar Coun., Women's City Club of N.Y. Home: 164 E 61st St New York NY 10021-8539 Office: Cahill Gordon & Reindel 80 Pine St 17th Fl New York NY 10005

BURKART, ROBERT EDWARD, trade association executive; b. Newark, Nov. 24, 1943; s. Albert and Edna (Billitz) B.; m. Elaine Doris Fowler, June 19, 1965; children: Dawn Michael, Heather Lynn. BA, Trenton (N.J.) State Coll., 1965, MA, 1967; PhD, Purdue (Ind.) U., 1973. Asst. prof. Camden County Coll., Blackwood, N.J., 1967-70, U. Md., College Park, 1973-74; dept. head U. Wis., Platteville, 1975-77; mgr. sales tng. Am. Hoechst Corp., Murray Hill, N.J., 1978-82; mgr. human resources Am. Hoechst Corp., Branchburg, N.J., 1983-87; dir. mgmt. devel. svcs. Indsl. Rsch. Inst., Inc., Washington, 1988—. Home: 18709 Shremor Dr Derwood MD 20855-1455 Office: Indsl Rsch Inst 1550 M St Ste # 1100 Washington DC 20005-1708

BURKE, ANDREW JOHN, chemicals executive; b. Paterson, N.J., May 14, 1955; s. Edward F. Burke and Mary Joan (Thoma) Muench; m. Mary Eileen Byrne, July 2, 1977; children: Daniel Michael, Scott Andrew, Erin Patricia. BS, Villanova U., 1977; MBA, Manhattan Coll., 1983. CPA, N.J. Staff acct. Price Waterhouse & Co., Hackensack, N.J., 1977-80; fin. coord. Beecham, Inc., West Paterson, N.J., 1980-83; mgr. acctg. Degussa Corp., Ridgefield Park, N.J., 1983-84, controller, 1984-86, dir. human resources, 1986-87, v.p. mktg. svcs., 1987-88, v.p., chief fin. officer, 1988-92, exec. v.p. Chem. Group, 1992—. Mem. AICPA, N.J. Soc. CPAs, Fin. Exec. Inst. (internat. bus. com.). Home: 50 Sturr St Haledon NJ 07508-2845 Office: Degussa Corp 65 Challenger Rd Ridgefield Park NJ 07660-2104

BURKE, ANN MCFARLAND, nonprofit corporation executive; b. Galion, Ohio, Feb. 14, 1952; d. Ralph Clinton and Mary Patricia (Harley) McFarland; m. Michael Henry Burke, Jan. 31, 1981; children: Allison McFarland Burke, Andrew Michael. BA, Miami U., 1974; M of Urban and Regional Planning, George Washington U., 1982. Med. social worker Norfolk (Va.) Gen. Hosp., 1974-76; jr. planner Dept. of Interior, Washington and Claremont, N.H., 1977; sr. planner Hist. Am. Engring. Record, Washington and Butte, Mont., 1978; assoc. dir. Springfield (Mass.) Cen., Inc., 1978-84; pres. Greater Holyoke (Mass.), Inc., 1984—; cons. City of Longmeadow, Mass., 1978, others. Bd. dirs. Stagewest Regional Theatre, Springfield, 1985—; bd. dirs. Children's Mus., Holyoke, 1990—, Volleyball Hall of Fame, 1992, Am. Heart Assn., Holyoke, 1987—, Holyoke Hosp., 1987-90, bd. dirs., past chmn. Holyoke Vis. Nurses Assn., 1985-90; steering com. Mass. Spl. Olympics, Springfield, 1990. Named to Volleyball Hall of Fame, 1992. Mem. Rotary (bd. dirs. 1986-89, 92), Holyoke Merry-Go-Round (bd. dirs. 1988—). Democrat. Office: Greater Holyoke Inc 187 High St Ste 203 Holyoke MA 01040-6527

BURKE, DANIEL BARNETT, communications corporation executive; b. Albany, N.Y., Feb. 4, 1929; s. J. Frank and Mary (Barnett) B.; m. Harriet Shore, Aug. 31, 1957; children: Stephen, J.Frank, Sarah, William. A.B., U. Vt., 1950; M.B.A., Harvard, 1955. Various positions product mgmt. and devel. Jell-O div. Gen. Foods Corp., 1955-61; gen. mgr. WTEN-TV, Albany, 1961-64; corp. v.p. WTEN-TV, 1962; gen. mgr. WJR AM/FM, Detroit, 1964-69; corporate exec. v.p., dir. WJR AM/FM, 1967; pres. pub. div. Capital Cities Broadcasting Corp., N.Y.C., 1969-72; pres., chief oper. officer Capital Cities Broadcasting Corp., 1972-85; pres., chief oper. officer Capital Cities ABC Inc., 1986-90, pres., chief exec. officer, 1990—; bd. dirs. Rohm & Haas Co., Avon Products, Inc., Conrail. Bd dirs. Cities in Schs. Inc., Nat. Urban League, Am. women's Econ. Devel. Corp., Am. Film Inst.; past chmn. bd. trustees U. Vt.; past chmn. bd. trustees Med. Mission Sisters, Phila. Served to 1st lt., inf. AUS, 1951-53, Korea. Mem. Phi Delta Theta. Office: Capital Cities/ABC Inc 77 W 66th St New York NY 10023-6201*

BURKE, DANIEL VALENTINE, art educator, visual artist; b. Erie, Pa., Apr. 21, 1942; s. Joseph and Joanne (Wisniewski) B.; m. Jane Mary Craig, Sept. 9, 1970; children: Katherine, Ellen, Timothy, Matthew. Student, Columbus Coll. of Art and Design, 1960-62; BA in Art, Mercyhurst Coll., 1969; Med in Art, Edinboro (Pa.) State U., 1972. Instr. art Mercyhurst Coll., Erie, 1969-71, asst. prof. art, 1971-74, assoc. prof. art, 1974-82, dir. Dept. of Art, 1982-88, prof. art, 1982—; mem. Associated Artists of Pitts., 1987—; juror Panorama '84 Erie Summer Festival of the Arts Regional Art Exhabit, Erie, 1984; slide juror 14th Washington & Jefferson, Washington, Pa., 1982. One man show include Williams Coll. Mus. of Art, 1981; exhibited in group shows Hallways Buffalo, 1990, Spaces, Cleve., 1991, Pitts. Ctr. for Arts, 1991. With U.S. Army, 1962-65. Fellow Mid Atlantic Arts Found., 1988, visual arts fellow Pa. Coun. on the Arts, Pa., 1986, fellow MacDowell Colony, Peterborough, N.H., 1970; recipient Traveling show honor Assn. Artists of Pitts., Carnegie Mus. of Art, 1990. Mem. Northwestern Pa. Artist's Assn. (Painting award 1988, co-exec. dir. 1975—). Home: 223 E 6th St Erie PA 16507-1523 Office: 18 N Park Row 3d Fl Art Studios Erie PA 16501

BURKE, GRACE R., medical/surgical nurse; b. Lakewood, Pa., Mar. 24, 1925; d. Carroll George and Esther Lena (Lloyd) Reynolds; m. C. Grafton Burke Jr., Nov. 22, 1956; children: Daniel, David. Diploma in nursing, Wilson Meml. Hosp. Sch. Nursing, Johnson City, N.Y., 1948; BA, Roberts Wesleyan Coll., 1952. RN, Pa.; cert. tchr., correctional health profl., 1991, HIV/AIDS edn. instr., 1991, Pa. Instr. med./surg. nursing Pottstown (Pa.) Meml. Ctr. Sch. Nursing, 1964-71; tchr. Western Montgomery Vocat. Tech. Sch., Limerick, Pa., 1977-81; staff nurse Correctional Med. Systems, Graterford, Pa., 1984-90; AIDS edn. nurse State Correctional Instn., Graterford, 1990—; dir. health svcs. Valley Force Christian Coll., Phoenixville, Pa., 1987-88. Mem. C. S. Wilson Nursing Alumnae.

BURKE, HARRY BRIAN, podiatrist; b. Pitts., Oct. 22, 1940; s. Harry Martin and Margaret Mae (Kelly) B.; m. Alice Rita Gurman, Aug. 15, 1965; children: Brian, Tracy. Grad., Duquesne U., 1967; D. of Podiatric Medicine, Ohio Coll. Podiatric Medicine, 1972. Diplomate Am. Bd. Podiatric Surgery. Pvt. practice Monaca, Pa., 1972—; dir. Residency Program, Beaver, Pa. Contbr. articles to profl. jours. Mem. Am. Podiatric Med. Assn., Am. Coll. Foot Surgeons, Pa. Podiatric Med. Assn. Roman Catholic. Office: 1256 Brodhead Rd Monaca PA 15061-2522

BURKE, J. GRANT, foreign service officer; b. Boston, Feb. 18, 1943; s. Major Arthur W. and Mona M. (Grant) B. BS in Fgn. Service, Georgetown U., 1964. With U.S. Fgn. Service, 1966—; vice consul Sydney, Australia, 1968-69; polit. officer, ad interim charge d'affaires Malabo, Equatorial Guinea, West Africa, 1969-70; mem. staff Pres.'s Commn. on UN, 1970-71; with Internat. Orgn. Bur. U.S. State Dept., Washington, 1971-77; polit. and econ. officer U.S. Consulate Gen. Hamilton, Bermuda, 1977-79; econ. anlyst Bur. Intelligence and Research, 1979-84; editor Sec. of State's Daily Report on Congress Office of Legis. Affairs, 1984-87; 1st sec. U.S. Embassy New Delhi, 1987-90; legis. affairs officer Econ. Bur., 1990—. Club: City Tavern (Washington). Home: 2400 Virginia Ave NW Apt 622C Washington DC 20037-2612

BURKE, JACQUELINE YVONNE, telecommunications executive; b. Newark, Apr. 10, 1949; d. Trim and Viola (Smith) Russell; m. Harry Clifford Burke Jr., Aug. 20, 1968 (div. 1977); 1 child, Terence Christopher. Student, Howard U., Washington, 1966-67. Teaching asst. Barringer High Sch., Newark, 1967; course developer Prudential Property and Casualty Ins., Newark, 1968-74; exec. Ad-A-System, Avenel, N.J., 1974-77; staff mgr. AT&T, Basking Ridge, N.J., 1977-83; quality assurance mgr. ops. and engring. Bell Communications Rsch., Morristown, N.J., 1984-86, dir. traffic routing adminstr., mem. tech. staff, 1986-91, tng./devel. specialist, 1991—; instr. Summer Tech. Edn. Program, Morristown, 1987; pres. Jacqueline Burke Enterprises, 1991—. Instr. Youth for Christ, Fanwood, N.J., 1984-86; cons., instr. Black Achievers/YMCA, Newark, 1985; pres. Archway Pregnancy Ctr., Elizabeth, N.J., 1985-89; mem. Faith Fellowship Ministries World Outreach Ctr., 1987—, tchr. neighborhood Bible study, 1989—; mem. bd. advisors Bros. and Sisters, Inc., 1989—; apptd. bd. advisors Am. Biog. Inst. Rsch., 1989; sec. Women Aglow, 1991-92, pres. Plainfield chpt. fellowship, 1992—. Recipient Tribute to Woman in Industry award YWCA, 1985, Black Achiever award, 1985, Sojourner Truth award Nat. Assn. Negro Bus. and Profl. Women, 1989, Bellcore Synergy III cert., 1989, Recognition award YWCA, 1986, Cert. of Recognition Urban Women's Ctr., 1990, Bellcore Software Devel. and Software Com. Quality award, 1991; named Outstanding Young Woman Am., 1985; Proclamation from City Mayor of Plainfield, 1990. Mem. NAFE, Nat. Assn. Negro Bus. and Profl. Women's Club, Inc., Career Options/YWCA, Am. Mgmt. Assn., Tribute to Women and Industry (speaker, mem. mgmt. forum 1985—), Internat. Platform Assn., Am. Biog. Inst. (rsch. bd. advisors 1989—). Democrat. Home: 229 West Ave South Plainfield NJ 07080-1924 Office: Bell Communications Rsch 435 South St Rm 1246A Morristown NJ 07960-6422

BURKE, JOHN FRANCIS, surgeon, educator, researcher; b. Chgo., July 22, 1922; s. Frank A. and Mary V. Burke; m. Agnes Redfearn Goldman, June 24, 1950; children: John Selden, Peter Ashley, Ann Campbell, Andrew Thomas. B.S., U. Ill., 1947; M.D., Harvard U., 1951. Intern Mass. Gen. Hosp., Boston, 1951-52; resident in surgery Mass. Gen. Hosp., 1952-54, 56-57; rsch. fellow Lister Inst., London, 1955; vis. surgeon Mass. Gen. Hosp., Boston, 1968—; chief trauma services Mass. Gen. Hosp., 1980—; program dir. Burn Trauma Research Center, 1973—; assoc. prof. surgery Harvard Med. Sch., 1969-75, prof. surgery, 1975-76, Helen Andrus Benedict prof. surgery, 1976—; chief of staff Shriners Burns Inst., Boston, 1969-80; vis. prof. MIT, 1977—; pioneer in development of artificial skin; developer concept antibiotic use to prevent post-operative infection; vis. fellow Baliol Coll. Oxford U., 1990; program dir. New Eng. Burn Demonstration Program, 1977-80; chmn. bd. dirs. Boston Med. Flight. Co-editor 12 books in field; contbr. articles to profl. jours. Served with USAAF, 1942-45. Moseley Traveling fellow, 1955. Mem. Am. Burn Assn. (pres. 1982-83), Boston Surg. Soc. (pres. 1983), N.Y. Acad. Scis., AMA, Am. Thoracic Soc., Mass. Med. Soc., A.C.S., Soc. Univ. Surgeons, Infectious Disease Soc. Am., Am. Surg. Assn., New Eng. Surg. Soc. (pres. 1989), Am. Assn. Surgery of Trauma, Surg. Infection Soc. (founding mem., pres. 1985), Internat. Soc. Burn Injuries, Am. Trauma Soc. (founding mem.). Home: 216 Prospect St Belmont MA 02178-2616 Office: Mass Gen Hosp Harvard Med Sch Trauma Svc Trauma Svc Boston MA 02114

BURKE, J(OHN) MICHAEL, environmental company executive; b. Takoma Park, Md., Apr. 27, 1946; s. John Richard and Doris Jean (Waltman) B.; m. Mary Jane Elenewski, May 24, 1975; children: Alexander, Mairead. AB, Thomas More Coll., 1966; PhD, Case Western Res. U., 1971. Staff scientist U.S. Army Missile Command, Redstone Arsenal, Ala., 1971; presdl. intern Nat. Bur. Standards, Gaithersburg, Md., 1972-73; rsch. assoc. Princeton (N.J.) U., 1973-77; project leader Procter and Gamble Co., Cin., 1977-87; v.p. Roslon Internat. Corp., Point Pleasant, N.J., 1987-91; pres. Pyrogenics of N.J., Ringoes, 1991-92; dir. environ. projects Tiger Constrn. Svc. Corp., Ringoes, 1992—; chmn. Environ. Commn., Spring Lake, N.J., 1991—; mem. Spring Lake Planning Bd., 1991—; adj. instr. Brookdale Community Coll., Lincroft, N.J., 1992—. Contbr. articles to environ. jours. Pres. Spring Lake/Spring Lake Heights Soccer, 1992. NSF fellow, 1965; NASA trainee Case Western Res. U., 1968; NIH postdoctoral fellow, 1976. Mem. Am. Chem. Soc., N.J. Fedn. Planning Ofcls., Nassau Club. Home: 309 Jersey Ave Spring Lake NJ 07762

BURKE, JOHN PATRICK, university educator; b. L.A., Oct. 16, 1953; s. Donald Edward and Eleanor Sutherland (Van Dorn) B. AB, Stanford U., 1975; MA, Princeton U., 1979, PhD, 1982. Asst. prof. U. Vt., Burlington, 1984-88, assoc. prof., 1988—, chmn. dept. polit. sci., 1991—. Author: Bureaucratic Responsibility, 1986, The Institutional Presidency, 1992; coauthor: How Presidents Test Reality, 1989. Williams Coll. fellow, Williamstown, Mass., 1982-84. Mem. Phi Beta Kappa. Office: U Vt Dept Polit Sci Burlington VT 05405

BURKE, JOSEPH ELDRID, materials scientist; b. Berkeley, Calif., Sept. 1, 1914; s. Charles Eldrid and Ruth (Hadcock) B.; m. Kathleen Mary Wilson, Sept. 16, 1939; children: Charles Robert, Margaret VanDecar. BA, McMaster U., Hamilton, Ont., 1935; PhD, Cornell U., 1940. Metallurgist Internat. Nickel Co., Bayonne, N.J., 1940-41; chemist Norton Co., Worcester, Mass., 1941-43; group leader Manhattan Dist. Project, Los Alamos, N.Mex., 1943-46; assoc. prof. U. Chgo., 1946-49; mgr. metallurgy Knolls Atomic Power Lab., Schenectady, 1949-54; mgr. ceramics GE Corp. Rsch. & Devel. Ctr., Schenectady, 1954-79; cons. in matls. sci. Burnt Hills, N.Y., 1979—; adj. prof. Rensselaer Poly. Inst., Troy, 1960-85; cons. Gillette Co., Boston, 1980—. Author (with A. Seybolt) Procedures in Experimental Metallurgy, 1955; editor rev. vols. Progress in Ceramic Science, Vols. 1-4, 1961, 62, 64, 66; contbr. articles to profl. jours. Chmn. Zoning Bd. Appeals, Ballston, N.Y., 1970-74. Recipient Frenkel Prize, Internat. Inst. of Simtering, Belgrade, 1981. Fellow ASM, Am. Nuclear Soc., Am. Ceramic Soc. (pres. 1974-75, Jeppson award 1981); mem. Nat. Acad. Engring. Home: 33 Forest Rd Burnt Hills NY 12027-9743

BURKE, KATHLEEN MARY, lawyer; b. N.Y.C., Dec. 8, 1950; d. Hubert J. and Catherine (Painting) B. BA magna cum laude, Marymount Manhattan Coll., 1972; JD, U. Va., 1975. Bar: N.Y. 1976, Calif. 1979, U.S. Dist. Ct. (so. and ea. dists.) N.Y. 1977, U.S. Ct. Appeals (2d cir.) 1977. Assoc. Donovan Leisure Newton & Irvine, N.Y.C., L.A., 1975-81, Kelley Drye & Warren, N.Y.C., 1981-84; assoc. counsel Soc. N.Y. Hosp., 1984-87, sec. and counsel, 1987—; sec. Joint Bd. N.Y. Hosp.-Cornell Med. Ctr., N.Y. Hosp.-Cornell Med. Ctr. Fund, Inc., Soc. N.Y. Hosp. Fund, Inc., Royal Charter Properties, Inc., Royal Charter Properties-East, Inc., Royal Charter Properties-Westchester, Inc., Exec. Registry, Inc., N.Y. Hosp. Downtown, Inc.; faculty Concern for Dying, N.Y.C., 1985—. Contbr. articles to profl. jours. Trustee Marymount Manhattan Coll., N.Y.C., 1990—. Mem. ABA, N.Y. State Bar Assn. (health law com. 1989-91), Assn. of Bar of City of N.Y. (children and law com. 1986-89, law and medicine com. 1991—), Am. Acad. Hosp. Attys. (speaker annual confs. 1987—), Health Care Exec. Forum, Nat. Health Lawyers, Greater N.Y. Hosp. Assn. Legal Adv. Com. Roman Catholic. Office: Soc NY Hosp 525 E 68th St Rm Whitney 109 New York NY 10021-4873

BURKE, PATRICIA, not-for-profit association executive; b. Boston, Apr. 30, 1943; d. Frederick Joseph and Dorothy (Thomas) Whateley; m. Paul W. Burke, Dec. 7, 1963 (div.); 1 child, Matthew A. Grad. high sch., Stoneham, Mass. Mktg. adminstr. Textron, Wilmington, Mass., 1966-76; contract adminstr. Kollsman Instruments, Merrimac, N.H., 1977-78; sec. gen. Internat. Desalination Assn., Topsfield, Mass., 1978—; sales rep. Internat. Conf. & Exhbn., London, 1988-90; pub. Water Internat. Industry News, London, 1988-90; pres. Compass Point, Inc. Vol. Ipswich (Mass.) Planning Coun. Recipient excellence and achievement awards Internat. Desalination Assn. Mem. Nat. Water Supply Improvement Assn. (bd. dirs. 1989-91, excellence and achievement awards), Water Resources Export Coun. (bd. dirs. 1988-90). Roman Catholic. Office: Internat Desalination Assn PO Box 387 Topsfield MA 01983-0587

BURKE, RICHARD THOMAS, writing educator; b. Jersey City, N.J., Oct. 5, 1947; s. Richard Patrick and Dorothy Florence (Golden) B. BA, U. Colo., 1969; MA, SUNY, Buffalo, 1971. Lectr. U. Hawaii, Honolulu, 1977-78; tchr. Punahou Sch., Honolulu, 1978-80; instr. Brookdale Community Coll., Lincroft, N.J., 1986—; freelance editor/writer, Newark, Navesink, N.J., 1980—; instr. Poets in the Schs., Honolulu, 1975-77. Author published essays, poetry; editor: (textbook) Pentech IV, 1990; editor/founder (literary jours.) Raport, Hanai; asst. editor Choice. V.p. Art Alliance of Monmouth County, Red Bank, N.J., 1991; active Big Bros./Big Sisters Am., Providence, 1966, Honolulu, 1975-80; assoc. mem. Navesink Fire Co., 1988—. Lt. cpl. USMC, 1965-68. Recipient Writing award City and County of Honolulu, 1977, Jean Townsend award Art Alliance of Monmouth County, 1990, 91. Fellow NEA. Home: RD 192 Chapel Hill Rd PO Box 574 Atlantic Highlands NJ 07716 Office: Brookdale Community Coll Newman Springs Rd Lincroft NJ 07738-1329

BURKE, RITA DENISE, engineering manager; b. Woonsocket, R.I., Aug. 21, 1950; d. Edward A. and Lucille G. (Lussier) Poirier; m. Richard Sousa, June 27, 1970 (div. Nov. 1979); children: Jennifer A., Lori J.; m. Russell A. Burke, Aug. 11, 1983. BSME, Roger Williams Coll., 1985; postgrad. in bus. adminstrn., Southeastern Mass. U., 1991. Draftsperson Mossberg/Hubbard, Cumberland, R.I., 1968-73; cons. Univis Frame, North Attleboro, Mass., 1974-76; draftsperson Carlton Mfg., Central Falls, R.I., 1976-77, Fram Corp., East Providence, R.I., 1977-81; supr. Thomson Nat. Press, Franklin, Mass., 1981-85; design engr. Taft Pierce, Cumberland, 1985-86; product design mgr. Cumberland Engring., South Attleboro, Mass., 1986—. Sec. Parent Adv. Com. for Spl. Edn., Somerset, Mass., 1990-91; mem. Supt.'s Parent Adv. Com., Somerset, 1991. Mem. Soc. of Plastics Engrs. Roman Catholic. Home: 39 Antrim St Somerset MA 02726-1413 Office: John Brown Cumberland Engring Div PO Box 6065 Providence RI 02940-6065

BURKE, RITA HOFFMANN, educational administrator; b. N.Y.C., Dec. 22, 1925; d. George William and Beatrice (Kearney) Hoffmann; m. Francis Joseph Burke, Oct. 4, 1952; children: Francis J., Patrick G., Joseph P., Rosemary Childs, Jeanmarie R., Gerard W., Christopher M., Maurita B. BA in Econs., Hunter Coll., N.Y.C., 1951; postgrad., Corning (N.Y.) Community Coll., 1985. Cashier Bloomingdale's Dept. Store, N.Y.C., 1943; jr. actuary Equitable Life Assurance Soc., N.Y.C., 1944-48; jr. acct. Steuben Glass, N.Y.C., 1948-53; controller E. R. Wolcott, Inc., Big Flats, N.Y., 1973-78; library asst. Notre Dame High Sch., Elmira, N.Y., 1978-85, bus. mgr., 1985—. Mem. sch. bd. St. Mary our Mother Sch., Horseheads, N.Y., 1970-76; mem., sec. parish coun. St. Mary Ch., Horseheads, 1973-76; historian Cinderella, 1973. Mem. Nat. Newman Hon. Soc. Democrat. Roman Catholic.

BURKE, SHAWN PATRICK, securities analyst; b. Jackson Heights, N.Y., July 6, 1958; s. Gerard A. and Pauline (Minarchi) B. BA, U. Rochester, 1980; MBA, Providence Coll., 1982. Bus. systems analyst Time Inc., Chgo. and Washington, 1982-84; sr. fin. analyst Shearson Lehman Brothers, Inc., N.Y.C., 1984-85; asst. v.p. Standard & Poor's Corp., N.Y.C., 1985-90; v.p. capital markets credit Merrill Lynch & Co., N.Y.C., 1990—; cons. Time, Inc., Washington, 1985, Chelsea Home Pubs., N.Y.C., 1987-88; staff researcher Rudolph Giuliani Rep. Mayoral Campaign, N.Y.C., 1989. President 132d Joralemon Assocs., Bklyn. Heights, N.Y., 1988-91. Mem. Inst. Mgmt. Scis., MENSA, Appalachian Mountain Club. Home: 4 Clover Ln Rumson NJ 07760-1849 Office: Merrill Lynch & Co World Financial Ctr South Tower 7th Fl New York NY 10080

BURKE, VIRGINIA EILEEN, small business owner; b. Willow Grove, Pa., Jan. 15, 1948; s. William David Coffin and Virginia Rullo; m. Edward Francis Burke, Nov. 18, 1960; children: Kimberly Ann, Hiya Blu, Sarah, John. Assoc. Early Childhood Edn., Keystone Jr. Coll., 1989—. Tchr. asst. Mayfield, Pa., 1986-92; owner, pres. Me-Alone Inc., Forest City, Pa., 1991—. Author: The 911 Project, 1990. Home and Office: Me-Alone Inc 603 Susquehanna St Forest City PA 18421

BURKET, PATRICIA KRISE, lawyer; b. McKeesport, Pa., Mar. 16, 1952; d. David Leo and Ruth Elizabeth (Lostetter) Krise; m. Wallace Charles Burket, Feb. 14, 1989. BS, Pa. State U., 1974, postgrad., 1974-76; postgrad., SUNY, Buffalo, 1976-77; JD, Franklin Pierce Law Ctr., 1986. Bar: Pa. 1986. Asst. counsel Pa. Unemployment Compensation Rev. Bd., Harrisburg, 1986-88, Pa. Pub. Utility Commn., Harrisburg, 1988—. Mem. AAAS, ABA, Pa. Bar Assn., N.Y. Acad. Sci., MENSA, Pa. State U. Alumnae Assn. Home: 97 N Hershey Rd Harrisburg PA 17112-9750 Office: Pa Pub Utility Commn PO Box 3265 Harrisburg PA 17105-6532

BURKETT, MARY FRANCES (MARY FRANCES ST. ONGE), art educator; b. Indiana, Pa., Feb. 24, 1939; d. George Kelly and Bertha (Ness) B.; m. Peter David St. Onge, May 20, 1972; 1 child, Anne. BS, Ind. U. Pa., 1961; MEd, U Pitts., 1964; PhD, Pa. State U., 1977. Art tchr. S.W. Butler (Pa.) Sch. Dist., 1961-63; art supr. Shippensburg (Pa.) Sch. Dist., 1963-64; grad. asst. U. Pitts., 1964-65, instr., 1965; art tchr. Penn Hills (Pa.) Sch. Dist., 1965-66; prof. Kutztown (Pa.) U., 1966—, chair art edn. and crafts, 1985—. Mem. Nat. Art Edn. Assn, Pa. Art Edn. Assn. (bd. dirs.), co-editor newsletter 1987—, Outstanding Art Educator Pa. award 1991). Office: Kutztown U Dept Art Edn and Crafts Kutztown PA 19530

BURKHAMMER, STEWART CURTIS, construction and engineering company executive; b. Long Beach, Calif., Dec. 27, 1943; s. Henry Bland and Edith Marie (Jones) B.; m. Cheryl Ernestine Fisher, June 28, 1969; children: S. Christopher, Wendy Lynette. Student, U. Wis., Whitewater, 1962-65, cert. in safety engring., 1967. Registered safety engr., Calif.; cert. safety profl., safety and health technician, safety mgr. With Bechtel Constrn., Inc., 1966—, regional mgr. safety, San Francisco, 1977-85, Gaithersburg, Md., 1985-86, asst. mgr. safety, 1986-88, mgr. safety svcs., 1988-89, v.p., mgr. safety svcs., 1989—. Mem. bd. advisors Ctr. Excellence, W.Va. U. Mem. Am. Soc. Safety Engrs. (profl.), World Safety Orgn., Nat. Constructors Assn. (vice chmn. safety and health com. 1987-88, chmn. 1988-89), U.S. Govt. Safety and Health delegation to People's Republic of China, Nat. Erectors Safety and Health Com., Meth. Men's Club. Republican. Home: 9212 Woodvale Dr Damascus MD 20872-1062 Office: 15740 Shady Grove Rd Gaithersburg MD 20877-1435

BURKHARDT, CHARLES HENRY, professional society executive, author, lecturer, consultant; b. Bklyn., June 17, 1915; s. Adolph Michael and Mildred (Herman) B.; m. Lillian Sanders, Jan. 31, 1942; children: Gregory Charles, Christopher Michael. BS, St. John's U., 1938; postgrad., Pratt Inst., 1947-48. Svc. mgr., asst. sales mgr. Concord Oil Corp., N.Y.C., 1939-43; instr. heat engring. Walter Hervey Jr. Coll., N.Y.C., 1947-49; dir. edn. Perfex Corp., Milw., 1949-51; gen. mgr. Paragon Maintenance Co., Mineola, N.Y., 1951-55; mng. dir., sec.-treas. Oil Heat Inst. Am., N.Y.C., 1955-60; v.p. Nat. Oil Fuel Inst., N.Y.C., 1960-62; exec. v.p. New Eng. Fuel Inst., Boston, 1962-81, pres., 1981-86; cons. Standard Oil Co., N.J., 1957-58, Bacharach Instrument Co., 1947, Richfield Mfg. Co., 1948, Arthur D. Little Inc., Global Petroleum Inc., Centennial and Atlantic Mutual Ins. Cos., Scully Signal Co., Nutter, McClennan & Fish, Boston, Rich, May, Bilodeau & Flaherty, Boston, Hinshaw, Culbertson, Moelmann, Hoban & Fuller, Chgo., CNA Ins. Co., New London (Conn.) Mut. Ins. Co., Sentry Ins. Co., Liberty Mut. Ins. Co., Robins, Kaplan, Miller and Ciresi, Minn., Morrison, Mahoney and Miller; mem. fuel oil mktg. adv. com. U.S. Dept. Energy, residential conservation task force; del. New Eng. Energy Congress, 1978, White House Conf. on Small Bus.; chmn. fuel oil marketers' fin. viability task force SBA; mem. Mass. state residential conservation adv. com. Author: Residential and Commercial Air Conditioning, 1959, Baseboard Heating, 1952, Domestic and Commercial Oil Burners, 1969. The Oil Heating Technician, 1957. Trustee St. Elizabeth's Hosp., Brighton, Mass., 1985-89; nat. coord. Oil Heat Centennial Celebration, 1985; pres. New Eng. Fuel Inst. Edn. Found., 1983-86, cons., 1987-90; chmn. Prudential Ctr. Residents Assn., 1989-91. Capt. AUS, 1943-46. Granted Knighthood Equestrian

Order of the Holy Sepulchre, Jerusalem, 1986; recipient Disting. Achievement award New Eng. Oil Heat Industry, 1972; certs. of commendation Conn. Petroleum Assn., 1974, 80; Oil Man of New Eng. award Better Home Heat Council N.H., 1975; Certificate of Appreciation, Soc. Mfg. Engrs., 1976; 15th Anniversary commendation New Eng. Fuel Inst., 1977; Man of Yr. award Met. Energy Council, 1984. Mem. ASHRAE (life), ASTM, Am. Soc. Assn. Execs., Nat. Soc. Bus. Economists. Republican. Roman Catholic. Home: 770 Boylston St Ste 23B Boston MA 02199-7725

BURKHARDT, JOHN LEONARD, JR., engineering executive; b. Bethlehem, Pa., Apr. 4, 1937; s. John Leonard Sr. and Miriam Cushman (Payrow) B.; m. Beverly Kathryn Eggers, Apr. 29, 1964; children: Julianne Carr, Andrew Payrow. AB, Dartmouth Coll., 1959. Spl. asst. Pa. Dept. of Transp., Harrisburg, 1967-69; exec. dir. Rep. Fin. Com. of Pa., Harrisburg, 1969-72; dep. exec. v.p. Am. Rd. & Transp. Builders Assn., Washington, 1973-75; mktg. mgr. TAMS Group, Washington, 1975-79; v.p. STV Group, Inc., Pottstown, Pa., 1979-90, Urban Engrs., Inc., Phila., 1990—. Sgt. U.S. Army, 1959-62, ETO. Mem. Am. Soc. Hwy. Engrs., Vesper Club. Republican. Episcopalian. Home: 39 Sylvan Dr # 4 Pottstown PA 19464-8321 Office: Urban Engrs Inc 300 N 3d St Philadelphia PA 19106-1193

BURKHART, JENNIFER ELLEN, business psychologist; b. Marietta, Ohio, Nov. 24, 1955; d. Michael Nicholas and Bertha (Christman) B. BA, Ohio State U., 1978, MA, 1980, PhD, 1987. Psychology intern Ohio State U., Columbus, 1979-81, Profl. Counseling Svc., Columbus, 1981-82, Franklin County Bd., Columbus, 1982; staff psychologist Western Psychiat. Inst. & Clinic, Pitts., 1983-87; pres. J.E. Burkhart, P.C., Pitts., 1988—. Author: (chpt.) Advances in Development Disorders, 1987; co-author: (chpt.) Advances in Mental Retardation and Developmental Disabilities, 1983, Current Issues and Practices in Special Education, 1987, Advances in Developmental Disorders, 1987, Treating Childhood and Adolescent Psychopathology: A Handbook, 1988; contbr. articles to profl. jours. Member steering com. Gourmet Gala, March of Dimes, Pitts., 1989—, Sta. WQED Priceless Auction, Pitts., 1990—; mem. Pitts. Ballet Theatre Guild, 1989—; mem. membership com. Pitts. Opera, 1989—. Mem. APA, Vocat. Rehab. Ctr. Pitts. (planning, mktg. and exec. coms. 1989—, bd. dirs.), Wesley Inst., Inc. (nominating and devel. coms. 1990—, bd. dirs, vice chair residential com. 1991—), Pitts. Pers. Assn., N.Y. Acad. Scis., Psi Chi.

BURKOWSKY, MITCHELL ROY, speech and language pathology educator; b. Cooperstown, N.Y., Aug. 11, 1931; s. Edward and Fannie (Gertz) B.; m. Diane Francine Benowitz, June 24, 1956; children: Ruth, Joel, Rena. BA, SUNY, Albany, 1952; PhD, Wayne State U., 1960. Asst. prof. Detroit Inst. Tech., 1959-61; asst. prof., clin. dir. U. N.D., Grand Forks, 1961-65; postdoctoral resident Med. Ctr. U. Fla., Gainesville, 1965-66; asst. prof. Syracuse (N.Y.) U., 1966-72; from assoc. prof. to disting. svc. prof. SUNY, Fredonia, 1972—; cons. VA Med. Ctr., Buffalo, 1983-92. Author: Teaching American Pronunciation to Foreign Students, 1969; author, editor: Parents' and Teachers' Guide to the Care of Autistic Children, 1970, Orientation to Language and Learning Disorders, 1973; co-author: Contemporary Voice Therapy-Children and Adults, 1987. Mem., pres., bd. visitors J.N. Adam Devel. Ctr., Perrysburg, N.Y., 1978—. With U.S. Army, 1952-54. Mem. Soc. Preservation and Encouragement of Barbershop Quartet Singing in Am. (office holder), Jamestown Area Swim Ofcls. Home: 164 Temple St Fredonia NY 14063-1757 Office: SUNY Fredonia NY 14063

BURKS, ARDATH WALTER, Asian studies educator; b. Covington, Ky., May 1, 1915; s. Alonzo Edwin and Clara Grace (McCracken) B.; m. Jane Virginia Lyle, Nov. 15, 1941 (dec.); 1 child, Riki Stephen. BA, U. Cin., 1939; MA, U. Minn., 1941; PhD, Johns Hopkins U., 1949. Asst. prof., assoc. prof., prof. Rutgers, The State U. N.J., New Brunswick, 1948-81, chmn. dept. polit. sci., 1961-65, dir. internat. programs, 1966-73, assoc. v.p. acad. affairs, 1973-77, prof. emeritus Asian studies, 1981—; bd. dirs. Coun. on Internat. Ednl. Exch., N.Y.C., 1971-73; cons. Frost & Sullivan, N.Y.C., 1985-90. Author: Japan, A Postindustrial Power, 3 edits., 1981, 84, 90; contbr. articles to encys. Mem. sister-cities com. New Brunswick-Fukui, Japan, 1985—. Lt. USNR, 1943-46, PTO. Sr. rsch. Fulbright scholar U.S.-Japan Binat. Commn., Kyoto, 1958-59; recipient Order of the Rising Sun with neck ribbon Govt. Japan, 1990. Mem. Assn. Asian Studies (bd. dirs. 1972-75), Japan Soc. N.Y., Internat. Ho. Japan, Phi Beta Kappa. Democrat. Home and Office: 120 Chelsea Way Bridgewater NJ 08807-3441

BURKS, JACK D., investment executive; b. San Antonio, Apr. 1, 1951; s. D.C. and Inez M. (Lyons) B.; m. Sheila Ann Nero, July 17, 1947. BA, Ind. U., 1972, MBA, 1979. V.p. Pitts. Nat. Bank, 1973-84; mgr. dir. Offitbank, N.Y.C., 1984—.

BURLAGA, LEONARD FRANCIS, astrophysicist; b. Superior, Wis., Oct. 1, 1938; s. Edward W. and Helen M. (Plachta) B.; m. Catherine Mary McDonough, Mar. 18, 1972; children: Anna-Marie, David. BS, U. Chgo., 1960; MS, U. Minn., 1962, PhD, 1966. NAS/NRC postdoctoral resident rsch. assoc. NASA/Goddard Space Flight Ctr., Greenbelt, Md., 1966-68, astrophysicist, 1968—. Mem. Am. Geophys. Union, Internat. Astron. Union (pres. commn. 49 1988-91, v.p. 1984-88), Internat. Assn. of Geomagnatism and Aeronomy (chmn. solar wind and interplanetary magnetic field div. 1977-83). Office: NASA/GSFC Code 692 Greenbelt MD 20771

BURLAGE, MATTHEW JAMES, nonprofit institution executive, investment banker; b. Cambridge, Mass., Apr. 10, 1963; s. James Edward and Virginia Catherine (Everett) B. Cert., Sophia U., Tokyo, 1983; BA, Yale Coll., 1985; MBA, Harvard Bus. Sch., 1991. Assoc. Lehman Bros., N.Y.C., 1985-86, Hong Kong, 1986, Tokyo, 1986-89; pres. The Makoto Found., Cambridge, Mass., 1991—; dir. The Makoto Found. Vol. tchr. Pauline Shaw Sch., Dorchester, Mass., 1991—. Named Youth of Yr. Lexington Town, 1981, Most Valuable Oarsman Yale Lightweight Crew, New Haven, Conn., 1982. Mem. Harvard Club. Roman Catholic. Home and Office: 324 Huron Ave Cambridge MA 02138

BURLAND, J(OHN) ALEXIS, psychoanalyst; b. N.Y.C., Sept. 17, 1931; s. Elmer Granville and Catherine Alexander (Dobrushina) B.; m. Patricia Ruth Millar, Mar. 30, 1963. BA, Colgate U., 1952; MD, Columbia U., 1956; MSc, Temple U., 1962. Intern Mary Hitchcock Meml. Hosp., Hanover, N.H., 1956-57; resident in psychiatry Temple U. Hosp., Phila., 1957-58, 60-61; resident in child psychiatry St. Christopher's Hosp., Phila., 1961-63; pvt. practice Bala Cynwyd, Pa., 1963—; assoc. prof. psychiatry Temple U. Hosp., St. Christopehrs Hosp., Phila., 1963-79; clin. prof. Jefferson Med. Coll., Thomas Jefferson U., Phila., 1979—; tng.-supervising psychoanalyst Phila. Psychoanalytic Inst., 1983—, pres., 1991—; chmn. bd. dirs. Phila. Psychoanalytic Found., 1988—. Editor: Rapprochement: Critical Phase of Separation-Individuation, 1980, Self & Object Constancy, 1985. Lt. comdr. USNR, 1958-60. Fellow Am. Psychiat. Assn.; mem. Am. Psychoanalytic Assn., Internat. Psychoanalytic Assn., Assn. Child Psychoanalysis, Pa. Psychoanalytic Soc. (pres. 1977-80), Union League, Phi Beta Kappa, Delta Upsilon. Home and Office: 15 Colwyn Ln Bala Cynwyd PA 19004-2308

BURLEY, DEXTER LISHON, gerontologist; b. Boston, Feb. 18, 1944; s. Harry Benjamin and Phyllis (Lishon) B.; m. Stephanie Lovejoy, June 22, 1969 (div. 1984); children: Jane Winchester, Benjamin Thomas. Student, Haile Sellassie I U., Addis Ababa, Ethiopia, 1967; BA, Marlboro Coll., 1968; MA, U. N.H., 1973, PhD, 1976. Dir. Augusta (Ga.) Inst. on Aging, 1979-81; assoc. prof. Augusta Coll., 1981-86; dir. gerontology Augusts Resource Ctr. on Aging, 1987-88; pres. Gerontology Assocs., Augusta, 1987-88; dir. gerontology and geriatrics U. Md., Balt., 1988-90; cons. Newbury, N.H., 1990—; adj. faculty Dartmouth Med. Sch., U. N.H., 1992; dir. gerontology U. Hosp., Augusta, 1986-87. Author: (newspaper column) Concord Monitor, 1990; co-author: Evliven, 1989; contbr. articles to profl. jours. Trustee Historic Augusta, 1978-87, Marlboro (Vt.) Coll., 1986-89; pres. bd. Augusta Symphony, 1980-86; bd. dirs. Augusta Ballet, 1986-88. Recipient Miteau award for innovation Am. Assn. State Colls. and U., 1981; fellow NEH, 1977, Am. Coun. Edn., 1981; Ga. Endowment for Humanities grantee, 1977-81. Mem. Am. Gerontol. Assn., So. Gerontol. Soc. (chair com., Disting. Gerontologist award 1987), New Haven Lawn Club, Lake Sunapee Yacht Club, Chilton Club. Republican. Episcopalian. Home: PO Box 328 Between The Mountains Rd Newbury NH 03255-0328

BURLEY, TIMOTHY ALAN, accountant; b. Jamestown, N.Y., Jan. 3, 1958; s. William George and Sarah Bernadette (McGonagle) B.; m. Ann Elizabeth Harling, June 7, 1980; children: Brendon, Owen, Ruth, Katherine, Eileen. BS, Canisius Coll., 1980. Staff mgr. Ernst & Whinney, Buffalo, 1980-84; from mgr. to sr. mgr. Ernst & Whinney, S.A., Geneva, 1984-87; chief operating officer, chief fin. officer Marctech S.A., Neuchatel, Switzerland, 1987-89; sr. mgr. Ernst & Young, Phila., 1989—; tech. advisor Wharton Export Network, Phila., 1989—. Mem. Chester County Devel. Coun. Internat. Initiative, Exton, Pa., 1990-91; vol. parent aide Chester County Family and Youth Svcs., West Chester, Pa., 1991. Mem. AICPA, N.Y State Soc. CPA's, French-Am. C. of C. Democrat. Roman Catholic. Office: Ernst & Young Wyomissing Profl Ctr 875 Berkshire Blvd Reading PA 19610

BURLING, DANIEL JAMES, pharmacist, drug company executive; b. Batavia, N.Y., Jan. 11, 1947; s. James Edward and Joyce Mae (Crane) B.; m. Jean Marie Dunckel, July 10, 1970; children: Mary Jean, David Marc. Cert., Riverside Sch. Aeros., 1971; student, Empire State Mil. Acad., 1976; Assoc. degree, Herkimer County Community Coll, 1977; BS in Pharmacy, SUNY, Buffalo, 1980. Aircraft mechanic Nellis Air Field, Ft. Plain, N.Y., 1972-75; project mgr., engr. Systems Rsch. Labs. Inc., Dayton, Ohio, 1975-77; mgr., pharmacist Wyo. Rexall Drug, Attica, N.Y., 1981-87; owner Medicine Man Charters, Lake Ontario, N.Y., 1985—; owner, chief exec. officer, pres. Burling Drug of Corfu (N.Y.) Inc., 1991—, Burling Drug Inc., Attica, 1987—; cons. pharmacist Genesee County Nursing Home, Batavia, N.Y., 1980-81. Bd. dirs. Jaycees, Ilion, N.Y., 1975. Sgt. USMC, 1965-69, Viet Nam; maj. Res. Mem. VFW, Lions (bd. dirs., pres. 1990), Am. Legion, Aircraft Owners Assn., Elks. Republican. Roman Catholic. Home: 3414 Pike Rd Batavia NY 14020 Office: Burling Drug Inc 29-31 Main St Attica NY 14011

BURMAN, KENNETH DALE, physician; b. St. Louis, Aug. 9, 1944; s. Philip and Henrietta Burman; m. Mary Eileen Schmidt, Sept. 23, 1973; children: Ed, Steve, Andrew, David, Emily. AB, Washington U., St. Louis, 1966; MD, Mo. U., 1970. House officer med. dept. Barnes Hosp., St. Louis, 1970-72; fellow in endocrinology Walter Reed Army Med. Ctr., Washington, 1972-74, asst. chief endocrinology dept., 1974-91, chief, endocrinology, 1991—. Mem. editorial bd. Jour. Clin. Endocrinology, Thyroid Jour. Col. U.S. Army, 1972—. Fellow ACP. Office: Walter Reed Army Med Ctr Washington DC 20307-5001

BURN, HELEN JEAN, writer, educator; b. Eugene, Oreg., Jan. 11, 1926; d. Claude Herbert and Mary Edna (Watson) Riggs; m. James McAllister Burn Jr., Dec. 19, 1952 (div. 1974); children: Angela Burn Gerken, Claudia, Melissa, James M. III, Robert. BA, Western Md. Coll., Westminster, Md., 1949; postgrad., Towson State U., Balt. Head writer Md. Pub. TV, Owings Mills, 1967-87, producer, 1988-90; vis. lectr. Towson State U., Balt., 1980—; vis. prof. Johns Hopkins U., Balt., 1990—; instr. screenwriting Warner Bros. TV, div. New Writer Recruitment, Burbank, Calif., 1990—. Author: Better Than the Birds, 1969, Savannah, 1981; author of short stories in Redbook, McCall's Seventeen, others. Recipient Cine Golden Eagle, Coun. Internat. Non-theatrical Events for Outdoors Maryland, 1990, Internat. Iris Nat. Assn. Pub. TV Program Execs. for Too Young to Parent, 1990, Emmy for a Region Dividend, NATAS, 1990, Gold Medal for Best Writing, N.Y. Internat. Festivals, 1992.

BURNACZ, KORNEL ANTHONY, market research analyst; b. N.Y.C., Dec. 17, 1957; s. Kornel Ernest and Martha Edith (Molnar) B.; m. Joanne Marie Griffin, Sept. 15, 1984; 1 child, Stephen. BS in Biology, St. John's U., Jamaica, N.Y., 1980; MA in Psychology, Hofstra U., Hempstead, N.Y., 1981, PhD in Psychology, 1984. Cons. L.I. Jewish-Hillside Med. Ctr., New Hyde Park, N.Y., 1980-84, Hilson Rsch., Kew Gardens, N.Y., 1981-83; consumer test analyst Lever Bros. R&D, Edgewater, N.J., 1984-89; sr. mkt. rsch. analyst J. Walter Thompson, N.Y.C., 1989-90; mkt. rsch. analyst BBDO, N.Y.C., 1990—; instr. Local 638 Steamfitters Pipes & Drums, L.I., 1988—. Home: 92-42 246th St Bellerose Terrace NY 11001 Office: BBDO 1285 Ave of the Americas New York NY 10019-6028

BURNES, KENNETT FARRAR, chemical company executive; b. Washington, Feb. 23, 1943; s. Richard M. and Ruth (Carney) B.; m. Barbara Jackson; children: Jennifer, Nathaniel, Lisa, Alison. AB, Harvard U., 1965, LLB, 1968. Ptnr. Choate, Hall & Stewart, Boston, 1968-87; v.p., gen. counsel Cabot Corp., Waltham, Mass., 1987-88; exec. v.p. Cabot Corp., Waltham, 1988—; bd. dirs. Neozyme Corp., Renaissance Properties Inc., Boston, White Flower Farm, Inc., Litchfield, Conn., Cabot Corp. Chmn. bd. Park Sch., Brookline, Mass., 1971-82. Office: Cabot Corp 75 State St Box 9073 Boston MA 02109-1806

BURNESS, JAMES HUBERT, chemistry educator; b. Phila., Nov. 20, 1949; s. James Hubert and Josephine Elizabeth (MacDonald) B.; m. Mary Regel, Dec. 11, 1971; children: Monika Leigh, Allison Nicole. BA in Chemistry, Rutgers U., 1971; PhD in Inorganic Chemistry, Va. Poly. Inst. & State U., 1975. Quality control chemist Harshaw Chem. Co., Gloucester, N.J., 1969-71; quality control supr. GAF Corp., Gloucester, 1971; instr. Lansing (Mich.) Community Coll., 1976; postdoctoral fellow Mich. State U., East Lansing, 1975-76; instr. U. Md., Munich, 1983-85; asst. prof. chemistry Pa. State U., York, 1976-92, assoc. prof. chemistry, 1992—; computer cons., York, 1985—; software reviewer DC Heath and Co., 1990. Referee Jour. of Chem. Edn., 1989—; contbr. articles to profl. jours. Recipient J. Shelton Horsley award Va. Acad. Sci., 1973, Student Appreciation award York Campus, 1979, York Campus Annual Teaching award Pa. State U., 1986, George W. Atherton award for Excellence in Teaching, 1990. Mem. Am. Chem. Soc. (chmn. southeastern Pa. sect. 1991), Sigma Xi (rsch. award 1975). Office: Pa State U 1031 Edgecombe Ave York PA 17403-3398

BURNETT, FRANCIS ALLAN, secondary education educator, consultant; b. Whitingham, Vt., Jan. 7, 1932; s. Wilbur L. and Lena D. (Kenney) B.; m. Mary Jean Herzig, Nov. 7, 1964; children: Sherry, Chad, Shawna. Student, Westfield State Coll., 1985-87. Mechanic Mohawk Chevrolet, Greenfield, Mass., 1950-60, Hartwin Motor Sales, Greenfield, Mass., 1960-62, 64-85, Bostley Motors, Greenfield, Mass., 1962-64; vocat. tchr. Franklin County Tech. High Sch., Turners Falls, Mass., 1985—; tech. expert Better Bus. Bur., Mass., 1991—. Elder Watchtower Soc. Jehovah's Witnesses, Greenfield, 1958—. Mem. Nat. Inst. Automotive Service (cert.). Home: 132 Log Plain Rd Greenfield MA 01301-1027 Office: Franklin County Tech High Sch Industrial Blvd Turners Falls MA 01376-1607

BURNETT, ROGER MACDONALD, biology, biochemistry and biophysics educator; b. London, Jan. 10, 1941; came to U.S., 1964; naturalized, 1991; s. John Edward Burnett and Patience Lena (Hatchard) Pumphrey; m. Ingrid-Karola Schuller, Dec. 8, 1990; children: Stephanie, Daniel V. BS in Physics, U. London, 1964; PhD in Protein Crystallography, Purdue U., 1970; Habilitation in Structural Biology, U. Basel, Switzerland, 1975. Assoc. rsch. biophysicist Biophysics Rsch. div. U. Mich., Ann Arbor, 1970-73; vollassistent dept. structural biology Bioctr., U. Basel, 1973-75, asst. prof., 1975-82, project leader, 1977-80; assoc. prof. dept biochemistry and molecular biophysics Columbia U., N.Y.C., 1980-88; prof., chmn. structural biology program The Wistar Inst., Phila., 1988—; Wistar Inst. prof. chemistry U. Pa., Phila., 1988—; Wistar Inst. prof. biochemistry and biophysics Sch. Medicine, U. Pa., 1989—; reviewer Cornell High Energy Synchrotron Source; reviewer NIH, mem. computer image analysis spl. study sect., 1983, mem. biophys. chemistry study sect., 1984, participant neurological disorders program project site visit, 1989; reviewer NSF, mem. biophysics program adv. panel Div. Molecular Bioscis., 1986-90; mem. biotech. resource adv. panel U. Ariz., Tucson, 1987-89; vice chmn. viral assembly summer conf. Fedn. Am. Socs. Exptl. Biology, Saxtons River, Vt., 1990, chmn., 1992; presenter profl. and ednl. instns. Co-contbr. chpt. to: The Molecular Replacement Method, 1972, Structure and Conformation of Nucleic Acids and Protein-Nucleic Acid Interactions, 1975, Flavins and Flavoproteins, 1976, The Rotation Method in Crystallography, 1977, Structural Aspects of Recognition and Assembly in Biological Macromolecules, 1981, Biological Macromolecules and Assemblies, Vol. I, Virus Structures, 1984, Crystallography in Molecular Biology, 1987, Biological Organization: Macromolecular Interactions at High Resolution, 1987; referee profl. publs. including European Molecular Biology Orgn. Jour., Jour. Biol. Chemistry, Jour. Virology, Proteins, Sci.; contbr. articles to profl. jours including Jour. Biol. Chemistry, Jour. Applied Crystallography, Jour. Molecular Biology, Biophysics, Jour. Gen. Virology, others. Dir. Washington Sq. West Project Action Com., Phila., 1990-91; mem. adv. coun. biophysics sect. N.Y. Acad. Scis., 1983-84. Recipient Irma T. Hirschl (Found.) Career Scientist award, 1981-85. Mem. AAAS, Am. Crystallographic Assn., Biophys. Soc., Harvey Soc. Home: 318 S 12th St Philadelphia PA 19107-5947 Office: The Wistar Inst 3601 Spruce St Philadelphia PA 19104-4265

BURNHAM, ROBERT ALAN, educator, academic administrator; b. Rochester, N.Y., July 4, 1928; s. J. Robert and Susan (Mason) B.; m. Shirley Semingson, Feb. 12, 1953 (div.); children: Teya, Jessica; m. Patricia Orr White, Feb. 23, 1980; 1 stepchild, Duncan. BA magna cum laude, U. Wash., 1955; PhD, Stanford U., 1972. Assoc. prof., assoc. dean Coll. of Edn. U. Ill., Urbana, 1969-76; research dir. Ill. Sch. Problems Commn., Springfield, 1974-77; prof., dean. Coll. Edn. Ill. State U., Normal, 1976-79; prof., dean. Coll. Edn. Ohio State U., Columbus, 1979-83, acting v.p. for communications and devel., 1982-83; prof., dean Sch. Edn., Health, Nursing and Arts Professions NYU, N.Y.C., 1983-89, prof., dir. Ctr. for Ednl. Tech. and Econ. Productivity, 1989—; v.p. Transitions Group, Inc., Wilton, Conn., 1989—; pres. Educator's Distance Learning Consortium, Inc., 1990—; mem. nat. edn. adv. com. Statue of Liberty-Ellis Island Commn., 1985-90, tech. adv. bd. High Sch. of Telecommunication Arts and Tech., Bklyn., 1985-91; frequent workshop presenter, lectr. Contbr. articles to profl. jours. Trustee, chair adminstrv. com. Ctr. for Pub. Edn., Columbus, 1980-83. With U.S. Army, 1948-52. Grantee U.S. Office Edn., 1966. Mem. Am. Assn. Colls. of Tchr. Edn. (instnl. rep., bd. dirs. 1981-85), Am. Ednl. Rsch. Assn., Am. Soc. for Tng. and Devel., Tchr. Edn. Conf. Bd. (pres. Albany, N.Y. 1984-89), Soc. for Applied Learning Tech., Phi Beta Kappa. Presbyterian. Office: NYU Ctr Edn Tech Econ Prod 239 Greene St Ste 300 New York NY 10003-6601

BURNS, ALLAN FIELDING, chemical company executive; b. Washington, Nov. 22, 1936; s. John Fielding and Louisa Page (Saegmuller) B.; m. Asenath Emily Payne, Aug. 16, 1958; children: John, Robert, Thomas, Laurie. BS, Cornell U., 1958; MS, Purdue U., 1960, PhD, 1962. Rsch. chemist Johns-Manville (N.J.) Corp., 1962-66, sr. rsch. chemist, 1966-69, sect. chief basic chemistry rsch., 1969-71; pres. intern/sci. and engring. NSF Picatinny Arsenal, Dover, N.J., 1972-73; tech. mgr. PQ Corp., Valley Forge, Pa., 1973-78; mgr., corp. planning PQ Corp., Valley Forge, 1978-82, mktg. mgr., 1982-89, assoc. dir. R & D, 1989-91, tech. dir. R & D, 1991—. Patentee in field; contbr. articles to profl. jours. V.p. Jaycees, Hunterdon County, N.J., 1967-71; pres. Conservation Commn., Readington Twp., N.J., 1971; mem. bd. edn. Readington Twp., 1971-73; trustee Area Pub. Libr. Bd., Coatesville, Pa., 1983—, pres., 1986-90. Mem. Am. Chem. Soc., Indsl. Rsch. Inst. (rep.). Republican. Methodist. Home: RR 1 Box 457 Parkesburg PA 19365-9109 Office: PQ Corp R & D Ctr 280 Cedar Grove Rd Conshohocken PA 19428-2240

BURNS, ARNOLD IRWIN, lawyer; b. N.Y.C., Apr. 14, 1930; s. Herman Leon and Rose (Lauterstein) B.; m. Felice Bernstein, June 17, 1951; children: Linda Susan, Douglas Todd. A.B., Union Coll., Schenectady, 1950; LL.B., Cornell U., 1953; postgrad., Parker Sch. Internat. Law, 1960; JD, Hofstra U., 1986. Bar: N.Y. 1953, D.C. 1977. Ptnr. Burns Summit Rovins & Feldesman (and predecessors), N.Y.C., 1960-86; assoc. atty. gen. U.S. Govt., Washington, 1986; dep. atty. gen. U.S. Dept. Justice, Washington, 1986-88; mem. Proskauer Rose Goetz & Mendelsohn, N.Y.C., 1988—; counsel N.Y. State Joint Legis. Com. on Ethics, 1964. Note editor: Cornell Law Quar, 1952-53. Former chmn., life trustee Union Coll., Schenectady; former chmn., now vice chmn. bd. dirs. Freedoms Found., Valley Forge, Pa.; vice chmn. nat. bd. dirs. Boys and Girls Clubs Am.; pres. Nat. Ethnic Coalition; mem. Coun. Governing Bds.; mem. adv. coun., co-chmn. nat. capital campaign Cornell U. Law Sch., Ithaca, N.Y.; former nat. chmn. Cornell Law Sch. Fund; mem. adv. coun. Hofstra U. Sch. Law; mem., bd. dir. Nat. Victim Ctr. Capt. U.S. Army, 1953-57. Mem. ABA, AIPAC (nat. exec. bd.), ADL (assoc. nat. com.), Fed. Bar Assn., N.Y. State Bar Assn., Fed. Bar Coun., Assn. Bar City N.Y., Cornell Law Assn., Am. Arbitration Assn. (mem. nat. panel arbitrators), Met. Club, Army and Navy Club, Lawyers Club (Washington), N.Y. Athletic Club, Friars Club, Order of the Coif, Phi Kappa Phi, Kappa Nu, Alpha Phi Omega. Republican. Jewish. Home: 25 Sutton Pl S New York NY 10022-2441 also: 338 Dune Rd Westhampton Beach NY 11978 Office: Proskauer Rose Goetz & Mendelsohn 1585 Broadway New York NY 10036-8200

BURNS, BRIAN PATRICK, electrical engineer; b. Camden, N.J., Mar. 17, 1962; s. James Francis and Mary Margaret (Grogan) B.; m. Alison Carol Barwis, May 16, 1987. BSEE, Drexel U., 1985; MA in Psychology for Human Factors Engring., George Mason U., 1992, postgrad., 1992—. Team leader Coop. Employment Tn. Act, Stratford, N.J., 1980; estimator E.C. Ernst, Phila., 1981-82; coop. student jr. engr. Harris Govt. Systems Group, Melbourn, Fla., 1982; coop. student fed. systems div. IBM, Manassas, Va., 1983; coop. student systems product div. IBM, Boca Raton, Fla., 1984; assoc. engr./scientist fed. systems div. IBM, Gaithersburg, Md., 1985-87, sr. assoc. engr./scientist systems integration div., 1987-88, staff engr./scientist systems integration div., 1988-90; adv. engr./scientist U.S. mktg. and svcs. group IBM; lead systems engr./architect systems integration div. IBM, Gaithersburg, Md., 1988-89, exec. area tech. lab. coord., 1989, bus. solutions cons. project mgr./tech. lead U.S. mktg. and svcs. group, 1989-91, adv. engr./scientist U.S. mktg. and svcs. group, 1990-91; adv. human factors engr. Gen. Sector div. IBM, Bethesda, Md., 1992—; lab. coord., IBM, 1986-89, adv. devel. prototype investigator, 1987-88; resident tutor Drexel U., Phila., 1982-85. Background vocalist for Christian folk music album I Lift Up My Eyes, 1987. Enumerator 1980 Census Bur., Westmont, N.J., 1980; election poll judge and clk. Camden County, N.J. Bd. of Elections, 1981-85; assessment commr. Twp. of Cherry Hill, N.J., 1982; vocalist Queen of Heaven Cath. Ch., Cherry Hill, 1985—. Recipient Dean J. Peterson Ryder award Drexel U., 1985. Mem. AIAA, IEEE, Computer Soc. of IEEE (student v.p. 1984-85), Human Factors Soc. (presenter 35th ann. meeting 1991), Assn. Computing Machinery. Democrat. Roman Catholic. Home: 24701 Kings Valley Rd Damascus MD 20872-2230 Office: IBM Mail Drop 3061 10401 Fernwood Rd Bethesda MD 20817

BURNS, DENNIS RAYMOND, medical center administration executive; b. June 29, 1943; m. Joan Thomas, June 11, 1966; 3 children. BS in Liberal Arts, Alderson-Broaddus Coll., Philippi, W.Va., 1966; MS in Biology, Edinboro State Coll., 1971; postgrad., Pa. State U., 1974; MS in Health Svcs. Adminstrn., Gannon U., 1981. Adminstrv. asst. Hamot Patient Svcs., Pa., 1971-75; dir. materials mgmt. Hamot Patient Svcs., 1975-87, asst. v.p., 1985-87; pres. Residential Patient Svcs., Inc., 1986-87; v.p. Hamot Med. Ctr./Hamot Health Systems, Erie, Pa., 1987—; pres. Ind. Profl. Svcs. Inc., 1988-90; v.p. Hamot Health Systems, Erie, 1985—; pres. Ind. Profl. Svcs., Inc., Erie, 1988-90, Corry Meml. Hosp., 1991-92. Mem. numerous local healthcare related and civic orgns. Mem. Am. Coll. Healthcare Execs., Health Mgmt. Assn. Northwestern Pa. (pres.), Cert. Profl. Healthcare Materials Mgmt., Internat. Materials Mgmt. Soc., Hosp. Coun. Western Pa. (mem. com.), Purchasing Mgmt. Assn. Erie, Inc., Am. Hosp. Assn. (Soc. Hosp. Purchasing and Materials Mgmt. chpt.). Home: 1506 Sumner Dr Erie PA 16505-2644

BURNS, EDWARD CHARLES, infosystems specialist; b. Newark, Sept. 22, 1942; s. Edward Joseph and Anna Marie (Grim) B.; divorced; children: Annalisa, Edward. BS, St. Peter's Coll., 1964; MBA cum laude, Fairleigh Dickinson U., 1973. Assoc. programmer IBM, Cranford, N.J., 1969-70; tech. support mgr. Beneficial Data Processing Corp., Morristown, N.J., 1970-75; mgr. computer performance planning group Warner-Lambert Co., Morris Plains, N.J., 1975-82; mgr. tech. devel. Internat. Paper Co., Denville, N.J., 1982-83; v.p. data ctr ops. The CIT Group, Livingston, N.J., 1983—; adj. assoc. prof. computer tech. County Coll. of Morris, Randolph, N.J., 1973-87; assessment cons. Thomas Edison Coll., Trenton, 1978—, mem. bus. degree adv. coun., 1979—; evaluator Am. Council on Edn., Washington, 1980—. With AUS, 1960-68. Decorated Bronze Star. Mem. CAP. Roman Catholic. Avocation: flying. Home: 23 Molly Stark Dr Morristown NJ 07960 Office: The CIT Group Inc 650 Cit Dr Livingston NJ 07039-5703

BURNS, ELLEN BREE, federal judge; b. New Haven, Conn., Dec. 13, 1923; d. Vincent Thomas and Mildred Bridget (Bannon) Bree; m. Joseph Patrick Burns, Oct. 8, 1955 (dec.); children: Mary Ellen, Joseph Bree, Kevin James. BA, Albertus Magnus Coll., 1944, LLD (hon.), 1974; LLB, Yale U.,

1947; LLD (hon.), U. New Haven, 1981, Sacred Heart U., 1986, Fairfield U., 1991. Bar: Conn. 1947. Dir. legis. legal svcs. State of Conn., 1949-73; judge Conn. Cir. Ct., 1973-74, Conn. Ct. of Common Pleas, 1974-76, Conn. Superior Ct., 1976-78; judge U.S. Dist. Ct. Conn., New Haven, 1978—, chief judge, 1988—. Trustee Fairfield U., 1978-85, Albertus Magnus Coll., 1985—. Recipient John Carroll of Carrollton award John Barry Council K.C., 1973, Judiciary award Conn. Trial Lawyers Assn., 1978, Cross Pro Ecclesia et Pontifice, 1981, Law Rev. award U. Conn. Law Rev., 1987, Judiciary award Conn. Bar Assn., 1987. Mem. ABA, Am. Bar Found., New Haven County Bar Assn. Roman Catholic. Office: US Dist Ct 208 US Courthouse 141 Church St New Haven CT 06510-2030

BURNS, FREDRIC JAY, radiation biology educator; b. Wilmington, Del., Apr. 20, 1937; s. Horace Stephen and Evelyn (Owens) B.; m. Mosse Drebot, Dec. 5, 1988. AB, Harvard U., 1959; MA, Columbia U., 1961; PhD, NYU, 1967. Asst. resident scientist NYU Med. Ctr., N.Y.C., 1961-67; fellow Chester Beatty Cancer Inst., London, 1967-69; asst. prof. NYU, N.Y.C., 1969-75, assoc. prof., 1975-78, prof., 1978—. Editor: Radiation and DNA, 1986, Radiation and Cancer, 1986; contbr. 65 scientific papers. Mem. Am. Assn. Cancer Rsch., Radiation Rsch. Soc., N.Y. Acad. Scis. Home: 28 Sutton Dr Ho Ho Kus NJ 07423 Office: NYU Med Ctr 550 1st Ave Rm 213 New York NY 10016

BURNS, HAROLD W., state representative, insurance company executive; b. Dec. 4, 1926; m. Eleanor A. Tedesco; 3 children. Pres. Burns Ins. Agy., Whitefield, N.H., 1951—; rep. Coos County Dist. 5, speaker N.H. Ho. of Reps.; former dep. speaker, former asst. majority leader N.H. Ho. of Reps. Mem. State Govt. Issues and Orgns. Com., Am. Legis. Exchange Coun., Assembly on the Legislature; former dir. Whitefield Taxpayers Assn., Coos County Rep. Com.; past pres. Lancaster Fair Assn., N.H. State Fair Assn.; mem. adv. bd. Small Bus. Assn.; former chmn. Coos County Del. With U.S. Army, 1945-46. Mem. Nat. Conf. Ins. Legis. (pres.), Nat. Conf. State Legislatures, Am. Legion, Masons, Grange. Home: Burns Lake Whitefield NH 03598 Office: Ho of Reps State House Rm 309 Concord NH 03301

BURNS, SISTER JACQUELINE, college president; b. Kearny, N.J., Sept. 1, 1927; d. John Francis and Elizabeth Louise (Calmar) B. BA, Coll. St. Elizabeth, Convent, N.J., 1957; MA, Cath. U. Am., Washington, 1963; PhD in History, Cath. U. Am., 1967; LHD (hon.), Seton Hall U., 1987. Secondary sch. tchr. St. John Cathedral High Sch., Paterson, N.J, 1957-64; instr., asst. prof. Coll. of St. Elizabeth, Convent, N.J., 1967-71, asst. dean of studies, 1971-76, dean of studies, 1976-81, pres., 1981—; bd. dirs. Chestnut Hill Coll., Phila., 1990—. Trustee N.J. Ind. Coll. Fund (treas. 1985-87); mem. N.J. Com. for Humanities, New Brunswick, 1982-86; bd. dirs. N.J. Coun. on Econ. Education, Trenton, 1984-88, Morris County Consumer Credit Union, Morristown, 1984-88; mem. N.J. Bd. Higher Edn., Trenton, 1988—, exec. com., 1990—, chair acad. affairs com., 1990—; trustee St. Joseph Hosp. and Med. Ctr., Paterson, 1984-88; bd. dirs. Nat. Assn. Ind. Colls. & Univs., 1985-88. Recipient Pres.'s award for ednl. leadership Northeast Coalition of Ednl. Leaders, 1987, Woman of Achievement award Bus. and Profl. Women's Clubs N.J., Morris County, 1984, Fulbright scholarship, France, 1964. Mem. Am. Hist. Assn., Am. Cath. Hist. Assn., Am. Coun. on Edn., Am. Cath. Colls. and Univs., Am. Assn. Higher Edn., Nat. Assn. Ind. Colls. and Univs., Nat. Collegiate Honors Coun., Assn. Ind. Colls. and Univs. of N.J. (bd. dirs. 1978—, chmn. 1985-87), Morris County C. of C. (bd. dirs. 1988—). Office: Coll St Elizabeth Office of Pres 2 Convent Rd Morristown NJ 07960-6989

BURNS, JOHN JOSEPH, JR., mechanical, structural and aeronautical engineer; b. Chgo., Dec. 16, 1925; s. John Joseph and Catherine Henryetta (Hill) B.; m. Mary Jean Calvert, Feb. 11, 1950; children—John, Thomas, James, Nancy. B.S. in Mech. Engring., Ill. Inst. Tech., 1945; M.S. in Aero. Engring., Drexel Inst. Tech., 1953; postgrad Columbia U., 1956-58; Ph.D., U. Colo., 1968. Registered profl. engr., Pa., Fla., Calif. Br. chief missiles Republic Aviation Corp., Mineola, L.I., 1955-59; sect. leader Martin Marietta Corp., Denver, 1959-65; prof. engring. sci. U. Fla., Gainesville, 1965-71; prof. U. Ill., Urbana, 1971-74; sect. chief research U.S. Nuclear Regulatory Commn., Washington, 1974—; cons. in structural engring. Contbr. articles to profl. jours. Council committeeman Boy Scouts Am., 1985. Served with U.S. Army, 1946-47. NASA fellow, 1971; recipient Silver Beaver and Spurgen awards Boy Scouts Am., 1980. Fellow AIAA (assoc.), ASME (design div. com. chmn. 1981-84); mem. Am. Soc. Engring. Edn., Nat. Acad. Mechanics, Sigma Tau, Sigma Xi. Avocations: backpacking; skiing; canoeing; sailing; scuba. Home: 12304 Pueblo Rd Gaithersburg MD 20878-2062 Office: US Nuclear Regulatory Commn Washington DC 20555

BURNS, JOSEPH M., economist; b. N.Y.C., Aug. 2, 1938; s. Arthur F. and Helen (Bernstein) B. AB, Swarthmore Coll., 1960; MA, U. Chgo., 1961, PhD, 1967. Economist rsch. dept. Fed. Reserve Bank N.Y., N.Y.C., 1961-62; asst. prof. dept. econs. UCLA, 1966-71; assoc. prof. dept. econs. Rice U., Houston, 1971-74; sr. economist, dep. dir. monetary rsch. office asst. sec. for internat. affairs U.S. Dept. Treasury, Washington, 1974-76; sr. economist, assoc. dir. rsch. div. econs. and edn. Commodity Futures Trading Commn., Washington, 1976-79; sr. economist antitrust div. U.S. Dept. Justice, Washington, 1979—; vis. assoc. prof. dept. econs. Stanford (Calif.) U., 1973-74; profl. lectr. fin. dept. Georgetown U. Sch. Bus., Washington, 1979, 84. Author: Accounting Standards and International Finance, 1976, A Treatise on Markets, 1979; contbr. articles to profl. jours. Mem. adv. com. on pub. policy program Swarthmore Coll., 1991—. Nat. fellow Hoover Instn., 1973-74. Mem. Am. Econ. Assn. (census adv. com. 1972-75). Office: US Dept Justice Antitrust Div 555-4th St NW Rm 11-112 Washington DC 20001

BURNS, KERRY LEE, safety and loss prevention consultant; b. Balt., July 28, 1959; s. Roger M. and D. Elaine (Tribull) B.; m. Deborah L. East, Dec. 12, 1981; 1 child Kaitlyn M. AA, Catonsville Community Coll., 1979; BS, U. Balt., 1981. Cert. safety and security profl., hazard control mgr. Safety engring. aide David Taylor Naval Ship R&D Ctr., Annapolis, Md., 1978-80; safety dir. I.T.O. Corp., Balt., 1981-82; safety and ins. mgr. Maher Terminals, Inc., Balt., 1982-85; dir. safety, tng. and ins. Ceres Corp., Balt., 1986-88; loss control tng. specialist, acct. mgr. Nat. Loss Control Svc. Corp., Long Grove, Ill., 1988—; instr. Steamship Trade Assn., Balt., 1981-88; notary pub. State of Md., Balt. County, 1988—. Inst. ARC, Balt., 1981-87. Republican. Office: Nat Loss Control Svc Corp 7 Bucksport Ct Baltimore MD 21228-4014

BURNS, MARYLEE, rehabilitation counseling services administrator; b. Hartford, Conn.; d. Robert Fabian and Helen Leontine (Perednia) B. AA, Greater Hartford CommunityColl, 1974; BA in Psychology, Cen. Conn. State Coll., 1979; MEd in Psychol. Counseling, Columbia U., 1981, MA in Organizational Psychology, 1984. Cert. rehab. counselor. Day program dir. Fed. Employment and Guidance Svc., N.Y.C., 1986-87; Sunday clinic coord. Post Grad. Ctr. for Mental Health, N.Y.C., 1981—; dir. vocat. svcs. Phoenix House, N.Y.C., 1987-88; dir. dept. rehab. counseling Met. Hosp. Ctr., N.Y.C., 1988—. Mem. AACD, Nat. Rehab. Assn. Office: Met Hosp Ctr 1901 1st Ave # 43M New York NY 10029-7418

BURNS, MICHAEL KEITH, columnist; b. Nashville, Sept. 17, 1940; s. Lewis Eugene and Katherine Virginia (Boles) B.; children: Katherine Margaret, Emily Alice. BA, U. Mich., 1962; postgrad., U. Republic, Montevideo, Uruguay, 1970-71, Stanford U., 1980-81. Reporter Herald and Review, Decatur, Ill., 1963-65; asst. editor Bangkok (Thailand) World, 1965-67; freelance writer Saigon, Vietnam, 1968; reporter, columnist The Sun, Balt., 1969—; bur. chief The Sun, Bonn, Fed. Republic Germany, 1976-80; labor columnist The Sun, Balt., 1986—. Mem. U. Mich. Club Balt. (pres. 1988—), Padonia Park Club, Phi Gamma Delta, Sigma Delta Chi. Presbyterian. Office: Balt Sun 501 N Calvert St Baltimore MD 21278-0001

BURNS, REBECCA ANN, educator, librarian; b. Waynesboro, Pa., Dec. 28, 1946; d. John Albert and Betty Jane (Mason) Castelluccio; m. Terry Lee Burns, 1966; children: Todd Darin, Derick Jason. BS, Shippensburg U., 1968, postgrad., 1969, 70, 75; postgrad., Pa. State U., 1973-74, 87, 89, U. Wyo., 1989. Cert. elem. tchr., library sci. tchr., Pa. Migrant educator Waynesboro (Pa.) Sch. Dist., 1971-72, elem. tchr., 1968-71, 74-79; elem. tchr. Mifflin County Sch. Dist., Lewistown, Pa., 1972-74; test examiner Office Personnel Mgmt. U.S. Govt., State College, Pa., 1982-83; instr. Adult Basic Edn.- Gen. Edn. Devel. and Career Tng. Mifflin County Job Tng. Partnership Act, Lewistown, 1985-86; libr. State Correctional Inst.-Rockview, Bellefonte, Pa., 1983-85, Midd-West Sch. Dist., Middleburg, Pa., 1986-89; edn. adminstrn. assoc., pupil transp. specialist Pa. Dept. Edn., Harrisburg, 1989-90, edn. adminstrn. specialist, coord. non pub. sch. svcs., 1990—. Lobbyist for stamp commemorating adult edn.; educator for women's rights. Mem. NEA, Am. Fedn. Tchrs., Pa. Fedn. Tchrs., Pa. State Edn. Assn., Pa. Sch. Libr.'s Assn. Roman Catholic. Home: 134 Hillside Dr Reedsville PA 17084-9606 Office: Pa Dept Edn 333 Market St Harrisburg PA 17101-2210

BURNS, ROBERT AMBROSE, JR., portfolio manager; b. N.Y.C., Oct. 5, 1955; s. Robert Ambrose Sr. and Margaret Theresa (Lane) B. AB in English, Lafayette Coll., 1977; MBA in Fin. and Acctg., Washington U., St. Louis, 1983. Mcpl. bond trader Moseley, Hallgarten, Estabrook & Weeden, Inc., Phila., 1981-83; structured portfolio specialist E.F. Hutton & Co., Inc., N.Y.C., 1983-88; portfolio mgr. fixed income Midland Montagu, Inc./Thomas Cook, Inc., N.Y.C., 1988—. Vol. Cen. Park Conservancy, N.Y.C., 1990; active Money Marketeers of NYU, 1991, Rockville Centre (N.Y.) Rep. Club, 1990. Mcpl. Art Soc. fellow, 1990. Roman Catholic. Home: 322 W 57th St Apt 30J New York NY 10019-3727 Office: Midland Montagu Inc/Thomas Cook Inc 156 W 56th St Fl 5 New York NY 10019-3800

BURNS, ROGER GEORGE, mineralogist, educator; b. Wellington, N.Z., Dec. 28, 1937; s. Alexander Parker and Jean Gertrude (Rodgers) B.; m. Virginia Anne Mee, Sept. 7, 1963; children: Kirk George, Jonathan Roger. BSc (Sir George Grey scholar 1958, Emily Lilias Johnson scholar 1959), Victoria U. of Wellington, 1959, MSc, 1961; PhD (Sci. fellow), U. Calif., Berkeley, 1965; MA in Geology (Brit. Council scholar 1965-66, Natural Environ. Research Council, Eng. fellow 1966), Oxford U., 1968, DSc, 1984. Demonstrator chemistry dept. Victoria U. of, Wellington, 1959-60; sr. lectr. geochemistry Victoria U. of, 1967; sci. officer Dept. Sci. and Indsl. Research, Wellington, 1961; research asso. dept. engring. scis. U. Calif., Berkeley, 1965; sr. research visitor, dept. mineralogy and petrology Cambridge U., Eng., 1966; lectr. geochemistry Oxford U., 1968-70; asso. prof. geochemistry MIT, Cambridge, 1970-72; prof. mineralogy and geochemistry MIT, 1972—; vis. prof. Scripps Instn. Oceanography, La Jolla, Calif., 1976; UNESCO prof. Jadavpur U., Calcutta, India, 1981; Hallimond lectr. Mineral. Soc. Eng., 1987; Guggenheim prof. Manchester U., England, 1991; prin. investigator lunar sample analysis team Apollo program NASA, 1970—, mem. lunar and planetary proposal rev. panel, 1978-81; mem. exec. com. Manganese Nodule Project Seabed Assessment Program Internat. Decade Ocean Exploration NSF, 1974-80; mem. adv. panel Marine Minerals Office, 1976; mem. rev. panel Nat. Scis. and Engring. Rsch. Can., 1985; mem. steering com. NASA MSATT project, 1990—. Author: Mineralogical Applications of Crystal Field Thepry, 1970; editor: Chem. Geology, 1968-85, Canadian Mineralogist, 1988-90; assoc. editor: Geochimica et Cosmochimica Acta, 1978—; contbr. articles to profl. pubk. Fulbright travel grantee U.S. Govt., 1961; Sci. Research fellow Com. for Exhbn. of 1851, London, 1961-63; Pacific scholar English Speaking Union, San Francisco, 1961-63; fellow Wolfson Coll. Oxford U., 1970, Guggenheim fellow, 1990-91. Fellow Mineral. Soc. Am. (life; award 1976, councillor 1978-82, rep. for Geol. Soc. Am. abstracts rev. com. 1984-88); mem. Mineral. Soc. Gt. Britain; Mem. Am. Geophys. Union (mineral physics com. 1984-86), Geochem. Soc., N.Z. Geochem. Group. Presbyterian. Home: 7 Humboldt St Cambridge MA 02140-2804 Office: MIT 54-816 Dept Earth Atmospheric and Planetary Scis Cambridge MA 02139

BURNS, RONALD A. DUFFY, college basketball coach; b. Napoleon, Ohio, July 19, 1959; s. Ronald Ray and Martha Jean (Hummel) B. BS, Ball State U., 1985; postgrad., U. Pitts., 1986-88, Cen. Conn. U., 1991—. Asst. coach men's basketball Wapahani High Sch., Selma, Ind., 1981-84, Ball State U., Muncie, Ind., 1984-85, Ill. State U., Normal, 1985-86, U. Pitts., 1986-88; asst. coach men's basketball Cen. Conn. State U., New Britain, 1988-90, asst. basketball coach women's, 1990—; coach, lectr. Five Star Basketball Camp, Pitts., 1983-91, Mich. State Camp, East Lansing, 1988-91. Mem. Nat. Assn. Basketball Coaches, Women's Basketball Coaches Assn., Sigma Nu. Home: 70 Grove Hill St Apt 3S New Britain CT 06052-1347 Office: Ctrl Conn State U Kaiser Hall New Britain CT 06050

BURNS, RUSSELL MACBAIN, forester, plant physiologist, silviculturist; b. N.Y.C., Aug. 25, 1926; s. John Russell and Martha Sophia (Metzler) B.; m. Mildred Ann Nastasia, Dec. 22, 1948; children: Stephen MacBain, John Conrad, Russell Malcolm. AA, SUNY, Sampson, 1948; BS, Mich. State U., 1951; MS, U. Miss., 1959; PhD, U. Fla., 1971. Registered profl. forester, Fla. Rsch. forester Forest Svc., USDA, New Orleans, 1951-76; rsch. adminstr. USDA, Washington, 1976—. Disaster relief chmn. ARC, Marianna, Fla., 1974-76. With AUS, 1944-46, ETO. Named Rsch. Forester of Yr., Fla. Soc. Am. Foresters, 1974; recipient Forest Svc. award USDA, 1992. Fellow Soc. Am. Foresters; mem. Nat. Capital Soc. Am. Foresters (chmn. 1991-92, Disting. Svc. award 1990). Office: USDA Forest Svc PO Box 96090 Washington DC 20090-6090

BURNS, SANDRA FLYNN, science educator; b. Pittsfield, Mass., Oct. 3, 1939; d. George Francis and Katherine Elizabeth (Drummond) Flynn; children: Katherine, Geoffrey, Rebecca. BS, Fitchburg State Coll., 1961; MS, Cornell U., 1963; PhD, U. Conn., 1972. Sci. tchr. Hartford, Mansfield (Conn.), Groton (N.Y.) Pub. Schs., 1963-72; prof. earth sci., sci. edn. Cen. Conn. State U., New Britain, 1963-65, 70-72; cons. MAST, 1990—; workshop cons. Addison-Wesley Co., 1989—; sci. cons. New England schs., 1972—; sci. program evaluator Interstate Certification Compact. Assoc. editor: Quinnetukqut; contbr. articles to profl. jours. Named one of Outstanding Young Women Am., 1966, 77, 78, Outstanding Young Educator Hartford Jaycees, 1966. Mem. NSTA, Conn. Sci. Tchrs. Assn., Am. Nature Study Soc., Sigma Xi. Office: Cen Conn State U Physics Dept 1615 Stanley St New Britain CT 06050

BURNS, SARAH ROSE, administration and data processing professional; b. Bridgeport, Conn., Feb. 13, 1949; d. Robert John and Clara Lucy (Grosso) B. Student, Housatonic Community Coll., Bridgeport, 1974-75, Sacred Heart U., Bridgeport, 1980, U. Bridgeport, 1990. Various clerical positions Gen. Electric Co., Bridgeport, 1968-84; specialist sales computer systems Black & Decker, Shelton, Conn., 1984-89; dir. mgmt. info. systems City of Bridgeport, 1989—. Advisor Jr. Achievement, Bridgeport, 1978-88; mem. New Rep. Voice, Bridgeport, 1989—; bd. dirs., Salvation Army, 1989—, sec. 1990-92; bd. dirs. Greater Bridgeport Postal Customer Coun., 1990—, sec. 1990-92. Mem. Gen. Electric Wilson Club (pres. 1973). Roman Catholic. Home: 170 Sunburst Rd Bridgeport CT 06606-1730 Office: City of Bridgeport 45 Lyon Ter Rm 6 Bridgeport CT 06604-4023

BURNS, W. HAYWOOD, lawyer, dean, educator; b. Peekskill, N.Y., June 15, 1940; s. Junious Haywood and Josephine (Clark) B.; m. Jennifer Ellen Dohrn, May 1, 1988; children: Seth, Amilcar, Jeremiah, Haydee, Atariba. BA with honors, Harvard Coll., 1962; postgrad. fellowship, Cambridge U., 1962-63; JD, Yale U., 1966. Bar: N.Y. 1967, U.S. Supreme Ct. 1977. Assoc. Paul, Weiss, Rifkind, Whaston & Garrison, N.Y.C., 1966; law clk. U.S. Dist. Ct. Judge C. B. Motley, N.Y.C., 1966-67; asst. counsel NAACP Legal Def. and Edn. Fund, N.Y.C., 1967-69; nat. dir. Nat. Conf. of Black Lawyers, N.Y.C., 1970-73; vis. prof. SUNY at Buffalo (N.Y.) Law Sch., 1974-75; assoc. prof. NYU Law Sch., N.Y.C., 1975-77; vice provost and dean Ctr. for Legal Edn. CCNY, N.Y.C., 1977-87; dean CUNY Law Sch. at Queens Coll., N.Y.C., 1987—; v.p. Ctr. for Constnl. Rights, N.Y.C., 1981—; pres. Nat. Inst., N.Y.C., 1984—. Author: Voices of Negro Protest in America, 1963; contbr. articles, chpts. and poetry. Vice chair Prisoner Legal Svcs. N.Y.; dir. Vera Inst. for Justice, 21st Century Found., Boehm Found.; chmn. Neighborhood Defender Svc. Harlem, all N.Y.C. Recipient Pres.'s award Malcolm-King Coll., N.Y.C., 1983, Florina Lasker award N.Y. Civil Liberties Union, N.Y.C., 1986, Human Rights award Bronx Community Coll., N.Y.C., 1988, Lawyer for Justice award Bklyn. (N.Y.) Legal Svcs., 1988. Mem. ABA (pro bono profl. responsibilities award litigation sect. 1989), Nat. Bar Assn., Assn. of the Bar of the City of N.Y., Nat. Conf. Black Lawyers (chmn. 1982-85, Founders award 1973), Nat. Lawyers Guild (nat. pres. 1986-88), Queens County Bar Assn., Coun. on Fgn. Rels. Office: CUNY Law Sch at Queens Coll 65-21 Main St Queens NY 11367

BURNS, WILLIAM KENNETH, music educator; b. Sioux City, Iowa, Sept. 2, 1925; s. Harry Milton and Stella (Hopper) B.; m. Arlene Ardath Nelson, June 10, 1947; children: Vicki Susan Burns Swenor, Nelson W., Leslie E. Burns Franklin, Laurie Anne Burns Colman. BS, Morningside Coll., 1947; ThM, Boston U., 1950; student, St. Lawrence U., 1943-44. Cert. minister of music. Dir. of music 1st Bapt. Ch., Melrose, Mass., 1947-50; organist Boston U., 1947-50; minister of music Morrow Meml. United Meth. Ch., Maplewood, N.J., 1950-88; prof. music Seton Hall U., South Orange, N.J., 1968—. Contbr. articles to profl. publs.; composer sacred music. Chaplain Town of Maplewood, 1970-80. With USNR, 1943-46. Mem. AAUP, Am. Guild Organists (dean 1970-72), Nat. Fellowship of Meth. Musicians (pres. 1972-74), Rotary (pres. Maplewood club 1975). Home: 118 Neptune Pl Sea Girt NJ 08750-3209 Office: Seton Hall U S Orange Ave South Orange NJ 07079

BURR, CHARLES ROGER, association executive; b. Yonkers, N.Y., Apr. 19, 1948; s. Roberts D. and Mary (Baughman) B.; m. Asako Takagi, July 2, 1972; children: Megumi F., Mimosa S. SB, MIT, 1970, SM, 1973; MBA, Harvard U., 1977. Blood gas lab. asst. dept. head Peter Bent Brigham Hosp., Boston, 1973-75, dir. clin. engring., 1977-80; mktg. engr. Hewlett Packard Med. Products Group, Waltham, Mass., 1980-81, support logistics mgr., 1981-83; mktg. communications Hewlett Packard Med. Products Group, Andover, Mass., 1983-84, tech. support mgr., 1984-85; regulatory affairs mgr Hewlett Packard Imaging Systems, Andover, 1985—. Deacon 1st Congl. Ch., Winchester, 1991—. Mem. Med. Device Industry Computer Software Com. (chmn. 1991-92), Am. Inst. Ultrasound in Medicine (bd. govs. 1990—), Winchester Boat Club. Office: Hewlett Packard Imagin Syst 3000 Minuteman Rd Andover MA 01810-1099

BURR, DONALD CALVIN, company services executive; b. South Windsor, Conn., May 8, 1941; s. Lorna D. Whitney; m. Brigita Rupner, 1961; children: Cameron, Whitney, Kelsey, Andrew. B.A., Stanford U., 1963; M.B.A., Harvard U., 1965. With Nat. Aviation Corp., N.Y.C., 1965-73, pres., 1971-73; with Tex. Internat. Airlines, Houston, 1973-80, pres., 1979-80; founder, pres., chief exec. officer People Express Airlines, Newark, 1980-86; pres. Burr Inc., Bernardsville, N.J., 1987—; bd. dirs. N.J. Bell. Mem. Young Pres.'s Orgn., Conquistadores del Cielo, Harvard Club. Home and Office: Burr Inc 158 Childs Rd 74 Ballantine Rd Basking Ridge NJ 07920

BURRELL, E. WILLIAM, university administrator, education educator; b. Providence, Apr. 28, 1927; s. Edward John and Helene Agnes (Kelly) B.; m. Barbara Mary O'Connor, Apr. 18, 1953; children: Jason Edwin, Mary Elizabeth. Student, Providence Coll., 1945-47; AB, Fordham U., 1949; MA, Boston U., 1959; EdD, Harvard U., 1964. Tchr. Providence Sch. Dept., 1957-65; prof. English and edn. Salve Regina U., Newport, R.I., 1965—, chmn. dept. edn., 1967-73, dean of coll., 1974-77, v.p., dean of faculty and grad. studies, 1977—; mem. accreditation team, sometime chmn. New Eng. Assn. Schs. and Colls., Winchester, Mass., 1975-86. Mem. allocations panel United Way Southeastern New Eng., Providence, 1976-91; bd. dirs. Samaritans of R.I., Providence, 1985-90. Mem. R.I. Coun. Tchrs. English (life; founder 1959, pres. 1965-67), Barnard Club (pres. 1971-72), Phi Delta Kappa. Home: Pinard Cottages Newport RI 02840 Office: Salve Regina U Ochre Point Ave Newport RI 02840-6906

BURRIDGE, ROBERT, former mathematics educator, scientific consultant; b. Essex, Eng., Dec. 6, 1937; came to U.S., 1971; s. Sydney Stanmore and Phebe Mercy (Raven) B.; BA (Major scholar King's Coll.), U. Cambridge, 1959, MA, 1962, PhD, 1963, ScD, 1980; m. Elizabeth Nelson Bingham, Sept. 22, 1962 (dec.); children: Rosalind, Lucinda, Robert; m. Marylyn Louise Sexton, Aug. 29, 1987. Research fellow Calif. Inst. Tech., Pasadena, 1963-64; rsch. geophysicist UCLA, 1964-65; asst. lectr. U. Cambridge, 1965-67; research fellow U.K. Atomic Energy Authority, 1967-71; fellow King's Coll., Cambridge, 1965-71; assoc. prof. math. NYU, N.Y.C., 1971-75, prof., 1975-86; sci. advisor Schlumberger-Doll Rsch., Ridgefield, Conn., 1986—. Recipient Adams prize in math. U. Cambridge, 1971; NSF research contract in earthquake mechanism studies, 1971—. Mem. Soc. Exploration Geophysicists, Soc. Indsl. and Applied Math., Am. Math. Soc. Mem. editorial bd. Wave Motion (Internat.); contbr. papers on applied math., theoretical seismology and wave propagation to tech. jours. Home: 43 Rockwell Rd Ridgefield CT 06877-5006 Office: Schlumberger-Doll Rsch Old Quarry Rd Ridgefield CT 06877-4108

BURRIS, JAMES FREDERICK, academic dean, educator; b. Mauston, Wis., Apr. 15, 1947; s. James Duane and Margaret Katherine (Jones) B.; m. Christine Tuve, July 3, 1971; 1 child, Cameron William Tuve. AB, Brown U., 1970, ScB, 1970; MD, Columbia U., 1974. Diplomate Am. Bd. Internal Medicine, Subspecialty Bd. Geriatrics, Am. Bd. Clin. Pharmacology. Intern Roosevelt Hosp., N.Y.C., 1974-75; resident in internal medicine Georgetown U. Med. Ctr., Washington, 1977-79; fellow in hypertension VA Med. Ctr., Washington, 1979-81; asst. prof. Georgetown U. Med. Ctr., Washington, 1981-86, assoc. prof., 1986-91, prof., 1991—, asst. dean, 1987-90; assoc. dean, 1990—; bd. dirs. Inst. for Clin. Rsch., Washington, 1989-92; rsch. assoc. Hypertension Unit VA Med. Ctr., 1981—; vis. investigator Centre Hospitalier U. Vaudois, Lausanne, Switzerland, 1982-83; dir. clin. rsch. Cardiovascular Ctr. No. Va., Falls Church, 1988—. Contbr. over 175 articles to profl. jours. Bd. dirs. Nation's Capital affiliate Am. Heart Assn. fellow couns. on high blood pressure rsch., circulation, epidemiology, clin. cardiology. Lt. comdr. USPHS, 1975-77. Recipient Svc. award ARC, 1970, Outstanding Svc. citation Disabled Am. Vets., 1987; commd. officer student tng. and extern program scholar USPHS, 1973-74; rsch. fellow Found. pour la Recherche des Maladies Cardiovasculaires, Lausanne, 1983. Fellow ACP, Am. Geriatrics Soc., Am. Coll. Preventive Medicine, Am. Coll. Clin. Pharmacology (bd. regents 1990—), Am. Coll. Cardiology; mem. AMA (Physician's Recognition award 1982, 85, 88, 91), Sigma Xi. Democrat. Office: Georgetown U Sch Medicine Rm NE 120 Med Dent Bldg 3900 Reservoir Rd NW Washington DC 20007

BURROUGHS, MIGGS, graphic artist; b. Neptune, N.J., Jan. 5, 1946; s. Bernard and Esta (Freedman) B.; m. Mimi Orkin; 1 child, Brayden Conner. BFA, Carnegie Inst. Tech., 1967. Graphic designer Westport, Conn., 1967—; instr. Fairfield (Conn) U., 1978—. Inventor Spec-ulator, Board-Mate; designer postage stamp, flag of Westport; illustrator 4 covers Time mag.; producer, host (TV program) Miggs B on TV; writer, producer video on creative problem solving Ransack, Wrestle and Roll. Home and Office: 2 Old Hill Rd Westport CT 06880-3013

BURROUGHS, RICHARD HANSFORD, III, oceanography educator; b. New Haven, Conn., July 5, 1946; s. Richard Hansford and Mary Drummond (Page) B.; m. Nancy Rowe, Mar. 31, 1984; children: Nicholas Loring, Hannah Grinnell. AB with honors, Princeton U., 1969; PhD, MIT, 1975. Staff officer Nat. Acad. Scis.-NRC, Washington, 1974-77; sr. fellow Ecosystems Ctr. Marine Biol. Lab., Woods Hole, Mass., 1977-79, 81; sci. adviser to dir. Bur. Land Mgmt., U.S. Dept. of Interior, Washington, 1979-81; rsch. scientist John Gray Inst., Beaumont, Tex., 1982-83; asst. prof., then assoc. prof. dept. marine affairs U. R.I., Kingston, 1983—; vis. assoc. prof. sch. forestry and environ. studies Yale U., New Haven, 1990-91, adj. prof., 1991-92; mem. summer faculty Coll. of Atlantic, Bar Harbor, Maine, 1988-90, 92. Editor, author: Multimedia Management of Municipal Sludge, 1978, OCS Oil and Gas, 1978; contbr. articles to profl. jours. Bd. dirs. Save the Bay, Providence, 1988-90. Mem. AAAS, Am. Geophys. Union, Geol. Soc. Am., The Coastal Soc., Sigma Xi. Office: U RI Dept Marine Affairs Kingston RI 02881

BURROWS, ARTHUR ANDREWS, 3RD, publishing executive; b. Chgo., Jan. 5, 1942; s. Arthur Andrews Jr. and Laura (Moyer) B.; m. Elise Carlson, Aug. 10, 1974; children: Ingrid Elizabeth, Arthur Andrews 4th. AB, Yale U., 1964; MA in Teaching ESL, Sch. for Internat. Tng., 1971. Mng. editor Stephen Greene Press, Brattleboro, Vt., 1966-71; dir. Am. Lang. Acad. Northfield-Mt. Hermon (Mass.) Sch., 1973-76; pub., pres. Pro Lingua Assocs., Brattleboro, 1980—. Author, editor, designer and pub. (textbook) Grammar Exercises I, 1985. Vice pres. Brattleboro (Vt.) Mus. and Art Ctr., 1981-87; dir. Vt. Pub. Radio, 1986—. Mem. Nat. Assn. Fgn. Student Advisors, Tchrs. of English to Speakers of Other Langs. Episcopalian. Home: RR 3 Brattleboro VT 05301-9803 Office: Pro Lingua Assocs 15 Elm St Brattleboro VT 05301-3291

BURROWS, BRENDA LEE, public relations executive; b. Detroit, Nov. 16, 1960; d. Lyle A. and Sylvia (Liss) Wolcott; m. Scott Frederick Burrows, May 3, 1986; 1 child, Emily S. BA in Journalism, Mich. State U., 1982. News

prodn. asst. Sta. WKAR Radio, East Lansing, Mich., 1980-82; asst./account exec. PR Assocs., Inc., Detroit, 1983-84, Borman/Williams, Manhattan, N.Y., 1984-85; media specialist Girl Scouts of the USA, Manhattan, 1985-87; account supr./group head KCS&A Pub. Rels., Manhattan, 1987-90; account supr. Saatchi & Saatchi Pub. Rels. (div. Saatchi & Saatchi N.Am.), Manhattan, 1990—. Recipient Creativity in Pub. Rels. award Inside PR, 1990. Mem. Pub. Rels. Soc. Am. (accredited, Silver Anvil award 1987, Big Apple award 1990), N.Y. Cares, Compassionate Friends. Office: Saatchi & Saatchi 375 Hudson St New York NY 10014-3658

BURROWS, JOHN EDWARD, communications company executive; b. Englewood, N.J., Aug. 6, 1950; s. Laurence McCallum and Pauline Hannah (McClave) B. BA in Journalism, Rutgers U., 1972. From staff asst. to account exec. Ogilvy & Mather Inc., N.Y.C., 1977-80; mgr. sales devel. CBS Radio Spot Sales, N.Y.C., 1980-81; dist. dir. affiliate relations CBS Radio Network, N.Y.C., 1981-84, dir. affiliate relations, 1984-86, v.p. affiliate relations, 1986-87; v.p. news and sports affiliate relations CBS Radio Networks, N.Y.C., 1987-89; broadcast cons. Hackensack, N.J., 1989-91; broadcast cons., classical piano instr. Norfolk, Conn., 1991—. Author: A Country Heart, 1983. Episcopalian. Home: PO Box 623 10 Laurel Ln Norfolk CT 06058

BURRY, WILLIAM CHARLES, physician, surgeon; b. Pitts., Aug. 9, 1911; s. Edward John and Ada Elizabeth (Simon) B.; m. Virginia Price Swaine, Oct. 26, 1940; children: William Charles III, Ronald Swaine, James Richard. BA, Pa. State U., 1933; postgrad., U. Ariz., 1934, U. Pitts., 1935; MD, Jefferson Med. Coll., 1939; grad., Army War Coll., 1958. Intern Allegheny Gen. Hosp., Pitts., 1939-40; resident Walter Reed Army Inst., Washington; resident in surgery Gorgas Gen. Hosp., Ancon, Canal Zone, 1948-50; commd. 1st lt., M.C. U.S. Army, Ancon, Canal Zone, 1940, advanced through grades to col., 1950; dir. office sci. Dept. Def., Washington, Canal Zone, 1950-57; surgeon USEUCOM Dept. Def., Paris, Canal Zone, 1958-61; surgeon, comdr. USA Hosp. Dept. Def., West Berlin, Canal Zone, 1967-70, ret., 1970; mem. staff Pocono Med. Ctr., East Stroudsburg, Pa., 1979—; med. dir. Tobyhanna Army Depot, Pa., 1972-77; mem. Speakers Bur., Pocono Med. Ctr., 1985-90; chief sch. physician Pocono Mountain Sch. Dist., 1981-86; cons. sports medicine, hosp. adminstrn., Mountainhome, Pa., 1981—; chmn. med. com., cons. Belvoir Woods Health Care Ctr. The Fairfax, Ft. Belvoir, Va.; physician in attendance Flagler-Metzger Health Ctr., East Stroudsburg U., 1988-91. Author: History of the Mountainhome United Methodist Church, 1954—, History of The Third United States Army 94th AREHU operated by the 94th Medical Gas Treatment Batallion in World War II; mem. edit. com. of history Pocono Med. Ctr., 1990-92. Mem. med. exec. com. Pocono Hosp., 1979-84; v.p. Monroe County Hist. Assn., 1984-90; chmn. adminstrv. bd. Meth. Ch., Mountainhome, 1980-83; mem. planning com. arts and mus., 1973-75; mem. physicians' rev. com. Monroe County Nursing Homes, 1980—; med. cons. to planning bd. Army Retirement Found., Ft. Belvoir. Decorated Bronze Star, Legion of Merit with oak leaf cluster, Army Commendation medal with oak cleaf cluster, European medal (four battle stars), Vietnam Svc. medal (1 star). Fellow Chgo. Surg. Soc., Phila. Coll. Physicians; mem. AMA, Ret. Officers Assn. (pres. chpt. 1975), Monroe County Med. Soc. (pres. 1984-86, mem. exec. com.), Mountainhome Cemetery Assn. (treas. 1980-90), Fairfax Residents Coun. (chmn. med. com.), Masons, Shriners, Phi Mu Alpha, Sinfonia, Delta Sigma Pi, Phi Alpha, Sitma Pi, Alpha Kappa Kappa, Alpha Omega Alpha. Republican. Home: PO Box 605 Mountainhome PA 18342-0605 also: 9120 Belvoir Woods Pkwy Apt Madison 204 Fort Belvoir VA 22060-2723

BURSIEK, RALPH DAVID, information systems company executive; b. Cin., Dec. 7, 1937; s. Ralph Carl and Marjorie (deCamp) B.; m. Judith Ann Bauer, July 27, 1963; children: Brian, Suzanne, Elizabeth. BCE, U. Cin., 1961; MBA, Harvard U., 1963. Mgr. large account mktg. IBM, Chgo., 1970-72; br. mgr. IBM, Green Bay, Wis., 1972-74; dir. fed. mktg. ops. IBM, Bethesda, 1974-76, dir. pub. sector, 1976-77; dir. product mgmt. IBM, White Plains, N.Y., 1977-81, div. dir., 1981-83; v.p. systems and line of bus. Burroughs Corp., Detroit, 1983-84, v.p. worldwide product mktg., 1984-85; v.p., regional mgr. UNISYS, Berkeley Heights, N.J., 1985-89; v.p. sales and mktg. Synasort, Inc. Syncsort, Inc., Berkeley Heights, N.J., 1989—. Guides program Darien (Conn.) YMCA, 1977-81; soccer coach Town of Darien and Grosse Pointe (Mich.) 1979-85, Millburn (N.J.) Twp., 1986-91. Office: Syncsort Inc 50 Stewart Rd Short Hills NJ 07078

BURSON, HAROLD, public relations executive; b. Memphis, Feb. 15, 1921; s. Maurice and Esther (Bach) B.; m. Bette Ann Foster, Oct. 30, 1947; children: Scott, Mark. BA, U. Miss., 1940; DHL (hon.), Boston U., 1988. Corr., reporter Memphis Comml. Appeal, 1938-40; dir. Ole Miss News Bur., Oxford, Miss., 1939-40; dir. pub. relations H.K. Ferguson Co., N.Y.C., 1941-43; chmn. Burson-Marsteller, N.Y.C., 1953—; bd. dirs., mem. exec. com. Young & Rubicam, N.Y.C.; mem. adv. coun. Emory U. Bus. Sch., Medill Sch. Journalism Northwestern U., U. So. Calif. Sch. Journalism. Chmn. bd., mem. exec. com., Joint Coun. on Econ. Edn.; mem. exec. com. Young Astronauts Coun., 1984-88; bd. dirs., exec. com., v.p. pub. info. Nat. Safety Coun., 1968-76; bd. dirs. Kennedy Ctr. Prodns., Washington, Catalyst Inc., 1978-89; former trustee World Wildlife Fund, 1979-81, Found. for Pub. Rels. Rsch. and Edn.; trustee Hackley Sch., Tarrytown, N.Y., 1968-76; mem. Fine Arts Commn., 1981-85; chmn. pvt. sector pub. rels. com. USIA; mem. adv. bd. Bus. Coun. for Internat. Understanding; mem. pres.' coun. N.Y. Acad. Sci. Served with AUS, World War II. Named Public Relations Profl. of Year Public Relations News, 1977, 89; recipient Gold Anvil award Public Relations Soc. Am., 1980; Horatio Alger award, 1986; Arthur Page award U. Tex., 1986; named to U. Miss. Hall of Fame, 1980. Mem. Am., Internat. public relations assns., N.Y. Soc. Security Analysts, Am. Philatelic Soc., N.Y. Acad. Medicine (assoc.), Blue Key, Overseas Press, Marco Polo Club, Mid-Am. Club, Internat. Club, Scarsdale Golf Club, Econ. Club of N.Y. (dir., trustee), Horatio Alger Assn. (dir.), Omicron Delta Kappa. Office: Burson-Marsteller 230 Park Ave S New York NY 10003-1516

BURSON, LINDA, theatre director, playwright; b. Memphis, July 9, 1942; d. Leo R. and Josephine (Wainman) Burson; children: Lisa B. Kumin, Henry Burson Lewis. BA, U. Mich., 1964; MA, Memphis State U., 1974; PhD, U. Ga., 1983. Dir. theatre Ga. State U., Atlanta, 1977-81; dir., asst. prof. U. Ky., Lexington, 1981-83; chmn. dept. theatre Beloit (Wis.) Coll., 1983-86; gen. mgr. Festival Theatre, Beloit, 1984-85; theatre dir. Westbeth Theatre, Actors Outlet, N.Y.C., 1987-89; artist-in-residence Atlantic Community Coll., Atlantic City, 1988; edn. dir. Theatre for a New Audience, N.Y.C., 1988-91; theatre dir. Chatham (N.J.) Players, 1990-91, Don-Mar Prodns., N.Y.C., 1989—; adjudicator Assn. Am. Community Theatre, Am. Coll. Theatre Festival, 1978—; screening com. Nat. Music Theatre Network, N.Y.C., 1991—; artist-in-resident, U. Ga./Cortona (Italy) Studies Abroad, 1985; conductor workshops in field; cons. in field. Author: Play with Shakespeare, Poe Into the Night; author scripts: The Raven, The Black Cat, Alone, The Conqueror Worm, Spotlight on Brutus, The Three Caskets, The Witches' Tale, The Players' Play, The Lonesome Skunk, Masque of the Red Death, God's Trombones; contbr. articles to profl. jours.; plays directed include: A Matter of Tone, 1989, Henry Hudson's Better Half, 1990, Believe Me!, 1990, The Diary of Anne Frank, 1991, Fertile Deception, 1991, Full House, 1991, Equus, The Investigation, Peter Pan or the Boy Who Would Not Grow Up, Scapino!, Men-in-Waiting, 1992, many others. Mem. Gay Men's Health Crisis, 1989—; humanities scholar Arrowhead Libr. System, Beloit, 1986; exec. v.p. Hadassah, Memphis, 1964-75; vol. Stage Dirs. and Choreographers Found., 1987—. Beloit Coll. scholar, 1984; State Arts Commn. of Ga., Ky. and Tenn. grantee, 1978-79, 81, 68-71; named Outstanding Working Woman Sigma Delta Tau, 1976, others. Mem. Soc. Stage Dirs. and Choreographers, Southeastern Theatre Conf. (pres. 1976-77), Dramatists Guild, East Cen. Theatre Conf., Am. Theatre Assn. (nat. sec. 1975-76, Disting. Woman 1977), U. Mich. Alumni Assn., Zeta Phi Eta. Home: 375 S End Ave #20A New York NY 10280

BURSTEIN, ALAN STUART, lawyer; b. Detroit, Sept. 21, 1940; s. Harry S. and Florence (Rosen) B.; m. Margery G. Gordon, June 23, 1963; children: Mark Albert, Florence Beth, Robert Gordon. BA, U. Mich., 1962, JD, 1965. Assoc. counsel to majority leader N.Y. State Senate, Albany, 1971-73; ptnr. Hiscock & Barclay, Syracuse, N.Y., 1965-85, Scolaro, Shulman, Cohen, Lawler & Burstein, Syracuse, 1985—; bd. dirs. Penfield Mfg. Co., Syracuse Onondaga County Resource Recovery Agy., Syracuse. Bd. dirs. Pub. Broadcasting Coun., Syracuse, 1977-84; v.p. Temple Adath Yeshurun; past pres. Syracuse Jewish Fedn. Named Outstanding Young Man Syracuse Jaycees, 1976; recipient Community Leadership award Syracuse Jewish Fedn., 1980, Community Svc. award B'nai Brith. Mem. ABA, N.Y. State Bar Assn., Onondaga County Bar Assn. (past bd. dirs.), Century Club, Cavalry Club. Republican. Jewish. Home: 100 Old Farm Rd Fayetteville NY 13066 Office: 90 Presidential Plz Syracuse NY 13201

BURSTEIN, SHARON ANN PALMA, corporate communications specialist; b. Schenectady, N.Y., July 18, 1952; d. Harold Edward and Lois Ida (Hesner) Rieck; m. Joseph Carmen Palma, May 17, 1975 (div. Sept. 1982); m. Richard Lyle Burstein, Sept. 8, 1985; 1 child, Alexandra Blaire. BA, Nat. Coll. Edn., 1974; postgrad., Russell Sage Coll., 1974-78, Union Coll., 1980. Cert. tchr., N.Y. Elem. tchr. Saratoga Springs (N.Y.) Schs., 1974-80; ednl. cons. Whitcomb Assocs., Boston, 1980-81; ednl. mktg. specialist Monroe Systems for Bus., Newington, Conn., 1981-83; nat. mktg. mgr. Victor Techs., Hartford, Conn., 1983, Exclusives, Boston, 1984-85; dir. pub. rels. Lawrence Group, Albany, N.Y., 1985-87, dir. corp. communications, 1987-88; v.p. Lawrence Group, Albany, 1988-89; v.p investors rels. Lawrence Group, N.Y.C., 1987-89; pres. S.A. Burstein & Assocs., Albany, 1989—; cons. N.Y. Assn. Bus. Ofcls., 1982-83. Editor: Helpline newspaper, 1985, 87; co-producer: Playing It Safe, 1986 (Nori award 1987), To Be As Independent As You Can Be (Nori award 1989), Cookbook Capital Connoisseur (Nori award 1989); acted in TV comml., 1981 (Addy award 1982). Bd. dirs. Multiple Sclerosis Soc., Albany, 1986—, Mohawk Pathways Girl Scouts U.S.; active in N.Y. Spl. Olympics, 1987, Capital Women's Charity Found., Albany, 1987—. Mem. NAFE, Nat. Investor Relations Inst., Am. Mgmt. Assn., Assn. Profl. Communicators, Nat. Assn. Investment Clubs, Albany C. of C. (mem. women's bus. coun.), Kappa Delta Pi. Democrat. Clubs: Steuben, Womens Press. Home: 4 Birch Hill Rd Albany NY 12211-2004

BURSTON, RICHARD MERVIN, business executive; b. Brookline, Mass., Oct. 31, 1924; s. Mark and Anita (Andrews) B.; m. Phoebe Harvey Hopkins, Aug. 29, 1958; children: Abby Lyn, Seth Hopkins, Joshua Craig, Mark Andrews, Amanda Lee. BA, Bowdoin Coll., 1949; MBA, Harvard U., 1952. Mgr. beauty dept. Kendall Co., Boston, 1953-58; regional sales mgr. M. Pier Co., Ft. Lauderdale, Fla., 1958-59; nat. sales mgr. Ozon Products, Inc., Bklyn., 1959-63; v.p., co-founder Burston/Larkin Assocs., Stamford, Conn., 1964-88; pres., chief exec. officer Excalibur, Inc., Stamford, 1981-88; founder, pres. Burston Inc., Stamford, 1987—; dir. Nat. Beauty and Barber Reps. Assn., N.Y.C., 1973-74, Louv Yacht Yard, Norwalk, Conn., 1969-73; cons. Ruckel Mfg., Inc., N.Y.C., 1969-87. Dir. Roxbury Babe Ruth, Stamford, 1969-85; pres., dir. Roxbury-Riverbank Little League, Stamford, 1971-82; trustee Miramichi Rod & Gun Club, Lyttleton, New Brunswick, Can., 1980—; fund raiser Bowdoin Coll., Brunswick, Maine, 1984-90. Served to lt. USNR, 1943-46, PTO. Recipient Man of Yr. award United Beauty Supply Corp., Bridgeport, Conn., 1983. Mem. Beauty and Barber Supply Inst., Am. Beauty Assn. Republican. Jewish. Clubs: Landmark, North Stamford Exchange (dir. 1984-86), Miramichi Rod & Gun, Bowdoin (Southwest Conn.); Spartan. Lodge: Masons. Avocations: fly fishing; sailing, commemorative plates, oriental rugs. Home: 156 Riverbank Dr Stamford CT 06903-3517 Office: Burston Inc 45 Church St Stamford CT 06906-1709

BURT, DAVID SILL, sculptor, writer, musician; b. Evanston, Ill., Feb. 20, 1917; s. William Griswold and Katharine (Brown) B.; children: Katharine O'Dea, Marcy Burt Butz, James Jackson, Sarah Jackson. Copywriter Benton & Bowles Inc., N.Y.C., 1943-50; promotion writer Time Inc., N.Y.C., 1950-62. Sculptural works include Voyagers stabile at Bradley Airport, Denouement stabile at U.S. Art-in-Embassies, Crescendo mobile at U. Wis., numerous other pub. works; represented in pvt. collections. Lt. USN, 1941-45, MTO, PTO. Winner competition for sculpture for Bradley Internat. Airport, Hartford, Conn., 1986, several exhbn. awards. Mem. Silvermine Guild of Artists (trustee 1982-86), Stamford Art Assn. Home: 24 Covewood Dr Norwalk CT 06853-2001 Office: 200 Henry St Stamford CT 06902-5825

BURTLE, JAMES LINDLEY, economist, educator; b. Bremerton, Wash., July 18, 1919; s. James Andrew and Hazel (Lindley) B.; m. Vasanti Erulkar, Sept. 1952 (div. 1961); children: Anthea, Meriel. BA, U. Chgo., 1942, MA, 1948. Mem. staff Internat. Labour Office, Geneva, 1949-58; v.p. W.R. Grace & Co., N.Y.C., 1958-80; mng. editor Internat. Country Risk Guide Internat. Reports, N.Y.C., 1980-82; prof. econs. Iona Coll., New Rochelle, N.Y., 1982-90; dir. fgn. exch. svc. Wharton Econometric Forecasting Assocs., Bala Cynwyd, Pa., 1990—; chmn. editorial adv. bd. Internat. Reports, N.Y.C., 1983—. Author: (with Sydney Rolfe) The Great Wheel, 1974. Staff sgt. USAAF, 1942-46, PTO. Mem. Econometric Soc. of Am. Econ. Assn. Home: 25 W 13th St New York NY 10011-7926 Office: 401 City Ave Bala Cynwyd PA 19004

BURTNICK, RONALD, training technology executive; b. Stuttgart, Republic of Germany, Nov. 9, 1946; came to U.S., 1947.; s. Robert Brennan and Ellen (Wondratchek) B.; m. Alice Galofaro, June 21, 1975; children: Katherine, Megan, Michael. AAS, Middlesex County Coll., Edison, N.J., 1970; BA, Montclair State Coll., 1972, MA, 1973; EdS, Rutgers U., 1982. Cert. mgr. Inst. Cert. Profl. Mgrs. Asst. dir. student ctr. Montclair State Coll., 1972-73; from coord. reg. vet. training ctr. to dir. N.J. vet. edn. Kean Coll., Union, N.J., 1973-76; assoc. dir. ctr. adult devel. Rutgers U. Grad. Sch. Edn., 1976-79; coord. mgmt. inst. Adelphi U., Garden City, N.Y., 1979-80; mgmt. trainer Thomas J. Lipton, Inc., Englewood Cliffs, N.J., 1980-83; mgr. computer auditing training Deloitte, Haskins & Sells, N.Y.C., 1983-88; adjunct prof. Raritan Valley Community Coll., Somerville, N.J., 1989—, Northampton Community Coll., Bethlehem, Pa., 1989—; dir. training tech. KBI Systems, Mountainside, N.J., 1990—; cons. U.S. Office of Edn., Washington, 1975-76. Active mem. Clinton (N.J.) Pub. Sch. PTA, 1990-91; exec. com. Middlesex County Coll. Alumni Assn., Edison, N.J., 1989—, Rutgers U. Grad. Sch. Edn. Alumni Assn., New Brunswick, N.J., 1988—. With U.S. Army, 1966. Mem. ASTD (chair career counseling com. 1978—), Inst. Cert. Profl. Mgrs. Home: 23 Marudy Dr Clinton NJ 08809-1220 Office: KBI Systems 177 Mill Ln Mountainside NJ 07092-2987

BURTON, ANNA MEISTER, psychiatrist, psychoanalyst; b. N.Y.C.. AB, Wellesley (Mass.) Coll., 1944; MD, N.Y. Med. Coll., 1948; grad., N.Y. Psychoanalytic Inst., 1965. Resident in psychiatry Kings County Hosp., N.Y., 1950-53; clin. psychiat. prof. Robert Wood Johnson Medicine Sch., Piscataway, N.J., 1985—; assoc. clin. psychiat. prof. N.J. Sch. of Medicine, Newark, 1985—; mem. faculty NYU Psychoanalytic Inst., Bellevue Hosp., 1987—. Fellow Am. Psychiat. Assn.; mem. Am. Psychoanalytic Assn. (cert.), N.J. Psychoanalytic Assn. (pres. 1988-90), N.Y. Psychoanalytic Assn., Psychoanalytic Assn. N.Y. State. Office: 163 Engle St Bldg 2 Englewood NJ 07631-2530

BURTON, CHARLES ARTHUR, venture capitalist; b. Akron, Ohio, Nov. 10, 1945; s. John Charles and Frances (Dunn) B.; m. Melinda Chang, Sept. 28, 1968; children: Samantha, Meris. BA, Gettysburg Coll., 1967; MBA, U. Pa., 1974. Analyst DuPont Pension Fund, Wilmington, Del., 1974-80; pres. Cigna Venture Capital, Phila, 1980-84; mng. dir. Phila. Venture Mgmt., Inc., 1984—; bd. dirs. Rose Communications, Milpitas, Calif., Sherpa Corp., Milpitas, Anadigics, Warren, N.J., Diamonex, Trexlertown, Pa. Lt. USN, 1967-72, Vietnam. Mem. Fin. Analysts of Phila., Founders Club. Republican. Presbyterian. Office: Phila Ventures 200 S Broad St Philadelphia PA 19102-3803

BURTON, DONALD H., marketing director; b. Albany, N.Y., Aug. 31, 1937; s. Donald H. and Jane (M.) Sedon; divorced; 1 child, Laurie Ann Massey. BSChemE, Clarkson U., 1959. Prodn. supr. Hercules Incorp., Glens Falls, N.Y., 1959-62; design engr. Hercules Incorp., Port Ewen, N.Y., 1962-70; mktg. dir. Hercules Incorp., Wilmington, Del., 1970—. Bd. dirs. Wildlife Mgmt. Inst., Washingotn, 1985—; exec. com. Sporting Arms and Ammunition Mgrs. Inst., Wilton, Conn., 1985—; bd. govs. Nat. Shooting Sports Found., Wilton, 1986—. Mem. NRA, Nat. Reloading Mfrs. Assn. (bd. dirs. 1980—, pres. 1990-92), Wilmington Trap Shooting Assn. (bd. dirs. 1981—), Ducks Unltd., Hercules Sportsmens Club (bd. dirs. 1984—). Republican. Home: 105 Tower Point Rd Chesapeake City MD 21915 Office: Hercules Inc Hercules Plz Wilmington DE 19894

BURTON, MARY LOUISE HIMES, librarian; b. Altoona, Pa., Oct. 4, 1948; d. Paul Silas and Clara Marie (Bettwy) Himes; m. Carl Hansel Burton, Aug. 28, 1983; children—Michael, Edward, Carla. A.A., Mt. Aloysius Jr. Coll., Cresson, Pa., 1968; B.S. in Edn., Slippery Rock U., 1970; M.L.S. magna cum laude, U. Pitts., 1982. Cataloguer Slippery Rock U., Pa., 1968-70; cataloguer, children's librarian Altoona Area Pub. Library, Pa., 1970-71; dir. library service Altoona Hosp., 1971-83; project coordinator Coll. of Physician of Phila., 1983-84; med. librarian VA Med. Ctr., Coatesville, Pa., 1984-85, acting chief libr. svc., 1985-86, chief library service, 1986—; security officer Automated Info. Systems, 1988—; local resource librarian Mideastern Regional Med. Library Program, Phila., 1976-82, Greater Northeastern Regional Med. Library Program, N.Y.C., 1983—. Mem. Spl. Libraries Assn., Pa. Libr. Assn. (chmn. spl. librs. div. and bd. dirs. 1980-82, 85-86, 89-90), Med. Library Assn., Acad. Health Info. Profls. (sr.), VFW Aux., Assn. Health Info. Profls., Consortium Health Info. (pres. 1990—). Mem. United Church of Christ. Avocations: vocalist, organist, pianist. Home: Box 159 VAMC Coatsville PA 19320 Office: VA Med Ctr Libr Svc (142D) 1400 Black Horse Hill Rd Coatesville PA 19320-2097

BURTON, STEVEN BRUCE, writer, actor; b. Norwich, N.Y., May 3, 1950; s. Robert Krause and Jean Estelle (Benedict) Burton. BA in Liberal Arts, Wash. State U., 1972. Actor stage, film, TV, L.A., 1972-85, N.Y.C., 1986—, including Gen. Hosp., 1980-84; author: (screenplays) Song for Susan, 1985, (stageplay) Rounds, 1991. Reader Recording for Blind, 1973; vol. Meals on Heals, N.Y.C., 1989. Mem. AFTRA, SAG. Home and Office: 532 W 50th St # 1-BR New York NY 10019

BURTON, WILLIAM JOSEPH, engineering manager; b. Gaffney, S.C., Mar. 22, 1931; s. Emory Goss and Olivia (Copeland) B.; m. Joan Holland Burton, Sept. 26, 1987. BSME, U. S.C., 1957, MSME, 1964; PhDME, Tex. A&M U., 1970. Registered profl. engr., Tenn. Sr. dynamics engr. Lockheed-Ga. Co., Marietta, 1957-62; sr. project engr. Allison div. GM Corp., Indpls., 1964-67; asst. prof., researcher Tex. A&M U., College Station, 1968-70; asst. prof. U. Tenn., Knoxville, 1970-74; projects mgr. Tenn. Valley Authority, Chattanooga, 1974-79; program mgr. Dept. Navy, Washington, 1979—; chmn. equal employment opportunity com. Chesapeake div. Naval Facilities Engring. Command, Washington, 1982-83. Author: On the Heating Surface Effects of Nucleate Boiling Data Correlation, 1964, The Effects of Surface Roughness on the Wave Forces on a Circular Cylindrical Pile, 1970; contbr. articles to profl. jours. Secretary, mem. hospitality com. Exch. Club, Knoxville, 1975, bd. dirs., 1976; coord. campaign Naval Facilities Engring. Com., Washington, 1982. With U.S. Army, 1951-53. Recipient Antarctic Svc. medal U.S. Dept. of Navy, 1962. Fellow ASME (chmn. exec. com. ocean engring. div. 1985, Golden Cert. 1989), Va. Soc. Profl. Engrs. (No. Va. regional coun. 1988); mem. AAAS, Nat. Soc. Profl. Engrs. (pres. elect Fairfax chpt. 1988), Soc. Mfg. Engrs., Soc. Naval Architects and Marine Engrs. Baptist. Home: 307 Miramar Rd Lakeland FL 33803-2633 Office: Chesapeake Div FPO-1 Naval Facilities Engring Command 8th and M Sts SE Bldg # 212 Washington DC 20374

BUSATH, DAVID DON, biophysicist, educator; b. Salt Lake City, Aug. 5, 1952; s. Don Lamar and Donna Lenore (Richards) B.; m. Anne Castleton, Dec. 29, 1975 (div. June 1987); children: Meagan, Gavin, Lorna, Maren; m. Angela Varanese, May 18, 1991; stepchildren: Crystal Occhiuti, Bethany Occhiuti. BA, U. Utah, 1974, MD, 1978. Asst. prof. biophysics Brown U., Providence, 1983-89, assoc. prof., 1989—. Mem. Ch. of Jesus Christ of Latter Day Saints. Office: Brown U PO Box G-B302 PO Box G-B3 Providence RI 02912

BUSCEMI, MARY CATHERINE, executive recruiter; b. Balt., Sept. 8, 1959; d. Edward L. and Mary Frances (Dunn) McNeir; m. Joseph Robert Buscemi, Sept. 20, 1986. BS, Notre Dame of Md., Balt., 1983. Legal pers. recruiter Williamson & Neil, Balt., 1984-88, Holland & Assocs., Towson, Md., 1988-89; owner/pres. recruiter NcNeir Buscemi Assocs., Inc., Towson, 1989—; guest speaker Dundalk Community Coll., Balt., Seton Keough High Sch., Balt., 1991. Mem. Md. Assn. Profl. Recruiting Cons. Democrat. Roman Catholic. Office: NcNeir Buscemi Assocs 401 Washington Ave Ste 701 Towson MD 21204

BUSCH, ALLEN CYRIL, retired government official, consultant; b. Cin., Aug. 21, 1931; s. Walter Albert and Lillian (Voegtle) B.; m. Patricia L. Burr, Mar. 23, 1957; children: Michael A., Melany M., Eric C., Craig A. BA, Miami U., 1955, MA, 1958. Pers. psychologist Kroger Co., Cin., 1957-59; sect. chief human factors Rsch. & Devel. Div. Avco Corp., Wilmington, Mass., 1959-62; staff psychologist HRB Singer Inc., State College, Pa., 1962-64; rsch. psychologist L. G. Hanscom Field USAF, Bedford, Mass., 1964-67; br. chief analysis br. FAA Tech. Ctr., Atlantic City, N.J., 1967-86; pvt. practice cons. Pawlet, Vt., 1986—; lectr. Northeastern U., Boston, 1964-65, Emery Riddle U., Atlantic City, 1982-83. Contbr. articles to profl. jours. Elected sch. bd. Mainland Regional High Sch., Linwood, N.J., 1976-78. Cpl. USMC, 1951-52, with USN, 1952-53. Recipient Silver medal award Dept. Transp., Washington, 1982. Mem. APA, IEEE (sr. mem., local chmn. 1978), Human Factors Soc., System Safety Soc., Aviation Psychologist Assn., N.Y. Acad. Sci. Home: RR 1 Box 2388 Pawlet VT 05761-9303

BUSCH-ROSSNAGEL, NANCY ANN, psychology educator; b. Denver, May 29, 1951; d. Edwin J. and Eleanor (Edison) Busch; m. Stephen Mark Rossnagel, Aug. 24, 1978; children: Amy Margaret, Philip Kenneth. BA, Scripps Coll., 1972; postgrad., Merrill-Palmer Inst., 1972-73; MS, Wayne State U., 1973; PhD, Pa. State U., 1979. Lectr. U. Guelph (Ont., Can.), 1973-77; asst. then assoc. prof. Colo. State U., Ft. Collins, 1979-84; assoc. prof. Fordham U., Bronx, N.Y., 1986—, asst. chair dept. psychology, 1987-91; chair dept. psychology Fordham U., Bronx, 1991—; vis. lectr. Fordham U., N.Y.C., 1983-85; project dir. Hispanic Rsch. Ctr., Bronx, 1984-86; cons. N.Y.C. Bd. Edn., 1987—, Office of Substance Abuse Prevention, N.Y.C., 1991—. Co-editor: Individuals as Producers of Their Development, 1981; editor Research Monographs in Adolescence, 1990—; cons. editor Jour. Personality and Social Psychology, 1989-91; contbr. articles to profl. jours., chpts. to books. Grantee Bur. for Edn. of Handicapped, 1978, Colo. State U., 1980-83, Fordham U., 1987-90. Mem. Soc. Rsch. on Adolescence, Soc. for Rsch. on Child Devel., Am. Psyhol. Assn., Coun. Undergrad. Programs in Psychology, Coun. Grad. Depts. in Psychology. Office: Fordham U Psychology Dept Bronx NY 10458-5198

BUSEK, ROBERT HENRY, engineering executive; b. Bklyn., June 2, 1947; s. Henry C. and Ruth A. (Bernius) B.; m. Linda P. Calianese, Oct. 7, 1972; children: Robert P., Kristi L. BCE, CCNY, 1969; MSCE, Purdue U., 1971. Registered profl. engr., N.Y., N.J., Conn., Del., Mass., Fla., Maine, Md. Design engr. N.H. Bettigole Co., Paramus, N.J., 1969-78, project mgr., 1978-81; pres. Bettigole, Andrews & Clark, Hackensack, N.J., 1989—; sr. v.p. Steinman, Boyston, Gronquist and Birdsall, N.Y.C., 1981-88; dir. engring. URS Cons., N.Y.C., 1988-89. Mem. ASCE, NSPE, Chi Epsilon, Sigma Xi. Office: H Bettigole, Andrews & Clark 1 University Plaza Dr Hackensack NJ 07601-6201

BUSH, BARBARA PIERCE, wife of President of the United States; b. Rye, N.Y., June 8, 1925; d. Marvin and Pauline (Robinson) Pierce; m. George Herbert Walker Bush, Jan. 6, 1945; children: George Walker, John Ellis, Neil Mallon, Marvin Pierce, Dorothy Walker. Student, Smith Coll., 1943-44; hon. degrees, Stritch Coll., Milw., 1981, Mt. Vernon Coll., Washington, 1981, Hood Coll., Frederick, Md., 1983, Howard U., Washington, 1987, Judson Coll., Marion, Ala., 1988, Bennett Coll., Greensboro, N.C., 1989, Smith Coll., 1989, Morehouse Sch. Medicine, 1989. Hon. chair adv. bd. Reading is Fundamental; hon. mem. Bus. Coun. for Effective Literacy; mem. adv. coun. Soc. of Meml. Sloan-Kettering Cancer Ctr.; hon. mem. bd. dirs. Children's Oncology Svcs. of Met. Washington, The Washington Home, The Kingsbury Ctr.; hon. chmn. nat. adv. coun. Literacy Vols. of Am., Nat. Sch. Vols. Program; sponsor Laubach Literacy Internat.; nat. hon. chmn. Leukemia Soc. of Am.; hon. mem. bd. trustees Morehouse Sch. of Medicine; hon. nat. chmn. Nat. Organ Donor Awareness Week, 1982-86; pres. Ladies of the Senate, 1981-88; mem. women's com. Smithsonian Assocs., Tex. Fedn. of Rep. Women, life mem., hon. mem.; hon. chairperson for the Nat. Com. on Literacy and Edn. United Way, Barbara Bush Found. for Family Literacy, Washington Parent Group Fund, Girls Clubs of Am., 10th anniversay Harvest Nat. Food Bank Network; hon. chmn. Nat. Com. for the Prevention of Child Abuse and Childhelp U.S.A.; hon. pres. Girl Scouts U.S; hon. chair Nat. Com. for Adoption. Recipient Nat. Outstanding Mother of Yr. award, 1984, Woman of Yr. award USO, 1986, Disting. Leadership

award United Negro Coll. Fund 1986, Disting. Am. Woman award Coll. Mt. St. Joseph, 1987. Mem. Tex. Fedn. Rep. Women (life), Internat. II Club (Washington), Magic Circle Rep. Women's Club (Houston). Episcopalian. Address: White House 1600 Pennsylvania Ave Washington DC 20501*

BUSH, CARL GAGE, JR., physician, naval officer; b. Huntingdon, Pa., Jan. 21, 1944; s. Carl Gage and Beulah (Irene (Mench) B.; m. Penney Gail Robinson, July 2, 1966; children: Christopher, Andrew, Kate. BS, Juniata Coll., Huntingdon, Pa., 1965; MD, Hahneman Coll., Phila., 1969. Officer USN Med. Corps., 1969-74; head dept. anesthesia Sturdy Hosp., Attleboro, Mass., 1974-88; officer USN Med. Corps., 1988—; owner Sail-By-Night Software, Attleboro, Mass., 1985—; capt. Bits 'N Bites Sport Fishing, Jerusalem, R.I., 1985—. Author: Sight Reduction, 1990, Celestial Navigation, 1992. Commdr. USN, 1988—. Named Regional Champion New England Enduro, 1986, Trail Chief, New England Trailriders, 1987, Man of Yr., Gooseberry Island, R.I., 1991. Republican. Home: PO Box 5341 Wakefield RI 02880

BUSH, DAVID FREDERIC, psychologist, educator; b. Watertown, N.Y., July 12, 1942; s. Frederic Ralph and Charlotte Mary (Ellingworth) B.; m. Joanne Arena; 1 child, Lara A. BA, U. South Fla., 1965; MA, U. Wyo., 1968; PhD, Purdue U., 1972. Instr. psychology Hiram Scott Coll., Scottsbluff, Nebr., 1967-69, Purdue U., West Lafayette, Ind., 1971-72; asso. prof. psychology West Chester (Pa.) State Coll., 1972-73; asst. prof., chmn. grad. program psychology Villanova (Pa.) U., 1972-77, assoc. prof., 1978-84, prof., 1984—, assoc. dir. human resource devel., grad. program in human orgn. sci.; instr. seminar Am. Coll., Bryn Mawr, Pa., 1976—; ptnr. Quality Mgmt. Group; cons. in field. Mem. coun. Unitarian fellowship Lafayette, Ind., 1970-72; bd. dirs. Ars Moriendi, Dennis Burton Day Care Ctr., 1971-72, Life Guidance Services, Inc., 1977-82; pres. Bush Assocs. NDEA fellow 1969-71, David Ross summer fellow, 1972; Villanova U. grantee, 1974, 77, 83. Mem. Am., Ea. psychol. assns., Soc. Psychol. Study Social Issues, Am. Soc. Quality Control, Assn. of Mgmt., Internat. Human Resource Mgmt. Assn., Human Resources Profl. Assn. (pres.), Acad. Mgmt., Soc. for Human Resource Mgmt., Assn. for Quality and Participation, Sigma Xi, Psi Chi. Author: Human Development: The Psychology of the Life-Span, 1974; Canterbury Press Memory Improvement Course. Editor: Researcher decision making and communication, orgn. behavior, human resource mgmt., quality improvement programs. Home: 2392 Pineview Dr Malvern PA 19355-2310 Office: Villanova U Dept Psychology Villanova PA 19085

BUSH, GEORGE HERBERT WALKER, President of the United States; b. Milton, Mass., June 12, 1924; s. Prescott Sheldon and Dorothy (Walker) B.; m. Barbara Pierce, Jan. 6, 1945; children: George W., John E., Neil M., Marvin P., Dorothy W. BA in Econs., Yale U., 1948; LLD (hon.), U. Tex., 1990; numerous other hon. degrees. Co-founder, dir. Zapata Petroleum Corp., 1953-59; pres. Zapata Off Shore Co., Houston, 1956-64; chmn. bd. Zapata Off Shore Co., 1964-66; mem. 90th-91st Congresses from 7th Dist. Tex., 1967-71, Ways and Means com.; U.S. amb. to UN, 1971-72; chmn. Rep. Nat. Com., 1973-74; chief U.S. Liaison Office Peking, People's Republic China, 1974-75; dir. CIA, 1976-77; adj. prof. adminstrv. sci. Rice U., Houston, 1978; V.P. of U.S., 1981-89, Pres. of U.S., 1989—. Chmn. Rep. Party Harris County, Tex., 1963-64; del. Rep. Nat. Conv., 1964, 68; Rep. candidate U.S. senator from Tex., 1964, 70. Served to lt. (j.g.), pilot USN, World War II. Decorated D.F.C., Air medals (3). Home and Office: The White House 1600 Pennsylvania Ave NW Washington DC 20500-0002*

BUSH, KAREN MICHAËLA, psychologist, educator; b. Scarsdale, N.Y., Nov. 30, 1947; d. Jean Evans and Kathryn (Morgan) B. BS, St. Lawrence U., 1969; MS, U. Pitts., 1977, PhD, 1980. Dir. research and rehab. unit Walter E. Fernald State Sch., Waltham, Mass., 1973-74; instr. Washington (Pa.) and Jefferson Coll., 1977-80, asst. prof., 1980-86, assoc. prof. psychology, 1986—, dir. Freshman Forum, 1988-90, assoc. dean acad. affairs, 1991—. Bd. dirs. Group Home, Inc., Washington, Pa., 1979-81. Mem. APA, LWV (bd. dirs. Washington County chpt. 1991—), Assn. Behavior Analysis, Am. Assn. Higher Edn. Office: Washington and Jefferson Coll Lincoln St Washington PA 15301-6720

BUSH, MELINDA JOHNSON, publisher; b. Champaign, Ill., June 14, 1942; d. Maurice R. and Margaret B. Johnson. BS, U. Colo., 1962; postgrad., NYU, 1962-64, London Sch. Econs. and Polit. Sci., 1962-64; postgrad. Advanced Mgmt. Program, Harvard U., 1984. Cert. hotel adminstr. With J. Walter Thompson, Advt., N.Y.C., 1962-64; pub. rels. Paul Bradley Assns., N.Y.C., 1964-66; with Ziff-Davis Pub. Co., N.Y.C., 1966—, mktg. dir. photography div., 1966-74, asst. to pres., 1974-76; pub. Hotel & Travel Index, N.Y.C., 1976—, v.p. bus. div., 1983-85; v.p. Murdoch Mags. div., pub. Hotel & Travel Index, News Group Publs., Inc., N.Y.C., 1985—; sr. v.p., group pub. Murdoch Mags., News America, Inc., N.Y.C., 1987-89; exec. v.p. directories Reed Travel Group; mem. exec. bd. Reed Travel Group div. Reed Internat.; disting. lectr. Cornell Hotel Sch., 1989; advisor Cornell U. Hotel Sch., Lausanne Hotel Sch.; advisor tourism programs U. Mass., New Sch. for Social Rsch., Culinary Inst. Am. (also mem. corp. bd.); columnist, frequent speaker and panelist at industry assns. and convs.; chmn. N.Y.C. Real Estae Devel. Conf. Author articles in field. Pres.'s Coun. Model Cities Task Force, 1970-72; founder, chmn. Photography Youth Found., 1973-76; mem. nat. bd. dirs. Am. Univ., Washington, Sun Resorts Inc., Master Media, Inc. Named Woman of Year in Travel, Travel Industry Assn. Am., 1980. Fellow Inst. Cert. Travel Agts. (bd. dirs., trustee); mem. Hotel Sales Mgmt. Assn. Internat. (bd. dirs.), Am. Hotel and Motel Assn. (trustee, cert. hotel adminstr.), Ednl. Inst. (trustee), Com. of 200 Women Entrepreneurs. Home: 2394 Players Ct West Palm Beach FL 33414 Office: Reed Travel Group Div of Reed Internat PLC 500 Plaza Dr Secaucus NJ 07094-3602

BUSH, RICHARD WAYNE, research chemist; b. Cleve., Nov. 5, 1934; s. George Leonard and Alma (Millonig) B.; m. Mary E. Hart, Apr. 26, 1969; children: Joseph, Gregory. SB, MIT, 1956; PhD, U. Ill., 1960; M. Adminstrv. Sci., Johns Hopkins U., 1978. Rsch. chemist W.R. Grace & Co., Columbia, Md., 1960-64, sr. rsch. chemist, 1964-69, supr., 1969-72, rsch. assoc., 1972—. Patentee in field. Mem. Am. Chem. Soc., Soc. Plastics Engrs. Office: WR Grace & Co 7379 State Route 32 Columbia MD 21044-4098

BUSH, ROBERT THOMAS, shipping company executive; b. Newbury, Berkshire, Eng., May 18, 1928; came to U.S., 1968; s. Randolph George and Catherine Ellen (Benger) B.; m. Haydee Ojeda, Jan. 23, 1966; children: Allan David, Linda Martha, Grace Katherine. Master Mariner, Southampton (Eng.) U., 1953. Shipmaster Burmah Oil Co., Rangoon, Burma, 1955-60; marine surveyor Sydney, Australia, 1960-68; terminal supt. Exportadora De Sal, Cedros Island, Mex., 1968-70; marine mgr. Balfour Williamson, London, 1970-73; sr. marine advisor Aramco, Saudi Arabia, 1974-76; ops. mgr. Mercantile & Marine (Tex.) Inc., Houston, 1976-80; sr. marine advisor Phillips Petroleum Co., Bartlesville, Okla., 1980-86; gen. mgr. Universe Tankships (Del.) Inc., N.Y.C., 1986—. Contbr. numerous articles to profl. jours. Charter mem. Better World Soc., Washington, 1988; tutor Literacy Vols. Am., Edison, N.J., 1988—; founder Friends of the Sea, N.Y., 1991. Mem. N.Y. Acad. Sci., Nautical Inst. of London. Home: 70 Fairview Ave Edison NJ 08817-2406

BUSH-BROWN, ALBERT, architectural, educational and financial consultant; b. West Hartford, Conn., Jan. 2, 1926; s. James and Louise (Carter) Bush-B.; m. Frances Wesselhoeft, Aug. 28, 1948; children: David, Frances, Lesley, Martha. AB, Princeton U., 1947, MFA, 1949, PhD, 1958; LLD, Emerson Coll., 1965; HHD, Providence Coll., 1966; DFA, Mercy Coll., 1976. Instr. art and archaeology Princeton U., 1949-50; jr. fellow Soc. of Fellows, Harvard U., 1950-53; prof. art and architecture Western Res. U., Cleve., 1953-54; prof. architecture and humanities MIT, 1954-62; pres. R.I. Sch. Design, 1962-68; prof., v.p. SUNY, Buffalo, 1968-71; chancellor L.I. U., 1971-85; chmn. Barclays Bank of N.Y., 1981-88, chmn. regional adv. bd., 1989-91; sr. counselor Hill & Knowlton Internat., N.Y.C., 1988-91; sr. cons. Paul R. Ray Co., N.Y.C., 1987-90; chmn. bd. dirs. The Barrel Hill Group, 1983—; pres. Albert Bush-Brown Assocs., 1980—. Author: Louis Sullivan, 1960; (with J.E. Burchard) The Architecture of America: A Social Interpretation, 1961, Books, Bass, Barnstable, 1967, King Khalid Military City, 1978, Skidmore, Owings and Merrill 1973-83, 1983, (with Dianne Davis) Hospitable Design for Healthcare and Senior Communities, 1991; editor architecture sect. Ency. Brit., 1955—; contbr. articles to profl. jours. Active Providence City Planning Commn., 1962-67; spl. advisor to sec. Dept. of Housing and Urban Devel., 1968-69, U. Mass, 1970-71; mem. White House Nat. Council on Arts, 1965-70, Trilateral Commn., Bretton Woods Conf.; bd. govs. Sch. of Arts, U. Pa., 1975-85; bd. dirs. Recording for the Blind, 1976-81; bd. mng. dirs. Met. Opera, 1976-85. Woodrow Wilson fellow Princeton U., 1947-48; Howard Found. fellow Brown U., 1959-60; fellow Inst. Politics, J.F. Kennedy Sch. Govt., Harvard, 1968-69. Mem. AIA (hon.), Council on Fgn. Relations, N.Y. Acad. Scis. Clubs: Century Assn. Office: Albert Bush-Brown Assocs PO Box 975 Barnstable MA 02630-0975

BUSHINSKY, DAVID ALLEN, nephrologist, educator, researcher; b. Elizabeth, N.J., Mar. 16, 1949; s. Morris and Frieda (Price) B.; m. Nancy Sue Krieger, Aug. 29, 1976; children: Joshua Mark, Seth Michael. B-SChemE magna cum laude, Lehigh U., 1971; MD, Tufts U., 1975. Instr. medicine Tufts U., Boston, 1979-80; asst. prof. medicine U. Chgo., 1980-87, assoc. prof. medicine, 1987-89, attending physician hosps., 1982-89; assoc. prof. physiology, assoc. prof. medicine U. Rochester, N.Y., 1989—; attending physician Michael Reese Hosp. & Med. Ctr., Chgo., 1980-82; chief nephrology Strong Meml. Hosp., Rochester, 1989—, attending physician, 1989—. Contbr. 10 chpts. to books and 50 articles to profl. jours. on calcium, protons and bone. Andrew Mellon fellow; grantee NIH, Am. Heart Assn., NSF, Michael Reese Rsch. Inst., Nat. Kidney Found. Mem. Am. Soc. Nephrology, Am. Heart Assn., Am. Fed. Clin. Rsch., Am. Soc. Bone and Mineral Rsch., Am. Soc. Clin. Investigation, Am. Physiol. Soc., Internat. Soc. Nephrology, Cen. Soc. Clin. Rsch. Home: 123 Heatherstone Ln Rochester NY 14618-4864 Office: U Rochester 601 Elmwood Ave Rochester NY 14642-9999

BUSHKIN, YURI, immunologist; b. Riga, Latvia, Oct. 22, 1949; s. Isser and Margarita (Skovronek) B.; m. Sandra Demaria, June 15, 1991. MS, Latvian State U., 1971; PhD, Weizmann Inst. Sci., 1978. Postdoctoral fellow Sloan-Kettering Inst. Cancer Rsch., N.Y.C., 1977-81, rsch. assoc., 1981-86; assoc. Pub. Health Rsch. Inst., N.Y.C., 1986-88, asst. mem., lab. head, 1988—; rsch. assoc. prof. pathology NYU Med. Ctr., N.Y.C., 1989—. Contbr. articles to profl. jours. Recipient Milberg Women's Cancer Rsch. Fund award, 1985, Nat. Cancer Cytology Ctr. award, 1986; grantee NIH, 1984-87, 87-91, Am. Cancer Soc., 1987-88, Coun. for Tobacco Rsch. U.S.A., 1992—. Office: Pub Health Rsch Inst 455 1st Ave New York NY 10016

BUSHNELL, GEORGE EDWARD, III, lawyer; b. Detroit, Feb. 18, 1952; s. George Edward Jr. and Elizabeth (Whelden) B.; m. Eileen Mary Maguire, Sept. 16, 1989; children: Ann-Elizabeth, Emily Spears Bushnell. BA, Bucknell U., 1974; JD, Emory U., 1981. Bar: Ga. 1981, D.C. 1983, N.Y. 1986. Staff asst. to hon. Lucien Nedzi U.S. Ho. of Reps., Washington, 1977-78; assoc. Duncan, Allen and Mitchell, Washington, Ivory Coast, Zaire, 1981-85, Shearman & Sterling, N.Y.C., 1985-91; corp. counsel Joseph E. Seagram & Sons Inc., N.Y.C., 1991—. Mem. ABA, N.Y. State Bar Assn., Ga. Bar Assn., D.C. Bar Assn. Office: Joseph E Seagram & Sons Inc 800 3d Ave New York NY 10022

BUSKIRK, ELSWORTH ROBERT, physiologist, educator; b. Beloit, Wis., Aug. 11, 1925; s. Ellsworth Fred and Laura Ellen (Parman) B.; m. Mable Heen, Aug. 28, 1948; children—Laurel Ann Buskirk Wiegand, Kristine Janet. Student, U. Wis., 1943; B.A., St. Olaf Coll., Northfield, Minn., 1950; M.A., U. Minn., 1951, Ph.D., 1954. Lab. and teaching asst. Lab. Physiol. Hygiene, U. Minn., 1951-53; research fellow Life Ins. Med. Research Fund, 1953-54; physiologist Environ. Research Center, Natick, Mass., 1954-57, Nat. Inst. for Arthritis, Metabolic and Digestive Diseases, NIH, Bethesda, Md., 1957-63; prof. applied physiology Pa. State U., University Park, 1963-92, dir. Lab. Human Performance Research, 1963-92; Marie Underhill Noll prof. Human Performance Pa. State U., 1988-92, emeritus, 1992—; mem. sci. adv. com. Pres.' Coun. on Phys. Fitness, 1959-61; mem. applied physiology study sect. divsn. rsch. grants NIH, 1964-68, 76-80; mem. com. on interplay of engring. with biology and medicine NAS-NAE, 1968-74, 82-88; mem. rsch. com. Pa. Heart Assn., 1970-73, 82-86, 87-89, 90—; mem. Pa. Gov.'s Coun. on Phys. Fitness and Sports, 1978-82; mem. com. on mil. nutrition rsch. NAS/NRC, 1982-90; mem. clin. scis. study sect. divsn. rsch. grants NIHh, 1989-92. Sect. editor Jour. Applied Physiology, 1974-78, assoc. editor, 1978-84; co-editor Science and Medicine of Exercise and Sports, 1974; editor Medicine and Sports, 1973-75; editor in chief Medicine and Sci. in Sports and Exercise, 1984-88, cons. editor, 1989—; mem. editorial bd. Physician and Sports Medicine, 1974-85, Jour. Cardiopulmonary Rehab., 1980—, Am. Jour. Clin. Nutrition, 1982-92, Jour. Gerontology, 1982—, Exptl. Gerontology, 1989—; contbr. over 225 physiology articles , revs to sci jours. Bd. visitors Sargent Coll., Boston U., 1976—; bd. dirs. Center Community Hosp., Pa., 1966-70, sec., 1971-72, v.p., 1973, pres., 1974-75. Served with U.S. Army, 1943-46, ETO. Recipient Disting. Alumni award St. Olaf Coll., 1969; rsch. grantee NIH, 1963-92, U.S. Olympic Com., 1965-68, USAF, 1965-69, Pa. Dept. Health, 1966-67, Pa. Heart Assn., 1966, 76-80, NSF, 1968-70, Nat. Inst. Occupational Safety and Health, 1969-74; NATO sr. fellow in sci., 1977. Mem. AAASS, AAHPERD, ASHRAE, Aerospace Med. Assn., Am. Acad. Phys. Edn., Am. Coll. Sports Medicine (citations 1973, 75, Honor award 1984, editorial award 1989, Mid-Atlantic regional chpt. Svc. award 1991), Am. Inst. Nutrition, Am. Physiol. Soc. (pres. environ. and exercise sect. 1987-91, com. on coms. 1988-92), Am. Heart Assn. (coun. on epidemiology), N.Y. Acad. Scis., NIH Alumni Assn., Pa. Heart Assn. (rsch. com. 1988—), Am. Diabetes Assn., Coun. Biology Editors. Lutheran. Club: Centre Hills Country. Home: 216 Hunter Ave State College PA 16801-6947 Office: Pa State U 119 Noll Lab University Park PA 16802-6900

BUSNAINA, AHMED ALI, mechanical engineering educator; b. Benghazi, Sept. 2, 1953; s. Ali A. Busnaina and Fathia H. Belrassali; m. Zainab A. Shwaidhdi; children: Wedad, Ibrahim, Ali. BS with honors, Tripoli U., 1976; MS in Mech. Engring., Okla. State U., 1979, PhD in Mech. Engring., 1983. Maintenance engr. GE, Benghazi, 1976, Esso Oil Co., Briga, 1977; teaching and rsch. asst. Okla. State U., Stillwater, Okla., 1978-79; teaching and rsch. assoc. Okla. State U., Stillwater, 1980-83; visiting asst. prof. San Diego State U., 1983-84; asst. prof. Clarkson U., Potsdam, N.Y., 1984-88; assoc. prof. Clarkson U., Potsdam, 1988—; dir. Ctr. for Particulate Control in Process Equipment, Potsdam, 1990—; cons. IBM Corp., Burlington Vt., 1985—, Du Pont Co., Wilmington, Del., 1988; pres. Advanced Computational Scis., Potsdam, N.Y., 1986—; dir. Microcontamination Rsch. Lab., Potsdam, 1988—. Developer (software) General Flow, 1984, Clean Room Modeling, 1986, Swirl Flow, 1987; contbr. articles to profl. jours. Recipient Ralph R. Teetor award Soc. Automotive Engrs., 1986. Mem. AIAA (spl. svc. award 1986, faculty advisor award 1988), ASME, Am. Soc. Engring. Edn. (outstanding faculty 1988), Inst. Environ. Scis. (sr. mem.), Fine Particle Soc. Office: Clarkson U MIE Dept Potsdam NY 13676

BUSS, EDWARD GEORGE, geneticist; b. Concordia, Kans., Aug. 28, 1921; s. George E. and Kathryn (Luginsland) B.; m. Dorothy Ruth Arvidson, May 7, 1949; children: Ellen, Norman. BS, Kans. State Coll., 1943; MS, Purdue U., 1949, PhD, 1956. Grad. rsch. teaching asst. Purdue U., West Lafayette, Ind., 1946-49; asst. prof. Colo. A&M Coll., Ft. Collins, 1949-55; instr. Purdue U., 1955-56; assoc. prof., prof. Pa. State U., University Park, 1956-86; prof. emeritus Pa. State U., 1987—; cons. P.T. Anputraco Ltd., Surabaya Indonesia, 1987—; sr. scientist Biopore Inc., State College, Pa., 1987—. Co-author: Meat Production in Turkeys, 1990; contbr. articles to profl. jours. Capt. U.S. Army, 1943-46. Mem. Am. Genetic Assn. (coun. mem.), Am. Inst. Biological Scis. (gov. bd., exec. com.), AAAS (fellow 1962); Poultry Sci. Assn. (fellow 1988), World's Poultry Sci. Assn. Democrat. Home: 1420 S Garner St State College PA 16801-6330 Office: Pa State U Dept Poultry Sci 213 Henning Bldg University Park PA 16802

BUSSARD, DAVID ANDREW, federal agency administrator; b. Wilmington, Del., Jan. 22, 1955. BA, Harvard Coll., 1976; postgrad., Kennedy Sch. Govt., 1979-81. Policy analyst U.S. EPA, Washington, 1981-88, dep. div. dir., 1988-90, dir. div., 1990—. Rockefeller fellow Harvard U., 1976-77. Office: US EPA Office Solid Waste 401 M St SW Washington DC 20460

BUSSE, MICHAEL PHILIP, business executive; b. Syracuse, N.Y., Oct. 28, 1948; s. Harold Frederick and Arlene Bertha (Dietz) B.; m. Suzanne Mary Windhausen, June 26, 1971; children: Justin Michael, Heather Marie (dec.), Eric Michael. Student, Onondaga Community Coll., Syracuse U. Various positions Anaren Microwave, Inc., 1969-81; plant mgr. Communication Techniques, Inc., 1981-83; pres., C.O.O. Microwave Systems, Inc., 1983-85, pres., chief exec. officer, C.O.B., 1985-89; pres., C.O.O. Corvus Microwave, Inc., 1989-91; v.p. microwave tech. div. and indsl. supply div. JHP Indsl., Inc., 1991; founder, chief exec. officer Strategic Alliance Assocs., Syracuse, N.Y., 1991—; founding bd. mem., dir. Cen. N.Y. Tech. Devel. Orgn., 1988. Contbr. articles to profl. jours. Com. chmn. troop #215 Boy Scouts Am., 1983; del., chair N.Y. fin. com. White House Conf. on Small Bus., 1986; parish coun., chair long range planning com. St. Ann's Ch., 1988; bd. dirs., mem. fin. com., chmn. devel. com. Am. Lung Assn., 1988. With USAF Air Nat. Guard, 1967-73. Mem. Greater Syracuse C. of C. (chair commerce com. of the small bus. coun. 1988-89, govt. rels. com., leadership devel. com. 1988, appointed Speaking from Experience program 1991). Republican. Roman Catholic. Office: Strategic Alliance Assocs 3200 B Court St Syracuse NY 13206

BUSTARD, THOMAS STRATTON, engineering company executive; b. Balt., Feb. 18, 1934; s. Thomas Harrison and Helen Isabella (Slough) B.; m. Dorothy Lee Harrow, Aug. 27, 1957 (div. Sept. 1979); children: Richard Todd, Cara Lynn Bustard Clark; m. Dubra Doris Schoen, Jan. 7, 1983. BS in Chem. Engring., Johns Hopkins U., 1955; MSME, Drexel U., 1962; PhD in Chem. Engring., U. Md., 1965; Cert. in Bus. Mgmt., George Washington U., 1969. Registered profl. engr., Md. Chemist E.I. Dupont DeNemours & Co., Inc., Phila., 1955-56; process engr. Davison Chem. Co., Curtis Bay, Md., 1956-57; heat transfer/thermodynamic specialist The Martin Co./Nuclear Div., Middle River, Md., 1957-65; sr. engr. to chief engr. Hittman Corp., Columbia, Md., 1965-77; on-site cons. Dept. of Energy, Washington, 1977-79; founder, pres. Energetics, Inc., Columbia, 1979—; past instr. Essex Community Coll., Loyola Coll., Johns Hopkins U. Contbr. articles to profl. jours.; patentee in field. With USCG, 1957-65. Recipient four Purple Martin awards Martin-Marietta, Outstanding Grad. Student award U. Md., 1965. Mem. Sigma Xi. Republican. Lutheran. Office: Energetics Inc 7164 Columbia Gateway Dr Columbia MD 21046-2101

BUSUTTIL, JAMES JOSEPH, lawyer; b. Manhasset, N.Y., July 28, 1958; s. Joseph Michael and Pauline Sally (Grech) B. BA, Harvard U., 1979; JD, NYU, 1982. Bar: N.Y. 1983, D.C. 1984, U.S. Ct. Internat. Trade 1986. Atty. adviser U.S. Dept. State, Washington, 1982-83; assoc. Curtis, Mallet-Prevost, Colt & Mosle, N.Y.C., 1983-84, Shearman & Sterling, N.Y.C., 1984-86, Porter & Travers, N.Y.C., 1986-90; spl. asst. to gen. counsel NOAA, Washington, 1986, interagy. com. U.S. Govt Internat. Whaling Commn., 1986—; guest lectr. law schs. Harvard U., Yale U., NYU, Georgetown U., also others; bd. dirs. Trivestments Inc., N.Y.C.; advisor Union Afghanistan Lawyers, 1989—. Author: Towards the Rule of Law: Soviet Legal Reform and Human Rights under Perestroika, 1989; chmn. NYU Jour. Internat. Law and Politics, 1988-90; contbr. numerous book revs. to profl. jours. Mem. coun. St. John's U., Jamaica, N.Y., 1986—; mem. devel. coun. REgis High Sch., N.Y.C., 1989—; rapporteur Ind. Counsel in Internat. Human Rights, N.Y.C., 1986—, Helsinki Watch Com. Jursits, N.Y.C., 1988—; mem. Coun. on Fgn. Rels., 1990—. Recipient Recent Grad. award NYU Sch. Law, 19187; scholar Harvard U., 1977-79. Mem. ABA (vice chmn. inter-bar com. on terrorism 1984-86, internat. law com. 1984—, mem. internat. fin. law com. 1986-90, comml. fin. svcs. com. 1988-90, environ. control com. 1988-90), N.Y. State Assn. (vice chmn. com. on internat. human rights 1987-89), D.C. Bar Assn., Assn. of Bar of City of N.Y. (com. on internat. human rights 1989—), Am. Soc. Internat. Law (exec. coun. 1988-91), Internat. Law Assn. (multinational banking com. 1988—, terrorism com. 1984—), Coun. on Fgn. Rels., NYU Law Sch. Alumni Assn. (bd. dirs. 1988—), Cath. Lawyers Guild, Harvard Club, Grads. Club, Order of Coif. Roman Catholic.

BUTCHER, MARY ELLEN, association executive, consultant; b. Ottumwa, Iowa, May 26, 1935; d. Harold Sylvester and Mary Bernice (O'Brien) B. BA, Rosary Coll., 1958; PhD, Cath. U. Am., 1969. Secondary tchr. various orgns., various cities D.C., S.D., Ill., 1957-71; secondary adminstr. O'Gorman High Sch., Sioux Falls, S.D., 1971-74; asst. fin. officer Sinsinawa (Wis.) Dominicans, 1974-77, gen. fin. officer, 1977-85; asst. prof. fin. Providence (R.I.) Coll., 1985-88; exec. dir. Nat. Assn. Treas. of Religious Insts., Silver Spring, Md., 1988—; cons. Natri, Silver Spring, 1983-85; mem. bd. Interfaith Ctr. on Corp. Responbility, N.Y.C., 1989—. Contbr. articles to profl. jours. Trustee Rosary Coll., River Forest, Ill., 1977-85, 90—, Providence Coll., 1990—; bd. dirs. Washington Area Community Investment Fund, 1988—. Mem. Am. Econ. Assn. Democrat. Roman Catholic. Office: Nat Assn Treas Rel Insts 8824 Cameron St Silver Spring MD 20910-4113

BUTERAKOS, KATHLEEN ANN, assistant principal; b. Jamaica, N.Y., Feb. 28, 1951; d. William Michael and Ann Marilyn (Parrucci) Maurer; m. James Nicholas Buterakos, Aug. 18, 1973; 1 child, Sophia Anndrina. BA in English and Edn., Queens Coll., 1972, MS in Edn., 1977; postgrad., SUNY, Albany, 1978, Brigham Young U., 1978, McPherson Coll., 1978; Profl. Diploma in Ednl. Supervision, St. John's U., Jamaica, N.Y., 1982; postgrad., Adelphi U., 1983, U. Mont., 1986. Cert. tchr., adminstr., supr., N.Y. Tchr. Elijah Clark Jr. High Sch., South Bronx, N.Y., 1972-75, Intermediate Sch. 291, Bklyn., 1975; tchr., dean, asst. prin. Jean Nuzzi Jr. High Sch., Queens Village, N.Y., 1975-83; asst. prin. William Cowper Intermediate Sch., Maspeth, N.Y., 1983—. Doctoral fellow Hofstra U., 1990. Mem. ASCD, Doctoral Assn. N.Y. Educators, nat. Sci. Suprs. Assn., Nat. Sci. Tchrs. Assn., Nat. Coun. Tchrs. English, Internat. Reading Assn., Phi Delta Kappa. Roman Catholic. Office: William Cowper Intermediate Sch 70 02 54th Ave Maspeth NY 11378

BUTINA, MARY ANN, lead manufacturing supervisor; b. Greensburg, Pa., Sept. 19, 1949; d. Joseph Mark and Dora Louise (Boehme) M.; m. Charles Stephan Butina, Aug. 29, 1970; children: Jason Charles, Luka John, Matthew James, Benjamin Lee. BS in Psychol., Sociol., U. Pitts., 1970. Elem. tchr. Diocese of Greensburg, Greensburg, Pa., 1970-71; mgr. McDonald's Restaurant, Latrobe, Pa., 1974-75; quality control Westinghouse Electric Corp., Blairsville, Pa., 1984-85, mfg. supr., 1985, lead mfg. supr., 1985-87, sr. supr., 1987-90, lead mfg. supr. ops. engring. group, 1990-91, job redesign and tng., 1991, prin. human resources rep., 1992—. Mem. Westinghouse Foreman's Assn. Democrat. Roman Catholic. Office: Westinghouse SMP RR 4 Box 333 Blairsville PA 15717-8943

BUTLER, BRIAN, podiatric physician; b. N.Y.C., Mar. 30, 1949; s. William Leland and Mary Theresa (O'Leary) B.; m. Catherine Mary Collins; children: Irene, Matthew, Beth. BA, St. Francis Coll., Bklyn., 1970; MA, Manhattan Coll., Riverdale, N.Y., 1973; D in Podiatric Medicine, N.Y. Coll. Podiatric Medicine, 1981; fellow advanced mgmt. program for clinicians, NYU, 1987. Lic. podiatrist, N.Y., Va.; diplomate Am. Bd. Podiatric Orthopedics. Asst. to pres. govt. affairs N.Y. Coll. Podiatric Medicine, N.Y.C., 1979-82, asst. prof. community medicine, 1988—; resident in surgery Joint Diseases North Gen. Hosp., N.Y.C., 1982; ptnr. Butler & Trepal, D.P.M., P.C., Brooklyn Heights, N.Y., 1982—; adj. asst. prof. medicine N.Y. Med. Coll., Valhalla, 1984—; assoc. prof. community medicine N.Y. Coll. Podiatric Medicine, N.Y.C., 1991, chmn. pres. adv. bd., 1991, chmn. curriculum reform commn., 1992. Author: Woodrow Wilson's Entry Upon the American Political Scene, 1973; contbr. articles to profl. jours. Pres., chmn. bd. U.S. Cath. Hist. Soc., N.Y.C., 1984—; chmn. bd. trustees Nat. Cath. Mus., Washington, 1988—; bd. dirs. Rachmiel Levine Diabetes Found., Westchester County Med. Ctr., N.Y., 1984—, Angel Guardian Home for Children, Bklyn., 1988—; bd. trustees Cath. Charities, Roman Cath. Diocese of Bklyn., 1991; past chmn. Bishop's Lay Com. for Charity Diocese Bklyn. Named Outstanding Young Man in Am., U.S. Jaycees, Washingotn, 1981, Knight of Malta Sovereign, Mil. Order Malta, Rome, 1982; recipient The Franciscan Spirit award St. Francis Coll., Bklyn., 1990. Fellow Am. Coll. Foot Orthopedists; mem. Am. Podiatric Med. Assn., N.Y. State Podiatric Med. Assn. (peer rev. and pub. affairs and legis. coms., Disting. Svc. award student chpt. 1981), N.Y. Athletic Club, Pi Mu Delta (former nat. pres.). Democrat. Home: 77 Sagamore Rd Bronxville NY 10708-1506 Office: Butler & Trepal DPM PC 115 Henry St Brooklyn NY 11201-2517

BUTLER, CARL ERNEST, dairy company executive, consultant; b. Pittsfield, Mass., Oct. 31, 1938; s. Carl Edwin and Ruth (Cook) B.; m. Diane Birkett, Sept. 8, 1956; children: Richard, Teresa. BS, U. Conn., 1960. Dairy farmer Prospect Hill Farm, Pine Plains, N.Y., 1960-90; acting chief exec.

officer Holstein Assn., Brattleboro, Vt., 1990-91, pres., 1991—. Pres. Pine Plains Bd. Edn., 1976-77; mem. Bush '88 USA Com., 1988. Mem. Pine Plains Lions Club (pres. 1975-76), Dutchess County Agrl. Soc. (bd. dirs., nat. dairy promotion and rsch. bd. 1985-89, vice chmn. 1988, v.p. 1990—), United Dairy Industry Assn. (bd. dirs.), Dutchess County Farm Bur., Dutchess County Extension Svc., Ea. N.Y. Holstein Club (pres. 1970-72). Republican. Home: Rt 1 Box 510 A Pine Plains NY 12567 Office: Holstein Assn 1 S Main St Brattleboro VT 05302

BUTLER, DANIEL PATRICK, fundraising consultant; b. N.Y.C., Nov. 25, 1939; s. Patrick Joseph and Johanna (Healy) B.; m. Kathleen McGroder, Oct. 23, 1965; children: Patricia, Ann. BS, Fordham U., 1962, MBA, 1971. Unit dir. United Way of Tri-State, N.Y.C., 1966-69; dir. capital campaign Lincoln Ctr. for Performing Arts, N.Y.C., 1969-70; assoc. dir. devel. Fordham U., N.Y.C., 1970-71; spl. asst. to pres. Adelphi U., L.I., 1971-74; mng. ptnr. Jerold Panas & Ptnrs., N.Y.C., 1974-76; v.p. sales/mktg. Blyth, Paine, Webber Healthcare Funding, N.Y.C., 1976-77; pres. Daniel P. Butler Co., N.Y.C., 1977—; cons. Boys Clubs of Am., N.Y.; instr. N.Y.U. Contbr. articles to profl. jours. Served with U.S. Army, 1963-69. Club: Univ. Home: 440 E 23d St New York NY 10010 Office: 60 E 42d St New York NY 10165

BUTLER, EDWARD LEE, pastor, consultant; b. Frostproof, Fla., June 29, 1945; s. Willie and Lucinda (Hays) B.; m. Thelma Ruth Moore; children: Adina Zaneta, Edward Lee II. BA, Pacific States U., 1972; MDiv, Payne Theol. Sem., 1982. Ordained to ministry Episcopalian Ch., 1973. Pastor Bethel A.M.E. Ch., Mt. Union, Pa., 1973-74, St. Paul A.M.E. Ch., Uniontown, Pa., 1974-79, Quinn Chapel A.M.E. Ch., Wilmington, Ohio, 1979-82, Trinity A.M.E. Ch., Pitts., 1982-90, Ebenezer A.M.E. Ch., Aliquippa, Pa., 1990—; mem. edn. com., cons. Interdenominational Social Action Alliance, Pitts., 1984—; part-time chaplain Pa. Coun. Chs., 1990—, Western Ctr. Mental Health Facility, Canonsburg, Pa., 1990—. Mem. council Am. Cancer Soc., Pitts., 1985-86; mem. adv. bd. Black Adoption Services, Pitts., 1987—; mem. publicity com. Black Polit. Empowerment Project, Pitts., 1987—. Fellow Black Child Devel. Inst., Met. Crusade for Voters, Urban League; mem. NAACP. Democrat. Lodge: Kiwanis (bd. dirs. Uptown Hill club 1986—). Home: 1015 Davis St Aliquippa PA 15001-3121

BUTLER, FRANCIS JOSEPH, philanthropic educator; b. Alexandria, Va., Feb. 4, 1945; s. Albert Augustus and Jean (Semple) B.; m. Frances Farrell, Dec. 28, 1968; children: Ellen, Meghan, John. STB, Cath. U. Am., 1969; MA, U. San Francisco, 1969; STD, Cath. U. Am., 1972. Rsch. assoc. U.S. House Rep., Washington, 1971-72; dir. govt. rels. U.S. Cath. Conf., Washington, 1973-74; exec. dir. Office Domestic Policy U.S. Cath. Conf., Washington, 1974-79; pres. Found. and Donors Interested in Cath. Activities, Washington, 1980—; chmn. Com. Religion and Philanthropy Coun. on Foundations, Washignton, 1983-88; chmn., founder Support Our Aging Religions, Silver Spring, Md., 1987—; bd. mem. Cath. U. Am. Sch. Religious Studies, Washington, 1987—. Editor: Quest for Justice, 1981, Funding Churches in the Future, 1988, How To Save The Catholic Inner City School, 1990. Bd. mem. Gabriel Homes, Cath. Charities, Arlington, Va., 1982; cons. Pontifical Coun. for the Laity, Rome, 1987. Mem. Ind. Sector, Cath. Charities. Roman Catholic. Office: FADICA Inc Ste 303 1350 Connecticut Ave NW Washington DC 20036-1701

BUTLER, JAMES ALBERT, English educator; b. Pitts., May 18, 1945; s. F. Ralph and Myrtle Gray (Saxman) B.; m. Joanne Marie Buck, June 9, 1967; children: Christine Anne, Amy Lynn, Anne-Kate. BA, La Salle U., 1967; MA, Cornell U., 1970, PhD, 1971. Asst. prof. English La Salle U., Phila., 1971-76, assoc. prof. English, 1976-78, prof. English, 1978—, chair dept. English, 1985—; cons. Pa. Humanities Coun., 1991—. Editor (quarterly) Four Quarters, 1977-78; (books) Lyrical Ballads by Wordsworth, 1992, Ruined Cottage by Wordsworth, 1979; asst. editor Cornell Wordsworth Series, 1979—; contbr. articles to profl. jours. Assoc. trustee Wordsworth Libr. and Mus., Grasmere, Eng., 1979—. Danforth Found. fellow, 1967-71, Am. Philos. Soc. Rsch. grantee, 1979, Am. Coun. of Learned Socs. fellow, 1976, NEH fellow, 1983; recipient Lindback for Disting. Teaching award La Salle U., 1980. Mem. MLA, Phi Beta Kappa. Office: La Salle U Dept English 1900 W Olney Ave Philadelphia PA 19141

BUTLER, JAMES NEWTON, chemist, educator; b. Cleve., Mar. 27, 1934; s. Clyde Henry and Margaret (Manor) B.; m. Nancy Elizabeth Close, Aug. 31, 1957 (div.); 1 son, Christopher J.; m. Rosamond Hatch Bee, Dec. 10, 1966; stepchildren: Alden G. Bee, Kenneth M. Bee. B.S. (Alumni scholar), Rensselaer Poly. Inst., 1955; Ph.D. (NSF fellow, Gen. Electric fellow), Harvard, 1959. Staff scientist NACA Lewis Lab., Cleve., summers 1952-57, MIT Lincoln Lab., summer 1958; instr. U. B.C., Vancouver, 1959-61, asst. prof., 1961-63; sr. scientist Tyco Labs., Inc., Waltham, Mass., 1963-66, dept. head, 1966-71, cons., 1962-63, 71-73; lectr. Harvard U., 1970-71, Gordon McKay prof. applied chemistry, 1971—, mem. faculty geol. scis., 1972-86, mem. com. on oceanography, 1972—, mem. faculty earth and planetary scis., 1986—; mem. steering com. co-author report Petroleum in the Marine Environment, Nat. Acad. Scis.—NRC, 1973-75, 80-82; mem. tech. panel, report drafting com. Com. on Environ. Decision-Making, 1975-77; chmn. com. on effectiveness of oil spill dispersants, NRC, 1985-89; cons. EPA, 1978— , NOAA, 1981—. Author: Ionic Equilibrium, 1964, Solubility and pH Calculations, 1964, The Calculus of Chemistry, 1965, Problems for Introductory University Chemistry, 1967, Pelagic Tar from Bermuda and the Sargasso Sea, 1973, Carbon Dioxide Equilibria and Their Applications, 1982, reprinted, 1991, Studies of Sargassum and the Sargassum Community, 1983, Using Oil Spill Dispersants on the Sea,1 1989; also articles. Trustee Bermuda Biol. Sta., 1972—, v.p., 1985-86, 89—, pres., 1986-89. NSF Faculty Sci. fellow, 1977. Mem. Am. Chem. Soc., AAAS, Am. Soc. Limnology and Oceanography, Internat. Soc. Electrochemistry, Electrochem. Soc. N.Y. (chmn. Boston sect.), Gordon Research Conf. on Electrochemistry (chmn.), Assn. Harvard Chemists (pres.), Sigma Xi, Phi Lambda Upsilon. Office: Harvard U Div Applied Scis Pierce Hall 29 Oxford St Cambridge MA 02138-2901

BUTLER, JESSE LEE, bank officer; b. Greenwood, S.C., Apr. 21, 1953; m. Jannie Connor, June 2, 1984; children: Christian Jarad, Garrison Jay, Brittany Jelisa, Jennifer Taylor. BA, Lander Coll., 1977; MA, Howard U., 1982; diploma, Nat. Grad. Compliance Sch. Cert. bank compliance officer; cert. regulatory compliance mgr. Bank examiner Fed. Res. Bank N.Y., N.Y.C., 1980-85; compliance audit officer, cons. First Fidelity Bancorp, Newark, 1985—; cons., instr. Am. Inst. Banking, Bloomfield, N.J., mem. speaker network; instr. N.J. Bank Audit Group, Bank Adminstrn. Inst., Am. Bankers Assn., Nat. Compliance Sch. Contbr. Summit Edn. Found.; treas. Jefferson Sch. PTO; mem. Summit Bd. Edn. Mem. N.J. Bankers Assn., NAt. Urban Bankers Assn., Nat. Black MBA Assn., Am. Mgmt. Assn., North Jersey Compliance Officers Assn., Soc. Fin. Examiners, Am. Banking Assn., Inst. Cert. Bankers, Lander Coll. Alumni Assn., Howard U. Alumni Assn., Omega Psi Phi. Mem. N.J. Sch. Bds. Assn., N.J. Bankers Assn., Nat. Urban Bankers Assn., Nat. Black MBA Assn., Am. Mgmt. Assn., North Jersey Compliance Officers Assn., Soc. Fin. Examiners, Joint Ctr. Polit. Studies, Am. Banking Assn., Inst. Cert. Bankers, Lander Coll. Alumni Assn., Howard U. Alumni Assn., Omega Psi Phi. Democrat. Baptist. Home: 10 South St Summit NJ 07901-3946 Office: First Fidelity Bancorp 151 Centennial Ave PO Box 1351 Piscataway NJ 08855

BUTLER, MARY JANE, accountant; b. Orangeburg, S.C., Sept. 24, 1946; d. Woodrow and Mary (Smith) Dantzler; m. Young F. Butler, Mar. 16, 1968; children: Dwayne M., Darrell W. BS, S.C. State Coll., 1970, MEd, 1978. Cert. counselor; cert. Notary Pub. Sec. Fayetteville (N.C.) State U., 1972-73; retail ops. Army/Air Force Exchange, Ft. Benning, Ga., 1974-75; vol. counselor Briarwood Elem. Sch., Charlotte, N.C., 1977; acct. Comptr. Dept. of Army, Ft. Monmouth, N.J., 1980-83, unit chief in acctg., 1983-85, sect. chief in acctg., 1985-89, br. chief in acctg., 1989—; team leader fin. and acctg. div. Ft. Monmouth, 1990—. Chmn. social action com. Delta Sigma Theta, Monmouth County, N.J., 1988-90. Mem. NAFE, Assn. Govt. Accts. (sec. 1985-87, pres. 1988-90, 90—, Nat. award 1988-89), Am. Soc. Mil. Comptrs., Am. Soc. Notaries. Baptist. Home: PO Box 52 Middletown NJ 07748 Office: Hdqrs CECOM Comptr AMSEL CP FA G Fort Monmouth NJ 07703

BUTLER, PAUL WILLIAM, lawyer; b. N.Y.C., Feb. 17, 1961; s. William Joseph and Kathleen Elizabeth (Raftery) B. Student, Villanova U., 1979-81; BA, SUNY, Albany, 1983, MA in History cum laude, 1984; postgrad. in law, Trinity Coll., Dublin, Ireland, 1987; JD, St. John's U., 1988. Bar: Pa. 1988, N.Y. 1990. Mgmt. trainee Fed. Res. Bank N.Y., N.Y.C., 1984-85; assoc. Kelley Drye & Warren, N.Y.C., 1987; law clk. to chief judge U.S. Dist. Ct. (ea. dist.) Pa., 1988-90; assoc. Cahill Gordon & Reindel, N.Y.C., 1990—. Mem. St. John's U. Law Rev., 1987-88. St. Thomas More scholar, 1987-88; recipient Jessup Internat. Law Moot Ct. award. Mem. Am. Judicature Soc., Am. Soc. Internat. Law, Phila. Bar Assn. (internat. human rights com.), Bar Assn. of City of N.Y. Roman Catholic. Home: 275 Henry St # 1B Brooklyn NY 11201

BUTLER, WILLIAM LANGDON, women's accessories company executive; b. Indpls., Jan. 26, 1939; s. Edward Morris Jr. and Louise Hughes (Dyer) B.; m. Grace Caroline Gage, Dec. 28, 1961; children: Mary Dyer, William Langdon Jr. BA, Middlebury Coll., 1962. With J.J. Newberry Co., N.Y.C., 1961-63; owner Butler Sales Assocs., Summit, N.J., 1965-66; regional mgr. Hi-Fashion Inc., Atlanta, 1966-67; chief exec. officer, owner Butler Sales & Mktg. Inc., Summit, 1967-80; regional sales mgr. Trina Inc., Fall River, Mass., 1980-82, v.p. sales, 1982-87, v.p. gen. mdse. div., 1987—. Coach Jr. Raider Football League, Fanwood, N.J., 1968; trustee Summit Jaycee Found., 1970. Served to 1st lt. U.S. Army, 1963-65. Named One of Outstanding Young Man of Am. Jaycees, 1971. Mem. N.J. NG Assn., Summit Jaycees (Outstanding Dir. award 1970, Key Man award 1970), Soc. for Preservation Barbershop Quartet Singing in Am. (bd. dirs. Westfield 1972-74), Sigma Phi Epsilon. Republican. Presbyterian. Home: 125 Russell Rd Fanwood NJ 07023-1063 Office: Trina Inc 350 5th Ave Ste 1217 New York NY 10118-1284

BUTRY, PAUL JOHN, engineer; b. Niagara Falls, N.Y., Mar. 12, 1946; s. John Steven and Sophie (Zaczek) B.; m. Sharon Lee Wall, Oct. 14, 1968 (div. Nov. 1976); 1 child, Paul John II; m. Deborah Lynn D'Agostino, Aug. 16, 1980; children: Taylor Bethany, Piers Alexander. AS in Math. and Sci., Niagara Community Coll., 1981; BS in Indsl. Tech., Buffalo State U., 1988. Chem. technician SKW Alloys, Niagara Falls, 1968-84; chemist Bell Aerospace Textron, Wheatfield, N.Y., 1986-89; tech. svc. engr. Great Lake Carbon Corp., Niagara Falls, 1989—; cons., owner Butry Analytical Svcs., Niagara Falls, 1982—. Mem. Geraldine Mann Sch. Parents Edn. Group, 1991—, Cayuga Island Homeowners Assn., 1991—. With USN, 1966-67. Mem. Am. Soc. for Quality Control, Buffalo State Alumni Assn., Am. Running and Fitness Assn., Skip Barber Racing Assn. (racing cert. 1984), Pres. Coun. on Phys. Fitness (running award 1991). Home: 8630 Hennepin Ave Niagara Falls NY 14304-4430 Office: Gt Lakes Carbon 6200 Niagara Falls Blvd Niagara Falls NY 14304-1534

BUTSCHER, EDWARD JOHN, English educator; b. Flushing, N.Y., Sept. 30, 1945; s. Edward John and Lena (Cutillo) B.; m. Paula Trachtman, Apr. 10, 1976. BA, Queens Coll., 1968; MA, L.I. U., 1971; ABD, NYU, 1988. English tchr. John Bowne High Sch., Flushing, 1971—; mem. faculty New Sch. for Social Rsch., N.Y.C., 1978-80. Contbg. editor: Home Planet News, 1978-84, Poet Lore, 1982—; author: (biographies) Sylvia Plath, 1976, Conrad Aiken: Poet of White Horse Vale, 1988 (Poetry Soc. of America's Melville Kane award 1989), (book of poems) Amagansett Cycle, 1981, (novel) Faces on the Barroom Floor, 1984, (criticism) Peter Wild, 1992. Recipient Poetry award Acad. Am. Poets, C. W. Post Coll., 1971, NDEA study grant, Stony Brook Univ., 1970. Mem. Modern Lang. Assn., Poetry Soc. Am., Am. Pen Soc. Democrat. Home: 84-01 Main St Briarwood NY 11435

BUTTACI, SALVATORE MICHAEL, handwriting analyst; b. Corona, N.Y., June 12, 1941; s. Michael Salvatore and Josephine (Amico) B. BA, Seton Hall U., 1965; MBA, Rutgers U., 1981. Cert. tchr., N.J., psychology of handwriting, questioned document examiner. Tchr. St. Annes Sch., Fair Lawn, N.J., 1966-70, sch. prin., 1970-71; tchr. Saddle Brook (N.J.) Sch. System, 1972-80; list compiler Dependable Inc., N.Y.C., 1980-81; mktg. mgr. Hugo Dunhill Inc., N.Y.C., 1981-91; pres. AccuWrite Cons., Inc., Oakland, N.J., 1989—; pres. Am. Handwriting Analyst Found., Lodi, N.J., 1989-90; v.p. N.J. Poetry Soc., Inc., 1979-80. Editor: New Worlds Unlimited, 1974-88; contbr. numerous poems to pubs. Democrat. Roman Catholic. Office: AccuWrite Cons Inc PO Box 887 Rochelle Park NJ 07662-0887

BUTTERFIELD, CHARLES EDWARD, JR., educational consultant; b. Urbana, Ill., Mar. 31, 1928; s. Charles E. and Bessie J. (Winters) B.; BS, U. Ill., 1951, MS, 1953; postgrad. (NSF/AAAS fellow) Mich State U., 1959, 64-65, 72, Duke U., 1958, No. Ill. U., 1958-59, Knox Coll., 1962, Fla. State U., 1969, U. Colo., 1970; m. Gayle Coberley, Jan. 27, 1952; children: Jeffrey M., Carey J. Field exec. Nottawa Trails council Boy Scouts Am., Battle Creek, Mich., 1953-54; instr. sci. Gardner-South Wilmington Twp. High Sch., Gardner, Ill., 1954-59, Lake Park High Sch., Medinah, Ill., 1959-65; sr. sci. project editor Singer/Random House Pub. Co., 1965-68; sci. supr. Ramsey (N.J.) Public Schs., 1968-82; cons. Rand McNally Pubs., 1972-80; sci. edn. cons., 1981—; mem. sci. adv. bd. Raintree Pubs., Milw., 1981-86; assoc. Thomas A. Edison Found., 1981-88; condr. various workshops for sci. teaching, 1965-92. Pres., Bd. Edn., Gardner, Ill., 1956-57; pres. Foxwood Village FMO, 1988-90; co-project dir., fin. officer suprs. programs NSF/NSSA/PEEC, 1979-83. With USN, 1946-48. Recipient Allendale (N.J.) Community Lifesaving award, 1976; fellow 1st Southeastern NASA Aerospace Conf., 1961. Contbg. author: NSSA Sourcebook for Science Supervisors, 2nd edit., 1976, 3d edit., 1988. Fellow AAAS; mem. NEA, Nat. Sci. Suprs. Assn. (pres. 1977-78, mem. exec. com. 1974-80, mem. editorial adv. bd. 1986-91, sr. staff mem. various other confs.-U. Calif. 1979, U. Iowa 1979-80, Outstanding Svc. award 1990), Nat. Sci. Tchrs. Assn. (exec. bd. 1977-78, Disting. Svc. Sci. Edn. citation 1981), N.J. Sci. Tchrs. Assn., N.J. Sci. Suprs. Assn. (Disting. Svc. award 1982), Ramsey Suprs. Assn. (founding pres. 1980-81), Bergen County Sci. Suprs. Assn. (pres. 1971-73, Outstanding Svc. award 1974, 78), Sch. Sci. and Math. Assn., Am. Inst. Biol. Scis., Nat. Assn. Biol. Tchrs., Coun. Elem. Sci. Internat., Assn. Edn. Tchrs. Sci., N.J. Prins. and Suprs. Assn., Am. Assn. Notaries, Nat. Notary Assn., Mensa, Masons, DeMolay (chevalier), Order of Ea. Star, Psi Chi.

BUTTERFIELD, ELIZABETH STANFORD, stained glass artist and jewelry designer; b. Balt., Sept. 21, 1954. Owner, designer Elizabeth Butterfield Stained Glass, Westmoreland, N.H., 1979—; ptnr., designer Taika Jewelry (Thornfield Ltd.), Westmoreland, 1991—. Contbr. articles, rev. to profl. publs.; art commd. for Christa McAuliffe Planetarium, 1990. Bd. dirs. Vt./N.H. Belfast Kids, Brattleboro, Vt., 1986-91. Recipient Best of Show award Hollis Arts Soc., 1990. Mem. Brookfield Craft Ctr. Democrat. Home & Office: RR 1 Box 102 Westmoreland NH 03467-9709

BUTTERFIELD, STEPHEN ALAN, education educator; b. Middlebury, Vt., Sept. 10, 1948; s. Stewart Ellsworth and Mary Elizabeth (Coursey) B.; m. Jeanne Allison Zong, June 20, 1970; children: Sarah, Jason, Scott. BS, Springfield (Mass.) Coll., 1971; MEd, Keene State Coll., 1980; PhD, Ohio State U., 1984. Tchr. 4th grade Whitingham Sch., Jacksonville, Vt., 1971-72; prin., tchr. Halifax Sch., West Halifax, Vt., 1972-73; tchr. phys. edn. Austine Sch. for the Deaf, Brattleboro, Vt., 1973-81; assoc. prof. edn. and spl. edn., coord. health, phys. edn. and recreation programs U. Maine, Orono, 1984—. Editor Maine Jour. Health, Phys. Edn., Recreation and Dance, 1988—; contbr. articles to profl. jours. Bd. dirs. Bangor (Maine) YMCA, 1990—; mem. Gov.'s Coun. Phys. Fitness and Sports. Sgt. USAR, 1970-83. Mem. AAHPERD, Maine Assn. Health, Phys. Edn., Recreation and Dance (pres. 1986-87, Honor Award for Disting. Leadership 1989), Nat. Consortium Phys. Edn. Recreation for Handicapped. Home: 277 14th St Bangor ME 04401-4454 Office: U Maine College Ave Orono ME 04469-0001

BUTTERWORTH, KENNETH W., manufacturing company executive; b. Australia, 1925. Grad., Sydney Tech. Coll., 1955; A.M.P., Harvard Bus. Sch. Dir. sales The Timken Co., 1957-68; mng. dir. Bearings, Inc., 1968-76; corp. v.p. and pres. European region Loctite Corp., Newington, Conn., 1976-83, pres., chief operating officer, 1983-85, pres., chief exec. officer, from 1985, now chmn., chief exec. officer. Office: Loctite Corp 10 Columbus Blvd Hartford CT 06106-1976*

BUTTOLPH, DAVID DANIELS, banker; b. Mt. Kisco, N.Y., June 3, 1957. BA in Psychology, Boston U., 1979; MBA in Fin., Suffolk U., 1980. Loan officer Bank of Boston, 1981-86; v.p. Barclays Bank, N.Y.C., 1986-87; dist. mgr. Barclays, N.Y.C., 1987-91; v.p. Standard Chartered Bank Group, N.Y.C., 1991—; adj. lectr. grad. sch. bus. Fordham U., 1989—. Advisor SUNY, Albany, 1987—. Named Eagle Scout Boy Scouts Am., Westchester, N.Y., 1974. Mem. Assn. for Corp. Growth. Republican. Office: Stan Chart Bus Credit Inc 400 Madison Ave New York NY 10022

BUTTON, KENNETH RODMAN, international economist, consultant; b. Chgo., Nov. 17, 1946; s. Bland Ballard Jr. and Nancy (Nimmons) B.; m. Linda Kathryn Bartley, Dec. 21, 1948; children: Kathryn, Daniel. BA, Trinity Coll., 1968; MA, Tufts U., 1971, MA in Law and Diplomacy, 1974, PhD, 1981; MBA in Fin., George Washington U., 1987. Rsch. assoc. Haile Selassie I U., Addis Ababa, Ethiopia, 1973; rsch. fellow U. W.I., Port of Spain, Trinidad, 1974-75; internat. economist mid. east U.S. Dept. Commerce, Washington, 1976-78; internat. economist developing countries U.S. Dept. Treasury, Washington, 1978-79, mem. exec. secretariat, staff aide to sec., 1979-81; asst. to pres. Econ. Cons. Svcs. Inc., Washington, 1981-85, chief economist, 1985-88, v.p., 1988—. Contbr. articles on internat. trade to profl. jours. With M.I. Corps, U.S. Army, 1968-71. Shell Internat. Rsch. fellow, Tufts U., 1973. Mem. Am. Econs. Assn., Am. Fin. Assn., Assn. Bus. Economists, Beta Gamma Sigma. Home: 3700 Military Rd NW Washington DC 20015-1740 Office: Econ Cons Svcs Inc 1225 19th St NW Ste 210 Washington DC 20036-2419

BUTTON, RICHARD TOTTEN, television and stage producer, former figure skating champion; b. Englewood, N.J., July 18, 1929; s. George and Evelyn Bunn (Totten) B.; children: Edward Totten, Emily Rada. BA, Harvard U., 1952, LLB, 1956; LHD (hon.), Buena Vista Coll., 1988. Founder, pres. Candid Prodns., Inc., N.Y.C., 1959—; dir. Decorative Arts Trust, 1979-80; commentator ABC Sports; creator, owner The Superstars sports competitions, NBC, World Profl. Figure Skating Championships, NBC, World Challenge of Champions figure skating competitions, ABC; producer Broadway shows: Sweet Sue, 1987, Artist Descending a Staircase, 1989. Author: Dick Button on Skates, 1955, Instant Skating, 1964; contbr. articles to various mags. Pres. Richmondtown Restoration, Inc., 1968-77. U.S. figure skating champion, 1946-52; world figure skating champion, 1948-52; European figure skating champion, 1948; Olympic gold medalist, 1948, 52; recipient James E. Sullivan award, 1949, Emmy award for outstanding sports personality-analyst, 1980-81; named to U.S. Olympic Hall of Fame, U.S. Figure Skating Assn. Hall of Fame. Mem. Bar Assn. D.C., Skating Club N.Y., Skating Club Boston, Phila. Skating Club. Club: N.Y. Athletic. Office: 250 W 57th St Ste 1818 New York NY 10107-1818

BUTTON, ROBERT EASTON, communications executive; b. Englewood, N.J., July 25, 1915; s. John Conyers and Olive Lyle (Demarest) B.; m. Decima Knight, July 2, 1945; children: Phyllis Ann, Marilyn, Allyson. BA, Dartmouth Coll., 1936; LLB, Bklyn. Law Sch., 1939. Clk. Guaranty Trust Co., N.Y.C., 1936-39; program mgr. NBC, N.Y.C., 1939-41; col. U.S. Army, 1941-46; sales exec. NBC, N.Y.C., 1946-54; cons. Sec. Def., Washington, 1954-55; dir. Voice of Am., Washington, 1955-58; counselor of embassy U.S. Govt., Paris, 1958-64; exec. asst. to chmn. Comsat, Washington, 1964-73; dir. satellite ops. Teleprompter, N.Y.C., 1973-75; pres. Am. TransCom, Greenwich, Conn., 1975—; instr. in field. Contbr. articles to local publs. Mem. Res. Officers Assn., 1991—, Broadcast Pioneers, N.Y.C., 1991—; dir. Orch., Greenwich, N.Y., 1991—, Mens Chorus, 1991—. With U.S. Army, 1944-45. Recipient 2 Bronze Stars. Mem. Lions, Acacia Lodge F&AM, Univ. Club D.C., Capital Hill Club D.C., Ret. Men's Assn. Republican. Home: 7 Sylvan Ln Old Greenwich CT 06870-2318 Office: Am TransCom Inc 80 Field Point Rd Greenwich CT 06830-6416

BUTTRICK, HAROLD, architect; b. Bryn Mawr, Pa., Jan. 2, 1931; s. Charles Edgar and Constance (La Boiteaux) B.; m. Ann Octavia White, Sept. 3, 1955; children—John Ward, Jerome Chanler, Mary Constance, Sarah Elizabeth, Catherine. A.B., Harvard Coll. 1953, M.Arch., 1959. Registered architect, Calif., Conn., D.C., Ind., Md., Mass., N.J., N.Y., Vt., Va.; cert. Nat. Council Archtl. Registration Bds. Prin. Harold Buttrick & Assocs., N.Y.C., 1963-75; ptnr. Smotrich Platt & Buttrick, N.Y.C., 1975-76, Buttrick White & Burtis, N.Y.C., 1976—. Prin. archtl. works include: Corpus Christi Monastery, Nairobi, Kenya, 1967; Green Vale Sch., Iselin Ctr., Glen Head, N.Y., 1971; Trans World Airlines 747 Hangar, John F. Kennedy Airport, N.Y., 1971; Carter Giraffe House, Bronx Zoo, N.Y., 1978; St. Thomas Choir Sch., N.Y.C., 1987; Central Park, N.Y.C projects; Loeb Boathouse, 1986, Ballplayers Refreshment Stand, 1990; Restoration of the Pulitzer Fountain and Grand Army Pla., 1990, The Charles A. Dana Discovery Ctr. and Restaurant at Harlem Meer, 1992, North Meadow Ctr., 1992. Bd. dirs. N.Y. Soc. Libr. Recipient Preservation League of N.Y. State awards, 1991. Mem. AIA (Honor award 1972, Brick in Architecture award 1991), N.Y. State Assn. Architects (AIA award 1991). Clubs: Century Assn., Harvard (N.Y.C.). Office: Buttrick White & Burtis 475 10th Ave New York NY 10018-1120

BUTTS, BARBARA LORETTA, mathematics educator; b. Bronx, N.Y., Feb. 7, 1941; d. Lloyd Robert and Beryl Leotta (Roach) Rallos; m. Edward S. Butts Jr., May 16, 1964; 1 child, Jeffrey Steven. BS in Math. and Phys. Edn., Queens Coll., CUNY, 1963, MS in Edn. and Math., 1967. Cert. tchr. math., sch. adminstr. and supr., sch. dist. adminstr., N.Y. State. Coord. Queens Ednl. Guild, East Elmhurst, N.Y., 1963-65; math. instr. Oliver Weldell Holmes Jr. High Sch., Long Island City, N.Y., 1963-68, Summer YOuth ABC Program Corona, East Elmhurst, N.Y., 1966, DeWitt Clinton High Sch., Bronx, 1968-70, Our Lady of Victory Cath. Sch., Bronx, 1972-73; program coord. Office Human Resources Adminstrn., N.Y.C., 1973; math. instr. John F. Kennedy High Sch., Bronx, 1973—; asst. prof. Manhattan Coll., Bronx, 1989-91. Mem. Assn. Tchrs. Math. N.Y.C., Assn. Black Educators of N.Y. Home: 555 Kappock St Apt 25D Bronx NY 10463-6461

BUTTZ, CHARLES WILLIAM, outdoor advertising executive; b. Aberdeen, S.D., Aug. 8, 1932; s. Ward Leland and Mary Baker (Eddy) B.; m. Teresa Margarita Castro, July 28, 1956; children: Jean, Teresa, Charles, William, James. BCE, Rensselaer Polytech Inst., 1956; MBA, U. Conn., 1974. Registered profl. engr. N.Y., N.J. Chief engr. Kuala Lumpur (Malaysia) Transp. Study, 1963-64; project mgr. Tippetts Abbett McCarthy Stratton Engrs., N.Y.C., 1956-65; mgmt. cons. Booz, Allen and Hamilton, N.Y.C., 1965-67; dir. Knight, Gladieux and Smith Cons., N.Y.C., 1967-74; group mgr. Boeing Computer Svcs. Cons., N.Y.C., 1974-76; v.p. Middlesex Rsch. Ctr., Washington, 1976-77; pres. Eastern Shelter-All Inc., Mountainhome, Pa., 1977—, N.J. Shelter-All Inc., Columbia, N.J., 1980—, Regional Shelter-All Inc., Buck Hill Falls, Pa., 1985—; instr. mktg. U. Conn., Stamford, 1975-76. Pres. St. Paul's Housing Corp., Norwalk, Conn., 1974-77; com. mem. Alfred Dater Coun. Boy Scouts Am., Stamford, 1970-77; v.p., camp chmn. Darien (Conn.) United Way, 1974; v.p., sec. Darien Young Mens Christian Assn., 1974-77; dir. United Way Monroe County, Stroudsburg, Pa., 1984—. Maj. USAR, 1956-70. Recipient MBA Scholar award, Wall St. Jour., 1974. Mem. ASCE, Pa. Soc., Inst. Transp. Engrs., Am. Legion, Army and Navy Club, Buck Hill Golf Club. Episcopalian. Home: Cottage 266 Buck Hill Falls PA 18323 Office: Ea Shelter-All Inc PO Box 152 Mountainhome PA 18342

BUTZ, JEFFREY RALPH, mathematician, educator; b. Akron, Ohio, Aug. 27, 1947; s. Donald Ralph and Carol Arlene (Thompson) B. BA, Kenyon Coll., Gambier, Ohio, 1969; MA, Johns Hopkins U., Balt., 1973; PhD, Johns Hopkins U., 1975. Asst. prof. math. U. Okla., Norman, 1975-80, Fordham U., Bronx, 1980-85; prof. math. Bridgewater (Mass.) State Coll., 1985—. Reviewer Math. Revs., Ann Arbor, Mich., 1977—; contbr. articles to profl. jours. Woodrow Wilson fellow,. 1969. Mem. Am. Math. Soc., Math. Assn. Am., Pi Mu Epsilon. Republican. Episcopalian. Office: Bridgewater State Coll Dept Math Bridgewater MA 02325

BUXTON, DOUGLAS FRANCISCO, ophthalmologist; b. N.Y.C., Nov. 5, 1952; s. Jorge Norman and Amalia (Gonzalez) B.; m. Maria Del Pilar Uribe, Sept. 23, 1989. BA, Yale U., 1975; postgrad., Columbia U., 1977; MD, Cornell U., 1982. Diplomate Am. Bd. Med. Specialities, Am. Bd. Ophthalmology, Nat. Bd. Med. Examiners. Intern St. Vincent's Hosp. and Med. Ctr., N.Y.C., 1982-83; resident N.Y. Eye and Ear Infirmary, N.Y.C., 1983-86; fellowship Cornea and External Disease N.Y. Eye and Ear Infirmary, N.Y.C., 1986-88; assoc. attending staff N.Y. Eye and Ear Infirmary, 1986; clin. asst. dept. Ophthalmology Manhattan Eye, Ear and Throat Hosp., 1988; clin. asst. prof. ophthalmology N.Y. Med. Coll., 1991; med.

adv. bd. Eye-Bank for Sigt Restoration, Inc., 1990. Contbr. articles to profl. jours. Fellow Am. Acad. Ophthalmology; mem. AMA, Am. Coll. Eye Surgeons, Am. Soc. Cataract and Refractive Surgeons, Castroviejo Cornea Soc., Contact Lens Assn. of Opthalmologist-Internat. Soc. Refractive Keratoplasty, Eye Bank Assn. of Am., N.Y. County/State Med. Soc., N.Y. Intra-Ocular Lens Implant Soc., N.Y. State Ophthalmological Soc., Pan Am. Assn. of Ophthalmology, Sociedad Medica Hispano-Am. de Nueva York, Inc. Office: NY Eye and Ear Infirmary 310 E 14th St New York NY 10003-4200

BUXTON, ROBERT STEVENS, sales executive; b. Bklyn., Aug. 20, 1925; s. S. Stevens and Marie Louise (Jehle) B.; m. Dorothy Louise Miller, May 27, 1950; children: Virginia, Steven, Jeffrey, Blake. BSME, MIT, 1945; MS in Indsl. Engring., Lehigh U., Bethlehem, Pa., 1948. Indsl. engr. Armstrong Cork Co., Lancaster, Pa., 1948-49; sales engr. Alan A. Wood, Inc., Phila., 1949-58; dist. sales mgr. B-I-F Industries, Phila., 1958-61; mktg. mgr. B-I-F Industries, Providence, 1961-65; reg. sales mgr. Hays Corp., Michigan City, Ind., 1965-66; founder, pres., chmn. bd. Sys. Control Assocs., Media, Pa., 1966—. Chmn. Hays-Republic Rep. Council, Riveira Beach, Fla., 1986—; elder Presbyn. Ch. U.S.A., 1960—. Lt. (j.g.), USNR, 1943-46; PTO. Republican. Presbyterian. Home: 726 Pine Ridge Rd Media PA 19063-1720 Office: Systems Control Assocs 304 E Front St Media PA 19063-3583

BUYSKE, STEVEN GEORGE, mathematics educator; b. N.Y.C., July 19, 1961; s. Donald Albert and Jo (Kessel) B.; m. Ann Louise Jurecic, June 25, 1988. Student, Deep Springs Coll., 1978-80; BA, Haverford Coll., 1983; ScM, Brown U., 1986, PhD, 1988. Asst. prof. math. Lafayette Coll., Easton, Pa., 1988—. Contbr. articles to profl. jours. Recipient Clementine Cope fellowship, 1983. Mem. AAAS, Am. Math. Soc., Math. Assn. Am., Assn. Women in Math., Phi Beta Kappa, Sigma Xi. Office: Lafayette Coll Dept Math Easton PA 18042-1781

BUYUKATAMAN, KAYAALP, aircraft engine manufacturing company executive; b. Istanbul, Turkey, Apr. 11, 1941; came to U.S., 1968; s. Sedat and Muazzez (Savaskan) B.; m. Esin Gurocak, July 1, 1966; 1 child, Sedef M. MSME, Tech. U. Istanbul, 1964; MBA, U. Istanbul, 1965; MS in Marine Arch., Mil. Sch., Istanbul, 1966; MS in Indsl. Engring., Wayne State U., 1972. Vice mgr. indsl. planning Am. Standard Corp., Istanbul, 1967-68; project leader Ferro Mfg. Co., Detroit, 1968-72; rsch. engr. Chrysler Motor Co., Highland Park, Mich., 1972-78; project mgr. Ford Motor Co., LIvonia, Mich., 1978-80; mem. sr. staff Aircraft Engines div. GE, Boston and Cin., 1980-91; sr. staff exec. United Technologies Corp., East Hartford, Conn., 1991—; instr. night classes Istanbul Tech. Coll., 1968, Marmara Tech. U., Istanbul, 1967-68; vice chmn. Dept. Def. Instrumeted Factory, Chgo., 1990—. Contbr. 28 tech. papers to profl. jours.; patentee in field. Lt. Turkish Navy, 1965-67. Mem. ASME (chmn. Power Transmission and Wear 1990-91, chmn. Gear Dynamics 1991—), AIAA, Turkish Soc. Mech. Engrs., Am. Mgmt. Assn., Am. Soc. Indsl. Engrs., Auto. Engrs. Soc., Am. Gear Mfrs. Assn. (vice chmn. aerospace engring. com. 1989—, Excellent Tech. Achievement awards 1988, 89, 90), Assembly of Turkish Am. Assns. (v.p. 1988—), New Eng. Turkish Am. Assn. (bd. dirs. 1984-89), Mich. Turkish Am. Assn. (bd. dirs. 1974-80), Shriners, Masons (Master Chrysler Square Club 1976-78), Turkish Am. Friendship Assn. Ohio (founder, pres. 1989-90), Conn. Turkish Am. Friendship Assn. (pres. 1991—). Republican. Islam (Sunni-Hanefi). Home: 235 E River Dr Apt 606 East Hartford CT 06108-5019

BUZBY, GORDON P., surgeon, educator; b. Phila., June 25, 1948; s. Gordon and Margaret (McMichael) B.; m. Karen Buzby, Apr. 30, 1987; children: Sarah, Kathryn, Alexander. BS, U. Pa., 1970, MD, 1974. Assoc. prof. U. Pa., Phila., 1981—. Mem. Phi Beta Kappa, Alpha Omega Alpha. Office: Hosp of U Pa 3400 Spruce St Philadelphia PA 19104

BUZNEY, SHELDON MARC, retinal surgeon, researcher, ophthalmologist, educator; b. Cleve., Dec. 10, 1945; s. H.I. and D.P. Buzney. BA, Harvard U., 1968, MD, 1972. Diplomate Am. Bd. Ophthalmology, Am. Bd. Pediatrics. Intern, then resident Children's Hosp. Med. Ctr., Boston, 1972-74; resident in ophthalmology Mass. Eye and Ear Infirmary, Boston, 1976-79; rsch. assoc. NIH, Bethesda, Md., 1974-76; clin. asst. scientist Eye Rsch. Inst., Boston, 1976—; clin. instr. ophthalmology Harvard U., Boston, 1981—. Contbr. articles to profl. jours. Lt. comdr. USPHS, 1974-76. Recipient Honor award Am. Acad. Ophthalmology, 1989. Mem. Mass. Soc. Eye Physicians and Surgeons (pres. 1990-91), Mass. Med. Soc., New England Ophthal. Soc. (chmn. pub. health com. 1983—), Assn. Rsch. Vision and Ophthalmology, Retina Soc. Office: Retina Assocs 100 Charles River Plz Boston MA 02114

BY, ANDRE BERNARD, engineering executive, research scientist; b. Detroit, May 19, 1955; s. Bernard Joseph and Margaret (Voytish) B. BS in Aerospace Engring., U. Mich., 1977, BS in Mech. Engring., 1977; MS in Mech. Engring., MIT, 1979, postgrad., 1985. Mech./chem. engr. Motor Vehicle Emissions Lab. EPA, Ann Arbor, Mich., 1977; teaching asst., rsch. asst. MIT, Cambridge, 1977-79; engr., sr. engr., sr. project engr. Computer Aided Engring. Group, No. Rsch. and Engring. Corp., Woburn, Mass., 1979-84; mgr. automated sytems group No. Rsch. and Engring. Corp., Woburn, Mass., 1984-90; rsch. assoc., lectr. mech. engring. dept. Tufts U., Medford, Mass., 1990—; pres., tech. dir. Automation Engring. Inc., Wakefield, Mass., 1990—; seminar lectr., panel mem. Cell Contr. Seminar, Soc. Mfg. Engrs., Detroit, 1989. Contbr. articles to profl. jours. Mem. AIAA, ASME, Soc. Mfg. Engrs., Soc. Automotive Engrs. Office: Automation Engring Inc PO Box 350 Wakefield MA 01880-0950

BYALL, LYNNE ANN, marketing consultant; b. Lakewood, Ohio, Nov. 24, 1953; d. Robert Taylor and Mary-Elizabeth (Wolf) B.; m. Bruce Douglas Corey, Feb. 14, 1980 (div. 1985). BA in English, U. Ky., 1976. Mktg. support rep. IBM, Cleve. and Cin., 1977-78; mktg. rep. Xerox Corp., Cin., 1978-81; office cons. Loth Office Furniture, Cin., 1981-83; sales rep. Exec. Comm., Indpls., 1983-84; mktg. dir., cons. Architects Plus, Cin., 1986-87; mktg. dir. Kasler & Assocs., Cin., 1984-87; reginal bus. devel. mgr. Swanke Hayden Connell Architects, Washington, 1987-89; dir. mktg. Fox Seko Constrn., Vienna, Vt., 1989-90; mktg. dir. Ward-Hale Design Assocs., Washington, 1990-91; pvt. cons. Ithaca, N.Y., 1992—; exec. com. Comml. Real Estate Women, Inc., Washington, 1989-91. Mem. awards com. Nat. Assn. Indsl. and Office Parks Developers, No. Va. and Met. Washington, 1988-91; mem. mktg. com., mem. president's com. Greater Washington Bd. Trade, 1988-90; mem. steering com. Jubilee Support Found., Washington, 1988-91; vol. Ann. Fundraising Auction; mem. resource com. Planned Parenthood Tompkins County, N.Y.; project coordinator authors series Ken. Humanities Coun., 1986. 97. Mem. Soc. for Mktg. Profl. Svcs. (sec. 1988-89, v.p. 1989-90, pres. 1990-91), Women's Info. Network, U. Ky. Alumni Assn. (pres. Washington chpt. 1990), DAR. Democrat. Home and Office: 427 E Seneca St Ithaca NY 14850

BYAM, SEWARD GROVES, JR., financial executive; b. Bridgeport, Conn., Jan. 9, 1928; s. Seward Groves and Marjorie W. (Cotton) B.; student Princeton U., 1949, U. Del., 1951; m. Constance Patricia Randell, Feb. 28, 1981; children: Pamela E. Byam Tinsley, John T. Mktg. exec. duPont Co., 1951-67; bus. mgr. Dow Badische Co., 1967-76; mktg. dir. Borg Textile Corp., 1976-79; v.p. Tower Securities Inc., 1979-81; pres., prin. Seward, Groves, Richard & Wells, Inc., 1985—; pres. Randell-Byam Assocs., Inc., Rye, N.Y., 1987—; mng. dir. Fiduciary Counsel Inc., 1981—, Econ. Analysts, Inc., 1983—. Chmn. Williamsburg (Va.) Sch. Bd., 1973-76. With USMC, 1946-47, USMCR, 1947-51. Mem. SAR, Mensa, Union League, Princeton Club, Nassau Club, Apawamis Club. Episcopalian. Home: 40 Wall St Apt 47 New York NY 10005-2301 Office: Seward Groves Richard & Wells 40 Wall St New York NY 10005-1303

BYERLEY, CURT JOSEPH, printing company executive; b. Camden, N.J., Aug. 23, 1956; s. Edward Joseph and Joan Ann (Beach) B.; m. Joan Marie Pfeffer; children: Kathleen Meghan, Kristen Marie. BS, Villanova U., 1978. Sales rep. Wallace Computer Service, Phila., 1978-80; sr. sales rep. Fed. Bus. Products, N.Y.C., 1980-82; account exec. Courier Corp., Lowell, Mass., 1982-83; pres. Printing Mgmt. Systems, Collingswood, N.J., 1983—. Com. mem. Nat. Adoption Ctr., Phila., 1986—, Sports Outreach Svc., Bala Cynwyd, 1986—; bd. dirs. Pro Athlete's Against Drunk Driving; advisor Autisum Found., 1989. Mem. Printing Brokerage Assn., Phila. Direct Mktg. Assn., Nat. Assn. Printers and Lithographers. Republican. Roman Catholic. Clubs: Variety (advisor 1987—), The Down Town (Phila.) (gov. 1986—), Merchantville Country, Haddon Heights Tennis, Haddon Glen Swim. Office: Printing Mgmt Systems 604 Bettlewood Ave Collingswood NJ 08108-3045

BYERS, ROBERT ALLAN, entomologist; b. Latrobe, Pa., Dec. 6, 1936; s. Charles Victor and Elsie Ruth (Stewart) B.; m. Patricia Lee Andrews, Sept. 3, 1960; children: Lisa Joanne, Robert Allan Jr. Student, St. Vincent Coll., 1955-56; BS, Pa. State U., 1960; MS, Ohio State U., 1961; PhD, Purdue U., 1971. Entomologist USDA Agrl. Rsch. Svc., Tifton, Ga., 1961-66, West Lafayette, Ind., 1966-70, University Park, Pa., 1970—. Contbr. numerous articles to sci. jours. Mem. Entomol. Soc. Am., Entomol. Soc. Pa. (sec. 1980—). Lutheran. Office: Regional Pasture Rsch Lab Curtin Rd State College PA 16802

BYLEWSKI, ANTHONY WALTER, state agency administrator; b. Buffalo, N.Y., July 5, 1948; s. Walter B. and Lucy Helen (Pawarski) B.; m. Patricia Ann Zdrojewski, Sept. 12, 1970; children: Scott Anthony, Candace Lynn. BS in Mgmt., Canisius Coll., 1970. Right of way agt. N.Y. State Dept. Transp., Buffalo, 1970-75; asst. assessor Town of Cheektowaga, N.Y., 1976-77; sr. pers. administr. Buffalo (N.Y.) Psychiat. Ctr., 1977-80; adminstrv. officer N.Y. State Office Mental Health, Buffalo, 1980—; human resource, fin. con. State Psychiat. Ctrs., Buffalo, 1987—. Photographer one man show photo exhbn. WNED-TV, 1980. Regional disaster preparedness coord. N.Y. State, Western and Finger Lakes Areas, 1990-92. With U.S. Army, 1970-71. Named Outstanding Vietnam Era Veteran, U.S. Pres. and Mayor of Buffalo, 1980. Mem. Polish Union Am. (v.p. 1980-91), Trasit-Woodridge Assn. (bd. dirs. 1990-92). Democrat. Roman Catholic. Home: 6086 Wellesley Common East Amherst NY 14051 Office: Western Regional Office 570 Forest Ave Buffalo NY 14222

BYNOE, PHILIP EARL, musician, educator; b. Stoneham, Mass., Aug. 13, 1961; s. Dillon Smith and Gloria Helen (Alleyne) B. Student, Longie Sch., 1969-70, Berklee Coll., 1980-81. Bassist Sound Investment, East Lyme, Conn., 1978-80; bassist, vocalist Flash/Fast Forward/ABC, Medford, Mass., 1980-87, Rick Berlin, Boston, 1987-90, World Premiere, Boston, 1991—; freelance musician Hustle for your Dreams, Malden, Mass., 1985—; music tchr. Future Shaping Through Music, Everett, Mass., 1987—; bassist Steve Perry, Stoughton, Mass., 1991; TV appearance Bayside Jenny Show, Osaki, Japan, 1991. Musician with numerous ensembles; musician (stage prodns.) South Pacific, Wizard of Oz, Jesus Christ Superstar; composer (score) Incorruptible/Fearless; actor appearing in Spenser for Hire, Freddie G's Promo Video, Roxbury Outreach Shakespeare Experience, Above the Law. Named Boston's Best Rythym Section Bassist, Boston Area Live Entertainment, 1989, Best Unsigne Bassist, Bass Player mag., 1990. Home: 83 Lyme St Malden MA 02148-5817

BYRD, MARK ALAN, institutional researcher, educator; b. Little Rock, Dec. 3, 1957; s. Isaac Durham Jr. and Joellen Rae (Horne) B.; m. Martha Lee, July 1, 1978; children: Jonathan, Andrew. BA, Ouachita Bapt. U., Arkadelphia, Ark., 1982; postgrad., Henderson State U., Arkadelphia, 1982; MA, U. Ark., 1984. Grad. asst. U. Ark., Fayetteville, 1982-84; rsch. analyst Ark. Dept. Higher Edn., Little Rock, 1984-86; rsch. assoc., computer system adminstr. U. Ark. Cen. Adminstrn., Little Rock, 1986-87; dir. institutional rsch. U. Scranton, Pa., 1987—, adj. faculty, 1989—; telecommunication cons. U. Ark. Cen. Adminstrn., 1987; cons. Greater Scranton C. of C. Mem. Assns. for Institutional Rsch., Higher Edn. Data Sharing Consortium (institutional rep.), Am. Assn. for Higher Edn., Am. Amateur Racquetball Assn., Exec. INfo. Systems Spl. Interest Group, Alpha Kappa Delta. Republican. Home: 204 Layton Rd Clarks Summit PA 18411-9032 Office: U Scranton 800 Linden St Scranton PA 18510-2429

BYRD, WILLIAM THOMAS, JR., interior designer, educator; b. Lancaster, Pa., Feb. 14, 1942; s. William Thomas and Mary Catherine (Parker) B. BArch, Cath. U. Am., 1965, MFA, 1968. Sole proprietor Bill Byrd Jr., N.Y.C., 1970-78; assoc., project dir. Interspace Inc., Washington, 1978-82; sr. project mgr. Swanke Hayden Connell Architects, N.Y.C., 1982-87; sr. constrn. project mgr. Irving Trust Co., N.Y.C., 1987-89; sr. project mgr. PHH Environments, N.Y.C., 1989-90; sole propr. Bill Byrd Jr., N.Y.C., 1989—; asst. prof. Kean Coll. of N.J., Union, 1990—; instr. U. Notre Dame, Ind., 1968-70; asst. prof. Stockton State Coll., Pomona, N.J., 1972-74; trainer The Hannah Harrison Sch., Washington, 1980-81; guest lectr. Monmouth Coll., West Long Branch, N.J., Bklyn. Coll., Marymount Manhattan Coll., N.Y.C., Marymount Coll., Tarrytown, N.Y., Edward S. Gordon Co. Real Estate, N.Y.C. Mem. AIA (assoc.), Interior Design Educators Coun. Home: 145 W 71st St Apt 6B New York NY 10023-3820 Office: Kean Coll of NJ Morris Ave Union NJ 07083

BYRNE, DANIEL WILLIAM, computer specialist, medical researcher, educator; b. Bklyn., Jan. 21, 1958; s. Thomas Edward and L.M. (Collins) B.; m. Loretta Marie May, June 22, 1985; children: Michael, Virginia. BA in Biology, SUNY, Albany, 1983; MS in Biostatistics, N.Y. Med. Coll., 1991. Programmer, critical care software Dept. Surgery N.Y. Med. Coll., Valhalla, 1983-84; computer/data analyst N.Y. Med. Coll., Westchester County Med. Ctr. and affiliate hosps, 1984-87; rsch. asst. prof. Dept. Surgery N.Y. Med. Coll., Valhalla, 1988—; founder, rsch. cons. Byrne Research, Ridgefield, Conn., 1989—. Author: (tng. manual) Guidelines for Analyzing Clinical Research on a Microcomputer, 1986; author/programmer various software including Trauma Management System, 1990, Occupational Stress Database, 1990, Nuclear Disaster Evacuation Plan Database, 1990; contbr. numerous articles to med. jours. Grantee Centers Disease Control 1987-90, 89-92. Mem. Am. Statis. Assn., Inst. Math. Stats., Biometric Soc. Roman Catholic. Home and Office: 19 Rustic Dr Ridgefield CT 06877-2211

BYRNE, GEORGE DENNIS, mathematician; b. Earlham, Iowa, June 15, 1933; s. Alphonsus Dennis and Mary Maurine (Bricker) B.; m. Laura Joan Brindle, May 30, 1960; children: Elizabeth Byrne Hensley, Margaret Byrne Mixon, Stephen, Dennis (dec.), Michael, Karen, David, Mark. BS in Math., Creighton U., 1955; MS in Math., Iowa State U., 1961, PhD in Applied Math., 1963. Mathematician White Sands (N.Mex.) Proving Ground, 1955-56; staff mem. Sandia Corp., Albuquerque, 1956-58; grad. asst. dept. math. Iowa State U., Ames, 1958-59, 62-63; programmer-analyst Cyclone Computer Lab./Iowa State U., Ames, 1959-62; numerical analyst Collins Radio Co., Cedar Rapids, Iowa, 1962; asst. prof. dept. math. U. Pitts., 1963-67, assoc. prof. math., adj. assoc. prof. dept. chem. and petroleum engring., 1967-80; sr. staff mathematician Exxon Rsch. and Engring. Co., Annandale, N.J., 1980-82, rsch. assoc., 1982—; numerical analyst Lawrence Livermore (Calif.) Lab., 1973, cons., 1973-80; vis. scientist Argonne (Ill.) Nat. Lab., 1974-75, cons., 1975-80; co-developer software packages for solving differential equations. Contbr. to tech. publs. 2d lt. U.S. Army, 1956. Fellow Inst. Math. and its Applications; mem. IEEE (sr.), mem. Am. Math. Soc., Internat. Assn. Math. and Computers in Simulation, Am. Inst. Chem. Engrs. (Computing Practice award Computing and Systems Tech. div. 1990), Assn. Computing Machinery, Soc. Indsl. and Applied Math., Toastmasters Internat., Sigma Xi. Roman Catholic. Office: Exxon Rsch and Engring Co Rte 22 E Annandale NJ 08801

BYRNE, JAMES CURRAN, podiatrist; b. Pitts., June 17, 1947; s. John Joseph and Lorraine Helen (Curran) B.; m. Valerie Monica D'Agostini, Sept. 5, 1970; children: Erin, James, Colin, Ryan. Student, Duquesne U., 1965-67; MS, Pitts. Inst. Mortuary Sci., 1968; postgrad., Duquesne U., 1968-69; DPM, Ohio Coll. Podiatric Medicine, 1974. Diplomate Nat. Bd. Podiatric Examiners, Am. Bd. Podiatric Surgery, Internat. Coll. Podiatric Laser Surgery. Intern St. Michael's Med. Ctr., Newark, 1974-75, chief resident, 1975-76, surg. staff, 1976—; surg. staff Union Hosp., Union, N.J., 1977—, Roseland (N.J.) Surg. Ctr., 1983—, Surgicare Surg. Ctr., Watchung, N.J., 1985—; pvt. practice Union; dir. podiatry Dayton Community Health Ctr., Newark, 1977-86; guest lectr. CO2 Laser Course, Roseland, N.J., 1987. Contbg. author: Laser Surgery of the Foot, 1989; patentee in field. Parent vol. Boy Scouts Am., Maplewood, N.J., 1989-91; vol. Sr. Citizen Health Fair, Union Hosp., 1989. With USAR, 1971-76. Fellow Am. Coll. Foot Surgeons, Internat. Soc. of Podiatric Laser Surgeons; mem. Am. Podiatric Med. Assn., N.J. Podiatric Med. Soc. (Disting. Svc. award 1975). Roman Catholic. Office: 934 Stuyvesant Ave Union NJ 07083-6935

BYRNE, JAMIE MARIA, educator; b. Belleville, Ill., July 31, 1961; d. Charles Henry III and Betty Jean (Stokes) Doerge ; m. Charles Alan Byrne, Oct. 10, 1987. BS in English and Journalism, Murray (Ky.) State U., 1983, MS in Communications, 1985; postgrad., Pa. State U. Systems mgr. Murray State News, 1983-84; asst. prof. U. Wis., Platteville, 1984-88, Elizabethtown Coll., 1988-91, Millersville U. of Pa., 1991—; adj. prof. Millersville U. Pa., 1989-91. Big Sister Grant County (Wis.) Dept. Family Svcs., 1985-88; dir. Platteville Community Players, 1986; pub. rels. specialist Theatre of the Seventh Sister, Lancaster, Pa., 1990-91; publicity com. mem. Jamison Mus. Assn., Platteville, 1987-88. Journalism educator grant Gannett Found., 1990; grantee U. Wis., 1986-87; Jesse Stuart fellowship Murray State U., 1983. Mem. NAFE, Pub. Rels. Soc. Am. (sec. cen. Pa. chpt., 1990-91, bd. dirs. 1990-91, pres.-elect 1991-92), Nat. Broadcasting Soc. (nat. v.p. for regional devel. 1986-92, U. Wis. Platteville chpt., Outstanding Profl. mem. 1987), Coll. Media Advisors, Am. Culture Assn. Roman Catholic.

BYRNE, JEFFREY EDWARD, pharmacology researcher; b. Mpls., July 15, 1939; s. Maurice Charles and Edna F. (Kinney) B.; m. Janice Grove, Feb. 1, 1960 (dec. Apr. 1976); children: Christopher, Maura; m. Margaret Ann Kaiser, June 17, 1978; 1 child, Jason. BA, U. N.D., 1962; MA, U. S.D., 1964, PhD, 1966. Sr. rsch. assoc. Bristol-Myers Co., Evansville, Ind., 1969-81, prin. rsch. scientist, 1981-87; sr. rsch. scientist II Bristol-Myers Squibb Co., Wallingford, Conn., 1987—, Princeton, N.J., 1991—; adj. faculty Ind. U. Sch. Medicine, Evansville, 1972-81, Evansville U. Sch. Nursing, 1972-81. Contbr. articles to profl. jours.; author (with others) books. Mem. Am. Soc. for Pharmacology and Exptl. Therapeutics, Am. Heart Assn., Internat. Soc. for Heart Rsch., AAAS. Republican. Lutheran. Home: 590 Atkinson Ln Langhorne PA 19047-1462 Office: Bristol Myers Squibb Co PO Box 4000 Princeton NJ 08543-4000

BYRNE, KEVIN FRANCIS, insurance consultant; b. N.Y.C., Oct. 28, 1952; s. Frank C. and Vera (Ward) B.; m. Irene M. Pieretti, Jan. 18, 1986; 1 stepchild, Deborah Cicchino. B in Bus. Scis., Adelphi U., 1975. Asst. div. mgr. The Equitable Life Assurance Soc., Melville, N.Y., 1979-82; div. mgr. The Equitable Life Assurance Soc., Melville, 1982-83; regional ops. support mgr. The Equitable Life Assurance Soc., Garden City, N.Y., 1983-84; br. mgr. GAB Bus. Svcs., Inc., Parsippany, N.J., 1984-87, asst. v.p., 1988-89, pres. employee benefit svcs. div., 1989-91; pvt. practice cons. Landing, N.J., 1992—; chmn. dental rels. com. Health Ins. Assn. Am., Balt., 1978-79. With USCGR, 1972-78. Home and Office: 118 Orben Dr Landing NJ 07850

BYRNE, OLIVIA SHERRILL, lawyer; b. Trenton, N.J., Aug. 14, 1957; d. Stewart and Elizabeth (Sherrill) B. Student, Vanderbilt U., 1975-76; BA, Bowdoin Coll., 1979; JD, U. Toledo, 1982; LLM in Taxation, Georgetown U., 1987. Bar: Tex. 1982, Ohio 1984, Md. 1985. Assoc. Whiteford, Taylor & Preston, Balt., 1984-87, Linowes & Blocher, Silver Spring, Md., 1987-90, Weinberg & Jacobs, Balt., 1990—. Author: The At-Risk Rules Under the Tax Reform Act of 1986, The Door Closes on Tax Motivated Investments. Mem. adv. com. on planned giving Am. Heart Assn., v.p. Rockville (md.) Young Rep. Club, 1989-90. Mem. ABA (taxation sect., exempt orgn. com. 1991—), Balt. City Bar Assn. (chairperson speakers bur. young lawyers sect.), Comml. Real Estate Women, Lawyers for the Arts Washington, D.C. Bowdoin Coll. Alumni Assn. (pres. 1992—), Howard County C. of C. (legis. com. 1989). Home: 5919 Barbados Pl # 201 Rockville MD 20852-5479 Office: Weinberg & Jacobs One Central Plz 11300 Rockville Pike Rockville MD 20852

BYRNE, PATRICK MICHAEL, philosopher, educator, entrepreneur, farm worker; b. Ft. Wayne, Ind., Nov. 29, 1962; s. John Joseph and Dorothy (Cain) B. Cert., Beijing Normal U., 1984; BA in Chinese and Philosophy, Dartmouth Coll., 1985; MA, Cambridge (Eng.) U., 1989; postgrad., Stanford U., 1989—. Teaching fellow Stanford (Calif.) U., 1989—; operating mgr. Blackhawk Investment Co., 1992—. Author: Lao-ze's Dao De Jing. Mem. Dem. Chmn.'s Circle, 1990. Marshall Assn. scholar, Eng., 1988-90. Mem. ACLU, U.S. Chess Fedn., World Tae Kwon Do Fedn. (black-belt instr.). Home: 35 Ropeferry Rd Hanover NH 03755-1404

BYRNE, THOMAS RAY, international financial and emerging markets consultant; b. Westfield, N.J., Oct. 31, 1958; s. Robert L. and Maryanna (Ray) B. BA in U.S. History, Polit. Sci., Lynchburg Coll., 1981. Internat. banking specialist Irving Trust Bank, N.Y.C., 1981-82, precious metals trader, 1982-84; regional mgr. Fundamental Brokers Inc., N.Y.C., 1984-87; dir. internat. bus. devel. Euro Brokers Inc., N.Y.C., 1987-89; mgr. fgn. bonds Security Pacific Nat. Trust Co., N.Y.C., 1990-91; pres. Hanover Sq. Internat., Inc., N.Y.C., 1990—; v.p., treas. Hanover Sq. Assn., N.Y.C., 1987—; ptnr. joint ventures Os Tres Magos Ltd., Rio de Janeiro, 1989—, Braco Rio Ltd., Rio de Janeiro, 1991—; mng. dir. HanoverFirst Ltd., Cayman Islands, 1990—. Assoc. bd. dirs. Riverside Symphony, N.Y.C., 1990; asst. track coach The Collegiate Sch., N.Y.C., 1992. Republican. Roman Catholic. Home: 517 E 81st St New York NY 10028

BYRNES, KERRY JOSEPH, agricultural sociologist, consultant; b. Dayton, Ohio, Sept. 11, 1945; s. Francis C. and Ethel B. (Overholt) B.; m. Sonia Gomez, Aug. 30, 1969; 1 child, Shannon Alexander. BA, Mich. State U., 1967, MA, 1968; PhD, Iowa State U., 1975. Rsch. aide Mich. State U., Cali, Colombia, 1968-69; rsch. asst. dept. sociology and anthropology Iowa State U., Ames, 1969-70, rsch. assoc., 1972-75; vol. VISTA, Miami, Fla., 1970-72; sociologist Internat. Fertilizer Devel. ctr., Muscle Shoals, Ala., 1975-84; agrl. instns. analyst AID/S&T/RD, Washington, 1984-85; sr. social sci. analyst AID Ctr. for Devel. Info. and Evaluation, 1987-89; agrl. rsch. extension, and edn. advisor AID, Washington, 1989—; cons. to various orgns. including World Bank, 1987, Mgmt. Tng. and Devel. Inst., Washington, 1985—, Winrock Internat. Inst. for Agrl. Devel., Washington, 1987, Acad. for Edn. Devel., Washington, 1985-86. Author: Review of A.I.D. Experience with Farming Systems Research and Extension, 1990, A Cross-Cutting Analysis of Agricultural Research, Extension, and Education in AID-Assisted LAC Countries, 1992; contbr. articles to profl. jours. Mem. Rural Sociol. Soc., Internat. Rural Sociol. Assn., Assn. for Farming Systems Rsch.-Extension, Nat. Eagle Scout Assn., Soc. for Preservation of Film Music, Phi Kappa Phi, Gamma Sigma Delta, Alpha Kappa Delta. Democrat. Roman Catholic. Home: 2161 Greenskeepers Ct Reston VA 22091-3843 Office: Chemonics Internat/LAC TECH 2000 M St NW Ste 200 Washington DC 20036-3383

BYRNES, ROBERT CHARLES, JR., state legislative staff director; b. Rochester, N.Y., Dec. 8, 1958; s. Robert Charles Byrnes and Barbara Anne (Fisher) Nixon. BA, Union Coll., 1981. Legis. assoc. N.Y. State Assembly Commerce Com., Albany, 1982-88; chief of staff N.Y. State Assenbly dep. majority leader, Albany, 1988-91, N.Y. State Assemblyman Joseph E. Robach, 1991—. Mem. exec. com. Monroe County Conservative Party, Rochester, 1981—, vice chmn., 1984-89, 1991—; com. mem. N.Y. State Conservative Party, Rochester, 1984-88; mem. Monroe County Sales Tax Adjustment Act Commn., Rochester, 1986-87; bd. dirs. Northwest Hearing and Speech Ctr., Rochester, 1991—. Episcopalian. Office: 2300 Ridge Rd W Rochester NY 14626-2801

BYRON, BEVERLY BUTCHER, congresswoman; b. Balt., July 27, 1932; d. Harry C. and Ruth Butcher; m. Goodloe E. Byron, 1952 (dec.); children: Goodloe E. Jr., Barton Kimball, Mary McComas; m. B. Kirk Walsh, 1986. Student, Hood Coll., 1962-64. Mem. 96th-102nd Congresses from 6th Md. dist., 1979—; mem. armed services com., chmn. subcom. on military personnel and compensation. State treas. Md. Young Dems., 1962, 65; bd. assocs. Hood Coll.; bd. visitors U.S. Air Force Acad., 1980-87; trustee Mt. St. Mary's Coll.; bd. dirs. Frederick County chpt. ARC; sec. Grederick Heart Assn., 1974-79; mem. Frederick Phys. Fitness Commn.; chmn. Md. Phys. Fitness Commn., 1979-89; mem. Frederick County Landmarks Found.; bd. dirs. Am. Hiking Soc. Episcopalian. Home: 306 Grove Blvd Frederick MD 21701-4813 Office: 2430 Rayburn House Office Bldg Washington DC 20515

BYRON, JAMES STEPHEN, human resources professional; b. Northampton, Mass., May 15, 1957; s. John Stephen and Barbara Gertrude (Forbes) B.; m. Mary Wanda Horton, June 20, 1981; children: James, Keely, Katherine. BS, Springfield Coll., 1980, MEd, 1983. Tng. coord. W. W. Johnson Life Ctr., Springfield, Mass., 1980-83; instrnl. tech. Human Tech., Inc., McLean, Va., 1983-85; mgmt. devel. specialist Citibank, Sioux Falls,

S.D., 1985-87; tng. mgr. Citicorp, St. Louis, 1987-88; sr. orgn. devel. cons. Air Products and Chems., Inc., Allentown, Pa., 1988—. Democrat. Roman Catholic. Home: 918 N Richmond St Fleetwood PA 19522-1905 Office: Air Products & Chems Inc 7201 Hamilton Blvd Allentown PA 18195-9642

BYRON, WILLIAM JAMES, university president; b. Pitts., May 25, 1927; s. Harold J. and Mary I. (Langton) B. A.B. in Philosophy, St. Louis U., 1955, Ph.L., 1956, M.A. in Econs, 1959; S.T.B., Woodstock Coll., 1960, S.T.L., 1962; Ph.D. in Econs, U. Md., 1969; cert., Harvard U. Inst. Ednl. Mgmt., 1974. Joined S.J., 1950, ordained priest Roman Cath. Ch., 1961. Tchr. math. Scranton (Pa.) Prep. Sch., 1956-58; manpower rsch. fellow Dept. Labor, 1965-66; asst. prof. econs. Loyola Coll., Balt., 1967-69; assoc. prof. social ethics, rector Woodstock Coll., Woodstock Jesuit Community, 1967-73; dean Coll. Arts and Scis. Loyola U., New Orleans, 1973-75; pres. U. Scranton, 1975-82, Cath. U. Am., 1982—. Author: Toward Stewardship: An Interim Ethic of Poverty, Pollution and Power, 1975, Quadrangle Considerations, 1989; editor: Causes of World Hunger, 1982; contbr. numerous articles to profl. jours. Bd. dirs. Fed. City Coun., Joint Commn. on the Accreditation Healthcare Orgns., Medlantic Healthcare Group, Commn. on Nat. and Community Svc. With U.S. Army, 1945-56. Mem. Am. Econs. Assn., Am. Soc. Christian Ethics, Assn. Cath. Colls. and Univs., Phi Beta Kappa, Alpha Sigma Nu. Home: 3901 Harewood Rd NE Washington DC 20017-1596 Office: Cath U Am Office of Pres 620 Michigan Ave NE Washington DC 20064-0001

BYUN, HANG S., neurosurgeon, educator; b. Pyungyang, Korea, Nov. 14, 1940; came to U.S., 1965; s. Kisup and Bonghyuk B. MD, Korea U. Med. Sch., Seoul, 1965. Rotating internship Mt. Sinai Svcs. City Hosp. Ctr., Elmhurst, N.Y., 1965-66, attending neurosurgeon, 1985—; resident in general surgery Mt. Sinai Hosp., N.Y.C., 1966-69, resident in neurosurgery, 1969-73; asst. prof. neurosurgery Mt. Sinai Sch. Medicine, N.Y.C., 1986—. Mem. Am. Congress of Neurol. Surgeons, Am. Assn. Neurol. Surgeons. Office: Elmhurst Hosp Ctr 79-91 Broadway Elmhurst NY 11373

BYWATER, WILLIAM GLEN, JR., philosophy educator; b. Detroit, Feb. 15, 1940; s. William Glen and Elma Florence (Miller) B.; m. Ann Marie Philbin, June 12, 1966 (div. May 1979); children: Patrick, Duncan; m. Ruth J. Vander Veen, Aug. 13, 1983. BA, Lehigh U., 1962; PhD, U. Mich., 1969; MA, Edinboro U., 1982. From instr. to prof. philosophy Allegheny Coll., Meadville, Pa., 1967—; cons. Crawford County Mental Health/Mental Retardation Program, Meadville, 1987—. Author: Clive Bell's Eye, 1975; contbr. articles to profl. jours. Recipient Teaching Excellence award Sears-Roebuck Found., 1990. Mem. Am. Philos. Assn., Am. Soc. for Aesthetics, Am. Assn. on Mental Retardation, Am. Psychol. Assn. Home: 630 N Main St Meadville PA 16335-1951 Office: Allegheny Coll N Main St Meadville PA 16335-1111

CABALLERO, CARLO, music historian; b. Westwood, Calif., Jan. 15, 1964; s. Oscar Ezequiel and Rosalie (Bastone) C. BA, Pomona Coll., 1985; postgrad., U. Pa., 1986—. Libr. tech. asst. Occidental Coll., L.A., 1985-86; univ. fellow U. Pa., Phila., 1986-87, dean's fellow, 1987-88, teaching fellow, 1988-89, Finkelstein fellow, 1989-90, Fontaine fellow, 1989-90, Mellon Fellow, 1991-92; Booth-Ferris fellow, 1992-93. Recipient Blanchard prize Pomona Coll., Claremont, Calif., 1985, McCord prize, 1984, Pomona Coll. Scholar, 1981-85. Mem. MLA, Am. Musicology Soc., Am. Soc. Aesthetics, Internat. Machaut Soc., Phi Beta Kappa. Home: 23 Hutchinson St Cambridge MA 02138-1339 Office: U Pa Music Dept 201 S 34th St Philadelphia PA 19104-6313

CABLE, MABEL ELIZABETH, urban planner, artist; b. Sewickley, Pa., May 23, 1935; d. Andrew Lee and Josephine (James) Yeck; m. Charles Allen Cable, Dec. 19, 1955; children: Christopher A., Carolyn E. BS, Edinboro U., 1958; M in Urban-Rural Planning, U. Pitts., 1982. Tchr. Mount Union (Pa.) Jr.-Sr. High Sch., 1964-69; graphics illustrator Crawford County Planning Commn., Meadville, Pa., 1974-79, planner, 1979-86; asst. dir. planning Crawford County Planning Commn., Meadville, 1987—. Exhibitor Foothills Art Gallery, Golden, Colo., 1986-87, Pastimes Gallery, Meadville, Pa., 1987—. Bd. dirs. Penn Lakes coun. Girl Scouts U.S.A., Meadville, 1974-79; pres. John Brown Heritage Assn., Meadville, 1985-88; mem. adv. coun. Pa. Community Devel. Block Grant Com., Harrisburg, 1987—, chmn., 1990—. Mem. Am. Inst. of Cert. Planners, Am. Planning Assn., Pa. Planning Assn. Home: 199 Jefferson St Meadville PA 16335-1108 Office: Crawford County Planning Commn Courthouse Meadville PA 16335

CABOT, JOHN G. L., chemical manufacturing company executive; b. Rio de Janeiro, Aug. 8, 1934; (parents Am. citizens); s. John Moors and Elizabeth (Lewis) C.; m. Carroll Lloyd Trimble, July 9, 1960; children: John Ridgeway, Andrew Lowell. AB, Harvard U., 1956, MBA, 1960. Various positions Cabot Corp., Boston, 1960-72, v.p., 1972-77, sr. v.p., 1977-85; exec. v.p. Cabot Corp., Boston and Waltham, Mass., 1985-88, vice chmn., 1988—, also bd. dirs.; bd. dirs. Am. Oil and Gas Corp., Houston, Cabot Oil and Gas Corp., Houston, Hollingsworth & Vose Co., East Walpole, Mass., Eaton Vance Corp., Boston. Trustee Tufts U., Medford, Mass., 1983—, New Eng. Hist. Geneal. Soc., 1990—; coun. mem. Mass. Hist. Soc., 1990—; overseer, gov. New Eng. Med. Ctr., Boston, 1981—; mem. corp. Mass. Gen. Hosp., Boston, 1982—; bd. dirs. New Eng. Legal Found., Boston, 1977—, chmn., 1989—; mem. bd. overseers WGBH Ednl. Found., Boston, 1988—. Office: Cabot Corp 75 State St Boston MA 02109-1806

CABOT, LEWIS PICKERING, manufacturing company executive, art consultant; b. Hague, Netherlands, Sept. 6, 1937; s. John Moors and Elizabeth (Lewis) C.; m. Judith Ogden, July 1, 1960 (div. 1974); children: Elizabeth Lewis, Edward Ogden, Timothy Pickering; m. Susan Knight, July 15, 1978; children: James Eliot, Alexander Lee. AB, Harvard U., 1961, MBA, 1964. Trainee F.S. Moseley & Co., Boston, 1961-62; analyst John P. Chase, Inc., Boston, 1964-68; prin. Gardner & Preston Moss, Boston, 1968-73; chmn., pres. Artcounsel, Inc., Portland, Maine, 1973—; chmn., pres. ZY-AX Corp. (name formerly Southworth Corp.), Portland, 1977—, Shellback Corp., Portland, 1984—; bd. dirs. Hov-air Internat., Ltd., Newbury, Eng.; pres., dir. Maine Art Leasing Corp., 1988—; dir. Material Handling Edn. Found. Inc., 1989—; leader Material Handling Inst. Roundtable, 1991; trustee NE Pooled Common Fund, Princeton, N.J., 1972—. Trustee Mus. Fine Arts, Boston, 1966-90; mem. MIT Arts Council, Cambridge, 1969-86; trustee Portland Sch. Art, 1982-91; vis. com. Harvard U. Art Mus., Cambridge, 1982-88. Mem. Met. Club (Washington), Somerset Club (Boston), Manchester Yacht Club (Mass.), N.Y. Yacht Club (N.Y.C.). Office: ZY-AX Corp PO Box 1980 Portland ME 04104

CABOT, LOUIS WELLINGTON, chemical manufacturing company executive; b. Boston, Aug. 3, 1921; s. Thomas Dudley and Virginia (Wellington) C.; m. Mary Ellen Flynn de Pena Vera, Oct. 19, 1974; children by previous marriage: James Bass, Anne Cabot Alletzhauser, Godfrey Lowell, Amanda Cabot Kjellerup, Helen Reuter. AB, Harvard U., 1943, MBA, 1948; LLD (hon.), Norwich U., 1961. With Cabot Corp., 1948—, pres., 1960-69, chmn. bd., 1969-86, also bd. dir. emeritus; chmn. Brookings Instn., Washington, 1986-92, trustee, 1992—; bd. dirs. Kendall Sq. Rsch., Owens-Corning Fiberglas Corp., 1961-91, Wang Labs Inc., 1982-91, New Eng. Tel. & Tel., 1965-82, R.R. Donnelley & Sons Co., 1965-91, Fed. Res. Bank Boston, 1970-78, chmn., 1975-78; U.S. rep. 15th Plenary Session UN Econ. Commn. for Europe, 1960; mem. bus. ethics adv. coun. Dept. Commerce, 1961-63; dir., New Eng. chmn. Nat. Alliance Businessmen, 1970-72, Boston chmn., 1968-69; chmn. Sloan Commn. on Govt. and Higher Edn., 1977-80; mem. Pres.'s Blue Ribbon Commn. on Def. Mgmt., 1985-86; mem. Def. Sec.'s Commn. on Base Realignment and Closure, 1988. Overseer Harvard U., 1970-76; chmn. Harvard Coll. Fund Council, 1963-65; pres. Beverly (Mass.) Hosp., 1958-61; chmn. Com. Corp. Support Pvt. Univs., 1977-83; trustee Norwich U., 1952-77, Mus. of Sci., Boston; corp. mem. MIT; trustee Northeastern U.; co-chmn. pres.'s cir. NAS. Fellow Am. Acad. Arts and Scis.; mem. C. of C. of U.S. (dir., exec. com. 1978-83), Nat. Coun. for U.S.-China Trade (dir. 1978-82), Bus. Coun., Conf. Bd., Coun. Fgn. Rels., Phi Beta Kappa, Sigma Xi. Clubs: Somerset (Boston), Commercial (Boston) (pres. 1970-72), Harvard (Boston); Metropolitan (Washington); Wianno (Osterville, Mass.); N.Y. Yacht, River. Office: 75 State St Boston MA 02109-1807 also: Brookings Instn 1775 Massachusetts Ave NW Washington DC 20036

CABRANES, JOSÉ ALBERTO, federal judge; b. Mayaguez, P.R., Dec. 22, 1940; s. Manuel and Carmen (Lópe z) C.; m. Kate Stith, Sept. 15, 1984; children: Alexander Richard Stith, Benjamin José; children from previous marriage: Jennifer Ann, Amy Alexandra. AB, Columbia U., 1961; JD, Yale U., 1965; MLitt in Internat. Law, Cambridge (Eng.) U., 1967; LLD (hon.), Colgate U., 1988, Trinity Coll., Hartford, Conn., 1990; LHD (hon.), U. New Haven, 1990. Bar: N.Y. 1968, D.C. 1975, Conn. Fed. 1976. Assoc. Casey, Lane & Mittendorf, N.Y.C., 1967-71; assoc. prof. law sch. Rutgers U., Newark, 1971-73; spl. counsel to gov. P.R., head Office Commonwealth P.R., Washington, 1973-75; gen. counsel Yale U., New Haven, 1975-79; judge U.S. Dist. Ct. Conn., New Haven, 1979—; mem. Pres.'s Commn. Mental Health, 1977-78; founding mem. P.R. Legal Def. and Edn. Fund, 1972, chmn. bd. dirs., 1977-80; counsel Internat. League for Human Rights, 1971-77, v.p., 1977-80; cons. to sec. Dept. State, 1978; mem. U.S. del. Conf. Security and Cooperation in Europe, Belgrade, 1977-78; appointed by Chief Justice, Fed. Cts. Study Com., 1988-90. Author: Citizenship and the American Empire, 1979; also articles on law and internat. affairs. Trustee Yale U., 1987—, Am. Mus. Natural History, N.Y.C., 1991—, Yale-New Haven Hosp., 1978-80, 84-87, Colgate U., 1981-90, 20th Century Fund, 1983—, Fed. Jud. Ctr., 1986-90; bd. dirs. Aspira of N.Y., 1970-74, chmn., 1971-73; mem. Coun. on Fgn. Rels. Recipient Life Achievement award Nat. P.R. Coalition, 1987, John Jay award Columbia Coll., 1991, Life Achievement award Student div. Nat. Hispanic Bar Assn., 1991; Kellett Rsch. fellow Columbia Coll., 1965-67. Fellow Am. Bar Found.; mem. ABA, Conn. Bar Assn., Assn. of Bar of City of N.Y., Am. Law Inst. Roman Catholic. Office: US Dist Ct 141 Church St New Haven CT 06510-2030

CABRINETY, PATRICIA BUTLER, software company executive; b. Earlville, N.Y., Sept. 4, 1932; d. Eugene Thomas and Helen Sylvester (Fulmer) Butler; m. Lawrence Paul Cabrinety, Aug. 20, 1955; children: Linda Anne, Margaret Marie, Stephen Michael. BS in Elem. Edn. and Music, SUNY, Potsdam, 1954. Cert. tchr. N.Y., Pa., Minn., Mass. Asst. tchr. music Hamilton (N.Y.) Cen. Sch., 1948-50; tchr. Cherry Lane Sch., Suffern, N.Y., 1954-56; instr. music Towanda, Pa., 1960-63, Sayre, Pa., 1963-79; pres. Superior Software Inc., Mpls., 1981—, MIZEN Products, Inc., Mass., 1988—; poet and illustrator, Edina, Minn., 1981—; cons. in field. Composer, artist numerous compositions; inventor: Musical for Computer, 1981; author monthly column on Boy Scouts, 1975-78, also 154 pub. poems and 56 pub. illustrations; author: CHARIS series; composer of "Paulette Fry" and "Mi Cazone"; creator of The Professional Writers' MAIL-IT Kit and Name in Notes, Picture Poetry Series. Recipient Golden Poet award World of Poetry, 1985-91, Poet of Month award All Season's Poetry, 1986, Vantage Press Invitational award, 1985-90, Poet of Month award Editor's Desk, 1986, Internat. Poet award, 1986, Confederation of Chivalry degree DCMSS, MCC Australia. Mem. NAFE, AAUW, DAR, Am. Soc. Profl. and Exec. Women, Nat. Assn. Bus. and Profl. Women, Nat. Writers Assn., Am. Mgmt. Assn., internat Soc. Poets, Internat. Platform Assn., Pioneers, Computer History Inst. for the Preservation of Software (bd. dirs.), Legion of Mary, Third Order Carmelite, Mpls. Music Tchrs. Forum, Edina C. of C., Worcester County Music Assn., Worcester County Poetry Assn. Home: 925 Pearl Hill Rd Fitchburg MA 01420-1622

CADDELL, FOSTER, artist; b. Pawtucket, R.I., Aug. 2, 1921; s. Foster and Clara (Bamford) C.; student R.I. Sch. Design, 1940-43; pvt. study with Peter Helck, Robert Brackman, Guy Wiggins; m. June A. Kaufmann, Apr. 10, 1943 (dec. Feb. 1989). Artist, Providence Lithograph Co. (R.I.), 1939-52; free-lance illustrator, 1951-65; owner, instr. Foster Caddell's Art Sch., Voluntown, Conn., 1958—; one-man shows Providence Art Club, 1948, 63, South County (R.I.) Art Assn., 1967, Slater Mus., Norwich Acad., 1976, Heritage Plantations of Sandwich, 1985; group shows include Springfield Mus. Fine Arts, 1962-77, Am. Watercolor Soc., 1973, NAD, 1973, Am. Artists Profl. League (awards 1953, 71, 72, 89, 90, 91), Acad. Artists Am. (awards 1968, 73, 75), Slater Mus., Norwich Acad., 1975-80, Providence Art Club (award 1978, 79, 92), Nat. Arts Club, 1978, Internat. Soc. Artists (award 1978), Societe Des Pastellists De France, 1987, others; specialist in portraiture, 1965—. Served as artist USAAC, World War II. Recipient awards Norwich Acad., 1947, Ogunquit Art Center, 1949, Conservative Painters R.I., 1962, Salmagundi Club, 1973, 80. Mem. Providence Art Club, Am. Artists Profl. League, Acad. Artists Am., Am. Portrait Soc., Salmagundi Club, Pastel Soc. Am. (award 1990, 91, 92), Conn. Pastel Soc. (award 1990, 91), Internat. Soc. Artists. Author: Keys to Successful Landscape Painting, 1976; Keys to Successful Color, 1979; Keys to Painting Better Portraits, 1982, Oil Painting Techniques, 1983, Landscape Painting Techniques, 1984, The New American Impressionism, 1992. Address: Northlight RFD 1 Rt 49 Voluntown CT 06384

CADE, FRANCES RENEE, computer science educator; b. New Martinsville, W.Va., Sept. 15, 1946; d. Kenneth Odell and Frances M. (Tustin) Kirkland; m. Eugene Lawrence Cade, Nov. 29, 1969; 1 child, Anna Catherine. BS, W.Va. Wesleyan Coll., 1968; postgrad., Xavier U., 1969-70, Loyola U., Balt., 1984-85; MS, Johns Hopkins U., 1989. Tchr. Anne Arundel Schs., Annapolis, Md., 1968-70, tutor, 1971-86; tchr. Mount de Sales Acad., Balt., 1985-86; tchr. Severn Prep. Sch., Severna Park, Md., 1987—, computer coord., instr. computer sci., 1987—. Mem. Assn. Independent Md. Schs. Computer Group, Delta Psi Kappa. Republican. Methodist. Home: 779 Tobbin Ct Severn MD 21144-2202 Office: Severn Prep Sch Water St Severna Park MD 21146-4599

CADE, JOHN A., state senator; b. Charleston, S.C., July 2, 1929. BS, Xavier U., 1953; MBA, Northwestern U., 1954; postgrad., U. Md., 1959-60. Mem. charter bd. County of Anne Arundel, Md., 1962-63, mem. county council, 1965-70; mem. Md. State Senate, 1975—, minority leader, 1983—; profl. bus. mgr. Republican. Office: Md Senate Office Bldg Rm 407 Annapolis MD 21401

CADIEUX, PIERRE H., Canadian government official; b. Hudson, Que., Can., Apr. 6, 1948. Min. of labour Can., 1986-89, min. of Indian affairs and no. devel., 1989-90; solicitor gen. of Can., 1990-91; min. of state for youth, fitness and amateur sport House of Commons, Ottawa, Ont., 1991—, dep. leader, 1991—. Office: House of Commons, Parliament Bldg, Ottawa, ON Canada K1A 0A6

CADIGAN, RICHARD FOSTER, lawyer; b. Balt., May 9, 1930; s. Timothy Joseph and Edna (Foster) C.; m. Anne M. Smith, Sept. 5, 1953; children: Anne Cecelia, Richard Foster, Charles Smith, Timothy Joseph, John Arthur. J.D., U. Md., 1957. Bar: Md. 1957. Assoc. Cable & McDaniel, Balt., 1957-59, ptnr., 1959-67; ptnr. Richard F. Cadigan, Towson, Md., 1967-77; sr. ptnr. Beach, Cadigan & Martin, Towson, 1977—; dir. Valley Supply & Equipment Funkstown, Md., 1981—. Bd. rev. Atty. Grievance Commn., Annapolis, 1976-79, Jud. Nominating Commn., Commn. of Md., 1981—, chmn., 1989—; treas. Com. to Elect Sitting Judges, Baltimore County, Md., 1976, 82. Co-author: Creditor's Rights in Maryland, 1961. Counselor St. Andrew Soc., Balt., 1975—; bd. advisors Villa Julie Coll., Stevenson, Md., 1979—; chmn. Ladies and Gentlemen Jud. Bar Libr. Found., 1990—. Served with USAF, 1951-53. Mem. AMA, Baltimore County Bar Assn. (chmn. 1978-80, chmn. constn. and by-laws com. 1989—), Md. Bar Assn., St. George's Soc., St. Andrew's Soc., Hibernian Soc., St. Thomas More Soc. Democrat. Roman Catholic. Club: Engineering. Office: Beach Cadigan & Martin 22 W Pennsylvania Ave Baltimore MD 21204-5017

CADMAN, THEODORE WESLEY, chemical engineering educator; b. Osceola Mills, Pa., Feb. 28, 1940; s. Frank B. and Marjorie (Lutz) C.; m. Mary Lou Richardson, June 24, 1961; children—Suzanne, David Scott. B.S. in Chem. Engring., Carnegie-Mellon U., 1962, M.S., 1964, Ph.D., 1966. Instr. Carnegie-Mellon U., Pitts., 1963-65; asst. prof. U. Md., College Park, 1965-68, assoc. prof., 1968-73, prof., 1973-78, prof., chmn. dept. chem. and nuclear engring., 1978-85; prof. engring. U. Md. Baltimore County, Catonsville, 1985—; cons. State of Md. Air Quality, 1970-74, Icarus, 1970-78, SAI, 1980-82; v.p. ENSCI Inc., College Park, 1973—; cons. Univ. Research Found., 1983-86. Contbr. articles to profl. jours. NSF grantee, 1968-70; Water Resources Ctr. grantee, 1971-73; State of Md. grantee, 1976-77; NSF grantee, 1976-85. Mem. Am. Inst. Chem. Engring., Am. Chem. Soc., Am. Soc. Engring. Edn. Republican. Methodist. Home: 9110 St Andrews Pl College Park MD 20740-4026 Office: U Md Baltimore County Catonsville MD 21228

CADOW, WILLIAM SCHUYLER, JR., aerospace company executive; b. Iowa City, Nov. 17, 1936; s. William Schuyler and Mary Elizabeth (Aust) C.; m. Alice Freeze, July 10, 1964 (div. Sept. 1986); children: William S. III, Lani C. BBA, U. Miss., 1959; MSA, George Washington U., 1980. Registered profl. engr. Commd. ensign USN, 1959, advanced through grades to capt.; comdg. officer EOD Tech. Ctr. USN, Indian Head, Md., 1976-79; comdr. explosive ordnance disposal group USN, Ewa Beach, Hawaii, 1980-83; dir. ammo systems Naval Sea Systems Command USN, Washington, 1983-86, ret., 1986; program mgr. Hercules Aerospace Co., Washington, 1986—. Decorated Legion of Merit. Mem. Inst. Indsl. Engrs., Internat. Assn. Bomb Tech. and Investigators, Navy League of the U.S. Presbyterian. Home: 600 Water St SW Washington DC 20024-2471 Office: Hercules Aerospace Co 1800 K St NW Ste 710 Washington DC 20006-2202

CAESAR, PATRICIA LOUISE, management consultant; b. N.Y.C., July 1, 1946; d. Harry Edward and Sally Ann (Firetag) Cohen; m. Philip D. Caesar, June 9, 1968 (div. 1971); m. Arnold J. Schaab, Mar. 7, 1981; children: Emily Diana, Genevieve Elizabeth. MEd, Columbia U., N.Y.C., 1972; BA, Brandeis U., Waltham, Mass., 1967. Cert. Fund Raising Exec. Rsch. assoc. Columbia U., N.Y.C., 1971-73; exec. dir. Girls Club N.Y., N.Y.C., 1975-80; cons. Govt. Non Profit Orgns., N.Y.C., 1970-80; pres. Caesar Assocs., N.Y.C., 1980-88; chmn. Caesar & Washburn, Inc., N.Y.C., 1988—; mem., bd. dirs., Nat. Soc. Fund Raising Exec. Found., Washington, 1985-87. Contbr. articles to profl. jours. Chmn., bd. dirs. Gods Love We Deliver, N.Y.C., 1988—. Fellowship Ford Found., N.Y.C., 1969-72. Mem. Nat. Soc. Fund Raising Execs., Coun. Advancement and Support of Edn., Nat. Assn. Hosp. Devel., Old Chatham Hunt Club, Doubles, Columbia Country Club. Office: Caesar & Washburn Inc 1841 Broadway New York NY 10023-7603

CAFFIN, LOUISE ANNE, library media educator; b. N.Y.C., Feb. 15, 1943; d. Milton D. and Tinette C. Caffin. BS, NYU, 1964; MLS, L.I. U., 1965. Tchr. N.Y.C. Bd. Edn., 1966—. Author: (manuscripts) Outward Bound, 1984-85, California Vs. Caryl Chessman, 1948-60 and Beyond, The Untrammelled Road He Chose: William O. Douglas, 1984-85, Invictus, 1985-86, Automobiles, Alcohol Abuse and Traffic Safety Curriculum, 1986, Tribute to Anne Frank, 1986-87. Member B'nai B'rith. Mem. Schoolmen and Schoolwomen's Lodge. Office: Frank D Whalen Jr High Sch 135 2441 Wallace Ave Bronx NY 10467-9215

CAFFREY, ANDREW AUGUSTINE, federal judge; b. Lawrence, Mass., Oct. 2, 1920; s. Augustine J. and Monica A. (Regan) C.; m. Evelyn F. White, June 26, 1946; children: Augustine J., Andrew A., James E., Mary L., Francis J., Joseph H. AB cum laude, Holy Cross Coll., 1941; LLB cum laude, Boston Coll., 1948; LLM, Harvard U., 1948. Bar: Mass. 1948, U.S. Supreme Ct. 1958. Assoc. prof. law Boston Coll. Law Sch., 1948-55; asst. U.S. atty., chief civil div. Dist. Mass., 1955-59, 1st asst. U.S. atty., 1959-60, U.S. dist. judge, 1960—, chief judge, 1972-86, sr. ct. judge, 1986—; Mem. Jud. Panel on Multidist. Litigation, 1975-90, chmn., 1980-90. Served with AUS, World War II, ETO. Named Alumnus of Yr. Boston Coll. Law Sch., 1986. Mem. ABA, Jud. Conf. U.S. (exec. com. 1973-79), Fed. Bar Assn., Mass. Bar Assn., Boston Bar assn., Am. Law Inst., Harvard Law Sch. Assn. Mass., Order of Coif (hon.), Alpha Sigma Nu, Delta Epsilon Sigma. Clubs: Merrimack Valley, Holy Cross Alumni (past pres., dir.). Office: US Dist Ct John W McCormack PO & Courthouse Rm 1629 Boston MA 02109

CAFIERO, ALBERT F., retired engineer; b. Bklyn., Jan. 16, 1922; s. Claudio Cesaro and Luisa Maria Cafiero; m. Renata deGara, Aug. 20, 1961; 1 child, Peter. BS in Indsl. Engring., NYU, 1965. Master control engr. Office of War Info.-Voice of Am., N.Y.C., 1943-51; TV broadcast engr. CBS-TV, N.Y.C., 1951-68; mgr. systems and procedure ABC, N.Y.C., 1968-86; retired, 1986. Author: The Approaching Transportation Crisis; contbr. articles to N.Y. Times, Bergen Record. Chmn. Transit Com., Bergen County, N.J., 1981—, mem. Transp. Coordinating Com., 1986-90; mem. steering com. Com. on Alternate Transp. Solutions, N.J., 1990—. Mem. N.Y. Acad. Scis. (life), Toastmasters (v.p. 1981-82). Roman Catholic. Home: 27 W Clinton Ave Apt 1P Tenafly NJ 07670-2077

CAGNEY, WILLIAM ROBERT, psychologist; b. Pitts., Oct. 7, 1937; s. Edward Patrick and Pearl Barbara (Sebastian) C.; m. Vivian Antoinette Tartaglia, June 26, 1965; children: Lori Anne, Julie Alissa, Melissa Beth. BS, Duquesne U., 1960, MA, 1965, PhD, 1968. Lic. psychologist, Pa.; cert. Nat. Register Health Svcs. Providers in Psychology. Psychology intern, staff psychologist Dixmont State Hosp., Glenfield, Pa., 1962-68; staff psychologist South Hills Child Guidance Ctr., Pitts., 1968-69; asst. dir., psychol. svcs. Woodville State Hosp., Carnegie, Pa., 1968-70; chief psychologist Counseling Ctr. of South Hills, Pitts., 1970-72; clin. dir. Chartiers MH/MR Ctr., Bridgeville, Pa., 1972-79; pvt. practice Pitts., 1971—; cons. Outreach South, Mt. Lebanon, Pa., 1976—, South Hills Interfaith Ministries, Bethel Park, Pa., 1969—, Crisis Addiction Recovery Edn., Inc., Washington, Pa., 1984-88, YMCA South Hills, Pitts., 1977-78; field supr. psychology dept. U. Pitts., 1970-73, W.Va. U., Morgantown, 1973-78; resident psychologist Sta. KDKA-TV Pitts. Today, 1977-78; presenter seminars and workshops to profl. and community groups, 1972—. Cons. Twp. Upper St. Clair Adminstrn., Police, Schs., Family Resource Program, Upper St. Clair, Pa., 1986-89. Fellow Pa. Psychol. Assn.; mem. APA, Greater Pitts. Psychol. Assn. Office: 1725 Washington Rd Ste 509 Pittsburgh PA 15241-1207

CAHN, EDWARD N., federal judge; b. Allentown, Pa., June 29, 1933; s. Norman A. and Miriam H. C.; m. Alice W.; Dec. 7, 1963; children: Melissa, Jessica. B.A. magna cum laude, Lehigh U., 1955; LL.B., Yale U., 1958. Atty. Cahn & Roberts, 1971-75; judge U.S. Dist. Ct. (ea. dist.) Pa., 1974—. Office: US Dist Ct Old Lehigh County Courthouse 501 E Hamilton St Allentown PA 18101-1501*

CAHN, GLENN EVAN, psychologist; b. Washington, Jan. 10, 1953; s. Julius Norman and Ann (Foote) C.; m. Emily Zofnass, Sept. 2, 1990. BA, Washington U., St. Louis, 1975; MA, Calif. Sch. Profl. Psychology, San Diego, 1978, PhD, 1980. Psychologist The Arbour, Boston, 1980-82, Stoughton Counseling Ctr., Mass., 1982, Mass. Rehab., Boston, 1982—, Fuller Meml. Hosp., S. Attleboro, Mass., 1985-90, Hurst Assocs., Boston, 1990—; pvt. practice psychology Sharon, Mass., 1988—. Contbr. articles to profl. jours. Mem. Am. Psychol. Assn., Mass. Psychol. Assn., Internat. Neuropsychol. Soc., Nat. Acad. Neuropsychology, Omicron Delta Kappa. Home: 373 Massapoag Ave Sharon MA 02067-2716

CAHN, STANLEY ERIC OLLENDORFF, stock exchange executive, financial planner; b. N.Y.C., May 15, 1939; s. Erich and Anny (Ollendorff) C.; m. Stefanie Sandra Dosik, Jan. 4, 1964; children: Melissa, Ethan Howard. BS, NYU, 1962. Sr. editor UPITN Corp., Washington, 1967-73; so. regional dir. B'nai B'rith Found., 1973-77; Washington rep. Zionist Orgn. Am., 1977-79; v.p. Legg Mason Wood Walker, Inc., Washington, 1979—; instr. Okla. Ctr. for Continuing Edn., Norman, 1973-75, Nat. Inst. Fin., Newark, 1985. Bd. dirs., mem. exec. com. and fin. mgmt. con. Am. Lung Assn. No. Va. Mem. Internat. Computer Users Fellowship (chmn.), Internat. Assn. Fin. Planning, Nat. Fin. Planners, Army and Nacy Club, Springfield Golf Club (Va., membership chmn. 1987), Rotary (chmn. world fellowship activities com. dist. 7610, fellowship exch.). Jewish. Home: 7012 Hundsford Ln Springfield VA 22153-1260 Office: Legg Mason Wood Walker Inc 1747 Pennsylvania Ave NW Washington DC 20006-4604

CAHNERS, DAWN, financial analyst; b. N.Y.C., July 21, 1962; d. Ronald and Evelyn (Locke) Branson; m. John Joseph Cahners, Apr. 16, 1989; 1 child, Samuel Joseph. BS in Behavioral Scis., NYU, 1984; MBA in Fin., U. Mich., 1988. Sales clk. electronics dept. Sears, Roebuck & Co., N.Y.C., 1982-84; sales clk. Computerland, N.Y.C., 1984-86; cons. computer labs. U. Mich., Ann Arbor, 1986-88; summer intern strategic info. svcs. Dept. of the Navy, Washington, 1987; fin. analyst Werik Informational Computer Svcs., Syracuse, N.Y., 1988—; cons. Hewlett-Packard, N.Y.C., 1988—; Larson Comm., Niagara Falls, N.Y., 1989-91. Author: Man and Computers: An Unholy Alliance?, 1990, co-editor New York City Bytes, 1991—; contbg. editor (fan club mag.) Where's Elvis?. Vol. Syracuse Pub. Libr., 1988—, Goldstein Meml. Hosp., Syracuse, 1988-89; group leader Epiphany Youth Ctr., Syracuse, 1989-91. Named one of Outstanding Young N.Y. Women, 1990. Mem. NOW, ICCE, Am. Assn. Computer Profls., Internat. Computer

Soc., N.Am. Computer Network. Democrat. Presbyterian. Office: Werik Towers Ste 1 915 Boulevard E Syracuse NY 13210-1033

CAHOON, HERBERT THOMAS FULLER, former curator; b. West Chatham, Mass., Dec. 29, 1918; s. George Clark and Emma Regina (Jones) C. AB, Harvard U., 1940; SBLS, Columbia U., 1943. Asst. Harvard Coll. Libr., Cambridge, Mass., 1937-41; asst. rare books N.Y. Pub. Libr., N.Y.C., 1941-54; curator autograph manuscripts Pierpont Morgan Libr., N.Y.C., 1954-89. Author: (poetry book) Thanatopsis, 1949, The Overbrook Press Bibliography, 1963; co-author: A Bibliography of James Joyce, 1953. Hon. fellow Pierpont Morgan Libr., N.Y.C., 1989. Mem. Century Assn. N.Y., Grolier Club N.Y., Caxton Club Chgo. Office: Pierpont Morgan Libr 29 E 36th St New York NY 10016-3490

CAHOON, RICHARD STUART, biotechnology research and development executive; b. Salt Lake City, Apr. 28, 1954; s. Reynolds Fehring and Margaret (Mothersill) C.; m. J'Nelle Hathaway, June 28, 1980; children: Lauren E., Lindsey M. BA, U. Utah, 1976, BS cum laude, 1977; MS, Mont. State U., 1983. R&D tech. Pax Co. (Cenex), Salt Lake City, 1974-78; rsch. tech. II Biology dept. U. Utah, Salt Lake City, 1978-80; rsch. specialist U.S. Geol. Survey, Salt Lake City, 1980-81; rsch. assoc. Inst. for Bioprocess Analysis Mont. State U., Bozeman, 1981-83; pres. Assoc. Biotechs., Inc., Salt Lake City, 1983-85; sales/process engr. Monroe Food Process Machinery, Inc., Salt Lake City, 1985-87; dir. bus. devel. CCE, Inc., Bozeman, 1987-88; tech. transfer dir. The R&D Inst., Bozeman, 1989—; program devel. Inst. for Bioprocess Analysis, 1988—; new projects cons. Utah State Dept. Agr., Salt Lake City, 1986-87; asst. dir. tech. mktg. Cornell U., 1990; assoc. dir. indsl. rels. Nat. Engring. Rsch. Ctr. Mont. State U., 1989-90. Author (strategic plan) Tech./Transfer Devel., 1989, IPA , 1989; patentee in field. Vol. tchr. Montessori Sch., Bozeman, 1988—, Granite Sch. Dist., Salt Lake City, 1980-81; vol. therapist Children's Ctr. United Way, Salt Lake City, 1978-80; coord. Neighborhood Tree Planning Porject, Salt Lake City, 1978-81. Rsch. Commendation award U.S. Geol Survey, Salt Lake City, 1981; Rsch. fellow Chevron, Inc., Bozeman, 1981-83, Rsch. Creativity grantee, Mont. State U., Bozeman, 1982. Mem. Pi Kappa Alpha. Office: 20 Thornwood Dr # 105 Ithaca NY 14850-1265

CAICEDO, JUANA ESTHER, bank executive; b. Portoviejo, Ecuador, July 25, 1949; came to U.S., 1982; d. Miguel Felipe Caicedo Lamar and Orfa Cedeno. B in Econs., Catholic U., Guayaquil, Ecuador, 1974. Acctg. trainee Delloitte Haskins & Sells, N.Y.C., 1975-76; asst. mgr., sr. account officer Bank of Am., Guayaquil, 1976-80; gen. mgr. Asesores Financieros subs. Greyhound Leasing & Fin. Corp., Guayaquil, 1980-82; minister, counselor comml. affairs Ecuadorean Govt. Trade Office, N.Y.C., 1982-88; v.p., mgr. Cen. Bank of Ecuador, N.Y.C., 1986-88; v.p. Mfrs. Hanover World Trade Corp., N.Y.C., 1989—; mem. adv. bd. Cath. U. Sch. Econs., Guayaquil, 1971-74, instr. sources fin., 1979-80, instr. credit analysis Banking Sch., 1980-81. treas. Fundacion Para Pacientes Quemados, Guayaquil, 1979-82. Mem. Econs. Assn., Ecuadorean-Am. Assn. N.Y. (dir. 1984-88, v.p. 1988—), Pan Am. Soc. N.Y. (dir. 1985-88). Roman Catholic. Club: Guayaquil Tennis. Office: Mfrs Hanover World Trade Corp 8th Fl 270 Park Ave New York NY 10017-2014

CAIN, B(URTON) EDWARD, chemistry educator; b. Batavia, N.Y., Sept. 11, 1942; s. Burton Leo and Bettie S. (Williams) C. BA, SUNY, Binghamton, 1964; PhD, Syracuse U., 1971. Biochemist Onondaga County (N.Y.) Pub. Health Labs., Syracuse, N.Y., 1971-72; chemist O'Brien & Gere Cons. Engrs., Inc., Syracuse, N.Y., 1972-74; asst. prof. chemistry Nat. Tech. Inst. Deaf, Rochester (N.Y.) Inst. Tech., N.Y., 1974-80, assoc. prof. dept. chemistry, 1980-84, prof., 1984—; asst. dept. head Nat. Tech. Inst. Deaf, Rochester, N.Y., 1988—; reader Advanced Placement chemistry exams. Ednl. Testing Svc., June 1987, 88, 89, 90, 91, 92. Author: The Basics of Technical Communicating, 1988; contbr. articles to profl. jours. Reviewer grant proposals coll. sci. instrument program NSF, 1987, instrumentation and lab. improvement program NSF, 1992. Recipient Eisenhart Outstanding Tchr. award, 1980. Mem. Am. Chem. Soc., AAAS, AAUP, Nat. Sci. Tchrs. Assn., Nat. Assn. Deaf, Conf. Am. Instrs. for Deaf, Registry of Interpreters for Deaf, Sigma Xi, Phi Lambda Upsilon, Gamma Epsilon Tau (Tchr. of Year award 1983). Home: PO Box 40257 Rochester NY 14604-0257 Office: 1 Lomb Memorial Dr Rochester NY 14623-0887

CAIN, DAVID LEE, corporate executive; b. Morgantown, W.Va., Oct. 14, 1941; s. David Melvin and Dorothy Elanor (Burchinal) C.; m. Dawn Marie Parker, July 2, 1983; children: Diana Jo, Michael Allen, Mark Aaron. BSME, W.Va. U., 1965. Adminstrn. mgr. Value Engring. Co., Alexandria, Va., 1968-72; gen. mgr. Walker Iron Works, Woodbridge, Va., 1972-75; owner, mgr. Dyna Products, Richmond, Va., 1975-78; adminstrn. mgr. VSE Corp., Alexandria, 1978-83; sr. v.p. The Orkand Corp., Silver Spring, Md., 1983—. Vol. youth progs., various orgns., 1965—; head coach freshman wrestling team, W.Va. U., Morgantown, 1965, asst. coach varsity wrestling team, 1965; judge Miss Nat. Teenager Pageant, Virginia Beach, Va., 1986—; mem. Rep. Nat. Com., 1990—. Capt. U.S. Army, 1965-68. Recipient scholarship W.Va. U., 1961-64, Disting. Student grant, ROTC, 1963-64, Disting. Mil. Grad., 1964-65. Mem. Nat. Contracts Mgmt. Assn., Wellington Civic Assn. Methodist. Office: The Orkand Corp 8484 Georgia Ave Silver Spring MD 20910-5604

CAIN, GERRY DYKE, social services administrator; b. Red Bank, N.J., June 7, 1952; d. Wilmer John and Eleanor (Roth) Dyke; m. Anthony Allen Cain, Dec. 16, 1972; children: Jennifer, Matthew, Sarah. BBA, Upper Iowa U., 1987; M in Theol. Studies, Wesley Theol. Sem., 1991. Comptroller Chafitz, Inc., Rockville, Md., 1980-83; asst. dir. Friends in Action/Community Ministry Montgomery County, Rockville, 1990, dir., 1990—. Bd. dirs. Montgomery County Coalition for the Homeless, 1991. Chair human rels. com. PTA, Silver Spring, Md., 1990—; bd. dirs. Montgomery County Coalition for the Homeless, 1991. Office: Friends in Action Community Ministry Montgomery County 114 W Montgomery Ave Rockville MD 20850-4213

CAIN, WILLIAM STANLEY, psychologist, educator; b. N.Y.C., Sept. 7, 1941; s. William Henry and June Rose (Stanley) C.; m. Eileen Margaret Nugent, Jan. 25, 1964; children: Justin, Alison. BS, Fordham U., 1963; MSc, Brown U., 1966, PhD, 1968. From asst. fellow to fellow John B. Pierce Lab., New Haven, 1967—; from instr. to assoc. prof. depts. Epidemiology, Pub. Health, and Psychology Yale U., New Haven, 1967-84; prof. dept. Epidemiology, Pub. Health, Psychology Yale U., New Haven, 1984—; mem. sensory disorders study sect. NIH, Bethesda, Md., 1991—; sci. adv. bd. Ctr. Indoor Air Rsch., Linthicum, Md., 1991—. Editorial bd. Chem. Senses, 1985—; editorial adv. bd. Indoor Air, 1990—; editor 5 books, 1971—; contbr. over 150 articles to profl. jours. Recipient Crosby Field award ASHRAE, 1984, Jacob Javits/Claude Pepper award NIH, 1984, Sense of Smell award, Fragrance Rsch. Fund, 1986. Fellow APA, Am. Psychol. Soc., Acad. Indoor Air Rsch.; mem. Assoc. Chemoreception Scis. (exec. chmn. 1983-84), N.Y. Acad. Scis. (pres. 1986). Office: John B Pierce Lab Yale U 290 Congress Ave New Haven CT 06519

CAIRNS, SUZAN SIEKMANN, biology educator; b. Buffalo, Mar. 9, 1941; d. Theodore John and Carolyn Ann (Christiansen) Siekmann; m. Donald Joseph Cairns, May 29, 1961; 1 child, Christopher Carl. BS, St. Lawrence U., 1962; MA, Adelphi U., 1968; PhD, SUNY, Stony Brook, 1987. Cert. secondary edn. tchr., N.Y. Tchr. chemistry Princess Anne High Sch., Virginia Beach, Va., 1962-63; tchr. sci. Walt Whitman High Sch., South Huntington, N.Y., 1963-66, Three Village Cen. Sch. Dist., Setauket, N.Y., 1966—; coord. student rsch. Waldemar Med. Rsch. Found., Woodbury, N.Y., summer 1966; mem., cons. biosafety com. Brookhaven Inst., Upton, N.Y., 1990, 91. Contbr. articles to profl. jours. Ruling elder Setauket Presbyn. Ch., 1989-91. USDA grantee, 1980. Mem. Am. Chem. Soc., Nat. Assn. Biology Tchrs., Nat. Sci. Tchrs. Assn., N.Y. Acad. Sic., Sci. Tchrs. Assn. N.Y. State (local chpt. sec. 1966—). Home: PO Box 2854 East Setauket NY 11733-0865

CALABRESE, BRIAN PAUL, illustrator, graphic artist; b. Phila., Aug. 16, 1959; s. Daniel John Sr. and Florence Elizabeth (McMichael) C. Student, Gloucester County Coll., 1980, Art Inst. Phila., 1984-86. Paste-up artist Shopper's Guide, Cherry Hill, N.J., 1986-90; freelance illustrator Thorofare, N.J., 1988—; freelance screenwriter Haddonfield, N.J., 1987—; illuminator Soc. Creative Anach., ea. U.S., 1990—; freelance portrait painter, Thorofare, 1986—. Author: (screenplays) Injustice, 1987, The Legend, 1989, The Jersey Devil, 1990, There Came a Child, 1991; illustrator: Roberts Rhymes, 1987. Recipient Award of Arms Soc. Creative Anach., 1991. Home: 100 E 9th St Thorofare NJ 08086

CALABRESE, ROSALIE SUE, professional arts administrator, writer; b. N.Y.C., Feb. 17, 1938; d. Julius and Florence (Tuck) Hochman; m. Anthony J. Calabrese, June 15, 1960 (div.); 1 child, Christopher. BA in Journalism, CCNY, 1959. Asst. news editor Electronic News, N.Y.C., 1960; asst. to publicist Abner Klipstein, N.Y.C., 1963; asst. to producer Leonard Field, N.Y.C., 1964; mgr. Am. Composers Alliance, N.Y.C., 1969-85, exec. dir., gen. mgr., 1985—; dir. Rosalie Calabrese Mgmt., N.Y.C., 1983—; music advisor, bd. dirs. Phillis Rose Dance Co., N.Y.C., 1987—; sec. bd. dirs. Am. Composers Orch., N.Y.C., 1987—; bd. dirs. 1st Ave. Ensemble, 1990—, Friends Am. Composers, treas. bd. dirs., 1991—; adv. bd. Downtown Music Prodns.; bd. dirs. Joan Miller's Dance Players, N.Y.C. Author, lyricist: (musicals) A Hell of An Angel, Simone, Not in Earnest, Murdering MacBeth, Pop Life, Does Anyone Here Speak Arabic?, Friends and Relations, Double-Play; assoc. producer, treas. box office: (play) Courtyard, 1959, The Mime and Me; co-producer: various plays at White Lake (N.Y.) Playhouse, also packaged tours for Prodn. Assocs.; dir. night club acts for Florence Hayle; lyricist with various composers; contbr. short stories and poetry to lit. and nat. mags. Mem. Dramatists Guild, Broadcast Music Inc., Am. Music Ctr. Office: 170 W 74th St New York NY 10023-2350

CALABRO, JOSEPH JOHN, III, physician; b. Carbondale, Pa., Sept. 4, 1955; s. Joseph J. and Judith A. (Fidati) C.; m. Anne Wroblewski Calabro, Jan 25, 1985; children: Lia Jude, J. John. IV. Secondary cert., Scranton Prep. Sch., 1973; BS in Biology cum laude, U. Scranton, 1977; DO, Phila. Coll. Osetopathic Med., 1981. Commd. 2d lt. U.S. Army, 1977, advanced through grades to maj., 1987; resident in emergency medicine Madigan Army Med. ctr., Tacoma, Wash., 1984-86; chief dept. ambulatory care and emergency med. svcs. Letterman Army Med. Ctr., San Francisco, 1986-90; asst. clin. prof. U. Calif., San Francisco, 1987-89; attending physician San Francisco Gen. Hosp., 1987-91; asst. clin. prof. U. Calif. Sch. Medicine, San Francisco, 1987—; chmn. Dept. Emergency Medicine Jersey Shore Med. Ctr., Neptune, N.J., 1990-92; chmn. dept. emergency medicine Beth Israel Med. Ctr., Newark, 1992—; asst. clin. prof. U. Calif. Sch. Nursing, San Francisco, 1987-89, U. Medicine and Dentistry of N.J., 1991—; chmn. San Francisco City and County Emergency Med. Care Com., 1988-90; chmn. emergency med. care com. San Francisco chpt. Am. Heart Assn., 1989-90. Reviewer Jour. AMA, Jour. EMS. Mem. Am. Coll. Emergency Physicians (chmn. natural disaster com. 1990—, bd. dirs., nat. com. mem. 1988—), Am. Coll. Osteopathic Emergency Physicians (nat. com. chmn., com. mem.), Am. Med. Assn., Am. Osteopathic Assn., Assn. Mil. Osteopathic Physicians and Surgeons, Assn. Mil. Surgeons of U.S., Soc. Acad. Emergency Medicine, Nat. Assn. EMS Physicians, Phi Lambda Upsilon. Roman Catholic. Home: 18 Spier Ave Allenhurst NJ 07711

CALCAGNI, THOMAS FRANK, marketing professional; b. Burlington, Vt., Mar. 3, 1953; s. Frank Rinaldo and Marion (Davis) C.; m. Stephanie Stec, May 25, 1974 (div.); children: Deane V., Gretchen A., Thomas E. BA cum laude, Middlebury (Vt.) Coll., 1978; MSJ, Northwestern U., Evanston, Ill., 1980. Reporter NBC News, N.Y.C., 1980, Sta. WVEC-TV, Norfolk, 1980-81, Sta. WBTV-TV, Charlotte, 1982-83; press sec. U.S. Senator Robert T. Stafford, Washington, 1983-85; anchor, producer Sta. WPTZ-TV, Plattsburgh, N.Y., 1986-87; ptnr., dir. mktg. Market Rsch. div. Macro Internat. Inc., Burlington, Vt., 1987—. Communications com. Retired Sr. Vol. Program, Winooski, Vt., 1987-88; tutor Higher Achievement Program, Washington, 1984-85. Recipient Emma Willard scholarship Howard Bank, 1973. Mem. Greater Burlington Middlebury Alumni (chpt. pres. 1990—), Middlebury Coll. Alumni (exec. com., bd. dirs. 1991—), Kapa Tau Alpha. Republican. Episcopalian. Home: 20 W Canal St Apt 425 Winooski VT 05404-2135 Office: Macro Internat Inc 126 College St Burlington VT 05401-8456

CALDA, PAVEL, waste management/environmental services executive; b. Czechoslovakia, Aug. 16, 1932; came to Can., 1968; m. Jirina Miskova; 1 child, Daniel. Masters, Tech. U. Prague, Czechoslovakia, 1957. Engr. City of Halifax, N.S., Can., 1968-70, city mgr., 1978-89; pres., chief exec. officer Halifax Harbour Cleanup, Inc., 1990—. Mem. Can. Assn. Mcpl. Adminstrs., Internat. City Mgmt. Assn. Office: Ctrl Guaranty Tower Ste 1300, 1801 Hollis St, Halifax, NS Canada B3J 3N4

CALDAMONE, ANTHONY ANGELO, pediatric urologist; b. Providence, May 16, 1950; s. Carmine Nicholas and Antonetta (Fargnoli) C.; m. Barbara Ward, July 22, 1973; children: Amy Lynn, Matthew Ward. AB, Brown U., 1972, MMS, 1975, MD, 1975. Diplomate Am. Bd. Urology. Resident U. Rochester, 1975-81; fellow Children's Hosp. of Phila., 1981-82; cons. pediatric urology, lectr. Hosp. for Sick Children, Inst. of Urology, London, 1982; asst. prof., dir. pediatric urology Case Western Res. U./Rainbow Babies & Children's Hosp., Cleve., 1983-86; assoc. prof., dir. pediatric urology Brown U./R.I. Hosp., Providence, 1986—; dir. urology residency Brown U., 1988—. Editor: Decision Making in Urology, 1990; Practice of Urology, 1991; contbr. articles to profl. jours., chpts. to books. Upjohn Achievement awardee, 1975, Lange Med. Pub. awardee, 1975, Med. Libr. award, Rochester Acad. Medicine, 1979, Walter S. Kerr First prize, Am. Urology Assn., 1981, First prize for sci. exhibit, 1982. Fellow Am. Acad. Pediatrics, ACS; mem. Am. Urol. Assn., Soc. Pediatric Urology, Soc. Univ. Urologists, Italian Pediatric Urology Soc. Roman Catholic. Office: 90 Plain St Providence RI 02903-4826

CALDER, JOHN MACKENZIE, publisher, theatre director, writer; b. Montreal, Ont., Can., Jan. 25, 1927; s. James and Lucienna (Wilson) C.; divorced; children: Jamie, Anastasia. Mng. dir. Calder Publs., London, 1949—, Riverrun Press, N.Y.C., 1978—. Author about 20 books and plays. Candidate Brit. and European Parliament, 1970-80. Named Chevalier of Arts and Letters Republic of France, Chevalier of Merite Nationale. Mem. Caledonian Club, Scottish Arts. Office: Riverrun Press 1170 Broadway New York NY 10001

CALDER, KENT EYRING, educator; b. Salt Lake City, Apr. 18, 1948; s. Grant H. and Rose (Eyring) C.; m. Toshiko Matsuura; children: Mari, Ryan. BA with honors, U. Utah, 1970; AM, Harvard U., 1972, PhD, 1979. Staff mem. U.S. Ho. of Reps., Washington, 1968-69; teaching fellow Harvard U. Dept. of Govt., Cambridge, Mass., 1972-74; research economist U.S. Fed. Trade Commn., Washington, 1974-78; visiting fellow U. Tokyo, Japan, 1977-78; exec. dir. U.S.-Japan Program Harvard U., Cambridge, 1979-80, lectr., 1979-83; asst. prof. Woodrow Wilson Sch. Princeton (N.J.) U., 1983-89, assoc. prof., 1989—, dir. U.S.-Japan program, 1990—; internat. adv. bd. Japanese Ministry of Fin., Inst. of Fiscal and Monetary Policy, Tokyo, 1987—; Japan chair Ctr. for Strategic and Internat. Studies, Washington, 1989-91. Author: Crisis and Compensation, 1988 (Ohira and Arisawa Meml. prizes 1990), The Struggle for Strategy, 1992, Japan's Changing Role in Asia, 1992; co-author: The Eastasia Edge, 1982. Instr. Japan Soc. U.S.-Japan Leadership Program, N.Y.C., 1988-91, U. Pa. Wharton Sch. Internat. Forum, 1990—; trustee Princeton in Asia, 1987—; mem. Coun. on Fgn. Rels., 1990—; Japanese chair Ctr. for Strategic and Internat. Studies, Washington, 1989-91. 1st lt. U.S. Army, 1975-76. Named Fulbright Faculty Fellow and Doctoral Fellow, 1985-86, 75-76, Faculty Research Fellow The Japan Found., 1984, Graduate Prize Fellow Harvard U., 1970-74. Mem. Am. Polit. Sci. Assn., Assn. for Asian Studies, Phi Beta Kappa, Phi Kappa Phi (Sparks Fellow 1970-71, Gibbs Fellow 1970), OECD Tide 2000 Club. Home: 197 Shadybrook Ln Princeton NJ 08540-4135 Office: Princeton U Woodrow Wilson Sch 320 Bendheim Hall Princeton NJ 08544

CALDWELL, JOYCE M., business owner, management consultant; b. N.Y.C., Jan. 21, 1944; d. William McKinley and Ada Elizabeth (Belcher) Wright; m. Robert Alphons Hansen, Aug. 19, 1961 (div. Dec. 1964); children: Robert Eric, Kimberly Adris Hansen Payne; m. Levert Caldwell Jr., Mar. 30, 1967 (div. Sept. 1988); 1 child, Levert III; m. Raymond Cleveland Marshall, Nov. 3, 1989. Grad., Fashion Inst. Tech., N.Y.C., 1962; cert. electronics, ICS, 1967; MBA, Syracuse (N.Y.) U., 1977; AAS, Rutgers U., 1983. Cert. substance abuse counselor; lic. consumer credit counselor. With fashion merchandising dept. Zacharia's, N.Y.C., 1961-62; elec. quality control technician Jet Propulsion Labs./NASA Interdata, Oceanport, N.J., 1967-74; chief exec. officer, v.p. Caldwell Assocs., Ltd., Tinton Falls, N.J., 1977—; mgmt. cons. Continental Wingate, N.Y.C., 1983—; designer in field. Contbr. articles to profl. jours. Active various coms. Tinton Falls Schs.; vol. social svcs. Red Bank area hosps., nursing homes and pvt. clients; counselor substance abuse Northampton Health and Human Svcs.; news commentator for local radio sta. for print handicapped. Mem. MENSA, Deborah Hosp. Found. Office: Caldwell Assocs Ltd 33 Steven Ave Eatontown NJ 07724-2630

CALDWELL, SUSAN HANES, art dealer; b. N.Y.C., May 19, 1938; d. John Wesley and Hope (Yandell) Hanes; m. Peter R.B. Caldwell, June 18, 1960 (div. 1975); children: Gillian, Dylan, Bailey. BA, Sarah Lawrence Coll., 1962. Columnist Dayton (Ohio) Jour. Herald, 1963-66; archtl. designer Susan Caldwell, Inc., N.Y.C., 1967-73; real estate devel. assoc. Soho, N.Y.C., 1973-74; owner, dir. Susan Caldwell Gallery, N.Y.C., 1974-85; cons. World Monuments Fund, N.Y.C., 1985-86; dir. N.Y. Studio Sch., N.Y.C., 1988-89. Mem. Art Dealers Assn. Am. Democrat. Home: 27 E 22d St New York NY 10010

CALDWELL, WILLIAM WILSON, federal judge; b. Harrisburg, Pa., Nov. 10, 1925; s. Thomas D. and Martha B. C.; m. Janet W. Garber. A.B., Dickinson Coll., 1948, LL.B., 1951. Ptnr. Caldwell, Fox & Stoner, Harrisburg, 1951-70; 1st asst. dist. Atty. Dauphin County, 1960-62; counsel, chmn. Bd. Arbitration of Claims State of Pa., 1963-70; judge Common Pleas Ct., Dauphin County, 1970-82, U.S. Dist. Ct. (mid. dist.) Pa., 1982—. Office: Fed Bldg PO Box 11877 Harrisburg PA 17108-1877*

CALE, WILLIAM GRAHAM, JR., environmental sciences educator, researcher; b. Phila., Dec. 10, 1947; s. William Graham and Kathryn (Rowland) C.; m. Betty Jean Byrd, June 8, 1974. B.S., Pa. State U., 1969; Ph.D. in Zoology, U. Ga., 1975. Asst. prof. ecology and environ. scis. U. Tex.-Dallas, Richardson, 1975-80, assoc. prof. environ. scis., 1980-87, full prof. 1987-89, assoc. dean Sch. Natural Scis. and Math., 1983-85, chmn. dept. environ. scis., 1984-89; dean Coll Natural Scis. and Math. Ind. Univ. Pa., 1989—; vis. scientist Oak Ridge Nat. Lab., 1981, 84, 85. Mem. NSF grant adv. panel, 1985-88—, Dept. Energy grant rev. panel, 1989-90; contbr. articles to profl. jours. NSF grantee, 1978, 81, 83, 85. Mem. Ecol. Soc. Am., Am. Inst. Biol. Scis., Internat. Assn. for Ecology, Internat. Soc. for Ecol. Modelling, Sigma Xi. Democrat. Avocations: tournament bridge; jogging. Home: 1051 Mansfield Ave Indiana PA 15701-2415 Office: Ind U of Pa Coll of Natural Scis & Math 305 Weyandt Hall Indiana PA 15705-1087

CALFO, JASON PHILEMON, graphic design consultant; b. Forest Hills, N.Y., Sept. 13, 1954; s. George Constantine and Helen (Canell) C.; m. Janet Marie Vallochi; 1 child, Maxfield Janson. BFA, Syracuse U., 1977. Designer Herb Lubalin Assoc. Inc., N.Y.C., 1978-81; creative dir. Carnase, Inc., N.Y.C., 1981-84; prin. Calfo Assocs., N.Y.C., 1984—; pres. Calfo/Aron, Inc., N.Y.C., 1989—; vis. prof. and thesis advisor, Pratt Inst., N.Y.C., 1981—. Editorial design dir. Ligature, 1982-87. Active Mus. Modern Art, Cooper-Hewitt Mus. Recipient Silver medal The Art Dirs. Club N.Y., 1980-84, Communication Arts, Palo Alto, Calif., 1981, 83, The Type Dirs. Club, N.Y.C., 1981-83, Creativity award Art Direction, N.Y.C., 1980, 82-85, 88-91. Mem. Am. Inst. Graphic Arts, Internat. Ctr. Photography, The Type Dirs. Club. Office: Calfo Assocs 20 W 20th St New York NY 10011-4213

CALHOUN, JOHN ALFRED, social services administrator; b. Phila., Dec. 1, 1939; s. John Alfred and Helen Fordham (Webster) C.; m. Ottilia Klenota, May 29, 1971; children: Byron, Hollis. BA, Brown U., 1962; M in Div., Episcopal Div. Sch., Cambridge, Mass., 1965; M in Pub. Admnistrn., Harvard U., 1986. Tchr. Phila. pub. schs., 1965-66; program adminstr. Action for Boston Community Devel., 1966-70; v.p. Tech. Devel. Corp., Boston, 1970-73; exec. dir. Justice Resource Inst., Boston, 1973-76; commr. Mass. Dept. of Youth Svcs., Boston, 1976-79; then commr. U.S. Adminstrn. for Children, Youth and Families, Washington, 1979-81; dir. Ctr. for Govtl. Affairs Child Welfare League, Washington, 1981-83; exec. dir. Nat. Crime Prevention Coun., Washington, 1983—; bd. dirs. Youth Svcs. Am., Nat. Com. for Prevention of Child Abuse, Chgo., Nat. Ctr. Early Adolescence, Chapel Hill, N.C., Thomas Jefferson Forum, Boston, Nat. Parent Aide Assn., Chgo., Ctr. for Internat. Leadership, N.Y.; mem. adv. bd. Va. Dept. for Children, Tribal and Alaskan Native Juv. Justice System, planning group Internat. Conf. on Urban Safety, Drugs and Crime Prevention, N.Am. Commn. Chem. Dependency/Child Welfare; assoc. in edn. Harvard U., 1978; moderator Aspen Inst., 1980—; founder Pre-trial Diversion Programs, Mass., Urban Ct. Mediaton Community Sentencing, Mass., Youth As Resources, Mass. and Ind., Community Responses to Drug Abuse. Author: What, Me Evaluate?, 1986; editor: Crime in Urban Communities, 1986, Making a Difference, 1985, Reaching Out: School-based Community Service Programs, Teens Crime and the Community, others; contbr. articles to profl. jours. Coach McLean Youth, McLean, Va.; state chmn. Mass. Adolescent Task Force, 1978; chmn. Mass. State of the Family Task Force, 1979; pres. Franklin Flaschner Found., 1978; treas. Met. Beaverbrook Area Mental Health Bd.; bd. advisors U. Mass. Coll. Community Pub. Service, 1979; bd. dirs. Edna Stein Acad., Boston, Pekinese Island Sch., Woods Hole, Mass. Littauer fellow Harvard U. Kennedy Sch. of Govt., 1986; recipient award of Recognition Am. Arbitration Assn., 1978. Mem. Am. Probation/ Parole Assn. (project planning commn. 1986-88). Democrat. Episcopalian. Home: 921 Mackall Ave Mc Lean VA 22101-1617 Office: Nat Crime Prevention Coun 1700 K St NW Washington DC 20006-3817

CALHOUN, JOHN COZART, financial services marketing executive; b. Ft. Oglethorpe, Ga., Aug. 6, 1937; s. James Paul and Geneva F. (Fortson) C.; LLB, Blackstone Sch. Law, 1970; BA, Eastern Nebr. Coll., 1972; LLD (hon.), Edward Waters Coll., 1975, Morris Brown Coll., 1976, Daniel Payne Coll., 1976; PhD (hon.), Va. Coll., 1976, PhD Clayton U., 1977, postgrad. U. East Asia, Macau. Intelligence analyst NATO, Izmir, Turkey, 1959; corr. Stars and Stripes, Dept. Def., 1959-60; newspaper editor, Ft. Myer, Va., 1961-63; news editor Sta. VUNC, Okinawa, 1963-64; public affairs rep. Dept. Def., Maine-N.H.-Vt., 1964-67; Tokyo public affairs rep. UN, 1967-68; chief community relations Mil. Dist. Washington, 1969-70; dir. public affairs Nat. Farmers Union, 1970-71; dir. minority communications Peace Corps, 1971-73; staff asst., dep. spl. asst. to Pres. for minority affairs, 1973-74; spl. asst. to Pres., also dir. for media relations The White House, Washington, 1975-76; chmn. bd. Aaken Calhoun Group; pres. Calhoun Assocs., Counselors, Internat. Law, Bus. and Internat. Relations; dir. Am.-Asian Trading Co., Am. Bionics Enterprises. Bd. dirs. Bel-Pre Civic Assn., 1973-76; communications adv. Republican Nat. Com.; mem. Nat. Adv. Council on Edn. for Disadvantaged Children, World Affairs Council Washington D.C.; mem. Balt. Coun. on Fgn. Affairs. Served with U.S. Army, 1955-59. Decorated Army Commendation ribbon; recipient award Middle Atlantic Assn. Indsl. Editors, 1961; Clio award Am. TV and Radio Comml. Festival Group, 1971; Andy award Advt. Club N.Y., 1971; Nat. Man of Yr. award Nat. Inst. Rural Agrarian Life, 1976; Disting. Public Service award Prairie View A&M U., 1976. Mem. Internat. Communication Assn., Am. Mgmt. Assn., Acad. Polit. Sci., Balt. Coun. on Fgn. Affairs, DAV (life), Am. Legion (life), Am. Assn. Retired People, Assn. Internat. Practical Tng. (bd. dirs. U.S. affiliate), Nat. Press Club, Capital Press Club (dir. 1969—), Rep. Nat. Com. Assos. Republican. Club: Capital Office: PO Box 70620 Washington DC 20024-0620

CALHOUN-SENGHOR, KEITH, lawyer; b. Richmond, Va., June 14, 1955; s. Clarence Calhoun Jr. and Senegal Senghor; m. Sharon White. AB with honors, Stanford U., 1977; JD, Harvard U., 1981. Bar: D.C. 1981, U.S. Ct. Appeals (4th cir.) 1982. Law clk. to judge U.S. Ct. Appeals for 4th Cir., Richmond, 1981-82; assoc. Gibson, Dunn & Crutcher, L.A. and Washington, 1983-85; fgn. legal fellow Kreuz, Niebler & Mittl, Munich, 1986; v.p., gen. counsel Tech. Applications, Inc., Alexandria, Va., 1986-90; pres. Noma Internat. Enterprises, Inc., Washington, 1990—; of counsel Wood, Williams, Rafalsky & Harris, Washington, 1991—. Fulbright scholar U. Bonn., 1977-78, German Acad. Exch. Svc. Fgn. fellow, 1985-86. Mem. ABA (com. on internat. trade and devel., sub-com. on African trade and investment), D.C. Bar Assn. Office: Noma Internat Enterprises Inc 1429 Madison St NW Washington DC 20011-6805

CALIA, VINCENT FRANK, educator, psychologist; b. Somerville, Mass., June 25, 1926; s. Frank and Antonina (Blunda) C.; children: Paul,

Moira. BA, Northeastern U., 1949; MEd, Boston U., 1954, EdD, 1959. Lic. psychologist, Mass., R.I. Counselor, intern Bd. of Cooperative Ednl. Svcs., Westchester County, N.Y., 1951-52; instr. Boston U. Jr. Coll., 1952-57, asst. prof. to assoc. prof., 1957-64; assoc. prof. R.I. Coll., Providence, 1964-65, prof. psychology, 1966—, chmn. dept., 1966-72; cons. psychologist Raytheon Mfg. Co., Waltham, Mass., 1960-62, Espousal Ctr., Waltham, 1968-78; pvt. practice, Lincoln, R.I., 1987—. Sr. editor: Pupil Personnel Administration, 1970, Critical Incidents in School Counseling, 1972. Sgt. U.S. Army, 1943-45, ETO. Grantee, Nat. Def. Edn., R.I. Coll., 1968. Fellow Mass. Psychol. Assn.; mem. Am. Psychol. Assn., Am. Group Psychotherapy Assn., R.I. Personnel and Guidance Assn. (pres. 1968-70). Office: RI Coll 600 Mt Pleasant Ave Providence RI 02908-1924

CALKIN, PARKER EMERSON, geology educator, researcher, consultant; b. Syracuse, N.Y., Apr. 27, 1933; s. Frank George and Georgia (Spencer) C.; m. Joan Arlene Chace, Sept. 15, 1955 (div. 1978); children: Mark, Lisa; m. Harriet Rose Simons, Feb. 19, 1979. BS, Tufts U., 1955; MSc, U. B.C., Vancouver, Can., 1959; PhD, Ohio State U., 1963. Asst. prof. geology SUNY, Buffalo, 1963-68, assoc. prof., 1968-75, prof., 1975—; vis. scholar U. Cambridge, Eng., 1970-71, 86; vis. prof. U. Colo., Boulder, 1979; cons. Hayden-Wegmen Engrs., Buffalo, 1975—, N.Y. State Law Dept., Buffalo, 1988-89, numerous others. Editor, author Great Lakes Coastal Geol. Svcs., 1981-83, Geol. Soc. Can. Paper 30, 1989; contbr. articles to profl. jours. Lt. (j.g.) USN, 1955-57. Recipient Antarctic Svc. award 86th Congress, 1960. Fellow Geol. Soc. Am. (2d vice chair quaternary geology and geomorphology div. 1992—); mem. Internat. Glaciological Soc., Am. Quaternary Assn. (councilor 1985-88, N.Y. State Geol. Soc. (pres. 1982), Sigma Xi. Republican. Presbyterian. Office: SUNY Dept Geology 415 Fronczak Hall Buffalo NY 14260

CALKINS, DAVID ROSS, physician, medical educator; b. Kansas City, Kans., May 27, 1948; s. Leroy Adelbert and Emily Virginia (Kygber) C.; m. Susan Spalding Rice, Sept. 22, 1989. AB, Princeton (N.J.) U., 1970; MD and MPP, Harvard U., 1975. Diplomate Am. Bd. Internal Medicine. Intern in medicine U. Wash., Seattle, 1975-76; resident in medicine Beth Israel Hosp., Boston, 1976-78, from asst. to assoc. in medicine, 1981—; fellow The White House, Washington, 1978-79; spl. asst., dep. exec., sec. Office of the Sec. HHS, Washington, 1979-81; from instr. to asst. prof. dept. medicine Harvard U. Med. Sch., Boston, 1981—; from instr. to asst. prof. Harvard Sch. Pub. Health, Boston, 1985—, dir. profl. programs dept. health policy and mgmt., 1985—; chief div. gen. internal medicine, med. dir. ambulatory svc. New Eng. Deaconess Hosp., Boston, 1991—. W.K. Kellogg Found. fellow, 1987. Office: New Eng Deaconess Hosp One Autumn St Boston MA 02215

CALKINS, RICHARD LAURIN, company and non-profit association executive; b. Torrance, Calif., Jan. 4, 1944; s. Laurin and Velma Alice (Singer) C.; m. Debra Barton (div. 1975). BA, Westmont Coll., 1966; MA in Teaching, Calif. State U., 1967; MA, Whittier Coll., 1975; PhD, U. Houston, 1979. Dean Am. Coll., Leysin, Switzerland, 1978-84; v.p. spl. projects Nestle Corp., Switzerland, 1984-87; exec. dir. Tesol, Washington, 1987-88, CINE, Washington, 1988—; pres. Washington Film and Video Coun., 1988—. Editor Internat. Festival Dir., 1988-91, Cine Yearbook, 1988-91; contbr. articles to profl. publs. Mem. vestry, chair outreach com. St. Thomas Parish, Washington; bd. dirs. Jubilee Jobs and Housing, Joint Nat. Com. on Langs. U. Houston fellow, 1979. Mem. Internat. TV Assn., Am. Soc. Assn. Execs., Greater Washington Soc. Assn. Execs., Assn. Chief Exec. Coun., Guild Profl. Tour Guides (mem. exec. com. 1985-90), Assn. Internat. Colls. and Univs. (bd. dirs.). Episcopalian. Office: CINE # 1016 1001 Connecticut Ave NW Washington DC 20036

CALLAHAN, AILEEN LOUGHLIN, artist; b. Dayton, Ohio; d. John Gualbert and Mariel (Loughlin) C. BFA, Boston U., 1968, MFA, 1970; student, Skowhegan Sch. of Painting, Maine, 1968-69, Escuela Nacional de Pintura, Mexico City, 1970-72. Lincoln fellow Mex., 1970-72; artist mural East Boston Drug Rehab. Clinic, 1973-74; artist H.P. Harris Jr., Houston, 1975; tchr. Boston Coll./Regis Coll., Weston, Mass., 1979; lectr. in art Boston Coll., Chestnut Hill, Mass., 1979—, Regis Coll., Weston, Mass., 1979—, Lesley Coll., Cambridge, Mass., 1988-91, U. Mass., Boston, 1991—; speaker, lectr. in field. Exhibited in juried nat. group shows at Carlson Gallery, U. Bridgeport, 1991, Pratt Manhattan Gallery, 1991, Amos Enos Gallery, N.Y.C., 1990-91; exhibited in juried internat. Cen. Mo. State U., 1989; 30 drawings published in Tragic Psalms, 1987; contbr. articles to profl. mags.; compledted 10 murals., 1968-80. Recipient Lincoln Fellowship in Mural Painting, Mexican Govt., 1970-72, Blanche E. Coleman award Coleman Trust, 1984, Juror's award Amos Eno Gallery, 1990, Purchase prize Skowhegan Sch. Painting & Sculpture, 1968-69; named First Place winner Pindar Gallery, 1989. Mem. Women's Caucus for Art. Home: 1200 Massachusetts Ave 41W Cambridge MA 02138 Office: Boston Coll Fine Arts Dept 140 Commonwealth Ave Chestnut Hill MA 02167-3801

CALLAHAN, DAVID MICHAEL, psychologist; b. Methuen, Mass., June 25, 1958; s. William John and Virginia Ann (Pageau) C.; m. Gretchen Stecher, July 31, 1982; children: Peter, Daniel. BS in Psychology, Fitchburg State Coll., 1980; MA in Clin. Psychology, U. Rochester, 1983, PhD in Clin. Psychology, 1985. Psychologist Herbert Lipton Mental Health, Fitchburg, Mass., 1985-86; cons. psychologist Family Svc. Assn., Fall River, Mass., 1987—; psychologist Psychology Assocs., Plymouth, Mass., 1987—; dir. Psychology Assocs., 1991—. Mem. Cult Awareness Network, 1986—. Mem. Am. Psychol. Assn. Democrat. Episcopalian. Office: Psychology Assocs 71 Court St Plymouth MA 02360-3822

CALLAHAN, JAMES FRANCIS, chemist, researcher; b. Phila., Mar. 28, 1954; s. James Patrick and Mary Evelyn (Delaney) C. BS, St Joseph's U., Phila., 1976; PhD, Temple U., 1981. Rsch. fellow Temple U., Phila., 1976-80; postdoctoral rsch. assoc. Columbia U., N.Y.C., 1981-82; assoc. sr. investigator medicinal chemistry Smith Kline & French Labs., Phila., 1982-84, assoc. sr. investigator peptide chemistry, 1985-88; sr. investigator peptide chemistry Smith Kline & French Labs., King of Prussia, Pa., 1988-89; sr. investigator peptidomimetic rsch. SmithKline Beecham Pharms., King of Prussia, 1989—. Contbr. articles to profl. jours. Patentee in field. Recipient awards and scholarships. Mem. AAAS, Am. Chem. Soc., Royal Soc. Chemistry, Phila. Organic Chemists Club (asst. sec./sec. 1983-85). Republican. Roman Catholic. Office: SmithKline Beecham Pharms 709 Swedeland Rd King Of Prussia PA 19406-2799

CALLAHAN, JOAN, speech arts and communicative disorders educator; b. N.Y.C., May 7, 1939; d. Lewis B. and Etta P. (Perlmutter) Schwartz; m. William Callahan, Aug. 16, 1973; 1 child, Jennifer. BA, Adelphi U., 1960; MA, Columbia U., 1961; D. Arts, Adelphi U., 1982. Instr. Adelphi U., Garden City, N.Y., 1975-78, coord. deaf edn., 1978—, assoc. prof., 1986—. Contbr. chpt. to textbook: Language and Communication Disorders in Children, 2d edit. 1989. Pre-school hearing grantee Nassau County Bd. Health, 1989-91. Mem. Am. Speech Hearing Lang. Assn., Alexander Graham Bell Assn., N.Y. State Speech and Hearing Assn., Coun. Edn. Deaf, Long Island Speech and Hearing Assn. Office: Adelphi U Dept Speech Arts and Communicative Disorders Garden City NY 11530

CALLAHAN, KATHLEEN ELISABETH, artist; b. Woburn, Mass., Dec. 20, 1957; d. Robert Filmore and Dorothy Elisabeth (Sellar) Sheerin; m. Glenn Thomas Callahan, Aug. 17, 1984; 1 child, Justin Dean. AS, Commer-Endicott Coll., 1978; BA, Syracuse U., 1980. Tech. illustrator Ford Aerospace and Communications MIT Lincoln Labs., Lexington, 1981-88; freelance artist Fitchburg, Mass., 1986-91; artist, pres., co-founder Celebrity Fine Art Co., Fitchburg, 1991—. Numerous exhibits in permanent collections, corp. collections, and gallery shows. Home: 24 Harrison Ave Fitchburg MA 01420 Office: Celebrity Fine Art Inc 151 Tremont St Ste 27 A Fitchburg MA 02111

CALLAHAN, LINDA JEANNE, corporate and external relations executive; b. Lakewood, N.J., July 11, 1951; d. Herbert Butler and Clara (Frankenberger) C.; children: Scott Herbert Morris, Kevin Matthew Morris; m. Douglas Mark Elias, Sept. 8, 1990. BA, Cornell U., 1973. Freelance writer Ithaca, N.Y., 1978-80; reporter Ithaca Times, 1980-81; staff asst. to v.p. rsch. Cornell U., Ithaca, 1983-84, adminstrv. mgr. Theory Ctr., 1984-86, asst. dir. Theory Ctr, 1986-89, dir. corp. and external rels. Theory Ctr., 1989—; cons. Nysernet, N.Y.C., 1987-88, N.E. Parallel Architectures Ctr., Syracuse, N.Y., 1987-88. Editor: Jour. Nutrition Edn. Spl. Supplement, 1978; contbg. editor: (brochures) Science and Supercomputing, 1989, The NSF Supercomputing Centers, 1991, U.S. Business and The NSF Supercomputing Centers, 1991. Mem. Adv. Com. on the Status of Women, Cornell U., Ithaca; vol. Spl. Olympics, Ithaca, 1991-92. Mem. AAAS, N.Y. Acad. Sci., Tech. Transfer Soc. Democrat. Office: Cornell Theory Ctr Engring and Theory Ctr Bldg Ithaca NY 14853-3801

CALLAHAN, NORMAN MATTOCK, JR., paper company executive; b. Phila, Jan. 24, 1920; s. Norman Mattock and Edna Ruth (Stickler) C.; m. Frances Virginia Wilt, Aug. 16, 1941; children: Michael, Frederick, Scott, Rebecca, Norman III. BA, Ursinus Coll., 1942. Sales rep. Quaker City Paper Co., York, Pa., 1946-50; exec. v.p. W.B. Killhouse and Sons, York, Pa., 1950-64; pres. Colony Papers, Inc., York, Pa., 1964-84; chmn., chief exec. officer Colony Papers, Inc., York, 1984—; bd. dirs. York County Indsl. Devel. Corp., York, 1960—, Small Enterprise Devel. Corp. SEDCO, York, 1980—. Lt. USNR, 1942-45, ETO. Mem. York Club Printing House Craftsmen (pres. 1959-60), Lafayette Club, Country Club of York, Masons. Republican. Home: 2170 Winding Rd York PA 17404-4370 Office: Colony Papers Inc 1776 Stanley Dr York PA 17404-2248

CALLAHAN, PIA LAASTER, medical researcher; b. Chapelle-lez-Herlaimont, Belgium, Sept. 21, 1955; came to U.S., 1956; d. Heino and Helga (Sepp) Laaster; m. Lynn T. Callahan III, June 26, 1981 (div. June 1992). BS in Microbiology, Cornell U., 1977; M in Clin. Microbiology, Hahnemann U., 1979. Registered microbiologist. Research asst. Temple U. Med. Coll., Phila., 1979-80; microbiologist Thomas Jefferson Hosp., Phila., 1980-81; staff virologist Merck Sharp & Dohme Rsch. Labs., West Point, Pa., 1981-84, research virologist, 1984-90, rsch. assoc., 1990—. Contbr. articles to profl. jours. Mem. NAFE, Am. Soc. Microbiology. Republican. Lutheran. Home: 432 Sterners Rd Green Lane PA 18054 Office: Merck Sharp and Dohme Rsch Labs Sumneytown Pike West Point PA 19486

CALLAHAN, ROBERT F., JR., radio network executive. Pres. ABC Radio Networks, N.Y.C. Office: ABC Radio Networks 125 W End Ave 7th Fl New York NY 10023*

CALLAN, JAMES RUSKIN, advertising research company executive; b. Dallas, Nov. 5, 1932; s. John Ruskin and Lorena (Watts) C.; m. K. Callan, June 4, 1957 (div. 1968); children: James Patrick, Kelly, Kristi; m. Earlene Shewmaker, Aug. 17, 1973; 1 child, Diane Bailey. BA, St. Mary's U., 1954; MA, U. Okla., 1969, postgrad., 1979. Tchr. Jesuit High Sch., Dallas, 1955-60, Dallas Pub. Schs., 1961-64; cons. Aero Research Lab., Dayton, Ohio, 1966-67; research engr. Schlumberger Research Ctr., Ridgefield, Conn., 1970-82; v.p. C Systems, Ltd., Ridgefield, 1982—; bd. dirs. Admetrics, Tex. Editor (newsletter) Advantages, 1982—; writer (mag. column) Computers and Electronic Marketing, 1984-86; pub.: (advt. placement reference book) HiTap, 1983—, (booklet) AdFocus, 1985. Fellow NSF, 1963, 64-65, NASA, 1966-69; research grantee Data Processing Mgmt. Assn., 1968. Mem. Bus./Profl. Advt. Assn., IEEE. Office: C Systems Ltd PO Box 708 Winnsboro TX 75494

CALLAS, JOHN ALEXANDER, insurance agent; b. Kittanning, Pa., Oct. 21, 1953; s. James George and Jean (Millard) C.; m. Janet Marie Glus, June 19, 1976; 1 child, Courtney Marie. Student, Edinboro U. of Pa., 1971-75. Registered investment advisor. Owner various restaurants, Kittanning, 1975-83; assoc. Allmerica Fin., Pitts., 1983—; specialist, stockbroker Pension & Profit Sharing Svcs. Treas. St. Paul's Episcopal Ch., Kittanning, 1989. Mem. Nat. Assn. Life Underwriters (Nat. Quality award 1986, 91, Nat. Sales Achievement award 1990, Achievement Leader Corp. Pension Profit Sharing 1986, 89, 90, 91, Circle of Honor 1985, 86, 89, 90, 91), Butler Country Club, Rotary Internat., Elks. Office: 308 Market St Kittanning PA 16201-1527 also: 2000 Gateway 2 Pittsburgh PA 15222 also: Morgan Mgmt Bldg 165 Brugh Ave Ste 320 Butler PA 16001

CALLIERI, JUAN CARLOS, electrical engineer; b. Santiago, Chile, Oct. 31, 1943; came to U.S., 1987; s. Carlos and Betty (Muller) C.; m. Eugenia Larranaga, Jan. 2, 1970; children: Christian, Paola. MEE, U. Chile, Santiago, 1968; MBA in Mgmt., Pacific Western U., 1983. Tech. mgr. Sindelen S.A., Santiago, 1968-70; plant mgr. Philco-Ford, Mexico City, 1971-76; mfg. dir. Black & Decker, Sao Paulo, Brazil, 1977-80, Sperry Vickers, Sao Paulo, Brazil, 1981-84; gen. mgr. Robert Bosch, Campinas, Brazil, 1985-87; sr. engr. Internat. Fin. Corp., Washington, 1987—; restructuring cons. Hindustan Motors, Calcutta, India, 1989; restructuring cons. Alsa, Monterrey, Mex., 1990-92; seminar speaker Automotive Mgrs., Jakarta, Indonesia, 1990, Budapest, Hungary, 1991. Mem. Rotary Internat. Home: 12644 Carrington Hill Dr Gaithersburg MD 20878 Office: Internat Fin Corp World Bank 1818 H St NW Washington DC 20433

CALLISON, CHARLES STUART, federal official, development economist; b. Boonville, Mo., July 11, 1939; s. Charles Hugh Callison and Ruth Marie (Ecord) Woolsey; m.m Michelle My-Dung Pham, Sept. 29, 1965; children: Cynthia Thuy-Tien, Patricia Mong-Tuyen, Clarissa Thien-Huong. BS in Fgn. Svc., U. Md., 1961; MA in S.E. Asian Studies, Yale U., 1969; PhD in Devel. Econs., Cornell U., 1976. Asst. prof. econs. Ohio U., Athens, 1973-74; econ. advisor Office of Vietnam Affairs Agy. for Internat. Devel. (AID), Washington, 1974-76; econ. advisor Bicol River Basin Devel. program AID, Naga City, Philippines, 1976-79; program economist AID, Manila, 1979-82; program economist regional office AID, Nairobi, Kenya, 1982-84, chief analysis div., 1984-87; dep. assoc. asst. adminstr. Office Policy Devel. AID, Washington, 1987-90; counselor Sr. Fgn. Svc. AID, 1987; dep. exec. dir. bd. for internat. food and agrl. devel. AID, Washington, 1990-91, dep. exec. dir. Agy. Ctr. for Univ. Coop. in Devel., 1991—; bd. govs. Mgrs. Network, AID, Washington, 1990—. Author: Land-to-the-Tiller in the Mekong Delta, 1983; editor-in-chief 1960 Terrapin Yearbook, 1959-60; editorial bd. Fgn. Svc. Jour., 1990—. Bd. dirs. Internat. Sch., Makati, Manila, 1980-82. Capt. USAF, 1961-67, Vietnam. Recipient fellowships Yale U., New Haven, Conn., 1967-69, Cornell U., Ithaca, N.Y., 1969-71, 73, Ford Found., South Vietnam, 1971-73. Decorated Bronze Star, Air Force Commendation medal. Mem. Am. Econ. Assn., Am. Fgn. Svc. Assn., Phi Kappa Phi, Omicron Delta Kappa, Scabbard & Blade, Phi Eta Sigma, Sigma Alpha Epsilon (chpt. corres. sec. 1958-61). Democrat. Christian Ch. (Disciples of Christ). Home: 11551 Paramus Dr N North Potomac MD 20878 Office: AID/R&D/UC Dept State Rm 900 SA-38 320 21st St NW Washington DC 20523

CALLOWAY, D. WAYNE, food and beverage products company executive; b. 1935. BBA, Wake Forest U., 1959. Exec. v.p., chief fin. officer Pepsico Inc., Purchase, N.Y., 1983-85, pres., chief operating officer, 1985-86, chmn., chief exec. officer, 1986—; former chmn., pres., chief exec. and operating officer Frito-Lay Inc. (subs. Pepsico Inc.), Dallas. Office: PepsiCo Inc Anderson Hill Rd Purchase NY 10577-2002*

CALNAN, ARTHUR FRANCIS, ophthalmologist; b. Boston, Mar. 11, 1926; s. Augustine Francis and Mary Ellen (Callahan) C.; m. Jeanne Elizabeth Faber, Nov. 27, 1954; children: Kathleen, Diane, Barbara, Jeffrey, Douglas, David. BS, Tufts U., 1946, MD, 1950; MS, U. Pa., 1954. Diplomate Am. Bd. Ophthalmology, Am. Bd. Med. Examiners. Rotating intern St. Louis City Hosp., 1950-51; resident ophthalmology, rsch. fellow Wills Eye Hosp., Phila., 1954-55, resident, 1955-57; preceptorship Trygye Gundersen MD, Boston, 1957-65; chair ophthalmology dept. Lahey Clinic, Boston, 1965-70; sr. mem. South Suburban Ophthalmology, Hingham, Mass., 1970—; clin. instr. ophthalmology Tufts U. Sch. Medicine, 1958; mem. active staff ophthalmology South Shore Hosp., Weymouth, Mass., 1960—; jr. assisting surgeon ophthalmology Carney Hosp., Dorchester, Mass., 1963—; asst. ophthalmology Milton (Mass.) Hosp., 1973—. Mem. Plymouth County Rep. Club. Served to capt. USAF, 1950-53. Mem. AMA, Internat. Assn. Ocular Surgeons, Am. Acad. Ophthalmology, Am. Intra-Ocular Implant Soc., New Eng. Ophthalmol. Soc., Mass. Soc. Ophthalmic Physicians and Surgeons, Mass. Med. Soc., Norfolk-South Med. Soc., Am. Soc. Cataract and Refractive Surgeons, Am. Soc. Contemporary Ophthalmology, Contact Lens Assn. Ophthalmologists, Mass. Eye and Ear Infirmary Alumni Assn., Wills Eye Hosp. Alumni Assn., Erie Soc., Clan Gillean Assn., South Shore C. of C., Air Force Assn., Guild St. Luke. Roman Catholic. Home: 703 Bay Rd Duxbury MA 02332-5219 Office: S Suburban Ophthalmology 31 Derby St Hingham MA 02043-3706

CALO, JOSEPH MANUEL, chemical engineering educator; b. Newark, Nov. 9, 1944; s. Serafin and Carmen (Garcia) C.; m. Diane Helen Benimeli, July 14, 1968; children: Joseph Manuel Jr., Andrew Joseph. BS in Chem. Engring., Newark Coll. Engring., 1966; AM, Princeton U., 1968, PhD, 1970; M Ad Eundem (hon.), Brown U., 1983. Registered profl. engr., R.I., N.J. Rsch. engr. Exxon Rsch. and Engring. Co., Florham Park, N.J., 1974-76; asst. prof. chem. engring. Princeton (N.J.) U., 1976-81; assoc. prof. engring. Brown U., Providence, 1981-89, prof. engring., 1989—; vis. prof. U. Strathclyde, Glasgow, UK, spring 1992, U. Alicante, Spain, summer 1992; cons. chem. industry and govt. Contbr. numerous articles to sci. jours. Coach, Smithfield (R.I.) Youth Soccer Assn., 1985—. Capt. USAF, 1970-74. Mem. Am. Inst. Chem. Engrs., Am. Chem. Soc., Sigma Xi. Home: 16 Hawthorne Rd Greenville RI 02828-1306

CALTON, SANDRA JEANE, accountant; b. Portales, N.Mex., Feb. 3, 1945; d. Lloyd Paul and Nana Mae (Parris) Grant; m. Gary Jim Calton, Nov. 26, 1964; children: Deborah, April, Craig. BS, Ea. N.Mex. U., 1967, U. Md., 1984. CPA, Md. Comptr. Purification Engring. Inc., Columbia, Md., 1981-85, IBF Biotechnics Inc., Savage, Md., 1987-88; pres. Srchem, Inc., Elkridge, Md., 1988—; acct. Calton Rsch. Assocs., Elkridge, 1974—. Treas. Howard Coun. Extension Homemakers Coun., Ellicott City, Md., 1984. Mem. AICPA, Md. Assn. CPAs. Home: 5331 Landing Rd Baltimore MD 21227

CALUSDIAN, RICHARD FRANK, physics educator; b. Watertown, Mass., Feb. 6, 1935; s. Frank and Rose Sarah (Giragosian) C.; m. Linda Mae Lamphere, Apr. 15, 1962; children—Diana Lynn, Rebecca Susanne, Robert Frank. B.A., Harvard Coll., 1957; M.S., U. N.H., 1959; Ph.D., Boston U., 1965. Sr. research, teaching fellow Boston U., 1964; physicist U.S. Army Materials Research Agy., Watertown, Mass., 1965, U.S. Army Natick Labs. (Mass.), 1966; prof., chmn. dept. physics Bridgewater State Coll. (Mass.), 1966-87; NSF instr., 1968-66. Contbg. author: College Physics, 1974. Mem. Am. Assn. Physics Tchrs., Sigma Xi. Home: 17 Atkinson Dr Bridgewater MA 02324-3501

CAMACHO, HENRY STEPHEN, III, executive; b. N.Y.C., Jan. 18, 1947; s. Henry C. Jr. and June (Eads) Hendrix; m. Virginia C. Jones, Jan. 23, 1971; children: Henry S. IV, Dawn M. BS, SUNY, Albany, 1980; MS, West Chester U., 1983. Police officer Balt. City Police Dept., 1969-71; security supr. Wyeth Labs. Inc., Great Valley, Pa., 1978-83; lic. pvt. detective, owner CMM Investigations, Norristown, Pa., 1981-88; constable Pa. State Constable Office, Norristown, 1988—; pres. Nat. Assn. Traffic Accident Reconstructionists & Investigators, King of Prussia, Pa., 1988—; sec. N.A.T.A.R.I., Norristown, 1984-88, Montgomery County Constable Assn., Norristown, 1990—. With U.S. Army, 1971-78. Mem. Nat, Drug Enforcement Assn. (state rep. 1982-86), Internat. Narcotic Enforcement Officers Assn., Montgomery County Pvt. Detectives Assn. (v.p. 1986-88), Optimist Club.

CAMDEN, DAVID GEORGE, sales executive; b. Hinsdale, Ill., Jan. 21, 1951; s. Kenneth George and Jeanne Audrey (Finnegan) C.; m. Marilyn Lee Childress, July 10, 1976; 1 child, Christopher. BS, Western Ill. U., 1974. Field rep. GMAC, Westchester, Ill., 1974-76; various field and staff positions Chrysler Corp., Elk Grove, Ill., 1976-82; merchandising mgr. Toyota Motor Distbrs., Inc., Englewood, Colo., 1982-84; field ops. mgr. Toyota Motor Distbrs., Inc., Carol Stream, Ill., 1984-86, sr. field ops. mgr., 1986-87; asst. gen. mgr. Toyota Motor Distbrs., Inc., Englewood, 1987-88; sr. asst. gen. mgr. Toyota Motor Distbrs., Inc., West Caldwell, N.J., 1988—. Home: 49 Winay Ter W Long Valley NJ 07853-3569 Office: Toyota Motor Distbrs Inc 16 Henderson Dr West Caldwell NJ 07006-6677

CAMER, MARY MARTHA, secretary; b. McAdoo, Pa., Oct. 30, 1932; d. John Fiolich and Elizabeth (Chomo) Sussick; m. Kenneth Camer, Feb. 10, 1952; children: Kenneth, Curtis, Marybeth. AA in Bus. Mgmt., Bucks County Community Coll., 1982. Sch. sec. Neshaminy Sch. Dist., Langhorne, Pa., 1959-61; NCR bookkeeper Gen. Doors Corp., Bristol, Pa., 1962-65; jr. acct., NCR bookkeeper Lower Bucks Hosp., Bristol, Pa., 1965-68; office mgr., bookkeeper Archdiocese of Phila., Blessed J. Neumann Nursing Home, 1968-78; payroll coord. Warmer Lambert Co. Alphamedics Divsn., Levittown, Pa., 1979-81, human resouces pers. coord., 1978-86; sec. Rohm and Hass, DVI, Bristol, 1988—. Recipient Outstanding Adult award Pa. Assn. for Adult Continuing Edn., 1991. Democrat. Roman Catholic. Home: 94 Queenlily Rd Levittown PA 19057 Office: Rohm and Haas DVI Rt 413 and Rt 13 Bristol PA 19007

CAMERON, ALLAN WILLIAMS, government official, educator; b. Racine, Wis., June 21, 1938; s. Angus Ewan and Jane (Williams) C.; m. Rebecca Hancock, Apr. 25, 1992. AB with honors, Dartmouth Coll., 1956; AM with honors, Tufts U., 1964, MA in Law and Diplomacy, with honors, 1965, PhD, 1979. Instr. in govt. Bates Coll., Lewiston, Maine, 1965-68; sr. political analyst Abt Assocs., Inc., Cambridge, Mass., 1969-70; asst. dean Fletcher Sch. of Law and Diplomacy, Medford, Mass., 1970-76, assoc. dean, 1976-78; rsch. fellow Am. Enterprise Inst., Washington, 1978-79; exec. asst. Senator Jeremiah Denton, Washington, 1981-87; exec. dir. Commn. on Merchant Marine and Def., Washington, 1987-89; dep. asst. sec. for internat. policy Dept. of the Navy, Washington, 1991—. Author: Indochina: Prospects After "The End," 1976; author, editor: Viet-Nam Crisis: A Documentary History, 1971; contbr. book chpts. and articles to profl. jours. Lt. (j.g.) USN, 1960-63. Kent fellow Danforth Found., 1967. Mem. AAUP, Am. Polit. Sci. Assn., Phi Beta Kappa. Republican. Episcopalian. Office: Office of Sec of Navy The Pentagon Washington DC 20350-1000

CAMERON, DONALD, Canadian premier; b. Egerton, N.S., Can., May 20, 1946; s. William David and Helen C.; m. Rosemary Simpson, 1969; children: Natalie Dawn, William David, Chirstine Anne. Student, McGill U. Elected N.S. Legislature, 1974, re-elected, 1978, 81 84, 88; min. of fisheries and recreation, 1978-80, min. of industry, trade and tech., min. responsible for Adminstrn. of N.S. Rsch. Found. Corp. Act, 1988, min. responsible for Adv. Coun. on Applied Sci. and Tech., 1988; premier N.S., 1991—. Presbyn. Office: Province House, Office of Premier, Halifax, NS Canada B3J 2T3*

CAMERON, DUKE EDWARD, cardiac surgeon, educator; b. Miami, Fla., Mar. 9, 1952; s. Edward John and Joanne (Abbott) C.; m. Claudia Oppenheim; children: Danielle, Nicole. AB, Harvard Coll., 1974; MD, Yale U., 1978. Resident gen. surgery Yale-New Haven Hosp., 1978-84, resident cardiothoracic surgery, 1984-87; asst. prof. surgery Johns Hopkins Hosp., Balt., 1987—. Fellow ACS; mem. Soc. Thoracic Surgeons, So. Thoracic Surg. Assn. Home: 2209 South Rd Baltimore MD 21209 Office: Johns Hopkins Hosp 600 N Wolfe St Baltimore MD 21205

CAMERON, LUCILLE WILSON, university dean, library administrator; b. Nashua, N.H., Dec. 21, 1932; d. Hugh Alexander and Louise Perham (Baldwin) C.; children: Glenn A. Browning, Gail W. Browning, Valerie B. Cruickshank; m. James Robert Doris, Aug. 19, 1976. BA, U. R.I., 1964, MLS, 1972. Social caseworker R.I. Dept. Pub. Assistance, Providence, 1964-70; asst. circulation libr. U. R.I. Libr., Kingston, 1970-72, rsch. libr., 1972-73, reference libr., bibliographer, 1973-88, head reference unit, 1983-86, chmn. pub. svcs., 1988-89, interim dean, 1989-90, dean, 1990—, libr. adminstr., 1989—; bd. govs. Univ. Press New Eng. Co-author: Labor and Industrial Relations Journals and Serials, 1989; also articles. Recipient Distin. Alumna award U. R.I. Grad. Sch. Libr. and Info. Studies, 1991; grantee Champlin Founds., 1989, 90, 91, U.S. Dept. Edn., 1990. Mem. ALA, Assn. Coll. and Rsch. Librs., Consortium R.I. Acad. and Rsch. Librs., Higher Edn. Libr. Info. Network, Alpha Kappa Delta. Office: U RI Univ Libr Kingston RI 02881

CAMERON, NICHOLAS ALLEN, diversified corporation executive; b. Phila., Jan. 6, 1939; s. Nicholas Guyot and Katherine (Rogers) C.; m. Leslie Wood, Dec. 14, 1974; children: Christopher Wilson, Pamela Wilson. BS, Yale U., 1960. Treas. Allied Corp., Morristown, N.J., 1979-81, v.p. and treas., 1981-82, v.p. fin., 1982-83, v.p. planning and devel., 1983-85; sr. v.p. planning, devel. and adminstrn. Allied-Signal Inc., Morristown, N.J., 1985-86; sr. v.p. tech. and bus. devel. Bendix Aerospace-Allied-Signal, Inc., Arlington, Va., 1986-87; group pres. Allied-Signal Aerospace, 1988; sr. v.p. ops. svcs. Allied-Signal, Inc., Morristown, N.J., 1988-90, sr. v.p., gen. mgr.

chem. intermediates, 1990—. Bd. dirs. United Way of Morris County, Morristown, N.J., 1980-86, 90—, campaign chmn., 1991. Mem. Morris County C. of C. (bd. dirs. 1975-86, 1990—), Morris 2000 (bd. dirs. 1990—), Tau Beta Pi. Republican. Episcopalian. Clubs: St. Elmo Soc. (New Haven); Morris County Golf. Home: Five Noe Ave Madison NJ 07940 Office: Allied-Signal Inc Columbia Rd Morristown NJ 07960-4518

CAMERON, ROBERT GEORGE, utilities executive; b. North Bergen, N.J., July 9, 1931; s. Robert William Cameron and Frieda (Nungesser) Mory; m. Florence G. Reilly, Dec. 17, 1955 (div. Apr. 1978); children: Florence F., Robert William; m. Gwendolyn Hackett, July 26, 1978; 1 child, Elizabeth. BS in Indsl. Mgmt., Fairleigh Dickinson U., 1963, MBA, 1967. Registered profl. engr., N.J. Engr. Bell Telephone Labs., N.Y.C., 1954-62; prin. engr. N.J. Bell, Newark, 1962-72, pub. utilities mgr., 1972-75; asst. to v.p. AT&T Corp. Hdqrs., N.Y.C., 1975-77, mgr. legal dept., 1977-80; mgr. legal dept. AT&T Communications, N.Y.C., 1980-86; cons. AT&T Hdqrs., N.Y.C., 1985—. Author: Performance Rating, 1967; contbr. articles in telephony; designer Bell Labs. switchboards and pvt. br. exchanges. Asst. chmn. Dem. Party Hudson County, N.J., 1970. Served to cpl. USMC, 1952-54, Korea. Named Man of Yr., Luth. Ch. in Am., 1975. Mem. N.J. Profl. Engrs. Assn., State of N.J. Pub. Utilities Assn. Democrat. Lodge: Order of Turtles (Imperial Turtle 1970—). Home: 1209 Hupmobile Dr NE Albuquerque NM 87112-6214

CAMERON, RUTH ALLEN, English educator; b. Lisbon Falls, Maine, Jan. 15, 1929; d. Willis Curtis and Pauline (Margitan) Allen; m. James Reese Cameron, Aug. 26, 1950; children: James Allen, Laura Jean Cameron Spencer. BA, Eastern Nazarene Coll., 1950; MA, Boston U., 1964, PhD, 1972. Tchr. English and French Eastern Nazarene Acad., Quincy, Mass., 1950-52; instr. English Eastern Nazarene Coll., Quincy, 1953-54, 56-59, instr. French, 1961-64, asst. prof., 1964-68, assoc. prof., 1971-77, prof. English, 1977—, Munro prof. lit., 1987; tchr. English Abington (Mass.) High Sch., 1959-60; vis. prof. N.W. Nazarene Coll, Nampa, Idaho, 1968-69. Mem. Modern Lang. Assn, Nat. Coun. Tchrs. English, Conf. on Christianity and Lit., Quincy Hist. Soc. Democrat. Mem. Ch. of Nazarene. Office: Ea Nazarene Coll 23 E Elm Ave Quincy MA 02170-2999

CAMESAS, ADRIENNE MULLER, cardiologist; b. N.Y.C., Oct. 17, 1956; d. Joseph Robert and Barbara C. (Cella) Muller; m. Lazarus Camesas, May 16, 1982; 1 child, Christopher. BA, Brown U., 1978; MD, Columbia U., 1982. Diplomate Am. Bd. Internal Medicine, Am. Bd. Cardiology. Intern Columbia-Presbyn. Med. Ctr., N.Y.C., 1982-83, resident, 1983-85; fellow in cardiology L.I. Jewish Med. Ctr., 1985-87; cardiologist South Shore Cardiologists, P.C., West Islip, N.Y., 1987—. Fellow Am. Coll. Cardiology. Office: South Shore Cardiologists 735 Montauk Hwy West Islip NY 11795

CAMISA, KENNETH PETER, industrial relations specialist; b. N.Y.C., Aug. 26, 1938; s. George and Florence (Stone) C.; m. Joan P. Kraus, Sept. 5, 1959; children: Cheryl Ann, Glen James, Dorine Ann. BS in Econs., CUNY, 1961. Benefits cons. Martin E. Segal Co., N.Y.C., 1962-68; dir. research Internat. Orgn. Masters, Mates & Pilots AFL-CIO, N.Y.C., 1968-72; sr. v.p. Martin E. Segal Co., N.Y.C., 1972—; mem. adv. bd. N.Y. Inst. Tech. Ctr. Labor and Indsl. Relations, Westbury, 1981—; cons. Long Island Health Care Coalition, Westbury, 1985—; mem. employee benefit panel Am. Arbitration Assn., N.Y.C., 1984—. Served as sgt. USAR, 1961-67. Mem. Indsl. Relations Research Assn. Roman Catholic. Office: One Park Ave New York NY 10016-5895

CAMISHION, RUDOLPH C., physician; b. Riverside, N.J., July 16, 1927; m. Nancy Muzzarelli, June 28, 1952; children: Germain, Sandra, Lisa, Nancy, Janice. BS, St. Joseph's Coll., 1950; MD, Jefferson Med. Coll. of Phila., 1954. Cert. Am. Bd. Surgery, 1960, Bd. of Thoracic Surgery, 1961, Bd. Gen. Vascular Surgery, 1983. USNR Petty Officer, 1944-46; intern Cooper Hosp., Camden, N.J., 1954-55; resident in surgery Jefferson Med. Coll. Hosp., Phila., 1955-59; trainee Nat. Cancer Inst., 1958-59, 1959-62; asst. in surgery Jefferson Med. Coll., 1959-60, instr. in surgery, 1960-62, asst. prof. surgery, 1963-64; cons. thoracic surgery VA Hosp., Phila., 1963-66; assoc. prof. surgery Jefferson Med. Coll., 1964-67. Numerous medical presentations. Recipient Surgical Excellence award, 1991, rev. Clarence E. Shaffrey, S.J., award, 1991. Mem. Acad. Surgical Rsch., Am. Assn. Advancement of Sci., Am. Assn. for Thoracic Surgery, AAUP, Am. Coll. Chest Physicians, ACS, AHA, AMA, Am. Thoracic Soc., Am. Surgical Assn., Pa. Assn. for Thoracic Surgery, Phila. Acad. of Surgery, Camden County Med. Soc., Soc. of Univ. Surgeons, Soc. for Vascular Surgery, Vascular Soc. N.J., Eastern Vascular Soc., Soc. Clin. Vascular Surgery, Southeastern Surgical Cong., N.J. Chpt. Am. Coll. Surgeons, Alpha Omega Alpha. Office: R Wood Johnson Med Sch 3 Cooper Pla Ste 411 Dept of Surgery Camden NJ 08103

CAMM, ROBERT JAMES, printing company executive; b. Phila., May 6, 1923; s. Edward Joseph and Margaret Mary (Ketler) C.; m. Frances V. Fisher, May 21, 1952 (div. Aug. 1973); 1 child, Candyce Mary; m. Donnamae Burns, Dec. 11, 1974. BS in Econs., Wharton U., 1951. Salesman Pfaelzer Bros., Chgo., 1951-52, Sun Life of Can., Phila., 1952-53; prodn. mgr. Walter Camenisch, Inc., Phila., 1953-55; graphic arts buyer Burroughs Corp., Phila., 1955-58; asst. to pres. Goodway Printing, Phila., 1958-61, v.p. mktg., 1961-65, v.p., dir., 1965-74; pres., dir. Quadra Graphics, Inc., Pennsauken, N.J., 1974—; v.p., dir. Quadra Graphics Sales, Inc., Pennsauken, 1976—; bd. dirs. Candyco, Inc., Cherry Hill, N.J., Em-Kath, Inc., Phila., Cooper River Graphics, Inc., Pennsauken. Adv. pres.' adv. bd. Immaculata (Pa.) Coll., 1990-91; supporter Com. for an Affordable N.J., Somerville, N.J. With USNA 1943-46. Mem. Weightman Soc. (Univ. Pa.), Riverton Country Club, Stone Harbor Country Club (assoc.). Republican. Roman Catholic. Home: 495 Tearose Ln Cherry Hill NJ 08003-3461 Office: Quadra Graphics Inc 7120 Airport Hwy Merchantville NJ 08109-4393

CAMMARATA, ANGELO, surgical oncologist; b. Italy, 1936; s. Giuseppe and Giuseppina (Ruggiero) C.; m. Diane M. Donner, Apr. 25, 1965; children: Joseph, Marisa, Michael, Christina. BA, Upsala Coll., 1958; MD, N.Y. Med. Coll., 1962. Diplomate Am. Bd. Surgery. Intern N.Y. Polyclin. Hosp., N.Y.C., 1962; resident, chief resident Met. Hosp. N.Y.C., 1963-67, asst. surgeon, 1968—; resident in surgery Meml. Hosp. Cancer and Allied Diseases, N.Y.C., 1967-68; assoc. surgeon, attending surgeon Cabrini Med. Ctr., N.Y.C.; attending surgeon Beth Israel North Hosp., N.Y.C.; instr. surgery N.Y. Med. Coll., N.Y.C., 1968-74, clin. asst. prof. surgery, 1974—; vis. attending surgeon Met. Hosp. Ctr., N.Y.C. Contbr. articles to profl. jours. Fellow ACS, Internat. Coll. Surgeons; mem. AMA, N.Y. Cancer Soc., N.Y. Met. Breast Cancer Group, Meml. Alumni Soc., Alpha Club. Office: 55 E 87th St New York NY 10128

CAMMARATA, RICHARD JOHN, financial advisor; b. Boston, June 29, 1950; s. Dominic Joseph and Anna Mary (Masone) C. BA, Stonehill Coll., 1972. Mgr. Ace Fence Co., South Boston, 1972-83; fin. advisor, investor self-employed Randolph, Mass., 1983—; mem. Am. Security Coun., Nat. Adv. Bd., Boston, Va., 1988—. Mem. Rep. Presdl. Task Force, Washington, 1987—, Rep. Nat. Com., Washington, 1984—, GOPAC, Washington, 1984—. Mem. N.Y. Acad. Scis., AAAS. Republican. Roman Catholic. Home: 47 Eugenia St Randolph MA 02368-1950

CAMP, DONALD EUGENE, experimental photographer, educator; b. Meadville, Pa., July 28, 1940; s. Ira Guy and Martha Gladys (Irving) C.; m. Marie Josephé Dumont, Nov. 26, 1966; children: Stephanie Martha Helené, Dorothea Rae. BFA, Tyler Sch. Art, Phila., 1987; MFA, Tyler Sch. Art, 1989. Staff photographer Phila. Bulletin, 1972-81; asst. prof. Tyler Sch. of Art, Phila., 1989-91, Slippery Rock (Pa.) U., 1992—; dir. Future Faculty Fellowship Program Temple U., Phila., 1990-91. Photographs have appeared in many popular magazines including Ebony, News Week, People; representedin numerous public collections including the Phila. Mus. Art and Schaumberg Ctr. for Black Culture, N.Y.C. Mem. Spiritual Assembly of Bahai's of Phila., 1981—, Interfaith Support Group, Phila, 1989—. Recipient Future Faculty fellowship, Temple U., Phila., 1988, Eugene Feldman award The Print Club, 1983; named Pa. Visual Artist fellow, 1990, Smithsonian Am. Artist Oral History, 1991. Mem. Soc. Photographic Educators (bd. dirs. 1990—, chmn., founder multicultural caucus, 1990—, Recherché. Home: 4511 Spruce St Philadelphia PA 19139

CAMP, FRANCES SPENCER, retired nurse; b. Lake Charles, La., Feb. 8, 1924; d. Henry Wesley and Annie Erle (Allen) S.; m. John Clayton Camp, Nov. 3, 1944; children: John C., Elizabeth C., Martha L., Charles H. Student, So. Meth. U., Dallas, 1943-44; BSRN, McNeese State U., Lake Charles, La., 1957. Surg. nurse St. Patrick's Hosp., Lake Charles, La., 1963-65; founder, dir. Home Health Svcs. Inc., Lake Charles, 1969-80; pres., founding com. mem. Hosp. Aux. for Charity Hosp., Lake Charles; mem. task group on ethical dilemmas caused by med. tech. George Washington U. Med. Ctr., Washington, 1991—. Artist commissioned oil paintings. Active sustainer Jr. League of Am., 1957—; mem. Hospitality and Info. Svcs. of Meridian House, Washington, 1980—. Recipient Woman of Yr. award, Lake Charles, La., 1962. Mem. Nat. Presbyn. Ch. Women's Assn. (1st v.p. 1990-91), Congl. Country Club, City Club of Washington, Sigma Theta Tau. Home: Apt 510 5450 Whitley Park Ter Bethesda MD 20814

CAMP, HAZEL LEE BURT, artist; b. Gainesville, Ga., Nov. 28, 1922; d. William Ernest and Annie Mae (Ramsey) Burt; m. William Oliver Camp, Jan. 24, 1942; children: William Oliver, David Byron. Student, Md. Inst. Art, 1957-58, 62-63. One-woman shows at Ga. Mus. Art, Rockville Art Mus., Coll. Notre Dame (Balt.), U. Md., Balt. Vertical Gallery, Cleveland Meml. Gallery (Balt.), Unicorn Gallery, 1982, Hampton Ctr. for Arts and Humanities (Va.), 1985, others; exhibited in juried shows at Peale Mus., Balt., Wilmington (Del.) Fine Arts Ctr., Smithsonian Instn., Turner Gallery, Balt., Bendann Art Gallery, Balt., 1980, City Hall Gallery, Balt., 1982, Balt. Watercolor Soc., 1983, Miniature Painters, Sculptors and Gravers Soc. at the Arts Club, Washington, 1987, 88, 89, 90, 91 (Honorable Mention award 1991), Hampton Bay Days Raddison Hotel Gallery, 1988, Twentieth Century Gallery, Williamsburg, Va., 1989-91, D'Art Ctr., Norfolk, Va., 1989, Va. Watercolor Soc. at Va. Beach Ctr. for Arts, 1990, at Verona, Va., 1991, Yorktown Cultural Arts Ctr. Va., 1991-92, William King Ctr. for Arts, Abingdon, Va., 1992, others; represented in permanent collections Ga. Mus. Art, Athens, Peabody Inst., Balt., Rehoboth Art League, Del., numerous pvt. collections; works publ. in Artists of Mid-Atlantic, 1991; contbr. illustrations to mags., booklets. Recipient 1st prize Md. chpt. Artists' Equity, 1967, St. Marys County Art Assn., 1964, 67, 1st prize still life Cape May, N.J., 1969, Catonsville (Md.) Community Coll., 1969, Nat. League Am. Pen Women Exhibit at St. John's Coll., 1969, Best in Show York (Pa.) Art Assn. Gallery, 1972, 2d award Md. Inst. Alumni Founding Chpt., Balt., 1976, Best in Show Three Arts Club, Balt., 1978, Honorable Mention, Rehoboth Art League, Del., 1983, Purchase award Old Point Nat. Bank, Hampton, Va., 1985, Merit award Hampton (Va.) City Hall, 1986, Juror's Choice award Twentieth Century Gallery, Williamsburg, Va., 1987, Award of Excellence Md. State Biennial Eliminations of Nat. League Am. Pen Women at Essex Community Coll., 1989, Montgomery Coll., Rockville, Md., 1987, Honorable Mention award Nat. Miniature Show, Jackson, Tenn., 1991. Mem. Nat. League Am Pen Women (pres. Carroll br. 1968-70, editor The Quill 1975-76, editor for Carroll br. 1982-83, rec. sec. nat. exec. bd. 1979-80, nat. nominating com. 1982, Md. art chmn. 1982, 3d prize in oil at Nat. Biennial exhibit), Rehoboth Art League, Hampton Arts League, Va. Watercolor Soc. (signature artist mem.), Balt. Watercolor Sco. (signature artist life mem., hon mention 1992, sec. 1978-80), Peninsula Fine Arts Ctr., 20th Century Gallery, Hampton Arts League, Suffolk Art League. Methodist. Home: 2 Bayberry Dr Newport News VA 23601

CAMP, RUTH SUZANNE ADAMS, health care administrator, social worker; b. Wilmington, Del., June 15, 1937; d. William Hussey Jr. and Ruth (Fries) Adams; m. George Hayward Camp, III, July 25, 1959 (div. Mar. 1979); children: George Hayward IV, Christopher A., Stephen E., Daniel S. BA in Fine Arts, U. Del., 1959. Cert. tchr., employment counselor, Va.; lic. social worker, Va. Tchr. Am. Coop. Sch., Monrovia, Liberia, 1966-69; field supr. Starch Inra Hooper Rsch. Co., Mamaronac, N.Y., 1970-72; dir. advt. and sales Sta. WOHN, Herndon, Va., 1972-76; residential mgr. Door Systems, Inc., Lorton, Va., 1977-78; rsch. specialist human svcs. County of Loudoun, Leesburg, Va., 1978-80; dir. social svc. Heritage Hall Health Care, Leesburg, 1980-82; dir. resident svcs. Mt. Vernon Nursing ctr., Alexandria, Va., 1983-84; dir. vol. svcs. and chaplaincy Greater S.E. Healthcare System, Washington, 1984-89, dir. alt. resources, 1990-91; mgr. corp. program devel. S.E. Healthcare Systems, Washington, 1992—; presenter Am. Soc. Healthcare Human Resources, Am. Soc. Healthcare Edn. and Tng., Nat. Conf. on Literacy in the Workplace, 1990; trainer in field; convener, facilitator Nat. Vol. Conf., New Orleans, 1989; guest lectr. Am. U., Washington, 1988; cons., lectr. St. Vincent's Hosp., Worcester, Mass., 1989; keynote speaker Healthcare Inst. Vol. Banquet, Washington, 1991; mem. presenting panel Affiliated Group Leaders Ann. Meeting, Indpls., 1991. Artist, creator 32 artistic renderings and enhancements The Critter Collection, 1988—; contbr. articles and poetry to various publs. Coord. LINK, Loudoun and Fairfax Counties, 1975-82; chairperson steering com. Va. State Coun. for Transp. Disadvantaged, Richmond, 1978-79; mem. adv. com. Coun. Govts.-Transp. Planning Bd., Washington, 1979-80; mem. coun. Continuity of Care Coord. Coun., Washington, 1982-84; founding mem. No. Va. Social Workers Support Group, 1982-84; mem. vestry St. Matthew's Episcopal Ch., Sterling, Va., 1984-86; mem. Supt.'s Coun. on Bus. and Industry, Prince George's County, 1986—. Recipient Testimonial of Appreciation, Am. Hosp. Assn., Chgo., 1986, Nat. Program awards, 1987-89, 92, The Washington-Dix St. Acad. award D.C. Schs., 1986, Cert. of Honor, Head Start Program, 1990; winner Great Ideas Program, Am. Soc. Dirs. Vol. Svcs. of Am. Hosp. Assn., Chgo., 1990; Freedom grantee, 1988; nominee for Innovator of Yr., Soc. Health Care Planning and Mktg. of Am. Hosp. Assn., 1989. Mem. Am. Soc. Dirs. Vol. Svcs. (bd. dirs. 1992—, com. on legis. issues 1991, com. chair 1992—, mem. ednl. core faculty 1991, com. on mktg. & pub. rels. 1987, 88, 91, com. on publs. 1989), Assn. for Vol. Adminstrn. (com. on legis. and legal issues 1991, mem. internat. conv. faculty 1989, 91), Capital Area Hosp. Coun. (legis. chair 1988-91), Vol. Resources Coun. (sec. 1985, v.p. 1986, membership chair 1986-87, pub. info. com. 1987, legis. com. 1988), Am. Hosp. Assn., Soc. for Healthcare Planning and Mktg., Am. Soc. Healthcare Mktg. and Pub. Rels., Women in Broadcasting. Episcopalian. Home: 1003 S Greenthorn Ave Sterling VA 22170-5102 Office: Greater SE Community Hosp 1310 Southern Ave SE Washington DC 20032-4699

CAMPANA, ANA ISABEL, architect; b. Banes, Oriente, Cuba, Jan. 16, 1934; came to U.S., 1967, naturalized, 1974; d. Abelardo Joaquin and Amparo (Cabrera) C. BS, Instituto del Vedado, Havana, Cuba, 1953; postgrad., Havana U., 1962, Albany (N.Y.) Inst. History and Art, 1970. Registered architect, N.Y. With Ministry of Pub. Works Havana, 1962-67, architect designer various firms, 1967-74; sr. architect Gen. Electric Co., Schenectady, N.Y., 1974-89; architect LaBerge Group, Albany, 1989—. Recipient 1st nat. award Nat. Mus. Com., Havana, 1948, 1st Province award, 1948, several international archtl. performance awards. Mem. AIA. Roman Catholic. Home: 422 Sand Creek Rd Apt 506 Albany NY 12205-2725 Office: LaBerge Group 4 Computer Dr W Albany NY 12205-1607

CAMPANELLA, FRANCIS BARRY, management educator; b. Mass., June 6, 1936; s. Francis J. and Margaret (Foley) C.; children: Kathleen M., Patricia J., Maureen E. BS, Rensselaer Poly. Inst., 1958; MBA, Babson Coll., 1966; D Bus. Adminstrn., Harvard U., 1970; LHD (hon.), Le Moyne Coll., 1985. Sales engr., treas. Acoustical Contractors, Inc., Mass., 1961-66; asst. prof., assoc. prof. Sch. Mgmt., Boston Coll., Chestnut Hill, Mass., 1970-73, exec. v.p., 1973-91, prof., 1991—; mem. adv. bd. Inst. for Religious Edn. and Pastoral Ministry, 1976-91, Campus Sch. for Multi-Handicapped Children, 1977—, Algemene Bank Nederland, N.V., 1986-88, Edutech Internat., 1985—, Maguire Assocs., Inc., 1987—, Internat. Mktg. Inst., Chestnut Hill, 1990—; vis. prof. Ulster (No. Ireland) Bus. Sch., 1990—; mem, founder adv. bd. Devel. Entrepreneurs in Boston for Ireland, Chestnut Hill, 1988—; mem. com. on fin. and svcs. College Bd. Scholarship Svc. Coun., N.Y.C., 1987—. Lt. USMC, 1958-61. Office: Boston Coll Chestnut Hill MA 02167

CAMPANELLI, DAN, watercolor artist; b. Bronx, N.Y., Mar. 18, 1949; m. Pauline Eblé. Grad., Sch. Visual Arts, N.Y.C., 1969. Group exhbns. include El Paso Mus. Art, Albrecht Art Mus.-Mo. Mint Mus. Art., Charlotte, N.C., Newark Mus., others; represented in pub., corp. and pvt. collections: illustrator: Wheel of the Year, 1989, Ancient Ways, 1991; paintings featured in PBS TV State of the Art, 1984, various mags.; watercolors published by N.Y. Graphic Soc. publs.

CAMPANELLI, PAULINE EBLE, artist; b. N.Y.C., Jan. 25, 1943; d. Joseph and Dorothy Eble; m. Dan Campanelli, May 24, 1969. Grad., Ridgewood Sch. of Art, 1964; student, Art Students League, 1965-67. fine arts pub. N.Y. Graphic Soc. Represented in pub., corp. & pvt. collections throughout the U.S.; exhibited in groups shows including Am. Art Gallery, Greenwich, Conn., Temple U., Leaver House.; author: Wheel of the Year, 1989, Ancient Ways, 1991, Circles, Groves & Sanctuaries, 1992.

CAMPBELL, ALMA JACQUELINE PORTER, educator; b. Savannah, Ga., Jan. 5, 1948; d. William W. and Gladys B. Porter. BS in Elem. Edn., Savannah State Coll., 1969; MEd, SUNY, Brockport, 1971, cert. advanced study in adminstrn. magna cum laude, 1988. Cert. permanent elem. tchr., N.Y. Elem. tchr. Savannah, 1969-70, 71-74; tchr. intern project unique Rochester (N.Y.) City Sch. Dist., 1970-71, tchr., 1974-88, adminstrv. intern chpt. 1 office, 1988; basic skills cadre Francis Parker Sch., Rochester, 1988—, lead tchr. mentor, 1991—; lead tchr., mentor tchr., basic skills cadre John Walton Spencer Elem. Sch., 1992—; Distar demonstration tchr. Rochester City Sch. Dist., 1976-78, curriculum writer, 1987, 88, tchr. rsch. linker, demonstration tchr., 1987-88 active Effective Parenting Info. for Children program1987-89; active coop. tchr. program, Nazareth Coll. and Rochester City Sch. Dist., 1987; coord., presenter ednl. workshops. Author: (with McGriff) Quick Reference Manual for Teachers, 1989-90; co-author: A Quick Reference Manual for Teachers and Absolutely Jam-Packed With Super Teaching Tips, 1991-92. Mem. Martin Luther King Commn. on Edn., Rochester, 1988-89, Francis Parker Sch. PTA, 1988—; mental health asst. Curriculum Task Force, Rochester City Sch. Dist., 1991, coop. learning tchr., trainer, 1990, 91-92; asst. dir. Meml. A.M.E. Zion Ch., 1979-82, dir. summer camp, 1982-85, asst. sec. bd. Christian edn., 1987-89; bd. dirs. Hamm House, Jefferson Area Child Devel. Ctr., 1990-91. Mem. NAFE, Internat. Reading Assn., Assn. Curriculum and Supervision, Phi Delta Kappa, Alpha Kappa Alpha (chair nominating com. 1988-89, Ivy Leaf reporter 1992—, cert. achievement 1988). Democrat. Home: 40 Menlo Pl Rochester NY 14620-2718 Also: Meml AME Zion Ch Clarissa St Rochester NY 14604

CAMPBELL, BRUCE HENRY, chemist; b. Madison, S.D., Oct. 27, 1940; s. Frank Leonard and Orville Estelle (Fulwider) C.; m. Karen Kay Tosch, May 12, 1963; children: Byron, Brandon, Bryson, Karissa. BS, U. Kans., 1962; MA, U. S.D., 1964; PhD, U. Tex., 1967. Asst. prof., then assoc. prof. U. So. Miss., Hattiesburg, 1967-72; postdoctoral fellow Clarkson Coll. Tech., Potsdam, N.Y., 1972-74; rsch. chemist J. T. Baker Chem. Co., Phillipsburg, N.J., 1984-91, Am. Cyanamid, Stamford, Conn., 1981—; mem. food chems. codex com. NAS/Nat. Acad. Medicine, Washington, 1977-82. Editor, contbr.: Organic Electrochemistry, 1974; contbr. articles to profl. jours.; editor jour. Critical Revs. in Analytical Chemistry, 1972-83. Mem. Am. Chem. Soc. (chmn. Lehigh Valley sect. 1980, chmn. Western Conn. sect. 1991), Mensa, Masons (officer 1970-72). Home: 445 W El Norte Pky Apt 108 Escondido CA 92026-1984 Office: Am Cyanamid 1937 W Main St Stamford CT 06902-4580

CAMPBELL, CATHERINE JEANNE, newspaper publishing executive; b. Lynchburg, Va., May 20, 1958; d. John Robley and Susie (Clarke) C. BA with honors, U. N.C., 1980; MBA, U. Va., 1984. Dist. mgr. circulation Durham (N.C.) Morning Herald Co., 1980-81, asst. city mgr. circulation, 1981-82; mktg. rsch. intern Harte-Hanks Communications, Anderson, S.C., 1983; mgmt. intern Washington Post, Washington, 1984-85, asst. to pub., 1985-86, zone mgr. circulation, 1986-90, VA single copy mgr., 1990—. Mem. Interstate Circulation Mgrs. Assn., U. N.C. Alumni Ass., Quar. Club Am., Potomac Exec. Network, Alpha Pi Omega. Democrat. Episcopal.

CAMPBELL, DAVID GEORGE, ecologist; b. Decatur, Ill., Jan. 28, 1949; s. George Robert and Jean Blossom (Weilepp) C.; m. Karen S. Lowell; 1 child, Tatiana Claire. BA, Kalamazoo Coll., 1971; MS, U. Mich., 1973; PhD, Johns Hopkins U., 1984. Exec. dir. Bahamas Nat. Trust, Nassau, 1974-77; ecologist N.Y. Bot. Garden, Bronx, 1984-88, leader Amazon Expdns., 1974-92, research fellow, 1989—; Henry R. Luce prof. in Nations and the Global Environment Grinnell (Iowa) Coll., 1991—; cons. Internat. Union for Conservation of Nature, 1978-79; biologist and lectr. M.V. World Discoverer in Amazon and Antarctic, 1981-87; biologist Brazilian Antarctic Expdn., 1987-88. Author: The Ephemeral Islands, 1978, The Crystal Desert, 1992; editor: Floristic Inventory of Tropical Countries, 1989; contbr. articles to profl. jours. Fellow John Simon Guggenheim Found., 1989-90; recipient Fulling award Soc. Econ. Botany, 1987, Houghton Mifflin Lit. Fellowship, 1992. Fellow Linnean Soc. London. Home: 4069 Coquina Dr Sanibel FL 33957-5205 Office: Grinnell Coll Dept Biology Grinnell IA 50112

CAMPBELL, DAVID NORBERT, education educator; b. Chgo., Apr. 16, 1932; s. Walter and Veronica (Janke) C.; m. Karen Irene Shuster, Mar. 6, 1982. BEd, Southeastern La. U., 1958; MS, U. Ill., 1959, PhD, 1970. Tchr. Blue Island (Ills.) High Sch., 1959-61, Markham (Ill.) Sch. Dist., 1961-65, Am. Sch., London, 1967-69, Astronaut High Sch., Titusville, Fla., 1987-89; prof. U. Pitts., 1970-81; headmaster Campbell Acad., Tampa, Fla., 1981-86; prof. edn., chmn. dept. ednl. studies California U. Pa., 1989—; adj. prof. Brevard Community Coll., Titusville, 1987-89; dir. Sch. of the Future, Munhall, Pa., 1989—; cons. in field. Author: Practical Guide to Open Classroom, 1973, On the Sixth Day, 1977; contbr. articles to profl. jours. With U.S. Army, 1953-55. Grantee Pa. Acad. Found., 1990-91. Mem. ACLU, Am. Tchrs. Edn., Pa. Tchrs. Edn., Pa. Edn. Assn. (exec. bd. 1990-91), Assn. Middle Schs., Greenpeace, Kappa Delta Pi. Home: 153 Quarry Ln California PA 15419-1226 Office: Calif U Pa 75 Keystone Blvd California PA 15419

CAMPBELL, E. E., publishing executive; b. Calgary, Alta., Can., Jan. 22, 1949; s. Daniel Eldon Campbell and Mae Lorraine (Studer) Stewart; m. Joyce Alita (Dudar), Feb. 13, 1954; children: Tracy Anne, Bruce Alfred Eldon, Lisa Lorraine. BSc., U. B.C., Vancouver, Can., 1952. Tech. sales rep. Naugatuck Chem., Elmira, Ont., Can., 1958; coll. sales rep. Prentice-Hall Inc. (name now Prentice-Hall Can. Inc.), B.C., 1959-60; sales supr. Prentice-Hall Can. Inc., Toronto, Ont., 1960-62; dist. sales mgr. Prentice-Hall Can. Inc., Scarborough, Ont., 1963-66, sales mgr., 1967-75, v.p. sales, 1976-81, exec. v.p., 1982—, also bd. dirs., 1982—. Active Scarborough Civic Award Com., 1979-89. Lt. Army, 1953-57. Mem. Can. Profl. Sales Assn. (life), Royal Can. Legion, Scarborough East Fed. P.C. Assn. (v.p. 1989—, pres. 1979-83), Scarborough East Provincial P.C. Assn., Sales Rsch. Club Toronto (pres. 1986-87), Scarborough Rotary (pres. 1990-91, bd. dirs. 1986—, Paul Harris fellow 1991), Masons (Master 1978). Office: Prentice-Hall of Can Inc, 1870 Birchmount Rd, Scarborough, ON Canada M1P 2J7

CAMPBELL, EDWARD CLINTON, violin maker; b. Scranton, Pa., May 24, 1929; s. Raymond Pyne and Mercedes Ruth (Simmons) C.; m. Mary Ringwald Dunfee, Sept. 1, 1954. BS in Engring., Pa. State U., 1955. Supr. order sect. Square D Electric Co., Inc., Detroit, 1955-59; propr., master violin maker Chimneys Violin Shop, Boiling Springs, Pa., 1960; operator Chimneys Sch. Violin Making; lectr. various colls.; luthier in residence Internat. String Conf., Pa. State U. String Conf., N.J. chpt. Am. String Tchrs. Assn., Nat. Sch. Orch. Assn. Co-author: The Chimneys Violin Maker's Workshop-Book I, Book II, Book III; contbr. articles to Viol mag., Violin Soc. Am. Jour. Pres. bd. dirs., fundraiser Amelia S. Givin Libr., Mt. Holly Springs, Pa., 1980-89. With USN, 1946-50. Recipient Grand Prize (14), Gold medal (3), Cert. of Merit (11), Internat. Violin Makers Competition; violins made by Edward Campbell exhibited at Renwick Gallery, Smithsonian Instn., 1978-79 and Oberlin Mus., Oberlin U., Ohio, 1987-88. Mem. Violin Soc. Am. (bd. dirs. 1976—, sec., chmn., host 15th ann. conv., coord. activities with 1st World String Quartet Congress 1989, 1st Am. Violin Congress 1987, coord. activities with 1st World Cello Congress 1988, host 20th Ann. Conv. and 10th Internat. Competition 1992), Am. String Tchrs. Assn. (luthier in residence string conf.), So. Calif. Violin Makers Assn. (charter), Catgut Acoustical Soc. (prin. speaker 1992 conv.), Pa. String Tchrs. Assn., Boiling Spring Allenberry Club (pres. 1989), Lions (pres. Mt. Holly). Republican. Methodist.

CAMPBELL, EDWARD IRVING, learning resources director/educator; b. N.Y.C., July 6, 1942; s. Joseph Albert and Margaret (White) C. BA, SUNY, New Paltz, 1964; MSLA, Pratt Inst., 1967; MSA, George Washington U., 1972. Audio-visual libr. U.S. Mil. Acad., West Point, N.Y., 1964-67; post libr. Ft. Gulick, Canal Zone, Panama, 1967-69; brigade libr. USNA,

Annapolis, Md., 1969-72; dir. learning resource ctr. Frederick (Md.) Community Coll., 1972—. Author: (fiction) Outrage in Annapolis, 1980; contbr. articles to profl. jours.; columnist. Pres. Big Bros./Sisters, Frederick, 1977-82, Fredericktowne Players, Frederick, 1973-75, Candlelight Concerts Soc., Frederick, 1976; judge Tax Assessment Appeals Bd., Frederick, 1983—; fundraiser YMCA, Frederick, 1977; bd. dirs. Fine Arts Coun., Frederick; arbitrator Better Bus. Bur., Balt., 1988—; tutor coll. English Frederick County Detention Ctr., 1983-85; coun. mem. St. John's Cath. Ch., Frederick, 1985—; EMT Frederick Fire Dept., ARC Emergency Assn.; tutor Frederick Literacy Coun., 1982—. Named Outstanding Vol., State Legis., Md., 1983. Mem. Frederick Meml. Hosp. Aux., Lions. Republican. Roman Catholic. Home: 107 W 14th St Frederick MD 21701-4415 Office: Frederick Community Coll 7932 Opossumtown Pike Frederick MD 21702-2097

CAMPBELL, ELIZABETH PFOHL, association executive; b. Winston-Salem, Dec. 4, 1902; d. John Kenneth and Bessie (Whittington) Pfohl; m. Edmund Douglas Campbell, June 16, 1936; children: Edmund Douglas Jr., Virginia Campbell Holt, Bejamin P., H. Donald. AB cum laude, Salem Coll., 1923, DHL (hon.), 1991; MA, Columbia U., 1924; postgrad., U. Pa., 1929, U. Mich., 1931; DHL (hon.), Washington and Lee U., 1989, Mary Baldwin Coll., 1990, Salem Coll., 1991. Dean of women Moravian Coll. for Women, Bethlehem, Pa., 1928-29; dean Mary Baldwin Coll., Staunton, Va., 1929-36; pres. The Greater Washington Ednl. Telecommunications Assn., Inc., 1957-71, v.p. community affairs, 1971—. Mem. Com. of 100 United Ch. Women, 1962—; bd. dirs. Arlington YMCA, 1965-78; regional chmn. Va. Mental Retardation Planning Coun., 1966-69; bd. trustees YWCA, 1966-70, Salem Coll., Winston-Salem, 1969-73; 1st vice chair Nat. Friends of Pub. Broadcasting, 1970-75; adv. bd. Consortium for Higher Edn. in No. Va., 1973-78, Asia Soc., 1979-83; bd. dirs. Arlington Community TV, 1982-90; mem. Nat. Citizens Com. for Pub. TV; founder, past pres. Dem. Club No. Va. Recipient Centennial Medallion for dedicated nat. svc. DAR, 1991, Esther Van Wagoner Tufty award Washington Leadership in Community Svc. Excellence in Communication, Am. Women in Radio and TV, 1990, First Community Voice and Vision award Arlington Community TV, 1990, Commendation Gen. Assembly Legislators, 1989, Disting. Alumnae award Salem Acad., 1988, The Washington Woman, Lifetime Achievement award 1987, Silver Circle award Nat Acad. TV Arts and Scis., 1986, Bd. Govs. award (Emmy), 1981, Valiant Woman award Coun. of Ch. Women Arlington. Mem. AAUW, Acad. TV Arts and Scis., Am. Women in Radio and TV, Nat. Assn. Ednl. Broadcasters, Nat. Friends of Pub. Broadcasting, Quota Club (hon. mem.), 20th Century Club (Washington), Women's Nat. Dem. Club, League Women Voters, Delta Kappa Gamma. Office: WETA TV/26 FM/91 PO Box 2626 Washington DC 20013-2626

CAMPBELL, JAMES PHILLIP, minister; b. Middletown, Ohio, July 8, 1961; s. James Philip and Virginia Ann (Jenia) C. BA, Taylor U., 1984; MDiv, Ashland (Ohio) Theol. Sem., 1988; postgrad., Am. Inst., 1988, Drew U., 1991. Am. overseas program coord. youth for understanding Internat. Student Exch., Indpls., 1984-85; youth minister Christ United Meth. Ch., Ashland, 1985-86; edn. worker Attica (Ohio) Cir. United Meth. Chs., 1986-87; assoc. minister Ridgewood United Meth. Ch., Parma, Ohio, 1987—; bd. dirs. West Side Ecumenical Ministry, Cleve. Author poetry. Vol. Cleve. Coun. on World Affairs, 1988—, Internat. Student Host Family Program, Cleve., 1989—, Nat Improvisational Theater, N.Y.C.; ch. and sch. liaison Parma (Ohio) Community Schs., 1987—. Republican. Methodist. Home: 548 Farview Ave Wyckoff NJ 07481-1140

CAMPBELL, JOHN ELLIOT, real estate executive; b. Greenwich, Conn., Apr. 17, 1959; s. Ralph Page and Mary Helen (Emerson) C. BA, Boston Coll., 1981, MBA, 1988. Paralegal Reimer & Braunstein, 1982-83; asst. v.p. Shawmut Bank N.A., 1983-88; v.p. The Wellesley Cos., 1988-89; investment officer John Hancock Properties, Inc., Boston, 1989—; prin. Riverside Cos., Watertown, Mass., 1989—. Home: 8R Riverside St #2-2 Watertown MA 02172 Office: Hancock Realty Investors 200 Berkeley St 19th Fl Boston MA 02117

CAMPBELL, (JAMES) LAWRENCE, editor, educator, artist; b. Paris, May 21, 1914; came to U.S., 1914; s. James Lawrence II and Alice (Ormond) C.; m. Joan Malkenson (div. 1958); children: Richard Elihu, James Lawrence IV; m. Audrey Holzman; children: Ian Burwell Ruskin Campbell, Sarah Alice Ormond Campbell. Diploma, Academie de la Grande Chaumiere, Paris, 1938; diploma, London Cen. Sch. Arts/Crafts, 1935; student, Art Students League of N.Y., 1946-50. Editor William Collins Pubs., Glasgow and London, Eng., 1932-35; with Foyles Books shop, London, 1935-36; freelance translator Paris, 1937-39; editor, publs. Art Students League of N.Y., 1950—; prof. art dept. Bklyn. Coll., 1960-84, prof. emeritus, 1984—; vis. assoc. prof. art history Pratt Inst., N.Y.C., 1967—; editorial assoc. Art News mag., 1950-76; freelance art critic and writer, 1950—. One-man shows include N.Y.C. Contemporary Arts, 1952, Tanager Gallery, 1959, Kornblee Gallery, 1969, Green Mountain Gallery, 1976; prin. works include Mus. Modern Art Lending Svcs., Hirschhorn Mus., 1960's, also others; contbr. articles to Art in Am. and Arts mags.; author: (booklets) Chris, 1955, Thomas Sills, 1967, numerous others. With U.S. Army, 1941-45, Middle East. Mem. Internat. Assn. Art Critics, Modern Painters and Sculptors, Art Students League of N.Y., Elizabethans (alumni Westminster Sch., London), Am. Assn. U. Profs. Democrat. Home: Apt 5A 215 W 98th St New York NY 10025 Office: Art Students League of NY 215 W 57th St New York NY 10019-2193

CAMPBELL, LEVIN HICKS, federal judge; b. Summit, N.J., Jan. 2, 1927; s. Worthington and Louise (Hooper) C.; m. Eleanor Saltonstall Lewis, June 1, 1957; children: Eleanor S., Levin H., Sarah H. A.B. cum laude, Harvard U., 1948, LL.B., 1951; postgrad., Nat. Coll. State Judiciary, 1970; LL.D. (hon.), Suffolk U., 1975. Bar: D.C. 1951, Mass. 1954. Assoc. firm Ropes & Gray, Boston, 1954-64; mem. Mass. Ho. of Reps., 1963-64; asst. atty. gen. State of Mass., 1965-66, spl. asst. atty. gen., 1966-67, 1st asst. atty. gen., 1967-68; assoc. justice Superior Ct. of Mass., 1969-72; judge U.S. Dist. Ct. Mass., Boston, 1972; judge U.S. Ct. Appeals (1st cir.), Boston, 1972—, chief judge, 1983-90; fellow Inst. of Politics J.F. Kennedy Sch. Govt. Harvard U., 1968-69, study group leader 1980; faculty chmn. law session Salzburg Seminar in Am. Studies, 1981. Pres. Cambridge 9 Neighborhood Assn., 1960-62; treas. Cambridge Ctr. for Adult Edn., 1961-64; campaign chmn. Cambridge United Fund, 1965; mem. bd. overseers Boston Symphony Orch., 1969-75, 77-80; pres. bd. overseers Shady Hill Sch., 1969-70; mem. vis. com. Harvard U. Press, 1958-64; v.p. Cambridge Community Svcs.; corp. mem. SEA Ednl. Assn., 1982—; trustee Colby Coll., Waterville, Maine 1981-90, 91—, Asheville (N.C.) Sch.; mem. Nat. Commn. Jud. Discipline and Removal, 1991—, Long Range Planning Commn., 1991—. 1st lt. JAGC, U.S. Army, 1951-54, Korea. Mem. ABA, Am. Law Inst., Am. Bar Found., Mass. Bar Assn., Boston Bar Assn., U.S. Jud. Conf. (ct. adminstrn. com. 1975-83, chmn. subcom. on supporting pers. 1980-83, exec. com. 1985-90, chmn. com. to rev. cir. coun. conduct and disability orders 1990—, nat. commn. on jud. discipline and removal 1990, jud. conf. com. on long range planning 1990), Salzburg Seminar Alumni Assn. (bd. dirs. 1983—). Office: US Ct Appeals PO & Courthouse 1618 John W McCormack Boston MA 02109

CAMPBELL, MICHAEL JOSEPH, association executive; b. Ft. Hood, Tex., Nov. 19, 1964; s. Walter J. and Barbara R. (Shea) C.; m. Diana M. Salsgiver, Nov. 26, 1988. BA in Philosophy and Polit. Sci., Gannon U., 1986; M Internat. Affairs, U. Pitts., 1989. Legis. asst. Mfrs. Assn. Northwestern Pa., Erie, 1985-86; asst. to dir. Blue Cross Western Pa., Pitts., 1986-87; mgr. internat. div. Greater Pitts. C. of C., 1987-88; founder, dir. Greater Pitts. World Trade Assn., 1988-90; mng. dir. pub. affairs program devel. Pa. Tech. Coun., Pitts., 1990—; exec. dir., bd. dirs. Am.-Israeli C. of C., Pitts.; dir. internat. env. environment program U. Pitts.; mem. internat. mgmt. adv. bd. Duquesne U. Mem. Phi Sigma Tau (v.p. 1985-86). Roman Catholic. Office: Pa Tech Coun 4516 Henry St Pittsburgh PA 15213-3730

CAMPBELL, NANCY EDINGER, nuclear engineer; b. Washington, May 9, 1957; d. Ralph Joseph and Eleanor (Brabble) Edinger; m. Larry Alan Campbell, Feb. 25, 1984. BS in Nuclear Engring. with honors, Ga. Inst. of Tech., 1978; MBA, U. Pitts., 1985. Nuclear safety engr. Westinghouse Nuclear Tech. Div., Monroeville, Pa., 1978-81; nuclear fuel proposal engr. Westinghouse Nuclear Fuel Div., Monroeville, 1981-86; nuclear fuel project engr. Westinghouse Comml. Nuclear Fuel Div., Monroeville, 1986-90; reactor engr. U.S. Nuclear Regulatory Commn., Washington, 1990—; chmn. hospitality, rep. nuclear fuel div. Westinghouse Women's Career Devel. Com., Pitts., 1985-87. Assoc. advisor Westinghouse Explorer Post 258, Monroeville, 1980-81. Mem. Am. Nuclear Soc., Soc. Women Engrs., Nat. Trust Hist. Preservation, Engring. Soc. Balt., Phi Kappa Phi, Tau Beta Pi, Phi Eta Sigma. Episcopalian. Office: US Nuclear Regulatory Commn Washington DC 20555

CAMPBELL, PATRICIA FORSYTHE, mathematics educator; b. Joliet, Ill., Nov. 29, 1948; d. Donald J. and Magdalene (Long) Forsythe; m. Gregory Campbell, Aug. 18, 1973; children: David, Sarah. BS, Coll. St. Francis, Joliet, Ill., 1970; MS, Mich. State U., 1972; PhD, Fla. State U., 1976. Instr. Lakeland Community Coll., Mentor, Ohio, 1972-73; vis. asst. prof. Purdue U., West Lafayette, Ind., 1976-80, coord. advising in computer sci., 1979-82; asst. prof. U. Md., College Park, 1982-87, assoc. prof., 1987—, dir. Ctr. Math. Edn., 1985-90; dir. Project Impact, NSF, College Park, 1989—. Editor: Young Children and Microcomputers, 1986; contbr. articles to profl. jours., chpts. to books. Mem. Nat. Coun. Tchrs. Math. (chair rsch. adv. com. 1990-92), Am. Ednl. Rsch. Assn., Psychology Math. Edn. Office: U Md Benjamin Bldg College Park MD 20742-1175

CAMPBELL, RAYMOND MCKINLY, psychologist, educator, consultant, researcher; b. Detroit, Feb. 26, 1942; s. Raymond McKinly and Norma Elizabeth (Mitchell) C.; m. Eleanor Joan Coleman, Mar. 15, 1962 (dec. 1985); m. Linda Steward, Dec. 31, 1989; children: Elizabeth Syrkett, Debra Morgan, Cheryl Campbell, Catherine Williams. BS, Wayne State U., 1966, MEd, 1967; PhD, U. Mich., 1974, MPH, 1975. Lic. psychologist, Mich. Spl. edn. tchr., counselor Highland Park (Mich.) Pub. Schs., 1966-70; cons. supr. Macomb County Intermediate Sch. Dist., Mt. Clemens, Mich., 1970-75; asst. dir. spl. edn. Dallas Ind. Sch. Dist., 1976-79; expert in planning and adminstrn. UN, N.Y.C., 1979-86; sr. rsch. fellow dept. substance abuse svcs. Office of Narcotics and Drug Rsch., Inc., N.Y.C., 1986-88; clin. supr. Bowery Residence Com. Promesca, Inc., Bronx, N.Y., 1988-90; organizational cons. N.Y. Chem. Abuse Tng. Svc.-Brite Futures, Bklyn., 1987—; assoc. prof. SUNY, Bklyn., 1990-91; psychotherapist Blueberry Treatment Ctr./New Hope Guild, Bklyn., 1990-92; cons. Promesca, Inc., 1989-90, Vis. Nurses Svcs., N.Y.C., 1992—, Minority Task Force on AIDS, N.Y.C., 1991-92; mem. Martin Deporres Community Bd., Astoria, Queens, N.Y., 1992—. Mem. 100 Black Men In., N.Y.C., Dallas, 1979, 87. Fellow Am. Orthopsychiatric Assn.; mem. APA, Alpha Phi Alpha (v.p. 1984). Baptist.

CAMPBELL, REBECCA RENNO, college official, career counselor; b. Monogahela, Pa., Dec. 11, 1947; d. Victor Raymond and Vernice Ellen (Sharp) Renno; m. William Terry Campbell, Aug. 16, 1969; children: Marc Daren, Jay Scott. BA, Thiel Coll., 1969; MS in Edn., Duquesne U., 1990. Elem. tchr. various schs., Md., Pa., 1969-74; owner Blossoms by Becky, Greensburg, Pa., 1974—; dir. career devel., coop. edn. Seton Hill Coll., Greensburg, 1985—. Founder Women's Svcs. of Westmoreland County, Inc., Greensburg, 1974. Mem. Coop. Edn. Assn. Pa., Pa. Coll. Career Svcs. Assn. (v.p. 1992-93), Western Pa. Coll. Career Svcs. Assn. (pres., gen. chmn. 1990-91, past pres. 1991-92), Mid-Atlantic Placement Assn. Republican. Lutheran. Office: Seton Hill Coll Seton Hill Dr Greensburg PA 15601-1599

CAMPBELL, ROBERT H., oil company executive; b. Pitts., June 11, 1937; children--R. Douglas, Heather; m. Nancy Wertz, Feb. 27, 1976. B in ChemE, Princeton U., 1959; M in ChemE, Carnegie Mellon U., 1961; M in Mgmt., MIT, 1978. Various engring. positions Sun Co., Phila., 1960-75; mgr. refinery ops. Sun Co., Corpus Christi, Tex., 1975-77; v.p. human resources Sun Ship, Inc., Chester, Pa., 1978-80, pres., 1980; pres. Sun Refining and Mktg. Co., Phila., 1983—; exec. v.p. Sun Co. Inc., Radnor, Pa., 1988-91, pres., chief exec. officer, chief oper. officer, 1991—; bd. dirs. The Phila. Nat. Bank, Elwyn Insts. Apptd. mem. by Dep. Sec. of Energy W. Henson Moore to Alternative Fuels Coun., 1990. Mem. Am. Petroleum Inst. (bd. dirs. 1988). Republican. Office: Sun Co Inc Ten Penn Center 1801 Market St Philadelphia PA 19103*

CAMPBELL, ROSEMARY GARST, economic researcher; b. Coon Rapids, Iowa, Mar. 31, 1917; d. Goodwin and Lovena (Kline) Garst; m. Colin D. Campbell, June 18, 1949; children: William G., Janet A. BS, Iowa State U., 1938; MA, U. Chgo., 1947; postgrad. U. Wis., Iowa State U. Instr. econs. Iowa State U., 1948-51; freelance econ. researcher, 1951—. Mem. Am. Econ. Assn. Co-author: Money, Banking and Monetary Policy, 1987, The Fiscal Systems of New Hampshire and Vermont, An Update: 1975-87, 1989.

CAMPBELL, THOMAS JUSTIN, investment banker; b. Boston, Jan. 20, 1959; s. Nicholas Joshua and Margaret Ellen (Follmer) C.; m. Christina Bennett, Nov. 11, 1988. BS in Acctg./Fin., Lehigh U., Bethlehem, Pa., 1980. CPA, Conn. Tax mgr. Coopers & Lybrand; acquisition fin. Manufacturers Hanover; v.p. merchant banking Wasserstein Perella, N.Y.C.; bd. dirs. Maybelline Inc., Yardley of London, Wickes, Newgateway. Mem. AICPA's, Winged Foot Golf Club, Westchester Country Club. Roman Catholic.

CAMPBELL, THOMAS LOUIS, college administrator; b. Bethlehem, Pa., Feb. 27, 1959; s. Robert Kenneth and Alvina Louise (Oblinger) C.; m. Carla Beth Himelman, Nov. 17, 1985; children: Stephen Michael, Robert Maxwell. BSBA, U. Del., 1981, MS in Edn., 1987; MBA in Fin., Wilkes U., 1990. Sales rep. Josten's Inc., Allentown, Pa., 1981-82; sales and ops. mgr. AT&T, Jacksonville, Fla., 1982-88; devel. officer Allentown Coll. of St. Francis de Sales, Center Valley, Pa., 1988—. Team mgr. United Way, Allentown, 1988—; bd. dirs. Big Bros./Big Sisters, Jacksonville, 1985-88, Allentown, 1990—; chmn. fundraising com. St. Thomas More Sch. Mem. Allentown C. of C., Upper Bucks C. of C. (250th anniv. Bethlehem, edn. sub-com.), Rotary. Republican. Roman Catholic.

CAMPBELL, THOMAS RICHARDSON BROWN, banker; b. Albany, N.Y., Sept. 3, 1938; s. Eldridge H. and Eleanor Albert (Brown) C.; m. Barbara Hunt, May 19, 1962; children: Thomas, John, Elizabeth. BA, Princeton U., 1961. Trainee Brown Bros. Harriman and Co., N.Y.C., 1962-63, portfolio mgr., 1963-64, asst. dept. head instit. investment, 1964-73, mgr. asst. dept. head, 1973-78, mgr. dept. head, 1978-81, sr. mgr., 1982-89, sr. mgr. pvt. banking mktg., 1990—; bd. dirs. Nordic Union Reins., N.Y.C., Vesta Am. Ins., N.Y.C., Brown Bros. Harriman Trust Co., N.Y.C. Trustee, treas. Boy's Club; bd. govs., v.p. India House. Mem. Ausable Club, Ivy Club, Anglers Club. Office: Brown Bros Harriman and Co 59 Wall St New York NY 10005-2818

CAMPBELL, WILLIAM I., cigarette company executive; b. 1944. BA, U. Alta., 1965; MBA, U. Western Ont., 1967. With Benson & Hedges, Inc., 1967-74, v.p., 1974-77; exec. v.p. Philip Morris Asia/Can., N.Y.C., 1978-80, pres., 1980-83; exec. v.p Philip Morris USA, N.Y.C., 1983-89; sr. v.p. corp. planning Philip Morris Cos., Inc., N.Y.C., 1989-90, pres., CEO, 1990—, also bd. dirs. Office: Philip Morris Cos Inc 120 Park Ave New York NY 10017-5523*

CAMPEAU, JEAN, financial executive; b. Montréal, Qué., Can., July 6, 1931; m. Réjeanne Rouleau; 3 children. BA, St.-Ignace and Ste.-Marie Coll., 1952; license, École des Hautes Études Commerciales, 1955. Investment broker, 1955-63, mfg. co. exec., 1963-71; head debt mgmt. Dept. Fin., Qué., 1971, asst. dep. minister, 1977-80; chmn., gen. mgr. Caisse de dépôt et placement du Qué., Montréal, 1980-90; chmn. bd. dirs. Domtar, Inc., Montréal, 1990—. Office: Domtar Inc, 395 Blvd de Maisonneuve, Montreal, PQ Canada H3A 1L6

CAMPENNI, THOMAS F(ELIX), real estate executive; b. N.Y.C., June 14, 1953; s. Anthony D. and Hesper G. (Tyndall) C.; BA, Fordham U., 1975; cert. property mgmt., N.Y.U., 1977; m. Debra Lee Pena, June 9, 1973; children: Cara Marie, Thomas Louis. Exec. v.p., sec. Barhite & Holzinger, Inc., N.Y.C., 1974-82; pres., mng. dir. Italma Constrn. Corp., Flushing N.Y., 1978-81; sec.-treas. Deluxe Buttonhole Embroidery Co. Inc., N.Y.C., 1979-81; owner, operator Thomas F. Campenni & Co., Dee Lee Painting Co., 1978-82; pres., chmn. bd. Barhite & Holzinger, Inc., 1982-89; chief exec. officer Robert Thomas Co., 1989-92, pres. 1990-92; pres. Campwill Petroleum Corp, Ft. Lauderdale, Fla., Am-Camp Petroleum, 1991—; instr. Queensboro Coll., 1989—, NYU. Contbr. Real Estate Weekly, 1987—. Mem. N.Y. Bd. Realtors, Inst. Real Estate Mgmt. (Campaign mgr., 1978) Westchester Bd. Realtors; bd. dirs. Exodus House. Clubs: Lions (club Lion of Yr. 1977), Sons of Italy, 35th Assembly Dist. Democratic (life), Associated Builders and Owners of N.Y. Home: 2708 NE 29th St Fort Lauderdale FL 33306 Office: 21 W 46th St New York NY 10036-4119

CAMPION, CAROL-MAE SACK, librarian; b. Atlantic City, Apr. 8, 1950; d. Herman Forman and Frances Olivia (Trebing) Sack; m. Thomas E. Campion, June 29, 1974; children: Jesse, Christopher. BA, Georgetown U., 1972; MLS, Rutgers U., 1973; MA, U. Scranton, 1981. Cert. sch. libr., Pa., media specialist, N.J. Head libr. Lackawanna Jr. Coll., Scranton, Pa., 1977—. Office: Lackawanna Jr Coll 901 Prospect Ave Scranton PA 18505-1870

CAMPMAN, CHRISTOPHER KULLER, consulting company executive; b. Bryn Mawr, Pa., May 25, 1949; s. Curtis Oscar Campman and Agnes R. (Kuller) Baberick; m. Sarah Ann Gladish, July 15, 1972; 1 child, Kurt Christopher. AS in Bus. Administrn., Montgomery County Community Coll., 1987. Asst. dir. solid waste Montgomery County, Norristown, Pa., 1970-84; owner, pres. C.K. Campman, Inc., Cons., Lansdale, Pa., 1984—; pres. Campman/Williams Assocs., Inc., Oley, Pa., 1989—. Bd. dirs. park and recreation adv. bd. Upper Gwynedd Twp., Pa., 1986—. Mem. Am. Pub. Works Assn. (assoc.), Nat. Solid Waste Mgmt. Assn., Montgomery County Pub. Works Assn. (sec. 1978—). Republican. Lutheran. Home: 934 Patriot Dr Lansdale PA 19446-5529 Office: Campman/Williams Assocs Inc Bertolet Mill Rd RR2 PO Box 64C Oley PA 19547-0064

CAMPOLONGO, JAMES MICHAEL, public relations executive; b. Phila., Sept. 29, 1962; s. Attilio and Rose (Mairoto) C.; m. Debra Elaine McCarroll, Nov. 21, 1987. BA, U. Pitts., 1984. Community relations rep. U.S. Senator John Heinz, Pitts., 1983-84; spl. asst. U.S. Senator John Heinz, Washington, 1985; adminstrv. asst. Commr. Barbara Hafer, Pitts., 1985-86; campaign mgr. Buckman for Congress, Pitts., 1986; pub. affairs mgr. Pa. Mfrs. Assn., Phila., 1987—; cons. Small Bus. Assn. Delaware Valley, Phila., 1988—; speech writer for govt. officeholders and polit. candidates. Contbr. articles to profl. jours. Committeeman Republican Party Allegheny County, Pa., 1985-86. Mem. Pub. Relations Soc. am., Vesper Club. Roman Catholic. Home: 217 Roesch Ave Oreland PA 19075-1709 Office: Pa Mfrs Assn 925 Chestnut St Philadelphia PA 19107-4212

CAMPOS, MICHAEL JOHN, secondary education educator, martial arts teacher; b. N.Y.C., Feb. 22, 1944; s. Anna Rose (Javarone) Elliott; m. Anne Crown Steltmann, June 28, 1974; 1 child, Amy. AA, Fulton-Montgomery Community, 1966; BA, Albany State U., 1968; MEd, Ohio U., 1972. Tchr. Fonda (N.Y.)-Fultonville Cen. Sch., 1968—; dir. Zen-Do Kai Martial Arts Assn., Johnstown, N.Y., 1969—; adminstrv. dir. Def. Systems Internat., 1983—. Author: Women's Guide to Self-Defense, 1978. Fund raiser St. Jude Children's Rsch. Hosp., Memphis, 1988-92. With U.S. Army, 1961-64. Named TV 10 winner WTEN, Albany, 1986; named to Hall of Fame, World Martial Arts Assn., 1990. Mem. World Kempo Karate Assn. (sr. mem., 8th degree black belt). Office: Zen-Do Kai PO Box 186 Johnstown NY 12095

CANAVAN, BERNARD, pharmaceutical company executive, physician; b. Valleyfield, Fife, Scotland, 1936; s. Thomas and Helen (Toner) C.; m. Margaret Reid, Dec. 26, 1957; 1 child, Helen. B in Medicine, BChir, Univ. Edinburgh, Scotland, 1960. Licentiate Med. Council Can. Intern St. Joseph's Hosp., London, Ont., Can., 1960-61; general practice medicine Toronto, Ont., Can., 1961-69; med. dir. Wyeth Ltd. Can., Toronto, 1969-70, pres., 1970-75; exec. asst. to pres. Wyeth Internat. Ltd., Phila., 1975, group v.p., 1975-78, exec. v.p., 1978-80, pres., 1980-84; pres. Wyeth Labs., Phila., 1984-87; chmn. Wyeth-Ayerst Labs., Phila., 1987-90; exec. v.p. Am. Home Products Corp., N.Y.C., 1987-90; pres. Am. Home Products, N.Y.C., 1990—. Trustee Sch. Nursing U. Pa.; bd. dirs. Bryn Mawr Hosp. Roman Catholic. Club: Phila. Country. Office: Am Home Products Corp 685 3rd Ave New York NY 10017*

CANAVAN, JOHN JAMES, JR., temporary employment services executive; b. Weymouth, Mass., May 24, 1933; s. John James and Doris Frances (Alexander) C.; m. Mary Ellen Neelon, Apr. 3, 1965; children: Patricia Anne, Andrea Frances. BS, Boston U., 1960, postgrad., 1962-63; postgrad., Columbia U., 1968-69. Dir. pub. rels. Wheaton Coll., Norton, Mass., 1960-61; asst. to the pres. Lesley Coll., Cambridge, Mass., 1961-66; adminstrv. dir. N.Y. Acad. Scis., N.Y.C., 1966-71; v.p., adminstrn. CCNY, N.Y.C., 1971-76; pres. The New Engl. Acad. Medicine, Boston, 1976-77; exec. dir. Commonwealth Inst. of Medicine, Boston, 1976-77; dir. devel. Mus. of Fine Arts, Boston, 1977-79; pres. Springfield (Mass.) Libr. and Mus. Assn., 1979-84; chmn., chief exec. officer United Temporaries of New Eng., Springfield, 1985—. Trustee, exec. com. Better Bus. Bur. of No. Conn., 1986—; trustee, White Pines Condominium Assn., chmn. 1990; corporator Bay State Med. Ctr., 1980—, Stage West, 1986—. Mem. Am. Mgmt. Assn., Hartford Club, Colony Club, Temporary Inds. Profl. Soc. Internat. (bd. dirs. 1988—, bd. sec. 1989—), Tau Mu Epsilon. Roman Catholic. Home: 78 Caseland St Springfield MA 01107-1214 Office: United Temporaries New Eng 1537 Main St Springfield MA 01103-1420

CANAVAN, KEVIN EDWARD, non-profit organization executive; b. New Haven, Mar. 3, 1951; s. Francis Edward and Blanche Canavan; m. Linda McAllister, Nov. 15, 1972 (div. 1974). BA, Georgetown U., 1973; MPA, U. New Haven, 1984. Dep. dir. Community Progress, Inc., New Haven, 1973-78; dir. human svcs. planning City of Utica, N.Y., 1978; dir. domestic programs Save the Children, Westport, Conn., 1979-82; nat. field dir. UN Assn., N.Y.C., 1982-85; assoc. dir. New Haven Found., 1985-90; fin. dir. Morrison for Gov., New Haven, 1990; dir. of devel. Conn. Jr. Rep., Litchfield, 1990—. Candidate for mayor Dem. Party, East Haven, Conn., 1973; mem. Dem. Town Com., East Haven, 1974. Mem. Coun. for Advancement and Support of Edn. Roman Catholic. Home: 96 Filbert St Hamden CT 06517 Office: Conn Jr Rep PO Box 161 Litchfield CT 06759

CANCELLI, JOHN JOSEPH, food service equipment company executive; b. New Britain, Conn., Nov. 2, 1952; s. William Runognoli and Gertrude (Peoulx) C.; m. Carol Curran, May 3, 1980; 1 child, Melissa Marie. BS in Fin., Pa. State U., 1976. Mgr. acctg. Intert ICS, Scranton, Pa., 1974-76; sales mgr. Skotte Electronics Corp., Archbald, Pa., 1976-78; v.p. Bills Appliance Co., Plainville, Conn., 1978-84; pres. CenConn Svc. Corp, Plainville, 1984—; bd. dirs. Comml. Supply Co., Hilly Hill, Fla., 1990-91. Mem. PTA Diloreto Sch., New Britain, 1989-91, Edgewater (Fla.) Sch., 1991; mem. ch. coun. St. Jerome Parish, New Britain, 1990-91, Sacred Heart Ch., New Smyrna Beach, Fla., 1991. Recipient Cert. Merit, County of Lackawana, Scranton, Pa., 1976; named Parent of Yr., New Britain Bd. Edn., 1991, Girl Scouts Leader of Yr., Conn. Yankee coun., Farmington, Conn., 1991. Mem. Nat. Assn. Credit Mgrs. Democrat. Roman Catholic. Home: 1904 Victory Palm Dr Edgewater FL 32141-3720

CANCIENNE, DONALD PAUL, dean; b. Jamaica, N.Y., Dec. 5, 1933; s. Stanley and Anna (Noll) C.; m. Margaret Gannon, Dec. 15, 1973; children: Kevin, Annemarie. BA, Mary Immaculate Coll., 1962; PhL, Laval U., Que., Can., 1964, PhD, 1967. Asst. prof. philosophy St. John's U., Jamaica, N.Y., 1965-72; dir. labor rels. Bellevue Hosp., N.Y.C., 1972-74; dir. labor rels. and pers. Bronx (N.Y.) Community Coll., 1975-77, dean of adminstrn., 1978—; accreditation evaluator Mid States Regional Accreditation Assn., Phila., 1984—. Contbr. articles to profl. publs. Active Park Commn., Village of Lake Success, N.Y., 1987-90, mem. Planning Bd., 1991. Democrat. Roman Catholic. Office: Bronx Community Coll W 181st St & University Ave Bronx NY 10453

CANDAGE, HOWARD EVERETT, insurance agent, broker, consultant; b. Blue Hill, Maine, Sept. 23, 1952; s. Aubrey Llewellyn and Evelyn Edsley (Carter) C.; m. Jeri-Lynn Moore, Nov. 3, 1979; children, Chelsea Alyssa, Curran Aubrey. Cert., Am. Inst. Property and Liability Underwriters, 1984, Ins. Inst. Am., 1989, 90. Ind. comml. fisherman Blue Hill, Maine, 1970-79; ins. agt. J.T. Rosborough, Inc., Ellsworth, Maine, 1979-80, W.C. Ladd & Sons, Inc., Rockland, Maine, 1980-86; br. mgr. W.C. Ladd & Sons, Inc., Damariscotta, Maine, 1986-89; resident v.p. W.C. Ladd & Sons, Inc., Damariscotta, 1988-90; ptnr. Cole-Harrison Agy. of Maine, Inc./Atlantic Yacht Insurers, Ltd., Kennebunk, 1990—; pres., Maine Marine Industry

Assocs., Freeport, 1982-83. Mem. Soc. Chartered Property and Casualty Underwriters (treas. Maine chpt. 1990-92, v.p. 1992-93), Nat. Soc. of Chartered Property and Casualty Underwriters (nat. chpt. affairs com.), Ind. Ins. Agts. Assn. Maine (chmn. com. 1983-84, 91-92, bd. dirs. 1990-93, Young Agt. of Yr. 1987), Profl. Ins. Agts., Am. Mgmt. Assn., Round Top Ctr. for Arts, Maine Maritime Mus., Propeller Club U.S. Home: 6 Meadow Crossing Dr Gorham ME 04038 Office: Cole Harrison Ins PO Box 358 83 Main St Kennebunk ME 04043

CANDELA, FRANK MICHAEL, aviation management executive; b. Chgo., Aug. 17, 1951; s. Frank Vincent and Mary Ann (Melone) C. Student, Washburn Tech., 1977, M.J. Kennedy, 1978, U. S.C., 1986, Thomas Edison State Coll., 1992. Corp. pilot RCA Corp., Trenton, N.J., 1979-81; data specialist FAA, Chgo., 1981-83; aviation safety mgr. Damin Aviation Corp., Weehawken, N.J., 1983-87; helicopter div. mgr., aviation safety mgr. Page Flight Inc., Washington, 1987—; pres. Mid-Atlantic Distbrs. Corp., Reston, Va., 1991—. With U.S. Army, 1970—. Recipient Long and Honorable Svc. award State of Ill., 1980; 2 Aviation World Speed Records Fedn. Aero. Internat., 1988, 2 U.S. Nat. Speed Records, 1988. Mem. Army Aviation Assn. (pres. Chgo. chpt. 1978-79; Aces award 1988), Helicopter Assn. Internat., Nat. Aero. Assn., Mid-Atlantic Helicopter Assn. (instrument flight regulations com. chmn. 1988-90). Home: 1703 Sundance Dr Herndon VA 22070-5613 Office: Leesburg Mcpl Airport PO Box 2308 Leesburg VA 22075

CANDENQUIST, ARTHUR, railroad executive; b. Luray, Va., June 19, 1946; s. Eugene and Bernice Estelle (Noble) C. BS in Communications, Temple U., 1968. Tower operator Penn Cen./Conrail/Amtrak, 1974-79; train dispatcher Amtrak, Phila., 1979-84, asst. chief train dispatcher, 1984-86, safety engr., 1986-87; mgr. safety and environ. control Amtrak, Washington, 1987—. Contbr. articles to profl. jours. Firefighter, adminstrv. officer Broomall (Pa.) Fire Co., 1962—, New Baltimore Vol. Fire Co., Fauquier County, Va., 1987—. Capt. USAF, 1968-74, Vietnam. Mem. Am. Soc. Safety Engrs., Nat. Fire Protection Assn., Masons (32 degree). Office: Amtrak 400 N Capitol St NW Washington DC 20001-1511

CANELL, BEVERLY JUNE, school administrator, educator; b. New Haven, Dec. 12, 1949; d. Eric and Margaret (Sause) Capper; m. Edward Lawrence Canell, Nov. 20, 1971; 1 child, Brian Edward. BS in French and Spanish, So. Conn. State U., New Haven, 1971, MS in Bilingual Edn., 1974, cert. in adminstrn., 1989. With Hamden (Conn.) Pub. Schs., 1971—, chair fgn. lang. dept., 1987—, dir. fgn. lang. dept. and ESL, 1971—; mem. adj. faculty So. Conn. State U., 1992—. Mem. ASCD, Conn. Coun. Lang. Tchrs. (chair poetry contest 1989-90, Appreciation award 1982, bd. dirs., membership chair 1991—), Am. Coun. on the Teaching of Fgn. Langs., Com. Fgn. Lang. Coords., Teaching English for Speakers of Other Langs. Roman Catholic. Home: 250 Cook Hill Rd Wallingford CT 06492-3330 Office: Hamden Pub Schs 2040 Dixwell Ave Hamden CT 06514-2479

CANELLAKIS, ZOE NAKOS, research scientist, pharmacology educator; b. Lowell, Mass., Sept. 7, 1927; d. Arthur John and Sophia (Michaelidou) Nakos; m. E.S. Canellakis (div.); children: Thomas Nakos, Arthur John. BA in Econs., Vassar Coll., 1947; MS in Biochemistry, U. Calif., Berkeley, 1951; PhD in Physiol. Chemistry, U. Wis., 1954. Postdoctoral fellow Yale U., New Haven, Conn., 1954-55, instr. biochemistry, 1955-59, rsch. assoc. pharmacology, 1959-67, sr. rsch. assoc. pharmacology and internal medicine, 1967-82, asst. dean grad. sch., 1972-77, sr. rsch. scientist, 1982—; rsch. scientist West Haven (Conn.) VA Med. Ctr., 1977—; vis. scientist Karolinska Inst., Stockholm, 1967, Athens (Greece) Med. Sch., 1976, Inst. de Invest. Citolog., Valencia, Spain, 1977; guest lectr. Japan, People's Republic of China, Helsinki (Finland), Jerusalem. Contbr. articles and book revs. to profl. publs., 1956—. Am. Cancer Soc. scholar NYU, 1988-89. Mem. Internat. Assn. for Women Bioscientists (bd. dirs. 1985-89), Am. Soc. Biol. Chemists, Am. Soc. Biochemistry and Molecular Biology (co-chmn. com. for equal opportunity for women, organizer internat. and nat. panels on women in sci. 1986—), Fedn. Am. Socs. for Exptl. Biology's Vis. Scientists for Minority Instns. Program, Greek Biochem. and Biophys. Soc., Profl. Resources Greece Orgn., Modern Greek Studies Assn., The Enzyme Club, Phi Beta Kappa, Sigma Xi. Mem. Soc. of Friends. Home: 206 Livingston St New Haven CT 06511-2210 Office: Yale U Dept Pharmacology Med Sch Cedar St New Haven CT 06519-2315

CANFIELD, ANDREW TROTTER, legal writer, lawyer; b. N.Y.C., Apr. 30, 1953; s. Edward Francis and Janet Powell (Trotter) C.; m. Marguerite Southworth Dove, May 30, 1987; children: Augusta Phillips, Lilian Sinclair. BA in History, U. Va., 1976; JD, Am. U., 1991. Bar: Pa. 1991. Legal writer on solar energy, environ. law, manufactured housing, computer products liability and govt. timber contracts, 1976—; rsch. assoc. Planning Rsch. Corp., McLean, Va., 1977-79; legal asst. Casey, Scott & Canfield, P.C., Washington, 1979-88; law clk. Casey, Scott, Canfield, and Heggestad, P.C., Washington, 1988-91; assoc. Casey, Scott, Canfield & Heggestad P.C., Washington, 1991—. Republican. Episcopalian. Home: 4924 Westway Dr Bethesda MD 20816-1728 Office: Casey Scott Canfield & Heggestad PC 805 15th St NW Ste 600 Washington DC 20005-2298

CANFIELD, DOROTHY MAY, engineering company official; b. Cortland, N.Y., Apr. 17, 1963; d. Charles Kennard and Doris Margaret (Lighthall) C. AS in Exec. Secretarial Tng., Cen. City Bus. Inst., Syracuse, N.Y., 1983; cert. in human resources mgmt., LeMoyne Coll., 1991. Fin. aid officer Cen. City Bus. Inst., 1983-86; human resources asst. Marsellus Casket Co., Syracuse, 1986-87; pers. asst. O'Brien & Gere Engrs. Inc., Syracuse, 1987-89, coord. tng., 1989—. Bd. dirs., officer Muscular Dystrophy Assn., Syracuse, 1983-90. Mem. ASTD (membership chmn. Syracuse 1991—, Most Active New Mem. award 1990), Profl. Secs. Internat. (pres. Syracuse chpt. 1988-89, Sec. of Yr. award N.Y. State div. 1989). Methodist. Office: O'Brien & Gere Engrs Inc 5000 Brittonfield Pky Syracuse NY 13221

CANGEMI, MICHAEL PAUL, accountant, financial executive; b. Bklyn., May 5, 1948; s. Ignatius and Mary (Chimento) C.; m. Maria D. Ruscitti, Nov. 23, 1974; children: Michael Jason, Marc Ignatius. BBA, Pace U., 1970. CPA, N.Y.; cert. info. systems auditor. Asst. to v.p. ops. Blair & Co., N.Y.C., 1966-70; prin. Arthur Young & Co., N.Y.C., 1970-80; v.p. Phelps Dodge Corp., N.Y.C., 1980-88; ptnr., nat. dir. EDP auditing BDO Seidman, 1988-92; sr. v.p., CFO Etienne Aigner Inc., Edison, N.J., 1992—; lectr. in field. Contbg. author: The Handbook fo EDP Auditing, 1986; co-author: Auditing in an EDP Environment; assoc. editor EDPACS, (newsletter) The EDP Audit, Control and Security; contbr. articles to profl. jours. Mem. AICPA, N.Y. State Soc. CPAs (data processing com. 1979-80, computer usage and data processing com. 1980-82), EDP Auditors Assn. (internat. bd. dirs. 1982-89, trustee 1982-89, v.p. edn. 1982-84, exec. v.p. 1984-85, assn. and found. pres. 1985-86, pres. N.Y. chpt. bd. dirs. 1978-86, 2d v.p., 1979-80, 1st v.p. 1983, mem. nominating com. 1982-86, conf. site selection com. 1981-82, editor The EDPAuditor Jour. 1987—, J.J. Wasserman award 1987, Eugene M. Frank award 1989), Fin. Execs. Inst., Inst. Internal Auditors (bd. dirs., program delvel. com. for 1986 conf. 1984-86. bd. govs. N.Y. chpt. 1986-92, pres. N.Y. chpt. 1989-90), Internat. Bd. Rsch. Advisors, Soc. for Info. Systems Quality (bd. dirs. 1987-88), Arthur Young Businessmen's Assn. (bd. dirs. 1982-89, v.p. 1985-89), Mining Club, Metuchen (N.J.) Golf and Country Club. Roman Catholic. Home: 18 Fishel Rd Edison NJ 08820-3217 Office: 47 Brunswick Ave Edison NJ 08818-3111

CANIGLIA, RICHARD GARY, retail executive; b. Providence, Aug. 4, 1948; s. Umberto Mario and Mary Ann (Aiello) C.; m. Mary Ellen Feeney, June 14, 1968; children: Richard, Christine. BS summa cum laude, Johnson & Wales Coll., 1979. Sr. service technician Bell & Howell, E. Providence, R.I., 1972-75; v.p., owner Northeast Office Supplies, Inc., Cranston, R.I., 1975-77; pres., owner Marel Creations Inc., Cranston, 1977-81; v.p., dir. Jay B. Rudolph, Inc.-Jordan Marsh, Boston, 1981-89, Jay B. Rudolph, Inc.-Bloomingdales, N.Y.C., 1989—. With U.S. Army, 1968-71. Mem. Gemological Inst. Am. Republican. Roman Catholic. Home: 140 Bald Hill Rd New Canaan CT 06840-2403 Office: Bloomingdales 1000 3d Ave New York NY 10022-1210

CANIKE, ANTHONY CHRISTOPHER, small business owner; b. Phila., Dec. 12, 1946; s. Anthony Harry and Helen Laura (Valence) C.; m. Heather H. O'Connor, Sept. 27, 1978 (div. June 1986); children: Anthony II, Kay Ellen. Degree in Hotel Adminstrn., Pa. State U., 1962; postgrad., Temple U., 1990, Pa. State U., 1992—. Pres. Country Host Inc., New Hope, Pa., 1965—. Bd. dirs. Aldie Found., Doylestown, Pa., 1988-91, Lenape Valley Found., Doylestown, 1989—; group leader Bucks County Coun. on Alcoholism, 1989—, bd. dirs., 1991—; sponsor Little League Baseball, New Hope, Pa., 1991—. Recipient vol. award United Fund, Doylestown, 1990, ann. vol. award Bucks County Coun. on Alcoholism, 1991. Mem. Bucks County Restaurant Soc. (pres. 1965-66), Cen. Bucks C. of C. (bd. dirs. 1988-91, v.p. 1992, chmn. ann. art show 1988-91), James Mitchen Art Mus., Exch. Club (pres. New Hope 1964-66), Eastport Yacht Club (Annapolis, Md.), Pa. State U. Bucks County Club. Home and Office: Box 135 Carversville PA 18913

CANIZARES, CLAUDE ROGER, astrophysicist; b. Tucson, June 14, 1945; s. Orlando and Stephanie (Bolan) C.; m. Jennifer Wilder, Aug. 31, 1968; children: Kristen, Alexander. BA, Harvard U., 1967, MA, 1968, PhD, 1972. Rsch. staff MIT, Cambridge, 1971-74, asst. prof. physics, 1974-78, assoc. prof. physics, 1978-84, prof. physics, 1984—, deputy dir. Ctr. for Space Rsch., 1989-90, dir. Ctr. for Space Rsch., 1990—; assoc. dir. NASA-AXAF Sci. Ctr.; chair Space Sci. Applicatin adv. com. NASA, 1992—, mem. Space Earth Sci. adv. com., Washington, 1986-88, mem. adv. coun. NASA, 1992—; mem. Astron. Astrophysics Survey Com. NRC, Washington, 1989-91. Contbr. over 100 articles to profl. jours. Royal Soc. vis. fellow, Cambridge, Eng., 1981-82, Alfred P. Sloan Found. fellow, 1980-84; NASA grantee, 1975-. Fellow Am. Phys. Soc.; mem. AAAS, Am. Astron. Soc., Internat. Astron. Union, Phi Beta Kappa, Sigma Xi. Office: MIT Rm 37-241 Cambridge MA 02139

CANLAS, LUZANO PANCHO, SR., writer, researcher; b. Tarlac, The Philippines, July 4, 1940; came to U.S., 1988; s. Juan Patio and Baltazara (Pancho) C.; m. Rosario Supan, Mar. 4, 1966; children: Luzano Jr., Richard, Jenny. Student, U. of East, Manila, 1957-61. Land adminstr. The Philippines, 1961-87, writer, researcher, 1967—. Author: Concise History of The Philippines, 1991, (med. guide) What You Need to Know about Arthritis and Rheumatism, 1991, (Pilipino proverbs) Book of Wisdom, 1991, (English proverbs) 1001 Proverbs-Guide for a Better Life, 1991, (med. guide) Hypertension-The Silent Killer, 1991, (med. guide) What You Need to Know about Your Heart and 34 Other Related Topics, 1992. Pres. Ch. of Christ Orgn., The Philippines, 1964-87, Ch. of Christ Parents Orgn., 1988—. Recipient Most Prolific Writer/Researcher, Lira Pampanguena, 1985. Home: 3831 Ste 101 Saint Barnabas Rd Suitland MD 20746

CANNALIATO, VINCENT, JR., investment banker, mathematician; b. Bklyn., July 12, 1941; s. Vincent and Margaret (Mancuso) C.; m. June A. Marino, Apr. 8, 1967; children: Amy June, Kimberly Dawn, Douglas Vincent. BS in Math., Fordham U., 1963; MA in Math., Bklyn. Coll. CUNY, 1964; grad. cert. in system design, U. Pa. Sch. Bus., 1970. Systems analyst N.Y. Telephone Co., N.Y.C., 1969-70; account exec. CIT Leasing Corp., N.Y.C., 1970-72; v.p. Kidder Peabody & Co., Inc., N.Y.C., 1972-80, head leasing and project financing group corp. fin. dept., 1977-80; sr. v.p., mng. dir. and head leasing/project fin. grp. Smith Barney, Harris Upham & Co., Inc., N.Y.C., 1980-90; mng. dir., first v.p., head Merchant Banking Group Sanwa Bus. Credit Corp., N.Y.C., 1990-91; founder, pres. Cannaliato & Assocs., investment bankers, N.Y.C., 1991—; bd. dirs. Nortankers, Inc., mem. audit com., 1989-90; vis. instr. Southwestern Grad. Sch. Banking, 1976-77; speaker law jour. seminars equip. leasing industry, 1986-87; adv. bd. U.S. Mcht. Marine Acad., 1974-90, chmn., 1977-90; instr. math. U. Md., 1966-69; mem. maritime adv. com. Dept. Transp., 1982-84, chmn. fin. subcom., 1983-84. Co-author: U.S. Taxation of International Operations, 1975, 77, 87; Oil and Gas Taxes/Natural Resources Service, 1979; World Leasing Yearbook, 1980, 81. Exec. bd., curriculum chmn. Gifted Child Soc., 1975-82; nation chief Rampo Indian Guides and Princesses, Western Hills YMCA, 1980-83; bd. dirs. Tomorrow Children's Fund, 1987—, exec. bd. 1989—; mem. parish coun. St. Elizabeth Roman Cath. Ch., 1986-88, pres., 1987-88. Capt. AUS, 1963-69. Decorated Bronze Star. Mem. Am. Assn. Equipment Lessors (bd. dirs. exec. and nominating coms., fed. legis. com. 1975-84, chmn. keyman com. 1977-83, chmn. mem. com. 1982-83, chmn. academia awareness task force 1988-92), Acad. Magical Arts, Inc. (life), Met. Club (N.Y.C.), Indian Trail Club (Franklin Lakes, N.J.). Home: 501 Alexis Ct Franklin Lakes NJ 07417-1050 Office: Sanwa Business Credit Corp 140 E 45th St Fl 36 New York NY 10017-3155

CANNELLA, JOHN MATTHEW, federal judge; b. N.Y.C., Feb. 8, 1908; s. Joseph and Laura (Gullo) C.; m. Ida Rutnik, Dec. 26, 1938; children: Lauretta (Mrs. Alfred Kushay), Christine (Mrs. John J. Phelan 3d), John Matthew. B.S., Fordham U., 1930, LL.B., 1933. Bar: N.Y. 1934. Gen. practice N.Y.C., 1934-40; asst. U.S. atty., 1940-42; commnr. Water Supply Gas and Electricity, N.Y.C., 1946-48, Dept. Licenses, 1948-49; mem. Ct. Spl. Sessions, N.Y.C., 1949-59, Ct. Gen. Sessions, N.Y.C., 1957-58, City Ct., N.Y.C., 1959-61, Criminal Ct., N.Y.C., 1963; U.S. judge So. Dist. N.Y., 1963—, sr. judge, 1977—. Comdr. USCGR, 1942-45. Mem. Catholic Lawyers Guild, Columbian Lawyers Assn. Office: US Dist Ct US Courthouse Foley Sq New York NY 10007-1501

CANNING, JOHN BECKMAN, corporate lawyer; b. Chgo., Dec. 29, 1943; s. John Albert and Katherine Marie (Beckman) C.; m. Janet Elizabeth Scovill, Aug. 3, 1968; children: William, Katherine. AB magna cum laude, Princeton (N.J.) U., 1965; LLB cum laude, Columbia U., 1968. Bar: N.Y., 1969, Conn. 1980, U.S. Dist. Ct. (so. dist.) N.Y. 1975, U.S. Dist. Ct. Conn. 1987, U.S. Ct. Appeals (2d cir.) 1975. Assoc. White and Case, N.Y.C., 1968-77; assoc. gen. counsel, fin. atty. ITT Rayonier Inc., Stamford, Conn., 1977-85, copr. sec., assoc. gen. counsel, 1985—; sec., dir. Sentry Savs. and Loan, Stamford, 1984-92; v.p., dir. Beckman Bros., Des Moines, 1986—. Moderator, ch. coun., Saugatuck Congl. Ch., Westport, Conn., 1990-92. 1st lt. USAR, 1968-73. Mem. ABA, Columbia Law Sch. Alumni Assn. Home: 9 Mortar Rock Rd Westport CT 06880-5055 Office: ITT Rayonier Inc 1177 Summer St Stamford CT 06905-5522

CANNISTRACI, ANTHONY, automotive executive; b. Torre Forte, Messina, Italy, Dec. 4, 1951; came to U.S., 1966; s. Santo and Carmela (Isgro) C.; m. Lisa T.M. Schaller, June 16, 1973 (div. 1978); 1 child, Casey Lynn. Assoc. with honors, Jr. Coll. Albany, 1973. Owner, pres. Village Auto Body Shop, Inc., Albany, N.Y., 1973—. Faculty scholar Jr. Coll. Albany, 1972, 73. Mem. Village Soccer Club (owner), Village Spring Soccer League (founder), Capital Dist. Soccer League (pres. 1980-85), Capital Dist. Women's Soccer League (founder). Home: 38 Grandview Dr Latham NY 12110-3826 Office: Village Auto Body Shop Inc 1691 Central Ave Albany NY 12205-4021

CANNIZZARO, PAUL PETER, food products executive; b. N.Y.C., Jan. 31, 1925; s. Pietro and Anna (Nicolini) C.; m. Dolores Cecile della Cella, Apr. 15, 1950; children: Diane, Linda, Peter. BS in Econs., U. Pa., 1948. Salesman Cannizzaro Wine Co., Inc., N.Y.C., 1948-50, dir. mktg., 1955-58; treas., gen. mgr. Continental Cigar Co., Inc., N.Y.C., 1951-54; treas. L. Della Cella Co., Inc., N.Y.C., 1959-62; pres. Westbury, N.Y., 1963—; proprietor Cordova Sales Co., Garden City, N.Y., 1970—, Agnesi Sales Co., 1975-81; pres. G. Nino Bragelli, Inc., Westbury, 1974—, Berona Trading Inc., 1964-74. Biography pub. in the Internat. Register of Profiles, Cambridge England, edit. X, 1990, included in 5000 Personalities of the World, edit. 2. Pres. Italy-Am. C. of C., N.Y.C., 1984, bd. dirs., 1980-85; treas. Malvern, N.Y. chpt. Com. for Preservation of Neighborhood Schs., Inc., 1966; mem. U.S. Power Squadron AP, 1971. Lt. (j.g.) USN, 1943-46. Mem. Cheese Importers Assn. Am., Inc. (pres., dir.-at-large 1971—), Beta Gamma Sigma. Republican. Roman Catholic. Club: Freeport (N.Y.) Yacht (vice-commodore 1979, commodore 1980). Home: 235 Brixton Rd Garden City NY 11530-1312 Office: L Della Cella Co Inc 1025 Old Country Rd # 303N Westbury NY 11590-5257

CANNON, DANIEL WILLARD, lawyer; b. Pitts., Sept. 3, 1920; s. Edgar Carl and Violet Jessie (Burke) C.; m. Ann Marshall Price, Sept. 30, 1943; children: Susan Ayres, David, Judith Lillie, Barbara, Ann Finch. AB, U. Pitts., 1941, JD, 1968. Bar: Pa. 1948, D.C. 1952, U.S. Supreme Ct. 1952. Atty., U.S. Steel Corp., Pitts., 1947-50; sec., gen. counsel Bituminous Coal Operators Assn., Washington, 1951-58; dir. Indsl. Devel. and Natural Resources, NAM, N.Y.C., 1958-74, dir. environ. affairs, Washington, 1974-84, dir. program devel., 1984—; lectr. in field. Mem. editorial adv. bd. Indsl. Wastes Mag., Air Quality Control, 1975; editor: Hazardous Waste Mgmt. Under RCRA: A Primer for Small Business, 1980, A Pollution Tax Won't Help Control Pollution, 1977, National Strength and the National Environmental Policy Act, 1972, Staying Out of Trouble: What You Should Know About the New Hazardous Waste Law, 1985, Preparing for Emergency Planning, 1987, Retroactive Emission Controls, 1987; NAM liaison Waste Minimization: Manufacturer's Strategies for Success, 1989. Served to 1st lt. USAAF, 1942-46. Recipient Moot Ct. award, U. Pitts. Law Sch., 1947; Award of Appreciation, Water Quality Rsch. Coun., 1974. Mem. ABA, Fed. Bar Assn., Bar Assn. D.C., Allegheny County Bar Assn., Air Pollution Control Assn., Water Pollution Control Fedn., Order of the Coif, Univ. Club, Army and Navy Club, Pa. Soc., Masons. Republican. Episcopalian. Home: 637 E Capitol St SE Washington DC 20003-1234 Office: Ste 1500 1331 Pennsylvania Ave NW Washington DC 20004-1790

CANNON, GRACE BERT, immunologist; b. Chambersburg, Pa., Jan. 29, 1937; d. Charles Wesley and Gladys (Raff) Bert; m. W. Dilworth Cannon, June 3, 1961 (div. 1972); children: Michael Quayle, Susan Radcliffe, Peter Bert Cannon. AB, Goucher Coll., 1958; PhD, Washington U., St. Louis, 1962. Fellow Columbia U., N.Y.C., 1962-64, Columbia U. Coll. Physicians and Surgeons, N.Y.C., 1964-65; staff fellow NIH Nat. Cancer Inst., Bethesda, Md., 1966-67; cell biologist Litton Bionetics, Inc., Kensington, Md., 1972-80, head immunology sect., 1980-85; dir. sci. ImmuQuest Labs., Inc., Rockville, Md., 1985-88; pres. Biomedical Analytics, Inc., Rockville, Md., 1988—; mgr. ATLIS Fed. Svcs., Inc., Rockville, Md., 1991—; Mem. contract rev. coms. Nat. Cancer Inst., 1983-87. Contbr. articles to profl. jours. Mem. Pub. Svc. Health Club, Bethesda, Md., 1984—, sec., 1990—. Grantee USPHS, 1959-65, NSF, 1959. Mem. AAAS, Am. Assn. for Cancer Research, N.Y. Acad. Sci., Sigma Xi. Republican. Presbyterian. Home and Office: 4905 Ertter Dr Rockville MD 20852-2203

CANNON, JOHN J(OSEPH), real estate sales and marketing executive; b. London, Jan. 29, 1954; came to U.S., 1963; s. Charles and Anne (Strogen) C.; m. Elena M. Manna; children: Ryan Scott, Taylor. Student, Pace U., 1972-74; BBA in Real Estate cum laude, Baruch Coll., 1976. Lic. real estate broker, N.Y. Corp. facilities rep. Volkswagen of Am., Englewood Cliffs, N.J., 1979-81; real estate negotiator The Chase Manhattan Bank, N.Y.C., 1981-82; regional mgr. real estate Pepsico, Pizza Hut, Inc., Wichita, Kans., 1983-85; regional dir. of real estate T.G.I. Fridays, Inc., Dallas, 1985; sales dir. The Beechwood Orgn., North Hills, N.Y., 1986, M.J. Raynes, Inc., N.Y.C., 1987-88; pres. Cannon Enterprises, N.Y., 1988-91; dir. sales The KLAR Orgn., East Meadow, N.Y., 1991-92; cons. real estate Audio Exchange, Inc., Hicksville, N.Y., 1984—. Named one of Outstanding Young Men of Am., 1985. Mem. L.I. Builders Inst. (treas. sales and mktg. coun. 1989, v.p. 1990-91), Nat. Assn. Home Builders, Inst. Residential Mktg., Beta Gamma Sigma. Republican. Roman Catholic. Home: 15 Farmington Ln Melville NY 11747 Office: The KLAR Orgn 2580 Hempstead Tpke East Meadow NY 11554

CANNON, LYNNE MARPLE, investment management company executive; b. Phila., Oct. 14, 1955; parents John and Edythe (Grebe) C. BA, Ohio Wesleyan U., 1977. Employee PRO Services Inc., Flourtown, Pa., 1979-82; asst. sec. PRO Services Inc., Blue Bell, Pa., 1982-86; v.p. AMA Investment Advisers Inc. (formerly PRO Svcs. Inc.), Blue Bell, 1986-92; v.p., sec. AMA Family of Funds, Inc., 1986-92; v.p. Independence Capital Mgmt., Inc., Horsham, Pa., 1992—, Independence Capital Group of Funds, Inc., 1992—. Vol. Plant Ambler Inc., Ambler, Pa., 1983—. Mem. Mut. Fund Edn. Alliance (bd. govs. 1990-91), Phila. Saddle Club (sec.). Republican. Episcopalian. Home: 122 N Ridge Ave Ambler PA 19002-4506 Office: Independence Capital Mgmt Inc 600 Dresher Rd Horsham PA 19044

CANNON, RICHARD DYSON, automotive executive; b. Boston, Oct. 4, 1928; s. James Leo and Mary E. (Beehman) C.; m. Mary Esther Kelley, June 14, 1954; children: Michael, Judith, James, Patricia, Richard L. BSBA, Boston U., 1954. Fin. analyst Metal Stamp Ford Motor, Cleve., 1954-66; fin. controller Tractor Ops. Eng. (Ford of Eng.), 1966-70; mfg. mgr. Tractor Equip, Plant (Ford of Iowa), 1970-72; plant mgr. Tractor Plant (Ford of Romeo), 1972-76; ops. mgr. Tractor0Ford Motor, Turkey, 1976-81; dir. mfg. Standard Motor Products, N.Y.C., 1982-86; v.p. ops. P.R., Hong Kong, N.Y.C., 1986—. Staff sgt. USMC, 1946-48, 50-51. Home: 169 Hidden Ridge Dr Syosset NY 11791

CANON, ROBERT MORRIS, opera producer; b. Winona, Miss., July 26, 1941; s. Booma Sharp and Elizabeth Pauline (Harrison) C. BA, U. Miss., 1964, MA, 1967. Artistic dir. Panola Playhouse, 1962-70; instr. opera theatre U. Miss., 1964-66, coordinator performing and fine arts, 1966-72; dir. Galveston (Tex.) Arts Ctr., 1972-74; exec. dir. Arts Council San Antonio, 1975-83; dir. Nat. Endowment for Arts, Washington, 1983-87; pres., chief exec. officer Opera Co. Boston, 1987-89; exec. dir. Boston Opera Theater, 1989—; program dir., cons. Miss. Arts Commn., Jackson, 1970-72; dir. The Joffrey Workshop, 1973-74; U.S. del. AITA-UNESCO Conf., Monaco, 1969; pres. Nat. Assembly Local Arts Agys., 1981-83; mem. nat. council U.S. Internat. Ballet Competition, 1981—; dir. Hispanic Telecommunications Network, 1984-90, mem. Miss. Arts Commn., 1967-70; bd. dirs. Tex. Assembly Arts Councils, 1976-79; mem. urban affairs com. Tex. Arts Commn., 1979-82. Contbr. articles to arts jours. Mem. Miss. Theatre Assn. (pres. 1966-68), Southeastern Theatre Conf. (gov. 1969-72), Assn. Am. Dance Cos. (exec. com. 1975-77), Houston Soc. Performing Arts (dir. 1978-81). Office: Boston Opera Theater 300 Massachusetts Ave Boston MA 02115-4544

CANTELMO, PATRICIA ANN, principal; b. Jersey City, N.J., Feb. 13, 1944; d. Joseph Anthony and Josephine Elizabeth (Parisi) C. BA in Elem. Edn., Jersey City State Coll., 1965, MA in Early Childhood, 1974; postgrad., William Paterson Coll., 1976. Team tchr. Teaneck (N.J.) Twp. Pub. Schs., 1965-77, team coord., 1977-78, elem. prin., 1978-84, primary prin., 1986-88, elem. prin., 1988—; middle sch. prin. East Hanover (N.J.) Pub. Schs., 1984-86; adj. tchr. Jersey City State Coll., 1981-82, Fairleigh Dickinson U., Teaneck, 1982-83; workshop leader Macmillan Pubs., 1978-80. Vol. Englewood Cliffs (N.J.) Dem. Assn., 1972—. Mem. Assn. for Supervision and Curriculum Devel., Nat. Assn. Elem. and Secondary Sch. Prins., Nat. Prins. and Suprs. Assn., Phi Delta Kappa. Home: 235 Prospect Ave Hackensack NJ 07601-2510

CANTLIFFE, JERI MILLER, art educator, artist; b. Alliance, N.C., Nov. 25, 1927; d. Rufus Faye Miller and Viola Elizabeth (Ireland) Miller Smith; m. Lawrence R. Cantliffe Jr., Sept.1, 1949; children: Eileen M., David L., Geri Lyn, Lisa Ann, Jonathan M. BA, Meredith Coll., 1949; M in Art Teaching, Wesleyan U., 1967; postgrad., Paier Sch. Art, New Haven, 1974-76. Designer Stephenson Appliance Co., Raleigh, N.C., 1949-50; lab. asst. N.C. State Coll., Raleigh, 1950, Hoffman-LaRoche Pharms., Clifton, N.J., 1951-52; art tchr. Horace Wilcox Tech. Sch., Meriden, Conn., 1962-66; workshop tchr. Park & Recreation Dept., Haddam and Wallingford, Conn., 1970-84, YWCA, Meriden, 1970-85, Middletown (Conn.) Art Guild, 1970-90, instr. in arts and crafts, 1989; workshop tchr. Community Art Ctr., Kensington, Conn., 1977-79; freelance artist specializing in home portraits, 1980—. One-woman shows include Cen. Bank, Meriden, 1977, 79, 82, Meriden Pub. Libr., 1981, 84 (commd. artists, Woman of Yr. in Arts award 1979), Cheshire (Conn.) Pub. Libr., 1982, Phoenix Mut. Life Inst. Co., Hartford, Conn., 1982, New Haven Pub. Libr., 1983, 86, Greene Art Gallery, Guilford, Conn., 1984, Meredith Coll., Raleigh, 1984, Lord Proprietor's Inn, Edenton, N.C.; juried mem. shows include Salamagundi, N.Y.C., New Haven Paint & Clay, Friends of New Britain (Conn.) Mus., Meriden Arts & Crafts (Frederick Flatow award 1979, Butler Paint award 1980, Alan Reid Meml. prize watercolor 1986), Middletown (Conn.) Art Guild (1st prize watercolor 1977, 78), Brush & Palette, New Haven, Milford (Conn.) Fine Arts, Mt. Carmel Art Assn., Hamden, Conn., Wis. Watercolor Show, Glastonbury (Conn.) Art Guild, The New Group, New Haven, Conn. Classic Arts, Conn. Acad. Fine Arts, Am. Penwomen, Fairfield, Conn.; invitational shows include Jewish Home for the Aged, New Haven, Art-on-the-Mountain, Wilmington, Vt., Wesleyan Showcase, Middletown Showcase (Most Popular award 1979), Glastonbury C. of C., AAUW Art Show, Soundview Ann. Art Show, Greeley Nat. Art Show, 1990, Brownstone Group, Meriden, 1990-92, Art Cache Gallery, Vt., 1990-92, Ariz. Arts & Crafts Market Gallery, 1990-92; illustrator Meriden Calendar, Meriden City Hall Christmas Card. Co-chmn. Commn. on Arts, Meriden, 1975-76; membership chmn. for the arts Nat. Art Bd., 1992—, chmn. art awards 1992—. Recipient Redstone Mfg. award Mum Art Festival, Bristol, Conn., 1978, Best in Show award Middletown Annual Winter Show, 1978, Judges

Tri-color award Community Art League, Kensington, 1978, Most Popular Vote award Middletown Showcase, 1979, Middletown Art Guild, 1992, Rick Ciburi 1st prize award Cheshire Art League, 1981, Best in Show (watercolor) Bridgeport Art League, 1982; named Woman Yr. in Arts Meriden Girls Club, 1982, Meriden-Record Jour., 1981, Meriden YWCA, 1992, Meredith Coll., 1984. Mem. Nat. League Am. PEN Women (nat. asst. memberhsip for the arts, bd. dirs., sec. 1990-92, pres. Fairfield County br. 1988-92, nat. art membership chair 1992—), PEN Women (state art co-chair 1988-89, Colo. Artists Assn., Rotary (youth exch. com., internat. com. chair youth exch. officer Meriden club). Congregationalist.

CANTOR, ELEANOR WESCHLER, medical association executive; b. N.Y.C., Dec. 30, 1913; d. Samuel Peter and Anna (Rauchwerger) W.; m. Alfred Joseph Cantor, June 9, 1938; children—Pamela Corliss, Alfred Jay. B.A., Hunter Coll., N.Y.C., 1938. Producer radio quiz show CBS, N.Y.C., 1936-41; exec. officer Internat. Acad. Proctology, N.Y.C., 1948—, Internat. Bd. Proctology, 1950—; co-founder Acad. Psychosomatic Medicine, 1954.

CANTOR, HARVEY IRA, immunologist, pathology educator; b. N.Y.C., Sept. 26, 1942; s. Albert and Blanche C.; m. Anne F. Harney, June 10, 1983; children: Andrew, Elizabeth. AB, Columbia U., 1963; MD, N.Y. U., N.Y.C., 1967; MA (hon.), Harvard U., 1979. Intern in medicine Jackson Meml. Hosp., Miami, Fla., 1967-68; resident in medicine Stanford U. Med. Ctr., Palo Alto, Calif., 1972-73; staff fellow NIH, Bethesda, Md., 1968-70; NIH special fellow Nat. Inst. Med. Rsch., London, 1970-72; asst. prof. medicine Harvard Med. Sch., Boston, 1974-76, assoc. prof., 1976-79, prof. pathology, 1979—; chief lab. of immunopathology Dana-Farber Cancer Inst., Boston, 1979—; mem. sci. adv. bd. Cancer Rsch. Inst., N.Y., 1977—, Biocyte Corp., N.Y., 1985. Mem. editorial bd. Immunology, 1975-79, Immunogenetics, 1982-85, Jour. Cellular and Molecular Immunology, 1984-90; contbr. more than 150 sci. papers to profl. publs. Recipient Borden Rsch. prize, Borden Co., 1967; scholar Leukemia Soc. Am., 1974, Karl Beyer lectureship, Leukemia Soc. Am., U. Wis., 1983. Office: Dana Farber Cancer Inst 44 Binney St Boston MA 02115-6084

CANTOR, JEROME OWEN, pathology educator, researcher; b. N.Y.C., Nov. 14, 1949; s. Morris and Helen (Resnick) C.; m. Linda Ellen Gultz, May 10, 1980. BA, Columbia U., 1971; MD, U. Pa., 1975. Diplomate Am. Bd. Pathology, Nat. Bd. Med. Examiners. Fellow Roche Inst. Molecular Biology, Nutley, N.J., 1975; intern Presbyn. Hosp., N.Y.C., 1975-76, resident, 1976-80; asst. prof. Coll. Physicians and Surgeons Columbia U., N.Y.C., 1980—; rsch. assoc. St. Luke's/Roosevelt Inst. for Health Scis., N.Y.C., 1987—; attending pathologist Arden Hill Hosp., Goshen, N.Y., 1990—, Horton Meml. Hosp., Middletown, N.Y., 1990—; cons. dept. pediatrics U. Medicine & Dentistry of N.J., Newark, 1987-91. Editor: Handbook of Animal Models of Pulmonary Diseases, 1989; contbr. numerous articles to profl. jours. Grantee Measey Found., 1973, NIH, 1976, Am. Lung Assn., 1978, N.Y. Lung Assn., 1987; recipient Bausch and Lomb Sci. award, 1967. Fellow Coll. Am. Pathologists; mem. Am. Assn. Pathologists, Am. Thoracic Soc. Office: St Lukes/Roosevelt Hosp Ctr 428 W 59th St New York NY 10019-1105

CANTOR, LESTER IRVING, musician; b. N.Y.C., Jan. 15, 1932; m. Jean Kershaw, Aug., 1964. BS, Julliard, 1957. Prin. bassoon Dallas Symphony, 1957-59, NBC Opera, N.Y.C., 1959-60, St. Louis Symphony, 1960-64; bassoonist pvt. practice N.Y.C., 1964-75; bassoonist N.Y.C. Ballet, 1975—, Joffrey Ballet, 1989—, Am. Ballet Theater, 1989—; woodwind instr. So. Meth. U., Dallas, 1957-59, So. Ill. U. St. Louis, 1960-64; dir. Greenwich House Music Sch., N.Y.C., 1975-80; chamber music dir. Composers Conf., Wellesley, Mass., 1980—. Performer with Radio City Music Hall Orch., N.Y.C. Opera Co., Symphony of the Air, Canadian Ballet, Martha Graham Dance Co., The 92nd ST. Y Orch., N.Y. Pops, Skitch Henderson, Broadway Shows, Recordings and Radio and TV Commercial Jingles. With U.S. Army, 1952-54, Korea. Mem. Am. Fed. Musicians, Local 802. Home: 302 W 79th St Apt 3B New York NY 10024-6115

CANTOR, MIRA, artist, educator; b. N.Y.C., May 16, 1944; d. Milton and Sara (Hochhauser) C.; m. Otto Piene, July 18, 1976 (div. 1983); 1 child, Chloe. BFA, U. Buffalo, 1966; MFA, U. Ill., 1969. Instr. U. Hawaii, Honolulu, 1970-71; with Northeastern U., Boston, 1983—, lectr. art, 1987-88, asst. prof., 1988-90, assoc. prof., 1991—. Ctr. for Advanced Visual Studies MIT fellow, 1978-80. Mem. Uban Arts (com. 1989, 90), Artists' Found. (com. 1989, 90, grantee 1978). Office: Northeastern U 360 Huntington Ave Boston MA 02115-5096

CANTOR, MORTON B., psychiatrist; b. St. Louis, June 21, 1924; s. William and Sarah (Goldberg) C.; m. Cecilia Lola Gersch; children: Jonathan, David. BA in Chemistry, U. N.C., Chapel Hill, 1943; MD, St. Louis U., 1947. Diplomate Am. Bd. Psychiatry and Neurology, Nat. Bd. Med. Examiners. Intern Morrissania City Hosp., Bronx, N.Y., 1947-48, resident in neurology, 1948-49; resident psychiatrist Bklyn. State Hosp., 1949-52; lectr., supr. Karen Horney Inst. and Clinic, N.Y.C., 1955-59; faculty, asst. dean Postgrad. Ctr. Mental Health, N.Y.C., 1959-69; faculty supr. Westchester Ctr. For Study of Psychoanalysis and Psychotherapy, White Plains, N.Y., 1973—; faculty, clin. assoc. prof. N.Y. Med. Coll., Valhalla, N.Y., 1975—; assoc. attending psychiatrist Westchester County Med. Ctr., Valhalla, 1972—. Contbr. articles to profl. jours.; co-editor: Affect: Psychoanalytic Theory and Practice, 1983, Psychoanalysis and Severe Emotional Illness. Capt. U.S. Army, 1952-54. Fellow Am. Psychiat. Assn. (life), Am. Acad. Psychoanalysis (treas. 1967-72, jour. editor 1978—); mem. Assn. Advancement of Psychoanalysis (pres. 1965-67). Home and Office: 4 Tory Ln Scarsdale NY 10583-2315

CANTOR, RICHARD IRA, physician, corporate health executive; b. N.Y.C., Jan. 25, 1944; s. Jacob Alvin and Sarah (Sanderow) C.; m. Patricia Ann Honeycutt, June 7, 1970. AB, NYU, 1965; MD, Med. Coll. Va., 1970; postgrad., Bellevue Hosp. Ctr., N.Y.C., 1970-73. Diplomate Am. Bd. Internal Medicine. Intern Bellevue Hosp. Ctr., N.Y.C., 1970-71, resident, 1971-73; practice medicine specializing in internal medicine N.Y. Med. Group, N.Y.C., 1973-76; asst. med. dir. substance abuse programs Bellevue Hosp., 1973-76, med. dir. substance abuse programs, 1976-79; med. dir. Med Plan, N.Y.C., 1979-84; employee health unit Equitable Life Assurance Soc. U.S., N.Y.C., 1984-87; v.p., dir. health and med. svcs. Citibank, N.Y.C., 1988-89, v.p., dir. health, med. and staff svcs., 1989—; teaching asst. in medicine N.Y.U. Med. Ctr., N.Y.C., 1970-73, asst. prof. clin. medicine, 1983—; attending physician Cabrini Med. Ctr., N.Y.C., 1973-76, Bellevue Hosp. Ctr., 1973—; chmn. policy adv. bd. N.Y.C. Methadone Maintenance Treatment Programs, 1976-77; med. cons. Am. Fedn. State, County, and Mcpl. Employees, N.Y.C., 1979-84. Columnist "Ask Your Med Plan Doctor", Pub. Employee Press, 1980-84. NIH trainee in endocrinology Med. Coll. Va., 1968. Mem. Am. Acad. Med. Dirs., Med. Soc. County N.Y., Am. Occupational Med. Assn. Med. Soc. State N.Y., Am. Coll. Physicians, NYU Club, Phi Beta Kappa, Alpha Omega Alpha, Sigma Zeta. Office: Citibank 399 Park Ave New York NY 10043-0001

CANTRIL, ALBERT H(ADLEY), public opinion analyst; b. N.Y.C., June 17, 1940; s. Hadley and Mavis Katherine (Lyman) C.; m. Susan Bradford Davis, June 30, 1973. AB, Dartmouth Coll., 1962; PhD, MIT, 1966. Asst. to Bill Moyers The White House, Washington, 1965-67; cons. to dir. Bur. of the Budget, Washington, 1967; spl. asst. to asst. sec. East Asian and Pacific affairs Dept. of State, Washington, 1967-69; exec. sec., com. on def. social sci. rsch. Nat. Acad. Scis., Washington, 1969-70; cons. Dem. Nat. Com. and candidates, Washington, 1971-74; dir. rsch. Commn. Op. of U.S. Senate, Washington, 1975-76; pres. Nat. Coun. on Pub. Polls, Washington, 1976-81, Bur. Social Sci. Rsch., Inc., Washington, 1981-86; fellow and rsch. fellow Inst. of Politics Harvard U., Cambridge, Mass., 1986-88; pvt. practice cons. in pub. opinion and survey rsch. Washington, Boston, 1989—; mem. editorial adv. bd. Pub. Opinion Quarterly, Chgo., 1985-89; trustee Nat. Coun. on Pub. Polls, 1982—; adj. prof. internat. politics, Fletcher Sch. Law and Diplomacy, Tufts U., Medford, Mass., 1991—. Author: The Opinion Connection: Polling, Politics and the Press, 1991; co-author: Hopes and Fears of the American People, 1971, Polls: Their Use and Misuse in Politics, 1972, 2d edit., 1980; editor: Polling on the Issues, 1980, Psychology, Humanism and Scientific Inquiry: The Selected Essays of Hadley Cantril, 1988. Recipient Mecklin award Dartmouth Coll., 1962. Mem. Am. Assn. Pub. Opinion Rsch. Democrat.

CANTWELL, LOIS, writer, editor; b. Jersey City, June 16; m. Robert Sefcik, Oct. 3, 1981; children: Teddy, Zoe. BA, U. Wis., 1973. Editor Ideal Pub., N.Y.C., 1977-78; editor-in-chief children's div. Parents mag., N.Y.C., 1978-81; editor-in-chief Careers mag. E.M. Guild Inc., N.Y.C., 1987-89; freelance writer N.Y.C., 1981-87; v.p., dir. internal communications Kidder, Peabody and Co., Inc., N.Y.C., 1989-90; mgr. internal communications Sony Corp Am., Park Ridge, N.J., 1990—; cons. AT&T, Morristown, N.J., 1985, CNR Ptnrs., N.Y.C., 1987. Author: Money and Banking, 1984, Freedom, 1985, Modeling, 1986, Blackstone's Magic Adventures, 1986. Pres. Midtown Manor Coop., N.Y.C., 1985, treas., 1986. Mem. Soc. Profl. Jours., Nat. Acad. TV Arts and Scis., Internat. Assn. Bus. Communicators, Fred Lewis Allen Room, Writers Room, Sigma Delta Chi. Home: 42 Walnut Ave Millburn NJ 07041-1512

CANTY, JAMES JOSEPH, JR., psychologist; b. Boston, July 26, 1931; s. James Joseph and Kathleen (McDonnell) C.; m. Eileen Maxwell, Sept. 3, 1960; children: Anne, Kathleen (dec.), James III, Edward. BS, Boston Coll., 1955; MA, Fordham U., 1962, PhD, 1970. Lic. psychologist. Counselor Cath. Charities, N.Y.C., 1960-61, Seton Hall U., South Orange, N.J., 1961-65; dir. counseling ctr. Manhattan Coll., Bronx, N.Y., 1965-73; clin. psychologist VA Med. Ctr., N.Y.C. and Montrose, N.Y., 1973—; pvt. practice clin. psychology N.Y. Office: FDR VA Hosp Montrose NY 10548

CAOUETTE, DAVID PAUL, insurance company executive; b. Sanford, Maine, Aug. 6, 1960; s. Paul Henry and Barbara (Stackpole) C. BA with distinction, U. Maine, Orono, 1983. Editor employee communications Union Mutual Life Ins. Co., Portland, Maine, 1981-84, pub. rels. acct. exec., 1984-85; mgr. employee communications UNUM Life Ins. Co., Portland, 1985-87; v.p., mgr. communications Integrated Resources, Inc., N.Y.C., 1987-89; asst. dir. corp. communications Fin. Guaranty Ins. Co., N.Y.C., 1989—; ptnr., co-founder Interactive Communications, Inc., Merrick, N.Y., 1989—. Recipient 1st place bronze award Fin. World Ann. Report Competition, 1990, 91. Mem. Internat. Assn. Bus. Communicators, Pub. Rels. Soc. Am. Democrat. Roman Catholic. Home: 666 Greenwich St Apt 814 New York NY 10014 Office: Fin Guaranty Ins Co 175 Water St New York NY 10038-4918

CAOUETTE, JOHN BERNARD, insurance company executive; b. New Bedford, Mass., Oct. 5, 1944; s. Bernard Adrian and Constance Mary (Donahue) C.; m. Margaretta Johnson, Jan. 30, 1966; children: Tristen Michelle, Brian Willis. BA, Calif. State U., Long Beach, 1969; MBA, U. Calif., Berkeley, 1970. With Citibank, San Francisco, 1970-71; mgr. swaps and global securities, v.p. Citibank, Jakarta, Indonesia, 1971-72, Hong Kong, 1972-79, N.Y.C., 1979-82; mgr. fgn. exch. and money markets Continental Grain Co., N.Y.C., 1982-86; pres., chief exec. officer Capital Markets Assurance Corp., N.Y.C., 1986—; chmn. Assn. Fin. Guaranty Insurors, 1990-91. Contbr. articles to various publs. With U.S. Army, 1965-67, Vietnam. Office: Capital Markets Assurance 885 3d Ave New York NY 10022

CAPANNA, MARK ANTHONY, carpenter, song writer; b. Elmer, N.J., Jan. 28, 1963; s. Carmen and Lucy Rose (Reach) C. Student, Glassboro State Coll., 1988. Lic. real estate agt. Cook, waiter Joann's Pizza, Egg Harbor, N.J., 1981-83; carpenter Capjohn Constrn., Pitman, N.J., 1983-90; real estate agt. Spinosi Real Estate, Pitman, 1991—; painter Sottile Enterprises, Pitman, 1991-92; carpenter Julian & Karen Capanna Builders, Pitman, 1992—. Song writer, 1978—. Republican. Roman Catholic.

CAPECELATRO, MARK JOHN, lawyer; b. New Haven, June 2, 1948; s. Ralph Ettore and Elaine (Scialla) C.; m. Jane Beals, June 19, 1971; children: Christopher Beals, Kate Rowley, Jonathan Mark. BA, Colgate U., 1970; JD, U. Conn., 1973. Bar: Conn. 1973. Assoc. Ells, Quinlan, Eddy & Robinson, Canaan, Conn., 1973-77; ptnr. Ells, Quinlan & Robinson, Canaan, 1977-90, Capecelatro & Nelligan, Canaan, 1991—; bd. advisors Canaan Nat. Bank, 1982—; mortgage counsel People's Bank, Canaan and Hartford, Conn., 1983—; trustee Sharon (Conn.) Hosp., 1984-91, vice chmn., 1990-91, chmn. exec. com. 1990-91; trustee Salisbury Congl. Ch., 1990—, vice chmn., 1990—. Bd. dirs. Housatonic Homemaker Health Aide, West Cornwall, Conn., 1977-80, Housatonic Day Care Ctr., Inc., Lakeville, Conn., 1981-90, Salisbury Pub. Health Nursing, Lakeville, 1983-85, Salisbury Winter Sports Assn., 1983-87, Salisbury (Conn.) Congl. Ch.; mem. adv. com. Parkside Med. Svcs. Corp., 1988—. Mem. ABA, Conn. Bar Assn., Litchfield County Bar Assn., Assn. Trial Lawyers Am., Conn. Assn. Trial Lawyers, Nat. Assn. Criminal Def. Lawyers. Republican. Home: 196 Belgo Rd Lakeville CT 06039 Office: Capecelatro & Nelligan 117 Main St Canaan CT 06018

CAPELLAN, ANGEL, computer systems executive; b. Zorraquin, Spain, Apr. 10, 1942; s. Sotero and Damasa Capellan; m. Sonia C. Guadalupe, Aug. 27, 1971; children: Carlos Manuel, Amaya Isabel. Licentiate degree, U. Madrid, 1968; MA, NYU, 1969, NYU, 1970; PhD, NYU, 1977. Tchr. Colegio Santa Maria, Spain, 1962-66; instr. Spanish Hunter Coll., N.Y.C., 1969-78; dir. lang. arts South Bronx campus Sch. New Resources, Coll. New Rochelle, N.Y.C., 1978-83; assoc. dean Eugenio Maria de Hostos Community Coll., N.Y.C., 1983-84; pres. LEA, Book Distbrs. & Links-Lazos, Internat. Computer Systems, N.Y.C., 1984—; judge CEPI Literary Prizes, N.Y.C., 1972-89. Contbr. articles to profl. jours.; author of book revs., poems, and stories; author: Hemingway and the Hispanic World, 1985, Paisajes renacidos, 1982; contbg. author: Gran enciclopedia Rialp, Tomo 20, 1974, Tomo 23, 1974. Juan March fellow Juan March Found., Madrid, 1969-70, Fulbright scholar Fulbright Found., 1968-69; Elias Ahuja fellow Fulbright Found., Madrid, 1968-69. Mem. MLA, Am. Assn. Tchrs. Spanish and Portuguese, Am. Booksellers Assn. Roman Catholic. Home and Office: 17023 83d Ave Jamaica NY 11432-2101

CAPIE, SUSAN ALVERA, import export company executive; b. Tokyo, July 26, 1953; d. Robert Mansfield and Alvera Frederick (Legerlotz) C.; m. Kenneth Michael Monda, July 11, 1981; 1 child, Katlin Mansfield Monda. BA in Anthropology, U. Calif., Santa Barbara, 1975, MA in Chinese History, 1980. Mgr. Triumphant Affiliates, Taipei, 1980-82; translator Taipei Lang. Inst., Taiwan, 1981-82; pres. asst. Kanjin Internat., N.Y.C., 1984-85; asst. to gen. mgr. China dept. MWM Chem., N.Y.C., 1985-86, mgr., 1986-87; gen. mgr. China Zetapharm, Inc., N.Y.C., 1987—. Stanford Ctr. grantee, Taipei, 1982-83. Mem. Phi Beta Kappa. Office: ZetaPharm Inc 70 W 36th St New York NY 10018-8007

CAPIZZI, TRACEY LEIGH QUANTE, infosystems specialist; b. Colorado Springs, Colo., Aug. 31, 1959; d. Frank Jr. and M. Virginia (Lanus) Quante; m. Jerry J. Capizzi, Feb. 13, 1987. Student, No. Va. Community Coll., Alexandria, 1976-79, U. Md., 1985-86, George Mason U., 1984-85, 87—. Traffic engrng. analyst TDX Systems Inc., Vienna, Va., 1977-78; lead operator TDX Telecommunications Inc., Vienna, 1978-79; prodn. coordinator Chilton Corp., Dallas, 1979-82; advt. coordinator Wall St. Jour., Dallas, 1982-84; adminstrv. asst. Oxford Devel. Corp., Bethesda, Md., 1984-85, systems coordinator, 1985-86; systems adminstr. Mintz, Levin, Cohn, Ferris, Glovsky & Popeo, Washington, 1986-87; info. systems mgr. Vinson & Elkins, Washington, 1987-88; cons. Gen. Analytics Corp., Vienna, Va., 1988-90, ASTRA, Inc., Bethesda, Md., 1990—. Mem. NAFE, Assn. Systems Mgmt. Republican. Episcopalian. Home: 110 N Johnson Rd # 101 Sterling VA 22170-2624

CAPLAN, CONSTANCE ROSE, real estate executive; b. Phila., Dec. 28, 1935; d. Morton M. and Esther (Hauptman) Rose; m. Caswell J. Caplan, June 21, 1955 (dec. 1986); children: Mark, Catherine, Jonathan. BA, Goucher Coll., 1957; MA, Johns Hopkins U., 1978. Criminal justice planner Md. Gov.'s Commn. on Law Enforcement and Adminstrn. Justice, Balt., 1972-76; criminal justice coord. Baltimore County, Towson, Md., 1976-86; pres. The Time Group, Balt., 1986—; managing dir. Caswell J. Caplan Charitable Trusts, Balt., 1987—; trustee The Am. Fedn. Arts, N.Y.C., 1990—, Balt. Community Found., 1990—, Balt. Mentoring Inst., 1990—. Editor: Bawlamer, 1971. Trustee, officer Balt. Mus. Art, 1987—, Walters Art Gallery, Balt., 1988—; bd. dirs. Balt. City Pvt. Industry Coun., 1989—, Preservation Md., 1989—, Washington/Balt. Regional Assn., 1991—, Downtown Partnership Balt. Inc., 1991—; overseer Balt. Sch. for Arts, 1990—. Democrat. Jewish. Office: Time Group 701 Cathedral St Baltimore MD 21201

CAPLAN, RALPH, design writer, consultant; b. Sewickley, Pa., Jan. 4, 1925; s. Louis and Ruth (Hirsch) C.; m. Deborah Frank, Sept. 9, 1956 (div. 1978); children: Aaron, Leah; m. Judith Ramquist, Aug. 20, 1985; stepchildren: Stacy Ramquist, Michael Ramquist, Stephen Ramquist. BA, Earlham Coll., 1949; MA, Ind. U., 1950. Editor-in-chief Indsl. Design, 1952-56; prof. Wabash (Ind.) Coll., 1957-62; cons. Ralph Caplan & Co., 1962—; bd. dirs. Internat. Design Conf., Aspen, Co., 1967-91; cons. com. on coll. physics, SUNY, Stonybrook, 1964-68. Author: By Design, 1982; co-author: The Design Necessity, 1972; editor: Design in America, 1969; contbr. articles to profl. jours. Mem. adv. bd. Childesign, N.Y.C., 1987—; advisor Innovative Design Fund, N.Y.C., 1986-90, Pratt Inst. Grad. Program. Cpl. USMCR, 1943-44. Recipient Disting. Alumnus award Earlham Coll., 1990, Bronze Apple award Indsl. Design Soc., 1985, Gold medal Art Dirs. Club, 1979, Jesse Neal award Bus. Publ. Soc., 1960; grantee NEA, 1974-90. Mem. Indsl. Designers Soc. Am. (hon.), Soc. of Typographic Arts (hon.), Soc. of Environ. Designers (hon.), Am. Inst. Graphic Arts (bd. dirs. 1985-90).

CAPLIN, JERROLD LEON, health physicist; b. Phila., Jan. 25, 1930; s. Samuel Harry and Katherine (Socloff) C.; children: Sally C. Daniels, Patricia Graham Reed. AB, Temple U., 1951, postgrad., 1952-53; postgrad. Vanderbilt U., 1951-52. Supervisory health physicist U.S. Army C.E., Fort Belvoir, Va., 1959-61; health physicist AEC, U.S. Nuclear Regulatory Commn., Washington, 1961-81, ret., 1981; cons., 1981—; guest lectr. radiation sci. Georgetown U. Grad Sch., 1987—. Photographer, newspaper editor, sci. writer, 1983—. Co-author, editor Manual Respiratory Protection Against Airborne Radioactive Materials, 1976. Active Nat. Mus. of Women in Arts, Friends of the Nat. Zoo, Friends of the Kennedy Ctr. Lt. USNR, 1953-58. AEC radiol. physics fellow Vanderbilt U., 1951-52; mem. Am. Nat. Standards Inst., Health Physics Soc., Am. Conf. Gov. Indsl. Hygienists, (chmn. com. 1977-83), Internat. Radiation Protection Assn., Am. Assn. Physics Tchrs., AAAS, ASTM, U.S. Naval Inst., Am. Film Inst., Nat. Wildlife Fedn., Nat. Geog. Soc., Smithsonian Instn. (resident assoc. 1970—). Home and Office: 9 Goodport Ln Gaithersburg MD 20878-1001

CAPODILUPO, ELIZABETH JEANNE HATTON, public relations executive; b. McRae, Ga., May 3, 1940; d. Lewis Irby and Essee Elizabeth (Parker) Hatton; m. Raphael S. Capodilupo, Jan. 21, 1967. Grad., Dale Carnegie Inst., 1976. Sec. A.R. Clark Acct., Fernandina Beach, Fla., 1958-59; receptionist, girl Friday Sta. WNDT-TV, N.Y.C., 1960-62, Coy Hunt and Co., N.Y.C., 1962-69; clk. Woodlawn Cemetery, Bronx, N.Y., 1969-71, historian, community affairs coord., 1971—, editor newsletter, 1979—, asst. to pres., 1984, dir. pub. rels., 1984; grad. asst. Dale Carnegie Inst., 1977-78. Researcher Woodlawn Cemetery's Hall of Fame. Chairwoman Ann. Adm. Farragut Honor Ceremony, Bronx, 1976—; founder, chairperson Toys for Needy Children, 1983-91; bd. dirs. Bronx Mus. Arts, v.p., 1983-84; pres. Bronx Coun. Arts, 1987-90; mem. adv. bd. Salvation Army, 1985, Bronx Arts Ensemble, 1985; bd. mgrs. Bronx YMCA, 1985, life mem.; bd. dirs. Bronx Urban League, 1985, Bronx Coun. on the Arts, 1985, pres. 1987-90. Recipient award citation VFW, 1976, Voice of Democracy Program judge's citation, 1980, Disting. Community Service award N.Y.C. Council, II Leone di Sanmarco award Italian Heritage & Culture Com. Bronx, 1989; named Woman of Yr., YMCA, Bronx, 1986, Woman of Yr., Network Orgn. of Bronx Women, 1986, Jeanne and Ray Capodilupo named as Mr. & Mrs. Bronx 1989-90 proclaimed by Borough Pres., named Pioneer of the Bronx, 1992; cert. appreciation Dale Carnegie Inst., 1977; Outstanding Citizenship award Bronx N.E. Kiwanis Club, 1981; Service to Youth award YMCA of Bronx, 1983; recipient proclamation City Council of N.Y., Italian Heritage and Culture Com. of the Bronx, 1989; Outstanding Cemeterian award Am. Cemetery Assn., 1987-88; Citation of Merit Bronx Borough Pres.'s Office, 1988; Spl. Hons. for Outstanding Vol. Work Ladies Aux. Our Lady of Mercy Med. Ctr.; named Hon. Grand Marshall Bronx Columbus Day Parade, 1987-89, Bronx Meml. Day Parade, 1989; apptd. to commn. celebrating 350 yrs. of the Bronx by Borough Pres., recipient Pioneer award for Women's History Month for Outstanding Humanitarian Svcs., 1991. Mem. Bronx County Hist. Soc., Network Orgn. Bronx Women, Women in Communication, Bronx C. of C. (sec. 1988), YMCA (life mem.), N.Y. Press Club, Italian Big Sisters Club, Women's City Club, Order Eastern Star. Methodist. Office: Woodlawn Cemetery PO Box 75 Bronx NY 10470-0075

CAPOLARELLO, JOE R., photojournalist; b. Bklyn., Sept. 6, 1961; s. Carmelo and Grace (Auditore) C. Cert. news prodn. and tech., Inst. New Cinema Artists, N.Y.C., 1980; cert. TV News Video Workshop, U. Okla., Norman, 1986; cert. TV News Feature Workshop, Internat. Film & TV Workshops, Rockport, Maine, 1987; cert. Leadership in Broadcast Photojournalism, The Poynter Inst. for Media Studies, St. Petersburg, Fla., 1992. Photojournalist, videotape editor, field producer W.Va. Jour. Sta. WSWP-TV, Beckley, W.Va., 1981-82; photojournalist Eyewitness News Sta. WABC-TV, N.Y.C., 1982; photojournalist Bus. Times, ESPN, N.Y.C., 1983, Broadcast News Svc., N.Y.C., 1983, Cable News Network, Inc., N.Y.C., 1983—, Entertainment Tonight, Paramount Pictures Corp., N.Y.C., 1988—, Fox News at Seven, The Ten O'Clock News, Sta. WNYW-TV, N.Y.C., 1988—, USA Today: The Television Show, Grant Tinker/Gannett East Prodns. Inc., N.Y.C., 1988-89, Preview: the best of the new, TV Program Enterprises, N.Y.C., 1990; photojournalist Personalities Twentieth Century Fox Film Corp., N.Y.C., 1991. Mem. Acad. TV Arts and Scis., Nat. Hon. Broadcasting Soc., TV and Radio Working Press Assn., Nat. Press Photographers Assn. Democrat. Roman Catholic. Home: 1 Liberty St Little Ferry NJ 07643-1708 Office: Cable News Network 5 Penn Plz New York NY 10001-1878

CAPONE, ANTONIO, psychiatrist; b. Afragola, Naples, Italy, Feb. 18, 1926; came to U.S., 1954; s. Giulio and Giovanna (Fico) C.; m. Maria Morello, Mar. 21, 1957; children: Antonio Jr., John, Walter. MD, U. Naples, 1953. Diplomate Am. Bd. Med. Psychotherapists, Am. Bd. Psychiatry and Neurology, Internat. Acad. Behavioral Medicine. Intern Ospedale Incurabili, Naples, 1953-54, St. Francis Hosp., Jersey City, 1954-55; resident physician St. Clare's Hosp., Denville, N.J., 1955-56; courtesy staff Butler Hosp., Providence, 1959—; chief psychiatry John E. Fogarty Meml. Hosp., North Smithfield, R.I., 1969-79, Pawtucket (R.I.) Meml. Hosp., 1971-80, St. Joseph Hosp., Providence, 1971—; dir. Psychiat. Svcs., Inc., Providence, 1970—; clin. asst. prof. psychiatry and human behavior Brown U. Med. Sch., Providence, 1980—; med. dir. psychiat. unit St. Joseph Hosp., Providence, 1987—; cons. psychiatrist Pawtucket Meml. Hosp., 1980—, John E. Fogarty Meml. Hosp., North Smithfield, 1979; chief psychiat. cons. R.I. Div. Vocat. Rehab., Providence, 1967-72; med. advisor Dept. HEW, 1967—; clin. elective course leader Brown Med. Sch., Providence, 1982—. Contbr. articles to profl. jours. Various presentations on mental health and alcoholism, Lions Club, Kiwanis, TV, and radio. Fellow Am. Psychiat. Assn. (pres. R.I. dist. br. 1968-70, mem. peer rev. com. 1982—, mem. fellowship com. 1984—, mem. ad hoc on referral svc. 1987-88); mem. AMA, R.I. Med. Soc., Providence Med. Assn., Psychiatry and Neurology, Pan Am. Med. Assn., Am. Soc. Vienna. Roman Catholic. Office: Psychiat Svcs Inc 911 Smith St Providence RI 02908-2789

CAPORALE, ROBERT STEPHEN, engineering company executive, elevator consultant; b. N.Y.C., May 29, 1945; s. Stephen and Virginia (Patafio) C.; m. Theresa Angela Riccio, Jan. 1, 1967; children: Anthony Christian, Robert Stephen Jr. AAS in Elec. Tech., SUNY, Farmingdale, 1980. Cert. elevator safety inspector. Draftsman Jaros Baum & Bolles, N.Y.C., 1964-75, designer, 1975-80, assoc., 1980-90; dir. engrng. D.T.M., Inc., N.Y.C., 1990; v.p. Syska & Hennessy, Inc., N.Y.C., 1990—; dir. Transp. Systems Group, Div. of Syska & Hennessy, N.Y.C., 1990—. Author: (computer programs) Eletran, Deletran, Raildata, Escada, 1985. Cub master Boy Scouts Am., Bay Shore, N.Y.; asst. coach Bay Shore Soccer Club. Mem. Am. Soc. Mech. Engrs., Nat. Assn. Elevator Safety Authorities, Elevator Cons. Forum. Office: Syska & Hennessy Transp Sys 115 5th Ave New York NY 10003-1004

CAPOSELA, ERNEST MICHAEL, lawyer; b. Paterson, N.J., May 31, 1953; s. Carmen and Florence (Mendello) C.; m. Eve Selma Atamian. BS, Fairleigh Dickinson U., 1975; MPA, NYU, 1977; JD, U. Louisville, 1981. Bar: N.J. 1983, U.S. Dist. N.J. 1983; cert. criminal trial atty. Legis. cons. Coun. of State Govt., N.Y.C., 1976-78; law clk. to presiding justice N.J. Superior Ct., Paterson, 1981-82; ptnr. Sala and Caposela, Clifton, N.J., 1983—; legal counsel Libr. Bd. Trustees, Paterson, 1983—; zoning bd. legal counsel Bd. Adjustment, Passaic, N.J., 1983; legal counsel Paterson

Restoration Corp., 1988—; lectr. on criminal trial preparation, N.J. Inst. of Continuing Legal Edn., 1987—. Sustaining mem. Passaic County Dem. Orgn., Passaic County, 1986. Named Outstanding Young Man Am. Jaycees, 1982. Mem. Assn. Trial Lawyers Am., N.J. Bar Assn., Passaic County Bar Assn., Assn. Criminal Def. Lawyers N.J. Democrat. Roman Catholic. Club: Hamilton (Paterson). Home and Office: 388 Lakeview Ave Apt 1C Clifton NJ 07011-4091

CAPPALLO, ROGER JAMES, astronomer; b. Cleve., Sept. 30, 1949; s. Roy Foster and Elizabeth Lynn (Harman) C.; m. Nancy Lynn Crispin, Oct. 16, 1971; children: Rigel Crispin, Trevor Austin, Spencer Harman. SB, MIT, 1971, PhD, 1980; postgrad., Calif. Inst. Tech., 1971-72. Rsch. scientist MIT Haystack Obs., Westford, Mass., 1980—. Contbr. articles to profl. jours. Registrar Groton-Dunstable Soccer Club, Groton, Mass., 1988-89. Recipient Group Achievement award NASA, 1986. Mem. Nashoba Chess Club. Home: 654 Longley Rd Groton MA 01450-1023 Office: Haystack Obs Rt 40 Westford MA 01886

CAPPEL, C. ROBERT, environmental scientist, chemist; b. Connersville, Ind., Nov. 17, 1942; s. Carl Henry and Mary F. (Tingle) C.; m. Linda Masterson, July 18, 1981; children: Robert, Lora, Craig. BS, Ball State U., 1969; MS, U. Ill., 1972, PhD, 1973. Sr. rsch. scientist Eastman Kodak Co., Rochester, N.Y., 1973-90, dir. environ. health and safety support svcs., 1990—. Patentee yellow dye stability in process K-14. Mem. IS&T, AQSC, Sigma Xi, Sigma Pi Sigma.

CAPPER, ALOYSIUS JOSEPH, III, banker; b. Phila., June 10, 1955; s. Aloysius Joseph Jr. and Jane Margaret (Cabrey) C. Student, Villanova U., 1974-75, Northwestern U., 1980; lic. real estate sales, Funk Inst., Pennsauken, N.J., 1976; student, Neumann Coll., 1992—. Distbn. mgr. Media Sales, Inc., Phila., 1975-76; sales rep. Tolz Realtors, Inc., Wildwood, N.J., 1976-77, 1st Ea. Realty, Inc., Avalon, N.J., 1977-79; charter supr. Five Mile Beach Bus Co., North Wildwood, N.J., 1980-84; sales coord. Advanced Hotel Mktg. Corp., Aurora, Colo., 1986-87; customer svc. rep. Chase, USA, N.A., Wilmington, Del., 1987-88, consumer credit analyst, 1988-89; credit analyst Chase, USA, N.A., 1989-91; ops. supr. Chase USA, N.A., Wilmington, 1991—; investment cons., Claymont, Del., 1988—. Vice pres. North Wildwood Dem. Club, 1978-79; coach Greater Wildwood Little League, 1980-85. Mem. Am. Assn. Individual Investors, Nat. Assn. Bankers, Sigma Phi Epsilon. Democrat. Roman Catholic.

CAPPITELLA, MAURO JOHN, architect; b. N.Y.C., July 11, 1934; s. Gaetano and Maria (D'Errico) C.; m. Christine Wilhelmine Otte, Oct. 11, 1964; children: Mark, Christina, Nicole. BS in Architecture, CCNY, 1956; postgrad., Columbia U., 1960-62; M in Urban Planning, NYU, 1967. Registered architect, N.Y., N.J.; lic. Nat. Coun. Archtl. Registration Bds.; profl. planner, N.J. Designer Garfinkel & Marenberg, N.Y.C., 1956-57; architect Western Electric Co., Inc., N.Y.C., 1957-68; cons. architect Norwood, N.J., 1968-76, Upper Saddle River, N.J., 1976—. Served to 1st lt. U.S. Army, 1957-59. Mem. AIA, N.Y. Soc. Architects, N.J. Soc. Architects (bd. dirs. 1983-84, 87-89), Architects League Northern N.J. (bd. dirs. 1980-83, 89-91, sec. 1984-85, v.p. 1985, 1st v.p. 1986, pres.-elect 1987, pres. 1988, Dir. of the Yr. award 1981, 82), Soc. 3d U.S. Inf. Div. U.S. Army, Saddle River Tennis Club, Windham Ridge Resorts Country Club, Rotary (Park Ridge Club). Republican. Roman Catholic. Office: 332 E Saddle River Rd Saddle River NJ 07458-2108

CAPPO, JOSEPH C., publisher; b. Chgo., Feb. 24, 1936; s. Joseph V. and Frances (Maggio) Caciopppo; m. Mary Anne Cappo, May 7, 1967; children: Elizabeth, John. BA, DePaul U., 1957. Reporter, Hollister Publs., Wilmette, Ill., 1961-62; reporter Chgo. Daily News, 1962-68, bus. columnist, 1968-78; columnist Crain's Chgo. Bus., 1978-79, pub., 1979-89; v.p. Crain Communications, Inc., 1981-89, sr. v.p. group. pub., 1989—; pub. Advt. Age, 1989—, publishing dir, 1992—; dir. Assn. Area Bus. Publs., 1982-88. Bd. dirs.: Off the Street Club, Chgo., 1981—, Chicago Advt. Fedn., 1987—, Mus. of Broadcast Communications, 1984-1990, Ill. Coun. on Econ. Edn., 1990—. With U.S. Army, 1959-61. Recipient award Ill. Press Assn., 1962, (with other Daily News staffers) Nat. Headliner award, 1966, Disting. Alumni award DePaul U., 1975, Page One award Chgo. Newspaper Guild, 1978, Peter Lisagor award Sigma Delta Chi, 1978, Outstanding Achievement award in Communication, Justinian Soc. Lawyers, 1979. Author: Future Scope: Success Strategies for the 1990's and Beyond, 1990. Mem. Econ. Club (Chgo.), Bus. and Econ. Writers (bd. govs. 1984-89), Ill. Small Business Advisory Comm., 1986-90, DePaul U. Alumni Assn. (bd. dirs. 1984-86), Delta Mu Delta (hon.). Roman Catholic. Office: Crain Communications Inc 740 N Rush St Chicago IL 60611-2590

CAPPON, ANDRE ALFRED, management consultant; b. Bucharest, Romania, Mar. 26, 1948; came to U.S., 1965; s. Otto and Frederica (Steuermann) C. BSc, MIT, 1970; MS, Columbia U., 1971. Analyst OECD, Paris, 1971-77; mgr. Arthur Andersen & Co., N.Y.C., 1977-80; v.p. Booz, Allen & Hamilton, Inc., N.Y.C., 1980-87; ptnr. Oliver, Wyman & Co., N.Y.C., 1987-91; mgmt. cons. N.Y.C., 1991—; prof. Lycee Francais N.Y., N.Y.C., 1970-71; lectr. Am. Coll., Paris, 1974-76. Home and Office: 531 Main St Apt 602 New York NY 10044-0109

CAPRICCI, SAMUEL CLEMENT, healthcare executive; b. Harrisburg, Pa., Jan. 10, 1955; s. Clement N. and Doris (Howell) C.; m. Theresa Elaine Apa, May 17, 1975. BS in Nursing cum laude, York (Pa.) Coll., 1987. RN, Pa. Machinist Bethlehem Steel Co., Steelton, Pa., 1973-84; ICU nurse Harrisburg Hosp., 1987-88; rehab. specialist Intracorp, Camp Hill, Pa., 1988; unit coord. Blue Ridge Haven West, Camp Hill, 1988-89; health care cons. Capital Blue Cross, Harrisburg, 1989—; mem. nursing adv. com. Pa. Emergency Health Svcs. Coun., Camp Hill, 1985-86. Mem. com. AIDS Edn. York City Sch. Dist., 1986-87; race dir. Blue Ridge Run to Benefit Arthritis, 1988. Mem. Sigma Theta Tau. Democrat. Lutheran. Home: 65 Chain Saw Rd Dillsburg PA 17019-9439 Office: Capital Blue Cross 100 Pine St Harrisburg PA 17101-1228

CAPRIO, NICHOLAS FRANK, pension fund administrator, accountant, educator; b. Trenton, N.J., Oct. 15, 1939; s. Earl and Josephine Mapps; m. Julia R. Caprio, Nov. 7, 1959; 1 child, Julie Caprio Stilwell. AA, Mercer County Community Coll., Trenton, 1972; BA, Trenton State U., 1974; MA, Rider Coll., 1977. Chief fiscal officer State of N.J., Trenton, 1972-83, dep. dir. div. pensions, 1983—; prin. Nicholas F. Caprio CPA, Trenton, 1980—; prof. Rider Coll., Lawrenceville, N.J., 1980—, Mercer County Community Coll., Trenton. Trustee Hamilton Ballet Theatre, Trenton; ptnr. Ballet Technique, Trenton. With USAF, 1961-65. Fellow N.J. Soc. CPAs; mem. AICPA. Home: 315 Sylvan Ave Trenton NJ 08610-5124 Office: State of NJ Div Pensions 50 W State St Trenton NJ 08608-1220

CAPRIOLO, JOHN ANTHONY, dentist; b. N.Y.C., May 29, 1957; s. Sam Martin and Blanche Ann (Hopewood) C.; m. Angela Sue Grabiel, May 2, 1987; children: John Anthony II, Nicholas David. BA in Psychology, U. Md., Balt., 1979, DDS, 1984. Resident VA, Martinsburg, W.Va., 1984-85; mem. staff, quality assurance coordinator, dir. dental student program VA, Martinsburg, 1986-90; gen. practice dentistry Balt., 1985; mem. staff Stockley Ctr. State of Del., Georgetown, 1985-86; asst. clin. prof. U. W.Va., Morgantown, 1986-90; pvt. practice gen. dentistry Glen Burnie, Md., 1990—; mem. adv. bd. U. Md. Dental Sch., 1983-84. Campaigner Paul Capriolo for Md. Ho. of Dels., 1986; dir. youth ministry, mem. coun. Holy Family Cath. Ch., Randallstown, Md., 1979-84; lector St. Joseph's Cath. Ch., Martinsburg, 1986-90, coord. home svc. team min., 1989-90; pres. Pikeview West Homeowners Assn., 1989-90, Falcon Ridge Homeowners Assn., 1990-91. Mem. ADA, Acad. Gen. Dentistry, Moose. Democrat. Home: 8801 Falcon Ridge Dr Randallstown MD 21133-4031

CAPUA, JAMES VINCENT, foundation executive; b. Ossining, N.Y., Sept. 22, 1949; s. Anthony Dominic and Josephine (Trapasso) C. BA with high honors, U. Rochester, 1971; MA, U. Chgo., 1972, PhD in History, 1976. Spl. asst. to chancellor, asst. prof. history U. Rochester (N.Y.), 1978-82; v.p. Inst. Ednl. Affairs, N.Y.C., 1982-85; dir. sec.'s discretionary fund U.S. Dept. Edn., Washington, 1985-87; pres. William H. Donner Found., Inc., N.Y.C., 1987—. Contbr. articles to profl. publs. Mem. N.Y.C. Commn. on Bicentennial of U.S. Constitution, 1988—. Danforth Found. fellow, 1971-75. Mem. Am. Soc. Marine Artists (bd. dirs. 1979—, v.p. 1984-86). Office: William H Donner Found 500 5th Ave Rm 1230 New York NY 10110-0180

CAPUTO, DANIEL VINCENT, psychologist; b. N.Y.C.; s. Pasquale and Hortense C.; A.B., Bklyn. Coll., 1954; Ph.D., U. Ill., 1961. Prof. med. psychology Washington U., St. Louis, 1959-64; prof. psychology Queens Coll., CUNY, Flushing, 1964—; research asso. St. Vincent's Med. Center, S.I., N.Y.; pvt. practice clin. psychology, 1973—. Registered psychologist, Nat. Register of Health Providers in Psychology; cert. psychologist, N.Y.; research grantee NIMH, 1963. Fellow N.Y. Acad. of Sci.; mem. N.Y. Acad. Scis., Am. Psychol. Assn., Eastern Psychol. Assn., N.Y. State Psychol. Assn. (rep. exec. com. 1981-83), Biofeedback Soc. Am. (cert.). Roman Catholic. Contbr. to Infants Born at Risk, 1979, Pre-term Birth: Relevance to Optimal Psychological Development, 1981. Home: 16-07 150th St Whitestone NY 11357 Office: Queens Coll Dept of Psychology Kissena Blvd Flushing NY 11367

CAPUTO, JOSEPH ANTHONY, university president; b. Jersey City, May 10, 1940; s. Anthony and Virginia (Bennett) C.; m. Linda Mary Ryan, Sept. 4, 1965; children: Christine D., David R. B.S., Seton Hall U., 1962; M.S., Seton U., 1964; Ph.D., U. Houston, 1967. Research assoc. Duke U., Durham, N.C., 1967-68; prof. dept. chemistry SUNY Coll.-Buffalo, 1968-77, chmn. dept. chemistry, 1974-77, v.p. acad. affairs, 1979-81; dean sch. sci. and math. S.W. Tex. State U., San Marcos, 1977-79; pres. Millersville (Pa.) U., 1981—; bd. dirs. Acad. for the Profession of Teaching, Harrisburg, Pa., 1987—, Harrisburg Univ. Ctr. Consortium, 1987—; cons. Pearsall Chem. Corp., 1978, Nat. Bur. Standards, 1973. Author: The Thermal Catalytic Equilibration of Cis and Trans Decalone-2, 1964, Studies in Electronic Transmission, 1967. Chmn. bd. Pa. State Athletic Conf., 1983; bd. dirs. Lancaster Area Arts Coun., 1987-90, Lancaster Gen. Hosp. Found., 1989—. SUNY Research Found. fellow, 1969; grantee, 1968-70; NSF grantee, 1972-73; Am. Chem. Soc. grantee, 1969-72. Fellow AAAS, Am. Chem. Soc., Commn. for State Colls. and Univs., Sigma Xi, Phi Kappa Phi; mem. Am. Assn. State Colls. and Univs. (bd. dirs. 1984-87), Pa. Assn. Colls. and Univs. (bd. dirs. 1991—), Lancaster (Pa.) C. of C. (bd. dirs. 1985-87). Home: 10 Hemlock Ln Millersville PA 17551-1701 Office: U Pa Office of Pres Millersville PA 17551

CAPUTO, WAYNE JAMES, surgeon podiatrist; b. Newark, Feb. 18, 1956; s. James Vincent and Jennie (DeMaio) C.; m. Phyllis A. Grillo, Nov. 20, 1984; children: Karla, Stefanie. BS in Biology, Syracuse (N.Y.) U., 1978; DPM, N.Y. Coll. Podiatric Medicine, 1982. Diplomate Am. Bd. Podiatric Surgery. Chief dept. podiatric surgery Clara Maass Med. Ctr., Belleville, N.J., 1987—; dir. residency in podiatric surgery Union (N.J.) Hosp., 1990—. Contbr. articles to profl. jours. Fellow ACS. Office: Clara Maass Profl Med Ctr 5 Franklin Ave Belleville NJ 07109-3532

CARANFA, ANGELO, philosophy educator; b. Rotello, Campobasso, Italy, May 24, 1942; came to U.S., 1957; s. Ermete Ugolino and Filomena (Terzano) C. BS, Stonehill Coll., 1966; MA, Boston Coll., 1971; PhD, U. Florence, Italy, 1972; MLS, Simmons Coll., 1987. Tchr. Bishop Stang High Sch., North Dartmouth, Mass., 1966-69, Archbishop Williams High Sch., Braintree, Mass., 1969-71, St. Columbkille High Sch., Brighton, Mass., 1974-75; adj. instr. Newbury Jr. Coll., Boston, 1975-76, Boston State Coll., 1976-78, Bridgewater (Mass.) State Coll., 1985-87, Stonehill Coll., North Easton, Mass., 1978-85, 90—. Author: Machiavelli Rethought, 1978, Claudel: Beauty and Grace, 1989, Proust: The Creative Silence, 1990; co-editor anthology of readings on human nature, 1984; contbr. articles to scholarly publs. Mem. MLA, APA. Roman Catholic. Home: 27 Sprague Ave Brockton MA 02402-3619 Office: Stonehill Coll Dept Philosophy North Easton MA 02357

CARAVASOS, NIKOLAOS, air transportation executive, educator; b. Sparta, Laconia, Greece, Feb. 28, 1938; came to U.S., 1951; s. Anastasios Constantine and Eugeniki (Kostolambros) C.; m. Maria Papaspiridakou, Aug. 15, 1962; 1 child, NiaLena. BSME, W.Va. U., 196; MS in Mgmt., U. Pa., 1988. Sr. engr. Boeing Comml. Airplane/Boeing Helicopter, Seattle, 1961-62; sr. engr. Boeing Helicopter, Phila., 1963-65, tech. specialist, 1965-83, tech. mgr., 1984—; guest lectr. Naval Postgrad. Sch., Monterey, Calif., 1989-91; lectr. Greece's NATO Forces, Athens, 1989. Contbr. numerous articles to profl. jours. Mem. AIAA (chmn. com.), Am. Helicopter Soc. Home: 70 Forest Ln Swarthmore PA 19081-1203 Office: Boeing Helicopter PO Box 16858 Philadelphia PA 19142-0858

CARBARY, JAMES FRANKLIN, space physicist; b. Corry, Pa., June 5, 1951; s. Richard J. and Sarah E. (Shaver) C.; m. Judith E. Greenblatt-Blum, June 8, 1991. BS, U. Ill., 1973; MS, Rice U., 1976, PhD, 1977. Postdoctorate Applied Physics Lab. Johns Hopkins U., Laurel, Md., 1978-83; staff Mission Rsch. Corp., Albuquerque, 1983-84; sr. staff Applied Physics Lab. Johns Hopkins U., 1985—. Contbr. articles to profl. jours. Mem. Howard County Striders, Columbia, Md., 1978—; triathlete Tri-Md.-Tri-Fedn., Balt., 1990—. Mem. Am. Geophys. Union, Am. Phys. Soc. Office: Johns Hopkins U Applied Physics Lab Johns Hopkins Rd Laurel MD 20723

CARBAUGH, JOHN EDWARD, JR., lawyer; b. Greenville, S.C., Sept. 4, 1945; s. John Edward and Mary Lou (McCarley) C.; m. Mary Middleton Calhoun; children: John, Martha. BA, U. of South, 1967; JD, U. S.C., 1973, postgrad., 1967-69; postgrad., Georgetown U., 1977-79. Bar: S.C. 1973, U.S. Ct. Appeals (4th cir.) 1982, U.S. Supreme Ct. 1982. With White House Staff, Washington, 1969-70; campaign dir. re-elect Thurmond campaign Washington, 1970-73; legis. asst. U.S. Senate, Washington, 1974-82; pvt. practice Washington, 1982—; bd. dirs. Argotech, Inc., Report from Am., Inc., Washington Watch, Inc., Advanced Diagnostics Labs., Inc., Mountain Brook Labs., Inc., Splty. Materials and Mfg. Inc.; mem. Pres. Commn. on Econ. Justice, Washington, 1985-87. Author: The Revisionists, 1991, New American Thinking About Japan, 1992, Japan Is Not the Enemy, 1992; co-author: A Program for Military Independence, 1980; contbr. articles to profl. jours. Rep. Nat. Platform Staff, 1976, 80, 84, 88, 92; Presdl. Transition Team, 1980-81. Sgt. USAR, 1969-77. Mem. Met. Club. Republican. Presbyterian. Office: Attorney-at-Law 1701 Pennsylvania Ave NW Washington DC 20006-5805

CARBERRY, MICHAEL GLEN, public relations executive; b. N.Y.C., Nov. 8, 1941; s. Glen Michael and Grace (Brennan) C.; m. Dianne Helen Riggs, Oct. 18, 1969; children—Glen, John, Catherine. BS, Manhattan Coll., 1963; MBA, Columbia U., 1968. Account exec. SSC&B, N.Y.C., 1968-69; account supr. Wells, Rich & Greene, N.Y.C., 1969-71; advt. mgr. U.S. Postal Svc., Washington, 1971-72; v.p., dir. Porter, Novelli & Assocs., Washington, 1972-79; chmn., chief exec. officer Henry J. Kaufman & Assocs., Washington, 1979—; adj. prof. Georgetown U., Washington, 1984—. V.p. exec. bd. Am. Cancer Soc., D.C. div., 1988—. 1st. lt. USMC, 1963-66, Vietnam, col. USMCR, 1968-92. Mem. Marine Corps Res. Officers Assn. (nat. v.p. 1985-86), Marine Corps Assn. (bd. dirs. 1987-91), N.Y. Athletic Club, Kenwood Country Club (Washington). Roman Catholic. Avocations: running, scuba diving. Office: Henry J Kaufman & Assocs 2233 Wisconsin Ave NW Washington DC 20007-4104

CARBONELL, RAMIRO M., lawyer; b. Astoria, N.Y., Sept. 9, 1962; s. Ramiro and Rosa Maria (Perez) C.; m. Michele G. Morgera, Apr. 28, 1989. BS, NYU, 1984; JD with tax honors, Rutgers U., 1987; LLM, Temple U., 1990. Bar: Pa., 1987, N.J., 1987. Assoc. Myers, Matteo, Rabil, Norcross & Langraf, Cherry Hill, N.J., 1987-89, Montgomery, McCracken, Walker & Rhoads, Cherry Hill, N.J., 1989—. Law Review Rutger's U., Camden, N.J., 1985-87. Mem. ABA, Nat. Assn. Bond Lawyers, Rotary Club of Cherry Hill. Republican. Roman Catholic. Office: Montgomery McCracken Walker & Rhoads 1010 Kings Hwy S Cherry Hill NJ 08034-2524

CARBONELLO, KAREN DELSPINA, administrator, consultant, educator; b. Orange, N.J., Sept. 16, 1956; d. Anthony C. and Frances A. (De Rosa) DelSpina; m. Gary Allen Carbonello, Dec. 10, 1978; children: Justin, Lyndsey. BA in Sociology, Seton Hall U., 1977; MA in Sociology, Fordham U., 1984. Dir. criminal justice planning County of Morris, Morristown, N.J., 1978-82, asst. trial ct. adminstr., 1982-88; exec. adminstrv. asst. to dep. dir. N.J. Adminstrv. Office of the Cts., Trenton, 1988-91; adj. prof. Caldwell (N.J.) Coll., 1984-85, Seton Hall U., South Orange, N.J., 1986-88, 92—, Fairleigh Dickinson U., Madison, N.J., 1988. Vol. Spl. Olympics; past mem. bd. trustees Jersey Battered Women Svcs., Morristown; past mem. social detoxification adv. bd. St. Clare's Hosp., Denville, N.J.; mem. adv. com. N.J. Judiciary EEO/AA, 1988-91. Recipient Resolution award Morris County Bd. Freeholders, 1988. Fellow Inst. for Ct. Mgmt.; mem. Nat. Assn. Ct. Mgrs., Am. Sociol. Assn., Children's Def. Fund, N.J. Assn. for Children. Republican. Roman Catholic.

CARD, ANDREW H., JR., government official; b. Brockton, Mass., May 10, 1947; s. Andrew Hill and Joyce (Whitaker) C.; m. Kathleene Marie Bryan; 3 children. BS in Engring., U. S. C., 1971; MA, LLD (hon.), Mount Ida Coll. and Assumption Coll.; MA, DPA (hon.), Curry Coll. Structural design engr. Maurice Reidy Engrs., Inc., 1971-72, David M. Berg, Inc., 1972-75; held several elected and appointed offices Holbrook, Mass., 1971-82; rep. Gen. Ct. of Commonwealth of Mass., 1975-82; v.p. CMIS Corp., Vienna, Va., 1983; spl. asst. to Pres. Ronald Reagan for Intergovtl. Affairs The White House, 1983-87; N.H. campaign mgr. for George Bush, 1987-88; dep. asst. to Pres. Ronald Reagan, dir. Office of Intergovtl. Affairs, 1988; asst. to Pres. and dep. chief of staff The White House, 1989-92; sec. of transp. Dept. of Transp., Washington, 1992—; mem. adv. commn. on intergovtl. relations, 1988. Candidate for gov., Mass., 1983. With USN, 1965-67. Named one of Nation's Outstanding Legislators, Nat. Rep. Legislators' Assn., 1982. Office: Dept Transp Room 10200 400 7th St SW Washington DC 20590*

CARD, DAVID NOEL, software engineer; b. Washington, June 14, 1952; s. Joseph David and Pauline Noel (Miller) C.; m. Marilza Emmanuel Novaes, Aug. 8, 1979; children: Simone, Michelle. BS in Interdisciplinary Scis., Am. U., 1975. Rsch. asst. Am. U., Washington, 1975-77; sr. programmer Litton Bionetics, Inc., Kensington, Md., 1977-78; dir. software process and measurement Computer Scis. Corp., Calverton, Md., 1978—. Author: Measuring Software Design Quality, 1990; mem. editorial adv. bd. Info. and Software Tech., 1988—; assoc. editor Jour. Systems and Software, 1990—; mem. editorial bd. Software Mag., 1991—; contbr. articles to profl. jours. With USN, 1970-71. Recipient Group Achievement award NASA, 1980, Tech. Innovation award, 1982, Profl. Activity award NSF, 1986. Mem. AIAA, IEEE, Am. Soc. for Quality Control. Office: Computer Scis Corp 4061 Powder Mill Rd Beltsville MD 20705-3149

CARD, RICHARD OTIS, business information consultant; b. Bath, Maine, Oct. 31, 1932; s. Otis Norris Edgar and Mildred Lucretia (Payne) C. BA, Bowdoin Coll., 1954; postgrad., Harvard U., 1956-57; diploma, Stonier Grad. Sch. Banking, 1976. From trainee to sr. systems cons. Bank of Boston, Mass., 1957-90; pvt. practice bus. info. cons. Boston, 1991—. Contbr. articles to local newspapers. Chmn. Rep. Ward Com., Boston, 1976-84. 1st lt. U.S. Army, 1954-56. Named Grand Bostonian, City of Boston, 1980. Mem. South End Hist. Soc. Inc. (bd. dirs., historian, pres. 1966-69), Boston Ctr. for the Arts (bd. dirs., chmn. 1984-85), Maine Maritime Mus. (bd. corporators mem.), Victorian Soc. in Am., Bostonian Soc., Soc. for the Preservation New Eng. Antiquities, Phi Beta Kappa. Methodist. Home: 183 W Brookline St Boston MA 02118-1279

CARDAMONE, RICHARD J., federal judge; b. Utica, N.Y., Oct. 10, 1925; s. Joseph J. and Josephine (Scala) C.; m. Catherine Baker Clarke, Aug. 28, 1946; 10 children. BA, Harvard U., 1948; LLB, Syracuse U., 1952. Bar: N.Y. 1952. Pvt. practice law Utica, 1952-62; judge N.Y. State Supreme Ct., 1963-71, Appelate div. 4th Dept. N.Y. State Supreme Ct., 1971-81, U.S. Ct. Appeals (2d cir.), Utica, 1981—. Trustee Slocum Dickson Found., Utica, St. Luke Hosp. Ctr., New Hartford, N.Y. Served as lt. (j.g.) USNR, 1943-46. Mem. Am. Law Inst., N.Y. State Bar Assn., Oneida County Bar Assn. Roman Catholic. Office: US Ct Appeals 10 Broad St Utica NY 13501-1233

CARDELLINA, JOHN HENRY, II, chemistry educator; b. Washington, Oct. 18, 1947; s. John H. and Gertrude P. (Grote) C. BA in Russian, BS in Chemistry, Pa. State U., 1968; PhD, U. Hawaii, 1979. Analytical chemist McNeil Labs., Ft. Washington, Pa., 1973-74; from asst. prof. to assoc. prof. chemistry Mont. State U., Bozeman, 1980-89; assoc. prof. Ctr. Marine Biotech., U. Md., Balt., 1989—; supervisory rsch. chemist Nat. Cancer Inst., 1988—. Served to lt. USN, 1968-72. Mem. Am. Chem. Soc., Am. Soc. Pharmacognosy, Mont. Acad. Sci. Office: U Md Ctr Marine Biotech Baltimore MD 21202

CARDI, VINCENZO, pharmacist; b. Formia, Italy, June 10, 1948; came to U.S., 1956, naturalized, 1962; s. Alfredo Armando and Marietta (Faiola) C.; divorced; children: Christine Marie, Danielle Patricia, Matthew Vincent. BSc, U. R.I., 1972; MPharm, Mass. Coll. Pharmacy, 1979. Resident in hosp. pharmacy R.I. Hosp., Providence, 1972-73, acting asst. to dir. pharm. svcs., 1973, pharmacy supr., 1974-76, acting asst. dir. pharmacy svcs., acting dir. cen. ops., 1976-79, asst. dir. pharmacy svcs., dir. cen. ops., 1979-81, dir. edn. and tng., 1981-85; pharmacist Brooks Drugs, Coventry, R.I., 1986-88; assoc. dir. pharmacy Day Kimball Hosp., Putnam, Conn., 1988-92; regional v.p. Primerica Fin. Svcs., 1989—. Contbr. articles to profl. jours. Active Muscular Dystrophy campaign. Mem. AAAS, R.I. Soc. Hosp. Pharmacists, Am. Soc. Hosp. Pharmacists, Am. Pharm. Assn., New Eng. Coun. Hosp. Pharmacists, Am. Inst. History of Pharmacy, Hosp. Assn. R.I., Am. Assn. I.V. Therapy, Nat. Alliance Bus., Am. Mgmt. Assn., Catholic Pharmacists Guild U.S., Societa di Maria Della Civita, Kappa Psi. Roman Catholic. Home: 149 Greenwood Rd North Kingstown RI 02852-6922 Office: Day Primerica Fin Svcs 911 Pontiac Ave Cranston RI 02420

CARDILE, PAUL JULIUS, fine arts dealer; b. N.Y.C., July 30, 1948; s. Julius Joseph and Mary Lola (Contrucci) C. BA, Queens Coll., N.Y.C., 1969, MA, 1971; MPhil, Yale U., 1974, PhD, 1976. Asst. prof. SUNY, Albany, 1975-76, Newcomb Coll., New Orleans, 1976-77, Cleve. State U., 1977-78; asst. prof., mus. dir. Denison U., Granville, Ohio, 1978-84; owner Cardile Galleries, N.Y.C., 1984—; appraiser Assn. of Am., N.Y.C., 1985—. Author: Paintings in Churches and Sacred Places in Cortona, 1982; contbr. articles to profl. jours. Humanities fellow NEH, 1982-83. Mem. Portuguese Heritage Found. (adv. coun. 1991—). Republican. Roman Catholic. Home: 880 5th Ave # 6H New York NY 10021-4951

CARDILLO, JOE (ALFRED), poet, novelist; b. Norwich, N.Y., Aug. 1, 1951; s. Alfio and Josephine (Pino) C.; m. Darlene Schlussel, Aug. 6, 1978. BA, Siena Coll., 1973; MA, SUNY, Albany, 1978. Cert. tchr., N.Y. Asst. prof. Hudson Valley Community Coll., Troy, N.Y., 1979—; freelance poet and rec. artist Troy, 1983—; performer, lectr. Internat. Tours, Averill Park, N.Y., 1988—; artist-in-residence Ragdale Artists Colony, Lake Forest, Ill., 1987, Sask. (Can.) Writers Guild, Emma Lake, 1988, 89. Author: A Legacy of Desire, 1983, Turning Toward Morning, 1984, 85, No Denials, 1986, Artifact, 1988, The Rock 'N' Roll Journals, 1989, Pulse, 1993; rec. artist (album) The Rock 'N' Roll Journals, 1989, (disco version) Freewill, 1990, (compact discs) First Light, 1991, Sharp, 1992, Be Wild, 1992. Roman Catholic. Office: Hudson Valley Community Coll Troy NY 12180

CARDILLO, ROBERT FRANCIS, JR., photographer; b. Pitts., Oct. 29, 1952; s. Robert Francis Sr. and Marianne Grace (Logiodice) C.; m. Sue Ann Leary, Sept. 2, 1984. BS, Pa. State U., 1975. Rsch. preparator Carengie Inst. Dept. Paleontology, Pitts., 1976-78; info. specialist Franklin Inst. Rsch. Ctr., Phila., 1979-80; herbarium technician Acad. Natural Scis., Phila., 1981-83; tech. dir. Visual Resources Ornithology, Phila., 1983-88; photography editor Organic Gardening Rodale Press, Emmaus, Pa., 1988—. Co-author: The Birds Around Us, 1987. Home: 6729 N 8th St Philadelphia PA 19126 Office: Rodale Press 33 E Minor St Emmaus PA 18098

CARDILLO, SUSAN MARIA, public relations professional; b. Pitts., May 7, 1958; d. Alfred Dominic Cardillo and Mary Josephine (Filipone) Perschetti. Student, U. Pitts., 1986-89; BA, Carlow Coll., 1991. Pediatric residency program coordinator Children's Hosp. of Pitts., 1981-85, adminstrv. asst., 1985-87, publs. specialist, 1987-89, sr. pub. rels. specialist, 1989-91, dir. pub. rels., 1991—. Recipient Effie award, 1992, Matrix award Pitts. chpt. Women in Communications, 1992, award of excellence Pitts. chpt. Internat. Assn. Bus. Communicators, 1991, PRSA Renaissance award, 1991. Mem. Pub. Rels. Soc. Am., Pub. Rels. Soc. Health Care Orgns., Am. Soc. Health Care Mktg. and Pub. Rels., Hosp. Assn. Pa. (3 superior awards

1990, Merritorious award 1991). Office: Children's Hosp of Pitts 3705 5th Ave Pittsburgh PA 15213-2524

CARDIN, BENJAMIN LOUIS, congressman; b. Balt., Oct. 5, 1943; s. Meyer M. and Dora (Green) C.; m. Myrna Edelman, Nov. 24, 1964; children: Michael, Debbie. B.A. cum laude, U. Pitts., 1964; J.D. (1st in class), U. Md., 1967. Bar: Md. 1967. Pvt. practice law Balt., 1967—; mem. Md. Ho. of Dels., 1966-86, chmn. ways and means com., 1974-79, speaker of house, 1979-86; mem. 100-102nd Congresses from 3d dist. Md., 1987—; asst. majority Whip; chmn. Md. Legal Svcs. Corp.; mem. Ways & Means Com., Health and Social Security subcoms. Contbr. articles to profl. publs. Trustee Balt. Mus. Art, Balt. Coun. Fgn. Affairs, Park Sch., St. Mary's Coll. Recipient U. Md. Law Sch. Alumni Assn. Cardin Pro Bono award, 1990, Ann Hogan Meml. award Common Cause of Md., Friend of Psychiatry award Md. Psychiat. Soc., Pub. Svc. Achievement award Waterfront Workers of Balt., MACO Legislator of Yr. award, 1984, Hadassah award Dr. Herman Seidel Humanitarian award, B'nai B'rith Menorah Lodge award, also several humanitarian awards. Mem. ABA, Md. Bar Assn., Balt. City Bar Assn., U. Md. Alumni Assn. (trustee), Order of the Coif, Omicron Delta Epsilon. Democrat. Jewish. Office: Cannon House Office Bldg Rm 117 Washington DC 20515

CARDINAL, JOHN ROBERT, pharmaceutical scientist, executive; b. Flint, Mich., Dec. 24, 1943; s. John Baptist and Daisy Myrtle (Solmonson) C.; m. Sharon Ruth Bonkoski, June 14, 1970; children—Michelle Marie, Suzanne Nicole. B.S., U. Mich., 1967; M.S., U. Wis.-Madison, 1969, Ph.D., 1973. Research asst. U. Wis.-Madison, 1967-71; asst. prof. U. Utah, Salt Lake City, 1972-79, assoc. prof., 1979-82, adj. assoc. prof., 1982-89; project leader Pfizer, Inc., Groton, Conn., 1982-83, mgr., 1983-88; dir. Merck & Co., Inc., 1988-90, sr. dir., 1990—; vis. prof. Upjohn Co., Kalamazoo, Mich., 1980. Holder several patents; contbr. articles to profl. jours. Bd. dirs. Cottenwood Inc., Salt Lake City, 1979-81. Fellow AAAS, Acad. Pharm. Scis. (vice-chmn., 1985), Am. Assn. Pharm. Scientists (chmn. pharmaceutics drug delivery sect., 1988) Am. Assn. Adv. Sci.; mem. Am. Chem. Soc., N.Y. Acad. Scis., Controlled Release Soc. (bd. govs. 1991—), Sigma Xi, Rho Chi Soc. Roman Catholic. Club: Indian Valley Country. Avocations: golf, bridge, cross-country skiing. Home: 1617 Stonington Cir North Wales PA 19454 Office: Merck Rsch Labs West Point PA 19486

CARDINAL, ROGER JOSEPH, banker, tax professional; b. Thompson, Conn., Apr. 25, 1950; s. Gerard O. and Adrienne (Lafleur) C.; m. Vivian Beauregard, June 12, 1971; children: Jason, Daniel. BS in Acctg., U. Mass., Dartmouth, 1978; MS in Taxation, Bentley Coll., 1985. CPA, Mass. Sr. tax acct. Arthur Andersen & Co., Boston, 1978-81; mgr. corp. tax State St. Bank & Trust Co., Boston, 1981-90, v.p. product tax, 1990—; appointed charter mem. IRS Info. Reporting Program Adv. Com., 1991—; speaker, lectr. Bank Tax Inst., N.Y.C., 1987—, Bank Adminstrn. Inst., Rolling Meadows, Ill., 1985—, Mass. Bankers Assn., Boston, 1983—; adj. assoc. prof. Bentley Coll., Waltham, Mass., 1986. Treas. Friends of the Holmes Libr., Halifax, Mass., 1989, 91. Sgt. USMC, 1969-73. Mem. AICPA, Tax Execs. Inst., Mass. Soc. CPAs, Mass. Bankers Assn. (ad hoc tax com.). Home: 95 Cranberry Dr Halifax MA 02338-1374 Office: State St Bank & Trust Co 225 Franklin St Boston MA 02110-2804

CARDINALE, KATHLEEN CARMEL, medical center administrator; b. Donegal, Ireland, July 13, 1933; came to U.S., 1958, naturalized, 1966; d. Denis and May (Cannon) O'Boyle; m. Anthony Cardinale, Aug. 28, 1965; BA, Jersey City State Coll., 1971, MA, 1973; RN, N.Y., U.K. nurse Walton Hosp., Liverpool, Eng., 1955; staff nurse, acting-in-charge Manhattan Gen. Hosp., N.Y.C., 1958-59; charge nurse, acting-in-charge, Met. Hosp., N.Y.C., 1959-60; charge nurse, relief supr. Manhattan Gen. Hosp., N.Y.C., 1960-64, asst. dir. nursing, 1964-68, staffing coord., 1968-70; acting assoc. dir. nursing Bernstein Inst., N.Y.C., 1970; clin. supr., clin. specialist Beth Israel Med. Ctr., N.Y.C., 1971-73; asst. dir. nursing Cabrini Med. Ctr., N.Y.C., 1974-77, assoc. DON, 1977-78, v.p. nursing svcs., 1978—. Mem. ANA, Greater N.Y. Hosp. Assn. (mem. mental hygene com.), Am. Hosp. Assn., Am. Orgn. Nurse Execs., Dean and Dirs. Home: 545 E 14th St New York NY 10009-3020 Office: Cabrini Med Ctr 227 E 19th St New York NY 10003

CARDUCCI, ELEANOR WHALEN, English educator; b. Pottsville, Pa., Dec. 5, 1942; d. John Francis and Eleanor (Doyle) Whalen; m. Joseph Anthony Carducci Jr., Oct. 11, 1975; 1 child, Erin Maureen. BS in secondary edn., Stroudsburg (Pa.) State Coll., 1964; MA in secondary edn., Seton Hall U., 1968; EdD, Rutgers U., 1979. Cert. tchr., N.J. Tchr. English Dover (N.J.) Pub. Schs., 1964-80; asst. prof. English, Edn. Centenary Coll., Hacketts Town, N.J., 1986-92; asst. prof. English, coord. liberal arts Sussex County C.C., Newton, N.J., 1992—; coord. Acad. Alliance N.W. N.J. Acaademic Collaborative, 1987—, N.J. Master Faculty Program, Centenary Coll., 1989—. Contbr. articles to profl. jours. Recipient Sears Roebuck award Centenary Coll., 1991. Mem. Assn. Tchr. Educators, Nat. Coun. Tchrs. of English, N.J. Coll. English Assn. Office: Sussex County Community Coll College Hill Newton NJ 07860

CARDWELL, NANCY LEE, editor; b. Norfolk, Va., Apr. 2, 1947; d. Joseph Thomas Cardwell and Martha (Bailey) Underwood. B.A. in Econs., Duke U., 1969; M.S. in Journalism, Columbia U., 1971. Copy editor Wall Street Jour., N.Y.C., 1971-73, reporter, 1973-76, editor fgn. dept. and Washington bur., 1977-80, night news editor, 1981-83, nat. news editor, 1983-87, asst. mng. editor, 1987-89; sr. editor Bus. Week mag., N.Y.C., 1989-91; editor Habitat World, Habitat for Humanity Internat., Americus, Ga., 1991—. Episcopalian. Office: Habitat for Humanity 121 Habitat St Americus GA 31709

CARDWELL, THOMAS AUGUSTA, III, air force officer; b. Oklahoma City, July 25, 1943; s. Thomas Augusta Jr. and Hilda Ogreta (Box) C.; m. T.J. Hopkins, 1992; children: Jill Suzanne, Mark Christopher. BBA, Tex. A&M U., 1965; MS, U. So. Calif., L.A., 1976; PhD, Pacific Western U., L.A., 1988. Commd. 2d lt. USAF, 1965, advanced through grades to col., 1982; F-4 fighter pilot 390th Tactical Fighter Squadron USAF, Da Nang Air Base, Republic of Vietnam, 1967; F-106 pilot 11th Fighter Interceptor Squadron USAF, Duluth, Minn., 1968-72; dep. chief staff for sys. and logistics, Fgn. Mil. Tng. Div. USAF, Washington, 1973-74; dir. acad. tng. and pubs. Interceptor Weapons Sch. USAF, Tyndall AFB, Fla., 1974-77; program and planning officer USAF, Washington, 1977-81; dep. comdr. ops. 323d Flying Tng. Wing USAF, Mather AFB, Calif., 1982-84; chief strategy div. Orgn. of Joint Chiefs of Staff, Washington, 1984-85; comdr. 601st Tactical Control Wing USAF, Semach Air Base, Fed. Republic Germany, 1985-87; asst. dep. chief staff for plans and prog. U.S. Air Forces in Europe, Ramstein Air Base, Fed. Republic Germany, 1987-88; dep. asst. chief staff and vice comdr. Air Force Ctr. for Studies and Analyses, Washington, 1988-90; comdr. Air Force Studies and Analyses Agy., Washington, 1990—; lectr. in field. Author: Quest for Unity of Command, 1984, 2d edit., 1991, Air Land Combat--An Organization for Joint Warfare, 1992; contbr. articles to profl. jours. Decorated Legion of Merit, DFC, Air Medal. Mem. Studies and Analyses Assn., Air Force Assn., Red River Valley Fighter Pilot Assn., Air Force Mus., Mil. Ops. Rsch. Soc., Assn. Former Students Tex. A&M U., Air War Coll. Alumni Assn., Armed Forces Communication and Electronics Assn., Tex. State Soc. Washington, Tex. Breakfast Club of Washington, Nat. Aviation Club, Assn. Old Crows, Am. Legion, VFW, Order of Daedalians (flight adjutant 1978-80, vice flight capt. 1987-88), Mil. Order of World Wars. Republican. Episcopalian. Home: 2385 N Danville St Arlington VA 22207-4923 Office: HQ USAF Studies/Analyses The Pentagon Washington DC 20330-5420

CARETTO, ALBERT ALEXANDER, chemist, educator; b. Baldwin, N.Y., May 16, 1928; s. Albert A. and Mary (Magnasco) C.; m. Virginia L. Ahman, Apr. 30, 1960; children—Joseph A., Ann M. B.S., Rensselaer Poly. Inst., 1950; Ph.D., U. Rochester, 1954. Postdoctoral research Brookhaven Nat. Lab., Upton, N.Y., 1954-56, U. Calif. at Berkeley, 1956-57; asst. prof. Carnegie Inst. Tech., Pitts., 1957-58, 59-64; asso. prof. Carnegie Inst. Tech., 1964-67; research chemist U. Calif. at Livermore, 1958-59; with CERN (European Lab. for Nuclear Research), Geneva, Switzerland, 1964-65; prof. Carnegie-Mellon U., Pitts., 1967—; chmn. dept. chemistry Carnegie-Mellon U., 1970-74; with European Lab. Nuclear Research, CERN, Geneva, Switzerland, 1974-75. Contbr. articles to profl. jours. Sch. Bd. dir., 1979-85; bd. dirs. Pa. Gov.'s Sch. for the Scis., 1982—. Mem. AAAS, Am. Chem. Soc., Am. Phys. Soc., Sigma Xi, Phi Kappa Phi. Home: 43B Bethany Dr Pittsburgh PA 15215-1207 Office: Carnegie-Mellon U Dept Chemistry Pittsburgh PA 15213

CAREY, JEAN LEBEIS, management consulting executive; b. Charleston, W.Va., June 2, 1943; d. Edward H. and Marian (Lendved) Lebeis; m. Robert W. Carey, Nov. 1971 (dec. Mar. 1990); 1 child, Megan Rose. BA, Pa. State U., 1965. Programmer Penn Mut. Life Ins., Phila., 1967-68; sr. analyst/programmer U. Pa., Phila., 1969-72; sr. systems analyst Acme Markets, Phila., 1972-74; programming mgr. Bryn Mawr Coll., Pa., 1976-77; project adminstr. Smith Kline Beckman, Phila., 1977-83; project mgmt. cons. Arco Chem. Co., Phila., 1983-87; chief exec. officer Carey Project Orgn., Ardmore, Pa., 1987—; chmn. Systems Methodology Users Mid-Atlantic, 1984-86, PMI Systems Tech. Papers, 1983; co-dir. Cobol project, U. Pa., Phila., 1969-72; Pa. Counc. on Children's Svcs., 1988—; lectr. in field. Author: Quality Management and Performance Measurement in Information Services, 1991, Making Quality Happen in Information Services, 1992; contbr. articles to profl. jours. Bd. dirs. Scan/Child Abuse Treatment Ctr., Phila., 1983-91, Danceteller/Dance Theater, Phila., 1985-88; mem. Leadership, Phila. vol. svcs. group, 1985—; exec. com. SCAN Devel. Fund, Inc., 1989—. Recipient Excel award, Arco, 1986. Mem. Project Mgmt. Inst. Soc. of Friends. Home and Office: Carey Project Orgn 663 Cricket Ave Ardmore PA 19003-1806

CAREY, KEVIN MICHAEL, military officer; b. White Plains, N.Y., Mar. 11, 1956; s. Neil James and Joan Marie (Gorman) C.; m. Margaret Therese Mall, July 22, 1989; 1 child, James Neil. BS in Resource Econs., U. R.I., 1978, M in Marine Affairs, 1991. Ensign USN, 1979, advanced through grades to lt. comdr., 1988, 1st lt. USS ENGLAND, 1979-81, navigator USS ENGLAND, 1981-82; mem. personnel exch. program Royal Belgian Navy, Zeebrugge, 1983-85; combat systems officer USS CURTS, 1986-88, USS HALSEY, 1988-89; instr. Surface Warfare Officers Sch. USN, Newport, R.I., 1990-92; exec. officer USS JARRETT, 1992—.

CAREY, MARTIN CONRAD, gastroenterologist, molecular biophysicist, educator; b. Clonmel, County Tipperary, Ireland, June 18, 1939; came to U.S., 1967; s. John Joseph and Alice (Broderick) C.; m. Gracia Antonieta Fernández, July 1, 1972 (div. 1987); children: Julian Albert, Dermot Martin. MB, BCh, BAO with 1st class honors, Nat. U. Ireland, 1962, MD, 1981, DSc, 1984; AM (hon.) Harvard U., 1989; LLD (hon.) Nat. U., Ireland, 1992. Intern, St. Vincent's Hosp., Dublin, Ireland, 1962-63, resident, 1965-67; resident Nat. Maternity Hosp., Dublin, 1963, St. Luke's Hosp., Dublin, 1964, Queen Charlotte's Hosp., London, 1964; postdoctoral fellow, rsch. assoc. Boston U. Sch. Medicine, 1968-73, asst. prof. medicine, 1973-75; asst. prof. medicine Harvard U. Med. Sch., Boston, 1975-79, assoc. prof., 1979-88 , Lawrence J. Henderson assoc. prof. health sci. and tech., 1979-88; faculty mem. Grad. Sch. of Arts and Scis., assoc. mem. Dept. of Cellular and Molecular Physiology, Harvard U. Med. Sch., Boston, 1983—, prof. medicine 1988—, Lawrence J. Henderson prof. health sci. and tech., 1988—; mem. staff Brigham and Women's Hosp., Boston, 1975—; cons. West Roxbury VA Hosp. and Dana-Faber Cancer Inst., Boston, 1975—, Calif. Biotech. Inc., Palo Alto, 1983-89, Dow Chem. Co., Midland, Mich., 1984-87, Oculon, Seattle and Cambridge, 1987—, Ciba-Geigy, Summit, N.J., 1988—. Author: Bile Salts and Gallstones, 1974, Hepatic Excretory Function, 1975; contbr. numerous articles to med. and sci. jours.; assoc. editor Jour. Lipid Rsch., 1978-81; mem. editorial bds. Am. Jour. Physiology, 1976-81, Gastroenterology, 1983-88, Hepatology, 1981-84. Recipient Acad. Career Devel. award NIH, 1976, also MERIT award, 1986, Adolf Windaus prize Falk Found., 1984; Guggenheim Found. fellow, 1974; Fogarty internat. fellow NIH, 1968; McIlrath guest prof., Royal Prince Alfred Hosp., U. Sydney, Australia, 1987. Fellow Royal Coll. Physicians Ireland; mem. Gastroenterology Rsch. Group (vice chmn., steering coms.), Am. Soc. Clin. Investigation, Am. Gastroent. Assn. (disting. achievement award 1990), Am. Oil Chemists Soc., Biophys. Soc., Interurban Clin. Club, Am. Assn. Physicians, Babson Club (Wellesley, Mass.). Democrat. Roman Catholic.

CAREY, WILLIAM PETER, financial executive; b. Abington, Pa., May 6, 1941; s. William George and Maria Joseph Sophia (Farley) C.; m. Sarah Walsh; children: William Peter Jr., Michael Francis. BS, Drexel Inst. Tech., 1964. CPA, Pa. Div. contr. Avebach Pub. Corp., Phila., 1970-74; treas. Braceland Bros. Inc., Phila., 1974-84; chief fin. officer ScanForms, Inc., Bristol, Pa., 1984—. Mem. AICPA, Pa. Inst. CPAs. Republican. Roman Catholic. Home: 805 Timber Ln Fort Washington PA 19025-1811 Office: ScanForms Inc PO Box 602 Bristol PA 19007-0602

CARFAGNO, SALVATORE PASQUALE, mechanical engineer, physicist, consultant; b. Norristown, Pa., Nov. 29, 1925; s. Vincent and Rose (DiDonato) C.; m. Ardea F. Dukich, Mar. 27, 1978; 1 child, Renato P. BSME, Drexel U., 1947; MS in Physics, U. Pa., 1949; PhD in Physics, Temple U., 1963. Head engring. dept. Franklin Rsch. Ctr., Phila., 1948-89; adj. prof. Drexel Evening & Univ. Coll., Phila., 1948—; tech. cons. Gladwyne, Pa., 1989—; mem. several adv. groups NRC. Contbr. articles to profl. jours. Mem. IEEE, Am. Phys. Soc., Am. Nuclear Soc., Sigma Xi. Home and Office: 1616 Riverview Rd Gladwyne PA 19035-1211

CARFORA, JOHN MICHAEL, economics and political science educator; b. New Haven, Conn., July 24, 1950; s. John Michael and Rose Mary (Mitro) C.; m. Linda Louise Palmer, July 22, 1972; 1 child, Rachel Ellen. BS, U. New Haven (Conn.), 1973, M in Pub. Adminstrn., 1975; MS in Econs. and Polit. Sci., London Sch. Econs. and Polit. Sci., 1978; AM, Dartmouth Coll., 1985. Vis. asst. prof. dept. def., 1979-80; vis. sr. lectr. Poly. of Central London, 1980; research asst. London Sch. Econs. and Polit. Sci., 1980-81; vis. asst. prof. internat. relations So. Conn. State U., New Haven, 1982; lectr. dept. polit. sci. Albertus Magnus Coll., New Haven, 1982-83; lectr. dept. econs. and quantitative analysis U. New Haven, 1982-83; program cons. Dartmouth Coll., 1984-85; asst. prof. internat. econ. Sch. Internat. Tng., 1985-90; v.p. rsch. and acad. affairs, dir. Soviet-Am. projects Global Consultancy Group, 1989-91, dir. east and west projects, 1992—; ednl. cons. USSR Acad. Mgmt., Moscow, 1991-92; cons. Commonwealth Acad. Mgmt., Moscow, 1992—; lectr. in field. Author book reviews; contbr. articles to profl. jours. Served with USAR, 1970-76. Recipient Roy E. Jenkins award, 1972; fellow Radio Free Europe-Radio Liberty, 1979, Internat. Research and Exchanges Bd., 1981-84. Mem. AAAS, NAFSA (internat. educators), Am. Acad. Polit. Sci., Am. Econ. Assn., Am. Polit. Sci. Assn., Acad. Polit. Sci., N.E. Slavic Assn., Royal Acad. Pub. Adminstrn. (eng.), Atlantic Econ. Soc., Am. Friends of the London Sch. Econs. (Conn. program chmn. 1981-85, N.H.-Vt. program chmn. 1985-87, alumni bd. dirs. 1983-92). Home: PO Box 964 Northampton MA 01061-0964 Office: Global Group Internat Cons PO Box 964 Northampton MA 01061-0964

CARGILL, LESLIE IRENE, marketing consultant; b. Beverly, Mass., Apr. 17, 1955; d. William R. and Mary Louise (Waters) C.; m. William F. Quigley, Jr., July 15, 1984. Cert., Katherine Gibbs Sch., 1976; postgrad., Simmons Coll. Grad. Sch. Sales mgr. Radisson Ferncroft Hotel, Danvers, Mass., 1976-80; asst. gen. mgr. Grand Teton Lodge Co., Jackson Hole, Wyo., 1980; advt., promotions, group sales dir. Boston Red Sox, 1980-85; pres., founder Cargill Communications, Topsfield, Mass., 1985—. Bd. dirs. Tri Town Coun. on Youth and Family Svc., Topsfield, 1985—; trustee Neurofibromatosis/Mass. Bay Area, Boston, 1990-91; chairperson Fall Foliage Classic, Topsfield, 1986—. Mem. Essex C. of C., Rotary. Office: Cargill Communications PO Box 39 Topsfield MA 01983-0039

CARIDEO, JAMES JOSEPH, counselor; b. Erie, Pa., Feb. 17, 1964; s. James Joseph and Patricia Mae (Milani) C. BS, Penn State U., 1987; MA, Edinboro U., 1991. Admission counselor Triangle Tech. Sch., Erie, Pa., 1988-89; residence hall coord. Edinboro (Pa.) U. of Pa., 1990-91; admission counselor Penn State U., Erie, 1991—. Mem. Am. Coll. Personnel Assn., Am. Assn. Counseling and Devel. Democrat. Office: Penn State U-Behrend Station Rd Erie PA 16563

CARIN, ARTHUR A., retired education and science educator; b. N.Y.C., Nov. 27, 1928; s. Samuel and Etta (Gaa) C.; m. Doris Terry Orkand, Dec. 23, 1951; children: Jill, Amy Carin Ohman, Jon. BS, SUNY, Oswego, 1951; MA, CUNY, 1954; EdD, U. Utah, 1959. Tchr. Gt. Neck (N.Y.) Pub. Schs., 1951-55; instr. U. Utah, Salt Lake City, 1955-58; prof. edn., assoc. dean tchr. edn., dir. environ. edn. Queens Coll., CUNY, Flushing, 1958-91, prof. emeritus, 1991—; evaluation dir. federally funded programs N.Y.C. Bd. Edn., 1976-81, sci. cons., 1991—. Author: Teaching Science Through Discovery, 1964, 6th edit., 1989, Teaching Modern Science, 1964, 5th edit., 1989, Guided Discovery Activities for Elementary School Science, 1980, 2d edit., 1989. Pres. Jericho (N.Y.) Bd. Edn., 1961-67. With U.S. Army, 1946-47. Recipient Disting. Alumni award SUNY, Oswego, 1985. Mem. NSTA, Phi Delta Kappa. Home: 12 Richmond Ave Jericho NY 11753-1933 Office: CUNY Queens Coll 65-30 Kissena Blvd Flushing NY 11367

CARL, SETH WILLIAM, machine operator; b. Point Pleasant, N.J., Mar. 31, 1961; s. James E.V. and Mary Lou (Brown) C. Student, Monmouth County Vocat. Inst., 1979-81. Machine operator Guardian Sprinkler Co., Elizabeth, N.J., 1982-91. Author pamphlet, 1991. With U.S. Army, 1981-82. Baptist.

CARLBERG, ROBERT JUDSON, college president; b. Allentown, Pa., Oct. 1, 1940; s. Robert Leonard and Helen Elizabeth (Thomas) C.; m. Janice Dawn Jensen, May 31, 1963; children: Heather, Chad. BA, Wheaton (Ill.) Coll., 1962; MDiv, Denver Sem., 1965; MA, Mich. State U., 1968, PhD, 1971. Asst. pastor Galilee Bapt. Ch., Denver, 1965-66; head resident advisor Mich. State U., East Lansing, 1966-69, dir. student affairs Lyman Briggs Coll., 1969-71, dir. advisement Lyman Briggs Coll., 1971-75, postdoctoral fellow, 1972-73; acad. provost John Wesley Coll., Owosso, Mich., 1975-76; dean of faculty Gordon Coll., Wenham, Mass., 1976-90, sr. v.p. devel., 1990-92, pres., 1992—; ednl. cons. numerous orgns., 1976—; chair Christian Coll. Consortium Dean's Coun., St. Paul, 1983-89, Coun. Ind. Colls. Dean's Task Force, Washington, 1985-89, Elder's Bd. Grace Chapel, Lexington, Mass., 1985-89; trustee Denver Sem., 1990—. Recipient Dean's award Coun. Ind. Colls., Washington, 1990. Mem. Am. Assn. Higher Edn. Mem. Evangelical Ch. Home: 27 Martel Rd South Hamilton MA 01982-2406 Office: Gordon Coll 255 Grapevine Rd Wenham MA 01984-1895

CARLETON, BUKK GRIFFITH, lawyer, investment counsel; b. N.Y.C., May 30, 1909; s. Bukk G. and Clarice (Griffith) C.; m. Mary Elizabeth Tucker, June 16, 1934; children: Elizabeth Holland, Bukk Griffith. AB magna cum laude, Harvard U., 1931, LLB, 1934. Bar: N.Y. 1935. Assoc. Larkin, Rathbone & Perry, N.Y.C., 1934-36; asst. counsel, asst. sec. Gen. Chem. Co., 1936-41; v.p., sec., dir. Perma-Bilt Homes, Inc., 1941-42; counsel RFC, 1942-44; head N.Y. law office Montgomery Ward & Co. 1944-46; mem. legal dept. Sinclair Refining Co., 1946-56; owner, investment counsel Griffith Carleton, 1946—. Pres., trustee Hicks-Stearns Mus. Mem. ABA, N.Y. Bar Assn., New Eng. Soc., Phi Beta Kappa. Quaker (com. nat. legis. 1957-58). Clubs: Met., Sleepy Hollow, Woodway Country (Conn.), Quinnatisset Country (Conn.), R.I. Country, New Canaan Country, Harvard (N.Y.), Phi Beta Kappa. Home and Office: 61 Parade Hill Ln New Canaan CT 06840-4120 also: Bukkskin East Killingly CT 06243

CARLEY, HAROLD EDWIN, plant pathologist, researcher; b. Syracuse, N.Y.; s. Harold Edison and Clara Elizabeth (Getman) C.; m. Mary Elizabeth Kersich, June 26, 1965; children: Michael Edward Carley, Donald Martin Carley, Jeanne Marie Carley. BS, Cornell U., Ithaca, N.Y., 1964; MS, U. ID, Moscow, 1966; PhD, U. Minn., St. Paul, 1969. Sr. biologist Rohm and Haas Co., Spring House, Pa., 1969-72, group leader, 1972-82; product devel. mgr. Rohm and Haas Co., Phila., 1983—. Contbr. articles to profl. jours.; patentee in field. Recipient Shevlin fellowship, grad. sch., U. Minn., Mpls., 1968; Caleb-Dorr award U. Minn., St. Paul, 1967. Mem. Am. Chemical Soc., Am. Phytopathological Soc., Sigma Xi. Rep. Presbyterian. Home: 11 Callowhill Rd Chalfont PA 18914-2101 Office: Rohm and Haas Co Independence Mall W Philadelphia PA 19105

CARLIN, DAVID R., JR., state senator, educator; b. Pawtucket, R.I., Apr. 9, 1938; AB, Providence Coll., 1960; MA, U. Notre Dame, 1962; MA, U. R.I., 1972; m. Maureen Brennan; children: David, Joshua, Margaret. Mem. R.I. State Senate, 1981—, senate majority leader, 1989-90. Columnist Commonweal mag. Mem. Newport (R.I.) Sch. Com., 1975-81; chmn. R.I. Film Commn., 1982-87, R.I. Sen. Fin. Com., 1987-89; mem. R.I. Pub. Telecommunications Authority, 1982-88, New Eng. Bd. Higher Edn., 1983—, R.I. Bd. Regents for Elem. and Secondary Edn., 1987-88. Democrat. Office: Coll of RI Social Scis Dept 400 East Ave Warwick RI 02886-1805

CARLIN, MICHELE DIANE (DUNCAN), marketing professional; b. Windber, Pa., Apr. 16, 1965; d. David James and Linda Diane (Blackburn) Duncan; m. Clayton G. Carlin, Apr. 4, 1992. BA in Communications, Juniata Coll., 1987. Mktg. intern Altoona (Pa.) Hosp., 1987; asst. pub. rels. dir. Wenzel and Co., Pennington, N.J., 1987-88; mktg. specialist BIOSIS, Phila., 1988-89; mktg. specialist ECRI, Plymouth Meeting, Pa., 1989-90, mktg. supr., 1990-91, mktg. and circulation supr., 1991—. Roman Catholic. Office: ECRI 5200 Butler Pike Plymouth Meeting PA 19462-1241

CARLINER, GEOFFREY OWEN, economist, director; b. Washington, Sept. 21, 1944; s. David and Miriam (Kalter) C.; m. Astrid Synnove Skrikerud, July 31, 1971; chilren: Anders Benjamin, Hannah Emily Brooke. AB cum laude, Harvard U., 1966; MA, U. Calif., Berkeley, 1968, PhD, 1972. Rsch. assoc. U. Wis., Madison, 1971-73; asst. prof. U. Western Ont., London, Ont., Can., 1974-80; sr. staff economist Coun. of Econ. Advisors, Washington, 1980-83, staff dir., 1983-84; exec. dir. Nat. Bur. of Econ. Rsch., Cambridge, Mass., 1984—; vis. asst. prof. U. Calif., Berkeley, 1976-77. Co-editor: Politics and Economics in the Eighties, 1991; contbr. articles to profl. jours. Recipient Joint Coun. of Econ. Edn. award, 1976. Mem. Am. Econ. Assn., Conf. for Rsch. on Income and Wealth (exec. com. 1985—), Internat. Seminar on Internat. Trade (steering com. 1988—). Office: Nat Bur Econ Rsch 1050 Massachusetts Ave Cambridge MA 02138-5302

CARLING, PAUL JOSEPH, psychologist; b. N.Y.C., Nov. 2, 1945; s. James Andrew and Mary Amelia (Lorenzo) C.; m. Anne Lois Borker, Jan. 13, 1968 (div. Sept. 1989); children: Oliver Samuel, Nathaniel Philip. BA, U. Pa., 1971, MS, 1972, PhD, 1977. Lic. psychologist, Pa., Vt. Gen. contractor Carling & Keitt, Phila., 1970-72; lectr. U. Pa., Phila., 1972-75; dir. program devel. Horizon House, Phila., 1974-78; bur. chief N.J. Dept. Mental Health, Trenton, 1978-79; spl. asst. to dir. NIMH, Rockville, Md., 1979-81; dep. commnr. Vt. Dept. Mental Health, Waterbury, 1981-83; rsch. assoc. prof. of rehab. Boston U., 1984-87; rsch. assoc. prof. of psychology U. Vt., Burlington, 1981—; prof. Trinity Coll. of Vt., 1992—; exec. dir., pres. Ctr. for Community Change, Burlington, 1987—; cons. South Burlington, Vt., 1988—; adj. prof. Union of Experimenting Cons., Cin., 1986—; cons. state and local mental health agys., 1975—. Author: Community Integration in Mental Health, 1992; editor: Community Living with Disability, 1991, Housing and Mental Health, 1981; contbr. chpts. in books, articles to profl. jours. and videotapes. Chair Vt. Advocacy Task Force, Waterbury, 1985. Recipient Switzer Scholar award Nat. Rehab. Assn. 1988; grantee fed. and state rsch. and dissemination 1975—. Fellow Am. Orthopsychiat. Assn.; mem. APA, Nat. Alliance for Mentally Ill, Nat. Mental Health Consumers Assn., Nat. Assn. Case Mgr. (bd. dirs.), Vt. Mental Health Assn. (bd. dirs.), Vt. Protection and Advocacy, Inc. (bd. dirs. Home: 70 Howard St Burlington VT 05401-4814 Office: IPD Trinity Coll of Vt Ctr for Community Change Colchester Ave Burlington VT 05401

CARLINI, JOHN LOUIS, musician; b. N.Y.C., Nov. 30, 1945; s. Louis A. and Phyllis (Mansfield) C.; m. Terry J. Triolo, July 23, 1983. Grad., Berklee Coll. Music, 1974. Music dir. Ice Capades, L.A., 1979-85; guitarist, writer David Grisman Quartet, San Francisco, 1986-89; orchestrator Song of Singapore, N.Y.C., 1991-92; pres. Garden Street Music, Inc., Summit, N.J., 1980—, The Jazz Alternative, Summit, 1991—. Orchestrator Tonight Show Band with D. Grisman, 1983, Kronos String Quartet, "Mondo Mondo," 1981; author: Arpeggio Cords for Guitar, 1984; composer musical works, 1980—. With USN, 1965-69. Grammy nomination guitarist David Grisman Quartet, 1990. Mem. Internat. Jazz Educator's Soc., N.J. Jazz Soc.. Roman Catholic. Office: Garden St Music Inc PO Box 1379 Summit NJ 07901

CARLL, ELIZABETH KASSAY, psychologist; b. May 4, 1950; d. Michael B. and Mary Kassay; m. Alan A. Carll, June 17, 1972. BA, Hofstra U., 1972, MA, 1976, PhD, 1978. Lic. psychologist, N.Y. Adj. asst. prof. Hofstra U., N.Y., 1978—; pvt. practice clin. psychologist Huntington and

Centerport, N.Y., 1979—; dist. psychologist Kings Pk. (N.Y.) Sch. Dist., 1981-86, chairperson psychol. svcs., 1986-89; guest speaker on family relationships and eating disorders numerous radio and TV programs. Contbr. articles to profl. jours. Fellow Am. Bd. Med. Psychotherapy (diplomate); mem. APA (task force for devel. nat. disaster response program), N.Y. State Psychol. Assn. (chair com. disaster/crisis relief), Suffolk County Psychol. Assn. (pres. elect 1989-91, pres. 1991—), Nat. Register Health Svc. Providers in Psychology, N.Y. Acad. Scis., Ea. Psychol. Assn., World Fedn. for Mental Health. Office: 4 Bittersweet Ct Centerport NY 11721-1703

CARLOUGH, EDWARD JOSEPH, executive; b. Bronx, N.Y., Apr. 10, 1932; s. Edward Francis and Florence (Sweeney) C.; m. June Mosburg, Sept. 11, 1954; children: Layne, Gail, Tracey, Christopher. BA in Polit. Sci., Am. U., 1955; LLD, Hofstra U., 1989. Apprentice Sheet Metal Workers' Internat. Assn., N.Y.C., 1949-51; staff mem. Labor's League Polit. Edn., Washington, 1955-56; dir. rsch. Sheet Metal Workers' Internat. Assn., Washington, 1957-60, dir. orgn., 1960-70, gen. pres., 1970—; v.p. AFL-CIO bldg. trades dept., Washington, mem. exec. bd. metal trades dept., maritime trades dept., gen. bd. dirs. Chmn. Dollars Against Diabetes, 1987—; sponsor Spl. Olympics, Washington, 1990; chmn. Dem. Congressional Campaign Com., mem. Dem. Nat. Com. Fin. Coun. Recipient Edward J. Small award Employee Assistance Profls. Assn., 1991, James Connolly award New Eng. Irish-Am. Labor Coalition, 1990, Gift of Sight award Internat. Guiding Eyes, 1989, medal of honor Assn. for Handicapped, 1992; Edward J. Carlough Chair of Internat. Labor Rels. established Am. U., Washington, 1992. Mem. Nat. Planning Assn. (bd. trustees), Nat. Ctr. Edn. and The Economy (bd. dirs.), Ams. Energy Independence (bd. dirs.), Nat. Bldg. Mus. (bd. dirs.), Com. changing Internat. Realities, Hassan-Fathy Inst. Democrat. Roman Catholic. Office: Sheet Metal Workers 1750 New York Ave NW Washington DC 20006-5301

CARLOZZI, CARLO, JR., sales professional; b. New Britain, Conn., Apr. 16, 1958; s. Carlo and Giuseppina (Ricciardi) C. BA in Politics, Washington & Lee U., 1980. Lic. property, casualty, life and health agt., Conn. Store mgr. Henry Miller, Inc., Hartford, Conn., 1982-85, 89-91; sales cons. The Hartford Ins. Group, 1985-89; acount exec. Arthur A. Watson & Co., Inc., Wethersfield, Conn., 1989; ins. agt. Sentry Ins., Farmington, Conn., 1991—. Bd. dirs. Neighborhood Housing Svcs., New Britain, 1987—, sec., 1991—, v.p. 1987-89, chmn. fin. com., 1988-91, mem. loan com., 1988—; lector St. Jerome Ch., New Britain, 1987%, mem. fin. com., 1988—, chmn., 1991—; commr. Civil Svc. Commn., New Britain, 1988; mem. Charter Oak Contbrs. Orgn., Hartford, 1988—; bd. dirs. Tri-State Italian-Am. Congress; commr. New Britain City Plan Commn., 1988—, chmn., 1988-89; mem. New Britain Dem. Town Com., 1987-90, rules and fin. com., 1987-90; del. Dem. Conf. Mem. Sons of Italy (pres. Angelo Tomasso Sr. Lodge, New Britain, 1987—, Conn. Grand Lodge state recording sec. 1991—, mem. ways and means com., social justic com. Conn. sect. 1989—, del. state conf., mem. pres.'s cabinet), Capitol Area Young Dems., Greater Hartford Architecture Conservancy, Conn. Hist. Soc., Chi Psi (nat. exec. coun. 1979-80), Hundred Club of Conn., Unico Internat., Wadsworth Atheneum. Roman Catholic. Home: 547 Slater Rd New Britain CT 06053-2645 Office: Sentry Ins 314 Farmington Ave Farmington CT 06032-1985

CARLSMITH, LAWRENCE ALLAN, management consultant; b. Terre Haute, Ind., June 12, 1928; s. Leonard Eldon and Hope (Snedden) C.; m. Dorothy Ann Libby, Sept. 4, 1951 (div. 1980); children: Laura Carlsmith Bast, Bruce, Duncan. BS, Stanford U., 1950; MS, MIT, 1953; cert. exec. program, Ind. U., 1974. Registered profl. engr., N.H. Project engr. Improved Machinery Inc., Nashua, N.H., 1953-69; chief engr. Impco div. Ingersoll-Rand Co., Nashua, 1969-81, v.p., tech. dir., 1981-86; ret., 1986; gen. mgr. Davidson Flight Svc., 1986-88; prin. cons., tech. cons. to pulp and paper industry Tailwind Cons., Amherst, N.H., 1988—; mem. adv. bd. exec. program Ind. U. Grad. Sch. Bus., Bloomington, 1974-89. Numerous patents in U.S. and fgn. countries. Bd. dirs., treas. Amherst Land Trust, 1974—. Mem. TAPPI, Can. Pulp and Paper Assn., Small Bus. Assn. New Eng., Qube Resources. Home and Office: Box 367 Amherst NH 03031

CARLSON, BRUCE ARNE, chemical company executive; b. St. Paul, Apr. 8, 1946; s. Arne Emmanuel and Ruth Serene (Goodwin) C.; m. Kathleen jackson Schmidt, Aug. 17, 1968; children: Brian Schmidt, Bradley Scott. AB, Cornell U., 1968; PhD, Purdue U., 1973. Rsch. chemist cen. rsch. dept. E.I. DuPont de Nemours & Co., Wilmington, Del., 1973-78, product specialist methanol products, 1978-80, product mgr. methanol/formaldehyde, 1980-82; asst. dist. mgr. chems. E.I. DuPont de Nemours & Co., Phila., 1982-84; asst. plant mgr. E.I. DuPont de Nemours & Co., Memphis, 1984-86, plant mgr., 1986-87; bus. mgr. Viton E.I. DuPont de Nemours & Co., Wilmington, 1987-88, dir. Americas Engring. Polymers, 1988-90, bus. engring. dir., 1990—; dir. DuPuy-DuPont Orthopaedics, Wilmington, 1988-90, Norcom-DuPont, Sao Paulo, Brazil, 1988-90, Solation Products, York, Pa., 1976-82; dir. Am. Rsch. Inst., Marcus Hook, Pa., 1987—. Contbr. articles to profl. jours.; patentee in field. Bd. dirs. Northridge Civic Assn., Wilmington, 1974-82, Memphis United Way, 1986-87, Christian Bros. Coll. Engring. Bd., Memphis, 1986-87; bd. dirs., treas. Courtney Sanford Fund-Cornell U., 1976—. Mem. AAAS, Am. Chem. Soc. (cuncilor 1976-82, treas. 1985-87), Sigma Xi, Phi Kappa Phi. Mem. Christian Ch.

CARLSON, CAROLIN MCCORMICK FURST, civic worker; b. Williamsport, Pa., Apr. 20, 1934; d. S. Dale and Esther Caroline (McCormick) Furst O'Brien; m. Elton Frederic Carlson, Sept. 15, 1956 (dec. 1970); children: Eric Dale, Margaret Cora, Dwight Leonard. BA, Smith Coll., 1955. Dir. First Nat. Bank of Port Allegany, Pa.; class fund sec. Abbot Acad., Phillips and Andover, Pa., 1951—; chmn. Abbot 40th Reunion, 1991. Contbr. articles to weekly paper Reporter-Argus, 1961-87. Jr. choir dir. Gethsemane Evang. Luth. Ch., Port Allegany, 1971-82, charter lay asst., 1972-74, 84-90, congl. sec., 1973—, Theos chpt. exec. dir. and grief counselor, 1972-76, chmn. bicentennial celebration com., 1975-76, pres. Luth Ch. Women, 1959-61, treas., 1962-65, 84-85, program chmn., 1976-80, sr. choir, 1983-86, Emporium Ministerium grief counselor, 1984-87; chmn. noon hour cultural series S.W. Smith Meml. Pub. Libr., 1972-74, 77-78, bd. dirs., 1977-89, v.p. spl. events, 1978-82, book selection, 1977-82, pres., 1985-88, adv. bd. McKean Literacy Team, 1991—; active Port Area Community TV, 1981-92; den mother Allegany Highland coun. Boy Scouts Am., Port Allegany, 1967-70, 76-79, sec., 1976-79, merit badge counselor, 1984—; asst. troop leader Keystone Tall Tree coun. Girl Scouts U.S., 1969-74; charter driver Meals on Wheels, 1972—; adv. bd. Charles Cole Meml. Hosp., 1988—, long-range planning, 1990-91; adv. bd. dirs. McKean County Children & Youth Svcs., 1980-83; v.p. Port Allegany High Sch. Band Boosters, 1982-85; chmn. United Way, 1984, 85; bd. dirs. Port Allegany Area Econ. Devel. Corp., 1984—, solicitation chmn. capital funds drive, 1987-90. Recipient award Luth. Ch. Am., 1975. Mem. Smith Coll. Alumnae Assn., Abbot Acad. Alumnae Assn., Indian Echo Country Club, Port Allegany Woman'sClub (treas. 1957-60, 66-67, auditor 1965, 82, sec. 1963-65, 70-71, 2d v.p. 1967-68, 71-72, pres. 1977-79, chmn. new community pool 1977-79, choir 1961—), McKean County Women's Club (sec. 1958-60, 66-68, treas. 1970-72, 1st v.p. 1972-76), Coudersport Golf Club, Order Ea. Star. Republican. Home: 45 Church St Port Allegany PA 16743-1133

CARLSON, DALE LYNN, lawyer; b. Buffalo, Feb. 21, 1946; s. Andrew Eugene and Edna Lucille (Atwell) Carlson. BSChemE, SUNY, Buffalo, 1968, MBA, 1969; JD, Syracuse U., 1975; LLM, NYU, 1979. Bar: N.Y. 1976, D.C. 1978, U.S. Supreme Ct. 1978, U.S. Ct. Appeals (fed. cir.) 1982, Conn. 1988. Mem. legal dept. Union Carbide Corp., N.Y.C. and Danbury, Conn., 1976-86; assoc. patent counsel Olin Corp., 1986-88, counsel, 1988-92, sr. counsel, 1992—; lectr. N.Y. Patent, Trademark and Copyright Law Assn., 1978, 87. Editor Internat. Law Rev., Syracuse, 1974-75; contbr. articles to profl. jours. Obtained state hist. designation Millplain Community Ch. of Danbury, 1983. Mem. ABA, Am. Intellectual Property Law Assn., N.Y. Patent, Trademark and Copyright Law Assn. (chmn. continuing legal edn. com. 1985-88, bd. dirs. nominating com. 1986-87, 1991-92, bd. dirs. 1988-91, chmn. lic. to practice requirements com. 1991-92), Internat. Legion of Intelligence, Mensa, Phi Alpha Delta. Home: 126 Aunt Hack Rd Danbury CT 06811 Office: Olin Corp 350 Knotter Dr Cheshire CT 06410-1118

CARLSON, DREW EMIL, physiology educator; b. Rochester, N.Y., Feb. 9, 1948; s. Norman Eric and Anita (Kimbark) C.; m. Susan Rudrow, Feb. 21, 1981; children: Erika Grace, Thomas John. BS, Cornell U., 1970; PhD, Johns Hopkins U., 1976. Fellow Johns Hopkins U., Balt., 1976-78, asst. prof., 1978-79; asst. prof. Brown U./R.I. Hosp., Providence, 1979-88, assoc. prof., 1988-89; assoc. prof. U. Md., Balt., 1989—. Contbr. articles to profl. jours. Mem. Am. Physiol. Soc., Endocrine Soc., Soc. for Neurosci., Soc. for Values in Higher Edn., Cornell U. Alumni Assn. (chair R.I. Ambs. 1987-89), Sigma Xi. Office: U Md MSTF 4-00 10 S Pine St Baltimore MD 21201-1192

CARLSON, ELVIN PALMER, military officer; b. Williston, N.D., Nov. 19, 1950; s. Palmer Elvin and Beulah Lorraine (McKay) C.; m. Berlinda Jo Gutierrez, Nov. 11, 1978. BA, N.Mex. State U., 1980; MS, Cen. Mich. U., 1988. Enlisted U.S. Army, 1970; pvt. Ft. Leonard Wood, Mo., 1970; pfc Ft. Devens, Mass., 1971; specialist 4th class Okinawa, Japan, 1972; specialist 4th class Ft. Devens, Mass., 1972-74; sgt. Kaiserslautern, Fed. Republic of Germany, 1974-76, Ft. Bliss, Tex., 1976-77; commd. 2nd lt., 1980, advance through grades to maj., 1992; comdr. of co. U.S. Army, Fed. Republic Germany, 1989-91; ops. officer Med. Bn., Ft. Meade, Md., 1991—. assoc. mem. Am. Coll. Health Care Execs. Democrat. Lutheran.

CARLSON, ERIC WALTER, retired English educator; b. Oskarström, Halland, Sweden, Aug. 20, 1910; came to U.S., 1916; s. John Fritjof and Hilma Victoria Carlson; m. Doris Gwendolyn Anderson, Dec. 29, 1938; children: Neal, Elinor, Carol. BS, Boston U., 1932, MA, 1936, PhD, 1947. Instr. English, Portland (Maine) U. Extension, 1934-36, Boston U., 1937-41, Babson Inst., Wellesley Hills, Mass., 1941-42; instr., asst. prof., assoc. prof., prof. U. Conn., Storrs, 1942-79, prof. emeritus, 1980—, course facilitator Ctr. for Learning in Retirement, 1990-91. Editor: Recognition of Edgar Allan Poe, 1966, Introduction to Poe: A Thematic Reader, 1967, Emerson's Literary Criticism, 1979; editor, contbr.; Critical Essays on Poe, 1987; also articles in World Book Ency., 1970—, Papers on Poe, 1972, Dictionary of Literary Biography Vols. 74, 102, Fifty Southern Writers before 1900, 1987. Editor newsletter World Federalists Mansfield, 1970-88, also mem. exec. com., archivist. Mem. MLA (life), Northeastern Modern Lang. Assn., Poe Studies Assn., (hon. life,founding mem., first pres.), Collegium. Democrat. Unitarian. Home: 18 Dunham Pond Rd Storrs Mansfield CT 06268-2009

CARLSON, HANNAH BICK, vocational rehabilitation counselor, program case manager; b. N.Y.C., July 13, 1963; d. Albert William David and Dale Elissa (Bick) C. BA in Psychology, U. Rochester, 1985; MA, Columbia U., 1986, MEd in Counseling Psychology, 1988; postgrad., Ctr. for Gestalt Psychotherapy, N.Y.C., 1986-88. Cert. rehab. counselor. Alcoholism counselor N.Y. Hosp., Payne Whitney Psychiat. Clinic, N.Y.C., 1986-87; sr. rehab. counselor NYU Med. Ctr. Rusk Inst., N.Y.C., 1988-91; vocat. rehab. counselor New Medico Rehab. Svcs., Great Neck, N.Y., 1991, program case mgr., 1991—; lectr. NYU Med. Ctr., Rusk Inst., 1989-91, Manhasset Pub. Schs., 1991—. Mem. APA, Nat. Rehab. Assn. Home: 101 Sport Hill Rd Easton CT 06612 Office: New Medico Rehab Svcs 150 Community Dr Great Neck NY 11021-5501

CARLSON, JOHN GREGORY, management consultant, writer; b. Amityville, N.Y., Mar. 20, 1951; s. John Edward and Frances (Pogorzelski) C.; m. May 20, 1979. BA, Bucknell U., 1973; MBA, U. Chgo., 1975. Fin. analyst N.Y.C., 1975-78; mgr. fin. analysis Gen. Instrument Corp., N.Y.C., 1978-82; v.p. fin., contr. Power Semiconductor div. Gen. Instrument Corp., Hicksville, N.Y., 1982-85; chief fin. officer, contr. Algorex Corp., Hauppauge, N.Y., 1985-87; chief fin. officer, v.p. fin., dir. Learning Svcs. Corp., Londonderry, N.H., 1987-89, pres., chief operating officer, 1989-91; pres., owner RHM Cons., Inc., Marlborough, Mass., 1991—. Contbr. articles to profl. jours. Mem. Nat. Head Injury Found., Risk and Ins. Mgmt. Soc., Self Ins. Inst. Am. Office: RHM Cons Inc 86 Pleasant St Marlborough MA 01752

CARLSON, JOSEPH MAXWELL, oil company executive; b. Atlanta, Apr. 10, 1942; s. Maxwell Daniel Carlson and Dorothy Mae (Mullis) Ring; m. Margaret Sue Finch, Apr. 6, 1973; 1 child, Sarah. BA, Nebr. Wesleyan Univ., 1963; MA in Econs., Kans. State U., 1964. Systems analyst/mgmt. intern US Atomic Energy Commn., Albuquerque, 1964-68; chief, dissemination and program evaluation NASA, Washington, 1968-73; v.p. Pub. Tech., Inc., Washington, 1973-78; asst. dir., tech. commercialization Solar Energy Rsch. Inst., Golden, Colo., 1978-79; mgr. fin. and planning Exxon Enterprises, Inc., Florham Park, N.J., 1979-81; sr. staff advisor Exxon Rsch. and Engring. Co., Florham Park, N.J., 1981-84, mgr. pub. affairs, 1984-90; sr. advisor pub. affairs Exxon Co., Internat., Florham Park, 1990—. Contbr. articles to profl. jours. Advisor Govs. Commn. on Sci. and Tech., Trenton, N.J., 1984-86; bd. dirs. Morris Mus., Morristown, N.J., 1985-87; chair, bd. trustees Community Ch., Mountain Lakes, N.J., 1986-88. Mem. AAAS.

CARLSON, MARY ANN, state legislator, hotel executive; b. Palo Alto, Calif., Jan. 22, 1944; m. Wesley H. Carlson; 5 children. BA, Marquette U., 1965; postgrad., Fordham U., 1977; MA in Psychology, Lesley Coll., 1991. Co-owner, operator West Mountain Inn, Arlington, Vt.; mem. Vt. State Senate, Montpelier, 1989—; Dem. leader Senate Rules/Joint Fiscal Com. Bd. dirs. Vt. Community Loan Fund; coord. Coun. of Vt. Interactive Television; adv. bd. HealthCare 2000. Mem. Women Bus. Owners Vt., Vt. Businesses for Social Responsiblity, Arlington Townscapes. Mem. Women Bus. Owners Vt., Northshire Women's Collective. Democrat. Home: PO Box 465 Arlington VT 05250-0465 Office: Vt State Senate State Capitol Montpelier VT 05602

CARLSON, NANCY BUSK, optometrist, educator; b. Derby, Conn., June 1, 1948; d. Clarence Elmer and Abigail Marie (Connors) Busk; m. Ronald Dennis Carlson, Sept. 27, 1969 (div. Sept. 1983); 1 child, Brian. BS, Cen. Conn. State Coll., 1970; OD, New Eng. Coll. Optometry, 1977. Staff optometrist Teamsters Local 25 Med. Ctr., Charlestown, Mass., 1978-88, Harvard Community Health Plan, Wellesley, Mass., 1988—; instr. New Eng. Coll. Optometry, Boston, 1977-81, asst. prof., 1981-85, assoc. prof., 1985—, chmn. dept. patient care mgmt., 1991—; chief of family practice New Eng. Eye Inst., Boston, 1991—. Author: (textbook) Clinical Procedures for Ocular Examination, 1990, (poster) Videotape: The Entrance Tests, 1986 (best edn. poster Am. Acad. Optometry, 1990). Exec. com. Seamark/Cotting Sch., Concord, Mass., 1985—. Recipient Seamark award Cotting Sch., Concord, 1988. Fellow Am. Acad. Optometry; mem. Am. Optometric Assn., Assn. Optometric Edn. (sec.-treas. 1987-89, pres. 1989-91), Mass. Soc. Optometrists, Beta Sigma Kappa. Home: 112 Beechnut Rd Westwood MA 02090-3304 Office: New Eng Coll Optometry 424 Beacon St Boston MA 02115

CARLSON, RICHARD WARNER, diplomat, journalist, federal agency administrator; b. Boston, Feb. 10, 1941; adopted s. W.E. and Ruth Miriam (Rafuse) C.; m. Patricia Caroline Swanson, Feb. 18, 1979; children: Tucker McNear, Buckley Peck; student U. Miss., 1961-62, LLD (hon.) Calif. Western U., San Diego, 1988. Editorial asst. L.A. Times, 1962-63; writer, columnist, freelance journalist UPI (TIME, LOOK, ABC-TV), San Francisco and Sacramento, 1964-65; investigative reporter, anchorman ABC-TV, San Francisco, 1966-71, anchorman, polit. editor, ABC-TV, L.A., 1971-75; anchorman Sta. KFMB-TV (CBS), San Diego, 1975-77; producer, writer, dir. documentary films NBC-TV, Burbank, Calif., 1974; anchorman, host Carlson & Co., CBS-TV, San Diego, 1975-76; sr. v.p. Gt. Am. First Bank, San Diego, 1977-84; dir. pub. affairs USIA, Washington, 1985; dir. USIA/Voice of Am., Washington, 1986-91; U.S. Ambassador to Republic Seychelles, 1991-92; pres., CEO Corp. for Pub. Broadcasting, 1992—; dir. Calif. Gen. Mortgage Assurance Corp., 1976-84, Calif. Community Bank, 1983—, Exec. Info. Svc., 1985—; lectr., cons. in field. Chmn. San Diego Coalition, 1980-81; co-chmn. Citizens for Open Space, 1978; pres. Rep. Bus. and Profl. Club, 1980, Actors and Others, Inc., 1971-75; bd. dirs. Sharp Hosp. Found., 1983—, Boy Scouts Am., 1984—, Arthritis Found., 1984—; mem. La Jolla Town Coun., 1983—; mem. Calif. State Rep. Cen. Com., 1982—; fin. adv. com. Jr. League San Diego, Inc., 1976-84; bd. dirs. NCCJ, 1980-83; co-chmn. com. on future San Diego Conv. & Visitors, 1982; appointed Pres.' Coun. on Peace Corps, 1982-84; commr. San Diego Crime Commn., 1984—; mem. La Jolla Planned Dist. Bd., 1982-84; fundraiser La Jolla Country Day Sch., 1976-83, St. George's Sch., Newport, R.I., 1981-87, Old Globe Theatre, San Diego, 1979-80; sponsor La Jolla Soccer League, 1978-79, La Jolla Bronco League. 1982; mem. housing industry task force State of Calif., 1982-83; chmn. Sta. KPBS-TV Ann. Auction, 1979; gov. Scripps Meml. Hosps., La Jolla, 1981—; adv. com. Sharp Meml. Hosps., La Jolla, 1982—; bd. dirs. Sharp Hosp. Found., 1981—; dir. Fund For Animals, N.Y.C., 1988—; trustee Fund for Am. Studies, 1988—; mem. Rosalind Russell Arthritis Found., 1985—. Recipient Broadcasting award documentary film San Francisco State Coll., 1967, investigative reporting awards AP, 1968, 76, 77, awards news analysis, 1968, 69, 75; Nat. Headliners award, 1968, Emmy award best investigative reporting, 1977, Golden Mike award best documentary, 1972, investigative reporting, 1975, best commentary, 1975; George Foster Peabody award, 1976, L.A. Press Club Grand award, 1976, San Diego Press Club award, 1976, 77, award merit San Diego Hist. Soc., 1979, Amigo de Distinction award Mexican-Am. Found., 1979, Friend of Lithuania award Knights of Lithuania, 1988, Jose Marti award Cuban Am. Polit. Soc., Miami, Fla., 1988. Mem. Nat. Press Club,. Univ. Club San Diego, Thunderbird Country Club (Rancho Mirage, Calif.), La Jolla Beach and Tennis Club, Mid-Ocean Club (Tuckerstown, Bermuda), Capitol Hill Club, Georgetown Club (Washington), Met. Club (Washington), DACOR (Washington), The Pilgrims (NYC), Sigma Delta Chi. Republican. Episcopalian. Author: History of Women in San Diego, 1978; also articles. ticks. Office: Corp Pub Broadcasting 901 E St NW Washington DC 20004-2006

CARLSON, ROBERT CHARLES, financial planner/publisher; b. West Hempstead, N.Y., Aug. 9, 1957; s. Edward Joseph and Muriel Catherine C. BS in Fin. Mgmt. with high honor, Clemson U., 1979; MS in Acctg., U. Va., 1982, JD, 1982. Bar: D.C. 1982; CPA, Md. Law clk. U.S. Dept. Justice, Washington, 1982, U.S. Dept. Edn., Washington, 1982-83; editor Tax Savs. Report, Balt., 1983-85, Fin. Independence, Balt., 1983-85, Tax Avoidance Digest, Balt., 1985—; prin. R.C. Carlson Advs., Falls Church, Va., 1988—; pres. Ctr. for Retirement Security, Inc., 1992—; mem. Va. Fiscal Alternative Commn., Richmond, 1989—; trustee Fairfax County, Va., Supplemental Retirement System, 1992—. Author: Retirement Tax Guide, 1989, 3d edit., 1991, How to Handle and Win a Federal Tax Appeal, 1988, 199 Loopholes That Survived Tax Reform, 1987, Tax Savings Through Short-Term Trusts, 1985, How to Slash Your Mutual Fund Taxes, 1990, 2d edit., 1991; editor Retirement Watch, 1991—. Treas. 10th Dist. Rep. Com., Fairfax, 1988-92; treas. No. Va. Rep. Bus. Forum, Alexandria, 1990—, Atoka Country Supper Com., Springfield, Va., 1989-92; chmn. Fairfax Area Young Reps., Annandale, Va., 1989-91. Named Outstanding Young Men of Am., U.S. Jaycees, 1983. Mem. D.C. Bar Assn., Conservative Club, Phi Kappa Phi, Phi Gamma Sigma. Roman Catholic. Home and Office: 3329 Grass Hill Ter Falls Church VA 22044-1232

CARLSON, THEODORE JOSHUA, lawyer, retired utility company executive; b. Hartford, Conn., Jan. 4, 1919; s. John and Hulda (Larson) C.; m. Jacqueline L. Coburn, Apr. 25, 1953; children: Stephanie, Christopher J., Victoria, Antoinette. A.B., Montclair State Coll., 1940; J.D., Columbia U., 1948, A.M., 1951; postgrad., U. Chgo., 1942. Bar: N.Y. 1948. Assoc. Gould & Wilkie, N.Y.C., 1948-54, ptnr., 1954—, sr. ptnr., 1970—; dir. Central Hudson Gas & Electric Corp., Poughkeepsie, N.Y., 1968-89, chmn., 1975-89, prin. officer, 1975-86; mem., chmn. fin. and audit com. N.Y. State Energy Rsch. Devel. Authority, 1980-88; dir. Empire State Electric Energy Rsch. Corp., Edison Electric Inst., 1976-79; chmn. exec. com. Energy Assn. N.Y. State, 1976-77, 82-83, N.Y. Power Pool, 1977-78; dir., mem. exec. com. Mid-Hudson Pattern, Inc., Poughkeepsie, N.Y.; chmn. bd. dirs. Christian Herald Assn. and related cos., 1985—. Author: A Design For Freedom. Pres. United Fund Rockville Centre, N.Y., 1966; chmn. adv. bd. Westchester County Salvation Army, 1977-80, STate of N.Y., 1977-83; chmn. Greater N.Y. Adv. Bd., 1988-91; chmn. bd. trustees King's Coll., 1982-89; chmn. bd. dirs. Christian Herald Assn., 1985—. Capt. USAAF, 1942-46. Mem. Am., N.Y. bar assns., Bar Assn. City N.Y. (chmn. pub. utility sect. com. on post admissions-legal edn. 1970-73). Lodge: Rotary (hon.). Office: Gould & Wilkie 1 Wall St New York NY 10005-2501

CARLSON, WILLIAM DWIGHT, government agency administrator; b. Denver, Nov. 5, 1928; m. Beverley Ann Bradshaw, 1950; children: Susan Elaine, Earl Dwight. D.V.M., Colo. State U., 1952, M.S., 1956; Ph.D. in Radiology and Radiation Biology, U. Colo., 1958. Prof., chmn. dept. radiology and radiation biology (founder) Colo. State U., 1964-68, pres. rsch. found., 1964-68, acting dir., 1966-68; prof. radiation biology, admistr. Am. studies program U. Wyo., Laramie, 1968-79, pres., 1968-79; pres. emeritus U. Wyo., 1989—; affiliate prof. radiology, radiation biology Colo. State U., Fort Collins, 1968-80; chief exec. officer St. John's Hosp., Jackson Hole, Wyo., 1980-84; assoc. adminstr. Office Grants and Program Systems USDA, Washington, 1984—; prin. vet. Cooperative State Research Service USDA, 1984-88; mem. USDA Nat. Agr. Research Com., 1985-87; joint coun. Food and Agr. Scis., 1985-87; nat. cons. vet medicine to surgeon gen. USAF, 1970-75; trustee Wyo. Blue Shield/Blue Cross, 1976-85, chmn. bd. trustees, 1982-83; adv. dir. Wyo. Indsl. Devel. Corp., 1966-79; commr. Wyo. Western Interstate Commn. Higher Edn., 1968-79; mem. pres. coun. and senate Assn. Land Grant Colls. and State Univs., 1968—; pres. coun. Western Athletic Conf., 1968-79; exec. com. Assn. Western Univs., 1970-79; regional adv. com. Inst. Internat. Edn., 1969-79; mem. scholarship com. Marathon Oil Co., 1977-79. Author: Veterinary Radiology, 3d edit, 1978; editor procs. Internat. Symposium on the Effects of Ionizing Radiation of the Reproductive System, 1964; contbr. articles to profl. jours. Mem. exec. com. Longs Peak council Boy Scouts Am., 1966-80, pres., 1974-76, v.p., North Central region, 1970-74; regional chmn. Nat. Eagle Scout Assn., 1975-80, Silver Beaver award, 1974; bd. dirs. U. Wyo. Found., 1968-79; bd. visitors Air U., Maxwell AFB, 1972-75; mem. Yellowstone Park Library and Mus. Bd., 1974-86, vice chmn., 1976-83. Named Outstanding Young Man of Year Colo. Jr. C. of C., 1960, Top Prof. Colo. State U., 1961, U.S. Vet. of Year Am. Animal Hosp. Assn., 1967, hon. alumni Colo. State U., 1971; recipient William E. Morgan award Colo. State U., 1989. Fellow AAAS; mem. AVMA (trustee ins. trust 1985-87), Nat. Acad. Practice (founding mem. vet. medicine 1986—, treas. 1988—), Am. Coll. Vet. Radiology (founding, diplomate), Nuclear Medicine Soc. Am. (nat. trustee 1964-68), Wyo. Med. Soc., Am. Vet. Radiology Soc. (charter, pres. 1965), Laramie C. of C. (bd. dirs. 1968-79), Wyo. Hosp. Assn. (dir. 1982-84, sec.-treas. 1983), Nat. Cowboy Hall of Fame (hon. life mem.). Lodge: Rotary (bd. dirs. 1965-83). Home: 1412B 12th St N Arlington VA 22209-3663 Office: USDA Aerospace Ctr Rm 328 Washington DC 20250

CARLSON-PICKERING, JANE, educator; b. Providence, Sept. 17, 1954; d. Arthur Julius and Laura Helen (Extovicz) Carlson; m. Allan Thomas Pickering, Nov. 2, 1980; children: Lauren, Taylor. BS in Art Edn., R.I. Coll., 1976, MEd in Art and Indsl. Arts Edn., 1983; cert. in lunar disc tchr. tng. program, NASA, 1991. Cert. elem. tchr. (life), R.I., gifted edn. tchr., NASA Lunar Disc tchr. Profl. photographer Ted Pickering Studios, Warwick, R.I., 1973—; calligraphy tchr. Warwick Adult Edn., 1978; secondary tchr. graphics arts Warwick Sch. Dept., 1976-78, secondary tchr. gifted program, 1978-83; elem. gifted program coordinator and tchr. Chariho Sch. System, Wyoming, R.I., 1983—; mem. Commr.'s Task Force on Vocat. and Indsl. Arts Edn., Providence, 1984-85, Commr.s' Task Force on Gifted and Talented Edn., 1991-92, Chariho K-12 Curriculum Coun.; aerial photographer Aerovisions. Recipient First Pl. award photography contest Warwick Arts Found., 1984, Tchr. award Invent Am., 1991, Lunar Disc Program Tchr. Tng. Cert. NASA, 1991. Mem. NEA, State Avocates Gifted Edn., Epsilon Pi Tau. Clubs: Nat. Student Art Edn. Assn. (treas. 1971-72). Home: 209 Blueberry Ln West Kingston RI 02892-1818 Office: Chariho Sch Dept Switch Rd Wood River Junction RI 02894-1301

CARLTON, CHARLES MERRITT, linguistics educator; b. Poultney, Vt., Dec. 12, 1928; s. Clarence Rann and Margaret Louise (Pennell) C.; m. Mary MacDonald, Aug. 31, 1957; children: David, John, Stephen. A.B., U. Vt., 1950; M.A., Middlebury Coll., 1951; Ph.D., U. Mich., 1963. Instr. Mich. State U., East Lansing, 1958-62; asst. prof. U. Mo., Columbia, 1962-66; prof. French and Romance linguistics U. Rochester, N.Y., 1966—; asst. dir. NDEA French Inst., U. Vt., Burlington, summer 1964; lectr. U.S. State Dept Seminars, Brasov, Romania, summer 1972, U. Ky., Cluj, Romania, summer 1977; reader NEH, 1974—; Fulbright lectr., 1971-72, Romania, 1986, Brazil. Author: Studies in Romance Lexicology, 1965, A Linguistic Analysis of a Collection of Late Latin Documents Composed in Ravenna between A.D. 445-700: A Quantitative Approach, 1973, Romanian Poetry in English Translation: An Annotated Bibliography and Census of 283 Poets in English (1740-1989), 1989; bibliographer: Romanian Language and Linguistics, 1973, 75-91, Comparative Romance Linguistics Newsletter; co-editor: Miorita:

Jour. Romanian Studies, 1977—; editor: Comparative Romance Linguistics newsletter, 1970-71. Fulbright fellow, Paris, 1950-51; fellow NSF, summer 1965, Nat. Def. Fgn. Lang., summer 1970; Fulbright grantee, 1974, 78, 82, 88, Romania, IREX grantee, 1982, 91. Mem. Am. Assn. Advancement of Slavic Studies, Am. Assn. Tchrs. of Spanish and Portuguese, Am. Romanian Acad., N. Am. Catalan Soc., Romanian Studies Assn. Am., Soc. Romanian Studies; mem. L'Amicale (Middlebury, Vt.), Fulbright Alumni Assn., Rochester Internat. Friendship Coun. (pres.), Sigma Delta Pi. Home: 3 Thornfield Way Fairport NY 14450-3023 Office: U Rochester Rochester NY 14627

CARLUCCI, FRANK CHARLES, III, former secretary of defense; b. Scranton, Pa., Oct. 18, 1930; s. Frank Charles, Jr. and Roxanne (Bacon) C.; m. Marcia Myers, Apr. 15, 1976; children: Karen, Frank, Kristin. AB, Princeton U., 1952; postgrad., Sch. Bus. Adminstrn., Harvard U., 1956; postgrad. hon. dr. degree, Wilkes Coll., Kings Coll., 1973; LLD (hon.), U. Scranton, 1989. With Jantzen Co., Portland, Ore., 1955-56; fgn. svc. officer Dept. State, 1956; vice consul, econ. officer Dept. State, Johannesburg, S. Africa, 1957-59; second sec., polit. officer Dept. State, Kanshasa, Congo, 1960-62; officer in charge Congolese polit. affairs Dept. State, 1962-64; consul gen. Dept. State, Zanzibar, 1964-65; counselor for polit. affairs Dept. State, Rio de Janeiro, Brazil, 1965-69; asst. dir. Office Econ. Opportunity, Washington, 1969, dir., 1970; assoc. dir. Office Mgmt. and Budget, 1971, dep. dir., 1972; undersec. HEW, 1972-74; ambassador to Portugal, 1975-78; dep. dir. CIA, Washington, 1978-81; dep. sec. Def. Washington, 1981-82; pres. Sears World Trade, Inc., Washington, 1983-84, chmn., chief exec. officer, 1984-86; asst. to the Pres. Nat. Security Affairs, Washington, 1986-87; Sec. Def. Washington, 1987-89; vice chmn. Carlyle Group, Washington, 1989—. Served as lt. (j.g.) USNR, 1952-54. Recipient Superior Svc. award Dept. State, 1972, Superior Honor award, 1969, HEW Disting. Civilian Svc. award, 1975, Def. Dept. Disting. Civilian award, 1977, Disting. Intelligence medal, 1981, Nat. Intelligence Disting. Svc. medal, 1981, Presdl. Citizens award, 1983, Woodrow Wilson award, 1988, James Forrestal Meml. award, 1988, Woodrow Wilson award, 1988, Herbert Roback Meml. award, 1989, George C. Marshall award, 1989. Office: Carlyle Group 1001 Pennsylvania Ave NW Washington DC 20004-2505

CARLUCCIO, FRANK, chemical engineer; b. Newark, Aug. 31, 1919; s. Anthony and Frances (DiGiacomo) C.; m. Mary Ebalda Scapicchio, July 9, 1959; 1 child, Frank Vincent. AS in Chem. Engring., Newark Tech. Sch., 1941; BS in Chem. Engring., Newark Coll. Engring., 1943; MS in Chem. Engring., Columbia U., 1947. Jr. scientist Atom Bomb Project, 1944-46; process group leader FMC Corp., Carteret, N.J., 1947-56; pilot plant engr. GAF Corp., Linden, N.J. and Easton, Pa., 1956-58; pilot plant mgr. GAF Corp., Easton, 1960-68, pilot plant supr., 1968-74; pilot plant supr. GAF Corp., Wayne, N.J., 1974-84. Patentee in field. With U.S. Army, 1943-46. Mem. Am. Inst. Chem. Engrs. Democrat. Roman Catholic. Home: 8 Gloria Dr Towaco NJ 07082-1112

CARMAN, ANNE, institute executive; b. Kansas City, Mo., Mar. 17, 1942; d. Martin Albert and Areleta Laynelle (Burditt) Utterback; m. Robert G. Stevens, Dec. 30, 1989; children: James Powell Carman Jr., Christopher Tully Carman. BS in Edn., U. Mo., 1965, MA, 1968, PhD, 1983. Coord. women's studies U. Mo., Columbia, 1977-81, mgr. ann. giving, 1981-83; dir. ann. giving Found., So. Ill. U. Found., Carbondale, 1983-85, dir. major gifts, 1985-86, pres., 1986-88; mem. bus. adv. com. So. Ill. U., Carbondale, 1987-88, 91—; v.p. Coun. for Advancement and Support Edn., Washington, 1988-90, The Aspen Inst., Washington, 1990—. Fellow NEH, 1980. Home: 104 Duke St Alexandria VA 22314-3804 Office: The Aspen Inst 1755 Massachusetts Ave NW Ste 501 Washington DC 20036-1511

CARMAN, GREGORY WRIGHT, federal judge; b. Farmingdale, N.Y., Jan. 31, 1937; s. Willis B. and Marjorie (Sosa) C. Exch. student, U. Paris, 1956-57; B.A., St. Lawrence U., 1958; J.D., St. John's U., 1961; Judge Adv. Gen. honors grad., U. Va. Law Sch., 1962. Bar: N.Y. 1961. Councilman Town of Oyster Bay, N.Y., 1972-81; mem. 97th Congress from 3d Dist. N.Y.; U.S. Congl. del. I.M.F. Cong., 1982; judge U.S. Ct. Internat. Trade, N.Y.C., 1983—. Served to capt. AUS, 1962-64. Mem. Am. Bar Assn., Nassau County Bar Assn., Nassau Lawyers Assn., Criminal Cts. Bar Assn., N.Y. State Defenders Assn., N.Y. State Bar Assn., St. John's Law Rev. Republican. Episcopalian. Club: Rotary. Office: US Ct Internat Trade 1 Federal Pla New York NY 10007*

CARMAN, WARREN EARL, JR., vocational school principal; b. Morristown, N.J., Nov. 21, 1948; s. Warren Earl and Pearl Lenore (Rosen) C.; m. Eileen Catherine Gill, June 27, 1970; children: Warren III, Brian Thomas. BA, Montclair State Coll., 1987; MA, Jersey City State Coll., 1988. Machinest apprentice Leslie Valve Co., Parsippany, N.J., 1968-70; machinist Solbern Corp., Fairfield, N.J., 1970-71; owner, operator Mt. Tabor (N.J.) Exxon, 1971-74; tchr. Parsippany (N.J.) Hills High Sch., 1974-79; supr. Singer Kearfott Corp., Little Falls, N.J., 1979-81; tchr. Sussex County Vo-Tech, Sparta, N.J., 1981-86; supr. Sussex County Vo-Tech, Sparta, 1986-88, dir. adult edn., 1988-90, prin., 1990—. Fireman Dist. Six, Parsippany, 1971-79. With USN, 1967-68. Mem. Hampton Rotary, KC. Republican. Roman Catholic. Home: 12 Chandoga Newton NJ 07860 Office: Sussex County Vo-Tech 105 N Church Rd Sparta NJ 07871-3203

CARMEN, DAVE, architectural designer; b. Holyoke, Mass., May 28, 1948; s. Irving and Virginia C.; m. Nancy Gregory, Mar. 25, 1968. Student Springfield Community Coll., 1972-74. Registered architect, Mass., Conn. Archtl. draftsman Heritage Homes, Westfield, Mass., 1969-71, Conlon Assoc., Westfield, 1971-73; archtl. designer Reinhardt Assocs., Springfield, Mass., 1973-78; prin. Dave Carmen, Architect, Granby, Mass., 1978—. Mem. AIA. Office: Carmen Assocs 15 Mary Lyon Dr Granby MA 01033-9437

CARMICHAEL, JUDY LEA, record industry executive, concert jazz pianist; b. Lynwood, Calif., Nov. 27, 1952; d. John Alvin and Jeanne Pauline (Boock) Hohenstein. Student, Calif. State U., Long Beach, 1970-73. Pianist, lectr. L.A., 1972-82, Steinway Artist, N.Y.C., 1984, USIA, L.A., N.Y., Zurich, Paris, and, Cannes, France, 1987-88, Carnegie Hall Concert, N.Y.C., 1988, Rio de Janiero, 1989; owner C&D Prodns., N.Y.C., 1989—; pianist, lectr. Peggy Guggenheim Concert, Venice, Italy, 1990, Concert Am. Acad. in Rome, 1991, USIA Tour of Portugal & Spain, 1991; chmn. jazz fellowships com. NEA, Washington, 1990-91; pianist USIA Tour of India, Tour of China, 1992. Author: (music) Judy Carmichael's Complete Book of Stride Piano, 1987; jazz editor Sheet Music mag., 1989-90; contbr. numerous articles to profl. jours. NEA fellow, grantee. Mem. Musician's Union. Office: C&D Prodns 21 E 4th St New York NY 10003-7012

CARMICHAEL, NANCY S., arts administrator; b. Albemarle, N.C., July 15, 1958; d. Philip Duncan and Betty Jane (Lisk) C. B. Music, Manhattan Sch. Music, 1980; MFA, Columbia U., N.Y.C., 1990. Adminstrv. dir. Harlem Sch. Arts, N.Y.C., 1979-86, Spanish Theatre Repertory, N.Y.C., 1986-90; exec. dir. Nat. Dance Inst., N.Y.C., 1990-91; sr. assoc. Caesar & Washburn, N.Y.C., 1992—; adv. bd. Riverside Symphony, N.Y.C., 1984-91; panelist N.Y. State Coun. Arts, 1986-90, site auditor, 1984—. Mem. Women Fin. Devel. Home: 166 E 96th St 16D New York NY 10128-5099 Office: Caesar & Washburn 1841 Broadway Ste 609 New York NY 10023

CARMICHAEL, ROBERT WILLIAM, medical group administrator; b. Lansdale, Pa., Dec. 22, 1958; s. Paul Louis and Pauline Cecilia (Lipsmire) C.; m. Ruth Maria Avendano, July 22, 1983; children: Diana Christina, Anna Maria. BS in Econs., U. Pa., 1980; MBA, U. Miami, 1987. Treas. AIESEC, U.S., N.Y.C., 1980-81; asst. to contr. Comfamiliar Andi Fenalco, Barranquilla, Colombia, 1981-82; asst. to v.p. ops. ICN Pharms., Covina, Calif., 1982-83; fin. mgr. Paulmarc Systems, Lansdale, 1983-85; ops. mgr. Coopervision Info. Systems, Lansdale, 1985-86; bus. mgr. Ophthalmic Assocs., Lansdale, 1987-90; cons. Mass. Eye and Ear Infirmary, Boston, 1990—; prtnr. Poolside Cons., Lansdale, 1985—; founder, v.p. Profl. Ophthalmic Adminstrs., Phila., 1989—; bd. advisors AIESEC, Long Beach, Calif., 1983. Acct. Mary Mother of Redeemer Ch., Montgomeryville, Pa., 1988—; bd. dirs. North Penn Symphony Orch., Lansdale, 1989. Named Outstanding Young Man of Yr., Lansdale Jaycees, 1990. Republican. Roman Catholic. Office: The Carter Eye Ctr 3310 Live Oak Ste 520 Dallas TX 75204

CARMODY, GEORGE EDWARD, lawyer, arbitrator, corporate director, executive; b. Mt. Vernon, N.Y., June 16, 1931; s. George Edward and Florence Alba (Liccione) C.; divorced; children: Elizabeth, Susan, Matthew, David. BA, U. Conn., 1955; JD, Fordham U., 1960. Bar: N.Y. 1961, U.S. Dist. Ct. (so. and ea. dists.) N.Y. 1962. Securities analyst Merrill Lynch Pierce Fenner & Beane, N.Y.C., 1955-60, assoc. law dept., 1960-62; counsel Van Alstyne, Noel & Co., 1962-64; ptnr. Stamer & Haft, N.Y.C. and London, 1964-70; prin. Carmody Law Office, N.Y.C. and Phila., 1970—; founder Telescis. Capital Corp., Marlboro, N.J., 1981—; pres. Leach Entertainment Enterprises, Inc.; bd. dirs. Leach Entertainment Enterprises, Inc., Danbury, Conn., Delta Switching Corp., Cherry Hill, N.J., Celebrity Concepts, Inc., Celebrity Prodns., Inc. Mem. Am. Assn. Arbitrators, Nat. Assn. Corp. Dirs., Fordham Law Alumni Assn. Libertarian. Home and Office: 888 8th Ave New York NY 10019

CARMODY, MARGARET JEAN, social worker; b. Wauwatosa, Wis., Aug. 5, 1924; d. Peter and Gertrude Francelia (Brown) Galijas; m. James Matthew Carmody, Apr. 3, 1971. BA, Marquette U., 1945; MA, U. Chgo., 1949. Social worker Denver Gen. Hosp., 1950-51; Fulbright fellow France, 1951-52; social worker, cons. U. Ill., Chgo., 1954-60; health scientist, adminstr. USPHS, Washington, 1961—; 1960—. Mem. Acad. Cert. Social Workers. Democrat. Roman Catholic. Home: 6130 31st St NW Washington DC 20015-1516 Office: Agy Health Care Policy Rsch 2101 E Jefferson St Exec Office Ctr Rockville MD 20852-4993

CARMODY, ROBERT EDWARD, human resource information systems professional; b. N.Y.C., Dec. 13, 1942; s. Henry Adrian and Lucille Dorothy (Dorsey) C.; m. Sara Jane Morris, Oct. 4, 1969; children: Jon Andrew, Heather Brooke. BA in Psychology, U. Va., 1964. CLU. Personnel systems supt. State Farm Ins. Co., Bloomington, Ill., 1966-78; exec. project dir. Info. Sci. Inc., Chgo., 1978-79; dir. human resources systems CIGNA Corp., Phila., 1979-88, asst. v.p., human resources info. services, 1988—; founding mem. Ins. Personnel Systems Group, 1987—. Contbr. articles to profl. jours. With Ill. N.G., 1964-70. Mem. Am. Mgmt. Assn., Soc. Human Resource System Profls., Conf. Bd., Info. Industry Assn., Ins. Personnel Systems Group (founding mem. 1987). Home: 118 Oak Ave Haddonfield NJ 08033-3978 Office: CIGNA Corp 1601 Chestnut St Philadelphia PA 19172-0001

CARNE, CAROLYN LEE, nursing home administrator; b. Washington, Nov. 20, 1943; d. William Francis and Ardith Geneveve (McCool) C. BS, James Madison U., 1965; MBA, Loyola Coll., Balt., 1982; postgrad., U. Md., 1983—. Registered dietitian, Md.; lic. nursing home adminstr., Md.; lic. dietitian, nutritionist, Md. Therapeutic dietitian Johns Hopkins Hosp., Balt., 1966-68; co-adminstr. St. Joseph's Nursing Home, Catonsville, Md., 1976-83, adminstr., 1983—; cons. registered dietitian, adminstrv. head dietetic dept. St. Joseph's Nursing Home, 1967—; cons. registered dietitian Sisters Servants of Mary Immaculate Day Nursery, Balt., 1967—; pres. CJS Assocs., Inc., Clinton, Md., 1981-83; part-time instr. dietetic tech. program Community Coll. Balt., 1980-83. Provincial treas. Sisters Servants of Mary Immaculate Inc., Catonsville, 1982-89, treas., bd. dirs., 1982-89, sec., 1989—, liaison to bd., Cleve., 1981-83. Mem. Am. Dietetic Assn., Md. Dietetic Assn., ADA Mems. with Mgmt. Responsibilities in Health Care Delivery Systems, Cons. Dietitians in Health Care Facilities, Am. Coll. Nursing Home Adminstrs., Hosp. Food Svc. Adminstrs. Soc., Am. Coll. Hosp. Adminstrs., Md. Cath. Health Care Consortium (chairperson-elect 1983, chairperson 1984), Md. Assn. Non-Profit Homes for Aging (reimbursement task force 1990-92). Democrat. Roman Catholic. Home and Office: St Josephs Nursing Home 1222 Tugwell Dr Catonsville MD 21228

CARNEY, JOSEPH PATRICK, government official; b. Bklyn., Jan. 10, 1939; s. Edward Francis and Marion Joan (Hickey) C.; m. Suga Fujino, Oct. 12, 1976. BA in Philosophy, Coll. of Holy Cross, 1960; MRE, MA in Theology, Maryknoll Sch. Theology, Ossining, N.Y., 1965; MA in History, Scranton U., 1968; PhD in African Studies, St. John's U., 1973. Adj. prof. African studies Notre Dame (Ind.) U., 1971-73; asst. prof. African studies, v.p. Maryknoll Sch. Theology, 1971-74; dir. adult edn. U. Dar es Salaam, Musoma, Tanzania, 1974-76, Coll. of New Rochelle (N.Y.), 1976-78; dir. edn. and human resources AID, Maseru, Lesotho, 1978-83, Kingston, Jamaica, 1983-87; chief edn. and human resources div. Latin Am.-Caribbean Bur. AID, Washington, 1987—; cons. on higher edn. Dem. Republic Yemen Ministry Edn., 1982; cons. internat. scholarship programs ministries edn., So. Africa, Latin Am. and Caribbean, 1978-92. Contbr. articles to various publs. Reicpient Meritorious Svc. award Lesotho Ministry Edn., 1983, Meritorious Leadership award Ptnrs. of Ams., Kingston, Jamaica, 1986, Higher Edn. Meritorious Svc. award U. W.I., 1986; scholarship Coll. of Holy Cross, 1956-60. Mem. Am. Hist. Soc., African Studies Assn., Latin Am. Studies Assn. Roman Catholic. Home: 13208 Coralberry Dr Fairfax VA 22033 Office: AID LAC Bur Edn Human Resources Div Dept State Rm 2239 Washington DC 20520

CARNEY, LYNN ROSE, accountant, real estate broker; b. Springfield, Mass., Jan. 28, 1955; d. Henry E. and Dolores R. (Delay) Yergeau; m. Terence M. Carney, May 28, 1983; children: Erin L., Michael T. BS in Acctg. cum laude, North Adams State Coll., 1977. Cert. real estate broker, Mass. Adminstrv. asst. Field, Eddy & Buckley Ins., Springfield, 1977-78; property acct. Westvāco US Envelope, Springfield, 1979-81, gen. acctg. supr., br. plant auditor, 1981-83, plant acct., 1983-85; pres., owner Carney Assocs., Belchertown, 1985—; broker assoc. Realty World Bay Path, Belchertown, 1989—. Treas. Belchertown Day Sch., 1987-90; mem. Tri-Lake Assn., Belchertown, 1988—, PTA, Belchertown, 1990—. Recipient Outstanding Svc. award Belchertown Day Sch., 1990. Mem. Nat. Soc. Tax Preparers, Mass. Assn. Realtors, Holyoke Chicopee Bd. Realtors. Home: 246 Bay Rd Belchertown MA 01007-9762 Office: Carney Assocs Stadler St Belchertown MA 01007-9448

CARNEY, ROGER FRANCIS XAVIER, retired army officer; b. Bklyn., Oct. 20, 1933; s. Frank Clement and Clara Helen (Muller) C.; m. Linda Ann Bowlus, Aug. 11, 1963; children—Kevin James, Stephen Jason, Brian Andrew. B.S., Purdue U., 1960, M.S. in Indsl. Adminstrn., 1963; grad. U.S. Army Command and Gen. Staff Coll., 1975, U.S. Army War Coll., 1979. Commd. 2d lt. U.S. Army, 1960, advanced through grades to lt. col., 1976; comdr. 583d Ordnance Co., Muenster, W.Ger., 1969-72; research and devel. coordinator Army Materiel Command Field Office, Kirtland AFB, N.Mex., 1972-74; logistic staff officer CENTAG Signal Support G.P. (NATO), Seckenheim, W.Ger., 1975-78, chief nuclear weapons logistic element G4, 1978; comdr. 15th Ordnance Battalion, Darmstadt, W.Ger., 1978-80; prof. head dept. Worcester Poly. Inst. (Mass.), 1980-84; prof. mil. sci., head dept. Fitchburg State Coll. (Mass.), 1980-84; prof. mil. sci., head dept. Nichols Coll., Dudley, Mass., 1982-84, dean student affairs, 1985—. Mem. Worcester Com. Fgn. Relations, Worcester Econ. Club, Mil. Adv. Council Ctr. for Defense Info. Decorated Legion of Merit, Bronze Star, 2 Meritorious Service medals, Army Commendation medal. Mem. Assn. U.S. Army, Nat. Assn. Student Personnel Adminstrs., Am. Coll. Personnel Assn. Purdue Alumni Assn., Alpha Sigma Phi (pres. Purdue U. chpt. 1959-60), Pi Lambda Theta. Democrat. Roman Catholic. Home: Center Rd Dudley Hill Dudley MA 01571

CARON, DONALD ALVIN, JR., financial consultant; b. Oyster Bay, N.Y., Sept. 9, 1966; s. Donald A. and Joan I. (Waters) C. BS in Fin., Pa. State U., 1988. Fin. asst. v.p. Kidder, Peabody & Co., Washington, 1988—. Mem. Greater Washington Bd. Trade. Republican. Home: 2217 McLean Park Rd Falls Church VA 22043 Office: Kidder Peabody 919 18th St NW #500 Washington DC 20006

CAROZZA, WILLIAM VICTOR, educator, director; b. Rochester, N.Y., July 3, 1961; s. Victor Lloyd and Jean Elizabeth (Rourke) C.; m. Marie Elizabeth Tanguay, Nov. 3, 1984; 1 child, Benjamin William. BA in Polit. Sci., U. N.H., 1983, MEd, 1987. Cert. tchr., N.H. Tchr. Deerfield Community Sch., Deerfield, N.H., 1983—; music dir., on-air person Sta. WDER, Derry, N.H., 1985—; Deerfield (N.H.) Community Sch., SD, SD; cooperating tchr. for coll. interns U. N.H., Durham, 1987—. Columnist Horizons, 1985—. Musician St. Paul Ch., Candia, N.H., 1981—. Mem. N.H. Coun. for Social Studies (pres. N.H. chpt. 1989—), Nat. Coun. for Social Studies (N.H. del. to ho. of dels.), Assn. for Supervision and Curriculum Devel. Democrat. Roman Catholic. Home: 28 Woodland Grn Rochester NH 03868-5716 Office: Deerfield Community Sch Rt 107 Deerfield NH 03037

CARPENTER, BARRY KEITH, chemistry educator, researcher; b. Hastings, Sussex, U.K., Feb. 13, 1949; came to U.S., 1973; s. George Henry and Gladys Mable Carpenter. BSc with honors, Warwick U., Coventry, Eng., 1970; PhD, U. Coll., London, 1973. Postdoctoral fellow Yale U., New Haven, 1973-75; asst. prof. Cornell U., Ithaca, N.Y., 1975-81, assoc. prof., 1981-85, prof., 1985—; cons. Hoffmann-La Roche, Inc., Nutley, N.J., 1985—, Astra AB, Sodertalje, Sweden, 1989—, Union Carbide, Linde Div., Tarrytown, N.Y., 1991; R.A. Welch Found. lectr., 1989, Bergmann lectr. Yale U., New Haven, 1992. Author: Determination of Organic Reaction Mechanisms, 1984; sr. editor Jour. Organic Chemistry, 1992—. NATO fellow, 1973, A.P. Sloan Found. fellow, 1980, J.S. Guggenheim Found. fellow, 1986, Av. Humboldt Found. grantee, 1990. Fellow AAAS; mem. Am. Chem. Soc., Royal Soc. Chemistry. Office: Cornell U Dept Chemistry Ithaca NY 14853-1301

CARPENTER, DELORES BIRD See BIRD, JUANITA DELORES

CARPENTER, EDMUND MOGFORD, manufacturing executive; b. Toledo, Dec. 28, 1941; s. Charles N. and Vivian (Mogford) C.; m. Mary Winterhoff, May 20, 1962; children: Susan, Edmund Mogford, Molly. BS in Indsl. Engring., U. Mich., 1963, MBA, 1964. Dist. plant mgr. Mich. Bell Tel. Co., Detroit, 1964-68; ptnr. Touche Ross & Co., CPA's, Detroit, 1968-74; pres. Fruehauf do Brasil, Sao Paulo, 1974-76; pres. auto truck group Kelsey-Hayes Co., Romulus, Mich., 1976-81; group gen. mgr. world wide automotive ops. ITT Corp., Southfield, Mich., 1981-83; v.p. ITT Corp., N.Y.C., 1983-85, pres., dir., 1985-88; chief oper. officer ITT Indsl. Products, N.Y.C., 1987-88; chmn., chief exec. officer Gen. Signal Corp., High Ridge Park, Stamford, Conn., 1988—; bd. dirs. Gen. Signal Corp., High Ridge Park, Stamford; bd. dirs. Campbell Soup Co., Camden, N.J., Dana Corp., Texaco, Inc., White Plains, N.Y. Bd. dirs. Jr. Achievement. Mem. Machinery and Allied Products Inst. (exec. com.). Office: Gen Signal Corp High Ridge Pk PO Box 10010 Stamford CT 06904-2010

CARPENTER, EDMUND NELSON, II, lawyer; b. Phila., Jan. 27, 1921; s. Walter S. and Mary (Wootten) C.; m. Carroll Morgan, July 18, 1970; children: Mary W., Edmund Nelson III, Katherine R.R., Elizabeth Lea; stepchildren: John D. Gates, Ashley du Pont Gates. AB, Princeton U., 1943; LLB, Harvard U., 1948. Bar: Del. 1949, U.S. Supreme Ct. 1957. Assoc. Richards, Layton & Finger, Wilmington, Del., 1949-53, ptnr., 1953-78, dir., 1978—, pres., 1982-85; dep. atty. gen. State of Del., 1953-54, spl. dep. atty., 1960-62; chmn. Del. Superior Ct. Jury Study Com., 1963-66, Del. Supreme Ct. Cts. Consolidation Com., 1985-87; mem. Del. Gov.'s Commn. Law Enforcement and Adminstrn. Justice, 1969; chmn. Del. Agy. to Reduce Crime, 1970-71, chmn. Del. Supreme Ct. Adv. Com. on Profl. Fin. Accountability, 1974-75; mem. Long Range Cts. Planning Com., 1976—. Trustee Wilmington Med. Ctr., 1965—, U. Del., 1971-77, Princeton U., 1974-85, 86-91, Winterthur Mus., 1991—, World Affairs Coun. Wilmington, 1968-80, Woodrow Wilson Found., 1985—; trustee Lawrenceville Sch., 1953-74, trustee Lawrenceville Sch., 1953-74, trustee emeritus, 1974—; bd. dirs. Good Samaritan Inc., 1973—; chmn. lawyers adv. com. U.S. Ct. Appeals (3d cir.), 1975-77; mem. Del. Health Care Injury Ins. Study Commn., 1976—. Fellow Am. Coll. Trial Lawyers, Am. Bar Found.; mem. ABA (ho. of dels. 1979-86), Del. State Bar Assn., Am. Judicature Soc. (dir. 1974—, exec. com. 1978-80, v.p. 1980-81, pres. 1981-83), Am. Trial Lawyers Assn. Home: 600 Center Mill Rd Wilmington DE 19807-1502 Office: PO Box 551 One Rodney Sq Wilmington DE 19899

CARPENTER, FRANK MASON, sales manager; b. Clearspring, Md., July 30, 1939; s. Frank M. and Ruth N. (Gruber) C.; children: Frank Jr., Stephen J., Scott A. Dir. internat. sales HIAC/Royco, Silver Spring, Md., Pacific Scientific, Silver Spring; dir. ops. Gardner-Neotec div. PS Co.; v.p. sales Neotec Corp., v.p. ops. Patentee in field. With USAF, 1960-64. Home: 4 Shipwright Ct Gaithersburg MD 20877-4319

CARPENTER, GENE BLAKELY, crystallography and chemistry educator; b. Evansville, Ind., Dec. 15, 1922; s. Leland A. and Juanita (Blakely) C.; m. Elizabeth E. Corkum, Apr. 15, 1949; children—Jonathan R., Anne E. B.A., U. Louisville, 1944; M.A., Harvard U., 1945, Ph.D., 1947. NRC fellow Calif. Inst. Tech., 1947-48, research fellow, 1948-49; instr. Brown U., 1949-52, asst. prof., 1952-56, asso. prof., 1956-63, prof., 1963-88, prof. emeritus, 1988—; Guggenheim fellow U. Leeds, Eng., 1956-57; vis. prof. U. Groningen, The Netherlands, 1963-64; Fulbright-Hayes lectr. U. Zagreb, Yugoslavia, 1971-72; vis. scientist Oak Ridge Nat. Lab., 1980, U. Göttingen, Fed. Republic of Germany, 1987, U. Canterbury, Christchurch, New Zealand, 1989. Author: Principles of Crystal Structure Determination, 1969; Contbr. articles to sci. jours. Mem. Am. Crystallographic Assn., Am. Chem. Soc. Home: 8 Angell Ct Providence RI 02906-4118 Office: Brown U Dept Chemistry Providence RI 02912

CARPENTER, HOYLE DAMERON, music educator emeritus; b. Stockton, Calif., Aug. 8, 1909; s. William Horace and Mabel (Hanna) C.; m. Rose Mick, Feb. 24, 1968. MusB, U. Pacific, 1930; Mus.M., U. Rochester, 1932; PhD, U. Chgo., 1951-57; postgrad. U. Calif., Berkeley, 1949-50. Instr. Ft. Hays (Kans.) State Coll., 1942-44; asst. prof. Grinnell Coll., 1944-57; faculty Glassboro (N.J.) State Coll., 1957—, asst. prof., 1957-60, assoc. prof., 1960-61, prof., 1961-76, prof. emeritus, 1976—. Treas. Gloucester County Mental Health Assn., 1963-68. Committeeman Glassboro Dem. Com., 1964; v.p. Glassboro Dem. Club, 1964-66. Mem. AAUP, Am., Internat. musicological socs., Music Tchrs. Nat. Assn. (sec. Eastern div. 1962-64), Music Educators Nat. Conf., Renaissance Soc. Am., Am. Guild Organists, N.J. Music Tchrs. Assn. (pres. 1961-63), Pi Kappa Lambda. Author: Teaching Elementary Music without a Supervisor, 1959; also edits. Holyoke's Instrumental Assistant, 1959, Crequillon Pisne me peult venir, 1962; also several poster sets on music, 1970, also articles; writer program notes for Hollybush Festival, Lenape Chamber Players, Craftsbury Chamber Players, 1980—, Allegro Soc., Glassboro State Coll. Home: 512 S Woodbury Rd Pitman NJ 08071-1636

CARPENTER, JAMES EDWARD, mathematics educator, academic administrator; b. Chgo., Dec. 11, 1946; s. James Joseph and Luella Mae (Ivers) C.; m. Linda Margaret Karkos, Jan. 27, 1973; children: Andrew, Carolyn, Thomas, John. BS, Ill. Benedictine Coll., 1968; MS, Chgo. State U., 1971; EdD, Columbia U., 1978. Tchr. St. Laurence High Sch., Burbank, Ill., 1968-74; prof. St. Mary of the Plains Coll., Dodge City, Kans., 1975-81, Iona Coll., New Rochelle, N.Y., 1981—; vis. acad. Trinity Coll., Dublin, Ireland, 1988-89. Contbr. articles to profl. jours. Mem. Nat. Coun. Tchrs. Maths., Math. Assn. Am. Office: Iona Coll 715 North Ave New Rochelle NY 10801-1890

CARPENTER, LISA DIANE, artist; b. Rochester, N.H., Mar. 30, 1960; d. Robert T. and Nancy J. (Spurling) Cramer; m. Jeffrey D. Carpenter, May 22, 1982; 1 child, Sean Michael. Student, U. N.H., 1979. Artist Barrington, N.H., 1986—; artist, owner Old Port Artisans, Portsmouth, N.H., 1991—. Pub. art prints; executed mural Four Seasons of Whippoorwill Farm, 1992; exhibited in permanent collection Bill W. Dodge Collection and Gallery, Carmel-by-the-Sea, Calif. Republican. Home: 216 Tolend Rd Barrington NH 03825 Office: Old Port Artisans 206 Market St Portsmouth NH 03801

CARPENTER, MICHAEL ALAN, securities firm executive; b. London, Mar. 24, 1947; came to U.S., 1971; s. Walter and Kathleen Mary C.; m. Mary Aughton, Mar. 1, 1975; children—Nicholas James, Abigail Lee. B.Sc. with joint honors, U. Nottingham, Eng., 1968; M.B.A., Harvard U., 1973. Bus. analyst Mond div. Imperial Chem. Industries, Runcorn, Eng., 1968-71; cons., mgr. Boston Cons. Group, 1973-78, v.p., 1978-83; v.p. Gen. Electric Co., Fairfield, Conn., 1983-86; exec. v.p. Gen. Electric Credit Corp., Stamford, Conn., from 1986; joined Kidder Peabody & Co. Inc., 1989, chmn., pres., CEO, 1990—; formerly chmn. Gen. Electric Venture Capital Corp. Baker scholar Harvard Bus. Sch., 1973. Office: Kidder Peabody & Co Inc 10 Hanover Sq New York NY 10005-3516*

CARPENTER, MICHAEL E., state official; b. Houlton, Maine, Sept. 3, 1947. BA, U. Maine, Orono, 1969; JD, U. Maine, 1983. Rep. State of

Maine, 1974-76, former senator dist. 33, asst. majority leader, from 1983, now atty. gen. Mem. YMCA. With U.S. Army, 1965-73; Abn Div., Vietnam, 1970-71. Decorated Combat Inf. badge, two Bronze Stars, two Air medals, Vietnamese Cross of Gallantry, Army Commendation medal; named one of Outstanding Young Men of Am., 1975, 78-82. Mem. VFW, KC, Elks. Democrat. Roman Catholic. Office: Office of Atty Gen State House Sta 6 Augusta ME 04333*

CARPENTER, PAUL SAMUEL, accountant, financial planner; b. Johnstown, Pa., June 29, 1956; s. Samuel C. and Josephine V. (Camut) C.; m. Kathy Ann Hammers, Oct. 21, 1978. BS magna cum laude, Indiana U. of Pa., 1978. CPA, Pa.; Cert. Fin. Planner. V.p. Carpenter & Carpenter CPAs, Johnstown, 1978—; pres. Carpenter Fin. Svcs. Inc., Johnstown, 1990—; registered rep. H.D. Vest Investment Securities Inc., Irving, Tex., 1989—. Mem. AICPA, Inst. Mgmt. Accts. (chpt. pres. 1985-86, Most Valuable Mem. 1979, 87), Pa. Inst. CPAs (treas. cen. chpt. 1989-90, sec. 1990-91), Internat. Assn. Fin. Planners, Inst. Cert. Fin. Planners, Registry Cert. Fin. Practitioners, Cambria-Somerset Estate Planning Coun. (pres. 1986-87), Rotary. Office: Carpenter & Carpenter CPAs 237 Johns St Johnstown PA 15901-1555

CARPENTER, STANLEY WATERMAN, paper company executive; b. Lowell, Mass., June 25, 1921; s. Daniel Albert and Edith May (Redfern) C.; m. Marie Kurth, May 12, 1957; children: Cheryl J., Mark S. Student, Lowell Textile Inst., 1939-42. With Thorp & Martin Co., Boston, 1947-49; self-employed distbr. Ditto, Inc., 1949-51; mktg. mgr. U.S. Envelope Co., Springfield, Mass., 1951-65; with N.Y. Nat. Envelope Corp., L.I. City, 1965—; v.p. sales N.Y. Envelope Corp., L.I., 1969-80, group v.p. mktg., 1980—. Asst. dir. CD, Bedford, Mass., 1946-49. With U.S. Army, 1942-46. Mem. Am. Mktg. Assn., So. Paper Trade Assn., Midwest Paper Trade Assn., Saugatuck Harbor Yacht Club, Conn. Gun Guild. Home: 14 Owenoke Pk Westport CT 06880-6832 Office: 29-10 Hunters Point Ave Long Island City NY 11101

CARPENTER, WILLIAM MORTON, English educator, writer; b. Cambridge, Mass., Oct. 31, 1940; s. James M. and Dorothy N. (Sauer) C.; m. Joanne Laventis, 1962 (div. 1987); 1 child, Matthew; m. Donna Gold; 1 child, Daniel. BA, Dartmouth Coll., 1962; PhD, U. Minn., 1967. Instr. U. Minn., Mpls., 1963-67; asst. prof. U. Chgo., 1967-72; mem. faculty dept. lit. Coll. of Atlantic, Bar Harbor, Maine, 1972—, faculty dean, 1983-89; bd. dirs. Maine Acad. Coalition, Augusta. Author: The Hours of Morning, 1981, Rain, 1986, Speaking Fire at Stones, 1992. Recipient Neruda prize U. Okla., 1979, Contemporary Poetry award Assoc. Writing Program, 1981, Black Warrior Rev. prize U. Ala., 1984, Morse prize Northeastern U., 1985; NEA fellow, Venice, Italy, 1985, Inst. for Human Ecology fellow 1989—, Yaddo Ctr., fellow 1984, MacDowell Colony fellow, 1985. Office: Coll of Atlantic 105 Eden St Bar Harbor ME 04609-1198

CARPENTER-MASON, BEVERLY NADINE, executive health care quality assurance nurse; b. Pitts., May 23, 1933; d. Frank Carpenter and Thelma Deresa (Williams) Smith; m. Sherman Robert Robinson Jr. (dec.), Dec. 26, 1953 (div. Jan. 1959); 1 child, Keith Michael; m. David Solomon Mason Jr., Sept. 10, 1960; 1 child, Tamara Nadina. RN, Shadyside Hosp. Sch. Nursing, Pitts.; BS, St. Joseph's Coll., North Windham, Maine, 1979; MS, So. Ill. U., 1981; postgrad., Columbia Pacific U., 1989—. Staff nurse med. surgery, ob-gyn neontology and pediatrics Pa., N.Y., Wyo., Colo. and Washington, 1954-68; mgr. clinician dermatol. svcs. Malcolm Grow Med. Ctr., Camp Spring, Md., 1968-71; pediatric nurse practitioner Dept. Human Resources, Washington, 1971-73; asst. dir. nursing Glenn Dale Hosp., Md., 1973-81; nursing coord. medicaid div. Forest Haven Ctr., Laurel, Md., 1981-83, spl. asst. to supt. for med. svcs., 1983-84; spl. asst. to supt. for quality assurance Burr. Habilitation Svcs., Laurel, 1984-89; exec. asst. quality assurance coord. Mental Retardation Devel. Disabilities Adminstrn., Washington, 1989-91; also bd. dirs., 1989—; asst. treas. Am. Bd. Quality Assurance Utilization Rev. Physicians, 1988—, chair exam. com., 1990—; ret. Mental Retardation Devel. Disabilities Adminstrn., Washington, 1991; bd. dirs. Quality Mgmt. Audits, Inc., 1991—; cons., lectr. in field; case study editor, mem. jour. editorial bd. Am. Coll. Med. Quality, 1985—, chmn. publs. com., 1987—, asst. treas., 1988—; mem. Am. Bd. Quality Assurance & Utilization Rev. Physicians, 1984—; owner, bd. dirs. Quality Mgmt. Audits, Inc., 1991—. Contbr. articles to profl. jours. Mem., star donor ARC Blood Drive, Washington, Md., 1975—; chair nominations com. Prince Georges Nat. Coun. Negro Women, Md., 1984-85. Recipient awards Dept. Air Force and D.C. Govt., 1966—, Della Robbia Gold medallion Am. Acad. Pediatrics, 1972, John P. Lamb Jr. Meml. Lectureship award East Tenn. State U., 1988, Woman of the Yr., 1990. Mem. NAFE, Am. Assn. Mental Retardation (conf. lectr. 1988), Am. Coll. Utilization Rev. Physicians, Assn. Retarded Citizens, Healthcare Quality Inst., Top Ladies of Distinction (1st v.p. 1986—), Internat. Platform Assn., Order Ea. Star (Achievement award Deborah chpt. 1991), Chi Eta Phi. Democrat. Baptist. Home and Office: 11109 Winsford Ave Upper Marlboro MD 20772-2378

CARPENTER-MEISTER, CAROLYN EVELYN, sexual assault counselor; b. Willimantic, Conn., July 23, 1946; d. David Joseph and Evelyn Emma (Brown) Loree; m. Kenneth Omar Carpenter, Jan. 31, 1963 (div. 1970); children: Julie Ann, Karen Marie; m. Gary Charles Meister, June 25, 1976. DDiv, The Aquarian Ch., Hermosa Beach, Calif., 1979. Lic. sexual assault counselor/domestic violence counselor, Conn. Singer, entertainer John Penny Ent./Gary Meister & Carolyn Carpenter Show, Watertown, Mass., 1973-80; proprietor/mgr. Family Corner Store/Luncheonette, Willimantic, 1981-82; founder, internat. cons. Love-N-Addiction Orgn., Willimantic, 1986—; sexual assault counselor/advocate supr. N.E. Conn. Sexual Assault Crisis Svcs., Willimantic, 1987—; spiritual/self-esteem cons. to families of alcohol and drug abusers, 1983—; facilitator, speaker, conductor workshops in field; mem. domestic violence adv. bd. United Svcs., Willimantic, 1988-90, Conn. Sexual Assault Crisis Svcs., 1991—. Author poetry: Only In My Mind, 1986, Nightfall, 1982, Yesterday's Child, 1986, Children of the Trees, 1987; contbr. articles to profl. jours. Recipient Golden Poet award World of Poetry, 1986, 87, Silver Poet award, 1990. Mem. Windham Photography Club. Republican. Home: PO Box 759 Willimantic CT 06226

CARPER, GERTRUDE ESTHER, artist, marina owner; b. Jamestown, N.Y., Apr. 13, 1921; d. Zenas Mills and Virgie (Lytton) Hanks; m. J. Dennis Carper, Apr. 5, 1942; children: David Hanks, John Michael Dennis. Student violinist, Nat. Acad. Mus., 1931-41; diploma fine arts, Md. Inst. of Art, 1950; voice student, Frazier Gange, Peabody Inst. Music, 1952-55. Interior decorator O'Neill's (Importers), Balt., 1942-44; auditor Citizens Nat. Bank, Covington, Va., 1945-46; owner, developer Essex Yacht Harbour Marina, Balt., 1955—, owner, developer St. Michael's Sanctuary wildlife preserve, 1965—. Jewelry designer, 1987—; portrait artist, 1947—; exhibited one-woman shows Ferdinand Roten Gallery, Balt., 1963, Highfield Salon, Balt., 1967, Le Salon des Nations a Paris, 1985, Ducks and Geese of North Am., 1986, Series of Lighthouses, 1991; exhibited group shows Md. Inst. Alumni Show, 1964, Essex Libr., 1981, Hist. Preservation of Am., Hall of Fame, 1989, others; works included in collections including Prestige de la Peinture d'Aujourd'hos dans le Monde, 1990, Artists and Masters of the Twentieth Century, 1991; Author: Expressions for Children, 1985; contbr. articles and poetry to ch. publs. and newspapers. Vol. tchr. of retarded persons, 1942—; leader Women's Circle at local Presbyn. chs., 1952-87, mem. 40 yrs. of choir svc. Mem. Md. Inst. Art Alumni Assn. (life), Grand Coun. World Parliament of Chivalry (Nobless of Humanity citation). Office: Essex Yacht Harbour Marina 500 Sandalwood Rd Baltimore MD 21221-5830

CARPER, THOMAS RICHARD, congressman; b. Beckley, W.Va., Jan. 23, 1947; s. Wallace Richard and Mary Jean (Patton) C.; m. Martha Stacy, Jan. 1, 1986; children: Christopher Thomas, Benjamin Michael. B.A. in Econs., Ohio State U., 1968; M.B.A., U. Del., 1975. Indsl. devel. specialist Del. div. Econ. Devel., Dover, 1975-76; state treas. State of Del., Dover, 1976-83; mem. 98th-102nd Congresses from Del., Washington, 1983—. Co-chmn. United Negro Coll. Fund Drive, Del., 1977; mem. adv. council Delmarva council Boy Scouts Am., 1983—; fund-raising chmn. Big Brothers-Big Sisters of Del., 1985; hon. chairperson Del Spl. Olympics, 1987-90. Comdr. USN, 1968-73, capt. Res., 1973—. Democrat. Presbyterian. Home: 600 W Matson Run Pky Wilmington DE 19802-1911 Office: 131 Cannon House Office Bldg Washington DC 20515*

CARPINELLI, R. ANTHONY, entrepreneur; b. Cleve., Nov. 14, 1963; s. Ralph R. and Patricia Carpinelli. AA in Communications, U. Akron, 1985, B in Mktg., 1987; cert. in entrepreneurship, Wichita State U., 1989; postgrad., Northeastern U., 1992—, Harvard U., 1992—. Pres. Neato Co., Cleve., Richfield, Ohio, 1979-90; lead svc. agt. Amtrak, Boston, 1989-90; asst. dir. tng. and devel. Eastern Airlines, Boston, Dallas, 1990; ops. mgr. Western Promotions, L.A., 1990—, TNC Mktg., Boston, 1990—. Vol. Boston Living Vtr., Dana Farber Cancer Inst., Boston. Mem. Boston Prof. Alliance, Greater Boston Bus. Coun. Home: 126 Pembroke St # 10 Boston MA 02118-1265 Office: TNC Mktg Corp Prudential Ctr 398 Columbus Ave Ste 115 Boston MA 02116

CARPINO, BARBARA ANN, mathematics educator; b. Springfield, Mass., Dec. 12, 1938; d. Lottie A. Nogosky; m. Louis A. Carpino, Aug. 30, 1958; children: Philip, Alexandra, Nicholas, Christine, Elizabeth, Margaret. BS, U. Mass., 1962; cert. in math., chemistry, Smith Coll., 1982. Pres. Carpino Tutoring Inst., Amherst, Mass., 1981—; prof. math. Holyoke (Mass.) Community Coll., 1990—; cons. Micklejohn Sch., Amherst, 1987-88; dir. sci. coun. Amherst Jr. High Sch., 1982-86. Mem. Amherst Women's Club. Home: 11 Mount Pleasant St Amherst MA 01002 Office: Holyoke Community Coll 303 Homestead Ave Holyoke MA 01040

CARR, DAVID WILDON, educator; b. Morristown, N.J., Apr. 4, 1945; s. Clifford Wildon and Marie (Schaible) C.; m. Carol Shearman, Mar. 25, 1966; children: Eve, Anna. BA, Drew U., 1967; MA, Columbia U., 1968; MLS, Rutgers U., 1973, PhD, 1979. Tchr. Princeton (N.J.) Regional Schs., 1968-71, East Brunswick (N.J.) Schs., 1971-73; libr. Douglass Coll., Rutgers U., New Brunswick, 1973-76; bibliographer Alexander Libr., Rutgers U., New Brunswick, 1976-80; assoc. prof. Grad. Sch. of Edn., Rutgers U., New Brunswick, 1980-87, Sch. of Communication, Info. and Libr. Studies, Rutgers U., 1987—; cons. W.K. Kellogg Found., Battle Creek, Mich., 1988-89, Strong Mus., Rochester, 1990-92, The Jewish Mus., N.Y.C., 1990, Children's Mus., Indpls., 1991. Contbr. articles to profl. jours. Trustee Christian and Teresa M. Dingler Found., Morristown, N.J., 1975—. Mem. ALA (Jesse Shera Award com. 1991—), Am. Assn. of Mus., Am. Ednl. Rsch. Assn. Home: 55 James St Morristown NJ 07960-5945 Office: SCILS Rutgers U 4 Huntington St New Brunswick NJ 08901-1071

CARR, EDWARD GARY, psychology educator; b. Toronto, Aug. 20, 1947; came to U.S., 1969; s. Saul Isaac and Anne (Goldsmith) C.; m. Ilene Wasserman, Aug. 2, 1987; 1 child, Aaron. BA, U. Toronto, 1969; PhD, U. Calif., San Diego, 1973. Lic. psychologist, N.Y. Asst. prof. psychology SUNY, Stony Brook, 1976-81, assoc. prof., 1981-85, prof., 1985—; cons. Devel. Disabilities Inst., Smithtown, N.Y., 1976—. Author: In Response to Aggression, 1981, How to Teach Sign Language, 1982; author monograph. Fellow Am. Psychol. Assn. Office: SUNY Dept Psychology Stony Brook NY 11794-2500

CARR, JAMES NORRIS, JR., advertising agency executive; b. West Chester, Pa., May 27, 1952; s. J. Norris and Elizabeth Ann (Phillips) C.; m. Audrey Lynn Radke, Nov. 30, 1985; 1 child, Amanda. BA in English, Washington and Lee U., Lexington, Va., 1974; MA in English, Villanova (Pa.) U., 1981. Auditor various hotels, 1975-79; v.p. J.N. Carr Transport Inc., Frazer, Pa., 1979-82, Norris Transport Inc., Devault, Pa., 1982-83; freelance copywriter King of Prussia, Pa., 1983-85; account exec. Ferguson Advt. Inc., Jenkintown, Pa., 1985-87; pres. Ferguson-Carr Advt., Inc., Jenkintown, Pa., 1988—. Mem. N. Penn C. of C. Republican. Presbyterian. Office: Ferguson-Carr Advt Inc Benson East #515 Jenkintown PA 19046

CARR, L(EWIS) CHARLES, clinical psychologist, management consultant; b. Boston, Aug. 17, 1946; s. Lewis Chapman and Mildred (Dodd) C.; m. Joan violet Wood, Aug. 5, 1967; children: Charles Christian, Jonathan Edward. BS, Gordon Coll., 1967; MDiv, Gordon-Conwell Sem., 1970; PhD, Rosemead Grad. Sch. Psychology, 1975. Pvt. practice N.Y.C., 1975-86, Atlanta, 1986-89; sr. staff psychologist The Inst. of Living, Hartford, Conn., 1989—. Mem. St. Paul's Episcopal Ch., Darien, Conn. 1975-86, Mt. Vernon Bapt. Ch., Sandy Springs, Ga., 1986-89. Mem. APA, Conn. Psychol. Assn. Congregationalist. Office: The Inst of Living 400 Washington St Hartford CT 06106-3351

CARR, MARK EDMUND, marketing professional; b. Woodbury, N.J., May 17, 1962; s. William John and Lorraine Ann (Applegate) C.; m. Lesley Derrickson, Aug. 8, 1990. BS in Textile Chemistry, Phila. Coll. of Textiles & Scis., 1984. Asst. chemist Gentex Corp., Carbondale, Pa., 1983; chemist Gentex Corp., 1984-85, product mktg. mgr., 1988—; project engr. ILC Dover Inc., Fredericka, Del., 1985-88. Loaned exec. United Way, Scranton Pa., 1989, allocations mem., 1990, 91, loaned exec. program chair, 1990. Mem. Am. Defense Preparedness Assn., Am. Chemical Soc., Am. Assn. of Textile Chemists and Colorists, Am. Soc. of Testing and Materials. Republican. Roman Catholic. Office: Gentex Corp PO Box 315 Carbondale PA 18407-0315

CARR, MICHAEL FABIAN, investment adviser-executive; b. Syracuse, N.Y., Apr. 7, 1935; s. Charles Francis and Genevieve Dorothea (La Flèche) C. BBA, U. Notre Dame, 1956; MBA, NYU, 1963. Portfolio analyst Merrill Lynch, Pierce Fenner & Smith, N.Y., 1959-62; analyst, portfolio mgr. Hayden Stone, Inc., N.Y.C., 1962-65; analyst Clark Dodge & Co., N.Y.C., 1965; sr. analyst Hirsch & Co., N.Y.C., 1966; v.p. Equity Rsch. Assoc., N.Y.C., 1967-70; sr. analsyt Shields & Co., N.Y.C., 1970-72; sr. v.p. Shearson Lehman Bros., N.Y.C., 1972-89; pres. Carr & Assocs. Inc., Lodi, N.J., 1989—; bd. dirs. Carr Rsch. Inc., Framingham, Mass., 1960-90. Comdr. Naval Order of the U.S., N.Y.C., 1985-88; pres. 3d dist. Naval Res. Assn., N.Y.C., 1989. Lt. (j.g.) USNR, 1956-59. Fellow Inst. Chartered Fin. Analysts; mem. Assn. for Fin. Mgmt. and Rsch. Roman Catholic. Home: 7200 Boulevard E North Bergen NJ 07047-5957

CARR, YVONNE DENISE, secretary; b. Hornell, N.Y., Apr. 9, 1970; d. Timothy Frank and Mary Ann (Kent) C. Diploma, Inst. Children's Lit., West Redding, Conn., 1991. Cashier Stop and Shop, Simpsbury, Conn., 1986—; office sec., asst. Power Access, Collinsville, Conn., 1989—. Author 10 poems, 1990—. Democrat. Baptist.

CARR-DERAMUS, DENISE, mental health counselor; b. Boston, Dec. 15, 1951; d. Gilman and Blanche (Francis) Carr. BA, Boston State Coll., 1981; MEd, U. Mass., 1983, CAGS, 1988, postgrad., 1988—. Lic. mental health counselor; cert. trauma counselor, addictions specialist, clin. mental health counselor, approved supr. Rehab. counselor Quincy (Mass.) Mental Health Ctr.; staff psychologist Wrentham (Mass.) State Sch.; psychologist III Mass. Treatment Ctr., Bridgewater. Mem. AACD, Nat. Acad. Clin. Mental Health Counselors, Assn. Multicultural Counseling and Devel., Am. Mental Health Counselors Assn., Internat. Assn. Addiction and Offenders Counselors, Nat. Hispanic Psychologists Assn., Internat. Assn. Trauma Counselors, Little People of Am., Vietnam Vets. Am.

CARREL, JEFFREY MACK, podiatrist; b. Buffalo, Mar. 7, 1942; s. Ralph and Gertrude (Rosen) C.; m. Sheila J. Rose, June 21, 1964; children: Aaron, Mitchell, David. Student, U. Buffalo, 1959-61; D Podiatric Medicine cum laude, N.Y. Coll. Podiatric Medicine, 1965. Diplomate Am. Bd. Podiatric Orthopedics, Am. Bd. Podiatric Surgery. Postgrad. trainee Civic Hosp., Detroit, 1965-66, Woodward Gen. Hosp., Highland Park, Mich., 1965-66; pvt. practice N.Y., 1966—; adj. clin. instr. Ill., Ohio, N.Y., Calif. and Pa. Colls. Podiatric Medicine; preceptor Family Medicine Ctr., Buffalo Gen. Hosp./Deaconess Hosp., 1977—; med. exec. com. Sheehan Emergency Hosp., 1986, chmn. podiatry adv. com., 1983—, bd. dirs., 1987—, chief podiatry, 1986-89; mem. N.Y. State Podiatry Bd., 1979-89, chmn., 1986-87; residency tng. com. Sheridan Park Hosp., 1978-89; chief podiatry St. Joseph Hosp., 1989—; presenter at profl. confs. mem. editorial bd. Jour. Am. Podiatric Med. Assn., 1975—; contbr. numerous articles to profl. publs. Fellow Am. Coll. Foot Orthopedists, Am. Coll. Foot Surgeons (exam. com. 1984-86, bd. dirs.), Am. Coll. Podiatric Radiologists, Am. Soc. Podiatric Dermatologists, Can. Podiatric Sports Acad.; mem. Am. Podiatry Assn., N.Y. State Podiatry Assn., Am. Assn. Hosp. Podiatrists. Office: 409 Brisbane Bldg Buffalo NY 14203

CARRERA, JOAN JUDITH, government agency official; b. N.Y.C., Feb. 20, 1928; d. Martin and Gertrude (Feibush) Totschek; m. Louis Carrera, Feb. 16, 1956. BA, Hunter Coll., 1950; MPA, NYU, 1951; MSW, Hunter Coll., 1966. Coord. program officer trainee program Office of Probation, N.Y.C., 1966-68; tng. cons. N.Y. State Dept. Social Svcs., Albany, N.Y., 1968-69, assoc. dir. manpower planning and devel., 1969-72, dir. manpower planning and devel., 1972-77; staff devel. specialist Office of Family Assistance U.S. Dept. Health and Human Svcs., Albany, 1977-80, program analyst office of family assistance, 1980-86, program analyst family support adminstrn., 1986-91, program analyst adminstrn. children & families, 1991—; cons. Pres.'s Commn. on Goals and Standards for Corrections, Washington, 1972. Editorial policy bd. Jour. of Continuing Edn., SUNY-Albany, 1981—; adv. com. Pub. Welfare Jour., 1987—; co-author: Income Maintenance Supervisor on the Firing Line, 1979; author: Surviving the Firing Line, 1985; contbr. articles to profl. jours. Mem. Am. Pub. Welfare Assn., Nat. Assn. Social Work, Nat. Staff Devel. and Tng. Assn. (sec. 1990-92, at-large bd. 1992—), Internat. Coun. of Social Welfare (U.S. com., bd. dirs. 1984-89, coun. social work edn. 1983-87).

CARRIG, JAMES JOSEPH, adult education educator; b. Little Falls, N.Y., Feb. 22, 1930; s. Timothy and Marie (Grau) C.; m. Mary Kathryn Chubbuck, Aug. 19, 1961; children: Timothy J., Kathryn M., James J. Jr. BA in English cum laude, Niagara U., 1952, MA in English, 1953; EdD in Adult Edn., Syracuse U., 1973. Instr. English Utica (N.Y.) Coll. of Syracuse U., 1956-68, asst. dir. continuing edn., 1968-70, dir. continuing edn., 1970-88, assoc. dean for continuing edn., 1988—. With U.S. Army, 1953-55. Mem. Assn. Continuing Higher Edn. (bd. dirs. 1961-65), Alpha Sigma Lambda (nat. counselor Alpha Omicron chpt.). Democrat. Roman Catholic. Home: 7219 Oriskany Rd Rome NY 13440 Office: Syracuse U Utica Coll 1600 Burrstone Rd Utica NY 13502-4857

CARRIGAN, DANIEL JAMES, management consultant; b. Boston, July 12, 1960; s. Robert Henry and Mary (McMullen) C.; m. Dawn L. Whitehad, July 18, 1980; children: Erin L., Daniel J. Jr. BA in Polit. Sci., St. Francis Xavier U., N.S., Can., 1982; MPA, U. Maine, 1985. NTL trainer cert.; psychol. type indicator cert. Ops. mgr. Nabisco Brands Inc., various locations, 1983-89; internal orgn. devel. cons. Hannaford Bros. Co., Portland, Maine, 1989—; cons. Scarborough (Maine) Sch. System, 1991—. Contbr. articles to profl. jours. Assn. of Atlantic Province Univs. scholar, 1983-84. Mem. Am. Soc. Tng. and Devel. Home: 15 Brookview Terr Portland ME 04102 Office: Hannaford Bros Co PO Box 1000 Portland ME 04104

CARRO, CARL RAFAEL, executive search consultant; b. N.Y.C., Mar. 16, 1961; s. John and Victoria (Eugenia) C.; m. Inna Liban, Nov. 17, 1984. BA in Polit. Sci., Econs., Columbia U., 1983. Cons. Korn Ferry Internat.; sr. exec. recruiter The Gap, Inc., N.Y.C.; v.p. Exec. Placement Consultants div. R.H. Macy & Co., N.Y.C., 1991—; cons. Korn Feray Internat., N.Y.C. Republican. Roman Catholic. Office: Exec Placement Consultants 11 Penn Pla Ste 602 New York NY 10001

CARROLL, ANTHONY QUENTIN, public relations and advertising executive; b. Allentown, Pa., May 12, 1944; s. Edward Quentin and Mary Delacroix (Cantlin) C.; m. Jean Marie Sullivan, Aug. 13, 1977; children: Sean Edward, Ryan Arthur. BA, Princeton U., 1966. Account exec. Fernley & Fernley, Phila., 1972-85; exec. dir. Resistance Welder Mfrs. Assn., Phila., 1974-85; pub. relations account exec. Contemporary Mktg., Inc., 1985-86; account exec., Target Communications, Inc., Plymouth Meeting, 1986-89, Norristown, Pa., 1989-90, sr. account exec., 1990—. Mem. Durham St. Town Watch, Mt. Airy, Phila., 1983. 1st lt. U.S. Army, 1969-71. Mem. Sierra Club (chmn. wildlife com. Ea. Pa. chpt. 1978-82). Democrat. Episcopalian. Office: Target Communications Inc 801 E Germantown Pike Ste F-1 Norristown PA 19401-2480

CARROLL, BETTY WILDER, treasurer; b. Stoneham, Mass., Nov. 23, 1921; d. Philip W. and Lucy Idabel (Jones) Potter; m. Dyer E. Carroll, May 8, 1943; children: Dyer E. Jr., Nancy W. Grad. high sch., Stoneham. Writer Stoneham Ind., 1938-45; editor What's New in Town, Boston, 1940-43; freelance writer, poet, freelance proofreader; founder, treas. Tech. Lab., Wakefield, Mass., 1965-68; incoroporator, treas. Carroll Engrs., Inc., Andover, Mass., 1968—. Member Rep. Town Com., Stoneham, United Meth. Episcopal Ch., Stoneham; dir. Stoneham Little League. Office: Carroll Engrs Inc 200 Andover St Andover MA 01810-5608

CARROLL, BRIAN DALE, commercial printing executive; b. Buffalo, Dec. 19, 1944; s. L. Stuart and Evelyn Irene (Wagner) C.; m. Linda Louise Stephens, July 6, 1968; children: Julie Louis, Brian William, Colleen Shannon. BS in Bus. Adminstrn., U. Buffalo, 1967; MBA in Fin., Canisius Coll., 1972. Asst. civil engr. Erie County Highway Dept., Buffalo, 1967; budget analyst Bell Aerosystems div. Textron, Inc., Wheatfield, N.Y., 1968-69; project cost analyst Twin Industries div. Wheelabrator, Buffalo, 1969-70; office mgr. Pfieffers Foods div. Internat. Salt Co., Buffalo, 1970-72; div. acctg. mgr. Internat. Salt Co., Clark's Summit, Pa., 1972-75; asst. to pres. Pfeiffer's Foods div. Internat. Salt Co., Buffalo, 1975-78; v.p. fin. Miken Cos., Inc., Cheektowaga, N.Y., 1978—. Vol. fireman Orchard Park (N.Y.) Vol. Fire Co., 1976—. Republican. Methodist. Home: 25 Bender Dr Orchard Park NY 14127-2330 Office: Miken Cos Inc 75 Boxwood Ln Buffalo NY 14227-2783

CARROLL, BRUCE E., library director; b. Beachville, Md., Mar. 15, 1951; s. James W. and Dorothy Cecilia (Carroll) G.; 1 child, Kimberly. BS, Morgan State U., 1974; MLS, Atlanta U., 1975. Asst. reference libr. Morgan State U., Balt., 1975-76; circulating libr. Community Coll. Balt., 1978, rsch. specialist, 1979-81, automation libr., 1987-89, dir. librs. and media svcs., 1989—; reference libr. Balt. County Libr., 1986-89. Living witness Balt. City Pub. Schs., 1989—. Named one of Outstanding Young Men Am., 1980. Mem. Am. Libr. Assn. Roman Catholic.

CARROLL, CYNTHIA LOUISE, marketing and advertising agency executive; b. Watertown, N.Y., Feb. 10, 1960; d. Joseph Patrick and Helen Marie (Arkles) C. BS, Syracuse U., 1982, MBA, 1988. Asst. claims adjuster A.T. Armstrong Ins. Co., Syracuse, N.Y., 1984-86; promotion coord. Latorra Advt., Syracuse, 1986-89; fin. analyst Central N.Y. Health Systems Agy., Syracuse, 1989-91; advt. account exec. Drumlins Advt. and Promotions, Syracuse, 1991; dir. grants Cazenovia (N.Y.) Coll., 1991—. Mem. Am. Mktg. Assn., Track and Racquet Club, Eta Pi Upsilon. Roman Catholic. Home: 254 Fellows Ave Syracuse NY 13210-2626

CARROLL, DYER EDMUND, mechanical engineer; b. Boston, June 4, 1921; s. Jerimiah Charles and Grace Mildred (Rice) C.; m. Betty Wilder Potter, May 8, 1943; children: Dyer Edmund Jr., Nancy Wilder. Cert. mech. engr., Lowell Inst., 1942; Assoc. in Mech. Engring., Northeastern U., BA, 1964. Registered profl. engr., Mass. Power engr. MIT, Cambridge, 1947-48; supr. rsch. engring. Mutual Boiler and Machinery Ins. Co., Waltham, Mass., 1948-51, supr. rsch., 1954-65; inspection engr. Commonwealth of Mass. Dept. Pub. Safety, Lowell, 1951-54; chief metall. engring. Factory Mutual Engring. Corp., Norwood, Mass., 1965-68; pres. Carroll Engrs., inc., Andover, Mass., 1968—; cons., instr. Mass. Bay Community Coll. Tech.; instr. U.S. Army Mechanic and Materials, Watertown, Mass., 1972-88, Lloyd's Register of Shipping, Crauley, Eng., 1971—. Author tng. manuals in field. Mem. recreation com. Town of Stoneham, Mass., 1952-55, chmn. bd. appeals; mem. com. Stoneham Little League. With USN, 1942-46. Mem. ASTM, ASME, Am. Soc. Non-Destructive Testing, Am. Soc. Metals, Am. Legion (comdr.). Republican. Home: 89 Spring St Stoneham MA 02180-1423 Office: Carroll Engrs Inc 200 Andover St Andover MA 01810-5608

CARROLL, JAMES F.L., educator, artist; b. Postville, Iowa, Sept. 4, 1934; s. Raymond J. and Genivieve (Wagoner) C.; m. Joanne Barbara Pardee, Apr. 27, 1938; children: Joel Raymond, Jeri Kae, James R.L., Jonelle. BA, Colo. State Coll., 1956, MA, 1962; MFA, U. Colo., 1966. Art tchr. Englewood Colo. Schs., 1957-58, Jefferson County Schs., Golden, Colo., 1958-66; fine arts prof. Kutztown Univ., Kutztown, Pa., 1966—; dir./pres. New Arts Program, Inc., Kutztown, 1974—; bd. dirs. Lehigh Valley Arts Coun., Allentown, Pa., 1987-91, East Pa. Emerging Arts, Kutztown, 1988-91; panel

mem./selection Pa. Coun. on the Arts, Harrisburg, Pa., 1990, 91, 92; nominator Awards in the Visual Arts, Winston-Salem, N.C., 1990. Author, pub.: (book) In & Out of Kutztown, 1981 (NEA grant 1980); contbr. essays to profl. catalogues. With U.S. Army, 1957, USAR, 1958-63. Recipient cert. of Recognition, Community Spirit Award, Morning Call, Allentown, 1989, cert. for Exceptional Acad. Svc., Commonwealth of Pa., Harrisburg, 1978. Mem. AAUP, Am. Assn. Mus., Assn. of Pa. State Colls. & Univs. Faculties, Internat. Sculpture Ctr., Artists Equity Assn., Pa. Arts Coalition. Office (Studio): New Arts Program PO Box 82 173 W Main St Kutztown PA 19530

CARROLL, JAMES JOSEPH, research chemist; b. Scranton, Pa., Dec. 12, 1935; s. Peter J. and Edith J. (Brace) C.; m. Marina La Belle, July 30, 1960; 1 child, Peter. BS in Chemistry, U. Scranton, 1957; MS in Phys. Chemistry, Pa. State U., 1960, PhD in Biochemistry, 1962; MBA in Internat. Bus., Fairleigh Dickinson U., 1978. Scientist Sandoz Pharm. Co., East Hanover, N.J., 1962-65; scientist, sr. scientist, sr. rsch. assoc. Warner Lambert Co., Morris Plains, N.J., 1965-76, mgr. bus. devel., 1976-78, product mgr. internat., 1978-85; pres., chief operating officer Am. Bioproducts Co., Parsippany, N.J., 1985-87; dir. R & D coagulation and chemistry Baxter Dade div. Baxter Healthcare Corp., Miami, Fla., 1987-89; dir. hemostasis R & D, Ortho Diagnostics div. Johnson & Johnson, Raritan, N.J., 1989—; adj. prof. Fairleigh Dickinson U., Madison, N.J., 1977-85; presenter at nat. and internat. sci. meetings on cardiovascular disease; industry rep. hematology and pathology device panel FDA, 1988—; mem. subcom. on coagulation Nat. Com. for Clin. Standards, 1989—. Contbr. articles to sci. jours.; patentee in U.S. and fgn. countries. Mem. Juvenile Delinquent Community Com., East Hanover, N.J., 1970-77, East Hanover Curriculum Steering Com., 1974-75; mem. adult edn. com. East Hanover Park High Sch., 1970-75. Mem. Am. Chem. Soc., Am. Assn. Clin. Scientists, Am. Heart Assn.

CARROLL, LEE FRANCIS, electrical engineer; b. Berlin, N.H., Oct. 14, 1937; s. Alton Francis and Mary Elizabeth (Cushing) C.; m. Judith Anne Magoun, Apr. 9, 1960; children—Shawn, Pamela, Bruce. B.S.E.E., Northeastern U., 1960. Registered profl. engr., Maine, N.H., Vt., Mass., N.Y., Pa., Va., Tex., La., N.J. Elec. engr. Fraser Paper Ltd., Madawaska, Maine, 1960-64; maintenance engr. Am. Optical Co., Southbridge, Mass., 1964-65; elec. engr. Ga. Pacific Corp., Lyons Falls, N.Y., 1965-66; chief elec. engr. central engring. dept. Brown Co., Berlin, 1966-70, Wright, Pierce Engrs., Topsham, Maine, 1970-73; prin. L.F. Carroll Elec. Cons., Gorham, N.H., 1973—. Commr. water sewer dept., Gorham, N.H., 1975—; pres. Gorham Devel. Corp., 1980-91; moderator town, Gorham, 1986—. Named N.H. Engr. of Yr., 1990. Mem. IEEE (sr.), Nat. Fire Protection Assn., Illuminating Engrs. Soc. Republican. Congregationalist. Avocations: flying; hunting; fishing; hiking. Home: PO Box F 43 Evans St Gorham NH 03581 Office: Elec Cons PO Box 357 1 Madison Ave Gorham NH 03581-0357

CARROLL, LUCY ELLEN, choral director, music coordinator; b. N.Y.C., Oct. 11, 1946; d. Edward Joseph and Lucy Sophie (Czapszys) C. B in Music Edn., Temple U., 1968; MA, Trenton State Coll., 1973; D in Musical Arts, Combs Coll. Music, Phila., 1982. Cert. tchr. music, N.J., Pa., Nat. Cert., 1991. Tchr. music Log Coll. Jr. High Sch., Pa., 1968-72, Ind. (Pa.) High Sch., 1972-73; tchr. music William Tennent High Sch., Warminster, Pa., 1973—, dir. mus. theater, 1973—; music coord. Centennial Schs., 1991; founder, dir. Madrigal Singers, Warminster, Pa., 1971—; choral dir. Cabrini Coll., Radnor, Pa., 1974-77, First Day Singers, Phila., 1979-83, Combs Coll. of Music, Phila., 1981-84, 1987-88; choral adjudicator various music festivals, 1973—; guest lectr. mus. seminars, convs., and writers' confs. Singer (operas Ambler Festival) Street Scene, 1970, Death of Bishop of Brindisi (premiere); (Robin Hood Dell) La Boheme; dir. (jazz theater piece N.Y.C.) Murder of Agamemnon, 1980, (musi. drama) Power of Love (1705), 1986, (outdoor music theater) Vorspiel (Pa. Historic Commn. 1989); contbr. articles to profl. jours., also sci. fiction to sci. fiction mags. and anthologies. Recipient awards Writers of the Future, 1985, '87, Andrew Ferraro award Combs Coll. of Music, 1989, Internat. Order of Merit IBA, 1991, plaque for Svc. to Music Bucks County Commr., 1991. Mem. Internat. Bus. and Profl. Women (Woman of Yr. 1982), Am. Choral Dirs. Assn., Theatre Assn. Pa., Delaware Valley Composers (choral cons. 1988-90); NEA, Pa. Edn. Assn. Centennial Edn. Assn., Bucks County Music Educators Assn., Hist. Soc. Pa., Smithsonian Assocs., Music Fund Soc. of Phila., The Sonneck Soc. for Am. Music, Pa. Music Educators Assn. (adv. bd., 1986-87), Theatre Assn. Pa., Friends of Pa. Hist. and Mus. Commn., Sigma Alpha Iota. Republican. Roman Catholic. Home: 712 High Ave Hatboro PA 19040-2418 Office: William Tennent High Sch Music Dept 333 Centennial Rd Warminster PA 18974-5400

CARROLL, MEGAN ELIZABETH, lawyer; b. Lake Forest, Ill., Sept. 7, 1967; d. Barry Joseph and Barbara (Pehrson) C. BA in Philosophy, French Lit., Boston Coll., 1989, JD, 1992; student, Middlebury Coll., Paris, 1987-88. Bar: Ill., Mass., 1992. Paralegal Holleb & Coff, Chgo., 1988; law clk. Middlesex County Probate & Family Ct., Cambridge, Mass., 1990-91; assoc. Powers & Hall, Boston, 1991; asst. dist. atty. Quincy, Mass., 1992—. Arts review writer various publs. Mem. Am. Ireland Fund, Boston, Chgo., 1985—, DAR, Chgo., 1985—, Phillips Acad. Alumni Coun., Andover, Mass., 1991—; trustee Regency Pk. Condominiums, Brookline, Mass., 1989-91; sec. Phillips Acad. Alumni Class of 1985, Andover, 1989—. Recipient Golden Key Nat. Honor Soc., Boston Coll., 1989, Order of the Cross and Crown, Scholar of the Coll. Mem. ABA, Arts and Media Law Assn. of Boston Coll. (pres., founder), Woman's Athletic Club of Chgo., Order of Malta Aux., Phi Delta Phi. Republican. Roman Catholic. Home: 55 Mayflower Rd Lake Forest IL 60045-3307 Other: 1731 Beacon St #320 Brookline MA 02146

CARROLL, OSCAR FRANKLIN, air force officer; b. Fairfield, Ala., Nov. 11, 1950; s. Gordon Diffley and Mavis Marie (Steele) Davis; m. Lilian Donaldson Ross, June 22, 1978; children: Joshua, Erin. BS in Latin Am. Studies, BS in History, U.S. Air Force Acad., 1972, BS in Math., 1972; MS in Systems Mgmt., U. So. Calif., 1988. Commd. 2d lt. USAF, 1972, advanced through grades to maj., 1984; systems engr. Lockheed SDI programs, Sunnyvale, Calif., 1984-85; systems analyst Hdqrs. Space Command, Colorado Springs, 1985, logistics program mgr. Boost-phase Surveillance and Tracking, 1987-89, logistics program mgr. Advanced Launch System, 1988-89, systems upgrade mgr. Pacer Frontier, 1989-90; wing flight evaluator 436 Mil. Airlift Wing, Dover AFB, Del., 1990—; cons. Lockheed Space Shuttle Ops. Ctr., Vandenburg AFB, Calif., 1985, Lockheed Fleet Ballistic Missile, Santa Clara, Calif., 1985, Lockheed Space Sta., Sunnyvale, 1985, Global Positioning Satellite, Colorado Springs, 1987. Writer logistics sect. Air Force Space Doctrine, 1987; editor logistics sect. Space Command Space Plan, 1987, Statements of Need, 1987-89, Systems Operation Requirements Documents, 1987-89. Directorate rep. Bd. Hdqrs. Space Command, Colorado Springs, 1986-89, Strategic Def. Panel, Colorado Springs, 1988-89; airspace mgr. Dover AFB/Dover local community/FAA, 1991-92. Decorated Air Force Commendation medal (2), Meritorious Svc. medal (2). Mem. Air Force Officers Club (rep. to adv. coun. 1982, 83, 84). Home: RD 1 Box 267 BC Dover DE 19901

CARROLL, ROBERT COURTNEY, lawyer, banker; b. N.Y.C., Sept. 9, 1946; s. Riley Courtney and Marie Veronica (Faust) C.; m. Joy C. Fields, Sept. 5, 1982; 1 child, Lauren. BBA, Manhattan Coll.; JD, Pace U., 1987. Bar: Conn. 1988. Asst. v.p., corp. records officer Chem. Bank Office of the Sec., N.Y.C., 1982—; v.p., sec. Chem. Internat. Fin., Ltd. and subs., N.Y.C., 1991—; pres. Broad Park Lodge Corp., White Plains, 1991—, bd. dirs., 1989—. Asst. coach Greenburgh (N.Y.) Little League, 1991. Recipient Outstanding Achievements award The Woods Schs., Langhorne, Pa., 1982. Home: 2 Westchester Ave White Plains NY 10601-3529 Office: Chem Bank 277 Park Ave New York NY 10172-0003

CARROLL, WAYNE DOUGLAS, insulation company executive; b. Richmond, Va., Apr. 30, 1938; s. Marion David and Virginia Mae (Horner) C.; m. Barbara Ann James, May 7, 1960; children: Diane Marie, Robin Lee. BSME, Duke U., 1961; MBA, Syracuse U., 1971. Project engr. Owens-Ill. Glass Co., Toledo, 1961-64; dept. foreman Corning Glass Works, Bradford, Pa., 1964-68; supr. process engring. Corning (N.Y.) Glass Works, 1968-69, supr. fiber optics, 1969-71; prodn. mgr. Union Carbide Co., Tuxedo, N.Y., 1971-78; mgr. prodn. Pitts. Corning Corp., 1978-79, works mgr., 1979-89, v.p., gen. mgr., 1990—. Mem. Edgewood Country Club. Home: 800 Limecrest Rd Pittsburgh PA 15221-2506 Office: Pitts Corning Corp 800 Presque Isle Dr Pittsburgh PA 15239-2799

CARROZZELLA, LOUISE BAILEY, government affairs consultant; b. Boston, Dec. 16, 1934; d. John Moran and Barbara (Leary) Bailey; m. Conrad J. Kronholm, Nov. 7, 1959 (div. 1978); children: Eric, Justin, John, Bailey; m. John A. Carrozzella, 1991. BA, Marymount Coll., Tarrytown, N.Y., 1956; postgrad., Boston U. Sch. of Law, 1956-57, Conn. State U., New Britian, 1957-58. Lic. ins. broker. Agt. John Hancock Ins. Co., Rocky Hill, Conn., 1985--; special events coord. Hartford Arts Council, Conn., 1984--. Staff mem. Dukakis Campaign, Hartford, Conn., 1988; sec. Conn. Law Enforcement Found., 1980—; trustee U. of Conn. Bd. of Trustees, 1978—; pres Hartford Ballet, 1974; lobbyist Masonic Home and Hosp., 1989. Recipient Alumnae Svc. award U. Conn., 1992, Yr. of the Women medal U. Conn. Mem. World Affairs Ctr., University Club, Hartford Club, March of Dimes. Democrat. Roman Catholic. Home: 178 Long Hill Rd Wallingford CT 06492-4934

CARRUBBA, EUGENE ROY, quality assurance professional, consultant; b. Melrose, Mass., Dec. 26, 1934; s. Sebastiano and Concetta (Calderaro) C.; m. Nancy Isabel Anderson, Sept. 5, 1965. BS in Mgmt., Boston U., 1956. Registered profl. engr., Calif. Engr. RCA, Needham, Mass., 1965-66; sr. engr. Avco Corp., Wilmington, Mass., 1966-70; engring. supr. GTE Sylvania Corp., Needham, 1970-75, engring. mgr., 1975-79; engring. mgr. Digital Equipment Corp., Maynard, Mass., 1979-83, sr. engring. mgr., 1983-85; dir. quality assurance Symbolics Inc., Cambridge, Mass., 1985-87; sr. dir. quality assurance Motorola Codex Corp., Mansfield, Mass., 1987-91, gen. mgr. corp. quality assurance, 1991—; pres. Product Assurance Learning Ctr., cons., Wayland, Mass., 1982—; lectr. Western New Eng. Coll., Bedford, Mass., 1986-87. Author: Assuring Product Integrity, 1975, Product Assurance Principles, 1988, Quality and the Consumer, 1992; also articles. Recipient Disting. Speaker award Gordon Inst., 1990. Mem. IEEE (sr., com. chmn. 1974-75, 80-85, lectr. 1976, 86, keynote speaker 1986), Am. Soc. for Quality Control, Mass. Coun. for Quality, Inc. (bd. dirs.). Home: 21 Cameron Rd Wayland MA 01778 Office: Motorola Codex Corp 20 Cabot Blvd Mansfield MA 02048

CARSKI, THEODORE ROBERT, physician, microbiologist; b. Balt., June 22, 1930; s. Theodore John and Katherine (Kocent) C.; m. Trudi Thau, July 10, 1954; children: Theodore Henry, Karen Anne, Christopher Robert, Gregory William. AB, Johns Hopkins U., 1952; MD, U. Md., 1956. Diplomate Am. Bd. Med. Microbiology; cert. med. and pub. health microbiology. Intern U. Md. Hosp., Balt., 1956-57; sr. asst. surgeon USPHS, Montgomery, Ala., 1957-60; dir. rsch. BBL Div., Balt., 1960-68; dir. microbiology Huntingdon Rsch. Ctr., Balt., 1968-69, asst. dir., 1970-72, dir., 1972-74; assoc. med. dir. Becton Dickinson & Co., Balt., 1974-76, corp. med. dir., 1976—. Contbr. articles to profl. jours. Mem. Am. Soc. for Microbiology (coun. policy com. 1976-79). Home: 14258 Baldwin Mill Rd Baldwin MD 21013-9003 Office: Becton Dickinson & Co 250 Schilling Cir Cockeysville Hunt Valley MD 21031-1103

CARSON, CHARLES HENRY, electronics engineer; b. Malden, Mass., July 18, 1930; s. Philip Stanley and Margaret (Mitchell) C.; m. Olivia Rose Marie Barto, Apr. 23, 1967; children: Cynthia, Craig. BSEE, Northeastern U., Boston, 1956, postgrad., 1966. Devel. engr. microwave Raytheon, Bedford, Mass., 1953-56; sr. engr., dept. mgr. Airtron Inc., Cambridge, Mass., 1956-58; co-founder, v.p., dir. ops. Ferrotec Inc., Newton, Mass., 1958-70; dir. corp. mkt. planning MA/COM, Burlington, Mass., 1970-75; chmn., founder, chief exec. officer Carson Assocs., Inc., Milford, Mass., 1975—; bd. dirs. Carson Assocs., Inc., Milford; co-founder, bd. dirs. Colonial Cablevision, Revere, Mass., 1976-86; co-founder, v.p. mktg., bd. dirs. Ferrotec Inc., Newton, 1958-70. Inventor in field; contbr. articles to profl. jours. Commr. Indsl. devel. Commn., Milford, 1968-70; minuteman Mass. Ind. Devel. Commn., 1969-73. With USN, 1948-53. Mem. U.S. Polo Assn. (del. 1986—), R.I. Tuna Tournament (dep. dir. 1973-77), Galilee Tuna Club (pres. 1976-77), Newport Polo Club (del. 1986). Office: Carson Assocs Inc 5 Kellett Dr Milford MA 01757-4013

CARSON, DAVID ALLEN, history educator; b. Newport, Tenn., June 10, 1956; s. Johnnie G. and Amarylis (Allen) C.; m. Sandra Bell, Aug. 20, 1977 (div. May 1989); 1 child, Jessica Miranda; m. Charlene Wojdan, July 20, 1991. BS, East Tenn. State U., 1977, MA, 1980; PhD, Tex. Christian U., 1983. Instr. Tarrant County Jr. Coll., Ft. Worth, 1981; assoc. prof., history SUNY, Buffalo, 1983—. Contbr. articles to profl. jours. New Faculty Devel. grantee, United U. Profs., 1985. Mem. Phi Alpha Theta (faculty advisor 1984—). Democrat. Mem. Christian Ch. Home: 4674 E River Rd Grand Island NY 14072-1141 Office: Buffalo State Coll Dept History 1300 Elmwood Ave Buffalo NY 14222-1095

CARSON, JOHN THOMPSON, JR., environmental consultant; b. Phila., Apr. 13, 1916; s. John Thompson and Agnes (Gillinder) C.; B.S., Haverford Coll., 1938; M.S., U. Pa., 1939; m. Margaret Evans, June 21, 1940; children: Frederick, Sylvia Hathaway. Tchr. sci. and math. Perkiomer Sch. Pennsburg, Pa., 1939-41; chmn. dept. biology George Sch., Newtown, Pa., 1941-64; exec. dir. Neshaminy Water Resources Authority, Doylestown, Pa., 1966-76; dir. Natural Resources Div., Bucks County, Doylestown, 1966-76; program dir. Delaware River Basin Commn., West Trenton, N.J., 1976-78; pres. John Carson & Assocs., Inc., Doylestown, 1978—; lectr. environ. law U. Pa., 1978-79; vis. prof. ecology Lehigh U., Bethlehem, Pa., 1977-78; adj. prof. environ. studies Delaware Valley Coll., 1990—. Pres. Coun. Rock Little League, 1950-56, Delaware River Watershed Assn., 1958-61, Neshaminy Valley Watershed Assn., 1957-64; chmn. Bucks County Water and Sewer Authority, 1962-65; vice chmn. Doylestown Twp. Bd. Suprs., 1980—; adv. com. Inst. for Research on Land and Water Resources, Pa. State U., 1975-82. Recipient Conservation award Soil Conservation Soc. Am., 1961, Pa. Forestry Assn., 1971, Samuel S. Baxter Meml. award Assn. Del. River Basin, 1987; named Watershed Man of Yr., Pa. Assn. Conservation Dists., 1974. Mem. Pa. Forestry Assn., Nat. Wildlife Fedn. Republican. Mem. Soc. of Friends. Contbr. articles to profl. jours. Address: 95 Cherry Ln Doylestown PA 18901

CARSON, RICHARD DEAN, food company executive; b. Bedford, Pa., May 23, 1956; s. Warren Harding and Shirley Jean (College) C.; m. Elizabeth Force, Aug. 26, 1978; children: Daniel R., Megan E. BA in Am. History, Indiana U. Pa., 1978; MDiv, Luth. Sem., Gettysburg, Pa., 1982; postgrad., Temple U., 1984-85. Ordained to ministry Luth. Ch.in Am., 1982. Pastor Luth. Ch., Red Lion, Pa., 1982-86; pers. adminstr. Cor-Box, Inc., York, Pa., 1986-87; v.p. human resources Round Hill Foods, Inc., New Oxford, Pa., 1987—; Motivational speaker Nat. Assn. Credit Mgmt., York, Pa., 1988-91, Indsl. Mgmt. Club, Hanover, 1990. Pres. Susquehanna Sr. Ctr., Craley, Pa., 1985; bd. dirs. ARC, Hanover, Pa., 1989-90; soloist St. Mathew Music Series, Hanover, 1990. Mem. Soc. for Human Resource Mgmt. (cert. sr. profl.), Hanover Area C. of C. (bd. dirs. 1991-93), Nat. Turkey Fedn. (health and safety task force 1991), Lions (chaplain West Manheim, Pa. 1989—). Office: Round Hill Foods Inc PO Box 38 New Oxford PA 17350-0038

CARSON, WILLIAM MORRIS, manpower planning consultant; s. Edward Belmont and Frances Lucretia (Powell) C.; children: Lincoln Bruce, Carson Adrien, Lee Allen, Anthony Lunt, Karen Tracy. BS, Columbia U.; MA, Johns Hopkins U.; postgrad. U. Chgo., London Sch. Econs. Indsl. rels. staff analyst ARAMCO, Dhahran, Saudi Arabia, 1964-70; mgr. mgmt. devel. and tng. Saudi Arabian Airlines, Jeddah, 1970-72; chief tng. sect. UN Devel. Programme, N.Y.C., 1973-75; mgr. mgmt. devel. and tng. Sylvania Tng. Ops., Waltham, Mass., 1975-76; dir. tng. Ingersoll-Rand Constrn. Services, Winston-Salem, N.C., 1977-79; sr. adv. manpower planning and devel. Internat. Human Resources Devel. Corp., Boston, 1979-83; gen. mgr. ITECO div., Saudi Tng. Svcs., Riyadh, Saudi-Arabia, 1983-84; mng. dir. Arab Resources Devel. Corp., Mass., 1984-87; mgr. Turkish tech. projects GE Internat. Svc. Corp., 1987—; cons. UN. Middle East Inst. fellow; Ford Found. area fellow; recipient Outstanding Performance award AID. Fellow Royal Anthrop. Inst. of Gt. Britain and No. Ireland; mem. Am. Soc. Profl. Cons., Soc. Advancement Mgmt., Assn. Internal Mgmt. Cons., Inst. Mgmt. Cons., Inst. Profl. Mgrs., Adult Edn. Assn. Co-author: International Manpower Planning: The Developing World, 1982; also articles. Office: GE Internat Svcs Corp Bldg 202-2 Cherry Hill NJ 08358 also: GE Internat Svc Corp, Resit Galip Cad 124/3 GO Pasa, Ankara Turkey

CARSWELL, LOIS MALAKOFF, cultural organization executive, consultant; b. N.Y.C., Mar. 2, 1932; d. Arthur and Dora (Krechevsky) Malakoff; m. Donald Carswell, Oct. 12, 1957; children: Anne Carswell Tang, Alexander, Robert Ian. AB magna cum laude, Radcliffe Coll., 1953; cert. in bus. adminstrn., Harvard U. and Radcliffe Coll., 1954. Editor Dell Pub. Co., N.Y.C., 1954-56; publicist Ruth E. Pepper Co., N.Y.C., 1957-58; vol. Bklyn. Botanic Garden, 1964—, co-chmn. plant sales, 1967—, co-chmn. capital campaign, 1984-88, chmn. bd. dirs., 1989—; chmn. Coalition Living Mus. N.Y. State, N.Y.C., 1980—; cons. N.Y. State Natural Heritage Trust, 1982—. Office: Bklyn Botanic Garden 1000 Washington Ave Brooklyn NY 11225

CARTA, FRANKLIN OLIVER, aeronautical engineer; b. Middletown, Conn., July 16, 1930; s. Salvatore and Anna (DeMauro) C.; m. Ann J. DiMauro, Sept. 25, 1954; children: Lisa Ann, Christopher Pace, Maura Ferragut. BS, MIT, 1952, MS, 1953. Rsch. asst. MIT Aeroelastics Lab., Cambridge, 1952-53; rsch engr. United Aircraft Rsch. Labs., East Hartford, Conn., 1953-60; aeroelastics engr. Cornell Aero. Lab., Buffalo, 1960; sr. engr./supr. aeromechanics United Tech. Rsch. Ctr., East Hartford, 1960—; lectr. aero von Karman Inst., Rhode-St-Genese, Belgium, 1970, 77, Iowa State U., 1975, 77, 80—; panel mem. Adv. Group for Aerospace Rsch. and Devel. of NATO, 1979-84. Assoc. editor Jour. of Fluids and Structures, 1985-87; contbr. articles to profl. jours., chpts. to books. Assoc. fellow AIAA; fellow ASME (v.p. 1992—, bd. dirs. Internat. Gas Turbine Inst. of ASME 1985-90, chmn. IGTI bd. dirs. 1988-89, Gas Turbine Power award 1967); mem. Sigma Xi, Tau Beta Pi, Gamma Alpha Rho. Office: United Tech Corp Silver Ln East Hartford CT 06118-1010

CARTEN, THOMAS FRANCIS, announcer, broadcast executive, priest; b. Apr. 13, 1942. BA in English, King's Coll., 1975; ThM, Notre Dame U., 1978. Lic. FCC 1st class broadcast engr., and amateur extra class. Announcer, engr. various radio stas., 1959—; dir., mgr., host radio reading service for the blind The Radio Home Visitor Sta. WRKC-FM King's Coll., Wilkes-Barre, Pa., 1974—, clergyman, 1979—; reader, narrator of talking books and mags. for the blind, including Worldradio, Sacramento, 1971—, Braille Circulating Library, Richmond, Va., 1974-85, QCWA News, Irving, Tex., 1986—; creator, mgr. radio reading service Pa. Assn. for the Blind, Wilkes-Barre, 1974—, also cons. to similar services, 1974—. Columnist Wilkes-Barre Citizens' Voice, 1979—; co-editor: The Big Band Era, 1986; editor various newsletters. 10-gallon donor ARC Blood Services, Wilkes-Barre, 1963—. Mem. Nat. Braille Assn. (Disting. Service award 1979), Assn. of Radio Reading Services. Clubs: Am. Radio Relay League (Newington, Conn.); Murgas Amateur Radio (Wilkes-Barre). Home and Office: 1602 E Kings Coll Wilkes Barre PA 18711

CARTER, CAROLYN MARIE, social work executive; b. Takoma Park, Md., Oct. 27, 1954; d. Cecil Frederick and Carolyn (Middleton) Ellingwood; m. Warren Grover Carter Jr., May 16, 1975; 1 child, Timothy Allen Carter. BA, U. Md., 1976; MSW, U. Pa., 1985. Lic. cert. social worker, Md. Employment counselor Md. Job Svc., Crisfield, 1978-82; social worker Worcester County Dept. of Social Svcs., Snow Hill, Md., 1982-87; social work supr. Ea. Correctional Instn., Westover, Md., 1987—; adj. instr. Univ. Md. Sch. of Social Work and Community Planning, Balt., 1988—. Recipient Can Do Service award, Gov. of Md., 1990. Mem. Nat. Assoc. Acad. Cert. Social Workers. Democrat. Presbyterian. Office: Ea Correctional Inst 30420 Revell S Nck Rd Westover MD 21871

CARTER, DAVID GEORGE, SR., university administrator; b. Dayton, Ohio, Oct. 25, 1942; s. Richard Walter and Esther Mae (Dunn) C.; m. Lena Faye Smith, Aug. 14, 1965; children: Ehrika Aileen, Jessica Faye, David George Jr. BS, Cen. State U., 1965; MEd, Miami U., 1968; PhD, Ohio State U., 1971. Cert. elem. tchr., Ohio. Prin. Dayton Pub. Schs., 1969-70, supr., 1970-71, unit facilitator, dist. supt., 1971-73; asst. and assoc. prof. Pa. State U., State College, 1972-77; assoc. dean and prof. edn. U. Conn., Storrs, 1977-82, assoc. v.p. acad. affairs, 1982-88; pres. East Conn. State U., Willimantic, 1988—. Contbr. articles to profl. jours. Bd. dirs. New England Regional Exch., Framingham, Mass., 1981-86, Haitian Health Found.; corporator Windham (Conn.) Meml. Community Hosp., 1982—; mem. Gov.'s Task Force on Jail and Prison Overcrowding. Named Young Man of Yr., Dayton C. of C., 1973. Mem. Nat. Orgn. Legal Problems of Edn. (bd. dir. 1980-83), Am. Edn. Rsch. Orgn., Phi Delta Kappa, Pi Lambda Theta, Phi Kappa Phi, Sigma Pi Phi. Home: 9 Charles Ln Storrs Mansfield CT 06268-2308 Office: East Conn State U 83 Windham St Willimantic CT 06226-2295

CARTER, GENE, chief judge; b. Milbridge, Maine, Nov. 1, 1935; s. K.W. and S. Loreta (Beal) C.; m. Judith Ann Kittredge, June 24, 1961; children: Matthew G., Mark G. B.A., U. Maine, 1958, LL.D. (hon.), 1985; LL.B., NYU, 1961. Bar: Maine 1962. Ptnr. Rudman, Winchell, Carter & Buckley (and predecessors), Bangor, Maine, 1965-80; assoc. justice Maine Supreme Jud. Ct., 1980-83; judge U.S. Dist. Ct. Maine, 1983-89, chief judge, 1989—; chmn. adv. com. on rules of civil procedure Maine Supreme Jud. Ct., 1976-80. Chmn. Bangor Housing Authority, 1970-77. Mem. Am. Trial Lawyers Assn., Internat. Soc. Barristers, Am. Coll. Trial Lawyers. Office: US Dist Ct 156 Federal St Portland ME 04101-4152

CARTER, GEORGE CARSON, lawyer, real estate broker; b. Lancaster, N.H., Sept. 15, 1957; s. George Francis and Sally Ann (White) C.; m. Diane Marie Gelineau, June 23, 1988; children: Catherine Morgan, George Christopher. BS, Plymouth State, 1979; JD, Franklin Pierce Law Ctr., 1982. Bar: N.H. 1982, U.S. Dist. Ct. N.J. 1982; lic. real estate broker, N.H.; justice of the peace. Assoc. Ingram & Ingram, Whitefield, N.H., 1982-86; owner, broker George C. Carter Real Estate, Lancaster, 1986—; pvt. practice law Lancaster; bail commr. Lancaster Dist. Ct. Fundraiser Weeks Meml. Hosp., Lancaster, 1987; treas. Weathervane Theatre, Whitefield, 1991—; bd. dirs. Weathervane Theatre Players, Inc., v.p., 1990-91; bd. dirs., sec. Col. Town Players, Inc., Lancaster; v.p. Weeks State Pk. Assn., 1990-91; chmn. Coos County George Bush for Pres. Campaign, 1987; county co-chairperson Bush-Quayle Re-election Campaign, 1992; town chmn. Robert Smith for Senate Campaign, 1990, Peter Spaulding for Congress Campaign, 1992. Mem. ABA (family law sect., mem. forum com. on sport and entertainment, criminal justice sect.), N.H. Bar Assn., Assn. Trial Lawyers Am., North Country Bd. Realtors (pres. 1987, 88, Realtor of Yr. 1986), N.H. Assn. Realtors (chmn. legal and consumer affairs com. 1986-90, v.p. region VI 1990, 91, chmn. bylaws com. 1990, 91, 92, bd. dirs. 1987-91, mem. exec. com. 1990-91), N.H. Trial Lawyers Assn., Coos County Bar Assn. (v.p.), Audubon Soc., Phi Alpha Delta. Home: Wedare Farm E Stebbins Rd Lancaster NH 03584 Office: 98 Main St PO Box 470 Lancaster NH 03584

CARTER, GERALD EMMETT, retired archbishop; b. Montreal, Que., Can., Mar. 1, 1912; s. Thomas Joseph and Mary (Kelty) C. BTh, Grand Sem. Montreal, 1936; BA, U. Montreal, 1933, MA, 1940, PhD, 1947, LTh, 1950; DHL, Duquesne U., 1963; LLD (hon.), U. Western Ont., 1966, Concordia U., 1976, U. Windsor, 1977, McGill U., Montreal, 1980, Notre Dame (Ind.) U., 1981; LittD, St. Mary's U., Halifax, 1980. Ordained priest Roman Cath. Ch., 1937. Founder, prin., prof. St. Joseph Tchrs. Coll., Montreal, 1939-61; chaplain Newan Club McGill U., 1941-56; charter mem., 1st pres. Thomas More Inst. Adult Edn., Montreal, 1945-61; mem. Montreal Cath. Sch. Commn., 1948-61; hon. canon Cathedral Basilica Montreal, 1952-61; aux. bishop London and titular bishop Altiburo, 1961; bishop of London, Ont., 1964-78; archbishop of Toronto, 1978-90, ret., 1990; elevated to cardinal, 1979; Chmn. Episcopal Commn. Liturgy Can., 1966-73; mem. Consilium of Liturgy, Rome, 1965, Sacred Congregation for Divine Worship, 1970; chmn. Internat. Com. for English in the Liturgy, 1971; appointee Econ. Affairs Coun. of Holy See, 1981; vice pres. Can. Cath. Conf., 1973, Cath. Conf. of Ont., 1971-73; pres. Can. Conf. Cath. Bishops, 1975; mem. coun. Synod of Bishops, 1977. Author: The Catholic Public Schools of Quebec, 1957, Psychology and the Cross, 1959, The Modern Challenge to Religious Education, 1961. Decorated companion Order of Can. Office: Chancery Office, 355 Church St, Toronto, ON Canada M5B 1Z8

CARTER, GRAYDON, editor; b. Canada, 1950. Co-founder Spy mag., 1986, former co-editor; editor New York Observer, 1991-92; editor-in-chief Vanity Fair mag., N.Y.C., 1992—. Office: Vanity Fair 350 Madison ave New York NY 10017*

CARTER, GREGG LEE, sociologist, educator; b. Missoula, Mont., July 15, 1951; s. Harley Willis and Betty Jo (Bell) C.; m. Lisa Diane Elias, June 11, 1988; children: Travis Harley, Kurtis Frederick. BA, U. Nev., 1973; MA, Columbia U., 1975, MPhil, 1978, PhD, 1983. Asst. prof. sociology Bryant Coll., Smithfield, R.I., 1983-88, assoc. prof. sociology, 1988—. Contbr. articles to profl. jours. Danforth Found. fellow, 1973-74, Leopold Schipp Found. fellow, 1975-79, Pres.'s fellow Columbia U., 1974-80, NSF fellow, 1988. Mem. Am. Sociol. Assn., Ea. Sociol. Soc., New Eng. Sociol. Assn. (v.p. 1990-91, newsletter editor 1989—). Home: 371 Sharon St Providence RI 02908-2221 Office: Bryant Coll 1150 Douglas Pike Smithfield RI 02917-1220

CARTER, HARRY ROBERT, fire chief; b. Neptune, N.J., July 29, 1947; s. Harry Barringer and Stella (Napiorkowski) C.; m. Jacalyn Roberta Miller, Apr. 29, 1972; children: Ellen, Kathleen, Todd. BA, Thomas Edison State Coll., 1975; BS magna cum laude, Jersey City State Coll., 1976; MA, Rutgers U., 1979; PhD, Western States U., 1984. Fire fighter Rahway (N.J.) Fire Dept., 1972-73; fire fighter Newark (N.J.) Fire Dept., 1972-77, fire capt., 1977-90, battalion fire chief, 1990—; adj. prof. Ocean County Coll., Toms River, N.J., 1977-81; pres. Carter Fire Protection, Inc., Adelphia, N.J., 1980—; fire marshal N.J. Army Nat. Guard, 1981-91. Author: Management in The Fire Service, 1989, Managing Fire Service Finances, 1989; contbr. numerous articles to profl. jours. Vol. fire fighter, officer Howell Twp. Fire Co. # 1, Adelphia, N.J., 1971—, tng. officer, 1978—, fire chief, 1991. Capt. USAR, 1966—. Mem. ISFSI (bd. dirs. 1989—), N.J. Soc. Fire Instrs. (bd. dirs. 1978-80, pres. 1980-82), Nat. Fire Protection Assn. (adv. coun. 1975-90), Internat. Assn. Fire Chiefs (schlarship 1975, 76), Internat. Assn. Fire Fighters, VFW, Am. Legion, Optimist Internat. Republican. Lutheran. Home: Box 100 Main St Adelphia NJ 07710 Office: Newark Fire Dept 34 Jersey St Newark NJ 07105

CARTER, JOHN MACK, publishing company executive; b. Murray, Ky., Feb. 28, 1928; s. William Z. and Martha (Stevenson) C.; m. Sharlyn Emily Reaves, Aug. 30, 1948; children: Jonna Lyn, John Mack II. Student, Murray State Coll., 1944-46, LL.D., 1971; B.J., U. Mo., 1948, M.A., 1949; LL.D., St. John's U., 1983. Reporter Murray Ledger & Times, 1945; asst. editor Better Homes & Gardens mag., 1949-51; mng. editor Household mag., Topeka, 1953-57, editor, 1957-58; exec. editor Together mag., 1958-59; editor Am. Home mag., 1959-61; exec. editor McCall's mag., 1961, editor, 1962-65; v.p. McCall Corp., N.Y.C., 1962-65; editor-in-chief Ladies Home Jour., 1965-74, pub., 1967-70; pres., chief operating officer Downe Communications Inc., 1972-73, chmn. bd., editor-in chief, 1973-77; pres. Am. Home Pub. Co., 1974-75; editor-in-chief Good Housekeeping mag., N.Y.C., 1975—; dir. new mag. devel. Hearst Corp., N.Y.C., 1980—. Bd. dirs. Future Homemakers Am., Am. Cancer Soc., Christian Ch. Found., Religion in Am. Life, Am. Bible Soc., Nat. Ctr. for Voluntary Action, Guideposts Mag. Served as lt. (j.g.) USNR, 1951-53. Recipient Walter Williams award for writing, 1949, Honor award for disting. service in journalism U. Mo., 1979, Faith and Freedom award Religious Heritage of Am., 1980, Quality of Life award for media Am. Lung Assn., 1986; named one of 10 Outstanding Men of Yr., U.S. Jr. C. of C., 1963, Pub. of Yr., Brandeis U., 1977, Headliner of Yr., Women in Communications, Inc., 1978, to Ky. Journalism Hall of Fame, 1983, Pub. of Yr., Mag. Pubs. Am., 1990. Mem. Kentuckians of N.Y. (pres.), Am. Soc. Mag. Editors (pres.), Sigma Delta Chi (pres. N.Y. chpt.). Office: Hearst Corp Good Housekeeping Mag 959 8th Ave New York NY 10019-3737

CARTER, LEWIS AARON, JR., public relations executive; b. N.Y.C., Jan. 12, 1941; s. Lewis A. Sr. and Gertrude E. C.; m. Beverly Ann Carter, Jan. 24, 1987; children: Eliza, Amanda. BA, U. Pa., 1963. Sr. v.p. Arthur Monks Assocs., Inc., Boston, 1965-72; dir. pub. rels. and advt. Boston 200, 1973-76; ptnr. Agnew, Carter, McCarthy, Inc., Boston, 1977—. Bd. dirs. Jobs for Youth, Boston, 1980, Copley Sq. Centennial Com., Boston, 1983, New Eng. Pollution Prevention Coun., Boston, 1989. Mem. Counselors Acad. Pub. Rels. Soc. of Am. (accredited). Office: Agnew Carter McCarthy Inc 222 Berkeley St Boston MA 02116-3748

CARTER, LINDA MICHELLE, English educator; b. Balt., Apr. 10, 1949; d. Frederick Benjamin and Helen (Green) C.; m. James Toney, Dec. 16, 1978. BA, Morgan State U., 1971, MA, 1973; PhD, U. Md., 1986. Substitute instr. English Morgan State U., Balt., 1973-76, instr. English, 1976-87, asst. prof. English, 1987—; judge Nat. Coun. of Tchrs. of English Achievement Awards in Writing, 1990-91. Editor: Reaching for the Moon, 1991; contbr. articles to profl. jours. Mem. Middle Atlantic Writers Assn., Inc. (treas. 1979-89, founder, bd. dirs. 1979—), Zora Neale Hurston Soc., Nat. Coun. of Tchrs. of English. Office: Morgan State U Dept English/Lang Arts Cold Spring Ln & Hillen Rd Baltimore MD 21239

CARTER, MARILYN JEAN, art educator; b. Neptune, N.J., Sept. 26, 1935; d. Elmer Cornelius and Lois Wendel (Woolman) Burdge; m. Donald E. Carter, Dec. 21, 1956; children: Douglas Mark, Brett Michael. BA magna cum laude, Georgian Ct. Coll., 1974; MA, Rutgers U., 1986. Cert. tchr. of art, tchr. English, N.J. Head humanities dept. St. Rose High Sch., Belmar, N.J., 1975-78; tchr. Chinese ink painting Middlesex County Coll., Edison, N.J., 1981-86; ink painter in Artist in Edn. Program Md. State Arts Coun., Talbot County, Calvert County, 1987—; resident artist Md. Hall for the Creative Arts, Annapolis; tchr. Chinese ink painting Anne Arundel Community Coll., Arnold, Md., 1987—; art/English tchr. exch. mem. Omiya Bd. Edn., Saitama Prefecture, Japan, 1981. Artist (ink paintings) Intertwined, 1982, Spring Flower 'n Bird, 1989. Vol. Freer/Sackler Galleries, Washington, 1991; pub. lectr. on Japanese architecture Kent Island (Md.) Fedn. Art, 1989. Mem. Nat. Sumi-e Soc. Am. (Spl. merit award 1991), Queen Anne's County Arts Coun., Smithsonian Assocs., Washington Asia Soc. Episcopalian. Office: Md Hall for the Creative Arts 801 Chase St Annapolis MD 21401-3534

CARTER, MARY, administrative assistant, painter; b. Hartsdale, N.Y., Apr. 12, 1931; d. Philip Moore and Edith (Woolfall) Carter; m. Peter Gould, Feb. 14, 1959 (dec. 1960); 1 child, Peter Carter Gould. Student, Art Students League of N.Y., 1951-55. With sales dept. New Am. Libr.; now adminstrv. asst. prodn. Simon & Schuster, N.Y.C. Exhibited Nat. Acad. Design, N.Y.C., 1956, 57, 72, Conn. Acad. Fine Arts at Hartford Athaneum, 1956, Pa. Acad. Fine Arts, 1957, Phila. Sketch Club, 1958, Ball State Art Gallery, 1958, 63, Springfield Art Mus., 1966, Del Mar Coll., Tex., 1967, Hudson Guild, N.Y., 1974—. Mem. Art Students League N.Y. Home: 253 W 16th St New York NY 10011-6006

CARTER, NANETTE CAROLYN, artist; b. Columbus, Ohio, Jan. 30, 1954; d. Matthew Gameliel and Frances (Hill) C. BA, Oberlin Coll., 1976; MFA, Pratt Inst. of Art, 1978. Tchr. art Dwight Englwood Prep Sch., Englwood, N.J., 1978-87; profl. artist, 1987—; artist-in-residence Triangle Workshop, Pine Plains, N.Y.C., 1991. One-woman shows include Ericson Gallery, N.Y.C., 1983, N'Namdi Gallery, Detroit, 1984, 86, 92, Birmingham, Mich., 1989, 92, Cinque Gallery, N.Y.C., 1985, Montclair (N.J.) Art Mus., 1988, Jersey City (N.J.) Mus., 1990, June Kelly Gallery, SoHo, N.Y., 1990; exhibited in group shows including Bklyn. Mus., 1981, Newark Mus., 1985, Pa. Acad. Fine Arts, Phila., 1986, Clocktower Gallery, N.Y.C., 1986, Associated Am. Artists Gallery, N.Y.C., 1986, Kenkelaba Gallery, N.Y.C., 1987, Fashion Moda Gallery, Bronx, N.Y., 1988, Studio Mus. in Harlem, N.Y., 1988, Louisa McIntosh Gallery, Atlanta, 1990, Sande Webster Gallery, Phila., 1990, Spacer Gallery, Cleve., 1991, Mary Ryan Gallery, N.Y.C., 1991, Bennington (Vt.) Coll., 1991, Bristol-Myers Squibb Co., Princeton, N.J., 1992; represented in permanent collections Planned Parenthood, N.Y.C., Jane Zimmerli Art Mus., Rutgers U., New Brunswick, N.J., Jersey City Mus., Libr. of Congress, Washington, ARCO, Phila., Reader's Digest, Pleasantville, N.Y., Schomburg Libr., N.Y.C., Salomon Bros., N.Y.C., Newark Mus., Herbert Johnson Mu., Art, Cornell U., Ithaca, N.Y., Studio Mus. Harlem, N.Y., MCI Telecomm., Chgo., Times Mirror, N.Y.C., AT&T, N.J., IBM, Stamford, Conn., Lang Comm., Randolph, Vt. Grantee Nat. Endowment for Arts, 1981, N.J. Coun. on Arts, 1985, N.Y. Found. for Arts, 1990. Mem. Artists Equity, Cinque Gallery (artistic bd. 1989-91).

CARTER, RAND, art educator, historian; b. Corpus Christi, Tex., Sept. 17, 1937; s. Noah Dilford and Lucy Violet (Pennington) C. AB, Columbia U., 1959; MFA, Princeton (N.J.) U., 1961; PhD, Coutauld Inst. of London, 1966; postgrad., Princeton (N.J.) U., 1966, Coutauld Inst. London, 1961-62. Asst. prof. McGill U., Mont., Can., 1962-70; prof. Hamilton Coll., Clinton, N.Y., 1970—; lectr. in field. Contbr. articles to profl. jours. Bd. dirs. Sculpture Space, Utica, N.Y., 1984—, pres., 1990—; bd. dirs. Players Theatre, Utica, 1979-81. Mem. Soc. Archtl. Historians, Reform Club of London, Sigma Phi. Democrat. Roman Catholic. Home: 1421 Oneida St Utica NY 13501-4311 Office: Hamilton Coll Clinton NY 13323

CARTER, RUSSELL WEBSTER, retired museologist, naturalist; b. Marmarth, N.D., May 29, 1918; s. Ernest Russel and Lola Ellen (Thompson) C.; m. Martha June Ball, Aug. 17, 1958. AA, Springfield (Ill.) Jr. Coll., 1939; BS, U. Ill., 1951. Chief park naturalist Ill. State Parks and Memls., Springfield, 1946-49; supr. museumobile Ill. State Mus., Springfield, 1951-54; curator natural sci. Schenectady Museum Assn., 1955-69; sr. exhibits planner in natural sci. N.Y. State Mus., Albany, 1969-89; co-chmn. Schenectady Moonwatch, 1956-61. Pres. Schenectady Astronomy Club, 1958-69. Mem. AAAS, Soc. Systematic Zoology, Am. Mus. Natural History, N.Y. Acad. Scis. Republican. Methodist. Home: 1428 Albany St Schenectady NY 12304-2706

CARTER, RUTH B. (MRS. JOSEPH C. CARTER), association executive; b. Charlotte, Vt.; d. Ira E. and Sadie M. (Congdon) Burroughs; m. Joseph C. Carter, June 28, 1935. PhB, U. Vt., 1931. Prin. Newton Acad., Shoreham, Vt., 1931-35; substitute tchr. Spaulding High Sch., Barre, Vt., 1931-35, Woodbury (Vt.) High Sch., 1935-36; tchr. Craftsbury Acad., Craftsbury Common, Vt., 1936-38; sales mgr., buyer Vt. Music Co., Barre, 1939-44; statistician Syracuse U., 1944-46; instr. English Temple U., Phila., 1946-47; records clk. sec. Phila., 1947-56; tchr. English Cen. High Sch., Phila., 1957, Springfield Twp. Sr. High Sch., Montgomery County, Pa., 1964-65; exec. dir. White-Williams Found., 1966-82, trustee, 1982—. Author: (with Joseph C. Carter) Anchors Aweigh Around the World with Ernest Vail Burroughs, 1960, Pilgrimage to the Lovely Lands of our Ancestors, 1984. Recipient Humanitarian award Chapel of Four Chaplains, 1981; city coun. citation City of Phila., 1982. Mem. AAUW (admissions chmn. Phila. chpt. 1959-61, sec. 1961-64, treas. 1965-67), DAR (treas., historian, com. chmn., budget dir., treas., historian, com. chmn., regent Germantown chpt., 1983-86, 89-92, treas. 1992—, registrar 1986-89, pub. rels. chmn. 1986—), Women for Greater Phila., New Eng. Historic Geneal. Soc., Geneal. Soc. Vt., Soc. Mayflower Descs. (bd. dirs. 1983-84, sec. 1985-91), Temple U. Faculty Wives Club (rec. sec. 1983-86, pres. Old York group), Temple U. Women's Club, The English Speaking Union, Regent's Club (Phila. chaplain 1986-88). Republican. Methodist. Home: 40 Mt Carmel Ave Apt 4 Glenside PA 19038-3438

CARTER, SYLVIA, journalist; b. Keokuk, Iowa; d. Charles Sylvester and Frances Elizabeth (Smith) C. B of Journalism, U. Mo., 1968. Intern Quincy (Ill.) Herald-Whig, 1966, Detroit Free Press, 1967; reporter The N.Y. Daily News, 1968-70; successively gen. assignment reporter, edn. reporter, food writer, restaurant critic Newsday, Melville, N.Y., 1970—, N.Y. Newsday, N.Y.C., 1970—; founder, editor Kidsday Newsday, Melville. Author: Eats: The Best Little Restaurants in New York, 1988. Trustee Anne O'Hare McCormick Scholarship Fund, N.Y.C., 1988—. Mem. Newswomen's Club N.Y. (pres. 1990-92, bd. dirs., Front Page award 1982). Democrat. Presbyterian. Home: 111 Waverly Pl New York NY 10011 Office: NY Newsday 2 Park Ave New York NY 10016

CARTER, TIMOTHY HOWARD, biochemist, educator; b. L.A., Nov. 6, 1944; s. Everett and Cecile (Doudna) C.; m. Jocklyn Armstrong, Dec. 31, 1976; children: Benjamin, Jonathan. AB, Harvard U., 1966; PhD, Princeton U., 1972. Postdoctoral fellow U. Pa. Med. Sch., Phila., 1972-74, Columbia U. Coll. Physicians and Surgeons, N.Y.C., 1974-75; asst. prof. Coll. Medicine Pa. State U., Hershey, 1975-78; asst. prof. St. John's U., Jamaica, N.Y., 1978-81, assoc. prof., 1981-92, prof. biochemistry, 1992—, chmn. dept. biol. scis., 1992—. Contbr. articles, chpts. to sci. publs. Pa. Plan Scientist, U. Pa., 1973; Mattheson fellow Columbia U., 1974; grantee NIH, 1978-90, NOAA, 1984-88, Am. Cancer Soc., 1991—. Mem. N.Y. Acad. Scis. (conf. com. 1991—), Am. Soc. Microbiology, Am. Soc. Biochemistry and Molecular Biology, Am. Soc. Cell Biology, Sigma Xi. Home: 71 Dover Pky Garden City NY 11530-3805 Office: St Johns U Dept Biol Sci Grand Central at Utopia Pky Jamaica NY 11439

CARTER, WARRICK LIVINGSTON, dean of faculty; b. Charlottesville, Va., May 6, 1942; s. Charles M. and Evelyn (Jones) C.; 1 child, Keisha Z. BS, Tenn. State U., 1964; MusM, Mich. State U., 1966, PhD, 1970. Cert. mgmt. adminstr., 1985. Asst. prof. U. Md., Princess Ann, 1966-71; assoc. prof. Northwestern U., Evanston, Ill., 1978-84; chmn. fine and performing arts Governors State U., University Park, Ill., 1971-84; dean of faculty Berklee Coll. Music, Boston, 1984—; cons. U. Santa Cantarina, Florianopolis, Brazil, 1980, U. Sao Paulo, Brazil, 1976, Nat. Endowment for Arts, Washington, 1983-87, Mich. Coun. for Arts, Detroit, 1988, U. V.I., St. Thomas, 1988, Mass. Coun. Arts, Boston, 1986-87. Music composer 1971—. Bd. dirs. Arts in Pub. Places, Chgo., 1976-82, Ptnrs. of Ams., 1975-84. Recipient Outstanding Svc. award Nat. Black Music Caucus, 1980, Composition grant, NEA, 1977, 82, 87; named Outstanding Music Educator, Sch. Musician mag., 1983, Best Drummer, Notre Dame, 1970. Mem. NEA (chmn. music 1982-85), Internat. Assn. Jazz Educators (pres. 1982-84), Music Educators Nat. Conf., Nat. Black Music Caucus (sec. 1974-78). Office: Berklee Coll Music 1140 Boylston St Boston MA 02215-3693

CARTER, WILLIAM HAROLD, SR., physicist, researcher, electrical engineer; b. Houston, Nov. 17, 1938; s. William Henry and Fannie (Augusta) C.; children: William Harold Jr., Elizabeth Lee. BSEE, U. Tex., 1962, MSEE, 1963, PhD, 1966. Rsch. asst. U. Tex., Austin, 1962-66; rsch. assoc. U. Rochester, N.Y., 1969-70; rsch. physicist Naval Rsch. Lab., Washington, 1971—; prof. U. Nebr., Lincoln, 1981-82; instr. Johns Hopkin's U., Balt., 1989—; vis. rsch. fellow U. Reading, Eng., 1976-77; vis. scientist applied physics lab. Johns Hopkin's U., Columbia, Md., 1991—. Contbr. numerous articles to profl. jours. Cellist Alexandria (Va.) Symphony, 1979-88, Georgetown Symphony, 1981-86. Capt. U.S. Army, 1967-69. Fellow Optical Soc. Am., Internat. Soc. for Optical Engring. (chmn. tech. coun. 1980-82, chmn. pub. com. 1981-83, chmn. fellows com. 1986); mem. IEEE (conf. chmn. 1988), Am. Phys. Soc., Cosmos Club. Home: 8301 Cherry Valley Ln Alexandria VA 22309-2117 Office: Naval Rsch Lab Code 4200 Washington DC 20375

CARTIER, DAVID ROBERT, hospitality sales and marketing consultant; b. Rochester, N.H., June 3, 1954; s. Robert Clement and Virginia (Came) C.; m. Elizabeth Apgar Hance, Apr. 30, 1977; children: Jessica, Monica, Darcy. BS in Hotel Adminstrn., U. N.H., 1976. Cert. hotel sales exec. Dir. sales Ramada Inn, Bath, N.Y., 1977-78; gen. mgr. Quality Inn, Binghamton, N.Y., 1978-80, Ramada Inn, Bennington, Vt., 1980-81; ptnr., dir. sales and mktg. Samoset Resort, Rockport, Maine, 1981-90; pres. Cartier & Assocs., Inc., Berwick, Maine, 1990—; instr. Ethan Allen C.C., Manchester, Vt., 1980-81; mem. Maine Tourism Commn., 1988-91, chair, 1989-90. Named Entrepreneur of Yr., Maine Soc. Entrepreneurs, 1989, Chamber Person of Yr., Rockland Area C. of C., 1989. Mem. Maine Innkeepers Assn. (bd. dirs., Community Svc. award 1989), New Eng. Innkeepers Assn. (bd. dirs. 1990-92, exec. v.p. 1992—), Hotel Sales and Mktg. Assn. Internat. (founder, pres. Maine chpt. 1989-91), Meeting Planners Internat., Am. Soc. Assn. Execs. Republican. Home: 16 Overlook Dr Berwick ME 03901 Office: Cartier & Assocs Inc PO Box 1125 Berwick ME 03901

CARTIER, GEORGE THOMAS, JR., chemistry consultant; b. Scranton, Pa., Jan. 26, 1924; s. George Thomas and Aline Merideth (Stier) C.; m. Constance Crittendon Lowry, June 13, 1946; children: George Thomas III, Constance Cartier Dube. AB in Biology, Haverford Coll., 1949. Organic chemist Smith, Kline Labs., Phila., 1949-51; head mktg. devel. Quaker Chem. Products Co., Conshohocken, Pa., 1951-55; dir. R&D Am. Collins div. Internat. Paper Co., Phila., 1955-61; pres. Keystone Filter Corp., Hatfield, Pa., 1961-74, Maine Shipping Room, Portland, 1980-88; dir. Cartier & Assocs., Cons., Falmouth, Maine, 1974—. Author: Water Purification, 1976; inventor hepa filter. With USNR, 1943-45. Mem. TAPPI, Am. Chem. Soc., Assn. Cons. Chemists and Chem. Engrs. Home and Office: 311 Middle Rd Falmouth ME 04105-1294

CARTO, WILLIS ALLISON, publishing executive; b. Ft. Wayne, Ind., July 17, 1926; s. Willis Frank and Dorothy Louise (Allison) C.; m. Elisabeth Waltraud Oldemeier. Student, Denison U., 1947-49. Treas., chief executive officer Liberty Lobby, Washington, 1955—; pub. The Spotlight, Washington, 1975—; cons. The Noontide Press, Torrance, Calif., 1960—. Founder: Jour. Hist. Rev., 1980; editor, author: Profiles in Populism, 1982, Conspiracy Against Freedom, 1986; contbr. articles to profl. jours. Founder, organizer Liberty Lobby, Washington, 1955, United Reps. Am., Washington, 1965, Inst. for Hist. Rev., Costa Mesa, Calif., 1979, Populist Party, Pitts., 1984, Populist Action Com., 1991. Cpl. U.S. Army, 1944-46. Decorated Purple Heart. Populist. Methodist. Office: Liberty Lobby 300 Independence Ave SE Washington DC 20003-1010

CARTWRIGHT, ALBERT THOMAS, association executive; b. Camden, N.J., June 20, 1917; s. Joseph and Clara (Edginton) C.; m. Mary Renninger, Apr. 6, 1940 (dec. 1983); children: Albert Jr., Mary Jane, Debbie, Laurie; m. Bette Moffet, June 14, 1986. Grad. high sch., Reading, Pa. Sportswriter Reading (Pa.) Times, 1933-42, Dayton Herald, 1942-44, Phila. Record, 1946-47; sports editor, columnist, features editor News-Jour., Wilmington, 1947-83; exec. dir. Internat. Assn. Sports Museums and Halls of Fame, Wilmington; cons. Phila. Phillies Baseball Club, 1970-71. Author: A La Carte, 1974, Tubby, 1980. With USN, 1944-45. Recipient Headliners Club Nat. Sportstory award, 1950, Thoroughbred Racing Assn.'s Column award, 1955; named Del. Sports Hall of Fame, 1980. Mem. Phila. Sportswriters Assn. (life). Home and Office: 101 W Sutton Pl Wilmington DE 19810-4115 Also: 1600 Gulf Blvd #418 Clearwater FL 34630

CARTWRIGHT, SCYRUS, physician, minister; b. Holly Grove, Ark., Feb. 3, 1953; s. Claude C. and Minnie Ruth (Jordan) C.; m. Lorenia Faye Gowder, Aug. 6, 1987; children: Sarah, Maria, Scyrus III, Rebekah. BA, Philander Smith Coll., 1975; MD, Yale U., 1982; MDiv, Harvard U., 1988, MPH, 1991. Ordained to ministry Ch. of God in Christ, 1973; diplomate Am. Bd. Internal Medicined. Intern U. Mich. Med. Ctr., Ann Arbor, 1982-83; instr. medicine Harvard Med. Sch., Boston, 1986—; resident in internal medicine U. Mich. Med. Ctr., Ann Arbor, 1983-85; dir. ambulatory emergency unit Brigham & Women Hosp., Boston, 1991—; instr. medicine U. Mich. Med. Ctr., Ann Arbor, summer 1985; instr. ACLS, Advanced Trauma Life Support; pastor Lord and Christ Ch., Boston. Pastor Am. Bapt. Ch., Valley Forge, Pa., 1990—. Mem. ACP, Am. Coll. Emergency Physicians. Home: 22 Rockridge Rd Natick MA 01760 Office: Brigham & Women Hosp 75 Francis St Boston MA 02215

CARTY, JOHN LYDON, financial services executive; b. Boston, Aug. 6, 1945; s. Arthur G. and Barbara A. (Lydon) C.; m. Lillian Hodges, Oct. 11, 1969; children: Melissa, Katherine. BA in Math., Tufts U., 1967. With tech. support fed. systems IBM Corp., Waltham, Mass., 1967-73; with sales and sales mgmt. IBM Corp., Waltham, 1973-82; product mgr. IBM Corp., White Plains, N.Y., 1982-85; mgr. svc. devel. and client svc. Boston Safe Deposit & Trust Co., 1985-87, dir. mktg., 1987-91, mng. dir. investment mgmt. svcs. div., 1991—. Bd. dirs. Boston Ctr. Blind Children, 1980-82; sponsor Jr. Achievement, Rochester, N.Y., bd. govs., 1977-80. Mem. Manchester Bath and Tennis Club (v.p. 1978-80), Bath and Tennis Club. Roman Catholic. Office: Boston Safe Deposit & Trust Co 1 Boston Pl Boston MA 02108-4401

CARUSO, DAVID R., marketing executive; b. N.Y.C., Mar. 20, 1956; s. Francis and Grace (De Roberts) C.; m. Nancie R. Spector, May 24, 1981; children: Rachel, Jonathan. BA, Colby Coll., Waterville, Maine, 1979; MA, Case Western Res. U., Cleve., 1982, PhD, 1983. Postdoctoral fellow Yale U., New Haven, 1983-85; group mgr. E. Marder Assocs., N.Y.C., 1985-86; sr. rsch. analyst Pitney Bowes, Stamford, Conn., 1986-89, mgr., 1989—. Contbr. articles to profl. jours., chpts. to books. Recipient Mensa Rsch. award, 1990; Apple Edn. Found. grantee, 1982. Office: Pitney Bowes 53-25 Walter Wheeler Dr Stamford CT 06926

CARUSO, NICHOLAS DOMINIC, protective services official; b. Wilmington, Del., Feb. 2, 1957; s. Nicholas Anthony and Philomena Marie (Pelaia) C. BA in Polit. Sci., U. Del., 1985; MA in Liberal Arts, Widener U., 1991. Sr. analyst Bank of N.Y., Newark, 1985-89; police officer Wilmington Police Dept., 1989—. With U.S. Army, 1975-78, USN, 1979-83. Mem. Nat. Intelligence Study Ctr., Internat. Assn. of Stategic Studies, Acad. of Polit. Sci. Democrat. Roman Catholic. Home: 1908 W 4th St Wilmington DE 19805-3422 Office: Wilmington Police Dept 300 N Walnut St Wilmington DE 19801-3936

CARUSO, VICTOR GUY, investment banker; b. Cleve., Jan. 20, 1948; s. Joseph Carl and Constance Christine (Dimitri) C.; m. Bonnie L.Kephart, July 21, 1973 (div. Jan. 1989); children: Nicholas Michael, Meredith Anne; m. Jeannine G. Smith, Oct. 5, 1991. BS, Miami U., Oxford, Ohio, 1970; MBA, U. Chgo., 1972. CPA, Minn., N.Y. Fin. analyst Ford Motor Co., Detroit, 1972-74; asst. v.p. First Chgo. Corp., 1974-80; v.p., treas. N.W. Bancorp, Mpls., 1980-82; v.p. Chem. Bank, N.Y.C., 1982-83; sr. v.p. Lehman Bros., N.Y.C., 1983—. Mem. AICPA, N.Y. Soc. CPAs, Am. Fin. Assn., Am. Bankruptcy Inst., Turnaround Mgmt. Assn., Darien Country Club, U. Chgo. Club. Republican. Roman Catholic. Home: 20 Carleton St Greenwich CT 06830-4626 Office: Lehman Bros World Fin Ctr World Fin Ctr 18th Fl New York NY 10285

CARUTHERS, DONALD MCILVAINE (BRICK MASON), artist, musician; b. Washington, July 11, 1953; s. Edward Graham and Margaret (Reiff) C. BA in Liberal Arts, Kalamazoo Coll., 1975. Graphic designer KTCA Pub. TV, St. Paul, 1976-77; prodn. illustrator, sketch artist various motion picture cos., 1981—; editorial illustrator, cartoonist various mags., jours., newspapers, 1975—; dir. ops. Plunge Prodns., N.Y.C., 1980—. Singer, songwriter, harmonica, trumpet (rock band) The K-Otics, appeared at N.Y. clubs and cabarets, 1981—. Mem. United Scenic Artists, Graphic Artists Guild. Home: 118 Bayview Dr Mastic Beach NY 11951 Office: Brick Mason 349 E 14th St # 3R New York City NY 10003

CARVER, GORDON HOWARD, feed manufacturing executive; b. Jamestown, N.Y., Aug. 21, 1953; s. Howard Lloyd Carver and Betty Jane (Martin) Crate; m. Roxanne Moore, Apr. 14, 1979 (div. Dec. 1982); 1 child, Annette Lee. Student, SUNY, Oswego, 1971-72, Jamestown Community Coll., 1980—. Truck driver Ashville and Jamestown, N.Y., 1973-77; airport lineman Interair Service, Clearwater, Fla., 1977-79; v.p., gen. mgr. C.V. Mills, Inc., Conewango Valley, N.Y., 1979-91; fin. planning agent Mondenhauer and Assocs., Buffalo, 1991—; bus. and estate planning specialist Moldenhauer & Assocs., 1992—. Republican. Lodge: Elks.

CARY, JAMES WILLIAM, safety specialist; b. Worcester, Mass., Apr. 3, 1941; s. Clifford Earl and Alberta May (Hall) C.; m. Judith Ann Schafer, Aug. 5, 1967; children: James, David. AAS in Machine Design, SUNY, Canton, 1962; BS in Edn., SUNY, Oswego, 1965; AIM in Mgmt., Ins. Inst. Am., 1979. Head indsl. arts Chadwicks (N.Y.) Union Free Sch., 1965-70; head driver edn. Whitesboro Cen. Sch., Yorkville, N.Y., 1970-76; sr. staff asst. Utica (N.Y.) Nat. Ins. Group, 1976-79, safety specialist, 1979—; cons. Printing Industry Am., Washington, 1985—; VDT task force mem. N.Y. State Bus. Coun. Legis. Com., 1989-90; DDC instr. Nat. Safety Coun., Utica, 1981-85. Active Oneida County Arson Task Force, Utica, 1986—; exec. mem. Oneida County Sch. Bds., 1974-78; pres. Chadwicks Union Free Sch. Bd., 1974-78; campaign leader retail United Way, Utica, 1978-85. Recipient Pub. Safety award Town of New Hartford, N.Y., 1982, Svc. award N.Y. State Sch. Bds. Assn., 1978, Loss Prevention award Long Island Loss Prevention Mgrs. Assn., 1982. Mem. Am. Soc. Safety Engrs. (sec. 1981-84), Ins. Loss Control Assn., N.Y. Sate Bus. Coun. (safety com. 1982—), Nat. Safety Coun. (printing and pub. sect. 1985—), Am. Nat. Standards Inst. (mem. B65 printing equipment safety standards com. 1991), Printing Craftsmen. Roman Catholic. Home: PO Box 342 Chadwicks NY 13319-0342

CARY, RICHARD, JR., retired insurance broker; b. Niagara Falls, N.Y., Sept. 27, 1918; s. Richard Leander Cary and Ambolena Huntington (Hooker) Robillard; m. Ursula Regina Luskey, July 29, 1944; children: Ursula Ann CAry, Mary Alice Cary Bourget, Martha Cary Evans. BA in English, Hobart Coll., 1942. Sales engr. Carborundum Co., Niagara Falls, N.Y., 1943-48; life ins. broker Aetna Life Ins. Co., Hartford, Conn., 1948-50; gen. ins. broker Western N.Y., 1950-89, ret., 1989. Historian Town

Lewiston, 1950—. With U.S. Army, 1942-43. Mem. The Niagara Club, Lewiston Queenston Rotary Club (pres. 1963-64). Republican. Roman Catholic. Home: 406 Aberdeen Rd Lewiston NY 14092-1023

CASABURRO, JOHN E., contracting, painting company executive; b. Bronx, N.Y., Oct. 14, 1951; s. Nicholas and Olympia (Vassallo) C.; m. Patricia J. McDerrmott, April 19, 1969 (div. May 1975); children: Anthony, Susan. Owner, propr. Casaburro Painting & Decorating Co., Yonkers, N.Y., 1979—; owner, cons., investor John Casaburro & Assocs., Yonkers, 1986—. Author: Men's Rights/ Women's Rights: The Inside Story, 1987. Community leader Govt. of Yonkers, 1979—; human rights adviser Yonkers Tenants Coalition, 1979—; human rights leader, Yonkers; mayoral cnadidate, Yonkers, 1988-89; co-founder, v.p. Equal Rights for Fathers, 1981-86; exec. sr. v.p. Nat. Orgn. for Men, nat. dir., 1983-91; liaison cons. NOW, 1982—, Nat. Orgn. for Men, 1984—; fathers' rights leader. Mem. Peoples Union (human rights advisor), Westchester Venture Capital Network (assoc.), Conbusters (founder). Home: 525 Bronxville Rd Bronxville NY 10708-1135

CASALE, PAUL PETER, construction company executive, consultant; b. Salem, Mass., Aug. 8, 1950; s. Peter Antonio and Mary Teresa (Sczybiak) C.; m. Elvira Tepedino, June 17, 1979. BS, U. Mass., 1974; MBA, Suffolk U., 1984. Project mgr. ACMAT Corp., East Hartford, Conn., 1977-84; freelance cons., 1985-86; exec. v.p. High Tech Interiors, Lynn, Mass., 1987-91; pres. Atlantic Interior Systems, Lynnfield, Mass., 1991—. Recipient Grad. Rsch. fellowship U. Suffolk, 1983-84. Mem. Am. Mgmt. Assn., Peabody Mus., Boston Mus. of Fine Art. Republican. Roman Catholic. Office: Atlantic Interior Systems Inc 3 Willard Ln Lynnfield MA 01940

CASANOVA, JEFFREY STEVEN, marketing professional; b. Bklyn., Sept. 6, 1971; s. Ralph and Joan (Wallace) C., 1988-89; Salesman Designer Brass, Forest Hills, N.Y., 1987-89; salesman Strictly Mint Baseball, Forest Hills, 1987-90, cons., 1990—; photographer's asst. Joseph Lang, Flushing, N.Y., 1988-89; founder Casanova Enterprises, Flushing, 1989—; cons. Strictly Mint Baseball, Forest Hills; merchandiser Anheuser-Busch, 1990—; founder Casnova Enterprizes, 1989. Editor The Forester newspaper, 1989. Democrat. Roman Catholic. Home and Office: Casanova Enterprizes 61-21 155th St Flushing NY 11367-1234

CASARINO, JOHN PHILIP, psychiatrist; b. Bklyn., Oct. 19, 1940; s. John Joseph and Grace Emily (Esposito) C. BS, U. Notre Dame, 1961; MD, Med. Coll. Ala., 1965. Intern Meadowbrook Hosp., East Meadow, N.Y., 1965-66; pediatric resident Meadowbrook Hosp., 1966-67; psychiatric resident St. Vincent's Hosp. & Med. Ctr. N.Y., 1967-69, 71-72; staff psychiatrist Luth. Med. Ctr., Bklyn., 1971-72; chief partial hospitalization svc. St. Vincent's Hosp., N.Y.C., 1972-83, attending physician, 1983—; pvt. practice N.Y.C., 1983—; attending physician Cabrini Med. Ctr., 1985—; cons., Archdiocese of N.Y., 1973-83, Mary Manning Home, N.Y.C., 1987—; clin. asst. prof. psychiatry N.Y. Med. Coll., 1978. Maj. USAF, 1969-71, Vietnam. Fellow Am. Psychiat. Assn.; mem. AMA. Home: 115 Central Park W New York NY 10023-4153 Office: 51 Fifth Ave Ste 1C New York NY 10003

CASAVIS, DAVID BINGHAM, systems consultant, residential and commercial developer; b. Irvington, N.J., June 10, 1952; s. James Nicholas and Alice Pauline (Bingham) C. BA, SUNY, Buffalo, 1975; MBA, Pace U., 1985; postgrad., NYU. Cert. secondary edn. tchr., N.Y. Tchr. East Ramapo Sch. Dist., Spring Valley, N.Y., 1977-80; data systems tour supr. U.S. Post Office, Mt. Vernon, N.Y., 1980-81, acct., 1981-82, product mgr. Express Mail service, 1982-86; systems cons. Chem. Realty Group div. Chem. Bank, N.Y.C., 1986-88; residential developer, owner Casavis Equities, Shipbottom, N.J., 1987-89; underwriter, systems cons. Pearce, Urstadt, Mayer & Greer Realty Corp. (name changed to Pearce, Mayer & Greer Realty Corp.), N.Y.C., 1988-90; dir. mktg., systems cons. Huberth & Peters, Inc., N.Y.C., 1988-90; dir. foreclosure sales Lyon's Den Properties, Ltd., N.Y.C., 1990-91; owner David Casavis Real Estate, N.Y.C., 1991—; adj. faculty NYU, 1990—. Contbr. articles to profl. jours. Recipient recognition of superior performance Express Mail Service, 1984. Mem. Real Estate Bd. N.Y., Met. Rep. Club of N.Y. Unitarian.

CASCIO, MICHAEL P., industrial hygienist; b. July 4, 1961; s. Salvatore Peter and Susan Victoria (Morrison) C.; m. Kim Patricia Palangi, Oct. 18, 1986; 1 child, Breanne. BS in Environ. Studies, Rutgers U., 1983. Cert. indsl. hygienist; registered environ. profl. Sr. indsl. hygienist Ethicon, Inc., a Johnson & Johnson Co., Somerville, N.J., 1983—. Mem. Am. Indsl. Hygiene Assn., Am. Soc. Safety Engrs. (profl.), Am. Acad. Indsl. Hygiene. Office: Ethicon Inc PO Box 151 Somerville NJ 08876-0151

CASE, ANNE CATHERINE, economics educator; b. Elmira, N.Y., July 27, 1958; d. James Joseph and Madeleine (Burns) Case; m. Edward Joseph Rhodes, Oct. 18, 1986. BS, SUNY, Albany, 1980; MPA, Princeton U., 1983, MA in Econs., 1986, PhD in Econs., 1988. Cons. World Bank, Washington, 1982-84; asst. prof. econs. Harvard U., Cambridge, Mass., 1988-91; asst. prof. Princeton (N.J.) U., 1991—. Contbr. articles to profl. jours. Ctr. for Internat. Studies fellow, 1986-87, Harold Willis Dodds Merit fellow in econs., 1983-84, Harbison Merit fellow, 1982-83. Mem. Am. Econs. Assn., Royal Econ. Soc., The Econometric Soc., Phi Beta Kappa. Home: 4 Symmes Ct Cranbury NJ 08512-2808 Office: Princeton U Woodrow Wilson Sch Princeton NJ 08544

CASE, JAMES VINCENT, JR., program manager; b. McKeesport, Pa., July 8, 1938; s. James Vincent and Anna Mae (Noonan) C.; m. I. Jeannine Billings, May 4, 1968; children: Monica Lynn, Vincent Michael, Christopher Anthony. BSEE, Va. Polytech, 1967; MSEE, U. Md., 1973. Electronics tech. FAA, Jamaica, N.Y., 1960-64; electronics engr. Tex. Instruments, Dallas, 1967-68; safety standards engr. Nat. Hwy. Traffic Safety Adminstrn., 1968-71; defects engr. Nat. Hwy. Traffic Safety Adminstrn., Washington, 1971-73; program engr. FAA, Washington, 1973-75, program mgr., 1975-85, 1990—, evaluation mgr., 1985-90. Contbr. to tech. reports and manuals. Pres. Golden Triangle Men's Golf, Crofton, Md., 1973-76; mem. Seton Parish Bldg. Com., Crofton, 1978-82; cub scout pack leader Boy Scouts Am., Crofton, 1980-82; chpt. chmn. Airway Engring. Soc., Camp Springs, Md., 1963-64. With USAF, 1956-59. Mem. Walden Golf Club, Gunpowder Golf Club. Roman Catholic. Home: 1303 Persimmontree Ct Crofton MD 21114

CASE, NAN BARKIN, psychologist; b. Brookline, Mass., Nov. 30, 1936; d. David and Libby (Hershon) Barkin; m. Robert B. Case, Nov. 9, 1973; 1 child, R. Miles Robert. BA, Radcliffe/Hunter Coll., 1959; MA, Columbia U., 1969, PhD, 1973. Psychology intern, clin. fellow Westchester div. N.Y. Hosp., White Plains, 1969-73; sr. psychologist N.Y. City Dept. Health Employee Counseling Svcs., 1973-74; supervising psychologist North Shore U. Hosp., Manhasset, N.Y., 1974—; clin. asst. prof. psychology in psychiatry Cornell U. Med. Coll., N.Y.C., 1990—. Mem. Am. Psychol. Assn. Home: 130 E 75th St New York NY 10021-3277

CASE, PAMELA JANE, data processing executive; b. Grand Rapids, Mich., July 12, 1944; d. Lester Austin and Janet Elisabeth (Roberts) Munson; m. William Ferguson Case, Nov. 1, 1969; children: Robin Elisabeth, Christopher Andrew. BS, Mich. State U., 1965, MS, 1968; postgrad., Am. U., 1971-72. Math. tchr. Charlotte (Mich.) High Sch., 1965-66; grad. resident advisor Mich. State U., East Lansing, Mich., 1966-68; mathemetician Dept. Def., Ft. Meade, Md., 1968-77; br. chief Dept. Def., Ft. Meade, 1977-78; sys. engr. Sys. Cons., Inc., Arlington, Va., 1979; project leader Sys. Cons., Inc., Arlington, 1979-80; sys. cons. Advent Systems, Inc., Greenbelt, Md., 1980-84, group leader, 1984-89; prin. Case Cons. Svcs., Davidsonville, Md., 1989—. Mem. IEEE, AFCEA, Assn. Old Crows. Presbyterian.

CASE, ROBERT BROWN, physician; b. Columbus, Ohio, July 19, 1920; s. William Lyman and Margaret (Brown) C.; m. Nan Barkin, Nov. 9, 1973; 1 child, Lisa Case. BA, Ohio Wesleyan, 1943; BS, MIT, 1943; MD, Columbia U., 1948. Diplomate Am. Bd. Internal Medicine. Intern and resident St. Luke's Hosp., N.Y.C., 1948-52, chief lab. of exptl. cardiology, 1956—, sr. attending physician, 1971—; rsch. fellow Havard Sch. of Pub. Health, Boston, 1952-54; rsch. assoc. Nat. Heart Inst., Bethesda, Md., 1954-56; prof. emeritus medicine Columbia U., N.Y.C., 1979—; chief cardiac consultation clinic N.Y.C. Dept. Health, 1962-70; mem. cardiovascular study sect. Nat. Heart Inst., 1970-74. Contbr. articles to profl. jours. With USPHS, 1954-56. Rsch. Career devel. grant NIH, 1962-72. Felow Am. Physiol. Soc., N.Y. County Med. Assn., N.Y. State Med. Assn., Am. Heart Assn., Am. Fedn. for Clin. Rsch. Home: 130 E 75th St New York NY 10021-3277 Office: St Lukes/Roosevelt Hosp 421 W 113th St New York NY 10025-1708

CASE, ROSALIND See AVRETT, ROZ

CASEBERE, JAMES EDWARD, artist; b. Lansing, Mich., Sept. 17, 1953; s. James Louis Casebere and Katherine Ann (Young) Kudreiko. Student, Mich. State U., 1971-73; BFA, Mpls. Coll. Art and Design, 1976; postgrad., Whitney Mus. Study Program, N.Y.C., 1977; MFA, Calif. Inst. Arts, Valencia, 1979. art prof. Rockland Community Coll., Suffern, N.Y., 1985-88; vis. artist Boston Mus. Sch., 1989, Calif. Inst. Arts, Valencia, 1984, R.I. Sch. Design, 1991. One-man shows include Neuberger Mus., SUNY Purchase, 1989, Art Mus., U. S. Fla., Tampa, 1989, Kuhlenschmidt/Simon Gallery, L.A., 1985, 88, Michael Klein, Inc., N.Y.C., 1987, Mpls. Coll. Art and Design, 1985, Diane Brown Gallery, N.Y.C., 1984, Sonnabend Gallery, N.Y.C., 1982, 84, St. George Ferry Terminal Installation, Staten Island, N.Y., 1983-84, Cepa Gallery, Buffalo, N.Y., 1982, Franklin Furnace, N.Y.C., 1981, Vreg Baghoomian Gallery, 1990, Urbi et Orbi, Paris, 1990, Fac-Simile Gallery, Milano, Itlay, 1990, Mus. Photographic Arts, San Diego, 1990, U. Iowa Mus. Art, 1991, Photographic Resource Ctr., Boston, 1991, Bruges (Belgium) La Morte Gallery, 1991, James Hockey Gallery, WSCAD Farnham, Eng., 1991, Birmingham (Ala.) Mus. Art, 1991; numerous group exhibits including Whitney Mus. Biennial, 1985, Nat. Mus. Am. Art, Washington, 1989, Mus. Modern Art, N.Y.C., 1991. Fellow N.Y. Found. for the Arts, 1985, 89, NEA, 1982, 86, 90. Studio: 175 Ludlow St New York NY 10002

CASEMENT, WILLIAM ROWLEY, humanities educator; b. Rochester, N.Y., Feb. 26, 1947; s. William Brown Casement and Marilyn Elberta (Rowley) Nowak; m. Andrea Ilona Szabo; children: Christopher James, Alexander John. BS in Social Scis., Edn., SUNY, Brockport, 1968; MS in Student Pers. Svcs., SUNY, Albany, 1969; MA in Philosophy, SUNY, Brockport, 1976; PhD in Philosophy, Georgetown U., 1980. Cert. permanent tchr. in secondary social studies, N.Y. Vocat. counselor Herkimer County Community Coll., Herkimer, N.Y., 1972-73; grad. fellow philosophy Georgetown U., Washington, 1976-80; instr. philosophy several univs., community coll., 1977-80; asst. prof. philosophy St. Thomas U., Miami, Fla., 1981-86, philosophy area coord. (dept. head), 1981-86, cofounder, tchr. honors program, 1982-86, acting chairperson humanities div., 1983-84; vis. researcher philosophy dept. Georgetown U., Washington, 1986-87; asst. prof. dept. ednl. studies SUNY, New Paltz, 1987—. Contbr. articles to profl. jours. With U.S. Army, 1969-71. Mem. Am. Philos. Assn., N.Am. Soc. for Social Philosophy, Philosophy of Edn. Soc., History of Edn. Soc., Am. Ednl. Studies Assn., Nat. Collegiate Honor Coun.

CASEY, COLEMAN HAMPTON, lawyer; b. Bryn Mawr, Pa., Mar. 14, 1947; s. Herbert Stephen Casey Jr. and Margaret Evelyn (Coleman) Dean; m. Jo Champlin, July 29, 1978; 1 child, Eleanor Champlin. BA magna cum laude, Amherst Coll., 1969; JD, Yale U., 1973. Bar: Conn. 1973, Mass. 1984. Assoc. Shipman & Goodwin, Hartford, Conn., 1973-78, ptnr., 1979—; reviewer Conn. Pub. Radio; mem. Conn. Pub. Radio Adv. Bd.; bd. editors Yale Law Jour., 1972-73. Pres. Mark Twain Meml., Hartford, Conn., 1983-85, trustee emeritus, 1990; 1st v.p. Hartford Symphony Orch., 1983-85, pres., 1985-87, bd. dirs., 1980—; bd. dirs. Cedar Hill Cemetery Assn., Hartford, 1982—, Hartt Sch. Music, 1982-86, Pump House Gallery, Hartford, 1988-90; bd. dirs. Greater Hartford Arts Coun., 1985-87, 90—, sec., 1992—; bd. dirs. Hartford Coll. Women, 1987—, vice chmn., 1990-92; trustee Helen M. Saunders Charitable Found., Wadsworth Atheneum, 1990—, Bushnell Meml. Hall, 1990—;. Mem. ABA, Conn. Bar Assn. (real property sect.), Am. Coll. Real Estate Lawyers, Hartford County Bar Assn., Hartford Club, Twentieth Century Club, Twilight Club, Farmington Field Club, Phi Beta Kappa. Democrat. Congregationalist. Address: 31 Woodside Circle Hartford CT 06105 Office: Shipman & Goodwin One American Row Hartford CT 06103-2819

CASEY, ELIZABETH JANE, counselor; b. Batavia, N.Y., Dec. 20, 1941; d. Philip Burton and Helen Marie (Anderson) Corcoran; m. Joseph Michael Casey Sr., Nov. 5, 1966; children: Mary Catherine, Joseph Michael Jr., Eileen Cecelia. BA, Pa. State U., 1962; MS in Edn., SUNY, Brockport, 1984, cert. advanced study, 1990. Nat. cert. counselor, nat. cert. sch. counselor; cert. sch. counselor, N.Y. Probation officer Genesee County, Batavia, N.Y., 1962-66, 83-86; counselor Genesee Wyoming BOCES, Batavia, 1986—; mem. residential svcs. admission/discharge com. Genesee Counmty Assn. for Retarded Children, Inc., Batavia, 1989—. Past pres. Batavia (N.Y.) Players, Inc., 1980; past pres., co-founder Upstage Theatre Collective, Batavia, 1986-90; co-chair Genesee County Fighting Back Consortium, Batavia, 1990—; bd. dirs. Genesee Arts Coun.; sec. bd. dirs. Wyoming County Bicentennial Signers. Mem. AACD, Chi Sigma Iota (Nu chpt., pres. 1990-91, awards chairperson 1987—, newletter co-editor 1991—, student rep. 1988-89, Leadership Fellowship 1989). Democrat. Roman Catholic. Home: 8975 Batavia Stafford Trial Rd Batavia NY 14020

CASEY, JOSEPH MICHAEL, government official, consultant; b. St. Louis, Jan. 6, 1948; s. John and Sara (Ford) C.; m. Cynthia Lynn Kerr, Oct. 21, 1972; children: Michael, John. BSBA, U. Mo., 1970. Sr. bank examiner FDIC, Washington, 1970-82; sr. rev. officer Farm Credit Banks St. Louis, 1983-85; sr. cons. WBK Ltd., Fairfax, Va., 1985-87; sr. regulatory analyst Office Thrift Supervision, Washington, 1988—. Bd. dirs. Henry George Found. Am., Columbia, Md., 1985—, Pub. Revenue Edn. Coun., St. Louis, 1982—, Common Ground/USA, Columbia, 1985—, League for Urban Land Conservation, Washington, 1986—; trustee The Georgist Registry, Columbia, 1989—. Democrat. Roman Catholic. Office: Office Thrift Supervision 1700 G St NW Washington DC 20552-0001

CASEY, KAREN ANNE, banker; b. Bklyn., Oct. 5, 1955; d. Stanley Joseph and Helen Katherine (Kosowski) Mozeleski; m. Dennis Joseph Casey, May 14, 1977; 1 child, Christopher Sean. BBA, Baruch Coll., CUNY, 1977. CPA, N.Y., CFP. Jr. acct. Coopers & Lybrand, N.Y.C., 1977-78, sr. acct., 1978-79, supr., 1979-81; asst. fin. contr. Gulf Internat. Bank, N.Y.C., 1981-82, fin. contr., 1982; v.p., fin. contr. Allied Irish Banks plc, N.Y.C., 1982-87, sr. v.p., fin. contr., 1988-89, sr. v.p. mgmt. support svcs., 1989—; bank rep. to Bank Adminstrn. Inst., 1983—, Inst. Fgn. Bankers, 1984—, Com. of Banking Insts. on Taxation, 1984—. Mem. Am. Inst. CPAs. Roman Catholic. Avocations: gardening, golf, tennis, reading. Office: Allied Irish Banks plc 405 Park Ave New York NY 10022-4405

CASEY, LAWRENCE DAVID, guidance director, counselor; b. Postdam, N.Y., Apr. 27, 1946; s. William Bernard and Marion Agnes (Maroney Strader) C.; m. Allyson Casey, Apr. 12, 1969 (div.); children: Brendan, Meghan, Donal. LeMoyne Coll., 1968, St. Lawrence U., 1973. Cert. NBCC, NCSC. Social studies, english tchr. Morristown Cen. Sch., N.Y., 1968-71; guidance dir. Morristown Cen. Sch., 1971-79, Canton Cen Sch., 1979—; chmn. Agati Scholarship Com., N.Y., 1986-91, Coll. Adv. Counc., Ogdensburg, N.Y., 1986-88. Bd. Edn. Notre Dame Sch., Ogdensburg, 1969-71, Morristown Cen. Sch., 1982-85; little league coach, Potsdam, Morristown, Canton, 1959—. Mem. NYSACD (past exec. coun.), NYSUT, AACD, NYACD, ACD (No. Zone counselor of the yr. 1971). Democrat. Roman Catholic. Home: 20 Cleaveland Ave Canton NY 13617-1104 Office: Hugh C Williams Sr High Sch 99 State St Canton NY 13617-1099

CASEY, MICHAEL JOSEPH, employee benefit consultant; b. Wilmington, Del., Mar. 22, 1949; s. William J. and Cecilia (Connor) C.; m. Margaret M. Murphy, Feb. 12, 1972; children: Kate, Mac, Maggie. BS, U. Del., 1971; MBA, Temple U., 1978. Asst. adminstr. Am. Benefit Plan Adminstrs., Wilmington, 1971-73, regional mgr., 1974-81; pension specialist Penn Mut. Life Ins., Phila., 1973-74; cons. Martin E. Segal Co., Washington, 1981-86, Williams, Thacher & Rand, Indpls., 1986-88; cons., prin. Williams, Thacher & Rand, Phila., 1988—; instr. fin. and labor rels. George Washington U., Washington, Wilmington (Del.) Coll., 1979-82. Vice-chmn. Del. Found. for Retarded Children, Wilmington, 1983. Mem. Cert. Employee Beneft Specialists. Roman Catholic. Office: Williams Thacher & Rand 650 Sentry Pky Blue Bell PA 19422-2318

CASEY, ROBERT J., international trade association executive; b. Youngstown, Ohio, July 18, 1923; s. Michael Francis and Anna Barbara (Siefert) C.; m. Phyllis Lou Lewis, May 20, 1950; children: Kathleen Ann, Robert J. II, Susan Elizabeth. BA, Kent State U., 1948; LLB, Youngstown U., 1954; JD, Ohio State U., 1956. Asst. dir. Ohio Bar Assn., Columbus, 1949-56; account exec. Ketchum, Inc., Pitts., 1956-60; v.p. Western Pa. Nat. Bank (Equibank), Pitts., 1960-65; dir. spl. svcs. PPG Industries, Pitts., 1965-69; dir. pub. info. Westinghouse Air Brake Co., Pitts., 1969-74, Amtrak, Washington, 1975-78; exec. dir. Ohio Rail Transp. Authority, Columbus, 1978-83; founder, exec. dir., pres. High Speed Rail Assn., Pitts., 1983—. Contbr. articles on bank mktg. and transp. to profl. jours. Rep. candidate for Ho. of Reps., Pitts., 1976; del. Rep. Nat. Conv., Miami, Fla., 1972. 1st lt. USAAF, 1943-45, MTO. Recipient Chmn.'s award High Speed Rail Assn., 1991. Mem. Am. Legion, Delta Upsilon. Office: High Speed Rail Assn McKnight Vilage Ste 501A 500 McKnight Park Dr Pittsburgh PA 15237

CASEY, THOMAS WARREN, graphic design company executive; b. Columbus, Ohio, Dec. 9, 1942; s. Warren Vale and Martha Elizabeth (Green) C.; m. Susan Henrietta Davis, Oct. 1, 1966. BArch, Ohio State U., 1966. Registered architect, N.Y. Draftsman Skidmore Owings & Merrill, Chgo., 1964-66; architect U.S. Peace Corps, Tanzania, 1966-69; designer Brooks Barr Graeber & White, Austin, Tex., 1969-71, Hardy Holzman Pfeiffer, N.Y.C., 1971-73; design dir. Paul Arthur & Assoc., N.Y.C., 1973-74; designer Page, Artibrio & Resen, N.Y.C., 1974-79; ptnr. Greenboam & Casey Assocs., Inc., N.Y.C., 1979—; juror Print Casebook Awards, N.Y.C., 1988, Hotel Sales & Mktg. Assoc., N.Y.C., 1987-90; adj. prof. N.J. Sch. of Architecture, Newark, 1980-82; guest lectr. Harvard U., Boston, 1982, U. Cin., 1990. Recipient Award for Print Casebook 7, 1987. Mem. AIA, Soc. Environ. Graphic Designers (bd. dirs. 1985-90, pres. 1988-89), SW Parks and Monuments Assn. (life). Democrat. Office: Greenboam & Casey Assoc 335 Greenwich Ave Greenwich CT 06830-6505

CASHEN, J. FRANK, professional baseball team executive; m. Jean Cashen; children: Blaise, Stacey, Sean, Brian, Timmy, Terry, Greg. B.A., Loyola Coll.; J.D., U. Md. Formerly sportswriter and columist Balt. News-Am.; gen. mgr. Balt. Raceway and Bel Air Race Track; exec. asst. to pres., dir. advt. Nat. Brewing Co., Balt., 1962-65; exec. v.p. Balt. Orioles, Am. League, 1965-75; sr. v.p. mktg. and sales Carling Nat. Breweries, Balt., 1975-79; adminstr. baseball Commr.'s Office, N.Y.C., 1979-80; exec. v.p., gen. mgr., chief operating officer N.Y. Mets, Nat. League, 1980—; mem. exec. com. Nat. League; bd. dirs. Major League Baseball Promotions Corp. Office: care NY Mets Roosevelt Avenue St Flushing NY 11368-2132

CASHIER-CORSO, MARIA ANNE, university administrator; b. Syracuse, N.Y., May 1, 1946; d. Emelio Ernest and Manuela (Biancardi) Cashier; m. Samuel Frank Corso, May 2, 1970. BS, Syracuse U., 1982, MBA, 1985, postgrad., 1987—. Adminstrv. asst. to dean Syracuse U. Sch. Mgmt., 1980-87; mgr. Info. Ctr. CIS Corp., Syracuse, 1987-88; adj. instr. LeMoyne Coll., Syracuse, 1988—; lectr., dir. Bus. Adminstrn. Student Adv. Ctr. SUNY, Oswego, 1990—; cons., trainer Bristol-Myers Squibb Co., Syracuse, 1988—. Contbr. articles for ednl. confs. in field. Mem. Assn. Computing Machinery (chmn. 1990-91, profl. devel. chair 1991—, publicity chair 1988—), Internat. Mgmt. Coun. (student liaison com. 1991), Beta Gamma Sigma, Phi Lambda Theta. Roman Catholic. Office: SUNY-Oswego Bus Adminstrn Student Adv Ctr 16 Swetman Hall Oswego NY 13126

CASHIN, FRANCIS JOSEPH, engineering executive; b. Bklyn., June 3, 1924; s. Frank Joseph and Mary Regina (Genoese) C.; m. Katherine E. Cullen, Apr. 20, 1947; children: Francis, Katherine, James, Mary, Michael, Aidan, Christopher, Thaddeus; divorced; m. Jean Louise Anderson, Dec. 15, 1989, stepchildren: Diane, Madeline. BSME, Stevens Inst. Tech., 1947, M in Engring., 1986, D in Engring., 1990; postgrad., Harvard U. Registered profl. engr., N.Y. Project engr. DeFlorez Co., Inc., N.Y.C., 1947-53; gen. mgr. The Huck Co., N.Y.C., 1954-59; pres. Cashin Assoc., N.Y.C., 1959-87, chmn., 1987—. Contbr. articles to profl. jours. and patentee in field. Active U.S. Trade Commn., Washington, 1988-90; pres. Accreditation Bd. Engring., N.Y.C., 1988-89; comdr. USNR, 1941-71. Fellow Inst. Engrs. Ireland, Nat. Acad. Forensic Engrs.; mem. ASME, IEEE, ASCE, Am. Acad. Environ. Engrs. (diplomate), Am. Cons. Engrs. Coun., Am. Pub. Works Assn., Constrn. Specifications Inst., Illuminating Engring. Soc., Inst. Mcpl. Engring., Inst. Solid Waste, L.I. Sanitation Ofcls. Assn. (trustee), Nat. Soc. Profl. Engrs., N.Y. State Assn. Solid Waste Mgmt., N.Y. State Soc. Profl. Engrs., Soc. Am. Mil. Engrs., City Midday and Drug and Chem. Club, Regency Whist Club, Halifax Club, Spruce Creek Country Club. Republican. Roman Catholic. Office: Cashin Assocs PC 255 Executive Dr Plainview NY 11803-1707

CASHMAN, MICHAEL EDWARD, small business owner; b. Bklyn., Apr. 3, 1935; s. Timothy and Margaret (Costello) C.; m. Jean Lento, June 29, 1957; children: Mary Elizabeth, Deborah, Kathleen, Patricia, Janet. BS, Fordham U., 1957; MBA, Pace U, 1965. Mgr. Western Electric, N.Y.C., 1959-67; v.p. Am. Mgmt. Assn., N.Y.C., 1967-70; mgr. Avon, Wilmington, Del., 1970-72; dir. Sandoz, East Hanover, N.J., 1972-75; chmn. bd. dirs., pres. Cashman Cons. Corp., Morristown, N.J., 1975—; lectr., cons. on mgmt. practices, strategic planning, mktg., negotiations, etc. Author: Management Development, 1990, Executive Development, 1991; contbr. articles to profl. pubs. Served to Lt. Col. USMCR, 1957-82, ret. Home: 135 Van Houton Ave Chatham NJ 07928 Office: Cashman Cons Corp 4 Perry St Morristown NJ 07960

CASIDA, LESTER EARL, JR., microbiologist, educator; b. Columbia, Mo., Aug. 25, 1928; s. Lester Earl and Ruth (Barnes) C.; B.S., U. Wis., 1950, M.S., 1951, Ph.D., 1953; m. Mardelle Elizabeth Baumgartner, Aug. 22, 1953; children—Nancy Ann, Sharon Ann. Research asst. Abbott Labs., North Chicago, Ill., 1951; microbiologist Pabst Labs., Milw., 1953; fermentation biochemist Pfizer Corp., N.Y.C., 1954-57; asst. prof. microbiology Pa. State U., State College, 1957-62, assoc. prof., 1962-66, prof., 1966—; cons. Recipient numerous research grants. Fellow Am. Acad. Microbiology; mem. Am. Soc. Microbiology, Am. Chem. Soc., Soc. Gen. Microbiology. Methodist. Author: Industrial Microbiology, 1968; contbr. articles on microbial ecology to profl. jours.; patentee indsl. fermentations. Home: 1364 Greenwood Cir State College PA 16803-3232 Office: Pa State U Dept Molecular & Cell Biology Eberly College Sci University Park PA 16802-4500

CASKEY, GARY MILTON, psychologist; b. Lancaster, Pa., Mar. 9, 1952; s. Aaron Milton and Elizabeth Ann (Morrison) C.; m. Mary Dorothy Griffin, Aug. 25, 1976 (div. Aug. 1978); 1 child, Erin; m. Beth Ann Schneider, Jan. 21, 1984; children: Ethan, Alexander. AB, Temple U., 1975; postgrad., U. So. Calif., 1976; MA, Clark U., 1978, PhD, 1986. Clin. psychologist Human Resource Inst., Norton, Mass., 1982-83; admissions officer Worcester (Mass.) State Hosp., 1980-83; clin. psychologist Attleboro (Mass.) Area Mental Health Ctr., 1983-85; program coord. cutler counseling Ctr., Norwood, Mass., 1985-86; program dir. Eliot Community Mental Health Ctr., Concorc, Mass., 1986-87; pvt. practice clin. psychology Lowell and Westford, Mass., 1987—; cosn. psychologist North Shore Childrens Hosp., Lowell, 1986-87; court psychologist Dept. Forensic Mental Health State Mass., 1989-91; cons. United Cerebral Palsy Found.; dir. Apple Valley Counseling Ctr., Westford, 1988—. Contbr. articles to profl. jours. Mem. APA (ind. practice div., clin. psychology div., forensic psychology div., exptl. analysis behavior div.), Mass. Psychol. Assn., Jean Piaget Soc., Nat. Register of Health Svc. Providers in Psychology, Psi Chi. Office: Apple Valley counseling 319 Littleton Rd Westford MA 01886-4133

CASO, ADOLPH, publishing company executive; b. Mirabella, Avellino, Italy, Jan. 7, 1934; came to U.S., 1947; s. Raffaele and Prisca (DeLuca) C.; divorced; children: Richard Anthony, Robert Ralph, Liana Cristina. BA, Northeastern U., 1957; AM, Harvard U., 1965. Dir. binlingual edn. Waltham (Mass.) Pub. Schs., 1964-83; pres., editor Branden Pub. Co. Inc., Boston, 1983—; teaching fellow Harvard U., Cambridge, Mass., 1964. Author: The Straw Obelisk, 1973, Lives of Italian Americans, 1976, Water and Life, 1979, America's Italian Founding Fathers, 1984, Bilingual Two Language Battery of Tests, 1985, Mass Media vs. The Italian Americans, 1986, Issues in Foreign Language and Bilingual Education, 1987, Pages and Windows, 1991, (with Joseph Kinney) Young Rocky--The Life of Rocky Castellani, 1983; contbg. editor: Dante in the 20th Century, 1985: editor: On Crimes and Punishments (Cesare Beccaria), 1985, Romeo and Ju-

liet—Original Text, 1992; also others. Pres. PTA, Newton, Mass., 1965, Waltham Overseas Studies, 1966-69; founder, pres. Dante U. Found., Boston, 1976—. With Signal Corps, U.S. Army, 1957-62; col. U.S. Army Res., 1963-87. Decorated cavaliere Republic of Italy; Fulbright scholar, 1966. Mem. Sons of Italy (commr.). Roman Catholic. Office: Branden Pub Co Inc 17 Station St # 843 Brookline MA 02146-7303

CASON, JUNE MACNABB, musician, educator, arts administrator; b. Phila., June 21, 1930; d. Vernon C. and Eleanor (Scarlet) Macnabb; m. Roger Lee Cason, June 12, 1952; children: David Alan, Diane Louise, Nancy Lynn. Student, Eastman Sch. Music, Rochester, N.Y., 1948-52; grad., U. Houston, 1965-69; postgrad. in bus., U. Pa., 1984. Dir. youth chorus St. John's Episcopal Ch., Charleston, W.Va., 1956-63; soloist ch. and music groups, Charleston, 1957-63; founder, dir. music summer camp Episcopal Diocese W.Va., 1961-62; soloist Christ Ch. Cathedral, Houston, 1963-71, Gilbert and Sullivan Soc., Houston, 1970; pvt. tchr. voice, Houston, 1965-71, Wilmington, Del., 1971—; tchr. voice San Jacinto Coll., Pasadena, Tex., 1969-71; founder, gen. mgr., soloist Minikin Opera Co., Wilmington, 1972-87; mem. faculty Wilmington Music Sch., 1973-77; mem. Del. Pro Musica, Wilmington, 1973-77, chmn., 1975-77; dir. music Immanuel Episcopal Ch., Wilmington, 1973-75; instr. music Albert Einstein Acad., Wilmington, 1975-76; v.p. Resource Ctr. for Performing Arts, 1982-86; chmn. Music Consortium New Castle County, 1982-84; devel. dir. OperaDelaware, 1988-92; trainer, cons. Nonprofit Mgmt. Devel. Ctr., La Salle U., 1989—; devel. assoc. arts and humanities, U. Del., 1992—. Contbr. articles to profl. jours. Recipient Theta Eta award U. Rochester, 1952. Mem. Music Tchrs. Nat. Assn. (nat. conv. chmn. vocal progarms 1989—), Nat. Assn. Tchrs. Singing, Del. Music Tchrs. Nat. Assn., Nat. Soc. Fundraising Execs., Met. Opera Guild, Nat. Opera Service, Sigma Alpha Iota (Sword of Honor 1971). Republican. Home and Office: 1125 Grinnel Rd Wilmington DE 19803-5125

CASON, ROGER LEE, chemical company executive, consultant; b. Madison, Wis., Aug. 13, 1930; s. Hulsey and Eloise (Boeker) C.; m. June Ely Macnabb, June 12, 1952; children: David Allan, Diane Louise, Nancy Lynn. BS in Mech. Engring. with high distinction, U. Rochester, 1951, MS, 1952; MBA, U. Del., 1977. Registered profl. engr., Del., W.Va. With E.I. DuPont de Nemours & Co., various locations, 1955—, sr. mech. engr., prodn. supr., mech. supr., Houston, 1963-70, staff bus. analyst, Wilmington, Del., 1971-75, bus. analysis mgr., 1975-83, prin. cons., 1983—. Contbr. articles to profl. publs. Served with C.E.C., USN, 1952-55. Mem. Fin. Mgmt. Assn. (instl. dir. 1987-89), Wilmington Power Squadron (instr. courses 1977-80, 83-89, sec. 1985-86, exec. officer 1987-88, comdr. 1988-89), Columbia Sailing Assn., Georgetown Racing Fleet, Beta Gamma Sigma, Phi Beta Kappa, Sigma Xi (asso. mem.), Tau Beta Pi. Republican. Episcopalian. Home: 1125 Grinnell Rd Green Acres Wilmington DE 19803 Office: DuPont Co Chems Dept Wilmington DE 19898

CASPE, LYNDA WENDY, artist, educator, poet; b. N.Y.C., July 3, 1939; d. Saul and Helen (Lazaras) C.; 1 child, Daniel. BA, U. Chgo., 1961; MFA, U. Iowa, 1964; postgrad., Atelier 17, Paris, 1964-65, N.Y. Studio Sch., 1966-68. Instr. U. Alberta, Edmonton, Can., 1966, U. Chgo., 1967, Newark State Coll., Union, N.J., 1968-72, Newark Sch. of Fine and Indsl. Art, 1973-77, Parson's Sch. of Design, N.Y.C., 1977-89, Borough of Man Community Coll., N.Y.C., 1977—, N.Y.C. Tech. Coll., 1974—. Author poetry; one women shows include Bowery Gallery, 1973, 76; group shows include Bowery Gallery, 1968-85, Cooper Hewitt Mus., 1978, Virelin Mus., Oslo, 1979, Inst. of Contemporary Art, London, 1980. Yaddo fellow, 1973; Creative Artist grantee, 1974. Home: 150 Franklin St New York NY 10013-2913 Office: Borough of Man Community Coll 199 Chambers St New York NY 10007-1006

CASS, APRIL LORRAINE, graphic designer; b. N.Y.C., Apr. 5, 1957; d. William and Catherine (Bouhouris) C. BFA in Graphic Design, Carnegie Mellon U., 1980. Freelance graphic artist Hoechstetter Printing Co., Pitts., 1981; graphic design and prodn. asst. Dennis Hatton Graphic Design, Pitts., 1982-83; graphic designer, prodn. asst. Jim Prokell Studio, Pitts., 1984-85; graphic designer Communication Works, Inc., Pitts., 1985-87; owner, mgr., graphic designer April Cass Design, S.I., N.Y., 1987—. Work exhibited So. Alleghenies Mus. Art, Johnson, Pa., 1981, Guild Book Workers 75th Anniversary Exhbn., N.Y.C., co. stationery in design publ. Am. Corp. Identity/4, designed a baby shower invitation and announcement which appear in the book Storks and Bonds. Mem. Am. Inst. Graphic Arts, Guild Book Workers, Bus. and Profl. Women, Daus. of Penelope Callicolone, Salt and Pepper Novelty Shakers Club, Mortar Bd. Democrat. Greek Orthodox. Home and Office: 199 Clarke Ave Staten Island NY 10306-1115

CASS, E. R. PETER, electronic publishing executive; b. La Porte, Ind., Nov. 21, 1941; s. Edward Smith and Shirley (Mazor) C.; m. Marilyn Brooks Cass, Apr. 1, 1967; children: Edward, Alexander. AB, Hamilton Coll., 1964; MBA, Syracuse U., 1970. Dir. mktg., gen. sales mgr. Mohawk Airlines, Inc., 1964-71; sr. v.p., gen. mgr. Travel Industry Assn. Am., Washington, 1971-78; gen. mgr., chief operating officer Tri County Met. Transp., Portland, Oreg., 1978-81; pres. Cablebus System Corp., Beaverton, Oreg., 1981-82; v.p. unregulated activities Pacific Telecom, Inc., Vancouver, Wash., 1982-83; chmn. bd. dirs., pres. Transax Data Corp., Falls Church, Va., 1983-85; pres. Transax Data, Bridgewater, 1985—, chief exec. officer, 1991—. Office: Transax Data 721 Rt 202/206 Bridgewater NJ 08807

CASS, THOMAS RICHARDSON, laboratory science executive; b. Peabody, Mass., Nov. 2, 1930; s. Thomas Edward and Alice (Richardson) C.; m. Marjorie Anne Perry, June 30, 1962; children: Meredith Richardson, Thomas Edward. BS in Chemistry, Merrimack Coll., Andover, Mass., 1952. Sales engr. Hercules, Inc., Wilmington, Del., 1956-58; prodn. supr. Nat. Sugar Refining Co., N.Y.C., 1958-59; plant mgr. Friend Bros., Inc., Malden, Mass., 1959-64; process engr. Bostik div. Emhart, Middleton, Mass., 1964-67; mfg. mgr. Comodore Foods, Inc., Lowell and Westboro, Mass., 1967-70; pres. Aqua Labs., Inc., Amesbury, Mass., 1970—; incorporator Provident Inst. Savs., Amesbury, 1987—. Mem. sch. bd. Masconomett Regional High Sch., Boxford, Mass., 1964-65. Lt. USN, 1952-56. Mem. Nat. Assn. Corrosion Engrs., Internat. Water Treatment Mfrs. Assn. (pres. 1974—), Assoc. Water Technologies, Small Bus. Assn. New Eng., Assoc. Industries Mass., Water Pollution Control Fedn., Sales and Mktg. Execs., Rotary (pres. local chpt. 1985-86). Home: 2 Taylor River Rd Hampton Falls NH 03844-2012 Office: Aqua Labs Inc 8 Industrial Way Amesbury MA 01913-3223

CASSADAY, MICHAEL MILLIET, engineering company executive, consultant,; b. New Orleans, July 21, 1944; s. George C. and Ella Rita (Milliet) C.; m. Jackie C. Williamson (div.); 1 child, Michael Edward; m. Corinne T. Catalano, Oct. 16, 1981; 1 child, Thomas George. BSME, U. Miss., 1969. Engr. Pratt & Whitney Aircraft, Hartford, Conn., 1970-73; project mgr. Milton Roy Co., St. Petersburg, Fla., 1973-78; sr. engr. R&D Technicon Instruments, Tarrytown, N.Y., 1978-88; prin. Micor Engring., Valhalla, N.Y., 1988—. Contbr. articles to profl. jours.; patentee on reaction cuvette, apparatus for non-invasive mixing, sample transport system, liquid level adjusting and filtering device, zero dead volume connector, isolation liquid layer retention device, chem 1 system patent, minimu carry over container. Office: Micor Engring 188 Prospect Ave Valhalla NY 10595-1831

CASSAR, RICHARD DOUGLAS, industrial hygiene consultant; b. Wilmington, Del., Oct. 21, 1930; s. G. Douglas and Dorothy S. (Siebecker) C.; m. Ann M. Welk, June 23, 1956; children: David D., Thomas E., James R. BS, Albright Coll., 1954; MS, U. Del., 1964. Chem. lab technician U.S. Army Chem. Corps, Anniston, Ala., 1954-56; rsch. chemist Sun Oil Co., Marcus Hook, Pa., 1956-60, Avisun, Marcus Hook, Pa., 1960-62, Suntech, Inc., Marcus Hook, Pa., 1962-77; indsl. hygienist Stewart-Todd Assocs., King of Prussia, Pa., 1977-81; ptnr. Cassar Tech. Svcs., Thornton, Pa., 1981—. Patentee 23 patents in field. Dist mem.-at-large Valley Forge (Pa.) Coun. Boy Scouts Am., 1965—. With U.S. Army, 1954-56. Mem. Am. Chem. Soc. Home: 319 Brinton Lake Rd Thornton PA 19373-1054 Office: Cassar Tech Svcs 319 Brinton Lake Rd Thornton PA 19373-1054

CASSARO, IRENE DOLORES, securities trader; b. N.Y.C., June 30, 1951; d. Mario Joseph and Rosalie (Calandrino) C. BA, CUNY, 1973; MA, New Sch. for Social Rsch., 1977; student in nursing, Westchester Community Coll., Valhalla, N.Y., 1991—. Cert. tchr., N.Y., 1973. Elem. sch. tchr. N.Y.C. Pub. Schs., 1973-74; treas. govt. securities White Weld & Co., N.Y.C., 1974-78; money market trader Merill Lynch & Co., N.Y.C., 1978-81; v.p., securities trader Morgan Stanley & Co., N.Y.C., 1981-88. Author: Money Market Instruments, 1978. Recipient scholarship N.Y. Dept. Edn., 1969. Mem. Nat. Student Nurses Assn. Roman Catholic. Home: 224 Commerce St Hawthorne NY 10532-2039

CASSEL, EDITH HERTHA SOPHIE, physicist; b. Aachen, Germany, May 9, 1940; d. Albrecht Carl Richard and Hertha Edith (Schröder) Tielsch; m. David Giske Cassel, Oct. 15, 1966; children: Erik Stefan, Monika Irene. PhD, U. Heidelberg, Germany, 1966. Rsch. assoc. Cornell U., Ithaca, N.Y., 1967-70, 74-78, lectr., 1978—. Mem. Am. Assn. Physics Tchrs. Office: Cornell U 105 Clark Hall Ithaca NY 14853

CASSELL, DEAN GEORGE, aerospace executive; b. Bklyn., Sept. 25, 1928; s. George James and Blanche Mary (Duffy) C.; m. Roberta Francis Reed, June 5, 1954; children: Gerald, Leslie Ann, Geoffrey. BS, Georgetown U., 1951; postgrad., MIT, 1977. Support mgr. early warning program Grumman Aerospace, Bethpage, N.Y., 1963-69, progaram mgr., 1969-75, asst. to sr. v.p. aircraft and space, 1975-77, v.p. ops., 1977-81, dir. comml. devel. ctr., 1981-85, v.p. product integrity and environ. affairs, 1986—; bd. dirs. Grumman Ohio Corp. Member execs. recycling rev. com. Suffolk County, Hauppauge, N.Y., 1990. With USN, 1953-60. Mem. L.I. Assn. (environ. com. 1986—), U.S. C. of C. Republican. Roman Catholic. Home: 764 Pat Dr West Islip NY 11795-3538 Office: Grumman Corp 1111 Stewart Ave Bethpage NY 11714-3533

CASSELMAN, WILLIAM E., II, lawyer; b. Washington, Pa., July 8, 1941; s. William E. and Lucy (Bobbs) C.; m. Caroline Murfitt, Dec. 16, 1967; children: Katharine Carr, Lee Wilson. BA, Claremont Men's Coll., 1963; postgrad., U. Madrid, 1963-64; JD, George Washington U., 1968. Bar: Va. 1968, D.C. 1972, U.S. Supreme Ct. 1975. Legis. asst. to Robert McClory U.S. Ho. of Reps., 1965-68; staff asst. Office of Pres., 1969, dep. spl. asst. to Pres., 1969-71, counsel to Pres., 1974-75; gen. counsel Gen. Svcs. Adminstrn., 1971-73; legal counsel to Vice Pres. U.S., 1973-74; ptnr. Ambrose & Casselman, P.C., 1975-79; pvt. practice Washington, 1979-82; ptnr. Dorsey & Whitney, 1982-84, Popham, Haik, Schnobrich & Kaufman, Ltd., Washington, 1985—; mem. adminstrv. conf. U.S., 1971-73; adv. mem. Nat. Conf. Commrs. on Uniform State Laws, 1975; mem. Gerald R. Ford Commemorative Com., 1977-82; bd. dirs., gen. counsel, mem. fin. com., fellow Georgetown U. Ctr. for Internat. Bus. and Trade, 1983—. Recipient Alumni Achievement award George Washington U., 1975. Mem. ABA, Fed. Bar Assn. (chmn. gen. counsels com. 1973-74, nat. coun. 1974-79, Disting. Svc. commendation 1974), George Washington Law Assn. (dir. 1976-80), Nat. Trust for Hist. Preservation (mem. com. on legal svcs. 1978-80), Franklin Square Club, Nat. Lawyers Club, Army-Navy Country Club, Delta Theta Phi, Theta Chi. Republican. Office: Popham Hawk Schnobrich & Kaufman Ltd 1300 I St NW # 600 Washington DC 20005-3314

CASSELS, PETER ANDREW, public relations consultant, educator; b. Providence, Sept. 23, 1943; s. Andrew and Mary Ann (Markey) C. BA, U. R.I., 1965; MA, Syracuse U., 1966. Mgr. pub. relations Lockheed Corp., Plainfield, N.J., 1966-68; various positions in pub. rels. mgmt. AT&T, various locations, 1966-89; pub. rels. dir. AT&T, Providence, 1986-89; adj. faculty Sch. Journalism Northeastern U., 1990-91, Boston U., 1991; pvt. practice San Francisco, R.I., 1991—. Bd. dirs. Jr. Achievement, Providence, 1988-90, Pub. Edn. Fund, Providence, 1988-91; chmn. Task Force on the Arts, Providence, 1988, R.I. Job Svc. Employers Com., 1988; mem. R.I. Task Force. Mem. Pub. Rels. Soc. Am. (pres. Boston chpt. 1988-89), Fed. Club Boston. Roman Catholic. Home and Office: 471 W Shore Rd Unit 5 Warwick RI 02889

CASSERLY, CHARLEY, professional football team executive; b. Feb. 27, 1949; m. Bev Casserly; 1 daughter, Shannon. BS in Edn., Springfield Coll., M. in Guidance. Asst. coach Cathedral H.S., Springfield, Mass., 1969-72; athletic dir. Cathedral H.S., 1974-75; asst. Springfield Coll., 1973-74; tchr., football coach Minnechaugh H.S., Mass., 1975-76; joined Washington Redskins, NFL, 1977, went from intern in scouting dept., to full-time scout, to asst. gen. mgr., 1977-89, gen. mgr., 1989—. Office: Washington Redskins Dulles Internat Airport PO Box 17247 Washington DC 20041-0247*

CASSESE, JOHN, medical equipment leasing company executive; b. N.Y.C., May 30, 1934; s. Albert and Nancy (Forzese) C.; m. Patricia Messina, Oct. 10, 1959; children: Karen, Lorraine, John Albert. Student, CCNY, 1952-53, C.W. Post Coll.-Long Island U., 1960, Hofstra U., 1968, Empire State Coll., 1973-74. Field tech. to field supr. missile installation and modification ARMA Corp., Garden City, N.Y., 1958-64; repairman, then. mgr. sales and service Packard Instrument Corp., Downers Grove, Ill., 1964-75; service mgr. Docutel Corp., Irving, Tex., 1975-76; with sales and mktg. staff Unirad/Ohio Nuclear, Solon, Ohio, 1976-77; mktg. mgr., regional sales mgr. Elscint, Inc., Hackensack, N.J., 1977-81; project mktg. mgr., dir. nat. and internat. sales Fonar Corp., Melville, N.Y., 1981-89; v.p. EquiMed Leasing, Inc., 1989—; vice-chmn. bd. Medi-Scan Health Systems, Inc., Commack, N.Y.; presenter papers various confs., seminars, workshops. Contbr. articles to profl. jours. Served to staff sgt. USAF, 1953-57. Office: EquiMed Leasing Inc 2 Executive Campus Cherry Hill NJ 08002-4102

CASSEY, JOHN CALVIN, JR., recreational facility director; b. Camden, N.J., Aug. 3, 1951; s. John Calvin and Norma Dorothy (Christie) C.; m. Jeannine Jinkner, Aug. 28, 1976; children: Andrew J., Jamie A. BA in Psychology, Grove City Coll., 1973; MA in Psychology, West Chester U., 1975. Mktg. rep. Aetna Casualty & Surety, Pitts., 1973-74; dir. Christian Edn. Westminster Presbyn. Ch., Auburn, N.Y., 1975-77; aquatics dir. Ransburg YMCA, Indpls., 1977-79; dir. aquatics, mktg. Kalamazoo (Mich.) Family YMCA, 1979-84; exec. dir. Fargo (N.D.)-Moorhead Family YMCA, 1984-86, Western YMCA of Del., Newark, 1986—; cons. YMCA of U.S.A., King of Prussia, Pa., 1989—. Contbr. articles to profl. jours. Vol. Jr. Achievement of Del., Wilmington, 1991. Mem. New Castle County C. of C. Presbyterian. Office: Western YMCA of Del 2600 Kirkwood Hwy Newark DE 19711-7299

CASSIDY, GEORGE THOMAS, international business development consultant; b. Jamaica, N.Y., Apr. 13, 1939; s. George Leo and Vivia P.M. (Sharpe) C.; m. Eileen Mary O'Shea, Nov. 25, 1967; children: George, Eileen, Patrick, Martin. BA, St. John's U., 1960. Officer Detroit Police Dept., 1964-66; fin. analyst Esso Internat., Inc., N.Y.C., 1966-69; asst. treas. Am. Standard, Inc., N.Y.C., 1969-74; dir. bus. devel. St. Regis Paper Co., Inc., N.Y.C., 1974-85; pres. SC Mgmt. Svcs. Corp., Wilton, Conn., 1985—; chmn. SC Mgmt. Svcs. Corp., Wilton, 1989—. Author: International Financial Management, 1987, Handbook of Budgeting, 1989. Lt. USCG, 1960-64. Mem. L.I. Assn. (internat. trade advisor 1991—). Republican. Roman Catholic. Home: 60 Evergreen Rd New Canaan CT 06840 Office: SC Mgmt Svcs Corp PO Box 7458 Wilton CT 06897

CASSIDY, LEE M., nonprofit association executive, marketing consultant; b. N.Y.C., Feb. 16, 1933; s. John J. and Lea F. (Schreiber) C.; children: Nancy, Allison, Jeannette. BBA, Adelphi U., 1955. Direct mktg. mgr. Allied Stores, N.Y.C., 1958-66; mktg. com. group supr. Dupont Co., Wilmington, Del., 1966-78; chmn. Del. Pub. Svc. Com., Dover, Del., 1975-78; exec. dir. U.S. Pres.'s Commn. on Exec. Exchange, Washington, 1978-81; v.p. Paul Stafford Assocs., Washington, 1981-82; mng. dir. Chinn & Cassidy Assocs., Washington, 1982-87; pres. Mature Market Inst., Washington, 1987-90; exec. v.p. Internat. Assn. for Seminar Mgmt., Washington, 1990-91; exec. dir. Nonprofit Mailers Fedn., Washington, 1991—; pres. Forty Plus Found., Washington, 1989—; founder, pres. Mature Market Inst., Washington, 1987-90; co-founder Internat. Assn. for Seminar Mgmt., Washington, 1990. Contbr. articles to profl. jours. Candidate Del. House of Reps., Wilmington, 1974, 75; del. Dem. Nat. Conv., 1976; chmn. Del. Com. for Carter for Pres., 1975-76. Mem. Am. Soc. Assn. Execs., Washington Soc. Assn. Execs.

CASSIDY, WILLIAM ARTHUR, geology and planetary science educator; b. N.Y.C., Jan. 3, 1928; s. John and Nellie (Briel) C.; m. Beverly J. Griffith, Aug. 29, 1959; children: Shauna Lynne, Laura Dawn, Brian John. B.S. in Geology, U. N. Mex., 1952; Ph.D. in Geochemistry, Pa. State U., 1961. Seismic computer Superior Oil Co. of Calif., Midland, Tex., 1952-53; research scientist Lamont Geol. Obs., Palisades, N.Y., 1961-67; assoc. to prof. geology and planetary sci. U. Pitts., 1968-80, prof., 1981—; trustee Univ. Space Research Assn., Columbia, Md., 1975-82, chmn., 1978-79; chmn. meteorite working group Lunar and Planetary Sci. Inst., Houston, 1977-83. Contbr. articles to profl. jours. Served with USNR, 1945-46. Recipient Antarctic Service medal NSF, 1978; Fulbright fellow, 1953-54; grantee NSF, NASA. Mem. Am. Geophys. Union, Meteoritical Soc. Clubs: Explorers (N.Y.C.); Antarctican (Washington). Office: U Pitts 321 Old Engineering Hall Pittsburgh PA 15260-3332

CASSIDY, WILLIAM DUNNIGAN, III, industrial company executive; b. Bluefield, W.Va., Aug. 4, 1941; s. William D. Jr. and Josephine Elizabeth (Williams) C.; m. Beverly Ann Lisk, Nov. 25, 1967; children: William IV, Michael, Sean. BS, Hampden-Sydney (Va.) Coll., 1963; MS, George Washington U., 1966; PhD in Psychology, Clayton U., St. Louis, 1987. With human resources dept. ITT, N.Y.C., 1965-82; sr. v.p. adminstrn. Warburg, Paribas, Becker, N.Y.C., 1982-84; v.p. adminstrn. The Genlyte Group, N.Y.C., 1984-86, Penn Cen. Industries Corp., Woodcliff Lake, N.J., 1986-90; v.p. and chief adminstrv. officer Concurrent Computer Corp., Oceanport, N.J., 1990—. Elder West Side Presbyn. Ch., Ridgewood, N.J., 1986. Mem. Internat. Assn. Corp. and Profl. Recruiters (bd. dirs.), The George Jr. Rep. Sch. N.Y. (bd. dirs.), Union League (N.Y.C.). Republican. Home: 274 Phelps Rd Ridgewood NJ 07450-1421 Office: Concurrent Computer Corp 2 Crescent Pl Oceanport NJ 07757

CASTAGNO, ANTHONY JOSEPH, utility company executive; b. Bklyn., May 27, 1949; s. Rowe Anthony and Marion Katherine (Macdonald) C.; m. Karen Marie Sczcepaniak, Oct. 17, 1987; 1 child, Katherine Amelia. BS, Trinity Coll., Hartford, Conn., 1971, MA, 1973. Editor, pubr. Hartford's Other Voice, Wild Raspberry, Hartford, Conn., 1969-72; tchr. sci. East Hartford High Sch., 1972-76; youth substance abuse counselor Hartford, 1969-76; adminstr. Waco (Tex.) State Home, 1976; mgmt./polit. cons. Hartford, 1986—; mgr. nuclear info. Northeast Utilities, Berlin, Conn., 1981—. Contbr. articles to encys. and profl. jours. Mem. Portland Econ. Devel. Commn., 1989—; bd. dirs. Literacy Vols., 1987—, Portland Dem. Election Com., 1989—, Portland Agrl. Fair, 1989; chmn. New Eng. Nuclear Info. Mgrs. Com., 1986—; Dem. candidate Conn. Senate, 1990. Mem. AAAS, Conn. Audubon Soc., Artista da Firenze, Conn. Jazz Confedn., Hartford Jazz Soc., Trinity Club, Lions. Democrat. Roman Catholic. Home: PO Box 25 Portland CT 06480-0025 Office: NE Utilities PO Box 270 Hartford CT 06141-0270

CASTALDO, PETER JAMES, telecommunications professional, lecturer; b. S.I., N.Y., Apr. 13, 1948; s. Peter Edward C.; m. Diane Frances Gottfied; children: Alicia, Peter James, Jr. Student, DeVry Inst., N.J., 1971, Brookdale (N.J.) Coll. Mgr. N.Y. Telephone, N.Y.C., 1979-81, O.S.P. engr., 1981-87; tech. staff Bell Communications Rsch., Red Bank, N.J., 1987—. Bd. dirs. ARC, S.I., 1980; chmn. ARC Small Craft Safety Com., S.I., 1980. Republican. Roman Catholic. Home: 17 Monmouth St Hazlet NJ 07730-2125 Office: Bell Communication Rsch Schultz Dr Red Bank NJ 07701

CASTANO, ELVIRA PALMERIO, art gallery director, art historian; b. Cin., July 23, 1929; d. John and Josephine C.; m. Carlo Palmerio, June 1, 1958 (dec.); 1 child, Marina. B. Literary Interpretation, Emerson Coll., Boston, 1950; postgrad., Pius XII Inst., Florence, Italy, 1954-55. Curator Castano Art Gallery, Boston, 1965-78; dir. Castano Art Gallery, Needham, Mass., 1978—; researcher Archives of Am. Art Smithsonian Instn., Boston, 1988-89; Vatican translator; interpreter Italian art, specialist in Macchiaioli art; Italian lang. translator. Mem. Nat. Rep. Congl. Com. Presdl. Task Force, Archives of Am. Art; bd. dirs. Needham Hist. Soc.; mem. Rep. Senatorial Inner Circle. Cardinal Spellman scholar. Mem. Boston Mus. Fine Artts, Brockton Art Mus. (adv. bd.), Fogg Art Mus. Harvard U., Friends Needham Libr., Needham Hist. Soc. (bd. dirs.), Archives Am. Art Boston, Alliance Francaise Boston. Republican. Roman Catholic. Address: 245 Hunnewell St Needham MA 02194

CASTANO, GREGORY JOSEPH, lawyer; b. Kearny, N.J., Feb. 17, 1929; s. Nicholas and Marianna (Prestinaci) C.; m. June Dwyer, Oct. 15, 1966; children: Gregory, Christopher, John, Timothy. BS, Seton Hall U., 1950; JD, Fordham U., 1953; LLM, NYU, 1956. Bar: N.J. 1956, U.S. Ct. Appeals (3d cir.) 1957, U.S. Supreme Ct. 1959, U.S. Tax Ct. 1974, N.Y. 1985. Pvt. practice Harrison, N.J., 1959-78; atty. Bd. Adjustment, Harrison, 1978; judge Superior Ct. N.J., Jersey City, 1978-85; ptnr. Tompkins, McGuire & Wachenfeld, Newark, 1985-88, Waters, McPherson & McNeill, Secaucus, N.J., 1988—; asst. atty. Town of Harrison, 1959-64; asst. prosecutor County of Hudson, N.J., 1963-71; atty. Town of West New York, N.J., 1977-78; adj. prof. Seton Hall U. Sch. Law, Newark, 1988—. Tax assessor Town of Harrison, 1964-78; mem. juvenile conf. com. Twp. West Caldwell, N.J., 1977-78; trustee Caldwell (N.J.) Coll., 1985-91, chmn. acad. affairs com. bd. trustees, 1987-91; mem. Hudson County Community Coll. Blue Ribbon Task Force, 1992—. With U.S. Army, 1953-55. Named Man of Yr., Kearny Jaycees, 1963, Alumnus of Yr., Dorf Feature Service, 1987. Fellow Am. Bar Found.; mem. ABA, N.J. Bar Assn., Hudson County Bar Assn. (Justice medallion 1985), Essex County Bar Assn., West Hudson Bar Assn. (pres. 1977-78), Assn. Fed. Bar N.J., Essex Fells Country Club. Home: 19 Sunset Rd West Caldwell NJ 07006-6540 Office: Waters McPherson & McNeill 300 Lighting Way PO Box 1560 Secaucus NJ 07096

CASTEEL, THOMAS JOSEPH, law office manager; b. Jamaica, N.Y., June 25, 1948; s. Lloyd Hamill and Agnes Teresa (Cain) C.; m. Mary Ann DelBuono, Oct. 23, 1971; children: Peter Lloyd, Amy Teresa. BA, Marist Coll., 1969; MBA, U. New Haven, 1976. Programmer, analyst Uniroyal, inc., Middlebury, Conn., 1969-87; systems and programming mgr. Waterbury (Conn.) Hosp., 1987-90; law office mgr. John DelBuono, Esq., Watertown, Conn., 1990—; v.p. ASRS User Group, 1971-72. Pres. Uniroyal Men's Club, Middlebury, Conn., 1979-80, Parish Home & Sch. Assn., Oakville, Conn., 1984-86; chmn. Parish Sch. Bd., Oakville, 1986-87; coach Watertown-Oakville Little League, Watertown, 1980-87. Mem. Am. Trial Lawyers Assn., Data Processing Mgmt. Assn. Home: 177 Charter Oak Dr Watertown CT 06795 Office: Atty John DelBuono 680 Main St Watertown CT 06745

CASTELLANOS, JULIO J(ESUS), banker; b. Havana, Cuba, Mar. 7, 1910; came to U.S., 1960, naturalized, 1967; s. Manuel de Jesus and Virginia (Justiniani) C.; B of Arts and Letters, De La Salle Coll., Havana, 1927; JD, Tulane U., 1933; DCL, U. Havana, 1934; student Fed. Res. System Examiner's Sch., 1964-65; m. Irene Machado, Dec. 27, 1976; children: Julio J., Maria, Ana Maria, Carlos. Bar: Cuba 1934. Tax commr. City of Havana, from 1934; sr. ptnr. Lopez Munoz & Castellanos, Havana; sec. gen. Banco de la Construccion, Havana, 1959-60; analyst Morgan Guaranty Trust Co. N.Y., N.Y.C., 1960-63; examiner Fed. Res. Bank N.Y., N.Y.C., 1963-66; v.p. Marine Midland Bank, N.Y.C., 1966-71; founder, organizer, sr. v.p., mgr. First Wis. Internat. Bank, N.Y.C., 1971-76; pres. Pan Am. Nat. Bank, Union City, N.J., from 1976; exec. rep. Banco de Intercambio Regional, N.Y.C., 1976-80; pres. Banco del Estado Holding Co. Inc., Atlanta, 1982-84; adviser Banco de Reservas de la Republica Dominicana, N.Y.C., 1982-84; N.Y.C. rep. Banco del Estado, Bogota, Colombia, 1978-84; N.Y. rep. Banco Hipotecario Dominicano, 1983-85; banking cons. law firm Reid & Priest, 1983-86; v.p. BHD Corp., real estate investments, 1984-86; pres., chief cons. Castellanos Cons. Group Inc., 1984—; v.p. IDOSA N.Y. Inc., 1984-85. Bd. dirs. Colombian-Am. Assn. Pan Am. Soc. of U.S., 1984-85 . Recipient retirement recognition diploma First Wis. Internat. Bank, 1976, pub. recognition diploma Dr. Guillermo Belt, former Mayor Havana, 1979. Republican. Address: 510 E 85th St New York NY 10028

CASTELLI, LEO, art dealer; b. Trieste, Italy, Sept. 4, 1907; came to U.S., 1941; s. Ernest Krauss and mother nee Castelli; m. Ileana Schapira (div.); 1 child, Nina; m. Toiny Castelli. (dec. Sept. 1987); 1 child, Jean-Christophe. Law degree, U. Milan; student, Columbia U., 1942-43; PhD (hon.), Sch. Visual Arts, N.Y.C.; LHD (hon.), Brenau U., 1991. Early career in internat. banking; opened Galerie Rene Drouin, Paris, 1939-49; worked in knit-goods mfg.; owner Leo Castelli Gallery, 1957—. Served with AUS, 1943-45. Decorated chevalier de l'Ordre Nat. de la Legion d'Honneur (France), 1987, officier, 1990; recipient Mayor's award of honor for arts and culture N.Y.C., 1976; Manhattan Cultural Awards prize, 1980; 150th Ann. award, Disting. New Yorker award Bowery Savs. Bank, 1984, Butler medal

Butler Inst. Am. Art, 1987, Adam Elsheimer Preis award City of Frankfurt, Germany, 1992. Office: Leo Castelli Gallery 420 W Broadway New York NY 10012-3764

CASTELLINO, RONALD AUGUSTUS DIETRICH, radiologist; b. N.Y.C., Feb. 18, 1938; s. Leonard Vincent and Henrietta Wilhelmina (Geffken) C.; m. Joyce Cuneo, Jan. 26, 1963; children: Jeffrey Charles, Robin Leonard, Anthony James. Student, Creighton U., Omaha, 1955-58, M.D., 1962. Diplomate: Am. Bd. Radiology. Rotating intern Highland Alameda County Hosp., Oakland, Calif., 1962-63; USPHS/Peace Corps physician Brazil, 1963-65; resident in diagnostic radiology Stanford U. Hosp., 1965-68, chief resident, 1967-68; asst. prof. radiology Stanford U. Med. Sch., 1968-74, assoc. prof., 1974-81, prof., 1981-90, chief diagnostic oncologic radiology, 1970-89, chief CT body scanning, 1979-89, dir. div. diagnostic radiology and assoc. chmn. dept. radiology, 1981-86, acting chmn. dept. diagnostic radiology and nuclear medicine, 1986-89; Carroll and Milton Petrie chair dept. radiology Meml. Sloan Kettering Cancer Ctr., N.Y.C., 1990—; mem. U.S. Cancer del., People's Republic China, 1977. Co-editor: Pediatric Oncologic Radiology, 1977; assoc. editor: Lymphology, 1973—, Investigative Radiology, 1985—, Radiology, 1986—, Postgraduate Radiology, 1986—; contbr. numerous rsch. papers to profl. jours., chpts. to books. Recipient T.F. Eckstrom Fund award, 1978; Guggenheim fellow, 1974-75. Mem. Internat. Soc. Lymphology, Am. Coll. Radiology, Assn. Univ. Radiologists (exec. com. 1984-86), Radiol. Soc. N.Am., Soc. Cardiovascular Radiology (charter), Am. Roentgen Ray Soc., Western Angiography Soc. (charter), Calif. Med. Assn. (adv. panel sect. radiology 1972-89), Calif. Radiol. Soc., Soc. Thoracic Radiology (charter), Soc. Cancer Imaging (charter), N.Am. Soc. Lymphologyg (charter, exec. com. 1982-86), Calif. Acad. Medicine, N.Y. Roentgen Soc., N.Y. Acad. Medicine, Alpha Omega Alpha. Office: Meml Sloan Kettering Cancer Ctr Dept Radiology 1275 York Ave New York NY 10021

CASTEN, RICHARD FRANCIS, physicist; b. N.Y.C., Nov. 1, 1941; s. Daniel F. and Constance Mary (Bell) C.; m. Jo Ann Daly, June 6, 1964. BS magna cum laude, Coll. of the Holy Cross, 1963; PhD, Yale U., 1967. Postdoctoral fellow Niels Bohr Inst., Copenhagen, Denmark, 1967-69, Los Alamos (N.Mex.) Sci. Lab., 1969-71; asst. scientist Brookhaven Nat. Lab., Upton, N.Y., 1971-73, assoc. scientist, 1973-76, scientist, 1977-81, sr. scientist, 1981—, group leader nuclear structure group, 1981—; chmn. N.Am. Steering Com. for a Radioactive Beam Facility, 1990—; guest prof. U. Cologne, Germany 1984—. Author: Nuclear Structure from a Simple Perspective, 1990; contbr. more than 200 articles to profl. jours. Danforth fellow, 1963-67; recipient Sr. Alexander von Humboldt prize, 1983. Fellow AAAS, NAS (panel on basic nuclear data 1990-92), Am. Phys. Soc. (exec. com. div. nuclear physics 1991-92), NSAC (long range plan working group 1989, subcom. on implementation long range plan), Sigma Xi. Office: Physics Dept Brookhaven Nat Lab Upton NY 11973

CASTER, BERNARD HARRY, artist; b. Wolcott, N.Y., May 27, 1921; s. Edward Everett and Effie Armenia (Reed) C.; m. Katherine Jane Capron, Nov. 29, 1941; children: Carol Sue (Mrs. Karl Schantz III), Cyril Everett, Allan David. A.A., Syracuse U., 1956, B.A., 1960. One-man shows at Galerie Paula Insel, N.Y.C., Univ. Coll. Syracuse (N.Y.) U., Edinborough (Pa.) State Tchrs. Coll.; exhibited in group shows at Syracuse Mus. Fine Arts, Rochester (N.Y.) Meml. Art Gallery, Albright Art Gallery, Buffalo; represented in permanent collections at St. Lawrence U., Canton, N.Y., Newark Pub. Library, Newark, Savannah Elem. Sch., Comstock Foods Corp., Rochester. Served with USAAF, 1942-45; PTO. Recipient Wilner award Cayuga Mus. History and Art, Auburn, 1962, Ceramic award, 1966, Crafts prize, 1972. Home: PO Box 154 House # 13083 South Butler NY 13154

CASTIGLIONE, LAWRENCE VIRGIL, JR., education educator; b. Port Chester, N.Y., Sept. 29, 1938; s. Lawrence Virgil and Mildred (Ruvo) C.; m. Tanya Shriver, Sept. 20, 1965; children: Jennifer, Lawrence V. III. BS, NYU, 1961, MA, 1962, PhD, 1965. Lectr. CUNY, N.Y.C., 1965-66, asst. prof., 1966-69, prof., chairperson dept. secondary edn. and youth svcs., 1972—, v.p. for sr. colls. Italian-Am. faculty and staff adv. com., 1989-90; asst. prof. Pace U., N.Y.C., 1969-72; cons. N.Y.C. Bd. Edn. Author: Questioning Techniques for Gifted Students, 1988. Pres. Bernard Schenck Meml. Math. Fund, N.Y.C., 1991; bd. dirs. Italian-Am. Legal Def. and Higher Edn. Fund, N.Y.C., 1990, chmn., 1991—, pres., 1992—. J.D. Clandra I-A Inst. CUNY fellow, 1991-92. Roman Catholic. Home: 82-67 165th St Jamaica NY 11432 Office: CUNY/Queens Coll Flushing New York NY 11367

CASTILLO, JENNY MARIA TERESA, foreign language professional, educator; b. Lima, Peru, Aug. 8, 1959; came to U.S., 1968; d. Jose Estanislao and Maria Teresa (Sayan) C. BA magna cum laude, Queens Coll., 1982, MA, 1985; postgrad. student, CUNY, 1991—. Literary translator Queens Coll., N.Y.C., 1982-85, instr., lectr., 1983-85; instr. Holy Cross Coll., Flushing, N.Y., 1985-88; asst. prof. Bernard Baruch Coll., N.Y.C., 1987—; treas. Mktg. Com. Holy Cross Coll., Flushing, 1985-88; adj. prof. Hunter Coll., N.Y.C., 1988—. Author: La mia voce, 1979, La sombra, 1980. Sec. Campus Ministry Soc., N.Y., 1991—. CUNY fellow, 1990—. Mem. N.E. MLA, Spanish HOnor Soc. (sec. 1982-86), Hispanics and Peruvians Assn. (spokesperson 1991—), Am. Mus. Natural History (assoc.). Office: Hunter Coll Dept Romance Langs 695 Park Ave New York NY 10021-5085

CASTILLO, RAYMOND ADOLPH, physicist; b. Albany, N.Y., June 7, 1935; s. Raimondo Felix and Helen (Schmigel) C.; m. Frances Ellen Jadick, May 6, 1961; children: Jennifer, Raymond, Allison, Sara. BS in Physics, Albany State U., 1957; MS in Physics, U. Maine, 1959; PhD in Atmospheric Sci., SUNY, Albany, 1979. Grad. asst. physics U. Maine, Orono, 1957-59; instr. physics R.I. Coll., Providence, 1959-62; asst. prof. physics Indiana (Pa.) State Coll., 1962-63; instr. sci. SUNY, Albany, 1966-69; prof. and chmn. tech. Schenectady County Community Coll., 1969-81; asst. dir. Atmospheric Scis. Rsch. Ctr., Albany, 1981-83, assoc. dir., 1983-87, head air pollution and aerosol sci., 1984-87; prof. Western Conn. State U., Danbury, 1987—, chair physics and astronomy, 1991—; cons. in field; bd. dirs. CSU Rsch. Found., 1988-89. Contbr. articles to profl. jours. Active in past Boy Scouts Am., Rep. Party. NOAA, NSF grantee, 1981-87; State of Conn. grantee, 1987—. Mem. Am. Meteorol. Soc., Am. Geophys. Union, N.Y. Acad. Scis., Sigma Pi Sigma, Sigma Psi. Office: Western Conn State U 181 White St Danbury CT 06810-6885

CASTLE, MICHAEL N., governor of Delaware, lawyer; b. Wilmington, Del., July 2, 1939; s. J. Manderson and Louisa B. Castle. B.A., Hamilton Coll., 1961; J.D., Georgetown U., 1964. Bar: Del. 1964, D.C. 1964. Asso. firm Connolly Bove and Lodge, Wilmington, 1964-73; partner firm Connolly Bove and Lodge, 1973-75; dept. atty. gen. State of Del., 1965-66; partner firm Schnee and Castle (P.A.), 1975-80; lt. gov. State of Del., Wilmington, 1981-85; prin. Michael N. Castle (P.A.), 1981—; gov. State of Del., 1985—; mem. Del. Ho. of Reps., 1966-67, Del. State Senate, 1968-76, minority leader, 1976. Bd. dirs. Boys Club of Wilmington. Mem. Del. State Bar Assn., ABA, Council State Govts., Nat. Gov.'s Assn., Rep. Gov.'s Assn., Southern Gov.'s Assn. Republican. Roman Catholic. Office: Office of Gov Legislative Hall Dover DE 19901

CASTLEMAN, ALBERT WELFORD, JR., physical chemist, educator; b. Richmond, Va., Jan. 7, 1936; s. Albert W. and Mildred L. Castleman; m. Heide Gisela Engel, Mar. 10, 1976; children: Sharon Beth, Robert Gill, Clifton Carl. BChemE, Rensselaer Poly. Inst., 1957; MS, Poly. Inst. Bklyn., 1963, PhD, 1969; D honoris causa, U. Innsbruck, Austria, 1987. Leader chemistry rsch. group Brookhaven Nat. Lab., 1958-75; adj. prof. atmospheric chemistry depts. earth and space sci. and mechanics SUNY, Stony Brook, 1973-75; prof. chemistry, CIRES fellow U. Colo., Boulder, 1975-82; prof. chemistry Pa. State U., University Park, 1982—, Evan Pugh prof. chemistry, 1986—, mem. adv. bd. Ctr. Particle Sci. and Engring., 1987—; vis. prof. Physics Inst., Leopold-Franzens U., Innsbruck, Austria, 1981, 84; mem. rev. com. chem. physics programs, Oak Ridge Nat. Lab., 1979, adv. com. to lab. dir. chem. physics programs, Health and Safety Div., 1987-90, chmn., 1990, mem. Dept. Energy rev. com. for chem. physics and radiol. physics program, 1985, Fulbright guest prof., 1990; adv. to Dept. Energy on chem. physics pertaining to energy related atmospheric pollution programs, 1980; mem. ad hoc. panel on atmospheric chemistry Com. on Atmospheric Scis., NRC, NAD, 1980; mem. rev. com. for radiol. and environ. rsch. div. Argonne Univs. Assn. Argonne Nat. Lab., 1977-81, chemistry div., Argonne, 1988; mem. various rev. and adv. coms. Nat. Ctr. for Atmospheric Rsch., U.S. Dept. Energy U.S. Nuclear Regulatory Commn.; cons. Mfg. Chemists Assn., 1975-80, nuclear div. Oak Ridge Nat. Lab., 1976-86, E.I. Dupont de Nemours, 1989—; chmn. subcom. on ions, aerosols and radioactivity Internat. Commn. Atmospheric Electricity, 1976-80; sr. scientist von Humboldt awardee Tech. Hochschule Darmstadt, 1987, Philipps U., Marburg, Germany, 1988. Mem. editorial bd. Jour. Phys. Chemistry, 1985-88, assoc. editor, 1988-90, sr. editor, 1991—; co-editor, mem. editorial bd. Zeitschrift fér Physick D, 1987—; mem. editorial bd. Internat. Jour. Mass Spectrometry and Ion Proc., 1987-90, Jour. Chem. Physics, 1985-87, Jour. Atmospheric Chemistry, 1982—, Aerosol Sci. and Tech., 1982-86, monograph series Understanding Chemical Reactivity, D. Reidel Pub. Co., 1986—. Recipient Sr. Scientist Alexander von Humboldt award, 1986, Sr. Scientist Fulbright award, 1990, Sherman Fairchild Disting. Scholar award, Calif. Inst. Tech., 1977; NSF Creativity Award grantee, 1985-87; Japanese Soc. for Promotion Sci. fellow, 1983. Fellow AAAS, Am. Phys. Soc., Am. Chem. Soc. (Creative Advances in Environ. Sci. and Tech. award 1988), Am. Geophys. Union, Am. Assn. Aerosol Rsch., Deutsche Bunsen-Gesellschaft Soc., N.Y. Acad. Scis., Materials Rsch. Soc., Sigma Xi, Phi Lambda Upsilon. Home: 425 Hillcrest Ave State College PA 16803-3419 Office: Pa State U Dept Chemistry University Park PA 16802

CASTRIGNANO, ROBERT ANTHONY, dean, retired broadcasting company executive; b. L.A., Aug. 10, 1920; s. Rocco and Catherine (Catogge) C.; m. Rose Mary Baffa, Aug. 14, 1949; children: Robert P., Marie A., Theresa M. BS in Elec. Engring., CCNY, 1949; MEE, Poly. Inst. of Bklyn., 1956. Registered profl. engr., Conn. From technician to v.p. CBS, Inc., N.Y.C. and Stamford, Conn., 1938-86; dean profl. devel. Bridgeport Engring. Inst., Fairfield, Conn., 1987—. Contbr. chpts. to tech. handbooks, articles to tech. jours. 1st lt. U.S. Army, 1942-46, ETO. Fellow Soc. Motion Picture and TV Engrs.; mem. IEEE (sr.), Assn. Info. and Image Mgmt., Conn. Soc. Profl. Engrs. (pres. S.W. chpt. 1975-76), Am. Legion, VFW, KC (navigator, grand knight). Roman Catholic. Home: 157 Idlewood Dr Stamford CT 06905-2407 Office: Bridgeport Engring Inst 785 Unquowa Rd Fairfield CT 06430-5001

CASTRO, VINCENT ROBERT, management consulting firm administrator; b. Bakersfield, Calif., July 19, 1948; s. Robert M. C. and Lilous (Robinson) Morganson; m. JoAnne Latoracca (div. 1974). Student, Bakersfield Community Coll., Bakersfield, Calif., 1968; student, Fresno State U., 1971; cert. in mgmt. evaluation, U. Calif., Santa Cruz, 1975. Dir. mgmt. info. system, Planning Dept. City of Fresno, 1971-73; administrv. svcs. officer U. Calif., Santa Cruz, 1973-75; dep. dir. ops. Am. Indian Commn., Denver, 1975-76; assoc. dir. Pacific Inst. for Rsch. and Evaluation, Bethesda, Md., 1978-87; pres. The CDM Group, Inc., Chevy Chase, Md., 1987—, also chmn. bd. dirs.; political cons. Charlene Drew Jarvis, Washington, 1982—. Chair Statewide Health Coordinating Coun., Washington, 1984-85; mem. AIDS Task Force, Washington, 1985. Democrat. Home: 1325 13th St NW #50 Washington DC 20005 Office: The CDM Group Inc Ste 1660 5530 Wisconsin Ave Chevy Chase MD 20815

CASTRO-KLAREN, SARA, Latin American literature educator; b. Arequipa, Sabandia, Peru, June 9, 1942; d. José Andrés and Zoila Rosa (Rivas) Castro-Valdivia; m. Peter F. Klaren, Sept. 3, 1962; 1 child, Alexandra. BA, UCLA, 1962, MA, 1965, PhD, 1968. Asst. prof. Dartmouth Coll., No. Hampshire, N.H., 1970-84; chief Hispanic div. Lib. of Congress Fed. Govt., Washington, 1984-86; prof. Latin Am. lit. Johns Hopkins U., Balt., 1986—. Author: El Mundo Magico de J.M. Arquedas, Lima, 1973, Mario Vargas Llosa, Analisis Introductorio, Lima, 1988, Escritrua Sjueto y Transgresión, Mexico, 1989, Understanding Mario Vargas Llosa, U. S.C., 1990, Women's Writing in Latin America, Westview Press, 1991. Fellow Woodrow Wilson Ctr. for Scholars, Washington, 1977-78. Mem. MLA, Latin Am. Studies Assn., Ibero-americana, Soc. of Hispanists. Office: Johns Hopkins U Hispanic and Italian Study 34 Charles St Baltimore MD 21201-3707

CASTRONOVO, DAVID, English educator; b. Bklyn., Oct. 30, 1945; s. Anthony John and Doris Loretta (Oliver) C. BA, Bklyn. Coll., 1967; MA, Columbia U., 1968, PhD, 1975. Reader Columbia U., N.Y.C., 1969; adj. asst. prof. Bklyn. Coll., 1972-76; adj. asst. prof. Pace U., N.Y.C., 1976-79, asst. prof., 1979-86, assoc. prof., 1986-88, prof. English, 1988—; mem. adv. bd. Peter Lang Pub., Inc., N.Y.C. Author: Edmund Wilson, 1984 (N.Y. Times Notable Book 1985), Thornton Wilder, 1986, The English Gentleman, 1987, The American Gentleman, 1991; contbr. Colliers Ency., N.Y.C., 1977—, Ency. of World Lit. in the 20th Century, N.Y.C., 1980; reviewer: (jours.) America, Commoweal, N.Y.C., 1980s. Fellow Columbia U., 1967-71. Mem. PEN, MLA. Democrat. Roman Catholic. Home: 1619 3d Ave New York NY 10128

CASTURO, DON JAMES, banker; b. McKeesport, Pa., Nov. 9, 1942; s. Charles and Elizabeth B. (Barno) C.; B.A., Mich. State U., 1964; M.B.A., U. So. Calif., 1965; m. Judith K. Erkman, Aug. 22, 1964; children—Don J.E., Christian D.E. Participant mgmt. devel. program Mellon Bank, Pitts., 1966-67, investment researcher, 1967-69, asst. investment officer, 1969-71, investment officer, 1971-73, asst. v.p., 1973-82, v.p., 1982-88; mgr. Venture Capital Investments, 1989—; gen. ptnr. Point Venture Ptnrs.; Pitts. co-chmn. enrichment program Mich. State U.; bd. dirs. Upper St. Clair Athletic Assn. Mem. Pitts. Soc. Fin. Analysts (past pres., chmn. exec. com., dir.), Fin. Analysts Fedn. (chartered fin. analyst), Nat. Venture Capital Assn., Pitts. Venture Capital Assn. (founding mem.), Sigma Nu. Republican. Orthodox Catholic. Home: 2339 Morton Rd Pittsburgh PA 15241-3301 Office: Point Venture Ptnrs 2970 USX Tower Pittsburgh PA 15219

CASWELL, ROBERT STEARNS, public relations director; b. Damariscotta, Maine, July 24, 1952; s. Stearns Dana and Gloria (Naylor) C.; m. Diane Lapointe, Aug. 23, 1975; children: Aimee Elizabeth, Jenna Leigh. BA, U. So. Maine, Gorham, 1974. Reporter The Courier Gazette, Rockland, Maine, 1975-80; pub. relations staff mem. Univ. So. Maine, Portland, 1980-83; media & univ. relations dir. Univ. So. Maine, 1983—; pres. Maine Pub. Relations Coun., Portland, 1988-89; dir. Maine Press Assn., Orono, 1984—. Producer Maine Pub. Broadcasting Network, Portland, 1982—; mem. United Way Campaign Cabinet, Portland, 1991-92. Mem. Gorham C. of C. (pres. 1990-92). Office: U So Maine 96 Falmouth St Portland ME 04103-4899

CATACOSINOS, WILLIAM JAMES, utility company executive; b. N.Y.C., Apr. 12, 1930; s. James and Penelope (Paleologos) C.; m. Florence Maken, Oct. 16, 1955; children: William, James. BS, NYU, 1951, MBA, 1952, PhD, 1962. Asst. editor 20th Century-Fox, N.Y.C., 1951-52; asst. dir. bus. mgmt. and adminstrn. Brookhaven Nat. Lab., Upton, N.Y., 1956-69; pres. Applied Digital Data Systems, Inc., Hauppauge, N.Y., 1969-77; chmn. and chief exec. officer Applied Digital Data Systems, Inc., 1977-82; chmn., chief exec. officer L.I. Lighting Co., Hicksville, N.Y., 1984—, also bd. dirs., 1978—; adj. asst. prof. NYU, 1962-64; mgmt. counselor, 1962-69; chmn. bd. Corometrics Med., 1968-74; bd. dirs. Utilities Mut. Ins. Co., Ketema Inc.; mem. adv. com., policy com. on strategic planning, bd. dirs. Edison Electric Inst., 1990—. Bd. dirs. Brookhaven Town Indsl. Commn., 1956-77, Suffolk County chpt. Am. Cancer Soc., 1969-77, Stony Brook Found., 1978-85; trustee Poly. Inst. N.Y., 1981-85; nat. chmn. Am. Soc. Prevention of Cruelty to Children, 1981-83; With USN, 1952-56. Mem. Edison Electric Inst. (bd. dirs., mem. advt. com., policy com. on strategic planning, 1990—).

CATALANO, EDUARDO FERNANDO, architect; b. Buenos Aires, Dec. 1, 1917; came to U.S., 1951; s. Fernando and Maria Catalano; divorced; Alejandrina, Adrian. Architect diploma, U. Buenos Aires, 1936-40; MArch, U. Pa., 1944, Harvard U., 1945. Prof. U. N.C., Raleigh, 1951-56, MIT, Cambridge, Mass., 1951-77; prin. Eduardo Catalano Architects and Engrs., Inc., Cambridge, 1951—. Author: Structure of Warped Surfaces, 1962, Eduaurdo Catalono Buildings and Projects, 1976, Structure and Geometry, 1986; prin. works include Peace Garden Nat. Meml., Washington. Recipient 3 1st prizes Nat. Archtl. Competitions; fellow U.S. Dept. States, Brit. Council, Fulbright Commn. for Exchange Scholars. Home: 44 Grozier Rd Cambridge MA 02138-3315 Office: 300 Franklin St Cambridge MA 02139-3796*

CATALANO, LOUIS WILLIAM, JR., neurologist; b. Bklyn., Apr. 20, 1942; s. Louis William and Aileen (Bobb) C.; m. Kathleen Jamea Ferrari, Oct. 1, 1966; children: Louis W. III, Jamea E. BS cum laude, U. Pitts., 1963, MD, 1967. Diplomate Am. Bd. Neurology, Am. Bd. Electroencephalography, Am. Bd. Medical Examiners. Intern Presbyn.-St. Luke's Hosp., Chgo., 1967-68; rsch. assoc. NIH, Bethesda, Md., 1968-70; fellow neurology The Neurol. Inst., N.Y.C., 1970-73; clin. asst., prof. neurology U. Pitts. Sch. Med., 1973—; pvt. practice Greensburg, Pa., 1973—; staff Latrobe (Pa.) Area Hosp., 1973—, Westmoreland Hosp., Greensburg, 1973—, Torrance (Pa.) State Hosp., 1978—, Indiana (Pa.) Hosp., 1983—; cons. Jeannette (Pa.) Hosp., 1984—, Frick Community Health Ctr., Mt. Pleasant, Pa., 1991—; lectr. in field. Contbr. articles to profl. jours. With USPHS, 1968-70. Spl. fellow Columbia U., NIH, 1970-73, epilepsy minifellow, Bowman Gray Sch. Medicine, Winston-Salem, N.C., 1988. Fellow Royal Soc. Medicine, Am. Acad. Neurology; mem. AMA, Am. Med. Electroencephalographic Assn., Am. Soc. Neuroimaging, Am. Acad. Clin. Neurophysiology, Am. Sleep Disorders Assn., Pa. Med. Soc., Westmoreland County Med. Soc., Latrobe Acad. Medicine, Pittsburgh Neurosci. Soc., Sigma Xi, Alpha Omega Alpha. Office: Cen Med Arts RD 7 Old Rte 30 Greensburg PA 15601

CATALANO, PETER, financial executive; b. Bklyn., Oct. 11, 1961; s. Vito Anthony and Geraldine (Sinacore) C.; m. Carol Ann Catoggio, Feb. 17, 1991. BBA in Acctg., Adelphi U., 1983. CPA, N.Y. Staff acct. Lawson Holland CPA, Great Neck, N.Y., 1981-82; sr. acct. Alan J. Kreitzman, P.C., Commack, N.Y., 1982-86; sr. acct. BDO Seidman, N.Y.C., 1986-88, mgr., 1988-89; contr. Kohn Pedersen Fox Assocs., P.C., N.Y.C., 1989—. Mem. AICPA, N.Y. State Soc. CPAs. Roman Catholic. Office: Kohn Pedersen Fox Assocs PC 111 W 57th St New York NY 10019-2211

CATALANO, ROBERT ANTHONY, ophthalmologist, hospital administrator, writer; b. Albany, N.Y., Nov. 24, 1956; s. Anthony Joseph and Ida Santa (Muscolino) C.; m. Madeline Faye Kalmer, Aug. 6, 1978; children: Christopher, Ruth, Thomas, Matthew. BS, Union Coll., Schenectady, 1978; MD, U. Va., 1982; MBA, Rensselaer Poly. Inst., 1992. Resident in ophthalmology Albany Med. Coll., 1983-86, vice-chmn. dept. ophthalmology, 1989-90, acting chmn., 1990-91; fellow in pediatric ophthalmology Wills Eye Hosp., Phila., 1986-87; v.p. med. affairs Olean (N.Y.) Gen. Hosp., 1991—. Author: Atlas of Ocular Motility, 1989, Ocular Emergencies, 1992; contbr. articles to profl. jours. Recipient Nat. Found. award March of Dimes Found., 1978, Robert D. Reinecke award Albany Med. Coll., 1985, Shannon award U. Va., 1986; Heed Found. fellow, 1986. Fellow Am. Acad. Ophthalmology; mem. AMA, Asm. Assn. Pediatric Ophthalmology and Strabismus, N.Y. State Ophthalmol. Soc. (bd. dirs. 1990-92), Soc. Heed Fellows, Alpha Omega Alpha. Roman Catholic. Office: Olean Gen Hosp 515 Main St Olean NY 14760

CATALANO, VINCENT PATRICK, safety professional; b. Albany, N.Y., Mar. 17, 1935; s. Antonio and Rosa (Cambarie) C.; m. Ellen B. Flanagan, June 4, 1956 (div. 1972); children: Eileen R., Vincent P.; m. JoAnne Linda McCoy, Oct. 15, 1975; children: Jennifer L., Connie F., Anthony J. Grad. high sch., Albany. Laborer Niagara Mohawk Power Corp., Albany, 1953-58, electrician, 1958-68, chief maintenance, mechanic, 1968-72, dir. constrn./maint., 1972, dir. safety, 1978—; mem. NE Safety and Health Coun., Albany, 1988-91. Mem. safety com. Town of Colonie. With N.G. Army Res., 1952-63. Mem. Am. Soc. Safety Engrs., Am. Fedn. Musicians, AFL-CIO (bus. agt. local 14, 1978-80, v.p. 1983-85, pres. 1986-87), West Albany Neighborhood Assn., Am. Legion, KC. Roman Catholic. Home: 452 Albany Shaker Rd Albany NY 12211-1835 Office: Niagara Mohawk Power Corp Albany Steam Sta Glenmont NY 12077

CATALFO, ALFRED, JR. (ALFIO CATALFO), lawyer; b. Lawrence, Mass., Jan. 31, 1920; s. Alfio and Vincenza (Amato) C.; m. Caroline Joanne Mosca (dec. Apr. 1968); children: Alfred Thomas, Carol Joanne, Gina Marie; m. Gail Varney, 1988. BA, U. N.H., 1945, MA in History, 1952; LLB, Boston U., 1947, JD (hon.), 1969; postgrad., Suffolk U. Sch. Law, 1955-56, Am. Law Inst., N.Y.C., 1959. Bar: N.H. 1947, U.S. Dist. Ct. 1948, U.S. Ct. Appeals 1978, U.S. Supreme Ct. 1979. Pvt. practice Dover, N.H., 1948—; ptnr. Catalfo, McCarthy, Catalfo and Catalfo, Dover, 1980—; county atty. Strafford County, Dover, N.H., 1949-50, 55-56; mem. bd. immigration appeals U.S. Dept. Justice, 1953—; football coach Berwick Acad., South Berwick, Maine, 1944, Mission Catholic High Sch., Roxbury, Mass., 1945-46. Author: Laws of Divorces, Marriages, and Separations in New Hampshire, 1962, History of the Town of Rollinsford, 1623-1973, 1973. Pres. Young Dems. of Dover, 1953-55; 1st vice-chmn. Young Dems., N.H., 1954-56; mem. Strafford County Dem. Com., 1948-75; vice chmn. N.H. Dem. Com., 1954-56, 1st chmn., 1956-58, chmn. spl. activities, 1958-60; del. Dem. Nat. Conv., 1956, 60, 76; chmn. N.H. Dem. Conv., 1958, conv. dir., 1960; mem. Dem. stte exec. com., 1960-70; Dem. nominee for U.S. Senate, 1962; vice chmn. Dover Cath. Sch. Com., 1969-71; mem. Dover Bd. Adjustment, 1960-65. Served as pilot AC, lt. comdr. USNR, 1942-44. Recipient keys to cities of Dover, Somersworth, Concord, Berlin and Manchester, N.H., 5 nat. plaques DAV, 3 disting. svc. awards Am. Legion, Am. Legion Life Membership award, spl. recognition award Berwick Acad., 1985. Mem. ABA, N.H. Bar Assn., Strafford County Bar Assn. (v.p. 1966-67, pres. 1968-69), Assn. Trial Lawyers Am., N.Y. State Trial Lawyers Assn., Mass. Trial Lawyers Assn., N.H. Trial Lawyers Assn., Tex. Trial Lawyers Assn., Nat. Assn. Criminal Def. Lawyers, N.H. Assn. Criminal Def. Lawyers, Am. Judicature Soc., Phi Delta Phi, DAV (judge adv. N.H. dept. 1950-56, 57-68, 72—; comdr. chpt. 1953-54, comdr. N.H. 1956-57), Am. Legion (life, chmn. state conv. 1967, 77, 84), Navy League, N.H. Hist. Soc., Dover Hist. Soc., Rollinsford Hist. Soc. Clubs: Eagles (Somersworth, N.H.), Sons of Italy (Portsmouth, N.H.). Lodges: Lions, Elks, K.C. (grand knight 1975-77), Moose, Lebanese (Dover). Home: 20 Arch St Dover NH 03820-3602 Office: 450 Central Ave Dover NH 03820-3451

CATALFO, BETTY MARIE, health service executive, nutritionist; b. N.Y.C., Nov. 2, 1942; d. Lawrence Santo and Gemma (Patrone) Lorefice; children—Anthony, Lawrence, Donna Marie. Grad. Newtown High Sch., Elmhurst, N.Y., 1958. Sec., clk. ABC-TV, N.Y.C., 1957-60; lectr., nutritionist Weight Watchers, Manhasset, N.Y., 1976-75; founder, pres. Every-Bodys Diet, Inc. dba Stay Slim, Bronx, N.Y., 1976—; dir. in-home program N.Y. State Dept. Health, N.Y.C., 1985—; founder, pres. Delitegul Diet Foods, Inc., 1988—; lectr. in field. Author: 101 Stay-Slim Recipes, 1983, Get Slim and Stay Slim Diet Cook Book, rev. ed., 1987. Author, dir., producer: (video) Dancersize for Overweight, 1986, Get Slim and Stary Slim Diet Cook Book, Eating Right for Your Life, Hello It's Me and I'm Slim; author, editor: (video) Eating Right For Life, 1985, Isometric Techniques for Weight Reduction, Dance Your Calories A-Weigh; author, producer: (video) Eating Habits, 1986—, (video) Isometric Techniques for Weight Reduction, 1986, (video) Patience Is a Virtue When Weight Loss is the Goal, 1986; producer, dir.: (video) Positive and Negative Diet Forces, 1987, (video) Hello It's Me and I'm Thin, 1987, (video) Dance Your Calories A-Weigh, 1987, (video) Positive and Negative Diet Forces, 1987. Sponsor, lectr. St. Pauls Ctr., Bklyn., 1981—, Throgs Neck Assn. Retarded Children, Bronx, 1985—; active ARC, LWV, Am. Italian Assn., United Way Greenwich, Council Chs. and Synagogues, Heart Assn., N.Y. Meals on Wheels, 1985—, Health Assn. Fairfield County. Named Woman of Yr., Bayside Womens Club, N.Y., 1983, O, PK Woman of Yr., 1986—, Woman of Yr. Richmond Boys Club, 1987, Woman of Yr. Bronx Press Club Assn., 1987; recipient Merit award for Service Catholic Archdiocese of Bklyn., 1985, Community Service award Sr. Citizens Sacred Heart League Bklyn./Queens Archdiocese. N.Y. State Nutritional Guidance for Children Nat. Assn. Scis. Mem. Nat. C. of C. for Women (Woman of Yr. 1987, 90), Pres.'s Coun. on Nutrition, Roundtable for Women in Food Service, Bus. and Profl. Women's Club, Pres. Council for Phys. Fitness, Nat. Assn. Female Execs., Assn. for Fitness in Bus. Inc., Nat. Assn. Female Bus. Owners. Democrat. Roman Catholic. Club: Mothers Sacred Heart Sch. (chairperson 1979-82). Avocations: reading; travel, golf, family. Home: 20805 15th Rd Flushing NY 11360-1117 also: 58 Riverside Ave Greenwich CT 06878 also: 100-05 101st Ave Ozone Park NY

CATANDELLA, KENNETH F., dentist, nutritionist; b. Bridgeport, Conn., May 21, 1936; s. Joseph Francis and Constance Marie (Florentino) C.; children: Kenneth M., Melinda A., Jolynn M., Gregg C. BS in Biology, Fairfield U., 1957; DDS, Fairleigh Dickinson U., 1962; MS in Nutrition, U. Bridgeport, 1981. Chief dental sci., capt. Ft. Lee (Va.) Army Hosp., 1962-64; chmn. alumni assn. Fairfield (Conn.) U., 1968-69; instr. U. of Bridgeport, Conn., 1970; asst. clin. prof. Fairleigh Dickinson Dental Sch., Teaneck, N.J., 1970-90; peer rev. com. Bridgeport, 1985-89; chmn. health dept. Trumbull,

Conn., 1988-90; lectr. Cosmetic Dentistry Soc., 1980-91; cons. Trumbull Sr. Citizen Group. Contbr. articles to profl. jours. Named Fairfield U. Alumnus of Yr., U. of Bridgeport Disting. Alumnus. Fellow Acad. Gen. Dentistry; mem. Bridgeport Dental Assn., Conn. Dental Assn., Am. Dental Assn., Acad. Gen. Dentistry. Home and Office: 4746 Madison Ave Trumbull CT 06611

CATANIA, A(NTHONY) CHARLES, psychology educator; b. N.Y.C., June 22, 1936; s. Charles John and Elizabeth (Lattarulo) C.; m. Constance J. Britt, Feb. 10, 1962; children: William John, Kenneth Charles. BA in Psychology with highest honors, Columbia U., 1957, M.A., 1958; Ph.D. (NSF fellow), Harvard U., 1961. Postdoctoral research fellow Harvard U., 1961-62; sr. pharmacologist Smith, Kline & French Labs., Phila., 1962-64; asst. prof. NYU, 1964-66, asso. prof., 1966-69, prof., chmn. dept. psychology, 1969-73; prof. dept. psychology U. Md. Baltimore County, Catonsville, 1973—; mem. psychobiology com. NSF, 1982-85. Author: Learning, 1979, 2d edit., 1984, 3d edit., 1992; co-author: (with E. Shimoff and B.A. Matthews) Behavior on a Disk, 1989; editor: Contemporary Research in Operant Behavior, 1968; co-editor: (with T.A. Brigham) Handbook of Applied Behavior Analysis, 1978, (with S. Harnad) The Selection of Behavior: The Operant Behaviorism of B.F. Skinner, 1988; editor: Jour. Exptl. Analysis Behavior, 1966-69, rev. editor, 1969-76, 83-91; assoc. editor: Behavioral and Brain Scis., 1980—; mem. bd. editors various jours.; contbr. articles to profl. jours.; contbr. chpts. to textbooks. Fulbright sr. research fellow U. Coll. North Wales, Bangor, 1986-87; recipient James McKeen Cattell Sabbatical award, 1986-87; grantee NSF, 1965-67, 74-79, 82-88, USPHS, 1967-73, 79-83. Mem. Assn. Behavioral Analysis (pres. 1982-83), Eastern Psychol. Assn. (dir. 1979-82), Soc. Exptl. Analysis of Behavior (pres. 1966-67, 81-83), Phi Beta Kappa. Home: 10545 Rivulet Row Columbia MD 21044-2420 Office: U Md Balt County Dept Psychology 5401 Wilkens Ave Baltimore MD 21228-5398

CATANIA, VITO CHARLES, newspaper publishing executive; b. Bronx, N.Y., Dec. 20, 1951; s. Sebastian Charles and Laura (Cuomo) C.; m. Christine L. Altman; 1 child, Joseph. BA in Math., Fordham Coll., 1973; MBA in Fin., Fordham U. Grad. Sch. Bus. Adm, 1977. Circulation acct. N.Y. Daily News, N.Y.C., 1974-75, market analyst, 1975-77, asst. to prodn. mgr., 1977-79, asst. to dir. ops., 1979-82, adminstrv. mgr. prodn., 1982-86, mgr. prodn. planning & adm., 1986-89; bus. mgr. N.Y. Post, N.Y.C., 1989—. Office: NY Post New York NY 10002

CATELL, ROBERT BARRY, gas utility executive; b. Bklyn., Feb. 1, 1937; s. Joseph Daniel and Belle (Mishkind) Cicatelli; m. Joan Katherine Weigand, June 25, 1971; children—Laura Ann, Erica Ann; children by previous marriage—Robert Edward, Carla Ann, Donna Theresa;. B.M.E., CCNY, 1958, M.M.E., 1964. Registered profl. engr. Asst. v.p. Bklyn. Union Gas Co., 1974-78, v.p., 1978-82, sr. v.p., 1982-84, exec. v.p., 1984-86, exec. v.p., chief operating officer, 1986-90, pres., chief operating officer, 1990-91, pres., chief exec. officer, 1991—; trustee Independence Savs. Bank, Bklyn., 1984—, Inst. of Gas Tech., 1986, Gasresearch Inst., 1992—; mem. adv. com. CCNY, 1986—; regional adv. com. Chem. Bank. Bd. dirs. Bklyn. Bur. Comml. Svc., 1988, Bklyn. Botanic Garden, 1989; mem. N.Y. Serda Bd., N.Y.C. Partnership, N.Y. State Bus. Coun.; chmn. N.Y. Gas Group, Gas Rsch. Inst. Mem. Am. Gas Assn., Soc. Gas Lighting. Office: Bklyn Union Gas Co One Metrotech Ctr Brooklyn NY 11201-3684

CATES, DALTON REEDE, international marketing manager, quality management consultant; b. Durham, N.C., July 10, 1933; s. Jesse Phillip and Clair Florine (Sorrell) C.; m. Joan Gery, Dec. 23, 1956; children: Mark Reede, Carol Lynn, Jesse Phillip. BS in Elec. Engring., Duke U., 1958; postgrad., N.C. State U., 1972, Internat. Inst. Mgmt. Devel., Geneva, Switzerland, 1979. Engr. Fla. Power & Light Co., Miami, 1958-63; quality control supr. Corning Electronics, Raleigh, N.C., 1963-72; telecommunications mktg. mgr. Corning (N.Y.) Electronics, 1972-74, product mktg. mgr., 1974-76, mktg. svcs. mgr., 1976-79, internat. bus. devel. mgr., 1979-88; mgr. total quality Corning Sci., 1988-89, mgr. internat. sales, 1989-90; mgr. quality systems Corning Quality Systems, 1990—; bd. dirs. Universal Scientific Instruments, Taichung, Taiwan, 1986-88; mem. Corp. Quality Coun., Corning, 1988-91; chmn. Quality Milestone Confs., Corning, 1988-91; cons. Legis. Commn. Sci. and Tech., Albany, N.Y., 1991. Pres. Corning Community Found., 1985-91; chmn. Osuka Japan Sister Cities, Corning, 1990-91; pres. United Way of Southeastern Steuben County, Corning, 1978-80. Maj. USAFR, 1955-56. Fellow Rotary Club (Paul Harris award 1990); mem. Hist. Soc. Republican. Baptist. Home: 7 Sage St Corning NY 14830-3736

CATEURA, LINDA BRANDI, writer; b. New Haven; d. Albert and Alice (Capobianco) Brandi; m. Henry Joseph Cateura; 1 child, Patricia. BA, Albertus Magnus Coll., New Haven, 1944. Assoc. lit. editor Harper's Bazaar Mag., N.Y.C., 1949-57; assoc. editor Woman's Day Mag., N.Y.C., 1957-60, Family Circle Mag., N.Y.C., 1961-63; free lance book reviewer N.Y. Times, Sat. Rev., N.Y.C., 1957-61; adminstrv. aide State Sen. William Giordano, N.Y.C., 1969-73; press aide N.Y. Sec. of State, N.Y.C., 1977-79; pub. info. officer Dept. State, State of N.Y., N.Y.C., 1979-82. Author: Oil Painting Secrets from a Master, 1984, Growing Up Italian, 1987, Catholics U.S.A., 1989 (books). Mem. Oral History Assn., The Nature Conservancy. Democrat. Roman Catholic. Home: 136 Willow St Brooklyn NY 11201-2202

CATEY, ERIC BRIAN, software engineer; b. Topeka, Mar. 18, 1962; s. David Leroy and Marylyn Shirley (Callahan) C.; m. Catherine Ellen Massias, Aug. 25, 1985. BS in Maths., U. Conn., 1985; postgrad., U. New Haven, 1990—. Software/test engr. Norden Systems, Norwalk, Conn., 1985-90; sr. software engr. Nielsen-Monitor Plus, Wilton, Conn., 1990—. Mem. IEEE Computer Soc., Medieval Acad. Am. Home: PO Box 5020 Brookfield CT 06804-5020 Office: Nielsen-Monitor Plus 187 Danbury Rd Wilton CT 06897-4003

CATHEY, MARY ELLEN JACKSON, religious educator; b. Florence, S.C., Jan. 12, 1926; d. John William and Mary Ellen (Heinrich) Jackson; m. Henry Marcellus Cathey, May 31, 1958; children: Mary Emily Cathey Ewell, Henry Marcellus Jr. AB, Winthrop Coll., 1947; MRE, Presbyn. Sch. Christian Edn., Richmond, Va., 1953. Cert. Christian educator. Tchr. English, drama Jenkins Jr. High Sch., Spartanburg, S.C., 1947-51; dir. Christian edn. First Presbyn. Ch., Anderson, S.C., 1953-56, Bethesda (Md.) Presbyn. Ch., 1956-59; organizer, dir. Co-op Nursery Sch., Bethesda Presbyn. Ch., 1967-70; dir. Christian edn. Potomac Presbyn. Ch., Potomac, Md., 1977-83, Bethesda Presbyn. Ch., 1983-85, Nat. Presbyn. Ch., Washington, 1985-88; freelance cons. and educator Nat. Capital Presbytery, Washington, 1988—; edn. cons. Covenant Presbyn. Ch., Arlington, Va., 1987, First Presbyn. Ch., Arlington, 1989-91, Lewinsville Presbyn. Ch., McLean, 1990; elder Nat. Presbyn. Ch., 1990—; elder commr. Gen. Assy., Presbyn. Ch., Milw., 1992. Author hymn text: God Almighty, God Eternal, 1956, others, numerous poems; co-author: Confirmation Guidebook, 1988, The Circle of Wholeness, 1991. Active in past various civic orgns. Recipient Sparkler Award Presbyn. Sch. of Christian Edn. Alumni/ae Coun., 1991. Mem. Hymn Soc., Presbyn. Writers' Guild, Presbyn. Assn. Musicians, Assn. Presbyn. Ch. Educators, Nat. Capital Presbytery Educators. Home and Office: 1817 Bart Dr Silver Spring MD 20905

CATO, ROBERT GEORGE, financial company manager; b. Portland, Oreg., Mar. 30, 1933; s. Archie Barnes and Etta Marie (Yager) C.; BA, U. Portland, 1954; postgrad. Portland State Coll., 1959-60, U. Portland, 1959-60, Johns Hopkins U., 1983; m. Nancy Louise Foord, Sept. 18, 1954; children: Cheryl, Sandra, Sharon. With Eastman Kodak Co., Portland, 1950-55; field rep. Gen. Motors Acceptance Corp., Portland, 1957-62, credit rep., Boise, Idaho, 1962-65, dist. rep., The Dalles, Oreg., 1965-66, credit supr., Seattle, 1966-69, credit mgr., 1969-72, sales mgr., 1972-74, staff asst., N.Y.C., 1974-77, asst. br. mgr., Norfolk, Va., 1977-79, Balt., 1979-85, control br. manager, Buffalo, 1985-86, Pitts., 1986-89, Mpls., 1989-92, ret., 1992. Served with U.S. Army, 1955-57. Mem. Mendakota Country Club, Lost Spur Country Club, Elks, Masons, Shriners. Republican. Home: 1902 South Ln Mendota Heights MN 55118 Office: 3600 West 80th St Ste 300 Minneapolis MN 55431

CATT, STEPHEN RICHARD, college administrator, consultant, educator; b. Butler, Pa., July 17, 1955; s. Richard Walter and H. Joyce (Curry) C.; m. Robin Jean McFate, Jan. 19, 1985. AA in Gen. Studies magna cum laude, Butler County Community Coll., 1975; BA in Edn. with honors, Mich. State U., 1977; MS in Human Resource Mgmt., La Roche Coll., 1985. Tchr. Butler Area Sch. Dist., 1977-78; with Servistar Corp., East Butler, Pa., 1978-86; dir. student activities Butler County Community Coll., 1986—; freelance organizational change cons., Butler, 1984—; instr. in mgmt. Butler County Community Coll., 1985—; pres., videographer Proven Image, Inc., Butler, 1985—. Author: (booklet) Student Living in Butler, 1990. Representative Commn. on the Status & Role of Women in the United Meth. Ch., Chgo., 1984-88; mem. Animal Friends of Butler County, 1987-91; pres. bd. dirs. Transitional Living, Inc., Butler, 1988-90. Mem. ASTD, Nat. Coun. on Student Devel., Pa. Coll. Pers. Assn. (exec. bd. 1989-91, New Profl. of the Yr. 1991), Mus. Theatre Guild of Butler. Democrat. Office: Butler County Community Coll College Dr Oak Hills Butler PA 16003-1203

CATTANI, RICHARD J., newspaper editor; b. Detroit, June 17, 1936; s. Primo and Emma (Ries) C.; m. Jacqueline P. Hunter, Jan. 23, 1960; children: Jeremy, Ruth, Gabriel. BA, Harvard U., 1958, MA, 1959. Editor Christian Sci. Monitor, Boston; bd. dirs. Roper Ctr., U. Conn., Storrs, 1987—. Home: 25 Granite St Wellesley MA 02181-4606 Office: Christian Sci Monitor 1 Norway St Boston MA 02115-3122*

CATTERSON, JAMES MICHAEL, lawyer; b. Jamaica, N.Y., Dec. 19, 1958; s. James Maxwell and Lola Fae (Hartwig) C. BA, Colgate U., 1980; JD, St. John's U., Jamaica, N.Y., 1985. Bar: N.Y., U.S. Dist. Ct. (ea. and so. dist.) N.Y., U.S. Ct. Appeals (2nd cir.). Legis. asst. U.S. Sen. Alfonse D'Amato, Washington, 1980-82; asst. county atty. Suffolk County Atty., Hauppauge, N.Y., 1985-87; asst. U.S. atty., chief asset forfeiture unit U.S. Atty., Ea. Dist., Bklyn., 1987—; legal writing instr. Cardozo Law Sch., N.Y.C., 1990; instr. U.S. Dept. Justice, Washington, 1988—. Campaign coord. Campaign 80, Reagan for Pres., Suffolk County, 1980. Mem. Civil War Round Table. Republican. Roman Catholic. Office: US Atty EDNY 1 Pierrepont 11th Plz # F Brooklyn NY 11201-2776

CAULFIELD, THOMAS JAMES, educational counseling educator; b. Buffalo, Mar. 14, 1932; s. Thomas Fabian and Lillian Frances (Coyle) C.; m. Camille Therasa Massaro, Aug. 27, 1957; children: Rena, Jennifer. BS, Canisius Coll., 1954, MS, 1962; EdD, SUNY, Buffalo, 1969. Firefighter City of Buffalo, 1954-55; tchr. English Buffalo Pub. Schs., 1960-65; sch. counselor Hamburg (N.Y.) Cen. Schs., 1965-68; prof. counseling Canisius Coll., Buffalo, 1969—. Contbr. articles to profl. jours. Capt. USN, 1960-65, USNR, 1955-79. Mem. N.Y. State Assn. Counseling and Devel., N.Y. State Assn. Counselor Educators and Suprs. (pres. 1989-91, Disting. Profl. Svcs. award 1988), Western N.Y. Assn. Counseling and Devel. (pres. 1972-73), Assn. Counseling Educators and Suprs., Nat. Acad. Cert. Clin. Mental Health Counselors. Roman Catholic. Office: Canisius Coll 2001 Main St Buffalo NY 14208-1098

CAUM, SARA JANE, counselor; b. Pitts., Sept. 9, 1928; d. Wallace Blair and Charlotte Anna (May) C. AB, Syracuse (N.Y.) U., 1950; MEd, Pa. State U., 1963. Lic. counselor, Pa. Tchr. Harrisburg (Pa.) Sch. Dist., 1951-63; counselor P. McCaskey High Sch., Lancaster, Pa., 1963-70, Cen. Dauphin High Sch., Harrisburg, 1970—. Chair com. Derry St. United Meth. Ch., Harrisburg, 1989-91. Mem. Am. Sch. Counselors Assn., Pa. Sch. Counselors Assn. (exec. com. constn. and by-laws, Recognition award 1967), Pa. Assn. Coll. Admissions Counselors (Recognition award 1989), Keystone Counseling Assn. (pres. 1967).

CAVADA, ABBY See HERNANDEZ, ABISAIL

CAVALCONTE, CHARLES C(ARMINE), management educator, consultant, engineer; b. N.Y.C., July 16, 1917; s. Rocco and Carmela (Potenza) C.; m. Margaret Flaherty; children: Charles C. Jr., John J. BEE, Manhattan Coll., 1939; BPh, Cath. U. Am., 1945; MPh, Fordham U., 1956; MS in Applied Sci., Adelphi U., 1961; PhD, St. John's U., 1971. Registered profl. engr., N.Y. Asst. profl. engr. Manhattan Coll., N.Y.C., 1949-55; R & D engr. Rep. Aviation Corp., Farmingdale, N.Y., 1955-65; prof. mgmt., emeritus C.W. Post Coll./L.I. U., Greenvale, N.Y., 1965-87; tech. cons. S.B. Bowne & Son Cons. Engr., Mineola, N.Y., 1965-78. Inventor plasma switch. Commr. Mineola Village Planning Commn., 1976-80, Mineola Village Zoning Commn., 1982—. Fulbright fellow, 1968; recipient Svc. award N.Y. State Air Force Assn., 1982. Mem. N.Y. Soc. Profl. Engrs., Alpha Phi Delta.

CAVALET, JAMES ROGER, engineering executive, consultant; b. Dean, Pa., Jan. 5, 1942; s. Irvin Gordon and Elizabeth Ann (Nevling) C.; m. Margaret Joan Burkey, June 17, 1961; children: Peggy Ann, James Jr., Beth Ann, Deborah. Assoc. Mech. Engring., Pa. State U., 1964; MCE, U. Pitts., 1981. Registered profl. engr., Pa., Ohio, W.Va., Minn., La., Tex., Va., WIs., Ala., N.J. Chief engr. Acme Design Co., Pitts., 1966-67; asst. mgr. civil engring. Auburn Engring., Inc., Pitts., 1967-69; asst. chief civil engr. Dravo Corp., Pitts., 1969-76; chief engr. Emp Projetos div. Dravo Corp., Belo Horizonte, Brazil, 1976-77; asst. chief facility engring. Dravo Corp., Pitts., 1977-80, chief design engr., 1980-82; div. mgr. Sci. Applications Internat., San Diego, 1982-88; v.p., gen. mgr. SEI Engrs. & Cons., Inc., Pitts., 1988-90, pres., 1990—; bd. dirs. SEI Engrs. & Cons., Inc. Contbr. articles to profl. jours. Mem. ASCE, Soc. Mining Engrs., Nat. Assn. Investment Clubs, Nat. Rifle Assn. Home: 1438 Swede Hill Rd Greensburg PA 15601-4748 Office: SEI Engrs & Cons Inc 300 6th Ave Pittsburgh PA 15222-2511

CAVALIERI, DONALD JOSEPH, physical scientist; b. N.Y.C., May 5, 1942; s. Emil Elias and Marie Catherine (DeClemente) C.; m. Letitia Alice Harrington, June 19, 1970; 1 child, Letitia-Marie. BS, CCNY, 1964; MA, CUNY, 1967; PhD, NYU, 1974. Instr. physics Queens Coll., CUNY, 1965-66; physicist U.S. Naval Applied Sci. Lab., N.Y.C., 1966-67; asst. prof. SUNY, Farmingdale, N.Y., 1967-70, Drexel U., Phila., 1976-77; postdoctoral resident assoc. NRC, Washington, 1974-76; staff scientist Systems and Applied Scis. Corp., Riverdale, Md., 1977-79; phys. scientist NASA Goddard Space Flight Ctr., Greenbelt, Md., 1979—. Mem. Am. Meteorol. Soc., Am. Geophys. Union, Internat. Glaciological Soc. Office: NASA Goddard Space Flight Ctr Code 971 Greenbelt MD 20771

CAVALLON, BETTY GABLER, interior designer; b. Waverly, N.Y., July 17, 1918; d. Wallace Frederick and Harriet (Heaton) Gabler; grad. Parisien Sch. Design, Detroit, 1939; m. Michel Francis Cavallon, Dec. 26, 1946 (dec. 1981); children: Claire, Carol (dec.); stepchildren: Michel, Mary; m. John W. Crist, Nov. 20, 1982. Lic. interior designer, Conn. Fabric coordinator Montgomery Ward, 1940-46; interior designer Betty Cavallon Interiors Ltd., Stamford, Conn., 1946—. Mem. Am. Soc. Interior Designers (corp.). Republican. Episcopalian. Home and Office: 69 Riverside Ave Stamford CT 06905-4413

CAVANAGH, CARROLL JOHN, business advisor, lawyer; b. N.Y.C., Nov. 11, 1943; s. Carroll and Mona (Schmid) C.; m. Valerie Ives Mixter (div.); children: Dorothy, Carroll III; m. Candida N. Smith, June 22, 1991. BA, Yale U., 1964; JD cum laude, U. Pa., 1970; cert., Hague (The Netherlands) Acad. Internat. Law, 1969. Bar: D.C. 1979, Conn. 1970, N.Y. 1970. Assoc. Sullivan & Cromwell, N.Y.C., 1970-79; sec., gen. counsel Nat. Gallery of Art, Washington, 1979-85, mem. trustee's coun., 1984—; prin. asst. Paul Mellon, Upperville, Va., 1985—; bd. dirs. Mellon Bank Corp. Lt. USNR, 1964-71. Clubs: Metropolitan (Washington), Union (N.Y.C.). Home: 1058 Leigh Mill Rd Great Falls VA 22066 Office: Rokeby Farms 1729 H St NW Fl 4 Washington DC 20006-3904

CAVANAGH, PAUL GUERARD, veterinarian; b. San Francisco, Feb. 21, 1948; s. Paul Thomas Cavanagh and Dorothy Patricia Lenus Erickson; m. Linda Bennett (div. 1975); m. Irena Cavanagh, Jan. 28, 1978; 1 child, Kaja. AA, N.Mex. Mil. Inst., 1968; BS, DVM, U. Minn., 1973. Diplomate Am. Coll. Vet. Internal Medicine. Intern Animal Med. Ctr., N.Y.C., 1973-74, med. resident, 1974-76, assoc. staff, 1976-78; staff Rondout Valley Animal Hosp., S.I., N.Y., 1978-81, Park East Animal Hosp., N.Y.C., 1981-84; co-owner, staff veterinarian Westside Vet. Ctr., N.Y.C., 1985—. Contbr. articles to profl. jours., chpts. to books. Mem. Am. Vet. Med. Assn., Am. Animal Hosp. Assn., Acad. Vet. Dentistry, Am. Coll. Vet. Internal Medicine (dir. 1983), N.Y.C. Vet. Assn. Republican. Roman Catholic. Office: Westside Vet Ctr 220 W 83d St New York NY 10024

CAVANAGH, RICHARD EDWARD, academic administrator, consultant, writer; b. Buffalo, June 15, 1946; s. Joseph John and Mary Celeste (Stack) C. BA, Wesleyan U., Middletown, Conn., 1968; MBA, Harvard U., 1970. Assoc. McKinsey & Co. Inc., Washington, 1970-77, sr. cons., 1979, ptnr., 1980-87; exec. dir. fed. cash mgmt. U.S. Office Mgmt. and Budget, Washington, 1977-79; exec. dean Kennedy Sch. Govt. Harvard U., Cambridge, Mass., 1987—; mem. staff Carter-Mondale Policy Planning, 1976; cons. Carter-Mondale Presdl. Transition, 1976-77; domestic coord. Pres.' Reorgn. Project, The White House, Washington, 1978-79; mem. exec. com. Pres.' Pvt. Sector Survey on Cost Control, Grace Commn., 1982-83; mem. bus. adv. com. advanced study program Brookings Instn., 1983-86; adviser to nat. govts., EEC, N.Y.C. Partnership, Am. Bus. Conf. Co-author: (with Donald K. Clifford Jr.) The Winning Performance: How America's High-Growth Midsize Companies Succeed, 1985, 2d edit., 1988 (pub. in 11 fgn. langs.); contbr. articles to Wall Street Jour., Mgmt. Rev., Fin. World, Planning Rev., N.Y. Times. Mem. bd. judges Dively Award, Harvard U., 1984—; mem. bd. visitors Georgetown U. Sch. Bus., 1985—; trustee Ctr. for Excellence in Govt., 1985, Wesleyan U., 1989—. With U.S. Army, 1968. Recipient Presdl. commendation, 1979, 80, 83; John Reilly Knox fellow, 1979, Clark fellow, 1979. Mem. Am. Soc. Pub. Adminstrn., Acad. Polit. Sci., Raimond Duy Baird Assn., Wesleyan U. Alumni Assn. (chmn. 1985-87), Harvard Club (N.Y.C.), Beta Theta Pi. Democrat. Roman Catholic. Home: 2 Ware St Cambridge MA 02138-4022 Office: Harvard U John F Kennedy Sch Govt 79 John F Kennedy St Cambridge MA 02138

CAVANAGH, RONALD JEROME, physician, consultant; b. N.Y.C., Jan. 28, 1940; s. Edward Jerome and Theresa Mary C.; m. Linda Junia, Mar. 30, 1964; children: Patrick, Michael, Marie, Thomas. BA, St. John's U., 1961; MD, N.Y. Med. Coll., 1965; MPH, Boston U., 1987. Diplomate Am. Bd. Psychiatry and Neurology. Rotating intern, resident in psychiatry Nat. Naval Med. Ctr., Bethesda, Md., 1965-69; chief, psychiatry Naval Regional Med. Ctr., Newport, R.I., 1970-72; pvt. practice Med. Ctr., Tiverton, R.I., 1973-91; cons. psychiatryst to underserviced rural health populations, 1991—; spl. fellow in community psychiatry Boston U., 1980-81; teaching cons. Dr. John Corrigan Ctr., Fall River, Mass.; psychiat. cons. Edgehill, Newport, 1987-91; mem. clin. faculty Brown U., Providence, 1973-85; dir. Bridge of Hope, Inc., health cons. to communities in developing countries. With USN, 1969-72. Mem. AMA, Am. Psychiat. Assn., Am. Pub. Health Assn., Nat. Coun. for Internat. Health, Am. Acad. Psychosomatic Medicine, Am. Soc. Addiction Medicine, Am. Soc. Tropical Medicine and Hygiene. Home: Penny Pond Winnisimet Farm Tiverton RI 02878 Office: Med Ctr 1334 Main Rd Tiverton RI 02878-4420

CAVANAGH, THOMAS EDGAR, political scientist, researcher, educator; b. Glen Ridge, N.J., Nov. 26, 1953; s. Robert Terrance and Ethel Adelle (Ball) C.; m. Shirley Ann Bickoff, Aug. 16, 1991. BA, Yale U., 1975, MPhil, 1978. Rsch. analyst Peter D. Hart Rsch. Assocs., Washington, 1976; asst. survey rsch. dir. Commn. on Adminstrv. Rev., U.S. Ho. of Reps., Washington, 1977; vis. lectr. polit. sci. dept. Trinity Coll., Hartford, Conn., 1979-80; vis. instr. govt. dept. Wesleyan U., Middletown, Conn., 1980-81; guest scholar Brookings Instn., Washington, 1981-82; rsch. assoc., sr. rsch. assoc. Joint Ctr. for Polit. Studies, Washington, 1982-84, 84-85; sr. rsch. assoc. Com. on Status of Black Ams., NRC, Washington, 1985-88; dir. Ctr. for the Study of Am. Govt., Johns Hopkins U., Balt., 1988-91; lectr. polit. sci. dept. Yale U., New Haven, 1991—. Author: Inside Black America, 1985, (with others) A Common Destiny, 1989; editor: Race and Political Strategy, 1983, Strategies for Black Voter Mobilization, 1987;. Danforth grad. fellow Danforth Found., 1978. Mem. Am. Polit. Sci. Assn., Midwest Polit. Sci. Assn. Democrat. Presbyterian. Home: 3230 Whitney Ave # 803 Hamden CT 06518 Office: Yale U Polit Sci Dept New Haven CT 06520

CAVANAUGH, JOHN RICHARD, English educator, priest; b. Rochester, N.Y., June 10, 1929; s. William and Helen Louise (Kavanaugh) C. BA, U. Western Ont., London, Can., 1952; STB, U. St. Michael's, Toronto, Ont., Can., 1955; MA, U. Toronto, 1956; PhD, St. Louis U., 1969. Joined Congregation of St. Basil, Roman Cath. Ch., 1946, ordained priest, 1955. Instr. English, St. John Fisher Coll., Rochester, 1956-59, asst. prof., 1962-64, assoc. prof., 1965-69, prof., 1970—, chmn. dept., 1964-69, 72-80, trustee, 1986—. Trustee emeritus Aquinas Inst., Rochester; bd. dirs. Friends Rochester Pub. Libr., 1983-88, Sister City Com. Waterford and Rochester, 1986—; chmn. Rochester chpt. Irish Am. Cultural Inst., 1989—. Mem. MLA, Renaissance Soc. Am., Am. Conf. for Irish Studies, Delta Epsilon Sigma. Democrat. Home: 3497 East Ave Rochester NY 14618-3577 Office: St John Fisher Coll 3690 East Ave Rochester NY 14618-3597

CAVANAUGH, MAXINE CORNELL, clinical psychologist; b. Phila., Mar. 18, 1931; d. David and Jeanette (Willensky) Cornell; m. David K. Cavanaugh, Feb. 8, 1953; children: David Charles, Carolyn Jeanne Claire. BS, Pa. State U., 1952, MS, 1953; PhD, U. Buffalo, 1958. Lic. psychologist N.Y. Intake supr. U. Buffalo Psychiat. Clinic, 1958; part-time staff psychologist Buffalo Psychiat. Ctr., 1958; chief psychologist Psychiat. Clinic, Jewish Family Svc., Buffalo, 1958-61; pvt. practice Tonawanda, N.Y., 1961—; cons. Office of Vocat. Rehab., Buffalo and Albny, 1972-85; instr. U. Buffalo, 1958-67; panelist TV show AM-Buffalo, 1979—. Mem. APA, Psychol. Assn. Western N.Y. (chmn. ethics com. 1982—, Disting. Achievement in Psychology award 1989). Home and Office: 161 Sweetbriar Rd Tonawanda NY 14150-7511

CAVANAUGH, PAUL FRANCIS, JR., biochemical pharmacologist; b. Rochester, N.Y., Oct. 23, 1955; s. Paul Francis and Ann Marie Cavanaugh; m. Kathleen Anne Vastola, Apr. 9, 1983; children: Anthony, Samuel. BS in Chemistry, Boston Coll., 1977; PhD in Biochem. Pharmacology, SUNY, Buffalo, 1983. Cancer rsch. scientist Roswell Park Meml. Inst., Buffalo, 1982-86; sr. rsch. investigator Eastman Kodak Co./Sterling Winthrop Inc., Malvern, Pa., 1986-92; Health Care Div., Proctor and Gamble Co., Cin., 1992—. Mem. Am. Assn. Cancer Rsch., Am. Chem. Soc., N.Y. Acad. Sci., Rho Chi. Office: Procter & Gamble Health Care Divsn 11511 Reed Hartman Hwy Cincinnati OH 45241-1369

CAVAZOS, LAURO FRED, former U.S. secretary of education, former university president; b. King Ranch, Tex., Jan. 4, 1927; s. Lauro Fred and Tomasa (Quintanilla) C.; m. Peggy Ann Murdock, Dec. 28, 1954; children: Lauro III, Sarita, Ricardo, Alicia, Victoria, Roberto, Rachel, Veronica, Tomas, Daniel. B.A., Tex. Tech U., 1949, M.A., 1951; Ph.D., Iowa State U., 1954. Teaching asst. Tex. Tech U., Lubbock, 1949-51, pres. health scis. ctr., 1980-88, prof. biol. sci., 1980-88, prof. anatomy Health Scis. Ctr., 1980-88; instr. anatomy Med. Coll. Va., 1954-56, asst. prof. anatomy, 1956-60, assoc. prof., 1960-64; prof. anatomy Tufts U. Sch. Medicine, Boston, 1964-80, chmn. dept., 1964-72, assoc. dean, 1972-73, acting dean, 1973-75, dean, 1975-80; spl. and sci. staff New Eng. Med. Ctr. Hosp., Boston, 1974-80; sec. U.S. Dept. Edn., Washington, 1988-90; fellows program adv. com. Nat. Bd. Med. Examiners, 1978; project site vis. Nat. Libr. of Medicine, 1978-80, mem. biomed. libr. rev. com., 1981-85; cons. coun. med. edn., Tex. Med. Assn., 1980-87; active Pan Am. Health Orgn.; bd. regents Uniformed Svcs. U. Health Scis., 1980-85; bd. dirs. Diamond R&M Inc. Mem. editorial bds. Anat. Record, 1970-73, Med. Coll. Va. Quar., 1964—, Tufts Health Sci. Rev., 1972-80, Jour. Med. Edn., 1980-85; contbr. articles to profl. jours., chpts. to books. Bd. dirs. campaign chmn. Tex. Tech U. United Way, 1980-88; mem. Tex. Gov.'s Task Force on Higher Edn., 1980-82; mem. Tex. Gov.'s Higher Edn. Mgmt. Effectiveness Coun., 1980-81, chmn., 1981-82; trustee S.W. Rsch. Inst.; chmn. Lubbock Boy Scoouts Am. Campaign, 1981, S.W. Athletic Conf. Coun. Pres., 1987-88. Served with U.S. Army, 1945-46. Named Disting. Alumnus Tex. Tech U., 1977; recipient edn. and teaching awards from graduating med. class, 5 yrs., Alumni Achievement award Iowa State U., 1979, Lauro F. Cavazos award Tex. Tech U., 1987, LULAC Nat. Hispanic Leadership award, 1988, medal of Merit Pan Am U., 1988, pres. medal A for Disting. Achievement CCNY, 1989, medal of Honor U. Calif., 1989, Midby-Byron Disting. Leader award U. Nev., 1989; named to Hispanic Hall of Fame League of United Latin Am. Citizens Hispanic Bus. Mag.,1987. Mem. AAAS, Am. Assn. Anatomists, Endocrine Soc., Histochem. Soc., Assn. Am. Med. Colls., Pan Am. Assn. Anatomy (founding, councilor from U.S., rep. Am. Assn. Anatomy 1974), Philos. Soc. Tex., Tex.

Sci. and Tech. Coun. (chmn. edn. com. 1984-85), Lubbock C. of C. (bd. dirs. 1980-88), Tufts Med. Alumni Assn. (hon. 1976), Sigma Xi. Roman Catholic. Office: 173 Annursnac Hill Rd Concord MA 01742

CAVENDER, PATRICIA LEE, chemist; b. Warren, Ohio, Sept. 26, 1950; d. Grant Lee and Phyllis Ruth (Lowrie) C.; m. Lawrence K. White, Jan. 8, 1977; children: Katherine, Andrew, Daniel. BS, Allegheny Coll., 1972; PhD, U. Ill., 1977. Rsch. chemist Schering Plough, Bloomfield, N.J., 1977-79; rsch. chemist FMC Corp., Inc., Princeton, N.J., 1980-89, sr. rsch. chemist, 1989—.

CAVICCHI, LESLIE SCOTT, health facility administrator; b. Plymouth, Mass., May 22, 1954; s. Alphonso John Jr. and Mary Louise (Brookings) C.; m. Christine Anne Lafayette, Apr. 9, 1977; children: Douglas Clifton Cushing, Jarrod Scott. BS, Stonehill Coll., 1976; MPA, Suffolk U., 1988. Lic. nursing home administrator, Mass. Respiratory therapist Mass., 1976-77; supr. South Shore Hosp., Weymouth, Mass., 1978; mgr. Brockton (Mass.) Hosp., 1978-83, dir. purchasing, 1984; dir. Start program Lakeville (Mass.) Hosp., 1984-86, assoc. dir., 1986-89; sr. mgr. Health Care Svcs. of N.E., Braintree, Mass., 1989-91; material adminstr. HMO Blue Cross/Blue Shield, Framingham, 1991—; cons., distbr. Success Motivation Inst., Waco, Tex., 1987-90. Contbr. articles to profl. jours. Mem. exec. bd. Am. Cancer Soc., 1984—, chmn. pub. issues com., 1992, Mass. unit pres., 1986-88. Mem. Hosp. Purchase Assn. Mass., Health Care Material Mgmt. Soc. (pres. 1991). Home: 60 Indian Pond Rd Kingston MA 02364 Office: HMO Blue 492 Old Connecticut Path Framingham MA 01701-4583

CAVICCHIO, CAROLYN C., association executive, management consultant; b. Phila., Dec. 31, 1963; d. Alfonzo Carlo and Julia Teresa (Del Raso) C. BA, Temple U., 1986; M of Govt. Adminstrn., U. Pa., 1991. Promotion dir. WRTI-FM, Phila., 1985-86; dir. pub. rels. Steelworks, Phila., 1986-88; assoc. The Conservation Co., Phila., 1988—. Mem. West Mt. Airy Neighbors, Phila., 1990—, Young Women's Alliance, Women's Way, Phila., 1991—, Weavers' Way Coop., Phila., 1990—; vol. Action AIDS, Phila., 1988—. Mem. Phila. Women's Network (assoc.). Democrat. Office: The Conservation Co 1 Penn Ctr Fl 1390 Philadelphia PA 19103-1813

CAVILL, RONALD WILLIAM, financial advisor; b. Escanaba, Mich., July 8, 1944; s. Robert Hugh and Lorraine (Kondory) C. BA, U. Md., 1971. Cert. fin. planner. Regional v.p. Am. Gen. Corp., Houston, 1973-75; pres. Corp. Benefit Cons., Inc., Denver, 1975-80, Cavill and Co., Washington, Md., 1980—; bd. advisors Tax Mgmt. Fin. Planning (BNA), Washington, 1985-88. Pres. Jefferson County Assn. for Retarded Citizens, Denver, 1977; bd. dirs. Good Shepherd Life Care Ctr., Silver Spring, Md., 1985, Ronald McDonald House, Washington, 1989—; chmn. Nat. Coun. on Aging, bd. dirs., 1991—; chmn. Nat. Inst. on Fin. Issues and Svcs. for Elders, 1991—. Mem. Internat. Assn. Fin. Planning (v.p. nat. capital chpt. 1984-86), Mem. Inst. Cert. Fin. Planners. Office: Cavill & Co 1225 I St NW #1200 Washington DC 20005-3914

CAVIN, SUSAN ELIZABETH, sociologist, writer; b. Trion, Ga., Mar. 18, 1948; d. John Charles and Mary (Risk) C.; 1 child, Julian Samuel Cavin-Zeidenstein. BA, Vanderbilt U., 1970; MA, Rutgers U., 1973, PhD, 1978. Teaching asst., sociology Rutgers U., Newark, N.J., 1970-75; typesetter SoHo News, N.Y.C., 1976; asst. prof. sociology Green Mountain Coll., Poultney, Vt., 1979-83; lectr. women's studies Rutger's U., New Brunswick, N.J., 1984-91, asst. dir. women's studies, 1988-91; adminstr. women in engring. sci. tech. program; cons. Gov.'s Study Commn. on Discrimination, Trenton, N.J., 1992; adj. asst. prof. sociology NYU, 1990—. Author: Lesbian Origins, 1985, poetry book, 1973; founding editor: (newspapers) Radical Chick, 1992—, Big Apple Dyke News (B.A.D. News), 1981-88, Green Mountain Dyke News, 1980, (jour.) Tribad, 1977-79. Named Outstanding Tchr. of Yr., Green Mountain Coll., Poultney, 1982-83, winner Declamation awards, Ga. High Sch. Assn., 1965, 66. Mem. Nat. Writers Union, Am. Sociol. Assn., Nat. Women's Studies Assn., Women in Engring. (adminstr. sci. and tech. N.J. Inst. Tech.). Democrat.

CAWLEY, LANCE COOPER, investment banker, entrepreneur; b. Easton, Md., Sept. 18, 1958; s. Wayne Archie and Barbara (Cooper) C.; m. Nancy Birch, Jan. 25, 1988. BS in Bus. Adminstrn., Washington & Lee U., 1984; MBA in Fin., Loyola Coll., 1990. Analyst Mercantile Bank, Balt., 1984-86; asst. v.p. First Nat. Bank of Md., Balt., 1986-89; v.p. Schelle Cellular Group, Inc. Ruxton Capital Group, Inc., Balt., 1989—, Am. Personal Communications, Balt., 1989—; owner Cawley Consulting, Balt., 1988—. Co. chairperson United Way Cen. Md., Balt., 1984-92. Republican. Home: 12806 Bridlepath Rd Reisterstown MD 21136 Office: Schelle Cellular Group Inc 2212 Old Court Rd Baltimore MD 21208

CAWLEY, THOMAS ANDREW, turnaround management company executive; b. Pitts., Apr. 16, 1956; s. Charles Raymond and Martha Ann (Kordich) C. BS in Econs., Pa. State U., 1978; MBA, U. N.C., 1982. Fin. analyst GE, N.Y.C., 1978-80; intern in corp. fin. Mellon Bank, Pitts., 1981; corp. fin. assoc. Irving Trust Co., N.Y.C., 1982-84; cons. Touche Ross & Co., N.Y.C., 1984-86; v.p. R.F. Stengel & Co., Inc., Valley Forge, Pa., 1986—; also bd. dirs. R.F. Stengel & Co., Inc., Wayne, Pa. Associate dir. Greater N.Y.C. United Way campaign, 1983. Mem. Turn Around Mgmt. Assn., U.S. Yacht Racing Union. Home: 3 Dreycott Ln Haverford PA 19041-1511 Home: 155 E 31st St New York NY 10016-6800 Office: RF Stengel & Co Inc PO Box 765 780 Yellow Springs Rd Valley Forge PA 19482

CAWLY, ROBERT HOUSTON, marketing executive; b. Batesville, Ark., Oct. 15, 1950; s. Porter Houston and Mary (Flinn) C.; m. Patricia Anne Teiber, Oct. 1, 1983; 1 child, Katherine Ashley. BS in Acctg., Strayer Coll., Washington, 1976. Mgmt. cons. Price Waterhouse, Bethesda, Md., 1977-86; nat. dir. applied tech. ctr. cons. div. Price Waterhouse, 1987-91, nat. dir. mktg. cons. div., 1991—. Contbr. articles to profl. jours.; inventor knowledge base software, 1990. With USMC, 1970-74. Mem. AICPAs, Info. Tech. Assn. of Am. (membership com. 1991—). Democrat. Lutheran. Home: 17123 Old Baltimore Rd Olney MD 20832

CAYWOOD BEAUREGARD, JANICE EILEEN, secure systems engineer; b. Pitts., May 15, 1955; d. William Parkes Jr. and Jane Elaine (MacFadden) C.; m. William C. Beauregard, Jr. BSCE, Carnegie-Mellon U., 1979; CAS in Mgmt., Radcliffe Coll., 1985. Prodn. supr. Polaroid Corp., Cambridge, Mass., 1979-81; quality engr. Polaroid Corp., Waltham, Mass., 1981-83; computer security engr. MITRE Corp., Bedford, Mass., 1983-89; systems engr. Infotec Devel., Inc., Wakefield, Mass., 1989-91; software engring. supr. Digital Equipment Corp., Merrimack, N.H., 1991—; chief exec. officer, owner Spectrum Aerial Enterprises, Lexington, Mass., 1981—. Editor, author newsletter, 1986-88. Vol., Boston Symphony Assn. Vols., Boston, 1981—. Recipient Community Svc. award Rotary Internat., 1973. Mem. Internat. Swift Assn., Armed Forces Communications and Electronics Assn., Aircraft Owners and Pilots Assn., Nashua AirPort Assn. (bd. dirs. asst.), Radcliffe Alumni Assn., Bellanca-Champion Club. Home: 9 Blackstone Dr Apt 82 Nashua NH 03063-5051 Office: Digital Equipment Corp PO Box 9501 MK02-1 Merrimack NH 03054-9501

CECERE, MICHAEL LEWIS, III, career naval officer; b. Geneva, N.Y., Dec. 26, 1952; s. Michael Lewis Jr. and Stella Adeline (Felice) C.; m. Susan Carol Wood, Mar. 31, 1978; children: Michael Lewis IV, Thomas Ryan. BSME, U.S. Naval Acad., 1975; MS in Naval Architecture/Marine Engring., MIT, 1983, Ocean Engr., 1983. Commd. ensign USN, 1971, advanced through grades to commdr., 1990; boiler officer U.S. S. Albany, Norfolk, Va. and Gaeta, Italy, 1975-76, 76-78; machinery inspector Bd. of Inspection of Survey, Atlantic, Norfolk, 1978-80; docking officer U.S. Naval Ship Repair Facility, Subic Bay Naval Sta., Philippines, 1983-85; main propulsion officer U.S.S. Coral Sea, Norfolk, 1986-89; weapons elevator prog. officer Naval Sea Systems Command, Washington, 1989-91, integrated electric drive program test coord., chief engr., 1991—. Ednl. asst. vol. Cen. Elem. Sch., Edgewater, Md., 1990-91. Democrat. Roman Catholic. Home: 3902 River Club Dr Edgewater MD 21037-3802 Office: Naval Sea Systems Command Navy Dept Washington DC 20362-5101

CECI, ANTHONY THOMAS, executive secretary; b. Wilmington, Del., May 21, 1917; s. Romano and Ersilia (Filichetti) C. Student, U. Del., 1948-51. Exec. sec. Baldwin Locomotive Works, Eddystone, Pa., 1940-46; with VA Hosp., Wilmington, Del., 1946—, ret., 1976. Recipient Citation, Gov. State of Del., 1975. Mem. Rodney Sq. Club, St. Anthony's Club. Republican. Roman Catholic. Home: 14 Stone Hill Rd Augustine Hills Wilmington DE 19803

CECIL, ALEX THOMSON, travel executive; b. Birmingham, Ala., May 5, 1930; s. Alex Thomson and Martha (Lamar) C.; m. Jennifer Brown, Dec. 2, 1962 (div. 1976); children: Thurston, Lila; m. Jacqueline Bottger, May 10, 1980; children: Julia, Caroline. Student, Ohio State U., 1950-52. Pres. Auto-Europe, Inc., N.Y.C., 1953—. Mem. Camden Yacht Club. Home: 160 Chestnut St Camden ME 04843-2224 Office: Auto-Europe Sharps Wharf Camden ME 04843

CEDARBAUM, MIRIAM GOLDMAN, federal judge; b. N.Y.C., Sept. 16, 1929; d. Louis Albert and Sarah (Shapiro) Goldman; m. Bernard Cedarbaum, Aug. 25, 1957; children: Daniel Goldman C., Jonathan Goldman C. BA, Barnard Coll., 1950; LLB, Columbia U., 1953. Bar: N.Y. 1954, U.S. Dist. Ct. (so. dist.) N.Y. 1956 U.S. Ct. Appeals (2d cir.) 1956, U.S. Ct. Claims 1958, U.S. Supreme Ct. 1958, U.S. Dist. Ct. (ea. dist.) N.Y. 1980, U.S. Ct. Appeals (5th and 11th cirs.) 1981. Law clk. to judge Edward Jordan Dimock U.S. Dist. Ct. (so. dist.) N.Y., 1953-54, asst. U.S. atty., 1954-57; atty. Dept. Justice, Washington, 1958-59; part-time cons. to law firms in litigation matters, 1959-62; 1st asst. counsel N.Y. State Moreland Act Commn., 1963-64; assoc. counsel Mus. Modern Art, N.Y.C., 1965-79; assoc. litigation dept. Davis, Polk & Wardwell, N.Y.C., 1979-83, sr. atty., 1983-86; acting justice Village of Scarsdale, N.Y., 1978-82, justice, 1982-86; judge U.S. Dist. Ct. (so. dist.) N.Y., 1986—; co-counsel Scarsdale Open Soc. Assn., 1968-86. Mem. adv. com. on labor rels. Scarsdale Bd. Edn., 1976-77; mem. Scarsdale Bd. Archtl. Rev., 1977-79. Recipient Medal of Distinction Barnard Coll., 1991. Mem. Am. Law Inst., ABA (chmn. com. on pictorial graphic sculptural and choreographic works 1979-81), N.Y. State Bar Assn. (chmn. com. on fed. legislation 1978-80), Assn. of Bar of City of N.Y. (com. on copyright and literary property, 1982-84, com. on the Bicentennial), Fed. Bar Coun., Copyright Soc. U.S.A. (trustee, mem. exec. com. 1979-82). Jewish. Office: US Dist Ct US Courthouse 40 Foley Sq New York NY 10007-1581

CEDDIA, ANTHONY FRANCIS, university president; b. Boston, Mar. 4, 1944; s. Antonio John and Marie (Loungo) C.; m. Valerie Ann Mulkern, Apr. 15, 1966; children: Ann-Marie, Michael. BS in Edn., Northeastern U., 1965, MEd, 1968; EdD, U. Mass., 1980; postgrad. John F. Kennedy Sch. Govt., Harvard U., 1990; LLD (hon.), North Adams State Coll., 1990; cert. sr. exec. program in local govt., Harvard U., 1990; LLD (hon.), North Adams State Coll., 1990. Cert. counselor, secondary sch. tchr., Mass. Tchr. social studies, counselor Melrose High Sch., Mass., 1965-70; fin. aid and admissions ofcl. North Adams State Coll., Mass., 1970-73, dean of adminstrn, 1973-78, exec. v.p., 1978-81; acting pres. North Adams State Coll., Mass., 1979; pres. Shippenburg U., Pa., 1981—; chmn. bd. Univ. Ctr., State System Higher Edn., Harrisburg, 1987-90; chmn. Commn. Univs. of Pa., 1986-88; mem. Sico Found., Sico Oil Corp., 1983—; mem. adv. bd. Orrstown Bank, Shippenburg, 1984-87. Mem. Cumberland County Transp. Bd., 1990; trustee Chambersburg Hosp. Bd., 1989—; mem. exec. com. South Cen. Pa. coun. Boys Scouts Am., 1982—, adv. panel Nat. Army ROTC, 1984—, chairperson, 1988—; bd. dirs. Ams. for the Competitive System, 1981-87; chair div. II steering com. NCAA, 1990-92. Recipient Disting. Alumni Northeastern U., 1979. Mem. Am. Assn. State Colls. and Univs. (editor 1982-86, chmn. com. rsch. and liaison, com. on policy and purpose 1987-90), Am. Assn. Higher Edn., Mid. States Assn. Colls. and Schs. (commn. on higher edn. 1986—), Nat. Intercollegiate Athletic Assn. (coun.). Home: PO Box 606 Shippensburg PA 17257-0606 Office: Shippensburg U Office of Pres Prince St Shippensburg PA 17257-1316

CEDRONE, MARIE C., university administrator. B in in Applied Scis., Boston U., 1979; M in Liberal Arts, Harvard U., 1983, M in Edn., 1988. Mem. div. Applied Scis. Harvard U., Cambridge, Mass., 1968-85, dept. adminstr. anthropology, 1985-88; mgmt., human resource cons. Network Dynamics, Inc., Cambridge, 1983-85; adminstrv. officer leaders for mfg. program MIT, Cambridge, 1988-90, contract adminstr., Office Sponsored Programs, 1990—. Mem. Harvard U. Art Mus. Mem. APA (assoc.), Mass. Assn. for Women in Higher Edn., Mass. Psychol. Assn. (assoc.), Eastern Psychol. Assn., New Eng. Soc. Applied Psychologists, New Eng. Bus. Educators Assn., Nat. Coun. Univ. Rsch. Adminstrs. Office: MIT 77 Massachusetts Ave Rm E19-702 Cambridge MA 02139-4307

CELENTANO, LINDA NANCY, industrial designer; b. Englewood, N.J., May 11, 1958; d. Edward and Ruth (Meyers) C. Student design, Copenhagen, 1978; B Indsl. Design, Pratt Inst., 1980. Indsl. designer Lebowitz/Gould Design, N.Y.C., 1979-81; indusl. designer Smart Design, N.Y.C., 1981-85; product design dir. Medin Corp., Wallington, N.J., 1985—; lectr. Pratt Inst. Alumni Series, Bklyn., 1986-87. Designer Product Design, 1987, Indsl. Design Mag., 1986, 90, Product Design II, 1987, Internat. Design Yearbook, 1988, 89, N.Y. Times, 1990, New and Notable Product Design, 1991, also salad servers; represented in permanent collection Cooper-Hewitt Collection, N.Y.C. Vol. Libr. for Recording for Blind, N.Y.C., 1990; co-founder Rowena Reed Kostellow Fund, 1990—, active exec. com.. Recipient Excellence award Indusl. Design Mag., 1986. Mem. Indusl. Designer Soc. Am. Lutheran. Home: 325 Haywood Dr Paramus NJ 07652

CELENTI, DAN NICHOLAS, electrical engineer; b. Bucharest, Romania, May 16, 1952; s. Xenophon Spyros and Cornelia (Poppa) C.; m. Romy Sylvia Sfintescu, Mar. 6, 1976; 1 child, Anna Maria. BSEE, MSEE, Bucharest Poly. Inst., 1976; PhD, SUNY, Buffalo, 1985. Research engr. Enterprise for design and Mfg. of Elevators, Bucharest, 1976-79; design engineer Hoechst AG, Cologne, Fed. Republic Germany, 1979-80; research asst. elec. & computer engring. dept. SUNY, Buffalo, 1981-84, teaching asst. elec. & computer engring. dept., 1984-85; systems analyst HHB Systems, Inc., Mahwah, N.J., 1985-86; asst. prof. elec. engring. dept. Fairleigh Dickinson U., Teaneck, N.J., 1986-90; mem. tech. staff AT&T Bell Labs., Middletown, N.J., 1990—; vis. and adj. prof. N.J. Inst. Technology, Newark, 1990—; dir. V.L.S.I. program Fairleigh Dickinson U., Teaneck, 1987-90; speaker at various confs. Contbr. articles to profl. jours. Mem. IEEE, Am. Soc. Engring. Edn., Eta Kappa Nu. Greek Orthodox. Home: PO Box 142 Holmdel NJ 07733 Office: AT&T Bell Labs 480 Red Hill Rd Middletown NJ 07748

CELLA, BETH ANN, business official; b. Holliston, Mass., Sept. 10, 1969; d. Albert Andrew and Jean Beverly (Demma) C. BBA, U. Miami, 1991. Cons. Systems Cons. Group, Miami, Fla., 1990; with sales and mktg. dept. Royal Horseguard, London, 1990; regional sales rep. Boston Capital Ptnrs., Inc., Boston, 1992—. Mem. Eastern Mass. Women's Soccer League, Lambda Chi Alpha. Home: 101 Donna Rd Holliston MA 01746

CELLER, GEORGE K., physicist; b. Walbrzych, Poland, Mar. 27, 1947; came to U.S., 1970; s. Karol and Lucja (Wolin) C.; m. Adeline Marie Heyman, May 27, 1975; children: Mark, Catherine. MS, Warsaw U., 1969; PhD, Purdue U., 1976. Rsch. scientist physics dept. Vienna (Austria) U., 1969-70; computer scientist Internat. Atomic Energy Agy., Vienna, 1970; mem. rsch. staff Western Electric Engring. Rsch. Ctr., Princeton, N.J., 1976-79; mem. tech. staff AT&T Bell Labs., Murray Hill, N.J., 1979-84, rsch. supr., 1984—, disting. mem. tech. staff, 1992—. Editor: Laser and Electron Beam Processing of Electronic Materials, 1980, Laser and Electron Beam Interactions with Solids, 1982, ULSI Science and Technology, 1991; referee Applied Physics Letters, others; contbr. 140 articles to profl. jours. Fellow Am. Phys. Soc.; mem. IEEE (conf. chair 1985-86), Electrochem. Soc. (mem. exec. com. electronics divsn. 1985—, vice-chmn. conf. chair 1991—), Materials Rsch. Soc. Office: AT&T Bell Labs Rm 6F-217 Murray Hill NJ 07974-0636

CELLIERS, PETER JOUBERT, public relations specialist; b. Vogelfontein, S. Africa; s. Bartilimy and Elsie Blanche (Goldberg) C.; ed. Eng., Continent; m. Helen Rassaby, Sept. 10, 1949; children: Gordon A.J., Jennefer A.J. Editor, to 1959; cons. to fgn. govts., internat. corps. Peter J. Celliers Co., N.Y.C., 1958-68; chief fgn. press svcs. Olympic Organizing Com., Mexico, 1968; dir. for N.Am., Mexican Nat. Tourist Coun., 1962-72; owner Ellis Assos., N.Y.C., 1969-91. Tech. adviser internat. market devel. to UN, hotels, carriers, govts. Mem. Soc. Am. Travel Writers (past pres.), N.Y. Assn. Travel Writers, Am. Soc. Journalists and Authors. Clubs: Nat. Press (Washington); Overseas Press, Dutch Treat (N.Y.C.). Home and Office: 240 Garth Rd Scarsdale NY 10583-3962

CELLUCCI, ARGEO PAUL, state official; b. Marlboro, Mass., Apr. 24, 1948; s. Argeo R. and Prisicilla Rose C.; m. Janet Garnett, 1971; children: Kate, Anne. BS, Boston Coll., 1970, JD, 1973. Atty. Kittredge, Cellucci and Moreira, Hudson, Mass., 1973-90; mem. charter commn. Hudson, 1970-71; selectman, 1971-77; state rep. Third Middlesex Dist., Mass., 1977-84; state senator Middlesex and Worcester Dists., Mass., 1985-90; lt. gov. Mass., 1991—. Capt. USAR. Recipient Haskins and Fells Found. award, 1969. Mem. ABA, Mass. Bar Assn., Elks, Sons of Italy. Republican. Roman Catholic. Office: State House Rm 259 Boston MA 02133*

CELOTTA, BEVERLY KAY, psychologist; b. Monroe, La., June 16, 1944; d. Morton and Geraldine (Hermalin) Lauter; m. Robert James Celotta; children: Jennifer Ann, Daniel Wayne. BA in Psychology, Queens Coll., 1965; MS, Bkyln. Coll., 1967; PhD in Ednl. Psychology, U. Colo., 1971. Lic. psychologist, Md. Research asst. Inst. for Devel. Studies, NYU, 1967; sch. psychologist Bur. of Child Guidance, N.Y.C., 1967-69, Head Start Program, N.Y.C., 1968-69; sch. psychologist Montgomery County Pub. Schs., Rockville, Md., 1973-74, ednl. researcher, 1976-77; sch. psychologist Fairfax (Va.) County Pub. Schs., 1975-76; asst. prof. counseling and personnel services dept. U. Md., College Park, 1977-83, asst. chair, 1982-83; pres. Celotta, Jacobs & Assocs., Inc., Darnestown, Md., 1983-91; pvt. practice Darnestown, 1991—; lectr. psychology Montgomery Coll., Rockville, 1975-76; cons., speaker in field. Contbr. articles to profl. jours. Mem. ACA, APA (editorial bd. div. cons. psychology 1989—), Assn. for Measurement and Evaluation in Counseling and Devel. (chmn. membership and program coms., mem. editorial bd. 1989-91). Home and Office: 13517 Haddonfield Ln Gaithersburg MD 20878-3622

CENKO, ALEXIS, aerospace engineering educator; b. Lvov, Ukraine, USSR, Jan. 4, 1944; came to U.S., 1949; s. Mykola and Volodymyra (Gardetsky) C.; m. Martha Diana Kuzmowych, June 30, 1950; children: Alexander Vladimyr, Andrew Trevor. BS, Pa. State U., 1965; M of Engring. in Aerospace Engring., Cornell U., 1967; PhD, W.Va. U., 1970; MBA, Dowling Coll., 1978. Assoc. engr. Boeing Div. Vertol, Morton, Pa., 1965-66; engr. Grumman Aerospace, Bethpage, N.Y., 1969-72, sr. engr., 1977-85; asst. prof. Dowling Coll., Oakdale, N.Y., 1972-77; assoc. prof. Hofstra U., Hempstead, N.Y., 1985-87; aerospace engr. Naval Air Devel. Ctr., Warminster, Pa., 1987—; mem. Joint Ordnance Commdrs. Group, Washington, 1988—. Contbr. articles to profl. jours., 1980—. Named Faculty fellow NASA, Am. Soc. for Engring. Edn., Langley, Va., 1975, navy Am. Soc. for Engring. Edn., Phila., 1986. Fellow AIAA (assoc. fellow). Republican. Greek Catholic. Office: NADC Code 6053 Warminster PA 18974-5000

CENTAFONT, RICHARD ALAN, pharmacist, hospital administrator; b. Trenton, N.J., Feb. 11, 1955; s. Anthony Lawrence and Lois Mae (Black) C.; m. Lucy Ann Alexander, May 13, 1978; children: Ryan Alan, Jeffrey Richard, Lauren Ann. BS in Pharmacy, Temple U., Phila., 1978, MBA, 1988. Pharmacist Med. Coll. Hosps.-Elkins Park (Pa.) Campus, 1978-79, asst. dir. pharmacy, 1979-83, dir. pharmacy, 1983-92, asst. v.p., 1992—. Baseball coach Southampton Sports Club, 1989-92, basketball coach, 1990-92. Mem. Am. Soc. Hosp. Pharmacists, Pa. Pharm. Assn. (hosp. del.), Rho Chi, Beta Gamma Sigma. Office: Med Coll Hosps Elkins Park Campus 60 Township Line Rd Elkins Park PA 19117-2249

CENTEIO, JOSE COUTO, lawyer; b. Atalaia, Fogo, Cape Verde Islands, May 1, 1960; came to U.S. 1971; s. Jose Couto and Dalia (Goncalves) C. BS in Psychology, Tufts U., Medford, Mass., 1984; JD, Boston Coll., 1988. Bar: Mass. 1989. Hearing officer, lawyer Dept. Social Svcs., Boston, 1988-90; pvt. practice law Boston, 1991—. Co-founder, bd. dirs. Cape Verdean Assn. New Eng., Boston, 1989—; bd. dirs. Dudley St. Neighborhood Initiative, 1991—. Mem. Mass. Bar Assn., ABA. Democrat. Roman Catholic. Office: 109 State St Boston MA 02109-2903

CERASIA, MARCELLA LO CASTRO, accountant; b. Passaic, N.J., Mar. 29, 1952; d. Anthony Lo Castro and Angelina (Chiavetta) Broward; m. Charles Robert Cerasia III, Aug. 25, 1979; children: Nichola Anne, Charles Robert IV, Natalie Allison. BA, Montclair State Coll., 1974; MBA, Fairleigh Dickinson U., 1977. Sr. acct. Wiss & Co., East Orange, N.J., 1974-76; mgr. Arthur Andersen & Co., Roseland, N.J., 1977-83, dir. bus. systems cons., 1991—; mgr. J.H. Cohn & Co., Roseland, 1983-85, ptnr., 1985-91; pres. J.H. Cohn Software Assocs., Roseland, 1988-91. Bd. dirs. Park Ridge Estates Homeowners Assn., Cedar Grove, N.J., 1991; trustee Holy Angels Ch., Little Falls, N.J., 1991. Recipient Woman of Achievement award YWCA of Essex and West Hudson, East Orange, N.J., 1987, Bus. Watch award Bus. Jour. N.J., Morganville, 1988. Mem. AICPA, Am. Women's Soc. CPAs (regional dir. 1989-90, pres. N.J. chpt. 1987-89), N.J. Soc. CPAs (v.p. 1990-91, vice chair CPE exec. com. 1991-92, chair 1992—), N.J. Assn. Women Bus. Owners (pres. Morris chpt. 1991-92), West Essex C. of C. (bd. dirs. 1992—). Roman Catholic. Home: 176 Eileen Dr Cedar Grove NJ 07009-1353 Office: Arthur Andersen & Co 101 Eisenhower Pky Roseland NJ 07068-1028

CEREGHINO, JAMES JOSEPH, health facility administrator, neurologist; b. Portland, Oreg., Oct. 27, 1937; s. Joseph Thomas and Amelia E. (Arata) C. BS, Portland State Coll., 1959; MD, U. Oreg., 1964; MS in Neurophysiology, Linfield U., 1971. Intern Good Samaritan Hosp., Portland, 1964-65; resident Good Samaritan Hosp. and Med. Ctr., Portland, 1965-68; rotating resident in neuropathology Sch. of Medicine U. Wash., 1967; rotating resident in child neurology U. Calif. Med. Ctr., San Francisco, 1968; rotating resident in psychiatry Med. Sch. U. Oreg., 1968; nerol. cons. pub. health svc.-health svcs. and mental health adminstrn.-neurol. and sensory disease control program HEW, Rockville, Md., 1968-70; staff neuroglogist epilepsy br. NIH HEW, Bethesda, Md., 1970-85; chief epilepsy br. convulsive, devel. and neuromuscular disorders program Nat. Inst. Neurol. Disorders and Stroke, Bethesda, Md., 1985—; speaker in field. Editor-in-chief Epilepsia; contbr. numerous articles to profl. jours. Capt. USPHS. Fellow Am. Electroencephalographi Soc. (pub. rels. com. 1980-81); mem. Am. Acad. Neurology, Am. Epilepsy Soc. (constn. com. 1970-74, chmn. 1975, membership com. 1975, chmn. 1976, 77 chmn. edn. com. 1978, 79, 80, dir. continuing med. edn. 1981-83, 1st v.p. 1982-83, pres. 1983-84, v.p. to ILAE 1985-86, coun. 1985—), Am. Neurologic Assn., Epilepsy Found. of Am. (profl. adv. bd. Washington chpt. 1969—, v.p. 1973-75, speaker's bur. 1972—, Epilepsy Internat. (libr. devel. com. 1981, chmn. 1981-85), U. Oreg. Med. Sch. Alumni Assn., Internat. Leage Against Epilepsy (edn. com. 1985—; coun. 1985—), Med. Soc. D.C. (sect. neurology and neurol. surgery 1971—), Uniformed Svcs. Orgn. Neurologists (chmn. awards com. 1984-85), World Fedn. Neurology (epidemiology rsch group 1978—). Home: 4998 Battery Ln Apt 317 Bethesda MD 20814-4961 Office: Dept Health & Human Svcs Nat Inst Neurol-NIH Fed Bldg Rm 114 Bethesda MD 20892

CERENZIA, JOSEPH ANTHONY, public relations executive; b. Canonsburg, Pa., May 8, 1954; s. Joseph Mark and Philomena (Aloia) C.; m. Lisa Marie Mark, Feb. 15, 1986; children: Kaitlin C., Mark Joseph C., Eva Roman, Adam Roman. BS, W.Va. U., 1977. Dir. pub. rels. Washington (Pa.) County Tourism, 1979-80; coord. pub. rels. Consolidation Coal Co., Pitts., 1980-87, supr. pub. rels., 1987-88, mgr. pub. rels., 1988—. Bd. dirs. Assn. for Retarded Citizens, Washington, 1982-83, Cath. Charities, Canonsburg, 1982-85; active St. Patrick's Parish Coun., Cbgs., 1992—. Recipient Pub. Rels. award W.Va. Press Assn., 1984. Mem. Consolidated Fed. Credit Union (supervisory com. 1991—, bd. dirs. 1992—), W.Va. Coal Assn. (pub. rels. com. 1985—), Ohio Mining and Reclamation Assn. (pub. rels. com. 1982—). Democrat. Home: 223 Mcgregor Dr Canonsburg PA 15317-2266 Office: Consol Coal Co 1800 Washington Rd Pittsburgh PA 15241-1421

CERF, JULIE MICOU, philanthropy consultant; b. San Francisco, Nov. 16, 1957; d. Paul and Ann (McKinstry) Micou; m. William Montgomery Cerf, Sept. 7, 1985; children: Olivia Micou Cerf, Charlotte Montgomery Cerf. BA, Smith Coll., 1980; MA in Law and Diplomacy, Tufts U., 1983.

Program asst. U.S. Agy. for Internat. Devel., Conakry, Guinea, 1981-82; asst. v.p. J.P. Morgan & Co. (Morgan Guaranty Trust Co.), N.Y.C., 1983-87; exec. dir. Schumann Fund for N.J., Montclair, 1988-91; philanthropy cons. Assn. for Children of N.J., Newark, 1991—. Mem. bd. overseers, chair fin. com. Govs. Sch. of N.J., Long Branch, 1989—; trustee, chair program and grant making com. Montclair Fund for Ednl. Excellence, 1991—; mem. community adv. bd. Jr. League of Montclair/Newark, 1990-92; mem. exec. com. Newark Collaboration Group, Newark, 1990-91; soprano Oratorio Soc. N.J.

CERINI, COSTANTINO PETER, research virologist; b. Phila., Nov. 19, 1931; s. Joseph and Rita Lillian (Cruciani) C.; m. Lydia Grace De Angelis, June 18, 1960. BA, La Salle Coll., 1953; MS, Lehigh U., 1960, PhD, 1964. Tchr. Secondary Sch. System, Phila., 1958-59; rsch. virologist Lederle Labs/ Am. Cyanamid, Pearl River, N.Y., 1964-70, group leader, 1970-81, sr. researcher/project leader, 1981-88; tech. coord. Lederle-Praxis/Am. Cyanamid, Pearl River, 1988—. Contbr. articles to sci. jours. With Med. Corps, U.S. Army, 1955-57, Korea. Mem. Am. Soc. for Microbiology. Office: Lederle Praxis Biols 401 N Middletown Rd Pearl River NY 10965-1263

CERINO, ANGELA MARIE, business law educator, lawyer; b. Phila., Mar. 17, 1950; d. Salvatore and Mary Rose (Falivene) C. BA in Polit. Sci., Temple U., 1972, JD, 1976. Bar: Pa. 1976, U.S. Dist. Ct. (ea. dist.) Pa. 1982, Internat. Ct. Trade, 1988, U.S. Ct. Appeals, 1988. Assoc. Stein & Silverman, Phila., 1975-77; staff atty. Camden (N.J.) Regional Legal Services, 1977-78; sole practice Phila., 1978-83; asst. prof. Villanova (Pa.) U., 1980—; arbitrator Phila. Ct. of Common Pleas, 1978-84. Contbr. articles to profl. jours. Mem. Variety Charity for Handicapped Children, Phila., 1985—. Mem. ABA (internat. law and labor law coms.), Mid-Atlantic Regional Bus. Law Assn. (exec. dir. 1986-89, sec.-treas. 1989-90, 2d v.p. 1990—, 1st v.p. 1991—), Am. Bus. Law Assn. Roman Catholic. Office: Villanova U Bartley Hall Villanova PA 19085

CERKANOWICZ, ANTHONY EDWARD, mechanical engineering educator, environmentalist; b. Bayonne, N.J., Feb. 19, 1941; s. Anthony Joseph and Clara Cerkanowicz; m. Elizabeth M. Cardillo, Aug. 27, 1966; children: Kirk Anthony, Mary Ellen, Leah Elizabeth, Andrea, James Anthony. BSME, Stevens Inst. Tech., 1962, MSME and Heat and Power, 1964, PhD in Mech. Engring. and Thermodynamics, 1970. Engr., cons. Lockheed Electronics, Plainfield, Newark, 1963-64; engr. Vitro Labs., West Orange, N.J., 1967-69; tech. v.p. Photochem Industries, Fairfield, N.J., 1969-74; sr. staff engr. Exxon Rsch. & Enging., Clinton, N.J., 1974-87; assoc. prof. mech. engring. N.J. Inst. Tech., Newark, 1987—; engr. NASA Goddard Space Ctr., Greenbelt, Md., summer 1962; cons. Engelhard Industries, Menlo Park, N.J., 1991. Numerous patents on photochem. combustion, fluidized bed heat transfer, charge induced separations. Vice pres. Lochada Taxpayers Assn., Glen Spey, N.Y., 1991. Recipient Outstanding Alumni award Stevens Inst. Tech., 1987. Mem. ASME, Combustion Inst., Stevens Inst. Tech. Alumni Assn., Sigma Xi. Republican. Roman Catholic. Home: 8 Fieldstone Dr Livingston NJ 07039-3309 Office: NJ Inst Tech King Blvd Belleville NJ 07109-1654

CERNA, CHRISTINA MONICA, lawyer; b. Munich, Fed. Republic Germany, Oct. 9, 1946; came to U.S., 1951; d. Eduardo Joseph and Marija (Vogel) C. BA, NYU, 1967; MA, U. Munich, 1970; JD, Am. U., 1973; LLM, Columbia U., 1974. Bar: D.C., U.S. Ct. Appeals (D.C. cir.), U.S. Supreme Ct. With Fried, Frank Harris, Shriver and Kampelman, Washington, 1974; with solicitor's office U.S. Dept. Labor, Washington, 1976-79; human right specialist Inter Am. Commn. on Human Rights, OAS, Washington, 1979—; vis. fellow St. Antony's Coll., Oxford U., 1989-90. Mem. Am. Soc. Internat. Law. Democrat. Office: OAS 1889 F St NW Washington DC 20006-4413

CERNY, FRANK JOSEPH, JR., physical therapy educator, consultant; b. Dayton, Ohio, June 10, 1946; s. Frank Joseph Sr. and Viola (McNeil) C.; m. Nancy Cerny, June 15, 1968; children: Hans Joerg, Peter Joseph, Scott Gordon. BA in Biology and Chemistry, MacAlester Coll., 1968; PhD in Phys. Edn./Physiology, U. Wis., 1972; postgrad., Medizinisches Universitats Klinik, Freiberg, Fed. Republic Germany, 1972-74. Instr. U. Wis., Madison, 1968-70, rsch. asst., NIH pulmonary trainee, 1969-72, asst. cadiac rehab. program, 1972-74; instr. in exercise physiology for sports medicine students Med. Coll., Freiburg, Fed. Republic of Germany, 1972-74; dir. rsch. Ont. Exercise-Heart Collaborative Study Satellite Centre, Windsor, Can., 1974-76; asst. prof., mem. faculty human kinetics U. Windsor, 1974-76; assoc. dir. Children's Lung Ctr. Children's Hosp. of Buffalo, 1976-85; rsch. asst. prof. dept. pediatrics U. Buffalo, 1976—; asst. prof. dept. phys. therapy and exercise sci. SUNY, Buffalo, 1985-91, assoc. prof. dept. phys. therapy and exercise sci., 1991—; rsch. assoc. Windsor Western Hosps., 1974; Alexander von Humboldt Found. fellow in rsch. metabolism and muscle physiology Bonn-Bad Godesberg, Fed. Republic of Germany, 1973-74; cons. City of Buffalo, 1989-91, County of Erie, Buffalo, 1990-91; presenter in field. Contbr. articles to profl. jours., including Jour. Clin. Investigation, Brit. Jour. Sports Medicine, Jour. Applied Physiology, Jour. Sports Medicine and Phys. Fitness, Jour. Pediatric Surgery, others; manuscript reviewer Annals of Allergy, Pediatric Pulmonology, Pediatric Rsch.; mem. editorial bd. Pediatric Exercise Sci. Grant reviewer Cystic Fibrosis Found., 1983-85, Can. March of Dimes, 1986, 87, Hosp. for Sick Children Found., 1986, 88. Grantee NIH, The Buffalo Found., Cystic Fibrosis Found., Am. Lung Assn. Fellow Am. Coll. Sports Medicine (membership com.); mem. Am. Physiol. Soc., Am. Lung Assn. (pediatric lung disease and adult patient care coms. Western N.Y. chpt., state del., occupational and environ. health com.). Office: SUNY 411 Kimball Tower Buffalo NY 14214

CERNY, LAWRENCE CHARLES, chemistry educator; b. Cleve., Mar. 5, 1929; s. Albert Frank and Bertha Josephine (Svoboda) C.; m. Elaine Louise Rose, Sept. 24, 1955; children: Louise Alfredson, Mary, Charles. BS, Case Inst., 1951, MS, 1952; postgrad., Cornell U., 1952-55; PhD, Ghent U., Belgium, 1956. Asst. prof. John Carroll U., Cleve., 1956-60; assoc. prof. Syracuse U., Utica (N.Y.) Coll., 1960-65, prof., 1965—; investigator MAsonic Med. Rsch. Lab., Utica, 1972-86; vis. prof. U. L'Aquila, Italy, 1990. Patentee in field; contbr. articles to profl. jours. Mem. Am. Heart Assn., Utica, 1962-72; mem. Clinton Rd. Sch. PTA, treas. 1968-72. Fulbright scholar, 1955-56; U.S.-Czech Acad. Sci. Exch. fellow, Prague, 1967, Sr. fellow Fogarty Internat. award, Kiryu, Japan, 1989; Rsch. Travel grantee, Oxford, England, 1980, 83; recipient Pub. Health Svc. Career Devel. award, Utica, 1967-72, Key to City of Utica, 1976. Mem. Am. Inst. Chemistry, The Red Band, Utica Coll. Band, KC, Alpha Chi Sigma, Tau Beta Pi, Sigma Xi. Roman Catholic. Home: 19 Genesee Ct Utica NY 13502 Office: Utica Coll Syracuse U Burrstone Rd Utica NY 13502

CERNY, RONALD NEAL, operations director; b. Passaic, N.J., Jan. 6, 1952; s. Anthony F. and Rosemarie (Litchenberger) C.; m. Alida Vangolen, Jan. 19, 1974; children: Kimberly, Corinne, Douglas. BSME, Lafayette Coll., 1973; postgrad., Villanova U., 1992—. Rsch. engr. Johns Manville Corp., Denver, 1973-79, rsch. mgr., 1979-82, product mgr., 1982-83; sales mgr. Specialty Glass Corp., Willow Gorve, Pa., 1983-86; mktg. mgr. Johnson Matthey, inc., West Chester, Pa., 1986-88, dir. sales and mktg., 1988-90, dir. ops., 1990—. Patentee in joint assembly, high-temperature conduit vent, improved slurry processing. Mem. ASME. Avocations: skiing, tennis, landscape. Office: Johnson Matthey Inc 1401 King Rd West Chester PA 19380

CERRA, LUIS R., psychiatrist; b. Humacao, P.R., Apr. 7, 1955; s. Gerardo Cerra Montilla and Rosa L. Ortiz-Sandoz. MD, Cayey (P.R.) Sch. Medicine, 1981. Intern dept. surgery San Juan City Hosp., 1981-82; resident dpet. psychiatry N.Y. Med. Coll.-Met. Hosp. ctr., N.Y.C., 1985-88; assoc. attending physician Woodhull Med. and Mental Health Ctr., Bklyn., 1988—; unit chief, inpatient psychiatry unit Woodhull Med. and Mental Health Ctr., N.Y.C., 1990—. Mem. Am. Psychiat. Assn. Roman Catholic. Home: 315 E 86th St New York NY 10028-4714 Office: 30 W 60th St Ste 1P New York NY 10023

CERUL, SANDRA MARY, community health nurse administrator; b. Bayshore, N.Y., Apr. 12, 1940; d. James Stewart Scott and Carlotta Marion (Adams) Breier; m. Edward Joseph Cerul, Apr. 16, 1966; children: Edward Jr., Heather, James, Thomas, Sara. BSN, Hartwick Coll., 1961; postgrad., Columbia U., 1964-66. RN, N.Y. Field coord. St. Denis, St. Columbia St. Vincent de Paul Soc., Hopewell, N.Y., 1980-83; field instr. Dutchess County Community Coll., Poughkeepsie, N.Y., 1966, 84-85; pub. health nurse Dutchess County Health Dept., Beacon, N.Y., 1966-67, 85-87, Ulser County Dept. Health, Kingston, N.Y., 1987; adminstr., dir. Tri-Cities and Helpmates, Inc., Cert. Home Health Agy., Kingston, N.Y., 1987—; owner, pres. Med Hx, Mt. Marion, N.Y., 1990—, My Nurse, Mt. Marion, N.Y., 1992—. Roman Catholic. Home and Office: PO Box 750 Mount Marion NY 12456

CERVIERI, JOHN ANTHONY, JR., real estate company officer; b. Suffern, N.Y., Jan. 28, 1931; s. John A. and Elizabeth Mildred (Kuester) C.; married; children: Stephen A., Christina L., Michael J., Peter A. BA, Columbia Coll., 1951; MBA, Harvard U., 1959. Real estate broker Albert B. Ashforth, Inc., N.Y.C., 1959-62; pension fund investment mgr. Textron, Inc., Providence, 1962-66; owner Capital for Real Estate, Inc., N.Y.C., 1967-69; chmn., chief exec. officer Property Capital Assocs., Boston, 1986—; mng. trustee Property Capital Trust, Boston, 1969—; bd. dirs. BayBanks, Inc., Boston; chmn., chief exec. officer Americana Hotels & Realty Corp., Boston, 1983—. Bd. dirs. Mass. Housing Fin. Agy., Boston, 1976., Dana-Farber Cancer Inst., Boston, 1980—; mem. Gov.'s Mgmt. Task Force Commonwealth Mass., Boston, 1990; trustee New Eng. Med. Ctr., Boston, 1991—. 1st lt. USAF, Korea. Named Baker scholar, Harvard U., 1959. Mem. Am. Soc. Real Estate Counsellors (chmn. New Eng. chpt. 1984-85), Nat. Assn. Real Estate Investment Trusts (pres. 1978-79), Nat. Realty Com. (chmn. exec. com. 1982-85), Urban Land Inst., Am. Stock Exchange. (chmn. co. adv. com. 1985), Boston Econ. Club. Roman Catholic. Office: Property Capital Assocs 1 Post Office Sq # 2100 Boston MA 02109

CERVONE, MICHELE BERNADETTE, industrial property clearance specialist; b. Bridgeport, Conn., Aug. 1, 1964; d. Edward Francis and Veronica Marie (Gentile) Board; m. Michael Angelo Cervone Jr., May 7, 1988. BS, Sacred Heart U., 1987; cert., Army Logistics Mgmt. Coll., 1990, Air Force Inst. Tech., 1991. Indsl. property cleanrance specialist Def. Contract Mgmt. Area Opers., U.S. Dept. of Def., Stratford, Conn., 1983—. Home: PO Box 26 Monroe CT 06468-0026 Office: Def Contract Mgmt Area Opers Bridgeport 555 Lordship Blvd Stratford CT 06497-7124

CESA, MICHAEL PETER, cardiologist, consultant; b. N.Y.C., Sept. 4, 1946; s. John J. and Catherine R. (Brunialti) C.; m. Barbara A. Perrelli, June 21, 1969; children: Christopher, Thomas, Gregory, Meredith. BS, Manhattan Coll., 1968; MD, SUNY, Bklyn., 1972. Diplomate Am. Bd. Internal Medicine, Am. Bd. Cardiovascualr Disease. Intern dept. medicine Kings County Hosp., Bklyn., 1972-72, med. resident dept. medicine, 1973-75, cardiology fellow dept. medicine, 1975-77; pvt. practice Bruckstein & Lerner, Smithtown, N.Y., 1977-78, North Suffolk Cardiology Assocs., P.C., Stony Brook, N.Y., 1978—; pres., chief exec. officer North Suffolk Cardiology Assocs., Stony Brook, 1984—; pres. med. staff St. Johns Hosp., Smithtown, 1984. Fellow AMA (Coun. on Clin. Cardiology), Am. Coll. Cardiology, Am. Coll. Chest Physicians. Roman Catholic. Office: North Suffolk Cardiology 2500-1 Nesconset Hwy Stony Brook NY 11790

CESARE, DENNIS ANTHONY, guidance counselor; b. Bridgeton, N.J., Nov. 26, 1954; s. Peter Lawrence and Marie Rita (Moffa) C.; m. Barbara Jean Burton, Apr. 29, 1978; children: Gregory, David. BA in Edn., Glassboro State Coll., 1976, MA, 1982. Cert. student pers. svcs., N.J. Elem. tchr. Bridgeton (N.J.) Pub. Schs., 1976-77; elem. tchr. Voorhees (N.J.) Twp. Pub. Schs., 1977-90, elem. counselor, 1990—; coord. Camden County Coll. Summer Day Camp, Blackwood, 1990, 91. Coach Magnolia (N.J.) Little League, 1987—; com. chmn. Cub Scouts Am., Magnolia, 1990—. Recipient Tchr. of the Yr. award N.J. Gov., 1987. Mem. AACD, N.J. Edn. Assn., Am. Sch. Counselor Assn. Methodist. Office: Osage Sch Guidance Ofc 112 Somerdale Rd Voorhees NJ 08043-1901

CHA, SE DO, internist; b. Seoul, Korea, Dec. 17, 1942; came to U.S., 1966, naturalized, 1977; s. Young Sun and Hee Joo (Chang) C.; m. Elsa Jane Greene, Dec. 21, 1974. M.D., Yon Sei U., 1966. Diplomate Am. Bd. Internal Medicine. Intern Presbyn.-U. Pa. Med. Ctr., Phila., 1966-67; resident in medicine Harrisburg (Pa.) Hosp., 1967-70; chief resident in medicine Roger Williams Gen. Hosp., Providence, 1970-71, cardiologist, 1973-75; fellow in cardiology Deborah Heart and Lung Center, Browns Mills, N.J., 1971-73, cardiologist, 1975—, asst. dir. adult cardiac catheterization lab., 1975-86, dir., 1987—; clin. asst. prof. U. Medicine and Dentistry N.J., 1987; instr. Brown U., Providence, 1973-75. Contbr. articles to profl. jours. Fellow ACP, Am. Coll. Angiology, Soc. for Cardiac Angiography; mem. AMA, Fedn. Clin. Rsch., Am. Heart Assn. Office: Deborah Heart and Lung Ctr Trenton Rd Browns Mills NJ 08015-3206

CHABE, ALEXANDER MICHAEL, education educator, photographer; b. Gary, Ind., Jan. 12, 1923; s. Michael Ivanovich and Barbara (Lysak) Chabai; m. Mary Janice Gilbert, Apr. 7, 1951; children: Daniel Stafford, David Gilbert. AB in History, Mich. State U., 1948; MS in Edn., Ind. U., 1950, EdD, 1959; postgrad. in Russian, Norwich U., 1986, 87, 88, Middlebury Coll., 1949, 85, 91. Tchr. elem. Calumet Twp. Schs., Gary, Ind., 1950-51, San Bruno (Calif.) Sch. System, 1951-52, Benton Harbor (Mich.) Sch. System, 1952-54; elem. sch. supr. Ottawa County Bd. of Edn., Grand Haven, Mich., 1954-56; asst. prof. edn. Park Coll., Parkville, Mo., 1956-58; prof. SUNY, Fredonia, 1959—. Author: Democracy and Communism, 1973, How People Live in France, 1976; author filmstrips in English and Russian, sound slide set; contbr. articles to profl. jours. 1st lt. U.S. Army, WWII. Mem. NEA (life), Am. Assn. Tchrs. of Slavic and Eastern European Langs., Am. Coun. Tchrs. of Russian, Am. Edn. Studies Assn. Russian Orthodox. Home: 126 Central Ave Fredonia NY 14063-1134 Office: SUNY Coll of Fredonia Fredonia NY 14063

CHACE, WILLIAM MURDOUGH, university president; b. Newport News, Va., Sept. 3, 1938; s. William Emerson and Grace Elizabeth (Murdough) C.; m. JoAn Elizabeth Johnstone, Sept. 5, 1964; children: William Johnstone, Katherine Elizabeth. BA in English, Haverford Coll., 1961; MA in English, U. Calif., Berkeley, 1963; PhD in English, U. Calif., 1968; LLD (hon.), Amherst Coll., 1990, William Coll., 1992. Instr. Stillman Coll., Tuscaloosa, Ala., 1963-64; teaching asst. U. Calif., Berkeley, 1964-66, acting instr., 1967-68; asst. prof. English Stanford (Calif.) U., 1968-74, assoc. prof., 1974-80, prof., 1980, assoc. dean Sch. Humanities and Scis., 1981-85, vice provost for acad. planning and devel., 1985-88; pres. Wesleyan U., Middletown, Conn., 1988—; cons. to Hewlett-Packard, Hallmark Cards Inc., Hawaiian Ednl. Fund, Midwestern Mgmt. Assn.; vis. prof. The Coll. Aboard the Delta Queen, 1979, 80, 82, The Coll. in We. Europe and Brit. Isles, 1985; lectr. to Libr. Assocs. of Stanford U., 1976, Sixth Internat. James Joyce Symposium, Dublin, 1977, Thirteenth Internat. James Joyce Symposium, Dublin, 1992, MLA Ann. Conv., 1977, 78, Tufts U. Symposium, 1978, English Conf. of U. Calif., Berkeley, 1979, Eighth Internat. James Joyce Symposium, Dublin, 1982, Thirteenth Internat. James Joyce Symposium, Dublin, 1992, Ann. Meeting of Midwest Placement Assn., Kansas City, 1983, IBM Internat. Bus. and Acad. Conf., Monte Carlo, 1984, Ezra Pound Centennial Colloquium, San Jose State U., 1985, Ann. Meeting of the Assn. of Grad. Liberal Studies Programs, St. Louis, 1986, Chico State U., La. State U., 1987, U. Utah Sch. of Medicine Pub. Lecture series, 1987, Northern Calif. Sci. Meeting of Am. Coll. Physicians, Monterey, Calif., 1987; mem. Conn. Acad. Arts and Scis., 1989—; corporator Middlesex Meml. Corp., 1990—; presenter Joyce and History conf. Yale U., 1990. Author: James Joyce: A Collection of Critical Essays, 1973, The Political Identities of Ezra Pound and T.S. Eliot, 1973, Lionel Trilling: Criticism and Politics, 1980, (with others) Graham Greene: A Revaluation, 1990; editor: (with Peter Collier) Justice Denied: The Black Man in White America, 1970, An Introduction to Literature, 1985, (with JoAn E. Chace) Making It New, 1972; contbr. numerous scholarly articles, revs. to profl. jours. Mem. resource devel. com. Middlesex United Way, 1989—; trustee Conn. River Trust, 1989—. Home: 269 High St Middletown CT 06459-0290 Office: Wesleyan U Office of Pres 600 S College Middletown CT 06459-0290

CHACKO, SUNIL, health professional, research administrator; b. Trivandrum, Kerala, India, June 1, 1959; came to U.S., 1986; s. John and Anna (Chandi) C. MD, Med. Coll., Trivandrum, 1983; MPH, Harvard U., 1987. Cert. in pub. health. Asst. dir. Internat. Commn. on Health Rsch., Boston, 1987-90; advisor Mexican Acad. Medicine, Mexico City, 1991—; praoject dir. Harvard Ctr. for Population and Devel., Cambridge, Mass., 1991—; cons. UNICEF, Florence, Italy, 1990. Editor Kerala Jr. Drs.' Jour., 1984. Recipient Internat. award Aga Khan Found., Geneva, 1986; Harvard fellow, 1987. Home: 12/306 Plamood Pattom, Trivandrum Kerala India 695 004 Office: Harvard U Ctr for Population Cambridge MA 02138

CHADWICK, GEORGE FREDERICK, engineering manager; b. Buffalo, N.Y., July 11, 1930; s. George M. and Edna E. (Schmidt) C.; m. Shirley J. Bellinger, June 28, 1952; children: Sharyl L., John F., Peggy A., David R. BA, U. Buffalo, 1951; MS, Pa. State U., 1956. Rsch. chemist Airco Speer Electronics, 1957-61, rsch. supr., 1961-65, devel. supr., 1965-69, devel. mgr., 1970-77; project engr. Mesch Engring., 1978-82; dir. process devel. Recra Environ., Buffalo, 1982-83; sr. process engr. Wilson Greatbatch Ltd., Clarence, N.Y., 1983-84, Harmac Industries, Buffalo, 1984-85; sr. process engr. Ethox Corp., Buffalo, 1985-90, engring. supr., 1990-91; engring. mgr. E-Three Inc., Buffalo, 1991—. Author: (chpt.) Flammability of Plastics; inventee in field. Plastic Inst. fellow, 1975. Mem. Am. Chem. Soc. (sr. chair 1980-81), Soc. Plastics Engr. (sr. chair 1972-73, internat. dir. 1974-75, internat. treas. 1976-77), Soc. Mech. Engrs. Robotics Inst. (sr.), Computer and Automated Systems Assn. (sr., chair 1991-92). Republican. Methodist. Home: 133 Pin Oak Dr Buffalo NY 14221-1532 Office: E-Three Inc 440 Lawrence Bell Dr # 12 Buffalo NY 14221-7080

CHADWICK, LYNN, communications executive; b. Santa Monica, Calif., Dec. 21, 1950; d. James Paul and Lenna Chadwick; m. David M. LePage. BA in English, U. Va., 1973; M in Pub. Policy, U. Calif., Berkeley, 1987. Writer, editor U.S. Dept. Transp., Washington, 1973-75; freelance writer Washington, 1975-81; pres. Feminist Radio Network, Washington, 1976-81; mng. dir. Western Pub. Radio, San Francisco, 1981-85; pres., chief exec. officer Nat. Fedn. Community Broadcasters, Washington, 1987—; cons. All India Radio, Delhi, 1988, N.W. Area Found., St. Paul, 1990. Office: Nat Fedn Community Broadcasters 666 11th St NW Washington DC 20001-4542

CHAFEE, JOHN HUBBARD, senator; b. Providence, Oct. 22, 1922; s. John S. and Janet (Hunter) C.; m. Virginia Coates, Nov. 4, 1950; children: Zechariah, Lincoln, John, Georgia, Quentin. B.A., Yale U., 1947; LL.B., Harvard U., 1950; LLD (hon.), Brown U., 1964, Providence Coll., 1965, U. R.I., 1965, Jacksonville U., 1970, Bryant Coll., 1979. Bar: R.I. 1950. Practice law Providence, 1952-62, 73-76; mem. R.I. Ho. of Reps. 3d Dist. Warwick, 1957-62, minority leader, 1959-62; gov. State R.I., 1963-69; sec. Navy, 1969-72; mem. U.S. Senate from R.I., 1977—. Chmn. Rep. Gov.'s Assn., 1967; Mem. corp. Yale, 1972-78; trustee Deerfield Acad., 1970-79. Served to capt. USMCR, 1942-45, 51-52. Chubb fellow Yale, 1965. Mem. R.I. Bar, Fed. Bar Assn. Episcopalian. Office: US Senate 567 Dirksen Senate Bldg Washington DC 20510*

CHAFFART, ROBBY GHISLAIN, French language educator; b. Oostende, Belgium, Aug. 5, 1958; came to U.S., 1981; s. Achille Jimmy and Regine Irene (Germonprez) C.; m. Lynona Ann Gordon, June 3, 1984. BA, Faculté du Salève, Collonges, France, 1981; MA, Andrews U., 1983; postgrad., U. Ariz., 1986. Instr. French Walla Walla Coll., College Place, Wash., 1983-86; tchr. French Walla Walla Valley Acad., College Place, Wash., 1984-86; instr. French Golden Ave Sch Dist., South Porcupine, Ont., Can., 1988-90; French immersion tchr. Niagara South Bd. Edn., Niagara Falls, Ont., Can., 1990—; sponsor, counselor French Club, College Place, 1984-86, leader French Sabbath Sch., 1983-86; youth leader Niagara Falls, 1991—. Mem. MLA, Alpha Mu Gamma. Republican. Adventist. Home: PO Box 2254 NMS Niagara Falls NY 14301 Office: Niagara South Bd Edn, 250 Thorold Rd W, Welland, ON Canada L3C 3W3

CHAFFEE, KEVIN ST. CLAIR, writer, public relations specialist; b. Erie, Pa., June 2, 1952; s. Clair Edgar and Madelyn R. (von Lindenberg-Bruder) C. Student, U. Nice, France, 1973; AB, MA in History, Georgetown U., 1974; postgrad., U. Bologna, Italy, 1975; MA in Internat. Rels., Johns Hopkins U., 1977. Researcher Washington bur. Balt. Sun, 1973; asst. to press sec. Rep. Marc L. Marks, Washington, 1976-77; researcher, fundraiser Radii Found. for Energy Research, Washington, 1977-78; asst. to pres. Internat. Mgmt. Resources Corp., Washington, 1978-79; editor, asst. pub. Encore mag., Washington, 1979-80, City Life mag., Washington, 1980-81; editorial cons., bus. mgr. Almanac Am. Politics, Washington, 1981-83; speechwriter, cons. Office of Pub. Affairs HUD, Washington, 1984-89; Washington editor Spade and Archer Pubs. Simon & Schuster; assoc. editor Washington Times, 1991—; cons. Arab Republic Egypt, Washington, 1979-80, Govt. of Nigeria, 1989-90, Ctr. for Pub. Integrity, Washington, 1990; cons. pub. rels. Congl. Quarterly, Inc., Washington, 1990, Citizens Rsch. Found., L.A., 1989; mng. editor, editorial cons. Campaigns and Elections Jour., Washington, 1980; pub. rels., editorial cons. Washington Bur. Quotidien de Paris, 1982-85; exec. producer Election Night 1986 Coverage C-Span Cable Network, Washington; cons. Paradine TV, London, L.A., 1989-90, Electronic Industries Assn., Washington, 1990, Campaign Rsch. Ctr., Washington, 1990-91, Ctr. for Pub. Integrity, Washington, 1990-91. Author: 50 Maps of Washington, D.C., 1991, Saving For a Rainy Day: How Congress Turns Campaign Cash into Golden Parachutes, 1990; assoc. editor Campaign Industry News, 1988, Life sect. of The Washington Times, 1991—; editor About Town; contbr. articles, editorials to newspapers. Researcher Reagan for Pres. campaign, 1980; bd. dirs. Source Theatre, Washington, 1982-90, Montesquieu Found., Paris, 1988—; fundraiser J.F. Kennedy Ctr. for the Performing Arts, Very Spl. Arts, Met. Opera, Am. Ballet Theatre, Dance Theatre Harlem, 1984—. Mem. Am. Assn. Polit. Cons., Washington Ind. Writers, English Speaking Union, Nat. Press Club. Home: 1536 15th St NW Washington DC 20005-1922

CHAFIN, SARA SUSAN, primary education educator; b. Huntington, W.Va., Mar. 24, 1952; d. William Albert and Margaret Irene (Stigall) C. BA, Coll. William and Mary, 1977. Tchr. The Woods Acad., Bethesda, Md., 1982-83; head tchr. Children's House Washington, 1983, The Vera Gander Montessori Sch., N.Y.C., 1984-85; adminstr., pres. The Manhattan Montessori Sch., 1985-88; tchr. St. Michael's Montessori Sch., N.Y.C., 1988-90, Children's House of Washington, 1990—; instr., speaker Internat. Montessori workshop, N.Y.C., 1986. Active N.Y.C. Friends and Advocates of Mentally Ill, 1985—, also newsletter, legis. coms. Mem. N. Am. Montessori Tchrs. Assn., Assn. Montessori Internat. (cert. adminstr.). Home and Office: 4923 Brandywine St NW Washington DC 20016-4330

CHAGNON, JOSEPH V., school system administrator; b. Newark, Mar. 28, 1929; m. Placidia Irma Rodriguez; children: Elaine, Joseph, David, Raymond, John. BS in Edn., N.J. State Tchr. Coll., 1954; MA, Columbia U., 1958; Cert in Pub. Sector Mgmt. Labor Relations, Rutgers U., 1983, Cert. in Equal Employment Opportunity, 1984, Cert. in Human Resource Mgmt., 1987. Tchr. Newark Pub. Schs., 1954-65, adminstr., 1965—; assessor N.J. Assessment Ctr. for Prins.; pres. Coun. of Union Employees Bd. Edn., Newark, 1990—. Commr. East Brunswick, N.J. Sewage Authority, 1970-88, sec. 1971, 79-81, vice chmn. 1972, 81, chmn. 1974, 82-88; pres. East Brunswick Mus. Corp., 1978-81, trustee, 1978—; trustee East Brunswick Pub. Library, 1978—, sec. 1986—; mem. East Brunswick Recreation and Pks. Adv. Bd., 1966-80, chmn., 1974-80; mem. East Brunswick Planning Bd., 1988-91. With USMC, 1946-48, 50-51. Recipient Ednl. Leadership award Benedette Crocé Ednl. Soc., 1982; Ednl. Svc. award Essex County and State N.J., 1991. Mem. NEA (life), NAESP (life), City Assn. Suprs. and Adminstrs. (pres. 1983—, treas. 1976-82, founding trustee 1975), Assn. for Curriculum and Devel., Indsl. Rels. Rsch. Assn., Am. Fedn. Sch. Adminstrs. (v.p. 1984-91, treas. 1991—, N.J. Prins. and Suprs. Assn. (mem. legis. com. 1984—), Am. Arbitration Assn. Home: 7 Carol Ct East Brunswick NJ 08816-4405 Office: Newark Bd Edn G W Carver Sch 333 Clinton Pl Newark NJ 07112-1599

CHAGNON, MARY B. BERGEN, anesthesiologist, educator; b. Carbondale, Pa., Mar. 15, 1946; d. William Joseph and Mae Elizabeth (Dietz) Bergen; m. Denis E. Chagnon, May 13, 1972; children: Denis J., Christopher J. BS in Biology, Marywood Coll., 1968; MD, Georgetown U., 1972. Diplomate Am. Bd. Anesthesiology. Resident anesthesia St. Joseph Hosp., Syracuse, N.Y., 1972-75; attending anesthesiologist Ellis Hosp., Schenectady, 1975-79; mem. faculty, attending physician Albany (N.Y.) Med. Coll., Albany Med. Hosp., 1979-90; dept. chair anesthesia Century

Same Day Surgery, Latham, N.Y., 1991—; v.p. Albany Ambulatory Anesthesia Assocs., P.C., 1991—; lectr. anesthesia residency Albany Med. Sch., 1979-90, Sch. Nurse Anesthesia, Albany, 1979-90; instr. ACLS, Albany, 1983-88. Religious edn. instr. St. Clares Ch., Colonie, N.Y., 1987, 88; active PTO, St. Gregorys Sch., 1979—. Mem. Am. Soc. Anesthesiologists, Soc. Ambulatory Anesthesia, N.Y. State Soc. Anesthesiologists, Windstar Found. Democrat. Roman Catholic. Office: Century Same Day Surgery 7 Century Hill Latham NY 12110

CHAIKA, ELAINE OSTRACH, linguistics educator; b. Milford, Mass., Dec. 20, 1934; d. Harry and RoseMary Ostrach; m. William Young Chaika, 1960; children: Eric Andrew, Daniel Ethan, Jeremy David. B of Edn., R.I. Coll., 1960; MAT in English, Brown U., 1965, PhD in Linguistics, 1972. Tchr. rural schoolhouse, Eastbrook, Maine, 1954-55, Vet.'s Meml. High Sch., Warwick, R.I., 1960-61, Roger Wms. Jr. High Sch., Providence, 1961-62; instr., English Bryant Coll., Smithfield, R.I., 1965-66; instr. R.I. Sch. of Design, Providence, 1967-68; spl. lectr. Providence Coll., 1971, asst. prof. linguistics, 1971-73, assoc. prof., 1974-78, prof. linguistics, 1979—. Author: Language: The Social Mirror, 1st and 2nd Edits., 1982, 89, Understanding Psychotic Speech, Beyond Freud and Chomsky, 1990; editorial bd.: College Communication and Composition, 1981-89, Interfaces, 1984; rev. books for publ.; contbr. articles to profl. jours. Recipient full tuition scholarship Pembroke Coll., Providence, 1952-54, NDEA scholarship, 1960-61, NDEA fellowship, Brown U., Providence, 1967-70. Fellow Brain and Behavior Scis., Linguistic Soc. Am. Office: Providence Coll Linguistics Dept Providence RI 02918

CHAIKIN, ALYCE, artist; b. N.Y.C., Apr. 14, 1923; d. Morris and Sara (Kunin) C.; m. Harold Louis Kleinman, Sept. 10, 1944 (dec. Dec. 1986); children: George Michael, Thomas John. Cert., Parsons Sch. Design, N.Y.C., 1943; student, Bennington Coll., 1941, Fairfield U., 1962. Cartoonist Famous Studios subs. Paramount, N.Y.C., 1943-44; freelance illustrator various dept. stores, Bridgeport, Conn., 1948-52; freelance artist, 1952—; represented by Capricorn Galleries, Bethesda, Md., 1979—, Silvermine Galleries, New Canaan, Conn., 1979—; cons. interior decorator Fairfield (Conn.) U., 1963-64. Group shows include Invitational Conn. Gallery, Marlborough, 1990, Invitational Munson Gallery, New Haven, 1989, Hon. Artist Conn. Commn. on Arts, Hartford, 1988, Invitational Drawing Show, Huntsville (Ala.) Mus., 1987, Philip Desind Collection of Contemporary Realism, Butler Inst. of Am. Art, Youngstown, Ohio, 1987; represented in permanent collections Town of Fairfield, New Haven Paint and Clay, U. Conn. Health Ctr., Meml. Sloan-Kettering Cancer Ctr.; executed murals Park Ave., Temple, Bridgeport, 1958-59. 1st pres. Park City Hosp. Aux., Bridgeport, 1952-53. Recipient numerous awards for drawings including two best-in-show awards. Mem. Conn. Women Artists, Silvermine Guild Artists, New Haven Paint and Clay Club, Inc., Art/Place Coop. Gallery. Home and Studio: 192 Glengarry Rd Fairfield CT 06430

CHAIKLIN, HARRIS, social work educator; b. Bridgeport, Conn.; s. David and Victoria (Spector) C.; m. Sharon Udren, June 5, 1955; children: Seth, Matthew, Martha, Nina. BA with distinction, U. Conn., Storrs, 1950; MA in Sociology, U. Conn., 1952; MS in Social Work, U. Wis., 1953; postgrad. in Sociology, NYU, 1953-55; PhD, Yale U., 1961. Lic. social worker, Md., Acad. Cert. Social Workers. Psychiat. social worker, case worker Jewish Bd. of Guardians, N.Y.C., 1953-56; instr. sociology U. Conn., 1959-60; asst. prof. Smith Coll. Sch. for Social Work, Northampton, Mass., 1960-62, Sch. of Social Work U. Md., Balt., 1962-64; assoc. prof. Sch. of Social Work U. Md., College Park, 1964-71, prof., 1971—, asst. dean for Informatics, 1990—; caseworker Jewish Family Svc., New Haven, Conn., 1958-59, Jewish Family and Children's Svc., Balt., 1963-76; social worker pvt. practice, Balt., 1977—, John F. Kennedy Inst. Family Ctr., 1984-86; clin. assoc. prof. psychiatry U. Md. Med. Sch., 1974—; assoc. John F. Kennedy Inst. for Handicapped Children; vis. prof. Haifa U., 1976-77, '80-81, '86-87, Morgan State U., 1977-78; summer, part-time teaching U. Calif, Berkeley, U. Conn. Sch. Social Work, Hartford Coll., U. Mass., U. Vt. and others. Editor: Marian Chace: Her Papers, 1975, Inventory of Research, 1963-65 (with others) Aides for Research Teachers: I-IV, 1969 (with Ralpha Segalman), Symbolic Interaction and Social Welfare, 1979; contbr. numerous articles to profl. jours.; mem. adv. or editorial bds. of many profl. jours. Recipient Harry Greenstein award Balt. Associated Jewish Charities, 1986, Md. Higher Edn. Assn. award of Merit, 1991; named Commonwealth Fund fellow, Yale U., 1956-58, Sr. Fulbright Hays lectr., Haifa U., 1976-77. Mem. NASW (Social Worker of Yr., Md. 1973), Am. Sociol. Assn., Am. Orthopsychiat. Assn., Am. Pub. Health Assn., Clin. Sociology Assn., Coun. on Social Work Edn., Soc. Applied Sociology, Soc. for Study Social Problems. Home: 5173 Phantom Ct Columbia MD 21044-1318 Office: U Md Sch of Social Work 525 W Redwood St Baltimore MD 21201-1777

CHAIT, LAURENCE PHILLIP, management consultant; b. Albany, N.Y., Mar. 20, 1942; m. Ann Weiner, Mar. 15, 1964; children: Jonathan, David. BA, Cornell U., 1963; MBA, Harvard U., 1965. Mdse. info. coord. Jordan Marsh Co., Boston, 1964-68; cons. Philip Hankins Inc., Arlington, Mass., 1969-69; dir. Wang Labs., Inc., Arlington, Mass., 1969; v.p., dir. Comml. Info. Corp., Arlington, Mass., 1969-72; chmn., pres. Jonathan David Inc., Lexington, Mass., 1972-78; dir. Arthur D. Little, Inc., Cambridge, Mass., 1978—. Author: Information Technology: Its Impact on the Insurance Industry, 1986, INformation Technology: Achieveing the Potential, 1990, Human Resources-Today and in the Future, 1989; contbr. articles to profl. jours. Mem. Lexington Transp. Adv. Com., 1976—, Lexington Cen. Bus. Dist. Com., 1976-77, Lexington Ctr. Revitalization Com., 1977-78. Mem. Lexington C. of C. (pres. 1977-80). Office: Arthur D Little Inc Acorn Pk Cambridge MA 02140

CHALAL, JO ANN, physician; b. Phila., May 22, 1954; d. Kenneth and Lorraine (Rudnitsky) C.; m. Bruce E. Engleman, June 28, 1986; children: Rachel, Sara. BA in Psychology, U. Pa., 1976; MD, Temple U., 1982. Diplomate Am. Bd. Internal Medicine. Resident in internal medicine U. Ill. Hosp., Chgo., 1982-85; fellow in hematology-oncology NYU Med. Ctr., N.Y.C., 1985-87; resident in radiation/oncology Albert Einstein Med. Ctr., Phila., 1987-90; sr. clin. instr. dept. radiation oncology Hahnemann U. Hosp., Phila., 1990—. Corr. sec. Hakol chpt. Hadassah, Phila., 1989-90. Mem. Am. Soc. Clin. Oncology, Am. Soc. of Therapeutic Radiology and Oncology. Office: Hahnemann U Hosp Dept Radiation Oncology Philadelphia PA 19102

CHALFANT, RICHARD DEWEY, hypnotherapist, insurance consultant; b. Muncie, Ind., Mar. 14, 1924; s. Dewey Franklin and Mary Lorraine (Hance) C.; m. Beatrice Buechler, Dec. 28, 1948 (dec. 1980); m. Eva Silvia Chalfant, Oct. 14, 1990. MA, NYU, 1962; BA in Edn., Fairleigh Dickinson U., 1972, MA in Human Devel., 1975. Asst. mgr. adminstrn. Chubb & Son, N.Y.C., 1947-50; self-employed musician N.J., 1950-58; dept. head Trenton (N.J.) Conservatory, 1958-69; sr. researcher career edn. U.S. Office Edn., Teaneck, N.J., 1970-75; gen. agt. Chalfant Ins. Agy., Point Pleasant, N.J., 1978-89, Whiting, N.J., 1989; pvt. practice hypnotherapy, 1989—; rsch. coord. N.J. Dept. Edn., Newark, 1966-78; pvt. practice as music tchr., composer, 1955-70. Commr. Ocean County Task Force on Elder Abuse, Toms River, N.J., 1986-91; cons. N.J. Coalition for Protection Vulnerable Adults, 1989-91; ins. advisor Somebody Cares, Inc., Whiting, 1984-91. Cpl. U.S. Army, 1942-46. Mem. Am. Assn. for Counseling and Devel., Nat. Assn. for Neurolinguistic Programming, Ocean County Bus. Assn. (bd. dirs. 1991—), Toms River Ocean County C. of C. (bd. dirs. 1983-87), Masons (master 1975), Shriners. Episcopalian.

CHALFEN, RICHARD MEGSON, anthropologist; b. Cambridge, Mass., July 16, 1942; s. Samuel Edward and Gladys Elizabeth (Megson) C.; m. Kirsten Roelling, July 29, 1967 (div. Nov. 1990); children: Leah, Claire. BA in Anthropology, U. Pa., 1964, MA in Communications, 1967, PhD in Communications, 1974. Instr., lang. & lit. Drexel U., Phila., 1967-69; rsch. assoc. Phila. Child Guidance Clinic, 1968-73; asst. prof., assoc. prof. Temple U., Dept. Anthropology, Phila., 1972-91, prof., 1991—; dir. MA program visual anthropology, Temple U., 1979-91. Author: Snapshot Versions of Life, 1987, Turning Leaves-The Photograph Collections of Two Japanese American Families, 1991; contbr. articles to profl. jours. Nat. Inst. Mental Health grantee, 1967-71, NSF grantee, 1980-81. Mem. Am. Anthrop. Assn. (bd. dirs. 1989-91), Internat. Visual Sociology Assn., Soc. Visual Anthropology (pres. 1989-91). Democrat. Office: Temple U Dept Anthropology Philadelphia PA 19122

CHALK, ROSEMARY ANNE, study analyst; b. Cin., May 25, 1948; d. John Henry and Virginia R. (Kamphaus) Chalk; m. Michael Anthony Stoto, June 28, 1986; children: Anna Murilius, Benjamin John. BA, U. Cin., 1970; postgrad., George Washington U., 1970-72. Policy analyst Libr. of Congress, Washington, 1972-75; rsch. fellow MIT, Cambridge, Mass., 1982-83; program dir. AAAS, Washington, 1976-86; cons. Harvard Sch. Pub. Health, Boston, 1986-87; study dir. Inst. of Medicine, Washington, 1987-89, Nat. Acad. Sci., Washington, 1989—; cons. The Field Found., N.Y.C., 1986-87, The Acadia Inst., Bar Harbor, Maine, 1988-91; adv. com. on ethics and values studies NSF, 1984-87. Editor: Science, Technology and Society: Emerging Relationships, 1988; contbr. articles to profl. jours. Fellow AAAS (coun. and section officer 1987—), Fedn. Am. Scientists (coun. mem. 1982-90), Student Pugwash USA (bd. dirs. 1988—). Roman Catholic. Home: 4404 Windom Pl NW Washington DC 20016 Office: Nat Acad Sci 2101 Constitution Ave NW Washington DC 20418

CHALKER-SCOTT, LINDA KAY, plant physiologist, educator; b. Oak Harbor, Wash., July 7, 1957; d. Raymond Lloyd and Charlotte Rae (Nygren) Chalker; m. James Douglas Scott, July 10 1982; 1 child, Charlotte. BS, Oreg. State U., 1978, MS, 1981, PhD, 1988. Postdoctoral assoc. forest products Oreg. State U., Corvallis, 1988-89; asst. prof. biology SUNY, Buffalo, 1989—. Author: (with others) Low Temperature Stress Responses in Crops, 1989, Condensed Tannins, 1989. Mem. AAAS (Robert I. Larus award 1988, nat. award in organismic biology 1989), Am. Soc. Hort. Sci. (1st place award 1988), Am. Soc. Photobiology, Am. Soc. Plant Physiologists, Sigma Xi. Office: SUNY Coll Buffalo Dept Biology 1300 Elmwood Ave Buffalo NY 14222-1095

CHALL, JEANNE STERNLICHT, psychologist, educator; b. Shendishov, Poland, Jan. 1, 1921; came to U.S., 1927;; d. Hyman and Eva (Kreinik) Sternlicht; m. Leo P. Chall, June 8, 1946 (div. 1964). BBA cum laude, CCNY, 1941; MA, Ohio State U., 1947, PhD, 1952; MA (hon.), Harvard, 1965; HLD, Lesley Coll., 1972. Rsch. asst. Ohio State U., Columbus, 1945-47, rsch. assoc., instr., 1947-49; instr. CCNY, 1950-54, asst. prof., 1954-62, assoc. prof., 1962-65, prof., 1965; vis. assoc. prof. Harvard U. Grad. Sch. Edn., Cambridge, Mass., 1963, prof., 1965-91, prof. emeritus, 1991; readability cons., 1950—; faculty summer sessions Tchrs. Coll., Columbia U., N.Y.C., 1958, 60, 61; mem. Nat. Com. on Dyslexia and Related Reading Disorders, 1968-69, steering com. Project Literacy, U.S. Office Edn.; sec.-treas. Nat. Conf. on Rsch. in English, 1962, v.p. 1964-65, pres. 1965. Author: Readability: An Appraisal of Research and Application, 1958, Learning to Read: The Great Debate, 1967, updated edit., 1983; co-author: (with Dale) A Formula for Predicting Readability, 1948, (with Roswell) Roswell-Chall Diagnostic Reading Test of Word Analysis Skills, 1956, Stages of Reading Development, 1983, Diagnostic Assessments of Reading with Trial Teaching Strategies, 1992, (With Jacobs and Baldwin) The Reading Crisis: Why Poor Children Fall Behind, 1990, (with Conrad) Should Textbooks Challenge Students? The Case for Easier or Harder Books, 1991, (with Roswell) Diagnostic Assessments of Reading with Trial Teachings Strategies, 1992; contbr. articles to profl. jours. Recipient Andre Favat award Mass. Coun. Tchrs. Eng., 1979, Am. Ednl. Rsch. Assn. award, 1982, 96, Edward L. Thorndike award APA, 1982; named to the Reading Hall of Fame, 1979, Nat. Acad. Edn., 1979. Fellow APA; mem. Nat. Assn. Remedial Teaching (chmn. program com. 1955), Nat. Reading Coun., Internat. Reading Assn. (dir. 1961-65, chmn. pre-conf. inst. 1959-61, membership com. 1958-60, Citation of Merit 1979), Am. Ednl. Rsch. Assn., Nat. Soc. for Study of Edn. (dir. 1972-74), Pi Lambda Theta, Beta Gamma Sigma, Phi Delta Kappa. Home: 1558 Massachusetts Ave Cambridge MA 02138-2913 Office: Harvard U Grad Sch Edn Larsen Hall Appian Way Cambridge MA 02138

CHALLIS, NORMA JEAN, educator; b. New Brighton, Pa., Oct. 23, 1934; d. Albert Orm and Elizabeth Freda (Handle) Franklin; m. George Ellery Douds, July 16, 1975 (dec. July 1982); m. Thomas Harold Challis, Mar. 10, 1984; 1 stepchild. BS, Maryville (Tenn.) Coll., 1956; MS, Pa. State U., University Park, 1968. Tchr. elem. edn. Highland Suburban Jointure, Beaver Falls, Pa., 1956-66, tchr. reading, 1966-73; reading specialist Blackhawk Sch. Dist., Beaver Falls, 1973-88; lectr. math. Geneva Coll., Beaver Falls, 1968-75; lectr. reading Community Coll. Beaver County, Monaca, Pa., 1975-77; gifted and talented elem. resource tutorial educator Blackhawk Sch. Dist., Beaver Falls, 1988—; guest lectr. Big Beaver Falls Sch. Dist., Highland Suburban, Beaver Falls, Beaver Valley Intermediate Unit, Monaca, Pattersen PTA, Beaver Falls. Bd. dirs. Greater Beaver Valley Cultural Alliance, 1990; deacon, elder 1st Presbyn. Ch. Beaver Falls. Mem. AAUW (sec. 1981), NEA, Pa. State Edn. Assn., Blackhawk Edn. Assn. (past pres.), Pa. Assn. Gifted Edn., Order Rainbow Girls (grand worthy assoc. advisor 1954), Delta Kappa Gamma (pres. 1982-83). Republican. Home: 1440 River Rd Beaver PA 15009-2410 Office: Blackhawk Sch Dist 402 Shenango Rd Beaver Falls PA 15010-1657

CHALMERS, GEOFFREY TEALE, lawyer; b. Evanston, Ill., Dec. 30, 1935; s. Gordon K. and Robert Teale (Swartz) C.; 1 child, Christopher L. BA cum laude, Harvard U., 1957; LLB, Columbia U., 1961; MBA in Fin., NYU, 1971. Bar: N.Y. 1961, Mass. 1973. Assoc. Cravath, Swaine & Moore, N.Y.C., 1961-65, Casey, Tyre, Wallace & Bannerman, N.Y.C., 1968-72; atty. SEC, Washington, 1965-66, Lehman Bros., N.Y.C., 1966-68; gen. counsel Continental Investment Corp., Boston, 1972-80; ptnr. Gray, Wendell, Chalmers & Dahlen, Boston, 1980-87; gen. counsel Liberty Real Estate Group, Inc., Boston, 1987—; assoc. prof. Suffolk Law Sch., N.Y.C., 1975-79. Office: Liberty Real Estate Group Inc 600 Atlantic Ave Boston MA 02210-2211

CHALMERS, RUTH, association executive; b. White Plains, N.Y., July 17, 1922; d. Alan Reid and Ruth Sylvester (Nash) C. AB, Smith Coll., 1944. Exec. dir. Jane Addams Peace Assn., N.Y.C., 1952—; coord. Conf. of Soviet and U.S. Women, Bryn Mawr, Pa., 1961; bd. dirs. Women's Internat. League for Peace and Freedom, Phila., 1962-69. Mem. Westchester County N.Y. Dem. Com., 1954-61; bd. dirs. Wespac Found. (chmn. bd. 1986-89). Episcopalian. Office: Jane Addams Peace Assn 777 United Nations Plz New York NY 10017

CHAMBERLAIN, ROBERT WAYNE, investment advisor; b. Flint, Mich., Feb. 28, 1951; s. Wayne J. and Elaine E. (Scheidler) C.; m. Janet Munoz Ching, Aug. 1, 1987; 1 child, Andrea Kristin. Student, Flint Jr. Coll., 1969, Honolulu Community Coll., 1975, N.Y. Inst. Fin., 1976, Coll. Fin. Planning, 1981. Cert. fin. planner; registered investment adviser. Registered rep. Blyth Eastman Dillon & Co., Inc., Honolulu, 1976-78; registered rep., regional dir. personal fin. mgmt. E.F. Hutton & Co., Inc., Honolulu, 1978-81; pres. Chamberlain & Assocs., Inc., Honolulu, 1981-90; br. mgr. Investmnt Mgmt. & Rsch., Inc., Sewickley, Pa., 1991—; dir. securities prin. Associated Planners Securities Corp., L.A., 1983-88; br. mgr. Investment Mgmt. & Rsch., INc., Sewickley, Pa., 1990—; owner Robert W. Chamberlain, Sewickley, 1990—; adj. faculty Coll Fin. Planning, Denver, 1981-86; sole proprietor Robert W. Chamberlain, CFP, 1990—. Author: The 1990's: Decade of Depression, 1990. Staff sgt. USAF, 1970-74. Named one of Best Fin. Planners in the nation Money Mag., 1987. Mem. Internat. Assn. Fin. Planning (bd. dirs. 1985-87, registry appeals bd. 1985-87, chmn. 1986-87, legis. liaison Honolulu chpt. 1984-90), Inst. Cert. Fin. Planners (ethics com. 1985-86, legis. liaison Honolulu chpt. 1984-85), Am. Arbitration Assn. (panel mem. 1983—), Hawaii C. of C. (chmn. small bus. coun. 1983-87, v.p. 1984-87), Pitts. Airport Area C. of C. (bd. dirs., chmn. legis. affairs 1991—).

CHAMBERLIN, MARK ANDREW, finance executive; b. New Milford, Conn., Oct. 19, 1962; s. John Edward and Margaret Lois (Benson) C.; m. Donna Marie Ferrara, June 12, 1988; children: Mark Andrew II, Stefan Ciro. BS, Marist Coll., 1984. CPA, N.Y. Audit mgr. Peat Marwick Main & Co., Stamford, Conn., 1985-89; mgr. fin. reporting Nestle Foods Corp., Purchase, N.Y., 1989-90, mgr. fin. planning and analysis, 1990-91, mgr. fin. control, 1991—. Mem. AICPA, N.Y. State Soc. Certified Pub. Accountants (scholastic award 1987). Republican. Roman Catholic. Home: Gobblers Knob Rd Pawling NY 12564-2111 Office: Nestle Food Corp 100 Manhattanville Rd Purchase NY 10577-2198

CHAMBERS, DANIEL WARREN, mathematics educator; b. South Bend, Ind., Dec. 29, 1952; s. Warren D. and Joyce E. (Kalahar) C.; m. Doreen Mary Arcus, Oct. 9, 1982; 1 child, Patrick. BS, U. Notre Dame, 1975; MA, U. Md., 1977, PhD, 1983. Instr., math. Boston Coll., Chestnut Hill, Mass., 1982-83, asst. prof. math., 1982-89, assoc. prof. math., 1989—. Contbr. articles to profl. jours. Mem. Am. Math. Soc., Inst. Math. Stats., AAAS, Pi Mu Epsilon. Office: Boston Coll Math Dept Chestnut Hill MA 02167

CHAMBERS, GORDON ANTHONY, magazine editor; b. Bronx, N.Y., Oct. 12, 1969; s. Byron George and Valerie DeRuth (Ellis) C. BA, Brown U., 1990. Asst. editor Essence Mag., N.Y.C., 1990—; hotline operator A.B.C. Broadcast Co., Hackensack, N.J., 1987-90; tchr. retarded children Teaneck (N.J.) Sch. System, 1985-86. Contbr. articles to mags. Democrat. Episcopalian. Home: 1021 Phelps Rd Teaneck NJ 07666-5623

CHAMBERS, J. RICHARD, education educator; b. Hanover, N.H., Dec. 16, 1930; s. John R. and Eva (Monica) C.; m. June, Aug. 13, 1960; children: Scot Alan, Tod Richard. BEd, Keene State Coll., 1952; EdM, Boston U., 1953, EdD, 1956. From asst. prof. to assoc. prof. U. Miami, Coral Gables, Fla., 1958-62; assoc. prof., dir. Ednl. Clinic Boston U., 1962—. Mem. Internat. Reading Assn., Mass. Reading Assn. (past pres.), Mass. Assn. Coll. and Univ. Reading Educators (past pres.). Office: Boston U Sch Edn 605 Commonwealth Ave Boston MA 02215-1605

CHAMBERS, LETITIA PEARL CAROLINE, public policy consulting firm executive; b. Alva, Okla., Feb. 1, 1943; d. E. Wade and Anita (Sims) Chambers; m. Stephen Morelock, Mar. 1964 (div. 1970); 1 child, Melissa. BA, U. Okla., 1965; MS, Okla. State U., 1971, EdD, 1973. Tchr. Oklahoma City Pub. Schs., 1965-70, adminstr., 1973-74; dir. fed. programs N.Mex. State Edn. Agy., Santa Fe, 1974-75; sr. analyst US Senate Budget Com., Washington, 1976-77; staff dir. US Senate Spl. Com. on Aging, Washington, 1978, US Senate Com. on Labor & Human Resources, Washington, 1979-81; pres. Chambers Assocs., Inc., Washington, 1982—; pres. Coalition of Publicly Traded Partnerships, Washington, 1987—; dir. Adams Nat. Bank, Washington; treas. Nat. Infrastruction Bond Coalition. Author various senate reports, policy studies. Edler Chevy Chase (Md.) Presbyn. Ch., 1986—; mem. Dem. Leadership Coun., Potomac Group, Dem. Nat. Com. Mem. Coun. for Excellence in Govt. (prin.), Nat. Assn. Women Bus. Owners, City Club. Office: Chambers Assocs Inc 1625 K St NW # 200 Washington DC 20006-1682

CHAMBERS, MARY ANNE BEEMAN, economist; b. Manchester, N.H., Aug. 10, 1958; d. John Francis and Evelyn Catherine (McDonald) Beeman; m. Daniel Nels Chambers, Feb. 29, 1984 (dec. June 21, 1989). BA in Econs., Merrimack Coll., 1980; MS in Econs., Syracuse U., 1982. Economist Cahner Pub. Co., Newton, Mass., 1982-83; sr. economist Assn. Am. R.R., Washington, 1983-86; dir. rsch. Nat. Assn. Convenience Stores, Alexandria, Va., 1986-90; economist, analyst State of N.H. Govt., Concord, 1990—. Author: Measuring Distance, 1990, Off on a Jetty, 1991. Mem. Widowed Persons Svcs., Seabrook, N.H., 1990—. Recipient Presdl. Point of Light to Widowed Persons Svc. award, 1991. Mem. Am. Econ. Assn., Nat. Assn. Bus. Economists, Am. Soc. Assn. Execs. Democrat. Roman Catholic. Home: 236 Winding Pond Rd Londonderry NH 03053-3378 Office: Legis Budget Asst Office State House Rm 102 Concord NH 03301

CHAMBERS, STEVEN MICHAEL, psychologist; b. Vineland, N.J., May 27, 1960; s. Howard Everett and Karen Eleanor (Shene) C.; m. Laurie Lee Schneck, June 5, 1982. BA summa cum laude, Eastern Nazarene Coll., Quincy, Mass., 1982; MA, Biola U., 1984, PsyD, 1987. Lic. psychologist, Pa. Psychology asst. Harford Psychol. Ctr., Fallston, Md., 1986-87; psychologist Acute Psychiatric Unit Dept. Vets. Affairs, Coatesville, Pa., 1987-89; psychologist, program coord. Dept. Vets. Affairs, Coatesville, 1989—; pvt. practice King of Prussia, Pa., 1990—; psychologist Metro Md. Counseling Ctr., Timonium, 1987-89. Youth group tchr. Ch. of Nazarene, Fairview Village, Pa., 1990—, bd. dirs. 1990—, Jr. High coord. 1990. Mem. Phi Delta. Home: 134 Forge Rd Kng Of Prussa PA 19406-3057 Office: Dept Vets Affairs 1400 Blackhorse Hill Rd Coatesville PA 19320-2040

CHAMETZKY, BARRY I., French language educator; b. Bklyn., Feb. 9, 1961; s. Leslie and Florence (Victor) C. BS in Piano Performance, Bklyn. Coll., 1983, MA in Music History, 1985; MA in French, Middlebury Coll., 1990; postgrad., U. Pitts., 1990—. Teaching asst. U. Pitts., 1990—. Composer: Symphony No. 1 in C minor, 1981, Symphony No. 2, 1985, Sympnohy No. 3 Kol Nidrei, 1991. Grantee U. Louisville, 1987, Middlebury Coll., 1989, 90, U. Pitts., 1990—. Mem. Am. Assn. Tchrs. French, Pi Delta Phi, Phi Sigma Iota. Home: 403 S Aiken Ave # 2 Pittsburgh PA 15232-1207

CHAMPOUX, DAVID HAROLD, administrator; b. Syracuse, N.Y., Nov. 7, 1948; s. Homer David and Jacqueline Alberta (Smith) C.; m. Marueen F. Brophy, June 27, 1970; children: John David, Michael Patrick. BA in Psycholoyg, St. John Fisher, 1970; MS in Communications, Syracuse U. Supr. Xerox Corp., Rochester, N.Y., 1970-71; prof. Herkimer County (N.Y.) Community Coll., 1972-86, div. chmn., 1986—. Mem. BEA, NAB, Elks. Democrat. Roman Catholic. Home: 12 Forge Hill Dr Ilion NY 13357 Office: Herkimer Community Coll Herkimer NY 13350

CHAN, CLARA SUET-PHANG, physician; b. Swatow, Guandong, People's Republic of China, Sept. 23, 1949; came to U.S., 1969; d. Hon-Kwong and Suet-Hing (Wong) C. BS, Mary Manse Coll., 1972; MD, George Washington U., 1976. Diplomate Am. Bd. Internal Medicine, Am. Bd. Hematology, Am. Bd. Oncology. Intern U. Miami (Fla.) Hosp., 1976-77, med. resident, 1977-79; fellow hematology, oncology George Washington U., 1979-81; fellow oncoloy research City of Hope Med. Ctr., Duarte, Calif., 1981-83, instr. medicine, 1982-83; asst. chief hematology VA Med. Ctr., Washington, 1983-91; with Hematology/Oncology Cons., Greenbelt, Md., 1991—; asst. prof. medicine George Washington U., 1983-88, assoc. prof., 1988—; prin. investigator stem cell lab. VA Med. Ctr., Washington, 1983-91; physician Hematology Oncology Cons., Greenbelt, Md., 1991—; project chmn. S.E. Cancer Study Group, Birmingham, Ala., 1982-85; mem. med. staff George Washington U., 1983—. Contbr. articles to profl. jours. Del. cancer update Citizen Ambassador program People to People Internat., 1986. Recipient Internat. Peace scholarship George Washington U. 1972-76; Med. Student Research grantee Pan Am. Health Orgn., 1974; Reader's Digest Internat. fellow United Christian Hosp., Hong Kong, 1976; research fellow VA Career Devel. program, Washington, 1981. Fellow ACP; mem. Am. Soc. Clin. Oncology, Am. Soc. Hematology, N.Y. Acad. Sci., William Beaumort Med. Soc. Home: 7001 Bybrook Ln Bethesda MD 20815-3166 Office: Hematology Oncology Cons 7525 Greenway Center Dr Ste 205 Greenbelt MD 20770-3532

CHAN, DONALD PIN-KWAN, orthopaedic surgeon, educator; b. Rangoon, Burma, Jan. 21, 1937; s. Charles Y.C. and Josephine (Golamco) C.; m. Dorothy Chan, July 31, 1966; children: Joanne, Elaine. BS, U. Rangoon, Burma, 1955, MD, 1960. Intern medicine U. Hong Kong, 1960-61, resident surgery and orthopaedics, 1961-68; resident orthopaedic surgery U. Vt., 1968-71; assoc. orthopaedist Strong Meml. Hosp., Rochester, N.Y., 1972-80, sr. assoc. orthopaedist, 1980-86, attending orthopaedist, 1986—; asst. prof. U. Rochester, 1972-80, assoc. prof., 1980-87, prof., 1987—; dir. Goldstein Fellowship, Rochester, Orthopaedic Clin. Svcs., Rochester; chief sect. spine surgery dept. orthopaedics, Rochester. Contbr. articles on clin. rsch. related to the spine. Bd. dirs. Rochester Chinese Assn., 1991. Traveling fellow Scoliosis Rsch. Soc. Fellow ACS, Am. Acad. Orthopaedic Surgeons, Am. Orthopaedic Assn., Scoliosis Rsch. Soc.; mem. AMA, N.Am. Spine Soc., Am. Spinal Injury Assn., Ea. Orthopaedic Assn. Office: U Rochester Sch Medicine 601 Elmwood Ave Rochester NY 14642

CHAN, ERIC PING-PANG, industrial designer; b. Canton, Peoples Republic of China, Sept. 1, 1952; came to U.S., 1978; s. Chung-Po and Kit-Jon (So) C.; m. Juliana Po-Ying Young, Sept. 18, 1985; 1 child, Kevin Yu-Hinn. Diploma in indsl. design, Hong Kong Polytechnic, 1976; MFA, Cranbrook Acad. Art, 1980. Sr. designer Henry Dreyfuss Assocs., N.Y.C., 1980-84; design assoc. Emilio Ambasz Assocs., N.Y.C., 1984-87; prin. designer Wang Lab, Lowell, Mass., 1987; pres., design dir. Chan & Dolan Design, Inc., N.Y.C., 1987-90, Ecco Design, Inc., N.Y.C., 1990—; guest

lectr. Parson Sch. of Design, N.Y.C., 1990—; cons. Chinese History Mus., N.Y.C., 1988-91. Design exhbns. Arango Internat. Design Exhbn., 1987, Milw. Art Mus., 1988; represented in permanent collections Denver Mus. Art, London Design Mus., Israel Mus.; contbr. articles to profl. jours.; patentee in field. Recipient Forma Finlandia Internat. Design award, Finland, 1989, award Internat. Furniture Design Competition, Progressive Architecture, 1982, Best Product Design award Accent on Design, N.Y., 1987, Best Product award in Good Office, Arango Design Exhbn., Mus. of Art, Fla., 1989, Best Product Design of 1989 Bus. Week, Best Product of 1990 Design News, Design Plus award Frankfurt (Germany) Fair, 1990, Highest award Design Innovation 90, Germany, others. Mem. Indsl. Design Soc. Am. (Bronze award 1989, 90). Office: Ecco Design Ste 600 89 Fifth Ave New York NY 10003

CHAN, JACK-KANG, anti-submarine warfare engineer, mathematician; b. Toyshan, China, Oct. 20, 1950; came to U.S., 1975; s. David En-Shek and Yip-Ching (Yuen) C.; m. Suet-Fong Ng, June 3, 1982; children: Me-Fun, Kang-Ray. PhD in Elec. Engring., Poly. U., 1982, PhD in Math., 1990. Microwave engr. Sedco Systems div. Raytheon, Melville, N.Y., 1979-80; sr. mem. tech. staff Norden Systems div. United Tech., Melville, 1980—. Author papers in field. Mem. IEEE (reviewer signal processing 1989-90), Am. Math. Soc., Math. Assn. Am., Soc. Indsl. and Applied Math. Office: Norden Systems United Tech 75 Maxess Rd Melville NY 11747-3182

CHAN, STEVEN K.S., systems development executive; b. Singapore, Singapore, Sept. 29, 1941; s. Chee Nam Chan and Swee Chow Yong; m. Lucy K.C., Aug. 7, 1966; children: Teren, Kit-Lun. BS, U. Singapore, 1966; diploma, Singapore Poly., 1966-67; MIBA, Inst. of Bus. Adminstrn., Melbourne, y. Programmer ICL, Singapore, 1966-67; programmer Catepillar, Singapore, 1967-69, data processing supr., 1969-73, sr. system analyst, 1973-83; asst. dir. Inst. of Advanced Computer Technology, Singapore, 1983-84; MIS mgr. Pata Gen. Mfg. Ltd., Singapore, 1984-85; cons. AGS Computer Ltd., N.Y.C., 1985—; systems cons. Am. Express hdqrs., N.Y.C., 1986-90, IBM Poughkeepsie (N.Y.) main plant, 1991—. Mem. Brit. Inst. Mgmt., Singapore Inst. Mgmt., Singapore Computer Soc., Inst. Bus. Adminstrn. Home: 36 Hudson Harbour Dr # B Poughkeepsie NY 12601-5378 Office: AGS Computers Inc 15 Myers Corners Rd Wappingers Falls NY 12590-4117

CHAN, WING-CHI, cultural organization administrator, musicologist; b. Hong Kong, Aug. 10, 1952; came to U.S., 1979; s. Hing and Mui-Fung (Leung) C.; m. Mina Chan, Jan. 1, 1979; children: Tidings, Leona, Dexter. BA, Chinese U., Hong Kong, 1978; MMus, Ill. U., 1981; postgrad., U. Amsterdam, 1991. Pres. Chinese U. Student Union, Hong Kong, 1977; rsch. asst. U. S.W. La., Lafayette, 1979; mgr. Charm's Trading Co., Houston, 1982; asst. to dir. coll. honors program U. Md., Catonsville, 1984-85; dir. devel. Washington Youth Orch., 1985—; broadcaster Voice of Am. Radio, Washington, 1989-90; lecture speaker U. Md., College Park, 1983, 84, Tenri (Japan) U., 1986, Kingston Poly., London, 1988, Hong Kong U., 1990; tour coord. Washington Youth Orch. to China, Hong Kong, Taiwan, Korea and Russia, 1986-88; cons. NEA, Washington, 1989—; vis. assoc. prof. ShenYang Conservatory, China, 1992—. Recipient Supr. Svc. award Mayor of Washington, 1987. Mem. Assn. for Asian Studies, Am. Symphony Orch. League, Cultural Alliance Greater Washington. Office: Washington Youth Orch Brightwood Sta Box 56198 Washington DC 20011

CHANATRY, FRANCIS, surgeon; b. Utica, N.Y.; s. Raymond and Bahia Margaret (Ghariba) C. AB, Hamilton Coll., 1946; MD, Albany Med. Coll., 1948. Diplomate Am. Bd. Surgery, Am. Bd. Medical Examiners. Intern USPHS, Staten Island, N.Y., 1948-49; sr. surgeon USPHS, Washington, 1949-50; surg. resident Upstate Med. Ctr., Syracuse, N.Y., 1950-55, chief resident in surgery, instr., 1954-55; attending surgeon St. Luke's Meml. Hosp., Utica, N.Y., 1955—, St. Elizabeth Hosp., Utica, N.Y., 1955—, Faxton Hosp., Utica, N.Y., 1955—. Fellow Am. Coll. Surgeons (gov. 1989—); mem. AMA, N.Y. State Med. Soc., N.Y. Acad. Medicine, Oneida County Med. Soc. (pres. 1981-82), Cen. N.Y. Surgical Soc. (pres. 1984-86). Roman Catholic. Home: 1109 Parkway E Utica NY 13501 Office: Francis Chanatry MD PC 103 Pleasant St Utica NY 13501

CHANCE, PAUL BRADLEY, writer; b. Glen Burnie, Md., Sept. 15, 1941; s. Edward George and Dorothy Emily (Kendall) C.; m. Diane Elizabeth Pfeiffer, Nov. 7, 1960. BS, Towson (Md.) State U., 1963; MA, U. No. Colo., 1966; PhD, Utah State U., 1973. Tchr. Marley (Md.) Middle Sch., 1963-64, Cortez (Colo.) Middle Sch., 1964-65; articles editor Psychology Today Mag., Del Mar, Calif., 1972-74; asst. mng. editor Psychology Today Mag., Del Mar and N.Y.C., 1974-76; contbg. editor, cons. Psychology Today Mag., Washington, 1986-89; writer, editor Federalsburg, Md., 1976-86; writer Laurel, Del., 1989—; editorial cons. various textbook pubs., 1980—; media cons. Assn. for Behavior Analysis, Kalamazoo, Mich., 1988—. Author: Learning and Behavior, 1987, Thinking in the Classroom, 1986; co-editor: Best of Psychology Today, 1989; contbr. articles to profl. jours. Del. White Ho. Conf. on Librs., Washington, 1991, Govs. Conf. on Librs., Dover, 1991; workshop leader Laurel Libr. Lt. USN, 1967-69. Grantee Nat. Inst. Edn., 1984; recipient Citation of Merit Md. Dept. Edn., 1982. Mem. Am. Psychol. Assn. Democrat. Home and Office: RR 3 Box 210A Laurel DE 19956-9541

CHANCELLOR, JOHN WILLIAM, news correspondent; b. Chgo., July 14, 1927; s. Estil Marion and Mollie (Barrett) C.; m. Constance Herbert; 1 child, Mary; m. Barbara Upshaw, Jan. 25, 1958; children: Laura, Barnaby. Student, DePaul Acad., Chgo., U. Ill. Reporter Chgo. Sun-Times; staff NBC News, 1950-65, newswriter, gen. assignment reporter U.S., 1953-58, Vienna corr., 1958, with London bur., 1959-60, Moscow corr., 1960-61, staff N.Y.C. office, 1961-63, Brussels corr., 1963-65; communicator TV program Today, 1961-62, staff corr., 1962-65; dir. Voice of Am., Washington, 1966-67; network nat. affairs corr. NBC, 1967—; anchorman NBC Nightly News, 1970-82; commentator NBC News, 1982—. Author: Peril and Promise: A Commentary on America, 1990. Address: care NBC 30 Rockefeller Plz New York NY 10020

CHANDLER, ELISABETH GORDON (MRS. LACI DE GERENDAY), sculptor, harpist; b. St. Louis, June 10, 1913; d. Henry Brace and Sara Ellen (Sallee) Gordon; m. Robert Kirkland Chandler, May 27, 1946 (dec.); m. Laci de Gerenday, May 12, 1979. Grad., Lenox Sch., 1931; pvt. study sculpture and harp. Mem. Mildred Dilling Harp Ensemble, 1934-45; instr. portrait sculpture Lyme Acad. Fine Arts, 1976—; dir. Abbott Coin Counter Co., Inc., 1941-55. Exhibited sculpture NAD, Nat. Sculpture Soc., Allied Artists Am., Nat. Arts Club, Pen and Brush, Lyme Art Assn., Mattatuck Mus., Catherine Lorillard Wolfe Art Club, Am. Artists Profl. League, Hudson Valley Art Assn., USIA, 1976-78, Lyme Art Ctr., 1979, retrospective exhbn. Lyme Acad. Fine Arts, 1987, Madison Gallery, 1987, Old State House, Hartford, Conn., 1989, Mellon Art Ctr., Wallingford, Conn., 1989, Fairfield U. Walsh Gallery, 1991; represented in permanent collections Aircraft Carrier USS Forrestal, Gov. Dummer Acad., James Forrestal Research Ctr. of Princeton U., Lenox Sch., James L. Collins Parochial Sch., Tex., Storm King Art Ctr., Columbia U., Pace U., White Plains, N.Y., St. Patrick's Cathedral, N.Y.C., McAuley Ctr., St. Joseph's Coll., West Hartford, Conn., Forrestal Meml. Medal, Timoschenko Medal for Applied Mechanics, Benjamin Franklin Medal, Albert A. Michelson Medal, Jonathan Edwards Medal, Shafto Broadcasting Award Medal, Woodrow Wilson Sch. of Princeton U., Ga. Pacific Bldg., Atlanta, Messiah Coll., Grantham, Pa., Adlai E. Stevenson High Sch., Ill., Queen Anne's County Courthouse Square, Md., pvt. collections. With mus. therapy div. Am. Theatre Wing, 1942-45; trustee The Lenox Sch., 1953-55; chmn. Associated Taxpayers Old Lyme, 1969-72; mem., trustee Brookgreen Gardens, S.C., 1989—. Recipient 1st prize Bklyn. War Meml. competition, 1945; 1st prize sculpture Catherine Lorillard Wolfe Art Club, 1951, 58, 63, Gold medal, 1969; Founders prize Pen & Brush, 1954, 76, 78, Gold medal, 1957, 61, 63, 69, 74, 76, Am. Heritage award, 1968, Solo Show award, 1961, 69, 75; Thomas R. Proctor prize NAD, 1956, Dessie Geer prize, 1960, 79, 85; Sculpture prize Nat. Arts Club, 1959, 60, 62, Gold medal, 1971; Gold medal Am. Artists Profl. League, 1960, 69, 73, 75, prize, 1981, Anna Hyatt Huntington prize, 1970, 76, Harriet Mayer Meml. prize, 1961; Gold medal Hudson Valley Art Assn., 1956, 69, 74, Mrs. John Newington award, 1976, 78; Lindsey Morris Meml. prize Allied Artists Am., 1973, Gold medal, 1982; sculpture prize Acad. Artists, 1974; Sydney Taylor Meml. prize Knickerbocker Artists, 1975; New Netherlands DAR Bicentennial medal, 1976, named Citizen of Yr., Town of Old Lyme, Conn., 1985. Fellow Nat. Sculpture Soc. (council 1976-85, Tallix Foundry award 1979, John Spring Founder's award 1986, John Cavanaugh Meml. prize 1991, Silver medal, citation 1992), Am. Artists Profl. League, Internat. Inst. Arts and Letters; mem. Federation International de la Medaille, Nat. Arts Club, Allied Artists Am., Am. Medallic Soc., Pen and Brush, Catherine Lorillard Wolf Art Club, Lyme Art Assn. (pres. 1973-75), Council Am. Artists Socs. (dir. 1970-73), Am. Artists Profl. League (dir. 1970-73), NAD, Lyme Acad. Fine Arts (trustee 1976—). Home and Studio: 2 Mill Pond Ln Old Lyme CT 06371

CHANDLER, KENNETH A., newspaper editor; b. Westcliff-on-Sea, Essex, Eng., Aug. 2, 1947; came to U.S., 1974; s. Leonard Gordon and Beatrix Marie (McKenzie) C.; m. Linda Kathleen, Mar. 22, 1975; children—Bethany, Benjamin, Kathryn. Mng. editor N.Y. Post, N.Y.C., 1978-86; exec. editor Boston Herald, 1986—. Office: News Group Boston Inc 1 Herald Sq Roxbury MA 02118-2297

CHANDLER, KENNETH ASHTON, psychologist; b. Fitchburg, Mass., Feb. 11, 1921; s. Luther Shattuck and Cora May (Cross) C.; m. Helen Hammond, Nov. 1, 1942; children: Kendra Hammond, Hilarie Kevala. AB, Clark U., 1948, MA, 1949, PhD, 1953. Diplomate Am. Bd. Clin. Psychology. Asst. prof. U. Del., Newark, 1953-54; assoc. prof. Bridgeport (Conn.) U., 1954-58; postdoctoral fellow Yale U., West Haven, Conn., 1958-60; asst. prof. depts. of psychology and psychiatry Yale U., 1960-65; from assoc. prof. to prof. Vassar Coll., Poughkeepsie, N.Y., 1965-86; prof. emeritus Vassar Coll., Poughkeepsie, 1986—; cons. Laurel Heights State Chronic Rehab. Hosp., Shelton, Conn., 1962-70, New Britain (Conn.) Mem. Hosp. Chronic Care and Rehab. Hosp., 1965-90. Author: Experimental Laboratory Manual, 1969; contbr. articles to profl. jours. With U.S. Army, 1943-45, ETO. Mem. AAAS, APA (vis. scientist 1964-67), Ea. Psychol. Assn., Sigma Xi. Home: 14 Kings Ln Essex CT 06426

CHANDLER, RACHEL EDEN, nursing educator; b. Fall River, Mass., Sept. 25, 1941; d. Elmer H. and Margaret L. (Hutchinson) Allen; widowed. BSN, U. Mass., 1962, MS in Psychiat.-Mental Health Nursing, 1974, PhD in Pub. Health, 1990. Cert. clin. specialist/adult psychiat.-mental health nursing. Coord. adult svcs. Westfield (Mass.) Mental Health Clinic, 1974-77; asst. prof., dir. div. nursing Am. Internat. Coll., Springfield, Mass., 1977-84, assoc. prof., 1984—; dir. day treatment dept. psychiatry Baystate Med. Ctr., 1970-72; clin. specialist Brightside Counseling Assocs., West Springfield, Mass., 1985—; cons., workshop facilitator We. Mass. Hosp., Westfield, 1991, Northampton (Mass.) State Hosp., 1990-91. Contbg. author: Managing the Critical Care Unit, 1987. Mem. West Springfield Sch. Com., 1985—, chmn., 1986-88. Mem. ANA, NLN, Mass. Assn. Sch. Comms., PEO (chpt. pres. 1976-78), Pioneer Valley Area Health Edn. Ctr. (adv. bd.), Sigma Theta Tau (Rsch. award 1990). Home: 57 Harbey Rd West Springfield MA 01089-4322

CHANDLER, ROBERT LESLIE, public relations executive; b. Phila., Mar. 3, 1948; s. Joel Leslie and Evelyn Laney (DeLaney) C.; AS, Atlantic Community Coll., 1969; BS, Bowling Green State U., 1971; MS, Ohio U., 1972; MBA in Hosp. Adminstrn., Wagner Coll., 1980; m. Maureen O'Keefe, Mar. 21, 1970. Dir. pub. rels. Athens Mental Health Ctr., Ohio, 1972; internal communications editor, pub. affairs dept. Owens-Corning Fiberglas Corp., Toledo, 1972-74; dir. community rels. Wyandotte Gen. Hosp., Mich., 1974-76; v.p. asst. adminstr. mktg./pub. affairs Meth. Hosp., Bklyn., 1976-82; exec. v.p. Burson-Marsteller Pub. Rels., N.Y.C., 1982—. Mem. budget com. United Way Mich., 1975-76. N.J. State scholar, 1969. Mem. Pub. Rels. Soc. Am., Am. Soc. Hosp. Mktg. and Pub. Rels., Am. Hosp. Assn., Hosp. Pub. Rels. Soc. Greater N.Y., Sigma Delta Chi, Kappa Tau Alpha. Home: 2 Horatio St Apt 2M New York NY 10014-1637 Office: Burson Marsteller Pub Rels 230 Park Ave S New York NY 10003-1513

CHANDONNET, CHRISTOPHER HENRY, public relations executive; b. Washington, Sept. 23, 1961; s. Noel Andrew and Sandra June (Shebell) C.; m. Kathleen Marie McNally, Sept. 21, 1986; 1 child, Kaitlyn Marie. BS, L.I. U., 1984; postgrad., Fordham U. Consumer affairs rep. Ins. Info. Inst., N.Y.C., 1985-88; mgr. corp. communications KPMG Peat Marwick, N.Y.C., 1988—. Author, editor (newsletters) Insurance Update, Insurance News; contbr. articles to profl. jours. Mem. Pub. Rels. Soc. Am., Internat. Assn. Bus. Communicators. Roman Catholic. Office: KPMG Peat Marwick 767 5th Ave New York NY 10153-0002 Home: 15 Gaines Pl Huntington NY 11743-1520

CHANEY, WILLIAM R., former cosmetic company executive; b. Satanta, Kans., July 31, 1932; s. Alva Ross and Irene (Reeves) C.; m. Carolyn Keenan; children: Carole Babette, Diana. B.A. in Bus. Adminstrn., U. Kans., 1953. With Avon Products, Inc., N.Y.C., 1955-85, dir. personnel adminstrn., 1966-67; v.p. personnel Avon Products, Inc., 1967-68, group v.p. field ops., 1968-69, sr. v.p. ops., 1969-72, exec. v.p., 1972-77, pres., 1977-85, also dir.; chmn. bd. Tiffany & Co., N.Y.C.; dir. Tiffany & Co., Bank of N.Y., New Hampton, Inc., FAO Schwartz, Fifth Ave. Assn. Chmn., Nat. Minority Supplier Devel. Council. Served to 1st lt. AUS, 1953-55. Mem. Advt. and Sales Execs. Club, Lambda Chi Alpha. Office: Tiffany & Co 727 5th Ave New York NY 10022-2503*

CHANG, ARNOLD, artist, Chinese painting expert; b. N.Y.C., Feb. 19, 1954; s. Gerard and Sheila (Liu) C.; m. Jillian Wang, Feb. 14, 1976; 1 child, Christopher. BA, U. Colo., 1974; MA, U. Calif., Berkeley, 1976. V.p. Sotheby's, N.Y.C., 1980—; bd. dirs.Sotheby's Hong Kong, Sotheby's Taiwan. Author: Painting in The People's Republic of China, 1980; contbr. numerous articles to profl. jours.; curator exhbn. The Mountain Retreat, 1986. Office: Sotheby s 1334 York Ave New York NY 10021

CHANG, BIANCA, elementary educator; b. Shanghai, China, June 26, 1939; came to U.S., 1956; d. Kuo Shuen and Soo Yee (Yu) C. BA, Colo. State Coll., 1962; MA, SUNY, Stony Brook, 1974. Tchr. Anaheim (Calif.) Sch. Dist., 1962-63, Port Washington (N.Y.) Sch. Dist., 1963-64, South Huntington (N.Y.) Sch. Dist., 1964—. Republican. Office: Countrywood Elem Sch Old Country Rd South Huntington NY 11746

CHANG, CHIA-LIN, accounting professional; b. Taipei, Republic of China, Oct. 20, 1959; came to U.S., 1969; s. Cheng H. and Ruby I.F. (Chuang) C. AS in Bus., Onandaga Community Coll., Syracuse, N.Y., 1979; BS in Acctg., SUNY, Binghamton, 1980, MBA in Human Resource Mgmt., 1983. Quality control lab. technician Bristol Labs., Syracuse, 1981; benefits analyst CIGNA Corp., Syracuse, 1983-85; v.p. Chia Enterprises, Inc., Syracuse, 1985—; acctg. asst. Empire State Life Ins. Co., Syracuse, 1985-90; fin. reporting analyst Unity Mut. Life Ins. Co. (parent co. Empire State Life), Syracuse, 1990-91; mgr. fin. reporting Columbian Mut. Life Ins. Co., Binghamton, N.Y., 1991—; photographer, photog. cons. March of Dimes, Syracuse, 1985-91. Vol. March of Dimes, 1983-91. Mem. Nat. Small Bus. United, Assoc. Photographers Internat. Republican. Office: Columbian Mut Life Ins Co Jack R Manning Plz PO Box 1381 Binghamton NY 13902-1381

CHANG, JIM C. I., aerospace researcher; b. Kiangsu, China, July 14, 1939; came to U.S., 1964; s. Jin-Chih and Shien-Wei (Hsiung) C.; m. Sue-Ying Hsu, May 1, 1987; 1 child, Dean C. BS, Taiwan Cheng Kung U., 1963; MS, Mich. Tech. U., 1966; PhD, Cornell U., 1971. Sr. scientist McDonald Douglas Co., Huntington Beach, Calif., 1973-74; group leader Westinghouse Co., Madison, Pa., 1974-78; br. chief materials div. Naval Rsch. Lab., Washington, 1978-88; mgr. materials, structures and space vehicles NASA, Washington, 1988-89; chief scientist Naval Air Systems Command, Arlington, Va., 1989-90; dir. aerospace scis. directorate Air Force Office of Sci. Rsch., Washington, 1990—; chmn. sci. engring. coms. on materials, structures, fluid mechanics, propulsion and U.S. sci. and tech. policy Dept. Def., Washington; inveited keynote and guest speaker in field. Assoc. editor Jour. Theoretical and Applied Fracture Mechanics; contbr. numerous articles to profl. jours. Chairman Asian-Am. EEO com. Naval Air Systems Command, 1990. Named Profl. Engr. of 1972, Memphis Engrs. Coun., 1972; recipient Invention award Ingersoll-Rand Co., 1967, Performance award, 1978-91. Mem. AIAA, ASME. Home: 7205 Greentree Rd Bethesda MD 20817-1507

CHANG, JOSEPH YOON, health products company executive; b. Ipoh, Perak, Malaysia, Oct. 22, 1952; came to U.S., 1978; s. Chee Kong and Philomena (Wong) C.; m. Wan Ping Wong, Oct. 16, 1974; children: Colin, Christopher. BSc with honors, Sch. of Pharmacy, Portsmouth, Eng., 1974; PhD, U. London, 1978. Postdoctoral fellow Johns Hopkins U., Balt., 1978-80, rsch. assoc., 1980-81; sr. rsch. scientist Wyeth Labs., Radnor, Pa., 1981-85, assoc. dir., 1985-87; dir. Wyeth-Ayerst Rsch., Princeton, N.J., 1988-91; OsteoArthritis Scis., Inc. Osteoarthritis Scis. Inc., Boston, 1991—, also bd. dirs. Editor: Pharmacological Methods in the Control of Inflammation, 1990; inventee in field; contbr. numerous articles to profl. jours. Board dirs. The Arthritis Found., Md., 1979. Bain Meml. fellow Brit. Pharmacology Soc., 1976; Med. Rsch. Coun. scholar, 1974-77. Mem. AAAS, Am. Coll. Rheumatology, Am. Soc. Pharmacology and Exptl. Therapeutics, Am. Thoracic Soc., N.Y. Acad. Scis., Inflammation Rsch. Assn., Reticuloendothelial Soc. Office: OsteoArthritis Scis Inc One Kendall Sq Bldg 200 Cambridge MA 02139

CHANG, LING WEI, marketing professional; b. Taiwan, China, July 27, 1960; came to U.S., 1976; d. Thomas T.P. and Hou Hsin (Wang) C. BE, Cooper Union, 1982; MS, Syracuse U., 1989. Engr. Data Systems div. IBM Corp., Poughkeepsie, N.Y., 1982-83; assoc. engr., 1983-85; systems engr. Nat. Accounts div. IBM Corp., N.Y.C., 1985-87, account systems engr. North Cen. Mktg. div., 1987-89, adv. systems engr. U.S. Mktg. and Svcs., 1990; adv. mktg. rep. N.Y. govt. br. IBM U.S., N.Y.C., 1991—. Vol. City Hosp. Ctr. at Elmhurst, N.Y., 1978; jr. judge Nat. Energy Found., 1979-82; bd. mgrs. Queens Ctr. Pla. Condominium, 1990—. Mem. Tau Beta Pi, Eta Kappa Nu. Home: 87-08 Justice Ave 10D Elmhurst NY 11373 Office: IBM Corp 590 Madison Ave New York NY 10022-2505

CHANG, PAUL KEUK, aerospace engineering educator; b. Inchon, Kyongi, Korea, Apr. 8, 1913; came to U.S., 1947; s. Leo Kibin and Lucia (Huang) C.; m. Frances W.S. Min, Nov. 25, 1955; children: Sophia W.S., Teresa W.S. Diploma in engring., Technische Hochschule, Berlin, 1940; D Engring., Technische U., 1963; M Aero. Engring., NYU, 1947; MS, Harvard U., 1948; DSc, U. Notre Dame, 1951. Aero. engr. Siebel Flugzeugwerke, Halle, Germany, 1940-41, Daimler Benz Motoren, Genshagen, Germany, 1941-42; mech. engr. Brown Boveri Cie Baden, Switzerland, 1946-47; instr. U. Notre Dame, South Bend, Ind., 1950-51; design engr. Airesearch Mfg. Co., L.A., 1952-54; rsch. specialist Lockheed Aircraft Corp., Van Nuys, Burbank, Calif., 1954-58; prof. Cath. Univ. of Am., Washington, 1958-79; invited prof. Korea Advanced Inst. of Sci & Technology, Seoul, Korea, 1979-88; prof. emeritus Cath. Univ. of Am., Washington, 1979—; exch. scientist NAS, 1977-78, 82; cons. in field. Author: Separation of Flow, 1970, Otrivnie Techeniya, 1972-73, Control of Flow Separation, 1976, Upralinie Otrivom Potoka, 1979, Recent Development in Flow Separation, 1985; also over 50 articles. Fulbright-Hayes grantee, 1963-65, 90-91. Fellow AIAA (assoc.); mem. Sigma Xi, Tau Beta Pi. Roman Catholic. Home: 8005 Falstaff Rd Mc Lean VA 22102-2726 Office: Cath U of Am Michigan Ave NE Washington DC 20064-0001

CHANG, RICHARD KOUNAI, physics educator; b. Hong Kong, June 22, 1940; came to U.S., 1956; s. Chia-Chu and Siao-Mei C.; m. Sung-Wen Pu Chang, Sept. 30, 1961; children: Pang-Hua, Pang-Mei, Pang-Yuan. BS, MIT, 1961; MS, Harvard U., 1962, PhD, 1965. Postdoctoral fellow Harvard U., Cambridge, Mass., 1965-66; asst. prof. Yale U., New Haven, 1966-70, assoc. prof., 1970-76, prof., 1976—, dir. Ctr. for Laser Diagnostics, 1981—; Henry Ford II prof. of applied physics, 1991; cons. Texaco, Inc., Beacon, N.Y., 1991. Co-editor: Surface Enhanced Raman Scattering, 1982, Optical Effects Associated with Small Particles, 1988. Chmn. Gordon Rsch. Conf. on Laser Diagnostics, Plymouth, N.H., 1989. Alfred P. Sloan fellow, 1967-69. Fellow Am. Phys. Soc., Optical Soc. Am. (dir.-at-large 1983-86). Office: Yale U PO Box 2157 New Haven CT 06520-2157

CHANG, WINSTON WEN-TSUEN, economist, educator; b. I-lan, Taiwan, Aug. 1, 1939; came to the U.S., 1963; s. Tsan-chin and Sheu-feng (Chen) C.; m. Shanyong Kuo, June 11, 1966; children: David, Jacqueline. BA, Nat. Taiwan U., 1962; MA, U. Rochester, 1966, PhD, 1968. Asst. prof. econs. SUNY, Buffalo, 1967-70, assoc. prof. econs., 1970-78, prof. econs., 1978—; dir. Ph.D. program in econs. dept. econs. SUNY, Buffalo, 1991; project specialist Chinese U. Devel. Project U.S. Nat. Acad. Scis., 1987, 89, 90. Contbr. numerous articles to profl. jours. NSF grantee, 1969. Mem. Am. Econs. Assn. Office: SUNY Dept Econs Buffalo NY 14260

CHANT, DAVIS RYAN, real estate broker, consultant; b. Port Jervis, N.Y., Dec. 15, 1938; s. B. Ryall and Miriam C. (Cathy) C.; m. Judith E. Gahm, Nov. 6, 1982; children: Tamara, Holley. BA, Belmont Coll., 1960. Constrn. materials salesman, architect service U.S. Gypsum Co., Chgo., 1960-62; chmn. bd. Davis R. Chant, Inc., realtors, Milford, Pa., 1962—; chmn. Davis R. Chant Assoc., Inc., realtors, Lords Valley, Pa., Davis R. Chant, Inc. Realtors N.J.; prin. DRC Group of Cos. Chmn., Econ. Devel. Council NE Pa.; mem. Pres.'s Com. on Leisure Housing. Bd. dirs. Pike County Conservation Dist.; trustee Milford Reservation, Inc. Recipient nat. award for advt. Nat. Assn. Real Estate Brokers, 1971. Mem. Nat. Assn. Review Appraisers, Nat. Time Share Council, Internat. Inst. Valuers, Am. Right of Way Assn., Nat., N.Y. assns. real estate bds., Nat. Inst. Real Estate Brokers, Pa. Vacation Land Developers Assn., Pa., N.Y. assns. Realtors, Internat. Real Estate Fedn., Sullivan County, Delaware County bds. Realtors, Pike County (past dir.), Wayne County, Port Jervis, N.Y. chambers commerce, Pike-Wayne County Bd. Realtors (past pres.), Pike Builders Assn., Urban Land Inst., Realtors Land Inst. (chmn. legis. com.), Am. Resort & Residential Devel. Assn., Nat. Assn. Home Builders, Pocono Mountain Vacation Bur., Community Assn. Inst. Am. (charter, dir.). Clubs: Masons, Lions.; Masons, Lions. Home: Clove Rd Montague NJ 07827 Office: 106 E Harford St Milford PA 18337-1002

CHANT, DIXON S., company executive; b. Toronto, Ont., Can.; s. Christopher William and Minnie Jane (Butler) C.; m. Marion K. Macnaughton; children: Brian William (dec.), Murray James. Pres. Argus Corp. Ltd., Toronto; pres., chmn. Sugra Ltd., Toronto; chmn. VS Svcs. Ltd., Argcen Inc.; dep. chmn. The Ravelston Corp. Ltd., Hollinger Inc; exec. v.p., dir. Am. Pub. Co., Saturday Night Mag. Inc., Valley Cable TV Inc.; bd. dirs. Sterling Newspapers Ltd., Cayman Free Press, Jerusalem Post, Western Dominion Investment Co. Ltd. Bd. govs. Pickering Coll. Mem. Granite Club, Toronto Club, Rosedale Golf Club, Can. Club, Bd. Trade, Empire Club, Muskoka Lakes Golf and Country Club, Royal and Ancient Golf Club, St. Andrews Club, Fife Club. Mem. United Ch. Home: 167 Coldstream Ave, Toronto, ON Canada M5N 1X7 also: PO Box 212, Port Carling, ON Canada P0B 1J0 Office: 10 Toronto St, Toronto, ON Canada M5C 2B7

CHAO, ELAINE L., federal official; d. James S. C. and Ruth M. L. (Chu) C. AB, Mt. Holyoke Coll., 1975; MBA, Harvard U., 1979; LLD (hon.), Villanova U., 1989, Sacred Heart U., 1991, St. John's U., 1991; LHD (hon.), Niagara U., 1992; HHD (hon.), Drexel U., 1992. Assoc. Gulf Oil Corp., Pitts., summer 1978; sr. lending officer Citicorp, NA, N.Y.C., 1979-83; v.p. capital markets group BankAmerica, San Francisco, 1984-86; dep. maritime adminstr. U.S. Dept. Transp., Washington, 1986-88; chmn. Fed. Maritime Commn., Washington, 1988; dep. sec. U.S. Dept. of Transp., Washington, 1989-91; dir. Peace Corps of U.S., Washington, 1991-92; adj. asst. prof. Grad. Sch. Bus. Adminstrn., St. John's U., 1984. Recipient Young Achiever award Nat. Coun. Women U.S., Inc., 1986; Eisenhower Fellow Assn. fellow, 1984; named. one of 10 Outstanding Women of Am., 1988. Mem. Coun. on Fgn. Rels., Inc., Am. Coun. Young Polit. Leaders (bd. dirs. 1989), Harvard Bus. Sch. (vis. com. 1989), Harvard Club (N.Y.C.), Harvard Bus. Sch. Club Washington, D.C. (bd. dirs.). Office: United Way of Am 701 N Fairfax St Alexandria VA 22314

CHAO, XIULI, industrial engineer; b. Zibo, Shandong, China, Apr. 15, 1964; came to U.S., 1985; s. Fuzhu Zhao and Hongyan Wang. BS, Shandong U., Jinan, 1983; PhD, Columbia U., 1989. Rsch. asst. Columbia U., N.Y.C., 1985-89; asst. prof. N.J. Inst. Tech., Newark, 1989—. Contbr. articles to profl. jours. Mem. Ops. Rsch. Soc. Am.

CHAPELLE, CLAIRE DANIEL, writer, playwright; b. Atlanta, May 31, 1949; d. Harold Turner and Mary Pearl (Rowan) Daniel; m. Richard John Chapelle, June 15, 1991; stepchildren: Kristen, Michael, Nicole. BS in Edn.,

U. Ga., 1971, MEd, 1977. 0 Bolton; tchr. Clayton County Schs., Jonesboro, Ga., 1972-75; ednl. therapist, cons. DeKalb (Ga.) County Sch. Dist., 1977-83; editor Holt, Rinehart & Winston, N.Y.C., 1983-85; project editor Scribner Ednl. Pubs., N.Y.C., 1985-86; sr. editor Silver Burdett & Ginn, Needham, Mass., 1986-89; freelance writer, editor Newton, Mass., 1990—; founder, mem. Stagewrights, Inc., N.Y.C., 1983-85. Author: ednl. children's stories, 1987—; author children's plays; playwright Sawdust in My Shoes, produced in Oxford, Miss., 1991 (finalist Festival of So. Theatre, semi-finalist Shiras Inst./ Mildred and Albert Panowski Playwriting award); playwright Cinnamon in Spaghetti, N.Y.C., 1985 (finalist Nat. Playwriting Competion), The Night Ride (Harold C. Crain award in Playwriting); contbr. articles to profl. jours. Mem. Internat. Reading Assn., Dramatists Guild, Kappa Delta Pi. Democrat.

CHAPIN, DAPHNE HEATH, psychotherapist; b. Balt., Apr. 4, 1935; d. George Widemeyer and Emily (Dimock) Health; m. Anthony van Dyke Chapin, Nov. 29, 1959; children: Timothy, Nathaniel, Matthew, Hugh. BFA, U. Colo., 1957; MEd, Cambridge Coll., Mass., 1989. Staff clinician The Haitian Clinic, Mass., 1989—; clin. fellow in psychology Dept. Psychaitry, Harvard Med. Sch., Cambridge, 1989—. Country coord. Amnesty Internat., N.Y.C., relief officer. Democrat. Episcopalian. Office: Haitian Clinic 1493 Cambridge St Cambridge MA 02139-1099

CHAPIN, DIANA DERBY, city official; b. St. Joseph, Mich., Nov. 15, 1942; d. David Norman and Gladys Ruth (Henke) Derby; B.A. cum laude (Woodrow Wilson fellow), U. Mich., 1964; M.A., Cornell U., 1966, Ph.D. (Woodrow Wilson dissertation fellow), 1971; m. James Burke Chapin, Mar. 16, 1968; children—James Derby, David Sheffield. Asst. prof. Queens Coll., N.Y.C., 1969-74; dist. adminstr. 8th Congl. Dist., N.Y.C., 1974-76; asst. commr. N.Y.C. Dept. Parks and Recreation, 1978-81, Queens Borough commr., 1981-86 ; dep. commr. planning Dept. Parks and Recreation, N.Y.C., 1986-90, dep. commr. planning and capital projects, 1990—. Del. Democratic Nat. Conv., Miami, Fla., 1972; dist. leader 35th Assembly Dem. Dist., N.Y.C., 1972-78; mgr. various campaigns, 1977-78. Recipient ann. employee award N.Y.C. Dept. Parks and Recreation, 1982. Congregationalist. Contbr. articles to profl. publs. Home: 35-46 79th St Jackson Heights NY 11372 Office: 830 Fifth Ave New York NY 10021

CHAPIN, DOUGLAS SCOTT, science foundation administrator; b. Muskegon, Mich., July 14, 1922; s. Ernest Knight and Lillian A. (Yuill) C.; m. Margaret Jane Gordon, Jan. 29, 1944; children: Jane E., Ruth E., Julia J., Ernestine L. BS in Chemistry, Kans. State U., 1944; MS in Gas Tech., Ill. Inst. Tech., 1948; PhD in Phys. Chemistry, Ohio State U., 1954. Asst. to assoc. prof. of chemistry U. Ariz., Tucson, 1954-66; assoc. program dir. of grad. fellow and traineeships NSF, Washington, 1966-68, program dir., 1968-73, head fellowships and traineeships sect., 1973-77, dir. faculty oriented programs, 1977-78, staff assoc. sci. personnel improvement div., 1978-82, program dir. grad. fellowships, 1982-90, sr. staff assoc., 1990—; staff mem. Lincoln Lab., Lexington, Mass., 1963-64; sr. rsch. scientist Jet Propulsion Lab., Calif. Tech. Inst., Pasadena, 1965. Contbr. articles to profl. jours. With U.S. Army, 1944-46. Rsch. grantee Am. Chem. Soc. Atomic Energy Commn., 1955-62, NSF, 1959-66, Petroleum Rsch. Fund, 1959-66. Mem. AAAS, Am. Chem. Soc. (sect. chair), Faraday Soc., Phi Kappa Phi, Phi Lambda Upsilon, Sigma Xi (sec., v.p., pres.), Sigma Pi Sigma. Home: 9303 Fernwood Rd Bethesda MD 20817-2340 Office: Nat Sci Found 1800 G St NW Washington DC 20550-0002

CHAPIN, SUZANNE PHILLIPS, psychologist; b. Syracuse, N.Y., Aug. 9, 1930; d. Harold Bridge and Charlotte Virginia (Warner) Phillips; m. Richard Hilton Chapin, June 13, 1953 (div. 1964); children: Bruce Phillips Chapin, Linda Chapin Fry. BA, Syracuse U., 1952; MA, Columbia U., 1965. Statis. asst. Syracuse Bd. of Edn., 1952-53; psychol. examiner Stamford (Conn.) Pub. Schs., 1965-68, psychologist Head Start program, 1967-68; psychologist Southbury (Conn.) Tng. Sch., 1968-74, Onondaga Assn. for the Retarded, Syracuse, 1974, Harlem Valley Psychiatric Ctr., Wingdale, N.Y., 1974—. Mem. Danbury Women's Ctr., Nature Conservancy. Democrat. Club: Sierra. Home: 29 Cornell Rd Danbury CT 06811-3717 Office: Harlem Valley Psychiat Ctr Rt 22 Wingdale NY 12594

CHAPMAN, ALLEN FLOYD, management educator; b. Dawson, N.Mex., Apr. 14, 1930; s. Thomas and Velma (Sylva) C.; married; children: Margaret Ann, Nancy Elizabeth. BS, U. Colo., 1951; D of Bus. Adminstrn., Harvard U., 1965; MBS, Hartford Grad. Ctr., 1982. Commd. ensign USN, 1951, advanced through grades to lt., resigned, 1960; rsch. assoc. Harvard U., Boston, 1961-63; dean grad. sch. bus. C.W. Post Ctr., Long Island U., Greenvale, N.Y., 1963-77; prof. mgmt. Hartford (Conn.) Grad. Ctr., 1977—, dean Sch. of Mgmt., 1977-79, 81-84, 87-89; pres., founder various pvt. corps., N.Y., Conn., 1965—; cons. to various corps. and depts. and agys. of U.S. Govt. Patentee in field. Recipient Cert. for Patriotic Civilian Svc. U.S. Army, 1973. Home: 64 Great Hl Pond Rd Portland CT 06480-1315

CHAPMAN, CLARA FELLOWS, psychologist; b. Worcester, Mass., July 29, 1944; m. Edward Chapman, 1967; children: Richard, Joanne, James. BA, Brown U., 1966; MS, U. Conn., 1969, PhD, 1972. Lic. psychologist, Conn. Pvt. practice Middletown, Conn., 1973—. Mem. Am. Psychol. Assn., Conn. Psychol. Assn. Office: Profl Bldg 79 Mill St Middletown CT 06457-4447

CHAPMAN, GEORGE BUNKER, biology educator; b. Bayonne, N.J., June 10, 1925; s. George Bunker and Ella (Greer) C. AB magna cum laude, Princeton U., 1950, AM, 1952, PhD, 1953. Asst. instr. dept. biology Princeton (N.J.) U., 1950-52, asst. rsch. dept. biology, 1952-53, rsch. asst. dept. biology, 1953-54, rsch. assoc. dept. biology, 1954-56; rsch. biologist RCA Labs., Princeton, 1953-56; asst. prof. dept. biology Harvard U., Cambridge, Mass., 1956-60; assoc. prof. anatomy Cornell U. Med. Coll., N.Y.C., 1960-63; prof., chmn. dept. biology Georgetown U., Washington, 1963-90, prof. dept. biology, 1990—; editorial bd. Jour. Bacteriology, Washington, 1960-69. Contbr. over 100 articles to profl. jours. With USNR, 1944-46. Mem. Am. Soc. Microbiology, Am. Microscopical Soc. (bd. reviewers 1966—), Sigma Xi (pres. chpt. 1967-68, historian 1968—), Phi Beta Kappa (pres. chpt. 1988-90). Republican. Office: Georgetown U Biology 37th and O Sts NW Washington DC 20057

CHAPMAN, JOHN ADKINSON, systems analyst; b. Chgo., Aug. 31, 1940. BA in Math. and Psychology, Knox Coll., 1962; postgrad., Carnegie Mellon U., 1963-67; MA in Exptl. Psychology, Hollins Coll., 1964. Rsch. psychologist U.S. Army, Natick, Mass., 1967-69; systems analyst Eye Rsch. Found., Bethesda, Md., 1971-74; tech. assoc. Ctr. for Visual Sci. U. Rochester, N.Y., 1975-86. Mem. AAAS, Nat. Conf. for On-Line Use of Computers in Psychology, Psi Chi, Sigma Xi. Address: 822 Thurston Rd Rochester NY 14619-3321 Office: U Rochester Visual Sci Ctr Rochester NY 14627-0270

CHAPMAN, JOHN HAVEN, lawyer; b. Norfolk, Va., Nov. 7, 1943; m. jane; children: John, Thomas. BA and BS, Brown U., 1966; JD, Boston U., 1969; MBA, U. So. Calif., L.A., 1974; MPhil, PhD, Columbia U., 1984, 88. Bar: Mass. 1969, R.I. 1969, U.S. Patent Office 1970, Calif. 1975, U.S. Dist. Ct. (cen. dist.) Calif. 1975, U.S. Supreme Ct. 1975, N.Y. 1980, U.S. Dist. Ct. (ea. dist.) N.Y. 1980, U.S. Ct. Appeals (2d cir.) 1980, D.C. 1981, U.S. Dist. Ct. D.C. 1981, U.S. Ct. Appeals (D.C. cir.) 1981. Sr. trial atty. Antitrust div. U.S. Dept. Justice, Washington, 1977-80; v.p., gen. counsel Chapman Moran Hubbard Glazer & Zimmermann, Washington, 1980-82; v.p. telecom Gartner Group, Stamford, Conn., 1981-83; dir. telecom rsch. Paine Webber, Inc., N.Y.C., 1983-84; founder, pres. Strategic Rsch., Stamford, 1985—; founder, first exec. dir., rsch. fellow Ctr. for Telecom & Info. Studies, Columbia U., N.Y.C., 1983—; founder, sr. ptnr. Chapman Moran Hubbard Glazer & Zimmerman, Stamford, 1983—; adj. prof. N.Y. Law Sch., N.Y.C.; rsch. fellow Columbia U. Treas. Xerox Community Involvement Program, Stamford, 1974-75. Mem. Computer Law Assn., Fed. Bar Assn. Office: Chapman Moran Hubbard et al 3 Landmark Sq Stamford CT 06901

CHAPMAN, JUDITH GRIFFIN, psychology educator; b. Kane, Pa., Oct. 22, 1949; d. Leon B. and Shirley J. (Winslow) Griffin; m. Robert J. Chapman, Jan. 16, 1971; children: Jessica Lynn, Joshua Griffin. BA cum laude, St. Bonaventure, N.Y., 1971, MA, 1975; PhD with distinction, Syracuse (N.Y.) U., 1987. Psychology instr. U. Pitts., Bradford, 1972-74; pscyhology instr. Empire State Coll., Buffalo Reginal Learning Ctr., 1976-77, Jamestown Community Coll., Olean, N.Y., 1975-83; cons. Syracuse Rsch. Corp., 1984-85; lectr. SUNY, Oneonta, 1987-88; asst. prof. St. Joseph's U., Phila., 1988—. Contbr. articles to profl. jours. PHEA Acad. scholarship, 1967-71. Mem. APA, Am. Psychol. Soc. (charter), Eastern Psychol. Assn., Soc. for Personality and Social Psychology (divsn. 8), Soc. for the Advancement of Social Psychology, Psi Chi, Sigma Xi. Office: St Josephs U Dept Psychology 5600 City Ave Philadelphia PA 19131-1376

CHAPMAN, PAUL LINDSEY, investment banker, hotel and restaurant consultant; b. Bklyn., Aug. 15, 1943; s. Percival Sherwood and Violet Marie (Bolduc) C. BS in Fgn. Svc., Georgetown U., 1965; postgrad., U. Teheran, Iran, 1966-68, U. Va., Charlottesville and Arlington, 1972-74. With Hilton Internat., 1967-71; gen. mgr. Georgetown Inn, Washington, 1971-72; v.p., gen. mgr. Howard Johnson, Washington, 1972-75; mng. dir., CEO Embassy Hotel Corp., Washington, 1975-78; regional v.p. Treadway Corp., Williamstown, Mass., 1978-82; founder, exec. v.p. Food Tech Internat., Alexandria, Va., 1982-86; asst. prof. of hotel, restaurant, and tourism mgmt. George Washington U., Washington, 1985-87; v.p. food and beverage, devel. York-Hannover Hotels Ltd., Toronto, Can., 1986-88; pres. The Lindsey Group, Washington, 1988—; bd. dirs. Berkshire Hills Conf., 1978-81; mem. exec. com. Met. Washington Bd. Trade. Contbr. restaurant revs. and wine lists to various publs. Bd. dirs. D.C. chpt. March of Dimes, 1980-87, Am. Ballet Theatre; mem. U.S. Army adv. com. to Teheran, Iran, 1966-67, Vietnam, 1967. Mem. Am. Hotel and Motel Assn. (affiliate), Am. Theatre Assn. (chmn pub. rels. and mktg. com. 1979-84), Hotel Assn. Washington D.C. (hon., bd. dirs. 1973-76), Sommelier Soc., Confrerie de Rotisseurs (bailli honoraire, founder/bailli 1984-87, charge des missions 1982-84, maitre de table restaureur 1975), Brotherhood Knights of Vine (founder, vice commdr. mid. Atlantic chpt. 1987—), Hotel Security Dirs. Assn. (founder), Beethoven Soc. (bd. dirs. 1981-86), U.S. Tennis Assn., Georgetown U. Alumni Assn., The George Town Club. Republican. Episcopalian. Office: The Lindsey Group 200 L St NW Ste 702 Washington DC 20036

CHAPMAN, PETER HERBERT, bank executive; b. Stockton, Calif., Mar. 6, 1953; s. Duff Gordon and Emalee (Sala) C.; m. Diane Chapman Clark; children: Charlotte Moseley, Alexander Clark. AB, Columbia U., 1977. V.p. Salomon Bros., Inc., N.Y.C., 1977-86, The First Boston Corp., N.Y.C., 1986-88; dir. Girozentrale Vienna, N.Y.C., 1989-91; sr. vp. Bessemer Trust Co., N.Y.C., 1991—; bd. dirs. C.D. Stimson Co., Seattle. Bd. dirs. Am. Internat. Sch., Florence, Italy, 1982—. Mem. The Links Club, Racquet and Tennis Club, Piping Rock Club. Republican.

CHAPMAN, RONALD THOMAS, musician, educator; b. Bklyn., Dec. 16, 1933; s. William Leon and Rosamond (Walker) C.; m. Joyce Elaine Chase, Dec. 1966 (dec. May 1973); adopted child, Debra Anne; m. Virginia Marie Knochenhauer, Feb. 14, 1975 (dec. July 1989); stepchildren: Suzanne, Michael. BS cum laude, CUNY, 1982; MA in Teaching, Lehman Coll., 1983; PhD in Music in Higher Edn., NYU, 1989. Cert. tchr. music, N.Y., tchr. Spanish, N.Y. Toured with Leonard dePaur Infantry Chorus, 1953-55; mem. trio The Versatones, U.S. and Can., 1955-59; vocalist, 1978—; asst. dir. men's choir Kingsborough Community Coll., 1980-82; asst. to dir. mixed chorus Lehman Coll., CUNY, 1982-83; instr. voice NYU, N.Y.C., 1986—; instr. computer music for music teachers N.Y. Inst. Tech., N.Y.C., 1987; pvt. instr. voice, piano, guitar, computerized music, music theory, sight singing and music lit., 1980—; substitute tchr. Hempstead (N.Y.) Sch. Dist., 1983-85, mem. faculty, 1988-89; mem. Music Educators Nat. Conf.; instr. voice, NYU, 1986—; bd. dirs. Cultural Environ, Queens, N.Y. Performed in Spain, Japan, Thailand, The Philippines, Eng., Jamaica, Can., Vietnam, P.R., Fed. Republic of Germany, Laos, Portugal and U.S. including N.Y.C., Atlanta and Miami; TV appearances on Johnny Carson Show, Arthur Godfrey Talent Scouts, Gary Moore Show, Tex and Jinx Falkenburg Show, many others; rec. artist for Columbia Records, RCA Records, Island in the Sun soundtrack; appeared in Broadway play Kwamina; appearing nightly Fox Hollow, Caterer/Restaurant, Woodbury, N.Y., 1978—; starred in Playboy Club and Hotel Chain, 1960-67, (movies) Rueda de Sospechosos, 1963, (revue) The Ronnie Chapman Show, 1968-69; debuted by singing and accompanying himself on piano a medley of Broadway Show Tunes and Internat. Art Songs in various langs. Carnegie Hall, 1991, 92. Bd. dirs. Cultural Environment, Queens, N.Y., 1978—; apptd. dep. gov. Am. Biog. Inst. Rsch. Assn., 1992. Mem. Internat. Assn. for Rsch. in Singing (rsch. assoc. Found. for Rsch. Singing), Nat. Assn. Tchrs. of Singing, N.Y. Singing Tchrs. Assn., N.Y. State Sch. Music Assn., Internat. Assn. Jazz Educators, Chopin Found. N.Y., Am. Assn. Choral Dirs., Music Educators Nat. Conf., Music Tchrs. Nat. Assn., Internat. Platform Assn., Phi Delta Kappa (v.p. programs NYU chpt. 1988-89) Pi Kappa Lambda, Kappa Delta Pi. Home and Office: 108 Glenmore Ave Hempstead NY 11550-6630

CHAPPELL, RAYMOND EDWARD, real estate company executive; b. Washington, Dec. 2, 1941; s. Raymond Elmer and Nancy (King) C.; m. Cynthia Laurenbach, Oct. 3, 1981; children: Brian, Ashley. BSBA, U. Md., 1964. Lic. real estate broker; cert. residential broker, Md. With sales and mgmt. depts. xerox, Washington, Md., 1965-78, Chris Coile & Assocs., Annapolis, Md., 1978-80, Merrill Lynch Realty, Washington, Md., Va., 1980-89; pres., chief exec. officer, owner Prudential Preferred Properties, Bethesda, Md., 1989—. Bd. dirs. Ronald McDonald House, Washington, 1982—. With U.S. Army, 1965, mem. Res. Republican. Roman Catholic. Office: Prudential Preferred Properties 7830 Old Georgetown Rd Bethesda MD 20814

CHAPPELL, SHIRLEY ANN, elementary school educator; b. Montgomery, Ala., June 23, 1951; d. Abe and Laura (Brown) Ch. AA, Springfield (Mass.) Tech. C.C., 1974, Holyoke (Mass.) C.C., 1987; BA magna cum laude, Am. Internat. Coll., 1989; cert., Nat. Acad. for Paralegal Studies, 1990. Clerical temp. mortgage dept. S/S Bank, Springfield, 1985; telemarketer ARC, Springfield, 1988-89; substitute tchr. Springfield Pub. Schs., 1992—. Contbr. articles to newspapers. Vol. Ted Kennedy Senate Campaign, Springfield, 1970, Youth Voters Participation, Springfield, 1971; organizer Crime Watch Group Seymour Ave., Springfield, 1990; vol. English tutor Holyoke Community Coll., 1987. Polit. scholar Am. Internat. Coll., Springfield, 1989; recipient Silver Poet award World Poetry-Calif., Orlando, Fla., 1986. Mem. Am. Internat. Coll. Alumni Assn. (com. mem. 1989-90). Democrat. Baptist. Home: 53 Seymour Ave Springfield MA 01109

CHAPPEN, EDWARD PETER, physician; b. Carbondale, Pa., July 8, 1925; s. Peter E. and Amelia E. (Kouloumpy) C. BS, Pa. State U., 1946; MD, Jefferson Med. Coll., 1952. Diplomate Am. Bd. Psychiatry and Neurology, Am. Bd. Psychiatry. Intern Jefferson Med. Coll. Hosp., Phila., 1953; gen. practice psychiatry, Trenton, N.J., 1955—; resident in psychiatry Menninger Sch. Psychiatry, Topeka, Kans., 1967-70; staff psychiatrist Cen. Santa Clara County Mental Health Ctr., San Jose, Calif., 1970-71; mem., then chmn. staff St. Francis Hosp.; cons. in psychiatry Hamilton Hosp., Union Indsl. Home, Trenton. Mem. Trenton Mayor's Com. for Selection of Trenton Sister City, 1961, Trenton Landmarks Commn. for Hist. Preservation, Trenton Civic Improvements Com.; mem. spl. groups div. Del. Valley United Fund, 1958; treas. local chpt. Am. Assn. UN, 1960-61; mem. exec. bd. Greater Trenton chpt. People to People; exec. council, chmn. pub. relations com. Parnassos Greek Cultural Soc. of N.Y. Inc., 1963; mem. adv. com. for study sociology, death and dying Mercer County; mem. fine arts com. Anglican Cathedral of the Trinity, Trenton; bd. govs. Greater Trenton Symphony Assn., 1966-67; trustee Friends of Trenton Free Pub. Library, Vis. Nurse Assn. Trenton; bd. mgrs. Donnelly Meml. Hosp.; trustee Greek Orthodox Ch., 1962-64. Served to lt. (j.g.) USMC, 1954. Menninger Sch. Psychiatry fellow, 1970. Mem. N.Y. Acad. Scis., AMA, Am. Psychiat. Assn., Santa Clara-Monterey Counties Psychiat. Soc., Mercer County Med. Soc. (chmn. physician placement service com.), Navy League U.S., Internat. Platform Assn., Byzantine Fellowship, Pa. Soc., Assn. Mil. Surgeons U.S., UN Assn. U.S.A. (chpt. pres. 1966), Alumni Assn. Menninger Sch. Psychiatry, Princeton Soc. Archeol. Inst. Am., Trenton Mus. Soc., State House Dist. Assn., Douglass House Commn., Archeol. Inst. Am., Nat. Hist. Soc., Trenton Hist. Soc., Hist. Soc. Hamilton Twp., Nat. Trust Hist. Preservation, Trent House Assn., Met. Mus. Art, Friends of Art Mus. Princeton U., Phi Alpha Sigma. Clubs: Architectoniki (Athens, Greece); Commd. Officers U.S. Naval Base (Phila.). Lodges: Rotary, Soc. of Mary, Masons (32 deg.), Shriners. Office: 476 Hamilton Ave Trenton NJ 08609-2797

CHARABATI, VICTORIA FRANCE, writer, editor, publishing executive; b. East Stroudsburg, Pa., Mar. 18, 1954; d. Donald D. and Barbara (Shaffer) France; m. Jihad Charabati, Oct. 13, 1981. BA in French Lang. and Lit. cum laude, N.C. State U., 1975; MA in Linguistics, Oakland U., 1981. Mem. faculty English Lang. Inst. Wayne State U., Detroit, 1981-82; copywriter Percivall Advt. & Mktg. Inc., Raleigh, N.C., 1982-83; acct. rep. Offset Paperback Mfrs., Inc., Dallas, Pa., 1986-87; dir. classes French Alliance, St. Paul, 1984; contbg. editor Newsmakers series, Detroit, 1985—; prodn. mgr. Bookmakers, Inc., Wilkes-Barre, 1987-89; freelance writer, editor, book prodn. mgr., 1989—. Contbg. editor Maicya series, Detroit, 1991—; contbr. articles to Times Leader newspaper. Active Wyoming Valley Art League, Cider Painters of Am. Mem. NAFE, Greater Wilkes-Barre C. of C. (exec. women's coun., diplomatic corps, visitation com.), Ad Club of NE Pa., Am. Advt. Fedn., Mensa. Home and Office: 33 Druid Hills Dr Wilkes Barre PA 18708-1102

CHARACHE, PATRICIA, physician, consultant; b. Newark, Dec. 26, 1929; d. Harold S. Connamacher and Carye-Belle Henle; m. Samuel Charache, June 11, 1951; 1 child, Barbara Elizabeth Coleman. Student, Oberlin Coll.; BA, Hunter Coll., 1952; MD, NYU, 1957. Diplomate Am. Bd. Med. Microbiology, Am. Bd. Med. Virology. Postdoctoral fellow in rsch. medicine U. Pa. Sch. Medicine, Phila., 1958-60; fellow infectious diseases Johns Hopkins U. Sch. Medicine, Balt., 1960-62, instr. then asst. prof. medicine and pathology, 1964-73, assoc. prof., 1973-92; prof. lab. medicine, prof. medicine Johns Hopkins U. Sch. Medicine, 1992—; dir. microbiology labs. Johns Hopkins Hosp., Balt., 1973—; rsch. assoc. Children's Hosp., Boston, 1962-64; rsch. assoc. Harvard U. Sch. Medicine, 1962-64; mem. bd. sci. counselors NIH, Bethesda, Md., 1972-76, Dept. Def. Contract Rev. Bds., Washington, 1984—; cons. BOSTID program NAS, Washington, 1985—; internat. cons. in med. microbiology and infectious diseases. Author 5 book chpts.; editor 3 books; contbr. over 75 articles to profl. jours. Recipient Career Devel. award NIH, Bethesda, 1968, Alumni Key Pin award, NYU, 1957. Fellow Infectious Disease Soc. Am.; mem. Am. Soc. Microbiology (past pres. Md. br.). Office: Johns Hopkins Hosp 600 N Wolfe St Baltimore MD 21205-2104

CHARISH, HOWARD ELLIOTT, social worker; b. Passaic, N.J., Mar. 14, 1945; s. Abraham Larry and Minnie (Mirsky) C.; m. Sharon Lynn Greenwald, June 16, 1968; children: Michael, Jessica, Rachel. BA, Rutgers U., 1967; MSW, U. Pa. Sch. Social Work, 1969. Asst. dir., community svcs. div. Jewish Ctrs. Assn., L.A., 1974-76; dir., women's div. Greater Hartford (Conn.) Jewish Fedn., 1976-77, dir., planning, 1977-78, asst. dir., 1978-80; dir., planning and budgeting Jewish Fedn. Coun., L.A., 1980-82; exec. v.p. United Jewish Fedn. MetroWest, East Orange, N.J., 1982—. Mem. steering com. U. Pa. Campaign to Raise One Billion Dollars, 1991; mem. bd. overseers U. Pa. Sch. Social Work, 1991. Recipient Louis Kraft award, Conf. Jewish Communal Svc., 1975. Office: United Jewish Fedn 910 Rt 10 E Whippany NJ 07981-1156

CHARLES, FAITH HARRIS, psychotherapist; b. Phila., Jan. 13, 1939; d. David Stedman and Martha Ann (Russell) H.; m. Robert Lowry Patten, June 11, 1961 (div. Jan. 1974); children: Jocelyn Soames, Christina Stedman; m. Oscar Charles, July 13, 1984. BA, Swarthmore Coll., 1961; MA, Rutgers U., 1963, PhD, 1967; cert., U. Houston, 1980. Cert. alcoholism and drug abuse counselor. Instr., assoc. prof. Tex. So. U., Houston, 1971-84; therapist, pub. rels. dir. The Bridge, Phila., 1984-85; therapist, supr. The Consortium, Phila., 1985-86; dir., therapist Freedom Counseling, Phila., 1985—. Chmn. counseling com. Unity Ch. of Christ, Phila., 1985-87. Mem. Nat. Assn. Alcoholism and Drug Abuse Counselors. Democrat. Hindu. Home and Office: 2325 N 52d St Philadelphia PA 19131

CHARLES, JUDITH KOREY, professional association executive; b. N.Y.C., Feb. 23, 1925; d. Harold Richard and Rose Kay (Boren) Korey; m. Alfred W. Charles, July 1, 1962; 1 child, Frederic Korey Charles. AB, Brown U., 1945. Advt. copy chief Sears, Roebuck and Co., N.Y.C., 1952-59, Saks 34th St, N.Y.C., 1959-61; account exec. Jesse Kram Advt., N.Y.C., 1961-63, Markland Advt., N.Y.C., 1963-65; pres. Creative Communication, N.Y.C., 1965-89; exec. dir. Roundtable for Women in Foodservice Inc., N.Y.C., 1989—; guest lectr. NYU Inst. Retail Mgmt., Women's Food Svc. Inst.; adj. prof. Barbizon Sch. Fashion Merchandising, N.Y.C., NYU Sch. Continuing Edn. Recipient Brown Bear award Associated Alumni of Brown U., 1991. Mem. Brown U. Club. Democrat. Home and Office: Roundtable Women in Foodservice 425 Central Park W New York NY 10025-4328

CHARLES, MICHAEL HARRISON, architectural interior designer; b. Fort Lauderdale, Fla., Feb. 8, 1952; s. Melvin Mowrer and Sylvia Ann (Cookus) C. BA, U. Fla., 1976; AS, Fla. Jr. Coll., 1982. Cert. interior designer, Fla. Ptnr., v.p. St. Johns Lighting Design, St. Augustine, Fla., 1978-81; archtl. interior designer KBJ Architects, Inc., Jacksonville, Fla., 1982-86; owner Michael H. Charles Assocs.-Comml. & Residential Interior Design, N.Y. and Fla., 1988—; dir. interior design DeWolff Ptnrship. Architects, Rochester, N.Y., 1986-88; cons. in field, St. Augustine, Fla., 1984—. Author: Interior Designers of the United States of america, 1991. Mem. Inst. Bus. Designers, Am. Soc. Interior Designers, English Speaking Union, Soc. Colonial Wars, N.Y. and Fla. Colonial Soc. of the Acorn, SAR (v.p. Fla. chpt. 1982-86), Colonial Soc. Pa., Gen. Soc. War 1812 (Fla. State sec. 1991-92), Nat. Soc. Sons and Daughters of Pilgrims, Descendants of Colonial Clergy, Order Stars and Bars, Nat. Huguenot Soc. (life), Pa. Huguenot Soc., Order Ams. Armorial Ancestery (life), Nat. Soc. CAR (chpt. organizing pres. 1963, sr. Fla. officer 1985-86), St. David's Soc. N.Y., St. Andrew's Soc. N.Y., Alliance Francaise, Glagon and Trencher (life), Pa. Soc. Sons of Revolutin, Descs. of Early Quakers (life), Royal Scottish Automobile Club. Republican. Episcopalian. Clubs: St. Augustine (Fla.) Yacht (gharial), Ponte Vedra, Sovereign Mil. Order Temple Jerusalem. Avocations: skiing, boating, genealogy. Home: 111 East Ave Ste 100 Rochester NY 14604-2520 Office: 1824 Penfield Rd Penfield NY 14526-1487 also: 18 Carrera St Saint Augustine FL 32084-3621

CHARLES, MICKEY, sports communications executive, sportswriter, editor. Columnist The Phila. Enquirer; sports commentator, host Mickey Charles Show Sta. WCAU/CBS Radio; writer Night-life; writer, travel editor, sports and special features editor N.Y. Update; prin. Comm. Team Inc.; founder, pres. The Sports Network; Sports commentator NFL pre-game shows Mut. Broadcasting, 1989-90; co-host sports/entertainment talk show Caesars World Entertainment; speaker in field. Author: Sportshots; contbr. aricles and books in field. Mem. Nat. Nightclub and Bar Assn. (adv. bd.), Mid. Atlantic Blind Golf Assn. (pres., ann. tournament orgn. for United Way and St. Jude's). Address: care Beth S Dietz 701 Mason's Mill Bus Pk Huntingdon Valley PA 19006

CHARLES, NORMAN C., ophthalmologist; b. Schenectady, N.Y., June 4, 1937; s. Milton and Ann Charlotte (Applebaum) Chodikoff; m. Barbara Jane Breinin, June 29, 1969; 1 child, Lauren Allegra. AB, Yale Coll., 1959; MD, NYU, 1963. Intern NYU-Bellevue Med. Ctr., N.Y.C., 1963-64; resident in ophthalmology NYU Med. Ctr., N.Y.C., 1966-70; Assoc. attending surgeon N.Y. Eye and Ear Infirmary, N.Y.C., 1972-85, attending surgeon, 1985—; instr. ophthamology N.Y. Med. Ctr., N.Y.C., 1970-73, dir. ophthalmic pathology, 1973—, clin. asst. prof., 1973-78, clin. assoc. prof., 1978-83; clin. prof. NYU Med. Ctr., N.Y.C., 1983—; cons. Manhattan VA Med. Ctr., N.Y.C., 1981—. Contbr. articles to profl. jours. Mem. nat. program com., bd. dirs. N.Y. Assn. for Blind, 1989—. Lt. USNR, 1964-66. Fellow Am. Coll. Surgeons, Am. Acad. Ophthalmology; mem. Am. Assn. Ophthalmic Pathologists, Eastern Ophthalmic Pathology Soc., Theobald Ophthalmic Pathology Soc., N.Y. Ophthalmology Soc., N.Y. Soc. Clin. Ophthalmology, Med. Socs. of N.Y. County and N.Y. State, Soc. Alumni of Bellvue Hosp., Phi Beta Kappa, Alpha Omega Alpha. Home: 180 W 58th St New York NY 10019 Office: 620 Park Ave New York NY 10021

CHARLES, REID SHAVER, municipal official; b. Wichita, Kans., Sept. 16, 1940; s. Harry Lytton and Margaret Virginia (Shaver) C.; m. Mary Elizabeth Rouland, June 1, 1963; children: Reid Shaver II, Rouland Shannon. BA, U. Wichita, 1964, postgrad., 1964-65; postgrad., Tulane U., 1968-69; MA, Wichita State U., 1970. Grad. fellow Wichita State U., 1965; asminstrv. asst. to city mgr. City of Newton, Kans., 1965-66; planning assoc. City of New Orleans, 1966-69; adminstrv. asst. to exec. sec. devel. Town of Brookline, Mass., 1969-73; chief systems planning City of Kansas City, Mo., 1973-74,

acting. dep. dir. city devel., 1974-75; prin. CHJ Assocs., Kansas City, 1975-78; adminstrv. dir. City of Lincoln, Nebr., 1976-79; chief adminstrv. officer City of Shreveport, La., 1979, mgmt. cons., 1980-83; city mgr. City of Ankeny, Iowa, 1983-84; town mgr. Town of Agawam, Mass., 1985-88; town adminstr. Town of Easthampton, Mass., 1989—; lectr. in field; participant Nat. Urban Policy Roundtable IV, 1977; mem. tech. adv. group Urban Econ. Policy and Mgmt. Group, U.S. Conf. Mayors-Nat. League Cities, 1977-82. Author mcpl. budgeting manuals. With USAAF, 1961. Mem. Am. Polit. Sci. Assn., Am. Inst. Cert. Planners, Am. Acad. Polit. and Social Scis., Internat. City Mgmt. Assn., Am. Planning Assn., Am. Soc. Pub. Adminstrn., Pi Sigma Alpha. Soc. of Friends. Home: 239 Main St Easthampton MA 01027-2024 Office: 43 Main St Easthampton MA 01027-2034

CHARM, JOEL BARRY, manufacturing company executive. BA in Chemistry, U. Mass., 1965; MS in Radiation Biology and Environ. Health, U. Mich., 1967; cert. advanced mgmt. program Columbia U., 1977. With Dow Chem. Co., Midland, Mich., 1968-73, radiation safety officer, 1968-73, chief indsl. hygienist dept. chem. prodn., 1970-72, research specialist in indsl. hygiene, 1972-73; corp. mgr. indsl. hygiene Miles Labs., Elkhart, Ind., 1973-75; mgr. occupational health and toxicology Allied Corp., Morristown, N.J., 1975-77, dir. corp. product safety and integrity, 1977—; speaker, lectr. on toxic substances control, indsl. hygiene, OSHA, radiation, pollution control at univs., profl. meetings. Author profl. reports and papers. NIH fellow, 1967. Mem. Am. Acad. Indsl. Hygiene (diplomate), Am. Indsl. Hygiene Assn. (chmn. com. product safety and health), Ind. Indsl. Hygiene Soc. (bd. dirs.), Mich. Indsl. Hygiene Soc. (bd. dirs. 1969-70), Health Physics Soc., ASTM (rec. sec. air sampling methodology and occupational safety and health criteria), Am. Soc. Safety Engrs. (profl.), N.J. Indsl. Hygiene Soc. Office: Allied Signal Inc Corp Health Safety Environ Scis PO Box 1013 Morristown NJ 07962-1013

CHARNIN, JADE HOBSON, magazine executive; b. N.Y.C., Mar. 12, 1945; d. John Louis Campo and Elizabeth (Anne) Stanton; m. David Alan Hobson, Dec. 30 (div. 1972); m. Martin Charnin, Dec. 18, 1984. BA, NYU, 1967. Asst. editor Glamour mag., N.Y.C., 1970; accessory editor Vogue mag., N.Y.C., 1970-78, fashion editor, 1978-81, fashion dir., 1981-86, creative dir. fashion, 1987-88; v.p., dir. creative svcs. for fashion and design group Revlon, Inc., 1988; exec. creative dir. Mirabella Mag., 1988—; cons. editor Self mag., N.Y.C., 1979-81. Costumer coord. for off broadway shows Laughing Matters, 1989, Martin Charnin, the Hits and the M.S.'s, 1990. Mem. NAFE, Am. Horticultural Soc., Horticultural Soc. N.Y. (bd. dirs.), Humane Soc., Animal Protection Inst. Democrat. Avocations: gardening, opera, ballet, theater, skiing. Office: Mirabella Mag 200 Madison Ave New York NY 10016

CHARNOFF, SCOTT DENNIS, cost analyst; b. Reading, Pa., Apr. 30, 1964; s. Lance Dennis and Patricia Ann (Harakal) C. BS in Fin., Pa. State U., 1986; MBA in Internat. Bus., St. Joseph's U., Phila., 1992. Fin. analyst Pa. Savs. Bank, Wyomissing, 1986-88; fin. analyst KB Alloys, Inc., Sinking Spring, Pa., 1988-90, cost analyst, 1990—, export credit specialist, 1991—. Mem. Travelers Protective Assn., Reading Fgn. Trade Assn. Home: 317 Spruce St West Reading PA 19611 Office: KB Alloys Inc 2917 Windmill Rd Sinking Spring PA 19608

CHAROCHAK, DALE MICHAEL, chief contract administrator; b. Pitts., Apr. 18, 1955; s. Michael and Alice (Nazak) C.; m. Kathleen Gallagher. BS in Biochemistry, U. Pitts., 1977. Contr. County Controller's Office, Pitts., 1977-80; contract supr. Dept. Aviation, Pitts., 1980-84, chief property adminstr., 1984-91. Dem. committeeman Moon, pa., 1982-83, sch. bd. dir., legis. rep., 1983-85; bd. trustees Montour (Pa.) Football Orgn., 1979-81; Pa. state commr. Am. Wallyball Assn.; asst. scoutmaster Boy Scouts Am., Montour. Mem. Am. Assn. Airport Execs., Pa. State Commissioner, Am. Wallyball Assn. Byzantine Catholic. Home: 131 Greenlea Dr Coraopolis PA 15108-2609 Office: Dept Aviation Rm 134M Terminal Bldg Pittsburgh PA 15231

CHAROS, EVANGELOS NIKOLAOU, economics educator; b. Larnaca, Cyprus, Sept. 13, 1953; s. Nicos Demetriou Charos and Alexandra (Tyllerou) Charou; m. Maryann Andrews, Oct. 2, 1976; children: Nikolas, Alexandra, Melanie. Bs in Math., U. N.H., 1975, MA in Econs., 1978, PhD in Econs., 1984. Instr. Nasson Coll., Springvale, Maine, 1980-83; asst. prof. Merrimack Coll., North Andover, Mass., 1983-88; assoc. prof. econs. Merrimack Coll., 1988—; dir. computer svcs. U. N.H., Durham, 1976-80. Asst. editor, data base mgr. Internat. Bus. Conditions Digest, 1980-83. Mem. Am. Econ. Assn., Northeast Bus. & Econs. Assn., Internat. Assn. Bus. Forecasters, Omicron Delta Epsilon. Greek Orthodox. Home: 1 Center Dr Dover NH 03820-4646

CHARPENTIER, CELESTE JEANNETTE, counselor; b. Manville, R.I., Dec. 21, 1956; d. Raoul and Jeannette (Gervais) C. BA, Providence Coll., 1979; MA, Lesley Coll., 1990. Religious edn. coord. West Bay Cath. Youth Orgn. Ctr., Charlestown, R.I., 1979-81; exec. dir. West Bay Cath. Youth Orgn., Warwick, R.I., 1981-83; vol. Jesuit Vol. Corps., Seattle, 1984-85; tchr. Seattle Preparatory High Sch., 1985-86; vocat. dir. Alternative Workshop, Lynn, Mass., 1986-88; student intern Bay Cove Mental Health Ctr., Boston, 1989-90; asst. dir. Haverhill (Mass.) Clubhouse, 1990—. Bd. mem. Dominic Savio Youth Ctr., Peacedale, R.I., 1979-81; mem. Nat. Pledge Resistance, Seattle, Boston, 1985-89, Mass. Audubon Soc., Ipswich, 1991—. Mem. AACD, Assn. for Religious and Value Issues in Counseling, Mass. Mental Health Counselors Assn. Roman Catholic. Office: Haverhill Clubhouse 217-219 Washington St Haverhill MA 01832

CHARPENTIER, KEITH LIONEL, school system administrator; b. Attleboro, Mass., Mar. 6, 1959; s. David L. and Matilda (Marchand) C.; m. Catherine Joan Fleming, July 29, 1989. AS, Mitchell Coll., 1980; BS, Plymouth State Coll., 1982, MEd in Guidance and Counseling, 1992. Cert. phys. edn. and health sci. tchr., N.H.; cert. reality therapist. Health, sci. tchr. SAU #23 Sch. System, Woodsville, N.H., 1982-84; counselor F.L. Chamberlain Sch., Lyman, N.H., 1984-86; spl. edn. tchr. Blue Mt. Union Sch., Wells River, Vt., 1985-86; dean of students, counselor Pike (N.H.) Sch. Inc., 1986—; instr. Crisis Prevention Inst., Brookfield, Wis., 1989—, Drug/Alcohol Edn., Meredith, N.H., 1988—, Life Skills Edn., Granville, Ohio, 1987—. Recipient Mitchell Coll. Athletic Trainers award, 1980. Mem. Nat. Athletic Trainers Assn., Am. Assn. Counseling and Devel., Assn. Supervision and Curriculum Devel. Home: RR # 151 Rockcreek Acres North Haverhill NH 03779 Office: Pike Sch Inc PO Box 299 Pike NH 03780-0299

CHARRAD, MOUNIRA, sociologist, educator; b. Sfax, Tunisia; d. Aly and Andrea (Doyen) C.; m. Michael Brenner, Mar. 25, 1979. BA, Sorbonne U., 1964; PhD, Harvard U., 1980. Lectr. sociology Harvard U., Cambridge, Mass., 1978-79; vis. prof. U. Pitts., 1980-82; rsch. assoc. U. Pa., Phila., 1982-83; asst. prof. U. Calif., San Diego, 1983-90; rsch. assoc. Ctr. Middle East Studies Harvard U., Cambridge, Mass., 1990-91; vis. asst. prof. Dept. of Sociology U. Pitts., 1991—; cons. Ctr. Population Activities, Washington, 1982, PPG Industries, Pitts., 1982, Westinghouse Corp., Pitts., 1981; organizer Internat. Conf. on Gender, State and Devel., Tangier, Morocco, 1991. Faculty fellowship U. Calif., 1985; recipient Rsch. award Am. Inst. Maghrebi Studies, L.A., 1990, Travel to Collections award NEH, 1991-92, Mellon award 1992—; grantee AAUW, 1992. Mem. Am. Sociol. Assn., Sociologists For Women InSoc., Mideast Studies Assn. Office: U Pitts Dept of Sociology Pittsburgh PA 15260

CHARRIER, MICHAEL EDWARD, investment banker; b. Columbia, S.C., July 6, 1945; s. Raymond Joseph and Anne Mary (Toth) C.; m. Elizabeth Andrea Alexandra Thyssen, June 17, 1967. Grad., Anson Acad., 1963; BA, Columbia U., 1967, MA, 1968; postgrad., Harvard U., 1977, Yale U., 1988. Cert. regional croquet referee; cert. croquet instr. With strategic planning and devel. TWA, N.Y.C., 1970-73; dir. devel. City Fed. Savs. Bank, Elizabeth, N.J., 1974-76; fin. cons. Pan Am., N.Y.C., 1976; chief fin. officer Jet Aviation Internat., N.Y.C., 1976, pres., 1977—; also bd. dirs.; chief exec. officer Hardwick, Wells & Winthrop, N.Y.C., 1978-84; also bd. dirs.; sr. ptnr. Ardsley, Milbank & Co., Inc., N.Y.C., 1985—; also bd. dirs.; pres. Hamilton Sci. Corp., Greenwich, Conn., N.Y.C., 1986—; also bd. dirs.; pres. Hamilton Chem. Corp., N.Y.C., 1988—; also bd. dirs. N.Y.C.; bd. dirs., mem. exec. com. Hamilton Chem. Internat., 1990—; bd. dirs. Hamilton Chem. Ltd., London, 1990—; cons. Columbia U., N.Y.C., 1985. Pub. Yale Croquet Manual, USCA Collegiate Manual, 1991, Collegiate Croquet Coaching Manual, 1992; contbr. articles to mags. Dir. Rep. Speakers Bur., N.Y.C., 1986; strategist Reagan-Bush Campaign, N.Y.C., 1984; mem. adv. bd. Def. Fire Protection Assn., 1987—; advisor Urban Design & City Planning, City of N.Y., 1973—; head coach Yale Croquet Team, 1988—, U.S. Naval Acad. Croquet Team, 1990, Nat. Collegiate Croquet Championship Team, Yale U., 1990, 91, World Collegiate Croquet Championship Team, Yale U., 1991. With U.S. Army, 1968-70, ETO. Recipient Proclamation City of N.Y., 1978, Citation for Bus. Devel. City of N.Y., 1978, Medal of Merit Presdl. Task Force, Washington, 1983. Mem. AIAA, AAAS, ASTM, Naval Inst., Navy League, N.Y. Acad. Scis., Am. Acad. Sci. & Tech. (sci. judge 1987—), Soc. for Advancement of Material & Process Engring., Global Econ. Action Com., Am. Chem. Soc., Defense Mfrs. and Suppliers Assn. Am., Nat. Fire Protection Assn., U.S. Croquet Assn. (Palm Beach, Fla., chmn. collegiate div.), N.Y. Croquet Club (bd. dirs. 1989, chmn. lawn com. 1990—), Yale Club of N.Y.C., N.Y. Stock Exch. Club, New England Soc., Columbia U. Faculty Club, LeClub, Ivy League Social Club (N.Y.C.). Home: 1520 York Ave New York NY 10028-7008 Home (summer): Barclay Dr Southampton NY 11963 Office: Hamilton Chem Corp 230 Park Ave New York NY 10169-0005

CHARRIEZ, BLANCA NOELIA, social worker; b. Bayamon, P.R., Sept. 27, 1947; d. Luis and Juanita (Robles) C. Student, Barnard Coll., 1965-66; BA, Brandeis U., 1969; MS in Social Svcs., Boston U., 1971. Lic. ind. clin. social worker, Mass. Group worker Roxbury (Mass.) Comprehensive Community Health Ctr., 1971-72; counselor-lectr. Herbert Lehman Coll., CUNY, Bronx, 1972-75; social worker Family Svc. Assn. Greater Boston, 1975-79; family svcs. coord. follow through prog. Cambridge (Mass.) Sch. Dept., 1979-81; counselor Boston U. Counseling Ctr., 1982-86; project dir. Hispanic mentoring program Boston U., 1984-86; sr. counselor U. Mich. Counseling Ctr., Ann Arbor, 1987-88; sr. clin. social worker Boston U. Counseling Ctr., 1989—. Grantee, Hispanic, Asian and Native-Am. Ministries, United Meth. Ch., 1984-86. Mem. NASW (com. on racial and ethnic affairs Mass. chpt. 1990—), AACD, Assn. for Multicultural Devel. Democrat. Home: 26 Rindge Ave Cambridge MA 02140-1907 Office: Boston U Counseling Ctr 19 Deerfield St Boston MA 02215-1995

CHARRON, MAUREEN JOAN, molecular biologist; b. Bklyn., Aug. 28, 1959; d. Joseph Ellsworth and Marie Ann (Sena) C. BA in Biology, CUNY, Queens Coll., Flushing, 1981, MA in Biology, 1983; PhD in Biology, CUNY, N.Y.C., 1987. Asst. prof. Albert Einstein Coll. Medicine, Bronx, 1990—. Contbr. articles to profl. jours. Postdoctoral fellow Whitehead Inst. Biomed. Rsch., Cambridge, Mass., 1987-90, Jane Coffin Childs fellow, 1987-89; Belle Zeller scholar CUNY, 1984-86; Diabetes Rsch. Edn. Found. grantee, 1991, Life and Health Ins. Med. Rsch. Fund grantee, 1991-94. Mem. Am. Diabetes Assn., Am. Soc. Biochemistry & Molecular Biology, AAAS, Diabetes Ctr. Albert Einstein Coll. Medicine. Office: Albert Einstein Coll 1300 Morris Park Ave Bronx NY 10461-1924

CHARTERS, ANN, language professional, educator; b. Bridgeport, Conn., Nov. 10, 1936; d. Nathan Danberg and Kate (Schultz) Danberg; m. Samuel B. Charters, Mar. 14, 1959; children: Mallay, Nora Lili. A.B., U. Calif.-Berkeley, 1957; M.A., Columbia U., 1960, Ph.D., 1965. Mem. faculty Colby Jr. Coll., New London, N.H., 1962-64; lectr. Columbia U., 1964-65; asst. prof. Am. lit. N.Y.C. Community Coll., 1967-70; assoc. dean of the coll. Brown U., 1989-90; prof. Am. lit. U. Conn., Storrs, 1974—. Author: Nobody-Life and Times of Bert Williams, 1967, Kerouac, 1973, 2d edit. 1986, I Love-Story of Vladimir Mayakovsky and Lili Brik, 1979, The Story and Its Writer, 1983, 3d edit., 1990, The Beats: Literary Bohemians in Post-War America, 1983, Beats and Company: A Portrait of a Literary Generation, 1986, The Viking Portable Beat Reader, 1992; author: (intro. Penquin Classic edit.) Three Lives and Q.E.D. (Gertrude Stein), On the Road (Jack Kerouac). Office: U Conn Dept English Storrs CT 06268

CHARTOCK, HYMAN, psychiatrist, neurologist; b. Bklyn., Aug. 26, 1912; s. Meyer and Zlata (Pressman) C.; m. Laurette Y. Friedman, Dec. 16, 1951; children: Robert, David. BA, NYU, 1933; MB, Royal Coll. Physicians and Surgeons, Edinburgh, Scotland, 1939. Intern Maimonides Hosp., Bklyn., 1939-40; mem. staff Bklyn. State Hosp., 1940-41; resident in neurology, psychiatry and neurosurgery City Hosp., Welfare Island, N.Y., 1941, asst. chief neuropsychiat. svc., 1946-57; postgrad. in neurology and psychiatry Columbia U., N.Y.C., 1946-48, mem. faculty Coll. Physicians and Surgeons, 1949-64; pvt. practice, N.Y.C., 1945—; staff neurologist, psychiatrist Hempstead Gen. Hosp., 1960-65; asst. attending psychiat. clinic Presbyn. Med. Ctr., 1949-64; neurologist L.I. Jewish Hosp., 1954-55; adj. prof. Union Grad. Sch., Yellow Springs, Ohio, 1972; pres. Bio-Phoresis Rsch. Found. Inc., 1979-81; cons. vocat. guidance div. B'nai B'rith, 1961; cons. psychiatrist and neurologist vocat. rehab. div. N.Y. State Bd. Edn., 1957, Commn. of Blind, N.Y. State Dept. Social Welfare, 1958; lectr. in field. Author: Road to Normalcy, 1947. Maj. M.C., U.S. Army, World War II. Mem. Med. Soc. State N.Y. (50 Yr. svc. citation 1989). Home: PO Box 431 46 Oak Dr Highland Mills NY 10930 Office: 103 E 86th St Apt 9D New York NY 10028-1058

CHARTON, BARBARA, librarian; b. Bklyn., Sept. 12, 1936; d. Joseph and Luba (Wolfman) Israel; m. Marvin Charton, Aug. 28, 1955; children: Michael, Sarah, Deborah. BA, Bklyn. Coll., 1958; MS, Pratt Inst., Bklyn., 1967, MLS, 1974. Tchr. biochemistry Packer Coll. Inst., Bklyn., 1965-70; rsch. editor Grolier Inc., N.Y.C., 1970-75; adj. prof. Pratt Inst., Bklyn., 1976-81; rsch. editor, librarian Reader's Digest, N.Y.C., 1976-81; asst. prof. Hofstra U., Uniondale, N.Y., 1981-82; asst. prof. L.I. U., Bklyn., 1982-86, assoc. prof., 1986-88; assoc. prof. and librarian Hunter Coll., N.Y.C., 1988—. Mem. Am. Chem. Soc., Internat. QSAR Soc., Internat. Union of Pure and Applied Sci. (div. history of chemistry), Spl. Librs. Assn. Democrat. Jewish. Home: 492 Sylvania Dr Bridgeville PA 15017

CHARTRAND, MARK RAY, astronomer, telecommunications consultant; b. Miami, Fla., Aug. 2, 1943; s. Mark Ray, Jr. and Barbara Dunaway (Wilkins) C. BS in Astronomy, Case Inst. Tech., Cleve., 1965; PhD, Case Western Res. U., 1970. Asst. to dir. Mueller Planetarium, Cleve., 1965-66; research asst. Warner and Swasey Obs., Cleve., 1966-70; edn. coordinator, asst. astronomer Am. Museum-Hayden Planetarium, N.Y.C., 1970-74; chmn., asso. astronomer Am. Museum-Hayden Planetarium, 1974-80; dir. Scientia, Inc.; speaker colls., public groups; presenter in field; cons., 1984—; editor-in-chief Satellite Systems Handbook, 1992—. Co-author: Astronomy, 1975, Stars, 1985; author: Skyguide, 1982, Planets, 1990, Exploring Space, 1991, Audubon Field Guide to the Night Sky, 1991; columnist: Omni mag, 1979-81, Space World mag., 1982-88, Ad Astra mag., 1989—; contbr. articles to mags., newspapers; host, producer: radio program What's Up?, 1977-78. Fellow Brit. Interplanetary Soc.; mem. AAAS, Nat. Space Club, Cosmos Club. Home: 19333 Hottinger Cir Germantown MD 20874-1503 Office: 19751 Frederick Rd Ste 349 Germantown MD 20876-1300

CHARY, MUDUMBAI SRNIVAS, social research educator; b. Nellore, Andhra Pradesh, India, Sept. 22, 1934; came to U.S., 1972; s. Venkata and Sitamma Chary; m. Nagarathna Kedda; children: Seshadri, Raghu. BA with honors, Andhra U., Waltair, India, 1955, MA, 1958; PhD, Kans. State U., 1975. Asst. prof. Narsapur (India) Coll., 1956-63, head dept. history and polit. sci., 1963-64; prof., head dept. history Adoni Coll., 1964-65; assoc. prof. Osmania U., Hyderabad, India, 1965-75; vis. scholar Sch. Internat. Affairs Columbia U., N.Y.C., 1975-78; vis. faculty fellow Princeton U., N.Y.C., 1978-79; mem. faculty New Sch. Social Rsch., N.Y.C., 1983—; faculty rep. students union Narasapur Coll., 1961-62, dir. dormitories, 1962-63; vis. scholar Paul Nitze Sch. Advanced Internat. Studies Johns Hopkins U., Washington, 1983-86. Author: United States Foreign Policy Toward India 1947-55, 1980; contbr. articles to profl. jours.; presenter in field. Mem. Tenants Union, N.Y.C., 1982-84; vol. soup kitchen St. John the Divine, N.Y.C., 1983—. Rsch. grantee Harry S. Truman Libr., 1973, Eleanor Roosevelt Inst., 1976, Harry S. Truman Inst. Internat. Affairs, 1990; NEH travel grantee, 1985; Lyndon Johnson Found. Moody grantee, 1985; Hoover scholar Herbert Hoover Libr. Assn., 1980. Fellow Asian Rsch. Svc.; mem. Asian Studies Assn. Home: 206 W 104th St Apt 8 New York NY 10025

CHASALOW, LEWIS CRAIG, manufacturing network designer; b. Washington, July 11, 1956; s. Ivan G. and Carol (Silver) C. BS in Indsl. Engring., Lehigh U., 1978, MS in Indsl. Engring., 1979, MBA, 1982. Mfg. control engr. Western Electric, Reading, Pa., 1979-81; forecasting analyst AT&T Long Lines, Bedminster, N.J., 1981-83, forecasting mgr., 1983-85; nat. account mgr. AT&T, Parsippany, N.J., 1985-88; industry mgr. AT&T, Bridgewater, N.J., 1988-89; sr. engr. AT&T Network Systems, Berkeley Heights, N.J., 1989-91, disting. mem. tech. staff, 1991—. Contbr. articles to profl. jours. Mem. Computer Automated Systems Assn./Soc. Mfg. Engrs. (sr.), Ops. Rsch. Soc. Am. Office: AT&T 2 Oak Way Berkeley Heights NJ 07922

CHASE, GARY ANDREW, statistician, educator; b. N.Y.C., Jan. 5, 1945; s. Allen Leonard and Janet Elaine (Rubensohn) C.; m. Anne M. Hirschfeld, May 28, 1968 (div. 1980); 1 child, Alexander Anthony; m. Carol S. Weisman, Nov. 21, 1980. AB magna cum laude, Harvard U., 1966; PhD, Johns Hopkins U., 1970. Rsch. fellow Johns Hopkins U., Balt., 1970-71, asst. prof., 1971-78, assoc. prof., 1978-85, prof., 1985—; cons. Armed Forces Inst. Pathology, Washington, 1984-85, NIMH, Rockville, Md., 1986-90. Co-author: Principles of Genetic Counseling, 1975; contbr. articles to profl. jours. Fellow Am. Psychopathol. Assn.; mem. Am. Statis. Assn. (bd. dirs. 1981-84), Soc. for Epidemiologic Rsch., Am. Pub. Health Assn. Jewish. Home: 801 Chestnut Glen Gth Baltimore MD 21204-3710 Office: Johns Hopkins Sch Pub Health 624 N Broadway Baltimore MD 21205-1999

CHASE, RICHARD HAZEN, real estate investment analyst; b. Holyoke, Mass., Oct. 19, 1953; s. Hazen P. and Dorothy (Tucker) C.; m. Cheryl Ann Parks, June 26, 1982; children; Daniel, Amy. BSM in Engring., Duke U., 1975; MS in Fin., U. Mass., 1977. Investment analyst Mass. Mut. Life Ins. Co., Springfield, 1977-80; investment officer Phoenix Mutual, Hartford, Conn., 1980-83; v.p. investments Cigna Ins. Co., Bloomfield, Conn., 1983—. Mem. Internat. Counsel Shopping Ctrs., Mortgage Bankers Assn., Urban Land Inst. Office: Cigna Investments Inc 900 Cottage Grove Rd Hartford CT 06152-0001

CHASE, SAMUEL BROWN, economics consultant; b. Great Falls, Mont., Feb. 21, 1932; s. Samuel Brown and Thelma (Wright) C.; m. Martha Trippet, July 11, 1953; children—Christy Lynn, Candace, Colleen Amy, Cathryn Ann. B.A., Dartmouth Coll., 1954; Ph.D., U. Calif.-Berkeley, 1960. Instr. in econs. U. Ill., 1957-59; mem. staff Office Sec. Treasury, Washington, 1962-63; mem. staff research dept. Fed. Res. Bank Kansas City (Mo.), 1959-62; dir., Md. Tax study, 1963-64; assoc. prof. econs. U. Md., 1963-65; mem., sr. staff Brookings Inst., 1964-67; dir. Mont. econ. study, 1968-69; prof. econs. U. Mont., 1967-71; assoc. dir. research Fed. Res. Bd. Washington, 1971-74, adviser to bd., 1974-75; pres. Samuel Chase & Co. Ltd., Washington, 1983—; assoc. economist Fed. Open Market Com., 1974-75; cons. fin. instns., 1975—, Hunt Commn., 1971; dir. several Dreyfus mut. funds. Author: Asset Prices in Economic Analysis, 1966. Contbr. articles to profl. jours. Recipient Buchanan Prize U. Calif., Berkeley, 1962. Mem. Am. Econ. Assn., Phi Beta Kappa. Office: Samuel Chase & Co Ltd Ste 408 4410 Massachusetts Ave NW Washington DC 20016-8000

CHASEN, EDITH ANDREA, geology and physics educator; b. N.Y.C., Dec. 29, 1947; d. Albert and Charlotte (Lapidus) C. MA, Boston U., 1968, AM, 1970. Adj. lectr. Hunter Coll. CUNY, 1971-75, Coll. S.I., 1978-79, N.Y. Tech. Coll. CUNY, 1980-86; adj. instr. Bloomfield (N.J.) Coll., 1976-80; asst. adj. prof. St. John's U., Jamaica, N.Y., 1980—; adj. lectr. Hunter Coll. CUNY, 1971-75, Coll. S.I. CUNY, 1978-79, N.Y.C. Tech. Coll. CUNY, 1980-86; remote info. provider Am. Online Computer Inc., Vienna, Va., 1986—. Contbr. articles to profl. jours. Mem. AAAS, Am. Crystallographic Assn., Geol. Soc. Am., Mineral. Soc. Am., N.Y. Acad. Scis. Office: St John's U Dept Physics Grand Central & Utopia Pkys Jamaica NY 11439

CHASEN, MIGNON CHARNEY, psychiatrist; b. Moscow, Jan. 5, 1911; came to U.S., 1938; d. Daniel and Anna-Chaya (Kissin) Charney; m. William Henry Chasen, Apr. 10, 1942; children: Barbara Z. Chasen-Joskow, Laura R. Chasen-Cohen. Student, U. Berlin and Leipzig, 1929-33; MD, Royal U. Palermo, Italy, 1935. Diplomate, Am. Bd. Psychiatry & Neurology. Intern Memonides Hosp., Bklyn., 1940-42; resident St. Francis Hosp., Honolulu, 1942-43; sch. physician N.Y. Health Dept., 1944-46; asst. physician Boston State Hosp., 1946-49; asst. in psychiatry Boston VA Hosp., 1949-54, sr. resident in psychiatry, 1954-55; clin. asst. in psychiatry Mass. Gen. and McLean Hosps., Boston, 1956-79; asst. in psychiatry Harvard U. Med. Sch., 1957-79; attending psychiatrist and cons. Brockton (Mass.) VA Hosp.; cons. Boston State Hosp. and VA Clinic., asst. in psychiatry Tufts U. Med. Sch.; frequent lectr. Author: articles in profl. jours. Active in resettling Russian immigrants in Boston. Fellow: AMA, Am. Psychiatric Assn. (dist. counsellor), Mass. Psychiatric Assn. Jewish. Home and Office: 250 Hammond Pond Pky Chestnut Hill MA 02167-1533

CHASIN, DANA JAMES, lawyer, political consultant; b. Boston, Jan. 4, 1960; s. Richard Melvin and Helen Alice (Seitzman) C. BA, Yale U., 1983; JD, Harvard U., 1988. Bar: N.Y. bar 1989, Mass. bar 1989, D.C. bar 1991. Assoc. Kaye, Scholer, Fierman, Hays & Handler, N.Y.C., 1989-90; cons. Europolitics Cons., N.Y.C., 1990—; bd. dirs. Internat. Policy Roundtable, N.Y.C., 1990—. Publisher (newsletter) New Europe News Weekly, 1990. Bd. dirs. Rockefeller Family Fund, N.Y.C., 1988—. Mem. Coun. Fgn. Rels.

CHASIN, MARK, pharmaceutical company executive; b. N.Y.C., Feb. 20, 1942; s. Philip Johann and Florence (Friedman) C.; m. Rena Bleiweiss Chasin, June 19, 1963; children: Jeffrey, Larry, Marni. AB, Cornell U., 1963; PhD, Mich. State U., 1967. Rsch. investigator Squibb Inst., Princeton, N.J., 1967-74; dir. biochemistry Ortho Pharm. Corp., Raritan, N.J., 1974-78; dir. INPD Intercorp. New Product Devel., Raritan, 1978-80; dir. clin. devel. Ortho Pharm. Corp., Raritan, 1980-81; dir. RIS Rsch. Info. Svcs., Raritan, 1981-85; dir. tech. devel. Nova Pharm. Corp., Balt., 1985-90; v.p. Purdue Frederick Rsch. Ctr., Yonkers, N.Y., 1990—; adj. prof. pharmacy U. Md. Sch. Pharmacy, Balt., 1989—. Contbr. articles to profl. jours. Mem. Am. Soc. for Biochemistry and Molecular Biology, Am. Soc. for Pharmacology and Exptl. Therapeutics, Am. Soc. for Clin. Pharmacology and Therapeutics, Controlled Release Soc., Drug Info. Assn. Office: Purdue Frederick Rsch Ctr 99-101 Sawmill River Rd Yonkers NY 10701

CHASIN, MARTIN, art gallery director, consultant, educator; b. Bklyn., July 17, 1938; s. Saul and Frances M. (Rosenfeld) C.; m. Jessica Wolf, Nov. 12, 1989; 1 stepchild, Jonah Gelbach. Student, Bklyn. Coll., 1956-60, U. Pa., 1960-66, Oxford U., Eng, 1962, Free U. Berlin, 1962-63. Mem. faculty history Howard U., Washington, 1966-69; Am. Coun. Learned Socs. fellow Princeton U., 1969-73; mgr. Hannoch, Weisman, Stern & Besser, Newark, 1973-77; gen. mgr. Western Union Internat./Airsignal, N.Y.C., 1977-82; dir. mktg. Center Art Galleries, Honolulu, Hawaii, 1982-85; dir. ops. Greenwich Workshop, Trumbull, Conn., 1985. Author: (with others) History of the Crusades Vol. VI, 1990. Named Harrison fellow, Univ. fellow, U. Pa., 1963-66; recipient Fulbright Grant, Fulbright Commn., Washington, 1962. Fellow Royal Soc. Arts (London); mem. Am. Hist. Soc., Princeton Club of N.Y.

CHASSE, JOHN DENNIS, economics educator; b. Kalispell, Mont., July 30, 1934; s. Clarence Harry and Aurice Rose (Weller) C.; m. Linda Marie Negus, Jan. 2, 1977; children: Matthew, Paul. BA, Gonzaga U., 1961; MA, Regis Coll., 1968; PhD, Syracuse U., 1974. Rsch. asst. Syracuse (N.Y.) U., 1968-70; intern UN Devel. Programme, New Delhi, 1971; from asst. to assoc. prof. Savannah (Ga.) State Coll., 1973-79; pub. health advisor U.S. Office Internat. Health, Rockville, Md., 1976; assoc. prof. SUNY, Brockport, 1979—; vis. prof. U.S. Bur. Labor Stats., Washington, 1974. Contbr. articles to profl. jours. Home: 234 S Main St Brockport NY 14420-2247 Office: SUNY Dept Bus and Econs Brockport NY 14420

CHAST, ROZ, cartoonist; b. Bklyn., Nov. 26, 1954; d. George and Elizabeth (Buchman) C.; m. William Franzen, Sept. 22, 1984; children: Ian, Nina. BFA, RISD, 1977. Contract artist The New Yorker Mag., N.Y.C., 1979—. Author: (cartoon collections) Unscientific Americans, 1982, Parallel Universes, 1984, The Four Elements, 1988, Proof of Life on Earth, 1991. Office: care New Yorker Cartoonists 25 W 43d St New York NY 10036

CHATOFF, MICHAEL ALAN, lawyer, editor; b. N.Y.C., Aug. 18, 1946; s. Alexander Zelig and Leona Rhoda (Weiss) C. BA, CUNY, 1967; JD, Bklyn. Law Sch., 1971; LLM, NYU, 1978. Bar: N.Y. 1971, U.S. Dist. Ct.

(so. and ea. dists.) N.Y. 1978, U.S. Ct. Appeals (2d cir.) 1980, U.S. Supreme Ct. 1980. Reader Chgo. Title Ins. Co., N.Y.C., 1972; sr. editor West Pub. Co., Westbury, N.Y., 1972—; cons. office bus. devel. N.Y. Sch. for Deaf, N.Y.C. Mayor's Office for Disabled, Westchester County Legis.; lectr. N.Y. State Dept. of Edn. Vocat. Ednl. Svcs. for Individuals with Disabilities, N.Y. Sch. Deaf, Lexington Sch. for Deaf, Parents for Dear Awareness, Am. Profl. Soc. for Deaf, N.Y. Ctr. for Law and the Deaf, Coun. on Jewish Deaf Edn. and Rehab., Nat. Coun. on Deaf People and Deafness, NYU. Assoc. law editor Ency. on Deaf People and Deafness; contbr. articles to Nat. Law Jour., N.Y. Law Jour., Able Adv., Communication Outlook, Deaf Spectrum. Counsel, bd. dirs. Westchester Community Svcs. for Hearing Impaired; counsel Conn. African-Am. Deaf Advocate; mem. Supreme Ct. Hist. Soc., Found. for Sci. and the Deaf, 1981-83, bd. dirs.; del. nominee Dem. Nat. Conv., 1992. Mem. ABA, Queens County Bar Assn., Assn. of Bar of City of N.Y., Nat. Assn. Deaf, Am. Contract Bridge League. Home: 260 09T Grand Central Pky Floral Park NY 11005

CHATTERJEE, PRONOY K., chemistry research scientist; b. Varanasi, U.P., India, Oct. 26, 1936; came to U.S., 1963; s. Rameshwar and Nanibala (Ganguli) C.; m. Swapna Chatterjee, Dec. 24, 1962; children: Gargi, Partha. MS, Banaras H U., Varanasi, 1958; PhD, Calcutta (India) U., 1962, DSc, 1973. Postdoctoral rsch. assoc. SRRL, U.S. Dept. Agr. and Princeton (N.J.) U., 1963-65; sr. rsch. chemist personal products Johnson & Johnson, Milltown, N.J., 1966-74, mgr. rsch. personal products, 1974-87; rsch. fellow Chicopee Johnson & Johnson, Dayton, N.J., 1987—; Nat. Acad. Sci. rsch. fellow, 1963-65. Mem. adv. bd. editors Nonwoven Rsch. Jour., 1988—; editor: Absorbency, 1985; editor Natas Notes, 1972-74; contbr. articles to profl. jours. Recipient Oustanding Rsch. Achievement award Johnson & Johnson, 1973, Ednl. Svc. award Plastic Inst. Am., Hoboken, N.J., 1976. Fellow Am. Inst. Chemists; mem. TAPPI, AAAS, Am. Chem. Soc., Fiber Soc. Home: 6 Marcin Ct Spotswood NJ 08884-1230 Office: Johnson & Johnson 2351 US Rt 130 Dayton NJ 08810

CHATTERTON, RAYMOND EDWARD, economics educator; b. Springfield, Mo., July 27, 1946; s. David Paul and Fern Katherine (Stotts) C.; children: Paul Allen, Robert Emerson. BA, SW Mo. State Coll., 1968; PhD, Washington State U., 1980. Lic. pvt. pilot. Asst. prof. econs. Randolph-Macon Woman's Coll., Lynchburg, Va., 1975-80; assoc. prof. Lock Haven (Pa.) U., 1982-88, prof., 1988—. Capt. AUS, 1968-71, Vietnam. H.L. Mednick Found. grantee, Lynchburg, Va., 1976. Mem. Am. Econs. Assn., Rotary Club (bd. dirs. 1987-91, v.p. Lock Haven chpt. 1988-89, pres. 1989-90). Unitarian. Democrat. Home: 3 Campus Vw Lock Haven PA 17745-1001 Office: Lock Haven U Lock Haven PA 17745

CHATTLER, ZACHARY LEE, podiatrist; b. Chgo., Mar. 24, 1952; s. Raymond Bear and Shirley (Franklin) C.; m. Jo Ellen Secker, Aug. 21, 1977; children: Jonathan Raymond, Daniel Jacob. BA, Sangamon State U., 1975, MA, 1977; DPM, Ill. Coll. Podiatric Medicine, 1985. Asst. headmaster City Day Sch., Springfield, Ill., 1977-79; sch. psychologist Wheaton (Ill.) Pub. Sch. Dist., 1979-81; resident in podiatry State of Md., Balt., 1985-87; podiatrist Podiatry Assocs., Balt., 1987—; instr. Md. Podiatric Residency Program, Balt., 1987—. Contbg. author: Podiatry for the Assistant, 1989. Den leader Boy Scouts Am., Owings Mills, Md., 1989—. Mem. Am. Podiatric Med. Assocs., Md. Podiatric Med. Assn. (v.p. 1991—). Office: Podiatry Assocs 300 E Joppa Rd Baltimore MD 21204-3020

CHATURVEDI, RAMA KANT, academic administrator, educator; b. Kanker, India, July 7, 1933; came to U.S., 1965; s. Chaturbhuj S. and Asarfi (Devi) C.; m. Veena Chaturvedi, May 28, 1958; children: Sanjiv, Kalpana, Seemant. BSc, Agra (India) U., 1954, MSc, 1956, PhD, 1960. Rsch. assoc., chem. dept. Ind. Univ., Bloomington, 1965-66; rsch. assoc., biochemistry dept. Yale U., New Haven, 1966-70; assoc. prof. chemistry Greater Hartford (Conn.) Community Coll., 1970-76, prof. chemistry, 1976-77, chair nat. sci. dept., 1977-82, dir. sci., math., psychology, and edn. div., 1982—. Contbr. articles to profl. jours. Founding pres. India Assn., New Haven, 1966-67. Recipient Sr. Rsch. fellowship Govt. of India, New Delhi, 1957-60, Fulbright grant Inst. Internat. Edn., N.Y.C., 1965-68, Meritorious Svc. award Bd. Conn. Community Colls., Hartford, 1990-91. Mem. AAUP, Conn. Congress Community Colls. (del. 1976-77). Democrat. Home: 39 Beacon St Newington CT 06111-4703 Office: Greater Hartford Community Coll 61 Woodland St Hartford CT 06105-2326

CHAUHAN, NARINDER SINGH, physics educator; b. Ambala, India, Jan. 10, 1952; came to U.S., 1986; s. Jaswant Singh and Chand (Kaur) C.; m. Sandip Rani, Oct. 11, 1980; children: Parneet, Divnaseem. BS in Physics, Punjabi U., Patiala, India, 1970, MS in Physics, 1972, PhD in Physics, 1979; ME in Computer Sci. with hons., Thapar Inst., Patiala, 1984. Rsch. fellow Punjabi U., 1973-78, asst. prof., 1978-86; asst. prof. George Washington U., 1986-88, assoc. prof., 1988—. Contbr. numerous articles on space physics, astrophysics and remote sensing to profl. jours. Mem. Am. Geophysical Soc., IEEE. Sikh. Home: 7715 Glenister Dr Springfield VA 22152-2005 Office: George Washington U Elec Engring & Computer Sci Washington DC 20052

CHAVE, ALAN DANA, oceanographer; b. Whittier, Calif., May 12, 1953; s. Keith Ernest and Georgiana Ruth (Steen) C. BS, Harvey Mudd Coll., 1975; PhD, MIT, 1980. Postdoctoral researcher geophysics Scripps Instn. of Oceanography, La Jolla, Calif., 1980-82; asst. rsch. geophysicist Scripps Instn. of Oceanography, La Jolla, 1982-85, assoc. rsch. geophysicist, 1985-86; tech. staff mem. AT&T Bell Labs., Murray Hill, N.J., 1986-91; assoc. scientist Woods Hole (Mass.) Oceanographic Instn., 1991—; guest scientist Los Alamos (N.Mex.) Nat. Lab., 1983—; assoc. adj. prof. Scripps Inst. Oceanography, La Jolla, 1986-90. Contbr. over 50 articles to sci. publs.; editor Revs. of Geophysics, 1991—. Recipient J. Robert Oppenheimer fellowship Los Alamos Nat. Lab., 1985. Mem. Am. Geophys. Union, IEEE, AAAS, Am. Meterol. Soc. Office: Woods Hole Oceanog Instn Falmouth MA 02543

CHAVERIAT, ANDREW JOHN, foreign currency trader; b. Chgo., Jan. 26, 1963; s. John Walter and Dorothea (Eissfeldt) C. BA, U. Chgo., 1985, MBA, 1987. Funding trader Citibank Investment Bank, N.Y.C., 1987-88, fgn. currency trader, 1988-92; Paribas Capital Markets, N.Y.C., 1992—. Republican. Lutheran. Home: 156 Newark St Hoboken NJ 07030-3548 Office: Paribas Capital Markets 787 7th Ave New York NY 10019

CHAYA, HENRY JOHN, JR., electrical engineering educator; b. Newburgh, N.Y., July 2, 1951; s. Henry John and Ruth Marie (King) C. BS, Manhattan Coll., 1973; MA, Princeton (N.J.) U., 1975, PhD, 1981. Instr. Christian Bros. Acad., Lincroft, N.J., 1978-80; assoc. prof. Manhattan Coll., Riverdale, N.Y., 1981—. Contbr. articles to profl. jours. Mem. IEEE, Am. Soc. Elec. Engrs., Bros. of the Christian Schs., Phi Beta Kappa, Tau Beta Pi (chief advisor N.Y. chpt. 1988—). Roman Catholic. Office: Manhattan Coll Dept Elec Engring Riverdale NY 10471-4099

CHAZEN, DAVID FRANKLIN, II, toy company executive; b. Detroit, Nov. 27, 1960; s. Jerome A. and Simona (Chivian) C. BS, U. Pa., 1982; MBA, Columbia U., 1986. Buyer The Broadway Stores, L.A., 1982-84; investment broker Goldman Sachs & Co., N.Y.C., 1986-88; pres. Good Stuff Corp., L.I. City, N.Y., 1988—; bd. dirs. Coastal Banc Savs., Houston. Mem., sponsor Youth at Risk Program, N.Y.C., 1988-89; mem. collectors circle Am. Crafts Mus., N.Y.C., 1988-90. Jewish. Home: 201 E 69th St PHF New York NY 10021-5471 Office: Good Stuff Corp 47-00 33d St Long Island City NY 11101

CHAZEN, JEROME A., apparel company executive; b. N.Y.C., Mar. 21, 1927; s. David and Rose (Mark) C.; m. Simona Chivian, June 26, 1949; children: Kathy Ann, Louise Sharon Chazen Banon, David Franklin. BA, U. Wis., Madison, 948; MBA, Columbia U., Madison, 1950. Security analyst Sutro Bros., N.Y.C., 1950-51; salesman/mgr. Rhea Mfg. Co., Milw., 1951-52, buyer Milw. Boston Stores, 1952-54; buyer Milw. Boston Stores Lit Bros., Phila., 1954-57; v.p. Winkelman Stores, Detroit, 957-68; v.p. sales Westwood Textiles, N.Y.C., 1968-73, Eccobay Sports Wear, N.Y.C., 1973-77; chmn. bd. dirs. Liz Claiborne, Inc., N.Y.C., 1977—; bd. dirs. Fashion Inst. Tech., Shenkar Coll. Vice chmn. Internat. Peace Park/Jewish Nat. Fund, Israel, 1987; bd. dirs. Greater N.Y. council Boy Scouts Am., 1983-84, Rockland Ctr. for Arts, Nyack, N.Y., 1983—, Lupus Found., N.Y.C., 1984, Ednl. Found., Am. Craft Mus., 1989; bd. dirs., chmn., div. leader Fedn. United Jewish Appeal, N.Y.C., 1983-86. Served with USN, 1945-46. Jewish. Office: Liz Claiborne Inc 1441 Broadway New York NY 10018-2002*

CHE, TRACEY ALLISON, podiatrist; b. N.Y.C., Mar. 12, 1962; d. John K. and Alice (Chin) C. BS, Cornell U., 1984; D Podiatric Medicine, N.Y. Coll. Podiatric Medicine, 1988. Diplomate Nat. Bd. Podiatric Examiners. Podiatric surgeon Francis Lewis Footcare, Bayside, N.Y., 1989—; attending surgeon St. Joseph's Hosp., Flushing, N.Y., 1989—. Associate Am. Coll. Foot Surgeons. Office: Francis Lewis Footcare 32-07 Francis Lewis Blvd Bayside NY 11358

CHECCHI, VINCENT VICTOR, economist; b. Calais, Maine, Nov. 25, 1918; s. Arthur R. and Dina I. (Pisani) C.; m. Mary E. Pate, Aug. 2, 1941; children: Dina Ann, Mary Jane, Vincent Arthur. AB, U. Maine, 1940; postgrad., Harvard U., 1941; MA, George Washington U., 1942. Statistician-economist WPB, 1941-45; dep. dir. requirements br. Allied Mil. Govt. in Italy, 1945-46; dir. program coordination UNRRA, Italy; then asst. to chief mission in China UNRRA, 1946-47; loan officer Internat. Bank Reconstrn. and Development, 1947; dir. China econ. br., later dir. East-West trade br. ECA, 1947-49, spl. rep. in Philippines, 1950-51; econ. editor Reporter mag., 1950; founder, 1951, since chmn. bd., chief exec. officer Checchi and Co., Washington; also dir. various subs. Co-author: Honduras, A Problem in Economic Development; author articles on econs. Home: 9206 Watson Rd Silver Spring MD 20910-4136 Office: Checchi and Co 1730 Rhode Island Ave NW Washington DC 20036-3101

CHECKETTS, DAVE, professional basketball team executive; b. Bountiful, Utah, 1956; m. Deb Checketts; children: Spencer, Katie, Nathaniel, Andrew, Ben. B in Comm. and Fin., U. Utah; MBA, Brigham Young U. Formerly with Bain and Co., Boston; with Utah Jazz, NBA, 1983-84, pres., 1984-89; v.p. devel. NBA, N.Y.C., 1990-91; pres. N.Y. Knickerbockers, NBA, N.Y.C., 1991—; cons. NBA, 1989-90. Office: NY Knickerbockers Madison Sq Garden 1 Pennsylvania Pla New York NY 10001*

CHECKLIN, VLADIMIR N., economist; b. Moscow, USSR, Oct. 20, 1941; s. Nikolai Ivanovich and Ana Alekseevna (Zakharova) C.; m. Tamara Mikhailova, Jan. 17, 1974; children: Anna, Ekaterina. Student, Moscow State Inst. Internat. Rels., 1965; PhD in Economy, Moscow State Inst. Internat. Rels., 1977. Desk officer Dept Trade Rels We. Countries Ministry of Fgn. Trade of USSR, Moscow, 1965-70, exec. sec. Joint Intergovtl. Commn. on Trade & Econ. Cooperation USSR, U.K, Austrialia, New Zealand, 1973-79, head dept. internat. econ. orgns., 1984-88; sr. econ. advisor USSR Trade Del. to U.K., London, 1970-73, dep. trade rep., 1979-84; dep. pres. U.S.-USSr Trade & Econ. Coun., N.Y.C., 1988—. Author: The USSR-U.K. Business Opportunities, 1978. Office: The US-USSR Trade & Econ Coun 805 3d Ave New York NY 10022-7513

CHEEK, DENNIS WILLIAM, educator, minister, consultant; b. Harrisburg, Pa., Apr. 13, 1955; s. Clarence William Jr. and Laura Priscilla (Rockey) C.; m. Kim Anita Douglas, Mar. 9, 1980; children: Carol Annette, Michael William. BA, Towson State U., 1979; MA, U. Md., 1984; BS, U. State N.Y. Regents Coll., 1988; PhD, Pa. State U., 1989; postgrad., Grad. Theol. Found., 1992—, SUNY, Albany. Cert. sci. and social studies tchr., sch. adminstr., N.Y.; ordained to minstry Assemblies of God Ch., 1979. Assoc. evangelist Don Summers Evangelistic Assn., Bristol, Eng., 1976-78; asst. pastor Gospel Tabernacle Balt., Inc., 1978-83; pastor Rhaunen (Fed. Republic Germany) Tabernacle, 1983-84; chmn. high sch. sci. dept. Dept. Def. Dependents Sch., Bitburg, Fed. Republic Germany, 1984-87; rsch. asst. sci., tech. and society program Pa. State U., University Park, 1987-88; project coord. Nat. Sci., Tech. and Soc. Network, University Park, 1988-89; coord. curriculum devel. N.Y. Sci., Tech. Soc. Edn. Project, State Edn. Dept., Albany, 1989—; tchr. Tabernacle Christian Sch., Balt., 1978-80; lectr. history European div. U. Md., Heidelberg, Fed. Republic Germany, 1985-87; aux. protestant chaplain USAF, Buechel, Fed. Republic Germany, 1984-87; field tester, reviewer nat. security in nuclear age series Mershon Ctr., Ohio State U., Columbus, 1986-87; advisor Nat. Bd. for Profl. Teaching Stds., 1992; advisor div. high level radioactive waste disposal U.S. Dept. Energy, Fed. Interagy. Task Force on Environ. Cancer, Heart and Lung Disease, Transformations media project AIME, 1990—; mem. task force on teaching anthropology in sch. Am. Anthropol. Assn., 1991—; cons. on sci., tech. and society edn. to numerous sch. dists. and nat. orgns.; cons. on ch. growth and Christian edn. to numerous chs.; mem. task force on sci. and tech. Evang. Luth Ch. in Am., 1989—. Author: Thinking Constructively about Science, Technology and Society Education, 1992; editor: STS Reporter, 1988-89, Proc. 5th Ann. Tech. Lit. Conf., 1990, Proc. 6th Ann. Tech. Lit. Conf., 1991, Proc. 7th Ann. Tech. Lit. Conf., 1992; co-editor Proc. 4th Ann. Tech. Lit. Conf., 1989; mem. editoral bd., book rev. editor Jour Tech. Edn., 1989—; cons. editor Odyssey; contbr. numerous articles, essays and curriculum for publ. Troop coord. Dulaney dist. Boy Scouts Am., Balt., 1979-83. U. Md. gen. univ. fellow, 1983. Mem. AAAS (reviewer Sci. Books & Films 1987—), NSTA (task force on scope, sequence and coordination secondary sch. sci. 1989, chmn. task force on NSTA-Sponsored presentations at non-NSTA convs. and meetings, task force on articulation with sch. adminstrs.), ASCD (facilitator network for sci., math. and tech. edn. 1990—, nat. adv. panel U.S. math. and sci. achievement 1991, internat. polling panel 1992—), Soc. for History Tech. (advisor Discovering Sci. and Tech. through Am. History project), Am. Anthropol. Assn. (task force on teaching anthropology in schs.), Nat. Assn. Sci., Tech. and Soc. (chmn. site and confs. liaison com., chmn. subcom. on STS assessment position paper, com. on STS evaluation, chair publs. com.), Acad. Parish Clergy (book reviewer), Alban Inst. (book reviewer), Religious Rsch. Assn., Am. Ednl. Rsch. Assn. (liaison spl. interest group edn. in sci. and tech. to ASCD and Coun. State Sci. Suprs.), Nat. Coun. Social Studies (manuscript reviewer, book reviewer 1991—, vice-chair sci. and soc. com. 1991—), Nat. Mid. Sch. Assn. (manuscript & book rev. bd. 1991—), Internat. Network for Info. in Sci. and Tech. Edn., UNESCO, Nat. Mid. Level Sci. Tchrs. Assn., Coun. of State Sci. Suprs., Sci. Tchrs. Assn. of N.Y., Kappa Delta Pi (assoc. counselor Sigma Mu chpt.), Phi Alpha Theta, Epsilon Pi Tau. Republican. Office: NY Sci Tech Soc Edn Project Edn Bldg Rm 228 EB Albany NY 12234

CHEEMA, MOHAN KRISHAN SINGH, internist; b. Lassoi, Punjab, India, Jan. 13, 1936; came to U.S. 1964; s. Anokh Singh Cheema and Jagir Kaur Tawana; m. Sheila Fairlie, Sept. 9, 1966; children: Ariana, Ranji. FSc, Mahandra Coll., India, 1955; MD, Med. Coll. Patiala, India, 1960. Diplomate Am. Bd. Internal Medicine and Pulmonary Disease. Intern Fordham Hosp., Bronx, N.Y., 1964-65, resident in internal medicine, 1965-66; resident in internal medicine L.I. (N.Y.) Coll. Hosp., 1966-67, VA Hosp., Bklyn., 1967-69; pvt. practice New Rochelle, N.Y.; Chief pulmonary sect. New Rochelle Hosp. Med. Ctr. Fellow Am. Coll. Chest Physicians, Am. Coll. Cardiology (assoc.); mem. AMA. Office: 158 Lockwood Ave New Rochelle NY 10801

CHEEVER, ALLEN WILLIAMS, pathologist; b. Brookings, S.D., June 4, 1932; s. Herbert E. and Margaret Haynes (Williams) C.; m. Jane Ellen Gilkerson, Aug., 1953; children: Carol, Erik, Laura, Angela. BS, Carleton Coll., 1954; MD, Harvard U., 1958. Diplomate Am. Bd. Pathology. Commd. 2d lt. USPHS, 1960, advanced through grades to capt., 1968; researcher NIH, Bethesda, Md., 1960—. Contbr. articles to profl. jours. Capt. USPHS, 1960—. Home: 4507 Conifer Ln Bethesda MD 20814-4009 Office: NIH Bldg 4 Rm 126 Bethesda MD 20892

CHEIMETS, SHEILA, association administrator; b. N.Y.C., May 4, 1936; d. David and Anna (Norman) Greenblatt; m. David Cheimets, Dec. 17, 1955; children: Peter, Steven, Alex. BA, Brandeis U., 1958. Reporter, editor Canton (Mass.) Reporter Newspaper, 1971-75; pub. info. officer Mass. League of Cities and Towns, 1975-77; dir. legis. office Mass. Mcpl. Assn., Boston, 1977-87, exec. dir., 1990—; guest lectr. Boston U.-Framingham State Coll., 1973-75. Contbr. articles to profl. publs. Surrogate scheduler Dukakis for Pres. Campaign, Mass., 1988; selectman Town of Canton, 1972-75; chair com. on edn. youth svcs. LWV, Canton, 1964-67. Recipient Best Story, Feature, Editorial and Makeup awards, New Eng. Press Assn., 1967-72; Loeb fellow Harvard U., 1980. Home: 540 Massachusetts Ave Roxbury MA 02118-1402 Office: Mass Mcpl Assn 60 Temple Pl Boston MA 02111-1306

CHELIUS, JAMES ROBERT, economics educator; b. Chgo., Apr. 24, 1943; s. Robert Edward and Ruth Winnifred (Anderson) C.; m. Maureen O'Brien, June 11, 1967; children: Karen, Lori. BS, U. Ill., 1965, MBA, 1967; PhD, U. Chgo., 1974. Economist Nat. Commn. on State Workmen's Compensation Laws, Washington, 1971-72; prof. Purdue U., Lafayette, Ind., 1972-81; prof. econs. Rutgers U., New Brunswick, N.J., 1981—; cons. U.S. SBA, Washington, 1985-88, Major League Baseball, N.Y.C., 1986-90, N.FL, N.Y.C., 1989, Assn. Am. RRs., Washington, 1989. Author: Workplace Safety and Health, 1976, Current Issues in Workers Compensation, 1987, The New Jersey Economy, 1988, 89, 90. Lt. USN, 1969-71. Grantee U.S. SBA, 1985-88. Mem. Am. Econ. Assn., Indsl. Rels. Rsch. Assn. Office: Rutgers U New Brunswick NJ 08903

CHEN, ALEXANDER YU-KUANG, robotics and automation systems specialist, manufacturing technology and computer application consultant; b. Taipai, Taiwan, Republic of China, Sept. 10, 1954; came to U.S., 1980; s. Ming-Mean and Be-Ing (Yu) C. BS, Nat. Taiwan U., 1976; MS, Nat. Chiao Tung U., Taiwan, 1978; MA, Princeton U., 1982, PhD, 1987. Field engr. Nat. Railroad Electrification Project, Taiwan, 1976; sci. instr. First Sargeant Acad., Taiwan, 1979; rsch. asst. Princeton (N.J.) U., 1980-82, asst. in instruction, 1982-84; sr. automation engr. Mactronix, Inc., Dallas, 1984-86; dir. advanced robotics group, rsch. scientist Sci. Rsch. Assocs., Inc., Glastonbury, Conn., 1986-91; analytic engr. United Techs. Rsch. Ctr., East Hartford, Conn., 1991—; adj. lectr. elec. engring. dept. Hartford Grad. Ctr. affiliate Rensselaer Poly. Inst., 1991—. Author: Forecasting Air Transport Demand, 1978, Classical Chinese Poetry, 1978, Optimal and Suboptimal Control of Robotic Systems, 1987, Spatial Planning for Space Robots, 1988, Intelligent Manipulation Technology for Mobile Multi-Branches Robotic Systems, 1991; contbr. articles on multiple computer platforms, computer graphics, sensor-actuator network devel., knowledge engring. and system integration to profl. jours. 1st Lt. Trans. Taiwan, 1978-80. MEM, IEEE, ASME, AIAA, Internat. Soc. Optical Engring., Chinese Culture Ctr. (bd. dirs. 1987-89, pres. 1988). Office: United Techs Rsch Ctr 411 Silver Ln MS 129-85 East Hartford CT 06108

CHEN, CHARLES CHIH-TSAI, aeronautical engineer, researcher; b. Kaohsiung, Taiwan, May 5, 1958; came to U.S., 1984; s. Feng-Chen and Yu-Fu (Yang) C.; m. Herng-Jen Lin, May 30, 1987; children: Richard J., Albert J. BS, Nat. Taiwan U., Taipei, 1980, MS, 1982; PhD, Purdue U., 1990. Teaching asst. Nat. Taiwan U., Taipei, 1980-81, rsch. asst., 1981-82; rsch. asst. Purdue U., West Lafayette, Ind., 1984-89; rsch. scientist Galaxy Sci. Corp., Mays Landing, N.J., 1990-91, program mgr., 1991—. Lt. Chinese Marine Corp, 1982-84. Mem. AIAA, Phi Kappa Phi, Tau Beta Pi, Phi Tau Phi. Home: 8 Drexel Gate Dr Sicklerville NJ 08081-2803

CHEN, DANIEL YIP CHING, securities company executive; b. Chungking, People's Republic China, Nov. 11, 1943; came to U.S., 1975; s. H.S. and Phylis (Kwok) C.; children: Kuni, Yumi. BA, Internat. Christian U., Tokyo, 1967, MA, 1969. Project economist Asian Devel. Bank, Manila, 1969-75; v.p. Salomon Bros., N.Y.C., 1975-79, Morgan Stanley & Co., N.Y.C., 1979-82; v.p., mgr. Salomon Bros. Inc., N.Y.C., 1982-89; exec. v.p. Kankaku Securities (Am.) Inc., N.Y.C., 1989—. Author: Shorinji Kempo, 1968. Bd. dirs., asst. treas. Japan Internat. Christian U. Found., N.Y.C., 1982—. Republican.

CHEN, DAVIDSON TAH-CHUEN, aerospace systems scientist; b. Wenling, Chekiang, China, Apr. 1, 1942; came to U.S., 1964; s. Pon-hwa and Helen (Ha) C.; m. Isabel Shaung-lin Chow, Aug. 13, 1966; children: Edgar Yung-chong, Ingrid Yung-i. BS, Nat. Taiwan U., Taipei, 1963; MS, U. Calif., Berkeley, 1966; PhD, N.C. State U., 1972. Rsch. oceanographer space sci. divsn. Naval Rsch. Lab., Washington, 1974-79, rsch. physicist, 1979-83, project mgr. space systems and tech. dept., 1983-90, program mgr., 1990-91, chief spl. projects, 1991—. Recipient outstanding performance award Naval Rsch. Lab., 1987-91. Mem. Am. Geophys. Union, Chinese-Am. Profls. Assn. Met. Washington (bd. dirs. 1987, pres. 1988), Phi Kappa Phi. Home: 7506 Nevis Rd Bethesda MD 20817-4742 Office: Naval Rsch Lab Code 4205 4555 Overlook Dr Washington DC 20375-5000

CHEN, EDWARD CHIH-HUNG, physician; b. Taiwan, Aug. 21, 1954; came to U.S. 1980; MD, Taipei (Taiwan) Med. Coll., 1980; MPH, Harvard U., 1981. Mem. AMA, Am. Coll. Gastroenterology, Am. Gastroenterological Assn. Office: 35 E Elizabeth Ave Bethlehem PA 18018

CHEN, GUAN SHANG, English educator; b. Ningbo, Peoples Republic of China, Apr. 5, 1919; came to the U.S., 1987; s. Zhang Hong and Xiu Lin (Lee) C.; m. Bao Ji Ying, Mar. 15, 1953 (dec. 1987); children: Chen Ping Jian, Chen Luo Lin. BA, Peking U., 1947; MA, Shanghai Tchrs. U., 1978, PhD, 1982. Instr. Shanghai Tchrs. Coll., 1957-77, head fgn. langs. and lits. dept., 1977-84; advisor Ningbo U., Zhejiang, Peoples Republic of China, 1986—; vis. rsch. scholar CUNY, 1987—. Editor: Literary Gems for Recitation, 1983, Afro-American Short Stories, 1983; translator: Knights of the Cross, 1978. 2d lt. Chinese Army, 1937-38. Recipient Honorary medal and cert. Polish Culture Polish Ministry Culture, 1983. Mem. China Assn. for Study Am. Lit. (coun. 1978—). Home: 1st Fl 3765 63d St Flushing NY 11377-2625 Office: Bernard M Baruch Coll Dept English 17 Lexington Ave New York NY 10010-5526

CHEN, HILO CHAO-HUNG, artist; b. Yee Nun, Taiwan, Republic of China, Oct. 15, 1942; came to U.S., 1968; s. Yion Ho and Wun (Yee) C.; m. Mei-Wan Fu, Nov., 1979; 1 child, Inten. BS in Architecture, Chong-Yieun U., Taiwan, 1966. Museum collections include Guggenheim Mus., N.Y.C., Taiei Fine Arts Mus., Taipei, Taiwan, Republic of China. Office: 302 Bowery New York NY 10012-2802

CHEN, HO-HONG H. H., industrial engineering executive, educator; b. Taiwan, Apr. 11, 1933; s. Shui-Cheng and Mei (Lin) C.; m. Yuki-Lihua Jenny, Mar. 10, 1959; children: Benjamin Kuen-Tsai, Carl Joseph Chao-Kuang, Charles Chao-Yu, Eric Chao-Ying, Charmine Tsuey-Ling, Dolly Hsiao-Ying, Edith Yi-Wen, Yvonne Yi-Fang, Grace Yi-Sing, Julia Yi-Jiun. Owner Tai Chang Indsl. Supplies Co., Ltd., 1967—; pres. Pan Pacific Indsl. Supplies, Inc., Ont., Can., 1975—, Maker Group Inc., Md., 1986—, Wako Internat. Co., Ltd., Md., 1986—; prof. First Econ. U., Japan. Author: 500 Creative Designs for Future Business, 1961; A Summary of Suggestions for the Economic Development in Central America Countries, 1979; Access and Utilize the Potential Fund in Asia, 1980. Mem. Internat. Club (Washington), Kenwood Golf & Country Club (Bethesda, Md.). Office: PO Box 5674 Friendship Sta Washington DC 20016

CHEN, JYH-HONG, materials scientist; b. Taipei, Taiwan, Republic of China, Dec. 1, 1951; came to U.S., 1977; s. Jong and Art-Ju (Lee) C.; m. Lee-Yuan Liu, Aug. 11, 1979; children: Justin K., Isaac E. BS, Nat. Taiwan U., 1975; MS, U. Conn., 1980; PhD, MIT, 1982. Rsch. leader Diligence Synthetic Leather Co., Taipei, 1975-76; mem. rsch. staff Nat. Sci. and Tech. Ctr., Taipei, 1976-77; teaching asst. chem. engring. U. Conn., Storrs, 1977-78, teaching asst. math., 1978-79; rsch. asst. materials sci. and engring. MIT, Cambridge, 1979-81, teaching instr. chem. engring., 1981-82; group leader W.R. Grace, Cambridge, 1982-84; rsch. assoc. fiber dept. E.I. Dupont, Wilmington, Del., 1984—; adj. prof. U. Del., Newark, 1992. Editor: (book) Interfaces in Composites, 1990; contbr. articles to profl. jours. Patentee in field. Recipient Best Paper award Internat. Conf. on Composite Interface, 1990. Mem. Materials Rsch. Soc., Soc. Plastic Engring., Sci. of Advanced Materials and Process Engring. Home: 492 S Feathering Ln Media PA 19063 Office: E I Dupont Chestnut Run Plz MAG 2217 Wilmington DE 19880-0702

CHEN, LIHTORNG ROBERT, lawyer, educator; b. Taiwan, Republic of China, Sept. 6, 1952; came to U.S., 1983; s. Su-Kuo and Su-Lien (Wu) C.; m. Ruei-Chu Catherine Li; children: Teresa, Anne. LLB, Soochow U., Taipei, 1977; MS, Mo. U., 1984; LLM, U. Miami, Fla., 1985; PhD, U. Wales, Eng., 1990. Researcher Republic of China Ministry of Econ. Affairs, Taipei, 1980-82; pvt. practice, 1985-90; assoc. prof. law Soochow U., 1991—.

CHEN, MICHAEL CHIEN-KUO, communications company developer; b. Taiwan, Sept. 29, 1955; came to U.S., 1979; s. C.C. and C.C. (Wu) C.; m. Evon Y. Lai, June 9, 1984. BS, Chiao Tung U., Hsinchu, Taiwan, 1978; MS,

Northwestern U., 1981, PhD, 1984. Mem. tech. staff Bellcore, Red Bank, N.J., 1984-88, AT&T Bell Labs., Middletown, N.J., 1988—. Mem. Chinese Inst. Engrs. (treas., sec. 1988-91, Inst. Svc. award 1990). Home: 60 Munch Rd Red Bank NJ 07701 Office: AT&T Bell Labs 200 Laurel Ave Middletown NJ 07748

CHEN, ROBERT CHIA-HUA, computer scientist; b. Shanghai, Jiangsu, People's Republic China, Oct. 26, 1946; s. Kang and Sylvia Tung-Huan (Lin) C.; m. I-Yu Tung, Mar. 6, 1971; children: Clara An-Ru, David I-Chung. BEE, Rensselaer Poly. Inst., 1966; SM, MIT, 1968; PhD, Carnegie Mellon U., 1974. Asst. prof. U. Pa., Phila., 1974-78; mem. tech. staff Bell Labs., Holmdel, N.J., 1978-81; software cons. engr. Digital Equipment Corp., Nashua, N.H., 1981—. Mem. Assn. for Computing Machinery, IEEE, Tau Beta Pi, Eta Kappa Nu, Pi Delta Epsilon, Sigma Xi (assoc.). Office: Digital Equipment Corp ZK03-4Y02 110 Spit Brook Rd Nashua NH 03062-2698

CHEN, SHIUM ANDREW, psychologist, educator; b. Tsunjiang, Jaingsu, China, Sept. 17, 1931; came to U.S., 1954; s. Ten and Quison (Hu) C.; m. Veronica Ling Koo, Aug. 28, 1964; children: Thomas, Herald, Andrea. BEd, Nat. Taiwan Normal U., Taipei, 1953; MEd, U. Oreg., 1956; MA, Columbia U., 1962; PhD, U. Pitts., 1970. Lic. psychologist, Pa. Rsch. asst. Bur. Applied Social Rsch. Columbia U., N.Y.C., 1956-61; instr. dept. edn. Hofstra U., New Hemstead, N.Y., 1961-62; asst. prof. psychology Emporia (Kans.) State U., 1963-66; prof. dept. counseling and ednl. psychology Slippery Rock (Pa.) U., 1966—, chair dept., 1980-87; ednl. specialist Tainjiang U., 1990; vis. prof. Oxford (Eng.) U., summer, 1986, Nat. Taiwan Norman U., 1973-74. Mem. steering com. English Plus Info. Clearinghouse, 1988—; chair Asian Am. adv. coun. Pa. Heritage Affairs Commn., Harrisburg, 1988—. Recipient Heritage Achievement award Chinese Assn. of Fairfield County, Conn., 1986. Fellow Am. Psychol. Assn.; mem. Asian Am. Psychol. Assn. (bd. dirs. 1973-91), Orgn. Chinese Americans (pres. 1985-86, chair anti-Asian violence task force 1989—, Disting. Leadership award 1986). Home: 107 Mohawk Dr Butler PA 16001-1249 Office: Slippery Rock U Dept Counseling & Ednl Psychology Slippery Rock PA 16057

CHEN, YONG-ZHUO, mathematics educator; b. Shanghai, China, Aug. 12, 1949; came to U.S., 1983; MS, Shanghai Normal U., 1981; MA, U. Pitts., 1985, PhD, 1988. Lectr. Shanghai (China) Normal Univ., 1982-83; teaching fellow Univ. Pitts., Pa., 1984-88; vis. asst. prof. Bowling Green (Ohio) State Univ., 1988-89; asst. prof. Univ. Pitts., Bradford, Pa., 1989—. Named Andrew Mellon Predoctoral fellow Univ. Pitts., 1985. Mem. Am. Math. Soc. Home: 89 Boylston St Bradford PA 16701-2010 Office: U Pitts 300 Campus Dr Bradford PA 16701-2898

CHEN, YU WHY, mathematician, educator; b. Nantong, China, Apr. 1, 1910; came to U.S., 1945; s. Yun Ke and Chiu Shu (Woo) C.; m. Susan Cho-Tchin Tsiang, Oct. 21, 1938; 1 child, Victor Kai-Hwa. PhD, Georg August U., Goettingen, Germany, 1934. Prof. Nat. U. Peking, Beijing, 1936-37, South-West Associated U., Kunming, China, 1938-45; rsch. assoc. Courant Inst., N.Y.C., 1946-49; temp. mem. Inst. Advanced Study, Princeton, N.J., 1949-50; assoc. prof. U. Okla., Norman, 1950-52; prof. Wayne State U., Detroit, 1952-65; prof. U. Mass., Amherst, 1965-82, prof. emeritus, 1982—. Contbr. numerous articles to profl. jours. Named hon. prof. U. Jilin, Changchun, China, 1982. Mem. Am. Math. Soc., Math. Assn. Am., Soc. Indsl. and Applied Math., Academia Sinica Taipei (hon.). Home: 149 Pomeroy Ln Amherst MA 01002-2909

CHEN, YUKI Y. KUO, industrial supplies company executive; b. Taipei, Taiwan, Apr. 16, 1930; came to U.S., 1975; parents: Shui-Lin and Chao-Dee (Lin) Kuo; m. Ho-Hong Chen, Mar. 10, 1959; children: Benjamin, Charmine, Carl. Student, Taihoku Acctg. Coll., Taipei, 1945. Pres. Hello Garments Corp./Hello Apparel Co., Ltd., Taipei, 1956-63, Am. Home Appliance Co., Taipei, 1965-74, China Ancient and Modern Decorative Products Co., Ltd., Taipei, 1972-75; v.p. Chung-Yang Environ. Protection Co., Ltd., Taipei, 1973-75, Riverond Internat. Assocs. Co., Ltd., Washington, 1975-87; exec. v.p. U.S. div. Pan Pacific Indsl. Supplies, Inc., Toronto, Ont., Can., 1982—. Mem. Kenwood Golf and Country Club. Office: Pan Pacific Indsl Supplies PO Box 5674 Washington DC 20016-1274

CHEN CHI, artist; b. Wusih, China, May 2, 1912; s. Shih-Pei and Shih Tsai C.; m. Alice Zu Min Huang, Oct. 5, 1962. Mem. faculty St. John's U., Shanghai, China, 1942-46, Pa. State U., 1959-60; artist in residence Ogden, Utah, 1967, Utah State U., 1971; Pres. Chen Chi Found. First one-man exhbn. Shanghai, China, 1940; others at various U.S. museums and art galleries in N.Y.C., Boston, N.H., R.I., Conn., Vt., Maine, R.I., Fla., Ariz., Phila., Allentown, Washington, Chgo., New Orleans, Iowa, Houston, Dallas, Fort Worth, San Antonio, Denver, Boulder, Seattle, San Francisco, Los Angeles, San Diego, Columbus, Ga., Anchorage, Alaska, Okla., Kans., Mo., S.C., W.Va., Santa Fe, N.Mex., Youngstown, Ohio, Ogden, Utah, Logan, Utah, Wusih, Peking, Shanghai, Taipei, Tai-chung, China; retrospective exhbn. at Gilcrease Mus., Tulsa, 1992; group exhbns. include Met. Art Mus., AAAL, Whitney Mus. Am. Art, Bklyn. Mus., Pa. Acad. Fine Arts Phil., Springfield Art Mus., Mo., Contemporary Chinese Am. Artists, San Diego, County Mus. L.A., Corcoran Gallery, Washington, Butler Inst., Am. Art, Ohio, New Brit. Mus. Am. Art, Conn., numerous others; painter series Am. city scenes, Colliers, Olympic Winter Games, Squaw Valley, Sports Illustrated, also other publs.; works represented in permanent collections Met. Mus. Art, Pa. Acad., Nat. Acad., Butler Inst., Cleve., Allentown Mus., Charles & Emma Frye Mus., Washington, New Britain Mus. Conn., Columbus Mus. Ga., Nat. Mus. of History, Taipei, Taiwan Art Mus., Taichun, China Jiangsu Art Mus., Wuxi Art Acad. Shanghai Mus., China, IBM Corp., Ford Motor Co., Gen. Mills, numerous museums, univs., pvt. collections: jury selection and awards Butler Inst. Am. Art, Frye Mus., Seattle, Am. Watercolor Soc., Allied Artists, Audubon Artists, sole judge ann. N.W. Coast Art Exhibit, Seattle, Washington, Pitts., Birmingham, Ala., San Diego, Columbia, S.C., Wilmington, Del., Detroit, Anchorage, N.J., Conn., also others. Author: Watercolors by Chen Chi, 1942, China, Chen Chi Paintings, Switzerland, 1965, Two or Three Lines from Sketchbooks of Chen Chi, 1969, China from the Sketchbooks of Chen Chi, 1974, Chen Chi Watercolors, Drawings, Sketches, 1980, Chen Chi Watercolors, 1981, China, Heaven and Water-Chen Chi, 1983, Chen Chi Nat. Mus. History, Taiwan, 1988 (medal of honor 1988), East Meets West Chen Chi Watercolors, Columbus (Ga.) Mus., 1989; Chen chi retrospective Gilcrease Mus., Tulsa, 1992, Chen Chi retrospective exhbn. The Nat. Arts Club, N.Y.C., 1993. Mem. Nat. Mus. of History, Taiwan, 1988. Recipient numerous awards, gold medals NAD, Am. Watercolor Soc., Nat. Arts Club, Salmagundi Club, Knickerbocker Artists, Audobon Artists, Phila. Watercolor Club; gold medal ann. watercolor exhbn. Nat. Arts Club, 1954, gold medal oil, 1954, Adolph and Clara Obrig prize NAD, 1955, Spl. $1000 award for watercolor 88th Exhbn. Am. Watercolor Soc., 1955; 1st watercolor prize, Butler Inst. Art, 1955, also Chautauqua Art Assn., 1955; Gold medal for Watercolor, 14th ann. Audobon Artists, 1956, spl. $1000 award 21st ann. exhbn.; $1500 grant Nat. Inst. Arts and Letters; gold medal honor, 47th ann. Allied Artists Am., 1960; Samuel Finley Breese Morse medal NAD, 1961; spl. award and medal Audubon Artists, 1963; John Singer Sargent Meml. award Springfield Art Mus.; medal honor Nat. Arts Club, 1966; 99th Ann. $600 Grand award and gold medal of honor Am. Watercolor Soc.; Winslow Homer Meml. award Watercolor U.S.A., Springfield Art Mus.; Gold Medal Honor, Nat. Arts Club, 1967, Audubon Artists, 1968; Thomas Hart Benton award, 1968, Saltus Gold medal or merit NAD, 1969, Silver medal Nat. Arts Club, 1970, Pres.'s award Audubon Artists, 1974, Benjamin West Clinedinst meml. medal, 1976, medal Acad. Western Art, 1990. Mem. NAD (William P. Schweitzer prize 1989), Internat. Inst. Arts and Letters, Am. Watercolor Soc. (hon., High Winds award 1972, 74, Bicentennial Gold medal 1976, Dolphin Fellowship medal 1990, Gold medal 1990, 91, inducted in the Cowboy Hall of Fame), Nat. Acad. Western Art, Nat. Arts Club, Audubon Artists, Allied Artists, Century Club, Dutch Treat Club, Salmagundi Club. Clubs: Century, Dutch Treat, Salmagundi, Nat. Arts. Home: 23 Washington Sq N New York NY 10011-9169 Studio: 15 Gramercy Park S New York NY 10003

CHENEY, CAROLYN LYNDS, personnel director; b. Houlton, Maine, Jan. 29, 1945; d. William R. and Janet (Brewer) Lynds; m. Joseph W. Cheney, July 13, 1968; 1 child, Lyndsey J. AA, Westbrook Coll., 1965. Lic. real estate broker, Maine. Adminstrv. asst. Ricker Coll., Houlton, 1965-68; pers. asst. Army & Air Force Exch. Svc., Ft. Dix, N.J., 1969-71; dir. pers. U. Maine, Presque Isle, 1972—. V.p. Cen. Aroostook Humane Soc., Presque Isle, 1980—; com. chair Varsity Swim Team Parents, Presque Isle, 1990—. Mem. Presque Isle Snowmobile Club.

CHENEY, DICK (RICHARD BRUCE CHENEY), secretary of defense, former congressman; b. Lincoln, Nebr., Jan. 30, 1941; s. Richard Hebert and Marjorie Lauraine (Dickey) C.; m. Lynne Anne Vincent, Aug. 29, 1964; children: Elizabeth, Mary Claire. B.A., U. Wyo., 1965, M.A., 1966; postgrad., U. Wis., 1966-68. Staff aide to Gov. Warren Knowles, Wis., 1966; mem. staff Congressman William A. Steiger, 1969; spl. asst. to dir. OEO, Washington, 1969-70; dep. to counsellor to Pres. The White House, Washington, 1970-71; asst. dir. Cost of Living Council, 1971-73; dep. asst. to Pres. The White House, Washington, 1974-75, asst. to Pres., 1975-77; ptnr. Bradley, Woods and Co., 1973-74; mem. 96th-100th Congresses from Wyo., 1979-89, Rep. Whip, 1987-88; sec. U.S Dept. of Defense, Washington, 1989—; chmn. Rep. Conf., 1981-87; chmn. Rep. Policy Com. Named One of 10 outstanding young men in Am., U.S. Jaycees, 1976; Congl. fellow Am. Polit. Sci. Assn., 1968-69. Republican. Office: US Dept Def The Pentagon Washington DC 20301*

CHENEY, PHILIP WARREN, engineering executive; b. Portland, Oreg., Dec. 3, 1935; s. Percy Jack and Lilian May (Emery) C.; m. Leslie Dineen, May 21, 1958; children: Stephen, Christopher, Pamela. BSEE, MIT, 1957, MSEE, 1958; PhD, Stanford U., 1961. Digital lab. mgr. Raytheon Co., Bedford, Mass., 1961-74; Bedford labs. mgr. Raytheon Co., 1974-81; asst. program mgr. Patriot programs Raytheon Co., Andover, Mass., 1981-83, dep. program mgr. HAWK program, 1983-85; AMRAAM program mgr. Raytheon Co., Bedford, 1985-90; v.p. engring. Raytheon Co., Lexington, Mass., 1990—; Bd. dirs. Emerson Hosp., Concord, Mass., NJRC, Tokyo. Mem. AIAA, IEEE, Aerospace Industries Assn., Am. Def. Preparedness Assn. Office: Raytheon Co 141 Spring St Lexington MA 02173-7899

CHENEY, RICHARD EUGENE, public relations executive; b. Pana, Ill., Aug. 30, 1921; s. Royal F. and Nelle E. (Henke) C.; m. Betty L. McCray, Oct. 17, 1943; children: R. Christopher, Elyn G. Cheney MacInnis; m. 2d, Virginia B. Burns, Jan. 23, 1966; children: Benjamin, Anne. AB, Knox Coll., Galesburg, Ill., 1943; MA, Columbia U., 1960. Assoc. editor Tide Mag., 1953; dir. pub. relations Tri Continental Corp., 1953-55; asst. mgr. pub. relations dept. Mobil Corp., 1955-60; chmn. bd. to emeritus chmn. Hill & Knowlton, Inc., N.Y.C., 1987-91, 91—, chmn. bd., 1987-91, chmn. emeritus, 1991—; bd. dirs. Chattem Inc., Chattanooga, C.R. Gibson Co., Norwalk, Conn., Alphabet Inc., Warren, Ohio, Rowe Furniture, Holopak Techs. Served to lt. (j.g.) USNR, 1943-47, PTO. Clubs: University, Dutch Treat (N.Y.C.); Edgewood (Tivoli, N.Y.); Castalia (Ohio); Century Assn. (N.Y.C.). Home: 25 W 81st St Apt 5A New York NY 10024-6023 Office: Hill & Knowlton Inc 420 Lexington Ave New York NY 10170-0002

CHENG, ALEXANDER HUNG-DARH, engineering educator, consultant; b. Taipei, Taiwan, May 25, 1952; came to U.S., 1976; s. Chia-hua and Yu-Chuen (Chwang) C.; m. Daisy T. Cheng, Nov. 23, 1979; children: Jacqueline, Julia. BS, Nat. Taiwan U., Taipei, 1974; MS, U. Mo., 1978; PhD, Cornell U., 1981. Asst. prof. Cornell U., Ithaca, 1981-82, Columbia U., N.Y.C., 1982-85; assoc. prof. U. Del., Newark, 1985—; vis scientist Schlumberger Cambridge (U.K.) Rsch., 1991; cons. Dowell Schlumberger Inc., Tulsa, 1985—. Editor: Computational Engineering, 1990; contbr. over 75 articles to profl. jours. Recipient awards, NSF, 1983, Gas Rsch. Inst., 1987, Agy. for Internat. Devel., 1991. Mem. ASCE, Am. Geophysical Union, Soc. Petroleum Engrs., Internat. Assn. Hydrological Rsch., Am. Acad. Mechanics, Internat. Assn. Bounding Element (sec. 1990). Office: U Del Dept Civil Engring Newark DE 19716

CHENG, ALEXANDER LIHDAR, computer scientist, researcher; b. Taichung, Taiwan, Aug. 1, 1956; came to U.S., 1980; s. Pei-Kao and Kuang-Kun (Shiong) C.; m. Wei-Hong Mao, Feb. 16, 1988; children: Alexander Raymond, Bernard King. BS, Nat. Taiwan U., 1978; MS, U. Ky., 1982; PhD, Poly. U., Bklyn., 1992. Rsch. asst. Taiwan Hydraulic Bur., Taichung, 1978; teaching asst. U. Ky., Lexington, 1981-82; sci. programmer Megadata Corp., Bohemia, N.Y., 1982-83; sr. software engr. Siemens Data Switching, Inc., Hauppauge, N.Y., 1983-87; tech. staff NYNEX S&T, Inc., White Plains, N.Y., 1987—; bd. dirs. C&M First Svcs., Inc., N.Y.C. V.p. Woodcrest Hts. Assn., White Plains, 1991-92. Mem. IEEE, IEEE Computer Soc., Assn. Computing Machinery, Upsilon Pi Epsilon. Home: 11 Springdale Ave White Plains NY 10604

CHENG, ANDREW FRANCIS, physicist; b. Princeton, N.J., Oct. 15, 1951; s. Sin I. and Jean S. Cheng; m. Linda S. Hu; children: Caroline, Matthew. AB, Princeton U., 1971; PhD, Columbia U., 1977. Postdoctoral fellow AT&T Bell Labs., Murray Hill, N.J., 1976-78; asst. prof. physics Rutgers U., New Brunswick, N.J., 1978-83; supr. theoretical space physics Johns Hopkins U., Laurel, Md., 1983—; mem. com. for planetary and lunar exploration Nat. Acad. Scis., 1987-90. Editor Transactions of the Am. Geophys. Union jour., 1989-91; contbr. over 90 articles to profl. jours. Named Outstanding Young Scientist Md. Acad. Sci., 1985; recipient Group Achievement awards NASA 1986, 91. Office: Johns Hopkins U Applied Physics Lab Laurel MD 20723

CHENG, DAVID TA LING, cardiologist; b. Sibu, Malaysia, Sept. 16, 1945; came to U.S., 1971; s. Tsu Yu and Kwee Choo (Ting) C.; m. Chu Jung Chang, Apr. 21, 1974; children: Mimi, Eugene. MB, BS, U. Singapore, 1969. Diplomate Am. Bd. Internal Medicine, Am. Bd. Cardiology. House officer Outram Road Gen. Hosp., Singapore, 1969-70; intern Cook County Hosp., Chgo., 1971-72; resident NYU-Bellevue Hosp., N.Y.C., 1972-73; instr. Rush-Presbyn.-St. Luke's Med. Ctr. Chgo., 1974-75; pvt. practice family medicine, Oak Park, Ill., 1975-79; resident Rutgers U. Med. Sch., New Brunswick, N.J., 1979-80, Bergen Pines County Hosp., Paramus, N.J., 1980-81; fellow Grad. Hosp., Phila., 1981-83, Univ. Hosp.-U. Mich., Ann Arbor, 1983-84; pvt. practice cardiology, Monroeville, Pa., 1985—; pres. Keystone Heart Inst., Monroeville, 1986—. Contbr. articles to med. jours. Mem. Orgn. Chinese Am., 1986—. Fellow Am. Coll. Cardiology, Am. Coll. Angiology; mem. ACP, AMA, Pa. Med. Soc., Allegheny County Med. Soc. Republican. Office: 4318 N Pike Monroeville PA 15146

CHENG, EDWARD HSIN-YI, gastroenterologist, researcher; b. Tokyo, Feb. 28, 1955; came to U.S., 1959; s. Charles Kang and Shirley Sui-Lan (Lau) C.; m. Sue-Fong Leong, Sept. 19, 1981; 1 child, Wesley. BS, SUNY, Stony Brook, 1976; MD, NYU, 1980. Diplomate Am. Bd. Internal Medicine, Bd. Gastroenterology. Resident in medicine U. Calif., San Diego, 1980-83; gastroenterology fellow SUNY, Stony Brook, 1983-85; attending physician SUNY/VA Hosp. Northport, Stony Brook, 1985—; asst. prof. medicine SUNY, Stony Brook, 1989—. Contbr. articles to profl. jours. Named Assoc. Investigator, VA Career Devel., 1983-85. Fellow Am. Coll. Physicians; mem. Am. Gastroent. Assn., Am. Coll. Gastroenterology. Office: VA Med Ctr Northport 79 Middleville Rd Northport NY 11768

CHENG, EMILY, artist; b. Manhattan, N.Y., July 28, 1953; d. Chi Kuan and Elizabeth Cheng; m. David Aiken Humphrey, July 20, 1980; 1 child, Simone. BFA, R.I. Sch. Design, 1975; student, N.Y. Studio Sch., N.Y.C., 1974, 77, 78. One person exhbns. include Pitts. Plan for Art, 1983, White Columns, N.Y.C., 1985, Lang & O'Hara Gallery, N.Y.C., 1987, 88, 90, The Bronx Mus., 1989, Schmidt/Dean Gallery, Phila., 1990, David Beitzel Gallery, N.Y.C., 1992; group exhbns. include Security Pacific Galleries, L.A., 1988, 90, New Visions Gallery, Ithaca, N.Y., 1989, Bard Coll., 1989, Blum Helman, 1989, Hillwood Art Gallery, 1989, Richard Anderson Gallery, 1991, many others. NEH fellow, 1982-83.

CHENG, VIC M., physicist; b. Kowloon, Hong Kong, June 27, 1945; came to U.S., 1965; BS, Lafayette Coll., 1968; MA, Princeton U., 1970, PhD, 1972. Postdoctoral fellow U. Ill., Urbana, 1972-73; asst. prof. Lafayette Coll., Easton, Pa., 1973-74; scientist GE Space Scis. Labs., King of Prussia, Pa., 1974-76; sr. rsch. assoc. Mobil R & D Corp., Paulsboro, N.J., 1976—. Office: Mobil R&D Corp Paulsboro NJ 08066

CHERICI, COLEEN ANN, pharmacist, educator; b. Uniontown, Pa., Mar. 8, 1950; d. John Shoaf and Eleanor Louise (Kaas) O'Brien; m. Pier Raoul Cherici, May 31, 1970; 1 child, Kristen Lara. BS in Pharmacy, St. John's U., 1972; MBA, LaSalle U., 1990. Lic. pharmacist, Conn. Pharmacist C. Fox Pharmacy, Hartford, Conn., 1972-73, Uncas Pharmacy, Norwichtown, Conn., 1973-74, Pevner's Drugs, Putnam, Conn., 1974-76; pharmacist Day Kimball Hosp., Putnam, 1976-83, dir., pharmacy, 1983—; assoc. clin. prof. U. Conn., Storrs, 1988—; chmn. Conn. State Ad Hoc Coalition of Pharmacists, 1990-91; bd. dirs. Conn. State Drug Utilization Rev. Recipient Syntex Preceptor of Yr. award U. Conn., 1991; named Hon. Alumnus U. Conn., 1991. Mem. Am. Soc. Hosp. Pharmacists (del. 1989-91), Conn. Soc. Hosp. Pharmacists (sec. 1987, pres. 1989-91, Pharmacists Concerned for Pharmacists com. 1991—, Innovative Achievement award 1988), Conn. Pharm. Assn. (exec. bd. 1992), Am. Soc. Parenteral and Enteral Nutrition, Windham County Kennel Club. Home: Rt 6 Hampton CT 06247 Office: Day Kimball Hosp 320 Pomfret St Putnam CT 06260-1836

CHERIM, STAN MARSHALL, chemist, educator; b. Phila., Sept. 13, 1929; s. Herman and Betty (Kaufman) C.; m. Solveig Gregersen, July 16, 1955; children: Greg, Lise. BA, U. Pa., 1951, MS, 1965. Tchr. Atlantic City (N.J.) Friends Sch., 1953-54, Tarsus (Turkey) Am. Coll., 1954-57, Friends Cen. Sch., Phila., 1957-69; chemistry prof. Delaware County Community Coll., Media, Pa., 1969—. Author: Chemistry for Lab Technicians, 1971, Preliminary Chemistry, 1974, Joy of Chemistry, 1978, Introductory Chemistry, 1981, Chemistry One and Chemistry Two, 1986. Bd. dirs. United Cerebral Palsy, Media, 1992, Friends Cen. Sch., Phila., 1991; chair Chemistry Conf., Washington, 1992, com. mem. Athletics Cong., Phila., 1992. Mem. Am. Chem. Soc. (regional dir. 1972—), Delaware County Road Runners, Phila. Masters Track Assn., Danish Brotherhood, Sierra Club. Democrat. Mem. Soc. of Friends. Home: 213 Wallingford Ave Wallingford PA 19086 Office: Del County Community Coll Media PA 19063

CHERKES, JOSEPH KENNETH, toxicologist, consultant; b. Woonsocket, R.I., Apr. 10, 1952; s. Joseph and Mildred (Petrowicz) C.; m. Rita Marianne Cotugno, July 19, 1980. BS, Marquette U., 1974; MA, R.I. Coll., 1982. Orthopedic technician West Allis (Wis.) Meml. Hosp., 1974-75; biochemist Med. Coll. Wis., Milw., 1975; chemist Rogor Williams Gen. Hosp., Providence, 1975-76; biochemist Pawtucket (R.I.) Meml. Hosp., 1976-77, VA Med. Ctr., Providence, 1977-80; chemist R.I. Hosp., Providence, 1981-85, toxicologist, 1985—. Contbr. articles to profl. jours. Mem. AAAS, N.Y. Acad. Sci., Nat. registry Clin. Chemistry, Am. Assn. Clin. Chemistry. Ukranian Orthodox. Home: 420 Auburn St Cranston RI 02910-4403 Office: RI Hosp 593 Eddy St APC 1146 Providence RI 02903-4923

CHERKSEY, BRUCE DAVID, physiology educator; b. Phila., Oct. 3, 1946; s. Arthur C. and Jeanne (Braslow) C. MS, NYU, 1973, PhD, 1980. NIH trainee ophthalmology NYU Med. Ctr., N.Y.C., 1980-81, asst. prof. physiology, 1985-90, assoc. prof. physiology, 1990-92, assoc. prof. psychiatry, 1992—. Contbr. articles to profl. jours. Mem. Soc. Neurosci., Assn. for Rsch. in Vision & Ophthalmology, Am. Chem. Soc., N.Y. Acad. Scis., Soc. Exptl. Biology and Medicine. Home: 608 Garden St Hoboken NJ 07030-3904 Office: NYU Med Ctr 550 1st Ave New York NY 10016-6402

CHERN, PAUL, actuary; b. Shang-hai, China, Aug. 27, 1940; came to U.S., 1949; s. Shiing Shen and Shih Ning (Na) C.; m. Susan Patricia Schofield, Aug. 23, 1969; children: Melissa, Theresa. BS in Math., U. Calif., Davis, 1962; MS in Math., U. Oreg., 1964; MS in Statistics, U. Calif., Berkeley, 1967; MS in Actuarial Sci., Northeastern U., 1972. Actuarial asst. New England Life Ins. Co., Boston, 1968-73; assoc. actuary Connell Co., Waltham, Mass., 1973-77; actuary Meidinger Inc., Boston, 1977-84, William M. Mercer, Boston, 1984-85; v.p. Pentad Corp., Waltham, 1985—. Mem. Am. Acad. Actuaries, Soc. Actuaries. Office: Pentad Corp 260 Bear Hill Rd Waltham MA 02154-1018

CHERNAK, ROBERT A., academic administrator; b. Boston, Aug. 25, 1946; s. Jack and Belle Florence (Wilensky) C.; m. Linda Ellen Fox, Aug. 27, 1972; 1 child, Jaclyn Ashley. BS, Boston U., 1968; MEd, Boston State Coll., 1975. Lic. real estate broker, Mass. Mem. faculty Bryant and Stratton Jr. Coll., Boston, 1970-72, dir. student pers. and alumni svcs., 1972-75; spl. asst. to v.p. student affairs Boston U., 1975-76, asst. to v.p. acad. svcs., 1976-77; exec. asst. to pres. U. Hartford (Conn.), 1977-79, asst. v.p., 1979-82, assoc. v.p., 1982-83, v.p., asst. provost acad. svcs., acting v.p. bus. and fin., 1983-85, v.p. adminstrn. and student svcs., 1985-88; v.p. student and acad. support svcs. George Washington U., Washington, 1988—. Coord. Greater Hartford United Way Campaign, 1987; mem. coll. adv. com. Hartford Jewish Community Ctr., 1988; bd. mem. ARC, Washington. With USN, 1968-70. Recipient Award of Excellence, Conn. Art Dirs. Club, 1990. Mem. Am. Assn. Univ. Adminstrs. (bd. mem. 1988—), Am. Mtkg. Assn., Nat. Assn. Student Pers. Adminstrs., Nat. Assn. Collegiate Dirs. Athletics, Tournament Players Club/Avenel, West Hartford C. of C. (bd. mem. 1987). Democrat. Jewish. Home: 8121 Autumn Gate Ln Bethesda MD 20817-4117 Office: George Washington U 2121 I St NW Ste 403 Washington DC 20052-0001

CHERNICK, MICHAEL LOUIS, religious studies educator; b. Bklyn., Dec. 8, 1943; s. Samuel and Sara (Roskin) C.; m. Miriam Chernick, Oct. 23, 1966; children: Jeremy, Saul. BA, Yeshiva U., 1965; MA, Bernard Revel Grad. Sch., 1969, PhD, 1978. Ordained rabbi, 1969. Prof. rabinic lit. Jewish Inst. of Religion Hebrew Union Coll., N.Y.C., 1974—; mem. faculty Wexner Heritage Found., N.Y.C., 1987—; cons., mem. com. Wexner Instnl. Grants Found., Columbus, Ohio, 1991—. Author: Hermeneutical Studies, 1984; contbr. articles to profl. jours. Founder Task Force on Jewish Women, Teaneck, N.J., Intra-Communal Jewish Dialogue, Teaneck; bd. dirs., bd. govs. Mazon, L.A., 1991. Meml. Found. for Jewish Culture grantee, 1981-82, 91. Mem. Am. Acad. Religion/Soc. Bibl. Lit., Assn. for Jewish Studies (bd. dirs. Cambridge, Mass. chpt. 1989-90), Am. Acad. Jewish Rsch. (Pub. grantee 1992), World Union of Jewish Studies. Office: Hebrew Union Coll Jewish Inst of Religion 1 W 4th St New York NY 10012-1186

CHERNOW, FRED BARNET, educator; b. Bklyn., Nov. 2, 1932; s. Barnet and Mabel (Rosenthal) C.; m. Carol Grossman, Apr. 10, 1954; children: Barbara Farber, Lynne Inwald. BA, Bklyn. Coll., 1953, MA, 1954. Supr. guidance N.Y.C. High Sch. Office, Bklyn., 1966-72; prin. John Tyler Sch., S.I., N.Y., 1972-83; assoc. prof. St. John's U., S.I., N.Y., 1983—; adj. prof. N.Y.C. Tech. Coll., Bklyn., 1990-92; mediator alternate dispute resolution, McKee High Sch., S.I., 1992—. Author: Classroom Discipline, 1990, Principal's Handbook, 1992. Dir. Snug Harbor Cultural Ctr., S.I., 1981-89; v.p. Temple Israel, 1980-82. With U.S. Army, 1954-56. Democrat. Jewish. Home: 60 Vassar St Staten Island NY 10314-6004 Office: St John's U 300 Howard Ave Staten Island NY 10301

CHERRY, JOHN PAUL, research center director, researcher; b. Rhinebeck, N.Y., Jan. 31, 1941; s. John and Susan (Borovsky) C.; m. Janet Carrol Day, Aug. 22, 1964; children: Jamie Paulette, Janine Collette. BS, Furman U., 1963; MS, W.Va. U., 1966; PhD, U. Ariz., 1970. NRC postdoctoral rsch. assoc. So. Regional Rsch. Ctr., Agrl. Rsch. Svc., USDA, New Orleans, 1970-72, supervisory rsch. chemist, rsch. leader, 1976-82, assoc. dir. Eastern Regional Rsch. Ctr., Phila., 1982-84, dir., 1985—; postdoctoral rsch. assoc. Tex. A&M U., College Station, 1972-73; asst. prof. U. Ga. Exptl. Sta., Experiment, 1973-75. Editor 3 books; contbr. chpts. to books and more than 120 articles to profl. jours. Recipient Excellence in Govt. Mgr. of Yr. award, Phila. Fed. Exec. Bd., 1991, Presdl. Rank award of Meritorious Exec., 1991. Mem. Am. Chem. Soc., Am. Assn. Cereal Chemists, Am. Oil Chemists Soc., Assn. Ofcl. Analytical Chemists, Am. Peanut Rsch. Edn. Assn., Inst. Food Technologists, Sigma Xi. Methodist. Avocations: travel, gardening. Home: 360 Dundee Dr Blue Bell PA 19422-2436 Office: Ea Regional Rsch Ctr ARS USDA 600 E Mermaid Ln Philadelphia PA 19118

CHERRY, PAUL STEPHEN, lawyer; b. Phila., Oct. 6, 1943; s. Herbert Israel and Toby (Ring) C.; m. Hilary Kirwan, Apr. 8, 1972. BA, Temple U., 1966; JD, Widener U., 1982. Registered sanitarian; cert. sewage enforcement officer, Pa. Sci. tchr. Cen. High Sch., Phila., 1966-67; physiology instr. Regional Sch. of Nursing, Owen Sound, Ont., 1967-68; natural sci. tchr. Sir Sanford Fleming Coll., Peterborough, Ont., 1968-69; sanitarian Dept. Pub. Health, Phila., 1972-73, Chester County Health Dept., West Chester, Pa., 1974-79; pvt. practice lawyer Wayne, Pa., 1983—; operating engr. Sound and Light Show at Independence Hall, Phila., 1961-82; bd. dirs. Hist. Soc. of the U.S. Dist. Ct. for the Ea. Dist. Pa., Phila., 1985—. Chaplain B'nai B'rith Freedom Valley Lodge (Valley Forge, Pa.), 1986—; mem. Tredyffrin Twp.

Traffic com., Berwyn, Pa., 1991. Recipient Annual recognition Women Against Abuse, Phila., 1986. Fellow Lawyers in Mensa (main line coord. 1985—); mem. Pa. Bar Assn., Chester County Bar Assn. Republican. Jewish. Home and Office: 151 Sullivan Dr Wayne PA 19087-1433

CHERVIN, PAUL N., neurologist; b. Boston, Oct. 11, 1941; s. Albert and Eva (Hurwitch) C.; children: Bradford, Amy. BA, U. Vt., 1963; MD, Duke U., 1967. Lic. physician, N.C., Mass., Calif.; diplomate Am. Bd. Pediatrics, Am. Bd. Psychiatry and Neurology. Intern Strong Meml. Hosp. of U. Rochester, 1967-68; resident in pediatrics Children's Hosp. Med. Ctr., Boston, 1968-70; resident in neurology Peter B. Brigham Hosp., Children's Hosp., Beth Israel Hosp., Boston, 1970-73; clin. fellow in neurology Harvard Med. Sch., Boston, 1970-73; pvt. practice specializing in neurology Woburn, Mass., 1973—; attending physician Univ. Hosp. of San Diego, 1973-76; child neurologist Children's & Adolescent's Unit, San Diego County Mental Hlth, 1975-76; attending physician VA Hosp., LaJolla, Calif., 1975-76; teaching fellow in pediatrics Harvard Med. Sch., Boston, 1968-70; clin. asst. prof. neurosci. U. Calif., san Diego, 1973-76; instr. neurology Harvard Med. Sch., 1976—; staff Children's Hosp., Boston, Mt. Auburn Hosp., Cambridge, Winchester Hosp., Lawrence Meml. Hosp., Medford, Symmes Hosp., Arlington; examiner Am. Bd. Psychiatry and Neurology. Lt. comdr. M.C., USNR, 1973-76. Mem. AMA, Mass. Med. Soc., Am. Acad. Neurology, Child Neurology Soc., Mass. Neurol. Assn. (pres. 1986-87). Office: 604 Main St Woburn MA 01801-2993

CHERWIN, JOEL IRA, lawyer; b. Winthrop, Mass., Apr. 29, 1942; s. Melvin Arthur and Martha (Baer) C.; m. Sherry Lenore Cherwin, July 5, 1970; children: Alison, Matthew, Joshua. BS in Econs., U. Pa., 1963; JD, Boston U., 1966. Bar: Mass. 1966, U.S. Dist. Ct. Mass. 1968, U.S. Tax Ct. 1969. Ptnr. Cherwin & Glazier, Boston, 1967-77, Cherwin & Glickman, Boston, 1977—. Mem. ABA, Mass. Bar Assn. Democrat. Jewish. Office: Cherwin & Glickman One International Pl Boston MA 02110

CHESIN, SORRELL ELY, university official; b. N.Y.C., July 16, 1932; s. Max and Cecil (Steuer) C.; m. Lorraine Barbara Schechter, Oct. 4, 1975. BS, SUNY, Geneseo, 1958; MA, Syracuse U., 1960; PhD, Mich. State U., 1967. Dir. men's housing U. Bridgeport, Conn., 1960-61; head resident advisor Mich. State U., East Lansing, 1961-65; assoc. dean students SUNY, Albany, 1965-71, asst. v.p. univ. affairs, 1971-82, assoc. v.p. for devel., 1982—; reviewer books on higher edn., 1966, 68. Contbr. articles to profl. jours. Bd. dirs., v.p. Mohawk-Hudson Community Found., Albany, 1986-89; chmn. bd. dirs. N.Y. State div. Am. Cancer Soc., Syracuse, 1987-88. Mem. Kappa Delta Pi, Phi Delta Kappa. Jewish. Home: 24 Pinedale Ave Delmar NY 12054-3013 Office: SUNY 1400 Washington Ave Albany NY 12222

CHESNUT, EDWARD B., JR., senior project staff/systems engineer. BS in Indsl. Engring. and Indsl. Mgmt., Purdue U., West Lafayette, Ind., 1972; M in Engring. Adminstrn., George Washington U., 1988; diploma, Def. Systems Mgmt. Coll., 1991. Indsl. engr. Westinghouse Electric Corp., Pitts. and Balt., 1972-75, Communications div. Bendix Corp., Balt., 1975-77; sr. indsl. engr. Gould Incorp., Glen Burnie, Md., 1977-81; prodn. mgr. Xerox Corp., Arlington, Va., 1981-83; engring. cons. Mclaughlin RSch.Corp., Alexandria, Va., 1983-84; sr. project staff/systems engr., cons. ARC Profl. Svcs. Group, Inc., Rockville, Md., 1984—. Vol. Youth at Risk Program, Washington, 1990-92; mem. Spl. Olympics Program, Washington, 1982. Recipient Pres.'s Club award Soc. Mfg. Engrs., 1979, cert. appreciation Spl. Olympics, Washington, 1982. Mem. Security Indsl. Assn., Def. Systems Mgmt. Coll. Alumni Assn., George Washington U. Alumni Assn. (bd. dirs. 1990, 91, exec. com., treas. 1991, v.p. 1992), Purdue Alumni Assn., Charles J. Givens Orgn., Kappa Alpha Psi (life). Home: 14229 Twig Rd Silver Spring MD 20905

CHESSON, MICHAEL BEDOUT, history educator; b. Richmond, Va., Sept. 5, 1947; s. Wesley Earle and Virginia Winborne (Ramsey) C.; A.B. with high honors in History, Coll. William and Mary, 1969; postgrad. (Gilman fellow) Johns Hopkins U., 1972-73; Ph.D. in History (Grad. fellow), Harvard U., 1978. Clk., R.F. & P. R.R., Richmond, 1966-69; park ranger-historian Colonial Nat. Hist. Park, Nat. Park Service, Yorktown and Jamestown, Va., 1969-70, 72, 73; teaching fellow Harvard U., 1975-78; asst. prof. history U. Mass., Boston, 1978-82, assoc. prof., 1982—. Served to comdr. USNR, 1969—. Mem. Am., So., Va. hist. assns., Orgn. Am. Historians, Naval Res. Assn. Democrat. Author: Richmond After the War, 1865-1890, 1981.

CHESTER, DOUGLAS BARRY, criminal defense lawyer; b. Hudson, N.Y., June 14, 1952; s. Albert William and Marjorie (Kahlmeyer) C.; m. Margaret Jane McMath, June 21, 1954. Assoc. degree, U. Leningrad, USSR, 1974; BA, Dartmouth Coll., 1975; JD, New Eng. Sch. Law, 1979. Bar: Mass. 1979, Pa. 1981, U.S. Supreme Ct. 1988. Pvt. practice lawyer Spring Mills, Pa., 1981—; trustee Kahlmeyer Found., Spring Mills, 1988—. Mem. Centre County Bar Assn. Home and Office: Maple St Spring Mills PA 16875

CHESTER, NORMAN CHARLES, bank executive; b. Glen Ridge, N.J., Dec. 7, 1953; s. Norman Harding Chester and Barbara Wanda (Barber) Tessier; m. Vivian Leslie Tarallo, Aug. 15, 1987; 1 child, Alfred Eduardo. BBA, Bucknell U., 1976; MBA, Rutgers U., 1981. Adj. instr. Bergen Community Coll., Paramus, N.J., 1983-85; rep. Equitable Life, E. Orange, N.J., 1976-77; mgmt. trainee U.S. Life Ins. Co., N.Y.C., 1977-79; acct. Chase Manhattan Bank, N.Y.C., 1979-82, asst. treas., 1982-85, second v.p., 1985—. Bd. trustees Westwood (N.J.) United Meth. Ch., 1988—, fin. chmn. 1989—, sec. adminstrv. coun. 1988-89; publicity chmn. Hillsdale Vol. Ambulance Svc., 1986—. Mem. Inst. of Mgmt. Accts. Methodist. Home: 782 Martin Ave Oradell NJ 07649-2338 Office: Chase Manhattan Bank 101 Park 17th Ave New York NY 10178-0002

CHESWORTH, E(DWARD) THOMAS, physicist, business executive; b. North Charleroi, Pa., Feb. 28, 1937; s. Edward Thomas and Gladys Eula (Mountser) C.; m. Josephine Rider, Feb. 6. 1959; children: Cynthia Chesworth Adams, Michael, Jennifer Chesworth Keal. BS in Meteorology, Pa. State U., 1960, MS in Physics, 1969, PhD in Physics, 1974. Registered profl. engr., Pa.; cert. electromagnetic compatibility engr. Engring. aide Radio Astronomy and Ionosphere Rsch. Labs. Pa. State U., University Park, 1959-66, posdoctoral scholar, 1974-75; rsch. engr. HRB-Singer, Inc., State College, Pa., 1966-70; staff physicist LOCUS, Inc., State College, 1975-79; pres. Seven Mountains Sci. Inc., Boalsburg, Pa., 1979—; tech. expert Nat. Inst. Sci. and Tech. Nat. Vol. Lab. Accreditation Program, Gaithersburg, Md., 1989—. Tech. editor Electromagnetic News Report, 1989—; contbr. articles to profl. jours. Mem. IEEE, IEEE Electromagnetic Compatibility Soc., dB Soc., Am. Radio Relay League (life), Phi Kappa Phi. Office: Seven Mountains Sci Inc PO Box 650 Boalsburg PA 16827-0651

CHEW, ELIZABETH, mathematician; b. Washington, May 12, 1959; d. Harry and Jane (Chu) C. BS in Math., U. Md., 1981. Math. aid U.S. Dept. Agr., Hyattsville, Md., 1979-81; programmer Vitro Corp., Silver Spring, Md., 1981-84; mathematician Vitro Corp., 1984-87, section leader, 1987-90; computer applications specialist U.S. Pharmacopeia, Rockville, Md., 1990—. Recipient Recognition award, Vitro Corp., 1986.

CHEYNEY, CURTIS PAUL, III, lawyer; b. Phila., Oct. 19, 1942; s. Curtis Paul Jr. and Bernice Edna (Thompson) C.; m. Barbara Yvonne Benjamin, Apr. 20, 1974; 1 child, Curtis Paul IV. BA, Gettysburg Coll., 1964; JD, Wake Forest U., 1968; postgrad., Acad. of Internat. Law, Holland, 1967. Bar: Pa. 1968, U.S. Dist. Ct. (ea. dist.) Pa. 1968, U.S. Supreme Ct. 1974. Assoc. Swartz, Campbell & Detweiler, Phila., 1968-74, ptnr., 1974-80, mng. ptnr., 1980—; lectr. Com. on Edn., San Francisco, 1986-90, Va. Def. Inst., 1984, Pa. Corp. Coun. Assn., 1988, Pa. Def. Inst., 1989, Phila. Claims Inst., 1989, lectr. profl. litigation seminar, 1992, Pa. Credit Union League, 1991; bd. dirs. Phila. Bail fund-Bailcare Program, 1988—; lectr. Pa. Bar Inst., comml. litigation seminar speaker, 1990, 92. Contbg. author: Workmen's Compensation, 1988. Bd. dirs., pres. St. John's Luth. Ch., Phila., 1978—; bd. dirs. Paul's Run Luth. Retirement Home, Phila., 1978-90; troop leader Cub Scouts Am., Boy Scouts Am., Haverford, Pa., 1988; mem. Delaware County Commn. BiCentennial, 1987. Mem. ABA, Pa. Bar Assn. (com. mem. employment sect. 1982—), Am. Soc. Internat. Law, Maritime Law Assn. U.S., Nat. Assn. R.R. Trial Counsel, Internat. Assn. Def. Counsel, Pa. Def. Inst. (faculty trial advocacy 1990-92, lectr.), Pa. C. of C. (ins. com. 1987-88), Union League Club (membership com. 1982), Pa. Soc. Sons Revolution (bd. mgrs. 1989-92), Quaker City Farmers Club, Corinthian Yacht Club, Aston Martin Owner's Club, Sigma Chi, Phi Delta Phi, Internat. Legal Fraternity. Republican. Home: 205 Whitemarsh Rd Ardmore PA 19003-1712 Office: Swartz Campbell & Detweiler 100 S Broad St Philadelphia PA 19110-1024

CHIACCHIERINI, RICHARD PHILIP, federal agency administrator; b. Elmira, N.Y., Mar. 21, 1943; s. Frank Andrew and Grace Rose (Spallone) C.; m. Kathleen Doris O'Grady, Aug. 14, 1965; children: Paul Thomas, Lisa Marie. BS, St. Bonaventure U., 1965; MES, N.C. State U., 1967; PhD, Va. Tech. Inst., 1973. Jr. statistician bioeffects div. Nat. Ctr. Radiol. Health, Rockville, Md., 1967-72; chief stats. sect. Office Radiation Programs EPA, Washington, 1972-73; sr. statistician epidemiol. studies br. BRH Bur. Radiol. Health-FDA, Rockville, Md., 1973-79, chief stats. sect., 1979-83; chief ionizing rad. and statis. br. FDA, Rockville, Md., 1982-84, chief stats. br. Ctr. Devices and Radiol. Health, 1984-85, dir. biometric sci. div., 1985—; chief scientist USPHS Commd. Corps, Rockville, 1987-91; chair USPHS Epidemiol. Tng. Commn., Bethesda, Md., 1989—. Mem. editorial bd. Statistics in Medicine, 1991—. Chmn., bd. dirs. Bennington, Gaithersburg, Md., 1978. Capt. USPHS, 1967—. Recipient Exemplary Svc. medal Surgeon Gen. USPHS, 1990, Outstanding Svc. medal, 1987, Commendation medal, 1987, 91, Citation, 1985, 87. Mem. Am. Stats. Assn., Am. Coll. Epidemiology, Biometrics Soc., Commd. Officers Assn. (bd. dirs., chmn. 1991—), Phi Kappa Phi. Roman Catholic. Office: FDA Ctr Devices and Rad Health 5600 Fishers Ln Rockville MD 20857-0001

CHIANG, EDWARD TSUNG-TING, engineering consultant; b. Anhwei, China, Nov. 15, 1936; s. Y.T. and Daisy (Yang) C.; m. Alice M.F. Shih; children: Vincent W.S., Victor W.Y. BS in Hydraulic Engring., Chung Yuan Coll. Sci. and Engring., Chung Li, Taiwan, 1960; MS in Civil Engring., Va. Poly. Inst. and State U., 1963, PhD in Civil Engring., 1968. Registered profl. engr., Mass., Maine, Vt., Conn., N.Y., Va., N.H., Fla., Nebr. Hydraulic engr. Metcalf & Eddy, Inc., Boston, 1967-69; water resource and hydraulic engr. Chas. T. Main, Inc., Boston, 1969-71; chief hydraulic engr., asst. v.p. Whitman & Howard, Inc., Wellesley, Mass., 1971-83; pres. H2O Engring. Cons. Assn., Inc., Woburn, Mass., 1980—; cons. Sudbury (Mass.) Water Dist., 1988—; water supply adv. bd. Mass. Dept. Environ. Protection, 1980-86. Bd. dirs., pres. Greater Boston Chinese Cultural Assn., Weston, Mass., 1975-88; vice chmn. bd. dirs. Boston Chinese Econ. Devel. Coun., 1988—; co-moderator Boston South Cove and China Town Neighborhood Coun., 1987—. Fellow ASCE; mem. Am. Water Works Assn., Am. Water Resources Assn., N.E. Assn. Chinese Profls. (chmn. bd. dirs. 1988—), Internat. Water Resources Assn. Office: H2O Engring Consulting Assn Inc 6 Page Pl Woburn MA 01801

CHIANG, GEORGE DJIA-CHEE, engineer, educator; b. Shanghai, China, Sept. 29, 1938; came to U.S., 1963; s. Tai Yei and Wai Yui (Lai) C.; m. Betty Theresa Doue, June 11, 1965; children: Andrew H., Audrey H. BS, Harbin (China) Inst. Tech., 1961; MS, U. Calif., Berkeley, 1965; PhD, Ariz. State U., 1971. Registered profl engr. Ariz., Washington, Tex. Asst. engr. Harbin Steel Co., 1961-62; research asst. U. Calif., 1964-66; sr. project engr. Sperry Rand Corp., Phoenix, 1966-70; faculty assoc. Ariz. State U., Tempe, 1970-71; head, prof. engring dept. U.S. Army Intern Tng. Ctr., Texarkana, Tex., 1971-77; litigation, tech. cons. Nat. Hwy. Traffic Safety Adminstn., Washington, 1977—; adj. prof. engring. U. So. Calif., Washington, 1977—; cons. Sperry Rand Corp., Phoenix, 1970-71, Edgewood (Md.) Arsenal, 1972-77. Contbr. articles to tech. jours. Active local PTA; bd. dirs. Potomac Chinese Sch., 1978-81. NASA fellow, 1970-71. Mem. ASME (tech. adv. com. 1980—), Profl. Engring. Soc., Tau Beta Pi. Democrat. Home: 8620 Tuckerman Ln Rockville MD 20854-3159 Office: Nat Hwy Traffic Safety Adminstrn 400 7th St SW Washington DC 20590-0002

CHIANG, PETER K., science administrator; b. Hong Kong, Oct. 20, 1941; came to U.S., 1961; s. Wing K. and Kwei Y. (Lee) C.; m. Sabrina C. Hung, May 1, 1966; children: Michelle Stephanie, Denise. BSc, U. San Francisco, 1965; MSc, U. Alta., Edmonton, Can., 1967, PhD, 1971. Postdoctoral fellow Johns Hopkins U., Balt., 1971-72; vis. fellow NIH, Balt., 1972-74; sr. staff fellow Johns NIH, Bethesda, Md., 1974-80, rsch. chemist, 1980-81; sect. head Walter Reed Army Inst. of Rsch., Washington, 1981-85, dept. chief, 1985—; assoc. editor Pergamon Press, Oxford, Eng., 1991—. Editor: Tumor Cell Differentiation, 1987. Treasurer NIH Day Care Ctr., Bethesda, 1979; v.p. Orgn. of Chinese Ams., Washington, 1982-87. Recipient Inventor's award U.S. Dept. Commerce, 1966, U.S. HHS, 1967. Mem. Am. Soc. Pharm. and Therapeutics, Am. Soc. Biochemistry and Molecular Biology, Soc. of Neurosci. Roman Catholic. Home: 9509 Starmont Rd Bethesda MD 20817-2307 Office: Walter Reed Army Inst Rsch Div of Biochemistry Washington DC 20817-5100

CHIAPELLA, ANNE PAGE, epidemiologist; b. Oakland, Calif., Oct. 12, 1942; d. Karl Josef and Anne Elizabeth (Gorrill) C. BA in Polit. Sci., Stanford U., 1964, PhD in Neurosci., 1982, MS in Stats., 1985; MPH in Epidemiology, Johns Hopkins U., 1986. Rsch. technician Stanford (Calif.) U., 1966-75, postdoctoral fellow, 1983-85; postdoctoral fellow Johns Hopkins U., Balt., 1986-88; program officer Inst. Medicine NAS, Washington, 1989-91; sr. analyst Nat. Inst. on Alcohol and Alcohol Abuse, Rockville, Md., 1991—; statis. and intellectual property cons. various orgns., Washington, 1983—. Writer humorous, tech. and travel speeches, 1985—; contbr. articles to profl. jours., 1980—. Pres. Nebr. Ave. Neighborhood Assn., Washington, 1987-89; assoc. Smithsonian Instn., Washington, 1987—; active in Friends of Kennedy Ctr., Washington, 1987—, Friends of Nat. Zoo, Washington, 1987—, Textile Mus., Washington, 1986—. Grantee and fellow NIH, 1975, 77, 83, 86; fellow Delta Gamma Soc., 1983; grantee Environ. Health Sci. Ctr., 1986. Mem. Am. Pub. Health Assn., Soc. Epidemiologic Research, N.Y. Acad. Scis., Toastmaster Internat. (officer 1987-89). Home: 5126 Nebraska Ave NW Washington DC 20008-2047

CHIAPPERINI, PATRICIA BIGNOLI, real estate appraiser, consultant; b. N.Y.C., Jan. 16, 1946; d. Gennaro and Giovanna (Resburgo) Bignoli; m. Joseph M. Chiapperini, Dec. 14, 1968. BS in Acctg. and Econs., St. John's U., 1968; postgrad., U. Ala., 1969, Rutgers U., 1980, Am. Inst. Real Estate Appraisers, 1983. Cert. gen. real property appraiser, N.J. Staff acct. Cleary, During & Co., N.Y.C., 1967-69; chief acct. Montgomery Bapt. Hosp. (Ala.), 1969-70; internal auditor Scottex Corp., N.Y.C., 1970-73; office mgr. Mid-Jersey Realty, East Brunswick, N.J., 1973-79; self-employed real estate appraiser, North Brunswick, N.J., 1979—; guest lect. Middlesex County Coll., 1979—; adj. prof. Jersey City State Coll. Chmn. Arts and Cultural Com., Milltown, N.J., 1979-83; active Am. Legion Aux., Milltown, 1973—. Recipient John Marshall award St. John's U., 1968. Mem. Nat. Assn. Ind. Fee Appraisers, Cen. Jersey Ind. Fee Appraisers (treas., 1982-83, v.p., 1984), Milltown C. of C. (v.p. 1987). Roman Catholic. Office: 735 Georges Rd North Brunswick NJ 08902

CHIARAMIDA, ANGELJEAN, chamber of commerce administrator; b. Lawrence, Mass., Apr. 12, 1949; d. Angelo and Isabel Veronica (Torrisi) C. BA in History, Merrimack Coll., 1970. History tchr. secondary schs. Reading, North Andover, Mass., 1971-76; adminstrv. asst. to v.p. devel. Merrimack Coll., North Andover, 1977-78, resident staff dir., 1978-79; dir. pub. rels. Notre Dame Coll., Manchester, N.H., 1979-80; dir. community rels. N.H. Lung Assn., Inc., Manchester, 1980-83; exec. v.p., chief exec. officer N.H. Hospitality Assn., Inc., Concord, 1983-84; dri. restaurants Dunfey Mgmt. Co. at Sheraton Wayfarer, Manchester, 1984-85; exec. dir., chief exec. officer Martha's Vineyard C. of C. Inc., Vineyard Haven, Mass., 1985—; pres. Martha's Vineyard C. of C. Edn. and Charitable Found., Inc., 1988—. Contbr. articles to Cape Cod Bus. Jour. Bd. dirs. Job Tng. and Edn. Corp., New Bedford, Mass., 1988—; coun. mem. Mass. Gov. Coun. on Tourism, Boston, 1985—; chair Martha's Vineyard (Mass.) Airport Adv. Com., 1988—. Named Alumna of Yr., Merrimack Coll., 1980. Mem. Nat. Assn. Bus. Economists, Am. Soc. Assn. Execs., Merrimack Coll. Alumni Assn. (class chair 1970), Zonta Internat. (pres. Martha's Vineyard chpt. 1991-93), Martha's Vineyard Rotary Club (charter). Office: Martha's Vineyard C of C PO Box 1698 Beach Rd Vineyard Haven MA 02568-1698

CHIARELLI, JOSEPH, accountant, banker; b. N.Y.C., Sept. 23, 1946; s. Biagio John and Mary Teresa (Cancellieri) C.; m. Eileen Mary Cook, Sept. 7, 1968; children: Claire Marie, Matthew Joseph, Christopher Joseph. BBA, Manhattan Coll., 1968; MBA, U. Hawaii, 1973. CPA, N.Y., Mont. Auditor Coopers & Lybrand, N.Y.C., 1973-77, audit mgr., 1977-81; asst. comptroller Morgan Guaranty Trust Co., N.Y.C., 1981-82, dep. comptroller, 1982-83; v.p., comptroller Morgan Bank Del., Wilmington, 1983-86, Morgan Securities Services Corp., N.Y.C., 1986-89; v.p., funds mgr. Morgan Guaranty Trust Co., N.Y.C., 1990—; chmn. adv. bd. acctg. dept. U. Del., Newark, 1985-87, mem. adv. bd., 1985—. Mem. sch. bd. Most Blessed Sacrament Sch., 1991—. Capt. USAF, 1968-73, lt. col. USAFR. Mem. sch. bd. Most Blessed Sacrament Sch., 1991. Capt. USAF, 1968-73, lt. col. USAFR. Named Outstanding Res. Officer of Yr., Air Force Audit Agy., 1980. Mem. AICPA, N.Y. Soc. CPAs, Fin. Execs. Inst. (founding dir. Del. chpt. 1985-87), Air Force Assn. Roman Catholic. Home: 510 Farview Ave Wyckoff NJ 07481-1110 Office: Morgan Guaranty Trust Co NY 60 Wall St New York NY 10260-0001

CHICCO, GIACOMO FRANCO, public relations executive; b. Maracay, Venezuela, Apr. 9, 1958; came to U.S., 1977; s. Giuseppe and Maria (Stagno) C.; m. Kathryn Cordes. BA, Kalamazoo Coll., 1980; MS, Boston U., 1982. Rsch. engr. biomechanic's lab. Brigham & Women's Hosp., Boston, 1980-82; sr. account supr. Daniel J. Edelman, Inc., N.Y.C., 1982-86; v.p. Ruder-Finn, N.Y.C., 1986-88; sr. v.p. The Rowland Co., N.Y.C., 1988-90; v.p., CSM Burson-Marstellar, N.Y.C., 1990-91; dir. client svcs., 1991—. Recipient Big Apple award Pub. Rels. Soc. Am., 1988, Creativity in Pub. Rels. award, 1991.

CHICKERING, F. WILLIAM, college dean, consultant; b. Atlanta, May 4, 1953; s. Frank Wilbur and Mary Alice (House) C. BA in English, Ga. State U., 1973; M of Librarianship, Emory U., 1974; Cert. Advanced Librarianship, Columbia U., 1978. Head of sales Rich's, Inc., Atlanta, 1970-76; media specialist Rockdale County High Sch., Conyers, Ga., 1974-76; teaching asst. Columbia U., N.Y.C., 1976-77, media svc. librarian, 1977-81; dir. multi media svcs. Pratt Inst., Bklyn., 1988, acting assoc. dean librs., 1989, dean of libraries, 1989—, acting assoc. provost, 1991—; vis. asst. prof. Pratt Inst., 1981-87, vis. assoc. prof., 1987—. Author, lectr. on mass media and manipulation; coord. workshop Multiple Choice in Film and Video, 1986, Laser Disks and the World of Info., 1986. Chair METRO Film Coop., 1983-87, mem. resources devel. com., 1987-88; jury chair Am. Film Festival, 1987, chair, 1986. Hubbard scholar Ga. Libr. Assn., 1973, Lee Found. scholar Ga. State U., 1970. Mem. ALA, Times Squares (pres. 1989-90). Home: 232A Willoughby Ave Brooklyn NY 11205-3805 Office: Pratt Inst Libr 200 Willoughby Ave Brooklyn NY 11205-3899

CHICKERING, HOWARD ALLEN, insurance company executive, lawyer; b. San Francisco, Mar. 21, 1942; s. Allen Lawrence and Caroline Cranford (Rogers) C.; m. Elizabeth Douglas Dalton, June 29, 1968; children: Philip Dalton, Caroline Howe. BS in Econs., U. Pa., 1966; JD, Stanford U., 1971. Bar: Calif. 1972. Assoc. Chickering & Gregory, San Francisco, 1971-76; sr. counsel Itel Corp., San Francisco, 1976-79; v.p., gen. counsel, bd. dirs. Clarendon Ins. Co. (Bermuda) Ltd., N.Y.C., 1979-81; pres. Clarendon Group Svcs. Inc., N.Y.C., 1981-85; exec. v.p., bd. dirs. Clarendon Ins. Group, N.Y.C., 1985-88; chmn., chief exec. officer R.V.I. Svcs. Co., Stamford, Conn., 1989—, R.V.I. Guaranty Co., Ltd., Hamilton, Bermuda, 1989—. Contbr. articles to profl. publs. Co-author, acting campaign chmn. San Francisco Proposition C (Open Space), 1974; campaign sec. Proposition J (Open Space and Park Renovation), 1974; mem. San Francisco Open Space Citizens Adv. Commn., 1976-78. Lt. (j.g.) USNR, 1966-68, Vietnam. Mem. State Bar Calif., Racquet and Tennis Club, N.Y. Yacht Club, Univ. Club (San Francisco), Belle Haven Club (Greenwich, Conn.). Republican. Episcopalian. Home: 80 Otter Rock Dr Greenwich CT 06830-7029 Office: RVI Svcs Co 1 Canterbury Grn Stamford CT 06901-2032

CHIDDICK, GERALD KEVIN, underwriter, consultant; b. N.Y.C., Apr. 9, 1967; s. Calvin Cecil and Leslie Sharon (Heartwell) C. BS, St. John's U., 1990. Underwriter Chubb & Son Inc., Uniondale, N.Y., 1990—; cons., bd. mem. Comfort Ride Inc., Deltona, Fla., 1992—. Songwriter Analogies, 1990, Check the Clock, 1992; songwriter, performer New York (is an Allusion), 1991. Mem. ASCAP, Black Alumni Assn. St. John's U. Baptist. Home: 49 Lafayette St Huntington NY 11743 Office: Chubb & Son Inc 333 Earle Ovington Blvd Uniondale NY 11552

CHIDESTER, JACK JOSEPH, sales executive; b. Bloomsburg, Pa., July 29, 1958; s. John J. and Patricia (Ritz) C.; m. Sharon Marie Doyle, Nov. 24, 1978; children: Kirstin, Kara, Jack IV. BS, Pa. State U., 1980. Mgr. Host Internat., Washington, 1980-81; account exec. MCI Telecommunications, Inc., Phila., 1981-83, sales mgr., 1983; br. mgr. MCI Telecommunications, Inc., Pitts., 1984-85, Washington, 1985-86; dir. sales MCI Telecommunications, Inc., Phila., 1986-1991; v.p. sales and mktg. MCI Telecommunications, Inc., Stamford, Conn., 1991—. Home: 10 Old Stone Ct Ridgefield CT 06877 Office: MCI Telecommunications Inc 2777 Summer St Stamford CT 06905

CHIEN, KUEI-YUAN, aerodynamicist, researcher; b. Chung Ching, Szechuan, China, Jan. 15, 1941; came to U.S., 1963; s. Huan-Wen and Jiang-Jen (Tso) C.; m. Shirley Ping Chou, Feb. 3, 1968; 1 child, Homer I-Chung. BS, Nat. Taiwan U., 1962; MS, MIT, 1965, PhD, 1968. Rsch. asst. MIT, Cambridge, Mass., 1963-68; rsch. assoc. Ames Rsch. Ctr. NASA, Moffett Field, Calif., 1968-71; sr. aerospace engr. Naval Surface Warfare Ctr., Silver Spring, Md., 1971—; lectr. U. Md., College Park, 1985—; assoc. prof., lectr. George Washington U., Washington, 1981; presenter nat. and internat. profl. meetings. Contbr. articles to profl. jours. Gerald Swope fellow MIT, 1964-65. Assoc. fellow AIAA (various tech. coms.); mem. Chinese Am. Profls. Assn., Sigma Xi, Sigma Gamma Tau.

CHIET, ARNOLD, lawyer; b. N.Y.C., June 18, 1930; s. Harry and Rose (Golofsky) C.; m. Marilyn Sally Cohen, May 22, 1955 (div. Apr. 1984); children: Richelle M. Chiet Sabia, Clifford S., Bradley A.; m. Wanda Flora Deeths, Sept. 1, 1984. BBA, CCNY, 1952; JD, NYU, 1959, LLM, 1962. Bar: N.Y. 1959. Acct., auditor Peat, Marwick, Mitchell & Co., N.Y.C., 1956-59; tax atty. Allied Signal Corp., N.Y.C., 1959-62, Stone & Webster Svc. Corp., N.Y.C., 1962-65; tax atty. Martin Marietta Corp., N.Y.C., 1965-68, asst. tax dir., 1968-76; dir. taxes Martin Marietta Corp., Bethesda, Md., 1976-86, v.p., gen. tax counsel, 1986—. Chmn. tax com. Nat. Crushed Stone Assn., Washington, 1978-84. Lt. USN, 1952-56. Mem. N.Y. State Bar Assn., Fin. Execs. inst., Tax Execs. Inst. (v.p. 1962—, pres. 1986-87), Aerospace Industries Assn. (chmn. tax com. 1989—). Office: Martin Marietta Corp 6801 Rockledge Dr Bethesda MD 20817-1836

CHIKOFSKY, ELLIOT JAY, software engineering researcher, consultant; b. N.Y.C., June 20, 1955; m. Julie M. Michutka, May 30, 1981; 2 children. BS in Computer and Communications Sci., U. Mich., 1975, MS in Indsl. and Ops. Engring., 1978. Sr. rsch. assoc. ISDOS project U. Mich., Ann Arbor, 1976-83, instr. indsl. engring., 1981-82; v.p. ISDOS Inc., Ann Arbor, 1983-86; dir. rsch. and tech. Index Tech. Corp., Cambridge, Mass., 1986-91; dir. CASE devel. Progress Software Corp., Bedford, Mass., 1991—; lectr. indsl. engring. Northeastern U., Boston, 1987—; presenter in field; pres. Radius Systems Inc., cons., Lake Odessa, Mich., 1980—; founding pres., sec., Internat. Workshop on Computer Aided Software Engring., Cambridge, 1987—. Author: Computer-Aided Software Engineering, 1989, IBM Ad/Cycle Enterprise Model Tool Builder's Guide, 1990, Reverse Engineering and Design Recovery, 1991 (software) Weltab Election Tabulation System, 1978, 86, Excelerator Extended Analysis, 1988, Excelerator Design Recovery, 1990; assoc. editor-in-chief IEEE Software mag., 1989—, guest editor, 1988, 90; contbr. articles to profl. jours. Chmn. Ann Arbor Cable TV Commn., 1981-82. Recipient cert. of merit Internat. Workshop on Computer Aided Software Engring., 1988. Mem. IEEE Computer Soc. (sr., vice chair tech. com. software engring. 1988—), Assn. for Computing Machinery, Masons. Office: Progress Software Corp 14 Oak Park Dr Bedford MA 01730-1485

CHILCOTE, SAMUEL DAY, JR., association executive; b. Casper, Wyo., Aug. 24, 1937; s. Sam D. and Juanita C. (Cornelison) C.; m. Ellen Sheridan Spear, Nov. 11, 1966. B.S., Idaho State U., 1959. Adminstrv. asst. Continental Oil Co., Glenrock, Wyo., 1960-63; asst. supt. public instrn., dir. Wyo. Surplus Property Agy., Wyo. Sch. Lunch Program, Cheyenne Wyo. Dept. Edn., 1963-67; supr. N. Central region Distilled Spirits Inst., Denver, 1967-71; exec. dir., chief operating officer N. Central region Distilled Spirits Inst., Washington, 1971-73; exec. v.p., chief operating officer Distilled Spirits

Council, Inc., Washington, 1973-77, pres., chief exec. officer, 1978-81; pres. Tobacco Inst., Washington, 1981—; mem. industry sect. adv. council consumer goods, Dept. Commerce. Pres. Sky Ranch Found. for Boys, 1975-81, pres. emeritus, 1981—; treas. Ford's Theatre, 1984-88, vice chmn., bd. trustees, 1988—; bd. dirs., exec. com. Art Barn; chmn. Awards Dinner Com., 1989—, USO Met. Washington, v.p. Capt. U.S. Army, 1959-60. Recipient Profl. Achievement award Idaho State U. Coll. Bus., 1986, Man of Yr. award Anti-Defamation league, 1986, Humanitarian of the Yr. award Tobacco and Confectionery Div. Dinner for the UJA-Fedn. 1991 campaign. Mem. U.S. C. of C. Clubs: George Town, Congressional Country (past pres., exec. com., bd. govs.), Burning Tree; Nat. Press, Capitol Hill, City, F Street, TPC Avenel (Washington); Jefferson Islands (bd. govs.). Lodges: Masons, Elks, Shriners. Office: Tobacco Inst 1875 I St NW Washington DC 20006-5409

CHILD, EDWARD TAYLOR, technology licensing executive; b. Richmond, Va., July 9, 1930; s. Roger Sherman and Martha Elizabeth (Taylor) C.; m. Beverly Jane Croft, June 25, 1955; children: Christopher, Jonathan, Martha, Benjamin, Frederic. BSChemE, Yale U., 1952; MSChemE, U. Del., 1954, PhDChemE, 1956; MBA in Bus. Mgmt., Pepperdine U., 1972. Rsch. chem. engr. Texaco Inc., Beacon, N.Y., 1956-62, group leader, 1962-67; rsch. supr. Texaco Inc., Montebello, Calif., 1967-73; strategic planning coord. Texaco Inc., Harrison, N.Y., 1982-83; project mgr. Texaco Devel. Corp, N.Y.C., 1973-82; licensing mgr. Texaco Devel. Corp, Harrison, 1983—. Patentee in field. Treas., dir. Tarryhill Homeowners Assn., Tarrytown, N.Y., 1981-84. Fellow Am. Inst. Chem. Engrs.; mem. Sigma Xi, Tau Beta Pi. Office: Texaco Inc 2000 Westchester Ave White Plains NY 10650

CHILD, IRVIN LONG, psychologist, educator; b. Deming, N.Mex., Mar. 11, 1915; s. Arthur Henry and Martina Avila (Long) C.; m. Alice Dukes Blyth, Mar. 29, 1941; children: Richard Blyth, Pamela Colman. B.A., UCLA, 1935; Ph.D., Yale U., 1939. Instr. psychology Harvard U. and Radcliffe Coll., 1939-41; with Yale U., 1941—, successively Latin-Am. research fellow, asst. prof., assoc. prof., prof. psychology, 1954-85, prof. emeritus, 1985—. Author: Italian or American?, The Second Generation in Conflict, 1943, Child Training and Personality: A Cross-Cultural Study, (with J.W.M. Whiting), 1953, Humanistic Psychology and the Research Tradition: Their Several Virtues, 1973. Mem. APA, Parapsychol. Assn., Am. Psychol. Soc., Phi Beta Kappa, Sigma Xi. Home: 2 Cooper Rd North Haven CT 06473-3001 Office: 2 Hillhouse Ave New Haven CT 06520-7447

CHILD, JACK, Spanish and Latin American studies educator; b. Buenos Aires, Argentina, Jan. 27, 1938; (parents Am. citizens); s. Roger Sherman and Martha (Taylor) C.; m. Sally Mann, Dec. 16, 1961 (div. 1977); children: Andrew, Eric; m. Leslie Morginson-Eitzen, Feb. 20, 1989. B in Engring., Yale U., 1960; MA, Am. U., 1966, PhD, 1978. Enlisted U.S. Army, 1960, advanced through grades to lt. col., 1980, ret., 1980; prof. Am. U., Washington, 1980—. Author: Geopolitics in South America, 1985, Antarctica, 1988, Inter-American Military System, 1980, Introduction to Spanish Translation, 1992; contbr. chpts. to books and articles to profl. jours. Office: Am U Dept Lang & Fgn Study Washington DC 20016

CHILD, JOHN SOWDEN, JR., lawyer; b. Lansdale, Pa., July 22, 1944; s. John Sowden and Beatrice Thelma (Landes) C. BS in Polit. Sci., MIT, 1967; BSChemE, 1967; JD, U. Pa., 1973; BLit in Politics, Oxford U., 1974. Bar: Pa. 1974, N.Y. 1977, U.S. Dist. Ct. (ea. dist.) Pa. 1978, U.S. Dist. Ct. (ea. dist.) N.Y. 1978, U.S. Patent and Trademark Office 1978, U.S. Ct. Appeals (2d cir.) 1978, U.S. Ct. Appeals (fed. cir.) 1981, U.S. Ct.Appeals (3d cir.) 1986. Assoc. Davis Hoxie Faithfull & Hapgood, N.Y.C., 1974-78, Synnestvedt & Lechner, Phila., 1978-88; of counsel Dann, Dorfman, Herrell and Skillman, Phila., 1988—; arbitrator Pa. Ct. Common Pleas, Phila., 1979—, U.S. Dist. Ct., Ea. Dist.) Pa., Phila., 1983—. Firm coord. United Way Southeastern Pa., 1983-88. Mem. Am. Intellectual Property Law Assn., N.Y. Patent, Trademark and Copyright Law Assn., Phila. Bar Assn., Phila. Patent Law Assn. (chmn. program com. 1981-85, editor, co-editor newsletter 1980—, gov. 1985-87, sec. 1987-89), Mil. Order Fgn. Wars, Com. of Seventy, Soc. Colonial Wars (treas. 1989-91, councilor 1991—), English Speaking Union, Colonial Soc. Pa., Phila. Oxford and Cambridge Soc. (sec. 1985—). Republican. Mem. Soc. of Friends. Clubs: Union League, Phila. Club, Cricket (Phila.). Home: 8221 Seminole St Philadelphia PA 19118-3929 Office: Dann Dorfman Herrell & Skillman 1310 Fidelity Bldg 123 S Broad St Philadelphia PA 19109-1030

CHILDERS, THOMAS ALLEN, information studies educator, consultant; b. Chillicothe, Ohio, July 2, 1940; s. William Allen and Jeannette Marie (Kohlrusch) C. BA, U. Md., 1961; MLS, Rutgers U., 1963, PhD, 1970. Sr. libr. Baltimore County Pub. Libr., Towson, Md., 1963, 65-67, spl. project dir., 1974; prof. Coll. Info. Studies Drexel U., Phila., 1970—, dir. Ctr. for Info. Rsch., 1980-87; A.B. Kroeger prof. info. studies, 1992—; adj. instr. Rutgers U., New Brunswick, N.J., 1970; mem. vis. faculty Syracuse (N.Y.) U., 1970; freelance cons. to pub. and pvt. librs. Author: Information Service in Public Libraries, 1971, The Information Poor in America, 1975, Information and Referral: Public Libraries, 1984; editor: Information Organizations: Management Perspectives for the 80s, 1981; contbr. articles to profl. jours. With U.S. Army, 1963-65. Brit. Libr. fellow, 1978; recipient Rsch. Achievement award Drexel U., 1985. Mem. ALA (coun. 1972-74, dir. libr. rsch. round table 1972-75, chair, mem. com. on program evaluation and support 1973-77, dir. reference and adult svcs. div. 1978-81), AAUP, ACLU, Am. Soc. Info. Sci., Am. Mgmt. Assn. Home: 231 S 42d St Philadelphia PA 19104 Office: Drexel U Coll Info Studies Philadelphia PA 19104

CHILDRESS, FAY ALICE, university administrator; b. Annapolis, Md., Nov. 23, 1929; d. John Douglas and Winifred Lee (Stevens) Howard; m. Larry Brownlow Childress, June 7, 1949; children: Patricia, Peter, Mary, Charles. AA, Montgomery Coll., Takoma Park, Md., 1979; BS, U. Md., 1982, postgrad., 1984—. Program technician NSF, Washington, 1972-78, sr. program technician, 1978-82, adminstrv. officer, 1982-86; asst. to exec. v.p. and equal opportunity officer Cath. U. Am., Washington, 1986—. Contbr. articles to profl. jours. Mem. steering com. Washington Area Affirmative Action Group, 1988—; mem. Washington Area Higher Edn. Liaison Group, 1989—; chief election judge Montgomery County Election Bd., Silver Spring, 1976-92; mem. Seven Oaks-Evanswood Citizens Assn., Silver Spring, 1980—; vol. Montgomery County Mental Health Assn., Rockville, 1982-84. Mem. Am. Assn. Affirmative Action, Coll. and Univ. Pers. Assn., Montgomery Coll. Alumni Assn. (bd. govs. 1985-87), Alpha Sigma Lambda (pres. Tau chpt. 1988-90). Office: The Cath U of Am 620 Michigan Ave NE Washington DC 20064-0001

CHILDRESS, JAN C., gas industry administrator; b. White Sulphur Springs, W.Va., July 7, 1954; s. Lorenzo and Grace (Swan) C.; m. Glenda Colon; 1 child, Jan Lucanus. BA in Indsl. Labor Rels., SUNY, N.Y.C., 1981; cert. in labor studies, Cornell U., 1982; cert. in real estate fin., NYU, 1990. Edn. dir. R-T-P, Inc., N.Y.C., 1974-76, project dir., 1977-78; spl. asst. for health 14th Congl. Dist. U.S. Ho. of Reps., Bklyn., 1979-83; employee benefits and svcs. coord. Bklyn. Union Gas Co., 1983-84, asst. to chmn. bd. dirs., 1984-87, dir. area devel. fund, 1988—; dir. Nonprofit Facilities Fund, N.Y.C., 1990—, Leviticus Alternative Fund, Ossining, N.Y., 1989—; trustee Jeannie L. Grant Found., Bklyn., 1981—. Secretary, trustee Cancer Care, Inc., N.Y.C., 1985—; bd. dirs. Navy Yard Boys & Girls Club, Bklyn., 1980—, Bklyn. chpt. ARC, 1982—, Bklyn. Psychiat. Ctrs., 1981—. David Rockefeller fellow N.Y.C. Ptnrship., 1989-90; named one of Outstanding Young Men of Am., 1985. Mem. Coun. Community Devel., Bklyn. Mgmt. Club (pres. 1981-82), Rotary (bd. dirs., pres. 1982-83). Home: 82 Pierrepont St Brooklyn NY 11201-2406 Office: Bklyn Union Gas Co 166 Montague St Brooklyn NY 11201-3524

CHILIAN, WILLIAM JOSEPH, analyst, consultant; b. Haworth, N.J., Apr. 3, 1965; s. Henry Joseph and Norma Dean (Harnden) C. BS in Econs. and Polit. Sci., Northeastern U., 1988; MBA in Internat. Fin. and Mktg., Fordham U., 1990. Owner, operator Party Pros, event catering svc., Boston, 1985-87; asst. to v.p. fin. ATA Internat., exporters, Moonachie, N.J., 1987-90; planning analyst Matsushita Electric Corp. Am. (Panasonic), Secaucus, N.J., 1990—. cons. on fin. matters, principally real estate, Haworth, N.J., 1990—. Mem. Omicron Delta Epsilon. Republican. Home: 309 Pleasant St Haworth NJ 07641 Office: Matsushita Electric Corp Am One Panasonic Way Secaucus NJ 07094

CHIMERA, PAUL ROBERT, writer, editor; b. Buffalo, Nov. 11, 1949; s. Joseph Charles and Mary Maureen (Lauria) C.; children: Catherine Renee, Kristy Lynn. BS in Journalism, Ohio U., 1971; MS in Social Scis., SUNY, Buffalo, 1985. Reporter Niagara Gazette, Niagara Falls, N.Y., 1972-73; publicity dir. Salvador Dali Mus., Beachwood, Ohio, 1973-74; br. coord., editor ARC, Cleve. and Buffalo, 1974-78; arts editor U. at Buffalo News Bur., 1978-80; newsletter editor Twin Fair Corp., West Seneca, N.Y., 1978-80; product promotion specialist Mennen Med., Inc., Clarence, N.Y., 1982-84; chief copywriter Creative Resource Group, Buffalo, 1984-85; pub. rels. coord. Barrister Info. Systems, Buffalo, 1985-86; writer, editor Chimera Communications, Buffalo, 1986—; adj. prof. Buffalo State Coll., 1986-89, Erie Community Coll., Buffalo, 1987; editor-in-chief Salvador Dali Collectors Newsletter, 1991—. Chmn. Claremont Neighborhood Watch Group, Kenmore, N.Y., 1989; assoc. mem. Salvador Dali Mus. Home and Office: 103 Thistle Lea Williamsville NY 14221

CHIMPLES, GEORGE, lawyer; b. Canton, Ohio, Oct. 8, 1924; s. Mark and Katherine (Hines) C.; m. Margaret Joanna Cavalaris, July 31, 1949; children: Alicia Candace, Mark II, John Hines, Katherine Hines. AB, Princeton U., 1951; LLB, Harvard U., 1954. Bar: Pa. 1955, U.S. Dist. Ct. (ea. dist.) Pa. 1955, U.S. Ct. Appeals (3d cir.) 1955, U.S. Ct. Claims, 1965, U.S. Tax Ct., 1965. Assoc. Stradley, Ronon, Stevens & Young, Phila., 1954-61, gen. ptnr., 1961—; adj. prof. law U. Pa., Drexel U. Grad. Sch. Bus.; co-authored establishment of overseas infrastructure for securities mktg. in Europe and the Antilles. Trustee Christ Church Preservation Trust; bd. dirs. Citizens Crime Commn. S.E. Pa.; permanent assoc. Phila. Mus. Art. Served to capt. USSAF, 1942-46, ETO. Decorated D.F.C., Air medal with four oak leaf clusters, Air Force Commendation medal, Victory medal, four Battle Stars. Mem. ABA (chmn. subcom. regulated investment cos.), Phila. Bar Assn. (tax sect.), Internat. Bar Assn., Internat. Fiscal Assn. (tax treaty sect.), Mid-Atlantic Coun., Commanderie de Bordeaux (maitre Phila. chpt.), Newcomen Soc. U.S. (com. chmn., nat. trustee) Army and Navy Club (Washington), Penn Club (life, bd. dirs., historian) Athenaeum of Phila. (life), Libr. Co. of Phila. (life), Phila. Mus. Art (permanent assoc.), Phila. Club, Princeton Club N.Y., Cannon Club (Princeton chpt.), Merion Cricket Club. Home: 1179 Lafayette Rd Wayne PA 19087-2110 Office: Stradley Ronon Stevens & Young 2600 One Commerce Sq Philadelphia PA 19103

CHIN, ALLEN E., SR., secondary educator; b. Arlington, Va., Oct. 21, 1950; s. Tung Ock and Hai Ock (Moy) C.; m. Amy Yung, Jan. 24, 1971; children: Allen Jr., Denise Maria Michelle. BA, George Washington U., 1972, MA, 1974, EdD, 1980. Cert. secondary social studies educator, D.C. Tchr. D.C. Pub. Schs., Washington, 1972-87, 88-91, dir. athletics, 1987-88, 91—; exec. cons. D.C. Coaches Assn., Inc., Washington, 1988—; exec. dir. AEC-10 Found., Inc., Washington, 1988—. Mem. Jefferson Club, Richmond, Va., 1990-91, Dem. Nat. Com., Washington, 1984—, Dem. Senatorial Campaign Com., Washington, 1984—. Recipient Coach of Yr. award, 1986, 87, 88, Athletic Dir. of Yr., 1974, Golf Coach of Yr., 1975. Mem. D.C. Coaches Assn., Washington Tchrs. Union, D.C. Coun. for Social Studies, Nat. Geog. Soc., Met. Police Boys & Girls Clubs, Nat. Coun. for Social Studies, Nat. Interscholastic Athletic Adminstrs. Assn., Am. Soc. Notaries. Democrat. Roman Catholic. Home: 6150 Windward Dr Burke VA 22015-3832 Office: Roper Sch 4800 Meade St NE Washington DC 20019-3999

CHIN, ALVIN JUILIN, cardiologist, pediatrician, educator, researcher; b. Urbana, Ill., Oct. 6, 1953; s. Te Ning and Mary (Kao) C.; m. Catherine Norton Marchand, June 18, 1978; children: Fiona Clare, Meredith Marchand. AB magna cum laude, Harvard U., 1973; MD, Stanford U., 1977. Diplomate Am. Bd. Pediatrics, subsidiary bd. pediatric cardiology. Intern medicine Children's Hosp., Boston, 1977-78, cardiology fellow, 1979-82; resident pediatrics Dartmouth-Hitchcock Med. Ctr., Hanover, N.H., 1978-79; instr. pediatrics Harvard Med. Sch., Boston, 1982-83; asst. prof. pediatrics UCLA Sch. Medicine, 1983-84; asst. prof. pediatrics U. Pa. Sch. Medicine, Phila., 1984-89, assoc. prof. pediatrics, 1989—; cons. Hewlett Packard Imaging Systems Div., Andover, Mass., 1989—. Contbr. articles to profl. jours. Mem. Baldwin Sch. Father's Assn., Bryn Mawr, Pa., 1988—, Md. Sci. Ctr., Balt., 1989—. Nat. Merit Scholar, 1970-73; grantee Harvard Coll. Scholarship, 1970-73, Ethel Brown Foerderer Fund Children's Hosp. Found., 1986-89, NIH 1987-88. Mem. AAAS, Am. Soc. Echocardiography, Am. Heart Assn., N.Y. Acad. Sci., Harvard Club Phila. Office: Children's Hosp 34th St and Civic Ctr Blvd Philadelphia PA 19104

CHIN, DAVID CHIU KWAN, health maintenance organization executive; b. Boston, June 16, 1949; s. David C. K. and Donna (Wong) C.; m. Carolyn Joan McCane-Chin, Aug. 20, 1978; 1 child, Lesley. AB, Harvard Coll., 1971, MD, 1975; MBA, Stanford U., 1980. Diplomate Am. Bd. Internal Medicine. Operating mgr. Harvard Community Health Plan, Brookline, Mass., 1981-83; health ctr. dir. Harvard Community Health Plan, Brookline, 1983-85, assoc. med. dir., 1985-86, deputy med. dir. for ops., 1986-87, pres., med. dir., health ctrs. div., 1987—; adv. coun. Grad. Sch. Bus., Stanford (Calif.) U., 1990—; bd. dirs. Baxter Internat., 1992—. Named Robert Wood Johnson Found. Clin. scholar Robert Wood Johnson Found., 1978-80. Mem. Am. Coll. Physician Execs., Young Pres.' Orgn. Home: 87 Sylvan Ln Weston MA 02193-1027 Office: Harvard Community Health 10 Brookline Pl W Brookline MA 02146-7215

CHIN, DER-TAU, chemical engineer, educator; b. Zhejiang, China, Sept. 14, 1939; came to U.S., 1963, naturalized, 1977; s. Tsu-Kang and Shou-Chen (Chen) C.; B.S. in Chem. Engring., Chungyuan Coll. Sci. and Engring., 1962; M.S. in Chem. Engring., Tufts U., 1965; Ph.D. in Chem. Engring., U. Pa., 1969; m. Lorna Fe Gencianeo, July 17, 1971; children—Janet G., Lynn G. Plant engr. Lungyen Sugar Factory, 1962-63; sci. programmer U.S. Air Force Cambridge (Mass.) Research Lab., Lexington, Mass., 1965; sr. research engr. research labs. Gen. Motors Corp., Warren, Mich., 1969-75; prof. Clarkson U., Potsdam, N.Y., 1975—; vis. scientist Brookhaven Nat. Lab., Upton, N.Y., summers 1977, 80, U.S. Army Belvoir Research Devel. Ctr., Ft. Belvoir, Va., summer 1985, U.S. Army Electronics Tech. and Devices Lab., Ft. Mammouth, N.J., summer, 1986; vis. prof. U. Calif., Berkeley, 1981, Swiss Fed. Inst. Tech., Zurich, 1981, Nat. U. Singapore, 1982, 87, Nat. Tsing Hua UNI, 1989—; cons. Centro de Pesquisas do Energia Electrica, Rio de Janiero, Brazil, summer 1979, Los Alamos Nat. Lab., 1981—, Hooker Chem. Devel. Center, Niagara Falls, N.Y., 1981—, Inst. Hydrogen Studies, U. Toronto, 1983—, St. Joe Minerals Corp., Monaca, Pa., 1983. Mem. Electrochem. Soc. (Young Authors award 1971), Am. Inst. Chem. Engrs., Am. Electroplaters Soc., Am. Chem. Soc., Inst. Colloid and Surface Sci., Sigma Xi. Office: Clarkson U Chem Engring Dept Potsdam NY 13699

CHIN, JEFFREY, educator; b. Boston, Jan. 31, 1953; s. Robert and Ai-li (Shen) C.; m. Margaret Sullivan, June 12, 1983; children: Anne, Honora. BA, Trinity Coll., Hartford, Conn., 1976; AM, U. Mich., 1978, PhD, 1983. Instr. Cen. Mich. U., Mt. Pleasant, 1980-82; asst. prof. Le Moyne Coll., Syracuse, N.Y., 1983-89; assoc. prof. Le Moyne Coll., 1989—. Editor: (book) Teaching Social Psychology, 1990, (jour.) Teaching Sociology, 1991; contbr. numerous articles to profl. jours. Office: Le Moyne Coll Syracuse NY 13214-1399

CHIN, JOHN PATRICK, experimental psychologist; b. West Islip, N.Y., Apr. 17, 1962; s. Dan and Betty Y. (Lee) C. BA, Colgate U., 1984; MS in Psychology, U. Md., 1986, PhD in Psychology, 1989. Asst. prof. of Psychology Lewis & Clark Coll., Portland, Oreg., 1989-90; mem. tech. staff Bell Core, Red Banks, N.J., 1990—. Mem. Am. Psycholog. Soc., Assn. for Computing Machinery, Human Factors Soc. Office: Bellcore NVC 1F329 331 Newman Springs Rd Red Bank NJ 07701-5699

CHIN, LOUIS, engineering educator; b. Brookline, Mass., Aug. 6, 1944; s. Yock Wing and Dong (Dik) C.; m. Victoria Louise Diehl, July 29, 1976; children: Anne, Sarah. BSChemE, Tufts U., 1966, MSChemE, 1968; MBA, Boston U., 1983, DBA, 1986. Registered profl. engr. Mass. Cons. E.I. DuPont DeNeMours, Wilmington, Del., 1968-70; engr. Stone & Webster Engring. Corp., Boston, 1970-72; cons. engr. Algonquin Gas Transmission, Boston, 1972-88; prof. Bentley Coll., Waltham, Mass., 1988—. Member Scituate (Mass.) Sch. Com., 1989—, YMCA, Quincy, Mass., 1991—; coach Scituate Soccer Club, 1986—; pres. YMCA Strypers Swim Team Boosters Club, Quincy, 1991—. Mem. Am. Inst. Chem. Engrs. Roman Catholic. Office: Bentley Coll 175 Forest St Waltham MA 02154-4705

CHIN, WILLIAM WAIMAN, biomedical research scientist, physician; b. N.Y.C., Nov. 20, 1947; s. James Gampoy and Yoke Ting (Chu) C.; m. Denise Jean-Claude, Mar. 28, 1981; children: Samantha, Daniel. AB, Columbia U., 1968; MD, Harvard U., 1972. Assoc. investigator Howard Hughes Med. Inst., Boston, 1979-84, investigator, 1984—; asst. prof. Med. Sch., Harvard U., Boston, 1981-84, assoc. prof., 1984—; chief div. genetics Brigham & Women's Hosp., Boston, 1987—, sr. physician, 1991—. Lt. comdr. USPHS, 1974-76. Mem. Am. Soc. Biochemistry and Molecular Biology, Am. Physiol. Soc. (Bowditch lecture 1984), Am. Thyroid Assn. (Van Meter-USV award 1986), Am. Soc. Clin. Investigation (coun. 1988-92, v.p. 1991-92), Endocrine Soc. (coun. 1989-92), Am. Fedn. Clin. Rsch. (award for clin. rsch. 1988). Office: Brigham & Womens Hosp 75 Francis St Boston MA 02115-6195

CHINN, HAROLD, paralegal; b. Medina, N.Y., Mar. 22, 1965; s. Jimmie Lee and Glennis (Hammonds) C.; m. Shellonnee Baker, Sept. 22, 1990; 1 child, Phatima Nicole English. BA, SUNY, Fredonia, 1988. Paralegal Cleary, Gottlieb, Steen & Hamilton, N.Y.C., 1989-90, Manville Personal Injury Settlement Trust, Washington, 1990-91, Zuckerman, Spaeder, Goldstein, Taylor & Kolker, Washington, 1991—. Mem. ABA, Nat. Assn. Legal Assts. Democrat. Baptist. Home: 52 15th St NE Washington DC 20002-8408

CHIODI, CHARLES KAROLY, publishing executive, advertising executive; b. Sopron, Hungary, Aug. 4, 1932; came to U.S., 1956; s. Karoly and Paula (Lehner) C.; m. Violetta Nozdroviczky, Dec. 15, 1951 (div. 1975); children: Charles Jr., Letty, George D., Gina, Roger; m. Ava Marie Mallwitz, Jan. 11, 1984. Student, U. Budapest (Hungary), 1948-51. Writer Army Newspaper, Hungary, 1951-53, The Patriot Ledger, Quincy, Mass., 1957-67; prin. Chiodi Advt., Quincy, 1967-75; pres. Chiodi Advt. and Publ., Inc., Quincy, 1975—; editor and pub. Multihulls Mag., Quincy, 1975—; dir. Internat. Multihull Symposium, various locations, 1976, 85, 88. Editor and pub.: The Symposium Book I, 1977, The Symposium Book II, 1986, The Capsize Bugaboo, 1980, Parachute Anchoring, 1982. Active on Rep. Presdl. Task Force, Washington, 1989. With Hungarian Comm., 1951-53. Named hon. citizen La Rochelle, France, 1984. Mem. Boating Writers Internat., Chesapeake Cruising Assn. (hon. life mem.), New Eng. Multihyll Assn. (commodore 1975-79). Office: Multihulls Mag 421 Hancock St Quincy MA 02171-2435

CHIODO, VINCENT ROBERT, consumer products company executive; b. N.Y.C., Aug. 18, 1955; s. Rudolph John and Mary Ann C. BA, NYU, 1979; MBA, Fordham U., 1987. Project dir. AHF Mktg. Research, N.Y.C., 1977-79; acct. exec. Decisions Ctr., Inc., N.Y.C., 1979-80; supr. market research Colgate-Palmolive, N.Y.C., 1980-84; mgr. group research Bristol-Myers Products, N.Y.C., 1984-86, mgr. group product, new products, 1986-90, dir. mktg., new products, 1990-91; category dir. analgesics, 1991—. Mem. Am. Mktg. Assn. (treas. 1982-84, bd. dirs. 1984-86). Home: 571 Fairmount Ave Chatham NJ 07928-1372

CHIOGIOJI, MELVIN HIROAKI, government official; b. Hiroshima, Japan, Aug. 21, 1939; came to U.S., 1939; s. Yutaka and Harumi (Yamasaki) C.; m. Eleanor Nobuko Oura, June 4, 1960; children: Wendy A., Alan K. B.S. in Elec. Engring., Purdue U., 1961; M.B.A., U. Hawaii, 1968; D.Bus. Adminstrn., George Washington U., 1972. Registered profl. engr., Hawaii. Head weapons gen. component div. Quality Evaluation Lab., Oahu, Hawaii, 1965-69; dir. weapons evaluation and engring. div. Naval Ordinance Systems Command, Washington, 1969-73; dir. Office Indsl. Analysis Fed. Energy Adminstrn., Washington, 1973-75; asst. dir., div. bldg. and community systems Dept. Energy, Washington, 1975-79, dir. fed. program div., 1980—, dep. asst. sec. state and local assistance program, 1980-85, dir. office of transp. systems, 1985-90, constrn. mgr. Office of New Prodn. Realtors, 1990—; pres. EFC, Inc., 1980—, Precision Auto Care, Inc., 1989—; prof. mgmt. sci. George Washington U., 1972—. Author: Industrial Energy Conservation, 1979, Energy Conservation in Commercial and Residental Buildings, 1982; contbr. articles to profl. jours. Mem. Md. State Adv. Com. on Civil Rights, 1976—; mem. Nat. Naval Res. Policy Bd., 1977—; vestryman Grace Episcopal Ch., Silver Spring, Md., 1982—. Served with USN, 1961-65; rear adm. USNR. Decorated Navy Commendation medal, Meritorious Svc. medal, Legion Merit medal. Mem. IEEE (sr.), Nat. Soc. Profl. Engrs., Acad. Mgmt., Naval Res. Assn., Assn. for Sci., Tech. and Innovation (pres. 1979-81), Soc. Am. Mil. Engrs., Armed Forces Mgmt. Assn., Purdue U. Alumni Assn. Home: 15113 Middlegate Rd Silver Spring MD 20905-5720 Office: 1000 Independence Ave SE Washington DC 20585-0001

CHIORAZZI, NICHOLAS, immunologist educator; b. Weehawken, N.J., Oct. 2, 1945; s. Joseph P. and Mary L. (Ippolito) C.; m. M. Lorraine Dziadowicz, June 19, 1971; children: Anne, Michael. BA, Holy Cross Coll., 1966; MD, Georgetown U., 1970. Intern Cornell Cooperating Hosps., Manhasset, N.Y., 1970-71, resident in medicine, 1971-74; post doctoral fellow in immunology Harvard U. Med. Sch., Boston, 1974-76; post doctoral fellow in clin. immunology Rockefeller U., N.Y.C., 1976-77; asst. prof. The Rockefeller U., 1977-82, assoc. prof., 1982-87, dep. head lab. immunology, 1984-87; prof. medicine Cornell U., N.Y.C., 1987—; chief rheumatology and immunology North Shore U. Hosp., Manhasset, 1987—. Contbr. 75 articles to profl. jours. NIH grantee, 1980—. Fellow ACP, Am. Coll. Rheumatology; mem. Am. Soc. for Clin. Investigators, Am. Assn. Immunologists. Office: North Shore Univ Hosp 300 Community Dr Manhasset NY 11030-3800

CHIPKEVICH, EDWARD ALBERT, JR., counselor; b. Hazleton, Pa., Dec. 9, 1946; s. Edward Albert and Mary Agnes (Ragan) C. AAS in Criminal Justice, Luzerne County Community Coll., Nanticoke, Pa., 1984; AAS in Fire Sci. Technol., LCCC, Nanticoke, Pa., 1985; BA in Criminal Justice, King's Coll., 1991. Program clk. USDA, Sybertsville, Pa., 1985-89; asst. health officer Dept. of Health, Hazleton, Pa., 1990; peer counselor Anthracite Region Ctr. for Ind. Living, Ltd., Hazleton, Pa., 1990—; rehab. counselor trainee Rehab. Svcs. Adminstrn., Scranton, Pa., 1991—; dir. ARCIL, Ltd., Hazleton, 1991—; parish advocate Diocese of Scranton, 1991—. Mem. Holy Name Soc., Hazleton, 1970, Knight of Lithuania, 1988. Recipient Eagle Scout award Boy Scouts of Am., 1963, Cert. of Merit, USDA, 1989, Acad. award Act 101 King's Coll., 1991, Cert. of Achievement, Operation Overcome, 1991, Rehab. Counseling stipend, 1991. Mem. Am. Assn. for Counseling and Devel. Republican. Roman Catholic. Home: 858 N Locust St Hazleton PA 18201 Office: Anthracite Region Ctr for Ind Living Ltd 40 N Church St Hazleton PA 18201

CHIRBAN, JOHN THOMAS, psychologist, theologian, educator; b. Chgo., June 24, 1951; s. Thomas Angelo and Georgia (Kappos) C. BA, Hellenic Coll., Brookline, Mass., 1973; MDiv, Holy Cros Sch. Theology, 1976; ThM, Harvard U., 1976, ThD, 1980; PhD, Boston U., 1990. Lic. psychologist, Mass.; diplomate and fellow Am. Bd. Med. Psychotherapists. Researcher Harvard U., Cambridge, Mass., 1974-75; geriatric tng. specialist Dept. Mental Health, Boston, 1978-79; cons. Mass. Disabilities Commn., Boston, 1979-84; psychologist Andover (Mass.) Psychol. Svcs., 1986-89, Mass. Corrections Inst., Boston, 1986-88; sr. lectr. Northeastern U., Boston, 1979—; cons. Mass. Rehab. Commn., Boston, 1980—; dir. Cambridge Counseling Assocs., 1983—; assoc. Harvard U., Cambridge, 1980—; co-dir. counseling and spiritual devel. Hellenic Coll. Holy Cross, 1978—, prof., 1975—; prof. Hellenic Coll. Holy Cross, 1975—. Mem. APA, Mass. Psychol. Assn., also others. Greek Orthodox. Home: 103 Potter Pond Lexington MA 02173-8251 Office: 1105 Massachusetts Ave Apt 3E Cambridge MA 02138-5207

CHIRLIAN, PAUL MICHAEL, electrical engineering educator; b. N.Y.C., Apr. 29, 1930; S. Gustave and Leonora (Morrison) C.; m. Barbara Ellen Schein, Aug. 27, 1961; children: Lisa Emily, Peter Jonathan. BEE, NYU, 1950, MEE, 1952, DSc in Engring., 1956. Instr. NYU, N.Y.C., 1951-57, asst. prof. elec. engring., 1957-60; assoc. prof. elec. engring. Stevens Inst. Tech., Hoboken, N.J., 1960-65, prof., 1965-85, Anson Wood Burchard prof. elec. engring., 1985—; cons. in field. Author: Analysis and Design of Integrated Electronic Circuits, 1986; author 30 textbooks and contbr. numerous articles to profl. jours. Recipient Great Tchr. award Stevens Inst.

Tech. Fellow IEEE; mem. Am. Soc. Engring. Edn., Sigma Xi, Tau Beta Pi, Eta Kappa Nu. Office: Stevens Inst of Tech Castle Pt Hoboken NJ 07030

CHISHOLM, CAROL LEE, research psychologist; b. Abington, Pa., Mar. 19, 1938; d. Lawrence and Gertrude Evelyn (Macdonald) Christianson; m. Franklin Donald Chisholm, June 10, 1956 (dec. May 1978); children: Jennifer Anne, Stephen Donald. BS in Edn., State Tchrs. Coll., Towson, Md., 1962; MA in Psychology, Towson State U., 1981; PhD in Psychology, U. Del., 1986. Elem. sch. tchr. Balt. County Bd. Edn., 1962-66, tutor, home tchr., 1966-68; instr. Towson State U., 1979-81, U. Del., 1981-85; psychologist, cons. Balt. Gas and Electric Co., 1980-87, computer applications coordinator, 1987-88; rsch. psychologist U.S. Govt., Washington, 1988—. Mem. Friends Nat. Zoo, Washington, Smithsonian Resident Assocs., Washington; screening com. Am. Field Svc., Balt.; workshop presenter Lutheran Ch. Named Outstanding Grad. Student in Psychology, Towson State U., 1981, Faculty award, Psychology Dept., 1981. Mem. Am. Psychol. Assn., Ea. Psychol. Assn., Soc. for Indsl./Orgnl. Psychology, Pers. Testing Coun. Met. Washington, Phi Kappa Phi. Home: 12423 Wolbert Way Bradshaw MD 21021-1950

CHISM, JOHN ROSS, author; b. Chgo., Mar. 19, 1954; s. Lafayette Ross and Miriam Joan (Beckman) C. BS, Northwestern U., 1976; pvt. study acting, Alvina Krause, Bloomsburg, Pa., 1976-77. Word processor operator Cahill Gordon Reindel, N.Y.C., 1984—. Author: Two Seasons, 1985, Secrets in a Young Man's Heart, 1989, The Narcissus Flower Has Many Colors, 1989, Narcissus, Chrysippus, Achilles, 1990-91; actor Bloomsburg Theatre Ensemble, 1978, 84, dir., 1980. Activist, writer AIDS Project/L.A., 1983; archivist Am. AIDS Found., N.Y.C., 1987, AIDS Coalition to Unleash Power, N.Y.C., 1989. Home: 63 Montague St 1-R New York NY 11201

CHITTICK, DAVID RUPERT, telecommunications executive; b. Boston, Jan. 2, 1934; s. Rupert Addison and Evelyn Florence (Bradley) C.; m. Eileen Elizabeth Ashley, Oct. 12, 1957; children: Bradley David, Allison Ashley. BSEE, U. Vt., 1955; MS, MIT, 1969. Divestiture v.p. We. Elec. Co., Morristown, N.J., 1983-84; gen. mgr. engring. design and constrn. AT&T, N.Y.C., 1984-86; sr. v.p. Resource Mgmt. Corp. AT&T, Basking Ridge, N.J., 1985-86, engring. v.p., 1986—; pres., chmn. bd. Industry Coop. for Ozone Layer Protection, Inc., 1990—; bd. dirs. AT&T Resource Mgmt. Corp., 1987—, Am. Ridge Ins. Co., 1990—, Environ. Law Inst., 1991—. Mem. Stratospheric Ozone Protection Adv. Coun. EPA, 1989—, Corp. Conservation Coun. Nat. Wildlife Fedn., 1990—; bd. dirs. World Environment Ctr., 1991—, Mgmt. Inst. for Environment and Bus., 1991—. A.P. Sloan fellow, 1986. Mem. Environ. Mgmt. Roundtable (chmn. steering com.), World Environment Ctr., Mgmt. Inst. Environ. & Bus., Aircraft Owners and Pilots Assn. Republican. Episcopalian. Office: 131 Morristown Rd Basking Ridge NJ 07920-8700

CHIU, HUNGDAH, lawyer, legal educator; b. Shanghai, China, Mar. 23, 1936; came to U.S., 1960; s. Han-ping and Ming-non (Yang) C.; m. Yuan-yuan Hsieh, May 14, 1966; 1 son, Wei-hsueh. LLB, Nat. Taiwan U., 1958; MA with honors, L.I. U., 1962; LLM, Harvard U., 1962, SJD, 1965. Assoc. in rsch. East Asian Research Center; asso. in research Harvard U., 1964-65; assoc. prof. internat. law Nat. Taiwan U., 1965-66; rsch. assoc. in law Harvard U., 1966-70, 72-74; vis. prof. law Nat. Chengchi U., Taipei, Taiwan, 1970-72; assoc. prof. law U. Md., Balt., 1974-77; prof. U. Md., 1977—. Author: The Capacity of International Organizations to Conclude Treaties, 1966, The People's Republic of China and the Law of Treaties, 1972, (with J.A. Cohen) People's China and International Law, 2 vols, 1974 (certificate of merit Am. Soc. Internat. Law 1976), Normalizing Relations with China: Problems, Analysis and Documents, 1978, China and the Taiwan Issue, 1979, Agreements of the People's Republic of China, 1966-80, A Calendar of Events, 1981; (with S.C. Leng) China: 70 years after the 1911 Hsin-Hai Revolution, 1984, Criminal Justice in Post-Mao China, 1985, (with Y.C. Jao and Y.L. Wu) The Future of Hong Kong, 1987, The Draft Basic Law of Hong Kong: Analysis and Documents, 1988, (with G. Knight) International Law of the Sea: Cases, Documents and Readings, 1991; contbr. numerous articles to profl. jours., chpts. to books; gen. editor: Contemporary Asian Studies, 1976—; editor in chief Chinese Yearbook of Internat. Law and Affairs, 1981—. Del. UN Conf. Law of the Sea, 1976-82 Served to 2d lt. Chinese Army, 1958-60. Named One of 10 Outstanding Young Men Jr. C. of C. of Republic of China, 1971; Social Sci. Research Council fellow, 1968; recipient Cultural award Inst. Chinese Culture, 1980, Toulmin medal Soc. Am. Mil. Engrs., 1982; Nat. Reconstrn. award Chinese Profl. Assn. Mid-Am., 1980. Mem. Am. Soc. Internat. Law (panel on China and internat. order 1969-74, chmn. interest group on law Pacific region 1987—), Assn. for Asian Studies (com. on Asian law 1976-79), Am. Assn. for Chinese Studies (v.p. 1982-84, pres. 1985-87), Assn. Am. Law Schs. (chair internat. legal exchange sect. 1986-88), Assn. Chinese Social Scientists, N.A. (pres. 1984-86). Home: 6168 Devon Dr Columbia MD 21044-3821 Office: U Md Law Sch 500 W Baltimore St Baltimore MD 21201-1786

CHIU, JEN-FU, biochemistry educator; b. Tungshi, Taichung, Taiwan, Sept. 30, 1940; came to U.S., 1972; s. Kuo-Feng and Ching-Leon (Yu) C.; m. Lucia Chi-Kai Yin, May 30, 1970; children: Rosaleen I-Hsuen, Cynthia I-Tyng. B Pharmacy, Taipei (Taiwan) Med. Coll., 1964; MS in Biochemistry, Nat. Taiwan U., Taipei, 1967; PhD in Biochemistry, U. B.C., 1972. Asst. biochemist U. Tex. System Cancer Ctr. M.D. Anderson Hosp. & Tumor Inst., Houston, 1974-75; asst. prof. Vanderbilt U., Nashville, 1975-78; assoc. prof. U. Vt., Burlington, 1978-87, prof. biochemistry, 1987—; cons. NIH, Bethesda, Md., 1983-86; dir. grad. studies in biochemistry U. Vt., Burlington, 1982—, dir. cancer biology program, 1983—; rsch. fellow Chinese Nat. Sci. Coun., Taiwan, 1966, Rosalie B Hite Found., Houston, 1972. Author, editor: The Basic of Cancer Molecular Biology, 1989; contbr. more than 126 sci. papers to pubis. Lt. Chinese ROTC, 1966-67, Taiwan. Rsch. grantee NIH, Bethesda, Md., 1975—, March of Dimes, Whiteplain, N.Y., 1978-80. Mem. Am. Soc. Biochemistry and Molecular Biology, Am. Soc. Cell Biology, Am. Assn. Cancer Rsch., Am. Soc. Microbiology, Soc. Chinese Biochemists in Am. (pres. Vt. chpt. 1989—). Office: U Vt Coll Medicine Dept Biochemistry Burlington VT 05405-0068

CHIU, PETER JIUNN-SHYONG, pharmacologist; b. Miao-LI, Taiwan, China, June 9, 1942; came to U.S., 1967; s. Uh-Tsuen and May-May (Hsu) C.; m. Peggy Tsui-Fang Tseng, Aug. 31, 1967; children: Vivian, Faye, Peter. BS in Pharmacy, Taipei Med. Coll., 1964; MS in Pharmacology, Nat. Taiwan U., 1966; PhD in Pharmacology, Columbia U., 1972. Postdoctoral fellow U. Pa., Phila., 1972-74; from sr. scientist to sr. prin. scientist Schering Corp., Bloomfield, N.J., 1974-85; sect. leader Schering-Plough Corp., Bloomfield, 1986-89; rsch. fellow Schering-Plough Rsch. Inst., Bloomfield, 1989—. Contbr. articles to profl. jours. Lt. Chinese Paratroopers, 1966-67. Mem. Am. Soc. Pharmacol. Exptl. Therapists, Am. Physiol. Soc., Am. Soc. Nehprology, Am. Heart Assn. (kidney coun. 1985—, hypertension coun. 1987—), Am. Fedn. Clin. Researchers, Soc. Chinese Bioscientists Am. Republican. Office: Schering-Plough Rsch Inst 60 Orange St Bloomfield NJ 07003

CHIVERS, JAMES LEEDS, lawyer; b. Pitts., Jan. 8, 1939; s. Joseph Hobart and Lorraine Anna (Silhol) C.; m. Patricia Ann Dolan, Sept. 3, 1960; children: Catherine Ann, Christopher John, Matthew Leeds. AB, Colgate U., 1960; LLB cum laude, Union U., Albany, N.Y., 1967. Bar: N.Y. 1967, U.S. Dist. Ct. (no. dist.) N.Y. 1967, U.S. Ct. Appeals (2d cir.) 1982, Fla. 1987, U.S. Dist. Ct. (so. and ea. dists.) N.Y. 1988, U.S. Supreme Ct. 1989. Assoc. Hinman, Howard & Kattell, Binghamton, N.Y., 1967-75, ptnr., 1975—, ptnr.-in-charge dept. litigation, 1981—; mem. arbitration panel Binghamton City Ct. Past pres. Vol. Am., Binghamton, bd. dirs. 1969—. Lt. USNR, 1960-64, Vietnam. Mem. ABA (tort and ins. practice sect.), Internat. Def. Counsel, Am. Arbitration Assn. (panel arbitrators), Assn. Trial Lawyers Am., Def. Rsch. Assn., N.Y. State Bar Assn. (ins., negligence and compensation, trial lawyers, environment, comml. and fed. litigation sects.), Broome County Bar Assn., Broome County C. of C., Justinian Soc., Binghamton Club (pres. 1987-89), Found. of SUNY-Binghamton, Harpur Forum, Am. Legion. Republican. Roman Catholic. Office: Hinman Howard & Kattell 700 Security Mutual Bldg Binghamton NY 13901

CHIZMADIA, STEPHEN MARK, lawyer, educator; b. Perth Amboy, N.J., June 19, 1950; s. Stephen Thomas and Madeline Cecilia (Vojack) C.; m. Gail Farina, June 23, 1988; 1 child (stepson) Keith. BA in Econs., U. Pa., 1971; MS in Mgmt., N.J. Inst. Tech., 1975; JD with honors, N.Y. Law Sch., 1977. Bar: N.J. 1977, U.S. Dist. Ct. N.J. 1977, Fla. 1978, N.Y. 1980, U.S. Dist. Ct. (so. and ea. dists.) N.Y. 1981. Assoc. Hampson & Millet, P.C., Somerset, N.J., 1978; pvt. practice law New Brunswick, N.J., 1979-80; counsel Home Ins. Co., Short Hills, N.J., 1980-81; assoc. John M. Downing, P.C., N.Y.C., 1981-84, Schneider, Kleinick & Weitz, P.C., N.Y.C., 1984-90; pvt. practice N.Y.C. and, N.J., 1990—; arbitrator small claims N.Y.C. Civil Ct., 1986—, arbitrator U.S. Dist. Ct. (ea. dist.) N.Y., 1987—; hearing officer small claims assessment rev. N.Y. State Supreme Ct. (9th jud. cir.), 1989—; lectr. legal topics profl. seminars; adj. instr. law and bus. mgmt. Middlesex County Coll., 1978-80; instr. paralegal program Sobelsohn Sch., N.Y.C., 1989—. Bd. dir. Raritan Bay (N.J.) Area YMCA, 1980-86, N.J. Inst. Tech. Alumni Coun., 1987—. Recipient Am. Jurisprudence award, 1977, several community svc. awards. Mem. N.J. Bar Assn., N.Y. State Bar Assn., Fla. Bar Assn., Am. Judicature Soc., Internat. Platform Assn., Toastmasters Internat., N.J. Inst. Tech. Alumni Coun. Home: 125 Sun Dance Rd Stamford CT 06905-1714 Office: 599 Amboy Ave Perth Amboy NJ 08861-2577

CHMARA, PAUL NICHOLAS, assistant principal; b. East Liverpool, Ohio, Jan. 14, 1954; s. Paul and Mary (Chuldenko) C.; m. Sherry Dianne Smith, June 19, 1982; 1 child, Kara Dianne. BS in Art Edn., Edinboro U., 1976; M in Art Teaching, Carnegie-Mellon U., 1979; elem. prin. cert., Youngstown U., 1979; PhD in Edn. Adminstrn., U. Pitts., 1989. Tchr. art. Seneca Valley Sch. Dist., Harmony, Pa., 1976-89, instr. staff devel., 1989; grad. asst. U. Pitts., 1987-89; asst. prin. North Allegheny Sch. Dist., Pitts., 1989—; cons. supt. stress and conflict U. Pitts., 1989-90. Represented in permanent collection; author lithograph Teachers Wardrobe (merit award 1990); exhibited in two-person show, 1992. Bd. dirs. Historic Harmony Inc., 1989—. Recipient numerous nat. and regional art awards, 1985. Mem. ASCD, Pa. Elem. Prin. Assn., Associated Artists Pitts., Nat. Elem. Prin. Assn., Phi Delta Kappa, Kappa Delta Phi. Democrat. Home: 755 Spring St Harmony PA 16037 Office: North Allegheny Sch Dist 500 Cumberland Rd Pittsburgh PA 15237

CHMIELINSKI, EDWARD ALEXANDER, electronics company executive; b. Waterbury, Conn., Mar. 25, 1925; s. Stanley and Helen C.; m. Elizabeth Carew, May 30, 1946; children: Nancy, Elizabeth, Susan Jean. BS, Tulane U., 1950; postgrad. Colo. U., 1965. V.p., gen. mgr. Clifton Products, Litton Industries, Colorado Springs, Colo., 1965-67; pres. Memory Products div. Litton Industries, Beverly Hills, Calif., 1967-69, Bowmar Instruments, Can., Ottawa, Ont., 1969-73; gen. mgr. Leigh Instruments, Carleton Pl., Ont., 1973-75; pres., dir. Lewis Engring. Co., Naugatuck, Conn., 1975-85; pres., dir. Liquidometer Corp., Tampa, Fla., 1975-85; pres. Lewis div. Colt Industries, 1985-90; ret. Pres., Acad. Water Bd., 1963-65; bd. dirs. United Way, Colorado Springs, 1965-67; fellow Tulane U. Pres.'s Council. Served with USN, 1943-46. Mem. C. of C., Pres.'s Council, Nat. Mfrs. Assn., IEEE, Air Force Assn., Navy League, Nat. Aero. Assn., Am. Helicopter Soc.

CHO, SUNG YOON, law librarian; b. Shinuiju, Pyongan Pukto, Republic of Korea, Sept. 10, 1928; came to U.S., 1955; s. Bong Soon Cho and Yong Soon Kim; m. Won Kyung Bae, Oct. 20, 1962 (dec. Nov. 1982); children: David, Margaret; m. Kyung Soo Kim, Aug. 31, 1985. LLB, Seoul (Republic of Korea) Nat. U., 1953; MA, Tulane U., 1957, PhD, 1963; M in Comparative Law, George Washington U., 1966. Korean atty. Civil Assistance Command UN, Seoul, 1953-55; legal specialist Korean and Japanese law Far Ea. Law div. Libr. of Congress, Washington, 1959-68, sr. legal specialist, 1968-77, asst. to chief, 1977-83, asst. chief, 1983—; cons. Rsch. Analysis Corp., McLean, Va., 1968-71. Author: Asian Survey, 1971, Japanese Writings on Communist Chinese Law, 1977, Law and Legal Literature of North Korea: A Guide, 1988; contbr. articles to profl. jours. Chmn. bd. trustees Korean Ch. Greater Washington, McLean, 1980-82, chmn. adminstrv. bd., 1988-90. Mem. Internat. Assn. Law Librs., Am. Soc. Internat. Law, Am. Assn. Law Librs. (com. fgn. law indexing 1973-79), Assn. Asian Studies (com. Asian law 1982-86), Japanese-Am. Soc. Legal Studies. Methodist. Office: Libr Congress Far Ea Law Div 101 Independence Ave SE Washington DC 20540-0001

CHO, YOUNG IL, mechanical engineering educator; b. Seoul, Nov. 26, 1949; came to U.S., 1976; s. Sungshik and Keunsook (Oh) C.; m. Sunyoung Uhm, Oct. 6, 1973; children: Joseph, Daniel. BS, Seoul Nat. U., 1972; MBA, Korea U., 1975; MS, U. Ill., Chgo., 1977, PhD, 1980. Rsch. fellow Energy Resources Ctr., U. Ill., Chgo., 1980-81; mem. tech. staff Jet Propulsion Lab., Calif. Inst. Tech., Pasadena, 1981-85; prof. dept. mech. engring. and mechanics Drexel U., Phila., 1985-91, prof., 1992—. Author: Advances in Heat Transfer, 1982, Handbook of Heat Transfer, 1985; editor Advances in Heat Transfer, 1991—; contbr. articles toprofl. jours. Awardee NASA, 1988; Lindback award of Excellence in Teaching; grantee NSF, 1987, NASA, 1988, Dept. Energy, 1989-91. Mem. ASME, Am. Electrophoresis Soc., Electrochem. Soc. Am., Am. Physics Soc., Korean Scientists and Engrs. in Am. Home: 8 Niamoa Dr Cherry Hill NJ 08003-1219 Office: Drexel U Dept Mech Engring 32d and Chestnut Sts Philadelphia PA 19104

CHOATE, ALBERT GEORGE, research physicist, science administrator; b. Buffalo, Apr. 28, 1947; s. Wilson S. and Bernice J. (Stephan) C.; m. Julie A. Gayk, July 17, 1976; children: Antares G., Bethany J. BS in Optics, U. Rochester, 1969. V.p. R&D Optical Gaging Products, Rochester, 1973—. Author: Core of Creation, 1982, Fundamental Geometrical Formulations of the Universe, 1989. Democrat. Home: PO Box 428 Rush NY 14543-0428 Office: Optical Gaging Products 850 Hudson Ave Rochester NY 14621-4839

CHOCK, ALVIN KEALI'I, retired botanist; b. Honolulu, June 18, 1931; s. Hon and Eleanor Kam Hoon (Au) C.; AA, Hannibal-LaGrange Coll. (Mo.), 1949; BA, U. Hawaii at Manoa, 1951, MS in Botany, 1953; postgrad. U. Mich., 1953-55, U.S. Dept. Agr. Grad. Sch., 1959, Pacific Asian Mgmt. Inst., U. Hawaii at Manoa, 1990; m. Yona Nahenahe Bielefeldt, June 18, 1962; children: T. Makana, D. 'Alana, D. Malama. Tech. adminstrv. asst. European Exchange Svc., Katterbach bei Ansbach/Mfr., Fed. Republic Ger., 1958-59; plant quarantine insp. Agrl. Rsch. Svc., U.S. Dept. Agr., N.Y.C., 1959-60, Honolulu, 1961-67, supervisory insp., Balt., 1967-70; program specialist Office of Pesticide Programs, EPA, Washington, 1970-71, supervisory program specialist, 1971-74, supervisory biologist, 1975; agrl. officer (plant quarantine) FAO, Rome, 1975-78, also tech. sec. Near East Plant Protection Commn. and Caribbean Plant Protection Commn., 1976; supervisory biologist, registration div. Office of Pesticide Programs, EPA, Washington, 1978-81; acting coord. internat. programs Plant Protection and Quarantine, Animal and Plant Health Inspection Svc. Dept. Agr., Hyattsville, Md., 1981-82, dir. Region II (Europe, Near East and Africa), 1981-82, The Hague, Netherlands, 1982-88; dir. region III (Asia and Pacific), Hyattsville, Md., 1988-92; lectr. botany U. Hawaii, Manoa, 1961-67, 69, 72, 79, 84, 86, 88, 90, 93; asst. botanist B.P. Bishop Mus., Honolulu, 1961-65; botanist Kokee Natural History Mus., Hawaii, 1953-55; bot. cons. Nat. Park Svc., 1962-63; mem. work panels European and Mediterranean Plant Protection Orgn., Paris, 1976-78. Mem. governing bd. Nat. Conf. State Socs., Washington, 1972-75, dep. dir. gen., 1973-74, 2d v.p., 1974-75; governing bd. Asian Pacific Am. Heritage Council, Inc., 1979-81, 88-92; sec. PTA, Overseas Sch. Rome, 1976-77; USDA rep., 1988, observer, 1990-91, governing bd. Am. Fgn. Svc. Assn. Served with inf. U.S. Army, 1955-57. Plant species Cyanea chockii named in his honor; recipient other awards in field. Mem. Hawaiian Acad. Sci. (dir. jr. acad. 1963-64), Lloyd Shaw Found., Assn. Tropical Biology (charter), Hawaiian Bot. Soc. (sec. 1962, dir. 1963, 65, pres. 1964), Internat. Assn. Plant Taxonomists, Pacific Sci. Assn., Soc. Econ. Botany, FAO Assn. Profl. Staff (appeals and procedures com. 1976-77, standing com. career devel. 1976-78), Nat. Capital Area Square Dance Leaders Assn. (editor newsletter 1980-81), Callerlab (traditional dance com., contra com. 1981—), Mediterranean Area Callers and Tchrs. Assn. (founder; publicity dir. 1977-78), European Callers and Tchrs. Assn., Hawaii State Soc. of D.C. (dir. 1968-69, 88-91, 1st v.p. 1969-71, pres. 1971-72, adv. 1978-79, 2d v.p. 1979-80), Am. Square Dance Soc., Folklore Soc. Greater Washington, Consumers Union, Bishop Mus. Assn., Bairich und Steirisch, Sigma Xi. Club: Ramblin' Romans Sq. Dance (founder). Founding editor Hawaii Bot. Soc. newsletter, 1962-63, 66; editor Fed. Plant Quarantine Insps. Nat. Assn. newsletter, 1963-65, Ka Nupepa, 1968-71; chmn. editorial com. FAO Plant Protection Bull., 1976-78; contbg. author books; editor: (with G. L. Addicott) Favorite Songs of the Hawaii State Society, 1973; contbr. articles to profl. jours. Home: 1515 Farrington St Honolulu HI 96822-3321

CHOCK, P. BOON, chemist researcher; b. Medan, Sumatra, Indonesia, Mar. 26, 1939; came to U.S., 1959; s. Ngiap Tjing and Djoei (Tjang) C.; m. Phyllis Ann Pease; 1 child, Johanna Y. BA, Northwestern U., 1963; MS, Stanford U., 1965; PhD, U. Chgo., 1967. Postdoctoral fellow Max-Planck Inst. für Biophysikalishe Chemie, Göttigen, Fed. Republic of Germany, 1968-71; postdoctoral fellow in chemistry U. Chgo., 1968; vis. scientist Nat. Heart & Lung Inst./NIH, Bethesda, Md., 1971-73, rsch. chemist, 1973-80, chief sect. on metabolic regulation, 1981—. Editor: Modulation by Coolant Modification, 1985, Enzyme Dynamics and Regulation, 1988, (series) Current Topics in Cellular Regulation, 1988—; contbr. over 100 articles to profl. jours. Office: NIH Bldg # 3 Rm 202 Bethesda MD 20892

CHODOROW, MARC, public relations executive, educator; b. Buffalo, Jan. 26, 1951; s. Wilfred and Claire (Harnick) C.; (div.); 5 children. BA, SUNY, Buffalo, 1973. Assoc. dir. Media Study of Buffalo, 1973-77; news dir. Sta. WBFO-FM, Buffalo, 1977-81; exec. producer Sta. WEBR/News Radio, Buffalo, 1981-83; v.p. corp. communications Goldome, Buffalo, 1983-89; pres. Chodorow Assocs. Ltd., Buffalo, 1989—; adj. prof. SUNY, 1981—. Bd. dirs. Life Transition Ctr., Buffalo, 1991—, Torah Temimah Sch., Buffalo, 1991—, Greater Buffalo Coun. on Alcoholism, 1986—, also v.p. Named Journalist of Distinction, AP, 1982, UPI, 1983. Mem. Greater Buffalo Coun. on Alcoholism (v.p. 1986—). Jewish. Office: Chodorow Assocs Ltd 1576 Sweet Home Rd Baird Rsch Park Amherst NY 14228

CHOI, JONGMOO JAY, finance educator; b. Seoul, Korea, Dec. 4, 1945; arrived U.S., 1969; s. Hyung Joon and Tai Im (Kim) C.; m. B. Eunyup Lee, Mar. 20, 1971; children—Raymond, Jason. B.B.A., Seoul Nat. U., 1968; M.B.A., NYU, 1974, Ph.D., 1980. Instr., NYU, 1979-80; vis. asst. prof. Columbia U., 1980-81; economist Chase Manhattan Bank, N.Y.C., 1981-82; adj. assoc. prof. fin., internat. bus. NYU, 1982-87; prof. fin. Temple U., 1983—; vis. faculty U. Pa., U. Hawaii, Internat. U. of Japan, 1987-91; cons. to various corps.; research asst. and assoc. Nat. Bur. Econ. Research, 1978-79; fin. analyst N.Y.C. Govt. Agy., 1973-75; internat. banking officer Korea Exchange Bank, 1968-73. Assoc. editor Internat. Jour. of Fin., Jour. of Econ. and Bus.; contbr. articles to scholarly jours. Korean-Am. Found. fellow, NYU Multinat. Corps. Project grant, Temple U. Disting. Faculty Rsch. fellow. Mem. Am. Econ. Assn., Am. Fin. Assn., Fin. Mgmt. Assn., Acad. Internat. Bus. Home: 516 Lexington Ln Norristown PA 19403-1207 Office: Temple U Sch Bus Adminstrn Philadelphia PA 19122

CHOLAKIS, CONSTANTINE GEORGE, judge; b. Troy, N.Y., Oct. 6, 1930; s. George Nicholas and Katine (Dukas) C.; m. Dassie Michaels, June 16, 1957; children: George D., Catherine, Gregory D. BA in Sociology, Siena Coll., 1955; JD, Albany Law Sch., 1958. Bar: N.Y., 1958. Pvt. practice law Troy, 1958-70; dist. atty. County of Rensselaer, Troy, 1968-74, judge county Ct., 1974-77; justice N.Y. Supreme Ct. (3d jud. dist.), Troy, 1978-86; judge U.S. Dist. Ct. (no. dist.) N.Y., Albany, 1986—; asst. dist. atty. County of Rensselaer, 1963-65, asst. pub. defender, 1966-67. Served to sgt. USMC, 1951-53, Korea. Republican. Greek Orthodox. Home: 17 Pasture Ln Troy NY 12180-7720 Office: US Dist Ct 445 Broadway PO Box 278 Albany NY 12201

CHOLODOWSKI, SISTER ANTONIA MARIE, religious organization administrator; b. Norwich, Conn., Aug. 8, 1932; d. Dominic Francis and Joanna Mary (Przekop) C. BA, Holy Family Coll., 1962; MS Counselor of Edn., Marywood Coll., 1973. Joined Sisters of the Holy Family of Nazareth, Roman Cath. Ch., 1950; cert. elem. tchr. Tchr. St. John Cantius Sch., Phila., 1953-60, St. Mary Sch., Ambler, Pa., 1960-67; child care worker St. Mary Villa for Children, Ambler, 1960-67; prin. Queen of Peace Sch., Ardsley, Pa., 1967-73, Our Lady Calvary Sch., Phila., 1973-79; dir. ministry Sisters of the Holy Family of Nazareth, Phila., 1979-90; asst. adminstr. St. Mary Villa for Children, Ambler, Pa., 1990—, trustee, 1979-90. Trustee Nazareth Hosp., Phila., 1979-90, Holy Family Coll., Phila., 1979-90, Nazareth Acad., Phila., 1979-90. Home and Office: St Mary Villa for Children Bethlehem Pike Ambler PA 19002

CHOMAN, THOMAS BOHDAN, trade association executive; b. Hackensack, N.J., Jan. 20, 1959; s. Bohdan Russell and Theresa Marie (Burchock) C.; m. Michelle Maria Acculto, Oct. 4, 1986; 1 child, Sara Lucinda. BA, U. Del., 1981; MA, Am. U., 1982. Assoc. editor Coal Outlook Newsletter, Arlington, Va., 1984-86; editor Energy Report, Arlington, 1986-90; dir. Congl. and pub. rels. Nat. Assn. Regulatory Utility Commrs., Washington, 1990—. Vol. tutor No. Va. Literacy Coun., Fairfax, 1983, St. Charles Cath. Ch., Arlington, 1985-86. Mem. Soc. Profl. Journalists, Alpha Phi Omega (sec. Zeta Sigma chpt. 1979-80). Roman Catholic. Office: Nat Assn Regulatory Utilities Commrs 12th and Constitution NW Washington DC 20044

CHONG, SHUI-FONG, graphic designer; b. Canton, China, Dec. 19, 1954; came to U.S., 1971; s. Muk-Wing and Kau-Mui C. BA, CUNY, 1978; postgrad., Sch. Visual Art, CNYC, 1978-79, Parsons Sch. Design, NYC, 1979-82. Asst. art dir. Schein/Blattstein Advt., Inc., N.Y.C., 1978-79; asst. art dir. Creative Decisions, Inc., N.Y.C., 1979-81, H/T Graphic Design, Inc., N.Y.C., 1981-82; graphic designer H/T Graphic Design, Inc., Kwasha Lipton, N.J., 1982-87; prin., graphic designer Shui-Fong Chong Design, N.Y.C., 1982—. Recipient Excellence award N.Y. Internat. Assn. Bus. Communication, N.Y.C., 1985, Best of Sch. winner Visual Art Competition, N.Y.C., 1973. Mem. Art Dirs. Club, Graphic Artists Guild, Am. Inst. Graphic Arts.

CHOPE, ROBERT WILLIAM, state official; b. Phila., July 14, 1952; s. Theodore William and Mary Elizabeth (Davies) C.; m. Elizabeth Ann Hodgkinson, Aug. 16, 1975; 1 child, Susan Elizabeth. BA, Rider Coll., 1974, MA, 1982. Project adminstr. County of Bucks, Pa. Office Community Devel., Doylestown, 1974-80; contract analyst III Southeastern Pa. Trans. Authority (SEPTA), Phila., 1980-85, mgr. spl. contracts, 1985—. Bd. dirs. Southampton Environ. Bd., 1972-75; pres. Southampton Dem. Party, 1974, Ivy Meadows Homeowners Assn., 1980; v.p. Hilltown Hist. Soc., 1985. Lutheran. Home: 229 Oak Hill Dr Hatboro PA 19040-1929 Office: SEPTA 714 Market St Philadelphia PA 19106-2312

CHOPPIN, PURNELL WHITTINGTON, research administrator, virology researcher, educator; b. Baton Rouge, July 4, 1929; s. Authur Richard and Eunice Dolores (Bolin) C.; m. Joan Harriet Macdonald, Oct. 17, 1959; 1 dau., Kathleen Marie. MD, La. State U., 1953; DSc (hon.), Emory U., 1988, La. State U., 1988, Tulane U., 1989, Washington U., 1991; D Medicine (hon.), U. Cologne, 1988. Diplomate: Am. Bd. Internal Medicine. Intern Barnes Hosp., St. Louis, 1953-54, asst. resident, 1956-57; postdoctoral fellow, rsch. assoc. Rockefeller U., N.Y.C., 1957-60, asst. prof., 1960-64, assoc. prof., 1957-60, prof., sr. physician, 1970-85, Leon Hess prof. virology, 1980-85, v.p. acad. programs, 1983-85; dean grad. studies Rockefeller U., 1985; v.p., chief sci. officer Howard Hughes Med. Inst., 1985-87, pres., 1987—; chmn. sect. 43 microbiology and immunology NAS, 1989-92, chmn. class IV med. scis., 1983-86, mem. com. on reorganization structure, 1985-86; coun. Inst. Medicine, 1987—, exec. com., 1988-91; mem. virology study sect. NIH, 1968-72, chmn. virology study sect., 1975-78; bd. dirs. Royal Soc. Medicine Found. Inc., N.Y.C., 1978—; mem. adv. com. fundamental rsch. Nat. Multiple Sclerosis Soc., 1979-84; chmn. adv. com. fundamental rsch., 1983-84; mem. adv. coun. Nat. Inst. Allergy and Infectious Diseases, 1980-83; mem. bd. scis., cons. Meml. Sloan-Kettering Cancer Ctr., N.Y.C., 1981-86; chmn. bd. scis., 1983-84; mem. commn. on life scis. NRC, Washington, 1982-87; mem. sci. rev. com. Scripps Clinic and Rsch. Found., La Jolla, Calif., 1983-85, chmn. sci. rev. com., La Jolla, Calif., 1984; mem. coun. for rsch. and clin. investigation Am. Cancer Soc., N.Y.C., 1983-85; mem. com. priorities for vaccine devel. Inst. Medicine, Washington; mem. governing bd. NRC, 1990-92. Contbr. numerous articles to profl. pubs., chpts. on virology, cell biology, infectious diseases to profl. pubs., 1958—; editor: Procs. Soc. Exptl. Biology and Medicine, 1966-69; assoc. editor Virology, 1969-72, editor, 1973-86; assoc. editor: Jour. Immunology, 1968-72, Jour. Supramolecular Structure, 1972-75; mem. editorial bd. Jour. Virology, 1972-85, Comprehensive Virology, 1972; mem. overseas adv. panel Biochem. Jour., 1973-77. Served as capt. USAF, 1954-56, Japan. Recipient Howard Taylor Ricketts award U. Chgo., 1978; Waksman award for excellence in microbiology Nat. Acad. Scis., 1984; named to alumni Hall of Distinction La. State U., Baton Rouge, 1983. Fellow AAAS; mem. NAS, Am. Acad. Arts and Scis., Am. Philos. Soc., Assn. Am. Physicians, Am. Soc. Clin. Investigation, Am. Soc. Microbiology (chmn. virology div. 1977-79, div. group councilor 1983-85),

Harvey Soc., Am. Assn. Immunologists, Soc. Cell Biology, Infectious Diseases Soc. Am., Practitioners Soc. N.Y., Am. Clin. and Climatological Assn., Am. Soc. Virology (pres. 1985-86), Sigma Xi (chpt. pres. 1980-81), Alpha Omega Alpha. Office: Howard Hughes Med Inst 6701 Rockledge Dr Bethesda MD 20817-1813

CHOQUETTE, KEITH ALAN, psychologist; b. Southington, Conn., Nov. 10, 1954; s. Vincent Arthur and Mabel Fern (Allen) C. BA, Cen. Conn. State U., 1976; MS, Tex. Christian U., 1980, PhD, 1982. Rsch. psychologist U.S. Army Rsch. Devel. Labs., Natick, Mass., 1984-85; psychologist Paul A. Dever State Sch., Taunton, Mass., 1985-88; social sci. analyst VA Med. Ctr., Brockton, Mass., 1988—. Contbr. articles to profl. jours. Post Doctoral fellow U. Conn. Health Ctr., 1982-84. Mem. Am. Psychol. Soc., Ea. Psychol. Assn. Democrat. Roman Catholic. Office: VA Med Ctr 918 Belmont St Brockton MA 02401-5562

CHOROSTECKI, GENE JOSEPH, urologist; b. Cooksville, Ont., Can., Mar. 19, 1933; came to U.S., 1960; s. Joseph and Michalina (Kurowska) C.; m. Helen Josephine Kowalski, Aug. 17, 19157; children: Kathleen, Lesley. MD, U. Toronto, Ont., Can., 1960. Diplomate Am. Bd. Urology. Intern Grace Hosp., Detroit, 1960-61, resident in gen. surgery, 1961-63; resident in urology Wayne State U.-Detroit Receiving Hosp., 1963-66; pvt. practice, Plattsburgh, N.Y., 1966-90. Fellow ACS; mem. Am. Urol. Assn., N.E. Sect. Am. Urol. Assn., N.Y. State Med. Soc. Home: 34 Eaglesfield Way Fairport NY 14450-4402

CHOTINER, BENNETT, ophthalmologist; b. McKeesport, Pa., May 13, 1941; s. Morris and Evelyn (Hirz) C.; m. Inez Marlene Luxemberg, Dec. 15, 1968; children: Kenneth, Eric, Melissa. BA, Kenyon Coll., 1963; MD, Pa. State U., Hershey, 1972. Diplomat Am. Bd. Ophthalmology. Internship Harrisburg (Pa.) Hosp., 1972-73; residency U. Pitts., 1973-76, pediatric ophthalmology fellowship, 1976-77; pres. Pa. Eye Assoc., Harrisburg, 1980—; med. dir. Pa. Eye Surgery Ctr., Harrisburg, 1985—; chief exec. officer Meml. Eye Inst., Harrisburg, 1985—. Contbr. articles to profl. jours. Fellow Am. Coll. Surgeons; mem. Am. Acad. Opthalmology, Pa. Med. Soc., Pa. Acad. Ophthalmology, Pa. Ambulatory Surgery Assn. (v.p. 1990—), Dauphin County Med. Soc., Outpatient Ophthalmic Surgery Soc., Federated Ambulatory Surgery Assn. Republican. Home: 3800 Laraby Dr Harrisburg PA 17112 Office: Meml Eye Inst 4100 Linglestown Rd Harrisburg PA 17112-6006

CHOU, NELSON SHIH-TOON, veterinarian; b. Taipei, Taiwan, Oct. 17, 1935; came to U.S., 1962; s. Ting-Kieng and Yuh (You) C.; m. Doris Yuh-Yuh Chen, July 2, 1966; children: Grace, Jennifer. BSc, Nat. U. Taiwan, 1959; MSc, U. Hawaii, 1964; PhD, U. Manitoba, 1967; DVM, U. Guelph, 1973. DVM Md., Mich., Ontario. Lectr. Ontario Vet. Coll., Guelph, 1967-69, asst. prof., 1969-71; rsch. vet. Ralston Purina Co., St. Louis, 1973-80; vet. med. officer FDA, Rockville, Md., 1980—; FDA rep. Joint Subcom. on Aquaculture, Washington, 1980—. Co-author: Diets for Largo Morphs Handbook/Nutrition and Food, 1977; patentee in field; contbr. articles to profl. jours. Pres. Taiwanese Assn. Can., 1968, v.p., 1977; pres. N.Am. Taiwanese Profs. Assn., Washington, 1990; v.p. Home Owners Assn., Gaithersburg, Md., 1989. 2d lt. Chinese Army, 1959-61. Recipient Rsch. grants Nat. Rsch. Coun., Ottawa, Can., 1968-71, Ontario Ministry of Agriculture, Ontario, 1968-70, scholarship East-West Ctr. for Cultural Exchange, Honolulu, 1962-64. Mem. Am. Vet. Med. Assn., Can. Vet. Med. Assn., Am. Inst. Nutrition, Am. Fisheries Assn., Nat. Assn. Fed. Vet., Fedn. Am. Soc. for Exptl. Biology, Chinese Bioscientist in Am. Home: 12161 Mcdonald Chapel Dr Gaithersburg MD 20878-2250 Office: Food and Drug Adminstrn CVM 7500 Standish Pl Rockville MD 20855

CHOVANEC, MICHAEL JUSTIN, secondary school educator; b. Blairsville, Pa., Dec. 25, 1968; s. Steven Andrew and Dolores Veronica (Soler) C. BS in Edn. and Physics magna cum laude, Indiana U. of Pa., 1990. Cert. secondary sci. tchr., Pa. High sch. sci. tchr. Hempfield Area Sch. Dist., Greensburg, Pa., 1990—. Mem. Pa. Sci. Tchrs. Assn., Am. Assn. Physics Tchrs., Nat. Sci. Tchrs. Assn. Home: 1A W Hills Dr Greensburg PA 15601-2015

CHOW, MICHAEL, financial analyst; b. Boston, May 8, 1965; s. Chok Wing and Wai Kim Chow. BS in Fin., Bentley Coll., 1987. Credit analyst BayBanks Credit Corp., Waltham, Mass., 1984-86; fund acct. Putnam Cos., Boston, 1987-88; fin. reporting analyst Cognex Corp., Needham, Mass., 1988—. Office: Cognex Corp 150 Gould St Needham MA 02194

CHOW, STEPHEN Y(EE), lawyer; b. Cleve., Miss., Sept. 8, 1952; s. Chester H. and June (Eng) C.; m. Lynn Elin Anderson, May 4, 1981; children: Astrid Crockett, Augustus Stephen. AB cum laude, SM in Applied Physics, Harvard U., 1975; JD, Columbia U., 1979. Bar: N.Y. 1980, Mass. 1983, U.S. Supreme Ct. 1983, U.S. Patent Office 1984. Assoc. Donovan Leisure Newton & Irvine, N.Y.C., 1979-82, Gaston Snow & Ely Bartlett, Boston, 1982-85, Cesari and McKenna, Boston, 1985-88; ptnr. Nutter, McClennen & Fish, Boston, 1988-90, Cesari and McKenna, Boston, 1990—. Bd. editors Mass. Law Rev., 1991—. Trustee Hawthorne Pl. Condominium Trust, Boston, 1985—; spl. asst. dist. atty. N.Y. County, 1980-82. Mem. ABA, IEEE, Am. Intellectual Property Law Assn., Mass. Bar Assn. (chmn. uniform comml. code project 1990—), Licensing Execs. Soc. (chmn. uniform comml. code com. 1991—), Boston Bar Assn. (chmn. intellectual property com. 1991—), N.Y.C. Bar Assn., Boston Patent Law Assn. (chmn. com. on computer law 1991—), Assn. Computing Machinery (chmn. ad hoc com. on software patenting 1991—), Boston Racquet Club, Union Boat Club. Republican. Home: 9 Hawthorne Pl Boston MA 02114-2344 Office: Cesari and McKenna 30 Rowes Wharf Boston MA 02110-3326

CHOW, YING-WEI, physics educator; b. Guangdong, China, Oct. 24, 1935; s. Raymond and Mary (Lau) C.; m. Kam-Ping Cheung, Aug. 15, 1981; children: James Chow, Jerry Chow. BS, Tshing-Hua U., Beijing, China, 1955; PhD, MIT, 1965. Rsch. assoc. MIT, Cambridge, Mass., 1965-66, Columbia U., N.Y.C., 1966-72; asst. prof. physics H. Lehman Coll., CUNY, Bronx, 1972-77; assoc. prof. physics M. Evers Coll., CUNY, Bklyn., 1977-83, prof. physics, 1983—. Contbr. articles to profl. jours. Rsch. fellow AEC, 1964-66, 66-72, NSF, 1973-76, NIH, 1977-82. Mem. Am. Phys. Soc., Sigma Xi. Home: 1220 Doone Ct Brooklyn NY 11235-4275

CHOY, DANIEL SHU JEN, physician, research scientist; b. Shanghai, Shangai, Republic of China, May 29, 1926; came to U.S., 1941; s. Jun Ke and Jessie (Wu) C.; m. Rhea Brown, Dec. 27, 1985; children: Martha, DAniel Jr. BA, Columbia Coll., 1944, MD, 1949. Intern Meadowbrook Hosp., 1949-50; resident Francis Delafield Hosp.-Columbia U., N.Y.C., 1951-54; fellow Am. Cancer Soc., 1951-54; dir. laser lab. St. Luke's-Roosevelt Hosp. Ctr.-Columbia U., N.Y.C.; asst. clin. prof. med. Columbia U., N.Y.C.; chief tumor svc. French Hosp., N.Y.C., 1962-74; attending physician Lenox Hosp., N.Y.C.; assoc. attending physician, rsch. scientist cardiology lab. St. Luke's Roosevelt Hosp., N.Y.C., dir. laser lab. Inventor Aeroplast, 1950, Laser Angioplasty, 1980, Percutaneus Laser Disc Decompression, 1986. Fellow ACP, Explorers Club; mem. Am. Soc. Clin. Oncology (founding, Am. Bd. Laser Surgery (founding, bd. dirs. 1985—). Home: 892 Riverbank Rd Stamford CT 06903-3114 Office: 170 E 77th St New York NY 10021-1912

CHRETIEN, MARGARET CECILIA, public administrator; b. Tupper Lake, N.Y., Jan. 19, 1953; d. William Lawrence and Catherine Eileen (Dowdle) LaGasse; m. Thomas J. Chretien, Oct. 1, 1977. BA, Siena Coll., 1975; MPA, SUNY, Albany, 1983, postgrad., 1992—. Program coordinator Saratoga County Office for Aging, Ballston Spa, N.Y., 1977-80; crime prevention specialist N.Y. State Div. Criminal Justice Svcs., Albany, 1980-84, pub. info. officer, 1984-86, criminal justice program rep., 1986—; publicity chair Nat. Mus. Dance, Saratoga Springs, N.Y., 1987-90. Mng. editor Crime Prevention Update, 1980-84; mem. editorial rev. bd. Mng. N.Y. State, 1987-89. Campaign worker N.Y. State Dem. Party, Albany, 1986; spl. events vol. City of Albany, 1986—; bd. dirs. Vol. Ctr. Albany, 1988—, sec., 1992; fundraising vol. St. Cecilia's Orch. Mem. Women's Press Club N.Y. State, Inc. (v.p. 1984-86). Democrat. Roman Catholic. Home: 8 Wagner Rd Saratoga Springs NY 12866-3744 Office: NY Div Criminal Justice Svc Executive Pk Albany NY 12203

CHRISLER, JOAN C., psychologist, educator; b. Teaneck, N.J., Jan. 1, 1953; d. Eugene Reed and Anna Mary (Whalen) C.; m. Christopher Bishop, Nov. 20, 1976. BS in Psychology, Fordham U., 1975; MA, PhD in Exptl. Psychology, Yeshiva U., 1986; cert. in behavior therapy, L.I. U. Adj. instr. Mercy Coll., Dobbs Ferry, N.Y., 1979-85, Coll. of Mt. St. Vincent, Riverdale, N.Y., 1979, Monroe Bus. Inst., Bronx, N.Y., 1980, Iona Coll., New Rochelle, N.Y., 1980, Ramapo Coll., Mahwah, N.J., 1980-84, Upsala Coll., East Orange, N.J., 1981-85, St. Thomas Acquinas Coll., Sparkill, N.Y., 1984, SUNY, Purchase, 1984-87, Coll. New Rochelle, N.Y., 1984-85, Bergen Community Coll., Paramus, N.J., 1984-85; asst. prof. Conn. Coll., New London, 1987—; asst. to dir. Internat. English Language Inst. Hunter Coll., N.Y.C., 1978-80; asst. to coordinator Media Ctr. Payne Whitney Psychiatric Clinic, N.Y.C., 1980-82; fieldwork in behavior therapy Creedmoor Psychiatric Ctr., Queens Village, N.Y., 1982; group therapist Health Improvement Systems, Cin., 1982-84. Author: (with others) New Directions in Feminist Psychology, Gender in Academe, Menstration, Health and Fitness, Feminist Perspectives on Addictions, Overcoming Fear of Fat; contbr. numerous articles to profl. jours. Dist. leader New Rochelle Dem. Com., N.Y., 1985-87; mem. Westchester County Dem. Com., White Plains, N.Y., 1985-87; v.p. Westchester NOW, White Plains, 1985-87; state bd. mem. Conn. NOW, 1988—; mem. exec. com. Westchester Women's Polit. Caucus, Mt. Vernon, N.Y., 1985-87. Named Woman of Yr., Westchester County, N.Y., 1987; recipient Susan B. Anthony award Westchester NOW, 1987. Mem. Assn. Women in Psychology (spokesperson 1985-88, conf. coord. 1990), APA, Soc. Menstrual Cycle Rsch., New Eng. Psychol. Assn. (steering com. 1991—, sec.-treas. 1992—), New Eng. Women's Studies Assn., AAUP (mem. Conn. exec. com. 1990—), Psi Chi. Home: 1006 Grassy Hill Rd Orange CT 06477-1103 Office: Conn Coll Dept of Psychology New London CT 06320

CHRISMAN, DIANE J., librarian; b. Lackawanna, N.Y., June 20, 1937; d. Floyd R. and Elizabeth R. (Nowakowski) Schutta. B.A., U. Vt., 1959; M.S.L.S., Simmons Coll., 1960. Asst. head Crane br. Buffalo & Erie County Pub. Library, 1961-64, asst. head young adult dept., 1964-65, asst. head order dept., 1965-68, coordinator children div., 1968-79, dep. dir., 1979—; lectr. SUNY-Buffalo, 1966-68, 80, 90, 91, 92. Contbr. articles to profl. jours. Mem. ALA, N.Y. Libr. Assn., Zonta (bd. dirs. 1983-84, 87-88, rec. sec. 1989-91, v.p. 1991—). Home: 78 Rainbow Ter Orchard Park NY 14127-2517 Office: Buffalo & Erie County Pub Libr Lafayette Sq Buffalo NY 14203-1821

CHRISMER, RONALD MICHAEL, federal agency administrator; b. Washington, May 4, 1954; s. Michael Joseph and Phyllis Ann (Long) C.; m. Dorothea May Shifflett, Sept. 20, 1986; 1 child, Jeffrey Ronald. BS magna cum laude, Towson State U., 1976; M. Gen. Adminstrn., Mgmt. Info. Systems, U. Md., 1987. Cert. purchasing mgr. Sr. proofreader Am. Assn. Life Ins., Washington, 1976-77; asst. supr. Coopers & Lybrand, CPAs, Washington, 1978-83; supr. Coopers & Lybrand, Washington, 1983-85; purchasing mgr. Am. Psychol. Assn., Washington, 1985-87; buyer U. Md., Balt., 1988; contract specialist IRS, Washington, 1988—; mem. telecommunications adv. coun. Bell Atlantic, Washington, 1983-85. Block capt. Neighborhood Watch, Cardinal Forest Devel., 1987—; mem. World Affairs Coun., Washington, 1983-85, Nat. Trust for Hist. Preservation, Washington, 1983-85; mem. sch. bd. St. Mary's Sch., Laurel, Md., 1990—, mem. parish coun., 1991-92, chmn., 1992-93. Mem. Nat. Assn. Purchasing Mgmt., Purchasing Mgmt. Assn. Md. (chmn. edn. com. 1988), Purchasing Mgmt. Assn. Washington, Nat. Honor Soc., Psi Chi. Roman Catholic. Home: 8810 Cardinal Ct Laurel MD 20723-1241

CHRIST, ALBERT HOWARD, metallurgist; b. Geistown, Pa., Nov. 22, 1941; s. Robert Straub and Helen Agnes (Dorotzak) C.; m. Vicki Ann Werder, June 24, 1967; children: Todd S., Bryan S. BSMetE, U. Pitts., 1963. Rsch. metallurist Pitts. Steel (Thomas Strip), Warren, Ohio, 1963-64; engr. Bethlehem Steel Corp., Johnstown, Pa., 1964-67, supr. non destructive testing, 1967-68, systems coord., 1968-69, metall. supr. specifications, 1969-75, chem. lab. supr., 1975-82, metall. supr., 1982-83, mktg. assignments, 1983-84, chief mktg. metallurgist, 1984-85, sr. metallurgist, 1985—. pres. Richland Music Boosters, Johnstown, 1988—; chief YMCA Indian Guides, 1985; bd. dirs. Johnstown Symphony, 1992—. Mem. Nat. Screw Machine Product Assn., Am. Soc. Metallurgists. Republican. Baptist. Home: 120 Weimer St Johnstown PA 15904-9672

CHRIST, DUANE MARLAND, computer systems engineer; b. Lakota, Iowa, Jan. 5, 1932; s. George Andrew and Esther Gertrude (Franke) C.; m. Lily Esther Shih, Sept. 14, 1963; 1 son, Wesley Anzo. B.S., Iowa State U., 1953; M.A., U. Minn., 1960. Sci. programmer United Aircraft Corp., Hartford, Conn., 1960-63; computer systems analyst IBM, N.Y.C., 1963-68, staff instr., 1968-76, adv. systems engr., 1976-82, sr. systems engr., 1982-87; prin., 1987—. 1st lt. USAF, 1953-56. IBM Resident Study fellow, 1966-68, S.E. Regional Dir. award, 1983; named Area Specialist of Yr., 1986. Mem. Assn. Computing Machinery, Soc. Indsl. and Applied Math., Math. Assn. Am. Lutheran.

CHRISTENSEN, CARL WILLIAM, family therapist, trainer and consultant; b. Indpls., Mar. 25, 1946; s. William Carl and Helen (Thuesen) C.; m. Sonya Marie Hruschka, Sept. 22, 1968; children: Candace Marie, Benjamin Ray, Michael Andrew, Sally Helen. BA, Antioch Coll., 1969; MSW, Portland State U., 1983. Cert. social worker, N.Y. Vol. U.S. Peace Corps, Jamaica, 1969-71; community organizer Southwest Oreg. Community Action, North Bend, Oreg., 1971-73; clin. dir. Southwest Oreg. Community Action, North Bend, 1983-87; supr. Coos County Juvenile, Coquille, Oreg., 1973-81; prin. clinician Coastal Ctr. for Counseling, North Bend, 1983-87; mgr. Family Svc. Rochester, N.Y., 1987-90; ind. practice Linden Oaks Family Therapy Inst., Rochester, 1990—; bd. dirs. Ctr. Systemic Rsch., North Bend, 1984-87. Fellow Am. Orthopsychiat. Assn.; mem. ACLU, Northwest Steelheaders, Acad. Cert. Social Workers, Nat. Assn. Social Workers (dist. chmn. 1985-86), Am. Assn. Marriage and Family Therapists (clinician, approved supr.). Democrat. Romany Catholic. Home: 218 Navarre Rd Rochester NY 14621-1042 Office: Linden Oaks Family Therapy Inst 100 Linden Oaks Ste 200 Rochester NY 14625-2831

CHRISTENSEN, DONNA RADOVICH, crafts consultant, educator; b. Midvale, Utah, Sept. 16, 1925; d. Daniel and Clara Ellen (Turley) Radovich; B.A., U. Utah, 1947; M.A. Columbia U., 1951; m. John Whittaker Christensen, Feb. 2, 1952; children: Carlyn M. Christensen Szalanski, John Chipman, Craig Whittaker. Tchr. and guidance counselor Jordan High Sch., Sandy, Utah, 1947-50; sec. Placement Bur. of Columbia U. Tchr.'s Coll., N.Y.C., 1950-51; free-lance designer of needlecrafts, 1970—; tchr. of needlecraft, 1965—; tchr. 18th Century painted finishes Isabel O'Neil Found. for Art of Painted Finish, N.Y.C., 1975-77; cons. in crafts, 1965—. V.p. Silvermine Guild of Artists, 1965-68, hospitality chmn., 1958-65. Recipient Service award Silvermine Guild, 1963, Journeyman's medallion O'Neil Studio, 1974. Mem. Embroider's Guild of Am., Needle and Bobbin Club (v.p. 1977-82, pres. 1982-89, bd. dirs. 1989-91), New Canaan Sewing Group (exec. bd. 1977-81), Phi Kappa Phi, Pi Lambda Theta, Kappa Delta Pi. Mormon. Club: New Canaan Garden (exec. bd. 1972-77, v.p. 1987-89, pres. 1989-91), Federated Garden of Conn. Inc. (asst. civic devel. chmn. 1991—) Home: 788 Ponus Rdg New Canaan CT 06840-3412

CHRISTENSEN, HENRY, III, lawyer; b. Jersey City, Nov. 8, 1944; s. Henry Jr. and M. Louise (Brooke) C.; m. Constance L. Cumpton, July 1, 1967; children: Alexander, Gustavus, Elizabeth, Katherine. BA, Yale U., 1966; JD, Harvard U., 1969. Bar: N.Y. 1970, U.S. Tax Ct. 1973, U.S. Ct. Appeals (2d. cir.) 1973, U.S. Supreme Ct. 1975. Assoc. Sullivan & Cromwell, N.Y.C., 1969-77, ptnr., 1977—; adj. assoc. prof. NYU, N.Y.C., 1985-88. Contbr. articles to profl. jours. Chmn. Prospect Park Alliance, Bklyn., 1985—; trustee, vice chmn. Peddie Sch., Hightstown, N.J., 1986—; trustee Am. Fund for the Tate Gallery, 1987—; dir., sec. Freedom Inst., N.Y.C., 1980—, The Friends of Jiangnan U., 1987—; dir., v.p. Am. Friends of Whitechapel Art Gallery Found., 1991—. Fellow Am. Coll. Probate Counsel; mem. N.Y. State Bar Assn. (chmn. estate and gift tax com. 1983-84, chmn. exempt orgn. com. 1986, chmn. income taxation of trusts com. 1984-85, 87-89, exec. com. tax sect. 1983-89), Internat. Acad. Estate and Trust Law (academician). Home: 61 Prospect Park W Brooklyn NY 11215-3021 Office: Sullivan & Cromwell 125 Broad St New York NY 10004-2400

CHRISTENSEN, KATHARINE ELEANOR, education educator; b. Camden, N.J., Sept. 20, 1929; d. Werner Paul and Agatha Ruth (Raisbeck) Meyer; m. John Paul Christensen, July 5, 1952; 1 child, Carrie Joan. BA, Mich. State U., 1951, MA, 1958; PhD, U. Del., 1972. Tchr. various pub. sch. systems Mich., 1951-62; dir. pvt. kindergarten, nursery sch. Newark, Del., 1965-67; dir. tutoring program for early readers Newark, 1967-70; supr. student tchrs. U. Del., Newark, 1971-72; assoc. prof. West Chester (Pa.) U., 1972-90, prof. edn., 1990—, asst. chair, grad. coord., 1980—; cons. in field; presenter at profl. confs. Contbr. articles on reading to edn. publs. Grantee Commonwealth of Pa., 1987. Mem. Internat. Reading Assn., Pa. Reading Tchr. Educators Coun., Chester County Reading Assn., Keystone State Reading Assn., Phi Delta Kappa, Delta Kappa Gamma. Office: West Chester U Dept Childhood Studies West Chester PA 19382

CHRISTENSEN, WALTER FREDERICK, JR., information systems specialist; b. New Brunswick, N.J., Aug. 2, 1949; s. Walter Frederick Sr. and Alyce Rose (Nomejko) C.; m. Andrea Marie Fay, June 5, 1971; children: Nicole Marie, Daniel Jordan. BS, U. Del., 1971; MS, U. Md., 1973. Dir. GTE, Silver Spring, Md., 1974-79; sr. dir. GTE, Mt. Laurel, N.J., 1979-87, Quotron (subs. Citicorp), N.Y.C., 1987-89; v.p. product engrng. Automatic Data Processing, Mt. Laurel, 1989-91; v.p. systems devel. Dow Jones/Telerate, Jersey City, 1991—; pres. WFC Cons., Mt. Laurel, 1985-90. Author: Optimum Teaching Assembly Language, 1971. Bd. dirs. South Jersey chpt. Am. Cancer Soc., Mt. Laurel, 1990. Capt. USAR, 1973-79. Recipient Excellence award Automatic Data Processing, 1987. Office: Dow Jones/Telerate Harborside Fin Ctr 600 Plaza Two Jersey City NJ 07311

CHRISTENSEN, WENDY ANN, illustrator, software engineering consultant; b. St. Paul, June 11, 1952; d. Donald Day and Jacqueline Marie (Davis) C.; m. Jeffrey C. MacGillivray, May 2, 1987. AA, Los Angeles Valley Coll., 1972; cert. in programming, UCLA, 1977. Auditing examiner Prudential Ins. Co., L.A., 1972-74; programmer Singer-Librascope, Glendale, Calif., 1974-78; sr. mem. tech. staff Transaction Tech., Inc., Santa Monica, Calif., 1978-81; software engr. Wang Labs., Inc., Lowell, Mass., 1981-83, Apollo Computer, Inc., Chelmsford, Mass., 1983-87; freelance illustrator New Ipswich, N.H., 1987—. Contbg. editor Cat Fancy mag.; contbr. book revs. to local newspapers and other publs. Office: PO Box 301 New Ipswich NH 03071-0301

CHRISTENSON, PAUL J., surgeon; b. L.A., Jan. 16, 1953; s. Luther B. and Velda Ruth (Johnson) C.; m. Melissa L. Rosado, May 23, 1980; children: E. Jon, Jennifer Ruth, Heather Kathleen. BS magna cum laude, Brigham Young U., 1972; MD, U. Utah, 1976. Cert. Nat. Bd. Med. Examiners, Am. Bd. Urology. Commd. ensign USN, 1972, advanced through grades to capt.; intern Naval Regional Med. Ctr., Portsmouth, Va., 1976-77; battalion surgeon 1st Div. 9th Marines, Okinawa, Japan, 1977-78; urology resident Nat. Naval Med. Ctr., Bethesda, Md., 1978-82, staff urologist, 1982-84; dir. surg. svcs., chief urology 13th Air Force Med. Ctr., Clark AFB, Philippines, 1984-88; chief urology div. USNS Comfort, Persian Gulf, 1990-91; asst. chief urology Nat. Naval Med. Ctr., Bethesda, 1988—; assoc. prof. surgery Uniformed Svcs. Univ. of Health Scis., Bethesda, 1988—. Contbr. urology articles to profl. jours.; co-producer 4 films in the fields of urology and wound ballistics. Fellow ACS; mem. Am. Urol. Assn., Phi Kappa Phi. Republican. Mem. LDS Church. Office: Nat Naval Med Ctr Urology Bethesda MD 20814

CHRISTENSON, PHILIP LAWRENCE, government foreign policy executive; b. Ely, Nev., May 18, 1947; s. Donald Philip Christenson and Marie (Leonard) Connolly; m. Martha Ann Vanier, Oct. 8, 1982 (div. 1988). BSFS, Georgetown U., 1971. Adminstrv. officer Dept. of State, Washington, 1966-70; foreign svc. officer Dept. of State, overseas, 1970-74; internat. trade specialist Dept. of Comm., Washington, 1974-79; assoc. dir. U.S.-S. Africa Leader Exchange Program, Washington, 1979-81; sr. profl. staff mem. U.S. Senate Com. on Foreign Relations, Washington, 1981-89; asst. adminstr. U.S. Agy. for Internat. Devel., Washington, 1989—. Contbr. articles to profl. jours. Del. Va. 8th Dist. Rep. Conv., Fairfax, Va., 1980; mem. Bush for Pres. Foreign Policy Study Group, 1988, Mandate III Task Force, Heritage Found., 1988. Episcopalian. Home: 2705 Unicorn Ln NW Washington DC 20015-2233 Office: Bur for Food Peace & Voluntary Assistance USAID Washington DC 20523

CHRISTENSON, WILLIAM NEWCOME, physician; b. Biltmore Forest, N.C., Dec. 2, 1925; s. William Lambert and Beth (Newcome) C.; B.S., U. N.C., 1949; M.D., Johns Hopkins U., 1948; m. Elizabeth Chandler White, Aug. 9, 1957; children: Lisa Ann, Laurie E., Susan. Intern, asst. resident Mass. Gen. Hosp., Boston, 1948-50; asst. resident N.Y. Hosp., N.Y.C., 1953-55; dir. personnel health svc., 1960-85, asst. attending physician, 1961-64, assoc. attending physician, 1964-85; attending physician Westchester County Med. Ctr., 1985—, physician Employee Health Svc., 1985—; postgrad. rsch. fellow USPHS; Postgrad. Med. Sch. London, 1955-56; instr. medicine Cornell U. Med. Coll., N.Y.C., 1956-59, asst. prof. medicine, 1959-65, clin. assoc. prof. medicine, 1965-79, assoc. prof. clin. medicine, 1979-85; dir. Office Grad. Med. Advising, N.Y. Med. Coll., 1985-88, 1988—, prof. clin. medicine, 1986—, assoc. dean, 1988—; cons. N.Y. Blood Center, 1976—; practice medicine specializing in internal medicine and occupational medicine, N.Y.C., 1960-85. With USNR, 1950-52. Fellow ACP, Am. Coll. Occupational Medicine; mem. Am. Fedn. Clin. Rsch., Am. Soc. Hematology, Am. Pub. Health Assn., Phi Beta Kappa, Alpha Omega Alpha, Delta Kappa Epsilon. Research in hematology and human ecology. Home: 4 Leggett Rd Bronxville NY 10708-4914 Office: NY Med Coll Sunshine Cottage Valhalla NY 10595

CHRISTIAN, EDWIN ERNEST, English educator; b. Portsmouth, Va., Dec. 28, 1953; s. Edwin Ernest and Gloria (DeBruin) C.; m. Margaret Foster, Dec. 19, 1982; children: Mary Elizabeth, James Paul, Edwin Peter. BS in Communications, Union Coll., 1977; MA in English, Loma Linda U., 1979; PhD in English, U. Nebr., 1983. Instr. English U. Nebr., Lincoln, 1982-83, 85-86, Loma Linda U., Riverside, Calif., 1984-85; exch. prof. English Beijing Langs. Inst., 1983-84; asst. prof. English Kutztown U. Pa., 1986—; del. Assn. Pa. State Coll. and Univ. Faculties, Modern Lang. Assn., 1992-94. Author: Joyce Cary's Creative Imagination, 1989; contbr. articles to profl. and scholarly publs. Fulbright scholar Oxford (Eng.) U., 1981-82. Mem. Joyce Cary Soc. (pres.), Soc. Detective Fiction (founder). Republican. Seventh-day Adventist. Office: U Pa Dept English Kutztown PA 19530

CHRISTIAN, HOWARD JOSEPH, retired pathologist; b. Cambridge, Mass., Sept. 17, 1923; s. Howard and Ruth Louise (Malaney) C.; m. Marjorie Scanlan, Mar. 9, 1945; children: Carol, Howard, David, Emily, Mark, Magdellan, John, Dorothy. BS, Tufts U., 1948, MD, 1952. Intern, resident Mallory Inst. Pathology, Boston City Hosp., 1952-56; pathologist St. Elizabeth Hosp., Brighton, Mass., 1956-57; pathologist-in-chief Carney Hosp., Boston, 1957-85; cons. Mass. Hosp. Sch., Canton, Mt. Pleasant Hosp., Lynn, Mass. Contbr. articles to profl. jours. Pres. Norfolk Med. Soc., 1971, Tufts Alumni Assn. 1st lt. U.S. Army, 1940-46, ETO. Commonwealth Fund fellow, 1963-64. Roman Catholic. Home: 37 Elm St Canton MA 02021-1243

CHRISTIAN, MARY JO DINAN, educator, real estate professional; b. Denver, May 7, 1941; d. Joseph Timothy and Margaret Rose (Ryan) Dinan; m. Ralph Poinsett Christian, Aug. 27, 1966. BA, Loretto Heights Coll., Denver, 1964; MA, George Washington U., 1983. Cert. English educator, adminstrn. and supervision secondary edn. English tchr. Denver Pub. Schs., 1964-67, Prince George's County Pub. Sch., Md., 1967-81; vice-prin. Prince George's County High Sch., Md., 1981—; presenter gender/ethnic expectations and student achievement Nat. Conf. Columnist: WomenSpeak, 1981-91. Md. Ho. of Dels. recognition. Mem. NAFE, ASCD, NEA (chair adminstrs. caucus 1991-92, adminstr.-at-large resolutions com. 1986-92, polit. action com. 1984-86, coord.-at-large women's caucus 1981-91, chair adminstr.'s caucus 1991—, Creative Leadership award 1989), Md. State Tchrs. Assn. (state coord. Sen. Sarbane campaign 1982, state voter registration coord. 1984, issue coord. Tom McMillen campaign 1986, Women's Rights award 1988), Vail Racquet Club, Capitol Hill Garden Club, Phi Delta Kappa, Alpha Delta Kappa. Home: 504 Independence Ave SE Washington DC 20003-1143 Office: Prince Georges County 5211 Boydell Ave Oxon Hill MD 20745-3700

CHRISTIAN, MICHAEL BEAUREGARD, military career officer; b. Valparaiso, Ind., Feb. 24, 1964; s. William Beauregard and Cynthia Anne (Cole) C.; m. Heather Karen Therese Stanley, Jan. 19, 1988; 1 child, Chantal Jacqueline Therese. BS, U.S. Coast Guard Acad., 1986; MSc, U. Southampton, Eng., 1988. Commd. ensign USCG, 1986, advanced through grades to lt., 1990; adminstrv. officer Coast Guard Acad., New London, Conn., 1986; Fulbright scholar U. Southampton, Eng., 1986-87; ops. officer USCGC, Cape May, N.J., 1987-89, Internat. Ice Patrol, Groton, Conn., 1989-92; commdg. officer USCG Loran Sta., Marcus Island, Japan, 1992—; mem. Human Rels. Coun., Coast Guard Acad., New London, 1989—, Climate Assessment Group, 1990—. Big brother Big Brothers, Sisters of Am., Groton, Conn., 1990; vol. Literacy Vols., Norwich, Conn., 1990. Recipient Fulbright scholarship, Fulbright Commn., Washington, 1986-87. Democrat. Home: 450 Edgewood Ave New Haven CT 06511-4051 Office: USCG Loran Sta Marcus Island PSC 484 FPO AP 96382-0006

CHRISTIE, DONALD MELVIN, JR., physician; b. Lewiston, Maine, May 5, 1942; s. Donald Melvin and Dorothy Carolyn (Doble) C. A.B., U. Rochester, 1964, M.D., 1968; D.L.F.C., U. Paris, 1963. Med. intern U. Iowa Hosps. and Clinics, Iowa City, 1968-69, resident, 1969-70, 73, chief med. resident, 1973-74; asst. prof. preventive medicine and medicine Sch. Medicine, U. Rochester (N.Y.), 1974-77; univ. physician, dir. clin. services Princeton (N.J.) U. Health Services, 1977-83; clin. instr. family medicine U. Med. and Dentistry N.J., Rutgers U., 1978-83; internist Community Health Plan, Poughkeepsie, N.Y., 1983—; contract escort-interpretor (French), U.S. Dept. State, 1964-70; coord. Robert Wood Johnson Found. grant, primary care tng. evaluation U. Rochester, 1974-77. Trustee Gould Acad., Bethel, Maine, 1984—; coord. internal medicine Mid-Hudson Family Practice Residency St. Francis Hosp., Poughkeepsie, 1989—; dir. dept. internal medicine Vassar Bros. Hosp., Poughkeepsie, 1992—. Served with M.C., U.S. Army, 1970-72. Diplomate Am. Bd. Internal Medicine. Fellow Am. Coll. Sports Medicine; mem. Am. Pub. Health Assn., ACP, Am. Med. Soc. Sports Medicine. Democrat. Home: Apt 1 15 S Clover St Poughkeepsie NY 12601-3004 Office: 160 Union St Poughkeepsie NY 12601

CHRISTIE, JEANNE MARIE, designer, consultant; b. Madison, Wis., Sept. 26, 1944; d. Edward and Edith (Morhoff) Bokina; m. Frederick Christie, Dec. 7, 1970; children: Heather, Sarah. BS with honors, U. Wis., 1967; MEd with honors, Miami U., Oxford, Ohio, 1969. Unit and program dir. ARC, Vietnam, 1967-68; assoc. dir. USO, Guam, 1969-70; asst. curator Jacksonville (Fla.) Children's Mus., 1971-72; instr. Fla. Jr. Coll., Jacksonville, 1972-73, No. Va. Community Coll., Woodbridge, 1973-74, Milford (Conn.) Sr. Citizen Ctr., 1978-82; instr. adult edn. Milford Bd. Edn., 1974—; pres. J. M. Christie, Inc., Milford, 1986—; regional chmn. Assn. Jr. Leagues Internat., N.Y.C., 1989-91; cons. TV program China Beach, Burbank, Calif., 1989-91. Contbg. editor Jr. League Rev., 1991; participant in video China Beach "Vets", 1990, So. New Eng. Telephone, 1990, VietNam: A Chance to Understand, 1990; writings selected for N.Y.C. Vietnam Vets. Meml., 1985. Vol., fundraiser congl. campaign, New Haven, 1989-91, fin. dir., 1992—; treas. Milford Oyster Festival, Inc., 1991; bd. dirs. Isaiah House, Bridgeport, Conn., 1991—, Jr. League Greater New Haven, 1987-88, 1991—; class agt. Hotchkiss Sch., Lakeville, Conn., 1988-91; spl. events coord. N.Y.C. Welcome Home Parade, 1985; mem. Gov.'s Task Force on Women Vets., 1988; guide, coord., researcher Yale African Outreach, 1989. Recipient Civilian Svc. medal U.S., 1967, Women Building the Future award New Haven C. of C., 1991. Mem. Ams. Overseas Assn., Nat. Soc. Performance and Instrn., Am. Med. Resources Found., Conn. Valley Vizsla Club (chair nominating com. 1991). Office: J M Christie Inc 101 Clark Hill Rd Milford CT 06460-6762

CHRISTIE, LINDON EDWIN, JR., academic administrator; b. Milo, Maine, Aug. 23, 1932; s. Lindon Edwin and Ethelyn (Pierce) C.; m. Jean Frumerin, July 31, 1954; children: David, Marc. BA, Colby Coll., 1954; MEd, U. Maine, 1960, cert. advanced study, 1966. Cert. sch. adminstr., Maine. Tchr., coach Bucksport (Maine) High Sch., 1956-59; submaster Lee (Maine) Acad., 1959-61; prin. East Corinth (Maine) Acad., 1961-63, Mt. Desert High Sch., Northeast Harbor, Maine, 1963-64, Mexico (Maine) High Sch., 1964-72, Mt. Ararat Sch., Topsham, Maine, 1972-79; dir. Husson Coll. South, Portland, Maine, 1980—; bd. dirs., treas. Maine Vision Plan Corp., 1979—; cons. Sci. Rsch. Assocs., Chgo., 1979-81. Dir. aerospace edn. Maine Wing CAP, 1977—. With U.S.Army, 1954-56. Recipient Gil Robb award CAP, 1989. Mem. NEA (life), Lions (treas. Brunswick, Maine club 1975-90). Home: RR2 Box 98 1 Birch Ridge Ave W Buxton ME 04093 Office: Husson Coll South 222 St John St Portland ME 04102-3000

CHRISTINE, PETER CARROLL, investor; b. Hartford, Conn., Oct. 23, 1952; s. Richard Joseph and Barbara Diane (Weed) C.; m. Kris Lowe, Aug. 26, 1978; 1 child, Cole Parker. BSBA, Boston U., 1974. Co-owner Studio-B Inc., Boston, 1974-83; investor pvt. practice, Alna, Maine, 1971—. Pub. advisor North Atlantic Salmon Conservation Orgn., Newton Corner, Mass., 1984-90. Hon. mem. Maine Coun. Atlantic Salmon Fedn. (lobbyist 1985); mem. Sheepscot River Salmon Club (pres. 1987-89), Wawenock Country Club. Republican. Home and Office: Rt 194 Head Tide Village Alna ME 04535

CHRISTMAN, IRENE RANCK, music education association administrator; b. Lancaster, Pa., Nov. 27, 1918; d. David Garfield and Kathryn Elizabeth (Mentzer) Ranck; m. Russell Berlin Christman, Dec. 12, 1949; children: Robert Randolph, John David. BS in Music Edn. and Music Supervision, Lebanon Valley Coll., 1939; cert., U. Pa., 1940; postgrad., U. R.I., 1951, Pa. State U., 1953. Cert. educator, Pa. Music supr. Warwick (Pa.) Schs., 1939-49, Middletown (Pa.) Schs., 1949-53; chmn. music edn. Cen. Dauphin Schs., Harrisburg, Pa., 1953-84; exec. sec. Pa. Music Educators Assn., Harrisburg, 1953-84, exec. dir., 1984—; bd. dirs., edn. com. Symphony Orch., Hershey, Pa., 1991—; organist, band/choral dir., vocal soloist Pa. State U.. Contr. articles to profl. jours. Fund-raiser cancer and heart assns.; ch. choir mem. Recipient Nat. award Music Industry Conf., 1991. Mem. Music Educators Nat. Conf. (chmn. nat. coun. state sects. 1981-83, state sec. div. 1953—, Nat. award 1990), Pa. Soc. Assn. Execs., Dauphin County Music Educators Assn. (pres. 1953-55), Pilot Club of Harrisburg, Pi Gamma Mu. Republican. Presbyterian. Home and Office: Pa Music Educators Assn 3512 Cloverfield Rd Harrisburg PA 17109-2029

CHRISTMAS, WILLIAM ANTHONY, internist, educator; b. Montreal, Que., Can., June 5, 1939; came to U.S., 1946; s. William Richard and Marcelle (Hudon) C.; m. Maribeth Hanson, July 14, 1962; children: William, Ann, Gillian, Ira. AB, Bowdoin Coll., 1961; MD, Boston U., 1965. Diplomate Am. Bd. Internal Medicine. Mixed medicine intern Sinai Hosp., Balt., 1965-66; resident in internal medicine Med. Ctrs. Hosps. Vt., Burlington, 1966-68; pvt. practice, Bennington, Vt., 1972-77; med. dir. univ. health svcs., asst. prof. medicine U. Rochester, N.Y., 1977-81; NIH fellow in infectious diseases U. Vt., Burlington, 1968-69, dir. Student Health Ctr., 1981—, clin. asst. prof. medicine, 1983-89, clin. assoc. prof., 1989—. Cons. editor Jour. Am. Coll. Health, 1985—; contbr. articles to med. jours. Pres., bd. dirs. State Com. Vt. YMCA, Burlington, 1983-91; bd. dirs. Greater Burlington YMCA, 1990—, Vt. Epilepsy Assn., Rutland, 1990— mem. Vt. Coalition for Disability Rights, 1991—. Fellow ACP, Am. Coll. Health Assn. (pres. 1987-88, Ruth Boynton award 1989); mem. Infectious Diseases Soc. Am., New Eng. Coll. Health Assn. (pres. 1985-86), Vt. Med. Soc. Home: 186A Browns Ter Jericho VT 05465 Office: U Vt Student Health Ctr 425 Pearl St Burlington VT 05401-3308

CHRISTODOULOU, ARIS PETER, pharmaceutical executive, investment banker; b. Athens, Greece, Feb. 23, 1939; came to U.S., 1945; s. Peter and Angeline (Magafas) C.; m. Marilena Lyratzakis, Aug. 23, 1975; 1 child, Peter. B.S. in Chem. Engring., MIT, 1960; M.S. in Nuclear Engring., Columbia U., 1963, Indsl. Engr., 1965; Ph.D. in Chem. Engring., CUNY, 1967. Sr. scientist Booz, Allen and Hamilton, N.Y.C. and Washington, 1967-70; sr. chem. analyst Lehman Bros. Inc., N.Y.C., 1970-72; sr. chem. analyst Blyth Eastman Dillon, N.Y.C., 1972-74, 1st. v.p., 1976-80; industry specialist Merrill Lynch, N.Y.C., 1974-76; pres., chief exec. officer Mayfair Capital Ptnrs. Inc., N.Y.C., 1980—; chmn., pres., chief exec. officer Penick Corp., Newark, 1988—. Contbr. numerous articles to profl. jours. Mem. N.Y. Acad. Scis., Planning Forum, Comml. Devel. Assn., Chem. Mktg. Research Assn., Am. Inst. Chem. Engrs., N.Y. Soc. Security Analysts, Am. Chem. Soc., Inst. Cert. Fin. Analysts. Club: MIT (N.Y.C.). Home: 137 E 66th St New York NY 10021-6130 Office: Penick Corp 158 Mt Olivet Ave Newark NJ 07114-2178

CHRISTOFFERSON, KIMBERLEE KILLMER, college official, fundraiser, researcher; b. Erie, Pa., June 12, 1959; d. Robert Edward and Gretchen (Fuellhart) Killmer; m. Scott Milligan Christofferson, June 19, 1988. BA, Westminster Coll., 1981, MEd, 1986. Staff asst. U.S. Senator John Heinz, Washington, 1981-82; with Westminster Coll., New Wilmington, Pa., 1982—, dir. alumni and ann. giving, 1986-87, dir. devel., 1987—; dir. research Westminster Coll., New Wilmington, 1989—; speaker CASE Dist. II Conf., Great Gorge, N.J., 1987—; equal opportunity officer Westminster Coll., New Wilmington, 1988—. Mem. Coun. for Advancement and Support Edn., Nat. Soc. Fund Raising Execs., Am. Mgmt. Assn., Am. Prospect Rsch. Assn., Nat. Coun. Univ. Rsch. Adminstrs., Nat. Assn. Women Deans, Adminstrs. and Counselors, New Castle C. of C., New Castle Jaycees. Republican. Presbyterian. Home: 313 E Edgewood Ave New Castle PA 16105-2165 Office: Westminster Coll North Hall Maple St New Wilmington PA 16172

CHRISTOPH, FRANK HENRY, JR., architect; b. Cranston, R.I.; s. Frank Henry and Marie Bertha (Leschke) C. BFA, R.I. Sch. Design, 1943; MArch, Harvard U., 1949. Registered architect, R.I., Mass. Owner, architect Christoph Assocs., Warwick, R.I., 1949—; panelist Am. Arbitration Assn., Boston, 1972—; bd. dirs. Urban Realty Co., Warwick; chmn. bd. dirs. Centerville Investments Inc., Warwick. Mem. Rep. City Com., Warwick, 1960-65; mem. Bldg. Code Revision Com., City of Warwick, 1957-67, chmn., 1966-67, mem. bd. rev., 1970-71. With AUS, 1943-45, ETO. Mem. Am. Inst. Architects, Constrn. Specifications Inst. (pres. 1971-73), Lions (East Greenwich) (pres. 1966-67). Home: 1279 Stowe Ln North Kingstown RI 02852-2907 Office: Christoph Assocs 130 Meadow St Warwick RI 02886-6909

CHRISTOPHER, JAMES ROY, executive director; b. Fort Worth, Aug. 4, 1942; s. Roy Leslie and Mary Ruth (Hudson) C. Student, U. Tex., 1962-64, UCLA, 1978-79. Program dir. Priority One Outpatient Treatment Ctr., Beverly Hills, Calif., 1987-89; founder, exec. dir. SOS/Secular Orgns. for Sobriety, Buffalo, 1986—; lectr. in field. Author: How to Stay Sober: Recovery Without Religion, 1988, Unhooked: Staying Sober and Drug Free, 1989, SOS Sobriety: The Proven Alternatives to 12 Step Programs, 1992; contbr. articles to profl. jours. Mem. Am. Coun. on Alcoholism. Unitarian. Office: Secular Orgns for Sobriety Sos Internat Clearinghouse Box 5 Buffalo NY 14215-0005

CHRISTOPHER, RAYMOND J., computer services executive; b. Toronto, Ont., Can., June 1, 1945; m. Karen Vanessa Toope, Jan. 22, 1983; children: Neal, Darren. Diploma in Bus. Adminstrn., Ryerson Poly. Inst., Toronto, 1966. Systems analyst GE, Toronto, 1966-68; instr. Honeywell Info. Systems, Toronto, 1968-70, mgr. edn., 1970-72, sales rep., 1972-74, br. sales mgr., 1974-79; dir. mktg. Global Travel Computer Svcs., Toronto, 1979-81, pres., 1981—. Mem. Met. Toronto Bd. Trade, Ont. Club. Office: Global Travel Computer Svcs, 365 -2000 Bloor St E, Toronto, ON Canada M1S 4C3

CHRISTOPOULOS, ANNA LOUISE, psychologist; b. Athens, Greece, Aug. 12, 1955; came to U.S., 1973; d. Athanassios and Jane (Basle) C. BA magna cum laude, Brown U., 1977; PhD, NYU, 1984. Lic. psychologist, N.Y. Teaching asst. Brown U., Providence, 1976-77, NYU, N.Y.C., 1978-80; intern in psychology Bronx (N.Y.) Psychiat. Ctr., 1981-82; staff psychotherapist Child & Family Counseling Ctr., Queens, N.Y., 1982-87; staff psychotherapist New Hope Guild, Bklyn., 1982-86; staff psychologist Bronx Children's Psychiat. Ctr., 1984-85; dir. child partial hosp. program Jersey City Med. Ctr., 1985-86; sr. psychologist North Cen. Bronx Hosp., N.Y.C., 1986—; pvt. practice, N.Y.C., 1985—; psychologist Brearley Sch., N.Y.C., 1986—; clin. asst. prof. NYU, 1986-91. Mem. APA, N.Y. State Psychol. Assn., Greek Am. Behavioral Scis. Inst. (chair 1988-90), Phi Beta Kappa, Sigma Xi. Office: 7 Patchin Pl New York NY 10011-8341

CHRISTY, JAMES THOMAS, chemicals executive, lawyer; b. Cin., Nov. 2, 1947; s. Thomas Perry and Mary (Vatsures) C.; m. Grace Thunborg, May 10, 1975; children: James, Diane, Caroline, Elizabeth, John. BBA, U. Cin., 1969, JD, 1972. Legis. asst. U.S. Ho. of Reps., Washington, 1973-75, adminstrv. asst., 1975-76; pvt. practice atty. Milford, Ohio, 1976-81; counsel U.S. Ho. of Reps. Com. on Energy & Commerce, Washington, 1981-84; legis. counsel U.S. Dept. of Interior, Washington, 1984-85; mgr. fed. rels. Air Products & Chems. Inc., Washington, 1985-86, dep. dir. fed. rels., 1986-88, dir. fed. rels., 1988—; bd. dirs. Nat. Assn. Bus. Polit. Action Coms., 1988—. Candidate 6th Congl. Dist., U.S. Congress, Ohio, 1980. Mem. NAM (pub. affairs steering com. 1989—), Bus.-Govt. Rels. Coun., The Pa. Group (founder), U.S. C. of C. (pub. affairs com. 1987—, taxation com. 1990—). Home: 1406 Kurtz Rd Mc Lean VA 22101-4019 Office: Air Products & Chems Inc 805 15th St NW # 330 Washington DC 20005-2207

CHROUSOS, GEORGE PANAGIOTIS, biomedical researcher; b. Patras, Greece, July 18, 1951; came to U.S., 1976; s. Panagiotis George and Spyridula (Karaiskos) C.; m. Georgia Antonakou, June 5, 1976; children: Phaedra, Ione, Thalia. MD, Athens U., 1975, ScD, 1976. Diplomate Am. Bd. Pediatrics/Endocrinology. Resident NYU Med. Ctr., 1976-78; fellow NIH, Bethesda, Md., 1978-81, sr. investigator, 1981-89; sect. chief, dir. Pediatric Endocrinology, NIH, Bethesda, 1989—; asst. prof. Georgetown U. Med. Sch., Washington, 1981-83, assoc. prof., 1983-85, prof., 1985—. Author 4 books; contbr. articles to profl. jours. Fellow ACP, Am. Acad. Pediatrics; mem. Soc. for Pediatric Rsch., Am. Soc. for Clin. Investigation, Endocrine Soc. (R. Weitzman Meml. award 1987), Soc. for Neuroscience. Office: NIH 9000 Rockville Pike Bethesda MD 20892

CHRYSSIS, GEORGE CHRISTOPHER, business executive; b. Crete, Greece, May 21, 1947; came to U.S., 1966; naturalized U.S. citizen; s. Christopher and Ourania (Kamisakis) C.; m. Margo Sayegh, May 21, 1978; children: Rania, Lilian, Alexander. AS in Elec. Engring., Wentworth Inst., 1969; BEE, Northeastern U., 1972, MEE, 1977. Electronic engr. Orion Rsch., Boston, 1977-78; sr. engr. Datel, Inc., Mansfield, Mass., 1978-79; co-founder, v.p. ops. and engring. Power Gen. Corp., Canton, Mass., 1979-85; pres., founder, chief fin. officer Intelco Corp., Acton, Mass., 1985-90, also chmn. bd. dirs.; pres., treas. G & M Enterprises, Inc., 1991—; trustee Hellenic Coll./Holy Cross; bd. dirs. Nat. Coun. Northeastern U., Nat. Coun. Wentworth Inst.; corporator Northeastern U., Wentworth Inst., chmn. 1989 fund campaign; lectr. in field. Author: High Frequency Switching Power Supplies, 1984, 89; contbr. articles to profl. jours. Bd. dirs. St. Demetrios Ch., Weston, Mass.; fellow Orthodox Stewart of Boston Diocese; active numerous community and civic orgns. Recipient New Englander award Smaller Bus. Assn. of New Egland (SBANE), 1989, Golden Leopard award Wentworth Inst.,1991; named Entrepreneur of Yr. Arthur Young Inc., 1989. Mem. Pancretan Assn. Am. (pres. Boston chpt. 1987-89, co-chmn. 30th nat. conv. 1988, gov. dist. I 1990—), Northeastern U. Huntington Soc., Press Club, 500 Club of Northeastern U., Alpha Omega Coun. Greek Orthodox.

CHU, BENJAMIN THOMAS PENG-NIEN, chemistry educator; b. Shanghai, China, Mar. 3, 1932; came to U.S., 1953; s. Charles C. and Gladys (Chen) C.; m. Louisa King, Mar. 30, 1959; children: Peter, Joanne, Laurence. BS magna cum laude, St. Norbert Coll., 1955; PhD, Cornell U., 1959. Research assoc. Cornell U., Ithaca, N.Y., 1958-62; asst. prof. U. Kans., Lawrence, 1962-65, assoc. prof., 1965-68; prof. chemistry SUNY, Stony Brook, 1968-88, Leading prof. chemistry, 1988-92, Disting. prof., 1992—, chmn. chemistry dept., 1978-85, prof. materials sci. and engring., 1982—; vis. prof. Wayne State U., Hokkaido U., 1975-76; cons. Calgon, Pitts., 1978-80, E.I. DuPont de Nemours, Wilmington, Del., 1979—, Brookhaven Instruments, L.I., 1981, USRA, Microgravity Sci. and Applications Div., NASA, 1988, Bristol-Myers Squibb Co., 1990—. Author: Molecular Forces, 1967, Problems in Chemical Thermodynamics, 1967, Laser Light Scatterings, 1974; editor: NATO ASI series B: Physics, Vol. 73, 1981, SPIE Milestone series: Selected Papers on Quasielastic Light Scattering by Macromolecular, Supramolecular, and Fluid Systems, Vol. MS 12, 1990, Laser Light Scattering: Basic Principles and Practice, 2d edit., 1991; patentee prism light scattering cells, method and apparatus for determining viscosity, light scattering and spectroscopic detector, magnetic needle rheometer. Sloan Research fellow, 1966-68, John Simon Guggenheim fellow, 1968-69, Japan Soc. Promotion Sci. fellow, 1975-76, 92-93; recipient Humboldt award 1976-77, 92-93, Disting. Achievement award St. Norbert Coll., 1981. Fellow Am. Phys. Soc., Am. Inst. Chemists; mem. Am. Crystallographic Assn., Am. Chem. Soc.

CHU, DAVID YUK, chemical engineer; b. Canton, People's Republic China, May 12, 1945; came to U.S., 1962; s. Kwok Tsing and Yuet Moi (Ma) C.; m. Margaret Po Yee, June 29, 1969; children: David Yue, William, Randolph. BSChemE, Lowell Tech. Inst., 1969, BS in Paper Engring., 1969. Tech. svc. engr. Westvaco, Mechan, N.Y., 1969-7l; lab. supr. Boston Insulated Wire and Cables Co., Boston, 1971-76, materials specialist, 1977-84; mgr. materials tech. svc. BIW Cable Systems, Inc., Plymouth, Mass., 1985-86; mgr. materials devel. BIW Cable Systems, Inc., North Dighton, Mass., 1987—. Fellow Am. Chem. Soc.; mem. Soc. Plastics Engrs., TAPPI, Am. Inst. Chem. Engring., Boston Rubber Group, Jackson Park Club (pres. 1984-86). Office: BIW Cable Systems Inc 22 Joseph E Warner Blvd North Dighton MA 02764-1345

CHU, FOO, physician; b. N.Y.C., Feb. 3, 1921; s. Fook Chu and Jan Hong; m. Nannie Marguerite Hanje, Mar. 27, 1948; children: Janice, David, Carol. BA, Oberlin Coll., 1942; MD, Cornell U., 1945. Diplomate Nat. Bd. Med. Examiners, 1945, Am. Bd. Pathology, 1962, Am. Bd. Quality Assurance and Utilization Review Physicians. Intern Bellevue Hosp. Cornell div., N.Y.C., 1945-46; resident in medicine Lincoln Hosp., Bronx, N.Y., 1948-50; pvt. practice N.Y.C., 1950—; personnel health asst. N.Y. Hosp., N.Y.C., 1950-51; asst. pathologist Lincoln Hosp., Bronx, 1951-64, pathologist, 1964-81, physician cons. dept. quality assurance, 1987—; assoc. med. dir. Comprehensive Med. Review, Inc., Bronx, 1982-87; instr. in medicine Cornell Med. Coll., N.Y.C., 1950-62; clin. instr. Albert Einstein Coll. of Medicine, Bronx, 1967-74, asst. clin. prof. pathology, 1974-76; mem. Minority Adv. Com. N.Y. State Dept. Mental Health, 1979-91. Contbr. articles to profl. jours. Chmn. Chinatown Health Coun., N.Y.C., 1969-73, Asian-Am. Mental Health Task Force, 1979-91; trustee Chinatown Community Health Ctr., 1979-91, Community Family Planning Coun., 1982—; trustee Hamilton Madison House, 1988; mem. adv. bd. Asian Am. Mental Health Project, 1983—, trustee, 1989. With U.S. Army, 1946-48. Recipient Community Service award Hamilton Madison House, 1985. Mem. AMA, N.Y. State Med. Soc., N.Y. County Med. Soc. Home: 116 Altamont Ave Tarrytown NY 10591-4203

CHU, HOI L., graphic designer, consultant; b. Szechwan, People's Republic of China, May 7, 1947; s. Quen Shang and Ping Ying (Wang) C.; m. Lillian C. Walters, Sept. 16, 1983; children: Lea A., Lucas Q. BS, U. Oreg., 1971; BFA, The Cooper Union, N.Y., 1974. Designer Lubalin, Smith, Carnase, N.Y.C., 1974; assoc. art dir. Avant Garde Mag., N.Y.C., 1974; designer Chermayeff & Geismar Assoc., N.Y.C., 1974-79; pres. H.L. Chu & Co. Ltd., N.Y.C., 1979—; designer various visual identities BF Goodrich, 1975; wrangler Prudential Securities Ziff-Davis Publ. Co., 1977, Diawa Bank Ltd., 1988, Key Coffee, Inc., 1988. Recipient One Show award 1975, Bronze medal Biennale Graphic Design, 1982, award of excellence, 1986, Gold Quill award Internat. Assn. Bus. Communicators, 1986. Mem. Am. Inst. Graphic Arts (various awards 1977-87), N.Y. Art Dirs. Club (various awards 1977-84). Office: 39 W 29th St New York NY 10001-4208

CHU, RODERICK GONG-WAH, management consultant; b. N.Y.C., Jan. 17, 1949; s. Norton Yuen and Frances (Liang) C. BS, U. Mich., 1969; MBA with honors, Cornell U., 1971. Staff analyst Arthur Andersen and Co., N.Y.C., 1971-75, mgr., 1975-81, ptnr., 1981-83; commr. Taxation and Fin., pres. State Tax Commn. State of N.Y., Albany, 1983-88; ptnr. Andersen Cons., N.Y.C., 1988—, worldwide mng. ptnr., state and local govt. practice, 1989-91, worldwide mng. ptnr., govt. practice, 1991-92; bd. dirs. Housing Fin. Agy., Med. Care Facilities Fin. Agy., Project Fin. Agy., Affordable Housing Corp., 1983-88, N.E. States Tax Ofcls. Assn, 1983-88, Fedn. Tax Adminstrs., 1985-88, Nat. Tax Assn.-Tax Inst. Am., 1986-88, mem. adv. bd. Coun. for Excellence in Govt., 1991—. Bd. dirs., bd. overseers Jacob's Pillow Dance Festival, Becket, Mass., 1984—; trustee SUNY, 1990—; mem. pres.'s adv. coun. China Inst. Am., 1990—. Recipient Man of Yr. award Chinese-Am. Planning Coun., 1984, N.Y.C. Police Dept., Asian Jade Soc., 1984, Disting. Achievement award United Chinese Am. League, 1985, Spl. Recognition award Asian Ams. for Affirmative Action, 1986, Champion of Excellence award Orgn. Chinese Ams., 1986; Paul Harris fellow Rotary Internat., 1988. Mem. Am. Soc. Pub. Adminstrn. (hon.), Cornell Club (N.Y.C.), Albany Country Club, Met. Opera Club. Democrat. Office: Andersen Consulting 1345 Ave of the Americas New York NY 10105-0099

CHU, VALENTIN YUAN-LING, author; b. Shanghai, Republic of China, Feb. 14, 1919; came to U.S., 1956, naturalized, 1961; s. Thomas V.D. and Rowena S.N. (Zee) Tsu; m. Victoria Chao-yu Tsao, Sept. 25, 1954; 1 son, Douglas Chi-hua. BA, St. John's U, Shanghai, 1940. Asst. Shanghai Mcpl. Coun., 1940-42; asst. mgr., pub., printer Thomas Chu & Sons, Shanghai, 1943-45; chief reporter China Press, Shanghai, 1945-49; pub. rels. officer Cen. Air Transport Corp., Shanghai and Hong Kong, 1949; Hong Kong corr. Time & Life mags., Shanghai and Hong Kong, 1949-56; with Time, Inc., N.Y.C., 1956-76; writer, asst. editor Time-Life Books, N.Y.C., 1968-76; assoc. editor Reader's Digest Gen. Books, N.Y.C., 1978-83; lectr. on China. Author: Ta Ta, Tan Tan—Fight Fight, Talk Talk, 1963. Thailand Today, 1968; (with others) U.S.A., A Visitor's Handbook, 1969; contbr. articles to popular mags. Recipient spl. award UN Internat. Essay Contest, 1948. Mem. Authors League Am., Authors Guild, China Inst. in Am., Inst. Noetic Scis. Presbyterian. Home: 10 Oconnor Ct Montrose NY 10548-1508

CHUA, KIAT, aerospace scientist; b. Kuala Lumpur, Selangor, Malaysia, May 8, 1962; came to U.S., 1984; s. Kia-Hong and Chi-Tai (Fong) C. BSME, U. Western Ontario, Can., 1984; MS in Aeros., Calif. Inst. Tech., 1985, PhD in Aeros., 1990. Rsch. asst. Calif. Inst. Tech., Pasadena, 1984-90; rsch. assoc. Continuum Dynamics, Inc., Princeton, N.J., 1990—. Contbr. articles to profl. jours. Sml. Bus. Innovative Rsch. grantee Dept. Energy, 1991. Mem. AIAA, Am. Helicopter Soc. Office: Continuum Dynamics Inc James Forrestal Campus Bldg 9A Princeton NJ 08540

CHUANG, CYNTHIA, artist; b. Taiwan, Yun-lomg, China, Oct. 15, 1951; Came to U.S., 1981; d. Sin-Shai and Hsiu-Chun (Lin) C.; m. Erh-Ping Tsai, July, 1983; children: Sue-San, Ron-Han. BA, Nat. Taiwan Acad. Art, Taipei, 1978; MFA, Parsons Sch. Design, N.Y.C., 1984; postgrad., N.Y. Studio Sch., N.Y.C., 1986; studied with William Tucker, Ronald Bladen. Owner Jewelry 10, Inc., Forest Hills, N.Y., 1985—. Two-person shows with Erh-Ping Tsai: Lincoln Ctr. Cork Gallery, N.Y.C., 1985, Lincoln Ctr. Crafts Show, N.Y.C. (chosen for program cover photograph 1988, citywide poster 1989), Galeria Mesa, Mesa, Ariz., 1990, Arrowmont Sch. Arts & Crafts, Gatlinburg, Tenn., 1990, San Angelo (Tex.) Mus. Fine Arts, 1990, Luckenbach Mill Gallery, Bethlehem, Pa., 1990, Zoller Gallery, Pa. State U. (recipient sculpture prize), 1990, Three Rivers Arts Festival, Pitts. (recipient indoor sculpture prize for outstanding artistic accomplishment, 1990, Mark Milliken Gallery, N.Y.C, 1990, Kleinert Art Ctr., Woodstock, N.Y., 1990; featured on Taiwan TV in "Two Taiwanese Artists Create A Fantasy in New York," 1991; contbr. articles to profl. publs. Recipient Niche award for outstanding craft design in wearable mixed media, Niche Mag., 1990, featured in profile article, 1992; winner 1st prize Columbus (Ohio) Arts Festival, 1992. Office: Jewelry 10 Inc 30 Markwood Rd Forest Hills NY 11375

CHUBB, HENDON, psychologist; b. N.Y.C., Mar. 1, 1933; s. Percy and Corinne Roosevelt (Alsop) C.; m. Nita Colgate, 1958 (div. 1981); children: Amber, Oliver; m. Phyllis Lancaster Nauts, June 12, 1982. BA, Yale U., 1954; MA, Adelphi U., 1976, PhD, 1978. Chief fin. officer Chubb Corp./ Chubb & Son, Inc., N.Y.C., 1957-74; sr. psychologist Kings County Med. Ctr., Bklyn., 1977-80; psychologist Kaiser Permanente, Martinez & Pleasanton, Calif., 1980-88; pvt. practice psychology Torrington and Cornwall, Conn., 1988—; dir. Brief Therapy Inst., West Cornwall, Conn., 1986—. Translator: If You Love Me, Don't Love Me, 1990; contbr. articles to profl. jours. Pres. Lexington Dem. Club, N.Y.C., 1970-72; mem. Bd. Fin., Cornwall, Conn., 1991—. With U.S. Army, 1954-56. Mem. Coun. on Fgn. Rels., Am. Family Therapy Assn., Am. Psychol. Assn. Democrat. Home and Office: Brief Therapy Inst 65 Johnson Rd West Cornwall CT 06796-1623

CHUCK, HARRY COUSINS, retired army officer; b. Bklyn., Mar. 10, 1904; s. Harry and Emily (Cousins) C.; B.A., Colgate U., 1926; J.D., N.Y. U., 1930, J.S.D., 1932; m. Amy May Blakeney, Jan. 16, 1943. Admitted to N.Y. bar, 1932; practiced in N.Y.C., 1932-40; commd. 2d lt., U.S. Army Res., 1925, advanced through grades to col., 1944, ret., 1959. Decorated Legion of Merit. Mem. Am. Bar Assn., N.Y. County Lawyers Assn., Assn. U.S. Army, Ret. Officers Assn., Phi Delta Phi, Pi Delta Epsilon. Baptist. Home: 1047 Sandy Ridge Rd Doylestown PA 18901-2434

CHUDOBIAK, WALTER JAMES, electronics company executive, electronics engineer; b. Gliechen, Alta., Can., Apr. 2, 1942; s. John and Clara (Suchy) C.; m. Mary Annetta Budarick, Oct. 11, 1969; children—Michael, Anne. B.Sc. in Elec. Engring., U. Alta., Edmonton, 1964; M.Eng. in Electronic Engring., Carleton U., Ottawa, Ont., Can., 1965, Ph.D. in Electronic Engring., 1969. Research officer Def. Research Bd., Ottawa, 1965-69; group leader, research scientist Communications Research Centre, Dept. Communications, Ottawa, 1969-75; assoc. prof. Carleton U., 1975-81; pres., founder Avtech Electrosystems Ltd., Ottawa, 1975—, also dir. U. Alta. scholar, 1960-64; Carleton U. scholar, 1964-65. Mem. IEEE, Assn. Profl. Engrs. (Ont.). Conservative. Contbr. numerous articles to profl. jours.; patentee in field; inventor nanosecond pulse circuits. Home: 12 Timbercrest Ridge, Nepean, ON Canada K2H 7V2 Office: Ste 205, 55 Grenfell Crescent, Nepean, ON Canada K2G 0G3

CHUDOW, SCOTT R., physician, surgeon; b. Flushing, N.Y., Mar. 20, 1953; s. Julius and Roslyn (Moskowitz) C.; m. Gail Baustin Chudow, June 13, 1976; children: Eileen, Eric, Joel, Jay, Sheri. BS, SUNY Stony Brook, 1974; MD, Albert Einstein Coll. Medicine, 1976. Internship, surgery Einstein Bronx (N.Y.) Mcpl., 1976-77; residency, surgery Einstein Hosp. Ctr., Bronx, N.Y., 1977-80, chief residency surgery, 1980-81; surgical attending St. Anthony Community Hosp., Warwick, N.Y., 1981-87, Arden Hill Hosp., Goshen, N.Y., 1981—; diplomate Am. Bd. Surgery, Phila., 1985, Soc. Am. Gastro Endosigsic Surgeons, 1990. Office: 30 Matthews St Goshen NY 10924-1963

CHUDZIK, DOUGLAS WALTER, internist; b. Newark, Dec. 18, 1946; s. Stanley Anselm and Irene Victoria (Winkler) C.; m. Jeanmarie Murphy, Jan. 18, 1975; children: Douglas, Jeanmarie, Gregory. BS in Biology, Xavier U., 1968; MD, U. Autonoma de Guadalajara, Mex., 1972. Intern St. Barnabas Med. Ctr., Livingston, N.J., 1974, resident in internal medicine, 1975-77; attending physician dept. medicine Bayshore Community Hosp., Holmdel, N.J., 1977—, dir. medicine, 1988-89; assoc. attending physician Riverview Med. Ctr., Red Bank, N.J., 1977—. Fellow Internat. Coll. Physicians, Am. Coll. Internat. Physicians. Democrat. Roman Catholic. Home: 88 Mallard Rd Middletown NJ 07748-2950 Office: 31 Village Ct Hazlet NJ 07730-1533

CHULACK, LARA TERESA, promotional representative; b. Mt. Lebanon, Pa., June 12, 1967; d. Peter George and Mary Rosary (Schwartz) C. BSBA, N.H. Coll., 1990. Mgr. trainee Weathervane Seafoods, Salem, N.H., 1986-89; waitress Ninety Nine Restaurant and Pub, Salem, 1989-91; gen. mgr. Windham (N.H.) Farms, 1991; fin. planner Primerica Fin. Svcs., Bedford, N.H., 1991—; promotional rep. R.J. Reynolds Tobacco Co., Hopkinton, Mass., 1991—. Mem. Salem Athletic Club. Republican. Roman Catholic. Home: 24A Crescent St Derry NH 03038

CHUN, HON MING, aerospace engineer; b. Hong Kong, Nov. 23, 1960; came to U.S., 1965; s. Bing Yit and Lai Ping (Wong) C.; m. Barbara Yu-Fong Wan, Sept. 1, 1984; 1 child, Stephanie. BS, MIT, 1981, MS, 1982, PhD, 1986. Engring. trainee Dryden Flight Rsch. Ctr., NASA, Edwards, Calif., 1978; engring. intern Charles Stark Draper Lab., Inc., Cambridge, Mass., 1979-81, Draper fellow, 1981-85; staff scientist Photon Rsch. Assocs., Inc., Cambridge, Mass., 1985—. Contbr. articles to profl. jours. V.p. of ch. coun. St. James the Greater Ch., Boston, 1991-92. Recipient Spl. Achievement award NASA, 1978. Mem. AIAA. Roman Catholic. Home: PO Box 397 Kendall Square Br Cambridge MA 02142

CHUNG, CONNIE See CHUNG, CONSTANCE YU-HWA

CHUNG, CONSTANCE YU-HWA (CONNIE CHUNG), broadcast journalist; b. Washington, Aug. 20, 1946; d. William Ling and Margaret (Ma) C.; m. Maurice Richard Povich. B.S., U. Md., 1969; D.J. (hon.), Norwich U., Northfield, Vt., 1974; LHD, Brown U., 1987. TV news reporter WTTG-TV, Metromedia Channel 5, Washington, 1969-71; corr. CBS News, Washington, 1971-76; TV news anchor sta. KNXT-TV, CBS, L.A., 1976-83; anchor NBC News, NBC News at Sunrise, NBC Nightly News (Saturday), NBC News Digests, NBC News, N.Y.C., 1983-86, NBC News Digest, NBC Nightly News (Saturday), NBC News Mag. 1986, 1986-87, NBC News Digests, NBC Nightly News (Saturday), NBC New Spls., 1987-89, Saturday Night With Connie Chung (CBS-TV), CBS Evening News (Sunday ed.), from 1989, CBS Evening News With Connie Chung (Sundays), 1992—. Recipient Emmy award for individual achievement Nat. Acad. TV Arts and Scis., 1978, 80, 87; Metro Area Mass Media award AAUW, 1971; cert. of achievement for series of broadcasts which enhanced pub. awareness of cruelties of seal harvesting U.S. Humane Soc., 1969; award Atlanta chpt. Nat. Assn. Media Women, 1973; Oustanding Excellence in News Reporting and Pub. Service award Chinese-Am. Citizens Alliance, 1973; nominated for Woman of Yr. award Ladies Home Jour., 1975; named Outstanding Young Woman of Yr., 1975; recipient award for best TV reporting Los Angeles Press Club, 1977; award for outstanding TV broadcasting Valley Press Club, 1977; Women in Communications award Calif. State U., L.A., 1979; George Foster Peabody award for programs on environment Md. Center Public Broadcasting, 1980; hon. mem. Pepperdine U. Broadcast Club, 1981; Newscaster of Yr. award Temple Emanuel Brotherhood, 1981; Portraits of Excellence award B'nai B'rith, Pacific S.W. Region, 1980; First Amendment award Anti-Defamation League of B'nai B'rith, 1981. Office: CBS 414 E 65th St Apt 3G New York NY 10021-7145*

CHUNG, JUNG GIT, aerospace engineer; b. Sun Wai, Moy Kok, Canton, Republic of China, Apr. 12, 1922; s. Pak Wing and Yow Fun (Dong) C.; m. Fay Yung Ma, May 3, 1951; 1 child, John Gingkeong. BAE, NYU, 1949, MAE, 1951. With Fairchild Republic, Farmingdale, N.Y., 1951-86, airloads and performance engr., 1962-64; airloads and performance engr. M-30 Aerospace Plane Fairchild Republic, Farmingdale, 1964-66; design air loads engr. Boeing 757, Boeing Aircraft, Seattle, 1979; preliminary design and performance FRC/SAAB Transport, Swearingen Aviation, San Antonio, 1980; loads and dynamics engr. Grumman E-2C, Grumman Aircraft, Bethpage, 1981, preliminary design of aerial refueling tank, 1982; missile ejection and separation dynamics Grumman F-14, Bethpage, 1983, with ASW-340 store carriage and separation, F-15 dispenser tech., 1984, with A-10 performance maintenance, capacity acctg., interface mgmt., aircraft accident analysis, 1985, T-46 aeroperformance, quality control flying surfaces, 1986; mem. faculty N.Y. Inst. Tech., 1969; instr. H&R Block, 1986. Vol. IRS Outreach, Retired Sr. Vol. Program, Medicare/Medicaid Assistance Program, Sr. Connections in Farmingdale; instr. Vol. Income Tax Assistance; coord. and instr. Tax Counseling for the Elderly; vol. Am. Fedn. Arts; mem. adv. bd. Sr. Connections Adelphi U. Sch. Social Work; 1st v.p. AARP Farmingdale chpt., 1988-89,legis. com. 1990—; program and membership chmn. Fairchild Republic Retirees, 1986-91. Mem. AAAS, Met. Mus. Art, Mus. Natural History, Am. Fedn. Arts, U.S. Coast Guard Aux., CAP, AIAA, Data Processing Mgmt. Assn., Air Force Assn., Am. Def. Preparedness Assn., N.Y. Acad. Sci., Nat. Assn. Tax Practitioners, Nat. Mgmt. Assn., Portrait Inst., Internat. Platform Assn. Republican. Presbyterian. Home: 17 Roberts St Farmingdale NY 11735-4553 Office: Sr Connections South Farmingdale Libr Farmingdale NY 11735

CHURCH, KATHRYN CANTEY, employee assistance counselor; b. Savannah, Ga., Aug. 22, 1954; d. Bryant Whitfield and Bricelyn (Johnston) Cantey; m. L.W. Preston Church, June 14, 1986; 1 child, Elizabeth Chandler. BA, Clemson (S.C.) U., 1976; MS in Clin. Psychology, Ea. Ky. U., 1978. Assoc. psychologist Greater Manchester (N.H.) Mental Health Ctr., 1978-81; cons./trainer Manchester, 1980-82; employee assistance coord. Cobb-Douglas Community Mental Health Svc. Area, Austell, Ga., 1982-86; pvt. cons. Poulsbo, Wash., 1986-87; sr. counselor Navy Family Svc. Ctr., Yokosuka, Japan, 1987-90; employee assistance counselor Montgomery Gen. Hosp., Olney, Md., 1990—; author/trainer workshop: Stress Mgmt., 1987—. Mem. Citizen's Adv. Coun. to Mayor, Greenville, S.C., 1971-72. Mem. Nat. Acad. Counselors and Family Therapists. Office: Montgomery Gen Hosps EAPS 18101 Prince Philip Dr Olney MD 20832-1512

CHURCH, PHILLIP BRENT, service executive; b. Kingsport, Tenn., Oct. 9, 1960; s. Gary H. and Betty (Bullis) C.; m. Rebecca Elizabeth Brien, Jan. 24, 1986. BBA in Mktg. cum laude, East Tenn. State U., 1984. Sports columnist Johnson City Press Chronicle, 1981-85; account mgr. Terry Bath Products div. J.P. Stevens & Co., Wagram, N.C., 1985-90; profl. rep. Pharmaceuticals & Imaging Agts. div. E.I. DuPont, Wilmington, Del., 1990—. Mem. U.S. Jaycees. Home: 4020 Oakbrook Ct Springfield IL 62707-8121 Office: EI DuPont de Nemours PO Box 80026 Barley Mills Plz Wilmington DE 19880-0026

CHURCH, RICHARD DWIGHT, electrical engineer; b. Ogdensburg, N.Y., June 27, 1936; s. Dwight Perry and Carmeta Elizabeth (Walters) C.; m. Vernice Naomi Ives, Aug. 26, 1961; children: Joel, Benjamin. BEE, Clarkson Coll. Tech., 1963. Electronic design engr. IBM, Owego, N.Y., 1963-69; prin. engr., pres. ASL Systems, Inc., Afton, N.Y., 1969—, chmn. bd. dir.; sr. electronic design engr. Magnetic Labs., Inc., Apalachin, N.Y., 1980-82; power supply engring. cons., 1982—. Patentee in field. Treas., trustee Candor Congregational Ch., 1972-84; vice chmn. Town Planning Bd. Candor, 1975-82; rep., mem. Candor Fire Co., 1972-87; bd. dirs., treas. Candor Community Club, 1970-72. With USAF, 1955-59. Recipient Dr. Carl Michel award Clarkson Coll. Tech., 1960. Mem. N.Y. Assn. Fire Chiefs, Assn. Energy Engrs. (sr.), Afton Bd. Fire Commrs., Candor Coin Club (pres. 1978-81). Republican. Home: RD 1 Box 702 Long Hill Rd Afton NY 13730 Office: PO Box 110 Afton NY 13730-0110

CHURCH, ROBERT LINDSAY, management consultant; b. Kingsville, Tex., Jan. 5, 1949; s. Walter Lee and Catherine (Barker) C.; m. Hollis Symonds, May 21, 1971 (div. 1983); m. Marlene Zolciak, Nov. 11, 1989; 1 child, James Robert. BSEE, U. Tex., 1972; MBA, U. Chgo., 1979. Sr. assoc. Booz Allen & Hamilton, N.Y.C., 1980-86; pres. Church & Co., Washington, 1986-89; prin. N.R.E.C.A., Washington, 1989—. Lt. USN, 1972-78. Home: 4709 Colorado Ave NW Washington DC 20011-3729 Office: NRECA 1800 Massachusetts Ave NW Washington DC 20036-1806

CHURCHILL, BERNARDITA REYES, history educator; b. Manila, Mar. 5, 1938; came to U.S., 1959; d. Benito Medina and Elvira Luna (Abueg) Reyes; m. Malcolm H. Churchill, Dec. 22, 1962; children: Paul Reyes, Cristina Reyes. BA magna cum laude, U. Philippines, Quezon City, 1958; MA, Cornell U., 1961; PhD in S.E. Asian History, The Australian Nat. U., Canberra, 1982. Asst. instr. dept. history U. Philippines, Quezon City, 1959-61, instr. dept. history, 1961-66, 72-74, asst. prof. dept. history, 1974-82, assoc. prof. dept. history, 1982-86, chmn. dept. history, 1984-87, prof., 1987-89, professorial lectr., 1990—; professorial lectr. De La Salle U., Manila, 1990—; lectr. Fgn. Svc. Inst. Dept. of State, Arlington, Va., 1985-92. Author: The Philippine Independence Missions to the United States 1919-1934, 1983; (with others) University of the Philippines The First 75 Years, 1985; author/editor: (with others) History of the Filipino People, 1990; editor Philippine Social Sciences Rev., 1988, (monograph) Philippine-China Relations, 1975-88, An Assessment, 1990; author book revs.; contbr. articles to profl. jours. Fellow in Philippine studies The Australian Nat. U., 1981. Fellow Philippine Assn. for Advancement of Sci.; mem. Manila Studies Assn. (pres. 1990—, charter), Philippine Nat. Hist. Soc. (life), Philippine Arts, Letters and Media Coun. (v.p. 1990—), Philippine Assn. Chinese Studies (v.p. external affairs 1990, dir. rsch./publs. 1991, v.p. internal affairs 1992), Philippine Hist. Assn. (life), Am. Studies Assn. of the Philippines (life), Philippine Coun. Fgn. Rels., Nat. Rsch. Coun. Philippines, Asian Studies Assn. Australia, Philippine Studies Assn. Australia, The Asia Soc., Assn. for Asian Studies (U.S., bd. dirs. Philippine Studies Group), Sci. and Tech. Adv. Coun. Washington. Home: 4715 47th St NW Washington DC 20016-4438 Office: U of Philippines, Dept History (CSSP), Diliman, Quezon City 1101, The Philippines

CHURCHILL, JOAN RUSSELL, marketing executive; b. Greenfield, Mass., Dec. 9, 1931; d. Rolfe Spalding Russell (dec.) and Hilda (Belknap) Stoddard; m. Frederick Deana Churchill, May 1, 1954; children: Rolfe Russell (dec.), Katherine Deane, Lucius Bradford. BA, U. Vt., 1953. Editor Carrier Air Conditioning Co., N.Y.C., 1955-56, Home Furnishings Publs., Mt. Vernon, N.Y., 1956-58; dir. Moore & Co., Stamford, Conn., 1958-63; pres. Churchill-Byrum Pub. Rels., Pelham, N.Y.C., N.Y., 1963-73; dir. pub. rels. Mt. Ascutney Hosp., Windsor, Vt., 1973-86, Valley Regional Hosp., Claremont, N.H., 1982-86; v.p. mktg. Valley Regional Healthcare, Inc., Claremont, 1986—; bd. dirs. Windsor (Vt.) Regional Home Health Care. Pres. Hist. Windsor (Vt.) Inc., 1979-81. Recipient Silver Anvil award Pub. Rels. Soc. Am., N.Y.C., 1970; named Citizen of Yr., Smith Mowry award Windsor (Vt.) C. of C., 1978. Mem. Am. Soc. for Health Care Mktg. and Pub. Rels., New Eng. Assn. for Mktg. and Pub. Rels. Home: PO Box 66 Windsor VT 05089-0066

CHURCHILL, JOHN WILLIAM, leisure studies educator; b. Homer, N.Y., Feb. 12, 1931; s. Neil Sylvester Churchill and Sarah Elizabeth (Cottrell) Churchill-Pike; m. Jule Marie Beaudry, Dec. 26, 1960; children: John Beaudry, Seth Cottrell. BS cum laude, SUNY, Cortland, 1958; MS, U. Ill., 1959; PhD, U. Wis., 1968. Cert. leisure profl.; registered recreation adminstr., N.Y., Md., rep. SEC. Asst. prof. SUNY, Cortland, 1958; asst. dir. recreation Sch. Dist. 11, Oceanside, N.Y., 1959-61; instr. U. Wis., Madison, 1961-64; dir. summer sch. recreation office U. Md., College Park, 1964-72, assoc. prof., 1964—; assoc. Internat. Money Mgmt. Inc., Greenbelt, Md., 1986—. Commr. Md. Nat. Capital Park and Plannng Commn., Upper Marlboro, 1972-82; v. chmn. Prince George's County Planning Bd., Upper Marlboro, 1974-82; convenor, 1st acting chmn. Md. Park and Recreation Citizen/Bd. Mem. Br.; convenor 1st County Travel and Tourism Com.; chmn. swimming pool task force Prince George's County; incorporator Prince George's County Park and Recreation Found., Riverdale, Md., 1982; founder, 1st sec. Prince George's Travel Promotion Council, Riverdale, 1978. Served with USN, 1950-54. Mem. Am. Planning Assn. (charter), Nat. Recreation and Pk. Assn., Md. Recreation and Pks. Assn., Am. Legion, Phi Delta Kappa (pres. Phi chpt. 1962), Kappa Delta Phi, Delta Psi Omega. Republican. Mem. Unitarian Universalist Assn. Home: 104 Lynbrook Ct Greenbelt MD 20770-1618 Office: U Md 2359 HHP Bldg College Park MD 20742

CHURCHILL, TIMOTHY ANDREW, hospital administrator; b. Lewiston, Maine, Apr. 21, 1948; s. Amos F. and Beulah (Way) C.; divorced; children: Amy, Melissa; m. Donna Jamison, May 18, 1991. BA, King's Coll., 1970; MBA, U. Maine, 1972. Comptr. nat. hdqs. Orthodox Presbyn. Ch., Phila., 1972-76; cost and budget analyst Hosp. of Med. Coll. Pa., Phila., 1976-78, dir. budgets and cost reimbursement, 1978-79, asst. adminstr., 1979-83; assoc. adminstr. Warminster (Pa.) Gen. Hosp., 1983-87; dir. regional ops. Mediq Care, Inc., Pennsauken, N.J., 1987-88; exec. dir. St. Joseph's Hosp., Phila., 1988-90; exec. dir., chief exec. officer Hosp. Phila. Coll. Osteo. Medicine, 1990—. Mem. govt. rels. com. Delaware Valley Hosp. Coun., Phila., 1991—. Home: 705 Spice Bush Ambler PA 19002-5057 Office: Hosp Phila Coll Osteo Medicine 4150 City Ave Philadelphia PA 19131-1610

CHURCHMAN, DAVID JOHN, education administrator; b. Chester, Pa., July 27, 1951; s. Paul and Michalina (Kane) C.; m. Diana Lynn Damer, Aug. 6, 1988; children: Sara Mrie, John Michael. AD, Williamson Sch., 1972; BS, Pa. State U., 1979, MEd, 1984. Cert. tchr., vice-prin. Masonry contractor State College, Pa., 1976-86; masonry instr. State Correctional Instn. at Rockview, Bellefonte, Pa., 1986-90; masonry instr., basketball coach Williamson Sch., Media, Pa., 1986-90; vice prin. Wicomico Applied Tech. Ctr., Salisbury, Md., 1990—; masonry cons., Salisbury, 1986—. Co-worker Food Drives for Salvation Army and St. Joseph's House, Salisbury, 1991-92; campaign worker Buckson for Gov.-Del., Dover, 1972. With U.S. Army, 1972-75. Mem. Am. Vocat. Assn., Assn. Pub. Sch. Adminstrs. and Suprs., ASCD, Nat. Brick Masonry Instrs. Assn., Vocat. Indsl. Clubs Am., Phi Delta Kappa, Iota Lambda Sigma. Home: 1 Kirknewton Dr Salisbury MD 21801 Office: Wicomico Applied Tech Ctr 607 Morris St Salisbury MD 21801

CIANCI, VINCENT ALBERT, JR., lawyer, mayor; b. Providence, Apr. 30, 1941; s. Vincent Albert and Esther (Capobianco) C. Grad., Moses Brown Sch., Providence, 1958; B.S., Fairfield (Conn.) U., 1962, Dr. Pub. Service (hon.), 1978; M.A. in Polit. Sci, Villanova U., 1965; J.D., Marquette U., 1966; LL.D. (hon.), Roger Williams Coll.; D.B.A. (hon.), Johnson and Wales Coll. Bar: R.I. bar 1967. Spl. asst. atty. gen. R.I., Providence, 1969-73; spl. asst. atty. gen. in charge of organized crime unit, 1973-74; mayor Providence, 1975-84, 91—, pvt. practice; host Sta. WHJJ-Radio, Providence, 1984-90; polit. commentator Sta. WJAR-TV, 1987, Sta. WLNE-TV (CBS), 1988-90; lectr. in govt. Bryant Coll., Providence, 1969-74. Trustee R.I. Hosp., Womens and Infants Hosp., Providence Pub. Library, Greater Providence C. of C. Served to 1st lt. U.S. Army, 1966-69. Decorated Order Merit Italy). Mem. R.I. Bar Assn., Bar U.S. Ct. Mil. Appeals, Bar U.S. Dist. Ct., Nat. Dist. Attys. Assn., Am. Judicature Soc., Phi Delta Phi. Clubs: Turks Head, Aurora, Providence Art, Italo-Am. (Providence); K.C. Address: 33 Power St Providence RI 02903

CIANFROCCA, FRANCIS, software company executive; b. Syracuse, N.Y., Nov. 14, 1960; s. Celestino and Mafalda (Barseti) C.; m. Paula Hostetter, Nov. 2, 1991. Student, Eastman Sch. Music, 1979-82, U. Mich., 1985-87. Software engr. Integrated Design Co., Ann Arbor, Mich., 1987-88; asst. music adminstr. N.Y.C. Opera, 1988-89; software engr. Bank of N.Y., N.Y.C., 1989-90, N.Y. Life Ins., N.Y.C., 1990-91; pres. Heldenleben Systems, Inc., N.Y.C., 1991—; cons. McDonnell-Douglas Co., N.Y.C., 1989, Colgate-Palmolive Co., N.Y.C., 1989. Office: Heldenleben Systems Inc 41-02 48th Ave New York NY 11104

CIANGIO, SISTER DONNA LENORE, religious organization administrator; b. Newark, Feb. 2, 1949; d. Nicholas Gabriel and Elizabeth Helen (Cwikla) C. BA, Caldwell (N.J.) Coll., 1971, 82; MA, NYU, 1980. Joined Sisters of St. Dominic of Caldwell, N.J., Roman Catholic Ch., 1967. Tchr. Blessed Sacrament Sch., Bridgeport, Conn., 1971-73, St. Ann Sch., Newark, 1973; chairperson art dept. St. Dominic Acad., Jersey City, 1974-78; art instr., gallery dir. Caldwell Coll., 1978-80; art dept. chairperson St. Cecilia High Sch., Englewood, N.J., 1979-81; assoc. dir. internat. office RENEW, Plainfield, N.J., 1981—; also coord. for internat. tng. and planning RENEW, Planfield, N.J.; cons. in art for secondary schs. Archdiocese of Newark, 1976-79. Recipient awards for paintings and drawings. Office: RENEW Internat Office 1232 George St Plainfield NJ 07062-1717

CIAO, FREDERICK J., principal, educator; b. Phila.; married; 3 children. BA, LaSalle U., 1962; MEd, Temple U., 1965; PhD, Southwest U. (La.), 1990. From tchr. to counselor to dept. chmn. N.E. Cath. High Sch., Phila., 1962-73; vice prin. Archibishop Wood High Sch., Warminster, Pa., 1973-85; prin. Bishop McDevitt High Sch., Wyncote, Pa., 1985—; mem. adj. faculty St. Agnes Hosp. Nursing Sch., Phila., 1963-71, Spring Garden Coll., Phila., 1971-73, Gwynedd Mercy Coll., Gwynedd Valley, Pa., 1976-84, LaSalle U., 1980—; presentor Nat. Diffusion Network. Named Man of the Yr., N.E. Cath. Alumni Assn., 1972, Educator of the Yr., Millay Club, 1986; named to Legion of Honor, Chapel of Four Chaplains, 1980; recipient John Neumann medal St. John Neumann High Sch., 1985. Mem. Nat. Assn. Secondary Sch. Prins., Nat. Cath. Edn. Assn., Nat. Coun. Tchrs. of Maths., Maths. Assn. Am., Nat. Assn. Curriculum Devel., Nat. Coun. for Self Esteem, Mid. States Assn. of Colls. (chair). Office: Bishop McDevitt High Sch 125 Royal Ave Wyncote PA 19095-1198

CIARULA, THOMAS ALAN, naval officer; b. Pottstown, Pa., July 6, 1948; s. Patrick Joseph and Gloria (Royal) C.; m. Nancy Ann Duruttya, Sept. 1, 1979; 1 child, Cristina Marie. BS in Aircraft Maintenance Engring., Northrop U., 1971. Commd. ensign USN, 1972, advanced through grades to comdr., 1987; aircraft div. officer Attack Squadron 37, NAS Cecil Field, Fla., 1973-75; maintenance control officer Naval Air Facility Kadena, Okinawa, Japan, 1975-77; line div. officer Antarctic Devel. Squadron 6, Pt Mugu Ca, Antarctica, 1977-79; maintenance control officer USS Forrestal, FPO Miami, Fla., 1979-82; wing maintenance officer Tng. Air Wing 3, NAS Chase Field, Tex., 1982-85; aircraft intermediate maintenance dept. officer Naval Air Sta., Key West, Fla., 1985-88; TASM class desk officer, cruise missiles project Navair Systems Command, Washington, 1988-89, dir. logistics, cruise missiles project, 1989-92; with PMA-205 NAVAIRSYS COM, Washington, 1992—. Vol. emergency med. technician Sugarloaf Vol. Fire Dept., Sugarloaf Key, Fla., 1985-88, Burke Vol. Fire Dept., 1988—. Republican. Roman Catholic. Home: 10924 Middlegate Dr Fairfax VA 22032-3018 Office: ATTN PE (CU)-C4 Cruise Missiles Project Washington DC 20361-1014

CIBOROWSKI, PAUL JOHN, psychology educator; b. N.Y.C., Jan. 15, 1943; s. Paul J. and Mary (Deptuch) C.; m. Doris E. Carlo, June 24, 1973; children: Philip Alan, Kevin Michael. BA, U. Dayton, 1965; MA, NYU, 1969; PhD, Fordham U., 1979. Cert. counselor. Counselor Christ the King High Sch., Queens, N.Y., 1967-70; coordinator drug edn. Sachem Sch. Dist., Holbrook, N.Y., 1971-73, sr. counselor/grant coordinator Sachem Schs., 1973-89; mental health counselor, 1980—; assoc. prof. counseling and psychology L.I. U., 1989—; pres. Stratmar Ednl. Systems; pvt. practice marriage and family therapy; cons., trainer Family Life Bur., Diocese of Rockville Centre. Author: The Changing Family I, 1984, 2d edit., 1986, Survival Skills for Single Parents, 1987; contbr. articles to profl. jours. Mem. parish council St. Mark's Roman Cath. Ch., also chmn. fin. com.; bd. dirs. Soundview Civic Assn.; fellow Ctr. for Study of the Changing Family, Port Chester, N.Y.; chair Brookhaven, N.Y. Youth Bd., Western Suffolk Coalition on child Abuse & Neglect. Grantee in field. Mem. N.Y. State Assn. for Counseling and Devel. (legis. chmn. 1989—, v.p., state curriculum com. 1981-82), Am. Assn. Counseling and Devel. (com. on children, youth and families), Am. Mental Health Counselors Assn. (chmn. spl. interest network on children and adolescents, coord. Child Adv. Network, exec. bd., nat. com. for the rights of children 1992—), Western Suffolk Counselors Assn. (past treas., past v.p.), Phi Delta Kappa. Home: 38 Mary Pitkin Path PO Box 284 Shoreham NY 11786

CICALA, JOSEPH JOHN, academic administrator, counselor; b. Phila., July 25, 1955; s. Joseph R. and Diana A. (Danesi); M. Joanne C. Conlon, June 22, 1985. BA, LaSalle U., 1979; MS, West Chester U. Pa., 1982. Cert. nat. counselor, nat. career counselor. Resident dir. Office of Residence Life West Chester U. Pa., 1980-82; residence hall dir. Office of Residence Svcs. Syracuse (N.Y.) U., 1982-85, acad. counselor Office of Supportive Svcs., 1985-86, assoc. dir. acad. advising and counseling svcs. Coll. Arts & Scis., 1986-90, dir. career exploration svcs. Coll. Arts and Scis., 1990-92. Steering com. spl. project N.Y. State Edn. Dept., 1985-86; planning com. mem. Cen. N.Y. Minority Forum on Grad. Edn., 1989-90. Mem. ACA, Am. Coll. Pers. Assn. (bd. dirs. Commn. VI 1990—), Am. Coll. Counseling Assn., Nat. Career Devel. Assn., Nat. Acad. Advising Assn., Nat. Assn. of Pre-Law Advisors. Home: 240 Main St PO Box 275 Stony Brook NY 11790-0275 Office: NYU Program In Higher Edn East Bldg Ste 300 Washington Sq New York NY 10003

CICERO, SOLOMON CHADWELL, artist, educator; b. Pittsfield, Conn., July 23, 1944; s. Solomon and Harriet (Dewitt) C.; m. Gloria Gail Jenkins, Aug. 16, 1969; children: India, Ceylon, Solomon Jr. BS in Edn., Hampton U., 1966; MS in Art Edn., Cen. Conn. State U., 1977. Fine arts tchr. Bloomfield (Conn.) Bd. Edn., 1966-70, 1974—; instr. U. Hartford Art Sch., West Hartford, Conn., 1970-73; teaching fellow art dept. Howard Univ., Washington, 1973-74; jurer Greater Hartford (Conn.) Youth Renaisance Exhibition, 1984—; prin. Vortex Design Systems, Hartford, 1988—. Artist: (graphic design patent) Keeping Jazz Alive, 1984. Sponsor Greater Hartford (Conn.) Urban League. Mem. NEA, Conn. Edn. Assn., Nat. Art Edn. Assn., Black Filmmakers Found. Home: 96 Canterbury St Hartford CT 06112

CICHELLI, MARIO THOMAS, chemical engineering consultant; b. Balt., Jan. 28, 1920; s. John and Candida (Grue) C.; m. Genevieve Bernadette Buettner, June 26, 1943; children: Richard, Joanne Cichelli Hill, David, John. BS summa cum laude, Loyola Coll., Balt., 1940; PhD in Chem. Engring., Johns Hopkins U., 1945. Registered profl. engr., Del. From rsch. engr. to mgr. engring R & D Du Pont, Wilmington, Del., 1950-65; supr., mgr. fibers R & D Du Pont, Wilmington and Richmond, Va., 1965-79; mgr. patent div. Du Pont, Wilmington, 1979-84; pres. M. T. Cichelli, Inc., Wilmington, 1990—. Contbr. to book: Graphical Presentation of Data, 1954, also articles to profl. pubs.; editor series: Heat Transfer -- Storrs, 1960; patentee in field. Bd. dirs. STEHM, Inc., Wilmington, 1988—. Mem. Am. Inst.

Chem. Engrs., Am. Chem. Soc. Roman Catholic. Home and Office: M T Cichelli Inc 10 Chilton Rd Wilmington DE 19803-1602

CIERNIEWSKI, JOSEPH WALTER, electrical engineer; b. Hartford, Conn., Nov. 7, 1957; s. Waclaw Jozef and Maria (Lysy) C. Student, U. Conn., 1975-78; BSEE, U. Hartford, 1980; MSEE, Western New Eng. Coll., 1986. Registered profl. engr., Conn. Nuclear engr. I Nuclear Power Systems/Combustion Engring. Inc., Windsor, Conn., 1981-85; exptl. engr. Hamilton Standard div. United Tech. Corp., Windsor Locks, Conn., 1985; mem. tech. staff Missile Systems div. Raytheon Co., Lowell, Mass., 1986—. Mem. IEEE, Assn. Computing Machinery. Republican. Roman Catholic. Home: 22 Roosevelt Ave Apt 14 Hudson NH 03051-2869 Office: Raytheon Co Missile Systems Div Woburn St # 311 Lowell MA 01852-5528

CIFFA, JOSEPH R., public relations executive; b. Buffalo, Apr. 19, 1950; s. Joseph Paul and Connie Grace (Alessi) C.; m. Bonnie Lynn Myers, Aug. 11, 1979; adopted children: Joel, Sara, Briana. BA, U. Buffalo, 1973. Pub. rels. asst. Niagara Frontier Transp. Authority, Buffalo, 1974-80, community rels. specialist, 1980-84, sr. community rels. specialist, 1984-88, acting mgr. pub. affairs, 1988-89; dir. pub., community rels. Millard Fillmore Hosps., Buffalo, 1989—; pub. rels. dir. Twin City Geminis Football Team, Tonawanda, N.Y., 1976-78, Ea. State Umpire Tng. Sch., Buffalo, 1976-77, Atlantic Football Conf., Tonawanda, 1977-78; news correspondent Tonawanda News, 1976-77. Gen. chmn. A Taste of Buffalo, 1988, mem. exec. bd., 1984—; mem. local organizing com. Empire State Games, Buffalo, 1984-86; mem. steering com. U.S./Can. Friendship Festival, Buffalo, 1987-88. Recipient Young Achievers award Fedn. of Italian Am. Socs. of Western N.Y., 1990. Fellow Pub. Rels. Soc. Am., Am. Soc. Hosp. Mktg. and Pub. Rels., Niagara Frontier Editors Assn. (pres. 1976-77). Republican. Home: 126 Delton St Tonawanda NY 14150-5364 Office: Millard Fillmore Hosps 3 Gates Cir Buffalo NY 14209-1194

CIMINO, ANN MARY, education educator; b. Easton, Pa.; d. John and Melina (Castelluzzo) C. BS, Pa. State U., State College, MEd; cert. reading, Lehigh U. Elem. tchr. State College; instr. Sonoma (Calif.) State U.; asst. prof. U. Md., College Park, Pa., Muhlenburg Coll., Allentown, Pa., 1968-72, Towson State U., Balt.; assoc. prof. dept. edn. Kutztown (Pa.) State U. Mem. Pa. State U. Coll. Edn. Alumni Assn. (dir.). Home: 1429 Andrew Dr Whitehall PA 18052-4311

CIMMET, GERALD, psychologist, hospital administrator; b. Wilkes-Barre, Pa., Sept. 13, 1941; s. Harold and Betty (Zerinski) C.; divorced; children: Lauren, Deena. BA, U. Pa., 1963; MS, U. Pa., Phila., 1966; MA, Temple U., 1970; PhD, Columbia Pacific U., 1989. Lic. psychologist, Pa.; cert. neuro-linguistic programming. Psychologist Family Coart, 1973-74, Community Mental Health, Phila., 1974-78; dir. West Park Sch. Community Mental Health, Phila., 1978-80; psychologist, dir. adolescent edn. Northwestern Inst. Psychiatry, Ft. Washington, Pa., 1980-90; pvt. practice Ft. Washington, 1984—. Author: Tales for Growing Up, 1989. Mem. Pa. Edn. Network for Eating Disorders (bd. mem.), Mindworks (cert.), Phi Delta Kappa. Democrat. Home: 1403 Basswood Grove Ambler PA 19002 Office: 7237 Hollywood Rd Fort Washington PA 19034-1298

CINALLI, JOSEPH P., JR., lighting company executive; b. Fairmont, W.Va., Oct. 23, 1942; s. Joe Paul and Evelyn (LoFiego) C.; m. Michele Nadine Ryan, Aug. 2, 1986; children: Lisa, Joseph III, Mike, Kelly, Maria. BSChemE, W.Va. U., 1965. Engr. Westinghouse Elec. Corp., Fairmont, W.Va., 1965-67, supr., 1967-69, gen. supr., 1969-79; capital program mgr. Westinghouse Elec. Corp., Bloomfield, N.J., 1979-81; mgr. mfg. Westinghouse Elec. Corp., Fairmont, 1981-83; plant mgr. Philips Lighting, Salina, Kans., 1983-89, Phnilips Lighting, Bath, N.Y., 1989—. Pres. bd. dirs. Mary Mount Coll., Salina, Kans., 1987-88, United Way, Salina, 1986-87; bd. dirs. St. John's Hosp., Salina, 1985-89. Mem. Illuminating Engring. Soc., Univ. Ind. Pub. Partnership for Econ. growth (bd. dirs.), Salina C. of C. (v.p. bd. 1988-89), Corning Country Club. Home: 12 Knollbrook Ln E Painted Post NY 14870-9345 Office: Philips Lighting 7265 State Rt 54 Bath NY 14810-8398

CINCOTTA, JOSEPH JOHN, analytical chemist; b. N.Y.C., Sept. 15, 1931; s. Thomas and Mary (Moleta) C.; m. Elaine M. Beck, Aug. 21, 1955; children: Jay J., Thomas C., Douglas J. BS, Columbia U., 1953; MS, CUNY, 1966. Analytical chemist Am. Molasses Co., Bklyn., 1953-59; analytical rsch. chemist Am. Cyanamid Co., Stamford, Conn., 1959-68, M. W. Kellogg Co., Piscataway, N.J., 1968-69; sr. analytical chemist Vista Chem. Co., Balt., 1969—. Home: 5025 Cloudburst Hl Columbia MD 21044-1501 Office: Vista Chem Co 3441 Fairfield Rd Baltimore MD 21226-1592

CINDRICH, RALPH EDWARD, sports agent, lawyer; b. Avella, Pa., Oct. 29, 1949; s. Anthony Joseph and Stella (Sfara) C.; m. Mary Rose; children: Michael Edward, Christina Marie. BA, U. Pitts., 1972; JD, South Tex. Coll. Law, 1978. Bar; Tex. 1978, Pa. 1981, U.S. Tax Ct., 1978. Profl. football player New Eng. Patriots, Foxboro, Mass., Houston Oilers, 1972-75; pvt. practice law Houston, 1978-81; sports agt., atty. Pitts., 1981-88; sports agt., atty. Internat. Mgmt. Group, Pitts., 1988-90, pres. football div., 1988-90; self-employed sports agt., lawyer Pitts., 1990—. Recipient Pro Golden Helmet award Coca Cola Co.; inducted into Western Pa. Sports Hall of Fame, 1989; named AP Pro Player of Week New Eng. Patriots vs. Miami Dolphins game. Mem. ABA, Pa. Bar Assn., Allegheny County Bar Assn., Allegheny County Lawyer Referral Svc., NFL Players Assn. Office: 552 Washington Ave Carnegie PA 15106-2894

CINQUEMANI, JOSEPH ROBERT, computer company manager; b. N.Y.C., Aug. 27, 1952; s. Charles Anthony and Joan (Howard) C.; m. Vinneann Paruolo, Jan. 2, 1972; children: Michael, Robert, Christopher. AS in Computer Tech., Control Data Inst., 1974; AAS in Bus. Mgmt., Pace U., 1989; MBA, Columbia U., 1991. Program support engr. IBM Corp., N.Y.C., 1974-76; unit mgr. Digital Equipment Corp., N.Y.C., 1976-78, product support mgr., 1978-80, br. mgr., 1980-83, dist. mgr., 1983-85, vendor equipment mgr., 1985-86, network bus. mgr., 1986-88, industry group mgr., 1988-90, bus. mgr., 1990-91, U.S. systems integration sales support mgr., 1991-92, U.S. facilities mgmt. svcs. mgr., 1992—. Pace U. scholar, 1986. Mem. Phi Sigma Eta. Home: 220 Dante Ave Tuckahoe NY 10707-3015

CIOLLI, ANTOINETTE, librarian, retired educator; b. N.Y.C., Aug. 20, 1915; d. Pietro and Mary (Palumbo) C.; A.B., Bklyn. Coll., 1937, M.A., 1940; B.S. in L.S., Columbia U., 1943. Tchr. history and civics Bklyn. high schs., 1943-44; circulation librarian Bklyn. Coll. Library, 1944-46; instr. history Sch. Gen. Studies, Bklyn. Coll., 1944-50, asst. prof. library dept., 1965-73, assoc. prof., 1973-81, prof. emerita, 1981—; reference librarian Bklyn. Coll. Library, 1947-59, chief sci. librarian, 1959-70, chief spl. collections div., 1970-81, hon. archivist, 1981—. Mem. ALA, Am. Hist. Assn., Spl. Libraries Assn. (museum group chpt. sec. 1950-51, 52-54), N.Y. Library Club, Beta Phi Mu. Author: (with Alexander S. Preminger and Lillian Lester) Urban Educator: Harry D. Gideonse, Brooklyn College and the City University of New York, 1970; contbr. articles to profl. jours. Home: 1129 Bay Ridge Pky Brooklyn NY 11228-2337

CIOROIU, MICHAEL GELU, surgeon; b. Brasov, Romania, July 27, 1947; came to U.S., 1978; s. Marin and Margareta (Juranescu) C.; m. Monica Moca, Aug. 4, 1978; 1 child, Monica Comana. BS, Nr 1 Liceum, Romania, 1965; MD, Faculty of Medicine, Romania, 1971. Diplomate Am. Bd. Surgery. Instr. clin. surgery Inst. Medicine & Pharmacy, Cluj, Romania, 1971-77; resident in surgery Cabrini Med. Ctr., N.Y.C., 1980-85, attending physician, surgeon, coordinator nutrition support services, 1985—, dir. surg. research, 1987—; assoc. prof. clin. surgery N.Y. Med. Coll., Valhalla, 1985—. Contbr. articles to profl. jours. Recipient cert. appreciation Bayley Seton Hosp., 1984. Fellow ACS, Internat. Coll. Surgeons, Am. Soc. Abominal Surgeons; mem. AMA (award 1987, 90), Surg. Soc. N.Y. Med. Coll. Republican. Office: 247 3d Ave L-3 New York NY 10010

CIRELLO, JOHN, waste management company executive; b. Bound Brook, N.J., Apr. 17, 1943; s. FioreAvanti and Assunta C.; m. Sherron Anne Thomas, July 31, 1965; children: Assunta Anne, Elizabeth Rose, Sherron Marie. BS, Rutgers U., 1965, MS, 1971, PhD, 1975. Registered profl. engr., N.J., Pa. Engr. Calif. Dept. Water, L.A., 1965-66, U.S. Army Corps of Engrs., Ft. Belvoir, Va., 1966-68, Balt. Gas and Elec., 1968-69; researcher Rutgers Water Resources Inst., New Brunswick, N.J., 1969-71; asst. prof. Rutgers U., New Brunswick, 1971-80; pres. Princeton Aqua Sci., Edison, N.J., 1980-85; v.p. IT Corp., Edison, N.J., 1985-88; v.p. ea. region Chem. Waste Mgmt., Inc., Princeton, N.J., 1988—. Editor (tng. manuals) Land Application of Effluents & Sludges, 1976, Ultimate Disposal of Organic and Inorganic Sludges, 1976, Water and Wastewater Polishing and Rennovation Techniques, 1976; co-editor (tng. manual) Construction and Environmental Inspectors Training Manual, 1977; contbr. articles to profl. jours. Mem. Bd. Adjustment, Bound Brook, N.J., 1976-81; councilman, pres., Bound Brook Town Coun., 1981-87; chmn. Dem. com. Bound Brook, 1982-86. Capt. U.S. Army Engr. Corps, 1966-68. Recipient award N.J. Water Pollution Control Assn., 1990. Mem. ASCE, Water Pollution Control Fedn., Am. Chem. Soc. Roman Catholic. Home: 620 Watchung Rd Bound Brook NJ 08805-1746 Office: Chem Waste Mgmt Inc 100 Nassau Park Blvd Princeton NJ 08540-5932

CIRINCION, MARCO VINCENT, dean of students; b. Hoboken, N.J., Mar. 29, 1938; s. Philip and Amelia (Della Volpe) C.; m. Patricia Wagner, July 6, 1963; children: Regina, Dayna, Philip. BA, Jersey City State Coll., 1963, MA, 1965; EdD, Fairleigh Dickinson U., 1974; DDiv (hon.), Universal Life, 1969. Tchr. Cliffside Park, N.J., 1963-64; dir. of residence Jersey City (N.J.) State Coll., 1964-69, assoc. dean, 1970-78, dean of students, 1978—. With USMC, 1951-59. Named Italian Am. Educator of Yr., 1985. Mem. Nat. Assn. Student Personnel Adminstrn. (chief student affairs officer, middle region, pres., v.p.). Office: Jersey City State College 2039 Kennedy Blvd Jersey City NJ 07305

CISTARO, PETER ANTHONY, utility executive; b. Elizabeth, N.J., June 20, 1946; s. Peter and Margaret (Oriscello) C.; m. Josephine A. Ciccone, July 29, 1973; children: Robert, Joseph. BS in Indsl. Engring., Newark Coll., 1968; MBA, Fairleigh Dickinson U., 1981. Engr. Pub. Svc. Electric and Gas Co., Summit, N.J., 1968-72; dist. mgr. Pub. Svc. Electric and Gas Co., Summit and Jersey City, N.J., 1972-80; asst. mgr. indsl. rels. Pub. Svc. Electric and Gas Co., Newark, 1980-86, mgr. indsl. rels., 1986-88; gen. mgr. region ops. Pub. Svc. Electric and Gas Co., Clifton, N.J., 1988-90; gen. mgr. mktg. svcs. Pub. Svc. Electric and Gas Co., Newark, 1990-91; gen. mgr. corp. quality Pub. Svc. Electric & Gas Co., Newark, 1991—. Mem. Parsippany (N.J.) Troy Hills Planning Bd., 1989—, Parsippany Rep. Club; bd. dirs. Essex chpt. ARC, East Orange, 1991—. Mem. Am. Gas Assn., Edison Electric Inst., Alpha Pi Mu. Roman Catholic. Office: Pub Svc Electric & Gas Co PO Box 570 Newark NJ 07101-0570

CITRIN, JAMES MICHAEL, management consultant; b. Great Neck, N.Y., Nov. 2, 1959; s. Harold Lee and Glenna (Green) C.; m. Gail Sarner, Aug. 14, 1988; children: Theodore, Oliver. AB, Vassar Coll., 1981; MBA with distinction, Harvard U., 1986. Fin. analyst Morgan, Stanley & Co., Inc., N.Y.C., 1981-84; assoc. Goldman, Sachs & Co., N.Y.C., 1986-87; sr. engagement mgr. McKinsey & Co., Stamford, Conn., 1987—. Founder, chmn. Vassar Coll. 21st Century Com., 1987-91. Mem. Phi Beta Kappa. Home: 2905 Long Ridge Rd Stamford CT 06903 Office: McKinsey & Co 3 Landmark Sq Stamford CT 06901

CITRON, RICHARD IRA, management consultant; b. Chgo., Apr. 1, 1944; s. Irving I. and Ruth (Katz) C.; m. Phyllis Sarah Kalifey, Dec. 26, 1971; children: Brian Todd, Dana Ann. BS, Roosevelt U., Chgo., 1966; MS, Ill. Inst. Tech., 1968, PhD, 1972. Enrolled Actuary. Consulting prin. A.S. Hansen, Inc., Chgo., 1972-79; mng. prin. A.S. Hansen, Inc., N.Y.C., 1979-82; exec. v.p. Frank B. Hall Consulting Co., N.Y.C., 1982-86; pres., chief exec. officer W F Corroon, Inc., Stamford, Conn., 1986-92; pres. Hogg Robinson, Inc., 1992—; CEO Penn Gen. Svcs., Inc., 1992—, Pension Planning, Inc., 1992—, Group Plan Cons., Inc., 1992—; bd. dirs. Employee Benefit Rsch. Inst., Washington, HRI, Inc., N.A. Author articles in profl. jours. Trustee Optometric Ctr. of N.Y., mem. Coll. Council of SUNY; cons. State of Ill. Pension Laws Commn. 1974-78. Recipient: Blum-Kolver Found. grant 1963-66, Nat. Sci. Found. grant 1968-70. Mem. Am. Acad. of Actuaries, Internat. Found. Employee Benefits (chmn actuaries com. 1981-82), Assn. of Private Pension and Welfare Plans, Am. Soc. for Advancement of Sci., Boardroom, Landmark, Elmwood Country Club. Office: W F Corroon Inc 2777 Summer St APO AE 09601-5000

CIVAN, MORTIMER M., physiology investigator, educator; b. N.Y.C., Nov. 13, 1934. AB, Columbia Coll., 1955; MD, Columbia U., 1959. Diplomate Am. Bd. Internal Medicine. Med. intern, then resident in internal medicine Presbyn. Hosp., N.Y.C., 1959-62; staff assoc. Nat. Inst. Arthritis and Metabolic Diseases/NIH, 1962-64; clin. and rsch. fellow in medicine Mass. Gen. Hosp./Harvard U. Med. Sch., 1964-65; instr. in medicine Med. Sch. Harvard U., 1965-68, asst. prof. physiology Med. Sch., 1969-72; assoc. prof. physiology U. Pa., Phila., 1972-77, prof. physiology, 1977—; assoc. prof. medicine U. Pa. Sch. Medicine, Phila., 1972-88; prof. of medicine U Pa Sch. Medicine, Phila., 1988—; vis. scientist dept. polymer rsch. Weizmann Inst. of Sci., 1970-71, Imperial Cancer Rsch. Fund Labs., London, 1984-85, 91-92; vis. prof. zoology U. Cambridge, Eng., 1978-79; established investigator Am. Heart Assn.; faculty scholar Josiah Macy Jr. Found., 1978-79; cons. NIH/NSF, 1972—; Harold Chaffer Meml. lectr. faculty medicine U. Otago, Dunedin, New Zealand, 1990. USPHS fellow, 1964-65, 70-71. Fellow AAAS; mem. Am. Physiol. Soc. (steering com. cell and gen. physiology sect. 1981-83, chmn. steering com. cell and gen. physiology sect. 1982-83), Am. Soc. Clin. Investigation, Am. Soc. Nephrology, Assn. for Rsch. in Vision & Ophthalmology, Internat. Soc. Nephrology, Soc. Gen. Physiologists (sec. 1981 1981-84), John Morgan Soc., Biophys. Soc., Nat. Kidney Found., Salt and Water Club, Phi Beta Kappa, Alpha Omega Alpha. Office: U Pa Dept Physiology Richards Bldg A-303 Philadelphia PA 19104-6085

CLACK, JERRY, classics educator; b. N.Y.C., July 22, 1926; s. Christopher Thrower and Mildred Taylor (VanDyke) C. A.B., Princeton U., 1946, M.A., 1958; Ph.D., U. Pitts., 1962; M.A., Duquesne U., Pitts., 1977. Documents officer U.S. Nat. Commn. for UNESCO, 1946-52; exec. dir. Allegheny County chpt. Nat. Found., Pitts., 1953-68; asst. prof. dept. classics Duquesne U., Pitts., 1968-71, assoc. prof., 1971-75, prof., 1975—, chmn. dept., 1973-75, 80-83, mem. preprofl. health com., 1970-76, mem. univ. library com., 1979—, mem. univ. due process, core curriculum, arts and scis. curriculum coms., 1986—, mem. univ. promotion and tenure com., 1988-90. Editor: The Classical World, 1977—, Anthology of Hellenistic Poetry, 1982, Meleager: The Poems, 1992; mem. editorial bd. Duquesne Univ. Press, 1991—; author books, articles, revs. in field. Pres. Western Pa. Pub. Health Conf., 1967; v.p. Western Pa. Council World Federalists, 1965-88, treas., 1987—; mem. U.S. del. to 3d UNESCO Gen. Conf., Florence, Italy, 4th UNESCO Gen. Conf., Paris. Mem. Classical Assn. Pitts. and Vicinity (treas. 1970-78, sec. 1988—), Pa. Classical Assn. (treas. 1977—), Classical Assn. Atlantic States (pres. 1987, exec. com. 1974—, 2d v.p. 1975, 1st v.p. 1976), Am. Philol. Assn. (chmn. working group editors classical jours., chmn. com. regional classical orgns. 1986—), Vergilian Soc. Am. (trustee 1985-87), Phi Sigma Iota, Delta Phi Alpha, Alpha Epsilon Delta, Phi Alpha Theta. Home: 5920 Kentucky Ave Pittsburgh PA 15232-2824 Office: Duquesne U Dept Classics Pittsburgh PA 15282

CLADIS, PATRICIA ELIZABETH, physicist; b. Shanghai, China; m. George H. Cladis, Dec. 29, 1962; children: Harrison Moule, Franklyn Paul. BA in Math. and Physics, U. B.C., 1959; MA in Physics, U. Toronto, 1960; PhD in Physics, U. Rochester, 1968. Meteorologist Dept. of Transport, Edmonton, Alta., 1960-62; lectr., dept. of physics Western Conn. State Univ., Danbury, 1963-64; responsible for fundamental rsch. Univ. Paris, Orsay, France, 1969-72; mem. tech. staff, rsch. physics div. AT&T Bell Labs., Murray Hill, N.J., 1972—; Kreeger Wolf Disting. prof. Northwestern Univ., 1976; adj. prof. dept. physics Univ. Del., Newark, 1977-78, Kent (Ohio) State Univ., 1989-91; vis. prof. sect. de la Vie, Ecole Pratique des Hautes Etudes, Paris, 1983, Groupe de Physique des Solides, Ecole Normale Superieure, Paris, 1985-86, Physique des Solides Univ. Paris-Sud, Orsay, 1985-86, dept. nuclear physics, Weizmann Inst., Rehovot, Israel, 1986. Mem. editorial bd. Liquid Crystals, 1986—, Sci. Instruments and Methods, 1988—; contbr. more than 100 articles to profl. jours. including Phys. Rev. Letters, Molecular Jour. Liquid Crystals, Jour. de Physique, Jour. Applied Physics. Fellow Am. Phys. Soc. (com. on the status of women in physics 1980-82, com. chair 1982, nominating com. 1982, Maria Goeppert-Mayer award com. 1987-88, com. vice chair 1987, com. chair 1988, task force for the Joseph A. Burton award 1988), Am. Inst. Physics (com. on the history of physics 1984—). Office: AT&T Bell Labs 600 Mountain Ave New Providence NJ 07974-2010

CLAGETT, BRICE MCADOO, lawyer, writer; b. Washington, July 6, 1933; s. Brice and Sarah Fleming (McAdoo) C.; m. Virginia Lawrence Parker, Sept. 18, 1965; children: John Brice, Ann Calvert Brooke; m. Diana Wharton Sinkler Knop, July 26, 1987. A.B. summa cum laude, Princeton U., 1954; postgrad. U. Allahabad (India), 1954-55; J.D. magna cum laude, Harvard U., 1958. Bar: D.C. 1958, U.S. Supreme Ct. 1962. Assoc., Covington & Burling, Washington, 1958-67, ptnr., 1967—; jud. counsellor Cambodian delegation to Internat. Ct. Justice, 1960-62; legal advisor Transition Team U.S. Dept. State, 1980-81; mem. nat. steering com. U.S. Iran Claimants Com., 1982—; adv. bd. Inst. for Transnat. Arbitration, 1989—. Bd. advisors Nat. Trust for Hist. Preservation 1978-81; Clagett family com. Chesapeake Bay Found., 1982—; trustee Md. Hist. Trust, 1971-78, chmn., 1972-78, Md. State House Trust, 1972-76, Md. Environ. Trust, 1978—, vice chmn., 1981-85, chmn. 1985-89; mem. Internat. Human Rights Law Group del. to Romania, 1990; bd. dirs. Chester-Sassafras Found., 1985-89; trustee New Eng. Hist. Geneal. Soc., 1989—, Tudor Place Found., 1992—; counsellor to the Pres. Gen., Soc. of the Cin., 1988—; mem. adv. coun. Accokeek Found., 1989—, trustee, 1991—; trustee Mt. Clare Plantation Found., 1990—; mem. arbitration com. U.S. Coun. Internat. Bus., 1989—. Commdr. Royal Order Cambodia, 1962. Recipient Cert. Disting. Citizens State of Md., 1978. Mem. ABA, Am. Soc. Internat. Law, Am. Law Inst., Am. Arbitration Assn. (panel of arbitrators 1990—), Internat. Law Assn., Washington Inst. Fgn. Affairs, Federalist Soc., Sons Confederate Vets., Mil. Order Stars and Bars, So. Md. Soc., Phi Beta Kappa. Episcopalian. Clubs: Met., City, City Tavern, Harvard (Washington), Chevy Chase, Harvard (N.Y.C.), Soc. Cin. Md., Marlborough Hunt (Upper Marlboro, Md.), Radnor (Pa.) Hunt. Co-author: The Valuation of Property in International Law, vol. 4, 1987, An Illustrated History of St. Albans School, 1981; bd. editors: Harvard Law Review, 1956-58; contbr. numerous articles to legal, geneal. and hist. jours. Home: Holly Hill Friendship MD 20758 also: 3331 O St NW Washington DC 20007 Office: Covington & Burling PO Box 7566 1201 Pennsylvania Ave NW Washington DC 20044

CLAGETT, DIANA WHARTON SINKLER, educator; b. Phila., Aug. 24, 1943; d. James Mauran Rhodes and Sarah Brinton (Wentz) Sinkler; m. Peter John Knop, Nov. 23, 1966 (div.); children: Alexandra Brinton, Peter Rhodes Quast, William James Wharton; m. Brice McAdoo Clagett, July 26, 1987. BA, George Wash. U., 1966. Rsch. asst. Nat. Investigations Com. on Aerial Phenomena, Washington, 1966-69; docent Asia Hall Smithsonian Instn., Washington, 1982-83, docent Sackler Gallery, 1989—; proprietor Georgian Antiques and Decorative Arts, Washington, 1983—. Mem. bd. devel. Hosp. for Sick Children, Washington, 1980—, vice chmn. bd. devel., 1985-86, co-chmn. flower and garden festival, 1988-90; mem. bd. devel. Children's Hearing and Speech Ctr., Washington, 1988—; mem. women's com. Phila. Acad. Fine Arts, 1980—; mem. alumni bd. Foxcroft Sch., Middleburg, Va., 1983-86. Mem. City Tavern Club (mem. bd. govs. 1990—), Radnor Hunt Club (mem. racing com.), Acorn Club, Evermay Club Georgetown, New Scotland Garden Club, Docent Coun. (sec. 1990—). Address: 3331 O St NW Washington DC 20007

CLAGETT, DONALD CARL, chemist; b. Madison, Wis., Dec. 31, 1939; s. Carl Owen and Mary Alice (Kauffman) C.; m. Lucile Morrison Sharp, Feb. 14, 1959 (div. Apr. 1968); children: Cynthia Lucile, Curt Owen, Charles Donald; m. Charlotte Ann Hollister, June 18, 1968; children: Jennifer Alison, Emma Mary, Sarah Ellen. BS, Pa. State U., 1961; MS, Yale U., 1963, PhD, 1965. Asst. prof. chem. and medicinal chemistry Northeastern U., Boston, 1968-73; sr. group leader W.R. Grace, Lexington, Mass., 1973-78; product devel. specialist GE Plastics, Pittsfield, Mass., 1978-81, mgr. process devel., 1981-86; mgr. process safety GE Plastics, Pittsfield, 1986—. Author: (with others) Engineering Plastics, 1986, Synthesis of Polycarbonates, 1988; contbr. articles to profl. jours. Bd. dirs. Berkshire Ballet, Pittsfield, 1978-88; mem. Boston Symphony Orch. Vol., Pittsfield, 1978—. Col. USAR, 1961—. Damon Runyon grantee Damon Runyon Found., N.Y.C., 1969-72, NIH grantee USPHS, 1970-73. Fellow Royal Chem. Soc.; mem. Am. Chem. Soc. (chemistry prize chmn. NE sect. 1972-73), N.Y. Acad. Sci., Chem. Mfrs. Assn. (CWD work group 1986—), Sigma Xi. Republican. Episcopalian. Home: 193 Bartlett Ave Pittsfield MA 01201-6919 Office: GE Plastics One Plastics Ave Pittsfield MA 01201

CLAGETT, GALEN RONALD, real estate broker; b. Brunswick, Md., Feb. 9, 1942; s. Lawrence Heeter Clagett and Pauline (White) Weddle; m. Elizabeth Patton Conley, July 4, 1988; children: Michele, Marcie, Thomas. BS, Frostburg State U., 1964, MS, 1972; postgrad., Western Md. Coll. Cert. tchr., real estate broker, Md. Adult edn. tchr. Frederick (Md.) County Pub. Schs., tchr., guidance counselor, sch. adminstr.; acad. instr. II Md. Dept. Corrections; instr. St. Mary's Coll., Emmitsburg, Md.; mktg. and sales v.p. Fed. Stone Corp., Thurmont, Md.; pres. Antietam Pharmacy Corp., Frederick, Clagett Enterprises, Inc., Frederick; chmn. bd. dirs. Clagett Realty, Inc., Frederick. County commr. Frederick County Govt.; pres. Frederick County Bd. Commrs.; mgr. Byron for Congress, 6th Congrl. Dist. Mem. NRA, Bd. Realtors, Humane Soc., Arts Coun., Frederick C. of C., Elks, Optimists. Democrat. Episcopalian. Home: 203 Grove Blvd Frederick MD 21701 Office: 45-G Waverley Dr Frederick MD 21702

CLAIBORNE, JACK E., communications executive; b. Newell, N.C., Oct. 19, 1931; s. Henry Goode and Minnie (Harton) C.; m. Margaret Watkins, 1957; children: Margaret Louise, Jack E. AB in English, U. N.C., 1957; MA, U. Chgo., 1960; DHL, U. N.C., Charlotte, 1991. Sports writer Charlotte Observer, 1948-58, reporter, 1959-65; city editor Charlotte Reporter, 1965-70, assoc. editor, 1970-90; v.p. Park Communications, Ithaca, N.Y., 1990—; lectr. Am. Press Inst., Columbia U., 1968-70, N.C. Ctr. for Advancement of Teaching, Cullowhee, 1989. Author: Unto the Least of These, The Story of the Alexander Children's Center, 1888-1988, 1988, The Charlotte Observer Its Time and Place, 1986, (anthology) Discovering North Carolina. A Tar Heel Reader, 1991; author editorial columns. Chmn. N.C. Humanities Coun., 1979-85; mem. Pub. Broadcasting Authority, Charlotte/Mecklenburg, 1980-84; vice chmn. Bioethics Resource Group, Charlotte, 1984-88; mem. exec. com. N.C. Lit. and Hist. Assn., 1989-90. With U.S. Army, 1953-55. Recipient Law Day Liberty Bell award Mecklenburg Bar Assn., 1986. Home: 12 Logans Run Dryden NY 13053-9782 Office: Park Communications Terrace Hill Ithaca NY 14850

CLAIBORNE, LIZ (ELISABETH CLAIBORNE ORTENBERG), fashion designer; b. Brussels, Mar. 31, 1929; came to U.S., 1939; d. Omer Villere and Louise Carol (Fenner) C.; m. Arthur Ortenberg, July 5, 1954; 1 son by previous marriage, Alexander G. Schultz. Student, Art Sch., Brussels, 1948-49, Academie, Nice, France, 1950; DFA, R.I. Sch. Design, 1991. Asst. Tina Lesser, N.Y.C., 1951-52, Omar Khayam, Ben Reig, Inc., N.Y.C., 1953; designer Juniorite, N.Y.C., 1954-60, Dan Keller, N.Y.C., 1960-76, Youth Guild Inc., N.Y.C., 1976-89; designer, pres., chmn. Liz Claiborne Inc., N.Y.C., 1985-89, pres., 1976-89, chmn., chief oper. officer, until 1989; chmn. Liz Claiborne Cosmetics, 1985-89; guest lectr. Fashion Inst. Tech., Parsons Sch. Design; bd. dirs. Coun. of Am. Fashion Designers, Fire Island Lighthouse Restoration Com. Recipient Designer of Yr. award Palciode Hierro, Mexico City, 1976, Designer of Yr. award Dayton Co., Mpls., 1978, Ann. Disting. in Design award Marshall Field's, 1985, One Co. Makes a Difference award Fashion Inst. Tech., 1985, award Coun. Fashion Designers, 1986, Gordon Grand Fellowship award Yale U., 1989, Jr. Achievement award Nat. Bus. Hall of Fame, 1990, Frederick A.P. Barnard award Barnard Coll., 1991, Hon. Doctorate, R.I. Sch. of Design, 1991; named to Nat. Sales Hall of Fame, 1991. Mem. Fashion Group. Roman Catholic. Office: 650 5th Ave New York NY 10019-6108

CLAIRE, THOMAS ANDREW, treasurer; b. Cleve., Feb. 13, 1951; s. William Henry and Dorothy Helen (Taylor) C. BA, Kenyon Coll., 1973; MA, Brown U., 1977; MBA, Columbia U., 1978. Account adminstr. Irving Trust Co., N.Y.C., 1978-80; dir. fin. planning and analysis W.R. Grace & Co., N.Y.C., 1980-83; asst. treasurer Harper & Row Publishers, Inc., N.Y.C., 1983-87; treas., asst. sec. Moët-Hennessy U.S. Corp., N.Y.C., 1987—. Mem. Greenwich Village Soc. for Hist. Preservation, N.Y.C., 1986-87. Recipient Fulbright scholar Acad. Coms., Paris, 1974-75, Nat. Merit scholar, Ohio,

1969-73. Mem. Phi Beta Kappa, Beta Gamma Sigma. Democrat. Roman Catholic. Clubs: Brown (N.Y.C.), Victorian Soc. of Am. (N.Y.C.). Home: 59 W 12th St New York NY 10011-8529 Office: Moët-Hennessy US Corp 2 Park Ave New York NY 10016

CLAIRE, WILLIAM FRANCIS, company executive; b. Northampton, Mass., Oct. 4, 1935; s. William Cahil and Vena Marie (Lasonde) C.; m. Sedgeley Mellon SChmidt, Nov. 23, 1973 (div. 1985); 1 child, Mark Andrew. BA, Columbia Coll., 1958; MLS, Georgetown U., 1979. Chief legis. asst. U.S. Rep. Silvio O. Conte, Washington, 1961-64; dir. Washington Office Am. Paper Inst., N.Y.C., 1965-69; exec. dir. World Federalsits U.S.A., Washington, 1969-71; dir. Washington office SUNY, 1971-85; sr. ptnr., pres. Washington Resources, Inc., 1985—; pres. Voyages Books and Art, Washington, 1987—; founding dir. Simenon (Georges) Festival, 1987-88; bd. dirs. various founds., D.C., N.Y. Author: To Break Marbleshell, From a Southern France Notebook, 1975; editor: Essays of Mark Van Doren 1924-1978, 1982; editor Voyages: Nat. Lit. Mag., 1967-73; bd. editors Lit. and Medicine, 1980—; contbr. articles to profl. jours. Chair Students for Stevenson, N.Y.C., 1956; state dir. Humphrey for Pres., Wash., Maine, Calif., 1968. With U.S. Army, 1959-61. Fellow Yaddo, Saratoga, N.Y., 1975, Macdowell Colony, Peterborough, N.H., 1977; residency fellow Rockefeller Found., Bellagio Italy, 1979-80; recipient Editor's award Nat. Endowment for Arts, Washington, 1972. Mem. Cosmos Club (Washington), Rolling Rock Club (Ligonier, Pa.), Nat. Press Club (Washington), Pen Am. Home: 4705 Butterworth Pl NW Washington DC 20016-4459 Office: Washington Resources Inc 1250 24th St NW Washington DC 20037-1124

CLAIRJEUNE, YUAN SAINTANGE, psychology consultant, educator; b. Haiti, Mar. 7, 1945; came to U.S., 1972; s. Joseph M. Adelina and Saintage C. Thelizene. BA in Law, Sch. Law and Econs., Haiti, 1966, ethnology degree, 1970; MEd, Laval u., 1976; PhD in Psychology, U. Toronto, 1990. Lawyer Haitian Civil Ct., 1966-70; prof. Bd. Edn., Quebec City, Que., Can., 1970-72; lectr. Bd. Edn., N.Y.C., 1972-75; prof. Govt. of Zambia, 1976-79; cons. Lucha Inc., N.Y.C., 1988-89; psychologist Health and Hosp. Corp., Bklyn., 1989—. Community advisor for Haitians in Bklyn.; mem. UN Assn., N.Y.C. Mem. United Fedn. Tchrs., Am. Psychol. Assn., Can. Assn. Social Work. Roman Catholic. Home: 26A Brighton Beach Ave # 10 Brooklyn NY 11235-8002 Office: Ste 13 136 Eastern Pky Brooklyn NY 11238

CLAMPITT, MARTHA REDDING, interior designer; b. North Wilkesboro, N.C., Jan. 11, 1947; d. Dewey Wayne and Pansy Lucille (Sale) Redding; m. Otis Clinton Clampitt, Jr., Apr. 3, 1971. BS, U. N.C.-Greensboro, 1971; MA in Art summa cum laude, Miss. Coll., 1985. Advt. copywriter Jordan Marsh, Greensboro, N.C., 1971-73; interior designer Oldtown Drapery, Winston-Salem, N.C., 1973-76, interior design mgr. Shade Shop, Inc., Columbia, S.C., 1976-80; interior designer Warren Wright's, Jackson, Miss., 1981-83; with Architects Plus, Jackson, 1985-89; assoc. ptnr., head interior design dept., sr. designer Interior Concepts, Inc., Annapolis, Md. 1989-90, Contract Interior Svcs., Annapolis, 1990-91; prin., design cons. Martha R. Clampitt Interior Design, 1991—; juror N.C.I.D.Q. Exam, 1991-92. Sec. Treasure Cove Homeowners Assn., Madison, Miss., 1983-84; mem. choir 1st Bapt. Ch., Jackson, 1982-89; sect. leader, 1983-84, exec. com., 1985-86; mem. handbell choir, 1987-89; former mem. Miss. Mus. Art Aux., Miss. Ballet League, Miss. Mus. Art, Miss. Craftsman's Guild, Miss. Artists Guild; active Smithsonian Assocs., 1988—, Balt. Mus. Art, 1990—, Nat. Trust for Hist. Preservation, 1988—, Miss. Coll. Renaissance Soc., 1989—; nominee to citizens amb. program People-to-People, 1988, 89; vol. Am. Cancer Soc., 1976—; vol. English as Second or Other Lang., 1992. Mem. Am. Soc. Interior Designers (profl.), Md. Coalition Interior Designers, Miss. Assn. (chmn. STEP program 1984-86, chmn. community svcs. com. 1984-86, sec. 1986-88, vice chmn. 1989, art auction com. Md. chpt. 1991-92, Chmn's. Citation for Outstanding Svc. 1988). Democrat. Avocations: sailing, skiing, painting, photography, antiques.

CLAMPITT, MARY O'BRIANT, government official; b. Connehatti, Miss., Feb. 18, 1931; d. Theron Russell and Ola Belle (Thompson) O'Briant; m. William Henry Clampitt, May 7, 1955; children: Russell, Henry, Amy, James. BS, U. Md., 1978, MA, 1982. Cert. quality analyst. Editor Chief State Sch. Officers, NEA, Washington, 1976-77; editor NAS, Washington, 1977-78; owner Clampitt Editorial Assocs., Chevy Chase, Md., 1970—; specialist White House Conf. on Aging, Washington, 1980-82; analyst Office Insp. Gen., Washington, 1982-84; analyst, mgr. Fed. women's program Food Safety Inspection Svc., Washington, 1984—; bd. dirs. Am. Fed. Credit Union. Bd. dirs. USDA Childcare Found., 1990—; mem. bd. reps. Greentree Home for Children, 1986—; mem. steering com. Forums on Aging, 1987, mem. adv. com. for ctr. planning, 1987—. Mem. Federally Employed Women, Interagy. Fed. Women's Program Mgrs., Woman's Action Taskforce (pres.), Bus. and Profl. Women's Club, Phi Kappa Phi. Republican. Baptist. Home: 7114 Edgevale St Bethesda MD 20815-5906 Office: Food Safety Inspection Svc 14th and Independence Ave Washington DC 20250

CLAMPITT, OTIS CLINTON, JR., health agency executive; b. Burlington, N.C., Nov. 17, 1947; s. Otis Clinton and Audrey Mae (Brafford) C.; m. Martha Jane Redding, Apr. 3, 1971. BA in English, Guilford Coll., 1971. Unit exec. dir. N.C. div. Am. Cancer Soc., Winston-Salem, 1972-73, area rep., 1973-74, met. area dir., 1974-75; dir. pub. edn./info. S.C. div. Am. Cancer Soc., Columbia, 1976-78, dir. devel., 1978-79, dep. exec. v.p., 1979-81; exec. v.p. Miss. div. Am. Cancer Soc., Jackson, 1981-89; nat. v.p. Am. Cancer Soc., Washington, 1989—; faculty, cons. Am. Cancer Soc. Acad., Atlanta, 1989—. Co-founder, pres. Forsyth County Interagy. Health Coun., Winston-Salem, 1975; chmn. Miss. Combined Fed. Campaign, Jackson, 1987-89, Miss. Com. on Indigent Patient Care, Jackson, 1989; appointed Govs. Task Force on Agy. Registration, Jackson, 1989; bd. dirs. Miss. Seatbelt Coalition, Jackson, 1986-90. Mem. Miss. Soc. Assn. Execs., Nat. Soc. of Fund Raising Execs. Home: 1712 Woodlore Rd Annapolis MD 21401-6568 Office: Am Cancer Soc PO Box 6640 Annapolis MD 21401-0640

CLAPP, JOHN MCMAHON, finance educator, real estate consultant; b. Washington, Apr. 5, 1944; s. Philip Fanshawe and Evelyn Patricia (McMahon) C.; m. Margaret Mason, June 25, 1966; m. Leslie Donna Elstein, Oct. 4, 1985; children: Jeremy E., Corey E. BA magna cum laude, Harvard Coll., 1967; MBA, Columbia U., 1969, MPh, PhD in Bus. Econs., 1974. Assoc. economist First Nat. Citibank, N.Y.C., 1969-74; asst. prof. UCLA, 1974-79; Brookings Instn. econ. policy fellow U.S. Acctg. Office, Washington, 1979-81; assoc. prof. U. Conn., Storrs, 1981-86, prof. fin., 1986—; cons. Am. Inst. Real Estate Appraisers, Chgo., 1989, Tomasso Bros., Inc., New Britain, Conn., 1989—. Author: Underwriting Income Property Mortgages, 1987, Handbook for Real Estate Market Analysis, 1987, (with others) Federal Economic Development Programs: An Econometric Analysis of Their Employment Effects, 1984, (with Mitchell) Legal Constrains on Youth Employment: A New Look at Child Labor and School Leaving Laws, 1977; bd. editors AREUEA Jour., Jour. Regional Sci., 1987—; editor, coeditor several publs.; contbr. numerous articles to profl. and scholarly jours. Harvard Coll. scholar, 1966. Mem. Beta Gamma Sigma. Home: 65 Auburn Rd West Hartford CT 06119-1304

CLAPP, LEE IRVING, research analyst; b. Gary, Ind., Feb. 28, 1941; s. Harlan F. and Denise Virginia (Davy) C.; m. Mary Dawn Pearson, Feb. 2, 1963; children: Dori Denise, Brian Lee. Student, Purdue U., 1958-59, 65, Ind. U., Gary, 1959-63, 70-71, U. Md., 1975, 80. Intelligence analyst Nat. Security Agy., Ft. Meade, Md., 1971-83, br. chief, 1981-83; sr. intelligence analyst GTE, Rockville, Md., 1983-84; mgr. Crofton (Md.) Office, Tech. Svc. Corp., 1984-90; cons. Crofton, 1990—. Contbr. articles to profl. publs. With U.S. Army, 1966-70. Recipient best tech. writer award Nat. Security Agy., 1981, cryptologic lit. award, 1981. Home: 1647 Eton Way Crofton MD 21114

CLARENDON, JOHN MARSDEN, youth program director; b. Greenwich, Conn., Aug. 27, 1946; s. Jean Knight and Katherine Eleanor (Marsden) C.; m. Patricia Marie Vetrone, June 26, 1982; 1 child, Colin McHugh. BA in English, Bucknell U., 1968; MEd in Counseling Psychology, Cambridge Coll., 1991—. Dir. youth programs Selectman's Com. on Youth and Human Resources, Westport, Conn., 1970-72; dir. Open Line (crisis ctr.), Westport, Conn., 1973-75; tng. dir. Hotline of Greenwich, Inc., Conn., 1976-78; exec. dir. Hotline of Greenwich, Inc., 1978-88; youth program dir. Barnstable (Mass.) County Sheriff's Office, 1988—; trainer Alternative to Violence project, Greenwich, 1978-84, Community Mediation Svcs., Stamford, 1985-88; founder Pers. Devel. Workshops, 1990. Dep. sheriff Barnstable County, 1989; bd. dirs. Samaritans, 1990. Mem. Assn. for Humanistic Psychology. Democrat. Roman Catholic. Home: 176 Main St Sandwich MA 02563-2269

CLARK, BILLY PAT, physicist; b. Bartlesville, Okla., May 15, 1939; s. Lloyd A. and Ruby Laura (Holcomb) C. BS, Okla. State U., 1961, MS, 1964, PhD, 1968. Grad. asst. dept. physics Okla. State U., 1961-68; postdoctoral rsch. fellow dept. theoretical physics U. Warwick, Coventry, Eng., 1968-69; sr. mem. tech. staff Booz-Allen Applied Rsch., 1969-70; sr. mem. tech. staff field svcs. div. Computer Scis. Corp., Leavenworth, Kans., 1970-73, sr. mem. tech. staff field svcs. div., Hampton, Va., 1973-76, head quality assurance engring. Landsat project Goddard Space Flight Center, NASA, Greenbelt, Md., 1976-77, quality assurance sect. mgr., 1977-79, sr. staff scientist engring. dept., 1979-80, sr. staff scientist image processing ops., 1980-82, sr. prin. engr./scientist GSFC sci. and application operation, system scis. div., 1982-83, sr. adv. staff CSC/NOAA Landsat Operation, 1983-91; sr. scientist Computer Scis. Corp. Ctr. Excellence in Geographic Info., 1991—; tech. rep. internat. Landsat Tech. Working Group (representing USA Landsat operation). Author tech. publs. Recipient undergrad. scholarships Phillips Petroleum Co., 1957-61, Am. Legion, 1957-58, Okla. State U., 1957-58. Mem. AAAS, IEEE, Am. Acad. Polit. and Social Sci., Internat. Platform Assn., Am. Phys. Soc., N.Y. Acad. Scis., Soc. Photo Optical Instrumentation Engrs., Internat. Soc. for Photogrammetry and Remote Sensing (organizer and dir. plenary sessions XVII congress meeting 1992), Am. Soc. for Photogrammetry and Remote Sensing, Victory Hills Golf and Country Club, Crofton Country Club, Pi Mu Epsilon, Sigma Pi Sigma. Home: 5811 Barnwood Pl Columbia MD 21044-2811

CLARK, CAROL CANDA, art historian, educator; b. N.Y.C., July 21, 1947; d. Henry G. Canda and Dolores C. Adam; m. Jon D. Clark, May 24, 1969 (div. Apr. 1983); m. Charles Parkhurst, July 1986. B.A. with distinction, U. Mich.-Ann Arbor, 1969, M.A., 1971; Ph.D., Case Western Res. U., Cleve., 1981. Registrar, U. Mich. Mus. Art, Ann Arbor, 1971-72; instr. Tex. Christian U., Ft. Worth, 1975-77; curator Amon Carter Mus. Ft. Worth, 1977-84; exec. prendergast fellow Williams Coll., Williamstown, Mass., 1984-87, lectr. art history, 1984-87; assoc. prof. fine arts Amherst (Mass.) Coll., 1987—; prof. fine arts and Am. studies; adj. prof. art history So. Methodist U., 1982-83; adj. curator of Am. Art, Clark Art Inst., Williamstown, Mass., 1984-87. Mem. adv. com. Hist. Deerfield. Author: Thomas Moran's Watercolors, 1980, Robert Lehman Collection VIII: American Drawings and Watercolors, 1992; (catalogue) American Impressionist and Realist Paintings, 1978; co-author Maurice and Charles Prendergast, 1990. Mem. art and architecture adv. panel Tex. Commn. on the Arts, 1981-83. Kress Found. fellow, 1972-75. Office: Amherst Coll Fayerweather Hall Amherst MA 01002-5000

CLARK, CHARLES JOSEPH (JOE CLARK), Canadian government official, former prime minister; b. High River, Alta., Can., June 5, 1939; s. Charles A. and Grace R. (Welch) C.; m. Maureen McTeer, June 30, 1973; 1 dau., Catherine Jane. B.A. in History, U. Alta., 1960, M.A. in Polit. Sci., 1973; LL.D. (hon.), U. N.B., 1976, U. Calgary, 1984. Lectr. polit. sci. U. Alta., 1965-67; journalist CBC Radio and TV, Calgary Herald, Edmonton Jour., 1966; exec. asst. in Ottawa to Robert L. Stanfield, 1967-70; M.P. for Rocky Mountain, 1972-79; M.P. for Yellowhead Alta., 1979—; leader Progressive Conservative Party, 1976-83; prime minister Can., 1979-80; leader of opposition, 1976-79, 80-83, sec. of state for external affairs, 1984-91, minister for constitutional affairs, 1991—; pres. Queen's Privy Coun. Roman Catholic. Office: House of Commons, Rm 165 E Block, Ottawa, ON Canada K1A 0A6

CLARK, CHARLES MICHAEL ANDRES, economics educator; b. West Islip, N.Y., May 16, 1960; s. John Edward and Carol Marilyn (Andres) C.; m. Lisa Mary McCarthy, Sept. 20, 1980; children: Meghan, Kaitlin, Charles. BA, Fordham U., 1982; PhD, New Sch. for Social Rsch., 1990. Instr. St. John's U., Jamaica, N.Y., 1984-89, asst. prof., 1989-91, assoc. prof., 1991—. Contbr. articles to profl. jours., chpts. to books. Bus. Rsch. Inst. grantee, 1990, 91. Mem. Am. Econ. Assn., History Econs. Soc., Assn. for Evolutionary Econs., Assn. for Institutionalist Thought. Roman Catholic. Office: St John's U Dept Econs Jamaica NY 11439

CLARK, CHESTER DODGE, actuary, consultant; b. Gloucester, Mass., July 3, 1938; s. James Parker and Marion Cummings (Dodge) C.; m. Ellen Katherine Hussey, Nov. 24, 1962; children: Amy D. Clark Huber, Victoria H. BA, Amherst Coll., 1959. Enrolled actuary. Actuary John Hancock Ins. Co., Boston, 1959-69; group actuary New Eng. Life Ins. Co., Boston, 1969-72; v.p. Towers, Perrin, Forster & Crosby, L.A., 1972-83; mng. dir. William M. Mercer Co., Boston, 1983—. Co-author monograph: Understanding Corporate Pension Plans, 1983. With U.S. Army Res., 1961-67. Fellow Soc. Actuaries, Conf. of Actuaries in Pub. Practice; mem. Am. Acad. Actuaries, Algonquin Club. Home: 2 Commonwealth Ave #8G Boston MA 02116 Office: William M Mercer Co 200 Clarendon St Boston MA 02116

CLARK, DAVID RIDGLEY, language professional, retired English educator; b. Seymour, Conn., Sept. 17, 1920; s. Ridgley Colfax and Idella May (Hill) C.; m. Mary Adele Matthieu, July 10, 1948; children: Rosalind Elizabeth, John Bradford, Matthew Ridgley, Mary Frances. Student, Reed Coll., 1940-41; BS, Wesleyan U., 1947; MA, Yale U., 1950, PhD, 1955. From instr. to prof. English, chmn. dept. U. Mass., Amherst, 1951-85, prof. emeritus, 1985—; vis. prof. U. Iceland, Reykjavik, 1960-61, Univ. Coll. Dublin, Ireland, 1965-66, Syracuse (N.Y.) U., 1968, U. Victoria, B.C., Can., 1971-72, 83, SUNY-Stony Brook, 1977, Williams Coll., Williamstown, Mass., 1989-90; vis. fellow Cambridge (Eng.) U., 1978; vis. prof., chmn. St. Mary's Coll., Notre Dame, Ind., 1985-87. Co-author: W.B. Yeats: The Writing of Sophocles' King Oedipus, 1989, (textbook) Reading Poetry, 1968, (poetry) A Curious Quire, 1962; author: Yeats at Songs and Choruses, 1983, Lyric Resonance, 1972, That Black Day, 1980, (poetry) Dry Tree, 1966, W.B. Yeats and the Theatre of Desolate Reality, 1965; editor: Critical Essays on Hart Crane, 1982, Twentieth Century Interpretations of Murder in the Cathedral, 1971, Studies in the Bridge, 1970, Riders To the Sea, 1970; mem. editorial bd. Cornell Yeats series, Irish Dramatic Texts series, Yeats: An Annual of Critical and Textual Studies; contbg. editor Mass. Rev.; gen. editor Manuscripts of W.B. Yeats series; contbr. articles to jours.. Society of Friends. Home: 330 Market Hill Rd Amherst MA 01002-1243

CLARK, DONALD GRAHAM CAMPBELL, surgeon, gynecologic oncologist; b. Airdrie, Scotland, May 9, 1920; came to U.S., 1945; s. Archibald Campbell and Alice Graham (Smillie) C.; m. Ann Beveridge Kiersted; children: Donald Graham Campbell, Michael Archibald Campbell, Alison Clark Zorman, Peter Fraser Campbell. BS, St. Andrews (Scotland) U., 1941, MB CHB, 1944; MD, Yale U., 1943. Diplomate Am. Bd. Surgery. Clin. attending surgeon N.Y. Med. Coll., N.Y.C.; dir. gynecol.-oncology Met. Hosp., N.Y.C.; pres. Meml. Hosp. Gen. Staff, N.Y.C., 1985-87; attending surgeon emeritus Meml. Sloan Kettering Cancer Ctr. Author: (with others) Gynecologic Oncology, 1982; contbr. articles to profl. jours. Pres. Greenville Community Coun., Scarsdale, N.Y., PTA Edgemont Sch. Dist., Scarsdale. Surgeon Merchant Marine, 1944-45. Mem. Soc. Pelvic Surgeons, Soc. Surg. Oncology, N.Y. Athletic Club, Scarsdale Golf Club. Home: 145 Old Army Rd Scarsdale NY 10583-2612 Office: Met Hosp New York NY 10028

CLARK, DONALD JUDSON, academic administrator; b. North Adams, Mass., Oct. 27, 1932; s. Judson Elmer and Mildred (Swan) C.; m. Ruth Pruyn, July 18, 1956 (div. 1970); children: Craig, Geoffrey, Bradford; m. Christina Welty, June 28, 1970 (div. 1983); 1 child, Matthew; m. Suemi Tanaka, Aug. 27, 1983. BA, Williams Coll., Williamstown, Mass., 1954; M in Divinity, Union Seminary, N.Y.C., 1957. Assoc. minister Mathewson St. Meth. Ch., Providence, 1957-60; minister First Meth. Ch., Pawtucket, R.I., 1960-64; dean, dir. Rolling Ridge Conf. Ctr., North Andover, Mass., 1964-67; nat. program dir. Inst. Cultural Affairs, Sydney, Australia, 1967-70; regional dir. Singapore, 1970-72, Miami, 1972-73; area dir. southeastern U.S. Houston, 1973-78; area dir. Tokyo, 1978-83; research dir. Hong Kong, 1982-83; lectr. Sagami Women's U., Sagamihara City, Japan, 1983-86, Sangyo Bus. U., Isehara City, Japan, 1983-86; dir. dept. continuing edn. for bus. U. So. Maine, Portland, 1986—; ptnr. The COS Group Internat., 1990—; bd. dirs. Intermediate Tech. Devel. Group N. Am. Mem. Am. Soc. for Quality Control, Japan Am. Soc. Maine (bd. dirs. 1987), Portland C. of C. (bd. dirs. 1992—). Home: 15 Oak Dale Dr Scarborough ME 04074-9097 Office: U So Maine 68 High St Portland ME 04101-3819

CLARK, DONALD MALIN, association executive; b. Buffalo, Feb. 11, 1929; s. Jack Merritt Malin and Louise Mary C.; m. Joan Marie Coyle, Dec. 27, 1958; children—Kevin Malin, Michael John, Elizabeth Anne. B.S. magna cum laude, Canisius Coll., Buffalo, 1950, M.A., 1952; Ed.D., SUNY, Buffalo, 1961; grad., U.S. Army Command and Gen. Staff Coll., 1969, U.S. Army War Coll., 1975. Administrv. asst. Traveler's Ins. Co., Buffalo, N.Y., 1950-57; mem. faculty Orchard Park (N.Y.) Sr. High Sch., 1957-66; dir. Ctr. Econ. Edn. SUNY, Buffalo, 1966-70; exec. dir. Industry-Edn. Coun., Niagara Falls, N.Y., 1970-79; pres., chief exec. officer Nat. Assn. Industry-Edn. Cooperation, Buffalo, 1979—; pres. Consumer Credit Counseling Svc., Buffalo, 1973, edn. chmn.; radio and TV public info. news commentator, 1962-78; adj. prof. Canisius Coll. Grad. Sch., Buffalo, 1962-63. Author: Meeting the Challenge of a Free Society, 1965; also handbooks, articles, guides; producer film on industry-edn. cooperation. Appointed by Pres. Reagan to Nat. Adv. Coun. on Ednl. Rsch. and Improvement, 1988-90; lectr. St. Michael's Roman Cath. Ch., Buffalo. With U.S. ANG, col. USAR, 1948—. Recipient Kazanjian Found. teaching award, 1968, Freedoms Found. medal, 1965; Presdl. Citation for Pvt. Sector Initiatives, 1985; fellow NAM, 1965. Mem. Am. Soc. Tng. and Devel., Western N.Y. Export Coun. (assoc.), U.S. Dept. Commerce, Active Corps Execs., U.S. SBA, Ret. Officers Assn., Buffalo Tennis Club, Amherst Dance Club (pres. 1987-88), Phi Delta Kappa. Republican. Roman Catholic. Home: 235 Hendricks Blvd Buffalo NY 14226-3304

CLARK, DONALD OTIS, lawyer; b. Charlotte, N.C., May 30, 1934; s. Otis and Ruby Lee (Church) C.; m. Jo Ann Hager, June 15, 1957 (div. 1980); children: Deborah Elise, Stephen Merritt; m. Anja Maria Smith, Nov. 5, 1983. A.B., U. S.C., 1956, J.D. cum laude, 1963; M.A., U. Ill., 1957. Bar: S.C. 1963, Ga. 1964. Practice law Atlanta, 1963-83; mem. Candler, Cox, McClain & Andrews, 1968-70, McClain, Mellen, Bowling & Hickman, 1970-75; ptnr. King & Spalding, 1975-78; sr. ptnr. Hurt, Richardson, Garner, Todd & Cadenhead, 1978-83; ptnr. Bishop, Liberman, Cook, Purcell & Reynolds, Washington, 1983-86, Kaplan Russin & Vecchi, Washington, 1986—; mem. dist. export council U.S. Dept Commerce, 1974—; adj. prof. law Emory U., 1970—, U.S.C., 1974; lectr. Ga. State U., 1972; lectr. numerous internat. trade seminars and workshops. Author: German govt. study on doing bus. in Southeastern U.S., 1974; editor-in-chief: S.C. Law Rev., 1963; contbr. articles to profl. jours. Served to capt. USAF, 1957-60. Decorated knight Order St. John of Jerusalem, Knights of Malta, knight and minister of justice Order of New Aragon, Sungrye medal Korea; recipient Nat. Leadership medal Air Force Assn., 1956, Coll. award Am. Legion, Outstanding Sr. award U. S.C., 1956, hon. consul Republic of Korea, 1972—. Mem. Atlanta Bar Assn., ABA, S.C. Bar Assn., Ga. Bar Assn., Lawyers Club Atlanta, Am. Judicature Soc., Am. Soc. Internat. Law, Atlanta C. of C., Ga. C. of C. (exec. com. Internat. Councils), Inst. Internat. Edn. (chmn. Southeastern regional adv. bd. 1974—, nat. trustee), So. Consortium Internat. Edn. Inc. (dir.), Wig & Robe, Sigma Chi (pres. 1956 Province Balfour award), Omicron Delta Kappa, Kappa Sigma Kappa, Phi Delta Phi (pres. 1963 Province Grad. of Yr. award).

CLARK, DUNCAN WILLIAM, physician, educator; b. N.Y.C., Aug. 31, 1910; s. William H. and Lillian (Keating) C.; m. Carol Dooley, Jan. 30, 1943 (dec. 1971); children: Carol Ann, Duncan William, James Fenton (dec.).; m. Ida O'Grady, June 10, 1972. A.B., Fordham U., 1932. Diplomate: Am. Bd. Internal Medicine, Am. Bd. Preventive Medicine. Intern Bklyn. Hosp., 1936-38; resident in medicine coll. div. Kings County (N.Y.) Hosp., 1938-40; fellow in medicine Yale U., 1940-41; dir. student health L.I. Coll. Medicine, 1941-49, dean, 1948-50, asst. prof. medicine, 1948-50; prof., chmn. dept. environ. medicine and community health SUNY Health Sci. Ctr., Bklyn., 1951-78; prof. preventive medicine State U. Coll. Medicine at N.Y.C., 1978-82, prof. emeritus, 1982—; cons. USPHS, 1961-81; cons. NIH, 1961-65, NRC, 1965-68; chmn. health services research tng. com. USPHS, 1965-69, mem. health services research study sect., 1961-65, 73-77; WHO traveling fellow, 1952; vis. prof. Med. Sch., U. Birmingham, Eng., 1961. Co-editor, co-author: Textbook of Preventive Medicine, 1967, 2d edit., 1981; Contbr. articles on med. edn., pub. health and medicine. Bd. dirs. Health Ins. Plan N.Y.C., 1953-71; chmn. N.Y. Study Com. Rsch. Accident Prevention in Children, 1958-60, Assn. Aid Crippled Children; bd. dirs. Health Systems Agy., N.Y.C., 1980-88, Kings County Health Care Rev. Orgn., 1980-84; mem. Gov.'s Adv. Coun. on AIDS to N.Y. State Health Dept., 1984—; chmn. Nat. Adv. Com. on Local Health Depts., 1960-61; mem. N.Y. State Commn. on Grad. Med. Edn., 1985; mem. distbn. com. N.Y. Community Trust, 1983-85; bd. dirs. Med. and Health Rsch. Assn., N.Y.C. Recipient Fordham Alumni award, 1958, Fordham Coll. Encaenia award, 1962; Frank L. Babbott award Downstate Med. Center Alumni Assn., 1974; 1st Duncan W. Clark award Assn. Tchrs. Preventive Medicine, 1974; medallion for disting. service to Am. medicine SUNY Coll. at N.Y.C., 1982. Fellow ACP, Am. Pub. Health Assn., N.Y. Acad. Medicine (trustee 1975, 85-89 , v.p. 1976-78, coun. 1975-89, pres. 1983-84, Disting. Svc. plaque 1986), Am. Coll. Preventive Medicine; mem. AMA (alt. del. 1983-88, 92, del 1989-91), AAAS, N.Y. Pub. Health Assn. (bd. dirs. 1951-55, 86-88, pres. 1954-55), Conf. Profs. Preventive Medicine (chmn. 1953-54), Assn. Tchrs. Preventive Medicine (pres. 1954-56, editor Newsletter 1959-70), Com. to Protect Our Children's Teeth (pres. 1957-60), N.Y. State Med. Soc. (del. 1978—), Kings County Med. Soc. (chmn. community medicine com. 1975-83, pres. 1983-84, trustee 1978—, v.p. 1981-82, censor 1991-92, chmn. pub. health com. 1990—), Harvey Soc., N.Y. Acad. Sci., Internat. Epidemiological Assn., Alpha Omega Alpha (faculty councillor 1948-76). Roman Catholic. Home: 35 Prospect Park W Brooklyn NY 11215-2369 Office: 450 Clarkson Ave Brooklyn NY 11203-2098

CLARK, ERIC SHANNON, psychotherapist; b. Buckingham, Pa., May 8, 1963; s. Paul and Shirley C.; m. Lori Sue Heffner, Dec. 5, 1987. BA, West Chester U., 1985; MEd, Temple U., 1986; postgrad., Wright State U., 1991—. Counselor Community Committment, Inc., Doylestown, Pa., 1986-87; psychotherapist Achievement Through Counseling and Treatment, North Philadelphia, Pa., 1987, Aldie Counseling Ctr., Doylestown, 1987—; pvt. practice Doylestown, 1990—; presenter at profl. confs. Contbr. articles to profl. publs. Mem. AACD. Home: 5155 Hollow Wood Ct # C Saint Louis MO 63128-4326

CLARK, FRED, legal writer, editor; b. Limón, Costa Rica, Dec. 12, 1930; came to U.S., 1968; s. Thomas and Irene (Penney) C.; m. Dorothy Hyacinth James, Aug. 4, 1956; children: Paul, Fred Jr., Lydia Ramona. Student Central Am. Acad., 1944-49; BLitt, U. Costa Rica, 1951; postgrad. Stafford Coll., 1956-57; barrister-at-law, Inner Temple, London, 1960. Bar: Eng., 1960, Jamaica, 1960; cert. in law Council Legal Edn. Master of langs. Merl Grove Sch., 1951-55; trust officer Govt. of Jamaica, 1960-61; individual practice law, Kingston, Jamaica, 1961-67; legal editor Corp. Trust Co., N.Y.C., 1968-69; sr. legal editor Prentice-Hall, Inc., Englewood Cliffs, N.J., 1969-91; cons. commonwealth law. Editor: The Corp. Jour., 1968-69. Trustee, United Ch. of Christ, 1970-78; spl. adviser U.S. Congl. Adv. Bd.; mem. nat. adv. bd. Am. Security Council. Recipient Disting. Leadership award, 1984, Presdl. medal of Merit, 1986. Mem. Am. Mgmt. Assn., Internat. Platform Assn., Internat. Commn. Jurists, Am. Mus. Natural History, Nat. Geog. Soc., AAAS, N.Y. Acad. Scis., Am. Ballet Theatre, Met. Opera Guild, U.S. Naval Inst., Freeport Bus. Promotion (bd. dirs.), U.S. Power Squadron (asst. sec.), Inter-Am. Soc. Lodge: Rosicrucians. Home: 39 W 4th St Freeport NY 11520-5709

CLARK, GORDON HOSTETTER, JR., physician; b. New Haven, Aug. 5, 1947; s. Gordon Hostetter and Elizabeth Master (Mapes) C.; m. Gail Marie Theroux, July 23, 1988; children from previous marriage: Emily Blakeslee Clark, Christopher Robert. BA, Yale U., 1970; MDiv, Pacific Sch. Religion, 1973; MD, George Washington U., 1977. Diplomate Am. Bd. Psychiatry and Neurology. Intern, then resident, then fellow Dartmouth-Hitchcock Med. Ctr., Hanover, N.H., 1977-81; staff psychiatrist Lakes Region Med. Health Ctr., Laconia, N.H., 1981-82, med. dir., 1982-86; dir. psychiat. unit Lakes Region Gen. Hosp., Laconia, 1986-89; med. dir. behavioral svcs. St.

Vincent Health Ctr., Erie, Pa., 1990—; adj. asst. prof. clin. psychiatry Dartmouth Med. Sch., Hanover, 1983-90; clin. asst. prof. psychiatry U. Pitts. Sch. Medicine, 1990—; chmn. com. psychiatrists in N.H. Community Mental Health Ctrs., Concord, 1982-86. Exec. v.p. Erie Phiharm., 1991-92. Recipient Exemplary Psychiatrist award, 1992; Falk fellow, 1979-81; recipient Benjamin Manchester award George Washington U., 1977. Fellow Am. Psychiat. Assn. (com. to develop guidelines for psychiat. practice in community mental health ctrs., Falk fellow 1979-81, cert., com. on state and community psychiat. systems 1990, cert. adminstrv. psychiatry 1992), Am. Coll. Mental Health Adminstrn., Am. Assn. Social Psychiatry; mem. AMA, Am. Assn. Community Psychiatrists (com. to develop guidelines for psychiat. practice in community mental health ctrs., pres. 1984-90, Disting. Svc. award 1990), Am. Assn. Psychiat. Adminstrs., Am. Assn. Gen. Hosp. Psychiatrists, Am. Coll. Physician Execs., Am. Coll. Psychiatrists, Pa. Med. Soc. (coun. on med. practice, physician execs. liaison com.), Nat. Psychiatry Alliance (chmn. med. staff com. 1992—, exec. com. 1992—), Psychiat. Physicians Pa. (coun., govt. rels. com., fed. legis. rep.), Western Pa. Psychiat. Soc. (pres. elect. 1992—). Democrat. Home: 203 Hunter Willis Rd Erie PA 16509-3701 Office: St Vincent Health Ctr 232 W 25th St Erie PA 16502-2701

CLARK, HALLIDAY, marketing executive; b. Bklyn., May 15, 1918; s. David Hatfield and Elizabeth C.H. (Halliday) C.; m. Hazel J. Frost, June 28, 1941; children: Halliday Clark, Jr., Elizabeth F. Kubie, Deborah G. Reinhart. Student NYU, 1938-41; LLB, LaSalle Law Sch., Chgo., 1966; MBA, Calif. Coast U., Santa Ana, 1982, PhD, 1983. Assoc. editor Variety Store Merchandiser Publs., N.Y.C., 1945-48; nat. accounts mgr. Best Foods Inc., N.Y.C., 1948-55; gen. sales mgr. Yale & Towne Mfg. Co., White Plains, N.Y., 1955-63; gen. mgr. Towne Hardware div., N.Y.C., 1963-68; v.p. sales Arrow Fastener Corp., Saddle Brook, N.J., 1968-72; pres., chmn. What to Do County Publs., Chappaqua, N.Y., 1972-78; pres. Halliday Clark & Assoc., Chadds Ford, Penn., 1978—; v.p. sales and mktg. Quaker City Mfg. Co., Sharon Hill, Pa., 1990—; pres., dir. Westchester Sales Execs., White Plains, N.Y., 1955-57; v.p. Sales, Mktg. Execs. Internat., N.Y.C., 1964-67; chmn. bd. UCP of Westchester, Harrison, N.Y., 1965-74. Author, publisher: What to do in Connecticut, 1973; What to do on Long Island, 1975; What to Do in New Jersey, 1976. Pres. bd. visitors Wassaic Devel. Ctr. (N.Y.), 1966-78; mem. U.S. Olympic Adv. Com., 1967-68. Served as capt. USAF, 1942-45, ETO. Recipient Civic Virtue award, UCP of Westchester, 1964. Mem. Scarsdale Alumni Assn. (pres. 1988—). Republican. Episcopalian (lic. lay reader).

CLARK, JAMES JOSEPH, electrical engineering educator; b. Vancouver, B.C., Can., May 6, 1957; came to U.S., 1985; s. James Joseph and Mary Patricia (Winfield) C. BASc, U. B.C., Vancouver, 1980, PhD, 1985. Rsch. asst. Nat. Sci. Coun. Can., Ottawa, Ont., 1979; rsch. scientist McDonald Detwiler & Assocs., Richmond, B.C., 1985; postdoctoral fellow, instr. elec. engring. Harvard U., Cambridge, Mass., 1985-86, asst. prof., 1986-90, assoc. prof., 1990—; vis. assoc. Calif. Inst. Tech., 1992. Author: Data Fusion, 1990. Recipient award for paper IEEE Acoustics, Speech and Signal Processing Soc. Roman Catholic. Office: Harvard U 29 Oxford St Cambridge MA 02138-2901

CLARK, JANE ELIZABETH KNALL, work and family consultant, educator; b. Cleve., Jan. 20, 1961; d. Robert Andrew and Betty Jean (Norris) Knall; m. Paul Bernard Clark, Nov. 5, 1988. BA in Psychology, Wittenberg U., 1982; MS in Sch. Psychology, Miami U., 1983; PhD in Counselor Edn., Kans. State U., 1992. Cert. sch. psychologist, Ohio, Pa.; nat. cert. sch. psychologist Nat. Sch. Psychology Cert. Bd., 1989. Sch. psychologist PSI, Inc., Cleve., 1985; sch. psychologist, guest lectr., inservice presenter Madeira (Ohio) City Schs., 1985-89; sch. psychologist Milford (Ohio) Exempted City Schs., 1985-86; career cons. Ctr. for Career Svcs., Phila., 1991; instr. Community Coll. of Phila., Pa., 1990—; work and family cons. Phila., 1992—; parent educator Manahattan (Kans.) Sch. Dist., 1989. Recipient grad. fellowship Miami Univ., Oxford, Ohio, 1982-84. Mem. AACD, Nat. Career Devel. Assn., Greater Phila. Counseling Assn., Sierra Club, Phi Kappa Phi.

CLARK, JERE WALTON, economics educator, researcher; b. Rex, Ga., Jan. 31, 1922; s. Grover Cleveland and Jessie Beatrice (Butler) C.; m. Juanita Stone, June 13, 1947; children: Merrilyn, Melissa Clark Vickers. Student, Berry Coll., 1941-43; BBA, U. Ga., 1947, MA, 1949; PhD, U. Va., 1953. Asst. prof. W.Va. U., Morgantown, 1952-55; assoc. prof. U. Chattanooga, 1955-62; prof. econs. So. Conn. State U., New Haven, 1962-91, prof. emeritus econs., 1991—, chmn. econs. dept., 1962-71, '85-91; cons. Ctr. for Interdisciplinary Creativity, 1966-91; pres. Quality Optimizer Assocs., 1991—. Author 10 book chpts., 1965-89; co-author: Full Circle...of Unified Science, 1974; editor nat. yearbook Enterprising Teachers, 1963, 64, 65; mem. editorial bd. Jour. Creative Behavior, 1965—, Gen. Systems Bull., 1968-72, Internat. Assns., 1970-72; contbr. articles to profl. jours. Moderator 12 TV panels on edn. Nat. League of Nursing, Chattanooga, 1961; author, narrator 60 radio econ-o-grams Nat./Joint Coun. Econ. Edn., New Haven, 1966; chmn. internat. task force on Gen. Systems Edn., SGSR, 1967-72. With U.S. Army, 1943-45, ETO. Recipient Best Coll. Course in Econs. for Tchrs. award Nat./Joint Coun. on Econ. Edn., 1963, 5 grants Kazanjian Found., 1967-80, grant USOE/HEW, 1975-76, 1st State Acad. Freedom award, 1992. Mem. Am. Econs. Assn., World Press Assn. (hon.), New England Bus. Adminstrn. Assn. (bd. dirs. 1987—), World Future Soc. Conn. (pres. 1975-76), Creative Edn. Found. (collegue 1956—).

CLARK, JERRY A., sign designer, artist; b. Bradford, Pa., Mar. 20, 1954; s. Richard John and Joann L. (Sparks) C.; m. Joann Keverline, Apr. 15, 1985; 1 child, Kristie. Student, U. Md., 1972-73, Western Ky. U., 1974-75, U. Pitts., 1975-78. Asst. mgr. The Rusty Nail, Ellicottville, N.Y., 1975-76; asst. mgr. The Rusty Nail, Limestone, N.Y., 1976-78, mgr., 1978-80; mgr. The Westline (Pa.) Inn, 1980-85, 88-90, The Limestone Grill, 1985-88; owner Sign Design of Westline, 1990—; art dir. Seneca Highlands Tourist Assn., McKean County, Pa., 1991—, Pa. Forest Industry Assn., Bradford, Pa., 1990—; corp. artist Bradford Hosp., Allegheny Particle Board, Kane Hardwood; bd. dirs. Seneca Highlands Tourist Assn., Pa. Forest Industry Assn. Pres. U. Pitts. Ski Club, 1977. With U.S. Army, 1972-75. Mem. VFW, Kinzua Valley Cross Country Ski Club (pres. 1984-85), Nat. Fedn. Ind. Bus. Republican. Presbyterian. Home: PO Box C Kinzua Dr Westline PA 16751 Office: Sign Design of Westline Big Shanty Rd C Westline PA 16751

CLARK, JOE See CLARK, CHARLES JOSEPH

CLARK, JOE HALLER, retired pharmaceutical company executive; b. Nashville, Ark., Nov. 26, 1913; s. August Barney and Jennie (Haller) C.; m. Edith Cummin, Sept. 13, 1947; children: William Cummin, James Gaylord, George Thomas. BA, U. Tex., 1935, MA, 1937; PhD, U. Ill., 1940. Rsch. chemist Eastman Kodak Co., Rochester, N.Y., 1940-42, Am. Cyanamid Co., Stamford, Conn., 1942-55; group leader Lederle Labs., Pearl River, N.Y., 1955-58; dir. tech. info. svc. Lederle Labs., Pearl River, 1958-70, dir. med. rsch. coord., 1971-75, dir. adminstrv. svcs., R&D, 1975-76. Contbr. articles to profl. jours.; patentee in field. Mem. Woocliff Lake (N.J.) Planning Bd., 1961-73, chmn., 1969-73; mem. Woodcliff Lake Bd. Adjustment, 1967-75, chmn., 1968. Mem. AAAS, Am. Chem. Soc., N.Y. Acad. Scis.,. Democrat. Unitarian. Home: 100 Lexington St Apt A6 Belmont MA 02178-1357

CLARK, JOHN HOLLEY, III, lawyer; b. N.Y.C., May 31, 1918; s. John Holley, Jr. and Mary (Angus) C.; m. Eleanor Jackson, June 4, 1964; children: Benjamin Hayden, Christopher Angus. BA with high honors, Princeton U., 1939; JD, Columbia U., 1942; MA, NYU, 1965. Bar: N.Y. 1942, U.S. Dist. Ct. (so. dist.) N.Y. 1949, U.S. Ct. Appeals (2d cir.) 1952, U.S. Ct. Mil. Appeals 1986. Assoc. Cahill, Gordon, Reindel & Ohl, N.Y.C., 1946-54; atty. Antitrust div. U.S. Dept. Justice, N.Y.C., 1954—. Vice pres. N.Y. Young Republican Club, 1953-54; mem. sch. com. Cathedral Ch. St. John the Divine, N.Y.C., 1979-81. Served with USAAF, 1942-46, PTO. Mem. NYU Grad Sch. Arts & Sci. Alumni Assn. (pres. 1983-85), NYU Alumni Council, Assn. Bar City N.Y., Am. Sociol. Assn., Am. Anthropol. Assn., Law and Soc. Assn. Democrat. Episcopalian. Home: 375 Riverside Dr Apt 9C New York NY 10025-2145 Office: Dept Justice Antitrust Div 26 Federal Plz Rm 3630 New York NY 10278

CLARK, KELLY, small business owner; b. Grosse Pointe, Mich., Apr. 19, 1953; d. Leo James and Marie Victoria Magdeline (Ulanowicz) Kelly; m. William Lee Clark, June 22, 1973 (dec. Jan. 1986). Student, Boston U., 1975; BA in Sociology, Wayne State U., 1976. Tchr. Community Action Program for Juvenile Offenders, South Boston, Mass., 1976; prodn. artist Reporter Pub. Co., Marblehead, Mass., 1977; copywriter McDougall Assocs., Salem, Mass., 1977-79; v.p., creative dir. Andrew Curcio Inc., Boston, 1980-86, account supr., 1982-86, exec. v.p., 1983-86; pres., co-founder Alden & Clark, Inc. (formerly Alden and Kelly, Inc.), Boston, 1986—, Kelly Clark Communications, Boston, 1988—. Pres. William Lee Clark Meml. Found., 1986—; mem. Women Affirming Life, Brighton, Mass.; chair Cotting League of Athletic and Sci. Ptnrs., Cotting Sch. for Spl. Needs Students, Lexington, Mass.; chair William Lee Clark Sci. Edn. Fund, Lexington; mem., sec. Ward Rep. Com., City of Boston; cons. Jr. Achievement Spl. Program for borderline students Boston High Sch. Mem. Nat. Mus. Women in the Arts, New Eng. Women Bus. Owners (chair speakers bur.), Internat. Platform Assn., Friends of Mass. Coll. of Art, Women of Wayne, Wayne State U. Alumni Assn., Amnesty Internat., Am. Women Entrepreneurs, Women Affirming Life, Adcraft Club Detroit, New Eng. Direct Mktg. Assn., Scarab Club. Roman Catholic. Office: Alden & Clark Inc 110 W Concord St Boston MA 02118-1508

CLARK, KENNETH BANCROFT, psychologist, educator; b. Canal Zone, July 24, 1914; s. Arthur Bancroft and Miriam (Hanson) C.; m. Mamie Phipps, Apr. 14, 1938 (dec. 1983); children: Kate Miriam, Hilton Bancroft. A.B., Howard U., 1935, M.S., 1936; Ph.D., Columbia U., 1940; LLD (hon.), CCNY, CUNY, 1987; Hon. degree, N.C. State U., 1986. Staff psychology dept. CCNY, 1942-75, prof., 1960-70, Disting. U. prof., 1970-75, prof. emeritus, 1975—; vis. prof. psychology Columbia U., summer 1955, U. Calif.-Berkeley, summer 1958, Harvard U., summer 1965; research dir. Northside Center for Child Devel., 1946—; social sci. cons. legal and ednl. div. NAACP, 1950—; cons. personnel div. U.S. Dept. State, 1961-68, 76-77, mem. com. on fgn. affairs personnel, 1961-62; Pres. Met. Applied Research Center Corp., 1967-75; chmn. bd., pres. Clark, Phipps, Clark & Harris Inc., 1975-86; pres. Kenneth B. Clark & Assocs., Inc., 1986—; bd. dirs. Presdl. Life Ins. Author: Desegregation: An Appraisal of the Evidence, 1953, Prejudice and Your Child, 1955, Dark Ghetto, 1965, A Possible Reality, 1972, The Pathos of Power, 1974; co-author: A Relevant War Against Poverty, 1968, How Relevant is Education in America Today, 1970; co-editor: The Negro American, 1966. Bd. regents State of N.Y., 1966-86; trustee U. Chgo., Woodrow Wilson Internat. Center for Scholars, 1980-87. Recipient Spingarn medal, 1961, Kurt Lewin award, 1965, Sidney Hillman Prize Book award, 1965, Coll. Bd. medal for disting. service to edn., 1980, Franklin Delano Roosevelt Four Freedoms award, 1985, Nat. Medal for Liberty, 1986, McGraw prize for edn., 1989. Fellow Am. Psychol. Assn. (dir. 1969, pres. 1970-71); mem. Soc. Psychol. Studies Social Issues (council 1954—, pres. 1959-60), Phi Beta Kappa, Sigma Xi. Episcopalian. Club: Century Assn. Home: 17 Pinecrest Dr Hastings On Hudson NY 10706-3701 Office: 615 Broadway Hastings On Hudson NY 10706-1039

CLARK, KEVIN ANTHONY, communications executive; b. Kansas City, Mo., Dec. 10, 1956; s. Harley Leon and Virginia Lee (Magee) C.; m. Heidi Jean Sawyer. BS, U. Tulsa, 1978. Producer, announcer Sta. KWGS-FM, Tulsa, 1976-78; assoc. communications specialist IBM Corp., Charlotte, N.C., 1979-80; communications specialist IBM Corp., Tarrytown, N.Y., 1981-82; staff communications specialist IBM Corp., White Plains, N.Y., 1983-84; corp. speak up adminstr., sr. communications specialist IBM Corp., Armonk, N.Y., 1985-87; info. rep., program adminstr. IBM Corp., White Plains, 1988-90, mgr. svcs. and mktg. media rels., 1991—; dir. corp. communications Okla. Intercollegiate Legislature, Oklahoma City, 1977. Author: IBM Speak Up Manual, 1986; editor: (brochure) IBM in Real Estate and Construction, 1984 (Excellence award IBM 1984, cert. Merit Printing Industries Am. 1984). Named one of Outstanding Young Men of Am., 1985. Mem. Pub. Rels. Soc. Am., Am. Mgmt. Assn. Home: 48 King St Danbury CT 06811-3439 Office: IBM Corp 1133 Westchester Ave White Plains NY 10604

CLARK, MARY KATHLEEN, nurse, educator; b. Teaneck, N.J., Feb. 22, 1956; d. Edward Albert and Kathleen Frances (Mulqueen) C. BS in Nursing, Seton Hall U., 1978; MA in Nursing, NYU, 1984. RN, N.J., N.Y. Staff nurse U. of Medicine & Dentistry, Newark, 1978-79, St. Barnabas Med. Ctr., Livingston, N.J., 1979-81; staff nurse med. intensive care unit The N.Y. Hosp., N.Y.C., 1981-83; cardiovascular rsch. nurse Cornell U. Med. Coll., N.Y.C., 1983-88; rsch. nurse The Burke Rehab. Ctr., White Plains, N.Y., 1988-89; clin. instr. The Presbyn. Hosp. in the City of N.Y., 1989—; assoc. faculty Columbia U. Sch. Nursing, N.Y.C., 1991—; adj. faculty The Coll. New Rochelle, N.Y., 1992—. Author: (with others) Standards of Critical Care, 1988, Principles and Practice of Adult Health Nursing, 1990; contbr. articles to profl. jours. Mem. AACN, Am. Nephrology Nurses Assn., N.Y. State Nurses Assn., The N.Y. Acad. Scis., Sigma Theta Tau. Office: The Presbyn Hosp City of NY Atchley Pavilion Rm 8-801 Fort Washington Ave New York NY 10032

CLARK, MATTHEW HARVEY, bishop; b. Troy, N.Y., July 15, 1937; s. M. Harvey and Grace (Bills) C. Student, Coll. Holy Cross, Worcester, Mass.; BA, St. Bernard's Sem., Rochester, N.Y.; STL, N. Am. Coll., Rome; JCL, Gregorian U., Rome. Ordained priest Roman Catholic Ch., 1962—; vice chancellor Diocese of Albany, N.Y.; Cath. chaplain Albany Law Sch.; mem. faculty Vincentian Inst.; chmn. personnel bd. Diocese of Albany; spiritual dir. N. Am. Coll.; bishop Diocese of Rochester, 1979—. Office: Chancery Office 1150 Buffalo Rd Rochester NY 14624-1823

CLARK, MATTHEW SCOTT, business executive; b. Bangor, Maine, Nov. 26, 1962; s. James Milford and Patricia Ann (Haynes) C. BSE, Princeton U., 1985; MSE, U. Pa., 1989. Sr. programmer Innovative Programming Assn., Princeton, 1981-84; technician Princeton U., 1985-86; assoc. mem., tech. staff David Sarnoff Rsch. Ctr., Princeton, 1986-90; v.p. devel. World View, Inc., Ithaca, N.Y., 1990—. Office: World View Inc 17 Main St # 313 Cortland NY 13045-2667

CLARK, MELVILLE, JR., physicist, electrical engineer; b. Syracuse, N.Y., Dec. 19, 1921; s. Melville and Dorothy Drew (Speich) C. S.B., M.I.T., 1943, postgrad., 1943-44; postgrad. U. N.Mex., 1945-46, Princeton U., 1946; A.M., Harvard U., 1947, Ph.D., 1949. Mem. staff Radiation Lab., M.I.T., Cambridge, 1942-45; mem. staff Manhattan dist. U. Calif., Los Alamos, N.Mex., 1945-46; physicist Brookhaven Nat. Lab., Upton, N.Y., 1949-53; mem. staff Radiation Lab., U. Calif., Livermore, 1953-55; dir. Clark Music Co., Syracuse, N.Y., 1948-60, v.p., 1957-60; pres. Meldor Corp., Cazenovia, N.Y., 1960-66; sr. engring. specialist Sylvania Electric Products, Waltham, Mass., 1962-64; sr. cons. scientist Avco, Wilmington, Mass., 1964-67; sr. scientist NASA, Cambridge, 1967-70; sr. devel. engr. Thermo Electron, Waltham, 1970-73; sr. cons. engr., sr. tech. strategist Combustion Engring., Windsor, Conn., 1973-83; pres. Melville Clark Assocs., Wayland, Mass., 1949—; bd. dirs. 416 South Salina St. Corp., Syracuse, 1957-60; cons. Raytheon Mfg. Co., Waltham, 1955-58, United Shoe Machinery Co., Beverly, Mass., 1955-56, Arthur D. Little, Cambridge, 1957-58, Aerodyne Research, Inc., Billerica, Mass., 1983-84; tech. expert witness Pennie and Edmonds, N.Y.C., 1984—; trustee Inst. for Sci. Rsch. in Music, Wayland, Mass., 1991—; assoc. prof. nuclear engring. M.I.T., Cambridge, 1955-62; adviser to Congressman Robert Drinan. Author: (with Rose) Plasmas and Controlled Fusion, 1961; (with Hansen) Numerical Methods of Reactor Analysis, 1964; translator, editor (with B. Daniel) Introduction to the Theory of Ionized Gases, 1960; contbr. articles to profl. jours. MIT Scholar, 1939-43; NRC predoctoral fellow Harvard U., 1946-49, NRC predoctoral and Hercules Powder Co. fellow Princeton U., 1946. Registered profl. engr., Mass. Mem. Am. Phys. Soc., Am. Inst. Physics, Fusion Power Assocs., AAAS, Acoustical Soc. Am., IEEE, Am. Assn. for Artificial Intelligence, Boston Computer Soc., Assn. Computing Machinery, Soc. Music Perception and Cognition, Sigma Xi. Patentee in field. Home and Office: 8 Richard Rd Wayland MA 01778-4099

CLARK, MERRELL MAYS, management consultant; b. Clifton Springs, N.Y., Feb. 8, 1935; s. Arthur Tillotson and Ruthanna Frame (Anderson) C.; m. Lynne Ruth Butcher, June 14, 1957; children: Elisabeth Lynne Clark Jenks, Aimee Ruthanna Clark Peterson, Catherine Merrell Clark Seda. BA, Yale U., 1957, MA in Religion, 1970. Asst. to advt. mgr. Armstrong Rubber Co., West Haven, Conn., 1959-60; mktg. analyst SSC & B, N.Y.C., 1960-62, account exec., 1962-64, v.p., account supr., 1964-68, v.p. mgmt. supr., 1968-70; prin. Knight, Gladieux & Smith, N.Y.C., 1970-72; v.p. Edna McConnell Clark Fedn., N.Y.C., 1972-77; exec. v.p. Acad. for Ednl. Devel., N.Y.C., 1977-81; prin. Clark Co., Scarsdale, N.Y., 1981—. Contbr. articles to profl. jours. Bd. dirs. Westchester Community Svcs. Coun., White Plains, 1965-72, Elderhostel, Boston, 1977—, pres. Elderworks, Scarsdale, 1978—, Nat. Sch. Vol. Program, Alexandria, Va., 1977-89, chmn. nat. adv. bd., Coun. for the Arts in Westchester, White Plains, 1978-83, Scarsdale Found., 1981-90; advisor Nat. Exec. Svc. Corps, N.Y.C., 1977-87, United Way Scarsdale-Edgemont, 1989—. Mem. Yale Club (N.Y.C.), Scarsdale Golf Club, Fox Meadow Tennis Club. Republican. Presbyterian. Office: PO Box 1385 Scarsdale NY 10583-9385

CLARK, MICHAEL ERIK, civic organization administrator; b. San Francisco, June 27, 1943; s. Thomas Arthur and Wilma (Bach) C.; m. Sondra Lee Weindorf, Nov. 22, 1963 (div. 1986); children: Michael Erik, Jr., Stephanie Leigh; m. Marcia Bard Isman, Aug. 9, 1987; stepchildren: Jamie, Jeffrey. BA in Sociology, U. Tulsa, 1965, MA in Sociology, 1967; postgrad., Cornell U., 1970. Instr. sociology U. Tenn., Martin, 1966-68, CUNY, Brooklyn, 1971-74; health cons. N.Y.C., 1974-76; sr. policy analyst Health Policy Adv. Ctr., N.Y.C., 1976-78; health planning , research specialist Community Service Soc. N.Y., N.Y.C., 1978-80, dir. ctr. health and human services, 1980-82, acting dir. dept. comml. devel., 1982-83, dir. program devel., 1983-86; exec. dir. Citizens Com. for N.Y.C., 1986—; pres. elect, v.p. Pub. Health Assn. N.Y.C., 1986-87, pres. 1988-89. Bd. dirs. Nonprofit Coord. Com.; mem. various block, neighborhood assns., Bklyn. Mem. Am. Pub. Health Assn., Pub. Health Assn. N.Y.C. Democrat. Roman Catholic.

CLARK, NANCY RANDALL, state legislator; b. Portland, Maine, May 6, 1938; d. Willis Shaw and Marthajane (Lund) Randall; B.S., Husson Coll. with high honors, 1962; M.Ed., U. Maine, 1968. Tchr. bus. edn. Scarborough High Sch., 1962-67, Freeport High Sch. Maine, 1968—; mem. Maine Ho. of Reps., 1972-78; mem. Maine Senate, 1978—, senate majority leader, 1986—. Maine bd. dirs. Arthritis Found., Maine chpt.; trustee Husson Coll., Freeport Conservation Trust. Recipient Vets. Service award Am. Legion Maine, 1978; named Outstanding Legislator, 1977, Woman of Yr., Bus. and Profl. Women's Club, 1982. Mem. NEA, Nat. Order Women Legislators, LWV, AAUW, Maine Tchrs. Assn. (pres. 1974-75), Nat. Bus. Edn. Assn., Bus. Edn. Assn. Maine, New Eng. Bus. Educators Assn., Brunswick Bus. and Profl. Women's Club, Maine Vocat. Assn., Freeport Tchrs. Assn., Freeport Hist. Soc., Tau Epsilon. Democrat. Congregationalist. Lodge: Order Eastern Star. Home: 6 Randall Rd Freeport ME 04032-6127 Office: Maine State Senate State Capitol Augusta ME 04333

CLARK, NORTON DWIGHT, museum executive; b. Newton, Mass., Sept. 23, 1932; s. Lawrence Norton and Alice (Babbitt) C.; m. Susan M. Wainwright, June 1, 1963; children: Kimberely, Wendy Lynne, Lawrence Norton. Grad. high sch., Newton. Drafter Bettinger Enamel Corp., Waltham, Mass., 1949-51; mem. test lab. staff Minn. Honeywell Co., Newton, 1951-60; asst. mgr. Equipment Renatl Co., Watertown, Mass., 1960-90; dir., clk. Edaville R.R. Corp., South Carver, Mass., 1960—; owner, pres. Nat. Fire Mus., Newton, 1960—; cons. mayor's adv. bd. transp., Newton, 1981—. Co-author: Boston's Commuter Rail, the First 150 Years, 1985, Boston's Commuter Rail, Second Section, 1986. Cpl. U.S. Army, 1953-55. Mem. Nat. Ry. Hist. Soc. (pres., Man of Yr. 1955), Suburban Middlesex R.R. Soc., Mass. Bay R.R. Enthusiasts, Cen. Electric Railfans' Assn., Mystic Valley R.R. Soc., Middlesex County Fire Wardens Assn., Boston St. Ry. Assn.

CLARK, PAUL FREDERICK, educator; b. Millville, N.J., Aug. 18, 1954; s. Frederick John and Bertha (Mahaney) C.; m. Darlene Ann Gates, Jan. 2, 1977; children: Molly Mahaney, Bryan Patrick. BA, Bucknell U., 1976; MS, Cornell U., 1979; PhD, U. Pitts., 1986. Researcher United Mine Workers of Am., Washington, D.C., 1975; labor extension assoc. Cornell U.-NYSSILR, Ithaca, N.Y., 1979; instr. Labor Studies Dept. Penn State U., New Kensington, 1979-82, asst. prof. Labor Studies Dept., 1982-89; assoc. prof. Labor Studies Dept. Penn State U., University Pk., 1989—; editorial bd. mem. Labor Studies Jour., New Brunswick, N.J., 1990—. Co-Editor: (book) Forging A Union of Steel, 1986; author: (book) Miners' Fight for Democracy, 1981; author/producer (video tape) Changing Labor's Image, 1987; contbr. articles to profl. jours. Recipient Rotary Found. fellowship, 1977-78; Research grant, Nat. Endowment for the Humanities, 1990-91, Program grant, Pa. Humanities Coun., 1986. Mem. Indsl. Relations Rsch. Assoc. (Nat.), Indsl. Relations Rsch. Assoc. (Western Pa. chpt. pres. 1989-90), Univ. & Coll. Labor Edn. Assoc., Am. Fedn. of Tchrs. Democrat. Protestant. Office: Pa State U Labor Studies Dept Old Botany Bldg University Park PA 16802

CLARK, PHILIP HART, urban and regional planner; b. Hartford, Conn., May 23, 1938; s. Raymond Gilbert and Phyllis Angeline (Hart) C. BArch, Cornell U., 1961, M in Regional Planning, 1968. Asst. project mgr. W.R. Grimshaw Co., Denver, 1964-65; project coord. U. Pa., 1968-69; sr. planner County of Fairfax, Va., 1969-72; urban planner Hellmuth, Obata & Kassabaum, Washington, 1972-73; chief air transp. planning Met. Washington Coun. Govts., 1973-77; urban planning cons. Reston, Va., 1977-78; with Gordian Assocs., Washington, 1978-79; program mgr. base comprehensive planning USAF Engring. and Svcs. Ctr., Tyndall AFB, Fla., 1979-81; program mgr. base comprehensive planning Sta. Hdqrs. USAF Pentagon, Washington, 1981-92, environ. restoration program mgr., 1992—; vis. lectr. George Washington U., 1975, Am. U. 1976-77, Air Force Inst. Tech., 1979—, USAF Acad., 1989; speaker Soc. Am. Mil. Engrs. Mtgs., aviation assn. meetings. Mem. Paul Hill Chorale, 1970-76, Choral Arts Soc., 1977-79, 81-83, Reston Chorale, 1983—, Kaleidoscope Theatre, Panama City, Fla., 1980-81. Capt. USAF, 1961-64. Mem. Am. Inst. Cert. Planners, Am. Planning Assn., Theta Chi. Democrat. Office: Hdqrs USAF/CEV Washington DC 20332

CLARK, R. THOMAS, lawyer; b. Milw., Dec. 22, 1951; s. Al T. and Sophie A. (Rakowski) C.; m. Mary Coldagelli, July 1, 1978; children: Rachael Mary, Elizabeth Mary. BS cum laude, Marquette U., 1975; JD, William Mitchell Coll. Law, 1979. Bar: Minn. 1979, U.S. Dist. Ct. Minn. 1980, U.S. Ct. Appeals (8th cir.) 1980, U.S. Mil. Ct. 1981, U.S. Mil. Ct. Appeals 1983, U.S. Supreme Ct. 1983, Conn. 1985, U.S. Dist. Ct. Conn. 1985, U.S. Ct. Appeals (2d cir.) 1985. Regional mgr. Security Schs., Inc., Mpls., 1979-81; instr. law Mohegan Community Coll., Norwich, Conn., 1983—; pvt. practice law New London, Conn., 1985—; instr. Acad. of Accountancy, Mpls., 1979; assoc. faculty Mitchell Coll., New London, 1984—; asst. prof. Eastern Conn. State U., Willimantic, 1985—; adj. faculty Teikyo Post U., 1990—; Jud. Hearing Officer, Ea. Conn. State U., 1990—. Co-author: Legal Assistance Guide for Members of Armed Forces in Connecticut, 1984; contbr. articles to mil. newspaper. Bd. dirs. Covenant Shelter of New London, Inc., 1991—. Lt. USNR, 1981-85. Mem. Conn. Bar Assn., New London County Bar Assn., Assn. Trial Lawyers Am., Conn. Trial Lawyers Assn., Judge Advocates Assn., Am. Bus. Law Assn., Guild of Cath. Lawyers, Alpha Sigma Nu, Beta Gamma Sigma. Roman Catholic. Office: PO Box 495 New London CT 06320-0495

CLARK, RANDALL LIVINGSTON, tire manufacturing company executive; b. Syracuse, N.Y., Sept. 13, 1943; s. Chester Edmond and Ruth Alice (Randall) C.; m. Suzanne Drane Jones, Jan. 8, 1966; children: Randall L., Karen Ann, Robert Dewitt. B.A., U. Pa., 1965; M.B.A., Wharton Sch., 1968. Mktg. assoc. B.F. Goodrich Co., Akron, 1968-70, product mgr., 1971-73; dir. mktg. Dunlop Tire and Rubber Corp., Buffalo, 1973-75, v.p. mktg. and sales, 1975-80, pres. tire div., 1980-83; pres. tire div., exec. v.p. corp., 1983-91; exec. v.p., COO Pratt & Lambert, Buffalo, 1992—; chmn., CEO, dir. Dunlop Tire Corp., Buffalo, 1985—; bd. dirs. Marine Midland, Mchts. Mut. Ins.; bd. dirs., past chmn. Upstate Roundtable on Mfg. Mem. Young Pres.'s Orgn., U.S. C. of C., Greater Buffalo C. of C. (chmn.), Park Country Club, Country Club Buffalo. Home: 177 Halston Pky East Amherst NY 14051-1891 Office: Dunlop Tire Corp PO Box 1109 Buffalo NY 14240-1109*

CLARK, ROBERT JENKINS, economist, educator; b. Chgo., May 19, 1913; s. Edward Perry and Maud Marion (Hugus) C.; m. Marilynne Burnette, Dec. 27, 1936 (div. 1947); children: Robert Jenkins Jr., Penelope Marilynne Marion; m. Scarlett Fried, Sept. 23, 1950. AB in Psychology, Stanford U., 1934; MS in Mech. Engring., Harvard U., 1940; PhD in Econs., NYU, 1953. Mech. engr. Texaco, Beacon, N.Y., 1940-42; asst. to pres. Am. Express Co., N.Y.C., 1947-56; econ. cons. Lionel D. Edie & Co., N.Y.C.,

1956-60; econs. cons., v.p. Econometric Inst., N.Y.C., 1960-63; export promotion advisor Ministry of Commerce, Govt. India, New Delhi, 1964, 65, Ministry of Commerce, Govt. Portugal, Lisbon, 1967; cottage industries expert, dept. indsl. promotion Ministry of Industry, Govt. Thailand, Bangkok, 1970-73; pvt. investor Southampton, N.Y., 1973—. Co-author: Korean Karate, 1968, Black Belt Korean Karate, 1975; contbr. over 2000 articles to jours. With USNR, 1942-46. Mem. Nat. Assn. of Scholars, Harvard Club of N.Y. Episcopalian.

CLARK, ROSALYN DAVIDA PIERCE, rehabilitation company owner, vocational expert; b. Phila., Sept. 2, 1952; d. Thomas Waudell and Geraldine (McKissick) Pierce; m. John R. Clark Jr., Oct. 7, 1973 (div. Jan. 1992); children: Adrienne Jenel, Jason John Thomas. BS in Rehab. Counseling, Pa. State U., 1973; MA, U. Md., 1975. Cert. rehab. counselor, ins. rehab. specialist; nationally cert. counselor; cert. Dept. Labor Office of Workers Compensation Programs. Mental health worker Charles R. Drew Community Mental Health/Mental Retardation, Phila., 1975-77; placement supr. Phila. Corp. for Aging, 1977-80; community program developer Faith United Ch. of Christ, Phila., 1981-83; mgr. Vocat. Rehab. Svc., Norristown, Pa., 1983-88; vocat. expert Social Security Adminstrn. Office Hearings and Appeals, Phila., 1986—; pres., vocat. rehab. cons. Target Rehab. Co., Glenside, Pa., 1988—. Bd. dirs. Charles R. Drew Community Mental Health/Mental Retardation Ctr., 1977-79, Stotesbury Community Assn., Wyndmoor, Pa., 1991—; chair Salem Bapt. Ch., Jenkintown, Pa., 1986—. Fellow Am. Bd. Vocat. Experts; mem. Nat. Assn. Rehab. Profls. in Pvt. Sector, Am. Assn. Counseling and Devel., Phila. Claims Assn., Buxmont Claims Assn., Del Chester Claims Assn., Nat. Ins. Industry Assn. Democrat. Home: 8534 Trumbauer Dr Wyndmoor PA 19118 Office: Target Rehab Co 1601 Church Rd Glenside PA 19038

CLARK, TOM, advertising executive. Vice chmn. BBDO Worldwide, N.Y.C., chmn. N. Am., also dir. Office: BBDO Worldwide 1285 Ave Of The Americas New York NY 10019-6028*

CLARK, WILLIAM HOWARD, JR., lawyer; b. Phila., Apr. 10, 1951; s. William H. and Alice Kimes (Metts) C.; m. Cristine D. Merkel, Aug. 18, 1973; children: Matthew, Alison, Daniel. BA summa cum laude, Amherst Coll., 1973; MA in Religion, Westminster Sem., 1979; JD magna cum laude, Temple U., 1983. Bar: Pa. 1983. Assoc. Morgan, Lewis & Bockius, Phila., 1983-89; ptnr. Klett Lieber Rooney & Schorling, Pitts., 1989—; chmn. corp. bur. advisory com. Pa. Dept of State, 1991—; cons. rules disciplinary bd. Supreme Ct. Pa., Harrisburg, 1983—. Mem. ABA, Pa. Bar Assn. (assoc. draftsman, lobbyist, corp. law com. 1984—, coun. sect. corp. banking and bus. law 1989—), Allegheny County Bar Assn. (coun. sect. corp. banking and bus. law 1991—), Dauphin County Bar Assn., Phi Betta Kappa. Republican. Presbyterian. Office: Klett Lieber Rooney & Schloring 1 Oxford Ctr 40th Fl Pittsburgh PA 15219

CLARK, WILLIAM ROGER, artist, educator; b. Altoona, Pa., July 27, 1949; s. Bernard A. and Marion H. (Suter) C.; m. J.C. Lee, Oct. 25, 1986. BFA, Md. Coll. Art, 1971; MEd, Temple U., 1974; MFA, U. Idaho, 1979. Cert. tchr., Pa., N.J. Tchr., coach Cen. Bucks High Sch., Doylestown, Pa., 1974-76; owner, artist Art Art Internat., N.Y.C., 1979-84; sculptor Cath. Fgn. Mission Soc. Am., Seoul, South Korea, 1984-87; adminstr. Mercyhurst Coll., Erie, Pa., 1987-90; prof. Camden County Coll., Blackwood, N.J., 1990—, Montgomery County Coll., Blue Bell, Pa., 1990—, Camden County Coll., Blue Bell, 1990-91, Bucks County Coll., Newtown, Pa., 1992—; dir. Cummings Art Gallery, Erie, 1987-90; art cons. St. Justin Martyr Soc., Valley Stream, N.Y., 1991; artist-in-residence Pa. State Correctional Instn. Graterford, 1992. Contbr. articles, illustrations to various publs. Vol. dir. Emmaus Soup Kitchen, Erie, 1987-90, Erie Geriatric Ctr., 1987-90; vol. St. Justin Soc. for Homeless, Valley Stream, 1990—. Mem. Nat. Art Edn. Assn., Pa. Art Edn. Assn., Coll. Art Assn., World Wildlife Fund, Oxfam Internat., Wilderness Soc. Roman Catholic. Home: 48 Kingwood Ln Levittown PA 19055-2406

CLARKE, ANDREW GERARD, playwright, filmmaker; b. Bronx, N.Y., June 4, 1961; s. Andrew Jerod and Mary Kate (Whyte) C. BS, Syracuse U., 1983. Freelance lighting dir., gaffer, 1984—. Author (play) Nobody's Hero, 1984, McNulty's Bar and Grill, 1990. Home and Office: 635 E 9th St #16 New York NY 10009

CLARKE, GARVEY ELLIOTT, educational association administrator, lawyer; b. Christ Church, Barbados, May 13, 1935; came to U.S., 1941; s. Elliott and Marion (Gibbs) C.; m. Yvonne E. Hayling, 1961; children: Wendy Y., Garvey H. AB, Dartmouth Coll., 1957; JD, N.Y. Law Sch., 1961. Bar: N.Y. 1963. Attorney legal dept. NBC, N.Y.C., 1963-65; v.p. A Better Chance, Inc., N.Y.C., 1965-75; pres. Nat. Fund for Minority Engring. Students, N.Y.C., 1975-82; v.p. Nat. Action Coun. for Minorities in Engring., N.Y.C., 1982-83; sr. assoc. Right Assocs., N.Y.C., 1983-85; dir. Morehouse Coll. Campaign The Oram Group, Inc., N.Y.C., 1985-86; dir. devel. Project Orbis, N.Y.C., 1986-87; dir. capital campaign United Negro Coll. Fund, N.Y.C., 1987-89; pres. Leadership Edn. and Devel. Progam in Bus., Inc., N.Y.C., 1989—; cons. Edn. Assoc., Washington, 1968-70, Frantzreb and Pray, N.Y.C., 1968-71. Pres. Stuyford Action Coun., Bklyn., 1963-70, Black Alumni of Dartmouth Assn., Hanover, N.H., 1976-78; mem. Dartmouth Alumni Coun., Hanover, 1977-79; bd. dirs. Boys Club of N.Y., N.Y.C., 1970-92. Mem. N.Y. County Lawyers Assn., Dartmouth Lawyers Assn. Mem. A.M.E. Zion Ch. Home: 33 Jordan Rd Hastings On Hudson NY 10706 Office: Lead Program in Bus Inc Ste 1112 1120 Ave of the Americas New York NY 10036-6700

CLARKE, JERROLD, architect; b. N.Y.C., Apr. 29, 1942; s. Fred and Gussie (Cohen) C.; m. Eileen Sue Friedson, Nov. 23, 1965; children: Michael, David, Steven. BS, Pratt Inst., N.Y.C., 1966. Registered architect, N.Y. Asst. architect N.Y.C. Bd. Edn., 1964-67; architect Schuman, Lichtenstein, Claman & Efron, N.Y.C., 1969—. Coach L.I. Jr. Soccer League, 1977-90, Jericho Athletic Assn., 1978, 79; bd. dirs. Birchwood Civic Assn., Jericho, 1981-83; bd. dirs. Temple Or Elohim, Jericho, 1982—, pres., 1985-87, chmn. bd. dirs., 1987-89; bd. trustees Queens (N.Y.) Museum of Art. Served to capt. U.S. Army, 1967-69, Vietnam. Decorated Bronze Star with one oak leaf cluster; honoree United Jewish Appeal, 1988. Mem. AIA, Constrn. Specifications Inst. Home: 58 Marion Ln Jericho NY 11753-1841 Office: Schuman Lichtenstein Claman 841 Broadway New York NY 10003

CLARKE, JIMMY CARLTON, producer, protective services officer; b. Trinidad and Tobago, Mar. 29, 1967; came to U.S., 1975; s. Cecil Clarke and Yvonne (Edwards) Modeste. Grad. high sch., Bronx, N.Y. Exec. producer Dr. York's Recording Studio, Bklyn., 1987-89; role model Flash Model and Talent, Inc., N.Y.C., 1989—; composer Hollywood Artists Record Co., Hollywood, Calif., 1990—. Vocalist at The Apollo Theatre, N.Y.C., 1990—; model for various movies. Recipient Cert. Achievement Hollywood Song Jubilee, 1990.

CLARKE, KELAH NANETTE, financial consultant; b. San Diego, Aug. 16, 1956; d. F. Richard and Anita Rita (Clara) Lambert; m. Gary A. Clarke, May 29, 1976; 1 child, Tara Kate. Diploma in nursing, Community Hosp. Roanoke Valley, 1976; BBA magna cum laude, Roanoke Coll., 1986. Staff nurse Lewis Gale Hosp., Salem, Va., 1976-81; fin. cons. Merrill Lynch, Pierce, Fenner and Smith, Inc., Roanoke, Va., 1984-90; fin. cons., asst. v.p. Merrill Lynch, Pierce, Fenner and Smith, Inc., Balt., 1990—; steering com. Roanoke Coll. Assocs., Salem, 1988—; chair Balt. area devel. com. Roanoke Coll., 1990—. Home: 2239 Laurel Woods Dr Salem VA 24153 Office: Merrill Lynch Pierce Fenner & Smith Inc Equitable Bank Ctr 100 S Charles St Baltimore MD 21201

CLARKE, NORMA JEAN KORNEGAY, human resources specialist; b. Trenton, N.C., Sept. 28, 1947; d. Judge Nero and Linnie Viola (Randall) Kornegay; m. Alan Clarke, Dec. 3, 1977; 1 child, Alan Kornegay. BS in History cum laude, Hampton (Va.) U., 1968; MEd in Rehab. Counseling, Boston U., 1970; PhD in Social Psychology, Boston Coll., 1981. Program coord. Bridge Fund, Inc., Boston, 1970-74; edn. and tng. specialist Commonwealth of Mass., Boston, 1974-75; dir. personnel Transitional Employment Enterprises, Boston, 1975-76; tng. rep. Harvard U., Cambridge, 1976-79; dir. human resources Mitre Corp., Bedford, Mass., 1979-88; v.p. human resources Open Software Found., Cambridge, 1988—; adj. instr. Sch. Mgmt. Suffolk U., Boston, 1990—; mng. tng. City of Boston, 1978-79; career planning cons. Harvard U., 1978-79; freelance trainer, Mass., 1970—; pers. auditor Smithsonian Astrophys. Observatory, Cambridge, 1981. Contbr. articles to profl. jours. Vice chairwoman bd. trustees Salem (Mass.) State Coll., 1984—; chairwoman bd. dirs. Roxbury Dental and Med. Group, Boston, 1976-78, Bridge Fund, Inc. 1974—, Advent Sch., Boston, 1991—; sec. to bd. Circle Assocs., Boston, 1971-74; vice-chairwoman Human Resource African Am. Alliance, Boston. Mem. N.E. Human Resources Assn. (bd. dirs., com. mem. 1990—), Internat. Assn. Personnel Women, Soc. for Human Resources, Am. Psychol. Assn., Alpha Sigma Nu, J.A. Everett Nat. Honor Soc., Delta Sigma Theta. Home: 32 E Springfield St Boston MA 02118 Office: Open Software Found 11 Cambridge Ctr Cambridge MA 02142-1405

CLARKE, PETER PARLEE, English educator; b. Milton, Mass., Dec. 18, 1943; s. Philip Hyde and Beatrice (Bull) C.; m. Elaine Giustina, June 11, 1966; children: Brock, Colin, Lonnie. BA, Amherst (Mass.) Coll., 1966; MA, U. Mass., 1967, PhD, 1971. Tchr. English Wilbraham (Mass.) Acad., 1967-70, Plymouth (Mass.) Carver High Sch., 1971-72; prof. Herkimer (N.Y.) County Community Coll., 1972—, chmn. humanities dept., 1977-80; adj. prof. Inst. of Tech., SUNY, Utica, 1981—. Author poems; contbr. numerous articles to profl. jours. Mem., pres. Little Falls (N.Y.) City Sch. Bd., 1977-83; founder, coach, treas. Little Falls Youth Soccer, 1978—; mem. Manheim (N.Y.) Zoning Bd. Appeals, 1989—; trustee, pres. bd. trustees Little Falls Pub. Libr., 1989—. Mem. Phi Kappa Phi. Democrat. Mem. Christian Ch.

CLARKE, STEPHAN PAUL, English educator, writer; b. Watertown, N.Y., Jan. 18, 1945; s. Albert John and Marjory Ruth (Grieb) C.; m. Mary Elizabeth Hawley, May 23, 1970; 1 child, Erin Elizabeth. BS in Edn., SUNY, Geneseo, 1966; MA, Bowling Green State U., 1968. Cert. secondary tchr., N.Y. English tchr. E. J. Wilson High Sch., Spencerport, N.Y., 1970—; speaker N.Y. State Edn. Dept. Writer's Conf., Albany, 1982, 87. Author: The Lord Peter Wimsey Companion, 1985 (Edgar Allan Poe Spl. award 1985), Crimes and Clues, 1977. Rec. sec. Ch. and Ministry Com. Genesee Valley Assn., United Ch. of Christ, Rochester, 1983-88. Lt. USNR, 1968-70. Recipient Excellence in Secondary Sch. Teaching award U. Rochester Grad. Sch. of Edn. and Human Devel. 1991. Mem. N.Y. State English Coun. (speaker 1975), Nat. Coun. Tchrs. of English (speaker 1978), Mystery Writers of Am., Stratford Shakespearean Festival Found. Can., Dorothy L. Sayers Soc. U.K. (speaker 1985). Republican. Home: 148 Greenway Blvd Churchville NY 14428-9210 Office: EJ Wilson High Sch 2749 Lyell Rd Spencerport NY 14559-2009

CLARKE-KUDLESS, DIANNE LOCH, educational marketing business specialist/consultant; b. Sharon, Pa., Aug. 4, 1951; d. William James and Marjorie (Loch) Clarke; m. James Webster Kudless, Dec. 28, 1973. BA, Allegheny Coll., 1973; MA, Montclair State Coll., 1976; MBA, Fairleigh Dickinson U., 1983; postgrad., Rutgers U., 1991—. Cert. tchr., N.J. Regional dir. Girl Scouts USA, Westfield, N.J., 1975-76; nat. mgr. Chubb & Son, Inc., Warren, N.J., 1976-80; mgr. tgn. Sea-Land Industries, Elizabeth, N.J., 1980-83; dir. tgn. Dun & Bradstreet, Inc., Murray Hill, N.J., 1983-86; dir. sales devel. On-Line Software, Ft. Lee, N.J., 1986-88; mng. dir. Enterprise Svcs., Califon, N.J., 1985—; prof., instr. Rutgers U., New Brunswick, N.J., 1991—; cons. dir. Edinboro (Pa.) State Coll., 1976; bd. dirs. Tech. Publs. adv. Bd., Chgo., 1985-88; program dir. Environ. Exposition Inc., Springfield, N.J., 1986—. Co-author: Communication in Corporate Settings; author mag. column, 1981-82; editor newsletter articles; contbr. articles to profl. jours. Founding bd. dirs. Goodwill Data Processing Sch. for Handicapped, Harrison, N.J., 1980-90, South Orange-Maplewood (N.J.) Ednl. Found., 1986-88, Access to Arts, 1990—, Environ. Edn. Found., 1991—; mktg. dir. Coldbrook Theatre and Arts Ctr., Oldwick N.J., 1989-90. Alden scholar, 1972; selected Young Career Woman Nat. Fedn. Bus. and Profl. Women, 1981; selected as Protege for Nat. SBA Program (WNET) for women entrepreneurs. Mem. ASTD (nat. dir. women's network 1991—), Nat. Soc. for Performance and Instrn., Maplewood Civic Assn. (pres.). Office: Enterprise Svcs RR 3 Box 96D Califon NJ 07830-9803

CLARKEN, ELIZABETH ANN, association executive; b. Newark, July 9, 1935; d. Joseph Austin and Josephine Angela (Gless) C. BA, Coll. St. Elizabeth, Morristown, N.J., 1956. Copywriter Hahne & Co., Newark, 1956-59; editor Newark Evening News, 1960-72; editor, reporter The Herald News, Passaic, N.J., 1972-78; exec. dir. Coll. St. Elizabeth Alumnae Assn., Morristown, N.J., 1978—. Recipient N.J. Food Communicator of the Yr. N.J. Dept. Agr., 1978, Mother Xavier award Coll. St. Elizabeth, 1989. Mem. Coun. for Advancement and Support Edn., N.Y. Metro Area Alumni Devel. Consortium, N.J. Consortium Alumni Profls. Roman Catholic. Office: Alumnae Assn Coll St Eliz 2 Convent Rd Morristown NJ 07960-6989

CLARNER, WALTER J., factoring company executive; b. N.Y.C., Aug. 8, 1947; s. George Christopher and Nora Winifred (Johanesen) C. Student, Queens Coll., N.Y. Inst. of Credit. Collector for Crompton Richmond Factors, N.Y.C., 1969-71, James Talcott Factors, N.Y.C., 1971-74; collector and jr. credit exec. for factoring div. Chemical Bank, N.Y.C., 1974-80; asst. sec. Security Pacific Bus. Credit, N.Y.C., 1980-84; asst. v.p. Century Bus. Credit, N.Y.C., 1984-86; asst. v.p. Amb. Factors div. Fleet Factors Corp. unit Fleet-Norstar Fin. Group, N.Y.C., 1986-92, v.p. Amb. Factors div., 1992—. Mem. Contemporary Credit Club. Democrat. Roman Catholic. Office: Ambassador Factors 1450 Broadway New York NY 10018-2201

CLAUSEN, JERRY LEE, psychiatrist; b. Wausau, Wis., Nov. 5, 1939; s. Douglas William and Florence Jean (Amidon) C.; m. Nancy Eileen Longdon, Aug. 3, 1962; children: Keith Russell, Pamela Dawn. BA, Wesleyan U., Middletown, Conn., 1961; MD, Albany Med. Coll., N.Y., 1965. Diplomate Am. Bd. Psychiatry and Neurology; cert. Am. Soc. Addiction Medicine, N.Y. State Alcoholism Counselor. Psychiatry intern Upstate Med. Ctr., Syracuse, N.Y., 1965-66; psychiatric resident Upstate Med. Ctr., 1966-67, 69-71, asst. attending, 1971-72, attending, 1972-80; staff psychiatrist Onondaga Mental Health Clinic, Syracuse, 1971-72; courtesy staff Benjamin Rush Psychiatric Ctr., Syracuse, 1971-84, active staff, 1984—; pvt. practice psychiatry Syracuse, 1971—; clin. asst. prof., 1972—; staff psychiatrist Onondaga Pastoral Counseling Ctr., Syracuse, 1971-73, 81—, psychiatric dir., 1973-81; cons. psychiatrist Loretto Rest Geriatric Ctr., Syracuse, 1972-74. Tchr. First Universalist Ch., Syracuse, 1966—. Lt. comdr. USN, 1967-69. Fellow Am. Psychiat. Assn. (chmn. ins. mktg. com. 1979-88); mem. Onondaga County Med. Soc., N.Y. State Med. Soc. Universalist-Unitarian. Office: 1014 State Tower Bldg Syracuse NY 13202

CLAUSON, FRANK LEVIN, JR., city planning consultant; b. Chgo., Oct. 20, 1944; s. Frank L. and Ethel (Emrich) C.; m. Judith Johnson, Aug. 3, 1968; children: Max, Elli, Fritz Per. Student, U. Vienna (Austria), 1964-65; BA, Denison U., 1966; MA, U. Wis., 1971; M. Landscape Architecture, Harvard U., 1978. Asst. prof. Western Ill. U., Macomb, 1971-73; instr. U. Wis.-Extension, Madison, 1973-74; planner Leo Jacobson, AIP, Madison, 1974-75; project mgr. Roxbury/Dorchester Community Program, Boston, 1977-78; urban designer City of Newton (Mass.), 1978-81; owner, prin. Stan Clauson Assocs., Cambridge, Mass., 1981-88; dir. planning and devel. City of Montpelier (Vt.), 1988-91; owner, prin. Stan Clauson Assocs., Montpelier, 1991—; sabbatical researcher street lighting and pub. spaces, Lausanne, Switzerland, 1986-87. Editor: Harvard Architects Rev., 1978; contbr. articles to Urban Innovation Abroad newsletter, 1986. Trustee Vt. Symphony Orch., Burlington, 1990—; mem. Montpelier Design Rev. Com., 1991—, Vt. Coll. Adv. Com., Montpelier, 1990-91, Cambridge (Mass.) Bd. Zoning Appeals, 1980-86; pres. Mass. Assn. Cons. Planners, Boston, 1984-85. Recipient Cert. of Nat. Merit, U.S. Dept. HUD, 1988, Recognition award Vt. Soc. Landscape Architects, 1991, honorable mention Montpelier Heritage Soc., 1989, 91; named for Outstanding Achievement in Community Devel., Vt. Dept. Housing and Community Affairs, 1988, for Best Planning Project, Vt. Planners Assn., 1990. Mem. Am. Inst. Cert. Planners, Nat. Coun. Urban Econ. Devel., Am. Planning Assn., Vt. Soc. Landscape Architecture, Vt. planners Assn., Montpelier Rotary Club (chmn. "Community Projects" 1989-90). Office: Stan Clauson Assocs 5 State St Montpelier VT 05602

CLAUSON, SHARYN FERNE, consulting company executive, educator; b. Phila., Oct. 4, 1946; d. Eugene and Gertrud Jayn (Besser) C. BA in English, Temple U., 1968; MEd in Psychology, Beaver Coll., 1979; MBA in Marketing, Drexel U., 1982; postgrad. in law, Temple U., 1987. Market analyst Epstein Research, Bala, Pa., 1967-69; cons. Ednl. Testing Service, Princeton, N.J., 1979-80; chief exec. officer CCX, Narberth, Pa., 1978-79; tchr. Cheltenham Twp. Sch. Dist., Elkins Park, Pa., 1969-86; dir. Sharyn Clauson Bus. Communications, Narberth, Pa., 1975-85; pres. S. Clauson & Assocs., Inc., King of Prussia, Pa., 1985—; dir. Execuwriter, King of Prussia, 1985—; mem. adj. faculty Drexel U., Phila., 1979—, Phila. Coll. Textiles & Sci., 1985-89, St. Joseph's U., Phila., 1986-92, Phila. Ctr. of Great Lakes Coll. Assn., 1988; talk show host Sta. WDVT-AM, Phila., 1985; bd. dirs. Site Selex, Inc., jenkintown, Pa., dir. communications/pub. rels., 1988—. Editor: Curriculum for Optacon Music Reading, 1984; mem. editorial adv. bd. Bus. Communications and Concepts, 2d edit., 1985. Mem. com. Women's Polit. Caucus, Phila.; mem. Phila. Art Alliance; mem. exec. bd., arts and scis. alumni bd. Temple U. Women's Law Caucus. Mem. Am. Mktg. Assn., Nat. Speakers Assn. (chair 1985), Nat. Assn. Profl. Saleswomen, (honoree 1982—), Nat. Council Tchrs. English, Assn. for Supervision and Curriculum Devel., Del. Valley Writing Council, Wallenberg Communicators, Phi Delta Kappa. Office: 2000 Valley Forge Cir Ste 1036 King Of Prussia PA 19406

CLAUSS, WAYNE FRANCIS, court clerk; b. Rockaway Beach, N.Y., Jan. 5, 1947; s. Milton Leroy and Ruth Margaret (Van Seldan) C.; m. Linda Veronica Scavetti, Nov. 9, 1977. BA, CCNY, 1970. Cert. peace officer, N.Y. Ct. officer N.Y.C. Criminal Ct., 1974-79; sr. ct. officer N.Y. State Supreme Ct., Queens, 1979-81; sr. ct. clk. N.Y. State Supreme Ct., 1981-87; assoc. ct. clk. N.Y. State Supreme Ct., Queens, 1987—. Maj. USAR, 1970—. Mem. N.Y. State Supreme Ct. Officers Assn. (alt. del. 1978), DAV (judge advocate 1984—, chpt. comdr. 1980-83, life mem.); Dept. N.Y. State Legis. Com. Office: NY State Supreme Ct 88-11 Sutphin Blvd Jamaica NY 11435

CLAUSSEN, ERIC WALTER, graphic designer, artist; b. Pottstown, Pa., Sept. 18, 1964; s. Walter August Helmut and Edeltraut Marie (Hess) C. Student, Art Inst. Phila., 1984-86; BFA, Indiana U. Pa., 1986. Prodn. mgr. Type-A-Graphics, King of Prussia, Pa., 1987-88; graphic artist, designer Stahl Advt. Design, New Berlinville, Pa., 1989; asst. prodn. and design dir. Am. Law Inst., Phila., 1989—. Mem. Oley Valley Hounds Fox-Hunting Club (Oley, Pa.), Alpha Tau Omega. Republican. Lutheran. Home: 19 E 4th St Boyertown PA 19512-1116 Office: Am Law Inst 4025 Chestnut St Philadelphia PA 19104-3019

CLAWSON, PATRICK LYELL, editor; b. Alexandria, Va., Mar. 30, 1951; s. Marion Robert and Mary (Montgomery) C. BA, Oberlin Coll., 1973; PhD, New Sch. for Social Rsch., N.Y.C., 1978. Adj. prof. Hunter Coll., N.Y.C., 1977; asst. prof. Seton Hall U., South Orange, N.J., 1978-81; economist Internat. Monetary Fund, Washington, 1981-85; sr. economist World Bank, Washington, 1985-89; vis. fellow Washington Inst. for Near East Policy, 1989, fellow in econs., 1992—; rsch. scholar Fgn. Policy Rsch. Inst., Phila., 1989; editor Orbis Fgn. Policy Rsch. Inst., 1990—; Washington agt. Scientists Inst. for Pub. Info., N.Y.C., 1983—; cons. World Bank, 1989—; mem. panel fiscal experts Internat. Monetary Fund, Washington, 1990—. Author: Syria's Military Building and Economic Crisis, 1989, Economic Consequences of Peace for Israel, Palestinians and Jordan, 1991, Uprooting Leninism, Cultivating Liberty, 1992; adv. editor Middle East Jour., 1988—; contbr. articles to profl. jours. John M. Olin Found. grantee, 1989, U.S. Inst. Peace grantee, 1990. Mem. Am. Econs. Assn., Soc. For Iranian Studies, Mid. East Studies Assn., Mid. East Inst., Phi Beta Kappa. Republican. Home: 2122 Locust St Apt 2A Philadelphia PA 19193-0001 Office: Fgn Policy Rsch Inst 3615 Chestnut St Philadelphia PA 19104-6006

CLAWSON, ROXANN ELOISE, college administrator, computer company executive; b. Dallas, Oct. 15, 1945; d. Robert Wellington Clawson and Jeannette Irene (Rodenhauser) Clawson Clayton. BFA, Mich. State U., 1968. Library asst. Cooper Union, N.Y.C., 1970-75, asst. librarian, 1976-82, asst. to dean, 1985—; pres. Standing By Wordprocessing, N.Y.C., 1982—; v.p. Word Group, N.Y.C., 1984—; computer cons., 1986—. Acting appearance in The Dragon's Nest, La MaMa Theatre, 1989. Mem. Nat. Assn. Female Execs., N.Y. Personal Computer Group. Democrat. Lutheran. Avocation: administration.

CLAYDON, CHARLES THOMAS, physician; b. Mt. Vernon, N.Y., Apr. 25, 1935; s. Frank Joseph and Ethel Catherine (Wynne) C. MA, Coll. Holy Cross, 1952-56; MD, Johns Hopkins Med. Sch., 1956-60. Intern Johns Hopkins Hosp., Balt.; resident Grady Meml. Hosp., Atlanta; chief of surgery Martha's Vineyard Hosp., Oak Bluffs, Mass., 1967—; clin. assoc. Mass. Gen. Hosp., Boston, 1969—, Harvard Med. Sch., Boston, 1969—; trustee, dir. Martha's Vineyard Hosp. Found., Oak Bluffs, Mass., 1986—. Capt. U.S. Army, 1962-63. Home: 54 Cooke St Edgartown MA 02539 Office: Box 1166 Oak Bluffs MA 02557

CLAYMAN, LAWRENCE ALAN, optician; b. Boston, Apr. 8, 1955; s. George William and Jeannette Diana (Balansky); m. Phyllis Elaine Kagan, Oct. 11, 1981; children: Gregory Jon, Julie Anne. BBA, U. Mass., 1977. Lic. optician, Mass. Sales rep. Interoptic Eyewear, Elmsford, N.Y., 1977-79; optician For Eyes Optical Co., Boston, 1979-80, Precision Vision, Boston, 1980-81; mgr. Optique Ltd., Canton, Mass., 1981-83, Univ. Vision, Boston, 1983-84; supr. optical svc. Harvard Community Health Plan, Boston, 1984-88; mgr. Opticians 3, Woburn, Mass., 1989—; interpreter Opticians 3, Woburn, 1989—, Harvard Community Health Plan, Boston, 1984-88. Mem. Delta Chi. Home: 24 Sturbridge Dr Mansfield MA 02048 Office: Opticians 3 300 Mishawum Rd Woburn MA 01801

CLAYTON, CHARLES STELLING, writer, editorial consultant; b. Teaneck, N.J., Mar. 20, 1951; s. Charles Lindsay Clayton and Doris (Stelling) Smith; m. Susan Margaret Oehler, May 31, 1981. AB, Bard Coll., 1973; MFA, U. Iowa, 1980. Editorial asst. Bantam Books, Inc., N.Y.C., 1974; asst. dir., lang. arts specialist Bard Coll., Annandale, N.Y., 1975-77; freelance writer, editorial cons. N.Y.C., 1977—; adj. lectr. Rutgers U., New Brunswick, 1982-84, John Jay Coll. Criminal Justice, CUNY, N.Y.C., 1982—; lectr. and cons. in field. Author: Creative Writing, 1980; author short stories, 1973—; contbr. articles to profl. jours. Mem. Nat. Coun. Tchrs. English, Part-Timers United (mem. steering com. 1988—).

CLAYTON, CONSTANCE, school system administrator. BA in Elem. Edn., U. Pa., MA in Elem. Sch. Adminstrn., PhD, 1981. Tchr. Harrison Elem. Sch., Phila.; dir. U.S. Dept. Labor Women's Bur., 1971-72; dir., exec. dir. Early Childhood Programs; assoc. supt. Phila. Sch. Dist., supt., 1982—. Office: Phila Sch Bd Office of Supt Parkway at 21st St Philadelphia PA 19103*

CLAYTON, DAVID RUSSELL, sales executive; b. East Waterford, Pa., Mar. 19, 1943; s. Roy Jacob and Estella Grace (Love) C.; m. Martha Jane Bauserman, July 17, 1966; 1 child, Erica Quinn. Student, Hagerstown Bus. Coll., 1966-68; AAS in Acctg., Letters, Arts & Scis., Pa. State U., 1974. Purchasing agt. Nitterhouse Concrete Products, Inc., Chambersburgh, Pa., 1968-74; steel sales Forbes Steel Corp., Wilmington, Del., 1974-80; steel broker Lancaster, Pa., 1980-89; sales mgr. U.S.A. Wire and Wire Products, Ivaco Steel Mills, Ltd., Montreal, Que., Can., 1989—. Founder Upper Tuscarora Scholarship Assn., East Waterford, Pa., 1985, Friends of Upper Tuscarora Presbyn. Ch., East Waterford, 1988, Tuscarora Soc. ARts, 1988; mem. Nat. Rep. Com., Pres. Bush's Task Force. Mem. Internat. Wire Assn., Nat. Hist. Soc., Pa. State Alumni Assn., Nittany Lion Club, Lancaster Aquatic Club (U.S. swimming official, club rep.), Juniata County Hist. Soc. (bd. dirs.). Republican. Presbyterian. Office: 1104 Mill Mar Rd Lancaster PA 17601-1623

CLAYTON, JOANN CLEVELAND, aerospace analyst; b. Ft. Smith, Ark., Dec. 8, 1935; d. James Wooley and Rachel (McLaughlin) C.; m. John David Clayton (dec.); children: Rachel Diana, David Edward. BA, U. Tulsa, 1958; MA, George Washington U., 1990. Chief legis. asst. U.S. Ho. Reps., Washington, 1974-79; analyst NRC/NAS, Washington, 1979—; dir. aeronautics and space engring. bd. NRC, 1990—. Pres. Turkish-Am. Cultural Soc., Ankara, Turkey, 1972-73. Recipient Outstanding Achievement award Women in Aerospace, 1991, Disting. Profl. Staff award NRC, 1990; McClure

scholar U. Tulsa, 1955. Mem. AIAA, AAAS, Am. Astron. Soc., Internat. Inst. Space Law, Women in Aerospace (v.p. 1990, Outstanding Achievement award 1991), Kappa Alpha Theta. Office: NRC 2101 Constitution Ave NW Washington DC 20418-0001

CLAYTON, JOHN MIDDLETON, JR., university administrator; b. West Grove, Pa., May 4, 1941; s. John Middleton and Esther Marion (Myers) C.; m. Norma Louise Towne, Aug. 17, 1968; 1 child, Signe Louisa. BS, West Chester U., 1963; MS, Drexel U., 1966. Librarian Penn's Grove (N.J.) High Sch., 1963-66; tchr. Avon-Grove High Sch., West Grove, 1966-67; reader svcs. librarian U. Del., Newark, 1967-69, archivist, 1969-89, dir. records mgmt., 1975-89, asst. dir. univ. devel., 1989—; acting dir. devel., cons. Bloomsburg (Pa.) U., 1988-89. Mem. revenue sharing screening com. City of Newark, 1985-88; sec., bd. dirs. Oaklands Civic Assn., Newark, 1988-89; clk. of session 1st and Cen. Presbyn. Ch., Wilmington, Del., 1988. Mem. Presbyn. Hist. Soc. (bd. dirs. 1979-85). Republican. Home: 234 Cheltenham Rd Newark DE 19711-3682

CLAYTOR, GRAHAM, JR., transportation executive; b. Roanoke, Va., Mar. 14, 1912; m. Frances Murray Hammond; children: Frances Murray, William Graham III. BA, U. Va.; JD summa cum laude, Harvard U. Bar: N.Y. 1937, D.C. 1938. Law clk. to Judge Learned Hand U.S. Ct. Appeals (2d crct.), 1936-37; law clk. to Justice Louis Brandeis, 1937-38; assoc. Covington and Burling, 1938-47, ptnr., 1947-67, of counsel, 1981-82; v.p. law dept. So. Rlwy. Co., 1963-67; CEO So Rlwy. Co. and System, 1967-77; sec. of the navy, 1977-79, acting. sec. transp., 1979; dep. sec. Dept. Def., 1979-81; chmn. of bd. dirs., pres. Nat. R.R. Passenger Corp. (Amtrak), Washington, 1982—. Lt. comdr. USNR, 1941-46. Office: Amtrak-Nat RR Passenger 60 Massachusetts Ave NE Washington DC 20002-4225*

CLEARFIELD, ANDREW MARK, pension fund administrator; b. Chgo., Aug. 25, 1949; s. Leon Edward and Zena Madeleine (Zibelman) C.; m. Janis Callen Bell, Dec. 20, 1969 (div. 1982); 1 child, Lisa-Maria; m. Barbara Ruth Grossman, Oct. 8, 1983; 1 child, Evan Francis. AB, U. Pa., 1971; PhD, Harvard U., 1980. Securities analyst Mabon Nugent & Co., N.Y.C., 1980-81; sr. securities analyst Coll. Retirement Equities Fund, N.Y.C., 1981-84, investment officer, 1984-86, v.p. internat. investments, 1986—; bd. dirs. Cref Holdings, B.V., Amsterdam, The Netherlands. Author: These Fragments I Have Shored, 1984. Active Met. Opera Guild, N.Y.C., 1983—. Mem. Modern Lang. Assn., N.Y. Assn. Internat. Investments. Republican. Roman Catholic. Home: 35 Woodland Ave Glen Ridge NJ 07028-1230 Office: Coll Retirement Equities Fund 730 3d Ave New York NY 10017

CLEARY, JAMES CHARLES, JR., audio-visual producer; b. N.Y.C., Mar. 15, 1921; s. James Charles and Elizabeth Adelaide (Anglin) C.; grad. Scarsdale (N.Y.) High Sch., 1940; m. Adele Lillian Coe, Nov. 28, 1954. Lithographer, cameraman Advt. Lit. Inc., N.Y.C., 1940-41; advt. copy writer Grosset & Dunlap, book pubs., N.Y.C., 1942-44; advt. copy writer, editor Baker & Taylor, book wholesalers, N.Y.C., 1945-46; asst. mgr. sales Camera Craft Inc., retail photog. sales, White Plains, N.Y., 1946-50, Colortone Camera Inc., White Plains, 1950-57; producer, lectr. Ansco div. Gen. Aniline & Film Corp., Binghamton, N.Y., 1959-61; lab. photographer Nevis Lab. Nuclear Research, Columbia U., 1959-75; audio-visual specialist Edgemont Sch. Dist., Scarsdale, 1975-83; owner-producer Cleary Sound-Slides, New Rochelle, N.Y., 1950—. Mem. Scarsdale Camera Club (pres. 1948-49), Color Camera Club Westchester N.Y. (dir. 1958-59), Am. Security Council (advisory bd. 1970—), U.S. Air Force Assn., Am. Def. Preparedness Assn., Westchester County Grand Jurors Assn., The Baker Street Irregulars, Three Garridebs, Sherlock Holmes Socs., Thomas Wolfe Soc. Patentee of complete sound-synchronized, dissolving slide projection control system, 1966; pioneer in use of dissolve projection and synchronized sound in presentation of color slide continuities. Address: Cleary Sound-Slides 28 Pengilly Dr New Rochelle NY 10804

CLEARY, MANON CATHERINE, artist, educator; b. St. Louis, Nov. 14, 1942; d. Frank and Crystal (Maret) C. BFA, Washington U., St. Louis, 1964; MFA, Tyler Sch. Art, Temple U., 1968. Instr. fine arts SUNY, Oswego, 1968-70; from instr. to assoc. prof. D.C. Tchrs. Coll., Washington, 1970-78; from assoc. prof. to prof. art U. D.C., Washington, 1978-92, acting chmn. dept., 1985-86, 90-91. One woman shows include Mus. Modern Art Gulbenkian Found., Lisbon, Portugal, 1985, Iolas/Jackson Gallery, N.Y.C., 1982, Osuna Gallery, Washington, 1974, 77, 80, 84, 89, Univ. D.C., 1987, Tyler Gallery SUNY at Oswego, 1987, J. Rosenthal Fine Arts, Washington, 1991, others; group exhibits include Twenthieth Century Am. Drawings: The Figure in Context, Traveled Nat. Acad. Design, 1984-85, others. Artist-in-residence Herning Hojskole, Denmark, 1980, Ucross Found., Wyo., 1984. Recipient Faculty Rsch. award, U. D.C., 1983, 89. Mem. NEA, Coll. Art Assn., Pi Beta Phi. Democrat. Presbyterian. Home: 1736 Columbia Rd NW Washington DC 20009-2833 Office: U DC Art Dept 4200 Connecticut Ave NW Rm 4942 Washington DC 20008-1174

CLEAVER, CAROLE ANNAMAY, writer; b. Ridgewood, N.J., May 21, 1934; d. Earl Atherton and Carroll (Amos) C.; m. Selden Rodman, Nov. 7, 1962; children: Carla Pamela Rodman Mendoza, Van Nostrand. Student, Douglas Coll., 1952-53, Columbia U., 1955-57. Asst. beauty editor Mademoiselle mag., N.Y.C., 1954-59; news editor Wyckoff (N.J.) News, 1959-62. Co-author: Horace Pippin, The Artist As a Black American, 1970, Spirits of the Night, 1992; contbr. articles, revs. to profl. publs. Home: 659 Ramapo Valley Rd Oakland NJ 07436-2813

CLEGHORN, CHEREE BRIGGS, public relations executive, consultant; b. Phoenix, June 25, 1945; d. Dale Sheaffer and Jeannetta Jeanne (Sebaugh) Briggs; m. George Reese Cleghorn, Mar. 15, 1975; stepchildren: Nona Elizabeth, John Michael. BA, Tulane U., 1966; BJ, U. Mo., 1969. Reporter The Charlotte (N.C.) Observer, 1969-72; dir. pub. affairs Sch. Medicine U. N.C., Chapel Hill, 1972-75; spl. asst. to pres. Queens Coll., Charlotte, 1975-76; dir. pub. affairs WSU Health Care Inst., Detroit, 1976-79; cons. pub. affairs Detroit Med. Ctr. Corp., 1979-81, Johns Hopkins Sch. Pub. Health, Balt., 1982-83; v.p. pub. affairs Washington Healthcare Corp., 1983-86; pres. Cleghorn Health Communications, Bethesda, Md., 1986-88; pres. pub. rels. div. Rosenthal, Greene & Campbell, Bethesda, 1988-90; pres. Cleghorn/McNeill & Assocs., Bethesda, 1990—. Mem. communications com. Greater Washington Bd. Trade, 1988-90. Mem. Soc. Profl. Journalists, Am. News Women's Club, Pub. Rels. Soc. Am., Assn. Am. Med. Coll.'s Group on Pub. Affairs. Democrat. Presbyterian. Home and Office: Cleghorn McNeill & Assocs 10910 Bloomingdale Dr North Bethesda MD 20892

CLELAND, ANDREW WALLACE, veterinarian; b. Washington, Sept. 24, 1946; s. Andrew Wallace Cleland and Helen Azile (Wolford) Lindeman; m. Donna Jean Palmer, Mar. 8, 1975; children: Jessica Jean, Nathan Andrew, Kenneth Ryan. BS, Bucknell U., 1968; MS, Pa. State U., 1978; VMD, U. Pa., 1982. Veterinarian Concord Pike Animal Hosp., Chadds Ford, Pa., 1982-85; veterinarian Carlton Animal Hosp., Upper Darby, Pa., 1986-87, prin., 1987—. Sustaining mem. Rep. State Com. of Pa., 1978—. Command pilot with USN, 1968-73; with USNR, 1976-86; with Air NG, 1986—. Mem. Am. Vet. Assn., Pa. Veterinary Med. Assn., Va. Vet. Med. Assn., N.C. Vet. Med. Assn., Sussex Fitness Ctr. Club, Gamma Sigma Delta. Presbyterian. Home: 35 Brookside Rd Media PA 19086-6208 Office: Carlton Animal Hosp 137 S State Rd Upper Darby PA 19082-3094

CLELLAND, RICHARD COOK, statistics educator, university administrator; b. Camden, N.Y., Aug. 23, 1921; s. Ford John and Beryl (Cook) C.; m. Anne Chapin Buel, June 16, 1963; children: Richard Buel, Susan Elizabeth. B.A., Hamilton Coll., 1944; A.M., Columbia U., 1949; Ph.D., U. Pa., 1956. Asst. prof. U. Pa., Phila., 1956-61; assoc. prof. U. Pa., 1961-66, prof., 1966—, chmn. dept. stats. and ops. research, 1966-71; acting dean Wharton Sch. U. Pa., 1971-72, assoc. dean, 1975-80; acting assoc. provost U. Pa., 1981, dep. provost, 1982-92; statis. cons. bus., govt. and research orgns.; trustee Presby-U. Pa. Med. Ctr., 1982-85. Author: (with M.W. Tate) Nonparametric and Shortcut Statistics, 1957, (with J.B. O'Hara) Effective Use of Statistics in Accounting and Business, 1964, (with others) Basic Statistics with Business Applications, 1966, 2d edit., 1973, (with others) Library Planning and Decision Making Systems, 1974. Served with Signal Corps, AUS, 1944-46. Fellow Am. Statis. Assn.; mem. AAUP, Inst. Mgmt. Scis., Inst. Math. Stats. Home: 530 Hilaire Rd Wayne PA 19087-4413

CLEMEN, JOHN DOUGLAS, lawyer; b. Mineola, N.Y., Dec. 18, 1944; s. John Douglas and Amy Gertrude (Ackerson) C.; m. Judith Anne Davis, June 3, 1967; children: Elizabeth, Jennifer. BA, Hobart Coll., 1966; JD, Seton Hall U., 1974. Bar: N.J. 1974, U.S. Dist. Ct. N.J. 1974, U.S. Ct. Appeals (3d cir.) 1980, U.S. Supreme Ct. 1982, N.Y. 1984, U.S. Dist. Ct. (so. dist.) N.Y. 1985, U.S. Dist. Ct. (ea. dist.) N.Y. 1989, U.S. Ct. Appeals (2d cir.) 1989. Law sec. to assoc. justice N.J. Supreme Ct., Trenton, 1974-75; assoc. Shanley & Fisher, Newark, 1975-83; ptnr. Shanley & Fisher, P.C., Newark, 1983—; arbitrator U.S. Dist. Ct. N.J., 1985—, N.J. Superior Ct., Morristown, 1986—; guest lectr. Acad. Medicine N.J., 1980-82. Contbg. editor Seton Hall Rev., 1973-74. Served to capt. USAF, 1966-71, Vietnam. Decorated Air medal. Mem. ABA, N.J. Bar Assn. (chmn. aviation sect.), N.Y. State Bar Assn., Trial Attys. N.J., Bergen County Bar Assn., Morris County Bar Assn. (chmn. continuing legal edn.), Commerce & Industry Assn. N.J. (bd. dirs., counsel 1988—). Clubs: Essex (Newark); Morristown. Home: 574 Colonial Rd Westwood NJ 07675-6107 Office: Shanley & Fisher PC 131 Madison Ave Morristown NJ 07960-6097

CLEMENDOR, ANTHONY ARNOLD, obstetrician, gynecologist, educator; b. Port-of-Spain, Trinidad, West Indies, Nov. 8, 1933; s. Anthony Arnold and Beatrice Helen (Stewart) C.; came to U.S., 1954, naturalized, 1959; A.B., NYU, 1959; M.D., Howard U., 1963; m. Elaine Browne, May 31, 1958 (dec. May, 1991); children—Anthony Arnold, David Alan. Intern, USPHS, S.I., N.Y., 1963-64; resident Met. Hosp. Ctr., N.Y.C., 1964-68, chief outpatient dept. ob-gyn, 1969-73; med. dir. family planning Human Resources Adminstrn., N.Y.C., 1973-74; assoc. dean student affairs, dir. office of minority affairs N.Y. Med. Coll., Valhalla, N.Y., 1974—, assoc. clin. prof. dept. ob-gyn., 1978-90, prof. clin. ob-gyn, 1990—. Bd. dirs. Elmcor, Caribbean-Am. Ctr. N.Y.C.; mem. Nat. Urban League, N.Y. Urban League; life mem. NAACP. Diplomate Am. Bd. Ob-Gyn. Fellow Am. Coll. Ob-Gyn, Am. Pub. Health Assn.; mem. Royal Soc. Medicine, Nat. Med. Assn., N.Y. State Med. Soc., N.Y. County Med. Soc. (sec. 1989, v.p. 1990, pres. elect 1991, pres. 1992—), N.Y. Gynecol. Soc. (v.p. 1986, pres. 1988).

CLEMENS, MARK GEORGE, physiologist; b. St. Louis, Jan. 29, 1950; s. William J. and Norma L. (Mense) C.; m. Deborah J. Farmer, Apr. 1973 (div. 1983); 1 child, Regina Alice; m. Elizabeth A. Miescher, June 21, 1986; 1 child, Elene Alexis. BS, St. Louis U., 1974, PhD, 1979. Postdoctoral fellow Yale U., New Haven, 1980-81, rsch. scientist, 1981-86; asst. prof. Johns Hopkins U., Balt., 1986-91, assoc. prof. dept. surgery, 1991—, dir. pediatric surgery rsch., 1986—. Contbr. articles to profl. jours. Recipient Charles Ohse award Yale U., 1981; Robert Garrett scholar, 1986—. Mem. Assn. Acad. Surgeons, Biophys. Soc., Microcirculatory Soc., Am. Physiol. Soc., The Shock Soc. (pub. com. 1990—). Office: Johns Hopkins U CMSC 7-113 600 N Wolfe St Baltimore MD 21205

CLEMENT, J. ROBERT, management consultant; b. Cohoes, N.Y., Feb. 23, 1944; s. John H. and Edna M. (Bariteau) C.; m. Marilyn J. Powell, Sept. 7, 1968; children: Kimberly A., Derek S. BS in Math., Siena Coll., 1967. V.p. Hosp. Assn. N.Y. State, Albany, 1969-77; pres. Trebor Health Assoc., Albany, 1977-83; ptnr. Ernst & Whinney, Rochester, N.Y., 1983-90; pres. Enterprise Mgmt., Rochester, 1990—; chmn. Rytown Millwork, Rochester, 1990—; pres. Sci. Radio Systems, Inc., Rochester, 1990—; cons. chief exec. officer Erie County Med. Ctr., Buffalo, 1985-88; exec. dir. Maxicap Inc., Rochester, 1977-80; chmn. fin. com. Genessee Region Home Care Assn., Rochester, 1984; chmn. future financing health care Bus. Coun. N.Y. State, Albany. Mem. U. Club. Home: 791 Avon Crest Blvd Niskayuna NY 12309 Office: Enterprise Mgmt Rochester NY 14606

CLEMENTE, ROBERT STEPHEN, lawyer; b. Bklyn., May 5, 1956; s. Hugo and Mildred (Wilinsky) C.; m. Mary Martin, June 8, 1985. AA, St. John's U., 1976; BFA, NYU, 1978; JD, Southwestern U., 1981. Bar: N.Y. 1982, U.S. Dist. Ct. (ea. and so. dists.) N.Y. 1982, U.S. Supreme Ct. 1988. Counsel Composto & Longo, Bklyn., 1981-86; arbitration counsel N.Y. Stock Exch., N.Y.C., 1986-88, mgr. arbitration, 1988-91, dir. arbitration, 1991—; arbitrator N.Y.C. Civil Ct., 1988—. Mem. ABA, N.Y. State Bar Assn., Am. Arbitration Assn., Assn. of Arbitrators, Am. Judges Assn. Office: NY Stock Exch Inc 11 Wall St New York NY 10005-1916

CLEMENT-O'BRIEN, KAREN, nurse educator; b. Saratoga Springs, N.Y., Aug. 24, 1956; d. William S. and Evelyn J. (Botlock) Clement; m. Thomas Jay O'Brien, Nov. 24, 1979; children: Kelli, Morgan, Ian. RN, Samaritan Hosp. Sch. Nursing, Troy, N.Y., 1977; BSN, SUNY, Plattsburgh, 1979; MSN, Russell Sage Coll., 1984. Charge nurse Champlain Valley Physicians Hosp., Plattsburgh, N.Y., 1978-79; instr. nursing Samaritan Hosp. Sch. Nursing, Troy, 1979-84; instr. nursing Adirondack Community Coll., Queensbury, N.Y., 1984-88, asst. prof. nursing, 1988—; staff nurse Med. Personnel Pool, Albany, N.Y., 1988, 91. Course developer method of instrn. for medication calculations, 1989. Mem. Samaritan Hosp. Sch. Nursing Alumni Assn., Sigma Theta Tau. Home: 31 Nicklaus Dr Gansevoort NY 12831-1761 Office: Adirondack Community Coll Bay Rd Queensbury NY 12804

CLEMENTS, BRIAN MATTHEW, computer company executive, educator; b. Glens Falls, N.Y., May 4, 1946; s. Robert Edward and Lois Jennie (Gubitz) C.; m. Rene Ann Hammond, Apr. 18, 1970; children: Chad Aaron, Andrew Hammond. BA in Edn. and Math., Potsdam Coll., 1969; postgrad., Adirondack Community Coll., Queensbury, N.Y., 1971-82, SUNY, Plattsburgh, 1971-82; MS in Edn. and Microcomputers, SUNY, Albany, 1984. Cert. ednl. specialist IBM; cert. nursery, kindergarten, elem. and higher edn. educator, N.Y. Instr. elem./mid. sch. Glens Falls (N.Y.) City Sch. Dist., 1969-84; instr. high sch. Southern Adirondack Ednl. Ctr., Hudson Falls, N.Y., 1984-87; under-grad. instr. Saratoga extension The New Sch. for Social Rsch., N.Y.C., 1987—; pres. computer div. Foothills Computer, Inc., Queensbury, N.Y., 1982—, pres. Xerox div., 1984—; ptnr. Clements Assocs., Glens Falls, 1988—; pres., chief exec. officer Foothills Computer Inc., Glens Falls, 1989—; grad. instr. Wilton extension The New Sch. for Social Rsch., N.Y.C., 1990—; founder, dir., instr. Adirondack Computer Camp, Glens Falls, 1982-85; dir., presenter microcomputers in banking N.Y. State Bankers Assn., Syracuse, 1983; cons. computer systems Bd. Coop. Edn. Svcs., Hudson Falls, N.Y., 1984—, Lower Adirondack Regional Arts Coun., Glen Falls, 1989—; v.p. Queensbury All-Sports Booster Club, 1990—. Author: (manual/software) CAI Elementary Astronomy, 1983, CAI Geometric Transformations, 1983; author, editor: (manual/software) Basic Basic Plus, 1983, software WWSC Election Coverage, 1983-89. Presenter Instrument Soc. Am. (Adirondack), Research Triangle Park, N.C., 1983; sponsor computer svc. Am. Diabetes Assn., Queensbury, 1983, Am. Heart Assn., Queensbury, 1984—; supporter, presenter internship program Adirondack Community Coll., Queensbury, 1984—, mem. adv. bd., 1986—. Named Tchr.-of-the-Yr., Glens Falls Schs. & Tchr. Assn., 1981, Hon. Life Mem., N.Y. State Congress of Parents & Tchrs., 1982, Best Spot News Election Coverage award, UPI NY/NJ in conjunction with Normandy Broadcasting, 1985. Mem. Vocat. Indsl. Clubs Am. (chmn. N.Y. state skills olympics data processing 1986, advisor 1985-87), N.Y. State United Tchrs. (local chpt. bldg. rep., treas., negotiating team, grievance chmn. 1969-87), N.Y. State Assn. Ednl. Data Systems, N.Y. State Assn. for Computers and Techs. in Edn., Queensbury Parent-Tchr.-Student Assn., ABCD: The Microcomputer Industry Assn., Adirondack Regional C. of C. (edn. com.), Rotary, Elks. Republican. Home: 70 Cronin Rd Queensbury NY 12804-1419 Office: Foothills Computer Inc 21 Ridge St Glens Falls NY 12801-3608

CLEMENTS, DOUGLAS HARVEY, mathematics educator; b. Buffalo, July 22, 1950; s. Harvey Clements and Alberta (Hamister) Reilly; m. Holly Perna; 1 child, Ryan. MEd, U. Buffalo, 1977; PhD, SUNY, Buffalo, 1983. Tchr. kindergarten Wilson (N.Y.) City Schs.; asst. prof. Kent (Ohio) State U.; assoc. prof. math. SUNY, Buffalo; cons. IBM, Boca Raton, Fla., 1989—, Scott Foresman & Co., Ill., 1988—. Author: Computers in Early and Primary Education, 1985, Computers in Elementary Mathematics Education, 1989, Logo Geometry, 1991; chair Jour. for Rsch. in Math. Edn., 1988-90; contbr. articles to profl. jours. Grantee NSF 1986, 90, 91. Mem. Am. Ednl. Rsch. Assn., Nat. Coun. Tchrs. Math. Office: SUNY 593 Baldy Hall Buffalo NY 14260

CLEMENTS, JONATHAN DAVID, journalist; b. London, Jan. 2, 1963; s. Richard Lionel Clements and June Elizabeth (Hamilton) Dosik; m. Molly Greene, June 13, 1987; 1 child, Hannah. BA, Cambridge U., Eng., 1985. Writer, researcher Euromoney Mag., London, 1985-86; staff writer, reporter Forbes Mag., N.Y.C., 1986-90; staff reporter Wall Street Jour., N.Y.C., 1990—. Editor: Stock Answers: A Guide to the International Equities Market, 1988. Recipient award for Excellence in Fin. Writing, N.Y. State Soc. CPAs. Office: Wall St Jour 200 Liberty St New York NY 10281-1003

CLEMENTS, LYNNE FLEMING, family therapist, programmer; b. Bklyn., Aug. 8, 1945; d. Daniel Gillies and Dorothy Frances (Zitzmann) Fleming; m. Louis Myrick Clements, Feb. 19, 1972; children: Ryan Louis, Glenn Fleming. BA in Sociology, Bradley U., 1967; MSW, Fordham U., 1973; post-grad. studies, Columbia U., 1970-71; cert. family therapy, Inst. for Mental Health Edn., 1990. Computer programmer Employer's Comml. Union Group Ins. Cos., Boston, 1967-69, Harvard Bus. Sch., Cambridge, Mass., 1969-70, Volkswagon of Am., Englewood Cliffs, N.J., 1971; psychiatric social worker Associated Cath. Charities Family and Children's Svcs., Paramus, N.J., 1973-74, Christian Health Ctr., Wyckoff, N.J., 1976; owner, mgr. Wicker Wagon, Bergenfield, N.J., 1977-85; psychotherapist The Psychotherapy Counseling Ctr., Bergenfield, N.J., 1982-89; programmer, analyst Atlas Computing Svcs., Secaucus, N.J., 1984-86; program coord., family therapist Div. of Family Guidance, Hackensack, N.J., 1986-91; admnstv. dir. Corp. Family Resources, Ridgewood, N.J., 1989—; part-time family therapist N.J. Ctr. for Psychotherapy Inc., Ridgefield Park, 1990. Sunday Sch. Tchr. All Saints Ch., 1982-89, chmn. bd. community play ctr., 1977-78; mem. Twin-Boro Youth Ministry Coun., 1989—, Bergen County Family Day Care Coalition, 1989—. Recipient 1st and 2nd pl. awards Bergenfield 1980 Art Contest; NIMH grantee, 1973. Mem. AAUW, Gifted Child Soc. (parent workshop coord. 1989—), Nat. Assn. Social Workers, Acad. Cert. Social Workers, Am. Orthopsychiat. Assn., Fordham U. Alumni Assn., N.J. Commerce and Industry Assn. (child care com. 1990—, human resources com. 1990—), N.J. Soc. Clin. Social Workers, Zonta (Amelia Earhart chmn. 1987-88), Women of Accomplishment (founder, pres. 1991—). Episcopalian. Home: 148 Harcourt Ave Bergenfield NJ 07621-1917 Office: Corp Family Resources 201 E Ridgewood Ave Ridgewood NJ 07450-3817

CLEMENTSON, JUDITH ANN, academic administrator, psychology educator; b. Milw., Oct. 26, 1951; d. Harry Arnold Clementson and Ruth Jeannette (Hansen) Stefferud; m. Donald Michael Mohr, Oct., 1977 (div. Sept. 1986); m. Donald Wallace Helmuth, Jan. 6, 1989. BA, St. Olaf Coll., 1972; MA, U. Minn., 1975, PhD, 1978. Diplomate Am. Bd. Profl. Psychology; lic psychologist, Mass. Staff psychologist Dennison U., Granville, Ohio, 1978-79; asst. dir. psychol. svcs. Purdue U., West Lafayette, Ind., 1979-84, dir. psychol. svcs., 1984-86; dir. Counseling & Testing Ctr. Northeastern U., Boston, 1986—, instr. counseling psychology, 1988—; asst. adj. prof. psychology dept. Purdue U., 1979-86; guest examiner Ind. State Bd. Exam. in Psychology, Indpls., 1985. Contbr. articles to profl. jours. U.S. Dept. of Edn. grantee, 1988. mem. APA (accreditation site visitor 1981—), AACD, Internat. Assn. Counseling Svcs. (bd. dirs. colls. and univ. ctrs. 1990—). Office: Northeastern U 302 Ell 360 Huntington Ave Boston MA 02115

CLEMMER, LEON, architect, planner; b. Phila., Feb. 11, 1926; s. Leon and Mary Colton (Steele) C.; m. Mary Jane Bertolet, 1955, Nov. 19, 1955; children: Catherine C. Pickell, Leon Jr. BArch, U. Pa., 1951. Registered architect, Pa., N.J., Fla. Architect Vincent G. Kling, FAIA, Phila., 1951-56, Nolen & Swineburne, Phila., 1957, Gleeson & Mulrooney, Phila., 1958-62; pvt. practice Phila./Jenkintown, 1962--. Vice chmn. Abington Township Planning Commn.; mem. Phila., Glenside, Jenkintown C. of C., Independence Hall Assn.; mem. bd. of mgrs. Abington YMCA; bd. dirs. Friends of Historic Rittenhouse Town, Historic Bartram Gardens. With USN, 1943-46, PTO. Recipient Disting. Bldg. award Pa. Soc. Architects, MacArthur award Carpenters' Co. of Phila., 1988, Juvenile Justices Penna/'s Best, 1990, Juvenile Justices Nation's Best, 1991. Mem. AIA, Pa. Soc. Architects (bd. dirs.), Engrs. Club, Found. for Architecture, Carpenters Co. City and County Phila. (pres.), Am. Soc. Planning Ofcls., Am. Soc. Ch. Architecture, Nat. Trust for Hist. Preservation, Soc. for Indsl. Archaeology (bd. dirs.), Pa. Hist. Soc., Old York Road Hist. Soc. (bd. dirs., pres.), Victorian Soc., Union League Phila. (bd. dirs.), Mennonite Historians Ea. Pa., Clinkers Club, Athenaeum of Phila., Seaview Country Club, Mfrs.' Country Club, Huntingdon Valley Kennel Club (pres.), Rotary. Republican. Episcopalian. Home: 160 Woodpecker Rd Jenkintown PA 19046-3922 Office: Leon Clemmer AIA Architect 591 Skippack Pike Blue Bell PA 19422-2160

CLENDENNING, BONNIE RYON, healthcare administrator; b. Quincy, Mass., Dec. 30, 1945; d. Edward George and Mildred Audrey (Raynor) Bottenus; m. Philip Hamlin Clendenning, May 18, 1968 (div. Dec. 1988); 1 child, Max Hamlin. BA, Smith Coll., Northampton, Mass., 1967; cert. degré supérieur, U. Paris, 1973; MA, Tufts U., 1986. Tchr. English as fgn. lang. Kayhan Sch. Journalism, Tehran, Iran, 1968-69; bookseller Oriental and African dept. Heffer's, Cambridge, Eng., 1969-72; documentalist Internat. Coun. Museums, UNESCO, Paris, 1972-73; head info. svcs. World Fedn. of Friends of Museums, Brussels, 1976-79; asst. dir. Fletcher Sch. Law and Diplomacy, Tufts U., Medford, Mass., 1980-83, dir. external rels., 1983-85; dir. external rels. Tufts U. Sch. Medicine, Medford, 1985-88, Boston U. Sch. Law, 1988-89; v.p. Univ. Hosp., Boston, 1989—. Mem. Assn. for Healthcare Philanthropy, Women in Devel. (bd. dirs. 1986-88, 92—), New Repertory Theatre (bd. dirs. 1990—). Home: 489 Walnut St Newton MA 02160 Office: Univ Hosp 88 E Newton St Boston MA 02118

CLERISME, JOSEPH ROOSEVELT, physician; b. Arniquet, Cayes, Haiti, Mar. 12, 1950; came to U.S., 1979; s. Theodore and Rosita (Lenescar) C.; m. Marie Nicole Nicolas, Aug. 6, 1977; children: Yves Rony, Jasmine, Tania Regine. MD, State U. of Haiti, Port-Au-Prince, 1976. Resident in psychiatry Mars and Kline Psychiat. Ctr., Port-Au-Prince, 1976-79; resident in psychiatry Creedmoor Psychiat. Ctr., Queens, N.Y., 1979-83, attending psychiatrist, 1983-84; fellow in psychogeriatrics Downstate Med. Ctr., Bklyn., 1984-85; attending psychiatrist Creedmoor Psychiat. Ctr., Queens, 1985-88, chief psychiatrist, 1988-89, assoc. med. dir., 1989—. U.S. Govt. grantee, 1984. Mem. Am. Psychiat. Assn., Internat. Psychogeriatric Assn., Assn. Haitian Physicians Abroad (pres. 1988). Roman Catholic. Home: 175 Salem Rd Westbury NY 11590-1226 Office: 19726 Hillside Ave Jamaica NY 11423-2127

CLERK, JAYANA JASHWANTLAL, English educator; b. Bombay, Sept. 26, 1936; came to U.S., 1970; d. Jashwantlal C. and Nirmala (Dalal) C.; m. Anil Sheth, Feb. 8, 1973 (div. Oct. 1985). BA with honors, Gujarat U., India, 1956; MA, Gujarat U., 1958; BA with honors, U. London, 1963; PhD, MPh, Columbia U., 1977. Asst. prof. English M.T.B. Coll., Gujarat U., Surat, India, 1958-60, asst. prof., 1963-67; assoc. prof. Mithibai Coll. Bombay U., 1967-70; instr. Baruch Coll., CUNY, N.Y.C., 1971-77, asst. prof., 1977—, asst. chair dept. English, 1988—. Author: Law and Liberty in Literature: Antecedent or Antithesis, 1978, Women's Liberator Buddhism or the Buddha?, 1979, Munshi: Self Sculptor, Bombay, 1979. Mem. exec. com. Bharatiya Vidya Bhavan, N.Y., 1972—. Am. Inst. Indian Studies fellow, 1978-79, NEH fellow, 1983, 85. Mem. Assn. for Asian Studies. Office: CUNY Baruch Coll 17 Lexington Ave New York NY 10010-5526

CLEVENGER, CHARLES, dean; b. N.Y.C., June 26, 1941; s. Thomas and Ann (Ragone) C.; m. Jeanne Meschi, Oct. 4, 1969; children: David, Elizabeth. BS, Fordham U., 1965; MA, SUNY, Brockport, 1973; PhD, SUNY, Buffalo, 1982. Various adminstrv. positions SUNY, Brockport, 1970-82; dir. planning and program rev. Dept. Higher Edn. State of Conn., Hartford, 1983-84; dean, prof. orgn. and policy Shippensburg (Pa.) U., 1984-88, v.p. acad. affairs, 1987-88; exec. dean Univ. Ctr. at Harrisburg (Pa.), State System of Higher Edn., 1988—; founding dir. Pa. Acad. for the Profession of Teaching, Harrisburg, 1987-90; cons. schs., agencies and businesses; presenter in field. Author: (book) Market Profile, 1969; contbr. articles to profl. publs. Active gov.'s Vocat. Edn. Adv. Coun., Hartford, 1983-84, Cumberland County (Pa.) Children and Youth Svcs. Bd., 1985-88, Task Force on AIDS Policy for Human Svc. Agys., 1987-88, gov.'s schs. cooperation com., Harrisburg, 1988-90, cen. steering com. Pa. Child Welfare Inst., 1989, Allied Arts Fund Allocation com., 1989, 90, speaker's bd. Legislative Office for Rsch., 1990—, ann. Jail Bail campaign Cen. Pa. chpt. AHA, 1991; bd. dirs. Coun. for Pub. Edn., Harrisburg METROARTS, Met. Harrisburg Project: Enterprise. Mem. Am. Assn. State Colls. and Univs., Assn.

Study of Higher Edn., Rotary (prog. chair 1991, bd. dirs. 1992-95), Pi Sigma Alpha, Phi Delta Kappa. Democrat. Office: Univ Ctr at Harrisburg 2986 N 2d St Harrisburg PA 17110

CLEVENGER, RAYMOND C., III, lawyer; b. Topeka, Aug. 27, 1937; s. Raymond C. and Mary Margaret (Ramsey) C.; m. Celia Faulkner, Sept. 9, 1961 (div. Mar. 1987); children: Winthrop, Peter. BA, Yale U., 1959, LLB, 1966. Ptnr. Wilmer Cutler & Pickering, Washington, 1975-90; judge U.S. Ct. Appeals (Fed. Cir.), Washington, 1990—. Office: Fed Cir Ct 717 Madison Pl NW Washington DC 20439-0002*

CLEVENGER, ROY EDWARD, credit and collections manager; b. Kansas City, Kans., Nov. 24, 1953; s. Roy J. and Rosa E. (Johnson) C.; m. Judith Ann Elizabeth Kowalski, Aug. 25, 1976; 1 child, Judith Ann. BJ, U. Kans., 1975. Exec. dir., trustee Washington Crossing (Pa.) Found., 1973-76; with credit and collections dept. Milton Roy Co., Ivyland, Pa., 1979-82; asst. credit mgr. McGraw-Hill Publs., Hightstown, N.J., 1982-83, mgr. credit and collections, 1984-89; mgr. credit and collections Wood Textures, Inc., Edison, N.J., 1989-91; mgr. collections div. HIAS Inc., N.Y.C., 1991—; vol. Independence Nat. Hist. Park, Phila., 1983—. Mem. Media Credit Assn., Nat. Assn. Credit Mgmt., Ea. Nat. Park and Monument Assn. Home: PO Box 33 Washington Crossing PA 18977

CLIFFORD, CARMELLA MARIE, medical illustrator, artist; b. Balt., Oct. 23, 1955; d. Thomas Edward and Mildred Diane (Depasquale) C. BS in Biology, Loyola Coll., 1978; postgrad., Md. Inst. Coll. Art, 1979, Schuler's Sch. Fine Arts, 1980; MA in Med. Illustration, Johns Hopkins U., 1982. Med. illustrator dept. art as applied to medicine Johns Hopkins U., Balt., 1982-88; freelance med. illustrator Balt., 1984—; guest lectr. Johns Hopkins U., Md. Inst. Art, Atlantic Bio Communicators, Towson State U.; master of ceremonies, coord. Ann. Conf. Mid-Atlantic Bio-Communicators, Balt., 1985, 86, 87, 88, 90. Contbr. articles to profl. jours. Mem. Assn. Med. Illustrators (chair student affairs com. 1986, workshop com. 1987, regional orgns. com. 1987-90), Mid-Atlantic Bio-Communicators (pres. 1985-90, Salon awards 1984, 87, Book award 1990, regional orgns. com. 1990, 91), Md. Masters Swim Team, Crabtowne Skiers, Guild Natural Sci. Illustrators. Office: 14 W Mt Vernon Pl Baltimore MD 21201-5125

CLIFFORD, CLARK MCADAMS, lawyer; b. Fort Scott, Kans., Dec. 25, 1906; s. Frank Andrew and Georgia (McAdams) C.; m. Margery Pepperell Kimball, Oct. 3, 1931; children: Margery Pepperell Clifford Lanagan, Joyce Carter Clifford Burland, Randall Clifford Wight. LL.B., Washington U., St. Louis, 1928. Assoc. Holland, Lashly & Donnell, St. Louis, 1928-33; assoc. Holland, Lashly & Lashly, 1933-37; ptnr. Lashly, Lashly, Miller & Clifford, 1938-43; sr. ptnr. Clifford & Miller, Washington, 1950-68; sec. Dept. Def., Washington, 1968-69; sr. ptnr. Clifford & Warnke, Washington, 1969-91; dir. emeritus Knight-Ridder Newspapers; spl. counsel to Pres. U.S., 1946-50. Served to capt. USNR, 1944-46; naval aide to Pres. U.S. 1946. Recipient Medal of Freedom from Pres. U.S. Mem. ABA, Mo. Bar Assn. , D.C. Bar Assn., St. Louis Bar Assn., Kappa Alpha. Clubs: Burning Tree (Washington), Metropolitan (Washington), Chevy Chase (Washington). Home: 9421 Rockville Pike Bethesda MD 20814-3911 Office: Law Offices 815 Connecticut Ave NW Washington DC 20006-4004

CLIFFORD, JOHN EDMUND, town official; b. Hornell, N.Y., July 14, 1943; s. John Edmund Clifford and Helen Marie Rawady Bossard; m. Kaye Frances Mehlenbacher, Oct. 10, 1970; 1 child, Bridget. County legislator Steuben County, Bath, N.Y., 1981—; town supr. Town of Hornellsville, N.Y., 1981—; exec. com. Steuben County Rep. Com.; com. mem. Senator John R. Kuhl. With USAR, 1966—. Recipient Sebago award Hornell Camp Fire, 1989, Congl. letter of recognition for 25 yrs. svc. with USAR, 1991; named Rep. of the Yr. (Lincoln Day award), 1986. Republican. Home: RR 3 Box 7 Hornell NY 14843-9402 Office: Town of Hornellsville PO Box 1 Arkport NY 14807-0001

CLIFFORD, JOHN STEPHEN, psychologist; b. Hackensack, N.J., Dec. 27, 1951; s. John Patrick and Elizabeth Dorothy (Hanson) C.; m. Terry Janette Griswold, Oct. 6, 1979; children: Sean Michael, Tracy Elizabeth. BA, Skidmore Coll., 1973; MEd, Northeastern Univ., 1976; PhD, N.Mex. State U., 1983. Lic. psychologist, R.I., Mass. Rsch. asst. McLean Hosp., Belmont, Mass., 1974-76; clin. specialist Sangre De Cristo Community Mental Health Ctr., Santa Fe, N.Mex., 1977-80; psychology intern North Charles Gen. Hosp., Balt., 1982-83; sr. assoc. Social Sci. Cons., Inc., New Orleans, 1983-85; chief psychologist Edgehill Newport, Inc., Newport, R.I., 1985—; dir. Sakonnet Psychol. Assocs., Tiverton, R.I., 1990—; clin. cons. Bristol Community Coll., Fall River, Mass., 1986-89, Stanley St. Treatment and Resource Ctr., Fall River, 1990—; book reviewer Jour. of Substance Abuse Treatment, N.Y., 1985-90. Author: Dual Diagnosis, 1989, Cocaine Addiction, 1989. Clin. adv. com. Counseling for Ind. Living, Middletown, R.I., 1990—. Mem. Am. Psychol. Assn., Nat. Acad. Neuropsychology, R.I. Psychol. Assn., Mass. Psychol. Assn., New Eng. Psychol. Assn. Office: Sakonnet Psychol Assocs 1061 Fish Rd Tiverton RI 02878

CLIFFORD, LEON ALBERT, real estate developer; b. Sherrill, N.Y., Mar. 6, 1919; s. Cloyse Leon and Kathleen Mabel (Knefley) C.; AB in Econs., Colgate U., 1941; attended Air War Coll., 1979. m. Mary E. Schneck, June 1, 1946; children: Charles Lewis, Thomas Arthur. Pres., Clifford Realty, Inc., Rome, N.Y., 1955-82 , Clifford Appraisers and Cons., Rome, 1963—, Clifford Rental Mgmt., Inc., Rome, 1971-82, Hudson-Mohawk Devel. Corp., Rome, 1971—; v.p. Rome Indsl. Corp., 1975-86. Pres., Rome United Way, 1965; vice chmn. bldg. fund Rome YMCA, 1970; chmn. mil. affairs com. Griffiss AFB, N.Y., 1977; trustee Mitchell Coll., New London, Conn., 1976—. Recipient various service awards; Paul Harris fellow Rotary Internat., 1979. Mem. Soc. Real Estate Appraisers (vice gov. 1977-78, cert. instr.), N.Y. Soc. Real Estate Appraisers (pres. 1985-86), Rome Area C. of C. (pres. 1979-80), The Vineyards Country Club, N.Y. Real Estate Bd. (dir. legis. com. 1972—), Rome Bd. Realtors (past pres.), N.Y. State Assn. Real Estate Brokers, Colgate U. Alumni Corp. (bd. dirs. 1990—, Colgate Maroon citation 1991), Rome Club, Teugega Country Club, Rotary (pres. Rome chpt. 1966). Republican. Methodist. Home: Teugega Point Rd Rome NY 13440-7553 also: 3115 Gulf Shore Blvd Naples FL 33940 Office: 219 W Thomas St Rome NY 13440-5098

CLIFFORD, PETER BULKELEY, dentist; b. Hartford, Conn., Mar. 12, 1931; s. Eugene Mathew and Majorie (Kellam) C.; m. Cynthia Brewester, Apr. 4, 1959; children: James, Jonathan. BS, Trinity Coll., 1953; DDS, U. Mich., 1957. Gen. practice dentistry Hartford, 1957—. Active West Hartford Rep., 1965—, Conn. Rep., 1970—; sustaining mem. Nat. Rep., 1981—; class agt. alumnus fund., 1984—. Recipient 150th Anniversary award Trinity Coll., 1975. Mem. ADA (alt. del. 1969), Conn. State Dental Assn. (coun. dental health 1965-73, chmn. 1971-73), Hartford Dental Soc. (pres. 1969-70, Svc. award 1973), Horace Wells Club Conn. (pres. 1976-77, sec., treas. 1978—, chmn. centennial com.), Founders of Hartford (life), Mayflower Soc. Conn. (life), Conn. Hist. Soc., The Old State House Assn., Hartford Club (life), Civitan, SAR (life), Delta Sigma Delta (life). Episcopalian. Home: 30 Pleasant St West Hartford CT 06107-1623 Office: 106 Niles St Hartford CT 06105-2395

CLIFFORD, SIDNEY, JR., lawyer, judge; b. Providence, Jan. 3, 1937; s. Sidney Sr. and Mary Elizabeth (Freeman) C.; m. Irene Kulpa, Sept. 23, 1989. BA, Marlboro (Vt.) Coll., 1959; JD, U. Va., 1962. Bar: R.I. 1962, U.S. Dist. Ct. R.I. 1963, Mass. 1985. Law clk. to assoc. justice Supreme Ct. R.I., Providence, 1963-64; chief examiner div. taxation State of R.I., Providence, 1964-66; ptnr. Quinn & Quinn, 1966-70; chief dep. clk. U.S. Dist. Ct. R.I., 1970-74; atty. legal dept. Commonwealth Land Title Ins. Co., 1980-84; title atty., head title dept. Old Colony Coop. Bank, 1980-82; assoc. Rustigian, Rosenfield, Portnoy & Nasif, 1984-85; legal counsel real estate R.I. Dept. Transp., 1985—; probate judge Little Compton, R.I., 1978—. Pres. Episcopal Charities Rhode Island, 1989-91. Mem. ABA (exec. coun. young lawyers sect. 1987-89), SAR (v.p. R.I. soc. 1991—), Legal Aid Soc. (sec. Providence charitable fuel soc. bd. dirs.), Legal Aid Soc. R.I. (bd. dirs., sec. 1985—), Marlboro Coll. Alumni Assn. (pres., trustee 1969-71), Moses Brown Sch. Alumni Assn. (bd. dirs. 1979—), Warrens Point Beach Club (treas. 1969-74, sec. 1973—), Agawam Hunt and Hope Club, Univ. Club, Providence Art Club, Sakonnet Golf Club, Masons (grand marshal 1977-81). Republican. Episcopalian. Home: 124 Congdon St Providence RI 02906-1413 Office: RI Dept Transp Office Chief Counsel 251 State Office Bldg Providence RI 02903

CLIFFORD, STEWART BURNETT, banker; b. Boston, Feb. 17, 1929; s. Stewart Hilton and Ellinor (Burnett) C.; m. Cornelia Park Woolley, Apr. 26, 1952; children—Cornelia Lee Wareham, Rebecca Lyn Mailer-Howat, Jennifer Leggett Danner, Stewart Burnett. A.B., Harvard U., 1951, M.B.A., 1956. Asst. cashier Citibank, N.A., N.Y.C., 1958-60, asst. v.p., 1960-63; exec. v.p., gen. mgr. Merc Bank, Montreal, Que., Can., 1963-67, v.p. planning Overseas div., 1967-68; v.p., adminstr. comml. banking group Citibank, N.Y.C., 1969-72; v.p. head world corp. dept. Citibank, London, 1973-75; sr. v.p. domestic energy Citibank, N.Y.C., 1975-80, sr. v.p., head pvt. banking and investment div., 1981-87, div. exec., head investment div., 1987—; bd. dirs. Cititrust Ltd., Bahamas. Pres., 120 East End Ave. Corp., Woolley-Clifford Found.; life trustee Spence Sch.; vice chmn. Neighborhood Com. for Asphalt Green; elder Brick Ch.; trustee YWCA, N.Y.C. 1st lt. arty. U.S. Ar.y, 1951-54. Republican. Clubs: Pilgrims, Union, University (N.Y.C.); Duxbury Yacht (Mass.). Home: 120 E End Ave New York NY 10028-7552 Office: Citibank NA 153 E 53d St New York NY 10043

CLIFT, ELAYNE G., writer; b. Woodbury, N.J., Mar. 20, 1943. BA in English, U. Md., 1979, MA in Communication, 1986. Social worker George Washington U. Hosp., Washington, 1970-75; program dir. Nat. Women's Health Network, Washington, 1979-81; mid-Atlantic dir. B'nai Brith Women, Washington, 1981-82; cons. Washington, 1982-85; dep. dir. Healthcom Project Acad. for Ednl. Devel., Washington, 1985-90; writer, cons. Rockville, Md., 1990—; chair Women and Health Roundtable, Washington, 1981-83; founding chair Health Action Network, Montgomery County, Md., 1983-85; v.p. Women in Transition, Inc., Chgo., 1991—. Author: Telling It Like It Is, 1991, (essays) And Still the Women Weep, 1990; contbr. poetry to publs.; contbr. more than 100 articles to profl. jours. and other periodicals. Chair Spl. Need Com. Montgomery County PTA, Rockville, 1989-90. Mem. Am. Pub. Health Assn., Am. Med. Writers Assn., Internat. Womens Writers Guild. Home and Office: 11320 Roven Dr Potomac MD 20854

CLIFTON, ANNE RUTENBER, psychotherapist; b. New Haven, Dec. 11, 1938; d. Ralph Dudley and Cleminette (Downing) Rutenber; 1 dau., Dawn Anne. BA, Smith Coll., 1960, MSW, 1962. Diplomate in Clin. Social Work. Psychiat. case worker adult psychiatry unit Tufts-New Eng. Med. Ctr., Boston, 1962-68, supr. students, 1967-68; pvt. practice psychotherapy, Cambridge, Mass., 1966—; supr. med. students, staff social workers outpatient psychiatry Tufts New Eng. Med. Ctr., 1973—, also mem. exec. bd. Women's Resource Ctr., interim co-dir., 1986-88. Lic. clin. social worker, Mass. asst. clin. prof. psychiatry Tufts U. Med. Sch., 1974—, research dept. psychiatry, 1966-68, 73, 77—. Mem. Acad. Cert. Social Workers, Nat. Assn. Social Workers, Phi Beta Kappa, Sigma Xi. Clubs: Cambridge Tennis, Mt. Auburn Tennis. Contbr. articles to profl. jours. Home: 126 Homer St Newton MA 02159-1518 Office: Ste 4 59 Church St Cambridge MA 02138-5756

CLIMO, LAWRENCE HANON, physician; b. New Haven, Jan. 5, 1938; s. Samuel and Esther (Levitin) C.; m. Diane June Schwartz, July 16, 1967; children: Alison Heather, Amy Catherine, Elana Dawn. BA, Yale U., 1959; MD, Albert Einstein Coll. Medicine, 1964. Diplomate Am. Bd. Psychiatry and Neurology. Dir. edn. Austen Riggs Ctr., Stockbridge, Mass., 1977-80; cons. and supervising psychiatrist Mass. Dept. Mental Health, Lawrence, 1980-91, Mass. Dept. Pub. Health, Tewksbury, 1988-90; sr. assoc. psychiatry Beth Israel Hosp., Boston, 1982—; mem. teaching faculty Harvard U. Med. Sch., Boston, 1985—; dir. DMH Psychopharmacology Clinic, Consulting Forensic; emergency svcs. psychiatrist Greater Lawrence Mental Health Ctr. Capt. U.S. Army, 1965-67. Decorated Bronze Star. Mem. Am. Psychiat. Assn., Am. Acad. Psychiatry and the Law. Office: PO Box 405 Andover MA 01810-0007

CLINE, JANICE CLAIRE, educator; b. Wausau, Wis., Aug. 22, 1945; d. George Leroy Cline and Irma Olga (Brummond) Doering; m. Brent Buell, Jan. 28, 1979. BS, U. Wis., 1967; MA, NYU, 1972; student of Eli Siegel, 1978—; student of Ellen Reiss, Aesthetic Realism Found., N.Y.C., 1977—; student of Aesthetic Realism Teaching Method, 1977—. Tchr. Hyde Park High Sch., Chgo., 1967-69; instr. Chase Manhattan Bank JOB Tng. Program, N.Y.C., 1969-71; evaluator York Coll. Title I Evaluation Team, Jamaica, N.Y., 1972; adj. lectr. N.Y.C. Community Coll., CUNY, Bklyn., 1971-72; lectr. York Coll., CUNY, Jamaica, 1972—; Aesthetic Realism cons.-in-tng., N.Y.C., 1977—; guest speaker WVON, Chgo., 1980. Contbr. articles to profl. jours. Coord. Conf. in Support of the Liberation of S. Africa and Namibia, York Coll., Jamaica, N.Y., 1985, Student/Faculty Consortium on Central Am., York Coll., 1986. Recipient Outstanding Contribution award Afro-Am. Club, York Coll., 1985, Outstanding Contribution award Conf. of African People, Jamaica, N.Y., 1986. Mem. AAUP, Profl. Staff Congress, Internat. Reading Assn. (Manhattan coun.), CUNY Women's Coalition. Democrat. Office: CUNY York Coll 94-20 Guy R Brewer Blvd Jamaica NY 11451

CLINE, JOHN CARROLL, clinical psychologist; b. Staunton, Va., Sept. 6, 1955; s. Carroll Hubert and Naomi Edith (Hevener) C.; m. Diane Jeannette Goudreau, May 21, 1983; 1 child, Virginia Goudreau Cline. BA, U. Va., 1977; PhD, U. Toledo, 1984. Lic. psychologist, Conn.; cert. biofeedback clin. assoc. Am. Bd. Med. Psychotherapists; diplomate Am. Acad. Pain Mgmt. Psychology intern U. Toledo, 1980-81; predoctoral intern VA Med. Ctr., New Haven, 1981-82; clinician Alcohol Svcs. Orgn., New Haven, Conn., 1982-85; attending psychologist VA Med. Ctr., West Haven, Conn., 1984-85; team leader, staff psychologist Elmcrest Hosp., Portland, Conn., 1985-86, asst. unit chief, 1986, dir. behavioral medicine svc., 1986-90; pvt. practice psychologist Hamden, Conn., 1986—; dir. adult outpatient svcs. Inst. of Living, Hartford, Conn., 1990—; clin. supr. Yale Psychol. Svcs. Clinic, Yale U., New Haven, 1985—; cons. psychologist VA Med. Ctr., West Haven, 1985-91; asst. prof. clin. psychiatry U. Conn. Med. Sch., Farmington, Conn., 1991—. Mem. mission study com. 1st Presbyn. Ch., New Haven, 1990-91. Mem. Am. Psychol. Assn., Conn. Psychol. Assn. (chair hosp. practice com. 1990—), N.Y. Acad. Scis., Soc. for Psychotherapy Rsch., AAAS, Assn. for Applied Psychophysiology & Biofeedback, Soc. Behavioral Medicine. Home: 4 Lamkin St Hamden CT 06517-3309 Office: Inst Living 400 Washington St Hartford CT 06106-3351

CLINE, MARLIN GEORGE, agronomy educator; b. Bertha, Minn., Dec. 31, 1909; s. Sampson and Amy Elizabeth (Smith) C.; m. Agnes Irene Israelson, Aug. 17, 1936; children: Richard, Mary Cline Harris, Carol Cline Powers. BS, N.D. State U., 1935; PhD, Cornell U., 1942; DSc (hon.), Trinity Coll., Dublin, Ireland, 1965, N.D. State U., 1965. Jr. soil surveyor USDA, N.D., Hawaii, Tenn., 1935-38; asst. soil scientist USDA, Tenn., 1941-42; agt. USDA, Washington, 1942-54, 56-74; asst. prof. Cornell U., Ithaca, N.Y., 1942-43, assoc. prof., 1943-45, prof., 1945-74, prof. emeritus, 1974—; cons. U.K. Colonial Office, Africa, 1949; soil scientist USGS Mil. Geology Unit, Washington, 1944-45; prof., cons. U. Philippines, Los Banos, 1954-56; cons. to USSR, USDA, 1958. Author: Soils of Hawaii, 1956; contbr. articles to profl. jours. Mem. Dryden (N.Y.) Sch. Bd., 1952-54. Recipient Cert. of Merit Soil Conservation Svc. USDA, 1974. Fellow AAAS, Soil Sci. Soc. Am.; mem. Am. Soc. Agronomy (hon.), N.Y. State Agrl. Soc. (Disting. Svc. Citation 1964). Democrat. Home: 107 Brandywine Dr Ithaca NY 14850-1747

CLINE, RANDALL KENT, youth organization administrator; b. Celina, Ohio, Nov. 17, 1948; s. William Ora and Marjoria Ellen (Clark) C.; m. MaryAnne Morrison, July 14, 1973; children: Michael Aaron, Paul Andrew. BA, Otterbein Coll., 1971. Dist. exec. Miami Valley Coun. of Boy Scouts, Dayton, Ohio, 1973-74; exec. dir. Treaty Line Girl Scout Coun., Richmond, Ind., 1974-79, Singing Sands Girl Scout Coun., South Bend, Ind., 1979-89, Hemlock Girl Scout Coun., Harrisburg, Pa., 1989—; treas. Tri-County Children's and Youth Coordinating Coun., Harrisburg, 1990—; trainer Girl Scouts of the USA, N.Y., 1991—. Vice chmn. Nat. Order of the Arrow Com., Boy Scouts of Am., Irving, Tex., 1990—, advisor Report of the Nation, Washington, 1988, 92, mem.-at-large exec. bd. Keystone Area Coun., Boys Scouts of Am., 1989—. Recipient Silver Beaver award No. Ind. coun. Boy Scouts of Am., 1984, Disting. Svc. award Order of the Arrow, Boy Scouts of Am., 1973. Mem. Nat. Eagle Scout Assn. (Eagle award 1964), Rotary. Home: 5284 Strathmore Dr Mechanicsburg PA 17055 Office: Hemlock Girl Scout Coun Inc 350 Hale Ave Harrisburg PA 17104

CLINGER, WILLIAM FLOYD, JR., congressman; b. Warren, Pa., Apr. 4, 1929; s. William Floyd and Lella May C.; m. Julia Whitla, Aug. 2, 1952; children: Eleanore, William Floyd, James, Julia. BA, Johns Hopkins U., 1951; LLB, U. Va., 1965. Bar: Pa. 1965, U.S. Supreme Ct. 1975. Advt. exec. New Process Co., Warren, 1955-62; ptnr. Stone and Harper, and successor firm Harper, Clinger & Eberly, Warren, 1965-78; mem. 96th-102d Congresses from 23d Pa. dist., mem. com. on public works and transp., 1979—; com. on govt. ops. 96th-102d Congresses from 23d Pa. dist., 1981; vice chmn. aviation subcom., vice chmn. energy, environment and natural resources subcom. 96th-102d Congresses from 23d Pa. dist.; chief counsel Econ. Devel. Adminstrn., 1975-77; del. Pa. Constl. Conv., 1968; chmn., bd. dirs. Ripon Ednl. Fund, Inc. Editorial bd.: U. Va. Law Rev, 1964-65. Chmn. Kinzua Dam Dedication Com., 1966; del. Republican Nat. Conv., 1972, 88; pres. Warren Library Assn., 1957-62, 67-70, Warren Hosp. Bd., 1971-75. Served to lt. USN, 1951-55. Decorated Spirit of Honor medal; named Man of Year Pa. Jaycees, 1960. Mem. ABA, Pa. Bar Assn., Warren County Bar Assn., Warren Jaycees (pres. 1959-60), House Wednesday Group (former chmn.), The Rep. Study Com. Presbyterian. Office: 2160 Rayburn House Office Bldg Washington DC 20515

CLINGERMAN, ROGER BRIAN, insurance company sales executive; b. Ossining, N.Y., May 17, 1961; s. Roger William and Jane Ann (Bost) C.; m. Sondra Lee Smith, Mar. 29, 1986; 1 child, Brandon Roger. AAS, Mercy Coll., Dobbs Ferry, N.Y., 1981. CLU; ChFC; ordained to ministry Jehovah's Witnesses, 1987. Account rep. Met. Life Ins. Co., Flushing, N.Y., 1983-85; sales mgr. Met. Life Ins. Co., Lake Success, N.Y., 1985-87; br. mgr. Met. Life Ins. Co., Mineola, N.Y., 1987-90; sales mgr. N.Y. Life Ins. Co., Rye, N.Y., 1990-92; assoc. br. mgr. MetLife, Larchmont, N.Y., 1992—; moderator Life Underwriters Tng. Coun., Rye, 1991—. Freelance theater critic Trader Publs., 1991—; mktg. mgr. Theatre Info., 1990—. Apptd. elder Congregation of Jehovah Witnesses, Sommers, N.Y., 1992. Mem. Nat. Assn. Life Underwriters (Nat. Sales Achievement award 1985, 86, Nat. Quality award 1985, 86), Gen. Agts. and Mgrs. Conf., Am. Soc. CLUs and ChFCs, Nat. Assn. Securities Dealers (registered rep.), Estate Planning Coun. Westchester County. Home: 8 Old County Rd Mahopac NY 10541 Office: MetLife 2365 Boston Post Rd Larchmont NY 10538

CLINGMAN, STEPHEN ROY, English educator, writer; b. Johannesburg, Transvaal, S. Africa, Apr. 23, 1954; came to U.S., 1989; s. Reginald and Madge (Friedman) C.; m. Moira Miller, July 18, 1978; children: Amelia, Rebecca. BA, U. Witwatersrand, Johannesburg, S. Africa, 1976, BA with honors, 1977; DPhil, Oxford U., Eng., 1983. Vis. fellow S. African Rsch. Program Yale U., New Haven, Conn., 1983-84; postdoctoral fellow African Studies Inst. U. Witwatersrand, Johannesburg, 1984-87; jr. fellow Soc. for Humanities, Cornell U., Ithaca, N.Y., 1987-88; asst. prof. U. Mass., Amherst, 1989-91, assoc. prof. English, 1991—. Author: The Novels of Nadein Gordimer, 1986, 2d edit., 1992; editor: The Essential Gesture (by Nadine Gordimer), 1988, Regions and Repertoires, 1991. Mem. Anti-censorship Action Group, S. Africa, 1986—, Amnesty Internat., 1990—. Recipient scholarships, fellowships U. Witwatersrand, Johannesburg, 1975-77, Annell Trust Bursary, 1977-79, Ford Found. fellowship, Yale U., New Haven, 1983-84. Mem. Modern Lang. Assn. Office: U Mass Dept English Amherst MA 01003

CLINKENBEARD, PAMELA RAE, educational psychologist, researcher, educator; b. Richmond, Ind., June 10, 1955; d. Harold Nelson and Willodean Eileen (Smith) C. BA, DePauw U., 1977; MS, Purdue U., 1980, PhD, 1984. Asst. dir. ednl. programs Talent Identification Program Duke U., Durham, N.C., 1983-85; asst. prof. ednl. psychology U. Ga., Athens, 1986-90; assoc. rsch. scientist Dept. Psychology Yale U., New Haven, 1990—. Contbr. chpts. to books, articles to profl. jours. Funding coord. New Haven Youth at Risk, 1991. Sarah Moss Faculty fellow U. Ga., 1988-89, Edn. Policy fellow Inst. Ednl. Leadership, 1991-92. Mem Am. Psychol. Soc., Am. Ednl. Rsch. Assn., Nat. Assn. for Gifted Children (rec. sec. 1987-88, bd. dirs. 1990—, parliamentary sec. 1991—, Early Scholar award 1991), Phi Delta Kappa. Office: Yale U Dept Psychology Box 11A Yale Sta New Haven CT 06520

CLINTON, LAWRENCE PAUL, psychiatrist; b. Lubbock, Tex., Apr. 27, 1945; s. Lewis Paul Clinton and Dorothy E. (Higgins) Clinton-Billingslea; m. Bonnie Gail Orenstein, June 22, 1969; children: Kerry Elizabeth, Andrew James, Alexander Geoffrey, Kaylin Lee. BA with honors, So. Conn. State Coll., 1966; postgrad., Ohio State U., 1966-68; MD, Hahnemann U., 1972. Diplomate Am. Bd. Psychiatry and Neurology. Teaching asst. Ohio State U., Columbus, 1966-68, research fellow, 1966-68; clin. instr. psychiatry Hahnemann U., Phila., 1975-82, asst. clin. prof., 1982—; chief exec. officer Bldg. Mgmt. Group, Vineland, N.J., 1986—; psychiat. dir. James Guiffre Med. Ctr., Phila., 1976-79; cons. Superior Ct. N.J., 1975—, Ranch Hope, Alloway, N.J., 1989-92. Contbr. articles to profl. jours. Mem. Am. Security Coun., 1975—, Rep. Senatorial Com., 1978—, Rep. Nat. Com., 1978, The Pres.'s Club, 1990—. Recipient awards Am. Security Coun., 1982, Buena Regional Sch. Dist., N.J., 1983, Vineland Parent Support and Adv. Group, 1990; decorated Chevalier Comdr. Ordre Souverain et Militaire de la Milice du Saint Sepulcre, 1990—. Mem. AMA, Am. Psychiat. Assn., Internat. Assn. Group Psychotherapy, N.J. Psychiat. Soc., Phila. Coll. Physicians and Surgeons, Internat. Platform Soc., Med. Club Phila., World Fedn. Mental Health, InterAm. Coll. Physicians and Surgeons, Hahnemann Undergrad. Rsch. Soc. (treas. 1971-72), Confedn. of Chivalry, Am. Chem. Soc., Phi Lambda Kappa (v.p. 1972), Societe d'Chemie (pres. 1965-66), SPQR Club (pres. 1961-62) (Milford, Conn.). Office: 1138 E Chestnut Ave Bldg 6 Vineland NJ 08360-5053

CLINTON, MICHAEL, magazine publisher. Pub. Gentleman's Quarterly, N.Y.C. Office: Gentlemen's Quarterly 350 Madison Ave New York NY 10017-3704*

CLINTON, RICKY JOHN, computer software executive; b. Elizabeth, N.J., May 27, 1954; s. Bertram John Clinton and Gladys Louise (Friese) Krasse; m. Veronica Hague, May 14, 1982 (div. Apr. 1990); 1 child, Edward Hague. BA, Rutgers U., 1976; M. Internat. Mgmt., Am. Grad. Sch. Internat. Mgmt., Glendale, Ariz., 1977. Regional mgr. Autodynamics, Inc., London, 1977-82; area mgr. Beckman Instruments, Inc., Al Khobar, Saudi Arabia, 1982-84; mktg. mgr. Combustion Engring. Inc., Edison, N.J., 1984-89; pres., founder IntelliPro, Inc., New Brunswick, N.J., 1989—. Office: IntelliPro Inc 100 Jersey Ave # 5D New Brunswick NJ 08901-3200

CLIZBE, JOHN ANTHONY, psychologist; b. Council Bluffs, Iowa, June 28, 1942; s. Harold George and Margaret Jane (Fariday) C.; m. Rebecca Rose Maddox, Jan. 30, 1965; children: Mark Andrew, Diane Christine. BA, William Jewell Coll., Liberty, Mo., 1964; PhD, Washington U., St. Louis, 1967. Clin. psychology resident Norfolk (Nebr.) State Hosp. and Northeast Mental Health Clinic, 1967-68; cons. psychologist Nordli, Wilson Assocs., Worcester, Mass., 1968—, gen. ptnr., 1975—, resident mgr., 1978—, mng. ptnr., 1983—; pres. PCMS, Inc., 1984—; dir., treas., PSI, Inc., 1983—, Human Interface Group, Inc., 1986—; dir., v.p., treas. Student Achievement Inst., Worcester, 1973—; instr. psychology Washington U., 1967; vis. lectr. Worcester Poly. Inst., 1973-78; vis. tchr. Jr. Achievement Inst., 1988-90; cons., researcher in field; commentator on mgmt. psychology Sta. WNCR, Worcester. Columnist Bus. Times. Pres. Malboro-Westboro Community Mental Health and Mental Retardations Area Bd., 1970-74; v.p. Mass Region V Mental Health and Mental Retardation Adv. Coun., 1972-73; dir. Dimensions in Human Devel. Series Northboro, 1973-78; dir., treas., pres. Nat. Psychol. Cons. to Mgmt.; mem. bd. edn. Town of Madison, Conn., 1980-86; trustee Calvin K. Kazanjian Econ. Found., Inc., 1986—; mem. standing com. Unitarian Ch., 1970-73, pres. congregation, 1974-76; chmn. Conn. Red Cross Disaster Mental Health Com., 1992—. NDEA fellow Washington U., 1967. Mem. APA (membership com. div. 14), Mass. Psychol. Assn., Am. Mgmt. Assn. (faculty President's Assn. 1987—), New Haven C. of C. (bd. dirs. 1989—), Sigma Xi, Pi Gamma Mu, Pi Kappa Delta. Home: 53 Granby Dr Madison CT 06443-1800 Office: 110 Whitney Ave New Haven CT 06510-1238

CLOCK, KATHLEEN ELIZABETH, secondary education educator; b. Bklyn.; d. Peter and Catherine (Crossey) Mooney; m. Robert R. Clock, Mar. 2, 1963; 1 child, Gerard P. BA, St. John's U., 1960, MA, 1967. Cert. English tchr., N.Y. Tchr. English Intermediate Sch. 293, Bklyn., 1962—, dir. corrective reading ctr., 1976-81, co-chair com. for sch. improvement, 1988-89, mentor for tchr. internship program, 1988-90; instr. in English and adult edn. Plainfield (N.J.) High Sch., 1971-73; adj. asst. prof. English Kean Coll. of N.J., Union, spring 1990. Author (play) A Ghostly Visitor Saves the Bald Eagle, 1966 (Afro-Mediterranean award for best writing of a play). N.Y. State Regents scholar, 1956. Mem. MLA, United Fedn. Tchrs., St. John's U. Alumni Assn. Roman Catholic. Office: Intermediate Sch 293 284 Baltic St Brooklyn NY 11201-6542

CLOSE, KAREN DOUGLASS MOTT, elementary school guidance counselor; b. N.Y.C., Mar. 25, 1951; d. Willard Sherwood and Charlotte Ollave (Douglass) Mott; m. Richard Alan Close, June 24, 1973; twins: Jillian Leigh, Kimberly Ann. BA, Quinnipiac Coll., 1973; MEd, U. Maine, 1989. Cert. guidance counselor, edn. specialist, Maine, Nat. Receptionist Oak Mgmt. Co., Inc., East Hartford, Conn., 1973-74; social work asst. Manchester (Conn.) Bd. Edn., 1974-75; acct. corr. State Conn. Support Svcs., East Hartford, 1976-78; welfare worker Brunswick (Maine) Welfare Dept., 1978-79; support svcs. staff Brunswick Police Dept., 1979-81; typist Nuclear Regulatory Commn., Wiscosset, Maine, 1985-86; adminstrv. asst. Maine Sch. Adminstrv. Dist. 75, Spl. Edn. Dept., Topsham, 1986-88; guidance counselor Sch. Union 30, Lisbon, Maine, 1989—; workshop leader; mem. Drop-Out Prevention Com., Lisbon, 1990—, coord. student assistance team, 1990—. Founding mem. Merry Meeting Counseling Network, Topsham, 1991—. Mem. Am. Sch. Counselor Assn., Maine Sch. Counselors Assn. Episcopalian. Home: RR 1 Box 1477 Richmond ME 04357-9732

CLOSSET, GERARD PAUL, forest products company executive; b. Longwy, France, Nov. 17, 1943; came to U.S., 1965, naturalized, 1976; s. Robert Joseph and Renee (Jacquemet) C.; m. Nicki Lynn Okin, June 29, 1968; children: Juliette, Jennifer. BS, U. Pitts., 1966, MS, 1968, PhD, 1973. Engr. Allied Chem. Corp., Morristown, N.J., 1968-69; research engr. Westvaco Corp., Laurel, Md., 1973-77; mgr. coating St. Regis Paper Co., West Nyack, N.Y., 1977-83, dir. materials, 1983-85; dir. papermaking Champion Internat., 1985-87, v.p. tech., 1987—. Contbr. articles to profl. jours. Pres. Rockland Suburban Symphony, 1984-89; bd. dirs. Rockland County Assn., 1987—. Mem. TAPPI (bd. dirs.), Am. Inst. Chem. Engrs. Avocations: Photography, skiing, scuba diving.

CLOSSON, WILLIAM DEANE, chemistry educator, researcher; b. Remus, Mich., Feb. 3, 1934; s. Charles William and Dorothy Lucette (Plumton) C.; m. Elizabeth Joan Aldrich, Aug. 30, 1969; 1 child, Adam P. B.S., Wayne U., 1956; Ph.D., U. Wis.-Madison, 1960. NSF postdoctoral fellow Harvard U., 1960-61; instr. Columbia U., N.Y.C. 1961-63, asst. prof., 1963-66; assoc. prof. chemistry SUNY-Albany, 1966-71, prof. 1971—. Contbr. articles on organic chemistry to profl. jours., 1956-82. Grantee Petroleum Research Found., 1962-65, NSF-NIH, 1966-74; A.P. Sloan Found. fellow, 1968-72. Mem. Am. Chem. Soc., AAAS. Office: SUNY Dept Chemistry Albany NY 12222

CLOTHIER, JOANNE NICOLAI, English educator; b. Phila., Aug. 5, 1951; d. Charles Wesley and Bernese Irene (Brahl) Nicolai; m. Robert Kenneth Clothier, Aug. 24, 1974; children: Amanda Elizabeth, Allison Jean. BA, Holy Family Coll., 1973; MA in Edn., Beaver Coll., 1977. Cert. English edn. tchr., Pa. Tchr. Archbishop Ryan High Sch., Phila., 1973-84; lectr. Holy Family Coll., Phila., 1981—; tchr. Disston Presbyn. Nursery Sch., Phila., 1990-91; chmn. steering com. self-evaluation study for mid. states assoc. accreditation Archbishop Ryan High Sch., 1979-81. Mem. Nat. Coun. Tchrs. of English, Playmasters Theatre Workshop, Inc. (sec. 1984-88, pres. 1988-90, bus. mgr. 1990—), Lambda Iota Tau. Office: Holy Family Coll Grant & Frankford Aves Philadelphia PA 19114

CLOUD, MARK DAVID, psychology educator; b. Trenton, N.J., Aug. 25, 1958; s. Fred Enos Cloud and Jeane Ann (White) Spoor; m. Suzan Claudette Roeger, Sept. 1, 1979; children: Jaime Marie, Joshua David. BS in Psychology, Ohio State U., 1979, MA in Psychology, 1981, PhD in Psychology, 1984. Vis. asst. prof. U. Mo., Columbia, 1985-86; asst. prof. Lock Haven (Pa.) U., 1986-90, chmn. dept. psychology, 1989—, assoc. prof., 1990—. mem. editorial bd. Jour. of the Pa. Acad. of Scis., 1988—; contbr. articles to profl. jours. Pres. Woolrich (Pa.) Elem. PTO, 1991. Profl. Devel. grant Pa. State System of Higher Edn., 1987-88, Lock Haven U., 1988-91. Mem. Am. Psychol. Soc. (charter), Midwestern Psychol. Assn., Pa. Acad. Scis., Psychonomic Soc. (assoc.). Office: Lock Haven U Fairview Ave Lock Haven PA 17745

CLOUTIER, CHARLOTTE BERUBE, management consultant; b. St. Denis, Canada, Aug. 3, 1942; came to U.S., 1965; d. Louis J. and Therese (Jean) Berube; m. Rene Cloutier, Sept. 2, 1961; 1 child, Robert L. AB, U. Manitoba, Winnipeg, Can., 1965; MA in Sociology, Northeastern U., Boston, 1974, PhD in Law, Pub. Policy, 1988; MPA in Adminstrn., Harvard U., 1981. Tchr. of languages various high schs., Tex./Mass., 1966-70; sec., chief exec. officer Bd. Medicine, Commonwealth of Mass., Boston, 1976-80; assoc. project mgr. Medicine in the Pub. Interest, Boston, 1980-82; fellow Northeastern U., Boston, 1982-88; cons., pvt. bus. Boston and Lexington, Mass., 1986—; lectr. in health policy and politics Coll. Pharmacy/Allied Health Professions, Northeastern U., Boston, 1989—; cons. Office of Inspector, U.S. Govt., Boston, 1989—, Cast/China, Kunming, Yunnan, 1982-85, Commonwealth of Mass. Legislature, Boston, 1980-82. Contbg. author: Social Controls and the Medicial Profession, 1985. Mem. People-to-People Internat. Med. Rehab. Delegation, 1982. Recipient Cert. Appreciation Fed. of State Med. Bds., Ft. Worth, Tex., 1981, First Prize Philosophy, U. Manitoba, 1965. Fellow Fedn. State Med. Bds.; mem. Am. Society Assn., Mass. Bar Assn. Home and Office: 16 Wilmor Rd Topsfield MA 01983-1021

CLOVIS, DONNA LUCILLE, educator; b. East Orange, N.J., Aug. 22, 1957; d. Clarence M. and Annye Brown; m. James R. Clovis III; children: Justin, Matthian, Michaela. BA, Trenton (N.J.) State Coll., 1978, LittD (hon.), 1991. Cert. in English as a second lang., elem. edn. Tchr. New Brunswick (N.J.) Bd. Edn., 1981-86; tchr. North Brunswick (N.J.) Bd. Edn., 1986-88, Voorhees (N.J.) Bd. Edn., 1989-91, Princeton Regional Schs., Princeton (N.J.) Bd. of Edn., 1991—; presenter ESL workshop, Burlington City, N.J., 1990, N.J. Fedn. Program Adminstrs., Atlantic City, TESOL Conv., N.Y.C., Cen. Jersey African Am. Bookfair, 1991, Borders Bookshop, Marten, 1992. Author: Metamorphosis, 1988 (N.J. Inst. Tech. 1990), Survival Through These Hard Times, 1990; author of poetry. Presenter Voorhees Women's Club, 1990, Echelson Towers Assn., Vorhees, 1990; mem. Princeton Arts Coun. Recipient 3rd Place award poetry Poet's Press, Tex., 1987, Success award Scholastic Mag., N.Y.C., 1990, Southern Poetry Blue Ribbon award Southern Poetry Soc., 1989, Citation award-writer's N.J. Inst. Tech., 1990. Mem. Tchrs. English to Students of Other Langs., Poet's and Writer's Guild, Soc. for Poet's and Writer's Guild, Soc. for Poets of Southern N.J., World Acad. Arts and Culture, World Congress of Poets, Conservatory Am. Letters, N.J./Penn TESOL, N.J, Poetry Soc., IPA Washington, NCTE (membership com. for publishing). Home: PO Box 0741 Princeton Junction NJ 08550 Office: Princeton Regional Schs PO Box 711 Princeton NJ 08544-0999

CLOVIS, JAMES S., research chemist; b. Waynesburg, Pa., Aug. 14, 1937; s. Roy W. and May (Phillips) C.; m. Constance Shane, Apr. 11, 1970; children: Nicole, Christie. BS in Chemistry and Math., Waynesburg Coll., 1959; PhD in Chemistry, Calif. Inst. Tech., 1963; postgrad., U. Munich, 1963. Scientist in plastics rsch. Rohm and Haas Co., Bristol, Pa., 1963-70; lab. head process rsch. Rohm and Haas Co., Phila., 1970-74, lab. head pollution rsch., 1974-76; mgr. R & D indsl. chems. and plastics Rohm and Haas Co., Valbonne, France, 1976-79; mgr. indsl. chems. Rohm and Haas Co., Phila., 1979-81; rsch. dir. indsl. chems. Rohm and Haas Co., Spring House, Pa., 1981-83, rsch. dir. new tech., 1983-86, rsch. dir. agrl. chems., 1986—, rsch. dir. separation tech., 1988-92; rsch. dir. toxicology Rohm and Haas Co., Spring House, Pa., 1992—. Contbr. articles to sci. and religion jours.; patentee in field. Founder, participant USTA/Nat. Jr. Tennis League Trenton, N.J., 1974—; trustee, chmn. George Sch., Newtown, Pa., 1980—. Mem. Am. Chem. Soc., Royal Soc. London. Mem. Soc. of Friends. Home: 207 Penn Valley Ter Morrisville PA 19067-1028 Office: Rohm and Haas Co 727 Norristown Rd Spring House PA 19477

CLOWNEY, SHIRLEY CARR, secondary education educator; b. Maryville, Tenn., July 25, 1936; d. James Andrew and Mary Pearl (Nicely) Carr; m. Cato Clowney Jr., Mar. 17, 1958; children: R. Lisa C. Brown, E. Lamarr, C. Raynard. BS, Tenn. State U., 1960. Cert. elem., secondary home econ., sci. and Eng. tchr., N.J. Tchr. Lincroft (N.J.) Elem. Sch., 1963-65, Bayshore Jr. High Sch., Leonardo, N.J., 1965-69, Middletown (N.J.) High Sch., 1965-66, Monmouth Regional High Sch., Tinton Falls, N.J., 1969—. Mem. NEA, N.J. Edn. Assn., Monmouth County Edn. Assn., Monmouth Regional Edn. Assn. (dept. rep.), Vocat. Home Econ. Assn. (v.p., pres. 1989-91), Monmouth County Home Econ. Assn. (v.p., pres. 1985-87), Delta Sigma Theta (v.p. 1985-88, sec., chaplain, com. chair). Home: 4 Kenneth Dr Asbury Park NJ 07712-2804 Office: Monmouth Regional High Sch 535 Tinton Ave Eatontown NJ 07724-3299

CLOWNEY, WILLIAM CLARKE, employee benefits manager; b. Cleve., Nov. 18, 1957; s. William Daniel and Mary (Seaman) C.; m. Isidora Konstantina Lagos, Aug. 24, 1985. BA in Russian and Polit. Sci., Rice U., 1980; MBA in Mktg., Ind. U., 1984. Group sales rep. Met. Life, Houston, 1980-82, Equitable Life Assurance, Overland Park, Kans., 1985-87; sr. group rep. NWNL Cos., Overland Park, 1987-88, asst. regional group mgr., 1988-89; regional group mgr. NWNL Cos., N.Y.C., 1989—. Fulbright Found. fellow, 1983; Am. Field Svc. Internat. scholar, 1984. Mem. Cert. Employee Benefit Specialist Orgn. of N.Y. Republican. Christian Orthodox. Home: 239 Jackman Ave Fairfield CT 06432-1727 Office: NWNL Cos 14th Fl 52 Vanderbilt Ave New York NY 10017-3808

CLUFF, CONSTANCE SOCKMAN, mental health services professional; b. Tuxedo, N.Y., Apr. 7, 1941; d. Bruce Earle and Gertrude Letitia (Stewart) Sockman; m. Philip Witonsky, Dec. 31, 1963 (div. Nov. 1976); children: Trudi D., Sharon G., Laura A.; m. Edward Fuller Cluff, Aug. 27, 1988. BS, Tufts U., 1963; MS, U. Wis., 1965. Cert. clin. mental health counselor, nat. cert. counselor. Social worker II Wilmington (Del.) Mental Health Clin., 1975-85; counselor Tressler Ctr., Wilmington, 1985-89; pvt. practice Wilmington, 1989—; instr. Goldey Beacom Coll., Wilmington, fall, 1975; counselor Tressler Ctr., 1980-85; chmn. Personal Growth Assoc., Wilmington, 1990-91. Chmn. adult religious edn. 1st Unitarian Ch., Wilmington, 1989-91, mem. children's religion com., 1984; chmn. day care study LWV, Dallas, 1971-72, chmn. bd. dirs., Richardson, Tex., 1970-71; Brownie leader Girl Scouts U.S.A., Richardson, 1973. Mem. ACA, Am. Mental Health Counselors Assn., Del. Mental Health Counselors Assn. (bd. dirs. 1990-91). Home: 706 Hertford Rd Wilmington DE 19803-1618 Office: 300 Foulk Rd Ste 104 Wilmington DE 19803-3819

CLYMER, ARTHUR BENJAMIN, consulting engineer, retired; b. Cleve., Aug. 7, 1920; s. William Ruhl and Lulu (Jackson) C.; m. Gayla Tarbill Gerwin, Dec. 3, 1953 (div. 1972); children: Mark Gerwin, Paul Jackson. BA, Oberlin Coll., 1941; MS, Ohio State U., 1946, MIT, 1948. Jr. design engr. Sperry Corp., L.I., N.Y., 1942-45; math. engr. Owens-Ill. Glass Co., Toledo, Ohio, 1949-53; rsch. coord. Bituminous Coal Rsch., Inc., Columbus, Ohio, 1953-55; sr. tech. specialist N.Am. Aviation, Inc., Columbus, 1955-61; environ. engr. Ohio EPA, Columbus, 1972-76; simulation engr. Electronic Assocs., Inc., W. Long Branch, N.J., 1977-81; dir. tng. Autodynamics, Inc., Freehold, N.J., 1981-83; cons. engr. Clymer Tech., Inc., Columbus, 1961-72, 76-77, Ocean, N.J., 1983-88; dir. Soc. Computer Simulation, San Diego, 1960-90 (Sr. Scientific Simulation award 1970). Home: 32 Willow Dr Apt 1B Asbury Park NJ 07712-2825

COAKLEY, JAMES FREDERICK, academic administrator; b. Rochester, N.Y., May 6, 1945; s. W. Roger and Ruth L. (Lunger) C.; m. Susan G. Gantz, June 6, 1970; children: Lynn, Beth, John. AB, Dartmouth Coll., 1967; MBA, Plymouth (N.H.) State Coll., 1973. Tchr. Kimball Union Acad., Meriden, N.H., 1967-71; asst. bus. mgr. Dartmouth Coll., Hanover, N.H., 1971-81; dean adminstrn. Vt. Tech. Coll., Randolph Center, 1981-86; v.p. Daniel Webster Coll., Nashua, N.H., 1986—. Home: 17 Waterview Dr Amherst NH 03031-2109 Office: Daniel Webster Coll University Dr Nashua NH 03063-1300

COATE, DAVID EDWARD, acoustician consultant; b. Kansas City, Mo., Sept. 10, 1955; s. Arthur Dale and Martha (Goodrich) C.; m. Sheryl Marie Luebbert, Aug. 8, 1981; children: Allison Marie, Brian Joseph. BA in Math/Chemistry/Physics cum laude, Westminster Coll., 1978; MS, MIT, 1980. Rsch. staff scientist MIT Energy Lab., Cambridge, 1980-81; energy auditor Volt Energy Systems, Boston, 1981-82; owner Turning Point Records, Boston, 1982-85; sr. scientist Bolt, Beranek, and Newman, Cambridge, 1986-89; sr. cons. Acentech Inc., Cambridge, 1989—. Albums include Time Keeps on Running, 1980, State of the Heart, 1985, Still Small Voice, 1990. Mem. Acoustical Soc. Am., Inst. Noise Control Engring. (assoc.), Transp. Rsch. Bd. Presbyterian. Office: Acentech Inc 125 Cambridge Park Dr Cambridge MA 02140-2327

COATES, ARTHUR DONWELL, chemist, consultant; b. Steubenville, Ohio, June 14, 1928; s. Arthur Raymond and Margaret June (Thompson) C.; m. Marie Maslin Silver, Apr. 6, 1957; children: Arthur Donwell Jr., Randolph Silver, Stephen Thompson. BS in Chemistry, Coll. Steubenville, 1950; MS in Chemistry, U. Del., 1961. Practice engr. Wheeling Steel Corp., Steubenville, 1950-51; chemist, rsch. chemist Terminal Ballistics Lab., Aberdeen Proving Ground, Md., 1951-55; chief ignition sect. Terminal Ballistics Lab., 1955-60, chief radiation damage sect., 1960-70, chief methodology sect., 1970-75; tech. asst. to chief Terminal Ballistics Div., 1975-78; spl. asst. to dir. U.S. Army Ballistic Rsch. Lab., 1978-86; pres. Silver Farms, Inc., Aberdeen, Md., 1979—; cons. in fields of applied chemistry and ballistic tech. Pfc. U.S. Army, 1951-53. Fellow Am. Inst. Chemists; mem. AAAS, Am. Chem. Soc., N.Y. Acad. Scis., Aberdeen C. of C. (planning com. 1989—), Sigma Xi. Methodist. Home and Office: 311 N Osborn Ln Aberdeen MD 21001-1918

COATES, CARROL F., language educator, researcher; b. Oklahoma City, July 22, 1930; s. B. Franklin and Maida Lenore (Sipe) C.; m. Clarisse Rahajamanarivo, June 20, 1952. B.A., U. Okla., 1951, M.A., 1954; Ph.D., Yale U., 1964. Instr. Ohio U., Athens, 1960-62; asst. prof. Lycoming Coll., Williamsport, Pa., 1962-63; asst. prof. SUNY-Binghamton, 1963-67, assoc. prof., 1967—, master Dickinson Coll., 1969-74, dir. basic langs. program, 1981-82; vis. assoc. prof. U. de Provence, Aix-en-Provence, France, 1980, 83-84; resident dir. program in French Studies SUNY, Aix-en-Provence, 1980, 83, 84. Collaborator 2 scholarly bibliographies (French and Que. lit.), 1973, 80. Contbr. numerous articles to scholarly jours. Assoc.-editor Callaloo jour. African-Am. and African Arts and Letters; translation and introduction René Depestre, The Festival of the Greasy Pole, U. Va., 1990. Served with U.S. Army, 1954-57. Recipient Research award SUNY Research Found., 1965; Que. Provincial Govt. fellow, 1978; Fulbright student grantee, 1952-53, vis. lectr. grantee, 1980. Mem. MLA, Am. Assn. Tchrs. of French, Am. Translators Assn. (accredited translator French-Eng.), Assn. for Can. Studies in U.S., Am. Council for Que. Studies. Avocation: piano playing. Office: SUNY Dept Romance Langs Binghamton NY 13902-6000

COATES, EDWARD MALCOLM, III, economist; b. Newport News, Feb. 10, 1966; s. Edward and Barbara (Howell) C. BS in Econs., U. Wis., 1989. Economist U.S. Dept. Labor - BLS, Washington, 1989—. Mem. Wis. State Soc. Republican. Home: 7330 Dartford Dr # 8 Mc Lean VA 22102 Office: 2 Massachusetts Ave Rm 4168 Washington DC 20212

COBAUGH, STEPHEN MARCUS, editor, photojournalist; b. Lancaster, Pa., Nov. 6, 1955; s. Charles Melvin and Shirley Anne (Querry) C. BA, Millersville U., 1977; MA, Indiana U. of Pa., 1979. Editor Space Age Times Mag., Elizabethtown, Pa., 1974—; art dir., acct. exec. Mark A. Vogel Advt., Lancaster, 1984-87. Asst. pub. affairs officer Pa. wing USAF Aux., Phila., 1990—; rsch. analyst Rep. staff Senate Pa., Harrisburg, 1980-81; art dir. Senate Rep. Comm. Office, Harrisburg, 1981-84; dir. vol. coordination Rep. State Com. Pa., Harrisburg, 1984; chmn. Elizabethtown Area Rep. Com., 1981-86, committeeman, 1980-88; adv. com. Lancaster County Rep. Com., Elizabethtown, 1980-86. Mem. Nat. Assn. Sci. Writers, U.S. Space Edn. Assn. (internat. pres. 1973—), Aviation/Space Writers Assn. (Photojournalism Still Photo/Space Industry Comm. award 1989, 90). Home and Office: Space Age Times 746 Turnpike Rd Elizabethtown PA 17022-1161

COBB, DAVID KEITH, accounting manager; b. Calhoun City, Miss., Mar. 2, 1941; s. Bayne and Frances (Clements) C.; m. Dorothy Hill, June 15, 1963; children: Paul J., John D., Mark F. BS, U. So. Miss., 1963. CPA, Miss., Fla., Md., Pa. Mng. ptnr. KPMG Peat Marwick, Phila., 1963—. Bd. dirs. Pa. Econ. League, Phila., 1991, Balt. Mus. Art, 1991, Balt./Washington Regional Assn., 1991, Internat. Visitors Ctr., Washington, 1991, bd. dirs., sponsor Sellinger Sch. of Bus., Loyola Coll., Balt., 1991; mem. Union League, Phila., 1991. Republican. Presbyterian. Home: 845 Mt Moro Rd Villanova PA 19085-2059 Office: KPMG Peat Marwick 1600 Market St Philadelphia PA 19103-4201

COBB, MARGARET MARY, research physician; b. Binghamton, N.Y., Nov. 7, 1948; d. John William and Margaret Mary (Jones) Menta; m. Fredrick Donald Cobb, June 5, 1971; 1 child, Heather Edith. MS, Syracuse U., 1977; PhD, Cornell U., 1981; MD, N.Y. Med. Coll., 1985; MPH with distinction, Yale U., 1990. Diplomate Nat. Bd. Med. Examiners. Rsch. assoc. E.R. Squibb & Sons, Princeton, N.J., 1970-73; rsch. asst. Syracuse (N.Y.) U., 1973-77; sr. rsch. assoc. Cornell U., Ithaca, N.Y., 1977-79; postdoctoral fellow Upstate Med. Ctr., Syracuse, 1980-81; med. intern Yale U. Affiliate, New Haven, Conn., 1985-86, postdoctoral fellow, resident pub. health, 1986-87; rsch. assoc., physician Rockefeller U., N.Y.C., 1987-90; assoc. dir. profl. med. svcs. Am. Cyanamid Corp., Pearl River, N.Y., 1990—; pvt. practice N.Y.C. Eucharistic minister St. Catherine's Ch., Riverside, Conn. Mem. AAAS, AMA, APHA, N.Y. Lipid Club, Sigma Xi. Roman Catholic. Home: 2 Glen Rd Greenwich CT 06830-4632 Office: 1735 York Ave Ste 2F New York NY 10128-6855

COBB, MILTON TERRY, theater educator; b. Anniston, Ala., Apr. 30, 1949; s. Ruben Arnold and Irene Krissie (Smith) C. BA, Auburn U., 1972; MA, Humboldt State U., 1976, MFA, 1980. Shop foreman theater dept. Auburn (Ala.) U., 1972-74; prodn. technician Santa Rosa (Calif.) Jr. Coll., 1976-79; sound and lighting designer Summer Repertory Theatre, Santa Rosa, 1978, 79; instr., now asst. prof. dept. theater U. Md. Baltimore County, Balt., 1980—; tech. cons. Qual-A-Wa-Loo Comedy Festival, Eureka, Calif., 1975; tech. dir. Balt. Internat. Theatre Festival, 1981. Mem. U.S. Inst. Theatre Tech. Office: U Md Baltimore County Dept Theater Baltimore MD 21228

COBBS, JOHN LEWIS, educational consultant; b. N.Y.C., Jan. 5, 1943; s. John Lewis III and Phyllis Conway (White) C.; m. Kathryn Ann Wixon, Aug. 8, 1981; 1 child, Kathryn. BA, Haverford Coll., 1965; PhD, U. N.C., 1975. Prof. Elizabeth City (N.C.) State U., 1976-81, U. Louisville, 1981-84, Jefferson Community Coll., Louisville, 1983-84, Ursinus Coll., Collegeville, Pa., 1984-90; cons., writer Valley Forge, Pa., 1990—; cons. Ednl. Testing Svcs., Princeton, N.J., 1991—. Fiction editor Carolina Quar., 1971-74; mem. editorial bd. 3 jours.; author: Owen Wister, 1984; editor, author (with others): Film Criticism: Introduction, 1973; contbr. articles to profl. jours. NEH Fellowship grantee U. Pa., 1985. Republican. Episcopalian. Home and office: 24 Acoma Ln Collegeville PA 19426-1702

COBEN, DANIEL PAUL, outplacement counselor, career consultant; b. Newark, Aug. 3, 1959; s. Melvin Stanley and Elaine Ruth (Gershen) C.; m. Vicki Marcia Schorr, Nov. 5, 1989. BA in Journalism, NYU, 1981, MA in Counseling Psychology, 1988; postgrad., Seton Hall U., 1991—. Broadcast journalist ABC News, N.Y.C., 1982-84, CBS News, Phila., 1984-85; recruiter Exec. Search Group, N.Y.C., 1985-86; asst. dir. career planning and placement N.J. State Coll. System, Jersey City, 1986-87; sr. outplacement cons. Chem. Banking Corp., N.Y.C., 1987—; cons. assoc. Drake, Beam, Morin, Inc., N.Y.C., 1988-90, Manchester, Inc., Parsippany, N.J., 1988-90, Lee Hecht Harrison, Inc., N.Y.C., 1990—. Author: (manual) Networking for Career Mobility, 1986. Vol. Spl. Olympics, Somerset County, N.J., 1990-91. Mem. Internat. Assn. Outplacement Profls. (charter), Human Resources Network (charter). Home: 15 Crown Rd Somerset NJ 08873-4130

COBERT, BARTON LEWIS, physician, pharmaceutical researcher; b. N.Y.C., Feb. 6, 1950; s. Henry and Ruth Cobert; m. Josiane Claude Weisbluth, Nov. 1, 1981; children: Emilie, Julien. BA, NYU, 1970, MD, 1974. Diplomate Am. Bd. Internal Medicine. Teaching asst. NYU Med. Sch., 1977—; dir., med. rsch. Hoechst Roussel Pharmaceuticals, Inc., Somerville, N.J., 1985—; teaching asst. U. Medicine and Dentistry of N.J., 1991—. Fellow Am. Coll. Physicians, Am. Coll. Gastroenterology; mem. Am. Gastroenterology Assn., Phi Delta Kappa. Office: Hoecht Roussel Pharms Inc Rt 202-206 N Somerville NJ 08876

COBERT, WENDY LYNN, small business owner; b. Abington, Pa., May 10, 1963; d. Roger William and Helen Barbara (Morris) C.. Lic., Becks Tech. Inst., 1981, Levittown Beauty Acad., 1981. Asst. to stylists Village Cuts, Langhorne, Pa., 1979-81, stylist, 1981-82; stylist Great Lengths, Langhorne, 1982-84, Super Hair, Fairless Hills, Pa., 1984-86; stylist, mem. design team Internat. Hair Design, Langhorne, 1986-88; owner, operator Concentrix Design, Tullytown, Pa., 1988—. Mem. KMS Hair Cosmetics. Home: 183 Aquetong Rd New Hope PA 18938-1129 Office: Concentrix Design 258 Main St Ste 13 Bristol PA 19007-6115

COBURN, JOHN, JR., real estate executive; b. Boston, Aug. 1, 1941; s. John and Jane (Shaw) C.; m. Abigail Lasbury, Mar. 5, 1966 (div. Mar. 1976); children: John III, Tristran Coffin; m. Elizabeth Bishop, July 24, 1976; children: Timothy Gage, James Bishop. AB, Harvard U., 1963. V.p., founder Coburn Bros. Corp., Wareham, Mass., 1961-71, New England Whalers, Boston, 1971-73, World Sports Ltd., Geneva, Switzerland, 1973-76; v.p. LandVest, Boston, 1977—; mem. FIABCI, N.Y.C., 1990-91. Trustee Dedham (Mass.) Country Day Sch., 1985-87; mem. planning bd. Town of MArion, Mass., 1969-71; mem. Econ. Devel. Com., Wareham, 1968-70. Mem. The Country Club, The Field Club, The Winter Club. Republican. Home: 35 Logan Rd New Canaan CT 06840-2102 Office: LandVest 10 Post Office Sq Boston MA 02109-4699

COCCAGNA, FRED JOSEPH, JR., flooring manufacturing executive; b. Phila., July 26, 1945; s. Fred Joseph and Helen J. (Ventrola) C.; m. Adrienne Speranza Imbrogno, July 1, 1972; children: Fred Franco, Michelle Adrienne. BS in Mgmt., Phila. Coll. Textiles & Sci., 1967. Gen. mgr. Indsl. Floor Corp., Jenkintown, Pa., 1967-69; pres., chief exec. officer Indsl. Floor Corp., 1981—; v.p. Indcon-Indsl. Corp., Jenkintown, 1969-81; cons. in field. Vol. Young Reps., Phila., 1960, 63, Com. to Re-elect The Pres., 1972. Mem. Phila. Mus. Art, Am. St. Corridor Bus. Assn., Rolls Royce Owner's Club, Abington Club, Ocean Club Majority Owners Assn. Inc. (treas.), N.J. Bus. and Commerce Assn. Roman Catholic. Office: Indsl Fl Corp Ste 418 Fox Pavilion Jenkintown PA 19046

COCCARI, RANDALL C., motor lodge company executive; b. Charleroi, Pa., Apr. 13, 1947; s. Joseph C. and Marie J. (Usher) C.; m. Sherry L. Williams, June 9, 1966; children: Kimberly J., Jodi M., Christopher J. ASBA, Point Park Coll., 1967; BSBA summa cum laude, Calif. U. of Pa., 1989, MSBA summa cum laude, 1991. Cert. multi-line ins. agt. Asst. to chief acct. Screw & Bolt Corp., Pitts., 1967-69; sales rep. Prudential Ins. Co., Monessen, Pa., 1967-71; sales mgr. Hub Real Estate Devel. Corp., Belle Vernon, Pa., 1971-73; gen. mgr. Motor Lodge Devel. Co., Belle Vernon, 1973—. Author: We Send You Our Love, 1990, The True Secret of Fantastic Wealth, 1977. Mem. Pa. Home Builders Assn., Rostraver Businessmen's Assn., Mon Valley Realtors Assn., Mon Valley Home Builders Assn., Pa. Notary Assn., Elks, Phi Sigma Pi. Home: 5 Crescent Dr Monessen PA 15062-2511

COCCO, ALEX MARK, surgeon; b. Wheeling, W.Va., Sept. 8, 1952; s. Leo P. and Betty (Pelectlette) C.; m. Nancy L. Cocco; 1 child, Abagail. AB in Biology, W.Va. U., 1974; MD, U. Aut. de Guad., Mexico, 1979. Diplomate Am. Bd. Surgery. Surg. resident Mercy Hosp., Pitts., 1981-86. Office: Hillcrest Med Ctr Grove City PA 16127

COCHÉ, JUDITH ABBE, psychologist, educator; b. Phila., Sept. 2, 1942; d. Louis and Miriam (Nerenberg) Milner; m. Erich Coché, Oct. 16, 1966; 1

child, Juliette Laura. BA, Colby Coll., 1964; MA, Temple U., 1966; PhD, Bryn Mawr Coll., 1975. Diplomate Am. Bd. Profl. Psychology. Rsch. asst. Jefferson Med. Coll., 1965-66; diagnostician Law Ct., Aachen, Germany, 1967-68; staff psychologist N.E. Community Mental Health Ctr., Phila., 1969-74; family clinician Inst. Pa. Hosp., 1974-76; instr. psychology Drexel U., 1976-77; lectr. Med. Coll. Pa., 1977-78; asst. clin. prof. Hahnemann Med. Coll., Phila., 1979—; pvt. practice Phila., 1974—, N.J., 1985—; assoc. prof. psychiatry U. Pa., 1985—; mem. faculty Family Inst. of Phila., 1990—; sr. cons. Phila. Child Guidance Clinic, 1992—; clin. cons. Hilltop Prep Sch., 1977-86; clin. supr. Am. Assn. Marriage and Family Therapy. Contbr. articles to profl. jours., chpts. to books. Bd. dirs. Whitemarsh Art Ctr., 1977-78; mem. profl. adv. bd. Parents Without Ptnrs., 1977-86.. Grantee Del. Children's Bur. Bryn Mawr Coll., 1974-75, Pa. Hosp., 1975-77. Fellow Am. Group Psychotherapy Assn.; mem. APA, Am. Assn. Marriage and Family Therapists, Phila. Soc. Clin. Psychologists (pres. 1980-81), Family Inst. Phila., Pa. Psychol. Assn. (chmn. legis. com. 1982), Soc. Rsch. in Psychotherapy. Address: 2037 Delancey Pl Philadelphia PA 19103

COCHRAN, GEORGE VAN BRUNT, physician, surgery educator, researcher; b. N.Y.C., Jan. 20, 1932; s. George Gilfillan and Mary Lott (Van Brunt) C.; m. Caroline Winston, June 13, 1970; children: Linsay, Alexander, John. AB magna cum laude, Dartmouth Coll., 1953; MD, Columbia U., 1956, ScD, 1967. Diplomate Am. Bd. Orthopaedic Surgery. Intern in surgery Presbyn. Hosp., N.Y.C., 1956-57; asst. resident, then resident N.Y. Orthopaedic Hosp., N.Y.C., 1961-63; NIH rsch. fellow dept. orthopaedics Columbia U., N.Y.C., 1964-69, prof. clin. orthopaedic surgery, 1981—; dir. orthopaedic rsch. St. Lukes Hosp., N.Y.C., 1970-80; dir., founder biomechs. rsch. unit Helen Hayes Hosp., West Haverstraw, N.Y., 1972-80, dir. and founder orthopaedic engring. and rsch. ctr., 1980—; attending orthopaedic surgeon rsch. svc. VA Med. Ctr., Castle Point, N.Y., 1975—; adj. prof. biomed. engring. Rensselaer Poly. Inst., Troy, N.Y., 1981—; dir. Charles A. Lindbergh Fund, Mpls., 1983-86, Health Rsch. Inst., Albany, N.Y., 1981-85. Author: A Primer of Orthopaedic Biomechanics, 1982; contbr. numerous articles to profl. jours. Capt. USAF, 1957-59, ETO. HEW/Social and Rehab. Svcs. fellow, 1968-69, A.O. Lab. for Exptl. Surgery/Arctic Inst. N.Am. fellow, 1967, USPHS fellow and grantee, 1964-66; NIH/VA grantee. Fellow N.Y. Acad. Scis., Am. Acad. Orthopaedic Surgeons, The Explorers Club (pres. 1981-85); mem. Bioelec. Repair and Growth Soc. (pres. 1990), Internat. Soc. Orthopaedic Surgery and Traumatology, Orthopaedic Rsch. Soc., Soc. for Exptl. Stress Analysis, Am. Congress Rehab. Medicine, Am. Orthopaedic Assn., Phi Beta Kappa, Kappa Delta (Orthopaedic Rsch. award 1968, Nicholas Andry co-award 1975, Spl. Achievement award 1987). Republican. Office: Helen Hayes Hosp RR 9 West Haverstraw NY 10993

COCHRAN, MAURA MCNALLY, real estate company executive, consultant; b. N.Y.C., July 30, 1948; d. George P. and Ellen (Carley) McNally; m. William J. Cochran, July 17, 1982. BFA, Art Inst. Chgo., 1970. Pres. Design Loft, Avon, Conn., 1976-79; v.p. Farley Co., Hartford, Conn., 1979-87; v.p. Bartram & Cochran, Hartford, 1987-90, prin., 1991—. Author: Understanding Construction, 1991; co-author: Strategies in Tenant Representation, 1990. Chmn. YMCA of Hartford, 1990-91, Read to Succeed, Hartford, 1990-92. Mem. Am. Soc. Real Estate Counselors (cert. real estate, vice chair Conn. chpt.), Soc. Indsl. and Office Realtors (cert., chair conv. edn. com. 1992), Real Estate Exch. (founding pres. 1987-89), Conn. Bd. Realtors (pres. Hartford chpt. indsl. div. 1982), Univ. Club (bd. mem., chair membership 1990—). Home: 1 Gold St Apt 20C Hartford CT 06103-2908 Office: Bartram & Cochran 64 Pratt St Hartford CT 06103-1608

COCHRAN, NATHAN MICHAEL, college administrator, art curator; b. Marion, Ohio, June 24, 1957; s. Blaine Richard and Ruth Edna (Roach) C. BA in Religious Studies, Pontifical Coll. Josephinum, Columbus, Ohio, 1980; MDiv, St. Vincent Sem., Latrobe, Pa., 1985. Entered St. Vincent Archabbey (Benedictine Soc. of Westmoreland County, Pa.), 1982. Curator St. Vincent Archabbey Art Coll., Latrobe, Pa., 1983—; registrar St. Vincent Coll., Latrobe, 1986—, St. Vincent Sem., 1989—; pub. rels. exec. St. Vincent Archabbey, 1989—. Mem. Am. Assn. Coll. Registrars and Admissions Officers, Middle State Assn. Coll. Registrars and Officers of Admission, Am. Assn. Mus., Constantian Soc. Republican. Home: St Vincent Archabbey Latrobe PA 15650 Office: St Vincent Coll Fraser Purchase Rd Latrobe PA 15650-2667

COCKER, TEDD, computer science company executive; b. Phila., Aug. 28, 1941; s. John William Cocker and Florence Mary (Maier) Moore; m. Frances Alberta Pope, Sept. 12, 1963; children: John, Angela Cocker Blackmon, Donna, Christopher, Kathleen. BS in Bus. and Mgmt., U. Md., 1984; BS in Gen. Bus., SUNY, Albany, 1984; MS in Gen. Adminstrn., Cen. Mich. U., 1987. Enlisted U.S. Army, 1961, advanced through grades to chief warrant officer, 1971, served in Korea, Vietnam, ret., 1983; mem. tech. staff Electrospace Systems, Inc., McLean, Va., 1983-86; mem. tech. staff Electrospace Systems, Inc., Greenbelt, Md., 1986, dept. mgr., 1986-87; dept. mgr. Electrospace Systems, Inc., McLean, 1987; mem. exec. staff Computer Scis. Corp., Hanover, Md., 1987-89, project dir., 1989—. Pres. Better Community Rels. Com., Pyongtaek, South Korea, 1976-77, 79-80. Decorated Bronze Star. Mem. Am. Mgmt. Assn., Armed Forces Communications and Electronics Assn. (symposium coord. Cen. Md. chpt. 1989—), U.S. Army Warrant Officers' Assn., Ft. Meade Officers' Club. Office: Computer Scis Corp 7471 Candlewood Rd Hanover MD 21076-3102

COCKSHAW, PETER ALBERT, publishing executive; b. East Orange, N.J., Mar. 25, 1934; s. Albert Barlow and Beatrice Florence (Drabble) C.; m. Constance LaRue Barkdoll, May 25, 1961; children: Cindy Beatrice, Peter Eric. BA, Gettysburg Coll., 1959. Pub. rels. assoc. Pub. Svc. Electric/Gas, Newark, N.J., 1960-63; editor Finishers Mgmt. Mag., Montclair, N.J., 1963-65; editor-in-chief Contractor News, Radnor, Pa., 1965-69; supr. pub. rels. Gray & Rogers, Inc., Phila., 1969-71; pres. Communications Counselors, Inc., Newtown Square, Pa., 1971—; pub. Cockshaw's Constrn. Labor News & Opinion, Newtown Square, 1971—; cons. Dept. Civil Engring. U. Md., College Park, 1985—, Constrn. Labor Rsch. Coun., Washington, 1981—. Contbg. author: Business Handbook, 1978; author: Bargaining Guide for Contractors, 1981, How to Avoid Labor Problems, 1985, How to Improve Productivity, 1988, Profit-Oriented Employee Relations Techniques, 1989. Special asst. U.S. Rep. Lawrence Williams, Washington, Media, Pa., 1973-74; judge of elections, Radnor Twp., 1973-77; chmn. Radnor Twp. Ethics Bd., 1986—; mem. Rep. U.S. Senatorial Inner Circle, Washington, 1988—, Senatorial Commn., 1991. With U.S. Army, 1954-56. Recipient Tom Campbell award Chilton Pub. Co., Radnor, 1967, Man-of-Yr. award Internat. Assn. W&C Contractors, Washington, 1971, Man-of-Yr. award Indsl. Constrn. Mag., Cleve., 1976, Outstanding Journalist award Nat. Assn. Women in Constrn., Washington, 1976, Journalism Excellence award Gen. Bldg. Contractors Assn., 1989. Mem. Constrn. Writers Assn. (bd. dirs. 1967-71), Newsletter Assn. of Am. (bd. dirs. 1979-83), Briarlin Civic Assn. (pres. 1985—), Sigma Delta Chi. Episcopalian. Home: 641 Lakeview Cir Newtown Square PA 19073-2608

COCKWELL, JACK LYNN, financial services company executive; b. East London, Republic of South Africa, Jan. 12, 1941; s. William Henry and Daphne (Cound) C.; children: Linda, Lorie, Leslie, Tessa, Malcolm, Gareth. M.Com., U. Cape Town, 1964, postgrad. with distinction, 1966. Chartered Acct. Mgr. Touche Ross & Co., Montreal, Que., Can., 1959-67; exec. v.p., chief oper. officer Edper Enterprises Ltd., Toronto, Ont., Can., 1968-90; exec. v.p., chief oper. officer Brascan Ltd., Toronto, 1979-91, pres., 1991—, also bd. dirs.; vice chmn., bd. dirs. Hees Internat. Bancorp, Inc.; bd. dirs. Astral Bellevue Pathe Ltd., Bramalea Ltd., Brookfield Devel. Corp., Brascade Resources, Inc., Continental Bank Can., Gt. Lakes Group, Inc., London Life Ins. Co., Noranda, Inc., Noranda Forest, Inc., Trilon Fin. Corp., Trizec Corp. Ltd., John Labatt Ltd., Norcen Energy Resources Ltd., Coscan Devel. Corp., Carena Devels. Ltd.; mem. adv. bd. Fin. Post. Office: Brascan Ltd/BCE Pl PO Box 762, 181 Bay St Ste 4400, Toronto, ON Canada M5J 2T3

CODA, JOHN R., insurance company executive; b. Phila., June 22, 1941; s. Thomas Peter and Grace (DeSantis) C. BSBA, St. Joseph's U., 1967, MBA in Bus. Mgmt., 1981. Cert. systems profl., property casualty underwriter. Methods and procedures analyst, programmer, systems analyst Fidelity Bank, Phila., 1968-70; systems analyst Food Fair, Inc., Phila., 1970-71; systems analyst, indsl. engr., sr. indsl. engr. First Pa. Bank, Phila., 1971-77; mgr. systems devel. Pa. Hosp., Phila., 1977-79; cons. structured analysis design technologist Softech, Inc., Waltham, Mass., 1979-80; mgr. data processing planning and adminstrn. Cen. Penn Nat. Bank, Phila., 1980-82; supt., mgr., asst. v.p. Gen. Accident Ins., Phila., 1982—; speaker in field. Co. chmn., United Way, Phila., 1986, co. loaned exec., 1989. With USAF, 1959-63, Okinawa. Mem. Am. Mgmt. Assn., Soc. Cert. Property and Casualty Underwriters, ISO (data quality com.), Assn. Systems Mgmt. (past Del. Valley chpt. pres., v.p., sec., program dir., newsletter editor, Keystone chpt. dir.). Home: 6425 Morris Pk Rd Philadelphia PA 19151

CODDINGTON, STEWART GOULD, sales manager; b. N.Y.C., Jan. 20, 1940; s. Clifford and Winifred Dana (Gould) Coddington; m. Jane Ann Bell, Apr. 17, 1965; children: James Stewart, Kimberly Ann. BSBA, U. Ariz., 1962; MS, Ill. State U., 1972. Sales mgr. Pac-Kit Safety, Norwalk, Conn. Home: 4 Bedford Ct Bloomington IL 61704-6270

CODEGA, MICHAEL P., II, automotive executive, consultant; b. Utica, N.Y., Sept. 18, 1953; s. Michael P. and Helen (Strife) C.; m. Marilyn Hamann, Apr. 30, 1977; children: Eric Michael, Colin James. Student, Ea. Sch. Music, 1968-70; BS, Rochester (N.Y.) Inst. Tech., 1979. Freelance musician Rochester, 1971-73; distbn. mgr. LaTouraine Coffee Co., Rochester, 1974-78; ops. mgr. Greenwich Mills, Rochester, 1978-80; inventory mgr. Bausch & Lomb, Rochester, 1980-83, materials mgr., 1983-85, 87-88, distbn. mgr., 1985-87, mgr. systems devel., 1988-90; dir. materials Purolator Products Co., Elmira, N.Y., 1990—; cons. CMS, Rochester, 1989, M. Codega Cons., Elmira, 1990-92. Mem. Home Sch. Orgn., Elmira, 1991; rep. Rochester C. of C., Henrietta, N.Y., 1978-80; bd. dirs. Jr. Achievement of Chemung County, Elmira, 1992—. Mem. Am. Prodn. Inventory Soc., Nat. Assn. Purchasing Mgrs., Assn. Systems Devel., Internat. Materials Mgmt. Soc., Logistics Coun., Ctr. for Inventory Mgmt. Congregationalist. Home: 205 Pine Forest Dr Horseheads NY 14845

CODEN, MICHAEL HENRI, fiber optic computer network manufacturing executive; b. N.Y.C., Mar. 6, 1947; s. William and Ruth (Carmel) C. BSEE, MIT, 1967; MS in Bus., Columbia U., 1975; MS in Math., NYU, 1979. Engr., Hewlett Packard Co., Palo Alto, Calif., 1967-69; mktg. mgr. Digital Equipment Corp., Maynard, Mass., 1969-72; v.p. data processing Maher Terminals Co., Jersey City, 1972-75; div. mgr. Exxon Enterprises, Inc., N.Y.C., 1975-79; pres., chief exec. officer Codenoll Tech., Yonkers, N.Y., 1979—. Patentee compound semiconductor and communications equipment, computer local network equipment; contbr. articles to profl. jours. Mem. adv. bd. Polytech. U. of N.Y. Recipient Distinction cert. Laser Inst. Am., Am. Chem. Soc. Mem. AAAS, IEEE (sr., tech. com. on computers and communications), Optical Soc. Am., Am. Electronics Assn. (mem. exec. coun.), N.Y. Acad. Sci., Inst. Mgmt. Sci., Columbia Club, Beta Gamma Sigma. Jewish. Office: Codenoll Tech Corp 1086 N Broadway Yonkers NY 10701-1107

CODY, JAMES R. CRONIN, designer, art educator; b. Litchfield, conn., Nov. 7, 1944; s. J. J. and M. V. Cody. BFA, Syracuse (N.Y.) U., 1969, MFA, 1975. Interior designer Colefax & Fowler, London, 1964-65; ind. interior decorator N.Y.C., Boston, 1969; co-dir. Mountebank Ltd., Syracuse, 1974-80; pres. Cody & Wolff Inc., Syracuse, 1980—; prof. of art Onondaga Community Coll., Syracuse, 1970—; gallery installation Assoc. Artists Gallery, Syracuse, Syracuse U.; designers' showhouse Jr. League of Syracuse, 1981, 90, 92. Record album cover design Riverside Ch., Mirrosonic Records, N.Y.C., 1974; invitational brochure design Zonta Internat., Weisbader, Germany, 1976; design and execute panels for aploytych for the Raredos St. John's Episcopal Ch., Ithaca, 1977; work in glass studio asst. stained glass for numerous churches with Prof. Richard E. Wolff, Syracuse U., 1968-78; exhibited at St. David's Celebration of the Arts, Dewitt, N.Y., 1970—; fabric and surface pattern designs for cos. and individuals, 1978—. Mem. Nat. Trust of Hist. Preservation. Republican. Home and Office: 103 Bradford Heights Rd Syracuse NY 13224

CODY, ROGER ALLEN, computer scientist; b. N.Y.C., Sept. 12, 1944; s. Philip and Margaret (Horvath) C. BA, Adelphi U., 1965, MS, 1967; PhD, Pa. State U., 1974. Cons. Lockwood, Kessler & Bartlett, Syosset, N.Y., 1965-68; lectr. Adelphi U., Garden City, N.Y., 1968-71; systems analyst Adelphi U., Garden City, 1968-71; mem. tech. staff Bell Labs., Piscataway, N.J., 1974-79; project mgr. Network Analysis Corp., Great Neck, N.Y., 1979-81, ITT Worldcom., N.Y.C., 1981-82; product mgr. Progressive Systems, Inc., N.Y.C., 1982-85; tech. dir., ptnr. BFT, Ltd., London, Eng., 1985-87. Home: 117 Abijah Bridge Rd Weare NH 03281-4805

COE, MICHAEL DOUGLAS, anthropologist, educator; b. N.Y.C., May 14, 1929; s. William Rogers and Clover (Simonton) C.; m. Sophie Dobzhansky, June 5, 1955; children—Nicholas, Andrew, Sarah, Peter, Natalie. AB, Harvard, 1950, PhD, 1959. Asst. prof. U. Tenn., 1958-60; mem. faculty Yale U., 1960—, prof. anthropology, 1968-90, Charles J. MacCurdy prof. anthropology, 1990—; adviser Robert Woods Bliss Collection Pre-Columbian Art, Dumbarton Oaks, Harvard, 1963-80. Author: La Victoria, An Early Site on the Pacific Coast of Guatemala, 1961, Mexico, 1962, The Jaguar's Children: Pre-Classic Art of Central Mexico, 1965, The Maya, 1966, (with Kent V. Flannery) Early Cultures and Human Ecology in South Coastal Guatemala, 1967, America's First Civilization, 1968, The Maya Scribe and his World, 1973, Classic Maya Pottery at Dumbarton Oaks, 1975, Lords of the Underworld, 1978, (with Richard A. Diehl) In the Land of the Olmec, 1980, Young Lords and Old Gods, 1982; (with Dean R. Snow and Elizabeth P. Benson) Atlas of Ancient America, 1986, Breaking the Maya Code, 1992; contbr. articles to profl. jours. Pres., chmn. bd. Planting Fields Found., 1985—; pres. Heath Hist. Soc., Mass., 1984-90. Fellow Royal Anthrop. Soc.; mem. NAS, Soc. Am. Archaeology, Mex. Soc. Anthropology, Soc. for Hist. Archaeology, Conn. Acad. Arts and Scis., Conn. Acad. Sci. and Engring., Limestone Trout Club, Sigma Xi. Home: 376 St Ronan St New Haven CT 06511-2251

COELHO, JOSEPH RICHARD, educator; b. Evanston, Ill., Apr. 27, 1946; s. Richard Joseph and Helene Christine (Lindquist) C.; m. Pauline Gloria Bailey, May 21, 1971 (div.). BS, Mich. State U., 1968; BA, U. Minn., 1975; MDiv, Yale U., 1978; postgrad., Columbia U., 1980-82. Research asst. U. Minn., Mpls., 1972-75; mgr. Meridian Mall, Okemos, Mich., 1978-79; cons. Gen. Motors, Detroit, 1979-80; mgr. Am. Mgmt. Assn., N.Y.C., 1981-82; cons. Pitney Bowes Inc., Stamford, Conn., 1982-85; exec. Bridgeport (Conn.) Deanery, 1985-88; adj. prof. philosophy Sacred Heart U., Fairfield, Conn., 1985-86; pres. Isaiah 61:1 Inc., Bridgeport, Conn., 1985—; lectr. applied ethics Fairfield (Conn.) U., 1986-90. Author, editor various works in art history, strategy and mgmt. Served to comdr. USNR, 1965—. Mem. Yale Club (N.Y.C.), Coasters Harbor Navy Yacht Club (Newport, R.I.), Phi Kappa Phi. Republican. Episcopalian. Home: 11 Main St Newtown CT 06470-2105 Office: Isaiah 61:1 Inc Bridgeport CT 06604

COELHO, RUI FREDERICK WILSON, quality assurance engineer; b. Louisville, June 12, 1956; s. Julio N. and Karin A.W. Coelho; m. Caroline N.D. Dealy. BS in Engring., U. Conn., 1984; MBA, Rensselaer Poly. Inst., 1990. Process engr. U. N.C. Naval Products, Uncasville, Conn., 1984-87, quality assurance coord., 1987-90; sr. engring., quality assurance Black & Decker Household Products Group, Shelton, Conn., 1990—. Mem. Am. Soc. for Quality Control (assoc.; seminar coord. 1988-90). Republican. Office: Black & Decker Household Products Group 6 Armstrong Rd Shelton CT 06484

COFFEY, JENNESS HALL, biologist, natural resource specialist; b. Washington, Apr. 1, 1951; d. Kenneth Delos and Jane (Thoma) Hall; m. Michael Allen Coffey. BS, U. Md., 1976; grad. natural resource specialist masters program, Nat. Park Service, 1986. Park ranger C&O Canal Nat. Hist. Park, Sharpsburg, Md., 1978-82; supr. White House tours and spl. events Nat. Park Svc., Washington, 1982-83; resource mgr. Nat. Park Svc., Triangle, Va., 1983-84; natural resource specialist Nat. Park Svc., Twentynine Palms, Calif., 1986-88, Boulder City, Nev., 1988-89; spl. park coord. ranger activities div. Nat. Park Svc., Washington, 1989—; leader Interagy. Task Force on Natural Resources, Dept. Interior and Dept. Navy, Quantico, Va., 1984; symposium presenter various natural resource couns.; agy. rep. interagy. work group Dept. of Interior and Dept. of Agr., 1989—. Contbr. articles to profl. journals. Member Enjoy Outdoors Am., Recreational Initiative Task Force, 1990—. Fellow Phi Kappa Phi; mem. Nat. Parks and Conservation Assn., George Wright Soc., Assn. Nat. Park Rangers, Park Arts Assn., Wilderness Soc. Office: Nat Park Svc Div Ranger Activities MIB 3310 PO Box 37127 Washington DC 20013-7127

COFFEY, TIMOTHY, physicist; b. Washington, June 27, 1941; s. Timothy and Helen (Stevens) C.; m. Paula Marie Smith, Aug. 24, 1963; children: Timothy, Donna, Marie. B.S. in Elec. Engring. (Cambridge scholar 1958), MIT, 1962; M.S. in Physics, U. Mich., 1963, Evening News Assn. fellow, 1964, Ph.D., 1967. Rsch. physicist Air Force Cambridge Rsch. Lab., 1964; theoretical physicist EGG, Inc., Boston, 1966-71; head plasma dynamics br., then supt. plasma physics div. Naval Rsch. Lab., Washington, 1971-80; assoc. dir. rsch. for gen. sci. and tech. Naval Rsch. Lab., 1980-83; dir. rsch. Naval Research Lab., 1983—. Recipient award Naval Rsch. Lab., 1974, 75, Disting. Civilian award Dept. Defense, 1991. Fellow Am. Phys. Soc., Washington Acad. Scis.; mem. AAAS, Franklin Inst. (Delmer S. Fahrney medal 1991 com. for sci. and arts), Am. Inst. Physics. Office: Naval Research Lab 4555 Overlook Ave SW Washington DC 20375-0001

COFFIN, ANNE GAGNEBIN, editor, consultant; b. Neptune, N.J., Aug. 2, 1939; d. Albert Paul and Genevieve (Hope) G.; m. John Devereux Coffin, Apr. 7, 1962; children: Samuel Devereux, Thomas Huguenin. BA, Smith Coll., 1961. Asst. editor, feature writer Look mag., N.Y.C., 1961-71; freelance writer and editor Downtown, N.Y.C., 1979-82, Archtl. Digest, L.A., 1982-84; N.Y. rep., newsletter editor Villa I Tatti, Harvard U. Ctr. for Italian Renaissance Studies, Florence, 1984—. Curator, exhbn. organizer Am. ARt: The Last 4 Decades, London, 1977. Bd. dirs., v.p. N.Y. Landmarks Conservancy, N.Y.C., 1981—; bd. dirs., pres. Chamber Music Soc. Lincoln Ctr., N.Y.C., 1984—; bd. dirs. Lincoln Ctr. for Performing Arts, 1991—, Leopold Schepp Found., 1991—; bd. dirs., pres. Brit.-Am. Arts Assn., 1985—, mem. Art Table. Mem. Brit.-Am. Arts Assn. (bd. dirs., pres. 1985—), Art Table. Home and Office: 1192 Park Ave Apt 16A New York NY 10128-1314

COFFIN, BEATRIZ DE WINTHUYSEN, landscape architect; b. Madrid, July 20, 1930; came to U.S., 1952; d. Jairer de Winthuysen and Maria Hector; m. Lawrence E. Coffin Jr., Jan. 4, 1958; children: Thomas A., Alisa W. BS, Furman U., Greenville, S.C., 1954; M in Landscape Arch., Harvard U., 1957. Cert. landscape architect, Md., Va. Landscape architect A. Carl Stelling, N.Y.C., 1957-58, Vorhees-Walker-Smith-Haines Architects, N.Y.C., 1958-60; ptnr. Coffin & Coffin, Washington, 1963—; landscape architect U.S. Navy, Washington, 1968; instr. George Washington Univ., Washington, 1974, Univ. Md., 1985; pres. Internat. Inst. of Site Planning, Washington, 1976—; lectr. Univ. Guanajuato, Mex., 1959; lectr. and cons. City of Quito, Ecuador (sponsored by U.S. Info. Agy.), 1990. Co-author: A Maryland New Town Turns 50, Arquitectura Paisajista, Quito, Conceptos y diseños, 1991; contbr. numerous articles to profl. publs. Mem. Dist. Columbia Commn. on the Arts and the Humanities (Design Adv. Steering Com.), 1986—. Mem. Latin Am. Mgmt. Assn. (treas. 1991, 92). Office: Internat Inst of Site Planning 715 G Street SE Washington DC 20003

COFFIN, DAVID LINWOOD, specialty chemicals and nonwoven materials manufacturing company executive; b. Windsor Locks, Conn., Dec. 15, 1925; s. Dexter Drake and Elizabeth (Dorr) C.; m. Marie Jeanne Cosnard des Closets, Sept. 15, 1973; children by previous marriage: Deborah Lee, David Linwood, Robert George. Student, Trinity Coll., Hartford, Conn., New Eng. Coll. With Dexter Corp., Windsor Locks, Conn., 1947—, asst. sec., asst. treas., asst. sales mgr., 1949-51, v.p., asst. treas., asst. sales mgr., asst. gen. mgr., 1951-52, v.p., asst. gen. mgr., sales mgr., 1952-55, v.p., gen. mgr., 1955-58, pres., chief exec. officer, from 1958, former chief exec. officer, now chmn., dir.; bd. dirs. Bank of New England Corp., Boston, Conn. Health Systems Agy., Hartford, Conn., Conn. Mut. Life Ins., Hartford, Life Technologies Inc., Gaithersburg, Md. Bd. dirs. Horace Bushnell Meml. Hall, Hartford, Conn. Hist. Soc., Hartford, Conn. Trust for Hist. Preservation, Hartford, The Inst. of Living, Hartford, Mystic Seaport Mus. and Stores, Mystic Conn. Served with USNR, World War II. Clubs: Hartford Golf (West Hartford, Conn.); Hartford; Lake Sunapee Yacht (N.H.); Links (N.Y.C.). Office: Dexter Corp 1 Elm St Windsor Locks CT 06096-2334*

COFFIN, JOHN MILLER, molecular biologist, educator; b. Boston, Apr. 20, 1944; s. Louis Fussell and Mary Elizabeth (McCarthy) C.; m. Marion Clair Szurek, June 22, 1968; children: Erica Mary, Heather Rachel. BA, Wesleyan U., 1967; PhD, U. Wis., 1972. Fellow U. Zurich (Switzerland), 1972-75; asst. prof. molecular biology Tufts U., Boston, 1975-78, assoc. prof., 1978-82, prof., 1982—; mem. virology study sect. NIH, Bethesda, Md., 1980-84; mem. scientific adv. bd. Viagene, Inc., San Diego, 1988. Editor: RNA Tumor Viruses, 2 vols., 1985; mem. editorial bd. Jour. Virol, Virology, Oncogene, Oncogene Res., Leukemia; editor Jour. Virol, 1991—; contbr. over 80 articles to profl. jours. Trustee Leukemia Soc. Am., N.Y., 1987. Recipient Outstanding Investigator award Nat. Cancer Inst., 1987. Mem. Am. Soc. Microbiology, Am. Assn. Advancement of Sci. Office: Tufts Med Sch 136 Harrison Ave Boston MA 02111-1800

COFFIN, LOUIS FUSSELL, JR., mechanical engineer; b. Schenectady, Aug. 30, 1917; s. Louis Fussell and Laura C. (Glen) C.; m. Mary Elizabeth McCarthy, Apr. 24, 1943; children—John, Sarah (Mrs. Joseph Fitzgerald), Laura (Mrs. Thomas Koch), Robert, Patricia (Mrs. Jeffrey Mullen), Deborah (Mrs. Patrick Higgins), Louis Fussell III, Margaret. B.S., Swarthmore (Pa.) Coll., 1939; Sc.D., Mass. Inst. Tech., 1949. From asst. to asst. prof. mech. engring. Mass. Inst. Tech., 1939-49; research asso., then supr. mech. metallurgy Knolls Atomic Power Lab., Gen. Electric Co., 1949-54; mech. engr. Corp. Research and Devel. Gen. Electric Co., Schenectady, 1954-86; adj. prof. mech. engring. Rensselaer Poly. Inst., Troy, N.Y., 1955-60, Disting. Research prof. 1986—; Union Coll., Schenectady, 1965—; vis. fellow Clare Hall Cambridge U., 1976; cons. in field. Author. Recipient Alfred E. Hunt award Am. Soc. Lubrication Engrs., 1958; award excellence Carborundum Co., 1974; Francis Clamer medal Franklin Inst., 1984 Clayton lectr. Inst. Mech. Engrs., London, 1974; Coolidge fellow, 1974. Fellow ASME (Nadai award 1979), Am. Soc. Metals (Albert Sauveur Achievement award 1980), ASTM (chmn. E9 com. on fatigue 1974-78, Dudley award 1975, award of merit 1978, Kroll zirconium medal 1991); mem. Nat. Acad. Engring., Am. Inst. Metall. Engrs. (Disting. Career award 1978), Sigma Xi, Pi Tau Sigma, Sigma Tau. Home: 1178 Lowell Rd Schenectady NY 12308-2512

COFFIN, TRISTRAM, writer, editor; b. Hood River, Oreg., July 25, 1912; s. Clarence Eugene and Lenora (Smith) C.; m. Margaret Avery, June 26, 1933; children: Lynne, Stephen Avery. AB, DePauw U., 1933. Reporter Indpls. Times, 1933-37; asst. to gov. Ind., 1937-41; with Office Facts and Figures, OWI, 1941-44; White House corr. CBS, 1945-47; newspaper columnist, 1948-51, free-lance writer and broadcaster, 1951-68; editor Washington Spectator, 1975—. Author: Missouri Compromise, 1947, Your Washington, 1954, Not to the Swift, 1961, The Passion of the Hawks, 1964, Mine Eyes Have Seen the Glory, 1964, The Sex Kick, 1966, Senator Fulbright, 1966; contbr. Washington Watch Newsletter, 1968-74; editor: Washington Spectator, 1974—. Mem. P.E.N. Home: 5601 Warwick Pl Bethesda MD 20815-5503 Office: Washington Spectator PO Box 70023 Washington DC 20088-0023

COFFMAN, CHARLES BENJAMIN, agronomist; b. Balt., Dec. 19, 1941; s. Benjamin Powell and Lucille Virginia (Blose) C.; m. Jane Victoria Wilhide, Apr. 10, 1971; children: Kristen Rebecca, Kathleen Marie. BS, U. Md., 1966, MS, 1969, PhD, 1972. Teaching asst. U. Md., College Park, 1969-71, instr., 1972; rsch. agronomist USDA-ARS, Beltsville, Md., 1972—. Contbr. articles to profl. jours. Mem. Northeastern Weed Sci. Soc. (chmn. various coms. 1975—, mem. exec. com., editor 1980-85), Sigma Xi, Alpha Zeta. Home: 7920 Frst & Strm Clb Detour MD 21725 Office: USDA-ARS Weed Sci Lab 10300 Baltimore Ave Beltsville MD 20705-2325

COFFMAN, DALLAS WHITNEY, financial planner; b. Louisville, Sept. 18, 1957; s. Lawrence DuWaine and Jean (Smith) C.; m. Deborah Joan Schneider, May 18, 1980 (div. July 1987); 1 child, Robert Smith; m. Francine R. Coffman, Dec. 26, 1987. AS in Bus. Mgmt., No. Essex Community Coll., Haverhill, Mass., 1977; BS in Mktg. Mgmt., Bentley Coll., 1979. CLU; chartered fin. cons.; registered investment advisor.; lic. ins. adviser, Mass. Mgr. McDonalds Corp., Westwood, Mass., 1975-79; fin. salesman Gold Assocs., Chestnut Hill, Mass., 1979-84; propr., fin. planner Whitman Fin. Svcs., Wakefield, Mass., 1984—; prin. gen. securities N.Y. Stock Exchange,

1987; adj. faculty Am. Coll., Bryn Mawr, Pa., 1986—, Northeastern U., Boston, 1986—, Coll. for Fin. Planning, Denver, 1986—; enrolled agt. IRS, 1989; br. mgr. Office of Supervisory Jurisdiction for LINSCO/Pvt. Ledger, 1990—; former mem. Boston chpt. Am. Soc. CLUs and ChFCs, Mass. and Boston chpts. Nat. Assn. Life Underwriters. Pub. Who's Who in Life Ins., 1982-84; contbr. articles to profl. jours. Test participant Project PIPER IRS, 1990-92; sponsor Wakefield Little League. Mem. HALT, Nat. Assn. Securities Dealers (bd. arbitrators 1990), Internat. Assn. for Fin. Planning, Registry Fin. Planning Practitioners, Boston Estate Planning Coun., Bentley Coll. Reps. for Admissions Vol. Orgn. Office: Whitman Fin Svcs 233 Albion St Wakefield MA 01880-3122

COFFMAN, JAY DENTON, physician, educator; b. Quincy, Mass., Nov. 17, 1928; s. Frank David and Etta (Kline) C.; m. Louise G. Peters, June 29, 1955; children: Geoffrey J., Joanne K., Linda J., Robert B. A.B., Harvard U., 1950; M.D., Boston U., 1954. Med. intern Univ. Hosp., Boston, 1954-55; asst. resident in medicine Univ. Hosp., 1955-56, chief resident in medicine, 1957-58, fellow in cardiovascular disease, 1956-57, sect. head peripheral vascular dept., 1960—; asso. in medicine Boston U. Med. Sch., 1960-65, mem. faculty, 1965—, prof. medicine, 1970—. Author: Raynaud's Phenomenon, 1989; co-author: Ischemic Limbs, 1973. Trustee Solomon Carter Fuller Mental Health Center, Boston, 1975-81. Served to capt. M.C. USAR, 1958-60. Diplomate Am. Bd. Internal Medicine; Mem. Am. Soc. Clin. Investigation, Am. Fedn. Clin. Research, Am. Physiol. Soc., Am. Heart Assn., A.C.P., Begg's Soc., Phi Beta Kappa, Alpha Omega Alpha. Office: 88 E Newton St Boston MA 02118-2347

COFFRIN, ALBERT WHEELER, judge; b. Burlington, Vt., Dec. 21, 1919; s. Morris Daniel and Florence Belle (Browe) C.; m. Elizabeth Ann MacCornack, May 14, 1943; children: Peter S., Albert W., III, James W., Nancy (Mrs. Michael G. Furlong). AB, Middlebury Coll., 1941, LLD, 1990; LLB, Cornell U., 1947. Bar: Vt. bar 1948. Assoc. Black & Wilson, Burlington, 1947-51, 52-56, Black, Wilson, Coffrin & Hoff, 1956-60; ptnr. Coffrin & Pierson, 1962-68, Coffrin, Pierson & Affolter, 1968-72; judge U.S. Dist. Ct. Vt., 1972—. Trustee Middlebury Coll., 1973-88, overseer, 1988—. With USN, 1942-45, 51-52; comdr. Res. 1952-66. Fellow Am. Bar Found.; mem. ABA, Vt. Bar Assn., Chittenden County Bar Assn., Burlington Tennis Club, Phi Delta Phi, Kappa Delta Rho. Republican. Unitarian. Office: US Courthouse PO Box 522 Burlington VT 05402-0522

COFRANCESCO, DONALD GEORGE, health facility administrator; b. New Haven, May 29, 1953; s. George William and Marie Teresa (Marra) C. BS in Chemistry and Life Scis., Worcester Poly. Inst., 1975; MA in Gerontology, U. New Haven, 1979; MPH, Yale U., 1992. Lic. nursing home adminstr., Conn. Asst. in rsch. Sch. Medicine, Yale U., New Haven, 1975-77; dir. biostats. and health planning Dept. of Health, New Haven, 1980; adminstr. Golden Manor Convalescent Home, New Haven, 1980-81, West Haven (Conn.) Nursing Ctr., 1981-85, Independence Manor, Meriden, Conn., 1986-87, Hillside Manor, Hartford, Conn., 1987-88; asst. adminstr., fin. analyst Sch. Medicine Yale U., New Haven, 1990—; cons. Hospice: Project Care, Inc., Watertown, Conn., 1989-90; v.p., chief fin. officer Environ. Health Corp., Hamden, Conn., 1991—. Bd. dirs. Partnerships Ctr. for Adult Day Care, Inc., Hamden, 1991—; mem. Health Systems Agy. South Cen. Conn., Inc., Woodbridge, 1982-87. Mem. NRA (cert. firearms instr., light rifle expert, air pistol sharpshooter), APHA, Am. Chem. Soc., Conn. Pub. Health Assn., Am. Coll. Health Care Execs., Planetary Soc., Peabody Mus. Yale U. Roman Catholic. Home: 104 Hillfield Rd Hamden CT 06518-1810 Office: Yale U Sch Medicine 330 Cedar St New Haven CT 06510-3218

COGAN, KENNETH GEORGE, quality assurance engineer; b. Neptune, N.J., Sept. 10, 1960; s. Kenneth Leonard Cogan and Mary Anne (Stevens) Taylor; m. Maureen Patricia Flanagan, Oct. 6, 1990. BS in Indsl. Mgmt., U. Lowell, 1988. Cert. quality engr. Mech. insp. M/A-COM Semicondr. Products, Burlington, Mass., 1979-87, quality assurance engr., 1988-90; quality assurance engr. Paramax Systems, Lanham, Md., 1990—. Editor newsletter Quality Nexus, 1991-92; mem. editorial review bd. Quality Progress. Mem. Am. Soc. for Quality Control (sr., treas. 1991, chair-elect 1991-92, chair 1992—, mixed media review bd.). Home: 3305 Parkford Manor Ter Silver Spring MD 20904-6143 Office: Paramax Systems 10265 Aerospace Rd Lanham MD 20706

COGAN, MARSHALL S., entrepreneur; b. Boston, 1937. Grad., Harvard U., 1959, MBA, 1962. With Carter Berlind Weill, 1962-67; vice chmn. Cogan Weill & Levitt, 1968-71, CBWL Hayden-Stone, 1973; chmn., chief exec. officer Knoll Internat. Holdings Inc., N.Y.C., 1989-90, 21 Internat. Holdings, Inc., N.Y.C., 1989—. Office: 21 Internat Holdings Inc Ste 5901 153 E 53d St New York NY 10022

COGHLAN, ANNE EVELINE, dean, biology educator; b. Boston, Mar. 29, 1927; d. William Henry and Alice Eveline (Blake) C. BS, Simmons Coll., 1948; MEd, Boston U., 1953; MS, U. Vt., 1957; PhD, U. R.I., 1965. Instr. Colby Jr. Coll., New London, N.H., 1949-59; asst. prof. Simmons Coll., Boston, 1962-65, assoc. prof., 1965-70, prof., 1970—, dean of scis., 1977—; chmn., bd. dirs. Milton (Mass.) Hosp., 1980-86; trustee Regis Coll., Weston, Mass., 1979-84, Fontbonne Acad., Milton, 1983-88. Mem., chair Warrant Commn., Milton, 1971-75; trustee Cunningham Found., Milton, 1989—. Fellow NSF, 1959-62. Democrat. Home: 65 Belcher Cir Milton MA 02186-5129 Office: Simmons Coll 300 The Fenway Boston MA 02115

COGHLAN, DAVID BUELL, chemical engineer; b. Cleveland Heights, Ohio, Apr. 14, 1920; s. Owen and Ava (Buell) C.; m. Gladys Mason, July 20, 1942 (div. 1967); children: Jill, David, Jeremy, Ross; m. Carolyn Farquhar, July 27, 1969; 1 child, Elisa. BE, Yale U., 1941. Registered profl. engr., Pa. Devel. engr. Allied Chems., Cleve., 1941-42, Point Pleasant, W.Va., 1942-43, Claymont, Del., 1943-46; mgr. devel. Foote Mineral, Exton, Pa., 1949-88; mgr. spl. projects Cyprus Foote, Malvern, Pa., 1988—. Designer lithium carbonate plant. Mem. Am. Inst. Chem. Engrs., Am. Chem. Soc., Soc. Mining Engrs., Soc. Indsl. and Applied Maths., Elk River Yacht Club. Home: 582 Grubbs Mill Rd West Chester PA 19380-1031

COGLIANDRO, JOHN ANTHONY, manufacturing manager, engineer, entrepreneur; b. Conn., May 20, 1964; s. Dominick Joseph and Mildred C. BS, U. Cin., 1987; postgrad., U. Conn., 1991—. Cert. in systems integration. Mfg. engr. Joint Med. Products, Stamford, Conn., 1987-88; chromalloy rsch. & technol. project mgr. Orangeburg, N.Y., 1989—; design engr. TRW-Hartzell Propellers, Piqua, Ohio; pres., small bus. product devel. cons. Mancog Industries Inc., Riverside, Conn., 1986—. Patentee in field. Vol. for ch. children's groups, Ohio, Conn., 1985—. Mem. IIE. Office: Maycog Industries Riverside CT 06878

COHALAN, PETER FOX, state supreme court justice; b. Sayville, N.Y., Jan. 10, 1938; s. John P. Jr. and Marion Caroline (Fox) C.; children: Pierce F., Mary A. BA, Manhattan Coll., 1959; JD, Fordham U., 1963; LLD (hon.), Dowling Coll., 1977; DHL (hon.), N.Y. Inst. Tech., 1982. Bar: N.Y. 1964. Pvt. practice Sayville, 1968-72; pres., pub. Suffolk County News, 1968-72; supr. Town of Islip, N.Y., 1972-79; exec. County of Suffolk, 1980-87; justice N.Y. State Supreme Ct., Riverhead, 1987—. Mem. Presdl. Commn. on Drunk Driving, Washington, 1981-84; del. Rep. Nat. Conv., 1980, 84, alternate del., 1972. Recipient Tree of Life award Jewish Nat. Fund, 1985. Mem. N.Y. State Bar Assn., Suffolk County Bar Assn. (chair mcpl. law com. 1970). Roman Catholic. Office: NY Supreme Ct Chambers 200 Railroad Ave Sayville NY 11782-2712

COHEN, ABRAHAM EZEKIEL, health company executive, retired; b. Calcutta, India; married. With Merck & Co. Inc., 1957-92, now sr. v.p.; mng. dir. Merck Sharp and Dohme Internat. Div., Patistan, 1962-64; retired, 1992; regional dir Merck Sharp and Dohme Internat. Div., S. Asia, 1964-67, No. Europe, 1967-69; v.p. Merck Sharp and Dohme Internat. Div., Europe, 1969-74; exec. v.p. Merck Sharp and Dohme Internat. Div., 1974-77, pres., 1977—. Office: Merck Sharp & Dohme Internat Div PO Box 2000 Rahway NJ 07065-0900

COHEN, ABRAHAM HAFT, public relations counselor; b. Preluka, USSR, Apr. 15, 1900; came to U.S., 1905; s. Isaac and Chernia (Haft) C.; m. Dora Hackman, 1925 (dec.); children: Elihu Shami, Matanah. In actuarial dept. Mutual Life Ins. Co., 1917-19; mgr. Navy Knitting Mills and Camel Sportswear, 1921-24; exec. dir. L.I. Pal Found. Fund, 1924-27; dir. Jewish Edn. Assn., 1927-32; exec. dir. Am. Jewish Congress, 1932-34; counsel in pub. rels., 1934-75; asst. to pres. Hebrew Home for Aged, Riverdale, N.Y., 1975-89; ret., 1989; bd. dirs. Am. Assn. for Jewish Edn.; founder New Bldg. Found. Fund Hebrew Home for Aged, Harlem, N.Y., Riverdale. Contbr. articles to De Haas Ency. of Jewish Knowledge. Chmn., admissions com. JBCA, exec. bd., 1940—; bd. dirs. JWB, N.Y.C., bd. trustees Tchrs. Sem. and Peoples U.; Herzlia Tchrs. Inst., Am. Mus. Jewish Culture. Mem. Am. Pub. Rels. Assn. (founding), Gerontol. Assn., N.Y. Assn. Homes and Svcs. for the Aging, Am. Assn. Fundraising Execs.

COHEN, ADELE R., artist; b. Buffalo, N.Y., May 5, 1922; d. Theodore and Etta (Siegel) Rieger; m. Paul Lenard, 1943 (wid.); children: Henry, Tina. Diploma, Art Inst., 1939, Parsons Sch. of Design, 1940. Tchr. instnl. drawing SUNY, Buffalo, 1974-75; artist, sculptor N.Y.C. Exhibited in one-woman shows Towson State Coll. Art Gallery, Balt., 1962, 74, Bodley Gallery, N.Y.C., 1963, Zuni Gallery, Buffalo, 1964, Albright Knox Art Gallery, Mem.'s Gallery, Buffalo, 1965, Phoenix Gallery, N.Y.C., 1968, 71, 74, 77, 80, New Gallery, Tel Aviv, 1974, Duns Scotus Gallery, Daemen Coll., Amherst, N.Y., 1977, Artists Gallery, Ashford Hollow Found., Buffalo, 1977, More Rubin Gallery, Buffalo, 1979, Burchfield Art Ctr., State U. Coll. at Buffalo, 1981, Waltuch Gallery, Tenefly, N.J., 1988, Transforming Images, poetry & rare book collection, SUNY at Buffalo, 1989; traveling exhbn. 10 Plagues, color etchings, 1987; group exhbns. include Albright Knox Art Gallery, Buffalo, 1957, 60, 64, 65, 69, 87, Inst. Contemporary Art, Boston, 1965, Michael C. Rockefeller Gallery State U. Coll., Fredonia, N.Y., 1975, Xerox Corp., Rochester, N.Y., 1975, Fgn. Inst., Dortmund, Fed. Republic Germany, 1976, Burchfield Gallery, Buffalo, 1976, 77, Artpark, Lewiston, N.Y., 1978, Inst. de Santiago, Chile, 1979, Pratt Inst. Gallery, N.Y.C., 1983, 14 Sculptors Gallery, N.Y.C., 1983, Artists Gallery, Buffalo, 1984, Bethune Gallery, SUNY at Buffalo, 1985, Contemporary Sculpture at Chesterwood, Stockbridge, Mass., 1985, 88, 90; represented in collections including Western N.Y. Forum Am. Art, Burchfield Ctr., Buffalo, Newark Mus., Mus. Arts & Scis., Evansville, Ind., U. Mass, Amherst, Towson Coll., Balt., John F. Kennedy Libr., Boston, Charles C. Penny Collection, Lockport, N.Y., SUNY at Buffalo, others; author: Gorge Legend Arbor, 1978, Sticks and Stones and Nuts and Bones, 1979, Diary of an Exhibition, 1983. Recipient Buffalo Courier Express award Albright-Knox Art Gallery, 1969, award for graphics NAWA, N.Y.C., 1977.

COHEN, ALAN BARRY, foundation executive; b. Bklyn., Nov. 3, 1952; s. Max B. and Blanche (Katz) C.; m. Helaine Francine Hartman, Dec. 22, 1973; children: Jeremy Todd, Bradley Daniel, Melanie Ann, Brandon Adam. BA, U. Rochester, 1973; MS, Harvard U., 1975, ScD, 1983. Rsch. asst. Beth Israel Hosp. and Harvard Med. Sch., Boston, 1974-75; sr. analyst Urban Systems Rsch. & Engring. Inc., Cambridge, Mass., 1975-79; rsch. assoc. Harvard Sch. Pub. Health, Boston, 1979-81; rsch. assoc. Johns Hopkins Sch. Hygiene and Pub. Health, Balt., 1981-82, asst. prof., 1982-84; assoc. dir. John Hopkins Ctr. for Hosp. Fin. and Mgmt., Balt., 1983-84; program officer Robert Wood Johnson Found., Princeton, N.J., 1984-87, sr. program officer, 1987-88, v.p., 1988—; chmn. commr.'s cardiac svcs. com. State of N.J., Trenton, 1990—; mem. Inst. Medicine, Tech. Monitoring Panel on Access to Care, 1989-91; cons. D.C. State Health Planning and Devel. Agy., 1984, Nat. Ctr. Health Svcs. Rsch., 1984. Mem. editorial bd. Inquiry, Quality Rev. Bull.; contbr. articles to profl. jours. Bd. dirs. ARC, Princeton, N.J., 1991—. Recipient Charles F. Wilinsky award Harvard Sch. Pub. Health, 1979; Kaiser fellow in health policy and mgmt., 1973-74; Dissertation grantee Nat. Ctr. Health Svcs. Rsch., 1979-80. Mem. APHA, Soc. for Med. Decision Making, Assn. for Health Svcs. Rsch., Internat. Soc. for Tech. Assessment in Health Care, Zeta Beta Tau (pres. Gamma Pi chpt. 1972-73, treas. 1970-72). Jewish. Office: Robert Wood Johnson Found PO Box 2316 Princeton NJ 08543-2316

COHEN, ALEXANDER H., theatrical and television producer; b. N.Y.C., July 24, 1920; s. Alexander H. and Laura (Tarantous) C.; m. Jocelyn Newmark, Jan. 12, 1942; 1 child, Barbara Ann; m. Hildy Parks, Feb. 24, 1956; children: Gerald Parks, Christopher Alexander. Attended, NYU, Columbia U. Exec. producer Stamford Ctr. for the Arts; Conceived and administered First Am. Congress of Theatre, Princeton U. Producer plays, 1941—; starting with Angel Street, other prodns. include At the Drop of a Hat, An Evening with Yves Montand, Victor Borge's Comedy in Music, An Evening with Mike Nichols and Elaine May, Beyond the Fringe, Maurice Chevalier at 77, Hamlet (Richard Burton), The Homecoming, Baker Street, Marlene Dietrich, Home, Little Murders, La Tragedie de Carmen, Dear World, Ulysses in Nighttown, The Devils, The School for Scandal, Ivanov, The First Gentleman, King Lear, Black Comedy, At the Drop of Another Hat, Dear World, The Madwoman of Chaillot, 6 Rms Riv Vu, Words and Music, 1974, Who's Who in Hell, 1974, Good Evening, 1974, Comedians, Hellzapoppin, 1976, Anna Christie, 1977, I Remember Mama, 1979, A Day in Hollywood/A Night in the Ukraine, 1980, 84 Charing Cross Road, 1982, Ben Kingsley as Edmund Kean, Peter Brook's Carmen, 1983, Play Memory, 1984, Dario Fo's Accidental Death of an Anarchist, 1985; also numerous plays presented in West End of London, including Come as You Are, 1976, The Happy Apple, Who Killed Santa Claus?, Harvey, The Price, Plaza Suite, Halfway Up the Tree, Man and Boy, Merchant of Venice, The Rivals, Applause, The Unknown Soldier and His Wife; for TV has produced ann. Antoinette Perry (Tony) Awards Show, 1967-86; other TV prodns. include A World of Love; CBS-TV Spl. for UNICEF, 1970, Marlene Dietrich's I Wish You Love, 1972, CBS: On the Air, A Celebration of Fifty Years, 1978, Emmy awards, 1978, 85, 86, Night of 100 Stars, 1982, Parade of Stars, 1983, The Best of Everything, 1983, The Placido Domingo Special, 1985, Night of 100 Stars II, 1985, NBC's 60th Anniversary Special, 1986, Happy Birthday Hollywood, 1987, ACE Awards, 1987, Classical Music Awards show, 1988, Sam Found Out: A Triple Play starring Liza Minnelli, 1988; Walt Disney Theme Park Spl., 1989, Night of 100 Stars III, 1990; supervised design and redesign of numerous theatres including O'Keefe Ctr., Toronto, Can., New Mechanic Theatre, Balt., Erlanger and Locust St. Theatres, Phila.

COHEN, ALLAN, gastroenterologist; b. N.Y.C., Mar. 11, 1953; s. Benjamin and Alice Cohen; married, July 7, 1976. BS, Bklyn. Med. Coll., 1975; MD, Downstate Med. Ctr., 1979. Mem. staff Community Med. Ctr., Toms River, N.J., 1984—; asst. mem. staff Kimbak Med. Ctr., Lakewood, N.J., 1984—. Office: 477 Lakehurst Rd Toms River NJ 08755

COHEN, AMY, mathematics educator, college dean; b. Madison, Wis., Nov. 22, 1942; d. Leon W. and Isabel (Ackerman) C.; m. M. Murray (dec. 1977); m. Lawrence J. Corwin (dec. 1992); 1 child, Nathan. BA, Harvard U., 1964; PhD, U. Calif., Berkeley, 1970. Vis. asst. prof. Cornell U., Ithaca, N.Y., 1971-72; asst. prof. Rutgers U., New Brunswick, N.J., 1972-78; assoc. prof. Rutgers U., New Brunswick, 1978-86, prof., 1986—; dean Univ. Coll., Rutgers U., New Brunswick, 1988—; pres. CAC Evening Childcare Inc., New Brunswick, 1988—. Contbr. articles to profl. jours. Mem. Am. Math. Soc., Math. Assn. Am., Assn. for Women in Math. Office: University Coll Rutgers U 35 College Ave New Brunswick NJ 08901-1164

COHEN, ARTHUR, fashion retail executive; b. N.Y.C., Mar. 3, 1927; s. Samuel Louis and Frances (Wallman) C.; m. Lenore B. Friedman, Jan. 29, 1949; children: Roni Ellen, Mitchell Mark. BS in Commerce, NYU, 1950. Mdse. coord. Lerner Stores, N.Y.C., 1950-81; dress merchandiser Cent. Buying Co., N.Y.C., 1981-84; v.p. adminstrn., ops. and mdse. control TSS, N.Y.C., 1984-89; cons. G.C. Svcs., N.Y.C., 1985-89. Cons. at small bus. devel. ctr. L.I.U., 1990—, Bklyn. Navy Yard Indsl. Coalition, 1991—. Served with USAF, 1945-47, PTO. Mem. Eta Mu Pi, Beta Gamma Sigma. Republican. Home: 13909 84th Dr # 310 Jamaica NY 11435-1800

COHEN, ARTHUR ABRAM, lawyer; b. Newport, R.I., July 4, 1917; s. Nathan and Clara (Jaffe) C. LLB, Boston U., 1941, JD (hon.), 1991. Bar: R.I. 1947, U.S. Dist. Ct. R.I. 1948, U.S. Ct. Claims 1961, U.S. Tax Ct. 1953, U.S. Ct. Mil. Appeals 1953, U.S. Supreme Ct. 1951; cert. judge advocate 1951. Pvt. practice Newport, 1947—; pres., legal advisor Local 529 Am. Fedn. Musicians, Newport, 1964-74. Contbr. articles to profl. jours. Lt. USNR, 1942-45, PTO. Decorated Purple Heart. Mem. R.I. Bar Assn., Mil. Order of the Purple Heart, PT Boats, Inc. Home and Office: 10 Middleton Ave Newport RI 02840-3642

COHEN, BARRY HOWARD, psychology educator; b. Bklyn., June 8, 1949; s. Michael and Mona (Franzblau) C.; m. Leona Gizzi, June 22, 1991. BS, SUNY, Stony Brook, 1970; MA, Queens (N.Y.) Coll., 1975; PhD, NYU, 1983. Phys. sci. technician U.S. Geol. Survey, Mineola, N.Y., 1970-72; rsch. asst. Queen's Coll., 1972-75; teaching asst. NYU, 1977-80, adj. asst. prof., 1985-87, asst. prof., 1987—; asst. dir. MA program in psychology NYU, 1987—. Author: (chpt.) Motor Theory of Voluntary Thinking, 1986. NIMH fellow, 1976-78, 83-85. Mem. Am. Psychol. Soc. (charter), Soc. for Psychophysiol. Rsch. Democrat. Office: NYU Dept of Psychology 6 Washington Pl New York NY 10003-6603

COHEN, BERNARD B., management specialist; b. N.Y.C., Jan. 31, 1927; s. Isidore and Esther (Nussbaum) C.; m. Janet L. Cohen; children: Suzanne (Cohen) Blacher, Roberta, Adam. Chmn. Hempstead Electronics, Inc., Hempstead, N.Y., 1958-62, Midway Industrial Elect. Inc., Rockville Ctr., N.Y., 1963-86; chmn., prin. cons. Profl. Marketers, Inc., Brentwood, N.Y., 1986-87; pres. Profl. Marketers, Inc. Asst. state dir. AARP, N.Y., 1988-90, dist. dir. Fla., 1990—. Mem. N.Y. RR Club. Home: 11258 Green Lake Dr Boynton Beach FL 33437-1411

COHEN, BERNARD LEONARD, physicist, educator; b. Pitts., June 14, 1924; s. Samuel and Mollie (Friedman) C.; m. Anna Foner, Mar. 30, 1950; children: Donald, Judith, Frederick, Ernest. B.S., Case Inst. Tech., 1944; M.S., U. Pitts., 1948; D.Sc., Carnegie Inst. Tech., 1950. With Oak Ridge Nat. Lab., 1950-58; prof. physics U. Pitts., 1958—; dir. Sarah Mellon Scaife Nuclear Physics Lab., 1965-78; on leave with Gen. Atomic Lab., San Diego, 1959-60, Inst. for Def. Analysis, Washington, 1962, Brookhaven Nat. Lab., 1965, Los Alamos Sci. Lab., 1969, Inst. Energy Analysis, Oak Ridge, 1974-75, Argonne Nat. Lab., 1978-79; cons. numerous govtl. agys. and pvt. corps. Author: Heart of the Atom, 1967, Concepts of Nuclear Physics, 1971, Nuclear Science and Society, 1974, Before It's Too Late: A Scientist's Case for Nuclear Power, 1983, A Homeowner's Guide to Radon, 1987, The Nuclear Energy Option: Alternative For The Nineties, 1990; contbr. numerous articles to profl. jours. Fellow Am. Phys. Soc. (chmn. div. nuclear physics 1974-75, Bonner prize for nuclear physics 1981), AAAS; mem. Am. Assn. Physics Tchrs. (nat. council 1973-78), Am. Nuclear Soc. (chmn. div. environ. scis. 1980-81), Soc. Risk Analysis, Health Phys. Soc. Home: 5414 Albemarle Ave Pittsburgh PA 15217-1133

COHEN, BRUCE LOUIS, association executive; b. Atlantic City, Mar. 9, 1955; s. Charles Neil and D. Patricia (Garfield) C.; m. Debra Eisenberg, Jan. 6, 1991. BA cum laude, Union Coll., 1978. Cert. tchr., Pa. Pianist, composer Kol Simcha Choral Ensemble, Phila., 1979-91; tchr., then prin. Chalutzim Acad., Phila., 1980-88; devel. chmn. Messianic Jewish Alliance Am., Phila., 1988—, internat. rep. to Israel, South Africa, 1985—; dir., writer Messianic Video Prodns., Phila., 1987; exec. producer Messianic Records, Inc., Phila., 1989; definition editor Am. Heritage Dictionary, Phila., 1982. Composer, lyricist over 30 songs; author course booklet: Israel, Arabs and Middle East, 1991. Republican. Jewish. Office: Messianic Jewish Alliance PO Box 417 Wynnewood PA 19096-0417

COHEN, DIANA LOUISE, mental health administrator, psychology, educator; b. Phila., Apr. 8, 1942; d. Nathan and Dorothy (Rubin) Blasberg; m. Jules L. Frankel, July 3, 1987; 1 child, Jennifer. BA, Temple U., 1964, MEd, 1969. Lic. psychologist, Pa., N.J.; nat. cert. counselor. Caseworker Phila. Gen. Hosp., 1964-69, staff psychologist, 1969-70; staff psychologist Atlantic Mental Health Ctr., McKee City, N.J., 1970-80, unit dir., 1980-87, v.p. profl. svcs., 1987-91; pvt. practice Pa., N.J., 1991—; mem. adj. faculty Glassboro (N.J.) State Coll., 1988—; community mediator Community Justice Inst., Atlantic County, N.J., 1990—. Com. chmn. Atlantic County Commn. for Missing and Abused Children, 1984—. Grantee N.J. Dept. Edn., 1988-89, N.J. Job Tng. Partnership Act, 1990. Mem. AACD, APA (assoc.), Pa. Psychol. Assn., N.J. Psychol. Assn. (assoc.). Home: 569 Gravelly Run Rd Mays Landing NJ 08330-1654 Office: 2106 New Rd Linwood NJ 08221 also: 1718 Welsh Rd Philadelphia PA 19115

COHEN, GAD JACQUES, lawyer; b. Meknes, Morocco, June 1, 1964; s. Raphael Aaron and Georgette (Kessous) C. BCL, LLB, McGill U., Montreal, 1987; DES/DEC, Jean de Brebeuf Coll., Montreal, 1983. Bar: N.Y. 1987. Assoc. White & Case, N.Y.C., 1987—. Mem. ABA, Can. Bar Assn., Am. Soc. Internat. Law, Can. Coun. Internat. Law, N.Y. Bar. Jewish. Home: 240 W 75th St New York NY 10023-1723 Office: White & Case 1155 Ave of the Americas New York NY 10036-2711

COHEN, GEOFFREY MERRILL, theater executive; b. Cleve., Jan. 20, 1954; s. Marvin Robert and Phyllis (Fossberg) C.; m. Deborah Ann Mackey, May 31, 1986; children: Zachary Erroll, Jillian Rebecca. BS in Edn., Miami U., Oxford, Ohio, 1978; MFA, Yale U., 1983. Asst. co. mgr. Yale Repertory Theatre, New Haven, 1980-81, co. mgr., 1982; asst. gen. mgr. Va. State Co., Norfolk, 1981-82; mng. dir. Yale Cabaret, New Haven, 1982-83; founding mgr. Am. Ibsen Theatre, Pitts., 1983; gen. mgr. George St. Playhouse, New Brunswick, N.J., 1983-88, Paper Mill Playhouse, Millburn, N.J., 1988—; grants evaluator N.J. State Coun. on Arts, Trenton, 1985, 86, 88, 90, 91, 92; speaker Trenton State Writers Workshop, 1988; lectr. Rutgers U., New Brunswick, 1988, Yale U., New Haven, 1987; mem. bd. advisors Lehigh Savs. Bank, Union, N.J., East Lynne County, Secaucus, N.J. Adviser Jersey City Performing Arts Ctr.; rep. Art Pride, Newark, 1988—; mem. Millburn (N.J.) Downtown Revitalization Com., 1991—. Mem. N.J. Theatre Group (bd. dirs. 1983-90, pres. 1986-88). Jewish. Home: 7 Maplewood Ave Edison NJ 08837-2505 Office: Paper Mill Playhouse Brookside Dr Millburn NJ 07041-1605

COHEN, GLORIA ERNESTINE, educator; b. Bklyn., July 6, 1942; d. Victor George and Marion Theodosia (Roberts) C. BS in Edn., Wilberforce U., 1965; MA in Elem. Edn., Adelphi U., 1975; Profl. Diploma in Ednl. Adminstrn., L.I. U., 1984; MS in Edn., Bklyn. Coll., 1986. Tchr. Bd. Edn., Bklyn., 1965—; case worker Dept. Welfare, Bklyn., 1965—; mem. comprehensive sch. improvement program Pub. Sch. 149, mem. open corridor planning com., mem. consultation com. Mem. Northwest Civic Assn., Freeport, N.Y., 1973—. Mem. NAFE, ASCD, Nat. Alliance of Black Sch. Educators, Inc., Bklyn. Reading Coun. Internat. Reading Assn., N.Y. State Reading Assn., Assn. Black Educators N.Y., Freeport Indoor Tennis Club, Rockville Racquet Club, Zeta Phi Beta, Kappa Delta Pi. Democrat. Roman Catholic. Home: 4 Sterling Pl Freeport NY 11520-1126 Office: Bd Edn PS 149 700 Sutter Ave Brooklyn NY 11207-4299

COHEN, HARVEY JAY, history and physical education educator; b. Brookline, Mass., Mar. 18, 1949; s. Charles E. and Esther (Abadoff) C.; m. Barbara Iris Epstein, June 20, 1970; children: Charlie Gayle, Matthew Ian. AA in Bus. Adminstrn., Manhattan Community Coll., 1970; BA in Econs., Bklyn. Coll., 1972; MA in Phys. Edn., NYU, 1981. Cert. tchr. social studies, phys. edn., gen. bus., N.J., cert. supr., N.J. Tchr., coach Chatham Twp. Sch., Chatham, N.J., 1973—; ice hockey coach Chatham Twp. High Sch., 1973-88, High Sch. of the Chathams, 1989—, athletic dir., 1976-79; co-jr. div. leader Camp H.E.S., Bklyn., 1979, asst. dir., program dir., 1980-83, 84; div. leader N.J. "Y" Camps, 1985, Fairfield, N.J.; sr. div. leader Pine Forest Camp, Jenkintown, Pa., 1988; group leader Na Sh Pa, Bloomingburg, N.Y., 1989, 90, athletic dir., 1991; head ice hockey coach John Jay Coll. Criminal Justice, N.Y.C., 1972. Author: Ice Hockey Playbook, 1990. Ice hockey coach Morris County Colonials Club, 1989, 91, 92. With U.S. Army Res., 1968-73. Named Area Ice Hockey Coach of Yr., Daily Record, 1982, N.J. Ice Hockey Coach of Yr., Newark Star Ledger, 1987. Mem. Knights of Pythias. Jewish. Home: 16 Fleetwood Dr Rockaway NJ 07866 Office: Chatham High Sch 255 Lafayette Ave Chatham NJ 07928

COHEN, HARVEY MARTIN, chemist, industrial hygienist; b. Boston, Sept. 8, 1936; s. Archie and Bella C.; m. Dorothy Keller, Aug. 30, 1958; children: Michael, Susan, Cheryl. AB, Harvard Coll., 1958; PhD, MIT, 1963. Cert. indsl. hygienist. Analytical chemist Avco Rsch. & Adv. Devel. Div., 1959-61; sr. chemist Nat. Rsch. Corp., 1962-69; sr. engr. Norton Co., 1969-70; v.p., pres. Tech. Assocs., Inc., 1970-76; adj. asst. prof. chemistry Northeastern U., 1978-83; indsl. hygienist, consultant Needham, Mass., 1976—; dir. Cambridge Tech. Assocs., 1976—. Contbr. articles to profl. jours. Mem. Am. Chem. Soc. (div. health and safety, div. environ. chemistry), Am. Indsl. Hygiene Assn. (New Eng. sect.), Am. Acad. Indsl. Hygiene,

Soc. Fire Protection Engrs. (New Eng. sect.). Office: Cambridge Tech Assocs PO Box 113 Needham MA 02192-0001

COHEN, HERMAN NATHAN, humane society executive; b. Bklyn., June 3, 1949; s. Stanley and Hannah (Persky) C.; m. Carolyn P. Grillo, Jan. 8, 1989. BA, Bklyn. Coll., 1970; MS in Ednl. Adminstrn., Hofstra U., 1975. Investigator IRS, N.Y.C., 1970-72; adminstrv. intern IRS, Washington, 1972-73; employee devel. specialist IRS, Uniondale, N.Y., 1973-75; tng. officer IRS, Bklyn., 1975-79; pers. officer Home Ins. Co., N.Y.C., 1979-81; asst. v.p. City Investing Co., N.Y.C., 1981-85; prin. H.N. Cohen Enterprises, Inc., N.Y.C., 1985-86; human resources dir. Empire Blue Cross Blue Shield, N.Y.C., 1986-89; v.p. adminstrn. ASPCA, N.Y.C., 1989-90, sr. v.p., 1990, exec. v.p., 1990-91, chief adminstrv. officer, 1991-92, chief of law enforcement, 1992—; arbitrator Am. Arbitration Assn., 1986—; bd. dirs. Ashfield Corp. Bd. dirs. Owen Sch. Mem. Am. Soc. Pers. Adminstrn. (treas. 1987-89, bd. dirs. 1988-93), Soc. Human Resource Mgmt. (bd. dirs.), Soc. Animal Welfare Adminstrn., Vet. Corps of Artillery. Democrat. Jewish. Office: ASPCA 424 E 92d St New York NY 10128-6803

COHEN, IRA MYRON, aeronautical and mechanical engineering educator; b. Chgo., July 18, 1937; s. Harry Nathan and Esther (Lenchner) C.; m. Linda Barbara Einstein, June 12, 1960; children: Susan Ellen Bolstad, Nancy Beth. B. in Aero. Engring., Poly. Univ., Bklyn., 1958; M.A., Princeton U., 1961, Ph.D. in Aero. Engring, 1963; M.A. (hon.), U. Pa., 1971. Mem. tech. staff Sandia Labs., Albuquerque, summers 1971, 74, 77; asst. prof. engring. Brown U., Providence, 1963-66; asst. prof. mech. engring. U. Pa., Phila., 1966-67, assoc. prof., 1967-76, prof., 1976-92, chmn. dept., 1992—; guest prof. Technische Hochschule Aachen, W. Ger., 1966; cons. fluid mechanics related problems to industry, 1966—, attys., 1966—; Mem. bd. The Sch. in Rose Valley, Moylan, Pa., 1969-74. Contbr. articles to various publs. Recipient Fulbright Travel grant, 1966. Assoc. Fellow AIAA (sect. sec. 1977-80, 85—); mem. AAUP, ASME, Am. Phys. Soc., Internat. Soc. for Hybrid Microelectronics, Sigma Xi. Office: U Pa Dept Mech Engring and Applied Mechanics 297 Towne Bldg Philadelphia PA 19104-6315

COHEN, IRVING ELIAS, real estate executive; b. Bklyn., Nov. 7, 1946; s. Daniel Arthur and Shirley B. (Kanner) C.; m. Adriane Pinsker, Aug. 22, 1976; 1 child, Jonathan D. BA in Psychology, CCNY, 1968; MBA in Fin., NYU, 1973, 1968. Mut. fund cashier Investors Funding Corp., Inc., 1968-69; syndication cashier Eastman Dillon, Union Securities, Inc., 1969-70; registered rep. Steiner, Rouse & Co., Inc., N.Y.C., 1970-72; instl. rep. Shearson Hayden Stone, Inc., N.Y.C., 1972-74; exec. v.p. Howard P. Hoffman Assos., Inc. subs. Lehman Bros. Kuhn Loeb, Inc., N.Y.C., 1974-81; sr. v.p. Security Pacific Realty Adv. Group, 1981-83; exec. v.p. E.F. Hutton Properties Inc., 1983-87; trustee, chmn. investment com. Mellon Participating Mortgage Trust, 1988-89; mng. dir. Real Estate Cons. Svcs. Group, Price Waterhouse, N.Y.C., 1989-90; mng. ptnr. Fuller Corp. Realty Ptnrs., 1990—. Mem. Am. Soc. Real Estate Counselors, Turnaround Mgmt. Assn., N.Y. State Biotech. Assn. Jewish. Home: 110 Riverside Dr Apt 5E New York NY 10024-3731

COHEN, IRWIN, economist; b. Bronx, N.Y., Feb. 29, 1936; s. Samuel and Gertrude (Levy) C.; B.S. in Accounting, N.Y. U., 1956, M.B.A. in Finance, 1964, M.A. in Econs., 1969; B.S. in Math., CCNY, 1970. Financial analyst U.S. SEC, N.Y.C., 1965-67, Fed. Res. Bank N.Y., N.Y.C., 1967-72, Prudential Ins. Co. Am., 1973-74, SEC, N.Y.C., 1974—. Life Fellow Internat. Biog. Assn., Am. Biog. Inst. Research Assn. (dep. gov.), World Acad. Scholars, World Literary Acad., World Inst. Achievement; mem. Internat. Biographical Ctr. (dep. dir. gen.), Internat. Platform Assn (life), Math. Assn. Am., Am. Finance Assn., Econ. History Assn. Home: 372 Central Ave Apt 2K Scarsdale NY 10583-1303

COHEN, ISAAC LOUIS (IKE COHEN), data processing executive; b. N.Y.C., Sept. 15, 1948; s. Louis and Dora (Dostis) C.; m. Lucille Competello, June 3, 1982 (div.); children: Janice, Matthew. AAS in Bus. Adminstrn., Kingsborough Community Coll., 1977. Asst. v.p. Mfrs. Hanover Trust Co., N.Y.C., 1966-87; data processing ops. mgr. First Boston Corp., Princeton, N.J., 1987—; owner ILC Liquidators Co., South Bound Brook, N.J., 1990—, ILC Vending Co., South Bound Brook, N.J., 1991—, ILC 900 Co., South Bound Brook, N.J., 1991—, ILC Fin. Mktg. Co., 1991—. Editor booklet: Annadale Memorial Day Parade, 1985, 86, 87. Asst. v.p. Annadale Community Assn., 1982-89; umpire S.I. High Sch. League & Semi-Pro Baseball, 1985—; assoc. scout Kansas City Royals Profl. Baseball Team, 1988—. With USNR, 1967-74. Mem. U.S. Submarine Vets., Am. Legion, Jewish War Vets., Vietnam Vets. Home: 5 Koehler Dr South Bound Brook NJ 08880-1304 Office: First Boston Corp 700 College Rd E Princeton NJ 08540-6689

COHEN, JAMES SIMON, structural engineer; b. N.Y.C., May 4, 1956; s. Edward and Elizabeth Belle (Cohen) C.; m. Sonya Ruth Freeman, Dec. 28, 1988. BSc in Engring. with distinction, Cornell U., 1978; MSc, Imperial Coll. Sci. & Tech., London, 1985. Registered profl. engr., N.J., N.Y., Pa.; chartered engr. U.K.; European engr. Jr. engr. Grumman Aerospace Corp., Bethpage, N.Y., 1978; structural engr. Ammann & Whitney Civil and Cons. Engrs., N.Y.C., 1978-80, Flint & Neill Partnership, London, 1981-84; project engr. Ove Arup & Ptnrs., London, 1985-91; sr. engr. Wiss, Janney, Elstner Assocs., Inc., Princeton Junction, N.J., 1991—. Contbr. articles to profl. jours. Ambulance mem. St. John Ambulance, London, 1988-91; mem. Friends of Hopewell Valley (N.J.) Open Space, 1992; active Multiple Sclerosis Soc., London, 1985—, Cancer Rsch. Soc., London, 1985—, Occupation and Rehab. Therapy, 1991—. Mem. ASCE (mem. pubs. com. 1991, mem. ANSI 58.1 com. 1989, chmn. TAC com. 1991, mem. com. Nat. Hazard REduction, 1992, mem. com. Elec. Trans. Struct., 1990, founder com. Telecom. Facilities, 1992), Instn. of Structural Engrs., N.Y. Acad. Scis., AEDR Am. Engrs. for Disaster Relief (founder), AEDR (UK) Engrs. for Disaster Relief (mgmt. com. 1988-91), Jr. Liaison Orgn. (treas. 1986-90). Jewish. Home: 258 Pennington Rocky Hill Pennington NJ 08534-1817 Office: Wiss Janney Elstner Assocs 14 Washington Rd # 501 Princeton Junction NJ 08550

COHEN, JEFFREY ALAN, financial executive, management consultant; b. Atlantic, N.J., Apr. 7, 1953; s. Jack W. and Ethel (Adams) C.; m. Patricia Hetzel Cohen, Sept. 25, 1983; children: Lisa Beth, Debra Lynne. BS, Fairleigh Dickinson U., 1975; MS, Pace U., 1982; cert. for advanced grad. study, Yale U., 1983. CPA, N.J. Tax and audit staff Touche Ross & Co., Gateway I, Newark, 1975-78, sr. mgmt. cons., 1986-88; chief fin. officer Charlex Prodns., Inc., Charlex Inc., Printbox Graphics Inc., Printbox Graphics Inc, 1990-91, Artists of the Computer Era, N.Y.C., 1988-90; sr. fin. analyst N.J. Casino Control Commn., Trenton, N.J., 1978-80, supr., 1980-82, mgr. fin. evaluation and control, 1982-83, dep. dir. fin., 1983-86; mem. faculty Sch. Bus., Rutgers U., part-time 1985—; staff mem. Atlantic City Conv. Hall Blue Ribbon Panel, 1982. Yale U. fellow, 1983. Fellow N.J. Soc. CPAs (gaming conf. com.); mem. AICPA, N.J. State Soc. CPAs, Am. Acctg. Assn., Internat. Teleproduction Soc., Tau Epsilon Phi. Jewish. Home: 273 Maple Point Dr Langhorne PA 19047-1449 Office: Touche Ross & Co Gateway I Newark NJ 07102 also: 2 W 45th St New York NY 10036

COHEN, JOAN LEBOLD, art historian, photographer; b. Highland Park, Ill., Aug. 19, 1932; d. Samuel N. Lebold and Patricia Louise (Aloe) Tucker; m. Jerome Alan Cohen; children: Peter Lebold, Seth Aloe, Ethan Randolph. AB, Smith Coll., 1954. Asst. slide and photograph collection dept. art Yale U., New Haven, 1954-55; registrar Corcoran Gallery Art, Washington, 1955-56; TV writer, on-camera person dept. pub. edn. Mus. Fine Arts, Boston, 1965-66, lectr. in art history, 1965-72; lectr. art history Tufts U.; lectr. Sch. Mus. Fine Arts Tufts U., Boston, 1968—; guest curator Sarah Lawrence Coll. Art Gallery, 1987, Smith Coll. Mus. Art, Northampton, Mass., 1982, 90, mem. vis. com., 1967—; curator CCIC Fin. Co., Hong Kong, 1984—. Author: Buddha, 1969; Angkor, Monuments of the God-Kings, 1975. Author, photographer: The New Chinese Painting, 1949-86, Yunnan School, A Renaissance in Chinese Painting, 1988; co-author, photographer: China Today and her Ancient Treasures, 1974, 3d revised edit., 1985; photographer solo exhbns. including Cambridge Trust Co., 1973-74, Northwestern U. Law Sch., 1976, Harvard Law Sch., 1976, Art/Asia, Boston, 1977, 79, Cambridge Sch., Weston, Mass., 1978, Detroit Inst. Art, 1981, Sch. House Gallery, Truro, 1982, Benton & Bowles, N.Y., 1983, Alisan Fine Arts & Societe Generale, Hong Kong, 1987, Am. Club Hong Kong, 1989, Smith Coll., Northampton, Mass., 1990, Kendall Gallery, Wellfleet, Mass., 1991; represented in permanent collections including Smith Coll. Mus. Art, Harvard Law Sch. ARCO, NYNEX, and pvt. collections. Trustee Pan Asian Repertory Theatre, N.Y.C., 1982-89, Truro Ctr. for Arts at Castle Hill, Mass., 1982—; mem. pres.'s council Asia Soc., N.Y.C., 1984; mem. adv. bd. Indo-China Arts Project, 1989—; mem. cultural exchange N.Y. Beijing Sister City Com., N.Y.C., 1983, co-chmn. exhbn. com., 1984-85. Mem. China Inst. (mem. sch. com. 1982-89), Fgn. Corrs. Club (journalist). Home and Office: 50 E 89th St New York NY 10128-1225

COHEN, JOYCE ARNOFF, career volunteer; b. Cleve., Aug. 21, 1925; d. Morris Saadia and Hilda (Fieldman) Arnoff; m. Robert J. Corday, Sept. 1948 (div. June 1953); m. Murray Cohen, July 1, 1958; children: Hollis Cohen Osman, Thomas, Amy Elizabeth. BA, Northwestern U., 1947. Author: (radio play BBC) The Dream Come True, 1952. Mem. working group Memorandum of Understanding, 1984—, chair subcom. children at risk; bd. dirs. Jewish Theol. Sem. of Am., 1985—, exec. com., 1985-91, mem. acad. affairs, devel. and Israel affairs coms., installed Pledge Redemption program, 1991 Chancellor's Coun.; bd. dirs. World Coun. Synagogues, 1985—, Mercaz, 1985—; trustee Robert Lee Kohns Found., 1987-91; v.p. United Jewish Appeal Fedn. of Jewish Philantropics of Greater N.Y., 1986-91, chair N.Y. Com. Jewish Agy. for Israel, 1988-91, co-chair cash campaign, 1979-89, exec. commn., 1986—, bd. overseas & domestic divs., 1985—, Project Renewal com., 1978—, Women's Campaign cabinet, 1977—; mem. campaign cabinet nat. United Jewish Appeal, 1982-88; trustee Columbia Grammar and Prep. Sch., 1970-83, United Israel Appeal, 1982—; bd. dirs. Coun. Jewish Fedns., 1985—, HIAS, 1976—, NYANA, 1976-84; trustee Park Ave. Synagogue, 1972—, Congregation Or Zarua, 1989—, Nat. Found. Jewish Culture; many other civic roles in various orgns. Jewish. Home: # 4F 8 E 83d St New York NY 10028-0418

COHEN, JUDITH W., academic administrator; b. N.Y.C., May 14, 1937; d. Meyer F. and Edith Beatrice (Elman) Wiles; BA, Bklyn. Coll., 1957, MA, 1960; cert. advanced studies Hofstra U., 1978; MA Columbia U., 1986, postgrad. 1986—. m. Joseph Cohen, Oct. 19, 1957; children: Amy Beth (dec.), Lisa Carrie, Adam Scott Frank, Elyssa Lily. Tchr. N.Y.C. Pub. Schs., Bklyn., 1957-60; tchr. Mid. Country Sch. Dist., Centereach, N.Y., 1970—, Title IX compliance officer, 1980-86, team leader 1987-91. Bus. adv. Women's Equal Rights Congress, Suffolk County Human Rights; chmn. bd. edn., Temple Beth David, trustee, 1975-79; pres. CHUMS, 1979-82; Tchr. of Gifted Post-L.I. U. Saturday Program; L.I. Writing Project fellow, Dowling Coll., 1979—; cert. sch. dist. adminstr., supr., adminstr., N.Y. State. Mem. Nassau Suffolk Coun. Adminstrv. Women in Edn. (pres. 1979—), Assn. for Supervision and Curriculum Devel., Assn. Gifted/Talented Edn., Women's Equal Rights Congress Com. (exec. bd.), Suffolk County Coordinating Council Gifted and Talented, Phi Delta Kappa, Delta Kappa Pi. Author: Arts in Education Curriculum in Social Studies and Language Arts, 1981. Home: 35 Gaymore Ln Commack NY 11725-1305 Office: Middle Country Sch Dist Adminstrn 43d St Centereach NY 11720

COHEN, LEEBER, ophthalmologist; b. Queens, N.Y., June 28, 1957; s. Eugene J. and Ada (Twersky) C.; m. Shelley Karen Franklin, Feb. 8, 1981; children: Tova Gail, Yaakov. BA, Yeshiva U., N.Y.C., 1979; MD with distinction, Downstate Med. Ctr., Bklyn., 1983. Diplomate Am. Bd. Ophthalmology. Intern in Ophthalmology Downstate Med. Ctr., Bklyn., 1983-84, resident in Ophthalmology, 1984-86, chief resident in Ophthalmology, 1986-87; pvt. practice N.Y.C., 1987—; mem. staff St. Vincent's Hosp., N.Y.C., N.Y. Eye and Ear Infirmary, N.Y.C., Beth Israel Med. Ctr. Editor (books) Dawn of a New Age, 1990, Rescue, 1991. Bd. dirs. Yeshurun, Kew Gardens, N.Y., 1991. Fellow Am. Acad. of Ophthalomology, Am. Bd. of Ophthalomology; mem. Am. Bd. Med. Specialists. Home: 123-35 82 Rd Kew Gardens NY 11415 Office: 11 Fifth Ave New York NY 10003

COHEN, LEONARD DAVID, physics educator; b. Phila., Aug. 7, 1932; s. Benjamin Herman and Hilda Reva (Sach) C.; m. Frances Lieberman, Apr. 15, 1957; children: Sara, Judith, Benjamin. AB, U. Pa., 1954, MS, 1956, PhD, 1959. Nuclear physicist G.E. Knolls Atomic Power Lab., Schenectady, N.Y., 1959-62; physicist G.E. Space Scis. Lab., King of Prussia, Pa., 1962-64; prof. Drexel Univ., Phila., 1964—; cons. G.E. Space Scis. Lab., King of Prussia, 1964-66. Contbr. over 50 articles to profl. jours. Commr. Home Rule Charter Commn., Plymouth Twp., Pa., 1975; chmn. Air Pollution Bd., Plymouth-Conshohocken, Plymouth Twp., 1977-81. Dept. of Def. grantee, 1968, U.S. Army, 1968, NOAA, 1968. Mem. Sigma Xi. Office: Drexel U 32d Chestnut Philadelphia PA 19118-3744

COHEN, LOIS JEAN, child psychologist, retired; b. Grand Rapids, Mich., Feb. 12, 1924; d. Francis Canfield Carl and Violet Morine (McCurdy) Ford; m. H. George Cohen, June 30, 1952 (dec.); children; Martha Jean, Sarah Rachel. BA, U. Mich., 1944; MA, State U. of Iowa, 1947; PhD, State U. Iowa, 1949. Instr. in psychology Smith Coll., Northampton, Mass., 1949-54, asst. prof., 1955-57, researcher, 1963-66, class dean, 1966-81, rsch. assoc., 1981-84. NIMH grantee, 1963, NSF grantee, 1966. Mem. Am. Psychol. Assn., LWV, Sigma Xi.

COHEN, MARGO PANUSH, internist; b. Detroit, Oct. 28, 1940; d. Louis and Tillie (Lipsitz) Panush; m. Perry Mandell Cohen, June 8, 1961; children: Michael Howard, Daniel Arthur, Jonathan Alan. BS, U. Mich., 1960, MD, 1964; PhD, U. Buenos Aires, 1970. Diplomate Am. Bd. Internal Medicine, Am. Bd. Endocrinology/Metabolism. Instr. U. Buenos Aires, 1970-71; asst. prof. Wayne State U., Detroit, 1971-75, assoc. prof., 1975-78, prof., 1978-82; prof. U. Med. & Dentistry of N.J., Newark, 1982-87, U. Pa., Phila., 1990—; pres. Exocell, Phila., 1988—; chmn. bd. sci. counselors NIH, 1976-80, 86-90. Author: Diabetes and Protein Glycosylation, 1986, The Polyol Paradigm and Complications of Diabetes, 1987, others; contbr. more than 100 articles to profl. jours. Fulbright scholar, 1987; recipient Probus award Probus Club, 1978, Wellcome award Burroughs Wellcome, 1980. Fellow ACP; mem. Am. Diabetes Assn., Endocrine Soc., Am. Soc. Clin. Investigators, Am. Soc. Biol. Chemists, Am. Physiol. Soc. Office: Exocell Inc 3508 Market St # 420 Philadelphia PA 19104-3377

COHEN, MARION CANTOR, immunologist, researcher; b. Bklyn., Feb. 14, 1940; d. Joseph and Sadie (Rosenband) Cantor; m. Stanley Cohen, Aug. 30, 1959; children: Laurie Ellen, Ronald Nelson, Kenneth Stuart. AB, Barnard Coll., 1960; MA, SUNY, Buffalo, 1974; PhD, U. Conn., 1978. Instr. U. Conn. Health Ctr., Farmington, 1978-81, dir. monoclonal antibody facility, 1980-87, asst. prof., 1981-87; assoc. prof. Hahnemann U., Phila., 1987—; with immunological scis. study sect. NIH, Bethesda, Md., 1986-88, with allergy, immunology, transplantation rsch. com. study sect., 1991—, with tobacco related disease rsch. program study sect., Berkeley, Calif., 1991, 92. Editor: Clinical Immunology and Immunopathology, 1989—; contbr. chpts.: Lymphokines and the Immune Response, 1990, Cellular Immunity and the Immunotherapy of Cancer, 1990. Office: Hahnemann U Micro/Immunology MS410 Philadelphia PA 19102

COHEN, MARK DANIEL, communications company executive; b. Perth Amboy, N.J., July 31, 1951; s. Joseph George and Florence (Schwartzman) C. BA with distinction, U. Mich., 1973; Teaching Cert., Kean Coll., Union, N.J., 1974; postgrad., U. Wis., 1974-75. Substitute tchr. Perth Amboy (N.J.) Sch. System, 1975-76; creative dir., copy writer Tri-Chem, Inc., Harrison, N.J., 1976-78; tchr. English Colonia (N.J.) High Sch., 1979-80; creative cons., copy writer Marin Rabkin Advt./Pub. Rels., Hackensack, N.J., 1980-83; investment counselor/bookkeeper D. Cohen & Sons, Inc., Perth Amboy, N.J., 1983-86; creative cons. Advanstar Communications, N.Y.C., 1986—. Author (play): Cubicle Wars, 1981; author (poetry): Coarctate, 1985, The Eyes Lear Never Lost, 1990; translator poetry collection: Georg Trakl: Poems, 1987. Home: 104 Village Dr Basking Ridge NJ 07920 Office: Advanstar Communications 270 Madison Ave New York NY 10016

COHEN, MARK N., business executive; b. Camden, N.J., July 14, 1947; s. Morris and Esther (Sobel) C.; m. Rhoda Posner, Dec. 19, 1971; children: Michele Rebecca, Gregory Leighton. BS, U. Mo., Kansas City, 1969; postgrad., N.Y. Med. Coll., 1969-70; MS, Am. Western U., Tulsa, 1972, PhD, 1976. Cert. state advisor U.S. Congl. Adv. Bd. Founder, pres., chmn. Nat. Recall Alert Ctr., Marlton, N.J., 1973—; founder, pres., chmn. Acad. Guidance Svcs., Marlton, 1975—, Nat. Corp. Svcs., Marlton, 1977—, Nat. Pub. Corp., Marlton, 1979—; pres. Am. Bus. Opportunity Commn., N.J., 1975; bd. dirs., chmn. Health Sytems Agy., Bellmawr, N.J., 1982; treas., bd. dirs. Perinatal Coop./South N.J., Camden, 1983; mem. bd. advisors Free Enterprise, Marlton, 1985; pres. Cohenterprises, Inc., Marlton, 1986, Am. Profl. Copy-Quick Printing Corp., Marlton, 1985, Nationwide Wats Telephone Answering Service, Inc., Marlton, 1985; mem. exec. com. Deborah Hosp. Author: 100 Best Spare Time Business Opportunities Today, 1990; columnist newsletter Executive Edge. Bd. dirs. Beth Israel Synagogue; trustee Cooper Found./Cooper Hosp. U. Med. Ctr.; assoc. advisor post 65 Explorer Scouts. Recipient Young Exec. of Yr. award Jim Walter Corp., Tampa, Fla., 1972, Disting. Leadership award Am. Security Council Found., 1984, Annual Register award Esquire mag.; named one of 50 Bus. People to Watch, N.J. Bus. Jour. U.S. C. of C., Am. Assn. Fin. Profls., Nat. Council on Patient Info. and Edn., Nat. Health Lawyers Assn., N.J. Assn. Commerce and Industry (chmn. 1974), Am. Assn. Sch. Adminstrs., Am. Assn. Univ. Adminstrs., Am. Assn. Indiv. Investors, Mensa. Republican. Jewish. Home: 6 Alluvium Lakes Dr Voorhees NJ 08043-4816 Office: Acad Guidance Svcs Inc PO Box 609 Marlton NJ 08053

COHEN, MARK ROBERT, writer, foundation administrator; b. Bklyn., Dec. 18, 1947; s. David and Sylvia (Rubin) C.; m. Sarah Ann Crary, Oct. 6, 1977; children: Rachel Colette, Zachary Abraham. BA in English, SUNY, Buffalo, 1968. Musician, writer N.Y.C., 1971-81; adminstr. capital gifts campaign Union Am. Hebrew Congregations, N.Y.C., 1981-84; campaign exec. United Jewish Appeal-Fedn. Jewish Philanthropies, N.Y.C., 1984-86; exec. dir. Holocaust Publs., N.Y.C., 1986-90; regional dir. Am. Jewish Congress, N.Y.C., 1990-91; dir. nat. cultural svcs. Nat. Found. for Jewish Culture, N.Y.C., 1991—. Composer, performer record albums; assoc. producer film short Fragments of Greatness; contbr. articles to mags., poems to jours. Press liaison Presdl. Primary Campaign of Senator Ernest F. Hollings, N.Y.C., 1983. Mem. ASCAP, Assn. Holocaust Orgns. (chmn. publs. com. 1989). Home: PO Box 186 Dobbs Ferry NY 10522-0186 Office: Nat Found Jewish Culture 330 7th Ave New York NY 10001-5010

COHEN, MARK STEVEN, dentist; b. N.Y.C., Dec. 10, 1948; s. Lawrence and Yetta (Grossman) C.; m. Arlene Debbie Deutsch, Aug. 23, 1970 (div. May 1984); 1 child, Aaron Philip; m. Donna Lynn Poissonnier, Nov. 27, 1985. BS, CCNY, 1971; DDS, Columbia U., 1975, cert. in Pedodontics, 1976. Practice dentistry Yonkers, N.Y., 1975-76, Bristol, Conn., 1976-79, Brookfield, Conn., 1977—; dir. dental service N.Y. Inst. for the Edn. Blind, Bronx, 1976-78; assoc. attending dentist Danbury (Conn.) Hosp., 1976-82, Blythdale Children's Hosp., Valhalla, N.Y., 1986-87; assoc. clin. prof. dentistry Columbia U., N.Y.C., 1976—, mem. quality assurance com., 1982-85. Patentee in field. Active Dental Guidance Council for Cerebral Palsy, N.Y.C., 1976-81. Chemistry fellow NSF, Washington, 1969-71, research fellow NIH, 1971, United Cerebral Palsy, 1975-76. Mem. ADA, Conn. State Dental Assn., Greater Danbury Dental Soc., Am. Dental Vols. for Israel, OKU Dental Honor Soc. Democrat. Jewish. Home: 4 Yale Dr New Fairfield CT 06812-3617 Office: Cohen Metcalf & Fitzgerald 304 Federal Rd Brookfield CT 06804-2418

COHEN, MARSHALL, diversified conglomerate executive. BA, U. Toronto, Can., 1956; LLB, Osgoode Hall Law Sch., Toronto, 1960; LLM, York U., Toronto, 1963, LLD (hon.), 1986. Pvt. practice, 1960-70; dep. minister Depts. Fin., Industry Trade and Commerce, and Energy and Mines and Resources, Govt. of Can., 1970-85; pres. Olympia and York Enterprises Corp., 1985-86; chmn. Gulf Can. Resources Ltd., 1986-88; pres., chief exec. officer Molson Cos. Ltd., Toronto, 1988—, also bd. dirs.; bd. dirs. Abitibi-Price Inc., Am. Barrick Resources Corp., Am. Internat. Group, Inc., Consumers' Gas Co. Ltd., Groupe Val Royal Inc., Gulf Can. Resources Ltd., Lafarge Corp., Toronto-Dominion Bank. Chmn. Ont. Ctr. for Internat. Bus.; bd. dirs. Bus. Coun. on Nat. Issues, C.D. Howe Inst.; bd. dirs. Jr. Achievement Can.; bd. govs., chmn. adv. coun. Faculty of Adminstrv. Studies, York U.; mem. adv. coun. Baycrest Ctr. for Geriatric Care, Mt. Sinai Hosp.; chmn. Internat. Trade Adv. Com., Govt. of Can. Mem. Brit.—N.Am. Com. (exec. com.), Ctr. for Strategic and Internat. Studies (intenat. councillor), Trilateral Commn., Investment Dealers Assn. Can. (pub. bd. dirs.). Office: Molson Cos Ltd, 40 King St W Ste 3600, Toronto, ON Canada M5H 3Z5

COHEN, MARTIN F., chemical company executive; b. Columbus, Ohio, Apr. 9, 1939; s. Isaac and Jeanette (Kapowitz) C.; m. Rochelle Pilzer, Aug. 20, 1962; children: Leslie Renee, Brian Allan. B Chem. Engring., MS in Engring., Ohio State U., 1962. Registered profl. engr., W.Va. Engr. Union Carbide Corp., Charleston, W.Va., 1962-75; market mgr. Union Carbide Corp., N.Y.C., 1975-86; bus. mgr. Union Carbide Corp., Danbury, Conn., 1986-91, bus. dir., 1991—. Pres. bd. trustees Temple Beth Am, Yorktown, N.Y., 1978-80; mem. Lakeland Bd. Edn., Yorktown, N.Y., 1980-86, mem. mgmt. com., 1986—. Office: Union Carbide Corp 39 Old Ridgebury Rd Danbury CT 06817

COHEN, MARVIN WILLIAM, periodontist; b. N.Y.C., Mar. 16, 1936; s. Abe O. and Sadie (Faust) C.; M. Honi Carol Prybutok, June 18, 1961; children: Rachelle Ruth, Alisa Beth, Sara Perle. BS, L.I. U., 1956; DDS, Temple U. Sch. Dentistry, 1961; postgrad., Georgetown U. Grad. Sch., 1970. Commd. mil. dental officer U.S. Army, 1961, advanced through grades to capt., 1964; comdr. dental svc. U.S. Army R & D Ctr., Ft. Belvoir and Camp Tuto, Va. and Greenland, 1964-67; chief Stone Dental Clinic, Ft. Ord, Calif., 1967-68; periodontal resident Fitzsimons Gen. Hosp., Denver, 1971; chief of periodontics 768th Dental Detachment, Augsburg, Federal Republic of Germany, 1971-74; mentor in periodontics Eisenhower Army Med. Ctr., Ft. Gordon, Ga., 1974-78; chief of periodontics Saloman Dental Clinic, Ft. Benning, Ga., 1978-81; pvt. practice in periodontics Utica, N.Y., 1981—; spl. lectr. U. Ga. Dental Sch., Augusta, 1974-78; attendee in periodontics St. Luke's Meml. Hosp., Utica, 1982—; lectr. in field. Bd. dirs. Bd. Edn., Temple Beth El, Utica, 1985, United Jewish Fedn. of Utica, 1988-89. Recipient cert. of achievement U.S. Army Materiel Command, 1967, Army Commendation medal, 1978, Meritorious Svc. award U.S. Army, 1981. Mem. ADA, Am. Acad. Periodontology, N.Y. Dental Soc. (appreciation award 1985, Bronze cert. 1986), Oneida-Herkimer County Dental Soc. (program chmn. 1984), Ret. Officers Assn. (Rome, N.Y.), Knights of Pythias, Alpha Omega (pres. Augusta chpt. 1976-78). Jewish. Home: 6 The Hills Dr Utica NY 13501-5514 Office: 286 Genesee St Utica NY 13502-4639

COHEN, MICHAEL, psychologist; b. Yonkers, N.Y., Mar. 14, 1950; s. Joseph and Mary (Harris) C.; m. Amy Beth Siskind, Nov. 1, 1987; 1 child, Laura Reneé. BA, SUNY, Binghamton, 1972; MA, PhD, CUNY, N.Y.C., 1992. Pvt. practice psychotherapist N.Y.C., 1973-89; rsch. cons. N.Y.C. (N.Y.) Bd. Edn., 1986-87; sr. rsch. analyst Kennan Rsch. and Cons., N.Y.C., 1987-90; dir. qualitive rsch. KRC Rsch. and Cons., N.Y.C., 1990-91, pres., 1992—; mem. adv. bd. Handprints Prodns., N.Y.C., 1990—. Editor: The Einstein Connection, 1979. Office: KRC Rsch and Cons 145 Ave of the Americas New York NY 10013-1515

COHEN, MILDRED THALER, art gallery director; b. N.Y.C., Oct. 30, 1921; d. William and Dora (Snow) Intner; m. Seymour R. Thaler, June 17, 1945 (dec. 1976); children: Frederic I., Joan Thaler Zimmer; m. Sidney Cohen, Mar. 20, 1982. BA, Hunter Coll., 1942; BLS, Pratt Inst., 1943. Librarian Queens Borough Pub. Libr., N.Y.C., 1943-44, Mus. of French Art, French Inst., N.Y.C., 1944-46; dir. Marbella Gallery, Inc., N.Y.C., 1971—. Author catalogues including Women Students of William Merritt Chase, 1973, Robert Hallowell, 1983, Eliot Clark, 1990; brochures Ethel Paxson, 1976, Three Generations of Wiggins, 1981, Samuel Rothbart, 1989, Rachel V. Hartley, 1991, Frank Kleinholz, 1992. Bd. dirs. Lenox Hill Settlement House, N.Y.C., 1955-77. Mem. Appraisers Assn. Am., Hunter Coll. Alumni (pres. Queens chpt. 1951-54, past bd. dirs., pres. scholarship and welfare fund 1958-60, name to Hall of Fame 1977). Democrat. Jewish. Home and Office: 28 E 72nd St New York NY 10021-4234

COHEN, NICHOLAS, microbiology and immunology educator; b. N.Y.C., Nov. 20, 1938; s. Saris and Frances (Pakett) C.; m. Jayne Sevin Rogal, July 1, 1962 (div. 1972); children: Jaime Anne, Jessica Sevin; m. Catharina Johanna van der Harst, Oct. 23, 1974; children: Misha Thomas, Mark Sebastian. AB, Princeton U., 1959; PhD, U. Rochester, 1965. Asst. prof. microbiology and immunology Sch. Medicine and Dentistry U. Rochester, N.Y., 1967-73, assoc. prof., 1973-80, prof. microbiology, immunology and

psychiatry, 1980—, dir. div. immunology, 1980—; vis. prof. Agrl. U., Wageningen, The Netherlands, 1982-83; mem. Basel Inst. for Immunology, Switzerland, 1975-76; mem. peer rev. bds. NIH, 1976-80; cons. NIH study sects., NIMH study sects., Elsevier Press, 1980—. Assoc. editor Brain, Behavior and Immunity Jour., Devel. Comparative Immunology; editor 4 books; contbr. articles to profl. jours. Postdoctoral scholar in immunology UCLA, 1965-67, Fulbright scholar, 1982-83; grantee NIH, NIMH, NSF, 1967—; recipient Rsch. Career Devel. award NIH, 1974-78. Mem. Am. Soc. Zoologists (chmn. div. comparative immunology 1977-79), Transplatation Soc., Am. Soc. Immunologists, Brit. Soc. Immunology, Internat. Soc. Devel. and Comparative Immunology. Democrat. Office: U Rochester Med Ctr Dept Microbiology & Immunology Box 672 Rochester NY 14642

COHEN, NOEL LEE, otolaryngologist, educator; b. N.Y.C., Sept. 20, 1930; s. Victor Max and Esther Lily (Schonfeld) C.; m. Baukje Philippina Boersma, June 1, 1957; 1 child, Mark Bennett. AB, NYU, 1951; MD, U. Utrecht, The Netherlands, 1957. Intern Stads-en Aacademish Ziekenhuis, Utrecht, 1955-57; resident in otolargyngology Bellevue Med. Ctr., NYU, 1959-62; instr. NYU Sch. Medicine, 1962-64, asst. prof., 1964-69, assoc. prof., 1969-73, clin. prof., 1973-80, prof. otolargyngology, 1980—, chmn. dept., 1980—; bd. dirs. N.Y. League for Hard of Hearing, 1985—; cons. cochlear implants Cochlear Corp., Englewoood, Colo., 1986—; mem. rsch. adv. bd. EAR Found., Nashville, 1987—. Mem. editorial bd. Am. Jour. Otology, 1986—; reviewer articles and books for profl. jours.; contbr. numerous articles to profl. jours., author chpts. in books. Lt. USNR, 1957-59. Fellow ACS, Am. Acad. Otolaryngology-Head-Neck Surgery (Honor award 1985), Am. Laryngol., Rhinol. and Otol. Soc., Am. Soc. Head and Neck Surgery, Am. Bronchoesophagol. Assn., Am. Otol. Soc., N.Y. Acad. Medicine, N.Y. State Soc. Otolaryngology-Head and Neck Surgery (pres. 1988-89), N.Y. Head and Neck Soc. (charter mem. Pres.' award 1984), Soc. Univ. Otolaryngologists, Soc. Acad. Depts. Otolaryngology, N.Y. Acad. Scis., Acoustic Neuroma Soc., Alexander Graham Bell Assn. (med. adv. bd.). Democrat. Jewish. Office: NYU Med Ctr 530 1st Ave New York NY 10016-6402

COHEN, PERRY D., management consultant; b. Atlanta, May 27, 1946; s. Bernard W. and Rae Alice (Bernstein) C.; m. Rosalie Mandelbaum, Aug. 16, 1975; children: Shayna K., Jonah B. BS, Carnegie-Mellon U., 1968; MS, MIT, 1971, PhD, 1979. Assoc. engr. Lockheed Ga. Co., Marietta, 1968-69; rsch. analyst Blue Cross-Blue Shield of Mass., Boston, 1971-72; instr. bus. MIT, Cambridge, 1972-75; rsch. assoc. Assn. Am. Med. Colls., Washington, 1975-77; sr. assoc. Urban Systems Rsch., Washington, 1977-79; pres. Perry Cohen Assocs., Washington, 1979—, Unison Corp., Bethesda, 1987-89; adj. assoc. prof. U. Md., 1991—. Contbr. articles to profl. jours. Chmn. fin. com. Group Health Assn., Washington, 1984-90, chmn. planning com., 1990-92, vice chmn. bd. trustees, 1986-89. MIT Spl. Rsch. fellow, 1972-75; grantee NIH, 1986-87, Nat. Cancer Inst., 1985-86. Mem. Am. Pub. Health Assn., Manpower Analysis and Planning Soc. (from v.p. to pres. 1981-83), Assn. Health Svcs. Rsch., Acad. Mgmt. Home: 3914 Harrison St NW Washington DC 20015-1938

COHEN, PETER ALAN, municipal official; b. Jersey City, July 24, 1954; s. Morton and Shirley (Aronson) C.; m. Jeanette Viruet, Dec. 11, 1989 (div. Apr. 1991). A in Fin., Englewood Cliffs Coll., 1974; BA in Mktg. and Mgmt., St. Peters Coll., 1977. Lic. real estate sales, N.J., investment broker, N.Y., N.J., Pa. Calif., Fla. Chief staff N.J. Senator David Friedland 32d Legis. Dist., Jersey City, 1978-79; office mgr. Carl Meinel Trading Co., N.Y.C., 1979-80; asst. dept. head govt. securities trading Bank N.Y., N.Y.C., 1980-84; investment broker Dean Witter Reynolds, N.Y.C., 1984-86; exec. dir. North Hudson Coun. Mayors, Guttenberg, N.J., 1986-87; chief staff Hudson County Exec., Jersey City, 1988-90; adminstrv. asst. Commnr. the Dept. Environ. Protection, Trenton, N.J., 1990—. Dep. exec. dir. Hudson County Dem. Orgn., Jersey City, 1990-91, Dem. county com., North Bergen dist., N.J., 1976-92. Mem. Nat. Assn. Noteries, Nat. Com. for the Support The Guard and Res. Dept. Defense, N.J. Gov. Coun. on Physical Fitness and Sports (dir. spl. events 1990—), Bedlington Terrier Club Am. Democrat. Jewish. Home: 8450 Blvd E North Bergen NJ 07047-6050

COHEN, REINA JOYCE (REINA), artist; b. N.Y.C., Mar. 28, 1931; d. Abraham Jack and Belle (Friedenberg) Lerman; m. Martin Alvo, 1950 (div. 1956); m. Albert Cohen, 1962; children: Alisa, Jordan. Student, Cooper Union Coll., 1952, The New Sch., 1964-66. Advt. dir. Ind. Printing Co., N.Y.C., 1960-63; advt. mgr. Tricolator Mfg. Co., Wantagh, N.Y., 1965-75; artist Print Portfolio, Inc., Glen Head, N.Y., 1975—; demonstrator various art orgns., Nassau County, N.Y., 1985-91. Recipient 1st prize Freeport (N.Y.) Arts Coun., 1979, 1st prize Arts Alive, 1986, award of excellence Ind. Art Soc., 1991; grantee Mid-Atlantic Arts Found., 1991. Mem. Nat. Assn. Women Artists. Home and Office: 29 Farmstead Ln Glen Head NY 11545-2601

COHEN, RICHARD STEVEN, podiatrist; b. Washington, Feb. 26, 1955; s. Herbert and Ruth (Freudberg) C.; m. Stacey Aileen Zuck, Aug. 20, 1977; children: Lindsey Rachel, Hillary Sara, Lauren Michelle. BS, U. Md., 1976; D of Podiatric Medicine, Ohio Coll. Podiatric Medicine, 1981. Diplomate Am. Bd. Podiatric Surgery. Pvt. practice Greenbelt, Md., 1982—; chief podiatric surgery Prince Georges Hosp. Ctr., 1987-91. Contbr. articles to med. jours. Mem. Am. Podiatric Med. Assn., Md. Podiatric Med. Assn., Am. Acad. Pain Mgmt. (diplomate), Am. Running and Fitness Assn. Jewish. Home: 5604 Griffith Farm Rd Rockville MD 20855-1666 Office: 7525 Greenway Center Dr Ste 112 Greenbelt MD 20770-3525

COHEN, ROBERT, mental health facility administrator; b. Bklyn., Aug. 16, 1932; s. Julius and Anna Cohen; m. Pearl Eimbinder, Dec. 19, 1952 (div. 1981); 1 child, Meryle; m. Beatrice Schwartz, Nov. 15, 1982. BA, NYU, 1953, JD, 1956; MSW, Fordham U., 1970. Cert. social worker. Assoc. Dreyer & Traub, Bklyn., 1954-58; parole officer N.Y. State, N.Y.C., 1958-71; social worker SE Nassau Guidance Ctr., Seaford, N.Y., 1971-80; adminstr. Sunrise Psychiat. Clinic, Inc., Amityville, N.Y., 1980—; pres. Suffolk Coalition Mental Health, 1985—; chmn. SE Regional Council Mental Health, Nassau County, 1987. Mem. agy. coun. United Way, Nassau/Suffolk, 1987, bd. dirs., 1988-89. Mem. Nat. Assn. Social Workers (diplomate), Lions (v.p. Amityville Club 1987). Home: 5 Club Dr Massapequa NY 11758-8532 Office: Sunrise Psychiat Clinic Inc 400 Broadway Amityville NY 11701-2711

COHEN, ROBERT (AVRAM), lawyer; b. Pitts., July 23, 1929; s. Max R. and Mollie (Segal) C.; m. Frances H. Steiner, Dec. 24, 1951 (div. Feb. 1974); children: Deborah E., David R.; m. Mary E. Connors, Mar. 11, 1974; children: Deborah A., Charles E., Chrisann. AB magna cum laude, Harvard U., 1951, JD, 1954. Bar: Pa. 1955, Fla. 1974, U.S. Dist. Ct. (we. dist.) Pa. 1955, U.S. Dist. Ct. (so. dist.) Fla. 1974, U.S. Tax Ct. 1983, U.S. Ct. Appeals (3d cir.) 1961, U.S. Supreme Ct. 1962. Assoc. Goldstock, Schwartz, Teitelbaum & Schwartz, Pitts., 1955-60; ptnr. Goldstock, Schwartz, Cohen & Schwartz, Pitts., 1960-67, Fine, Perlow, Stone & Cohen, Pitts., 1967-70, Cohen & Goldstock, Pitts., 1970-73; assoc. Herring, Evans & Fulton, West Palm Beach, Fla., 1974; from assoc. to ptnr. Rothman, Gordon, Foreman and Groudine, P.A., Pitts., 1974-86; pvt. practice Pitts., 1986—. Trustee We. Allegheny Community Libr., 1989—, pres., 1991—; v.p. County Libr. Assn. Serving the People; mem. Zoning Bd., Borough of Oakdale, 1991—. Mem. ABA, Assn. Trial Lawyers Am. (pres. we. Pa. chpt. 1972-73), Am. Judicature Soc., Pa. Bar Assn. (com. on ethics and profl. responsibility 1988—, com. on professionalism 1990—), Acad. Trial Lawyers Allegheny County, Pa. Trial Lawyers Assn., Allegheny County Bar Assn. (civil litigation coun. 1988—, coun. on professionalism 1990—, civil litigation sect. 1988-90, continuing legal edn. 1977—), Golden Triangle Lodge (v.p. 1966-69), B'nai B'rith. Democrat. Jewish. Home: 205 Oak Heights Dr Oakdale PA 15071-1137 Office: 819 Frick Bldg Pittsburgh PA 15219

COHEN, ROBERT LESLIE, social worker; b. Passaic, N.J., July 3, 1941; s. Rudolph and Goldie (Rosenberg) C.; m. Elaine Marsha Smith, Apr. 8, 1979; 1 child, Ryan Lee. BA, Rutgers U., 1963, MEd, 1964, MSW, 1973. Cert. social worker Acad. Cert. Social Workers. Employment counselor N.J. Dept. Labor, Jersey City, 1964-65; vocat., rehab. counselor N.J. Dept. Labor, Marlboro, 1965-66; caseworker Passaic County Bd. Social Svcs., Paterson, N.J., 1968-69; social worker Passaic County Bd. Social Svcs., Paterson, 1969--70, supr., 1970-85, asst. tng. supr., 1985—; mem. profl. adv. com. to Mental Health Bd. Passaic County, Paterson, 1983—; program dir. Health, Edn., Welfare Coun. of Passaic County, Paterson, 1988—; treas. Coalition on AIDS in Passaic County, Paterson, 1988—. Bd. dirs. Mental Health Assn. Passaic County, Paterson, 1984, pres. and chmn. of bd., 1987-89, v.p., 1987-89. With USN, 1967-72. Mem. NASW. Home: 53 Windsor Rd Clifton NJ 07012-2010 Office: Passaic County Bd Soc Svcs 80 Hamilton St Paterson NJ 07505-2017

COHEN, ROCHELLE LYNN, insurance agent; b. Bronx, N.Y., Jan. 12, 1963; d. Seymour Daniel and Elaine (Korman) Cohen. Grad. high sch., Rye, N.Y., 1981. Agt. Equitable Life Assurance Soc., Milford, Conn., 1991—. Mem. Nat. Assn. Security Dealers (rep. 1991—), Nat. Mus. Women in Arts (charter mem.). Republican. Orthodox. Office: Equitable Life Assurance Soc 303 Mill St Poughkeepsie NY 12601-3113 also: Equitable Barbetta Agy 612 Wheelers Farms Rd Milford CT 06460

COHEN, RONALD JAY, neurological surgeon; b. Pitts., Apr. 8, 1947; s. Albert K. and Dorothy (Fisher) C.; m. Margaret Callanan, June 11, 1972; children: Sarah, Jessica, Jacob. BA, U. Pitts., 1968; MD, Johns Hopkins U., Balt., 1972. Am. Bd. Neurological Surgery. Asst. resident gen. surgery Johns Hopkins Hosp., Balt., 1972-74; clin. assoc. Nat. Cancer Inst., Balt., 1974-76; asst. resident, Neurological Surgery Johns Hopkins Hosp., Balt., 1976-81; ast. prof. dept. Neurological Surgery Johns Hopkins Med. Inst., Balt., 1981—; neurological surgery pvt. practice, 1981—; chmn. Peer Review Mgmt. Com. Med. and Surgical Faculty of Md. Fellow Am. Coll. Surgeons, Am. Assn. Neurological Surgeons, Cong. Neurological Surgeons, Stroke Soc. of Am. Heart Assn. Office: East Bldg Ste 370 1777 Reisterstown Rd Baltimore MD 21208

COHEN, RONNY HELENE, creative consultant; b. N.Y.C., Apr. 19, 1950; d. Nathan B. and Rita (Falsberg) C. BA, Finch Coll., N.Y.C., 1972; MA, Inst. of Fine Arts, N.Y.C., 1974, PhD, 1979. Art critic Artforum, Art in Am., Art News, 1974—; ind. art curator Bristol Myers Squibb, 1989-91, P.S.I., 1981-91; lectr. various mus. and univs.; adj. asst. prof. Coll. S.I., CUNY, 1990-91. Editor: The Art Dealer's Newsletter, 1983-85; contbr. over 500 articles on contemporary modern art and design subjects to profl. jours. Danforth Found. fellow, 1972-79; Fulbright Hays fellow, 1976-77. Mem. NAFE, Internat. Assn. Art Critics. Home: 521 E 82d St New York NY 10028-7172

COHEN, SAMUEL ISRAEL, clergyman, organization executive; b. Asbury Park, N.J., Apr. 17, 1933; s. Meyer and Henrietta (Gershman) C.; m. Mira Hager, Sept. 5, 1960; children: Baruch Chaim, Michael Nachum, Miriam Rachel. BA, Bklyn. Coll., 1955; MRE, Yeshiva U., 1959, EdD, 1967. Ordained rabbi, 1956. Exec. dir. L.I. Zionist Youth Commn., Queens, N.Y., 1957-61; regional dir. Supreme Lodge B'nai B'rith, Queens, 1961-66; dir. membership dept. dist. 1 Supreme Lodge B'nai B'rith, N.Y.C., 1966-72; nat. dir. orgn. Am. Jewish Congress, N.Y.C., 1972-74; exec. dir. Am. Zionist Fedn., N.Y.C., 1974-77; exec. v.p. Jewish Nat. Fund, N.Y.C., 1977—; adj. asst. prof. sociology L.I. U., 1967; lectr. sociology Queensborough Community Coll., 1968, adj. asst. prof., 1971-74; lectr. Borough of Manhattan Community Coll., 1968, adj. asst. prof., 1970-72; adj. asst. prof. John Jay Coll. Criminal Justice, 1973—; lectr. Herzl Inst., N.Y.C., 1974-78. Contbr. articles to nat. publs. Chmn. edn. adv. bd. Yeshiva Toras Chaim, Woodmere, N.Y., 1971-74; mem. Religious Zionists Am., 1960—, Zionist Orgn. Am., 1960—, Nat. Coun. Jewish Edn., 1970—; mem. Conf. Jewish Communal Svc., 1970—; mem. Congregation Shaarei Tephila, Lawrence, N.Y., 1983-87, Congregation Kneseth Israel, 1983—; sec Olam Chadash, 1980—; bd. dirs. Union Orthodox Jewish Congregations Am., 1973—, United Israel Appeal, 1984—. Co-recipient Boneh Israel award, Mercaz Horav Kook. Mem. Adult Edn. Assn. (nat. com. on goals and objectives religious edn. sect. 1967-68), Educators Council Am., Young Israel of Wavecrest and Bayswater (v.p. 1973-75), Assn. Jewish Community Orgn. Profls., Nat. Council for Adult Jewish Edn., Nat. Soc. Fund Raising Execs, B'nai B'rith (v.p. Briarwood Lodge, 1964). Home: 112 Rand Pl Lawrence NY 11559-1327 Office: 42 E 69th St New York NY 10029

COHEN, SHELDON GILBERT, physician; b. Pittston, Pa., Sept. 21, 1918; s. Samuel H. and Dorthy (Goldberg) C. Grad., Wyo. Sem., 1936; student, Syracuse U., 1936-37; BA, Ohio State U., 1940; MD, NYU, 1943; DSc (hon.), Wilkes Coll., 1976. Diplomate Am. Bd. Allergy and Immunology. Intern Bellevue Hosp., N.Y.C., 1944; resident internal medicine VA Hosp., Balt., 1947-48; resident in allergy VA Hosp., Aspinwall, Pa., 1948-49, U. Pitts. Med. Ctr., 1948-49; research fellow U. Pitts. Sch. Medicine, 1949-50; practice medicine specializing in allergy Wilkes-Barre, Pa., 1951-72; research asso. Addison H. Gibson Lab. Applied Physiology U. Pitts., 1950-51; attending physician Allergy Clinic, Falk Clinics, 1950-51; chief of allergy Mercy Hosp., Wilkes-Barre, 1951-72; attending physician in allergy VA Hosp., Wilkes-Barre, 1951-60; cons. in internal medicine and research VA Hosp., 1960-72; asso. prof. biol. research Wilkes Coll., Wilkes-Barre, 1952-62; prof. biol. research Wilkes Coll., 1962-68, prof. exptl. biology, 1968-72; cons. extramural programs Nat. Inst. Allergy and Infectious Diseases, 1972-73, chief allergy and immunology br., 1973-76, dir. immunology, allergic and immunologic diseases program, 1977-88, sci. advisor div. of intramural rsch. office of dir., 1988—; bd. sci. advisors Allergy and Immunology Inst. of Internat. Life Scis. Inst., 1989—; adj. prof. medicine Northwestern U.; scholar in residence Nat. Library of Medicine, 1988—; regional med. cons. Children's Asthma Research Inst. and Hosp., Denver, 1969-72; mem. medico adv. bd. CARE, 1977-89; cons. to Ministry Public Health, State of Kuwait, 1981-83; mem. expert adv. panel on immunology WHO, Geneva, Switzerland, 1979—, dir. WHO Collaborating Ctr. for Allergy, 1985-89; bd. dirs. Asthma and Allergy Found. Am., 1969-81, mem. com. public edn., 1976-81; bd. dirs. Lupus Found. Am., 1978-85, exec. v.p., 1981-85, mem. med. council, 1978—; mem. aeroallergens com. NRC, 1976-80. Author books on history of medicine; mem. editorial bd. Jour. Devel. and Comparative Immunology, 1976-81, New Eng. and Regional Allergy Proc., 1983—; editor: Hist. Notes, Allergy Proc., 1988—; cons. editor: Am. Jour. Rhinology, 1986—; contbr. articles to profl. jours., chpts. to books. Trustee Marywood Coll., Scranton, Pa., 1983-89; bd. govs. adv. coun. Wilkes U., Wilkes-Barre, Pa., 1991—. Served to capt. M.C. USAAF, 1944-46. Recipient Disting. Svc. award Wyo. Sem., 1978, Asthma and Allergy Found. Am., 1981, Clemens von Pirquet award Georgetown U., 1981, NIH Centennial award, Terri Gotthelf Lupus Rsch. Inst., 1987, NYU Med. Alumni award in Health Sci., 1988, Achievement award Internat. Assn. Allergology and Clin. Immunology, 1988, Spl. Recognition award Am. Acad. Allergy and Immunology, 1989, recognition citation TLS Allergy and Immunology Inst., 1992. Fellow ACP, Am. Acad. Allergy (chmn. rsch. coun. 1963-66, historian 1963-69, v.p. 1979-80, Disting. Svc. award 1971), Am. Coll. Allergists; mem. Coll. Physicians Phila., Am. Assn. Immunologists, Assn. Am. Physicians, Clin. Immunology Soc., Am. Thoracic Soc., Soc. for Investigative Dermatology, Am. Coll. Rheumatology, Soc. for Exptl. Biology and Medicine, Collegium Internat. Allergologicum, Am. Fedn. Clin. Rsch., Alpha Omega Alpha (NYU alumni), Sigma Xi. Club: Cosmos. Home: Apt 1927N 5500 Friendship Blvd Bethesda MD 20815-7213 Office: NIH Rm 2C37 Solar Bldg NIAID Bethesda MD 20892

COHEN, STEWART ERIC, human resources executive; b. Springfield, Mass., Dec. 15, 1950; s. Jacob and Edith Barbara (Ascher) C.; m. Dorothy Jean Martin, July 10, 1977; children: Jennifer, Heather. BS in BA, Bryant Coll., Smithfield, R.I., 1972; MEd in Guidance, Springfield Coll., 1973. Indsl. rels. assoc. RCA, Cherry Hill, N.J., 1973-74; employee rels. specialist GE, Pittsfield, Mass., 1974; asst. personnel dir. Rsch. Found. of SUNY, Albany, 1975-77; reg. personnel mgr. Ethan Allen, Inc., Amherst, N.H., 1977-80; employee rels. mgr. Centronics, Hudson, N.H., 1980-81; personnel mgr. ECA, Manchester, N.H., 1981-84; dir. human resources Aerotronics, Contoocook, N.H., 1984-88; prin. Tanglewood Group, N.H., 1988; dir. human resources Burndy Corp., Manchester, N.H., 1988—; chmn. So. N.H. Survey Group; bd. dirs. Granite State Credit Union, 1983—. Bd. dirs. Temple Beth Jacob, Concord, N.H., 1990-91, 1st Night New Hampshire, Concord, 1990-91. Recipient George M. Parks award, Bryant Coll., 1972, Bryant Good Citizenship award, 1972. Mem. Soc. for Human Resource Mgmt., Manchester Area Human Resource Assn. (pres. 1991), Randolph Area C. of C. (pres. 1978), Psi Chi. Office: Burndy Corp 47 E Industrial Park Dr Manchester NH 03109

COHEN, THEODORE, chemistry educator; b. Arlington, Mass., May 11, 1929; s. Gideon and Lillian Sarah (Leight) C.; m. Pearl Bernice Silverman, July 22, 1954; children: Bret Ronald, Rima Jean. BS, Tufts Coll., 1951; PhD, U. So. Calif., 1955. Ramsay meml. postdoctoral fellow U. Glasgow, Scotland, 1955-56; prof. chemistry U. Pitts., 1956—. Contbr. articles to profl. publs. Home: 2825 Shady Ave Pittsburgh PA 15217-2740 Office: U Pitts Dept Chemistry Pittsburgh PA 15260

COHEN, WAYNE ROY, obstetrician-gynecologist, educator; b. N.Y.C., Apr. 27, 1946; s. Eugene Mark and Helene (Paul) C.; m. Marion Boardman, June 9, 1968 (div.); 1 child, Aaron Robert; m. Sharon Rose Ominski, Aug. 24, 1980; children: Daniel Paul, Giselle Rose. AB in Biology, U. Rochester, 1967; MD, Boston U., 1971. Diplomate Am. Bd. Ob-Gyn. Intern Mt. Auburn Hosp., Cambridge, Mass., 1972-73; resident Beth Israel Hosp., Boston, 1973-76; asst. prof. Harvard Med. Sch., Boston, 1976-82; assoc. prof. Albert Einstein Coll. Medicine, N.Y.C., 1983—. Editor: Management of Labor, 1983, 2d edit., 1989; contbr. chpts. to books, articles to profl. jours. Mem. Soc. for Gynecologic Investigation, Soc. Perinatal Obstetricians, Am. Fedn. for Clin. Rsch. Democrat. Jewish. Office: Albert Einstein Coll Med Dept Obstetrics 1300 Morris Park Ave Bronx NY 10461

COHEN, WILLIAM SEBASTIAN, senator; b. Bangor, Maine, Aug. 28, 1940; s. Reuben and Clara (Hartley) C.; children: Kevin, Christopher. AB cum laude, Bowdoin Coll., 1962; LLB cum laude, Boston U., 1965; LLD, St. Joseph's Coll., Windham, Maine, 1974; LL.D., U. Maine, 1975, Western New Eng. Coll., 1975, Bowdoin Coll., 1975, Nasson Coll., 1975, Thomas Coll., 1988, Colby Coll., 1988. Bar: Maine, Mass., D.C. Ptnr. Paine, Cohen, Lynch, Weatherbee & Kobritz, Bangor, 1966-72; instr. U. Maine, 1968-72; asst. county atty. Penobscot County, Maine, 1968-70; mem. 93d-95th Congresses fromMaine; U.S. Senator from Maine, 1979—; Mem. Bangor Sch. Com., 1970-71, Bangor City Council, 1969-72, mayor, Bangor, 1972; Trustee Unity Coll.; bd. overseers Bowdoin Coll., 1973-85. Author: Of Sons and Seasons, 1978, Roll Call, 1981, Getting the Most Out of Washington, 1982, A Baker's Nickel, 1986, One-Eyed Kings, 1991; co-author: (with Gary Hart) The Double Man, 1985, (with George Mitchell) Men of Zeal, 1988. Recipient Alumni award for disting. pub. service Boston U., 1976; named to N.E. Hall of Fame Basketball Team, 1962, Silver Anniversary award Nat. Collegiate Athletic Assn., 1987; Outstanding Young Man of Yr. Nat. Jaycees, 1975; James Bowdoin scholar, 1961-62; Alumni Fund scholar, 1962, selected for Balfour Silver Anniversary All-Am. Team, Nat. Assn. Basketball Coaches U.S., 1987. Office: US Senate 322 Hart Senate Office Bldg Washington DC 20510

COHEN-ROSENTHAL, EDWARD, labor educator, consultant; b. Balt., Aug. 16, 1952; s. Bernard Joseph and Bernice Helaine (Sachs) R.; m. Ellen Cohen, June 12, 1977; children: Janna, Mollie, Jacob. BA, Rutgers Coll., 1974; EdM, Harvard U., 1975. Mem. faculty Rutgers Labor Edn. Ctr., New Brunswick, N.J., 1976-78; assoc. dir. Am. Ctr. for Quality of Work Life, Washington, 1978-79; pres. ECR Assocs., Foster, Va., 1979—; asst. to pres. Bricklayers Internat. Union, Washington, 1987-91; sr. extension faculty Cornell U., Ithaca, N.Y., 1991—; cons. numerous corp. union, govt., internat. orgns., 1979—. Author: Mutual Gains: Guide to Union-Management Cooperation, 1987; (booklet) Doing the Best Job, 1990; contbg. editor Workplace Democracy; contbr. numerous articles to profl. jours. Chmn. Prevailing Wage Commn. State of Md., 1986-87. Mem. ASTD (network dir., Achievement award 1989), Assn. for Quality and Participation, Internat. Assn. Adult Edn. (assoc.). Home: 106 Woodcrest Ter Ithaca NY 14850 Office: Cornell U NYSSILR PEWS Ext Bldg Ithaca NY 14853

COHICK, JAMES ALLEN, JR., healthcare services executive; b. Mechanicsburg, Pa., Dec. 22, 1959; s. James Allen Sr. and Norma (Bloom) C.; m. Lynn Garden Harrison, July 4, 1981; children: Charles James, Sarah Bloom. BSBA, Shippensburg Coll., 1981. Claims adjuster Nationwide Ins., Harrisburg, Pa., 1981-83; bus. office mgr. Rehab. Hosp. York (Pa.), 1983-84; dir. data processing Rehab. Hosp. Svcs. Corp., Washington, 1984-88; chief info. officer Continental Med. Systems, 1988—. Republican. Mem. Evangelical Free Ch. Home: 346 Gettysburg Pike Mechanicsburg PA 17055-5170 Office: Continental Med Systems PO Box 715 Mechanicsburg PA 17055-0715

COHILL, MAURICE BLANCHARD, JR., district court judge; b. Pitts., Nov. 26, 1929; s. Maurice Blanchard and Florence (Clarke) C.; m. Suzanne Miller, June 27, 1952 (dec. may 1986); children: Cynthia Cohill Plattner, Jonathan, Jennifer, Victoria Cohill Rifai. A.B., Princeton U., 1951; LL.B., U. Pitts., 1956. Bar: Pa. 1957. Judge family div. Common Pleas Ct., Allegheny County, Pitts., 1965-76; judge U.S. Dist. Ct. Pa. (we. dist.), 1976-85, 92—, chief judge, 1985-92; bd. dirs. Pa. George Jr. Republic, Grove City; bd. visitors Grad. Sch. Social Work, U. Pitts.; chmn. bd. fellows Nat. Center for Juvenile Justice. Served to capt. USMCR, 1951-53. Mem. Am., Pa., Allegheny County bar assns., Nat. Council Juvenile Ct. Judges (v.p.), Pa. Council Juvenile Ct. Judges (past pres.), Pa. Conf. State Trial Judges, Phi Delta Phi. Republican. Presbyterian. Office: US Dist Ct 8th Fl Rm 3 Pittsburgh PA 15219

COHN, DANIEL ROSS, physicist; b. Berkeley, Calif., Nov. 28, 1943; s. Roy Wolfsohn and Betty (Black) C.; m. Helen Desfosses, Aug. 25, 1967 (div. 1974); 1 child, Adam Robsohn; m. Joanne Brecker, June 10, 1978. BA, U. Calif., Berkeley, 1966; PhD, MIT, 1971. Rsch. scientist Francis Bitter Nat. Magnet Lab., MIT, Cambridge, Mass., 1971-77; group leader Francis Bitter Nat. Magnet Lab., MIT, Cambridge, 1977-80; div. head Plasma Fusion Ctr., MIT, Cambridge, 1980—; sr. rsch. scientist Nuclear Engring. Dept., MIT, Cambridge, 1980—; cons. in field. Editor Jour. of Fusion Energy, 1984—; contbr. more than 100 articles to profl. jours. Mem. Fusion Energy Div., Am. Nuclear Soc., Am. Phys. Soc., Phi Beta Kappa. Home: 26 Walnut Hill Rd Chestnut Hill MA 02167-3125 Office: MIT Plasma Fusion Ctr 167 Albany St Cambridge MA 02139-4294

COHN, J. GUNTHER, retired research executive; b. Berlin, Germany, Mar. 6, 1911; came to U.S., 1941; s. Hermann and Gertrud (Stiasny) C.; m. Catherine Wolf, Feb. 25, 1940; 1 child, Miriam Viveka. PhD in Chemistry, U. Berlin, Germany, 1934. Rsch. fellow Nobel Inst. for Chemistry, Stockholm, 1934-36; instr. Chalmers Tech. U., Gothenburg, Sweden, 1936-41; Carnegie-M.W. Welch fellow U. Minn., Mpls., 1941-43; with Engelhard Industries Engelhard Minerals and Chems. Corp., Iselin, N.J., 1943-76, dir. rsch., 1955-72; v.p. Engelhard Minerals and Chems. Corp., now Engelhard Corp., Iselin, 1963-72, v.p. for rsch., 1972-76, sci. and tech. cons., 1976—; lectr. at univs. Contbr. articles to rsch. publs.; patentee in field. Recipient Disting. Achievement award Internat. Precious Metal Inst., 1987. Mem. Am. Chem. Soc., Electrochem. Soc., Metal Sci. Club of N.Y. Home: 20 Lincoln Ave West Orange NJ 07052-2312

COHN, JAN KADETSKY, college dean; b. Cambridge, Mass., Aug. 9, 1933; d. Allan Robert and Beatrice (Goldberg) Kadetsky; m. Donald S. Solomon, Feb. 6, 1955 (div. 1968); children: Cathy Rebecca, David Seth; m. William Henry Cohn, Mar. 9, 1969. BA, Wellesley Coll., 1955; MA, U. Toledo, 1961; PhD, U. Mich., 1964. From instr. to asst. prof. U. Toledo, 1964-68; assoc. prof. U. Wis., Whitewater, 1968-70, Carnegie Mellon U., Pitts., 1970-79; prof., dept. chair George Mason U., Fairfax, Va., 1979-87; dean faculty Trinity Coll., Hartford, Conn., 1987—; cons. in field. Author: The Palace or the Poorhouse, 1979, Improbable Fiction, 1980, Romance and the Erotics of Property, 1988, Creating America, 1989. Bd. dirs. Nat. Bldg. Mus., Washington, 1987-91; exec. bd. dirs. Conn. Pub. Broadcasting, Hartford, 1988-92. Fellow Am. Coun. Learned Socs., 1972, NEH, 1972-73. Mem. Modern Language Assn., Popular Culture Assn., Am. Culture Assn., Am. Studies Assn., Phi Kappa Phi. Democrat. Jewish. Office: Trinity Coll Dean Faculty 300 Summit St Hartford CT 06106-3100

COHN, JOSEPH DAVID, surgeon; b. N.Y.C., Jan. 26, 1937; s. Samuel Theodor and Gertrude (Emsheimer) C.; m. Barbara Ester Forst, July 27, 1966; children: Michael, Russell. SB, MIT, 1957; MD, NYU, 1961; postgrad., Rutgers U., 1990—. Diplomate Am. Bd. Surgery, Am. Bd. Thoracic Surgery. Intern Duke Hosp., Durham, N.C., 1961-62; surg. resident Bronx Mcpl. Hosp. Ctr., N.Y., 1962-67; thoracic surgery resident U. Calif., San Diego, 1969-71; from asst. dir. surgery to dir. St. Barnabas Med. Ctr., Livingston, N.J., 1971-83; thoracic surgeon Northfield Surg. Assn., Livingston, 1978—; clin. asst. prof. surgery UMDNJ, Newark, 1972-79, assoc. prof., 1979-90, prof., 1990—; bd. dirs. Daltex Corp., N.Y.C., 1983—. Editor: scientific jours.; author: software programs, 1988; contbr. articles to profl. jours. Capt. USAF, 1967-69. Fellow Am. Heart Assn. 1966-67, NIH

1964-66. Fellow Am. Coll. Surgeons, Am. Coll. Critical Care Medicine; mem. Sigma Xi, Phi Lambda Upsilon, Alpha Omega Alpha. Office: Northfield Surg Assocs 299 E Northfield Rd Livingston NJ 07039

COHN, ROBERT MARK, publishing executive; b. N.Y.C., June 21, 1945; s. Joseph and Cecile (Skvirsky) C. AB, Dartmouth Coll., 1966; MBA, Amos Tuck Sch., 1969. Exec. asst. CBS Inc., N.Y.C., 1970-71, mgr. product planning pub. group, 1971-73, dir. mktg. planning, analysis, 1973-74, dir. circulation mktg. mag. div., 1974-77; dir. planning and circulation N.Y. mag., N.Y.C., 1977-78; account supr. Wunderman Ricotta & Kline, N.Y.C., 1978-79; v.p. Policy Devel. Corp., N.Y.C., 1979-86; pres. Robert M. Cohn & Assocs., N.Y.C., 1986-87; exec. publisher American Health mag., N.Y.C., 1987-90; sr. v.p. Mag. Pubs. Am., N.Y.C., 1990-91; pres., pub. Horticulture Mag., Boston, 1991—; pres. Wicks Mag. Group, N.Y.C., 1991—; lectr. NYU, N.Y.C., 1985-90. Pres. Gramercy Owners Ltd., N.Y.C., 1988—; chmn. Battery Dance Co., N.Y.C., 1985-89. With US Army, 1969-70. Mem. Direct Mktg. Info. Exch., Direct Mktg. Assn. (mem. program adv. bd. 1986, chmn. Cirulation Coun. 1986—), Yale Club. Democrat. Jewish. Home: 44 Gramercy Park N New York NY 10010-6310 Office: Wicks Mag Group 405 Park Ave New York NY 10022-6102

COHN, STUART HARRIS, recording industry executive, consultant; b. New Haven, June 21, 1950; s. Joel and Rhoda Diana (Cohen) C.; m. Jill Maris Rosenfield, May 30, 1981; 1 child, Joelle. BS in Real Estate and Urban Devel., Am. U., 1972. Dir. Joseph Cohn & Son Inc., New Haven, 1972—; founder, organizer New Haven Mchts. Bank, 1983-87; founder Jill Cohn Ctr. for Head Injury Rehab., New Haven, 1988—; pres. Sugarcone/Nana Mary Records, New Haven, 1989—; mgr. Euclid's Bakery, N.Y.C., 1989—; mng. dir., founder Brother Monk's Monastary Recipes, New Haven, 1990—. Jewish. Home: 18 Temple Ct New Haven CT 06511-6819

COHNE, HERBERT WILLIAM, securities trader, consultant; b. Boston, Aug. 26, 1921; s. Robert L. and Martha E. (Coleman) C.; m. Bernice L. Fishman, Sept. 10, 1944; children: Malcolm S., Martin M., Carol L. Meirovitz. BBA, Boston U., 1948. Pres. Coleman Supply Co., Newton, Mass., 1950-56; spl. agt. Equitable Life Assurance, Boston, 1957-65; stockbroker Mann and Co., Medford, Mass., 1965-68; sales mgr. Security Investor Svcs. Investment Co., Boston, 1969-75; account cons. F.P. Putnam & Co., Boston, 1975-82; fin. sales cons. Advest Inc., Boston, 1983-88; account cons. Dickinson & Co., Boston, 1989—. Pres. Newton Corner Businessmen's Assn., 1954. Staff sgt. USAF, 1943-47. Mem. Boston Stockbrokers Assn. (bd. dirs., gov. 1972-75), Boston U. Alumni Assn., Amex Club of Boston, Temple Emanuel Brotherhood (life bd. dirs., Marcus Fineberg Trophy award 1980), B'nai B'rith, Masons, Phi Epsilon Pi (vice superior 1941-42). Jewish. Home: Box 534 Newton MA 02158 Office: Dickinson and Co 155 Federal St 13th Fl Boston MA 02110

COHN-HAFT, HERA MARIA, psychiatrist; b. N.Y.C., July 5, 1947; d. Louis and Athena Iris (Capraro) Cohn-H.; m. David Brian Cohn-Haft Johnston, May 4, 1969; children: Rebekah, Mariah, Alexander, Isaac. BA, Barnard Coll., N.Y.C., 1971; MD, Med. Coll. Pa., 1979. Resident in psychiatry U. Conn., Farmington, 1984; pvt. practice psychiatry West Hartford, Conn., 1984—; staff psychiatrist Manchester (Conn.) Meml. Hosp. Mental Health Clinic, 1984—; supr. Collaborative Counselling, Manchester, 1985—. Vol. Nat. Abortion Rights Action League, Hartford, 1983—; lectr. in field. Mem. Am. Med. Women's Assn., Am. Psychiat. Assn., Am. Assn. Women Psychiatrists. Home: 22 Beverly Rd West Hartford CT 06119-1710 Office: 10 N Main St West Hartford CT 06107-1901

COIA, ROBERT SALVATORE, biology educator, consultant; b. Phila., Dec. 1, 1944; s. Salvatore and Jennie (Capasso) C. BS, Pa. State U., 1967; MEd, Temple U., 1969, postgrad., 1975-80. Cert. secondary sci. edn., Pa. Biology tchr. Sch. Dist. Phila., 1967-71; assoc. prof. Community Coll. of Phila., 1972—; tchr. biology. Mem. Nat. Assn. Biology Tchrs., Am. Orchid Soc., Am. Hemerocallis Soc., Ctr. City Orchid Soc. (bd. dirs. 1987-90, guest speaker 1987-90), Southeast Pa. Orchid Soc. (v.p. 1985-86). Republican. Roman Catholic.

COIGNEY, RODOLPHE LUCIEN, retired public health service official; b. Paris, Oct. 14, 1911; s. Jacques and Marthe C.; m. Martha Wadsworth, Dec. 27, 1969; children by previous marriage: Arielle, Frederique, Joel. Baccalaureat, Sorbonne U., Paris, 1927; MD, Paris Med. Faculty, 1937, MA in Internat. Medicine, 1938; MPH, Columbia Sch. Pub. Health, 1963. Pvt. practice Paris, 1938-42; dir. med. svcs. for displaced persons UN Relief and Rehab. Adminstrn., London, 1944-47; dir. health Internat. Refugee Orgn., Geneva, 1947-52; dir. liaison office WHO with UN, N.Y.C., 1952-73; ret. WHO of UN, N.Y.C., 1973; lectr. Columbia Sch. Pub. Health, N.Y.C., 1965-73; assoc. prof. Mt. Sinai Sch. Medicine, N.Y.C., 1966-73. Maj. (hon.) Med. Corps, 1937-46. Recipient citations (3) with French Croix de Guerre, other French war awards; named commdr. French Legion of Honor. Mem. Fly Fishers' Club of London, Theodore Gordon Fly Fishers. Home: 1200 5th Ave New York NY 10029-5208

COINER, MARYROSE C., psychologist; b. Newark, Dec. 14, 1949; d. William J. and Margaret (Queenan) Carew; m. H. Michael Coiner, Mar. 8, 1975; children: John P., Thomas M. BS, St. Peter's Coll., Jersey City, N.J., 1971; PhD, Yale U., 1978. Lic. psychologist, Mass. Asst. prof. psychology Millersville (Pa.) State U., 1978-80; staff psychologist Framingham (Mass.) Union Hosp., 1980-90; pvt. practice Marlboro and Framingham, Mass., 1981—; bd. dirs. Together Inc., Marlboro, 1983—, Advocates Inc., Framingham, 1991—. NSF fellow, 1971-74. Mem. APA, Mass. Psychol. Assn. Office: 14 Vernon St Ste 206 Framingham MA 01701-4783

COLADARCI, THEODORE, educational psychology educator; b. Palo Alto, Calif., Nov. 16, 1953; s. Arthur Paul and Jane (Bottenfield) C.; m. Janet Spector, Nov. 24, 1978; children: Alison, Gregory. BA in Psychology and Sociology, Calif. State U., Chico, 1975; PhD in Ednl. Psychology, Stanford U., 1980. Teaching and rsch. asst. Stanford (Calif.) U. Sch. Edn., 1975-80; asst. prof. ednl. psychology U. Mont. Sch. Edn., Missoula, 1980-83; asst. prof. ednl. psychology U. Maine Coll. Edn., Orono, 1983-87, assoc. prof., 1987—; mem. adj. faculty U. San Francisco Sch. Edn., 1980; cons. ednl. measurement, Mont., Maine; mem. evaluation team Maine Tchr. Cert. Implementation Study, 1984-86; mem. evaluation team Augusta (Maine) Sch. System, 1987-88; conf. presenter in field; ad hoc reviewer in field for various pubs. Co-author: Elementary Descriptive Statistics, 1980; assoc. editor Jour. Rsch. in Rural Edn., 1989-90, editor, 1991—; adv. editor Jour. Ednl. Psychology, 1989-90, Jour. Exptl. Edn., 1991—; contbr. articles to profl. jours. Rsch. grantee U. Mont. Grad. Sch., 1983, U. Maine Grad. Sch., 1986. Mem. Am. Ednl. Rsch. Assn. Home: 71 Norfolk St Bangor ME 04401-3862 Office: U Maine Coll Edn Orono ME 04469

COLANGELO, ROCCO, JR., sales executive; b. Hazleton, Pa., Sept. 8, 1964; s. Rocco and Blanche (Farace) C. BSBA summa cum laude, Ind. (Pa.) U., 1986; MBA, U. Rochester, 1988. Salesman Quality Beverage Distr. Hazleton, Inc., 1988—; tng. for intervention procedures by servers of alcohol trainer Health Communications, Inc., Washington, 1990. Mem. Beta Gamma Sigma. Republican. Roman Catholic. Home: 1334 Bloom Rd Danville PA 17821 Office: Quality Beverage Distr 695 S Poplar St Hazleton PA 18201

COLANTONI, ALFRED DANIEL, newspaper executive; b. Plainfield, N.J., Apr. 1, 1952; s. Joseph and Susan Colantoni; m. Nicole A. Gamache; children: Terri, David, A.J. BS in Acctg., Rider Coll., 1974. Audit sr. Price Waterhouse, Morristown, N.J., 1974-77; with Asbury Park (N.J.) Press Inc., 1977—; v.p. corp. svcs. Asbury Park Press, Neptune, N.J., 1985-89, v.p. corp. svcs., chief fin. officer, 1989—; bd. dirs. Press Broadcasting Co., Neptune, Mattison Oper. Co., Neptune, Summerfield Oper. Co., Neptune; speaker Am. Press Inst. Bd. dirs. Monmouth County chpt. ARC, 1988—. Mem. Internat. Fin. Execs., Broadcast Fin. Mgmt. Assn. Office: Asbury Park Press 3601 Hwy 66 Neptune NJ 07753-2694

COLAO, RUDOLPH NICHOLAS, artist, educator; b. Peekskill, N.Y., Dec. 26, 1927; s. Rudolph Joseph and Marie Filomena (DeMaria) C.; m. Camila McRoberts, July 26, 1957 (div. 1986); children: William, Margaret, Marta. Student, Art Students League, N.Y.C., 1947-52. Instr. painting Art Students League of N.Y., N.Y.C., 1985-87, Scottsdale (Ariz.) Artists Sch., 1986, 87, 91. Exhbns. include Colao Gallery, Rockport, Mass., 1979-81, Harbor Gallery, Cold Spring Harbor, N.Y., 1970-86, Salmagundi Club, N.Y.C., 1982-84, Nat. Acad. Design, N.Y.C., 1985. With U.S. Army, 1946-47. Recipient Silver medal Rockport Art Assn., 1981, Gold medal of honor, 1985, Best Painter in any Medium, 1990. Mem. Artists Equity Assn. of N.Y., Allied Artists of Am. (John Young Hunter award 1984), Rockport Art Assn., Hudson Valley Art Assn. (Frank Dumond award 1982), Knickerbocker Artists of N.Y., Art Students League of N.Y. Home and Office: 15 W 67th St New York NY 10023-6226

COLARULLO, LOUIS ANTHONY, construction company executive; b. Bklyn., Oct. 21, 1948; s. Salvatore and Maria (Adipetro) C.; m. Adrianne Helene Talbot, Feb. 6, 1951. AAS, N.Y.C. Community Coll., 1977. With N.Y. Telephone Co., Bklyn., 1966-70; budget analyst Seagrams, N.Y.C., 1971-72; engr. Enrico & Sons Contracting Co., New Hyde Park, N.Y., 1972-80; project mgr. Enrico & Sons Contracting Co., New Hyde Park, 1981-84; pres. ALC Enterprises, Inc., Hauppauge, N.Y., 1982—, chmn., 1986—. Sgt. USMC, 1966-70, Vietnam. Mem. Am. Concrete Inst. Home and Office: 8 Bluff Cir Hauppauge NY 11788-3437

COLATRELLA, CAROL ANN, literature educator; b. Newark, Aug. 18, 1957; d. Peter Carmen Colatrella and Marie Rose (Juliano) Caulfield. BA, St. John's Coll., Annapolis, Md., 1979; MA in Comparative Lit., Rutgers U., 1983, PhD in Comparative Lit., 1987. Archival asst. Md. Hall of Records, Annapolis, 1979-80; reference asst. library Rutgers U., New Brunswick, N.J., 1982-86; lectr. Rutgers U., New Brunswick, 1983-86; asst. prof. Albany (N.Y.) Coll. Pharmacy, 1987-88; asst. prof. lit. Rensselaer Poly. Inst., Troy, N.Y., 1988—. N.J. Dept. Edn. scholar, 1975-79, fellow, 1979-83. Mem. MLA, Am. Comparative Lit. Assn., Northeast MLA, Soc. for Lit. and Sci. (chmn. pub. com. 1989—), Pine Hills Neighborhood Assn. Democrat. Roman Catholic. Home: 47 S Allen St Albany NY 12208-2203 Office: Rensselaer Poly Inst Dept Lang Lit & Communicati Troy NY 12180

COLAW, THOMAS ALLAN, real estate executive, consultant; b. Kansas City, Mo., Sept. 1, 1939; s. John Allan and Frances Mae (Thomas) C.; divorced; 1 child, Christopher Allan; m. Polly Patricia McGinniss, July 2, 1988. Student, Mich. Coll. Mining and Tech., 1957-58; BSBA, Kans. State U., 1962. Lic. real estate broker, Tex. Sales rep. Container Corp. Am., Arlington, Tex., 1965-67; sales mgr. Nat. Homes Corp., Tyler, Tex., 1967-71; project mgr. Mid-Continent Devel. Corp., Dallas, 1971-72, Blaylock Devel. Co., Dallas, 1974-75; mktg. dir. Advanced Property Rsch., Inc., Dallas, 1972-74; dir. real estate Church's Fried Chicken, Inc., San Antonio, 1975-83; comml. loan mgr. Gill Savs. & Loan, San Antonio, 1983-85; cons. San Antonio, 1985-86; dir. devel. systems Marriott Corp., Washington, 1986-90; pres. Thomas A. Colaw & Assocs. Real Estate Demographics Cons., Bethesda, 1990—; guest lectr. St. Mary's U., San Antonio, 1977-82; speaker Am. Mktg. Assn., San Antonio, 1977; mem. product design adv. com. Nat. Decisions Systems, Inc., 1989—; profl. musician, Kansas City and Las Vegas, 1954-85. 1st lt. USAF, 1962-65. Mem. Nat. Assn. Corp. Real Estate Execs. (restaurant coun., pres. 1989-91, Outstanding Achievement award 1980), Internat. Coun. Shopping Ctrs., Smithsonian Assocs., Nat. Assn. Eagle Scouts. Republican. Presbyterian. Home and Office: 15618 Moon Dust Dr Dallas TX 75248

COLBECK, SAMUEL CHARLES, geophysicist, educator, consultant; b. Pitts., Oct. 31, 1940; s. Samuel Charles and Edith (McManis) C.; m. Margaret Arnold, Dec. 28, 1969 (div. Aug. 1984); children: Eric, Craig, David; m. Muriel Magee, June 15, 1991. BS, U. Pitts., 1962, MS, 1965; PhD, U. Wash., 1970. Rsch. geophysicist U.S. Army Cold Regions Rsch. and Engring. Lab., Hanover, N.H., 1970—; adj. prof. Dartmouth Coll., Hanover, 1973—; cons. Am. Electric Power, Duke Power, 1973-83; expert witness snow and ice problems and skier injury suits, 1978—. Editor 5 tech. jours., also books and procs.; contbr. articles to profl. jours. Mem. various coms. Nat. Acad. Sci./Nat. Rsch. Coun., 1974-90. Fellow Am. Geophys. Union (various coms., Horton award 1980); mem. Internat. Glaciological Soc. (v.p. 1984-87, pres. 1987-90), Electromagnetic Acad., Am. Assn. Avalanche Profls. (Eastern rep. 1990—). Home: RR 2 Box 29 Norwich VT 05055-9709 Office: USA CRREL 72 Lyme Rd Hanover NH 03755-1290

COLBERT, DOUGLAS MARC, lawyer; b. N.Y.C., Feb. 8, 1948; s. Leonard M. and Estelle (Ginsberg) C.; m. Amy Jo Guryan, May 1, 1976 (div. 1977); m. Angel Mendez, Dec. 28, 1986. Student, Hunter Coll., N.Y.C., 1964-67; BBA cum laude, Bernard Baruch Coll., N.Y.C., 1969; JD, Bklyn. Law Sch., 1972. Bar: N.Y. 1974. Honor law intern N.Y. County Dist. Atty., N.Y.C., 1971; law asst. N.Y.C. Corp. Counsel, 1972-74; arbitrator N.Y.C. Civil Ct., 1979—; atty. Hauser & Rosenbaum Esq., N.Y.C., 1974-76; pvt. practice law N.Y.C., 1974—. Vol. atty. Vol. Lawyers for the Arts, N.Y.C., 1979-85; spl. investigator N.Y. State Bd. Elections, N.Y.C., 1981-84. Mem. N.Y. County Lawyers Assn., USCG Aux., Moot Ct., Sigma Alpha Mu (founder). Office: 350 5th Ave New York NY 10118-0110

COLBOURN, ANDREA MARIA, communications studies-management theory educator; b. Bklyn., May 6; d. Andrew Anthony and Margaret Catherine (Pirrone) Pilato; m. Frank E. Colbourn, May 29, 1981. BA, Pace U., 1977; MA, NYU, 1978, PhD, 1988. Lectr., instr. C.W. Post Coll., L.I. U., 1978-79; instr. communication studies and mgmt. theory Pace U., N.Y.C., 1978-85, asst. prof., 1986—, organizer, faculty advisor mass media course press conf., 1985, coach, judge, advisor speech intramurals, 1979-89; exec. v.p. Colbourn Communication Cons., Inc., 1981—; critic judge, speaker Downtown Athletic Club Speaker's Assn., N.Y.C., 1979-81; faculty advisor Toastmasters Internat., 1983-88. Assoc. editor Trans. of Soc. Fellows of Dyson Coll., 1989—; dir. Reader's Theatre, "A Christmas Tale", 1980. Recipient Debate award Pace U., 1977, 10th Rank Speaking Recognition Debate, Columbia U., 1976. Fellow Dyson Soc.; mem. Internat. Soc. Gen. Semantics, Speech Communications Assn.; Women's Studies Orgn. (advisor 1989—), Pace U. Publ. Com. (chmn. 1988—). Home: O/D Harbour Green Estates 145 Cedar Shore Dr Massapequa NY 11758-8133 Office: Pace U 1 Pace Plz New York NY 10038

COLBY, GEORGE VINCENT, JR., electrical engineer; b. Montpelier, Vt., Sept. 4, 1931; s. George Vincent and Clara Pauline (Tebbetts) C.; m. Barbara Ann Gardner, Sept. 5, 1955; children: George V. III, Ann G. Colby Cummings, Catherine M. Colby Fielding. BEE, MEE, MIT, 1954. Tech. staff engr. Gen. Electric Co., West Lynn, Mass., 1954-55; mgr. radar lab. L.F.E. Corp., Waltham, Mass., 1957-70; staff mem. MIT Lincoln Lab., Lexington, Mass., 1970-80; dep. dir. Textron Def. Systems, Everett, Mass., 1980—. Treas. troop 159 Boy Scouts Am., Lexington, 1970-76; dir. teen mass St. Brigid's Ch., Lexington, 1974-81. 1st lt. U.S. Army, 1955-57. Mem. IEEE (sr.). Roman Catholic. Home: 7 Hawthorne Rd Lexington MA 02173-1731 Office: Textron Def Systems 210 Lowell St Wilmington MA 01887

COLCHADO, EDMUNDO MOISES, JR., policy analyst; b. San Benito, Tex., Jan. 18, 1954; s. Edmundo Moises Colchado Sr. and Aurora Theresa (Leal) Nunez. BS, U.S. Mil. Acad., 1976; MS in Telecommunications-Computing Mgmt., Poly. U., 1986. Commd. 2d lt. U.S. Army, 1976, advanced through grades to capt., resigned, 1981; mgr. N.Y. Telephone, N.Y.C., 1981-87; regional ops. mgr. LIGHTNET, N.Y.C., 1988-89; pvt. practice telecommunications cons. Weehawken, N.J., 1989-90; telecommunications policy analyst N.Y. State Dept. Pub. Svc., Albany, 1990—; mem., chair subcom. N.Y.C. Mayor's Task Force on Network Reliability, 1990-91. Admissions rep. U.S. Mil. Acad., Albany, 1981; bd. dirs., program chmn. West Point Soc. of the Capitol Dist., Albany, 1990-93. Roman Catholic. Office: NY State Dept Pub Svc 3 Empire State Albany NY 12223-0999

COLCORD, HERBERT NATHANIEL, III, food company executive; b. Quincy, Mass., Mar. 21, 1951; s. Herbert Nathaniel Jr. and Audrey Louise (Gunn) C.; m. Deborah Sue O'Brien, Nov. 8, 1975; children: Heather Michele, Jared Scott, Devon Elizabeth. BA in Journalism (cum laude), Northeastern U., 1973; MA in Journalism, U. Mo., 1975. Accredited bus. communicator. Staff reporter The Patriot Ledger, Quincy, Mass., 1970-73, Columbia (Mo.) Daily Tribune, 1974-75; pub. affairs asst. Nat. Fire Protection Assn., Boston, 1975-77, mgr. editorial programs, 1977-79; mgr. pub. affairs Ocean Spray Cranberries, Inc., Plymouth, Mass., 1979-82, mgr. consumer affairs, 1982-89; mgr. mktg. communications Ocean Spray Cranberries, Inc., Lakeville, Mass., 1990—; bd. dirs. Plymouth County Devel. Coun., Pembroke, Mass., 1989-92; bd. dirs. Nat. Guest Rels. Assn., 1984-86, pres., 1984-85. Contbr. articles to profl. jours. Recipient Gold Quill award for Excellence Internat. Assn. Bus. Communicators, 1983, Writing Excellence award Coop. Communicators Assn., 1980-81, Writing Excellence award Nat. Coun. Farmer Coop., 1981-82; named to Kappa Tau Alpha, 1975. Mem. Internat. Assn. Bus. Communicators, Coop. Communicators Assn., Advt. Club Greater Boston. Home: 322 Nichols Dr Taunton MA 02780-4373 Office: Ocean Spray Cranberries Inc One Ocean Spray Dr Lakeville MA 02349

COLDWELL, PETER REID, volunteer organization executive; b. Clinton, Mass., Sept. 27, 1945; s. Robert Bassett and Barbara Wyman (Fitton) C.; m. Penelope Lee Taylor, June 18, 1977; children: Emma, Morgan. BA in Psychology, Am. Univ., Washington, 1967. Salesman Coldwell's Inc., Berlin, Mass., 1973-80; exec. dir. Vols. For Peace, Inc., Belmont, Vt., 1980—. Editor: International Workcamp Director (annual), Annual Internat. Workcamper newsletter, 1981—. Coord. Nuclear Weapons Freeze Campaign, Rutland County, Vt., 1982. Mem. Coordinating Com. for Internat. Voluntary Svc. UNESCO (exec. com. 1990—). Home and Office: Vols For Peace 43 Tiffany Rd Belmont VT 05730

COLE, CHARLES NORMAN, molecular biologist; b. N.Y.C., Oct. 28, 1946; s. Charles Norman Cole and Betty Jane (Heldman) Weil; m. Liz Ryan, June 15, 1969; children: Noah, Ethan, Silas, Jonas. AB, Oberlin Coll., 1968; PhD, MIT, 1972. Instr. MIT, Cambridge, Mass., 1972-73; postdoctoral fellow Stanford (Calif.) U. Med. Ctr., 1974-77; asst. prof. human genetics Yale U. Med. Ctr., New Haven, 1977-83; assoc. prof. biochemistry Dartmouth Med. Sch., Hanover, N.H., 1983-88, prof. biochemistry, 1988—; cons. NIH, Bethesda, Md., 1981—, NSF, Washington, 1982—, Howard Hughes Med. Inst., Bethesda, 1985—. Mem. editorial bd. Jour. of Virology, 1986—; contbr. articles to profl. jours. Bd. sch. dirs. Town of Thetford, Vt., 1988—; v.p. Thetford Water Coop., 1984-88. Rsch. grantee NIH, 1977—, NSF, 1981-85. Mem. AAAS, Am. Soc. Microbiology, Am. Soc. for Virology. Jewish. Office: Dartmouth Coll Med Sch Dept Biochemistry Hanover NH 03755

COLE, DAVID CHARLES, museum curator; b. Providence, R.I., July 9, 1948; s. Charles Francis and Mabel Genevieve (Matteson) C.; m. Nancy Marion Dodge, June 27, 1970; children: Elizabeth Ellen, Charles Christopher. BS, Boston U., 1970. Curator First Corps of Cadets Mus., Boston, 1969-72; adminstrv. tech. Dept. Army Mass. Army Nat. Guard, Cambridge, 1973-74; pvt. practice mus. cons. Saratoga Springs, N.Y., 1974; dir. Fort George G. Meade (Md.) Mus., 1975-85; mus. curator Office of the Chief of Mil. History, Washington, 1985—; cons., tech. advisor various TV/Film Prodns., Washington, 1979—; lectr., speaker in field, Washington, 1979—. Contbr. articles to profl. jours. Maj. U.S. Army, 1990-91. Decorated medal Freedom Found., Valley Forge, Pa., 1973, Md. Meritorious Svc. medal Md. Army Nat. Guard, Annapolis, 1980, Commdrs. award for civil svc. U.S. Army, Washington, 1988, Bronze Star medal U.S. Army, Saudi Arabia, 1991. Fellow Co. Mil. Historians; mem. Nat. Guard Assn. of the U.S., Capital Area Mil. Mus. Assn. (com. on military), Mus. in Am. (treas. 1980-85). Office: HQDA Attn DAMH-MDC 1099 14th St NW Washington DC 20005-3402

COLE, EDWARD LOGAN, JR., leasing executive; b. N.Y.C., Feb. 9, 1953; s. Edward Logan and Ernestine (Davis) C.; m. Susan Brennan, May 24, 1975, 1 child, Edward Logan III. BSBA, Western Conn. State U., 1976. Ops. mgr. Aamco Transmissions, Inc., Bala Cynwyd, Pa., 1983-84; sr. ops. mgr. Aamco Transmissions, Inc., Bala Cynwyd, 1984-85, regional ops. mgr., 1985-87, dir. ops. adminstrn., 1987-88; dir. human resources Tokai Fin. Svcs., Inc., Berwyn, Pa., 1988-89; v.p. adminstrn. Tokai Fin. Svcs., Inc., Berwyn, 1989-90, v.p. ops., 1990-91, v.p. nat. sales mgr., 1991—. Mem. Conn. Assn. Pers. Cons. (dir. 1980-82, newsletter editor 1981-82). Republican. Episcopalian. Office: 214 Southside Cir Downingtown PA 19335

COLE, ELBERT LEE, JR., electrical engineer; b. Charleston, W.Va., Nov. 11, 1940; s. Elbert Lee and Janice Erle (McCoy) C.; m. Marilyn Elizabeth Hayes, Jan. 8, 1966; children: Sarah L., Suzanne P., Melanie A., Cynthia L. BSEE, Va. Inst. Tech., 1962; MSEE, Johns Hopkins U., 1974; postgrad., Stanford U., 1975-76. Assoc. engr. Westinghouse, Balt., 1962-63, various engring. positions, 1965-88, sr. adv. engr., 1988—; lectr. Johns Hopkins U., Balt., 1986—, Westinghouse Sch. Applied Sci., Balt., 1974-87; course developer Johns Hopkins U., Balt., 1985-86. Patentee in field. Mem. area staff Am. Field Svcs., Balt., 1988-91; pres. Catonsville (Md.) Jr. High PTA, 1987. 1st lt. U.S. Army, 1963-65. B.G. Lamme fellow Westinghouse, 1975. Mem. IEEE. Republican. Baptist. Office: Westinghouse Electric Corp PO Box 18996 Baltimore MD 21206-0096

COLE, ELMA PHILLIPSON (MRS. JOHN STRICKLER COLE), social welfare executive; b. Piqua, Ohio, Aug. 9, 1909; d. Brice Leroy and Mabel (Gale) Phillipson; m. John Strickler Cole, Oct. 3, 1959. AB, Berea Coll., 1930; MA, U. Chgo., 1938. Various positions in social work, 1930-42; dir. dept. social svc. Children's Hosp. D.C., Washington, 1942-49; cons. pub. coop. Midcentury White House Conf. on Children and Youth, Washington, 1949-51; exec. sec. Nat. Midcentury Com. on Children and Youth, N.Y.C., 1951-53; cons. recruitment Am. Assn. Med. Social Workers, 1953; assoc. dir. Nat. Legal Aid and Defender Assn., 1953-56; exec. sec. Marshall Field Awards, Inc., 1956-57; dir. assoc. orgns. Nat. Assembly Social Policy and Devel., 1957-73; assoc. exec. dir. Nat. Assembly Nat. Vol. Health and Social Welfare Orgns., 1974; dir. edn. parenthood project Salvation Army, 1974-76, asst. sec. dept. women's and children's social svcs., 1976-78, dir. rsch. project devel. bur., 1978-92; mem. Manhattan adv. bd., 1975—, sec., 1984—, mem. hist. commn., 1978—, mem. exec. com., 1988—; cons. nat. orgns. Golden Anniversary White House Conf. on Children and Youth, 1959-60; mem. adv. coun. pub. svc. Nat. Assn. Life Underwriters & Inst. Life Ins.; mem. judges com. Louis I. Dublin Pub. Svc. awards, 1961-74; v.p. Blue Ridge Inst. So. Community Svc. Execs., 1977-79, mem. exec. com., 1979-81; mem. awards jury Girls Clubs of Am., 1981—; mem. adv. bd. Nat. Family Life Edn. Network, 1982—. Mem. com. pub. rels. and fund raising Am. Found. for Blind Commn. on Accreditation, 1964-67; mem. task force on vol. accreditation Coun. Nat. Orgns. for Adult Edn., 1974-78; mem. adv. bd. sexuality edn. project Ctr. for Population Options, 1977-86; sec., bd. dirs. James Lenox House and James Lenox House Assn., 1985-89, pres., 1989—; bd. dirs. Values and Human Sexuality Inst., 1980-85. Mem. Pub. Rels. Soc. Am. (cert.), Nat. Assn. Social Workers (cert.), Nat. Conf. Social Welfare (mem. pub. rels. com. 1961-66, 69-82, chair adminstrn. sect. 1966-67), Jr. League N.Y., Women's Club of N.Y., Pi Gamma Mu, Phi Kappa Phi. Home: 19 Washington Sq N New York NY 10011-9170

COLE, ERNEST GEORGE, human services executive, consultant; b. Newark, Dec. 29, 1940; s. George William Jr. and Grace Naomi (Raymond) C.; m. Noël May Wetzel, Aug. 27, 1961; children: Jennifer Noël, Amy Lin. BA, Montclair State Coll., 1972; MEd, William Paterson Coll., 1978; EdD, Rutgers U., 1984. Cert. sch. adminstr., prin., supr., tchr. of spl. edn. and vocat. edn., handicapped, indsl. arts, skilled trades, N.J. Spl. edn., vocat. tchr. Caldwell-West Caldwell (N.J.) Bd. Edn., 1972-75, Morris County Vocat. Sch., Denville, N.J., 1975-76; coord. vocat. programs for the handicapped Roselle (N.J.) Bd. Edn., 1976-80; supr. vocat. svcs. for the disadvantaged N.J. State Dept. of Edn., Trenton, 1980-83, edn. program specialist, 1983-86; dir. programs The Matheny Sch./ Hosp., Peapack, N.J., 1986-90.; exec. dir. Cerebral Palsy League of Union (N.J.) County, 1990—; cons. Community Coll. Morris, 1988, Montclair State Coll., 1971, 73, 79-80, Essex County Ednl. Svcs., 1979, others. Contbr. numerous articles to profl. jours. Recipient Excellence in Edn. Communications award Nat. Assn. State Edn. Dept. Info. Officers, 1984. Mem. Am. Vocat. Assn., Nat. Assn. Vocat. Edn. Spl. Needs Pers. (treas. N.J. chpt. 1981-83, v.p. 1983-84, pres. 1984-85), Nat. Assn. Spl. Needs State Adminstrs., Vocat. Assn. N.J., Masons (trustee Mountain View Lodge 1981-83, Worshipful master 1979-80, jr. warden 1977, sr. warden 1978, proxy to grandlodge 1976), North Jersey Past Mastoers Masonic Assn., Epsilon Pi Tau (treas. 1971-72, recipient Epsilon Pi Tau Fellowship award for rsch. devel., 1978), Omicron Tau Theta, Kappa Delta Pi. Home: 80 Woodvine Ave Trenton NJ 08610-1936 Office: Cerebral Palsy League of Union County 373 Clermont Ter Union NJ 07083-8028

COLE, HAROLD SAMUEL, health facility administrator, physician; b. Bklyn., Apr. 20, 1916; s. Morris and Celia (Lilienfeld) C. BS, U. Md., 1937;

postgrad., Princeton U., 1938; MD, NYU, 1942; postgrad., N.Y. Med. Coll., 1947-48. Intern New Rochelle (N.Y.) Hosp., 1942-43; resident Willard Parker Hosp., N.Y.C., 1946, Met. Hosp., 1947; pvt. practice in pediatrics Rutherford, N.J., 1948-65; prof. pediatrics N.Y. Med. Coll., N.Y.C., 1965-80, emeritus prof. pediatrics/community and preventive medicine, 1980—; med. dir. Flower-Fifth Ave. Hosp., N.Y.C., 1978-80, Bronx (N.Y.) Devel. Ctr., 1983—. Co-editor: Early Diabetes, 1972, Early Diabetes in Early Life, 1973, Vascular and Neurological Changes in Early Diabetes, 1973, Prediabetes, 1989. Capt. U.S. Army, 1943-46, PTO. Fellow Am. Acad. Pediatrics; mem. Am. Diabetes, Am. Pediatric Soc., Lawson Wilitins Pediatric Endocrine Soc. Home: 185 E 85th St New York NY 10028-2140 Office: Bronx Devel Ctr 1200 Waters Pl Bronx NY 10461-2798

COLE, JACK ELI, physician; b. Matamoras, Pa., Jan. 7, 1915; s. Eli Martin and Louise (Henneberg) C. m. Evelyn Gaston Darragh, Apr. 26, 1941; children: Jack Eli, Thomas, Beverly, Martin, Robert, Leslie, Christopher, Candace, Champa. BS, Pa. State U., 1937; MD, U. Pa., 1941. Diplomate Am. Bd. Family Practice. Intern Wilkes-Barre (Pa.) Gen. Hosp., 1941-42; practice medicine, specializing in family practice Matamoras, Pa., 1946-47; staff St. Luke's Hosp., Bethlehem, Pa., 1948—; practice medicine, specializing in family practice Bethlehem, 1952-68, 1973-89; sec. dept. family practice St. Luke's Hosp., Bethlehem, 1973-88; incorporator, mem. med. staff Muhlenberg Hosp., Bethlehem, 1960—; pres. med. staff St. Luke's Hosp., Bethlehem, 1961-62; student health physician Lehigh U., Bethlehem, 1948-52; physician Peace Corps, Afghanistan, Swaziland, India, 1968-73; leader mission med. team United Ch. Christ, Honduras, 1987; preceptor Temple U. Med. Sch., Phila., 1978-86. Charter mem. mission partnership com. N.E. Pa. conf. United Ch. of Christ, 1984. With U.S. Army, 1942-45. Decorated Purple Heart, Combat Medic badge; recipient Recognition award Temple U. Med. Sch., 1979; Boss of Yr. award Allentown Bus. Womens Assn., 1975. Fellow Am. Acad. Family Physicians; mem. Northampton County Med. Soc., Pa. Med. Soc., Lehigh Valley Acad. Family Physicians (v.p. 1979-81, pres. 1981-83), Pa. Acad. Family Physicians, Am. Acad. Family Physicians, Met. Opera Guild, Masons. Republican. Home: 782 Barrymore Ln Bethlehem PA 18017-2522

COLE, JEANETTE LINDA, artist; b. Lincoln, Nebr., Mar. 29, 1952; d. Paul Otto and Lydia Johanna (Fenske) Spehr; m. John Russell Cole, June 23, 1973 (div. 1981); m. William A. Childress, Apr. 29, 1983. BFA in Edn. with distinction, U. Nebr., 1973; MFA, Tex. Tech U., 1979. Vis. asst. prof. Murray (Ky.) State U., 1980-81, St. Lawrence U., Canton, N.Y., 1981-82; adj. asst. prof. Franklin & Marshall Coll., Lancaster, Pa., 1983-88; asst. prof. U. Mass., Amherst, 1989—; juror Art Ctr. Assn., Louisville, 1981, Ky. Art Coun., Frankfort, 1983, Francis Hook Scholarship, Mpls., 1990. One-person shows include John Gibson Gallery, N.Y.C., 1984, 85, 2d St. Gallery, Charlottesville, Va., 1991; exhibited in group show at Frumkin/Adams Gallery, N.Y.C., 1988. Faculty rsch. grantee U. Mass., 1990, 91; recipient Hon. Mention prize Va. Commn. on Arts, 1989. Mem. Archeol. Soc. Va. Home: PO Box 124 New York NY 10013-0124 Office: U Mass Art Dept Fine Arts Ctr Amherst MA 01003

COLE, LAURENCE ANTHONY, reproductive biology and cancer biology educator; b. Bournemouth, Eng., Feb. 8, 1953; came to U.S., 1977; s. Leonard Lewis and Estella (Pinkus) C.; m. Linda Sue Friedman, Mar. 30, 1977; children: Anna Eva, Daniel Levi. PhD in Biochemistry, Med. Coll. Wis., 1982. Postdoctoral fellow U. Mich., Ann Arbor, 1982-83, asst. rsch. scientist, 1983-85; prof. reproductive cancer biology Yale U., New Haven, 1986—. Contbr. over 50 articles to profl. jours. Nat. Cancer Inst. grantee, 1986—. Mem. Endocrine Soc., Am. Fedn. Clin. Rsch., Internat. Trophoblast Disease Soc. Democrat. Jewish. Office: Yale U Sch Medicine 333 Cedar St New Haven CT 06510-3289

COLE, LEON MONROE, government executive; b. Dallas, Apr. 4, 1933; s. Kenneth McCutchen and Cacy Ann (Robbins) C.; m. Jeannie Campbell Tudor, Apr. 1, 1961; children: Kenneth Tudor, Kevin Robbins, Susanna Ellis. BSCE magna cum laude, So. Meth. U., 1955; MSE, U. Wash., 1961; MCP, Harvard U., 1963, PhD, 1965. Asst. prof. planning and transp. Harvard U., 1965-67, assoc. prof., 1967-69; staff dir. U.S. Dept. HUD, Washington, 1967-68, div. dir., 1968-69; prof., dir. grad. program U. Tex., Austin, 1969-73; sr. specialist transp. Congl. Rsch. Svc. Libr. Congress, Washington, 1973-75, chief econs. div., 1975—; chmn. group I coun. NAS, NRC, Transp. Rsch. Bd., Washington, 1978-81, chmn. various coms. on transp. policy and rsch., 1970-85. Co-author, editor: Tomorrow's Transportation: New Systems for the Urban Future, 1969, Economic Policymaking in U.S. Government, 1988, Transportation in the United States: Perspectives on Federal Policies, 1989; contbr. chpts. to books and articles to profl. jours. Commr. Tex. State Urban Devel. Commn., Austin, 1970-72; chmn. Austin City Bd. Environ. Quality, 1972-73. Served to capt. with USNR, 1956-60. Recipient Meritorious Achievement award HUD, 1969; Spl. Resolution of Commendation City of Austin, 1974; Resident fellow Harvard U., 1962-64. Mem. ASCE, Am. Econ. Assn., Am. Inst. Cert. Planners, Am. Planning Assn., Edgemoor Club, Sigma Xi, Chi Epsilon, Sigma Tau. Democrat. Home: 7401 Fairfax Rd Bethesda MD 20814-1240

COLE, ROBERT CARLTON, English and journalism educator; b. Beaver, W.Va., June 2, 1937; s. Carlton Enfield and Naomi Ruth (Bowman) C.; children: Cathryn Alisa, Alan Robert; m. Nancy Elaine Knight, Mar. 14, 1973; children: Robin Matthew, Timothy Carlton. AB, Marshall U., 1959; MA, Wake Forest U., 1964; PhD, Lehigh U., 1971. Reporter Herald-Dispatch, Huntington, W.Va., 1957-59; reporter, columnist Jour. and Sentinel, Winston-Salem, N.C., 1959-64; from asst. to assoc. dir. of pubs. Lehigh U., Bethlehem, Pa., 1964-72; asst. prof. English Lehigh U., 1972-73, Trenton State Coll., Trenton, N.J., 1973-83; assoc. prof. English and journalism Trenton State Coll., 1983-91, prof. English, 1991—; cons. Edison State Coll., Trenton, 1985; dir. Dow Jones Newspaper fund N.J. Copyediting Intern Prog., Trenton, 1989; speaker N.J. Press Assn., AP Mng. Editors, Am. Soc. Newspaper Editors, 1980—. Contbr. articles to profl. jours. Mem. Planning Commn., Yardley, Pa., 1974-76; dir. social concerns Wesley United Meth. Ch., Bethlehem, Pa., 1969-71. Recipient nat. teaching award in journalism Am. Soc. Newspaper Editors and Poynter Inst. for Media Studies, 1984, 86; John Ben Snow fellow Am. Press Inst., 1983, 90. Mem. Am. Fedn. Teachers, N.J. Press Assn., Sigma Delta Chi. Democrat. Home: 198 S Canal St Morrisville PA 19067-1702 Office: Trenton State Coll Trenton NJ 08650

COLEMAN, ARLENE HAMLETT, reading consultant, freelance writer; b. Newark, Apr. 17, 1946; d. Edwin and Helen Hamlett; BA in Elem. Edn., William Paterson Coll., 1967; MS in Reading, Queens CUNY, 1977; m. Gregory D. Coleman, Jr.; children: Candice Arlene, Naniette Helene, Aaron Gregory. Elem. sch. tchr., East Orange, N.J., 1967-70; Fulbright-Hays exchange tchr., Halifax, N.S., Can., 1970-71; lang. arts tchr., East Orange, 1971-72; sch. svc. rep./cons. Westinghouse Learning Corp., N.Y.C., 1972-73; reading, writing specialist Westbury Pub. Sch. Dist. (N.Y.); talk show host, producer That's Interesting, Sta. WCWP, 1981-83; mem. editorial bd., asst. editor L.I. Courier, 1989-90. Pvt. reading cons., writer, Westbury, 1977—; instr. Adelphi U., 1980; adj. prof. SUNY Coll., Old Westbury, 1980-84, Molloy Coll., 1992—; evaluator Commn. Higher Edn., Middle States Assn. Colls. and Schs. V.p. Westbury chpt. LWV, 1979-80, membership/conf. dir., 1978-79, program dir., 1980-81, v.p. 1990-91; mem. membership com. Soc. Gifted and Talented Children, 1979-80; mem. Greater Westbury Coalition, Greater Westbury Arts Coun., Sherwood Civic Assn.; legis. chmn. Cen. Nassau chpt. Jack and Jill Club Am., 1983—, v.p., 1989-91, Jumoke Chairperson, 1990-92; bd. dirs. Nassau County Coun. Girl Scouts U.S., 1985-86; bd. dirs. Day Care Coun. Nassau County, 1981-83; mem. arts coun. Westbury Pub. Libr., 1982—; mem. gifted and talented com. Westbury Schs., 1978-79; trustee Westbury Libr. System; v.p. Westbury PTA Council. Recipient Woman of Yr. award Zeta Phi Beta, 1984; Westbury Sch. Improvement Council grantee, 1986. Mem. AAUW (dir., chairperson creative writing group, N.Y. state award for Excellence and Equity in Edn., 1987, membership com. N.Y. state div. , wide trainer, L.I. tng. coord. 1989-90, Intercounty Tchr. Resource Ctr. grantee 1989-90), Nat. Assn. Negro Bus. and Profl. Women's Clubs (dir. Westbury 1979-81, UN com., chpt. Pres.'s award 1980), Internat. Reading Assn., Internat. Women Writers Group, Soc. Children's Book Writers, Soc. Gifted and Talented Children (v.p. 1982-83), Nassau Reading Council, Nat. Writers Club, N.Y. State Reading Assn., Nat. Assn. Negro Bus. and Profl. Women's Clubs, Assn. Black Women in Higher Edn., Phi Delta Kappa, Kappa Delta Pi, Delta Sigma Theta (Nassau alumni chpt. exec. bd. corr. sec. 1987-88). Methodist. Author: (poetry) U.S. in Clover '76, 1976, The Clover Collection of Verse, 1975, Respite, A Days Work, Jubilee, Ebony Pearl, 1988; (plays) The Organ Grinder, 1982, We Are All America, 1985 (World of Poetry Gold Poet award 1989). Home and Office: 813 Eastfield Rd Westbury NY 11590-1429

COLEMAN, CY, pianist, composer, producer; b. N.Y.C.; s. Max and Ida (Prizent) Kaufman. Began playing piano at age four, classically trained pianist; grad., High Sch. of Music and Art; diploma, N.Y. Coll. Music, 1948; pupil, Rudolph Gruen, Adele Marcus, Bernard Wagenaar, Hall Overton. Pres. Notable Music Co., Notable Records Co. Began performing publicly at age six in N.Y.C.; pianist night clubs throughout U.S., 1948—; TV appearances on Dumont, 1947-48, Date in Manhattan, 1948-51, Kate Smith Show, 1951-52, Art Ford Greenwich Village Party, 1957-58; contbr. John Murray Anderson's Almanac, 1953; provided background music to Compulsion, 1957; appearances with Milw. Symphony Orch., Syracuse (N.Y.) Symphony Pops Orch., Detroit Symphony Orch., Indpls. Symphony Orch., San Antonio Symphony Orch., Ft. Worth, Edmonton (Can.), New Orleans, Toledo, Tulsa, Hartford Pops, Grand Rapids, Honolulu, Middletown and Spokane symphony orchs.; composer music for Broadway shows Wildcat, 1960, Little Me, 1962, Sweet Charity, 1963, also revival, 1986, See-Saw, 1973, I Love My Wife, 1977, On the Twentieth Century, 1978 (Tony award Best Original Score 1978), Barnum, 1980, City of Angels, 1989 (Tony award for Best Original Musical Score, 1990), Welcome to the Club 1989, The Will Rogers Follies, 1991 (Tony award for Best Score, 1991, Grammy award for Best Mus. Show Album, 1992, Grammy award for Record Producer and Composer, 1992), also lyrics; for motion pictures Heartbreak Kid, Sweet Charity, 1969, Power, 1986; rec. artist for Westminster, Capitol, Columbia, M.G.M., London records, (recipient Interborough awards Music Edn. League 1934, 35, 36, LaGuardia Meml. award 1961, 2 Emmy awards for TV spl. If They Could See Me Now 1974, Emmy award for Gypsy in My Soul 1975, Drama Desk award for best score I Love My Wife 1977, Cue mag. Golden Apple award for best score I Love My Wife 1977, Tony award Best Score for On the Twentieth Century 1977-78, for City of Angels, 1990); composer popular songs Why Try to Change Me Now, 1952, I'm Gonna Laugh You Out of My Life, 1955, Witchcraft, 1957, Firefly, 1958, It Amazes Me, 1958, You Fascinate Me So, 1958, The Best is Yet to Come, 1959, The Riviera, 1959, Play Boy Theme, 1960, Rules of the Road, 1961, Pass Me By, Pussy Cat, Hey Look Me Over, Big Spender, If My Friends Could See Me Now, Nobody Does It Like Me, I Love My Wife, Hey There Good Times. Mem. ASCAP (dir.), Acad. Motion Picture Arts and Scis., Dramatists Guild (dir.). Office: C C Enterprises 161 W 54th St New York NY 10019-5322

COLEMAN, DAVID CECIL, financial executive; b. Topeka, Sept. 7, 1937; s. Merrill Orda and Cecil Jennie (Warders) C. BS in Fin., Kans. U., 1959; PhD in Bus. Adminstrn., Calif. Western U., 1979. Registered investment advisor. Cost acct. Am. Electronics, Inc., Orange, Calif., 1963-65; fin. mgr. Univ. Calif. San Diego, La Jolla, 1965-67; v.p. fin. Aero Titanium Products, San Diego, 1967-69; contr. Gen. Tire, Tustin, Calif., 1969-70; fin. mgr. Hughes Aircraft, El Segundo, Calif., 1970-76; proprietor Concept Pub., York, N.Y., 1976—; realtor assoc. Mitchell Pierson Jr., Realtor, Mendon, N.Y., 1980—; instr. MBA prog. Rochester (N.Y.) Inst., 1982-86. Author: Management of the Firm, 1977, For the Long Term Investor, 1979, Consistency in Market Forecasting, 1982, How to Collect Bad Checks, 1989, Tax Tricks for the Proprietor, 1990. Fin. mgr. York (N.Y.) Hist. Soc., 1988. 1st Lt. USMC, 1959-63. Home: 2706 York Rd E York NY 14592-0500 Office: Concept Pub 2702 York Rd E York NY 14592-0500

COLEMAN, DAVID DENNIS, II, theater educator; b. Boston, Nov. 18, 1957; s. George Washington Smith and Sallie Lee Coleman; m. Marie Edith Elder, Oct. 11, 1986; children: David Dennis III, Brandon Nathaniel. BA, Boston Coll., 1979; MEd, Boston U., 1982; C.A.G.S., Harvard U., 1984; postgrad., Boston U. Cert. secondary tchr., speech tchr., spl. edn. tchr., Mass. Teaching intern Mass. Hosp. Sch. for Handicapped Children; studio technician Sta. WGBH-TV, Boston, 1982; assoc. prof. communications Bunker Hill Community Coll., Boston, 1985-87; chmn. dept. humanities, assoc. prof. theater Roxbury Community Coll., Boston, 1987—; instr. photography Digital Equipment Corp., Andover, Mass., 1985; asst. prof. English and lit., Roxbury Community Coll., 1982-85; tech. dir. Black Folks Theater Co., Boston, 1988—; adviser Roxbury Outreach Shakespeare Experience, Boston, 1988—; researcher sta. WGBH-FM, 1981; camera man TV show 10 O'Clock News, 1982; stage mgr. TV show Front Line, 1982, Masterpiece Theatre Mystery, 1982. Appeared in plays including Lookin' for an Echo, 1987, Macbeth, 1989; tech. dir. play Zooman and the Sign, 1988; writer, dir. play Words of Resistance, 1988. Instr. photography Hawthorne Youth Ctr., Boston; cinematographer Ops. Crossroads Africa; group leader, constrn. worker Assn. of Ghana. Mem. Performers Ensemble, Mass. Tchrs. Assn., Internat. Brotherhood Elec. Workers, Greater Boston Pan-Hellenic Coun. (v.p.), Phi Beta Sigma (state dir. 1982, area dir. 1983). Home: 11 Oak Ter Malden MA 02148-1109 Office: Roxbury Community Coll 1234 Columbus Ave Roxbury MA 02120-3400

COLEMAN, DAVID EDWARD, architect; b. N.Y.C., Sept. 20, 1956; s. John F. and Barbara E. (Riewold) C. BFA, R.I. Sch. Design, 1978, BArch, 1979; Grad. Dipl., Royal Danish Acad. Fine Arts, Copenhagen, 1980-82. Registered architect Vt. Designer/draftsman Davis Brody & Assocs., N.Y.C., 1979; planner H.P. Hoffman & Assocs., N.Y.C., 1979-80; project designer/planner Circus Studios, Waitsfield, Vt., 1981-83; project architect Michael Graves, Architect, Princeton, N.J., 1984-85; prin. David Coleman Arch., Burlington, Vt., 1986—. Contbr. articles to profl. jours. Mem. Waterfront Bd., City of Burlington, 1989—. Design Arts fellow Vt. Coun. on the Arts, 1984-85; recipient Design awards Home Bldrs. Assn. Vt., 1986, 90, Art award Am. Internat. Women's Club, Denmark, 1981, 82, Design award Govt. of the European Communities, 1982; Royal Danish Acad. Fine Arts scholar, 1980-82. Office: David Coleman Arch 9 Marble Ave Burlington VT 05401-4732

COLEMAN, DENIS PATRICK, JR., investment banker; b. N.Y.C., Jan. 6, 1946; s. Denis Patrick and Muriel (Clark) C.; m. Annabelle Giellerup, Sept. 15, 1972; children: Denis P. III, Nicholas A., Timothy W., Matthew T. BSBA, Georgetown U., 1967. Former exec. v.p. Bear Stearns Cos. Inc., N.Y.C., from 1967; now vice chmn. Discount Corp. N.Y., N.Y.C. Bd. dirs. Covenant House, N.Y.C., Canterbury Sch., New Milford, Conn. Mem. Mcpl. Bond Club N.Y., Bond Club N.Y. Roman Catholic. Home: PO Box 1328 Southampton NY 11969-1328 Office: Discount Corp NY 58 Pine St New York NY 10005-1519*

COLEMAN, JANE DWIGHT DEXTER, communications executive; b. Boston, Aug. 24, 1942; d. Franklin and Mianne (Palfrey) Dexter; m. Peter S. Coleman, Aug. 18, 1969; 1 child, Dan C. AB, Barnard Coll., 1965; MPhil, PhD, Columbia U., 1976. Adj. lectr. Hunter Coll., 1974-75; mgr. program analysis CBS Broadcast Group, 1976-77, dir. program analysis, east, 1977-80; mgr. Sta. WINS, N.Y.C., 1980-81; v.p., gen. mgr. Sta. WIND, Chgo., 1981; pres. Oberland Prodns., N.Y.C., 1982-84, 87—; assoc. dir. adminstrn. Gannett Ctr. for Media Studies (name now Gannett Found. Media Ctr.), 1985—. Mem. Nat. Acad. TV Arts and Scis., Internat. Radio and TV Soc. Office: Columbia U Gannett Found Media Ctr 2950 Broadway New York NY 10027-7004

COLEMAN, JOHN JERPEL (MIKE COLEMAN), manufacturing executive; b. Altoona, Pa., July 18, 1932; s. John Malcolm and Lena (Herpel) C.; m. Irma G. Hoover, Sept. 23, 1951; children: Donna Jean, Linda M. Coleman Tschoepe, Brenda Lee Coleman Scholtz, Brian E. BS in Bus., Pa. State U., 1959. Tool and die maker E.G. Budd Co., Phila., 1951-58; tool maker Insaco Inc, Quakertown, Pa., 1958-60, shop foreman, 1961-68, plant mgr., 1968—; cons. machining of ceramics and sapphire to numerous orgns.; instr. course on machining of ceramics and sapphire. Trustee Ch. of the Brethern, Ambler, 1955—; advisor, chmn. Upper Bucks Tech. Sch., 1968—. Mem. Soc. Mfg. Engring., Am. Ceramic Soc. Home: 905 Llanfair Rd Ambler PA 19002 Office: Insaco Inc PO Box 9006 Quakertown PA 18951

COLEMAN, JOHN JOSEPH, telephone company executive; b. Boston, Aug. 2, 1937; s. Martin Joseph and Anna Veronica (Leonard) C.; m. Carol Ann Holmes, May 6, 1961; children: Mark Christopher, Cara Romaine. BA cum laude, Boston Coll., 1964; postgrad., Harvard U., 1970. With New Eng. Telephone Co., 1955—; various supervisory positions plant, acctg., sales, mktg. New Eng. Telephone Co., Mass. and R.I.; now v.p. New Eng. Telephone Co., Boston; bd. dirs. Mchts. Nat. Bank, Manchester. Bd. dirs. United Way of Greater Manchester, chmn., 1980; chmn. Gov.'s Mgmt. Rev., 1981; chmn. fundraising campaign Manchester Crimeline, Inc., 1982; bd. dirs. Boston Mcpl. Rsch. Bur., 1984-86, Mass. Taxpayers Found. Inc., 1984-86; mem. New Spirit in Boston Com., 1984-85. With USN, 1956-58. Mem. Bus. and Industry Assn. of N.H. (dir.), N.H. Safety Coun. (adv. bd.), Am. Automobile Assn. Mass. (mem. adv. bd.), Greater Boston C. of C. (chmn. pub. safety com. 1985-86). Office: 745 Atlantic Ave Ste 500 Boston MA 02111-2735

COLEMAN, JOHN MICHAEL, lawyer, food products executive; b. Boston, Dec. 28, 1949; s. John Royston Coleman and Mary Norrington (Irwin) Murray; m. Susan Lee Lavine, Oct. 29, 1978; children: William L., Anne H. L. BA, Haverford (Pa.) Coll., 1975; JD, U. Chgo., 1978. Bar: N.Y. 1978, Pa. 1979, U.S. Ct. Appeals (3rd and 4th cirs.) 1979, U.S. Dist. Ct. (ea. dist.) Pa. 1979, U.S. Dist. Ct. (so. dist.) N.Y. 1981, U.S. Supreme Ct., 1982, N.J. 1988. Law clk. to judge U.S. Ct. Appeals, Richmond, Va., 1978-79; law clk. to chief justice Warren Burger U.S. Supreme Ct., Washington, 1980-81; assoc. Dechert Price & Rhoads, Phila., 1981-86, ptnr., 1986-89; v.p., gen. counsel Campbell Soup Co., Camden, N.J., 1989-90, sr. v.p. law and pub. affairs, corp. sec., 1990—; adj. prof. law U. Pa., Phila., 1985-88. Chmn. bd. trustees Campbell Soup Found., 1990—; trustee N.J. State Aquarium, 1991—, Food & Drug Law Inst., 1991—. Staff sgt. USAF, 1968-72, Vietnam. Mem. Order of Coif, Phi Beta Kappa. Mem. Soc. of Friends. Home: 840 Golf View Rd Moorestown NJ 08057-2027 Office: Campbell Soup Co Campbell Pl Camden NJ 08103-1702

COLEMAN, JOSEPH MICHAEL, transportation consultant; b. Washington, Mar. 6, 1945; s. Francis Thomas and Helen (Hile) C.; m. Dorothy Burke, Feb. 14, 1976; children: Caroline Dalton, Joseph Michael Jr., Elizabeth O'Keefe. BSBA, Georgetown U., 1971. Asst. to pres. Leaseway Transp. Corp., Cleve., 1971-73; pres. Leaseway Transp. Mktg. Corp., N.Y.C., 1973-77; v.p. Colorlab Corp., Rockville, Md., 1977-78; area dir. Hertz Corp., N.Y.C., 1978-82; nat. account exec. Hertz Penske Truck Leasing, Reading, Pa., 1982-86; v.p. Indsl. Fleet Mgmt., Towson, Md., 1986-88; pres. Friedman, Fuller & Coleman, Inc., Rockville, Md., 1988—. Mem. Md. Motor Truck Assn., N.Y. Athletic Club, Gentleman Afield Sporting Club. Republican. Roman Catholic. Office: Friedman Fuller & Coleman 8330 Boone Blvd Vienna VA 22182-2624

COLEMAN, KEVIN EDWIN, insurance agent; b. Hartford, Conn., July 15, 1960; s. Timothy Edwin and Maureen Elizabeth (Wolf) C.; m. Annette Gabriel, June 17, 1989. BSBA, Northeastern U., 1983; postgrad., U. Conn., 1986—. Fin. svcs. sales rep. Profl. Svcs. Am., West Hartford, Conn., 1986-90; Great West Life Assurance Co. West Life Assurance Co., West Hartford, 1990—; cons. Profl. Svcs. Am., West Hartford, 1990—. Capt. U.S. Army, 1983-86. Mem. Hartford Life Underwriters Assn., Am. Vets. Assn., N.G. Assn. U.S., Northeastern U. Conn. Alumni Assn. (pres. 1990—), Officers Club Conn. Home: 269 East St Suffield CT 06078-1907 Office: Gt West Life Assurance 433 S Main St Ste 214 West Hartford CT 06110-1670

COLEMAN, LINDA JANE, marketing educator; b. Charleston, W. Va., May 18, 1947; d. James Littleton and Mary Ellen (Atkins) C.; m. Gerald D. Smith, Jr., Aug. 9, 1969 (div. Nov. 1972). BS in Bus., W.Va. Wesleyan Coll., 1969; MS in Bus., Va. Commonwealth U., 1974. Tchr. Armstrong H.S., Richmond, Va., 1970-72; ops. officer Equitable Trust Co., Balt., 1974-77; asst. prof. U. Balt., 1977-84; assoc. prof. Salem (Mass.) State Coll., 1984—; counselor Sml. Bus. Devel. Ctr., Salem, 1991—; vis. faculty Alaska Pacific Univ., Anchorage, 1983; cons./workshop leader in field. Co-author conf. proceedings in field; contbr. articles to profl. jours; reviewer publs. in field. Bd. dirs. Howard County Rape Crisis Ctr., 1980-81, Am. Lung Assn., 1982-84; active numerous women's fairs, Balt.; actor Theatre East at Barton Square, Salem, 1985, Gloucester Stage Co. Acting Class, 1990; vol. V.A. Hosp., Loch Raven Blvd., 1982, Manchester Hist. Soc., 1984—, others. Named to Outstanding Young Women of Am., 1976, runner-up for Dean James Chair Disting. Teaching awards U. Balt., 1979, 80, named Outstanding Tchr. Sch. of Bus., 1980. Mem. Am. Mktg. Assn., Stage Source, Sierra Club, Manchester Hist. Soc., Internat. Soc. for Intercultural Edn. Tng. and Rsch., others. Office: Salem State Coll Sch of Bus and Econs Salem MA 01970

COLEMAN, NANCY CATHERINE, actress; b. Everett, Wash., Dec. 30, 1912; d. Charles Sumner Coleman and Grace Sharpless; m. Whitney French Bolton, Sept. 16, 1943 (dec. Nov. 1969); children: Charla Elizabeth, Grania Theresa. Student, U. Wash., 1930-34. Appeared in films including King's Row, 1941, Dangerously They Live, 1941, The Gay Sisters, 1942, Desperate Journey, 1942, The Edge of Darkness, 1943, In Our Time, 1944, Devotion, 1946, Her Sister's Secret, 1947, That Man From Tangier, 1953, Slaves, 1968; various TV shows including Valiant Lady, 1954-55; plays include Susan and God with Gertrude Lawrence, 1938, The Desperate Hours, 1955. Mem. AFTRA, SAG, Actors' Equity, Motion Picture Arts & Scis.

COLEMAN, PAUL DAVID, neurobiology researcher, educator; b. N.Y.C., Dec. 2, 1927; s. A. Barnett and Martha L. (Michaels) C.; m. Zinia J. Cereska, Mar. 13, 1955 (div. Sept. 1978); children: Laura A., Paul David; m. 2d Dorothy G. Flood, Feb. 26, 1983. AB, Tufts U., 1948; PhD, U. Rochester, 1953. Asst. prof., research assoc. Tufts U., Medford, Mass., 1956-59; assoc. Computer Ctr. MIT, Cambridge, 1957-59; spl. fellow Johns Hopkins Sch. Medicine, Balt., 1959-62; assoc. prof. Sch. Medicine U. Md., Balt., 1962-67; prof. neurobiology and anatomy Sch. Medicine, U. Rochester, N.Y., 1967—. Editor in chief Neurobiology of Aging, 1988—; contbr. articles to profl. jours. 1st lt. U.S. Army, 1953-56. Recipient award for leadership and excellence in Alzheimer's disease Nat. Inst. Aging, NIH, 1990; rsch. grantee NSF, 1958-67, NIH, 1963—; NIH spl. fellow Johns Hopkins U. Sch. Medicine, 1959-62. Mem. Soc. for Neurosci., Am. Assn. Anatomists, AAAS, Gerontol. Soc., Am. Psychol. Assn., Sigma Xi. Club: Yacht (Rochester, N.Y.) (bd. dirs. 1971-72). Home: 35 Atkinson St Rochester NY 14608-2247 Office: U Rochester Med Ctr PO Box 603 Rochester NY 14642-0001

COLEMAN, RICHARD WILLIAM, lawyer; b. Brookline, Mass., Dec. 9, 1935; s. Michael John and Mary Ellen (Motherway) C.; m. Mary M. Kilcommins, June 3, 1961; children: Lauren, Christopher. BS, Boston Coll., Newton, Mass., 1957; JD, Boston Coll., Brighton, Mass., 1960. Bar: Mass. 1960, U.S. Dist. Ct. Mass. 1961, U.S. Ct. Appeals (1st cir.) 1981. Field atty. NLRB, Newark, 1960-61; assoc. Segal & Flamm, Boston, 1961-69; labor rels. advisor Scott Paper Co., Phila., 1969-70; labor rels. mgr. Harvard U., Cambridge, Mass., 1970-72; ptnr. Segal, Roitman & Coleman, Boston, 1972—. Contbg. editor Development of Law Under National Labor Relations Act, 1988. Recipient Cushing award Cath. Labor Guild Boston, 1976. Mem. ABA, Indsl. Rels. Rsch. Assn., Mass. Bar Assn., Boston Bar Assn., AFL-CIO Lawyers Coord. Com. Democrat. Roman Catholic. Office: Segal Roitman & Coleman 11 Beacon St Boston MA 02108-3002

COLEMAN, ROGER LEWIS, psychiatrist; b. N.Y.C., Feb. 14, 1945; s. Jerome Byron and Evelyn Rose C.; m. Dalia Gelman; children: Jenifer Suzanne, Claire Elise, Jonathan Charles; stepchildren: Miri Laub, Avi Laub. BA cum laude, Harvard U., 1967; MD, Tufts U., 1971; MPH, U. Calif., Berkeley, 1976. Intern Mary's Help Hosp., Daly City, Calif., 1971-72; resident in psychiatry San Mateo (Calif.) Mental Health Service, 1971-72; asst. prof. psychology U. Alaska, Fairbanks, 1972-73, lectr. behavioral scis., 1973-74; asst. profl. health scis. Alaska Meth. U., Anchorage, 1974-75; resident, fellow dept. psychiatry Yale U., New Haven, 1976-78; dir. psychiatry inpatient unit Danbury (Conn.) Hosp., 1978-83; dir. psychiatry Meml. Hosp., Meriden, Conn., 1983—; asst. prof. psychiatry N.Y. Med. Coll., 1979-83; asst. clin. prof. psychiatry Yale U., 1983—. Served with USPHS, 1972-75. Mem. AMA (recipient Physicians Recognition award 1976, 79, 82, 85, 88), Am. Psychiat. Assn., Am. Assn. Gen. Hosp. Psychiatrists. Home: 8 Salem Rd Woodbridge CT 06525-2624

COLEMAN, STEPHEN, composer; b. Greenville, S.C., Jan. 29, 1973; s. Stephen Beasley Jr. and Alexandra Ophelia (Sammons) C. Student, N.C. Sch. Arts, Manhattan Sch. Music. music dir. mus. theatre prodns. throughout U.S. Composer film scores and concert works including (film

score) Welcome Stranger, (mus. compositions) Requiem, 1990, A Hero's Welcome, 1991, An American Epitaph, 1992.

COLEMAN, WILLIAM HARVEY, biology educator; b. Chestertown, Md., Mar. 6, 1937; s. Charles Parker Sr. and Sarah Myrtle (Usilton) C.; m. Joyce C. Vender, Aug. 31, 1968; children: John William, Thomas Andrew. BS, Wash. Coll., Chesterton, Md., 1959; MS, U. Chgo., 1962, Phd, 1967. Instr. U. Chgo., 1966-68; rsch. assoc. U. Colo., Denver, 1966-71; prof. biology dept. U. Hartford, West Hartford, Conn., 1971—. Contbr. articles and revs. to profl. jours. Chair Libr. Bd. Dirs., Bloomfield, Conn., 1975-79; vice-chair, sec., mem. Bd. Edn., Bloomfield, 1980-91. Higher Tech. grantee State of Conn., 1989; Nat. Insts. of Allegy and Infectious Diseases fellow NIH, 1987. Mem. Am. Soc. for Microbiology. Democrat. Home: 40 Hill Farm Rd Bloomfield CT 06002-1842 Office: U Hartford 200 Bloomfield Ave West Hartford CT 06117-1500

COLEN, FREDERICK HAAS, lawyer; b. Pitts., May 16, 1947; married, 1972. BSChemE, Tufts U., 1969; JD, Emory U., 1975. Bar: Pa. 1975, Ga. 1975, U.S. Patent Office 1976, U.S. Dist. Ct. (we. dist.) Pa. 1975, U.S. Dist. Ct. (no. dist.) Ga. 1975, U.S. Ct. Appeals (fed. and 3d cirs.) 1975, U.S. Supreme Ct. 1980. Chem. engr. Shell Oil Co., New Orleans, 1969-71; san. engr. USPHS, Morgantown, W.Va., 1971-73; patent atty. Mobay Chem. Corp., Pitts., 1975-79; assoc. Reed Smith Shaw & McClay, Pitts., 1979-86, ptnr., 1986—. Contbr. articles to profl. jours. Mem. ABA, Allegheny County Bar Assn., Pa. Bar Assn., Ga. Bar Assn., Am. Intellectual Property Law Assn. Home: 4940 Ellsworth Ave Pittsburgh PA 15213-2807 Office: Reed Smith Shaw & McClay James H Reed Bldg 435 6th Ave Pittsburgh PA 15219-1809

COLES, ROBERT, child psychiatrist, educator, author; b. Boston, Oct. 12, 1929; s. Philip and Sandra (Young) C.; m. Jane Hallowell; children—Robert, Daniel, Michael. A.B., Harvard U., 1950; M.D., Columbia U., 1954; M.D. (hon.), Temple U., Notre Dame U., Bates Coll., 1972, Wayne State U., 1973, Western Mich. U., Holy Cross Coll., 1974, Hofstra U., 1975, Coll. William and Mary, Bard Coll., U. Lowell, U. Cin., 1976, Stonehill Coll., Lesley Coll., Rutgers U., 1977, Wesleyan U., Columbia Coll., Knox Coll., Cleve. State U., Wooster Coll., 1978, U. N.C., Manhattan Coll., St. Peter's Coll., Coll. New Rochelle, Pratt Inst. and Sch. Design, 1979, Berea Coll., Bklyn. Coll., Emmanuel Coll., 1980, Colby Coll., 1981, Sienna Heights Coll., Salem State Coll., Williams Coll., 1983, Beloit Coll., 1984, Emory U., Fairfield U., Macalaster Coll., Colgate U., 1986, Dartmouth Coll., 1987. Intern U. Chgo. Clinics, 1954-55; resident in psychiatry Mass. Gen. Hosp., Boston, 1955-56, McLean Hosp., Belmont, Mass., 1956-57, Judge Baker Guidance Center-Children's Hosp., 1957-58; mem. staff children's Unit Met. State Hosp., Waltham, Mass., 1957-58; mem. staff alcoholic clinic Mass. Gen. Hosp.; teaching fellow in psychiatry, mem. psychiat. staff and clin. asst. in psychiatry Harvard Med. Sch., 1955-58; research psychiatrist Harvard U. Health Services, 1963—; lectr. gen. edn. Harvard U., 1966—, prof. psychiatry and med. humanities, 1977—; child psychiat. fellow Judge Baker Guidance Center, Children's Hosp., Boston, 1960-61; mem. Nat. Adv. Com. on Farm Labor, 1965—; cons. Appalachian Vols., 1965—, Rockefeller Found., 1969—, Ford Found., 1969—; mem. Inst. of Medicine, Nat. Acad. Scis., 1973-78; vis. prof. public policy Duke U., 1973—; cons. supr. dept. psychiatry Cambridge (Mass.) Hosp., 1976—; cons. Center for Study of So. Culture, U. Miss., 1979—; bd. dirs. Ctr. for Documentary Studies, Duke U.; vis. prof. psychiatry, Dartmouth Coll., 1989. Author: Children of Crisis: A Study of Courage and Fear, 1967, Dead End School, 1968, Still Hungry in America, 1969, The Grass Pipe, 1969, The Image is Yours, 1969; Wages of Neglect, 1969, Uprooted Children: The Early Lives of Migrant Farmers, 1970, Teachers and the Children of Poverty, 1970, Erik H. Erikson: The Growth of His Work, 1970, The Middle Americans, 1970, Migrants, Sharecroppers and Mountaineers, 1972, The South Goes North, 1972, Saving Face, 1972, Farewell to the South, 1972, A Spectacle Unto the World, 1973, Riding Free, 1973, The Darkness and the Light, 1974, The Buses Roll, 1974, Irony in the Mind's Life: Essays on Novels by James Agee, Elizabeth Bowen and George Eliot, 1974, Headsparks, 1975, The Mind's Fate, 1975, Eskimos, Chicanos and Indians, 1978, Privileged Ones, Vol. V of Children in Crisis book series, 1978, (with Jane Hallowell Coles) Women of Crisis Lives of Struggle and Hope, 1978, Walker Percy: An American Search, 1978, Flannery O'Connor's South, 1980, Women of Crisis; Lives of Work and Dreams, 1980, Dorothea Lange: Photographs of a Lifetime, 1982, (with Ross Spears) Agee, 1985, The Political Life of Children, 1986, Dorothy Day: A Radical Devotion, 1987, Simone Weil: A Modern Pilgrimage, 1987, Times of Surrender: Selected Essays, 1988, Harvard Diary, 1988, That Red Wheelbarrow, 1988, The Call of Stories: Teaching and the Moral Imagination, 1989, Rumors of Separate Worlds, 1989, The Spiritual Life of Children, 1990; contbg. editor: The New Republic, 1966—, Am. Poetry Rev, 1972—, Aperture, 1974—, Lit. and Medicine, 1981—, New Oxford Rev, 1981—; mem. editorial bd.: Integrated Edn., 1967—, Child Psychiatry and Human Devel., 1969—, Rev. of Books and Religion, 1976—, Internat. Jour. Family Therapy, 1977—, Grants mag., 1977—, Learning mag., 1978—, Jour. Am. Culture, 1977—, Jour. Edn., 1979—; bd. editors: Parents' Choice, 1978—; editor: Children and Youth Services Rev., 1978—. Bd. dirs. Field Found., 1968—; trustee Robert F. Kennedy Meml., 1968—, Robert F. Kennedy Action Corps, State of Mass., 1968—, Miss. Inst. Early Childhood Edn., 1968—, Twentieth Century Fund, 1971—; bd. dirs. Reading is Fundamental, Smithsonian Inst., 1968—, Am. Freedom from Hunger Found., 1968—, Am. Parents Com., 1971—; mem. corp. Boston Children's Service, 1970; mem. adv. council Inst. for Nonviolent Social Change of Martin Luther King, Jr. Meml. Center, 1971—, Ams. for Children's Relief, 1972—; mem. nat. com. for Edn. of Young Children, 1972—; mem. nat. adv. council Rural Am., 1976—; trustee Austen Riggs Found., Stockbridge, Mass., 1976—; mem. nat. adv. com. Ala. Citizens for Responsive Public Television, 1976—; mem. adv. com. Nat. Indian Edn. Assn., 1976—; visitor's com. mem. Boston Mus. Fine Arts, 1977; bd. dirs. Boys Club Boston, 1977; vis. com. Boston Coll. Law Sch., 1977; adv. Center for So. Folklore, 1978—; mem. children's com. Edna McConnell Clark Found., 1978—; bd. dirs. Lyndhurst Found., 1978—; mem. nat. adv. bd. Foxfire Fund, Inc., 1979—. Recipient Ralph Waldo Emerson prize Phi Beta Kappa, 1967; Anisfield-Wolf award in race relations Saturday Rev., 1968; Hofheimer award Am. Psychiat. Assn., 1968; Sidney Hillman prize, 1971; Weatherford prize Berea Coll. and Council So. Mountains, 1973; Lilliam Smith Award So. Regional Council, 1973; McAlpin medal Nat. Assn. Mental Health, 1972; Pulitzer prize, 1973 (all received for Children of Crisis, Vols. II, III); disting. scholar medal Hofstra U., 1974; William A. Shonfeld award Am. Soc. Adolescent Psychiatry, 1977; MacArthur Found. award, 1981; Josepha Hale award, 1986; fellow Davenport Coll., Yale U., 1976—. Fellow Am. Acad. Arts and Scis., Inst. Soc., Ethics and the Life Scis.; mem. Am. Psychiat. Assn., Am. Orthopsychiat. Assn. (past dir.), Acad. Psychoanalysis, Nat. Orgn. Migrant Children. Home: 81 Carr Rd Concord MA 01742-1852 Office: Harvard U Univ Health Svcs 75 Mt Auburn St Cambridge MA 02138-4901

COLETTI, JOHN ANTHONY, lawyer, furniture and realty company executive; b. Cherry Point, N.C., Sept. 22, 1952; s. Joseph Nicholas and Gloria Lucy (Fusco) C.; m. Barbara Nancy Carlotti, July 20, 1975; children: Lisa M., Kristen B. Student, Biscayne Coll., 1970-72; BA summa cum laude, Boston Coll., 1974, JD, 1977. Bar; R.I. 1977, U.S. Dist. Ct. R.I. 1977. Assoc. Resmini, Fornaro, Colagiovanni & Angell, Providence, 1979-81; ptnr. Coletti & Tente, Cranston, R.I., 1981—; pres. Coletti's Furniture, Inc., Johnston R.I., 1983—, Coletti's Realty, Inc., Johnston, 1983—. Legal counsel Cranston Housing Authority, 1988—; interviewer alumni admissions coun. Boston Coll., 1980—. Mem. ABA, R.I. Bar Assn., R.I. Conveyancers Assn., Phi Beta Kappa. Roman Catholic. Home: 20 Laurel Hill Dr Smithfield RI 02917-2126 Office: Coletti & Tente 311 Doric Ave Cranston RI 02910-2903

COLETTI, THEODORE A., counseling psychologist, educator; b. Bronx, N.Y., Mar. 24, 1965; s. George Edward and Virginia May (Palma) C.; m. Veronica Alicia Dengler, May 19, 1991. BS in Psychology, Fordham U., 1987; postgrad., Seton Hall U., 1989—. Rehab. coord. Altro Health Rehab., N.Y.C., 1987-88; counselor William Paterson Coll., Wayne, N.J., 1990-91, Fairleigh Dickinson U., Madison., N.J., 1991-92; instr. Ramapo Coll., Mohawk, N.J., 1990, Seton Hall U., South Orange, N.J., 1991, Kean Coll., Union, N.J., 1991-92, William Paterson Coll., 1992, Upsala Coll., 1992. Mem. APA, Am. Assn. Counseling and Devel., Am. Assn. Higher Edn., N.J. Psychol. Assn., N.J. Counseling and Devel. Assn., Doctoral Student Assn., (v.p.), Psi Chi, Kappa Delta Phi. Republican. Roman Catholic. Home: 68 Myrtle Ave Millburn NJ 07041

COLFIN, BRUCE ELLIOTT, video producer, lawyer; b. Bklyn., June 9, 1951; s. Abraham and Sylvia (Laykin) C.; m. Virginia Mary Faszczewski, Sept. 27, 1981. BA, Queens Coll., CUNY, 1977; JD, N.Y. Law Sch., 1980. Bar: N.Y. 1982, U.S. Dist. Ct. (so., ea. dists.) N.Y., 1987, U.S. Ct. Internat. Trade, 1990. Audio engr. Snowball Sound Systems, N. Bergen, N.J., 1974-77; producer, dir. cable TV program What's On, N.Y.C., 1976-84; stage mgr. Peter Tosh U.S. tour Rolling Stones Records, 1978; v.p., producer Upswing Artists Mgmt., N.Y.C., 1979-86; tour mgr. Inner Circle U.S. tour, 1980; pres., producer, dir. LegalVision, Inc., N.Y.C., 1982-87; ptnr. Jacobson & Colfin, N.Y.C. and Washington, 1985-90; mem. Jacobson & Colfin, P.C., N.Y.C. and Washington, 1990—; speaker Discovery Ctr., N.Y., 1st Ann. Musicians Seminar, L.I., N.Y. Law Sch. Media Law Soc., 1986; vis. lectr. SUNY, Oneonta, 1988—; counsel Mick Taylor Music, New Riders of the Purple Sage, 1985, Golden Legs, Inc., 1986, Dance Internat., Inc., 1986, Silk Club, 1986, Bridgewater-Wind, Ltd., 1987, Best Film and Video, Inc., 1988, Marty Balin, 1988, Johnny Winter, 1989, Cynthia Entertainment Inc., 1990, Andrew Tosh, 1990, Asociacion de Compositores y Editores de Musica Latino Americana, 1991, East Europe Records, 1992, Charly Records, 1992. Assoc. producer music video Blues Alive, 1982; exec. producer, dir. video series Entertainment Law Video Primer, 1984; contbr. articles to profl. jours. Mem. ABA (com. on entertainment sports law, subcom. chmn. patent, trademark and copyright com. 1989, subcom. chmn. internat. law and practice, internat. intellectual property rights com., editorial advisor pubs. com. internat. law sect. 1990—, exec. com. entertainment law circle 1989—), N.Y. State Bar Assn. (entertainment, arts and sports law sect., com. on talent agys. and talent mgmt.), Copyright Soc. U.S.A. (edit. bd. 1986-88, 90—). Jewish. Office: Jacobson & Colfin PC 156 5th Ave Ste 434 New York NY 10010-7002

COLGAN, PETER TRISTRAM, real estate company executive; b. Boston, Apr. 20, 1945; s. Edmund F. and Winifred Wentworth (Coffin) C.; m. Susan Faville Taylor, Mar. 29, 1971. Student, U. Mass., Boston, 1965-67. Broker, salesman Hunneman & Co. Inc., Boston, 1973-76, ptnr., v.p., 1977-81; ptnr., pres. The Gifford Group, Inc., Boston, 1982—. Author, editor The Tower Report, 1990-92. Mem. Realtors Nat. Mktg. Inst., Mass. Assn. Realtors, Greater Boston Real Estate Bd. (chmn. econs. and rsch. com. 1990-91), Soc. Colonial Wars, Univ. Club Boston. Office: The Gifford Group Inc 50 Congress St Boston MA 02109

COLGAN, SUMNER, manufacturing engineer, chemical engineer; b. Framingham, Mass., Sept. 11, 1934; s. Joseph and Leora C.; student Boston Coll., 1957-61, Boston U., 1961, Banff Climbing Sch.; married; 1 son, Scott Paul. Chem. engr. Beam Tube Corp., Western, Mass., 1962-63; reliability engr. Gen. Motors Corp., Framingham, 1963-86, mfg. engr., 1986-91; chemist Envirotech Operating Systems, North Haven, Conn., 1991—. Served in USAF, 1953-57. Mem. Hunting Ravine Avalanche Patrol, 1970-78. Mem. Matterhorn Climbers Assn. Zermatt, Pvt. Pilot Assn., Mt. Rainier Summit Climbers Assn. Clubs: Appalachian Mountain, Sea Urchins. Home: PO Box 138 Framingham MA 01701-0001 Office: 63 Western Ave Framingham MA 01701

COLINO, RICHARD RALPH, communications consultant; b. N.Y.C., Feb. 10, 1936; s. Victor and Caroline (Pauline) C.; m. Wilma Jane Rubinstein, June 10, 1962 (div. Oct. 1991); children: Stacey Anne, Geoffrey William. BA, Amherst Coll., 1957; JD, Columbia U., 1960. Bar: N.Y. 1961, D.C. 1973. Assoc. Sargoy & Stein, N.Y.C., 1960-61; atty. FCC, Washington, 1962-64, U.S. Info. Agy., Washington, 1964-65; dir. internat. affairs Communications Satellite Corp., Washington, 1965-68; dir. Europe Communications Satellite Corp., Geneva, 1968-69; asst. v.p. Communications Satellite Corp., Washington, 1969-75, v.p. and gen. mgr. internat. ops., 1975-79; pres., chief exec. officer Continental Home Theatre, Burlingame, Calif., 1979-80, DynaCom Enterprises Ltd., Chevy Chase, Md., 1980-83; dir. gen., chief exec. officer Internat. Telecommunications Satellite Orgn., Washington, 1983-86; v.p., cons. W.L. Pritchard & Co., Inc. Cons. Engrs., Bethesda, Md., 1990—; bd. dirs. CFS, Inc., 1983-87; com. mem. U.S. C. of C., 1973-76. Contbr. articles to profl. jours. Bd. dirs. Internat. Inst. Communication, London, 1985-86, Big Bros., Washington, 1975-77; co-chmn., chmn. Fund Raisers, Washington, 1983-89. With U.S. Army, 1961-62. Named one of top 15 people in U.S. communications Communications Week, 1986. Home: care C Kelly 326 Deerfield Irving CA 92714 Office: WL Pritchard & Co Inc 7315 Wisconsin Ave Bethesda MD 20814-3202

COLLARD, THOMAS ALBERT, transportation executive; b. Paterson, N.J., Nov. 9, 1942; s. Albert Garrison and Katherine Barbara (Adams) C.; BS in Bus. Adminstrn., U. Buffalo, 1964; m. Cynthia Louise Davis, Nov. 6, 1965; children: Elizabeth, Katherine. Various positions Pa. R.R., Cleve. and Buffalo, 1964-69; svc. analyst mktg. dept. Penn Central, Phila., 1969-70, supr. svc. quality control, 1971; mgr. svc. planning Cen. R.R. of N.J., Newark, 1972-74, dir. transp. planning, 1974-75, dir. stas. and intermodal operation, 1975; with Conrail Activation Task Force, 1975-76, dir. svc. planning and performance, 1976-80, dir. svc. devel., 1980-83, mgr. transp. svc. planning and costing, 1983-89; mgr. ea. ops. Nat. Salvage and Svc., 1989-90; mgr. Solid Waste Bus. Group, 1991—; chmn., chief exec. officer The Elise Corp./N.J. So. Coachways, 1983-90; mem. Transp. Rsch. Forum, 1981—; adv. S. Jersey Transp. Adv. Com., 1982-85. Author children's book: Diesels First, 1977; contbr. articles to tech. publs. Active Big Brother Orgn., Willingboro, N.J., 1972-81; v.p. Big Bros./Big Sisters of Burlington County (N.J.), 1975-76, pres., 1977-78; vol. juvenile probation counselor, 1978; adv. Concerned Citizens North Camden, 1981-85. Mem. Am. Soc. Traffic and Transp. (cert.), ICC Practitioners Assn. Episcopalian (vestryman, tchr., dir. ch. edn. 1970—). Home: 30 Topeka Ln Willingboro NJ 08046-4120 Office: 243 E Winslow Rd Bloomington IN 47401-8638

COLLESANO, WILLIAM JOSEPH, safety supervisor; b. Niagara Falls, N.Y., May 21, 1949; s. William Joseph Collesano and Irene (Heintzelman) Harrison; m. Janet Bovanizer, Mar. 21, 1970; children: Christopher Michael, Christina Lee. BS in Commerce, Niagara U., 1971; postgrad., Niagara U., SUNY, Buffalo, 1987—. Acting br. mgr. Permanent Savings Bank, Niagara Falls, 1971-73; environ. health tech. Niagara County Health Dept., Niagara Falls, 1973-76; pub. info. officer N.Y. Power Authority, Lowville, N.Y., 1976-78; safety and security supr. N.Y. Power Authority, Niagara Falls, 1978—. Vol. Youngstown (N.Y.) Vol. Fire Co., 1978-82, Am. Red Cross, Niagara Falls, 1978—, chmn., 1990—; cub scout leader Boy Scouts of Am., Youngstown, N.Y., 1981-82; asst. coach Niagara Frontier Soccer League, Youngstown, 1983-85; trustee Youngstown (N.Y.) Presbyn. Ch., 1983-85. Mem. Fed. Safety and Health Coun. (chmn.), Nat. Safety Coun., Am. Soc. Safety Engrs., Am. Mgmt. Assn., Am. Soc. for Indsl. Security, Nat. Fire Protection Assn., Youngstown Yacht Club (chairperson 1990—), Catalina Fleet 89 (officer, mem. 1979—). Republican. Home: 831 Youngstown Lockport Rd Youngstown NY 14174-1138 Office: NY Power Authority 5777 Lewiston Rd Lewiston NY 14092-1999

COLLETTE, BRUCE BADEN, ichthyologist; b. N.Y.C., Mar. 14, 1934; s. Raymond Hill and Agnes Helen (Larson) C.; m. Sara Elizabeth Foster, June 14, 1956; children: Karen Wiltse , Sheila Helen Collette Bell, Claire Elizabeth. BS, Cornell U., 1956, PhD, 1960. Rsch. asst. Cornell U., Ithaca, N.Y., 1956-57, teaching asst., 1957-60; systematic zoologist Systematics Lab. Nat. Marine Fisheries Svc., Washington, 1960-82, dir. Systematics Lab., 1982—, sci. editor, 1974-77; professorial lectr. George Washington U., Washington, 1978-79; vis. prof. Northeastern U., Nahant, Mass., summers 1967-85, adj. prof. biology, 1980—; instr. Bermuda Biol. Sta., summers 1984—; rsch. assoc. Smithsonian Instn., Washington, 1967—, Mus. Comparative Zoology, Harvard U., Boston, 1977—. Editor: Ecology of Coral Reef Fishes, 1972; contbr. over 140 articles to sci. jours. (awards Fishery Bull., 1969, 75, 84). Mem. exec. bd. Little Hunting Creek Citizens Assn., Mt. Vernon, Va., 1971-77; Mt. Vernon rep. Fairfax County Environ. Quality Adv. Coun., Fairfax County, Va., 1974-77; mem. natural resources com. No. Va. Planning Dist. Coun., 1974-77. Recipient Conservation award Internat. Wildlife Found., 1981. Fellow AAAS, Am. Inst. Fishery Rsch. Biologists; mem. Am. Soc. Ichthyologists and Herpetologists (ichthyology editor 1964-68, sec. 1974-78, pres. 1981, Frederick H. Stoye award 1956, 58, 59, Robert A. Gibbs Meml. award 1989), Biol. Soc. Washington (pres. 1976-77), Am. Assn. Zool. Nomenclature (pres. 1987), Soc. Systematic Zoologists (councilor 1986-88), Willi Hennig Soc. (councilor 1988-90). Home: Pageland Farm Casanova VA 22017 Office: Nat Marine Fisheries Svc Systematics Lab Nat Mus Natural History Washington DC 20560

COLLETTI, FRANCIS ANTHONY, JR., army officer; b. Hempstead, N.Y., Apr. 21, 1957; s. Francis Anthony and Marjorie Pauline (Kautz) C.; m. Sun Hwa Chon, Dec. 29, 1981; 1 child, Peter Francis. BS in Gen. Sci., U.S. Mil. Acad., 1979; MA in Social Psychology, U. N.C., 1989. Commd. 2d lt. U.S. Army, 1979, advanced through grades to maj., 1991; platoon ldr. 4th Squadron, 7th Cavalry, Korea, 1980-81; adjutant, then battalian maint. officer 1st Battalion, 77th Armor, Ft. Carson, Colo., 1982-84; troop comdr. 5th Squadron, 15th Cavalry, Ft. Knox, Ky., 1985-87; instr. Dept. Behavioral Scis. & Leadership, U.S. Mil. Acad., West Point, N.Y., 1989-90, asst. prof., 1990-91, assoc. prof., 1991—, dir. gen. psychology, 1991—. Officer-in-charge Cadet Theatre Arts Guild, West Point, 1990-91. Decorated Army Commendation medals (2), Meritorious Svc. medal. Mem. U.S. Army Armor Assn., Assn. U.S. Army. Roman Catholic. Office: US Mil Acad Dept Behavioral Sci & Leadership West Point NY 10996

COLLI, BART JOSEPH, lawyer; b. Englewood, N.J., Feb. 13, 1948; s. Bart Joseph and Marie (Burns) C.; m. Mary Ellen Diemer, May 20, 1972; 1 son, Michael John. B.A. summa cum laude, Fordham Coll., 1968; J.D. cum laude, Harvard U., 1971. Bar: N.Y. 1972, Tex. 1975, N.J. 1988. Assoc. firm White & Case, N.Y.C., 1971-75; ptnr. firm Hughes & Luce, Dallas, 1976-85, McCarter & English, Newark, 1985—; adj. prof. law Seton Hall U. Served to capt. M.I., U.S. Army Res., 1968-76. Contbr. articles to law rev. jours. Mem. ABA (fed. regulation of securities com.), N.Y. State Bar Assn., N.J. State Bar Assn. (securities law com.); adj. prof. law Seton Hall U. Mem. Phi Beta Kappa. Office: McCarter & English 4 Gateway Ctr 100 Mulberry St Newark NJ 07102-4096

COLLIER, DUAINE ALDEN, manufacturing-distribution company executive; b. Chambersburg, Pa., Aug. 19, 1950; s. Clyde Alden and Etta Jean (Browell) C.; m. Trudy Jean Shoap, Aug. 22, 1970; children: Patrick, Crystal. BS in Math., Shippensburg U., 1972. Product specialist ITT Domestic Pump, Shippensburg, 1972-77; pres., chief exec. officer College Town, Inc., Shippensburg, 1971—; gen. mgr. Shippensburg Pump Co., Inc., 1985—; bd. dirs., sec.-treas. Beidel Printing House, Inc., Shippensburg, 1975—, White Mane Pub. Co., Inc., Shippensburg, 1987—, Shippensburg Pump Co., Inc., 1985—. Committeeman Franklin County Republican Party, 1989—; pres. Shippensburg Area Devel. Corp., 1983-84, bd. dirs., 1982-84. Mem. The Wednesday Club, Masons (master Orrstown lodge 1979), Shippensburg Lions Club (pres. 1989-90), Sons of the Am. Legion. Methodist. Office: College Town Inc 17 W Burd St PO Box 337 Shippensburg PA 17257-0337

COLLIER, JOHN THORNTON, public relations consultant; b. Memphis, June 23, 1910; s. William Armistead Jr. and Lucile Moore (Pittman) C.; m. Blanche Hellickson Merry, Oct. 26, 1940 (dec. 1983); children: Louis William, Eleanor Collier McWaters; m. Jodell Mallory Reiter, July 26, 1986. Student, U. Ill., 1930-32; BS, Am. U., 1956. Pub. rels. trainee North Shore RR and affiliates, Chgo., 1930-33, 1929; rsch. asst., editor, dir. Fed. Emergency Relief Adminstrn., Chgo. and Milw., 1934-39; pub. rels. mgr. Spraywire Labs., Mpls., 1947; pub. affairs officer constituent units HEW, Washington, 1950-59; dir. planning and evaluation, injury control programs USPHS, Washington, 1960-67; dir. spl. projects HEW, Washington, 1967-72; cons. Washington, 1972—; freelance writer def. industries, advt. agys., 1951-59; chair pub. safety Nat. Safety Coun., Washington, 1969-71, v.p. pub. safety, 1972-74. Editor TV documentary films on safety; contbr. articles to profl., trade, and popular publs. Col. AUS, 1940-46, 48-50, 63. Decorated Silver Star, Bronze Star; recipient Disting. Svc. to Safety award Nat. Safety Coun., 1975. Mem. Res. Officers Assn. (dept. pres. 1947), Ret. Officers Assn., Am. Revolution Round Table (pres. 1976-77), D.C. Civil War Round Table (pres. 1980-81), U.S. Horse Cavalry Assn. (life, chair com. 1986—), Va. Soc. Cincinnati, Arts Club of Washington (emeritus life, bd. 1975-76), Kappa Sigma. Republican. Episcopalian. Home: 3821 N Tazewell St Arlington VA 22207-4569 Office: # 912 1300 Connecticut Ave NW Washington DC 20036

COLLIER, MAXIE TYRON, psychiatrist, writer, consultant, educator; b. Waverly, Tenn., Mar. 30, 1945; s. James R. and Pearlie (May) C.; m. Betty Collier (div. Oct. 1979); m. Katherine Grant, June 13, 1982; children: Letoynia, Maxie D., Mar-yoi, Lemoya, Zaitrarrio, Tara, Nonya. BA in Psychology, Vanderbilt U., 1967; postgrad., Howard U., 1968-71, 72-73; MD, U. Md., Balt., 1977. Diplomate Am. Bd. Psychiatry and Neurology. Intern South Balt. Gen. Hosp., 1977; resident in psychiatry U. Md. Hosp., Balt., 1977-79; fellow in community psychiatry U. Md. U. Md. Hosp., 1979-80; staff psychiatrist Montgomery County unit Springfield Hosp., 1980, asst. div. dir., 1980-81; dir. Bur. Mental Health, Balt. City Health Dept., 1981-84, assoc. commr. div. human behavior and community psychiatry, 1984-87; commr. of health Balt., 1987-90; chmn. Balt. Mental Health Systems, Inc., 1987-90; chmn. dept. community psychiatry Liberty Med. Ctr., Balt., 1991—; pvt. practice, Balt., 1980—; pres. Spectrum Devel. Svcs., Inc., 1984-91; chief psychiatry Johns Hopkins Health Plan, 1987; cons. Morgan Mgmt. Systems, 1983-84, West Balt. Health Care Corp., 1980-82; asst. prof. Johns Hopkins Hosp., U. Md.; lectr. in field; staff privileges Md. Gen. Hosp. Author: Phoenix Arising, 1990; contbr. articles to med. jours. Mem. Md. Gov.'s Coun. on Lead Poisoning, Balt. Mayor's Homeless Relief Adv. Bd., Balt. Mayor's Task Force on Food and Hunger; bd. dirs. ARC, Am. Visionary Art Mus., Threshold, Inc.; mem. exec. bd. Balt. Urban League; mem. Md. Mental Health Manpower Coun.; mem. substance abuse task force Md. Gov.'s Commn. on Minority Health. Recipient numerous awards. Fellow Am. Psychiat. Assn.; mem. APHA, Md. Psychiat. Assn., Med. and Chirurg. Faculty Md., Balt. City Med. Soc. (bd. dirs.). Home: 3915 Liberty Heights Ave Apt 3A Baltimore MD 21207-7536 Office: Liberty Med Ctr 3101 Towanda Ave Baltimore MD 21215-7891

COLLIER, MICHAEL THOMAS, news agency executive; b. N.Y.C., Oct. 17, 1950; s. Patrick and Eileen (Casey) C. BA, Hunter Coll., 1975. Dir. Riverdale Protection Group, N.Y.C., 1975-77; supr. cen. services B'nai Jeshurun Community Ctr., N.Y.C., 1975-76; pres. M.T.C.'s News Agy., Phila., 1976—; chief exec. officer M.T.C., 1978—; chmn. Grams Unltd., Inc., 1982. Active Nationalities Service Ctr., ednl. services, Phila., 1979; mem. Mus. Nat. History. Mem. AAAS, N.Y. Acad. Sci., Geog. Soc. Phila. Club: Vanderbilt Athletic. Address: PO Box 1733 Murray Hill Sta New York NY 10156

COLLIER, SUSAN STARR, chemist; b. Washington, Nov. 5, 1939; d. Melville C. and Dorothy S. (Atwood) Williams; 1 child, David L. Black. AB, Cornell U., 1961; PhD, U. Rochester, 1966. Postdoctoral fellow Ohio State U., Columbus, 1966-69; sr. chemist Eastman Kodak Co., Rochester, N.Y., 1969-74, rsch. assoc., 1975—. Fellow Soc. for Imaging Sci. and Tech.; mem. Am. Chem. Soc. (councilor 1976—, chmn. women chemists com. 1973-75, award Rochester sect. 1985). Office: Eastman Kodak Co Rsch Labs Rochester NY 14650-2104

COLLINGS, RICHARD JAMES, political science educator, academic administrator; b. Owensboro, Ky., Nov. 11, 1946; s. Milton H. and Jean Helen (Ladmore) C.; m. Marilyn Jane Linville, Nov. 24, 1967; children: Kelly Jean, Michael James, Kirsten Jane. A.B. in Internatl. Studies, U. Louisville, 1968; M.A. in Latin Am. Studies, Tulane U., 1972, Ph.D. in Polit. Sci., 1977. Prof. Southeast Mo. State U., Cape Girardeau, 1977, chmn. dept., 1979-85, asst. provost, 1985-89; dean liberal arts and scis. Kutztown (Pa.) U., 1989-91, provost and v.p. academic affairs, 1991—. Chmn. bd. Southeast Mo. Wesley Found., Cape Girardeau, 1980-87. Served with U.S. Army, 1969-71. NSF trainee Tulane U., 1973. Mem. Mo. Polit. Sci. Assn. (sec.-treas. 1980-85), Am. Polit. Sci. Assn., Am. Assn. Higher Edn., Latin Am. Studies Assn., Southeastern Coun. Latin Am. Studies, Phi Kappa Phi, Pi Sigma Alpha, Woodcock Soc. Home: 58 Miller Dr Reading PA 19608-1268 Office: Kutztown U 305 Stratton Adminstrn Kutztown PA 19530

COLLINS, CHARLES DILLARD, art historian, researcher; b. Rahway, N.J., Aug. 18, 1942; s. John Dillard and Elizabeth Woodson (Miller) C.; m. Somsri Athaso Collins, July 26, 1969; 1 child, Vasanta Andrew Collins. BA, Rutgers U., New Brunswick, N.J., 1964; MA, U. Iowa, Iowa City, 1972, PhD, 1980. Instr. Memphis State U., Memphis, 1973-78; asst. prof. Eisenhower Coll., Seneca Falls, N.Y., 1979-82; asst. Rochester (N.Y.) Inst.

of Tech., N.Y., 1982-87; assoc. prof. Rochester (N.Y.) Inst. of Tech., 1987-92; prof. Rochester (N.Y.) Inst. of Tech., N.Y., 1992—. Author: The Iconography and Ritual of Siva at Elephanta, 1988; contbr. articles to profl. jours. Vol. Peace Corps., Malaysia, 1968-69. 1st Lt. U.S. Army, 1965-67, Vietnam. Recipient Art History Essay Contest 1st prize, Rutgers U., New Brunswick, N.J., 1964, Travel grant-in-aid, Nat. Com. on U.S.-China Rels., 1975, Kearse Disting. Lecture, Rochester Inst. of Tech., N.Y., 1989. Mem. Coll. Art Assn. of Am., Assn. for Asian Studies, Am. Oriental Soc., Am. Com. for South Asian Art. Home: 139 Brightwoods Ln Rochester NY 14623-2744 Office: Rochester Inst of Tech One Lomb Memorial Dr Rochester NY 14623

COLLINS, CHRISTOPHER CARL, manufacturing executive; b. Schenectady, N.Y., May 20, 1950; s. Gerald Edward and Constance (Messier) C.; m. Margaret Elizabeth Busby Cox, May 20, 1972 (div. Apr. 1978); 1 child, Carly Elizabeth; m. Mary Sue Kuhn, Jan. 9, 1988; 1 child, Caitlin Christine. BS in Mech. Engring., N.C. State U., 1972; MBA, U. Ala., 1975. Sales engr. Westinghouse Elec. Corp., Birmingham, Ala., 1972-76; market rsch. analyst Westinghouse Elec. Corp., Buffalo, 1976-77, mgr. market planning, 1978-79, mgr. gearing div., 1980-82; pres., chmn., chief exec. officer Nuttall Gear Corp., Niagara Falls, N.Y., 1983—; mem. small bus. adv. coun. Fed. Res. Bank N.Y., 1992—. Bd. dirs. Kenmore Mercy Hosp., 1986—; mem. ho. of dels. United Way, Buffalo, 1986—; mem. Small Bus. Adv. Coun. Fed. Res. Bank N.Y., 1992—. Mem. Young Pres.'s Orgn. (chmn. edn. com. 1988-89, chmn. chpt. 1989-90, chmn. membership 1990-91, chmn. exec. com. 1991—), Brookfield Country Club. Republican. Roman Catholic. Home: 8 Ransom Oaks Dr East Amherst NY 14051-1299 Office: Nuttall Gear Corp PO Box 1032 Niagara Falls NY 14302-1032

COLLINS, DONALD FRANCIS, electrical contractor; b. Springfield, Mass., Oct. 6, 1928; s. William Paul and Helen Veronica (Foley) C.; m. Louise Marie Kelley, Oct. 2, 1954; 1 child, Brendan Anthony. BS, Coll. of Holy Cross, Worcester, Mass., 1949; MBA, Columbia U., 1951. Corp. clk. Collins Electric Co., Chicopee, Mass., 1950-52, treas., 1954—; Trustee Springfield (Mass.) Instn. for Savs., 1975—. Mem. elec. sect. Nat. Fire Prevention Assn., Boston, 1965—; assoc. trustee Coll. of Holy Cross, 1970—; trustee Mercy Hosp., Springfield, 1978-90, Clarke Sch. for Deaf, Northampton, Mass., 1982—. With C.E., U.S. Army, 1952-54. Fellow Acad. Elec. Contracting; mem. Nat. Elec. Contractors Assn. Democrat. Roman Catholic. Clubs: Colony (pres. 1978), Century, Holy Cross of Pioneer Valley (pres. 1968), The Club (Springfield). Lodges: Rotary, Knights of Malta, Knight Grand Cross Equestrian Order of the Holy Sepulchre. Office: Collins Electric Co 53 2d Ave Chicopee MA 01020

COLLINS, EDDIE LEE, educator; b. Newbern, Ala., Mar. 22, 1936; s. Hue J. and Janie B. (Martin) C.; m. Mildred Thrift, Mar. 26, 1977; 1 child, Sebastian Martinique. BA, Cen. State U., Wilberforce, Ohio, 1960; MA, Antioch-Putney, 1973. Cert. elem. history tchr., elem. and secondary counseling. Tchr. James Rhoads Elem. Sch., Phila., 1964-74; tchr. Pepper Middle Sch., Phila., 1974—; PhD equivalent Temple U., 1985. Mem. Democratic Club, Lawnside, N.J., 1977—, Lawnside Bd. Edn., 1979-82; chmn. Lawnside Bd. Health, 1979—, Lawnside Juvenile Conf. Com., 1980—. Sgt. USAF, 1960—. Recipient World Affairs Coun. award World Affairs Coun., Phila., 1971, Youth Leadership award Nat. Freedom Day Assn., 1974, Tchr. of Excellence award ARCO and Phila. Bd. Edn., 1991; William Ross Jr. scholar, 1988; named for Disting. Svc. Phila. City Edn. Assn., 1969. Mem. Nat. Coun. Math., Nat. Coun. Reading, Assn. for Supervision and Curriculum, Nat. Coun. Social Studies, Phila. Fedn. Tchrs. (assoc.), Educators to Africa (Phila., pres. 1980-84), Omega Psi Phi. Democrat. Baptist. Home: 224 JFK Blvd Lawnside NJ 08045 Office: Pepper Mid Sch 84th & Lyons Ave Philadelphia PA 19153

COLLINS, ERIK, psychologist, researcher; b. Grand Rapids, Mich., May 17, 1938; s. Kreigh Taylor and Theresa (Van Der Laan) C.; divorced; children: Brett and Brian; m. Janice Louise Lloyd, Dec. 19, 1987; children: Nicole, Ben, Toby. BBA, U. Mich., 1959, MA, 1963, PhD, 1969. Lic. psychologist, Pa., Del. Tchr. Plymouth (Mich.) Community Schs., 1963-67; vis. lectr. edn. Eastern Mich. U., Ypsilanti, 1967-69; asst. prof., rsch. project dir. SUNY, Fredonia, 1969-74; rsch. assoc., project dir. U. Md., Prinecess Anne, 1974-76; dir. rsch. Geneva Acad., Phila., 1976-77; ptnr. Greely, Collins & Assocs., N.Y.C., 1977-78; psychologist Embreeville Ctr., Coatesville, Pa., 1978-87, Haverford (Pa.) State Hosp., 1987-89, Del. State Hosp., New Castle, 1989—; cons. test devel. SUNY, Brockport, 1971-72, evaluation N.Y. Bd. Edn., 1974-78, rsch. projects and proposal devel. N.Y.C. Community Sch. Dists. Stoney Pointe, N. Y., U. Md., 1976-78; consulting psychologist Pinehill Rehab. Ctr., Phila., 1986-84; pvt. practice West Chester, Pa., Wilmington, Del., 1980—; consulting psychologist, Phila., Elwyn, 1991—. Author poetry; contbr. articles to profl. jours. Evalution grantee N.Y. State Ctr. for Migrant Studies, Geneseo, 1971-72, Innovative project grantee ESEA Title I and VII Appalachian Regional Commn., 1972-78, rsch. grantee Coop. State Rsch. Svcs., 1974-76, Innovative project gratee Dept. of Spl. Edn., Harrisburg, Pa., 1977. Mem. Am. Psychol. Assn., Lower Shore Assn. for Children Learning Disabilities (pres. Eastern Shore chpt. 1975-76), Dunkirk Yacht Club (fleet capt. 1971-72).. Democrat. Episcopalian.

COLLINS, ERIN PATRICK, risk management consultant; b. Orange, N.J., Dec. 25, 1962; s. Bernard Francis and Veronica Theresa (Mitchell) C.; m. Jane Marie Dougan, Jan. 2, 1983; children: Jessica Joan, Theresa Marie. BA in History, U. Idaho, 1983, BS in Secondary Edn., 1983, MPA, 1984. Cert. assoc. in risk mgmt. Ins. Inst. Am. Dir. pers. and risk mgt. County of Mohave, Kingman, Ariz., 1984-90; mgr. human resources City of Gresham, Oreg., 1990; cons. risk mgmt. Cashan Corp., Hammonton, N.J., 1990—. Mem. Pub. Risk and Ins. Mgmt. Assn., Phi Beta Kappa. Republican. Roman Catholic. Office: Cashan Corp 11 S 3d St Hammonton NJ 08037

COLLINS, FRANCIS WINFIELD, chemical company executive; b. N.Y.C., Jan. 5, 1927; s. Francis W. and Lillian A. (Schaeffler) C.; m. Rhoda Henry Collins, May 30, 1952; children: Sharon, Russell, Margaret, Cynthia, Wayne. BA cum laude, Amherst Coll., 1948; MA, Columbia U., 1949. From control chemist to asst. dept. head Merck and Co., Rahway, N.J., 1949-60; tech. rep. E.I. DuPont de Nemours, Wilmington, Del., 1960-65; supt. E.I. DuPont de Nemours, Gibbstown, N.J., 1965; sr. market researcher E.I. DuPont de Nemours, Wilmington, Del., 1985; pres. Brandywine Cons., Inc., Wilmington, 1985—. Chair Hanby Civic Assn., Wilmington, 1978-80, West Milford (N.J.) Adv. Commn., 1969, Svc. Corps. Ret. Execs. chpt. 42 chmn., 1991—; asst. chmn. bd. trustees Minikin Opera, Wilmington, 1985—. Home and Office: 2401 Dorval Rd Wilmington DE 19810-3528

COLLINS, FRANK MILES, microbiologist; b. Adelaide, Australia, Mar. 30, 1928; came to U.S., 1965; s. Frank Vernon and Ethelwyn (Littler) C.; m. Lorna Fay Hannaford, May 24, 1952; children: W. Mark, Michael J. BSc, U. Adelaide, South Australia, 1949, MSc, 1951; PhD, U. Adelaide, 1960, DSc, 1976. Asst. prof. U. Adelaide, 1955-65; assoc. mem. Trudeau Inst., Inc., Saranac Lake, N.Y., 1965-68, mem., 1969—; chmn. U.S. tuberculosis panel NIH U.S.-Japan Coop. Med. Program, Washington, 1986-90; mem. bacteriology and mycology study sect. NIH, Washington, 1987-91. Contbr over 160 articles to sci. jours. Chmn. Nursery Sch. Saranac Lake, 1968-91. Fellow Am. Acad. Microbiologists; mem. Soc. Leukocyte Biology (hon. life), Am. Assn. Immunologists, Soc. Gen. Microbiology, Am. Soc. Microbiology. Home: 41 Kiwassa Rd Saranac Lake NY 12983-2306 Office: Trudeau Inst Inc Algonquin Ave Saranac Lake NY 12983-2131

COLLINS, GERRI, college official; b. Sharon, Pa., Dec. 7, 1933; d. Robert William and Frances Winifred (Reagle) Kear; children: Cynthia Elaine George, Lisa Darlene Zay, Blaine Scott Collins. BA in English, Purdue U., 1969, MS in English Edn., 1974. Instr., acad. auditor Purdue U., Lafayette, Ind., 1969-74; mgr. Roy Meriwether Trio, Dayton, Ohio, 1974-76; acad. counselor Thomas Edison State Coll., Trenton, N.J., 1977-81; asst. to v.p. acad. affairs Thomas Edison State Coll., Trenton, 1981-82, exec. asst. to pres., 1982—; adj. prof. Union County Coll., Cranford, N.J., 1978-82, Mercer County Coll., West Windsor, N.J., 1982-84; v.p. ChumFun, Inc., Roosevelt, N.J., 1985—; cons. in basic skills Dept. Human Svcs., Trenton, 1977—. Author: (short stories) Having Fun with Punctuation, 1985, (children's story series) The Saturday Morning Furniture, 1991; composer song That Smile, 1989; composer/playwright (musical) We're Movin' On, 1990. Mem. Am. Assn. Affirmative Action Officers, N.J. Assn. Affirmative Action Officers, N.J. State Coll. Affirmative Action Officers Coun., Am. Assn. for Higher Edn., Songwriters Guild (assoc.), Dramatists Guild (assoc.). Home: PO Box 191 Roosevelt NJ 08555-0191 Office: Thomas Edison State Coll 101 W State St Trenton NJ 08608-1176

COLLINS, J. MICHAEL, public broadcasting executive; b. Buffalo, Feb. 17, 1935; s. John Lloyd and Celestine (Buhrle) C.; m. Marilyn Anne Mercer, Aug. 5, 1961; children: Kevin Michael, Timothy David, Sheila Anne, Jeanne Mary, Julie Lynn. BS in Social Scis., Canisius Coll., 1957, LHD (hon.), 1978; postgrad., Mich. State U., 1957-58. Promotion mgr. WNY Pub. Broadcasting Assn. (Stas. WNED-TV, WNEQ0TV, WEBR, WNED-FM, WNJA-FM), Buffalo, 1959-60; dir. devel. WNY Pub. Broadcasting Assn. Stas. WNED-TV, WNEQ-TV, WEBR, WNED-FM, WNJA-FM, Buffalo, 1961-62; asst. sta. mgr. WNY Pub. Broadcasting Assn. (Stas. WNED-TV, WNEQ-TV, WEBR, WNED-FM), Buffalo, 1963-65, gen. mgr., 1966-69, pres., 1970—. Contbg. author: ETV: The Farther Vision, 1967. Mem. Ho. Dels. United Way of Buffalo and Erie County, 1967—; trustee Ea. Ednl. Network, 1965—, treas., 1967-70, mem. exec. com., 1967-74, 78-81, 84-85, 1988-90, 92—, chmn. budget and fin. com., 1967-70, pres., 1971-72, chmn., 1973-74, v.p., 1980-81, 88-90, 92—, mem. adv. bd. interregional prog. svc., 1984-90; mem. CATV com. Ednl. TV Stas., mem. devel. adv. com.; exec. bd. Niagara Frontier coun. Boy Scouts Am., 1971-76; exec. com. Cantalician Ctr., 1978-85; trustee St. Joseph's Collegiate Inst., 1978-85; chmn. PBS Border Sta. Consortium, 1986-88; bd. dirs. PBS, 1972-78, 80-86, vice-chmn., 1975, mem. nat. program policy com., 1990—; bd. dirs. PBS Enterprises, 1985-90, Nat. Data Cast, Inc., 1989-90; trustee Nat. Assn. Pub. TV Stas., 1987—, mem. exec. com., 1989—, chmn. nominating com., 1989; mem. Kenmore-Tonawanda Pub. Schs. Bd. Edn., 1974-81, v.p., 1977, pres., 1978; trustee Chautauqua Instn., 1988—; mem. devel. com., 1989, program com., 1988—, exec. com., 1989—, pers. com., 1990—, chmn. edn./youth/recreation com., 1989—; mem., bd. dirs. Blue Shield of West N.Y., 1990; mem. fin. coun. St. Amelia Ch. Recipient Focus award Buffalo Courier Express, 1978, Signum Fidei award St. Joseph's Collegiate Inst., 1984, Man of Yr. award Nat. Columbus Day com., 1985, Matrix award Women In Communications, 1985. Mem. N.Y. State Ednl. Radio and TV Assn. (trustee, pres. 1964-65, treas. 1963, editor newsletter 1962), Pub. Rels. Assn. Western N.Y. (pres. 1966), Nat. Assn. Ednl. Broadcasters, Canisius Coll. Alumni Assn. (bd. govs. 1960-62, 70-73, named Outstanding Alumnus 1977), Exec. Club (Buffalo). Office: Sta WNED-TV PO Box 1263 Buffalo NY 14240-1263

COLLINS, JAMES EDWARD, engineer; b. Pasadena, Calif., Mar. 26, 1937; s. Hugh and Gertrude Lillian (Bundle) C.; m. Bette Jane MacGregor, Feb. 14, 1963; children: Lisa Lynn, James. BS in Engring., U.S. Naval Acad., 1959; MS in Computer Sci., Naval Postgrad Sch., 1970; MBA in Mgmt., Marymount U., 1989. Registered prof. nuclear engr., Calif., 1974. Commd. ensign USN, 1959, advanced through grades to capt., 1979, retired, 1986; tech. dir. Integrated Systems Analysis Inc., Arlington, Va., 1986-88, group mgr. adv. scis. group, 1988-90; corp. tech. dir. Integrated Systems Analysts Inc., New London, Conn., 1990—; instr. math, computer sic. U. S.C., Charleston, 1974-77, New Sch. Social Rsch., N.Y.C., 1981-82. Contbr. articles to profl. jours. Bd. dirs. YMCA, Saratoga Springs, N.Y., 1979-82; v.p., explorer Boy Scouts Am., Saratoga Springs, 1979-82; bd. dirs., dir. ARC, New London, 1991—. Mem. Am. Soc. Naval Engrs. (chmn. combat systems group 1986—), Naval Submarine League (pres. New England chpt. 1992—), Soc. Logistics Engrs., Navy League. Home: 35 Quanaduck Rd Stonington CT 06378 Office: Integrated Systems Analysts 210 Howard St New London CT 06320

COLLINS, JAY LEO, real estate broker, insurance executive; b. Revere, Mass., Feb. 28, 1938; s. James L. and Beatrice E. (Porcella) C.; m. Maureen B. O'Brien, Aug. 22, 1955 (div. 1964); children: James L., Kathleen M., John F. (dec.); m. Carol Ann Stinson, June 20, 1970; 1 child, Michael B. Student, Stanford U., Palo Alto, Calif., 1958-59, Boston U., 1965-67. Ins. agt. Metro. Life Ins. Co., Boston, 1959-64; asst. brokerage mgr. Occidental Life Ins. Co., Boston, 1964-69; mgr. Patriot Gen. Life Ins. Co., Boston, 1969-70; pres., chief exec. officer Patriot Real Estate Inc., Andover, Mass., 1970-84, Derry, N.H., 1970-84; owner Jay's Mountain Images, Whitefield, N.H., 1984—; broker, owner Collins Real Estate & Ins., Whitefield, N.H., 1984—. With USN, 1955-59. Mem. Am. First Day Cover Soc., Ski-Ski-Ski Club. HOme: Mtn Route Rd # 3 Whitefield NH 03598 Office: Jays Mountain Images PO Box 217 Whitefield NH 03598-0217

COLLINS, JOHN FRANCIS, humanities educator, consultant; b. Bklyn., July 16, 1937; s. John Francis and May Louise (Shear) C.; m. Patricia Anne Russell, July 23, 1960; children: John F., Kathleen P., James H., Michael A., Anne M., Margaret E., Stephen R., Daniel M., William L. AB, St. Peter's Coll., 1959; MA, Columbia U., 1960, PhD, 1967. Lectr. St. Peter's Coll., Jersey City, 1959-61; instr. Fordham U., Bronx, N.Y., 1961-67; adj. prof. Pace U., N.Y.C., 1964—; asst. prof. NYU, 1967-71; tchr. Loyola Sch., N.Y.C., 1971-77; prof., coord. liberal arts Five Towns Coll., Dix Hills, N.Y., 1991—; adj. assoc. prof. Bklyn. Coll., CUNY, 1970—; fellow Latin-Greek Inst., N.Y.C., 1978—; leader NEH sponsored seminar, Gt. Neck, N.Y., 1989-91; lectr. in field; cons. medieval and Renaissance texts. Author: A Primer of Ecclesiastical Latin, 1985; editor: Einhard's Life of Charlemagne, 1985, Erasmus' The Praise of Folly, 1991; translator: Kurt Vonnegut's Requiem, 1985. Mem. St. Agnes Sch. Bd., Rockville Centre, N.Y., 1972-75, lector at Mass. Mem. Classical Assn. Atlantic States, Alpha Sigma Lambda. Democrat. Roman Catholic. Home: 55 Burtis Ave Rockville Centre NY 11570-4203

COLLINS, PATRICIA, software engineer; b. Pittsfield, Mass., Oct. 31, 1962; d. Hugh McCullough and Marisa (Scarafoni) Daley; m. Tony Austin, June 20, 1985 (div. Oct. 1989); children: Rebecca Jean, Jesse James; m. Todd Solomon Collins, Feb. 15, 1991; 1 child, Lucinda Grace. Student, Williams Coll., 1980-81; BS in Computer Sci., Rensselaer Poly. Inst., 1984, MS, 1986. Design engr. Werik Data, Pitts., 1987-89, dir. product devel., 1989—; co-pres. Collins Designs, Inc., Shadyside, Pa., 1991—; cons. Fin. Tech. Corp., Phila., 1988—. Contbr. poetry to women's mags. Vol. Big Bros./Big Sisters, Albany, N.Y., 1983-85, Planned Parenthood, Pitts., 1987—. Mem. NOW, LWV (co-chmn. membership com. local br. 1988-89), Computer Soc. of IEEE, Am. Assn. Computer Profls., Assn. Computing Machinery (co-editor quar. jour. 1991—), Greenpeace. Democrat. Office: Werik Data 992 Perry Hwy Ste M Pittsburgh PA 15237-2107

COLLINS, RICHARD RAOUL, life insurance company executive; b. St. Agatha, Maine, Sept. 4, 1936; s. Raoul and Gladys (Michaud) C.; m. Anne Adams, June 24, 1961; children: Jennifer Anne, Pamela Jane. BA, U. Maine, 1959; postgrad., NYU, 1960-61. Agy. mgr. Travelers Ins. Co., Yonkers, N.Y., 1961-66; v.p. Am. Life Ins. Co., Beirut, 1968-69; asst. v.p. Am. Internat. Reinsurance, Hamilton, Bermuda, W.I., 1969-72; v.p. Am. Internat. Group, N.Y.C., 1972-75; sr. v.p. Iran Am. Internat. Ins. Co., Tehran, 1975-79; dep. gen. mgr. Am. Life Ins. Co., Tokyo, 1979-81; pres., chief exec. officer Am. Life Ins. Co., Wilmington, Del., 1981—; bd. dirs., Wilmington Trust; chmn. bd. trustees Goldey Beacom Coll., Wilmington; mem. pres.'s devel. coun. U. Maine. Trustee Am. Coll.; mem. Del. Bus. Roundtable, Wilmington, Del. Theatre Co., Del. Symphony Orch. Mem. Wilmington Country Club, Rodney Sq. Club, Del. Symphony Orch. (elected to pres's. devel. coun. U. Maine). Republican. Home: 115 Adams Dam Rd Wilmington DE 19807-1401 Office: Am Life Ins Co 600 N King St Wilmington DE 19801-3708

COLLINS, ROBERT EDWARD, management professional; b. Lynn, Mass., Feb. 26, 1949; s. Roland Collins and Marie (White) Crone; m. Sandra Lynn; 1 child, John Edward. BS, Husson Coll., 1979; MS, Am. Coll., 1987. CLU, Chartered Fin. Cons., FLMI. Mgr. R&D UNUM Life Ins. Co., Portland, Maine, 1980-83; info. specialist Unum Life Ins. Co., Portland, Maine, 1983-84, pension compliance analyst, 1986-88; chief compliance officer UNUM Sales Corp., Portland, Maine, 1989—. Treas. Trindle For State Rep., Portland, 1979; campaign mem. Longly for Gov., Portland. Mem. Am. Soc. CLU, Greater Boston FLMI Soc. (pres. 1980), Maine CLU Soc. (v.p. 1982, edn. chmn. 1976-81). Home: 87 Cottage Rd Windham ME 04062-4402

COLLINS, ROBERT ELLWOOD, surgeon; b. Cottage City, Md., Aug. 4, 1932; s. Edward Clarence and Edith (Blough) C.; m. Barbara Kauffmann Murray, June 28, 1964; children: Garret, Randy, Robin, Bill, Bruce, Brad, Beth. BS, Ea. Mennonite Coll., 1954; MD, Med. Coll. Va., 1958. Diplomate Am. Bd. Orthopaedic Surgeons. Intern Washington Hosp. Ctr., 1958-59, orthopaedic resident, 1961-64; pvt. practice medicine Broadway, Va., 1959-60; resident in gen. surgery Med. Coll. Va., Richmond, 1960-61; pvt. practice medicine specializing in orthopaedic surgery Washington, 1964—; acting orthopaedic chief Children's Hosp., 1970-72; chief orthopaedics Washington Hosp. Ctr., 1973-75, vice-chmn. dept. orthopaedics, 1975-80, bd. dirs., pres. med. and dental staff, 1981, 83-85; assoc. prof. Georgetown U. Hosp., 1975—; courtesy staff Sibley Meml. Hosp.; pres. med. staff Nat. Rehab. Hosp., Washington, 1988; bd. dirs. Medlantic Health Corp., Washington. Bd. dirs. Easter Seal Soc., Washington, 1986—. Recipient Teaching award Georgetown U., Washington, 1985; Children's Orthopaedic's fellow Children's Hosp., 1963, Cerebral Palsy fellow Children's Rehab. Inst. Johns Hopkins U., 1965. Fellow ACS (chmn. D.C. trauma com.), Am. Acad. Cerebral Palsy, Am. Acad. Orthopaedic Surgeons, Am. Acad. Orthopaedic Foot Surgeons; mem. Med. Soc. D.C. (pres. 1985-86), Washington Clin. Club (past pres.), Georgetown Club, Congl. Country Club (Bethesda, Md.), Columbia Country Club (Chevy Chase, Md.). Presbyterian. Home: 9311 River Rd Rockville MD 20854-4631 Office: Drs Collins Gordon Johnson PC 106 Irving St NW Ste 318 Washington DC 20010-2988

COLLINS, THOMAS MICHAEL, medical products executive; b. Phila., Dec. 1, 1934; s. Thomas Francis and Anna (Kallam) C.; m. Joanne Ross, May 6, 1961; children: Sharon A. Deakins, Thomas F., Patricia A. BS in Econs., U. Pa., 1956; DSc in Pharmacy (hon.), Mass. Coll. Pharmacy and Allied Health Scis., 1984. Dir. distbn. SmithKline Beckman Corp., Phila., 1969-71; v.p. mktg. USPP U.S. Pharm. Products, Phila., 1971-78, v.p. ops. USPP, 1978-79; gen. mgr. SmithKline & French Labs., Phila., 1979-80, pres., 1980-85, v.p. corp. affairs, 1985-89; chmn. SmithKline Beecham Found., Phila., 1989-91; corp. v.p. SmithKline Corp., Phila., 1973-89. Bd. dirs. Phila. Conv. and Visitors Bur., 1985—; chmn. Penjerdel Coun., 1987—; assoc. trustee U. Pa., 1985—. Lt. (j.g.) USN, 1956-58. Mem. Nat. Assn. Retail Druggists, Am. Pharm. Assn., C. of C. (bd. dirs. 1982—). Republican. Roman Catholic. Clubs: Union League of Phila., Phila. Country, Merion Cricket, Navy League, Coral Beach & Tennis. Office: Penjcrdel Coun 1234 Market St Ste 1800 Philadelphia PA 19107-3792

COLLINS, THOMAS STEPHEN, newspaper columnist; b. Chicopee, Mass., Feb. 21, 1961; s. Thomas Stephen and Carolyn Lavina (Dunbrack) C. BA, U. Va., 1983. Reporter, columnist The Citizen, Auburn, N.Y., 1987—. Recipient Selwyn Kershaw Profl. Standards award Syracuse Press Club, 1991. Democrat. Home: 65 South St Auburn NY 13021-3920 Office: The Citizen 25 Dill St Auburn NY 13021-3632

COLLINS, WALLACE EDMUND JAMES, III, lawyer; b. Bklyn., Aug. 11, 1955; s. Wallace E. J. and Aldona (Bar) C. BA in English, Fordham U., 1977; JD, Fordham Law Sch., N.Y.C., 1987. Bar: N.Y., N.J., Calif. Musician Rock Band "AM-FM", U.S. and Europe, 1973-84; assoc. Townley & Updike, N.Y.C., 1987-91, Kane, Dalsimer, Sullivan, N.Y.C., 1991—. Contbr. articles to profl. jours. Mem. N.Y. Bar Assn., N.J. Bar Assn., Nat. Acad. Rec. Arts and Scis., N.Y. Patent, Trademark and Copyright Assn., The Copyright Soc. U.S.A., Vol. Lawyers for the Arts. Home: 250 E 39th St Apt 9K New York NY 10016 Office: Kane Dalsimer Sullivan 711 3d Ave New York NY 10016

COLLINS, WINIFRED QUICK (MRS. HOWARD LYMAN COLLINS), organizational executive, retired navy officer; b. Great Falls, Mont.; m. Howard Lyman Collins (dec.). B.S., U. So. Calif., 1935; grad. Harvard-Radcliffe Program in Bus. Adminstrn., 1938; M.A., Stanford U., 1952. Commd. ensign U.S. Navy, 1942, advanced through grades to capt. 1957; personnel dir. Midshipman's Sch., Smith Coll., 1942-43; asst. chief Naval Personnel for Women, 1957-62; ret.; nat. v.p. U.S. Navy League, 1964-70, nat. dir. and chmn. nat. awards com., 1964—; nat. dir. Ret. Officers Assn.; former cons. HEW; former trustee Helping Hand Found.; former mem. Sec. Navy's Bd. Advs. and Tng. of Naval Personnel; dir. CPC Internat., Inc., 1977-84, chmn. employee investment com., mem. audit, exec. compensation and exec. coms.; bd. dirs. Interseas Fast Craft Co., Leadership Found.; trustee U.S. Naval Acad. Found., 1977—. First v.p. Republican Women of D.C. Decorated Legion of Merit, Bronze Star; recipient Navy's Disting. Civilian Pub. Service award, 1971, Disting. Service award Navy League of U.S., 1973; named to Hall of Fame Nat. Navy League, 1990. Mem. Harvard Grad. Bus. Sch. Washington Club (past dir.), Army Navy Town Club, Army Navy Country Club, Chevy Chase Club. Home: Harbour Sq 540 N St SW Washington DC 20024-4557

COLLINS-SCHEIFELE, LESA MAE, environmental company executive, educator; b. Hartford, Conn., Apr. 27, 1962; d. Harold Martin and Rita Jeanne (Daigle) Collins. AS in Exotic Animal Tng. and Mgmt., Moorpark Coll., 1984. Emergency vetinary trainer Animal Emergency Care Clinic, Hartford, Conn., 1986-87; marine mammal trainer Mystic (Conn.) Marinelife Aquarium, 1987-89; environ. educator Bd. of Edn., Norwich, Conn., 1989—; environ. educator The Lost Ark, Inc., Norwich, 1990—, pres., 1991—; independent animal trainer, Manchester, Conn., 1984—; spl. profl. Nat. Undersea Rsch. Ctr., Groton, Conn., 1990—; animal behaviorist Analysis and Tech., New London, Conn., 1990—. Author edn. guides in field; contbr. articles to mags. Merit badge counselor Boy Scouts Am., Norwich, 1990. Mem. Am. Assn. Zoo Keepers, Suspended Animation Juggling Activities (coord. 1986—), Internat. Jugglers Assn. Roman Catholic. Home and Office: The Lost Ark Inc 129 Hunters Rd Norwich CT 06360-1935

COLLYER, STEVEN GEORGE, advertising executive; b. Albany, N.Y., Apr. 11, 1950; s. George Clairville Collyer and Muriel Atwood (Matott) Powers; m. Pamela Ann Sturges, July 16, 1978; children: Douglas George Norman, Elizabeth Christine. AA in Art, Adirondack C.C., Glens Falls, N.Y., 1971; BFA in Graphic Design, Sir George Williams U., Montreal, Que., 1973. Art dir. Muncom Publs., Inc., Scotia, N.Y., 1973-74; graphic designer Churchill Assocs. Advt., Latham, N.Y., 1974-75; gen. mgr., art dir. Adirondack Press, Inc., Lake George, N.Y., 1975-80; asst. v.p. info. & comm. Advance Energy Techs., Inc., Clifton Park, N.Y., 1980-81; v.p., COO Lange, Collyer & Assocs., Inc., Glens Falls, 1981—; adj. instr. Adirondack C.C., Glens Falls, 1978-85. Mem. Glens Falls Civic Ctr. Authority, 1989—, City of Glens Falls Zoning Ordinance Rev. Com., 1991; chair, pub. rels. com. Adirondack Regional C. of C., Glens Falls, 1992—, mem. com. leadership adv. bd., 1991—, bd. dirs., 1992—, strategic planning com. 1992—; vol. cardiac arrest Am. Heart Assn., Glens Falls, 1988—; mktg. cons. Adirondack Girl Scout Coun., 1983—; drum major Galloway Gaelic Pipes & Drums, 1989—; civil self def. instr. Royal Can. Army Cadets, 1971-72. Recipient cert. of achievement Adirondack Balloon Festival, 1988, certs. of appreciation Am. Heart Assn., 1991, Adirondack Regional C. of C., 1992. Mem. Clan Donnachaidh Soc. of New Eng., Family of Bruce Soc. in Am., Can. 17th Rgt. Legion (hon.). Republican. Presbyterian. Office: Lange Collyer & Assocs Inc 509 Glen St Glens Falls NY 12801

COLMAN, RICHARD THOMAS, lawyer; b. Boston, Sept. 22, 1935; s. Albert Vincent and Marie Catherine (Henehan) C.; m. Marilyn Flavin, Dec. 1, 1962; children: Elizabeth B., Catherine B., Richard T. Jr., Patrick B. AB magna cum laude, U. Notre Dame, 1957; LLB cum laude, Boston Coll., 1962. Bar: Mass. 1962, D.C. 1966. Trial atty. Antitrust Div. U.S. Dept. Justice, Washington, 1962-66; ptnr. Howrey & Simon, Washington, 1970—. Mem. ABA, Internat. Bar Assn., Fed. Bar Assn., D.C. Bar Assn., Wianno Club, Beach Club. Democrat. Roman Catholic. Office: Howrey & Simon 1730 Pennsylvania Ave NW Washington DC 20006-4706

COLMAN, ROBERTA FISHMAN, chemistry and biochemistry educator. AB summa cum laude, Radcliffe Coll., 1959; PhD, Harvard U., 1962. Postdoctoral fellow NIH, Bethesda, Md., 1962-64; postdoctoral fellow Washington U. Sch. Medicine, St. Louis, 1964-66, asst. prof. dept. biol. chemistry, 1966-67; assoc. Harvard Med. Sch., 1967-69, asst. prof. dept. biol. chemistry, 1969-72, assoc. prof. dept. biol. chemistry, 1972-73; prof. dept. chemistry and biochemistry U. Del., 1973—. Editorial bd. The Jour. of Biol. Chemistry, 1982-87, Archives of Biochemistry and Biophysics, 1979-84, Protein Expression and Purification, 1990—; assoc. editor The Jour. of Protein Chemistry, 1981-87; editorial adv. com. Protein Sci., 1991—; exec. editor Archives of Biochemistry and Biophysics, 1985—; contbr. numerous articles to profl. jours. Mem. AAAS, Am. Soc. Biol. Chemists (treas., mem. coun. 1981-85, com. ednl. affairs 1976-78, com. women in biochemistry 1972-74,

87—), Am. Chem. Soc. (Carothers lectr. award com. Del. div. 1985-87), N.Y. Acad. Scis., Biophys. Soc., Protein Soc., Am. Soc. Biol. Chemistry and Molecular Biology (publs. com. 1988—, chmn. nominating com. 1987-88). Office: U Del Dept Chemistry/Biochemistry Newark DE 19716

COLMER, ROY DAVID, artist; b. London, Sept. 26, 1935; came to U.S., 1967; s. Arthur Frederick William and Daisy Winifred (Wanderpant) C.; m. Claudia Ann Tedesco, June 26, 1981. Hochschule fur Bildende Kunste, Hamburg, 1960-65. Asst. prof. painting U. Iowa, Iowa City, 1970-71; vis. lectr. fine arts U. Cin., 1972; art dir. freelance Grove Press, Inc., N.Y.C., 1978-87, Carroll & Graf Pubs., Inc., N.Y.C., 1982—, Kodansha Internat., U.S.A., N.Y.C., 1989—; instr. photography Parsons Sch. Design, N.Y.C., 1988—; Prin. work includes photo book by Roy Colmer, 1984-86. Recipient grant for Photographic Project, Found. for Contemporary Performance Art, Inc., 1990, Prize for Film, Ann Arbor Film Festival, 1976. Fellow John Simon Guggenheim Found.; mem. Canyon Cinema, Film-Maker's Cooperative, Blue Sky Gallery. Home and Office: 36 Walker St # A New York NY 10013-3514

COLOMBANI, PAUL MICHAEL, general pediatric and transplant surgeon; b. Salem, Mass., May 7, 1951; s. Louis Dante and Phyllis Marie (McLaughlin)úC.; m. Linda Anne Bresnahan, June 29, 1974. AB cum laude, St. Anselm's Coll., 1972; MD with distinction, U. Ky., 1976. Intern, resident in gen. surgery George Washington U. Hosp., Washington, 1976-80, chief resident in gen. surgery, 1980-81; resident in pediatric surgery Johns Hopkins Hosp., Balt., 1981-82, chief resident in pediatric surgery, 1982-83, pediatric surgeon-in-charge, 1991—; instr. in surgery sch. of medicine Johns Hopkins U., Balt., 1983-84, asst. prof. surgery, 1984-87, asst. prof. pediatrics, oncology, 1985—, chief pediatric transplantation, pediatrical surg. oncology, 1985—, assoc. prof. surgery, pediatrics, oncology, 1987—, chief pediatric surgery, 1991—; spl. cons. FDA, Rockville, Md., 1989-91; prin. investigator Pediatric Oncology Group, St. Louis, 1985—. Contbr. over 75 articles to profl. jours. and books. Nat. Cancer Inst. grantee, Am. Cancer Soc. grantee. Fellow ACS, Am. Acad. Pediatrics (vice-chmn. program com. 1991); mem. Transplantation Soc., Am. Pediatric Surg. Assn. (vice-chmn. transplant com. 1989—, publ. com. 1992—), Soc. U. Surgeons, Am. Soc. Transplant Surgeons, Pediatric Transplant Study Group (sec. 1990-91). Democrat. Roman Catholic. Office: Johns Hopkins Hosp 600 N Wolfe St Baltimore MD 21205-2104

COLONNA, JOSEPH GEORGE, urologist; b. Jersey City, Jan. 20, 1949; s. Joseph Anthony and Ednamae (Kuppler) C.; m. Maria Rotundo, Nov. 3, 1979; children: Laura, Kathrine, Christine. BA, Ohio No. U., 1973; MD, U. Autonoma de Guadalajara, Mexico, 1977. Diplomate Am. Bd. Urology. Fifth pathway Coll. Medicine and Dentistry N.J., Hackensack (N.J.) Hosp., 1978-79; gen. surgery resident Coll. Medicine and Dentistry N.J., Rutgers div., Piscataway, 1979-80; resident Hahnemann Med. Coll. and Hosp., Phila., 1980-81; urology resident W.Va. U. Med. Ctr., Morgantown, 1981-84; pvt. practice urology Waldorf, Md., 1985—; mem. active staff surgery/urology Physician Meml. Hosp., Laplata, Md., 1987—; mem. active staff surgery/urology St. Mary's Hosp., Lenardtown Md., 1989—, So. Md. Hosp., Clinton, 1985—, Doctors Community Hosp., Lanham, Md., 1987—. Fellow ACS; mem. AMA, Am. Urol. Assn., Am. Fertility Soc., Med. and Chirurgical Faculty Md., Charles County Med. Soc. Roman Catholic. Home: 1017 Suffolk Dr LaPlata MD 20646-3507 Office: Pembrooke Square Ste 214 5046 Hwy 301 S Waldorf MD 20603

COLONY-COKELY, PAMELA CAMERON, medical researcher; b. Boston, Apr. 18, 1947; d. Donald Gifford Colony and Priscilla (Adams) Pratley; m. E. Paul Cokely Jr., Apr. 26, 1986; children: Daniel Patrick, John Travis. BA, Wellesley (Mass.) Coll., 1969; PhD, Boston U., 1976. Rsch. asst. sch. medicine Boston U., 1969-71, U. Hosp., 1971-73, Peter Bent Brigham Hosp., Boston, 1973-75; instr. dept. medicine Harvard Med. Sch., 1975-77; assoc. staff in medicine Peter Bent Brigham Hosp., Boston, 1976-79; research asst. Harvard Med. Sch., Boston, 1975-77, sr. fellow, instr., 1979-81; asst. prof. anatomy and medicine Pa. State Coll. Medicine, Hershey, Pa., 1981-88; adj. assoc. prof., pre-health advisor Franklin and Marshall Coll., Lancaster, 1988-91; adj. assoc. prof. of surgery Pa. State Coll. Medicine, Hershey, 1988-92, sr. rsch. support assoc. surgery, 1992—; sr. rsch. support assoc. Dept. Surgery Pa. State Coll. Medicine, Hershey, 1992—; ind. assessor Nat. Health and Med. Rsch. Coun., Australia, 1985—; ad-hoc reviewer NIH, Nat. Cancer Inst., Bethesda, Md., 1986; lectr. Harrisburg Area Community Coll., 1991—. Contbr. articles to profl. jours. Fellow Nat. Found. Ileitis and Colitis, 1979-81; grantee Fed. Republic Germany, 1978, Cancer Rsch. Ctr., 1982-83, NIH, 1982-91. Mem. AAAS, Am. Soc. Cell Biology, N.Y. Acad. Sci., Am. Gastroent. Assn., Nat. Assn. Advisors Health Profls. Home: Shamrock Farm RR 2 Box 1760 Lebanon PA 17042-9254 Office: Pa State Coll Medicine Dept Surgery Div Gen Surg PO Box 850 Hershey PA 17033

COLTON, CLARK KENNETH, chemical engineering educator; b. N.Y.C., July 20, 1941; s. Sidney and Goldie (Chases) C.; m. Ellen Ruth Brandner, June 20, 1965; children: Jill Erin, Jason Adam, Michael Ross, Brian Scott. B of Chem. Engring., Cornell U., 1964; PhD, MIT, 1969. Asst. prof. chem. engring. MIT, Cambridge, 1969-73, assoc. prof., 1973-76, prof., 1976—, Bayer prof. chem. engring., 1980-85, dep. head dept. chem. engring., 1977-78, chmn. centennial chem. engring. edn., 1988; cons. to NIH, FDA, various indsl. orgns.; mem. adv. bd. mil. personnel supplies NRC, 1971-75. Mem. editorial bd. Jour. Membrane Sci., 1975-81, Jour. Bioengring., 1976-79, Preparative Chromatography, Trans. Am. Soc. Artificial Internal Organs, Cell Transplantation; contbr. articles to sci. jours. Ford found. fellow, 1969-70; recipient Tchr./Scholar award Camille and Henry Dreyfus Found., 1972. Mem. AAAS, N.Y. Acad. Scis., Am. Inst. Chem. Engrs. (dir. food, pharm. and bioengring. div. 1978-81, Allan P. Colburn award 1977), Am. Soc. Artificial Internal Organs (editorial bd. 1978-84), Am. Diabetes Assn., Am. Soc. for Engring. Edn. (Curtis W. McGraw rsch. award 1980), North Am. Membrane Soc., Am. Heart Assn., Internat. Soc. on Oxygen Transport to Tissue, Am. Chem. Soc., Internat. Soc. Articificial Organs, Internat. Soc. Blood Purification (Gambro award 1986), Biomed. Engring. Soc., Cornell Club, Sigma Xi, Tau Beta Pi, Phi Lambda Upsilon. Home: 279 Commonwealth Ave Chestnut Hill MA 02167-1012 Office: MIT Dept Chem Engring Cambridge MA 02139

COLUMBUS, JOHN CURTIS, film festival executive; b. Augusta, Ga., May 2, 1944; s. John Broas and Georgia Viannah (Hogan) C.; m. Ellen Winifred Caddoo, June 21, 1969; children: Erin, Gillian. BFA, U. Hartford, 1969; MFA, Columbia U., 1975. Ind. filmmaker West Orange, N.J., 1968—; asst. prof. film, arts and humanities Stockton State Coll., Pomona, N.J., 1975-80; program dir. Wildcliff Mus., New Rochelle, N.Y., 1980-81; exec. dir. Fairlawn (N.J.) Cultural Ctr., 1981; founder, exec. dir. Edison-Black Maria Film Festival Edison Nat. Hist., 1981—; adj. assoc. prof. Univ. of the Arts, Phila., 1982—; cons. Medgar Evers Community Coll. Film, 1974-75, Edison Papers Project, Rutgers U., 1985-87; cons. cinematographer The Americana Trail Film DeLavarre Prodns., 1975-76; chief exec. officer Media Arts Consortium, 1990—. Producer, dir. film Sweetwater, 1973, Down Jersey, 1978, Olive's Farm, 1989; collaborator, producer Barnegat, 1983. Trustee Friends of the Edison Nat. Hist. Site, 1984—; founder, bd. dirs. Atlantic Film Soc.; panelist, juror Film and Arts Forums, 1985—; bd. dirs. Internat. Film Seminars, 1991—; mem. Morris County Freewheelers Assn., 1991—. Democrat. Office: Edison Black Maria Film Festival Dept Media Studies Jersey City Coll 203 W Side Ave Jersey City NJ 07305-1444

COLWILL, RUTH MELANIE, psychologist; b. Kent, Eng., Apr. 6, 1956; came to U.S., 1982; d. Derek James Colwill and Mary (Ellson) Hornsey. BA with honors, York U., York, Eng., 1978; PhD, Cambridge U., Eng., 1982. Postdoctoral fellow U. Pa., Phila., 1982-84; rsch. assoc. Hughes Med. Inst., N.Y.C., 1984-85; lectr. U. Pa., Phila., 1986-88; asst. prof. Purdue U., West Lafayette, Ind., 1988-89, Brown U., Providence, 1989—; ad hoc reviewer for various psychol. jours., NSF, NIH. Contbr. numerous articles to profl. jours. Grantee NSF. Mem. APA, Animal Behavior Soc., Eastern Psychol. Assn., Psychonomic Soc., Sigma Xi. Office: Brown U Dept Psychology Box 1853 89 Waterman St Providence RI 02912

COMAN, WILLIAM LEROY, environmental engineer, consultant; b. Ft. Sam Houston, Tex., May 13, 1948; s. Charles Pitman and Theresa Arlys (Bailey) C.; m. Julie-Anne White, Mar. 2, 1951 (dec. Jan. 1990); 1 child, Heather Gloriana. BS, Harvey Mudd Coll., Claremont, Calif., 1970; MSCE, U. So. Calif., L.A., 1973, MSME, 1975. Cert. engr.-in-tng. Mem. tech. staff Hughes Aircraft Co., L.A., 1972-77; engr. III EG&G WASC, Rockville, Md., 1977-81, engr. IV, 1981—. Mem. Am. Soc. for Photogrammetry and Remote Sensing. Republican. Office: EG&G WASC 1396 Piccard Dr Rockville MD 20850-4323

COMBS, JAMES MILTON, educator; b. New Brunswick, N.J., Oct. 26, 1951; s. Albert M. and Dorothy J. (Bennett) C.; m. Joanne Ellen Forry, June 12, 1982. BA in Polit. Sci., Juniata Coll., 1973; JD, Ohio No. U., 1976; LLM in Taxation, Villanova U., 1984. Bar: Pa. 1977, N.J. 1978. Assoc. Trigg & Flynn Atty. at Law, Lancaster, Pa., 1977-78; instr. acctg./law Pa. State U. at Harrisburg, Middletown, Pa., 1978—; pvt. practice West Lawn, Pa., 1978—; tax cons. West Lawn, 1982—; pro bono legal cons. Pa. State U., Middletown, 1978—, local community, 1978—. Mem. Pa. Inst. CPAs. Home: 401 Dorchester Ave Reading PA 19609-2321 Office: Pa State U Rt 230 Middletown PA 17057

COMDEN, BETTY, writer, dramatist, lyricist, performer; b. Bklyn., May 3, 1919; d. Leo and Rebecca (Sadvoransky) C.; m. Steven Kyle, Jan. 4, 1942; children: Susanna, Alan. Student, Bklyn. Ethical Culture Sch., Erasmus Hall High Sch.; B.S., N.Y. U. Writer, performer nightclub act, Revuers; writer: (with Adolph Green) book and lyrics Broadway shows On The Town, 1944-45, Billion Dollar Baby, Two on the Aisle, Bells are Ringing, Fade-Out-Fade-In, Subways are for Sleeping, On the Twentieth Century, A Doll's Life, 1982 (Tony award), lyrics for Hallelujah, Baby!, lyrics for The Will Rogers Follies, 1991 (Tony award); screenplays Auntie Mame, Good News, The Barkleys of Broadway, Singin' in the Rain, The Band Wagon, others; screenplay and lyrics for On the Town, Bells are Ringing, Fade-Out-Fade-In, Subways are for Sleeping, A Doll's Life, 1982 (Tony award), It's Always Fair Weather, What a Way to Go; co-author: book for Applause, 1970; co-author (with Adolph Green) book for Lorelei, 1973, book and lyrics On the 20th Century, 1978; appeared in: On the Town, 1944; performed with Adolph Green, 1959, 77; also appeared in play Isn't it Romantic, 1983, in movie Garbo Talks, 1985, The Band Wagon. Recipient Donaldson award and Tony award for Wonderful Town, as co-lyricist Best Score 1983; Tony award for Hallelujah, Baby, as co-writer Best Score 1968, Tony award Applause 1970, Tony award Lyrics and Book On the 20th Century, A Doll's Life, Tony award for Best Original lyrics The Will Rogers Follies, 1991; Woman of Achievement award NYU Alumnae Assn. 1978; N.Y.C. Mayor's award Art and Culture 1978, Lifetime Achievement award Kennedy Ctr., 1991, Grammy award for Will Roger Follies, 1992; named to Songwriters Hall of Fame 1980, Theatre Hall of Fame. Mem. Dramatists Guild (council, v.p. Dramatists Guild Fund). Office: care The Dramatists Guild 234 W 44th St New York NY 10036-3909*

COMEAU, LOUIS ROLAND, electric power industry executive; b. Meteghan, N.S., Can., Jan. 7, 1941; s. Désiré Joseph and Antoinette Marie (Saulnier) C.; m. Clarice Marie Theriault, June 20, 1964; children: Louise Anne, Jacques, Martine. BSc, St. Mary's U., 1962; BEd, Dalhousie U., 1963; EdD, U. Ste-Anne, 1986. Prof. physics and math. Coll. Ste-Anne, 1963-65, 1967-68; elected to Ho. of Commons, 1968; pres. Coll. Ste-Anne, 1971-77, E.M. Comeau and Sons Ltd., 1977-83, Kingston Lumber and Bldg. Supplies Ltd., 1981-83; pres., chief exec. officer N.S. Power Inc., 1983—, also bd. dirs.; bd. dirs. Tidal Power Corp., Can. Elec. Assn. Mem. Clare Arts Coun., Soc. Historique de La Baie Ste Marie, Nat. Rsch. Coun.; bd. govs. St. Mary's U.; sr. mem. Conf. Bd. Can. Roman Catholic. Office: NS Power Inc, 1894 Barrington St/Box 910, Halifax, NS Canada B3J 2W5

COMEN, RONALD GARY, computer education educator, sportswriter; b. New Haven, Dec. 23, 1942; s. Sidney Morris and Shirley Ann (Winnick) C.; m. Shirley E. Dymarczyk, Aug. 24, 1968 (div. 1985); children: Gregory, Joshua. AS in Liberal Arts, Quinnipiac Coll., 1963, BA in History, 1966; MS in Edn., So. Conn. State U., New Haven, 1970; postgrad., So. Conn. State U. Tchr. math., English and history City of New Haven, 1966-85, computer lab. instr., 1985—. Sportswriter, Shoreline Newspapers, 1985—; actor, producer with local theater group, 1968-73. Chief umpire Branford (Conn.) Jr. Baseball, 1991-92. Mem. New Haven Fedn. Tchrs. (v.p. 1968-70). Home: 11A Bellview Rd Branford CT 06405 Office: Troup Magnet Acad Scis 259 Edgewood Ave New Haven CT 06511

COMER, DAN K., food scientist; b. Wolf City, Tex., Feb. 14, 1947; s. Robert Charles and Lucille Elizabeth Comer; m. Frances Elaine Cook, Dec. 6, 1974; 1 child, Ian Nathanial. BS in Food Sci., U. Minn., 1979. Food rsch. technician III, Gen. Mills Corp., Mpls., 1969-79; sr. food scientist Ralston-Purina, St. Louis, 1979-83; dir. R & D, dir. quality control Mavar Shrimp & Oyster Co. Inc., Biloxi, Miss., 1983-88; sr. food scientist Alpo Pet Foods, Allentown, Pa., 1988—; cons. Protocepts Unltd., Allentown, 1982—. Author manuals in field; patentee gravy forming intermediate moisture pet food. Recipient cert. for exptl. design U.S. Dept. Commerce, 1990, cert. quality optimization Rochester Inst. Tech., 1991. Mem. Inst. Food Sci. (profl., biotech., microbiology and seafood groups). Baptist.

COMER, M. MARGARET, biology educator; b. Jacksonville, Fla., Sept. 11, 1942; d. Stewart and Mary (Rauers) C. AB, Harvard U., 1964; PhD, Purdue U., 1972. Postdoctoral fellow U. Wis., Madison, 1972-75, U. Regensburg, Fed. Republic Germany, 1975-76; prof. biology Clark U., Worcester, Mass., 1976—. Home: 154 Uncatena Ave Worcester MA 01606-1845 Office: Clark U 950 Main St Worcester MA 01610-1473

COMER, NATHAN LAWRENCE, psychiatrist, educator; b. Phila., Nov. 10, 1923; s. Rubin L. and Fannie (Cassover) C.; m. Rita Ellis, June 19, 1949 (dec. Mar. 1978); children: Robert, Susan Comer Kitei, Debra R., Marc J. BA, U. Pa., 1944; MD, Hahnemann Med. Coll., 1949. Diplomate Am. Bd. Psychiatry and Neurology. Intern Hahnemann Med. Coll., Phila., 1949-50; NIMH fellow Inst. of Pa. Hosp., Phila., 1951-53, sr. attending psychiatrist, 1968—; chief of psychiatry Jefferson Park Hosp., Phila., 1978; clin. assoc. prof. Med. Coll. Pa., Phila., 1978—; emeritus sr. attending Phila. Psychiat. Ctr., 1988—, pres. med. staff, 1975-77; pres. med. staff Inst. of Pa. Hosp., 1983-85. Contbr. articles to profl. jours. Bd. dirs. Temple Adath Israel of Main Line, Merion, Pa., 1958-78. Fellow Am. Psychiat. Assn. (life); mem. AMA, Am. Soc. for Adolescent Psychiatry, Hahnemann Med. Coll. Alumni Assn. (pres. 1973-74), B'nai Brith. Republican. Jewish. Home: 1100 Hillcrest Rd Narberth PA 19072-1224 Office: Inst Pa Hosp 111 N 49th St Philadelphia PA 19139-2718

COMERFORD, PHILIP MICHAEL, banker, consultant; b. Toledo, Apr. 20, 1931; s. L.C. "Bill" and Regina (Heiler) C.; m. Diana Lange, Feb. 7, 1953; children: Philip M. Jr., Cynthia, David, Andrew. AS, Jackson Mich. Jr. Coll., 1950; BBA, U. Mich., 1952, MBA, 1953, grad. sch. of banking, 1980. CPA, D.C., Pa. Sr. mgr. Price Waterhouse, Phila., 1957-64; asst. treas. SPS Techs., Jenkintown, Pa., 1964-69; pres. Ea. Bancorp., Phila., 1970-77; chief, exec. officer, dir. Dominion Bank Md. (formerly State Nat. Bank of Md.), Bethesda, 1977-91; mng. dir. PMC Fin. Group, Inc., Bethesda, 1991—; trustee Dover Regional Fin. Shares, Phila., 1987—. Bd. visitors Sch. Pub. Affairs U. Md., College Park, 1988—; bd. dirs. Betheseda-Chevy Chase C. of C., 1982-85. Lt. j.g. USCG, 1953-56. Mem. AICPA (com. on banking 1985-88), D.C. Inst. CPAs (fin. instns. com. 1987—), Md. Bankers Assn. (bd. dirs. 1983-86), Montgomery County Bankers Assn. (pres. 1986), Rockville C. of C. Office: 4550 Montgomery Ave Ste 1215N Bethesda MD 20814

COMIS, ROBERT LEO, oncologist, educator; b. Troy, N.Y., July 16, 1945; s. James Carl and Mary (Casile) C.; divorced; children: Larissa, Robert Jr., Anthony. BS, Fordham U., 1967; MD, SUNY, Syracuse, 1971. Diplomate Am. Bd. Internal Medicine, Am. Bd. Internal Medicine-Med. Oncology. Intern SUNY Upstate Med. Ctr., Syracuse, 1971-72, resident, 1974-75, chief med. oncology, 1978-84; staff assoc. cancer evaluation program Nat. Cancer Inst., NIH, Bethesda, Md., 1972-74; dir. Cen. N.Y. Regional Oncology Ctr., N.Y.C., 1984-88; chmn. med. oncology Fox Chase Cancer Ctr., Phila., 1984-88, med. dir., 1984—, v.p. med. sci., 1987—; prof. medicine Temple U. Hosp., Phila., 1987—; staff assoc. cancer therapy evaluation program; asst. prof. medicine, chief solid tumor oncology svc., sect. hematology/oncology SUNY Upstate Med. Ctr., 1976-78, assoc. prof., 1978-83, prof. medicine, 1983-84, chief sect. med. oncology, 1978-84; chmn. respiratory disease com. Cancer and Leukemia Group, 1979-84; assoc. chmn. lab. sci. Eastern Coop. Oncology Group, 1991—; mem. cancer award selection com. Bristol Myers-Squibb, 1985-91; asst. in medicine Peter Pent Brigham Hosp., Boston, 1975-76. Contbr. articles to profl. publs. V.p. Am. Cancer Soc., Onodaga County, N.Y., 1981-82, pres., 1982, mem. med. affairs com. N.Y. State div. With USPHS, 1972-74. Grantee Eastern Coop. Oncology Group, 1985—, Bristol Myers, 1985-89, Small Instrumentation Program, 1989-90, Biomed. Rsch. Support, 1989-90. Mem. AAAS, Am. Soc. Clin. Oncology (program chair 1985-86, editorial bd. jour. 1985, chmn. program com. 1985, clin. trial com.), Am. Radium Soc. (resident awards com. 1990—, sci. program com. 1990-91), Am. Assn. Cancer Rsch., Inc., Internat. Assn. for Study of Lung Cancer, N.Y. State Cancer Programs Assn., Pa. Soc. Hematology/Oncology, Pa. Med. Soc., Phila. County Med. Soc., Soc. Biol. Therapy. Office: Fox Chase Cancer Ctr 7701 Burholme Ave Philadelphia PA 19111-2497

COMISKEY, DONALD GEORGE, manufacturing processes and quality asssurance executive, consultant; b. N.Y.C., Feb. 6, 1943; s. William Thomas and Evelyn Audrey (Beeny) C.; m. Carol Jane Fusti, Feb. 27, 1965; children: Susan Jane van der Meulen, Brian Donald. AS in Tool Tech., Norwalk State Coll. Tech., 1964; student, U. Bridgeport, 1965-68; BSME, Bridgeport Engring. Inst., Fairfield, Conn., 1972. Technician Handy & Harman, Fairfield, 1964-66, engr., 1966-67, gen. foreman quality control, 1967-69, gen. foreman mfg., 1969-71, gen. foreman inprocess and final inspection and test depts., 1971-73, sr. engr., 1973-77, mgr. quality control, 1977-89, adminstr. quality assurance and prodn. procedures, 1989—; assoc. prof., vice-chmn. Bridgeport Engring. Mem. ASME, Am. Soc. Quality Control (sr., chmn. 1974-75, Hy Stein award 1975), Soc. Mfg. Engrs. (sr. 1963—), Am. Soc. for Quality Control (sr.), Alumni Assn. Bridgeport Engring., Boat Owners Assn. of the U.S., NRA. Home: 123 Fairview Ave Fairfield CT 06430-5216 Office: Handy and Harman 1770 Kings Hwy Fairfield CT 06430-5399

COMITO, JOHN WILLIAM, artist, painter; b. Bklyn., Aug. 12, 1961; s. John and Carol (Cutinella) C. BFA, Sch. Visual Arts, N.Y.C., 1978-82. Illustrator John Comito Illustration, N.Y.C., 1982-86; design principle The Graphic Edge, N.Y.C., 1985-87; mural artist Eon Design, N.Y.C., 1988; artist John Comito Portraits, Bklyn., 1988—. Author: The Anatomy and Structure of the Head, 1991; contbr. articles to profl. jours. Recipient award Sch. Vis. Arts Illustration Competition, 1982, Silver award Soc. Illustrators Competition, 1983, 10th Pl. award Nat. Portrait Competition, 1989. Mem. Nat. Acad. Design, Art Students League. Home and Office: John Comito Portraits 24 Sutton St Brooklyn NY 11222-4422

COMIZIO-ASSANTE, DELVA MARIA, nurse; b. Yonkers, N.Y., Nov. 8, 1964; d. Vito Joseph and Delva Maria (Ciucci) Comizio; m. William J. Assante, Nov. 5, 1988. BSN, Coll. Mt. St. Vincent, Bronx, N.Y., 1986. RN, N.Y.; cert. med.-surg. nurse. Staff nurse St. Joseph's Med. Ctr., Yonkers, N.Y., 1986-87, sr. nurse, 1987-89, nurse clinician, 1989-90; med.-surg., ambulatory surgery-recovery rm. nurse Community Hosp at Dobbs Ferry, N.Y., 1991—; mem. quality assurance coun. St. Joseph's Med. Ctr., Yonkers, 1989, chmn. nurse practice coun., 1987-90, mem. leadership coun., 1987-90, mem. exec. coun., 1987-90, mem. documentation com., 1989, mem. com. for the system of nursing care delivery, 1989. Mem. ANA, Nat. League Nursing, Am. Soc. Post-Anesthesia Nurses, N.Y. State Nurses Assn., Dist. 16 Nurses Assn., All County Head Nurse Assn., Sigma Theta Tau (treas. chpt. 1987-92, v.p. 1992—). Republican. Roman Catholic. Home: 32 Prospect Dr Yonkers NY 10705-2453 Office: Community Hosp Dobbs Ferry 128 Ashford Ave Dobbs Ferry NY 10522-1896

COMIZZOLI, ROBERT BENEDICT, physicist; b. Jersey City, Apr. 22, 1940; s. Mario Arthur and Irene (Sonvico) C.; stepfather: Nino P. Diverio; m. Flora-Marie Ardito, Sept. 11, 1965; children: Sabrina G., Cara L. BS in Physics, Boston Coll., 1962; MA in Physics, Princeton U., 1964, PhD in Physics, 1967. Mem. tech. staff RCA Labs., Princeton, N.J., 1966-79; mgr. quality assurance RCA Solid State Tech. Ctr., Somerville, N.J., 1979-81; mem. tech. staff AT&T Bell Labs., Murray Hill, N.J., 1981-83, 85-88, Holmdel, N.J., 1983-85; disting. mem. tech. staff AT&T Bell Labs., Murray Hill, 1988—, supr., 1988—. Contbr. articles to profl. publs.; patentee in field. Mem. Montgomery Twp. (N.J.) Bd. Adjustment, 1989—. Fellow Electrochem. Soc. (div. chair 1986, Callinan award 1988); mem. IEEE (sr. mem.). Roman Catholic. Office: AT&T Bell Labs PO Box 636 New Providence NJ 07974-0636

COMPAGNON, ANTOINE MARCEL, French educator; b. Brussels, July 20, 1950; came to U.S., 1985; s. Jean and Jacqueline (Terlinden) C. Ecole, Nat. des Ponts et Chaussees, Paris, 1975; D es Lettres, U. Paris VII, 1985. Rsch. attache Centre Nat. de la Recherche Scientifique, Paris, 1975-78; lectr. Ecole Poly., Paris, 1978-85, French Inst., London, 1980-81, U. Rouen, France, 1981-85; vis. prof. U. Pa., Phila., 1986, 90; prof. U. Le Mans, France, 1989-90; prof. Columbia U., N.Y.C., 1985-91, 1991—. Author: La Seconde Main, 1979, Ferragosto, 1985, Proust entre deux Siecles, 1989; editor: Marcel Proust, Sodome et Gomorrhe, 1988. Fellowship Found. Thiers, 1975-78, Guggenheim Found., 1988. Mem. Acad. Lit. Studies. Office: Columbia U 517 Philosophy Hall New York NY 10027

COMPTON, GEORGE WILLIAM, JR., software engineer; b. Bristol, Pa., Feb. 4, 1965; s. George William Sr. and Lois Anna (Gring) C.; m. Smita Bhatia, Sept. 23, 1989. BS in Computer Sci., Drexel U., 1988. Computer scientist Naval Air Propulsion Ctr., Trenton, N.J., 1984-88; software engr. Unisys, Lebanon, N.J., 1988—.

COMSTOCK, ROBERT FRANCIS, lawyer; b. Lincoln, Ill., June 4, 1936; s. William Bryan and Mary Euceba (Durham) C.; m. Jean Joyce Herring, May 9, 1970; children: James, Michael, Kelly, Jennifer, Margaret. AB, Cath. U., 1958, LLB, 1964. Bar: U.S. Dist. Ct. 1965, U.S. Ct. Appeals (D.C. cir.) 1965, U.S. Tax Ct. 1971. Ptnr. Interdonato, Reilly & Comstock, Washington, 1965—; chmn. bd. dirs. Balt. Bancorp, 1991—, Met. Fed. Savs. & Loan, Bethesda, Md., 1986-87, ,Met Holding Co., Bethesda, 1985-87, First Continental Bank, Silver Spring, Md., 1983-86. Trustee Cath. U. Am., Washington, 1987—; bd. dirs. Cath. Cemeteries Washington, 1986—, Cath. Youth Orgn. Capt. USAF, 1958-61. Named Knight of Holy Sepulchre, Papal Award of Holy See, to Athletic Hall of Fame, Cath. U., 1985. Mem. ABA, D.C. Bar Assn., Cath. U. Alumni Assn. (bd. govs.). Roman Catholic. Clubs: Columbia Country (Chevy Chase, Md.); Univ. Md. M. Home: 7707 Brookville Rd Bethesda MD 20815-3933 Office: Interdonato Reilly & Comstock 4801 Massachusetts Ave NW Washington DC 20016-2069

COMTOIS, GEORGE SPENCER, musuem director; b. Glen Gove, N.Y., Feb. 19, 1940; s. George Spencer Sr. and Neenah Carlisle (Reynolds) C.; m. Louise Henry Orr, June 26, 1973; children: James MacNeil, Rebecca Ophelia. BA, Vassar Coll., 1975; MA, U. Del., 1979. Curator State of N.Y., New Windsor, 1967-71; preparator Old Mus. Village, Monroe, N.Y., 1970-71, curator, 1975-77; researcher, writer Lynch Mus. Svcs., Pennsauken, N.J., 1979; dir. Manchester (N.H.) Historic Assn., 1979—; mem. Manchester City Planning Commn., 1989-91, City Arts Commn., Manchester, 1989-91, N.H. Com. for Promotion of History, Concord, 1989-91; participating scholar N.H. Coun. for Humanities, Concord, 1990-91. Author: (foreword) Childish Things, 1988, (columns) Manchester Union Leader, 1988-91, Deerfield Country Ledger. Trustee Fitts Mus. Found., Candia, N.H., 1991—. With U.S. Army, 1959-61. Mem. Am. Assn. Mus., Am. Hist. Assn., Am. Assn. for State and Local History, Orgn. Am. Historians, New Eng. Mus. Assn., Nat. Trust for Historic Preservation, Kiwanis. Home: 9 Old Deerfield Rd Candia NH 03034-2729 Office: Lord Addison Travel PO Box 3307 Peterborough NH 03458-3307

CONABOY, RICHARD PAUL, federal judge; b. Scranton, Pa., June 12, 1925; m. Marion Hartnett; children: Mary Ann, Richard, Judith, Conan, Michele, Kathryn, Patrick, William, Margaret, Janet, John, Nancy. Student, U. Scranton, 1943-45; LL.B., Cath. U. Am., 1950. Bar: Pa. 1951. Ptnr. firm Powell & Conaboy, Scranton, 1951-54; dep. atty. gen., 1953-62; assoc. firm Kennedy O'Brien & O'Brien, 1954-62; judge Pa. Ct. Common Pleas, 1962-79, presiding judge, 1978-79; judge U.S. Dist. Ct. (mid. dist.) Pa., Scranton, 1980—, chief judge, 1989—; pres. Pa. Joint Council on Criminal Justice System, 1971-79; mem. Nat. Conf. Juvenile Justice, Nat. Conf. Corrections. Contbr. articles to legal jours. Bd. dirs. Marywood Coll., U. Scranton. Served with USAF, 1945-47. Mem. Pa. Conf. State Trial Judges (pres. 1976-77, v.p. 1973-76, sec. 1968-73), ABA, Pa. Bar Assn., Am. Judicature Soc. Office: US Dist Ct US Courthouse Box 189 Scranton PA 18501*

CONANT, ROGER SCOTT, insurance executive; b. High Point, N.C., July 17, 1950; s. Roger Corbin and Dorothy Jane (Leithold) C.; m. Karen Ann Kryvoruka, June 1, 1974; children: Jessica Kristen, Christopher Scott. BS in Bus. Adminstrn., Susquehanna U., Selinsgrove, Pa., 1972. Claims rep. Liberty Mut. Ins. Co., South Plainfield, N.J., 1972-75; claims supr. Liberty Mut. Ins. Co., Allentown, Pa., 1975-76; asst. claims mgr. Crum & Forster Ins. Co., Morristown, N.J., 1976-79; br. claims mgr. Crum & Forster Ins. Co., Pitts., 1980-82; casualty claims mgr. Crum & Forster Ins. Co., N.Y.C., 1982-84; regional claims mgr. Crum & Forster Ins. Co., Parsippany, N.J., 1984-89; v.p. legal claims Crum & Forster Ins. Co., Basking Ridge, N.J., 1990—; pres. North Jersey Claims Mgrs. Coun., Florham Park, N.J., 1986-87; pres. N.J. Def. Assn., Parsippany, 1987-88, chmn. bd., 1988-90. Recipient Disting. Svc. award Def. Rsch. Inst., 1988. Mem. Am. Ins. Assn. (claims automation com. 1990-91). Home: 145 Buffalo Hollow Rd Glen Gardner NJ 08826 Office: Crum & Foster Comml Ins 211 Mt Airy Rd Basking Ridge NJ 07920

CONARD, PAUL LEE, administration executive; b. Milton, Pa., Jan. 31, 1933; s. George W. and Ellen (Brown) C.; m. Elizabeth Ann Menges, Oct. 13, 1956; children: Dr. Holly Dagney, Paula Faus, Molly Gottstein. BS, Bloomsburg U., 1964. From parts and service mgr. to auto salesman Lincoln Mercury Corp., Bloomsburg, Pa., 1957-64; from asst. bus. mgr. to asst. v.p. Bloomsburg U., 1964—; active mem. Ea. Assn. Coll. & U. Bus. Officers. Campaign chmn. United Way, Bloomsburg, Am. Cancer Soc; treas. Am. Heart Assn.; chpt. chmn. ARC; with USMC, 1951-54. Recipient Distinguished Svc. award Bloomsburg U. Alumni Assn., 1987, Ray Calabrese award, Cancer Soc., 1991. Mem. Bloomsburg Kiwanis Club (lt. gov. 1985-86), Bloomsburg Elks Club. Democrat. Lutheran. Home: 707 Country Club Dr Bloomsburg PA 17815-8592

CONARTY, MURRAY ROGERS, electrical engineer; b. Anchorage, Alaska, June 11, 1963; s. Roger Leon and Anna May Campbell; m. Cheryl Marie Creasey, July 8, 1989. Diplome de Langue et civilization Françaises, U. Paris Sorbonne, 1985; BS in Elec. engring., U. New Mex., 1986, BA in French, 1986. Tchr. Coll. St. Michel, Paris, 1984-85; lead design engr. aviation div. Honeywell Co., Albuquerque, 1985-89; elec. engr. United Tech. Sikorskey Div., 1989-91, E-Systems, Dallas, 1991—; translator Immigration and Naturalization Service, Albuquerque, 1985. Author: Font Generation Techniques, 1987. Info. specialist Nat. Forest Service, Tijeras, N.Mex., 1985-87. Mem. Alliance Francaise (scholar 1985), Am. Inst. Individual Investors, Blue Key. Republican. Roman Catholic. Home: 16 Heritage Pl Allen TX 75002-5227 Office: United Techs Sikorsky Div 6900 Main St Stratford CT 06497-1361

CONBOY, KENNETH, judge; b. 1938. AB, Fordham Coll., 1961; JD, U. Va., 1964; MA in History, Columbia U., 1980. Trial atty., chief rackets bur., exec. asst. dist. atty. Manhattan Dist. Atty.'s Office, 1966-77; dep. commr., gen. counsel N.Y. Police Dept., 1978-83; criminal justice coord. N.Y.C., 1984-86, commr. of investigation, 1986-87; judge U.S. Dist. Ct. (so. dist.) N.Y., N.Y.C., 1987—; summer faculty Organized Crime Inst. Cornell Law Sch. Author: Grand Jury Examination of the Recalcitrant Witness, 1977; contbr. articles to profl. jours. Mem. N.Y. State Crime Control Planning Bd., N.Y. Sovern Commn.; dir. Cath. Interracial Coun. of N.Y. Capt. U.S. Army, 1964-66. Mem. Am. Soc. Legal History, N.Y. State Bar Assn., Assn. of Bar of City of N.Y. (criminal cts., judiciary, penology and police law policy coms.). Office: US Dist Ct So Dist US Courthouse Foley Sq New York NY 10007-1581*

CONCILIO, M. ALPHONSA, voice educator; b. Allentown, Pa., Sept. 22, 1932; d. August Charles and Anna Elizabth (Nolan) C. BA, Marywood Coll., 1959, BM, 1966; MA, St. Louis U., 1974, Marywood Coll., 1977. High sch. tchr. Immaculate Conception High Sch., Lock Haven, Pa., 1954-57, South Catholic High Sch., Scranton, Pa., 1957-58, Laurel Hill Acad., Susquehanna, Pa., 1958-59, St. Basil High Sch., Dushore, Pa., 1959-61, I. H. M. High Sch., Coeur d'Alene, Idaho, 1961-71; tchr. Pocono Cen. Catholic High Sch., Cresco, Pa., 1971-75; coll. prof. voice and related subjects Marywood Coll., Scranton, Pa., 1975—; Vocal Coach Marywood Drama/Music Dept., Scranton, Pa., 1976-90; workshop presentor various chs. and sch. groups, Scranton. Mem. Nat. Assn. Tchrs. of Singing (gov. 1985-87), MENC. Roman Catholic. Home and Office: Marywood Coll 2300 Adams Ave Scranton PA 18509-1598

CONCONI, DIANA ALEXIS, public relations executive; b. Alexandria, Va., Dec. 2, 1962; d. Charles Norman and Carole Ann (Rose) C. BA, U. Va., 1984. Free-lance media specialist Washington (D.C.) Inc., 1984, Anne Banville & Assocs., Washington, 1984; account rep. Burson-Marsteller Co., Washington, 1984-85, asst. account exec., 1985-86, account exec., 1986-87; asst. dir. mktg., ptnr. Events Mgmt. Inc., Washington, 1987-88; pres. Conconi Communications, Washington, 1988—; instr. media relations pub. relations cert. program George Washington U., Washington, 1986. Home: 1412 Taylor St NW Washington DC 20011-5510 Office: Conconi Communications 2033 M St NW # 502 Washington DC 20036-3305

CONDAX, KATE DELANO, marketing and public relations executive; b. Phila., Mar. 23, 1945; d. John and Laura Foster (Delano) C. Student, Sweet Briar Coll., 1965-67, U. St. Andrews, Scotland, 1966-67, U. Pa., 1975-76. Legis. aide to Sen. Samuel J. Ervin, Jr. Subcom. Separation of Powers, Com. on Judiciary U.S. Senate, Washington, 1970-73; ptnr. U.S. Trade Trip to People's Republic China, 1973; assoc. producer, asst. dir. KYW-TV, Phila., 1973-74; account exec. Aitkin, Kynett Pub. Rels., Phila., 1975-77, ICPR Pub. Rels., N.Y.C., 1977-79; dir. pub. rels. Am. Heritage Pub. Co., Inc., N.Y.C., 1979-81; account exec. Howard J. Rubenstein Pub. Rels., Inc., N.Y.C., 1981-82; rsch. assoc. Nordeman Grimm Exec. Search Firm, N.Y.C., 1982-84; prin. Kate Delano Condax & Assocs. Mktg., N.Y.C., 1984-89; nat. dir. mktg. and pub. rels. Allmilmo Corp., Fairfield, N.J., 1989—; mktg. and media cons.; exec. dir. Philadelphia 100. Author: Horse Sense: Cause and Correction of Problems, 1980, 2d edit., 1990, Rider's Guide: How to Ride with Safety and Good Form Right from the Start, 1980. Probono housing counselor to elderly, N.Y.C., 1980—; exec. dir. Phila. 100. Mem. Brit. Horse Soc. (instr.), Am. Horse Shows Assn. (judge), Soc. Mayflower Descendants, Nat. Soc. Colonial Dames Am., Coffee House Club. Office: 315 Chestnut St Moorestown NJ 08057

CONDICT, EDGAR RHODES, medical electronics, aviation instrument manufacturing and medical health care executive, inventor, mediator; b. Boston, Apr. 27, 1940; s. Clinton Adams and Elizabeth May (Lane) C.; m. Judith Pond, June 9, 1962; children: Edgar Rhodes Jr., Robert Adams, Carolyn Helen. Student, Bucknell U., 1962. Chmn. bd., pres. Bio-Tronics Rsch., Inc., 1962—, Kearsarge Healthcare, Inc., 1978—, Condict Instruments, Inc., 1985—; pres. Medel Corp., patent devel. investment, 1965—; cons. U. Tex. Med. Sch., 1968-70; cons. in med. electronics, electronics, biophysics, biofeedback, telecommunications, environ. health and welfare. Author: A Theory of Anesthesia, Feedback Anesthesia, Electronic Pain-Killing Devices, others. Patentee in med. electronics, telecommunications fields. Chmn. Mantowa dist., exec. bd. Daniel Webster coun. Boy Scouts Am., 1979-84; chmn. bd. World Mediators, 1990—; bd. dirs. Lake Sunapee Area Mediation Program, 1988-90, pres., 1990. Recipient various grants in neuro-brain scis.; numerous med. awards from fgn. countries. Mem. Sigma Chi. Baptist. Address: RR 2 Box 475 Main St New London NH 03257

CONDIT, DOUGLAS DODD, JR., physician assistant; b. Harrisburg, Pa., May 6, 1945; s. Douglas Dodd and Virginia Grey (Higgins) C. Student, Colo. State U., 1963-66; grad., U. Ala., Birmingham, 1972. Physician asst. Montefiore Med. Ctr., Bronx, N.Y., 1972—; instr. in surgery Touro Coll. Physician Asst. Program, N.Y.C., 1983-89; adj. faculty CUNY Physician Asst. Program, Harlem, N.Y., 1990—; clin. instr. Montefiore/Albert Einstein Coll. Postgrad. Surg. Physician Asst. Program, Bronx, 1975—. Clin. articles editor: Infections in Surgery, 1982-90; contbg. editor: Physician Asst., 1975-83; editor: APACVS Newsletter, 1990—; contbr. articles to profl. jours.; co-editor: Vietnam Experience, 1989. Steering com. Montefiore Tenants Assn., Bronx, 1989—; active 52 Precinct Community Coun., Bronx, 1989—, March of Dimes/Walk America Com., Bronx, 1989—. With USN, 1966-70, Vietnam. Recipient John W. Kirklin award for profl. excellence Am. Assn. Surgeons Assts., 1990. Mem. Am. Acad. Physician Asss. (chair surg. coun. 1982-85), Assn. Physician Assts. in Cardiovascular Surgery (bd. dirs. 1986—), N.Y Acad. Scis., Vietnam Vets. Am., Am. Heart Assn. Episcopalian. Home: 345013N Wayne Ave Bronx NY 10467-1587 Office: Montefiore Med Ctr 111 E 210th St Bronx NY 10467-2490

CONDON, THOMAS BRIAN (BRIAN CONDON), hospital executive; b. Beverly, Mass., June 1, 1942; s. Thomas William and Marguerite Mary (Welch) C.; m. Carol Therese Sicilliano, Apr. 29, 1969; children: Therese Beth, Tara Bridget, Colleen Marguerite, Caroline Susan. BA in English, Boston Coll., 1964; MPA, U. New Haven, 1973, MA in Community Psychology, 1975, MA in Indsl. and Organizational Psychology, 1977. Dir. unit mgmt. Yale New Haven Hosp., 1971—, asst. adminstr., 1975, v.p., 1980; pres., dir. Shirley Frank Found., New Haven, 1980—; chmn., dir. South Cen. Community Coll. Found., New Haven, 1988—; dir. Nat. Inst. Community Health Edn., Hamden, Conn., 1990—; bd. dirs. Hill Devel. Corp., New Haven; mem. adv. coun. New England Organ Bank, 1990—. Elected mem. Cheshire (Conn.) Planning & Zoning Commn., 1976-87; mem. Gov.'s Task Force on Student Aid, Hartford, Conn., 1986-87; chmn., dir. Conn. Student Loan Found., Rocky Hill, 1976—. Capt. U.S. Army, 1964-70. Recipient Community Svc. award Bd. Trustees Conn. State Coll., 1991. Roman Catholic. Home: 150 Hotchkiss Ridge Cheshire CT 06410 Office: Yale New Haven Hosp 20 York St New Haven CT 06504

CONE, EDWARD CHRISTOPHER, newspaper publisher; b. Montclair, N.J., Mar. 29, 1937; s. Edward della Torre and Patricia Clapp (Laurence) C.; married; children: David Christopher, Jennifer Lynn. BA, Princeton U., 1958. Missionary Holy Cross Mission, Bolahun, Liberia, 1958-63, commissary, 1984—; asst. to editor West Essex Tribune, Livingston, N.J., 1963-68, mng. editor, 1968-80, pub., pres., 1980—; cons. Vols. in Tech. Assistance, Washington, 1964—, Assn. Episc. Colls., 1985—. Author: Automotive Operation and Maintenance, 1973. Trustee North Essex United Way, Montclair, N.J., 1982—, Livingston Symphony Orch., 1978—; sole sponsor Korea-Vietnam Veterans Meml., Livingston, 1987; sponsor Occupational Ctr. Sheltered Workshop, Livingston, 1981; tech. mgr. Studio Players Theater, Montclair, 1963-68; vestryman Grace Episcopal Ch., Madison, N.J., 1991—. Mem. N.J. Press Assn. (editorial com. 1968—, bd. dirs. 1988—), Nat. Newspaper Assn., Livingston Coun. of the Arts, Livingston C. of C. (bd. dirs. 1981—). Republican. Episcopalian. Office: West Essex Tribune 495 S Livingston Ave PO Box 65 Livingston NJ 07039

CONE, ROBERT EDWARD, immunologist; b. Bklyn., Aug. 18, 1943; s. Joseph and Ruth C.; m. Michele Nash, Aug. 21, 1966; children: Jennifer, Laura. BS, Bklyn. Coll., 1964; MS, Fla. State U., 1967; PhD, U. Mich., 1970. Postdoctoral fellow Walter & Eliza Hall Inst., Melbourne, Australia, 1971-73, Basel (Switzerland) Inst. Immunology, 1973-74; mem. faculty Yale U., 1974-84, asst. prof. pathology, 1974-79, assoc. prof. pathology, 1979-84, asst. prof. surgery, 1974-79, assoc. prof. surgery, 1979-84; prof. pathology U. Conn. Health Ctr., 1985—; mem. histocompatibility com. New Eng. Organ Bank. Recipient Research award UpJohn, 1979; Horace Rackham fellow, 1968-69; Damon Runyon postdoctoral fellow, 1971-72; F. G. Novy fellow, 1969-70; NSF grantee, 1980-83; NIH grantee, 1974-77, 81—; Am. Cancer Soc. grantee. Mem. AAAS, Am. Assn. Immunologists, Soc. for Exptl. Biology and Medicine, N.Y. Acad. Sci., Sigma Xi. Contbr. numerous articles to profl. jours., 1969—. Office: U Conn Health Ctr Dept Pathology Farmington CT 06032

CONE, THOMAS EDWARD, JR., pediatrician, educator; b. Bklyn., Aug. 15, 1915; s. Thomas Edward and Helen (McMahon) C.; m. Barbara Cross, Dec. 5, 1939; children: Thomas Edward, Mary Cross, Elizabeth Gray. BA, Columbia Coll., 1936; MD, Coll. Physicians & Surgeons, 1939. Diplomate Am. Acad. Pediatrics. Resident Lenox Hill Hosp., N.Y.C., 1939-41; commd. med. officer USN, 1941, advanced through grades to capt., 1955; chief ambulatory svcs. Children's Hosp., Boston, 1963-66; prof. pediatrics Southwestern Med. Sch. U. Tex., Dallas, 1966-67; clin. prof. Harvard Med. Sch., Boston, 1967-82, ret., 1982; mem. nat. adv. coun. Inst. Child Health and Human Devel., Bethesda, Md., 1962-64. Author: History of American Pediatrics, 1980, History of Care and Feeding of Premature Infants, 1985; contbr. articles to profl. jours. Recipient Outstanding Svc. award Am. Acad. Pediatrics, 1984. Mem. Am. Pediatric Soc., Ambulatory Pediatric Soc., Soc. Med. Cons. Armed Svcs. U.S., N.Y. Acad. Sci., Irish and Am. Pediatric Soc. (founder, 1st pres.). Roman Catholic. Home: 5 Short Hill Rd Lincoln MA 01773-3803 Office: Harvard U Med Sch 25 Shattuck St Boston MA 02115-6092

CONESTABILE, FRANK ROCCO, human resource management director; b. Rome, N.Y., Aug. 18, 1956; s. Rocco Peter and Jean (Corasinitti) C.; m. Shari Ellen Clintsman, May 31, 1986; 1 child, Frank II. AAS, Mohawk Valley Community Coll., Utica, N.Y., 1976; B. Profl. Studies, SUNY, Utica, 1978. Employment counselor City of Rome (N.Y.), 1980, employment adminstr., 1980-81, dir. employee rels., 1981-90; dir. pers. Masonic Home (Nursing Facility), Utica, 1990-91, dir. human resource mgmt., 1991—; labor rels. cons., Rome, 1988—; adjutant prof. New Sch. of Social Rsch., Griffiss, N.Y., 1987. Com. person Republican Party, Rome, 1983-84; mem. Indsl. Labor Edn. Coun., Utica, 1991. Mem. Internat. Pers. Mgrs. Assocs., Cen. N.Y. Pers. Assn. Roman Catholic. Home: 8724 Maple Dr Lee Center NY 13363 Office: Masonic Home 2150 Bleecker St Utica NY 13501-1714

CONFALONE, PAT NICHOLAS, pharmaceutical company executive; b. Bethlehem, Pa., Oct. 6, 1945; s. Nicholas and Carmel (Romano) C.; m. Elizabeth Dianne Lollar, Jan. 6, 1979; children: Nicholas Stewart, Patricia Nicole. BS, MIT, 1967; MS, Harvard U., 1968, PhD, 1970, postgrad., 1971. Rsch. fellow Hoffmann-LaRoche, Nutley, N.J., 1971-81; dir. DuPont, Wilmington, Del., 1981-90; exec. dir. DuPont Merck, Wilmington, 1991—; adj. prof. Drew U., Madison, N.J., 1989—, Rutgers U., Newark, 1979-81; vis. prof. U. Colo., Boulder, 1977; R.A. Welch lectr. Welch Found., Tex., 1988; Esther Humphrey lectr. U. Vt., Burlington, 1990; S.M. McElvain speaker U. Wis., Madison, 1982. Patentee in field. Mem. Am. Chem. Soc. (chmn. 1988-91), Internat. Soc. Heterocyclic Chemists, Pharm. Mrs. Assn., Drug Info. Assn., Internat. Union Pure and Applied Chemists, Harvard Assn. Chemists, Alpha Chi Sigma, Phi Lambda Upsilon. Republican. Roman Catholic. Home: 722 Hertford Rd Wilmington DE 19803 Office: DuPont Merck Ex Sta E353-300 Wilmington DE 19880-0353

CONFUSIONE, MICHAEL JOSEPH, psychologist; b. Bklyn., Oct. 19, 1947; s. John and Francesca Rachael (Sardo) C.; m. Linda Elizabeth Otvas, Sept. 6, 1986; stepchildren: James, Virginia, Jennifer, Matthew, Thomas. BA, John Jay Coll., 1969; MA, New Sch. for Social Rsch., 1971; PhD, Calif. Sch. Profl. Psychology, 1979. Diplomate Am. Bd. Med. Psychotherapists; lic. psychologist, N.Y. Drug abuse counselor N.Y. State Drug Abuse Svcs., Bklyn., 1971-72; methadone clinic supr. Suffolk County Drug Abuse Svcs., Bayshore L.I., N.Y., 1972-75; clinics coord. Suffolk County Drug Abuse Svcs., Hauppauge L.I., 1975-76; psychology intern various agys., Calif., 1976-79; rsch. asst. SUNY, Stony Brook, 1979-80; cons. Comprehensive Home Care-Hospice, Smithtown, N.Y., 1979-81; psychologist Suffolk County Correctional Facility, Riverhead, N.Y., 1981-82; cons. Suffolk County Drug Abuse Svcs., Hauppauge, 1979-88; asst. prof. clin. family medicine SUNY Dept. Family Medicine, Stony Brook, 1980—; clin. psychologist pvt. practice Rocky Point, N.Y., 1983—; cons. in field. Contbr. articles to profl. jours. Hon. mem. North Shore Youth Coun., Rocky Point, N.Y., 1981—. Recipient Nat. Innovations in Clin. Teaching award, 1986, Achievement award for Drug Abuse Edn. and Prevention for Primary Care Physicians, 1983. Mem. APA, Am. Assn. Family Counselors/Mediators, Nat. Assn. Alcoholism and Drug Abuse Counselors. Office: Michael J Confusione PO Box 5011 Rocky Point NY 11778-0962

CONIFF KANE, MARGUERITE, counselor, consultant; b. Norwalk, Conn., Apr. 4, 1948; d. Edward Keating and Virginia (Johnson) Coniff; m. Peter Evans Kane, May 27, 1981; stepchildren: Emily, Ellen, Amy, Jake. BA in Liberal Studies, SUNY, Brockport, 1975; MS in Ednl. Counseling, SUNY, 1981; postgrad., Colgate Rochester Div. Sch., 1990-91. Tchr., supr. Escola Graduda, São Paulo, Brazil, 1971-74; assoc. for continuing edn. SUNY, Brockport, 1975-79, 80-81; counselor Am. Internat. Sch., Lisbon, Portugal, 1979-80; group counselor SUNY, Brockport, 1982-84; coll. counselor Genesee Community Coll., Batavia, N.Y., 1984—; cons. IDEA Ctr., Rochester, N.Y., 1986—; creator, facilitator Sharp Preventative Mental Health Program, SUNY, 1989. Founder, bd. dirs. Brockport Interagy. Coun., 1987—, Greater Rochester Communityof Churches, 1990—; vice moderator Diocesan Coun. Episcopal Diocese, Rochester, 1982—; chair Conv. of Rochester Diocese, Corning, N.Y., 1990-91; mem. Ecumenical Outreach Com., 1989—, Jud. Process Commn., 1988—. Recipient Chancellor's Prof. Svc. award SUNY, 1989. Mem. AACD, Nat. Bd. Cert. Counselors, N.Y. State Counseling Assn., Coll. Pers. Assn., Chi Sigma Iota. Home: 8 Chiswick Dr Churchville NY 14428-9407 Office: Genesee Community Coll College Rd Batavia NY 14020-9703

CONIGILARO, PHYLLIS ANN, retired educator; b. Ilion, N.Y., Nov. 27, 1932; d. Gus Carl and Jennie Margaret (Marine) Denapole; m. Paul Anthony Conigilaro, July 16, 1983. BS cum laude, SUNY, Cortland, 1955; MA in Edn., Psychology, Cornell U., 1961. Cert. tchr., N.Y. Elem. classroom tchr. Mohawk (N.Y.) Central Sch., 1955-88. Contbr. articles to profl. jours. Bd. dirs. United Fund of Ilion, Herkimer, Mohawk and Frankfort, 1984-86, pres., 1986; pres. bd. edn. St. Mary's Parochial Sch., 1978; mem. Herkimer County Hist. Soc., 1988. Mem. N.Y. State United Tchrs., Mohawk Tchrs. Assn. (past pres.), Retirees of the Mohawk Valley, AAUW (pres. Herkimer br. 1981-82), Herkimer County Hist. Soc., N.Y. State Ret. Tchrs. Assn. (Herkimer County legis chmn.), Rep. Women's Club, Kappa Delta Pi. Republican. Roman Catholic. Home: RR 1 Box 285 Frankfort NY 13340-0285

CONKLIN, C. AMY, employee involvement facilitator; b. Yorktown, Va., July 20, 1965. BA magna cum laude, Radford U., 1987; MA summa cum laude, Regent U., 1989. Tng. and employee involvement adminstr. Londontown Corp., Balt., 1990—. Named Beasley scholar Regent U., Virginia Beach, 1988-89. Mem. ASTD, Assn. for Quality Participation, Chesapeake Human Resources Assn. Office: Londontown Corp Londontown Blvd Eldersburg MD 21784

CONKLIN, D(ONALD) DAVID, college president; b. Waynesburg, Pa., Oct. 29, 1944; s. Donald David and Esther Louise (McCracken) C.; m. Kathleen Ann Fitzwilliam, Aug. 3, 1968; children: Donald David III, Elizabeth Ann. BA, Pa. State U., 1966, MEd, 1967; EdD, NYU, 1975. Asst. dean. instrn. SUNY, Farmingdale, 1970-72, exec. asst. to pres., 1972-78; spl. asst. N.J. Dept. Higher Edn., Trenton, 1978-80; dean for planning and devel. Mercer County Community Coll., Trenton, 1980-83, dean for adminstrn., 1983-86, dean for acad. affairs, 1986-92; pres. Dutchess Community Coll., Poughkeepsie, N.Y., 1992—; cons. AAA of No. N.J., Morristown, 1984, Harrisburg Area Community Coll., 1983, Ednl. Testing Svc., Princeton, N.J., 1990, Educom Cons. Svcs., Princeton, 1985-90. Contbr. articles to profl. jours., chpt. to book. Recipient Adminstrs. award for excellence in aviation edn. FAA, 1989. Mem. Hamilton Twp. C. of C., YMCA, Rotary, Phi Theta Kappa, Alpha Mu Gamma. Presbyterian. Home: 55 Pendell Rd Poughkeepsie NY 12601 Office: Dutchess Community Coll Pendell Rd Poughkeepsie NY 12601

CONKLIN, DONALD RANSFORD, pharmaceutical company executive; b. Bound Brook, N.J., Sept. 10, 1936; s. Walter Ransford and Dorothy Ann (Haase) C.; m. Louise Sealey, July 13, 1960; children: Elizabeth, Edward. BA, Williams Coll., 1958; MBA, Rutgers U., 1961; grad. program for mgmt. devel., Harvard U., 1970. Dir. mktg. Schering Corp. U.S.A. (name changed to Schering-Plough 1971), Kenilworth, N.J., 1970-74; dir. mktg. Europe div. Schering-Plough, Lucerne, Switzerland, 1975-76; v.p. internat. mktg. Schering-Plough, Kenilworth, 1977-79; regional dir., sr. v.p. Latin Am. div. Schering-Plough, Miami, Fla., 1980-83; sr. v.p. internat. hdqrs. Schering-Plough, Kenilworth, 1984—, pres., 1985, group v.p. pharm. ops., 1986, exec. v.p. pharm. ops., 1987-89, pres. pharm. ops., 1989—. Bd. dirs. Mt. Kemble Hosp., Morristown, N.J. Home: 9 Chandler Rd Chatham NJ 07928-1803 Office: Schering-Plough Corp 1 Giralda Farms Kenilworth NJ 07033

CONKLIN, JACK LARIVIERE, education educator; b. Pt. Jefferson, N.Y., Dec. 9, 1942; s. John Agustus and Jeanne (Lariviere) C.; m. Susan J. Kuceluk, July 25, 1981; children: Susanne, Danielle, Genevieve, Michelle. BA, Dowling Coll., 1967; MA, Adelphi U., 1970; PhD, U. So. Calif., L.A., 1972. Tchr. Comsewogue Sch. Dist., Pt. Jefferson Sta., N.Y., 1967-70; asst. principal intern Toll Jr. High Sch., Glendale, Calif., 1971-72; prof. edn. North Adams (Mass.) State Coll., 1972—, chmn. edn. dept., 1980-88, 91—, cert. officer, 1988—; chmn. Commonwealth Tchr. Edn. Consortium, 1981-83. Bd. dirs. Berkshire Ctr. for Families and Children, Pittsfield, Mass., 1977, South Forty Alternatives, North Adams, 1978; vestry mem. St. John's Episcopal Ch., Williamstown, Mass., 1983-84; cons. N.E. Regional Ctr. for Drug Free Schs., 1988—. Mem. Am. Assn. Colls. for Tchr. Edn. (adv. coun. state reps.), Mass. Assn. Colls. for Tchr. Edn. (pres. 1988-89), North Adams State Faculty Assn. (pres. 1980-83), Joint Task Force on Tchr. Preparation, Phi Delta Kappa, Pi Lambda Theta. Democrat. Home: 85 Hawthorne Rd Williamstown MA 01267-2700 Office: North Adams State Coll Hopkins Hall Church St North Adams MA 01247-4100

CONLAN, EDWARD FRANCIS, JR., physical education educator; b. Waterbury, Conn., July 25, 1939; s. Edward Francis and Mary Agnes (Corden) C.; m. Joyce Ann Koslowski, July 18, 1964; children: Terri Ann, Kristin Ann. BS, St. Bonaventure U., 1961; MS, U. Bridgeport, Conn., 1962; postgrad., So. Conn. State U., 1967. Instr. City of Waterbury, 1962—; playground supr. City of Waterbury, 1957-65; camp dir. Easter Seal Rehab. Ctr., Waterbury, 1969-71; football ofcl. Eastern Coll. Athletic Conf., Centerville, Mass., 1978—; instr. in CPR, Am. Heart Assn., Wallingford, Conn., 1978—. Recipient Merit award Golden Circle of Sports, 1991. Mem. NEA, Conn. Edn. Assn., Waterbury Tchrs. Assn. (sch. rep.), Elks. Democrat. Roman Catholic. Home: 101 Plainfield Dr Oakville CT 06779

CONLIN, JAMES FRANCIS, sales executive; b. Wilmington, Del., Dec. 14, 1949; s. James Francis and Catherine Ann (Twomey) C.; m. Margaret Mary McGrath, Sept. 21, 1974; 1 child, James. BA, Allentown Coll., 1972. Tchr. North Cath. High Sch., Phila., 1972-73; assembly line foreman Strick Trailers, Fairless Hills, Pa., 1973-74; data control specialist J.D. Morrissey Inc., Phila., 1974-78; salesman Managistics Inc., Phila., 1978-81; sales trainer Safeguard Bus. Systems, Ft. Washington, Pa., 1981—; cons. various banks and sales orgns., Phila., 1986—; mgmt. trainer Zenger Miller, Wayne, Pa., 1991—. Author Market Opportunity Sales Training course, 1990; co-author: Life of Thomas Garrett in Historical Society of Delaware, 1972. Organizer Rep. Party, Pitts., 1980-84; soccer coach Mayfair Shamrocks, Phila., 1989—. Democrat. Roman Catholic. Home: 3016 Fanshawe St Philadelphia PA 19149-2515 Office: Safeguard Bus Systems 455 Maryland Dr Fort Washington PA 19034-2594

CONLOGUE, JON ALAN, education administrator; b. Presque Isle, Maine, Jan. 22, 1959; s. Paul David and Emma Octavia (Gray) C.; m. Donna Lee Olson, Sept. 29, 1984; 1 child, Thomas Alan. BS in Indsl. Design, U. Bridgeport, 1982; MA in Communication, Fairfield U., 1986; postgrad., U. Pitts., 1988—. Purchasing agent Sterling Auto Parts, Presque Isle, 1977-78; resident asst. U. Bridgeport, Conn., 1981-82; head resident Fairfield U., Conn., 1982-84; resident dir. Ohio U., Athens, 1984-85, asst. coord. residence life, 1985-87; asst. dir. residence life U. Pitts., 1987—; mem. presdl. selection com. U. Pitts., 1990-91. Vice pres. Aroostook County Young Dems., 1976-77, pres., 1977-78; v.p. Maine Young Dems., 1978; del. Maine Dem. Conv., 1978. Charles Dana scholar U. Bridgeport, 1981. Mem. U. Pitts. Staff Assn. Council (v.p. 1989—), Am. Coll. Personnel Assn. (nat. conf. presenter 1986), Phi Kappa Phi. Democrat. Home: 315 E Swissvale Ave # 2 Pittsburgh PA 15218-1442 Office: U Pitts ORL Tower C Lobby Pittsburgh PA 15260

CONLON, BRIAN THOMAS, promotion executive; b. Oceanside, NY, Mar. 19, 1958; s. Thomas James and Joan Anna (Erickson) C.; m. Mary Jane Lewis, Nov. 12, 1988; 1 child, Brendan Lewis. BA in English, Hofstra U., 1979. Asst. account exec. DR Group, N.Y.C., 1981-82, account exec., 1982-83; account exec. D.L. Blair, Inc., Garden City, N.Y., 1983-85, v.p./account supr., 1985-90, sr. v.p., 1990-91, exec. v.p., 1991—; pres. Promotion & Merchandising, Inc., Garden City, 1990—. Roman Catholic. Office: DL Blair Inc 1051 Franklin Ave Garden City NY 11530-2931

CONLON, JOHN JOSEPH, English and theatre arts educator; b. Lowell, Mass., Mar. 23, 1945; s. John Joseph and Helen Theresa (Matthews) C.; m. Simonne Juliette Dufour, Feb. 17, 1973; children: Sean Joseph, Nicole Danielle. BA, Cath. U. of Am., 1968; MA, Tufts U., 1970, PhD, 1974. Tchr. English Malden (Mass.) Cath. High Sch., 1968-70; teaching asst. Tufts

U., Medford, Mass., 1971; prof. English Pine Manor Coll., Chestnut Hill, Mass., 1971; tchr. English Fall River (Mass.) Pub. Schs., 1972-74; dir. tchr. certification U. Mass., Boston, 1974-80, asst. dean arts and scis., 1980-83, assoc. dean arts and scis., 1983-90, assoc. prof. English, lectr. theatre arts, 1983—. Author: Walter Pater and the French Tradition, 1982; contbr. numerous articles to profl. jours. Woodrow Wilson fellow, 1968, Coll. scholar Cath. U. Am., 1968. Mem. MLA, Walter Pater Soc., Mass. Soc. Profs., New Eng. Victorian Studies Assn., Phi Beta Kappa. Roman Catholic. Home: 74 Crescent Dr Bridgewater MA 02324-2429 Office: U Mass Harbor Campus Boston MA 02125

CONMY, GEORGE FRANK, insurance company executive; b. Binghamton, N.Y., May 4, 1955; s. Eugene Gerald and Marjorie Ethel (Grube) C.; m. Suzanne White, Apr. 7, 1979; 1 child, Katherine Marjorie. BS, LeMoyne Coll., Syracuse, N.Y., 1980. Area mgr. Ashland Oil Corp., Syracuse, N.Y., 1978-80; sales rep. Whirlpool Corp., Syracuse, N.Y., 1980-82; pension analyst Braun Group, Syracuse, N.Y., 1982-83; d.c. pension analyst Am. Gen. Life Ins. Co., Syracuse, N.Y., 1983-84, d.b. pension analyst, 1984-85, sr. pension analyst, 1985-86, pension spr., 1986-88, asst. mgr., 1988-89, mktg. mgr., 1989-90, reg. dir., 1990—. Bd. dirs. Westcott Recycles, Syracuse, 1985. Mem. Syracuse Chpt. Life Underwriters. Home: 452 Brattle Rd Syracuse NY 13203-1103 Office: Am Gen Life Ins Co PO Box 1456 Syracuse NY 13201-1456

CONN, PAUL KOHLER, engineering executive, consultant; b. Akron, Ohio, July 25, 1929; s. Chester Orlo and Jennie Maye (Kohler) C.; m. Janice Jones, Sept. 12, 1954; children: David, Kathryn, Laura Beth. AB, Kenyon Coll., 1951; MS, Kans. State U., 1953, PhD in Phys. Chemistry, 1956; postgrad., Pa. State U., 1965. Sr. engr. GE, Cin., 1955-59, prin. engr., 1959-61, unit mgr., 1961-68; prin. scientist Bell Aerospace Textron, Niagara Falls, N.Y., 1969-75, staff prin. scientist, 1975-77, electroforming task force, 1977-78, program mgr., 1978-79, chief engr., 1980, dir. engring. labs., 1980-91, ret., 1991; materials cons. U. Buffalo Dental Sch., 1991—. Co-author: (chpt.) Hovercraft Technology, 1989. Member Environ. Mgmt. Coun. of Niagara County, 1983—; bus. solicitor United Appeal, Cin., 1968; co. advisor Jr. Achievement, Niagara Falls, 1972-82; bd. dirs. City of Niagara Falls, 1976-89. Mem. ASTM, Am. Chem. Soc., Masons, Sigma Xi, Delta Phi, Phi Lambda Upsilon. Republican. Lutheran. Home: 4682 W Park Dr Lewiston NY 14092-1112

CONN, REX BOLAND, JR., physician, educator; b. Marengo, Iowa, Aug. 3, 1927; s. Rex Boland Helena Dorothea (Schoenfelder) C.; m. Victoria Grace Sellens, Dec. 28, 1950; children: Elizabeth Marian, Victoria Anne, Mary Catherine. B.S., Iowa State U., 1949; M.D., Yale U., 1953; B.Sc., U. Oxford, Eng., 1955; M.S., U. Minn., 1960. Prof. pathology, dir. clin. labs. W.Va. Med. Center, Morgantown, 1960-68; prof. lab. medicine, dir. dept. Johns Hopkins Med. Instns., Balt., 1968-77; prof. pathology and lab. medicine, dir. clin labs. Emory U., Atlanta, 1977-87; prof. and vice chmn. dept. pathology and cell biology, dir. clin. labs. Thomas Jefferson Med. Coll., Phila., 1987—; mem. pathology tng. com. NIH, 1972-73, mem. pathology A study sect., 1968-72; cons. Walter Reed Army Med. Center, 1972-77; cons. Armed Forces Inst. of Pathology, 1984-88. Editor: Current Diagnosis, 1991, Yearbook of Pathology and Clinical Pathology, 1980. Served with USNR, 1945-46. Mem. Coll. Am. Pathologists, Am. Soc. Clin. Pathologists (dir. 1975-81, v.p. 1991—), Acad. Clin. Lab. Physicians and Scientists (pres. 1972). Office: Thomas Jefferson Univ Hosp 204 Pavilion Philadelphia PA 19107

CONN, WALTER EUGENE, religion educator, counselor; b. Providence, July 11, 1940; s. Earl Furness and Ethel Helen (Keough) C.; m. Joann Wolski, Oct. 14, 1972. BA, Providence Coll., 1962; MA, Boston Coll., 1966; PhL, Weston Coll., 1966; PhD, Columbia U., 1973; MS, Villanova U., 1988. Assoc. prof. Christian ethics St. Patrick's Sem., Menlo Park, Calif., 1973-78; prof. religious studies Villanova (Pa.) U., 1978—; counselor Cath. Social Svcs., West Chester, Pa., 1988—. Author: Conscience, 1981 (named Best Book Coll. Theology Soc. 1982), Christian Conversion, 1986 (Best Book award Cath. Press Assn. 1987); also articles; editor: Conversion, 1978, Mainstreaming, 1985; mem. editorial adv. bd. Religious Studies Rev., 1980—. Mem. Am. Acad. Religion, Cath. Theol. Soc. Am., Coll. Theology Soc. (bd. dirs., editor in chief Horizons jour. 1980—), Soc. for Christian Ethics, Amnesty Internat. USA, Bread for the World. Roman Catholic. Home: 25 Aldwyn Ln Villanova PA 19085-1435 Office: Villanova U Religious Studies Dept Villanova PA 19085

CONNELL, KATHLEEN SULLIVAN, state government official; b. Newport, R.I., May 24, 1937; d. Lawrence Francis and Margaret (Byrnes) Sullivan; m. Gerald Connell, June 11, 1960; children: Lawrence, Margaret, Kathleen. BS in Nursing magna cum laude, Salve Regina Coll., 1958; postgrad., Boston Coll., U. R.I., R.I. Coll. Registered nurse Newport Vis. Nurses Assn., 1958-61; health educator Newport Sch. Dept., 1970-86; sec. of state State of R.I., Providence, 1987—; pres., bd. dirs. Shake-a-Leg, Inc. Mem. Middletown Sch. Com. 1965-76, chmn. 1972-76; mem. Middletown Town Council 1977-83, vice-chmn. 1981-83; active Save the Bay, Aquidneck (R.I.) Goals Group, Aquidneck Ecology; mem. council nominating com. Newport Girl Scouts of U.S.; bd. dirs. Vis. Nurse Service of Newport County; vice-chmn. R.I. Dem. Com.; mem. Dem. Women's Caucus, Middletown Charter Rev. Commn.; mem. Dem. Nat. Com. Recipient awards R.I. Libr. Assn., Vol. Svcs. for Animals, John F. Kennedy Ctr. for Performing Arts, Very Spl. Arts Assn., John E. Fogarty award, 1991, Disting. Leader award R.I. Women's Polit. Caucus, 1989, Juliette Low award, 1989, RIPACEtter award NEA, 1987, Woman of Achievement award R.I. Fedn. Bus. and Profl. Women's Clubs, 1987; named Alumnus of Yr. Salve Regina Coll., 1987. Mem. Am. Nurses Assn., R.I. State Nurses Assn., R.I. Sch. Nurses Assn., NEA, R.I. Edn. Assn., LWV, Women's Network, Vietnam Vets. of Am. (assoc.), Newport Irish Heritage Soc. (bd. dirs.), Nat. Conf. State Legislatures (com. labor and edn.), Delta Kappa Gamma. Home: 233 Tuckerman Ave Newport RI 02840-6046 Office: Office Sec of State 217 State House Smith St Providence RI 02903

CONNELL, SHIRLEY HUDGINS, public relations professional; b. Washington, Oct. 5, 1946; d. Orville Thomas and Mary (Beran) H.; m. David Day Connell, Dec. 13, 1980 (div. 1985). BA, U. R.I., 1968, MA, 1970. Clk., editor MGM Studios, Culver City, Calif., 1970-72; scriptor, talent Monarch Records, Studio City, 1972-73; communications specialist U. So. Calif., L.A., 1973-81; dir. pub. rels. Six Flags Movieland, Buena Park, Calif., 1981-82, Donald J. Fager & Assocs., N.Y.C., 1982—; cons. Children's TV Workshop, N.Y.C., 1978; ind. beauty cons. Mary Kay Cosmetics, 1991—; instr. Princeton Rev., 1990-91. Contbr. articles to profl. jours.; contbg. editor Greater N.Y. Doctor's Shopper mag., 1987—. Pres. bd. trustees Oaks at North Brunswick Condominium Assn., 1987—; founding mem. Mcpl. Svcs. Com., North Brunswick; mgr. Animal Rescue Force, North Brunswick, 1988—, chair, 1990—; mem. environ. com. Twp. of North Brunswick, 1990—. Mem. NAFE, Marine Tech. Soc. (vice chmn. 1980-81), Mensa (pub. rels. adv. com. 1989—, pub. rels. coord. Ctrl. N.J. chpt. 1992—), Oceanic Soc. (bd. dirs. 1979-81).

CONNELL, WILLIAM FRANCIS, diversified company executive; b. Lynn, Mass., May 12, 1938; s. William J. and Theresa (Keaney) C.; m. Margot C. Gensler, May 29, 1965; children: Monica Cameron, Lisa Terese, Courtenay Erin, William Christopher, Terence Alexander, Timothy Patrick. BS magna cum laude, Boston Coll., 1959; MBA, Harvard U., 1963. Contr. Olga Co., Inc., Van Nuys, Calif., 1963-65; asst. treas. Litton Industries, Inc., 1965-68; pres. div. Marine Tech., Inc., 1965-68; treas. Ogden Corp., N.Y.C., 1968-69; v.p., treas. Ogden Corp., 1969-71, sr. v.p., 1971-72, exec. v.p., 1980-85; chief exec. officer, chmn. bd. Ogden Leisure, Inc.; chmn. bd., chief exec. officer Ogden Food Service, Inc., Ogden Recreation, Inc., Ogden Security, Inc., Ogden Svcs. Inc.; bd. dir. Ogden Corp., various Ogden subs., 1969-85; chmn., chief exec. officer, pres. Avondale Industries, Inc. 1985-87; chmn., chief exec. officer Connell Ltd. Partnership, 1987—. Active fund raising Boston Coll., trustee, 1974-86, 88—, chmn. bd. trustees, 1981-84; trustee St. Elizabeth Hosp., Boston, Boston 200 Corp. 1st lt. AUS, 1959-61. Mem. Greater Boston C. of C. (chmn. bd. dirs. 1988-90), Algonquin Club, Univ. Club (Boston), Tedesco Country Club, Knights of Malta Club, Beta Gamma Sigma, Alpha Sigma Nu, Alpha Kappa Psi. Roman Catholic. Home: 111 Ocean Ave Swampscott MA 01907-2413 Office: Connell Ltd Partnership One International Pl Boston MA 02110-2600

CONNELLY, CHUCK, artist; b. Pitts., Jan. 7, 1955; s. Ann Marie Adamson Connelly. BFA, Tyler Sch. Art, Phila., 1977. group exhbns. include: Museo Tamayo, Mexico City, 1984, Aldrich Mus. Contemporary Art, Ridgefield, Conn., 1984, 86, Annina Nosei Gallery, N.Y.C., 1984, 85, 86, 90, Indpls. Mus. Art, 1986, Lennon, Weinberg, Inc., N.Y.C., 1989, 90, 91, U. Ariz. Mus. Art, Tucson, 1989, Hofstra Mus., Hempstead, N.Y., 1989, Lehigh U. Art Gallery, Bethlehem, Pa., 1989. One man shows at Arno Kohnen, Dusseldorf, Germany, 1982, Serra di Felice Gallery, N.Y.C., 1984, Annina Nosei Gallery, N.Y.C., 1984, 85, 86, 87, No. Ill. U. Art Gallery, Chgo., 1984-85, Lawrence Oliver Gallery, Phila., 1985, Asher/Faure Gallery, L.A., 1986, Galleria La Planita, Rome, 1987, Thomas Segal Gallery, Boston, 1988, Lennon, Weinberg, Inc., N.Y.C., 1989, 90; permanent collections include Bklyn. Mus., Met. Mus. of Art, N.Y.C., Portland (Oreg.) Art Mus. Office: Lennon Weinberg Inc 2d Fl 580 Broadway New York NY 10012-3223

CONNELLY, JOHN EDWARD, education educator, consultant; b. Elmira, N.Y., Dec. 4, 1934; s. Edward F. and Margaret (Spillane) C.; m. Mary Claire Woodhouse, Dec. 28, 1957; children: John, Nancy, Joseph, Ellen, Anne. BS, SUNY, Cortland, 1957, MS, 1962; EdD, U. Buffalo, 1968. Cert. K-12 reading educator. Reading tchr. Corning (N.Y.) Pub. Schs., 1957-61, dir. reading, 1961-63; prof., dir. reading ctr. SUNY, Fredonia, 1963—; vis. prof. Ind. U., Bloomington, 1969, U. Ky., Lexington, 1975, West Glamorgan Inst., Swansea, Wales, 1990-91; clin. prof. Kent (Ohio) State U., 1971, Mich. Stae U., East Lansing, 1974; prof. Mico Coll., Kingston, Jamaica, 1986; bd. dirs. Exptl. Tchr. Fellowship, Fredonia, 1969-70; cons. HEW, Washington, N.Y. State Edn. Dept.; test developer Regents Coll., N.Y., 1987-92. Author: (with others) Reading in the Middle School, 1975. Bd. dirs. Nat. Right to Read, Cassadoga, N.Y., 1970-73, N.Y. State Edn. Dept. Right to Read, Belmont, 1976-78, Literacy Vols., Dunkirk, N.Y., 1984-86, N.Y. State Planning Fedn., Albany, 1984-90; coord. Fredinia-Hamburg Tchr. Ctr., 1984-88; trustee Fredonia, 1976-82, St. Joseph's Ch., Fredonia, 1989—; mem. bd. edn. No. Chautauqua Catholics, Dunkirk, 1989—; active Upward Bound, Fredonia, 1988-91. Mem. Ptnrs. of Am. (cons. 1986—), Internat. Reading Assn. (N.Y. state exec. bd., Chautauqua chpt. reading dir. 1970-84), Northeastern ERA. Home: 91 Water St Fredonia NY 14063-2016 Office: SUNY Thompson Hall Fredonia NY 14063

CONNELLY, JOHN JOSEPH, physicist, retired; b. Syracuse, N.Y., Apr. 14, 1925; s. John Joseph and Florence Wilhemena (Haas) C.; m. Jean Anne Cavanaugh, June 7, 1947; children: Robert John, Richard James, Roger Joseph. B in Aero. Engring., Rensselaer Poly. Inst., 1945; MS in Physics, U. Va., 1955, PhD in Physics, 1956. Commd. USN, 1942, advanced through grades to comdr., 1961; pilot USN, various, 1942-64; prog. mgr./direct energy conversion U.S. Atomic Energy Commn., Washington, 1956-60, Office of Naval Rsch., Washington, 1960-64; prof. physics State Univ./Coll. of Fredonia, N.Y., 1964-85; cons. USN, Washington, 1985—; guest prof. Eigenoschisse Tech. Hoch Schule, Zurich, 1972-84; mem. NASA com. on Space Power Plants, Washington, 1961-64, various other govtl. coms., 1959-64. Patentee in field; author lab. manual for basic physics course, 1974; contbr. articles to profl. jours./publs. Radiation officer Chautauqua County, Mayville, N.Y., 1975—; trustee Sinclairville (N.Y.) Vol. Fire Co., 1964—. Recipient grants Am. Assn. Physics, Fredonia, 1967, Rsch. Found., State of N.Y., 1968, summer insts., NSF, 1969, 70, 72. Mem. Am. Legion (comdr. 1984-85), Raven Soc., Sigma Xi (grant 1967). Republican. Roman Catholic. Home: Rt 1 Bernard Rd Cassadaga NY 14718

CONNELLY, JOHN ROBERT, JR., manufacturing company executive; b. Bethlehem, Pa., Mar. 13, 1936; s. John Robert and Martha Alice (Alvord) C.; m. Carolyn Yeagley, June 29, 1963; children: John Paul, Mark Andrew. BS in Bus. Adminstrn., Pa. State U., 1959, MS in Bus. Adminstrn., 1961. Cert. CPA, Pa. Supr. Coopers & Lybrand, Phila., 1961-69; sec./treas. Turbo Machine, Lansdale, Pa., 1969-73; fin. mgr. Warner & Swasey Co., New Phila., Ohio, 1973-79; dir. corp. planning The Warner & Swasey Co., Cleve., 1979-80; dir. bus. planning Bendix Automation Group, Cleve., 1980-84; bus. systems dir. Automatic Switch Co., Florham Park, N.J., 1984—; treas. No. Am. Soc. for Corp. Planning, Oxford, Ohio, 1982-83. Pres. United Way of Tuscaraway County, New Phila., 1978-79. Mem. AICPA, Penna Inst. of CPAs, Planning Forum. Home: 128 Parker Rd Long Valley NJ 07853-3053 Office: Automatic Switch Co 50-60 Hanover Rd Florham Park NJ 07932-1591

CONNELLY, JOHN THOMAS, security and investigation company executive; b. Boston, Dec. 31, 1952; s. John T. and Ella R. (Harrington) C.; m. Janet E. Gray, Sept., 1983; children: John, Maura, Bridget, Matthew. BA, Coll. of Holy Cross, 1974; JD, New Eng. Sch. Law, 1982. Bar: Mass. 1982; cert. protection profl. Dir. security Children's Hosp., Boston, 1975-80; mgr. safety and security Deaconess Hosp., Boston, 1980-86; pres. Longwood Security Svcs. Inc., Boston, 1986—; adj. prof. security mgmt. Northeastern U. Coll. Criminal Justice, Boston, 1989. Author: Civil Liability and The Supervisor, 1988; producer video Security: A Community Effort, 1987. Mem. Internat. Assn. Hosp. Security, Am. Soc. for Indsl. Security (chmn. Boston chpt. 1985, v.p. for New Eng. 1986), Mass. Bar Assn. Office: Longwood Security Svcs Inc 10 Brookline Pl W Brookline MA 02146-7215

CONNELLY, ROBERT JOHN, small business owner; b. Pitts., June 25, 1960; s. James Matthew and Anna Mae (Noonan) C.; m. Cynthia Perla, Mar. 5, 1988; children: Mara Grace, Zachary Robert. BS, St. Vincent Coll., 1982. Acct. Internat. Graphics, Hollywood, Fla., 1982-84; v.p. Gilbert Penrose & Assocs., Ft. Lauderdale, Fla., 1984-87; sole proprietor RJC Acctg. Svcs., Pitts., 1987-90; pres. Robert Connelly & Assocs. Inc., Murrysville, 1991—, CBCI, Inc., Murrysville, 1992—; bd. dirs. World Missions Assocs., 1990—;. Big Bro. Youth Guidance, Pitts., 1985-89; mem. Christian Bus. Ctr. Mem. Nat. Fedn. Ind. Bus. Republican. Office: Robert Connelly & Assocs 4091 Saltsburg Rd Ste G Murrysville PA 15668-9774

CONNER, HOLLY REID, military officer; b. St. John, New Bruns., Can., Oct. 20, 1951; d. William and Genevieve Ellna Marjorie (Smith) McLelland; m. Richard J. Baker, June 10, 1972 (div. Dec. 1979); m. Carl Watson Conner, Feb. 12, 1983. BA, U. LaVerne, 1978; MS, Air Force Inst. Tech., 1981; student, Command and Staff Coll., Air U., Maxwell AFB, Ala., 1992-93. Cert. profl. contracts mgr.; cert. advanced designation in logistics mgmt. Commd. 2d lt. USAF, 1978, advanced through grades to maj., 1989; contract negotiator Western Space and Missile Ctr., Vandenberg AFB, Calif., 1978-80; chief, contract ops. Def. Dissemination System/Space Div., L.A., 1981-84; instr., contract mgmt. Air Force Inst. Tech., Wright-Patterson AFB, Ohio, 1984-85, asst. prof., contract adminstrn. course dir., 1985-87, exec. officer, 1987-88; contracting staff officer Asst. Sec. of the Air Force (Acquisition)/Pentagon, Washington, 1988-90; chief acquisition mgmt. br., tactical programs Sec. of the Air Force (Acquisition)/Pentagon, Washington, 1990-92. Editor: Contract Administration, 1986. Fellow Nat. Contract Mgmt. Assn. (v.p. Dayton chpt. 1985-86, Blanche Witte award 1987, nat. bd. dirs. 1986-87); mem. Air Force Assn. (Svc. award Goddard chpt. 1980), Def. System Mgmt. Coll. Assn. Presbyterian. Home: 108 S Hiley Ct Bonaire GA 31005-1259 Office: ACSC/AU Maxwell AFB AL 36112

CONNER, JAMES JOHN, III, trade association executive; b. Du Bois, Pa., July 19, 1939; s. James John Jr. and Mary Louise (Bennett) C.; m. Rita M. Godino, Dec. 26, 1961; children: James John IV, Jason Bennett. BA in Journalism, San Diego State U., 1964; MBA, Ind. U., 1975. V.p. mktg. Nat. Home Furnishings Assn., Chgo., 1965-72; exec. dir. Home Ctr. Inst., Indpls., 1972-76; dir. of svcs. Motor and Equipment Mfrs. Assn., Teaneck, N.J., 1976-80; pres. Assn. Graphic Artists, N.Y.C., 1980-86; exec. v.p. Motor and Equipment Mfrs. Assn., Englewood Cliffs, N.J., 1986—. Cpl. USMC, 1959-63. Mem. Am. Soc. Assn. Execs., N.J. Soc. Assn. Execs. Office: Motor Equipment Mfrs Assn 300 Sylvan Ave # 1638 Englewood Cliffs NJ 07632-2517

CONNERS, JAMES, mayor. Mayor City of Scranton, Pa. Office: Muncipal Bldg Scranton PA 18503*

CONNOLA, DONALD PASCAL, JR., management consultant, educator; b. New Brunswick, N.J., Sept. 25, 1948; s. Donald Pascal and Josephine (Montalbano) C. AB, Rutgers U., 1970, MBA, 1973; JD, Bklyn. Law Sch., 1977. Mktg. control analyst Gen. Foods Corp., White Plains, N.Y., 1973-74, product analyst, 1974, sr. fin. analyst, 1974-75, fin. assoc., 1975-79, fin. specialist, 1979, internal mgmt. cons., 1979-82, mgmt. cons., 1983—; prof. mgmt. Fairleigh Dickinson U., Rutherford, N.J., 1983-86; dir. MBA program, dir. undergrad. student svcs., 1986—. Mem. N.J. State Bar Assn., Am. Soc. Tng. and Devel., Assn. MBA Execs., Soc. for Human Resource Mgmt. Home: 1896 Manor Dr Apt A Union NJ 07083-4514 Office: 223 Montross Ave Rutherford NJ 07070-1977

CONNOLLY, DAVID PAUL, surgeon; b. Pitts., Oct. 1, 1936; s. John Wray and Pauline (Rock) C.; m. Joeanne Clare Perrone, Oct. 2, 1965; children: Colleen A., David J., Meghan G., Cara M., Anne W. BA, John Carroll U., 1957; MD, Loyola U., Chgo., 1961. Diplomate Am. Bd. Surgery. Intern Akron (Ohio) Gen. Hosp., 1962; resident Mercy Hosp., Pitts., 1964-69; dir. surg. edn. St. Margaret Meml. Hosp., Pitts., 1976—, pres. med. staff, 1990-92; mem. exec. com. Am. Cancer Soc., Pitts., 1977-82, chmn. profl. edn. com., 1977-82; lectr. Am. Cancer Soc., Pitts; fellow Am. Cancer Soc., Meml.-Sloan-Kettering Inst., 1967-68. Maj. USAF, 1962-64. Fellow ACS (bd. govs. S.W. Pa. chpt. 1975-79, liaison fellow commn. on cancer 1977—), Soc. Surg. Oncology; mem. AMA, Pa. Med. Soc. (coun. edn./sci. 1976-78), Pitts. Surg. Soc. (pres.-elect 1992-94), Allegheny County Med. Soc., Internat. Coll. Surgeons, Am. Soc. Clin. Oncologists, Am. Soc. Gastrointestinal Endoscopy, Soc. Surgery of Alimentary Trace, Soc. Laparoscopic Surgeons, Am. Soc. Laser Medicine and Surgery. Roman Catholic. Office: 100 Delafield Rd Ste 203 Pittsburgh PA 15215

CONNOLLY, ELMA TROUTMAN, contractor artist; b. Middleburg, Pa., May 10, 1931; d. Benjamin F. and Eva Ellen (DeLong) Hollenback; m. Kenneth R. Troutman, Aug. 15, 1950; children: Kenneth, Linda, Robert; m. Jerome P. Connolly, Apr. 15, 1973. Student, Lock Haven State Tchrs. Coll., 1949. Cons. for exceptions unit Pa. Tax Bur., Harrisburg; pres. Arts ETC Co., Sunbury, Pa.; artist S.Am. Hall, Smithsonian Mus. Natural History, 1974; artist, contractr Govt. of Taipei, Taiwan; artist, contractor, sculptor George C. Page, Mus. of La Brea, L.A.; bus. cons. Cohen, Danville, 1970-72. Named Woman of Yr., ABI, 1991, recipient Am. Women's award. Mem. NAFE, Sunbury Mchts. Coun. (pres.), C. of C. (govt. affairs com.), Susquehanna Art League, Internat. Platform Assn. Republican. Home: 102 S U S # 1115 Selinsgrove PA 17870

CONNOLLY, JOHN MATTHEW, philosophy educator and administrator; b. N.Y.C., Sept. 20, 1943; s. John Clement and Alice Agnes (Joiner) C.; m. Marianne P. Kaul, June 28, 1969; children—Fiona, Sabine. B.A., Fordham Coll., 1965; M.A., Oxford U., 1967; postgrad. Princeton U., 1967-68; Ph.D., Harvard U., 1971. Instr. philosophy Elms Coll., Chicopee, Mass., 1971-73; asst. prof. Smith Coll., Northampton, Mass., 1973-81, assoc. prof., 1981-88, prof., 1988—, chmn. philosophy dept., 1984-87, sec. of faculty 1984-87, dir. Jr. Yr. in Germany, 1978-79, dean curriculum and faculty devel., 1992—; cons. Fern Universität Hagen, Germany, 1981-82. Author: (correspondence course) Handlungstheorie I, II, 1982, III, 1989. Translator/editor: Absicht, 1986, Hermeneutics versus Science ?, 1988. Contbr. articles to profl. jours. Recipient Open Exhbn. award Brasenose Coll., Oxford, Eng., 1966; Presdl. scholar, 1961-65; Danforth fellow, 1965-71, Humboldt fellow, 1977-82. Mem. Am. Philos. Assn. Democrat. Avocations: music; walking; reading; racquet sports; travel. Home: 72 Dryads Green St Northampton MA 01060-2914 Office: Philosophy Dept Smith Coll Northampton MA 01063

CONNOLLY, LYNDA MURPHY, lawyer; b. Washington, Feb. 29, 1948; d. John H. and Mary (McDonough) Murphy; m. Michael Joseph Connolly, Aug. 14, 1971; children: John, Justin, Allison, Lauren. AB, Coll. William & Mary, 1970; JD, Boston Coll., 1974. Bar: Mass. 1975, U.S. Dist. Ct. Mass. Spl. prosecutor Suffolk County Dist. Atty., Boston, 1975-76; assoc. Connolly & Johnson, Boston, 1976-78; mgr. Statewide Campaign for Sec. State, Boston, 1978; pvt. practice Boston, 1981-89; gen. counsel Gallagher & Gallagher, P.C., Boston, 1989—; adj. assoc. prof. Bentley Coll., Waltham, Mass., 1981-82; lectr. in law New Eng. Sch. Law., Boston, 1981-84. Author: (with others) Annual Survey of Mass Law, 1981. Elected del. Dem. State Conv., Mass., 1983-90; trustee Franklin Found., Boston, 1988—; dir. Franklin Inst., Boston, 1988—. Mem. Mass. Bar Assn. Roman Catholic. Office: Gallagher & Gallagher PC One Constitution Pla Boston MA 02129

CONNOLLY, MICHAEL JOSEPH, state official; b. West Roxbury, Mass., Apr. 20, 1947; s. Michael Joseph and Florence C.; m. Lynda Murphy, Aug. 14, 1971; children: John Ronan, Justin, Allison, Lauren. A.B., Holy Cross Coll., 1969; J.D., New Eng. Sch. Law, 1976. Tchr. math. Boston Latin Sch., 1972; mem. Mass. Ho. of Reps., 1973-79, chmn. spl. legis. com. on commuter traffic, 1973-79; Sec. of the Commonwealth of Mass., 1979—; Chmn. Mass. Hist. Commn.; chmn. Archives Adv. Commn. Mem. Marriage Encounter. Mem. Mass. Bar Assn., Nat. Assn. Secs. of State, Internat. Trade Adv. Bd. Club: Holy Cross (Boston). Office: State House Rm 337 Boston MA 02133*

CONNOLLY, SARAH WHETSTONE, health facility administrator, nurse; b. Phila., July 7, 1944; d. Sherman Gray and Phyllis (Rogan) Whetstone; m. Bryan J. McSweeney, Aug. 7, 1965 (div. 1972); children: Catherine, Bryan Michael II; m. Thomas Joseph Connolly, Feb. 9, 1991. RN, Presbyn. Sch. of Nursing, 1965; 20BS, Eastern Coll., 1978; MS, Villanova (Pa.) U., 1981. RN, Pa.; lic. counselor, Pa. RN Children's Hosp. of Phila., 1965-66, Phila. Bd. of Edn., 1966-68; RN Malvern (Pa.) Inst., 1975-78, dir. of nursing, 1984-88, quality assurance dir., 1990—; psychotherapist Inst. of Pa. Hosp., Phila., 1978-81; clinic dir. Help Counseling, West Chester, Pa., 1981-84; bd. dirs. Pastoral Counseling Ctr., Paoli, Pa., 1976-80, Pa. Episcopal Diocese Addiction Coun., Phila., 1985-90, Pa. Adult Children of Alcoholics, 1987-91. Volunteer Bryn Mawr Rehab. Aquatic Program, Malvern, 1991; chmn. ways and means com. Whitelands Coun. of Rep. Women, Malvern, 1975-87; mem. vestry St. Paul's Episcopal Ch., Exton, Pa., 1982-84, conv. del., 1987. Mem. Am. Mental Health Assn., Am. Assn. Counseling, Villanova U. Alumni Assn. (grad. div. 1981—). Home: 117 Putney Ln Malvern PA 19355-3208 Office: Malvern Inst 940 W King Rd Malvern PA 19355-3167

CONNOLLY, THOMAS EDWARD, lawyer; b. Boston, Nov. 7, 1942; s. Thomas Francis and Catherine Elizabeth (Skehill) C. AB, St. John's Sem., Brighton, Mass., 1964; JD, Boston Coll., 1969. Bar: Mass., 1969. Assoc. Schneider & Reilly, Boston, 1969-73; ptnr. Schneider, Reilly, Zabin, Connolly & Costello, P.C., Boston, 1973-85, Connolly Leavis & Rest, Boston, 1986-90; with Mass. Superior Ct., Boston, 1990—; instr. law Northeastern Law Sch., Boston, 1975-76. Mem. governing coun. Boston Coll. Law Sch. Alumni Coun., 1980—. Mem. ABA (vice chmn. products liability sect. 1978—), Trial Lawyers Assn. Am. (nat. gov. 1977-80), Mass. Acad. Trial Lawyers (gov. 1976—), Am. Coll. Trial Lawyers, Univ. Club (Boston), Algonquin Club (Boston). Democrat. Roman Catholic. Home: 253 Marlborough St # 4 Boston MA 02116 Office: The Superior Ct Boston MA 02108

CONNOLLY, WILLIAM GERARD, newspaper editor; b. Scranton, Pa., Oct. 12, 1937; s. William Gerard and Loretto Dorothy (Blewitt) C.; m. Clair Carmen Connor, Nov. 14, 1964; children: William Gerard III, Kathleen, Harold James. BS in English, U. Scranton, 1959; MS in Journalism, Columbia U., 1963. Reporter Houston Chronicle, 1963-65; copy editor, wire editor Detroit Free Press, 1965-66; copy editor, asst. real estate editor N.Y. Times, 1966-77, asst. nat. editor, 1977-79, 84-85, dep. editor week in review, 1985-86, sr. editor, 1987—; mng. editor The Virginian-Pilot, Norfolk, 1979-83; cons. Virginia Beach, Va., 1983-84; sr. faculty editing program for minority journalists, U. Ariz., Tucson, 1981—; sr. fellow Gannett Urban Journalism Ctr., Northwestern U., Evanston, Ill., 1983-88. Author: The N.Y. Times Guide to Buying or Building a Home, 1978; contbr. articles to popular mags. With U.S. Army, 1960-62. Mem. Asian Am. Journalists Assn., Nat. Assn. Black Journalists, Nat. Assn. Hispanic Journalists. Roman Catholic. Office: NY Times 229 W 43d St New York NY 10036

CONNOR, DAVID MICHAEL, psychologist; b. Manchester, Eng., Oct. 15, 1935; came to U.S., 1961; s. John Sewell and Edith Beatrice (Lockett) C.; m. Patricia Anne Kolk, Dec. 30, 1959 (div. 1979); children: Jennifer Clare, Leslie Ann. BA with honors, Cambridge U., 1956, MA, 1959; PhD, Yale U., 1969; EdD, Boston U., 1989. With Cornell U., N.Y., 1964-75, asst. dean Coll. Arts & Scis., 1970-74; dir. six yr. PhD program Cornell U., N.Y.C., 1972-75; guidance counselor Brookline (Mass.) Pub. Schs., 1980-83; dir. guidance dept. Wellesley (Mass.) Pub. Schs., 1983-86; clinician Sraight New Eng., Stoughton, Mass., 1986-87; dir. Access Program Mansfield (Mass.)

Pub. Schs., 1987—. Mem. Am. Assn. Counseling and Devel., Assn. Moral Edn., New Eng. Assn. Specialists in Group Work. Episcopalian. Home: 69A Cottage St Sharon MA 02067

CONNOR, GEOFFREY WARREN, wine merchant, wine writer; b. Balt., Oct. 23, 1946; s. Arthur Joseph and Sara Eugenia (Brown) C. BS, Rutgers U., 1968. Asst. mgr. Medco Fine Jewelry, East Brunswick, N.J., 1968-69; operating rm. orderly Robert Wood Johnson Univ. Hosp., New Brunswick, 1969-71; mgr. camera dept. Woolco, Union, N.J., 1971; mgr. Bottle King Liquors, Union and Hackensack, N.J., 1971-76; mgr. wine dept. Field's Pharmacy, Pikesville, Md., 1976-78; wine mgr. Wells Discount Liquors, Balt., 1978-80; wine salesman The Kronheim Co., Balt., 1980; pres. Calvert Discount Liquors, Hunt Valley, Md., 1981—. Author newspaper column From the Wine Cellar, 1989, Notes From the Wine Cellar, 1989—. Advisor Am. Heart Assn. Fine Wine Auction, Balt., 1989—. Mem. Am. Wine Soc., Soc. Wine Educators. Libertarian. Deist. Home: 6145 Parkway Dr Baltimore MD 21212 Office: Calvert Discount Liquors 10128 York Rd Hunt Valley MD 21030

CONNOR, PAUL EUGENE, social worker; b. Atchison, Kans., Aug. 11, 1921; s. Samuel Walters and Juanita Marie (Fry) C.; m. Louise Dorothy Schiddel, June 28, 1959 (div. 1964). BS in History with honors, Columbia U., 1962, MA, 1963; grad. cert. in social work, Fordham U., 1973. Lectr. Am. History Rutgers State U., 1966-67; lectr. S.E. Asian history New Sch. Social Rsch., 1967-68; caseworker Bergen Ctr., South Bronx, N.Y., 1970-73; caseworker Protective Svcs. Bur. of Child Welfare, Bronx, N.Y., 1973-76; caseworker preventive svcs. Spl. Svcs. for Children, N.Y.C., 1976-83; supr. I family program Crisis Intervention Svcs., N.Y.C., 1983-87; tchr. The Internat. Ctr., N.Y.C., 1977-86. Rec. sec. Bronx Coun. for Environ. Quality, 1981-83, bd. dirs., 1983—; docent Mus. of City of N.Y., 1988-91. Mem. Internat. Coun. Social Welfare, Asia Soc., Am. Hist. Assn., S.C. Hist. Soc., N.C. Lit. and Hist. Assn., Soc. of Boonesborough. Democrat. Home: 2755 Reservoir Ave Apt 5A Bronx NY 10468-2730

CONNOR, ROBERT T., former government official; b. Washington, 1919; ed. Boston Coll., U.S. Naval Acad.; BA, CUNY; LLD (hon.), St. Johns U.Ops. officer CIA, 1946-49; staff officer Fgn. Service, Dept. State, 1949-51, vice consul Mexico City; councilman-at-large, N.Y.C., 1963-65, borough pres. S.I., 1965-77; mem. N.Y.C. Bd. of Estimate, 1965-77; dep. asst. sec. Navy, 1977-81. Capt. USNR, ret. Home: 1610 Starling Dr Sarasota FL 34231-9118

CONNORS, EDWARD ANTHONY, mathematics educator; b. Holyoke, Mass., Oct. 30, 1940; s. James Jerome and Camillia (Gendron) C.; m. Mary Ann Theresa Corbo, June 7, 1969; children: James, Kathleen. AB in Math., Holy Cross Coll., Worcester, Mass., 1962; MA in Math., U. Mass., 1964; PhD in Math., U. Notre Dame, 1969. Instr. U. Notre Dame (Ind.), 1968-69; asst. prof. math. U. Mass., Amherst, 1969-74, assoc. prof., 1974-87, prof., 1987—; dir. Office Govt. and Pub. Affairs Joint Policy Bd. for Math., Washington, 1990-91; vis. scholar Inst. of Systems Sci., Beijing, China, 1985, Harvard U., Cambridge, 1983; guest assoc. prof. U. Notre Dame, 1976. Author Report on Annual AMS/MAA Survey,1 986-90. Mem. Sch. Supts. Adv. Com., East Hampton, Mass., 1988-90. Mem. Am. Math. Soc. (chmn. data and employment 1986-90), Commn. on Profls. in Sci. and Tech. (commr. 1986—). Home: 19 Sterling Dr Easthampton MA 01027-2504 Office: U Mass Math Dept Math Dept Lederle Tower Amherst MA 01003

CONNORS, JOHN FRANCIS, physician; b. Rahway, N.J., Oct. 5, 1958; s. John and Agnes C. BS in Health/Biology, West Chester U., 1982; DPM, Ill. Coll. Podiatric Medicine, 1987. Orthopedic/surg. resident N.Y. Coll. of Podiatric Medicine and Affiliate Hosp., 1987-88; prof. pediatric/orthopedic N.Y. Coll. of Podiatric Medicine, 1988—; pvt. practice N.Y.C., 1989—, Podiatric Medicine Surgery Sports Medicine, Little Silver, N.J., 1990—; prof. pediatric/orthopedic dept. N.Y. Coll. Podiatric Medicine, 1988—; team sports podiatrist various high schs., N.J., 1990—; sports doctor N.Y.C. Marathon, 1987; sports cons. N.Y. Road Runners Club; clin. adv. Am. Running and Fitness Assn. Mem. Am. Acad. Podiatric Sports Medicine (assoc.), Physician Sports Medicine, N.Y. Road Runners Club, Am. Podiatric Med. Assn., Eastern Monmouth C. of C. Roman Catholic. Office: 133 E 73d St New York NY 10021

CONNORS, ROBERT LEO, city official; b. Kings County, N.Y., June 11, 1940; s. John Leo and Emma Mae (Bayers) C.; m. Elaine Roscoe, July 21, 1979; children: Anne, Laura, Kathleen. B. Profl. Studies, Pace U., 1974, MS in Indsl. Labor Relations, 1976. Police officer, trustee, fin. sec. exec., 1st v.p. Patrolmen's Benevolent Assn., N.Y.C. Police Dept., 1965-77; dep. commr., dir. labor relations Dept. Gen. Services City of N.Y., 1977-83; dir. personnel adminstrn. City of Fall River, Mass., 1984-85, city adminstr., 1985—; lectr. in field. Co-author: Comprehensive Reorganization of Municipal Government, 1986. Mem. Fall River Regional Task Force, 1984—. Served with USAF, 1957-61. Recipient Community Relations Service award, U.S. Justice Dept., Boston, 1985. Mem. Am. Mgmt. Assn., Nat. League of Cities, Internat. City Mgmt. Assn., Greater Fall River Personnel Council, Internat. Personnel Mgmt. Assn., Soc. of Profls. in Dispute Resolution. Democrat. Lodge: Masons. Home: 4980 N Main St Apt 1-15 Fall River MA 02720 Office: City of Fall River One Government Ctr Fall River MA 02722

CONNORS, THOMAS EDWARD, English literature educator; b. Waltham, Mass., Jan. 21, 1929; m. Feiga Hollenberg, June, 1956; children: Thomas, David, Sarah. BA, Brandeis U., 1956; MA, Boston U., 1957. Prof. English Suffolk U., Boston, 1957—. Author short stories. With USMC, 1946-48, PTO. Mem. AAUP. Home: 320 Tappan St Brookline MA 02146-4309 Office: Suffolk U Boston MA 02114-4299

CONOBY, JOSEPH FRANCIS, chemist; b. Albany, June 12, 1930; s. Joseph Francis and Helen Emma (Brucker) C.; B.S., Union Coll., 1952; m. Mary Joan A. Ryan, June 21, 1958; children—James Francis, Mark Joseph. Sr. tech. service engr. Allied Chem. Corp., Syracuse, N.Y., 1956-66; research chemist Conversion Chem. Corp., Rockville, Conn., 1966-69; environ. engr., indsl. hygienist, mgr. environ. and health engring. Honeywell Bull, Billerica, Mass., 1969-87, mgr. environ. engring. Bull HN Worldwide Info. Systems, 1987—; mem. adv. bd. Mass. Water Resources Authority Sewer Use (rules and regulations, policy and procedures, and facilities planning task forces); cons. exptl. project course Mass. Inst. Tech., 1977-78. Served to lt. USN, 1952-56. Mem. Am. Electroplaters Soc. (chmn. project com.), Am. Electroplaters Soc. (pres. Merrimack br.), Am. Indsl. Hygiene Assn. Patentee in field, U.S., Germany. Contbr. articles to profl. jours. Home: 5 Samuel Parlin Dr Acton MA 01720-3206 Office: Bull H N Worldwide Info Systems Billerica MA 01821

CONOSCENTI, CRAIG STEPHEN, physician; b. Jersey City, Jan. 11, 1955; s. Gerald Raoul and Constance Theresa (Niosi) C.; m. Rosanne Denise Scarpa, June 27, 1982; 1 child, Stephen Joseph. BS, Fordham U., 1977; MD, St. Georges U., 1981. Diplomate Am. Bd. Internal Medicine. Resident in internal medicine Meth. Hosp., Bklyn., 1981-82; resident in internal medicine Hackensack (N.J.) Med. Ctr., U. Medicine and Dentistry N.J., 1982-84, chief resident, 1984-85; fellow in pulmonary critical care medicine Norwalk (Conn.) Hosp., Yale U. Sch. Medicine, 1985-87, chief hyperbaric medicine, 1991—; pvt. practice, Norwalk, 1991—; med. dir. Norwalk Hosp. Sch. Respiratory Therapy, 1987—, med. dir. advanced cardiac life support program, 1986—. Contbr. articles to profl. jours.; co-inventor bronchoscopy catheter. Orator Norwalk Sons of Italy, 1990—. Norman Brady Internat. fellow Brompton Chest Hosp., London, and Norwalk Hosp., 1986. Mem. ACP, Am. Coll. Chest Physicians, Am. Thoracic Soc., Undersea and Hyperbaric Med. Soc., Fairfield County Lung Assn. (bd. dirs. 1987—). Office: Norwalk Hosp Dept Pulmonary and Critical Care Medicine Maple St Norwalk CT 06856

CONOVER, LLOYD HILLYARD, retired pharmaceutical research scientist and executive; b. Orange, N.J., June 13, 1923; s. John Howard and Marguerite Anna (Cameron) C.; m. Virginia Rogers Kirk, Aug. 24, 1944 (dec. Dec. 1988); children: Kirk Howard, Roger Lloyd, Heather Cameron, Craig Scott; m. Marie Strauss Solomons, Oct. 18, 1990. BA, Amherst Coll., 1947; PhD, U. Rochester, 1950. Rsch. chemist Chas. Pfizer & Co., Bklyn. and Groton, Conn., 1950-58; supr., mgr. Chas. Pfizer & Co., Groton, 1958-68; dir. chem. rsch. and chemotherapy Pfizer Cen. Rsch., Groton, 1968-71; rsch. dir. Europe Pfizer Cen. Rsch., Sandwich, Eng., 1971-74; v.p. agrl. R & D Pfizer Cen. Rsch., Groton and Sandwich, 1975-84; drug rsch. cons. Sandwich, Conn., 1984-86. Contbr. articles to sci. jours.; patentee tetracycline. Chmn. Waterford Planning and Zoning Commn., 1964-68; trustee Waterford Library, 1965-71; inductee Nat. Inventors' Hall of Fame, 1992. Lt. (j.g.) USNR, 1943-46, PTO. Recipient Eli Whitney award Conn. Patent Law Assn., 1983, Third Century award Found. Creative Am., 1990. Fellow Royal Soc. Chemistry (chartered chemist), Royal Soc. Arts; mem. Am. Chem. Soc., Phi Beta Kappa, Sigma Xi. Republican. Home: 27 Old Barry Rd Quaker Hill CT 06375-1019

CONOVER, ROBERT FREMONT, artist, educator; b. Trenton, N.J., July 3, 1920; s. Norman Smith and Emily (Fox) C.; m. Ruth Hageman, July 1949 (div); 1 child, Christine. Cert., Phila. Mus. Sch., 1942; student, Art Students League N.Y., 1945-48, Bklyn. Mus. Sch., 1948-50, The Barnes Found., Merion, Pa., 1947-48. Tchr. New Sch. for Social Rsch., N.Y.C., 1957—, Bklyn. Mus. Art Sch., 1961—, Lenox Sch., 1961-66, Newark Sch. Fine and Indsl. Arts, 1966—. One-man shows include Laurel Gallery, The New Gallery (now E.V. Thaw), Zabriskie Gallery, The New Sch. for Social Rsch.; exhibited in group shows at Mus. Modern Art, Bklyn. Mus., Met. Mus., Chgo. Art Inst., Whitney Anns., Pa. Acad. Anns., Carnegie Internat., Phila. Print Club, other nat. and internat. exhbns.; represented in permanent collections Bklyn. Mus., Phila. Mus. Art., Balt. Mus., Nat. gallery Art., Rosenwald Collection., Walker Art Ctr., Mpls., Smithsonian Collection., Tokyo Mus. Modern Art, Everson Mus., Syracuse, N.Y., Whitney Mus. Am. Art., N.Y., USIA Collection, N.J. State Mus., Cin. Art Mus., Balt. Mus., Mus. Art, Skopje, Yugoslavia, other university and private collections. MacDowell Colony fellow, 1955-58, Yaddo fellow, 1959-60; N.Y. State C.A.P.S. fellow, 1976. Mem. Am. Abstract Artists, So. Am. Graphic Artists (coun. v.p., List prize 1967, others), Nat. Acad. Design. Democratic. Home: 162 E 33rd St New York NY 10016

CONRAD, BRUCE PHILLIPS, mathematics educator; b. Ann Arbor, Mich., July 2, 1943; s. John P. and Charlotte (Merchant) C.; m. Rebecca K. Smith, Dec. 22, 1964; children: Clinton, Esther, Jessica, Rosemary. BS, Harvey Med. Coll., 1964; PhD, U. Calif., Berkeley, 1969. Asst. prof. math. dept. Temple U., Phila., 1969-73; assoc. prof. Temple U., 1973—. Contbr. articles to profl. jours. Mem. Am. Math. Soc., Math. Assn. Am., Soc. Indsl. and Applied Math., AAAS, Fedn. Am. Scientists. Democratic. Home: 147 Pelham Rd Philadelphia PA 19119-2661 Office: Temple U Dept Math Box 038 16 Philadelphia PA 19122

CONRAD, CONRAD A., oil company executive; b. Pineville, Ky., Feb. 27, 1946; s. Boyd J. and Jeanette A. (Hill) C.; m. Patricia A. Chausse, June 24, 1947; children: Alison, Laura. BA in Acctg., Coll. of William & Mary, 1968. CPA. Sr. acct. Price Waterhouse & Co., Washington, 1968-73; asst. mgr. internal audit Quaker State Corp., Oil City, Pa., 1974-77, asst. controller, 1977-82, controller, 1982-85, formerly v.p. fin., chief fin. officer, from 1985, now pres., COO. Served with U.S. Army, 1969-71. Republican. Presbyterian. Clubs: Wanango Country, Oil City. Home: 6 Glenwood Ave Bradford PA 16701-1801 Office: Quaker State Corp PO Box 989 Oil City PA 16301-0989*

CONRAD, GEORGE JOHN, design engineer, planner; b. N.Y.C., Apr. 24, 1943; s. George John and Bridget Anne (Kelly) C.; m. Marita Margaret Teuber, Apr. 24, 1971; children: Tracey Lynn, Kimberly Ann, Christopher George. BEE, Manhattan Coll., 1965. With Phila. Naval Shipyard, 1965—, supr. field design, 1973-79, gen. engr., 1979-84, design br. head, 1984-85, asst. chief design engring., 1985-87, advance planning supr., 1987-90, waterfront supr., 1990—; chief exec. officer, Conrad Properties, Atco, N.J., 1973—. Coach Waterford twp. Athletic Assn., 1987-90; chief YMCA Indian Guides, Echelon, N.J., 1987—; founder Winslow Crossing Civic Assn., 1972. Mem. Fed. Mgrs. Assn. (v.p. chpt. 4 1984-90). Roman Catholic. Home: 464 Raritan Ave Atco NJ 08004-1830

CONRAD, KENNETH ALLEN, internal medicine research director; b. Reading, Pa., Sept. 30, 1946; s. Roger Stapleton and Margaret (Miller) C.; m. JoAnne Ruth Castonguay, Aug. 30, 1974; children: Heather, Allison. BS, Albright Coll., 1968; MD, U. Pa., 1972. Diplomate Am. Bd. Internal Medicine, Am. Bd. Clin. Pharmacology. Asst. prof. Med. Coll. Pa., Phila., 1976-77; asst. prof. U. Ariz., Tucson, 1977-83, assoc. prof., 1983-89; sr. dir. clin. rsch. Wyeth-Ayerst Labs., Phila., 1989—; vice chief staff U. Ariz. Med. Ctr., Tucson, 1987-88. Editor: Drug Therapy for the Elderly, 1982. Fellow ACP; mem. Am. Soc. Clin. Pharmacology and Therapeutics. Office: Wyeth-Ayerst PO Box 8299 Philadelphia PA 19101-8299

CONRAD, TERRY LEE, health services administrator; b. Wilkes-Barre, Pa., June 5, 1954; s. Philip Jacob and Mary E. (Bloss) C.; m. Doreen M. Faneck, Dec. 26, 1977; children: Christopher Lee, Janelle Elizabeth. AS summa cum laude, Lackawanna Jr. Coll., Scranton, Pa., 1978; BS cum laude, Wilkes U., 1979, M of Healthcare Adminstrn., 1987. Sr. staff acct. Parente, Randolph, et al, CPAs, Wilkes-Barre, 1979-80; acctg. mgr. Geisinger System, Wilkes-Barre, 1980-82; asst. contr. Nesbitt Meml. Hosp., Kingston, Pa., 1982-85; contr. Community Med. Ctr., Scranton, 1985-88; chief fin. officer Pocono Health System, Stroudsburg, Pa., 1988-89, CMC Healthcare System, Scranton, 1989—; Mem. mgmt. com. Northeastern Lithotripsy Assocs., Scranton, 1989-91, Health Care Corp. N.E. Pa., 1985-91, Northeastern Pa. Imaging Ctr., 1985-91, Scranton Regional Cancer and Imaging Ctr., 1989-91; treas. Duolith, Inc., Scranton, 1989—; sec./treas. Hosp. Cen. Svcs., Inc., 1984—, Community Med. Care, Inc., 1989, Med. Dimensions, Inc., 1989—; asst. treas. Community Med. Ctr. Found., Scranton, 1989-91; mem. chief fin. officer com. VHA Pa., Inc., Pitts., 1985-91; treas. Med. Svcs., Inc., Scranton, 1989—, Healthnet N.E. Pa., Inc., Scranton, 1989-91, Scranton Counseling Ctr., 1989—; adj. prof. U. Scranton, 1991-92. Mem. audit com. United Way Lackawanna County, Scranton, 1988-89; fin. advisor Northeastern Pa. Children's House, Inc., Scranton, 1988-91; treas. First Ch. of Christ, Wilkes-Barre, 1982-86, vice chmn., 1986-88, trustee, deacon, 1990-91. Named one of Outstanding Young Men in Am., Jaycees, 1980. Fellow Healthcare Fin. Mgmt. Assn. Office: CMC Healthcare System 1800 Mulberry St Scranton PA 18510-2369

CONRAD, TERRY LYNN, university administrator; b. Steubenville, Ohio, Dec. 14, 1947; s. Iris Roy and Susie Jane (Findling) C.; m. Eileen Marie Woldridge, Nov. 18, 1981; 1 child, Benjamin Clay. AS, Cuyahoga Community Coll., Cleve., 1970; BS, Plymouth (N.H.) State Coll., 1973. Dir. alumni affairs N.H. Coll., Manchester. Vice pres. League N.H. Craftsmen Found., Concord, 1990—. With USMC , 1966, Vietnam, ret. Home: 1315 Belmont St Manchester NH 03104-3467 Office: NH Coll 2500 River Rd Hooksett NH 03106-1045

CONRAD, THOMAS ROBERT, college administrator; b. Youngstown, Ohio, Jan. 10, 1940; s. Harold D. and Bernice (Waffler) C.; m. Patricia Brough, Sept. 1, 1962; children: Daniel J., Jill Conrad Smith. BA, Wittenberg U., 1962; MA, U. Mass., 1964, PhD, 1968. Prof. polit. sci. Mount Union Coll., Alliance, Ohio, 1965-74; exec. dir. E. Cen. Coll. Consortium, Hiram, Ohio, 1974-78; v.p. devel. Monmouth (Ill.) Coll., 1978-88; v.p. inst. advancement Muhlenberg Coll., Allentown, Pa., 1988—. Contbr. 10 articles to profl. jours. Bd. dirs. Community Music Sch., Allentown, 1989-91; pres. E. Stark Ct. Mental Health Clinic, Alliance, Ohio, 1974-78. Mem. Rotary (officer 1984-88). Methodist. Home: 119 N 31st St Allentown PA 18104-5305 Office: Muhlenberg Coll 2400 W Chew St Allentown PA 18104-5564

CONRATH, BARNEY JAY, astrophysicist; b. Quincy, Ill., June 23, 1935; s. Frederick Barney and Jayme Wilson (Cason) C.; m. Marjorie Ann Hilder, Sept. 3, 1962; children: Ann, Frederick, Susan. BA, Culver-Stockton Coll., Canton, Mo., 1957; MA, U. Iowa, 1959; PhD, U. N.H., 1966. Astrophysicist Goddard Space Flight Ctr., NASA, Greenbelt, Md., 1960-90, sr. fellow, 1990—. Co-author: Exploration of the Solar System by Infrared Remote Sensing, 1991; contbr. over 100 articles to profl. jours. Recipient Exceptional Sci. Achievement medal NASA, 1982, 90. Mem. Am. Astron. Soc., Am. Geophys. Union, Sigma Xi. Office: Goddard Space Flight Ctr Cod 693.2 Greenbelt MD 20771

CONROY, DAVID LORAM, executive director; b. Doylestown, Pa., Apr. 9, 1946; s. Robert B. C. and Mary Patricia (Loram) Stephenson. BA, Claremont Mens Coll., 1968; MA, U. Mass., 1972, PhD, 1974. Exec. dir. Suicide Prevention Resources, N.Y.C., 1988—. Author: Out of the Nightmare, 1991. Grantee Van Ameringen Found., 1990, N.Y. Community Trust, 1990, Mental Illness Found., 1991, Rapoport Found., 1991. Mem. N.Y. Assn. Suicidology. Office: Suicide Prevention Resource 347 E 61 # 1-RE New York NY 10021

CONROY, DENNIS PATRICK, human resources executive; b. Hartford, Conn., Apr. 8, 1945; s. Patrick Henry and Anna Marie (DePersia) C.; m. Karen Elizabeth DePersia, Sept. 14, 1968; children: Kevin P., Michael D. AAS, Hartford State Tech Coll., 1969; BA, U. Conn., 1986. Hwy. engr. Conn. Dept. of Transp., Wethersfield, 1964-71; dir. leasing Murphy, Inc., Bridgeport, Conn., 1971-76; fin. planner Travelers Ins. Co., Hartford, 1976-81; dir. human resources Bradley Meml. Hosp., Southington, Conn., 1981-90; mgr. human resources CDI Med. Scvs., Inc., Bloomfield, Conn., 1990—; commr. Cen. Conn. Tourism Dist., New Britain, 1986—; trustee Conn. Hosp. Assn. Workers Compensation, Wallingford, 1989-90; bd. dirs. Sheldon Community Guidance, New Britain. Mng. editor: (mag.) Healthstyle, 1986 (award). Chmn. Charter Revision Commn., Southington, Conn., 1977; sec. Zoning Bd. Appeals, Southington, 1978; bd. dirs. Greater Southington C. of C., 1982-84; vice chmn. Town Coun., Southington, 1983; active Planning and Zoning Commn., Southington, 1991. Mem. UNICO Nat., Soc. Human Resources Mgrs., Am. Soc. Healthcare Human Resources Adminstrn., First Co. Gov.'s Food Guard (adj. 1990—, Coldstream Guard medal). Democrat. Roman Catholic. Office: CDI Med Svcs Inc 1280 Blue Hills Ave Bloomfield CT 06002-1374

CONROY, TAMARA BOKS, business executive; b. Most, Bohemia, Czechoslovakia; came to U.S., 1947; d. Alois and Tatiana (Shapilova) Boks; m. John P. Conroy, Aug. 19, 1950 (dec. Oct. 1973); 1 child, Michael Thomas (dec.). Student, U. Graz, Austria, 1945-47; RN, New Rochelle (N.Y.) Med. Ctr., 1950; student, Coll. of William & Mary, 1958, 59, Cath. U. Am., 1960; BS in Nursing Edn., Columbia U., 1963, MA in Spl. Edn., 1965. RN, N.Y.; cert. spl. edn. tchr., N.Y. Nurse accident rm. New Rochelle Hosp./Med. Ctr., 1950-51; pub. health nurse Va. Dept. of Health, Richmond, 1958-59; tchr. spl. edn. Southern Westchester Bd. Coop. Edn. Svcs., Portchester, N.Y., 1965-83; freelance artist and painter N.Y.C. and Pelham, N.Y., 1969—; asst. to chmn. math. dept. Columbia U., N.Y.C., 1975-76. Author math. program Learning Numbers-Step by Step, 1977. Pres., founder Classical Music Lover's Exch., Pelham, 1980—. Mem. Am. Fedn. Tchrs., N.Y. State United Tchrs., BOCES Tchrs. Assn. (profl.), Women's Mus. Group, Mamaroneck Artists Guild, Silvermine Artists Guild, Westchester Musicians Guild (assoc.), Kappa Delta Pi. Office: Classical Music Lovers' Exch PO Box 31 Pelham NY 10803

CONROY-LACIVITA, DIANE CATHERINE, historic site director; b. Schenectady, N.Y., Aug. 22, 1965; d. William Edward and Bernice Mary (Paluch) Conroy; m. Joseph James LaCivita, Nov. 5, 1988; 1 child, Frances Catherine. BA in History, SUNY, Oswego, 1986; MA in History, SUNY, Albany, 1989; cert. in clowning, Hudson Valley Community Coll., 1988. Exec. dir. Shaker Heritage Soc., Albany, 1988—. Mem. Snyder Lake Improvement Assn., Wynantskill, N.Y., 1988—; mem. Capital Dist. Speed Skating Group, Albany, 1991; co-chair edn. com., planning com. Nat. Hist. Preservation Week, 1990-91. Mem. Fedn. Hist. Svcs., Mid Atlantic Assn. Mus. Office: Shaker Heritage Soc 1848 Shaker Meeting House Albany Shaker Rd Albany NY 12211

CONSIDINE, JOSEPH BYRNE, electrical engineer, regional sales manager; b. Bryn Mawr, Pa., June 12, 1961; s. John Michael and Jane (Byrne) C. BEE, Drexel U., 1984; MBA, Boston Coll., 1991. Asst. plant engr. Joseph E. Seagram & Sons, Inc., Relay, Md., 1980; programmer Leeds & Nothrup Co., North Wales, Pa., 1981; logic designer Burroughs Corp., Paoli, Pa., 1982-84; sales assoc. Tex. Instruments, Dallas, 1984-85; sales engr. Tex. Instruments, Waltham, Mass., 1985-88; regional sales engr. Cognex Corp., Needham, Mass., 1988—. Mem. Drexel U. Boston Alumni Club. Home: 3 Kings Grant Rd Weston MA 02193-2117 Office: Cognex Corp 15 Crawford St Needham MA 02194-2618

CONSIDINE, TIMOTHY JAMES, economics educator, researcher; b. Chgo., Mar. 16, 1953; s. Timothy James and Joan (McNamara) C.; m. Margaret E. Tait, Oct. 5, 1985; children: Nicholas, Maureen, John. BA with honors, Loyola U., Chgo., 1975; MS, Purdue U., 1977; PhD, Cornell U., 1981. Assoc. analyst U.S. Congl. Budget Office, Washington, 1981-83; economist Bank of Am., San Francisco, 1983-86; assoc. prof. mineral econs. Pa. State U., University Park, 1986—; cons. U.D. Dept. Energy, Washington, 1990-92. Contbr. articles to profl. jours. Recipient Young Scholar's award U.S. Dept. Interior, 1990-92. Mem. Am. Econ. Assn., Am. Assn. Agrl. Econs. Office: Pa State U Dept Econs 201 Walker University Park PA 16802

CONSTABLE, ROBERT LEE, educator, scientist; b. Detroit, Jan. 20, 1942; s. Wilfred Lee and Virginia (Tabor) C.; m. Carol E.; children: Amy E., Emily C. AB, Princeton U., 1964; MA, U. Wis., 1965, PhD, 1968. From asst. prof. to prof. computer scis. Cornell U., Ithaca, N.Y., 1968—. Author: A Programming Logic, 1980, Implementing Mathematics, 1986. Mem. Assn. for Symbolic Logic, Assn. for Computing Machinery. Office: Cornell U Computer Sci Dept Upson Hall Ithaca NY 14853

CONSTANTINIDES, SPIROS MINAS, food science educator; b. Thessaloniki, Greece, Nov. 4, 1932; came to U.S., 1961; s. Minas and Argiro (Paraskevaides) C.; m. Niovi Lazarides, Dec. 23, 1959; children: Minas, Dorothea. BS, U. Thessaloniki, 1957; MS, Mich. State U., 1963, PhD, 1966. Instr. U. Thessaloniki, 1957-61; grad. rsch. asst. Mich. State U., East Lansing, 1961-66, postdoctoral fellow, 1966-68; prof. food sci. U. R.I., Kingston, 1968—; dir. Midwest Rsch. Inst., Saudi Arabia, 1978-86, Internat. Ctr. Marine Rsch. Devel., Kingston, 1987—; vis. prof. U. Valparaiso, Chile, 1972, U. Campinas, Brazil, 1975; cons. in field. Contbr. articles to profl. publs. NIH fellow, 1967. Mem. Inst. Food Technologists. Greek Orthodox. Office: U RI Woodward Hall 126 Kingston RI 02881

CONSTANTINO, GARY JAMES, design and architecture consultant; b. Buffalo, N.Y., Nov. 23, 1954; s. Angelo Paul and Anne (Campisi) C. BPS in Architecture, SUNY, Buffalo, 1982; MArch, Syracuse U., 1985; cert. spl. programs, Harvard U., 1987, 1988. Asst. to engr. in charge N.Y. State Office of Gen. Svcs., Buffalo, 1983; designer Masque Design, Ithaca, N.Y., 1984-85, McDonald and Korman, Architects, Syracuse, 1985; project asst. N.Y. State Office of Mental Health, Albany, N.Y., 1985; designer Duchscherer-Oberst, Design, Kenmore, N.Y., 1986; assoc. Cannon Design, Inc., Grand Island, N.Y., 1986-90; designer Cannon Design, Inc., Boston, 1987-88; prin. EPISTE, Buffalo, 1990—; vis. critic SUNY, Buffalo, 1986—. Co-editor (design) Milieu Mag., 1981; contbr. (architecture) Modo Mag., 1986. Bd. dirs. Senecare Corp., Buffalo, 1987—; mem. housing adv. com. Am. Blind Assn, Buffalo, 1990. Recipient Fgn. Study grant Div. of Internat. Studies, Florence, Italy, 1983. Mem. AIA (assoc.), Nat. Trust for Hist. Preservation, ASID. Home: 345 N Park Ave Buffalo NY 14216-1937 Office: EPISTE 700 Main St Buffalo NY 14202-1909

CONSTANTINOU, CLAY, lawyer; b. N.Y.C., Sept. 4, 1951; s. Dan and Eleni (Maouris) C.; m. Eileen Calamari, Mar. 6, 1976; children: Jennifer, Dan. BA, Jersey City State Coll., 1973; JD, Seton Hall U., 1981; LLM, NYU, 1986. Ptnr. Constantinou & Carroll Law Offices, West Orange, N.J., 1981-86; pvt. practice Clay Constantinou Law Offices, West Orange, 1986—. Commr. N.J. Turnpike Authority, New Brunswick, 1990—; supreme pres. Cyprus Fedn. Am., N.Y.C., 1986-90; mem. Jersey City State Coll. Devel. Fund, 1991—; trustee Dem. Nat. Com., Washington, 1988-91; N.J. state fin. chair Dem. Primary and Gen. Election, 1988-89. Mem. N.J. State Bar Assn. Office: 50 Northfield Ave West Orange NJ 07052-5336

CONTE, JOHN MICHAEL, rheumatologist; b. New Haven, Conn., Feb. 17, 1951; s. Harold Sebastian and Irma-Linda (Rossi) C.; m. Olga Helen Harbar, Dec. 23, 1991. BS in Psychology, Trinity Coll., 1973; MD, U. Conn., 1978. Diplomate Am. Bd. Internal Medicine; cert. Rheumatology Bds., Geriatric Bds. Intern Washington Hosp. Ctr., 1978-79; resident Newton (Mass.)-Wellesley Hosp., 1979-81; clin. and rsch. fellow in medicine

Mass. Gen. Hosp., Boston, 1981-84; geriatric rsch. and edn. fellow E.N.R. Meml. Veterans Hosp., Bedford, Mass., 1984-86; pvt. practice Providence, 1986—; asst. prof. medicine Boston U., Bedford, 1986—, U. Mass., Worcester, 1989-91, Brown U., Providence, 1991—. Homeless van physician Travelers Aide Soc., Providence, 1991-92. Fellow ACP, Am. Coll. Rheumatology; mem. Pagets Disease Found. Roman Catholic. Office: Rheumatology Assocs 49 Seekonk St Providence RI 02906

CONTESTABILE, JOHN MICHAEL, highway engineer; b. Stoneham, Mass., June 20, 1956; s. John A. and Clara S. (Cuscuna) C.; m. Janice K. Rafferty, Mar. 21, 1981, children: Jenna D., Kaila B. BSCE, Worcester Poly. Inst., 1978; MBA, U. Balt., 1985. Project engr. project planning div. Md. State Hwy. Adminstrn., Balt., 1978-80, engr. group leader, 1980-84, project mgr., 1984-86, from sect. chief to asst. div. chief., 1986-90, div. chief engr. access permits div., 1990—. V.p. Md. Jr. Wrestling League, Balt., 1980; bd. dirs. Vill. 12 Tress Civic Assn., Randallstown, Md., 1985-90; co-chmn. long range planning com. Wards Chapel United Meth. Ch., 1989—. Mem. ASCE (assoc.), Assn. MBA Execs., Soc. for the Advancement Mgmt., Md. Soc. Engrs., Phi Gamma Delta, Delta Mu Delta (sec. 1984), Sigma Iota Epsilon, Beta Gamma Sigma. Republican. United Methodist. Office: Md State Hwy Adminstrn 707 N Calvert St Baltimore MD 21202

CONWAY, JAMES ARTHUR, educator; b. Westchester, N.Y., May 24, 1933; s. James Patrick and Florence (Simermeyer) C.; m. Linda Hyde, Aug. 31, 1963; children—James Hyde, Matthew Gerard, Christopher John. B.A., SUNY-Albany, 1954; M.A., Columbia U., 1955; C.E.A., SUNY-Albany, 1963, Ed.D., 1963. Vis. prof. U. Miami, Fla., 1966-67; exchange prof. Didsbury Coll., Manchester, Eng., 1973; vis. lectr. Univ. Coll., Galway, Ireland, 1974; assoc. prof. edn. U. Buffalo, 1969, chmn. ednl. adminstrn., 1979-82, coordinator ednl. adminstrn., 1982-89, vis. practitioner Prin's. Ctr. Harvard U., 1989; acting prin. Saratoga Jr. High Sch., N.Y., 1962; cons. Oxford Poly., Wheatley, Eng., 1982, 85; external examiner U. Hong Kong, Shatin, 1984, 91. Co-author: Understanding Communities, 1974, (with S. Jacobson) Educational Leadership in an Age of Reform, 1990; mem. editorial bd. Ednl. Adminstrn. Quar., 1982-86; contbr. articles to profl. jours. With U.S. Army, 1956-58. U. Albany fellow, 1960-63; NSF fellow, 1959. Mem. Univ. Council for Ednl. Adminstrn. (exec. com. 1979-82), Am. Ednl. Research Assn., Collegiate Assn. for Devel. of Ednl. Adminstrn. (sec.-treas. 1982-84). Phi Delta Kappa, Sigma Tau Rho. Avocations: bridge; tennis; golf; chess. Home: 161 Amherstdale Rd Buffalo NY 14226-4413 Office: U Buffalo 477 Baldy Hall Buffalo NY 14260

CONWAY, RICHARD FRANCIS, investment company executive; b. Greenwich, Conn., Jan. 4, 1954; s. Francis Xavier and Marie (Bohan) C.; m. Greta Weil, Oct. 29, 1988; 1 child, Signe Charlotte. BA, Harvard Coll., 1976; M of Pub. and Pvt. Mgmt., Yale U., 1981. Mgmt. trainee Citibank, N.Y.C., 1976-79; assoc. L.F. Rothschild, Unterberg, Towbin Inc., N.Y.C., 1981-83, v.p., 1983-86, prin., 1986-88; v.p. Salomon Bros. Inc., N.Y.C., 1988-90, Security Pacific Mcht. Bank, N.Y.C., 1990-91; sr. v.p. Needham and Co. Inc., N.Y.C., 1992—. Trustee Choate Rosemary Hall Sch., Wallingford, Conn., 1974-78; class com. Harvard Coll. Fund, Cambridge, Mass., 1991. Mem. Harvard Club N.Y.C. Roman Catholic. Home: 1361 MAdison Ave 1361 Madison Ave New York NY 10128 Office: Needham and Co Inc 400 Park Ave New York NY 10022

CONWAY DE MACARIO, EVERLY, immunologist; b. Buenos Aires, Argentina, Apr. 20, 1939; came to U.S., 1974; d. Delfin E. and Maria Gloria (Benatuil) Conway; m. Alberto J.L. Macario, Mar. 16, 1963; children: Alex, Everly. PhD in Pharmacy, Nat. U. Buenos Aires, 1960, PhD in Biochemistry, 1962. Rsch. fellow Nat. Acad. Medicine Argentina, Buenos Aires, 1962-63; head lab. oncology and immunology Argentinian Assn. against Cancer, Buenos Aires, 1966-67; chief immunology Sch. Medicine, Buenos Aires, 1967-68; research fellow dept. tumor-biology Karolinska Inst., Stockholm, 1969-71; sr. research scientist Lab. Cell Biology, NRC Italy, Rome, 1971-73; vis. scientist Internat. Agy. Research on Cancer, WHO, Lyon, France, 1973-74; vis. scientist Brown U., Providence, 1974-76; research scientist Lab. Immunology, N.Y. State Dept. Health, Albany, 1976—; prof. Sch. Pub. Health dept. Biomed. Scis., 1986—, mem. admissions com., 1986-89, pers. com., 1989-91, curriculum com., 1991—. Recipient Prof. J.M. Mezzadra award Nat. U. Buenos Aires, 1969; Travel award to Eng., 2d Internat. Immunology Congress, 1974; Gold medal Argentinian Soc. Biochemistry, 1980; Hans Osterman Found. grantee, Sweden, 1969; Sir Samuel Scott of Yews Trust grantee, Sweden, 1970; Winifred Cullis grantee Internat. Fedn. Univ. Women, 1972; NATO research grantee, 1975, 81; Dept. Energy grantee, 1981, 84; Travel awardee to China, 1985, Peru, 1987, Portugal, 1988, Germany, 1990. Mem. Scandinavian Soc. Immunology, Italian Assn. Immunologists, French Soc. Immunology (travel award 1974), Am. Assn. Immunologists (chmn. com. on status of women 1980-86, edn. com. 1982-87, awards com. 1991-92, travel award to Australia 1977), Am. Soc. Microbiology (sr. editor Manual Clin. Lab. Immunology 4th edit.). Co-editor: Monoclonal Antibodies Against Bacteria, 1985-86, Gene Probes for Bacteria, 1990; assoc. editor profl. jour., 1986—; contbr. articles to profl. jours. Achievements include patents in microcircle system, microsample holder and carrier; invention of ultrasensitive micro-immunoenzymatic assay and multipurpose modular system for use in lab. and field settings, of the antigenic fingerprinting method; creation of immunotechnology for rapid identification of microbes directly in samples of complex microbial mixtures; first to establish the antigenic cohesiveness of methanogenic and halophilic archaebacteria and demonstrate clusters overlapping phylogenetic branches. Home: 18 Carriage Rd Delmar NY 12054-3704 Office: Wadsworth Center Labs Empire State Plz Albany NY 12201

CONWILL, JOSEPH DILLARD, photographer; b. N.Y.C., Dec. 12, 1954; s. Allan Franklin and Arolyn Frances (Hodgkins) C. BA in Am. Culture, Northwestern U., 1979. U.S. agt. Soc. Quebecoise des Ponts Couverts, St. Eustache, 1981-92. Photographic works represented in permanent collections at Nat. Archives of Can., Can. Centre. for Architecture; editor Covered Bridge Topics, 1992—. Mem. Nat. Soc. Preservation Covered Bridges. Roman Catholic. Home: PO Box 829 Rangeley ME 04970 Office: E Philip Levine Inc 23 Dry Dock Ave Boston MA 02210

COOGAN, MICHAEL DAVID, religious studies educator; b. Madison, Wis., July 30, 1942; s. Daniel Francis and Inge (Bruns) C.; m. Pamela A. Hill, Aug. 21, 1982; children: Daniel, Elizabeth, Matthew. BA, Fordham U., 1966; PhD, Harvard U., 1971. Asst. prof. St. Jerome's Coll., Waterloo, Ont., Can., 1971-74; asst. prof. Harvard Div. Sch., Cambridge, 1976-80, assoc. prof., 1980-85, vis. prof., 1989-90; vis. prof. Wellesley (Mass.) Coll., 1986-89; prof. Stonehill Coll., North Easton, Mass., 1985—; assoc. trustee Am. Schs. of Oriental Rsch., Balt., 1981-90. Author: West Semitic Personal Names, 1976, Stories from Ancient Canaan, 1978; assoc. editor Cath. Bibl. Quar.; contbr. articles to profl. jours. Mem. Soc. Bibl. Lit. (pres. New Eng. region 1985-86), Archaeol. Inst. of Am., Bibl. Colloquium, Cath. Bibl. Assn., Israel Exploration Soc., Am. Schs. of Oriental Rsch. Home: 15 Whittemore St Concord MA 01742-3513 Office: Stonehill Coll North Easton MA 02357

COOK, ANTHONY JOHN RAINE, investment management associate; b. Sommerville, N.J., Aug. 5, 1963; s. John E. and Vivien R. (Taylor) C. BS in Econs., Carnegie-Mellon U., 1985; MBA in Fin./Internat. Bus., NYU, 1990. Investment mgmt. assoc. J.P. Morgan Investment Mgmt., N.Y.C., 1985-89, Brown Bros. Harriman, N.Y.C., 1990—. Baritone Grace Ch. Choir, N.Y.C., 1985-91; editor Owners Corp., Bklyn., 1986-89. Named to Dean's List, Carnegie Mellon U., 1985; named Stern scholar NYU, 1989. Mem. Beta Gamma Sigma, Boys Club of N.Y. (vol. leader 1990-91), Carnegie Mellon N.Y.C. Club. Episcopalian. Office: Brown Bros Harriman 63 Wall St New York NY 10005-3001

COOK, BOB, rare book dealer; b. Pitts., Oct. 25, 1948; s. Donald James and Anna Marie (Swope) C.; m. Nora Marie Sheehan, June 30, 1989; children: Emily, Melissa, Laurie, Dennis, Nicholas. Self-employed Buffalo, 1971—. Bd. dirs. Greater Buffalo Counseling Ctrs. (pres., 1990—, vol. counselor, 1986—); group leader Parents Anonymous, 1986—; vol. Suicide Hot Line, Buffalo Crisis Svcs., 1986-89. Home and Office: Box 129 North Java NY 14113

COOK, CHANDLER LEWIS, transportation executive; b. Chgo., Jan. 25, 1937; s. Wallace Lewis Cook and Elizabeth (Hodson) Ludwig; m. Marilyn Louise MacAulay, June 27, 1959; children: Elizabeth, Jennifer, Douglass. BA in Psychology magna cum laude, U. Utah, 1963; MBA, Pepperdine U., 1977. Line officer USN, 1963-72; asst. dir. Sch. of Work Study USN, Norfolk, Va., 1970-72; mem. tech. staff Hughes Aircraft Co., Fullerton, Calif., 1972-76; asst. to mgr., liaison Hughes Aircraft Co., Washington, 1976-87; mgr., Phila. dist. Hughes Aircraft Co., Trevose, Pa., 1988—. Pres. King's Park Civic Bd., Annandale, Va., 1980. Mem. Am. Soc. Naval Engrs. (chmn. combat systems symposium event subcom. 1983-87), Navy League U.S.A., U.S. Naval Inst., Assn. Old Crows (bd. dirs., chmn. scholarship com. 1988—), Calif. Scholarship Fedn. (life), Phi Kappa Phi. Republican. Home: 15 Country Club Dr Warrington PA 18976-1212 Office: Hughes Aircraft Co Three Neshaminy Interplex 3 Neshaminy Interplex Ste 301 Langhorne PA 19053-6939

COOK, DONALD MICHAEL, insurance agent; b. Washington, Feb. 21, 1953; s. Donald Andrew and Joan Alene (McLaughlin) C.; m. Diana Lynn Bischoff, Sept. 16, 1972 (div. Aug. 1985); children: Brendon Michael, Kelley Lynn, Kristie Lynn; m. Susan Elizabeth Kenney, June 1, 1986; step-children: Colleen Kenney, John J. Kenney III. Grad. high sch., Wanaque, N.J., 1971. LUTC; cert. realtor. Office mgr. Bischoff Ins. Agy., Inc., Ringwood, N.J., 1972-74; agt. The Prudential, San Antonio, Tex., 1975-78; agt. The Prudential, Oakland, N.J., 1981-86, sales mgr., 1986-87, agt., fin. planner, 1987—; real estate agt. Cook Agt. Real Estate, Ringwood, 1978-81; union leader/local union rep. Ins. Workers Am., Washington, 1982-84, local union/Pompton Plains, N.J., 1984-89. Chmn. Festival Day, Borough of Ringwood, 1984, 85. Mem. Pompton Associated Life Underwriters. Republican. Mem. Christian Ch. Home: 3 Choctaw Trail PO Box 371 Ringwood NJ 07456 Office: The Prudential 169 Ramapo Valley Rd Ste 2M Oakland NJ 07436-2509

COOK, FRANK XAVIER, JR., management consultant; b. Oak Park, Ill., Apr. 13, 1940; s. Frank X. Sr. and Margaret I. (Wilson) C.; m. Babrara Ann Kuzmick, Sept. 18, 1965; children: Barbara, Kathleen, Cynthia, Michael. B of Mechanical Engring., Manahttan Coll., 1961; M of Mechanical Engring., CUNY, N.Y.C., 1966; MS in Mgmt. Sci., Stevens Tech., 1972. Product devel. engr. Bulova Watch Co., N.Y.C., 1961-62; engr. Grumman Aerospace Corp., Bethpage, N.Y., 1962-68; dir. Mathematica Inc., Princeton, N.J., 1969-78; ptnr. Ayers, Whitmore & Co. Inc., N.Y.C., 1979-88, Cook, Holmlund & Co. Inc., Princeton, 1988—. Author: Financial Risk Analysis, 1972. Mem. APICS, Soc. Mfg. Engrs. Republican. Office: Cook Holmlund & Co Inc PO Box 7397 Princeton NJ 08543-7397

COOK, HARVEY CARLISLE, law enforcement official; b. Cambridge, Md., June 19, 1936; s. John Morrison and Lula Arbelia (Warfield) C.; m. Shirley Marie Cox, Aug. 4, 1973; children: Brenda, Claudine, John, Anne. AA in Police Sci., Charles Ct. Community Coll., LaPlata, Md., 1973; BBA, U. Md., 1979, cert. in paralegal, 1980; cert. in criminal justice, FBI Nat. Acad., Quantico, Va., 1983. USCG Masters lic., 1988. Inspector Tidewater Fisheries Dept., Hughesville, Md., 1958-61, dist. inspector, 1962-64; lt. Md. State Marine Police, Hughesville, 1965-69; capt. Md. State Marine Police, LaPlata, 1970-72, Md. Natural Resources Police, LaPlata, 1973-75; maj. Md. Natural Resources Police, Annapolis, 1976-86, dep. supt., 1986-88; dir. Hovercraft tng. and ops. Hover Systems, Inc., 1988—; liaison officer Emergency Mgmt. Agy., Pikesville, Md., 1974-86, USCG Aux., Balt., 1982-86. Bd. dirs. Charles County Fair, LaPlata, 1985. Recipient Ann. Safe Boating award USCG Aux., 1975, Disting. Svc. award, 1987; named Best Engring. Soldier Md. N.G. 121st Engr. Battalion, 1967, Disting. Citizen, Mass. Gov.'s Office, 1983; commd. Ky. Col., Gov. Ky., 1983. Mem. NRA (life), Nat. Police Officers Assn. Am. (charter), So. Md. Bd. Realtors, FOP, Hoverclub Am., Md. Chiefs Police Assn., Charles County Community Coll. Alumni Assn. (pres. 1984), Dr. Samuel A. Mudd Soc. Inc. (treas. 1987), U.S. Hovercraft Soc. Inc. (bd. dirs. 1987, v.p. 1990-92). Republican. Methodist. Home: 408 Briarwood Dr Media PA 19086-6503 Office: Hover Systems Inc 1500 Chester Pike Chester PA 19022-1337

COOK, HOWARD LAWRENCE, trade association executive; b. N.Y.C., July 27, 1925; s. Howard Alfonse and Agnes Veronica (Honohan) C.; m. Ann Hathaway, Apr. 18, 1964. BSChemE, Columbia U., 1950. Sr. design engr. RCA, Harrison, N.J., 1950-66; tech. and mktg. cons. Robertson & Assocs., Summit, N.J., 1966-68; asst. to the pres. Aluminum Assn., N.Y.C. (now Washington), 1968-76; exec. sec. Transp. Safety Equipment Inst., Englewood Cliffs, 1976—; group adminstr. Motor & Equipment Mfrs. Assn., Englewood Cliffs, 1976—, Automotive Chem. Mfrs. Coun., Englewood Cliffs, 1985—. Lt. USNR, 1951-54. Home: 105 Franklin St Cedar Grove NJ 07009-2209 Office: Automotive Chem Mfrs Coun PO Box 1638 300 Sylvan Ave Englewood Cliffs NJ 07632

COOK, JAMES HARRISON, insurance company executive; b. N.Y.C., Sept. 10, 1942; s. Zenas Dee and Ruth Hazel (Warringer) C.; m. Ann Catherine Madigan, Apr. 8, 1967; children: Julie Ann, Allison Jane, Jill Marie. BA, U. Pa., 1963; AS in Health Ins., Life Mgmt. Inst. CLU. Traffic asst. Ohio Bell Telephone Co., Youngstown, 1967-68; group ins. underwriter Conn. Gen. Life Ins. Co., Hartford, 1968-71; 2d v.p. Wis. Life Ins. Co., Madison, 1971-82, Cen. Life Assurance Co., Madison, 1982-87; mgr. med. and dental underwriter Combined Ins. Co. of Am., Trevose, Pa., 1987-88; v.p., A&H underwriting NEM Reinsurance Corp., Piscataway, N.Y., 1988-90; regional v.p. PERICO, Ltd., Willow Grove, Pa., 1990—. Capt. U.S. Army, 1964-67. Fellow Life Mgmt. Inst. Republican. Roman Catholic. Office: Perico Ltd 2300 Computer Rd Bldg G Willow Grove PA 19090-1732

COOK, JEANNINE SALVO, library director; b. N.Y.C., Apr. 11, 1929; d. Ernest August and Edith Agatha (Lombardo) S.; m. Donald Carter Cook, June 9, 1962; 1 child, Carter Steven. BA, Hunter Coll., 1951; MLS, Columbia U., 1958, postgrad., 1973. Chemist Charles Pfizer and Co., Inc., Bklyn., 1951-56, lit. chemist, 1956-58; cen. med. librarian Am. Cyanamid, N.Y.C., 1958-60; sr. profl. adminstr. Engring. and phys. scis. library Columbia U., N.Y.C., 1960-62; assoc. librarian SUNY, Stony Brook, 1962-63; dir. Emma S. Clark Meml. Library, Setauket, N.Y., 1966—; editorial adv. bd. Gale, Rsch. Pub., Detroit, 1989, adv. bd., 1986-88; design com. Gaylord Bros., Syracuse, N.Y., 1987. Pres. bd. dirs. 3 Village Community Youth Coun., Stony Brook, 1978-88; bd. dirs. Ministries Coun., Setauket, 1978-85, 3 V Schs.-Community Youth at Risk, Stony Brook, 1989—; co-chmn. edn. com. Assn. Community Univ. Cooperative, Stony Brook, 1973-80. Recognized for voluntarism Brookhaven Youth Bur., Setauket, 1984, for Outstanding Service Community Youth Services, Stony Brook, 1988; recipient Pub. Relations award Library Pub. Relations Coun., 1978. Mem. ALA (pub. relations award 1987), Brookhaven Library Dirs. (pres. 1976-80), Pub. Library Dirs. Assn. (exec. bd. 1976—), Spl. Library Assn., Med. Library Assn. Home: 40 Seabrook Ln Stony Brook NY 11790-3328 Office: Emma S Clark Meml Libr 120 Main St Stony Brook NY 11790-1932

COOK, JONATHAN BOYD, charitable organization administrator; b. Mpls., May 26, 1942; s. Stuart Wellford and Annabelle (Hurley) C.; m. G. Grace Newman, July 21, 1990. BA, Harvard U., 1964, LLB, 1967. Exec. dir. Pub. Interest Mgmt. Assocs., Washington, 1971-73; nat. exec. dir. Support Ctrs. Am., Washington, 1973—. Contbr. articles to profl. jours. Bd. dirs. Ctr. for Sci. in Pub. Interest, 1989—, Accts. for Pub. Interest, Washington, 1974-84, Nat. Coun. Philanthropy, N.Y.C., 1975-80. Named Washingtonian of Yr., Washingtonian Mag., 1991. Office: Support Ctrs Am 2001 O St NW Washington DC 20036-5955

COOK, JUDITH HELEN, elementary education educator; b. Yonkers, N.Y., May 3, 1942; d. Joseph Charles and Helen (Bobak) Cassino; m. Lawrence E. Cook, July 4, 1966; children: Matthew, Michael, David, Kathryn. BS, SUNY, New Paltz, 1964; MS, Iona Coll., 1992. Tchr., first grade Peekskill (N.Y.) City Sch. Dist., 1979—. Recipient Dr. Lolabel Hall scholarship. Mem. AAUW (sec. 1983-85, treas. 1986-87), Peekskill Faculty Assn. (treas. 1989-91, v.p. 1991—), Delta Kappa Gamma (sec. 1990-92). Roman Catholic. Home: 271 Buttonwood Ave Cortlandt Mnr NY 10566-4911 Office: Uriah Hill Elem Sch Pemart Ave Peekskill NY 10566-2208

COOK, LEAH MARIE, economic researcher; b. Beverly, Mass., Apr. 25, 1966; d. Robert Warren and Claire Ruth (Potter) C. BA in Econs. magna cum laude, Wellesley Coll., 1988. Cons. Monitor Co., Cambridge, Mass., 1988-89; rsch. asst. Fed. Res. Bank Boston, 1989-90, sr. rsch. asst., 1990—. Authjor: (with Alicia Munnell) Financing Capital Expenditures in Massachusetts, 1990, (with Karl Case) The Distributional Effects of Housing Price Booms: Winners and Losers in Boston, 1980-88, 1989, (with Richard Kopcke and Alicia Munnell) The Influence of Housing and Durables on Personal Saving, 1991, (with Alicia Munnell) Explaining the Postwar Pattern of Saving, 1991. Mem. Phi Beta Kappa. Democrat. Roman Catholic. Office: Fed Res Bank Boston 600 Atlantic Ave Boston MA 02106-2706

COOK, LEROY FRANKLIN, JR., physicist, educator; b. Ashland, Ky., Dec. 12, 1931; s. LeRoy Franklin and Dorothy (Williams) C.; m. Arrelle Janet Rapp, June 16, 1957; children: Nancy Grace, Laura Arrelle, Andrew LeRoy. B.A., U. Calif.-Berkeley, 1953, M.A., 1957, Ph.D., 1959. Instr. Princeton U., 1959-62, asst. prof., 1962-65; asso. prof. U. Mass., Amherst, 1965-68; prof. physics U. Mass., 1968—, acting head physics dept., 1969-71, head physics and astronomy dept., 1971-75, 79-85; cons. Inst. Def. Analyses, Arlington, Va., 1963-67; vis. fellow Clare Hall, Cambridge U., spring 1972. Contbr. articles profl. jours. Mem. exec. com. Gt. Trails council Boy Scouts Am., 1983-85. Served with AUS, 1953-55. Fellow Am. Phys. Soc. (vice chmn. New Eng. sect. 1989-90, chmn. 1990-91); mem. AAAS, Sigma Xi. Home: 48 Morgan Cir Amherst MA 01002

COOK, MICHAEL ANTHONY, financial services executive; b. Kingston, Jamaica, Jan. 10, 1956; came to U.S., 1979; s. Noel Keith and Edna Elaine (Walsh) C.; m. Maida E. Rivera, June 7, 1985; 1 child, Yvette. Diploma, Coll. Arts, Scis. and Tech., Kingston, 1976; BS, CUNY, 1982; MBA, Baruch Coll., 1984. Registered profl. engr., N.J., Jamaica; cert. fin. planner. Transmitter engr. Radio Jamaica Ltd., Kingston, 1976-79; acct. South Bklyn. Health Ctr., 1981-83; fin. cons. Tri-Star Fin. Svcs., Queens, 1983-85; fin. planner John Hancock, Queens, 1985-87; chief exec. officer M.A.C. Assocs., Queens, 1987—; cons. Tri-Star Fin. Svcs., 1985—; bd. dirs. Scudder's Trucking, Inc., Bronx, Expressways, Inc., Bklyn. Inventor high voltage, high frequency isolating transformer. Recipient Econs. award Am. Econs. Assn., 1982. Mem. Internat. Assn. for Fin. Planners, Inst. Cert. Fin. Planners, Nat. Soc. Pub. Accts., N.Y. Soc. Ind. Accts., IEEE, Masons, Rosicrucian. Home: 85-12 169th St Jamaica NY 11432 Office: MAC Assocs 89-32 210th St Queens Village NY 11428

COOK, PETER BIGELOW, television producer, screenwriter; b. N.Y.C., Apr. 17, 1939; s. Peter Geoffrey and Joan (Folinsbee) C.; m. Sarah Chapman Scott, Sept. 9, 1961; children: Anne F., Peter S., Elizabeth F., Caitlin B. AB, Princeton U., 1960; MAT, Harvard U., 1962. Tchr. English St. George's Sch., Newport, R.I., 1962-66, Princeton (N.J.) High Sch., 1966-68, Am. Sch., Paris, 1968-70; TV producer, writer WGBH-TV, Boston, 1970—. Producer, writer (docudrama) Concealed Enemies, 1984, (documentary) Edelin Conviction, 1976, Mexico: Revolution, 1988. Recipient Alfred I. DuPont award, 1974, Peabody award, 1976, Silver Gavel award ABA, 1976, Emmy award NATAS, 1984. Office: WGBH-TV 125 Western Ave Boston MA 02134

COOK, PHILIP GEORGE, artist, film director; b. Wegberg, Germany, Dec. 25, 1957; came to U.S., 1989; s. Brian Norman and Betty (Sheph) C.; m. Lauren Sandra Ackerman, Apr. 8, 1990. BA, Leeds (Eng.) Poly. Inst., 1980; MA, Royal Coll. of Art, London, 1985. From asst. film editor to film editor Uden Assocs., London, 1986-88; freelance film editor London, 1988; creative dir. Wolfcat Prodns., East Brunswick, N.J., 1989—. Producer, dir., writer, editor (film) The Ornithologist, 1982, Demons, 1984 (Chgo. Film Festival award, Fantasporto Portugal award), Dib & Dab, 1985; painter Truck Series, 1988—. Royal Coll of Art grantee, 1985; recipient Cert. of Merit, Chgo. Internat. Film Festival, 1985. Mem. Middlesex County C. of C. Office: Wolfcat Prodns PO Box 443 East Brunswick NJ 08816-0443

COOK, RALPH, alcohol/drug abuse services professional; b. Washington, Feb. 18, 1946; s. Dennis and Sallie (Hampton) C.; m. Margaret Elizabeth Kennedy, July 14, 1969; children: Tonya Jacquanette, Laurette Angelique, Brandy Nicole. BS in Sociology, D.C. Tchrs. Coll., 1969; MBA, U. N.C., 1971; drug tng., U. Thailand, Bangkok, 1972. Trouble shooter East Asian Pharm., Bangkok, 1971-73; analysis Govt. Saudi Arabia, Riyadh, 1973-74, Bur. of Prisons, Lewisburg, Pa., 1974-75; polit. organizer Nat. Reps., 1976-80; dir. mktg. U.S. Jefferson Mint, Washington, 1980-82; dir. Ea. Narcotic Coatition, Washington, N.Y.C., 1983-88; legal rsch. Narcotic Def. Tactics, Washington, 1988-89; researcher Md. Dept. Corrections, Westover, 1989—; cons. Internat. Narcotics Traffic, Interpol, 1988-90; analysis Drug-Currency Linkage Forum, Washington, 1988-90; researcher N.Y.C. Drug Task Force, 1990-91. Contbr. articles to profl. jours. dir. Minority Rep. Forum, Washington, 1991. Recipient First Fgn. Citizen award Arab-Am. League 1974, Achievement award Internat. Precious Metal Assn. 1982, Outstanding Svc. award Interpol 1989, Cert. of Appreciation City of N.Y. 1990. Home: PO Box 2277 Washington DC 20013 Office: Ste E 400 Peppermill Dr Capitol Heights MD 20743

COOK, RICHARD BURTON, military officer, comptroller; b. Johnson City, N.Y., Feb. 21, 1944; s. Burton Sargent and Eva Mae (Wagner) C.; m. Elizabeth Yates Lewis, June 10, 1967; children: Christopher, Donald, Jonathan. BS, U.S. Coast Guard Acad., 1967; MS, USN Postgrad. Sch., 1972. Commd. ensign USCG, 1967, advanced through grades to capt., 1988; shipboard asst. engr. Seattle, 1967-70, marine inspector, 1970-71; mem. research and devel. planning staff Washington, 1972-76, contract specialist, 1976-77; resident contracting officer Tacoma, 1977-80; procurement br. chief Washington, 1980-84; comptroller USCG Acad., New London, Conn., 1984-87, USCG Yard, Balt., 1987-89; commdg. officer USCG Supply Ctr. Curtis Bay, Balt., 1989-90; head contracting activity USCG Hdqrs., Washington, 1990—; supervisory com. Coast Guard Hdqrs. Credit Union, Washington, 1982-84; bd. dirs.Community Services Credit Union, New London, 1984-87. Vestry mem. Holy Trinity Ch., Bowie, 1974-77; bd. chmn. Holy Trinity Sch., 1976-77; cub master Boy Scouts Am., Tacoma, 1979-80, asst. scoutmaster, Arnold, Md., 1981-84, com. mem. Arnold and East Lyme, Conn., 1981-88, 89-91; treas. St. John's Niantic, Conn., 1985-86. Mem. Bowie Jaycees (Jaycee of Month 1975). Episcopalian. Office: USCG Hdqrs Washington DC 20593

COOK, ROBERT GEORGE, education educator; b. Iowa City, Iowa, Nov. 12, 1953; s. Desmond Lawrence and Helen-Louise (Jones) C.; m. Sherrill Ann Glidden, July 21, 1990. BS, Ohio State U., 1976; MA, U. Calif., Berkeley, 1980, PhD, 1983. Postdoctoral fellow U. Tex. Health Sci. Ctr., Houston, 1983-86; assoc. prof. Tufts U., Medford, Mass., 1986—. Contbr. articles to profl. jours. Grantee Nat. Eye Inst., 1984-86, NSF Rsch., 1989-92. Mem. Am. Psychol. Assn., AAAS, Psychonomic Soc., Am. Psych. Soc., Am. Ornithol. Union, Sigma Xi. Democrat. Office: Tufts U Psychology Dept Paige Hall Medford MA 02155

COOK, THOMAS HERBERT, consulting company executive; b. Tarrytown, N.Y., Sept. 6, 1936; s. Herbert Peter and Mary (Ronan) C.; m. Joan May Flasher; children: Mary, Thomas Jr., Michael, John. BA, U. Notre Dame, 1958, BSME, 1959; MS in Indsl. Adminstrn., Carnegie-Mellon U., 1961. Registered profl. engr., Pa.; cert. data processing. Dir. info. svcs., system and svcs. div. Westinghouse Electric Corp., Pitts., 1971-76, dir. mgmt. systems, learning group, 1976-79, dir. info. systems, industry products co., 1979-82; mgr., MIS Duquesne Light Co., Pitts., 1982-90; exec. Gateway Group, Pitts., 1990—; sec., treas. TJM & Assocs., Ltd., 1989—; instr. Carnegie-Mellon U., Pitts., 1959-63, Canisius Coll., Buffalo, N.Y., 1963-64; lectr. IBM Corp., Cin., 1982. Mem. com. Dan Marino Leukemia Golf Event, Pitts., 1988—; mem. Mcpl. Recreation Bd., Churchill, Pa., 1972-79. Mem. Pa. Soc. Profl. Engrs., Inst. for Cert. of Computer Profls., Edison Electric Inst. (info. systems com.). Republican. Roman Catholic. Home: 232 Thornberry Dr Pittsburgh PA 15235-5062 Office: Gateway Group Inc 1 Gateway Ctr Ste 440 Pittsburgh PA 15222-1416

COOK, TONY STANLEY, writer; b. Varnville, S.C., Nov. 7, 1960; s. Norris J. and Bridie (Stanley) C.; m. Donna Jean Capelle, June 24, 1989. AS in Bus., U. S.C., Allendale, 1982; BA in History, U. S.C., 1984; MA in History, U. Toledo, 1986. Editorial fellow The Historian profl. jour., dept. history U. Toledo, 1984-86, English instr., 1986-87; coll. rels. assoc. SUNY, Potsdam, 1987-90, dir. media rels., 1990; fellow Creative Writing program Syracuse (N.Y.) U., 1990—; fiction editor Blueline lit. mag., SUNY-Potsdam, 1988-90; editor Mark lit. mag., U. Toledo, 1985-87. Author: Summer Songs and Other Stories, 1987; contbr. articles to profl. jours. Mem. Nat. Coun. Tchrs. English, South Atlantic MLA, Phi Alpha Theta (Hammond Essay

prize 1986), Phi Beta Kappa. Home: 604 Kirkpatrick St Syracuse NY 13208-2106 Office: Syracuse U 239 HB Crouse Hall Syracuse NY 13244

COOKE, ALBERT CURTS, marketing and sales executive; b. Paterson, N.J., Mar. 10, 1960; s. Albert Curts and Geraldine Teresa (Campbell) C.; m. Kathleen T. Dwyer, Oct. 2, 1988. BS, Lehigh U., 1982. Sales rep. Russ Berrie and Co., Inc., Oakland, N.J., 1983-85, sr. acct. mgr., 1985; credit mgr. Russ Berrie and Co., Inc., Oakland, 1986-87; dir. adminstrn. Russ Berrie and Co., Inc., Chgo., 1985-86; adminstrv. mgr. Freelance, Inc., Willow Grove, Pa., 1987-88; dir. adminstn. Freelance, Inc., Dayton, N.J., 1988-89; mktg. rep. Mgmt. Dynamics, Inc., Lyndhurst, N.J., 1990-91; account mktg. rep. Mgmt. Dynamics, Lyndhurst, N.J., 1991-92; sr. mktg. rep. Digital Equipment Corp., Parsippany, N.J., 1992—. Methodist. Home: 75 Harmer Ter Wayne NJ 07470-2843 Office: Digital Equipment Corp 4 Gatehall Ste 100 Parsippany NJ 07054

COOKE, DONALD ALAN, educational association administrator, writer; b. Bryn Mawr, Pa., Feb. 3, 1953; s. Donald Ewin and Margaret (Nielson) C.; m. Sally Anne Freitas, Oct. 23, 1976; children: Alexis F., Brittany M. BS, Williams Coll., 1975. V.p. Haverford House Pubs., Wayne, Pa., 1976-80; planetarium dir. The Franklin Inst., Phila., 1981-84, dir. devel., 1985-91, v.p. external affairs, 1987-91, acting mus. dir., 1991-92, exec. v.p., 1992—. Author: Life and Death of Stars, 1985. Trustee Episcopal Acad., Merion, Pa., 1989-92, Cen. Phila. Devel. Corp., 1992—, PRIME, Phila., 1991—. Mem. Am. Assn. Mus., Mayors Cultural Adv. Coun., Assn. Sci. Tech. Ctr. Office: The Franklin Inst 20th and Pkwy Philadelphia PA 19103

COOKE, JACK KENT, diversified company executive; b. Hamilton, Ont., Can., Oct. 25, 1912; s. Ralph Ercil and Nancy (Jacobs) C.; m. Barbara Jean Carnegie, May 5, 1934 (div.); children: Ralph Kent, John Kent; m. Jeanne Maxwell Williams, Oct. 31, 1980 (div.); m. Marlena LVR Chalmers, May 5, 1990. Student, Malvern Collegiate. Joined No. Broadcasting and Pub. Ltd., Can., 1937; ptnr. Thomson Cooke Newspapers, 1937-52; pres. Sta. CKEY, Toronto, Ont., Can., 1944-61, Liberty of Can. Ltd., 1947-61, Toronto Maple Leaf Baseball Club Ltd., 1951-64, Micro Plastics, Ltd., Acton, Ont., Can., 1955-60, Robinson Indsl. Crafts, Ltd., London, Ont., Can., 1957-63, Precision Die Casting Ltd., Toronto, Ont., 1955-60, Consol. Frybook Industries, Ltd., 1952-61; chmn. bd., pres. Consol. Press Ltd., 1952-61; pres. Aubyn Investments, Ltd., 1961-68, Continental Cablevision Inc., 1965-68; chmn. Jack Kent Cooke Inc., 1976—; chmn. bd. Transamerica Microwave, Inc., 1965-69; chmn. Pro-Football Inc., Washington Redskins, NFL, 1960—; pres. Calif. Sports, Inc. (Los Angeles Lakers, NBA, Los Angeles Kings, NHL), 1965-79, The Forum of Inglewood, Inc., 1966-79; dir., chmn. exec. com. H&B Am. Corp, 1969-70; chmn., chief exec. officer Teleprompter Corp., 1974-81; chmn. Group W Cable Inc. (formerly Teleprompter Corp.), 1981-85, Cooke Properties Inc., 1966—, Chrysler & Kent Bldgs., N.Y.C., 1966—, Kent Farms, 1979—, Byrnley Farms, 1979-88, Cooke Media Group, Inc. (Daily News), Los Angeles, 1985—, Cooke CableVision Inc., Warner Ctr., Calif., 1986-89, Ercil Pub. Inc., 1976—, Kent Plaza, Phoenix, 1983-85, Elmendorf Farm, Inc., Lexington, Ky., 1985—, Video Tape Enterprises, 1976-85, Raljon Pub. Co., Inc., 1988—. Trustee Little League Found. Mem. Nat. Athletic Inst. (bd. dirs.). Office: Washington Redskins Dulles Internat Airport PO Box 17247 Washington DC 20041-0247 also: Daily News 21221 Oxnard St Woodland CA 91367

COOKE, PAUL PHILLIPS, writer, lecturer, consultant, researcher; b. N.Y.C., June 29, 1917; s. Louis Philip and Mamie Kathleen (Phillips) C.; m. Rose Clifford, Aug. 22, 1940; children: Kelsey C. Meyersburg, Paul C., Anne E., Katherine M. BS, Miner Tchrs. Coll., 1937; MA, NYU, 1941, Cath. U. Am., 1943; EdD, Columbia U., 1947; LLD (hon.), U. D.C., 1986. Tchr. English and history Pub. Sch. of D.C., Washington, 1941-44; instr. in English Miner Tchr.'s Coll., Washington, 1944-49, from asst. to assoc. prof., 1949-53; prof. Miner Tchrs. Coll., 1954-55, Dist. Columbia Tchr's Coll., Washington, 1955-74; acad. dean D.C. Tchr.'s Coll., Washington, 1962-64; dir. model sch. div. Pub. Schs. D.C., 1964-65; pres. D.C. Tchr.'s Coll., Washington, 1966-74; dir. internat. programs Am. Assn. State Colls. and Univs., Washington, 1974-75; cons. World Peace Through Law Ctr., Washington, 1974-78; writer, researcher, cons. physics, astronomy and spl. edn. depts. Howard U., Washington, 1976-81; cons., reader Anacostia Mus./Smithsonian Instn., Washington, 1979—. Author: Civil Rights in U.S., 1966, Mary Church Terrell, 1978, Normal Schools in D.C., 1983, Graduates of the District of Columbia and Predecessor Institutions, 1990, Perspectives on the Preparation of American Teachers and Educators, 1990; contbr. articles and revs. to profl. jours. Chair, mem. adv. com. U.S. Commn. on Civil Rights, Washington, 1978-87; Nat. chair Am. Vets. Com., 1963-65; dir. At Large Internat. Assn. Torch Clubs, 1982-85. With USAF. Recipient Bessie Levine medal Am. Vets. Com., 1960; Thomas Wyatt Turner award Office of Black Caths., 1983; His Holiness Pope John Paul II Pro Ecclesia Et Pontifice, 1984. Mem. Assn. for Study of Afro-Am. Life and History (editor, contbr. Washington chpt. 1987—), Kappa Alpha Psi (pres. Washington chpt. 1953-55). Republican. Roman Catholic. Home: 1203 Girard St NW Washington DC 20009-5325

COOKE, ROGER LEE, mathematician, educator; b. Alton, Ill., July 31, 1942; s. Ralph William and Helen Marie (Schweickhardt) C.; m. Catherine Hutton, Jan. 20, 1968; children: Catharine, Andrew, Hilary. AB, Northwestern U., Evanston, Ill., 1963; MA, Princeton U., 1965, PhD, 1966. Asst. prof. Vanderbilt U., Nashville, Tenn., 1966-68; asst. prof. U. Vt., Burlington, 1968-72, assoc. prof., 1972-77, prof., 1977—; spl. liaison with USSR, Math. Scis. Edn. Bd., Washington, 1990—; cons. Russian translator, Burlington, 1987—. Author (monograph) The Math. of Sonya Kovalevskaya, 1984. Interpreter Burlington-Yaroslavl Sister Cities, Burlington, 1988—. Recipient Internat. Rsch. and Exchanges Bd. award Am. Coun. Learned Soc., 1981, 88, Fulbright-Hays award Coun. Internat. Exchange of Scholars, 1984, 88. Mem. Am. Math. Soc., Math. Assn. Am., History of Sci. Soc., Can. Soc. for History & Philosophy of Math. Home: 500 S Union St Burlington VT 05401-4808 Office: U Vt Dept Math Burlington VT 05405

COOKUS, GERALD, university security administrator; b. Ashland, Pa., Sept. 16, 1938; s. Clarence and Ermina (Williams) C.; m. Louise Rodak, Oct. 23, 1965; children: Patricia, Gerald, John, Kellie and Kristen (twins). AS in Criminal Justice, King's Coll., Wilkes-Barre, Pa., 1976; postgrad., Pa. State U., 1978. Lt. of police Wilkes-Barre Police, 1965-86; agt. Best Locking Systems, Malvern, Pa., 1986-90; chief Wilkes U., Wilkes-Barre, 1990—. Mem. Fraternal Order Police (pres. chpt. 36 1974-76), Pa. Crime Prevention Officer (pres. 1984-86), Am. Assn. Indsl. Sec. Democrat. Roman Catholic. Home: 17 W Sunrise Dr Pittston PA 18640-1502 Office: Wilkes U PO Box 111 Wilkes Barre PA 18766-0001

COOLAHAN, JAMES EDWARD, JR., aerospace engineer; b. Balt., July 28, 1950; s. James Edward Sr. and Shirley Marie (Hill) C.; m. Elizabeth Venera Bakutis, Mar. 8, 1975; children: Theresa Marie, Patrick Bernard, Kathleen Elizabeth. BS in Aerospace Engring., U. Notre Dame, 1971; MS in Aerospace Engring., Cath. U. Am., 1975; MS in Computer Sci., Johns Hopkins U., 1980; PhD in Computer Sci., U. Md., 1984. Assoc. engr. Applied Physics Lab., Johns Hopkins U., Laurel, Md., 1972-77, sr. staff engr., 1977-81, prin. staff engr., 1981—, mgr. ocean data acquisition program, 1982-90, supr. system devel. and evaluation br., 1988-90, program area mgr. for space systems and tech. applications, 1990—; lectr. G.W.C. Whiting Sch. Engring., Johns Hopkins U., Balt., 1985-87, mem. computer sci. program com., 1988-92. Contbr. articles to profl. jours. Pres. Chapel View Improvement Assn., Ellicott City, Md., 1977, Resurrection-St. Paul Home and Sch. Assn., Ellicott City, 1990-92; baseball coach Howard County Youth Program, Ellicott City, 1988-91. Mem. AIAA, IEEE, IEEE Computer Soc. (chmn. Balt. chpt. 1984-86), Assn. for Computing Machinery, Notre Dame Club Md. (bd. dirs. 1988—, pres. 1992-93). Roman Catholic. Home: 3517 Belfont Dr Ellicott City MD 21043 Office: Johns Hopkins U Applied Physics Lab Johns Hopkins Rd Laurel MD 20723-6099

COOLER, WHEY, recording company executive, popular musician; b. Camden, N.J., Feb. 13, 1960; s. Andrew and Rita Elizabeth (Giraffo) Corea; m. Stephanie Whitehead, June 17, 1991. Owner Svengali Records, Merchantville, N.J., 1980—, Genetic Music Pub. Co., Merchantville, 1980—; founding mem. Pretty Poison, Merchantville, 1980-87. Albums include Catch Me I'm Falling, 1988, 2 Cool Thing, 1991, Better Be Good 2 Me, 1992, Sex & Violets, 1992. "Catch Me I'm Falling" named Song of Yr. Phila. Music Found., 1988, Album of Yr. Nat. Assn. Ind. Retailers and Distbrs. 1988; recipient Gold record for sales Virgin Records, 1989. Mem. ASCAP (recipient pop/film award for "Catch Me I'm Falling" 1989), AFTRA, Am. Fedn. Musicians. Home: 10 Church Rd Merchantville NJ 08109

COOLEY, IVORY LEE, civil servant; b. Lavrinburg, N.C., Apr. 25, 1951; s. Elijah Kimnon and Ollie Mae (McLean) C.; m. Sharon Lynne Raines, Dec. 16, 1972 (div. May 1984); children: Alkeim, Jamille. A in Journalism, Essex County Coll., 1984; student, Rutgers U. Transit clk. First Fidelity Bank, Newark, 1970-72; modified distbn. clk. U.S. Postal Svc., Newark, 1973—. Pres. Carmel Tower Community Assn., Newark, 1982, Fairview Homes Community Orgn., 1986; mem. Clean City Commn., Newark, 1985; dist. leader City of Newark, 1987, 89; v.p. Africa-Network Orgn., 1986-89; sponsor Cultural Day Festival Ann. Event. Named one of Outstanding Young Men of Am. Jaycees, 1980, Ambassador of Goodwill Gov. of Ark., 1980; recipient Brotherhood award Newark Human Rights Commn., 1984. Mem. Internat. Platform Assn. (cert. recognition 1986), Am. Biog. Inst. (bd. advisors 1987, cert. recognition 1986, 87), Newark African-Am. Diaspora Orgn. (pres. 1989—). Home: 74 17th Ave Newark NJ 07103-2528

COOLEY, JAMES LAWRENCE, aerospace engineer, mathematician; b. Northampton, Mass., Apr. 17, 1938; s. Edward Ericson and Evelyn Viola (Avery) C.; m. Brenda Ruth Brizzolari, Sept. 9, 1961; children: Deborah Celeste, Andrew Ericson. BS, U. Mass., 1960; MA, Pa. State U., 1962; postgrad., U. Md., 1962-66. Aerospace mathematician NASA Goddard Space Flight Ctr., Greenbelt, Md., 1963—, head mission design section, 1973-84, staff engr., 1984—. Contbr. articles to profl. jours. Mem. Am. Astron. Soc., Math. Assn. Am., Sigma Xi, Phi Kappa Phi, Pi Mu Epsilon. Home: 232 Lastner Ln Greenbelt MD 20770 Office: Goddard Space Flight Ctr Greenbelt MD 20771

COOLIDGE, GLORIA GEARY, foundation administrator; b. Pitts., Sept. 20, 1948; d. James F. and M. Gloria (Vetter) Geary; m. John H. Dyett Jr., June 13, 1969 (div. June 1978); children: John Hathaway III, Jason Matthew. BA, Wells Coll., 1971; MEd, Northeastern U., 1975; cert. in advanced studies, Harvard U., 1981; MBA, Simmons Coll., 1987. Lic. counselor, Mass. Tchr., cons. Brookwood Sch., Manchester, Mass., 1976-80; donor, advisor Coolidge Family Fund, Boston, 1984—; planning coord. Crittendon Hastings House, Brighton, Mass., 1987-88; mgr. resource devel. Boston Children's Svcs., 1988-90; mem. vis. com. Harvard U. Grad. Sch. of Edn., Cambridge, Mass., 1990—; counselor Planned Parenthood of Mass., Cambridge, 1983-86; pres., treas., dir. Am. Friends of Marva Pula Sch., North Edgecomb, Mass., 1983—. Trustee Old North Ch., Marblehead, Mass., 1990—. Recipient Weston Howland Jr. award Tufts U., 1991. Mem. Assn. for Grantmakers of Mass., Women and Founds./Corp. Philanthropy, Adirondack League Club. Home and Office: 7 Brown St Marblehead MA 01945-3701

COOMES, MARGUERITE WILTON, biochemist; b. Hertford, Eng., Dec. 26, 1942; d. Stanley Ralph and Joan Marguerite (Bent) Wilton; children: Mark, Stephen. BS, U. North Tex., 1973, MS, 1975; PhD, U. Tex. Health Sci. Ctr., Dallas, 1980. Staff fellow NIEHS, NIH, Research Triangle Park, N.C., 1980-83; instr. Coll. of Medicine Howard U., Washington, 1983-85, asst. prof. Coll. of Medicine, 1985-89, assoc. prof. Coll. of Medicine, 1990—; cons. EPA, Washington, 1987-88, Am. Petroleum Inst., Washington, 1990. Contbr. articles to profl. jours. Predoctoral fellow NSF, 1974-77, dissertation fellow AAUW, 1978-79. Mem. Am. Soc. Biochemistry and Molecular Biology, Grad. Women in Sci. (treas. Washington chpt. 1987-90). Office: Howard U Coll Medicine 520 W St Washington DC 20059

COON, THOMAS GARY, child care worker, writer; b. Schenectady, N.Y., Oct. 23, 1957; s. Gary Martin and Lois Mae (Singleton) C.; m. Meryl Jean Leone, May 10, 1991; stepchildren: Jennifer, Michael. AS, Am. Acad. Dramatic Arts, 1980. Aide to pvt. family N.Y.C., 1977-78; dir. childrens theatre Town of Colonie Recreation, Latham, N.Y., 1978-80; child care worker Northampton (Mass.) Ctr. for Children and Families, 1987-88, Berkshire Farms, Ctr. for Youth, Canaan, N.Y., 1988—; cons. Crossroads Drug & Alcohol Awareness Program for Teenage Boys, Canaan, 1989-90. Food coord. for participants Jerry Lewis Telethon, N.Y.C., 1982; fellow mem. Matt Talbot Group 20, 1990—, North Shore Animal League, 1990—, Legionaries of Christ, 1991—. Republican. Home and Office: County Rt 25 Kinderhook NY 12106

COONEY, J(OHN) GORDON, lawyer; b. Bklyn., Jan. 21, 1930; s. John Philip and Josephine (Gordon) C.; m. Patricia Ruth McEwen, June 8, 1957; 1 son, J. Gordon. A.B., St. John's U., 1951, LL.B., 1953. Bar: N.Y. 1953, Pa. 1962, D.C. 1970. Asso. Patterson, Belknap & Webb, N.Y.C., 1953-55; staff counsel U.S. Industries, N.Y., 1956-57; atty. SEC, Washington, 1957-59, FTC, 1959-61; ptnr. Schnader, Harrison, Segal & Lewis, Phila., 1962—; bd. dirs. PH II, Inc.; arbitrator Am. Arbitration Assn., 1964—; public mem. nat. com. on arbitration Nat. Assn. Securities Dealers, 1977-83; dir. Attys. Liability Assurance Soc., 1979-85. Dir., pres. Strafford Village Assn., 1969-70; bd. govs. N.Y.C. Young Republican Club, 1957. Recipient Superior Service award FTC, 1961. Fellow Am. Bar Found.; mem. Am. Law Inst. (adviser project on corp. governance 1980—), ABA (council sect. corp., banking and bus. law 1980-84), N.Y. State Bar Assn., Phila. Bar Assn. Roman Catholic. Clubs: Union League (Phila.); Overbrook Golf, Merion Cricket. Home: 320 Gatcombe Ln Bryn Mawr PA 19010-3628 Office: Schnader Harrison Segal & Lewis 1600 Market St Ste 3600 Philadelphia PA 19103-4247

COONEY, JUDITH LIFSHITZ, clinical psychologist; b. Queens, N.Y., Jan. 13, 1956; d. Martin A. and Renee (Jackera) Lifshitz; m. Ned L. Cooney, Aug. 21, 1983; children: Sarah Beth, Daniel Adam. BA in Psychology cum laude, SUNY, Stony Brook, 1977; MS in Psychology, U. Ga., 1979, PhD in Clin. Psychology, 1981. Lic. psychologist, Conn. Intern Brown U., 1979-80; psychologist Sunnyview Rehab. Hosp., Schenectady, 1981; psychologist, assoc. chief outpatient behavioral med. clinic VA Med. Ctr., Newington, Conn., 1981-86, dir. health psychology program, 1986—; asst. prof. psychiatry U. Conn. Med. Sch., Farmington, Conn., 1981—; cons. dept. mental retardation, region 5, State of Conn., Farmington, 1986—, New Britain Gen. Hosp.; adj. faculty, supr. Conn. Coll., New London, 1982—, psychology dept. U. Conn., Storrs, 1991; guest speaker numerous acad. and civic orgns., 1981—. Guest editor The Behavior Therapist, 1991; reviewer various jours., 1985—; contbr. articles to profl. jours., 1983—. Mem. Jewish Community Ctr., Greater Hartford, 1990—, Hartford Chorale, 1985—. USPHS fellow, U. Ga., 1977-79. Mem. APA, Assn. for Advancement of Behavior Therapy, Soc. Behavioral Medicine, Conn. Behavior Therapy Assn. (pres. 1989—). Office: VA Med Ctr Psychology Svc 555 Willard Ave Newington CT 06111-2600

COONEY, LENORE, public relations executive. V.p., then exec. v.p. D-A-Y Pub. Rels., N.Y.C.; now pres. Ogilvy, Adams & Rinehart (previously Ogilvy Pub. Rels. Group), N.Y.C. Office: Ogilvy Adams & Rinehart 708 Third Ave New York NY 10017*

COONEY, PATRICIA RUTH, civic worker; b. Englewood, N.J.; d. Charles Aloysius and Ruth Jeannette (Foster) McEwen; m. J. Gordon Cooney, June 8, 1957; 1 child, J. Gordon, Jr. Student, Fordham U., 1950-51; DHL honoris causa, Phila. Theol. Sem. St. Charles Boromeo, 1991. Blood bank chmn. Strafford Village Civic Assn., 1968-69, sec., 1970-71; vice chmn. Spl. Gifts Com. Cath. Charities Appeal of Archdiocese of Phila., 1980—, chmn., 1985. Mem. Coun. of Mgrs. Archdiocese of Phila., 1982-88, sec., exec. com., 1983-88; bd. dirs. Cath. Charities of Archdiocese of Phila., 1984—, sec., exec. com., 1988-90, v.p., exec. com., 1991—; bd. dirs. Village of Divine Providence, Phila., 1982—, sec., 1983-85, v.p. exec. com., 1990—; bd. dirs. St. Edmond's Home for Crippled Children, Phila., 1984—, v.p. exec. com., 1990—; bd. dirs. Don Guanella Village of Archdiocese of Phila., 1984—, v.p. exec. com., 1990— ; mem. Archdiocesan Adv. Com. on Renewal, 1991—; mem. Women's Com. Wills Eye Hosp., 1973—, mem.-at-large, 1st v.p.; mem. Women's Aux. St. Francis Country House, Darby, Pa., 1976—, treas., 1978-82; exec. com. United Way of Southeastern Pa., 1984-90, sec., 1986-88; bd. dirs. Chapel of Four Chaplains, 1984-89, Phila. Criminal Justice Task Force, 1989-90. Decorated Cross Pro Ecclesia et Pontifice, 1982. Republican. Home: 320 Gatcombe Ln Bryn Mawr PA 19010-3628

COONS, HELEN LOUISE, clinical psychologist; b. Harrisburg, Pa., Feb. 11, 1958; d. Albert and Louise (Lyons) C. BA with distinction, U. Wis., 1980, MS, 1985; PhD, Temple U., 1990. Lic. psychologist, Pa. Asst. prof. dept. mental health sci. Hahnemann U., Phila., 1990—. Bd. dirs. YWCA, Madison, Wis., 1982-84. Mem. APA (chair com. on women and health, div. health psychology 1989—), Pa. Psychol. Assn. Office: Hahnemann U 1427 Vine St MS 950 Philadelphia PA 19102-1192

COONS, RONALD EDWARD, historian, educator; b. Elmhurst, Ill., July 24, 1936; s. William A. and Madeline Louise (Theisen) C. B.A., DePauw U., Greencastle, Ind., 1958; A.M., Harvard U., 1959, Ph.D., 1966. Teaching fellow history Harvard U., 1961-62, 63-66; research fellow Inst. Europäische Geschichte, Mainz, W.Ger., 1962-63; mem. faculty U. Conn., Storrs, 1966—, prof. history, 1979—, dir. grad. studies, dept. history, 1983-87, 90—. Author: Steamships, Statesmen and Bureaucrats: Austrian Policy Towards the Steam Navigation Company of the Austrian Lloyd, 1836-1848, 1975, I primi anni del Lloyd Austriaco, 1983; mem. editorial bd. Austrian History Yearbook, 1992—; also articles. Mem. exec. com. St. Mark's Episcopal Chapel, Storrs, 1976-77, 77-82, 83-85, asst. organist, 1980-87, U. Conn. Friends of Soccer, 1989—, New Eng. Hosta Soc., 1989—, exec. com. Soc. for Habsburg and Austrian History, 1992—. Nat. Endowment Humanities summer fellow, 1969; Am. Council Learned Socs. grantee, 1974, Am. Philos. Soc. grantee, 1974; NIH grantee, 1979; Gladys K. Delmas Found. grantee, 1983-84; Am. Council Learned Socs. grantee, 1985. Mem. AAUP, Am. Hist. Assn., Conf. Group Cen. European History, New Eng. Hist. Assn., Conn. Acad. Arts and Scis., Verein Geschichte der Stadt Wien, Conn. Hort. Soc., Am. Hosta Soc., Phi Beta Kappa (chpt. sec. 1976-86, v.p. 1987-88, pres. 1988-89), Phi Alpha Theta, Phi Mu Alpha. Democrat. Home: 476 Prospect St Willimantic CT 06226-2028 Office: U Conn Dept History Storrs CT 06269-2103

COOPER, ARNOLD MICHAEL, psychiatrist; b. N.Y.C., Mar. 9, 1923; s. Morris and Clara (Aronow) C.; m. Madge Huntington, June 28, 1973; children by previous marriage: Andrew, Melissa, Thomas. AB, Columbia U., 1943, cert. psychoanalytic medicine, 1956; M.D., U. Utah, 1947. Research fellow in medicine Harvard U., 1947-48; asst. in medicine Thorndike Meml. Lab., Boston City Hosp., 1947-48; intern internal medicine Presbyn. Hosp., N.Y.C., 1948-50; psychiat. resident Bellevue Hosp., N.Y.C., 1950-53; mem. faculty Columbia U. Coll. Physicians and Surgeons, 1968—, clin. prof. psychiatry, 1971-74; lectr. Columbia U. Div. Humanities and Contemporary Civilization, 1964-79, adj. prof. comparative lit., 1985—; prof. psychiatry N.Y. Hosp.-Cornell U. Med. Ctr., 1974—, prof. consultation liaison psychiatry, 1992—; assoc. chmn. edn., dept. psychiatry N.Y. Hosp.-Cornell U. Med. Ctr.-Payne Whitney Clinic, 1974-88; supr., tng. psychoanalyst Columbia U. Psychoanalytic Ctr. Tng. and Research, 1961—; mem. instnl. rev. bd. Rockefeller U., 1990—. Editor: Psychoanalysis and Contemporary Thought, 1987, Psychoanalysis: The Second Century, 1989; editorial bd. Psychiatry Textbook, Am. Jour. Psychiatry, Jour. Am. Psychoanalytic Assn., 1988-91, Jour. Acad. Psychiatry; consulting editor: Jour. Psychotherapy Practice and Rsch.; contbr. articles on masochism, narcissism, applied psychoanalysis, psychoanalytic concepts, psychoanalytic technique, psychoanalytic and psychiat. edn. to profl. jours. Mem. Am. Psychoanalytic Assn. (pres. 1980-82), Am. Assn. Dirs. Psychiat. Residency Tng., Internat. Psychoanalytic Assn. (v.p. 1985-89, assoc. sec. 1989—), Am. Coll. Psychiatry, Am. Psychiat. Assn. (pres. N.Y. County dist. br. 1988-89), N.Y. Psychiat. Soc., Assn. Dirs. Med. Student Edn., Assn. Psychoanalytic Medicine (pres. 1975-77), Am. Coll. Psychoanalysis, Vidonian Soc., Century Club (N.Y.C.), Alpha Omega Alpha. Office: 525 E 68th St New York NY 10021-4873

COOPER, BARBARA JO, marketing professional; b. Bishop, Calif., Apr. 10, 1945; d. James Joseph and Inez E. (Fackrell) Carberry; m. Robert M. West, Oct. 1, 1972 (div. 1982); children: N. Dion, W. Todd; m. John Walton Cooper III, May 13, 1989; 1 child, Elizabeth Inez. BBA, Boise State U. Mktg. asst. H.J. Heinz Co., Boise, Idaho, 1973-74, asst. product mgr., 1975-78, product mgr., 1978-80, sr. product mgr. new products Ore-Ida Brand div., 1980-81, sr. product mgr. product devel. dept. Weight Watchers div., 1981-83; sr. product mgr. Am. Home Products, 1983-84; pres. Barbstac Corp., 1984-86; mgr. mktg./promotions Commtek Publ., 1986-87; dir. mktg. and promotions Commtek Pub., 1987-88; dir. sales promotion McCalls Mag., 1988-89; dir. corp. promotion Lang Communications, N.Y.C., 1989-91, dir. corp. mktg. 1991—. Advisor Jr. Achievement, Boise, 1976-77; pub. rels. dir. Idaho chpt. Cystic Fibrosis, 1979-80. Recipient Mktg. Achievement award Sales and Mktg. Execs., 1979; Jr. Achievement scholar, 1964. Mem. Am. Mktg. Assn., Idaho Advt. Fedn., Assn. Nat. Advertisers. Democrat. Roman Catholic.

COOPER, CAROL JOAN, healthcare marketing communications consultant; b. St. Louis, June 14, 1938; d. Norman Leonard and Ethel (Silver) Mistachkin; m. Malcolm P. Cooper, Aug. 25, 1962 (div. June 1977); children: Lawrence, Edward, Marcus. BS, U. Wis., 1959; MA, N.Y. Inst. Tech., 1992. Media buyer Lennen and Newell, Los Angeles, 1959-61; advt. mgr. Hartfield-Zodys, Los Angeles, 1961-62, Haggarty's, L.A., 1962-63; sales rep. Abbott Labs., Bklyn., 1974-75; edn. dir. N.Y. and N.J. Regional Transp. Program, N.Y.C., 1975-78; account exec. Med. Edn. Dynamics, Woodbridge, N.J., 1978-79; dir. program devel. Kallir, Phillips & Ross Info. Media, N.Y.C., 1979-81; exec. v.p. sales and mktg. Audio Visual Med. Mktg., N.Y.C., 1981-85; exec. v.p. Park Row Pubs./John Wiley & Sons Med. Div., N.Y.C., 1985-88; pres., prin. Park Row Pubs., N.Y.C., 1988-91; healthcare mktg. communications cons., Syosset, N.Y., 1991—; cons., prof. communications N.Y. Inst. Tech., 1991—; cons. Am. Acad. Physician Assts., Washington, 1986-87, Am. Soc. Anesthesiologists, Chgo., 1986-88, Am. Acad. Family Physicians, 1987-91, Am. Psychiat. Assn., 1988, Am. Coll. Gen. Practitioners, 1988, N.Am. Soc. Pacing and Electrophysiology, 1988-91. Editor pub. med. papers, med. films, med. jours. for pharmaceutical cos. Mem. Am. Women in Radio and TV, Soc. Tchrs. Family Medicine (cons.), Pharm. Advt. Council, Nat. Council Jewish Women, Hadassah. Home and Office: 87 Hidden Ridge Dr Syosset NY 11791-4315

COOPER, CHARLES GERSON, computer company executive; b. Elizabeth, N.J., Sept. 6, 1932; s. David S. and Mabel M. (Peiser) C.; m. Judith A. Kaplan, Dec. 23, 1962; children: Margo L., Brad A. BSEE, Rutgers U., 1954. Engr. IBM, Poughkeepsie, N.Y., 1954-55; asst. div. mgr. CEIR, Arlington, Va., 1957-60; pres., exec. v.p. Computer Applications Inc., N.Y.C., 1960-68; cons. Clifton, N.J., 1968-71; pres. Blair Systems, N.Y.C., 1971-73; v.p. Delta Resources, N.Y.C., 1973-75; pres. DIMIS, Ocean, N.J., 1975-83, Amarex Tech., N.Y.C., 1984—; v.p. Comar Mgmt., Edison, N.J., 1986—; cons. Poly Systems-Air Pollution Co., Ramsey, N.J., 1969-71. 1st lt. ASA, 1955-57. Home: 10 Ferrin Ct Middletown NJ 07748-3029

COOPER, CHARLES LEONARD, retail executive; b. Wilmington, Del., July 12, 1936; s. Charles Harvey and Wyomia (Johnson) C.; m. Doris S. Cooper, Feb. 14, 1959 (div. 1974); m. Brenda L. Barbouri, Oct. 25, 1975 (separated); children: Lear E. White, Kenya. Laborer Fairmount Park Commn., Phila., 1956-66; officer Phila. Police Dept., 1966-75; supr. armed guard svc. N.Y. Art Ctr. FAA, N.Y., 1975-79; detective Two Guys Dept. Store, Coram, N.Y., 1980-81; owner, mgr. C.L.C. Security Svcs., Medford, 1981—, Black Legacies Coop., Medford, 1990—; sign hand letterer L.I. State Pks. Historic and Recreation Commn., Babylon, N.Y., 1981—. Contbr. poems to profl. pubis. Recipient Obelist award World of Poetry, 1989, Golden Poet award, 1989, Cert. Recognition, Nat. Coun. Negro Women, 1991. Republican. Baptist. Office: Black Legacies Coop 495 Granny Rd Medford NY 11763-1651

COOPER, CHESTER LAWRENCE, research administrator; b. Boston, Jan. 13, 1917; s. Israel and Hannah (Levenson) C.; m. Orah Pomerance, July 23, 1917; children: Joan Laurence Gould, Susan Louise. BS, NYU, 1939, MBA, 1941; PhD, Am. U., Washington, 1960. Asst. dep. dir. CIA, Washington, 1947-62; sr. staff White House/NSC, Washington, 1962-66, U.S. Dept. State, Washington, 1966-70; dir. internat. div. Inst. Def. Analysis, Arlington, Va., 1970-72; fellow Woodrow Wilson Internat. Ctr. Scholars, Washington, 1972-75; dep. dir. Inst. Energy Analysis, Oak Ridge, Tenn., 1975-83; dep. dir., acting dir. Internat. Inst. Applied Systems Analysis, Laxenburg, Austria, 1983-85; coord. internat programs Resources for the Future, Washington, 1985-92; assoc. dir. Battelle Pacific N.W. Labs., Washington, 1992—; mem. adv. bd. Greyhaven Inst., Carmel, Calif.; cons. Aspen Inst.

Sci. Policy Assocs., Washington, Screenscope Films, Washington, Aspen Trust. Author: The Lost Crusade, 1971 (award 1971), The Lion's Last Roar, 1977; editor: Growth in America, 1976, Science for Public Policy, 1987. Bd. dirs. D.C. Tuberculosis Soc., Washington, 1960-62, D.C. Common Cause, Washington, 1970, Chevy Chase (Md.) Fire Dept., 1986—, Lester Cook Found., Washington, 1987-89. Nat. War Coll. scholar, Washington, 1952-53, Internat. Inst. Applied Systems Analyses hon. scholar, Laxemburg, Austria, 1986. Mem. Am. Com. U.S.-Soviet Rels., Coun. Fgn. Rels., Poets, Essayists, Novelists, Cosmos Club. Home: 7514 Vale St Bethesda MD 20815-4004 Office: Battelle Pacific NW Labs 1616 P St NW Washington DC 20036-1434

COOPER, DANIEL JOHN, decorative fabric stylist; b. Lancaster, Pa., Aug. 17, 1956; s. John C. and Jeanette E. (Norton) C. BA in Polit. Sci., Millersville U., 1979. Woven stylist Schumacher Fabrics, N.Y.C., 1981-86; nat. sales mgr. Jablan Fabrics, N.Y.C., 1986-89; dir. home textiles Weave Corp., N.Y.C., 1989-91; sales mgr. Continental Textiles, N.Y.C., 1992—. Recipient Product Design award ASID, 1986. Mem. Am. Soc. Interior Designers. Democrat. Home: 96-10 57 Ave 11K Rego Park NY 11368

COOPER, DAVID CLAYTON, environmental services executive, educator; b. Beverly Hills, Calif., Apr. 29, 1943; s. Clayton Harold and Virginia (Cobb) C.; m. Susan Stoneburner Hollis, Dec. 28, 1971 (div. Sept. 1981); children: Christopher E. Mason, Joshua A. Mason, Karen Kelty Cooper; m. Janice Peck, Sept. 24, 1987. BA, Lawrence Coll., 1965; MA and PhD, U. Tex., 1970; postgrad., Pa. State U., 1977. Asst. prof. SUNY, Binghamton, 1970-72; rsch. scientist Battelle Meml. Inst., Columbus, Ohio, 1972-73, prin. rsch. scientist, 1973-74, assoc. sect. mgr., 1974-76; mng. dir. Battelle New Eng. Marine Rsch. Labs., Duxbury, Mass., 1976-82; dir. environ. svcs. Briggs Assocs., Inc., Rockland, Mass., 1984—; vis. lectr. Harvard U., Cambridge, Mass., 1989—. Contbr. articles to profl. jours. and monographs. Board dirs. Mayflower Mental Health Clinic, Plymouth, Mass., 1983-86. Tex. Water Quality Bd. fellow, 1968; SUNY Found. grantee, 1970. Mem. Nat. Asbestos Coun. (pres. New Eng. chpt. 1987-89), Duxbury Yacht Club. Home: PO Box 2277 Duxbury MA 02331-2277 Office: Briggs Assocs Inc 400 Hingham St Rockland MA 02370-1298

COOPER, DENNIS LAMAR, engineering consultant; b. York, Pa., May 15, 1941; s. John H. and Theda E. (Reeser) C.; m. Patricia A. Gemmill, Aug. 27, 1961; children: Kimberly, Lynda, Scott. AS in Engring., Pa. State U., York, 1961; B in Profl. Studies, Elizabethtown Coll., 1987. Registered profl. engr., Pa., Ohio, Md. Design draftsman St. Onge, Ruff & Assocs., York, 1960-67; project mgr. Dentsply Internat., York, 1967-71; jr. elec. engr. McCrory Corp., York, 1971-72; assoc. engr. western div. Met-Ed Power Co., York, 1972-74; mgr. engring. P.A. & S. Small Co., York, 1974-76; engring. cons. Dept. Gen. Svcs., Commonwealth of Pa., Harrisburg, 1976—; adj. instr. engring. Pa. State U., York, 1972—; freelance writer. Past mem. ch. coun., active Christian edn. Mt. Zion United Ch. of Christ, York, 1961—. Recipient Good Citizenship award DAR, 1957. Mem. IEEE (Susquehanna chpt.), Nat. Soc. Profl. Engrs. (Lincoln chpt.), Nat. Assn. Broadcast and Ednl Radio (sr.), Inst. Certification of Engring. Technicians (sr.), Assn. Communication Technicians, Am. Radio Relay League (vol. examiner 1980, asst. tech. coord. 1985), York Amateur Radio Club (pres. 1979, tng. dir. 1978), Quarter Century Wireless Assn. (pres., historian chpt. #165 York 1987). Republican. Home: 1013 Ridgewood Rd York PA 17402-1757 Office: Commonwealth of Pa Dept Gen Svcs 18th & Herr Sts Harrisburg PA 17120

COOPER, DOUGLASS WILLIAM, architect, industrial designer; b. Pitts., July 10, 1956; s. John Coleman and Martha Jane (Douglass) C.; m. Sherry Lou McKibben, Oct. 2, 1985. Student, Technische Hochschule, Darmstadt, Fed. Republic Germany, 1977; BS, Pa. State U., 1978; MArch, Yale U., 1981. Designer, draftsman Pitts. History and Landmarks Found., 1978, Lucian Caste Architects, Pitts., 1978-81; project architect Jay Alpert Architect, Woodbridge, Conn., 1981; sr. designer Gruen Assocs., N.Y.C., 1982-85; designer Heller & Leake Architects, San Francisco, 1986; project architect William Turnbull Assocs., San Francisco, 1987-89; assoc. Eseman-McCallum Architects, Manchester, N.H., 1989; project architect MacLachlan, Cornelius & Filoni, Pitts., 1990—. Designer of sports car, 1984 (Runner-up Internat. Automotive Design Competition). Mem. Omicron Delta Kappa. Home: 7025 Edgerton Ave Pittsburgh PA 15208-2824 Office: MacLachlan Cornelius & Filoni 200 The Bank Tower Pittsburgh PA 15222

COOPER, GEORGE DAVID, psychologist; b. Hagerstown, Md., July 7, 1935; s. George Emmanuel and Mary Elva (Longanecker) C. BA, Sheperd Coll., 1958; PhD in Clin. Psychology, Duke U., 1962. Lic. psychologist, Va., W.Va., Md. Chief psychologist Petersburg (Va.) Tng. Sch., 1961-63; clin. psychologist Springfield Youth Ctr., Sykesville, Md., 1963-64, Newton D. Baker Vets. Ctr., Martinsburg, W.Va., 1964-73; assoc. prof. George Mason U., Fairfax, Va., 1973-79; clin. dir. Glaydin Sch., Leesburg, Va., 1979-83; chief psychologist MCTC Div. of Correction, Hagerstown, Md., 1984—; vis. assoc. prof. W.Va. U., Morgantown, 1968-69. Mem. APA, Kiwanis. Republican. Methodist. Office: Md Correctional Tng Ctr 18800 Roxbury Rd Hagerstown MD 21746

COOPER, HOWARD, plastic and reconstructive surgeon; b. N.Y.C., Jan. 24, 1934; s. Benjamin and Jean (Harrison) C.; m. Adela Lander; children: Stephanie Anne, Benjamin, Anna Laura. BS in Pharms., L.I. U., 1955; MD, Mcpl. U. Amsterdam, The Netherlands, 1962. Sr. attending surgeon plastic surgery Lenox Hill Hosp., N.Y.C., 1972—, Pennisula Hosp., N.Y.C., 1972—. Capt. U.S. Army, 1962-69. Office: Howard Cooper MD 911 Park Ave New York NY 10021-0337

COOPER, HOWARD NORVIN, psychiatrist, educator, consultant; b. Chgo., July 13, 1922; s. Benjamin and Gertrude (Coleman) C. BS, Northwestern U., 1945; MD, Columbia U., 1949. Diplomate Am. Bd. Psychiatry and Neurology. Intern in medicine Bellevue Hosp., N.Y.C., 1949-50; residency in psychiatry Payne Whitney Hosp. Cornell U., 1950-53; pvt. practice N.Y.C., 1953—; asst. prof. psychiatry Cornell U. Med. Sch., N.Y.C., 1957—; attending psychiatrist N.Y. Hosp., N.Y.C., 1957—; psychiatrist emeritus, 1991—; dir. N.Y.C. Community Mental Health Bd., 1960-62; med. dir. N.Y. Coun. on Alcoholism, N.Y.C., 1962-65; cons. N.Y.C. Bd. Edn., 1980—. Fellow Am. Psychiat. Assn. (life). Office: 450 E 63d St New York NY 10021

COOPER, IRVING BEN, federal judge; b. London, Eng., Feb. 7, 1902; came to U.S., 1912, naturalized, 1921; s. Max and Rachel (Shimansky) C.; m. Anita Bennett, Mar. 28, 1929; children—Richard Bennett, Benita H. (Mrs. Theodore Lee Marks). LL.B., Washington U., 1925. Bar: N.Y. bar 1927. Gen. practice civil law N.Y.C., 1927-38; asso. counsel ambulance chasing investigation Appellate div. N.Y. Supreme Ct., 1928; asso. counsel bar assns. disciplinary proc., 1928-30, spl. dep. atty. gen. to investigate improper med. practices, 1929, asso. counsel investigation Magistrates courts, 1930-31; asso. counsel to Judge Samuel Seabury in investigation N.Y.C. Govt., 1932-33; spl. counsel Dept. Investigation, N.Y.C., 1934-37; city magistrate, 1938-39; asso. justice Ct. Spl. Sessions, 1939-51, chief justice, 1951-60; U.S. dist. judge So. Dist. N.Y., 1961—, now sr. judge; lectr., cons. program of law and psychiatry Menninger Found., 1960; lectr. criminal law, 1960-61; Hon. pres. Univ. Settlement, N.Y.C.; trustee Nat. Council Crime and Delinquency, chmn. criminal courts sect., adv. counsel of judges, 1954-69. Trustee Reconstructionist Found. Recipient Silver Buffalo award Boy Scouts Am., 1965. Mem. Am. Judicature Soc., Assn. Bar City N.Y., N.Y. County Lawyers Assn., Am. Bar Assn. (chmn. com. on sentencing, probation and parole 1957-61). Office: US Dist Ct US Courthouse Foley Sq New York NY 10007-1501

COOPER, JAMES WILLIAM, chemistry professional; b. Buffalo, N.Y., Feb. 7, 1943; s. Charles William and Aleen (Neely) C.; m. Vicki Sue Kintner, June 14, 1969; children: Vaughn, Nicole. AB, Oberlin Coll., 1964; MS, Ohio State U., 1967, PhD, 1969. Instr. chemistry SUNY, Buffalo, 1969-70; applications programmer Digital Equipment Corp., Maynard, Mass., 1970-71; analytical applications mgr. Nicolet Instruments, Madison, Wis., 1971-74; asst. prof. chemistry Tufts U., Medford, Mass., 1974-80; v.p., software devel. Braker Instruments, Inc., Billerica, Mass., 1980-84; adv. engr. IBM Instruments, Inc., Danbury, Conn., 1984-88; rsch. staff mem. IBM T.J. Watson Rsch. Ctr., Yorktown Heights, N.Y., 1988-89, mgr. lab automation, 1989—. Author: Spectroscopic Techniques for Organic Chemists, 1980, Intro to Pascal for Scientists, 1984, Microcomputer in the Laboratory, 1986, Microsoft Quick Basic for Scientists, 1988, Writing Scientific Progs. under OS/2, 1990, others. Pres. Wilton (Conn.) Y Wahoo Swim Club, 1990-91, v.p. 1986-90; trustee Chelmsford (Mass.) Pub. Librs., 1978-84. Mem. Am. Chem. Soc. Democrat. Unitarian. Home: 48 Old Driftway Rd Wilton CT 06897-2315 Office: IBM TJ Watson Rsch Ctr Rt 134 PO Box 218 Yorktown Heights NY 10598

COOPER, JEFFREY STUART, orthodontist; b. Hackensack, N.J., Apr. 11, 1947; s. H. Miton and Gladys L. (Levitas) C.; m. Marcia G. Cohen, June 22, 1969; children: Jill, Karen, Greg. BS, U. Md., 1969, DDS, 1972; MS in Dentistry, Fairleigh Dickinson Coll., 1976. Diplomate Am. Bd. Orthodontics. Pvt. practice Ramsey, N.J., 1976—, Tenafly, N.J., 1976—. Lt. USNR, 1972-74. Mem. Coll. of Diplomates of Am. Bd. Orthodontics, N.J. Dental Assn., ADA, Am. Assn. Orthodontists, N.J. Assn. Orthodontists, Lions. Independant. Jewish. Home: 282 Pine St Wyckoff NJ 07481-2825 Office: 42 N Franklin Tpke Ramsey NJ 07446-2034

COOPER, JOHN PAUL, priest; b. N.Y.C.; s. Charles Tracy and Ruth Mary (Menefee) C. Student, SUNY, New Paltz, 1975-76; cert. in Edn., Duarte Costa Sch. of Religion, Altoona, Pa., 1988. Ordained priest, 1989. Missionary priest Servants Jerusalem Covenant, Cath. Apostolic Ch. in N.Am., Poughkeepsie, N.Y., 1989—; personal and home health aide Hudson Valley Home Care, Poughkeepsie; pastor Chapel of Christ the King, Poughkeepsie. Head usher Bardovon Theatre, Poughkeepsie, 1979-85; co-founder Mid-Huston chpt. UECAL, N.Y. Liberal. Independent Cath. Home: 77 Academy St Poughkeepsie NY 12601-4113

COOPER, LEON N., physicist, educator; b. N.Y.C., Feb. 28, 1930; s. Irving and Anna (Zola) C.; m. Kay Anne Allard, May 18, 1969; children: Kathleen Ann, Coralie Lauren. AB, Columbia U., 1951, AM, 1953, PhD, 1954, DSc, 1973; DSc hon. degrees; DSc, U. Sussex, Eng., 1973, U. Ill., 1974, Brown U., 1974, Gustavus Adolphus Coll., 1975, Ohio State U., 1976, U. Pierre et Marie Curie, Paris, 1977. NSF postdoctoral fellow, mem. Inst. for Advanced Study, 1954-55; rsch. assoc. U. Ill., 1955-57; asst. prof. Ohio State U., 1957-58; assoc. prof. Brown U., Providence, 1958-62, prof., 1962-66, Henry Ledyard Goddard U. prof., 1966-74, Thomas J. Watson Sr. prof. sci., 1974—; dir. Ctr. for Neural Sci., 1978—; lectr. pub. lectures, internat. conf. and symposia; vis. prof. various univs. and summer schs.; cons. indsl., ednl. orgns.; sponser Fedn. Am. Scientists; mem. Def. Sci. Bd.; co-chair Nestor Inc., assoc. Neuoscience Rsch. Program. Author: Introduction to The Meaning and Structure of Phsyics, 1968; Contbr. articles to profl. jours. Alfred P. Sloan Found. rsch. fellow, 1959-66, John Simon Guggenheim Meml. Found. fellow, 1965-66; recipient Nobel prize (with J. Bardeen and J.R. Schrieffer), 1972; award of Excellence, Grad. Facilities Alumni of Columbia, U., 1974; Descartes medal Acad. de Paris, U. Rene Descartes, 1977, John Jay award Columbia Coll., 1985, award for Disting. Achievement Columbia U., 1990. Fellow Am. Phys. Soc., Am. Acad. Arts and Scis.; mem. AAAS, Am. Philos. Soc., Nat. Acad. Scis. (Comstock prize with J.R. Schrieffer 1968), Soc. Neurosci, Internat. Neural Network Soc. (governing bd.), Phi Beta Kappa, Sigma Xi. Office: Brown U Dept Physics Providence RI 02912

COOPER, LOUIS ZUCKER, pediatrician, educator; b. Albany, Ga., Dec. 25, 1931; s. Jacob Harrison and Cecile (Berman) C. BS, Yale U., 1954, MD, 1957. Intern medicine Mass. Meml. Hosp., Boston, 1957-58; jr. asst. resident medicine Boston VA Hosp., 1958-59; fellow medicine (infectious disease) Tufts-New Eng. Med. Ctr., Boston, 1961-64; from instr. to assoc. prof. Sch. Medicine, NYU, N.Y.C., 1964-73; prof. pediatrics Coll. Physicians and Surgeons, Columbia U., N.Y.C., 1973—; dir. pediatrics Roosevelt Hosp., N.Y.C., 1973-81, St. Luke's-Roosevelt Hosp. Ctr., N.Y.C., 1981—. Capt. USAF, 1959-61. Office: St Luke's-Roosevelt Hosp Amsterdam Ave New York NY 10023-7409

COOPER, MARK ARTHUR, academic administrator; b. Farmington, Maine, May 9, 1949; s. Arthur Edward and Nora Margaret (Gerry) C. BA, St. Anselm Coll., 1971; MSA, U. Notre Dame, 1979. Ordained priest Roman Catholic Ch., 1976. Bus. office staff St. Anselm Coll., Manchester, N.H., 1976-79, treas., chief fin. officer, 1979—; bd. dirs. 1st Signature Bank, Portsmouth, N.H. Mem. Nat. Assn. Colls. and Univ. Bus. Officers. Republican. Roman Catholic. Home: St Anselm Abbey Manchester NH 03102 Office: St Anselm Coll 87 St Anselms Dr Manchester NH 03102-1310

COOPER, MARVIN MEYER, religious studies educator; b. Bklyn., Jan. 20, 1931; s. George Joseph and Betty (Galfon) C.; m. Muriel Jewel Hershman, June 19, 1954; children: Denise Nina, Sherri Beth. BA, L.I.U., 1954; MS, Bklyn. Coll., 1958; PD, Hofstra U., 1977. Cert. elem. tchr. Music tchr. North Country Sch., Lake Placid, N.Y., 1953-54, Bd. Coop. Edn. Svcs., Patchogue, N.Y., 1954-55; music, elem., English, reading tchr. Brentwood (N.Y.) Pub. Schs., 1955-84, reading cons., 1984-90, ret., 1990; religious tchr., principal Sinai Reform Temple, Bay Shore, N.Y., 1957-63; religious tchr. Temple Beth El, Huntington, N.Y., 1963-88; camp counselor Samuel Field YMHA, Queens, N.Y., 1954-58, camp supr. Mid Island YMHA, Wantagh, N.Y. 1958-68, adminstrv. asst., 1968-70. Contbr. articles to profl. jours. Recipient Master Tchr. award Jewish Bd. Edn., 1975. Mem. N.Y. State Tchrs. Assn. (bldg. rep. 1955-88). Republican. Jewish. Home: 295 Terry Rd Hauppauge NY 11788-1926

COOPER, MERRI-ANN, psychologist; b. N.Y.C., Dec. 22, 1946; d. Isidore and Florence (Koplick) C.; m. Stephan Kessler, Aug. 23, 1965 (div. 1971). BA in Psychology cum laude, Bklyn. Coll., 1967; PhD, U. Chgo., 1974; postdoctoral student, U. Minn., 1976-78. Rsch. asst. U. Chgo., 1969-71; asst. prof. Ill. State U., Bloomington, 1972-76; personnel researcher Hennepin County Dept. Personnel, Mpls., 1977-78; rsch. scientist Advanced Rsch. Resources Orgn., Bethesda, Md., 1979-81, sr. rsch. scientist, 1981-85, program mgr., 1985-87; project dir. Univ. Rsch. Corp., Bethesda, Md., 1988-90, dep. div. dir., 1990—; adj. assoc. prof. U. Md., College Park, 1985-86; expert witness litigation support-selection/promotion, 1986, 89; presenter in field; co-chair conf. on employment testing Bur. Nat. Affairs, 1988. Developer selection/promotion tests for spl. agts., R.R. engrs., others; contbr. articles to profl. jours. Recipient USPHS traineeship U. Chgo. Mem. Personnel Testing Coun. (recorder 1986-87, sec. 1985-86, pres. 1988-89), Soc. for Indsl./Organizational Psychology (edn. and tng. com. 1983-84, program com. 1985), Am. Psychology. Home: 8348 N Brook Ln Bethesda MD 20814 Office: Univ Rsch Corp 7200 Wisconsin Ave Bethesda MD 20814-4811

COOPER, MICHAEL R., opinion research company executive; b. Bklyn., Mar. 8, 1946; s. Sam and Shirley (Boris) C.; m. Ruth Mines, Sept. 7, 1969; children: Carolyn S., Jordan D. PhD, Ohio State U., 1972. Lic. psychologist, Mass.; diplomate Am. Bd. Adminstrv. Psychology. Sr. v.p. Opinion Rsch. Corp., Princeton, N.J., 1976-80; pres., sr. ptnr. The Hay Group, Phila., Washington, 1980-89; pres., chief exec. officer Opinion Rsch. Corp., Princeton, N.J., 1989—, also dir.; bd. dirs. Pub. Rels. News, Arthur D. Little Worldwide Quality Ctr. Bd. trustees Mktg. Sci. Inst. 1st lt. U.S. Army, 1972-76. Mem. Am. Mgmt. Assn. (pres. assoc.), Am. Psychol. Soc., Internat. Cons. Found. Office: Opinion Rsch Corp PO Box 183 Princeton NJ 08542-0183

COOPER, PAULETTE MARCIA, writer; b. Antwerp, Belgium, July 26, 1942; came to U.S., 1948; naturalized, 1951; d. Ted S. and Stella R. (Toepfer) C.; B.A. with honors, Brandeis U., 1964; M.A., CUNY, 1968. Free-lance writer, 1968—. Recipient Edgar Allan Poe spl. award Mystery Writers Am., 1975. Mem. NATAS, Am. Soc. Journalists and Authors (Spl. award 1988, Conscience in Media award 1992), Travel Journalists Guild. Author 6 books including: The Scandal of Scientology; The Medical Detectives; also 1000 articles. Address: 401 E 74th St New York NY 10021

COOPER, RICHARD LEE, journalist; b. Grand Rapids, Mich., Dec. 8, 1946; s. Harold Ralph and Elizabeth (DeSchipper) C.; m. Carol Jean Bonjernoor, Sept. 5, 1968; children—Jason Adam, Jessica Lynne. Student, Grand Rapids Jr. Coll., 1965-67; B.A., Mich. State U., 1969. Reporter Rochester (N.Y.) Times-Union, 1969-77; reporter Phila. Inquirer, 1977—, Neighbors editor, 1983—, asst. city editor, 1988-91, Main Line editor, 1991—; instr. journalism Temple U., 1980—. Recipient N.Y. State Asso. Press Spot News First Place award, 1972, 76; Pulitzer prize for gen. local reporting, 1972; Distinguished Alumni award Grand Rapids Jr. Coll., 1974; Outstanding Contbn. in Pub. Info. award N.Y. State Bar Assn., 1977; 1st prize for investigative reporting Gannett News, 1977; Mich. Journalism fellow, 1990—. Mem. Phila. Newspaper Guild, Pen and Pencil Club, Swan Creek Sailing Assn., Chesapeake Bay Triton Fleet, Rock Hall Sailing Club, Sigma Delta Chi. Presbyn. Office: Phila Inquirer 400 N Broad St Philadelphia PA 19130-4099

COOPER, ROBERT ALFRED, electrical engineer; b. Rotherham, Yorkshire, England, Feb. 24, 1938; came to the U.S., 1983; s. Douglas Dentith and Ann (Duffy) C.; m. Carol Hawkhead, Aug. 12, 1961; children: Mark Anthony, Richard John. BS in Engring., RAF Coll., 1969; BA in Physics, Open U., 1979; postgrad., Cambridge U., 1971, Cambridge U., 1976. Commd. 2d lt. RAF, 1953, advanced through grades to squadron leader, 1977, ret., 1983; mgr. European programs mil. scis. group Sci. Applications Internat. Corp., McLean, Va., 1983-89; chief engr. space physics div. Sci. Applications Internat. Corp., Washington, 1989—; chmn. NASA Space Physics Tech. Panel, Washington, 1989-90; co-chmn. U.S./United Kingdom Space Assets Working Group, 1979-82. Author: Space Physics Handbook, 1991; editor: Engring. Coll. Jour., 1968. Flight safety officer CAP, Fairfax, Va., 1984—. Fellow British Interplanetary Soc.; mem. IEEE, AIAA, Inst. Elec. and Electronic Inc. Engrs. (North Am. rep. 1984—), Royal Yachting Assn., Rotary (dir. programs Dulles, Va. chpt. 1991). Roman Catholic. Home: 10031 Glenmere Rd Fairfax VA 22032 Office: Sci Applications Internat 400 Virginia Ave SW Washington DC 20024

COOPER, ROBERT RODNEY, educational administrator; b. Brownstown, Pa., Sept. 11, 1938; s. Robert Yost and Mildred Grace (Mearig) C.; m. June Steller (div. 1980); children: Robert, Jon, Rebecca; m. Dorothy Ann Kempfle, Aug. 10, 1980; stepchildren: Robert, Michael, Thomas, Anita. BS in Edn., Millersville U., 1960, Med. Counselling, 1966. Cert. tchr., counselor, adminstr., Pa. Tchr. Pequea Valley Sch. Dist., Kinzers, Pa., 1960-64; counselor Cocalico Sch. Dist., Denver, Pa., 1964-66, Conestoga Valley Sch. Dist., Lancaster, Pa., 1966-68; adminstr. dist. Conestoga Valley Sch. Dist., 1968-69, high sch. prin., 1969—, dist. adminstr., 1969-92; commr.'s task force-student discipline Dept. Edn., Harrisburg, Pa., 1975-76; mem., pres. Lancaster Guidance Clinic; instr. Am. Mgmt. Assn., 1978. Editor for sch. publications. Committeeman Boy Scouts Am., Brownstone; dir. Civil Def., Brownstown; active Habitab; bd. dirs. Lancaster County Pub. Libr. Mem. Pa. Assn. Pupil Personnel Adminstrs. (pres. 1987-88), Pa. Sch. Public Relations Assn. (charter mem., exec. com. 1974), Ass. Energy Mgrs., Pa. Assn. Sch. Bus. Officials, Nat. Assn. Secondary Sch. Adminstrs., Pa. Assn. Secondary Sch. Administrs, Lions (pres. Brownstown). Republican. Lutheran. Office: Conestoga Valley Sch Dist 2110 Horseshoe Rd Lancaster PA 17601-6099

COOPER, SHARON ELIZABETH, clinical social worker; b. Chgo., Sept. 25, 1951; d. John Herbert and Ruth (Header) Cooper. BS in Nursing, Duke U., 1973; MSSW, Columbia U., 1975. Lic. clin. social worker, Del. Oncology social worker Meml. Sloan Kettering Cancer Ctr., N.Y.C., 1975-84; field instr. Hunter Coll. Sch. S.W., N.Y.C., 1979-84; clin. social worker Catholic Social Svcs., Phila., 1985-87; pvt. practice clin. social work Wilmington, Del., 1985—. Contbr. articles to profl. jours. Mem. Lic. Clin. Social Work Soc. Del. (sec. 1987-88), Nat. Assn. Clin. Social Workers. Office: 1704 Shallcross Ave Wilmington DE 19806

COOPER, SHELDON MARK, medical educator, immunology researcher, rheumatologist; b. N.Y.C., Dec. 5, 1942; s. Alex and Sylvia (Silverman) C.; m. Amy Diane Freedman, Nov. 23, 1966; 1 child, Jonas Eric. BS cum laude, Hobart Coll., 1963; MD, NYU, 1967. Diplomate Am. Bd. Internal Medicine, Am. Bd. Rheumatology. Intern, asst. resident in internal medicine King's County Hosp. Ctr., Bklyn., 1967-69; fellow rheumatic disease study unit NYU Med. Ctr., N.Y.C., 1970-72; asst. prof. medicine U. So. Calif. Sch. Medicine, L.A., 1974-80; assoc. prof., rsch. coord., 1980-82; assoc. prof. medicine, dir. rheumatology and clin. immunology unit U. Vt., Coll. Medicine, Burlington, 1982-86, prof. medicine, dir. rheumatology and clin. immunology unit 1986—; mem. staff L.A. County U. So. Calif. Med. Ctr., 1974-82, Med. Ctr. Hosp. of Vt., Burlington, 1982—. Contbr. articles to profl. jours. Mem. exec. com., Vt. chpt. Arthritis Found., Burlington, 1982—, chmn., trustee, 1990—; mem. panel gen. and plastic surgery devices FDA. Served to maj. USAF, 1972-73. NIH fellow, 1971; Nat. Cancer Inst. grantee, 1976, NIAMS grantee, 1984—, NIH grantee, 1984—. Mem. Am. Coll. Rheumatology, Am. Fedn. Clin. Research, Am. Assn. Immunologists, Reticuloendothelial Soc., Physicians for Social Responsibility, Union Concerned Scientists. Democrat. Jewish. Avocations: jogging, swimming, travel, cinema. Home: Barstow Rd Shelburne VT 05482-7263 Office: U Vt Given Bldg D301 Burlington VT 05405

COOPER, STEVE NEIL, art gallery owner, photographer; b. N.Y.C., July 19, 1944; s. Felix Cooper and Sybil Koff. AAS, Rochester (N.Y.) Inst. Tech., 1964, BFA, 1966; cert. in film, NYU, 1992. Owner Steve Cooper Studio, N.Y.C., 1972—, Sybille Art Gallery, N.Y.C., 1985—. Recipient NE Pocket Billiards Champion NCAA, 1966, award Soc. Publ. Designers, 1975, N.Y.C. Art Dirs. Club award, 1978, Award of Excellence Decor Mag., 1987; N.Y. State Regents Coll. scholar, 1962. Mem. Am. Soc. Mag. Photographers, Assn. Ind. Video and Filmmakers. Jewish. Home: 5 W 31st St New York NY 10001 Office: Sybille Gallery 316 Bleecker St New York NY 10014-3428

COOPER, WILLIAM THOMAS, retired air force officer, writer, educator; b. Itta Bena, Miss., Feb. 3, 1938; s. Singleton Moore and Vera Ernestine (Bussell) C.; m. Janet Faye Johnston, Mar. 8, 1960 (div. 1984); children: William Thomas Jr., Teryl Catherine, Jonathan Gregory; m. Joan Ellen Schulhafer, Aug. 17, 1985. BA, La. Tech. U., 1962; MA in Polit. Sci., U. Louisville, 1970. Commd. 2d lt., 1962, advanced through grades to col., 1983; chief internal info. Hdqrs. SAC, Offutt AFB, Nebr., 1973-75, chief pub. affairs 3902nd Air Base Wing, 1975-78; dir. pub. affairs Hdqrs. Eighth Air Force, Barksdale AFB, La., 1978-81; special asst. for B-1 Bomber Pub. Affairs USAF, Pentagon, Washington, 1981-83, chief, media rels., 1983-84, dir. internal info., 1984-86; tchr., dean of student life Montclair (N.J.) Kimberley Acad., 1987—. Author: Triad of Knives, 1984, Warmoon, 1985. Decorated Legion of Merit, Meritorious Service medal with 1 oak leaf cluster, Commendation medal with 1 oak leaf cluster. Baptist.

COOPERMAN, GENE DAVID, computer information scientist, researcher; b. Union, N.J., May 14, 1952; s. Philip and Elsie (Blumen) C.; m. Celeste Kostopulos, Apr. 1983; children: Adam, Sarah. BS, U. Mich., 1974; PhD, Brown U., 1978. Postdoctoral fellow Mich. State U., East Lansing, 1978-80; prin. mem. tech. staff GTE Labs., Waltham, Mass., 1980-86; assoc. prof. computer sci., Northeastern U., Boston, 1986—. Mem. editorial bd. CRC series, 1990—; contbr. chpt., articles to profl. publs. Co-patentee optical pulse generator. NSF grantee, 1989-92. Mem. Soc. Indsl. and Applied Math., Assn. Computing Machinery (sec. pl. interest group on symbolic and algebraic manipulation 1991—), Sigma Xi (br. treas. 1985-86). Office: Northeastern U Computer Sci 360 Huntington Ave Boston MA 02115-5096

COOPERMAN, JACK M., nutrition educator; b. N.Y.C., Jan. 13, 1921; s. Harry and Fanny (Wexler) C.; m. Ruth Eleanor Drucker, July 10, 1949; 1 child, Jonathan Keith. BS in Chemistry, CCNY, 1941; MS in Biochemistry, U. Wis., 1943, PhD in Biochemistry, 1945. Nutritionist Hoffmann-Laroche Inc., Nutley, N.J., 1946-57; asst. prof. N.Y. Med. Coll., N.Y.C., 1957-62, assoc. prof., 1963-72; prof. N.Y. Med. Coll., Valhalla, 1973—; per grant reviewer USDA, Washington, 1985—; Lederle lectr. in nutrition Israeli Dietetic Soc., Tel Aviv, 1988, Cath. Med. Coll. Korea, Seoul, Republic of Korea, 1989; vis. prof. U. West Indies, Jamaica, 1960, India Inst. Med. Sci., New Delhi, 1978; John P. McGrath lectr. C.W. Post Coll., 1987; lectr. nutrition Am. Coll. Gen. Practioners in Osteo. Med. and Surgery, 1985, Sigma Xi. Reviewer of articles Am. Jour. Clin. Nutrition, 1980—; author: (with others) Handbook of Vitamins, 1990, Encyclopedia of Nutrition and Technology; contbr. articles to profl. jours. Grantee NIH, 1958-90. Fellow AAAS, N.Y. Acad. Scis., 1976; mem. Am. Inst. Nutrition, Am. Soc. for Biochemistry and Molecular Biology, Am. Soc. Clin. Nutrition, Am. Chem. Soc., Biochem. Soc., Harvey Soc., Soc. Exptl. Biology and Medicine, Bi-

ochem. Soc. (Great Britian), Harvey Soc. Jewish. Office: NY Med Coll Munger Rm 509 Valhalla NY 10595

COOTS, FRANK SHEPHERD, III, public relations executive; b. Louisville, Ky., Oct. 12, 1949; s. Frank S. and Jean Ruddy C.; m. Ellen V. Blackmun, May 10, 1980 (div. Aug., 1990). BA in Journalism, U. Ky., 1972. Editor Ky. Kernel, Lexington, Ky., 1970-71; press aide Commonwealth of Ky., Frankfort, 1971-74; editor E. Suburban Press, Pitts., 1975-77, Standard Observer, Irwin, Pa., 1977-78; community relations mgr. Humana, Inc., Louisville, 1978-83; group mgr. Skaare Group, Pitts., 1988-89; pres. Frank Coots Communications, Pitts., 1989—; pub. rels. cons., 1984-88. Columnist: various newspapers, 1977-80; contbr. articles to mags., bus. jours., 1978-89. Mem. Pub. Relations Soc. Am. (accredited), Am. Mktg. Assn., Acad. of Health Svcs. Mktg. Democrat. Office: Frank Coots Communications 400 Penn Center Blvd Pittsburgh PA 15235

COPE, ALFRED HAINES, political scientist, educator; b. Oakbourne, Pa., May 29, 1912; s. Joseph and Ellen (Fussell) C.; m. Ruth Balderston, Aug. 23, 1937; 1 child, Joan. AB, Earlham Coll., 1934; PhD, U. Pa., 1948. Agt. Equitable Life Ins. Co., 1934-36; dir. Am. Friends Service Co., Chgo., 1936-38, War Relief Adminstrn., Spain, 1938-39; adminstrv. asst. U. Pa. Inst. Local and State Govt., 1940-42, instr., 1946-48; sr. adminstrv. aid. U.S. CSC, Phila., 1942-43; asst. prof. Syracuse (N.Y.) U., 1948-51, assoc. prof., 1951-56, asst. dean, prof. citizenship Utica Coll., 1956-60, asst. dean Coll. Liberal Arts, 1960-70, prof. citizenship Coll. Liberal Arts, 1956-75, prof. polit. sci. Coll. Liberal Arts, 1962-75, univ. registrar and mgr. student data systems, 1970-74, prof. emeritus Coll. Liberal Arts, 1975—. Author: Administration of Civil Service in Cities of the Third Class in Pennsylvania, 1948; (with Fred Krinsky) Franklin Roosevelt and the Supreme Court, 1952, rev. edit., 1969; Current Defense of the U.S., 1954; (with E.E. Palmer) The Dixon Yates Contract and the National Power Policy, 1955; The Basis for a New Legal System, 1973; Managing World Resources, 1975. Pres. bd. dirs. Child and Family Svcs., 1963-66; arbitrator Syracuse Better Bus. Bur.; trustee Oakwood Sch., Poughkeepsie, N.Y., 1974-90, treas., 1977-84, chmn. fin. com., 1984-87, pres. bd. mgrs., trustees, 1987-89; chmn. fin. com. Friends World Com., sect. of Ams., 1976-81, mem. world fin. group, 1975-81, del. triennial meeting Gwatt, Switzerland, 1980; Friends Assn. for Higher Edn.; co-clerk Task Force on Peace Studies, 1985-88; mem. cen. com. Friends Gen. Conf., 1978-84; chmn. devel. com., mem. exec. pers. and advancement coms.; mem. gen. svcs. com. N.Y. Yearly Meeting, Religious Soc. Friends, 1978-81, chmn. com. sharing of world resources, 1981-85; mem. gen. bd. Pendle Hill, Wallingford, Pa., 1982—; treas., trustee Syracuse Friends Meeting; trustee Lindley Murray Fund, 1984—, chmn., 1992—. Served to capt. AUS, 1943-46. Fellow AAAS; mem. Am. Acad. Polit. Sci., Friends Assn. Higher Edn. (assoc.), Acad. Polit. Sci., Am. Judicature Soc., Friends Hist. Soc., Genol. Soc. Pa., Chester County Hist. Soc. (life), Phi Delta Kappa. Club: Torch (Syracuse) (pres. 1969-70).

COPE, JAMES DUDLEY, association executive; b. Nelsonville, Ohio, Apr. 22, 1932; s. James Wesley and Flossie Lucinda (Barber) C.; m. Mary Ann Thress, Aug. 15, 1957 (div. Nov. 1960); 1 child, Derilyn Untied; m. Janet Parrett, Dec. 17, 1960; children: David Blaine, Brian Edward. BA, Denison U., 1954; student Inst. Organization Mgmt., Yale U., 1959. Exec. dir. Ohio State Pharm. Assn., Columbus, 1957-61; corp. sec. Nonprescription Drug Mfrs. Assn., Washington, 1961-66, v.p., sec., 1966-67, exec. v.p., 1967-73, pres., 1973—; bd. dir. 1st Am. Bank, 1985-91. Contbr. articles to profl. jours. Pres. Glen Mar Park Civic Assn., Bethesda, Md., 1963; pres. bd. trustees Faith United Meth. Ch., Rockville, Md., 1978; bd. dirs. Council on Family Health, N.Y.C., 1967—, First Am. Bank, 1985-91; pres. Nat. Drug Trade Conf., Washington, 1975, 83, 88. Served as cpl. U.S. Army, 1954-56. Recipient Achievement Medal Alpha Zeta Omega, 1960, Alumni Citation Denison U., 1979; named Man of Yr. Am. Druggist, 1959. Mem. Am. Soc. Assn. Execs. (dir. 1979-82), Greater Washington Soc. Assn. Execs., Denison U. Alumni Assn., World Fedn. of Proprietary Medicine Mfrs. (vice chmn. 1979-86, 89—). Republican. Clubs: Nat. Assn. Execs. (Washington) (pres. 1984); Met. (N.Y. and Washington); Sky (N.Y.C.); Congl. Country (Potomac, Md.). Home: 11836 Farmland Dr Rockville MD 20852-4304 Office: Nonprescription Drug Mfrs Assn 1150 Connecticut Ave NW Washington DC 20036-4104

COPE, JOHN R(OBERT), lawyer; b. San Angelo, Tex., May 30, 1942; s. Robert Lloyd and Meta (Young) C.; 1 child, Lloyd Chapman. BBA, U. Tex., 1964, JD, 1966. Bar: Tex. 1966, D.C. 1976. Ptnr. Bracewell & Patterson, Attys., Houston, 1966-76; ptnr. Bracewell & Patterson, Attys., Washington, 1976—, mem. adv. mgmt. com., 1987-90; joint venturer R/C Joint Venture (Cattle Joint Venture), Romney, W.Va., 1980—; vice chmn. bd. dirs., gen. counsel Century Nat. Bank, Washington, 1982—; bd. dirs., gen. counsel Columbia Nat. Bank, Washington, 1987-90; bd. dirs., v.p., gen. counsel Century Bancshares, Washington, 1985—; mem. fed. savs. and loan adv. coun. Fed. Home Loan Bank Bd., Washington, 1980-81; chmn., lectr. Practicing Law Inst. Seminars on Energy Litigation, Washington, 1980, 81; chief judge Wake Island Ct., Wake Island, North Pacific Ocean, 1989. Mem. devel. bd. Lon Morris Coll., Lake Jackson, Tex., 1974-76; mem. Southwest U. Spl. Edn. Found., San Marcos, Tex., 1973-76; v.p., dir. Harris County Easter Seal Soc., Houston, 1972-76; treas. Dem. Party Harris County, Houston, 1976-77; mem. nat. fin. coun. Dem. Nat. Com., Washington, 1976-80. Mem. ABA (mem. litigation sect.), D.C. Bar Assn. (mem. litigation and govt. contracts sect.), Tex. Bar Assn. (mem. litigation sect.), Houston Bar Assn. (mem. gen. litigation sect.), Nat. Cattlemen's Assn., W.Va. Cattlemen's Assn., Orton Soc. Republican. Methodist. Office: Bracewell & Patterson 2000 K St NW Washington DC 20006-1809

COPELAND, ANNE PITCAIRN, psychologist; b. Pitts., Sept. 3, 1951; d. James Dudley and Barbara (Findley) C.; m. James Potter Womack, Dec. 15, 1984; children: Caroline Copeland, Katherine Copeland. BA, Eckerd Coll., St. Petersburg, Fla., 1973; PhD, Am. U., 1977. Lic. psychologist, Mass. Med. psychology intern child devel. and rehab. ctr. Oreg. Health Scis. U., Portland, 1976-77; asst. prof. psychology Kent (Ohio) State U., 1977-79; asst. prof. psychology Boston U., 1979-85, assoc. prof. psychology, 1985—; acad. advisor, acting dir. British programmes Boston U., London, Oxford, 1988-89. Co-author: Studying Families, 1991; contbr. articles to profl. jours. Recipient Alumni Achievement award Eckerd Coll., 1988. Mem. Am. Psychol. Assn., New England Psychol. Assn. (pres. 1985), Soc. for Rsch. in Child and Adolescent Psychopathology, Soc. for Rsch. in Child Devel., AAUP, Sigma Xi, Phi Beta Delta Soc. Internat. Scholars. Office: Boston U Psychology Dept 64 Cummington St Boston MA 02215-2407

COPELAND, RITA LYNETTE, lawyer; b. Buffalo, June 26, 1960; d. Leon Scott and Bonnie Lee (Adams) C. BA, Boston U., 1980; JD, SUNY, Buffalo, 1983. Bar: N.Y. 1984. Asst. county atty. Erie County Dept. Law, Buffalo, 1984-87; dep. counsel N.Y. State Bd. Elections, Albany, 1987; assoc. counsel N.Y. State United Tchrs., N.Y.C., 1987-90; ptnr. Copeland & Aughtry, Bklyn., 1990-92; pvt. practice, Buffalo, 1992—; hearing officer N.Y.C. Transit Authority, Bklyn., 1990-91. Recipient svc. award Women's Aux., St. John Bapt. Ch., Buffalo, 1984, Community svc. award Albee Square Mall, Bklyn., 1991. Mem. N.Y. State Bar Assn., Bklyn. Bar Assn., Bar Assn. Erie County, Delta Sigma Theta Sorority Inc. Office: 482 Franklin St Buffalo NY 14202

COPELAND, ROBERT MARSHALL, music educator; b. Douglas, Wyo., Jan. 30, 1945; s. Wilbur Clyde and Arvilla Estella (Walkinshaw) C.; m. Louise Margaret Edgar, June 10, 1966; children: Thomas Edgar, Anne Louise, Kathryn Elizabeth. BS, Geneva Coll., 1966; MM, U. Cin., 1970, PhD, 1974; postgrad., Westminster Choir Coll., 1981-82, Emory U., 1988. Asst. prof. to prof. music Mid-Am. Nazarene Coll., Olathe, Kans., 1971-81; prof. music, chmn. dept. music, dir. choral activities Geneva Coll., Beaver Falls, Pa., 1981—; vis. lectr. U. Kans., Lawrence, 1977; trustee, sec. Ref. Presbyn. Theol. Sem., Pitts., 1981-93, vis. lectr., 1983-84. Author: Spare No Exertions, 1986; co-editor: The Book of Psalms for Singing, 1973; contbr. articles to profl. jours. Dir. music Internat. Covenanter Conf., Northfield, Minn., 1970, 76, 80, 84; ruling elder Ref. Presbyn. Ch., 1973—. With U.S. Army, 1966-68. NDEA fellow, 1968-71. Mem. AAUP (v.p. Kans. Conf. 1980-81), Am. Musicological Soc. (v.p. Allegheny chpt. 1987-89, pres. 1989-91, coun. mem. 1992—), Sonneck Soc. for Am. Music (founding mem., program com. 1982), Coll. Music Soc., Am. Choral Dirs. Assn. (co-editor Pa. Newsletter 1983-85, editor 1985-90), Huguenot Fellowship (bd. dirs. 1987—). Republican. Home: 3111 5th Ave Beaver Falls PA 15010-3616 Office: Geneva Coll 3200 College Ave Beaver Falls PA 15010-3557

COPP, ROBERT MECCA, financial consultant; b. Rochester, N.Y., Oct. 2, 1949; s. Richard Owen and Mary June (Luffman) C.; m. Florence Mecca-Copp, Mar. 22, 1975; children: Emily Rose, Joanna Lauren. BA, SUNY, Geneseo, 1971; MA, Bowling Green State U., 1972; MPA, Syracuse U., 1976. Supervising analyst City of San Jose, Calif., 1977-81; dir. fin. and adminstrn. Hearing and Speech Ctr. of Rochester, 1981-86; surgery adminstr. Strong Meml. Hosp., Rochester, 1986-90; fin. cons. CIGNA Individual Fin. Svcs., Fairport, N.Y., 1990—. Exec. dir. Eshmun Found., San Jose, 1981; elder Laurel Presbyn. Ch., Irondequoit, N.Y., 1985-88; trustee Presbytery of Genesee Valley, Rochester, 1987-92; bd. dirs. Presbyn. Found. Genesee Valley, 1992. Mem. Phi Alpha Theta. Democrat. Home: 43 Wildmere Rd Rochester NY 14617 Office: CIGNA 300 Cross Keys Office Pk Fairport NY 14450

COPPENS, THOMAS ADRIAAN, pharmaceutical manufacturing executive; b. Rotterdam, Netherlands, Feb. 2, 1923; came to U.S., 1927; s. Philip Adriaan and Evelyn (van Capelle) C.; m. Sylvia Helen Scofield, Feb. 26, 1944; children: Laura Kathryn, Carole Elizabeth, John Philip, Barbara Helen. Student, McGill U., 1941-43, Lafayette Coll., 1944; D LL (hon.), Inst. Applied Rsch., London, 1973. Internat. rep. Sharp & Dohme, Inc., Mediterranean area, 1946-52; mng. dir. Merck, Sharp & Dohme, Manila, 1952-57; v.p. Merck & Co., Inc., Rahway, N.J., 1957-77; pres. Merck, Sharp & Dohme, BV, Haarlem, Netherlands, 1977-82; cons. Merck & Co., Inc., Rahway, 1982-84; prin. Camelot Antiques, Cooperstown, N.Y., 1984-90. Contbr. articles to profl. publs. Sr. warden St. Andrews Episcopal Ch., Harrington Park, N.J., 1958-67; bd. dirs. Hubbard Farms, Walpole, N.H., 1975-77, Walden U., Naples, Fal., 1984—; trustee Naples Community Hosp., 1988—. Sgt. U.S. Army, 1943-46, ETO. Decorated Purple Heart. Mem. Rotary (Paul Harris fellow), Am. C. of C. of Hague, Netherlands (bd. dirs. 1977-83). Home and Office: 6075 Pelican Bay Blvd Naples FL 33963-8169

COPPER, ROBERT ARNOLD DE VIGNIER, architectural and interior designer; b. Waynesboro, Va., Nov. 3, 1938; s. William Thomas and Elizabeth Dalrymple (de Vignier) C.; m. Morinda Delores Anne Cree, Sept. 10, 1975 (div. Apr. 1981); 1 child, Rebecca Elizabeth de Vignier. Student, U. Richmond, 1954-56; BFA, Coll. of William and Mary, 1961. Pres. Arnold Copper & Co., N.Y.C., 1972—. Author: Psychic Summer, 1975; contbr. articles to profl. jours.; work featured include: (mags.) House and Garden's, 1988 (Best of Decoration 1988), Laura Ashley At Home, 1988, Period Style, 1989, Favorite Recipes of New Eng.; designed sets and costumes Regional Theatre, City Theatre, N.Y.C., Spoleto U.S. Bd. dirs. Am. Philharmonic Orchestra, 1981-83; pres. Children's Internat. Summer Villages UNESCO, 1980-82, Friends of Spoleto Festival, Charleston, S.C., 1984-86. Recipient 1st prize designer showcase House Beautiful Mag., 1985. Episcopalian. Office: Arnold Copper Inc 872 Madison Ave New York NY 10021-4121

COPPLESTONE, DAVID WESLEY, artist, small business owner; b. Newton, Mass., Feb. 29, 1952; s. Wesley and Elizabeth (Winchell) C. Diploma, Art Inst. of Boston, 1975. Owner Landscape Design, Wellesley, Mass., 1967-73, Home Improvement Contractor, Wellesley, 1973—, Copplestone Artworks, Wellesley, 1975—; product design, graphic artist Fun-N-Safe Inc., Natick, Mass., 1991. Inventor of games. Mem. Mus. of Fine Art, Boston. Mem. Wellesley Artist Assn., Cambridge Art Assn., Coply Soc., Italo Am. Ednl. Club. Home and Office: 6 Shadow Ln Wellesley MA 02181-4311

COPPOLA, LAWRENCE, computer analyst; b. N.Y.C., Nov. 16, 1958; s. Ronald and Jean (Di Pietrantonio) C. BA, CUNY, Queens, 1980; BS, N.Y. Inst. Tech., 1990. Staff acct. Aberdeen Mfg. Corp., N.Y.C., 1981-82; computer analyst N.Y. Acad. Medicine, N.Y.C., 1983—. Mem. AIAA, IEEE. Office: NY Acad Medicine 2 E 103d St New York NY 10029

COQUILLETTE-DEAN, DANIEL ROBERT, lawyer, educator; b. Boston, May 23, 1944; s. Robert McTavish and Dagmar Alvida (Bistrup) C.; m. Judith Courtney Rogers, July 5, 1969; children: Anna, Sophia, Julia. A.B., Williams Coll., 1966; M.A. Juris., Univ. Coll., Oxford U., Eng., 1969; J.D., Harvard U., 1971. Bar: Mass. 1974, U.S. Dist. Ct. Mass. 1974, U.S. Ct. Appeals (1st cir.) 1974. Law clk. Mass. Supreme Ct., 1971-72; to Warren E. Burger, chief justice U.S. Supreme Ct., 1972-73; assoc. Palmer & Dodge, Boston, 1973-75, ptnr., 1980-85; assoc. prof. law Boston U., 1975-78; dean, prof. Boston Coll. Law, 1985—; vis. assoc. prof. law Cornell U., Ithaca, N.Y., 1977-78; vis. prof. law Harvard Law Sch., 1978-79, 83-85; reporter com. rules and procedures Jud. Conf. U.S.; vis. assoc. prof. law Cornell U., Ithaca, N.Y., 1977-78. Author: The Civilian Writers of Doctors Commons, London, 1988; editor: Law in Colonial Massachusetts, 1985; bd. dirs. New England Quarterly, 1986—; contbr. articles to legal jours. Trustee, sec.-treas. Ames Found., Cambridge Friends Sch.; treas. Byron Meml Fund; propr., trustee Boston Athenaeum. Recipient Kaufman prize in English Williams Coll., 1966; recipient Sentinel of the Republic prize in polit. sci. Williams Coll., 1965; Hutchins scholar, 1966-67; Fulbright scholar, 1966-68. Mem. ABA (com. on profl. ethics), Am. Law Inst., Mass. Bar Assn. (task force on model rules of profl. conduct), Boston Bar Assn., Am. Soc. Legal History (bd. dirs. 1985—), Mass. Soc. Continuing Legal Edn. (dir.), Social Welfare Research Inst. (dir.), Selden Soc. (state corr.), Colonial Soc. Mass. (v.p., mem. council), Anglo-Am. Cathedral Soc. (dir.), Mass. Hist. Soc., Am. Antiquarian Soc., Phi Beta Kappa. emocrat. Quaker. Clubs: Curtis, Tavern, Country, Club of Odd Volumes. Home: 12 Rutland St Cambridge MA 02138-2503 Office: Boston Coll Sch Law 885 Centre St Newton MA 02159-1156

CORAH, NORMAN LEWIS, behavioral science in dentistry educator; b. Kenmore, N.Y., July 18, 1933; s. Leo Wesley and Alice Beulah (Congdon) C.; m. Patricia Ann Laney, June 21, 1958; children: Norman Lewis Jr., Joseph Leo. BA, U. Buffalo, 1955, PhD, 1960. Instr. U. Buffalo, 1959-60; rsch. instr. Washington U., St. Louis, 1960-61, asst. prof., 1961-65; assoc. prof. SUNY, Buffalo, 1965-71, prof., 1971—. Editor: Origins of Abnormal Behavior, 1971; contbr. 75 articles to profl. jours. Recipient Rsch. Career Devel. award Nat. Inst. of Dental Rsch., 1969, Disting. Scientist award Internat. Assn. for Dental Rsch., 1991. Mem. AAAS, APA, Am. Assn. Dental Schs., Am. Cut Glass Assn. (ea. bd. dirs. 1990-92). Home: 123 Ivyhurst Rd Buffalo NY 14226-3440 Office: SUNY Sch of Dental Medicine Squire Hall Buffalo NY 14214

CORAK, WILLIAM SYDNEY, consultant; b. Phila., Mar. 10, 1922; s. Henry Herbert Gottlieb and Minnie (Barofsky) C.; m. Hilda Ivker, June 9, 1946; children: Seth, David, Jonathan, Steven, Eric. BSChemE, U. Pa., 1943; MS in Chemistry, Ohio State U., 1947; PhD, U. Pitts., 1955. Chem. control engr. Davison Chem. Corp., Curtis Bay, Md., 1943-44; field engr. Chemistry Dept., Johns Hopkins U., Balt., 1944-45; rsch. assoc. Ohio State U. Rsch. Found., Columbus, 1945-46; univ. fellow Ohio State U., Columbus, 1946-47; sr. engr. Cen. Rsch. Lab., Westinghouse, Pitts., 1947-55; ops. mgr. Spl. Products Dept. Semiconductor Div., Youngwood, Pa., 1955-64; sr. adv. scientist Advanced Technology Div., Westinghouse, Balt., 1964-88; cons. Ctr. for Nondestructive Evaluation, Johns Hopkins U., Balt., 1988—; cons. in field; tech. adv. bd. mem. Semiconductor Rsch. Corp., Rsch. Triangle Pk., N.C., 1985-88. Co-editor: Integrated Electronic Systems, 1970; contbr. articles to profl. publs. V.p. Temple Beth Shalom, Arnold, Md., 1966-69; inst. rep. Boy Scouts of Am., Arnold, 1967. Mem. Am. Phys. Soc., IEEE, ASM Internat., Phi Lambda Epsilon, Sigma Xi.

CORAM, EDWARD CLINTON, information systems executive; b. N.Y.C., Jan. 4, 1947; s. Eugene Clinton and Alma Marie (Monsanto) C.; m. Deborah Aurellia Warren, Sept. 22, 1984; children: Lisa Michelle, Toosdhi Nicole. AAS, Manhattan Community Coll., 1973; BBA, Baruch Coll., N.Y.C., 1978; MBA, Baruch Coll., 1981. CLU, chartered fin. cons. Computer operator Met. Life, N.Y.C., 1967-69, ops. mgr., 1969-70, systems programmer, 1970-74; applications programmer Equitable Life Assurance Soc., N.Y.C., 1974-77, project mgr., 1977-83, dir., 1983-87, v.p. info. systems, 1987—; Bd. dirs. Louise Wise Svcs., Inc. Recipient Black Achiever award Harlem YMCA, 1985. Fellow Life Mgmt. Inst.; mem. Am. Soc. CLU's, Data Processing Mgmt. Assn., Assn. for Systems Mgmt., Minority Interchange Inc. (bd. dirs. 1981-86), Black Data Processing Assn. (N.Y. chpt. adv. bd. 1987—). Office: Equitable Life Assurance Co 2 Pennsylvania Plz New York NY 10121

CORAOR, JOHN EDWARD, museum director; b. Woodbury, N.J., Nov. 30, 1955; s. George Robert and Martha Geraldine (Wells) C.; m. Hanna Nekvasil, May 2, 1979. BFA, Syracuse U., 1977; MEd, Pa. State U., 1981, PhD, 1985. Cert. art edn., N.Y. Edn. asst. H.F. Johnson Mus. Art, Ithaca, N.Y., 1977-79; mng. editor The Museologist, State College, Pa., 1980-83; grad. asst., course instr. Pa. State U., State College, 1981-85; exec. dir. Tempe (Ariz.) Arts Ctr., 1985-88; dir. Heckscher Mus., Huntington, N.Y., 1988—; councillor N.Y. State Assn. Museums, 1992—; mem. Suffolk County, N.Y. Cultural Affairs Adv. Bd., 1990—; cen. region rep. Mus. Assn. of Ariz. Exec. Bd., 1987-88; mem. West Wing jury panel, Ariz. State Capitol, Phoenix, 1985-88. Recipient Mayoral Proclamation City of Tempe, 1988; Andrew V. Kozak fellow Phi Delta Kappa, 1984. Mem. Am. Assn. Mus., Mid-Atlantic Assn. Mus. (fellow 1980, vice chmn. publs. com. 1991—), N.Y. State Assn. Mus. (sec., councillor exec. coun. 1992—), L.I. Mus. Assn., Nat. Art Edn. Assn. (scholarship 1983). Office: Heckscher Mus 2 Prime Ave Huntington NY 11743-7702

CORATTI, JOHN EDWARD, judicial clerk; b. Jersey City, Nov. 17, 1950; s. Nicholas and Bernice (Johnson) C.; 1 child, Kathleen Mary. BA in English, Rutgers Coll., 1973; MA, Seton Hall U., 1981; postgrad., NYU, 1981-88, Trinity Coll., Dublin, Ireland, 1974; JD, U. Dayton, 1988. Pres. off-Broadway theater John a-Dreams Profl. Repertory Theatre, N.J., N.Y., 1973-84; instr. English Wright State U., Dayton, 1988, U. Dayton, 1986-88; legal adminstrv. asst. Ocean County Prosecutor's Office, N.J., 1988-91; jud. appellate clk. Superior Ct. Appellate Div., N.J., 1991—. Recipient Am. Jurisprudence award Lawyers Coop. Pub. Co., 1988, Award for Excellence, Italian Am. Bar Assn. Mem. W.E.B.A., Nat. Right to Life, Univ. Ctrs. for Rational Alternatives, Federalist Soc., Amnesty Internat., Am. Theatre Wing, Civil Liberties Union, Phi Theta Kappa. Democrat. Roman Catholic. Home: 617 Mistletoe Point Plesant NJ 08742 Office: Superior Ct of NJ Appellate Div 100 E Water St Toms River NJ 08754

CORBER, ROBERT JACK, lawyer; b. Topeka, June 29, 1926; s. Alva Forrest and Katherine (Salzer) C.; m. Joan Irene Tennal, July 16, 1949 (dec. July 1987); children: Janet, Suzanne, Wesley Sean, Robert Jack II; m. Deborah Perkins Corkey, Jan. 7, 1989. B.S. in Aero. Engring, U. Kans., 1946; J.D. cum laude, Washburn U., 1950; postgrad., U. Mich., 1950-51. Bar: Kans. 1950, D.C. 1951, U.S. Supreme Ct. 1964. Assoc. Steptoe & Johnson, Washington, 1951-57, ptnr., 1957-75, 80—; commr. ICC, Washington, 1975-76; ptnr. Conner, Moore & Corber, Washington, 1977-80. Author: Motor Carrier Leasing and Interchange Under the Interstate Commerce Act, 1977; contbr. legal and polit. articles to various publs. Chmn. Arlington (Va.) Republican Com., 1960-62; chmn. Va. 10th Congl. Dist. Rep. Com., 1962-64; state chmn. Rep. Party of Va., 1964-68. Served to lt. (j.g.) USNR, 1944-47. Mem. ABA (chmn. motor carrier com. pub. utility sect. 1983-86), Bar Assn. D.C. (chmn. adminstrv. law sect. 1978-79, chmn. continuing legal edn. com. 1979-83), Transp. Lawyers Assn., Assn. Trans. Practitioners. Methodist. Clubs: Met. (Washington), Washington Golf and Country (Washington).

CORBET, DAVID LEWIS, biomedical company executive; b. Plainfield, N.J., May 4, 1953; s. William Boice and Constance Lorraine (Melson) C.; m. Angela Jane Post, Sept. 17, 1977; children: Mary Constance, Patricia Jane. BS in Zoology, U. R.I., 1975. Tech. sales rep. Dade div. Am. Hosp. Supply Corp., Miami, Fla., 1976-78, product mgr., 1978-79; new product devel. mgr. Hyland div. Baxter Travenol Co., Deerfield, Ill., 1979-81; dir. mktg. Cooperbiomed., Malvern, Pa., 1981-85; dir. comml. devel. T Cell Scis., Inc., Cambridge, Mass., 1985-88, v.p., gen. mgr., corp. officer, 1988-91, pres., chief oper. officer, 1991—, also dir. Mem. Biomed. Mktg. Assn. Office: T Cell Scis Inc 38 Sidney St Cambridge MA 02139-4160

CORBETT, GERARD FRANCIS, electronics executive; b. Phila., Apr. 6, 1950; s. Eugene Charles and Dolores Marie (Hoffmann) C.; m. Marcia Jean Serafin, July 9, 1983; 1 child, Daniel Gerard. AA, Community Coll. of Phila., 1974; BA in Pub. Rels., San Jose State U., 1977. Sci. programmer Sverdrup Inc., NASA Ames Rsch. Ctr., Moffett Field, Calif., 1970-77; sr. writer Four-Phase Systems, Inc., Cupertino, Calif., 1977-78; with Nat. Semicondr. Corp., Santa Clara, Calif., 1978-79; sr. account exec. Creamer Dickson Basford, Providence, 1979-81; mgr. tech. and exec. communications Internat. Harvester Co., Chgo., 1981-82; mgr. corp. tech. communications Gould Inc., Rolling Meadows, Ill., 1982-83, dir. corp. pub. rels., 1983-86, bd. dir. corp. communications 1986-89; corp. communications exec., ASARCO Inc., N.Y.C., 1989—; pub. rels. and communications cons. on high tech. Recipient Vice Presdl. award of honor Calif. Jaycees, 1977. Mem. AIAA, Nat. Investor Rels. Inst., Pub. Rels. Soc. Am. (accredited, Pres.'s citation 1981), Am. Mining Congress (communications com.), LEAD Industries Assn. (chmn. pub. affairs com.), Nat. Assn. Sci. Writers, Internat. Coun. on Metals and the Environ., Kappa Tau Alpha. Republican. Roman Catholic. Clubs: Capital Hill, Commonwealth of Calif., Meadow (Rolling Meadows, Ill.). Home: 48 Woodland Ave Glen Ridge NJ 07028-1232 Office: ASARCO Inc 180 Maiden Ln New York NY 10038-4925

CORBETT, JACK ELLIOTT, mutual fund officer, clergyman, author; b. Oak Park, Ill., Nov. 27, 1920; s. Elliott Wesley and Clara Helen (Froelich) C.; m. Sarah Anne Rapp, July 1, 1945; children: Kathleen, Marjorie, Stephen. BS, Temple U., 1950; BD, Crozer Seminary, Chester, Pa., 1950; PhD in Internat. Relations, Am. U., 1967. Pastor Landenberg (Pa.)-Hamorton Ch., 1949-50, Community Meth. Ch., McHenry, Ill., 1950-58, Oregon (Ill.) Meth. Ch., 1958-61; ofcl. Bd. of Ch. and Society United Meth. Ch., Washington, 1961-80, Balt. Conf. United Meth. Ch., 1981-83; v.p. Pax World Fund, Portsmouth, N.H., 1971—; pres. Pax World Found., Bethesda, Md., 1971-90. Author: Prophets on Main Street, 1964, Christians Awake, 1970, Turned On By God, 1971, Becoming A Prophetic Community, 1980. Chmn. Nat. Coalition To Ban Handguns, 1974-75. Unitarian-Univ. Peace Fellowship award, 1991. Mem. UN Assn. (bd. dirs. Washington area 1975—, v.p. 1985-89, pres. 1990-91). Democrat. Home and Office: 6006 Milo Dr Bethesda MD 20816-1156

CORBETT, PETER FRANK, electrical engineer; b. Sault Ste. Marie, Ont., Can., Dec. 11, 1959; s. Ronald Roy and Shirley Irene (Fera) C. BASc, U. Waterloo, Ont., Can., 1983; MASc, U. Waterloo, 1985; MA, Princeton U., 1989, PhD, 1990. Elec. engr. GE Corp. R & D, Schenectady, N.Y., 1985-87; mem. rsch. staff IBM T.J. Watson Rsch. Ctr., Yorktown Heights, N.Y., 1990—. Inventor, author tech. articles. Mem. IEEE, Assn. Computing Machinery. Office: IBM TJ Watson Rsch Ctr PO Box 218 Yorktown Heights NY 10598-0218

CORBETT, RICHARD ALEXANDER, metallurgist; b. Hong Kong, Sept. 28, 1948; s. Richard Hayes and Martha Ellen (Barrett) C.; m. Barbara Elizabeth Gillespie, Aug. 19, 1972; children: Kristine Elizabeth, James David, Richard Andrew. BS, Va. Mil. Inst., 1970; MSc, Old Dominion U., 1975. Cert. corrosion specialist, cathodic protection specialist. Chemistry tchr. Norfolk (Va.) City Schs., 1970-75; sr. corrosion engr. Henkels & McCoy, Inc., Blue Bell, Pa., 1975-78, Amax Nickel Co., New Orleans, 1978-81; tech. svcs. engr. E.I. duPont de Nemours & Co., Wilmington, Del., 1981-86; pres. Corrosion Testing Labs., Inc., Wilmington, 1986—; dir. PE Corrosion and Materials Consultancy, Colts Neck, N.J.; cons. Condux, Inc., Newark, 1987—, Deltech Vocat. High Sch., Wilmington, 1990-91. Contbg. author: Metals Handbook-Corrosion, 1987. Fellow Inst. Corrosion; mem. ASTM, Nat. Assn. Corrosion Engrs. (cert. exams chmn. 1982—), Am. Soc. Metals Internat. Republican. Episcopalian. Office: Corrosion Testing Labs Inc 410 B & O Ln Wilmington DE 19804

CORBETT, RICHARD EDWARD, psychotherapist; b. Newton, Mass., Jan. 6, 1949; s. Edward J. and Ardrith A. (Cossaboom) C. BA in Psychology, Northeastern U., 1974; MA in Counseling Psychology, Assumption Coll., Worcester, Mass., 1977. Lic. mental health counselor; nat. cert. addictions counselor, cert. alcohol counselor. Mental health worker Framingham (Mass.) Union Hosp., 1974-78; prin. psychologist Wrentham (Mass.) State Sch., 1978-81; psychotherapist Marsalin Inst., Holliston, Mass., 1981-84; coord. dual diagnosis program Arbor Hosp., Boston, 1984-87; coord. outpatient addictions svcs. New Eng. Meml. Hosp., Stoneham, Mass., 1987—; mem. adv. coun. Middlesex County Driving Under the Influence of

Liquor Program, Waltham, Mass., 1990—. Fellow Am. Orthopsychiat. Assn.; mem. APA (assoc.), Nat. Assn. Alcoholism and Drug Abuse Counselors, Mass. Psychol. Assn. (assoc.), Mass. Com. Voluntary Cert. Alcoholsm Counselors, Mass. Assn. Alcoholism Counselors, Mass. Mental Health Counselors Assn. Office: New Eng Meml Hosp Dept Psychiat Svcs 5 Woodland Rd # 9102 Stoneham MA 02180-9102

CORBETT, ROY GILMAN, museum administrator; b. Colebrook, N.H., Jan. 4, 1932; s. Gerald Albert and Doris Imogene (Keene) C.; m. Jean Charlotte Greig, June 19, 1954; children: James Douglas, Kathryn Ann (Kelly), Pamela Jean. BS with highest honors, Springfield Coll., 1954; MS, Washington State U., 1955; cert. advanced grad. study, R.I. Coll., 1970. Commd. 2d lt. U.S. Marines, 1956, advanced through grades to col., 1978; art. battery comdr. 2d Marine Div., Camp LeJeune, N.C., 1964-65; rifle co. comdr., fire support coord. 1st Marine Div., Republic of Vietnam, 1966-67; asst. prof. Brown U., Providence, 1967-70; ops. officer 3d Marine Div., Okinawa, Japan, 1971-72; exec. officer, br. head Hdqrs. U.S. Marine Corps., Arlington, Va., 1972-76; art. bn. comdr., asst. chief staff 2d Marine Div., Camp LeJeune, N.C., 1976-79; dir. hdqrs. support div. Hdqrs. U.S. Marine Corps., Arlington, 1979-82; asst. dir. The Walters Art Gallery, Balt., 1982—. Decorated Legion of Merit, Meritorious Svc. Medal, Navy Commendation Medal with Combat "V". Mem. Ret. Officers Assn., Marine Corps Assn., Assn. Art Mus. Adminstrs. Republican. Baptist. Home: 1704 Woodlore Rd Annapolis MD 21401-6568 Office: The Walters Art Gallery 600 N Charles St Baltimore MD 21201-5185

CORCORAN, BERNADETTE ELLEN, school counselor; b. Buffalo, Nov. 15, 1947; d. M. Joseph and Bernadette Grace (Shyne) C. BA, Canisius Coll., Buffalo, 1969; EdM, SUNY, Buffalo, 1972; CAS, State U. Coll., Buffalo, 1985. Nat. cert. counselor; cert. secondary lang. arts and sch. counseling, N.Y. Secondary lang. arts tchr. Kensington High Sch., Buffalo, 1969-72; sch. counselor Buffalo Pub. Schs. Dist. 79 and St. Columba Sch., 1972-82; secondary lang. arts tchr. Triangle Acad. 28, Buffalo, 1982-84; sch. counselor Coll. Learning Lab./Campus West, Buffalo, 1984-85; sch. counselor and asst. to dir. guidance and counseling svc Buffalo Pub. Schs. Triangle Acad. 28, 18, 33, 1985—; mem. profl. advisement com. Monsignor Carr Inst., 1989—. Co-chmn. coll. day com. Community Action Orgn., Buffalo, 1985—; mem. career day com. Buffalo Urban League, 1985—; mem. exploring/career awareness com. Boy Scouts Am., Buffalo, 1988—. Recipient Exemplary Counseling Practice award N.Y. State Sch. Counselors Assn., 1987; named Counselor of the Yr. Coll. Edn., Niagara U., 1988, Outstanding Community Svc., Community Action Orgn., 1988. Mem. NEA, Am. Sch. Counselor Assn., Am. Assn. for Counseling and Devel., BuffaloSch. Counselors Assn. (pres. 1987-88), Western N.Y. Assn. for Counseling & Devel. (pres. 1987-88), N.Y. State Assn. for Counseling and Devel. (Region I chair 1987-89), N.Y. State Sch. Counselor Assn. (pres.-elect 1991—), Buffalo Tchrs. Fedn, N.Y. NEA, Phi Delta Kappa. Democrat. Roman Catholic. Home: 100 E Depew Ave Buffalo NY 14214 Office: Buffalo Pub Schs 807 City Hall Buffalo NY 14202-3308

CORCORAN, J. WALTER, communications executive; b. Rochester, N.Y., Apr. 24, 1938; s. Walter J. and Marguerite (McDermott) C.; m. Joan V. Melville, Aug. 21, 1965; children: Christine, Daniel, Denise. BA, St. Bernard's Coll., 1960; LLB, Cornell U., 1964. Pres. Philips Credit Corp., N.Y.C., 1976—. Bd. dirs. Boys Scouts Am., Greenwich, Conn., 1985—, Celutel, Inc., The New 42nd St., Inc.; chmn. O'Casey Theater Found. Mem. Union League Club. Office: Philips Credit Corp 100 E 42d St New York NY 10017

CORD, STEVEN B., foundation administrator; b. N.Y.C., July 22, 1928; s. Mandel E. and Bertha T. Cord; children: Emily, Louise, Daniel. EdD, Columbia U., 1962. Prof. Indiana U. of Pa., 1962-86; pres. Henry George Found. Am., Columbia, Md., 1986—; dir. Henry George Sch., N.Y.C., 1979—, Henry George Inst., N.Y.C., 1980—, Robert Schalkenbach Found., N.Y.C., 1981—; dir. rsch. Ctr. for the Study of Econs., 1980—. Author: Henry George: Dreamer or Realist?, 1965, rev. edit., 1984, Catalyst, 1979, Evidence for Land Value Taxation, 1987. Home: 6167 Llanfair Dr Columbia MD 21044 Office: Henry George Found Am 2000 Century Plz # 238 Columbia MD 21044

CORDARO, TOM ANTHONY, not-for-profit association executive, writer; b. Des Moines, Sept. 29, 1954; s. George S. and Angela L. (Sposeto) C.; m. M. Brigid Harren; 1 child, Angela Harren. BS, Iowa State U., 1978. Campus min. Cath. Student Ctr., Ames, Iowa, 1976-83; coord. adult edn. St. Wenceslaus Ch., Cedar Rapids, Iowa, 1985-86; dir. Ctr. for Nonviolent Studies, Omaha, 1986-88, Erie, Pa., 1988—; cons. issues of disarmament and local group devel. Pax Christi. Author: Faith & Resistance, 1985, To Wake the Nations: Nonviolent Direct Action for Personal & Social Transformation, 1990; (booklet) Critical Choices: The Moral Challenges Posed by the Persian Gulf War, 1991, A Shoot Shall Rise Up: Building an Alternative to the New World Order, 1991; (pamphlet) Securing the Nation: Threats to Our Future, 1990; editor: Dear Bishops, 1989; editor Voice of the Prophet, 1979-83, Midwest Resistance Newsletter, 1984-87, Faith & Resistance Newsletter, 1987—. Office: Ctr for Nonviolent Studies 226 Liberty Erie PA 16503

CORDTS, PAUL ROGER, surgeon; b. Cumberland, Md., Sept. 27, 1958; s. Harold J. and Jeanne (Moore) C. BA, Johns Hopkins U., 1980; MD, USUHS, 1984. Diplomate Am. Bd. Surgery. Commd. med. officer U.S. Army, 1980; intern, resident in surgery William Beaumont Army Med. Ctr., El Paso, Tex., 1984-89; advanced through grades to surgeon Munson Army Community Hosp., Ft. Leavenworth, Kans., 1989, mem. staff in surgery, 1989-90; fellow in vascular surgery Boston U. Med. Ctr., Boston, 1990-92. Fellow ACS (assoc.); mem. ODK Nat. Leadership Soc., USUHS Surg. Soc., The Am. Venous Forum. Home: 75 Glen Rd #R-5 Brookline MA 02146 Office: Boston U Med Ctr Dept Vascular Surgery D-5 88 E Newton St Boston MA 02118

CORETH, JOSEPH HERMAN, bank executive; b. San Antonio, Jan. 14, 1937; s. Rudolph C. and Eltha (Zipp) C.; m. Margaret Nowell Graham, June 18, 1960; 1 child, Elizabeth Moore. BS, U.S. Mil. Acad., 1959; MA, Cornell U., 1966; JD, George Washington U., 1989. Bar: Md. 1989, Tex. 1990, D.C. 1990, N.H. 1991. Commd. 2d lt. U.S. Army, 1959, advanced through grades to maj., 1967; assoc. prof. English U.S. Mil. Acad., West Point, N.Y., 1966-69; chief plans officer 4th Inf. Div., An Khe, Vietnam, 1969-70; resigned U.S. Army, 1970; exec. v.p. Nat. Mortgage Corp., Washington, 1970-78; pres. Stannard's, Inc., Silver Spring, Md., 1979-84; v.p., trust officer Riggs Nat. Bank, Washington, 1985—. former trustee, assoc. Grad. U.S. Mil. Acad. Clubs: Metropolitan (Washington); Chevy Chase (Md.). Home: 5508 Park St Chevy Chase MD 20815-7107 Office: Riggs Nat Bank 808 17th St NW Washington DC 20006-3910

COREY, ELIAS JAMES, chemistry educator; b. Methuen, Mass., July 12, 1928; s. Elias and Tina (Hashem) C.; m. Claire Higham, Sept. 14, 1961; children: David, John, Susan. BS, MIT, 1948, PhD, 1951; AM (hon.), Harvard U., 1959; DSc (hon.), U. Chgo., 1968, Hofstra U., 1974, Oxford U., 1982, U. Liege, 1985, U. Ill., 1985. From instr. to asst. prof. U. Ill., Champaign-Urbana, 1951-55, prof., 1955-59; prof. chemistry Harvard U., Cambridge, Mass., 1959—, Sheldon Emory prof., 1968—. Contbr. articles to profl. jours. Bd. dirs. phys. sci. Alfred P. Sloan Found., 1967-72; mem. sci. adv. bd. dirs. Robert A. Welch Found. Recipient Intrasci. Found. award, 1968, Ernest Guenther award in chemistry of essentials oils and related products, 1968, Harrison Howe award, 1971, Ciba Found. medal, 1972, Evans award Ohio State U., 1972, Linus Pauling award, 1973, Dickson prize in sci. Carnegie Mellon U., 1973, George Ledlie prize in sci. Harvard U., 1973, Nichols medal, 1977, Buchman award Calif. Inst. Tech., 1978, Franklin medal in sci. Franklin Inst., 1978, Sci. Achievement award CCNY, 1979, J.G. Kirkwood award, Yale U., 1980, Chem. Pioneer award, Am. Inst. Chemists, 1981, Wolf prize (chem.), Wolf Found., 1986, Japan prize, 1989, Nat. Med. Sci., 1988, Nobel prize in chemistry, 1990, Gold Medal Award, AIC, 1990, numerous others; fellow Swiss-Am. Exch., 1957, Guggenheim Found., 1957-58, 68-69, Alfred P. Sloan Found., 1956-59. Mem. Am. Acad. Arts and Scis., AAAS, Am. Chem. Soc. (award in synthetic chemistry 1971, Pure Chemistry award 1960, Fritzche award 1968, Md. sect. Remsen award 1974, Arthur C. Cope award 1976), Nat. Acad. Sci., Sigma Xi. Office: Harvard U Dept Chemistry Cambridge MA 02138

COREY, JOHN R., business executive; b. Charleston, W.Va., Apr. 23, 1946; s. Guy L. and Mabel F. (Grafton) C.; m. Sharon Eva Perrine, Mar. 29, 1970; children: John Thomas, Rebecca Lynn, Catherine Grace. BSJ, W. Va. U., 1969; MA in Law and Justice, U. Pitts., 1991; postgrad., W.Va. U., 1969-72. With sales Montgomery Ward, 1972-74; info. dir. W.Va. Air Pollution Control Commn., 1974-76; with ins. sales and brokerage Met. Life, Conn. Mut., 1976—; with real estate sales Northwood Better Homes and Gardens Realty, 1978—; dir. communication Metromountain Assocs., 1979—, pres., 1991—. Water safety instr. ARC, 1968—. Mem. Pub Rels. Student Soc. Am., Pub. Rels. Soc. Am., Soc. Profl. Journalists, USCG Aux. Flotilla 7-1, Am. Legion, Ancient Mystic Order Samaritans, Internat. Order Odd Fellows, Order of Arrow, Nat. Eagle Scouts Assn. (life), Tall Cedars Lebanon, Grottos of North Am., Gideons Internat., W.Va. Scenic Trails Assn., Warrior Trail Assn., King Solomon Single SideBand Radio Club, Masons (worshipful master 1991, most excellent high priest 1989-90, zernbbabel apron), Shriners (pres. Downtown Luncheon Club 1992). Methodist. Home: 937 Bridgewater Dr Pittsburgh PA 15216-1705 Office: Metromountain Assocs Ltd PO Box 14500 Pittsburgh PA 15234-0500

COREY, MELODY LANE, sales executive; b. Sewickey, Pa.; d. Frederick Hale Stierheim and Sue Ann (Taylor) Colburn; m. Robert Crimmins; children: Taylor Catherine, Alexander Crimmins. BA, Stone Hill Coll., 1986. Asst. circulation mgr. Progress Newspapers, Horsham, Pa., 1973-75; client svc. rep. Lab. Procedures, King of Prussia, Pa., 1975-78; customer svc. rep. Teaching Resources, Hingham, Mass., 1978-80; mdse. distbr. Commonwealth Trading, Stoughton, Mass., 1980-82; sr. analyst sales force automation Serono Labs., Norwell, Mass., 1982—; Chmn. Serono Software Com., Randolph, 1985-86, Town Computerization Study Com., Lakeville, Mass., 1987—. Active, bd. dirs. Pets Are Worth Saving, Inc., Lakeville, 1986; activities coach Socialization for Today's Adult Retarded, North Wales, Mass., 1975-76. Roman Catholic.

CORI, RONALD JOSEPH, human resources executive; b. Drexel Hill, Pa., July 24, 1956; s. Joseph Robert and Carmela N. (Monzo) C.; m. Kathryn Lee Campanella, Nov. 19, 1988; 1 child, Robert. BS, St. Joseph's U., Phila., 1978; MS, Radford (Va.) U., 1980. Occupational analyst Pa. Dept. Labor and Industry, Harrisburg, 1980-81; personnel coord. Donnelley Printing Co., Lancaster, Pa., 1981-84; employment specialist Eagleville (Pa.) Hosp., 1984-85; asst. personnel mgr. Kennedy Meml. Hosps., Stratford, N.J., 1985-88; dir. human resources Nazareth Hosp., Phila., 1988—. Mem. Phila. Hosps. Human Resources Soc., Am. Soc. Hosp. Human Resources Assn. Office: Nazareth Hosp 2601 Holme Ave Philadelphia PA 19152-2096

CORIATY, GEORGE MICHAEL, clergyman, vicar general, chancellor, cultural center executive; b. Sao Paulo, Brazil, Jan. 1, 1933; came to Can., 1960, naturalized, 1967; s. Michael A. and Marie (Nassif) C.; B.A., St. Savior's Sem., Saida, Lebanon, 1950; Ph.D. in Social Psychology and Polit. Sci., 1977; postgrad. in canon law Strasbourg U., France, 1986—; Ph.D. in Byzantine Studies (hon.), Internat. U. Found. Ordained priest Roman Catholic Ch., 1956; prof. St. Savior's Sem., Lebanon, 1952-56; asst. pastor Our Lady Annunciation Ch., Boston, 1957-60; pastor St. Savior's Ch., Montreal, Que., Can., 1960—; apostolic visitor, patriarchal vicar for Melkites in Can., 1972—; nominated judge for Ecclesiastical Maronite Tribunal in Can., 1987; chaplain Golden Age Assn., 1985; organizer, administrator Community Youth Club, 1986; superior Basilian Order in Can.; founder Our Lady Assumption Parish, Toronto, Ont., Can., Our Lady of Lebanon Parish, Quebec City, Que., St. George's Parish, Vancouver, B.C., Can., 1976; founder Middle-East Immigrant Aid Soc. Can., 1963; mem. multiculturalism Council Can., Que. Region; founder, pres. Centre Multicultural Bois de Boulogne, 1973—; mem. ecumenical movement. Decorated mem. Order of Can.; Highest Medal of Merit (Egypt); named First Citizen of Montreal, 1973; recipient Bronze medal for peace Albert Einstein Internat. Acad. Found., 1986. Mem. Can. Canon Law Soc., House of Trade of Montreal, Can. and Am. Hist. and Geog. Assn., U.S. Tennis Assn. (hon. life), Assn. Quebeçoise de la Solidarité Internationale (exec. mem.), Council of the Internat. Scholarship Found.-Que. Founder, pub., editor Trait D'Union Rev., 1964; founder Byzantine Mus., 1975. Office: 329 Viger St, Montreal, PQ Canada H2X 1R6

CORKERN, WILTON CLAUDE, JR., conservationist; b. Bogalusa, La., Sept. 19, 1946; s. Wilton Claude and Ruth Ann (Tynes) C.; m. Mary Bruce Batte, June 12, 1971; children: Mary Virginia Tynes, Sarah Ruthe Batte. BA, George Washington U., 1974, MPhil, 1981, PhD, 1984. Program asst. NEH, Washington, 1974-75, pub. info. specialist, 1975-76, spl. projects officer, 1976-79; editor Am. Studies Internat., Washington, 1979-82; assoc. dir. Consortium of Univs. of Washington Met. Area, 1982-87, v.p., 1987-90; sr. v.p., gen. mgr. Univ. Support Svcs., Washington, 1987; exec. v.p. Accokeek (Md.) Found., 1990—; pres. Galaxy, Inc., Accokeek, 1990—. Editor: Ecosystem Farm, 1990, The Nation's River, 1990. Trustee Corina Higginson Trust, Washington, 1989—, Ctr. for Advanced Study of Ams., Washington, 1987-89, D.C. Law Students in Ct., Washington, 1987-89; pres. Alexandria (Va.) Assn., 1984-87, Alexandria Libr. Co., 1987-90; treas. Lyceum Co., Alexandria, 1984-90; mem. Alexandria Archaeol. Commn., 1983-89, Alexandria Bicentennial Commn., 1979-83; mem. Leadership Washington, Inc., 1990. With USN, 1966-71. Am. Studies Internat. fellow, 1979. Mem. So. Md. Mus. Assn., Am. Studies Assn., Nat. Trust Hist. Preservation, Nat. Parks and Conservation Assn., Land Trust Alliance, Md. Mus. Com., City Club Washington. Democrat. Episcopalian. Office: Accokeek Found 3400 Bryan Point Rd Accokeek MD 20607-9654

CORLE, FREDERIC WILLIAM, II, computer manufacturing executive; b. Phila., June 20, 1945; s. Frederic William and Marjorie (Dudley) C.; m. Pamela Gaus White, Apr. 16, 1983 (div. May 1987); children: Alison Gaus, Louise Armour. BA, Marietta Coll., 1967; MBA, U. Denver, 1973. Supply mgmt. officer Fed. Deposit Ins. Corp., Washington, 1970-72; program analyst Exec. Office of Pres., Washington, 1973-77; dir. Commn. on Budget U.S. Ho. of Reps., Washington, 1977-78; v.p. City Sports Mgmt., Inc., Washington, 1978-82; asst. to adminstr. White House, Washington, 1983-84; dir. mktg. Interand Corp., Washington, 1984-85; spl. asst. Dept. of Interior, Washington, 1985-86; mgr. fed. mktg. Datapoint Corp., Washington, 1987-89; chief exec. officer Mktg. Solutions Internat., Inc., Washington, 1989—; bd. dirs., dir. fed. mktg. Sun Microsystems Fed. Inc., Washington, 1991—. Served as lt. (j.g.) USN, 1967-70. Mem. Armed Forces Communications and Electronics Assn., Am. Electronics Assn. (govt. and bus. com.), Nat. Assn. Mfrs., Calif. Policy Steering Com., City Tavern Club, Army Navy Country Club. Republican. Episcopalian.

CORLEY, FARRELL WAYNE, naval officer, test pilot; b. Elk City, Okla., Dec. 28, 1949; s. Elisha Almon and Erma Lenora (Brice) C. MS in Aerospace Engring., U. Okla., 1974; MS in Aero. Engring. with honors, Naval Postgrad. Sch., Monterey, Calif., 1983; grad. with distinction, U.S. Naval Test Pilot Sch., 1984. Commd. ensign USN, 1974; naval aviator, 1976; fighter pilot USS Independence, Virginia Beach, Va., 1976-79; F-14 fighter pilot USS Kitty Hawk, San Diego, 1979-82; test pilot, program mgr. Naval Air Test Ctr., Patuxent River, Md., 1984-86; F-14 fighter pilot, strike leader USS Carl Vinson, San Diego, 1986-89; chief test pilot U.S. Naval Test Pilot Sch., Patuxent River, 1989—; test pilot F-14 flight tests, 1985; F-14 program mgr. and chmn. F-14 Aircrew Systems Adv. Panel, 1984-86. Contbr. articles to profl. jours. Mem. AIAA., Soc. Exptl. Test Pilots, Tailhook Assn., Exptl. Aircraft Assn. Home: 99 Pine Needle Ct California MD 20619-9723 Office: US Naval Test Pilot Sch Patuxent River MD 20670

CORLEY, LESLIE M., investment banker; b. Chgo., May 14, 1946; s. Leslie T. and Lorena M. (Turner) C. BS in Aero. and Astronautical Engring., U. Ill., 1969; MBA, Harvard U., 1971. Fin. analyst Exxon Chemical Co., N.Y.C., 1969-71; securities analyst Fidelity Investments, Boston, 1972-75, sr. securities analyst, 1975-77; mgr. corp. planning and devel. Norton Simon Inc., N.Y.C., 1977-81; v.p. Kelso and Co., N.Y.C., 1981-82, gen. prtnr., 1982-88; pres. LM Capital Securities, Inc., N.Y., N.Y., Fla., 1992—; chmn. LM Foods, Inc., N.Y.C., 1990—, Roberts Bros., Inc., Winter Haven, Fla., 1990—. Adv. bd. 21st Century Polit. Action Com., N.Y.C., 1985; dir. Kelso and Co. Polit. Action Com., N.Y.C.,1986, Friends of Davis Ctr., Inc., N.Y.c., 1989—; treas. Urban Equities Mgmt. Corp., Boston, 1971-72; treas. Manhattan Community Bd. #9, 1991-92. Fellow Harvard Grad. Sch. Bus. Adminstrn., 1969, recipient scholarships, Pullman Found. Chgo., 1964, U. Ill., 1964; named James Scholar U. Ill., 1965. Mem. Harvard Club, Alpha Phi Alpha, Phi Eta Sigma, Sigma Gramma Tau. Home: 60 Hamilton Ter New York NY 10031-6403 Office: LM Capital Corp 730 5th Ave New York NY 10019-4105

CORMACK, ALLAN MACLEOD, physicist, educator; b. Johannesburg, South Africa, Feb. 23, 1924; came to U.S., 1957, naturalized, 1966; s. George and Amelia (MacLeod) C.; m. Barbara Jeanne Seavey, Jan. 6, 1950; children: Margaret, Jean, Robert. BS, U. Cape Town, South Africa, 1944, M.Sc., 1945; research student, Cambridge (Eng.) U., 1947-50. Lectr. U. Cape Town, 1946-47, 1950-56; research fellow Harvard U., 1956-57; asst. prof. physics Tufts U., Medford, Mass., 1957-60; assoc. prof. Tufts U., 1960-64, prof., 1964-80, University prof., 1980—; researcher nuclear and particle physics, computed tomography and related math. topics. Recipient Ballou medal Tufts U., 1978, Nobel prize in medicine and physiology, 1979, Medal of Merit U. Cape Town, 1980, Nat. Medal Sci., 1990. Fellow AAAS, Am. Phys. Soc., Am. Acad. Arts and Sci., Royal Soc. South Africa (fgn.); mem. South African Phys. Soc., NAS, Am. Assn. Physicists in Medicine (hon.), Inst. Medicine, Sigma Xi. Office: Tufts U Physics Dept Medford MA 02155

CORMIER, ROBERT JOSEPH, secondary education educator; b. Worcester, Mass., Aug. 3, 1941; s. Norman Paul and Anita Marie (Lambert) Bernard; m. Judith Hope Curran, Sept. 20, 1962 (div. Jan. 1989); children: Kenneth, Amy, Scott; m. Carol Lynn Tansey, Dec. 22, 1990. BA in History, Assumption Coll., 1969, MA in History, 1970, cert. of advanced grad. studies, 1976. Adminstr., tchr., coach Assumption Prep. Sch., Worcester, 1963-70; tchr. Grafton (Mass.) High Sch., 1970-91, Shrewsbury (Mass.) High Sch., 1991—; edn. cons. You. Inc. Intensive Probation Program, Worcester, 1971-77. Author: (computer program) HYPERTOWN, 1989. Member Shrewsbury Sch. Com., 1971-83; mem. exec. bd. Mass. Assn. Sch. Coms., Boston, 1977-81; chmn. Mass. Assn. Sch. Community Fed. Rels., Boston, 1977-80. With USAF, 1959-63. Named one of Outstanding New Eng. Tchr.'s, John F. Kennedy Libr., 1991. Mem. ASCD, Old Sturbridge Village Rsch. Libr. Soc., Nat. Coun. for Social Studies, Shrewsbury History Soc. (bd. dirs.).

CORN, JACK W., oil company executive; b. Cobb County, Ga., Oct. 8, 1929; s. Ezra and Sarah (Pruitt) C.; m. Ann McConnel; children: Dana Corn Crissey, William E., Beth Ann. BBA, U. Ga., 1953. Pres., chief exec. officer Quaker State Corp., Oil City, Pa., 1974-86, vice chmn. to pres., chmn. and chief exec. officer, 1988—; mem. emeritus Smyra Bank and Trust Co. Active 1st Bapt. Ch., Marietta, Ga. With USAF, 1953-56. Mem. Am. Petroleum Inst. (bd. dirs.), Allegheny Mountain Health Systems, Marietta Country Club, Georgian Club, Oil City Club, Wanango Country Club. Home: 9 Shady Oak Ln Oil City PA 16301-3045 Office: Quaker State Corp 255 Elm St Oil City PA 16301-1412*

CORN, MORTON, environmental engineer, educator; b. N.Y.C., Oct. 18, 1933; s. Julius and Sophie (Haber) C.; m. Jacqueline Karnell, Aug. 21, 1955; children—Matthew Irwin, Frederick Eliot. B.S. in Chem. Engring, Cooper Union, 1955; M.S., Harvard U., 1956, Ph.D., 1961. Asst. san. engr. USPHS, Cin., 1956-58; research asso. Harvard, 1960-61; asst. prof. U. Pitts., 1962-65, assoc. prof., 1965-66, prof. Grad. Sch. Pub. Health and Sch. Engring., 1967-79; prof. and div. head environ. health engring. Sch. Hygiene and Public Health, Johns Hopkins U., Balt., 1980—; pres. Morton Corn; Assocs., Cons. Engrs., 1977—; cons. div. biology and medicine AEC, 1965-74; chmn. air pollution rsch. grants com. EPA, 1968-71, mem. sci. adv. bd., 1978-84; mem. com. on biol. effects air pollution NAS, 1971, mem. com. risk assessment, 1982-83; mem. expert panel occupational health WHO, 1973—; asst. sec. labor for occupational safety and health U.S. Dept. Labor, 1975-77; mem. Allegheny County Air Pollution Adv. Com., 1967-72; mem. nat. adv. com. health vital stats. Dept. HHS 1979-81, mine health rsch. adv. com. Nat. Inst. Occupational Safety and Health, 1986-89, GM/UAW joint health and safety adv. com., 1988—; chmn. OTA Commn. Preventing Injury and Illness in the Workplace, 1982-84; chmn. tech. adv. bd. Clean Sites, Inc., Alexandria, Va., 1984-87; trustee Assoc. Univ., Inc., 1991. Editor: Adhesion of Dusts and Powders by A.D. Zimon, 1970; mem. editorial bd. Excerpta Medica, 1965, Internat. Jour. Air-Water Pollution, 1965-87, Am. Jour. Indsl. Medicine, 1982—, Jour. Applied Indsl. Hygiene, 1985—; contbr. articles to profl. jours. Chmn. Gov. of Md.'s Toxic Coun., 1986-89. NSF postdoctoral fellow U. London, 1961-62; WHO fellow, 1970; Guggenheim fellow, 1972. Fellow Am. Pub. Health Assn.; mem. Am. Inst. Chem. Engrs., Air Pollution Control Assn., Am. Indsl. Hygiene Assn., AAAS, Am. Conf. Govt. Indsl. Hygienists (chmn. 1983-84), Sigma Xi. Home: 1714 Eutaw Pl Baltimore MD 21217-3730 Office: Johns Hopkins U 615 N Wolfe St Baltimore MD 21205

CORNELIUS, CYNTHIA JEANNE, podiatrist; b. Oak Park, Ill., Aug. 17, 1952; d. George Paul and Lee Jeanne (Sponholz) Wnuck; m. Russell Lee Cornelius, Dec. 17, 1988. BA, Valparaiso U., 1973; D Podiatric Medicine, N.Y. Coll. Podiatric Medicine, 1989. Pvt. practice Brookfield (Conn.) Podiatry, 1990—; adj. staff Danbury Hosp. Vol. dir. Rye (N.Y.) City TV, 1991. Mem. Am. Podiatric Med. Assn. Republican. Mem. Soc. Friends. Office: Brookfield Podiatry 246 Federal Rd Ste 21C Brookfield CT 06804-2647

CORNELIUS, LESTER ERNEST, protective coating company executive; b. Jamaica, N.Y., July 27, 1953; s. Lester Henry Cornelius and Irene Veronica (Dupont) Fortin; m. Reinette Frances Galchus, July 25, 1981; children: Meredith Leigh, Dale Elaine, Lester Terence. AAS, N.Y.C. Community Coll., 1973. Cert. ophthalmic dispenser, mfg. engr. Gen. mgr. Davis Optical Lab., Mineola, N.Y., 1973-75; v.p. Davis Optical Lab., Mineola, 1975-79; sr. lab mgr. Eyeglasses, Inc., N.Y.C., 1979-85; v.p. research and devel. Eyeglasses, Inc., Long Island City, N.Y., 1986—; pres. Optical Technologies Corp., Long Island City, 1987—. Inventor protective coatings for optics. Fellow Nat. Acad. Opticians; mem. Am. Bd. Opticians, N.Y. Soc. Coating Tech., N.Y. Soc. Dispensing Opticians, Soc. Mfg. Engrs., Intertel Club (regional dir. N.E. chpt. 1980-83). Republican. Lutheran. Home: 297 Raff Ave Carle Place NY 11514-1119 Office: 47-00 33rd St Long Island City NY 11101

CORNELIUS, RICHARD DEAN, chemistry educator; b. Chgo., Sept. 18, 1947; s. Kenneth Cremer and Hollie (Tupper) C.; m. Beverly Babl, Sept. 5, 1970; children: Tamarine, Kimbrin, Quinn. BA, Carleton Coll., 1969; PhD, U. Iowa, 1974. Rsch. assoc. U. Wis., Madison, 1969-74; asst. prof. chemistry Wichita (Kans.) State U., 1977-82, assoc. prof., 1982-85; prof. chemistry, chmn. dept. Lebanon Valley Coll., Annville, Pa., 1985—; vis. assoc. prof. U. Nice, France, fall 1983. Contbr. articles to profl. jours.; author computer software for chemistry edn. Mem. Am. Chem. Soc. Office: Lebanon Valley Coll Garber Sci Ctr Annville PA 17003-0501

CORNELIUSSEN, PÅL, art director, graphic designer; b. Oslo, Norway, Dec. 28, 1964; s. Peter and Åse-Liv (Risdal) C. Student, Royal Norwegian Air Force Acad, 1984; grad. with distinction, London Sch. Fgn. Trade, 1985; BFA with honors, Parsons Sch. Design, 1991. Art dir. asst. Kampanje Plan Advt., Oslo, 1983-84; shipbroker Davies & Newman Ltd., London, 1985-86, R.S. Platou Shipbrokers, Oslo, 1987; designer Koppel & Scher, N.Y.C., 1990-91; art dir. Metzdorf/Stone Advt., N.Y.C., 1991, Rosenfeld, Sirowitz, Humphrey & Strauss, N.Y.C., 1991—. 2d lt. Norwegian Air Force, 1984. Named Most Valuable Instr., Royal Norwegian Air Force, 1984. Mem. Am. Inst. Graphic Artists. Home: 135 W 16th St Apt 21 New York NY 10011 Office: Rosenfeld Sirowitz Humphrey & Strauss 111 5th Ave 7th Fl New York NY 10003

CORNELL, ALAN, research and product development consultant; b. Fall River, Mass., May 4, 1929; s. Herman and Florence (Lipsky) C.; m. Marcia Persky, Sept. 14,1952; children: James S., Andrew P., Lawrence J. BS, U. Mass., 1951; PhD, MIT, 1961. Sr. scientist Philip Morris Rsch. Ctr., Richmond, Va., 1961-67; mgr. food sci. Ralston Purina, St. Louis, 1967-69; v.p. R&D Consol. Cigar Co., N.Y.C., 1969-85; mgmt. cons. in rsch. and product devel. Bloomfield, Conn., 1985—; also cons. in chem. products, 1985-92; sr. scientist Atlantic Environ. Svcs., Inc., Colchester, Conn., 1992—; cons. environmental chemistry, chem. products; cons. A.D. Little, Cambridge, Mass., 1988. Contbr. articles to profl. jours. Bd. dirs. MIT Enterprise Forum, 1990—. Cpl., U.S. Army, 1951-53. Home and Office: 10 Arnold Dr Bloomfield CT 06002-1608

CORNELL, HOWARD VERNON, ecology educator; b. Berwyn, Ill., Apr. 13, 1947; s. Howard V. and Mertle LaMerle (Worbington) C.; m. Sarah Rebecca Peterson, Aug. 24, 1971; 1 child, Christopher Richard. BA, Tufts U., 1969; PhD, Cornell U., 1975. Asst. prof. U. Del., Newark, 1975-83, assoc. prof., 1983—, prof., 1990—. Bd. editors, Ecology and Ecol. Monographs, 1979-81; contbr. articles to profl. jours. NSF grantee, 1979-90. Mem. Am. Soc. Naturalists, Ecol. Soc. Am. Office: U Del Sch Life and Health Scis Newark DE 19716

CORNELL, JOHN WILLIAM, construction company executive; b. Phila., June 6, 1929; s. John W. and Frances (Doriss) C.; grad. Germantown Acad., 1946; B.S. in Civil Engring., U. Pa., 1950; m. Nancy Fleming, Sept. 8, 1956; 1 child, Nina Frances. Draftsman Howard, Needles, Tamen & Bergendoff, Kansas City, Mo., 1950-51; engr., estimator J.S. Cornell & Son Inc., Phila., 1951-63, v.p., 1963-77, chmn. bd., 1977—; cons. Phila. area. Mem. bldg. adv. bd. Pa. Dept. Labor and Industry, 1964—, mem. Carpenters Co. City and County Phila., 1959—, pres., 1971; bd. dirs. Carson Valley Sch., Chestnut Hill Hist. Soc., Assn. Preservation Tech. Phila. chpt., Germantown (Pa.) Hist. Soc., Preservation Coalition, Phila.; trustee Beaver Coll. With AUS, 1954-56. Registered profl. engr., Pa. Mem. ASCE, Gen. Bldg. Contractors Assn. (dir. 1973-75), Union League. Republican. Episcopalian (vestryman). Home: 1107 Chestnut Ln Flourtown PA 19031-2032 Office: 1528 Cherry St Philadelphia PA 19102

CORNELL, KEITH ARTHUR, management consultant; b. Dhahran, Saudi Arabia, May 19, 1957; s. Vernon Arthur and Bonnie Lou (Richey) C.; m. Julie Jaye Lydon, May 3, 1980. B.S. in Engring., Harvey Mudd Coll., 1978; M.S. in Indsl. Engring., Carnegie-Mellon U., 1980. Mktg. coord. United Controls div. Envirotech, Santa Fe Springs, Calif., 1978; cons. Mgmt. Adv. Services, Price Waterhouse & Co., L.A., 1979, mgr. mgmt. adv. svcs., Ft. Worth, 1982-84; cons. Braxton Assocs., Boston, 1980; asst. to v.p. planning Western Co. of N.Am., Ft. Worth, 1981-82, contr. Pacesetter Tool div., Houston, 1982; pres. DSA Fin. Corp., Dallas, 1984-85; dir. mktg. and product svcs. Hall Fin. Group, Dallas, 1985-86; pres. MacDonald Masi Fin. Corp., Dallas, 1986-88; assoc. Marakon Assocs., San Francisco, 1989-90, mgr. Greenwich, Conn., 1990-92, sr. mgr., Stamford, Conn., 1992—; bd. dirs. Planned Investments, San Francisco, M-Power Inc., Dallas, Med. Indsl. Capital, Inc., Mpls. Active Project Bus., Jr. Achievement, 1983-88, 92—. Mem. Assn. MBA Execs., Nat. Soc. Profl. Engrs. Home: 184 Southgate Rd Southport CT 06490-1424

CORNELL, LAWRENCE EVERETT, school system administrator; b. Westport, Mass., Oct. 23, 1933; s. Everett William and Helen Marjorie (Tripp) C.; m. Shirley Reed Doane, June 24, 1956; children: Kathie Dawn, Gregg Doane, Laurie Beth, Scott Doane. BS, U. Mass., 1955; MEd, Bridgewater State U., 1962. Cert. math. tchr., administr., Mass. Math. tchr. Westport High Sch., 1957-59, Smith Sch., Lincoln, Mass., 1960-61; head math. dept. Old Rochester Regional High Sch., Mattapoisett, Mass., 1961-67; adminstrv. intern Concord-Carlisle (Mass.) High Sch., 1967-68; coord. Project COD, New Bedford, Mass., 1968-71; prin. Mullen-Hall Sch., Falmouth, Mass., 1971-77; asst. supt. Sch. Adminstrv. Unit 22, Hanover, N.H., 1977-82; supt. Burrillville Pub. Sch., Harrisville, R.I., 1982-87, Gardner (Mass.) Pub. Sch., 1987-91; cons. R.I. Schs., 1985-87; prof. R.I. Coll., Providence, 1985-87, Bridgewater ((Mass.) State Coll., 1971-77, Mass. Maritime Acad., 1976-77. Trustee Westport Libr., 1958-61; active Westport Sch. Com., 1963-69, chmn., 1965-66, 68-69; active Gardner United Way, bd. dirs., 1987-91; pres. Am. Cancer Soc., 1989-91. Capt. U.S. Army, 1955-63. Mem. Worcester County Supt. Assn. (pres. 1990-91), Mass. Assn. Sch. Supts. (exec. bd. 1990-91), Rotary (exec. bd. Gardner chpt. 1989-90, Disting. Svc. award 1990). Home: 700 Shore Dr Apt 605 Fall River MA 02721-1075

CORNELL, RALPH LAWRENCE, JR., publishing executive; b. Albany, N.Y., Nov. 26, 1951; s. Ralph Lawrence and Madeline (Hitchcock) C. Student, Purdue U., 1986-87. Mem. housekeeping staff Vets. Hosp., Albany, 1976-78; food svcs. supr. Univ. Aux. Svcs., Albany, 1981-89; owner, editor R.C. Publs., Albany, 1988—. Author: The Moods of Madness, 1985, Midnless Wanderings, 1986, Tales of the Streets, 1992; editor poetry newsletter Ralph's Rev., Opportunity Digest, RC's Stamp Hotline, RC's Mini Rev. With USN, 1971-74. Mem. NRA, Am. Philatelic Soc., Audubon Soc., Albany Art Gallery. Roman Catholic. Home and Office: RC Publs Ste 9 280 State St Albany NY 12210-2138

CORNISH, EDWARD SEYMOUR, magazine editor; b. N.Y.C., Aug. 31, 1927; s. George Anthony and Elizabeth Furniss (McLeod) C.; m. Sally Woodhull, Oct. 12, 1957; children: George Anthony, Jefferson Richard Woodhull, Blake McLeod. Diplome d'etudes, U. Paris, France, 1948; A.B., Harvard U., 1950. Copy boy, cub reporter Evening Star, Washington, 1950-51; staff corr. U.P. Assn., Richmond, Va., 1951-52, Raleigh, N.C., 1952-53, London, 1953-54, Paris, 1954-55, Rome, 1956; staff writer Nat. Geog. Soc., 1957-69; founder, pres. World Future Soc., Washington, 1966—; creator, editor The Futurist Mag., 1966—; editor World Future Soc. Bull., 1968-77; cons. to govt., bus. and ednl. orgns. Author: The Study of the Future, 1977; editor: Resources Directory for America's Third Century, 1977, The Future: A Guide to Information Sources, 1977, 1999: The World of Tomorrow, 1978, Communications Tomorrow, 1982, Global Solutions, 1984, The Computerized Society, 1985, Careers Tomorrow, 1988, The 1990s and Beyond, 1989; editorial cons.: Nat. Goals Rsch. Staff, 1970, White House Report Toward Balanced Growth, 1970. Bd. dirs. World Watch Inst., 1974—; adv. bd. Inst. for Alternative Futures. Mem. Internat. Sci. Writers Assn. Home: 5501 Lincoln St Bethesda MD 20817-3723 Office: World Future Soc 7910 Woodmont Bethesda MD 20814

CORNO, LYN, psychology educator; b. Williams, Ariz., May 25, 1950; d. Edward Eugene and Verla (Hornbacher) C.; m. William Fairfax Herbert, Aug. 4, 1984; children: William Fairfax Herbert Jr., Leigh Carter Herbert. BA, Ariz. State U., 1972; MA, Stanford U., 1977, PhD, 1978. Rsch. assoc. SWRL Edn. Rsch. and Devel., Los Alamitos, Calif., 1972-74, Ctr. for Edn. Rsch. at Stanford, Calif., 1974-77; asst. prof. edn. Stanford U., 1977-82; assoc. prof. edn., psychology Columbia U., N.Y.C., 1982—. Fellow APA, AAAS, Am. Psychol. Soc. Democrat. Episcopalian. Office: Columbia U Tchrs Coll PO Box 25 New York NY 10027-0025

CORNWALL, DEBORAH JOYCE, consulting firm executive, management consultant; b. Wilmington, Del., Dec. 9, 1946; d. Samuel and Norma (Bram) Handloff; m. Barry Newland Cornwall, June 22, 1968; 1 child, Deborah Leigh. BA, Mount Holyoke, 1968; MBA, Boston U., 1975. Editor Houghton Mifflin Co., Boston, 1967-69; editor Harbridge House, Inc., Boston, 1969-73, cons., 1973-74, assoc., 1974-75, sr. assoc., 1975-77, prin., 1977-79, v.p., 1979-81, v.p., div. mgr., 1981-83, sr. v.p., div. mgr., 1983-90; mng. v.p. Korn/Ferry Organizational Cons., Boston, 1991—; mem. mid. mgmt. excellence com. City of Boston, 1986. Mem. Phi Beta Kappa, Beta Gamma Sigma. Office: Korn/Ferry Organizational Cons 75 Federal St Boston MA 02110-1904

CORNWELL, TREVOR, service league executive; b. N.Y.C., June 26, 1964; s. Anthony Ewart Frank and Anne (Christake) C. BA, John Hopkins U., 1987. Scheduling deputy dir. Gary Hart for Pres., Washington, 1983-84; deputy polit. dir. Dem. Senatorial Campaign Com., Washington, 1987; field dir. Hamilton Fish for U.S. Congress, Westchester, N.Y., 1988; campaign dir. Richard Brodsky for County Exec., Westchester, 1989; trial preparation asst. N.Y. County Dist. Atty., N.Y.C., 1990; pres., founder National Service League, Irvington, N.Y., 1990—. Recipient Outstanding Community Svc. Rotary Club, Westchester, 1981, 82. Democrat. Presbyterian. Home: Shadowbrook Irvington NY 10533 Office: Nat Svc League Inc 821 N Broadway Irvington NY 10533

CORRADO, ANTHONY JOSEPH, JR., political science educator; b. Fall River, Mass., Feb. 4, 1957; s. Anthony Joseph and Jeanette Theresa (Drainville) C.; m. Lori Ann Cameron, June 7, 1987. BA, Cath. U. Am., 1979, MA, 1982; PhD, Boston Coll., 1990. Staff mem. Carter-Mondale Presdl. Com., Washington, 1979-80; exec. dir. Capitol Svcs., Washington, 1981-82; dept. to campaign mgr. Mondale for Pres. Com., Washington, 1984; campaign cons. James O'Neil, Atty. Gen. R.I., Providence, 1986; instr. Colby Coll., Waterville, Maine, 1986-89, asst. prof. polit. sci., 1989—; cons. Rolde for Senate Com., Portland, Maine, 1990, Dukakis for Pres. Com., Boston, 1988; project scholar Ctr. for Am. Founding Documents, Boston, 1989—; dir. Maine Humanities Coun. Constn. Inst., Waterville, 1987. Author: Creative Campaigning, 1992; contbr. articles to profl. jours. Nat. campaign coord. Kerrey for Pres. Com., Washington, 1992. Recipient Cath. U. Pres.'s award, 1979. Mem. Am. Polit. Sci. Assn., New Eng. Polit. Sci. Assn. (John C. Donovan prize 1990), Nat. Capitol Hist. Soc. Democrat. Roman catholic. Office: Colby Coll Dept Govt Waterville MD 04901

CORRAO, RICHARD GAETANO, scientist, pharmacist; b. Bklyn., Sept. 9, 1946; s. Antonio Salvatore and Salvatrice Caroline (Intoci) C.; m. Kathleen Anne Knapp, June 5, 1977; children: Carol Susan, Brandalyn Alyce, Jessica Katherine, Sarah Anne. BS in Pharmacy, St. John's U., 1969. Registered pharmacist, N.Y. Rsch. scientist Bristol Labs., Syracuse, N.Y., 1970-74; pharmacist Plaza 81 Pharmacy, Syracuse, 1974-80, Cazenovia (N.Y.) Pharmacy, 1980, Church Drugs, East Syracuse, 1980-90; sr. rsch. scientist Bristol-Myers Squibb Co., Syracuse, 1980—; pharmacist Fay's Pharmacy, Syracuse, 1990—. Mem. Am. Assn. Pharm. Scientists, Delta Sigma Theta (rec. sec. 1966-67, historian 1967-68). Roman Catholic. Home: 109 Teakwood Ln Minoa NY 13116-1125 Office: Bristol-Myers Squibb Co Thompson Rd East Syracuse NY 13057

CORREA, CRAIG ARTHUR, defense company executive; b. Washington, Aug. 30, 1959; s. Manuel Angel and Dolores Lucy (Salato) C.; m. Zita Antoinette Smith, Aug. 19, 1981; children: Sierra Antoinette, Raquel Ashley. BSEE, U. Md., 1984. Asst. staff MIT Lincoln Lab., Lexington, 1984-86; from cons. to sr. cons. Booz, Allen & Hamilton, Inc., Bethesda, Md., 1986-91, assoc., deputy program mgr., 1991; prin. rsch. and devel. initiatives Fairchild Defense Co., Germantown, Md., 1992—; cons. Stratiegic Defense Initiative Orgn., newsletter editor, 1990. Mem. IEEE. Republican. Roman Catholic. Office: Fairchild Def Co 20301 Century Blvd Germantown MD 20874-1182

CORREA-VILLASEÑOR, ADOLFO, epidemiologist, physician; b. Mazatlán, Sinaloa, Mex., Mar. 2, 1946; came to U.S., 1961; s. Adolfo and Estela (Villaseñor) Correa; m. Ana Isabel Alfaro, June 2, 1978. MS, U. Calif., San Diego, 1970, MD, 1974; MPH, Johns Hopkins U., 1981, PhD, 1987. Diplomate Am. Bd. Pediatrics, Am. Bd. Preventive Medicine. Intern San Francisco Gen. Hosp., 1974-75; resident in pediatrics U. Calif., San Francisco, 1975-77, chief resident in pediatrics, 1977-78; epidemic intelligence service officer Ctr. for Disease Control, Atlanta, 1978-80; resident in preventive medicine Johns Hopkins Sch. Hygiene and Pub. Health, Balt., 1980-83, asst. prof. epidemiology, 1987—, asst. prof. pediatrics, 1988-92, asst. prof. population dynamics, 1990—; cons. Pan Am. Health Orgn., Washington, 1984-85, NIH, Bethesda, Md., 1988, Population Dynamics, 1990—, World Bank, Washington, 1990. Mem. Soc. for Epidemiologic Rsch., Am. Acad. Pediatrics, Math. Assn. Am. Home: 419 Kensington Rd Baltimore MD 21229-2436 Office: Johns Hopkins U Dept Epidemiology 615 N Wolfe St Baltimore MD 21205

CORREIA, ALBERTO ABRANTES, marketing executive; b. Milford, Mass., Nov. 16, 1956; s. Alberto Filipe and Julia Abrantes (Simones) C.; m. Sharon Ann Haaf; 1 child, Alexis Abrantes. BS, Coll. Holy Cross, Worcester, Mass., 1978. With Waters, Milford, Mass., 1976-77; sales rep. Waters Assocs., Milford, Mass., 1978-79, sales mgr., 1980; dir. sales Millipore, Paris, 1981-84, Xydex Inc., Bedford, Mass., 1985-87; dir. product mgmt. Genex Co., Gaithersburg, Md., 1988-89; Zymark, Hopkinton, Mass., 1990-91, dir. engring., 1991-92; dir. sales Zymark, Hopkinton, 1992—. Home: 3 Leah Ln Milford MA 01757-1276 Office: Zymark Zymark Ctr Hopkinton MA 01748

CORREIA, CLAUDINE MARIA, program officer; b. Paramaribo, Suriname, Dec. 23, 1954; came to U.S., 1985; d. Napoleon and Romana (Flu) C. MS in Econ. cum laude, Cath. U. Brabant, Tilburg, The Netherlands, 1982. Jr. profl. officer UN Devel. Program, Kingston, Jamaica, 1984, 85; project officer UN Devel. Fund for Women, N.Y.C., 1986-88, program officer, 1988—. Author: Development of Production Relations in Central America, 1982. Mem. NAFE, Assn. Caribbean Econs., Caribbean Assn. for Feminist Rsch. and Action. Home: 171 Pearsall Dr #1G Mount Vernon NY 10552

CORREIA, JOHN ARTHUR, physicist; b. Boston, June 8, 1945; s. Arthur F. and Mary E. (Kenneally) C.; m. Dorothy E. Reddington, Sept. 8, 1967 (div.); 1 child, Gabe J. BS, U. Lowell, 1967, PhD, 1973. Rsch. fellow Mass. Gen. Hosp., Boston, 1973-75; rsch. assoc. dept. radiology Harvard Med. Sch. and Mass. Gen. Hosp., Boston, 1975-76; assoc. dir. Physics Rsch. Lab Mass. Gen. Hosp., 1980-83, dir. PET Cyclotion Labs., 1983—; asst. prof. dept. radiology Harvard Med. Sch., 1976-83; rsch. fellow dept. radiology Harvard Med. Sch., Boston, 1973-75; assoc. prof. Harvard Med. Sch., 1983—; mem. nat. rev. bds. NIH, Washington, 1978—, U.S. Dept. Energy, Washington, 1985—. Assoc. editor Jour. Nuclear Medicine, N.Y.C., 1989—; contbg. author textbook chpts., 1973—; contbr. articles to profl. jours. Grantee NIH, Dept. Energy, EPA. Fellow Am. Heart Assn., Am. Coll. Nuclear Physicians; mem. IEEE (adminstrv. com. 1987—), Soc. Nuclear Medicine, AAAS. Office: Dept Radiology Mass General Hosp 32 Fruit St Boston MA 02114-2698

CORREIA, JOHN FURIA, senator, plumbing supply company executive; b. Ponta Delgada, St. Michael, Azores, Portugal, Nov. 7, 1939; came to U.S., 1963; s. Joao F. Correia and Eteluina Sousa; m. Cidalia Avelar, Nov. 23, 1963; children: Richard, Deborah. Ed., Indsl. Trade Sch., St. Michael. Lic. master plumber. Owner, pres. J.F. Correia Plumbing and Heating, M & G Plumbing Supply, East Providence and Warren, R.I., 1981—; U.S. senator from State of R.I., 1983—, pres. pro tempore, sec. com. on spl. legis., mem. Senate Corp., joint com. on water resources, commn. to study state aid to local sch. dists., commn. to study feasibility of exclusive state fund for workers compensation. Trustee, coord. fundraising St. Francis Xavier Parish, 1974-81; pres. Casa Dos Acores, R.I.; treas. Holy Ghost Beneficial Brotherhood R.I., 1977-79; co-chmn. Castro for Senate Com., 1976-80; treas. Almeida for Coun. Com., 1976-78. Mem. Prince Henry Club, Holy Ghost Brotherhood of Charity. Democrat. Roman Catholic. Office: RI State Senate State Capitol Providence RI 02903

CORRESSEL, ROBERT HENRY, transportation executive; b. Evansville, Ind., Mar. 2, 1947; s. Florien Henry and Dorothy Raye (Erskine) C.; m. Patricia Helen Ilves, Dec. 26, 1969; children: Nicole Helene, Noelle Dorothea. BS in Bus. Econs., U. S.C., 1970; MA in Econs., Temple U., 1974. Econ., budgetry analyst Southeastern Pa. Transp. Authority, Phila., 1973-76; sr. planner, spl. svcs. Southeastern Pa. Transp. Authority, 1976-82, mgr. spl. svcs. and paratransit, 1982—; mem. adv. com. Boston Coll. Study Communication Techniques for Visually Impaired in Rail Rapid Stas., 1982-83; cons. in field. With USMC, 1971-75. Mem. Am. Pub. Transit Assn. (elderly and handicapped tasks force, Cert. of Recognition 1986), Nat. Trust Historic Preservation, Transp. Rsch. Bd., Greenpeace, Sierra Club. Office: SEPTA 714 Market St 25 S 9th St Philadelphia PA 19106

CORRIDORI, ANTHONY JOSEPH, executive engineer; b. Worcester, Mass., Sept. 27, 1961; s. Frank Joseph and Anita Louise (Ferdella) C. AS in Engring., Worcester Jr. Coll., 1983; BS in Engring, Cen. N.E. Coll., 1984; diploma, Worcester Indsl. Tech. Inst., 1981. Rsch. and devel. tech. Acumeter Labs., Marlboro, Mass., 1984-85; project engr. Hypertronics Corp., Hudson, Mass., 1985-86; sr. project engr. Augat Inc., Attleboro, Mass., 1986—; coll. coord. Am. Soc. of Mech. Engrs., Worcester, 1983-84. Inventor floatable surface mount terminal. Mem. Am. Soc. of Metals, NRA, Knights of Columbus, Worcester Vocat. Tech. AlumniAssn. Roman Catholic. Home: 727 Franklin St Worcester MA 01604-1758 Office: Augat Inc 33 Perry Ave Attleboro MA 02703-2400

CORRIGAN, JOHN EDWARD, III, electrical engineer; b. Evanston, Ill., Oct. 2, 1953; s. John Edward and Eileen (Williams) C.; m. Phyllis Kass, June 22, 1985; children: Brendan, Evan. BS in Engring., U. Mich., 1975; MSEE, Johns Hopkins U., 1981. Engr. Westinghouse Electric Co., Balt., 1975-78; mem. tech. staff MA-COM DCC (now Hughes Network Systems), Germantown, Md., 1978-83, dir. hardware devel., 1983-91, v.p. engring., 1991—. Patentee frequency control system. Mem. Washington Soc. Engrs. Home: 33 W Irving St Chevy Chase MD 20815 Office: Hughes Network Systems 11717 Exploration Ln Germantown MD 20876

CORRY, CHARLES ALBERT, steel and energy company executive; b. Wyoming, Ohio, Feb. 14, 1932; s. Charles Albert and Rella Marie (Ulrich) C.; m. Margaret Anna Stuve, Dec. 9, 1961; children: Lynne, Diane, Elizabeth. BS, U. Cin., 1955, JD, 1959. Bar: Ohio 1959. Tax atty. U.S. Steel Corp. (now USX Corp.), Pitts., Cleve. and N.Y.C., 1959-70; asst. comptr. Am. Bridge div. U.S. Steel Corp. (now USX Corp.), Pitts., 1970-71; mgr. acctg.-steel, parent co. U.S. Steel Corp. (now USX Corp.), Homestead, Pa., 1972-73; comptr. USS Engrs. and Cons., Pitts., 1974; gen. mgr. taxes U.S. Steel Corp. (now USX Corp.), Pitts., 1975-78; asst. comptr. U.S. Steel Corp. (now USX Corp.), Pitts., Pa., 1978; v.p. corp. planning U.S. Steel Corp. (now USX Corp.), Pitts., 1979-82; sr. v.p., comptr. U.S. Steel Corp. (now USX Corp.), Pitts., Pa., 1982-86; pres. USX Diversified Group, Pitts., 1987—, corp. pres., dir., 1987—, also chmn., chief exec. officer, 1989—; bd. dirs. Mellon Bank Corp., Mellon Bank, N.A. Bd. dirs. United Way So. Pa., Ind. Sector; trustee U. Pitts. Served to capt. USAF, 1955-57. Mem. ABA, Ohio Bar Assn., Am. Iron and Steel Inst., Duquesne Club, St. Clair Country Club, Laurel Valley Golf Club, Rolling Rock Club. Lutheran. Office: USX Corp 600 Grant St Pittsburgh PA 15219-2701

CORRY, EMMETT BROTHER, educator; b. N.Y.C.; s. Patrick Joseph and Bridget (Cosgrove) C. BA, St. Francis Coll., N.Y.C., 1960; MS, Columbia U., 1962; PhD, NYU, 1977. Tchr. Franciscan Bros. Schs., Bklyn., 1960-69; libr. St. Francis Coll., Bklyn., 1970-71, St. Anthony's High Sch., Smithtown, N.Y., 1971-77; assoc. prof. Div. of Libr. and Info. Sci. St. John's U., Jamaica, N.Y., 1977-88, dir., 1988—; cons. N.Y.C. Bd. Edn., 1984-88. Author: Grants for Libraries, 1982, 2d edit., 1986. Mem. Cath. Libr. Assn. (pres. 1989-91, Libr. of Yr. 1991). Address: Franciscan Bros St Gerard Majella 90-37 189th St Hollis NY 11423 Office: St Johns U Jamaica NY 11439

CORRY, JAMES MICHAEL, insurance executive, educator; b. N.Y.C., Apr. 27, 1947; s. Patrick Joseph and Bridget (Cosgrave) C.; m. Maureen Patricia Grogan; children: Matthew, Michael. BS, Manhattan Coll., 1968; MS, CUNY, 1971; PhD, U. Oreg., 1975. Health specialist N.Y.C. Bd. Edn., 1968-71; teaching asst. U. Oreg., Eugene, 1971-73; asst. dir. health Oreg. Bd. Edn., Salem, 1973-74; asst. prof. Worcester (Mass.) State Coll., 1974-76, U. North Tex., Denton, 1976-81; dir. health edn. dept. Mt. Sinai Med. Ctr., N.Y.C., 1981-88, asst. dean for continuing edn. Sch. Medicine, 1981-88; dir. health and fitness programs Met. Life Ins. Co., N.Y.C., 1988—; cons. Tex. Dept. Edn., Austin, 1975-76; grant dir., researcher State of Tex. Rsch. Fund, Denton, 1976-80. Author: Consumer Health: Facts, Skills and Decisions, 1983, Drugs: Facts, Alternatives, Decisions, 1984, Implementing Health/Fitness Programs, 1986; contbr. articles to profl. jours. Bd. dirs. Silvermine Community Assn., New Canaan, Conn., 1981-83, Mid Fairfield Hospice, Norwalk, Conn., 1982-84. Diocese of Bklyn. and U. of Oreg. scholar, 1964, 71. Fellow Nat. Ctr. for Health Edn.; mem. Assn. Adv. Health Edn. Educators, Am. Pub. Health Assn., Soc. for Pub. Health Edn., Assn. for Fitness in Bus., Roton Point Club. Democrat. Roman Catholic. Home: 47 Comstock Hill Rd Norwalk CT 06850-1008 Office: Met Life Ins Co 1 Madison Ave New York NY 10010-3603

CORSARO, ROBERT DOMINIC, physical chemist; b. Elizabeth, N.J., Nov. 5, 1944; s. Joseph Anthony and Clara (Olesinski) C.; m. Mary B. McCole, Aug. 12, 1967; children: Brigid, Michael. BS in Chemistry with honors, Lebanon Valley Coll., 1966; PhD in Chemistry, U. Md., 1971. Rsch. chemist Naval Rsch. Lab., Washington, 1970-81, sect. head, 1981—; lectr. in field. Editor: Sound and Vibration Damping with Polymers, 1990; patentee in field; contbr. over 40 articles to profl. jours. Recipient NRL Rsch. Pub. award Naval Rsch. Lab. Fellow Acoustical Soc. Am.; mem. Am. Chem. Soc., Sigma Xi. Office: Naval Rsch Lab Code 5135 Washington DC 20375-5000

CORTELL, JASON MERRILL, environmental consultant; b. Lowell, Mass., Feb. 18, 1936; s. Albert B. and Pearl (Weisberg) C.; m. Mary-Brenda Barber, June 15, 1958; children: Perry S., Karen G., Eric D. BA in Biology, Boston U., 1957, MA in Biology, 1958. Pres. Allied Biol. Inc., Wellesley, Mass., 1959-83; chief exec. officer, chmn. Jason B. Cortell & Assocs. Inc., Waltham, Mass., 1963—; dir. Cortell-Harris Environ. Svcs., The Hague, Netherlands, 1989—; environ. cons. AT&T, 1973—, Snowbird Ski Resort, Alta, Utah, 1978-82, 3d Harbor Tunnel-Cen. Artery Project, Boston, 1987—. Bus. leader Boston Symphony Orch. Recipient commendation Dept. Navy, 1985. Mem. Nat. Assn. Environ. Profls. (cert.), Internat. Engrs. Coun. (environ. quality com.), Nat. Assn. Corp. Real Estate Execs., Buzzards Yacht Club (Pocasset, Mass.), World Trade Club. Office: 244 2d Ave Waltham MA 02154

CORTESE, ARMAND FERDINAND, surgeon, educator; b. N.Y.C., Dec. 4, 1932; m. Patricia Lange, 1975; children: Amanda Lange, Kevin Armand. AB, Columbia U., 1954; MD, Cornell U., 1958. Intern N.Y. Hosp., Cornell U., N.Y.C., 1958, resident, 1959-66, Am./Nat. Cancer fellow, 1966-68, assoc. attending surgeon, 1976—; clin. assoc. prof. surgery Cornell Med. Coll., N.Y.C., 1976—. Author: (with others) Care of the Adult Patient, 1971; contbr. articles to profl. jours. Lt. USN, 1960-62. Rsch. grantee Josia and Macy Found., 1958. Mem. AMA, Am. Coll. Surgery, Am. Soc. Clin. Oncology, Harvey Soc., N.Y. Surg. Soc., N.Y. Cancer Soc., N.Y. Acad. Medicine. Office: 50 E 69th St New York NY 10021

CORTÉS-HWANG, ADRIANA, foreign language educator; b. Valparaíso, Chile, Nov. 9, 1928; came to U.S., 1963, naturalized, 1969; d. Luis and Sofía (Garcés) Cortés; 1 child, Verónica. BA, U. Chile, 1963; Lic. in English, Inst. Chile, 1963; BA in English, Portland State U., 1965; MA in Spanish Lit., U. Oreg., 1967, postgrad., 1968; postgrad. U. N.C., 1970, Inst. de Filología Hispánica U. Madrid, Spain, 1971, Duke U. Liaison officer, Chilean Inst. Culture and U. Chile, 1961-63; instr. Spanish Portland State U., 1963-64, Grants Pass (Oreg.) Sr. High Sch., 1964-65, U. Oreg., Eugene, 1965-67, Wilson Coll., Chambersburg, Pa., 1967, Pa. State U., Mont Alto; asst. prof. modern langs. Shippensburg (Pa.) State Coll., 1968-80, adviser internat. studies, 1971-80, Fulbright adviser, chmn. Latin Am. studies, 1970-80; asst. prof. fgn. langs. Bloomsburg (Pa.) State Coll., 1980-81, Kutztown (Pa.) U., 1981—, mem. univ. senate, coord. lower div. courses, 1984-85, mem. com. internat. affairs, com. of sixteen, rep. fgn. lang. dept. to APCUF Coun., rep. for faculty exchange programs with S.Am. univs., cons. lang. programs for Bloomsburg Pub. Sch. Dist., 1980-81, student acad. advisor, 1981-88; guest speaker Inst. Pedagógico, U. Chile, Engring. Sch., U. Buenos Aires, 1988-89; lectr. series Sch. Engring. Buenos Aires, 1989, Univ. Tecnica, Santa María Valparaíso, Chile, 1989, Instituto Chileno N.Am. de Cultura, 1989, Kean Coll. Union City, N.J., 1989. Contbr. articles to profl. jours. Recipient Gold medal Ateneo Cervantes, Valparaíso, Chile, 1947. Mem. MLA, AAUP, Latin Am. Studies Assn., Sociedad Nacional Hispanica, Sigma Delta Pi. Home: 590 Upper Mountain Ave Montclair NJ 07043-1623 Office: De Francesco 204 Kutztown State U Kutztown PA 19530

CORVA, ANGELO FRANCIS, architect; b. N.Y.C., Apr. 9, 1948; s. Frank John and Angelina (Di Gennaro) C.; m. Susan Aiuto, May 3, 1973; children: Christopher Francis, Katherine Mary. BA in Sci., N.Y. Inst. Tech., 1972. Registered architect, Calif., Conn., Ill., La., Maine, Mass., Mich., Minn. N.J., N.Y., Ohio, Pa., Vt., Va., Wis., Fla., Ga. Project architect Gencorelli & Salo, Mineola, N.Y., 1968-77; prin., founder Angelo Francis Corva Assoc. Architects, Garden City, N.Y., 1977—; Cons. architect N.Y. State Thoroughbred Racing Capital Investment Fund. Contbr. articles on architecture to N.Y. Times, 1984. Committeeman Nassau County Rep. Orgn., Merrick, Garden City, 1978-85; past v.p. Merrick Rep. Com.; mem. Garden City Rep. Com., Rep. Pres. Task Force, Rep. Sentorial Inner Circle; adv. bd. mem. State Bank L.I., 1983—, N.Y. State Transp. Com.; chmn. Town of Hempstead Landmarks Preservation Com.; vice chmn. North Hampstead Landmarkers Com.; mem. Heart Fund Ball Com., St. Francis Hosp. Challenge Fund. Recipient Masonry Inst.award. Mem. AIA (L.I. chpt., Bldg. Design award 1984), Construction Specifications Inst., N.Y. C. of C. (Bldg. Design award Quens chpt. 1983, Bldg. Design award Riverhead chpt. 1985), Merrick Hist. Soc., Roslyn Hist. Soc., Nat. Trust Hist. Preservation, Queens C. of C. Roman Catholic. Lodges: Kiwanis, KC. Office: Angelo Francis Corva & Assoc 141 Eab Plz Uniondale NY 11556-3803

CORVINO, FRANK ANTHONY, hospital executive; b. N.Y.C., Mar. 13, 1949; s. Grace (Stiso) Fata; children: Timothy, Aimee; m. Virginia Valente,

Sept. 1, 1985. BS in Pharmacy, Fordham U., 1971; MS, St. Johns U., 1973. With Our Lady of Mercy Med. Ctr., Bronx, N.Y., 1976-88; exec. v.p. profl. svcs. Our Lady of Mercy Med. Ctr., 1986-88; pres., chief operating officer Greenwich (Conn.) Hosp., 1988—; asst. prof., N.Y. Med. Coll., Valhalla, 1987—. Recipient Recognition award, N.Y. State Bd. Pharmacy, Albany, 1989. Mem. Am. Coll. Healthcare Execs., N.Y. State Coun. Hosp. Pharmacists, N.Y.C. Soc. Hosp. Pharmacists (award of merit 1987), Rotary. Roman Catholic. Home and Office: Greenwich Hosp Perry Ridge Rd Greenwich CT 06830

CORY, JEFFREY, TV, film, stage, event and creative director; b. Johannesburg, Rep. of South Africa, Oct. 10, 1945; came to U.S., 1990; s. Isaac and Flora (Moshal) Kwitz. BS, Jerusalem U., 1967. Freelance stage and event dir. U.K. and Israel, 1963-68; dir. ITC TV Sta., Israel, 1969-74; chief exec. officer, dir. Jeffricory Prodns., Israel, 1974-75; chief exec. officer San Hill Prodns., Rep. of South Africa, 1975-78; founder, exec. dir. Performing Arts Workshop Coll., Rep. of South Africa, 1983-87; chief exec. officer Screen Machine Prodns., Rep. of South Africa, 1978-90; chief exec. officer, dir. Scene Internat., N.Y.C., 1990—; exec. dir. Performing Arts Workshop Coll., Rep. of South Africa, 1983-87. Dir.: (TV/film prodn.) Loerie (award 1990), N.Y. Film Festival (Bronze award 1985). Recipient Gold Statue award Houston Film Festival, 1989; finalist N.Y. Film Festival, 1984, 85, Israels Citizen's award for TV, 1971. Mem. Mtg. Planners Internat., S.A. Film and TV Technicians Union, Assn. of Comml. Producers, WIZO (hon. life). Jewish. Office: Scene Internat 51 West 14th St 4th Flr New York NY 10011

CORY-SLECHTA, DEBORAH ANN, neurotoxicologist; b. St. Paul, Minn., Jan. 31, 1950; d. Donald Joseph and Olive Gayle (Brantseg) Cory; m. Thomas Fredrik Slechta, Sept. 6, 1975; children: Christopher Thomas Slechta, Amy Elizabeth Slechta. BS magna cum laude, West Mich. U., 1971, MA with honors, 1972; PhD, U. Minn., 1977. Postdoctoral fellow Nat. Ctr. for Toxic Rsch., U. Rochester, 1979-82; rsch. assoc. U. Rochester Med. Sch., 1982-84, asst. prof., 1984-90, assoc. prof. toxicology and pediatrics, 1990—; cons. Nat. Inst. Environ. Health Sci., Research Triangle Park, N.C., 1985—, EPA, Washington, 1987, Agy. for Toxicology Sub. and Disease Reg., Atlanta, 1987, 90; program co-chair 9th Internat. Neurotoxicology Conf., Little Rock, Ark., 1991. Assoc. editor Neurotoxicology; mem. editorial bd. Fundamental and Applied Toxicology, Neurobehavioral Toxicology and Teratology; author 7 book chpts. Com. mem. Dept. Parks and Recreation Adv. com., Pittsford, N.Y., 1988—. Rsch. grantee NIH, 1985-92; postdoctoral fellowship, 1979-82; recipient New Investigator award NIH, 1982-85. Fellow Am. Psychol. Assn.; mem. Soc. for Neuroscience, Soc. of Toxicology (neurotoxicology specialty sect., councilor 1986-88, sec., treas. 1988-90, v.p. elect 1990-91, v.p. 1991-92, pres. 1992—). Office: U Rochester Med Sch PO Box EHSC Rochester NY 14642

COSBY, BILL, actor, entertainer; b. Phila., July 12, 1937; s. William Henry and Anna C.; m. Camille Hanks, Jan. 25, 1964; children: Erika Ranee, Erinn Chalene, Ennis William, Ensa Camille, Evin Harrah. Student, Temple U.; MA, U. Mass., 1972, EdD, 1977. Pres. Rhythm and Blues Hall of Fame, 1968—. Appeared in numerous night clubs, including The Gaslight, N.Y.C., Hungry I, San Francisco, Shoreham Hotel, Washington, Basin St. East, N.Y.C., Hilton, Las Vegas, Nev., Harrah's Lake Tahoe; guest appearances on numerous TV shows, including The Electric Co, 1972, Capt. Kangaroo; co-star: TV show I Spy, 1965-68; star: TV show The Bill Cosby Show, 1969, 72-73, The Cosby Show, 1984—; exec. producer TV show A Different World, 1987—; recs. include: Revenge (Grammy award Nat. Acad. Performing Arts and Scis. 1967), To Russell, My Brother, With Whom I Slept, Top Secret, 200 M.P.H, Why Is There Air, Wonderfulness, It's True, It's True, Bill Cosby is a Very Funny Fellow: Right, I Started Out as a Child, 8:15, 12:15, Hungry; Reunion, 1982, Bill Cosby...Himself, 1983, Those of You With or Without Children, You'll Understand; films include Hickey and Boggs, 1972, Man and Boy, 1972, Uptown Saturday Night, 1974, Let's Do It Again, 1975, Mother, Jugs and Speed, 1976, Aesop's Fables, A Piece of the Action, 1977, California Suite, 1978, Devil and Max Devlin, 1979, Leonard: Part VI, 1987, Ghost Dad, 1990; recipient 4 Emmy awards 1966, 67, 68, 69, 8 Grammy awards, named number 1 in comedy field Top Artists on Campus Poll (album sales) 1968; author: The Wit and Wisdom of Fat Albert, 1973, Bill Cosby's Personal Guide to Power Tennis, Fatherhood, 1986, Time Flies, 1988, Love and Marriage, 1989, Childhood, 1991. Served with USNR, 1956-60.

COSENZA, VINCENT JOHN, accountant; b. Bklyn., Aug. 12, 1962; s. Vincent James and Rosalie Theresa (Ferraro) C. BS in Acctg., NYU, 1984. CPA, N.Y. Mgr. fin. adminstrn. Jr. Achievemnt N.Y. Inc., N.Y.C., 1984-85; staff acct. Rosenshein, Neiman & Weiss, CPA's, N.Y.C., 1985-87, Pepper, Gelbord, Roth & Co., N.Y.C., 1987—; assoc. acct. Sheldon Plotnick, Bklyn., 1986-88. Mem. AICPA, N.Y. State Soc. CPAs, Citizens Choice. Democrat. Roman Catholic. Home: 1393 E 53d St Brooklyn NY 11234-3226 Office: Pepper Gelbord Roth & Co Ste 1201 60 E 42d St New York NY 10165

COSEO, DAVID PAUL, university official; b. Watertown, N.Y., Oct. 29, 1936; s. Earle Charles and Mary C. (Ash) C.; m. Debra Ann Stauffer, Nov. 28, 1958; children: Elizabeth, William Brian. BA, St. Lawrence U., Canton, N.Y., 1960, MEd, 1972. Commd. 2d lt. U.S. Army, 1960, advanced through grades to lt. col., 1976; ret., 1980; mgmt. analyst U. Vt., Burlington, 1980-82, dir. fin. aid, spl. asst. to asst. v.p., 1982-90, sr. adminstrv. analyst, 1990—; testifier U.S. Congress, 1986-88; mem. Coll. Bd.; mem. ea. regional coun. Am. Coll. Testing Svc. Decorated Legion of Merit. Mem. Soc. Coll. and Univ. Planning, Nat. Assn. Coll. and Univ. Bus. Officers, Nat. Assn. Student Fin. Aid Adminstrn., Ea. Assn. Student Fin. Aid Adminstrn. Republican. Roman Catholic. Home: 38 Wildwood Dr Essex Junction VT 05452-3816 Office: U Vt 109 S Prospect St Burlington VT 05405-0016

COSLOW, RICHARD DAVID, electronics company executive; b. N.Y.C., Feb. 28, 1942; s. Charles Louis and Beatrice (Hoffman) C.; m. Rona Elaine Koslow, Feb. 18, 1967; children: Bari, Todd. BS in Acctg., NYU, 1963. CPA, N.Y., N.J. Audit mgr. Touche Ross & Co., N.Y.C., 1967-80; v.p. controller MEGO Internat. Inc., N.Y.C., 1980-82; v.p. fin. The Fulham Capital Group, Inc., N.Y.C., 1982-83, Endless Energy, Inc., N.Y.C., 1983-84; v.p. controller Toshiba Am., Inc., Wayne, N.J., 1984—. Mem. Fin. Execs. Inst., Tax Execs. Inst., Am. Inst. CPA's, N.Y. State Soc. CPA's, N.J. Soc. CPA's. Home: 16 Cavan Ln Hazlet NJ 07730-1131 Office: Toshiba Am Inc 82 Totowa Rd Wayne NJ 07470-3114

COSTA, ERMINIO, pharmacologist, cell biology educator; b. Cagliari, Italy, Mar. 9, 1924; s. Oreste and Gigina (Murgia) C.; divorced; children: Max, Robert Henry, Michael John; m. Ingeborg Hanbauer, July 13, 1973. MD, U. Cagliari, 1947, PhD in Pharmacology, 1953; PhD in Biol. Sci. (hon.), U. Cagliari, Italy, 1986; DSc (hon.), Georgetown U., 1992; MD (hon.), U. Tampere, Finland, 1992. Asst. prof., assoc. prof. U. Cagliari, 1948-54, prof. pharmacology, 1954-56; physician II, med. rsch. assn. Thudichum Psychology Rsch., Galesburg, Ill., 1956-60; vis. scientist NIH, Bethesda, Md., 1960-61; dep. chief lab. chem. pharmacology Nat. Heart Inst., Bethesda, 1961-63, head sect. clin. pharmacology, 1963-65; assoc. prof. pharmacology Columbia U., N.Y.C., 1965-68; chief lab. preclin pharmacology St. Elizabeth's Hosp., Washington, 1968-85; dir. Fidia-Georgetown Inst. for the Neurosci. Georgetown U., Washington, 1985—. Editor Neuropharmacology, 1967, Advance Biochem Psychopharmacology, 1968; contbr. articles to profl. jours. Recipient Bennet award and Gold medal Soc. Biol. Psychiatry, Gold medal Fed. II Univ., Naples, 1990, Premio Fiuggi award Fiuggi Rsch. Found., 1988. Mem. NAS, Academia Nazionale Lincei, Am. Soc. Pharmacology and Exptl. Theareutics., Am. Soc. Physiology., Am. Soc. Biol. Chemistry and Molecular Biology, Cosmos Club, Pepipathetic Club. Office: Fidia-Georgetown Inst Neurosciences 3900 Reservoir Rd NW Washington DC 20007-2187

COSTAGLIOLA, FRANCESCO, former government official; b. Cranston, R.I., Aug. 24, 1917; s. Luigi and Rose (Lubrano) C.; m. Agnes Mary Ross, June 14, 1952; children: Francesca Gensler, Marisa Consoli, Antonia Burns, Roseanne Rubin. Student U. R.I., 1935-37; BSEE, U.S. Naval Acad., 1941; postgrad. Naval Postgrad. Sch., 1946-47, MIT, 1947-49, Cath. U. Am., 1967-71; MBA, Am. U., Washington, 1974. Commd. ensign U.S. Navy, 1941, advanced through grades to capt., 1960; served in U.S.S. Phoenix in 24 ops. PTO, 1941-46; comdg. officer U.S.S. Halsey Powell, Korea, 1951-52; various positions naval sea and shore assignments involving atomic energy, 1952-64; mil. asst. to asst. to Sec. Def., 1964-67; ret., 1968; commr. AEC, 1968-69; engr. RCA, 1974-76; staff mem. Joint Congressional Com. on Atomic Energy, Washington, 1967-68, 69-71, 76-77; staff mem. Office of Sec. of Senate, Washington, 1977-86; mem. Md. Radiation Control Adv. Bd., 1973-81. Contbr. articles to profl. jours. Decorated Legion of Merit, Bronze Star with Combat V. Mem. Am. Nuclear Soc., Ops. Rsch. Soc. Am., U.S. Naval Inst., Pearl Harbor Survivors Assn., Naval Acad. Alumni Assn., MIT Alumni Assn., Mil. Order World Wars, Army and Navy Club (Washington). Roman Catholic. Home: 307 Gibbon St Alexandria VA 22314-4129

COSTANTINO, GIUSEPPE, clinic director, research associate; b. Nocera Terinse, Catanzaro, Italy, Dec. 25, 1937; came to U.S., 1961; s. Gaetano and Erminia (Tomaino) C.; m. Maryse Borges-Costantino, Aug. 4, 1968; 1 child, Erminia. BS, CUNY, 1968, MS, 1971; PhD, NYU, 1975. Caseworker N.Y.C. Dept. Social Svcs., 1968-72; psychology intern Coney Island Hosp., Bklyn., 1973-74; assoc. psychologist South Beach Psychiat. Ctr., Staten Island, N.Y., 1974-76; chief psychologist Sunset Park Mental Health Ctr., Bklyn., 1977-84, clin. dir., 1984—; rsch. assoc. Hispanic Rsch. Ctr., Fordham U., Bronx, N.Y., 1978—; clin. cons. St. John's U., Queens, N.Y., 1990—, clin. supr., 1990—; reviewer 9th and 10th Mental Measurements Yearbook, Buros Inst., Lincoln, Nebr., 1988, 89. Author: (projective test) TEMAS (Tell-Me-A-Story), 1988, (book) Cuento Therapy, 1985, (textbook) Psychology, 1989; cons. editor: Jour. of Personality Assessment, 1988—; contbr. articles to psychology jours. Jr. lt. Infantry, 1958-60, Italy. NIMH (Cuento Therapy) grantee, 1980-83, 84-85, NIMH (Hero/Heroine Modeling Therapy) grantee, 1988-90, William T. Grant Found. grantee, 1985-86, Fordham U. Biomedical Rsch. Support grantee, 1989-90. Mem. APA, N.Y. State Psychol. Assn. Democrat. Roman Catholic. Home: 14340 Ash Ave Flushing NY 11355-2113 Office: Sunset Park Mental Hlth Ctr 514 49th St Brooklyn NY 11220-2098

COSTAS, PETER LOUIS, lawyer; b. Binghamton, N.Y., Mar. 7, 1931; s. Louis George and Demetria (Bounacos) C.; m. Joan Bennett, June 28, 1953; children: George, Carol, Barbara. BS, Syracuse (N.Y.) U., 1951, JD, 1954. Bar: N.Y. 1954, U.S. Dist. Ct. (no. dist.) N.Y. 1954, U.S. Supreme Ct. 1958, D.C. 1959, Conn. 1959, U.S. Ct. Appeals (2d and 1st cirs.) 1961, U.S. Dist. Ct. (so. and ea. dists.) N.Y. 1965, U.S. Ct. Appeals (fed. cir.) 1977. Atty. Aluminum Co. of Am., Pitts., 1956-59; assoc. Lindsey & Prutzman, Hartford, Conn., 1959-62; prin. Law Offices of Peter L. Costas, Hartford, 1962—; ptnr. Costas, Montgomery & Dorman, Hartford, Costas & Montgomery, Hartford; prin. Law Offices of Peter L. Costas, Hartford. Contbr. articles to profl. jours. Counsel Conn. Acad. Sci. & Engring., 1976—, Conn. Citizens for Jud. Modernization, 1971-83; vice chmn. Conn. Drug Adv. Coun., 1967-71 Sgt. U.S. Army, 1954-56, ETO. Mem. ABA, N.Y. State Bar Assn., Am. Intellectual Property Law Assn., Conn. Bar Assn. (John Eldred Shields Meml. award for disting. profl. svc. 1987), U.S. Trademark Assn. Office: 3 Lewis St Hartford CT 06103-2554

COSTAS, ROBERT QUINLAN (BOB COSTAS), sportscaster; b. N.Y.C., Mar. 22, 1952; s. John George and Jayne (Quinlan) C.; m. Carole Randall, June 24, 1983; children: Keith Michael, Taylor. Student, Syracuse U., 1970-74. Sportscaster Sta. KMOX-AM, St. Louis, 1974-81; sportscaster, host sports programs NBC Sports, N.Y.C., 1980—; Host of show, Later (gen. interest late night interview program); host prime-time coverage for NBC-TV Summer Olympics, Barcelona, Spain, 1992. Named Nat. Sportscaster of Yr. Nat. Assn. Sportscasters and Broadcasters, 1985, 87, 88; recipient Emmy awards for oustanding host play by play announcing, 1987, 88. *

COSTELLO, ALBERT JOSEPH, diversified consumer products executive; b. N.Y.C., Sept. 4, 1935; s. John and Lena (Compiani) C.; m. Barbara Theresa Antolotti, May 31, 1958; children: Gregory A., Peter M., Albert Joseph. B.S., Fordham U., 1957; M.S., NYU, 1964. With Am. Cyanamid Co., 1957—; asst. mng., mng. dir. Am. Cyanamid Co., Mexico City, Madrid, Spain, 1974-77; div. v.p. Am. Cyanamid Co., Wayne, N.J., 1977-82, pres. agrl. div., 1982, group v.p., 1982-83, exec. v.p., 1983-90, pres., 1990—. Patentee in field. Served with U.S. Army, 1959-61. Mem. Nat. Agrl. Chems. Assn. (dir. 1982—, chmn. 1984-85), Chem. Mfrs. Assn. (bd. dirs. 1987—), Soc. Chem. Industry (exec. com. 1991—), Nat. Assn. Mfrs. (bd. dirs. 1992—). Office: Am Cyanamid Co 1 Cyanamid Dr Wayne NJ 07470-4000

COSTELLO, AMELIA FUSCO, educator; b. Schenectady, Apr. 12, 1946; d. Alfonso and Adele (D'Andrea) Fusco; m. Thomas Michael Costello, July ll, 198l; l stepchild, Jason Sean. BA in English, Russell Sage Coll., 1971, MS in Elem. Edn., 1973. Cert. tchr., N.Y. Tchr. English, theater arts Averill Park (N.Y.) Cen. Schs., 1971—. Contbr. to various profl. publs. Sec. Troy (N.Y.) Charter Revision Com., 1978; mem. Rensselaer Dem. Com., Troy, 1978-82; admissions vol. Russel Sage Coll., 1992—. Named Labor Person of Yr., Troy Labor Coun., 1982. Mem. AFL-CIO (pres. Troy area labor coun. 1980-82), LWV (pub. rels. chair 1981), Am. Fedn. Tchrs., N.Y. State United Tchrs., Averill Park Tchrs. Assn. (v.p. 1989—, greivance chmn. 1990—), St. Jude's Rosary Soc., Russell Sage Troy Club (v.p. 1977-78), Russell Sage Alumni (admissions vol. 1992—). Roman Catholic. Home: 28 Goodman Ave Troy NY 12180-8814 Office: Averill Park High Sch Gettle Rd Averill Park NY 12018-9760

COSTELLO, CYNTHIA ANN, textile stylist; b. St. Paul, Jan. 26, 1952; d. Harry George and Mary Margaret (Alexander) C. BA, Knox Coll., 1974; MFA, BKlyn. Coll., 1980; AAS, Fashion Inst. Tech., 1982. Textile designer Waverly Fabrics, N.Y.C., 1981-82, Covington Fabrics, N.Y.C., 1982-83; freelance textile designer N.Y.C., 1983-84, Burston Fabrics, N.Y.C., 1984, Anju Woodridge, N.Y.C., 1985-89; wallcovering stylist F. Schumacher, N.Y.C., 1989-91. Charles G. Shaw Meml. scholar Bklyn. Coll., 1979, Skowhegan Sch. of Drawing scholar, 1980. Mem. Prince St. Gallery. Roman Catholic. Home and Office: 15 Bergen St # 2S Brooklyn NY 11201-6377

COSTELLO, ROBERT MICHAEL, public relations executive; b. Scranton, Pa., Feb. 11, 1940; s. Peter Francis and Catherine C. (Meehan) C.; m. Anne Elizabeth Dempsey, June 8, 1968; children: Colleen A., Ellen M. Student, Girard Coll., 1948-58; BS in English and Philosophy, U. Scranton, 1963. Reporter, editorial asst. Cath. Light, Scranton, 1966-67; press sec. Mayor James J. Walsh, Scranton, 1968-70; pub. rels. dir. Scranton (Pa.) Redevelopment Authority, 1970-72; reporter The Scranton (Pa.) Times/The Sunday Times, 1972-73; dep. press sec. Pa. Gov. Milton J. Shapp, Harrisburg, Pa., 1973-75; press sec. Pa. Health Sec. L. Bachman, MD, Harrisburg, 1975-78; pub. rels. dir. Pa. Turnpike Commn., Harrisburg, 1978-79; pub. info. dir. U.S. Dept. Health & Human Svcs., Phila., 1979-80; pub. rels. dir. Mercy Hosp. Scranton, Pa., 1980—; blood svcs. coord. ARC, Scranton (Pa.) chpt., 1980—; chmn. communications Diocesan Synod II, Scranton, 1982-85; vice chmn. Diocesan Communications Com., Scranton, 1986-89. Editor: (quarterly hosp. publ.) Mercy News, 1987—. Dep. press sec. Pa. Gov. Milton Shapp for Re-election Campaign, Harrisburg, 1973; press spokesman Pa. Health Dept., Harrisburg, 1976; bd. dirs. Lackawanna United Way, Scranton, 1982-85; pub. rels. cons. Judge James J. Walsh for Pa. Supreme Ct. Justice Election, 1988. With U.S. Army, 1963-66. Recipient citation of appreciation Diocese of Scranton (Pa.) Synod II, 1985, Patriotic Svc. award U.S. Savs. Bonds, Sec. of the Treasury, Washington, 1990; named Outstanding Community Blood Svcs. Coord., ARC, Scranton, 1990. Mem. Am. Soc. for Hosp. Mktg. and Pub. Rels. (cert.), Pub. Rels. Soc. Hosp. Assn. Pa., Irish Am. Men's Assn., Univ. Scranton Alumni, Girard Coll. Alumni. Democrat. Roman Catholic. Home: 1404 Delaware St Scranton PA 18509-2022 Office: Mercy Hosp 746 Jefferson Ave Scranton PA 18501

COSTENBADER, CHARLES MICHAEL, lawyer; b. Jersey City, Dec. 9, 1935; s. Edward William and Marie Veronica (Danaher) C.; m. Barbara Ann Wilson, Aug. 1, 1959; children: Charles Michael Jr., William E., Mary E. BS in Acctg., Mt. St. Mary's Coll., 1957; JD, Seton Hall U., 1960; LLM in Taxation, NYU, 1968. Bar: N.J 1960; U.S. Tax Ct. 1961, U.S. Ct. Appeals (3d cir.) 1973, U.S. Supreme Ct. 1983. Trial atty. office regional counsel IRS, N.Y.C., 1961-69; tax assoc. Shanley & Fisher, Newark, 1969-76; tax ptnr. Stryker, Tams & Dill, Newark, 1976—. Mem. N.J. State and Local Expenditure and Revenue Commn., 1985-88, bd. policy advisors Pub. Affairs Rsch. Inst. N.J. Mem. ABA, N.J. Bar Assn. (chmn. taxation sect. 1984-85), N.J. State C. of C. (chmn. cost of govt. com. 1988—), Am. Coll. Tax Counsel, Essex Club. Republican. Roman Catholic. Home: 8 Neptune Pl Colonia NJ 07067-2502 Office: Stryker Tams & Dill 2 Penn Plaza E 33 Washington St Newark NJ 07105

COSTIKYAN, GREG, writer, game designer; b. N.Y.C., July 22, 1959; s. Edward N. and Frances (Holmgren) C.; m. K. Louise Disbrow, Sept. 4, 1986; children: Elizabeth, Victoria. BS in Geophysics, Brown U., 1982. Game designer Simulations Publs., Inc., N.Y.C., 1976-82; dir. rsch. and design West End Games, Inc., N.Y.C., 1985-87; v.p. Eric Goldberg Assocs., Inc., N.Y.C., 1987-88; pvt. practice Jersey City, 1988—; pres. Game Designer's Guild, N.Y.C., 1985-86. Author: Another Day, Another Dungeon, 1990 (Sci. Fiction Book Club selection 1991); game designer Supercharge, 1976, Swords & Sorcery, 1978, The Creature That Ate Sheboygan, 1979 (Origins award Best Sci. Fiction or Fantasy Boardgame 1979), Vector 3, 1979, DeathMaze, 1979, Barbarian Kings, 1980, Return of the Stainless Steel Rat, 1981, Trailblazer, 1981, Bug-Eyed Monsters, 1983, Paranoia, 1984 (Origins award Best Roleplaying Game 1984), 2nd edit., 1987, Toon, 1984, Web and Starship, 1984 (Origins award Best Sci. Fiction Boardgame 1984), Star Trek: The Adventure Game, 1985, Star Trek III, 1985, Pax Britannica, 1985 (Origins award Best Pre-20th Century Boardgame 1985), Acute Paranoia, 1986, The Price of Freedom, 1986, Your Own Private Idaho, 1987, Star Wars: The Role Playing Game, 1987 (Origins award Best Roleplaying Rules 1987, Gamer's Choice award Best Sci. Fiction Roleplaying Game 1988), The Willow Game, 1988, MadMaze, 1989; contbg. editor Reason mag., 1991—, The Gamer mag., 1991—; contbr. short stories to mags. including Isaac Asimov's Sci. Fiction Mag., Amazing Stories, articles to publs. including New York. Mem. Sci. Fiction Writers Am. Libertarian.

COSTLE, DOUGLAS MICHAEL, retired law school dean; b. Long Beach, Calif., July 27, 1939; m. Elizabeth Rowe; 1 son, 1 dau. AB, Harvard U., 1961; JD, U. Chgo., 1964. Bar: D.C. 1965, Calif. 1968. Trial atty. civil rights div. U.S. Dept. Justice, 1964-65; atty. Econ. Devel. Adminstrn., U.S. Dept. Commerce, 1965-67; assoc. firm Marshall, Kaplan, Gans & Kahn, San Francisco, 1968-69; sr. staff assoc. Pres.'s Adv. Council on Exec. Orgn., 1969-70; fellow Woodrow Wilson Internat. Center for Scholars of Smithsonian Instn., 1971; dep. commr. Conn. EPA, 1972-73, commr., 1973-75; asst. dir. Congressional Budget Office, 1975-77; adminstr. EPA, 1977-81; chmn. U.S. Fed. Regulatory Coun., 1978-81, Radiation Policy Coun., 1980-81; of counsel Wald, Harkrader & Ross, Washington, 1981-85, Updike, Kelley & Spellacy, Hartford, Conn., 1981—; dean Vt. Law Sch., South Royalton, 1987-91, ret., 1991; vis. scholar Sch. Pub. Health, Harvard U., 1981; bd. dirs. Clean Sits, Inc., Washington, Air and Water Techs., Inc., Somerville, N.J., Niagra Mohawk Power Co. Bd. dirs. Freedom Environ. Fund, Boston, Keystone (Colo.) Ctr. Home: RR #2 PO Box 480 Woodstock VT 05091

COTELINGAM, JAMES DWARKANATH, pathologist; b. Mysore, India, Dec. 26, 1941; came to the U.S., 1973; s. James Dinanath and Mercy Lily (Purshotam) C.; children: Monica, James Jr. Degree, Ewing Christian Coll., Allahabad, India, 1960; MD, Christian Med. Coll., Ludhiana, India, 1966. Diplomate Am. Bd. Anatomic and Clin. Pathology and Hematopathology. Intern Christian Med. Coll., Ludhiana, Panjab, India, 1966; demonstrator, then lectr. in pathology Christian Med. Coll., 1967-73; resident in pathology Ohio Valley Med. Ctr., Wheeling, W.Va., 1973-74, Presbyn. Hosp., Pitts., 1974-76; staff pathologist Naval Regional Med. Ctr., Orlando, Fla., 1977-79, head lab. svc., 1979-81; fellow hematopathology Nat. Naval Med. Ctr., Bethesda, Md., 1981-82, staff hematopathologist, 1982-85, head anatomic pathology, 1985-87, head hematopathology, 1987—; program dir. tri-svc. hematopathology fellowship U.S. DOD, 1987—. Contbr. articles to profl. jours. Ruling elder Presbyn. Ch., Gaithersburg, Md., 1980—. Capt. USN, 1987—. Decorated Commendation medal, Desert Storm Unit Citation; recipient Alumni award Christian Med. Coll., 1966. Fellow Am. Soc. Clin. Pathologists, U.S.-Canadian Acad. Pathologists, Coll. Am. Pathologists; mem. Indian Med. Assn., Christian Med. Assn. India, N.Y. Acad. Sci., Washington Soc. Pathologists, Am. Coll. Physician Execs. Home: 2322 Fort William Dr Olney MD 20832 Office: Nat Naval Med Ctr Box 213 Naval Hosp Bethesda MD 20814

COTHREN, MICHAEL WATT, art educator; b. Nashville, Ark., Apr. 9, 1951; s. Virgil Watis and Mildred Ellen (Lofton) C.; m. Susan Lowry; children: Emma, Nora. BA, Vanderbilt U., 1973; MA, Columbia U., 1974, PhD, 1980. Asst. prof. Swarthmore (Pa.) Coll., 1978-83, assoc. prof., 1983-92, chair art dept., 1983—, prof., 1992—; mem. com. at large Corpus Vitrearum, 1981—. Mem. Internat. Ctr. Medieval Art (bd. advisors 1987-90), Phi Beta Kappa. Home: 611 Strath Haven Ave Swarthmore PA 19081-2308 Office: Swarthmore Coll Dept Art Swarthmore PA 19081

COTI, RALPH, lawyer; b. N.Y.C., Oct. 16, 1952; s. Armand Anthony and Anne (Martemucci) C.; m. Mary Alice Freehill, Nov. 19, 1977. BA, Columbia U., 1974, MBA, JD, 1977. Bar: N.Y. 1977. Researcher Columbia U., N.Y.C., 1974-76; legal asst. Haight, Gardner, Poor & Havens, N.Y.C., 1976-77, assoc., 1977-79; atty. Tiger Internat., Inc., N.Y.C., 1979-80; assoc. Lovejoy, Wasson & Ashton, N.Y.C., 1980-83; pvt. practice, N.Y.C., 1983-84; ptnr. Coti & Flicker, N.Y.C., 1984-91, Coti & Sugrue, N.Y.C., 1991—. Roman Catholic. Home: PO Box 712 Ridgewood NJ 07451-0712 Office: 20th Fl 575 Lexington Ave New York NY 10022-6183

COTIER, RALPH, psychotherapist; b. N.Y.C., Jan. 20, 1936; s. Richard Joseph and Alida (Dubé) C.; children: Vance Richard, Yvonne, Yvette. BS, St. John's U., 1962; MS, L.I.U., 1986. Nat. cert. counselor, nat. cert. addictions counselor II; credentials alcoholism counselor, N.Y. Alcoholism counselor South Oaks Psychiat. Hosp., Amityville, N.Y., 1980-81; alcoholism counselor Mercy Hosp. New Hope, Garden City, N.Y., 1981; cons. L.I. Ctr., Huntington Station, N.Y., 1981-86; alcoholism group counselor leader Plainview (N.Y.) Rehab. Ctr., 1981-85; dir. Dorothy Young Recovery House, Plainview, 1985—; coord. alcoholism counselor tng. Queensborough Community Coll., Bayside, N.Y., 1986-89, lectr., 1986—; lectr. Hofstra U., Hempstead, N.Y., 1990, 92, Adelphi U., 1992, Nassau Community Coll., Garden City, N.Y., 1990, Queens Coll., 1990—, South Oaks Inst. Alcohol Studies, Amityville, 1987; mem. L.I. Counsel on Alcoholism, 1992. Contbr. articles to profl. jours. including a column in N.Y. Fedn. Alcoholism and Chem. Dependency Counselors' newsletter. With U.S. Army, 1955-58. Mem. N.Y. Fedn. Alcoholism and Chem. Dependency Counselors (bd. dirs. 1986-91, sec. 1988-89, v.p. 1989-90), L.I. Alcoholism and Chem. Dependency Counselors Assn. (regional rep. 1986-91, v.p. 1984-85, pres. 1985-86, Yev Gardiner award for outstanding achievement 1990), Am. Assn. for Counseling and Devel., N.Y. State Assn. for Counseling and Devel., Am. Mental Health Counselors Assn., Nat. Assn. Alcoholism and Drug Abuse Counselors, Soc. Ams. for Recovery, Am. Legion. Home: 9 Richlee Ct Mineola NY 11501-3629 Office: Dorothy Young Recovery House 1425 Old Country Rd Plainview NY 11803-5015

COTIGNOLA, DESIREE ROSE, investigator; b. Freeport, N.Y., Nov. 17, 1959; d. Patrick Anthony and DeLores June (Schnieder) C.; children: Jaimilee Schnieder (dec.), Samantha Mileti. AAS, Broome Coll., 1985. Investigator pre-trial release program State of N.Y., 1985-87; title clk. Miller Motor Corp., Vestal, N.Y., 1987-88; self-employed investigator N.Y., 1988-90, 91—; v.p. Jaimilee Enterprizes, N.Y.C., 1990-91. Treas. Martha Lyons Judge, Johnson City, N.Y., 1990-91; mem. Jim Moran Assembly, Johnson City, 1991. Home: PO Box 494 Montrose PA 18801

COTLER, MARVIN AARON, small business owner; b. Frackville, Pa., Sept. 17, 1932; s. Morris and Fay (Tenenholz) C.; m. Frieda Nemerowsky Dec. 21, 1958; children: Gregg, Douglas. BA, Pa. State U., 1954. Asst. buyer John Wanamaker's, Phila., 1956-57; asst. buyer to buyer Gimbel's, Phila., 1957-58; tchr. Phila. Sch. System, 1958-60; owner, operator Marvin Cotler Bowling Supplies, Phila., 1960-90; owner Product Specialities, Inc., Phila., 1990—; announcer, color man Sta. WTAF TV Bowling Show, 1970-81; cons. to English bowling instr., 1986—. Chmn. USA Bowling Team, World Maccabiatt Games, 1993. With U.S. Army, 1954-56. Mem. Bowling & Billiard Inst. Am., Bowling Writers' Assn. Am. Office: Product Specialties Inc PO Box 37 Wyncote PA 19095

COTRUVO, JOSEPH ALFRED, federal agency administrator; b. Toledo, Aug. 3, 1942; s. Nicholas and Angela (Campanale) C.; m. Marcia J. Ramm,

Dec. 28, 1968 (div. 1970); m. Karen Shrum, June 18, 1983; 1 child, Joseph Alfred Jr. BS in Chemistry, U. Toledo, 1963; PhD, Ohio State U., 1968; postdoctoral, U. Bologna, Italy, 1969. Mgr. R & D Chem. Samples Co., Columbus, Ohio, 1970-72; programs analyst EPA, Washington, 1973-76, dir. criteria and standards div., 1976-90, dir. health and environ. rev. div., 1990—; mem. Coun. Pub. Health Cons., Nat. Sanitation Found., Ann Arbor, Mich. Co-editor: Ozone/Chlorine Dioxide, 1978, Water Chlorination, 1983; chmn., editor book series NATO/CCMS Drinking Water Pilot, 1980; contbr. articles to jours. in field. Recipient Environ. Leadership award Nat. Sanitation Found., Ann Arbor, 1988, Donald R. Boyd award Assn. Met. Water Agys., 1990; named Meritorious Exec., Pres. U.S., 1983. Mem. Am. Chem. Soc., Am. Water Works Assn. (mem. editorial adv. bd. Jour. Am. Water Works Assn. 1987—). Roman Catholic. Office: EPA Health & Environ Rev Toxic Substances Office 401 M St SW Washington DC 20460-0002

COTTEN-HUSTON, ANNIE LAURA, psychologist, educator; b. Oxford, N.C., Nov. 18, 1923; d. Leonard F. and Laura Estelle (Spencer) Cotten; diploma Hardbarger Bus. Coll., 1944; AB, Duke U., 1945; MEd, U. Hartford, 1965; PhD, Union Grad. Sch., 1979; children: Hollis W., Rebecca Ann, Laura Cotten. Asst. to pres. So. Meth. U., 1953; rsch. asst. Duke U., 1947-49; exec. sec. Ohio Wesleyan U., 1955-56, Conn. Coun. Chs., 1958-60; adj. prof. U. Hartford, 1976-78; clin. pastoral counselor Hartford Hosp., 1962-65; asst., then asso. dir. social svcs. Hartford Conf. Chs., 1965-67; teaching fellow U. N.C., 1970-71; adj. prof. U. Hartford, 1976-78; assoc. prof. Cen. Conn. State U., New Britain, 1967—; cons. Somers Correctional Ctr. (Conn.), 1980-81, instr./researcher, 1980-81; cons. Life Ins. Mktg. Rsch., 1981—; amb. to China, spring, 1986; presenter 3d Internat. Interdisciplinary Cong. on Women, 1987; vis. prof., scholar Duke U., 1989; vis. prof. Conn. Coll. New London, Conn., 1990; dir. Ctr. Adult Learners Cen. Conn. State U., 1991—. Elder hostel dir. Cen. Conn. State U., 1987—. Mem. AAUW, Am. Personnel and Guidance Assn., Am. Assn. Marriage and Family Therapists (cert.), Am. Psychol. Assn. (presenter conf. 1987), Nat. Coun. Family Rels., Am. Assn. Sex Educators, Counselors and Therapists (cert.), Conn. Psychol. Assn., Conn. Council Chs. (dir.), Hartford Women's Network. Contbr. articles to profl. jours. Home: 193 Westland Ave West Hartford CT 06107-3057 Office: Ctrl Conn State Coll Dept Psychology New Britain CT 06050

COTTER, DOUGLAS ADRIAN, healthcare executive; b. Brockport, N.Y., Aug. 15, 1943; s. Adrian Edwards and Rita Elizabeth (Marshall) C.; m. Rosalyn DeVaughn, June 12, 1965 (div.); children: Elizabeth D., Anne R.; m. Anne Holmes Thompson, Oct. 4, 1986. BS, Duke U., 1965; MS, N.C. State U., 1967, PhD, 1970. Rsch. engr. Corning Glass Works, Raleigh, N.C., 1966-69, mem. rsch. and devel., 1970-78; bus. devel. mgr. Corning Med. Europe, Halstead, Essex, England, 1978-80; portfolio mgr. Corning (N.Y.) Glass Works, 1980-83; dir. info. systems Corning Med., Medfield, Mass., 1984-85; pres. Healthcare Decisions Inc., Cambridge, Mass., 1986—; adj. prof. Boston U., 1985—, N.C. State U., 1973-76; dir. Respironics Inc., Murrysville, Pa., 1989—. Inventor/patentee in field. Mem. Inst. Elec. Engrs. (sr. mem.), Assn. Corp. Growth, Licensing Exec. Soc. Office: Healthcare Decisions Inc 1600 Providence Hwy Walpole MA 02081

COTTER, JAMES MICHAEL, lawyer; b. Providence, May 12, 1942; s. James Henry and Marguerite Louise (Clark) C.; m. Melinda Irene Tighe, Feb. 6, 1971; children: Elizabeth, Heather, Kathryn. AB, Fairfield U., 1964; LLB, U. Va., 1967. Bar: N.Y. 1967. Assoc. Simpson Thacher & Bartlett, N.Y.C., 1967-75, ptnr., 1975—. Served as lt. comdr. USNR, 1968-71. Mem. ABA, N.Y. State Bar Assn., N.Y. Law Inst. (treas., bd. dirs. 1984—), Met. Golf Assn. (pres., bd. dirs. 1972—), Met. Golf Assn. Found. (chmn. bd. dirs. 1991—), Greenwich Country Club (Conn.). Office: Simpson Thacher & Bartlett 425 Lexington Ave New York NY 10017-3903

COTTER, PAUL BARRY, JR., physician; b. Buffalo, N.Y., Sept. 26, 1949; s. Paul Barry and Mary Elizabeth (Maghran) C.; m. Margaret Olivia Barres, June 29, 1974; children: Nathaniel Barnes, John Oliver, Paul Barry III. BA, U. Toronto, 1972; MD, SUNY, 1976. Cert. Am. Bd. Ophthalmology, 1982. Physician pvt. practice, 1981—. Fellow Am. Acad. Ophthalmology; mem. New England Ophthalmological Soc., Mass. Soc. Eye Physicians and Surgeons. Office: 179 Quincy St Brockton MA 02402

COTTLE, ROBERT DUQUEMIN, plastic surgeon, otolaryngologist; b. Montreal, Que., Can., May 10, 1935; s. Melvin Wheeler and Lilian Louise (Butt) C.; m. Mildred Isabel Cave, 1960 (div. 1968); children: Stephen, Michael, Sean, Scott; m. Suzanne Kern, 1969; 1 child, Melanie Catherine. BA magna cum laude, Loyola Coll., Montreal, 1956; MD, C.M., McGill U., Montreal, 1960. Diplomate Am. Bd. Otolaryngology. Intern, then resident in gen. surgery Henry Ford Hosp., Detroit, 1960-62; rsch. fellow in otology Columbia U., N.Y.C., 1964; asst., resident surgeon in otolaryngology/head and neck surgery Columbia-Presbyn. Med. Ctr., N.Y.C., 1965-67; pvt. practice medicine specializing in facial plastic surgery, head and neck surgery, otolaryngology Stamford, Conn., 1967—; pres., med. dir. Stamford Hearing and Speech Ctr., Stamford; pres. SKC AIR, Inc., White Plains, N.Y., 1972—; chmn. bd. dirs., chief exec. officer Maple Leaf Petroleum, Dallas, 1982-85; chief div. otolaryngology/head and neck surgery St. Joseph Hosp., Stamford, 1979—; mem. staff Stamford Hosp. Bd. dirs. United Way Stamford, PSRO Conn., Fairfield Health Plan, Physicians Health Svcs. Conn. (bd. chmn. IPA 1986-87). Capt. M.C., USAF, 1962-64. Recipient Gov.-Gen. of Can. medal, 1956. Fellow ACS, Am. Acad. Cosmetic Surgery, Am. Acad. Otolaryngology/Head and Neck Surgery, Am. Acad. Facial Plastic Surgery; mem. AMA, Am. Coll. of Surgeons (sec. Conn. state coun. 1987-88, pres. elect 1989-90), N.Y. Acad. Scis., Fairfield County Med. Assn. (trustee 1986—, chmn. bd. trustees 1988-90), Conn. State Med. Soc. (del. 1979—, assoc. councilor 1990—), Stamford Med. Soc. (pres. 1978-79), Internat. Platform Assn., Landmark Club. Republican. Office: 22 Long Ridge Rd Stamford CT 06905-3803

COTTLE, WILLIAM ANDREW, music educator, choirmaster; b. Clovis, N. Mex., June 17, 1941; s. Lorenzo Warren and Rhea (Vaughter) C.; m. Sandra Jo Williams, June 30, 1962 (div.); children: William Andrew Jr., Katherine Joe; m. Rebecca Jane Taylor, Mar. 27, 1987. B in Music Edn., Ea. N. Mex. U., 1964, MA, 1964; ArtsD, U. No. Colo., 1979. With choral, band Carlsbad (N. Mex.) City Schs., 1964-66; chmn. fine arts dept. Napa (Calif.) Valley Unified Schs., 1966-79; asst. prof. U. Ill., Champaign, Urbana, 1979-81; assoc. prof. U. Del., Newark, 1981—; Bd. dirs. Bay Sect. Calif., Music Educators Assn., 1976-78; mem. Univ. Del. Senate. Editor Choral Courier, 1987—; contbr. articles to profl. jours. Named Tchr. of Yr. Nat. Honor Soc., Carlsbad, N. Mex., 1966, Jr. C. of C., Napa, Calif., 1970, CA Congress Parents & Tchrs., 1974; recipient Medal of Honor, Finnish Ministry Edn., 1988, Meritorious Svc. award Del. State Supt., 1989, Order of Excellence, Del. State Bd. Edn., 1990. Mem. Am. Choral Dirs. Assn. (bd. dirs. ea. div. 1987—), Del. Music Educators Assn. (bd. dirs. 1986-88), Soc. Mayflower Descendants. Office: U Del Music Dept Newark DE 19716

COTTONE, FRANCIS JOHN, physician; b. Trenton, N.J., Apr. 24, 1929; s. Rosano John and Martha (Broad) C.; m. Irene Mae Yuhas, May 18, 1963; children: Peter, Mary, Elizabeth, Thomas, Ellen. BS, Georgetown U., 1950, MD, 1954. Diplomate Am. Bd. Surgery. Ptnr. Fares Surg. Assocs., Trenton, 1965-91; dir. surgery St. Francis Med. Ctr., Trenton, 1991—; assoc. prof. Hahneman U., Phila., 1972—; clin. asst. prof. surgery Robert Wood Johnson U., 1991—. Lt. USNR, 1957-79. Fellow Am. Coll. Surgeons (liaison); mem. AMA, Alpha Omega Alpha. Roman Catholic. Office: Saint Francis Med Ctr 601 Hamilton Ave Trenton NJ 08629

COTTS, ROBERT MILO, physics educator; b. Green Bay, Wis., Aug. 22, 1927; s. Milo Miles and Myrtle Ruth (Williams) C.; m. Barbara Ann Meyer, June 17, 1950; children: David R., Eric J., Stuart M., Steven L. BSEE, U. Wis., 1950; PhD in Physics, U. Calif., Berkeley, 1954. Instr. Stanford (Calif.) U., 1954-57; asst. prof. Cornell U., Ithaca, N.Y., 1957-63; assoc. prof. Cornell U., Ithaca, 5, 1963-68, prof. physics, 1968—; mem. advanced placement examining com. Coll. Entrance Examining Bd., Princeton, N.J. and N.Y.C., 1965-70, chmn., 1968-70; vis. physicist metallurgy div. Nat. Bur. Standards, Washington, 1963-64; vis. prof. physics U. B.C., 1970-71; S.R.C. sr. vis. fellow U. Warwick, Eng., 1978; SERC vis. fellow chem. lab. Cambridge (Eng.) U., 1986. Contbr. articles to profl. publs. Mem. Am. Phys. Soc. (mem. edn. com. 1980-83), Am. Assn. Physics Tchrs. (mem. resource letters editorial bd. 1972-75, 92—). Home: 115 Northview Rd Ithaca NY 14850-6039 Office: Cornell U Dept Physics Clark Hall Ithaca NY 14853-2501

COUCH, ROBERT FRANKLIN, military officer, geologist, environmental program manager; b. Kokomo, Ind., Feb. 15, 1947; s. Robert Franklin Sr. and Virginia Jean (Lorts) C.; m. Alice Ann Stemen, Jan. 1972 (div. Mar. 1979); m. Gloria Archuleta, Feb. 6, 1982. BS, Capital U., 1969; MS, Ohio State U., 1971. Commd. 2d. lt. USAF, 1969, advanced through grades to lt. col., 1985; spl. scientist and analyst DCS Devel. Plans Air Force Systems Command, Holloman AFB, N.Mex., 1971-73; nuclear weapons rsch. officer and geologist Air Force Weapons Lab., Kirtland AFB, N.Mex., 1973-74, chief earth phenomology, 1979-82; sect. chief microscopy lab. McClelland Central Lab., McClelland AFB, Calif., 1974-79; dir. nuclear surety and warhead integration Joint Cruise Missle Program, Crystal City, Va., 1982-84; program mgr. Def. Nuclear Agency Hdqs., Alexandria, 1984-87; dep. div. chief Strategic Nuclear div. Office of Asst. Sec. AF Acquisition, Pentagon, Washington, 1987-90; program mgr. PRC Environ. Mgmt., Inc., 1990—. Contbr. articles to profl. jours. Youth leader Luth. Ch., Roseville, Calif., 1974-79, Boy Scouts Am., Roseville, 1979; pastorial intern advisor Luth. Ch., Fairfax, Va., 1983-90. Mem. Kappa Iota Lambda. Republican. Home: 156 Desert Willow Rd Corrales NM 87048-7531 Office: 2021 Girard Blvd Albuquerque NM 87106

COUCH, WILLIAM GARRANT, JR., digital performance analyst; b. Dallas, May 10, 1952; s. William Garrant and Marion Estelle (Lyons) C.; m. Linda Margaret LaForge, July 7, 1979; children: David, Kristin, Rebecca. BS in Math., U. Tex., Arlington, 1973, MA in Math., 1975. Adj. prof. Trenton State Coll., Ewing, N.J., 1979-81; stats. analyst AT&T Mkt. Rsch., Basking Ridge, N.J., 1982-87; mem. tech. staff Bell Communications Rsch., Morristown, N.J., 1987—; vice chair performance working group T1 com. Integrated Svcs. Digital Network, 1991—. Mem. Am. Math. Soc., Inst. Math. Stats., Phi Kappa Phi, Pi Mu Epsilon. Republican. Episcopal. Home: 38 Manor Dr Belle Mead NJ 08502-1422 Office: Bell Communication Rsch 435 South St Morristown NJ 07960-6422

COUCHMAN, PETER ROBERT, materials science educator; b. London, England, Jan. 5, 1947; came to U.S., 1969; s. Clifford Robert and Pamela (Izzett) C.; m. Signe Mary Lund, July 3, 1977; children: David Peter, Christopher Ian. BS in Physics, U. Surrey, Guildford, England, 1969; MS in Materials Sci., U. Va., 1972, PhD in Materials Sci., 1975. Asst. prof. materials sci. Rutgers U., Piscataway, N.J., 1978-81, assoc. prof., 1981-87, prof., 1987—. Contbr. articles to profl. jours. Recipient Newcomb fellowship U. Va., Thorton fellowship, U. Va. Fellow Am. Phys. Soc., Soc. Plastic Engrs. Roman Catholic. Home: 12 High Ct High Bridge NJ 08829-1620 Office: Rutgers U PO Box 909 Piscataway NJ 08855-0909

COUDERT, RENÉ JOHN, leasing company executive, consultant; b. Greenwich, Conn., Sept. 9, 1936; s. Victor Raphael and Anita Marie (Ohmer) C.; m. Cheryl Fisher, June 20, 1969. BA in English, U. Va., 1960. Sr. mgr. pers. IBM Corp., Armonk, N.Y., 1960-80; v.p. human resources Moore McCormack Resources, Stamford, Conn., 1980-87; chmn., chief exec. officer Nat. Pers. Svc. Network, Inc., Stamford, Conn., 1988—; chmn. Pers. Roundtable, 1984-86; noted authority on the changing workplace and orgnl. restructuring. Bd. dirs. Family and Children's Svcs., 1980-85. Mem. N.Y. Yacht Club, Indian Harbor Yacht Club (rear commodore 1987-89). Republican. Roman Catholic. Home: 76 Sturbridge Hill Rd New Canaan CT 06840-4239 Office: Nat PSN Inc 1234 Summer St Stamford CT 06905-5510

COUDERT, VICTOR RAPHAEL, JR., marketing and sales executive; b. Dayton, Ohio, Mar. 8, 1926; s. Victor Raphael and Anita Marie (Ohmer) C.; m. Virginia Beach, Sept. 1, 1956; children: Anne, Victor III, Margaret, Catherine, Matthew, Paul, Lucy. AB in Econs., Yale U., 1946; postgrad., Stanford U., 1947-48; MBA, Harvard U., 1950. Sales trainee Hollingsworth & Whitney Co., Inc., Boston, 1950-52; salesman, exec. v.p. Montmorency Paper Co., N.Y.C., 1952-73; pres. Coudert Assocs. Inc., Greenwich, Conn., 1973—; from v.p. to exec. v.p. and gen. mgr. Irvine Forest Products, Inc., Greenwich, Conn., 1978-92; ret.; pres. United-Coudert, Inc., Pawtucket, R.I., 1992—. Published booklet on Soviet Union; contbr. articles to profl. jours. and newspapers. Chmn. Greenwich Bd. Ethics, 1977—, St. Mary Council, 1986-87; mem. Conn. Ethics Commn., 1984-85; bd. dirs. YMCA, 1975-81; trustee Sacred Heart U., 1975—, Convent Sacred Heart, Greenwich, 1985—. Lt. (j.g.) 1943-47, PTO. Mem. Assn. Am. Woodpulp Importers (pres. 1970-71), Tech. Assn. Pulp and Paper Industry, Millbrook Club, Exch. Club, Harpoon Club, N.Y. Yacht Club, Indian Harbor Yacht Club, Knights of Malta, Knights of St. Gregory. Republican. Roman Catholic. Home: 55 Indian Field Rd Greenwich CT 06830-7210 Office: Coudert Assocs Inc 15 Vallely Dr Greenwich CT 06831

COUDRIET, CHARLES EDWARD, banker; b. Richmond, Va., Sept. 18, 1946; s. Edward Ambrose and Annie Jeannette (Smith) C.; m. Kathrine Ann Furlong, May 2, 1970; children: Kathrine Ann, Charlotte McCauley, Charles Edward. A.B. in Econs., U. N.C., 1968; postgrad., U. Richmond, 1969-71. Cert. comml. lender. Asst. v.p. United Va. Bank (name now Crestar Bank), Richmond, 1968-74; sr. v.p. Sovran Bank (now Nations Bank), Richmond, 1974-77; v.p. Am. Security, Richmond, 1977-81, Dominion Bank N.A., Roanoke, Va., 1981-85; sr. v.p., regional exec. officer Equitable Bank N.A., Rockville, Md., 1985-90; sr. v.p. Md. Nat. Bank, 1990—; bd. dirs. Richmond Indsl. Corp.; mem. Robert Morris Assocs. Served with US Army, 1969-74. Mem. Commonwealth Club (Richmond), Univ. Club (Washington), Congl. Country Club, Kenwood Golf and Country Club, Duck Woods Country Club (Kitty Hawk, N.C.). Roman Catholic. Home: 1813 Thornton Ridge Rd Baltimore MD 21204 Office: Md Nat Bank 10 Light St Mail Stop 021508 Baltimore MD 21202

COUGHLIN, CAROLINE MARY, library director, educator; b. Bronx, N.Y., Dec. 6, 1944; d. Daniel Anthony and Antoinette (Aponte) C.; m. William Martin Weinberg, Oct. 3, 1981; 1 child, Nora Harie Weinberg. BA, Mercy Coll., 1966; MLS, Emory U., 1967; PhD, Rutgers U., 1976. Teaching asst. Rutgers U., New Brunswick, N.J., 1961-74; reference libr. First Nat. City Bank, N.Y.C., 1967-68; instr. Emory U., Atlanta, 1968-71; children's libr. Phillipsburg (N.J.) Pub. Libr., 1972-73; asst. prof. libr. sci. Simmons Coll., Boston, 1974-78; asst. dir. libr. Drew U., Madison, N.J., 1978-86, dir., 1986—, assoc. prof. bibliography and rsch., 1986—; cons. to librs., 1974—; team membership for site visits Middle State Assn., 1979—; dir. Assn. Ind. Colls. and Univs. of N.J. Librs. Group, 1986-89; reviewer of grants U.S. Office Edn., 1987—; bd. dirs. Ctr. for Rsch. Librs., Chgo., 1987-92, N.J. Ctr. for the Book., N.J.; vis. faculty mem. Rutgers U., 1988, 90. Editor: Recurring Library Issues, 1978; co-author: Administration of College Library, 1992; contbr. articles to profl. publs. Bd. dirs. Women's Project of N.J., 1984—; mem. Women's Polit. Action Caucus, N.J., 1985—. Mem. ALA (councillor 1977-81), Assn. Libr. and Info. Sci. Educators (various coms.), N.J. Libr. Assn. (pres. coll. sect. 1974-75). Democrat. Home: 304 Grant Ave Highland Park NJ 08904-1828 Office: Drew U Libr Rt 24 Madison Ave Madison NJ 07940

COUGHLIN, FRANCIS RAYMOND, JR., surgeon, educator, lawyer; b. N.Y.C., Feb. 22, 1927; s. Francis Raymond and Isabel (Archibald) C.; B.S., Fordham U., 1948; M.D., Yale, 1952; M.S. (Hosmer Teaching fellow), McGill U., Montreal, Que., Can., 1955, diploma in surgery, 1959, J.D., U. Bridgeport, 1988; m. Barbara Ann Blunt, June 9, 1951; children—Hilary, Mary, Patricia, Christopher Francis, Geoffrey Blunt, Daniel Taylor, Isabel, David Carleton. Intern, N.Y. Hosp., N.Y.C., 1952-53; resident in surgery McGill U. Teaching Hosp., Montreal, 1953-57; resident in thoracic surgery Overholt Thoracic Clinic, Boston, 1958-60; practice medicine, specializing in thoracic surgery, Stamford, Conn., 1960-88; medico-legal cons., 1988—; teaching fellow Harvard U., 1958; dir. div. thoracic and vascular surgery Stamford Hosp., 1970-73; dir. thoracic and vascular surgery St. Josephs Hosp., Stamford, 1970-73, 80-85, assoc. chief surgery, 1971-73, chief surgery, 1973-77; assoc. prof. clin. surgery N.Y. Med. Coll., 1981—; mem. staff Norwalk Hosp.; vice chair Conn. State Commn. on medicolegal investigations, 1990—. With U.S. Maritime Svc., 1945-46. Recipient Encaenia award Fordham U., N.Y.C., 1958. Diplomate Am. Bd. Surgery, Am. Bd. Thoracic Surgery. Fellow ACS (sec.-treas. Conn. chpt. 1966-70), Royal Coll. Surgeons (Can.), Am. Coll. Cardiology, Am. Coll. Chest Physicians, Royal Soc. Health, Royal Soc. Medicine, Am. Coll. Legal Medicine; mem. Soc. Thoracic Surgeons (founding mem.), N.Y. Acad. Medicine, Conn. Heart Assn. (dir. 1961-64), Conn. Lung Assn. (dir. and exec. com. 1963-69, v.p. 1967-69), Lung Assn. So. Fairfield County (pres. 1963-68, dir. 1960-70), Soc. Med. Jurisprudence (v.p. N.Y.C. chpt. 1992—), English-Speaking Union, Scottish-Am. Found., Canadian Soc., Stamford Yacht Club, Yale Club N.Y. Republican. Roman Catholic. Office: 20 Mead St New Canaan CT 06840-5701

COUGHLIN, LAWRENCE, congressman; b. Wilkes-Barre, Pa., Apr. 11, 1929; s. R. Lawrence and Evelyn (Wich) C.; m. Susan MacGregor; 4 children. A.B., Yale U.; M.B.A., Harvard U.; LL.B., Temple U. Former mem. Pa. Senate; mem. 91-102d Congresses from 13th Pa. dist. U.S. Ho. of Reps., 1969—; mem. appropriations com. 91-102nd Congresses from 13th Pa. Dist., 1969—; vice chmn. select com. narcotics abuse and control. Bd. dirs. Easter Seal Soc.; bd. dirs. Big Bros. Assn., Montgomery County Opportunities Industrialization Ctr., Med. Coll. Pa. Served to capt. USMC, Korea. Recipient first human rights award Interreligious Task Force on Soviet Jewry; recipient first human rights award Montgomery County Opportunities Industrialization Ctr.; named outstanding young man Main Line C. of C. Mem. Am. Legion, Mil. Order of Fgn. Wars, Marine Corps League. Office: Rayburn House Office Bldg Rm 2309 Washington DC 20515

COUGHLIN, PETER JOSEPH, economics educator, researcher; b. Hackensack, N.J., July 3, 1952; s. Joseph J. and Doris M. (Walcott) C.; children: Kathleen, Charles. BA in Math. magna cum laude, SUNY, Albany, 1973, MA in Econs., 1974, PhD in Econs., 1976; MS in Math., U. Vt., 1978. Instr., then asst. prof. dept. econs. Middlebury (Vt.) Coll., 1976-78; postdoctoral fellow Harvard U., Cambridge, Mass., 1978-79, Stanford U., Calif., 1979-80, Oxford (Eng.) U., 1980-81, Carnegie-Mellon U., Pitts., 1981-82; asst. prof. dept. econs. U. Md., College Park, 1982-85, mem. faculty applied math., 1982—, assoc. prof. dept. econs., 1985—; vis. scholar dept. econs. Case Western Res. U., Cleve., 1986-87; fellow Ctr. Advanced Study in Behavioral Scis., Stanford U., 1987-88; referee profl. jours. Contbr. articles in field to profl. jours., encys. and books. Recipient James L. Barr award in pub. econs. Assn. Pub. Policy Analysis and Mgmt., 1984; Pew grantee, U. Md., 1987-90, NSF grantee, 1984-87. Mem. Am. Econ. Assn., Ea. Econ. Assn., Econometric Soc., Pub. Choice Soc., So. Econ. Assn. Office: U Md Dept Econs College Park MD 20742

COUKIS, PETER GEORGE, musician, composer; b. Waterbury, Conn., Jan. 15, 1955; s. George Peter and Antoinette (Kachulis) C. BA, Western Conn. State U., 1978; AS, Mattatuck Community Coll., Waterbury, 1987. Musical arranger, composer Waterbury Children's Found., 1977-78; arranger, songwriter Youth Theatre Ensemble, Watertown, Conn., 1985-87; producer, performer Laurel Cablevision, Litchfield, Conn., 1988—; recording artist Coukis/Calvo, Waterbury and Wallingford, Conn., 1990—. Composer, keyboardist The Nutmeg Ballet, Torrington, Conn., 1988; songwriter World Star Prodns., New Haven, 1988; keyboardist South Mich. Ave, Wolcott, Conn., 1980-86; synthesizer player Angels and Co. (Nunsense), N.Y.C. and Waterbury, 1989; artist, proucer cable In Performance, 1988, Repertoire, 1989 (Laurel award 1989), Kaleidoscope, 1991, 13-week cable series, 1991, cable spl., 1992; released cassette single Girl, 1992. Talk show guest Barbara Davitt's Coffee Break, Sta. WATR, Waterbury, 1990; feature guest Lifestyles with Dr. Kotler, Sta. WCAT-13, Waterbury, 1990. Mem. Conn. Songwriters Assn. (Three-year award 1985, Five-year award 1987). Democrat.

COULOMBE, LYNN CATHERINE, counselor; b. Providence, Aug. 12, 1956; d. Normand William and Mary Louise (Bogetti) C.; m. Richard Ronald Sewchuk, Dec. 26, 1976; 1 child, Meredith Catherine. BA, Clark U., 1978; MA, R.I. Coll., 1988. Social caseworker State of R.I. Dept. Social & Rehab. Svcs., Providence, 1978-79; rsch. asst. Ctr. for Rsch. in Writing, Brown Univ., Providence, 1980-81; writing instr. R.I. Coll., Providence, 1981-83; counselor Planned Parenthood of R.I., Providence, 1987-87; English tchr. Sch. One, Providence, 1988-89, counseling coord., 1989—. Author: (poetry) Close to Home, 1978. V.p. Lupus Assn. of R.I., Providence, 1981, pres., 1982. Mem. AACD, Assn. Counselor Educators and Suprs., R.I. Govs. Com. on Youth, Alcohol & Substance Abuse, Providence Substance Abuse Prevention Coun. Democrat. Home: 3 Quaker Ln Greenville RI 02828-2110 Office: Sch One 75 John St Providence RI 02906-2033

COULSON, JACK RICHARD, entomologist; b. Manhattan, Kans., Jan. 31, 1931; s. Emery Jack and Esther Marie (George) C.; married 1955 (div. 1959); 1 child, Susan Jane Rowland; m. Ursula E. M. Cobb, July 2, 1964; 1 child, Andrew McKenzie. BS in Zoology, Iowa State U., 1952. Entomologist Agr. Rsch. Svc. USDA, Paris and Moorestown, N.J., 1963-67; asst. to chief and rsch. leader Agr. Rsch. Svc. USDA, Beltsville, Md., 1968-85, dir. Agr. Rsch. Svcs. Biol. Control Documentation Ctr., 1982—. Contbr. book chpts. and over 50 articles to profl. jours. Sgt. USMC, 1952-56. Mem. Internat. Orgn. Biol. Control (pres. nearctic regional sect. 1987-88, pres. global body 1988-92)), Entomol. Soc. Am., Entomol. Soc. Washington. Home: RR 1 Box 355 Bluemont VA 22012-9503 Office: USDA Bldg 476 BARC-E Beltsville MD 20705

COULSON, ROBERT, association executive; b. New Rochelle, N.Y., July 24, 1924; s. Robert Earl and Abby (Stewart) C.; m. Cynthia Cunningham, Oct. 16, 1961; children: Cotton Richard, Dierdre, Crocker, Robert Cromwell, Christopher. BA, Yale U., 1949; LLB, Harvard U., 1953; DSc in Bus. Adminstrn. (hon.), Bryant U., 1985; LLD (hon.), Hofstra U., 1987. Bar: N.Y. 1954, Mass. 1954. Assoc. Whitman, Ransom & Coulson, N.Y.C., 1954-61; ptnr. Littlefield, Miller & Cleaves, N.Y.C., 1961-63; exec. v.p. Am. Arbitration Assn., N.Y.C., 1963-71; pres. Am. Arbitration Assn., 1971—; Cons. N.Y. State Div. Youth, 1961-63; pres. Youth Consultation Service of N.Y., 1970. Author: How to Stay Out of Court, 1968, Labor Arbitration: What You Need to Know, 1973, Business Arbitration: What You Need to Know, 1980, The Termination Handbook, 1981, Fighting Fair, 1983, Arbitration in Schools, 1986, Business Mediation, 1987, Alcohol and Drugs in Arbitration, 1988, Empowered at Forty, 1990; editor: Racing at Sea, 1958; contbr. articles to profl. jours. Bd. dirs. Fedn. Protestant Welfare Agys., pres., 1982-84, chmn. 1985-87; bd. dirs. Internat. Coun. for Comml. Arbitration, Fund for Modern Cts. Mem. ABA, Assn. of Bar of City of N.Y. (sec. 1960-62), Am. Soc. Assn. Execs., N.Y. Soc. Assn. Execs. Clubs: New York Yacht, Riverside (Conn.) Yacht. Home: 9 Reginald St Riverside CT 06878-2522 Office: Am Arbitration Assn 140 W 51st St New York NY 10020-1203

COULTER, WILLIAM GODDARD, journalism educator; b. Clinton, Mass., Feb. 12, 1928; s. Craven Houghton and Barbara (Goddard) C.; m. Joyce Irene Mallar, Feb. 28, 1954; children: James, Carolyn, Constance, Candace, Christopher, Catherine. AA, Boston U., 1949, BS in Journalism, 1951. Reporter Quincy (Mass.) Ledger, 1953-55; editor Clinton (Mass.) Daily Item, 1955-86; co-pub. Clinton Daily Item, 1969-86; columnist Telegram & Gazette, Worcester, Mass., 1986-89; adj. prof. journalism Northeastern U., Boston, 1989—. Author: Profiles of Nypro, 1990. Trustee Clinton Hosp., 1971—, chmn. bd., 1983—; pres. Clinton Citizen's Coun., 1973-75. With U.S. Army, 1951-53. Recipient Outstanding Citizen award Grange, Berlin, Mass., 1981. Mem. Rotary (pres. Clinton 1965-66, Paul Harris award 1990). Episcopalian. Home and Office: 337 Central Ave Marshfield MA 02050-6152

COUREY, NORMAN LEON, anesthesiologist; b. Montreal, Que., Can., July 4, 1942; came to U.S., 1982; s. Leon and Laurice Courey; m. Susan Silverman, Nov. 27, 1971. BSc, McGill U., Montreal, 1963, MD, 1966, diploma in anesthesia, 1971. Diplomate Am. Bd. Anesthesiology. Intern Jewish Gen. Hosp., Montreal, 1966-67; resident Royal Victoria Hosp., Montreal Children's Hosp., 1967-71, Montreal Chest Hosp., Montreal Neurol. Inst., 1967-71; anesthesiologist Grace Hosp., Ottawa, Ont., Can., 1971-73, St. Mary's Hosp., Montreal, 1973-82, Royal Victoria Hosp., Montreal, 1980-81, Newton-Wellesley Hosp., Boston, 1982-90, St. Margaret's Hosp., Boston, 1991—. Fellow Royal Coll. of Physicians; mem. Mass. Med. Soc. Eastern Orthodox.

COURIC, KATHERINE, broadcast journalist; b. Arlington, Va., 1957; m. Jay Monahan. Grad., with Am. Studies major, U. Va. Began career with reporting and producing jobs NBC affiliates, Miami, Washington; joined NBC Network News, 1989; former nat. corr. Today, NBC, Washington; co-

anchor Today, NBC, 1991—. Address: NBC TV Today Show 30 Rockefeller Pla New York NY 10112*

COURRIER, KATHLEEN K., publishing executive; b. Albert Lea, Minn., June 4, 1949; d. Ralph Henry and Lois Marcella (Trytten) C.; m. Erik Peter Eckholm, Sept. 5, 1972 (div. 1981); m. Kevin Joseph Finneran, July 18, 1985; children: Anna Livia, Eamon Anders. BA, Occidental Coll., L.A., 1971; MA, Georgetown U., 1974. Instr. Marymount U., Arlington, Va., 1974-77; editor Worldwatch Inst., Washington, 1974-77; editor, writer Clearinghouse on Devel. Communication, Washington, 1977-79; communications dir. The Solar Lobby, Washington, 1979-82; acting dir. Ctr. for Renewable Resources, Washington, 1982; pub. cons. Orgn. Am. States, Washington, 1982-83; publs. dir. World Resources Inst., Washington, 1983—; mem. editorial adv. bd. Eco-Decision mag., 1991—. Editor: Life After '80: Environmental Choices We Can Live With, 1980; co-author: The Greenhouse Trap, 1990; editorial bd. Brick House Pubs., 1982-83; co-editor Guides to the Environment, 1989—; book columnist Sierra Mag., 1991—; editorial adv. bd. Internat. Union for Conservation of Nature, 1991—; free-lance book critic, 1978—. Mem. adv. bd. Theater IV, Richmond, Va., 1990—; mem. Friends of Mt. Pleasant Libr., Washington, 1990—. Fellow 21st Century Leaders Conf., The Aspen Inst., Wye, Md., 1990. Mem. Soc. Scholarly Pub., Nat. Bd. Women's Assn. Democrat. Unitarian. Home: 1636 Hobart St NW Washington DC 20009-3705 Office: World Resources Inst 1709 New York Ave NW Washington DC 20006-5206

COURSEN, CHRISTOPHER DENNISON, lawyer; b. Mpls., Dec. 6, 1948; s. Richard Dennison and Helen Wilson (Stevens) C.; m. Pamela Elizabeth Lynch, June 3, 1978; children: Cameron Dennison, Matthew Ashbolt, Madeline Messurier. BA, Washington & Lee U., 1970; JD, George Washington U., 1975. Bar: D.C. 1975, U.S. Dist. Ct. D.C., 1976, U.S. Ct. Appeals (D.C. Cir.) 1976, U.S. Ct. Mil. Appeals 1976, U.S. Supreme Ct. 1978. Sole practice Washington, 1975-78; assoc. Dempsey & Koplovitz, Washington, 1978-80; majority communications counsel U.S. Senate Com. Commerce, Sci., and Transp., Washington, 1980-83; ptnr. O'Connor & Hannan, Washington, 1983-87; pres. The Status Group, Washington, 1988-90, The Coursen Group, Washington, 1990—; adj. prof. law The George Washington U., Washington, 1983. Team mem. Pres.-Elect Reagan's Transition Team, Washington, 1980; atty. adv. Reagan-Bush 1984, Washington; telecomms. advisor Bush/Quayle presdl. campaign, 1988; mem. Pres.' Adv. Bd. for Cuba Broadcasting, 1991; mem. nat. fin. com. Bush-Quayle 1992; mem. adv. bd. Blue Ribbon Commn. on Reconstruction of Cuba; mem. bd. Children's Hosp. Found. Mem. D.C. Bar Assn., Chevy Chase Club. Roman Catholic. Home: 5006 Nahant St Bethesda MD 20816-2463 Office: The Coursen Group 1133 Connecticut Ave NW # 900 Washington DC 20036-4305

COURTEMANCHE, LEO MAURICE, silk screen printer and designer; b. Lowell, Mass., Apr. 18, 1959; s. Leo J. and Jeanette C. (Frechette) C.; m. Christina Maria Vallante, Dec. 18, 1962; children: Katrina Elaina, Kyle Anthony. Grad. tech. high sch., Tyngsboro, Mass. Sprayer Congress Tech. Spray Co., Dracut, Mass., 1977-81; silkscreener Wang Labs., Lowell, Mass., 1981-87; pres. Merrimack Valley Screen Printing, Inc., Lowell, 1987—. Republican. Roman Catholic. Office: Merrimack Valley Box 1145 528 Broadway St Lowell MA 01853-1145

COURTENAY, IRENE DORIS, nursing consultant; b. Regina, Sask., Can., July 1, 1920; d. Thomas Greer and May Elizabeth (York) C. BS in Nursing, U. Western Ont., 1956, MPH (IH), U. Mich., 1957. RN. Occupation health nurse Chrysler of Can., 1948-50, 52-55; cons. occupational health nursing N.C. Bd. Health, 1958-61; occupational health nursing specialist Nat. League for Nursing, 1961-64; cons. occupational health nursing Dept. Nat. Health and Welfare, Ottawa, Ont., 1966-69; asst. prof., dir. grad. program occupational health nursing U. N.C., Chapel Hill, 1971-75; assoc. prof., dir. grad. program occupational health profls. NYU, 1975-78; pvt. practice cons. occupational health nursing, 1978—. Author several publs. Mem. Am. Nurses Assn., Nat. League Nursing, Am. Assn. Occupational Health Nurses, Am. Bd. Occupational Health Nurses (bd. dirs.), Am. Indsl. Hygiene Assn. (assoc.), Permanent Commn. and Internat. Assn. Occupational Health, AAUP, Am. Pub. Health Assn., Can. Council Occupational Health Nurses (bd. dirs., chmn. exam. com.). Mem. Anglican Ch. Home: # X14, 5110 Wyandotte St E, Windsor, ON Canada N8S 1L2

COURTER, JEANNE LYNN, materials scientist; b. Flushing, N.Y., May 7, 1953; d. Harry Melvin Jr. and Ruth Jane (Rieben) C. B in Engring. Sci., SUNY, Stony Brook, 1975; PhD in Materials Sci., MIT, 1981. Research sci. Am. Cyanamid Co., Stamford, Conn, 1981-83; materials section projects mgr. Am. Cyanamid Co., Stamford, Conn., 1983-90, quality asst. to the div. dir., 1990—. Inventor epoxy resin compound; patentee in field (with others), 1978-86. Mem. Am. Soc. for Quality Control, Am. Chem. Soc., Tau Beta Pi. Methodist. Lodge: N.Am. Guild Change Ringers. Office: Am Cyanamid Co 1937 W Main St Stamford CT 06902-4580

COURTNEY, SUZAN LEE, artist, educator; b. Mobile, Ala., Sept. 6, 1947; d. Douglas Grant Courtney and Betty (Ennette) Petty; m. George F. Hritz, July 6, 1982; 1 child, Amelia Courtney Hritz. Diploma in art, Kingston-Upon-Hull Coll. Art, Hull, England, 1973; student, Whitney Mus. Ind. Study Progra, N.Y.C., 1974-75; MFA, Yale U., 1977. Asst. to sculptor Sol LeWitt, N.Y.C., 1974-75, 78-79; instr. Univ. South Fla., Tampa, Fla., 1977-78, R.I. Sch. Design, Providence, R.I., 1979-82; adj. prof. Southampton Coll., Southampton, N.Y., 1983-84, Rutgers Univ., New Brunswick, N.J., 1985--; adj. prof. Parsons Sch. Design, N.Y.C., 1987—; exhbn. curator Galerie Gordon Pym, Paris, 1992, Fine Arts Mus. of the South, Mobile, Ala., 1987, Ericson Gallery, N.Y.C., 1982. Artist numerous paintings, set and costume designs. Program dir. N.J. Summer Arts Inst., Rutgers Univ., New Brunswick, N.J., 1985-87. Recipient Susan Whedon Prize for Painting, Yale U., 1977, Edward Albee Found. Grant, Edward Albee Found., Montauk, N.Y., 1980. Studio: 530 Canal St # 3W New York NY 10013-1334

COUSER, GRIFFITH THOMAS, English educator; b. Melrose, Mass., Sept. 22, 1946; s. William Griffith and Ann (Van Stelten) C.; m. Margaret Ann Jackson, Aug. 21, 1974 (div. 1980); m. Barbara Beth Zabel, Dec. 29, 1984. BA, Dartmouth Coll., 1968; PhD, Brown U., 1977. Asst. prof. English Conn. Coll., New London, 1976-82; from asst. prof. to full prof English Hofstra U., Hempstead, N.Y., 1982—. Author: American Autobiography: The Prophetic Mode, 1979, Altered Egos: Authority in American Autobiography, 1989; editorial bd. Auto/Biography Studies, 1990—. NEH fellow, 1986. Home: PO Box 227 Quaker Hill CT 06375-0227 Office: Hofstra U Dpet English Hempstead Tpke Hempstead NY 11550

COUTURIER, LANCE CORNELIUS, psychologist; b. Ardmore, Pa., May 17, 1948; s. Gerard Morency and Jean (Cornelius) C.; m. Katherine Jean Devlin, Dec. 26, 1976; children: Graham, Gregory, Anna. BA, U. Md., 1970; MA, Temple U., 1974, PhD, 1980. Teaching assoc. Temple U., Phila., 1972-76; tng. inst. dir. Juvenile Justice Ctr. Pa., Phila., 1976-80; clin. dir. Southeast Secure Treatment Unit, West Chester, Pa., 1980-85; chief psychologist Pa. Dept. Correction State Correctional Instn., Graterford, 1985-92, Pa. Dept. Corrections, Camp Hill, 1992—; cons. United Cerebral Palsy Assn., Pottstown Drug and Alcohol Rehab. Program, Collegeville, Pa., 1985-88, Pub. Mgmt. Info. Systems, Washington; vis. lectr. Neumann Coll., Aston, Pa., 1983. Contbr. articles to profl. jours. Den leader Cub Scouts, Ardmore, 1988—; bd. dirs. Crime Prevention Assn., Phila., 1980-86; mem. adv. bd. South Phila. Unemployment Peoject, 1977-80, Family Resource Ctr., Graterford, 1989—. Sgt. USNG, 1976-80. Mem. Am. Psychol. Assn., Family and Correctins Network, Phi Kappa Phi. Home: 641 Woodcrest Ave Ardmore PA 19003-1919 Office: PO Box 246 Collegeville PA 19426-0246

COVELL, CHRISTOPHER GREENE, management executive; b. Providence, R.I., Apr. 14, 1947; s. Walter Howard and Harriette Francis (Tabakin) C. Founding pres. Ballet Who, Inc., N.Y.C., 1987—; resident fellow Abuse Rsch. Inst., N.Y.C., 1985—.

COVER, DAVID JOSEPH, trust company executive; b. Windber, Pa., July 30, 1962; s. Guy Richard and Ellen (Scaglione) C.; m. Marlene Frances Beatty, Sept. 12, 1987. BS in Acctg., Pa. State U., 1984; cert. in trust ops., Cannon Fin. Inst., 1989. Cert. trust ops. specialist. Acct. Olmes & Dickson CPAs, Titusville, Pa., 1984-85; trust ops. officer Johnstown (Pa.) Bank & Trust Co., 1985-90; asst. v.p. BT Mgmt. Trust Co., Johnstown, 1990—. Mem. Nat. Assn. Trust Ops. Specialists (vice chmn. 1989—), Inst. Mgmt. Accts. (dir. 1987-90), Mid-Atlantic Securities Transfer Assn., Am. Bankers Assn., Am. Fedn. Musicians, Greater Johnstown C. of C. Republican. Baptist. Home: 1903 Willett Dr Johnstown PA 15905 Office: BT Mgmt Trust Co 551 Main St Johnstown PA 15901

COVERT, EUGENE EDZARDS, aerophysics educator; b. Rapid City, S.D., Feb. 6, 1926; s. Perry and Eda (Edzards) C.; m. Mary Solveig Rutford, Feb. 22, 1946; children: David H., Christine J., Pamela M., Steven P. BS, U. Minn., 1946, MS, 1948; ScD, MIT, 1958. Registered profl. engr., Mass.; chartered engr., U.K. Preliminary design group USNADC, Johnsville, Pa., 1948-52; mem. staff MIT Aerophysics Lab., 1952-63, assoc. dir., 1963-75, assoc. prof. aeronautics and astronautics, 1963-68, prof., 1968—, head dept. aeronautics and astronautics, 1985-90; cons. Bolt, Beranek & Newman, Inc., Govt. Israel, Pratt and Whitney Aircraft div. United Techs, Hercules, Inc., MIT Lincoln Lab., Sverdrup Tech., U.S. Army Research Office; chief scientist USAF, 1972-73; mem. panel Naval Aeroballistic Adv. Com., 1965-75; mem. NASA Aeronautical Adv. com., 1985-89, Aeronautics and Space Engring. Bd., 1986—; mem., chmn. USAF Sci. Adv. Bd., 1975-86, 90—; chmn. Power, Energetics and Propulsion panel Adv. Group for Aerospace Research and Devel. NATO, 1982-86; aero. policy com. Office Sci. and Tech. Policy, 1976—; dir. Rohr Industries Inc., Chula Vista, Calif., Allied Signal Inc., Morristown, N.J., Phys. Scis. Inc., North Andover, Mass.; mem. Pres.' commn. for investigation of space shuttle accident. Served with USNR, 1943-47. Recipient Exceptional Civilian Sci. award USAF, 1973, 86, Univ. Educator of Yr. award Am. Soc. Aerospace Edn., 1980, Pub. Service award NASA, 1981, von Karman medal Adv. Group for Aerospace R & D, 1990. Fellow AIAA (dir., Ground Testing award 1990, W.F. Durand lectureship 1992), AAAS, Royal Aero. Soc.; mem. N.Y. Acad. Sci., Nat. Acad. Engring., Sigma Xi. Office: MIT 77 Massachusetts Ave Cambridge MA 02139-4307

COVI, LINO, psychiatrist; b. Trento, Italy, Mar. 19, 1926; came to U.S., 1956, naturalized, 1965; s. Giuseppe and Giuseppina (Mariotti) C.; m. Beverly A. Yeutsy, Dec. 30, 1958 (dec.); children: Lisa Martina, Michelle Peppina, Gina Albina, Tina Maria. Student in philosophy, U. Florence, Italy, 1945-47, Sch. Social Work, Trento and Rome, 1949-51; MD, U. Rome, 1955. Asst. U. Rome Neuropsychiat. Clinic, 1955-56; intern Albert Einstein Med. Ctr., Phila., 1956-57; resident fellow psychiatry Johns Hopkins Hosp., Balt., 1957-60, dir. outpatient clin. rsch. unit, 1968-83, dir. Cognitive Therapy Clinic, 1982—, dir. treatment assessment rsch. unit, 1983—; assoc. clin. prof. U. Md. Med. Sch., Balt., 1986—; instr. psychiatry Johns Hopkins U., 1960-67, asst. prof., 1967-72, assoc. prof., 1972—; vis. psychiatrist Balt. City Hosp., 1960-80; vis. scientist Nat. Inst. Drug Abuse-Addiction Rsch. Ctr., Balt. 1988—; psychiatrist Francis Scott Key Med. Ctr., Balt., 1988—; staff psychiatrist Patuxent Instn., Jessup, Md., 1960-62; chief out-patient dept. Gundry Hosp., Balt., 1962-86, pres. bd. dirs., 1972-84, rsch. dir., 1973-86; mem. bd. govs. Cen. Md. Health Systems Agy., 1978-83; rsch. psychiatrist NIMH Collaborative Studies, 1962-64, co-prin. investigator, 1964-65, prin. investigator, 1965-83, prin. investigator clin. trials of new drugs for depression and anxiety, 1970—, studies of group cognitive therapy in depression, 1980—; teaching assoc. Sheppard and E. Pratt Hosp., 1973-79; cons. Pharm. Rsch. Labs., 1971—, Centro Psicologia Clinica, Milan, 1981—. Editor: The Md. Psychiatrist, 1974-80, Today's Psychiatry, Md. Med. Jour., 1985—; contbr. articles to profl. jours. Mem. human rights com. Coop. Studies Program, VA, 1981-84. Mem. AMA (profl. staff drug evaluation coun. on drugs 1968-71), AAAS, Am. Assn. Psychoanalytic Physicians, Am. Coll. Neuropsychopharmacology (coms.), Md. Psychiat. Soc. (coms.), Am. Psychiat. Assn. (nat. coms., dep. rep. Md., Newsletter award 1977), Am. Psychosomatic Soc., World Fedn. Mental Health, Johns Hopkins Med. Soc., Am. Group Psychotherapy Assn., Assn. Advancement Behavior Therapy, Md. Med. Soc., Balt. Med. Soc. (chmn. coms.), Collegium Internat. Neuropsychopharmacologicum, Italian-Am. Hist. Assn. Democrat. Roman Catholic. Home: 501 Columbia Ct Baltimore MD 21228-5864 Office: 1777 Reisterstown Rd Baltimore MD 21208-1313

COVIELLO, ROBERT FRANK, retail executive; b. Hartford, Conn., Dec. 20, 1941; s. James Joseph Coviello and Ann Frances (Links) Leary; m. Anne Elizabeth Lomasney, Oct. 22, 1966; 1 child, Michael James. Student, U. Conn., 1960-61, U. Madrid, 1961-62; graduated, Machine Accts. Tng., 1963; student, Northeastern U., Boston, 1969. Data processing mgr. Chadwick-Miller, Inc., Boston, 1964-66; systems design analyst nat. accts. KeyData Corp., Watertown, Mass., 1969-70; systems designs mgr. KeyData Corp., N.Y.C., 1970-72; western regional mgr. KeyData Corp., Chgo., 1972-73; pres. Gallery of Gifts Shoppes, Inc. (doing bus. as Kitchen Etc.), No. Hampton, N.H., 1973—; Chmn. Downtown Bd. of Trade, Dover, N.H., 1975-77, 82-83; pres. Merchants Assn. of Lilac Mall, Rochester, N.H., 1982-83. Dir. C. of C., Dover, 1983-86. With U.S. Army, 1966-68. Recipient buyer's award of recognition Housewares Club New Eng., 1986, Potter's Club award Pfaltzgraff Co., 1986, 89. Mem. Retail Mchts. Assn. N.H. (past pres. 1985-87, dir. 1980—, named Retailer of Yr. 1988), Am. Mgmt. Assn. (Pres.'s Assn. div.), Gift Assn. Am. (dir. 1981—), World Club (St Paul). Office: Gallery of Gifts Shoppes Inc 820 Lafayette Rd #1 Hampton NH 03842-9800

COVILL, KEITH, SR., marketing executive; b. Danbury, Conn., Nov. 5, 1948; s. George Webb Sr. and Lillian Katherine (Madden) C.; m. Diane Raymond, July 30, 1968; children: Dawn Lee, Carol Ann, Keith Jr. Grad. high sch., 1966. Tester/insp. Arrowhead Enterprises Inc., Bethel, Conn., 1972; svc. mgr. Arrowhead Enterprises Inc., New Milford, Conn., 1973, sales engr., 1974-76, 79-81, regional salesman, 1976-78, tech. dir., 1981-89; tech. dir. Arrowhead Enterprises Inc., Medway, Mass., 1987-89; product mgr. Arrowhead Enterprises Inc., Stockton, Calif., 1990-91; mktg. mgr Scantronics USA Inc., Stockton, Calif., 1991—. Cub master Boy Scouts Am., Brookfield, Conn., 1985, 86. Sgt. USAF, 1968-72. Republican. Congregationalist. Office: Scantronic USA Inc 1 Charlesgate Rd Hopedale MA 01747

COWAN, BARTON ZALMAN, lawyer; b. Cleve., Mar. 3, 1934; s. Milton Jerome and Clara (Umans) C.; m. Teri Anne Thomas, June 25, 1961; children: Pamela B., Cynthia R., Susan L. AB with honors, U. Mich., 1955; JD cum laude, Harvard U., 1958. Bar: Pa., Ohio, U.S. Dist. Ct. (we. dist.) Pa., U.S. Ct. Appeals (3d, 5th and D.C. cirs.), U.S. Supreme Ct. Assoc. Eckert Seamans Cherin & Mellott, Pitts., 1961-68, ptnr., 1968—; chmn. lawyers com., mem. policy com. Atomic Indsl. Forum, Washington, 1981-87; chmn. layers com. Nuclear Mgmt. and Resource Coun., Washington, 1988-90. Pres. Pitts. chpt. Am. Jewish Com.; mem. bd. overseers Hebrew Union Coll., Jewish Inst. Religion, Cin.; treas., bd. dirs. Jewish Edn. Svc. N.Am., Inc.; sr. v.p. Rodef Shalom Cong., Pitts.; v.p. Jewish Edn. Inst. Pitts.; bd. dirs. United Jewish Fedn. Pitts., Jewish Healthcare Found. Pitts.; mem. nat. exec. coun. Am. Jewish Com. 1st lt. USAF, 1958-61. Recipient Clyde A. Lilly award Atomic Indsl. Forum, Inc., 1985. Mem. ABA (chmn. energy resources law com., tort and ins. practice sect. 1986-87), Pa. Bar Assn., Ohio Bar Assn., Allegheny County Bar Assn., Am. Judicare Soc., Internat. Nuclear Law Assn., Am. Nuclear Energy Coun., AAAS, N.Y. Acad. Sci., Duquesne Club, Westmoreland Country Club. Republican. Office: Eckert Seamans Cherin & Mellott 600 Grant St Ste 42 Pittsburgh PA 15219-2703

COWBURN, DAVID (ALAN), scientist; b. Sale, Cheshire, Eng., July 13, 1945; came to U.S., 1970; s. Thomas Alan and Grace Muriel (Seagrief) C.; m. Elizabeth Stoner, Sept. 25, 1977; children: Adam, Leah. BSc with honors, U. Manchester Inst. Tech., 1965; PhD, London U., 1970, DSc, 1981. Postdoctoral fellow Coll. of Physicians and Surgeons of Columbia U., N.Y.C., 1970-73; asst. prof. structural biology and chemistry Rockefeller U., N.Y.C., 1973-79, assoc. prof., 1979—, head of lab., 1992—; cons. Meml. Sloan Kettering Cancer Ctr., N.Y.C., 1983—. Contbr. numerous articles to sci. jours. Recipient sci. grants NIH, NSF, Am. Heart Assn., 1976—. Office: Rockefeller U 1230 York Ave New York NY 10021-6341

COWEN, JILL BERNICE, educator; b. Phila., Nov. 27, 1943; d. Robert B. and Bernice B. (Staschke) Dobie; m. David Raymond Heacock, June 5, 1968 (div. 1972); 1 child, Todd Dobie Heacock; m. Joseph Henry Cowen, Aug. 24, 1978. BA, Glassboro Coll., 1965, MA, 1977; postgrad., Rutgers U., 1986, U. Del., 1990. Cert. elem. tchr., N.J., Md., Del. Tchr. Woodlynne N.J. Pub. Schs., 1972-84, IV coord., 1984—. Head coach Hadden Top Athletic Assn., Hadden Twp., N.J., 1979-82; mem. Priscilla, Faith Luth. Ch., 1986-91. Mem. NEA, N.J. Edn. Assn., Woodlynne Edn. Assn. (sec., team mem. 1975-80, chair negotiating team 1985, Gov.'s Tchr. of Yr. award). Republican.

COWEN, PHILIP RICHARD, wire manufacturing company executive; b. N.Y.C., July 7, 1942; s. Arthur S. and Elsie (Smerling) C.; m. Gloria Rene Perlo, June 21, 1964; children: David, Andrew, Ellen. BS, NYU, 1963, MBA, 1965. Mgr. Arthur Andersen & Co., N.Y.C., 1964-70; v.p. Gen. Dynamics Corp., St. Louis, 1970-80, LTV Corp., Dallas, 1980-82; CEO Kentron Internat., Dallas, 1982-86; CEO, chmn. Alpha Wire Corp., Elizabeth, N.J., 1986—. Office: Alpha Wire Corp 711 Lidgerwood Ave Elizabeth NJ 07207

COWEN, ROBERT E., federal judge; b. Newark, Sept. 4, 1930; s. Saul and Lillie (Selzer) C.; m. Toby Cowen, Dec. 21, 1973; children: Shulie, Eve. BS, Drake U., 1952; LLB, Rutgers U., 1958. Assoc. Schreiber, Lancaster & Demos, Newark, 1959-61; asst. prosecutor Essex County, N.J., 1969-70; dep. atty. gen. organized crime Criminal Justice Dept., N.J., 1970-72, dir. Div. Ethics and Profl. Svcs., 1972-78; magistrate U.S. Dist. Ct. N.J., Newark, 1978-85; judge U.S. Dist. Ct. N.J., Trenton, 1985-87, U.S. Ct. Appeals (3d cir.), Trenton, 1987—; pvt. practice, Newark, 1961-69. Office: US Ct Appeals 3d Cir 402 E State St Rm 103 Trenton NJ 08608-1507

COWETT, RICHARD MICHAEL, pediatrician; b. N.Y.C., Sept. 20, 1942; s. Allen Abraham and Sylvia (Kazin) C.; m. Katherine Manz, June 25, 1966; children: Beth Ellen, Allison Ann, Allen Manz. BA cum laude, Lawrence Coll., 1964; MD, U. Cin., 1968; MA ad eundem (hon.), Brown U., 1982. Cert. Am. Bd. Pediatrics. Internship in pediatrics Cleve. Met. Gen. Hosp., Case Western Res. U. Sch. Medicine, 1968-69; jr. asst. resident in pediatrics Cleve. Met. Gen. Hosp., 1969-70; asst. resident in medicine Children's Hosp. Med. Ctr., Harvard U. Med. Sch., Boston, 1970-71; teaching fellow dept. pediatrics Harvard Med. Sch., Cambridge, Mass., 1970-71; teaching fellow div. biology and med. scis. Brown U., Providence, 1974-76, asst. prof. pediatrics div. biology and med. scis., 1976-81, assoc. prof. pediatrics div. biology and med. scis., 1981-89, prof. pediatrics div. biology and med. scis., 1989—; attending staff pediatrics Women & Infants' Hosp., R.I. Hosp., Providence, 1976—; adj. clin. instr. pediatrics Brown U., Providence, 1975-76; adv. coun. mem. Providence Sch. Com., 1981-85; reviewer NIH, Bethesda, Md.; mem. med. adv. com. Maternal and Child Health Div., State of R.I., 1977. Editor: Principles of Perinatal/Neonatal Metabolism, 1991; contbr. articles to profl. jours. Mem. bd. trustees Temple Beth El, Providence, 1981-85. Major USAF, 1971-73. Recipient Rsch. Career Devel. award Nat. Inst. Child Health and Devel., 1980-85, grantee, 1977-92. Mem. Am. Acad. Pediatrics (sect. of perinatal pediatrics), R.I. Acad. Pediatrics, New Eng. Neonatology Soc., AAAS, New Eng. Perinatology Soc. (counselor 1977, pres. 1978), Am. Fedn. for Clin. Rsch., Soc. for Pediatric Rsch., Am. Diabetes Assn., Am. Inst. Nutrition, Perinatal Rsch. Soc., Am. Soc. for Clin. Nutrition, Am. Pediatric Soc., Ea. Soc. for Pediatric Rsch. Office: Women & Infants Hosp of RI 101 Dudley St Providence RI 02905-2499

COWHER, BILL, professional football coach; b. Pitts., May 8, 1957; m. Kaye Cowher; children: Meagan Lyn, Lauren Marie, Lindsay Morgan. Degree in edn., N.C. State. Football player Cleve. Browns, 1980-82, spl. teams coach, 1985-86, secondary coach, 1987-88; football player Phila. Eagles, 1983-84; def. coord. Kansas City Chiefs, 1988-92; head coach Pitts. Steelers, 1992—. Office: Pitts Steelers 300 Stadium Cir Pittsburgh PA 15212

COWLES, FREDERICK OLIVER, lawyer; b. Steubenville, Ohio, Oct. 18, 1937; s. Oliver Howard and Cornelia Blanche (Regal) C.; m. Christina Monica Muller, Sept. 9, 1961; children—Randall, Eric, Gregory, Cornelius. A.B. magna cum laude, Yale U., 1959; J.D., Harvard U., 1962. Bar: R.I. 1963, Mich. 1967, Ill. 1969. Assoc. Hinckley, Allen, Salisbury & Parsons, Providence, 1962-67; internat. atty. Upjohn Co., Kalamazoo, Mich., 1967-69; chief internat. atty. Am. Hosp. Supply Crp., Evanston, Ill., 1969-71; internat. atty. Kendall Co., Boston, 1971-73; chief internat. counsel, Colgate Palmolive Co., N.Y.C., 1973-86, assoc. gen. counsel, asst. sec., 1986-90, assoc. gen. counsel, asst. sec., v.p. legal ops., 1990—; dir. various cos. Deacon, South Salem Presbyn. Ch.; mem. com. Lewisboro Boy Scouts; co-founder Internat. House R.I. Inc.; group leader Operation Crossroads Africa, Gambia. Mem. ABA, Westchester Fairfield Corp. Csl. Assn., Internat. Lawyers Assn., Phi Beta Kappa. Home: Oscaleta Rd South Salem NY 10590 Office: 300 Park Ave New York NY 10022

COWLES, ROGER WILLIAM, government audit executive; b. Ft. Madison, Iowa, July 5, 1945; s. Arthur William and Enid Francis (Smith) C. BBA cum laude, Tex. Wesleyan Coll., 1968; MA, Cen. Mich. U., 1980. Cert. cost analyst, Va. Contract auditor Def. Contract Audit Agy., Ft. Worth, 1967-76; course mgr. Def. Contract Audit Inst., Memphis, 1976-78; program mgr. hdqrs. Def. Contract Audit Agy., Alexandria, Va., 1978-80, chief mgmt. info. branch, 1980-81, chief spl. audits, 1982-86; auditor dir. contract mgmt. Office of Asst. Sec. Def., 1986-88; chief audit liason div. Office Dept. Def. Compt., Washington, 1988-89, dir. for contract audit and analysis directorate, 1990—; mem. congl. staff U.S. Congress, Washington, 1981-82. Creator toothpick sculpture (Spl. Merit award 1975); contbr. articles to profl. jours. Mem. adminstrv. bd. Franconia United Meth. Ch., 1989-91. Mem. Assn. Govt. Accts. (facilitator 1985-87, Tng. Program award 1981), Am. Soc. Mil. Compts., Sr. Exec. Svc., Nat. Contract Mgmt. Assn., Inst. Cost Analysis, Mgmt. Devel. Program, Sr. Exec. Svc. Assn., Smithsonian Assocs., Fed. Execs. Inst. Alumni Assn., Nat. Trust for Hist. Preservation, Colonial Williamsburg Found., Nat. Cathedral Found. Republican. Methodist. Office: Office of Dept Def Compt The Pentagon Rm 3C965 Alexandria VA 22301

COWPERTHWAITE, JOHN MILTON, JR., architect, construction consultant; b. Bridgeport, Conn., Nov. 3, 1912; s. John Milton Sr. and Anna Emalia (Osterberg) C.; m. Eula Mae Lunny, Sept. 5, 1936; 1 child, John Milton III. Cert., U. Bridgeport, 1944; student, Yale U., 1945. Registered architect, N.Y., Pa., Conn. Project architect Ashiem & Wilkens, Bridgeport, Conn., 1946-47, Lyons & Mather, Bridgeport, 1947-48, Andrew Euston, New Haven, 1949-50, Schilling & Goldbecker, New Haven, 1950-51; co-owner Aubin & Cowperthwaite, Hartford, Conn., 1951-53, Eaton & Cowperthwaite, Stratford, Conn., 1953-55; designer Carl Segerberg, Middltown, Conn., 1955-56; assoc. William Cram, Norwalk, Conn., 1957-59; owner Stratford, 1960—; clk. of works City of Milford, Conn., 1974-76; owner, developer Milton Reed Assoc., Inc., Stratford, 1980—. Mem. Conservation Commn., Stratford, 1970, chmn., 1973-76; mem. Bd. Appeals Bldg. Dept., Stratford, 1975—. Mem. Conn. Soc. Genealogists. Republican. Episcopalian. Clubs: Classic Jaguar Assn. (Calif.) (chartered); Conn. Classic Jaguar Assn. Home and Office: 941 E Broadway Stratford CT 06497-5909

COX, CHRISTOPHER, statistician; b. Pitts., May 22, 1944. BA, Brown U., 1966; PhD, U. Ill., 1973. Postdoctoral trainee, div. biostatistics U. Rochester (N.Y.) Med. Ctr., 1975-79, asst. prof. biostatistics, 1979-86, asst. prof. toxicology, 1983-86, assoc. prof. biostatistics and toxicology, 1987—; cons. NIH rsch. grants. Contbr. numerous rsch. articles to statis. and biomedical rsch. jours. Mem. Am. Statis. Assn., Biometric Soc., Sigma Xi. Office: U Rochester Med Ctr Dept Biostatistics Box 630 601 Elmwood Ave Rochester NY 14642-0002

COX, DIANE STEIGER, health care fundraiser, public relations executive; b. Pitts., Aug. 31, 1948; d. William Joseph and Betty (Molek) S.; m. Jeffrey Ellis Cox, May 23, 1970. BA, Carnegie Mellon U., 1970; MA, Duke U., 1974. Feature writer, copy editor Howard County News, Ellicott City, Md., 1977; pub. rels. asst. Melwood Hort. Tng. Ctr., Upper Marlboro, Md., 1977-78; dir. pub. rels. and devel. Peninsula Gen. Hosp. Med. Ctr., Salisbury, Md., 1978-84; v.p. devel. and community rels. Geneva (N.Y.) Gen. Hosp., 1984-91; v.p. devel. Waterbury (Conn.) Hosp., 1991—. Author: 101 Fund Raising Letters, 1984; contbr. articles to profl. jours. Bd. dirs. United Way of Geneva, 1990-91. Recipient 1st pl. Best News Feature Writing award Md., Del. and D.C. Press Assn., 1977. Mem. Am. Soc. for Hosp. Mktg. and Pub. Rels. (cert.), Assn. for Hosp. Philanthropy, Conn. Hosp. Pub. Rels. Coun. Office: 590 100th Ave N Naples FL 33963

COX, ERIC FREDERICK, professional society administrator; b. Balt., July 20, 1932; s. Cecil Rhodes and Elvira Viola (Bile) C. BA, Dickinson Coll., 1954. In real estate bus. Cox and Co., Washington, 1954-66; exec. dir. Washington Metro. chpt. United World Federalists, 1966-68; projects. dir. Bronx Community Coll., Bronx, N.Y., 1969-72; cons. N.Y.C., 1972-74; exec. dir. Campaign for U.N. Reform, Wayne, N.J., 1975-76; exec. dir. Campaign for U.N. Reform, Washington, 1988—, legisl. dir., 1976-87; field dir. World Federalist Assn., Washington, 1975-90, dep. dir., 1990-91; mem. core com. Support the UN Stamp Campaign, 1990-91; lectr. in field. Page writer guest columns St. Louis Dispatch, Cleveland Plain Dealer; editor newsletter Campaign for U.N. Reform, 1985-88; contbr. articles to profl. jours. Testified twice before Senate Fgn. Relations Com., D.C., 1964-65, before the Subcom. on Poverty of the Senate Labor Com., 1965, before the House Com. on banking fin. and urban affairs, 1990; mem. Washington Crim Coun., 1965, Mayor's Vol. Coun., N.Y.C., 1972; chmn. fgn. relations com. Young Democrats U.S., 1964; publicity chmn Internat. Platform Assn., Washington, 1964. With AUS, 1954-56. Mem. Citizens for Clean Air (founder D.C. area), Metro. Athletic Assn. (founder 1963-66). Democratic. Unitarian. Home: 3133 Connecticut Ave NW Apt 516 Washington DC 20008-5107 Office: Campaign for UN Reform 713 D St SE Washington DC 20003

COX, GERARD ANTHONY, academic director; b. N.Y.C.; s. Anthony Vincent and Margaret Agnes (Horan) C.; m. Margaret Mary Bellino, Dec. 26, 1970; children: Stephen Anthony, Anthony James, Anne Marie. BA, Marist Coll., 1956; MA, CUNY, Hunter Coll., 1960; newspaper fund fellow, Columbia U.; cert., RCA Inst. Lic. tchr., N.Y., Fla. Tchr. Scanlon High Sch., N.Y.C., 1956-62; dept. head English Christopher Columbus High Sch., Miami, Fla., 1962-67; asst. prof. Marist Coll., Poughkeepsie, N.Y., 1967—; assoc. acad. dean Marist Coll., Poughkeepsie, v.p., dean for student affairs; pres. N.Y. Archdiocesan Cath. Forensic League, N.Y.C., 1958-62, Miami (Fla.) Archdiocesan Cath. Forensic League, 1963-67, Nat. Cath. Forensic League, 1964-68. Playwright: (short plays) For Second Springs, 1989, (full length plays) The Angel's Share, 1991, The Penny Stealers, 1992. Pres. bd. Community Exptl. Repertory Theatre, Poughkeepsie, 1975-85. Recipient 1st Prize one act playwriting City Lights Inc., Poughkeepsie, 1986. Office: Marist Coll 82 North Rd Poughkeepsie NY 12601-1387

COX, JOE MANSFIELD, II, financial services company executive, consultant; b. Columbia, Mo., Oct. 6, 1958; s. Joe Mansfield and Jane Faye (Brown) C.; m. Terri Ann Haacke, June 26, 1982; 1child, Michael Haacke. BA in Biochemistry, Johns Hopkins U., 1981. Sales rep. Abbott Labs, White Plaines, N.Y., 1981-83; sales mgmt. CIGNA, Tarrytown, N.Y., 1983-87; prin. Fleming, Relyea & Cox, Inc., Greenwich, Conn., 1987—. Chmn. Wilton Conn. High Sch. Planning, 1985; com. vice chmn. Wilton Parks & Recreation, 1989. Office: Fleming Relyea & Cox Inc 68 Arch St Greenwich CT 06830-6525

COX, MARY BLANCHE, psychologist; b. Orange, N.J., May 10, 1945; d. William Roe and Mary Sophia (Bilinski) C.; m. Stanley Winter, July 18, 1971 (div. Nov. 1977); m. Csaba Bázsa, Apr. 25, 1983 (div. May 1990). Lic. psychologist, N.Y. Psychology trainee VA Hosp., N.Y.C., 1969-70, psychology intern outpatient clinic, 1971-72, staff psychologist outpatient clinic, 1972-76; pvt. practice N.Y.C., 1974—; psychologist New Hope Guild, N.Y.C., 1991. Mem. APA, N.Y. State Psychol. Assn. (task force on AIDS, 1989—, treas. 1992), Am. Soc. for Psychical Rsch., Nat. Coun. for Register of Health Svc. Providers in Psychology. Republican. Episcopalian. Office: 46 E 83d St Ste # B New York NY 10028

COX, MARY LATHROP, child psychologist; b. N.Y.C., June 5, 1930; d. Charles Stelle and Mary Jay (Schieffelin) Brown; m. Maxwell Evart Cox, June 30, 1950; children: Rachel, Elizabeth, Ann, Robert. AB, Barnard Coll., N.Y.C., 1952; MA, NYU, N.Y.C., 1972; PhD, CUNY, 1987. Cert. sch. psychologist; lic. psychologist, N.Y. Psychol. worker Brookdale Hosp. & Med. Ctr., Bklyn., 1973-77; sch. psychologist N.Y.C. Bd. Edn., Bklyn., 1978-86; psychologist Home Clinic/Hosp. Ctr. Ednl. Programs, Inc., Bklyn., 1986-88, Schneider Children's Hosp. Med. Ctr., New Hyde Park, N.Y., 1988—; pvt. practice, 1980—. Bd. dirs. Alfred T. White Community Bldg., 1963-68; pres. bd. PAES, Inc., Bklyn., 1978-82, dir., 1982—. Mem. APA, Assn. Play Therapy, Nat. Ctr. for Clin. Infant Programs, Heights Casino. Office: 81 Remsen St Brooklyn NY 11201

COX, RACHEL DUNAWAY, psychologist; b. Murray, Ky., Jan. 20, 1904; d. Enoch T. and Khadra (Fergeson) Dunaway; m. Reavis Cox, Feb. 18, 1928; children: David J., Rosemary Cox Masters. BA, U. Tex., 1925; MA, Columbia U., 1930; PhD, U. Pa., 1943. Lic. psychologist, Pa. Reporter Amarillo (Tex.) Globe News, 1925; reporter, editorial writer N.Y. Herald Tribune, 1926-33; tchr., chmn. dept. edn. West Side YWCA, N.Y.C., 1927-35; hosp. case worker Walter Reed Hosp., Washington, 1945; from. asst. prof. to prof. psychology and edn. Bryn Mawr (Pa.) Coll., 1945-71; psychologist Manchester Royal Infirmary, U.K., 1971-72; pvt. practice clin. psychology Swarthmore, Wallingford, Pa., 1973-89; dir. rsch. project devel. personality in adult yrs., N.Y.C., 1948—. Author: Counselors and Their Work, 1945, Youth Into Maturity, 1970; contbr. articles to profl. jours. W.T. Grant Found. grantee, N.Y.C., 1947-91; recipient Disting. Svc. award Pa. Psychol. Assn., 1988, Jerome Bruno award Please Touch Mus., 1988, others. Fellow Soc. for Personality Assessment (sec. 1950). Republican. Presbyterian. Home: 3300 Darby Rd Haverford PA 19041-1061

COX, ROBERT, management consultant; b. Phila., 1931; m. Virginia Skelly, 1960. BS in Engring., Drexel U., 1951; MBA, Wayne State U., 1958. Registered profl. engr., Mich., Pa. Sr. mfg. engr. Ford Motor Co., Dearborn, Mich., 1953-57; co-owner, pres. Leon Chem. Industries, Inc., Grand Rapids, Mich., 1957-60; mfg. cons. Robert Heller Assocs., Cleve., 1960-64; div. gen. mgr. Bendix Corp., Detroit, 1964-68; v.p., gen. mgr. Joy Mfg. Co., Ozone Park, N.Y., 1969-71; sr. v.p. mfg. Iverson Cycle Co., Bklyn., 1974-75; pres., chief exec. officer Pitts. Brewing Co., 1978-79; pres., chief operating officer Choice-Vend Ind., Hartford, Conn., 1980-81; exec. v.p. Norton-Lilly, Inc., Secaucus, N.J., 1984-85; chief exec. officer Bldg. Techs. Inc., Cin., 1988; pres. Cox & Southard Assocs. Inc., N.Y.C., 1973—; instr. U. Detroit, 1958. Author: Crisis Management, A Growing Need. Bd. dirs. YMCA, Detroit, 1964-66, Smithtown, N.Y., 1971-73. 1st lt. C.E., U.S. Army, 1951-53. Recipient award Am. Meat Inst., 1955, Nissan Motor Co., 1959. Mem. Drexel Varsity Club, Huntington Country Club, Theta Chi. Office: 12 Westview Dr Lloyd Harbour Huntington NY 11743-1635

COX, ROBERT THORNTON, international futures executive; b. Ill., Oct. 24, 1953; m. Gail Joy McCarthy, Aug. 17, 1985; children: Julia Olden, Elliott Rutledge. BA, Northwestern U., 1975. Mktg. mgr. Collins Commodities, Chgo., 1976-80; ind. trader MidAm. Commodity Exch., Chgo., 1980-84; v.p., gen. mgr. Continental Ill. Fin. Futures, Singapore, 1984-87; v.p., mgr. Goldman Sachs (Japan) Corp., Tokyo, 1987-89, Goldman Sachs (Asia) Ltd., Hong Kong, 1989—; mng. dir. Goldman Sachs Futures Pte. Ltd., Singapore, 1991—; bd. dirs. Singapore Internat. Monetary Exch. (SIMEX). Mem. Union League Club of Chgo., The Am. Club of Hong Kong, Manila Polo Club. Office: Goldman Sachs (Asia) Ltd 85 Broad St New York NY 10004-2434

COX, ROGER LINDSAY, English educator; b. Manson, Iowa, Mar. 23, 1931; s. Roy Harvey and Ruth Mae (Lindsay) C.; m. Joan Rae Damerow, Aug. 5, 1951; children: Julie, Laura, Stephen, Allan. BA, Morningside Coll., 1951; MA, UCLA, 1952; PhD, Columbia U., 1961. Instr. Bates Coll., Lewiston, Maine, 1958-61; from asst. prof. to assoc. prof. DePauw U., Greencastle, Ind., 1961-71; from assoc. prof. to prof. U. Del., Newark, 1971—. Author: Between Earth & Heaven, 1969, Shakespeare's Comic Changes, 1991. Cpl. U.S. Army, 1952-54. Recipient Fulbright Scholarship, 1955-56; fellow Lydia Roberts Fellowship, Columbia U., 1956-58, Am. Coun. Learned Socs., 1967-68, Mellon Found., 1969-70. Home: 404 Vassar Dr Newark DE 19711-3163 Office: U Del Dept English Newark DE 19716

COX, TERRENCE GUY, manufacturing automation executive; b. Revere, Mass., Feb. 29, 1956; s. Thomas Ambrose and Jennie Constance (Meli) C.; m. Therese Marie Paone, Sept. 15, 1979. BS in Fin. cum laude, Babson Coll., 1976, MBA, 1977. Asst. to pres. Standard Bldg. Systems, Inc., Point of Rocks, Md., 1977-80; sr. fin. analyst Nortek, Inc., Cranston, R.I., 1980-82; mgr. new bus. devel. Compo Industries, Waltham, Mass., 1982-83; founder, v.p., chief fin. officer, treas. CAD/CAM Integration, Inc., Woburn, Mass., 1983—, also bd. dirs.; treas., bd. dirs. Encode, Inc., Nashua, N.H. Contbr. articles to profl. jours. Founder Revere track league, 1974, pres., 1974-77; coach Revere little league, 1969-77; bd. dirs. Revere Parks and Recreation Commn., 1972-74, Boy's Club of Revere, 1974-77. Roman Catholic. Office: CAD/CAM Integration Inc 76 Winn St Woburn MA 01801-2898

COX, WALTER THOMPSON, III, federal judge; b. Anderson, S.C., Aug. 13, 1942; s. Walter Thompson and Mary (Johnson) C.; m. Victoria Grubbs, Feb. 8, 1963; children: Lisa, Walter. BS, Clemson U., 1964; JD, U. S.C., 1967. Bar: S.C. 1967, U.S. Ct. Mil. Appeals 1984, U.S. Dist. Ct. S.C., U.S. Ct. Appeals (4th cir.), U.S. Supreme Ct. 1987. Commn. capt. U.S. Army, 1964, atty., 1964-73; ptnr. Jones, McIntosh, Threlkeld, Newman & Cox, Anderson, S.C., 1973-78; trial judge 10th cir. State S.C., Anderson, 1978-84; appellate judge U.S. Ct. Mil. Appeals, Washington, 1984—. Mem. ABA, Fed. Bar Assn., S.C. Bar Assn. (del.), Army Navy Club, Wild Dune Golf & Racquet Club. Episcopalian. Home: 107 Sparrow Dr Isle Of Palms SC 29451-2504 Office: US Ct Mil Appeals 450 E St NW Washington DC 20442-0002

COX, WILLIAM MARTIN, lawyer, educator; b. Bernardsville, N.J., Dec. 26, 1922; s. Martin John and Nellie (Fotens) C.; m. Julia S. Cox, June 14, 1952; children: Janice Cox Walker, William Martin, Joann Cox Cahoon, Julieann Cox Allen. AB, Syracuse U., 1947; JD, Cornell U., 1950. Bar: N.J., U.S. Dist. Ct. Mem. Dolan & Dolan, Newton, N.J., 1950—; mem. faculty, tchr. zoning adminstrn. Rutgers U.; gen. counsel N.J. Fedn. Planning Ofcls.; bd. dirs. Newton Cemetery Assn.; pres. N.J. Inst. Mcpl. Attys., 1982-84; mem. Land Use Law Drafting Com., 1970—. Recipient Pres.'s Disting. Service award N.J. League Municipalities, 1981. Mem. ABA, N.J. Bar Assn., Sussex County Bar Assn., Am. Planning Assn. Baptist. Clubs: Rotary (Newton). Author: Zoning and Land Use Administration in New Jersey, 11th edit., 1992. Office: 1 Legal Ln Newton NJ 07860-8799

COX, WINSTON H., television executive; b. Montclair, N.J., 1941. Student, Princeton U., 1963; postgrad. Bus Sch. of Bus., Harvard U., 1965. Chmn., chief exec. officer Showtime Networks Inc., N.Y.C.; bd. dirs. Lifetime Cable TV Network. Mem. Nat. Cable TV Assn. (bd. dirs.). Office: Showtime Networks Inc 1633 Broadway New York NY 10019

COYLE, MARA GENEVIEVE, physician, pediatrician; b. Pompton Plains, N.J., Feb. 14, 1961; d. James Butler and Frances Genevieve (Senger) C. BS, Boston Coll., 1982; postgrad., Dartmouth Coll., 1982-84; D of Medicine, Brown U., 1986. Pediatric intern Children's Hosp. of Phila., 1986, pediatric resident, 1987-89; neonatology fellowship Womens & Infants Hosp., Providence, 1989-92; staff neonatalogist Huntington Meml. Hosp., Pasadena, Calif., 1992—. Fellow Am. Acad. Pediatrics (bd. cert. pediatrics); mem. Sigma Xi, Sci. Rsch. Soc., Phi Beta Kappa. Roman Catholic. Home: 300 LaFollette Dr Los Angeles CA 90042

COYNE, CHARLES COLE, lawyer, chemical company executive; b. Abington, Pa., Dec. 3, 1948; s. James Kitchenman and Pearl (Black) C.; m. Paula J. Latta, May 15, 1976; 1 child, Anna Elizabeth. BS in Econs., U. Pa., 1970; JD, Temple U., 1973. Bar: Pa. 1973, U.S. Supreme Ct. 1982, N.J. 1985. Ptnr. Fell & Spalding, Phila., 1987—; dir., sec., mem. mgmt. com. George S. Coyne Chem. Co., Inc., Croydon, Pa. Assoc. editor Temple Law Quar., 1972-73. Chester County (Pa.) rep. Del. Valley Regional Planning Commn., 1982—; bd. dirs. Chester County Hosp. & Edn. Facilities Authority, 1982—, sec., 1984-89, vice-chmn, 1989—; bd. suprs. East Fallowfield Twp., Chester County, 1982-83; mem. Panel of U.S. Bankruptcy Trustees, 1991—. AIESEC Exch. fellow, U. Melbourne, 1968; recipient Disting. Young Rep. award Greater Phila. Young Reps., 1976. Mem. ABA, Pa. Bar Assn., Phila. Bar Assn. (chmn. sub-com. local bankruptcy rules 1974-75), Chester County Bar Assn., Temple Law Sch. Alumni Assn. (chmn. 10th reunion com.), U. Pa. Gen. Alumni Soc. (exec. bd. organized classes, pres. Class of 1970). Clubs: Union League (Phila.), Racquet, Right Angle (bd. control 1984-85), Nat. Steeplechase and Hunt Assn. Lodge: Masons (master 1982). Home: Sycamore Run Farm Box 155 Unionville PA 19375 Office: 8th Fl 211 S Broad St Philadelphia PA 19107

COYNE, WILLIAM JOSEPH, congressman; b. Pitts., Aug. 24, 1936; s. Phillip and Mary (Ridge) C. B.S., Robert Morris Coll., 1965. Mem. Pa. Ho. of Reps., 1970-72; mem. Pitts. City Council, 1973-80, 96th-102nd Congresses from 14th dist. Pa., 1979—. Served with AUS, 1955-57. Democrat. Roman Catholic. Office: 424 Cannon House Office Bldg Washington DC 20515*

COZZARELLI, FRANCIS ANTHONY, mechanical engineer; b. Jersey City, Apr. 8, 1933; s. Nicholas and Katherine (Meluso) C.; m. Kathleen Burke, June 7, 1958; children: Catherine, Isabelle, Delia, Julia, John, Claire. ME, Stevens Inst. Tech., 1955, MS in Applied Mechanics, 1958; PhD in Applied Mechanics, Poly. Inst. Bklyn., 1964. Stress analyst Gibbs & Cox., Inc., N.Y.C., 1955-57; instr. engrng. sci. Pratt Inst., 1957-61, asst. prof., 1961-62; asst. prof. interdisciplinary studies and rsch. SUNY, Buffalo, 1962-66, assoc. prof., 1966-71, prof., 1971-80, dir. grad. studies dept. engrng. sci., 1971-74, 78-80, acting chmn., 1975-76, prof. civil engring., 1980-82, prof. mech. and aerospcae engring., 1982—; vis. prof. Lab. Applied Mechanics, Technische Hogeschool, Delft, Netherlands, 1968-69, Inst. Mechanics, Politecnico di Milano, Italy, 1976-77; vis. scientist materials div. Joint Rsch. Centre, Euratom, Ispra, Italy, 1977. Contbr. 60 articles to profl. jours.; co-author four books in field; contbg. author books in field. NSF Sci. Faculty fellow, 1968-69; Fulbright-Hays rsch. scholar, 1976-77; grantee SUNY Rsch. Found., 1963, NSF, 1972, 80-83, 87—, SUNY, Buffalo Instnl. Funds, 1974-75, Office of Naval Rsch., 1964-82. Mem. ASME, Engring. Sci. Soc., Am. Acad. Mechanics, Sigma Xi, Tau Beta Pi. Home: 393 Starin Ave Buffalo NY 14216-2030 Office: SUNY Dept Mech and Aerospace Engring Buffalo NY 14260

COZZI, RONALD LEE, antiquarian bookseller, rare book appraiser; b. Wellsville, N.Y., Dec. 29, 1943; s. Glenn Murray Cozzi and Almina (Rogers) Thornton; m. Marilee Ann Banas, Apr. 8, 1989; 1 child: Deborah Ann, stepchildren: Charles F. Banas III, William D. Banas. Diploma in acctg., Bryant Stratton Bus. Inst., Buffalo, 1972-73. Technician IBM, Buffalo, 1967-69, A-M Corp., Buffalo, 1969-71; with U.S. Post Office, Buffalo, 1971-75; owner, mgr. Old Editions Book Shop, Buffalo, 1976—. With U.S. Army, 1965-67. Mem.. University Heights Bus. Assn. (bd. dirs. 1989—). Republican. Methodist. Office: Old Edits Book Shop 3124 Main St Buffalo NY 14214

CRABTREE, ROBERT HOWARD, chemistry educator, consultant; b. London, Apr. 17, 1948; came to U.S., 1977, naturalized, 1985; s. Arthur and Marguerite (Vaniere) C. B.A., Oxford U., 1970; Ph.D., Sussex U., Eng., 1973, D.Sc. (hon.), 1985. Attache De Recherche Centre Nationale de la Recherche Scientifique, Paris, 1975-77; asst. prof. chemistry, Yale U., New Haven, Conn., 1977-83, assoc. prof., 1983-85, prof., 1985—; cons. Air Products, Allentown, Pa., 1984—. Contbr. articles to sci. jours. Fellow Royal Chemistry Soc. (Corday-Morgan medal 1984, Organometallic Chemistry medal 1991); mem. Am. Chem. Soc.

CRAFT, DIANE, speech therapist, educator; b. Pownal, Vt., Oct. 10, 1955; d. Kirk and Tonya (Clark) Brewer; m. Howard Craft, June 21, 1980; children: Adam Clark, Adrienne Blake, Evan Anderson. BS, U. Vt., 1976; MS in Comm. Scis. and Disorders, Northwestern U., 1978. Speech therapist, audiologist Westchester (Pa.) Pub. Schs., 1981-83, Hall's Sch., Phila., 1984-85; speech therapist Jacobs and Assocs., Phila., 1985-88, Daly Pub. Health Ctr., Lancaster, Pa., 1986—; pvt. practice Phila., 1988—; mem. adj. faculty U. Pa., Phila., 1990—; condr. workshops and seminars in field. Author: (fiction) When No One Understands, 1983, (non-fiction) How You Can Help Your Child Communicate, 1989, (with others) The Pragmatic Function of Communication, 1986; contbr. articles to profl. jours. Trustee Franklin Carson Found., 1988—; mem. coun. Shea Congl. Ch., 1992—, summer day camp leader, 1986-88. Grantee Northwestern U., 1977-78. Mem. APHA, Nat. Assn. Hearing and Speech. Democrat. Address: Werik Pl Ste 101 1709 S Broad St Philadelphia PA 19148-1505

CRAGG, ERNEST ELLIOTT, insurance trade association executive; b. Franklin, Minn., Aug. 12, 1927; s. Loren Elliott and Inga Annette (Hanson) C.; m. Doris Laverne Anderson, July 5, 1957; children—Lauren Carol, Jeffrey Elliott, Karyn Kristen. B.A., Carleton Coll., 1948. CLU. Sales mgr. Washington Nat. Ins. Co., Washington, 1948-59; dir. sales Washington Nat. Ins. Co., Evanston, Ill., 1959-68, v.p., chief mktg. officer, 1968-74, exec. v.p., 1974-75, pres., 1975-83; pres. Washington Nat. Corp., Evanston, Ill., until 1983; pres., chief exec. officer Life Ins. Mktg. and Research Assn., Farmington, Conn., 1983—; chmn. Life Insurers Conf., Richmond, Va., 1983, Life Underwriters Tng. Council, Washington, 1979; gov. Nat. Assn. Securities Dealers, Washington, 1978-81. Author: The Cragg Commentaries, 1979, Learning From the Funny, The Profound, The Unassailable, 1988. Trustee, Chgo. Theol. Sem. 1980-83; sgt. at Arms Young Republicans, Washington, 1956. Served with USN, 1944-45. Named Huebner scholar Am. Soc. C.L.U.s, Chgo., 1983; recipient John Newton Russell Meml. award, 1989. Fellow Life Mgmt. Inst. Lodge: Rotary Internat.

CRAHEN, DANIEL EDWARD, priest; b. Buffalo, N.Y., Dec. 19, 1944; s. Edward Henry Crahen and Agnes Grace (Swiatkowski) Louis. AA, Our Lady of Hope Coll., 1966; MA in Philosophy, Oblate Coll., 1971. Ordained priest Roman Catholic Ch., 1971. Oblate father, missionary order Oblates of Mary Immaculate, Lowell, Mass., 1964—; Spanish apostolate dir. Immaculate Conception Ch., Lowell, 1971-79; founder Unitas, Inc., Lowell, 1971—; Spanish apostolate Miami (Fla.) Archdiocese, 1979-90; curate St. Timothy Ch., Miami, 1979-81, St. Monica Ch., Opa Locka, Fla., 1981-82, St. Stephen Ch., Miramar, Fla., 1982-85, St. Michael's Ch., Miami, 1988-90. Mem. Parent's Adv. Bd., Lowell, 1977-79, Lowell Mental Health Bd., 1972-79. Named Man of Yr. Mass. Jaycees, 1975. Home and Office: 486 Chandler St Tewksbury MA 01876

CRAIG, ALAN DANIEL, chemical executive; b. Hempstead, N.Y., Feb. 11, 1935; s. Robert Russell and Margaret (Rankin) C.; m. Eleanor Duguid, June 25, 1960; children: Robert R., Bruce A., Jeffrey B., Jeannette R. BA in Chemistry, Hofstra U., 1956; PhD in Chemistry, U. Pa., 1961. Rsch. chemist Hercules Inc., Wilmington, Del., 1961-66; rsch. mgr. Hercules Inc., Wilmington, 1967-70, mktg. mgr., 1979-81, dir. labs., 1982-84; dir. devel. No. Am. Biologicals Inc., Miami, Fla., 1971-72; v.p. Adria Labs Inc., Wilmington, Del., 1973-78; dir. rsch. Hercules Splty. Chems., Wilmington, 1984-85; dir. acquisitions and planning Hercules Engineered Polymers Co., Wilmington, 1986-89; dir. bus. devel. Hercules Advanced Materials Co., Wilmington, 1989—; bd. dirs. Tex. Alkyls Inc., Deer Park, Tex., BHC Labs Inc., Warsaw, Ind. Contbr. articles to profl. jours. Bd. dirs. Girls Clubs of Delaware, Inc., 1975—, pres. 1986-88; bd. dirs. Med. Ctr. of Delaware, 1987—, chmn. strategic planning com.; trustee Wilmington Friends Sch., 1989—. Mem. Am. Chem. Soc., Wilmington Country Club. Office: Hercules Inc Hercules Plz Wilmington DE 19894

CRAIG, CHARLES SAMUEL, marketing educator; b. Atlantic City, May 6, 1943; s. Charles Hays and Catherine Sara (McMullen) C.; m. Elizabeth Anne Coyne, Aug. 10, 1985; 1 child, Mary Catherine. BA, Westminster Coll., 1965; MS, U. R.I., 1967; PhD, Ohio State U., 1971. Mktg. rep. IBM, Providence, 1966-68; asst. dir. Mechanized Info. Ctr., Columbus, 1971-73; asst. prof. lib. adminstrn. Ohio State U., Columbus, 1971-73, asst. prof. mktg., 1972-74; asst. prof. mktg. Grad. Sch. Bus. and Pub. Adminstrn., Cornell U., Ithaca, N.Y., 1974-77, assoc. prof., 1977-79; vis. assoc. prof. mktg. Stern Sch. of Bus., N.Y.U., 1979-81, assoc. prof. mktg., 1981-84, prof. mktg., 1984-88, assoc. dean acad. affairs, 1984-88, prof. mktg. internat. bus., 1988—, chmn. mktg. dept., 1991—; dir. Presbyn. and Reformed Pub. Co., Phila., 1973—; mem. exec. bd. Jour. Retailing, 1985—. NDEA fellow, 1969-71. Mem. Am. Mktg. Assn., Assn. Consumer Rsch., Acad. Internat. Bus., Phi Kappa Phi, Omicron Delta Epsilon, Psi Chi. Presbyterian. Co-author: Consumer Behavior: An Information Processing Perspective, 1982; International Marketing Research, 1983; co-editor: Personal Selling: Theory, Research and Practice, 1984, The Development of Media Models in Advertising, Repetition Effects over the Years, The Relationship of Advertising Expenditures to Sales, 1986; mem. editorial bd. Jour. Mktg. Research, 1978-85, Jour. Retailing, 1980-85; contbr. articles to profl. jours. Home: 100 Bleecker St Apt 28D New York NY 10012-2202 Office: NYU 44 W 4th St New York NY 10012-1106

CRAIG, DOUGLAS WARREN, food service industry executive; b. Woodbury, N.J., Nov. 22, 1942; s. John Galbraith Craig and Vivian (Rundquist) Morris; m. Carolyn Louise McCans, Nov. 22, 1964 (div. Oct. 1984); children: Carl Douglas, Jeffray Alan, Eric John; m. Helen Mae Reisner, June 29, 1985; 1 child, Whitney Reisner. BA, Gettysburg Coll., 1964; MBA, Loyola Coll., Balt., 1982. With Svc. Am. Corp., Stamford, Conn., 1960-75; regional v.p. Svc. Am. Corp., Greenwich, Conn., 1972-75; pres. Food Svcs. Internat. Inc., Ft. Lauderdale, Fla., 1975-77; div. v.p. Marriott Corp., Washington, 1977-88; pres. Whitco Corp., Alexandria, Va., 1988-89, Am. Window and Bldg. Cleaning, Inc., Washington, 1989-90, Scott's Mgmt. Svcs., Inc., Markham, Ont., Can., 1991—; bd. dirs. CFEP, Inc.; sec., treas., dir. Chesapeake Computer Solutions, Inc., Middleburg, Va., 1985-88. Fin. sec. Good Shepherd Luth. Ch., Reston, Va., 1983-85, treas., 1985-87. Mem. Loyola Coll. Exec. Alumni Assn. (pres. 1985-88), Am. Philatelic Soc. Republican. Home: 7 Logan Ct RR # 4, Stouffville, ON Canada L4A 7X5 Office: Scott's Mgmt Svcs Inc, 500 Hood Rd, Markham, ON Canada

CRAIG, GENE MARTIN, small business owner; b. Cortland, N.Y., July 28, 1957; s. Gilbert William and Lillian Juva (Stafford) C.; m. Barbara Leah Bennett, Aug. 5, 1978; children: Geoseph Martin, Jennifer Leah. AAS with honors, SUNY, Morrisville, 1977. Mechanic Internat. Harvester Co., Cortland, N.Y., 1977; gen. mgr. Tractor Supply Co., Cortland, 1978-85; parts mgr. Lucas Case-IH Farm Equipment, Cortland, 1985-91; owner, mgr. Craig's Supply & Svc., Homer, N.Y., 1992—; grad. asst. Dale Carnegie Course, Syracuse, N.Y., 1991. Trustee Scott (N.Y) United Meth. Ch., 1983—; bd. dirs. Cortland County Fair, 1985—; first responder Spafford (N.Y.) Vol. Fire Dept., 1975—; chmn. Homer Future Farmers Am. agrl. consulting bd., 1980—; mem. BOCES Future Farmers Am. consulting bd., 1988—, Scott Town 150 yr. Heritage Day com., 1990; instr. Cortland County Farm Tractor Safety program, 1980—. Named hon. chpt. farmer Homer Future Farmers Am., 1982. Mem. Morrisville Coll. Alumni Assn. Home: RD #1 Homer NY 13077 Office: Craigs Supply & Svc 210 S Main St Homer NY 13077

CRAIG, JOHN TUCKER, development economist, consultant; b. Bklyn., June 17, 1926; s. Clarence Tucker and Rena (Stebbins) C.; m. Ruth Doris Weiler, Aug. 5, 1950; children: Daniel, Thomas, Andrew, Paul. BA, Oberlin Coll., 1948; MPA, Princeton U., 1950; postgrad., Tufts U., 1966-67. With AID, 1950-80; A.I.D. career and program officer AID, Tunis, Tunisia, 1967-68; program officer AID, Kathmandu, Nepal, 1968-71; internat. rels. officer Latin Am. Bur. AID, Washington, 1971-74; program officer AID, Port-au-Prince, Haiti, 1974-78; asst. dir. AID, Georgetown, Guyana, 1978-80; cons. Silver Spring, Md., 1980-83; economist for agr. survey U. Md./Rwanda Agrl. Ministry, Kigali, Rwanda, 1983-86; chief party Assocs. in Rural Devel., Proje Sove Te, Burlington, Vt. and Camp Perrin, Haiti, 1988-90; cons. Washington, 1986-88, 90—. Editor: Haiti: Development Assistance Program, 1976, Guyana: Country Development Strategy Statement, 1980. With USNR, 1944-46. Recipient Superior Honor award AID, 1980. Mem. Soc. for Internat. Devel., Am. Econ. Assn. Methodist. Home and Office: PO Box 407103 Fort Lauderdale FL 33340-7103

CRAIG, PETER STEBBINS, historian; b. Bklyn., Sept. 30, 1928; s. Clarence Tucker and Rena (Stebbins) C.; m. Lois Achor, June 9, 1950 (div. 1969); children: Stephen Tucker, Carolyn Alden, Jennifer Stebbins; m. Sally Love Banks, Feb. 14, 1970; 1 child, Katherine Love. BA, Oberlin (Ohio) Coll., 1950; JD, Yale U., 1953. Bar: D.C. 1953, U.S. Supreme Ct. 1959. Assoc. Covington & Burling, Washington, 1953-63; commerce counsel So. Rwy., Washington, 1964-67, gen. atty., 1969-84; asst. gen. counsel litigation U.S. DOT, Washington, 1967-69; assoc. gen. counsel Amtrak, Washington, 1984-89; historian 17th Century Scandinavian immigrants to Del. River, 1982—; speaker and cons. to various authors, mus., hist. socs. and geneal. socs. Author: The Stille Family in America, 1641-1772, 1986, 1693 Census of the Swedes on the Delaware, 1991; co-author: The Yocums of Aronameck, 1983, Membership of Holy Trinity Church in Wilmington-1764, 1985, Membership of Swedish Lutheran Churches at Raccoon and Penns Neck-1771, 1985; contbg. editor Swedish Am. Genealogist, 1989—; contbr. articles

to profl. jours. Trustee Com. of 100 on the Federal City, Washington, 1965-85. Named Washingtonian of Yr., Washintonian Mag., 1972; recipient Cert. Appreciation Swedish Nat. Com. of New Sweden, 1988, study grant to Sweden, Bicentennial Swedish-Am. Exchange Fund, 1991. Fellow Am. Soc. Genealogists, Geneal. Soc. Pa.; mem. Am. Hist. Assn., Hist. Soc. Pa., Hist. Soc. Del., N.J. Hist. Soc., Md. Hist. Soc., Hist. Soc. of Washington, Swedish Colonial Soc., Del. Swedish Colonial Soc., Am. Swedish Hist. Found., Swedish Am. Hist. Soc., Am. Scandinavian Assn., Nat. Geneal. Soc., Del. Geneal. Soc., Geneal. Soc. N.J., Md. Geneal. Soc. Democrat. Soc. of Friends. Home and Office: 3406 Macomb St NW Washington DC 20016-3160

CRAIG, PHILIP JOEL, engineering executive; b. Ft. Worth, Sept. 2, 1949; s. Homer Dallas and Adele (Smith) C.; m. Besa H., June 24, 1976; children: Shawn P., Michael J., Shannon B. BS in Aerospae Engring., U. Mo., 1971; MBA, U. Pitts., 1991. Field svc. engr. Westinghouse Elec. Corp., St. Louis, 1972-74; startup engr. Westinghouse Elec. Corp., Taipei, Taiwan, 1974-75; power plant installation engr. Westinghouse Elec. Corp., St. Louis, 1975-76, Joplin, Mo., 1976-77; regional mech. engr. Westinghouse Elec. Corp., Kansas City, Mo., 1977-81, maintenance program mgr., 1981-83, diagnostic svc. product line mgr., 1983-88; product line mgr. Westinghouse Elec. Corp., Pitts., 1988-91, mgr. advanced product devel., 1991—. Patentee in field; contbr. articles to profl. jours. Mem. Am. Soc. Non-destructive Testing, Econ. Club of Pitts., Boy Scouts of Am. (asst. scoutmaster 1989—). Office: Westinghouse Elec Corp 841 Old Frankstown Rd Pittsburgh PA 15239

CRAIG, RICHARD JAMES, civil engineer; b. Phila., July 2, 1959; s. William Richard and Jean Alberta (Kortenhoff) C.; m. Gail Elizabeth Cromie, May 1, 1982; children: Jennifer Elizabeth, Shannon Amy. BS in Civil Engring., U. Pitts., 1981. Registered profl. engr., Pa. Resident engr. Chester County, West Chester, Pa., 1981-85, bridge engr., 1985-87, asst. county engr., 1987—. Bd. trustees Forks of the Brandywine Presbyn. Ch., Glenmore, Pa., 1987-90, elder, 1990—; bd. trustees Beverly Hills Presbyn. Ch., Upper Darby, Pa., 1983-85. mem. ASCE, Am. Soc. Hwy. Engrs., West Caln Sportsmen's Club (Wagontown, Pa.) (fin. sec. 1988—). Republican. Office: Chester County Engrs Office 15 E Gay St West Chester PA 19380-3144

CRAIG, WILLIAM GLENN, academic administrator; b. Jersey City, N.J., Feb. 4, 1952; s. John L. and Lydia C. (Reinke) C.; m. Marian J. Killops, Aug. 20, 1977; children: Ian C., Robin A., Kelly J. BSBA, Seton Hall U., 1974. CPA, N.J. Asst. acct. Peat Marwick Mitchell & Co., Trenton, N.J., 1974-75, sr. acct., 1975-77, supervising sr. acct., 1977-78; chief acct. Rutgers U., New Brunswick, N.J., 1978-79, asst. controller, 1979-81; controller Monmouth Coll., West Long Branch, N.J., 1981-86; assoc. v.p., controller Monmouth Coll., West Long Beach, N.J., 1986-88, v.p. fin., controller, 1988—. Named Outstanding Young Man Am., 1987. Home: 317 Grandview Ave Piscataway NJ 08854-2219 Office: Monmouth Coll West Long Branch NJ 07764-1898

CRAIG, WILLIAM OOLEY, research specialist; b. Springfield, Mo., Dec. 31, 1931; s. William Jasper and Coral Mae (Ooley) C.; m. Mary Ellen Towle, Oct. 3, 1959; children: William Frederick, Douglas Allen, Thomas Ooley. BJ, U. Mo., 1953. Reporter-photographer Kansas City (Mo.) Star, 1956-58; editor Traffic World, Washington, 1958-69; editor, info. officer Smithsonian Instn., Washington, 1969-76; publs. dir. NEH, Washington, 1976-82; dir. Office Pub. Affairs, U.S. Patent and Trademark Office, Washington, 1982-90; rsch. specialist, 1990—. Editor: Increase and Diffusion, 1970, also mus. directories, 1970-76, numerous other publs. With CIC, U.S. Army, 1954-55, Korea. Mem. Pub. Rels. Soc. Am., Masons, Kappa Alpha. Methodist. Home: 6125 9th Rd N Arlington VA 22205 Office: 1701 Pennsylvania Ave NW Washington DC 20006-5889

CRAIGLOW, JAMES HAWKINS, graduate school official; b. Harrisburg, Pa., Nov. 21, 1941; s. James Hawkins and Jeanette (Sweeney) C.; m. Elizabeth Blatz, Aug. 31, 1964 (div. Nov. 1978); children: Alison, Hilary; m. Shelley Whittier, Aug. 22, 1981; 1 child, Brittany. BA, Lafayette Coll., 1963; MEd, Antioch N.E Grad. Sch., Keene, N.H., 1977. Secondary tchr. social studies Walton (N.Y.) Cen. Sch., 1963-66; elem. tchr. Transfiguration Day Sch., Freeport, N.Y., 1966-70; dept. chmn., adminstrv. intern Emma Willard Sch., Troy, N.Y., 1970-77; assoc. dean Antioch New England Grad. Sch., 1977-86, provost, chief exec. officer, 1986—; mgmt. cons.; presenter numerous confs. Contbr. numerous articles to profl. jours. Bd. dirs. Monadnock Children's Mus., Keene, 1987-91, Monadnock United Way, 1989—, Monadnock Family Svcs., 1989—. Mem. Nat. Assn. Coll. and Univ. Bus. Officers, Coun. for Adult and Experiential Edn., Greater Keene C. of C. (bd. dirs.), Rotary. Democrat. Office: Antioch New Eng Grad Sch Roxbury St Keene NH 03431-3265

CRAIN, DARRELL CLAYTON, JR., physician; b. Washington, Mar. 29, 1910; s. Darrell Clayton Sr. and Annie Augusta (Rau) C.; m. Leslye Louise Moore, July 12, 1934; children: Barbara Jean, Lillian Anne, Darrell Clayton III. MD, George Washington U., 1932. Diplomate Am. Bd. Internal Medicine. Practice medicine specializing in arthritis and rheumatic diseases Washington, 1937-87; founder, sr. physician Arthritis Rehab. Ctr., Washington, 1966-87; founder, dir. Rheumatology Clinic, Georgetown U. Hosp., Washington, 1947-72; clin. prof. Georgetown U. Sch. Medicine, Washington, 1971-87, ret., 1987; cons. in arthritis and rheumatic diseases Office of Surgeon Gen. U.S. Army, Washington, 1947-72, Surgeon Gen. U.S. Pub. Health, Bethesda, Md., 1947-69. Author: Help for Ten Million, 1959, The Arthritis Handbook, 1971; com. chmn. for booklet The Arthritis Primer, 1959. Bd. dirs. Westminster Found. at Annapolis, Md., 1947—; co-founder Arthritis and Rheumatism Assn. of Met. Washington, 1947, pres., 1948-49, bd. dirs., 1948-72; mem. medals subcom. Ofcl. Inaugural Coms., 1980, 84, 88. Served to maj. U.S. Army, 1942-45, PTO. Fellow ACP, Washington Acad. Scis.; mem. AMA, Acad. Medicine of Washington (pres. 1980-84), Med. Soc. D.C. (pres. 1972). Republican. Presbyterian. Home: 6422 Garnett Dr Bethesda MD 20815-6616

CRAIN, THEODORE SCOTT, JR., lumber company executive; b. Altoona, Pa., Jan. 30, 1955; s. Theodore Scott Sr. and Mary Jane (Wagner) C.; m. Nancy Renee Kuhn, June 20, 1981; children: Elyse Brittany, Whitney Alison. BS in Mktg., Pa. State U., 1976. Yardman, driver Crain Lumber Co., Port Matilda, Pa., 1970-76, counter salesman, 1976-80, gen. mgr., 1980—; tech. cons. Sunn Classic Pictures, Salt Lake City, 1977. Author: UFOs, MJ-12 and the Government, 1991; contbr. articles to publs. Pa. notary pub. Pa. Assn. Notaries, Pitts., 1981—; bd. trustees Centre County Community Hosp., State College, Pa., 1982-86, chmn. bylaws com., 1986. Recipient Supervision cert. Keye Productivity Ctr., Kansas City, Mo., 1979, Voice of Democracy Cert. of Merit, VFW, 1972; rsch. grantee Sunn Classic Pictures, 1977. Mem. Pa. Assn. for the Study of the Unexplained (field investigator 1984—), Mut. UFO Network Inc. (state sect. dir. 1977—). Republican. Home: 103 Julie Cir Port Matilda PA 16870-9580 Office: Crain Lumber Co 201 North St Port Matilda PA 16870

CRAIR-SCHLEGER, STACEY ESS, foot physician; b. Bklyn., May 15, 1961; d. Melvin and Shirley Jean (Blustein) Crair; m. Jeffrey Keith Schleger, Nov. 4, 1990. BA in Psychology, Bklyn. Coll., 1981; DPM magna cum laude, N.Y. Coll. Podiatric Medicine, 1985. Diplomate Am. Bd. Podiatric Orthopedics. Pvt. practice Middle Village, N.Y., 1987—; asst. chairperson med. ethics and bd. rev. com. Deepdale Gen. Hosp., Little Neck, N.Y., 1990—. Lectr. various sr. citizen ctrs., N.Y.C., 1987—. Fellow Am. Coll. Foot Orthopedists; mem. Am. Podiatric Med. Assn. Office: 73-05 Metropolitan Ave Middle Village NY 11379

CRAKES, GARY MICHAEL, economics educator; b. Southington, Conn., July 2, 1953; s. Harry Fremont and Frances Katherine (Koth) C.; m. Deborah Jean MacArthur, Aug. 14, 1976; children: Andrew David, Jeffrey Alan, Timothy Scott. BA in Econs., Cen. Conn. State U., 1975; MA in Econs., U. Conn., 1976, PhD in Econs., 1984. Rsch. asst. Health Ctr. U. Conn., Farmington, 1976-79, vis. prof. Health Ctr., Sch. Dental Medicine, 1988; instr. U. Conn., Hartford, 1979-80; asst. prof. So. Conn. State U., New Haven, 1980-85, assoc. prof., 1985-89, prof., 1989—; chmn. dept. econs. and fin. So. Conn. State U., Hartford, 1991—; pres. Maher, Crakes & Assocs., Cheshire, Conn., 1987—; econ. expert witness. Contbr. articles to profl. jours. Mem. State of Conn. Sr. Economist Exam. Com., Hartford, 1987. Richard D. Irwin fellow Irwin Publ. Co., Homewood, Ill., 1983-84, U. Conn. fellow, 1983; recipient Univ. Tchr. of the Yr. award, 1987. Mem. Am. Econ. Assn., Ea. Econ. Assn. Nat. Assn. Forensic Econ., AAUP, Omicron Delta Epsilon (chpt. advisor). Democrat. Home: 860 Ward Ln Cheshire CT 06410-3363 Office: So Conn State U 501 Crescent St New Haven CT 06515-1355

CRAMER, CATHERINE PATRICIA, neuroscience educator; b. L.A.; m. John Francis Pfister, May 23, 1986; children: Noah Christopher, Benjamin Edward. BA, Johns Hopkins U., 1976, MA, PhD, 1982; MA, U. Calif., Berkeley, 1982. Asst. prof. Dartmouth Coll., Hanover, N.H., 1982-88; assoc. prof. Dartmouth Coll., Hanover, Mass., 1988—; councilor Assn. for Women in Sci., Washington, 1989-91. Contbr. articles to profl. jours. and books. Office: Dept Psychology Dartmouth Coll Hanover NH 03755-3459

CRAMER, JAMES PERRY, association executive, publisher, educator, architectural historian; b. Aberdeen, S.D., Aug. 7, 1947; s. Harry John and Carol B. (Bickel) C.; m. Corinne M. Aaker, Dec. 21, 1969; children: Ryan James, Austin Michael. BS, No. State U., Aberdeen, 1969; MA, St. Thomas U., St. Paul, 1974; planning cert., U. Minn., Mpls.-St. Paul, 1976; bus. mgmt. cert., Wharton Sch. Bus., U. Pa., 1987. Dir., teaching faculty U. Minn., Mpls., 1974-76; dir. St. Louis Park Community Svcs., Minn., 1976-78; exec. v.p. Minn. Soc. AIA, Mpls., 1978-82; pres., chief exec. officer AIA Svc. Corp., Washington, 1982-86, also bd. regents; pres. Am. Archtl. Found. and Octagon Mus., Washington, 1986-89; chief exec. officer AIA, Washington, 1988—; group pub. Architecture Mag., 1982-89, pub. chmn., 1990—; with Archtl. Tech. Mag., 1983-89. Pres. Coun. Archtl. Components Washington, 1980-81; pres. Greenway Civic Assn., McLean, Va., 1986-88; bd. trustees Nat. Bldg. Mus., Washington, 1989—; chmn. United Way Assn., Washington div., 1992. Mem. AIA (hon., chmn. 1981-82, chief exec. officer 1989—, spl. award 1982), Am. Soc. Assn. Execs. (cert. assn. exec.), Mag. Pubs. Am., Octagon Soc. (life hon.), Am. Archtl. Found. (life, pres. 1986-89, regent 1981-82, 86—), Am. Design Coun. (founder, bd. dirs. 1988—). Home: 8300 Riding Ridge Pl Mc Lean VA 22102-1316 Office: AIA 1735 New York Ave NW Washington DC 20006-5209

CRAMER, JOHN SANDERSON, health care executive; b. Butte, Mont., Feb. 22, 1942; s. John Dale and Angela Rita (Sanderson) C.; m. Ellen E. McGrath, Apr. 15, 1968; children: Jennifer, Jon. BBA in Small Bus. Adminstrn., Adelphi U., 1964; MBA in Hosp. Adminstrn., George Washington U., 1969. Asst. to assocs. John G. Steinle and Assocs., Garden City, N.Y., 1960-64, jr. assoc., 1964-67, assoc., 1969-70; adminstrv. resident Harrisburg (Pa.) Hosp., 1968-69, asst. dir., 1970-73, dir. planning, 1973-78; v.p. corp. planning Capital Health System, Harrisburg, 1978-84, sr. v.p. corp. planning, 1984-88, pres., chief exec. officer, 1988—. Author: (with others) Organizational Theory, Cases and Applications, 1990. Mem. Coun. for Pub. Edn., Harrisburg, 1991—. Fellow Am. Coll. Healthcare Execs.; mem. Am. Hosp. Assn. (bd. dirs. 1990—, Nat. Recognition award 1985), Hosp. Assn. Pa. (mem. Blue Ribbon Vision 2000 Panel 1990—, bd. dirs. 1991—, Ann. Creative Energy award 1981), Vol. Hops. Am./Pa., Inc. (sec. 1991—), Colonial Country Club, The Tuesday Club.

CRAMER, LEE H., accountant, treasurer; b. Pitts., Nov. 18, 1945; s. Walter C. and Eleanor J. Cramer, Jr.; m. Kathryn M. Martin, July 24, 1971; children: Julie, James. BS in Acctg., Pa. State U.; MBA in Acctg., So. Meth. U. CPA, Pa. Treas. Rockwell Internat. Corp., Pitts., from 1981, now v.p. and treas., 1988—. Home: 1391 Candlewood Dr Pittsburgh PA 15241-2905

CRANDALL, ARLENE BERNADETTE, school psychologist, special education coordinator and director; b. Bklyn., Feb. 22, 1956; d. Walter Brooks and Agnes (Fink) C. BA, Marywood Coll., 1978; MEd, St. John's U., Jamaica, N.Y., 1981, MS, 1983; PD in Ednl. Adminstrn., Long Island U., 1988. Nat. cert. sch. psychologist. Instr. Holy Trinity High Sch., Hicksville, N.Y., 1978-82; instr. psychology Marywood Coll., Scranton, Pa., 1982; sch. psychologist Shield Inst. for Mentally Retarded, Flushing, N.Y., 1983-85, Smithtown (N.Y.) Cen. Sch. Dist., 1985-90; coord. spl. edn. Middle Country Sch. Dist., Centereach, N.Y., 1990-91; dir. spl. svcs. Ctr. Moriches Sch. Dist., N.Y., 1991—; presenter N.Y. State conventions, Nat. Sch. Psychologists conventions on suicide prevention, 1985—. Pres. coun. Pupil Svc. Orgn. N.Y. State, 1989—. Mem. NAFE, NOW, AAUW, N.Y. Assn. Sch. Psychologists (pres. 1988-90), Nat. Assn. Sch. Psychologists, Nassau County Psychol. Assn., Am. Assn. Suicidology, Mensa. Democrat. Home: 26 Smith St Glen Cove NY 11542-3925 Office: Ctr Moriches Sch Dist 511 Main St Center Moriches NY 11934-2299

CRANDALL, ROBERT MASON, pharmaceutical executive; b. Muskegon, Mich., Apr. 10, 1928; s. Clarence Albert and Mary Ann (Mason) C.; m. Joeanne Lee Drews, Apr. 6, 1951; children: Robin Lee, Robert Mason II, Michael Drew, Jill Hunter. BS, Bowling Green (Ohio) U., 1951; MBA, U. Toledo, 1953. Adminstrv. asst. John Wood Co., Muskegon, 1954-56; from salesperson to group v.p. Richardson-Vicks Div., N.Y.C., 1956-70; internat. dir. Schering Co., Bloomfield, N.J., 1970-72; sr. v.p. USV Pharms., Tuckahoe, N.Y., 1972-75; pres. internat. div. The Mentholatum Co. Inc., Buffalo, 1975-88, pres., chief operating officer, 1988—, also bd. dirs.; bd. dirs. Barett Co., S.A., Paris, Magedoma, B.V., Amsterdam, Netherlands. Bd. dirs. Juvenile Diabetes Found., Buffalo, 1979-85. 1st lt. USAF, 1951-53. Mem. Saturn Club, Cragburn Golf Club. Home: 91 Troon Rd East Aurora NY 14052 Office: The Mentholatum Co Inc 1360 Niagara St Buffalo NY 14213

CRANDLEMERE, ROBERT WAYNE, engineering executive; b. South Weymouth, Mass., Mar. 5, 1947; s. Robert Winton and Elizabeth Mildrede (Smith) C.; m. Cynthia Robin Stoddard, May 18, 1980; children: Donna Marie, Raina Lee. A.E. in Chem. Tech., Franklin Inst. Boston, 1967; BS in Chemistry, Suffolk U., 1970, MS in Analytical Chemistry, 1975. V.p., chief chemist, lab. dir., dir. Briggs Engring. & Testing Inc., 1973-83; founder, prin., pres., chief exec. officer Cert. Engring. & Testing Co., Weymouth, Mass., 1983—; former instr. environmental and phys. chemistry Suffolk U. Contbr. articles to profl. jours. Mem. Nat. Inst. Bldg. Scis. (com. on asbestos ops. and mgmt. programs), ASTM (comml. real estate transactions environ. due diligence subcom.), Am. Inst. Chemists (chair dist. VI com. on chemistry and environ. concerns). Home: 423 S Franklin St Holbrook MA 02343-1855 Office: Cert Engring & Testing Co 25 Mathewson Dr Weymouth MA 02189-2364

CRANE, ANN ROBINSON, interior designer; b. Bklyn., Sept. 26, 1930; d. Willard Marshall Law and Genevieve (James) Robinson; m. Alfred M. Crane, Oct. 31, 1953. BA, Mt. Holyoke Coll.; postgrad., N.Y. Sch. Interior Design, 1960. Interior designer William Grey Schaefer Interiors, Darien, Conn., 1969-70, Decorator's Choice, Darien, 1970-73, Studio of Interiors, Darien, 1973-76; pvt. practice interior design Darien, 1976—; advisor Interior Design Mag., 1978. Staff aide, v.p. ARC Vols., Darien, 1960-65; v.p. publicity, v.p. ways and means, v.p. programs Mt. Holyoke Alumnae Assn., 1968. Republican. Home: 57 Edgerton St Darien CT 06820-4124

CRANE, BONNIE LOYD, art gallery owner, director, author; b. Mpls., Aug. 24, 1930; d. Frank Riley and Evelyn (Davis) Loyd; m. David Alford, Oct. 23, 1954 (div. May 1992); children: Melinda Crane Engel, Matthew Loyd, Lauren Amanda. BA, Sweet Briar (Va.) Coll., 1950; MA, Bryn Mawr (Pa.) Coll., 1972. Lectr. Kinkaid Sch., Houston, 1975-76, Mus. Fin. Arts/Sch. of Arts, Houston, 1975-76, Rice U., Houston, 1976; tchr. Cairo Am. Coll., 1978-79; curator Clark Gallery, Lincoln, Mass., 1980-82; curatorial asst., dir. edn. Brockton (Mass.) Art Mus., 1982; freelance dealer Dedham and Dover, Mass., 1983-84; owner, dir. Crane Collection Gallery, Boston, 1985—. Author: Blanche Ames, Artist & Activist, 1982, The Gentle Art of Still Life, 1989. Donor, mem. Channel 2 Auction, Boston, 1985—; mem. Newbury St. League, Boston, 1985—; tour guide Trinity Ch., Boston, 1988-89; spl. gifts solicitor United Way, Back Bay, Boston, 1988; bd. dirs. Handel and Haydn Soc., Boston, 1988—, Friends of Art Sweet Briar Coll., 1992—. Mem. Archives of Am. Art, Internat. Art Gallery Assn., New Eng. Appraisers Assn. Episcopalian. Office: Crane Collection 218 Newbury St Boston MA 02116-2504

CRANE, DIANA MARILYN, sociology educator; b. Toronto, Ont., Can., Apr. 5, 1933; d. John Halliday and Lorna Margaret (Somerville) Crane; m. Michel E.A. Herve, Sept. 13, 1965; 1 child, Adrienne Marcelle. AB, Radcliffe Coll., 1949; MA, Columbia U., 1961, PhD, 1964. Asst. prof. sociology Yale U., New Haven, 1964-68; asst. to assoc. prof. Johns Hopkins U., Balt., 1968-72; assoc. to full prof. sociology U. Pa., Phila., 1973—; vis. prof. sociology U. Poitiers, France, 1989-90; cons. Orgn. For Econ. Coop. and Devel., Paris, 1971-72, 74. Author: Invisible Colleges, 1972, The Sanctity of Social Life, 1975, The Transformation of the Avant-Garde, 1987, The Production of Culture: Media Industries and Urban Arts, 1992. Guggenheim fellow, 1974-75, Fulbright grantee, 1987-88. Mem. Am. Sociol. Assn., Internat. Sociol. Assn., Sociology of Culture Sec. of Am. Sociol. Assn. (chair 1991-92). Democrat. Home: 13 rue Cassette, 75006 Paris France Office: U of Pa Dept Sociology 113 McNeil Philadelphia PA 19104-6299

CRANE, EDWARD M., publishing executive; m. Jean Drummond. BA in History, Princeton U., 1945. V.p., sec. D. Van Nostrand Co., Inc., 1958-63, pres., 1963-68; pres. D. Van Nostrand Reinhold Co., 1968-69, Litton Internat. Pub. Co., 1969-70; founder, pres. Boutwell-Crane-Moseley Assocs. Mgmt. Cons., 1970-73; pres. Pitman Pub. Corp. U.S., 1973-75; v.p. Coun. fin. Aid to Edn., 1978-89; exec. vice chmn. Taylor & Francis Pubs., Inc., 1988—; trustee Curran Found., Wilmington, Del.; sec. Nat. Schs. Com., Greenwich, Conn.; v.p. Aerospace Edn. Found., Washington; past pres. Morven Found. Trustee McCarter Theater; chmn. Nat. Schs. Com., 1992—. With USMC, World War II. Home: 647 Rosedale Rd Princeton NJ 08540-2217

CRANE, JOHN WILLIAM, funeral home executive; b. Holden, Mass., Nov. 13, 1940; s. Edward J. and Louise E. (Dumont) C.; m. M. Patricia O'Donnell, Feb. 19, 1966; children: John W. Jr., Catherine L., Stephen J. BA in Biology, Providence Coll., 1962; postgrad., U. N.H., 1962-63, Boston Coll., 1968-72; AS in Funeral Svc., New Eng. Inst., Boston, 1975. Sales rep. Fisher Sci. Co., Pitts., 1967-71, sales mgr., 1971-73, div. mgr., 1973-74; funeral dir., treas., v.p. James F. O'Donnell & Sons, Lowell, Mass., 1974—; sec. Mass. Bd. Registration in Funeral Directing, 1988—, chmn., 1990-92; instr. Mt. Ida Coll., Newton, Mass., 1991; bd. dirs. Lowell Five Cents Savs. Bank. Active devel. com. Merrimack Valley Cath. Charities, 1975—; mem. Men's Guild, St. John's Hosp., Lowell, 1975—, pres., 1980-81; active Lowell Girl's Club, 1974-77; chmn. profl. div. campaign United Fun, 1975, 81; campaign co-chmn. Am. Heart Assn., 1977; chmn. pub. rels. com. Cath. Charities, Lowell, 1982-84; fund raiser Oblate Mission Guild, 1979—. Lt. comdr. USN, 1964-67, with Res. 1967-73. Mem. Mass. Funeral Dirs. Assn. (legis. com. 1987), Vesper Country Club (Tyngsboro, Mass.), Quechee Club (Vt.). Home: 726 Andover St Lowell MA 01852-2036 Office: James F O'Donnell & Sons 276 Pawtucket St Lowell MA 01854-3497

CRANE, LAURA JANE, research chemist; b. Middletown, Ohio, Nov. 2, 1941; d. David R. and Frances T. (Watkins) Scott; B.S., Carnegie Inst. Tech., 1963; M.S., Harvard U., 1964; Ph.D., Rutgers U., 1972; postdoctoral fellow Roche Inst. Molecular Biology, 1972-74, research asso., 1974-75; m. Robert K. Crane, Apr. 13, 1972. Analytical chemist Eastman Kodak Co., Rochester, N.Y., 1962; asst. scientist Warner-Lambert Co., Morris Plains, N.J., 1965, 67-68; English tchr. Am. Sch., Manila, 1966; assoc. scientist W. R. Grace & Co., Clarksville, Md., 1969; sr. scientist diagnostic enzymology Warner-Lambert Co., 1975, group leader coagulation research, 1976-79; mgr. lab. products research J. T. Baker Inc., Phillipsburg, N.J., 1979, asst. dir. research and devel., 1980-85, dir. research and devel., 1986—; mem. faculty Seton Hall U., 1979; participant profl. symposia. Mem. R&D Coun. N.J., state sci. adv. coun. Rutgers U. Armco Corp. scholar, 1959-63; Women's Dorm. Council scholar; William Connelly scholar; Nat. Merit scholar; NSF fellow; DuPont fellow; NDEA fellow, 1969-72; others. Mem. Am. Chem. Soc., AAAS, U.S. Dressage Fedn., Arabian Horse Registry Am., Al Khamsa Arabian Horse Breeders Assn. (pres.). Contbr., editor sci. articles and books. Home: PO Box 160 Crane's Ln at Mill Rd Buttzville NJ 07829 Office: J T Baker Inc 222 Red School Ln Phillipsburg NJ 08865-2200

CRANFORD, WILSON HESSBURG, JR., management consultant; b. Spartanburg, S.C., Jan. 31, 1916; s. Wilson Hessburg and Myrtle (Bostian) C.; m. Florence Ann McGlinchey, Apr. 27, 1939 (dec. Mar. 1990); children: Wilson Hessburg III, Patricia Ann Murray; m. Margaret Ann Mulkern, Nov. 24, 1990. MBA, Bryant Coll., 1941. Credit mgr. Goodrich Oil Co., Pawtucket, R.I., 1941-43; shipfitter Walsh-Kaiser Shipyard, Providence, 1943-45; asst. treas. H. & B. Am. Machine Co., Pawtucket, 1948-51; credit mgr. Trafari, Krussman & Fisher, Providence, 1951-52; bus. mgr. Hartford (Conn.) Hosp., 1952-57; office and credit mgr. A.G. Spalding Bros., Chicopee, Mass., 1957-59; bus. mgr. So. Conn. State Coll., New Haven, 1959-62; adminstrv. dir. Southbury Tng. Sch., State of Conn., 1962-79; chief cons. Cons. Unltd., Wethersfield, Conn., 1985—; pres. Managerial Group Conn. State Employees Assn., Hartford, 1976-79, Local 2213, United Steelworkers of Am., Providence, 1941-43; dir. Brandywine Condo Assn., Wethersfield, 1985—. Mem. Aux. Conn. State Police, Troop A, Southbury, 1977-79; mem. Bd. Tax Rev., Wethersfield, 1990—; vice chmn., commr. Barnstable Airport Commn., Hyannis, Mass.,1981-84; mem. Rep. Town Com., Wethersfield, 1986—; bd. dirs. Wethersfield Taxpayers Assn., taught course in supervision Adult Edn. Program, Wethersfield schs., 1990, 92. Methodist. Home: 8C Barrington Dr Wethersfield CT 06109-2431 Office: Cons Unltd Wethersfield CT 06109

CRANNEY, MARILYN KANREK, lawyer; b. Bklyn., June 18, 1949; d. Sidney Paul and Aurelia (Valice) Kanrek; m. John William Cranney, Jan. 1, 1970 (div. June 1975); 1 child, David Julian. BA, Brandeis U., 1970; MA in History, Brigham Young U., 1975; JD, U. Utah, 1979; LLM in Tax Law, NYU, 1984. Bar: N.Y. 1980, U.S. Dist. Ct. (so. and ea. dists.) N.Y. 1992. Assoc. Cravath Swaine & Moore, N.Y.C., 1979-81; v.p., asst. gen. counsel InterCapital Div. Dean Witter Reynolds Inc., 1981—. Mem. N.Y. County Lawyers Assn., Order of the Coif. Democrat. Jewish. Home: 1830 E 23d St Brooklyn NY 11229 Office: Dean Witter Reynolds Inc InterCapital Div Two World Trade Ctr New York NY 10048

CRARY, SHARON ANNE, needlework designer; b. Morristown, N.J., Jan. 17, 1953; d. Randolph and Virginia Bette (Joostema) Smith; m. John Gerald, July 8, 1972; children: Laura, Megan, Benjamin. Grad. high sch., Saranac Lake, N.Y. Sec. U. of the Ozarks, Clarksville, Ark., 1972-76, 2d Bn. 42d FA, Crailsheim, Germany, 1978-80, Swisher & Ackerson Attys., St. Petersburg, Fla., 1982-83; sec., asst. Cardinal Industries, College Park, Ga., 1984-85; designer, owner The Crary Collection, Wahiawa, Hawaii, 1985-87, Sharon Anne Designs, Ft. Leavenworth, Kans., 1989-90; designer, owner, needlework tchr. Sharon Anne Designs, Evans Mills, N.Y., 1990—; needlework adviser Ft. Drum (N.Y.) Officers Wives Club, 1990—. Designer original needlework designs The Stitchery, 1990, 91, 92. Asst. sec. 1/7 Leaders Wives Group, Ft. Drum, 1990-91, Sunday Sch. substitute Ft. Drum Main Post Chapel, 1990-91; 2d grade asst. Evans Mills Primary Sch., 1990-91; ways and means chairperson Ft. Drum Officers Wives Club, 1991-92. Mem. Heartland Stitch Counters Soc. (sec. 1989-90). Republican. Home and Office: Sharon Anne Designs 3176 Anabel Ave Evans Mills NY 13637

CRASSWELLER, ROBERT MICHAEL, pomology educator; b. Wyandotte, Mich., July 11, 1954; s. Roger Edwards and Rosemary Margaret (Reeber) C.; m. Sherry Ann Ferris, July 31, 1976; children: Michael, Kristine. BS, Miami U., Oxford, Ohio, 1976; MS, Ohio State U., 1978, PhD, 1980. Asst. prof. U. Ga., Griffin, 1980-82, Athens, 1982-83; assoc. prof. pomology Pa. State U., University Park, 1984—; cons. AID, Swaziland, 1986, 88. Editor Pa. Fruit News, 1988—; also articles. Mem. Ferguson Twp. Indsl. Devel. Commn., State College, Pa., 1987-89; vice chmn. Ferguson Twp. Planning Commn., 1989—; mem. Centre Region Planning Commn., State College, 1991—. Recipient svc. award Ga. Apple Coun., 1983; fellow group XII, Kellogg Nat. Fellowship Program, 1991-94. Mem. Am. Pomological Soc. (treas., bus. mgr. 1990—), Am. Soc. for Hort. Sci., Phi Kappa Phi, Gamma Sigma Delta. Office: Pa State U 102 Tyson Bldg University Park PA 16802

CRATE, STEPHEN CHURCH, vocational rehabilitation specialist, consultant, author; b. Doylestown, Pa., Aug. 2, 1952; s. Douglas Willits and Sally (Alexander-Church) C.; m. Allison Catherine Ferris, Aug. 23, 1975; children: Matthew Stephen, Daniel Church. Assoc., U. Me., Augusta, 1977; BA, U. Me., Farmington, 1980; postgrad., Northeastern U., 1981. Fellow Am. Bd. Vocat. Experts; State of Me. Approved Rehab. Provider; Cert. Rehab. Counselor. Counselor Halcyon House Emergency Shelter, Hinckley, Me., 1978-80; activities dir. Hinckley Home Sch. Farm, 1980-82; employ-

ment, tng. specialist Me. Dept. Labor, Skowhegan, 1982-83; vocat. evaluator Waterville (Me.) Sch. Dept., 1983-85; chief exec. officer Employee Devel. Corp. of New England, Waterville, 1986—; rehab. cons. N.E. Occupational Cons., Waterville, 1984-86. Co-author: I Lost My Job, Now What Do I Do?, 1990; syndicated columnist The Changing Workplace, Allied Feature Syndicate. Bd. dirs. Waterville Mcpl. Airport; v.p. Opera House Assn. Fellow Am. Bd. Vocat. Experts; mem. Nat. Rehab. Assn., Rehab. Profls. Maine, Am. Arbitration Assn., Better Bus. Bur. (consumer div.), Ctrl. Maine C. of C. (bd. dirs.). Office: Employee Devel Corp New Eng PO Box 256 179 Main St Waterville ME 04903-0256

CRAUGH, JOSEPH PATRICK, JR., insurance company executive, lawyer; b. Yonkers, N.Y., Oct. 21, 1934; s. Joseph Patrick and Lucille Maxine (Gruber) C.; m. Ellen Maria Roesser, Sept. 5, 1959; children: Joseph Patrick III, Elizabeth Anne. BS, Coll. of Holy Cross, 1956; LLB, Syracuse U., 1959. Bar: N.Y. 1961, N.H. 1971. Counsel Inter-County Title Guaranty Co., White Plains, N.Y., 1959-61; dist. claims mgr. Utica (N.Y.) Mut. Ins. Co., 1961-70; staff lawyer Nat. Grange Mut. Ins. Co., Keene, N.H., 1970-75, gen. counsel, v.p., bd. dirs., 1975-81; sr. v.p., gen. counsel Harleysville (Pa.) Mut. Ins. Co., 1981—; instr. profl. courses. Chmn. Cheshire County Republican Com., 1979. Mem. N.Y. State Bar Assn., N.H. Bar Assn., Internat. Assn. Def. Counsel, Am. Corp. Counsel Assn., Fedn. Ins. Counsel, Assn. CPCU, Am. Soc. Corp. Secs., Am. Arbitration Assn., K.C. Republican. Roman Catholic. Home: 236 Elm Dr Lansdale PA 19446-2638 Office: Harleysville Mut Ins Co 355 Maple Ave Harleysville PA 19438-2200

CRAVER, DONALD H., English language educator; b. Winston-Salem, N.C., Dec. 22, 1935; s. Roy Howard and Fairy (Carter) C. BS, Wake Forest U., 1956; MA, Duke U., 1959; MPh, George Washington U., 1969, PhD, 1972. Instr. in English U. Cin., 1959-62; prof., co-chmn. English dept. Towson (Md.) State U., 1962—. Contbr. articles and reviews to profl. jours. Mem. theater panel Md. State Arts Coun., Balt., 1982-85. Recipient NDEA fellowship, George Washington U., 1969. Mem. Modern Lang. Assn., Nat. Coun. Tchrs. of English, Phi Beta Kappa, Omicron Delta Kappa, Alpha Sigma Lambda. Home: 2307 Eastridge Rd Lutherville Timonium MD 21093-2504 Office: Towson U Dept English Towson MD 21212

CRAWFORD, ALBERT GENE, health services analyst; b. Phila., Jan. 27, 1950; s. Chalres Stockton and Rosalind (Earnshaw) C.; m. Donah Zack, July 16, 1988; children: Gordon Zack Languell, Kathryn Zack C., William Stuart Zack C. BA in Sociology, Temple U., 1971; PhD in Sociology, U. Pa., 1976; MBA in Health Adminstrn., Widener U., 1985; advanced profl cert. mgmt. info. systems, Drexel U., 1990. Rsch. assoc. U. Pa., Phila., 1971-82; asst. prof. sociology Widener U., Chester, Pa., 1982-84; systems analyst Grad. Hosp., Phila., 1984-91; chief analyst Independence Blue Cross, Phila., 1991—. Contbr. articles and papers to profl. publs. Democrat. Methodist. Home: 4116 Terrace St Philadelphia PA 19128-5012 Office: Independence Blue Cross 1901 Market St Philadelphia PA 19103-1400

CRAWFORD, HUNT DORN, JR., military career officer; b. Louisville, Dec. 25, 1948; s. Hunt Dorn Sr. and Carrol Frank (Watson) C.; m. Kate Kerr Delano, Aug. 1, 1970; children: Scott Holden, Carolyn Hunt. BS, U.S. Mil. Acad., 1970; MA and MS, Stanford U., Palo Alto, Calif., 1978; MPh, Columbia U., 1980; MMAS, Command & Gen. Staff Coll., 1985. Commd. 2d lt. U.S. Army, 1970, advanced through grades to lt. col., 1987; staff officer, comdr. 1st Inf. Div. Forward, Augsburg, Germany, 1970-73; staff officer Hdqrs. III Corps, Ft. Hood, Tex., 1974-75; from instr. to asst. prof. U.S. Mil. Acad., West Point, N.Y., 1978-81; staff prin. 1st Inf. Div. Forward, Goppingen, 1981-84; instr. Command & Gen. Staff Coll., Ft. Leavenworth, Kans., 1985-88; strategic analyst U.S. Army Concepts Analysis Agy., Bethesda, Md., 1988-91; mil. advisor U.S. Arms Control & Disarmament Agy., Washington, 1991—; mem. NATO arms control analysts group SHAPE Tech. Ctr., The Hague, Netherlands, 1988—; mem. conv. arms control work group Ctr. for Strategic & Internat. Studies, Washington, 1989-90; mem. arms control ad hoc study group Carnegie Endowment for Internat. Peace, Washington, 1990—. Contbr. articles to profl. jours. Member World Wildlife Fund, Washington, 1989—; assoc. Woodrow Wilson Ctr., Washington, 1985—. Decorated M.S.M. Mem. Am. Polit. Sci. Assn., Acad. Polit. Sci., Assn. of U.S. Army, Internat. Inst. for Strategic Studies, Internat. Studies Assn., Ops. Rsch. Soc. (bd. dirs. 1991—), Amnesty Internat., Phi Kappa Phi. Republican. Episcopalian. Home: 7301 Centennial Rd Rockville MD 20855-1906 Office: US Arms Control Disarmament Agy 320 21st St NW Washington DC 20451-0002

CRAWFORD, JAY BRUCE, business management consultant, protection services consultant; b. Toledo, June 17, 1946; s. Byron G. and Ruth P. (Liefer) C.; m. Karen G. Crawford, Mar. 26, 1966; children: Michael Jay, Stephen Jay. AS, Community Coll. Allegheny Cty., 1978. Cert. protection profl. Supr. investigations and security Pinkerton's Inc., Toledo, Pitts., 1968-76; dist. mgr. Pinkerton's Inc., Pitts., 1979-88; v.p. Firm Electronics, Pitts., 1976-79; br. mgr. Wells Fargo, Pitts., 1988—; pres. Jay Crawford & Assocs., Pitts., 1990—; internat. security inventions judge, 1991, 92. Contbr. articles to publs. Sgt. USMC, 1964-68, Vietnam. Recipient numerous awards Bethel Pk. Jaycees. Mem. Am. Soc. Indsl. Security Western Pa. (vice chmn. 1988-89, chmn. 1989-90, past chmn. 1990-91), Am. Soc. Safety Engrs. Western Pa. (membership chmn. 1990-91, v.p. 1991-92), Rotary. Office: Jay Crawford & Assocs PO Box 765 Bethel Park PA 15102

CRAWFORD, LINDA SIBERY, lawyer, educator; b. Ann Arbor, Mich., Apr. 27, 1947; d. Donald Eugene and Verla Lillian (Schenck) Sibery; m. Leland Allardice Crawford, Apr. 4, 1970; children: Christina, Lillian, Leland. Student, Keele U., 1969; BA, U. Mich., 1969; postgrad., SUNY, Potsdam, 1971; JD, U. Maine, 1977. Bar: Maine 1977, U.S. Dist. Ct. Maine 1982, U.S. Ct. Appeals (1st cir.) 1983. Tchr. Pub. Sch., Tupper Lake, N.Y., 1970-71; asst. dist. atty. State of Maine, Farmington, 1977-79; asst. atty. gen. State of Maine, Augusta, Maine, 1979—; ptnr. The Forensic Cons. Group, Lexington, Mass., 1988—; legal advisor U. Maine, Farmington, 1975; legal counsel Fire Marshall's Office, Maine, 1980-83, Warden Svc., Maine, 1981-83, Dept. Mental Health, 1983-89, litigation div., 1989—; teaching team trial advocacy Law Sch. Harvard U., Cambridge, Mass., 1987—, lectr. Sch. Medicine, 1991. Mem. Natural Resources Coun., Maine, 1985-90; bd. dirs. Diocesan Human Rels. Coun., Maine, 1977-78, Arthritis Found., Maine, 1983-88. Named one of Outstanding Young Women of Yr. Jaycees, 1981. Mem. ABA, Maine Bar Assn., Kennebec County Bar Assn., Assn. Trial Lawyers Am., Maine Trial Lawyers Assn., Nat. Assn. State Mental Health Attys. (treas. 1984-86, vice chmn. 1987-89, chmn. 1989-91). Home: 25 Winthrop St Hallowell ME 04347-1150 Office: State of Maine Dept of Atty Gen State House Sta #6 Augusta ME 04333

CRAWFORD, MARY E., psychology educator; b. Pottsville, Pa., Aug. 16, 1942; d. Wallace Barckley and Mary c. (Drummer) Crawford; m. M.B. Whipple, June 3, 1962 (div. 1969); children: Mark, Mary; m. Roger J.S. Chaffin, Jan. 12, 1974; 1 child, Benjamin Crawford Chaffin. BS, West Chester (Pa.) Coll., 1963; MA, U. Del., Newark, 1972, PhD, 1975. Asst. prof. Buena Vista Coll., Storm Lake, Iowa, 1974-78; asst. prof. psychology West Chester U. of Pa., 1978-81, assoc. prof., 1981-84, prof. psychology, 1984—; vis. prof. Trenton (N.J.) State Coll., 1989-90, Hamilton Coll., Clinton, N.Y., 1986-88. Book rev. editor Psychology of Women Quar., 1990—; editorial adv. bd. Feminism and Psychology, 1990—; co-editor: Gender and Thought, 1989; co-author: Women and Gender: A Feminist Psychology, 1992; contbr. articles to profl. jours. Fellow APA, Am. Psychol. Soc.; mem. Nat. Women's Studies Assn., Ea. Psychol. Assn., Sigma Xi. Office: West Chester U Dept Psychology West Chester PA 19383

CRAWFORD, NANCY CORRINE, clinical social worker, psychology educator; b. Pitts., Nov. 11, 1938; d. Kermit George and Ida Mae (Swoger) Davis; m. Donald Jones Crawford, Feb. 9, 1962; children: Suzanne Lyn Crawford Rubins, Cynthia Lee Crawford Christopher. BA in Psychology, Canisius Coll., 1977; MSW, SUNY, Buffalo, 1979. Lic. clin. social worker, N.Y.; diplomate Am. Bd. Examiners in Clin. Social Work. Exec. dir. Elderly & Family Counseling Svcs., Buffalo, 1983—; adj. asst. prof. Hilbert Coll., Hamburg, N.Y., 1985—; clin. asst. prof. SUNY, Buffalo, 1988-89; mem. adv. bd. Daemen Coll. Sch. Social Work, Buffalo, 1990—. Bd. dirs. Ctr. for Women in Mgmt., D'Youville Coll., Buffalo, 1991—. Grantee Buffalo Found., 1987. Mem. NASW (profl. practices com. 1988—), Nat. Assn. Pvt. Geriatric Care Mgrs. (co-chmn. grievance com. 1990—). Office: Elderly & Family Counseling Svcs 200 Macarthur Dr Buffalo NY 14221-3735

CRAWFORD, RICHARD JAY, aeronautical engineer; b. Miami, Fla., Nov. 18, 1947; s. Kenneth E. and Jacqueline D. (Ducharme) C.; m. Camille A. Markey, Aug. 3, 1968; children: Stephen K., Megan A. BS in Engring., Cath. U. Am., 1969; MS In Sci. Adminstrn., George Washington U., 1980. Wind tunnel engr. Grumman Aerospace Co., Bethpage, N.Y., 1969-70; flight test engr. Calverton, N.Y., 1970-71; rocket motor engr. Naval Ordnance Sta., Indian Head, Md., 1971-73, asst. program mgr., 1973-75; facilities engr. Strategic Systems Program Office, Washington, 1975-78, facilities sect. head, 1978-83, mgr. facility projects, 1983-85, dep. mgr. facilities acquisition, 1985-88, mgr. facilities acquisition, 1988—. Mem. civic affairs com. City of Bowie, Md., 1978. Mem. Am. Mgmt. Assn., Golden Hill Gun Club, Inc. (bd. dirs., sec. 1986-88, pres. 1988-91).

CRAWFORD, SHIRLEY ANN, biology educator; b. Erie, Pa., July 2, 1933; d. Karl C. and Nellie M. (Fairburn) Eagley; m. Jack R. Crawford, Feb. 25, 1956; children: Kathleen, Jonathan, Mary. BS, Pa. State U., 1955; MAT, Rollins Coll., Winter Park, Fla., 1965; PhD, SUNY, Syracuse, 1975. Biology, chemistry, ecology tchr. Mid-Fla. Tech., Orlando, 1965-68, Valencia Community Coll., Orlando, 1968-73; prof. gen. biology, cancer biology and environ. sci. SUNY, Morrisville, 1973—; mem. NSF rev. panels, Washington, 1977—; presenter various confs. Contbr. articles to profl. jours.; inventor in field. Vice pres. Madison County Health Systems Coun., Morrisville, 1979-82; chmn. Madison County Task Force on Hazardous Wastes, Wampsville, 1981-83, Madison County Environ. Mgmt. Coun., 1983-86; mem. SUNY Task Force on Entry Level Criteria for Freshmen, Albany, 1991—. Recipient Chancellor's Award for Excellence in Teaching, 1980, Morrisville Coll. Disting. Faculty award, 1990, SUNY Disting. Teaching Prof., 1991. Mem. Phi Theta Kappa, Delta Kappa Gamma, Phi Kappa Phi. Episcopalian. Office: SUNY Morrisville NY 13408

CRAWFORD, WILLIAM DAVID, equipment company executive; b. Tuscaloosa, Ala., Jan. 19, 1947; s. Clarence W. and Louise (Hatcher) C.; m. Elaine Randall, July 21, 1977; 1 child, John Samuel. BS in Indsl. Mgmt., U. Ala., 1972; MBA, Jacksonville State U., 1974. Prodn. supr. Goodyear Tire & Rubber Co., Gadsden, Ala., 1972-77; mgmt. instr. U. Ala., Gadsden, 1975-77; proj. mgr. Posting Equipment Corp., Buffalo, N.Y., 1977-80; adminstrv. mgr. Posting Equipment Corp., Buffalo, 1980-84; v.p. Posting Equipment Corp., Buffalo, N.Y., 1985-91, pres., chief exec. officer, 1991—; v.p. Mead-Hatcher, Inc., Buffalo, 1985-91, chief exec. officer, 1991—. Coach Lou Gehrig Youth Baseball, Amherst, N.Y., 1979-89; bd. dirs. Oakbrook Condominium, Williamsville, N.Y., 1978-80, 87-90, pres., 1989-90; bd. dirs., treas. Christian Found. for Performing Arts, 1992—. With USNR, 1964-69, Vietnam, 1967-68. Mem. Am. Prodn. and Inventory Control Assn. (bd. govs. 1989—, treas. 1990-91, v.p. 1992—), Nat. Office Products Assn. (bd. govs. young execs. forum 1983-88, budget and fin. com. 1990-91), SAR, U. Ala. Alumni Assn., Rotary. Republican. Protestant.

CRAWLEY, JOHN BOEVEY, group publisher; b. N.Y.C., Mar. 1, 1946; s. Charles John and Katherin Marie (Dowd) C.; m. Ann Auwerda, June 28, 1969; children: John, Mark, Brian, Jean. B.A., Coll. Santa Fe., 1968. Advt. salesman N.Y. Daily News, N.Y.C., 1968-73; L.I. (N.Y.) advt. mgr. N.Y. Daily News, 1973-75; western advt. mgr. N.Y. Daily News, Chgo., 1975-80; city circulation sales mgr. N.Y. Daily News, N.Y.C., 1980-81; advt. sales mgr. N.Y. Daily News, 1981-82; advt. sales rep. Time, Inc./People mag., N.Y.C., 1982-83; pub. Times Mirror Mags./Outdoor Life mag., N.Y.C., 1983-88; group pub. Times Mirror Mags., N.Y.C., 1988—; cons., pres. J. Blair & Co., N.Y.C., 1981. Sgt. U.S. Army, 1967-68. Mem. N.Y. Athletic Club, Tokeneke Club (Darien, Conn.), Darien Country Club. Republican. Roman Catholic. Home: 10 Pheasant Run Darien CT 06820-4813 Office: Times Mirror Mags 2 Park Ave New York NY 10016-5603

CREAMER, NELSON GLENN, mechanical and aerospace engineer, researcher; b. Waco, Tex., Apr. 20, 1959; s. Walter Joe and Margaret Nell (Glenn) C.; m. Ruth Ann Shubock, June 15, 1991. BS, Tex. A&M U., 1981; MS, Va. Poly. Inst. and State U., 1982, PhD, 1987. Teaching asst. engring. mechanics Va. Poly. Inst. and State U., Blacksburg, 1981-82, rsch. and teaching asst., 1983-85; engr. Gen. Dynamics, Ft. Worth, 1982-83; rsch. assoc. instr. aerospace engring. Tex. A&M U., College Station, 1985-87; mem. tech. staff Gen. Rsch. Corp., Arlington, Va., 1987-88; satellite control engr. Swales and Assocs., Inc. at Naval Rsch. Lab., Washington, 1989—. Contbr. articles to profl. jours. Mem. Md. Pub. Interest Rsch. Group, College Park, 1991, Vols. in Tech. Assistance, 1991. Mem. AIAA (reviewer Jour. Guidance, Control and Dynamics 1988, '90, '91), IEEE, ASME (assoc.), Sigma Gamma Tau. Democrat. Home: 6012 Harbor Seal Ct Waldorf MD 20603-4329 Office: Swales and Assocs Inc Beltsville MD 20705

CREASEY, DAVID EDWARD, physician, psychiatrist, educator; b. Santa Barbara, Calif., Aug. 26, 1944; s. Edward Louis Aja and Ruth (Bryan) Creasey; m. Beverly Dewolfe, Apr. 8, 1972. BA cum laude, Tufts U., 1966, MD, 1970. Surgical intern, then OB/GYN resident Tufts-New England Med. Ctr., Boston, 1970-72; gen. med. officer Newport (R.I.) Naval Hosp., 1972-74; resident in psychiatry Boston VA Hosp., Boston, 1974-77; fellow in psychiatry Mt. Auburn Hosp., Cambridge, Mass., 1977-78; staff psychiatrist Westwood (Mass.) Lodge Hosp., 1978-79, Mass. Mental Health Ctr., Boston, 1979—; psychiat. dir. New Eng. Psychiat. Rehab. Tng. program, Cambridge, Mass., 1978—; cons. Mass. Rehab. Com. and Com. for the Blind, Boston, 1984—; clin. instr. psychiatry Harvard Med. Sch., 1984—; adj. assoc. prof. Boston Univ., 1986—; assoc., pre-med adv. North House Harvard Univ., 1982—. Contbr. articles to profl. jours; reviewer Am. Jour. Psychiatry, Hosp. and Community Psychiatry; author interactive videodisc teaching program, 1985. Mem. various community orgns. Lt. cmdr. USN, 1972-74. Mem. Am. Psychiat. Assn. (physician's recognition award 1978, 82, 85, 88, 91), Mass. Psychiat. Soc. Office: 8th Fl 1101 Beacon St Brookline MA 02146-5502

CREASEY, WILLIAM ALFRED, pharmacologist, administrator; b. London, May 12, 1933; came to U.S., 1959; s. William John and Elsie Elizabeth (Huxley) C.; m. Stella Nicolaou, Apr. 13, 1957; 1 child, Maria. BA, Oxford U., 1955, MA, PhD, 1959. Asst. prof. pharmacology Yale U., New Haven, 1964-68, assoc. prof. pharmacology, 1968-76; rsch. prof. pharmacology and pediatrics U. Pa., Phila., 1976-82; assoc. dir. clin. pharmacology Squibb Inst. for Med. Rsch., Princeton, N.J., 1982-86; dir. biol. rsch. VRG Internat./Roberts Pharms., Eatontown, N.J., 1986-87; dir. biomed. info. svcs. Info. Ventures, Inc., Phila., 1987—. Author: (textbooks) Drug Disposition in Humans, 1979, Cancer, An Introduction, 1981, Diet and Cancer, 1985; contbr. articles to profl. jours. Fellow Am. Coll. Clin. Pharmacology; mem. Am. Assn. for Cancer Rsch., Am. Soc. for Pharmacology and Experimental Therapeutics, Am. Soc. Clin. Oncology, Am. Fedn. for Clin. Rsch., Am. Soc. Biochemistry and Molecular Biology, Am. Soc. for Clin. Pharmacology and Therapeutics, N.Y. Acad. Sci. Office: Info Ventures Inc 1500 Locust St Ste 3216 Philadelphia PA 19102

CREEGAN, KEVIN PAUL, psychologist; b. Scranton, Pa., Oct. 31, 1950; s. Robert Paul and Clare Ann (Kane) C.; m. Joan Elizabeth Hauber, July 11, 1980. BS, U. Scranton (Pa.), 1972, MS, 1975; PhD, SUNY, Albany, 1984. Lic. psychologist, Pa. Drug abuse counselor Chenango County Drug Abuse Coun., Norwich, N.Y., 1977-79; postdoctoral fellow, grad. asst. Dept. Counseling Psychology, SUNY, Albany, 1979-83; psychology intern Coatesville (Pa.) VA Med. Ctr., 1983-84; asst. dir. psychology Allied Svcs., Scranton, 1984-88; staff psychologist VA Med. Ctr., Wilkes-Barre, Pa., 1988—; instr. Dept. Psychology, Marywood Coll., Scranton, 1990—; instr. Dept. Human Resources, U. Scranton, 1986—. Mem. Am. Psychol. Assn., 1985—.

CREEL, FRANK WARNER, civil servant; b. Tulsa, June 13, 1941; s. Francis Milton and Florence Lucile (Moore) C.; m. Ender Ones, Jan. 18, 1967; children: Derya Melissa, Berna Melinda, James Timur. BA, St. Josephs Coll., 1963; MA, U. Chgo., 1973, PhD, 1978. U.S. civil servant U.S. Dept. Commerce, Washington, DC, 1973—. Contbr. articles to various publs. Vol. Peace Corps, Turkey, 1963-65; nat. membership adv. com. Ams. for Legal Reform, Washington, 1988. 1st lt. U.S. Army, 1965-68, Vietnam. Decorated Bronze Star; recipient Fulbright-Hays fellowship, 1971-72. Republican. Roman Catholic. Home: 2509 N Quantico St Arlington VA 22207-1053 Office: SIPS/IA/ITA Rm 211 14th Constitution Ave NE Washington DC 20230-0001

CREENAN, KATHERINE HERAS, lawyer; b. Elizabeth, N.J., Oct. 7, 1945; d. Victor Joseph and Katherine Regina (Lederer) Petervary; m. Edward James Creenan; 1 child, David Heras. BA, Newark State Coll., 1968; JD, Rutgers U., 1984. Bar: N.J. 1984, U.S. Dist. Ct. N.J. 1984. Various teaching positions including, Union and Stanhope, N.J., 1968-81; law clk. to presiding judge Superior Ct. of N.J. Appellate Div., Newark, 1984-85; assoc. Lowenstein, Sandler, Kohl, Fisher & Boylan, Roseland, N.J., 1985-88, Kirsten, Simon, Friedman, Allen, Cherin & Linken, Newark, 1988-89, Whitman & Ranson, Newark, 1989—. Mem. ABA, N.J. State Bar Assn., Union County Bar Assn., Essex County Bar Assn. Office: Whitman & Ransom One Gateway Ctr Newark NJ 07102

CREEVEY, LUCY ELLSWORTH, political science educator, director women's studies program; b. Cambridge, N.Y., July 2, 1940; d. Kennedy and Margaret (Brundage) C.; children: Kennedy Robert Behrman, Ari Creevey de Wilde. BA in Russian Civilization magna cum laude, Smith Coll., 1962; MA in Govt., Boston U., 1963, PhD, 1967. Asst. prof. polit. sci. U. Pa., Phila., 1967-72; assoc. prof. polit. sci. Rutgers U., New Brunwick, N.J., 1972-74; dir. urban studies U. Pa., Phila., 1974-78, assoc. prof. city and regional planning, 1974-80, prof. city and regional planning, 1980-87, dir. program in appropriate technol. and energy mgmt. devel., 1983-86; dir. women's studies program U. Conn., Storrs, 1987—, prof. polit. sci., 1987—; bd. dirs. Food Corps USA, Waltham, Mass., Sarvodaya Shramadana Rsch. Inst. Ratmalana, Sri Lanka. Author (book): Muslim Brotherhoods and Politics in Senegal, 1970; editor (book): Women Farmers in Africa, 1986. Danforth fellow, 1964-67, Social Sci. Rsch. Coun. fellow, 1965-66; recipient State Dept. Am. Experts Program award 1976, 81; faculty rsch. grant U. Conn., 1991. Mem. AAUP, Am. Inst. Collegiate Planners, Am. Planning Assn., Am. Polit. Sci. Assn., African Studies Assn., Nat. Women's Studies Assn., New Eng. Women's Studies Assn. Democrat. Office: U Conn Women's Studies Program U Box 181 Storrs CT 06268

CREIGHTON, DOUGLAS GEORGE, French educator; b. Toronto, Ont., Can., July 8, 1923; s. Henry Robinson and Marjorie (Douglas) C.; m. Margaret Ona West, Aug. 6, 1953; children—Geoffrey, Sheila, Rhonda. Instr. French, Brown U., Providence, 1947-49, U. Sask., Saskatoon, Can., 1950-53; asst. d'anglais Lycee Chaptal, Paris, 1953-54; asst. prof. Beloit Coll., Wis., 1955-59; asst. prof., assoc. prof., prof. French, U. Western Ont., London, 1959-89, prof. emeritus, 1989—. Author: Diderot's Refutation of Helvetius, 1952; J.-F. De Luc of Geneva and .....Rousseau, 1982. Editor: A Travers Les Siecles, 1967. Mem. Am. Assn. Tchrs. of French, Am. and Can. Socs. for 18th Century Studies. Avocation: philately. Home: 24 Longbow Pl, London, ON Canada N6G 1Y3 Office: U Western Ont, Dept French, London, ON Canada N6G 3K7

CREMER, LEON EARL, federal agent, lawyer; b. Cin., Dec. 30, 1945; s. Walter H. and Beatrice (Campbell) C. BS, Calif. State U., 1973, MA, George Washington U., 1976, JD, Rutgers U., 1982. Bar: Pa. 1983. Officer, U.S. Secret Service, Washington, 1975-77; spl. agt. U.S. Bur. Alcohol Tobacco and Firearms, U.S. Dept. Treasury, Phila., 1977-83; spl. agt. FBI, U.S. Dept. Justice, N.Y.C., 1983—. Served with U.S. Army, 1968-69. Mem. ABA, FBI Agts. Assn., Phila. Bar Assn., Pa. Bar Assn., Am. Trial Lawyers Assn., Internat. Platform Assn., Am. Mensa Soc. Avocations: yachting, aviation, skiing, tennis, long-distance running. Office: FBI 26 Federal Pla New York NY 10278

CRESAP, CHARLES NASH, manufacturing company executive; b. Washington, June 7, 1919; s. Logan and Nancy Collins (Nash) C.; m. Joan W. Wilmarth, Aug. 1956 (div.); children: Nancy Nash, Caroline deWolfe, Frank Mc., Joan Marshall; m. May Standfast Henson, Feb. 3, 1982 (dec. Feb. 1989). BS, MIT, 1942; MA, Johns Hopkins U., 1949. Engr. chemist Westvaco, Charleston, W.Va., 1942-44; engr. Am. Cyanamid, Pitts., 1946-68; owner, founder Cresap R&D Inc., Ardsley, N.Y., 1951—; cons. in field. Patentee in field. Lt. (j.g.) USN, 1944-46. Republican. Episcopalian. Home and Office: Silver Mt Millerton NY 12546

CRESPI, TONY D., psychologist; b. Plattsburgh, N.Y., Oct. 19, 1955; s. David Emanuel Crespi and Hope Gloria (Leeger) Pinkerton; m. Cheryl Susan Raudis, June 22, 1984. BA, U. Hartford, 1975; MA, Western State Coll., 1976; EdD, U. Mass., 1985. Lic. psychologist, Conn. Sch. counselor Wallingford (Conn.) Bd. of Edn., 1977-79; sch. psychologist Dept. Children & Youth Svcs., Conn., 1979—; mem. vis. faculty U. Mass., Amherst, summers 1985-86; cons. div. rehab. Conn. State Dept. Edn., 1986-87. Consulting editor Profl. Psychology: Rsch. and Practice, 1992—. Mem. APA, Nat. Assn. of Sch. Psychologists (contbg. editor), Am. Assn. Marriage and Family Therapy (clin. reader). Home: 420 Swain Ave Meriden CT 06450-7220

CRESS, KEVIN BRUCE, electric power industry professional; b. Denver, Apr. 24, 1957; s. Hal J. and Joann (Heselton) C.; m. Marie Adel DeCollibus, Dec. 8, 1985; children: Nicole, Marie. BS in Energy Mgmt., Eastern Ill. U., 1982. Energy auditor DMC Energy, Inc., Boston and Chgo., 1982-83; sr. mktg. analyst DMC Energy, Inc., Boston, 1983-85; area mgr. DMC Energy, Inc., Woburn, Mass., 1985; conservation and load mgmt. rep. Mass. electric, Hopedale, 1987; energy auditor New Eng. Power Svc. Co., Leominster, Mass., 1986-87; team leader New Eng. Power Svc. Co., Westboro, Mass., 1987, coord. standby gen. program, 1987-89, coord. lighting program, 1989—; charter mem. Speaker's Bur. Elder United Presbyn. Ch. of Whitensville, Mass., 1990—. Mem. Assn. Energy Engrs., Assn. Demand Side Profls., Toastmasters (local pres. 1990-91, award 1990). Office: New Eng Power Svc Co 25 Research Dr Westborough MA 01582-0001

CREUTZ, MICHAEL JOHN, physicist; b. Los Alamos, N.Mex., Nov. 24, 1944; s. Edward Chester and Lela Gudrun Marie (Rollefson) C.; m. Carol Ann Russell, May 7, 1966; 1 child, Lela. BS, Calif. Inst. Tech., Pasadena, 1966; PhD, Stanford (Calif.) U., 1970. CTP fellow U. Md., College Park, 1971-72; asst. physicist Brookhaven Nat. Lab., Upton, N.Y., 1972-74, assoc. physicist, 1974-76, physicist, 1976-85, sr. physicist, 1985—; High Energy Physics adv. panel Dept. Energy, Washington, 1984-88; program adv. panel for Div. Advanced Sci. Computing, NSF, Washington, 1987-89. Author: Quarks, Gluons, and Lattices, 1983; contbr. over 100 articles to profl. jours. Fellow Am. Phys. Soc. (DPF exec. com. 1986-88, fellowship 1986). Office: Physics Dept Brookhaven Lab Upton NY 11973

CREVELING, CYRUS ROBBINS, chemist, educator; b. Washington, May 30, 1930; s. Cyrus Robbins and Edith Lois (Hill) C.; m. Cornelia Mills Rector, Sept. 3, 1954; children: Victoria Anne Creveling Mariano, Diana Rector Creveling Mears. AA, George Washington U., 1952, BS, 1954, MS, 1955, PhD, 1962. Rsch. assoc. Naval Ordinance Rsch. Lab., Washington, 1953-54; chemist Oscar B. Hunter Labs., Washington, 1955-57, Nat. Heart Inst., NIH, Bethesda, Md., 1957-62, Nat. Inst. Diabetes and Digestive and Kidney Diseases, NIH, Bethesda, 1964—; rsch. assoc. Harvard Med. Sch., Boston, 1962-64; adj. prof. of pharmacology Howard U. Sch. Medicine, Washington, 1967-86; affiliate prof. pharmacology and toxicology Med. Coll. Va., Richmond, 1985—; mem. editorial bd. Jour. Med. Chemistry, ASC, Washington, 1967-70. Editor: Transmethylation. 1979, 3d edit., 1984; contbr. more than 200 rsch. articles and papers to profl. jours. Chmn. Bethesda Meth. Ch., 1979-84, Libr. Adv. Com., Kensington Park, Md., 1985-90, Balt. Ann. Conf. United Meth. Ch., 1979—. Grantee NIH, 1966-70, Eli Lilly, 1984, E.I. duPont, 1985; Am. Diabetes Soc. fellow, 1955. Mem. Am. Fedn. Scientists, Am. Chem. Soc., Am. Soc. Pharmacol. Exptl. Therapeutics, Soc. Exptl. Biology and Medicine (pres. 1977-78, 90-91), Washington Acad. Scis. (chair awards com. 1989—, v.p. 1991—), Fdn. Advanced Edn. in Scis. (chair scholarship com. 1989—), Catecholmine Club (pres. 1980-81), Soc. Neurosci., Gordon Conf. on Cyclic Nucleotides, Chem. Soc. Washington, Internat. Soc. Study Xenobiotics, Internat. Union Physiol. Scis., Internat. Union Pure and Applied Chemistry (affiliate), Internat. Narcotics Rsch. Conf. 1989—, Internat. Union Physiol. Sci. Republican. Office: NIDDK NIH Lab Bioorg Chem 9000 Rockville Pike Bethesda MD 20892-0001

CREVOISERAT, PATRICIA JILL, special education educator; b. Freeport, N.Y., Dec. 11, 1955; d. Russell Ritchie and Dorothy A. (Gallinagh)

C. BS in Edn., SUNY, Geneseo, N.Y., 1978; MS, Adelphi U., 1981, L.I. Univ., 1986; postgrad., Hofstra U., 1987—. Cert. in spl. edn., reading, math., nursery, and elem. edn., N.Y. Freelance tutor, 1979—; learning disabilities therapist Adelphi U. L.D. Clinic, Garden City, N.Y., 1979-81; field supr. Adelphi U., Garden City, N.Y., 1980; spl. edn. tchr. Brentwood Pub. Schs., 1980, in-svc. instr., 1982-83, resource room tchr., 1980—; freelance computer programmer, 1980—; club advisor Brentwood Pub. Schs., 1982-84, swim team timer and scorekeeper, 1982-88, sch. improvement team mem., 1991—. Contbr. writer Study Skills Pack--Jr. Coll. Level, 1978-79; line editor Basal reading series, 1980-81. Sponsor Spl. Olympics, Washington, 1986—, U.S. Olympic Com., Colorado Springs, Colo., 1986—; mem. Cousteau Soc., Norfolk, Va., 1982—, World Wildlife Fund, Washington, 1983—, Nat. Wildlife Found., Vienna, Va., 1983—, Nat. Audubon Soc., N.Y.C., 1987—, Nature Conservancy, Balt., 1988—; sponsor Geneseo Found., Geneseo, N.Y., 1980—, Adelphi U. Fund, Garden City, N.Y., 1982—, Human Resources Ctr., Albertson, N.Y., 1987—, Am. Printing House for the Blind, Pleasantville, N.Y., 1986—. Mem. Coun. for Exceptional Children, AAUW, N.Y. Assn. for Learning Disabled, Assn. for Children with Learning Disabilities, Internat. Reading Assn., Nassau/Suffolk Reading Coun., Assn. for Supervision and Curriculum Devel., Nat. Coun. Tchrs. English, Am. Ednl. Rsch. Assn., Kappa Delta Pi. Republican. Office: Freshman Ctr Leahy Ave Brentwood NY 11717-1012

CREWDSON, JOHN MARK, journalist, author; b. San Francisco, Dec. 15, 1945; s. Mark Guy and Eva Rebecca (Doane) C.; m. Prudence Gray Tillotson, Sept. 11, 1969; children: Anders Gray, Oliver McDuff. A.B. with great distinction in Econs., U. Calif., Berkeley, 1970; postgrad. studies in politics, Oxford U., Eng., 1971-72. Reporter N.Y. Times, Washington, 1973-77; nat. corr N.Y. Times, Houston, 1977-82; nat. news editor Chgo. Tribune, 1982-83, met. news editor, 1983-84; west coast corr. Chgo. Tribune, L.A., 1984-90; sr. nat. corr. Chgo. Tribune, Washington, 1990—. Author: The Tarnished Door, 1983, By Silence Betrayed, 1988. Recipient Bronze medallion Sigma Delta Chi, 1974; Goldberg award N.Y. Deadline Club, 1977; Page One award N.Y. Newspaper Guild, 1977; Pulitzer prize, 1981; Polk award for med. reporting, 1990. Office: Chgo Tribune 1615 L St NW Washington DC 20036-5610

CRIARES, NICHOLAS JAMES, obstetrician and gynecologist; b. Bronx, N.Y., Apr. 2, 1934; s. James George and Christina (Brim) C.; M.D., St. Louis U., 1960; D.Sc., U. Pa., 1963; m. Helen Athos, July 3, 1966; 1 son, Peter. Diplomate Am. Bd. Ob-Gyn. Commd. 2d lt. U.S. Air Force and U.S. Army, 1960-88, advanced through grades to brig. gen., 1960-88, ret.; intern Meadowbrook Hosp., 1960-61; resident in ob-gyn Met. Hosp., N.Y.C., 1961-62, Misericordia Hosp., Phila., 1962-65, Johns Hopkins U., 1965-66; asst. attending staff Montefiore-Morrisania Affiliation, Bronx, N.Y., 1966-69; asst. prof. ob-gyn Upstate Med. Ctr., Syracuse, N.Y., 1969-72; surgeon N.Y. State Troopers Med. Evacuation, 1983-85, surgeon gen., 1985—; pres. Nicholas J. Criares, M.D., P.C., Hartsdale, N.Y., 1972-88, ret.; asst. attending staff Hosp. of Albert Einstein Coll. Medicine, Bronx Mcpl. Hosp. Ctr., Keller Army Hosp. of U.S. Mil. Acad.; clin. asst. prof. ob-gyn Albert Einstein Coll. Medicine. Mem. Soc. Urban Physicians, 1968-69, Doctors Council, 1978-80. Fellow Am. Coll. Obstetricians and Gynecologists, Internat. Coll. Obstetricians and Gynecologists, Am. Coll. Quality Assurance and Utilization Rev. Physicians (cert.); mem. Bronx Ob-Gyn Soc., Assn. Mil. Surgeons U.S., AMA (Physicians Recognition award), Med. Soc. State N.Y., Westchester County Med. Soc., Am. Coll. Legal Medicine. Greek Orthodox. Club: West Point Officers. Contbr. articles profl. jours. Research on alkaline phosphatase during pregnancy, teratology, the Feto-Placental Unit, anomalies in gynecology. Office: 34 Andover Rd Hartsdale NY 10530-2003

CRIDER, ANDREW BLAKE, psychologist; b. Cleve., June 11, 1936; s. Blake and Doris (Towne) C.; m. Anne Horrocks, Apr. 25, 1964; children: Juliet Gage, Jonathan Andrew. BA, Colgate U., 1958; MS, U. Wis., 1960; PhD, Harvard U., 1964. Lic. psychologist, Mass. Research assoc. Harvard Med. Sch., Boston, 1964-68; asst., then assoc. prof. psychology Williams Coll., Williamstown, Mass., 1968-77, prof., 1977-84, Warren prof. psychology, 1984—, chmn. dept., 1986-91, dir. Oxford program, 1991—; cons. Berkshire Med. Ctr. Psychiatry Dept., Pittsfield, Mass., 1979-85. Author: Schizophrenia, 1979; (with others) Psychology, 1983; contbr. articles to profl. jours. Bd. dirs. No. Berkshire Mental Health Assn., 1982-91. Fulbright scholar U. Brussels, 1958-59; NIH research grantee, 1964-74. Mem. Am. Psychol. Assn., Soc. Psychophysiol. Research, Assn. for Applied Psychophysiology and Biofeedback. Home: 770 Hancock Rd Williamstown MA 01267-3016 Office: Williams Coll Dept Psychology Williamstown MA 01267

CRIDER, JEAN MARIE, employee communications specialist; b. Arlington, Va., Jan. 27, 1963; d. William Alton and Irma Virginia (Kemp) C. BA in Journalism, Ind. U., 1985. Assoc. editor Potomac Elec. Power Co., Washington, 1985-87, supr. employee communications, 1987—. Mem. Montgomery County High Tech. Coun. Communications Com., 1990—. Recipient Silver award United Way Am., 1990, Honorable Mention, 1991. Mem. Internat. Assn. Bus. Communicators. Office: Potomac Elec Power Co 1900 Pennsylvania Ave NW Rm 501 Washington DC 20068-0002

CRIDER, RUDYARD LEE, psychotherapist; b. Abilene, Kans., Oct. 16, 1942; s. Clarence A. and Myrtle (Cox) C.; m. Doris Elaine Heisey, Aug. 3, 1962; 1 child, Michele Renee. BA, Messiah Coll., 1971; MS, Shippensburg U., 1978. Cert. clin. mental health counselor. Mental health worker King's View Hosp., Reedley, Calif., 1966-68; crisis intervention counselor Holy Spirit Hosp. Mental Health, Camp Hill, Pa., 1974-78; psychotherapist Holy Spirit Hosp. Mental Health, Camp Hill, 1978—, asst. coord. outpatient svcs., 1989—; sr. peer reviewer Holy Spirit Hosp. Mental Health, Camp Hill, 1990—, quality assurance com., 1990—, clin. site supr., 1983—. Mem. Nat. Acad. Cert. Clin. Mental Health Counselors, Am. Assn. Counseling and Devel., Am. Mental Health Counselors Assn., Pa. Counselors Assn., Pa. Psychol. Assn. Lutheran. Home: 438 Parkside Rd Camp Hill PA 17011 Office: Holy Spirit Hosp 21st St Camp Hill PA 17011

CRILLEY, JOSEPH JAMES, artist; b. Phila., Jan. 8, 1920; s. James John and Anna (Spoerl) C.; m. Marion Gertrude Haly, Jan. 31, 1948 (div.); children: Pamela, Geraldine, Candace, Joseph; m. Suzanne Corlette, Aug. 16, 1982. Student, Phila. Coll. Art, 1938-39, 41-42, Phila. Coll. Art, 1956-61. Art tchr. New Hope (Pa.)-Solebury High Sch., 1955-60; photographer William J. Keller, Inc., Buffalo, 1960-71. Photographer: New York, Island of Islands, 1965; one-man shows at Lambertville (N.J. Ho., 1976-80, 82-85, Coryell Gallery, Lambertville, 1981, The Kiski Sch., Saltsburg, Pa., 1985, Genest Gallery, Lambertville, 1986-90, The Phila. Sketch Club, 1990; exhibited in group shows at Nat. Acad. Design, N.Y.C., Art. Alliance, Phila. Mus. Art, Michener Art Mus., Doylestown, Pa., others; represented in permanent collections at The Kiski Sch., Atlantic Salmon Mus., Cape Breton, N.S., Can., others. Capt. AUS, 1942-45, ETO. Recipient 1st prize Shad Festival Art Exhbn., Lambertville, 1987, Sienkeiwicz award Phillips Mill Art Assn., New Hope, Pa., 1990, 2d prize in oils Coryell Gallery, Lambertville, 1981, 2d prize in oils Yardley (Pa.) Art Assn., 1977, 80. Mem. Am. Soc. Marine Artists, Da Vinci Art Alliance (Jules Scallela award 1981, 88, Toastmasters award 1986), Salmagundi Club (Calvary Hosp. award 1986, Philip Isenberg award 1985), Audubon Artists, Phila. Sketch Club (3d prize 1985), Mystic (Conn.) Internat. (achievement award 1991).

CRIMLISK, JANE THERESE, judicial secretary; b. Boston, Dec. 2, 1945; d. Herbert Leo and Grace Beatrice (McGilvray) C. AS, Aquinas Coll., Newton, Mass., 1968; BA in Sociology cum laude, Boston Coll., 1974; MS in Bus. Edn., Suffolk U., Boston, 1978; MEd in Rehab. Counseling, U. Mass., 1991. Tchr. religious edn., 1965-68; legal sec. Hale, Sanderson, Byrnes & Morton, Boston, 1968-69; sec. Boston Coll. Law Sch., Chestnut Hill, 1969-74, Life Resources, Inc., Boston, 1974-75; tchr. Archbishop Williams High Sch., Braintree, Mass., 1975-78; exec. sec. Cramer Electronics, Newton, Mass., 1978-79; tchr. adult edn., 1979—; jud. sec. Com. of Mass. Ct. Systems, Boston, 1979—; tchr. adult edn. Hickox, 1979-88, Aquinas Coll., Milton, 1989—. Vol. counselor Pregnancy Help, Brighton, Mass., 1988-89, 92, Arthur Clark for U.S. Congress campaign, Newton, 1980, Marian Walsh for State Senate campaign, 1992, Mass. Citizens for Life. Mem. Am. Assn. Counseling and Devel., Am. Rehab. Counseling Assn., Nat. Career Devel. Assn., Boston Coll. Alumni Assn. (bd. dirs. 1982-84), Boston Coll. Evening Coll. Alumni Assn. (bd. dirs., past pres.), Aquinas Coll. Alumni Assn. Democrat. Roman Catholic. Home: 113 Sherman Rd Chestnut Hill MA 02167-3181 Office: Supreme Jud Ct 1300 New Courthouse Boston MA 02108

CRISONA, GEORGE JOSEPH, JR., insurance company executive; b. Far Rockaway, N.Y., Dec. 8, 1949; s. George Joseph and Ann (Quagliana) C.; m. Sue Sirlin, Sept. 16, 1974; children: Michael, Mallory. BS, U. Hartford, 1971; JD, Bklyn. Law Sch., 1975. Pres. Garden City Brokerage Inc., Carle Place, N.Y., 1973—. Coach Little League, Merrick, N.Y. Mem. Nassau Life Underwriters Assn. (membership v.p. 1989-90, pres. 1991-92), N.Y. State Life Underwriters Assn. (vice chmn. membership 1992-93). Office: Garden City Brokerage Inc 340 Westbury Ave Carle Place NY 11514

CRIST, CHRISTINE MYERS, consulting executive; b. Harrisburg, Pa., Feb. 5, 1924; d. John Eyster and Eunice Horton (Ingham) Myers; m. Robert Grant Crist, June 25, 1949; children: Catherine Ingham Crist Marcson, Jessica Rogers Crist, Robert Jeffrey Myers Crist. BA, Dickinson Coll., 1946. Reporter The Patriot, Harrisburg, Pa., 1946-49; editor West Shore Times, Lemoyne, Pa., 1964-65; adminstr. arts in edn. Pa. Dept. Edn., Harrisburg, 1974-77, dir. leadership in arts edn., 1977-79; press sec. gov.'s office Pa. Commn. for Women, Harrisburg, 1980-83, dir. Gov.'s Commn. for Women, 1983-87; exec. dir. com. for women Evang. Luth. Ch. in Am., Chgo., 1987-90; ptnr. Crist and Crist, Cons., Camp Hill, Pa., 1990—. Editor: Song As A Measure of Man, 1975 (excellent pub. 1975). Pres. Camp Hill (Pa.) Civic Club, 1970-72; mem. Camp Hill Sch. Bd., 1967-73, Capital Area Intermediate Bd., Lemoyne, Pa., 1970-73; mem. coun. Trinity Congregation, 1991—; mem. Harrisburg Choral Soc.; mem. Dickinson Alumni Coun., 1992—; bd. dirs. Women's Polit. Network of Pa. Mem. Monday Club. Luthern. Home and Office: Crist and Crist 1915 Walnut St Camp Hill PA 17011-3854

CRIST, DARLENE TREW, public relations executive; b. Pitts., Feb. 4, 1954; d. Ralph Lou and Isabel Marie (Nostis) Trew; m. Robert wylie Crist, Aug. 27, 1977 (dec. 1983); m. Steven Richard DeToy, May 25, 1986; children: Marishka, Cydnee. BA, Am. U., Washington, 1975. Edn. specialist Nat. Pk. Svc., Washington, 1974; pub. info. specialist U.S. EPA, Washington, 1975-76; rsch. analyst Heidelberg, Clary & Assocs., Inc., Providence, 1976-78; campaign coord. Com. to Elect Claudine Schneider, Providence, 1978; ind. cons. Narragansett, R.I., 1979-80; fed. programs liaison, press sec. U.S. Rep. Claudine Schneider, Cranston, R.I., 1980-82; pub. info. specialist CIBA-Geigy Inc., Cranston, 1992—; co-dir. pub. rels. Duffy & Stanley, Inc., Providence, 1984-87; exec. v.p. Collins & Crist Pub. Affairs, Providence, 1987—. Author Heathwire Quar., 1990. Commr. Narragansett Bay Commr., Providence, 1987—; chair Long Range Planning Com., Narragansett Bay Commn., Providence, 1991—; mem. pub. edn. com. Narragansett Bay Project, 1989, Save the Bay/Long Range Planning Edn. Project, 1991. Mem. Pub. Rels. Soc. Am. Office: Collins & Crist Pub Affairs 184 Waterman St Providence RI 02906

CRIST, M. GRACE, administrative executive, food program executive; b. Dunkirk, N.Y., May 23, 1957; d. Paul Anthony and Marygrace (Giambrone) DeJoe; m. Carl Jeffrey Crist, Nov. 12, 1983; children: Gregory A , Vanessa M., Jonathan J. AS, Jamestown Coll., 1984. Cert. elderly and low income tax counselor. Actress Mutuus Mime Co., Inc., Chautauqua County, 1982-85; adminstrv. asst. Chautauqua Art Assn., 1988-90, Southwestern Ind. Living, Jamestown, N.Y., 1989-91; food pantry coord. Southwestern Ind. Local Coll., Jamestown, 1989—, grants and devel. 1989—. Writer numerous grants. Bd. advisors Food Bank of WNY, 1989-90, Museum Without Walls Internat., Jamestown, 1991. Republican. Roman Cahtolic.

CRISTELLA, ARLEEN KARIMA, artist, consultant; b. Phila., Dec. 20, 1941; d. Michael Amerigo and Helen Peter (Azar) C. Student, Phila. Coll. Textiles & Sci., 1962-65, U. Okla., 1967-69. Solo exhbns. include Ocean Nat. Bank, Beach Haven, N.J., 1989, Diplomat Hotel, Atlantic City, 1989, Art Gallery, Barnegat, N.J., 1990; represented in permanent collections including Annenberg collection. Office: PO Box 948 Tuckerton NJ 08087

CRISTINI, ANGELA, biology educator; b. Englewood, N.J.; d. Joseph and Florence (Desideratti) C.; m. Robert Lazell, Sept. 18, 1983; 1 child, Jeffrey. BA, Northeastern U., 1971; PhD, CUNY, 1977. Asst. prof. Ramapo Coll. of N.J., Mahwah, 1977-83, assoc. prof., 1983-88; prof. N.J. Dept. Environ. Protection, Trenton, 1988—, asst. dir. environ. rsch., 1987-89; dir. Inst. of Environ. Studies, Mahwah, 1991—. Contbr. articles to profl. jours. Nat. Marine Fisheries Svc. grantee, 1987, U.S. EPA grantee, 1990, N.J. Dept. Environ. Protection grantee, 1990-91. Mem. AAAS, Am. Soc. Zoologists, Soc. Environ. Toxicology and Chemistry (pres. N.J. chpt. 1989—), Estuarine Rsch. Found., Crustacern Soc. Office: Ramapo Coll of NJ 505 Ramapo Valley Rd Mahwah NJ 07430-1623

CRITTENDEN, GARY, retail executive; b. Ogden, Utah, July 13, 1953; s. Charles L. and Ruth (Fowers) C.; m. Catherine Jean Cox, Dec. 19, 1975; children: KelliAnn, Stephanie, Spencer. BS, Brigham Young U., 1976; MBA, Harvard U., 1979. V.p. Bain and Co., Boston, 1979-90; sr. v.p. ops. Filene's Basement, Inc., Wellesley, Mass., 1990—. Home: 76 Claflin St Belmont MA 02178 Office: Filene's Basement Inc 40 Walnut St Wellesley MA 02181

CROAN, ROBERT JAMES, music critic, singer; b. N.Y.C., Apr. 30, 1937; s. Sydney Joseph and Sylvia (Zorn) C. BA, Columbia U., 1958, MA, 1959; PhD, Boston U., 1968. Prof. voice Duquesne U. Sch. of Music, Pitts., 1962—, chmn., 1983—; music critic Pitts. Post-Gazette, 1963—. Mem. Music Critics Assn. (chmn. ednl. activities 1978-90), Nat. Assn. Tchrs. of Singing. Democrat. Office: Pitts Post-Gazette 50 Blvd Of The Allies Pittsburgh PA 15222-1208

CROCCO, JOHN ANTHONY, physician; b. Bklyn., Dec. 31, 1934; s. Anthony B. and Angelica Louisa (Garbarino) C.; m. Mary Arlene Setzer, Nov. 22, 1942; children: Robert J., Mary Grace, Elizabeth A., Kathleen A., John A. BS cum laude in Biology, Georgetown U., 1956; MD, SUNY, Bklyn., 1961. Intern, resident in medicine St. Vincent Hosp. & Med. Ctr., N.Y.C., 1961-63; med. resident to chief resident/fellow pulmonary SUNY, Bklyn., 1963-66; asst. instr. medicine SUNY, 1964-65, instr. medicine, 1965-69, asst. prof. medicine, 1969-73, asst. clin. prof. medicine, 1973-78; assoc. prof. medicine to prof. clin. medicine N.Y. Med. Coll., Valhalla, N.Y., 1978-88; clin. prof. medicine UMDNJ, Robert Wood Johnson Sch. Medicine, Piscataway, N.J., 1988—; dir. Jersey Shore Med. Ctr., Neptune, 1988—; dir. pulmonary svc. St. Vincent Hosp. and Med. Ctr., 1973-88, assoc. dir. medicine, 1978-88. Cons. editor Am. Jour. Medicine, 1974; editorial bd. Critical Care Medicine, 1975-89. Trustee Our Lady of Help Christians Ch., Bklyn., 1970-81; bd. govs. Cath. Guardians Soc. Bklyn., 1974-85. Maj. USAR, 1967-71. Named Prof. of the Yr., SUNY, 1969. Fellow ACP, Am. Coll. Chest Physicians, N.Y. Acad. Medicine; mem. AMA, Am. Lung Assn., N.Y. Lung Assn. (bd. govs. 1984—, bd. dirs. 1986—), Alpha Omega Alpha. Home: 20 Dorothy Ln Milltown NJ 08850-2109 Office: Jersey Shore Med Ctr 1945 State Rt 33 Neptune NJ 07753-4859

CROCIATA, FRANCIS J., academic program director; b. Rochester, N.Y., Aug. 4, 1948; s. Joseph S. Crociata Sr.; m. Linda F. Joffe, June 4, 1989. BA, St. John Fisher's Coll., 1970. Dir. pub. rels. Eastman Sch. of Music, Rochester, 1974-78; exec. dir. Va. Symphony, Norfolk, 1978-80; pres. Gibbs St. Artists Mgmt., Rochester, 1980-85; dir. alumni rels. Keuka Coll., Keuka Park, N.Y., 1985-89, dir. major gifts and planned giving, 1989—. Contbr. articles to profl. jours. Exec. v.p. The Leo Sowerby Found., 1971—; mem. Rochester Folk Art Guild, 1985—; artistic dir. Park Keyboard Concerts, 1985—. Mem. Rotary. Democrat. Home: 135 Wintergreen Way Rochester NY 14618-4831 Office: Keuka Coll Keuka Park NY 14478

CROCKER, CHESTER ARTHUR, diplomat, scholar; b. N.Y.C., Oct. 29, 1941; s. Arthur M. and Clare V.; m. Saone Baron, Dec. 18, 1965; children—Bathsheba, Karena, Rebecca. B.A., Ohio State U., 1963; M.A. in Internat. Studies, Johns Hopkins U., 1965, Ph.D., 1969. News editor Africa Report, 1968-69; lectr. Am. U., 1969-70; staff officer Nat. Security Council, 1970-72; dir. M.S. in Fgn. Svc. program Georgetown U., Washington, 1972-78, dir. African studies Ctr. for Strategic-Internat. Studies, 1976-81, Landegger Disting. rsch. prof. Sch. Fgn. Svc., 1989—; asst. sec. state African affairs, 1981-89; bd. dirs. U.S. Inst. Peace, 1991—; cons. in strategy and negotiation; chmn. Africa working group Reagan campaign, 1980; coord. for Africa Bush campaign; bd. dirs. Minorco, Luxembourg, U.S. Africa Airways. Author: High Noon in Southern Africa, 1992, also others; contbr. articles to profl. jours. counsellor Fgn. Student Svc. Coun. Recipient Disting. Svc. award Sec. State, 1988, Presdl. Citizen's award, 1989. Mem. Coun. Fgn. Rels., African Studies Assn., Internat. Inst. Strategic Studies, Am. Acad Diplomacy, Cosmos Club, Tahawus Club. Office: Georgetown U Sch Fgn Svc Washington DC 20057

CROCKER, JANE LOPES, library director; b. Mass., Sept. 19, 1946; d. Joseph Barros and Mary (Faria) Lopes; m. Lowell Steven Crocker, Feb. 14, 1976; children: Susan J., Jennifer L., Jacqueline M. BA in English, Bridgewater State Coll., 1968; MS in Libr. Sci., Simmons Coll., 1971. Cert. libr., Mass.; cert. secondary edn. tchr., Mass. Libr. New Bedford (Mass.) Pub. Libr., 1968-71; pub. svcs. libr. Simmons Coll. Libr., Boston, 1971-73; head libr. Boston City Hosp., 1973-76; libr. dir. Gloucester County Coll., Deptford, N.J., 1976—. Editor Bay State Libr., 1974-76; contbg. author: Reference and Information Service, 1978, N.J. Libraries, 1984, 89-90. Recipient Ray Murray award N.J. Assn. Libr. Assts., 1991. Mem. ALA, N.J. Libr. Assn. (pres. elect 1991-92, pres. 1992—), South Jersey Regional Libr. Coop. (pres. 1988-90, Resolution of Appreciation award 1990). Roman Catholic. Office: Gloucester County Coll Tanyard Rd RR 4 Box 203 Sewell NJ 08080

CROCKETT, RICHARD HAYDEN, architectural firm executive; b. Camden, Tenn., May 8, 1947; s. Edward Hugh and Jo Sue (Melton) C.; m. Mary Jane Schmell, Nov. 8, 1949; children: Michael Edward, Joshua William. BA in Music & History, Goshen (Ind.) Coll., 1970. Trade mgr. Herald Press, Scottdale, Pa., 1970-71; mktg. mgr. Herald Press, 1971-73; retail mgr. Provident Bookstore, Bloomington, Ill., 1973-77; gen. mgr. Provident Bookstore, Lancaster, Pa., 1977-87; owner/operator Bridgewater Interiors, Lancaster, Pa., 1987—; dir. bus. and devel. Gilbert Architects, 1988—. Editor: Jesus Life Songbook, 1971. Named Sales Man of the Yr. Herald Press, 1973. Democrat. Mennonite Ch. Home: 2393 Debra Ave East Petersburg PA 17520-1404

CROES, ROBERT ALLEN, training program administrator; b. Wilmington, Del., Aug. 16, 1948; s. Allen E. and Wanda (Jagodzinski) C.; m. Susan Marion McMahan, Dec. 21, 1974; children: Julia E., Sara E. BA, U. Del., 1970. Biol. technician Pavlovian Inst., Perryville, Md., 1971-73; instr. Marshallton Elem. Sch., Wilmington, Del., 1973-74; mgr. Concord Pike Sound Studio, Inc., Wilmington, 1975-77; sales agt. Northwestern Mutual Life Ins. Co., West Chester, Pa., 1977-80; technician DuPont Agrl. Products, Wilmington, 1981-87, tng. program adminstr., 1987—. Home: 113 Norris Rd Wilmington DE 19803-4516 Office: Dupont Agrl Products PO Box 80402 Wilmington DE 19880-0402

CROFT, ROXANNE GAYLE FRALLEY, clinical psychologist; b. Honolulu, Jan. 24, 1947; d. George harry and Jacqueline Arkin (Snedeker) Fralley; m. Mark Clyde Croft (div. Feb. 1992). BA in Biol. Scis. cum laude, Goncher Coll., 1970; MA in Clin. Psychology, U. Rochester, 1976, PhD in Clin. Psychology, 1977. Lic. clin. psychologist, N.J. Asst. prof., rsch. assoc. U. Rochester, N.Y., 1976-77; staff psychologist counseling ctr. Rutgers U., New Brunswick, N.J., 1977-78, field supr. Grad. Sch. for Applied and Profl. Psychology, 1977—; pvt. practice Highland Park, N.J., 1977—. Mem. APA, N.J. Psychol. Assn., N.J. Acad. Psychology. Office: 114 S 1st Ave # B Highland Park NJ 08904-2114

CROGHAN, GARY ALAN, cancer research scientist, physician; b. Ft. Wayne, Ind., Oct. 2, 1954; s. Robert Thomas and Catherine Marie (Krantz) C.; m. Ivana Tallerico, July 3, 1982. BA, Wabash Coll., Crawfordsville, Ind., 1977; PhD, SUNY, Buffalo, 1982; MD summa cum laude, Buffalo Sch. Med., 1990. Rsch. asst. dept. diagnostic immunology rsch. and biochemistry Nat. Breast Cancer Project Lab., Roswell Park Meml. Inst., SUNY, Buffalo, 1980-82, rschr., 1982-84, rschr. cancer rsch. sci., 1984—, prin. investigator ovary and breast cancer lab, Diagnostic Immunology Rsch., 1985—, asst. rsch. prof. pathology, 1986—; intern gen. internal medicine Millard Fillmore Hosp., Buffalo, 1990-91; resident internal medicine Mayo Grad. Sch. Medicine, Rochester, Minn., 1991—; cons., lectr. in field. Contbr. articles in field. N.Y. State Cancer Predoctoral fellow, 1978-82, postdoctoral fellow, 1983-84, Cancer Immunology fellow Cancer Research Inst., 1984-86. Mem. AAAS, AMA, N.Y. Acad. Sci., Am. Assn. Clin. Chemists, Internat. Assn. Breast Cancer Research, Med. Soc. N.Y. State, Am. fertility Soc., Assn. Scientists RPMI, Union Concerned Scientists. Am. Soc. Microbiology, Sigma Xi, Alpha Omega Alpha. Democrat. Office: Mayo Grad Sch Medicine Dept Internal Medicine 666 Elm St Rochester MN 55902

CROKE, PRUDENCE (ANNE MARY CROKE), religious studies educator; b. Woonsocket, R.I., Oct. 27, 1926; d. James Vincent and Prudence Anne (Wadsworth) C. BEd, Cath. Tchrs. Coll., 1953; AB, Salve Regina U., 1956; MA, Cath. U. of Am., 1968; PhD, Boston U., 1975. Tchr. St. Mary's Sch., Pawtucket, R.I., 1947-56; tchr., missionary St. Catherine Acad., Belize City, Belize, 1956-58, Maria Regina, LeCeiba, Honduras, 1958-59; tchr. St. Mary Acad.-Bay View, Riverside, R.I., 1960, St. Xavier Acad., Providence, 1960-68; instr. Salve Regina U., Newport, R.I., 1968-71, asst. prof., 1977-80, assoc. prof., 1980-83, religious studies prof., 1983—. Author: Eucharist and Spiritual Growth, 1975; contbr. articles to profl. jours. Mem. Cath. Theol. Soc. Am., Coll. Theology Soc., Mercy's Assn. Scripture and Theology, Mercy Higher Edn. Colloquium. Roman Catholic. Home: 147 Center Ave Newport RI 02840-6003 Office: Salve Regina U 100 Ochre Point Ave Newport RI 02840-4192

CRONAS, PETER CHRIS, company executive; b. Bklyn., Jan. 16, 1945; s. Chris Peter and Caroline Rose (Battinelli) C.; m. Adrianne Marie Vigueras, June 22, 1968; children: Johanna, Chris. BA, St. John's U., Bklyn., 1968; cert. in systems, NYU, 1974, cert. in programming, 1977. Cert. systems profl. Underwriter USF & G, N.Y.C., 1968-69; office mgr. State Mut. Ins. Co., N.Y.C., 1969-71; systems analyst Marine Office Appleton & Cox, Inc., N.Y.C., 1971-74; mgr. systems and procedures Am. Fgn. Ins. Assn., Wayne, N.J., 1974-77; MIS project mgr. AIG Ins., N.Y.C., 1977-78; MIS project leader Gen. Reins. Corp., Greenwich, Conn., 1977-78, Pepsi-Cola Co., Purchase, N.Y., 1979-81; asst. v.p. MIS reins. div. Frank B. Hall & Co., Briarcliff Manor, N.Y., 1981-87; v.p., dir. MIS, Duncanson & Holt, Inc., N.Y.C., 1987—; bd. dirs. Rochdale Ins. Co., N.Y.C. Emergency Med. Tech., Monroe (N.Y.) Vol. Ambulance Corps, 1972-78; pres. Monroe Jaycees, 1975; cub scout master pack 47, coun. Boy Scouts Am., Westwood, N.J., 1985, Career Day speaker, N.Y.C., 1991. Mem. Assn. for Systems Mgmt., Ins. Acctg. and Systems Assn., Smithsonian Assocs., Nat. Trust for Hist. Preservation. Office: Duncanson & Holt Inc One Liberty Plz New York NY 10006

CRONAUER, ADRIAN, lawyer; b. Pitts., Sept. 8, 1938; s. George DeSales and Elizabeth Marcella (Dean) C.; m. Melba Jeane Steppe, Oct. 18, 1980. BA, New Sch. for Social Rsch., 1985, MA in Media Studies, 1987; JD, U. Pa., 1989. News anchor Sta. WIMA-TV, Lima, Ohio, 1966-67; ops. mgr. Sta. WRFT-TV, Roanoke, Va., 1967-73; sr. mgmt. cons. Raymar Assocs., Belmont, Calif., 1973; mgr. Sta. WPVR-Radio, Roanoke, 1973-75; prin. Adrian Cronauer Advt. Agy., Roanoke, 1976-79; ind. broadcaster N.Y.C., 1979-86; assoc. LeBoeuf, Lamb, Leiby & MacRae, Washington, 1990-91; of counsel Weadon & Assocs., Washington, 1991—; instr. New Sch. for Social Rsch., N.Y.C., 1981-86. Author: (film script) Good Morning, Vietnam!, 1988; How to Read Copy, 1989; spl. projects editor U. Pa. Law Rev., 1989. Vice chmn. Vietnam Vets. Inst., Washington, 1989—. Sgt. USAF, 1962-66. Recipient Spl. Svc. award FCC, 1989, Sch. Bell award Va. Edn. Assn., 1972, 70. Mem. Fed. Communications Bar Assn., ABA, Bar. Assn. D.C. (chair communications law com. 1991). Home: 3800 N Fairfax Dr # 805 Arlington VA 22203

CRONBACH, ROBERT M., sculptor; b. St. Louis, Feb. 10, 1908; s. Lee and Ruby (Lowenhaupt) C.; m. Maxine Judd Silver, Oct. 12, 1934; children: Paula, Michael Theodore, Lee. Student, St. Louis Sch. Fine Arts, 1925-26, Pa. Acad. Fine Arts, 1927-30; European travel, Cresson scholarship, 1929-30. Exhibited sculpture, Mus. Modern Art, N.Y. C., Nat. Inst. Arts and Letters, Bertha Schaefer Gallery, Whitney Mus., Phila. Art Mus., St. Louis Art Mus., AAAL, other mus., galleries; one man shows, Bertha Schaefer

Galleries, N.Y., 1956, 67, 70, 74; two-person show Humphrey Gallery, 1988; exhbn. group show, Hemisfair, San Antonio, 1968, Kouros Gallery, 1985; retrospective exhbn. Humphrey Gallery, 1992; sculptor decorations lime stone, St. Louis Municipal Auditorium, 1932, tamped concrete decorations, Willerts Park Housing Project, Buffalo, 1939, two bronze statues, Social Security Bldg., Washington, 1940, 120 foot bronze screen, Dorr-Oliver Bldg., Stamford, and bronze wall sculpture for, UN Gen. Assembly Bldg., 1960, Reynolds Metal Corp. Ann. Award Trophy, 1961; Fifteen-foot fountain, St. Louis Fed. Bldg., 1963, fountain for plaza, Charleston (W.Va.) Pub. Library, 1967, Stainless Steel Sculpture, L.I. Assn. Hall of Fame, 1972, sculpture, Fashion Inst. Tech., N.Y.C., 1976, sculpture fountain, James Madison Meml. Library, Library of Congress, Washington, 1973-79, 13 foot outdoor hwy. sculpture, East Hills, N.Y., 1981, decorations pub. and pvt. bldgs.; fountains; commd. to design medal Soc. of Medalist, 1987. Mem. Nat. Council on Arts and Govt.; Chmn. bd. govs. Skowhegan Sch. Painting and Sculpture., 1982. With Mcht. Marine, World War II. Recipient Henry Hering Meml. medal Nat. Sculpture Soc., 1985, medal award Conn. chpt., 1991; Gold medal of honor for sculpture Audubon Artists, 1989, Silver medal of Honor for sculpture, 1990, Lewine Meml. award, 1992, Medal for Sculpture Audubon Artists, 1992. Mem. Sculptors Guild, Inc., Fedn. Modern Painters and Sculptors, Century Assn. Address: 420 E 86th St New York NY 10028

CRONENWETT, JACK LEMOYNE, vascular surgeon educator; b. Ludington, Mich., Dec. 13, 1946; s. Jack L. and K. Marie (Grundmark) C.; m. Linda R. Houk, 1969 (div. 1980); children: Sara, Molly; m. Debra A. Cote, Sept. 26, 1981. BS, U. Mich., 1969; MD, Stanford U., 1973. Diplomate Am. Bd. Surgery. Resident in gen. surgery U. Mich., Ann Arbor, 1973-79; resident in vacsular surgery U. Tenn., Memphis, 1979-80; asst. prof. surgery U. Mich., Ann Arbor, 1980-84; assoc. prof. surgery Dartmouth Coll., Hanover, N.H., 1984-89, prof. surgery, 1989—. Mem. New Eng. Soc. Vascular Surgery (sec. 1991—), Soc. for Vascular Surgery, Soc. of Univ. Surgeons, Internat. Soc. for Cardiovascular Surgery, Ea. Vascular Soc., Midwestern Vascular Soc., New Eng. Surg. Soc. Office: Dartmouth-Hitchcock Med Ctr 1 Medical Center Dr Lebanon NH 03756

CRONKITE, WALTER, radio and television news correspondent; b. St. Joseph, Mo., Nov. 4, 1916; s. Walter Leland and Helen Lena C.; m. Mary Elizabeth Maxwell, Mar. 30, 1940; children: Nancy Elizabeth, Mary Kathleen, Walter Leland III. Student, U. Tex., 1933-35; LL.D., Rollins Coll., 1966, Bucknell U., Syracuse U.; L.H.D., Ohio State U.; hon. degree, Am. Internat. Coll., Harvard U. News writer, editor Scripps-Howard, also UP, Houston, Kansas City, Dallas, Austin, El Paso, Tex., N.Y.C.; UP war corr., 1942-45, fgn. corr., reopening burs. in Amsterdam, Brussels, chief corr. Nuremberg war crimes trials, bur. mgr., Moscow, 1946-48, lectr., mag. contbr., 1948-49, CBS-News corr., 1950-81, spl. corr., 1981—; mng. editor CBS Evening News with Walter Cronkite, 1962-81. Host spl.: Universe, CBS; anchor for: TV news spls. Vietnam: A War That Is Finished, 1975, In Celebration of US, 1976, Our Happiest Birthday, 1977, The President in China, 1975, Solzhenitsyn: 1984 Revisited; Author: Challenges of Change, 1971. Recipient Peabody award, 1962, 81, several Emmy awards; William A. White award for journalistic merit, 1969; George Polk Journalism award, 1971; Gold medal Internat. Radio and TV Soc., 1974; Alfred I. DuPont-Columbia U. award in Broadcast Journalism, 1978, 81; Presdl. medal of Freedom, 1981. Mem. Acad. TV Arts and Scis. (pres. nat. acad. N.Y. chpt. 1959, Govs. award 1979), Assn. Radio News Analysts, Chi Phi. Clubs: Nat. Press, Overseas, Writers, N.Y. Yacht, Players. Office: CBS Inc 51 W 52d St New York NY 10019

CROOKE, EDWARD A., utility company executive; b. 1938. BS, U. Md., 1960; MBA, Loyola, 1971. With Balt. Gas & Electric Co., 1960—, assoc., fin. analyst, 1968-71, estimates analyst, 1971-72, sr. estimates analyst, 1972-73, supr. fin. planning, 1973-78, asst. sec., asst. treas., 1978, v.p., sec., 1978-88, pres., chief oper. officer, 1988—, also bd. dirs. With USAR, 1956-64. Office: Balt Gas & Electric Co PO Box 1475 Baltimore MD 21203-1475*

CROOM, JOHN HENRY, III, utility company executive; b. Fayetteville, N.C., Dec. 12, 1932; s. John Henry and Mary Dalice (Howard) C.; m. Verna Arlene Willetts, June 21, 1953; children: Mary, Karen, Elizabeth, John. BS in Mech. Engring., N.C. State Coll., 1954. Engr. United Fuel Gas Co., Charleston, W.Va., 1954-69; indsl. sales mgr. Charleston Group Cos., 1969-73; indsl. utilization mgr. Columbia Distbn. Cos., Columbus, Ohio, 1973-74; v.p. engring. and planning Columbia Distbn. Cos., Columbus, 1974-79; sr. v.p. Columbia Gas System, Wilmington, Del., 1979-80; exec. v.p., dir. Columbia Gas System, Wilmington, 1981-82, pres., bd. dirs., 1982-84, chmn., pres., chief exec. officer, 1984—; bd. dirs. Associated Electric & Gas Ins. Svcs. Bd. dirs. Med. Ctr. Del.; dir., v.p. Opportunities Ctr. Inc., Wilmington; dir. YMCA of Del.; bd. dirs., past pres. N.E. region Del.-Md.-Va. coun. Boy Scouts Am.; dir. N.E. Region Boy Scouts of Am.; dir., past chmn. bd. Gas Rsch. Inst., Chgo. With AUS, 1954-56, Korea. Mem. NSPE, Del. Roundtable (bd. dirs., past chmn.), Wilmington Country Club (bd. dirs.), Am. Gas Assn. (bd. dirs., past vice chmn.), Nat. Eagle Scout Assn. (bd. regents). Home: 255 Pondview Chadds Ford PA 19317 Office: Columbia Gas System Inc 20 Montchanin Rd Wilmington DE 19807-3094

CROPPER, M. ELIZABETH, art history educator; b. Dewsbury, Yorkshire, Great Britain; came to U.S., 1967; d. John Theodore Ingham and Helena Isabel (Allen) C.; m. Charles G. Dempsey, Nov. 15, 1975. BA with honors, Cambridge U., Eng., 1967; PhD, Bryn Mawr Coll., 1972. Leverhulme fellow Cambridge U., U.K., 1971-72; from asst. prof. to prof. Temple U., Phila., 1973-85; prof. art history Johns Hopkins U., Balt., 1985—, dir. Villa Spelman, 1987—; Slade prof. Cambridge U., 1992-93. Author: The Ideal of Painting, 1984, (catalogue) Pietro Testa: 1612-1650, 1988. Fulbright fellow, 1967; recipient fellowships English Speaking Union, 1967, Villa I Tatti, Florence, Italy, 1978, CASVA nat. Gallery, Washington, 1984, Inst. for Advanced Study, Princeton, N.J., 1989. Mem. Coll. Art Assn., Renaissance Soc. (nominating com. 1991). Office: Johns Hopkins U History of Art Baltimore MD 21218

CROPPER, SUSAN PEGGY, veterinarian; b. N.Y.C., Feb. 11, 1941; d. Eli and Ruth (Rader) Abrahams; divorced; 1 child, Tracy Lynn. BS, Kans. State U., 1962, DVM, 1964. Assoc. veterinarian Asbury Park (N.J.) Animal Hosp., 1964-65; instr. in Vet. Sci. Kans. State U., Manhattan, 1965-66; owner, veterinarian Markle (Ind.) Vet. Clinic, 1966-71, Meisels Animal Hosp. Clinic, Elmwood Park, N.J., 1971-73, Ridgewood (N.J.) Animal Hosp., 1973-75, Cropper House Call Practice, Wyckoff, N.J., 1975—; editor Nat. Assn. Women Vets., 1966-68; mem. Audibon Soc. Mus. Natural History. Editor WJMA Jour., 1973; photographer: Best Diving Spots in Western Hemisphere, 1987. Leader Brownie troop Girl Scouts of Am., Glen Rock, N.J., 1976-77, Wyckoff, 1977-83; chair No. Jersey Tridents, Ridgefield, N.J., 1985-86. Mem. AVMA, Soc. Aquatic Vet. Medicine (treas.), No. N.J. Vet. Med. Assn. (pres. 1972-73), Met. Vet. Med. Assn., N.Y. Zool. Soc., Van Saun Zool. Soc., N.J. Acad., Ski and Scuba Club of Westwood, North Jersey Tridents Club (Ridgefield, chair 1985-86). Office: 310 Newtown Rd Wyckoff NJ 07481-2608

CROSBIE, JOHN CARNELL, Canadian government official; b. St. John's, Nfld., Can., Jan. 30, 1931; s. Chesley Arthur and Jessie (Carnell) C.; m. Jane Furneaux, Sept. 8, 1952; children: Chesley, Michael, Beth. BA in Polit. Sci. and Econs., Queen's U., Kingston, Ont.; LLB, Dalhousie U., 1956; postgrad., London Sch. Econs. Bar: Nfld. 1957. Practice in St. John's, 1957-66; mem. St. John's City Coun., 1965-66, dep. mayor, 1966; min. Nfld. Dept. Mcpl. Affairs and Housing, 1966-67, Dept. Health, 1967-68; rep. Nfld. Ho. of Assembly from St. John's West, as Liberal, 1966-68; as Progressive Conservative, after 1971, govt. house leader, 1974-75; min. of fin., pres. Treasury Bd., also min. econ. devel. Nfld., 1972-74; min. fisheries, 1974-75, min. intergovtl. affairs Nfld., 1974-76, min. mines and energy, 1975-76; mem. Canadian Ho. of Commons for St. John's West, 1976—, chmn. Progressive Conservative caucus on energy, after 1977, also parliamentary critic for industry, trade and commerce; min. of fin. for Can., 1979-80; min. of justice, atty. gen. Can., 1984-86, min. of transp., 1986-88, min. internat. trade, 1988-91; min. fisheries and oceans, min Atlantic Can. Opportunies Agy Atlantic Can. Opportunities Agy., 1991—. Office: Min Fisheries and Oceans, Atlantic Can Opportunities Agy, Ottawa, ON Canada

CROSBY, GORDON EUGENE, JR., insurance company executive; b. Remsen, Iowa, Nov. 14, 1920; s. Gordon E. and Florence (Plummer) C.; m. Betty Jo Hubbard, May 2, 1942; children: Gordon Eugene III, Douglas H. Grad., Kemper Mil. Sch., 1938; student, U. Mo., 1938-40. Agt. New Eng. Mut. Life Ins. Co., Knoxville, Tenn., 1945-47; supr. New Eng. Mut. Life Ins. Co., Oakland, Calif., 1946; agy. mgr. New Eng. Mut. Life Ins. Co., Seattle, 1947, gen. agt., 1948-59; v.p., dir. agys. U.S. Life Ins. Co., N.Y.C., 1959-62, sr. v.p., dir. agys., 1962-64, exec. v.p., 1964-66, pres., chief exec. officer, 1966-67; pres., dir., mem. exec. com. USLIFE Corp., N.Y.C., 1966, chmn., chief exec. officer, 1967—; chmn. U.S. Life Ins. Co., N.Y.C., U.S. Life Ins. of Calif., Pasadena, All Am. Life Ins. Co., Chgo., U.S. Life Credit Ins. Co., Schaumburg, Ill., U.S. Life Equity Sales Corp., N.Y.C., U.S. Life Advisers, Inc., N.Y., The Old Line Life Ins. Co. Am., Milw., U.S. Life Systems Corp., N.Y., U.S. Life Income Fund, Inc., U.S. Life Real Estate Svcs. Corp.; bd. dirs. Life Ins. Coun. of N.Y.; mem. adv. bd. Mfrs. Hanover Trust, Manhattan. Member tax data base subcom. of steering com. on fed. taxation Am. Coun. Life Ins.; past trustee Pace U.; past pres., bd. trustees Fifth Ave Presbyn. Ch.; past bd. dirs. The Anglers Club of N.Y. Lt. USNR, World War II, PTO. Decorated Bronze Star medal. Mem. Econ. Club of N.Y., Manhattan's India House, Royal Palm Yacht Club, Beta Gamma Sigma, Sigma Chi (Significant Sig award 1977). Presbyterian. Clubs: Anglers, Brook, India House (N.Y.C.); Long Island (N.Y.). Office: USLIFE Corp 125 Maiden Ln New York NY 10038-4912

CROSBY, JOHN GRIFFITH, investment banker; b. Bayshore, N.Y., Feb. 10, 1943; s. Gordon Josiah and Ruth Louise (Plante) C.; m. Joan Louise Kelly; July 10, 1965; children: Bruce, Brian, David. Grad. Wm. Penn Charter Sch., 1961; AB with distinction, Lafayette Coll., 1965; MBA, Harvard U., 1969. V.p., stockholder, dir. Kidder, Peabody & Co. Inc., N.Y.C., 1969-80; mng. dir. Merrill Lynch & Co., N.Y.C., 1980-90; ptnr. The Lodestar Group, 1990—; bd. dirs. Am. Bankers Ins., TCI, Inc., Exec. Re, Inc. Author: Private Placement Market Review, 1975-81. Class fund mgr. Lafayette Coll., 1969-90; bd. deacons Presbyterian Ch., Madison, N.J., 1972; campaign chmn. Madison YMCA, 1975; coach Little League, 1977-84; treas. Troop 125, Boy Scouts Am., 1984-87; bd. dirs., asst. treas. Am. Coun. for Arts, 1987-90; pres. PTO, 1979-80. 1st lt. U.S. Army, 1965-67, Vietnam. Decorated Bronze Star medal. Mem. Bond Club of N.Y., Securities Industry Assn. (chmn. corp. fin. com. 1984-85). Clubs: Noe Pond, Madison Golf. Office: The Lodestar Group 110 E 59th St New York NY 10022-1304

CROSBY, RALPH WOLF, communications executive; b. Annapolis, Md., Dec. 16, 1933; s. Raymond Thomas and Lillian Sylvia (Wolf) C.; m. Carlotta Stafford, June 16, 1958; children: Laura Crosby Avallone, Raymond, Belinda Crosby Butler. BS in Journalism, U Md., 1956. Reporter, editor Balt. News-Am., 1956-60; bur. editor Iron Age Mag., Washington, 1960-65, Med. Econs. mag., Washington, 1966-67; assoc. editor Kiplinger's Changing Times, Washington, 1967-70; exec. v.p. Annapolis Harbour House, Inc., 1970-86; pres. Crosby Communications, Annapolis, 1972—; owner Severn Valley Racquet Club, Millersville, Md.; bd. dirs. DeRand Real Estate Investment Trust, Arlington, Va., Annapolis Bank and Trust Co. Editor (book) Person to Person Management, 1966; contbr. articles to numerous mags. including N.Y. Times Mag. Recipient Jesse H. Neal editorial award, 1966. Mem. Md. Direct Mkgt. Assn., Advt. Assn. Balt., Greater Annapolis C. of C. (pres. 1975-76), Annapolis Bus. Coalition (pres. 1983-84), U. Md. Colonnade Soc. (bd. dirs.), Nat. Press Club, Annapolis Touchdown Club (pres. 1976), U. Md. Dean's First Edit. Club (chmn. 1986—), Annapolitan Club. Democrat. Home: 139 Wallace Manor Rd Edgewater MD 21037-1205 Office: Crosby Communications Inc 647 Ridgely Ave Annapolis MD 21401-1069

CROSBY, RUSSELL UDELLIUS, trust fund executive; b. Vallejo, Calif., Oct. 8, 1951; s. Russell U. and Dorothy M. (Godwin) C. BA, Coll. William and Mary, 1973; M in Internat. Bus. Studies, U. S.C., 1976. Tng. instr. So. Nat. Bank, Lumberton, N.C., 1977-79; asst. v.p. Bank of N.C., Raleigh, 1979-80; mng. dir. Fed. Express Corp., Memphis, 1980-86; dir. Cadmus Communications, Springfield, Va., 1986-88, UMWA Health & Retirement Fund, Washington, 1988—. Office: UMWA Health and Retirement Funds 4455 Connecticut Ave Washington DC 20008-2302

CROSBY, THOMAS ANTHONY, radio producer, broadcaster; b. New London, Conn., July 25, 1947; s. Franklin Clifton and Dorothy Rose (Perkins) C.; m. Sheryll Ann Bellotti, Jan. 4, 1970; children: Sunny Marie, Kevin Franklin, Michael Thomas, Matthew Stephen. BA, U. R.I., 1969; MA, Am. U., 1979. News anchor, reporter WSAV/TV/AM, Savannah, Ga., 1971-73; news dir., anchor WSPA/TV/AM/FM, Spartanburg, S.C., 1973-77, Assoc. Press Radio Network, Washington, 1979-80; bur. chief, corr. WLOS TV/FM, Asheville, N.C., 1977-78; grad. asst. Am. U. Sch. Communication, Washington, 1978-79; broadcaster, writer WAMU-FM, Washington, 1978-79; broadcaster, producer Voice of Am., Washington, 1979—; narrator audio-visual presentations Wheeler Industries, Washington, 1978. Writer, producer, anchor documentary Vietnam Vets. Syndrome, 1979. 1st lt. U.S. Army, 1969-71, Vietnam. Decorated Bronze Star. Mem. North Springfield Racquet and Swim Club. Unitarian. Home: 5751 Heming Ave Springfield VA 22151-2714 Office: Voice of Am 330 Independence Ave SE Washington DC 20547-0001

CROSS, ALLAN JOSEPH, security software company executive, educator; b. Syracuse, N.Y., Mar. 6, 1944; s. Kenneth J. and Mary Ann (Polinski) C.; m. Martha Balon, Oct. 11, 1980; 1 child, Danielle. BA in Sociology/Criminology, Syracuse U., 1965; BA in Bus., U. Wyo., 1970, MBA, 1972; postgrad., Air Force Inst. Tech., 1972, Air Command and Staff Coll. Commd. 2d lt. USAF, 1965, advanced through grades to maj.; comdr. minuteman missile crew, 90th SMW UTAPAO RTNAB, Security Police Squadron, Thailand, 1968-74; comdr. Rhein Main AFB Security Police Squadron, Frankfurt, Fed. Republic of Germany, 1975-78; regional dir. Def. Investigative Svc., Phila., 1978-82; dir. security joint cruise missiles project USAF, Washington, 1982-84; chief ops. USAF/Def. Nuclear Agy., Washington, 1984-85; ret. USAF, 1985; mgr. RCA/GE, Camden, N.J., 1985-87; dir. assets protection Wall to Wall Sound & Video, Inc., Cinnaminson, N.J., 1987-89; v.p. PPM 2000, Inc., Edmonton, 1989—; Merchantville, N.J., 1989—; instr., lectr. U. Md., various locations, 1974-78, U. Del., Wilmington, 1985-88; pres. Cross Check Inc., Merchantville, N.J., 1987-89. Contbr. articles to profl. jours. Mem. Merchantville Hist. Soc., Better Bus. Bur., South Jersey, 1987-88. Fellow Quintillion Group; mem. Phila. C. of C., Am. Soc. Indsl. Security, Internat. Assn. Chiefs of Police, Acad. Security Educators and Trainers, Police Chiefs Assn. of S.E. Pa., VFW (cert. protection profl.), Beta Gamma Sigma. Home: 218 E Maple Ave Merchantville NJ 08109-2662 Office: PPM 2000 Inc, 10010-107 A Ave, Edmonton, AB Canada T5H 4H8

CROSS, JOHN WILLIAM, foreign language professional, educator; b. Franklin, Pa., June 1, 1943; s. William Robert and Madaline Ann (Maurin) C.; m. Beverly Jean Boor; 1 child, Catherine Elizabeth. BA, W.Va. U., 1965, MA, 1967; PhD, U. Conn., 1974. Instr. French U. N.C., Asheville, 1967-68; asst. Lycee Louis-Le-Grand, Paris, 1972-73; instr., asst. prof. French SUNY, Geneseo, N.Y., 1969-75; asst. prof. SUNY-Potsdam Coll., Potsdam, N.Y., 1976-84; chair modern langs. SUNY-Potsdam Coll., Potsdam, 1985-86, 90-91, assoc. prof., 1984-91, prof. modern langs., 1991; dir. for lang. programs MLA of Am., N.Y.C., 1991—; advanced placement reader Ednl. Testing Svc., Princeton, N.J., 1983-87; cons. in field. Editor Assn. Depts. of Fgn. Langs. Bull.; contbr. articles and revs. to profl. jours. Recipient French Govt. scholarship Svcs. Culturels Francais, 1990; grantee NEH, 1977, 85, 88, Office des Universites, 1972-73. Mem. MLA of Am., Am. Assn. Tchrs. French, N.Y. State Assn. Fgn. Lang. Tchrs., Societe d'Analyse de la Topique du Roman. Home: 60 E 9th St New York NY 10003-6402 Office: MLA 10 Astor Pl New York NY 10003-6935

CROSS, LAURA ELIZABETH, lawyer; b. Lathrop, Mo.; d. Pross T. and Nina (Peel) C.; A.B., Lindenwood Coll., 1923; B.Litt., Columbia Sch. Journalism, 1925; J.D., George Washington U., 1939. Bar: D.C. 1940. Bibliog. rsch. Libr. of Congress, Washington, 1931-42; atty. Office Chief of Engrs., U.S. Army, 1942-73; practiced in Washington, 1973—. Mem. ABA, Fed. Bar Assn., D.C. bar assns., Am. Judicature Soc., Women in Communications, Kappa Beta Pi, Theta Sigma Phi. Dec. Feb. 7, 1992. Home: 2500 Wisconsin Ave NW Apt 709 Washington DC 20007-4522

CROSS, RONALD, musicologist, educator; b. Fort Worth, Feb. 18, 1929; s. John Butler and Verna (Bailey) C. BA, Centenary Coll. La., 1950; MA, NYU, 1953, PhD, 1961; Fulbright scholar, U. Florence, U. Vienna, 1955-57. Mem. faculty Notre Dame Coll., S.I., 1958-68; assoc. prof. music Wagner Coll., S.I., 1968-75, prof., 1975—, chmn. music dept., 1981-84; dir. Collegium Musicum, S.I., 1968—; chair Kurt & Auguste Reimann, 1984—. Organist, choirmaster various chs.; recorded and directed Songs and Dances of the Renaissance (Lieder und Tänze der Renaissance) Collegium Pro Musica FSM Pantheon, 1984; author: Mathaeus Pipelare: Opera Omnia, 3 vols., 1966-67; reviewer Renaissance recs. for Music Quar., 1971-76; video: The Harpsichord Today: An Interview With Ronald Cross, 1991; contbr. articles to profl. jours. Am. Coun. Learned Socs. grantee, 1954, performance grantee Staten Island Coun. on the Arts, 1986, 87, 88, 89, 90, 91, 92; recipient Founders Day award NYU, 1962, Alumni Achievement award, 1988. Mem. Am. Guild Organists (asso.), Internat., Am. Musicol. Socs., Coll. Music Soc., Soc. for Ethnomusicology, Am. Recorder Soc. Home: 221 Ward Ave Staten Island NY 10304-2140

CROSS, THOMAS GARY, executive search consultant; b. Bayonne, N.J., July 17, 1947; s. Louis F. Jr. and Muriel B. (Burnett) C.; m. Lynda A. Armitage, June 15, 1968; children: Brian T., Jason S., Jonathan A. BA, Seton Hall U., 1969. CLU. Mgmt. trainee Chem. Bank, N.Y.C., 1969-70; sales mgr. Met. Life Ins., Hillside, N.J., 1970-74; employee benefits cons. Corroon & Black, N.Y.C., 1974-77; asst. v.p. Bayley Martin & Fay, N.Y.C., 1977-78; mktg. specialist Merrill Lynch, N.Y.C., 1978; sr. v.p., corp. life specialist Rollins Burdick Hunter, Roseland, N.J., 1978-87; v.p. exec. planning svcs. Alexander & Alexander, N.Y.C., 1987-88; pres. Cross & Assocs., Inc., Long Valley, N.J., 1988—. Asst. coach Long Valley (N.J.) Soccer Assn., 1982-84. Served with U.S. Army, 1969-75. Home: 15 Falcon Ln Long Valley NJ 07853-3345 Office: PO Box 370 Long Valley NJ 07853-0370

CROSSAN, DONALD FRANKLIN, educator; b. Wilmington, Del., Apr. 8, 1926; s. Samuel Davis and Anna Bertha (Spinken) C.; m. Ruth Hilda Swanson, June 11, 1948; children: Connie Christine, Donna Christine, Eric Richard. BS, U. Del., 1950; MS, N.C. State U., 1952, PhD, 1954. Asst. prof. U. Del., 1954-59, assoc. prof., 1959-65, prof., 1965—, assoc. dean/dir. Coll. Agr., 1969-71, asst. v.p., 1971-72, v.p., 1972-76, dept. chm., 1976-77; dean and dir. Coll. Agr. Sci. and Del. Agr. Experiment Sta., 1977-91; prof. emeritus U. Del., 1991—. Author numerous articles in profl. jours. Chmn. Del. Coastal Zone Indsl. Control Bd., Del. Farmland Preservation Found. Recipient Excellence in Teaching award U. Del., 1961. Mem. Potomac Div. Am. Phytopathological Soc., Longwood Gardens, Inc., (trustee 1979—). Republican. Home: 38 Sunset Rd Newark DE 19711-5236 Office: U Del Coll Agrl Scis Newark DE 19717

CROSSETT, KEVIN STEPHEN, lawyer, accountant; b. Phila., Sept. 20, 1960; s. Robert Harold and Dorothy Margaret (Shortall) C.; m. Joan Patricia Domaszewicz, Mar. 2, 1985. BS, Phila. Coll. Textiles and Sci., 1982; JD, Villanova (Pa.) U., 1989. Bar: Pa., U.S. Dist. Ct. Pa (ea. dist.) Pa. 1989, Supreme Ct. Pa. 1989, Supreme Ct. N.J. 1989, U.S. Dist. Ct. N.J. 1989; CPA, Pa. Assoc. Drinker, Biddle & Reath, Phila. Mem. AICPAs, Pa. Inst. CPAs. Republican. Roman Catholic. Home: 720 Maple Hill Dr Blue Bell PA 19422-2026 Office: Drinker Biddle & Reath Broad and Chestnut Sts Philadelphia PA 19107

CROSSLEY, FRANCIS RENDEL ERSKINE, engineering educator; b. Derby, Eng., July 21, 1915; came to U.S., 1937; s. Erskine Alick and Edith Mary (Helme) C.; m. Mary Eleanor de Lacy Coyne, Aug. 23, 1941; children: Phyllis de Lacy Crossley Mervine, Michael Francis Erskine Crossley. BA, Cambridge (Eng.) U., 1937, MA, 1941; D of Engring., Yale U., 1949. Lab. asst. GM Rsch. Labs., Detroit, 1937-38; designer Ford Motor Co., Dearborn, Mich., 1939-41; instr. in drafting U. Detroit, 1942-44; asst. prof. Yale U., New Haven, 1944-55, assoc. prof., 1955-65; vis. fellow U. Manchester (Eng.)/Inst. of Sci. & Tech., 1965; prof. mech. engring. Ga. Inst. Tech., Atlanta, 1966-69; prof. mech. and civil engring. U. Mass., Amherst, 1970-80; adj. prof. U. Fla., Gainesville, 1988-91; Fulbright lectr. Tech. U., Munich, 1962-63; U.S. mem. delegation forestry energy div. Internat. Energy Agy., Washington, 1977-79. Author: (textbook) Dynamics in Machines, 1954; editor, founder Jour. of Mechanisms, 1966-71; editor-in-chief Jour. Mechanism and Machine Theory, 1971-73. Member Town of Branford (Conn.) Bd. of Edn., 1987-92, chmn. solid waste mgmt. com., 1986-87; staff scientist, legis. fellow Conn. State Legislature, Hartford, 1981-83; bd. dirs. U.S. nat. com. Internat. Assn. for Exch. Students for Tech. Experience, 1963-65, 68-70. Von Humboldt Found. Sr. Scientist award, 1975-76. Fellow ASME (life, chmn. mechanisms conf. Atlanta 1967-68, policy bd. gen. engring. 1979-80, Centennial medal 1980, Machine Design award 1991); mem. Internat. Fedn. for Theory of Machines and Mechanisms (hon., v.p. elect 1967-75), Verein Deutscher Ingenieure (corr., hon.). Republican. Episcopalian.

CROSSLEY, GARY EXLEY, organization executive; b. Charleston, S.C., Oct. 6, 1951; s. Gilbert Franklin and Elsie Neal (Exley) C.; m. Debra Ann Hulon, Aug. 8, 1976 (div. Nov. 1982); m. Sharon Louise Hiers, Nov. 9, 1985. BS in Mktg., U. S.C., 1973. Labor market analyst S.C. Employment Security Commn., Columbia, 1973-85; labor market info. and rsch. dir. Interstate Conf. of Employment Security Agys., Inc., Washington, 1985—; cons. Army Transition Labor Market Info. Project, Washington, 1988-91. Editor, contbr. newsletter Labor Market Inform-the-Nation, 1985—; co-editor Workforce; contbr. articles to profl. publs. Bd. dirs. Consortium on Adolescent Pregnancy, Washington, 1987-90; asst. treas. St. Mark's Episcopal Ch., Washington, 1988—. Recipient contbr.'s award Nat. Occupational Info. Coordinating Com., 1988. Mem. Internat. Assn. Pers. in Employment Security (bd. dirs. S.C. chpt. 1980-81, nat. bd. dirs. 1987—, S.C. Employee of Yr. award 1982, Individual Merit award S.C. 1989), Soc. Nat. Assn. Publs., Partnership for Employment & Tng. Careers, Assn. Pub. Data Users. Democrat. Home: 1226 Walter Pl SE Washington DC 20003 Office: Interstate Conf Employment 444 N Capitol St NW Washington DC 20001-1512

CROSSMAN, WILLIAM WARREN, computer company executive; b. Oakland, Calif., Feb. 15, 1946; s. Malcolm Earl and Verge (Richter) C.; m. Maria Katherine Voltz, Dec. 23, 1971; children: Christopher, Karen. BS, U.S. Mcht. Marine Acad., 1969; MBA, U. Calif., Berkeley, 1974. Pres. Matrix Enterprises, San Francisco, 1973-75; v.p. Moore Mc Cormack Transport Inc., Stamford, Conn., 1975-83; mgr. fin. planning United Techs. Corp., Hartford, Conn., 1983-86; chief fin. officer Pacific ops. Otis Elevator Co., Farmington, Conn., 1986-91; pres. Computer Search, Inc., Canton, Conn., 1991—; bd. dirs. Otis India, Bombay, Otis Australia, Sydney, Otis Singapore, Otis Thailand, Bangkok, Pernas Otis, Kuala Lumpur, China Tianjin, Otis Export Corp., Hong Kong. Lt. USNR, 1969-76. Republican. Roman Catholic.

CROSSWHITE, DAN ELSWORTH, safety/environmental services executive; b. Ontario, Oreg., May 16, 1944; s. Claude Crosswhite and Louise M. (Jones) Crosswhite Schultz; m. Jennifer S. Stephens, Apr. 6, 1964 (div. June 1978); children: Carol M., Teresa L., Larry C. AS, Treasure Valley Community Coll, 1975; BS, Boise State U., 1984. Clerical U.S. Army Security Agy., 1964-68; store clk. Sherwin Williams Paints, Arlington, Va., 1968; pers. clk. Ore-Ida Foods Inc., Ontario, Oreg., 1968-72; pers. mgr. Ore-Ida Foods Inc., Ontario, 1972-77; plant mgr. Ore-Ida Foods Inc., Massillon, Ohio, 1977-78; new offices coord. Ore-Ida Foods Inc., Boise, 1978; pers. mgr. Northwest Agrl. Coop. Assn., Ontario, 1979-82; safety/indsl. rels. supr. Morrison-Knudsen Corp., Boise, 1982-86; mgr. safety and indsl. rels. Morrison-Knudsen Corp., Hornell, N.Y., 1986-90; mgr. safety and environ. svcs. Morrison-Knudsen Corp., Hornell, 1990—. Pres. Payette (Idaho) Jaycees, 1975-76, Treasure Valley Kiwanis Club, Ontario, 1976-77. Sgt. U.S. Army, 1964-68. Office: Morrison Knudsen Corp Morrison Knudsen Dr Hornell NY 14843-2268

CROUCH, CEDRIC VINCENT, musician, producer; b. Allentown, Pa., Dec. 6, 1967; s. Gordon Howard and Althea Irene (Bear) C.; 1 child, Andrew Ryan. Auditor Inventory Control Systems, North Hampton, Pa., 1985-87; accounts mgr. C.D.M. Counselling, Inc., Pottstown, Pa., 1989-91; bass player With Band DeFault, Thorndale, Pa., 1991—. Writer, performer: (albums) The Road Never Ends, 1990, DeFault, 1991, (single) DeFault, 1992. Republican. Home: RD 1 Box 9 Bechtelsville PA 19505

CROUGH, DANIEL FRANCIS, lawyer, insurance company executive; b. Syracuse, N.Y., Feb. 2, 1936; s. Vincent Leo and Sarah Jane (McMahon) C.; m. Domenica Dolores Cappadozy, July 27, 1957; children: Sara, Deborah, Maura, Deanne, Daniel. B.A., LeMoyne Coll., 1957; J.D., Syracuse U., 1960. Bar: N.Y. 1961, Pa. 1969, U.S. Supreme Ct. 1981. Sole practice Syracuse, 1961-63; staff atty. Reliance Ins. Co., Phila., 1963-69, asst. gen. counsel, 1969-71, sec., assoc. gen. counsel, 1971-72; v.p., gen. counsel Colonial Penn Ins. Co., Phila., 1972-74; v.p., corp. counsel Colonial Penn Group, Inc., Phila., 1975-78, sr. v.p., sec., gen. counsel, 1978-83, pres., 1983-86, chief exec. officer, 1985-86; pres., chief exec. officer, trustee The Mutual Assurance Co., Phila., 1988—; bd. dirs. Green Tree Ins. Co., Valley Ins. Co., Am. Loyalty Ins. Co., Keystone State Life Ins. Co., Citizens Crime Commn. of Delaware Valley, World Affairs Coun., Ins. Fedn. Pa.; bd. dirs. Ins. Soc. Phila., chmn., 1990—. Trustee LeMoyne Coll., chmn. 1991—. Mem. ABA, Internat. Assn. Def. Counsel, N.Y. State Bar Assn., Pa. Bar Assn., Phila. Bar Assn., Nat. Assn. Corp. Dirs., Aronimink Golf Club, Down Town Club, Sunday Breakfast Club. Republican. Roman Catholic. Office: The Mut Assurance Co 414 Walnut St Philadelphia PA 19106-3703

CROUSE, LLOYD ROSEVILLE, lieutenant governor; b. Lunenburg, N.S., Can., Nov. 19, 1918; s. Kenneth Eleazer and Mary Bertha (Lantz) C.; m. Marion Cavell Fraser, Oct. 7, 1942; children: Marilyn, Stephen. Grad. in bus. adminstrn., Lunenburg County Acad., 1935. Fishing fleet owner Crouse Fisheries Ltd., Viking Fisheries Ltd., Atlas Fisheries Ltd., Lunenburg, 1945-67; M.P. from Queens-Lunenburg dist., also mem. Privy Coun. Parliament of Can., Ottawa, 1957-88; now lt. gov. of N.S. Halifax; Mem. Lunenburg Town Coun., 1950-52; mem. coun. Lunenburg Bd. Trade, 1946-56; chmn. Can. del. Commonwealth Parliamentary Conf. in U.K., 1962, del., 1973, del. to 26th Commonwealth Parliamentary Conf., Lusaca, Zambia, 1980, del. 22d Can. Regional Commonwealth Parliamentary Conf., N.W.T., 1982, leader Commonwealth Parliamentary Del., Isle of Man, 1987; bd. govs. Waterloo Lutheran U., Kitchener, Ontario, 1960-69; del. to NATO Parliamentary Conf., Paris, 1963, 64, 66, to Brussels, 1967; del. to Internat. Parliamentary Union Conf., Paris, 1971; del. CPAs Conf., Jamaica, 1978, New Zealand, 1979; chmn. standing com. on pub. accounts, 1974, 75; del. to UN Conf. at Colombo, Sri Lanka, 1981; chmn. bd. trustees Pub. Archives Nova Scotia; served on House Standing Coms. External Affairs and Nat. Def., Fisheries and Regional Expansion; mem. Shadow Cabinet, responsible for fisheries policies for Can. Mem. Lunenburg Sch. Commrs., 1950-52; chmn. Luth. Youth Bd., 1950-54; chmn., master ceremonies N.S. Fisheries Exhbn., 1946-56; mem. bd. govs. Waterloo Luth. U., Kitchener, Ont., 1960-69. Pilot RCAF, WWII. Fellow N.S. Royal Commonwealth Soc.; mem. Commonwealth Parliamentary Assn. (pres. Can. br. 1984, chmn. 1985, 86, 87, 88), Can. Legion (past pres. Lunenburg br.), Knight of Grace, Order St. John of Jerusalem. Progressive Conservative. Lutheran. Home and Office: 1451 Barrington St, Halifax, NS Canada B3J 1Z2

CROUSE, ROGER LESLIE, information analyst, consultant; b. Medford, Mass., Mar. 24, 1944; s. Mahlon Dale and Doris Mabel (Butman) C.; m. Judy Avis Wiley, May 10, 1969; children: Alison, Erin. BS, U. Mass., 1966; MS, U. Vt., 1977. Programmer, analyst positions IBM, Essex Junction, Vt., 1966-77; adv. systems analyst IBM, 1977-80, devel. mgr., 1980-82, adv. edn. analyst, 1982-83, adv. info. ctr. analyst, 1983-91, distributed computing cons., 1991—; ptnr. in edn. Burlington (Vt.) Area Vocat. Ctr., 1986-88; pub. software specialist IBM, Burlington, 1988-89; adj. prof. U. Vt., 1990. Contbr. articles to profl. jours. Treas. Nat. Guard Assn. Vt., Burlington, 1980-86; bd. dirs. Lake Iroquois Action Commn., Hinesburg, Vt., 1980—; 8-gallon blood donor ARC, Burlington, 1966—; bd. dirs. Make-A-Wish Found. of Vt., Burlington, 1989—. With Vt. Air N.G., 1967—. Mem. Masons (Worshipful Master local chpt. 1976-77). Office: IBM Corp 1000 River St Essex Junction VT 05452-4299

CROUT, JOHN J., risk management consultant; b. Phila., May 16, 1937; s. Robert M. and Marie (Kuhn) C.; m. Joan E. Pampanin, Oct. 1, 1966; children: David Alan, Philip John. BS, Rutgers U., 1976. Casualty underwriter Comml. Union Ins. Co., Phila., 1954-62; ins. salesperson Kressler, Wolf & Miller Ins. Agy., Easton, Pa., 1962-68; risk mgmt. cons. Blades & Macaulay, Union, N.J., 1968-79, ptnr., 1979-91; ptnr. Blades, Macaulay, Crout & Myers, Union, N.J., 1991—. Mem. Soc. Risk Mgmt. Consultants (sec. 1989-90). Office: Blades Macaulay Crout & Myers 2444 Morris Ave PO Box 188 Union NJ 07083-0188

CROWE, VIRGINIA MARY, librarian; b. Meadville, Pa., Mar. 8, 1933; d. Harold Augustus and Daisy Lee (Ervin) Shartle; m. Robert William Crowe, Mar. 22, 1951; children: Thomas Robert, David William, Steven Michael. BS in Edn., Edinboro U. of Pa., 1965; MLS, U. Pitts., 1967, PhD, 1973. Elem. sch. librarian Saegertown (Pa.) Area Schs., 1965; elem. sch. librarian Gen. McLane Sch. System, Edinboro, 1965-67, sec. sch. librarian, 1967-68; asst. prof. libr. sci. Edinboro Univ. of Pa., 1968-72, dept. chair of libr. sci. and assoc. prof., 1972-82; asst. dir. outreach svcs. U. Libr. Svcs., Va. Commonwealth U., Richmond, 1982-83, assoc. dir. for pub. svcs., 1983-87; dean libr. and media svcs Shippensburg U. of Pa., 1987—; adj. faculty Cath. U. Am., Washington, 1984-87; cons. Weston Woods Studios, Conn., 1980-85. Contbr. articles to profl. jours. Pres. Venango (Pa.) Borough Coun., 1973-79; dir. Cambridge Springs Joint Sch. Bd., 1958-69; trustee Venango Pub. Libr., 1975-80. U.S. Office of Edn. grantee, 1975, 77, 79. Mem. ALA, Pa. Libr. Assn., State System of Higher Edn. Librs. Coun. (chair 1989-91). Home: 395 Briar Ln Chambersburg PA 17201-3144 Office: Shippensburg U Shippensburg PA 17257

CROWELL, RICHARD LANE, microbiology educator; b. Springfield, Mo., Sept. 27, 1930; s. Thomas Rolla and Addie Malinda (Lane) C.; m. Arlene Mildred Prell, June 27, 1953; children—Steven Richard, Kathleen Margaret Crowell Miller, Barbara Lane, Wendy Jane. B.A., U. Buffalo, 1952; M.S., U. Minn., 1954, Ph.D., 1958. Instr. microbiology U. Minn. Med. Sch., Mpls., 1958-60; asst. prof. Hahnemann U. Sch. Medicine, Phila., 1960-64, assoc. prof., 1964-71, prof., 1971—, chmn. microbiology and immunology, 1979—; research cons. Smith Kline Corp., Phila., 1975-77, Lehn and Fink Co., Montvale, N.J., 1976-80; ad hoc reviewer NIH, Bethesda, Md., 1966—. Editor: Tumor Virus Infections and Immunity, 1976; Virus Attachment and Entry into Cells, 1986; assoc. editor Jour. Microbial Pathogenesis, 1985-91, mem. editorial bd., 1991—. Recipient Lindback award Hahnemann U. Sch. Medicine, 1967-68; NIH research career devel. awardee, 1962-72. Fellow Am. Acad. Microbiology; mem. Am. Soc. Virology, Am. Soc. Microbiology (pres. 1991-92, pres. eastern Pa. br. 1974-76), Assn. Med. Sch. Microbiology Chairmen (pres. U.S. and Can. 1986), Am. Assn. Immunologists, Phi Beta Kappa, Sigma Xi. Democrat. Presbyterian. Avocations: camping; fishing. Home: 407 Hutchins Dr Ambler PA 19002-2822 Office: Hahnemann U Sch Medicine Dept Microbiology & Immunology Broad & Vine Sts Philadelphia PA 19102

CROWLEY, DENNIS W., university administrator, quality management consultant; b. Rochester, N.Y., Oct. 19, 1941; s. Jerome Arthur and Jeannette Eleanor (Davis) C.; m. Linda Marie Lange, May 23, 1964; children: Bradford, Gwen. BA, Va. Mil. Inst., Lexington, 1963; MEd, U. Rochester, 1973. Cert. quality improvement facilitator Eastman Kodak Co. Asst. registrar Smithsonian Inst., Washington, 1966-67; computer programmer Eastman Kodak Co., Rochester, 1967-68; asst. registrar St. John Fisher Coll., Rochester, 1968-71, dir. fin. aid, 1971-76, registrar, asst. dean, 1976-88, registrar, asst. dean, asst. to pres. for quality mgmt., 1988—; Mem. N.E. Quadrant Governance Bd., 1990—; mem. Bishop's Commn. on the Reorgn. of Cath. Schs., 1989-90; chmn. Christian Formation Com., 1986—. Contbr. articles to profl. jours. Mem. Monroe County Div. Youth, Rochester, 1984. Maj. U.S. Army, 1964-66, Res., 1966-85. Mem. Am. Soc. for Quality Control (sec. 1990—, Outstanding Speaker 1990). Roman Catholic. Home: 71 Fairlawn Dr Rochester NY 14617-3201 Office: St John Fisher Coll 3690 East Ave Rochester NY 14618-3597

CROWLEY, KEVIN JOHN, psychologist; b. N.Y.C., Mar. 29, 1956; s. John B. and Margaret B. (Croughan) C.; m. Susan T. Hackeling, Apr. 13, 1985; children: Brian, Colleen. BA, SUNY, Stony Brook, 1978; MS, CUNY, Flushing, 1980; PhD with distinction, Pace U., N.Y.C., 1989. Lic. psychologist, N.Y., Md.; cert. sch. psychologist, N.Y., Md. Sch. psychologist Edgemont Sch. Dist., Scarsdale, N.Y., 1980-82, Bedford Cen. Sch. Dist., Mt. Kisco, N.Y., 1981-90; psychology intern L.I. Jewish/Hillside Med. Ctr., Glen Oaks, N.Y., 1986-87; clin. psychologist Ctr. for Applied Activation, Rockville, Md., 1990-92; psychologist pvt. practice Rockville, Md., 1991—. Author: Evaluation of Good Touches/Bad Touches - A Program to Prevent Child Sexual Abuse, 1989. Chairperson Citizens Adv. com. on dist.-wide testing, North Salem, N.Y., 1989-90. Mem. APA, N.Y. State Psychol. Assn., Md. Psychol. Assn., Psi Chi. Home: 7820 Moorland Ln Bethesda MD 20814

CROWLEY, SHARON BURKE, technical center director; b. Rutland, Vt., Sept. 22, 1945; m. Phillip F. Crowley, July 22, 1972; children: Colleen, Kelly. BS in Home Econs. Edn., U. Vt., 1967, MEd in Adminstrn. and Planning, 1979. Cert. tchr., adminstr., Vt. Dept. chair, instr. home econs. Rutland High Sch., 1968-74; asst. dir. Rutland Area Vocat.-Tech. Ctr., 1974-84, housemaster, 1984-87; dir. Stafford Tech. Ctr., Rutland, 1987—; mem. Vt. coun. U. Vt., Burlington, 1985-89; adv. com. U. Vt. Extension Svc. Rutland County, 1983-86. Active citizen's adv. com. Rutland Town-Hwy., 1989-91, Police Com., 1990-91; incorporator Rutland Regional Med. Ctr., 1988-92. Named one of Vt. Women Who Make A Difference Castleton State Coll., 1991. Mem. Rutland City Administrv. Assn., Vt. Vocat. Dirs. Assn. (pres. 1989, treas. 1987-89), Am. Vocat. Assn., Vt. Vocat. Assn. (assoc. v.p. 1972-74). Home: N Grove St Rutland VT 05701 Office: Stafford Tech Ctr Stratton Rd Rutland VT 05701

CROWN, JUDITH ANN, logistics company executive; b. South Bend, Ind., Nov. 13, 1952; d. William Eugene and Margaret Irene (Carroll) Hay; m. Gerrit John Schutte III, Aug. 11, 1974 (div. Nov. 1983); 1 child, Gerrit John IV; m. Francis Joseph Crown Jr., Jan. 1, 1986. BS, SUNY, Albany, 1978; MA, Cen. Mich. U., 1979. Intern Stock Fund Br., Fort Dix, N.J., 1978-81, dir., 1981-85; chief Installation Supply Div., Fort Dix, 1985-89; dep. dir. Directorate of Logistics, Fort Dix, 1989-90; chief Logistics Data Mgmt. Team, dir. maj. item info. program Systems Integration and Mgmt. Activity, Chambersburg, Pa., 1990—. Home: 620 Kittatinny Dr Chambersburg PA 17201-9292 Office: SIMA D/MIIP Attn AMXSI-MSS-L Letterkenny Army Depot Chambersburg PA 17201

CROWN, WILLIAM HARRY, statistics educator; b. Middlebury, Vt., June 14, 1954; s. Merle Wesson and Minnie (Balch) C.; m. Robin East, June 7, 1975; 1 child, Sarah Anne. BA in Econs., U. Vt., 1976, MA in Econs., 1979; PhD in Urban and Regional Planning, MIT, 1982. Rsch. asst. Nat. Econ. Rsch. Assocs., Boston, 1977-78; regional econ. analyst MIT, Cambridge, 1978-82; assoc. rsch. prof., sr. rsch. assoc. Brandeis U., Waltham, Mass., 1982—; vis. lectr. Gerontology Inst., U. Mass., 1988-89; ptnr. Analytic Resources, Needham, Mass., 1990—; cons. Boettner Rsch. Found., Bryn Mawr, Pa., 1990—, Ctr. on Aging and Devel., U. Miami, Fla., 1990-91, Boston Estate Planning Coun., 1991-92. Author: (with J.H. Schulz and A. Borowski) Economics of Population Aging: The "Graying" of Australia, Japan and the United States, 1991, (with C.F. Longino Jr.) Old Money, 1989, (chpt.) Economic Roles for Older People in Maturing Societies, 1988; contbr. articles to profl. jours. Chair adv. com. Minuteman Home Care Corp., Burlington, Mass., 1985—. Mem. Am. Econ. Assn., Gerontol. Soc. Am., Regional Sci. Assn. Office: Brandeis U Florence Heller Grad Sch Waltham MA 02254

CROWTHER, G(EORGE) RODNEY, III, writer, photographer, television production company executive; b. Asheville, N.C., Jan. 11, 1927; s. G. Rodney Jr. and Martha Maria (Lewis) C. Grad., Boys' Latin Sch., Balt., 1944; student, Sch. Modern Photography, N.Y.C., 1949-50. Fashion photographer Amos Parrish & Co., N.Y.C., 1950-53; ind. comml. photographer Chevy Chase, Md., 1956-61; free-lance writer Washington, 1962—; pres. The Carrollian Age, Washington, 1987—. Author: Surname Index to Sixty-Five Volumes of Colonial and Revolutionary Pedigrees, 1964; contbr. articles to Nat. Geneal. Soc. Quar., 1962—; photograph Sputnik and the Big Dipper in Modern Mus. Art, N.Y.C., Echo I satellite in Smithsonian Inst., Where 'KONG' Stood, UN, N.Y.C., 1951. Served with USN, 1945-46, PTO. Episcopalian. Office: PO Box 369 Ben Franklin Sta Washington DC 20044

CRUICE, WILLIAM JAMES, chemist, consultant; b. N.Y.C., Aug. 22, 1937; s. DeCourcy Vincent and Margaret (Fleming) C.; m. Gregoria Restivo, Aug. 14, 1965; children: William G., Danielle N. BS in Chemistry magna cum laude, St. John's U., Queens, N.Y., 1960, BA in English magna cum laude, 1961, MS in Chemistry, 1964. Teaching fellow N.Y. State Regents St. John's U., N.Y.C., 1960; tchr. Xaverian High Sch., Bklyn., 1961-62; teaching asst. St. John's U., 1962-63; rsch. chemist Thiokol Corp., Denville, N.J., 1963-69; asst. v.p. rsch. and engring. U.S. Banknote Corp., N.Y.C., 1969-70; v.p., assoc. chief scientist Hazards Rsch. Corp., Mt. Arlington, N.J., 1969—. Author: (with others) Fire Protection Handbook, 17th edit., 1991; contbr. articles to books in field. Recipient N.Y. State Regents scholarship, 1955, Manhattan Coll. scholarship, 1955, Cath. U. Am. scholarship, 1955; NSF fellowship, 1960. Fellow Am. Inst. Chemists; mem. ASTM, Am. Inst. Chem. Engrs., Nat. Fire Protection Assn. Roman Catholic. Office: Hazards Rsch Corp 200 Valley Rd Mount Arlington NJ 07856-1316

CRUM, ALBERT BYRD, psychiatrist, consultant; b. Omaha, Nov. 17, 1931; s. J. Rufus and Alberta (McCreary) C.; m. Rosa Maria Hennessy y Sinclair; children: Rosa Maria Crum O'Brien, Elsie A., Alberta Crum Fousek. BS, U. Redlands, Calif., 1953; MD, Harvard U., 1957; MS, NYU, 1987; DS (hon.), U. Redlands, 1974. Med. intern Columbia U. div. Bellevue Med. Ctr., N.Y.C., 1957-58; rsch. fellow, psychiat. resident Creedmoor Inst. for Psychol. Studies, Queens Village, N.Y., 1958-59; chief, neuropsychiatric svcs., Continental Air Command USAF Hosp., 1959-61; psychiat. resident Columbia U. Psychiat. Inst. of Columbia-Presbyn. Hosp., N.Y.C., 1961-63; pvt. practice Brooklyn Heights, N.Y., 1963—; active attending staff Gracie Sq. Hosp., N.Y.C., 1963—; med. dirs. Psychiatric Svcs. Internat. P.C., Brooklyn Heights, 1980—; ednl. dir. med. and health seminars Internat. Inst. for Human Behavior, Inc., Brooklyn Heights, 1983—; advisor Office of Tibet, N.Y.C., 1984—; clin. prof. behavioral scis. NYU, N.Y.C., 1987—; pres., dir. behavioral scis. Way of Life/N.Y., Ltd., Brooklyn Heights, 1989—; pres. Y.F. One/N.Y., Ltd., Brooklyn Heights, 1991—, Y.F. Nationwide, Inc., Brooklyn Heights, 1991—; co-chmn. U.S. Coordinating Commn. for Nomination of His Holiness the Dalai Lama of Tibet for the Nobel Peace Prize, Brooklyn Heights, 1986—; adj. prof. anatomy and neuroanatomy, NYU, 1987—; ptnr. Burdick Assocs. Investment Firm, Brooklyn Heights, 1976—; pres. Burdick Assocs. Owners Corp., Brooklyn Heights, 1983—; chmn. Human Behavior Found., Brooklyn Heights, 1968—; chmn. selection com. Human Behavior Found.'s Albert Schweitzer Humanitarian Award, Brooklyn Heights, 1986—. Author (chpt.) The Triumphant Person, 1989. Bd. dirs. Albert Schweitzer Fellowship, N.Y.C., 1982—; chmn. William James Found., Brooklyn Heights, 1989—; bd. dirs. Burdick Internat. Ancestry Library, Sarasota, Fla., 1985—; mem., chn., bd. advisors NYU's Coll. of Dentistry, N.Y.C., 1988—; mem. Brooklyn Heights Assn., 1970—. Capt. USAF, 1959-61. Recipient Disting. Svc. award Bklyn. Jr. C. of C., 1966, Bicentennial award Nat. Jogging Assn., 1976. Fellow Royal Coll. Physicians and Surgeons in Psychiatry; mem. Pan Am. Med. Assn., Nat. Bd. Med. Examiners, Med. Coun. of Can., Am. Acad. Clin. Psychiatrists, Am. Orthopsychiatric Assn., Am. Psychiat. Assn., AMA, Med. Soc. State of N.Y., Kings County (N.Y.) Med. Soc., World Med. Assn., World Fedn. Mental Health, Am. Physicians Art Assn., Harvard Med. Soc., English Speaking Union, Harvard Club of N.Y., Bklyn. Club, Heights Casino and Racquet Club, MENSA (life, nat. coord. 1980-84), Phi Beta Kappa (councillor 1981-84). Home and Office: Psychiat Svcs Internat PC 77 Remsen St Brooklyn NY 11201-3400

CRUM, SUSAN WEY, marketing executive; b. Brockton, Mass., Jan. 3, 1957; m. William C. Crum, Sept. 4, 1982. BA in Physics, Wellesley Coll., 1978; MSEE, Northeastern U., 1982; MBA, Harvard U., 1984. Process engr. GTE Sylvania, Needham, Maa., 1978-80; sr. devel. engr. Honeywell Electro-Optics, Lexington, Mass., 1980-82; product mgr. Teradyne, Boston, 1984-88; sr. product mgr. Racal Datacom, Boxborough, Mass., 1988-90; mgmt. cons. various cos., 1990-91; sr. product mktg. mgr. Xyplex, Boxborough, Mass., 1991—. Mem. Wellesley Coll. Club of Boston (sec. 1982-87).

CRUZ, ALBERT RAYMOND, consumer affairs coordinator; b. Mora, N.Mex., Oct. 4, 1933; s. Barney Fred and Gertrude Virginia (Branch) C.; m. Patricia Ann Aragon, Oct. 4, 1957; children: Albert Jr., John. BA in Psychology, N.Mex. Highlands U., 1958, MS in Clin. Psychology, 1958; postgrad., George Washington U., 1959-63. Sch. psychologist D.C. Pub. Schs., 1959-62; rsch. psychologist U.S. Dept. Labor, Washington, 1962-63, counseling rsch. specialist, 1963-67, manpower analyst, 1967-69, spl. asst., adminstr., 1969-74, internat. program officer, 1974-75, asst. to under sec., 1975-82, consumer affairs coord., 1982—; cons. and asst. to White House, Interagy. Commn. on Mexican-Am. Affairs, Washington, 1966-69; manpower and psychology test advisor Bur. of Internat. Affairs, U.S. Dept. Labor, Washington, 1967-75. Baseball coach N.Mex. Highlands U., Las Vegas, 1958; pres. Dept. of Labor Recreation Assn., 1964-66. Sgt. U.S. Army, 1954-56, Korea. Mem. Am. Psychol. Assn. (Psi Chi Nat. Svc. award 1958), Fed. Exec. Inst. Alumni Assn., N.Mex. Highlands U. Alumni Assn. (chpt. pres. 1977-89). Home: 4116 Havard St Silver Spring MD 20906

CRUZE, KENNETH, surgeon; b. Takoma Park, Md., Oct. 10, 1927; s. Conrad Ellis and Claudia Eleanore (Carpenter) C.; B.A., Columbia Union Coll., 1949; M.D., Loma Linda U., 1955; m. Jean Anna Hansen, June 13, 1948; children: Wendy Jean, Lori Ann, Barbara Lee. Intern, Los Angeles County Gen. Hosp., 1955-56; resident in surgery Wadsworth Gen. Med. and Surg. Hosp., West Los Angeles, 1956-60; resident in pediatric surgery Children's Hosp. Los Angeles, 1958-59; fellow in thoracic and cardiovascular surgery U. Fla., Gainesville, 1960-62; practice medicine specializing in thoracic and cardiovascular surgery, Takoma Park, Md., 1962-89; mem. staff Washington Adventist Hosp., Takoma Park, 1962-89, dir. open heart surgery program, 1970-89; ret. Mem. exec. com., bd. trustees D.C. Blue Shield, Columbia Union Coll., Takoma Park. Served to capt. M.C., U.S. Army, 1956-63. Fellow A.C.S., Am. Coll. Chest Physicians, Am. Coll. Angiology; mem. Am. Thoracic Soc., Am. Trauma Soc., Med. and Chirurg. Faculty Md., Md. Heart Assn., Soc. Thoracic Surgeons. Republican. Club: Civitan. Mem. editorial bd. Md. State Med. Jour., 1972-77; contbr. articles to med. jours. Home: 12804 Gaffney Rd Silver Spring MD 20904-3517

CRYER, THEODORE HUDSON, ophthalmologist; b. Chgo., May 8, 1946; s. Arthur William and Maxine Ritter C.; A.B. in Chemistry, Taylor U., 1968; M.D., U. Md., 1972; children: Timothy Hudson, Jordan Tinley, Megan Elizabeth, Rebecca Jeanne. Straight med. intern South Balt. Gen. Hosp., 1972-73; jr. asst. resident, 1973-74; asst. resident U. Md. Hosp., Balt., 1974-76, resident, 1976-77; practice medicine specializing in ophthalmology, Waynesboro, Pa., 1977—, Westminster, Md., 1977-85; instr. U. Md. Sch. Medicine, 1979-91, clin. asst. prof. Sch. Medicine, 1991—; chmn. com. on ethics Waynesboro Hosp., 1984, chmn. com. quality assurance, 1987—, v.p. med. staff, 1987-89, pres. med. staff, 1989-91, trustee, 1991—. Clk. session Westminster Reformed Presbyn. Ch., 1980-83. Mem. AMA, Am. Acad. Ophthalmology, Pa. Med. Soc., Franklin County Med. Soc., Md. Eye Physicians and Surgeons, Pa. Acad. Otolaryngology and Ophthalmology, AAAS, Nat. Soc. to Prevent Blindness (charter mem.), Ophthal. Assn. Rsch. to Prevent Blindness, Ind., 1978. Republican. Methodist. Office: 45 Roadside Ave Waynesboro PA 17268

CRYSTAL, JAMES WILLIAM, insurance company executive; b. N.Y.C., Oct. 9, 1937; s. I. Frank and Evelyn G. Crystal; m. Jean Crystal; children: James F., Sanford F., Jonathan F. B.S., Trinity Coll., 1958. With Royal Globe Ins. Group, N.Y.C., 1956; underwriter Home Ins. Co., N.Y.C., 1957; spl. agt. Home Ins. Co., San Francisco, 1958-59; chmn., chief exec. officer Frank Crystal & Co. Inc., N.Y.C., 1960—; chmn. bd. F.F.H. Ins. Co., Northeast Inst. Co.; bd. dirs. Atlantic Internat. Ins. Co., Century Air Rail and Land Ins. Co., Donkenny, Inc. Bd. dirs. Auto Resources, Inc.; trustee Mt. Sinai Hosp., N.Y.C. Mem. Nat. Assn. Casualty and Surety Agts., Harmonie Club, N.Y. Stock Exch. Lunch Club, Century Country Club, Wings Club N.Y. Republican. Home: 875 Park Ave New York NY 10021-0341 Office: Frank Crystal & Co 40 Broad St New York NY 10004-2315

CRYSTAL, ROBERT ABRAHAM, pharmacist; b. Liberty, N.Y., Mar. 13, 1956; s. David Sydney and Harriet Frances (Tofel) C.; m. Elizabeth Anne DeMeo, Apr. 12, 1981; children: Joshua Michael, Allison Rebecca. BS in Pharmacy, Mass. Coll. Pharmacy, Boston, 1979. Pharmacist, asst. mgr. Peoples Drug Stores, Alexandria, Va., 1979-80; pharmacist Potomac (Md.) Village Pharmacy, 1980-83, Rodman's Drug, Silver Spring, Md., 1983-85; pharmacist, asst. mgr. Drug Fair, Cleve., 1985-86, Rite Aid Corp., Harrisburg, Pa., 1986-91; pharmacist mgr. Wal-Mart, Milford, Del., 1991—. Bd. dirs. Congregation Beth Sholom, Dover, Del., 1989—, pres., 1991—. Named Congregant of Yr., Congregation Beth Sholom, 1987-88. Mem. Planetary Soc., Couples Club of Gaithersburg Hebrew Congregation (co-chmn. 1985-86). Democrat. Home: 817 Sunset Ter Dover DE 19901-6801

CSENCSITS, CHRISTOPHER JOSEPH, naval officer; b. Allentown, Pa.; s. Joseph Frank and Sonia Anne (Zaharchuk) C. BSEE, Boston U., 1987. Commd. ensign USN, 1987, advanced through grades to lt., 1991; assigned to Naval Nuclear Power Sch., Orlando, Fla., 1987, Nuclear Power Tng. Unit, Windsor, Conn., 1987-88, Naval Submarine Sch., Groton, Conn., 1988; chemistry and radiol. controls asst. USS Dallas (SSN-700), Portsmouth, N.H., 1989-90, Groton, Conn., 1990-91; ptnr. CS Assocs., Northampton, Pa., 1991—. Republican. Home: 282 Steeple Rd Northampton PA 18067-9243 Office: CS Data Assocs 282 Steeple Rd Northampton PA 18067

CSERMELY, THOMAS JOHN, computer engineer, physicist; b. Szombathely, Hungary, June 25, 1931; s. Janos and Maria (Szarvas) C.; diploma in engring. Tech. U. Budapest, 1953; Ph.D., Syracuse U., 1968; m. Tiiu Vaharu, June 17, 1962; 1 son, Erik Thomas. Instr., Inst. Theoretical Physics, Tech. U. Budapest (Hungary), 1953-56; nuclear engring. cons. Design Bur. Power Stas., Budapest, 1956; research engr. Carrier Corp., Syracuse, N.Y., 1957-67; research assoc. physics Syracuse U., 1967-68, assoc. prof. elec. and computer engring., 1976-88, assoc. prof. bioengring., 1988—; asst. prof. physiology SUNY Upstate Med. Center, Syracuse, 1968-76; asst. prof. physics LeMoyne Coll., Syracuse, 1976-77. Recipient Wolverine Diamond Key award ASHRAE, 1964. Mem. Am. Phys. Soc., IEEE, Biophys. Soc., N.Y. Acad. Scis., Am. Assn. Physics Tchrs., Soc. Computer Simulation, AAAS, Sigma Xi. Club: Tech. Syracuse. Contbr. articles to profl. publs. and orgns. on control, heat exchange dynamics, quantum biochemistry, brain functions and computer simulation neuronal network dynamics, computer applications in medicine. Home: 149 Humbert Ave Syracuse NY 13224-2251

CSERR, HELEN FITZGERALD, physiologist; b. Boston, June 23, 1937; d. Joseph Harold and Ruth Knowles (Milliken) FitzGerald; m. Robert Cserr, May 28, 1962; 1 child, Ruth. BA, Middlebury Coll., 1959; PhD, Harvard U., 1965. Fellow in physiology Harvard U., Boston, 1965-67, instr. physiology, 1967-70; lectr. med. sci. Brown U., Providence, 1970-71, asst. prof. med. sci., 1971-76, assoc. prof. med. sci., 1976-82, prof. med. sci., 1982—; mem. physiology study sect. NIH, Bethesda, Md., 1975-79. Editor: Fluid Environment of the Brain, 1975, The Neuronal Microenvironment, 1986; contbr. 62 articles to profl. jours. Trustee Mt. Desert Island Biol. Lab., Salsbury Cove, Maine, 1971-76, 83-86, The Grass Found., Quincy, Mass., 1990—. Postdoctoral fellow in brain rsch. United Cerebral Palsy Rsch., 1964-67; recipient Rsch. Career Devel. award NIH, 1973-78, Javitz Neurosci. Investigator award, NIH, 1987-94. Mem. Am. Physiol. Soc., Soc. for Neurosci., The (Brit.) Physiol. Soc. Office: Brown U Dept Physiology PO Box G-B3 Providence RI 02912-0001

CUBAS, JOSE M(ANUEL), advertising agency executive; b. Matanzas, Cuba, Mar. 1, 1930; came to U.S., 1960; s. Jose M. and Luisa M. (Ruiz) C.; m. Edith Perez, Apr. 26, 1952; children: Mercedes, Alina. Student, U. Havana Law Sch. Pres. Publicidad Siboney, S.A., Havana, 1953-60, San Juan, P.R., 1962-84; pres. Internat. Mktg. and Advt. Services Corp., Fla., 1979-84; exec. v.p. Foote Cone & Belding-Latin Am., N.Y.C., 1985-86, pres., 1987—. Mem. Internat. Advt. Assn., U.S.-Hispanic C. of C. (recipient awards). Republican. Roman Catholic. Office: Foote Cone & Belding LAm 18th Fl 400 Madison Ave New York NY 10017

CUBBERLEY, WILLIAM CHARLES, publishing company executive, lawyer; b. Durham, N.C., June 6, 1945; s. Charles Lamb and Catherine (Brabble) C. BA, Wofford Coll., 1967; JD, U. N.C., 1972; LLM in Internat. Law, NYU, 1978. Bar: D.C. 1973. Asst. trust officer Nat. Savs. & Trust Co., Washington, 1973-77; polit. affairs officer UN, N.Y.C., 1978-80; adminstrv. editor Clark Boardman Co., Ltd., N.Y.C., 1980-83; dir. hardcover pub. and audio-video prodn. Practising Law Inst., N.Y.C., 1983—; cons. Commn. To Study Orgn. of Peace, N.Y.C., 1979. Contbg. author: Human Rights in Third World Perspective, 1983. With U.S. Army, 1969-71. Carnegie En-

dowment for Internat. Peace fellow, 1978. Mem. ABA, D.C. Bar, Am. Soc. Internat. Law, Union Internat. Avocats. Office: Practising Law Inst 810 7th Ave New York NY 10019

CUCCARO, RONALD ANTHONY, insurance adjusting company executive; b. Utica, N.Y., Dec. 14, 1944; s. Pasquale and Rose (Pepe) C.; m. Sheila Jane McCarthy, Apr. 1, 1967; children: Stephanie Ann, Elizabeth Ann. BS, Syracuse U., 1966. Cert. sr. profl. pub. adjuster. Adjuster, br. mgr. Gen. Adjustment Bur., Utica and Plattsburg, N.Y., 1966-71; sec., treas. Basloe, Levin & Cuccaro, Ltd., Utica, 1971—; pres., chief exec. officer Adjusters Internat., Utica, 1985—; cons. Govt. Kuwait for UN claims program for Iraqi war reparations. Pub. Adjusting Today; contbr. articles to profl. jours. Pres. Oneida County Assn. Retarded Citizens, 1976-79, JCI senator Utica Jaycees, Cen. N.Y. Community Arts Coun., 1982-85, Friends in Deed of the Retarded Found., 1991; bd. dirs. Better Bus. Bur., Utica, 1980-81, Downtown Utica Devel. Assn., 1991. Recipient Chpt. Service award Oneida County Assn. Retarded Citizens, 1979, Coll. Services award Utica Coll., 1983; named Dirs. Emeritus, Cen. N.Y. Arts Council, 1986, Top 40 Alumni of Achievement, Utica Coll., 1987. Mem. N.Y. Assn. Pub. Adjusters, Nat. Assn. Pub. Ins. Adjusters (v.p. 1985-90, pres. 1990-91), Alpha Phi Delta Alumni (pres. 1971-72). Roman Catholic. Club: Ft. Schuyler. Home: 2230 Douglas Cres Utica NY 13501-5907 Office: Adjusters Internat PO Box 90 Utica NY 13503-0090

CUCCI, LOUIS ANTHONY, layout engineer; b. Mt. Vernon, N.Y., Sept. 10, 1943; s. Anthony Louis and Teresa M. (Silvestri) C.; m. Marie Louise Torraca, Apr. 15, 1967. AAS, Ulster Coll., 1976; student, Marist Coll., Poughkeepsie, N.Y., 1977-78. Market rep. Visual Graphics, N.Y.C., 1979-82; layout engr. IBM, Poughkeepsie, 1983—. Cons. Heart Assn., Poughkeepsie, Cancer Soc., Poughkeepsie; advisor Spackenkill High Sch. Leo Club, Poughkeepsie, 1981—. Mem. KC (grand knight 1982-92), Lions (Poughkeepsie chpt. pres. 1981-82, 91-92, Lion of Yr. award 1982, Lion of Decade award 1992), Elks. Home: 33 Forest Valley Rd Pleasant Valley NY 12569 Office: IBM South Rd Poughkeepsie NY 12602

CUDDIHY, ROBERT VINCENT, JR., marketing executive; b. Rochester, N.Y., July 15, 1959; s. Robert Vincent Sr. and June Marie (Tuck) C.; m. Michele Pittenger; children: Brendan, Shea. BA in Acctg., Franklin and Marshall Coll., Lancaster, Pa., 1981. CPA, N.Y. Sr. mgr. Peat, Marwick, Main & Co., N.Y.C., 1981-87; pres., chief fin. officer, chief operating officer, sec. MarkitStar, Inc., N.Y.C., 1987—, bd. dirs., 1988—; chief oper. officer MarkitStar, Inc., 1989—, pres., 1990—; Cons. in field. Mem. Am. Inst. CPA's, N.Y. State Soc. CPA's, Nat. Assn. Accts. Republican. Office: MarkitStar Inc 475 10th Ave New York NY 10018-1120

CUDLIP, CHARLES THOMAS, investment banker, real estate company executive; b. Detroit, July 13, 1940; s. William Byrnes and Lynwood (Bope) C.; m. Frances Farrar, Apr. 21, 1964 (div. 1976); children—Charlotte Luxmore, Jeffrey Rockwell (dec.); m. Mary Brittain Bardes, Apr. 15, 1983; 1 child, Mary Brittain; stepchildren: Blakely, Merrill. B.A., U. Va., 1963; postgrad., U. Mich. Grad. Bus. Sch., 1965-66. Legis. planning mgr. Ford Motor Co., Dearborn, Mich., 1970-73; mgr. sales Johns Island Co., Vero Beach, Fla., 1973-76; dir. congl. relations USDA, Washington, 1976-77; exec. asst. chmn. Republican Nat. Com., Washington, 1977-78; pres. Hannibal Assocs., Washington, 1978-81; corp. v.p. Chrysler Corp., Washington, 1981-83; chmn. Historic Properties Inc., Washington, 1983—; chmn. Hannibal Ptnrs. Inc., Washington; bd. dirs. No. Va. Banking Corp., Nat. Bank No. Va.; instr. Polit. Sci., U. Detroit, 1971-73. Cons. presdl. campaigns, 1968, 72, 76, 80, 84; staff mem. Nat. Platform Com. Rep. Nat. Conv., 1980, Pres. Transition Team, U.S. Trade Reps. Office, 1980; mem. Nat. Fin. Com. Presdl. Inaugural, 1985; alt. George Bush for Pres. Com., 1988; del. Rep. Nat. Conv., 1988; past treas., bd. dirs. Washington Tennis Found.; bd. dirs. Internat. Tennis Hall of Fame, Newport, R.I. Episcopalian. Home: Meryvale Rt 1 Box 63A Middleburg VA 22117 Office: Hannibal Ptnrs Ste 882 1919 Pennsylvania Ave NW Washington DC 20006-3404

CUDMORE, BOB, radio personality; b. Amsterdam, N.Y., Nov. 9, 1945; s. Clarence Henry and Julia Harriet (Cook) C.; m. Mary Rose Pritchard, Aug. 20, 1966; children: Robert Jr., Kathleen. BA, Boston U., 1967, MA, 1968. Announcer Sta. WCSS, Amsterdam, 1962-63, Sta. WBUR, Boston, 1966-67, Sta. WCAS, Cambridge, Mass., 1967-68; program host Sta. WBEC, Pittsfield, Mass., 1968-80; talk show host Sta. WGY, Schenectady, N.Y., 1980—. Producer radio documentary Creating Radio: The People Who Made WGY, 1992. Lector St. Joseph's Ch., Scotia, N.Y., 1980-92. Recipient Media award Albany Kiwanis, 1986, N.Y. State Bar Assn., 1987; named finalist Internat. Radio Festival, 1985. Democrat. Roman Catholic. Office: WGY 1430 Balltown Rd Schenectady NY 12302

CUDNOHUFSKY, WALTER LEE, landscape architect; b. Pontiac, Mich., July 15, 1940; s. Walter and Gertrude (Degroot) C.; m. Irene K. Koster, June 4, 1964 (div. 1975); children: Craim William, Niels Walter; m. Susan Cudnohufsky, Aug. 9, 1986. BS in Landscape Architecture with honors, Mich. State U., 1962; MLA with honors, Harvard U., 1965. Registered landscape architect, Mass., Conn., N.J. Designer East Detroit (Mich.) Pub. Works, 1960-62; landscape architect Sasaki Strong Assn., Toronto, Ont., Can., 1962-63, 65-66, The Architects Collaborative, Cambridge, Mass., 1963-66; ptnr. landscape architecture Rsch. Planning and Design Assocs., Amherst, Mass., 1966-72; landscape architecture cons. Conway, Mass., 1972-80; ptnr., landscape architect Conway Design Assocs., 1980-90; prin. Walter Cudnohufsky Assocs., Conway, 1990—; founder, dir. Conway Sch. Landscape Design, 1972—; asst. prof. grad. faculty U. Mass., 1966-72; vis. prof., critic 25 programs of landscape architecture through U.S. and Can., 1966-76; appeared in workshops and guest critic programs at landscape architecture and architecture for students and faculty, 1976—; co-dir. S.E. New Eng. Study, 1972; co-dir. visual and social subproject A Multivariate Model for the Study of Fresh Water Wetlands in Mass., 1969-72; workshop leader Hariot Watt U., Edinburgh, Scotland, 1982. Co-author: Designing Your Corner of Vermont, 1991; contbr. articles to profl. jours. Organizer, cofounder Deerfield (Mass.) Land Trust, 1989-90. Recipient Regional award for Outstanding Comprehensive Planning, Am. Planning Assn., 1991, Regional award for Planning Implementation, Am. Planning Assn., 1991, Merit awards for Landscape Planning, Boston Soc. Landscape Architects, 1991, AIA Regional Honor award, 1982, Award of Excellence, Design and Environment Mag., 1973, Jacob Weidenman Traveling fellowship, 1965; named Outstanding Educator in Conservation, 1981; faculty growth and faculty rsch. grantee U. Mass., Amherst, 1966-67. Mem. Am. Soc. Landscape Architects. Office: Walter Cudnohufsky Assocs Box 264 Main St PO Box 264 Conway MA 01341

CUETARA, PAUL SAVAGE, education consultant; b. Boston, Jan. 27, 1947; s. Jose Phillip and Barbara (Savage) C.; m. Joan A., Aug. 2, 1969; children: Kimberly, Gregory. BS in Edn., U. Maine, 1970; MEd, U. N.H., 1980. Tchr. North Hampton (N.H.) Pub. Schs., 1970-73; tchr. tech. Newmarket (N.H.) High Sch., 1974-88; vocat. dir. Salem (N.H.) Sch., 1988-90; ednl. cons. North Hampton, 1990—; coord. Seacoast Tech. Prep. Consortium, Stratham (N.H.) Tech. Coll., 1991-92; project dir. McAuliffee Sabbatical, North Hampton, 1987-88. Author: A Guide for Change Making Transition From IA to TE, 1985. Moderator Town of North Hampton, 1981, Sch. Dist. North Hampton, 1981. Mem. Am. Vocat. Assn., N.H. Tech. Edn. Assn. (sec.), Internat. Tech. Edn. Assn., N.H. Vocat. Assn. (pres. 1985), N.H. Baseball Umpires Assn., N.H. Soccer Ofcls. Assn., Internat. Assn. Approved Basketball Ofcls., Women's Basketball Ofcls. for North Atlantic Conf. (Eluba supr. 1991—). Home and Office: 58 Winnicut Rd North Hampton NH 03862-2014

CUFFIN, B. NEIL, biomedical research scientist, electrical engineer; b. McKeesport, Pa., Apr. 21, 1941; s. Benjamin and Emma (Fuls) C. BS, Pa. State U., 1963, MS, 1965, PhD, 1974. Antenna design engr. RCA, Moorestown, N.J., 1965-66; instr. elec. engring. Pa. State U., University Park, 1969-74; staff scientist MIT, Cambridge, Mass., 1974—. Contbr. numerous articles to profl. jours. With U.S. Army, 1966-68. Office: MIT (NW14-2224) 77 Massachusetts Ave Cambridge MA 02139-4307

CUHAJ, GEORGE STEPHEN, numismatist, sculptor; b. Long Island City, N.Y., Jan. 8, 1960; s. George and Eileen (Petrow) C. AAS, CUNY, 1978, BBA, 1985. Systems operator Am. Numismatic Soc., N.Y.c., 1981-88; chief usher St. Patrick's Cathedral, N.Y.c., 1988-89; catalogue prodn. mgr. Stack's Rare Coins, N.Y.c., 1990—; archivist Bklyn. Tech. Rsch. Found., 1989—. Mem. Am. Medallic Sculptor Assn. (treas.1986-92, sec. 1992—), Nat. Sculpture Soc. Home: PO Box 6021 Long Island City NY 11106-0021

CULBERT, KENNETH EDWARD, software engineer; b. Cold Spring, N.Y., Feb. 17, 1948; s. Edward Webber and Muriel Aimee (Mosher) C.; m. Patricia Ann Kozlowski, July 31, 1976; children: Amanda Mei, Christie Elizabeth. BA, SUNY, New Paltz, 1974; MA, SUNY, 1976; postgrad., Boston U., 1978-81. Software engr. Indsl. Computer Controls, Inc., Cambridge, Mass., 1981-82, Micom Systems, Inc., Newton, Mass., 1982-84; group mgr. Micom Systems, Inc., 1984-86; software engr. Cullinet Software, Westwood, Mass., 1986-88; group ldr. Cullinet Software, 1988-89; modem software mgr. Microcom, 1989—. Bd. trustees United Ch. Christ, Canton, 1989, chmn. 1988-90, mem. 1987—; active Canton Junction Civic Assn. Mem. Boston Computer Soc. Mem. United Ch. of Christ. Home: 175 Chapman St Canton MA 02021-2067 Office: Microcom Inc 500 River Ridge Rd Norwood MA 02062-5028

CULBERTSON, JUDI C., writer, social worker; b. Norfolk, Va., Mar. 1, 1941; d. Hubert Roe and Charlotte Eleanor (Hess) Chaffee; m. Paul Culbertson, June 23, 1962 (div. Feb. 1971); 1 child, Andrew William; m. Thomas Randall, June 22, 1974. BA, Wheaton Coll., 1962; postgrad., Vt. Coll. Editorial asst. Eternity Mag., 1962-64; various teaching positions; sr. caseworker Suffolk County Dept. Social Svcs., Ronkonkoma, N.Y., 1970—. Author: Games Christians Play, 1967, Little White Book on Race, 1970, Permanent Parisians, 1985, Permanent New Yorkers, 1987 (named One of 25 Best Rsch. Books of 1988, N.Y. Pub. Libr., 1988), Permanent Californians, 1988, Permanent Londoners, 1991; also articles. Mem. AAUW, Nat. Writers Union. Democrat. Home: 211 Hawthorne St Port Jefferson NY 11777

CULHANE, JOHN WILLIAM, journalist, author; b. Rockford, Ill., Feb. 7, 1934; s. John William and Isabel June (Fissinger) C.; m. Hind Noel Rassam, Aug. 27, 1960; children: Michael Noel, T.H. BS, St. Louis U., 1956; cert. in advanced internat. reporting, Columbia U., 1966. Reporter St. Louis (Mo.) Globe Dem., 1955; daily columnist, reporter Rockford Register-Republic, 1956-61; reporter, feature writer, fgn. corr. Chgo. Daily News, 1962-66; assoc. editor Newsweek mag., N.Y.C., 1966-71; freelance journalist N.Y. Times mag., others, N.Y.C., 1971-85; roving editor Reader's Digest, Pleasantville, N.Y., 1985—; moustro-of-ceremonies Mickey Mouse's 50th Birthday Retrospective and Whistle-Stop Train Tour Across the U.S., 1978; guest clown Ringling Bros., Barnum and Bailey Circus, 1974-84. Author: Special Effects in the Movies, 1981, Walt Disney's Fantasia, 1983, Backstage at Disney's, 1983, The American Circus: An Illustrated History, 1990 (Washington Irving Book Selection Westchester Libr. Assn. 1991), Disney's Aladdin: The Making of an Animated Film, 1992; co-author: The Art of the Muppets, 1980, (TV specials) Noah's Animals, 1974, King of the Beasts, 1976, Last of the Red Hot Dragons, 1980, voice of cartoon dragon; moderator: A Forum on Animation and Fantasy Filmmaking, 1981; co-producer (documentary) Circus!, 1983; narrator (documentary) Fantasia: The Making of a Masterpiece, 1991; model for Mr. Snoops character Walt Disney's The Rescuers, 1977. Master-of-ceremonies Winnebago County Sesquicentenniel, Rockford, 1968; mem. Clearwater Assn. (author: PCB's: The Poison That Won't Go Away). Recipient 4 1st Prize awards Ill. AP., 1960, 61, 63, 64; Ford fellow Columbia U., 1965-66; Ill. Humanities Coun. grantee, 1991. Mem. Alpha Sigma Nu, Sigma Delta Chi (2 awards for pub. service journalism 1964, 69). Office: Readers Digest Pleasantville NY 10570

CULLARI, SALVATORE SANTINO, clinical psychologist, educator; b. Caroniti, Calabria, Italy, Apr. 1, 1952; came to U.S., 1955; s. Carmelo and Carmela (Cullari) C.; m. Kathryn Plesce, Apr. 26, 1985; children: Catherine, Dante. BA, Kean Coll., 1974; MA, Western Mich. U., 1976, PhD, 1981. Lic. psychologist, Pa., W.Va. Dir. psychology White Haven (Pa.) Ctr., 1982-83; psychologist Danville (Pa.) State Hosp., 1983-84; coord. of psychology Harrisburg (Pa.) State Hosp., 1984-86; assoc. prof. Lebanon Valley Coll., Annville, Pa., 1986—; cons. Harrisburg State Hosp., 1986—, Bur. Disability Determination, Harrisburg, 1987—. Author acad. questionnaire acad. social evaluation scales, 1990; contbr. numerous articles to profl. jours. Mem. APA, Assn. Advancement of Behavior Therapy, Assn. Behavior Analysts. Office: Lebanon Valley Coll Psychology Dept Annville PA 17003

CULLEN, JAMES PATRICK, international trading company executive; b. Balt., Nov. 28, 1944; s. James Patrick and Frances Ann (Lanza) C. Cert., U. Madrid, 1964; BA, Johns Hopkins U., 1966; LLB, U. Pa., 1969. Bar: D.C., 1971. Trust officer First Am. Bank, N.A., Washington, 1970-74; spl. counsel U.S. Securities & Exchange Commn., Washington, 1974-80; corp. sec. COMSAT Gen. Corp., Washington, 1980-83; pres. Universal Export Ltd., Balt., 1983—. Author: The Fieldstone Affair, 1988; inventor hand-held computer, 1987. Mem. World Trade Inst., Md. Club, Met. Club, City Tavern Club, Loch Raven Skeet & Trap Club (gov.), Delta Phi Club Md. (bd. dirs.). Home: 109 Thicket Rd Baltimore MD 21212-2442 Office: Universal Export Ltd PO Box 27606 Baltimore MD 21285-7606

CULLEN, STEPHEN LEONARD, JR., electrical engineer; b. Manchester, N.H., Feb. 16, 1940; s. Stephen Leonard and Margaret (O'Connor) C.; m. Elizabeth Ann Jutras, Aug. 26, 196l; children: Kathleen E., Judith A., Sandra J., Susan L. BEE, Rensselaer Poly. Inst., 196l; MSEE, U. N.H., 1968. Engr. Sprague Electric Co., Concord, N.H., 196l-65; mgr. engring. IBM, East Fishkill, N.Y., 1965-74; dir. testing Codex, Newton, Mass., 1974-80; sr. mgr. product mgmt. Digital Equipment Corp., Maynard, Mass., 1980—; panelist Internat. Testing Conf., 1979. Patentee test method. Mem. Medfield (Mass.) Energy Commn., 1974. Mem. IEEE. Republican. Roman Catholic. Office: Digital Equipment Corp 333 South St Shrewsbury MA 01545-4195

CULLEN, VINCENT ALBERT, athletic director, basketball coach; b. Providence, Mar. 23, 1934; s. Vincent A. and Edith Elise (Miner) C.; m. Ann Winslow Cornell, Sept. 1, 1962 (dec. Apr. 1989); children: Carol, Kevin, Steven, Patricia. EdB, R.I. Coll., 1955; MA, Wesleyan U., 1964. Tchr. Calef Jr. High Sch., Johnston, R.I., 1955-56, Park View Sch., Cranston, R.I., 1960-62, 63-64; athletic dir., coach Community Coll. of R.I., Warwick, 1965—. Contbr. articles to profl. jours. Lt. (j.g.) USCG, 1956-60. Named Nat. Basketball Coach of Yr., Nat. Jr. Coll. Athletic Assn., 1991, R.I. Coach of Yr. Words Unltd., 1978, 89, AHEPA, 1973; recipient Charles B. Willard Achievement award R.I. Coll. Alumni Assn., 1982, Disting. Svc. award R.I. Bd. Govs. of Higher Edn., 1990, Bert Summer Meml. award R.I. Jewish Bowling Congress, 1982, William Kutneski award R.I. Bd. of Basketball Officials, 1980. Mem. Nat. Assn. of Collegiate Dirs. of Athletics (jr. coll. rep. to nat. exec. com. 1978-82, sec. 1985-89, chmn. continuing edn. 1990—, nat. exec. com. 1978-82), Nat. Alliance of Two-Yr. Coll. Athletic Adminstrs. (nat. exec. com. 1988—), NJCAA New England Soccer Com., Nat. Assn. of Basketball Coaches, R.I. Assn. of Intercollegiate Athletics for Women (sec. 1980—), NJCAA Basketball Coaches Assn., R.I. Assn. of Health, Phys. Edn., Recreation and Dance, Kappa Delta Pi. Home: 12 Ionia St Cranston RI 02921-1120 Office: Community Coll of RI 400 East Ave Warwick RI 02886-1805

CULLEY-FOSTER, ANTHONY ROBERT, lobbyist, international business consultant; b. Londonderry, Ireland, July 31, 1947; came to U.S., 1971; s. Allen Foster and Eileen Louisa Culley; m. Heidi Rubroeder; children: Joshua, Daniel, Valentina. Diploma, Reading U., 1969, Coll. Preceptors, U.K., 1971; BA magna cum laude, Roosevelt U., Chgo., 1973, MA, 1979. Cert. tchr., U.K. High sch. tchr. London, 1969-71; dir. Boys & Girls Clubs of Chgo., 1971-77; personal asst. to chmn. Combined Internat. Corp., Chgo., 1977-81; founding dir., chief exec. officer The Congl. Award, Washington, 1981-85; pres. Culley-Foster & Co., Washington, 1985—; cons. W. Clement Stone Enterprises, Chgo., 1978—, Brit. Multinat. Corps. Nat. organizer Run Across Am. program Am. Bicentennial Com., 1976, Run for Ireland program Olympic Coun. Ireland, 1980; co-founder Congl. Award-U.S., 1979, President's Award for Youth, Ireland, 1983; founding chmn. No. Ireland Partnership U.S., 1990; mem. Nat. Boys Club U.K., 1966—; trustee Internat. Fedn. Keystone Youth Orgns., World Meml. Fund for Disaster Relief. Recipient Duke of Edinburgh's Gold Award, 1966, Pub. Service commendations Office of Pres. of U.S., 1976, 79, 83, Congl. award U.S. Congress, 1981, Nat. Achievement award Pres.'s Council on Phys. Fitness and Sports, 1976, Nat. Achievement award Olympic Council Ireland, 1980. Mem. Brit.-Am. C. of C., Am. C. of C.-U.K., C. of C. of the U.S., Am. League of Lobbyists, Brit.-Am. Bus. Assn., U.S.-Irish Rowing Union (hon. life), Royal Automobile Club. Office: Culley-Foster & Co PO Box 17370 Washington DC 20041-0370

CULLIGAN, JANE TERESA, counselor; b. Newark, Mar. 16, 1933; d. Joseph Philip and Jane (Wallace) C. BA in English, St. Elizabeth Coll., Convent Station, N.J., 1963; MA in Edn., Seton Hall U., 1966; MA in Counseling, Iona Coll., 1985; postgrad., NYU, 1970-72. Entered Sisters of Charity, Roman Cath. Ch., 1955—. Tchr. Sisters of Charity, Convent Station, N.J., 1958-72; dance therapist Essex County Hosp. Ctr., Cedar Grove, N.J., 1972-82, St. Vincent Nursing Home, Montclair, N.J., 1983-84; counselor Sacred Heart Sch., South Plainfield, N.J., 1984-85; youth minister Epiphany Ch., Cliffside Park, N.J., 1985-86; spiritual dir. Our Lady of Peace Spiritual Life Ctr., Narragansett, R.I., 1986-87; counselor, spiritual dir. Cornerstone Counseling Ctr., Cranston, R.I., 1987—; dance therapist Free Lancer, Cranston, R.I., 1987—; retreat dir. Medjugorje in Am., Fitchburg, Mass., 1990—; region dir. Medjugorje in Am., 1990—, lectr., 1988—; conductor dance workshops. Mem. Dance Therapy Assn., Assn. for Counseling and Devel., Christian Therapy Assn., Am. Dance Therapy Assn. (bd. dirs. 1984-86), Religious Issues Assn. of Counseling and Devel. (rep. for Religious 1987). Democrat. Roman Catholic.

CULLINGWORTH, LARRY ROSS, residential and commercial real estate development company executive; b. Toronto, Ont., Can., Sept. 26, 1939; s. Allan Joyce and Ethel Alexandra (Davis) C.; m. Betty Kathleen Hughes, July 9, 1966; children: Lisa, Kevin. B.A.Sc., U. Toronto, 1963, P. Eng., 1965; M.B.A., York U., Toronto, 1972. Cons. engr. Proctor & Redfern, Toronto, 1963-68; regional mgr. George Wimpey Can. Ltd., Toronto, 1968-72; mgr. corp. devel. Coscan Devel. Corp. (formerly Costain Ltd.), Toronto, 1973-74, v.p. fin., sec., 1975-78, sr. v.p., chief fin. officer, sec., 1979, exec. v.p., chief fin. officer, sec., 1980-82, pres., chief operating officer, 1983-85, pres., chief exec. officer, 1986-92; pres., chief exec. officer Coscan Devel. Corp., Toronto, 1992—; bd. dirs. Coscan Devel. Corp. Bd. dirs. RP Eye Rsch. Found., Consol. Carma Corp., Can. Inst. Pub. Real Estate Cos. Mem. Assn. Profl. Engrs. Ont., National Club, Bayview Club, Granite Club (Toronto). Home: 23 York Valley Crescent, Willowdale, ON Canada M2P 1A8 Office: BCE Pl, 181 Bay St Ste 4200, Toronto, ON Canada M5J 2T3

CULLITY, JOHN PATRICK, economics educator; b. Jersey City, N.J., Nov. 3, 1928; s. Patrick Leo and Gertrude Bernadette (Lambert) C. BS cum laude, St. Peter's Coll., 1952; MA, Columbia U., 1955, PhD, 1963. Prof. Rutgers U., Newark, 1963—. Contbr. to books, articles to profl. jours, mags. With U.S. Army, 1952-54. Salzburg Seminar scholar, 1957; Faculty Rsch. fellow, 1972. Roman Catholic. Office: Rutgers U Dept Econs Newark NJ 07102

CULP, MICHAEL, securities company executive, research director; b. N.Y.C., June 17, 1952; s. Robert Walter and Anna Lee (Filtzer) C. BA in Econs. magna cum laude, CUNY, 1973. Securities analyst Standard & Poor's, N.Y.C., 1974-79; v.p., securities analyst E. F. Hutton & Co., Inc., N.Y.C., 1979-82; v.p., sr. securities analyst Prudential Securities Inc., N.Y.C., 1982-86, sr. v.p., mng. dir. rsch., 1986—, bd. dirs., 1986-91, oper. coun., 1991—, chmn. stock selection com., 1989—, chmn. equity devel. coun., 1991—; chartered fin. analyst U. Va. Mem. N.Y. Soc. Security Analysts, Fin. Analysts Fedn., Inst. Chartered Fin. Analysts, Phi Beta Kappa, Omicron Delta Epsilon. Home: Chastellux Tuxedo Park NY 10987 also: Chastellux Tuxedo Park NY 10987 Office: 1 Seaport Plz New York NY 10292-0001 also: Chateau Chastellux Tuxedo Park NY 10987

CULVER, ERNEST WAYNE, marketing professional; b. Urbana, Ill., Nov. 3, 1938; s. Lawson Blaine and Sunray Lillian (Cooper) C.; m. Betty-Faye Williams (Oct. 1966); 1 child, Dawn Wynette; m. Carol Louise Skoog; children: Anita Lynn, Sheri Leigh, Ernest Wayne. Student, U. Ill., 1957-58, 1963-66, Armstrong Jr. Coll., Savannah, Ga., 1959-62. Sr. technician Space & Reentry Systems, Philco-Ford, Newport Beach, Calif., 1966-67; jr. elec. engr. Lear Jet Research & Devel., Santa Ana, Calif., 1967-68; tech. tng., field engr. Hughes Aircraft Co., Fullerton, Calif., 1968-73; asst. dist. mgr. Hughes Aircraft Co., Lexington, Mass., 1973-74, 77-78, sr. mgr. corp. mktg., 1982—; regional mgr. Hughes Aircraft Co., Lawton, Okla., 1974-77; dist. mgr. Hughes Aircraft Co., Huntsville, Ala., 1978-82; chmn. curriculum adv. council Inst. Aviation U. Ill., Urbana, 1983—. Served with USAF, 1958-62. Mem. Air Force Assn., Am. Def. Preparedness Assn., Armed Forces Communications Engring. Assn. Republican. Home: 13 Greenbriar Cir Andover MA 01810-3269 Office: Hughes Aircraft Co 420 Bedford St Lexington MA 02173-1502

CUMINGS, EDWIN HARLAN, biology educator; b. Washington, Mar. 2, 1933; s. Glenn Arthur and Winifred (Wenkheimer) C. AB magna cum laude, DePauw U., Greencastle, Ind., 1954; AM in Zoology, Dartmouth Coll., 1956; AM in Biology, Harvard U., 1958, postgrad., 1978—. Teaching asst. in zoology DePauw U., 1953-54; teaching fellow in Zoology Dartmouth Coll., Hanover, N.H., 1954-56; teaching fellow in Biology Harvard U., Cambridge, Mass., 1956-57; tutor in zoology George Washington U., Washington, 1963-64, teaching assoc. in zoology, 1964; lectr. in Biology Boston U., 1965-66, 67, 68-73; instr. in Biology Northeastern U., Boston, 1966-68; asst. in Biology Harvard U., Cambridge, 1976-77. Rector scholar DePauw U., 1950-54; Jeffries Wyman scholar in Anatomy Harvard U., 1956-57; predoctoral research fellow NIH, 1957-61. Mem. AAAS, AAUP, Am. Mus. Natural History, N.Y. Smithsonian Inst., Mus. Fine Arts, Harvard U. Art Mus., N.Y. Acad. Scis., Soc. Study Amphibians and Reptiles, Nat. Geog. Soc., New England Hist. Geneal. Soc., Faculty Club, Harvard, Phi Sigma, Sigma Xi, Phi Eta Sigma, Phi Beta Kappa. Democrat. Presbyterian. Home: 28 Wendell St Apt 4 Cambridge MA 02138-1825

CUMMIN, ALFRED S(AMUEL), chemist; b. London, Sept. 5, 1924; came to U.S., 1940, naturalized, 1948; s. Jack and Lottie (Hainesdorff) C.; m. Sylvia E. Smolok, Mar. 24, 1945; 1 dau., Cynthia Katherine. B.S., Poly. Inst. Bklyn., 1943, Ph.D. in Chemistry, 1946; M.B.A., U. Buffalo, 1959. Rsch. chemist S.A.M. labs., Manhattan Project, Columbia U., 1943-44; plant supr. Metal & Plastic Processing Co., Bklyn., 1946-51; rsch. chemist Gen. Chem. div. Allied Chem. & Dye Corp., N.Y.C., 1951-53; sr. chemist Congoleum Nairn, Kearny, N.J., 1953-54; supr. dielecs-advance devel. Gen. Elec. Co., Hudson Falls, N.Y., 1954-56; mgr. indsl. products rsch. dept. Spencer Kellogg & Sons, Inc. (Textron), Buffalo, 1956-59; mgr. plastics div. Trancoa Chem. Corp., Reading, Mass., 1959-62; assoc. dir. product devel. service labs. chem. div. Merck & Co., Inc., Rahway, N.J., 1962-69; dir. product devel. Borden Chem. div. Borden Inc., N.Y.C., 1969-72; tech. dir. Borden Chem. div. Borden Inc., 1972-73; tech. dir. Borden Inc., 1973-78, v.p. product safety and quality, 1978-81, v.p. sci. and tech., 1981-89, sr. v.p. sci. and tech., 1989—; researcher in polymers, electrochemistry, and food packaging; mem. exec. com. Food Safety Council, 1976-81, trustee, chmn. membership com., 1976-81; bd. dirs. Formaldehyde Inst., 1977-86, vice chmn., 1982-86, mem. exec. com., 1981-86, mem. med. com., 1977-86, steering com., 1977-86; bd. dirs. Internat. Life Scis. Inst., 1986—, Nutrition Found., 1986—, Risk Assessment Inst., 1986—, Rsch. Inst., 1986—; bd. dirs., treas. Health and Environ. Sci. Inst., 1990—; instr. Poly. Inst. Bklyn., 1946-47; asst. prof. Adelphi Coll., 1952-54; prof. math. sci. U.S. Merchant Marine Acad., 1954; seminar leader Am. Mgmt. Assn.; prof. mgmt. N.Y. U. Sch. Mgmt., 1968—. Contbr. articles to profl. jours. Recipient cert. award Fedn. Socs. Paint Tech., 1965. Mem. Am. Chem. Soc. Fedn. Coatings Tech., Inst. Food Tech., ASTM, Synthetic Organic Chems. Mfg. Assn. (dir. 1977-84), Paint Research Inst., Delta Sigma Pi, Gamma Sigma Epsilon, Beta Gamma Sigma, Phi Lamda Upsilon.

CUMMINGS, FRANK, lawyer; b. N.Y.C., Dec. 11, 1929; s. Louis and Florence (Levine) C.; m. Jill Schwartz, July 6, 1958; children: Peter Ian, Margaret Anne. BA, Hobart Coll., 1951; MA, Columbia U., 1955, LLB, 1958. Bar: N.Y. 1959, D.C. 1963. Adminstrv. asst. to U.S. Senator Javits, 1969-71; minority counsel com. labor and pub. welfare U.S. Senate, 1965-67, 71-72; assoc. firm in N.Y.C. and Washington, 1958-63, 67-68; ptnr. Gall, Lane & Powell, Washington, 1972-75, Marshall, Bratter, Greene, Allison & Tucker, Washington, 1976-82, Nossaman, Krueger & Knox, 1982-83, Cummings & Cummings, P.C. and predecessor firm (Cummings & Kershaw, P.C.), 1983-86, LeBoeuf, Lamb, Leiby & MacRae, Washington, 1986—; lectr. law Columbia U. Law Sch., 1970-74; adj. prof. Georgetown U. Law

Sch., 1983-86; chmn. Am. Law Inst.-ABA Ann. Course Employee Benefits Litigation, 1989—; mem. pub. adv. coun. employee welfare and pension benefit plans Dept. Labor, 1972-74; mem. adv. bd. Pension Reporter Bur. Nat. Affairs. Author: Capitol Hill Manual, 1976, 2nd edit., 1984, Multiemployer Plans, 2nd edit., 1986; articles editor Columbia U. Law Rev., 1957-58. Mem. ABA (chmn. com. pension, welfare and related plans 1976-79), Am. Law Inst.; Bar Assn. D.C. (chmn. com. labor rels. law 1972-73), Cosmos Club, Nat. Press Club, Phi Beta Kappa. Articles editor Columbia U. Law Rev., 1957-58. Home: 4305 Bradley Ln Bethesda MD 20815-5232 Office: LeBoeuf Lamb Leiby & MacRae 1875 Connecticut Ave NW Washington DC 20009-5728

CUMMINGS, GARY DAVID, marketing executive; b. Norwich, N.Y., Jan. 15, 1950; s. Raymond W. and Kathrine L. (Satterlee) C.; m. Joy E. Spangenberg, June 12, 1970; children: Charity, Matthew. AAS in Mech. Tech., Mohawk Valley Community Coll., Utica, N.Y., 1970; BS in Indsl. Tech. cum laude, SUNY, Buffalo, 1972; MBA, Syracuse U., 1987. Prodn. supr., jr. indsl. engr. Chesebrough Ponds, Sherburne, N.Y., 1976; design engr. Liquidometer, Norwich, 1976; from sales engr. to applications engr. Simmonds Precision Engine Systems, Norwich, 1977-82, from market mgr. to program mgr., 1982-85, from mgr. engring. to mgr. mfg., 1985-87, dir. quality control, 1987-89, v.p. program and bus. mgmt., 1989-91, v.p. mktg., 1991—. Mem. New Berlin (N.Y.) Sch. Bd., 1990. With U.S. Army, 1972-75.

CUMMINGS, NANCY BOUCOT, nephrologist; b. Phila., Feb. 21, 1927; d. Arthur B. Guest and Katharine (Rosenbaum) Sturgis; m. Milton Curtis Cummings Jr., July 1959 (div. 1985); children: Christopher Ronald, Jonathan Benton, Susan Sturgis. BA, Oberlin Coll., 1947; postgrad., Radcliffe Coll., 1947; MD, U. Pa., 1951. Rotating intern Pa. Hosp., Phila., 1951-52; resident in internal medicine Hosp. of the U. Pa., Phila., 1952-54; rsch. and clin. asst. Royal Hosp. St. Bartholomew, London, 1954-55, Manchester (Eng.) Royal Infirmary, 1955; rsch. fellow in internal medicine, nephrology Harvard Med. Sch., Boston, 1955-58; asst. medicine Peter Bent-Brigham Hosp., Boston, 1955-58; rsch. fellow in biochemistry Harvard Med. Sch., Boston, 1958-59; guest worker Lab. Intermediary Metabolism Nat. Inst. Arthritis and Metabolic Diseases, Bethesda, 1959-62; rsch. med. officer Walter Reed Army Inst., Washington, 1962-66; exptl. medicine researcher USN Med. Rsch. Inst., Bethesda, Md., 1966-72; clin. instr. medicine Georgetown U., Washington, 1960-70, clin. asst. prof. medicine, 1970-81, clin. assoc. prof. medicine, 1981-88, clin. prof. medicine, 1988—; officer Kidney Disease Collaborative Program Nat. Inst. for Arthritis, Metabolism and Digestive Diseases (now Nat. Inst. of Diabetes and Digestive and Kidney Diseases)/NIH, Bethesda, 1972-73, spl. asst. to dir., 1973-74, acting assoc. dir. for kidney, urologic and blood diseases, 1974-76, assoc. dir. for kidney, urologic, and blood diseases, 1976-84, assoc. dir. for research and assessment, 1984—; nephrological cons. NIH, 1972—, USN Hosp., Bethesda, 1966-72. Editor: Prevention of Kidney and Urinary Tract Diseases, 1978, Immune Mechanisms in Renal Disease, 1982, Chronic Renal Failure, 1985. Lay reader Cathedral St. Peter and Paul, Washington, 1976—; vestrywoman St. Albans Ch., Washington, 1975-79, 89-92, chmn. Sunday Forum, 1986-89; chmn. com. on med. ethics Episcopal Diocese of Washington, 1990—; mem. Standing Commn. on Health, Gen. Conv. Episcopal Ch., 1992—; bd. dirs. Collington Episcopal Life Care Community,1991—. Recipient Jacob Ehrenzeller award Pa. Hosp., 1986, Hall of Fame award Cheltenham High Sch. Alumni Assn., 1984. Mem. Am. Soc. Nephrology, Internat. Soc. Nephrology, Am. Fedn. for Clin. Rsch., Nat. Kidney Found. (sci. adv. bd. 1973-79, Disting. Svc. award 1981), Washington Acad. Medicine (bd. dirs. 1989-92, v.p. 1992—), European Dialysis and Transplant Assn., Exec. Women in Govt. (treas. 1978-79), Women in Nephrology (program chmn. 1987—, sec. 1990—), Cosmos Club. Episcopalian. Home: 3900 Connecticut Ave NW Washington DC 20008-2418 Office: NIH Nat Inst Diabetes Digestive & Kidney Diseases Bethesda MD 20892

CUMMINGS, PAUL, author, editor, publisher; b. Detroit Lakes, Minn., Jan. 24, 1933; s. C.C. and Rose (Vollrath) C. Student, U. Minn., 1951-53, Goldsmith Coll., U. London, 1953-54. Ind. corp. cons. N.Y.C., 1961-69; dir. oral history Archives Am. Art, N.Y.C., 1966-77, editor Jour. Archives Am. Art, 1970-77; founder Print Collectors Newsletter, 1970; adj. curator drawings Whitney Mus. Am. Art, N.Y.C., 1976-87; pres. The Drawing Soc., N.Y.C., 1977—; editor Drawing, N.Y.C., 1978—; pub. Catchword Papers, N.Y.C., 1988—; mem. Friends Bd., The Poetry Project, Century Assn. Home and Office: 420 E 72d St New York NY 10021

CUMMINGS, RALPH WALDO, JR., federal agency administrator; b. Ithaca, N.Y., July 20, 1938; s. Ralph Waldo and Mary Catherine (Parrish) C.; m. Emilie Ann Anderson, July 22, 1961; children: Kiran Beckley Harrill, John Kennan. BA with honors in Econs., U. N.C., 1960; PhD, U. Mich., 1965. Instr. U. Mich., Ann Arbor, 1965; asst. prof. U. Ill., Urbana, 1965-67, 69-70; asst. dir. Midwest Consort for Internat. Devel., Urbana, 1966-67; chief AG Econ. div. Agy. for Internat. Devel., New Delhi, India, 1967-69; advisor in agr. econs. Harvard Devel. Adv. Svc., Jakarta, Indonesia, 1970-72; agrl. economist Rockefeller Found., N.Y.C., 1972-82; vis. fellow Woodrow Wilson Sch.-Princeton U., N.J., 1982-83; agrl. economist Agy. for Internat. Devel., Washington, 1982-91, coord. IARC staff, 1991—; lectr. in field; advisor land adv. bd. Epcot Ctr., Walt Disney, Orlando, Fla., 1977—. Co-author: To Feed this World, 1978, Policy Planning for Agricultural Development, 1979; editor: Beyond the Bottom Line, 1982; co-editor: Land Clearing and Development in the Tropics, 1985. Treas. River Place West Coop., Arlington, Va., 1984—; alumni bd. visitors Econs. Dept., U. N.C., 1987—. Fulbright fellow, 1963-64. Mem. Am. Agrl. Econs. Assn., Phi Eta Sigma, Phi Beta Kappa, Phi Kappa Phi. Episcopalian. Home: 1880 Massachusetts Ave McLean VA 22101 Office: Agy for Internat Devel Washington DC 20523

CUMMINGS, ROBERT LAWRENCE, JR., insurance-employee benefits consultant; b. Richmond, Va., Nov. 14, 1959; s. Robert L. and Carol (Wise) C.; m. Sara Pond, June 14, 1980; children: Clayton, Chelsea. BS, U. Mass., 1982. CLU. Ins. broker, cons., prin. Am. Benefits Group, Northampton, Mass., 1985—. Columnist: Western Mass. Bus. Jour., 1988-90. Bd. dirs. Northampton (Mass.) Ctr. for the Arts, 1988—, Hampshire County YMCA, Northampton, 1991. Mem. Western Mass. Estate Planning Coun., Am. Soc. CLU, Million Dollar Round Table, Employers Coun. Flexible Compensation. Office: Am Benefits Group PO Box 1209 88 King St Northampton MA 01060

CUMMINGS, WILLIAM KENNETH, sociology educator; b. Raleigh, N.C., Oct. 18, 1943; s. Ralph Waldo and Mary Catherine (Parrish) C.; m. Fumiko Kimura, Jan. 26, 1969; children: Yujin K., Seijin K. BA, U. Mich., 1965; MA, Harvard U., 1968, PhD, 1972. Assoc. prof. U. Chgo., 1972-77, 81; project officer Ford Found., 1977-81; sr. fellow East-West Ctr., 1982-84; sr. analyst NSF, 1984-86; project coord. Harvard Inst. Internat. Devel., Cambridge, Mass., 1987—. Author: Education and Equality in Japan, 1980, Educational Policies in Crisis, 1987, Profiting from Education, 1990. Rsch. grantee Social Sci. Rsch. Coun., 1973, Japan Found., 1975, Nat. Inst. Edn., 1975, U.S.-Japan Friendship Commn., 1989. Office: Harvard Inst Internat Devel 1 Eliot St Cambridge MA 02138-5781

CUMMINS, GARY STEVEN, security official; b. Bryn Mawr, Pa., Apr. 25, 1950; s. Charles Morris and Kathryn Arlene (Fisher) C.; m. Joan Velma Lewis, Dec. 12, 1970 (div. Sept. 1980); m. Jeryl Dawn Brodsky, Oct. 7, 1989; children: Christian, Shannon. Student in criminal justice, Pa. State U., 1975-76, U. Del., 1976-78; BA in Pub. Adminstrn., West Chester U., 1988. Cert. protection profl. Police officer West Chester (Pa.) Bur. of Police, 1975-80, police cpl., 1980-86, platoom comdr., 1986-89; security supr. Johnson Matthey, Inc., West Deptford, N.J., 1989-90, supt. of security, 1990—. crime prevention specialist Pa. Commn. on Crime and Delinquency, Harrisburg, 1979—; police instr. Pa. Mcpl. Police Officers Tng. Commn., Hershey, 1982-89; instr. substance abuse U.S. Dept. Transp./Bur. Traffic Safety, Washington, 1983-89. Asst. scoutmaster Boy Scouts Am., Willistown-Malvern, Pa., 1980—; bd. dirs. Chester County March of Dimes, West Chester, 1981-83, Big Bros./Big Sisters of Am., West Chester, 1982-83; pres. Chester County Coun. Boy Scouts Am., West Chester, 1967-68. Mem. Fraternal Order of Police, Am. Soc. Indsl. Security. Republican. Methodist. Home: 27 May Apple Dr Downingtown PA 19335 Office: Johnson Matthey Inc 2001 Nolte Dr West Deptford NJ 08066

CUMMINS, GEORGETTE JABER, political consultant; b. Ramallah, Palestine, Dec. 3, 1931; came to U.S., 1955; d. Hanna Salem and Hilweh (Muhawi) Jaber; m. John M. Cummins Jr. (dec.); children: John, Flavia. AB, U. Calif., Berkeley, 1958; postgrad., Harvard U., 1958-60. Teaching fellow Harvard U., Cambridge, Mass., 1958-60; instr. NYU, N.Y.C., 1968-69; writer, cons. middle east and European affairs Chatham, N.J., 1970—. Mem. Harvard Club (N.Y.C.), Princeton Club (N.Y.C.). Republican. Roman Catholic. Home: 23 Glenmere Dr Chatham NJ 07928-1305

CUMMINS, JULIE ANN, children's library services specialist; b. Mansfield, Ohio, Nov. 15, 1939; d. Donald Snively and Mozelle Alene (Fisher) Fulmer; m. A. Blair Cummins, June 9, 1962. BA, Mt. Union Coll., 1961; MLS, Syracuse (N.Y.) U., 1963. Br. children's libr. Rochester (N.Y.) Pub. Libr., 1963-66, bookmobile libr., 1966-69, head cen. ch. rm., 1969-76; children's svcs. cons. Monroe County Libr. System, Rochester, 1976-87; coord. ch. svcs. N.Y. Pub. Libr., N.Y.C., 1987—; voting cons. children's catalog 14th edit., 1982-85. Author: (chpt.) Managers & Missionaries, 1989; editor: Choices vol. 2, 1990, Children's Book Illustration & Design, 1992; contbr. articles to profl. jours. Recipient City Employee award City of Rochester, 1983. Mem. ALA (councilor-at-large nationwide 1985-89, N.Y. chpt. councilor 1990—, planning com. 1991—, chair nominating com. 1991), N.Y. Libr. Assn. (pres. youth svcs. sect. 1978-79, pres. N.Y.C. chpt. 1987-88, Pied Piper award 1987, chair empire state award com. 1990-92), Assn. for Libr. Svc. to Children (bd. dirs. nationwide 1985-88, chair Newbery award com. 1985, chair notables revision com. 1990-92). Home: 264 Lexington Ave # 8B New York NY 10016-4182 Office: NY Pub Libr 455 5th Ave New York NY 10016-0109

CUMMINS, WALTER MERRILL, English language educator; b. Long Branch, N.J., Feb. 1936; s. Jacob and Pearl (Lichstenstein) Caminsky; m. Judith Gruenberg, June 14, 1957 (div.); children: Pamela, Jennifer; m. Alison Elizabeth Cunningham, Feb. 14, 1981. BA, Rutgers U., 1957; MA, U. Iowa, 1962, MFA, 1962, PhD, 1965. Editor Gen. Electric Co., Schnectady, N.Y., 1957-59; instr. U. Iowa, Iowa City, 1962-65; asst. to full prof. Fairleigh Dickinson U., Madison, N.J., 1965—; communication cons., 1969—. Author: (story collections) Were We Live, 1983, Witness, 1975; co-author: Managing Management Climate, 1972; editor-in-chief: Literary Review, Madison, 1985—; contbr. short stories to jours. With U.S. Army. Recipient Fiction Fellowship, N.J. State Coun. on the Arts, Trenton, 1982. Mem. AAUP (chpt. pres. 1974-76), Coll. English Assn., Nat. Coun. Tchrs. of English. Office: Fairleigh Dickinson U 285 Madison Ave Madison NJ 07940-1099

CUNEO, JOHN ANDREW, JR., health facility administrator; b. N.Y.C., May 5, 1929; s. John A. Sr. and Adele (Neive) C.; m. Gloria Britting, June 28, 1952; children: Susan, Richard. BS, Fordham U., 1951; M, Columbia U., 1955. Asst. adminstr. Mid Island Hosp., Beth Page, N.Y., 1955-59; adminstr. Pelham Bay Gen. Hosp., Bronx, N.Y., 1959-74; exec. dir. Parkway Hosp., Forest Hills, N.Y., 1974-87; sr. v.p. LaGuardia Hosp., Forest Hills, 1987-92. Capt. USAF, 1951-53. Fellow APHA, Royal Soc. Health, Am. Coll. Healthcare Execs.; mem. Am. Hosp. Assn., Assn. Pvt. Hosp. Inc. (sec., v.p., pres.), Pub. Health Assn. N.Y.C.

CUNNINGHAM, ANN MARIE, information association executive; b. S.I., June 2, 1947; d. John Aloysius and Katherine Marguerite (Zauner) C. BA, Notre Dame Coll., 1968; MSLS, Villanova U., 1971. Dept. head Villanova (Pa.) Univ. Libr., 1971-79; mgr. edn. and tng. Inst. for Sci. Info., Phila., 1979-84; sect. chief Biosis, Phila., 1984-85, head product planning and promotion dept., 1985-91; exec. dir. Nat. Fedn. Abstracting and Info. Svcs., Phila., 1991—. Editor: Information Industry Human Resources Survey, 1991, National and International Information Policies, 1991. Mem. ALA, Am. Soc. for Info. Scis., Am. Soc. Assn. Execs. Office: NFAIS 13th Fl 1429 Walnut St Philadelphia PA 19102-3202

CUNNINGHAM, EARLENE BROWN, biochemistry educator; b. Cleve., Aug. 27, 1930. BS, U. Ill., 1949; MS, UCLA, 1951; PhD, U. So. Calif., 1954. Research assoc. Ind. U. Sch. Medicine, Indpls., 1954-59; asst. prof. Howard U. Coll. Medicine, Washington, 1959-63, assoc. prof., 1963-64; research assoc. U. Calif.-Berkeley, 1964-67; lectr. chemistry U. S.C., Columbia, 1968-71, assoc. prof. Med. U. S.C., Charleston, 1971-78; assoc. prof. U. Medicine and Dentistry N.J., N.J. Med. Sch., Newark, 1978—. Author: Biochemistry: Mechanisms of Metabolism, 1978; contbr. articles, abstracts to sci. publs.; conducted research, biochemistry and molecular biology of signal transduction mechanisms. Recipient Lederle Med. Faculty award Howard U., 1961, Career Advancement award NSF, 1991; spl. fellow NIH, 1964. Mem. Sigma Xi. Office: U Medicine and Dentistry NJ Med Sch 185 S Orange Ave Newark NJ 07103-2714

CUNNINGHAM, JOEL LUTHER, university president; b. Mooresville, N.C., Jan. 11, 1944; s. Elbert Claxton and Ruth Morton (Journey) C.; m. Trudy Bender, June 12, 1965; children: Nancy Elizabeth, Susan Ruth. BA, U. Tenn., Chattanooga, 1965; MA, U. Oreg., 1967, PhD, 1969. Asst. prof. math. U. Ky., Lexington, 1969-74; dean continuing edn. U. Tenn., Chattanooga, 1974-79; acad. v.p. Susquehanna U., Selinsgrove, Pa., 1979-84, pres., 1984—. Mem. adv. bd. World Trade Inst., N.Y.C., 1984-89; bd. dirs. Sunbury (Pa.) Hosp., 1984—, Coun. Ind. Colls., 1987-92, Pa. Campus Compact, 1987—, Soc. Values in Higher Edn., 1992—. Woodrow Wilson fellow, 1965, Am. Council on Edn. fellow, 1976-77. Mem. Am. Math. Soc., Math. Assn. Am., Am. Assn. for Higher Edn., Cen. Susquehanna Valley C. of C. (bd. dirs. 1985—), Sigma Chi (chmn. bd. leadership tng. 1977-87, treas. 1987-89, v.p. 1989-91, pres. 1991—, Internat. Balfour award 1965), Sigma Xi. Lutheran. Home: 501 University Ave Selinsgrove PA 17870-1163 Office: Susquehanna U Office of Pres Selinsgrove PA 17870-9989

CUNNINGHAM, JOHN JAMES, academic administrator; b. Portland, Maine, June 4, 1941; s. John Jerome and Shirley Eleanor (Sears) C.; m. Jane Blandin, June 27, 1964; children: John James, Amos Blandin, Elizabeth Sears. BA cum laude, U. Notre Dame, 1963; MA with honors, Columbia U., 1965; postgrad., Vanderbilt U., 1980-83; EdD with distinction, Calif. Coast U., 1990. Asst. dir. admissions Tchrs. Coll. Columbia U., N.Y.C., 1963-65; dir. admissions Keene (N.H.) State Coll., 1965-81, dean student svcs., 1977-81, acting dean of students, 1976-77; asst. to v.p. and treas. Franklin Pierce Coll., Rindge, N.H., 1982-83, asst. to pres. and coord. strategic planning, 1983-92, v.p., dean student affairs, 1992—; chmn. Univ. System of N.H. Admissions Coun., 1979-81, N.H. Admissions Consortium, 1976-78; sec. New Eng. Regional Coun. of Coll. Entrance Examination Bd., 1974-75. Chmn. Bd. Edn. for Diocese of N.H., 1976-81; chmn. St. Joseph Regional Sch. Bd., Keene, 1971-76; incorporator Cheshire Med. Ctr., Keene, 1988—. Recipient Disting. Svc. award N.H. Coll. and Univ. Coun., 1981, Coll. Entrance Exam. Bd., 1976, Community Svc. award Keene Family YMCA, 1974; named one of Outstanding Young Men in Am., U.S. Jaycees, 1969. Mem. New Eng. Assn. Coll. Admissions Counselors (bd. dirs. 1978-81), New Eng. Assn. Collegiate Registrars and Admissions Officers (bd. dirs. 1975-78), Nat. Coun. for Cath. Edn. (bd. dirs. 1982—), The Samaritans (bd. dirs. 1985-89), Kappa Delta Pi, Phi Delta Kappa. Roman Catholic. Home: 22 Gilsum St Keene NH 03431-2721 Office: Franklin Pierce Coll College Rd Rindge NH 03461-3114

CUNNINGHAM, KAREN ANN, professional association administrator; b. Bklyn., Nov. 10, 1954; d. Calvin Michael and Alice Marie (Shemanski) C. AA, Suffolk County Community Coll., Selden, N.Y., 1974; BS, Buffalo U., 1976; MS, Columbia U., 1978. Dir. of mem. svcs. N.Y. State Assn. of Counties, Albany, 1978-88; exec. dir. Hospice Assn. of Ulster County, Kingston, N.Y., 1988-89, Hospice of Dutchess County, Poughkeepsie, N.Y., 1989-90; mng. dir. Empire State Conf. Group, Albany, 1990—; cons. Girl Scouts Am., Albany, 1982-84; mem. adv. bd. Sta. WMHT, 1988-90. Bd. dirs. Unity House of Troy, N.Y., 1981-88, pres., 1984-85; mem. allocations com. United Way of Northeast N.Y., 1985—. Named one of Outstanding Young Women in Am., 1983. Mem. NAFE, Nat. Assn. Bus. and Profl. Women. Home: 355 State St Apt # B Albany NY 12210 Office: Empire State Conf Group 132 State St Albany NY 12207

CUNNINGHAM, KEITH ALLEN, II, computer services company executive; b. Belington, W.Va., Aug. 1, 1948; s. Keith A. and Jeanne Antionette (Viquesney) C.; m. Barbra Anne McCoy, 1991. Student Oakland U., 1972; BA, Mich. State U., 1973. Asst. mgr. Joseph Lucas N.Am., Inc., Detroit, 1973; distbn. ctr. mgr. Lucas Industries, Inc., San Francisco, 1974-78; export mgr. Primark, Inc., San Mateo, Calif. and Reno, Nev., 1978-79; operational planning mgr. United Nuclear Corp., Falls Church, Va., 1979-80; pres., chief exec. officer, dir. Unicore, Inc. subs. United Nuclear Corp., North Haven, Conn., 1980-82; dir. bus. devel. UNC Resources, 1982; pres., chief exec. officer, dir. UNC Teton Exploration Drilling Co., a UNC Resources co., 1982-84; prin., dir. Atlis Systems, Inc., Vienna, Va., v.p. fin. and adminstrn., chief fin. officer, 1985-87, pres., chief oper. officer, 1987—; dir. McFarland Graphics and Design, Dilsburg, Pa., 1989. Mem. Mich. State U. Alumni Assn. Home: 6 Coral Gables Ct N Potomac MD 20878 Office: Atlis Systems Inc 6011 Executive Blvd Rockville MD 20852-3804

CUNNINGHAM, MARK FRANCIS, researcher, chemist; b. Olean, N.Y., Mar. 9, 1959; s. George Henry and Catherine Dolores (Gallery) C. BA in Physiol. Psychology, U. Wis., 1986; hon. degree in physiology, SUNY, Buffalo, 1988. Mktg. analyst Technocraft, Ltd., McEllbattan, Pa., 1987; quality control chemist McCreath-Gannett Flemming Labs., Harrisburg, Pa., 1989; chem. analyst Amp., Inc., Harrisburg, 1990; ind. chem.-data analyst, cons., Harrisburg. Campaign aide Ind. Voters Racine, Wis., 1973-77, Anderson for Pres., Madison, Wis., 1980; active Rep. Presdl. Task Force. Roman Catholic.

CUNNINGHAM, MERCE, dancer; b. Centralia, Wash.. Student, Cornish Sch.; hon. doctorate, U. Ill. Own dance co., 1953—; tchr. Sch. Am. Ballet, 1948-51; propr. own dance sch. N.Y.C., 1959—. Soloist Martha Graham Co., 1939-45; 1st solo concert, 1944, many tours including U.S. and Europe, 1949, 58, 60, 66, 69, 70, 72, 76, 77, 79-91, world tour 1964, S.Am., 1968, 76, 82, Mideast, 1972, 76, Australia, 1976, Japan, 1976, 87, Far East, 1984, India, 1990; prin. works choreographed include The Seasons, 1947, Sixteen Dances for Soloist and Company of Three, 1951, Septet, 1953, Minutiae, 1954, Suite for Five, 1956, Nocturnes, 1956, Antic Meet, 1958, Summerspace, 1958, Rune, 1959, Crises, 1960, Aeon, 1961, Story, 1963, Winterbranch, 1964, Variations V, 1965, How to Pass, Kick, Fall and Run, 1965, Place, 1966, Walkaround Time, 1968, RainForest, 1968, Canfield, 1969, Tread, 1970, Second Hand, 1970, Signals, 1970, Landrover, 1972, Changing Steps, 1973, Solo, 1973, Un Jour ou Deux, 1973, Sounddance, 1974, Rebus, 1975, Torse, 1976, Squaregame, 1976, Travelogue, 1977, Inlets, 1977, Fractions, 1977, Exchange, 1978, Locale, 1979, Duets, 1980, Channels/Inserts, 1981, Trails, 1982, Quartet, 1982, Coast Zone, 1983, Roaratorio, 1983, Pictures, 1984, Doubles, 1984, Phrases, 1984, Native Green, 1985, Arcade, 1985, Points in Space, 1986, Fabrications, 1987, Shards, 1987, Five Stone Wind, 1988, Cargo X, 1989, Field and Figures, 1989, Inventions, 1989, August Pace, 1989, Polarity, 1990, Neighbors, 1991, Trackers, 1991, Beach Birds, 1991, Loosestrife, 1991, Change of Address, 1992. Decorated comdr. Order of Arts and Letters (France), 1982, Legion of Honor (France), 1989; recipient Gold medal Internat. Festival Dance, 1966, Grand prix Belgrade Internat. Theatre Festival, 1972, Creative Arts award Brandeis U., 1973, Capezio award, 1977, Samuel H. Scripps/Am. Dance Festival award, 1982, N.Y.C. Mayor's award of honor for arts and culture, 1983, Kennedy Ctr. honors, 1985, Laurence Olivier award, 1985, Meadows award for Excellence in the Arts, So. Meth. U., 1987, Nat. Medal of Arts, 1990, Digital Dance Premier award, 1990; MacArthur Found. fellow, 1985. Mem. Am. Acad. and Inst. Arts and Letters (hon.). Office: 55 Bethune St New York NY 10014-1703

CUNNINGHAM, M(URRAY) HUNT, JR., aerospace company executive, mechanical engineer, author; b. Vicksburg, Miss., Aug. 6, 1942; s. Murray H. and Hannah (Jacobs) C.; m. Linda Barbara Adler, Aug. 15, 1964; children: Keli Barbara, Jennifer Ann. BSME, La. State U., 1965, MSME, 1967; postgrad., Fla. Inst. Tech., 1980-81. Registered profl. engr., La. Engr., sr. engr. Martin Orlando, Orlando (Fla.), Cumberland (Md.), 1966-71; staff engr. Martin Marietta Corp., Orlando, 1971-74; resident engr. Martin Marietta Aerospace div. Martin Marietta Corp., Dayton, Ohio, 1974-75; group engr. Martin Marietta Corp., Orlando, 1975-77; chief resident engr. Martin Marietta Aerospace, Van Nuys, Calif., 1977-79; dep. program mgr. Martin Marietta Aerospace, Orlando, 1980-82; mgr. advanced programs Martin Marietta Aerospace, Balt., 1982-88, dir. weapon systems advanced and internat. programs, 1988-91, dir. advanced programs and environ. remediation/waste mgmt., 1992—; v.p. naval surface warfare programs Martin Marietta, Bethesda, Md., 1988—; chmn. joint internat. agreement surface ship vertical launching system Martin Marietta/FMC, 1987-91. Fundraiser Rep. Coms., Orlando, Balt., 1968—, PTA; asst. coach Cockeysville Recration Coun., 1986—; v.p. polit. affairs Young Reps., 1968-70. Mem. AIAA (sec. 1976-77, judge student papers 1971-80), ASME (judge U.S. Naval Acad. sr. design projects 1987—), Nat. Security Indsl. Assn. (chmn. com. 1980-83, leader launcher com. 1985-87, study leader destroyer variant affordability 1991-92), Am. Soc. Naval Engrs., U.S. Naval Inst., U.S. Navy League, Nat Coun. Corvette Clubs. Methodist. Office: Martin Marietta Aero & Naval Systems 103 Chesapeake Park Plz Baltimore MD 21220-4201

CUNNINGHAM, RANDALL, professional football player; b. Santa Barbara, Calif., Mar. 27, 1963; s. Samuel and Mabel Cunningham. Student, U. Nev., Las Vegas. With Phila. Eagles, 1985—; player NFL Pro Bowl, 1989. Named N.F.L. Player of Yr., 1991. Office: Phila Eagles Veterans Stadium Philadelphia PA 19148*

CUNNINGHAM, THOM W., interior designer; b. Bethlehem, Pa., Sept. 26, 1943; s. John Edward and Eleanor Catherine (Brugger) C.; m. Michelle Lorain, Sept. 16, 1971 (div. May 1988). BA, Moravian Coll., 1969. Set decorator CBS-TV, N.Y.C., 1970-79; pres. Thom W. Cunningham, Inc., N.Y.C., 1979-85; dir. spl. events SESAC, N.Y.C., 1985—; producer Lormas Prodn., N.Y.C., 1979-83; lectr. in field. Fund raiser, lectr. Rape Crisis Intervention Ctr., St. Vincent's Hosp., N.Y.C., 1983. With U.S. Army, 1965-67. Recipient Emmy Nominations Nat. Acad. TV Arts & Sci.; Mayflower descendant. Democrat.

CUNNINGHAM-RUNDLES, CHARLOTTE, physician, immunobiology educator, researcher; b. Ann Arbor, Mich., July 12, 1943; d. R. Wayne Rundles and Mary Alice (Cunningham) Cunningham-Rundles; m. James B. Bussel, Nov. 13, 1982; 1 child, A. Christine. BS, Duke U., 1965; MD, Columbia U., 1969; PhD, NYU, 1974. Diplomate Am. Bd. Internal Medicine. Intern Bellevue Hosp., NYU, N.Y.C., 1969-70, resident, 1970-72; with dept. immunology NYU Med. Ctr., 1972-74; assoc. Sloan Kettering Inst., N.Y.C., 1974-86, dir. biochem. immunology, 1982-86; assoc. attending physician Meml. Hosp., N.Y.C., 1978-86, adj. assoc., 1986—; assoc. prof. medicine and pediatrics Mt. Sinai Med. Ctr., N.Y.C., 1986—, assoc. prof. Immunobiology Inst., 1986—; bd. dirs. Immunodeficiency clinic; speaker various nat. and internat. mtgs. on immunology. Contbr. numerous articles to sci. and med. jours., chpts. to books. Rsch. grantee NIH, Nat. Cancer Inst., Am. Cancer Soc., Nat. Found. March of Dimes, Multiple Sclerosis Soc. Fellow ACP; mem. Nat. Immunodeficiency Found. (bd. med. advisors 1988—), Modell Found. (bd. med. advisors 1989—, Lifetime Achievement award), Am. Fedn. Clin. Rsch., Am. Assn. Immunologist, Mucosal Immune Soc., Clin. Immunology Soc., The Harvey Soc. Episcopalian. Office: Mt Sinai Med Ctr 1 Gustave L Levy Pl New York NY 10029-6504

CUOMO, MARIO MATTHEW, governor of New York; b. Queens County, N.Y., June 15, 1932; s. Andrea and Immaculata Cuomo; m. Matilda Raffa; children: Margaret Cuomo Perpignano, Andrew, Maria Cuomo Cole, Madeline, Christopher. B.A. summa cum laude, St. John's Coll., 1953; LL.B. cum laude, St. John's U., 1956. Bar: N.Y. 1956, U.S. Dist. Ct. (no. dist.) N.Y. 1957, U.S. Supreme Ct. 1960, U.S. Dist. Ct. (ea. dist.) N.Y. 1962, U.S. Ct. Appeals (2d cir. 1967). Confidential legal asst. to Hon. Adrian P. Burke, N.Y. State Ct. Appeals, 1956-58; assoc. Corner, Weisbrod, Froeb and Charles, Bklyn., 1958-63; ptnr. Corner, Cuomo & Charles, 1963-75; sec. of state State of N.Y., 1975-79, lt. gov., 1979-83, gov., 1983—; mem. faculty St. John's U. Sch. Law, 1963-73; counsel to community groups, including Corona Homeowners, 1966-72; charter mem. First Ecumenical Commn. of Christians and Jews for Bklyn. and Queens, N.Y.; former profl. baseball player Pitts. Pirates Orgn. Author: Forest Hills Diary: The Crisis of Low-Income Housing, 1974, Diaries of Mario M. Cuomo, Campaign for Governor, 1983; co-author: Lincoln on Democracy, 1990; contbr. articles to legal publs. Speaker keynote address Dem. Nat. Conv., San Francisco, 1984. Recipient Rapallo award Columbia Lawyers Assn., 1976, Dante medal Italian Govt.-Am. Assn. Tchrs. Italian, 1976, Silver medallion Columbia

Coalition, 1976, Pub. Adminstr. award C.W. Post Coll., 1977; Theodore Roosevelt award Internat. Platform Assn., 1984. Mem. Am., N.Y. State Bar Assn., Bklyn. Bar Assn., Nassau Bar Assn., Queens County Bar Assn., Assn. of Bar of City of N.Y., Am. Judicature Soc., St. John's U. Alumni Fedn. (chmn. bd. 1970-72), Cath. Lawyers Guild of Queens County (pres. 1966-67), Skull and Circle. Office: Office of Gov Albany NY 12224

CUPPLES, JOHN EUSTACE, health facility administrator; b. Berkeley, Calif., Mar. 11, 1944; s. John Theetus and Francis Ida (Toews) C.; m. Adrienne Sherrill, Sept. 3, 1944; children: Amy C., Alison S. AB, U. of the Pacific, 1965; M Theol. Studies, Harvard U., 1968; cert., Yale Sch. Mgmt., 1984. Ordained to ministry United Ch. of Christ. Regional staff Clergy and Laity Concerned, Boston, 1968-74; dir. So. Jamaica Plain Health Ctr., Boston, 1974-77; asst. v.p. Peter Bent Brigham Hosp., Boston, 1977-82; acting dir. community health improvement program Harvard Sch. Pub. Health, Boston, 1978-79; v.p. Brigham & Women's Hosp., Boston, 1982-87; sr. v.p., chief operating officer hebrew Rehab. Ctr. for Ages, Boston, 1987—; lectr. Harvard Sch. Pub. Health, Boston, 1977—. Incorporator Urban Edge, Boston, 1977; pres. Mass. Pub. Health Assn., Boston, 1988. Rockefeller Bros. fellow, 1965. Mem. Mass. Health Edn. and Rsch. Found. (trustee, v.p. 1985—), Assn. Mass. Homes for Aging (trustee 1989—), Rogerson House Found. (trustee 1980—), Blue Key Honor Soc. Home: 14 Olmstead St Boston MA 02130 Office: Hebrew Rehab Ctr for Aged 1200 Centre St Boston MA 02131

CURAZZATO, RONALD SAMUEL, mail handler, poet; b. Rochester, N.Y., Sept. 12, 1955; s. Joe and Grace (Comella) C. Grad. high sch., West Covina, Calif. Barker Checceni & Checceni traveling fairs, L.A., 1976-79; security guard St. Mary's Hosp., Rochester, N.Y., 1979-81; mail handler U.S. Post Office, Rochester, N.Y., 1981—. Author: (poems) Treasured Poems of America, 1989, Many Voices Many Lands, 1989, Days of Future's Past, 1989 (Editors Choice award). With U.S. Army, 1974-76. Recipient Poet of Merit award Am. Poetry Assn., Santa Cruz, Calif., 1989, Editors Choice award Nat. Libr. Poetry, Owings Mills, Md., 1989. Home: PO Box 17184 Rochester NY 14617

CURCHOE, CARL A., printing company executive; b. Williamsport, Pa., Apr. 26, 1944; s. Eugene A. and Adelyne T. (Cioffi) C.; m. Marguerite L. Kase; 1 child, M. Josie. MS, Mich. State U., 1966, MBA, 1973. Regional adminstrv. mgr. Hilti Fastening Systems, Stamford, Conn., 1973-74; asst. to pres. Curchoe's Food Inc., Williamsport, 1974-78; svc. cons. Beiters, Williamsport, 1978-80; pres. Pa. Kwik-Kopy, Inc., Williamsport, 1978—; cons., chmn. internat. negotiating com., nat. dir. Kwik-Kopy Corp., Houston, 1987—. Councilman City of Williamsport, 1976-79, 84-87, 90—; v.p. City Coun., Williamsport; bd. dirs. Lycoming County Nat. Coun. Christians, Williamsport, 1980—, chmn., 1992; bd. dirs. Lycoming County Hist. Soc., Williamsport Water and Sanitation Authority, 1982-84; mem. exec. com. Lycoming Rep. Com.; mem. State Rep. Com. 1st lt. U.S. Army, 1967-69. Scholar Johnson's Wax, 1966, H.J. Heinz, 1965. Mem. West Br. Mfrs. Assn., Williamsport-Lycoming C. of C., Greater Williamsport Bus. Assn., Exch. Club (pres. 1983-84, bd. dirs. 1984-85), Jaycees (bd. dirs. 1975-77), Ross Club.

CURCIO, CYNTHIA DAVIES, banker; b. Allentown, Pa., Aug. 30, 1947; d. William Vaughan and Jean (Benner) Davies; m. Ronald E. Hofmann, Jan. 4, 1963 (div. Oct. 1985); children: Michael T., Dena M.; m. Carl A. Curcio Jr., Jan. 5, 1986. BA, Allentown Coll. of St. Francis de Sales, 1983; MBA, Wilkes Coll., 1988. Sr. profl. in human resources. Purchasing dir. Lehigh County Community Coll., Schnecksville, Pa., 1977-78; dir. human resources Lehigh County Community Coll., Schnecksville, 1978-83; recruiter AT&T Techs., Reading, Pa., 1983-84; employee rels. coord. AT&T Techs., Reading, 1984-86; strategic planner AT&T Techs., Allentown, 1986-87; asst. v.p. quality assurance Lehigh Valley Bank, Bethlehem, Pa., 1987-89; asst. v.p. quality and human resources mgmt. Lehigh Valley Bank, Bethlehem, 1989-90; v.p. human resources Ind. Bancorp, Perkasie, Pa., 1990—; cons. Northampton Area Community Coll., Bethlehem, 1982, Pvt. Industry Council, Allentown, 1983; commencement speaker Allentown Coll., 1987—; chairperson personnel bd. Lehigh County, Allentown, 1983-84. Pres. No. Lehigh PTA, Slatington, Pa., 1978; sec. No. Lehigh Community Adv. Bd., Slatington, 1979; exec. bd. dirs. Valley Youth House, Bethlehem, 1986—. Mem. Soc. Human Resources Mgmt., Am. Soc. Quality Control (v.p. East Cen. Pa. chpt.), Assn. for Quality and Participation, Allentown Coll. Alumni Assn. (bd. dirs.), No. Lehigh Jaycettes (pres. Slatington br. 1978-79). Democrat. Home: 3710 Miller St Bethlehem PA 18017-2923 Office: Independence Bancorp 1 Hillendale Rd Perkasie PA 18944

CURFMAN, DAVID RALPH, neurological surgeon, musician; b. Bucyrus, Ohio, Jan. 2, 1942; s. Ralph Oliver and Agnes Mozelle (Schreck) C.; m. Blanche Lee Anderson, June 6, 1970. Student, Capital U., 1960-62; AB, Columbia Union Coll., 1965; MS, George Washington U., 1967, MD, 1973. Diplomate Nat. Bd. Med. Examiners. Asst. organist, choirmaster Peace Luth. Ch., Galion, Ohio, 1956-62; bus. mgr. Mansfield/Galion Ambulance Svc., Galion, Ohio, 1962-66; with news div. Sta. WTOP-TV, Washington, 1965; choirmaster, assoc. organist Grace Luth. Ch., Washington, 1966-73, historian, curator, 1969—; teaching fellow in anatomy George Washington U., Washington, 1966-67, gen. surgery intern, 1973-74, resident in neurol. surgery, 1974-78; resident in neuropathology Armed Forces Inst. Pathology, Washington, 1975; resident in pediatric neurol. surgery Children's Hosp. Nat. Med. Ctr., Washington, 1976; teaching fellow in anatomy Georgetown U., Washington, 1967-69, clin. instr. neurol. surgery, 1978—, practice medicine specializing in neurol. surgery, 1978—; chief Div. Neurol. Surgery, Jefferson Hosp., Alexandria, Va.; panelist for Am. Assn. Neurol. Surgery ann. meeting "Ethical Issues in Neurol. Surgery." Chmn., chief author: Physician's Reference Guide for Medicolegal Matters, 1982. Elected mem. D.C. Rep. Com. Mem. AMA (Phys. Recognition award 1983—), Assn. Am. Med. Colls. (nat. student chmn. rules and regulations com. 1971-73), Med. Soc. D.C. (chmn. medicine and religion com. 1981-83, chmn. medico-legal com. 1986-88), Pan Am. Med. Soc., Congress Neurol. Surgeons, Am. Coll. Legal Medicine, Washington Acad. Neurosurgery, Galion Hist. Soc. (charter), Children Am. Revolution (pres. Ohio 1963-64, hon. pres.), SR, U.S. Capitol Hist. Soc. (founding supporting mem.), Nat. Cathedral Assn., Cathedral Choral Soc. (v.p. bd. trustees 1981-83, pres. 1984-86), Am. Guild Organists (dean D.C. chpt. 1974-76, publicity chmn. nat. conv. 1982, state chmn. 1984-91), Internat. Congress Organists (Washington program chmn. 1977), Royal Sch. Ch. Music (Eng.), English-Speaking Union, Luth. Laymen's Fellowship, Pilgrim Soc. (Plymouth chpt.), Hymn Soc. Am., Sovereign Mil. Order Temple of Jerusalem, Loyal Legion U.S., Sons of Union Vets. Civil War, Crawford County Coin Club, George Washington U. Club, Elks (Galion Lodge No. 1191, Sigma Xi (pres. chpt. 1981-82), Phi Delta Epsilon. Home: 4201 Massachusetts Ave NW Washington DC 20016-4701 Office: 3301 New Mexico Ave NW Ste 210 Washington DC 20016-3658

CURIEL, IMMA JACINTA, mathematics educator; b. Willemstad, Curacao, Nov. 6, 1960; d. Ina B. C. BS, U. Nymegen, The Netherlands, 1982, MS, 1984, PhD, 1988. Rsch. asst., instr., dept. math. Univ. Nymegen, 1984-88; asst. prof. dept. math. and stats. Univ. Md., Baltimore County, 1988—. Contbr. articles to profl. jours. Mem. Women in Sci. com., U. Md., Baltimore County, 1990—; mentor Leadership 2001/Circle of Women Mentoring Prog., 1990—. AAAS/EPA environ. sci. and engring. fellow, 1992. Office: U Md Dept Math Baltimore County Catonsville MD 21228

CURKO, KATHLEEN ANN, educator, real estate investor; b. Jersey City, Aug. 3, 1950; d. Bernard Joseph and Louise K. (Pinto) Vandermark; m. John Mark Curko, Aug. 9, 1970; 1 child, Jared Mark. BA summa cum laude, Parsons Coll., 1971. Tchr. Bergenfield (N.J.) Bd. Edn., 1970—; pres. Curko Enterprises, Inc., Oakland, N.J., 1985—. Bd. dirs. Our Lady of Perpetual Help Ch., Oakland, 1988—; chmn. fund raising Dogwood Sch. PTA, Oakland, 1987—. Mem. NEA, N.J. Edn. Assn., Kappa Delta Pi. Roman Catholic.

CURL, VINCENT STUART, biology educator, water sports company executive; b. Norfolk, Va., Mar. 9, 1947; s. Vincent Lee and Phyllas (Enenbach) C.; m. Margaret Elaine Sherman, 1970 (div. 1980); m. Tracy E. Burke, Sept. 19, 1987; 1 child, Vincent Lee. BA, Frostburg State U., 1969; JD, U. Baltimore, 1982. Tchr. P.G. County Bd. Edn., Upper Marlboro, Md., 1969-70; tchr., biology P.G. County Bd. Edn., Upper Marlboro, 1973—; spl. agt. U.S. Secret Svc., Washington, 1970-71; pres. Bay County Water Sports, Bowie, Md., 1973—; mgr. Alben-Daniel Chem. Corp., Washington, 1971-75; asst. dir. Wisp Ski Sch., Deep Creek Lake, Md., 1977-80; ptnr. Pinnacle Ski Shop, Deep Creek Lake, 1984-90; instr. P.G. County Community Coll., Largo, Md., 1990—. Pres., capt. P.G. County Underwater Rescue, 1965—; vice chmn. P.G. County Park and Recreation Bd., 1983—; pres. Tall Oaks Home Owners Assn., 1989—; instr. life sav. and first aid P.G. County. ARC, Profl. Dive Instr. Corp., Safe Boating Md. Dept. of Natural Resources. Named Rescue Squad Man of Yr., P.G. County, 1965. Democrat. Roman Catholic. Home: 15101 Partridge Ct Bowie MD 20721-3002

CURLEY, ARTHUR, library director; b. Boston, Jan. 22, 1938; s. Alphonsus Matthew and Lillian (Norton) C.; children: Susan, Ellen. A.B., Harvard U., Cambridge, 1959; M.S., Simmons Coll., Boston, 1962. Dir. Avon Pub. Library, Mass., 1961-64; dir. Palatine Pub. Library, Ill., 1964-68, Montclair Pub. Library, N.J., 1968-75, Cuyahoga County Library, Cleve., 1975-76; dep. dir. Detroit Pub. Library, 1977-80, N.Y. Pub. Library, N.Y.C., 1980-85; dir. Boston Pub. Library, 1985—; lectr. Rutgers Univ., New Brunswick, N.J., 1971-75, Univ. Mich., Ann Arbor, 1978-79; pres. Harvard Libr., N.Y.C., 1982-85; pres. Assn. Rsch. Librs., 1991—. Author: Modern Romance Literatures, 1967; Simple Library Cataloging, 1977, 84; Building Library Collections, 1985. Editor jour. Collection Building, 1978—. Recipient Alumni Achievement award Simmons Coll., 1984. Mem. ALA (council 1970-74, 1981-87, exec. bd. 1983-87), Assn. Rsch. Librs. (pres. 1991—), Mass. Libr. Assn., New Eng. Libr. Assn. Clubs: Harvard (N.Y.C., Boston), St. Botolph, Odd Volumes, Badminton and Tennis, Longwood Cricket. Office: Boston Pub Libr Copley Sq Waltham MA 02154-8112

CURLEY, JOHN FRANCIS, JR., securities company executive; b. Wollaston, Mass., July 24, 1939; s. John Francis and Ann (Omar) C.; m. Loretta Mae O'Keeffe, Oct. 20, 1962; children: William Laurance, Edward Reid, David Neil. Grad., Phillips Acad.; AB, Princeton U., 1960; MBA, Harvard U., 1962. With Paine, Webber, Jackson & Curtis, Inc., N.Y.C., 1964—, gen. ptnr., 1969-72, exec. v.p., 1972-77, pres., 1977-80, chmn. fin. com., 1980-82; vice-chmn. bd. Legg Mason, Inc., Balt., 1982—, Legg Mason Wood Walker, Inc., Balt., 1982—; pres., dir. Legg Mason Value Trust, Inc., 1982—; gov. Investment Co. Inst.; bd. dirs. ICI Mutual Ins. Co., Western Asset Mgmt. Co. Bd. dirs. Balt. Opera Co., Sellinger Sch. Bus. 1st lt. AUS, 1962-64. Mem. Securities Industry Assn. (dir., exec. com. 1978-80), Investment Assn. N.Y. (past pres.), Bond Club N.Y.C., Bond Club Balt., Princeton Club (N.Y.C), Center Club, L'Hirondelle Club, Maryland Club. Office: Legg Mason Wood Walker Inc 111 S Calvert St Baltimore MD 21202-6174

CURLEY, JOHN J., diversified media company executive; b. Dec. 31, 1938; m. Ann Conser; two sons. BA, Dickinson Coll., 1960; MS, Columbia Univ., 1963. Reporter, editor AP, 1961-66; with Gannett Co. Inc., Arlington, Va., 1969—; former pres. Mid-Atlantic newspaper group, sr. v.p. Gannett Co. Inc., Washington, 1982-84, pres., 1984—, chief operating officer, 1984-86, chief exec. officer, 1986—, chmn., 1989—, also bd. dirs. Lt. U.S. Army, 1960-62. Office: Gannett Co Inc 1100 Wilson Blvd Arlington VA 22234-0001

CURLEY, JUDITH MARIE, student affairs professional; b. Nyack, N.Y., Mar. 13, 1949; d. George Joseph and Edith Marie (Bennison) Foden; m. Stephen R. Curley, Sept. 26, 1970; children: Kevin Joseph, Gregory Mark. BA in Spanish, Pa. State U., 1970, MEd in Counselor Edn., 1989, postgrad., 1991—. Small bus. owner Dressmaking Specialties, State College, Pa., 1975-85; sr. teller Unitas Nat. Bank, Pine Grove Mills, Pa., 1985-86; office mgr. Pa. State U., University Park, 1986-88, grad. intern, 1988-89, acad. advisor, 1989-90, student devel. coord., 1990—; project coord. Project WISE, Coll. Engring., Pa. State U., 1989-92. Editor: (tng. manual) Workplace Integration Skills for Engineers, 1989. Den leader, pack leader Boy Scouts Am., State College, 1979-84; clothing coord. Birthright, State College, 1983-85. Mem. Am. Coll. Pers. Assn., Pa. Coll. Pers. Assn. (chair govt. rels. 1990—), Nat. Assn. Student Pers. Adminstrs., Assn. for Multicultural Counseling and Devel., Am. Assn. Counseling and Devel., Phi Sigma Iota. Democrat. Roman Catholic. Office: Pa State U 215 Hetzel Union Bldg University Park PA 16802

CURLOOK, WALTER, mining company executive; b. Coniston, Ont., Can., Mar. 14, 1929; s. William and Stephanie (Acker) C.; m. Jennifer Burak, May 28, 1955; children: Christine, William Paul, John Michael, Andrea. BA in Sci., U. Toronto, 1950, MA in Sci., 1951, Ph.D., 1953; D.Sc. (hon.), Laurentian U., 1983. Postdoctoral fellow Imperial Coll. Sci. and Tech., London, 1954; rsch. metallurgist Inco, Sudbury, Ont., Can., 1954-59; supr. rsch. sta. Inco, Port Colborne, Ont., 1959-60; supr. rsch. Inco, Copper Cliff, Ont., 1960-64, asst. to gen. mgr., 1964-69; v.p. adminstrv. and engring. svcs. Inco, Copper Cliff, 1973-74; v.p. Inco, N.Y.C., 1974-77; sr. v.p. prodn. Inco Metals Co., Toronto, 1977-80, pres., chief exec. officer, 1980-82; exec. v.p. Inco Ltd., Toronto, 1982-91, vice chmn., 1991—; dir. Inco Ltd., 1989; pres. Inco Gold Co., Toronto, 1987-89; dir. Technique of Cofimpac, Paris, 1969-72, v.p. adminstrn., 1972-73; bd. dirs. Great-West Life Assurance Co., Winnipeg, Man., TVX Gold, Inc.; mem. Nat. Adv. Com. on Mining Industry, 1980—; mem. Premier's Coun. for Econ. Renewal, 1991—. Patentee in field. Bd. dirs. Foundation Cambrian Found., Sudbury, 1983; first chmn. bd. Cambrian Coll. Applied Arts and Tech., Sudbury, Ont., 1980. Recipient Mc Charles prize U. Toronto, 1989. Fellow Can. Acad. Engring.; mem. Assn. Profl. Engrs. of Ont., Metall. Soc. of Can. Inst. Mining and Metallurgy (Airey 1979), AIME, Mining Assn. Can. (bd. dir. and past chmn.), Sci. North (hon. life Sudbury chpt. 1988), Ont. Mining Assn. (past pres.). Roman Catholic. Club: Board of Trade (Toronto). Home: 25 Cluny Dr, Toronto, ON Canada M4W 2P9 Office: Inco Ltd, Royal Trust Tower Box 44, Toronto, ON Canada M5K 1N4

CURRAN, J. JOSEPH, JR., lawyer, state official; b. West Palm Beach, Fla., July 7, 1931; s. J. Joseph Sr. and Catherine (Clark) C.; m. Barbara Marie Atkins, 1959; children: Mary Carole, Alice Ann, Catherine Marie, J. Joseph III, William A. (dec.). LLB, U. Balt., 1959. Bar: Md., U.S. Dist. Ct. Md., U.S. Supreme Ct. State senator from Md., 1963-83; lt. gov. State of Md., 1983-86; atty. gen. State of Md., Balt., 1987—; mem. Md. Regional Planning Council, 1963-82. Mem. Md. Bar Assn., Balt. Bar Assn. Office: Office of Atty Gen 200 St Paul Pl Baltimore MD 21202-2004*

CURRAN, JOHN J., lawyer; b. N.Y.C., Jan. 27, 1931; m. Patricia Curran; children: John, Elizabeth, Joseph, Patricia. BS, Fordham U., 1953, JD, 1961. Gen. counsel, sec., chmn. exec. com., dir. Prudential Securities, N.Y.C., 1955-87; arbitrator N.Y. Stock Exch., 1970—, Nat. Assn. of Securities Dealers, N.Y.C., 1968—. Trustee Wilton (Conn.) Libr. Home: 1B Middlebrook Farm Rd Wilton CT 06897-2015

CURRAN, JOHN JUDE, journalist; b. N.Y.C., Nov. 21, 1953; s. John Francis and Catherine (Farrell) C.; m. Joan Marino. BA, Bard Coll., 1975. Staff writer The Wall St. Transcript, N.Y.C., 1977-78; reporter Fortune Mag., N.Y.C., 1978-83, assoc. editor, 1983-88, bd. of editors, 1988—. Recipient Best Fin. Reporting from Abroad award Overseas Press Club, 1988. Office: Fortune Mag 1271 Ave of the Americas New York NY 10020-1300

CURRAN, JUDITH ELLEN, mathematics educator; b. Fitchburg, Mass., Sept. 7, 1953; d. Harry Jaques and Ruth (Bennett) Tucker; m. James R. Curran, July 1, 1978 (dec. Dec. 1984); children: James T., Jack B. BS, Bridgewater State Coll., 1977; MA in Math., SUNY, Stony Brook, 1978. Cert. tchr., Mass., N.H. Tchr. Calvary Christian Sch., Derry, N.H., 1979-88; grad. assoc. U. N.H., Durham, 1988—. Mem. Nat. Coun. Tchrs. Math. Am. Ednl. Rsch. Assn.

CURRERI-ALIBRANDI, GAETANO, artist; b. Rome, Dec. 22, 1927; came to U.S., 1965; s. Giuseppe and Anita (Alibrandi) Curreri; m. Erminia Spina, May 7, 1952 (div. Sept. 1971); children: Daniela, Vincenzo, Loredana; m. Patricia Ann Binette, Jan. 28, 1972; 1 child, Tania Loren. Student, Acad. Fine Arts, Rome, 1950-54; M Art Edn., Mass. Coll. Art, 1974. Asst. to gen. dir. fine arts and antiquities Govt. of Italy, Rome, 1950-62; asst. prof. architecture U. Rome, 1962-65; dean New Eng. Sch. Art, Boston, 1967-70; dir. art program Univ. Ctr., Boston, 1974-84; instr. painting Sch. Danforth Mus., Framingham, Mass., 1975-85. Solo exhbns. from 1956-64 include Rome, Paris, France, Lyon, France, Salzburg, Austria, Bologna, Italy, Venice, Italy, N.Y.C., 1966-71, Corcoran, Miami, Fla., 1972, Buffalo, N.Y., 1962, U. Lowell, Mass., 1977, Boston Archtl. Ctr., 1982, Rome and Venice, 1986; represented in permanent collection, Rome Mus. Modern Art; group art shows include Union Carbide Bldg, N.Y.C., 1974, Florence, Italy, 1986, Quadr. Naz.d'Arte, Rome, 1987; author: Beyond the Vanishing Point, 1989, also books and articles in Italian. Decorated Knight of Merit Republic of Italy. Republican. Home and Studio: 15 Windsor Rd Milford MA 01757

CURREY, PATRICIA LOU, trust officer; b. Youngstown, Ohio, May 20, 1954; d. Robert George and Betty Lou (Stiver) Alm; m. John Douglas Potter, June 21, 1975 (div. Feb. 1987); m. J. Raymond Currey III, Aug. 17, 1991. BSBA, Miami U., 1976; MS in Gen. Adminstrn., U. Md., 1989. Profit sharing analyst Booke & Co., Winston-Salem, N.C., 1977-78; indsl. engring. tech. Cons. and Designers, Inc., N.Y.C., 1978-79; allocations unit supr. Wachovia Bank & Trust Co., Winston-Salem, 1979-80, asst. v.p. employee benefit plans dept., 1980-82, 84-85; v.p., group head, employee benefit trust group Security Trust Co., Balt., 1985-90, v.p., new bus. devel. mgr., trust unit, 1991—. Mem. Hunt Meadow Homeowners Assn., Annapolis, Md., 1990-91. Mem. Internat. Found. Employee Benefit Plans (moderator round table meeting 1991), Meml. Hosp. Easton (planned gifts com.). Republican. Home: 789 Sonne Dr Annapolis MD 21401-7120 Office: Security Trust Co 36 N Washington St Easton MD 21601-3126

CURRIE, KENNETH MAX, military officer; b. Shenandoah, Iowa, Aug. 23, 1947; s. Max Robert and Dorothy Darlene (Aldrich) C.; m. Dawn M. Campbell, Oct. 5, 1991; 1 child, Sean Kristen. BS, Iowa State U., 1969; MA, Ind. U., 1976; PhD, George Washington U., 1987. Commd. 2d lt. USAF, 1970, advanced through grades to lt. col., 1986; chief strategic studies div. Air Force Intelligence Agy., Washington, 1987-89, dir. rsch. and Soviet studies, 1989-90; asst. nat. intelligence officer Nat. Intelligence Coun., Washington, 1990—. Author: Soviet Military Politics: Contemporary Issues, 1991; author chpt.: Gorbachev and the Soviet Military, 1989; editor: Soviet Union: What Lies Ahead?, 1985. Mem. AAASS, Air Force Assn. (life). Republican. Episcopalian. Home: 9603 Lake Braddock Dr Burke VA 22015 Office: Nat Intelligence Coun Washington DC 20505

CURRIE, RICHARD ALAN, English educator; b. Bklyn., Dec. 15, 1941. BA, Kans. U., 1963; MA, NYU, 1965, MPhil, 1980, PhD, 1988. Instr. S.I. Community Coll., 1968-72, asst. prof., 1972-76; asst. prof. Coll. of S.I., 1976-89, assoc. prof. English, 1990—. Co-editor Victorian Studies Bull., 1988—; contbr. articles to profl. jours. NEH fellow, 1982, 88, 91, Mellon fellow, 1989. Home: 500 Howard Ave Staten Island NY 10301-4411 Office: Coll of SI 715 Ocean Ter Staten Island NY 10301-4547

CURRIE, ROBERT, procurement professional; b. Plainfield, N.J., July 30, 1959; s. Ashton Markoe and Evelyn Margaret (Gautreau) C.; m. Suzanne Jean Morris, Oct. 18, 1987; 1 child, Claire MacPherson Currie; 1 stepchild, Hilary Buchanan Boller. BS in Mktg. cum laude, Fairleigh Dickinson U., 1991. Journalist Foster Pubs., Scotch Plains, N.J., 1979-81; internat. specialist Hoechst Celanese Corp., Bridgewater, N.J., 1981-89; procurement specialist Hoechst Celanese Corp., Summit, N.J., 1989—; v.p. HCC Sci. and Tech. Co., Inc., Bridgewater, 1989—. Producer/dir. film: Trade Secrets and Technology, 1991 (Disting. Achievement award Am. Soc. Indsl. Security); editor (book): With Sword and Harp, 1992. Comdr. The Clan Currie, Glasgow, 1991—; pres. Clan Currie Soc. N.Am., Summit, N.J., 1990—; dir. Bonnie Brae Scottish Games, Millington, N.J., 1985-88, U.S. Equestrian Team - Horse Trials, Gladstone, N.J., 1990-91. Recipient James S. Cogswell Outstanding Indsl. Security Achievement award Dept. Def., 1992. Mem. Nat. Classification Mgmt. Soc., Am. Soc. for Indsl. Security (Disting. Achievement award 1991), St. Andrew's Soc. of N.Y. Home: PO Box 541 Summit NJ 07902-0541 Office: Hoechst Celanese Corp 86 Morris Ave Summit NJ 07901

CURRIE, ROBERT RAYMOND, mechanical engineer; b. Baldwinsville, N.Y., Oct. 14, 1921; s. Robert and Maude Lillian (Weigand) C.; m. Evelyn Margaret Meyers, May 29, 1946; children: Robert Raymond III, Margaret Kimberly. BSME, U. Rochester, 1948. Registered profl. engr. Mich. Sales prop engr. GE, Schenectady, N.Y., 1948-52; sales engr. indsl. sales GE, Detroit, 1952-59; sales engr. of sml. AC motors GE, Schenectady, 1959-66, sales trainer, 1966-70; mgr. ednl. program adminstrn. Mgmt. Devel. Inst. GE, Croton-on-Hudson, N.Y., 1970-83; pres. Productive Bus. Meetings Inc., Burnt Hills, N.Y., 1983—. Bd. dirs. SCCC Found. Inc., Schenectady, 1987—; mem. com. Union Coll. Adult L.L., Schenectady, 1988—. Capt. USAAF, 1943-61. Mem. Schenectady Sr. Elfun (chmn. 1990-91), AARP (55 Alive instr. 1988—), Masons, Shriner, Kiwanis (pres. 1968), Toastmasters (pres. 1959). Republican. Methodist. Home: 37 Forest Rd Burnt Hills NY 12027-9743 Office: Productive Bus Meetings Inc 37 Forest Rd Burnt Hills NY 12027-9743

CURRIE, STEVEN RAY, artist; b. Flint, Mich., Sept. 1, 1954; s. Richard Lee and Gwen Laurie (Cummings) C.; m. Annette Marie Davidek, July 27, 1985. BFA, U. Mich., 1977; MFA, Yale U., 1984. One man show includes Borgenight Gallery, N.Y.C., 1988, 90, 92, Ctr. Contemporary Art, Chgo., 1989, 91; represented in various mus. collections. NEA fellow, 1988, N.Y. Found. Arts fellow, 1990.

CURRY, JOHN ANTHONY, JR., university administrator; b. Lynn, Mass., May 12, 1934; s. John Anthony and Margaret (Connors) C.; m. Marcia E. Mudge, Aug. 18, 1956; children: Robert, Susan Brown, Timothy. BA, Northeastern U., 1956, MEd, 1963; EdD, Boston U., 1980. Tchr., prin. elem. and secondary schs. Bourne, Saugus, Newton, Mass., 1957-63; dir. edn. placement, then dir. admissions Northeastern U., Boston, 1963-70, dean of admissions, 1972-74, dean of adminstrn., 1974-75, v.p. adminstrn., 1975-79, sr. v.p. adminstrn., 1979-84, exec. v.p., 1984-89, pres., 1989—. Contbr. articles to profl. jours. Chmn. Saugus Sch. Com., 1967; pres. Saugus Am. Little League, 1970; trustee Forsyth Rsch. Ctr., Boston, 1986—, Boston Mus. Sci., 1989—, Plan for Excellence for Boston, 1990—; chair edn. div. United Way Mass., 1990. Recipient Positive Force award Nat. Black Students Assn., 1985, appreciation Mass. Spl. Olympics, 1985, Quality Edn. award Freedom House, 1985, Auerbach Community Svc. award Boston Celtics, 1986, Educator of Yr. award Commonwealth of Mass., 1986. Mem. Nat. Assn. Career Edn. (pres. 1982), Nat. Assn. Ind. Colls. and Univs., Assn. Ind. Colls. and Univs. Mass., Mass. Tchr. Assn. (founding), Phi Kappa Phi, Phi Delta Kappa. Democrat. Roman Catholic. Home: 1 Spearfield Ln Lynnfield MA 01940-2554 Office: Northeastern U 110 Churchill 360 Huntington Ave Boston MA 02115-5096*

CURRY, JOHN MICHAEL, investment banker; b. Buffalo, Dec. 30, 1942; s. John Vincent and June (Eisele) C.; m. Thea Adrian Kirk, July 12, 1969 (div. 1982); children: John Adrian, James Prescott; m. Margaretta Buckley, Mar. 17, 1990. BA, U. San Francisco, 1968; MBA, Harvard U., 1970; postgrad., Suffolk U., 1971. Cert. property mgr.; registered rep. and gen. securities rep.; registered fiduciary and investment adviser, registered securities prin. Developer Devel. Corp. Am., Boston, 1970-73; founder John M. Curry & Co., Inc., Boston, 1973—; founder, chmn. APT Fin. Svcs., Inc., Boston, 1977—, APT Asset Mgmt., Boston, 1992—, Curry Capitao Corp. (name changed to Apt. Asset Mgmt.), Boston, 1987—; chmn. Curry Asset Mgmt., 1985-92; bd. dirs. 11 corps.; Bd. dirs. Taylor Woodrow PLC, London, 1983-85. Vol. various fed., state, local polit. orgns. and campaigns. Sgt. U.S. Army, 1961-64. Recipient Modernization award Building Mag., 1980-81, Outstanding Restoration award Lowell C. of C., 1981, Nat. Jewish Life award, 1987. Mem. Harvard Club (Boston), Harvard Faculty Club (Cambridge), various securities firms orgns. Home: 75 Algonquin Rd Chestnut Hill MA 02167-1001 Office: Apt Asset Mgmt 150 Federal St 26th Fl Boston MA 02110

CURRY, RICHARD ORR, history educator and freelance writer; b. White Sulphur Spring, W.Va., Jan. 26, 1931; s. Ernest Chalmers and Ida Mitt (Atkinson) C.; m. Patricia Leist, Apr. 6, 1954 (dec. 1967); children: Kimberly, Andrea, Jonathan; m. Patricia Montenegro, Feb. 11, 1968; 1 stepson, Michael Del Rosario. B.A., Marshall U., 1952, M.A., 1956; Ph.D., U. Pa., 1961; postdoctoral fellow, Harvard Div. Sch., 1965-66. Instr. European history Morris Harvey Coll., Charleston, W.Va., 1959-60; instr. Am. history Pa. State U., 1960-62; vis. asst. prof. Am. history U. Pitts.,

1962-63; asst. prof. Am. history U. Conn., Storrs, 1963-66, assoc. prof., 1966-71, prof., 1971—, Fulbright lectr., 1981—; lectr., participant numerous seminars and symposia U.S., Philippines, Australia, New Zealand; assoc. dir. NDEA Inst. for High Sch. Tchrs. Am. History, (U. Conn.), summers 1965, 66; cons., critic Holt, Rinehard and Winston, Little, Brown & Co., Dodd, Mead & Cook, Allyn & Bacon, Dryden Press, Prentice-Hall, Iowa State U. Press, U. Mo. Press, La. State U. Press, Can. Research Council, NEH, others. Author: A House Divided: A Study of Statehood Politics and the Copperhead Movement in West Virginia, 1964, (with others) The Shaping of America, 1972, The Shaping of American Civilization, 2 vols., 1972; editor: The Abolitionists, 1965, 1973, 1985, (with others) Slavery in America: Theodore Weld's American Slavery As It Is, 1972, 3d edit., 1985; contbg. editor: Radicalism, Racism and Party Alignment: The Border States During Reconstruction, 1969 (award 1971), Conspiracy: The Fear of Subversion in American History, 1972, Freedom at Risk: Secrecy, Censorship and Repression in the 1980's, 1988 (award 1989), American Chameleon: Individualism in Trans-National Context, 1991, An Uncertain Future: Thought Control and Repression During the Reagan-Bush Era, 1992; contbr. articles to profl. jours. With USN, 1952-54. Recipient Disting. Alumnus award Marshall U., 1986, 8th ann. H.L. Mencken award Free Press Assn., 1989, Outstanding Book award Gustavus Myers Ctr., 1989; fellow Am. Assn. State and Local History, 1964, Soc. for Values in Higher Edn., 1965-66, Ludwig von Mises fellow, 1982-83, Social Sci. Rsch. Coun., 1966, NSF, 1966, NEH, 1967, Am. Philos. Soc., 1967, 70; Fulbright lectr., 1981. Fellow Soc. Values Higher Edn., Conn. Acad. Arts and Scis.; mem. Orgn. Am. Historians, Am. Hist. Assn., So. Hist. Assn., New Eng. Hist. Assn., Fulbright Alumni Assn., Soc. Historians of Early Republic (bd. editors jour. 1991—).

CURTIN, DOREEN T., graphic design company executive, artist; b. Flushing, N.Y., Feb. 24; d. Francis P. and Nancy T. (Taschetta) C.; m. Paul G. Kalka. BA, SUNY, Binghamton; postgrad., USDA Grad. Sch., Washington. Artist, preparator Ross Park Zool. Gardens, Binghamton; artist Nat. Zool. Park, Washington; freelance illustrator, designer Clinton, N.J.; pres. Tundra Conservation Communication Studio, Clinton; cons. Hiram Blauvelt Art Mus., Oradell, N.J., 1989-90, dir. devel., 1990—; cons. pro bono Endangered and Nongame Species Program N.J., Trenton, 1984-91; cons. Nat. Audubon Soc., Harlequin Nature Graphics, 1988-91, Cape May County Park Zoo, 1989-91, Kamper Park Zoo, 1990-91, Western Hemisphere Shorebird Res. Network, N.J. Endangered and Nongame Species Program, 1984—, Henson Robinson Zoo, Springfield, Ill., 1992, Aquarium at Jenkinson's, Point Pleasant, N.J., 1992, others. Illustrator: (book) Finding Birds in the National Capitol Area, 1983; illustrator NAS edml. series on wildlife and conservation; contbg. author: 59 More Studio Secrets for the Graphic Artist, 1989; producer, dir. TV pub. svc. announcement on endangered species. Mem. NAFE, Am. Assn. Mus., Nat. Assn. Mus. Exhibitionists, Graphic Artists Guild, Am. Assn. Zool. Parks and Aquariums (conf. procs. 1986, 90). Office: Tundra Conservation Communication Studio PO Box 5453 Clinton NJ 08809-0453

CURTIN, FRANCIS MICHAEL, government official, scientist; b. Phila., Sept. 16, 1951; s. John Joseph and Helen (Toole) C.; m. Mary Elizabeth Niles, Mar. 26, 1977. BA in History, BA in Logic-Philosophy, Pa. State U., 1974, MPA, 1976. Rsch. asst. Pa. Transp. Inst., University Park, 1974-76; systems engr. System Devel. Corp., Santa Monica, Calif., 1976-78; systems analyst II, Auerbach Assocs., Rosslyn, Va., 1978-80; chief litigation support and econ. analysis FTC, Washington, 1980—, agy. rep. Office Tech. Assessment, 1981—; guest lectr. Washington semester program Am. U., Washington, 1985—; cons. on fed. and state info. systems devel. Author: Information Processing for Attorneys and Economists, 1989. Recipient commendation FTC, 1985, Outstanding Productivity award, 1989. Mem. Am. Soc. for Pub. Adminstrn., Am. Soc. for Info. Scis. Roman Catholic. Home: 6223 Cheryl Dr Falls Church VA 22044-1806 Office: FTC 6th St and Pennsylvania Ave NW Washington DC 20580

CURTIS, ALTON KENNETH, film company executive, clergyman; b. Pawtucket, R.I., June 14, 1939; s. Alton T. and Althea A. C.; m. Dorothy Stevenson, Aug. 27, 1961; children: William Kenneth, Karen Althea. BA, Gordon Coll., 1961; MDiv, Gordon Conwell Theol. Sch., 1964, DD, 1987; PhD, Walden U., 1976; postgrad. Boston U., 1966-69, Pa. State U., 1971. Ordained to ministry Am. Bapt. Chs., 1964. Dir. communications City Mission Soc., Boston, 1967-68; media cons. Am. Bapt. Chs., 1968-70; gen. mgr. Creative Venture Assocs., Valley Forge, Pa., 1970-72; pres. Gateway Films, Inc., Valley Forge, 1972—; chmn. Curtis Mark Communications, Lansdale, Pa., 1980-85, Vision Video, Inc., Worcester, Pa., 1981—; adj. faculty Ea. Coll., St. Davids, Pa., 1974—; adj. faculty, prof. ch. history Ea. Bapt. Theol. Sem., Pa., 1986-87, chmn., pres. Friends of the Libr., 1991—; vis. prof. Inst. Youth Ministries, Colorado Springs, Colo., 1991; bd. dirs. Christianity Today Inc., 1992—; cons. Strategic Careers Project, 1990—. Mem. adv. bd. Episcopal Radio-TV Found., 1991—. Author: Festival, 1974, Dates With Destiny, 1991, From Christ to Constantine, 1991, Dates with Destiny, 1992; founder, pub., editor Christian History mag., 1982-89, sr. editor, 1990—; editor, pub. (periodicals) Glimpses, Pastor's Notes, 1990—; writer, producer (film) First Fruits, 1982; producer, dir., author The Good Seed, 1985; assoc. producer Shadowlands, 1986 (Internat. Emmy); writer, producer Comenius, 1987, (TV documentary series) The Trial and Testimony of the Early Church, 1989 (Gold meal Houston Internat. Film Festival, Chris award Columbus Film Festival, Angel award Religion in Media, Best Series award Christian Visual Media Internat.); prodn. assoc., cons. (TV documentary series) Mine Eyes Have Seen the Glory, 1992; contbr. articles on mass media and religion to mags. Sr. pastor Lower Providence Bapt. Ch., Collegeville, Pa., 1977-80; pres. Christian History Inst., 1983—; instr. YMCA Handicapped Persons Swimming Program, Lansdale, Pa., 1986—. Recipient Best Screenplay of Yr. award and Best Film of Yr. award Acad. Christian Cinemagraphic Arts, 1983, A. Jack Good Community Svc. award Gordon Coll., 1986. Mem. Soc. Cinema Arts and Sci., Phi Alpha Chi. Office: Gateway Films Inc PO Box 540 Worcester PA 19490-0540

CURTIS, EDWARD JOSEPH, JR., gas industry executive, management consultant; b. Boston, May 26, 1942; s. Edward Joseph and Violet Ella (Upton) C.; m. Virginia Carolyn Fye, May 6, 1976; children: Jane Mercedes, Sherri Jean, Virginia Amy. BSChemE, Worcester Polytech., 1964, MSChemE, 1966. Engr. Cabot Corp., Boston, 1966-68; mgr. corp. devel. Distrigas Corp., Boston, 1968-72; pres. E.J. Curtis Assocs., Inc., York Harbor, Maine, 1972—; pres. Pine Hill Assocs., Inc., Hollis, N.H., 1976-80; ptnr. ABC Mgmt. Systems, Bellingham, Wash., 1977-82; chmn. gas New England Energy Congress, Boston, 1978-80; mem. N.H. Energy Policy Adv. Com., Concord, 1978-80; mng. ptnr. Essex Cons. Svcs., Boston, 1981-82. Pres. York Harbor Neighborhood Assn., 1989—. Mem. Am. Inst. Chem. Engrs., Am. Gas Assn., New Eng. Gas Assn. (dir. 1988-91), Soc. Gas Lighting, Soc. Energy Engrs., York Golf and Tennis Club, Twenty Assocs. Club (pres. 1985-86), Theta Chi. Republican. Mem. Congl. Ch. Office: E J Curtis Assocs Inc Box 1000 York Harbor ME 03911

CURTIS, FRANCIS HENRY, education educator; b. Angels, Pa., Mar. 21, 1934; s. Francis Henry and Letha Gertrude (Crossman) C.; m. Ann Louise Franc, July 4, 1959; children: Kyra Jo, Francis Henry. BS, Pa. State U., 1956, MEd, 1963, postgrad., 1964-71. Cert. agr., biol. sci., gen. sci. and social studies tchr., elem. and secondary prin., asst. to supt. for instrn., asst. to supt. for bus. affairs. Agr. tchr. Blue Ridge High Schs., New Milford, Pa., 1956; army edn. specialist Army Edn. Ctr., Korea, 1957-58; tchr. spl. edn. Wayne County Schs., Honesdale, Pa., 1959-62, Cambria County Schs., Ebensburg, Pa., 1962-64; grad. asst. Pa. State U., Cornwells Heights, 1964-66; adminstrv. intern Bensalem Sch. Dist., Cornwells Heights, 1965-66; prof., dir. secondary edn. U. Scranton, Pa., 1966-91, chmn. dept. edn., 1991—. Pres. Sterling (Pa.) Cemetery Corp., 1985—; chair Sterling Twp. Planning Commn., Wyo. Conf. Coun. on Ministries, Binghamton, N.Y. With U.S. Army, 1956-58, Korea. Senator Crow scholar State of Pa., 1952. Mem. Nat. Sci. Tchrs. Assn., Pa. Sci. Tchrs. Assn., Pa. Assn Colls. Tchr. Educators, Assn. Tchr. Educators, Phi Delta Kappa (sec. 1966-68), Alpha Tau Alpha. Methodist. Office: U Scranton Dept of Edn Linden at Jefferson Scranton PA 18510

CURTIS, GREGORY DYER, investment company executive, foundation administrator, author, poet, playwright; b. Mechanicsburg, Ohio, Jan. 14, 1947; s. Vernon L. and Jean (Dyer) C.; m. Lynne Everett, June 29, 1968 (div. 1989); m. Simin Yazdgerdi, June 7, 1991; children: Sarah E., Alice D., Peter A.D.. AB cum laude, Dartmouth Coll., 1969; JD cum laude, Harvard U., 1974. Bar: Pa. 1974, U.S. Dist. Ct. (we. dist.) Pa. 1974. Assoc. Reed, Smith, Shaw & McClay, Pitts., 1974-79; counsel Roldiva, Inc., Pitts., 1979-81, v.p., bd. dirs., 1981-83; fin. adv. C.S. May Family Interests, Pitts., 1983—; pres. Laurel Found., Pitts., 1983—; pres., bd. govs. Laurel Assets Group, Pitts., 1983—; pres. C.S. May Assocs., Pitts., 1983—; bd. dirs. Enrecon, Inc., Golden, Colo., L.C. Holdings, Inc., Boulder, Key West Holdings, Ltd., Pitts., Phoenix Technologies, Inc., Denver, Tenir, Inc., Pitts., Winding River Properties, Inc., St. George, Utah, Investment Fund for Founds., 1991—. Recipient Acad. Am. Poets prize, 1986. Mem. legal com. ACLU, Pitts., 1974-78; bd. dirs. Neighborhood Legal Svcs. Assn., Pitts., 1976-79, The Ellis Sch., 1987—, Investment Fund for Founds., 1991—; bd. dirs. Grantmakers Western Pa., Pitts., 1986—, pres. 1989-91; bd. dirs. Investment Fund for Founds., 1991—, St. John's Coll., 1992—. Sgt. U.S. Army, 1970-72. Mem. ABA, Allegheny County Bar Assn., Duquesne Club (Pitts.), Rolling Rock Club (Ligonier). Author: (plays) Jungle Music, 1969 (Frost prize), LBO, 1991, Marginally Retared Delinquents: A Protocol for Independence, 1970.; The Essential Liberal, 1990; co-author: (with T. Szabo) Marginally Retarded Delinquents: A Protocol for Independence, 1970, The model Cities Experience, 1972, Federal Revenue Sharing: A Comparative Analysis, 1975, The Essential Liberal, 1990, Popular Culture and Moral Seriousness, 1991, (plays) Jungle Music, 1969 (Frost award); contbr. articles to profl. jours. Home: 8 Dunmoyle Pl Pittsburgh PA 15217-1029 Office: Laurel Found 3 Gateway Ctr Pittsburgh PA 15222

CURTIS, JAMES L., psychiatrist; b. Jeffersonville, Ga., Apr. 27, 1922; s. Will and Francis (Hall) C.; m. Vivian Alzine Rawls, Dec. 11, 1948; children: Lawrence, Paul. BA, Albion Coll., 1943; MD, U. Mich., 1946; cert. psychoanalysis, Columbia U., 1954. Diplomate in psychiatry Am. Psychiatry and Neurology. Intern Wayne County Gen. Hosp., Eloise, Mich., 1947, resident in psychiatry, 1948; resident in psychiatry SUNY, Bklyn., 1949-50; from instr. to clin. asst. prof. SUNY Dowstate Med. Ctr., Bklyn., 1954-68; assoc. dean, assoc. prof. psychiatry. Cornell U. Med. Ctr., N.Y.C., 1968-80; clin. prof. psychiatry N.Y. Med. Coll., N.Y.C., 1980-82, Columbia U. Coll. Physicians & Surgeons, N.Y.C., 1982—; dir. dept. psychiatry Harlem Hosp. Ctr., N.Y.C., 1982—. Author: Blacks, Medical Schools and Society, 1971; contbr. articles to profl. jours. Capt. USAF, 1952-54. Fellow Am. Psychiat. Assn., Am. Orthopsychiat. Assn., Am. Psychoanalytic Assn., Am. Acad. Psychoanalysts. Democrat. Congregationalist.

CURTIS, JAMES THEODORE, lawyer; b. Lowell, Mass., July 8, 1923; s. Theodore D. and Maria (Souliotis) Koutras; m. Kleanthe D. Dusopol, June 25, 1950; children: Madelon Mary, Theodore James, Stephanie Diane, Gregory Theodosius, James Theodore. BA, U. Mich., 1948; JD, Harvard U., 1951; Sc.D., U. Mass., 1972. Bar: Mass. 1951. Assoc. Adams & Blinn, Boston, 1951-52; legal asst., asst. atty. gen. Mass., 1952-53; pvt. practice law, Lowell, 1953-57; sr. ptnr. firm Goldman & Curtis, and predecessors, Lowell and Boston, 1957—. Chmn. Lowell and Greater Lowell Heart Fund, 1967-68; mem. adv. bd. Salvation Army, sec., 1956-58; mem. Bd. Higher Edn. Mass., 1967-72; elected mem. Lowell Charter Commn., 1969-71; del. Dem. Party State Convs., 1956-60; trustee U. Lowell, 1963-72, chmn. bd., 1968-72; bd. dirs. U. Mass. Rsch. Found., 1965-72, Merrimack Valley Health Planning Coun., 1969-72. Served with AUS, 1943-46. Decorated Knight Order Orthodox Crusade Holy Sepulcher. Mem. ABA, Mass. Bar Assn., Middlesex County Bar Assn., Lowell Bar Assn., Assn. Trial Lawyers Am., Mass. Trial Lawyers Assn., Mass. Acad. Trial Lawyers, Am. Judicature Soc., Harvard Law Sch. Alumni Assn., U. Mich. Alumni Assn., Lowell Hist. Soc., DAV, Delta Epsilon Pi, Harvard Club of Lowell (pres. 1969-71, bd. dirs.), Masons. Democrat. Greek Orthodox. Home: 111 Rivercliffe Rd Lowell MA 01852-1434 Office: 144 Merrimack St Lowell MA 01852

CURTIS, KENNETH M., lawyer; b. Leeds, Maine, Feb. 8, 1931; s. Archie M. and Harriet (Turner) C.; m. Pauline B. Curtis, Nov. 17, 1956; children: Susan L. (dec.), Angela Curtis Hall. BS, Maine Maritime Acad., 1952; JD, U. Maine, 1958. Sec. state State of Maine, Augusta, 1965-66, gov., 1967-74; ptnr. Curtis, Thaxter, Stevens, Micholeau & Broder, Portland, Maine, 1975—; ambassador to Can. Ottawa, 1979-81; bd. dirs. New Eng. Telephone Co., Boston. Chmn. Dem. Nat. Com., Washington, 1977-78; trustee Susan Curtis Found., Portland, 1973—. Served to lt. comdr. USNR, 1953-65. Mem. Maine Bar Assn. Home and Office: Maine Maritime Acad Castine ME 04112

CURTIS, LAWRENCE HENRY, real estate developer; b. N.Y.C., May 7, 1958; s. Joseph Kenneth and Marge (Mandell) C.; m. Marla Glanzer, Aug. 30, 1981; children: Meade, David. BArch, The Cooper Union for the Advancement of Sci. and Art, 1981; MArch in Urban Design and Planning, Harvard U., 1983. Project prin. Boylston Devel. Group, Boston, 1983-86; v.p. The Catamount Corp., Chelsea, Mass., 1986-87; sr. v.p. WINN Devel. Co., Boston, 1987—; bd. dirs. Comml. Mortgage Corp. of Am. Club: Harvard (Boston). Home: 156 Washington St West Boxford MA 01885-9999 Office: WINN Devel Co Boston MA 02109-0409

CURTIS, ROBERT KERN, lawyer, physics educator; b. N.Y.C., June 11, 1940; s. Sargent Jackson and Phyllis (Kern) C.; m. Beverley Meadows, Dec. 26, 1971; 1 child, Phyllis. AB in Physics, Fordham U., 1964, MS in Edn., 1970; Lic. in Philosophy, Woodstock Coll., 1965; JD, Seton Hall U., 1985. Tchr. Bklyn. Prep. Sch., 1965-67; dir. Jesuit Sem. and Mission Bur., N.Y.C., 1967; tchr. Xavier High Sch., N.Y.C., 1967-69, Hackensack (N.J.) High Sch., 1969—; sole practice Hackensack, 1985—; tchr. law Hackensack Evening Sch., 1980, law for tchrs. Hackensack Pub. Schs., 1986. Mem. Am. Phys. Soc., Assn. Trial Lawyers Am., ACLU, N.Y. Acad. Scis., Am. Assn. Physics Tchrs., Math. Assn. Am., Hackensack Edn. Assn. (pres. 1979-81). Home and Office: 287 Hamilton Pl Hackensack NJ 07601-3614

CUSACK, THOMAS JOSEPH, banker; b. N.Y.C., Aug. 12, 1938; s. Thomas Joseph and Josephine (Mingalone) C.; m. Elizabeth Mary McAuliffe, June 4, 1960; children: Thomas, Elizabeth, Bridget. BBA, St. Francis Coll., 1968; grad., Stonier Grad. Sch. Banking, New Brunswick, N.J. Asst. v.p. Irving Trust Co., N.Y.C., 1959-79; v.p., sr. ops. mgr. Mellon Bank Internat., N.Y.C., 1979-83; gen. mgr. Mellon Bank Internat., 1983-85; v.p., sr. ops. mgr. Creditanstalt, 1985-90, v.p. planning and devel., 1990—; U.S. rep. Swift Documentary Credit Working Group, Brussels, Belgium, 1983-85; mem. Payments and Settlement Systems Com., Bankers Assn. Fgn. Trade, 1983-85. Mem. fin. com. St. Vincent DePaul Roman Cath. Ch., Elmont, N.Y., 1988—. Mem. U.S. Council on Internat. Banking (chmn. 1987-88), K.C. (4th deg.). Home: Ten John Ave Elmont NY 11003

CUSANO, ANTHONY JOHN, union administrator; b. Newark, Sept. 23, 1950; s. Anthony and Rose Veronica (Paglia) C.; m. Maryann J. Tavolacci, Feb. 28, 1953; children: Christine Maria, Anthony John, Patrice Veronica. BS, Strayer Coll., 1973; postgrad., Fairleigh Dickenson U. Purchasing agt. S.J. Groves & Sons, Minn., 1974-77; adminstr. welfare, pension, legal svcs. and annuity funds Local 408 Teamsters, Union, N.J., 1977—, cons. for employee benefits, 1992—; cons. profit sharing plans, investments, human resources. Active Mountainside Little League. Mem. Assn. Benefit Adminstrs. (bd. dirs. 1986—, v.p.), Internat. Found. Employee Benefits, N.J. Labor Mgmt., Health Care Coalition. Democrat. Roman Catholic. Home: 310 Garret Rd Mountainside NJ 07092 Office: Teamsters Local 408 Benefit Funds 1907 Morris Ave Union NJ 07092

CUSHING, KAY SMITH, public relations executive; b. Pitts., Feb. 21, 1944; d. George Byron and Margaret Elizabeth (Smith) C.; m. Kenneth Neuhausen, May 16, 1981. BA, Lindenwood Coll., 1965. Gen. mgr. Pitts. Ballet Theatre, 1975-78; account supr. Ketchum Pub. Relations, Pitts., 1978-79, v.p., 1979-82, group mgr., 1982—, sr. v.p., 1984—. Trustee Am. Fed. Aging Research; bd. dirs. Pitts. Pub. Theater, Winchester-Thurston Sch., Performing Arts Com. of Carnegie; chair Friends of Carnegie's Performing Arts. Recipient Matrix award Women in Communications, Pitts., 1983-84, Bus. and Leadership award YWCA Pitts., 1990. Mem. Pub. Relations Soc. Am. (pres. Pitts. chpt. 1986-87; Vic Barkman award 1984), Fedn. Girls Sch. Socs. Republican. Roman Catholic. Club: Rivers (Pitts.). Office: Ketchum Pub Rels 6 Ppg Pl Pittsburgh PA 15222-5406

CUSICK, J. AMBLER, stockbroker; b. Washington, Apr. 29, 1961; s. Ralph A. Jr. and Jaquelin Carter (Ambler) C. BA, Washington & Lee U., 1983. Account mgr. ITT World Communications Inc., N.Y.C., 1983-86; sr. account mgr. Internat. Communication Consortium, N.Y.C., 1987-88, Weston Union Corp., Washington, 1988-90; investment rep. Alex Brown & Sons, Inc., Washington, 1990—. Mem. Young Reps., Montgomery County, Md., 1992—. Mem. Washington & Lee U. Alumni Assn. (chpt. v.p. 1991—), Met. Club, Chevy Chase (Md.) Club, Union League Club, Capital Club (bd. dirs. 1990-92). Episcopalian. Office: Alex Brown & Sons Inc 1440 New York Ave NW # 500 Washington DC 20005

CUSIMANO, ADELINE MARY, educational administrator; b. Jamestown, N.Y., Apr. 18, 1939; d. Joseph and Rose (Bivona) Miletti; m. John Leo Cusimano, Sept. 24, 1960; children: Judith Ann Cusimano Pancio, John Anthony. BS, Elmira Coll., 1961, MS, 1976. Cert. reading specialist, N.Y. Tchr. Horseheads (N.Y.) Sch. Dist., 1961-62; diagnostician, clinician Horseheads, 1962-76; reading specialist Elmira Heights Schs., N.Y., 1976-78; dir. Achievement Ctr., Horseheads, 1978—; presenter ednl. N.Y. St. Reading Conf., Kiamesha Lake, N.Y., 1982, Bd. Coop. Ednl. Svcs. Tchrs. Tng., Horseheads, 1978-80; researcher learning disabilities, Horseheads, 1962—. Author: ACHIEVE Visual Memory Teaching Material, 4 Vols., 1980. Mem. pub. affairs edn. home life Chemung Valley Jr. Women's Club, 1968-78, 1st v.p., 1971-72; asst. treas. Horseheads Women's Club, 1983-85. Recipient Outstanding Jr. Women's Club award, 1975. Mem. Nat. Assn. Learning Disabilities, N.Y. State Head Injury Assn., Chemung Valley Reading Assn., Horseheads Women's Club (asst. treas. 1983, corr. sec. 1990-91). Republican. Roman Catholic. Office: Achievement Ctr 104 Ridge Rd Box 315 Horseheads NY 14845

CUSTER, JOHN CHARLES, small business owner; b. Chgo., Aug. 30, 1934; s. John Howard and Irene Lillian (McGovern) C.; m. Barbara Ann Welcher, Sept. 5, 1959; 1 child, John Thomas. AB, Ind. U., 1956; MHA, U. Minn., 1966; student Advanced Mgmt. Program, Harvard U., 1975. Asst. adminstr. Johns Hopkins Hosp., Balt., 1966-67; clin. adminstr. Kaiser Permanente Med. Care Program, Oakland, Calif., 1967-69, dir. materials, 1969-70; mgr. health plan Med. Care Program, Oakland, 1970-74, v.p., health plan mgr., 1974-79; v.p. Kaiser Permanente Adv. Services, Oakland, 1979-84; pres., chief exec. officer Keystone Health Plan, Camp Hill, Pa., 1984-85; pres. chief exec. officer Custer & Assocs., Hummelstown, Pa., 1986—; lectr. U. Minn. Grad. Sch. of Pub. Health, Mpls., 1983-88, Harvard U. Grad. Sch. of Pub. Health, Boston, 1977-80. Chmn. Pa. Assn. HMO's, Harrisburg, 1984-86. 1st lt. U.S. Army, 1956-58, col. USAR. Mem. Am. Coll. Health Care Execs., Am. Pub. Health Assn., Am. Hosp. Assn., Med. Group Mgmt. Assn., Internat. Fedn. of Employee Benefit Plans, Pa. State C. of C. (health care cost contain com.), Pa. State Dept. of Pub. Welfare (health care adv. subcom. 1984-85), Delta Upsilon. Episcopalian. Clubs: Cosmos (Washington), Army-Navy (Washington). Lodge: Elks. Home and Office: 589 Lovell Ct Hummelstown PA 17036-9156

CUSTER, RICHARD LEWIS PAYZANT, fire protection engineering educator, consultant; b. Phila., July 19, 1940; s. Richard Philip and Clare (Phyzant) C.; m. Pamela A. Powell, July, 1979. BA in Geology, U. Pa., 1960; MS in Geol. Engring., N.C. State U., 1964; postgrad., George Washington U., 1967-70. Engring. geologist N.C. Hwy. Commn., Raleigh, 1966-67; lectr. Fire Protection Engring. U. Md., College Park, Md., 1967-71; fire protection engr. Ctr. for Fire Rsch. Nat. Bur. Stds., Gaithersburg, Md., 1971-75; chief fire detection & control Ctr. for Fire Rsch. Nat. Bur. Stds., Gaithersburg, 1975-78, assoc. dir, 1978-81; energy legislative aide Office U.S. Senator John Culver, Washington, 1979-80; exec. dir. Nat. Ctr. for Tech. in Lw, Rockville, Md., 1981; assoc. prof., assoc. dir. Ctr. for Firesafety Studies, Worcester Polytechnic Inst., Mass., 1982-91; adj. assoc. prof. fire protection engrng. Worcester (Mass.) Poly. Inst., 1991—; prin. Custer Powell Inc., Wrentham, Mass., 1991—; prin. Richard L. P. Custer & Co., Wrentham, 1981-91. Editor: Engineering Methods Sect. Society Fire Protection Engineers Handbook of Fire Protection Engineering; contbr. articles to profl. jours on Geology and Firesafety. Named Hon. mem. Salamander Fire Protection Honor Soc., College Park, Md., 1967, Man of Yr., 1991; fellow U.S. Dept. Commerce, 1979. Mem. ASTM (mem. fire test com. 1983—), Soc. Fire Protection Engrs. (Dir.'s award 1989), Internat. Assn. Arson Investigators, Nat. Fire Protection Assn. (chmn. fire investigation com. 1984—, vice chair fire tech. educators sect. 1991—), Nat. Assn. Fire Investigators, Internat. Assn. Fire Safety Sci. Office: Custer Powell Inc 155 South St # 741 Wrentham MA 02093-1525

CUTLER, ARNOLD ROBERT, lawyer; b. New Haven, Mar. 20, 1908; s. Max Nathan and Kate (Harder) C.; m. Hazel Lourie, Apr. 8, 1942; 1 son, David. B.A., Yale U., 1930, J.D., 1932; LLD (hon.), Brandeis U., 1984. Bar: Conn. 1932, Mass. 1946. Mem. staff Office Gen. Counsel Pub. Works Adminstrn., Washington, 1933-36; chief counsel Pub. Works Adminstrn. State of Wash., 1937-38; spl. asst. to chief counsel IRS, 1939-44, trial counsel New Eng. div., 1945-47; ptnr. Lourie & Cutler, Boston, 1947—; lectr. on taxation. Contbr. to books articles to legal jours. Trustee Beth Israel Hosp.; trustee emeritus Brandeis U.; trustee, past mem. exec. com. Combined Jewish Philanthropies Greater Boston; past. bd. dirs. Nat. Jewish Welfare Bd.; past pres. Brookline, Brighton and Newton Jewish Community Ctr.; past. treas. Associated Jewish Community Ctrs. of Greater Boston; past chmn. bd. Yale Law Sch. Fund; past chmn. bequest com. Yale Law Sch. Lt. comdr. USCG, 1942-45. Fellow Am. Coll. Tax Counsel, Mass. Bar Found.; mem. ABA (com. on govt. submissions 1987—, past chmn. spl. adv. exempt orgns. com. tax sect.), Mass. Bar Assn., Boston Bar Assn. (past chmn. fed. tax com., past mem. council), Am. Law Inst. Clubs: New Century (past pres.), Greater Boston Brandeis (past pres.), Yale, Harvard, Wightman Tennis, Rotary (past bd. dirs.). Office: Lourie & Cutler 60 State St Boston MA 02109-1803

CUTLER, JAY B., psychiatric association executive; b. N.Y.C., Sept. 7, 1930; s. Murray and Shirley (Salkin) C.; m. Randy Handelsman, Apr. 5, 1952; children: Hollie, Perri. BS, NYU, 1951; JD, Bklyn. Law Sch., 1956; PHD (hon.), So. Coll. Optometry, Memphis, 1978. Bar: N.Y. 1956, D.C. 1958. Atty., pub. affairs TV producer Theodore Granik Law Office, Washington, 1958-68; minority counsel U.S. Senate Health Subcom. Alcoholism and Narcotics, Washington, 1969-77; counsel, staff dir. U.S. Senate Human Resources Com. (Minority), Washington, 1974-77; spl. counsel and dir. govt. relations Am. Psychiatric Assn., Washington, 1977—; tech. cons. on corp. affairs White House Conf. on Children and Youth; lectr. med. grand rounds Downstate Med. Ctr., Bklyn., N.Y. Coll. Medicine, Columbia U. Coll. Physicians and Surgeons, U. Md. Med. Coll., Cleve. Clin., Western Psychiat. Inst., Pitts. Author: Analysis for Comprehensive Health Manpower Training Act in Health/Environment Manpower 1984, Federal Health Care Financing of Mental Illness in the New Economics and Psychiatric Care. Pres. Md. Assn. for Learning Disabled, Coalition for Health Funding, 1978-81,lvice presdl. campaign Hubert H. Humphrey, 1964. With U.S. Army 1951-53. Recipient Award of Excellence Am. Soc. of Assn. Execs., 1985, 87. Mem. Am. Psychiat. Assn. (pres. 1956, Presdl. Commendation, 1985. Office: Am Psychiat Assn 1400 K St NW Washington DC 20005-2403

CUTLER, LESLIE STUART, academic administrator, dentistry educator; b. New Brunswick, N.J., Jan. 20, 1943; s. Norman Jack and Marian (Lazerowitz) C.; m. Terry Ruth Grubman, July 30, 1966; children: Adam, Matthew. Student, UCLA, 1960-62, Los Angeles Valley Coll., Van Nuys, Calif., 1962, Calif. State U., Northridge, 1962-64; DDS, Washington U., St. Louis, 1968; PhD, SUNY, Buffalo, 1973; M in Mgmt., Hartford Grad. Ctr., 1984. Asst. prof. dept. oral biology U. Conn. Health Ctr., Farmington, 1973-77, assoc. prof. depts. oral diagnosis and pathology, 1977-83, prof., chmn. dept. oral diagnosis, 1977-87, assoc. v.p. adminstrn. and rsch., 1987-91, assoc. v.p., assoc. provost heath affairs, 1991-92, interim v.p., provost for health affairs, exec. dir., 1992—; speaker Am. Dental Assn., 1988-89. Editor, contbr. chpts. to books, articles to profl. jours. Mem. Internat. Assn. Dental Rsch. (pres. salivary rsch. group 1985-86), Histochem. Soc. (councilor 1990—), Assn. Acad. Health Ctrs. (task force on sci. policy 1990—). Office: U Conn Health Ctr 263 Farmington Ave Farmington CT 06030-0001

CUTLER, RHODA, psychologist; b. N.Y.C.; d. Samuel and Sophia (Petrushinsky) C. AB in Physiology/Psychology, Hunter Coll.; AM in Psychology, NYU; postgrad., Yeshiva U.; PhD, NYU. Lic. psychologist, N.Y. Counseling psychologist N.Y. Assn. for New Ams., N.Y.C., 1947-60; asst. instr. psychiatry N.Y. Med. Coll., N.Y.C., 1961-65; sch. psychologist Bur. of Child Guidance, N.Y.C., 1964-65; psychol. cons. Bur. Child Welfare, Div. Adoption Svcs., N.Y.C., 1965—; psychotherapist Mental Health Cons.

Ctr., N.Y.C., 1967-70; rsch. assoc. prof. Inst. for Developmental Studies, NYU, 1966-68, vis. assoc. prof., 1969; asst. prof. psychiatry N.Y. Med. Coll., N.Y.C., 1968-69; rsch. psychologist Child Devel. Ctr., N.Y.C., 1969-70; asst. prof. clin. psychiatry Mt. Sinai Coll. Medicine/Beth Israel Med. Ctr., N.Y.C., 1970—. Contbr. articles to profl. jours. Mem. Am. Psychol. Assn., N.Y. Psychol. Assn., N.Y. Soc. Clin. Psychologists, N.Y. Acad. Sci., Soc. of Clin. and Exptl. Hypnosis. Home: 230 E 88th St Apt 10A New York NY 10128-3382

CUTLER, ROBERT STEVEN, computer scientist; b. East Cleveland, Ohio, Dec. 12, 1962; s. Robert Alan and Margaret (Evanoff) C.; m. Heather Jean Blair, Oct. 26, 1991; 1 child, Elizabeth Margaret Blair. BA in German, BA in Computer Sci., Dartmouth Coll., 1984; postgrad., Plymouth State Coll., 1990—. Pres. The Vt. Software Co., Inc., Groton, 1987—. Computer com. Town of Groton, 1989, lister, auditor, 1992—. Recipient Thayer Math. award Dartmouth Coll., 1981. Mem. IEEE, ACM, Am. Prodn. and Inventory Control Soc. (chpt. exec. v.p. 1991-92), Urban and Regional Info. Systems Assn. (SDS-SIG leader 1991-92). Office: The Vermont Software Co PO Box 233 Groton VT 05046-0233

CUTLER, RONNIE, artist; b. N.Y.C.; d. Leo and Sarah (Saks) C.; m. Mar. 1, 1951 (dec. May 1990). Student, Columbia U., 1955-56, Bklyn. Mus. Art, 1958, Art Students League, N.Y.C., 1959-60. Exhibited in group shows Whitney Mus. Am. Art, N.Y.C., 1954, Delgado Mus. Art, New Orleans, 1955, Berkshire Mus. Art, Pittsfield, Mass., 1956, Bklyn. Mus., 1956, 58, Riverside Mus. Art, N.Y.C., 1957, Springfield (Mass.) Mus. Art, 1957, Nat. Acad. Art, N.Y.C., 1958. Recipient Sherwood prize in oil Silvermine Guild Artists, 1955, 1st prize Riverside Mus. Art, 1957, alumni purchase award Art Students League, 1960, 1st prize in oil So. Berkshire Assn., 1979, 80, Painters and Sculptors Soc., 1955. Home and Studio: 175 W 12th St Apt 11J New York NY 10011

CUTTER, DAVID L., advertising specialty executive; b. Waltham, Mass., Mar. 10, 1941; s. Howell G. and Marion E. (Nickerson) C.; m. Kathryn Ann Pombriant, July 31, 1965; children: Mary C., Susan Beth. BSBA, Ohio State U., 1963. Cost acct. Honeywell Info. Systems, Waltham, Mass., 1969-70; cost acct., pers. mgr. Geiger Bros., Lewiston, Maine, 1970-76, data processing mgr., pers. mgr., 1976-83, v.p. human resources and mgmt. info. systems, 1983—. Bd. dirs. United Way, Lewiston, 1985-90; bd. dirs. Pathways, Inc., Auburn, Maine, 1977-84, mem. pers. com., 1977-91; mem. Citizens Evaluation Commn., Lewiston, 1986-87. Lt. USN, 1963-69. Office: Geiger Bros Mount Hope Ave Lewiston ME 04241

CUTUGNO, LEONARD F., diversified financial services executive; b. Bklyn., Jan. 9, 1952; s. Leonard and Rose (Bongiorno) C.; m. Victoria Amato, May 18, 1975; 1 child, Michael L. BS, St. Johns U., N.Y.C., 1973, MBA, 1976. Trust officer Chase Manhattan Bank, N.Y.C., 1973-78; treas. investment officer Empire Savings Bank, N.Y.C., 1978-81; investment officer N.Y. State Ins. Fund, N.Y.C., 1981-82; v.p. Home Life Ins. Co., N.Y.C., 1982-87; sr. v.p. Integrated Resources, N.Y.C., 1987—; dir. Harvest Real Estate Trust, N.Y.C., 1988--, Delta Govt. Options Corp., N.Y.C., 1988--. Republican. Roman Catholic. Office: Integrated Resources 10 Union Sq E New York NY 10003-3314

CYBYK, BOHDAN ZYNOWIJ, aerospace engineer; b. Cleve., June 22, 1961; s. Roman Lubomyr and Ulana Eugenia (Wolynec) C. BS in Aero. Engring., U. Cin., 1984; MS in Aero. Engring., U. Mo., Rolla, 1987. Engring. trainee GE, Cin., 1981, NASA Lewis Rsch. Ctr., Cleve., 1981-83; sr. engr. McDonnell Aircraft Co., St. Louis, 1984—; grad. fellow U. Md., College Pk., 1990—. Mem. The Washington Group, 1991; counselor Boy Scouts Am., Ukrainian Scouting Group, Cleve., 1976-79. Recipient U. Md. grad. fellowship, 1970-91, Schneider, Fleishman and Herfurth scholarships U. Cin., 1980-84. Mem. AIAA. Home: 10217 Parkwood Dr Kensington MD 20895-4131

CYPHER, THOMAS W., educator; b. Saxton, Pa., May 10, 1944; s. Joe R. and Elizabeth (McIntire) C.; m. Kay Spencer, July 30, 1966; children: Kristin, Tricia, Mark. BS, Shippensburg (Pa.) U., 1966, MEd, 1969; EdD, Pa. State U., 1983. Tchr. Forbes Rural Schs., Harrisonville, Pa., 1966-77; asst. prin. Peters Twp. Schs., McMurrey, Pa., 1977-79; prin. Greenwood Schs., Millerstown, Pa., 1979-84; dir. secondary edn. Dallas (Pa.) Schs., 1984-88; assoc. prof. ednl. adminstrn. founds. dept. Shippensburg U., 1988—; asst. dir. Pa. Sch. Study Coun., University Park, 1982-83. Contbr. articles to profl. jours. Com. chmn. Boy Scouts Am., 1988—; active PTA. Mem. Assn. for Supervision and Curriculum Devel., PAC-TE, Acacia (sec.), Masons, Phi Delta Kappa. Republican. Methodist. Office: Shippensburg Univ 208 Horton Hall Shippensburg PA 17257

CYR, CONRAD KEEFE, federal judge; b. Limestone, Maine, Dec. 9, 1931; s. Louis Emery and Kathleen Mary (Keefe) C.; m. Judith Ann Pirie, June 23, 1962 (dec. Mar. 1985); children: Keefe Clark, Jeffrey Louis Frederick; m. Diana Kathleen Sanborn, Sept. 25, 1987. BS cum laude, Holy Cross Coll., 1953; JD, Yale U., 1956; LLD (hon.), Husson Coll., 1991, Husson Coll., 1991. Bar: Maine 1956. Pvt. practice Limestone, 1956-59; asst. U.S. atty., Bangor, Maine, 1959-61; judge U.S. Bankruptcy Court, Bangor, 1961-81; judge U.S. Dist. Ct., Bangor, 1981-83, chief judge, 1983-89; judge U.S. Fgn. Intelligence Surveillance Ct., 1987-89, U.S. Ct. Appeals (1st cir.), Bangor, 1989—; standing spl. master U.S. Dist. Ct., Maine, 1974-76; chief judge Bankruptcy Appellate Panel Dist., Mass., 1980-81; mem. Jud. Council for the 1st Circuit, 1987—, com. on adminstrn. of the bankruptcy system Jud. Conf. U.S., 1987—. Editor-in-chief Am. Bankruptcy Law Jour., 1970-81; contbg. author, editor: Collier on Bankruptcy, Vol. 10. Treas. Limestone Republican Com., 1958; chmn. Town of Limestone Budget Com., 1959. Recipient cert. of appreciation Kans. Bar Assn., 1979, U. Maine, 1983; Nat. Judge's Recognition award Nat. Conf. Bankruptcy Judges, 1979; Key to Town Limestone, 1983; named one of Outstanding Young Men of Maine, 1963. Mem. Maine Bar Assn., Penobscot Bar Assn., Nat. Conf. Bankruptcy Judges (pres. 1976-77), Nat. Bankruptcy Conf. (exec. bd. 1974-77), Am. Judicature Soc., Limestone C. of C. (pres.). Roman Catholic.

CZAJKA, JAMES VINCENT, architect; b. Lackawanna, N.Y., Dec. 6, 1950; s. Joseph Martin and Livia Maria (Jengo) C. BS in Art and Design, MIT, 1972, MArch, 1975. Registered architect, N.Y. Asst. prof. architecture SUNY, Buffalo, 1975-79; architect Ehrenkrantz Group Architects and Planners, N.Y.C., 1979-84, Beyer, Blinder, Belle Architects and Planners, N.Y.C., 1984-91; assoc. Beyer, Blinder, Belle Architects & Planners, N.Y.C., 1987-91, studio dir., 1988-91; prin. pvt. practice, N.Y.C., 1991—. Prin. works include Baird Point Amphitheater, SUNY, Buffalo, 1978, Social Security Adminstrn. Bldg., Queens, N.Y., 1982, Paul Klapper Hall Queens Coll., 1986, N.Y. Hall of Sci. Master Plan, 1990, Riverside South Master Plan, Manhattan, 1992. Mem. AIA, Nat. Coun. Archtl. Registration Bds. (cert.). Home and office: 303 E 84th St Apt 2F New York NY 10028-4435

CZAPNIK, SHELDON JACOB, publishing executive; b. N.Y.C., Dec. 4, 1947; s. Bernard and Anna (Mass) C.; m. Tobie Rabinowitz; children: Dana, Karyn. BA, CCNY, 1969; MA, NYU, 1971; MBA, Columbia U., 1979. Sr. editor Prentice Hall Inc., Englewood Cliffs, N.J., 1974-77; editorial contr. Newsweek Inc., N.Y.C., 1979-83, asst. to editor, 1983-84; asst. mng. editor adminstrn. Sports Illustrated, N.Y.C., 1984-88; fin. asst. to editor-in-chief Time Warner Inc., N.Y.C., 1988-92; dir. editorial adminstrn., 1992—. Home: 250 W 82d St New York NY 10024 Office: Time Inc Time-Life Bldg Rockefeller Ctr New York NY 10020

CZIN, JERRY WOLF, securities broker; b. Budapest, Hungary, Oct. 31, 1938; came to U.S., 1949; s. Ernest and Seren (Kasser) C.; m. Carol Gilbert, Apr. 1, 1966 (div. Sept. 1974); 1 child, Jennifer; m. Maria Bongiorno, Mar. 15, 1975. BSME, Drexel U., 1962. Pres. Northfield Investments, Roseland, N.J., 1978-86; exec. v.p. Domestic Arbitrage Group, Pompton Plains, N.J., 1986-87; stockbroker Josephthal Lyon & Ross (and predecessor firms), Wayne, N.J., 1988—; teaching asst. Rutgers U., New Brunswick, N.J., 1963; option coord. Philips Appel & Walden, N.Y.C., 1974-76; seminar speaker option strategies, 1975—. Contbr. articles to profl. jours. Life mem. Rep. Presdl. Task Force, Washington. Drexel U. scholar, 1958-59. Fellow Masons. Home: 206 Highland Ave Upper Montclair NJ 07043 Office: Josephthal Lyon & Ross 30 Galesi Dr Wayne NJ 07470

CZINKOTA, MICHAEL RUDOLF, business educator; b. Augsburg, Bavaria, Germany, Oct. 5, 1951; came to U.S., 1975; s. Michael and Ursula (Magerl) C.; m. Ilona Rosa Vigh, Aug. 10, 1984. Vordiplom, U. Erlangen-Nuremberg, Fed. Rep. Germany, 1974; MBA, Ohio State U., 1976, PhD, 1979. Ptnr., owner Fellwa GmbH, Ingolstadt, Germany, 1972-75; lectr. Ohio State U., Columbus, 1977-79; prof. Georgetown U., Washington, 1980—; sr. trade advisor U.S. Dept. Commerce, Washington, 1986; dep. asst. sec. Internat. Trade Adminstrn., U.S. Dept. Commerce, Washington, 1987-89; head U.S. delegation OECD Industry Com., Paris, 1987-89. Co-author: International Marketing, 1990, International Business, 2d edit., 1992, 3d edit., 1993, Unlocking Japan's Market, 1991. Recipient Dr. Wernher v. Braun award Soc. Logistics Engrs., 1979; Fulbright grantee, 1975, 76; Acad. Mktg. Sci. disting. fellow, 1991. Mem. Am. Mktg. Assn. (v.p., bd. mem.), Acad. Mktg. Sci. (bd. govs.), Cosmos Club. Home: RR 4 Box 370 Luray VA 22835-9038 Office: Georgetown U 37th and O Sts NW Washington DC 20057

CZUJ, CHESTER FRANCIS, JR., food service professional; b. Greenfield, Mass., Apr. 28, 1955; s. Chester Francis and Mary Theresa (O'Sullivan) Matthews; m. Joanne M. Divece, Nov. 25, 1989; 1 child, Chester Francis III. B in Math., Worcester State Coll., 1978. Food svc. mgr. Dining and Kitchen Adminstrn. Inc., Wakefield, Mass., 1973-81; asst. food svc. adminstr. Quincy City (Mass.) Hosp., 1981-84; owner, operator Parkar Bros. Inc., Weymouth, Mass., 1984-86; food svc. mgr. Seiler Corp., Waltham, Mass., 1986-88; resident dist. mgr. Seiler Corp., Phila., 1988-90; dist. mgr. All Seasons Svcs., Inc., Mid-Atlantic, 1990—; instr. Quincy (Mass.) Jr. Coll., 1985-86. Democrat. Roman Catholic. Home and Office: 314 Langford Rd Broomall PA 19008-2811

DABAH, HAIM, apparel executive; b. Jerusalem, Israel, June 18, 1951; s. Morris and Ivette (Marcos) D.; m. Barbara Haddad, Feb. 15, 1976; children: Morris, Mac, Michael. Mgr. Big D Discount Stores, N.Y.C., 1971-73; v.p. The Orit Corp./Gitano, N.Y.C., 1973-77; exec. v.p. The Gitano Group Inc., N.Y.C., 1977-88, pres., chief oper. officer, 1988—, also bd. dirs.; bd. dirs. Isaac Mizrahi & Co., N.Y.C. Trustee Am. Assocs. Ben Gurion U. in the Negev, N.Y.C., 1986—; bd. dirs. Internat. Sephardic Edn. Found., N.Y.C., 1986—, Yeshiva of Flatbush, Bklyn., 1986—. Jewish. Office: The Gitano Group Inc 1411 Broadway New York NY 10018*

DABAH, MORRIS, apparel company executive; b. 1925. Self-employed, until 1970; mdse. & credit mgr. Sutton & Sutton Ltd., N.Y.C., NY, 1970-71; with Orit Imports Inc. N.Y.C., NY, 1971—; chmn. bd., chief exec. officer Gitano Group Inc., N.Y.C., NY, 1987—, also bd. dirs. Office: Gitano Group Inc 1411 Broadway New York NY 10018-3404*

D'ABATE, JANINA MONICA, library administrator; b. Providence, June 20, 1921; d. John Lawrence and Marya Ann (Swiatlowski) Barlowski; m. John D'Abate, Apr. 10, 1943; children: Marya Ann, John G., Janina V. BA, Brown U., 1943; MLS, U. R.I., 1977. Br. libr. Cranston (R.I.) Pub. Libr., 1966-70; dir. North Scituate (R.I.) Pub. Libr., 1974—; mem. steering com. Gov. Conf. on Libr. and Info. Sci., 1977-79. Pres. bd. trustees Mohr Meml. Libr., Johnston, R.I., 1964-69; bd. dirs. R.I. Philharm., chmn. childrens concert com., 1976-78; bd. dirs. Nickerson House, Providence, 1947—, sec., 1952-72; bd. dirs. Camp Fire Inc. R.I., 1980—, sec., 1980-86, pres., 1987. Mem. R.I. Libr. Assn., Beta Phi Mu. Home: 28 Reservoir Ave Johnston RI 02919-2900 Office: Greenville Rd North Scituate RI 02857

DACEY, BRIAN FRANCIS, real estate executive; b. Boston, Dec. 12, 1951; s. John Morrissey and Mary Elizabeth (Mullin) D.; m. Beth Ann DiBuono, Sept. 19, 1976; children: Ann, Sara. BA in Polit. Sci., Boston Coll., 1974; MBA, Boston U., 1984. Asst. to v.p. Sverdrup Corp., Boston, 1974-75; staff dir. Mass. State Senate, Boston, 1975-76; project mgr. Mass. Lt. Gov., Boston, 1976-77; dep. dir., then dir. fed. regs. Mayor's Office, City of Boston, 1977-79; dir. Econ. Devel. and Indsl. Corp. of Boston, 1979-84; exec. v.p. Combined Properties, Inc., Boston, 1984-89, John Drew Co., Boston, 1989—; bd. dirs. Boston Local Devel. Corp., founder revolving loan fund for local businesses, 1980; bd. dirs. Boston Pvt. Industry Coun., 1980-84. Bd. dirs. Morgan Meml. Goodwill Industries, 1986—, chmn., 1991—; sub-com. chair Artery Bus. Com., Boston, 1989—. Mem. Greater Boston Real Estate Bd. (mem. fin. div.), Urban Land Inst. Office: John Drew Co World Trade Ctr Boston MA 02210

DACH, LESLIE ALAN, public relations executive; b. N.Y.C., Apr. 17, 1954; s. Joseph and Edith (Lipsyzc) D.; m. Mary Ann Dickie, Nov. 19,1983; 1 child, Jonathan Alexander. BS in Biology, Yale U., 1975; MPA, Harvard U., 1981. Staff scientist Environ. Def. Fund., Washington, 1977-79; mem. scheduling staff Kennedy for Pres., Washington, 1979-80; assoc. dir. Nat. Audubon Soc., Washington, 1981-84, legis. dir., 1984-87; dir. scheduling Mondale-Ferraro campaign, Washington, 1984; spl. asst. to chmn. U.S. Senate Agr. Com., Washington, 1987; dir. communications Dukakis for Pres., Boston, 1987-88; sr. v.p. Edelman Pub. Rels., Washington, 1989-90, exec. v.p., 1990—. Office: Edelman Pub Rels 1420 K St NW Washington DC 20005

DACK, SIMON, physician; b. N.Y.C., Apr. 19, 1908; s. Isidore and Rebecca (Beitch) D.; m. Jacqueline Rosett, Jan. 23, 1949; children: Jerilyn Beth, Leonard. B.S., CCNY, 1928; M.D., N.Y. Med. Coll., 1932. Intern Mt. Sinai Hosp., N.Y.C., 1932-33; research fellow cardiology Mt. Sinai Hosp., 1934-38, clin. staff cardiology, 1938—, adj. physician cardiology, chief cardiac clinic, 1945-58, attending physician, 1966—; lectr. cardiology Columbia U.; asso. prof. medicine N.Y. Med. Coll., 1959—; asso. clin. prof. medicine Mt. Sinai Sch. Medicine, 1966-70, clin. prof. medicine, 1970-76, clin. prof. emeritus, 1976—; chief cardiac clinics Met. Hosp., N.Y.C., 1955-62; attending vis. physician Met. Hosp., 1962—; asso. physician in cardiology Mt. Sinai Hosp., N.Y.C., 1958-70; attending physician cardiology Mt. Sinai Hosp., 1970-76, acting chief cardiology, 1972-74, cons. cardiologist, 1976—; attending physician Flower Fifth Ave. Hosp., 1966—; hon. prof. medicine U. Santo Tomas, Manila, 1961—. Contbr. articles to profl. jours.; editor-in-chief: Am. Jour. Cardiology, 1958-82, Jour. Am. Coll Cardiology, 1982—. Served as maj. M.C., AUS, 1942-45. Recipient Disting. Fellow award Am. Coll. Cardiology, 1969; presdl. citation Am. Coll. Cardiology, 1972; Jacoby medal Alumni Assn. Mt. Sinai Med. Ctr., 1979, Medicine and Edn. award Alumni Assn. N.Y. Med. Coll., 1987, Lester Gabrilov award for contbns. to medicine Alumni Assn. Mt. Sinai Med Ctr., 1990. Fellow ACP, Am. Med. Writers Assn. (editorial cons.), Am. Coll. Cardiology (trustee 1952—, pres. 1956-57, Spl. award 1961), N.Y. Cardiol. Soc. (hon.); mem. N.Y. Acad. Scis., A.M.A., Am. Heart Assn. (council on clin. cardiology 1962—), Am. Fedn. Clin. Research, Am. Coll. Chest Physicians, Philippine Heart Assn. (hon.), Alpha Omega Alpha. Home: 85 E End Ave New York NY 10028-8020

DACRE, JACK CRAVEN, toxicologist; b. Auckland, New Zealand; came to U.S., 1970; s. George Craven and Grace (Piper) D.; m. Jean Rosina Olney, Dec. 10, 1950; children: Kenneth J.C., Terrence M., Paul C. BS, U. New Zealand, 1943, MS with honors, 1946; PhD, U. London, 1950, DS, 1982. Sr. rsch. biochemist Toxicology Rsch. Unit/NZ Med. Rsch. Coun., Dunedin, New Zealand, 1954-61, head of unit, 1968-70; chief toxicologist pathol. rsch. dept. U. Otago Med. Sch., Dunedin, 1961-67; assoc. prof. Lab. Environ. Medicine Tulane U. Med. Sch., New Orleans, 1970-74; rsch. toxicologist U.S. Army Med. Bioengring. R & D Lab/Ft. Detrick, Frederick, Md., 1974-84, mgr. chem. weapons, 1985—; expert mem. Joint WHO/FAO Expert Com. on Food Additives, Geneva, Rome, 1968-84. Contbg. author: Metabolic Aspects of Food Safety, 1969, Environmental Risk Analysis of Chemicals, 1981, Cholinesterases--Fundamental and Applied Aspects, 1983, Lewisite: Its Chemistry, Toxicology and Biological Effects, 1989. Recipient Chem. Essay prize New Zealand Inst. Chemistry, 1959, 68, ICI Silver medal and prize Imperial Chem. Industries, New Zealand, 1974, Commr.'s Spl. Citation award and medal FDA, Nat. Ctr. for Toxicol. Rsch., 1990. Fellow Acad. Toxicological Scis. Home: 7209 E Sundown Ct Frederick MD 21702-2950 Office: US Army Biomedical Rsch and Devel Lab Fort Detrick Frederick MD 21702-5010

DADDONA, JOSEPH S., mayor; b. Allentown, Pa., Aug. 14, 1933; m. Ann Burton. Grad. in engring., Lehigh U., 1960. Engr. Western Elec. Co., 1956-65; charter commr., Allentown, 1966; city councilman, 1967-74; mayor, 1974-78, 81—; bd. dirs. Nat. League of Cities. Active Jr. Achievement. With USN. Mem. Allentown-Lehigh County C. of C., Jaycees, Sertoma Club. Democrat. Roman Catholic. Office: 435 W Hamilton St Allentown PA 18101-1603*

DADEZ, EDWARD WILLIAM, dean; b. Balt., Oct. 24, 1956; s. Ricarte and Dorothy Elaine (Koutz) D.; m. Teresa Grace Leitch, Sept. 15, 1979; children: Michael, Robert. BS, Va. Commonwealth U., 1980; MA, Ohio State U., 1982; PhD, Mich. State U., 1991. Resident dir. U. Dayton, Ohio, 1982-84; complex dir. Mich. State U., East Lansing, 1984-88; assoc. dean Bucknell U., Lewisburg, Pa., 1988—, instr., 1989—. Contbr. articles to profl. jours.; editor: (newsletter) Wellness Commission VIII, 1987-88. Named Eagle Scout Boy Scouts Am., 1972, Vigil Honor, 1975. Mem. Am. Coll. Personnel Assn. (program presenter, Outstanding Young Prof., 1987), Assn. Coll. and U. Housing Officers, Assn. Fraternity Advisors (N.E. Interfraternity Conf. Adv. of Yr. 1992), Assn. Student Jud. Affairs, Nat. Assn. Student Personnel Adminstrs. (program presenter), Pa. Coll. Personnel Assn. (exec. bd. 1991—, program presenter). Democrat. Roman Catholic. Office: Bucknell U 207 Langone Ctr Lewisburg PA 17837

DAEHNICK, WILFRIED W., associate provost, physics educator; b. Berlin, Germany, Dec. 30, 1928; came to U.S., 1955; s. Adolf F. W. and Adelheid E. (Janke) D.; m. Claire Fullerton, Jan. 30, 1960; children: Christian C., Michael J., Karen S. BS, Tech. U. Munich, Munich, Fed. Republic of Germany, 1951; MSc, Hamburg U., Hamburg, Fed. Republica of Germany, 1955; PhD in Physics, Washington U., St. Louis, 1958. Rsch. assoc. Princeton (N.J.) U., 1959-60, instr., 1960-62; asst. prof. U. Pitts., 1962-65, assoc. prof., 1965-69, prof., 1969—, assoc. provost, 1989—; vis. prof. Max Planck Inst. for Kernphysik, Heidelburg, Fed. Republic of Germany, 1973-74; dir. Scaife Nuclear Physics Lab., Pitts., 1978-79; cons. to various orgns., 1957-89; bd. dirs. Mellon-Pitt-Carnegie Corp., Ben. Franklin Tech. Ctr. S.W. Pa., Bituminous Coal Rsch. Nat. Lab., Pitts.; chmn. Univ. Rsch. Coun., U. Pitts., 1989—; chmn. Exec. Com. for Acad. Computing, 1976-79, 84—. Author: Residual Interaction of Bound Nucleons, 1983; Contbr. numerous articles to profl. jours., conf. abstracts and proc. Nat. Merit fellow, Studienstiftung Germany, 1949-54, U.S. Exch. fellow, 1951-52, Washington U. Grad. fellow, 1957-58. Fellow Am. Phys. Soc.; mem. Am. Phys. Soc. (div. nuclear physics), NASULGC, Sigma Xi. Office: Univ of Pittsburgh 801 C of L Pittsburgh PA 15260

DAELHOUSEN, SCOTT GLENN, construction executive, photographer; b. Warren, Pa., Apr. 17, 1950; s. Glenn Lester and Ruth Elizabeth (Brocklehurst) D.; m. Brenda Althea Bachman, Oct. 19, 1974; children: Kim Noel, Eric Scott. BS, Pa. State U., 1972, MCE, 1977. Registered profl. engr. Pa., N.J., Fla. Field engr. Chantilly (Va.) Constrn. Corp., 1972-74, Herbert R. Imbt, Inc., State Coll., Pa., 1976-81; constrn. engr. Stone & Webster Engring. Corp., Boston, 1982-90; constrn. mgr. Gilbert Commonwealth, Inc., Reading, Pa., 1990—; prin. author for U.S. Doe. Stone & Webster Engring. Corp., Boston, 1987-90. Photographer: (color photos) New Orleans View, 1984 (1st pl.), Camden, Maine, 1989, (2nd pl.), Christmas Lights, 1990 (2nd pl.), Cover Photo 25th Anniversary Issue, 1985; (b&w photos) NMP2, 1985, (hon. mention), NMP2, 1989 (1st pl.). Mem. Nat. Soc. Prof. Engrs., Pa. State Alumni Assn. (life), Delta Mu Sigma (v.p. 1969-70), Chi Epsilon (treas.). Baptist.

DAFOE, CHRISTOPHER RANDY, marketing education professional; b. Wilkesboro, N.C., Oct. 26, 1962; s. Alfred Walter Brett and Verna Irene Dafoe. LLB, Somerset, Ilminster,, 1985-89; BEd, York U., North York, Ont., Can., 1991; MEd, Greenwich U., 1992; DD (hon.), United Luth. Ch. Sem., Modesto, Calif., 1989. Ordained to ministry Luth Ch., 1990; lic. primary/jr. level tchr., psychotherapist, Ark., Ontario, Can., Brazil, Mo. Dir. mktg. Info. Interchange Co. Ltd., Freehold, N.J., 1983—; chair. Profl. Paralegal Assn., Ont., Can., 1985—; cons. Internat. Mktg. Inst., London, 1989—. Named Prince of Medina by Patriarch of Antioch, Baron of San Nicandro by Coun. of Westphalia. Mem. Internat. Lawyers Assn., Internat. Bar Assn., World Jurist Assn., Soc. Psychotherapy and Psychodrama, Notary Assn., Knights Templar (adjutor gen., adjutor 1987-91, Duke of Tyre, 1989), Coun. Seven Sages (H.S.H. sovereign grand master of the order). Home: 3001 Salena St Saint Louis MO 63118 Office: Info Interchange Co Ltd 25-5 Broad St Ste 233 Freehold NJ 07728

DAGA, ANDREW WILLIAM, aerospace research company executive, architect, inventor; b. N.Y.C., July 18, 1957; s. Lorenzo Mario and Gloria Valentine (Bloom) D.; m. Meryl Ann Towarnicki, June 4, 1988. BArch magna cum laude, Spring Garden Coll., 1985. Pres., prin. researcher space exploration initiative Integrated SpaceSystems Corp., Collegeville, Pa., 1987—; pres., chief exec. officer Travel Techs., Inc., Collegeville, Pa., 1991—; bd. tech. dirs. Starnet Structures, Inc., West Babylon, N.Y.; instr., lectr. Spring Garden Coll., Phila., 1985—; promoter Internat. Space U., Cambridge, Mass., 1987. Inventor system for forming structural concrete, lunar base architecture, novel architecture for undeveloped nations, inertially-based surveying instrument, concrete bladdercasting technique, Lugvelope Luggage Protector. Mem. ACI, Spacepac, Spacecause, Space Studies Inst., Nat. Space Soc., AIAA.

DAGAVARIAN-BONAR, DEBRA AGHAVNI, college administrator; b. N.Y.C., Oct. 26, 1952; d. Harry H. Dagavarian and Norma Siran (Cazanjian) Hansen; m. James B. Bonar, Dec. 26, 1988. BA, SUNY, New Paltz, 1973; MA, SUNY, Albany, 1975; EdD, Rutgers U., 1986. Transfer admissions counselor Mercy Coll., Dobbs Ferry, N.Y., 1976-79, asst. dir. spl. sessions, 1979-81, dir. evening programs, 1981-86, dir. acad. advising, 1986-87; from. instr. to asst. prof. Mercy Coll./Empire State Coll., Dobbs Ferry, Hartsdale, N.Y., 1979-89; asst. dean for assessment Empire State Coll., Hartsdale, 1987-88; dir. testing and assessment Thomas Edison State Coll., Trenton, N.J., 1988—; cons. New Eng. Assn. Schs. and Colls., Winchester, Mass., 1989—, North Cen. Assn. Colls. and Schs., Chgo., 1991, Middle States Assn. Colls. and Schs., various colls. in U.S. and Gt. Britain, 1988—; dir., founder Nat. Inst. on the Assessment in Experiential Learning, Princeton, N.J., 1988—. Author: Saying It Ain't So: American Values as Revealed in Children's Baseball Stories, 1987; editor: A Century of Children's Baseball Stories, I, 1990, II, 1992, A Century of Children's Sports Stories, 1993; also articles. Mem. AAUP, Am. Sociol. Assn., Nat. Continuing Edn. Assn., N.J. Coll. and Univ. Coalition on Women's Edn., Soc. for Am. Baseball Rsch. Democrat. Home: 105 Baylor Rd Trenton NJ 08610-4108 Office: Thomas Edison State Coll 101 W State St Trenton NJ 08608-1176

DAGHER, AZAR PETER, radiologist; b. Beirut, Oct. 20, 1960; came to U.S., 1973; s. Fuad Joseph and Malak (Nahhas) D. BS in Engring., Loyola Coll., Balt., 1981; postgrad., McGill U., Montreal, Can., 1984-85; MD, U. Md., 1989. Assoc. engr. Westinghouse Electric, Balt., 1981-83; intern Dartmouth Hitchcock Med. Ctr., Hanover, N.H., 1989-90; resident in radiology Johns Hopkins Hosp., Balt., 1990—. Mem. AMA, Radiol. Soc. N.Am., Soc. Magnetic Resonance in Medicine. Home: 2515 Boston St Apt 602 Baltimore MD 21224 Office: Johns Hopkins Med Instn Dept Radiology 600 N Wolfe St Baltimore MD 21205

DAGHLIAN, JOHN EDWARD, advertising agency executive; b. Hoboken, N.J., Jan. 23, 1946; s. John and Mildred (Gross) D.; m. Linda Parker, Aug. 14, 1976. BS, Fairleigh Dickinson U., 1970; MBA, Fordham U., 1974. Market research mgr. McGraw-Hill Publs., N.Y.C., 1964-71; mortgage cons. J.I. Kislak Mortgage Corp., Newark, 1972; v.p. account supr. Compton Adv., Inc., N.Y.C., 1973-80; group brand dir. Lorillard, Inc., N.Y.C., 1980-90; v.p. strategic mktg. Campbell-Mithun-Esty Advt., N.Y.C., 1991—. Mem. Packanack Lake Golf Club (pres. 1989-90). Office: Campbell-Mithun-Esty Advt 405 Lexington Ave New York NY 10174-0002

D'AGOSTINO, ANTHONY CARMEN, anthropologist, educator; b. Rochester, N.Y., Mar. 1, 1939; s. Antonino and Maria (Plutino) D'A. BA, U. Buffalo, 1962; MA, SUNY, Buffalo, 1965, PhD, 1974. Teaching fellow, then instr. anthropology SUNY, Buffalo, 1964-67; asst. prof. anthropology U. Fla., Gainesville, 1967-68; assoc. prof., now prof. St. John Fisher Coll., Rochester, N.Y., 1969—; chmn. dept. anthropology St. John Fisher Coll., 1980—; ethnographic fieldwork with San Carlos Apache Indians, Ariz., 1962. Writer, producer, narrator TV series Science Today, WHEC-TV, Rochester, 1976-77; contbr. articles to profl. jours. Trustee, East Rochester Pub. Libr., 1976-90; bd. dirs. Opera Theatre Rochester, 1980-88. Fellow

Am. Anthropol. Assn., Am. Assn. Phys. Anthropologists; mem. N.Y. State Archaeol. Assn., Rochester Acad. Scis., AAAS, Hajji Baba Club (N.Y.C.). Home: 1000 East Ave Rochester NY 14607-2260 Office: St John Fisher Coll Rochester NY 14618

D'AGOSTINO, JOSEPH SALVATORE, government official; b. Providence, Apr. 3, 1928; s. Luigi and Julia (Lonardo) D'A.; m. Mary Ellen Grealish, Nov. 23, 1972; children: Lawrence Martin, Joy Marie. BS, Manhattan Coll., 1951; MA, NYU, 1954, PhD, 1966. Dir. devel. Christian Bros. (New England), 1966-72; dean alumni coll. Hofstra U., Hempstead, N.Y., 1972-78; dir. alumni rels. Am. U., Washington, 1978-83, George Mason U., Fairfax, Va., 1984-91; program officer Eisenhower math. and sci. program U.S. Dept. Edn., Washington, 1991—. Fellow Westinghouse Co., 1956, GE, 1957, NSF, 1959, Shell Oil Co., 1960. Mem. Nat. Sci. Tchrs. Assn. (life), Coun. Advancement and Support of Edn., Phi Delta Kappa (pres. NYU chpt. 1966-67), Kappa Delta Pi, K.C., Kiwanis (pres. 1977-78). Roman Catholic. Home: 2529 Bull Run Ct Vienna VA 22180-6901 Office: US Dept Edn Elem and Secondary Edn 400 Maryland Ave SW Rm 2040 Washington DC 20202-0002

D'AGOSTINO, MAE A., lawyer; b. Albany, N.Y., Dec. 18, 1954; d. Salvatore and Teresa (Occhialiano) D'A. BA, Siena Coll., 1977; JD, Syracuse U., 1980. Bar: N.Y. 1981. Assoc. Maynard, O'Connor & Smith, Albany, 1981-85, ptnr., 1985—; lectr. Albany Med. Ctr. Hosp., Soc. Profl. Engrs., 1985, 86, Benedictine Hosp., Kingston, N.Y., Brandeis U., 1985, 86; instr. civil ligitation Jr. Coll. Albany; instr. Siena Coll., Loudonville, N.Y.; adj. prof. law Albany Law Sch., 1988; lectr. to ins. cos. on def. in automobile negligence case. Vice chmn. assoc. bd. trustees Siena Coll. Recipient cert. of appreciation Am. Soc. Safety Engrs., 1984, 85. Mem. N.Y. State Bar Assn. (chair trial lawyers sect., outstanding young lawyers awards ins., negligence, compensation sect. 1989), Albany County Bar Assn. (bd. dirs.), Inns of Ct. (mem. program com.). Office: Maynard O'Connor & Smith 80 State St Albany NY 12207-2543

D'AGOSTINO, MATTHEW PAUL, bakery executive; b. Yonkers, N.Y., Apr. 15, 1948; s. Paul Francis and Mary Cristina D'A.; m. Kathleen Marie Karpinski, July 17, 1951; children: Carolyn, Paul. BA in English, Polit.Sci., Nathaniel Hawthorne Coll., Antrim, N.H., 1970. Bakery mgr. Pathmark Supermarkets, Woodbridge, N.J., 1971; gen. mgr. La Bonbonniere Bake Shoppes, Edison, N.J., 1972—. Mem. Am. Soc. Bakery Engrs., Tri-County Bakers Assn. (pres. 1986-88), N.J. Bakers Bd. Trade (pres. 1988-90), Retail Bakers Am. (dir.-at-large 1988, mem. exec. com. 1990—, N.J. dir. 1990—), N.J. Environ. Soc., Kiwanis, Elks. Roman Catholic. Home: 16 Huntington Rd Edison NJ 08820 Office: La Bonbonniere Bake Shoppes PO Box 981 Edison NJ 08818-0981

D'AGOSTINO, RALPH BENEDICT, mathematician, statistician, educator, consultant; b. Somerville, Mass., Aug. 16, 1940; s. Bennedetto and Carmela (Piemonte) D'A.; m. Lei Lanie Carta, Aug. 28, 1965; children: Ralph Benedict, Lei Lanie Maria. A.B., Boston U., 1962, M.A., 1964; Ph.D., Harvard U., 1968. Lectr. math. Boston U., 1964-68, asst. prof., 1968-71, assoc. prof., 1971-76, prof. math. and stats., 1976—, chmn. dept. math., 1986-91, dir. stats. cons. unit, 1986—, dir. stats. unit Framingham Heart Study, 1985—, dir. Biostats MA/PhD Program, 1988—, lectr. law, 1975-91, prof. pub. health, 1982—, assoc. dean Grad. Sch., 1976-78, prof. law, 1991—; vis. lectr. Am. Statis. Assn., 1975-86, 88—; spl. scientist Boston City Hosp., 1981—, New Eng. Med. Ctr., 1990—; mem. Health Inst. New Eng. Med. Ctr., 1991—; cons. stats. United Brands, 1968-76, Diabetes and Arthritis Control Unit, Boston, 1971-75, City of Somerville, Mass., 1972, ednl. div. Bolt, Beranek & Newman, 1971, Harvard U. Dental Sch., 1969, Lahey Clinic Found., 1973-85, Walden Rsch., 1974-79, FDA Biometrics Div. and Over-the-Counter Div., 1975—, Cardio and Renal Div. FDA, 1987—, Arnold & Porter, 1980, Bedford Rsch. Assn., 1976-81, Corneal Scis., 1976, Biotek, 1979-88, GCA, 1979-87, Lever Bros., 1982-87, Conrail, 1981, FBI, 1984, Ctr. Psychiat. Rehab., Boston U., 1985—, NIMH, 1985, Dade Clin. Assays, 1986—, Millipore, 1983—, VLI Corp., 1985—, New England Coll. Optometry, 1985—, Dupont corp., 1985, Bristol Myers, 1986, Cheseborough Ponds, 1987—, med. decision making div. and health svcs. rsch. unit Tufts New England Med. Ctr., 1986—, Am. Inst. Rsch. in Social Scis., 1983-88, New England Rsch. Insts., 1987—, Thompson Med., 1987—, Merck, Sharpe and Dohme, 1988—, Carter Ctr. Emery U., 1989—, Unilever, 1991—, Miles, 1991—, Ultra Fem., 1991—, Health Effects Inst., 1992—, other rsch. insts.; mem. various FDA coms. including fertility and maternal health drugs adv. com., 1978-81, life support subcom., 1979-81, drug abuse adv. com., 1987-90, gastrointestinal drugs adv. com., 1990—; mem. task force on design and analysis in dental and oral rsch., 1979—, health tech. com. Harvard U., 1986-90; mem. Honolulu Heart Study adv. com. NIH, 1989—, Balt. Longitudinal Study of Aging adv. com., 1990, Consensus Panel on Liver Transplantation, 1983, Consensus Panel on Fresh Frozen Plasma, 1984, Consensus Panel on Geriatric Assessment Methods for Clin. Decision Making, 1987; mem. study sect. Agy. Health Care Policy and Rsch., 1990—; mem. task force Office Tech. Assessment, 1980; mem. consensus panel on intraoral techniques ADA, 1990; mem. study sect. Agy. for Health Care Policy and Rsch., 1990—; prin., co-prin. investigator or sr. statistician on grants Nat. Ctr. Health Svcs. Rsch., 1976-82, USAF, 1980-85, Nat. Cancer Inst., 1985—, Nat. Inst. Criminal Justice, 1982-85, Nat. Ctr. Child Abuse and Neglect, 1982-85, Robert Wood Johnson Found., 1981-85, Social Security Adminstrn., 1982-86, 90—, Motor Vehicle Mem. Assn., 1987, NIOSH, 1985, Nat. Insts. Aging, 1986—; grant and contract reviewer NAS, 1979—, Nat. Ctr. Health Svcs. Rsch., 1976, 89, NIH, 1983, NSF, 1987—, AHCPR, 1990—. Author: (with E.E. Cureton) Factor Analysis, An Applied Approach, 1983, (with Shuman and Wolfe) Mathematical Modeling, Applications in Emergency Health Services, 1984, (with Stephens) Goodness of Fit Techniques, 1986; assoc. editor: Am. Statistician, 1972-76, Statistics in Medicine, 1981-91; editor: Emergency Health Service Rev., 1981-88; mem. editorial bd. Biostatistica, 1990—; book reviewer Houghton Mifflin, Holden-Day, Duxbury Press, Prentice Hall, 1969—; contbr. articles to profl. jours.; co-developer instrument for predicting acute ischemic heart disease and stoke health risk appraisal function. Recipient Spl. citation FDA Commr., 1981, Metcalf awrd for excellence in teaching Boston U., 1985; Am. Heart Assn. fellow, 1991. Fellow Am. Statis. Assn. (pres. Boston chpt. 1972, v.p. 1971, mem. nat. coun. 1973-75, vis. lec(cardiovascular epidemiology coun.), Inst. Math. Stats., Am. Soc. Quality Control, Biometrics Soc. (regional adv. com. 1989—), Am. Pub. Health Assn. (chmn. sect. emergency health svcs. 1982-83, governing coun. 1983-85), Phi Beta Kappa, Sigma Xi. Home: 5 Everett Ave Winchester MA 01890-3523 Office: Boston U Dept Math 111 Cummington St Boston MA 02215-2411

DAHBANY, AVIVAH, psychologist; b. Bklyn., Jan. 3, 1951; d. Hyman and Esther (Levy) D.; BA, CCNY, 1974, MS, 1978. Fellow in Clin. Psychology Albert Einstein Coll. Medicine, 1976-77; psychologist Adams Sch., N.Y.C., 1977-78; dir. spl. edn., psychologist Dov Revel Yeshiva, Forest Hills, N.Y., 1978-79; psychologist Franklin Twp. Public Schs., Somerset, N.J., 1979—; adj. lectr. CCNY, 1977-78; adj. instr. Monmouth Coll., 1981, 88-92, Raritan Valley Community Coll., 1987-88; psychol. cons. Robert Wood Johnson Meml. Hosp., Laurie Devel. Inst., 1985-89, Child Evaluation Ctr., 1985-89. Mem. NEA, N.Y. Assn. Sch. Psychologists (chairperson student certification task force 1977-78), Am. Psychol. Assn., Nat. Assn. Sch. Psychologists. Office: Pupil Personnel Services 1755 Amwell Rd Somerset NJ 08873-2793

DAHL, ARLENE, actress, author, designer, cosmetic executive; b. Mpls., Aug. 11, 1928; d. Rudolph and Idelle (Swan) D.; m. Marc A. Rosen; children: Lorenzo Lamas, Carole Christine Holmes, Stephen Andreas Schaum. Student, U. Minn., 1943-44, Mpls. Inst. Art, 1945, Minn. Coll. Music, Minn. Bus. Coll. Pres. Arlene Dahl Enterprises, 1952-77; v.p. Kenyon & Eckhart, 1967-72; pres. Woman's World div. Kenyon & Eckhart Advt. Agy., 1967-72; nat. beauty and health advisor Sears Roebuck Co., 1970-75; internat. dir. Sales and Mktg. Execs. Internat., 1972-75; fashion dir. O.M.A., 1975-78; pres. Dahlia Parfums, Inc., 1975-80, Dahlia Prodns., Inc., 1978-81, Dahlmark Prodns., 1981—, Scandia Cosmetics, Ltd., 1978-80; pres., chmn. Lasting Beauty Ltd., 1986—. Author: Always Ask a Man, 1965, 12 Beautyscope books, 1968, rev. edit., 1978, Arlene Dahl's Secrets of Hair Care, 1970, Arlene Dahl's Secrets of Skin Care, 1972, Beyond Beauty, 1980, Arlene Dahl's Lovescopes, 1983, Arlene Dahl's 1991 Astro Forecast, Arlene Dahl's 1992 Astrological Forecast, Arlene Dahl's 1993 Astrological Forecast; actress: (Broadway plays) including Mr. Strauss Goes to Boston, Questionable Ladies, Cyrano de Bergerac, Applause (Tony award musical), (films) including (debut) My Wild Irish Rose, The Bride Goes Wild, Reign of Terror, A Southern Yankee, Ambush, The Outriders, Three Little Words, Watch the Birdie, Scene of the Crime, Inside Straight, No Questions Asked, Desert Legion, Slightly Scarlet, Sangaree, Caribbean Gold, Jamaica Run, Diamond Queen, Here Come the Girls, Bengal Brigade, Kisses for My President, Woman's World, Journey to the Center of the Earth, Wicked as They Come, She Played with Fire, Les Poneyettes, Du Blé Enliases, The Land Raiders, The Way to Kathmandu, Fortune is a Woman, The Big Bank Roll, Who Killed Maxwell Thorn?, Midnight Warrior, 1991, (TV shows) Lux Video Theatre, 1952-53; guest starring appearances on The Love Boat, Fantasy Island, Love American Style, One Life to Live, 1981-84, Night of 100 Stars, 1983, Happy Birthday Hollywood, 1987; hostess (TV series): Pepsi-Cola Theatre, 1954, Opening Night, 1958, Arlene Dahl's Beauty Spot, 1966, Arlene Dahl's Starscope, 1979-80, Arlene Dahl's Lovescope, 1980-82, One Life to Live, 1981-84; played throughout U.S. in One Touch of Venus, The Camel Bell, Blithe Spirit, Liliom, The King and I, Roman Candle, I Married an Angel, Bell, Book and Candle, Applause, Marriage Go Round, Pal Joey, A Little Night Music, Forty Carats, Life With Father, Murder Among Friends, Dear Liar; (nightclub acts) Flamingo Hotel, Las Vegas, Latin Quarter, N.Y.C.; internat. syndicated beauty columnist, Chgo. Tribune/ N.Y. News Syndicate, 1950-70, Arlene Dahl's Lucky Stars Column, Globe Communications, 1988-90, Arlene Dahl's Astroscope Mag., 1991, 92, 93; designer sleepwear for A.N. Saab & Co., 1952-57, In Vogue with Arlene Dahl (Vogue Patterns), 1980-85; Arlene Dahl Pvt. Collection Jewelry, 1989—. Hon. life mem. Father Flannagan's Boys Town; internat. chair Pearl Buck Found.; bd. dirs. Hollywood Mus. Recipient 10 Laurel awards Box Office mag., Hollywood Walk of Fame Star, Coup de Chapeau Deaville Film Festival award, 1982; named Best Coiffed, Heads of Fame awards 1967-72, 80, Woman of the Yr., Adv. Club of N.Y.C., 1969, Mother of the Yr., 1982. Mem. UNIFEM, Acad. TV Arts and Scis., Author's Guild, Acad. Motion Piction Arts and Scis., Acad. TV Arts and Scis. (bd. govs.), Commanderie des Bontemps du Medoc et Graves, Internat. Platform Assn., Sierra Club, Nat. Trust Hist. Preservation, Vesterheim Norwegian/ Am. Found., The Film Soc., Smithsonian Instn. Office: Dahlmark Prodns PO Box 116 Sparkill NY 10976-0116

DAHL, CHRISTOPHER CURTIS, academic dean, author; b. Brattleboro, Vt., Aug. 26, 1946; s. Edward Curtis and Anna (Kurko) D.; m. Ruth Ann Rowse, Aug. 24, 1974; 1 child, George Edward. AB, Harvard U., 1968; MPhil in English, Yale U., 1972, PhD, 1978. Inst. English U. Mich., Dearborn, 1973-78, asst. prof., 1978-82, assoc. prof., 1982-89, chair dept. humanities, 1983-89; dean sch. humanities and social scis. Millersville (Pa.) U., 1989—; dir. Rsch. Soc. for Victorian Periodicals, 1982—; vice-chair exec. com. Project 30 Alliance for Tchr. Edn., 1991—. Author: Louis Auchincloss, 1986; contbr. articles to profl. jours. Dir. Planned Parenthood of Lancaster County, Pa., 1991—. Woodrow Wilson fellow 1968-69. Mem. MLA (Victorian Division Bibliography Com.), Midwest Victorian Studies Assn., Elizabethan Club of Yale U., Phi Beta Kappa. Democrat. Presbyterian. Home: 427 N George St Millersville PA 17551-2023 Office: Millersville Univ E Frederick St Millersville PA 17551

DAHLEN, ROGER WAYNE, health science administrator; b. Iola, Wis., Sept. 7, 1935; s. Orin E. and Marian (Tobie) D.; m. Karen Hackleman, may 3, 1986; children: Peggy A., Garth M., Todd S., Tara L. BA, Luther Coll., 1956; MS, U. Iowa, 1958, PhD, 1960. Instr. Boston U. Sch. Medicine, Boston, 1960-62; asst. prof. N.J. Coll. Medicine, Jersey City, 1962-68; program officer Nat. Heart Lung & Blood Inst., Bethesda, Md., 1968-71; chief biomed. info. Nat. Libr. Medicine, NIH, Bethesda, 1971—; bd. regents Upsala Coll., East Orange, N.J., 1964-68. Contbr. 15 sci. articles to profl. jours. Grantee NIH, Am. Heart Assn., N.J. Heart Assn. Home: 10958 Trotting Ridge Way Columbia MD 21044-2834 Office: Nat Libr Medicine 8600 Rockville Pike Bethesda MD 20894-0001

DAHM, ALFONS GEORGE, investment company executive; b. N.Y.C., July 4, 1942; s. Alfonse and Berta (Schmider) D.; m. Jacqueline Ann Jones, June 27, 1965; 1 child, Jeremy Matthew. BA, Hunter Coll., 1964; MBA, Baruch Coll., 1973. Cert. fin. planner, advanced studies fin. planner; registered investment advisor; registered rep. Nat. Assn. Security Dealers. Acct. United Parcel Service, N.Y.C., 1965-67; fin. analyst, adminstr. RCA Corp, N.Y.C., 1967-69; with Mobil Corp., N.Y.C., 1969-90, sr. fin. systems cons., 1981-83, mgr. systems and computer services, records services, 1983-90; pres., chief exec. officer, chmn. bd. dirs. Alfons G. Dahm & Co., Garden City, N.Y., 1982—; assoc. prof. CUNY, N.Y.C., 1973—; chief exec. officer, bd. dirs. Kildare Adminstrv. Services Co., Inc., N.Y., 1986—; bus. advisor INROADS, Inc., NYC, 1986-90. Solicitor United Way, N.Y.C., 1983-86, campaign organizer, 1986-87. Served with USAR, 1965-71. Recipient Disting. Service award CUNY, 1988. Mem. Inst. Cert. Fin. Planners, Assn. for Image and Info. Mgmt., Assn. Records Mgrs. and Adminstrs., Am. Mgmt. Assn. Roman Catholic. Home and Office: Alfons G Dahm & Co Inc 118 Kildare Rd Garden City NY 11530-2502

DAIDONE, DONALD, librarian; b. Detroit, May 12, 1942; s. John and Sophie Daidone; m. Elizabeth Earp, Jan. 2, 1982; children: Giovanni, Mari-a. AS, Macomb Coll., Warren, Mich., 1967; BA, Wayne State U., 1969; postgrad., Eastern Mich. U., 1970-72; MLS, Western Mich. U., 1976. Social sci. libr. Va. Tech. U., Blacksburg, 1976-83; owner, operator Explorers Attic, Gatlinburg, Tenn., 1983-86; collection devel. libr. Rutgers U., New Brunswick, N.J., 1986—. Author: Serials Publications in Geography, 1980. Mem. North Am. Cartographic Info. Soc. (pres. 1981-82). Office: Rutgers U Alexander Libr New Brunswick NJ 08903

DAIDONE, LEWIS EUGENE, financial services company executive; b. Perth Amboy, N.J., Aug. 6, 1957; s. Eugene John and Gertrude Rose (Sawyer) D.; m. Kathleen Eleanor Ward, May 11, 1985; children: Eugene Joseph, Brittany Nicole. BA, Rutgers U., 1979, MBA, 1980. CPA, N.Y., N.J. Sr. acct. Ernst & Young, N.Y.C., 1980-82; asst. controller Reserve Group, N.Y.C., 1982-84; mgr. commodity acctg. Dean Witter Reynolds, N.Y.C., 1984; v.p., treas., sec. Cortland Distbrs., Inc., Hackensack, N.J., 1984-89; sr. v.p., chief fin. officer Cortland Fin. Group, Inc., Hackensack, N.J., 1984-89; also bd. dirs. Cortland Distbrs., Inc., Hackensack, N.J.; mng. dir., chief fin. officer mutual funds Smith Barney, Harris Upham & Co., Inc., N.Y.C., 1990—; sr. v.p., dir. Smith Barney Advisors, Inc., N.Y.C., 1990—, Mutual Mgmt. Corp., N.Y.C., 1990—; sr. v.p., treas. Smith Barney Funds., Inc., N.Y.C., 1990—, Smith Barney Equity Funds, Inc., N.Y.C., 1990—, Smith Barney Money Funds, Inc., N.Y.C., 1990—, Smith Barney Muni Bond Funds, N.Y.C., 1990—, Smith Barney World Funds, Inc., N.Y.C., 1990—, Smith Barney Tax-Free Money Fund, N.Y.C., 1990—; v.p., treas. Cortland Trust, Inc., Hackensack, 1984-89; cons. in field. Trustee Wyndmoor Condominium Assn., Woodbridge, N.J. Named one of Outstanding Young Men Am., U.S. Jaycees, 1979. Fellow N.J. State Soc. CPAs; mem. AICPA, N.Y. State Soc. CPAs, Woodbridge Racquet and Fitness Club, Beta Gamma Sigma. Office: Smith Barney Harris Upham 1345 Ave Of The Americas New York NY 10105-0099

DAIL, PATRICIA KEYES, counselor; b. Cambridge, Md., Feb. 6, 1967; d. Donald Hamilton and Elizabeth Ann (Yoor) K.; m. Jeffrey Scott Dail, Jan. 6, 1990. BA in Psychology, Salisbury State U., 1988; MA in Counseling, U. Md., 1991. Rehab. specialist ReVisions, Inc., Catonsville, Md., 1989-90; psychiat. technician Arlington (Va.) Hosp., 1990—; group co-leader Eastern Shore Hosp. Ctr., Cambridge, 1987-88; addictions counselor Prince George's County Drug and Alcohol Program, Riverdale, Md., 1990-91. Mem. AACD, Phi Eta Sigma, Phi Kappa Phi, Psi Chi. Home: 6926 Hanover Pky Greenbelt MD 20770-2210

DAILEY, LEE KENNETH, human resource executive; b. Bklyn., Oct. 5, 1940; s. Leander Agustin and Lillian Amalia (Johnson) D.; m. Bridget Ann Papa; children: Kristin Lee, Erin. BA/Eng., Psychology, Colgate U., 1963. Spl. agt. Atlantic Mut. Ins. Co., N.Y.C., 1964-70; dir. sales and tng. Agway, Inc., Syracuse, N.Y., 1970-78, v.p. mktg. and sales, 1978-81; dir. human resource devel. Carrier Corp., Syracuse, 1981-85; dir. employee devel. United Tech. Corp., Hartford, Conn., 1985—; adj. prof. Syracuse U. Bus. Sch., 1981-85; cons. human resource devel., 1978-86. Mem. Conn. Employment and Tng. Coun., Hartford, 1988-89; bd dirs. U. Conn. Bus. Sch., Storrs, 1988-89. 1st lt. U.S. Army, 1964-70. Mem. Am. Soc. Tng. and Devel. Republican. Roman Catholic. Office: United Techs 4 Farm Springs Rd Farmington CT 06032-2526

DAILEY, PRISCILLA FIEDER, manufacturing executive, nurse; b. Passaic, N.J., Nov. 27, 1947; d. Frederick William and Margaret Brisbane (Collison) Fieder; m. Robert Cole Dailey, Aug. 26, 1978; children: Robert Cole II, Cole Major III, Margaret Collison. Cert., St. Margaret's Sch. of Nursing, Montgomery, Ala., 1969. RN. Co-founder Christian Fantasy Collectibles, Rutherford, N.J., 1985—. Author: Legend of the Prayer Bear; producer ltd. edit. porcelain plates in field. Capt. Nurse Corps, USAF, 1972-78. Republican. Home and Office: Christian Fantasy Collectibles 125 Woodland Ave Rutherford NJ 07070-2744

DAILEY, THOMAS HAMMOND, surgeon; b. Orange, N.J.; s. Louis Bird and Evelyn (Hammond) D.; m. Denise Benzacar Dailey, Aug. 22, 1959; children: Andrea, Erika, Seth. AB, Princeton U., 1957; MD, Cornell U. Med. Coll., 1961. Assoc. clin. prof. surgery Coll. Physicians and Surgeons, N.Y.C., 1991; sr. attending dept. surgery St. Luke's-Roosevelt Hosp. Ctr., N.Y.C., 1982, dir. div. colon and rectal surgery, 1990; pres. med. bd. St. Luke's-Roosevelt Hosp., N.Y.C., 1989-91; v.p. Rsch. Found. of Am. Soc. Colon and Rectal Surgeons. Capt. U.S. Army Med. Corps., 1966-68, Vietnam. Mem. Med. Strollers, Physician's Sci. Soc., N.Y. Soc. of Colon and Rectal Surgeons (pres. 1979-81). Office: Madison Surgical Assocs 53 E 67th St New York NY 10021

DAILEY, VICTORIA ANN, economist, policy analyst; b. San Antonio, Aug. 30, 1945; d. John Thomas and Helen (Bass) D. BA, Swarthmore Coll., 1967; PhD, U. Va., 1973. Economist FTC, Washington, 1972-79, U.S. Dept. Transp., Washington, 1979—. Brookings Econ. Rsch. fellow Brookings Instn., 1971-72. Office: US Dept Transp 400-7th St SW Washington DC 20590

DAILY, THOMAS V., bishop; b. Belmont, Mass., Sept. 23, 1927. Student, Boston Coll., St. John's Sem., Brighton, Mass. Ordained priest Roman Cath. Ch., 1952; missionary Peru as mem. Soc. St. James the Apostle; ordained titular bishop of Bladia and aux. bishop Boston, 1975-84; first bishop Palm Beach, Fla., 1984-90; bishop Diocese of Bklyn., 1990—. Address: Chancery Office 75 Greene Ave Box C Brooklyn NY 11202

DAISAK, STEPHEN THEODORE, writer; b. N.Y.C., Apr. 1, 1957; s. Stephen and Jennie D. BA cum laude, St. John's U., 1979; MA in Politics, NYU, 1982; postgrad., CUNY, 1987-88; postgrad. in law, Am. U., 1989-90. Freelance writer S.I. (N.Y.) Eagle newspaper, 1987-89. Recipient scholarship, NYU, 1981. Mem. Internat. Platform Assn. Roman Catholic. Home: 63 Albright St Staten Island NY 10304-4203 Office: Staten Island Eagle 37 New Dorp Plz Fl 2D Staten Island NY 10306-2983

DAIUTE, COLETTE AGNES, education educator, researcher; b. Nov. 30, 1948; d. Joseph Francis and Doris Daiute; m. Patrick Wright, May 26, 1984; 1 child, Jack Joseph. BA, Syracuse U., 1970; EdD, Columbia U., 1980. Instr., supr. writing program in basic skills Fashion Inst. Tech., N.Y.C., 1975-79; adj. asst. prof., rsch. assoc. Tchr.'s Coll. Columbia U., N.Y.C., 1980-83; asst. prof. grad. sch. edn. Harvard U., Cambridge, Mass., 1983-88, assoc. prof., 1988—; sr. ednl. evaluation advisor, nat. adv. bd. dirs. Children's TV Workshop, Ghostwriter, N.Y.C., 1988—. Author: Writing and Computers, 1985; co-author: (computer software) The Personal Media Studio, 1991. Rsch. grantee The Spencer Found., 1983-88, Harvard U., 1989-91, Apple Computer, Inc., 1990. Mem. Am. Ednl. Rsch. Assn., Nat. Coun. Tchrs. English (rsch. grantee 1990—, Promising Rsch. award 1980), Internat. Reading Assn. Office: Harvard U Grad Sch Edn Appion Way Cambridge MA 02138

DAKIN, ARTHUR HAZARD, writer; b. Boston, Jan. 25, 1905; s. Arthur Hazard and Emma Frances (Sahler) D.; A.B., Princeton U., 1928, M.A., 1929, Ph.D., 1933; D. Phil., Oxford U., 1938. Author: Von Hügel and the Supernatural; Man the Measure; chpts. in Audiovisual Aids to Instruction (edited by W. Exton) and The Heritage of Kant (edited by G.T. Whitney and D.F. Bowers); A Paul Elmer More Miscellany; Paul Elmer More. Comdr., USNR ret.; exec. officer U.S. Naval Tng. Sch., Hampton, Va., and officer-in-charge Advance Base Reshipment Depot Battalion, Iroquois Point, Oahu, T.H., World War II. Mem. Am. Philos. Assn., Huguenot Soc., Soc. Colonial Wars, Saint Nicholas Soc. City N.Y., Metaphys. Soc. Am., Phi Beta Kappa. Clubs: Algonquin (Boston); Century, Princeton, University (N.Y.C.). Home: 355 S Pleasant St Amherst MA 01002-2541

DALE, CHARLENE BOOTHE, international health administrator; b. Washington, June 10, 1942; d. John Edward and Frances Elizabeth (Jett) Boothe; children: Cynthia Lee, Anthony John, Jennifer Elizabeth. AA with high honors, Howard Community Coll., 1977; BA magna cum laude, U. Md., 1979. Asst. dir. univ. relations, alumni dir. U. Md., Catonsville, 1977-81; assoc. dir. univ. relations and devel. U. Md., College Park, 1982-83; sr. devel. officer Internat. Ctr. Diarrhoeal Disease Research, Dhaka, Bangladesh, 1984-86; exec. v.p. Internat. Child Health Found., Columbia, Md., 1985—; organizer internat. symposium on food-based oral rehydration therapy Aga Khan U., Pakistan, 1989; cons. to organize symposium oral rehydration therapy Nat. Coun. Internat. Health, Washington, 1987. Editor: Proceedings, Oral Rehydration Therapy Symposia, 1987, 89; contbr. articles to profl. jours. Pub. affairs chmn. United Way, Washington Capital Area, Prince Georges County, 1981-83; pres. Windstream Assn., 198-89; mem. pub. relations com. Md., Del. Cable TV Assn., Balti., 1981-83. Mem. Nat. Council Internat. Health, Am. Pub. Health Assn., AAUW, U. Md. Balti.County Alumni Assn. (bd. dirs. 1979-83), Women's Internat. Pub. Health Network. Democrat. Club: Columbia Assn. Athletic (Md.) (capt. women's traveling racquetball team 1979-83). Home: 10441 Waterfowl Ter Columbia MD 21044-2465 Office: Internat Child Health Found Am City Bldg PO Box 1205 Columbia MD 21044-0205

DALE, DIANNA COCUZZA, university administrator; b. Newark, Feb. 19, 1952; d. Donald Joseph and Anna (Curcione) Cocuzza; m. John Dale Jr., May 31, 1980; children: John III, Jenna Leigh. BA, Curry Coll., 1974; MA, Seton Hall U., 1976. Resident dir. Curry Coll., Milton, Mass., 1976-77; asst. dir. resident living Drexel U., Phila., 1977-85, dir. resident living, 1985—; sec.-treas. Mid-Atlantic Coll. and Univ. Housing Officers, 1985, pres., 1990. Office: Drexel U 101 N 34th St Philadelphia PA

DALE, JAMES ALEXANDER, psychology, educator; b. Toronto, June 6, 1942; came to U.S., 1970; s. Geoffrey Butler and Margaret Alexandra (Cummings) D.; m. Sharon Sitt, Dec. 7, 1979; children: Geoffrey, Peter, Steven, Elliot. BA, Wilfred Laurier U., 1965, BA with honors, 1966; MA in Psychology, U. Waterloo, 1968, PhD in Psychology, 1971. Lic. psychologist, Pa. Sr. teaching asst. Univ. Waterloo, Ont., 1969-70; asst. prof. Allegheny Coll., Meadville, Pa., 1970-77; assoc. prof. Allegheny Coll., Meadville, 1977-84, health professions advisor, 1974-88, prof. psychology, 1984—; vis. fellow Western Australia Inst. Tech., Perth, 1979; vis. scientist Neuropsychiatric Inst. UCLA, Santa Monica, Calif., 1979-80; psychol. fellow anaesthesiology Univ. Va. Med. Sch., Charlottesville, Va., 1987; psychologist Meadville (Pa.) Med. Ctr., 1974-88; pvt. practice Psychology Assocs. of Meadville, 1988—. Contbr. articles to profl. jours. Past pres. Northwestern Pa. Psychol. Assn., Meadville, 1972, Lake Area Health/Edn. Consortium, Erie, Pa., 1985; past commodore Pymatuning Sailing Club, Linesville, Pa., 1983; v.p. Western Pa. Sigma Xi Club, Meadville, 1991. Recipient Ontario fellowship, Ont., 1967. Mem. Am. Psychol. Assn., Soc. for Behavioral Medicine, Soc. for Psychophysiological Rsch., Kiwanis. Home: 477 Cole Dr Meadville PA 16335-1306 Office: Allegheny College Meadville PA 16335

DALE, MADELINE HOUSTON MCWHINNEY, banker; b. Denver, Mar. 11, 1922; d. Leroy and Alice Barse (Houston) McWhinney; m. John Denny Dale, June 23, 1961; 1 son, Thomas Denny. B.A., Smith Coll., 1943; M.B.A. in Fin, NYU, 1947. With Fed. Res. Bank N.Y., 1943-73; pres. First Women's Bank, N.Y.C., 1974-76; vis. lectr. N.Y. U. Grad. Sch. Bus., 1976-77; pres. Dale, Elliott & Co., Inc., N.Y.C., 1977—; dir. Carnegie Corp. N.Y., 1974-82, vice chmn. bd., 1980-82; asst. dir. Whitney Mus. Am. Art, 1983-86; mem. adv. bd. N.Y. U. Grad. Sch. Bus. Adminstrn., 1974-85, U. Denver Grad. Sch. Bus. and Public Adminstrn., 1974-86; dir. Atlantic Energy Inc., 1983—. Adv. bd. Banking Law Jour., 1973-83. Trustee Retirement System

Fed. Res. Banks, 1955-58, Mgrs. Funds, 1983—, Inst. Internat. Edn., 1976—, treas., 1979-85, 88—; bd. dirs. Investor Responsibility Rsch. Ctr., 1975-80, Charles F. Kettering Found., 1975—, chmn., 1987-91; mem. Pres.' Commn. on White House Fellows, 1975-77; bd. govs. Am. Stock Exch., Inc., 1977-81; commr. N.J. Casino Control Commn., 1980-82; mem. adv. com. profl. ethics N.J. Supreme Ct., 1983—; mem. N.J. Com. for Humanities, 1988—. Recipient medal Smith Coll., 1971, Alumni Achievement award N.Y. U., 1971. Mem. Am. Fin. Assn. (dir. 1955-57), Alumni Assn. N.Y. U.-Grads. Bus. Adminstrn. (pres. 1957-59), Money Marketeers (pres. 1960-61), Am. Econ. Assn., Women's Bond Club, Nat. Assn. Bank Women, Fin. Women's Assn., Women's Econ. Round Table (chmn. 1987-88), Soc. Meml. Center, Phi Beta Kappa Assos. Home: PO Box 458 Red Bank NJ 07701-0458

DALE, ROBERT FRANCIS, engineer; b. St. Louis, Apr. 17, 1949; s. Ralph E. and Ruth (Anderson) D. BS in Civil Engring., U. Mo., Rolla, 1971; ME in Civil Engring., Tex. A&M U., 1972. Registered profl. engr., N.J., Mo. Rsch. asst. Tex. Transp. Inst., College Station, 1971-72; asst. traffic engr. N.J. Turnpike Authority, New Brunswick, 1973-77, traffic engr. ops., 1977-83, dir. ops., 1983—. Mem. Nat. Com. on Uniform Traffic Devel., 1990—. Mem. Inst. Transp. Engrs., Am. Soc. Civil Engrs., Am. Soc. safety Engrs., Internat. Bridge, Tunnel and Tpk. Assn., Transp. Rsch. Bd. (chmn. com. on travelers' svcs. 1988-91), Indsl. Fire Chief's Assn., Tau Beta Pi (Acad. award 1971), Chi Epsilon (Acad. award 1971). Office: NJ Turnpike Authority PO Box 1121 New Brunswick NJ 08903-1121

D'ALESSANDRIS, PAUL DAVID, physics educator; b. Baden, Pa., Mar. 31, 1965. BS in Physics, Carnegie Mellon U., 1987; AM in Physics, Harvard U., 1989. Rsch. physicist Lawrence Livermore Nat. Lab., Livermore, Calif., 1985-87; asst. prof. Monroe Community Coll., Rochester, N.Y., 1990—; participant Pa. Gov.'s Sch. for the Scis., Pitts., 1984-85, Applied Physics Summer Inst., Livermore, 1985, NSF Faculty Devel. Workshop, Buffalo, 1991. Recipient grad. fellowship NSF, 1987-89, Andrew Carnegie scholarship Carnegie Mellon U., Pitts., 1987. Office: Monroe Community Coll 1000 E Henrietta Rd Rochester NY 14623-5780

D'ALESSIO, NATALIE MARINO, artist; b. Elizabeth, N.J., July 4, 1951; d. John T. and Stefana (Sarullo) Marino; m. Anthony Paul D'Alessio, Aug. 28, 1968; 1 child, Stephanie Elsbeth. BA, NYU, 1969; postgrad., New Sch., N.Y.C., 1969-72; cert., N.J. Ctr. Visual Arts, 1977. One woman shows include Exxon Corp., Linden, N.J., 1985, Florence Gallery, Dallas, 1985; exhibited in group shows at N.J. State Mus., 1979, Bergen Community Mus., Paramus, N.J., 1980, Nat. Art Club, N.Y.C., 1981, Phila. Port of History Mus., 1984, Lincoln Ctr., N.Y.C., 1983, Cork Art Gallery, N.Y.C., 1983, numerous others; represented in permanent collections Rosalyn Sailor Gallery and Mus. Fine Art, Margate, N.J., Phila.; contbr. illustrations to books; author: (screenplay) The Successor, 1989; illustrator: Art Lovers Cookbook, 1975; producer, dir. video & TV programs. Vol. cons. N.J. Ctr. for Visual Arts, Summit, 1989; trustee TV 36, Communities on Cable, Summit, 1989; judge for sr. citizen art shows, Newark, 1989. Recipient Bee Co. award Pastel Soc. Am., 1981, European Banner of Arts, Accademia d'Europa, 1984, award-artists grant Union County Div. of Art and Cultural Affairs; N.J. state Coun. for Arts grantee Union County Cultural Commn., 1985-86, Lugwig Vogelstein Found. grantee, 1989. Fellow Artists Equity, Women's Caucus for Art, Riker Hill Art Park (exec. com.); mem. N.J. Ctr. Visual Art (award 1979). Home: PO Box 225 Springfield NJ 07081-0225

DALITZKY, MARTHA OKUN, interior designer; b. Springfield, Mass., Aug. 6, 1932; d. Morris and Esther (Chase) Okun; m. Milton Dalitzky, July 4, 1955; children: Scott David, Nancy Beth. BS, U. Mass., 1954. Pres. Studio East Inc., East Longmeadow, Mass., 1963—; chmn. DataPix Pub. Inc., Raleigh, N.C., 1989-90. Designer Solo Showhouse, Am. Cancer Soc., Longmeadow, Mass., 1983; designs shown in various mags. Recipient 1st Prize for Residential Kitchen, DuPont Corian, 1989. Mem. Am. Soc. Interior Designers. Office: Studio East Inc 15 Benton Dr East Longmeadow MA 01028-3111

DALLAS, DONALD EDWARD, JR., marketing executive; b. East Cleveland, Ohio, Sept. 17, 1931; s. Donald Edward and Zella Gwynn (Rogers) D.; m. Marianne Mock, May 25, 1968 (dec. 1981); children: Susan, Benjamin. BS, U. Cin., 1954; postgrad., MIT, 1958-61. Rsch. engr. Ludlow Corp., Needham Heights, Mass., 1961-63; sales rep. J. M. Huber Corp., Westwood, Mass., 1963-69; mktg. mgr. J. M. Huber Corp., Edison, N.J., 1969-73; pres. D.E. Dallas & Assocs. Inc., Balt., Wellesley, Mass., 1972—; mktg. mgr. Allis-Chalmers Corp., West Allis, Wis., 1974-87; pres. Hoult Engring. & Mfg. Co., Wayland, Mass., 1987-88; mktg. mgr. Allis Mineral Systems (formerly Boliden Allis, Inc.), West Allis, Wis., 1987-92; v.p. mktg. and tech. svcs. Electro/Magnetic Solutions, Inc., Denver, 1992—; lectr. mktg. MIT, 1988—. Contbr. articles to profl. jours. With USNR, 1954-64. Mem. ASME, Engrs. Soc. Western Pa.

DALLISON, FRANK KEITH, transportation company executive; b. Montreal, Que., Can., Dec. 20, 1940; s. Leonard and Olga (Schonberg) D.; m. Beverly Ross Cooke, Apr. 23, 1964; children: Heather, Patricia, Karen. Student, McGill U., Montreal, 1959-65. Chartered acct. V.p., gen. mgr. TNT Alltrans, Mississauga, Ont., Can., 1976-87; v.p. Can. Pacific Express, Toronto, Ont., 1987-88; president, chief exec. officer Day and Ross Transp., Hartland, N.B., 1988—; chmn. Day & Ross Inc., St. John's, Nfld., Can., 1988—; bd. dirs. Right-O-Way Inc., Tustin, Calif.; mem. industry adv. forum Transport Can., Ottawa, 1990—. Mem. Can. Inst. Chartered Accts. Home: 1713 Mazo Crescent, Mississauga, ON Canada L5J 1T9

DALLOS, LISA KAY, broadcasting executive; b. N.Y.C., Dec. 25, 1961; d. Robert Emanuel and Carol (Griffenhagen) D. BA in English, Boston U., 1983. Publicity coord. Turner Broadcasting System, Inc., N.Y.C., 1985-87; mgr., pub. rels. Turner Broadcasting System, Inc., Washington, 1987-88, dir. pub. rels., 1988-91, v.p., 1991—; bd. dirs. Cable TV Adminstrn. and Mktg. Soc. Mem. NATAS, Am. Women in Radio and TV. Office: Turner Broadcasting 820 1st St NE Washington DC 20002-4205

D'ALO, FREDERICK ANTHONY, management information systems director; b. Bklyn., Apr. 13, 1949; s. Frederick Dennis and Flavia (Castiglione) D.; m. Linda Rose Portoghese, Apr. 30, 1972; children: Marisa Rose, Allegra Grace. BA, CCNY, 1971; MBA, Baruch Coll., 1978. Systems analyst N.Y.C. Dept. Pers., 1973-87, mgmt. info. systems dir., 1987—; cons. Am. Mgmt. Systems, N.Y.C., 1985; guest lectr. Baruch Coll. Grad. Sch., N.Y.C., 1990; mem. Mcpl. Data Processing Coun., 1987—. Contbr. articles to profl. jours. Active PTA, Oceanside, N.Y., Drug Adv. Coun., Oceanside, 1991. Capt. U.S. Army, 1971-73. Mem. Assn. Computer Trainers.

DALTO, MICHAEL, medical microbiologist; b. N.Y.C., Nov. 19, 1956; s. Cono and Emanuela (Asaro) D. BS, St. John's U., Jamaica, N.Y., 1978, MS, 1982, M in Philosophy, 1986, PhD in Biology, 1989. Cert. of qualification for clin. lab. dir., N.Y.C. Biology dept. technician St. John's U., 1981-82, instr. gifted children program, 1981-88; asst. attending microbiologist Queens Hosp. Ctr., Jamaica, 1989—; adj. faculty mem. Elizabeth Seton Coll., Yonkers, N.Y., 1987-88; substitute tchr. St. John's U., 1988. Capt. United Way Fund, L.I. Jewish affiliation Queens Hosp. Ctr., 1990. Mem. AAAS, Am. Soc. Microbiology (N.Y.C. br.), Am. Soc. for Med. Tech., Am. Soc. for Clin. Pathologists, N.Y. Acad. Sci., Soc. for Indsl. Microbiology, Phi Theta Kappa. Home: 1494 Sweetman Ave Floral Park NY 11003-3012 Office: Queens Hosp Ctr Div Microbiology Bldg H 82-68 168th St Jamaica NY 11432

DALTON, ARTHUR JOSEPH, research administrator; b. Joussard, Alta., Can., June 28, 1936; s. Joseph and Germaine (Fortin) D.; children: Cynthia, Jennifer. BSc, U. Alta., 1957, BA, 1959, MA, 1962; PhD, McMaster U., Hamilton, Ont., Can., 1968. Diplomate Ont. Bd. Examiners in Psychology. Spl. lectr. U. Toronto, Ont., 1969-73, rsch. assoc., 1973-77, assoc. prof., 1983-87; rsch. assoc. Toronto Gen. Hocp., 1976-77; rsch. dir. Surrey Pl. Ctr., Toronto, 1974-87; dep. dir., head aging lab. N.Y. State Inst. for Basic Rsch., N.Y.C., 1986—; pres. Rsch. Innovations Internat., N.Y.C. and Toronto, 1987—; U.S. mktg. mgr. ADL, Inc., Mississauga, Ont., 1991—. Contbr. articles to sci. publs. Co-founder Alzheimer Soc. Can., Toronto, 1977, pres., 1981-84, v.p., 1982-86, bd. dirs., 1982-85; v.p. Neurolog. Diseases Coalition, Toronto, 1983-86. Recipient Ontario Bi-Centennial medal for Community Svc., Premier of Ont., 1984, Cert. of Merit, Ont. Nursing Home Assn., 1985, Founders award Alzheimer Soc. Can., 1986; U.S. Nat. Inst. on Aging rsch. grantee, 1991. Mem. S.I. Alzheimer Assn. (sci. advisor 1990—), N.Y. State Assn. for Retarded Children (cert. 1988), Nassau/Suffolk Alzheimer Assn. (sci. advisor 1990-91, cert. 1987). Office: NY State Inst Basic Rsch 1050 Forest Hill Rd Staten Island NY 10314-6399

DALTON, DANIEL JOSEPH, state official; b. Woodbury, N.J., Aug. 8, 1949; s. William Lawrence and Margaret Mary D.; m. Suzanne Garvey, July 17, 1982; children: Jason, Ryan, Caitlin, William. BA, King's Coll., 1971; MPA, Memphis State U., 1974. Job specialist N.J. Dept. Labor, Woodbury, 1974-75; adminstrv. asst. Rep. James Florio, Washington, 1975-76; grants coord. Hon. James Florio, U.S. Ho. of Reps., Glassboro, N.J., 1976-78; v.p., agt. William Dalton Ins. Agy., Glassboro, 1978-92; mem. N.J. Assembly, 1980-82; mem. N.J. Senate, 1982-92, majority leader, 1990-92. Vol. Peace Corp, Upper Volta, West Africa, 1971; coach basketball St. Mary's Grammar Sch., Williamstown, N.J., 1972-73; com. mem. Democratic County Com., Gloucester County, N.J., 1977; campaign coord. U.S. Senator William Bradley, Gloucester County, 1978. Recipient N.J. Recycling award N.J. Recycling Forum, New Brunswick, 1981, Outstanding Svc. award March of Dimes, N.J., 1983; named State Legislator of Yr., Vietnam Vets. Post 512, Riverside, N.J., 1982, Legislator of Yr., Nat. Energy Jour., N.J., 1982, N.J. Farm Bur., 1989, Senator of Yr. N.J. Coun. of Chs., 1990; recipient Spirit of South Jersey award So. N.J. Devel. Coun., 1992, Environ. Legis. Leadership award N.J. Environ. Fedn., 1992. Democrat. Roman Catholic. Office: NJ Office of Sec of State 125 W State St Ln 300 Trenton NJ 08625-0300

DALTON, PATRICK JAMES, accountant; b. Ogdensburg, N.Y., Feb. 17, 1949; s. Thomas Albert and Eileen M. (Finnin) D.; m. Linda Susan Mayer, Sept. 16, 1972; children: Shawn Adam, Nicholas Aaron, Alicia Eileen, Justin William. BSBA, SUNY, Albany, 1972. Office mgr. Quail Linen Supply Inc., Albany, 1970-74; owner Good Vibrations, Massena, N.Y., 1974-75; asst. mgr. Ames Dept. Store, Massena, 1976-77; v.p., controller Wormuth Bros. Foundry Inc., Athens, N.Y., 1977—. Democrat. Roman Catholic. Home: 62 Patridge St Albany NY 12206

DALTON, THOMAS FRANCIS, funeral director; b. Mineola, N.Y., Oct. 13, 1928; s. Thomas Francis Sr. and Irene Marie (Harper) D.; m. Mary Esther Spedding, June 5, 1951; children: Beth Carol Dalton Costello, Pamela Anne D. Mola. BA, Syracuse U., 1951. Lic. funeral dir., N.Y. Funeral dir. Thomas F. Dalton Funeral Homes, Inc., Floral Park, N.Y., 1954-57; pres., bd. dirs. Thomas F. Dalton Funeral Homes, Inc., Levittown, N.Y., 1957—; bd. dirs. Andromeda, Oyster Bay, N.Y. Pres., bd. dirs. Floral Park Lions, 1968; campaign dir. Town Councilman, Levittown, 1968; bd. dirs. Exch. Club, Levittown, 1970's. Capt. USAF, 1952-54. Recipient Jerusalem award St. Francis Episcopal Ch., 1990. Mem. Levittown C. of C. (bd. dirs., pres. 1975—, Businessman of Yr. 1988), N.Y. State Funeral Dirs. Assn., Am. Legion, K. of C., Kiwanis, Elks. Republican. Roman Catholic. Home: 5 South Rd Oyster Bay NY 11771-1905 Office: Thomas Dalton Funeral Home 2786 Hempstead Tpke Levittown NY 11756-1335

DALY, CHARLES ULICK, foundation executive, investor; b. Dublin, May 29, 1927; came to U.S., 1934, naturalized, 1940; s. Ulick deBurgh and Violet (Sealy-King) D.; m. Mary Larmonth, June 11, 1949 (dec.); children: Michael, Douglas, Charles, Kevin; m. Christine Sullivan, Nov. 11, 1988. B.A. Internat. Relations, Yale U., 1949; M.S. Journalism, Columbia U., 1959. Mgr. then v.p. Mexican subs. Pacific Molases Co., San Francisco, 1949-50, 52-58; congl. fellow Am. Polit. Sci. Assn., 1959-60; editor Stanford U., Calif., 1961; staff asst. Pres. Kennedy and Pres. Johnson, 1962-64; v.p. pub. affairs U. Chgo., 1964-67, v.p. devel. and pub. affairs, 1967-71; v.p. govt. and communtiy affairs Harvard U., Cambridge, Mass., 1971-76; editor Media and the Cities, The Quality of Inequality, Urban Violence; pres. Joyce Found., Chgo., 1978-86; dir. John F. Kennedy Libr., Boston, 1988—; mem. Lloyd's of London, 1977—; free lance writer, 1958—. Mem. Commn. on Admistrv. Rev., U.S. Ho. of Reps.; chmn. Donor's Forum, Chgo., 1980; bd. dirs. Joint Ctr. for Polit. Studies, Washington, Santa Fe Inst., Am. Ireland Fund, Southwest Voter Rsch. Inst., San Antonio. With USNR, 1945-46; USMCR, 1950-52. Decorated Silver Star, Purple Heart. Mem. Chgo. Club, Bantry Golf Club (Ireland), St. Botolph Club (Boston), Hibernian Club (Dublin). Office: John F Kennedy Libr Columbia Point Dorchester MA 02125

DALY, DENNIS FRANCIS, city officer; b. Salem, Mass., Apr. 19, 1948; s. Richard Edward and Louise (McCarthy) D.; m. Joanne M. Maciejewska, Nov. 19, 1977; children: Jennifer, Karen, Colleen, Patrick. BS in Acctg., Boston Coll., 1970; MA in English Lit., Northea. U., 1975. Freelance writer, 1975—; laborer Gen. Electric Co., Lynn, Mass., 1980-87; steward Internat. Union Elec. Workers Local 201, Lynn, 1985-87, union leader, 1987-89; purchasing agt., chief procurement officer City of Salem, 1990—. Mng. editor Elec. Union News, 1987-89; pub., editor North Shore Union Leader, 1989—; contr. articles, poetry to various jours., newspapers; translator play. Democrat. Roman Catholic. Home: 41 Appleton St Salem MA 01970-1627 Office: City of Salem City Hall Salem MA 01970

DALY, T(HOMAS) F(RANCIS) GILROY, federal judge; b. N.Y.C., Feb. 25, 1931; s. Paul Gerard and Madeleine (Mulqueen) D.; m. Stuart Stetson, Jan. 16, 1960; children: Timothy Francis Gilroy, Matthew M., Loan, Anna L. B.A., Georgetown U., 1952; LL.B., Yale U., 1957. Bar: Conn. bar 1957, N.Y. bar 1959. Assoc. Simpson Thacher and Bartlett, N.Y.C., 1957-61; asst. U.S. atty. U.S. Dept. Justice, So. Dist. of N.Y., 1961-64; pvt. practice Fairfield, 1964-77; dept. atty. gen. State of Conn., 1967-71; spl. asst. to atty. gen. State of Conn., Conn., 1971-75; dep. state treas. State of Conn., 1976-77, ins. commr., 1975-76; judge U.S. Dist. Ct., Conn., 1977—; chief judge U.S. Dist. Ct. Conn., Bridgeport, 1983-88, mem. subcommittee on supporting personnel, 1983-87, mem. subcommittee jud. stats. and resources com. jud. conf., 1987—. Trustee Leukemia Soc. Am., chmn., 1971; 1st lt. Rangers, U.S. Army, 1952-54. Recipient Disting. Svc. award Fairfield Jr. C. of C., 1967. Mem. Am., Conn., Fed. bar assns., Assn. of Bar of City of N.Y., Am. Judicature Soc., Fed. Bar Coun., Am. Legion, Phi Delta Phi. Democrat. Roman Catholic. Office: US Dist Ct 915 Lafayette Blvd Bridgeport CT 06604-4706

DAMAN, HARLAN RICHARD, allergist; b. N.Y.C., Nov. 1, 1941; s. D. Leon and Frances (Weissler) D.; AB cum laude, Harvard U., 1963; MD, Albert Einstein Coll. Medicine, 1967. Diplomate Am. Bd. Pediatrics, Am. Bd. Allergy and Immunology. Intern, then resident Yale-New Haven Hosp./Med. Ctr., 1967-69; fellow in allergy and clin. immunology Nat. Jewish Hosp. Research Ctr./U. Colo. Med. Ctr., Denver, 1971-73, instr., 1974-81; clin. asst. prof. pediatrics Albert Einstein Coll. Medicine, N.Y.C., 1981—; dir. pediatric allergy clinic Bronx Mcpl. Hosp. Ctr., 1982-92; mem. Med. Ctr./Sch. Medicine, 1976-90. Co-editor: Psychobiologic Aspects of Allergic Disorders, 1986; contbr. chpt. to Outpatient Medicine, 1980; contbr. articles on pulmonary function testing in asthmatic disorders. Served to maj. M.C., USAF, 1969-71. Fellow Am. Acad. Pediatrics, Am. Coll. Allergists, Am. Coll. Chest Physicians, Am. Acad. Allergy; mem. N.Y. Allergy Soc., Westchester Allergy Soc. (ednl. program dir. 1978-89, treas. 1980-81, pres. 1982-83), Westchester Acad. Medicine. Office: 769 Kimball Ave Yonkers NY 10704-1598

D'AMATO, ALFONSE M., senator; b. Bklyn., Aug. 1, 1937; m. Penelope Ann Collenburg, 1960; children: Lisa, Lorraine, Daniel, Christopher. B.S., Syracuse U., 1959, J.D., 1961. Bar: N.Y. 1962. Adminstr. Nassau County, N.Y., 1965-68; receiver of taxes Town of Hempstead, L.I., 1971-77, presiding supr., vice chmn. County bd. suprs., 1977-80; U.S. senator from N.Y., 1980—; mem. various subcoms. Appropriations Com., Banking, Housing and Urban Affairs Com., Select Com. on Intelligence; co-chmn. Senate Caucus on Internat. Narcotics Control, 1987—; chmn. Internat. Commn. on Security and Cooperation in Europe; mem. Helsinki Commn.; founder, co-chmn. Senate Anti-Terrorism Caucus. Mem. Island Park Vol. Fire Dept. Republican. Roman Catholic. Clubs: K.C., Lions, Sons of Italy.

D'AMATO, ANTHONY S., food products company executive; b. Brooklyn, N.Y., 1930. BSChemE, Poly. Inst. of Brooklyn, 1952. With Borden, Inc., N.Y.C., 1959—, exec. v.p., from 1985; pres. Borden Packaging and Indl. Products (officer Borden Chem. Div.), Columbus, Ohio, from 1985; chmn., chief exec. officer Borden Packaging and Indl. Products (formerly Borden Chem. Div.), Columbus, until 1990; pres. Borden, Inc., N.Y.C., 1990—, CEO, 1991—, chmn. bd., 1992—. Office: Borden Inc 180 E Broad St Columbus OH 43215-3707*

D'AMATO, MICHAEL ANGELO, management consultant; b. Waukesha, Wis., Dec. 21, 1953; s. Lawrence Samuel and Ione (Husman) D'A.; m. Susan Gail McIntosh, Oct. 8, 1978; children: Katherine, Laura, Alexander. BS, MIT, 1975; MBA, Harvard U., 1977. Cons. Bain & Co., Boston, 1977-80, mgr., 1980-82, ptnr., 1982-85, v.p., 1985-92, dir., 1992—. Baker scholar, 1977. Mem. Tau Beta Pi, Pi Tau Sigma. Presbyterian. Home: 1753 Wexford Way Vienna VA 22182-2151 Office: Bain & Co 20 Copley Pl Boston MA 02117-0897

D'AMATO, ROSEMARY, interior designer, lighting designer; b. Norwalk, Conn., Mar. 3, 1956; d. Joseph Peter and Eleanor (Atanas) D'A. BFA, N.Y. Sch. Interior Design, N.Y.C., 1978. Lic. interior designer, Conn. Designers asst. Ralph Kuhn Interiors, Greenwich, Conn., 1976-78; interior designer Ethan Allen Nat. Hdqrs., Danbury, Conn., 1978-81; lighting designer Alfred Scholz Assocs., New Canaan, Conn., 1981-83; tchr. Parsons Sch. Design, N.Y.C., 1990-91; pres., owner RD Designs, Greenwich, 1983—. Mem. Nat. Assn. Women in Constrn. (dir. 1989—, Career Day chair 1990-91), Ptnrs. in Progress, Am. Soc. Interior Designers (assoc.), Allied Bd. Trade, NAFE, Entrepreneurial Women's Network. Office: RD Designs 55 Old Field Point Rd Greenwich CT 06830-6149

D'AMBOISE, CHRISTOPHER, ballet dancer, artistic director, choreographer; b. N.Y.C., Feb. 4, 1960; s. Jacques and Carolyn (George) d'A. Mem. co. N.Y.C. Ballet, 1978—; artistic dir. Pa. Ballet, 1990—. Debut in The Nutcracker, appearances also include Stars and Stripes, Four Temperaments, Mozartiana, Tango, Interplay, Fancy Free, Dancers at a Gathering, Piano Pieces, The Gershwin Concerto, On Your Toes, Song and Dance; author: Leap Year: A Year in the Life of a Dancer, 1982. Office: Richard Boehm Agy 737 Park Ave New York NY 10021 also: Pa Ballet 1101 S Broad St Philadelphia PA 19147*

D'AMBROSIO, JOSEPH ANTHONY, dentist; b. Bklyn., May 20, 1954; s. Joseph and Rose (Ambrosio) D'A. BA, Columbia U., 1976; DDS, SUNY, Buffalo, 1980, MS, 1986. Diplomate Am. Bd. Oral Medicine. Coord. dental residency Erie County Med. Ctr., Buffalo, 1981-87; asst. prof. dentistry SUNY, Buffalo, 1983-87; vice chmn. dentistry Michael Reese Hosp./Med. Ctr., Chgo., 1987-89; asst. prof. dental medicine U. Conn., Farmington, 1989—, dir. grad. oral medicine, 1991—; attending staff John Dempsey Hosp.; cons. ADA, Chgo., 1988—. Editorial rev. bd. Oral Surgery, Oral Pathology, Oral Medicine Jour., St. Louis, 1988—; contbr. articles to sci. publs. Mem. ADA, Am. Acad. Oral Medicine, Am. Assn. Hosp. Dentists (newsletter editor), Orgn. Tchrs. Oral Diagnosis (pres. 1992), Am. Assn. Dental Schs., Omicron Kappa Upsilon. Office: Univ Conn Health Ctr 263 Farmington Ave Farmington CT 06030-1605

DAME, SAMUEL, booking agency executive; b. Lynn, Mass., Oct. 13, 1917; s. Louis and Dora (Dubrow) D.; m. Corinne K. Dame, June 29, 1947; children: Evan, Douglas. BS in Bus. Adminstrn., Boston U., 1940. Office mgr., salesman Marshard Music and Vaughn Monroe Prodns., Boston, 1946-53; pres. Lordly & Dame, Inc., Boston, 1954—. Served to lt. col. U.S. Army, 1942-46. Fellow Meeting Planners Internat. (bd. dirs. 1977-80); mem. Internat Group Agts. and Burs. (bd. govs. 1985-87), Am. Soc. of Assn. Execs. Republican. Jewish. Lodge: Masons. Home: 75 Cambridge Pky Cambridge MA 02142-1237 Office: Lordly & Dame Inc 51 Church St Boston MA 02116-5417

DAME, WILLIAM PAGE, III, banker; b. Balt., July 6, 1940; s. William Page and Harriet Carrington (Brent) D.; m. Laura Jacqueline Cordier, June 28, 1968 (div. 1975); children: William Page IV, Laura Alexandra. BA, U. Va., 1963. Ofcl. asst., asst. treas. Bankers Trust Co., N.Y.C., 1963-68; dep. rep. Bankers Trust Co., Tokyo, 1968-70; asst. treas. Bankers Trust Co., N.Y.C., 1970-71; asst. v.p. Franklin Nat. Bank, N.Y.C., 1971-72; regional rep. Franklin Nat. Bank, Singapore, 1972-74; v.p. Riggs Nat. Bank, Washington, 1974-76; v.p. Security Pacific Nat. Bank, L.A., 1976-77, San Francisco, 1977-79, Sydney, Australia, 1979-80; v.p. J. Henry Schroder Bank and Trust Co., N.Y.C., 1981-82; sr. v.p. Palmer Nat. Bank, Washington, 1982-84; v.p. Sovran Bank, Arlington, Va., 1985-86; chief fin. officer DITT, Inc. subs. Electricité de France, Washington, 1986-88; v.p. Am. Security Bank, Washington, 1988-91; internat. fin. cons. Washington, 1991—. Mem. Washington Internat. Trade Assn., Am. Bus. Coun.-Singapore (founding mem.), World Affairs Coun., Asia Soc., Old Asian Hands Soc., BT Alumni Assn., The Soc. of the Cin., North Hatley Canoe Club, Tanglin Club, Singapore Cricket Club. Republican. Episcopalian. Home: 1308 21st St NW Washington DC 20036-1508 Office: 1828 L St NW Ste 600 Washington DC 20036-5183

DAMESHEK, H(AROLD) LEE, physician; b. Balt., Mar. 16, 1937; s. Samuel and Rose (Rudick) D.; m. Michelle Zubasic, Sept. 12, 1965; children: Lynne R. Shine, Amy, David, Deborah. BS in Chemistry, Franklin and Marshall Coll., 1959; MD, Tufts U., 1963. Diplomate Am. Bd. Internal Medicine. Intern Presbyn.-Univ. Hosp., Pitts., 1963-64, resident in internal medicine, 1966-68; hematology fellow Ohio State U. Hosp., Columbus, 1968-69; practice medicine specializing in hematology and oncology Pitts., 1969—; clin. instr. medicine U. Pitts., 1969-74, clin. asst. prof., 1974-81, clin. assoc. prof., 1981—; instr. West Penn Hosp., Pitts., 1969-77; chmn. cancer com. Presbyn.-Univ. Hsop., 1980—; cons. various hosps.; bd. dirs. Physicians' Healthg Plan Pa., 1986—. Contbr. articles to med. jours. Bd. dirs. Leukemia Soc. West Pa., 1971—, v.p., 1977-79, Am. Cancer Soc.; treas. Presbyn.-Univ. Hosp., 1984-86, v.p., 1986-88, pres. med. staff, 1988-90; mem. med. adv. com. Cancer Support Ctr., 1987—. Capt. U.S. Army, 1964-66. Fellow ACP; mem. AMA, Am. Soc. Hematology, Allegheny County Med. Soc. (treas. 1980-81, v.p. 1982, pres. 1984, bd. dirs. 1985—, peer rev. bd. 1991, Frederick Jacob award 1988), Pa. Med. Soc., Pitts. Acad. Medicine (treas. 1981—), Westmoreland Country Club (sec., bd. dirs. 1987-89), Univ. Club (Pitts.). Home: 421 Radcliffe Dr Pittsburgh PA 15235 Office: 3471 Fifth Ave Pittsburgh PA 15213

D'AMICO, MARY BARBARA, nurse; b. Hope, Kans., Dec. 19, 1940; d. James Vincent Mullin and Rosyln Beverly (Page) McFarland; m. Vincent Mario D'Amico, Aug. 26, 1967; children: Michael Anthony, Matthew Morris. BS, Grove City Coll., 1962; MS in Nursing, N.Y. Med. Coll. Grad. Sch., 1966, MS in Neurol. Nursing, 1969. Sci. tchr. Peace Corps, Sierra Leone, West Africa, 1962-63; rsch. asst. Metabolic Rsch. Ctr./Highland Hosp., Oakland, Calif., 1963-64; med.-surgical nurse Georgetown U. Hosp./Mt. Sinai Hosp., Washington and N.Y.C., 1966-67; clin. instr. N.Y. Med. Coll. Grad. Sch. of Nursing, 1967-68; clin. specialist in neurosurg. Met. Hosp., N.Y.C., 1969-73; instr. Grad. Sch. of Nursing/Pace U., Pleasantville, N.Y., 1973-74, 76-77. Editor/author: (procedure book) Metropolitan Hospital Nursing Procedures, 1971. Bd. dirs., sec. United Way of Greater White Plains, N.Y., 1988-91; pres. beautification com. Elmsford (N.Y.) Beautification Com., 1989-92; bd. dirs. Westchester's Tchr.'s Ctr., Hartsdale, N.Y., 1988-92; pres. Greenburgh Cen. Sch. Dist. PTA, Hartsdale, 1992. Mem. N.Y. Acad. Sci., N.Y. Zool. Soc. Home: 14 Crescent Dr Elmsford NY 10523

DAMICO, NICHOLAS PETER, lawyer; b. Chester, Pa., June 29, 1937; s. Ralph A. and Mary C. (Ametrane) D.; m. Patricia Ann Swatek, Aug. 26, 1967; children—Christine, Gregory. B.S. in Acctg. St. Joseph's U. 1960, LL.B., U. Pa., 1963; LL.M., Georgetown U., 1967. Bar: Pa. 1963, D.C. 1967, Md. 1986. Tax law specialist IRS, Washington, 1963-66; assoc. Silverstein and Mullens, Washington, 1966-72, ptnr. 1972-76; prin. Damico & Assocs., Washington, 1976—; adj. prof. Georgetown U. Law Ctr., Washington, 1973-75. Mem. ABA, Fed. Bar Assn. Author: Qualified Plans-Taxation of Distributions, Tax Management Portfolio, 1978. Office: 1225 I St NW Ste 1050 Washington DC 20005-3946

D'AMICO, THOMAS F., economist, educator; b. N.Y.C., Aug. 20, 1948; s. Lawrence J. and Anita (Mingione) D'A.; m. Franca Paola Paniccia, Sept. 1970; children: Diana Christina, Gina Maria. BA, Fordham Coll., 1970; MA, NYU, 1979, MPhil, 1981, PhD, 1983. Econ. analyst Con Edison, N.Y.C., 1970-72; program dir. East Harlem Community Corp., N.Y.C.,

1972-75; instr. St. Peter's Coll., Jersey City, N.J., 1975-78, from assoc. prof. to prof. econs., 1981—, chair dept. econs., 1989—; asst. prof. Manhattan Coll., Riverdale, N.Y., 1978-81; cons. various pvt. firms and non-profit agys., N.Y. Met. area, 1975—. Author: The Economics of Market and Non-Market Racial Discrimination, 1983; contbr. articles to scholarly jours.; referee various scholarly jours. Mem. AAUP, Am. Econ. Assn., Ea. Econ. Assn., Assn. Social Econs. Roman Catholic. Office: St Peter's Coll Dept Econs Jersey City NJ 07306

DAMJANOV, IVAN, pathologist; b. Subotica, Yugoslavia, Mar. 31, 1941; came to U.S., 1967; s. Milenko and Ana (Pavkovic) D.; m. Andrea Zivanovic, Jan. 18, 1964; children: Nevena, Ivana, Milena. MD, U. Zagreb (Yugoslavia), 1964, PhD, 1971. Lic. physician, Yugoslavia; diplomate Am. Bd. Pathology. Intern Gen. Hosp., Zagreb, Yugoslavia, 1964-65; resident in pathology U. Zagreb, 1966-67; intern in pathology Cleve. Met. Gen. Hosp., Cleve., Phila., 1967-68; resident in pathology Mt. Sinai Hosp., N.Y.C., 1968-69; asst. in pathology U. Zagreb, 1969-71; postdoctoral fellow Fels Rsch. Inst., Temple U., Phila., 1971-72; asst. prof. pathology U. Zagreb, 1972-73; from asst. prof. to assoc. prof. U. Conn., Farmington, 1973-77; from assoc. prof. to prof. Hahnemann Med. Coll. and Hosp., Phila., 1977-86; prof. pathology Jefferson Med. Coll. of Thomas Jefferson U., Phila., 1986—; cons. pathologist VA Hosp., Newington, Conn., 1975-77, Cancer Info. Dissemination and Analysis Ctr. for Virology, Immunology and Cancer-Related Biology, Franklin Inst., Phila., 1977-82; mem. group for rsch. in pathology edn. U. Iowa, 1977-82; ad hoc reviewer, mem. site vis. teams and study sects. NIH, Bethesda, Md., 1978—; mem. basic sci. merit award bd. VA, 1989-92. Editorial bd. Ultrastructural Pathology, 1985—, Virchows Archiv A, 1986—, In Vivo, 1988—, Hosp. Physician, 1990—, Human Pathology, 1991—; assoc. editor Lab. Investigation, 1982—; regional editor for North Am. Differentiation, 1985—. Recipient Christian R. and Mary F. Lindback award for disting. teaching Jefferson Med. Coll., Phila., 1988. Mem. Am. Assn. Pathologists, Am. Assn. for Cancer Rsch., Internat. Acad. Pathology, Internat. Soc. Differentiation, Developmental Biology Soc., Am. Soc. for Cell Biology. Home: 129 Edgewood Rd Ardmore PA 19003-2507 Office: Thomas Jefferson U 1025 Walnut St Philadelphia PA 19107-5083

DAMMINGER, MARYANNE MARGARET, food products executive; b. Camden, N.J., Sept. 7, 1949; d. Bernard Vincent and Margaret Elizabeth (Shields) Houlihan; m. George Logan Damminger Jr., Aug. 12, 1972; children: George L. III, Elizabeth Ann, Christopher Louis. Clk. typist The Bank of N.J., Camden, 1967-71; payroll clk. Campbell Soup Co., Camden, 1971-79, sr. lead clk., 1979-80, payroll supr., 1980-89, payroll mgr., 1989-92, project mgr. human resources info. system, 1992—. Treas. St. Mary's PTA, Gloucester, N.J., 1983, 84. Mem. NAFE, Am. Payroll Assn., Northeastern Users Payroll Pers., N.J. Users Payroll Pers. Home: Rt 2 Box 257 Thorofare NJ 08086 Office: Campbell Soup Co Campbell Pl Camden NJ 08103

D'AMORE, VICTOR, director, choreographer, dance educator; b. Bronx, N.Y., May 31, 1943; s. Victor and Angela (Cavolina) D.; m. Donna Marie Apple, Oct. 12, 1968. B.A., Adelphi U., 1976. Pres., Vic D'Amore Studio Dance, Deer Park, Coram, Patchogue, N.Y., 1976—. Dir./choreographer 60 mus. comedy prodns.; choreographer 5 ballets, 200 short works. Served to sgt. U.S. Army, 1964-68. Mem. Soc. Stage Dirs. and Choreographers, Dance Masters Am. (bd. dirs.), Dance Educators Am. (bd. dirs.), Brookhaven Theatre Dance Guild (v.p.). Roman Catholic. Home: 41 Roosevelt Blvd Hauppauge NY 11788-4436 Office: Vic D'Amore Studio of Dance 721 Acorn St Deer Park NY 11729-3202 also: 30 Grove Ave Patchogue NY 11772

D'AMOUR, CLAIRE MARIE, marketing professional; b. Holyoke, Mass., Aug. 13, 1956; d. Gerald Emil and Jeanne Eva (Fontaine) D'A. BA, U. Mass., 1978. Dir. advt. Big Y Foods, Inc., Springfield, Mass., 1978-85, v.p. advt. and media ops., 1981—, v.p. advt. and pub. rels., 1985-89, v.p. mktg., 1989-91; v.p. corp. affairs Big Y Foods, Inc., Springfield, 1991—; bd. dirs. Multibank West, Pittsfield, Mass.; adj. instr. bus. Bay Path Coll., Longmeadow, Mass. Bd. dirs. ARC, Springfield, 1989—, United Way, Pioneer Valley, Springfield, 1988-91, Pvt. Industry Coun./Regional Employment bd., Mercy Hosp., Springfield, 1988—, Mass. Easter Seal Soc. 1991—, Springfield Coll., 1992—; corporator MacDuffie Sch. Brightside for Families and Children, West Springfield, Mass.; chmn. Easter Seals Telethon, We. Mass., 1990,'91, '92. Mem. Advt. Club Western Mass., Greater Hartford Ad Club, Rotary Club Springfield, Greater Springfield C. of C. Office: Big Y Foods Inc PO Box 7840 280 Chestnut St Springfield MA 01104

DAMPIER, FREDERICK WALTER, electrochemist; b. Winnipeg, Manitoba, Can., Oct. 1, 1941; s. Walter Lloyd and Helen (Kram) D. BS in Chemistry, U. Manitoba, Winnipeg, Can., 1962; MS in Chemistry, Rensselaer Poly. Inst., 1964, PhD in Phys. Chemistry, 1968. Postdoctoral fellow U. Calif., Berkeley, 1968-70; sr. scientist ESB Inc., Yardley, Pa., 1970-75, EIC, Inc., Newton, Mass., 1975-78; tech. staff GTE Labs., Waltham, Mass., 1978-86; program mgr. secondary battery GTE Govt. Systems, Waltham, Mass., 1986-88; pres. Lithium Energy Assocs., Inc., Watertown, Mass., 1988—. Patentee in field; contbr. 12 sci. papers to profl. jours. Mem. Am. Chem. Soc., Electrochem. Soc. Office: Lithium Energy Assocs Inc 225 Crescent St Waltham MA 02154

DAMUCK, WALTER EDWARD, JR., sales executive; b. New Haven, Aug. 22, 1949; s. Walter Edward and Laura Mary (Mantilia) D.; m. Christine M. Anderson, June 18, 1972 (div. mar. 1978); m. Sandra Lou Weigh, Apr. 21, 1979 (div. Nov. 1987); m. Patricia Ann Flynn, Oct. 14, 1989. BS in Physics, Lehigh U., 1972; MBA, U. New Haven, 1983. Applications engr. Veeder-Root Co., Hartford, Conn., 1979-80, supr. mktg., 1980-82, product mgr., 1983-85; nat. sales mgr. EOTec div. 3M, West Haven, Conn., 1985-87, Baumer Electric Co., Southington, Conn., 1987—; speaker Instrument Soc. Am., Research Triangle Park, N.C., 1980-85. Contbr. articles to popular mags. Recipient Leadership Dynamics and Personal Dynamics award U.S. Jaycees, 1976. Mem. Conn. Marine Model Soc., Soc. Am. Magicians, Sigma Alpha Mu. Office: Baumer Electric Co 122 Spring St Southington CT 06489

DANA, F(RANK) MITCHELL, theatrical lighting designer; b. Washington, Nov. 14, 1942; s. John Daskum Mitchell and Elizabeth Francis (Woods) D.; m. Wendy Karen Bensinger, Dec. 31, 1967; children: Scott Cameron, Ian Michael. B.F.A., Utah State U., 1964; M.F.A., Yale U., 1967. Asst. to Jo Mielziner N.Y.C., 1968-69; tech. dir. Yale Drama Sch., New Haven, Conn., 1970-71; assoc. lighting dir. Ferd Manning, N.Y.C., 1978—; guest lectr. U. Wash., So. Meth. U., San Francisco State U.; lectr. Rutgers U., 1982—. Prodn. mgr.: Stratford Festival, Pitts. Civic Light Opera; prodn. supr. Yale Repertory Theatre; lighting designer: Broadway Plays include The Freedom of the City, 1974, Once in a Lifetime, 1978, Inspector General, 1978, Man and Superman, 1978, The Suicide, 1980 (Drama Logue award), Mass Appeal, 1981, Monday After the Miracle, 1982, The Babe, 1984, Oh Coward, 1986; off-Broadway Plays include Three Acts of Recognition, 1982, A Coupla White Chicks, 1980, Mass Appeal, 1980, Oh Coward, 1981, Calling in Crazy, 1969, Songs My Mother Never Sang Me, 1982, Husbandry, 1984, A Hell of a Town, 1984, The Ninth Step, 1984, Daughters, 1986, Cold Sweat, 1988, Other People's Money, 1989, King Fish, 1991; operas Turandot, Royal Opera, Covent Garden, 1984, La Rondine, N.Y.C. Opera, 1984, Magic Flute, 1985, Merry Widow, 1986, Cleve. Symphony, 1985, Harriet, The Woman Called Moses, Un Ballo in Maschera Va. Opera, 1985, Mikado, Marriage of Figaro, 1989, Don Giovanni, Die Fledermaus, 1990, Falstaff Abductum From the Seraglio, 1991, June Opera Assn, Falstaff, Abduction From The Seraglio, 1991, Turandot, Wembly Arena, Carmen. L.A. Opera, Carmen for L.A. Opera and Seville Expo92, La Traviata for Barcelona Opera, 1992; also Pitts. Civic Light Opera, 1973-74, 79, 84-87; tours Hello Dolly, 1981, Mass Appeal, 1982, Guys and Dolls, 1984, George M., Jesus Christ Superstar, 1985, Stop the World, 1986, Other People's Money, Okla., 1990; regional theaters Am. Conservatory Theatre, 1972-80, BAM Theatre Co., 1977, 78, 80, 81, Goodman Theatre, 1973-82, McCarter Theatre, 1969-71, 82, 86-90, Nat. Arts Ctr., Ottawa, 1982-84, others including Mark Taper Forum, Phila. Drama Guild, Va. Mus. Theatre, Geva Theater, Folger Theater, Hartford Stage Festival, Ala. Shakespeare Co., Cin. Playhouse, Syracuse Stage, 1984, 87, Seattle Repertory, Stratford Shakespeare Festival, Studio Arena Theatre, Roundabout Theatre, 1987, 88. Mem. Internat. Alliance Theatrical Stage Employees, United Scenic Artists (trustee 1970-72). Republican. Office: 221 W 82nd St New York NY 10024-5406

DANAHAR, DAVID C., university dean, history educator; b. Dobbs Ferry, N.Y., Sept. 29, 1941; s. Walter Vincent and Catherine Marie (Charles) D.; m. Cecelia Upritchard, Aug. 24, 1985; children: Deirdre Modesta, Rebecca Rima. BA, Manhattan Coll., Bronx, N.Y., 1963; MA, U. Mass., 1965, PhD, 1970. Instr. U. Mass., Amherst, 1969-70; asst. prof. SUNY, Oswego, 1970-73, assoc. prof., 1973-83, prof., 1983-85; dean Coll. Arts and Scis., prof. history Fairfield (Conn.) U., 1985—; vis. prof. U. Pisa, Italy, 1971-72. Contbr. articles on Habsburg and Austrian history to profl. jours. Mem. Fairfield County Regional Planning Com., 1987-89. Univ. fellow U. Mass., 1966-69, rsch. fellow Am. Coun. Learned Socs., 1975-76; grantee SUNY Rsch. Found., 1971-73, NEH, 1983-88, also numerous others from founds. and corps., including Ford Found., Mellon Found., Keck Found., IBM, GE, 1985—. Mem. Am. Hist. Assn., Am. Conf. Acad. Deans, Coun. Colls. Arts and Scis., Conf. on Cen. European History. Office: Fairfield U N Benson Rd # 101 Fairfield CT 06430-5152

DANATOS, MICHAEL ROSS, data processor; b. Jersey City, Apr. 30, 1954; s. Steven and Catherine Lillian (Clark) D.; m. Cathleen Ann Martineau, June 30, 1990. BS, Montclair State Coll., Upper Montclair, N.J., 1982; MBA, Fairleigh Dickinson U., 1989. Cert paralegal ABA. Graphic arts cons. DBS, Lodi, N.J., 1978-80; supr. computer photo-typesetting Pub.'s Phototype Inc., Carlstadt, N.J., 1980-83; adminstr. corp. local area networks J.M. Huber Corp., Edison, N.J., 1983-89; mgr. local area network systems support Automatic Data Processing, Roseland, N.J., 1989—. With USAF, 1975-78. Mem. Microcomputer Mgrs. Assn., Aircraft Owners and Pilots Assn., Outward Bound Alumni Assn., Nat. Trust Historic Preservation, Smithsonian Assocs., Am. Mus. Natural History. Roman Catholic. Home: 36 Stratford Rd East Brunswick NJ 08816-2022 Office: Automatic Data Processing 1 A D P Blvd Roseland NJ 07068-1728

DANBERG, JAMES E(DWARD), aerospace engineer, educator; b. Wallingford, Conn., Oct. 13, 1927; s. August Edward and Loretto Margaret (Kennedy) D.; m. Mary Alouise Conlon, June 6, 1953; children: James Edward Jr., Mary Paula Wylie, Mark Edward, Karen Margaret Chase, Carl Christian. B in Aero. Engring., Cath. U. Am., 1949, M in Aero. Engring., 1952, D in Mech. Engring., 1964. Aero. devel. engr. tech. evaluation dept. U.S. Naval Ordnance Lab., Silver Spring, Md., 1951-55, aero. rsch. engr. aerophysics div., 1956-60, chief hypersonics group aerophysics div., 1960-62; aerospace technologist rsch. div. Office Advanced Rsch. & Tech., NASA Hdqrs., Washington, 1962-67, chief fluid physics br. rsch. div., 1967; assoc. prof. mech. and aerospace engring. dept. U. Del., Newark, 1967-72, assoc. dean engring. Coll. of Engring., 1969-72, prof. mech. and aerospace engring. dept., 1972-85, acting chmn. mech. and aerospace engring. dept., 1979-80; aerospace engr. launch and flight div. U.S. Army Ballistic Rsch. Lab., Aberdeen Proving Ground, Md., 1985—; cons. U.S. Army Ballistic Rsch. Lab., 1967-85, Thiokol Chem. Corp., Elkton, Md., 1969-70, NASA/Langley Rsch. Ctr., Hampton, Va., 1978, ILC Dover, Inc., Frederica, Del., 1984-85, Dyna Structures, Inc., Phila., 1983. Contbr. articles to profl. jours. Fellow AIAA (assoc.); mem. Sigma Xi. Office: US Army Ballistic Rsch Lab Aberdeen MD 21005-5001

DANBURY, RICHARD S., III See OLMSTED, ROBERT WALSH

DANCE, JAMES WALTER, management consultant; b. New Castle, Pa., Apr. 12, 1951; s. Walter Strayer and Evelyn Frances (McGrath) D.; m. Patricia Lynn Grassi, May 26, 1973; children: Caitlin Ann, Christine Kanella. Student, Mohawk Valley Community Coll., 1969-71, SUNY, Cortland, 1971-73. Media programmer SUNY at Cortland, N.Y., 1973-78; bus. owner Crown Graphics/Frame Shop, Cortland, 1978-83; account exec. WKRT/WOKW, Cortland, 1983-87; sales mgr. WNDR/WNTQ, Syracuse, N.Y., 1987-89; gen. sales mgr. WNYP, Cortland, 1989-90; mgmt. cons., pres., founder The Walter Strayer Group, Cortland, 1990—; speaker Speakers U.S.A., Pigeon Forge, Tenn., 1990—; assoc. Carlson Learning Co., Mpls., 1991—; distbr. TTI Mgmt. Software, Phoenix, 1991—; presenter in field. Author: The Great Sales Meeting System, 1990, How To Get the Most Out of Sales Meetings, 1991; contbr. articles to profl. jours. Group leader Coll. Student Outreach Program, Cortland, 1987-91; 2nd chair horn Community Orch., Cortland, 1988—. Mem. Greater Syracuse C. of C. Home: 31 Cedar St Cortland NY 13045-3005 Office: The Walter Strayer Group PO Box 5635 Cortland NY 13045-5635

DANDO, GEORGE WILLIAM, professional association executive; b. Balt., May 24, 1935; s. Llewellyn Stewart and Mariester (Anderson) D.; m. Diane Mills, Sept. 1, 1976; 1 child, Ross Stewart. BA, Baylor U., 1960; MDiv, Pitts. Theol. Sem., 1963. Ordained to ministry Presbytery of New Castle, 1963. Pastor 1st Presbyn. Ch., Greenfield, Iowa, 1963-65; commd. ensign USNR, 1962; advanced through grades to lt. comdr. USN, 1969, chaplain, 1965-83, ret., 1983; interim minister Presbytery of Carlisle, Pa., 1984-90; exec. dir. Mil. Chaplains Assn. U.S.A., Washington, 1990—. With U.S. Army, 1957-60. Mem. Kiwanis (lt. gov. Pa. dist. 1989-90). Home: 18 Gladys Trl Fairfield PA 17320-8177 Office: Mil Chaplains Assn US PO Box 42660 Washington DC 20015-0660

D'ANDREA, CAROL DOROTHY, customer service administrator; b. Jersey City, Sept. 7, 1959; d. Victor P. and Alice (Beam) D'A. BS, Montclair (N.J.) State Coll., 1981. Customer svc. supr. Media Communications, Inc., Englewood Cliffs, N.J., 1980-82; asst. dir. telecommunications CallCtr. Svcs., Inc., Cresskill, N.J., 1982-88; dir. customer svc. Publishers Circulation Fulfillment, Hackensack, N.J., 1988—. Home: 363 Greenmount Ave Cliffside Park NJ 07010-1607 Office: PCF Inc 433 Hackensack Ave 11th Fl Hackensack NJ 07601-6335

DANDY, ROSCOE GREER, clinical psychotherapist, educator; b. L.A., Dec. 20, 1946. BA, Calif. State U., 1970; M in Social Work, U. So. Calif., 1973; MPH, U. Pitts., 1974, MPA, 1975, DrPH, 1981; cert., Harvard U., 1981. Lic. clin. social worker. Youth counselor Calif. State Youth Authority, Ontario, Calif., 1971; pub. health intern Colo. State Dept. Health, Denver, 1974; health planning intern Green Engring Corp., Pitts., 1975; adminstrv. health intern Kane Hosp., Pitts., 1979; assoc. dir. U.S. Pub. Health Clinic, Washington, 1980-81; asst. chief trainee VA Hosp., Washington, 1981-83; asst. chief med. adminstrn. svc. VA Hosp., Ft. Howard, Md., 1983-85, social worker, 1985—; psychotherapist Columbia Inst. of Psychotherapy, Inc., 1989-91, D.A. Wynne & Assocs. Inc., 1991—; instr. U. Pitts., 1977-80, Grad. Sch. Washington ext. campus Cen. Mich. U., 1980—, Columbia Pacific U., San Rafael, Calif., 1990—, Nova U., Ft. Lauderdale, Fla., 1991—; vis. instr. Andrews AFB, Washington, Walter Reed Army Med. Ctr. Hosp., Washington, Aberdeen Proving Ground, Md., Ft. Meade, Md., Ft. Hamilton, N.Y.; mem. Nat. Rev. Panel for Substance Abuse Contracts, 1991—. Author: (book) Board and Care Homes in Los Angeles County, 1976. Police community liaison Howard County Police Dept., 1989. With USAF, 1965-68, USPHS, 1980-81, with Res., 1982-83. Nat. Martin Luther King Jr. fellow, Woodrow Wilson Found., 1971-73; named Am. Biog. Inst. Man of Yr. 1990; scholar U. So. Calif., 1971-73, U. Pitts., 1976, citation Dept. Vets. Affairs Sec. Edward Derwenski, 1992. Fellow Am. Biog. Inst.; mem. Am. Pub. Health Assn., Fed. Am. Scientists, Am. Coll. of Health Care Execs. Home: PO Box 2213 Columbia MD 21045-1213

DANEL, JEAN-BAPTISTE, diplomat; b. Boulogne, France, Sept. 18, 1947; came to U.S., 1990; s. Georges-Edouard and Claire (Briene de la Hossezaye) D.; m. Claire J. Chretien, Oct. 7, 1972; children: Pauline, Sophie, Grégoire, Matthias. Agrl. engring. degree, Inst. Nat. Agro., Paris, 1970; agr. economy degree, ENGREF, Paris, 1972. Head of div. Agr. Svc., Paris, 1973-76; agr. economist Ministry of Fgn. Trade, Paris, 1976-79; agrl. counsellor French Embassy, London, 1979-83; adviser Minister of Fgn. Trade, Paris, 1983-85; dep. dir. Office Nat. Interprofl. de Cereales, French Grain Bd., Paris, 1985-88; staff counsellor Minister for European Affairs, Paris, 1988-89; agrl. counsellor French Embassy, Washington, 1990—. Roman Catholic. Office: French Embassy 4101 Reservoir Rd NW Washington DC 20007

DANELLO, TIMOTHY FRANCIS, lawyer; b. Cambridge, Ohio, July 24, 1956; s. Frank Louis and Lillian T. (Krizek) D.; m. Grace Rathkamp, May 2, 1987; 1 child, John. AB, Dartmouth Coll., 1978; JD, Case Western Res. U., 1981. Bar: Ohio 1981, D.C. 1985. Assoc. Baker & Hostetler, Cleve., 1981-84, Wiley, Rein & Fielding, Washington, 1984-87; v.p., gen. counsel Oxford Realty Svcs. Corp., Bethesda, Md., 1987—. Mem. ABA, Am. Corp. Coun. Assn., D.C. Bar Assn., Washington Area Corp. Coun. Assn. Office: Oxford Realty Svcs Corp 7316 Wisconsin Ave Ste 300 Bethesda MD 20814

DANESH, ABOL HASSAN, sociologist, educator; b. Gazvin, Tehran, Iran, May 14, 1952; came to U.S., 1975; s. Abol Ghasem and Fatemeh (Beigom) Danesh; m. Sholeh Ghedari, Jan. 15, 1982; children: Shabnam, Sheida. BA in Acctg., Tehran U., 1974; PhD in Sociology, U. Calif., Riverside, 1985. Vis. asst. prof. Colby Coll., Waterville, Maine, 1985-89; asst. prof. sociology U. R.I., Kingston, 1989-92, assoc. prof., 1992—. Author: Rural Exodus and Squatter Settlement, 1987, The Informal Economy, 1991; contbr. articles to profl. jours. Mem. Am. Sociol. Assn., Eastern Sociol. Soc. Islamic. Office: U RI Dept Sociology & Anthrop Kingston RI 02881-0808

DANFORD, RICHARD OTTO, radiologist; b. Cleve., Mar. 24, 1938; s. Otto F. and Nancy (Weil) D.; m. Arleen Relles, June 19, 1961; children: Gregory, Laura, Natalie. BA, Yale U., 1960; MD, Western Reserve U., 1964. Intern surgery Grace New Haven Hosp., 1964-65; Cushing fellow Yale U., New Haven, 1965-66, NIH fellow in radiology, 1967-70; resident surgery Yale New Haven Hosp., 1966-67; assoc. radiology and nuclear medicine prof. U. Mass., Worcester, 1982—; chief fin. officer Worcester Radiologists, Inc., 1982—; radiology dept. chmn. Med. Ctr. of Cen. Mass., Worcester, 1989—. Maj. U.S. Army, Vietnam, 1970-72. Mem. Am. Coll. of Radiology. Office: Worcester Radiologists Inc 121 Lincoln St Worcester MA 01605-2402

DANFORTH, ARTHUR EDWARDS, finance executive; b. Cleve., Jan. 23, 1925; s. Arthur Edwards and Jane (Hillyard) D.; m. Elizabeth Wagley, Mar. 17, 1956; children: Hillyard Raible, Nicholas Edwards (dec.), Jonathan Ingersoll, Elizabeth Wagley, Michael Stowe. B.A., Yale, 1949. With Hayden Miller Co., Cleve., 1949-54, First Nat. City Bank (predecessor to Citibank N.A.), N.Y.C., 1954-63; asst. mgr. Buenos Aires office First Nat. City Bank (predecessor to Citibank N.A.), 1959-61; treas. Bunge Corp., N.Y.C., 1963-65; sr. v.p., treas. Colonial Bank & Trust Co., Waterbury, Conn., 1965-70; chmn., chief exec. officer Farmers Bank of Del., Wilmington, 1970-76; prin. Danforth Group, New Canaan, Conn., 1976—. Former bd. dirs. United Way of Del., Boys Club of Wilmington, Grand Opera House Inc. of Del., NCCJ, Audubon Soc. Conn., Greater Wilmington Devel. Council. Served as ensign USNR, 1945-46. Clubs: Sankety Head Golf (Nantucket, Mass.), Nantucket Yacht; Yale (N.Y.C.). Home: 260 Whiting Pond Rd Fairfield CT 06430-1742 Office: 21 Locust Ave New Canaan CT 06840-4735

DANFORTH, DAVID NEWTON, JR., physician, scientist; b. N.Y.C., June 25, 1942; s. David Newton and Gladys Margaret (Blaine) D.; m. Anne Walker Nickson, Apr. 13, 1985. BA, Northwestern U., Evanston, Ill., 1965; MD, Northwestern U., Chgo., 1971; MS, U. N.Mex., Albuquerque, 1967. Diplomate Am. Bd. Surgery. Intern, then resident Cornell Med. Ctr., N.Y.C., 1971-74, 77-79; clin. assoc. NIH, Bethesda, Md., 1974-77; surg. fellow M.D. Anderson Hosp., Houston, 1979-80; sr. staff fellow NIH, Bethesda, 1980-82; sr. investigator Nat. Cancer Inst., NIH, Bethesda, 1982—. Editor: Diagnosis and Management of Breast Cancer, 1988; contbr. articles to profl. jours. Served to lt. comdr. USPHS, 1974-76. Fellow Am. Cancer Soc., 1979-80. Fellow ACS, Soc. Surg. Oncology, Am. Soc. Clin. Oncology, Am. Assn. Cancer Research, Endocrine Soc. Republican. Episcopalian. Home: 4701 Willard Ave Apt 406 Bethesda MD 20815-4611 Office: Nat Cancer Inst Surgery Br Bldg 10 Rm 2B38 Bethesda MD 20892

DANG, THONG QUOC, aerospace engineering educator; b. Saigon, Vietnam, Apr. 18, 1959; s. Dang Van and Uyen Thi D. BS, U. Calif., Davis, 1981; MS, MIT, 1983, PhD, 1985. Sr. scientist McDonnell Douglas Corp., Long Beach, Calif., 1985-88; mem. tech. staff Rockwell Internat. Corp., Canoga Park, Calif., 1988-89; asst. prof. Syracuse U., N.Y., 1989—; cons. in field. Mem. AIAA, ASME. Office: Syracuse U 151 Link Hall Syracuse NY 13244

D'ANGELO, ANTHONY WILLIAM, marketing communications executive; b. Newark Valley, N.Y., Oct. 30, 1960; s. Domenico and Jane (Salwoski) D'A.; m. Deborah Ann Tomazin, June 11, 1983; 1 child, Alison Marie. BA, Syracuse U., 1982. Dist. exec. Hiawatha coun. Boy Scouts Am., Syracuse, 1982-83; promotions asst. sch. edn. Syracuse U., 1983-84; communications mgr. Syracuse U. News Svcs., 1984-85; account exec. Sage Marcom, Inc., Syracuse, 1985-89, dir. pub. rels., 1989—; adj. prof. S.I. Newhouse Sch. Pub. Communications Syracuse U., 1990—. Contbr. articles to newspapers and mags. Mem. communications com. United Way Cen. N.Y., Syracuse, 1987-88; communications chmn. exploring exec. com. Hiawatha coun. Boy Scouts Am., 1987—. Recipient Gold medal for excellence in newswriting Coun. for Advancement and Support of Edn., 1985, EFFIE award Am. Mktg. Assn., 1990. Mem. Pub. Rels. Soc. Am. (pres. cen. N.Y. chpt. 1989—), Phi Beta Kappa. Roman Catholic. Home: 157 North Way Camillus NY 13031-1253 Office: Sage Marcom Inc 717 Erie Blvd W Syracuse NY 13204-2225

D'ANGELO, DOLORES AMIDON, English educator; b. Phila., Apr. 27, 1947; d. Donald Harris and Doris Elwood (Barton) Amidon; m. Lawrence James D'Angelo, June 2, 1973; children: Marisa, Michael. BA, Simmons Coll., 1969, MA, 1972; AGS, U. Md., 1983, PhD, 1987. Cert. tchr., Mass., N.C., Md., Ga. Tchr. North Reading (Mass.) High Sch., 1969-72, Chapel Hill (N.C.) High Sch., 1972-73, Montgomery Blair High Sch., Silver Spring, Md., 1973-76, Open Campus West High Sch., Atlanta, 1977-79; substitute tchr. Montgomery County (Md.) Pub. Schs., 1980-87; instr. English U. Md., College Park, 1987—. Contbr. articles to profl. jours. Mem. Phi Delta Kappa, Phi Kappa Phi, Sigma Tau Delta. Home: 6409 Fallen Oak Ct Bethesda MD 20817-3249 Office: U Md English Dept College Park MD 20742

D'ANGELO, ERNEST EUSTACHIO, brokerage house executive; b. Jersey City, Jan. 21, 1944; s. Eustachio and Catherine (Valentino) D'A.; m. Carol Abramowitz, Apr. 23, 1966; 1 child, Ernest E. Jr. BS in Acctg., Rutgers U., 1972. Contract officer N.Y. State Urban Devel. Corp., N.Y.C., 1972-75; fin. dir. Cen. Essex Health Plan, Orange, N.J., 1975-79, New Community Corp., Newark, 1979-81; first v.p. corp. services Prudential Bache Securities Group, Inc., N.Y.C., 1981—. Active Worldwide Marriage Encounter, Montclair, N.J., 1975-81; bd. dirs. United Scleroderma Found., Watsonville, Calif., 1987. Mem. Nat. Assn. Accts., Nat. Purchasing Mgrs. Assn., Assn. Corp. Travel Execs. (bd. govs.). Roman Catholic. Home: 57 Eastern Dr Kendall Park NJ 08824-1321 Office: Prudential Securities 100 Gold St New York NY 10292

D'ANGELO, RITA YVONNE, psychologist, educator; b. N.Y.C., Apr. 21, 1928; d. J. Anthony and Alice (Mignona) D'A. BA, Hunter Coll., N.Y.C., 1948; MA, Fordham U., N.Y.C., 1950, PhD, 1961. Lic. psychologist, N.Y. Clin. psychologist Cath. Charities Mental Health Clinic, N.Y.C., 1950—; asst. prof. psychology Marymount Coll., Tarrytown, N.Y., 1953-57; supr. clin. psychology St. Germaines Residential Treatment Ctr., Peekskill, N.Y., 1957-62; asst. prof. L.I. U., N.Y.C., 1962-64, Hunter Coll., 1964-68; asst. assoc. full prof. Lehman Coll. CUNY, N.Y.C., 1968-91, prof. emerita, 1991—; acting dir. Italian-Am. Studies CUNY, 1975-80; psychology dept. chairperson CUNY, N.Y.C., 1976-88; acting dean Coll. Social Scis. CUNY, 1977-78; mental health cons. HEW, NIMH, 1973-77. Recipient Disting. Tchrs. award CUNY, 1973. Mem. Am. Psychol. Assn., Eastern Psychol. Assn., N.Y. Soc. for Clin. Psychologists.

D'ANGELO, RONALD HOLMES, priest, psychotherapist; b. Perth Amboy, N.J., Oct. 16, 1933; s. Sabatino John and Ruth Marie (Coley) D'A.; m. Robin Angell Ranahan, Nov. 24, 1990; stepchildren: Suzanne H. Rioux, Adam Rioux. BS in Acctg., Seton Hall U., 1955, BA in Classical Studies, 1962; STM in Pastoral Counseling, N.Y. Theol. Sem., 1974; MDiv in Theol. Studies, Darlington Sem., 1975. Ordained priest, 1966; cert. minister Fedn. Christian Ministries, 1978; cert. instr. concept. therapy, pastoral counelor, marriage and family therapist, psychoanalyst. Assoc. pastor Roman Cath. Ch., Union City, N.J., 1966-85; staff therapist Pastoral Counseling Svcs. of No. N.J., Bergenfield, N.J., 1976—, D'Angelo, Daly & Gilson, Rutherford, 1990—; clin. supr. Shelter Our Sisters, Teaneck, 1983-87. Trustee, chair Union City Free Pub. Libr., 1971-91, Shelter Our Sisters, Teaneck, 1981-86. With USAF, 1955-59.

DANGINIS, VASSILIS ARISTIDIS, quality assurance engineer; b. Athens, Greece, June 16, 1960; came to U.S., 1980; s. Aristidis V. and Efpraxia (Spyropoulos) D.; m. Kim Theresa Beck, Oct. 18, 1985; 1 child, Aristidis V. BSChemE, SUNY, Stony Brook, 1984, MS in Material Engring., 1987; postgrad., K-W U., L.A. Technician Evepy S.A. Plastic Industry, Athens, Greece, 1978-80; R&D engr. Brookhaven Nat. Lab., Upton, N.Y., 1984-86; R&D and process engr. Vactronic Lab. Equipment Inc., Bohemia, N.Y., 1986-88; quality assurance and lead project engr. Standard Microsystems Corp., Hauppauge, N.Y., 1988—; teaching asst. SUNY, Stony Brook, 1984-86. Contbr. articles to profl. jours. Mem. Am. Soc. for Quality Control, Electrochem. Soc., Materials Sci. and Engring. Club, Hellenic Soc. Clubs. Mem. Greek Orthodox Ch. Home: 91 Crown St Port Jefferson Sta NY 11776 Office: Standard Microsystems Corp 35 Marcus Blvd Hauppauge NY 11788

DANIEL, CAROL GENE, infosystems specialist; b. Minden, La., Nov. 2, 1945; d. William Adolphus and Edna Ruth (Hearron) D.; m. Kenneth Joseph Gingras, June 4, 1977, (div. June 1984). BA, Northwestern State U. of La., 1967; MEd, Boston U., 1976. Cert. tchr. Ma., La., Kans., Calif., Colo. Educator U.S. Forces Dept. of Def. Dependent Schs., W. Germany, 1968-76, State of Calif., U.S. Army, Monterey, 1976-79, Leavenworth (Kans.) Sch. Dist., 1979-80; analyst U.S. Army Europe, 1st Personnel Command, Schwetzingen, W. Germany, 1980-82; tng. mgr. McDonnel Douglas/Inco, Inc., Colorado Springs, Colo., 1983-85; sr. systems analyst Syscon Corp., Colorado Springs, 1985-87; engr. CTA, Inc., Bedford, Mass., 1987-88; systems analyst Input, Output Computer Svcs., Inc., Waltham, Mass., 1988-90; prin. The Network Trainer, Revere, Mass., 1990—; cons. v.p., Tech. Svcs., Inc., Colorado Springs, 1986-87, cons. tng., Daniel Agy., Morgan City, La., 1980-83. Pub. relations dir. Star/Bar Amateur Theater Group, Colorado Springs, 1984; active campaigns, Nat. Rep. Women, Colorado Springs, 1985, recruitment Colorado Springs C. of C. 1983-87. Recipient fellowship, U. Calif., Santa Cruz, 1978. Mem. Nat. Assn. Female Execs. (panel spkr. 1986), Am. Soc. Tng. and Devel., Boston U. Alumni Assn., NOW (Heidelberg, W. Germany chpt., v.p. 1981-82). Democrat. Episcopalian.

DANIEL, DANIEL SALMAN, research chemist; b. Basrah, Iraq, July 1, 1934; came to U.S., 1960; naturalized, 1971; s. Salman D. E. and Munira (Shabi) D.; m. Elizabeth Goldstein, Aug. 22, 1965; children: David S., Michael J., Ameera H. BSc, U. London, 1955, PhD, 1959. Rsch. assoc. Carnegie-Mellon U., Pitts., 1960-63; sr. rsch. chemist Eastman Kodak Co., Rochester, N.Y., 1964-69, rsch. assoc., 1969—; mem. adj. faculty Rochester Inst. Tech., 1979—. Mem. Royal Chem. Soc., AAAS, Am. Chem. Soc., N.Y. Acad. Scis., Am. Assn. Clin. Chemistry, Sigma Xi. Home: 3051 St Paul Blvd Rochester NY 14617-3442 Office: Eastman Kodak Co Rsch Lab 1669 Lake Ave Rochester NY 14650

DANIEL, ELEANOR SAUER, economist, real estate executive; b. N.Y.C., Feb. 8, 1917; d. Charles Peter and Elsie Edna (Dommer) Sauer; m. John Carl Daniel, Dec. 31, 1952; children: Victoria Ann, Charles Timothy. BA magna cum laude (Bardwell fellow), Mt. Holyoke Coll., 1936; MA (Perkins fellow), Columbia U., 1937. Economist, U.S. Steel Co., N.Y.C., 1938; lectr. econs. Bklyn. Coll., 1939-40; with Mut. Life Ins. Co. N.Y., N.Y.C., 1940-74, asst. v.p., 1972-74, sr. econ. adviser, 1972-74; economist Fed. Home Loan Bank, N.Y.C., 1974-75; v.p., dir. Daniel Realty Co., N.Y.C., 1975—; pres. Midtown Daniel, 1986—; former dir., chmn. fin. com. Atlantic City Electric Co.; past chmn. fin. com. Atlantic Energy, Inc.; former mem. bd. mgrs. U.S. Savs. Bank Newark; mem. Pres's. Task Force Fed. Credit Programs, 1968-69; mem. N.J. Gov's. Econ. Recovery Com., 1975-76; mem. econ. adv. bd. U.S. Sec. Commerce, 1971-73; mem. bus. research adv. council U.S. Bur. Labor Statistics, 1966-86. Author: (with J.J. O'Leary and S.F. Foster) Our National Debt and Our Savings; contbr. articles to profl. jours. Former trustee Blue Shield of N.J., trustee fellow Mt. Holyoke Coll., also past vice chmn., mem. fin. com., trustee. Mem. Am. Econ. Assn., Am. Fin. Assn. (past dir.), Phi Beta Kappa. Home and Office: 34 North Dr East Brunswick NJ 08816-1122

DANIEL, GERARD LUCIAN, physician, pharmaceutical company executive; b. Swanton, Vt., May 6, 1927; s. Edward and Exzilia (Perron) D.; AB, St. Michaels Coll., 1950; MD, U. Vt., 1954; m. Armande Renee Messier, Nov. 24, 1949; children: Suzanne Beatrice Foley. Practice medicine, Brattleboro, Vt., 1955-59; chief clin. medicine Dept. Army, Washington, 1959-63, chief life scis. div., 1963-70; med. dir. Pacific Region, Sterling/Winthrop Internat., Minami Azabu, Tokyo, 1970-73, internat. dir. clin. research Winthrop Products Inc., N.Y.C., 1973-75; corp. med. dir. Rhone-Poulenc, Inc., N.Y.C., 1975-78; exec. v.p. Lipha Chems. Inc., N.Y.C. subs. Air Liquid, France, 1978-81, pres., 1981-90, chmn., pres., chief exec. officer, 1990-91; chmn., pres., chief exec. officer Lipha Pharms., Inc. subs. E. Merck, 1991—; pub. health officer State of Vt., 1958-59; mem. adv. com. Multiple Sclerosis, 1959-60; chmn. Pharm. Dels. Japan, Tokyo, 1972-73; mem. planning com. White House Conf. Aging, 1980-81. Recipient Achievement award NASA, 1963; Intelligence Merit medal, 1970. Mem. AMA, Am. Mgmt. Assn. (pres. assoc.), AAAS, Assn. Former Intelligence Officers, Med. Execs. Assn. N.Y.C., Washington Acad. Medicine, Fed. Execs. Alumni Assn. Home: Carnegie House Ste 2Q 100 W 57th St New York NY 10019-3327 Office: 9 W 57th St New York NY 10019

DANIEL, JONATHAN RUSSELL, special effects expert; b. N.Y.C., Apr. 2, 1961; s. D. Howard Daniel and Nina (Horne) Kelman; children: Jared Samuel, Jenniffer Rachael. BA/BS, CCNY, N.Y.C., 1984; Cert. Film Program, NYU, N.Y.C., 1989. Computer graphics cons. C.I.A.C., Wilmington, Del., 1976-83; spl. effects designer Phil Marco Prodns., N.Y.C., 1983-84; live action spl. effects designer Innovative Effects Co., Scarsdale, N.Y., 1984-88; dir. spl. effects Olympian Films Group, Bayside, N.Y., 1988—; chief exec. officer Olympian Entertainment East/West, N.Y. and Calif., 1991—; exec. dir. Found. for Arts Living Legacy, 1992; graphid systems con. to more than 240 clients in N.Y., N.J., Conn., 1976-83. Dir. documentary Technical Directors, 1987 (Golden Circle award 1987, 89, 90); dir. feature film Just One of Those Days, 1989; dir. spl. effects feature film Metamorphisis, 1988; comml. spl. effects dir. video and film over 30 nat. spots, 3 features, and 5 shorts, 1980-88; producer, dir. commls., features, 1988—. Office: Olympian Entertainment East/West 48 Eastview Ct Jericho NY 11361

DANIEL, RICHARD NICHOLAS, fabricated metals manufacturing company executive; b. Bklyn., Sept. 18, 1935; s. Louis V. and Jean (D'Andrea) D.; m. Elaine E. Sherman, Sept. 24, 1966; children: Matthew, Jeffrey. B.B.A., St. John's U., 1957; M.B.A., U. Pa., 1959. C.P.A., Tex. Planning assoc. Mobil Oil Corp., N.Y.C., 1962-70; v.p. fin. Laird Enterprises Inc., N.Y.C., 1970-71; v.p. ops. Wheelabrator-Frye, N.Y.C., 1971; v.p., controller Handy & Harman, N.Y.C., 1971-76, v.p.-fin., 1977-78, group v.p., 1978-79, pres., COO, 1979-83, pres., CEO, 1983-87, chmn., pres., chief exec. officer, 1988—, chmn., pres., CEO, 1988-92, chmn., CEO, 1992—. Home: 91 Hawthorne Pl Briarcliff Manor NY 10510-2226 Office: Handy & Harman 250 Park Ave New York NY 10177

DANIEL, STEPHEN JAMES, consultant, market researcher; b. Jersey City, Feb. 23, 1943; s. Lothar and Elizabeth (Lowenthal) D.; m. Deborah Sue Watsky, Jan. 18, 1969 (div. Apr., 1987); children: Matthew Lorin, Erica Dale. BS, Northeastern U., 1970; MBA, NYU, 1974. Corp. loan officer Mfrs. Hanover Trust, N.Y.C., 1970-74; investment analyst Prudential Ins. Co., Boston, 1975; sr. fin. analyst Inforex, Inc., Burlington, Mass., 1976; mktg. mgr. Data Gen. Corp., Westboro, Mass., 1976-83; pres. Eastern Edge Corp., Somerville, Mass., 1983-85, Daniel Assocs., Framingham, Mass., 1985—. Author: How to Buy a Small Business Machine, 1980; contbr. articles to profl. jours. Bd. dirs. Temple Beth Am Youth Basketball League, Framingham, Mass., 1980—. Mem. Boston Computer Soc., Am. Mktg. Assn. (v.p. computer mktg.), Materi (nat. pres.). Home and Office: Daniel Assocs 49 Hill Rd Ste 4 Belmont MA 02178-4302

DANIEL-DREYFUS, SUSAN B. RUSSE, civic worker; b. St. Louis, May 30, 1940; d. Frederick William and Suzanne (Mackay) Russe; m. Don B. Faerber, Nov. 27, 1962 (div. Nov. 1968); 1 child, Suzanne Mackay; m. Marc Andre Daniel-Dreyfus, Aug. 9, 1969; 1 child, Cable Dunster. Student, Smith Coll., 1958-60, Corcoran Sch. Fine Arts, 1960-61, Washington U., St. Louis, 1961-62. Mng. ptnr. Communications, Inc., 1980-82; asst. dir. Harvard Bus. Sch. Fund, Cambridge, 1982-86; pres. SCR Assocs. Corp., Cambridge, 1986—; mem. bd. advisors Odysseum, Inc.; bd. dirs. Future Mgmt. Systems. Mem. St. Louis-St. Louis County White House Conf. on Edn., 1966-68; mem. Mo. 1st Gov.'s Conf. on Edn., 1966, 2d Conf., 1968; bd. dirs. Tunbridge Sch., 1973-78, St. Louis Smith Coll.; hon. bd. dirs. New Music Circle; mem. woman's bd. dirs. Washington U., New Music Circle, 1963-67; mem. woman's bd. Mo. Hist. Soc.; bd. dirs. Non-Partisan Ct. Plan for Mo., Young Audiences Inc., 1967-69; bd. dirs. Childrens Art Bazaar, 1968-70; founder St. Louis Opera Theater; chmn. Art. Mus. Bond Issue election St. Louis, 1966; jr. bd. dirs. St. Louis Symphony, 1966-68, Opportunities Indsl. Center, Boston; legis. chmn. bd. dirs. Boston LWV, 1969-72; mem. council, bd. dirs. Jr. League Boston, 1970-72, 74-76, v.p. Bd. of Family Counseling Services-Region West, Boston, 1979—; pres. Family Counseling Bd., Brookline, Mass.; trustee Chestnut Hill Sch., Boston, Brookline Friendly Soc.; mem. steering com. ann. fund Boston Children's Hosp. Med. Center, 1980-84; v.p. Nat. Friends Bd., Joslin Diabetes Found., 1980-83; mem. corp. bd. Joslin Diabetes Ctr.; v.p. bd. dirs. Boston Ctr. Internat. Visitors, 1979-82; Boston bd. dirs. Mass. Soc. Prevention of Cruelty to Children, 1980-84; exec. v.p. Ctr. for Middle East Bus., 1978-82; pres. bd. Brookline Community Fund, 1984—; overseer Old Sturbridge Village, 1987—. Mem. Colonial Dames, Soc. Art Historians. Clubs: Women's City (dir.) (Boston); Vincent (dir.). Home: 120 Middlesex Rd Chestnut Hill MA 02167-1841

DANIELL, ROBERT F., diversified manufacturing company executive; b. Milton, Mass., 1933; married. Grad., Boston U. Coll. Indsl. Tech., 1954; DSc (hon.), U. Bridgeport; LLD (hon.), Trinity Coll., Boston U. With Sikorsky Aircraft, Stratford, Conn., 1956-82, design engr., from 1956, program mgr., 1968-71, comml. mktg. mgr., 1971-74, v.p. comml. mktg., 1974-76, sr. v.p. mktg., 1976-77, exec. v.p., 1977-80, chief exec. officer, 1980-82, pres., 1981-82; with United Techs. (parent co.), Hartford, Conn., 1982—; v.p. United Technologies (parent co.), Hartford, Conn., 1982-83, sr. v.p. def. systems, 1983-84, pres., COO, 1984-92, dir., 1984—, chief exec. officer, 1984—, chmn. bd. dirs., 1987—; bd. dirs. The Travelers Corp., Hartford, Conn., Shell Oil Co., Houston. Bd. trustees Boston U., Naval Aviation Mus. Found., Inc., Falcon Found.; corporator Inst. of Living Svcs. Corp., mem. Conf. Bd. Fellow U. Bridgeport. Mem. The Bus. Coun., Bus. Roundtable, Conn. Bus. for Edn. Coalition, Inc. Mem. Wings Club (N.Y.C., former pres.). Office: United Techs Corp United Techs Bldg Hartford CT 06101

DANIELS, BARBARA JOYCE, English educator; b. Sioux City, Iowa, June 27, 1945; d. Henry George and Viola Octavia (Wik) Bossman; m. David Isaac Daniels, Dec. 22, 1983. BA, Buena Vista Coll., 1966; MA, NYU, 1972. Spanish and English tchr. Lawrence High Sch., Lawrenceville, N.J., 1966-69; English tchr. Rutherford (N.J.) Jr. High, 1969-71, Camden County Coll., Blackwood, N.J., 1976—. Author: (with David I. Daniels) English Grammar, 1991. Mem. N.J. Coll. English Assn. (pres. 1989-90). Office: Camden County College PO Box 200 Blackwood NJ 08012-0200

DANIELS, CECIL EDWIN, III, producer, director; b. Stamford, Conn., Nov. 14, 1961; s. Cecil E. Jr. and Ann Marie (Booker) D. BA, Ashland U., 1984. Prodn. asst. Pro Video Prodn., Darien, Conn., 1984-85, dir., 1985-86; producer, dir. Double C Entertainment, Stamford, 1985—; video tech. Group W Communications, Stamford, 1985-87; dir. TV prodn. svcs. Commonwealth of Mass., 1990—; producer, dir. Wilton (Conn.) Bd. Edn., 1987-88; unit prodn. mgr. Praxis Media, South Norwalk, Conn., 1988-89; cons. Ray Proof Shielding Systems, Norwalk, 1986-87. Prin. works include We Create Silence, 1987, Strip Life Down to the Bone, 1987, Pre-School, 1988, AIDS, 1988, The Elder Connection, 1991, Swim Across the Sound, 1990, Behind the Scenes, 1989. Youth leader Stamford YMCA, 1985-89; ski leader Greenwich (Conn.) YMCA, 1985-91; camera operator Dem. Cen. Com., Stamford, 1988. Mem. Internat. TV Assn., Am. Film Inst., United Brotherhood Carpenters. Baptist. Home: 55 Oak Ridge St Greenwich CT 06830-5224 Office: Double C Entertainment 486 Chandler St Studio A Park Sq Worcester MA 01602

DANIELS, CHARLES JOSEPH, III, electrical engineer; b. L.A., July 1, 1941; s. Charles Joseph and Madeline Anna (Baldassare) D.; m. Joan Reichhold, Oct. 10, 1965; 1 child, Charles Joseph. BSEE, U. Md., 1971, MS in Physics, 1976. Draftsman Hazen & Sawyer Engrs., N.Y.C., 1960-62; technician EMR Corp., Greenbelt, Md., 1966-68; rsch. engr. Naval Rsch. Lab., Washington, 1971-73; sanitary engr. FDA, Rockville, Md., 1973-77; head of prodn. testing Digital Communications Corp., Germantown, Md., 1977-78; mem. tech. staff Watkins-Johnson, Gaithersburg, Md., 1978-79; sr. engr. Digital Communications Corp., Germantown, 1979-80; sr. staff engr. Frederick (Md.) Electronics, 1980-81; disting. mem. tech. staff AT&T Bell Labs., Allentown, Pa., 1981—. Patentee in field; contbr. over 20 articles to profl. jours. Cpl. USMC, 1962-66. Mem. Am. Phys. Soc., Tau Beta Pi (pres. 1970-71), Sigma Xi, Phi Kappa Phi, Omicron Delta Kappa (sec. 1970-71), Sigma Pi Sigma. Office: AT&T Bell Labs 555 Union Blvd Allentown PA 18103-1229

DANIELS, EDMOND, writer, publisher, entertainer; b. Richmond, Va., Mar. 1, 1953; s. Eugene and Sally (Daniels) Gaskins. A in Mgmt., C.C. Phila., 1975; cert. in music interpretation, Music I, Phila., 1984. Sponger Modern Sponge & Cloth Co., Phila., 1971-77; sales rep., writer, entertainer Ozart Enterprise, Phila., 1978-86; mgr. Jean Joint/Big Store, Phila., 1980-83, Club LaZorra, Phila., 1985-90; asst. mgr. Oak Tree, Phila., 1983-84, S&H Shoe Outlet, Phila., 1985-86; writer, entertainer, arranger, prodr. T.S.W. Records, Phila., 1988-91, Soc. Hill Records, Phila., 1991—; pub. Edmond F. Daniels Songs, Inc., Phila., 1989—; jingle composer, Phila., 1988, product leader Team F.A.D. (Fight Against Drugs), King of Prussia, 1987—. Author: (play, short story) I Just Can't Seem to Forget, 1991, (animated mus.) The King That Never Was, 1992; composer: All Fall Down, 1992, Just Friends, 1992. With USMC, 1969-70. Recipient Appreciation award Power 99FM, 1989. Mem. ASCAP, BMI. Home: 1142 A South St Philadelphia PA 19147

DANIELS, JANET DELUCA, college administrator, accounting educator; b. Wilmington, Del., Apr. 14, 1939; d. Samuel Joseph and Ruth Veronica (Minors) DeLuca; m. Craig Evan Daniels, June 11, 1959; children: Scott Evan, Eric Douglas, Lynn Heather, Laird Kevin. BS, Tufts U., 1959; MEd, U. Del., 1966; MS in Acctg., U. Hartford, 1980; MBA, Boston U., 1982, D in Bus. Adminstrn., 1988. CPA, Md. Tchr. Brown Tech. High Sch., Wilmington, 1965-67; customer rep. Hartford (Conn.) Fed. Savings & Loan, 1974-77; account exec. Bache Halsey Stuart Shields, Inc., Hartford, 1977-78; lectr. in acctg. U. Hartford, West Hartford, Conn., 1981-83, asst. prof. acctg., 1983-89, dir. grad. studies, 1985-88, chair of acctg., 1986; assoc. prof. Bryant Coll., Smithfield, R.I., 1989—, assoc. dean of faculty, dir. grad. sch., 1989—, interim chair acctg., 1992—. Contbr. articles to profl. publs. Mem. Bloomfield (Conn.) Town Coun., 1976-79. Doctoral consortium fellow Health Care Adminstrn. div. Acad. of Mgmt., 1984. Mem. Am. Inst. CPAs, Am. Acctng. Assn. (N.E. coord. govt. and non-profit sect. 1989—, doctoral consortium fellow 1983), N.E. Bus. and Econs. Assn. (bd. dirs. 1990—), Conn. Soc. CPAs, Beta Gamma Sigma. Office: Bryant Coll 1150 Douglas Pike Smithfield RI 02917-1220

DANIELS, JENNIFER, physician; b. Buffalo, N.Y., Mar. 11, 1957; d. Matthew Clifford and Lillian Ethel (Mitchell) D.; children: Lillian Nicole, Benjamin Banneker. AB cum laude, Harvard U.-Radcliff Coll., 1979; MD, MBA, U. Pa., 1983. Intern Chestnut Hill Hosp., Phila., 1983-84; house physician Rolling Hill Hosp., Phila., 1984-85; med. dir. Lac Courte Oreilles Community Health Ctr., Hayward, Wis., 1985-86; clin. dir., physician Ft. Totten (N.D.) Indian Health Svc. Clinic, 1987-88; resident in family practice St. Joseph's Family Practice Residency, Syracuse, 1989-91; med. specialist I Hutchings Psychiatric Ctr., Syracuse, 1990—; physician, owner Family Medicine, Syracuse, 1991—; med. cons., Phila., spring 1982; emergency physician Nat. Emergency Svcs., Stanley and Woodruff, Wis., 1985-86, Spectrum Emergency, Inc., Hayward, 1985-86. Bd. dirs. Syracuse Model Neighborhood Corp., 1991; vol. Syracuse Women's Commn., 1990, Clinic for the Homeless, 1991—, City of Syracuse Bd. Ethics, 1991, Syracuse U. Health Sci. Ctr. Mentor program for minority med. students, 1991. Mem. AMA, Am. Med. Women's Assn. (pres. br. 18), Am. Assn. Family Physicians, N.Y. State Med. Soc. Home and Office: 3100 S Salina St Syracuse NY 13205-1848

DANIELS, JOANNE P., education educator; b. Norwich, Conn., June 16, 1947; d. George and Helen (Piechta) Pugatch; m. David W. Morton, June 22, 1974 (div. Jan. 1981); m. Lloyd Keith Daniels, Oct. 24, 1986. BS, Eastern Conn. State U., 1976; MA, U. Conn., 1983, diploma in edn., 1986, PhD, 1989. Patent law sec. Law Offices Peter L. Costas, Hartford, Conn., 1971-75; adminstrv. asst. Westinghouse Electric Supply Co., East Hartford, Conn., 1975-78; tchr. Halls Hill Elem. Sch., Colchester, Conn., 1978-86; supr. student tchrs. U. Conn., Storrs, 1986-89; lectr. Eastern Conn. State Coll., Williamantic, 1989; asst. prof. edn., coord. edn. field experience New Eng. Coll., Henniker, N.H., 1989—. Mem. Internat. Reading Assn., New England Reading Assn., Granite State Reading Assn., Eastern Conn. State U. Alumni Assn. (bd. dirs., chmn. awards com.), Phi Delta Kappa, Pi Lambda Theta. Roman Catholic. Office: New Eng Coll 23 Bridge St Henniker NH 03242-3296

DANIELS, JOHN MAYNARD, marketing professional; b. Binghamton, N.Y., Aug. 17, 1935; s. Horace Maynard and Elma (Trimmer) D.; m. Diana Petronella Manassero, Aug. 16, 1958 (div. 1983); children: Lisa M., Douglas J., Heather E.; m. Sheila Marjory Brady, June 22, 1985. BS in Chemistry, Trinity Coll., 1957; PhD in Chemistry, Brandeis U., 1965. Postdoctoral rsch. assoc. Nat. Bur. Standards, Washington, 1964-66; asst. prof. chemistry Union Coll., Schenectady, N.Y., 1966-72; pres. Capital Dist. Water Treatment, Inc., Schenectady, N.Y., 1971-80; mktg. dir. Encotech, Inc., Schenectady, N.Y., 1978—; bd. dirs. Tri-State Cogeneration Assn., N.Y.C. Mem. Adirondeck Mountain Club (white water chmn. 1986-88). Home: 722 Rankin Ave Schenectady NY 12308-3425 Office: Encotech Inc PO Box 714 Schenectady NY 12301-0714

DANIELS, JOSEPH JERARD, telecommunications engineer; b. Balt., Dec. 4, 1953; s. Reginald Daniels and Hilda (Payne) Ellison; m. Pearl Virginia Garrett; children: Jessica, Joshua. AA, Community Coll. Balt., 1978; student, U. Md., 1978-79; BS, Johns Hopkins U., 1985, postgrad. Coord., supt. Mayor's Office of Manpower, Balt., 1978; time-keeper Hilton Hotel, Inc., Balt., 1978; network engr. C&P Telephone Co./AT&T, Balt., 1979-83, engr. cen. office equipment, 1984—. Bd. dirs., Cen. Md. Com. on Sickle Cell, 1983; pres. Summitt Ridge Community Assn., Balt., 1987. With USAF, 1972-74. Mem. IEEE, Telephone Pioneers Am. (project co-chmn. 1982), Am. Legion. Republican.

DANIELS, MADELINE MARIE, psychotherapist, author; b. Newark, Oct. 14, 1948; d. William and Dorothy Barlow; BA cum laude, CCNY, 1971; PhD, Union Grad. Sch., Yellow Springs, Ohio, 1975, PhD, Union Grad. Sch., Cin., 1988; m. Peter W. Daniels, Oct. 18, 1976; children—Jonathan, Jedediah, Jeremiah. Lectr., Westchester Community Coll., also Bronx Community Coll., 1973-74; mem. adj. faculty SUNY, Purchase, 1974-76; data processing coordinator GTE Internat., 1976-78; lectr. div. continuing edn. U. N.H., 1979-87; exec. dir. Crossroads Center Human Integration, East Kingston, N.H., 1979-88; administrator Spectrum Cross-Cultural Inst. Youth Inc., East Kingston, 1988—; psychotherapist, lectr., cons. in field. Cert. ind. biofeedback practitioner, clin. mental health counselor. Mem. Internat. council Psychologists (area chair 1988), Am. Psychol. Assn., Biofeedback Soc. Am., Soc. Psychol. Athropology, N.H. Psychol. Orgn., Phi Beta Kappa. Author: Realistic Leadership, 1983, Living Your Religion in the Real World, 1985, A Culturally Different Perspective on Psychology, 1989. Office: Crossroads Center East Kingston NH 03827

DANIELS, ROBERT ALAN, marketing executive; b. Bklyn., Dec. 19, 1944; s. Louis and Sarah D.; m. Iris; 1 child, Jesse. BS, L.I. U., 1966. Regional sales mgr. Sperry Rand Corp., N.Y.C., 1966-72; internat. sales mgr. Wascator of Am., 1972-74; v.p. Incerator Systems Corp., 1974-76; v.p. mktg. Marland Systems/Allied Water Corp., Lake Geneva, Wis., 1976-82; v.p. internat. mktg. Univox Calif., Inc., Washington, 1982-84; pres., chief exec. officer Marland Environ. Systems, Inc., Lake Geneva, 1984-86; pres. Bob Daniels Internat., 1986-89; exec. v.p. Water-Jel Tech., Carlstadt, N.J., 1989—. Patentee in field; contbr. numerous articles to profl. jours. Mem. Soc. Naval Architects & Marine Engrs. Office: Water-Jel Tech 243 Veterans Blvd Carlstadt NJ 07072-2708

DANIELS, WILBUR, lawyer; b. Detroit, Jan. 23, 1923; s. Max and Dora (Miller) D.; m. Patricia Heyman, Dec. 22, 1963; 1 child, Ann G. B.S., CCNY, 1942; J.D., NYU, 1950. Bar: N.Y. 1950, U.S. Supreme Ct. 1951. Rsch., asst. dir. rsch. Internat. Ladies' Garment Workers' Union, N.Y.C., 1943-50; assoc. gen. counsel Internat. Ladies' Garment Worker's Union, N.Y.C., 1950-59, asst. to pres., 1959-61, dir. master agreements dept., 1965-87, v.p., 1969-73, exec. v.p., 1973-87; ptnr. firm Vladeck & Elias, N.Y.C., 1961-63; exec. dir. Nat. Bd. Coat and Suit Industry, N.Y.C., 1963-65, S.H. and Helen R. Scheuer Family Found., 1987—; assoc. adj. prof. grad. div. NYU Law Sch., 1979-84; vice chmn. N.Y. State Job Devel. Authority; mem. Nat. Commn. Unemployment Commn., 1977-80, U.S. Adv. Coun. on Employee Welfare and Pension Benefit Plans, 1961-69, Fed. Adv. Coun. Unemployment Inst., 1975-82. Bd. mng. dirs., chmn. exec. com. Met. Opera Assn.; mem. bd. visitors Grad. Ctr., CUNY; past bd. dirs. Lincoln Ctr. for Performing Arts; chmn. N.Y. State Adv. Coun. on Employment and Unemployment Ins.; bd. dirs. United Housing Found., 1977-87, N.Y. Urban Coalition, 1970-73; alt. mem. N.Y.C. Office Collective Bargaining, 1986-87. With U.S. Army, 1945-46. Mem. ABA, Assn. of Bar of City of N.Y., UN Assn. (bd. dirs.), Am Arbitration Assn. (bd. dirs.), Phi Beta Kappa. Home: 242 E 19th St New York NY 10003-2634 Office: SH & Helen R Scheuer Family Found 104E E 40th St New York NY 10016-1801

DANIELS, WILLIAM ALBERT, food products executive; b. Westboro, Mass., Dec. 7, 1937; s. Roy Oliver and Florine (Francesco) D.; m. Anne Farrell Richardson, Apr. 15, 1967; children: Paul, Kimberly, David. Student, Boston U., 1959-61. Lic. real estate broker. Pres. W.A. Daniels Real Estate Co., Peabody, Mass., 1959-64; with sales Sears, Roebuck and Co., Saugus, Mass., 1964-67; pres. Antech Chem. Co., Middleton, Mass., 1968-78; treas., co-owner Richardson Farms Inc., Middleton, 1978—; corporator Danvers (Mass.) Sav. Bank, 1984—. Mem. New Eng. Ice Cream Retailers Assn., Nat. Trust for Hist. Preservation, Middleton Hist. Soc. Republican. Roman Catholic. Home: 100 S Main St Middleton MA 01949-2211 Office: Richardson Farm Inc PO Box 715 Middleton MA 01949-2615

DANIELS, WILLIAM BURTON, physicist, educator; b. Buffalo, Dec. 21, 1930; s. William C. and Sophia (Penner) D.; m. Adriana A. Braakman, Sept. 2, 1958; children: Charlotte, William Fredrik, Donald Christopher. BS in Physics, U. Buffalo, 1952; MS, Case Inst. Tech., 1955; PhD, Case Int. Tech., 1957. Instr. to asst. prof. Case Inst. Tech., 1957-59; rsch. scientist Union Carbide Corp., 1959-61; mem. faculty Princeton U., 1961-72, prof. solid state scis., 1967-72; Unidel prof. physics U. Del., Newark, 1972—; rsch. collaborator Brookhaven Nat. Lab.; cons. U.S. Army Rsch. Lab.; guest scientist rsch. facility, Denmark, 1976; invité Coll. France, 1977; exchange prof. U. Paris, 1977; guest scientist IBM Zurich Lab., 1977/. Recipient Alexander von Humboldt Sr. Scientist award, 1981; John S. Guggenheim Meml. fellow, 1976-77. Fellow Am. Phys. Soc.; mem. AAAS. Office: U Del Physics Dept Newark DE 19716

DANIELS, WILLIAM JAMES, dean; b. Chgo., Mar. 3, 1940; s. William Hector and Ethel Cora (Dent) McCoy; m. Fannie Pearl Hudson, Aug. 25, 1963; 1 child, Twanda Delois. BA, Upper Iowa U., 1962; MA, U. Iowa, 1964, PhD, 1970. Asst. prof. Union Coll., Schenectady, N.Y., 1966-72; assoc. prof. Union Coll., 1973-81, prof., 1982-88, assoc. dean, 1983-88; Coll. of Liberal Arts dean Rochester Inst. of Tech., Rochester, N.Y., 1988—. Mediator Ctr. for Law, Order & Justice, Schenectady, 1985-88, chmn. bd. dirs., 1986-88. Alfred & Smith fellowship, N.Y. State Govt., Albany, N.Y. 1970-71, Fulbright Hays fellowship, Tokyo, 1973-74, Judicial fellow, U.S. Supreme Ct., 1978-79; Liberty Bell award, Schenectady County Bar Assn., 1988. Mem. Am. Polit. Sci. Assn. (v.p. 1990-91), Nat. Conf. of Black Polit. Sci. (pres. 1972-73, exec. coun., Disting. Svc. award 1984), Assn. of Am. Colls. (bd. dirs. 1992—). Home: 18 Audubon St Rochester NY 14610-1502 Office: Rochester Inst of Tech 1 Lomb Memorial Dr PO Box 9887 Rochester NY 14623-0887

DANIELSON, URSEL REHDING, psychiatrist; b. Hamburg, West Germany, Aug. 15, 1935; came to U.S., 1954; d. Martin George and Gerda Maria (Muller) Rehding; 1 child, Richard. BS, U. Vt., 1964, MD, 1967. Diplomate Am. Bd. Psychiatry and Neurology. Intern Robert Packer Hosp.,

Sayre, Pa., 1967-68; resident in psychiatry U. Vt., Burlington, 1968-71; chief resident McGill U. and Children's Hosp., Montreal, Quebec, Can., 1971-72; pvt. practice Burlington, 1972-86; med. dir. Vt. State Hosp., Waterbury, 1986-90; child psychiatrist Dept. Psychiatry U. Vt., Burlington, 1990—; cons. Franklin Grand Isle Mental Health Ctr., St. Albans, Vt., 1982-86, Essex Junction Sch. System, 1982-86, Chittenden Cen. Sch. Dist., 1972-86, Weeks Sch. , Vergennes, 1972-80, Ogdensburg (N.Y.) State Hosp. Children's Svcs., 1980-84; asst. prof. dept. psychiatry, U. Vt., Burlington, 1972-86, assoc. prof., 1986—, supr. psychiatric residents, 1972—. Treas., dir. Providence Island Assocs., South Hero, Vt., 1988—. Fellow APA; mem. Vt. Psychiat. Assn. (chair nominating com. 1984, 85, 88-91, pres. 1985-86, rep. to APA assembly and area coun. 1978-84, 89-90). Home: 29 Biscayne Hts Colchester VT 05446-1612

DANIS, MARCEL, Canadian government official, lawyer; b. Oct. 22, 1943; married; 2 children. Student, Loyola Coll., Fordham U., U. Paris, U. Montreal. Pvt. practice law; dir. Legal Aid Office Concordia U., prof.; prof. RCMP Coll., dep. speaker, 1984-90; minister of State for Youth House of Commons, minister of state for youth, also fitness and amateur sport, 1990-91, dep. leader of the Govt., 1990-91; min. of Labour, 1991—. Progressive Conservative. Office: House of Commons, Ottawa, ON Canada K1A 0A6

DANIS, ROY STEVEN, marketing professional; b. Freeport, N.Y., Apr. 30, 1956; s. Melvyn James and Lorraine Yvette (Kunken) D.; m. Susan Iris Feltheimer, Jan. 22, 1983; children: Lauren Beth, Rachel Blair. BS, Cornell U., 1978; MBA, Boston Coll., 1984. Asst. ops. mgr. Seagram, N.Y.C., 1978-79; sales rep. Seagram, Westwood, Mass., 1979-81; asst. state mgr. Seagram, Westwood, 1981-82; state mgr. Seagram, Albany, N.Y., 1982-85, Lake Success, N.Y., 1985-87; regional mgr. Seagram, Balt., 1987-88; nat. product mgr. Seagram, N.Y.C., 1988-90, sr. product mgr., 1990—. Pres. exec. bd., 1st vice pres. exec. bd., bd. mem. Assn. for Children with DownSyndrome, Bellmore, N.Y., 1991, 90, 89. Office: Seagram 800 3rd Ave New York NY 10022-7604

DANITZ, MARILYNN PATRICIA, choreographer; b. Buffalo. BS in Chemistry, Le Moyne Coll.; MS in Chem. Engring., Columbia U. Artistic dir. High Frequency Wavelengths/Danitz Dances, 1976—; assoc. prof. Tainan Cheng Chuan Coll., Taiwan, 1984; profl. dancer Ballet Mcpl. Strasbourg, France, Ballet Mcpl. Geneva, Switzerland; choreography commns. include The 11th Internat. Ballet Comp. Varna, Bulgaria, 1983, Tbilisi Ballet Co., USSR, Nat. Ballet of Colombia, Nat. Cheng Kung Dance Group, Taiwan, Cheng Chuan Dancers, Taiwan, others internationally; master choreography workshops include The Cen. Ballet, Beijing, Shanghai Ballet, People's Republic China, Nat. Inst. for Arts, Chinese Cultural U., Taipei, Taiwan, Nanatsudera Theatre and Okuda Studio, Nagoya, Japan, Ballet Philippines, Manila, New South Wales Coll. Dance, Sydney, Australia, The Ballet Sch., Bogota, Colombia, others internationally; video prodn. Real Art Ways Nat. Residency; founder NEA, 1990. TV prodns. of works include Nat. Broadcasting, Venezuela, Nat. Broadcasting, Colombia, Pub. Broadcasting, Albany, N.Y.C., Mpls.; works performed by Nat. Ballet with the Nat. Philharm. Orch. of Colombia Gala Performance, 1984; co. tours include China, Japan, Taiwan, Europe, Hawaii; contbr. articles to Jour. Colloidal Chemistry, Jour. Clin. Pathology, others. Recipient Gold medal, scholarships Conservatoire de Geneve, N.Y. State Regents award, one of 3 Outstanding Dance-Theater Works of 1986 award Dance Brew-ATV Cable Manhattan; NIH Fellow; N.Y. State Regents scholar, Le Moyne Coll. Chemistry scholar, others; chosen for Bessie Schonberg Lab. for Experienced Choreographers, Dance Theater Workshop. Mem. Nat. Assn. for Regional Ballet (Distinction award, mem. choreography conf.), Performance Project, Dance Theater Workshop, Am. Dance Guild (bd. dirs., nat. conf. planning com., seminars for choreographers com.), Albany League of Arts, Rensselaer League of Arts. Address: 560 Riverside Dr New York NY 10027 also: PO Box 216 Sand Lake NY 12153

DANKER, MERVYN KENNETH, director of education; b. Cape Town, South Africa, Mar. 27, 1944; came to U.S., 1989; s. David Barry and Nina (Selbo) D.; m. Rochelle Gould, Dec. 16, 1969; children: Dionne Bonita, David Jonathan, Gareth Saul. BA, U. Cape Town, 1965, BEd, 1974. Cert. secondary edn. tchr., South Africa, Australia. Tchr. Camps Bay High Sch., Cape Town, 1967-76; vice prin. Herzlia High Sch., Cape Town, 1977; headmaster Theodor Herzl Sch., Port Elizabeth, Republic of South Africa, 1978-86, Carmel Sch., Perth, West Australia, 1986-89; dir. of edn. Solomon Schechter Day Sch., West Hartford, Conn., 1989—. Author: History of Theodor Herzl School, 1986. Jewish. Home: 119 Mohegan Dr West Hartford CT 06117 Office: Solomon Schechter Sch 26 Buena Vista Rd West Hartford CT 06107

DANKO, WILLIAM DAVID, marketing educator; b. N.Y., May 21, 1952; m. Connie Christy, July 27, 1974. MBA, SUNY, Albany, 1976; PhD, Rensselaer Poly. Inst., 1983. Prof. mktg. Sch. Bus., SUNY, Albany, 1976—; mktg. cons. Niskayuna, N.Y., 1976—; instr. Taiwan Ministry Econ. Affairs., 1987—. Mem. Am. Mktg. Assn., Steuben Athletic Club (Albany). Republican. Roman Catholic. Office: SUNY 1400 Washington Ave Albany NY 12222-0001

DANNENBERG, ARTHUR MILTON, JR., experimental pathologist, immunologist, educator; b. Phila., Oct. 17, 1923; s. Arthur Mansbach and Marion (Loeb) D.; m. Aileen Rose Hart, Mar. 30, 1948; children: Arlene Jane, Andrew Loeb, Audrey Ann. A.B., Swarthmore Coll., 1944; M.D., Harvard U., 1947; M.A., U. Pa., 1951, Ph.D., 1952. Diplomate: Nat. Bd. Med. Examiners. Intern Albert Einstein Med. Ctr., Phila., 1947-48; research resident Children's Hosp., Phila., 1948-49; fellow Henry Phipps Inst. U. Pa., Phila., 1950-52, asst. prof., 1956-64; fellow U. Utah, 1952-54; assoc. prof. environ. health scis. Johns Hopkins U. Sch. Hygiene, Balt., 1964-73, prof., 1973—, prof. joint faculty Sch. Medicine, dept. pathology, 1976—. Assoc. editor: Am. Rev. Respiratory Diseases, 1979-84, mem. editorial bd., 1973-75; mem. editorial bd. Infection and Immunity jour., 1976-78; contbr. articles to profl. jours. and chpts. to books. Served as lt. comdr. Med. Research Unit 1, USN, 1954-56. Mem. Am. Assn. Pathologists, Histochem. Soc., Am. Soc. Microbiology, Soc. for Leukocyte Biology (sec. 1975-76), Am. Assn. Immunologists, Am. Thoracic Soc., Soc. Investigative Dermatology. Home: 12 Lake Manor Ct Baltimore MD 21210-1017 Office: Johns Hopkins U Sch Hygiene Baltimore MD 21205

DANNER, PAMELA JEAN, software engineering executive; b. Neptune, N.J., June 17, 1962; d. Gene Arthur and Lucy (DeGrande) Ravally; m. James J. Danner III, Aug. 16, 1986. B. Arts and Sci. in Computer Sci., Temple U., Phila., 1984. Software engr. Interactive Structures Inc., Bala Cynwyd, Pa., 1982; product mgr. DISC Systems Inc., Willow Grove, Pa., 1982-84; product support engr. Commodore Tech., West Chester, Pa., 1984-86; network engring. software devel. mgr. ADP, N.Y.C., 1986-90; staff engr. Catalyst Corp., Newtown, Pa., 1990—. Bd. dirs. Temple U. Arts & Scis. Alumni Assn., 1984-89; v.p. Washington Twp. (N.J.) Rep. Assn., 1989; youth svcs. commr. Washington Twp., 1989—. Recipient Landscape Design award Gloucester County (N.J.) Parks and Recreation, 1989. Mem. Phi Sigma Sigma (nat. chair chpt. adminstrn. 1990—). Roman Catholic. Home: 587 Heuton's Mill Dr Newtown PA 19047 Office: Catalyst Corp Catalyst Bldg 27 Blacksmith Rd Newtown PA 18940-1870

DANNIBLE, ANTHONY FRANK, public accountant; b. Syracuse, N.Y., Apr. 1, 1947; s. Louis Frank and Mary Anne (Louise) D.; m. Judith Anne Susco, May 16, 1970; children: Christine, Amy, Thomas. BS, Syracuse U., 1969. CPA, N.Y. state. Acct., tax expert Price Waterhouse & Co., Syracuse, N.Y., 1969-78; founder Dannible & McKee, CPAs, Syracuse, 1978—; cons. Dannible/McKee Assocs., Ltd., Syracuse, 1980—; chmn. N.Y. State Soc. CPAs Tax Conf., N.Y.C., Rochester, 1991; faculty Found. for Acctg. Edn., 1982—; dir. Syracuse U. Tax Adv. Com.,1 984—; valuation expert Tax Ct. Expert Witness, 1983—. Author: (course/workbook) Valuing a Design Firm, 1980, Tax Planning for Design Firms, 1972, Ownership Transition for the Design Professional, 1980, 89. Treas. Liverpool (N.Y.) Youth Soccer League, 1985—; pres. Estate Planning Coun. Cen. N.Y., Syracuse, 1990-91, dir., 1982—. Mem. AICPAs, N.Y. State Soc. CPAS, Tax Com. for Closely Held Bus., AICPAs Tax Div. Home: 4968 Lantern Cir Liverpool NY 13088-4721 Office: Dannible & McKee CPAs 499 S Warren St Syracuse NY 13202-2609

DANSEREAU, FRED EDWARD, JR., behavioral scientist, educator; b. Yeadon, Pa., Sept. 20, 1946; s. Fred Edward and Catherine (Kennedy) D.; B.S., St. Josephs Coll., 1968; M.A., U. Ill., 1970, Ph.D., 1972. NSF fellow in behavioral sci. U. Ill., 1968-72; asst. prof. organizational behavior City U.N.Y., 1972-73; asso. prof. organizational behavior State U.N.Y., Buffalo, 1973—; cons. various orgns. Mem. Am. Psychol. Assn., Acad. Mgmt., AAAS, AAUP, Phi Kappa Phi. Author: Theory Testing in Organizational Behavior: The Varient Approach, 1984; contbr. articles and chpts. to profl. publs. Home: 60 Groton Dr Buffalo NY 14228-2543 Office: SUNY 276 Jacobs Hall Buffalo NY 14260

DANTINI, JULIE ANN, educational administrator, director, counselor; b. Susquehanna, Pa., Dec. 9, 1947; d. Guilio and Anna Louise (Pingeralli) D. BS, Mansfield (Pa.) U., 1969; MS, SUNY, Oneonta, 1972. Cert. elem. and spl. edn. tchr., guidance counselor, N.Y.. Educaotr Binghamton (N.Y.) City Sch. Dist., 1969-73, social worker, tchr. in charge visually impaired, 1973-79; vocat. rehab. counselor N.Y. State Edn. Dept., Binghamton, 1979-81, sr. vocat. rehab. couselor, 1981-85; dir. counseling Binghamton and Elmira, N.Y., 1985—; advisor, cons. Broome Community Coll., Binghamton, 1983—; advisor N.Y. Assn. for Learning Disabled, Albany, 1985-89; mem. steering com. psychology dept. SUNY-Binghamton, 1984-86; advisor Peer Newtork NYU, N.Y.C., 1987; mgmt. team for rehab. svcs. adminstrn. grant Catskill Ind. Ctr., 1990—; project adv. com. Internat. Ctr. for Disabled, 1991—. Cons. book Vocational Rehabilitation for Learning Disables Adults, 1984. Recipient Cert. of Merit, Gov. of N.Y., 1985, 91, Nat. Disting. Svc. Registry, 1989. Mem. Nat. Rehab. Assn., Nat. Rehab. Counseling Assn. Home: 69 Moore Ave Binghamton NY 13903-3120 Office: NY State Edn Dept 92 Hawley St Binghamton NY 13901-3997

D'ANTONIO, ROBERT VINCENT, JR., mental health services professional; b. Upper Darby, Pa., Nov. 21, 1962; s. Robert Vincent Sr. and Ruth Ann (Runske) D'A.; m. Theresa Marie Dougherty, Apr. 15, 1989. BA in Behavioral Sci., Neumann Coll., 1987; MEd, West Chester (Pa.) U., 1991. Mental health therapist Media (Pa.) Child Guidance, 1987-89; mental retardation case mgr. Delaware County Offic of Mental Retardation, Media, 1989—. Named World Powerlifting champion World Corp. Games, 1988. Mem. AACD, Am. Drug Free Powerlifting Assn. Republican. Roman Catholic. Home: 5200 Hilltop Dr # 16Y Chester PA 19015-1204 Office: Delaware County Office Mental Retardation 1 E 9th St Chester PA 19013-4289

DANZIGER, RICHARD MARTIN, lawyer; b. N.Y.C., Feb. 18, 1938; s. Frederick S. and Louise (Paskus) D.; m. Peggy Block, June 11, 1962; children: Michael Paskus, Katherine Block. BA, John Hopkins U., 1960; postgrad., U. Va. Law Sch., 1960-61; LLB, Yale, 1963. Bar: N.Y. 1963. Assoc. Kupfer, Silberfeld, Nathan & Danziger, N.Y.C., 1963-69; ptnr. Danziger, Bangser & Klipstein, N.Y.C., 1970-80; counsel Danziger, Bangser & Weiss, N.Y.C., 1980-88, Richards & O'Neil, N.Y.C., 1988—; bd. dirs. Block Drug Co., Inc., Jersey City, N.J.. Trustee Spence Sch., N.Y.C., 1974-81; asian art vis. com. Met. Mus. of Art, N.Y.C., 1981—; bd. govs., exec. com. Yale U. Art Gallery, 1986—; bd. dirs. Japan Soc., 1982-88. Mem. Assn. of the Bar of the City of N.Y., N.Y. State Bar Assn., Yale Law Sch. Assn. (exec. com. 1987—), Yale Club, Century Country Club. Republican. Jewish. Home: 155 E 69th St New York NY 10021-5195 Office: Richards & O'Neil 885 3rd Ave New York NY 10022-4834

DAOUST, RAYMOND GEORGE, pharmaceutical scientist, company executive; b. Montreal, July 3, 1932; came to U.S., 1965; s. Georges Emmanuel and Ida Elizabeth (Dion) D.; m. Monique Musy, Aug. 22, 1955; children: Michelle, Madeleine, Daniel. BA, U. Montreal, 1952, B in Pharmacy, 1956, PharmM, 1957; PhD, Purdue U., 1960. Rsch. chemist ATLAS Chem. Industries, Wilmington, Del., 1960-63; asst. prof. U. Montreal, 1963-65; sr. rsch. scientist Bristol Labs., Syracuse, N.Y., 1965-67, asst. dir. product devel., 1967-72, mgr. devel. and prodn., 1972-75, devel. group mgr., 1975-80; mgr. pharmacy rsch. Bristol Myers Internat. Div., N.Y.C., 1980-85; assoc. dir. tech. affairs Bristol Myers Pharm. R&D, Wallingford, Conn., 1985-91; dir. Worldwide Reg. Affairs Bristol Myers Squibb Pharm. Rsch. Inst., Syracuse, 1991—; Mem. Pharmacy Examining Bd. Canada, 1963-65. Contbg. editor Internat. Pharm. Abstracts, Montreal, 1963-65; participant USA/UK Handbook of Pharm. Excipients, 1979-80; contbr. articles to profl. jours.; patentee in field. Grantee Purdue Rsch. Found., Lafayette, Ind., 1959. Mem. Am. Assn. Pharm. Scientists, Internat. Pharm. Fedn., Drug Info. Assn., Regulatory Affairs Profl. Assn. Roman Catholic. Home: 4600 Watergap Manlius NY 13104 Office: Bristol Myers Squibb Thompson Rd East Syracuse NY 13221

D'APOLITO, DAVID JOSEPH, dentist; b. Port Reading, N.J., Apr. 26, 1955; s. Michael Anthony and Helen (Bahush) D'A.; m. Nancy Elizabeth DePlacido. BS, Northeastern U. Coll. Pharmacy, 1978; DMD, U. Medicine and Dentistry of N.J., Newark, 1983. Lic. dentist, N.J., N.Y.; registered pharmacist, N.J. Staff pharmacist, pharmacy resident NIH USPHS, Bethesda, Md., 1978-79; pharmacist SupeRx Drugs, Carteret, N.J., 1980-83; pvt. practice dentistry N.J., N.Y., 1983-84, Woodbridge, N.J., 1984—; attending dentist, oral cancer screener John F. Kennedy Hosp., Edison, N.J., 1986—; resident in tempomandibular joint dysfunction Univ. Medicine Dentistry N.J., 1987-89. Lt. (j.g.) USPHS, 1978-79. Italian Dental Soc. N.Y. scholar, 1983; recipient Am. Coll. Stomatologic Surgeons award N.J. Dental Sch., 1983. Mem. Am. Dental Soc., Middlesex County Dental Soc., N.J. Dental Assn., Omicron Kappa Upsilon, Rho Chi. Office: 511 Rahway Ave Woodbridge NJ 07095-3404

D'ARCANGELO, MARCIA DIANE, educational video producer; b. Meadville, Pa., May 16, 1945; d. Terrence Benjamin and Eileene Marie (Judy) Darcangelo; m. Thomas Brown Andrews V, Sept. 16, 1989. BS in Chemistry, Grove City Coll., 1967. Info. specialist Eastman Kodak Co., Rochester, N.Y., 1967-68; singer/dancer Kids Next Door-Young Ams. Orgn. (Katand Prodns.), L.A., 1968-69, Stand Up and Cheer TV Show, The Johnny Mann Singers, L.A., 1970-74; singer, dancer, actor John Brown's Body AEA Nat. Tour, Fitzgerald Prodns., L.A., 1975-76; singer, dancer The Perry Como Show-Roncom Prodns., 1977-82; med. news journalist Physicians Radio Network, N.Y.C., 1983-84; prodn. asst., prodn. coord. ASCD, Alexandria, Va., 1985-86, producer, sr. producer, 1987-88, mgr. media prodns., 1989—; cons. Holbrook & Kellogg, Falls Church, Va., 1990, Developmental Studies Ctr., San Ramon, Calif., 1991, Soc. for Preservation of Social Security and Medicare, Washington, 1991. Composer 4 mus. pieces (words and music); co-author 12 tng. manuals; author/co-author 32 video-based tchr. tng. programs, article. Recipient medal of merit VFW, 1971, Jack Kennedy Alumni Achievement award Grove City Coll. Alumni Assn., 1984, Clarion award Women in Comm., 1991, 3 Cine golden Eagle awards Coun. on Internat. Nontheatrical Events, 1991, 92, Silver Apple award Nat. Ednl. Film and Video Festival, 1992. Mem. NAFE, ASCD, Women in Film and Video, Internat. TV Assn., Am. Soc. for Tng. and Devel. Republican.

DARCY, KEITH THOMAS, educator, finance company executive; b. N.Y.C., June 18, 1948; s. Donald and Geraldine (Kindermann) D.; m. Lynne Alison Cumming, June 17, 1972; children: Erin Lyn, Timothy James. BS in Econs., Fordham U., 1970; MBA, Iona Coll., New Rochelle, N.Y., 1974; postgrad., N.Y. Theol. Sem. With Bankers Trust Co., N.Y.C., 1970-77; v.p. Marine Midland Bank N.A., N.Y.C., 1977-82; chief exec. officer IGM div. of Frank B. Hall & Co., Inc., Briarcliff Manor, N.Y., 1982-83; dir. human resource div. Marine Midland Bank, N.Y.C., 1984-89; pres., chief exec. officer Found. For Leadership, Quality and Ethics Practice, N.Y.C., 1989—; adj. faculty mem. Marymount Coll., 1978—, Mercy Coll., 1975-82; mem. faculty consumer bankers Assoc. Grad. Sch. of Bank Mgmt., U. Va. Author: I Quit My Job Today, 1992; participating author Change Management; mem. editorial bd. At Work: Stories of Tomorrow's Workplace. Treas. Westchester County Rep. Com., White Plains, N.Y., 1979-89; asst. treas. N.Y. State Friends for Jim Buckley, 1976; dir NCCJ, 1977-85; trustee Bedford Presbyn. Ch., N.Y., 1982-87; mem. Westchester Blue Ribbon Commn. to Formulate County Housing Policy, 1979; trustee March of Dimes, Westchester, 1978-84, chmn. Exec. Walkathon, 1978-81. Mem. Delta Mu Delta. Club: Soc. Friendly Sons of St. Patrick (pres. 1985). Home: Horseshoe Hill W Pound Ridge NY 10576

DARDEN, JOSEPH SAMUEL, JR., health educator; b. Pleasantville, N.J., July 25, 1925; s. Joseph Samuel and Blanche Catherine (Paige) D.; A.B., Lincoln U., 1948; M.A., N.Y.U., 1952, Ed.D. (Danforth Found. fellow), 1963; m. Barbara Cassandra Sellers, Dec. 30, 1955 (div. July 1979); 1 dau., Michele Irene. Instr. biol. scis. Clark Coll., Atlanta, 1952-55; asst. prof. Albany (Ga.) State Coll., 1955-58, prof., 1959-64; asst. prof. Kean Coll. of N.J., Union, 1964-67, prof. health edn., 1970—, coord. of health, 1977-79, chmn. dept. health and recreation, 1979-84, coord. of health, 1984—, dir. minority enrollment, 1988—; adj. prof. health Wagner Coll., S.I., N.Y., 1965-88; cons. N.J. Dept. Edn., 1968-73, 76-88. Bd. advisors Marylawn of Oranges, 1971-73; bd. dirs. N.J. Council Family Relations, 1981-83; trustee Planned Parenthood of Essex County, N.J., 1985—. Served with AUS, 1944-46. Mem. Am. Alliance for Health, Phys. Edn., Recreation and Dance (Eastern dist. v.p. for health edn. 1971-72, dist. pres. 1974-75; Eastern dist. rep. 1979-82; honor award Eastern dist. 1976, nat. honor award 1985, Outstanding Tchr. award Eastern dist. 1983, Charles D. Henry award 1988, Edwin B. Henderson award 1991), Am. Sch. Health Assn. (governing council 1970-73, Disting. Service award 1971), Assn. Advancement Health Edn. (dir. 1975-78, Profl. Svc. award 1990), N.J. Health Edn. Council (founder 1967, honor award 1975), N.J. Assn. Health, Phys. Edn. and Recreation (v.p. health edn. 1967, Honor fellow award 1972, Disting. Leadership award 1975), Alpha Phi Alpha. Author: (with others) Growth Pattern and Sex Education, 1967, Updated Supplement to Growth Pattern and Sex Education, 1972. Home: 1416 Thelma Dr Union NJ 07083-6220 Office: Kean Coll NJ Union NJ 07083

DARDEN, MARGARET See BROOKS, MAGGIE

DAREHSHORI, NADER FARHANG, publishing company executive; b. Shiraz, Iran, Dec. 15, 1936; came to U.S., 1961, naturalized, 1972; s. Zaki F. and Rokhsar (Farsimadan) D.; B.A. in B.A., U. Wis., 1966, postgrad., 1966; m. Anne C. Wagnild, Dec. 14, 1968 (dec.); m. CynthiaMcGuffey, Aug. 3, 1991. Supt. village schs., Shiraz, 1959-61; salesman Houghton Mifflin Co., Geneva, Ill., 1966-75, field sales mgr., 1975-77, sales mgr. of Midwest, 1977-84, v.p., gen. mgr. Coll. div. Midwest, 1984-86, v.p., dir. Coll. Div., 1987-89, exec. v.p., bd. dirs., 1989-90, chmn, CEO, 1990-91, chmn., pres., CEO, 1991—, Houghton Mifflin Co., Boston. Democrat. Club: Kiwanis. Office: Houghton Mifflin Co One Beacon St Boston MA 02108

DARGAHI-NOUBARY, GHOLAMREZA, statistics educator; b. Tehran, Iran, Feb. 23, 1946; came to U.S., 1988; s. Abbasali and Zahra Dargahi-Noubary; m. Zohreh Garrousian, Aug. 16, 1973; children: Behzad, Farzad. BSc, Tehran U., 1966, MSc, 1968; MSc, Manchester U., Eng., 1975, PhD, 1978. Asst. prof. Iran U. Sci. & Tech., Tehran, 1968-74, assoc. prof., 1980-87; teaching asst. Manchester U., Eng., 1978-79; prof. U. Kaiserslautern, Germany, 1987-88; assoc. prof. U. Northern Ill., Dekalb, 1988-89, Bloomsburg (Pa.) U., 1989—; vis. prof. Cath. U. Louvain, Belgium, 1986, Wharton Sch., U. Pa., summers 1991, 92; vis. rsch. fellow UCLA, 1991; vis. scholar Princeton (N.J.) U., 1992-93; cons. Power Rsch. Ctr., Tehran, 1983-86. Contbr. articles to profl. jours. Grantee NSF, 1991—, Pa. State System of Higher Edn., 1990—. Fellow Alexander von Humboldt, Royal Statis. Soc., Iranian Math. Soc. (exec. com., bulletin editor 1983-86); mem. Am. Math. Soc., Math. Assn. Am., Am. Geophys. Union, Natural Hazard Soc. (Time Series and Forecasting Soc.), Assn. Math. Geology. Home: 1198 Franklin Dr Bloomsburg PA 17815-8879 Office: Bloomsburg U Bloomsburg PA 17815

DARGIS, JEAN ANTHONY, voluntary health agency executive; b. Mpls., Mar. 9, 1931; s. Henry Joseph and Josephine Marie (Violette) D.; m. Mary Ruth Buschman, July 2, 1956; 1 child, Melissa Jeanne Dargis Herzog. BA, St. Paul (Minn.) Sem., 1952; MusB, Universite Laval, Quebec, Can., 1954. Tchr. St. Anthony Acad., Mpls., 1954-59, Holy Childhood Sch., St. Paul, 1955-57; various positions March of Dimes Birth Defects Found., White Plains, N.Y., 1959—; v.p., dir. nat. office of vols. March of Dimes Birth Defects Found., White Plains, 1989—. Author: (handbook) Manual for Chapters, 1990; editor: (handbook) Volunteer Development Guide, 1991, (booklet) Basic Principles of Volunteer Development, 1989. Mem. Diocesan Commn./Devel., San Jose, Calif., 1983-90; dir. Diocesan Choir, San Jose, 1983-90, St. Victor's Parish Choir, San Jose, 1971-90. Mem. Mensa, Ind. Sector. Republican. Roman Catholic. Home: 3 Arborwood Ln White Plains NY 10603-3350

DARIEN, STEVEN MARTIN, pharmaceuticals executive; b. N.Y.C., Oct. 29, 1942; s. Leo and Laura (Kalish) D.; m. Susan Ruth Kinsley, Nov. 29, 1942; children: Jodi Ellen, Andrew Todd. AB, Rutgers Coll., 1963; MBA, Columbia U., 1966. Claims settler Equitable Life, N.Y.C., 1963-64; mgmt. trainee Merck & Co., Inc., Rahway, N.J., 1966-69, mgr. coll. rels., 1969-74, exec. dir. pers. resources, 1974-79, exec. dir. U.S. Pers., 1979-85, v.p. employee rels., 1985-89, v.p. worldwide pres., 1989-90, v.p. human resources, 1990—; chmn. adv. bd. Sta. WNET Channel 13, Newark, 1988—. Mem. Columia U. Bus. Sch. Alumni Assn. (v.p.). Office: Merck & Co Inc 126 E Lincoln Ave Rahway NJ 07065-4687

D'ARISTA, JANE WEBB, economic analyst; b. Jacksonville, Fla., July 28, 1932; d. Henry Toby Webb and Sarah Adella Green Renner; m. Robert Augustus D'Arista, Oct. 30, 1954 (dec. 1987); children: Carla, Peter, Thomas, Antonia. BA, Barnard Coll., 1954; postgrad., Am. U., 1964-65. Staff mem. Com. on Banking & Currency, U.S. Ho. of Reps., Washington, 1966-78; prin. analyst Congl. Budget Office, Washington, 1978-83; chief fin. economist Subcom. on Telecommunications and Fin., U.S. Ho. of Reps., Washington, 1983-86; assoc. dir. Morin Ctr. for Banking Law Studies, Boston U., 1986—. Author: Federal Reserve Structure and the Development of Monetary Policy, 1972, Financial Restructuring: The Major Policy Issues, 1986; contbr. articles to profl. jours., chpts. to books. Democrat. Episcopalian. Home: 4 Candle Light Way Ashland MA 01721-1065 Office: Boston Univ Sch Law 765 Commonwealth Ave Boston MA 02215-1401

DARLINGTON, HENRY, JR., investment broker; b. N.Y.C., Jan. 8, 1925; s. Henry and Dorothy (Stone-Smith) D.; m. Frances Elizabeth Richardson, June 5, 1948 (div. Feb. 1965); children: Henry Darlington III, Elizabeth Aldrich, Victoria Wilde Darlington Yoder; m. Dorothea Fiske Page, July 1965 (div. Dec. 1973); m. Carla P. Barratt-Brown, June 1990. Student, pvt. schs.; BA, Columbia U., 1949; LHD (hon.), St. Paul's Coll., Lawrenceville, Va., 1987. Salesman IBM, 1949-52; security salesman Cosgrave, Miller & Whitehead, 1952-55; gen. ptnr. Hill, Darlington & Co., 1955-62; registered rep. Cruttenden, Podesta and Miller, 1962; with syndicate dept. Loeb, Rhoades & Co., 1962-64, br. office adminstr., 1964-67, v.p., 1967-71, registered rep., 1972-79; investment exec. Shearson Loeb Rhoades, Inc. (now Shearson Lehman Bros.), 1979—; v.p. B. J. Van Ingen & Co., Inc., 1956-59. Trustee Hoosac Sch., Hoosick, N.Y., 1968-75, Ch. Heavenly Rest Day Sch., N.Y.C., 1974-84, Search and Care, N.Y.C., 1972-87; bd. dirs. Fedn. Protestant Welfare Agys., 1962-89, asst. treas., 1971-79; bd. dirs. Episcopal Mission Soc., 1979-89, St. Paul's Ch., Rome, St. James' Ch., Florence, Italy; trustee Bd. Fgn. Parishes; vestryman Ch. Heavenly Rest, 1969-75; warden Eglise Francaise du Saint Esprit, 1984-88. With USNR, 1943-46, lt. Res., 1946-65. Mem. SAR, St. Nicholas Soc. (pres. 1976-78), S.R., St. Andrews Soc., The Huguenot Soc. (pres. 1986-89), Soc. Colonial Wars, Mil. Order World War, N.Y. Soc. Mil. and Naval Officers World War, Navy League U.S. (past sec., treas. Western Conn. Coun.), Naval Order, Pilgrim Soc., Union Club, Univ. Club, Everglades Club, Piping Rock Club, Delta Psi (trustee Alpha chpt. 1953-58). Home: 1115 5th Ave New York NY 10128-0100 Office: 3 Corporate Park Dr White Plains NY 10604-3803

DARMAN, RICHARD GORDON, government official, former investment banker, former educator, business consultant; b. Charlotte, N.C., May 10, 1943; m. Kathleen Emmet, Sept. 1, 1967; children: William Temple Emmet, Jonathan Warren Emmet. B.A. cum laude, Harvard U., 1964, M.B.A., 1967. Dep. asst. sec. HEW, Washington, 1971-72; asst. to sec. Dept. Def., Washington, 1973; spl. asst. to atty. gen. Washington, 1973; fellow Woodrow Wilson Internat. Center for Scholars, Washington, 1974; prin., dir. ICF, Inc., Washington, 1975, 77-80; asst. sec. Dept. Commerce, 1976-77; lectr. public policy and mgmt. Harvard U., 1977-80; asst. to Pres. Reagan, The White House, Washington, 1981-85; dep. sec. Dept. Treasury, 1985-87; mng. dir. Shearson Lehman Hutton Inc., N.Y.C., 1987-88; dir. office mgmt. and budget, mem. Pres. Bush's Cabinet The White House, Washington, 1989—; vice chmn. U.S. del. UN Conf. on Law of Sea, 1977; mem. U.S. del. Summit of Industrialized Countries, 1981, 82, 83, 84, 85, 86; mem. ocean policy com. Nat. Acad. Scis., 1978-80. Editor: Harvard Ednl. Rev, 1970; contbg. editor

U.S. News & World Report, 1987-88; author various articles on bus. and public policy. Trustee Bennington (Vt.) Coll., 1974-75, The Brookings Inst., 1987-88. Office: Exec Office of Pres US Trade Rep 600 17th St NW Washington DC 20503-0001*

DARR, WALTER ROBERT, financial analyst; b. Phila., June 19, 1956; s. John Fluke Sr. and Lois Marilyn (Fry) D. BS in Commerce, Rider Coll., 1978, MBA, 1991. Collateral analyst First Nat. Bank & Trust Co., Beverly, N.J., 1978-84; collateral analyst First Peoples Bank of N.J., Westmont, 1984-88, loan rev. analyst, 1988—. Treas. Cinnaminson Bapt. Ch., 1983-87, deacon, 1988-89; mem. Lewis Shearer Chorale, 1982—. Recipient Sch. award Am. Legion Post, Medford, N.J., 1974. Republican. Baptist. Home: 416 Hemlock Rd Mount Laurel NJ 08054-2146

DARRETTA, JOHN LAWRENCE, English and communication arts educator; b. Yonkers, N.Y., Oct. 4, 1938; s. Anthony F. and Concetta A. (Mancini) D. AAS, Westchester Community Coll., Valhalla, N.Y., 1958; BA, Iona Coll., 1963; MA, Fordham U., 1966, PhD, 1972. Instr. Marian Coll., Indpls., 1965-67; prof. Iona Coll., New Rochelle, N.Y., 1967—, chair communication arts dept., 1976-78, 83-85; chair communication arts dept., 1992—; Fulbright prof., Milan, 1975-76. Author: Vittorio De Sica, 1983; co-author (screenplays) Holy Terror, 1987, Channel Crossing, 1989; contbr. articles to profl. jours. Ford Found. grantee Am. Film Inst., 1979, Iona Coll. grantee, 1980, 85. Mem. AAUP, Am. Film Inst., Modern Lang. Assn., Writers Guild Am. Fulbright Alumni Assn. (life). Roman Catholic. Home: 27 Sherman Ave Mount Vernon NY 10552-2008 Office: Iona Coll Communication Arts Dept 715 North Ave New Rochelle NY 10801-1890

DARRIGAN, ROBERT JOSEPH, JR., accountant; b. Newburgh, N.Y., June 17, 1958; s. Robert Joseph and Marie Regina (Ochietti) D.; m. Anne M. Mainey, Aug. 11, 1984 (div. Nov. 1989). BBA in Pub. Acctg., Hofstra U., 1980, MBA in Bus. Computer Info. Systems, 1990. Sr. acct. Alfred Sperber and Co., Lake Success, N.Y., 1980-84; asst. to the controller Nikon Inc., Melville, N.Y., 1984—; pvt. practice tax preparer Long Beach, N.Y., 1980—. Mem. Nat. Assn. Accts., Am. Mgmt. Assn. Republican. Roman Catholic. Home: 27 Georgia Ave Long Beach NY 11561-1232 Office: Nikon Inc 1300 Walt Whitman Rd Melville NY 11747-3064

DARROW, WILLIAM RICHARD, pharmaceutical company executive; b. Middletown, Ohio, Sept. 7, 1939; s. Richard William and Nelda Virginia (Darling) D.; B.A., Ohio Wesleyan U., 1960; M.D., Western Res. U., 1964; Ph.D. in Pharmacology, Case-Western Res. U., 1969; m. Janet Elizabeth Swan, June 20, 1964; children: James William, Susan Elizabeth, Margaret Ellen. Intern, Univ. Hosps., Cleve., 1964; sr. clin. rsch. assoc. CIBA Pharm. Co., 1969, asst. dir. clin. pharmacology, 1969-70; dir. clin. pharmacology CIBA-GEIGY Corp., 1970-75, exec. dir. clin. rsch., 1975-76; sr. v.p. rsch., med. dir. Wallace Labs. div. Carter Wallace, Inc., Cranbury, N.J., 1976-80; med. dir. Schering Labs. div. Schering-Plough Corp., Kenilworth, N.J., 1980, v.p. med. and regulatory affairs, 1981-82, sr. v.p. med. ops., 1982—. Chmn. rsch. com. N.J. Health Scis. Group, 1973-76, mem. exec. com., 1973-74, 76-86, treas. 1977-80, v.p., 1980-86, Bernards Twp. Bd. Health, 1979—, v.p., 1980, pres., 1981-85, 86—; bd. dirs. N.J. Arthritis Found., 1990—, exec. com., 1991—; mem. sci. adv. bd. Clin. Rsch. Ctr. Robert Wood Johnson Med. Ctr., 1990—. Recipient Roche award, 1962; USPHS postdoctoral fellow, 1965-69. Fellow Royal Soc. Medicine; mem. AMA, Drug Info. Assn., N.J. Acad. Scis., Pharm. Mfrs. Assn. (mem. steering com. med. section 1984—, program chmn. 1988-89, vice-chmn. 1989-90, chmn. 1990-92, past chmn. 1992—), Pharm. Mfrs. Assn. Found. (sci. adv. bd. 1990—, mem. U.S. del. Internat. Conf. on Harmonization 1991), Phi Gamma Delta, Phi Rho Sigma, Omicron Delta Kappa, Pi Delta Epsilon. Republican. Presbyterian. Home: 42 Palmerston Pl Basking Ridge NJ 07920-2524 also: 521 E Lake Rd Penn Yan NY 14527 Office: Galloping Hill Rd Kenilworth NJ 07033

DARST, DAVID MARTIN, investment banking company executive, writer, educator; b. Knoxville, Tenn., Nov. 14, 1947; s. Guy Bewley and Susan Mary (McGinnis) D.; m. Diane Wassman; children: Elizabeth Mathews, David Martin, Jr. BA, Yale U., 1969; MBA, Harvard U., 1971. Assoc. Goldman, Sachs & Co., N.Y.C., 1971-75, v.p., mgr., 1981—; v.p., resident mgr. Goldman, Sachs & Co., Zurich, Switzerland, 1975-81; vis. lectr. Coll. and Sch. Mgmt., Yale U., New Haven, 1981—, Bus. Sch., Harvard U., Boston, 1987—. Author: The Complete Bond Book, 1975, The Handbook of the Bond and Money Markets, 1981; contbr. articles to profl. jours. Bd. dirs. Deer Park Assn., 1985—, pres., 1989—. William H. Donaldson Disting. Faculty fellow Sch. Mgmt. Yale U., 1986-87. Mem. The Money Marketeers, The Phelps Assn. (v.p., gov. 1974—), Assn. Internat. Bond Dealers (edn. com.), Yale Club of N.Y.C. (coun. 1987—, chmn. fin. com. 1987—). Office: Goldman Sachs & Co 29th Fl 85 Broad St New York NY 10004-2434

DART, JACK CALHOON, chemical engineer; b. Concord, Mich., Aug. 14, 1912; s. James Laurance and Ethel Lenore (Calhoon) D.; m. Widder, June 16, 1940, (wid. May 1990); children: Dianne Gibson, Linda Dart, Janis Cook, James. AB, Albion Coll., 1934; BSE, U. Mich., 1935, MSE, 1937. Chem. engr. Pan Am. Ref., Texas City, Tex., 1937-44; chief engr. Esso Labs, Baton Rouge, 1944-47; mgr. rsch. lab. Houdry Process Corp., Phila., 1947-55, v.p., 1955-62; owner J.C. Dart and Assocs., Potomac, Md., 1962—. Mem. Sch. Bd. Nether Providence, Wallingford, Pa., 1961, 62. Recipient Disting. Alumni award Albion (Mich.) Coll., 1982. Fellow Am. Inst. Chem. Engrs. (Disting. Svc. award 1974, founder). Home and Office: 10101 Gary Rd Rockville MD 20854-4109

DART, JOHN ROBERT, horticulturist; b. Montour, N.Y., July 25, 1925; s. Russel S. and Helen M. (Bristow) D.; m. Maryann Alexander, Aug. 20, 1951 (div. Jan. 1974); children: Ralph, Richard, Christopher. Student, U. Conn.; U.S. Mcht. Marine Acad., Kings Point, N.Y. Commd. ensign U.S. Mcht. Marines, 1944; advanced through grades to 1st engr. $, $, $, 1957; with Pratt & Whitney Aircraft Exptl., 1957-68; pres. Dart Tree Farm Corp., Middle Haddam, Conn., 1960—; with bldg. dept. Conn. Nat. Bank, Hartford, 1968—; pres., sexton Union Hill Cemetery, Middle Haddam, 1959—. Mem. Rotary (pres. 1983), Masons. Republican. Home and Office: Easy St Middle Haddam CT 06456-9999

DAS, PRADIP KUMAR, polymer chemist; b. Boko, India, Dec. 1, 1951; came to U.S., 1980; s. Bhuban Chandra and Prafulla Bala Das; m. Krishna Saharia, Jan. 28, 1988. BSc with honors, Cotton Coll., Gauhati, India, 1971; MSc, Gauhati U., 1973; PhD, Va. Poly. Inst. and State U., 1984. Lectr. in chemistry Digboi (India) Coll., 1973-75, Sci. Coll., Jorhat, India, 1975-80; rsch. asst. Va. Poly. Inst. and State U., Blacksburg, 1980-84; sr. rsch. chemist Monsanto Chem. Co., Springfield, Mass., 1984-86; rsch. specialist Monsanto Chem. Co., Springfield, 1986-88, sr. rsch. specialist, group leader, 1988-91, ops. mgr., 1991, tech. mgr., 1991—. Contbr. articles on polymer chemistry to various publs. Bd. dirs. World Affairs Coun., Springfield, 1986—, Insights, Inc., Springfield, 1986-88; mem. Sci. Mus. Adv. Bd., Springfield, 1988—; coord. Springfield Sch. Tchrs. Program, 1989—. Fellow Am. Inst. Chemists; mem. Am. Chem. Soc., AAAS. Home: 8 Karen Dr Wilbraham MA 01095-2516 Office: Monsanto Chem Co 730 Worcester St Springfield MA 01151-1089

DAS, T. K., management educator, consultant; b. Calcutta, India, July 8, 1938; s. Kisori Mohan and Radha Rani Das. BS with honors, U. Calcutta, 1957; MS, Jadavpur U., Calcutta, 1959; M in Mgmt., Asian Inst. Mgmt., Manila, 1977; PhD, UCLA, 1984. Cert. Assoc. of the Indian Inst. of Bankers, 1964. Various exec. positions State Bank of India, 1960-76; asst. prof. mgmt. Calif. State U., L.A., 1980-83; asst. prof. strategic mgmt. Tex. Tech U., Lubbock, 1984-86; asst. prof. strategic mgmt. CUNY, 1987-89, assoc. prof., 1990—. Author: Operations Research for Decision Making in Commercial Banks, 1972, Understanding Our New Organizational Roles, 1972, Operations Research in Banking, 1973, The Area Superintendent: Role Design, Development, and Experience, 1975, Agricultural Financing by Commercial Banks, 1976, Marketing in Banks, 1976, Human Resource Management and Productivity: State of the Art and Future Prospects, Vol. I: Focus on the United States, 1984, Vol. II: International Perspectives, 1985, The Subjective Side of Strategy Making: Future Orientations and Perceptions of Executives, 1986, The Time Dimension: An Interdisciplinary Guide, 1990; assoc. editor SCIMA (Systems and Cybernetics in Mgmt.), 1990—; assoc. editor Rev. of Business Studies; mem. editorial bd. Jour. Managerial Issues; contbr. numerous articles to acad. and profl. jours. Recipient 1st prize Indian Inst. of Bankers Prize Essay Competition, 1964, Charat Ram Found. award All India Mgmt. Assn., 1968. Mem. World Future Soc. (profl.), Acad. of Mgmt., Inst. Mgmt. Scis., Strategic Mgmt. Soc., Planning Forum, Acad. Internt. Bus., Internat. Soc. Study of Time, Soc. Mgmt. Sci. and Applied Cybernetics (life), Indian Inst. Bankers (life), Beta Gamma Sigma. Home: 73-12 35th Ave Apt F61 Jackson Heights NY 11372 Office: CUNY Mgmt Dept 17 Lexington Ave New York NY 10010

DASH, BARRY HAROLD, pharmaceutical company executive; b. N.Y.C., June 9, 1931; s. Joseph and Anna (Levine) D.; m. Selma Magid, Dec. 19, 1953; children: Faith, Neil, Jeffrey. BS, Columbia U., 1952, MS, 1954; PhD, U. Fla., 1956. Asst. prof. Columbia U., N.Y.C., 1956-60; dir. rsch. and devel. Whitehall Labs., N.Y.C., 1960-70, v.p. sci. affairs, 1970-76; v.p., dir. labs. Am. Can Co., Greenwich, Conn., 1976-78; v.p. rsch. and devel. J.B. Williams Co., Div. Nabisco, N.Y.C., 1978-82; v.p. sci. affairs Whitehall div. Am. Home Products, N.Y.C., 1983-91, sr. v.p. sci. affairs, 1991—; indsl. cons., 1956-60; vis. staff Pfizer & Co., Bklyn., 1958; clin. prof. Coll. Podiatry, L.I. U., 1958-60; nat. seminar chmn. Soc. Cosmetic Chemists, N.Y.C., 1962. Contbg. editor: Remington's Practice of Pharmacy, 12th edit. 1960. Patentee in field. Mem. N.J. Fed. Bds. of Edn., Englewood Cliffs, 1965-68, v.p., 1965-68. Fellow Am. Found. Pharm. Edn., 1954-56; recipient Lascoff award, Columbia U., 1950, Merck award, 1952. Mem. AAAS, Am. Pharm. Assn., Acad. Pharm. Sci., N.Y. Acad. Sci., Soc. Cosmetic Chemists, Phi Kappa Phi, Rho Chi. Avocations: boating, tennis. Home: 168 Wood Rd Englewd Clfs NJ 07632-1625 Office: Whitehall Labs 685 3d Ave New York NY 10017

DASH, ROBERT (WARREN), artist, writer; b. N.Y.C., June 8, 1931; s. Emanuel and Shirley (Nisinson) D.; B.A. in Ethnology and English (State scholar), U. N.M., 1953. Works in Bklyn. Mus., Modern Art Mus. Munich (W.Ger.), N.Y. U., Chase Manhattan Bank, Phila. Mus. Art, Mus. Modern Art Traveling Exhibit, Am. Fedn. Arts Traveling Exhbn., Guggenheim Mus., Corcoran, Joslyn Art Mus., Hirschhorn Mus., Guild Hall, East Hampton, N.Y., Boston Mus. Fine Arts; commns. include: stage set for Port, 1964, Garden Lithographs with lines by James Schuyler, 1972, various covers vols. of poetry; adj. prof. advanced painting Southampton Coll., 1970, 75; columnist East Hampton Star, 1986-91; contbr. artices to Hortus, RHS Jor., Newday; art critic Arts and Art News. Trustee Group for Ams. South Fork; bd. dirs. The Land Found., Animal Rescue Fund, Internat. Commn. Relief of Suffering and Starvation; bd. govs. Peconic Land Trust; trustee The Nature Conservancy; adv. bd. Garden Book Club; adv. panel N.Y. State Council on Arts; founding mem. Garden Conservancy. Fellow Royal Hort. Soc.

DASHEFSKY, ARNOLD MARTIN, educator; b. Phila., Sept. 9, 1942; s. Leo and Sylvia (Effron) D.; m. Sandra Deborah Waldman, Feb. 11, 1968; children: Michael, Alisa. BHL, Gratz Coll., Phila., 1963; BA, Temple U., 1964, MA, 1966; PhD, U. Minn., 1969. Prof. sociology U. Conn., Storrs, 1969—, dir. Ctr. for Judaic Studies & Contemporary Jewish Life; cons. Am. Jewish Com., N.Y.C., 1974-76, R.I. Dept. Vocat. Edn. Sex Equity Project, Providence, 1977-78, Commn. on Jewish Edn. of the Greater Hartford Jewish Fedn., 1976—. Co-author: Ethnic Identification Among American Jews, 1974, Americans Abroad, 1992; editor: Ethnic Identity in Society, 1976, Contemporary Jenry, 1986, 87. Grantee Nat. Endowment for the Humanities, 1974; Meml. Found. for Jewish Culture fellowship, 1977-78. Mem. Assn. for Social Scientific Study of Jewry (pres. 1989—, v.p. 1975-77, sec., treas. 1971-73), Ea. Sociol. Soc. (papers com. 1988-90, Rogers award com. 1991), Am. Sociol. Assn. (Discipline grant award 1980-81), Soc. for the Scientific Study of Religion. Office: U Conn 344 Mansfield Rd Storrs Mansfield CT 06269-2068

D'ASTOLFO, FRANK JOSEPH, graphic designer, educator; b. Charleroi, Pa., July 19, 1943; s. Galderino Joseph and Gustina Evlyn (Petaccia) D'A. BA, Pa. State U., 1966; MA, U. Pitts., 1973. Graphic designer The United Fund, Pitts., 1968-69, Fisher Sci. Co., Pitts., 1969-73; instr. U. Pitts., 1972-76; graphic designer Pitt Studios, Pitts., 1973-74; design cons. Frank D'Astolfo Design, Pitts., 1974-77; instr. Tyler Sch. Art, Phila., 1977-80; design cons. Infield & D'Astolfo, N.Y.C., 1980-88; assoc. prof. Rutgers U., Newark, 1980—; design cons. Frank D'Astolfo Design, N.Y.C., 1988—; cons. in field; chmn. dept. art & design Rutgers U., Newark, 1989-92, dep. chmn. dept. visual and performing arts, 1992—; bd. dirs. Ringside Inc., N.Y.C., 1987—. Graphic designer Print Magazine, 1984, 86 (Fifty Best Ann. Reports 1984, 86), Graphis Diagrams I, 1988, Am. Corporate Identity 5-8, 1989-92 (Awards of Excellence 1989-92), Metropolis The Architecture and Design Magazine New York, 1985. Design cons. Architects, Designers and Planners for Social Responsibility, N.Y.C., 1985, ICIS Internat. Ctr. for Integrating Studies, N.Y.C., 1983; dir. Com. for Cultural Awareness and Discussion, Pitts., 1977; cons. Shelly Friedman for Judge Com., Pitts., 1977. Recipient Gold award Art Dirs. Club Phila., 1981, Distinctive award Merit Soc. Pub. Designers N.Y., 1983, Cert. of Distinction Creativity 19 Art Direction Mag., 1989, Silver award Case Coun. for Advancement and Support of Edn., 1985, Desi award Graphic Design U.S.A., 1982, 83, 85, 87, 88, 92, Typography 4 Print Mag. Regional Design Ann., 1982, 84, 89; Cert. of Merit Art Dirs. Club N.Y., 1978, 81, 85, Cert. of Excellence Art Dirs. Club N.J., 1981, 82, 83, 85. Mem. Am. Inst. Graphic Arts (Cert. of Excellence 1977, 83), Coll. Art Assn., Graphic Design Edn. Assn. Democrat. Roman Catholic. Home: 80 Warren St Apt 32 New York NY 10007-1038 Office: Rutgers U Newark NJ 07102

DASTOLI, DONALD ANTHONY, personnel administration director; b. Pittsfield, Mass., Oct. 24, 1950; s. Anthony C. and Angeleine A. (Schiavone) D.; m. Elaine M. Behaylo, June 18, 1972; children: Saralyn, Andrew, Nathan. BA in Chemistry, St. Anselm's Coll., 1972. With Stanhome, Inc., Easthampton, Mass., 1972—, pers. dir., 1986-88, dir. pers. adminstrn., 1989—. Treas. Easthampton Community Theater Assn., 1972-74; bd. dirs. Multi-Svc. Health for Addictions, Northampton, Mass., 1989—; mem. Sch. Bus. Partnership Com., Easthampton, 1990—. Mem. Am. Chem. Soc., Employers Assn. Western Mass., Pers. Mgmt. Assn. (bd. dirs. 1985—), Easthampton C. of C. (bd. dirs. 1986—). Roman Catholic. Home: 3 Hawthorne Dr Southampton MA 01073 Office: Stanhome Inc 116 Pleasant St Easthampton MA 01027

DATES, LOIS ANN, academic program director; b. Corning, N.Y., Aug. 29, 1952; d. Harold Frank and Anna (Kalinich) D.; m. Thomas P. Hultzman, Aug. 24, 1974 (div. 1981). BA in Sociology and Philosophy, Skidmore Coll., 1974; MPS in Community Svc. Adminstrn., Alfred U., 1979; cert., Oxford (Eng.) U., 1973. Edn. coordinator Corning (N.Y.) Mus. Glass, 1974-79; community devel. dir. Town of Millis, Mass., 1979-81; prodn. supr. Corning, Inc., 1981-83; prodn. planner Steuben Glass, N.Y.C., 1983-86; program mgr. Corning Glass Works Found., 1986-88; dir. corp., found. and govt. support Hobart and William Smith Colls., Geneva, N.Y., 1988-92; dir. corp., found. rels. Butler U., Indpls., 1992—. Bd. dris. Inst. for Human Svcs., 1986-92, Seven Lakes coun. Girl Scouts U.S.A., 1987-92, Smith Opera House for Performing Arts, 1988-92. Mem. Nat. Soc. Fund Raising Execs. (assoc.), Geneva C. of C. (bd. dirs. 1990-92), Semeca Yacht Club, Keuka Yacht Club, Rotary. Republican. Presbyterian.

DATILES, MANUEL BERNALDES, III, ophthalmologist; b. Manila, Feb. 26, 1951; came to U.S., 1979; s. Roberto Aguiling and Loretta (Bernaldes) D.; m. Jacqueline Romero, Mar. 13, 1976; children: Michelle, Joyce, Margaret, Jennifer, Manuel IV, Michael. BS cum laude, U. Santo Tomas, Manila, 1970; MD cum laude, U. Santo Tomas, 1974. Rsch. fellow Philippine Eye Rsch. Inst.-U. Philippines, Manila, 1975-76; resident in ophthalmology U. Philippines-Philippine Gen. Hosp., Manila, 1976-79; rsch. scholar, vis. scientist Lab. Vision Rsch. Nat. Eye Inst.-NIH, Bethesda, Md., 1979-82; clin. fellow corneal and cataract surgery Wilmer Eye Inst.-Johns Hopkins U. Hosp., Balt., 1982-83; sr. staff ophthalmologist Nat. Eye Inst.-NIH, Bethesda, 1983-88; acting chief cornea and cataract sect., clin. svc. br. Nat. Eye Inst.-NIH, 1989-92, chief, 1992—; vis. lectr. Wilmer Eye Inst.-Johns Hopkins U., Balt., 1984, Osaka (Japan) U., 1986, U. Munich, 1988. Editor cataract sect. Duane's Clinical Ophthalmology Textbook Series; contbr. articles to profl. jours., chpts. to ophthalmol. books. Mem. Assn. Rsch. in Vison and Ophthalmology, Am. Acad. Ophthalmology, Castroviejo Soc. Corneal Surgeons, Johns Hopkins Med. Surg. Assn., Internat. Assn. Ocular Surgeons, Washington Acad. Ophthalmology, Md. Soc. Eye Physicians and Surgeons. Roman Catholic. Office: Nat Eye Inst NIH Bldg 10 Rm 10N226 Bethesda MD 20892

DATSKOVSKY, BORIS ABRAMOVICH, mathematics educator; b. Moscow, USSR, Nov. 6, 1960; came to U.S., 1976; s. Abram B. and Tamara M. (Datskovsky) Aimbinder; m. Beth Weiner, July 24, 1983; children: Miriam Malka, Chana Yemima, Avital Sarah. BA summa cum laude, Columbia Coll., 1980; PhD, Harvard U., 1984. Asst. prof. math. Tufts U., Medford, Mass., 1984-86, Temple U., Phila., 1988-90; assoc. prof. math. Temple U., Phila., Mass., 1990—. NSF fellow Harvard U., 1986-88; NSF grantee, 1989. Mem. Am. Math. Soc., Math. Assn. Am., Phi Beta Kappa. Independent. Jewish. Office: Temple U Dept Math Philadelphia PA 19122

DATTA, RANAJIT KUMAR, financial planner; b. Munshigunj, Bangladesh, Apr. 1, 1933; came to U.S., 1965; s. Ramananda and Mahamaya D.; m. Bhakti Biswas, Dec. 12, 1964; 1 child, Rakhi. BSc with honors, Calcutta (India) U., 1956, MSc, 1958, PhD, 1963, DSc, 1975. Asst. prof. Bengal Vet. Coll., Calcutta, India, 1961-63; sr. rsch. officer USDA Projects, Calcutta (India) U., 1963-65; rsch. scientist N.Y. State Rsch. Inst. Neurochem. and Drug Addiction, N.Y.C., 1965-67; assoc. biophysicist Beth Israel Med. Ctr., N.Y.C., 1968-82; fin. planner N.Y. Life, N.Y.C., 1982—, mem. pres.'s coun., 1985-89, mem. exec. coun., 1984-85, 90-91; asst. prof. pathology Mt. Sinai Coll. Medicine, N.Y.C., 1971-82. Collaborator: (med. jour.) Clinician, 1970-82; pub., editor: (newspaper) Sangbad Bichitra, 1971—. Pres. Cultural Assn. Bengal, Pelham Manor, N.Y., 1971-78, East Coast Durga Puja, N.Y.C., 1972-73; v.p. Assn. Indians in Am., N.Y.C., 1980-81. Recipient svc. award Purba Queens Bangla Pathasala, N.Y.C., 1980, Disting. Svc. award N.Am. Bengali Conf., 1988. Home: 101 Iden Ave Pelham NY 10803-2122 Office: NY Life 411 Theodore Freund Ave Rye NY 10580

DATTILO, NICHOLAS C., bishop; b. Mahoningtown, Pa., Mar. 8, 1932. Educated, St. Vincent Sem., Latrobe, Pa., St. Charles Borromeo Sem., Phila. Ordained priest Roman Cath. Ch., 1958, apptd. Eighth Bishop of Harrisburg, 1989, ordained Bishop of Harrisburg, 1990. Home and Office: 4800 Union Deposit Rd Harrisburg PA 17105*

DATTILO, VINCENT JOSEPH, graphic designer; b. Bronx, N.Y., Sept. 2, 1967; s. Joseph and Jenny D. Student, Bridgeport U., 1985—. Asst. to art dir. Market Pl. Publs., Greenwich, Conn., 1984-85; graphics coord. Cahners Pub., Stamford, Conn., 1985-86; mech. artist Frank Fatta Graphics, Greenwich, 1986-87, Sims Freeman O'Brien, Elmsford, N.Y., 1987-88; freelance artist Benchmark, Westport, Conn., 1988-89, Clarion, Glenville, Conn., 1988—; freelance pacakge prodn. Zotos, Darien, Conn., 1989; prodn. cons. Solimar Communications, 1990-92; prodn. coord. PrintMark, Stamford, Conn., 1992—. Home and Office: 63 Angus Rd N Greenwich CT 06831-4307

DAUB, ALBERT WALTER, publishing executive; b. Westwood, N.J., July 2, 1931; s. Albert and Mary Josephine (Huber) D.; m. Martha Jane Jolly, Sept. 27, 1958; children: Steven Albert, David Hayes, Thomas William, Michael James. BA, Washington and Lee U., 1953; MLS, Rutgers U., 1968. Sales rep. IBM, Paterson, N.J., 1955-65; assoc. v.p. Scarecrow Press Inc., Metuchen, N.J., 1965-70, exec. v.p., 1970-75, pres., 1986—. Vice chmn. Planning Bd., Watchung, N.J., 1980—. 1st lt. U.S. Army, 1953-55, Korea. Mem. ALA (chair endowment fund 1982-91, mem. bd. pub. 1990-93). Home: 1 Hill Hollow Rd Watchung NJ 07060-6403 Office: Scarecrow Press Inc 52 Liberty St Metuchen NJ 08840-1279

DAUB, MATTHEW FORREST, artist, educator; b. N.Y.C., Aug. 29, 1951; s. Alan J. and Sara Ann (Goldman) D.; m. Barbara Crawford, Aug. 1, 1971; children: Joshua, Sarah. Student, Pratt Inst., 1969-70; BA, So. Ill. U., 1981, MFA, 1984. Asst. prof. Kutztown (Pa.) U., 1987-92, assoc. prof., 1992—. Author: A Charmed Vision: The Art of Carolyn Plochmann, 1990; one-person shows include Sherry French Gallery, 1984, 86, 88, 91, Jan Cicero Gallery, 1987-89; contbr. art to calendar Met. Mus. Art, 1991. Home: 920 N Richmond St Fleetwood PA 19522-1905 Office: Kutztown U Sharadin Art Bldg Kutztown PA 19530

DAUBEN, JOSEPH WARREN, history educator; b. Santa Monica, Calif., Dec. 29, 1944. AB, Claremont-McKenna Coll., 1966; AM, Harvard U., 1968, PhD in Hist. Sci., 1972. Teaching fellow hist. sci. Harvard U., Cambridge, Mass., 1967-72; from asst. prof. to assoc. prof. Lehman Coll. CUNY, 1972-81, prof. hist. sci., 1981—; mem. Inst. for Advanced Study Princeton U., 1977-78; vis. prof. ancient sci. Clark U., Worcester, Mass., 1971-72, hist. sci. Columbia U., N.Y.C., 1979-84, Oberlin (Ohio) Coll., 1980-81, N.Y. Bot. Garden, 1989—, NYU, 1989—. Author numerous hist. vols., biographies of Georg Cantor and Abraham Robinson; editor Historia Mathematica, 1976-86. Humanist fellow NEH, 1973-74, Guggenheim fellow, 1980-81, NEH fellow, 1991-94; recipient Bolzano medal Czechoslovak Acad. Sci., 1978, Lenin medal U. Tashkent, USSR, 1986. Fellow N.Y. Acad. Sci.; mem. AAAS, Internat. Acad. Hist. Sci., Internat. Commn. History Math. (chmn. 1985—), Hist. Sci. Soc., Sigma Xi, Phi Beta Kappa. Office: CUNY Grad Ctr PhD Program in History 33 W 42d St New York NY 10036-8099

DAUBERT, SCOTT DAVID, psychologist; b. Phila., Sept. 25, 1959; s. Wellington Brown and Janet Marie (Pileggi) D.; m. Karen Nina Molzahn, Aug. 15, 1981; 1 child, Emily Nina. BA, Muhlenberg Coll., 1981; MA, Ind. U., Pa., 1983. Lic. psychologist, Pa. Psychologist Gnaden Huetten Meml. Hosp., Lehighton, Pa., 1983-90; program dir. Gnaden Huetten Meml. Hosp., Stroudsburg, Pa., 1990—; pvt. practice, Nazareth, Pa., 1987—. Mem. Am. Psychol. Assn., Pa. Psychol. Assn., Nat. Alliance for Mentally Ill (profl. mem.), Phi Beta Kappa. Democrat. Lutheran. Office: Open Forum Gnaden Huetten Meml Hosp 51 N 2D St Stroudsburg PA 18360

DAUGHENBAUGH, TERRY L., water technology executive; b. Latrobe, Pa., July 20, 1939; s. Gladys Idella Hollobaugh; children: Thomas, Todd, Tracey. BS, U. Pitts., 1968; postgrad., Columbia U., 1985. With Kennemetal Corp., Latrobe, Pa., 1957-58; with Latrobe (Pa.) Steel Co., 1958-92, project engr., 1968-70, melt shop supt., 1970-73, mgr. primary ops., 1973-85, gen. mgr. mfg., 1985-88, gen. mgr. primary ops. and engring., 1988-92; pres. Innovative Water Tech., Inc. divsn. Innovative Group, Latrobe. Sec. exec. bd. Ea. Westmoreland Devel. Corp., Latrobe, 1984—, chmn. transp. com.; bd. dirs. Westmoreland County Blind Assn.; coach, mgr., commr. Latrobe-Derry Area Teener League, 1974-84; capt. sustaining mem. drive Boy Scouts Am., 1988. Mem. Am. Soc. for Metals, Am. Iron and Steel Inst., Assn. Iron and Steel Engrs., Touchdown Club. Republican. Lutheran. Home: 10 W Tacoma Ave Latrobe PA 15650-1145 Office: Latrobe Steel Co South Ligonier St Latrobe PA 15650

D'AUGUSTINE, ROBERT, university official; b. Tacoma, Apr. 22, 1947; s. Anthony Patrick and Marie Colette (Carofola) D'A.; m. Marcia June Morgan, June 6, 1970; children: Matthew Morgan, Allie Morgan. BA, U. Pa., 1968, MA, 1971; MBA, Rutgers U., Newark, 1982. Asst. dir. student fin. aid U. Pa., Phila., 1971-77; exec. asst. to dean U. Medicine and Dentistry N.J.-N.J. Dental Sch., Newark, 1977-83; asst. v.p. for acad. affairs U. Medicine and Dentistry N.J., Newark, 1983-87, assoc. v.p. for acad. adminstrn., 1987—; mem. governing bd. Consortium for Pre-Coll. edn., Newark, 1985—; trustee Med. Libr. Ctr. N.Y., N.Y.C., 1984—, sec.-treas., 1985—. Contbr. articles on ednl. and profl. practice mgmt. to profl. jours. Vice pres. Citizens for Quality Edn., Metuchen, N.J., 1987—. With U.S. Army, 1968-70. Mem. Beta Gamma Sigma. Home: 7 Delmar Pl Metuchen NJ 08840-2731 Office: U Medicine & Dentistry NJ 30 Bergen St Newark NJ 07107-3000

DAUKSHUS, A. JOSEPH, systems engineer; b. Tamaqua, Pa., Oct. 17, 1948; s. Anna Daukshus. BS in Aerospace Engring., Pa. State U., 1975. Devel. engr. Carl Zeiss Inc., Thornwood, N.Y., 1984-88; cons. Panasonic, Secaucus, N.J., 1988, Pratt & Whitney, E. Hartford, Conn., 1989; cons. AT&T, Largo, Fla., 1990, Somerset, N.J., 1990-91; cons. Torrington (Conn.) Co., 1990, Trecom Bus. Systems, Edison, N.J., 1990-91; systems engr. Canberra Industries, Meriden, Conn., 1991—. Mem. N.Y. Acad. Sci. Home: PO Box 8916 New Fairfield CT 06812-1776

DAULER, L. VAN V., JR., chemicals executive; b. Pitts., June 13, 1943; s. Lee V. Dauler and Margaret (Hodge) McPherson; m. Cynthia A. Adams,

Dec. 5, 1970 (div. Mar. 1983); 1 child, Cameron C.; m. Randi E. Kanuk, Apr. 17, 1983. BA, Yale U., 1966; MBA, U. Pa., 1968. Mgr. Peat Marwick Mitchell & Co., N.Y.C., 1968-78, Coopers & Lybrand, N.Y.C., 1978-79; mng. dir. Merrill Lynch Capital Markets, N.Y.C., 1979-88; dir. Neville Chem. Co., Pitts., 1979—, chmn., 1987—, chmn., pres., 1989—; bd. dirs. Nevcin Polymers, Uithoorn, The Netherlands, Nevco, Pitts.; pres., chmn. Vitae Investment Co.; trustee Western Pa. Sch. for Blind Children, Shadyside Hosp., Emma Clyde Hodge Found. Mem. Rolling Rock Club, Fox Chapel Golf Club, Duquesne Club, Laurel Valley Golf Club, Allegheny Club, Igloo Club. Office: Neville Chem Co 2800 Neville Rd Pittsburgh PA 15225-1496

DAUSTER, WILLIAM CHARLES, medical center administrator; b. Weehawken, N.J., Oct. 9, 1956; s. William George and Ines Josephine (Caputo) D.; m. Gail Frances Gilday, Oct. 22, 1983. BA, William Paterson Coll., 1979; MS, Polytechnic U., 1986; cert., Fairleigh Dickinson U., 1991. Asst. editor News Pub. Co., Palisades Park, N.J., 1980-82; pub. affairs assoc. St. Michael's Med. Ctr., Newark, 1982-85, dir. external affairs, 1987-91; dir. mktg. and pub. rels. Kennedy Meml. Hosp., Saddle Brook, N.J., 1985-87; v.p., devel. and pub. affairs Jersey City Med. Ctr., 1991—. dist. chmn. Boy Scouts Am., City of Newark, 1989-91; bd. trustees Ironbound Boys' and Girls' Club, Newark, 1987-91; mem. Washington Commons Devel. Corp., Newark, 1988-91; mem. steering com. Love Newark, 1987-91. Recipient 1st Pl. award North Jersey Press Club, 1984, 2d Pl. award, 1985, Single Achievement award, 1987, 1st Pl. award Am. Heart Assn., N.J. chpt. 1990, Dist. award of merit Boy Scouts Am., 1991. Mem. Am. Soc. Hosp. Mktg. and Pub. Rels., Nat. Soc. Fund Raising Execs., N.J. Hosp. Pub. Rels and Mktg. Assn., Rotary Club of Saddle Brook (pres. 1987). Office: Jersey City Med Ctr 50 Baldwin Ave Jersey City NJ 07304

DAUSTER, WILLIAM GARY, lawyer, economist; b. Sacramento, Nov. 25, 1957; s. William Joe and Marianne Dauster; m. Ellen Lisa Weintraub, May 10, 1986; children: Matthew Isaac, Natanya Miraim. BA in Econs., Polit. Sci. and Internat. Rels., U. So. Calif., 1978, MA in Econs., 1981; JD, Columbia U., 1984. Bar: N.Y. 1985, U.S. Dist. Ct. (so. and ea. dists.) N.Y. 1985, D.C. 1986. Assoc. Cravath, Swaine & Moore, N.Y.C., 1984-86; chief counsel com. on budget U.S. Senate, Washington, 1986—. Author: Congressional Budget Act Annotated, 1990, Budget Process Law Annotated, 1991; editor-in-chief Columbia Jour. Law and Social Problems, 1983-84; contbr. articles to profl. jours. Bd. visitors Columbia Law Sch. Recipient Order of Palm, 1978; U. So. Calif. Trustee scholar, 1974, Harlan Fiske Stone scholar, 1982-84. Mem. ABA, D.C. Bar Assn., N.Y. Bar Assn., Columbia Law Sch. Alumni Assn. of Washington, Skull and Dagger, Blue Key, Phi Beta Kappa, Phi Kappa Phi. Democrat. Jewish. Home: 9713 Connecticut Ave Kensington MD 20895-3528 Office: US Senate Com on Budget 621 Dirksen Office Bldg Washington DC 20510-6100

DAVE, RAJU S., scientist; b. Calcutta, India, Aug. 29, 1958; Came to U.S., 1981.; s. Shivprasad M. and Jaya D.; m. Aparna, July 9, 1983. BS with honors, Indian Inst. Technol., Kharagpur, India, 1981; MS, Wash. State U., 1983; DSc., Wash. U., 1986. Rsch. asst. Wash. U., 1983-86; instr., rsch. assoc. Mich. Molecular Inst., Midland, 1986-88, asst. rsch. prof., assoc. scientist, 1988-89; rsch. specialist Monsanto Chems. Co, Springfield, Mass., 1989—. Contbr. articles to profl. jours. Gen. sec., L.T.S.- A Social Welfare Orgn., Calcutta, India 1974-76. Recipient Nat. Grad. Student award Soc. for the Advancement of Materials and Processing 1986. Mem. Soc. for Plastics Engr., Am. Soc. Composites, Am. Inst. Chem. Engr., Sigma Xi. Home: 10B Paris Ave Worcester MA 01603-1643 Office: Monsanto Chems Co 730 Worcester St Bldg 43A Springfield MA 01151-1089

DAVENEL, GEORGE FRANCIS, educational consulting association executive; b. Woodhaven, N.Y., June 18, 1914; s. Edward Alfred and Elizabeth (Johanna) D.; m. Viola Ferraino, Aug. 22, 1940; children: George F., Ann Marie. BS cum laude, CCNY, 1935; MA in Guidance and Pers., Columbia U., 1943. Dean's asst. Queens Coll., N.Y.C., 1937-45, dir. career counseling and placement ctr., 1945-76, instr. student pers., 1952-57, asst. prof. student pers., 1958-64, assoc. prof. student pers., 1965-71, prof. student pers., 1972-76, prof. emeritus, 1977—; v.p. Nat. Ctr. Career Life Planning, N.Y.C., 1977-80; pres. George Davenel & Assocs., N.Y.C., 1981—; examiner N.Y. State Civil Svc.; asst. examiner N.Y.C. Bd. Examiners; vocat. expert Social Security Adminstrn. Author: Help Your Child Develop Career Talents, 1957, Make Your Life More Interesting, 1958, Learn to Succeed, 1961; author, editor: Merit Students' Encyclopedia, 1961-74; contbr. articles to profl. jours. Recipient Citation of Merit, Kiwanis, 1969, Honor Scroll, Placement Assn. CUNY, 1976, Citation for Retirement Counseling, CUNY, 1978; fellow Found. Econ. Edn., 1954-55, N.Y. Life Co., 1955-56. Mem. Career Devel. Assn., Nat. Vocat. Guidance Assn. (chairperson nat. placement sect. 1955-57), Career Counseling and Placement Assn. (chairperson 1972-75), N.Y. Pers. Assn. (dir. 1960-62), Coll. Fed. Agy. Coun. (bd. dirs. 1956-58). Roman Catholic. Office: George Davenel & Assocs 45-14 156th St Flushing NY 11355

DAVENSON, WENDY H., consultant, marriage and family therapist; b. Buffalo, May 20, 1943; d. Norman Wrigley and Vesta (Gow) Howard; m. Willian E. Bausch, July 9, 1966 (div. 1980); children: William H. Bausch, Jeffrey D. Bausch, Wendy E. Bausch; m. M. Lee Davenson, 1986 (dec. 1988). AA, Centenary Coll., 1963; BA, Kent State U., 1965; M. in Family Therapy, So. Conn. State U., 1986; cert. of advanced grad. study, U. Hartford, 1992. Cert. alcohol counselor, drug counselor, grief counselor, family life educator, prevention profl. Dir. Youth Svcs. Newtown (Conn.), 1986-87; dir. adolescent svcs. Arms Acres, Carmel, N.Y., 1987-88; dir. treatment planning RYSAP, Bridgeport, Conn., 1988-90; assoc. dir. Drugs Don't Work!, Hartford, Conn., 1990-91; pvt. practice marriage and family therapy Newtown, 1986—; cons. Coop. Ednl. Svcs., Fairfield, Conn., 1991—, Canterbury Sch., New Milford, Conn., 1987—. Author: (with others) Cocaine Solutions, 1990; author: (tng. manual) Grieving and Loss--Process of Growth, 1991. Republican. Episcopalian. Home: 88 Church Hill Rd Sandy Hook CT 06482 Office: CES 785 Unquowa Rd Fairfield CT 06430

DAVEY, CLARK WILLIAM, newspaper publisher; b. Chatham, Ont., Can., Mar. 3, 1928; s. William and Marguerite (Clark) D.; m. Joyce Gordon, Sept. 13, 1952; children: Richard Gordon, Kevin William, Clark Michael. BA in Journalism, U. Western Ont., 1948, LLD (hon.), 1986. With Chatham Daily News, 1948-51; mng. editor No. Daily News, Kirkland Lake, Can., 1951; hydro. seaway corr. Globe and Mail., 1951-55; mem. Parliamentary Press Gallery, Ottawa, 1956-60; fgn. editor Globe and Mail, 1960-63, mng. editor, 1963-78; pub. Vancouver (B.C., Can.) Sun, 1978-83, Montreal Gazette, 1983-89; pres., chmn. The Canadian Press, 1981-83; v.p. Southam Inc., 1983—, Ottawa Citizen, 1989—. Named to Can. News Hall of Fame, 1992. Mem. Can. Daily Newspaper Assn (dir.). Office: 1101 Baxter Rd, Box 5020, Ottawa, ON Canada K2C 3M4

DAVID, EDWARD JOSEPH, lawyer; b. Tarrytown, N.Y., Jan. 11, 1942; s. Joseph Michael and Mary (Babic) D.; children from previous marriage: Cynthia Lynne, Jennifer Lea.; m. Mary Ellen Marra. BA, King's Coll., Wilkes-Barre, Pa., 1965; JD, Villanova U., 1968. Bar: Pa. 1969. Assoc. law Broderick, Schubert & Fitzpatrick, Phila., 1968-71; assoc. law Liebert, Short, Fitzpatrick & Lavin, Phila., 1971-78; ptnr. law Mylotte, David & Fitzpatrick, Phila., 1978—. Author: (course manuals) Opening Argument 1978, Jury Selection in Asbestos Litigation, 1983, Medical Issues in Asbestos Litigation; contbr. articles to legal jours. Vol. Am. Heart Assn., Phila., 1987—, Save the Bay Found., 1989; mem. Pa. Wildlife Fedn., 1989. With USAF, 1959-60. Recipient svc. award Am. Heart Assn., Phila., 1988. Mem. ABA, Phila. Bar Assn., Pa. Bar Assn., Def. Rsch. Inst., Rolling Green Golf Club, Vesper Club. Republican. Roman Catholic. Home: 512 Flora Cir Media PA 19064-1363 Office: Mylotte David & Fitzpatrick 1800 John F Kennedy Blvd Philadelphia PA 19103-2925

DAVID, ROBERT PAINE, chemical engineer, manufacturing executive; b. Newton, Mass., June 12, 1939; s. Marshall Stetson and Dorothy (Paine) D.; m. Doris Eileen Wogatzke, Sept. 2, 1962; children: Elizabeth Jean, Deborah Irene. BAChemE, Rensselaer Poly. Inst., 1961; MBA, Babson Coll., 1963. Market devel. rep. new products DuPont Fibers, Wilmington, Del., 1965-70; sr. engr. mfg. DuPont Fibers, Chattanoog, Tenn., 1970-72, planning supr. mfg., 1972-74; planning cons. DuPont Corp. Plans, Wilmington, 1974-77; sr. planning cons. DuPont Internat., Wilmington, 1978-80; planning mgr. DuPont Polymers, Wilmington, 1980—; mem. Planning Forum. Author, editor, tchr. boating edn. safety course U.S. Power Squadrons, 1983-88. Chmn. com., adult advisor Boy Scouts of Am., Wilmington, 1965-70, Chattanooga, 1970-73. Capt. corps engrs. USAR, 1963-65. Mem. Am. Inst. Chem. Engrs., U.S. Power Squadrons (nat. officer 1983—, nat. ednl. officer 1990—), SAR. Home: 2605 Tonbridge Dr Wilmington DE 19810-1216 Office: DuPont Polymers D-13020 1007 N Market St Wilmington DE 19898-0001

DAVIDGE, ANNE MARJORIE, psychologist; b. Atlanta, Dec. 21, 1957; d. Edwin Baxter and Ingrid (Mellgren) D.; m. Stephen Bishop Chace, Sept. 8, 1990. BA, Roanoke Coll., 1979; PhD, U. S.C., 1989. Counselor Tinker Mt. Workshop, Roanoke, Va., 1979-80, Cedar Hills Hosp., Portland, Oreg., 1980-81; counselor, coord. Discovery Land Hosp., Bryan, TEx., 1982-84; grad. asst. USC Dept. Psychology, Columbia, 1984-87; psychology intern Child & Family Svcs., Inc., Hartford, Conn., 1987-88; children's crisis intervention coord. Corrigan Mental Health Ctr., Fall River, Mass., 1988-89; staff psychologist New Bedford (Mass.) Child & Family Svcs., 1989—; psychologist Tiverton (R.I.) Psychol. Svcs., 1990—; cons. Seekonk (Mass.) Sch. Dist., 1990—. Contbr. articles to profl. jours. Mem. Tiverton Substance Abuse Task Force, 1990. Mem. Am. Psychol. Assn., R.I. Psychol. Assn., S.E. Mass. Psychol. Assn., Nat. Register of Health Svc. Providers. Office: Tiverton Psychol Svcs 2128 Main Rd Tiverton RI 02878-4609

DAVIDOFF, E. MARTIN, lawyer, accountant; b. Suffern, N.Y., Jan. 27, 1952; s. Earle and Estelle (Topper) D.; m. Sheila Temkin, May 30, 1976; children—Sherri, Laura. S.B., MIT, 1974; M.B.A., Boston U., 1975; J.D., Washington U., St. Louis, 1978. Bar: N.J. 1981, N.Y. 1979; CPA, N.J., N.Y. Tax sr. Richard A. Eisner & Co., N.Y.C., 1978-80; tax mgr. Leonard C. Green & Co., Woodbridge, N.J., 1980-81; pres. E. Martin Davidoff, CPA, Dayton, N.J., 1981—; tax counsel Cullier, Cohen, Shields & Bock, Attys. at Law, N.Y.C., 1983—; del. White House Conf. on Small Bus., 1986. Contbr. articles to profl. jours. Mem. ABA, AICPAs (chmn. fed. tax com. 1988-90, trustee 1990-92, pres. 1991-92), N.J. Soc. CPAs, Am. Assn. Attys. and CPAs, N.J. Bar Assn., U.S. Jaycees. Home: 16 Independence Dr East Brunswick NJ 08816-3224 Office: 353 Georges Rd Ste K Dayton NJ 08810

DAVIDON, WILLIAM COOPER, physics and mathematics educator, scientist; b. Fla., Mar. 18, 1927; s. Jack and Ruth (Simon) D.; m. Maxine Libros; children: Alan, Ruth, Sarah, Martin. Student, Purdue U., 1943-44; B.S., M.S., Ph.D., U. Chgo. Engaged as research dir. Nuclear Chgo. Co., 1948-54; research asso. Fermi Inst., U. Chgo., 1954-56; asso. physicist Argonne Nat. Lab., 1956-61; asso. prof. physics Haverford Coll., 1961-69, prof. physics, 1969-82, chmn. dept., 1969-70, 72-75, prof. math., 1982-91, prof. emeritus, 1991—; vis. assoc. prof. U. Wash., 1958. Participant 3d, 10th, 17th and 22d Pugwash Confs. Scientists, 1958, 62, 67, 72. Named One of Ten Outstanding Young Men of Chgo., Chgo. Jaycees, 1960; Fulbright research scholar, 1966-67, 76-77. Mem. ACLU (bd. dirs. for Phila. 1971—), Soc. for Social Responsibility in Sci. (pres. 1965-67, edn. chmn.), Fedn. Am. Scientists (vice chmn. 1960-61). Home: 3900 Ford Rd Unit 17-0 Philadelphia PA 19131-2046

DAVIDOV, LOUIS PHILIP, systems analyst; b. Bklyn., Apr. 25, 1953; s. Benjamin and Rachel (Gingold) D.; m. Sandra Denise Haar, Dec. 16, 1979. BA in Econs., Coll. of S.I., 1988. Machimst Helm Machine, N.Y.C., 1975-80; supr. shipping and receiving Bebe Girdle & Jr. Forms, Bklyn., 1980-81; bus. rep. N.Y. Tele., N.Y.C., 1981-86; sr. programmer NYNEX Svc. Co., N.Y.C., 1986-89; systems analyst Telesector Resources Group, N.Y.C., 1989—. Mem. Tech. Excellence Soc. (Tech. Excellent Program award 1988). Democrat. Jewish. Home: 360 Montreal Ave Staten Island NY 10306-4412

DAVIDOVITS, PAUL, chemistry educator; b. Moldava, Czechoslovakia, Nov. 1, 1935; came to U.S., 1957; s. Imre and Rose (Braun) D.; m. Judith Taplitz, May 17, 1957; children: Michael, Deborah. BS, Columbia U., 1960, MS, 1961, PhD, 1964. Instr. Columbia U., N.Y.C., 1964-65; asst. prof. chemistry Yale U., New Haven, 1965-70, assoc. prof., 1970-74; prof. chemistry Boston Coll., Chestnut Hill, Mass., 1974—; cons. Arthur D. Little, Cambridge, Mass., 1978-80, Aerodyne Rsch. Inc., Billerica, Mass., 1980—. Author: Communication, 1972, Physics in Biology and Medicine, 1975, Alkali Halide Vapors (with D.L. McFadden) 1979; patentee in field; contbr. numerous articles to profl. jours. Mem. AAAS, Am. Chem. Soc., Am. Phys. Soc. Office: Boston Coll Dept Chemistry Chestnut Hill MA 02167

DAVIDOW, JOSEPH RUSSELL, psychologist; b. Vineland, N.J., Oct. 23, 1955; s. Israel and Angelica B. (Santoro) D. Student, Emerson Coll., 1973-74; BA, Glassboro State Coll., 1977, MA, 1980; MA, New Sch. Social Rsch., 1985. Cert. sch. psychologist, N.J. Asst. dir. Mental Health Assn. N.Y. and Bronx Counties, N.Y.C., 1988-90; therapist Washington Sq. Inst., N.Y.C., 1989—, Bklyn. Mental Health Clinic, 1990—; psychologist Ocean City (N.J.) Pub. Schs., 1990—; cons. in field. Contbr. to profl. publs. Mem. ASCD, Nat. Assn. Sch. Psychologists, N.J. Assn. Sch. Psychologists. Home: 417 Chestnut Ave Vineland NJ 08360

DAVIDSON, BARRY DANIEL, mechanical engineering educator; b. Buffalo, N.Y., Nov. 27, 1960; s. Melvin and Miriam (Ginsberg) D. BS in Aerospace Engring. summa cum laude, SUNY, 1981; MS in Aeronautics, Calif. Inst. Tech., 1983; PhD in Aerospace Engring., Tex. A&M U., 1988. Design engr. Rockwell Internat. Space Systems Div., Downey, Calif., 1981-82; project engr. Rockwell Internat. Space Systems Div., Downey, 1983-84; mem. tech. staff Jet Propulsion Lab., Pasadena, Calif., 1988-90; asst. prof. Syracuse (N.Y.) U., Dept. Mechanical Aerospace Engring., 1990—; lectr. Soc. Automotive Engrs., Warrendale, Pa., 1990—. Contbr. articles to profl. jours. Mem. AIAA (Outstanding Student award 1981), Am. Soc. Engring. Edn., Soc. Automotive Engrs., Soc. Advancement Material and Process Engring. Office: Syracuse U Dept Mechanical & Aerospace Engring 149 Link Hall Syracuse NY 13244

DAVIDSON, CLIFF IAN, civil engineering educator; b. Passaic, N.J., May 9, 1950; s. Sol M. and Penny (Goldfinger) D.; m. Megan Graae, Aug. 15, 1976; children: Ian, Jacob. BSEE, Carnegie-Mellon U., 1972; MS in Environ. Engring. Sci., Calif. Inst. Tech., 1973, PhD in Environ. Engring. Sci., 1977. Asst. prof. civil engring. Carnegie-Mellon U., Pitts., 1977-82, assoc. prof., 1982-86, prof., 1986—; com. mem. NAS, EPA, U.S. Dept. State, U.S. Dept. Energy. Co-editor: Toxic Metals in the Atmosphere, 1986; mem. editorial bd. Environ. Monitoring and Assessment, Chemosphere; contbr. over 100 articles to profl. jours.; patentee on detector for dry deposition of atmospheric contaminants. Recipient George Tallman Ladd award Carnegie-Mellon U., 1979, Ralph Teetor award Soc. Automotive Engrs., 1982. Mem. ASCE (Outstanding Prof. of Yr. award Western Pa. sect. 1989), Am. Assn. fo r Aerosol Rsch., Air and Waste Mgmt. Assn., Sigma Xi, Tau Beta Pi, Eta Kappa Nu. Office: Carnegie-Mellon U Pittsburgh PA 15213

DAVIDSON, DAN EUGENE, language educator, cultural exchange administrator; b. Wichita, Kans., Sept. 18, 1944; s. Clerin D. and Fay E. (Scott) D.; m. Maria D. Lekic, Apr. 20, 1976; children: Michael Scott, Paul Eugene. BA, U. Kans., 1966; MA, Harvard U., 1971, PhD, 1972. Asst. prof., then assoc. prof. Amherst (Mass.) Coll., 1971-76; prof. Russian Bryn Mawr (Pa.) Coll., 1976—; exec. dir. Am. Coun. Tchrs. of Russian, Washington, 1980—; adj. prof. U. Pa., Colombia U., Harvard U., 1975; vis. prof. U. Md., College Park, 1987-89; cons. UN, N.Y.C., 1987, 88, 91, U.S. Dept. Edn., NEH, Washington. Series editor: Soviet-American Textbook Series of Russian, 1974-91; author, co-author univ.-level textbooks on English and Russian; editor, co-editor scholarly collections, jours.; contbr. articles to scholarly publs. Room parent Washington Episc. Sch., 1989-90; bd. dirs. numerous non-profit ednl. orgns.; mem. Washington Mayor's Coun. on Internat. Activities. Woodrow Wilson Found. fellow 1966; recipient Medal Internat. Friendship, USSR, 1990. Mem. Am. Coun. Tchrs. of Russian (pres. 1975-79), Internat. Assn. Tchrs. of Russian Lang. and Lit. (v.p. 1975-80, 91—, Pushkin medal 1982), Harvard Club, Phi Beta Kappa, Delta Phi Alpha. Democrat. Episcopalian. Office: ACTR/ACCELS 1776 Massachusetts Ave NW Washington DC 20036-1904

DAVIDSON, DONALD WILLIAM, advertising executive; b. Toronto, Ont., Can., May 18, 1938; s. John Harvie and Harriet Gertrude D.; m. Olive Margaret Somerville, July 28, 1962; children: Scott, Susan. Student, Brantford Collegiate Inst., U. Toronto, York U. Adminstr. Gould Outdoor, Brantford, 1956; account exec. E.L. Ruddy, Toronto, 1957-68, Foster & Kleiser, Detroit, 1968-70; v.p. Outdoor Advt. Sales, 1971-72; v.p. Montreal, 1972-73, v.p. mktg. group, 1973-75, v.p. nat. sales Claude Neon Ltd., Toronto, 1975-77, exec. v.p., 1977-79; pres. Mediacom Inc., Toronto, 1979-80, chmn., pres., 1980-84; exec. v.p., chief operating officer Gannett Outdoor, N.Y.C., 1984-86, pres., chief exec. officer, 1986—. Bd. dirs., mem. exec. com. Traffic Audit Bur.; trustee Madison Sq. Boys and Girls Club. Mem. Outdoor Advt. Assn. Can. (past chmn. bd., bd. dirs), Outdoor Advt. Assn. Am. (mem. exec. com.), Can. Outdoor Measurement Bur. (past vice chmn.), The Advt. Council (bd. dirs.), Media-Advt. Partnership for a Drug Free America (mgmt. bd.), Lambton Golf and Country Club, Bronxville Field Club. Home: 305 Central Pky Mount Vernon NY 10552-1118 Office: Gannett Outdoor 535 Madison Ave New York NY 10022-4212

DAVIDSON, FRANK PAUL, macro-engineer, lawyer; b. N.Y.C., May 20, 1918; s. Maurice Philip and Blanche (Reinheimer) D.; m. Izaline Marguerite Doll, May 19, 1951; children: Roger Conrad, Nicholas Henry, Charles Geoffrey. BS, Harvard U., 1939, JD, 1948, DHL (hon.), Hawthorne Coll., 1987. Bar: N.Y. 1953, U.S. Dist. Ct. (so. dist.) N.Y. 1953. Dir. mil. affairs Houston C. of C., 1948-50; contract analyst Am. Embassy, Paris, 1950-53; assoc. Carb, Luria, Glassner & Cook, N.Y.C., 1953-54; pvt. practice law, N.Y.C., 1955-70; rsch. assoc. MIT, Cambridge, 1970—, also chmn. system dynamics steering com. Sloan Sch. Mgmt., coord. macro-engring. Sch. Engring.; pres. Tech. Studies, Inc., N.Y.C., 1957—; vice chmn. Inst. for Ednl. Svcs., Bedford, Mass. 1980-84; spl. lectr. Société des Ingénieurs et Scientifiques de France, 1991; Nat. Acad. Scis. del. to Renewable Resources Workshop, Katmandu, Nepal, 1981; governing bd. Channel Tunnel Study Group, 1957—; co-founder Channel Tunnel Study Group, London and Paris, 1957; appointed to NASA Exploration Task Force, Washington, 1989. Author: Macro: A Clear Vision of How Science and Technology Will Shape our Future, 1983, Macro: Big Is Beautiful, 1986; editor series of AAAS books on macro-engring., Tunneling and Underground Transport, 1987; co-editor Macro-Engineering, Global Infrastructure Solutions, 1992, Solar Power Satellites, 1992; mem. editorial bd. Interdisciplinary Sci. Revs., 1985—; mem. adv. bd. Tech. in Soc., 1979—, Mountain Research and Development, 1981-91, Project Appraisal, 1986—. Bd. dirs. Internat. Mountain Soc., Boulder, Colo., 1981-91; trustee Norwich (Vt.) Ctr., 1980-83; mem. steering com. Am. Trails Network, 1986-88; bd. dirs. Am. Trails, Washington, 1988-90; apptd. NASA Exploration Task Force, Washington, 1989. Capt. RCAC, 1941-46, ETO. Decorated Bronze Star; recipient key to City of Osaka, Japan, 1987; Lewis Mumford fellow Rensselaerville Inst., 1982. Mem. ABA, Internat. Assn. Macro-Engring. Socs. (bd. dirs. 1987—), Am. Soc. Macro-Engring. (bd. dirs. 1982—, vice chancellor 1983—), Assn. Bar of City of N.Y. (internat. law com. 1959-62). Clubs: Knickerbocker (N.Y.C.); St. Botolph (Boston). Home: 140 Walden St Concord MA 01742-3613 Office: MIT E40-294 Cambridge MA 02139

DAVIDSON, JEFF ALAN, science administrator; b. Midland, Mich., May 14, 1961; s. Clayton Leslie and Alice Mae (Mitchell) D.; m. Janet Kay Swim, Aug. 13, 1983. BSChemE, Purdue U., 1983; MBA, U. Minn., Mpls., 1988. Chem. engr. Corp. Rsch. div. Gen. Mills, Mpls., 1983-86; rsch. chem. engr. Corp. Rsch. div. GM, Mpls., 1986-87; process engr. New Ventures div. Continental Baking Co., St. Louis, 1987-88; mktg. mgr. Biotech. Inst. Pa. State U., University Park, 1988-91, exec. dir. Bioprocessing Resource Ctr., 1991—; also bd. dirs. Bioprocessing Rsource Ctr. Bioprocessing Resource Ctr., University Park; exec. dir. Pa. Biotech. Assoc., 1989—. Editor, pub.: Our World/Your World, 1992—; (newsletter) Pa. Biotech., 1989, 91; (mag.) Pa. Biotech. & Bus. Report. Mem. Inst. Chem. Engrs., Am. Mktg. Assn., Internat. Churchill Soc. Democrat. Home: 1010 Amelia Ave State College PA 16801 Office: Pa State U 519 Wartzik Lab University Park PA 16802

DAVIDSON, JOAN REBECCA LIPSON, art educator, artist; b. N.Y.C., Oct. 19, 1940; d. Jerome Irving and Ethel Emily (Brandstein) Lipson; m. Michael F. Davidson, Dec. 21, 1966; children: Sarah, Jonathan. BA, U. Miami, 1962; MFA, Columbia Tchrs. Coll., 1964; postgrad., NYU, 1979; advanced cert. adminstrn., supervision, CCNY, 1980. Art instr. U. Hawaii, Honolulu, 1967; art tchr. Wilbur Cross High Sch., New Haven, 1967-68, Milford High Sch., Milford, Conn., 1968-69, Intermediate Sch. 44, N.Y.C., 1963-87; asst. prin. art John Adams High Sch., Queens, N.Y., 1987—; dist. arts liaison Community Sch. Dist. 3, N.Y.C., 1984-85; dir., founder Pub. Sch. 87 After Sch. Ctr., N.Y.C., 1980-87; prodr., host New Ventures Manhattan Cable TV, N.Y.C., 1986—; N.Y.C. rep. Asia Soc. and TOK, summer 1983. Author: Research Management by Objectives Analysis, 1981; exhibitions include Viewpoint Gallery, N.Y.C., 1984, 86, Kenny Gallery High Sch. Art and Design, N.Y., 1985, Cork Gallery Lincoln Ctr., N.Y.C., 1986, 91, Bklyn. Union Gas Co., 1988, Berkshire Anthenaeum, Pittsfield, Mass., 1988, Marymount Manhattan Coll., N.Y.C., 1988, Columbia Tchrs. Coll., N.Y.C., 1989, Fordham U. Libr., 1989, Becket Art Ctr., 1989, 90, 91, Sotheby Galleries, N.Y.C., 1990, Wall Gallery John Hay Coll., 1990, Cork Gallery, Avery Fisher Hall, Lincoln Ctr., N.Y.C., 1991, Pace Coll. Gallery, 1992, Fed. Pla. Gallery, 1992. Mem. ASCD, Nat. Art Edn. Assn. (del. assembly 1990-91), United Fedn. Tchrs., N.Y.C. Art Tchrs. Assn. (pres., chmn. 1981—, N.Y.C. Art Educator of Yr. award 1985-89), N.Y. State Art Tchrs. Assn. (pres. 1990, N.Y. State Art Educator of Yr. award 1991), West Side Arts Coalition, Kappa Delta Pi. Office: John Adams High School 10101 Rockaway Blvd Jamaica NY 11417-2228 Studio: Tyne Rd Beckett MA 01223

DAVIDSON, JUDITH ANN, human resources specialist; b. Scotia, N.Y., Nov. 28, 1947; d. John Archer and Mary Alice (Travis) Howgate; m. Glenn Franklin Mitchell, Aug. 28, 1971 (div. 1981); m. Wesley Clarke Davidson, Jan. 29, 1983. BA in Sociology, Fordham U., 1975; MA in History, Western Conn. State U., 1983. Compensation benefits asst. Xerox, Greenwich, Conn., 1973-80; sr. compensation analyst Lone Star Industries, Greenwich, 1980-82; compensation officer Bankers Trust, N.Y.C., 1982-84; compensation specialist Reichhold Chems., White Plains, N.Y., 1984-86; mgr. pers. svcs. Nynex Mobile Communications, Pearl River, N.Y., 1986-87; compensation mgr. People's Bank, Bridgeport, Conn., 1987-89; sr. employee rels. adminstr. Norelco Consumer Products, Stamford, Conn., 1989—. Mem. Am. Compensation Assn., Pers. Roundtable, EEO Roundtable. Office: Norelco Consumer Products High Ridge Park PO Box 10166 Stamford CT 06904-2166

DAVIDSON, LARRY, psychologist; b. Bklyn., Dec. 31, 1960; s. Bernard and Faye (Bernstein) D.; m. Maryanne Loetterle, Oct. 28, 1990. BA, Emory U., Atlanta, 1982, MA, 1982; MA in Psychology, Duquesne U., Pitts., 1983, PhD, 1989. Counseling coord. Duquesne U. Health Svc., Pitts., 1985-86; predoctoral fellow Duquesne U. Psychology Dept., Pitts., 1986-87; predoctoral intern Danbury (Conn.) Hosp., 1987-88; predoctoral fellow Yale U. Med. Sch., New Haven, 1988-89; lectr. Yale U. Nursing Sch., New Haven, 1989; adv. resident Danbury Hosp., 1989-90, clin. cons., 1990; postdoctoral fellow Yale U. Med. Sch., 1990—. Cons. editor Jour. Phenomenological Psychology, Pitts., 1986—. Contbr. articles to profl. jours. Named Disting. Young Investigator, Soc. for Life History Rsch., 1990, Karl Jaspers prize, Assn. for Advancement of Philosophy and Psychiatry, 1991. Mem. APA, Conn. Psychol. Assn., Human Sci. Rsch. Conf., Internat. Soc. for Theoretical Psychology, Am. Assn. Applied and Preventive Psychology, Soc. for Phenomenology and Psychiatry (sec. 1990—). Democrat. Jewish. Office: Yale Univ Med Sch 34 Park St New Haven CT 06519

DAVIDSON, MICHAEL SAMUEL, health educator; b. Lawrence, Mass., June 21, 1938; s. Philip Israel and Lillian (Shavitsky) D.; m. Mary Knight Wickens, Dec. 17, 1967; children: Anthony S., Nicole L. AB, Brown U., 1959, MA, Columbia U., 1969, MEd, 1971, EdD, 1975. Program adminstr. Inst. Internat. Edn., N.Y.C., 1968-70; rsch. asst. Columbia U., N.Y.C., 1970-71; program officer World Edn., N.Y.C., 1971-72; asst. prof. health professions Montclair State Coll., Upper Montclair, N.J., 1972—, chmn. dept., 1992—. Contbr. articles to profl. jours. Bd. trustees N.J. Eyemobile Found., 1973-75, Mcburney Sch., N.Y.C., 1980-82; bd. dirs. Morningside Hts. Housing Corp., N.Y.C., 1988-89. With USAR, 1960-66. Mem. AAHPERD, Am. Coll. Health Assn. Home: 70 La Salle St Apt 13F New York NY 10027-4751 Office: Montclair State Coll Dept Health Professions Upper Montclair NJ 07043

DAVIDSON, PAUL MICHAEL, publishing executive; b. Cambridge, Mass., July 10, 1941; s. Harry and Ann (Ladinsky) D.; m. Fern Dana Schattner, June 20, 1964; children: Caryn, Keith, Heather. BS, NYU, 1964,

MS, 1966. Pres. Adams Book Co., N.Y.C.; pres. Tex. Ednl. Paperbacks, Dallas, A.T.S. Realty, N.Y.C. Mem. NSF, N.Y. Acad. Scis., Phi Delta Kappa. Home: 35 Herrick Dr Lawrence NY 11559-1527 Office: Adams Book Co Inc 537 Sackett St Brooklyn NY 11217-3099

DAVIDSON, ROBERT MICHAEL, computer services consultant; b. Phila., Aug. 14, 1941; s. William Maurice and Sarah Harrison (Frye) D.; m. Pamela Ann Hermann, Dec. 17, 1966; children: Andrew Michael, Eric Matthew, Kent McDonald, Ryan Harrison. BA, Lehigh U., 1963. Mktg. rep. IBM, Phila., 1965-68, adv. mktg. rep. Service Bur. Co. subs., Phila., 1969-74; pres., founder Timesharing Cons. Pa., Flourtown, 1975—, Ft. Washington Christian Businessmens Com., 1986—; founder TCI Software, 1981. Contbg. editor: Auerbach Computer Tech. Reports, 1974-79. Mem. Montgomery County Dem. Com., 1974-84; sec. Dem. Com. 148th Legis. Dist., 1978-81; chmn. Whitemarsh Dem. Com., 1982-83; pres. Colonial Jr. Wrestling League, 1980-83; mem. ch. sch. steering com. St. Thomas Ch. of Whitemarsh, 1982-84, sec. to vestry, 1985, stewardship chmn., 1984-85, evangelism chmn., 1986, del. to diocesan conv., 1986-87, diocesan stewardship com., 1986-92, chmn., 1989-90; active Univ. of South Edn. for Ministry Program, 1986-90; chmn. stewardship com. Episcopal Diocese Pa., 1989—, property and fin. com., 1989—. With inf., U.S. Army, 1963-65. Decorated Army Commendation medal. Mem. Digital Equipment Computer Users Soc., Asa Parker Soc. of Lehigh U., Chi Psi. Episcopalian.

DAVIDSON, ROGER H(ARRY), congressional researcher; b. Washington, July 31, 1936; s. Ross Wallace and Mildred (Younger) D.; m. Nancy Elizabeth Dixon, Sept. 29, 1961; children: Douglas Ross, Christopher Reed. A.B. magna cum laude, U. Colo., 1958; Ph.D., Columbia U., 1963. Asst. prof. govt. Dartmouth Coll., Hanover, N.H., 1962-68; assoc. prof. polit. sci. U. Calif.-Santa Barbara, 1968-71, prof., 1971-83, assoc. dean letters and sci., 1978-80; sr. specialist Congl. Rsch. Svc., Washington, 1980-88; prof. govt., politics U. Md., College Park, 1981—; profl. staff mem. U.S. House Reps., Washington, 1973-74; rsch. dir. U.S. Senate, Washington, 1976-77; cons. White House, 1970-71, U.S. Com. on Violence, Washington, 1968-69. Author: The Role of the Congressman, 1969; co-author: A More Perfect Union, 4th edit., 1989; Congress and Its Members, 3d edit., 1989, Governing, 2d edit., 1992; editor: The Postreform Congress, 1992; co-editor: Ency. of the U.S. Congress, 1989—; contbr. articles to profl. jours. Co-chmn. Upper Valley Human Rights Council, Hanover, N.H., 1966-68; chmn. Goleta Valley Citizens Planning Group, Santa Barbara, 1974-76; bd. dirs. Dirksen Congl. Ctr. Woodrow Wilson Nat. Found. fellow, 1958, Gilder fellow Columbia U., 1960, Faculty fellow Dartmouth Coll., 1965-66. Mem. Nat. Capital Area Polit. Sci. Assn. (pres. 1985-86), Legis. Studies Group (charter mem., nat. chmn. 1980-81), Am. Polit. Sci. Assn. (joint com. mem. Project 87-Am. Hist. Assn./Am. Polit. Sci. Assn., chmn. congl. fellowship com. 1990), Western Polit. Sci. Assn. (bd. editors 1977-78), Nat. Acad. Pub. Adminstrn. Baptist. Avocations: astronomy, music, history. Home: 3510 Edmunds St NW Washington DC 20007-1431 Office: 2141 LeFrak Hall College Park MD 20742

DAVIDSON, STEVEN J., emergency physician; b. Phila., Mar. 9, 1950; s. Jay Howard and Claire Beverly (Silverman) D.; m. Simone F. Mogul, June 21, 1987; 1 child, Zoey Samuel. AB in Chemistry, Temple U., 1971, MD, 1975; MBA, U. Pa., 1989. Diplomate Am. Bd. Emergency Medicine. Intern in acute care Med. Coll. Pa., 1975-76, resident in emergency medicine, 1976-78; instr., asst. prof., assoc. prof. surgery Med. Coll. Pa., Phila., 1978-84, assoc. prof. emergency medicine, 1984-89, prof. emergency medicine, 1989—, div. head emergency med. svc., 1988—; med. dir. Phila. Emergency Med. Svc., 1983—; oral examiner Am. Bd. Emergency Medicine, 1980—, bd. dirs., 1986—. Assoc. editor: Yearbook of Emergency Medicine, 1981—; guest reviewer Annals of Emergency Medicine, 1983—. Fellow Am. Coll. Emergency Physicians (bd. dirs. Pa. chpt. 1979-85Emeregency Med. Svc. award 1992), Soc. Acad. Emergency Medicine (pres. 1985-86), Nat. Assn. Emergency Med. Svc. Physicians, Phila. County Med. Soc., Pa. State Med. Soc. Office: Med Coll Pa 3300 Henry Ave Philadelphia PA 19129

DAVIDSON, WILLIAM FRANCIS, engineer; b. Bridgeport, Conn., Oct. 7, 1968; s. William Francis Jr. and Eleanor (Colandrea) D. BS in Materials Sci., Cornell U., 1990, MEng in Engring. Mechanics, 1992. Advt. exec. Red Ivy Pub., Stratford, Conn., 1988-92; engr. advanced materials Elec. Boat div. Gen. Dynamics, Groton, Conn., 1991—. Editor: A Student's Guide to Fairfield, 1988-92. Mem. AIAA, SAMPE, ASM, Delta Tau Delta. Home: 3 Waterside Rd Niantic CT 06357

DAVIE, BRUCE FENWICK, economist; b. L.A., June 17, 1936; s. Frank Edwin and Dorothy (Catlin) D.; m. Ann Duncan Rose, Aug. 17, 1958; children: Kathryn, Samuel, Dorothy Grace. BA, Pomona Coll., 1958; PhD, Harvard U., 1964. Teaching fellow Harvard U., Cambridge, Mass., 1960-63; asst. prof. econs. Georgetown U., Washington, 1963-67, assoc. prof., 1967-70, dir. Office of Instnl. Rsch., 1970-73, prof. econs., 1973-75; sr. economist Office of Mgmt. and Budget, Washington, 1973-78; chief tax economist Com. on Ways and Means U.S. Ho. Reps., Washington, 1978-89; prin. Arthur Andersen & Co., Washington, 1989—; lectr. Fgn. Svc. Inst., Washington, 1968-73; cons. various govt. progs., Washington, 1964-73. Co-author: Public Finance, 1971, Modern Political Arithmetic, 1969; contbr. articles to profl. jours. Elder/trustee N.Y. Ave. Presbn. Ch., Washington, 1970. Fellow Danforth Found., 1958-63, Woodrow Wilson Found., 1958. Mem. Am. Econ. Assn., Nat. Tax Assn., Econ. History Assn. Democrat. Office: Arthur Andersen & Co 1666 K St NW Washington DC 20006-2803

DAVIE, MALCOLM HENDERSON, retired city official; b. North Bay, Ont., Can., Oct. 11, 1918; s. William Malcolm and Vera (Henderson) D.; BA, U. Western Ont., 1945; MA, U. Toronto, 1945-47; B.D., Andover-Newton Theol. Sch., 1950; MA in Psychology, Boston U., 1959; m. Helen Marjorie Marsh, July 1948 (div. Oct. 1954). Salesman, Davie Cheese Co., Ilderton, Ont., 1932-41; with London (Ont.) Provincial Hosp., 1942-44; psychol. counsellor, bus. agent Gould Farm, Great Barrington Mass., 1948-51; attendant Hall-Brooke San., Westport, Conn., 1951; attendant Fernald State Sch., Waverly, Mass., 1954-56, acting night supr., 1959-61; ordained to ministry Congl. Ch., 1951; minister Congl. chs., Monroe, Conn., 1951-53, Chaplin, Conn., 1953-54, Boston, 1955-58; appeared as actor with Wellesley (Mass.) Players, Westport (Conn.) Community Theatre; toured in own musical program A Wee Bit of Bonnie Scotland, 1963-83; gym supr. Ridgefield (Conn.) Parks and Recreation Commn., 1984-92; sometimes lectr. Mem. Internat. Platform Assn. Lodge: Masons (life). Home and Office: 124 Tanton Hill Rd Ridgefield CT 06877-3208

DAVIES, ALMA, producer, playwright, lyricist, composer, designer, sculptor; b. Bloemfontein, South Africa; came to U.S., 1949; d. Walter David and Elizabeth (Van der Kar) D.; m. Lee Kaye, Dec. 9, 1956 (dec. 1967); children: Elena-Beth Kaye, Walter Ian Kaye; m. Edwin William Williams, June 22, 1985.

DAVIES, ANTHONY EDMUND JOSEPHS ADRIAN, economics educator; b. Savannah, Ga., Apr. 4, 1965; s. Alan George and Margaret Josephs (Hartnett) D.; m. Kristina Antolin. BS, St. Vincent Coll., 1987; PhD, SUNY, Albany, 1992. Instr. computer programming Penn State Tech. Coll., Williamsport, Pa., 1984-85; founder, pres. Paragon Corp., Greensburg, Pa., 1985-87; computer cons. Ullrich Copper, Inc., Kennilworth, N.J., 1985—; lectr. econs. dept. SUNY, Albany, 1987-92; asst. prof. W. Va. Wesleyan Coll., Buckhannon, 1992—. Author: (game) Economic Simulation, 1990, (computer software) Micro Word Processor, 1984. Actor Community Theatre League, Inc., Williamsport, 1976-86; dancer Judy Hakes, Montoursville, Pa., 1974-84. Recipient Grad. fellowship SUNY Albany, 1987; grantee SUNY Albany, 1990, 91. Roman Catholic. Office: W Va Wesleyan Coll Econs Dept Buckhannon WV 26201

DAVIES, BRYAN ALLEN, podiatrist; b. Chgo., Aug. 8, 1955; s. Frank and Delores (LeRoy) D.; m. Karen Ann Trent, July 2, 1983; 1 child, Michelle Ann. BA, SUNY, Oswego, 1977; D Podiatric Medicine magna cum laude, N.Y. Coll. Podiatric Medicine, 1988. Surg. resident Podiatry Hosp. of Pitts., 1988-90; pvt. practice podiatry Syosset, N.Y., 1990—; mem. staff Syosset Community Hosp., Cen. Gen. Hosp.; cons. Health Ins. Plan of N.Y., Suffolk County, 1990—. Capt. USAF, 1978-84. Mem. Am. Acad. Podiatric Sports Medicine, Am. Podiatric Med. Soc., Pi Delta. Office: 175 Jericho Tpke Syosset NY 11791-4501

DAVIES, DAVID LLEWELLYN, entrepreneur; b. Birkenhead, Eng., Mar. 22, 1941; came to U.S., 1971; s. Llewellyn Gwylym and Margaret (Woods) D.; m. Patricia Mary Grundy, Aug. 16, 1963; children: Claire Margaret, Helen Veronica, Oonagh, Imogen. BSc in Tech., Manchester (Eng.) U., 1964, BA in Econs., 1967; MBA in Fin., Ops. and Mgmt. Info. System, U. Pa., 1973. From rsch. engr. to mktg. mgr. Stone Plant Engring., Manchester, 1964-68; mktg. mgr. Ford Motor Co., Brentwood, Essex, Eng., 1968-71; fin. mgr. Ford of Europe (Eng.), 1969-71; chief fin. officer Radiation Mgmt. Corp., Phila., 1973-75; chief operating officer Wharton Econometric Forecasting Assocs., Phila., 1975-78; sr. cons. Gilbert Commonwealth, Reading, Pa., 1978-80, Booz Allen & Hamilton, Bethesda, Md., 1980-86; chief executive officer, owner Davies Assocs., Gaithersburg, Md., 1986—. Contbr. articles to profl. jours. Sir Walter Preston scholar, 1964-67, Ford scholar, 1971-73. Home: 13609 Query Mill Rd Gaithersburg MD 20878-3967

DAVIES, ELIZABETH ANN, physicist; b. Atlanta, Nov. 20, 1961; d. Alastair and Shirley (Carr) McLean. BA in Physics with honors, U. Cambridge, Eng., 1983, MA in Physics with honors, 1987; grad., U.S. Naval Test Pilot Sch., 1991. Physicist Raychem Ltd., Swindon, Eng., 1983-86; simulation scientist CAE Electronics Ltd., Montreal, Can., 1986-88; sr. engr. Paramax Electronics, Montreal, 1988-89; project leader Naval Air Test Ctr., Patuxent River, Md., 1989—. Tutor Navy Acad. Vols. for Youth, St. Mary's County, Md., 1989-90. Named NASA astronaut candidate finalist, 1992. Mem. AIAA, Soc. Flight Test Engrs. (sec. 1991—), Inst. of Physics. Anglican. Office: Naval Air Warfare Ctr Aircraft Divsn Patuxent River MD 20670

DAVIES, GEOFFREY, chemistry educator; b. Stoke-on-Trent, Eng., Feb. 6, 1942; came to U.S., 1966; s. Frank and Alice Ada (Boulton) D.; m. Elizabeth Florence, Jan. 16, 1965 (div. Dec. 1985); children: Warwick Harvey, Russell Howard, Claire Elizabeth. BS in Chemistry, Birmingham U., Birmingham, U.K., 1963, PhD in Chemistry, 1966, DSc in Chemistry, 1987. DSIR fellow Birmingham U., Birmingham, U.K., 1963-66; postdoctoral fellow Brandeis U., Waltham, Mass., 1966-68; rsch. assoc. Brookhaven Nat. Lab., Upton, N.Y., 1968-69; ICI rsch. fellow U. Kent, Canterbury, Kent, U.K., 1969-71; from asst. prof. to prof. Northeastern U., Boston, 1971-88, univ. disting. prof., 1988—; cons. Hi-Tech, Ltd., Salisbury, Eng., 1978—, James River Corp., South Hadley, Mass., 1989—, Jones, Day, Reavis, Pogue, Dallas, 1990—, Union Carbide Corp., Charleston, S.C., 1990—. Editor numerous books; contbr. articles to profl. jours. Ringing master Ch. of the Advent, Boston, 1971-82; chmn. planning com. North Am. Guild of Change Ringers, 1981-83, hon. mem., 1992—; mgr. Bell Restoration Proj. Old North Ch., Boston, 1981-83; librarian Guild of Bellringers, Ch. of the Advent, Boston, 1983--. Mem. Simon W. Robinson Lodge AF & AM (master 1988-89, marshall 1990-91). Republican. Episcopalian. Office: Northeastern U Chemistry Dept Boston MA 02115

DAVIES, JANE B(ADGER) (MRS. LYN DAVIES), architectural historian; b. Amboy, Ill., Sept. 9, 1913; d. Henry Harold and Clara May (Heermans) Badger; m. Lyn Davies, July 18, 1942. BA, Wellesley Coll., 1935; MA, Columbia U., 1942, BLS with high honors, 1944; postgrad., U. Mich., 1936, U. Wis., 1937, 38. Tchr. Monticello Prep. Sch., Godfrey, Ill., 1935-37, Kent Sch. Girls, Denver, 1937-41; reference libr. Columbia Univ. Librs., 1944-50, rare book cataloger, 1951-77; cons. Nat. Trust for Hist. Preservation, 1965, 87-88, 91-92, Smithsonian Inst., 1967, Greensboro (N.C.) Preservation Soc., 1967-70, Historic Green Springs, 1970-73, 82, Llewellyn Park Hist. Dist., 1982-84, Hist. Hudson Valley, 1986-88, Met. Mus. Art, N.Y.C., 1989-92; guest curator, author catalog A.J. Davis and Am. Classicism, Fed. Hall Mus., N.Y.C., 1989; lectr. on Am. archtl. history. Author: intro. Houston Mus. Fine Arts: The Gothic Revival Style in America, 1830-1870, 1976; intro. Alexander Jackson Davis: Rural Residences (1837), 1980; contbr. to Prophet with Honor, A.J. Downing, 1989, Alexander Jackson Davis, American Architect, 1992; editorial asst. Jour. Soc. Archtl. Historians, 1964-65; contbr. articles on Am. archtl. history to mags., jours., symposiums and reference books. Am. Coun. Learned Socs. grantee, 1970, Am. Philos. Soc. grantee, 1970-71; NEH fellow, 1978. Mem. Soc. Archtl. Historians (sec.-treas. N.Y. chpt. 1959-67), Victorian Soc. Am. (adv. com. 1966-76), Nat. Trust Historic Preservation, Friends of Lyndhurst, N.Y. Hist. Soc., Preservation League N.Y. State, Greensboro Preservation Soc. (hon.), Phi Beta Kappa, Beta Phi Mu. Presbyterian. Home: 549 W 123d St New York NY 10027

DAVIES, JO ANN, secondary school educator; b. Holland, Mich., Sept. 12, 1948; d. Fred and Helen (Doevieno) Gauthier; m. Donald R. Davies, Oct. 18, 1969; 1 child, Brian. BS, SUNY, Albany, 1970, MS, 1975. Lic. sch. dist. adminstr., coord. diversified coop. edn. Supr. occupational edn. Bethlehem Cen. Sch. Dist., Delmar, N.Y., 1979-84, 1985—; evaluator prior coll.-level learning Empire State Coll., Albany, N.Y., 1991—; vis. com. chmn. Mid. States Assn. Colls. and Schs., Commn. on Secondary Schs., Phila., 1989—; mem. steering com. Albany-Schoharie-Schenectady BOCES, Colonie, N.Y., 1984—. Weekly columnist Area Auto Racing News, 1986—. Treas. Village Stage, Inc., Delmar, N.Y., 1984-86. Mem. NEA (chmn. 1983-88), Internat. Tech. Edn. Assn., Nat. Bus. Edn. Assn., Am. Vocat. Assn., Suburban Coun. Occupational Edn. Suprs. Assn. (v.p., treas. Capital dist. region 1987—), N.Y. State Tech. Edn. Assn., N.Y. State Home Econs. Edn. Assn., Bethlehem C. of C. Methodist. Home: 4 Morningstar Ln Feura Bush NY 12067-9799 Office: Bethlehem Cen Sch Dist 700 Delaware Ave Delmar NY 12054-2499

DAVIES, RICHARD OWEN, pharmaceutical executive; b. Brantford, Ont., Can., July 28, 1931; came to U.S., 1976; s. Leonard Stanley and Mario F. F. (Owen) D.; m. Irma W. Bullock, Aug. 4, 1954; children: Graham, Blair, Mara. BS in Pharmacy, U. Toronto, 1954, MA, 1956, PhD in Pharmacology, 1958, MD, 1962. Lic. dr., Providence of Que. Lectr. U. Manitoba, Winnipeg, Can., 1963-65; dir. clin. pharmacology Ayerst Labs., Montreal, 1965-75; sr. dir. clin. pharm. Merck, Sharp & Dohme, West Point, Pa., 1975-81, group dir. clin. rsch., 1981-85; v.p. clin. and med. affairs I.C.I. Pharm. Group, Wilmington, Del., 1985-89; v.p. cardiovascular clin. rsch. Pharm. Rsch. Inst. Bristol-Myers Squib Co., Princeton, N.J., 1989—. Fellow Am. Coll. Cardiology; mem. Am. Soc. Clin. Pharm. and Therapeutics (v.p. 1972), Am. Soc. Hypertension, Am. Heart Assn. (coun. on cariodlogy, coun. on high blood pressure rsch.), Can. Cardiovascular Soc., Pharm. Mfrs. Assn. (chmn. Can. Med. sect. 1974). Home: 106 St Andrew's Pl Newtown PA 18940 Office: Bristol-Myers Squibb Co PO Box 4000 Princeton NJ 08543-4000

DAVIES, WILLIAM ROBERT, purchasing manager; b. Allentown, Pa., May 21, 1942; s. Lewis Thomas and Ella Veronica (McGinley) D. AA, Lehigh Community Coll., 1962; BA, Pa. State U., 1964. Cert. purchasing mgr. Dir. purchasing Internat. Minerals and Chems., Mundelein, Ill., 1962-76; mgr. purchasing Durkee French Foods, Bethlehem, Pa., 1976—. Served Pa. Coun. Econ. Edn. Student Project on Internat. Trade, arbitrator in contractual disputes Am. Spice Trade Assn. Mem. Nat. Assn. Purchasing Mgmt. (pres. 1989-90, dir. nat. affairs 1991-92, dir. pub. rels. 1992). Republican. Roman Catholic. Home: 731 N 8th St Allentown PA 18102 Office: Durkee French Foods 1001 Eighty Ave Bethlehem PA 18018

DAVIS, ALLEN FREEMAN, history educator, author; b. Hardwick, Vt., Jan. 9, 1931; s. Harold Freeman and Bernice Susan (Allen) D.; m. Roberta Hazel Green, June 16, 1956 (div.); children: Gregory Freeman, Paul Studley. A.B., Dartmouth Coll., 1953; M.A., U. Rochester, 1954; Ph.D., U. Wis., 1959. Instr. history Wayne State U., Detroit, 1959-60; asst. prof. history U. Mo., Columbia, 1960-63; assoc. prof. U. Mo., 1963-68; prof. Temple U., Phila., 1968—; vis. prof. U. Tex., Austin, 1983, U. Amsterdam, 1986-87, John Adams chair. Co-author: March of American Democracy, Vol. V, 1966, Spearheads for Reform, 1967, 84, American Heroine, 1973, The American People, 1986, 2d edit., 1990, (with Jim Watts) Generations, 1974, 78, 83, (with Fredric Miller and Morris Vogel) Still Philadelphia, 1983, Philadelphia Stories, 1988, also numerous articles; editor: (with Harold D. Woodman) Conflict and Consensus in American History, 1966, 8th edit., 1992, (with Mary Lynn McCree) Eighty Years at Hull House, 1969, (with Mark Haller) The Peoples of Philadelphia, 1973, Jane Addams on Peace, War and International Understanding, 1974, For Better or Worse, 1980, (with Mary Lynn Bryan) 100 Years at Hull House, 1990. Served with AUS, 1954-56. Danforth Grad. fellow, 1953-59, Am. Council Learned Socs. sr. fellow, 1971-72, Fulbright fellow, 1986-87; Am. Philos. Soc. grantee, 1962, 65. Mem. Am. Hist. Assn., Orgn. Am. Historians, Am. Studies Assn. (treas. 1971-72, exec. sec. 1972-77, pres. 1989-90), Soc. Am. Historians. Home: 2032 Waverly St Philadelphia PA 19146-1343 Office: Temple U History Dept Philadelphia PA 19122

DAVIS, ANDRÉ LEROY, cartoonist, recording artist; b. Bklyn., July 8, 1965. BFA, Sch. Visual Arts, N.Y.C., 1987. Artist: (children's book) Johnnie Tootite, 1992; artist: (The Last Word) The Source. Home: 1801 Dorchester Rd Brooklyn NY 11226

DAVIS, ANDREW FRANK, conductor; b. Hertfordshire, Eng., Feb. 2, 1944; s. Robert James and Florence Joyce (Badminton) D. Mus.B. (Organ scholar), King's Coll., Cambridge (Eng.) U.; M.A., Cambridge (Eng.) U., 1967; student, Franco Ferrara, Rome, 1967-68; Litt.D. (hon.), York U., Toronto, 1984. Pianist, harpsichordist, organist Acad. of St. Martin-in-the-Fields, London, 1966-70; debut with BBC Symphony Orch., 1970, Paris Opera, 1981; appeared with BBC Scottish Symphony Orch. (asst. conductor), Glasgow, 1970-72, Met. Opera, 1981, Covent Garden, 1983, Chgo. Lyric Opera, 1987, Frankfurt Radio Orch., 1988, Berlin Philharmonic Orch., 1988; music dir. Glyndebourne Festival Opera, 1988—; assoc. condr. New Philharmonia Orch., London, 1973-76; prin. guest condr. Royal Liverpool (Eng.) Philharm. Orch., 1974-77; chief condr. BBC Symphony Orch., 1989—; condr. tour in Japan and China, 1978, Europe, 1983, 86; condr. laureate Toronto Symphony, summer, 1988; chief condr. Chgo. Lyric Opera , 1987, Frankfurt Radio and Berlin Philharmonic, 1988, BBC Symphony Orch., from Oct., 1989; guest condr. world's maj. orchs.; has appeared with maj. internat. festivals including Berlin, Edinburgh and Flanders; also recs. including Sir Michael Tippett's The Mask of Time (Gramaphone Record of Yr. award 1987). Recipient 2 Grand Prix du Disque awards for rec. Requiem (Duruflé) with Philharmonia Orch. Office: care Hugh Kaylor Shaw Concerts Inc 1900 Broadway 2d Fl New York NY 10023

DAVIS, ANDREW HAMBLEY, JR., lawyer; b. Fall River, Mass., Feb. 10, 1937; s. Fall River, Mass., Feb. 10, 1937; s. Andrew Hambley and Doris (Baker) D.; m. Gail D. Perry, July 21, 1962; children: Andrew W., Katherine B., Joshua P. AB, Brown U., 1959; LLB, U. Va., 1962. Bar: R.I. 1963, Mass. 1962. Ptnr., Swan, Jenckes, Asquith & Davis, Providence, 1963-78; ptnr. Davis, Jenckes, Kilmarx & Swan, Providence, 1979—; sec., dir. Union Wadding Co., Uncas Mfg. Co., Potter Hazelhurst Advt. Co. Pres., Bethany Home of R.I., 1966; bd. dirs., exec. com. Bradley Hosp., 1974-91; bd. dirs. Moses Brown Sch., R.I. Philharmonic Orch., 1967—. Mem. ABA, R.I. Bar Assn., Boston Bar Assn., Estate Planning Council, Am. Coll. Probate Council. Clubs: University, Acoaxet Golf, Agawam Hunt, Elephant Rock Beach, Providence Art, Hope. Lodge: Masons. Home: 9 Harbour Rd Barrington RI 02806-4410 Office: Davis Jenckes Kilmarx & Swan 1420 Hosp Trust Tower 1 Hosp Pla Providence RI 02903

DAVIS, CHARLES HOWARD, II, real estate and wholesale hosiery companies executive; b. Melrose, Mass., May 19, 1944; s. Charles Howard and Libra (Vigiroli) D.; B.A., U. Ariz., 1971, postgrad., 1971-72. Gen. ptnr. Davis Properties and Investments, Los Angeles, 1966-76, pres., 1976—, Boston, 1982—; pres., founder The Davis Group, Los Angeles, 1980—, Boston, 1982—; cons. in field. Served to 1st lt. U.S. Army, 1965-69. Decorated Bronze Star. Republican. Roman Catholic. Office: The Davis Group 355 Beacon St Boston MA 02116-1003

DAVIS, CHRISTINA LINDA, parapsychologist, hypnotist; b. Phila., Aug. 29, 1940; d. Rocco Sabastian and Maureena Rita (Scuderi) Traina; m. Raymond Davis, June 3, 1961 (div. 1986); children: Donna Marie, Raymond M. Jr.; m. Anthony Di Domenico, Mar. 28, 1987. AS in Bus., Pa. Acad Bus., Phila., 1969; AS in Philosophy, Summit U., San Jose, 1979; Cert. in Hypnosis, Beaver Coll., Cedarbrook, Pa., 1977; D of Parapsychology, Interfaith Metaphys. Studies Ctr. and Sch. Ethical Hypnosis, 1988; ordination studies with Christ Light Ch., 1984-91. Cert. hypnotist. Adminstrv. asst. Sportsfilm, Inc., Phila., 1967-69; owner Internat. Bakeries, Horsham, Pa., 1974-79; adminstr. Exide Indsl. Battery, Horsham, Pa., 1978-80; office mgr. D'Gerald Ent., Inc., Willow Grove, Pa., 1980-82; pres. AAPHR Inc. Bucks County, Huntington Valley, Pa., 1983-87; tchr. Sch. Ethical Hypnosis, Sicklersville, N.J., 1986-90; lectr. Phila. Psychic Investigators, West Point, Pa., 1988-90; founder, pres. Stairs of Gold Rsch. Assocs., Southampton, Pa., 1989-91; chpt./county adminstr. Hypnosis Soc. Pa., Warminster, 1991—; parapsychologist Warminster; lectr. Moore Coll. of Art, Phila., 1988-89; cons. Bucks County Community Coll., 1988-90; lectr. Profl. Women of Pa., 1988—, Friends Libr. Soc. N.E., Mayfair, Pa., 1990-91; mem. Frontier Sci. Temple U., Quantum Physics Princeton U.; presented rsch. papers on psychic children Atlantic U., 1990. Contbr. articles to profl. jours. Troop cons. Girl Scouts U.S.A., Bucks County, Pa., 1983; v.p. Phila. PTA, 1968; treas. Marion Soc. OLGC Ch., Southampton, Pa., 1984; founder Ch. Golden Light; mem. Menninger Found., Topeka. Mem. Hypnosis Hall of Fame, Norristown, Pa., 1990; named Investigator of the Yr., Phila. Investigators Inc., 1990, Rookie of the Yr., Lady Lyons, 1990. Mem. Hypnosis Soc. Pa. (chpt. pres. 1991—), Ethical Hypnosis Soc., Assn. to Advance Parapsychology (past pres.), Am. Women in Radio and TV, Assn. to Advance Hypnosis (dir. 1987-91), Artisans Order of Mutual Protection (producer 1974—), Coll. Interfaith Metaphysical Studies. Republican. Roman Catholic. Home: 805 Henry Ave Warminster PA 18974-4366

DAVIS, CHRISTOPHER LYTH, trade association executive; b. Buffalo, N.Y., May 28, 1949; s. Paul Benning and Eunice Carolyn (Lyth) D. BA, U. N.C., 1971; JD, SUNY, Buffalo, 1975. Bar: N.Y. 1975, D.C. 1980. Adminstr. aide Mayor, Buffalo, 1972-74; legis. counsel City of Buffalo, N.Y., 1974-76; mgmt. assoc., Office of Mgmt. and Budget Exec. Office of the Pres., Washington, 1977-78; spl. asst. to the pres. The White House, Washington, 1979-81; assoc. Surrey & Morse, Washington, 1981-85; chief executive officer Investment Program Assn., Washington, 1986—; cons., advisor Cen. European Inst., Washington, 1990—. Mem. Nat. Skeet Shooting Assn. (dir. 1984—), Va. Skeet Shooting Assn. (pres. 1990—), Phi Beta Kappa. Office: Investment Program Assn 1100 Connecticut Ave NW Ste 500 Washington DC 20036-4112

DAVIS, CLARK BRYANT, JR., sales executive; b. Bronx, N.Y., May 30, 1964; s. Clark Bryant and Barbara Ann (Whitaker) D. BA in Polit. Sci., U. Rochester, 1986. Assoc. Rochester (N.Y.) Mgmt. Inc., 1984-85; supr. Serv-Rite Corp., Rochester, 1985-86; sales rep. Beecham Products U.S.A., Albany, N.Y., 1987-89; sr. sales rep. Bausch and Lomb, Edison, N.J., 1989-92, sales exec., 1992—; assoc. Nardone Assocs., N.J., 1991-92. Exhibited in group shows at Sailor's Snug Harbor, S.I., N.Y., 1979, Met. Mus. Art, N.Y.C., 1980. Vol. Red Cross Am., S.I., N.Y., 1979; counselor Baden St. Settlement, Rochester, 1984; dir. Com. of Leadership for New Am. 20th Century, Binghamton, N.Y. Named Coop. Edn. Vol. of Yr., ARC, S.I., N.Y., 1979; recipient Irwin Tobin award N.Y.C. Bd. Edn., 1982, Disting. Youth award Daily News, 1982. Mem. Theta Delta Chi (charge mgr. 1985-86). Episcopalian.

DAVIS, CLIVE JAY, record company executive; b. Bklyn., Apr. 4, 1934; s. Herman and Florence (Brooks) D.; children: Fred, Lauren, Mitchell, Douglas. BA magna cum laude, N.Y. U., 1953; LLB cum laude, Harvard U., 1956. Bar: N.Y. bar 1957. Assoc. firm Rosenman Colin Freund Lewis & Cohen, N.Y.C., 1958-60; gen. atty. Columbia Records, 1960-65, pres., 1966-73; pres. Arista Records, Inc., N.Y.C., 1974—. Author: Clive: Inside the Record Business, 1975. Recipient humanitarian award Anti-Defamation League, 1970; named Man of Year Am. Parkinson Disease, 1972, Record Co. Exec. of Year Nat. Assn. TV and Radio Announcers, 1973, Nat. Pop Music Survey, 1974, 78, 80, 84, 87, 90—, Pres. of Yr., Man of Yr. City of Hope, 1978, Man of Yr., Martell Found. for Cancer, Leukemia and Aids Rsch., 1980, Humanitarian of Yr. Am. Cancer Soc., 1985, Martin Luther King Humanitarian of Yr. award Congress Racial Equality, 1991, Man of Yr., Friars, 1992. Mem. Record Industry Assn. Am. (pres., chmn. bd. 1972-73, now dir.). Office: Arista Records Inc Arista Bldg 6 W 57th St New York NY 10019-3913

DAVIS, CURTIS CARROLL, writer, reviewer, critic; b. Balt., Feb. 18, 1916; s. Hoagland Cook and Mary Katharine (Carroll) D.; m. G. Margarete Davis (dec. May 1985). AB, Yale U., 1938; MA, Columbia U., 1939; PhD, Duke U., 1947. Commd. air corps U.S. Army, 1942, advanced through

grades to lt. col., ret., 1976; ops. officer CIA, Washington, 1947-49; dir. Star Spangled Banner Flag House Assn., Balt., 1959—; mem. exec. com. Edgar Allan Poe Soc., Balt., 1964—. Author: Chronicler of the Cavaliers, 1953, The King's Chevalier, 1961, That Ambitious Mr. Legaré, 1971, Revolution's Godchild, 1976; editor: John S. Wise's The End of an Era, 1965, Belle Boyd in Camp and Prison, 1968, William A. Caruthers' The Knights of the Golden Horse-Shoe, 1970. Narrator Soc. War of 1812 (Md.) ann. mcpl. "Cavalcade", Balt., annually. Decorated Bronze Star. Mem. Nat. Book Critics Circle, Am. Antiquarian Soc., Am. Hist. Soc., Md. Hist. Soc. (past chmn. libr. com.), Manuscript Soc., U.S. Commn. on Mil. History, Soc. Colonial Wars (past gov.), S.R. (past pres.), Cosmos Club, Capitol Hill Club Yale Club N.Y., Circumnavigators Club, Balt. Country Club. Roman Catholic. Home: 10 Overhill Rd Baltimore MD 21210-2916

DAVIS, DONALD GEORGE, guidance counselor; b. Wilmington, Del., Sept. 27, 1943; s. Thomas Norval and Winifred Marie (Van Skite) D.; m. Virginia Ellen Broom, Nov. 21, 1977; children: Zachary Andrew, Meredith Ellen. BS in Elem. and Spl. Edn., U. Del., 1974; MA in Human Svcs. and Counseling, DePaul U., 1976. Cert. tchr., spl. educator, guidance counselor. Spl. edn. tchr. Balt. City Schs., 1976-86; spl. edn. tchr. Balt. County Schs., Towson, Md., 1986-90, guidance counselor, 1990—; mem. Towson Support Line, 1990—. Dir. Neighborhood Transp. Inc., Balt., 1976-82. Mem. Tchrs. Assn. Balt. County Schs. (rep. 1991-92), NEA, AACD, Am. Sch. Counselors Assn., Md. Assn. Sch. Assistance Program Profls., Jaycees (bd. dirs. Balt. chpt. 1976-79, Outstanding New Mem. Balt. chpt. 1977, life Md. chpt. 1984, Assoc. Mem. of Yr. Monumental City chpt. 1984). Democrat. Roman Catholic. Home: 1606 Samantha Dr Forest Hill MD 21050-2801 Office: Towson High Sch 69 Cedar Ave Towson MD 21204

DAVIS, DORYNE SHARI See GERSTEIN, DORYNE SHARI

DAVIS, DREW MELVIN, lawyer; b. Trenton, N.J., Jan. 17, 1947; s. Melvin Albert and Lilliam (Buckalew) D.; m. Kathy Herrick, Sept. 3, 1977 (div. 1990). BA, Roanoke Coll., 1969; JD, George Washington U., 1972. Bar: D.C. 1973. Asst. legal counsel Nat. Soft Drink Assn., Washington, 1973-77, mgr. congl. affairs, 1977-80, dir. congl. affairs, 1980-91; v.p. fed. offices Nat. Soft Drink Assn., 1991—; pres. Washington Legis. Group, 1981-82. Mem. ABA, Fed. Bar Assn., D.C. Bar Assn. Office: Nat Soft Drink Assn 1101 16th St NW Washington DC 20036-4803

DAVIS, EDWARD BRADFORD, history of science-physics educator; b. Phila., Aug. 5, 1953; s. Edward Bradford and Margaret Edna (Sayers) D.; m. Kathryn Avis Freeman, June 24, 1978; children: Katherine Elizabeth, Julia Lynn. BS, Drexel U., 1975; MA, Ind. U., 1981, PhD, 1984. Vis. asst. prof. Vanderbilt U., Nashville, 1984-85; asst. prof. Messiah Coll., Grantham, Pa., 1985-90, assoc. prof., 1990—. Contbr. articles to profl. jours. Charlotte W. Newcombe Found. Fellow, 1983, Mellon fellow in Humanities, U. Pa., 1991; NSF rsch. grantee, 1989. Mem. Am. Sci. Affiliation, History of Sci. Soc. Office: Messiah Coll Grantham PA 17027

DAVIS, EVERETT M., accountant; b. Salem, Mass., Feb. 8, 1934; s. Bradford and Blanche (Martin) D.; m. Phyllis Joycelyn Davis, June 16, 1968; children: Scott Bradford, Douglas Andrew. BSBA, Bentley Coll., Waltham, Mass., 1954; BS in Bus. Adminstrn., Suffolk U., 1962. CPA, Mass. Staff acct. Spark, Mann & Co., Boston, 1954-62; controller Lauren Standard Wholesale Grocers, New Bedford, Mass., 1962-63; prin. Everett M. Davis, CPA, Marion, Mass., 1964—. Office: Everett M Davis CPA 163 Front St Marion MA 02738-1526

DAVIS, FRANCIS RAYMOND, priest; b. Washington, Feb. 10, 1920; s. Frank Raymond and Ruth Madeline (Donovan) D.; B.A., St. Bernard's Sem., Rochester, N.Y., 1941; M.L.S., Cath. U. Am., 1953. Ordained priest Roman Cath. Ch., 1945; asst. pastor St. Ambrose Ch., Rochester, 1945-50; prof. lit. St. Bernard's Sem., 1950-51, librarian, 1950-69, prof. speech., 1958-67; pastor Our Lady Lourdes Ch., Elmira, N.Y., 1969-78; pastor St. Mary's Ch., Dansville, N.Y., 1978-80, St. Patrick's Ch., Corning, N.Y., 1980-90. Mem. Chemung county gen. edn. bd. Diocese of Rochester, 1971-78; mem. exec. com. Chemung County (N.Y.) Council Aging, 1972-76; mem. adv. com. Chemung County Office for Aging, 1973-78; mem. exec. com. Ecumenical Preaching Mission, 1977-78; bd. dirs. All Saints' Acad., Corning, 1986-90, founder. Fellow Internat. Biog. Assn.; mem. ALA, Cath. Library Assn. (officer sem. sect. 1958-61), Ch. and Synagogue Library Assn. (nominating com. 1979), Elmira Vicinity Ministerial Assn. (officer 1972-73). Author articles and book revs. Address: St Vincent's Ch 222 Dodge Ave Corning NY 14830

DAVIS, FRANKLIN TARAVHONTY, composer; b. Phila., July 29, 1964; s. Roosevelt Carroll and Yvonne Lydia (Joseph) D. BA in Music Edn., Jersey City State Coll., 1989. Dorm counselor Jersey City State Coll., 1986, cheerleader coach athletic dept., 1986—; choreographer Fair Lawn (N.J.) High Sch., 1986; artist Big Beat Records, N.Y.C., 1987-89; composer Fox Channel 5, N.Y.C., 1988, Club Beat, Elizabeth, N.J., 1988; phys. instr. dance dept. Sports and Leisure, Jersey City, 1989—; pvt. trainee Newport Swim and Fitness, Jersey City, 1990-91; chief exec. officer Studio 4 Records, Newark, 1990—; chief exec. officer Studio Y Promo Perf, Newark, 1990—. Composer: Join Hands/Can't Hide, 1987, America's Most Wanter, 1988, Studio 4 Albus 1-2-3, 1990; composer movie sound track Resurection Bridge, 1991. Mem. Phi Beta Sigma (pres. 1984-85, brother 1983—). Home and Office: Studio Y Records 38 Rose Ter Newark NJ 07108-1619

DAVIS, GEORGE HIGHTOWER, psychologist; b. Atlanta, Apr. 30, 1944; s. Harry Jones and Martha (Hightower) D.; m. Deborah Everhart, June 15, 1980; children: Kevin Everhart, Ellen Harrison. BA, Yale Coll., 1967; MS, Yale U., 1972, MPhil, 1972, PhD, 1973. Lic. psychologist, Conn. Intern VA Hosp., West Haven, Conn., 1970-71, Yale Psycho-Ednl. Clinic, New Haven, Conn., 1971-72; postdoctoral fellow Yale Psychiat. Inst., New Haven, 1973-77, psychologist, 1975-77; intern Yale Health Svcs., New Haven, 1972-73; dir. psychology Yale Psychiat. Inst., New Haven, 1977-78; dir. counseling ctr. U. New Haven, 1978-82; asst. clin. prof. psychiatry Med. Sch. Yale U., New Haven, 1978—; dir. psychology Elmcrest Psychiat. Inst., Portland, Conn., 1982-87; clin. dir. Klingberg Family Ctrs., New Britain, Conn., 1987-90; exec. dir. Assocs. in Psychology, New Haven, 1990—. Author: Reparation and Change, 1978. Mem. Conn. Psychol. Assn. (pres. 1989-90), Am. Psychol. Assn., Am. Psychol. Soc., Soc. for Personality Assessment, Sigma Xi. Home: 144 Blake Rd Hamden CT 06517-3322 Office: Assocs Psychology 103 Whitney Ave Ste 4 New Haven CT 06510-1297

DAVIS, GLEN EDWARD, clinical psychologist; b. Oak Ridge, Tenn., July 25, 1956; s. James Wendell and Dorothy Gale (Bergman) D.; m. Catherine Jean Calahan, July 8, 1984; children: Emily Margaret, Timothy James. BA summa cum laude, Macalester Coll., 1978; PhD, U. Vt., 1985. Lic. clin. psychologist, Maine. Clin. psychologist Kennebec Valley Mental Health Ctr., Waterville, Maine, 1985-89, Mid-Maine Med. Ctr., Waterville, 1987—; cons. Vassalboro (Maine) Sch. System, 1989—; co-founder Pediatric Behavioral Medicine Clinic, Waterville, Maine, 1990—. Contbg. author: Prevention of Anti-Social and Delinquent Behavior, 1985; also articles. Pres. Kennebec Valley Big Bros., Big Sisters, Waterville, 1986-88. Mem. Phi Beta Kappa. Methodist. Home: RR 1 Box 424 Belgrade ME 04917-9723 Office: Mid Maine Med Ctr 30 Chase Ave Waterville ME 04901-4635

DAVIS, HARRY STEPHEN, counselor, consultant, substance abuse executive; b. Ashland, Pa., Dec. 2, 1952; s. Harry William and Anna Delores (Karas) D.; m. Carla Dee Kurtz, June 8, 1974; children: Benjamin Charles Davis, Bethany Leigh Davis. BA in Psychology, Millersville State Coll., 1974; MA in Counseling, Liberty U., 1992. Cert. chem. abuse counselor. Alcohol detox counselor St. Joseph's Hosp., Lancaster, Pa., 1976-77; drug and alcohol treatment specialist II Union/Snyder Community Counseling Svc., Lewisburg, Pa., 1977-80; clin. dir. White Deer Run Treatment Ctr., Allenwood, Pa., 1980-90; drug and alcohol and life skills instr. Intensive Confinement Ctr. and Fed. Penitentiary, Lewisburg, 1990-91; pvt. counselor Psychol. Svcs., Sunbury, Pa., 1990-91; drug and alcohol treatment mgr. Muncy (Pa.) State Correctional Instn., 1991—; drug and alcohol cons. Bethesda Day Treatment Ctr., West Milton, Pa., 1990—; corp. patient mgmt. com. mem. Koala Treatment Ctrs., Nashville, 1988-89; oral exam evaluator Pa. Cert. Addiction Counselor Bd., Harrisburg, 1988—. Asst. coach AYSO Soccer, Milton, 1986, 88, 89; asst. leader Boy Scouts Am., Kelly Crossroads, Pa., 1988-89. Mem. AACD, Am. Assn. Christian Counselors, Nat. Assn. Alcoholism & Drug Abuse Counselors, Internat. Assn. for Addictions and Offender Counselors. Republican. Mem. Assemby of God Church. Home: 20 Spottswood Dr Milton PA 17847-9644 Office: State Correctional Instn PO Box 180 Muncy PA 17756-0180

DAVIS, HELEN WHITE, psychotherapist, educator; b. Greensboro, N.C., July 30, 1939; d. Rufus and Katrine Reese (Smith) White; m. John Charles Davis, June 24, 1961; children: Donna Katrin, Anna Lynn, John Kenneth. BS in Religion and Sociology, Meredith Coll., 1961; MS in Counseling, U. Hartford, Conn., 1981. Cert. alcohol counselor, Conn. Sr. rehab. counselor E.B. Kuhn Tng. Ctr., Middletown, Conn., 1981-83; psychotherapist The Wheeler Clinic, Plainville, Conn., 1983-90; pvt. practice Hartford, 1990—; adj. prof. Manchester (Conn.) Community Coll., 1990—; clin. supr. Conn. Alcohol & Drug Cert. Bd., Glastonbury, 1990—. Mem. AACD, Employee Assistance Profl. Assoc., Inc. (assoc.), Elmcrest Hosp. Pvt. Practice Assn. Conn., Prospect Ave. Pvt. Practice Supervision Group. Home: 56 Millstone Rd Glastonbury CT 06033-2520 Office: 664 Prospect Ave Hartford CT 06105-4203

DAVIS, JAMES CARL, retired government official, government consultant; b. St. Louis, Jan. 13, 1945; m. Linda L. Coston, Dec. 22, 1976. AA, St. Leo, Fla., 1977; BS, SUNY, Albany, 1989. Cert. pilot. Commd. 2d. lt. U.S. Army, 1963, advanced through grades to maj., 1980, ret., 1984; pres. Knights of Malta Found., New Orleans, 1984-86; adminstrn. cons. McTernan, Parr & Rumage, New Orleans, 1986-87; spl. asst. to the comdg. gen. Hdqrs. D.C. N.G., Washington, 1987-90; cons. local and U.S. govt., 1990—. Author: Where's My Award, 1982. Decorated two Bronze stars, two Purple Hearts. Mem. NRA, Res. Officers Assn., The Ret. Officers Assn. Home: Rt 2 Box 118 Picayune MS 39466-9521

DAVIS, JAMES MICHAEL, JR., air force officer, human resources professional; b. Tucson, Sept. 9, 1954; s. James Palmer and Elva (Flores) D.; m. Linda Sue Wilmington, Apr. 10, 1977, (div. Mar. 1987); m. Paula Denise Bloomfield, Dec. 10, 1987; children: James F.M. V, Deidre Allyson. ADN, Community Coll. of Air Force, Maxwell AFB, Ala., 1979; BA, U. Md., 1980; MPA, U. Okla., 1982; M of Healthcare Adminstrn., Cen. Mich. U., 1986. Enlisted U.S. Air Force, 1972, advanced through grades to capt., 1988; med. svc. specialist 162 USAF Clinic (ANG), Tucson, 1972-75, 127 TAC Clinic, Selfridge Air Force Base, Mich., 1976; cryptologic lang. specialist 6912 Electronic Security Group, Tempelhof Cen. Airport, Berlin, 1978; supr. surveillance and warning ctr. 6912 Electronic Security Group, Tempelhof Cen Appt, Germany, 1979-81, NCOIC, current ops., 1981-82; chief cryptologic lang. support br. Nat. Security Agy., Ft. George G. Meade, Md., 1982-86; comdr. med. squadron 384th Strategic Hosp., McConnell AFB, Kans., 1986-88, dir. med. readiness and resource mgmt., 1988-89; chief fin. officer 842d Strategic Hosp., Grand Forks AFB, N.D., 1989-91; dir. aeromed. evacuation sect. 609 Contingency Hosp., Zweibrücken, Germany, 1991; mgr. health manpower resources Office of the Air Force Surgeon Gen., Bolling AFB, Washington, 1991—; regional coord. Nat. Disaster Med. System, Wichita, Kans., 1986-89; advisor subcom. on intelligence Nat. Security Coun., Washington, 1983-85; del. nat. intelligence com. ad hoc working group Dept. of Def., Washington, 1982-85. Rep. Hosp. Coun. of South Cen. Kans., Wichita, 1987-89; mem. Sedgwick County Disaster Coun., Wichita, 1986-89. Mem. Am. Coll. Healthcare Execs., Assn. Mil. Surgeons of the U.S., Am. Soc. Mil. Compts. (chmn. awards com. 1990-91). Democrat. Roman Catholic. Home: 9503 Sea Shadow Columbia MD 20146 Office: Office Air Force Surgeon Gen Bolling AFB Washington DC 20332-6188

DAVIS, JERRY BERNARD, education educator; b. N.Y.C., June 16, 1932; s. Samuel and Ray (Bennett) D.; m. Ruth Goode, Aug. 27, 1960; children: Steven, Gary, Richard. BA, Bklyn. Coll., 1954; MA, Columbia U., 1955, prof. diploma, 1957, EdD, 1961. Sci. tchr. N.Y.C. high schs., 1957-60; part-time instr. Columbia U., N.Y.C., 1960-61; assoc. prof. sci. edn. SUNY, Oswego, 1961-64; prof. secondary edn. Hofstra U., Hempstead, N.Y., 1964—; rsch. fellow Sci. Manpower Project Columbia U., 1960-61; curriculum cons. Coll. Discovery and Devel. Program CUNY, 1970s-80s; program devel. specialist Tchr. Corp. Project, 1980s; dir. NSF Inservice Insts. biol. scis. curriculum studies biology, Hofstra U., 1965-73. Contbr. articles to profl. jours. Mem. profl. adv. com. L.I. chpt. March of Dimes, 1980—. Recipient NSF grant for biol. sci. curriculum studies Biology Inservice Insts., 1965-73. Mem. Assn. for the Edn. Tchrs. Sci., Nat. Sci. Tchrs. Assn., N.Y. State Sci. Suprs. Assn., Coun. for Evolution Edn., Nassau County Sci. Suprs. Assn. (pres. 1974, mem. exec. com. 1970-85). Office: Hofstra U Hempstead NY 11550

DAVIS, JOEL ANTHONY, free-lance writer; b. Ventura, Calif., Oct. 11, 1948; s. Gerald Herbert and Antonia (Farkas) D. BA in English, Calif. Luth. U., 1970; MLS, U. Oreg., 1976. Registered profl. librarian, Wash. Librarian Spokane County Library System, Wash., 1977-78; reporter Spokane Community Press, 1978-79; free-lance writer Spokane and Olympia, Wash., 1979—. Author: Endorphins: New Waves in Brain Chemistry, 1984, Flyby: The Interplanetary Odyssey of Voyager 2, 1987, Defending the Body: Unraveling the Mysteries of Immunology, 1989, Mapping the Code: The Human Genome Project and the Choices of Modern Science, 1990, Journey to the Center of Our Galaxy, 1991; co-author: Mirror Matter; Pioneering Antimatter Physics, 1988; contbr. numerous articles to profl. jours. Recipient 1st place Sci. Writing award Soc. Profl. Journalists, 1985, U.S. Coun. for Energy Awareness Forum award, 1988. Mem. Authors Guild, Nat. Assn. Sci. Writers, Oak Soc., Sci. Fiction Writers Am. Democrat. Home: 1201 W 12th St Spokane WA 99204 Office: care Scott Meredith Lit Agy Inc 845 3rd Ave New York NY 10022-6601

DAVIS, JOHN ADAMS, JR., electrical engineer, roboticist, executive; b. Winston-Salem, N.C., May 26, 1944; s. John Adams and Jean Elizabeth (Bowles) D.; m. Sharon Kay Hammons, Dec. 19, 1965; 1 child, Heather Noelle. BSEE with honors, N.C. State U., 1971; MS in Engring., Fla. Tech. U., 1976; MBA, Loyola Coll., Balt., 1980. Design engr. Martin Marietta Corp., Orlando, Fla., 1971-76; sr. program mgr. Martin Marietta Corp., Glen Burnie, Md., 1988-89; sr. engr., project mgr. Gould, Inc., Glen Burnie, Md., 1976-79, program mgr., 1984-88; mgr. data systems Bendix Corp., Columbia, Md., 1979-81; corp. ops. mgr. Vector Automation, Inc., Balt., 1981-82; dir., div. mgr. Ill. Inst. Tech. Rsch. Inst., Chgo., 1982-83; gen. mgr. Marine Systems div., dir. corp. bus. area Eastport Internat., Inc., Upper Marlboro, Md., 1989-91, corp. bus. area dir., 1991—; pres., cons. Bustech Co., Severna Park, Md., 1982—; speaker profl. confs. Contbr. articles to profl. jours. Bd. dirs. Cape Arthur Community Improvement Assn., Severna Park, 1981-82, 89-90; mem. Md. Gov.'s Com. to Elect Sch. Bd., 1982. Sgt. USAF, 1965-68, Vietnam. Recipient USAF Commendation medal. Mem. AIAA, IEEE (bd. dirs. 1978-79), Am. Def. Preparedness Assn., Assn. U.S. Army, Am. Legion, Internat. Platform Assn., Marine Tech. Soc. (remotely operated vehicle com.), Assn. Unmanned Vehicle Systems (Mem. of Yr. 1991), Tau Beta Pi, Eta Kappa Nu. Republican. Presbyterian. Office: Easport Internat Inc 501 Prince Georges Blvd Upper Marlboro MD 20772-8760

DAVIS, JOHN EUGENE, restaurant owner; b. Buffalo, Aug. 27, 1948; s. Stanley and Dorothy (Svennson) D.; m. Carolyn Elizabeth Cummings, June 14, 1969; children: John, Jady. AA, Niagara County Community Coll., 1968; BA, Oneonta State U., 1970; MS, Russell Sage Coll., 1974. Tchr. Schenectady (N.Y.) City Sch. Dist., 1970-91; pres. PJ's Bar-B-Q, Inc., Saratoga Springs, N.Y., 1986—. Mem. Rep. Chairman's Club, Saratoga Springs. Mem. Nat. Restaurant Assn., N.Y. State United Tchrs., Schenectady Fedn. Tchrs., Greater Saratoga C. of C., United Restaurant Hotel Tavern Assn. of N.Y. State, Nat. Rifle Assn., N.Y. State Restaurant Assn., Lions (Lion of the Yr. 1984-85). Methodist. Home: 1 Kaydeross Ave Saratoga Springs NY 12866 Office: PJ's Bar-B-Q Inc Rt 9 South Broadway Saratoga Springs NY 12866

DAVIS, JUANITA JOHNSON, vocational guidance coordinator, educator; b. Florence, S.C., Nov. 7, 1942; d. Samuel Lee and Artis (Eagleton) Johnson; m. George Kenneth Davis, Apr. 4, 1970; children: Tanecia R., Jason N. BS, Claflin U., 1965; MS, George Washington U., 1973; EdD, Va. Poly. Inst. & State U., 1991. Cert. administrator, guidance, counseling. Dir. youth St. Mark Ch., N.Y.C., 1965-66; tchr. Washington DC Pub. Schs., 1966-72, sch. based specialist, 1972-75, compliance monitor, 1975-79, spl. edn. resource specialist, 1979-82, media specialist, 1982-84, guidance counselor, 1984-89, coord. vocat. guidance, 1989—; adj. prof. Va. Poly. Inst. & State U., Falls Church, Va., 1991—; testing coord. Booz, Allen & Hamilton, Washington, 1990-91; cons. New Adventures Counseling Ctr., District Heights, Md., 1980—. Task force leader Far N.E. Boys and Girls Club, Washington, 1982; troop leader Girl Scouts Am., Suitland, Md., 1985—; mem. Md. State Del. Campaign, Suitland, 1986, DC Ward Campaign, 1990-91. Named Educator of the Yr., DC Mayor's Office, 1979, Outstanding Spl. Educator, Exceptional Coun., Washington, 1983, Exemplary Counselor, Guidance and Counseling, Washington, 1985, Community Leader, Girl Scouts Am., Suitland, 1990; recipient Outstanding Community Svc. award Boys and Girls Club, Washington, 1984. Mem. DC Assn. Counseling (membership chair, 1991—), DC Career Devel. Assn. (bd. trustees, 1989-91), Am. Sch. Counselor Assn., AACD, No. Va. Alliance Sch. Educators, Nat. Coun. Negro Women, Inc. Democrat. Baptist. Home: 4307 Ridgecrest Dr Suitland MD 20746-3749 Office: DC Public Schools 415 12th St NW Washington DC 20004-1905

DAVIS, KENNETH IRA, advertising and marketing professional; b. Bronx, N.Y., July 24, 1941; s. Albert Coleman and Martha Lillian (Schneid) D.; m. Judy Ann Forman, Apr. 28, 1968; children: Meredith Paige. BS in Bus., NYU, 1959-63; student, CCNY, 1963-64. Office mgr. advt., prodn. mgr. advt. Ethan Allen Furniture, N.Y.C., 1965-68; co-mgr. advt. Bates Mfg. Co., Inc., N.Y.C., 1968-71; pres. Sales Communications Inc., Millburn, N.J., 1971—, Planned Kreative Promotions, Inc., N.Y.C., 1972-82; chmn. Rothenberg Winter and Davis Inc., N.Y.C., 1989—; sr. v.p. M.L. Grant Advt., N.Y.C., 1983-85, Douglas Turner, Inc., Newark, 1986-87; chmn. Rothenberg, Winter & Davis, Inc., N.Y.C., 1989—. Served with U.S. Army, 1963. Mem. 4A's. Jewish. Lodge: K.P.

DAVIS, LAWRENCE WILLIAM, radiation oncologist; b. N. Braddock, Pa., Sept. 5, 1935; s. William Paul and Julia Helen (Zukas) D.; children: James G., Karen E. BS, Juniata Coll., Huntington, Pa., 1957; MA, U. Pa., 1969; MBA, Temple U., 1984; MD, Georgetown U., 1961. Diplomate Am. Bd. Radiology (trustee 1981—); lic. physician Pa., Md., N.Y., Ga. Asst. instr. radiology U. Pa., Phila., 1962-66, instr. radiology, 1966, 68-69, asst. prof. radiology, 1969-72, assoc. prof. radiology, 1972-75; prof. radiation therapy Thomas Jefferson Sch. Medicine, 1975-84; prof. and chmn. radiation oncology Albert Einstein Coll. Medicine, Bronx, 1984-91, Emory U., Atlanta, 1991—; cons. Armed Forces Radiobiology Rsch. Inst., Bethesda, 1968-70; exec. com. of med. staff Montefiore Med. Ctr., 1984-87, 1990-91, div. coun., 1988-89; prof. svc. com. Phila. div. Am. Cancer Soc., 1970-75. Contbr. numerous articles to profl. jours.; assoc. editor Internat. Jour. Radiation Oncology, 1986—; editorial bd. Neuro Oncology, 1989—, assoc. editor, 1991—; editorial bd Am. Jour. Clin. Oncology, 1991—. Capt. USAF, 1966-68. Fellow Am. Cancer Soc., Phila., 1963-64, NIH, 1964-66, Am. Cancer Soc. traineeship, 1968-71. Fellow Am. Coll. Radiology; mem. AAAS, Am. Assn. Cancer Rsch., Am. Coll. rAdiology (commn. on radiation oncology chmn. 1981-90), Am. Soc. Therapeutic Radiology and Oncology (chmn. bd. 1988-89, pres. 1987-88), Am. Coll. Hosp. Adminstrs., Am. Mgmt. Assn., AMA, Am. Radium Soc. (pres. 1992—), Am. Soc. Clin. Oncology, DeKalb County Med. Soc., John Morgan Soc. of U. Pa., N.Y. Acad. Sci., Ga. State Med. Soc., Ga. State Radiol. Soc., N.Y. Roentgen Soc., Radiation Rsch. Soc., Radiol. Soc. N. Am., Alpha Omega Alpha. Office: Emory Clinic 1365 Clifton Rd NE Atlanta GA 30322

DAVIS, LYNN HARRY, educator; b. Jamestown, N.Y., Mar. 6, 1949; s. Harry Lynn and Marjorie Ellen (Greenwood) D.; m. Patricia Ann Carapella; 1 child, Matthew Michael. BS, SUNY, Fredonia, 1971. Cert. tchr., N.Y. Sci. tchr. West Genesee Sch. Dist., Camillus, N.Y., 1972—; adult edn. computer tchr. West Genesee Sch. Dist., 1985-91, Syracuse U. Teaching Ctr., 1984-86; tech. support specialist Teaching Ctr. Syracuse U., 1991—; chmn. Sci. Bldg., West Genessee Sch. Dist., 1983-88, coord. sci. curriculum, 1988—. Contbr. numerous articles to profl. jours. Strategic planning com. mem. West Genesee Cen. Schs.; fundraiser United Way, Syracuse, 1978-81, YMCA, Syracuse, 1981; mem. Friends of Zoo, 1987—. Mem. N.Y. State United Tchrs. (del. 1980-85), Am. Fed. of Tchrs., Nat. Sci. Tchrs. Assn., Assn. for Supervision and Curriculum Devel., West Genesee Tchrs. Assn. (v.p. for negotiations 1979-85, sec. 1986—). Avocations: golf, photography, computers. Home: 14 Blackwood Dr Liverpool NY 13090-3764 Office: West Genesee Cen Sch Dist Ike Dixon Rd Camillus NY 13031-9619

DAVIS, MACEO NATHANIEL, international marketing and financial executive; b. Manning, S.C., Sept. 10, 1948; s. Nathaniel Davis and Rosa Belle (June) Francis; m. Rita Jean Anderson; children: Paige Adia, Maceo Anderson. BA, Lincoln U., 1970; MBA, U. Pa., 1973. Mktg. rep. IBM, Phila., 1970-71; account mgr. Citibank Corp., N.Y.C., 1973-76; v.p. tech. svcs. Greater Phila. Community Devel. Corp., 1976-78; mgr. internat. programs Grumman Internat. Corp., Bethpage, N.Y., 1978-79; chmn., chief exec. officer Internat. Resources Exch. Corp., Houston, 1979-83; owner, mgr. Internat. Resources Exch. Corp., Phila., 1989—; mgr. internat. bus. devel. City of Phila., 1983-89; mem. Am. Friends Svc. Com. Nat. Pers. Com., 1989. Organizer, mem. exec. com. Phila. CARES for Africa, 1986; bd. dirs. Walnut St. Theatre, Phila., 1987-89; active Mt. Carmel Bapt. Ch., Phila., 1987—. Named Black Achiever of Yr. Citibank, N.Y.C., 1975, one of Outstanding Young Men in Am., 1978. Mem. Kappa Alpha Psi. Home: 5104 Nevada St Philadelphia PA 19131-2418 Office: Internat Resources Exch Corp 3 Penn Ctr Ste 820 1515 Market St Philadelphia PA 19102-1969

DAVIS, MARION PEASE (MRS. WERNER SALLAND), social work administrator, therapist; b. Derby, Conn., Oct. 9, 1918; d. John Wood and Myrtle Stowe (Humphrey) Pease; m. Paul Davis, Oct. 15, 1938; children: Linda Davis Looney, Robert, Richard. BA in Psychology, U. Bridgeport, 1964; MSW, U. Conn., 1969. Cert. Ind. social worker, Conn.; cert. hypnotherapist, past life therapist. Caseworker dept. welfare State of Conn., Bridgeport, 1964-65, social worker dept. protective svcs., 1965-67, supr. protective svcs. unit, 1969-73, sr. psychiat. social worker, 1973-75, supervisory psychiat. social worker, 1975-78; dir. psychiat. social workers Greater Bridgeport Community Mental Health Ctr., 1973-82, chmn. housing com., 1974-78, mem. accreditation com., 1974-78, chmn., 1978-81, chief psychiat. social work, 1978-82; pvt. practice psychiatric social worker, 1982-91; owner Winning Combinations, 1983-86. Contbg. author: The Courage to Grow Old. Mem. profl. adv. com. Vis. Nurses Assn., 1987-91; mem. Sr. Citizens Needs Assessment Com., 1987-89; sec., co-chair by-laws com. Washington Sr. Citizens Ctr. Coun., 1987-89; vice-chair Washington Srs. Coun., 1987-88; mem. profl. adv. bd. Rainbow Nursery Sch. Co-editor: Washington Sr. Ctr. News, 1987-89. Mem. Nat. Assn. Social Workers (diplomate, registered clin. social worker, mem. exec. com. 1974-75, editorial com. 1975-77), Am. Assn. Marriage Family Counsellors (assoc. 1978-80), Logos World Univ. Bd. (chair curriculum com. 1986-88), Huxley Inst. Biosocial Rsch. (v.p., bd. dirs. 1978-81), Conn. Assn. Human Svcs., Mental Health Svcs. Coordinating Com. (rec. sec., exec. com. 1975-82, corr. sec. 1978-82), Assn. for Rsch. and Enlightenment (rep. study group 1963-79, 84-92), Conn. Assn. Rsch. and Enlightenment (sec. 1986-88, v.p. 1987-88, chair Conn. coun. 1989-91, editorial com. 1989-91), Assn. for Past Life Rsch. and Therapy (accreditation 1988), Soc. for Clin. and Exptl. Hypnosis, Internat. Soc. Hypnosis, Nat. Guild Hypnotists (cert. 1988), Assn. for Study Dreams, LWV (bd. dirs. 1985-91, pres. 1986-88, chair agrl. study com. 1986-88, co-chmn. mem. com. 1988-91), Acad. of Certified Social Workers. Home: 47 Sunset Ln Washington Depot CT 06794-1018

DAVIS, MICHAEL ALLAN, radiology educator, consultant; b. Boston, May 19, 1941; s. Milton K. and Muriel A. (Swartz) D.; m. Rona Van Der Molen, June 9, 1963; children: Marla S., Marc A. BS, Worcester (Mass.) Poly. Inst., 1962, MS, 1964; MS, Harvard U., 1965, ScD, 1969; MBA, Northeastern U., 1979; MD, U. Mass., 1985. Prof. U. Mass. Med. Sch., Worcester, 1980—; cons. E-Z-EM, Inc., Westbury, N.Y., 1985—, Viomedics, Worcester, 1988—; sci. sentinel Macrochem, Inc., Lexington, Mass., 1989—. Active Town of Westwood (Mass.) Bd. of Health, 1989-91. Mem. Am. Chem. Soc., Am. Roetgen Ray Soc., Soc. Nuclear Medicine, Assn. Univ. Radiologists, Radiol. Soc. N.Am., Soc. Magnetic Resonance Imaging, Soc. Magnetic Resonance in Medicine. Office: U Mass Med Sch 55 Lake Ave N Worcester MA 01655-0001

DAVIS, MICHAEL PETER, philosophy educator, writer; b. Albany, N.Y., Dec. 19, 1947; s. John Mills and Clara (Spector) D.; m. Susan Heldt, June

28, 1969; children: Jessica Mills, Sarah Henning. BA, Cornell U., 1969; postgrad., Heidelberg U., Fed. Republic of Germany, 1971-72; MA, Pa. State U., 1973, PhD, 1974. Vis. asst. prof. Dickinson Coll., Carlisle, Pa., 1974-75, Conn. Wesleyan U., Middletown, 1975-76; asst. prof. Alfred (N.Y.) U., 1976-77; prof. Sarah Lawrence Coll., Bronxville, N.Y., 1977—; Author: Ancient Tragedy and the Origins of Modern Science, 1988, Aristotle's Poetics: The Poetry of Philosophy, 1992; mem. editorial bd. Ancient Philosophy, 1980; contbr. articles to profl. jours. Author: Ancient Tragedy and the Origins of Modern Science, 1988; mem. editorial bd. Ancient Philosophy, 1980—; contbr. articles to profl. jours. NDEA fellow, 1971-73, Richard Weaver fellow Intercollegiate Studies Inst., 1973-74, Earhart Found. fellow, 1986, 90-91. Mem. APA, Soc. for Ancient Greek Philosophy, Soc. for Greek Polit. Thought. Office: Sarah Lawrence Coll Philosophy Dept Bronxville NY 10708

DAVIS, MORTON DAVID, mathematics educator; b. N.Y.C., May 31, 1930; s. Harry and Fannie (Sobol) D.; m. Gloria Steinman, Aug. 18, 1963; children: Jeanne Rachel, Joshua Paul. AB, U. Colo., 1952; MA, U. Calif., Berkeley, 1956, PhD, 1961. Mathematician IBM, Oakland, Calif., 1959-61, Yorktown Heights, N.Y., 1959-61; rsch. assoc. Princeton (N.J.) U., 1961-63; asst. prof. Rutgers U., New Brunswick, N.J., 1963-65; prof. math. CCNY, 1965—. Author: Game Theory, 1970, Mathematically Speaking, 1980, Art of Decision Making, 1984. Lt. (j.g.) USN, 1952-55. Home: 25 Brinkerhoff Ave Teaneck NJ 07666-3125 Office: Math Dept CCNY 138th St and Convent Ave New York NY 10031

DAVIS, OSSIE, actor, author; b. Cogdell, Ga., Dec. 18, 1917; s. Kince Charles and Laura (Cooper) D.; m. Ruby Ann Wallace (Ruby Dee), Dec. 9, 1948; children: Nora, Guy, Hasna. Student, Howard U., 1935-38. Stage debut with Rose McClendon Players in Harlem, 1939; Broadway debut in Jeb, 1946; theatre appearances include A Raisin in the Sun, Purlie Victorious, I'm Not Rappaport, 1987; writer, dir., actor (films) The Cardinal, The Hill; TV appearances include All God's Children, The Eleventh Hour; narrator: Freedom Road, With Ossie & Ruby, King; appeared in TV series B.L. Stryker, Evening Shade, 1990—; dir. films Cotton Comes to Harlem, Black Girl, Countdown at Kusini, Gordon's War; actor (films) The Scalphunters, School Daze, Do The Right Thing (Best Supporting actor award, Image award for role DA Mayor NAACP), Jungle Fever, 1991; author: Escape to Freedom: The Story of Young Frederick Douglass, 1978, Langston, 1982, Purlie Victorious; co-producer (home videotape) Hands Upon the Heart, 1991. Named to NAACP Image Awards Hall of Fame with wife, Ruby Dee, 1989. Office: care Artists Agy 10000 Santa Monica Blvd Ste 305 Los Angeles CA 90067-7095

DAVIS, RANDALL EUGENE, clergyman; b. Covengiton, Ky., Nov. 13, 1947; s. Harold Lee Jr. and Mona Geneva (Curtis) D.; m. Sandra Patrica Asselin, Oct. 25, 1974; 1 child, Daniel Theodore. MA in Theology, Faith Bible Theol. Sem., Milton, Fla., 1992. Asst. pastor Calvary Bapt. Ch., 1964-66; pastor Bliss Bapt. Ch., 1966-67; evangelist, 1970—; staff evangelist Faith Bible Ch., Agawam, Mass., 1990—. Author: (book) Love Moves the North Pole, 1988, (poetry) Dear God, 1990 (Golden Poet 1990), 50th Wedding Anniversary, 1991 (Golden Poet 1991), Now the Time Has Come. With USMC, 1967-69. Republican. Baptist. Home and Office: 63 Ogden St Springfield MA 01151-1826

DAVIS, REX DARWIN, business consultant; b. Skiatook, Okla., June 11, 1924; s. Ivan Francis and Ruth Mae (Nabors) D.; m. Amelia Roberts Fry, Apr. 14, 1979; children by previous marriage: Deborah Ruth, Kathleen Marie. LLB, U. Okla., 1949; postgrad., Princeton U., 1966. Exec. asst. to asst. regional commr. Bur. Alcohol Tobacco and Firearms, Cin., 1962-66, asst. regional commr., 1966-70; dir. Bur. Alcohol Tobacco and Firearms, Washington, 1970-78; pres. Nat. Assn. Beverage Importers, Inc., Washington, 1978-85, Delta Cons., Inc., Washington, 1985—; pres., chief exec. officer New Europe Wines, Inc., 1991—; chmn. Lic. Beverage Info. Coun., Washington, 1981-85, Internat. Fedn. Wine & Spirits, Paris, 1982-85; bd. dirs. Am. Nat. Metric Coun., 1976-78, Internat. Assn. Chiefs of Police, Washington, 1975-78. Author: Federal Searches and Seizures, 1964. Vice chmn. Sky Ranch Found., Washington, 1983-85; pres. Treas. Hist. Assn., 1978-79. 1st lt. USAAF, 1943-45. Recipient Chevalier de Merite Agricole French Gov., 1983, award for exceptional svc. Dept. Treasury, 1978, Meritorious Svc. award 1977; named Fed. Employee of Yr. Cin. chpt. Fed. Bus. Assn., 1965; Meritorious award William A. Jump Found., 1959. Mem. Am. Soc. Assn. Execs., Okla. Bar Assn., Pi Kappa Alpha, Internat. Club, Princeton Club. Home and Office: Delta Cons Inc 311 10th St SE Washington DC 20003-2130

DAVIS, ROBERT JAMES, astrophysicst, computer software designer; b. Omaha, Oct. 26, 1929; s. Harry Cleve and Margaret Louise (Homan) D.; m. Ruth Cinnamon, May 16, 1953; children: Carolyn Hargis, Deborah Mossberg, Paul, Elizabeth Poimboeuf. BA, Harvard U., 1951, MA, 1956, PhD, 1960. Astrophysicist Smithsonian Instn., Cambridge, Mass., 1956—; mem. planetarium com. Boston Mus. of Sci., 1975—; mem. safety com. Smithsonian Astrophys. Obs., Cambridge, 1980-90. Sr. author: The Celescope Catalog of Ultraviolet Stellar Observations, 1972. Sr. deacon Park Ave. Congl. Ch., Arlington, Mass., 1976-80. Lt. (j.g.) USNR, 1951-54. Recipient Detur award Harvard U., 1949. Mem. Am. Astron. Soc., Internat. Astron. Union, Internat. Soc. for Philos. Enquiry (historian 1967-72, trustee 1986—). Mem. Christian Ch. Office: Smithsonian Instn Astrophysical Observatory Cambridge MA 02138

DAVIS, ROLAND HAYES, university official; b. Cleve., Feb. 9, 1927; s. Sylvester Sanford Sr. and Amaza (Weaver) D.; m. Jean Alston, Aug. 26, 1951 (div. Oct. 1979); children: Jeffrey Hayes, Leslie Suzanne, Kurt Bradley. Student, Case Western Res. U., 1945-46, Hofstra Coll., 1955-58; BA, L.I. U., 1961; MSW, Adelphi U., 1969. Social worker Nassau County (N.Y.) Dept. Social Svcs., 1966-79; ret., 1979; univ. adminstr. Hofstra U., Hempstead, N.Y., 1979-92; cons. to pres. Hofstra U., Hempstead, 1992—; bd. dirs. Vanguard/Guardian Bank, Hempstead, 1975-89, chmn. 1975-85. Past pres. Assn. Minority Enterprises Inc. of N.Y., 1980-85. Lt. U.S. Army, 1946-66. Recipient Unispan award Hofstra U., 1979, Bus. Leadership award L.I. Bus. Community, 1981, Legis. citation Legislature of State of N.Y., 1983, Community Svc. Recognition award Pres. of U.S., 1984, Man of Yr. Hempstead C. of C., 1986. Mem. NAACP (life), Blue Cross/Blue Shield of N.Y. (voting mem.), The Edges Group, Inc. (treas. 1990—), Health and Welfare Coun. of Nassau County (bd. dirs. 1982-91), Hempstead Gen. Hosp. Adv. Bd., 100 Black Men, Nassau/Suffolk, Inc. (pres. 1980-85, mem. 1978—). Office: Hofstra Univ 1000 Fulton Ave Hempstead NY 11550-1009

DAVIS, S. GARETH, publishing executive; b. Bar Harbor, Maine, July 27, 1921; s. Meyer and Hilda (Emery) D.; m. Esther Peter, June 4, 1962 (div.); children: Troy Alaric, Athena Veronica, Kim Gregory, Kristina Starr. D World Law, East-West U., Fernhill, India, 1987. Actor N.Y.C., 1940-52; founder, pres. Internat. Registry World Citizens, Paris, 1949; founder, world coord. World Govt. of World Citizens, Ellsworth, Maine, 1953; founder, mng. dir. NWO Publs., Burlington, Vt., 1992—; founder, pres. World Svc. Authority, Washington, 1954, cons., 1975—. Author: The World is My Country, 1960, World Government, Ready or Not!, 1985, Passport to Freedom, 1992. Candidate for mayor, Washington, 1986; candidate for U.S. president, 1988. 1st lt. U.S. Air Corps, 1941-46. Fellow Fortean Soc.; mem. Vets. for Peace. Home: 300 Maple St Burlington VT 05401 Office: World Svc Authority 1012 14th St NW Washington DC 20005

DAVIS, SHOSHANA TIKVA, nurse; b. Lincoln, Nebr., May 5, 1950; d. Elden Dwain and Darlene Levana (Hageman) McKenzie; m. Richard Lawrence Crews (div. Jan. 1986); m. Peter Arnold Davis, Oct. 24, 1987; 1 child, Aaron Alexander Crews Davis. BA in Humanities, New Coll. Calif., 1978; MPA, U. Okla., 1988; AS in Nursing, Regents Coll., Albany, 1990; postgrad., U. Conn., 1990—. RN, Conn. Maternity nurse Naval Hosp., Groton, Conn., 1988-89, ambulatory surgery nurse, 1989; psychiatry nurse Norwich (Conn.) Hosp., 1989-90; community health nurse Community Health and Home Care, Pomfret, Conn., 1990-91; nursing supr. Village Manor Health Care, Plainfield, Conn., 1991; staff relief nurse Staff Mates, Hebron, Conn., 1991—; grad. asst. Sch. Nursing U. Conn., Storrs, 1991-92; nursing supr. Natchaug Hosp., 1992—. Recipient award Guam Press Club, 1987. Mem. Conn. Nurses Assn., Intertel, Mensa, Clan MacKenzie Soc. Ams., B'nai B'rith Hillel Found. (chair grad. activities U. Conn. 1991), Sigma Theta Tau Internat. Nursing Honor Soc. Democrat. Jewish. Home: PO Box 207 Canterbury CT 06331-0207

DAVIS, STEPHEN EDWARD FOLWELL, banker; b. Auckland, N.Z., July 12, 1964; s. George Folwell and Elizabeth Ann (Strother) D. BA, Harvard Coll., 1987. Rsch. intern The Brookings Instn., Washington, 1984; sales intern Lotus Devel. Corp., Cambridge, Mass., 1986-87; fin. analyst Salomon Bros. Inc., N.Y.C., 1987-89; interest rate swap trader Kidder Peabody & Co., N.Y.C., 1989-90; spl. products trader Deutsche Bank AG, N.Y.C., 1990—. Researcher book: The Ultimate Insiders, 1989. Homesteading coord., dir. Crimson Impact Inc., N.Y.C., 1991—; jr. com. mem. The Quadrille Soc., N.Y.C., 1991—. JFK Sch. Govt. grantee, 1984; Lindsay Exeter Meml. scholar, 1983. Mem. Fgn. Policy Assn. (young profls. group, speaker's com.), Harvard Club of N.Y. Home: 27 W 44th St # 57 New York NY 10036-6645 Office: Deutsche Bank AG 31 W 52nd St New York NY 10019-6118

DAVIS, STEPHEN MARSHALL, political and economic analyst; b. N.Y.C., May 2, 1955; s. J. Sanford and Helen H. Davis; m. Carole A. Douglis, Aug. 29, 1982 (div. July 1990); m. Claudine Swidler, Sept. 22, 1991. Student, London Sch. Econs., 1975-76; BA, Tufts U., 1977, PhD, 1982. Mem. staff Senate Com. on Govt. Ops., Washington, 1975; asst. polit. officer U.S. Dept. State, Lusaka, Zambia, 1978; legis. dir. Conn. State Senate Dems., Hartford, 1982-86; cons. Washington, 1986-87; sr. analyst and dir. global program Investor Responsibility Rsch. Ctr., Washington, 1988—. Author: Apartheid's Rebels, 1987, Shareholder Rights Abroad, 1989; contbr. articles to Harpers Mag., Boston Globe, and other publs. Founding chmn., Battle for Madison (Conn.) Com., 1982-83, Phone Fairness Com., Madison, 1984-86; trustee, The Country Sch., Madison, 1985-86; pres., Deacon John Grave Found., Madison, 1985-86; prin. adviser South African policy, Dukakis for Pres. campaign, 1987-88. Mem. Coun. Fgn. Relations, African Studies Assn., Ams. for Dem. Action (mem. nat. bd. dirs.). Jewish. Home: 57 Hancock St Newton MA 02166 Office: Investor Responsibility Ctr 1755 Massachusetts Ave NW Washington DC 20036-2102

DAVIS, STEPHEN OLIVER, computer company executive; b. N.Y.C., Apr. 19, 1942; s. Marvin Buchannan and Dorothy Alma (Meighen) D.; m. Lorraine Lippold, Feb. 24, 1943; children: Tammy Leigh, Amanda Faith. BS in Sci., Lafayette Coll., 1964; MS in Engring., NYU, 1965. Registered profl. engr., Mass. Staff engr. Bendix Corp., N.J., 1965-66; cons. Conductron, St. Charles, Mo., 1966, M.I.T., Cambridge, Mass., 1966-70, Honeywell, Mass., 1970-80; chief exec. officer Real Time Software Systems, Meredith, N.H., 1980—, Real Time Engring. Inc., Holliston, Mass., 1981—.

DAVIS, SUSAN SMITH, museum director; b. Lewiston, Maine, Feb. 28, 1943; d. Abbott Pliny and Elizabeth Cooper (Saunders) S.; m. Daniel Bryant Davis, Oct. 19, 1968 (div. Aug. 1987); children: Sarah McIntire, Micum Saunders. BA, Bates Coll., 1965; MAT, Fairleigh Dickinson Coll., 1967; postgrad. student, U. Munich, West Germany, 1967-68. Tchr. Cranford (N.J.) High Sch., 1966-67; owner, founder Staples Natural Foods, Kingfield, Maine, 1971-75, One Stanley Ave. Restaurant, Kingfield, Maine, 1972-87; owner, prin. Flower Box Co., Kingfield, Maine, 1979-82; founder Stanley Museum, Kingfield, Maine, 1981, dir., 1985—; founder Maine Arts Sponsors Assn., 1981-85. Organizer, chmn. Kingfield Bicentennial Celebration, 1976, Save Stanley Sch. effort, 1981; co-chmn. Comprehensive Plan Com., Kingfield, 1988-89; bd. dirs. Western Mountains Alliance, Farmington, Maine, 1988-91. Mem. Am. Assn. Mus., Am. Assn. State and Local History, Maine Assn. Mus. (bd. dirs. 1981-85, v.p. 1989-91, founder). Democrat. Episcopalian. Office: Stanley Museum School St # 280 Kingfield ME 04947

DAVIS, TAMARA JEAN, financial manager; b. Danville, Ky., Mar. 10, 1964; d. Donald Lloyd and Johelen (Mayfield) D. Student, Hampton Inst., 1982-85; BA in Econs., U. Md., 1987. Cert. facility security officer. Systems operator The Barlow Corp., Chevy Chase, Md., 1987-88; acct. K-COM Micrographics, Inc., Vienna, Va., 1988-89; facility security officer K-COM Micrographics, Inc., Washington, 1990-91, fin. mgr., 1989—; property mgr. The Branden Equity Group, Washington, 1990—; bd. dirs. The Magma Group, Inc., Washington. Treas. Calvary Chapel-Young Adult Fellowship, Ft. Meade, Md., 1991. Mem. NAACP, Nat. Assn. Black Accts., U. Md. Alumni Assn., Alpha Kappa Alpha, Phi Beta Lambda. Democrat. Home: 13212 Warburton Dr Fort Washington MD 20744-6537 Office: K-COM Micrographics Inc 1353 H St NE Washington DC 20002-4406

DAVIS, THOMAS CHARLES, music educator, church musician; b. Pitts., July 12, 1938; s. Thomas Charles and Anna Mae (Shaffer) D. BFA in Music, Carnegie-Mellon U., 1961, BFA in Music Edn., 1961, MFA in Music, 1962. Dir. music Emanuel United Meth. Ch., Pitts., 1961—; tchr. div. prep. Carnegie-Mellon U., Pitts., 1962-83; tchr. Brentwood High Sch., Pitts., 1963—. Mem. Am. Matthay Assn. (pres. 1990—). Home: 46 Poplar St Pittsburgh PA 15205

DAVIS, THOMAS GENE, chemical instrumentation executive, consultant, engineer; b. Galena, Mo., Dec. 26, 1936; s. Thomas Warren and Ruba Fern (Stephens) D.; m. Betty Ellen McCabe, Oct. 1, 1982. BA in Physics, U. Calif., Riverside, 1958; MSEE, MIT, 1965, PhD in Elec. Engring., 1968. Asst. prof. MIT, Cambridge, Mass., 1968-73; mgr. novel systems Xerox Corp., Webster, N.Y., 1973-80; v.p. engring. and tech. AM Printer Systems, Livingston, N.J., 1980-82; dir. tech. Wang Labs., Lowell, Mass., 1982-83; chief scientist P.A. Tech., Princeton, N.J., 1983-86; pres. Scientifica, Princeton, 1986—; cons. Johnson & Johnson Corp., New Brunswick, 1987-91. Patentee in field; contbr. numerous articles to profl. jours. Mem. Soc. for Imaging Sci. and Tech., Soc. Photo-Optical Instrumentation Engrs. Office: Scientifica 340 Wall St Princeton NJ 08540-1518

DAVIS, WALTER BOND, minister; b. Balt., Jan. 16, 1930; s. Everett Fogg and Fanny-Fern (Smith) D.; m. Catherine Fixx, Sept. 18, 1934 (div. 1981); m. Barbara Buschmeyer, Nov. 24, 1928; children: Ward, Peter, Eric, Craig, Jean, Martha, Neil, Tom. BA with honors, Cornell U., 1951; MDiv, Yale U., 1954; postgrad., Harvard U., 1957-60. Ordained to ministry United Ch. of Christ, 1954. Assoc. pastor First Ch., Oberlin, Ohio, 1954-57, Cen. Congl. Ch., Newtonville, Mass., 1957-60; sr. pastor First Congl. Ch., United Ch. Christ, Verona, N.J., 1960-65, Santa Barbara, Calif., 1965-71, Winchester, Mass., 1971-89, Attleboro, Mass., 1989—; vis. scholar Claremont (Calif.) Sch. Theology, 1975, 86, Vienna, 1986; dean youth confs., United Ch. of Christ, Ohio, N.J., 1950-70; exec. com., bd. dirs. Mass. Conf., 1980; recording sec. United Ch. Bd. for World Ministries, 1982-86, steering com. FOCUS, 1988—; community rep. protocol com. Winchester Hosp., 1985-89. Contbr. articles to profl. jours. and newspapers; composer hymns. Chmn. Community Rels. Commn., Santa Barbara, Calif. 1966-70, Dept. Coll. and Univ. Ministries, N.J. Conn. Chs., 1962-65; founding pres. Winchester Interagy. Coun., 1975; founder Family to Family Fellowship, Santa Barbara, 1967; bd. dirs. United Way, 1990—, Habitat for Humanity, 1990—, Attleboro Area Literacy Coun., 1990—. Recipient Outstanding Program award Exch. Club, Outstanding Svc. award ABI. Mem. Congl. Christian Hist. Soc. (clk. 1981—, exec. bd.), Winchester Interfaith Coun. (pres. 1988-89), Theol. Study Mass. Coun. Chs., Winthrop Club Boston (pres. 1982-84), Rotary Club. Office: Second Congl Ch 50 Park St Attleboro MA 02703-2338

DAVIS, WALTER STANLEY, retired propulsion engineer; b. Auburn, Maine, Dec. 10, 1928; s. Leslie Milton and Irma B. (Davis) D.; m. Joyce Ann MacConnell, Oct. 17, 1953; children: Leslie I., Jan E., Walter C., Linwood B., Hope A., Beth A. BSME, U. Maine, 1952; MS in Engring., Princeton U., 1960. Rsch. asst. Princeton U., Princeton, N.J., 1952-56; sr. engr. Convair and Astronautics div. Gen. Dynamics Corp., San Diego, 1957-65; sr. engr. Textron Def. Systems, Wilmington, Mass., 1965-90, ret., 1990. Inventor, patentee electro thermal reactor; contbr. articles to profl. jours. Mem. AIAA, Tau Beta Pi. Republican. Home: 12 Wheeler Ave Salem NH 03079-3447

DAVIS, WILLIAM KRUGER, automotive executive; b. Binghamton, N.Y., Mar. 30, 1926; s. Charles Edson and Amelia (Parker) D.; m. Alma Marie Welcher, Sept. 5, 1948; children: Christine-Susan, Scott Charles, Jennifer Ann. BS, Hartwick Coll., 1949. V.p. Hotaling Sales & Svc., Inc., Sidney, N.Y., 1949-69; pres. Country Club Chevrolet, Inc., Oneonta, N.Y., 1969—; v.p. C.O.D. Realty Corp., Oneonta, 1969—, Otsego Automotive, Inc., Oneonta, 1974—; bd. dirs. Wilber Nat. Bank, Oneonta; trustee Hartwick Coll., Oneonta, 1985-91. Sr. warden St. James Episcopal Ch., Oneonta, 1987—. Sgt. USAF, 1943-46. PTO. Mem. Sidney (N.Y.) C. of C. (pres. 1965-68), Del. County C. of C. (bd. dirs. Stamford, N.Y. chpt. 1964-67), Rotary (pres. Oneonta chpt. 1976). Republican. Home: RR 2 Box 54 Otego NY 13825-9608 Office: Country Club Chevrolet Inc 70 Oneida St Oneonta NY 13820-2192

DAVIS-FULLER, ETHLYN ANITA, educator; b. Phila., Oct. 9, 1944; Mem. Phi Delta Kappa.; d. Ernest and Ruth Edna (Yates) Davis; 1 child, Chiara Anita Davis Fuller. BA, Cheyney U., 1966; MEd, Newton Coll. Sacred Heart, 1973; PhD, Boston Coll., 1988. Cert. tchr. elem./sec. edn. English, Pa., Mass.; cert. prin., Mass. Tchr. Phila. Pub. Schs., 1966-73, Newton Pub. Schs., 1973-81; assoc. prof. Cambridge (Mass.) Coll., 1977-83, prof. edn., 1983—; vis. prof. Simmons Coll., Boston, 1983-91; cons. Boston Pub. Schs., 1976—; lectr. Boston vicinity Calif. Pub. Schs., Pasadena, 1983—. Author: Cultural Diversity in the Classroom: Reaching Out to Cultural Diversity, 1991. Fundraiser Pierce Sch., Brookline, Mass., 1987—, active PTO, 1987—; youth coord. St. Paul AME Ch., Cambridge, Mass., 1976-80. Washington U. fellow, 1976; named Black Achiever Greater Boston YMCA, 1992; recipient Outstanding Black Educators award Charles St. AME Ch., 1990. Home: 8 Auburn Ct Brookline MA 02146 Office: Cambridge Coll 1 Mifflin Pl Cambridge MA 02138

DAVISON, CHARLES HAMILTON, financial executive; b. Providence, Dec. 20, 1926; s. Ernest H. and Margery C. (Crowell) D.; m. Lessie Hall Lang Busbee, Aug. 16, 1958; children: Charles Hamilton, James Lang, Andrew Burwell. A.B., Dartmouth Coll., 1950; M.B.A., N.Y. U., 1953. C.P.A. Accountant Hurdman & Cranstoun, N.Y.C., 1950-55; partner firm Comery, Davison & Co., Providence, 1955-64; mng. partner Peat, Marwick, Mitchell & Co., Providence, 1964-65; mng. partner New Eng. Area Peat, Marwick, Mitchell & Co., 1965-67, mng. partner Chgo. office, mem. exec. com. Midwest Area, 1967-77; dep. chmn. Peat, Marwick, Mitchell & Co., N.Y.C., 1977-80; vice chmn., chmn. fin. com., mem. exec. com. Smith Barney, Harris Upham & Co., N.Y.C., 1980-82; chmn., chief exec. officer Paramount Cards Inc., 1983—. Pres., bd. dirs. United Charities Chgo.; bd. dirs. Community Fund Chgo., Inc., R.I. Philharmonic; trustee Roosevelt U., Inst. on Man and Sci.; chmn. fin. com., mem. exec. com. Kenyon Coll.; mem. adv. council Northwestern U. Grad. Sch. Mgmt.; bd. overseers Amos Tuck Sch., Dartmouth Coll., NYU Grad. Sch. Bus.; mem. vis. com. Grad. Sch. Bus., U. Chgo. Serve with USAAF, 1944-46. Mem. Am. Inst. C.P.A.'s, Ill., N.Y. socs. C.P.A.'s, Chgo. Assn. Commerce and Industry (dir., v.p., policy com.). Republican. Congregationalist. Clubs: Commercial of Chgo; Round Hill (Greenwich, Conn.); Indian Hill, Belle Haven; Racquet and Tennis (N.Y.C.); To Kalon (Pawtucket, R.I.); Agawam Hunt, University, Hope (Providence); Chicago (Chgo.); Johns Island (Vero Beach, Fla.). Home: 124 Glenwood Dr Greenwich CT 06830-7015 Office: Paramount Cards Inc 400 Pine St Pawtucket RI 02863-2607

DAVISON, GLENN ALAN, podiatric surgeon; b. Newark, Sept. 18, 1963; s. Phillip Davison and Arlene Joan (Schwartz) Dubrovsky; m. Anne Frances Zebrowski, Oct. 7, 1991. BA, Skidmore Coll., 1985; D Podiatric Medicine, N.Y. Coll. Podiatric Medicine, 1989. Lic. in podiatric medicine, N.J., N.Y. Resident in podiatric medicine and surgery Union (N.J.) Hosp., 1989-90; assoc. in podiatry Hillside, N.J., 1990-91; pvt. practice Elizabeth, N.J., 1991—; founder Family Health Ctr. Union Hosp., Elizabeth, 1991—; mem. med. staff Union Hosp., Elizabeth Gen. Med. Ctr., Runnells Hosp., St. Elizabeth Hosp.; mem. intern and resident tng. com., preceptor of podiatry out-patient tng., mem. resident teaching staff, podiatric continuing med. edn. credit adminstr. Union Hosp.; guest lectr. various community hosps., nursing homes, civic orgns.; participant pedal screening programs and local health fairs. Contbr. article on foot surgery to profl. jour., numerous articles on diabetic foot care and common pedal ailments to newspapers. Active, com. mem. Shoes for the Homeless project, N.J., 1991. Recipient 1st prize OUM Group Podiatric Writing Contest, 1990, PICA Podiatric Writing Contest, 1990. Mem. Am. Podiatric Med. Assn., N.J. Podiatric Med. Soc. (cert. of achievement 1991, treas. exec. com.), Am. Coll. Foot Surgeons, Am. Podiatric Med. Postgrad. Soc.. Office: 315 Elmora Ave Elizabeth NJ 07208-1301

DAVISON, JAMES ERIC, psychologist; b. Washington, Aug. 18, 1953; s. Dexter Ralph and Janet (Arpert) D.; m. Janet Clare Hamilton, May 23, 1976 (div. Apr. 1983); m. Joanne Jean Parke, Dec. 27, 1987. BA in Anthropology, Coll. William & Mary, 1975; MEd in Counselor Edn., James Madison U., 1982; PhD in Counseling Psychology, Ind. State U., 1989. Correctional officer Va. Dept. Corrections, Barhamsville, 1976; lt. instr. Va. Dept. Corrections Acad., Waynesboro, 1976-78; correctional counselor Staunton (Va.) Correctional Ctr., 1978-85; doctoral student Ind. State U., Terre Haute, 1985-88; psychology intern U.S. Penitentiary, Terre Haute, 1988-89; staff psychologist, drug program coord. Fed. Correctional Instn., Loretto, Pa., 1989—; counselor home based family therapy project Ind. State U., 1986-88; vol. counselor Alternatives for Abused Adults, Staunton, 1982-84. Mem. The Chem. People Task Force, Staunton, 1984. Recipient Eugene Debs award E.V. Debs Found., Terre Haute, 1987. Mem. APA. Methodist. Office: Fed Correctional Instn PO Box 1000 Loretto PA 15940-1000

DAVISSON, WILLIAM SEARS, civil engineer; b. Seattle, Dec. 3, 1946; s. Harold Ford and E. Jane (Sears) D.; m. Ann W. Allred, June 5, 1972; 1 child, Douglas Eldon. BSCE, Va. Poly. Inst. & State U., 1974; MSCE, U. Pitts., 1983. Registered profl. engr., Pa. Engr. Am. Bridge Div. USS Corp., Pitts., 1974-83; sr. engr. Michael Baker Corp., Pitts., 1983-84; mgr. computer systems DuPont Regional Engring. Office, Bridgeville, Pa., 1984-90; sr. engr. E.I. DuPont DeNemours Inc., Newark, Del., 1990—. With USN, 1966-72. Rpublican. Presbyterian. Home: 3109 Albemarle Rd Wilmington DE 19808-2701 Office: EI DuPont De Nemours Inc PO Box 6090 Newark DE 19714-6090

DAWES, LYELL CLARK, publishing company executive; b. Balt., Apr. 10, 1931; s. Lyell Clark and Anne (Mehorter) D.; m. Patricia Clarke Clinton, July 1975; children: William, Elizabeth; m. Jessie Scott Pollock, Dec. 27, 1981; children: Sterling, Clement. AB, U.N.C., 1953. With McGraw Hill Pub. Co., 1956-65; pub. mgr. RCA Instrnl. Systems, Palo Alto, Calif., 1965-67; v.p., dir. Macmillan Info., N.Y.C., 1967-69; group v.p., dir. Westinghouse Learning Corp., N.Y.C., 1969-76; with ISI Press, Phila., 1978-80; pres. University City Info. Co., Phila., 1980-82; pres., chief exec. officer Cobblestone Pub., Inc., Peterborough, N.H., 1982—. Bd. dirs. N.H. Assn. for Blind, Concord, 1985-87, Monadnock Hospice, Peterborough, N.H., 1989; edn. com. Ridgewood (N.J.) Sch. Dist., 1973. Capt. USMC, 1953-55, Korea. Mem. IEEE, Rotary, Univ. Club, Naval War Coll. Found. Home: Box 116 Francestown NH 03043 Office: Cobblestone Pub Inc 7 School St Peterborough NH 03458

DAWKINS, WAYNE JESSE, journalist, newsletter editor; b. N.Y.C., Sept. 19, 1955; s. Edward Henry and Iris Carmen (McFarquhar) D.; m. Joyce C. Ingram, Oct. 16, 1982 (div. 1987); m. Allie Crump, Apr. 29, 1988; 1 child, Carmen Jamila. BA, L.I. U., 1977; MS in Journalism, Columbia U., 1980. Reporter Daily Argus, Mt. Vernon, N.Y., 1980-84; reporter Courier-Post, Cherry Hill, N.J., 1984-88, editorial writer, 1988—. Editor (monthly newsletter) Black Alumni Network, 1980—. Recipient 1st Pl. award Depth Reporting N.Y. State AP, 1983, Grand award Pb. Svc. Phila. Press Assn., 1986, 1st Pl. award Editorial Writing, 1991, 1st Pl. award Spot News Reporting N.J. Press Assn., 1987, Alumni Assn. award Columbia U. Sch. Journalism, 1990. Mem. Nat. Ass. Black Journalists (regional dir. 1984-89, scholarship chmn. 1985-87, mem. scholarship com. 1985-91, writer jours. 1985—, historian 1991—), Garden State Assn. Black Journalists (founding pres. 1988-90, treas. 1989—), Columbia U. Alumni Assn. (bd. dirs. 1980-84). Mem. Unitarian-Universalist Ch. Home: 5 Hopewell Ln Sicklerville NJ 08081 Office: Courier-Post 301 Cuthbert Blvd Cherry Hill NJ 08002

DAWLEY, ALAN CHARLES, historian, educator; b. Milw., Dec. 18, 1943; ss. Clarence F. and Thelma E. (Lee) D.; m. Katherine Louise Wechsler, Sept. 10, 1966; children: Aaron Michael, Evan Nicholas. BA, Oberlin Coll., 1965; MA, Harvard U., 1966, PhD, 1971. Editor Miss. Free Press, Jackson, 1963-64; asst. prof. Trenton (N.J.) State Coll., 1970-78, assoc. prof., 1979-84, prof., 1985—; exch. prof. Worcester (Eng.) Coll., 1976-77; vis. fellow Davis

Ctr. Princeton (N.J.) U., 1977-78, vis. prof., 1991-92; vis. sr. lectr. U. Warwick, Eng., 1982-83; tenure cons. Columbia U., U. N.C. Author: Class and Community, 1976 (Bancroft prize 1977), Struggles for Justice, 1991; co-author, editor: Working for Democracy, 1985; contbr. articles to profl. jours. Bd. pres. Bucks County (Pa.) Housing Group, 1988-89, bd. mem., 1985—; active Bucks County Cen. Am. Network, 1989—. NEH fellow, 1986-87; Mellon Found. grantee Schlesinger Libr., 1985, 86, Hagley Libr. grantee, 1984, Beveridge grantee Am. Hist. Assn., 1982. Mem. Am. Hist. Assn., Orgn. Am. Historians (Merle Curti prize com.), Pa. Labor History Soc. Democrat. Home: 123 E Marshall Ave Langhorne PA 19047-2115 Office: Trenton State Coll Dept History Trenton NJ 08650

DAY, IRVING MEADE, III, business writer; b. Phila., Aug. 4, 1938; s. Irving Meade Jr. and Jane (Smith) D.; m. Kathleen Kinney, July 24, 1971; 1 child, Irving Meade IV. BS in Govt. and Pub. Affairs, Columbia U., 1968. From mgr. client rels. and svcs. to dir. mktg. svcs. PHH Homequity, Inc., Wilton, Conn., 1973-87; prin. Irving M. Day III Bus. Writer and Communication Cons., Fly Creek, N.Y., 1987—. Contbr. articles to profl. jour. Councilman Town of Otsego, N.Y., 1992—, chmn. community resources commn., 1990—. With USAR, 1956-64. Mem. Internat. Assn. Bus. Communicators, Cooperstown C. of C. (1st v.p. 1988-89), Cooperstown Country Club (pres. 1991—, v.p. 1989-91), Rotary Club Cooperstown (bd. dirs. 1991—), Jesters Club. Republican. Episcopalian. Home and Office: Schoolhouse Rd PO Box 234 Fly Creek NY 13337

DAY, JAMES MEREDITH, psychologist, educator; b. Troy, Ohio, Feb. 26, 1955; s. J.M. and Geneva (Puterbaugh) D.; m. Ria Goris, July 24, 1985; 1 child, Julia Martina. AB, Oberlin Coll., 1977; postgrad., Yale U., 1978; EdM, Harvard U., 1981; PhD, U. Pa., 1987. Counselor, therapist Woodside S. Assistance Ctr., Queens, N.Y., 1979-80; researcher Lab. Human Devel. Harvard U., Cambridge, Mass., 1981-82; milieu therapist Human Resource Inst., Brookline, Mass., 1981-82; psychology intern Eromin Ctr., Phila., 1983-84; grad. teaching fellow U. Pa., Phila., 1983-85, instr., 1985-87; counselor Community Coll. of Phila., 1985-86; staff psychologist St. Joseph U., Phila., 1986-87; asst. prof. Sch. Edn. Boston U., 1987-89, assoc. prof., dir. grad. program in counseling overseas div., 1989—; sr. cons. Small Groups Conf., U. Pa., 1987; reviewer Jour. Counseling and Devel.; scholar-in-residence Katholiek U. te Leuven (Belgium, 1991); vis. fellow Princeton (N.J.) Theol. Sem. and U., 1987-88. Co-author, co-editor: Personality Theory, Moral Development and Criminal Behavior, 1983, Crime, Values, and Religion, 1987, Character in Young Adulthood, 1990; contbr. articles to profl. jours. Bd. dirs. Episc. Chaplaincy, Boston U., 1987-89. Internat. Religious Found. traveling fellow, 1984. Mem. Am. Psychol. Assn., AACD, Assn. for Moral Edn., Assn. Specialists in Group Work, Assn. Edn. Young Children, Assn. Religious and Values Issues in Counseling, Phi Delta Kappa. Home: Scheffelstrasse 5, No. 6, 6907 Nussloch 3, Germany Office: Boston U #29223 130th Hospital Edn Ctr APO AE 09102

DAY, JOHN MICHAEL, librarian; b. Cleve., Oct. 22, 1945; s. William I. and Marcella F. (Robinson) D.; m. Sheila D. Dougherty, Nov. 10, 1972; 1 child, Russell John. BA, Ind. U., 1969; MSLS, Cleve. Western Res. U., 1973. Mgr. pers. Chi Corp., Cleve., 1972-74; mgr. rsch. Mckinsey & Co., Cleve., 1974-77; mgr. Mgmt. Info. System Lake Erie Consortium, Painesville, Ohio, 1977-79; dir. libr. Lake Erie Coll., Painesville, Ohio, 1978-83; libr. Gallaudet U., Washington, 1983—; chair Libr. Coun., Washington, 1990. Editor: Guidelines of Library Services for Deaf People, 1991. Pres. bd. trustees Lake County Neighboring Project, Painesville, 1982-83. Mem. ALA (chair 1989—), Internat. Fedn. Libr. Assns. (sec. 1988—, chair Div. III 1991—). Office: Gallaudet U Libr 800 Florida Ave NE Washington DC 20002-3660

DAY, PETER RODNEY, geneticist; b. Chingford, Essex, Eng., Dec. 27, 1928; came to U.S., 1963; m. Lois Elizabeth Rhodes, May 26, 1951; children: Susan Catherine, Rupert Peter, William Rodney. BS in Botany, Birbeck Coll., Eng., 1950; PhD, U. London, 1954. Sr. scientific officer John Innes Inst., Norwich, Eng., 1957-63; assoc. prof. Ohio State U., Columbus, 1963-64; chief, genetics dept. Conn. Agrl. Expt. Sta., New Haven, 1964-69; dir. Plant Breeding Inst., Cambridge, Eng., 1979-87; prof. genetics, dir. Rutgers U., New Brunswick, N.J., 1987—; sec. Internat. Genetics Fedn., 1984—; trustee Internat. Ctr. for Maize and Wheat Improvement, Mexico City, 1986-92; chmn. Mng. Global Genetic Resources Bd. on Agr., NAS, Washington, 1986—. Author: Fungal Genetics, 1963, Genetics of Host-Parasite Interaction, 1974. Commonwealth Fund fellow U. Wis., 1954-56; Guggenheim Meml. fellow U. Queensland, 1972. Home: 394 Franklin Rd North Brunswick NJ 08902 Office: AgBiotech Ctr. Rutgers U College Farm Rd Cook Coll New Brunswick NJ 08903-0231

DAY, RONALD ELWIN, consulting executive; b. Randolph, Vt., Dec. 15, 1933; s. John Ellis and Esther Murle (Tabor) D.; A.A., Pasadena City Coll., 1958, student, 1958-59; B.A., U. Calif., Santa Barbara, 1961; M.B.A., UCLA, 1962; m. Elizabeth Jean McKeage, June 26, 1955; children—Gary Alan, Kathi Ellen, Judy Anne, Jeffrey Evan. Internal auditor North Am. Aviation, Downey, Calif., 1962-64; systems and procedures mgr. Proto Tool Co., Los Angeles, 1964-65; computer programmer First Nat. Bank, Boston, 1966-67; project mgr., 1967-73, systems analyst 1974-77, system planning com. chmn., trust div., 1977-89, trust info. mgmt. system adminstr., 1977-89; pres. Edge System Projects, Inc., North Reading, Mass., 1990—. With USAF, 1952-56. Mem. Soc. Advancement of Mgmt., Inst. Internal Auditors, Nat. Geog. Soc., Indsl. Mgmt. Club, Boston Computer Soc., Assn. Systems Mgmt., Alpha Gamma Sigma. Republican. Clubs: U.S. Ski Assn., Indian Guides. Home and Office: 2 Bigham Rd North Reading MA 01864-2904

DAY, RUSSELL CLOVER, federal agency administrator; b. Concord, N.H., June 29, 1943; s. Alan C. and Lois M. (Huntington) D.; m. Carol Ann Tasker, July 9, 1965; children: Jennifer Marie, Jeffrey Russell. BA, New England Coll., 1965; postgrad., Fairfield U., 1965, U. N.H., 1965-67; M of Human Svcs. Adminstrn., Antioch N.E. Grad. Sch., Keene, N.H., 1978. Examiner Soc. Security Disability Determination Svc., Concord, 1967-73, supr., 1973-81, dep. dir., 1981-85, adminstr., 1985—. Mem. Nat. Coun. Disability Determination Dirs. (exec. com. 1991—), N.H. Fed. Credit Union Supervisory Com., N.H. Lions Multiple Dist. 44-Health Coun (Gov.'s Cabinet 1991—). Republican. Congregationalist. Home: 73 Wallace Rd Goffstown NH 03045 Office: Social Security Disability Determination Svc PO Box 452 Concord NH 03301

DAY, STACEY BISWAS, physician, educator, retired health science administrator, author; b. London, Dec. 31, 1927; came to U.S. 1955, naturalized 1977.; s. Satis B. and Emma L. (Camp) D.; m. Ivana Podvalova, Oct. 18, 1973; 2 children. M.D., Royal Coll. Surgeons, Dublin, Ireland, 1955; Ph.D., McGill U., 1964; D.Sc., Cin. U., 1971. Intern King's County Hosp., SUNY Downstate Ctr., 1955-56; resident fellow in surgery U. Minn. Hosp., 1956-60; hon. registrar St. George's Hosp., London, Eng., 1960-61; lectr. exptl. surgery McGill U., Montreal, Que., Can., 1964; asst. prof. exptl. surgery U. Cin. Med. Sch., 1968-70; assoc. dir. basic med. research Shriner's Burn Inst., Cin., 1969-71; from asst. to assoc. prof. pathology, head Bell Mus. Pathobiology U. Minn., Mpls., 1970-74; dir. biomed. communications and med. edn. Sloan-Kettering Inst., N.Y.C., 1974-80; mem. Sloan-Kettering Inst. for Cancer Research, 1974-80; mem. adminstrv. council, field coordinator, 1974-75; prof. biology Sloan Kettering div. Grad. Sch. Med. Sci. Cornell U., 1974-80, ret., 1980; clin. prof. medicine div. behavioral medicine N.Y. Med. Coll., 1980—; prof. biopsychosocial medicine, chmn. dept. community health U. Calabar (Nigeria) Sch. Medicine, 1982-85; prof. internat. health, dir. Internat. Ctr. for Health Scis. Meharry Med. Coll., Nashville, 1985-89, dir. WHO Collaborating Ctr. ICHS, 1987-89; founding dir. WHO Collaborating Ctr., Nashville, 1987-89, emeritus dir., 1989; adj. prof. family and community medicine U. Ariz. Coll. Med. Scis., Tucson, 1985-89; univ. prof. internat. health U. Calabar, Nigeria, 1989—; Arris and Gale lectr. Royal Coll. Surgeons, Eng., 1972, vis. lectr., Ireland, 1972; vis. prof. U. Bologna, 1977, Saga, Japan, 1992; vis. prof. health communications U. Santiago, Chile, 1979-80; vis. prof. Oncologic Research Inst., Tallinn, Estonia, 1976, All India Insts. Health, 1976, Univ. Maiduguri, 1982, Kyushu, Japan, 1990; vis. prof. internat. health U. Mauritius, 1991; vis. prof. Bratislava U., 1991; moderator med. cartography and computer health Harvard U., 1978, Acad. Scis., Czechoslovakia, 1987, Australia, 1988; Fulbright prof. Charles U., Czechoslovakia, 1989; vis. prof. U. Mauritius, 1991, Kyushu, Japan, 1990, Saga, Japan, 1992; cons. Pan Am. Health Assn., 1974-90, U.S.-USSR Agreement for Health Cooperation, 1976, WHO Collaborating Centre Meharry Med. Coll., Nashville, 1985, liaison officer NAFEO/AID, 1986-89; mem. expert com. for health, manpower devel., WHO, 1986-90, cons. div. strengthening health care resources WHO, Geneva, 1987-90; cons. to UN-FSSTD, 1987; AID/Joint Memorandum of Understanding cons. West Africa, Kenya, Sudan. Southern Africa, 1985-89; pres., chmn., pub. Cultural and Ednl. Prodns., Montreal, U.S.A., 1966-85; advisor to dean Med. Coll., Faculty Medicine and Health Scis., ABHA, Province of Asir, Saudi Arabia, 1981; cons. advisor to rector Universidad Autonoma Agraria Antonio Narro, Saltillo, Mexico, 1987-89; cons. U.S. Dept. Edn. Office Spl. Edn. Region X, San Francisco, 1986-89; cons. Dictionary of Sci. Biography, Ency. Britannica; cons., advisor to dir. High Tatras symposia Post Grad. Med. Inst., Bratislava, 1990—; bd. dirs. Internat. Health, African Health Consultancy Service, Nigeria; bd. dirs., v.p. Am. sci. activities Mario Negri Research Found., 1975-80; hon. founding chmn., bd. dirs. Lambo Found. U.S.; v.p., trustee Cancer Relief Found., Calabar; pres., exec. dir. Internat. Found. for Biosocial Devel. and Human Health, 1978-86; cons. Inst. Health, Lyfford Cay, Bahamas, 1981, Govt. Cross River State, Nigeria, Itreto State and H.H. Obong of Calabar, Nat. Bd. Advs., Am. Biog. Inst., 1982—; cons. community health and health communications Navaho Nation, Sage Meml. Hosp., Ganado, Ariz., 1984; founder, cons. Primary Self-Health Clinics, Oban, Ikot Oku Okono, and Ikot Imo, Nigeria, 1982-84; appointed ambassador Gov. State of Tenn., 1986—; adj. clin. prof. medicine N.Y. Med. Coll.; researcher in field. Writer, 1965—; author: verse Collected Ls, 1966; play By the Waters of Babylon, 1966; verse American Lines, 1967; play The Music Box, 1967; Three Folk Songs Set to Music, 1967, Poems and Etudes, 1968; novel Rosalita, 1968; The Idle Thoughts of a Surgical Fellow, 1968, Edward Stevens-Gastric Physiologist, Physician and American Statesman, 1969; novella Bellechasse, 1970; A Leaf of the Chaatim, 1970, Ten Poems and a Letter from America for Mr. Sinha, 1971, Curling's Ulcer: An Experiment of Nature, 1972, Tuluak and Amaulik: Dialogues on Death and Mourning with the Innuit Eskimo of Point Barrow and Wainwright, Alaska, 1974, East of the Navel and Afterbirth: Reflections from Rapa Nui, 1976, Health Communications, 1979, The Biopsychosocial Imperative, 1981, What Is Survival: The Physician's Way and the Biologos, 1981; editor: Death and Attitudes Toward Death, 1972, Membranes, Viruses and Immune Mechanisms in Experimental and Clinical Disease, 1972, Ethics in Medicine in a Changing Society, 1973, Communication of Scientific Information, 1975, Trauma: Clinical and Biological Aspects, 1975, Molecular Pathology, 1975; (with Robert A. Good) series Comprehensive Immunology, 9 vols., 1976-80; Cancer Invasion and Metastasis-Biologic Mechanisms and Therapy, 1977, Some Systems of Biological Communication, 1977, Image of Science and Society, 1977, What Is a Scientist, 1978, Sloan Kettering Inst. Cancer Series, 1974-80; editor-in-chief, mem. editorial bd.: Health Communications and Informatics, 1974-80; editor in chief: The American Biomedical Network: Health Care System in America Present and Past, 1978, A Companion to the Life Sciences, Vol. 1, 1979, A Companion to the Life Sciences, Vol. 2, Integrated Medicine, 1980, A Companion to the Life Sciences, Vol. 3: Life Stress, 1981, Advance to Biopsychosocial Health, 1984; editor in chief, mem. editorial bd. Health Communications and Biopsychosocial Health; editor: (with others) Cancer, Stress and Death, 1979, 2d edit., 1986, Computers for Medical Office and Patient Management, 1981, Readings in Oncology, 1980, Biopsychosocial Health, 1981; editor: Primary Health Care Guidelines: A Training Manual for Community Health, 2d edit., 1986, (with T.A. Lambo) Contemporary Issues in International Health, 1989; sr. editor (with Salat and others): Health and Quality of Life in Changing Europe in the Year 2000, 1992; mem. editorial bd.: Annual Reviews on Stress; also co-editor various publs.; contbr. articles to profl. lit.; producer TV and radio health edn. programs, Nigeria, TV film River Blindness (Onchocerciasis) in Africa, 1988. Served with Brit. Army, 1946-49. Recipient Moynihan medal Assn. Surgeons Gt. Britain and Ireland, 1960, Reuben Harvey triennial prize Royal Coll. Physicians, Ireland, 1957, Disting. scholar award Internat. Communication Assn., 1980, Sama Found. medal, 1982; named to Hon. Order Ky. Cols.; named Chieftan Ntufam Ajan of Oban Ejagham People, Cross River State, Nigeria, 1983; recipient Chieftan Obong Nsong Idem Ibibio Nigeria, 1983, Mgbe (Ekpe) honor Nigeria, commendation WHO address Fed. Govt. Nigeria, Calabar, 1983, Leadership in Internat. Med. Health citation Pres. U.S., 1987, WHO medal, 1987, Agromedicine citation Commr. of Agr., State of Tenn., 1987, Assembly citation State of N.Y., 1987, Citation Congl. Record., 1987; Maestro Honorifo, U. Autonoma Agraria, Coahuila, Mex., 1987; presented Key to the City of Nashville, 1987; recipient Vice-Chancellor's Citation and Presentation for Primary Health Care Teaching in Nigeria, U. Calabar, 1988; Pamétni medal Postgrad. Med. Coll., Prague, 1991, Gold medal U. of Bratislava, 1991; addresses presented by people of Ikot Imo, Nsit Anyang, Oban, 1982-84, Commendation from King of Calabar, 1984; Ciba fellow Can., 1965; Stacey Day Ward named in his honor by Fed. Minister and Gov. of Cross River State, Calabar Med. Ctr., Nigeria, 1986; charter mem. U.S. Normandy Com., 1988; hon. mem. Hagakure Res. Soc. (Samurai), Kyushu, Japan, 1991. Fellow Zool. Soc. London Royal Micros. Soc., Royal Soc. Health, World Acad. Arts and Scis., Japanese Found. for Biopsychosocial Health (internat. hon. fellow and most disting. mem.), African Acad. Sci., African Acad. Med. Scis. (founder); mem. AAS, AMA, Am. Burn Assn., Internat. Burn Assn., Can. Authors Assn., N.Y. Acad. Scis., Am. Assn. History Medicine, Am. Inst. Stress (bd. dirs.), Am. Anthrop. Assn., Am. Rural Health Assn. (v.p. internat. sci. affairs, bd. dirs.), Soc. Med. Geographers USSR. Home: 6 Lomond Ave Chestnut Ridge NY 10977-6901

DAY, WILLIAM HOMER, entomologist, researcher; b. Wilmington, Del., Sept. 29, 1934; s. Frank Homer and Ann F. (Dangel) D.; m. Charlotte Anne Schempp, May 15, 1959; 1 child, Robert Steven. BS, U. Del., 1955; PhD, Cornell U., 1965. Rsch. entomologist Beneficial Insects Rsch. Lab., Agrl. Rsch. Svc., USDA, Moorestown, N.J., 1965-71, lab. dir., 1971-73; lab. dir. Beneficial Insects Rsch. Lab., Agrl. Rsch. Svc., USDA, Newark, Del., 1973-78, rsch. entomologist, 1978—. Author: (chpt.) Biological Control in Crop Protection, 1981, Economic Importance and Biological Control of Mirids in North America, 1987; contbr. articles to profl. jours. Mem. Am. Entomol. Soc. (pres. 1971-72, sec. 1970, governing coun. 1970—, chmn. fin. com. 1980—), Entomol. Soc. Am. (audit com. 1970-71, nominating com. 1976-78), Internat. Orgn. Biol. Control. Lutheran. Office: USDA Agrl Rsch Svc 501 S Chapel St Newark DE 19713-3800

DAYAN, RODNEY S., lawyer; b. Seattle, May 3, 1933; s. Jesse Charles Dayan and Thelma (Spencer) Dorsey; m. Barbara Heustis, Aug. 27, 1958; children: Christopher, Amanda. AB, Princeton U., 1955; LLB, Columbia U., 1961; LLM, NYU, 1967. Bar: N.Y. 1962. Assoc. Cadwalader, Wickersham & Taft, N.Y.C., 1961-69, ptnr., 1969—; Frequent chmn., panelist on legal or investment banking. Chmn. Bd. Examiners Montclair Dept. Pub. Safety, N.J., 1976-80; mem. Montclair Bd. Edn., 1971-75, Montclair Bd. Sch. Estimate, 1972-75. Keasby fellow New Coll. Oxford U., 1955-56. Mem. ABA (fed. regulation securities com. 1972-78), N.Y. State Bar Assn., Assn. of Bar of City of N.Y. (securities regulations com. 1973-76, commodities regulation com. 1976-77). Clubs: Down Town (N.Y.C.); Montclair Golf; Pennask Lake Fishing and Game (British Columbia, Can.). Office: Cadwalader Wickersham & Taft 100 Maiden Ln New York NY 10038-4818

DAYWALT, DANIEL GRAY, human resources professional; b. Norristown, Pa., Oct. 4, 1957; s. Daniel G. and June A. (Carline) D.; m. Carol L. Steffen, Aug. 25, 1979; 1 child, Christopher D. BA in Econs., U. Mich., 1979; MBA, Youngstown State U., 1986. Labor rels. staff asst. Jones & Laughlin Steel Co., Youngstown, Ohio, 1981-84; labor rels. supr. LTV Steel Co., Youngstown, 1984-86, Canton, Ohio, 1986-87; mgr. personnel Anchor Hocking Corp., Clarksburg, W.Va., 1987; mgr. human resources Anchor Hocking Indsl. Glass Co., Monaca, Pa., 1987-89, v.p. human resources, 1989-92, v.p. human resources and quality assurance, 1992—. Mem. Soc. for Human Resources Mgmt., Beaver Valley Personnel Assn. Office: Anchor Hocking Indsl Glass 400 9th St Monaca PA 15061-1862

DEA, DONALD DON, business executive; b. May 12, 1954; s. Kim Fun and Moy (Sleu) D.; m. Catherine L. Dea, Oct. 20, 1984; children: Erin Jennifer, Alexander Gregory. BA, Western Md. Coll., 1976; MBA, Duke U., 1978; postgrad., MIT, 1988. With Xerox Corp., 1978—; mgr. fin. and adminstrn. real estate ops. Xerox Corp., Rochester, N.Y., 1986-87, mgr. planning adn disposition real estate ops., 1987-89, mgr. market channel devel., 1989-90, gen. mgr. channel ops. (OEM/VAR) and devel., 1990—; gen. mgr. channel strategic ptnr. devel., 1992—; spl. asst. to atty. gen. dept. justice Pres.'s Exec. Exch. Program, Washington, 1982-83; gen. mgr. Channel Strategic Ptnr. Devel., 1992. Mem. bd. alumni advisors Duke U. Fuqua Sch. Bus., Durham, N.C., 1988—; pres., v.p., controller Assn. for Blind and Visually Impaired, Rochester, 1986—; bd. dirs. Salvation Army, Rochester, 1985—. Recipient John Seaman award Balt. Poly. Inst., 1968, Alumni Citizenship award Western Md. Coll., 1976, MBA award Pensions & Investment, 1988. Mem. Western Md. Coll. Alumni Assn. (pres. 1987—). Home: 128 Barrington St Rochester NY 14607-2904 Office: Xerox Corp Xerox Sq # 8 Rochester NY 14644-0001

DEAN, ANTHONY MARION, physical chemist; b. Savannah, Ga., Aug. 26, 1944; s. Anthony David and Anne (Mylod) D.; m. Linda Eunice Nicks, Aug. 27, 1966; children: Paul, Dianne, Melanie, David. BS, Spring Hill Coll., 1966; PhD, Harvard U., 1970. Asst. prof. U. Mo., Columbia, 1970-75, assoc. prof., 1975-79; sr. staff chemist Exxon Rsch. & Engring. Co., Linden, N.J., 1979-82; rsch. assoc. Exxon Rsch. & Engring. Co., Clinton, N.J., 1982-90, sr. rsch. assoc., 1990—; mem. PhD thesis com. MIT, Cambridge, Mass., 1987—, Rensselaer Poly. Inst., Troy, N.Y., 1990—. Reviewer publs. for govt. agys., 1970—; contbr. articles to Jour. Phys. Chemistry, Internat. Jour. Chem. Kinetics, Jour. Chem. Physics and symposiums. Mem. Union Twp. (N.J.) Bd. Edn., 1986—, v.p., 1989-90, pres., 1990-91. Grad. fellow NSF, Harvard U., 1966-70. Mem. Am. Chem. Soc., Combustion Inst. Democrat. Roman Catholic. Home: 67 Country Acres Dr Hampton NJ 08827-9744 Office: Exxon Rsch & Engring Co Rte 22 E Annandale NJ 08801

DEAN, DIANE D., youth service agency executive, management consultant; b. Detroit, Aug. 26, 1949; d. Edward Lesley and Ada V. (Spann) D. Student, Mich. State U., 1966-68; BS, N.C. Argl. and Tech. State U., 1971; MS, Ind. U., 1973; postgrad., Stanford U., summer 1981, UCLA, 1982-83. Area coord. U. Miami, Coral Gables, 1973-75; dir. housing Occidental Coll., L.A., 1975-78; asst. dir. admissions assistance and sch. rels. U. So. Calif., L.A., 1978-80; from asst. dir. to assoc. dir. admissions, dir. ops. UCLA, 1980-85; dir. incentive grants and scholarship programs Nat. Action Coun. Minorities in Engring., N.Y.C., 1985-90; mgmt. cons. Girl Scouts of the U.S.A., N.Y.C., 1990—; appointed rep. Grad. Mgmt. Admissions Coun., Santa Monica, Calif., 1981-85, co-chair Region VI, Nat. Assn. Student Pers. Adminstrs., 1984-85. Author and editor: Directory of Minority Pers. Associated with Admissions, 1979-85. Named to J & B Winners Circle, Paddington Corp., N.Y.C., 1984. Mem. NAACP, Nat. Assn. Student Pers. Adminstrn. (regional co-chair 1985), Corporate Women's Network, Trans Africa, Black Women's Forum, Girl Scouts of U.S.A. (life mem.), Schomberg Soc. for Preservation of Black Culture, Urban League, UCLA Alumni Assn. (life mem.), N.C. Agrl. and Tech. State U. Alumni Assn., Alpha Kappa Alpha (v.p. 1969-71). Office: Girl Scouts of the USA 830 3rd Ave New York NY 10022-7522

DEAN, HOWARD, governor of Vermont; b. N.Y.C., Nov. 17, 1948; s. Howard Brush and Andrea (Maitland) D.; m. Judith Steinberg; children: Anne, Paul. BA, Yale U., 1971; MD, Albert Einstein Coll. Medicine, 1978. Intern, then resident in internal medicine Med. Ctr. Hosp. Vt., 1978-82; practice medicine specializing in internal medicine Shelburne, Vt.; mem., house edn. com., mcpl. corps. and elections com., rules com. Vt. House of Reps., Montpelier, 1983-86, asst. minority leader, 1985-86; lt. gov. State of Vt., Montpelier, 1986-91; gov. State of Vt., 1991—; asst. clin. prof. medicine U. Vt. Coll. Medicine. Bd. dirs. Vt. Developmental Capabilities Council, U. Vt. Council, Vt. Adv. Commn. Intergovtl. Affairs, Vt. State Bd. Nat. Forests; founder Vt. Youth Conservation Corps; sponsor Long Trail Preservation Fund. Home: 325 S Cove Rd Burlington VT 05401-5447 Office: Office of Governor 109 State St Montpelier VT 05609-0101

DEAN, JAMES LEROY, executive recruiter; b. New Brunswick, N.J., Sept. 19, 1942; s. James E. and Elizabeth (Shipman) D.; m. Evelyn L. Kraus, Mr. 20, 1964 (div. Mar., 1979); children: Susanne Luisa, Elizabeth Ruth; m. Sara E. Van Sant, May 4, 1979. BS, Rider Coll., 1965. Recruiter various employment agys., N.J., 1965-73; employment mgr. Transam. Delaval, Inc., Trenton, N.J., 1973-77; human resources mgr. C.F. Braun & Co., Murray Hill, N.J., 1977-79; regional mgr. Fox Morris Assocs., various locations, 1979-86; pres. Dean-Wharton Assocs., Inc., Somerville, N.J., 1986—. Mem. Exchange Club, Somerville (pres. 1990-92, pres. elect N.J. Dist. Exchange Clubs 1991-92). Baptist. Office: Dean Wharton Assocs Inc 166 W End Ave Somerville NJ 08876-1835

DEAN, JEFFREY DAVID, aircraft mechanic; b. Pontiac, Mich., Mar. 7, 1960; s. James Warren and Evelyne Eileen (Jewette) D.; m. Carol Ann Gratton, June 29, 1984. Student, Community Coll. Air Force, 1988—. Aircraft mechanic USAF Civil Svc., Dover, Del., 1986—; founder, pres. A.R.M.E.D. Prodns., Dover, 1987—; producer, host The Coffee Shop radio show, Dover, 1991—; co-founder bamd Sunburst, Dover, 1990—. Author: Starstruck, 1987; composer over 100 songs; author 2 Star Trek episodes, 1990, 92. With USAF, 1981-85. Mem. Jireh Christian Ctr. Home: 4 Holly Cove Ln Dover DE 19901 Office: 512 EMS/Isochronal Inspect Bldg 711 Dover DE 19902

DEAN, LESLIE ALAN, foreign service officer; b. Indpls., June 18, 1940; s. Henry Lloyd and Margaret Ann (Pfafman) D.; m. Jeanne Louise Lambert, Apr. 14, 1962; children: David Richard, Laura Elizabeth. BA, U. Ill., 1963, MA, 1966; postgrad., U. Pitts., 1968-69. Officer, capt. USAF, Detroit, 1964-68; internat. loan analyst Bank of Calif., San Francisco, 1969; devel. officer AID, Washington, 1970, 77-79, Vientiane, Laos, 1971-75; devel. officer U.S. Govt., Kathmandu, Nepal, 1975-77, Islamabad, Pakistan, 1979-83, Dar Es Salaam, Tanzania, 1983-85; mission dir. U.S. Govt., Lusaka, Zambia, 1985-90; sr. fgn. svc., office dir. U.S. Govt., Washington, 1990-92; mission dir. AID, Pretoria, South Africa, 19926. Recipient Superior Honor award U.S. Agy. AID, 1981, Meritorious Honor award U.S. AID, 1983, 79, 75, Air Force Commendation award, 1968. Methodist. Home: 9505 Orion Ct Burke VA 22015-3241 Office: AID Dept of State AFR/SA Rm 3921 NS Washington DC 20523-0050

DEAN, NATHAN WESLEY, university administrator, physicist, educator; b. Johnson City, Tenn., Dec. 10, 1941; s. Everett Francis and Ethel (Garvin) D.; m. Mary Fetzer, Apr. 11, 1963; 1 child, Mary Ellen. BS, U. N.C., 1963; PhD, Cambridge U., Eng., 1968. U.S. Churchill scholar Cambridge U., 1965-66, NSF grad. fellow, 1966-68; vis. scientist CERN, Geneva, Switzerland, 1967-68; from instr. to asst. prof. physics Vanderbilt U., Nashville, 1968-70; from asst. prof. to prof. physics Iowa State U., Ames, 1970-80; mem. high energy physics staff U.S. AEC, Germantown, Md., 1973; asst. v.p. for rsch. U. Ga., Athens, 1980-84, acting v.p. for rsch., 1984-86, prof. physics, 1980-87; vice provost for grad. studies and rsch., prof. physics SUNY, Binghamton, 1987—; cons. Environ. Rsch. Lab., U.S. EPA, Athens, 1986-87; mem. doctoral coun. N.Y. State Edn. Dept., Albany, 1987—; mem. exec. com. Nat. Assn. Sate Univs. and Land-Grant Colls. Coun. on Rsch. Policy and Grad. Edn., Washington, 1989—. Author: Introduction to Strong Interactions, 1976; contbr. numerous articles to profl. jours. Mem. Ga. High Tech. Adv. Coun., Atlanta, 1983-86; mem. Tri-Cities Opera Coun., Binghamton, 1991—. Mem. Rotary Club, Phi Beta Kappa, Sigma Xi, Phi Kappa Phi. Home: 412 Clarkson Dr Vestal NY 13850-2706 Office: SUNY Binghamton PO Box 6000 Binghamton NY 13902-6000

DEAN, PETER, artist; b. Berlin, N.Y., July 9, 1941; s. William F. and Roza (Nathan) D.; m. Lorraine Otterson; 1 son, Gregory. Student, Cornell U., 1957-58; B.A., U. Wis., 1959. One man shows include Darthea Speyer Gallery, Paris, 1981, Allan Stone Gallery, N.Y.C., 1970, 73, 78, 80, Bienville Gallery, 1975, 77, 79, 81, Semaphore Gallery, N.Y.C., 1981, 86, Bellman Gallery, N.Y.C., 1984, Osuna Gallery, Washington, 1984, Struve Gallery, Chgo., 1984, Koplin Gallery, L.A., 1985, 88, 90, Traver-Sutton Gallery, Seattle, 1985, 89, Kerr Gallery, N.Y.C., 1986, San Antonio Art Inst., 1988, Katzen-Brown Gallery, N.Y.C., 1989, Rena Branstein Gallery, San Francisco, Ca., 1987, 89, N.D. Mus. Art, 1989, 90, Alt. Mus. N.Y., 1990, 91, Mus. Art, U. Ariz., Tucson, 1991, U. Wis. Art. Mus., Milw., 1992; exhibited in group shows Nat. Inst. Arts and Letters, N.Y.C., 1973, Corpus Christi Mus., 1981, Chrysler Mus., Norfolk, Va., 1981, Chgo. Art Inst., 1982, Venice Bienniale, 1984, Tucson Mus., U. Ariz., 1991; represented in permanent collection Nat. Collection, Washington, Chgo. Art Inst., Madison (Wis.) Art Center, New Orleans Mus., Gray Gallery, N.Y. U.; vis. artist, Yale U., La. State U., N.D. U., U. Wis., Skidmore Coll., U. Tex., Yale U., Princeton U., Cranbrook Acad. Founding mem. Rhino Horn Group, co-

chmn., 1969-79. Fellow Nat. Endowment for the Arts, 1981, 87; N.Y. Council Arts grantee, 1975-76. Address: 2 Spring St New York NY 10012

DEAN, ROBERT BRUCE, architect; b. Brockton, Mass., Jan. 15, 1949; s. Robert George and Marjorie Gertrude (O'Donnell) D.; m. Mary Hood Hoskinson, June 18, 1977; children: Robert Maxwell, Anne, Claire. BA, U. Pa., 1971; MArch, Columbia U., 1976. Registered architect, N.Y., Conn. Staff architect Skidmore, Owings & Merrill, Architects, N.Y.C., 1976-77; job capt. Stephen Jacobs & Assn., N.Y.C., 1977-78; staff architect Johnson-Burgee Architects, N.Y.C., 1978-79; pvt. practice architecture N.Y.C. and Syracuse, 1979-85; project architect Robert A.M. Stern Architects, N.Y.C., 1985-86; pres. Dean Design, Inc., New Canaan, Conn., 1986—; adj. assoc. prof. Columbia U., N.Y.C., 1978-83; asst. prof. Syracuse U., 1980-84. Contbr. articles to profl. jours. Trustee North Stamford Congl. Ch., 1986-87; governing coun. Redding (Conn.) Congl. Ch., 1991—; mem. Planning Commn. Town of Redding, Conn. Grantee Syracuse U., 1982, grantee Nat. Endowment Arts, 1983-84; William Kinne Fellow, 1976. Mem. AIA, Conn. Soc. Architects. Democrat. Congregationalist. Office: Dean Design Inc 111 Cherry St New Canaan CT 06840-5530

DEAN, RUTH J(OSEPHINE), retired French educator; b. N.Y.C., Mar. 10, 1902; d. Amos Carlton and Lovisa Vaughn (Mallory) D. BA, Wellesley Coll., 1922; BA with honors, Oxford (Eng.) U., 1924, MA, 1928, DPhil, 1938; LHD, U. Pa., 1979; DHL, Mt. Holyoke Coll., 1989. Mem. faculty Mt. Holyoke Coll., South Hadley, Mass., 1934—, Mary Lyon prof. French, 1966—, prof. emeritus, 1967—; mem. Inst. Advanced Study, Princeton, N.J., 1943-44, 50-51; lectr., vis. prof. U. Pa., Phila., 1969-75, prof. emeritus, 1975—; hon. rsch. fellow Inst. Romance Studies, U. London, 1990—; br. and state pres., mem. nat. coms. AAUW, 1940-61. Co-editor The Rule of St. Benedict, 1964; contbr. articles, revs. to numerous jours. Palmer fellow AAUW, 1943-44; Guggenheim fellow, 1948-49; sr. fellow NEH, 1967-68. Fellow Medieval Acad. Am. (past coun., com. mem., v.p., pres.), Brit. Acad. (corr.); mem. MLA (exec. coun., mem. bds., coms., v.p. 1958-80), Ordre des Palmes Academiques (France). Home: 165 W 66th St Apt 10C New York NY 10023-6521

DEAN, STEPHEN ODELL, physicist; b. Niagara Falls, N.Y., May 12, 1936; s. Stephen Odell and Marian Cecelia (Gammon) D.; m. Elizabeth Alice Wiles, July 21, 1962 (div. Sept. 1976); children: Stephen, Richard, Marcy. BS in Physics, Boston Coll., 1960; SM in Nuclear Engring., M.I.T., 1962; PhD in Physics, U. Md., 1971. Physicist U.S. Atomic Energy Commn., Washington, 1962-68, U.S. Naval Research Lab., Washington, 1968-72; dir. fusion research U.S. Dept. Energy, Washington, 1972-79; scientist Sci. Applications Internat. Corp., Gaithersburg, Md., 1979—; pres. Fusion Power Assocs., Gaithersburg, Md., 1979—, also bd. dirs.; cons. Bechtel Corp., San Francisco, 1982—, Oak Ridge (Tenn.) Nat. Labs., 1982—, Los Alamos (N.Mex.) Nat. Labs., 1985—. Editor: Prospects for Fusion Power, 1981; assoc. editor Journal of Fusion Energy, 1984—. Mem. Sec. of Energy's Fusion Adv. Com., 1991—. Recipient Cert. of Appreciation U.S. Dept. Energy, 1979, Disting. Assoc. award, 1988, Research Publ. award U.S. Naval Research Labs., 1971, Spl. Achievement awards U.S. Energy Research and Devel. Adminstrn., 1976, 77. Fellow Am. Nuclear Soc. (div. chmn. 1985, 86, exec. com. 1982-86); mem. Am. Physical Soc., Am. Soc. Assn. Execs., Am. Nuclear Soc. Office: Fusion Power Assocs 2 Professional Dr # 249 Gaithersburg MD 20879-3489

DEAN, THOMAS G., government official; b. Hartford, Conn., Apr. 11, 1967; s. Richard Stanley and Maxine Arnetta (Ross) D. Student, Howard U., 1989. Asst. shipper Fox Press, Inc., Windsor, Conn., 1986-88; sales assoc. Limited Express, W. Hartford, Conn., 1989; interviewer Covington-Burgess Mkt. Rsch., Washington, 1990; fiscal asst. U.S. Dept. State, Washington, 1989—; intern to program dir. WMMJ 102.3 FM, Washington, 1991—; cons. Blue Chip Entertainment, Hartford, 1989—; cons., co-founder Character's Ultimate Eye Fashions, Washington, 1989. Author song: First Glance, 1987; author collection of poems and stories: untitled Eponymy, 1986. Active Pacifica Radio Found., Berkeley, Calif., 1991. Democrat. Pentecostal Ch. Home: 931 Longfellow St NW Apt 105 Washington DC 20011-8223

DEANE, JOHN HERBERT, technologist; b. L.A., Feb. 3, 1952; s. Theodore E. and Marion Gail (Blake) D.; m. Linda Zampier, Nov. 22, 1973 (div. 1982); m. Anne N. Butler, June 13, 1987; children: Devon, Jennifer. BS, SUNY, Albany, 1976; MBA, SUNY, 1978. Sr. cons. Arthur Young & Co., N.Y.C., 1978-81; project mgr. Morgan Stanley & Co., N.Y.C., 1981-86; v.p. Asia Morgan Stanley & Co., Tokyo, Japan, 1986-87; v.p., dir. Salomon Bros. Asia Ltd., Tokyo, Japan, 1987-90; ptnr. Price Waterhouse, N.Y.C., 1990—. Sgt. USAF, 1970-74. Mem. Tokyo Am. Club, Glen Ridge Country Club, DAV (life), Nat. Eagle Scout Assn. (life), N.Y. Yacht Club. Methodist. Home: 126 Forest Ave Glen Ridge NJ 07028-2414 Office: Price Waterhouse 153 E 53d St New York NY 10022

DEANGELUS, RONALD PATRICK, lawyer; b. Schenectady, N.Y., May 31, 1935; s. Dominick and Edith (Matarazzo) DeA.; m. Arlene L. Blanchard, July 1, 1973. BA, Union Coll., 1957; JD, Albany Law Coll., 1960. Bar: N.Y. 1960, U.S. Dist. Ct. (no. dist.) N.Y. 1960. Law clk. to presiding justice U.S. Dist. Ct. Oreg., Portland, 1960-61; dep. pub. defender Schenectady County, N.Y., 1967-68, asst. county atty., 1968-69; asst. corp. counsel City of Schenectady, 1976-79; ptnr. DeAngelus & DeAngelus, Schenectady, 1965-88, Englert, DeAngelus, Stillman, McHugh & DeAngelus, Schenectady, 1989-90, DeAngelus & DeAngelus, Schenectady, 1990—. Mem. Am. Trial Lawyers Assn., Nat. Assn. Criminal Def. Lawyers, N.Y. State Bar Assn., N.Y. State Defenders Assn., Schenectady County Bar Assn., Capital Dist. Trial Lawyers Assn. Democrat. Office: DeAngelus & DeAngelus 224 State St Schenectady NY 12305-1897

DEANIN, RUDOLPH DRESKIN, plastics engineering educator, consultant; b. Newark, June 7, 1921; s. Zalman and Sonya (Dreskin) D.; m. Grace Rae Greif, 1946 (div. 1965); m. Joan Marie Berkoff, Dec. 1, 1966; children: Nancy, Alice. AB in Chemistry, Cornell U., 1941; MS in Organic Chemistry, U. Ill., 1942, PhD in Organic Chemistry, 1944. Rsch. asst. Regional Soybean Rsch. Lab., USDA, Urbana, Ill., 1941-42; spl. rsch. asst. Govt. Synthetic Rubber Program, Urbana, 1943-47; rsch. chemistry group leader Allied Chem. Corp., Morristown, N.J., 1947-60; dir. chem. R & D, DeBell & Richardson, Inc., Hazardville, Conn., 1960-67; prof., grad. coord. plastics engring. U. Mass., Lowell, 1967—; cons. on plastics materials to 500 cos. worldwide, 1960—; Meml. lectr. Am. Leather Chem. Assn., Pinehurst, N.C., 1989. Author 2 books; editor 9 books; also over 130 articles and chpts.; numerous patents in field. Rsch. award Plastics Inst. Am., 1989. Mem. Am. Chem. Soc. (chmn. symposia), Soc. Plastice Engrs. (meeting chmn., bd. dirs. Ea. New Eng. sect. 1967—, Edn. award 1985), New Eng. Soc. for Coatings Tech. (edn. chmn. 1985—). Home: PO Box 446 Westford MA 01886-0446 Office: Univ Mass at Lowell Plastics Engring Dept Lowell MA 01854

DEANS, GLENN NORFLEET, accountant; b. Elizabeth, N.C., June 6, 1947; s. Emma Marie (Bowe) Deans; m. Dorothea Vivian Pitcairn, Aug. 23, 1969; children: Jason Norfleet, Jazmine Nicole. AS, Nassau Community Coll., Garden City, N.Y., 1970; BS in Acct., NYU, 1972; MBA, Pace U., 1990. Sr. auditor Arthur Andersen & Co., N.Y.C., 1972-76; sr. acct. St. Joe Minerals, N.Y.C., 1976-78; planning analyst Pfizer, Inc., N.Y.C., 1978-80; ptnr. Mitchell, Titus & Co., N.Y.C., 1980-91; pvt. practice, 1991—; treas. Judea United Bapt. Ch., Bayside, N.Y., 1980—, N.Y. Urban League, N.Y.C., 1988—. Sgt. U.S. Army, 1966-68, Vietnam. Office: 13 Meadow Ln Freeport NY 11520

DEAN-ZUBRITSKY, CYNTHIA MARIAN, psychologist, reseacher; b. Urbana, Ill., Oct. 27, 1950; d. William Bonaparte and Lois (Doran) Dean; m. John Jay Zubritsky , Sept. 15, 1979; 1 child, Grant Doran. BA, Ind. U., 1972; M in Psychology, Pa. State U., 1978; PhD, Temple U., 1989. Counselor New Castle (Pa.) Youth Devel. Ctr., 1972-76; dir. Ill. Family Edn. Ctr., Danville, 1976-77; researcher Pa. State U., University Park, 1977-78, 89—; film cons. Ill. Devel. Disabilities Council, Springfield, 1978; psychologist Atkins House, York, Pa., 1978-82; quality assurance specialist Pa. Office Mental Retardation, Harrisburg, 1982-84; dir. tng. and staff devel. Pa. Office Mental Health, Harrisburg, 1984-89; pvt. practice psychology Harrisburg, 1989—; bd. dirs. children and youth svcs. Vermilion County Mental Health Program, Danville, 1975-77; psychologist Loysville (Pa.) Youth Devel. Ctr., 1981-82; tchr. Danville Community Coll., 1975; cons. U. Ill., Urbana, 1976, Danville Sch. System, 1975-76; faculty dept. psychiatry U. Pa., 1989—; rsch. alliance for mentally ill Pa., 1989-92. Vol. ARC, 1967-87, YWCA, 1970-89; mem. Pa. Task Force on Mental Health: Women, Harrisburg, 1986-87. Human Resource Devel. grantee NIMH, 1985—, Office of Substance Abuse Prevention grantee, 1992—. Mem. Internat. Psychogeriatric Assn., Nat. Assn. State Mental Health Program Dirs., Am. Horticulture Soc., Phi Delta Kappa, Phi Mu. Republican. Presbyterian. Office: Dept Psychiatry U Pa Philadelphia PA 19104

DEARBORN, DONALD EDWARD, school system administrator; b. Portland, Maine, June 21, 1939; s. Richard B. and Dorothy F. (Hagen) D.; m. Joan Davis, Aug. 13, 1966; children: Meg, Beth, Sara. BA, St. Anselm's Coll., 1961; MA, George Washington U., 1967, EdD, 1972. Cert. Supt., N.J., Pa., Va. Tchr. Alexandria (Va.) Pub. Schs., 1962-65, asst. prin., 1965-67, prin., 1967-68, dir., 1968-77, asst. supt., 1977-84; supt. Galloway Twp. Pub. Schs., Absecon, N.J., 1984—; cons. in field; spl. edn. adv. com. Spl. Svc. Sch. Dist., Atlantic County, N.J., 1989—; exec. dir. Galloway Twp. Edn. Found., Absecon, 1984—. Contbr. several articles to profl. jours. Named Outstanding Young Educator Alexandria Jaycees, 1972, Disting. Lecture Scholar Assn. for Supervision and Curriculum Devel., 1984. Mem. N.J. Assn. Sch. Adminstrs., Atlantic County Assn. Sch. Adminstrs., Atlantic County Assn. Sch. Adminstrs. (v.p. 1988-90, pres. 1990—), Am. Assn. Sch. Adminstrs., Assn. for Supervision & Curriculum, Phi Delta Kappa. Home: 506 E Oslo Ct Absecon NJ 08201-9624 Office: Galloway Twp Pub Schs 101 Reed Rd Absecon NJ 08201-2100

DEARIE, RAYMOND J., judge; b. 1944. AB, Fairfield U., 1966; JD, St. John's U., 1969. Pvt. practice law Shearman & Sterling, N.Y.C., 1969-71, Surrey & Morse, N.Y.C., 1977-80; chief Appeals div. U.S. Dept. Justice, 1971-74, chief gen. crimes sect., 1974-76, chief Criminal div., 1976-77; exec. asst. U.S. Atty.'s Office, 1977; asst. U.S. atty. U.S. Dist. Ct. (ea. dist.) N.Y., 1971-77, chief asst. U.S. atty., 1980-82, U.S. atty., 1982-86; judge U.S. Dist. Ct. (ea. dist.) N.Y., Bklyn., 1986—. Contbr. articles to profl. jours. Bd. dirs. Daytop Village. Mem. ABA, N.Y. State Bar Assn., Assn. of Bar of City of N.Y., Fed. Bar Coun. Office: US Dist Ct 225 Cadman Pla E Brooklyn NY 11201*

DEARSTYNE, BRUCE WILLIAM, archivist, history educator; b. Niskayuna, N.Y., June 11, 1944; s. Laurence William and Minnie (Mattice) D.; m. Susanna Vultaggio; children: Annmarie, Emily. BA in History, Hartnick Coll., 1966; PhD in History, Syracuse U., 1974. Cert. archivist. Instr. history SUNY, Potsdam, 1971-72; various offices State Hist. and State Archives, 1973-85; exec. dir. Nat. Assn. Govt. Archives and Records Adminstrs., 1983—; dir. external svcs. State Archives and Recores Adminstrn., Albany, N.Y., 1985—; adj. prof. history SUNY, Albany, 1983—. Author: Railroads and Railroad Regulation in New York City, 1984, Management of Local Government Records, 1988, The Archival Enterprise, 1992; co-author; New York: Yesterday, Today, Tomorrow, 1988. Office: NY State Archives & Records 10A46 Cultural Edn Ctr Albany NY 12230

DEARTH, JEFFREY L., magazine publisher; b. Pontiac, Mich., Sept. 10, 1950; s. Robert Alfred and Regina (Miller) D.; m. Marion Semple Oxford, Sept. 29, 1981; children: James Oxford, Alexander Miller. BA, U. N.C., 1973. Mgr. mktg. Time mag., N.Y.C., 1973-74; sales exec. Time mag., London, 1974-77, Amsterdam, Netherlands, 1977-78, Paris, 1978-79; dir. sales Vision mag., London, 1979-81; dir. mktg. Smithsonain mag., N.Y.C., 1981-84; pub. The New Republic mag., Washington, 1984-89, pres., 1986—; prof. pub. George Washington U., Washington, 1987; pres. C-Media, Boston, 1985—. Morehead scholar U. N.C., 1968; Internat. Schoolboy fellow, 1968, Richardson Leadership Inst. fellow, 1971. Mem. Mag. Pubs.' Assn. Office: New Republic 1220 19th St NW Washington DC 20036-2405

DEB, SANJAY KUMAR, surgeon; b. Calcutta, India, Apr. 23, 1938; came to U.S., 1968; s. Soroj Ranjan and Uma (Burahan) D.; m. Mary Szylinski, June 23, 1972 (dec. Feb. 1978); 1 child, Ravi; m. Mary Ann Fiordaliso, Jan. 3, 1981; 1 child, Anita. MD, Caclutta U., 1961; M Surgery, Delhi U., 1965. Diplomate Am. Bd. Gen. Surgery. Intern Med. Coll. Hosp., Calcutta, 1961-62; resident Maulana Azala Med. Coll. Group Hosps., Delhi, India, 1963-67, South Buffalo (N.Y.) Mercy Hosp., 1968-69; resident Sisters Hosp., Buffalo, 1969-72, attending surgeon, 1972—; attending surgeon St. Joseph Hosp., Buffalo, 1972—. Fellow ACS, Royal Coll. Surgeons Can. Office: 3527 Harlem Rd Buffalo NY 14225

DEBARTOLO, EDWARD J., SR., real estate developer; b. Youngstown, Ohio, May 17, 1919; s. Michael and Rose (Villani) DeB.; m. Maria Patricia Montani, Dec. 18, 1944 (dec.); children: Edward J., Marie D. Grad., U. Notre Dame; DSc (hon.), Fla. Inst. Tech., 1981. Registered profl. engr., registered surveyor. Ptnr. Michael DeBartolo Constrn. Co., Youngstown, 1936-41; pres. Michael DeBartolo Constrn. Co., 1946-48, Edward J. DeBartolo Corp., Youngstown, 1958-79; chmn. bd., chief exec. officer Edward J. DeBartolo Corp., 1979—; owner Thistledown Racing Club, Cleve., Louisiana Downs race tracks, Remington Pk., Oklahoma City. Mem. adv. coun. U. Notre Dame. 2d lt. C.E., U.S. Army, 1941-46, Okinawa. Decorated Order of Merit (Italy); named Man of Yr., Youngstown West Side Mchts. and Civic Assn., 1954, hon. citizen, St. Petersburg, Fla., 1972, Man of Yr., Fraternal Order Police, Boardman, Ohio, 1975, Mahoning Valley Econ. Devel. Corp., 1983, City of Pitts., 1983; recipient Ellis Island Medal of Honor, 1986, Gov.'s award State of Ohio, 1984, Disting. Citizen award Youngstown State U., 1984. Mem. Urban Land Inst., Nat. Realty Com., Thoroughbred Racing Assn. (Eclipse award 1989), Internat. Coun. Shopping Ctrs., Italian-Am. War Vets. (life). Roman Catholic.

DEBEVOISE, DICKINSON RICHARDS, federal judge; b. Orange, N.J., Apr. 23, 1924; s. Elliott and Josephine (Richards) D.; m. Katrina Stephenson Leeb, Feb. 24, 1951; children: Kate, Josephine Debevoise Davies, Mary Debevoise Rennie, Abigail D. Byrne. B.A., Williams Coll., 1948; LL.B., Columbia U., 1951. Bar: N.J. 1953, U.S. Supreme Ct. 1956. Law clk. to Hon. Phillip Forman, chief judge U.S. Dist. Ct. for Dist. N.J., 1952-53; assoc. firm Riker, Emery & Danzig, Newark, 1953-56; partner firm Riker, Danzig, Scherer, Debevoise & Hyland, Newark, 1957-79; judge U.S. Dist. Ct. for N.J., 1979—; pres. Newark Legal Services Project, 1965-70; chmn. N.J. Gov.'s Workmen's Compensation Study Commn., 1972-73; mem. N.J. Supreme Ct. Adv. Com. on Jud. Conduct, 1974-78; chmn. N.J. Disciplinary Rev. Bd., 1978-79; mem. Lawyers Adv. Com. for 3d Circuit, 1975-79, chmn., 1979; chmn. N.J. Legal Services Adv. Council, 1976-78. Asso. editor: N.J. Law Jour, 1959-79. Trustee Ramapo Coll., N.J., 1969-73, chmn. bd., 1971-73; trustee Williams Coll., 1969-74; trustee Hosp. Center at Orange, N.J., v.p., 1975-79; pres. Democrats for Good Govt., 1956-60, active various presdl., senatorial, gubernatorial campaigns. Served from sgt. to 1st lt. U.S. Army, World War II, Korean War. Decorated Bronze Star. Fellow Am. Bar Found.; mem. Am. Bar Assn., N.J. Bar Assn., Fed. Bar Assn. (v.p. 1976), Assn. Fed. Bar State N.J. (v.p. 1977-79), Essex County Bar Assn. (treas. 1960-64, trustee 1968-71), Am. Law Inst., Judicature Soc. Mem. United Ch. of Christ. Office: US Dist Ct PO Box 999 Newark NJ 07101-0999

DE BIASE, JOHN FRANCIS, financial executive; b. Elmhurst, N.Y., Jan. 15, 1952; s. Vincent Francis and Dolores Ann (Castoria) De B.; m. Sheila Abina Mullins, May 24, 1987; 1 child, Sean Michael. BS, St. John's U., 1973. From staff asst. to airport mgr. La Guardia Airport, Port Authority of N.Y. and N.J., Flushing, N.Y., 1974-81; sr. budget analyst Woodhull Hosp., Bklyn., 1982-89; chief fin. officer Ridgewood-Bushwick Home Care, Bklyn., 1989—. Pres. Middle Village (N.Y.) Dem. Club, 1981-84, Glendale (N.Y.) Human Svcs. Ctr., 1984-87; pub. rels. dir. Middle Village Bicentennial Com., 1975-76; race dir. 10K Race, 1981. Democrat. Roman Catholic. Home: 62-29 78th St Middle Village NY 11379 Office: Ridgewood Bushwick Home Care Coun Inc 280 Wyokoff Ave Brooklyn NY 11237

DEBLASIS, CELESTE NINETTE, novelist; b. Calif., May 8, 1946; d. Raymond and Jean (Campbell) DeB. BA in Eng. cum laude, Pomona Coll., 1968. Author: The Night Child, 1975, Suffer a Sea Change, 1976, The Proud Breed, 1978, The Tiger's Woman, 1981, Wild Swan, 1984, Swan's Chance, 1985, A Season of Swans, 1989, Graveyard Peaches, 1991. Mem. NOW, ACLU, Authors Guild, People for Am. Way, Novelists, Inc., Nature Conservancy, Calif. Hist. Soc., Calif. State Libr. Found.

DEBLASIS, DONNA MARIA, development executive; b. N.Y.C., July 6, 1946; d. John and Antoinette (Caldiero) Iraci; 1 child, Thomas John. BS in Edn., Duquesne U., 1968; postgrad., Carlow Coll., 1987-88. Cert. tchr., Pa. Tchr. North Allegheny Schs., Pitts., 1968-69, St. Teresa Sch., Pitts., 1977-86; dir. devel. Goodwill Industries Pitts., 1986-88, Hist. Soc. Western Pa., Pitts., 1988-91, Make-A-Wish Found. Western Pa., Pitts., 1991—; writing cons., Pa. Dept. Edn., Harrisburg, 1983-86. Mem. ad hoc com. on women C.C. Allegheny County, Pitts., 1972-77; bd. dirs. North Hills Affordable Housing Task Force, 1992—. Mem. AAUW, Women in Communication, Nat. Soc. Fund Raising Execs. (com. chair 1989-91, Bronze awards 1989, 90), Pitts. Planned Giving Coun. Republican. Roman Catholic. Home: 119 Inverness Dr Pittsburgh PA 15237-4757 Office: Make-A-Wish Found Western Pa Westin William Penn Hotal Ste 212 Pittsburgh PA 15219

DEBO, DAVID RAY, mechanical engineer; b. Marion, Ohio, June 21, 1955; s. Russell Lowell and Fay Delores (Mead) D.; m. Pamela Sue Young, July 3, 1975 (div. 1987); 1 child, Christopher Ray; m. Kimberly Ann DeSena, Dec. 31, 1987; 1 child, Tyler James. BS in Mech. Engring., Ohio State U., 1977; MS in Mech. Engring., Carnegie Mellon U., 1983. Registered profl. engr., Idaho. Devel. engr. Dresser Industries, Marion, 1977-79; mech. engr. Westinghouse-Bettis Lab., West Mifflin, Pa., 1979-83, sr. mech. engr., 1985—, design productivity com., 1990—; field engr. naval reactors facility Westinghouse, Idaho Falls, 1983-85. Coach Youth Basketball League, North Huntingdon, Pa., 1989-91; asst. coach Youth Baseball League, North Huntingdon, 1990-91. Mem. ASME, Ohio State U. Mech. Engring. Alumni Soc. (mem. awards com. 1989—), Ohio State U. Alumni Assn. Republican. Home: 10540 Farview Dr Irwin PA 15642-9761 Office: Westinghouse Bettis Lab PO Box 79 West Mifflin PA 15122-0079

DEBOER, GEORGE EDWARD, education educator; b. Paterson, N.J., Nov. 3, 1944; s. George and Lillian (Beekman) DeB.; m. Judith Ann Gindele, Sept. 27, 1969 (dec. 1990); children: Margo, Mark. BA, Hope Coll., Holland, Mich., 1966; MAT, U. Iowa, 1968; PhD, Northwestern U., Evanston, Ill., 1972. Tchr. secondary biology, chemistry, earth sci. Glenbrook South High Sch., Glenview, Ill., 1971-74; asst. prof. dept. edn. Colgate U., Hamilton, N.Y., 1974-82; assoc. prof., chmn. dept. Colgate U., Hamilton, 1982-91, prof., 1991—; dir. MA teaching program, dir. grad. summer session Colgate U.; numerous presentation in field. Author: A History of Ideas in Science Education, 1991; contbr. articles to profl. jours. Mem. Am. Ednl. Rsch. Assn., Nat. Assn. Rsch. in Sci. Teaching, Nat. Sci. Tchrs. Assn. Home: Box 142E Rambling Brook Rd Hamilton NY 13346

DE BOER, PIETER CORNELIS TOBIAS, mechanical and aerospace engineering educator; b. Leiden, Netherlands, May 21, 1930; s. Pieter and Willemina (Zuydam) deB.; m. Joan Lieshout, June 7, 1956; children: Maarten P., Claire E., Yvette E. MechE degree, Delft U. Tech., 1955; PhD in Physics, U. Md., 1962. Rsch. asst., assoc. Tech. U. Delft, 1954-55; rsch. assoc. U. Md., 1957-62, rsch. asst. prof., 1962-64; asst. prof. Cornell U., 1964-68, assoc. prof., 1968-74; prof. Sibley Sch. Mech. and Aerospace Engring., Cornell U., 1974—, assoc. dir., 1982-91; mem. tech. staff Aerospace Corp., summer, 1963, 65, 67; vis. prof. von Karman Inst. for Fluid Dynamics, Belgium, 1968, Cornell Aero. Lab., Buffalo, 1969, Tech. U. Delft, 1985-86; cons. Ford Motor Co., 1971-73, gas turbine div. GE Co., 1978-79, others; assoc. editor for N.Am. Applied Sci. Rsch., 1987—. Contbr. articles to profl. jours. With Dutch Army, 1955-57. NATO fellow, 1968. Assoc. fellow AIAA; mem. ASME, Am. Phys. Soc., Internat. Assn. Hydrogen Energy, Royal Inst. Ingenieurs Netherlands, Royal Netherlands Acad. Scis. (corr.), Golden Key Soc., Rsch. Club Cornell U., Finger Lakes Cycling Club, Finger Lakes Runners Club, Cayuga Nordic Ski Club (pres.), Sigma Xi, Pi Tau Sigma, Sigma Pi Sigma. Office: Cornell U Sibley Sch Mech Aerospace Upson Hall Ithaca NY 14853

DEBOLD, JOSEPH FRANCIS, psychology educator; b. Boston, Nov. 3, 1947; s. Joseph Francis and Patricia (Miltimore) DeB.; m. Carol Lynn Hook, Dec. 20, 1969. AB, UCLA, 1969; PhD, U. Calif., Irvine, 1976. Trainee U. Calif. NICHD Devel. & Reproductive Biology, Irvine, 1971-75; instr., rsch. assoc. Mich. State U., East Lansing, 1975-77; asst. prof. Carnegie-Mellon U., Pitts., 1977-79; asst. prof. Tufts U., Medford, Mass., 1979-83, assoc. prof., 1983-91, prof., chmn. dept. psychology, 1990—; vis. rsch. assoc. Children's Hosp. Med. Ctr., Boston, 1981-85; advisor NSF, Washington, 1989-92. Mem. editorial bd. Hormones and Behavior, 1987-92; contbr. articles to profl. jours., chpts. to books. Grantee NSF, 1986-94, Nat. Inst. Alcoholism and Alcohol Abuse, 1980-92, Biomed. Rsch. Support Program, 1990-91, Nat. Inst. Drug Abuse. Mem. Soc. for Neurosci., AAAS, Nat. Assn. Advisors for Health Prof., N.Y. Acad. Scis., Rsch. Soc. on Alcoholism, Psi Chi, Sigma Xi. Office: Tufts U Dept Psychology Paige Hall Medford MA 02155

DEBOLT, GARY PAUL, education educator, administrator; b. Penn Yan, N.Y., Feb. 4, 1951; s. Kenneth F. and Mary E. (Tobin), DeB.; m. Gwendolyn, Aug. 19, 1972; children: Daniel, Christopher, Jessica. BA, SUNY Cortland, 1973; MS in Edn., SUNY Geneseo, 1978; EdD, Syracuse, 1989. Cert. in secondary social studies, N.Y.; cert. sch. dist. adminstr., N.Y. Tchr. social studies Geneseo (N.Y.) Cen. Sch., 1973-86; teaching asst. Syracuse (N.Y.) U., 1986-88, instr., 1989-91; asst. prof. SUNY Coll. at Geneseo, 1989-91, asst. dir. Sch. of Edn., 1991—. Editor: Teacher Induction and Mentoring: Collaborative School Based Programs. Mem. ASCD, Assn. Tchr. Educators, Nat. Coun. Social Studies, N.Y. State Coun. Social Studies, Kiwanis Club (pres. Livonia, N.Y. 1989-91), Phi Kappa Phi, Pi Lambda Theta, Phi Delta Kappa, Kappa Delta Pi. Office: SUNY College at Geneseo Blake C Geneseo NY 14454

DE BORCHGRAVE, ARNAUD, editor, writer, lecturer; b. Brussels, Oct. 26, 1926; s. Count Baudouin and Audrey (Townshend) de B.; m. Dorothy Solon, Apr. 1950; 1 child, Arnaud; m. Eileen Ritchel, Mar. 31, 1959; 1 child, Trisha; m. Alexandra D. Villard, May 10, 1969. Student, Maredsous, Belgium, 1936-39, King's Sch., Canterbury, Eng., 1940-42. Free-lance writer Eastern Europe, 1946-47; staff United Press, Western Europe, 1947-51; mgr. Benelux Countries, 1949-51; European Corr. Newsweek, Paris, North Africa, Middle East, Indo-China, 1951-54; fgn. editor, sr. editor Newsweek, 1955-59, chief fgn. corr., 1959-62, mng. editor internat. edits., 1962-63, chief Newsweek Corr., 1964-80; columnist, TV host; sr. assoc. Ctr. for Strategic and Internat. Studies, 1981-85; editor in chief The Washington Times and Insight Mag., 1985-91; sr. advisor Ctr. for Strategic and Internat. Studies, Washington, 1991—. Served with Brit. Royal Navy, 1942-46. Decorated commandeur de l'Ordre de Leopold II, Medaille Maritime Belge; recipient Medal of Honor Def. Council, 1980, Medal of Honor World Bus. Council, 1981, Washington Dateline award Soc. Profl. Journalists, also numerous awards for fgn. reporting. Mem. Am. Soc. Newspaper Editors, Internat. Press Inst., Inter-Am. Press Assn., Council on Fgn. Relations., U.S. Global Strategy Council, Sigma Delta Chi. Clubs: Racquet and Tennis, Metropolitan, Econ. of Washington, Nat. Press, Cosmos. Home: 2141 Wyoming Ave NW Washington DC 20008-3916 Office: Ctr for Strategic and Internat Studies 1800 K St NW Washington DC 20006-2202

DE BRAGANÇA, MIGUEL, portfolio manager; b. N.Y.C., Sept. 25, 1951; s. John de Bragança and Winifred (Seyburn) Cheston; m. Barbara Fales, Sept. 27, 1980; children: Miguel Samuel, Annabel, Camilla. BA, U. Pa., 1972; MA, Yale U., 1976, MPhil, 1978. Curatorial asst. Mus. of Fine Arts, Boston, 1973-74; teaching fellow Yale U., New Haven, Conn., 1978-79; trust officer, portfolio mgr. State St. Bank & Trust, Co., Boston, 1980-84; portfolio mgr. Trinity Investment Mgmt. Corp., Cambridge, 1984-89, supervising portfolio mgr., 1989-92, mng. dir., 1992—. Author: (exhbn. cat.) Ancient Egypt: God, King, and Man, 1978. Bd. dirs. The Bostonian Soc., 1982—, asst. treas., 1982-85, treas., 1985—, Alliance Française of Boston, 1983-88, treas, 1983-88; overseer Mus. of Fine Arts, Boston, 1988—, vice chair of vis. city dept. Egyptian art, 1990—. Mem. Am. Bankers Assn. (cert. fin. svcs. counsellor 1983), Assn. for Investment Mgmt. and Rsch., Boston Security Analysts Soc., The Brook Club (N.Y.C.), Somerset Club (Boston), The Country Club (Brookline, Mass.). Republican. Episcopalian. Home: 301 Berkeley St Boston MA 02116-2013 Office: Trinity Investment Mgmt Corp 1 Memorial Dr Cambridge MA 02142-1301

DEBROT, PETER, industrial engineer; b. Bklyn., Aug. 20, 1960; s. Jacques Louis Debrot and Moira Margaret (Walsh) Modica; m. Noreen M. Feely, June 22, 1985. BS in Indsl. Engring., Va. Poly. Inst. & State U., 1982. Indsl. engr. Johns-Manville Corp., Manville, N.J., 1982-84; sr. indsl. engr. Internat. Paper Co., Cedar Knolls, N.J., 1984-87; supr. pharm. prodn. Sandoz Pharms., E. Hanover, N.J., 1987-90, mgr. prodn. planning, 1990—. Mem. Inst. Indsl. Engrs. (assoc.). Republican. Roman Catholic.

DEBS, BARBARA KNOWLES, academic administrator; b. Eastham, Mass., Dec. 24, 1931; d. Stanley F. and Arline (Eugley) Knowles; m. Richard A. Debs, July 19, 1958; children: Elizabeth, Nicholas. BA, Vassar Coll., 1953; postgrad., Radcliffe Coll., 1956-58; PhD, Harvard U., 1967; LLD, N.Y. Law Sch., 1979; LHD, Manhattanville Coll., 1985. Instr. art Vassar Coll., 1955-56; freelance translation editor Ency. of World Art div. McGaw-Hill Pub., N.Y.C., 1959-62; asst. prof. art history Manhattanville Coll., Purchase, N.Y., 1968-73, assoc. prof., 1973-77, prof., 1977-86, pres., 1975-85; trustee, chmn. collections com. N.Y. Hist. Soc., 1985-87, pres., chief exec. officer, dir., 1988-92; bd. dirs. AMF Inc., 1978-85. Contbr. articles on Renaissance and contemporary art to profl. publs. Mem. N.Y. Council Humanities, 1978-85; mem. Westchester Med. Ctr. Hosp. Implementation Bd., 1978-84; mem. Westchester County Bd. Ethics, 1979-84; trustee N.Y. Law Sch., 1979—; trustee Geraldine R. Dodge Found., 1985—; bd. dirs. Internat. Found. for Art Research, 1985—, trustee Com. Econ. Devel., 1985—, mem. council on fgn. relations, 1983—; mem. Commn. Ind. Colls. and Univs. of N.Y., 1977-79; mem. com. on higher edn., adv. council to Dems. N.Y. State Senate, 1979-85. AAUW Nat. fellow and Ann Radcliffe fellow, 1958-59; Am. Council Learned Socs. grantee, 1973; Fulbright fellow Scuola Normale, Pisa, Italy, 1953, U. Rome, 1954. Mem. Am. Coun. on Edn. (chmn. commn. acad. affairs 1977-79), Young Audiences (nat. dir. 1977-80), Hundred Club of Westchester (bd. dirs.), Renaissance Soc. of Am., Coll. Art Assn., Phi Beta Kappa. Club: Cosmpolitan, Century Assn. Office: NY Hist Soc 170 Central Park W New York NY 10024-5102

DECABIA, FRANCIS CARMEN, stock brokerage company executive; b. Elizabeth, N.J., Dec. 29, 1941; s. Carmen Francis and Antoinette (Ruggiero) DeC.; m. Joanne Louise Pagliaro, Mar. 22, 1981; children: Robert, Lisa, Michael. BS, U. Tampa, 1964. V.p. Masters Trucking Corp., Huntington, N.Y., 1965-71; sr. v.p. Kaufman Carpet, Yonkers, N.Y., 1971-80; chief oper. officer D&S Carpet, Huntington, 1980-84; sr. govt. bond specialist McLoughlin, Piven, Vogal, N.Y.C., 1984-86; v.p. Shearson, Lehman Hutton, White Plains, N.Y., 1986-88, Kidder, Peabody & Co., Inc., N.Y.C., 1988-90; exec. v.p., mng. dir. Josephthal & Co., N.Y.C., 1990—; dir. ATOMM Acquisitions Corp., Ft. Lauderdale, Fla.; mem. pres. adv. coun. Rochester (N.Y.) Funds. Mem. adv. bd. Hudson Valley Nat. Found., Inc., Yonkers, N.Y. Mem. Internat. Assn. Fin. Planning, Am. Mgmt. Assn., Wykagyl Country Club. Republican. Roman Catholic. Office: Josephthal Lyon & Ross Inc 300 Park Ave New York NY 10022-7402

DE CAPITANI, ALBERTO, personnel director; b. Casale Monferrato, Italy, Apr. 1, 1942; came to U.S., 1969; s. Carlo and Maria (Pasquino) de C.; m. Renata Serrafero, Sept. 15, 1968; children: Alessandro, Ilaria. JD, Universita degli studi di Milano, Italy, 1965; M of Philosophy in Econs., George Washington U., 1977. Div. chief energy dept. World Bank, Washington, 1985-86, asst. dir. industry dept., 1986-87, prin. adv., sr. v.p. external affairs and adminstrn., 1987-89, dir. pers. ops., 1989—. Contbr. articles to profl. jours. Recipient Luigi Einaudi award for best dissertation, 1965, Milano. Mem. Am. Mgmt. Assn. Home: 10405 Great Arbor Dr Rockville MD 20854-4216

DE CARO, LAURENCE THOMAS, secondary school educator; b. Springfield, Mass., May 24, 1945; s. Anthony A. and Maria C. (Ragno) De C.; m. Barbara Ann St. Lowell, July 28, 1973; children: Lawrence T. Jr., Scott Andrew. BS, Montclair State U., 1968, MA in Health, 1974. Cert. secondary sch. tchr. health, phys. edn., driver edn.; cert. family life educator. Tchr. Pascack Valley Regional High Sch., Hillsdale, N.J., 1971—; student asst. coord. Pascack Valley Regional High Sch., Hillsdale, 1985-86; co-dir. Adolescent Intervention Counsel for Suicide, Pascack Valley Regional High Sch., Hillsdale, 1983-86; author (curriculums) family life edn. grades 9, 11, 12; AIDS, grades 9-12. Co-pres. Bergen County Task Force Crimes Against Children, Hackensack, N.J., 1984-85; cubmaster Boy Scouts Am., Pack 108, Hillsdale, 1985-88; coach Hillsdale Baseball Recreation, 1985-88. With U.S. Army, 1968-70. Recipient award Am. Cancer Soc., 1991. Mem. NEA, N.J. Tchrs. Assn., Nat. Coun. Family Rels., Bergen County Edn. Assn., Bergen County Wrestling Coaches, Pascack Valley Region Edn. Assn. Roman Catholic. Home: 148 Riverdale St Hillsdale NJ 07642-1512

DÉCARY, ROBERT, appellate court judge; b. Montreal, Que., Can., May 26, 1944; s. Jacques M. Décary and Madeleine Toupin. BA, Coll. Brebeuf, Montreal, 1963; LLL, U. Montreal, 1966; LLM, U. London, 1968. Bar: Quebec 1967. Polit. asst. Sec. State External Affairs, Ottawa, Ont., Can., 1970-73; lawyer Deschênes, de Grandpré, Montreal, 1973-80, Noël, Décary & Assocs., Hull, Que., 1980-90; judge Fed. Ct. Appeal, Ottawa, 1990—. Contbr. essays to publs. Mem. Can. Bar Assn. (coun.). Office: Fed Ct Appeals, Supreme Ct Bldg, Ottawa, ON Canada K1A 0H9

DECATO, CLIFFORD MILES, psychology educator; b. Lebanon, N.H., Feb. 1, 1940; s. Harold H. and Yvonne R. (Beaudry) DeCato; m. Kathleen M. Orlando, Sept. 10, 1966; children: Leah A., Todd D. BA cum laude, U. N.H., 1963, MA, 1965; PhD, Temple U., 1971. Diplomate Internat. Acad. Behavioral Medicine, Am. Bd. Med. Psychotherapists. Postdoctoral fellow Irving Schwartz Inst., Phila., 1970-71; sr. instr. grad. edn. in psychology Hahnemann Med. Coll. and Hosp., Phila., 1971-72, asst. dir. grad. edn. in psychology, 1972-75, asst. prof., 1972-76, acting dir. div. of psychology, 1975-77; assoc. prof., assoc. dir. div. psychology Hahnemann U., Phila., 1977-85, prof., 1985-89; prof., assoc. dir. Inst. for Grad. Clin. Psychology Widener U., Chester, Pa., 1989—; chief psychologist Div. Mental Health Svcs., Phila. Prisons, 1977-84. Contbr. numerous articles to profl. jours. Recipient award for Outstanding Svc. to Pa. Psychol. Assn., 1984, award for Valuable Contributions to the Assn., 1977. Fellow Soc. for Personality Assessment, Am. Bd. Med. Psychotherapists; mem. APA, Am. Psychol. Assessment Exch., Assn. Advancement Psychology, Internat. Assn. Behavioral Medicine Coun. Psychotherapies, Internat. Rorschach Soc., Pa. Psychol. Assn., Phila. Soc. Clin. Psychologists, Sigma Xi. Roman Catholic. Office: Inst Grad Clin Psychology Widener Univ One University Pl Chester PA 19013

DECATOR, CARL J., transportation executive; b. Port Huron, Mich., Feb. 11, 1949; s. John Robert and Ruth Ann (Gorte) D.; m. Sandra Ann Lane, Aug. 23, 1974; children: Andrea Marie, Christopher John. BSBA, Bowling Green U., 1971; MBA, Fairleigh Dickinson U., 1982. Traffic supr. UniRoyal Inc., Oxford, Conn., 1971-74; account mgr. Ryder Truck Rental, Medford, Mass., 1974-76; mgr. corp. trucks NL Industries, Hightstown, N.J., 1976-79, Warner Lambert Co., Morris Plains, N.J., 1979-82; asst. v.p. Maher Terminals, Jersey City, 1982-89; sr. v.p. Penn Terminals, Eddystone, Pa., 1989—. Mem. Bd. Adjustment, Hillsborough, N.J., 1986; transp. team leader Govs. Mgmt. Improvement Plan, N.J., 1983-84. Recipient Golden 100 award Fleet Owner Mag., 1980. Mem. Nat. Assn. Stevedores, Coun. Bus. Logistics, N.J. Motor Truck Assn. (dir. 1980-84, pvt. carrier coun. pres. 1980-82), N.Y. Downtown Athletic Club, Forsygate Country Club. Republican. Lutheran. Home: 65 Royce Brook Rd Belle Mead NJ 08502 Office: Penn Terminals 1 Saville Ave Eddystone PA 19022

DECEW, JUDITH WAGNER, philosophy educator; b. Oberlin, Ohio, Nov. 19, 1948; d. Robert Wanner and Sally (Marsh) Wagner; m. Alan Edward DeCew Jr., Aug. 23, 1969; children: David Alan, Melissa Sue, Jeffrey Robert. BA, U. Rochester, 1970; MA, U. Mass., 1976, PhD, 1978. Asst. prof. MIT, Cambridge, 1979-87; asst. prof. Clark U., Worcester, Mass., 1987-90, assoc. prof., 1990—. Author: (with others) Moral Responsibility and the University, 1990; contbr. articles to profl. jours. Pres. Peirce Extended Day Program, Newton, Mass., 1991—, Cabot After Sch. Program, Newton, 1983-87. Higgins Faculty fellow Clark U., 1989-90; rsch. fellow Radcliffe Bunting Inst., 1988-89, Am. Coun. of Learned Soc., 1984-85; fellow Harvard Law Sch., 1980-81. Mem. AAUW (dissertation fellowship 1977-78), AAUP, Nat. Am. Philos. Assn. (com. on law and philosophy 1990-93), Am. Philos. Assn. Democrat. Office: Clark U 950 Main St Worcester MA 01610-1473

DE CHERNEY, ALAN HERSH, obstetrics and gynecology educator; b. Phila., Feb. 13, 1942; s. William Aaron and Ruth (Hersh) DeC.; m. Deanna Faith Saver, June 26, 1966; children: Peter, Alexander, Nicholas. BS in Natural Scis., Muhlenberg Coll., 1963; MD, Temple U., 1967; MA (hon.), Yale U., 1985. Diplomate Am. Bd. Ob-Gyn (examiner 1984—), Am. Bd. Reproductive Endocrinology (examiner 1987-88, bd. dirs. 1988—), Nat. Bd. Med. Examiners (examiner 1987-90). Intern in gen. medicine U. Pitts., 1967-68; resident in ob-gyn. U. Pa., Phila., 1968-72, instr. dept. ob-gyn, 1970-72; asst. prof. ob-gyn. Yale U. Sch. Medicine, New Haven, 1974-78, assoc. prof., 1979-84, prof., 1984-91, John Slade Ely prof. ob-gyn, 1987-92, dir. div. reproductive endocrinology, dept. ob-gyn, 1982-92, lectr. dept. biology, 1985-92; Louis E. Phaenof prof., chmn. dept. ob.-gyn. Tufts U. Sch. Medicine, 1992—. Assoc. editor Jour. In Vitro Fertilization and Embryo Transfer. Maj. U.S. Army, 1972-74. Recipient Disting. Alumni award Temple U., 1989. Fellow Am. Coll. Ob.-Gyns., Am. Fertility Soc., Soc. for Assisted Reproductive Tech. (pres. 1987-88), Am. Assn. History of Medicine, Soc. Reproductive Endocrinologists (pres. 1988), Soc. Reproductive Surgeons (charter, pres. 1991), Assn. Profs. Ob.-Gyn., Blockley Obs. Soc. (v.p. 1970), Endocrine Soc., European Soc., Human Reproduction and Embryology, Soc. Gynecologic Investigation (coun. 1989-91), Soc. Gynecologic Surgeons, Soc. for Study of Reproduction. Republican. Jewish. Office: Tufts U Dept Ob-gyn 750 Washington St Boston MA 02111

DECHI, DANIEL SALOMON, electrical draftsman; b. Buenos Aires, Argentina, Jan. 14, 1959; came to U.S., 1965; s. Djemil and Camila (Ezra) D. AS, Heald's Coll., 1981. Asst. mgr. McDonald's, Novato, Calif., 1975-78; chef Zim's Restaurants, San Rafael, Calif., 1978-82; elec. draftsman Otis Elevator Co., Bloomfield, Conn., 1983—. Author (humor manuscript) I Didn't Want to Pay for a Rent-A-Car, 1990; author (illustrated humor) Wilburn, The Flaming Gorrilla, 1992; author humor column Offsides, 1987-88. Vol. We are the Children, Hartford, Conn., 1989—, Symphony on Ice, Hartford, 1989—, San Francisco Food Drive, 1987, 88, Spl. Olympics, Hartford, 1989—. Named Most Valuable Player (goalie), San Francisco Recreational Soccer League, 1987, 88. Democrat.

DECI, EDWARD LEWIS, psychologist, educator; b. Clifton Springs, N.Y., Oct. 14, 1942; s. Charles Henry and Janice Margaret (Upchurch) D. AB, Hamilton Coll., 1964; postgrad., London Sch. Econs., 1965; MBA, U. Pa., 1967; PhD, Carnegie-Mellon U., 1970. Mem. faculty U. Rochester, N.Y., 1970—; prof. psychology U. Rochester, 1978—; pvt. practice psychotherapy, 1975—; orgnl. cons., 1970—. Author: The Psychology of Self-Determination, 1980, Intrinsic Motivation, 1975; co-author: Industrial and Organizational Psychology, 1977, Intrinsic Motivation and Self-Determination in Human Behavior, 1985. Trustee Monhegan (Maine) Conservation Assocs., 1982-89; pres. Monhegan Mus. Assn., 1984—. NIMH grantee, 1977-78, 89—, NSF grantee, 1981-83, Nat. Inst. Child Health and Human Devel. grantee, 1986-89, 90—. Fellow Am. Psychol. Assn., Am. Psychol. Soc. Office: U Rochester Psychology Dept Rochester NY 14627

DECKER, GARY ARDEN, real estate executive; b. Toledo, Ohio, Feb. 7, 1942; s. Glen Arden Decker and Sibyl Christine (Green) Beatty; m. Linda Lou Searle, Sept. 29, 1962 (div.); Scott Arden, Jeffrey Allen, Dana Lynn. BSEE, U. Toledo, 1967; MSEE, Rutgers U., 1969. Communications tech. Long Lines, Toledo, 1962-67; mem. tech. staff Bell Labs., Holmdel, N.J., 1967-71; various engring., pers. and ops. Long Lines, Chgo., 1971-74; dist. ops. mgr. Long Lines, Toledo, 1974-76; pers. Long Lines, Redminster, N.J., 1976-78; various engring., sales and ops. Long Lines, Chgo., 1978-82; gen. mgr., engring. AT&T Communications, Chgo., 1982-85; dir. consumer sales ops. AT&T, Basking Ridge, N.J., 1985-86; real estate v.p. AT&T, Basking Ridge, 1986—. Mem. Indsl. Devel. & Redevel. Corp. (bd. mem.), Somerset Alliance for the Future(bd. mem.), N.J. Alliance for Action (bd. mem.), Urban Land Inst. Home: 1537 Ocean Ave Mantoloking NJ 08738-1515 Office: AT&T 222 Mt Airy Rd Basking Ridge NJ 07920-2335

DECKER, ROBERT OWEN, history educator, clergyman; b. Lafayette, Ind., Nov. 6, 1927; s. Samuel Owen and Helen Dale (Noble) D.; m. Margaret Ann Harris, May 30, 1948; 1 child, Terry Lynn Decker DeIulis. AB, Butler U., 1953; AM, Ind. U., 1958; PhD, U. Conn., 1970. Ordained to ministry Congregational Church, 1990. Instr., Sch. City of LaPorte (Ind.), 1956-59; instr. Cen. Conn. State U., New Britain, 1959-63, asst. prof., 1963-73, assoc. prof., 1973-77, prof. history, 1977, prof., 1977-89, prof. emeritus, 1989; evaluator manuscripts Wesleyan U. Press, 1977-89; advisor Nat. Endowment for Humanities, 1977-89, Connecticut River Found. Mem. Christian Activities Council, Hartford, 1965—, pres., 1972-74, 76-78; dir. Hartford (Conn.) InnerCity Exchange, 1971-81, chmn. bd., 1977-80; chmn. state legis. adv. com. Conn. Developmental Disabilities Council, 1973-75; evaluator programs Conn. Humanities Coun.; Historian Christian Activities Coun., 1983—, Rocky Hill (Conn.) Congl. Ch., 1985-89, Conn. 350th Com., 1985-86, historian, 1985-89; justice of peace, 1985—, constable Rocky Hill, 1986—; apptd. town historian, 1990; pastor Eagle Rock Congl. Ch., 1989—; mem. UCC Hist. Com., 1989-92; dir. Old Towne Tourism Dist. Conn., 1989-90. Served with U.S. Army, 1946-48, 50-51. Asian Studies grantee, 1959; Am. Studies grantee, 1959; Danforth grantee, 1962; Munson Maritime grantee, 1961; Smithsonian Inst. grantee, 1963. Mem. Orgn. Am. Historians, Am., New Eng., Conn. hist. assns., Assn. for Study of Conn. History, AAUP, New London County Hist. Soc., Am. Waldensian Aid Soc. (pres. Hartford chpt. 1986-89), Phi Alpha Theta. Republican. Congregationalist (life deacon). Club: Masons. Author: Whaling Industry of New London, 1973; The Whaling City: A History of New London, 1976; A Student Guidebook to American History, 1983; Hartford Immigrants, 1987; The New London Merchants, 1986, Cromwell, Connecticut 1650-1990: The History of A River Port Town, 1991; contbr. articles and book revs. to profl. jours. Home: 2623 Main St Rocky Hill CT 06067-2507 Office: Eagle Rock Congregational Ch Thomaston CT 06787

DECLE, DENIS CHRISTOPHER, advertising executive; b. Montreal, Que., Can., May 24, 1951; s. Russell Cyril Carl and Kathleen Elizabeth (Cooke) D.; m. Carol Anne Marshall, Apr. 4, 1977; children: Jaclyn Elizabeth, Lana Patricia. Pres. Black Opal Enterprises Inc., Montreal, 1972-73; product devel. mgr. Robin Hood MultiFoods Ltd., Montreal, 1974-75, product group mgr., 1976-77; account supr. Grey Advt. Ltd., Toronto, Ont., Can., 1978-79, account dir., v.p., 1979-81, group dir., sr. v.p., 1982-84, dir. affiliate ops., sr. v.p., 1985-86, gen. mgr., sr. v.p., 1987—. Mem. Kenya Wildlife Fund, Greenpeace 2000 (charter). Office: Grey Advt Ltd, 1881 Yonge St, Toronto, ON Canada M4S 3C4

DECOCK, JENNIFER ELIZABETH, marketing representative; b. Bryn Mawr, Pa., July 3, 1965; d. Frederick Talbot and Priscilla Anne (Mitchell) DeC. BA in Journalism, U. W.Va., 1987. Payroll 1 Phila., Inc., Malvern, Pa., 1991—. Mem. Cath. Philopatrian Lit. Inst. (membership chmn. 1990-91, social chmn. 1991, pres. 1991-92), Greenpeace. Home: 404 West Ave Wayne PA 19087-3208 Office: 301 Lindenwood Dr Ste 100 Malvern PA 19301

DECOSTA, PETER F., chemical engineer; b. New Bedford, Mass.; s. Anthony and Deolinda (DeSouza) DeC. BS with distinction, U. Mass., Dartmouth, 1962; MA, U. Conn., 1966; cert., U. R.I., 1968; MS, MIT, 1970; cert., Boston U., 1979, Northeastern U., 1980; profl. engring. degree, U. Wis., 1981. Chemist Portsmouth Naval Shipyard, N.H., 1962-64; quality assurance engr. U.S. FDA, Boston, 1966-71; systems analyst U.S. EPA, Washington, 1971-75; ops. rsch. analyst U.S. Army Natick (Mass.) Rsch., Devel. and Engring. Ctr., 1976-83, phys. scientist, 1983-86, gen. engr., 1986—; part-time instr. Northeastern U., Boston, 1987—, Worcester (Mass.) Poly. Inst., 1984—, Mass. Bay Community Coll., Wellesley, 1983—. Contbr. articles to profl. jours. Planner, Planning Bd. City of New Bedford, Mass., 1975; mem. ch. activities, charities; mem. leadership circle Sta. WGBH-TV (PBS), Boston, 1992. Commonwealth scholar U. Mass., 1958-62, City of New Bedford scholar, 1958-62, Allied Chem. Co. scholar, 1960-62, U. Conn. teaching fellow, 1964-65, Advanced Engring. fellow MIT, 1969-70, NSF/AAAS fellow MIT, 1984; recipient Natick Comdr.'s award U.S. Army Natick Rsch., Devel. and Engring. Ctr., 1986. Fellow Am. Inst. Chemists; mem. Am. Chem. Soc., Am. Inst. Chem. Engrs. (cert. 1990), Mus. Sci., Children's Mus., MIT Faculty Club, MIT Club Southeastern Mass., Sigma Xi, Alpha Chi Sigma, Phi Lambda Upsilon. Office: US Army Natick Rsch Devel & Engring Ctr Kansas St Natick MA 01760-5015

DE COTRET, ROBERT RENE, Canadian government official; b. Ottawa, Ont., Can., Feb. 20, 1944; m. Diane Chenier; children: Lynne, Marc, Michel. BA, U. Ottawa, 1964; MBA, U. McGill, 1966; CPh, U. Mich., 1969. Teaching fellow; sr. economist to Pres. of U.S. Washington; with Conf. Bd. Can., 1972-78; minister industry and commerce Govt. Can., 1979; 1st v.p., dir. gen., exec. v.p. internat. affairs Nat. Bank Can., Montreal, Que., 1980-84; pres. Treasury Bd. Can., Ottawa, Ont., 1984-87; minister regional indsl. expansion, minister of State for sci. and tech. Govt. Can., Ottawa, 1987-89; pres., treas. bd. Can. Govt. Can., Ottawa, Ont., 1989-90, also min. environment, 1990-91; sec. state, minister responsible for status disabled persons Govt. Can., 1991—. Office: House of Commons, 337 W Block, Ottawa, ON Canada K1A 0A6

DE COURSEY, ROBERT WURTS, insurance agent, pension consultant; b. Phila., Aug. 18, 1927; s. George Earle and Marion W. (Wurts) De C.; m. Marjorie Ann De Coursey, Apr. 28, 1956; children: Samuel L., Mary E., Peter L., Ruth M. Student, Yale U., 1944-45, 48-50. Enrolled actuary, CLU. Asst. sales mgr. Prudential Ins. Co., Phila., 1950-68; mgr. Union Cen. Life Ins. Co., Phila., 1968-81, agt., 1981—; pres. Phila. Assn. Life Underwriters, 1979-80, Pa. Assn. Life Underwriters, Harrisburg, 1987-88, Assn. Health Ins. Agts., Washington, 1991-92. Sgt. U.S. Army, 1946-48, 50-51. Mem. Am. Soc. Pension Actuaries, Phila. Cricket Club, Yale Club of Phila. Office: 555 E City Ave Ste 900 Bala Cynwyd PA 19004-1160

DE COURT, BRUCE WAYNE, cable television executive; b. Nashville, Dec. 24, 1953; s. Albert Paul and Sherrie Ann (Hardwick) De C.; m. Jane Margaret Kennedy, Nov. 3, 1979. BA, Rutgers U., 1975. Adminstr. Cable Arts Found., N.Y.C., 1977-78; sales supr. UA-Columbia Cablevision, Oakland, N.J., 1978-79; sales mgr./dir. mkt. devel. Paradigm Communications, N.Y.C., 1979-80; mktg. dir. Pay TV of Greater N.Y., 1980-84; dir. mktg. and sales Cooper Wireless Cable, Inc., 1984-86; dir. mktg. Microband Wireless Cable, 1987-89; dir. bus. devel. Cablevision of N.Y.C., 1989—; pres. Kennedy DeCourt Mktg. Communications, Sparkill, N.Y., 1988—. Mem. AMA, Interactive Svcs. Assn. Home: 18 Burr St Easton CT 06612 Office: Cablevision of NYC 930 Soundview Ave Bronx NY 10473-3700

DECRANE, ALFRED CHARLES, JR., petroleum company executive; b. Cleve., June 11, 1931; s. Alfred Charles and Verona (Marquard) DeC.; m. Joan Elizabeth Hoffman, July 3, 1954; children: David, Lisa, Stacie, Stephanie, Sarah, Jennifer. BA, U. Notre Dame, 1953; JD, Georgetown U., 1959; LHD (hon.), Manhattanville Coll., 1990. Bar: Va. bar 1959, D.C. bar 1959, Tex. bar 1961, N.Y. bar 1966. Legal dept. Texaco, Inc., Houston, 1959-64, N.Y.C., 1964-66; asst. to vice chmn. bd. Texaco, Inc., 1965-67, asst. to chmn. bd., 1967-68, gen. mgr. producing dept. Eastern hemisphere, 1968-70, v.p., 1970-76, sr. v.p., gen. counsel, 1976-77, sr. v.p., dir., 1977-78, exec. v.p., 1978-83, pres., 1983-86, chmn. bd. dirs., 1987—; dir. CIGNA Corp. Trustee Com. for Econ. Devel., The Conf. Bd., U. Notre Dame. 1st lt. USMCR, 1954-55. Mem. ABA (sect. sec. 1964-67, co-founder Natural Resources Law Jour. mineral law sect.). Home: 55 Valley Rd Bronxville NY 10708-2211 Office: Texaco Inc 2000 Westchester Ave White Plains NY 10650-0001

DECROSTA, EDWARD FRANCIS, JR., former paper products company executive, consultant; b. Hudson, N.Y., Sept. 20, 1926; s. Edward F. and Anna Ruth (Crisci) DeC.; m. Annette Mae Powell, Sept. 20, 1953; children: Donna Marie, Lisa Ann. BCE, Rensselaer Poly. Inst., 1950; MS in Phys. Chemistry, Siena Coll., 1960; MBA, Rensselaer Poly. Inst., 1978. Plant chemist (process engr.) Universal Match Corp., Hudson, 1951-64; chemist Albany Felt Co., N.Y., 1965-69, mgr. tech. devel., 1969-72, dir. rsch. and devel., 1972-76; dir. rsch. and tech. devel. Papermaking Products Group, Albany Internat. Corp., N.Y.C. 1977-82, sr. scientist, 1982-83. Author: (booklet) Chemical and Physical Properties of the Elements, 1956; contbr. articles on tech. of paper to profl. jours.; patentee in field. With USAAF, 1944-45, 1950-51. Fellow Tech. Assn. Pulp and Paper Industry (chmn. engring. div. 1982-84, E.H. Neese award engring. div. 1987); mem. Am. Chem. Soc., Can. Pulp and Paper Assn., Internat. Assn. Sci. Papermakers, N.Y. Acad. Sci., Capital Dist. Research Dirs. Club, KC, Elks. Roman Catholic. Home and Office: 28 James St Hudson NY 12534-1310

DECROSTA, SUSAN ELYSE, graphic artist; b. Cambridge, Mass., Aug. 28, 1956; d. Joseph Mario and Gertrude Ermelinda (Galligani) DeC. BFA, Mass. Coll. Art, 1980. certified art tchr., supr. Graphic artist Nixdorf Computer Corp., Burlington, Mass., 1981-86; lead artist, illustrator Raytheon Co., Andover, Mass., 1986—; illustrator Rivers, Trainor, Doyle, Providence, 1987; freelance graphic artist, 1980—; guest speaker to design and illustration students Northeastern U., 1992. Vol. AIDS Action Com., Boston. Recipient Excellence award Soc. Tech. Communications & Art Direction, 1986. Mem. Arlington Ctr. Arts, Mass. Art Alumni Assn., Creative Club Boston, The Boston Computer Soc. Democrat. Office: Raytheon Co 350 Lowell St Andover MA 01810-4499

DE DELL, GARY JEROME, printing company executive, consultant; b. Syracuse, N.Y.; s. Harry Jerome and Mary Helen (Belge) DeD. Assoc. in Sci., Rochester Inst. Tech.; student, Syracuse U. Owner North Side Newspaper, Syracuse; technician IBM Corp., N.Y.C., 1959-61; salesman, then sales mgr. Kaufman De Dell Printing Inc., Syracuse and Washington, 1961-69; v.p. Kaufman De Dell Printing Inc., Syracuse and N.Y.C., 1969—; owner Kaufman Press, Syracuse, 1979—; pres. MaDe Corp., Silver Spring, Md., 1974—; owner Printcrafters, Syracuse, 1983—, cons., 1983—; dir. mktg. Campbell Corp., Syracuse, 1985-88; cons. Man and His World, Montreal, Que., Can., 1968, N.Y. World's Fair, Time-Life, N.Y.C., 1963-64; bd. dirs. Nat. Council on Crime and Delinquency, 1966-69; mem. businessmen's adv. group U.S. Dept. Commerce and Dept. Justice, 1978-82. Author: Poetry in U.S., 1965; editor (newspaper) Purple and Gold; patentee in field. Chmn. Syracuse Univ. Charter Governance Commn., 1972-73; mem. N.Y. State Legis. Adv. Com., Albany, 1967-71, Nat. Right to Work Com., Washington, 1968—; dir. Rep. Com. for Nixon, Syracuse, 1968, 72; cons. in advt. N.Y. State Gubernatorial campaign, N.Y.C., 1978, dist. mgr., 1982; congl. campaign mgr., 1978, asst. campaign mgr., 1980, 82; founder Neighborhood Watch, N.Y., 1977; bd. mem. Nat. Coun. on Crime and Delinquency; Northside chmn. Lake Ont. Water Com.; derby dir. 1969 Soap Box Derby; chmn. Get-Out-The-Vote campaign; chmn. City-County Reapportionment Com.; dir. Nat. Coun. on Crime & Delinquency. Served to lt. USAFR. Recipient Pres.'s Youth Opportunity Campaign award, 1965, Jacques Cousteau Soc. award, 1983, Life Saving award Sheriff's Dept., Award of Ams. Pan Am. Union; named Man of Yr. Nat. Leadership Coun., 1991. Mem. NRA, Nat. Def. Coun., UN Assn. U.S.A., Nat. Pilots. Assn., Nat. Small Bus. Assn., Nat. Space Inst., Nat. Trust Hist. Preservation, Nat. Fedn. Ind. Bus., Printing Industry Am., Am. Security Coun. (nat. adv. bd.), Am. Film Inst., Am. Mgmt. Assn., Am. Mus. Natural History, Nat. Audubon Soc., Internat. Security Studies Found., Internat. Platform Assn., Pres.'s Task Force (medal of merit 1983-89), U.S. Naval Inst., U.S. C. of C., U.S. Senatorial Club, Smithsonian Inst., Wilderness Assn., Nature Conservancy, Graphic Artists Guild, Olympic Com., Mensa, World Trade Coun., Air Force Officers Club. Republican. Roman Catholic. Home: 1010 Turtle St Syracuse NY 13208-1726 Office: Kaufman Press Printcrafters Syracuse NY 13207

DEE, RAYMOND CHARLES, aluminum company executive; b. Bronx, N.Y., Apr. 6, 1942; s. Coleman F. and Patricia (Sheridan) D.; m. Maureen Kane, July 11, 1964; children: Kathleen, Maureen, Denise, Michael, Mary Beth, Colleen. BS in Econ., Bonaventure U., 1964; MBA, Loyola U., 1972. Salesman Alumnium Co. Am., Chgo., 1968-70, account exec., 1970-75; br. mgr. Alumnium Co. Am., Garden City, N.Y., 1975-76; asst. dist. mgr. Alumnium Co. Am., N.Y.C., 1976-78; market mgr. Alumnium Co. Am., Massena, N.Y., 1978-79; v.p. sales Cressona (Pa.) Aluminum Co., 1979-90, exec. v.p., 1990—. Trusteee Alvernia Coll., Reading, Pa., 1985—; assoc. bd. St. Bonaventure U., Olean, N.Y., 1987—; pres. Parish Coun. St. John, Pottsville, Pa., 1991-92. Home: 1229 Mahantongo St Pottsville PA 17901 Office: Cressona Aluminum Co Pottsville St Cressona PA 17929

DEEGAN, E. GREGORY, III, sales manager; b. Attlebor, Mass., Mar. 15, 1948; s. E. Gregory II and Gloria A. (Benoit) D.; m. Jeannine M. York, Oct. 12, 1985. BSChemE, So. Meth. U., 1971; student, AirForce Acad., Colorado Springs, 1965, U. Miami, Fla., 1966. CE, CPESC. Gen. mgr. Unicorn Golf & Recreation ARea, Stoneham, Mass., 1971-77, Aeronomics Arabia, Ltd., Jecblah, Saudi Arabia, 1978-80; project mgr. Saudi Agy. Svcs.

Corp., Dahahram, 1981-82; European sales mgr. Weathermatie/Telseo Industry, Dallas, 1982-85; nat. export sales mgr. N.Am. Green, Sandwich, Mass., 1985—. Editor: Fundamentals of Plant Propogation for Erosion Control North American Green, 1991; designer, builder grass golf course, 1978. Mem. Am. Soc. Agronomy, Am. Soc. Conservation, Internat., Erosion Control Assn. (state rep. 1987-91), Soil Conservation Svc. (chpt. rep. 1989-91), Golf Course Supt. Assn. Am. Roman Catholic. Home: 6 Heather Hill Rd Sandwich MA 02563 Office: Po Box 1900 Sandwich MA 02563

DEELEY, EDWARD JOSEPH, office products company executive; b. Frankfurt, Germany, Aug. 24, 1956; s. Walter Gerald and Patricia Ann (McCarthy) D. Grad. high sch., Balt. Warehouse mgr. Lucky Stores Inc., Buena Park, Calif., 1974-77; mgr. material control Morrison-Knudsen, Saudi Arabia, 1977-80; distbn. mgr. Lucky Stores Inc., 1980-83; shipping mgr. Sysco, Jessup, Md., 1983-86; distbn. mgr. Gestener Corp., Savage, Md., 1986—; cons. Indsl. Integration Svc., Bethesda, Md., 1988-91, Brian Packing Co., Hicsville, N.Y., 1989-91; pres. Paragon Cons. Svcs., Inc., 1991—, Personal Devel. Assocs., Inc., 1992—; cons. Univ. Press of Am., 1991—, Nat. Book Network, 1991—. Programmer/author: (software) The Parts Locator, 1989, The Shipping Manager, 1991. Mem. Nat. Safety Coun., Am. Mgmt. Assn., Coun. Logistics Mgrs., Warehouse Edn. and Rsch. Coun. Home: 3626 Benson Ave Baltimore MD 21227-1005 Office: Gestetner Corp 8705 Bollman Pl Savage MD 20763-9775

DEEN, HAROLD EUGENE, retired chemical company executive; b. Detroit, Aug. 7, 1926; s. William Everett and Iva Jewel (Ponder) D.; m. Ruth Edith Watson, Aug. 28, 1948; children: Paul David, Robert Everett, Keith Charles, Susan Kathleen. BS in Chem. Engring., Wayne State U., 1949; MS in Chem. Engring., Purdue U., 1951. Asst. foreman Rinshed Mason Co., Detroit, 1948-50; engr. Standard Oil Devel. Co., Linden, N.J., 1951-62; sect. head Exxon Chem. Co., Linden, 1963-68, sr. engring. assoc., 1969-74, chief scientist, 1974-86. Patentee in field. With U.S. Army, 1944-46. Mem. Soc. Automotive Engrs. (chmn. fuel and lubricant tech. com. 1981-86, cert. of appreciation 1987). Methodist. Home: 216 Oak Ln Cranford NJ 07016-2042

DEEPHOUSE, CHRISTOPHER VAUGHN, computer software executive; b. Norfolk, Va., Jan. 29, 1954; s. James Russell and Lucy Larcom (Dayton) D.; m. Betty Rosenmann Mock, Sept. 12, 1982; 1 child, Nancy. BS in Engring. cum laude, Princeton U., 1976; MS, MIT, 1978. Transp. specialist Gen. Foods Corp., White Plains, N.Y., 1978-82; founder, ptnr. Sundance Software, Inc., Armonk, N.Y., 1982-91; pres. Software Forte Inc., Pitts., 1991—; info. systems rschr. Carnegie Mellon U., 1992—; speaker, cons. in field. Co-author: Software Reuse in Japan, 1992. Mem. IEEE, Assn. for Computing Machinery, Ind. Computer Cons. Assn., Madison Beach Club.

DEER, JAMES WILLIS, lawyer; b. Reading, Pa., Mar. 14, 1917; s. Irvin E. and Rosemary (French) D.; m. Marion M. Hawkinson, July 31, 1943 (dec. 1987); 1 child, Ann Marie. AB, Oberlin Coll, 1938; JD, U. Mich., 1941. Bar: Ohio 1941, N.Y. 1948. Legal staff SEC, 1942-45; practice in N.Y.C., 1945—; mem. firm Holtzmann, Wise & Shepard, 1954-92; bd. dirs. Arts Way Mfg. Co., Inc., Selvac Corp., Techsci. Industries, Allegheny & Western Energy Corp., Syntech Internat. Inc. Mem. ABA, N.Y. State Bar Assn., Phi Beta Kappa, Phi Alpha Delta. Home: 611 Shore Acres Dr Mamaroneck NY 10543-4012 also: Barr Terr 50 East Dr Delray Beach FL 33483 Office: 90 Secor Ln Pelham NY 10803

DEFEO, WILLIAM THOMAS, JR., podiatrist; b. Phila., Jan. 21, 1927; s. William Thomas and Thelma (Baglivo) DeF.; m. Patricia M. DeFeo, Oct. 8, 1971; children: Nicole, Heather. BS, Temple U., 1972; DPM, Pa. Coll. Podiatric Medicine, 1976. Diplomate Am. Bd. Podiatric Surgery. Resident John F. Kennedy Meml. Hosp., Stratford, N.J., 1976-77; pvt. practice podiatry, 1977-92; pvt. practice Nazareth, Pa., 1990—; ptnr. pvt. practice podiatry office, Allentown, Pa., 1986—; adj. prof. clin. faculty Pa. Coll. Podiatric Medicine, Phila., 1982—; mem. staff Sacred Heart Hosp., Allentown, Pa., 1977—, Allentown Osteo. Med. Ctr., Allentown, 1977—, Muhlenberg Med. Ctr., Bethlehem, Pa., 1977—; chief dept. of podiatry Lehigh Valley Hosp. Ctr., Allentown, 1977-87; co-chmn. dept. podiatry Lehigh Valley Hosp. Ctr./Allentown Hosp., 1987—. Recipient Recognition award Am. Coll. Podiatric Radiologists, 1976. Fellow Am. Coll. Foot Orthopedists, Am. Coll. Foot Surgeons (Ea. div. award 1976); mem. Am. Podiatric Med. Assn., Pa. Podiatric Med. Assn. (past pres. Lehigh Valley div.). Home: 3093 Chestnut Hill Rd Center Valley PA 18034-9747 Office: 3131 College Heights Blvd Allentown PA 18104-4858

DEFILIPPO, KATHLEEN BYRNE, academic administrator; b. Port Chester, NY, Oct. 5, 1943; d. Lawrence Sylvester Jr. and Mary Josephine (Matthews) Byrne; m. James J. DeFilippo, July 16, 1966; children: Elizabeth Ann, Sharon Marie, Kristen Leigh. BA in English, Coll. Mt. St. Vincent, 1965; MS in Edn., SUNY, New Paltz, 1976. Tchr., television instr. Wappingers Cen. Sch. Dist., Wappingers Falls, N.Y., 1965-68; owner, mgr. Silver Apple, Inc., Hopewell Junction, N.Y., 1980-83; freelance communications cons., 1983-88; dir. corp. and profl. edn. Marist Coll., Poughkeepsie, N.Y., 1988—; cons. leadership tng. edn. com. So. Dutchess C. of C., Wappingers Falls, 1988—, Poughkeepsie C. of C., 1991—. Sunday sch. tchr. Hopewell Reform Ch., 1974-85, youth adviser, 1985-88. Mem. NAFE, N.Y. State Assn. Women in Higher Edn., Am. Coun. Edn., N.Y. Assn. Continuing Community Edn. Republican. Home: 5 Brusk Dr Hopewell Junction NY 12533-6226 Office: Marist Coll Dyson Ctr Poughkeepsie NY 12601

DEFLEUR, LOIS B., university president, sociology educator; b. Aurora, Ill., June 25, 1936; d. Ralph Edward and Isabel Anna (Cornils) Begitske; m. Melvin L. DeFleur (div.). AB, Blackburn Coll., 1958; MA, Ind. U., 1961; PhD in Sociology, U. Ill., 1965. Asst. prof. sociology Transylvania Coll., Lexington, Ky., 1963-67; assoc. prof. Wash. State U., Pullman, 1967-74, prof., 1975-86, dean Coll. Arts and Scis., 1981-86; provost U. Mo., Columbia, 1986-90; pres. SUNY, Binghamton, 1990—; disting. vis. prof. U.S. Air Force Acad., 1976-77; vis. prof. U. Chgo., 1980-81; mem. sociology grad. record com. Ednl. Testing Service, 1980-86. Author: Delinquency in Argentina, 1965; (with others) Sociology: Human Society, 3d edit. 1981, 4th edit., 1984, The Integration of Women into All Male Air Force Units, 1982, The Edward R. Murrow Heritage: A Challenge for the Future, 1986; contbr. articles to profl. jours. Mem. Wash. State Bd. on Correctional Standards and Edn., 1974-77, State of N.Y. Edn. Dept. Curriculum and Assessment Coun., 1991—; bd. curators Stephens Coll., 1987—. Recipient Disting. Alumni award Blackburn Coll., 1991; grantee NIMH, 1969-79, NSF, 1972-75, Air Force Office, 1978-81. Mem. Am. Sociol. Assn. (pubs. com. 1979-82, nominations com. 1984-86, coun. mem. 1987-90), Pacific Sociol. Assn. (pres. 1980-82), Law and Society Assn., Inter-Univ. Seminar on Armed Forces and Soc., Coun. Colls. of Arts and Scis. (bd. dirs. 1982-84, pres. 1985-87), Aircraft Owners and Pilots Assn., Internat. Comanche Soc., Nat. Assn. State U. and Land-grant Colls. (exec. com. 1990-93), Assn. of Colls. and U. of N.Y. (bd. trustees). Office: Binghamton U Office of Pres PO Box 6000 Binghamton NY 13902-6000 also: SUNY Binghamton Vestal Pkwy E Binghamton NY 13901

DEFOREST, WALTER PATTISON, III, lawyer; b. Ft. Sill, Okla., Dec. 4, 1944; s. Walter P. Jr. and Mary E. (Miller) DeF.; m. Anna Thun. BA, U. Pitts., 1966; JD, Harvard U., 1969. Bar: U.S. Ct. Appeals (2d and 3d cirs.) 1973, U.S. Supreme Ct. 1974, U.S. Ct. Appeals (4th, 5th and D.C. cirs.) 1978, U.S. Ct. Appeals (10th cir.) 1981, U.S. Ct. Appeals (11th cir.), U.S. Ct. Appeals (7th cir.) 1986. Assoc. Reed, Smith, Shaw & McClay, Pitts., 1969-77, ptnr., 1978—; instr. Grad. Sch. Indsl. Adminstrn. Carnegie Mellon U., Pitts., 1974-75. Mem. adv. com. Big. Bros. and Big Sisters Western Pa., Pitts., 1984-91; bd. dirs. Pa. Small Bus. Advocacy Coun., Harrisburg, 1984-89, 92. Mem. ABA (litigation, labor sects.), Pa. Bar Assn. (litigation, labor sects.), Allegheny County Bar Assn. (litigation sect., fed. ct. sect.). Office: Reed Smith Shaw & McClay James H Reed Bldg 435 6th Ave Pittsburgh PA 15219-1809

DE FRANCESCO, JOHN KENNETH, foreign languages educator; b. Phila., July 26, 1932; s. John and Anna (Giove) de F. BA, LaSalle Coll., 1955; AM, Middlebury Coll., 1956; postgrad., U. Rome, 1961, U. Florence, Italy, 1962, Rutgers U., 1962-63, U. Perugia, Italy, 1990. Tchr. Phila. Pub. Schs., 1955-56; grad. asst. U. Wis., Madison, 1957-58; dir. lang. lab LaSalle U., Phila., 1958-60, asst. prof., 1959-67; assoc. prof. Camden County Coll., Blackwood, N.J., 1967-69; prof. Camden County Coll., Blackwood, 1969—; lectr. Cabrini Coll., Radnor, Pa., 1965-68. Named Tchr. of Yr., Camden County Coll., 1987; recipient award for teaching excellence U. Tex., Austin, 1989; scholar Middlebury Coll., 1952, 53, 55, 56, U. Wis., 1957-58, Rutgers U., 1962-63; Fulbright grantee, Rome and Florence, 1961-62, Fulbright-Hays grantee, 1965; Govt. of Italy study grantee U. Perugia, 1990. Mem. MLA-PV (bd. dirs. Phila. sect. 1979-83, 90—), Am. Assn. Tchrs. Spanish and Portuguese (pres. 1979-83, spl. award 1983), Am. Assn. Tchrs. Italian (pres. 1990—), Camden Coll. Faculty Assn. (pres. 1969-71, commencement speaker 1991), Sons of Italy, Overbrook Farms Club, Overbrook Italian-Am. Club, Pi Delta Phi. Roman Catholic. Home: 6491 Sherwood Rd Philadelphia PA 19151-2416 Office: Camden County Coll PO Box 200 Blackwood NJ 08012-0200

DEFRANCIS, SUELLEN MARIA, interior architect; b. Bklyn., Sept. 21, 1946; d. Joseph Agustino and Mary DeF.; m. James D. Block, Apr. 23, 1965 (div. 1983); children: Melissa, Louis, Maximillian. BS, CCNY, 1982; BArch, CUNY, 1982, M. Urban Design, 1983. Designer, dir. interiors Peter Gisolfi Architects, Hastings-on-Hudson, N.Y., 1983-85; designer John Burgee Architects, N.Y.C., 1985-86; prin., owner Suellen DeFrancis Archtl. Interiors, Scarsdale, 1986—. Prin. works include features in Asset Housing mag., Mitsubishi Home mag., N.Y. Times, Ku-Kan mag., Housing mag.; pvt. residences designed and built in Tokyo and N.Y.C. Recipient Del Gaudio award N.Y. Soc. Architects, 1982; AIA scholar, 1982. Mem. AIA (assoc.), Am. Soc. Interior Designers, Internat. House of Japan, Far East Assn. Architects and Engrs., Ardsley Country Club, Nippon Club. Office: PO Box 247 Scarsdale NY 10583

DE FRONDEVILLE, BERTRAND LAMBERT, management and engineering consultant; b. Marseilles, France, Sept. 18, 1934; came to U.S., 1966; s. Maurice Lambert and Anne-Marie (D'Alauzier) DeF.; m. Barbara Janice Fuller, Feb. 20, 1960; children: Tristan, Eric, Alexis. B in Math., Sci., Lycee Chasseloup-Laubat, Saigon, Vietnam, 1950; MS, Ec Polytech., Paris, 1955; MS Naval Architecture, ENSGM, Paris, 1958; MS in Nuclear Engring., U. Calif., Berkeley, 1959; postgrad., U. Columbia, 1978. Sr. engr. French Naval Architect Corps, Indret, France, 1959-63; dir. Metall. Rsch. & Quality Assurance, Indret, 1963-65; pres. Am. Techigaz Inc., Boston, 1965-67; sr. staff mem. Arthur D. Little, Inc., Cambridge, Mass., 1967-72; v.p., projects and engring. Burmah Oil Tankers Ltd., N.Y.C., 1972-75; mng. dir. BDF Internat. Co., Rye, N.Y., 1975-92; v.p. global project fin. group Deutsche Bank A.G., N.Y.C., 1992—; sr. advisor BNP, San Paolo Bank, N.Y.C., and other banks, 1986-92; v.p. and sr. engr. Deutsche Bank, Frankfurt and N.Y.C.; adj. prof. internat. bus. Pace U., N.Y.C.; tchr. ethics seminars Grad. Bus. Sch., Columbia U., 1990—; planning cons. U.S. C.E., Ft. Belvoir, Va., 1970-80. Com. mem. NAS, Washington, 1976-78, 79-80, Citizen Adv. Com. to N.Y. State Senators, Rye and Westchester, N.Y., 1982—; founder, instr. Manchester (Mass.) Sailing Assn. and Sea Scout Ship, 1967-72. Comdr. French Naval Res., 1975—. Mem. N.Y. Acad. Sci., Pres.'s Assn. of Am., Soc. Naval Architects, French Am. C. of C., Am. Yacht Club. Home: 19 Hook Rd Rye NY 10580-3715 Office: Deutsche Bank 31 W 52d St New York NY 10019

DEGATANO, ANTHONY THOMAS, educational adminstrator; b. Elizabeth, N.J., Apr. 2, 1950; s. Anthony James and Leonora (Malta) D.; m. Jeanne Marie Stevens, Apr. 15, 1972; 1 child, David. BA, Rider Coll., 1971; MA, Kean Coll., 1975. Cert. tchr., supr., prin., chief sch. adminstr. Elem. tchr. Elizabeth Bd. Edn., 1971-77, adult edn. instr., 1972-74, cons., 1977-81; dir. Union County Edn. Svc. Commn., Westfield, N.J., 1981-86, Ind. Child Study Teams, Inc., Jersey City, 1986—; bd. dirs. Ednl. In-Roads, Jersey City, 1988—. Author: (curriculum guide) Alternate Math Program, 1980, (guide books) Teacher Handbook, 1982, Teacher Resource Book, 1983; editor: Mathematics Series, 1992. 1st pres., founder Union County Commn. Adminstrs. Assn., 1983-86; pres. Herbert Hoover PTO, 1991-92; chmn. edn.-budget subcom. Citizen Adv. Com., Edison, N.J., 1992; mem. N.J. Edn. Commr.'s Adv. Com., Trenton, 1988-92, PTA/PTO Adv. Coun., Edison, 1991-92. Named Outstanding Young Man of Am., U.S. Jaycees, 1983; recipient Recognition for Svc., N.J. Commr. of Edn., 1990, Union County Edn. Svc. Commn. Adminstrs. Assn., 1986. Mem. N.J. Assn. Fed. Program Adminstrs., ASCD. Home: 148 Howard Ave Edison NJ 08837 Office: ICST Inc 377 Danforth Ave Jersey City NJ 07305

DEGRAFF, DAVID CHARLES, mechanical engineer; b. Rochester, N.Y., Mar. 17, 1954; s. Gerald Stuart and Elizabeth T. (DiLiddo) D.; m. Margaret M. Degraff. Machine designer Davenport Machine Tool, Rochester, N.Y., 1973-75; tool designer Jasco Tools Inc., Rochester, N.Y., 1976-80, Morgood Tool Corp., Rochester, N.Y., 1981-84; sr. engr. Jasco Precision Co., Rochester, N.Y., 1985—. Founder Med/Event Inc., Rochester, 1974; bd. dirs. N.Y. State Emergency Health Svcs. Coun., 1982-85, Empire Nine Regional Health Svcs., Upstate N.Y., 1980-85, Chili (N.Y.) Pub. Library, 1973-75, Nat. Kidney Found. of Upstate N.Y., 1989. Recipient Cert. of Merit Kodak Internat. Photo Competition, 1982; Community Svc. awad Empire Nine, Upstate N.YH., 1983, 84; Vol. Excellence award Nat. Kidney Found. Upstate N.Y., 1989, 92. Home: 4 Camden Ct Fairport NY 14450-9603 Office: Jasco Precision PO Box 60497 Rochester NY 14606-0497

DEGRANDE, GARY CHRISTOPHER, physician; b. West Long Branch, N.J., Aug. 14, 1949; s. Natale and Diana (Fingo) DeG.; m. Elaine Frances Smorra, Aug. 21, 1971; children: Laura, Michael. BS, Monmouth Coll., 1971; MD, U. Guadalajara, 1977. Diplomate Am. Bd. Obstetrics and Gynecology. Intern, resident SUNY, Syracuse, 1979-83; pvt. practice Montclair, N.J., 1983—; assoc. dir. dept. ob-gyn. Mountainside Hosp., Montclair, 1991—. Fellow Am. Coll. Obstetrics and Gynecology; mem. AMA. Office: 33 N Fullerton Ave Montclair NJ 07042

DE GRAZIA, SEBASTIAN, political philosopher, author; b. Chgo., Aug. 11, 1917; s. Alfred Joseph and Catherine Cardinale Lupo de G.; m. Miriam Lund Carlson; children: Alfred Joseph III, Margreta, Sebastian; m. Anna Maria d'Annunzio di Montenevoso; children: Marco, Tancredi; m. Lucia Heffelfinger. AB, U. Chgo., 1939, PhD, 1947. With FCC, 1941-43, OSS, 1943-45; mem. faculty U. Chgo., 1945-50; cons. bus. firms, state and U.S. Govt., 1947—; dir. research study time, work and leisure Twentieth Century Fund, 1957-61; prof. polit. philosophy Rutgers U., 1962-88; vis. prof. U. Florence, Italy, 1950-52, Princeton U., 1957, 91-92, U. Madrid, 1963, John Jay Coll. Criminal Justice, 1967-71, Inst. Advanced Study Princeton, 1983. Author: The Political Community, 1948, Errors of Psychotherapy, 1953, Of Time, Work and Leisure, 1962, Masters of Chinese Political Thought, 1973, Machiavelli in Hell, 1989 (Pulitzer Prize for Biography 1990). Grantee Am. Philos. Soc., Social Sci. Research Council, Am. Council Learned Socs.; Fulbright prof. Mem. Am. Polit. Sci. Assn., Am. Soc. Polit. and Legal Philosophy, Institut Internat. de Philosophie Politique. Clubs: Cosmos (Washington); Nassau, Prettybrook (Princeton); Century (N.Y.C.). Home: 914 The Great Rd Princeton NJ 08540 Office: Princeton U Robertson Hall Princeton NJ 08544-1013

DEGROAT, WILLIAM CHESNEY, pharmacology educator; b. Trenton, N.J., May 18, 1938; s. William Chesney and Margaret (Welch) deG.; m. Dorothy Marion Albertson, June 13, 1959; children: Allyson L., Cynthia L., Jennifer L. BSc, Phila. Coll. Pharmacy and Sci., 1960, MSc, 1962; Ph.D., U. Pa., 1965, postdoctoral, 1965-66; postdoctoral, Australian Nat. U., Canberra, 1966-67. Vis. research fellow John Curtin Sch. Med. Research, Canberra, 1967-68; asst. prof. U. Pitts. Med. Sch., 1968-72, assoc. prof., 1972-77, prof. pharmacology, 1977—, acting chmn. dept. pharmacology, 1978-80, adj. prof. pharmacy, 1978-88, prof. psychology, 1982-86, mem. ctr. of neurosci., 1984—, prof. in dept. of behavioral neurosci., 1986—; mem. neurobiology study sect. NIH, 1983-88; vis. scientist NIAAA-NIH, 1989-90. Mem. editorial bd. Jour. Pharmacology and Exptl. Therapeutics, 1975—, Jour. Autonomic Nervous System, 1979—, assoc. editor, 1985—, Neurology and Urodynamics, 1982—, Am. Jour. Physiology, 1983—; editorial cons. profl. jours.; contbr. articles to profl. jours., chpts. in books. NSF predoctoral fellow, 1962-63; pharmacology fellow Riker Pharm. Co., 1966-67; NSF postdoctoral fellow, 1966-67; recipient research Career Devel. award NIH, 1972-77. Mem. AAAS, N.Y. Acad. Scis., Am. Soc. Pharmacology and Exptl. Therapeutics, Soc. for Neurosci., Internat. Brain Rsch. Orgn., Am. Gastroent. Assn., Urodynamics Soc., Internat. Med. Soc. of Paraplegia, Soc. for Basic Urologic Rsch., Sigma Xi, Rho Chi. Republican. Methodist. Home: 6357 Burchfield Ave Pittsburgh PA 15217-2732 Office: U Pitts Med Sch W-1352 Biomed Sci Tower Terrace St Pittsburgh PA 15261-0001

DEGROFF, RALPH LYNN, JR., investment banker; b. Balt., Oct. 23, 1936; s. Ralph Lynn and Marion (Day) D.; m. Marion Parsons Sinwell, Feb. 4, 1989. AB, Princeton U., 1958; MBA, U. Va., 1960. With Dillon, Read & Co. Inc., N.Y.C., 1961-81, v.p., 1970-74, sr. v.p., 1974-81; mng. dir. Donaldson, Lufkin & Jenrette, 1981—; past bd. dir. The Ryland Group, Inc.; trustee Holland Soc. N.Y. With U.S. Army, 1960-61. Mem. Soc. of the Cin. Colonial Wars, Downtown Assn., Md. Club, Rockaway Hunting Club, Elkridge Club. Presbyterian. Home: 7 Gracie Sq New York NY 10028-8030 Office: Donaldson Lufkin & Jenrette Securities Corp 140 Broadway Fl 49 New York NY 10005-1101

DEGROSS, PIERCE EDWARD, III, real estate executive; b. Yonkers, N.Y., Sept. 1, 1964; s. Pierce Edward DeGross and Eleanor Jean Richter Netelle; m. Jennifer Elaine Stoll, Sept. 22, 1990. BS, Providence Coll., 1986. Data bank researcher Coldwell Banker Comml., Washington, 1986, available properties coord., 1986-87; asst. property mgr. Coldwell Banker Real Estate Mgmt. Svcs., Washington, 1987-88; real estate mgr. for comml. properties The Holladay Corp., Washington, 1988—. Mem. Internat. Coun. of Shopping Ctrs., Washington Golf and Country Club, Cosmopolitan Club Washington, D.C. Roman Catholic. Home: 814 N Woodrow St Arlington VA 22203

DEHART, RONALD DAVID, musician; b. Chelsea, Mass., Oct. 30, 1948; s. Raymond Curtis and Gertrude Mildred (Crossley) DeH.; m. (div. Oct. 1987); m. Elaine Ann Reardon, Feb. 10, 1988; 1 child, Jenny Martinez. BA in Alternative Edn. cum laude, U. Mass., 1976. Cert. secondary educator, Mass. English instr. Cape Cod Regional Tech. High Sch., Harwich, Mass., 1976-82; owner, craftperson Quandockamon, Brewster, Mass., 1982-86; disabled transp. staff U. Mass., Amherst, 1986—; sound engr. On-Line Prodns./Bella Records, Warwick, 1990—; meditation instr. Touchstone, Hyannis, Mass., 1985-86. Albums include Dharma Boogie, 1991 (Best Local Release of Yr. 1991), Live Dirty Die Clean, 1992 (Best Local Release of Yr. 1992), Hilltown Country, 1992; copywrites in field. Tchr. Dharma Seed Tape Libr., Northfield, Mass., 1991—; Long Term Yogi Insight Meditation Soc., Barre, Mass., 1990, Buddhist monk, 1984-85. Mem. Assn. State, County and Mcpl. Employees (columnist, writer AFL-CIO newsletter 1989-91), Broadcast Music, Inc. Buddhist. Home: 25 Quarry Rd Warwick MA 01364 Office: On-Line Productions Spooner Rd Warwick MA 01364

DEHN, JAMES THEODORE, physicist; b. N.Y.C., Oct. 24, 1930; s. Joseph William and Anne (McMahon) D.; m. Rosemary Guenot, June 1, 1968; children: Danielle, James, Annmarie. PhL, Bellarmine Coll., 1957; PhD, Georgetown U., 1963; ThL, Woodstock Coll., 1965; MBA, George Washington U., 1970. Mem. faculty St. Peter's Coll., Jersey City, 1965-66, Pa. State U., University Park, 1966-68; physicist Ballistic Rsch. Lab., Aberdeen, Md., 1968—. Home: 1224 Grafton Shop Rd Bel Air MD 21014-2423 Office: Ballistic Rsch Lab Aberdeen Proving Ground Aberdeen MD 21005

DEHOVITZ, JACK ALAN, physician, educator, health facility administrator; b. Oceanside, Calif., Aug. 12, 1952; s. Bernard and Ruth (Senturia) DeH. BS, U. Calif., Davis, 1974; MPH, U. Tex., Houston, 1975; MD, U. Tex., Galveston, 1980. Diplomate Am. Bd. Internal Medicine, Am. Bd. Preventive Medicine, Am. Bd. Infectious Disease. Intern medicine St. Vincent's Hosp. and Med. Ctr., N.Y.C., 1980-81; asst. resident medicine N.Y. Hosp.-Cornell Med. Ctr., N.Y.C., 1981-82; Strang fellow in pub. health Cornell U. Med. Coll., N.Y.C., 1983-85; fellow in internat. medicine, infectious diseases N.Y. Hosp., N.Y.C., 1983-85; asst. med. dir. Spellman Ctr. of HIV Disease, N.Y.C., 1985-88; asst. prof. Cornell U. Med. Coll., N.Y.C., 1985—; asst. prof. SUNY, Bklyn., 1985-91, assoc. prof., 1991—, dir. AIDS Prevention Ctr., 1988—; cons. infectious diseases N.Y. State Dept. Health, Albany, 1989-91; cons. Czech Min. Health, Prague, 1990—. Editor AIDS Manual, 1988; contbr. articles to profl. jours. Mem. organizing com. Czech-Am. Med. Com., Prague, 1990. Fellow ACP, N.Y. Acad. Medicine; mem. Infectious Diseases Soc. Am., Am. Pub. Health Assn., N.Y. Soc. Tropical Medicine, Internat. AIDS Soc. Jewish. Office: SUNY Health Sci Ctr Bklyn 450 Clarkson Ave # 43 Brooklyn NY 11203-2098

DEIBLER, WILLIAM EDWIN, newspaper editor; b. Altoona, Pa., Apr. 18, 1932; s. Edwin Howard and Elizabeth Grace (Sheehan) D.; m. Phyllis Maxine Gates, Jan. 17, 1953; children—Gail Marie, William Eric. B.A. in Journalism, Pa. State U., 1959. Staff writer Centre Daily Times, State College, Pa., 1958-60; editor Daily Messenger, Homestead, Pa., 1960-63; writer AP, 1964-68; legis. corr., then city editor Pitts. Post-Gazette, 1968-74, mng. editor, 1979—. Served with USAF, 1952-56, Korea. Decorated Commendation medal; recipient award disting. reporting public affairs Am. Polit. Sci. Assn., 1971, award for cultural affairs writing Golden Quill, 1983, award for news feature writing Keystone Press, 1983. Mem. Internat. Press Inst., Am. Press Inst., AP Mng. Editors Assn., Pa. Soc. Newspaper Editors Assn., Hemingway Soc., Soc. Profl. Journalists, Kappa Tau Alpha. Home: 1233 Satellite Cir Pittsburgh PA 15241-3620 Office: 50 Blvd Allies Pittsburgh PA 15222

DEILY, ANN BETH, special education educator; b. Albany, N.Y., Oct. 16, 1948; d. Ezra Jack and Sonya June (Balshan) Sarachan; m. William Edward Deily, Aug. 13, 1972. BA, U. Rochester, 1970; MA, Vanderbilt U., 1971, MS, 1972; PhD, SUNY, Albany, 1977. Speech-lang. therapist Children's Rehab. Ctr., Kingston, N.Y., 1972-73; pvt. practice Chatham, N.Y., 1973-79; teaching fellow SUNY, Albany, 1974-75; dir. dept./developer Speech Hearing Dept. St. Mary's Hosp., Troy, 1974-77; instr. communication disorders Coll. St. Rose, Albany, 1977-78, asst. prof. communication disorders, 1978-82, assoc. prof., 1982-87, prof., 1987-91; dir. rural edn. grant Coll. St. Rose, Albany, 1983-86; cons. State of N.Y. Dept. Edn., State of Conn. Dept. Edn., Wildwood Sch., Schenectady, N.Y., BOCES, East Greenbush, Albany, Columbia County Spl. Needs Group, d/b/a Deily Cons. Assocs., 1991—. Author: Working with Communication Disorders in Rural Settings, 1987; contbr. 15 articles to profl. jours. Founder Capital Area Network for Rural Speech-Lang. Pathologists, 1985; co-founder Capital Dist. Computer Users Group in Speech-Lang. Pathology, 1989, Columbia-Greene Rape Crisis Ctr. (edn. and tng. com., coord. com. 1981). Mem. Am. Speech-Lang.-Hearing Assn. (nat. site visitor, nat. computer tutor, nat. faculty-teleconf., Am. Coun. Rural Spl. Edn. (editorial rev. bd.), AG Bell Assn. for Deaf (editorial rev. bd.), Computer Users in Speech Hearing (pres.), Coun. Exceptional Children. Home: RD 3 Box 360 Merwin Rd Valatie NY 12184

DEITCH, IRA, civil engineer; b. Bronx, Jan. 24, 1942; s. Paul and Mae Deitch; m. Nancy Barbara Budde, Apr. 30, 1977; 1 child, Dara Paige. Student, Bklyn. Coll., 1959-61; B of Civil Engring., CCNY, 1964. Resident engr. N.Y. State Dept. Transp., N.Y.C., 1964-77, constrn. supr., 1977-81, Westway constrn. supr., 1981-85, structures supr., 1985-90; dir. structures N.Y. State Dept. Transp., N.Y.C. area, 1990—. Named Bridge Man of Yr. Assn. Bridge Constrn. and Design, N.Y., 1989. Home: 4108 Ocean Ave Brooklyn NY 11235 Office: NY State Dept Transp 47-40 21st St New York NY 11001

DEITCH, JAMES MICHAEL, banker, accountant; b. Hazleton, Pa., Feb. 2, 1954; s. James Aaron and Nancy Mae (Saylor) D.; m. Judith Ann Klucher, Aug. 25, 1977; children: Christina, Michael. BS with high honors, Lehigh U., 1976, MBA with high honors, 1978. CPA, Pa. Auditor Arthur Andersen & Co., Phila., 1976-77; corp. planner J.E. Baker Co., York, Pa., 1977-81; acctg. mgr. Air Products & Chems., Allentown, Pa., 1981-83; v.p, contr. Internat. Signal & Control Group, Lancaster, Pa., 1983-88; pres., chief exec. officer Parent Fed. Savs. Bank, Lancaster, 1988—; bd. dirs. 1st Capital Mgmt. Ltd., York. Bd. dirs. York County Literacy Coun., York, 1981-89, Jr. Achievement Lancaster, 1988—; mem. bd. advisors Millersville U., Lancaster, 1986—. William T. Morris Found. scholar, 1972. Mem. Fin. Execs. Inst., AICPA, Pa. Inst. CPA's, Mortgage Bankers Assn. (bd. dirs., secondary market com. 1988—). Republican. Roman Catholic. Home: 3405 Pebble Ridge Dr York PA 17402-4349 Office: Parent Fed Savs Bank 801 Estelle Dr Lancaster PA 17604

DEITCH, STEPHEN HOWARD, hazardous waste disposal company executive; b. N.Y.C., Aug. 20, 1945; s. Meyer and Rachel (Slopak) D.; m. Jacqueline S. Queller, June 10, 1967 (div. July 1988); children: Jonathan David, Rachel Mara, Shana Rebecca; m. Elizabeth Ann Boman, May 26, 1989; stepchildren: Mark Alan, David James. B Chem. Engring., CUNY, 1967; postgrad., Drexel U., 1969-72, Corpus Christi State U., 1977-78. Chem. engr. dyes and chems. DuPont Co., Deepwater, N.Y., 1967-72; sales rep. petroleum chems. DuPont Co., St. Louis, 1972-73; account mgr. DuPont Co., Pitts., 1973-75; process engr. DuPont Co., Corpus Christi, Tex., 1975-78; sales mgr. Browning Ferris Industries, Houston, 1978-80; field svcs. mgr. Rollins Environ. Svcs., Bridgeport, N.J., 1980-83; dir. mktg. Rollins Field Svcs., Wilmington, Del., 1983-84; nat. dir. Rollins Chempack, Wilmington, 1985—. Mem. Am. Inst. Chem. Engrs. Office: Rollins Chempak Inc PO Box 2349 Wilmington DE 19899-2349

DEITERS, SISTER JOAN ADELE, nun, chemistry educator; b. Cin., Apr. 28, 1934; d. Alfred Harry and Rose Catherine (Rusche) D. B.A., Coll. Mt. St. Joseph, Cin., 1963; M. Christian Spirituality, Creighton U., Omaha, 1985; Ph.D., U. Cin., 1967. Joined Sisters of Charity, Roman Cath. Ch., 1952; prof. chemistry Coll. Mt. St. Joseph, Cin., 1968-78; prof. chemistry, Vassar Coll., Poughkeepsie, N.Y., 1978—. Contbr. articles to profl. jours. Mem. Am. Chem. Soc., Sisters of Charity, Sigma Xi. Democrat. Home and Office: Vassar Coll Dept Chemistry PO Box 143 Poughkeepsie NY 12602-0143

DEITRICK, GEORGE ALBERT, III, biopharmaceutical executive; b. Ashland, Pa., Apr. 17, 1946; s. George Albert and Sabina Mary (Cortellini) D.; m. Tara Lynne Gleason, Nov. 28, 1981; 1 child, Taryn Christine. Student, U. Pa., 1964-66; AB, Gettysburg Coll., 1970; MD, Temple U., 1976. Cert. Am. Bd. Surgery, Nat. Bd. Med. Examiners. Various positions in industry, 1964-76; intern The Pa. Hosp., Phila., 1976-77, resident in surgery, 1977-81; gen. surgeon, asst. clin. prof. surgery U. Pa. Sch. Medicine, Phila., 1981-91; v.p. med. affairs Curative Technologies Inc., East Setauket, N.Y., 1991—; cons. W.L. Gore and Assocs., Flagstaff, Ariz., 1983-91. Mem. Union League of Phila., 1985—. Fellow ACS, Am. Coll. Physician Execs.; mem. Sigma Alpha Epsilon. Office: Curative Technologies 14 Research Way Box 9052 East Setauket NY 11733-9052

DEJONG, DAVID NEIL, economist, educator; b. Madison, Wis., June 4, 1963; s. Peter J. and Marcia A. (Baldwin) D.; m. Denise M. Delzell, Dec. 27, 1986; 1 child, Andrew D. BA, Cen. Coll., Pella, Iowa, 1985; PhD, U. Iowa, 1989. Asst. prof. econs. U. Pitts., 1989—. Contbr. articles to profl. jours. NSF grantee, 1990-91. Home: 4144 Saline St Pittsburgh PA 15217-2716 Office: U Pitts Dept Econs Pittsburgh PA 15260

DE JONG, DAVID SAMUEL, lawyer, educator; b. Washington, Jan. 8, 1951; s. Samuel and Dorothy (Thomas) De J. BA, U. Md., 1972; JD, Washington and Lee U., 1975; LLM in Taxation, Georgetown U., 1979. Bar: Md. 1975, U.S. Dist. Ct. Md. 1977, U.S. Tax Ct. 1977, U.S. Ct. Appeals (4th cir.) 1978, U.S. Supreme Ct. 1979, D.C. 1980, U.S. Dist. Ct. D.C. 1983, U.S. Ct. Claims, U.S. Ct. Appeals (fed. cir.) 1983; CPA, Md. Atty. Gen. Bus. Services Inc., Rockville, Md., 1975-80; ptnr. Stein, Sperling, Bennett, De Jong, Driscoll, Greenfeig & Metro P.A., Rockville, 1980—; adj. prof. Southeastern U., Washington, 1979-85, Am. U., Washington, 1983—; instr. U. Md., College Park, 1986-87, Montgomery Coll., Rockville, 1983. Co-author: (annual book) J.K. Lasser's Year-Round Tax Strategies, 1989-93; editor of Notes and Comments, Washington and Lee U. Law Rev., 1974-75. V.p. Seneca Whetstone Homeowners Assn., Gaithersburg, Md., 1981-82, pres. 1982-83. Mem. ABA, AICPA, Md. Bar Assn., Montgomery County Bar Assn. (chmn. tax sect. 1991-92), D.C. Bar Assn., Md. Assn. CPAs, D.C. Inst. CPAs, Am. Assn. Atty.-CPAs, Phi Alpha Delta. Office: Driscoll Greenfeig Metro et al 25 W Middle Ln Rockville MD 20850-2204

DEJONG, GERBEN, hospital research executive; b. Emmeloord, The Netherlands, June 19, 1946; s. Sidney and Jacoba (Oomkes) DeJ.; m. Janice May DeHaan, Apr. 24, 1971. BA in Econs., Calvin Coll., 1968; MPA, U. Mich., 1970, MA in Econs. and Policy, 1972; PhD in Pub. Policy, Brandeis U., 1980. Policy analyst Office of the Gov., Lansing, Mich., 1969-71; dir. program evaluation div. Mich. Dept. Social Svcs., Lansing, 1972-75; project dir. Levinson Policy Inst. Brandeis U., Waltham, Mass., 1976-77; rsch. assoc. Sch. Medicine Tufts U., Boston, 1978-80, dir. rsch. dept. phys. medicine, 1979-80, sr. rsch. assoc. Sch. Medicine, 1980-85; dir. rsch. Nat. Rehab. Hosp., Washington, 1985—; prof. community and family medicine Georgetown U., Washington, 1987—; cons. various pvt. and pub. orgns.; mem. study group on ethical issues in rehab. medicine Hastings Ctr., 1985-87; mem. com. for nat. agenda for prevention of disabilities Inst. Medicine, Washington, 1989-91. Mem. editorial bd. Archives of Physical Medicine and Rehabilitation, 1985-86, Jour. Neurologic Rehab., 1988-89, Jour. of Disability Policy, 1989—; contbr. articles to profl. jours. Mem. Interagy. Coun. on Ind. Living, Boston, 1978-80; bd. dirs. Boston Self-Help Ctr., Brookline, Mass., 1981-83. Fulbright scholar, 1984; recipient Licht award Am. Congress Rehab. Medicine, 1985; U. Mich. fellow, Brandeis U. fellow. Mem. Am. Congress Rehab. Medicine (com. chair 1978—), Am. Pub. Health Assn. (program chair 1988-89), Assn. for Health Svcs. Rsch., Soc. for Disability Studies. Home: 5301 Westpath Way Bethesda MD 20816-2212 Office: Nat Rehab Hosp 102 Irving St NW Washington DC 20010-2921

DEKOSKY, STEVEN TRENT, neurologist; b. Camden, N.J., Mar. 23, 1947; s. Aaron and Evelyn (Gorlen) DeK.; m. Sheila, June 20, 1971; children: Allison. Lauren. AB in Psychology, Bucknell U., 1968; MD, U. Fla., 1974. Post-doctoral fellow, instr. neurology U. Va. Sch. Medicine, Charlottesville, 1978-79; asst. prof. neurology, anatomy U. Ky. Coll. Medicine, Lexington, 1979-85; grad. faculty U. Ky. Grad. Sch., Lexington, 1981-90; assoc. prof. anatomy and neurology U. Ky. Coll. Medicine, Lexington, 1985-90, interim chmn. dept. neurology, 1985-87; prof. psychiatry U. Pitts. Sch. Medicine, 1990—, prof. neurology, neurobiology, anatomy, cell sci., 1990—, grad. faculty, 1991—; vis. prof. psychobiology U. Calif., Irvine, 1983; co-dir. Alzheimer's disease rsch. ctr. U. Pitts. Med. Ctr., 1990—, U. Ky. Med. Ctr., 1985-90; task force on Alzheimer's disease State of Ohio, Columbus, 1986—; dir. behavioral neurology of aging tng. program U. Pitts., 1990—. Mem. Am. Neurol. Assn. (Presdl. award 1988), Am. Acad. Neurology, Am. Soc. Neurochemistry, Am. Heart Assn. (stroke coun.), N.Y. Acad. Scis., Soc. Neurosci., Soc. Experimental Neuropathology (councillor 1990—), Behavioral Neurology Soc. Office: U Pitts 3600 Forbes Ave Ste 400 Pittsburgh PA 15213

DE LA BANDERA, ELNA MARIE, interpreter, translator; b. Rahway, N.J., Apr. 30, 1936; d. Laertes Gardner and Clara (Hansen) Fortenbaugh; m. Jorge Luis de la Bandera, Dec. 13, 1963; children: Jorge Luis Jr., Cristina Renee. BA in Spanish with honors, Colby Coll., 1958; MA in Spanish translation, Rutgers U., 1991. Cert. Spanish interpreter U.S. Cts., 1987; accredited translator Am. Translators Assn. Spanish-English, 1987, English-Spanish, 1988. Sec., translator U.S. Fgn. Svc., Argentina, Uruguay, 1959-63; translator Inter-Am. Coun. Commerce and Prodn., Montevideo, Uruguay, 1966-67; freelance interpreter, translator U.S. and Peru, 1968-86; sr. editor Princeton (N.J.) Internat. Translations, 1980-83; sec. Wysoker, Glassner & Weingartner, New Brunswick, N.J., 1984-86; translator, interpreter, test adminstr. N.J. Judiciary, Trenton, 1986—; temporary faculty Rutgers U., New Brunswick, 1986, 91; cons., coord. interpreting svcs. State of Mass., 1988; cons. on ct. interpreter cert. State of Wash., 1990; oral examiner Fed. Ct. Interpreter Cert. Project, 1989. Mem. Nat. Assn. Judiciary Interpreters and Translators, Am. Translators Assn., Phi Sigma Iota, Alpha Delta Pi. Republican. Presbyterian. Home: 103 Fairway Blvd Jamesburg NJ 08831-2712 Office: Adminstrv Office of Cts CN 988 Trenton NJ 08625

DE LA GUERONNIERE, RAPHAEL, securities firm executive. Chmn., CEO Discount Corp., N.Y.C. Office: Discount Corp NY 58 Pine St New York NY 10005-1519*

DE LA HABA, GABRIEL LUIS, biochemistry educator, researcher; b. Santurce, P.R., June 29, 1926; s. Gabriel and Teresa (Melia) de la H.; m. Dorothy Anne Kunz, Feb. 12, 1988. AB, Johns Hopkins U., 1946, PhD, 1950. Instr. biochemistry Yale U. Sch. Medicine, New Haven, Conn., 1953-54, asst. prof., 1954-55; sr. asst. scientist USPHS, NIMH, Bethesda, Md., 1955-58; rsch. assoc. Johns Hopkins U., Balt., 1958-59; assoc. in anatomy U. Pa., Phila., 1959—, asst. prof., 1961-68, assoc. prof., 1968—. Mem. Am. Soc. Biochemistry and Molecular Biology. Home: 2400 Beaver Rd Birchrunville PA 19421 Office: U Pa Philadelphia PA 19104-6058

DELAHUNTY, JOSEPH LAWRENCE, state senator, business investor; b. Portland, Maine, June 5, 1935; s. Joseph Edward and Jane (Faulkner) D.; m. Gail Ruth Ruppert, Sept. 2, 1961; children: Deborah Baker, Joseph Jr., Devin, Brian, William. Student, Bryant Coll., 1955-57. Store mgr. W.T. Grant Co., Wethersfield, Conn., 1957-75; dist. mgr. W.T. Grant Co., N.H., Vt., Mass.; regional mgr. W.T. Grant Co., N.E. U.S.; owner, pres. Windham Nurseries & Florist Inc., 1975-83; pres. Car-Del Property Mgmt. Co., 1983—; owner, pres. Fireside Inn motel, Salem, N.H., 1985-87, Delahuntys Auto-Wash, Salem, 1988—; mem. N.H. State Senate, Concord, 1986—; senate majority leader N.H. State Senate. Mem. Salem Bd. Selectmen. Served with U.S. Army, 1958-60. Republican. Roman Catholic. Home: 108 Hooker Farm Rd Salem NH 03079-1814 Office: N H State Senate State Capitol Concord NH 03301

DELAIN, NANCY BAUM, medical and technical documentation specialist; b. Norfolk, Va., June 23, 1956; d. Parker Bryant and Jane Ginn (Bailey) Baum; m. Gary E. Delain, June 9, 1990; 1 child, Teresa L. AB, Smith Coll., 1978; MS, Rensselaer Polytech. Inst., 1981. Tech. editor RCA, Princeton, N.J., 1981-82; assoc. editor Springer-Verlag N.Y. Inc., N.Y.C., 1982-84; cons., owner Stylus Sci. and Tech. Communications Cons., Inc., Ballston Spa, N.Y., 1984-89; sr. instr. Benchmark/Newkirk Products Inc., Albany, N.Y., 1989-90; owner Delain Assocs., Schenectady, N.Y., 1990—. Contbr. articles to profl. jours. Instr. Literacy Vols. of Am., Albany, 1988-89, Schenectady, 1989-90, 92—. Mem. Soc. for Tech. Communication (sr.). Home and Office: 505 Bedford Rd Schenectady NY 12308

DELAMATER, JEROME HERBERT, film studies educator; b. Camden, N.J., Aug. 2, 1943; s. Clayton and Eleanor (Richie) D. BA, Rutgers U., 1964; MA, Northwestern U., 1971, PhD, 1978. Tchr. Moorestown (N.J.) Friends Sch., 1964-70; instr. Wright State U., Dayton, Ohio, 1974-78; prof. Hofstra U., Hempstead, N.Y., 1978—; commentator Montage/Weekend Cinema, Woodbury, N.Y., 1979-81. Author: Dance in the Hollywood Musical, 1981. Office: Hofstra Univ Hempstead NY 11550

DELANEY, EDWARD NORMAN, lawyer; b. Chgo., Sept. 16, 1927; s. Frederick E. and Wynifred (Ward) D.; m. Carole P. Walter, May 31, 1950; children: Deborah Delaney Rogers, Kathleen Delaney Langan, Edward Norman II, Dorian A. LLB, Loyola U., Chgo., 1951; LLM, NYU, 1959. Bar: Ill. 1952, Minn. 1961, U.S. Supreme Ct. 1963, Mo. 1974, D.C. 1975. Staff Office Chief Counsel IRS, N.Y.C., 1955-60; atty. Investors Diversified Svcs., Inc., Mpls., 1960-73, v.p., gen. counsel investment adv. group, 1968-73; sr. v.p., gen. counsel Waddell & Reed and United Investors Life Ins. Co., Kansas City, Mo., 1974; ptnr. firm Bogan & Freeland, Washington, 1975-81; prin. Edward N. Delaney & Assocs., Washington, 1981—; chmn. tax com. Investment Co. Inst., 1963-74; mem. bus. adv. com. SEC Inter-Agy. Task Force Offshore Funds, 1970-71. Active fundraiser Ctr. for Performing Arts, Kansas City, Mo., 1974; bd. dirs., chmn. lawyers com., mem. exec. com. Washington Performing Arts Soc.; mem. exec. com. Ambs. Ball, Washington chpt. Nat. Multiple Sclerosis Soc.; bd. dirs., pres. Civic Orch., Mpls., 1963-68. Fellow Am. Bar Found.; mem. ABA (coun. tax sect. 1974-77, vice chmn. 1978-81, chmn. 1983-84), Fed. Bar Assn., Minn. Bar Assn., Hennipin County Bar Assn., Mo. Bar Assn., D.C. Bar Assn., Am. Law Inst., Am. Coll. Tax Counsel, Capitol Hill Club, Cong. Country Club, Univ. Club, Georgetown Club. Home: 9405 Tobin Cir Rockville MD 20854-4543 Office: 1629 K St NW Washington DC 20006-1602

DELANEY, HAROLD, association executive; b. Phila., Aug. 24, 1919; s. William Y. and Henrietta Pinkney Delaney; B.S., Howard U., 1941, M.S., 1943, Ph.D. in Chemistry, 1958, LHD (hon.), Towson State U., 1987, Frostburg State U., 1991; m. Geraldine East, Sept. 9, 1946; children—Milton Y., Doyle O. Chemist, Manhattan Project, U. Chgo., 1943-45; instr. chemistry Morgan State Coll., Balt., 1948-69, dean, 1967-69; vice chancellor, asso. provost central adminstrn. SUNY, Albany, 1969-72; v.p. gen. adminstrn. U. N.C., Chapel Hill, 1972-74; pres. Manhattanville Coll., Purchase, N.Y., 1974; assoc. dir. Nat. Inst. Edn., Washington, 1976-77; exec. v.p. Am. Assn. State Colls. and Univs., Washington, 1977-86, exec. v.p. emeritus 1986; spl. asst. to chancellor U. Md. System, 1988-89; acting pres. Chgo. State U., 1989-90; interim pres. Frostburg State U., 1991; instr. Chemistry N.C. Agrl. and Tech. U., 1945-48. Recipient Disting. Am. award Am. Found. Negro Affairs, 1976. Fellow Am. Inst. Chemists; mem. Am. Chem. Soc., Am. Assn. Higher Edn., Phi Beta Sigma. Office: 1 DuPont Cir Washington DC 20036

DELANEY, NANCY JO, statistician, consultant; b. Buffalo, N.Y., Sept. 15, 1941; d. Howard Joseph and Josephine Laura (Garguiolo) Klein; m. Thomas James Delaney; 1 child, Kathleen Grace Delaney. BS in Math., SUNY, 1962, MS in Math., 1963; MS in Stats., Rensselaer Poly. Inst., 1975, PhD in Stats., 1979. Math. tchr. various high schs. and jr. coll., Albany, Schenectady, N.Y., 1966-74; data analyst Space Astronomy Lab., Albany, 1974-76; asst. prof. Union Coll. Inst. Adminstrn. and Mgmt., Schenectady, 1978-82, Northeastern U. Coll. Bus., Boston, 1982-88; statis. advisor Mobil Solar Energy Corp., Billerica, Mass., 1988—; cons. Gen. Foods, Inc., Tarrytown, N.Y., 1978, Sterling Drugs, Albany, 1981, Bard Cardiosurgery, Billerica, 1985-86. Contbr. articles to profl. jours. Mem. Am. Soc. for Quality Control, Ops. Rsch. Soc. Am., Am. Statis. Assn. (Boston chpt., program chmn. 1984-85, treas. 1986—), Epsilon Delta Sigma. Office: Mobil Solar Energy Corp 4 Suburban Park Dr Billerica MA 01821-3904

DELANEY, ROBERT PATRICK, librarian, writer; b. Miles City, Mont., Mar. 16, 1961; s. Alfred John and Ann Lois (D'Ambrosia) D. AAS in Broadcast Communications, Suffolk County Community Coll., 1982; BA in English magna cum laude, Dowling Coll., 1985; MS in Library Sci., L.I. U., 1987. Grad. asst. Southampton (N.Y.) Campus Library L.I. U., 1986-87, librarian, 1987—; librarian Babylon (N.Y.) Pub. Library, 1987-88, Farmingdale (N.Y.) Campus Libr., Poly. U., 1988, C.W. Post Campus Libr., L.I. U., Brookville, N.Y., 1989—. Author: (short stories) Dreamfinder, 1986, Nightfawn and the Gleam, 1989, Brightblossom and the Gleam, 1990, The Sinking Star, 1990. Mem. Suffolk County Library Assn., Soc. Preservation Film Music, Internat. Arthurian Soc. Home: 34 University Dr Ronkonkoma NY 11779-1905

DELANEY, THOMAS FRANCIS, publishing executive; b. Rockville Center, N.Y., Feb. 2, 1948; s. Thomas Francis and Isabel (Sullivan) D.; m. Julia T. Igoe, Nov. 29, 1986. BA in English, Holy Cross Coll., 1970; MS, Syracuse U., 1972. News editor Gallagher Report, N.Y.C., 1974-83; account mgr. BBDO Advt., N.Y.C., 1983; sr. editor Adweek Mag., N.Y.C., 1983-89; pres., pub. The Delaney Report, N.Y.C., 1990—. Mem. Audit Bur. of Circulation. Home and Office: The Delaney Report 510 E 23rd St New York NY 10010-5012

DE LA PLANTE, WALTER SOWERBY, business consultant; b. Buffalo, Aug. 3, 1915; s. Walter Magliore and Ruth Louise (Sowerby) de la P.; m. Grace Bertha Rammacher, Apr. 27, 1946; children: Michelle Tauber, John Clark Hogarth. Student, U. Buffalo, Millard Fillmore Coll. Merchandise buyer Knott Stores, N.Y.C., 1940, J.B. White's, Augusta, Ga., 1940-42; with Am. Field Svc., Mid-East Europe, 1942-45; merchandise sr. buyer William Hengerer, Buffalo, 1945-49; pres. Chemo Co., Buffalo, 1949-57, W.S. de la Plante Assocs., Buffalo and Rochester, N.Y., 1950—. Mem. N.Y. State Club Assn. (pres. 1984—), The Buffalo Club (pres. 1980), Country Club of Buffalo. Democrat. Presbyterian. Home: 2 Hidden Pond Ln Buffalo NY 14226-3526 Office: WS de la Plante Assocs 3960 Harlem Rd Ste 7A Buffalo NY 14226-4706

DE LA RENTA, OSCAR, fashion designer; b. Santo Domingo, Dominican Republic, July 22, 1932; s. Oscar and Maria Antonia (deFiallo) de LaR.; m. Francoise de Langlade, Oct. 31, 1967 (dec. 1983); 1 adopted child, Moises Oscar; m. Anne E. de la Renta, Dec. 26, 1989. Student, Santo Domingo U., Academia de San Fernando, Madrid, Spain. Staff Balenciaga's AISA, Madrid; asst. to Antonio Castillo at Lanvin, Paris, 1961-63; designer, ptnr. Jane Derby, Inc., N.Y.C., from 1965; chief exec. Richton's Oscar de la Renta Couture, Oscar de la Renta II, Oscar de la Renta Furs, Oscar de la Renta Jewelry, also dir., 1969-73; designer, Elizabeth Arden, N.Y.C., 1963-65; now designer Oscar de la Renta, Ltd., N.Y.C., 1973—. Active Dominican Childhood Center, orphanage, Santo Domingo. Decorated Order Juan Pablo Duarte, Order Cristobal Colon (Dominican Republic); recipient Coty awards, 1967, 68, Golden Tiberius award, 1968, Received Lifetime of Achievement award The Coun. of Fashion Designers of Am., 1989, 90; Neiman-Marcus award, 1968; Fragrance Found. award 1978; named to Coty Hall of Fame, 1973. Mem. Council Fashion Designers Am. Office: 550 7th Ave New York NY 10018-3203*

DE LA TEJA, ELPIDIO LEONCIO, food products executive, educator; b. Cienfuegos, Cuba, June 18, 1943; came to U.S., 1962; s. Elpidio C. and Dolores Carolina (Medina) de la T.; m. Silvia Teresa Canton, Dec. 17, 1983; 1 child, Roland Thomas. AS, Bronx (N.Y.) Community Coll., 1968; BS in Chemistry, Fairleigh Dickinson U., 1972; MS in Chemistry, Stevens Inst. Tech., 1974. Rsch. technician Union Carbide, Elmsford, N.Y., 1968-69; assoc. scientist Thomas J. Lipton, Inc., Englewood Cliffs, N.J., 1969-74; group leader Thomas J. Lipton Inc., Englewood Cliffs, 1974-84; asst. mgr. Takeda USA, Inc., N.Y.C., 1984-85, mgr., 1985—; adj. prof. Chemistry Fairleigh Dickinson U. Contbr. articles to profl. jours. Bd. dirs. ARC, 1988—. Mem. Internat. Hydrolyzates Coun. (councilor), Am. Chem Soc., Am. Assn. Cereal Chems., Nat. Inst. Food Tech. (seminar chmn. 1985—, cert. appreciation 1986), Flavors and Extracts Assn., Lyons Internat. Roman Catholic. Home: 3624 Lincoln Ter North Bergen NJ 07047-2339 Office: Takeda USA Inc 8 Corporate Dr Orangeburg NY 07047

DELAURA, DAVID JOSEPH, English language educator; b. Worcester, Mass., Nov. 19, 1930; s. Louis and Helen Adeline (Austin) DeL.; m. Ann Beloate, Aug. 19, 1961; children: Michael Louis, Catherine, William Beloate. A.B., Boston Coll., 1955, A.M., 1958; Ph.D., U. Wis., 1960. Mem. faculty U. Tex. at Austin, 1960-74, prof. English, 1968-74; Avalon Found. prof. humanities, prof. English U. Pa., Phila., 1974—; chmn. dept. U. Pa., 1985-90. Author: Hebrew and Hellene in Victorian England: Newman, Arnold, and Pater, 1969; editor: Victorian Prose: A Guide to Research, 1973; contbr. chpts. to books, articles and revs. to profl. publs. Mem. Modern Lang. Assn. (ann. award for outstanding article 1964), AAUP. Home: 31 Orchard Ln Villanova PA 19085-1133 Office: U Pa Dept English Philadelphia PA 19104-6273

DELAURO, ROSA, congresswoman. Student, London Sch. Econs. & Polit. Sci., 1962-63; BA in History and Polit Sci. cum laude, Marymount Coll., 1964; MA in Internat. Politics, Columbia U., 1966. Tng. assoc. Community Progress Inc., New Haven, Conn., 1967-69; instr. in internat. rels. Albertus Magnus Coll., 1967-68; adminstrv. asst. Nat. Urban Fellows, 1969-72, asst. dir., dir., 1972-75; city coord. Carter-Mondale Presdl. Campaign, New Haven, 1976; exec. asst. Mayor Frank Logue, New Haven, 1976-77, campaign mgr., 1977; exec. asst., devel. adminstr. City of New Haven, 1977-79; campaign mgr. Chris Dodd for U.S. Senate, 1979-80, 86; adminstrv. asst. U.S. Senator Christopher J. Dodd, Washington, 1981-87; state dir. Mondale-Ferraro Presdl. Campaign, N.J., 1986; ptnr. DeLauro-Geller, 1987-88; regional dir. Dukakis for Pres. Campaign, N.Y., N.J., Con., 1988; exec. dir. EMILY's List, 1989; elected to U.S. Ho. of Reps., 1990; del. to Dem. Nat. Conv., 1984; bd. dirs. Pax Ams. Bd. dirs. Shubert Theater for Performing Arts, New Haven; past pres. New Haven Arts Coun. Assoc. fellow Timothy Dwight Coll., Yale U.; recipient Leadership award Am. Com. on Italian Migration. Mem. Nat. Italian-Am. Found., Dem. Women for Progress. Office: US House of Reps Offices of House Members Washington DC 20515

DE LA VARRE, ANDRÉ, broadcast executive; b. Vienna, Austria; s. Andre and Ilse (Laechle) De La V.; m. Gretl Sotona, Nov. 5, 1955; children: Rene, Byron, Trilawny. PhD in Music, Vienna Acad. of Music, Vienna, 1956. On tour piano concerts worldwide, 1955—; with publicity dept. Burton Holmes Travelogues, Chgo., N.Y., Hollywood, Calif., 1960-75; pres. Visual Pub. Rels., N.Y.C., 1970—; ptnr. Brompton Advt., 1991—; assoc. TMM Internat., 1991—. Writer, dir., producer travel documentaries, Edinburgh, Scotland, Venice, Italy, Atlanta. Recipient Cine Golden Eagle award. Home and Office: Piney Point Croton On Hudson NY 10520

DEL BORGO, NANCY W., alumni affairs executive; b. Watertown, N.Y., Nov. 4, 1946; d. Lawrence F. and Alice E. (Giblin) Withington; m. Elliot A. Del Borgo, June 20, 1970; children: Anne K., Laura N. BS, SUNY, 1968, MS, 1969. Tchr. Canton (N.Y.) Pub. Schs., 1969-71, Potsdam (N.Y.) Pub. Schs., 1971-72; dir. SUNY, 1985—. Liturgy Com. St. Mary's Cath. Ch., Potsdam, 1990—. Recipient Distinguished Svc. award Potsdam Coll. Alumni Assn., 1984. Mem. SUNY Confederation of Alumni (exec. coun. 1989—), Coun. Advancement and Support Edn. Democrat. Roman Catholic. Office: Alumni Office Potsdam Coll Pierrepont Ave Potsdam NY 13676-2027

DEL COLLIANO, GERARD ANTHONY, publisher; b. Hoboken, NJ, July 20, 1946; s. Gerard Victor and Adele (Visconti) Del Colliano; m. Judy Gallagher, Mar. 28, 1970 (div. June 1978); 1 child, Gerard R.; m. Laura Loro, Feb. 14, 1983; 1 child, Daria Rose. BS in Communications, Temple U., 1968. Announcer Sta. WDVR, Phila., 1965-66; announcer, personality Sta. WFIL-TV, AM/FM, Phila., 1966-68; personality Sta. WIBG Radio, Phila., 1968-69, program dir., 1972-74; announcer Sta. WIP Radio, Phila., 1969-71; program dir. Sta. WIFI Radio, Phila., 1971-72; publisher Inside Radio Inc., Cherry Hill, N.J., 1974—. Democrat. Roman Catholic. Office: Inside Radio Inc 1930 Marlton Pike E Ste 93S Cherry Hill NJ 08003-4210

DELEHANT, RAYMOND LEONARD, botanist, educator; b. New Haven, June 30, 1937; s. John Patrick and Dorothy Barbara (Luft) D. BS, So. Conn. State U., 1959, MS, 1964; postgrad., U. Colo., 1965, U. Calif., Berkeley, 1966, U. Vt., 1967. Permanent cert. tchr., Conn. Instr. botany So. Conn. State U., New Haven, part-time 1964-71; sci. tchr. jr. high sch. Bd. Edn., North Haven, Conn., 1959—; cons. textbook program Rand McNally Co., 1974. Camp dir. nature section Boy Scouts Am., summers 1953, 57, 64, merit badge counselor Quinnipiac Council New Haven, 1964-70; asst. ranger West Rock Nature Ctr., New Haven, 1956, 58; rep. Citizens Pk. Council, New Haven, 1974-75; chmn. bd. trustees Park Oaks Sr. Commr. Assn., New Haven, 1964—. NSF fellow 1966, 67; recipient Eagle Scout award Boy Scouts Am. 1955. Mem. Conn. Sci. Tchrs. Assn. (life; pres. 1979-83, John Prymack award 1975, Spl. Recognition award 1990), Conn. Sci. Suprs. Assn., Sequassen Alumni Assn. (sec. 1970-72), Ecol. Soc. Am., Park Oaks Sr. Commr. Assn. (chmn. bd. trustees, treas.). Roman Catholic. Home: 973 Sherman Ave New Haven CT 06511-1050 Office: North Haven Middle Sch 55 Bailey Rd North Haven CT 06473-2670

DE LEMOS, RUTH GEISLER, counselor, educator; b. N.Y.C., Sept. 1, 1907; d. Anthony and Bertha (Duncombe) Geisler; (dec.); children: Robert, Mrs. William Krupman. BCS, NYU, 1927; BS, Washington Sq. Coll., 1931; MA, Columbia U. Cert. counselor. Owner, dir., counselor Children's Summer Camps, 1937-67; educator Tchrs. Coll., Columbia Univ., 1960-75; dir. project Six City Sch. Dists. of Westchester, 1972-75; adj. prof. counselor edn. Grad. Sch. Edn., C. W. Post, L. I. Univ., 1975—; mem. bd. edn. Mt. Vernon, N.Y.; pres. Parent Tchrs. Assn., Mt. Vernon; adj. assoc. prof. counselor edn., C. W. Post. Home: 2 Stoneleigh Plaza Bronxville NY 10708

DELEON, ROBERT LOUIS, research chemist, chemistry educator; b. N.Y.C., Apr. 19, 1954; s. Robert Louis and Anna Marie (Anderson) DeL.; m. Donna Lynn Venezky, Oct. 24, 1981; children: Emma Elizabeth, Alyssa Marie. BS in Chemistry, SUNY, Stony Brook, 1976; MS in Phys. Chemistry, U. Rochester, 1978, PhD in Phys. Chemistry, 1981. Rsch. assoc. U. Rochester, N.Y., 1981-84; prin. chemist Arvin-Calspan, Buffalo, 1984—; vis. lectr. SUNY, Buffalo, 1986, 88-90, adj. assoc. prof., 1990—. Contbr. articles to profl. jours. Regents scholar, 1972-76. Mem. AIAA, Am. Chem. Soc., Sigma Xi (sec. Calspan chpt. 1988-90). Office: Arvin Calspan PO Box 400 Buffalo NY 14225-0400

DELFINER, JOEL STEVEN, neurologist; b. Phila., May 4, 1952; s. Herman and Bernice (Cohen) D.; m. Madeline Susan Ginzburg, July 31, 1977; children: Leslie, Alexandra, Matthew. AB magna cum laude, Franklin & Marshall Coll., 1973; MD, U. Pa., 1979. Diplomate Am. Bd. Psychiatry and Neurology, Am. Bd. Electro Diagnostic Medicine. Resident in neurology Neurologic Inst., N.Y.C., 1980-83, neuromuscular disease fellow, 1982-83; jr. attending neurologist Nassau County Med. Ctr., East Meadow, N.Y., 1983, asst. attending neurologist, 1984, assoc. attending neurologist,

1985—; asst. prof. clin. neurology SUNY, Stony Brook, 1983—; dir. M.D.A. Clinic, Nassau County Med. Ctr., 1985—, chief div. neuro/muscular disease, 1985—. Fellow Am. Assn. Electrodiagnostic Medicine; mem. AMA, AAS, AAN, N.Y. Acad. Scis., Phi Beta Kappa. Office: Nassau County Med Ctr 2201 Hempstead Turnpike East Meadow NY 11554

DELFINO, ASTRID DIANN, assistant marketing representative; b. Port Chester, N.Y., Dec. 31, 1966; d. Patrick John and Wenche Rigmor (Kvaerne) D. BA in Polit. Sci., Bates Coll., 1988; cert. in bus., SUNY, Purchase, 1992. Front office supr. Rye Town Hilton, Rye Brook, N.Y., 1988-92, restaurant mgr., 1989-92; asst. mktg. rep. Hobbs Group, Inc., Greenwich, Con., 1992—. Flutist Hudson Valley Wind Symphony. Mem. Bates Coll. Alumni Club (Fairfield County chpt. club leader, co-pres. 1989). Lutheran. Home: 115 Laura Joy Cir Mamaroneck NY 10543-3128 Office: Hobbs Group Inc 75 Holly Hill Lane Greenwich CT 06830

DELFYETTE, RAYMOND, labor union administrator; b. Bayside, N.Y., June 29, 1955; s. Raymond and Valerie (Morse) D.; m. Mary Rose Wade, Aug. 9, 1976 (div. Jan. 1991); children: Dawn, Timothy. AAS, Queens Borough Community Coll., 1980. Tng. and devel. mgr. Bayside (N.Y.) Fed. Savs., 1976-81; distbn. clk. U.S. Postal Svc., JFK Airport, Jamaica, N.Y., 1981-90; exec. v.p. APWU Queens Area Local, Ozone Park, N.Y., 1990—. Tex. league pres. Bayside Little League, 1991, 92, treas., 1992; mem. legis. adv. com. State Sen. Frank Padavan, Bellerose, N.Y., 1989—; basketball coach Bayside Boys Club, 1974-77. Democrat. Roman Catholic. Office: APUW Queens Area Local 98-11 101 Ave Ozone Park NY 11416

D'ELIA, GERARDO ANTONIO, JR., publishing company executive; b. N.Y.C., Sept. 17, 1942; s. Gerardo and Filomena Mary (Abbatantuono) D'E.; m. Roseanne Falcone, Sept. 2, 1944; children: Anthony, Mary. Grad. high sch., N.Y. With McGraw Hill, Inc., N.Y.C., 1961-76; prodn. coord. McGraw Hill, Inc., 1973-76; asst. prodn. mgr. People/Money Time, Inc., N.Y.C., 1976-78; prodn. mgr. Money Time, Inc., 1978-80; prodn. mgr. Cosmopolitan Hearst Corp., N.Y.C., 1980-83; opts. mgr. corp. Hearst Mags., 1983-87; dir. mfg. Good Housekeeping Hearst Corp., 1987-90, v.p., dir. printing and transp. svcs., 1990—; lectr. in field. Editorial bd., Pub. and Prodn. Exec., 1988-89. Named Prodn. Man of Yr. Assn. pub. Prodn. Mgrs., 1987; recipient Luminaires award Women in Prodn., 1992. Mem. Assn. Pub. Prodn. Mgrs. (pres. 1988-89), Hearst Prodn. Mgrs. Com. (chmn. 1985-87), McGraw Hill Prodn. Mgrs. Assn. (chmn. 1971-72), Specifications of Web Offset Publs. (dir. at large 1990-92), The Navigators (pres. 1969-70). Republican. Roman Catholic. Home: 1737 Pascal Pl Belmar NJ 07719-3749 Office: Hearst Mags 224 W 57th St 959 8th Ave New York NY 10019-3737

D'ELIA, JAMES JOSEPH, elementary school educator; b. Bklyn., Oct. 10, 1954; s. James Biagio and Theresa (Liguori) D'E. AA, Nassau Community Coll., 1973; BS, State Univ. Coll., Oneonta, 1974; MS in Lang. and Literacy, CUNY, 1992. Cert. elem. tchr., N.Y. Tchr. Briarcliff Manor (N.Y.) Pub. Schs., 1977—; salesperson real estate Fire Island Pines, N.Y., 1988—. Advisor Todd Sch. Garden Club. Mem. Nat. Sci. Tchrs. Assn. Home: 301 Cathedral Pky Apt 20C New York NY 10026-4065

DE LIMANTOUR, CLARICE B., food scientist; b. Allentown, Pa., Dec. 24, 1918; d. Joseph Robert and Laura (Wirthlin) Barr; m. Julio Edwardo Iturbide Limantour, Sept. 13, 1940 (dec. 1972); children: Jose' Ignacio, Julio Edwardo. BS, Rutgers U., 1938, MS, 1940; postgrad., U. Mexico, 1946-49, Rutgers U., 1949-50. Advisor Nat. Sch. Feeding Program, Mexico, 1947-49; pres. Factory Feeding Corp., Mexico, 1950-58; advisor Nat. Factory Feeding Program, Mexico, 1958-60; developer New Food Product-Gen. Foods, White Plains, N.Y., 1960-61, New Food Product-Gen. Mills, Reynolds, 1961-63, New Food Products-Miles Labs., 1963-64; cons. New Food Products-various cos., 1964-78; pres., researcher Limantour Devel. Corp., Pa., 1966-91, pres., 1988—; developer Cliffdale Farms, Palm, Pa., 1988—; inventor in field. Inventor in field. Mem. Bucks County Conservancy Assn., Doylestown, Pa., 1989-91, Fine Arts Club, N.Y.C., 1984-88, Republican Club, Pa., 1982-89, Citizens Against Govt. Waste, Washington, 1988-91. Republican. Episcopalian. Home: 905 Durham Rd Durham PA 18039-9999 Office: Cliffdale Farms Rt 29 Box 69 Palm PA 18070

DELIO, RICHARD MICHAEL, management consultant; b. N.Y.C., Aug. 25, 1948; s. Carmine J. and Mary (Ghigna) DeL.; m. Jeanne M. DiCesare, Sept. 4, 1976. BSEE, Rensselaer Poly. Inst., 1970, MSEE, 1971. Sr. cons. Arthur Andersen & Co., N.Y.C., 1971-77, Touche Ross & Co., Newark, N.J., 1977-80; ptnr. Retail Strategies, N.Y.C., 1980-83; mgr. systems devel. Lane Bryant, N.Y.C., 1983-84; ptnr. Retail Systems Mgmt., N.Y.C., 1984-88; sr. prin., dir. info. tech. retail and consumer products Arthur Young, N.Y.C., 1988-89; v.p. retail practice leader Tech. Solutions, N.Y.C., 1989-90; pvt. practice mgmt. cons. Ramsey, N.J., 1990—. MEm. Tau Beta Pi, Eta Kappa Nu. Roman Catholic. Home and Office: 31 Manor Dr Ramsey NJ 07446

DELIYANNIS, CONSTANTINE CHRISTOS, economist, mathematician, educator; b. Kallithea, Mesolongion, Greece, July 7, 1938; came to U.S., 1964; s. Christos Constantine and Theodora Constantine (Merantzis) D. BA in Econs. summa cum laude, Athens Grad. Sch. Econs. and Bus. Scis., Greece, 1960; MA in Econs., U. Notre Dame, 1965; PhD in Econs., Cath. U. Am., 1982. Lic. life ins. agt. Prodn. supr. Piraiki-Patraiki, Cotton Mfg. Co., Inc., Athens, Greece, 1962-64; prof. econs. So. Ill. U., Edwardsville, 1965-66; cons. in stats. Bur. Social Rsch., Cath. U. Am., Washington, 1967; economist Internat. Bank for Reconstrn. and Devel., Washington, 1967-69; prof. econs. George Mason U., Fairfax, Va., 1970-71; economist The Urban Inst., Washington, 1971-72; prof. math.. U. D.C., 1972-74; cons. health econs. Transcentury Corp., Washington, 1975; cons. on bus. investment, stabilization instruments, urban pub. fin., poverty and inequality, and fin. planning Washington, 1976—; prof. econs. No. Va. Community Coll., Annandale, 1986-88; ins. exec. Am. Fidelity Life Ins. Co., Washington, 1986-90. Author: (book) Capital and Growth: Theory and A Case Study of Greece, 1962; contbr. numerous articles on efficient exchs., employment, taxation, internat. competition, factor shares, and minimum wages to profl. pubs. 2d lt. Greek Army, 1960-62. Fellow Cath. U. Am., U. Notre Dame, Soc. Greek Studies. Mem. Am. Econ. Assn., Econometric Soc. Greek Orthodox. Home and Office: Apt 603 1101 New Hampshire Ave NW Washington DC 20037

DELL, DONALD LUNDY, lawyer, television and marketing executive; b. Savannah, Ga., June 17, 1938; s. Julian Peter Jr. and Margaret (Lundy) D.; m. Carole Marie Osche, Mar. 20, 1971; children: Alexandra Lundy and Kristina Osche (twins). BA in History, Yale U., 1960; LLB, U. Va., 1964; D in Comml. Scis. (hon.), St. John's U., 1983. Bar: D.C. 1964, Va. 1964. Assoc. Hogan & Hartson, Washington, 1964-67; spl. asst. to dir. R. Sargent Shriver OEO, Washington, 1967-68; sr. ptnr. Dell, Craighill, Fentress & Benton, Washington, 1968-72; chmn. ProServ, Inc., Washington, 1972—, ProServ TV, Inc., Washington, 1972—. Author: Minding's Other People's Business, 1990. Co-founder Assn. of Tennis Profls., Fla., 1972, Nat. Jr. Tennis League, N.Y.C., 1969, Sovran Bank Tennis Classic, Washington, 1969—; pres. Internat. Tennis Hall of Fame, Newport, R.I., 1989-90; mem. Cath. Youth Orgn., Washington, 1986—. Named to Hall of Stars Washington Redskins Orgn., 1985. Mem. ABA, D.C. Bar Assn., Va. Bar Assn., U.S. Tennis Assn. (U.S.A. Davis Cup capt. 1968-69), Washington Area Tennis Patrons Found., Columbia Country Club, City Club (Washington), Queen's Club (London), Yale Club (N.Y.C.), Farmington Country Club (Charlottesville, Va.), Les Ambs. Club (London). Democrat. Roman Catholic.

DELL, ERNEST ROBERT, lawyer; b. Vandergrift, Pa., Feb. 6, 1928; m. Karen D. Reed, May 8, 1965; children: Robert W., John D., Jane C. B.S., U. Pitts., 1949, M.Litt., 1953; J.D., Harvard U., 1956. Bar: Pa. 1957, U.S. Supreme Ct. 1961; C.P.A., Pa. Ptnr. firm Reed Smith Shaw & McClay, Pitts., 1956—; adj. prof. law Duquesne U. Law Sch., Pitts., 1960-86; bd. dirs. Atty's. Liability Assurance Soc. Inc., Chgo., Atty's. Liability Assurance Soc. (Bermuda) Ltd. Mem. ABA, Fed. Bar Assn., Pa. Bar Assn., Allegheny County Bar Assn., AICPAs, Pa. Inst. CPAs. Home: 119 Riding Trail Ln Pittsburgh PA 15215-1521 Office: Reed Smith Shaw & McClay Mellon Sq 435 6th Ave Pittsburgh PA 15219

DELL, RALPH BISHOP, pediatrician, researcher; b. Mt. Village, Alaska, July 31, 1935; s. Elwin B. and Elizabeth B. (Bishop) D.; m. Kathryn M. Bownass, June 17, 1957 (div. Dec. 1982); children: Laura, Kenneth; m. Karen K. Hein, Aug. 28, 1983; stepchildren: Ethan Hein, Molly Hein. BA, Pomona Coll., 1957; MD, U. Pa., 1961. Diplomate Am. Bd. Pediatrics. Intern and resident Children's Hosp. Med. Ctr., Boston, 1961-63; NIH postdoctoral fellow Coll. Physicians and Surgeons, Columbia U., N.Y.C., 1963-66, assoc., 1966-67, asst. prof. pediatrics, 1967-72, assoc. prof., 1972-78, prof., 1978—. Author 3 books, 100 research papers; co-inventor amino acid solution. Recipient Research Career Devel award NIH, 1966-71, Career Scientist award Health Research Council N.Y., 1972-75; Fogarty Sr. Internat. fellow NIH, 1975-76. Mem. Am. Pediatric Soc., Am. Physiologic Soc., Am. Soc. Clin. Investigation, Soc. for Pediatric Research, Assn. for Computing Machinery. Democrat. Home: 116 Pinehurst Ave New York NY 10033-1755 Office: Columbia U Coll Physicians & Surgeons 630 W 168th St New York NY 10032-3702

DELL, ROBERT CHRISTOPHER, geothermal sculptor, scenic artist; b. Nyack, N.Y., Feb. 22, 1950; s. Edward John and Laurel Jean (McGrath) D.; children: Robert Carroll, Terrence Edward; m. Siena Gillan Porta, May 30, 1986. BS in Edn., SUNY-Oneonta, 1972, MFA in Sculpture, SUNY, New Paltz, 1975. Selected exhibits: Md. Art Inst., Balt., 1980, Thronja Gallery, Springfield, Mass., 1984-92, 14 Sculptors Gallery, N.Y.C., 1985, Thorpe Intermedia Gallery, Sparkhill, N.Y., 1984, Everson Mus., Syracuse, N.Y., 1983, Lincoln Ctr., N.Y.C., 1983, A.B. Condon Gallery, N.Y.C., 1982, Vorpal Galleries, San Francisco, and N.Y.C., 1977-92, New Acquisitions Gallery, Syracuse, 1982-87, SUNY, New Paltz, 1987, MIT Mus., Cambridge, Mass., 1990-91, Lehigh U., Bethlehem, Pa., 1991-92, Perlan, Reykjavik, Iceland (permanent geothermal sculpture installation), 1991—; selected solo exhibits: SUNY-Oneonta, 1976, Vorpal Gallery, Chgo., 1978, N.Y.C., 1981, 88, Vorpal Gallery, San Francisco, 1985, New Acquisitions Gallery, Syracuse, 1983, Blue Hill Cultural Ctr., Pearl River, N.Y., 1987, Am. Cultural Ctr., Reykjavik, Iceland, 1988, Mid-Hudson Arts and Sci. Ctr., Poughkeepsie, N.Y., 1992; selected pub. collections: Syracuse U., Mus. Fine Art, Springfield, Mass., MacDowell Colony, Peterborough, N.H., SUNY, Town of Orangetown (N.Y.), Fulbright Comm., Reykjavik, Reykjavik Mcpl. Dist. Heating; mem. Architect and Community Appearance Bd. Rev., Orangetown, 1979—, vice chmn. 1987—; dir. visual arts Vriesland W. Hudson Art Ctr., Pearl River, N.Y., 1978-80, artist-in-residence, 1980; scenic artist motion pictures and TV including The Cotton Club, Heaven Help Us, Beat Street, The Ultimate Solution of Grace Quigley, also TV shows, master scenic artist One Life to Live, ABC, 1988—, others; subject of TV documentary Ugluspegill(worlds 1st geothermal sculpture), State Television, Reykjavik, Iceland, 1988, subject of video Hitavaetur at M.I.T., Circumstantial Prodns., Nyack, N.Y., 1991. MacDowell fellow, Peterborough, N.H., 1980, Collaboration, Art, Sci. and Tech. grant, Syracuse, N.Y., 1978; NYSCA grantee, 1986, Fulbright Rsch. grantee, 1988, Ptnrs. of the Ams. grantee, 1992. Home: 421 Washington St Tappan NY 10983-2703

DELL, STEPHEN OWEN, neurosurgeon; b. N.Y.C., June 13, 1944; s. Joseph Bernard and Laura Rachel (Lubowitz) D.; m. Julia Anne Walsh, Jan. 17, 1972; children: Elizabeth, Emily, Rebecca, Joseph. AB, Harvard U., 1964; postgrad., Oxford (Eng.) U., 1965-66; MA, Princeton U., 1967; MD, NYU, 1972. Intern, resident U. Calif., San Francisco, 1972-74; chief Friends' Hosp., Kaimosi, Kenya, 1974-75; resident N.Y. Neurol. Inst., N.Y.C., 1975-79; instr. Tufts U., Boston, 1979-82; neurosurgeon Spine Clinic New Eng., Epsom, N.H., 1992—, Brookdale Hosp., Bklyn., 1990-91; founder, dir. Med. Diagnostics, Burlington, Mass., 1984-92. Contbr. articles to sci. jours. Fellow Rockefeller Found., 1982. Mem. AMA, Am. Assn. Neurol. Surgeons, Congress Neurol. Surgeons, Soc. Pediatric Neurosurgery. Unitarian Universalist. Home: 19 Bagdad Rd Durham NH 03824 Office: Spine Clinic New England Epsom Circle Epsom NH 03234

DELL, WARREN FRANK, II, management consultant; b. Louisville, Aug. 8, 1945; s. George Justus and Opeal Lee (Roberts) D.; m. Theresa LoParco, July 11, 1970; 1 child, Stacy Lee. BS, Northeastern U., 1968; MBA, Iona Coll., 1973. Cert. mgmt. cons. Systems analyst Am. Can Co., Greenwich, Conn., 1968-69; cons. Info. Techniques, Inc., Norwalk, Conn., 1969-70; systems analyst Colgate Palmolive, N.Y.C., 1970-72, supr. mktg. stats., 1972-73, mgr. forecast and adminstrn., 1973-77; cons. Case and Co., Stamford, Conn., 1977-80, prin., 1980-83, sr. ptnr., dir., 1983-85; prin. Cresap, a Towers Perrin Co., N.Y.C., 1985-86, v.p., 1986-90; pres. Dellmart & Co., Stamford, Conn., 1990—. Contbr. articles to profl. jours. Mem. Coun. Logistics Mgmt., Warehouse Edn. Rsch. Coun., Food Distbn. Rsch. Soc., Am. Philatelic Soc., Internat. Soc. Planning and Strategic Mgmt., Inst. Mgmt. Cons. Planning Forum, Ye Old Post Rd. Stamp Club. Office: Dellmart & Co PO Box 16789 Stamford CT 06905-8789

DELL AQUILA, JOHN JOSEPH, technical pricing specialist; b. Schenectady, N.Y., Aug. 29, 1953; s. Vince and Christine (Calvenice) Dell A.; m. Gina J. Puglise, July 29, 1978. Student, Schenectady C.C., 1978, SUNY, Albany, 1991—. Machine tool operator GE, Schenectady, 1973-74, 77-78; pricing specialist GE, Schenectady, N.Y., 1989—; mech. draftsman Mech. Tech., Inc., Latham, N.Y., 1979-84; machine tool operator Watervliet (N.Y.) Arsonal, 1984-86; composites material technician U.S. Composites Corp., North Greenbush, N.Y., 1986-88; electronics tech. Brad Cable Electronics, Schenectady, N.Y., 1988-89; cons. in field. Sgt. USMC, 1970-73. Mem. Am. Mus. Natural History, Soc. for Advancement of Material and Process Engring., Navy League, Watervliet Rod and Gun Club. Republican. Home: PO Box 13179 Albany NY 12212 Office: GE I River Rd Schenectady NY 12345

DELLA SELVA, PATRICIA COUGHLIN, psychology educator, psychologist; b. Paterson, N.J., Sept. 19, 1954; d. James Dominic and Patricia (Sanglyn) Coughlin; m. Michael Pascal Della Selva, May 30, 1981; children: Megan, Katherine, Anthony. BS, Ohio U., 1976; MS, Syracuse (N.Y.) U., 1978, PhD, 1981. Lic. psychologist, N.Y. Asst. prof. Med. Sch. Northwestern U., Chgo., 1981-88; prin. psychologist Albany (N.Y.) Psychol. Assocs., 1989-90; asst. prof. Albany Med. Coll., 1989—; pvt. practice psychologist Albany, 1989—. Author: (chpt.) Sleep Disorder, 1986; contbr. to Preverbal Trauma (jour.). Mem. APA, Assn. Psychologists in Ind. Practice, N.Y. Psychol. Assn. Home: 2632 Troy Rd Niskayuna NY 12309-1410 Office: 435 New Karner Rd # 204 Albany NY 12205-3833

DELOCA, CORNELIUS EDWARD, JR., management consultant; b. Hollis, N.Y., Oct. 21, 1930; s. Cornelius Edward and Rita Katherine (Doherty) D.; m. Ann Marie Friel, Sept. 6, 1952; children: Edward, Catherine, Thomas, Jeanne, Matthew. BA in Social Sci., Bucknell U., Lewisburg, Pa., 1952; postgrad., Northwestern Grad. Sch., Switzerland, 1966, UCLA, 1977. Sales rep./mgr. sales sch. IBM Corp., Garden City, N.Y., 1953-57; various sales positions IBM Corp., N.Y.C., 1958-60, acctg. machine area dist. mgr., 1960-63; dir. sales/mktg. IBM World Trade Europe, Paris, 1964-66; midwestern reg. sales mgr. IBM Corp., N.Y.C., 1967, product mgr., 1967-72; various directorships IBM Corp., Franklin Lakes, N.J., 1976-81; dir. fin. and competitive IBM Corp., White Plains, N.Y., 1982-87; mgmt. cons., pres. C. Del Assocs., Franklin Lakes, 1987—; pres. D & K Book Co., Inc.; cons. mktg. and product mgmt. Mem. Ridgewood Country Club (v.p. 1990—), Met. Golf Assn. (exec. com.). Roman Catholic. Home: 232 Gregory Rd Franklin Lakes NJ 07417-2014

DE LONG, J. BRADFORD, educator; b. Boston, June 24, 1960; s. James V. De Long and Fonya (Lord) Helm; m. Ann Marie Marciarille, June 7, 1986; 1 child, Michael Marciarille De Long. BA, Harvard U., 1982, MA, 1985, PhD, 1987. Instr. MIT, Cambridge, Mass., 1986-87; asst. prof. Boston U., 1987-88; asst. prof. Harvard U., Cambridge, 1988-91, Danziger assoc. prof. econs., 1991—. Democrat. Office: NBER 1050 Massachusetts Ave Cambridge MA 02138

DE LONG, JACOB EDWARD, real estate broker; b. Syracuse, N.Y., Oct. 5, 1939; s. Jacob Edward and Eva Ann (Sposato) D.; children: Edward Andrew, Michael Anthony, Sean Michael (dec.); m. Diana J. Sondej, Dec. 21, 1985. Grad. high sch., Fayetteville, N.Y. Sales rep. Ill. Shade Div., Slick Airways, Chgo., 1963-67; dir. mktg. Bean Bros. Inc., Walton, N.Y., 1967-71; real estate sales Longley Jones Assoc., Syracuse, 1971-73, Radclif Real Estate, Syracuse, 1973-76; comml. real estate J. Edward De Long Real Estate, Syracuse, 1976-80, Eagan Real Estate Inc., Syracuse, 1980—; pres. bd. dir. The Andrew Nelson Self Help Ctr., Syracuse. Fund raiser, Friends of the Burnet Park 200, Syracuse, 1986. Sgt. USAF, 1957-62. Mem. N.Y. State Bd. Realtors, Onandaga Bd. Realtors, Onandaga Ski Club, Am. Legion. Republican. Roman Catholic. Home: 5100 Highbridge St Fayetteville NY 13066-2411 Office: Eagan Real Estate Inc 1200 Mony Plz Tower 1 Syracuse NY 13202-2720

DELPHIN, JACQUES MERCIER, psychiatrist; b. Cap Haitien, Haiti, Apr. 26, 1929; s. Alexander and Sonia (Bernadin) D.; came to U.S., 1959, naturalized, 1972; B.S., Lycee Nat. Phillipe Guerrier, 1950; M.D., Faculty Medicine Port-au-Prince, Haiti, 1957; m. Marlene Lavitola Mastroti, Aug. 26, 1967; children—Patrick, Barthold, Beverly, Miriam, Matthew, Janice. Intern, St. Luke's Hosp., Newburgh, N.Y., 1960; resident in psychiatry Hudson River Psychiat. Center, Poughkeepsie, N.Y., 1961-64; dir. psychiat. day hosp. Hudson River State Hosp., Poughkeepsie, N.Y., 1966-69; dir. psychiat. day hosp. Community Mental Health Center, Poughkeepsie, 1969-74, now supervising psychiatrist; attending physician St. Francis Hosp., Poughkeepsie, 1968—; med. dir. Mother Cabrini Home, West Park, N.Y., 1974—; practice medicine specializing in psychiatry, Poughkeepsie, 1968—. Commr., Dutchess County Dept. Mental Hygiene, Poughkeepsie, 1973-74. Fellow Am. Psychiat. Assn. (pres. Mid-Hudson br. 1974-76). Republican. Roman Catholic. Lodge: Kiwanis (dir. Poughkeepsie 1968). Author: Chants du Passe, poems, 1951; Rythmes et Fleurs, poems, 1953; Une Robe au Destin Librarie Garneau, 1972. Home: Schutzvill Rd Clinton Corners NY 12514-9999 Office: Community Mental Health Ctr 230 North Rd Poughkeepsie NY 12601-1328 also: 84 Haight Ave Poughkeepsie NY 12603

DELSON, ERIC, anthropology educator; b. N.Y.C., Jan. 18, 1945; s. Robert and Marjorie (Feldman) D.; m. Roberta Alice Marx, Sept. 17, 1967; 1 child, William Charles. BA, Harvard Coll., 1966; PhD in Geology, Columbia U., 1973. Asst. prof. anthropology U. Pitts., 1972-73; asst. prof. anthropology CUNY Lehman Coll. & Grad. Sch., 1973-75, assoc. prof. anthropology, 1975-79; prof. anthropology CUNY Lehman Coll. & Grad. Sch., N.Y.C., 1980—; prof. biology CUNY Grad. Sch., N.Y.C., 1986—; coord phys. anthropology grad. program CUNY Grad Sch., 1978-79, 83—; cons. N.Y. Zool. Soc., Am. Mus. Natural History, 1989—; mem. sci. exec. com. L.S.B. Leakey Found., Oakland, Calif., 1990—; exec. adv. bd. Ency. Human Biology and Dictionary of Sci. and Tech., 1988-92; sci. assoc. Inst. Human Origins, Berkeley, Calif., 1982-87; vis. prof. anthropology Yale U., New Haven, 1980; rsch. assoc. vertebrate paleontology Am. Mus. Natural History, N.Y.C., 1975—; dir. N.Y. Consortium Evolutionary Primatology, 1991—. Author, editor: Ancestors: The Hard Evidence, 1985; author: (with F.S. Szalay) Evolutionary History of the Primates, 1979; editor: Encyclopedia of Human Evolution and Prehistory, 1988, Paleoanthropology Annuals, 1990, Jour. Human Evolution, 1986-89, assoc. editor 1983-85, 90—; contbr. articles to profl. jours. Mem. Paleoanthropology Del. to People's Republic of China, 1975, Nat. Del. to Internat. Quaternary Assn. Congress, Moscow, 1982. Rsch. grantee NSF, 1974, 79-88, 91—; recipient CUNY Faculty Rsch. award, 1975-92, Wenner-Gren Found. Anthrop. Rsch. award, 1971, 78, 80, 83-84, Nat. Geog. Soc. award, 1971. Mem. AAAS, Paleoanthropology Soc., Soc. Vertebrate Paleontology, Internat. Assn. Human Paleontology, Am. Assn. Phys. Anthropologists, Am. Anthropol. Assn., Am. Soc. Primatologists, Internat. Primatological Soc., Internat. Quaternary Assn., Am. Soc. Mammalogists, Soc. Study Evolution, Soc. Systematic Biology, Paleontol. Soc. Office: CUNY Lehman Coll Dept Anthropology Bedford Park Blvd W Bronx NY 10468-1539 also: Am Mus Nat Hist Dept Vertebrate Paleontology New York NY 10024

DELTORTO, PAT ANN, fashion colorist, painter; b. Tuckahoe, N.Y., July 30, 1946; d. Mario Peter and Helen Anita (Luersen) D.; 1 child, Sarah Weaver. BS in Art Edn., Buffalo State Coll., 1968; postgrad., New Sch. for Social Rsch., 1970, Pace U., 1984. Various jobs Ameritex, N.Y.C., 1970-71; film retoucher Kwik Offset Plate Svc., N.Y.C., 1972-75; fashion colorist Texfi Industries, L.A., 1975-77; freelance fashion colorist, painter various cities, 1977—; mem. Screen Printing Assn., N.Y.C., 1972-75. Author: Guide for Abstract Artists, 1992; copyrighted fashion color cards. Unitarian Universalist. Home: PO Box 1217 North Falmouth MA 02556-1217

DEL TUFO, ROBERT J., lawyer, attorney general; b. Newark, Nov. 18, 1933; s. Raymond and Mary (Pellecchia) Del T.; children: Barbara, Ann, Robert, David. B.A. cum laude in English, Princeton U., 1955; J.D., Yale U., 1958. Bar: N.J. 1959. Law sec. to chief justice N.J. Supreme Ct., 1958-60; assoc. firm Dillon, Bitar & Luther, Morristown, N.J., 1960-62, ptnr., 1962-74; asst. prosecutor Morris County, N.J., 1963-65; 1st asst. prosecutor, 1965-67; 1st asst. atty. gen. State of N.J., 1974-77; dir. criminal justice, 1976-77; U.S. atty. Dist. of N.J., Newark, 1977-80; prof. Rutgers U. Sch. Criminal Justice, 1979-81; ptnr. firm Stryker, Tams & Dill, 1980-86, Hannoch Weisman, 1986-90; atty. gen. State of N.J., 1990—; mem. N.J. State Commn. of Investigation, 1981-84; instr. bus. law Farleigh-Dickinson U., 1964; mem. N.J. State Bd. Bar Examiners, 1968-74; mem. criminal law drafting com. Nat. Conf. Bar Examiners, 1972—; mem. com. on character N.J. Supreme Ct., 1982-84; spl. master,fed. jail overcrowding litigation, Essex County, 1989-90. Bd. editors Yale U Law Jour; contbr. articles to profl. jours. Mem. law enforcement adv. com. County Coll. of Morris, 1970-85; mem. Morris County Ethics Com., 1968-71, Morris County Jud. Selection Com., 1970-72, Essex County Jud. Selection Com., 1982-84; v.p., mem. exec. com. United Fund of Morris County, 1966-70; chmn. Morris Twp. Juvenile Conf. Com., 1963-74; bd. dirs. Nat. Found. March of Dimes, 1966-68, Vis. Nurse Assn. Morris County, 1963-70, Morristown YMCA, 1970-74; trustee Newark Acad., 1976—, pres. bd. dirs. 1983-87; bd. regents St. Peter's Coll., 1979-85. Fellow Am. Bar Found.; mem. Am., N.J., Morris County bar assns., Nat. Dist. Attys. Assn., Yale Law Sch. Assn. (exec. com. 1978-84), Order of Coif. Home: 30 Elm Rd Princeton NJ 08540 Office: Law & Pub Safety Dept Justice Complex CN 080 Trenton NJ 08625

DELUCA, ANTHONY BART, mental health commissioner, psychotherapist; b. Waterbury, Conn., Apr. 1, 1942; s. Joseph A. and Genevieve (Buckley) DeL.; m. Nancy Norkin. BA, U. Conn., 1964, MSW, 1970. Med. social worker Hartford (Conn.) Hosp., 1967-69; psychiat. social worker Conn. Dept. Mental Health, Hartford, 1970-77; commr. Tompkins County, Ithaca, N.Y., 1977—. Bd. dirs. Cen. Conn. Health Planning Commn., Waterbury, 1972-76, Health Planning Commn., 1978-84; pres. bd. dirs. R.S.V.P., Ithaca, 1979-82. 1st lt. U.S. Army, 1964-66. Mem. Nat. Assn. Social Workers, Conn. Soc. for Clin. Social Work Svc., Kiwanis (Bloomfield, Conn.) (pres. 1967-69). Republican. Office: Tompkins County Mental Health Dept 201 E Green St Ithaca NY 14850-5634

DE LUCA, ANTHONY JAMES, psychoanalyst, theologian; b. N.Y.C.; s. James Carl and Antoinette (Scarano) DeL. BA, St. John's U., 1957; STB, Catholic U. Am., 1961; BS, Queens Coll., 1963; MA, Fordham U., 1965; PhD, 1971; MA, St. John's U., 1973; cert. in psychoanalysis and psychotherapy Postgrad. Center Mental Health, 1975. Installed as Monsignor, Mercian Orthodox Cath. Ch., 1991; lic. psychologist, Pa., marriage counselor, N.J., sch. psychologist, N.Y., N.J. Asst. prof. philosophy and psychology Notre Dame Coll., N.Y.C., 1967-71, Fordham U., N.Y.C., 1972-73; exec. dir Am. Inst. for Creative Living Inc., Bklyn., S.I., N.Y., Morrisville, Pa., and East Brunswick, N.J., 1972—; assoc. pastor Bklyn Diocese, Roman Catholic Ch., 1961-67, cons. Marriage Tribunal, 1967—; bishop Mid-Atlantic Diocese of St. Nicholas Mercian Orthodox Cath. Ch.; chaplain to students Fedn. Christian Ministries; dean Internat. Sch. for Mental Health Practitioners, S.I. and Pa.; cons. N.Y.C. Police Dept., 1980—; dean Internat. Sch. Mental Health Practitioners, Morrisville, Pa.; dean St. Nicholas Deanery, Mercian Orthodox Cath. Ch., 1991—; dir., producer S.I. Community TV. Author: Freud and Future Religious Experience, 1976. Mem. S.I. Mental Health Council, 1975—. Fellow Am. Orthopsychiat. Assn.; mem. APA, Am. Philos. Assn., Am. Sociol Assn., Am. Group Psychotherapy Assn., Am. Assn. Marriage and Family Therapists (supr.), Am. Found Religion and Psychiatry, N.Y. Soc. Clin. Psychologists, Am. Assn. Psychoednl. Therapists (adv. bd.), Council Register Health Providers in Psychology. Home: 2295 Victory Blvd Staten Island NY 10314-6625 also: 78 N Pennsylvania Ave Morrisville PA 19067

DE LUCA, CARLO JOHN, biomedical engineer; b. Bagnoli del Trigno, Italy, Oct. 12, 1943; came to U.S., 1973; s. John and Josephine (De Blasio) De L.; B in Applied Sci. U. B.C., Can., 1966; MS, U. N.B., Can., 1968; PhD, Queen's U., 1972; m. Christine M. Rafferty. Lectr. U. N.B. Computing Ctr.,

Fredericton, 1968; lectr. biomed. engring. unit Queen's U., Kingston, Ont., Can., 1969-70, lab. instr. dept. anatomy, 1970-71, lectr. dept. anatomy, 1971-72, asst. prof. dept. anatomy, 1972-73; lectr. M.I.T., Cambridge, 1973—; rsch. assoc. in orthopaedic surgery Children's Hosp. Med. Ctr., Harvard U. Med. Sch., Boston, 1973-79, prin. rsch. assoc. in orthopaedic surgery, 1979-84, dir. Neuromuscular Rsch. Lab., 1980-84; adj. assoc. prof. biomed. engring. Boston U., 1977-84, prof. biomed. engring., 1984—, rsch. prof. neurology, 1985—, bd. dirs. NeuroMuscular Rsch. Ctr., 1984—, chmn. dept. of biomed. engring., 1986; dean Coll. of Engring., Boston U., 1986-89; cons. Liberty Mut. Rsch. Ctr., Hopkinton, Mass., 1973—; rsch. mem. Harvard-M.I.T. div. of health sci. and tech., 1978-84; affiliated scientist New Eng. Regional Primate Ctr., 1977-87; mem. nat. and internat. coms. Ont. Govt. fellow, 1969-70. Founding editor-in-chief Jour. Electromyography and Kinesiology, 1990; mem. editorial bds. sci. jours.; co-author: Muscles Alive; contbr. articles on biomed. engring. and neurophysiolgy to sci. publs. Founder, pres. Neuromuscular Rsch. Found., 1985—. RSA grantee, VA grantee, NIH grantee; Volvo award Internat. Soc. for Study of Lumbar Spine, 1989. Fellow IEEE; mem. Biomed. Engring. Soc., Internat. Soc. of Electrophysiol. Kinesiology (sec. gen. 1976-80, sec. 1980-84, v.p. 1985-88, pres. 1988—), Can. Med. and Biol. Engring. Soc., Soc. Neuro-sci., AAAS, Orthopaedics Rsch. Soc., Dante Alighieri Soc. (bd. govs. 1986-88), Mass. Tech. Park Corp. (bd. govs. 1987—), Sigma Xi. Club: Harvard of Boston. Home: 30 Yarmouth Rd Wellesley MA 02181-1249 Office: Boston U NeuroMuscular Rsch Ctr 44 Cummington St Boston MA 02215-2407

DE LUCE, VIRGINIA, entertainer; b. San Francisco, Mar. 25, 1921; d. George Arthur Dickinson Wilson and Hallie Virginia Wells. Student, Bishop-Lee Sch. of Theatre, Beacon Hill, Mass. Lic. real estate salesman. Model John Roberts Powers, Harry Conover; dir. New Wrinkle Theatre; actress 20th Century Fox Film Corp., Columbia Pictures, Paramount Pictures; actress commls.; pres. Soc. Prodns., Cosmic Sci. Inst., Earth Jazz, Texloid Products, Blue Dove Enterprises, Contessa Spring Prodns.; pres. de Virginia, Four Winds Prodns.; radio personality Sta. WCRB-FM, 1977; lectr. Master Class, Boston Conservatory, New Eng. Conservatory Music, Boston. Actress: (musicals and plays) including Kiss Me Kate, Brigadoon, Can Can, Pal Joey, Will Success Spoil Rock Hunter, Twelfth Night, Emperor Jones, Pygmalion and Galatea, White Iris, Leave It To Psmith, The Sacrifice, Bonanza, The Beggars' Opera, (Broadway play) Who Was That Lady at Martin Beck Theatre, (musical revues) Vaudeville at Palace Theatre, New Faces at Royale Theatre, New Faces at Shubert Theatre, Boston, Great No. Theatre, Chgo., Chic at Orpheum Theatre, Billy Barnes' Review at Carnegie Hall, Have A Heart at Madison Sq. Garden; producer: (concert) Blue Dove's Many Feathers; appeared in hotel shows and cabarets including Ritz Carlton Hotel, Montreal, Can., Le Cabaret, Toronto, Can., Copacobana Palace, Rio De Janeiro, Brazil, Copacobana, N.Y.C., Comedy Club, N.Y.C., Twelfth Night Club, N.Y.C., Waldorf Astoria, N.Y.C., Biltmore Bowl, L.A., Golden Horseshoe, Disneyland, Calif., Hotel Roosevelt, New Orleans, Scotch and Sirloin, L.A., #1 Fifth Avenue, N.Y.C., Di Maggio's Yacht Club, San Francisco, Armed Forces shows, Leon & Eddie's, N.Y.C., The Ballroom, N.Y.C., Mayfair, Boston, Pirates' Den, Hollywood, Calif., Trocadero, Hollywood, House of Vienna, N.Y.C., Blue Angel, N.Y.C., Lambs' Club, N.Y.C., Hollywood (Calif.) Canteen, Stage Door Canteen, N.Y.C., Hotel Brunswick, Boston, St. Francis Hotel, San Francisco, N.Y. World's Fair, San Francisco Exposition; advance "man" for Spike Jones Orch., Coast to Coast Tour; appearances in TV shows including Play of the Week (NTA), Repertoire Workshop, Tonight Show, Sgt. Bilko series, others, also radio shows, local and network telethons; appeared in rodeos Leo Carillo, Roy Rogers Rodeos, Coliseum, L.A.; author, composer: The Boston Nod, (scripts, songs and poetry), The Sun is Shining, Scuddy Wuddy-Boo!, Dallas Sal, Spider, Give All His Love to Her, Great Sun, Victory, Making Up-Silent Song, Pow Wow Smile, Saga of Jini, When Love is Near, The Thorns of Summer, JOBS!; author: Your Own Voice, My Learning Path, Crystal Gazing Lessons, Your Heart's Desire, Lucky Break; creator: Wood Spirits, also astrological paintings, datascope, delineations, Dog-O-Scope, Cat-O-Scope, character of Venus for radio program, 1977, Save A Bag and Save A Tree, Where Have the Birds Gone?, Concrete Drain, Georgia's Bank - For Savings DEPOSIT not WITHDRAWAL, Nuclear Freeze=Slave To Your Knees!, Romping 'Round, the Reservoir, Trash, Fair Snare & Teachers' Net, Human Life Question, Inter-Friends of the World, On Hunting or ON Hunting!, Mined Item Veto; creator documentary series for Four Winds Prodn., Hello Again, 1971; painter The Soul Hath Strength; also fashion designer and songwriter; vocalist with Bob Hardy Orch., Roly Rogers Orch. and Rudy Vallee Orch.; works in librs. of John F. Kennedy, Boston and UCLA; author numerous essays, polit. cartoons, caricatures. Co-chmn., sec. Rep. Town Com., Charlemont, Mass., 1989—; mem. Rep. Town Com., Weston, Mass., Girl Scouts U.S., 5 Civilized Tribes-Choctaw, Chickasaw, Cherokee, Creek, Seminole; alt. Senator Silver Haired Legis., Mass.; asst. to mgr. Eisenhower-Nixon Bandwagon Hdqtrs., N.Y.C.; creator theme, chmn. entertainment Inaugural Ball Pres. Nixon; asst. coord., bd. dir. pub. rels. Mass. Satellite Inaugural Ball for Pres. Reagan, 1980; precinct dir. Re-elect Pres. Reagan, 1984; coord. Dr. Richard A. Jones for Senator campaign, Weston; speaker, write LWV Candidate Night; apptd. election officer Town of Weston, also apptd. Fence Viewer; author Mass. Legis. House bills, proposals for proclamations for Native Am. History Month; bd. dirs. Arts and Crafts Assn.; mem. Environment Task Force, Mass., Rep. Nat. Com.; commd. as chartered Mass. del. to Presdl. Trust of Reps., 1992—; aux. police woman Office of Civil Def., City of N.Y.; field dep. registrar City of L.A., 1971-72; enumerator U.S. Bur. Census, 1980; past mem. numerous other civic orgns., bds.; delegate Presdl. Trust, Mass., 1992; guest delegate Rep. Nat. Conv., Houston, 1992; vol. worker, performer for charities; pres. Weston Rep. Women's Club; mem. USCG Aux., 1943-44; mem. Nat. Rep. Senatorial Com. Res. seaman first class USCG, 1944-45. Named to Times Square Hall of Fame, Miss Pan-Am. Coffee Bur. Girl of Yr., 1942; recipient Theatre World award, Yale U. Drama Salute. Mem. Am. Guild Variety Artists, Screen Actors' Guild, Actor's Equity Assn., AFTRA, Franklin County C. of C., Am. Legion, Mass. Fedn. Rep. Women (bd. dirs.), Nat. Rifle Assn., Am. Fedn. Astrologers, Gun Owners' Action League, Am. Indian Movement (former treas. L.A. chpt.). Episcopalian and Congregationalist. Office: care William Morris Agy 1350 Ave Of The Americas New York NY 10019-4701

DE LUCIA-WEINBERG, DIANE MARIE, systems analyst; b. Huntington, N.Y., Apr. 29, 1964; d. Salvatore Joseph and Margaret Ann (Baker) De L.; m. Bruce Weinberg. BA in Econs. and Spanish, Clemson U., 1986. Cons. O.I.T., Inc., Huntington, 1986-87; systems analyst Blackbaud Micro Systems, Huntington, 1987-88, Datability Software Systems, N.Y.C., 1988-89, Aetna Life & Casualty Co., Lake Success, N.Y., 1989-90; pres. Lazer Tech., 1990—. Mem. Dem. Exec. Com. Town of Huntington. Mem. NAFE, AAUW, Am. Mgmt. Assn., Nat. Assn. Women Bus. Owners, L.I. Networking Entrepreneurs, L.I. Assn. Office: Lazer Tech 11 W 23d St South Huntington NY 11746

DE LUCIE, VICTOR SCOTT, stockbroker; b. Bklyn., Jan. 15, 1965; s. Victor and Marie (Licciardi) De L. BS in Mktg., Ithaca Coll., 1987; MBA in Fin., St. John's U., 1993. Margin Pershing & Co., N.Y.C., 1987-88; ops. support exec. Prudential-Bache Securities, N.Y.C., 1988-89; broker Lehman Bros., N.Y.C., 1989-90, D.H. Blair & Co., N.Y.C., 1990—. Republican. Home: 237 Ardsley St Staten Island NY 10306 Office: D H Blair & Co 44 Wall St New York NY 10005

DELULLO, RALPH PATRICK, safety professional; b. Williamsport, Pa., Mar. 15, 1966; s. Ralph James and Jean Marie (Greenthaner) DeL. BS in Safety Sci., Ind. U. of Pa., 1989. Machinist D&M Tooland Machine Co., Montgomery, Pa., 1983-89; corp. safety trainee Internat. Paper Co., Moss Point, Miss., 1989-90; safety supr. Internat. Paper Co., Westfield, Ma., 1990—. Mem. Am. Soc. Safety Engrs. Republican. Home: 342 Southwick Rd Apt 77 Westfield MA 01085-4759 Office: Internat Paper Co 94 N Elm St Westfield MA 01085-1600

DELUSTRO, FRANK JOSEPH, financial officer, consultant; b. N.Y.C., June 30, 1947; s. Nicholas and Mary (Garafola) DeL.; m. Maria Palma, July 16, 1972. BS, L.I. U., 1970. Various mgmt. acct. and fin. positions, 1970-81, pvt. practice acct., tax cons., 1981-88; contr. VEP, West Caldwell, N.J., 1988-90; chief fin. officer Xaverian High Sch., Bklyn., 1990—; cons. various engring. firms and clients, N.Y.C., 1979—, income tax cons. Trustee Xaverian High Sch., 1990—; chmn. adv. bd. Salvation Army, Bklyn.; treas. Civil Ct. Judgeship, Campaign, 1991. Mem. Inst. Mgmt. Accts., Bayfort Benevolent Assn., Cathedral Club. Home: 4117 Ave S Brooklyn NY 11234 Office: Xaverian High Sch 7100 Shore Rd Brooklyn NY 11209-1098

DELUTY, ROBERT HILLEL, psychology educator; b. N.Y.C., May 12, 1954; s. David and Elise (Kreppel) D.; m. Barbara Medine, June 26, 1983; 1 child, Laura Mee-Ae. BA summa cum laude, NYU, 1975; MA, SUNY, Buffalo, 1978, PhD, 1980. Lic. psychologist, Md. Psychology intern, Div. of Child Psychiatry Children's Meml. Hosp., Chgo., 1979-80; asst. prof. psychology Univ. Md., Baltimore County, 1980-86, assoc. prof. psychology, 1986—, dir. clin. tng., dept. psychology, 1988—; field coord. Standardization of Wechsler Presch. and Primary Scale of Intelligence/rev., San Antonio, 1987-88; clin. psychologist, pvt. practice, Balt., 1988—, Sinai Counseling Ctr., Reisterstown, Md., 1986-88. Editorial cons. 11 jours. in field including Jour. of Consulting and Clin. Psychology, Arlington, Va., 1988-90; author book chpts., test and book revs.; contbr. articles to profl. jours. Mentor gifted and talented prog. Howard County Pub. Sch. System, Ellicott City, Md., 1989-90; presenter to community, sch. and ch. groups on topics of managing aggressive behavior in children, Balt., Reisterstown, 1987—. Recipient grants NIMH, 1982-83, Dept. of Health and Mental Hygiene, State of Md., 1985-86, Outstanding Faculty Mentor award U. Md. Chpt. Phi Kappa Phi, 1989. Mem. Am. Psychol. Assn., Ea. Psychol. Assn., Am. Assn. Suicidology, Am. Assn. Applied and Preventive Psychology, Phi Beta Kappa, Psi Chi. Office: Dept of Psychology Univ Md Baltimore County 5401 Wilkens Ave Baltimore MD 21228-5398

DELVAILLE, JOHN PAUL, physicist; b. Riverside, Calif., Oct. 5, 1931; s. Gilbert C. and Lorraine M. (Harvey) D.; m. Natalie L. Gundrey, Oct. 2, 1965 (div. 1978); 1 child, Christopher H. BA in Physics, U. Calif., Berkeley, 1954; PhD in Physics, Cornell U., 1962. Asst. prof. physics Cornell U., Ithaca, N.Y., 1963-70; physicist Smithsonian Astrophys. Obs., Cambridge, 1974-81; rsch. mem. Ctr. for Space Rsch., MIT, Cambridge, 1970-74; staff mem. Lincoln Lab., MIT, Lexington, 1982—; cons. Wang Labs., Tewksbury, Mass., 1981-82. Contbr. articles to Phys. Rev. Letters, Bull. Am. Astron. Soc., Astrophys. Jour., Applied Optics, Nature, Can. Jour. Physics, Jour. Phys. Soc. Japan, Sci. Am., Ency. Physics. Chmn., deacon, trustee 1st Ch. Unitarian, Littleton, Mass., 1980-89; trustee Rowe (Mass.) Camp and Conf. Ctr., 1989—. Mem. AAAS, Am. Phys. Soc., Am. Assn. Physics Tchrs. Office: MIT Lincoln Lab 244 Wood St Lexington MA 02173-6499

DEL VALLE, CEZAR JOSE, artist; b. Washington, Apr. 14, 1945; s. Cezar and Ida Marie (MacIntosh) Del V.; m. Irene Dorthea DuVal, Sept. 1963 (div. Aug. 1968); m. Darleen Jeanette Travers, Sept. 21, 1968; 1 child, Corinne. Grad. high sch., Suitland, Md. Co-owner Talking of Michaelangelo Gallery, Washington, 1973; concert promoter MacIntosh Prodns., Alexandria, Va., 1976-78; performers agt., Alexandria and N.Y.C., 1976-82; lectr. Smithsonian Instn., Washington, 1973, North Va. Community Coll., 1973; curator 11th Ann. Invitational Art Show, Annapolis, Md., 1973; lectr. Mus. of Holography, N.Y.C., 1988-91; bd. dirs. Nebreuko Theatre Co., 1984. Exhibited in over 17 solo exhbns., 61 group shows, including L.I. U., Bklyn., 1974, 89, Cameravision, L.A., 1981, Wolfe St. Gallery, Alexandria, Va., 1973-75, Belanthi Gallery, Bklyn., 1982, Monmouth Mus., Lincroft, N.J., 1992; group shows include Cleve. Photographic Workshop, 1981, 89, Mus. of Hudson Highlands, Cornwall-on-Hudson, N.Y., 1983, Transamerica's Celebrate the Athlete, L.A., 1984, Photospiva '91, Joplin, Mo., 1991, OIA Artists Salon, N.Y.C., 1991, Newark Mus., 1992; represented in permanent collections Kinsey Inst., Ind. U., Word Craft, Redwood City, Calif., Tampa (Fla.) Mus. of Art, numerous pvt. collections; work pub. in photographic annual. Columnist Alexandria Port Packet, 1976. Mem. Printmaking Coun. of N.J., Orgn. Ind. Artists, Arts Coun. of Greater New Haven, Friends of Dr. Who. Home and Studio: 433 16th St Brooklyn NY 11215

DEL VECCHIO, JOSEPH ANGELO, greeting company executive; b. Boston, Mar. 6, 1942; s. Frank and Adeline Eleanor (Giacoppo) Del V. BA, U. Mass., 1969; MA, U. Md., 1971. Grad. Fellow U. Mass., Amherst, 1964-65; Commonwealth Fellow Commonwealth of Mass., Boston, 1965-66; grad. asst. U. Md., College Park, 1966-71; spl. asst. U.S. Dept. Transp., Washington, 1968-76; v.p. Balloon Bouquets, Inc., Washington, 1976—; franchisor Balloon Bouquets, Inc., Washington, 1979—. Author: (trademark) Balloon Bouquets, 1981. Home and Office: Balloon Bouquets Inc 500 23rd St NW Washington DC 20037-2828

DELVENTHAL, BRUCE WARREN, college hockey coach; b. Englewood, N.J., Jan. 27, 1949; s. Warren Henry and Georgina Hamilton (Fraser) D.; m. Alice Maxfield Kissam, June 4, 1971; 1 child, Brent Warren. BA, Hamilton Coll, 1971; MDiv, Princeton (N.J.) Sem., 1975. Asst. hockey coach Princeton U., 1981-84; head coach Rochester (N.Y.) Inst. Tech., 1984-88; head coach, dir. Achilles Rink Union Coll., Schenectady, N.Y., 1988—; summer camp coach/instr. Pa. State U., 1981—, Bowdoin Coll., Brunswick, Maine, 1981—, Morris County Pks., 1981—; coach USA Hockey, St. Cloud, Minn., 1992. Mem. Am. Hockey Coaches Assn. (sec., treas. 1988—). Office: Union Coll - Achilles Rink Schenectady NY 12308

DE MACEDO, CARLYLE GUERRA, health administrator; b. Parnagua, Piaui, Brazil, Apr. 15, 1937; came to U.S., 1983; s. Julio Borges and Arquiminia (Guerra) de M.; m. Renee Salles de Asevedo, Dec. 2, 1957; children: Carlyle Guerra Jr. Med. degree, U. Pernambuco, Recife, Brazil, 1961; MPH, U. Chile, Santiago, 1968; profl. honoris causa, Nat. Sch. Pub. Health, Rio de Janeiro, 1984, Autonomous U. Santo Domingo, Dominican Republic, 1984, Cayetano Heredia U., Lima, Peru, 1985. Health sector chief Brazilian Devel. Agy., 1962-63, head of health div., 1964-65; sec. of health State of Piaui Dept. Health, 1965-70; mem. devel. coun. State of Piaui, 1966-69; tng. ofcl., head tng. div. Pan Am. Health Planning Ctr., Santiago, Chile, 1970-75; coord. strategic tng. of health pers. Pan. Am. Health Orgn., Brasilia, Brazil, 1976-83; dir. Pan. Am. Health Orgn., Washington, 1983—; vis. prof. sch. pub. health U. Argentina, U. Chile, U. Colombia, U. Peru, U. Brazil, U. Mexico, 1963-82; cons., instr. ILPES/PAHO, Santiago, 1969; cons. state health depts., univs., and ministries, Brazil, 1976-80; mem. nat. program for food and nutrition Nat. Inst. Food and Nutrition/World Bank, Brazil, 1978-82. Contbr. articles to profl. jours. Decorated Orden Rodolfo Robles, Govt. of Guatemala, 1983, Orden Merito Piauiense, State of Piaui, 1983, Orden Daniel Carrion, Govt. of Peru, 1985, Orden del Quetzal, Govt. of Guatemala, 1986, Orden Civil de Sanidad, Govt. of Spain, 1986; named Hon. Citizen, states of Ga., Va., cities of Miami and Hialeah, Fla., and Phoenix, countries of Uruguay, Bolivia, Colombia, Brazil, Guatemala, and Paraguay. Office: Pan Am Health Orgn 525 23rd St NW Washington DC 20037

DE MAILLE, LEON SCOTT, marketing executive; b. West Islip, N.Y., Apr. 9, 1963; s. Leon and Rose Marie (Caliendo) DeM.; m. Catherine Frances Howlett, Aug. 5, 1989 (div.). BBA, Hofstra U., 1985; postgrad., U. Conn., 1988—. Mktg. mgr. Vantage Computer Systems, Wethersfield, Conn., 1985-87; mktg. cons. Hartford, Conn., 1987-88; founder, pres. Synergy Mktg. Solutions, Hartford, 1988—. Water safety instr. ARC, Babylon, N.Y., 1985. Island Drafting Inst. scholar, 1981. Mem. Ad Club of Greater Hartford, Am. Mktg. Assn., Greater Hartford C. of C., Conn. Bus. and Industry Assn. Republican. Roman Catholic. Office: Synergy Mktg 190 Wethersfield Ave Hartford CT 06114-1100

DE MAIO, JAMES MICHAEL, corporate trainer; b. New Haven, Apr. 17, 1961; s. Edward Alfred and Angelina (Pastore) De M. BS, Quinnipiac Coll., 1983; MBA, U. New Haven, 1991. Records retention and control clk. Am. Nat. Bank, Hamden, Conn., 1984; tech. writer Am. Nat. Bank, Hamden, 1984-86, tech. writer, analyst, 1986-89, tng. specialist, 1989-90; dir. corp. tng. Lafayette Am. Bancorp, Hamden, 1990-91, asst. v.p., dir. corp. tng., 1991—. Editor: (co. newsletter) Current Interest, 1990—. Vol. March of Dimes, New Haven, 1987—; co-chairperson for cos. campaign United Way, Hamden, 1990. Mem. ASTD, Am. Inst. Banking (New Haven chpt. v.p. edn. 1990—, instr. 1990—), Delta Mu Delta. Office: Lafayette Am Bancorp 2992 Dixwell Ave Hamden CT 06518-3517

DE MAIO, MARIE ROSE, educator; b. Newark, July 23, 1940; d. Rocco and Carmelina (Goione) De Maio. BA, Newark State Coll., 1962, MA, 1966; MA in Adminstrn. and Supervision, Kean Coll., 1978. Tchr. elem. sch., West Orange, N.J., 1962-65, acting prin., 1985-86, prin. 1986—, tchr. summer exptl. learning lab., 1968-69, counselor Newark Dept. Recreation Summer Playground Program, 1966; speech correctionist Newark State Coll. Speech Clinic, 1962-66; asst. tchr. Dr. Joseph Hancock, Kean Coll., summer, 1977. Chairperson fundraising Cancer and Heart Funds, Essex County Civic Assn. Ladies Aux., 1968-77; trustee Community Mental Health Services, 1976-81; trustee Oakside-Bloomfield Cultural Ctr., 1985-87. Grantee for Ptnrs. In-learning N.J. State Dept. Edn., 1989-91. Mem. N.J. Edn. Assn., NEA, Essex County Edn. Assn., West Orange Edn. Assn. (co-chairperson negotiations com. 1976—, bldg. rep. 1963-68, chairperson tchr. edn. and profl. standards com. 1973, membership sec. 1968-72, sec. 1974-80, v.p. 1979—), Bloomfield Fedn. Music (v.p. bd. trustees 1979-87), AAUW, Nat. Assn. Elem. Sch. Prins., West Orange Adminstrs. Assn., Anthony Gallo Athletic Assn. (treas. 1979—, pres. 1983-85), Assn. for Supervision and Curriculum Devel. Roman Catholic. Office: Washington Sch West Orange NJ 07052

DEMAKIS, LOUISE WARD, archivist historian, writer; b. Jersey City, Apr. 11, 1935; d. William Joseph and Estelle Frances (Materna) Ward; m. George John Demakis, Sept. 2, 1961; children: George John Jr., Drew William, Deirdre Louise. BA in Humanities, Sarah Lawrence Coll., 1980; MA in History, NYU, 1988, cert. in archival mgmt., 1988. Exec. sec. Exxon Corp., Linden, N.J., 1953-61; homemaker, 1961-87; archivist, historian N.Y. Pub. Libr. for Performing Arts, Lincoln Ctr., N.Y.C., 1987-89; free-lance writer Westport, Conn., 1989—; cons. archivist Helen Keller Internat., N.Y.C., 1987. Contbr. articles to hist. publs. Mem. Westport Zoning Bd. Appeals, 1978-81, Rep. Town Com., 1990—. Mem. Soc. Am. Archivists, Westport Hist. Soc., Westport Women's Club, Westport Garden Club. Home: 1 Larch Tree Ln Westport CT 06880

DE MAR, LEODA MILLER, fabric and wallcovering designer; b. N.Y.C., May 26, 1929; d. Benjamin and Malvina (Altman) Miller; m. Robert Mathis de Mar, Dec. 30, 1955 (div. Jan. 1985); children: Victoria, Miller Mathis, Charles David. Diploma, Parson's Sch. of Design, N.Y.C., 1946-49; postgrad., Parson's Sch. of Design, Eng., France, Italy, 1949, NYU, 1950-53. Designer Joseph B. Platt, Indsl. Design, N.Y.C., 1950-53; instr. textiles Parson's Sch. Design, N.Y.C., 1953-55; freelance designer various companies, N.Y.C., 1956-62; designer Leoda de Mar, Inc., N.Y.C., 1962-74; designer, advt. cons. Woodson Wallpapers, N.Y.C., 1975-85, Richard E. Thibaut, Inc., Irvington, N.J., 1985—. Designer 1st wallpaper collection Pippin Papers, N.Y.C., 1954, 1st wallpaper collection Woodson Wallpapers, 1955, own collections Richard E. Thibaut, Inc., 1985—, fabric and wallcovering designs featured in various popular mags.; contbr. articles to mags. Recipient Creativity award Art Direction mag., 1981. Home and Office: 350 Riversville Rd Greenwich CT 06831-3255

DE MARCO, MICHAEL JOSEPH, podiatrist, consultant; b. Bklyn., Jan. 2, 1960; s. Michael Angelo and Dolores Theresa (Caraciola) De M.; m. Celeste Mary Magrino, Sept. 19, 1982; 1 child, Michael Daniel. BS, Wagner Coll., 1982; D Podiatric Medicine, Pa. Coll. Podiatric Medicine, 1986. Diplomte Nat. Bd. Podiatric Examiners. Podiatric resident Seton Hall U., 1986-88, fellow, 1988-89, chief resident, fellow in infectious disease, 1989; pvt. practice, Irvington, N.J., 1989—; asst. dir. podiatric residency, dir. external affairs, infectious disease cons. St. Michael's Med. Ctr., Newark, 1989—; attending podiatrist, specialist in wound care St. Mary's Wound Care Ctr., Orange, N.J., 1990—; lectr. in field; mem. staff Essex County Geriatric Ctr., 1988—. Contbr. articles to profl. jours. Mem. Am. Podiatric Med. Assn., Kiwanis. Republican. Roman Catholic. Office: Surg Podiatry Assocs APC 50 Union Ave Irvington NJ 07111-3262

DEMARCO, PETER ANTHONY, pianist, composer, arranger; b. Bridgeport, Conn., Feb. 21, 1961; s. Daniel Raymond and Lucille Ann (Giannini) DeM. BS in Acctg., U. Bridgeport, 1981; MusM, U. Miami, Coral Gables, Fla., 1983. Freelance musician Bridgeport, Conn. Composer symphony: DreamQuest: A Rhapsody for Orchestra, 1990; composer, producer jazz recording Kick'n' Off, 1986. Mem. ASCAP, Miami Fedn. Musicians. Roman Catholic. Home: 70 Ohio Ave Bridgeport CT 06610

DEMARCO, ROLAND R., foundation executive; b. Mt. Morris, N.Y., July 21, 1910; s. Marion and Mary (Scalzette) DeM.; m. Lydia Hees, June 23, 1934; children—Richard, Ronald, Lynn. Diploma, Geneseo State Tchrs. Coll., 1930; B.S., N.Y. State Coll. Tchrs., 1934; A.M., Columbia U., 1937, Ph.D., 1942; student, U. Munich, Germany, 1937, Shrivenham Am. U., Eng., 1945, Officers Candidate Sch., 1944, Air Intelligence Sch., 1944; LL.D., Chungang U., Seoul, Korea, 1959; D.Litt., Sung Kyun Kwan U., Seoul, 1969, Hanyang U., Seoul, 1974. Instr. Gowanda Pub. Schs., 1930-34; dir. social studies East Islip High Sch., N.Y., 1934-38; instr. social scis. Coll. Charleston, 1939, Columbia U., 1939-40; staff mem. Air Intelligence Sch., 1944-45; vis. prof. Columbia U., 1946-47; prof. history, head dept. social scis. Ala. State Tchrs. Coll., 1940-46, pres. dept., dean, 1949, adminstrv. head, 1949-50, pres., 1950-52; pres. Finch Coll., 1952-70, pres. emeritus, cons., 1970-75; chmn., chief exec. officer Internat. Human Assistance Programs, Inc., N.Y.C., 1973-82, hon. chmn., 1982-84, 85—, pres., chief exec. officer, 1984-85; head history dept. Finch Jr. Coll., 1947-49; curriculum cons. Jackson County Schs., Ala., 1940-43; mem. Nat. Adv. Coun. Edn. Disadvantaged Children, 1971-73; exec. vice chmn., chmn. ednl. adv. com. Am.-Korea Found., 1953-64, pres., 1964-68, 71-73, hon. chmn., 1968-71, chmn., chief exec. officer, 1973-75. Author: The Italianization of African Natives, 1943, The Comeback Country, Vol. I: Light of the East, an Insight into Korea, 1972. Contbr. articles to profl. jours. Founder Fathers of Am.-Korean Found., 1952; trustee Allen Stevenson Sch. Boys, pres., 1956-58; bd. dirs., treas. Council Higher Ednl. Instns., N.Y.C.; pres. All Am. Open Karate Championships, 1965-80, Karate Championships North Am., 1967-80; v.p. World Taekwan Do Fedn., 1973-82; trustee Universidad Politecnica de P.R., San Juan, 1974-85; bd. dirs. Am. Behavioral Scis., 1967-80; color commentator ABC-TV Wide World of Sports for Billiard Championship Match, 1962. Served to 1st lt. USAAF, 1943-46. Decorated Order Cultural Merit Nat. medal (Korea); named hon. citizen of Seoul, 1964; knight officer Order of Merit (Italy); recipient Disting. Alumni award SUNY, 1969, Disting. Alumni award Coll. Arts and Sci. at Geneseo, 1971. Mem. NEA, Nat. Coun. Social Studies, N.Y. Assn. Deans and Guidance, Soc. Advancement Edn., Acad. Polit. Sci., Academia Tiberna, Internat. Sports Fedn., Phi Delta Kappa, Kappa Delta Pi (scholar 1939-40). Home: 1400 East Ave Rochester NY 14610-1611 also: Avoca NY 14809

DEMARCO, THOMAS ANDREW, III, investment counselor; b. N.Y.C., Aug. 9, 1948; s. Thomas A. and Janet (Lefevre) DeM.; B.S. in Banking and Fin., 1970; postgrad. Sch. Banking, Williams Coll., 1976-77; M.B.A. Babson Coll.; m. Deborah E. Foster, June 29, 1974; children—Todd Shepherd, Robin Courtney, Chad Foster. Trust officer and portfolio mgr. State St. Bank and Trust Co., Boston, 1973-79; v.p., dir. personal mktg. and portfolio mgr. David L. Babson and Co., Boston, 1979—; v.p., portfolio mgr. Eaton Vance Mgmt., Boston, 1989—. Overseer Boston Mus. of Sci. Served to 1st lt. U.S. Army, 1971-72. Recipient Leadership medal Greater Boston C. of C., 1974. Mem. Boston Security Analysts Soc., Am. Assn. Individual Investors (chpt. pres.), Assn. Investment Mgmt. Sales Execs., Sigma Chi. Republican. Episcopalian. Club: Dedham Country and Polo. Home: 29 Eliot St Sherborn MA 01770-1540

DE MARGITAY, GEDEON, acquisitions and management consultant; b. Budapest, Hungary, Mar. 6, 1924; s. Joseph and Anne (de Bessenyei) de M.; came to U.S., 1953, naturalized, 1958; student U. Budapest Grad. Sch. Econs., 1941-44, Ecole des Scis. Politiques, Paris, 1946-48; m. Virginia Varet Martin, Dec. 30, 1963. With N.Y. Times, 1947-50, European info. div. Mut. Security Agy., 1950-53; with N.Y. Times, 1954-61; chief exec. Magnum Photos, Inc., N.Y.C., 1961-63; with Time Inc., 1964-75, dir. mktg. services Time/Life TV, 1975; dir. broadcast and corp. planning NBC, 1975-78; acquistions and mgmt. cons., N.Y.C., 1978—. Mem. The Planning Forum, Assn. for Systems Mgmt., Internat. Radio-TV Soc., World Future Soc., Am. Acad. Polit. and Social Sci. Republican. Co-author: Broadcasting: The Next Ten Years, 1977. Address: 65 E 96th St New York NY 10128

DEMARIA, SISTER JEAN DOMINICI, art educator; b. Bklyn., June 19, 1938; d. Thomas J. and Madeline (Londrey) DeM. BS in Art Edn., St. John's U., Jamaica, N.Y., 1970; MS in Art Edn., SUNY, Buffalo, 1974; MA in Fine Arts, L.I. U., 1981; PhD, NYU, 1991. Cert. K-12 art tchr., N.Y.; joined Sisters of St. Dominic, Roman Cath. Ch., 1956. Tchr. art St. Michael's High Sch., Bklyn. and L.I., 1968-72, St. John the Bapt. High Sch., West Islip, N.Y., 1972-80; assoc. prof. art Molloy Coll., Rockville Centre, N.Y., 1980—. Mem. Cath. Fine Arts Soc. (pres. 1988—), Cath. Artists of

90's (chief exec. officer 1989—), Phi Delta Kappa. Home and Office: 1000 Hempstead Ave Rockville Centre NY 11570-1199

DEMARIA, THOMAS PATRICK, psychologist; b. Long Beach, N.Y., Feb. 20, 1960; s. William and Margaret (Roche) D.; m. Mary Kate Magee, Sept. 8, 1990. BA, St. John's U., 1982; MA, Hofstra U., 1983, PhD, 1986. Lic. psychologist, N.Y. Staff therapist Inst. for Behavior Therapy, Manhattan, N.Y., 1984-87; sch. psychologist Rockville Centre (N.Y.) Sch. Dist., 1983-87; chief psychologist South Nassau Community Hosp. Mental Health Clinic, Oceanside, N.Y., 1987-89; asst. dir. South Nassau Community Hosp. Mental Health Ctr., Oceanside, N.Y., 1990—; trainer, cons. psychology, N.Y., 1985—. Contbr. articles to profl. jours. Chair svc. area coun. Nassau County Dept. Mental Health, 1990—, mem. community disaster task force, 1991—. Mem. Am. Psychol. Assn., Assn. Advancement Behavior Therapy, Nassau County Psychol. Assn. Roman Catholic. Office: South Nassau Community Hosp 2485 Oceanside Rd Oceanside NY 11572-1549

DEMARIE, LINDA ESTHER, sales executive; b. Liberty, N.Y., Jan. 2, 1960; d. Carryl Merritt Vail and Arline Margaret (Weitmann) McCarthy; m. Paul DeMarie, June 3, 1978 (dec. June 1980). Mgr. sales and customer svc. State of Newburgh, N.Y., 1981-85; contract sales mgr. Hunt Contract Furniture, Wingdale, N.Y., 1985-88, v.p. contract sales, 1988—. Home: 1 Richman Ave Newburgh NY 12550-4208 Office: Hunt Contract Furniture Webatuck Rd Wingdale NY 12594

DE MARINO, DONALD NICHOLSON, international business executive, former federal agency administrator; b. Greensburg, Pa., Sept. 28, 1945; s. Thomas C. and Sue Eleanor (Nicholson) De M.; m. Caroline Mack, Dec. 27, 1967 (div. 1981); children: Christopher Tyson, Benjamin Nicholson; m. Betsy Reiver, July 18, 1981; children: Alexander Reiver, William McCurdy. BA, U. Pa., 1967. Dir. Mack & Nicholson, West Chester, Pa., 1972-76; bus. cons. The Nicholson Group, Inc., N.Y.C., 1976-81; sr. project officer U.S.-Saudi Arabian Joint Commn. on Econ. Cooperation, Riyadh, Saudi Arabia, 1981-84; dir. U.S.-Saudi Arabian Joint Commn. on Econ. Cooperation, 1985-87; mgr. Litton Industries Offset Investment Programs, Riyadh, 1984-85; sr. project adviser The Arab Investment Co., Riyadh, 1985; internat. bus. cons., prin. Don N. De Marino, Coatesville, Pa., 1987-88; dep. asst. sec. Africa, Near East and South Asia U.S. Dept. Commerce, Washington, 1989-90; sr. U.S. rep. for Tata Group of India, Unionville, Pa., 1991—; chmn. Nat. U.S.-Arab C. of C., 1991—; mem. nat. adv. com., Am.-Arab Affairs Coun., Washington, 1987-88; sr. advisor to Huntsman Ctr. for Global Competitiveness Wharton Sch., U. Pa. Recipient disting. svc. award, Govt. of Saudi Arabia, 1987. Mem. Racquet Club, Mask & Wig Club. Republican. Presbyterian. Home: 18 Longview Rd Coatesville PA 19320-4311 Office: PO Box 791 Unionville PA 19375-0791

DEMARK, EUGENE F., accountant; b. Bklyn., Aug. 19, 1947; s. William and Adeline (Chirico) DeM.; m. Carol Ann DeMark; children: Dina, Christopher. BBA in Acctg., Hofstra U., 1969. CPA, N.Y. Ptnr.-in-charge audit KPMG Peat Marwick, Jericho, N.Y., 1985-88, mng. ptnr., 1988—. Chmn., pres. Nassau County coun. Boy Scouts U.S.A.; bd. dirs., chmn. nominating com. United Way L.I.; bd. overseers Tilles Ctr., L.I. U., Brookville, N.Y.; chmn. Multiple Sclerosis, Huntington Station, N.Y.; pres. East Meadow (N.Y.) Civic Assn. Mem. Nat. Assn. Accts., N.Y. State Soc. CPAs (chmn. com. coop. with bankers Nassau chpt.), L.I. Assn. (bd. dirs.). Office: KPMG Peat Marwick Jericho NY 11753

DE MARTINI, ALFRED E., graphic and industrial designer; b. Camden, N.J., Feb. 25, 1916; s. Frank and Rose (De Rago) De M.; m. Alberta Cianfrani, June 4, 1942; children: Alfred, Nina, Rosemary, Frank, Paul. Student, Phila. Coll. Art, 1937. Pres. De Martini Displays, Camden, N.J., 1935-40; adminstr. War Dept. Suggestion System, Phila., 1940-44; graphic designer Martin & Ladriere, N.Y.C., 1944-48, Parents Inst., N.Y.C., 1948-52; pres. De Martini Assocs., Inc., Phila., 1952-72, De Martini Ednl. Films, Haddon Heights, N.J., 1972-76, De Martini Plaza, Haddon Heights, N.J., 1976, De Martini Assocs., Inc., Haddon Heights, N.J., 1980—; pubr. Holiday Bazaar, Haddon Heights, 1959-69. Author ednl. film: Oxford: Bastion of Tradition (Gold award 1980); dir., writer film: Shakespeare: Man from Stratford. Chmn. Haddon Hts. Planning Bd. Recipient The Golden Cube Art Dirs. Club, 1968, Gold Medal N.Y. Internat. Film Festival, 1976, V.I. Internat. Film Festival, 1976. Mem. Art Dirs. Club of Phila. (treas. 1955-65, pres.). Home and Office: 414 4th Ave Haddon Heights NJ 08035-1392

DEMASO, DAVID RAY, psychiatrist; b. Battle Creek, Mich., Nov. 1, 1949; s. Harry A. and Mary Jayne (Hocott) D.; m. Josephine Marie Giancola, May 21, 1971; children: Christine Marie, Jeffrey David, Timothy David. BS with distinction, U. Mich., 1971, MD cum laude, 1975. Diplomate Am. Bd. Psychiatry and Neurology. Resident in pediatrics Mass. Gen. Hosp., Boston, 1975-76; resident in psychiatry Duke U. Med. Ctr., Durham, N.C., 1976-78; fellow in child psychiatry Judge Baker Children's Ctr. and Children's Hosp., Boston, 1980-81; cons.-liaison fellow Children's Hosp., Boston, 1980-81, assoc. in psychiatry and cardiology, 1983—; dir. cons. and emergency svcs., dept. psychiatry Children's Hosp., 1983, asst. clin. dir., 1990—; asst. prof. psychiatry Harvard Med. Sch., Boston. Mem. Alpha Omega Alpha. Roman Catholic. Office: Children's Hosp 300 Longwood Ave Boston MA 02115-5737

DEMASO, JEFFREY ANTHONY, lawyer, business owner; b. Derby, Conn., Apr. 10, 1964; s. Andrew Anthony and Mary Louise (Palmieri) DeM. BS in Fin., Boston Coll., 1986, JD, 1989. Bar: Conn. 1989, U.S. Dist. Ct. Conn. 1990. Assoc. Tarlow, Levy & Drancy, PC, Farmington, Conn., 1989-91; owner, ind. distbr. Double Eagle Distributorships, Middletown, Conn., 1991—. Mem. ABA, Conn. Bar Assn., Community Assn. Inst. (program com. Conn. chpt. 1989-90). Republican. Office: Double Eagle Distributorships 402 Cambridge Commons Middletown CT 06457

DEMATTEIS, THOMAS JAMES, secondary school educator; b. Wilmington, Del., Oct. 6, 1962; s. Mary Jane (Walker) DeM.; m. Theresa M. Collins, June 27, 1987; 1 child, Elizabeth Theresa. BA, Cabrini Coll., 1984. Cert. secondary edn. tchr., Del. Tchr., journalism instr. St. Mark's High Sch., Wilmington, 1984—, varsity soccer coach, 1986—. Reporter The Dialog, Wilmington, 1984-87. Instr. New Castle County Soccer Camp, Wilmington, 1987—, Middlestates Soccer Camp, Wilmington, 1987—; site coord. YMCA, Wilmington, 1988; dir. Spartan Soccer Camp, Wilmington, 1988—. Named Outstanding Soccer Coach, Nat. Fedn. Interscholastic Coaches Assn., 1988. Mem. Nat. Soccer Coaches Assn. Am. (Regional Coach of Yr. 1990), Del. High Sch. Soccer Coaches Assn. (conf. rep. 1986—, Coach of Yr. 1986). Roman Catholic. Home: 97 White Clay Cr Newark DE 19711

DEMBECK, MARY GRACE, artist, writer; b. N.Y.C., Oct. 29, 1931; d. August and Lucia Louisa (De Sanctis) Menghini; m. John Francis Dembeck, June 14, 1958; children: Christine Elizabeth, John Francis Jr. Student, St. John's U., N.Y.C., 1950-51, Fordham U., 1951-52, Fairfield U., 1982-83; studies with, Charles Reid, Daniel Green, John Mc Clelland, Leonard Everett Fisher, John C. Pellew and Mary Ann Hoberman, Conn., N.Y., 1974-82. Artist, pres. Pinafore, Ltd., Westport, Conn., 1987—. works exhibited at Eagle Tower Gallery, Stamford, Conn., 1979, 80, Nat. Acad. Design, N.Y.C., 1981, Westport Nature Ctr., Westport Ctr. Arts, 1983-85, Rowayton (Conn.) Arts Ctr., 1983-87 (acrylic award 1983, 89), Trumbull (Conn.) Library, 1985-87, Gallery Four, Norwalk, 1986, Norfield Art Show, Weston, Conn., 1987, Fairfield (Conn.) U., St. Vincent, Bridgeport Gallery, 1987, Portland Pl. Gallery, South Norwalk, Conn., Gallery 53, Meriden Ct. (art award Conn. Classic Arts 1990); one woman shows include St. Vincent's Bridgeport, Conn., 1989; contbr. light verse, humor and poetry to mags., newspapers including Nat. Wildlife Fedn's. Ranger Rick Mag., Westport News, 1979-83, Banker's Newsletter, 1985, Wall Street Jour., 1985—, Reader's Digest, 1988, NBC News, Steve Allen Radio Program, 1988, Garrison Keillor's Am. Radio Co. of The Air, 1990; creator cartoon character "Harriet"; mng. editor, staff artist Carousel Mag., 1988-89; panelist local radio, cable TV arts/humor discussions. Designer Mass book cover St. Patrick's Cathedral, N.Y.C., 1977—; judge children's poetry and short story Trumbull Arts Festival, 1986-89; mem. Westport Hist. Soc., Westport Women's Club (awards for acrylics 1985, 86, 87); artist mem. Italian Apostolate Archdiocese N.Y.C. Recipient Nat. Pub. Radio award, 1987. Mem. Rowayton Arts Ctr., Westport Ctr. for the Arts, So. Vt. Arts Ctr., Conn. Classic Arts, Trumbull (award 1987), Nat. League of Pen Women (poetry award 1983, best humerous poem 1984), Brontë Soc. Roman Catholic.

DEMBOWSKI, FREDERICK LESTER, educational administration educator, consultant; b. Syracuse, N.Y., July 17, 1948; s. Frederick L. and Jean Marie (Oswald) D.; m. Rhona Dembowski; children: Kirsten, Erika. BS, SUNY-Oswego, 1970, MS, 1972; EdD, U. Rochester, 1978. Asst. prof. SUNY-Albany, 1979-84, assoc. prof. ednl. adminstrn., 1984—, dir. Ednl. Mgmt. Inst., 1985—; cons. AID, Washington, 1984—; dep. chief party Somtad Project, Usaid/Somalia, Africa, 1988-90. Author: School Financial Management, 1983; School/Banking Relations, 1982. Editor: Administrative Uses of Microcomputers 3 vol. series, 1984; contbr. articles to profl. jours. and chpts. to books. Mem. Am. Sch. Bus. Ofcls. (chmn. mgmt. com. 1982—, outstanding researcher award N.Y. State assn. 1985), Am. Edn. Fin. Assn., Am. Ednl. Rsch. Assn., Phi Delta Kappa. Roman Catholic. Avocations: travel, fishing, diving. Office: SUNY-Albany Ednl Adminstrn ED 327 Albany NY 12222

DEMEIS, RICHARD ANTHONY, aerospace technology writer, aerospace engineer; b. N.Y.C., Aug. 10, 1945; s. Louis Joseph and Adeline Christina (Skalecki) DeM.; m. Mia Theresa Riedl, Aug. 24, 1968; children: Jude, Matthew. B in Engring., Rensselaer Poly. Inst., 1967, M in Astronautical Engring., 1970. Tchr. sci. Margaretville (N.Y.) Cen. Sch., 1970-71; aerospace engr. Grumman Aerospace, L.I., N.Y., 1971-75, Grumman Am., Savannah, Ga., 1975-77, Raytheon Missile Systems, Bedford, Mass., 1977-84; freelance writer, editor engring. Aerospace Am. Mag., Washington, 1984—. Editor, writer first ofcl. Russian Space Program Publs. in West; contbr. articles to profl. jours. Mem. town meeting Needham, Mass., 1986—; lector St. Joseph Ch., Needham. Recipient Excellence award, Regional Excellence awards Aviation/Space Writers Assn., 1987-90. Fellow AIAA (assoc., coun. New England sect. 1979—).

DEMELLO, LOUISE ANN, writer, singer; b. Providence, Sept. 8, 1948; d. Vincent and Marianna (Matarese) Russillo; m. Odorico Fernando DeMello, Nov. 11, 1970; 1 child, Anna. Grad., Mt. Pleasant High Sch., Providence, 1967, Katherine Gibbs Secretarial Sch., Providence, 1968. Sales sec., traffic mgr., continuity dir., comml. copy writer WICE Radio, Providence, 1967-74; comml. copy writer WEAN & WPJB Radio, Providence, 1974-81; advt. asst. Brassard Agy., Pawtucket, R.I., 1980-83; soloist singer Holy Ghost Ch., Providence, 1983—; singer R.I. Civic Chorale, Providence, 1987—; sing, act Trinity Ch. Players, Providence, 1986-87. Treas. The Opera Guild, 1984-87, pres., 1987—; mem. Da Vinci Opera Soc., 1988—, Italian Am. Hist. Soc., 1986—. Mem. Saturday Matinee Club, The Chaminade Club (1st v.p. 1991—). Roman Catholic.

DEMENTIS, KATHARINE HOPKINS, interior designer; b. Indpls., Dec. 20, 1922; d. Stephen Francis and Margaret Bell (Yeager) Hopkins; m. Gilbert X. Dementis, Feb. 1, 1953; children: Mary Margaret Dementis O'Dwyer, Stephen Ezra Hall. Student, John Herron Art Sch., 1941-44; BS, U. Wis., 1971. Interior designer L.A. Ayres and Co., Indpls., 1945-51; pres. Ariz. Questers, 1991--. Mem. DAR, Lakes Club, Union Hills Country Club, Passport Club. Republican. Presbyterian. Home: 12830 W Castlebar Dr Sun City West AZ 85375-3270 Office: Questers 210 S Quince St Philadelphia PA 19107-5534

DEMERS, ANDREA NANCY, critical care nurse; b. Providence, Dec. 9, 1965; d. Antimo and Rosalie (Porreca) D'Agostino; m. James Orin Demers. ADN, Community Coll. R.I., 1989; BSN, R.I. Coll., 1992; post-grad., U. R.I., 1992—. Cert. provider ACLS, Am. Heart Assn., cert. instr. BLS, Am. Heart Assn., cert. provider defibrillation Roger Williams Med. Ctr., R.I., cert. provider intra-aortic balloon pump Roger Williams Med. Ctr., R.I. RN Roger Williams Med. Ctr., Providence, 1989—; coord., presenter Nursing Grand Rounds, Providence, 1991; rsch. in collaboration with Roger Williams Med. Ctr. and U. R.I. Mem. ANA, Critical Care Nurses Assn., Critical Care Protocol Com., Surg. Oncology Com., Oncology Nurses Soc., Sigma Theta Tau. Home: 1179 Phenix Ave Cranston RI 02921

DEMERS, PAUL RENE, campus minister; b. Manchester, N.H., Jan. 5, 1937; s. Rene T. and Beatrice Alice (Vezina) D. BA in English, St. Michael Coll., Winooski, Vt., 1961, MA in Teaching, 1968; MA in Bibl. Studies, Providence Coll., 1981; D Ministry, Boston U., 1988. Joined Bros. of Sacred Heart, Roman Cath. Ch., 1955. Jr. and sr. high sch. tchr. Sacred Heart Acad., Central Falls, R.I., 1957-62, prin., 1968-70; tchr. Father MacDonald High Sch., St. Laurent, Que., Can., 1962-63; tchr. Mt. St. Charles Acad., Woonsocket, R.I., 1963-68, prin., 1970-74, tchr. English, dept. chmn., 1974-80; campus min. Bishop Guertin High Sch., Nashua, N.H., 1981-84; campus min., lectr. religious studies Notre Dame Coll., Manchester, N.H., 1985-88, Rivier Coll., Nashua, N.H., 1988—; trustee Bros. of Sacred Heart, Pascoag, R.I., 1970-73, 79-82; mem. Liturgical and Ecumenical Commns. Diocese of Manchester, 1986—; mem. Liturgical commn. Diocese of Providence; presenter Missionary Renewal Session, Lusaka, Zambia, 1982; staff Religious Renewal Program, Belvidere, N.H., 1981-82. Chaplain Dartmouth-Hitchcock Hosp., Hanover, N.H., summer 1986. Recipient Beyond War award, 1990. Mem. Cath. Campus Ministry Assn., nat. Campus Ministry Assn., New Eng. Campus Ministry Assn., Assn. Religion and Intellectual Life. Office: Rivier Coll 420 Main St Nashua NH 03060-5086

DEMETER, STEVEN, neurologist, publishing company executive; b. Budapest, Hungary, Jan. 12, 1947; came to U.S., 1957; s. Arpad and Ilona (Wiesner) D.; m. Diane Simkin, Jan. 8, 1984; children: Sara, Nikki. BS, CUNY, 1969; MD, N.Y. Med. Coll., 1973. Diplomate Am. Bd. Psychiatry and Neurology. Intern Beth Israel Med. Ctr., N.Y.C., 1973-74; neurology resident Albert Einstein Coll. Medicine, Bronx, N.Y., 1974-77; inst. neurology N.Y. Med. Coll., N.Y.C., 1977-79; fellow in behavioral neurology U. Iowa Coll. Medicine, Iowa City, 1979-81; fellow Ctr. for Brain Rsch., U. Rochester (N.Y.) Sch. Medicine, 1981-84, instr. neurology, 1982-84, asst. prof. Ctr. for Brain Rsch., 1984-87, asst. prof. neurology, 1987-89, clin. asst. prof., 1989-91, clin. assoc. prof., 1991—; pres. Arbor Pub. Corp., electronic pub., Rochester, 1990—; neurology cons. Rochester Psychiat. Ctr., 1985-91. Contbr. numerous articles to med. jours. Grantee Scottish Rite Schizophrenia Rsch. Found., 1987-90, Whitehall Found., 1990-93, NIH, 1991-94. Fellow Am. Acad. Neurology, Royal Soc. Medicine (London); mem. AAAS, Am. Assn. Anatomists, Soc. for Neurosci., Tourette Syndrome Assn. (med. com. 1985—, bd. dirs. 1987—). Office: U Rochester Med Ctr PO Box 605 Rochester NY 14642-0001 Office: Arbor Pub Corp 333 Metro Park Ste 208N Rochester NY 14623-2632

DEMETRION, JAMES THOMAS, art museum director; b. Middletown, Ohio, July 10, 1930; s. Tom and Susie (Tsifiklis) D.; m. Barbara Parrish, 1954; 1 child, Elaine. BS in Edn., Miami U., 1952; hon. doctorate, Simpson Coll., 1984. Curator Pasadena Art Mus., Calif., 1964-66; dir. Pasadena Art Mus., 1966-69, Des Moines Art Ctr., 1969-84, Hirshhorn Mus. & Sculpture Garden, Washington, 1984—; mem. Mus. adv. panel Nat. Endowment for Arts, 1973-76, co-chmn., 1974-76; mem. IRS Art Adv. Panel, 1983-86. Mem. art adv. panel 1st Nat. Bank Chgo. Mem. Assn. Art Mus. Dirs. (treas. 1976-77, pres. 1979-80). Office: Hirshhorn Mus-Sculpture Garden Independence Ave at 8th St SW Washington DC 20560

DEMETRIOU, MICHAEL, lawyer; b. N.Y.C., Nov. 4, 1927; s. Peter and Esther (Finkelstein) D.; m. Koula Rapton, Oct. 28, 1951; children: James P., Theodore, Diantha K., Paul. BS, NYU, 1948, MBA, 1952; JD, St. John's U., 1951; LLM, Bklyn. U., 1965. Bar: N.Y. 1953. Life ins. cons. Met. Life, N.Y.C., 1953-58; pvt. practice real estate mgmt. and investments cons. N.Y.C., 1948—; pvt. practice Demetriou and Demetriou, N.Y.C., 1953-79; ptnr. Demetriou & Demetriou Law Offices, N.Y.C., 1979—; counsel, dir. Queenschpt. ARC, Flushing , N.Y., 1986—; bd. mgrs. Long Island City YMCA, 1979—; adv. council paralegal studies N.Y. Inst. Tech., 1987—; adv. council Am. Title Ins. Co., 1984—, Long Island U. C.W. Post, 1985-86; judge Village of Brookville, N.Y., 1973—. Mem. devel. adv. com. Fiorello H. LaGuardia Community Coll., 1989; scoutmaster Boy Scouts Am. Troop 23, N.Y.C., 1945-51, chmn. bd. dirs. Troop 346, N.Y.C., 1965-69, ARC, Queens, N.Y., 1990-91; counsel St. Demetrios, Astoria, N.Y., Holy Trinity, Hicksville, N.Y., Holy Cross, Whitestone, N.Y.; trustee ARC Greater N.Y. Mem. Borough of Queens C. of C., N.Y. County Lawyers Assn., Queens County Bar Assn., Nassau County Bar Assn., Rotary, Parthenon F & AM, Ahepa. Republican. Greek Orthodox. Home: 20 Rolling Dr Glen Head NY 11545-2613 Office: Demetriou and Demetriou 29-14 Queens Pla East Long Island NY 11101

DEMIANCZYK, PAMELA J., real estate consultant; b. Salem, W.Va., Oct. 31, 1949; d. Harry Jr. and Grace Belle (Gain) Fetty; m. William Dennis Demianczyk, Jan. 27, 1976. Grad., Mountain State Coll., 1968; postgrad., W.Va. U., 1968-71. Mktg. dir. Comml. Banking & Trust, Parkersburg, W.Va., 1970-74; regional mgr. A-F Mgmt., Pitts., 1974-77, ManuLife, Dallas and Toronto, Can., 1978-79; chief adminstrv. officer Soc. Comml. Reassurance, Paris and Dallas, 1980-83; chief oper. officer RCS Investments, Dallas, 1983-88; pvt. practice cons. Dallas, 1988—; cons. Dai Tokyo Marine, 1983—, Belcourt Constrn., Montreal, Can., 1988—, Suit-Up, Dallas, 1988—, Rue De La Hollande, Corsica, France, 1990—. Interscholastic athletic ofcl. Home and Office: 3066 E Bardonner Rd 3066 E Bardonner Rd Gibsonia PA 15044

DEMICHIEI, ROBERT ALLEN, accountant; b. Pitts., Dec. 10, 1964; s. Raymond J. and Pauline E. (Koban) DeM.; m. Amy Lynn Zoltun, Aug. 19, 1989. BA in Bus. Econs., U. Pitts., Johnstown, 1987. CPA, Pa. Staff acct. Price Waterhouse, Pitts., 1987-90, sr. acct., 1990—. Chmn. Plum (Pa.) Borough Bd. Auditors, 1989—. Mem. AICPA, Pa. Inst. CPAs, Iota Alpha Alumni Assn. of Kappa Delta Rho (bd. dirs. 1987). Democrat. Byzantine Catholic.

DE MILLE, NELSON RICHARD, writer; b. N.Y.C., Aug. 23, 1943; s. Huron and Antonia (Lombardo) DeM.; divorced; children: Lauren, Alex; m. Ginny Sindel Witte, 1988. BA in Polit. Sci. and History, Hofstra U., 1970, Doctorate of Humane Letters, (hon.), 1989. Free-lance writer, Garden City, 1973—; author more than 12 novels, including By the Rivers of Babylon (Book-of-the-Month Club main selection, Readers Digest condensed book), 1978; Cathedral (Lit. Guild main selection), 1981; The Talbot Odyssey, 1984; Word of Honor (Book-of-the-Mo. Club main selection), 1985, The Charm School (Reader's Digest Condensed Book), 1988; The Gold Coast (Book-of-the-Mo Club main selection) 1990, The General's Daughter (Lit. Guild Main Selection), 1992; contbr. short stories to mags. 1st lt. U.S. Army, 1966-69. Decorated Air medal, Bronze Star, Vietnamese Cross of Gallantry; recipient Estabrook award Hofstra U. Mem. Mystery Writers Am., Author's Guild, Mensa. Roman Catholic. Office: 61 Hilton Ave Ste 23 Garden City NY 11530-2813

DEMING, IRA MICHAEL, podiatrist, consultant; b. Balt., Apr. 29, 1958; s. Martin Eugene and Esther Ruth (Levin) D.; m. Amy Lynn Tabach, Sept. 9, 1990; 1 child, Brian Jeffrey. BS in Pharmacy, U. Md., 1981; DPM, Pa. Coll. Podiatric Medicine, 1985. Diplomate Am. Coun. Cert. Podiatric Physicians and Surgeons. Pharmacist Peoples Drug, Oxon Hill, Md., 1981-83, Eckerd Drugs, Depford, N.J., 1983-87; resident Met. Hosp.-Parkview, Phila., 1985-86, chief resident in podiatric surgery, 1986-87; resident clinican, lectr. Pa. Coll. Podiatric Medicine, Phila., 1986-87; pvt. practice Silver Spring, Md., 1987—; cons. Fernwood House, Bethesda, 1988—, Bethesda Retirement & Nursing Ctr., Chevy Chase, Md., 1988—, The Westwood, Bethesda, 1988—, Gallaudet U., Washington, 1990—, The Pavillion-Suburban Hosp., Bethesda, 1991—; affiliate Holy Cross Hosp., Montgomery Gen. Hosp.; assoc. attending Suburban Hosp. Mem. Am. Coll. Foot Surgeons (assoc.). Home: 4108 Sandcastle Ln Olney MD 20832-2842 Office: 8201 16th St Silver Spring MD 20910-3240 Office: 5713 Bradley Blvd Bethesda MD 20814-1034

DEMIS, D. JOSEPH, dermatology and pharmacology educator; b. N.Y.C.; s. Joseph and Mary Theresa (Connolly) D. BS, Union U.; MD, Yale U.; PhD, U. Rochester, N.Y. Diplomate Am. Bd. Dermatology. Asst. prof. George Washington U., Washington, 1959-65; dir. dept. dermatology Walter Reed Army Hosp., Washington, 1961-64; prof. Sch. of Medicine Washington U., St. Louis, 1964-67; prof. Albany (N.Y.) Med. Coll., 1967—; bd. dirs. Dermatology Rsch. Assocs., Albany. Author, editor: Clinical Dermatology, 1972—. Board dirs. Albany Symphony Orch., 1977-82. Maj. U.S. Army, 1957-64. Fellow Am. Acad. Dermatology; mem. Am. Soc. Clin. Investigation, Am. Dermatology Assn., Histamine Club Internat., Phi Beta Kappa. Office: Dermatology Rsch Assocs 195 Delaware Ave Delmar NY 12054-1292

DE MITA, FRANCIS ANTHONY, mathematics educator; b. N.Y.C., Oct. 13, 1927; s. Michael Joseph and Rachel Catherine (Prudente) DeM.; m. Lois Marie Smith, Mar. 22, 1934; children: Francis Anthony Jr., Michael Spencer. BS, NYU, 1950, MA, 1951; diploma in mgmt., Cornell U., 1988. Tchr. math. Bedford Park Acad., N.Y.C., 1951-53; tchr. math. Valley Stream (N.Y.) Central High Sch., 1953—, chmn. dept. math., 1981—; adj. asst. prof. math. Queensborough Community Coll., N.Y.C., 1962—; pres., chmn. bd. Nassau Educators Fed. Credit Union, Valley Stream, 1971—. Contbr. articles to mags. Founder, pres. East Central Civic Assn., Valley Stream, 1967-69, 79-89. Cpl. U.S. Army, 1946-48. NSF grantee, 1958-65; named Vol. of Yr., Nat. Assn. Fed. Credit Unions, Denver, 1981, Dir. of Yr. Credit Union Execs. Soc., 1989; recipient Congl. Citation, U.S. Congress, 1982. Mem. Nat. Coun. Tchrs. Math., Nat. Assn. Credit Union Pres., N.Y. State Tchrs. Math., Nassau County Math. Suprs., Model A Club of L.I. (Hicksville, N.Y.), Elks, Lions (pres. 1973-74). Republican. Roman Catholic. Home: 108 E Euclid St Valley Stream NY 11580-4145 also: 55 Forest Dr Lake Monticello VA 22963

DEMLER, MARVIN CHRISTIAN, air force officer; b. North Tonawanda, N.Y., Oct. 23, 1909; s. Ernest Frederick and Bertha Wilhelmina (Krull) D.; m. Willena Mayverette Brown; children: James Carl, Roger Lee. BSME, NYU, 1931, Aero. Engr., 1934; MS in Aero. Engring., U. Mich., 1941; ScD (hon.), NYU, 1967. Commd. 2nd lt. U.S. Army Air Corps., 1938; advanced through grades to maj. gen. USAF, 1958, ret. 1971; sales and svc. engr. Lycoming div. Avco, Williamsport, Pa., 1934-38. Decorated D.S.M. with oak leaf cluster, Legion of Merit with 2 oak leaf clusters, Bronze Star medal, others. Fellow AIAA; mem. Planetary Soc., Order of Daedalians, Internat. Club, Mil. Order of the World Wars, Sigma Xi. Republican. Address: 7309 River Crescent Dr Annapolis MD 21401

DEMMLER, ALBERT WILLIAM, JR., editor, metallurgical engineer; b. Pitts., Feb. 21, 1929; Albert William and Hester Louisa (Dye) D.; m. Donna Lou Frederick, Feb. 16, 1957; children: Richard Frederick, Keith Alan (dec.), Diane Leslie, Debra Lynn. PhB in Liberal Arts, U. Chgo., 1948; BS in Metall. Engring., U. Mich., 1951, MS in Metall. Engring., 1952, PhD, 1955. Rsch. engr. Alcoa Rsch. Labs., New Kensington, Pa., 1955-68; registered rep. Butcher & Singer, Pitts., 1968-74; exec. searcher Reese Assoc., Pitts., 1974-76; assoc. editor Soc. Automotive Engrs. Inc. Mags., Warrendale, Pa., 1976-90, sr. editor, 1990—. Patentee in field. Mem. NRA, Soc. Automotive Engrs., Am. Soc. for Metals Internat., Hypnotism Soc. Pa., Tarentum Dist. Sportsmens Club, Pa. Rifle and Pistol Assn., Detroit Press Club, Crowfoot Rod and Gun Club, Mensa, Tau Beta Pi, Phi Lambda Upsilon, Sigma Xi. Democrat. Presbyterian. Home: 132 Glenview Dr New Kensington PA 15068-4900 Office: Soc of Automotive Engrs 400 Commonwealth Dr Warrendale PA 15096-0001

DE MOURA, PATRICIA BROWN, nurse; b. Fall River, Mass., Apr. 25, 1948; d. Albert Prescott and Dorothy (MacInnis) Brown; divorced; children: Joel David, Heidi Jean. RN diploma, St. Luke's Hosp., New Bedford, Mass., 1969; BS, Upsala Coll., 1990. RN, N.J., Mass., Conn.; cert. nurse oper. rm., orthopaedic nurse. Staff nurse Manchester (Conn.) Hosp., 1969, Morton Hosp., Taunton, Mass., 1970; staff nurse Mountainside Hosp., Montclair, N.J., 1977-88, edn. coord., 1988—; oper. rm. cons., 1991—; lectr. Howmedica, Rutherford, N.J., 1988, Johnson & Johnson Orthopedics, New Brunswick, N.J., 1988. Mem. Am. Oper. Rm. Nurses, Nat. Assn. Orthopedic Nurses. Home: 1664 Broad St Bloomfield NJ 07003-3110 Office: Mountainside Hosp Bay Ave Montclair NJ 07042

DEMPSEY, DANIEL THOMAS, surgeon, educator; b. Cambridge, N.Y., Mar. 30, 1953; s. Harry Francis and Jennie (Vairo) D.; m. Barbara Ann Seneca, Oct. 19, 1975; 1 child, Patrick. AB, Princeton U., 1975; MD, U. Rochester, 1979. Resident surgery U. Pa., Phila., 1979-86, lectr. surgery, 1987-88; asst. prof. surgery Temple U., Phila., 1986-87, 88—. Office: Temple U Hosp Broad and Ontario Sts Philadelphia PA 19140

DEMPSEY, OWEN ANDRE, biotechnology company executive; b. Crestwood, N.Y., Aug. 19, 1957; s. Wallace Guy and Monique (Samson) D. BA, Dartmouth Coll., 1979; MBA, Stanford U., 1984. Mktg. rep. IBM Corp., Boston, 1979-82; rsch. assoc. Internat. Mgmt. Devel. Inst., Lausanne, Switzerland, 1984-85; pres. Endogen, Inc., Boston, 1985—, also bd. dirs., 1985—. Contbg. editor: (ednl. video) Competing Through Manufacturing, 1985. Mem. Mass Biotech. Coun., Am. Assn. Immunology, Harvard Entrepreneurs (hon.), D.O.C. Office: Endogen Inc 451 D St Boston MA 02210-1950

DEMPSEY, RAYMOND LEO, JR., radio and television producer, moderator, writer; b. Providence, June 18, 1949; s. Raymond Leo Sr. and Louise Veronica (Gambuto) D.; m. Patricia Batchelder (div. 1984); children: Joab, Jahdeam, Deezsha, Nathaniel, Talitha. BA in Liberal Arts, R.I. Coll., 1973; Cert. in Bus., U. R.I., 1979; cert., Blake Computer Programming Inst., 1977, Billy Graham Sch. Evangelism, 1989. Lic. real estate aggt., R.I.; lic. radio sta. operator FCC; cert. secondary tchr., videographer, contractor, R.I. Writer local and nat. publs., 1980—; producer, moderator Chapter & Verse TV, RICA-TV, Providence, 1983—; tchr. R.I. Pub. High Schs., Providence and Cranston, 1988—; producer, moderator radio programs Ch. Focus and People, WRIB AM Radio, East Providence, R.I., 1989—; bd. dirs. Blessing, Inc., Providence; spl. corr. Songtime, U.S.A. Radio Network, 1988—, spl. reporter, spl. contbr., 1991; host Straight Talk, Sta. WKRI, 1989; co-host The Lighthouse, Sta. KOFL, Tacoma; prodr., co-host The Bible Answer Program, Sta. WARV, 1986; judge The Ace Awards, 1992; interviewer Gallup Poll, 1987; trainee N.E. Law Enforcement Officers Assn., 1991. Bd. dirs. R.I. Right to Life, Cranston, 1973—; witness R.I. Gen. Assembly, 1973—, R.I. Bd. Health, 1973—; vol. ARC, R.I. Hosp.; registrar voters, State of R.I., 1980, 91; sponsor World Vision, Pasadena, Calif., 1981—, Compassion Internat., Colorado Springs, Colo., 1989—; chief boys instr. Mattson Acad. Karate, Providence, 1969-71; del. Gov.'s Conf. on Libr. and Info. Svcs., 1991; elector White House Conf. on Libr. and Info. Svcs.; Justice of the Peace, 1991; R.I. state voter registrar, 1991, 92; regional rep. Students Against Vietnam War, 1971, Taxpayers Action Network, 1991; ptnr. Food for the Hungry, 1984—; del. Ellen McCormack for Pres., 1976. Named One of Top 4 Local Cable TV Prodrs. in Nation, Nat. Assn. Local Cable Programming, 1987, ofcl. Jerusalem Pilgrim, State of Isrrael, 1990; recipient 2 Internat. Angel awards for excellence in cable TV presentations, 1991, Neighborhood Diamond award, 1992, 1st prize for excellence in pub. affairs in R.I. and Mass., 1992. Mem. AAAS, ASCD, Am. Math Soc., Am. Soc. Oriental Rsch., Archaeol. Inst. Am., R.I. Assn. for Edn. Young Children, R.I. Assn. for Supervision and Curriculum Devel., Mental Health Assn. R.I., N.Y. Acad. Scis., Nat. Geog. Soc., Nat. Acad. Cable Programming, Near East Archaeol. Soc., Internat. Platform Assn., Jewish TV Inst. (charter), Smithsonian Air and Space, Bread for the World, Evangs. for Social Action, Mus. Heritage Soc., Mensa, USCG Aux., Phi Theta Kappa. Home and Office: PO Box 41000 75 Marion Ave Providence RI 02940-1000

DEMPSTER, (FRANK) CURT, artistic director and producer; b. Detroit, Nov. 1, 1938; s. Frank Dudley and Anna Jeanette (Miller) D. Artistic dir. Ensemble Studio Theatre, N.Y.C., 1965—; tchr., lectr. Smith Coll., Rutgers U., Hofstra U., Columbia U., Yale U.; assoc. prodr. First Internat Festival Arts, N.Y.C., 1988. Author: (plays) Mimosa Pudica, 1978 (Best Play award 1978), Wolf Point, 1991, (short play) Leonard Peltier, 1991. Instr. climbing N.Y. Outward Bound. Mem. SAG, Am. Alpine Club. Home: 26 Grove St New York NY 10014 Office: Ensemble Studio Theatre 549 W 52nd St New York NY 10019-5012

DEMSEY, DAVID BLACKSTONE, arts and sciences dean; b. Winchester, Mass., Apr. 7, 1955; s. Norton Eugene and Barbara (Blackstone) D.; m. Karen Boor, Aug. 16, 1980; 1 child, Laura. BS in Music Edn., U. Maine, 1977; MusM, Juilliard Sch. of Music, 1980; D in Mus Performance, Eastman Sch. of Music, 1989. Mem. music faculty U. Maine, Augusta, 1980-90, dean Coll. Arts & Scis., 1990-92; coord. jazz studies program William Paterson Coll., Wayne, NJ, 1992—; cons., clinician Tanglewood Coll., 1985, Great Woods Inst., 1986-87, Colgate U., 1988-91. Co-author: Alec Wilder: A Biobibliography; contbg. editor Saxaphone Jour., 1989-91. Clinician Selmer Co., 1988-91; bd. dirs. Forum-A Arts Coun., Augusta, 1983-91. Juilliard Sch. of Music scholar, 1980. Mem. N.Am. Saxophone Alliance, Internat. Assn. Jazz Educators, Maine Music Tchrs. Assn. (co-chair theory com. 1988-90). Home: 33 Brookdale Ter Wayne NJ 07470 Office: William Paterson Coll Dept Music Pompton Turnpike Wayne NJ 07470

DEMUTH, DONALD LYNN, management consultant; b. Phila., May 23, 1951; s. William Elmer and Emma (Baer) DeM.; m. Nancy Marwick DeMuth, Dec. 18, 1977; children: Drew Matthew, Lance Justin. BA, Franklin & Marshall Coll., 1972; MBA, U. Pa., 1976. CPA; cert. profl. bus. cons. CPA Touche Ross & Co., Phila., 1972-75; asst. prof. acctg. and fin. Pa. State U., Middletown, Pa., 1976-80; asst. prof. fin. and acctg. Franklin & Marshall Coll., Lancaster, Pa., 1976-78; proprietor Donald L. DeMuth Profl. Mgmt. Cons., Harrisburg, Pa., 1976—. Author: Physicians Guide to Tax Reform Act of 1986, 1987, 1988 Tax Planning Strategies for Dentists, 1988; contbr. articles to profl. jours. Mem. Inst. Certified Profl. Bus. Cons., Soc. Medical-Dental Mgmt. Cons. (regional dir.), Am. Inst. CPAs, Cen. Pa. Estate Planning Coun., Harrisburg Reds Men's Sr. Baseball Team. Republican. Presbyterian. Home: 129 Montsera Rd Carlisle PA 17013-9351 Office: 890 Poplar Church Rd Camp Hill PA 17011-2250

DEMYAN, DAVID BLAKE, consulting firm executive, consultant; b. Akron, Ohio, July 22, 1947; s. Andy William and Enol Reva (Cline) D.; m. Jeanne LaEtta Frank, Aug. 16, 1969 (div. Apr. 1984); children: Laura Jeanne, Jerilyn Sue; m. Joan Ann Daly, Apr. 26, 1986. BS, Akron U., 1974. Tech. writer Babcock & Wilcox Co., Barberton, Ohio, 1975-78, Diebold, Inc., Canton, Ohio, 1978-82; pres. Mendem Concord Inc., Warren, N.J., 1986-91; cons. AT&T, Morristown, N.J., 1982-91; v.p. Semi-Suites, Inc., Warren, N.J., 1989-91; owner PSL Publications, Warren, 1991—. Author: (newsletter) Print Shop Desktop Publisher, 1991. With USCGR, 1967-73. Mem. Soc. for Tech. Communication (newsletter editor 1989, program chair 1990, sr. mem.). Republican. Roman Catholic. Office: Mendem Concord Inc One Mountain Blvd Warren NJ 07059

DENARO, ANTHONY THOMAS, psychiatrist; b. N.Y.C., Aug. 9, 1929; s. Joseph and Maria (DeGennaro) Denaro; m. Mitsuru Suzuki, Nov. 23, 1963. BS, CCNY, 1960; MD, U. Okla., 1969; MPA, U. Hartford, 1981. Diplomate Nat. Bd. Med. Examiners, Am. Bd. Psychiatry, Am. Bd. Gen. Psychiatry and Child Psychiatry, Adminstrv. Psychiatry. Intern Nassau County Med. Ctr., East Meadow, N.Y., 1969-70; resident in child psychiatry U. Pa., Phila., 1970-72, resident in gen. psychiatry, 1972-74; dir. child psychiatry U. Conn. Health Ctr., Farmington, 1974-78; dir. adolescent unit Natchaug Psychiat. Hosp., Willamantic, Conn., 1978-80; assoc. dir. child and adolescent service Mt. Sinai Hosp., Hartford, Conn., 1980-82; assoc. dir. child and adolescent psychiatry Elmcrest Psychiat. Inst., Portland, Conn., 1982-84; dir. outpatient psychiatry Woodhull Med. and Mental Health Ctr., N.Y.C., 1984-85; dir. child and adolescent psychiatry First Hosp. Wyoming Valley, Wilkes-Barre, Pa., 1985—; asst. prof. dept. psychiatry U. Conn. Sch. Medicine, Farmington, 1974-83. With U.S. Army, 1947-49. Fellow Am. Acad. Child and Adolescent Psychiatry; mem. AMA, Am. Psychiat. Assn., Northeastern Pa. Psychiat. Soc. (pres. 1990-91), Phi Beta Kappa. Republican. Office: First Hosp Wyoming Valley 149 Dana St Wilkes Barre PA 18702-4899

DENBURG, DOROTHY URMAN, college dean; b. Paris, France, Mar. 17, 1949; came to U.S., 1951; d. Felix and Michelle (Golubczyk) Urman; m. Howard Seth Denburg, May 21, 1972; children: Michelle R., Elizabeth U., Abigail R. BA, Barnard Coll., 1970; MA, Columbia U., 1976, MEd, 1980, EdD, 1986. Admissions assoc. Barnard Coll., N.Y.C., 1971-72, asst. dir. admissions, 1972-75, assoc. dir. admissions, 1975-78, asst. dean, 1980-83, freshman dean, 1983-87, assoc. dean of studies and class dean, 1987—. Trustee Park Ave. Synagogue, N.Y.C., 1987-89, chair sch. bd., 1990—; mem. Nat. Acad. Adv. Coun., N.Y.C., 1990—, Anti-Defamation League of B'nai Brith, N.Y.C. Office: Barnard Coll 3009 Broadway New York NY 10027

DENBY, DAVID, film critic. Film critic N.Y. Mag. Editor: Film Seventy-Two ato Seventy-Three: An Anthology by the Nat. Assn. of Film Critics, 1973; contbr. articles to mags. Office: New York Mag 755 2nd Ave New York NY 10017-5906*

DENCKER, PETER ANTHONY, business owner, consultant; b. Huntington, N.Y., Aug. 4, 1947; s. Burton and Josephine (Coschignano) D.; m. Donna Rabenda, Sept. 16, 1988. BS in Engring., U.S. Mil. Acad., 1969; MA in Polit. Theory, Georgetown U., 1975. Commd. 2d lt. U.S. Army, 1969, advanced through grades to maj., served in Vietnam, 1970-72; instr. U.S. Mil. Acad., 1975-79; resigned U.S. Army, 1979; prin., v.p. Gardnertown Farms, Newburgh, N.Y., 1979—; exec. v.p. Ulster Internat. Inc., Highland, N.Y., 1981-85; v.p. mktg. M.B. O'Neil Assocs., Inc., Newburgh, 1985-89; prin., pres. C.B. Driscoll's Inc., Newburgh, 1989—; with liaison staff Admissions Office, U.S. Mil. Acad., West Point, N.Y., 1985. Composer numerous songs (hon. mention at Am. Song Festival). Bd. dirs. Orange Lake Civic Assn., Newburgh, 1987—. Decorated Sivler Star, Bronze star (7), Purple Heart. Home: 50 Odell St Newburgh NY 12550-3222 Office: CB Driscoll's Inc 1100 Union Ave Newburgh NY 12550-2910

DENEAU, RONALD ARTHUR, construction company executive; b. Elkhart, Ind., Oct. 4, 1938; s. Arthur Vilbon and Mildred Lenora (Lambert) D.; m. Mary Margaret Glenney, Sept. 2, 1961 (div. Aug. 1984); children: Teresa, David, Judy, William; m. Jayne Marlene Kaitis, Oct. 11, 1984. BSCE, U. Ill., 1962. Registered profl. engr., Md. Hwy. engr. County Kankakee Hwy. Dept., 1959-67; civil structural engr. Bechtel Corp., Gaithersburg, Md., 1967-73; pres. Deneau Constrn. Inc., Gaithersburg, 1973—; founding bd. dirs. 1st Montgomery Bank. Developer various shopping ctrs. Fundraiser YMCA, Upper Montgomery County, Md., 1984-85. Mem. ASCE, Gaithersburg C. of C., AIA, Nat. Utility Contractors Am., U. Ill. Alumni Assn. Roman Catholic. Lodge: Rotary (pres. Gaithersburg chpt. 1988—). Home: 6821 Capri Pl Bethesda MD 20817-4209 Office: Deneau Constrn Inc 7861 Beechcraft Ave Gaithersburg MD 20879-1545

DENEGALL, JOHN PALMER, JR., insurance company executive; b. Tarrytown, N.Y., Mar. 21, 1959; s. John P. Sr. and Edna D. (Kirkaldy) D.; m. Johnnie Lou Jarrett, Feb. 27, 1982 (div.); children: John P. III, Revisa Taylor. Student, Westchester Community Coll., Vahalla, N.Y., 1977-80. Mgr. Elmsford (N.Y.) Raceway Inc., 1976-80, Radio Shack, Yorktown Heights, N.Y., 1980-81; ins. claims adjuster Liberty Mut. Ins. Co., N.Y.C., 1981-85; sr. ins. claims rep. Crum & Forster Comml. Ins., N.Y.C., 1985—; abribrator Ins. Arbitration Forum, N.Y.C., 1986—; pres. Denegall Properties, Inc., Jamaica, N.Y., Eva's Laundry Inc. Democrat. Presbyterian.

DENENY, SÉAN FRANCIS, television executive; b. N.Y.C., May 18, 1951; s. John Francis and Anna May (Noone) D.; m. Elizabeth Clarke Overmyer, June 22, 1985; children: Séan Christopher, Kelly Elizabeth. BS in Mktg. and Mgmt., Fordham U., 1972, MBA, 1976. Nat. accounts mgr. Xerox Corp., N.Y.C., 1972-77; sales mgr. Eastman Kodak, N.Y.C., 1977-79; group sales mgr. Storer Communications, N.Y.C., 1979-85; v.p., gen. sales mgr. Viacom Internat., N.Y.C., 1985—. Mem. Pa. Assn. Broadcasters (assoc. bd. dirs. Harrisburg chpt. 1988-91). Office: Viacom Internat 1515 Broadway New York NY 10036-5702

DENES, MAGDA, psychologist; came to U.S., 1950; d. Gyula and Margaret (Indig) D.; m. Michel Radomisli, May 1963 (div. Jan. 1976); children: Gregory John, Timothy Evan. BA, CCNY, 1956; MA, Boston U., 1958; PhD, Yeshiva U., 1961; cert. psychoanalysis, psychotherapy, NYU, 1967. Lic. psychologist, N.Y. Pvt. practice psychoanalysis, psychotherapy N.Y.C., 1961—; clin. prof. supr. tng. analyst Inst. Psychol. Studies Adelphi U., Garden City, 1969—, Inst. Advanced Psychol. Studies, 1970—; sr. cons. VA, N.Y.C., 1971-73; assoc. clin. prof. supr. and tng. analyst NYU, N.Y.C., 1972—; cons. ABC-TV FYI Pub. Service program, 1980-84; mem. faculty, supr. dept. psychiatry Mt. Sinai Sch. Medicine, N.Y.C., 1981—. Author: In Necessity and Sorrow: Life and Death in an Abortion Hospital, 1976; contbr. articles to profl. jours., newspapers and mags. Fellow Am. Psychol. Assn. (various coms.); mem. N.Y. Soc. Clin. Psychologists (pres. 1978-79), N.Y. State Psychol. Assn. (pres. 1986-87). Club: Williams Coll. Home: 40 E 84th St New York NY 10028-1115 Office: 125 E 87th St New York NY 10128-1124

DE NESNERA, ALEXANDER PETER, psychiatrist; b. Montclair, N.J., Feb. 9, 1957; s. Peter and Olia (Donn) de N.; m. Susan Carter Jarvis, May 30, 1987; 1 child, Christopher Lewis. Student, Johns Hopkins U., 1974-75; BA in Biology, NYU, 1978; diploma med. scis., St. George's U., Grenada, 1983; MD, Dartmouth Coll., 1986. Diplomate Nat. Bd. Med. Examiners; bd. cert. Am. Bd. of Psychiatry and Neurology, 1991; lic. medicine, N.H. Escort interpreter U.S. Dept. State, Washington, 1978-86; research asst. Rockefeller U., N.Y.C., 1980-81; resident in psychiatry Dartmouth Hitchcock Med. Ctr., Hanover, N.H., 1986-90; asst. med. dir. Weekend Intoxicated Driver Intervention Program, Hanover, 1987-88; med. dir. Weekend Intoxicated Driver Intervention Program, 1988-89; cons. psychiatrist Hanover Terrace Nursing Home, 1988-89; cons. psychiatrist Alzheimer's disease clinic Mary Hitchcock Meml. Hosp., Hanover, 1988-89; staff psychiatrist Nashua (N.H.) Brookside Hosp., 1988-90; asst. prof. psychiatry Dartmouth Coll., 1990—; staff psychiatrist New Hampshire Hosp., 1990—; asst clerkship dir., med. student teaching Dartmouth Med. Sch., 1990—. Mem. Am. Psychiat. Assn., N.H. Psychiat. Soc., N.H. Med. Soc., Beta Lambda Sigma. Roman Catholic. Office: New Hampshire Hosp 105 Pleasant St Concord NH 03301-3861

DE NEUFVILLE, LAWRENCE EUSTACE, stock brokerage executive; b. London, Apr. 9, 1913; came to U.S., 1934; s. Eustace Charles and Elsie (Johnston) de N.; m. Adeline McCreary, Apr. 22, 1938 (dec.); 1 child, Richard Lawrence; m. Esther Bonter, July 27, 1974. BA, MA, Oxford (Eng.) U., 1934; postgrad., Harvard U., 1934-35. N.Am. corr. Reuters News Agy., 1935-40; mng. editor Young Am. News Weekly, 1941-44; with U.S. Govt., Eng., France, Germany, 1944-54; cons. on exec. selection and placement, McMurry Corp., N.Y.C., 1955-61; v.p. Plax Corp., Bloomfield, Conn., 1961-63; N.Y.C. as overseas mktg. mgr. Chemstrand div. Monsanto Corp., 1963-67; investment profl., Advest Inc., Hartford, Conn., 1967—. Mem. Vets. OSS, Spl. Forces Club (London). Office: Advest Inc 280 Trumbull St Hartford CT 06103-3501

DENGEL, DENNIS MICHAEL, computer programmer/analyst; b. Poughkeepsie, N.Y., Mar. 10, 1949; s. Chester D. and Eleanor C. Dengel. AAS, SUNY, Poughkeepsie, 1971. Programmer DeLaval Separator Co., Poughkeepsie, 1971-78; sr. programmer Vassar Coll., Poughkeepsie, 1978—.

DENGER, GEORGE ROBERT, aerospace engineer; b. Pottstown, Pa., Aug. 8, 1966; s. George P. and Sylvia J. (Holmes) D.; m. Tamara L. Craig, Sept. 22, 1990. BS, Pa. State U., 1988, MS, 1990. Rsch. aide Pa. State U. Applied Rsch. Lab., State College, 1988-90; aerospace systems engr. Gen. Electric Co., Valley Forge, Pa., 1990—. Mem. AIAA. Home: 546 Whetstone Rd Horsham PA 19044-1954

DENHARDT, DAVID TILTON, biochemistry and biology educator; b. Sacramento, Feb. 25, 1939; s. David Burton and Edith (Tilton) D.; m. Georgetta Louise Harrar, July 1, 1961; children—Laura Jean, Kristin Ann, David Harrar. B.A. in Chemistry with high honors, Swarthmore Coll., 1960; Ph.D. in Biophysics, Calif. Inst. Tech., 1965. Instr. biol. labs Harvard U., 1964-66, asst. prof., 1966-70; assoc. prof. biochemistry McGill U., Montreal, Que., Can., 1970-77; prof. McGill U., 1977-80; prof. biochemistry, microbiology and immunology, dir. Cancer Research Lab., U. Western Ont., London, 1980-88; prof., chmn. dept. biolog. scis. Rutgers U., New Brunswick, N.J., 1988—, dir. Bur. Biol. Rsch., 1988—; mem. sci. adv. bd. Ctr. for Advanced Biotech. and Medicine, Piscataway, N.J., 1988-91, 1988-91. Editor Jour. Virology, 1977-87, Gene, 1985—; mem. editorial bd. Jour. Cancer Rsch. and Clin. Oncology, In Vivo Internat. Jour. Fellow Royal Soc. Can.; mem. Am. Cancer Soc., Am. Soc. Biol. Chemists, Am. Microbiol. Soc., N.Y. Acad. Scis., Am. Soc. Cellular Biology, Phi Beta Kappa. Office: Rutgers U Nelson Labs PO Box 1059 Piscataway NJ 08855-1059

DENIĆ, SRDJAN, oncologist, hematologist; b. Belgrade, Serbia, Yugoslavia, Oct. 28, 1952; came to U.S., 1981; s. Mioljub and Jelena (Simić) D.;m. Danica Nikola Doślov, Dec. 6, 1989; children: Vladimir, Nikolas. MD, U. Belgrade, 1978. Diplomate Am. Bd. Internal Medicine, Am. Bd. Hematology, Am. Bd. Med. Oncology. Intern U. Hosps. Belgrade, 1979; clin. physician Children's Hosp., U. Belgrade, 1979-81; gen. physician Tjesno, Yugoslavia, 1978; resident, fellow hematology The Bklyn. Jewish Hosp., 1981-85; fellow oncology Mt. Sinai Hosp., N.Y.C., 1985-87; physician Inst. Oncology and Radiology, Belgrade, 1987-88; cons. oncology-hematology Ibn Al-Bitar Hosp., Baghdad, Iraq, 1988-90; pvt. practice oncology-hematology Lewistown (Pa.) Hosp., 1991—. Mem. ACP, N.Y. Acad. Scis. Mem. Orthodox Ch. Home: 79A Middle Rd Lewistown PA 17044

DE NICOLA, PETER FRANCIS, photographic manufacturer; b. N.Y.C., Oct. 28, 1954; s. Louis Joseph and Nancy Eleanor (Maddi) DeN. BS, NYU, 1976, MBA, 1978. Pres., founder P.F. DeNicola, Inc., Stamford, Conn., 1976-84; acct. Main Hurdman, N.Y.C., Conn., 1978-81; tax mgr. Gen. Signal Corp., Stamford, Conn., 1981-83, Emery Air Freight Corp., Wilton, Conn., 1983-85; dir. taxes A.I. Internat. Corp., N.Y.C., Conn., 1985-88; tax mgr. Siemens Corp., N.Y.C., 1989-91; sr. tax analyst Fuji Photo Film U.S.A., Inc., 1991. Author: Legal Liability of Tax Return Preparers, 1978; contbr. articles to tax and investment periodicals. Recipient Ferdinand W. Lafrentz acctg. award, 1977 CPA, Conn., N.Y. Mem. Tax Soc. NYU, Assn. MBA Execs., Am. Mgmt. Assn., Stamford Tax Assn. (sec.-treas. 1988-89, v.p. 1989-90), Nat. Assn. Accts., NYU Commerce Alumni Assn. (dir. 1978—, corr. sec. 1978-79, rec. sec. 1979-81, chmn. budget com. 1987-88, chmn. Annual Bus. Conf. 1988-89, chmn. alumni admissions coun. 1989—), AICPA (fed. tax and tax acctg. coms. 1984—), N.Y. Soc. CPAs (fed. and state tax com. 1983-85, depreciation and investment tax credit com. 1986-87), Conn. Soc. C.P.A.s, Tax Execs. Inst., Round Table Assn. of U.S. (co-founder 1986, nat. treas. 1987-88, 90-92, nat. pres. 1988-89, del. to internat. convention, 1987, 88), Estate Planning Council Westchester County, Round Table 3 of Greenwich (Conn.) (dir. 1984-90, 1985-86, pres. 1986-88), Internat. Platform Assn., Princeton Club, Rockefeller Ctr. Club (N.Y.C.), Landmark Club, Long Ridge Club (Stamford), Saw Mill River Racquet Club (Mt. Kisco, N.Y.), St. James's Club (Antigua), Capitol Hill Club (Washington), N.Y. Athletic Club, Pelham (N.Y.) Country Club. Republican. Roman Catholic. Home: PO Box 4637 Stamford CT 06907-0637 Office: Fuji Photo Film USA Inc 555 Taxter Rd Elmsford NY 10523-2314

DENIG, WILLIAM FRANCIS, physicist; b. N.Y.C., Apr. 17, 1953; s. Joseph Anthony and Marie (Smith) D.; m. Maureen Ann Purcell, May 22, 1982; children: Erin Marie, Jason William. BS, Siena Coll., 1975; MS, Utah State U., 1979, PhD, 1983. Geophysics scholar Air Force Geophysics Lab., Hanscom AFB, Mass., 1982-84; physicist Phillips Lab., Hanscom AFB, Mass., 1984—. Contbr. articles to profl. jours. Mem. Am. Geophys. Union. Roman Catholic. Office: Phillips Lab Geophys Dir Hanscom AFB Bedford MA 01731

DENINO, MARK JUSTIN, investment banker; b. Hartford, Conn., July 25, 1953; s. Justin Anthony and Elenaor Mae (Clark) DeN.; m. Leslie Gold, Aug. 5, 1987; children: Alexis, Lauren, Jessica, Danielle. BS, Boston Coll., 1975; MBA, Harvard U., 1979. Registered rep. NASD. Staff acct. Deloitte & Touche, Boston, 1975-77; asst. to chmn. Daniels Head & Assocs., Portsmouth, Ohio, 1979-80; chief fin. officer Biol. Energy Corp., Valley Forge, Pa., 1980-84, Ecogen, Inc., Langhorne, Pa., 1984-86; mng. dir. First Fidelity Bancorp., Phila., 1986-90; pres. CMS Corp. Fin. Inc., Phila., 1990-91; valuation com. mem. Radnor Venture Ptnrs., Wayne, Pa., 1989—, advisor SpaceVest, Washington, D.C., 1991—; bd. dirs. Pa. Pvt. Investment Group; bd. advs. Hamilton Lane Advisors and Delaware Capital Investments. Pres. Country Gate Civic Assn., Wayne, Pa., 1985-86; vol. Bus. Vols. for the Arts, Phila., 1987; bd. dirs. Patrons Found. Mem. Harvard Bus. Sch. Club of Phila. (bd. dirs. 1987—), Waynesborough Country Club, Beta Gamma Sigma. Office: Crossroads Capital Inc 435 Devon Park Dr Ste 804 Wayne PA 19087-1945

DENISON, RICHARD EUGENE, agricultural services company executive; b. Harrisburg, Pa., Aug. 24, 1932; s. Benjamin C. and Viola M. (Cramer) D.; m. Peggy A. Koskinas, Apr. 19, 1958; children: Richard E. Jr., Carol Denison Brame. BS, Pa. State U., 1954. Cert. agrl. cons. Asst. store mgr. Grange League Fedn., Youngsville, Pa., 1957-59; grain buyer Quaker Oats, Shiremanstown, Pa., 1959-62; assoc. editor, advt. salesman Pa. Farmer, Harrisburg, 1962-68, mgr., 1968-70; mgr. Pa. Farmers Assn. Farm Mgmt. Svcs., Camp Hill, Pa., 1970-86; gen. mgr. Pa. Farmers Assn. Mems. Svcs. Corp., Camp Hill, Pa., 1986—; pres. Pa. State Agrl. Adv. Coun., Univeristy Park, Pa., 1988-90, mem., 1984—; mem. Pa. Adv. Coun. on Vocat. Edn., Harrisburg, 1982-85, Pa. Farm Show Com., Harrisburg, 1970-82. Asst. coun. commr. Keystone area coun. Boy Scouts Am., Mechanicsburg, Pa., 1945—; trustee Shiremanstown United Meth. Ch., 1977-87, adminstrv. bd. mem., 1960-87; past mem., chmn. adv. bd. Mechanicsburg Rainbow Assn., 1975-80; past mem. Shiremanstown Borough Coun., 1970-74. Recipient Silver Beaver award Boy Scouts Am., 1977, Award of Merit, 1982, God and Svc. Recognition award, 1986, Grand Cross of Color award Internat. Order of Rainbow for Girls, 1979. Mem. Am. Soc. Agrl. Cons., Harrisburg Consistory, Masons, Zembo Shrine. Republican. Home: 211 Walnut St Shiremanstown PA 17011 Office: PFA Mems Svc Corp 510 S 31st St # 8736 Camp Hill PA 17011-5200

DENKER, SUSAN A., art historian; b. N.Y.C., Apr. 2, 1948. BA, Harvard Coll., 1970; MA, Wellesley Coll., 1972; ABD, Brown U., 1976. Chairperson art hist. dept. Sch. of Mus. Fine Arts, Boston, 1975—, mem. criticism faculty, 1979—; curatorial asst. List Art Gallery, Brown U., Providence, 1975-76; lectr. Tufts U., Medford, Mass., 1975—. Author: The Artist's Guide to Paris, 1989; (catalogues) French Watercolors and Drawings in the Collection of the Museum of the Rhode Island School of Design, 1975, Sandi Slone Paintings 1972-1981, 1981, Europe in Torment 1450-1550, 1974. Rsch. grantee Govt. of France, 1969, Cushman Found. grantee, 1991; fellow Kress Found., 1975. Mem. Am. Film Inst., Coll. Art Assn. Office: Sch of Mus Fine Arts Art History Dept 230 The Fenway Boston MA 02115

DENMARK, STANLEY JAY, orthodontist; b. Queens, N.Y., May 26, 1927; s. Jack and Frieda (Kirschenbaum) D.; m. Florence Levin, June 7, 1953 (div. June 1973); children—Valerie, Pamela and Richard (twins); m. Anita Goodman, Jan. 2, 1984. B.S., Queen's Coll., 1950; M.Sc., NYU, 1955; D.D.S., U. Pa., 1955, orthodontics cert., 1957. Diplomate Am. Bd. Orthodontics. Asst. prof. orthodontics Fairleigh Dickinson U., Hackensack, N.J., 1974-79; practice dentistry specializing in orthodontics, Westbury, N.Y., 1955—; clin. asst. prof. orthodontics Sch. Dentistry N.Y.U., 1991—. Served with USN, 1945-47. Mem. Am. Assn. Orthodontists, Northeastern Soc. Orthodontists, Coll. Diplomates of Am. Bd. Orthodontists, ADA, Sigma Xi. Jewish. Avocations: painting; woodcuts; tennis; cross-country skiing. Home: 209 Northwood Ct Jericho NY 11753-2826 Office: 675 Old Country Rd Westbury NY 11590

DENNIES, SANDRA LEE, city official; b. Buffalo, Dec. 26, 1951; d. Norman John and Shirley Edith (Dils) D.; m. Robert Francis Gilbane, Sept. 21, 1974 (div. Apr. 1987); children: Brandon Michael, Gianpatrick. AS in Dental Hygiene, U. Bridgeport, Conn., 1972, BS in Dental Hygiene Edn., 1973; MS in Health Scis., So. Conn. State U., 1979. Dental hygienist various orgns., New Haven, 1972-73, Leonard B. Zaslow, DDS, Westport, Conn., 1973-81; lectr. U. Bridgeport, 1973-76; planner City of Bridgeport, 1977-79, planning asst., 1979-81; grants dir. City of Stamford, Conn., 1981—; sec. Com. on Emergency Med. Disaster Planning, Bridgeport, 1978-79; dir., dep. dir. Stamford Coliseum Authority, 1982-91; dep. dir. Stamford Film Commn., 1986-88. Editor, chief: Hy-Light Jour., 1973-76. Mem. Stamford Youth Planning and Adv., 1981-91, Stamford Youth Svc. Bur., 1991—, United Way Corp., Stamford, 1986—; pres., sec. The Alcohol and Drug Abuse Coun., 1987-92; mem. NSCC bd. Christian Outreach, Stamford, 1988-92, Coun. of Chs. and Synagogues Assembly, Stamford, 1989; pres. Stamford Mcpl. Supervisory Employees Union, 1991—. Democrat. Congregationalist. Home: 171 Shadow Ridge Rd Stamford CT 06905-1813 Office: City of Stamford 888 Washington Blvd Stamford CT 06904-2152

DENNIN, ROBERT ALOYSIUS, JR., pharmaceutical research scientist; b. Newark, Mar. 5, 1951; s. Robert Aloysius Sr. and Elizabeth Jane (Cooney) D. B in Biology, Montclair State Coll., 1975, M in Biology, 1976. From asst. scientist II to clin. project coord. Hoffmann La Roche, Inc., Nutley, N.J., 1977-88; sr. clin. rsch. coord. Hoffmann La Roche, Inc., Nutley, 1988—. Contbr. chpt. in book and articles to profl. jours. Mem. AAAS, Am. Soc. for Microbiology, N.Y. Acad. Scis. Office: Hoffmann-LaRoche Inc 340 Kingsland St Nutley NJ 07110

DENNIS, BARBARA ANN, lawyer, criminal justice educator; b. Newark, July 28, 1950; d. Chandler Malcolm and Lois Venice (Brown) D. BA, Upsala Coll., East Orange, N.J., 1972; JD, Villanova U., 1976. Bar: Pa. 1976, N.J. 1978, U.S. Dist. Ct. N.J. 1978. Instr. criminal justice Trenton (N.J.) State Coll., 1976-78; spl. agt. FBI, N.Y.C., 1978-89; pvt. practice East Orange and West Orange, N.J., 1981—; asst. prof. criminal justice County Coll. Morris, Randolph, N.J., 1989—; mem. legal edn. and bar admission com. Pa. Bar, 1976-83. Contbr. articles to profl. jours. Speaker County Coll. Morris Speaker Bur., 1989—; mentor East Orange Entrepreneur Club, 1989—. Mem. NAFE, Greater Newark C. of C. (speaker 1990—), Order Eastern Star. Office: 659 Eagle Rock Ave West Orange NJ 07052-2138

DENNIS, BARRY WILLIAM, publisher, marketing professional; b. Balt., Feb. 9, 1942; s. Daniel D. and Iona Mae (Fechtig) D.; m. Maria I. Vargas, Nov. 1968 (div. 1978); children: Daniel, Scott; m. Sharon L. Becker Hudson, Oct. 22, 1985; 1 child, Aaron Z. BS in Bus., U. Balt., 1977. Pres. Stereo Equip. Sales, Inc., Elkridge, Md., 1974-79, Lifestyle Mktg. System, Inc., Owings Mills, Md., 1979-85, Cable Call Corp., Owings Mills, 1986-88, Omni Group, Timonium, 1986-91; pub./pres. Md. Maturity, Timonium, 1991—. Chpt. coord. Toughlove Internat., Timonium, 1989—. With U.S. Army, 1964-65. Office: Network Communications 1940A Greenspring Dr Lutherville Timonium MD 21093-4148

DENNIS, BENJAMIN FRANKLIN, III, lawyer, aerospace engineer; b. N.Y.C., June 1, 1942; s. Benjamin Franklin and Margaret Mary (Duggan) Dennis; m. Marilyn Ruth Scully, Aug. 14, 1971; children—Laura Meghan, Benjamin Franklin IV. BA magna cum laude, Fairleigh Dickinson U., 1979; JD Georgetown U., 1991. Bar: Md. Missile systems engr. Sperry Gyro, Lake Success, N.Y., 1966-69; computer programmer Litton Sweda ARS, Morristown, N.J., 1970-72; systems designer Digital Computer Controls, Fairfield, N.J., 1972-75; pres., cons. Dennis-Weingarten Assocs., Mt. Freedom, N.J., 1975-84; mgr. software engring. Conrac/Lear Siegler Avionics, Caldwell, N.J., 1980-82; mgr. engring. computer services Litton Amecom, College Park, Md., 1984-86; project mgr. FAA/DIA/DOJ programs Data Transformation Corp., Silver Spring, Md., 1986—. Leader Boy Scouts Am., 1989—, staff dist. tng., 1992—. With U.S. Army, 1963-66. Mem. Am. Inn of Ct. (sec./treas. 1990). Roman Catholic. Lodges: Sons of St. Patrick (life), Masons (jr. warden 1991). Office: Data Transformation Corp 8300 Colesville Rd Silver Spring MD 20910

DENNIS, CHARLES ERWIN, JR., professional association executive; b. Newport, R.I., Dec. 25, 1925; s. Charles Erwin Dennis and Catherine Helena (Pingley) Clelland; m. Marion Irene Kistler, Jan. 1, 1947; children: Kathleen I, Mary Ellen, Elizabeth Ann, Charles Erwin III. Student, George Washington U., 1947-48. Pres. Dennis Detective Agy., Inc., Severna Park, Md., 1955-87; exec. dir. World Assn. Detectives, Inc., Severna Park, 1987—; pres. Nat. Coun. Investigators and Security Svcs., Inc., 1980-82, treas., 1982—; pvt. security adv. coun. Law Enforcement Assistance Adminstrs., Washington, 1976-77; com. mem. tng. curriculum Model Security Guard Tng., 1977. Bd. dirs. Severna Park Health Ctr., 1964-68, Anne Arundel Trade Coun., 1976-78. Recipient Wayne Wunder award Nat. Coun. Investigators and Security Svcs., Inc., 1989, John J. Duffy award, 1990, Norman J. Sloan award World Assn. Detectives, 1991. Mem. DAV, SAR, World Assn. Detectives (pres. 1980-81, Investigator of Yr.), Severna Park C. of C. (past pres.) Kiwanis Club Severna Park (past pres.), Masons, Scottish Rite, Am. French Genealogical Soc., Newport (R.I.) Hist. Soc., R.I. Genealogical Soc., Annapolitan Club, Chartwell Golf and Country Club. Office: World Assn Detectives Inc 515 Benfield Rd PO Box 1049 Severna Park MD 21146

DENNIS, DONNA JEAN, human resources professional; b. Evanston, Ill., Dec. 21, 1937; d. Fay C. Archer and Adelaide Gertrude (Daus) Sohl; m. Richard Dennis, Feb. 2, 1957 (div. 1972); children: David, Deborah Meola, Douglas. BS in Edn., U. Ill., 1968, MS in Edn., 1975; PhD in Human and Organizational Devel., Fielding Inst., Santa Barbara, 1985. Trainer RCA Labs., Princeton, N.J., 1982-85; mgr. tng. RCA/GE Merger, Cherry Hill, N.J., 1985; mgr. employee rels. GE, Cherry Hill, 1985-87; dir. staffing and devel. Hosp. U. of Pa., Phila., 1987-89; mgr. tng. Chubb & Son, Inc., Warren, N.J., 1989—; speaker in field; workshop leader, 1989-91. Mem. Partnership for N.J., Somerset County, 1989-90. Mem. ASTD, Human Resources Planning Group (founder, pres. N.J. chpt.), Nat. Human Resources Planning Soc., Fielding Alumni Group. Lutheran. Home: 7 Railroad Pl Pennington NJ 08534-2214 Office: Chubb & Son Inc 15 Mountain Blvd Warren NJ 07059-5686

DENNIS, JOHN MURRAY, health facility administrator, radiologist; b. Willards, Md., Jan. 31, 1923; s. John Murray and Bettie Lee (Hearne) D.; m. Mary Helen France, Oct. 8, 1947; children: Lori Dennis Raneri, John M., Patrick F., Terry Dennis Passano. BS, U. Md., 1943; MD, U. Md., Balt., 1945. Cert. radiologist. Resident in radiology U. Md., Balt., 1948-50, instr., assoc. sch. medicine, 1951-53, prof., chmn. sch. medicine, 1953-74, dean sch. medicine, 1974-90, dean emeritus sch. medicine, 1990—; fellow in radiology U. Pa., Phila., 1950-51; chmn. of coun. Am. Coll. Radiology, N.Y., 1969-71, chmn. bd. chancellors, 1975-76, pres., 1976-77 (Gold medal 1980). Contbr. articles to profl. jours. Bd. dirs. Am. Cancer Soc., N.Y., 1963-69. Capt. USAF, 1946-48. Recipient Andrew White award Loyola Coll., 1982, Gold medal Am. Roentgen Ray Soc., 1990; named Outstanding Alumnus of Yr. U. Md., 1984, U. Md. Sch. Medicine, 1990. Mem. Md. Club, Balt. Country Club. Roman Catholic. Home: 803 Huntsman Rd Baltimore MD 21204-1456

DENNIS, LORRAINE BRADT, psychology educator; b. Norway, Mich., May 11, 1921; d. Maurice Lincoln and Mary Louise (Martini) Bradt; m. Lawrence Edward Dennis, Nov. 24, 1943 (div. 1972); children: Patrick, Brian, Deborah, Thomas. BSN, U. Minn., 1943; MS, Kans. State U., 1951; PhD, U. Fla., 1976. RN, R.I. Instr. Drake U., Des Moines, 1952-54; rsch. asst. Pa. State U., State College, 1957-60; asst. prof. Marymount Coll., Arlington, Va., 1961-64; cons. Child Study Ctr., Caracas, Venezuela, 1965-67; instr. Roger Williams Coll., Bristol, R.I., 1969—. Author: Psychology of Human Behavior for Nurses, 1960; co-author: Introduction Human Development and Health Maintenance, 1982. Home: 47 Seneca Rd Portsmouth RI 02871-4210 Office: Roger Williams Coll Bristol RI 02806

DENNIS, ROGER WILSON, retired museum conservator, artist; b. Norwich, Conn., Mar. 11, 1902; s. William Henry and Elin (Proctor) D.; m. Edith Wood (dec. 1983); 1 child, R.W. Dennis Jr.; m. Dorothy Richardson Thurber, Sept. 16, 1984. Student pub. schs., Norwich. Conservator of paintings, artifacts Lyman Allyn Mus., New London, Conn.; now ret. Landscapes and marine paintings exhibited in New Briton (Conn.) Mus., Old Lyme (Conn.) Art Assn., Florence Griswold Mus., Old Lyme; solo exhibit Lyman Allyn Mus., 1989, L.A. Mus., 1943-79; paintings and watercolors in collections at New Briton Mus. of Am. Art, pvt. collections. Home: 9 Columbus Ave Niantic CT 06357-3140 Office: Patricia Shippee PO Box 747 Old Lyme CT 06371-0747

DENNIS, STEPHEN NEAL, lawyer; b. LaFayette, Ga., Nov. 18, 1943. AB, U. N.C., 1965; PhD, Cornell U., 1969; JD, Duke U., 1974. Bar: N.C. 1974, D.C. 1979. Asst. dir. Inst. Govt., Chapel Hill, N.C., 1974-76; asst. gen. counsel Nat. Trust Historic Preservation, Washington, 1976-85; exec. dir. Nat. Ctr. Preservation Law, Washington, 1986—. Bd. dirs. Royal Oak Found., N.Y.C., 1990—. Mem. Phi Beta Kappa. Home: 3901 Connecticut Ave NW Washington DC 20008 Office: Nat Ctr Preservation Law 1333 Connecticut Ave NW Washington DC 20036

DENNISON, ALLEN MANSFIELD, internist; b. N.Y.C., Sept. 28, 1952; s. Ethan Allen Jr. and Frances (Ferry) D.; m. Jane Atkinson Mackenzie, May 26, 1979; children: Eric, Ethan Allen, Malcolm Thayer, John Francis. BA in Biology magna cum laude, Harvard U., 1975; MD, Columbia U., 1980. Diplomate Am. Bd. Internal Medicine. Intern in internal medicine R.I. Hosp., Providence, 1980-81, resident, 1981-83, asst. attending physician, 1983—; practice medicine specializing in internal medicine Providence, 1983—; asst. prof. medicine Brown U., Providence, 1984—. Mem. ACP, Am. Soc. Internat. Medicine, R.I. Hosp. House Staff Assn. (pres. 1982-83), West Chop Club (Vineyard Haven, Mass.). Episcopalian.

DENNISTON, MARJORIE MCGEORGE, educator; b. Coraopolis, Pa., Mar. 21, 1913; d. Chauncey Kirk and Elsie (George) McGeorge; m. Delbert Dicks Denniston, Dec. 25, 1942 (dec. 1973); 1 child, Robert Bruce. Student, Ohio U., 1931-33; BA, Westminster Coll., 1936; postgrad., U. Kans., 1959, Western Ill. U., 1962, 64. Elem. tchr. county schs. West Pittsburg, Pa., 1936-42, New Castle Sch. System, Pa., 1942, 51-78. Vol. aid Pa. Assn. Retarded Children, Jameson Hosp., Law County Home, 1983—; trustee, elder Presbyn. Ch., New Castle, 1986—. Named First Lady of New Castle, 1989, Outstanding Woman of Yr. for Community Svc. Jr. Woman's Club, 1990. Mem. AAUW, LWV (sec. New Castle chpt. 1986—), Coll. Club (parliamentarian), Woman's Club (parliamentarian Lawrence County fedn. 1984—, sec. 1986—), Woman's Club of New Castle (parliamentarian 1990—), Delta Kappa Gamma. Republican. Home: 331 Laurel Blvd New Castle PA 16101-2523

DENOON, CLARENCE ENGLAND, JR., business executive; b. Richmond, Va., Feb. 25, 1915; s. Clarence England and Blanche Williams D. BS, U. Richmond, 1934, MS, 1935, DSc (hon.), 1986; PhD, U. Ill., 1938; student, Harvard Bus. Sch., 1961. Research chemist DuPont Corp., Wilmington, Del., 1938-42; dir. research Landers Corp., Toledo, 1942-45; v.p., then dir. Rohm and Haas, Phila., 1945-76; ret., 1976; v.p. Tri Ex Oil and Gas Corp., Denver, 1978-84; mng. ptnr. Englehold Group, Newtown, Pa., 1982—; dir. Technology Service Corp., 1976-77, Leksi Corp., 1976-84. Contbr. articles to chem. jours.; patentee organic chemistry, plastics, synthetic rubber. Trustee Buckingham Friends Sch., George Sch., U. Richmond, Alderbaugh Found.; pres. Planned Parenthood of Bucks County; mem. Family Planning Council of Phila. DuPont fellow, 1937-38. Mem. Am. Chem. Soc., Comml. Devel. Assn., Phi Beta Kappa. Republican. Quaker. Club: Down Town (Phila.). Home and Office: Pennswood Village D105 Newtown PA 18940

DENSLOW, DEBORAH PIERSON, educator; b. Phila., May 2, 1947; d. Merrill Tracy Jr. and Margaret (Aiman) D.; m. James Tracy Grey III, Nov. 24, 1972 (div. Dec. 1980); 1 child, Sarah Elizabeth. BS, Gwynedd Mercy Coll., 1971. Tchr. Willingboro (N.J.) Bd. Edn., 1971—; union rep. Burlington County Edn. Assn., Willingboro, 1981-82; mem. task force for reoganization Morrisville Sch. Dist., 1991-92. Committeewoman 1st ward Morrisville (Pa.) Rep. Com., 1986—; mem. Borough Coun., Morrisville, 1988—; rep. candidate for Borough Coun., 1985; borough chmn. Am. Cancer Soc., 1986-87; sec. bd. dirs. Morrisville Free Libr., 1988-90, bd. dirs., 1988—. Mem. NEA, N.J. Edn. Assn., Willingboro Edn. Assn. (union rep. 1981-82, alt. union rep. 1988-89), Parents without Ptnrs. (bd. dirs. Mercer County chpt. 1981-82, sec. 1982-84), Bucks County Boroughs Assn. (bd. dirs. 1989—, v.p. 1990-92, pres. 1992-93). Presbyterian. Home: 1206 Ohio Ave Morrisville PA 19067-2417

DENSON, JOE RUSSELL, accountant; b. La Center, Ky., Sept. 15, 1930; s. William Isaac and Maxine (McElyea) D.; m. Doris Jean Milton, Sept. 9, 1949; children: Jacqueline Ann, Julia Lynn, Jeffrey Alan. BSBA, U. Charleston, 1963. Acct. B.F. Goodrich, Institute, W.Va., 1956-64; contr. J.M. Huber Corp., St. Albans, W.Va., 1964—. Assoc. dir. Boys Club Am., Portland, 1974-78, chmn. Cumberland (Maine) Parks and Recreation Com., 1973-83; pres. Little League, Cumberland, 1974-75. With U.S. Army, 1952-54. Recipient Outstanding Svc. award Boys Club Am., 1976; named to Hon. Order of Ky. Col., 1986. Democrat. Home: 14 Meadowview Rd # 407 Cumberland Center ME 04021-9511

DENTAI, ANDREW GOMPERZ, inorganic chemist; b. Budapest, Hungary, June 8, 1942. Diploma engineer chemistry, U. Veszprem (Hungary), 1966; MS, Rutgers U., 1973, PhD in Ceramics, 1974. Disting. mem. tech. staff AT&T Bell Labs., Holmdel, N.J., 1969—. Contbr. numerous articles to profl. jours.; patentee in field. Mem. IEEE (sr.).

DENTON, KEITH G., psychologist; b. Mansfield, Eng., Sept. 23, 1945; came to U.S., 1947; s. Peter Robert and Gertrude (Rosenstrauch) D.; m. Elaine Karten, Aug. 3, 1969; children: Michael, Amy. BA, Adelphi U., 1967; MA, New Sch. for Social Rsch., 1970; PhD, Hofstra U., 1977, postdoctoral cert. in clin. psychology, 1979. Nat. cert. sch. psychologist, 1989. Spl. edn. tchr. Queens (N.Y.) Public Schs., 1968-72; sch. psychologist Island Trees, N.Y., 1973-75, East Rockaway, N.Y., 1978-80, East Meadow, N.Y., 1981—; prof. spl. edn. C.W. Post Center, 1977—; pvt. practice clin. psychology, 1979—; psychologist L.I. Council Chs. Clinic, Albertson, N.Y., 1979—. Trustee Nassau Psychol. Svcs. Inst. Mem. APA, Nat. Assn. Sch. Psychologists, N.Y. State Psychol. Assn., Nassau County Psychol. Assn. (dir.), Round Robin Model R.R. Club. Jewish. Home and Office: 48 Melanie Ln Syosset NY 11791-5118

DENTZ, PAUL ALBERT, JR., guidance director; b. Paterson, N.J., Apr. 30, 1936; s. Paul Albert and Helen (Vitz) D.; children: Lori, Steven, Jon-Eric. BA, Union Coll., 1958; MA, Seton Hall U., 1963; profl. diploma, Manhattan Coll., 1985. Cert. tchr., N.J.; primary cert. rational-emotive theory & techniques, 1992. Tchr., coach, class advisor Ramapo High Sch., Franklin Lakes, N.J., 1958-64; guidance counselor, dir. Indian Hills High Sch., Oakland, N.J., 1964—; group leader Monsignor Wall Ctr., Hackensack, N.J., 1974-75; adj. prof. Edward Williams Coll., Fairleigh Dickinson U., Hackensack, 1974-91, Berkeley Coll. Bus., Totowa, N.J., 1990-92; speaker ann. meeting Middle States Assn. Collegiate Registrars & Officers of Admission, 1973; career cons. Sci. Rsch. Assocs., Chgo., summer 1974; keynote speaker Regional Learning Disabilities Conf., Bergen County, N.J., spring 1989, Chi Sigma Iota Inaugural Induction, Manhattan Coll., winter 1990. NDEA grantee Colgate U., 1963, Harvard Admissions Inst., 1989. Mem. AACD, Am. Sch. Counselors Assn., Assn. Humanistic Edn. and Devel., Nat. Assn. Secondary Sch. Prins. and Suprs., N.J. Prins. and Suprs. Assn., Bergen County Dirs. Guidance Assn. (pres. 1977-79), Bergen County Profl. Counselors Assn. (pres. 1975-76, Dir. of Guidance of the Yr. 1987), Union Coll. Alumni Assn. (admissions com.). Democrat. Episcopalian. Office: Indian Hills High Sch 97 Yawpo Ave Oakland NJ 07436-2770

DENVER, ANDREW MALCOLM, software company executive; b. London, Eng., Dec. 23, 1947; came to U.S., 1951; s. Sydney and Minnie (Goldman) D.; m. Gail E. Hazell, Aug. 27, 1977; children: Michelle Nicole, Traci Loraine. BSc with honors, U. Toronto, 1972. Systems analyst Mfrs. Life Ins., Toronto, 1972-74; sr. analyst Can. Tire Corp., Toronto, 1974-75, acctg. mgr., 1975-78, dir. fin. systems, 1978-79; fin. analyst Software Internat. Corp., Toronto, 1979-80; mgr. internat. ops. Software Internat. Corp., Andover, Mass., 1980-83; dir. internat. ops. Computer Corp. Am., Cambridge, Mass., 1983-84, Henco Software Corp., Waltham, Mass., 1984-86; dir. planning Cullinet Software, Westwood, Mass., 1987-89; pres., dir. internat. cons. DPSC, Internat., Wellesley, Mass., 1989-91; founder VI/Comp Mgmt. Inc., Lexington, Mass., 1991—. Pres. Condominium Assn., Toronto, 1980. Mem. Can. Info. Processing Soc. Office: VI/Comp Mgmt Inc 1 Militia Dr Ste 5 Lexington MA 02173

DENYSYK, BOHDAN, business executive; b. Kornberg, Germany, Feb. 13, 1947; came to U.S., 1949; s. John and Maria (Zelenewich) D.; m. Halina Bubela, June 28, 1969; children: Maria H., Danya L., Adrienne Y., Alexis M. BS, Manhattan Coll., 1968; MS, Cath. U. Am., 1971; PhD, Union Inst. (formerly Union for Experimenting Colls. and Univs.), Cin., 1981. Project mgr. Naval Weapons Lab., Dahlgren, Va., 1968-72; scientist Naval Med. Research Inst., Bethesda, Md., 1972-75; program mgr. Naval Surface Weapons Ctr., Dahlgren, 1975-78; dept. head E.G. & G. Inc., Rockville, Md., 1978-81; dep. asst. sec. U.S. Dept. Commerce, Washington, 1981-83; dir. civil programs IBM Corp., 1983-86; pres. DLR Assocs., Arlington, Va., 1972-80, 83—; sr. v.p. Global U.S.A., 1986—, also bd. dirs.; mem. Congl. Adv. Panel on China, 1985—; bd. dirs. Mazak Corp.; mem. Def. Sci. Bd., 1990—. Contbr. articles to profl. jours. Mem. Presdl. Transition Team, Washington, 1981; regional dir. Rep. Nat. Com., 1980; dir. pub. relations Ukranian Nat. Info. Service, 1976-80; mem. Pres.'s Export Council, 1981—, Presdl. Awards Commn., 1986-87; exec. dir. Md. Reagan-Bush Campaign, 1984; pres. Phi Mu Alpha Sinfonia, 1967-68; nat. dir. for coalitions Dole for U.S Pres. campaign. Navy fellow, 1969-72; Regents scholar, 1964-68. Fellow N.Y. Acad. Sci.; mem. AIAA, AAAS, Am. Def. Preparedness Assn., Am. Phys. Soc. Republican. Roman Catholic. Office: Global USA Inc 2121 K St NW Washington DC 20037-1801

DEORIO, DAVID JAMES, economist; b. Cleve., July 20, 1959; s. J. Clement and Lorayne (Fox) DeO. AB, U. Mich., 1982; M Pub. Policy, Harvard U., 1987; DPhil, Oxford (Eng.) U., 1991. Prin. economist UNDP/Micronesia, 1982-84; cons. economist World Bank, Washington, 1986—; fin. economist U.S. Treasury Dept., 1987-90; sr. economist United Nations, 1990-92; lead economist Price Waterhouse, Washington, 1992—. Author: (monograph) National Economic Management, 1986, Managing International Development, 1987, The Effects of Deposit Insurance on Risk Taking, 1991, Food Aid and Structural Adjustment, 1991, Food, Food Aid and Poverty, 1992. Mem. exec. com. Nat. Symphony Orch., Washington, 1987—, Kennedy Sch. Govt., Harvard U., 1989—. Recipient Meritorious Svc. award Govt. Micronesia, 1982, Presdl. Fellowship, 1988; UN fellow, 1980, Schepp fellow, 1986-87, OAS fellow, 1991-92. Mem. Am. Econ. Assn., Soc. for Internat. Devel., Royal Econ. Soc., Harvard Club (Boston), Univ. Club (Washington). Home: 2011 Hillyer Pl NW Washington DC 20009 Office: Price Waterhouse 1801 K St NW Washington DC 20006

DEORIO, GEORGE LOUIS, metals company executive; b. Schenectady, Aug. 5, 1945; s. Anthony Frank and Lena Helen (D'Amelio) DeO.; m. Sheri Santa, May 7, 1976; children: Chelsea Marie, Eric James. BA in Acctg., Hartwick Coll., 1967; MBA in Fin. Mgmt., Xavier U., Cin., 1969. Sr. auditor Allegheny Internat., Pitts., 1974-77, mgr. acctg., 1981-86; mgr. cost acctg. Allegheny Ludlum Steel Corp., Brackenridge, Pa., 1977-81; contr. Vista Metals, Inc., McKeesport, Pa., 1986-87, treas., 1987—, also bd. dirs.; sec./treas. Pitts. Nipple Works, Inc., 1992—; also bd. dirs. Mem. Berkeley Hills Civic Assn., Pitts., 1981—; mem. ptnrs. with youth com. North Hills YMCA. Mem. Nat. Assn. Accts., Soc. Carbide Engrs. Roman Catholic. Office: 1435 Spring Garden Ave Pittsburgh PA 15212

DEOUL, NEAL, electronics company executive; b. N.Y.C., Feb. 27, 1931; s. George and Pearl (Hirschfield) D.; B.S. in Physics, Coll. City N.Y., 1952; postgrad. Rutgers U., 1954-55; LL.B., Bklyn. Law Sch., 1959; m. Bernice Kradel, Dec. 25, 1955 (div.); children: Cara Jan, Stefani Neva, Evan Craig; m., Kathleen B. Davis, June 20, 1982; 1 child, Shannon Rae. Engr., Signal Corps, U.S. Army, Evans Signal Lab., Belmar, N.J., 1952-55; engr. Airborne Instruments Lab., Deer Park, N.Y., 1955-56; sales mgr. FXR, Inc., Woodside, L.I., 1956-60; admitted to N.Y. State bar, 1960; pres. Microwave Dynamics Corp., Plainview, L.I., 1960-61, Paradynamics, Inc., Huntington Station, N.Y., 1961-64; mgr. Servo Corp. Am., Hicksville, N.Y., 1964-66; v.p. Trio Labs., Inc., Plainview, N.Y., 1966-69; exec. v.p. Microlab/FXR, Livingston, N.J., 1969-74; pres. Neal Deoul Assocs., Owings Mills, Md., 1974—. Mem. IEEE (sr.), N.Y. State Bar Assn., Md. Bar Assn., Young Pres.'s Orgn., Profl. Group Engring. Mgmt., Am. Arbitration Assn. Home and Office: 3104 Caves Rd Owings Mills MD 21117-2912

DEPACE, NICHOLAS LOUIS, physician; b. Nutley, N.J., Oct. 18, 1953; s. Nicholas Frank and Rose (Piro) DeP.; m. Marilyn Tomaro, Jan. 17, 1981. BS, Seton Hall U.; MD, N.J. Sch. Medicine, Mt. Sinai, N.Y.C.; internal medicine cardiology, Hahnemann U., Phila. Diplomate Am. Bd. Internal Medicine and Cardiology. Intern in internal medicine Overlook Hosp., Summit, N.J., Columbia U., N.Y.C., 1978-79; resident internal medicine Hahnemann Med. Coll. and Hosp., Phila., 1979-81; practice medicine specializing in internal and cardiology medicine Phila., 1982—; pres. So. Phila. Cardiology Inst., Phila., 1982—, Cen. City Cardiovascular Inst., Phila., 1986; clin. prof. medicine Med. Coll. Pa., 1987-89; chief cardiology Benjamin Franklin Hosp., Phila., 1989—. Contbr. numerous chpts. to books and articles to profl. jours. Fellow Am. Coll. Cardiology; mem. AMA, N.Y. Acad. Scis., Pa. Med. Soc. Republican. Roman Catholic. Home: 109 Jefferson Ave Haddonfield NJ 08033-3411 Office: 2424 S Broad St Philadelphia PA 19145-4494

DEPALMA, RALPH GEORGE, surgeon, educator; b. N.Y.C., Oct. 29, 1931; s. Frank and Maria (Sibilio) DeP.; m. Maleva Tankard, Sept. 23, 1955; children: Ralph L., Edward F., Maleva B., Malinda G. A.B., Columbia U, 1953; M.D., NYU, 1956. Diplomate Am. Bd. Surgery, Am. Bd. Vascular Surgery. Resident in surgery Univ. Hosps., Cleve., 1962-64; instr. to assoc. prof. surgery Case Western Res. U., Cleve., 1964-80, prof. surgery, 1973-80; prof., chmn. surgery U. Nev., Reno, 1980-82, George Washington U. Sch. Medicine, Washington, 1982-92; Lewis B. Saltz prof. of surgery George Washington U. Med. Ctr., Washington, 1992—, Lewis B. Saltz prof. surgery, 1992—. Editor: (with J.M. Giordano) Reoperative Vascular Surgery, 1987, Basic Science of Vascular Surgery, 1988; assoc. editor: Haimovici Vascular Surgery: Principles and Techniques, 1989; mem. editorial bd. International Vascular Surgery, Jour. Impotence Research; contbr. articles to profl. jours. Served to capt. USAF, 1958-61. Grantee USPHS, 1974-82. Fellow ACS; mem. Cleve. Vascular Soc. (pres. 1977-78), Rocky Mt. Vascular Soc. (pres. 1981-82), Am. Surg. Assn., Soc. Vascular Surgery, Washington Acad. Surgery (sec. 1991-92, v.p. 1992—), Am. Venous Forum (sec. 1991—). Clubs: West River Sailing Club (Galesville, Md.); Cosmos (Washington) (membership com.).

DEPAMPHILIS, MELVIN LOUIS, laboratory director, educator; b. Pitts., Apr. 15, 1943; s. Emid and Grace (Deurlein) DeP.; m. Jean Baschnagel, Aug. 26, 1967; children: Kimberly, Christine. BS in Chemistry, U. Pitts., 1964; PhD in Biochemistry, U. Wis., 1970. Asst. prof. Med. Sch. Harvard U., Boston, 1978, assoc. prof. Med. Sch., 1978-85, prof. Med. Sch., 1985-86; full mem. Roche Inst. Molecular Biology, Nutley, N.J., 1986-87, lab. head, 1987—; adj. prof. Columbia U., N.Y.C., 1988—; disting. lectr. Roswell Park Cancer Inst., Buffalo, 1990; investigator Am. Heart Assn., 1974-79, mem. rsch. study sect., 1984-88; mem. virology study sect. NIH, 1981-85. Mem. editorial bd. Nucleic Acids Rsch., 1983—, Jour. Biol. Chemistry, 1985-91, Molecular Biology Reports, 1986-89, Biochimica et Biophysica Acta, 1990—. NIH fellow, 1970-73; NASA grantee, 1964-67. Mem. AAAS, Am. Soc. Microbiology, Am. Soc. Biochemistry and Molecular Biology. Office: Roche Inst Molecular Biology 340 Kingsland St Nutley NJ 07110-1199

DEPASQUALE, PETER GERARD, crisis intervention social worker; b. Huntington, N.Y., June 3, 1955; s. Frank L. and Ermine (Rabai) DeP.; m. Elizabeth A. McAlonen, Apr. 21, 1979; children: Peter John, Paul Francis, Alyssa Marie. BA, SUNY, Albany, 1977; MS, U. Hartford, 1978; MSW, SUNY, Stony Brook, 1982; PhD, Columbia Pacific U., 1991. Cert. social worker, N.Y. Program coord. Deer Park (N.Y.) Youth Found., 1978-79; dir. Holbrook (N.Y.) Youth Devel. Corp., 1979-84; program dir. Cath. Charities Community Support Svcs., Bay Shore, N.Y., 1984-85; crisis intervention program facilitator East Islip High Sch., Islip Terrace, N.Y., 1985—; pvt. practice psychotherapy, Setauket, N.Y., 1982—; field instr. Sch. Social Work SUNY-Stony Brook, 1989—; instr. Staff Devel. Ctr. of Islips, East Islip, N.Y., 1990—. Author: Family Therapy as a Treatment Modality, 1984. Mem. NASW, AACD, Am. Assn. Marriage and Family Therapy. Democrat. Roman Catholic. Home: 23 Willis Ave Ronkonkoma NY 11779-4151 Office: 15 Main St East Setauket NY 11733-2863

DEPASQUALE, ROBERT JOSEPH, business educator; b. Greensburg, Pa., Aug. 25, 1953; s. Daniel Frank and Ann (Cirelli) D.; m. Dawn K. Wilson, Aug. 7, 1987. BS, St. Vincent Coll., Latrobe, Pa., 1975; MBA, U. Pitts., 1977, PhD, 1992. CPA, Pa.; cert. mgmt. acct., Pa. Jr. acct. Dean W. Maschett, Jeanette, Pa., 1975-76; assoc. prof. St. Vincent Coll., Latrobe, Pa., 1978—; lectr. U. Pitts., 1977-78. Contbr. articles to profl. jours. Mem. Greensburg Mental Health Advs., 1990—; chmn. Latrobe Leadership Commn., 1989—. Mem. AICPA, Am. Acctg. assn., Inst. Mgmt. Accts., Pa. Inst. CPA's (editor Jour. 1989-91). Democrat. Roman Catholic. Office: St Vincent Coll Bus Adminstrn Dept Latrobe PA 15650

DEPETRIS, SUSAN ABRAHAMS, freelance science writer; b. N.Y.C., June 8, 1946; d. Harold L. and Sophie (Baum) Abrahams; m. Ronald Edward DePetris, Jan. 12, 1975; 1 child, Melissa Kate. A.B., Vassar Coll., 1967; Ph.D. in Biology, Columbia U., 1972; M.S. in Journalism, Poly. Inst. N.Y., 1985. Postdoctoral fellow Rockefeller U., N.Y.C., 1972-75; research scientist NYU Med. Ctr., N.Y.C., 1975-82; editor Imaging Quarterly, Poly. U., N.Y., 1983-86; contbg. editor Emergency Medicine, 1987—; contbr. chpts. to books, articles to profl. jours. Am. Cancer Soc. fellow, 1973-75. Mem. Soc. Tech. Communication, Sigma Xi. Clubs: Vassar of N.Y.; Southampton Bath and Tennis. Home: 1175 York Ave New York NY 10021-7169 Office: Emergency Medicine 249 W 17th St New York NY 10011-5300

DEPPE, SCOTT ALLEN, physician, educator; b. Omaha, Mar. 27, 1953; s. William Frederick and Elaine Maxine (Graham) D.; m. Tammy Kay Anderson, June, 1979; children: Heather Marie, Rachel Kay, Blake Allen. BA in Math., Baylor U., 1975; MD, U. Minn., 1979. Diplomate Am. Bd. Internal Medicine, Critical Care Medicine Subsplty. Bd; cert. Nat. Bd. Med. Examiners. Intern categorical medicine USPHS Hosp., San Francisco, 1979-80, resident in internal medicine, 1980-81; resident in internal medicine Children's Hosp. San Francisco, 1981-82; fellow critical care medicine Letterman Army Med. Ctr., San Francisco, 1982-84, asst. chief critical care medicine, co-dir. nutritional support svc., 1984-85; dir. surg. intensive care units Dept. Surgery Brooke Army Med. Ctr., Ft. Sam Houston, Tex., 1985-87; dir. med. ICU, med. dir. respiratory care Ben Taub Gen. Hosp., Houston, 1987-89; med. dir. parenteral and enteral nutrition svc. Meth. Hosp., Houston, 1988-89; assoc. dir. trauma/ICU Mercy Hosp. Pitts., 1989—; clin. instr. dept. medicine Sch. Medicine U. Calif., San Francisco, 1983-85; clin. asst. prof. medicine Uniformed Svc. U. Health Scis., 1985-87; asst. prof. medicine Baylor Coll. Medicine, Houston, 1987-89; clin. asst. prof. Dept. Anethesiology/Critical Care Medicine U. Pitts., 1990—; mem. critical care com. Mercy Hosp. Pitts., mem. div. gen. surgery com., mem. div. chiefs com., mem. trauma com., mem. nursing svc. com., mem. nutrional support com.; site visitor for internal medicine-critical care medicine tng. program Henry Ford Hosp. Accreditation Coun. Grad. Med. Edn., Detroit, 1989; instr. advanced trauma life support ACS, 1983—; presenter, invited lectr. numerous profl. confs. Author: (with others) Critical Care Medicine Review for Internal Medicine Bases Intensivists, 1989, Critical Care Burns, 1991; guest editor, author: (with N.P. Ninos) Nutrional Support of the Critically Ill Adult: Problems of Critical Care, 1988; contbr. articles to profl. jours. Mem. affiliate faculty advanced cardiac life support Am. Heart Assn., 1984—. Maj. MC US Army, 1982-87. Fellow ACP, Am. Coll. Critical Care Medicine, Am. Coll. Chest Physicians; mem. Soc. Critical Care Medicine (contbr. test questions and rationales 18th ann. ednl. and sci. symposium 1989), Pa. Soc. Critical Care Medicine (treas. 1992-93), Pa. Med. Soc., Soc. of Parenteral and Enteral Nutrition (pres.-elect greater Pitts. 1992). Office: Mercy Hosp Pitts 1400 Locust St Pittsburgh PA 15219

DEPREZ, GENE EDWARD, strategic business location and facilities consultant; b. Rochester, N.Y., Jan. 31, 1940; s. Jean Victor and Eleanor (Winnek) DeP.; m. Patricia Louise Donahue, June 23, 1962; children: Michel Jean, Therèsé Marie. BFA in Communications, Rochester Inst. Tech., 1962, MFA in Communications, 1968; postgrad. in community devel., pub. policy formation, Syracuse U., 1972-74. Head instl. design Rochester (N.Y.) Inst. Tech., 1962-65, dir. communications, 1971-78; producer/dir., asst. to gen. mgr. Eastman Kodak Co. Market Edn. Ctr., Rochester, 1965-70; dir. communications Rochester Mus. and Sci. Ctr., 1970-71; pres., chief exec. officer Urbanarium, Inc., Rochester, 1978-82; mng. ptnr. Concept Ventures, Rochester, 1982-84; pres., chief exec. officer Partnerships Data Net, Inc., Washington, 1984-87; v.p. PHH Fantus Corp., N.Y.C., 1987-90, v.p., prin., mem. exec. com., 1990—; chmn. strategic planning Health Maintenance Orgn., 1981-82; vis. lectr. Grad. Communications Program Rochester Inst. Tech., 1983-84. Co-host Real to Reel TV News mag., 1981-82. Trustee Lake Mohawk Country Club, 1990—; mem. exec. com. Arts for Greater Rochester, 1980-84; chmn., dir. Rochester Internat. Film Festival, 1972; chmn. exec. com. Rochester City Charter Commn., 1970-71; chmn. Monroe County Met. Arts Commn., 1974-77; bd. dirs., sec. Genesee Hosp. Health Svc., Rochester, 1975-80. Named one of Outstanding Young Men in Am.; recipient Gold award N.Y.C. Internat. Film and TV Festival. Mem. Am. Econ. Devel. Coun., Nat. Coun. fro Urban Econ. Devel. (mem. com.), Am. Soc. Assn. Execs., Pub. Rels. Soc. Am. (exec. com. Rochester 1980-84), Rochester/Monroe County Bar Assn. (chmn. long-range planning retreat 1982-83), Urban Land Inst., The Conf. Bd. (community and pub. issues coun.), Nat. Civic League (all-Am. city selection com.), Internat. Assn. Mgmt. Cons., Internat. Planning Forum, Internat. Assn. Corp. Real Estate Execs. Democrat. Roman Catholic. Lodge: Rotary (bd. dirs. Rochester 1978-80). Home: 14 Oakwood Trail Lake Mohawk Sparta NJ 07871-1502 Office: PHH Fantus Corp 590 5th Ave Ste 1700 New York NY 10036-4702

DEPTULA, NANCY MONTEITH, educational administrator; b. Milw., Jan. 28, 1928; d. Charles Monteith Ihrig and E. Alberta E. (Copeland) Bennett. m. George Deptula, Oct. 4, 1947; 1 child, George Copeland Deptula. AB, Wellesley (Mass.) Coll., 1980. Rsch. asst. Harvard U., Cambridge, Mass., 1954-58, adminstrv. asst., 1958-81, adminstrv. ofcr., 1981-91, exec. dir., 1991—. Author: Precedents of the Administrative Board of Harvard College, 1890-1970, The Early Years of Alexander I: A Reappraisal. Recipient Mei-ling Soong prize Wellesley Coll, 1978, Deborah Diehl prize, 1980. Mem. Concerns of Women in New England Colls. and Univs. Unitarian. Home: 89 Larch Rd Cambridge MA 02138-3316

DERAPELIAN, DOROTHY, psychotherapist; b. Bronx, N.Y., May 5, 1955; d. Charles and Gloria (Jefahirjian) D. BS, U. Tex., 1976; MEd, U. N.H., 1984. Family counselor Early Intervention Program, Laconia, N.H.; counselor in pvt. practice Meredith, N.H. Mem. Am. Mental Health Counselors Assn., AACD (N.H. chpt.). Home: 16 Lake St # 334 Meredith NH 03253-5818

DERBORT, JOHN JOSEPH, psychologist; b. Morristown, N.J., Sept. 22, 1959; s. F. Joseph and Miriam (Young) D.; m. Nancy Ruth Kressin, Sept. 8, 1990. BA, Franklin Marshall, 1981; MA, U. Dayton, 1983; PhD, Syracuse U., 1987. Lic. psychologist, Mass. Post-doctoral fellow Boston City Hosp., Boston, 1987-88; child psychologist South Shore Mental Health, Braintree, Mass., 1988-89; sr. psychologist, clin. prof. Boston U., 1989—; psychologist, pvt. practice Boston, 1990—; clin. supr. Boston City Hosp., 1989—; mem. editorial bd. Career Devel. Quarterly, 1990—. Mem. Am. Psychol. Assn. Office: The Counseling Ctr Boston U 19 Deerfield St Boston MA 02215-1995

DERCHIN, MICHAEL WAYNE, investment banker, financial analyst; b. N.Y.C., Aug. 17, 1942; s. James and Rose (Minenberg) D.; m. Dary Ingham, Dec. 29, 1970. B.A., Bklyn. Coll., 1964; M.B.A., CCNY, 1966; postgrad. Syracuse U., 1966-69. Sr. analyst Am. Airlines, N.Y.C., 1969-70; dir. mktg. Pan Am. World Airways, N.Y.C., 1970-74; dir. mktg. Am. Airlines, N.Y.C., 1974-79; v.p. Oppenheimer & Co. Inc., N.Y.C., 1979-82, First Boston Corp., N.Y.C., 1982-88; mng. dir. Drexel Burnham Lambert, N.Y.C., 1988-90; sr. v.p., dir. rsch., chmn. stock selection com. County Nat. West Securities, N.Y.C., 1990, dir. rsch., 1991—; columnist Travel Weekly, N.Y.C., 1984—; spl. guest Wall St. Week, Owings Mills, Md., 1982-90, guest MacNeil Lehrer Newshour, N.Y., 1985; expert witness U.S. Senate Aviation subcom., 1984; lectr. Travel Research Assn., N.Y.C., 1981-84. Named to first team All Am. Analysts Instnl. Investor mag., 1983, 90. Mem. N.Y. Soc. Security Analysts, N.Y. Airline Analysts Soc. (chmn. membership com. 1985, pres. 1986-87), Wings Club, Travel Tourism Research Assn. Club: Nat. Arts, University (N.Y.C.). Avocations: tennis; photography; reading. Office: County Nat West Securities 100 Wall St New York NY 10005-3701

DERENZO, EVAN GAINES, gerontologist, health services administrator, researcher; b. Chgo., June 17, 1951; d. Maurice H. and Suzanne R. (Rovee) Gaines; m. Flint A. Nelson, Feb., 1974 (div. Oct. 1980); m. Emil Vince DeRenzo, Aug. 13, 1983. BA in Polit. Sci., Wheaton Coll., 1973; MA in Edn. and Human Devel., George Washington U., 1976; PhD in Human Devel. Specialization in Gerontology, U. Md., 1986; spl. grad., Harvard U., 1977. Substitute tchr., libr. Brent Elem. Sch., Washington, 1974-75; head tchr. Clarendon Child Care Ctr., Arlington, Va., 1975; supervising pre-sch. tchr. Georgetown Children's House, Washington, 1976; spl. edn. asst. tchr. Walter E. Fernald Sch., Waltham, Mass., 1977; dir. fed. employee's coop. learning ctr. for preschoolers U.S. Dept. of Edn., Washington, 1977-79; asst. to dir. of pers. Am. Pharm. Assn., Washington, 1982-83; dir. rsch. admissions, pub. rels. and mktg. Collingswood Nursing Ctr., Rockville, Md., 1986-88; sr. staff researcher, cons. bioethics program Clin. Ctr. NIH, Bethesda, Md., 1988—; spl. asst. to the chief grad. student appointment NIMH, Washington, 1980-86, guest researcher, 1986-90; adj. lectr. gerontology and psychology Marymount U., Arlington, Va., 1987—; planner, adminstr. geriatric svcs. program, spl. projects cons. Balt. County Bur. of Mental Health, Towson, Md., 1988—, cons. psychotherapist Southwestern Community Mental Health Ctr., 1990—; cons. geriatric mental health designated bed project dept. health and mental hygiene Md. State Mental Hygiene Adminstrn., U. Md. Sch. of Nursing, Balt., 1989—; cons. Office of Senator George McGovern, Washington, 1978, Office of Gerontology and Aging Studies U. Ill., Urbana-Champaign, 1980, Dept. Leisure Studies, 1980, Alliance for Aging Rsch., Washington, 1987, 88, Baltimore County Dept. Aging, Towson, Md., 1988, The Futures Group, Washington, 1988, Serammune Physicians Lab., Ltd., Vienna, Va., 1987-89. Author (with others) Preretirement Needs of Working Midlife Women in the United States, 1990. Mem. adv. coun. Episcopal Congregation of the U. of Md., College Park, 1981-83. Mem. AACD, Am. Assn. Ret. Persons, Alzheimer's Assn. Greater Washington, Am. Soc. Aging, Balt.-Washington Soc. Psychogeriatrics (pres.), Gerontol. Soc. Am., Mental Health Assn. Montgomery County, Montgomery Hospice Soc., Nat. Coun. Aging, Josephson Inst. Ethics, Rose and Joseph Kennedy Inst. Ethics, Nat. Press Club. Democrat. Office: NIH Clin Ctr Bioethics Program 10/1C116 Rockville MD 20892

DE RISI, DWIGHT CARLTON, oncologist, surgeon; b. N.Y.C., Aug. 22, 1947; s. Joseph and Wanda (Sokolosky) De R.; m. Donna Cecile Serini, June 2, 1973; children: Darren Christian, Drew Carlton, Dara Christine, Deirdre Cara. BA, Seton Hall U., 1969; MD, Georgetown U., 1973. Diplomate Am. Coll. Surgeons. Intern in gen. surgery North Shore U. Hosp., Manhasset, N.Y., 1973-74, resident in gen. surgery, 1973-77, chief resident in trauma and gen. surgery, 1976, chief resident in surgery, 1977-78, resident in pathology, 1978-79; physician North Shore U. Hosp., Great Neck, N.Y., 1981—; fellow in surg. oncology Roswell Park Meml. Inst., Buffalo, 1979-80, chief fellow in surg. oncology, 1980-81; mem. med. records com. North Shore U. Hosp.; mem. cancer com. Flushing (N.Y.) Hosp.; assoc. attending surgery Flushing Hosp. Med. Ctr., 1982—; asst. clin. instr. in surgery Cornell U. Sch. Medicine, 1975-76, assoc. clin. instr. in surgery, 1976-78; surg. oncoloy fellow SUNY, Buffalo, 1979-81, clin. instr. in surgery, 1979-81; guest lectr. surg. treatment of Carcinoma of the tongue Cen. Oncology Tumor Conf. Schedule, 1982; guest lectr. dept. ob./gyn. Breast Cancer Conf., 1989, 90; presenter mastectomy reconstruction, Barcelona, Spain, 1992. Contbr. articles to profl. jours. Fellow ACS; mem. AMA, Am. Bd. Surgery, Am. Soc. Gastrointestinal Endocscopies (assoc.), Soc. Am. Gastrointestination Endoscopic Surgeons, Am. Soc. Clin. Oncology, Nassau Acad. Medicine, Roswell Park Soc. Roman Catholic. Home: 292 Lattingtown Rd Locust Valley NY 11560-1011 Office: North Shore Surg Oncology Assocs 600 Northern Blvd # 106 Great Neck NY 11021-5299

DE RISO, THOMAS NEIL, psychology educator, psychologist; b. Englewood, N.J., May 5, 1946; s. Walter Carl and Carla Margaret (Sondergaard) De R.; m. Carol Ann Abate, July 11, 1970; children: Karen, David. BA, Fairleigh Dickinson U., 1968, MA, 1973; PhD, Stevens Inst. Tech., 1984. Social caseworker Bergen County Welfare Bd., Hackensack, N.J., 1968-73; prof. psychology, dept. chmn. County Coll. of Morris, Randolph Twp., N.J., 1973—; indsl. psychologist De Riso Assocs., Denville, N.J., 1975—. Author: Racial Differences in Preferred Leadership Behavior, 1983. Coach Little League, Denville, 1984—. With USN, 1969-71. Mem. APA, N.J. Psychol. Assn. Home: 115 Cedar Lk W Denville NJ 07834-1763

DERKE, HANNS JOACHIM, sales and marketing executive; b. Bergisch Gladbach, Fed. Rep. Germany, Aug. 14, 1957; came to U.S., 1961; s. Waldemar and Vera L. (Wirth) D.; m. Cristina Marie Ross, May 8, 1981; 1 child, Nicholas A. Grad. high sch., Brownsville, Tex. V.p. Advanced Machinery Imports, New Castle, Del., 1976—, also bd. dirs.; nat. sales mgr. Renk Corp., Duncan, S.C., 1981-83. Bd. dirs. Wilmington (Del.) Montessori Sch., 1990—. Libertarian. Home: 107 Baynard Blvd Wilmington DE 19803-4241

DE ROSE, LOUIS JOHN, financial services executive; b. Elizabeth, N.J., Mar. 2, 1952; s. Ralph Anthony and Mary Rose (Di Leo) DeR.; m. Alejandrina Oriol, Jan. 20, 1982; children: Daniel A., Sandra M., Ralph A. III. AAS, Union Coll., 1972; BS, Rutgers U., 1980; postgrad., Pace U., 1980-84. Tax acct. U.S. Trust Co. N.Y., N.Y.C., 1972-79; tax acct. Fiduciary Trust Co., Inc., N.Y.C., 1979, asst. tax officer, 1979-80, tax officer, 1980-83; asst. v.p., dept. head Fiduciary Spl. Svcs., Inc., Jersey City, 1983-86, v.p., 1986—; mem. com. on banking instns. on taxation. Coach Rahway (N.J.) Youth Soccer Assn., 1984—. Mem. Nat. Soc. Notaries, Nat. Assn. Real Estate Planners, Nat. Youth Sports Coaches Assn. Democrat. Roman Catholic. Office: Fiduciary Spl Svcs Inc Journal Sq # Ii Jersey City NJ 07306-4006

DEROUCHEY, BEVERLY JEAN, investment company executive; b. Kenosha, Wis., Sept. 3, 1958; d. Dean Rodney and Doris May (Rasch) DeR. BS in Bus. Mgmt., U. Wis., 1982; MBA in Fin., Cornell U., 1984. Acctg. asst. Kenosha (Wis.)-News Pub. Corp., 1979-81; polit. intern Office of Congressman Les Aspin, Racine, Wis., 1982; staff cons. Peterson & Co., N.Y.C., 1984-86; assoc. Salomon Bros., N.Y.C., 1986-90, v.p., 1991; assoc. investment officer Dartmouth Coll., Hanover, N.H., 1992—. Alumni phonathons Cornell U., Ithaca, N.Y. and N.Y.C., 1982-87, co-chair new donor com., 1985-87; active Rep. Senatorial Inner Circle. Cornell U. scholar, 1982-84, BPW scholar, 1977, 82-83, AAUW scholar, 1981. Mem. ASCPA, Am. Film Inst., N.Y. Soc. Security Analysts, Assn. for Investment Mgmt. and Rsch. (chartered fin. analyst program N.Y.C. chpt. 1987—), Inst. Chartered Fin. Analysts, Bus. and Profl. Women (bd. dirs. 1991—), Film. Soc. Lincoln Ctr, Quechee (Vt.)-Lakes Landowners' Assn. Republican. Lutheran. Home: PO Box 1309 White River Junction VT 05001 Office: Dartmouth Coll 63 S Main St 3d Fl Hanover NY 03755

DERR, THOMAS SIEGER, religion educator; b. Boston, June 18, 1931; s. Thomas Sieger and Mary Ferguson (Sebring) D.; m. Virginia Anne Bush, June 9, 1956, (div. 1977); children—Peter Bulkeley, Laura Seely, Mary Williams; m. Janet Hackman, Apr. 12, 1980 (div. 1985); 1 child, Philip Henry; m. Linda Vincent, Feb. 14, 1986. AB, Harvard U., 1953; MDiv, Union Theol. Sem., 1956; PhD, Columbia U., 1972. Ordained to ministry, United Ch. of Christ, 1956. Researcher World Council Chs., Geneva, 1961-62; asst. chaplain Stanford U., Calif., 1956-59; asst. chaplain Smith Coll., Northampton, Mass., 1963-65, asst. prof. religion, 1965-71, assoc. prof., 1972-77, prof., 1977—; cons. World Coun. Chs., 1965—; dir. Inst. on Religion in Pub. Life, N.Y.C.; mem. complemental faculty Rush Med. Coll., Chgo., 1979-84. Author: The Political Thought of the Ecumenical Movement, 1972; Ecology and Human Need, 1975; Church State, and Politics, 1981; Barriers to Ecumenism: The Holy See and the World Council of Churches on Social Questions, 1983; Believable Futures of American Protesantism, 1988; contbr. articles to profl. jours. Danforth Found. grantee, 1959-60, 65-66; Inst. for Advanced Study of Religion, U. Chgo. fellow, 1981. Soc. for Christian Ethics. Home: 60 Harrison Ave Northampton MA 01060-2911 Office: Smith Coll Dept Religion Northampton MA 01063

DERRICK, KARLTON L., sales manager; b. N.Y.C., Aug. 28, 1960; s. Walter and Elizabeth (Greene) D. BSChemE, Stanford U., 1982. Rep. First Investors Corp., N.Y.C., 1982, sales supr., 1983-86, dist. mgr., 1987—; sales trainer First Investors Corp., 1989—. Bd. dirs. Reality House, N.Y.C., 1991. Home: 5010 Palisade Ave West New York NJ 07093 Office: First Investors Corp 2 Pennsylvania Pla New York NY 10121

D'ERRICO, DIANE FAVA, health educator; b. Providence, Nov. 15, 1946; d. Aldonio Arthur and Elena Victoria (Errico) Fava; m. John R. Golden Jr., June 22, 1968 (div. 1981); children: Elise Erica Golden, Keith Mitchell Golden. BA, Emmanuel Coll., 1968; MA, U. R.I., 1978. Family life educator Family Svcs., Inc., Providence, 1977-80; Lalor fellow Women and Infants Hosp., Providence, 1980-82; community liaison R.I. Hosp., Providence, 1982-89; health edn. coord. Women and Infants Hosp., Providence, 1990—; cons., trainer, 1980—. editor: Focus on Aging, 1987-89; contbr. articles to profl. jours. Bd. mem. ALS of R.I., 1989-91, R.I. Sch. Health Assn., Providence,; v.p. Advent House, Inc., Providence, 1989—. Recipient Lalor Fellowship in Reproductive Health, Lalor Found., Wilmington, Del., 1980-82. Mem. R.I. Women's Network, R.I. Assn. for Counseling and Devel. Office: Women and Infants Hospital 101 Dudley St Providence RI 02905

DERSH, JEROME, physician, ophthalmologist; b. N.Y.C., Mar. 27, 1928; s. Philip and Selma (Gallantry) D.; m. Rhoda E. Dersh, Dec. 23, 1956; children: Debra Lori, Jeffrey Jonathan. BS, Albright Coll., 1949, HHD (hon.), 1989; postgrad. in Bacteriology, U. Pa., 1949-50; MD, Thomas Jefferson U., 1954. Diplomate Am. Bd. Ophthalmology, Am. Bd. Med. Examiners. Intern St. Joseph Hosp., Reading, Pa., 1954-55;, 1956-58; resident in surgery Wills Eye Hosp., Phila., 1955-58; capt., chief ophthalmology Westover USAF, Springfield, Mass., 1958-60; pres. Eye Physicians Assocs. Ltd., Reading, Pa., 1960—; chief ophthalmology dept. St. Joseph's Hosp., Reading, pres. med. staff, 1977-79; cons. Reading Area C.C., 1976-79. Contbr. articles to profl. jours. Trustee Albright Coll., Reading, 1974—, chmn. fine arts commn., 1972—; fine arts bd. Reading Redevel. Authority, 1977-85, Reading Mus., 1977-82. Recipient Dist. Alumnus award Albright Coll., 1979. Fellow ACS (diplomate); mem. AMA (Physicians Recognition award 1977, 80, 83, 86, 89, 92), Am. Acad. Ophthalmology, Pa. Med. Soc., Pa. Acad. Ophthalmology and Otoloaryngology (editor-in-chief Transaction 1968-78, coun. mem. 1964-81, pres. 1980-81) Reading Ear, Nose, Throat Soc. (pres. 1969-70), Berks County Med. Soc. Home: RD 1 Box 1488 Mohnton PA 19540 Office: Eye Physicians Assoc Ltd 606 Court St Ste 200 Reading PA 19601

DERSH, RHODA E., management consultant, business executive; b. Phila., Sept. 10, 1934; d. Maurice S. and Kay (Wiener) Eisman; m. Jerome Dersh, Dec. 23, 1956; children: Debra Lori, Jeffrey Jonathan. BA, U. Pa., 1955; MA, Tufts U., 1956; MBA, Manhattan Coll., 1980. Interpreter Consul of Chile, 1954-57; various teaching and staff positions Albright Coll., Mt. Holyoke Coll., Amherst Coll., Marple Newtown Sch., 1957-64; systems designer Systems Inc., Reading, Pa., 1964-67; pres., chief exec. officer Profl. Practice Mgmt. Assocs., Reading, 1976—, Pace Inst., Reading, 1981—, Pace Mgmt., Inc., 1983—; chief exec. officer Pace Microcomputers Internat., 1986—; pres. Wordserv, 1984—; mem. regional adv. bd. Hamilton Bank. Author: The School Budget is Your Business, 1976, Business Management for Professional Offices, 1977, The School Budget: It's Your Money, It's Your Business, 1979, Improving Public School Management Practices, 1979, Part-Time Professional and Managerial Personnel: The Employers View, 1979; contbr. articles to profl. jours. Pa. State Bd. Pvt. Lic. Schs., 1987—; cons. dir. pub. sch. budget study project City of Reading, 1967-78, chmn. comprehensive community plan task force, 1973-75, chmn. pub. svc. cons. project, 1980—; panel chmn. budget allocations United Way, 1974-76; del. White House Conf. on Children Youth, 1970; co-founder World Affairs Coun., Reading and Berks County, 1963-65; chmn. Berks County Com. for Children Youth, 1968-72; commr. Trial Ct. Nominating Commn. of Berks County (Pa.), 1982-84; bd. dirs. United Way of Berks County, 1984-89; chmn. programs Leadership Berks, 1986-87; bd. dirs. Reading Ctr. City Devel. Corp., Bus.-Edn. Coalition Corp. Recipient Outstanding Womens award Jr. League Reading, Trendsetter award YWCA, 1985. Mem. AAUW (ednl. found. grant.), NAFE, LWV, Inst. Community Affairs (exec. com. 1975-79), Pa. Assn. Pvt. Sch. Bus. Adminstrs. (bd. dirs. 1985-89), Berks County C. of C. (bd. dirs. 1983-86, chmn. edn. com. 1983-85), Pa. Chamber of Bus. and Industry (edn. com.), Am. Mgmt. Assn., Am. Acad. Ind. Cons. (pres. 1978-80), Reading and Berks C. of C (bd. dirs., chmn. edn. com., Entrepreneur of Yr. 1985), Rotary (bd. dirs. Reading, Pa., chpt. 1989-90). Office: 606 Court St Reading PA 19601

DERWIN, JORDAN, lawyer, consultant, actor; b. N.Y.C., Sept. 15, 1931; s. Harry and Sadie (Baruch) D.; m. Barbara Joan Concool, July 4, 1956 (div. 1969); children: Susan Lee, Moira Ellen; m. Joan Linda Wolfberg, May 6, 1973. BS, NYU, 1953, JD, 1959. Bar: N.Y. 1959, U.S. Dist. Ct. (so. and ea. dists.) N.Y. 1960, U.S. Ct. Appeals (2d. cir.) 1960, U.S. Supreme Ct. 1962. Arthur Garfield Hays rsch. fellow NYU, 1958-59, rsch. assoc. Duke U. Sch. of Law, Durham, N.C., 1959-60; assoc. Brennan, London, Buttenwieser, N.Y.C., 1960-64; sole practice Jordan Derwin, N.Y.C., 1964-70; gen. counsel N.Y.C. Off Track Betting Corp., 1970-74; assoc. gen. counsel Gen. Instrument Corp., N.Y.C., 1974-79; cons., 1980—; instr. basic life support and advanced 1st aid ARC, 1988—, Am. Heart Assn., 1989—; emergency med. technician N.Y. State, 1990—; v.p., gen. counsel Cen. Park Med. Unit, N.Y.C., 1992—; v.p., gen. counsel Cen. Park Med. Unit, Inc., 1991—. Author (with F. Hodge O'Neal), Expulsion or Oppression of Business Associates: Squeeze Outs in Small Business, 1960; actor in various films including Stardust Memories, 1980, Rollover, 1981, I'm Dancing as Fast as I Can, 1982, Cotton Club, 1984, One Down Two to Go, 1986, Cadillac Man, 1990, McBain 1991, The Ambulance, 1991, TV programs including Nurse, Today's FBI, Another World, Guiding Light, All My Children, One Life To Live, Saturday Night Live, Late Night With David Letterman, TV commls. 1980—; contbr. articles to prof. jours. Lt. j.g., USNR, 1953-56, Korea, Vietnam. Mem. SAG (dir. nat. bd. 1982—, nat. exec. com., 1983—, sec. N.Y. br. 1983-87, 12th nat. v.p. 1984-87, 4th nat. v.p. 1987-89, 1st v.p. N.Y. br. 1987-89, 2d v.p. N.Y. br. 1989-91), AFTRA (dir. N.Y. local bd. 1980-83, 87-90, dir. nat. bd. 1981—), Am. Soc. Mag. Photographers, Nat. Press Photographers Assn., Motion Picture Players Welfare Fund (trustee 1987—), Actors Equity Assn., Associated Actors and Artistes Am. AFL-CIO (del. internat. bd. 1984—), Phi Delta Phi. Home and Office: 305 E 86th St New York NY 10028-4702

DERWINSKI, EDWARD JOSEPH, secretary of veterans affairs; b. Chgo., Sept. 15, 1926; s. Casimir Ignatius and Sophia (Zmijewski) D.; m. Bonita L. Margalus; children: Maureen Sue, Michael Stephen. BS in History, Loyola U., 1951. Rep. 24th dist. Ill. Gen Assembly, 1957-58; mem. 86th-97th Congresses from 4th Dist. Ill., 1959-83; mem. fgn. affairs, post office, civil svc. coms.; counselor U.S. Dept. State, Washington, 1983-87, undersec., 1987-89; adminstr. VA, Washington, 1989; sec. Vets. Affairs Dept. of Vets. Affairs, Washington, 1989—; chmn. exec. com. Am. Group Interparliamentary Union. Founder, 1st chmn. Rep. Study Com. With inf. AUS, 1945-46. Mem. VFW, Polish Highlanders, Cath. War Vets, Am. Legion, Polish Legion Am. Vets (past state vice cmdr.), Polish Roman Cath. Union, Polish Nat. Alliance, KC, Kiwanis. Office: Dept Vets Affairs 810 Vermont Ave NW Washington DC 20005

DESAI, BARIN G., psychiatrist; b. Bombay, India, Apr. 3, 1933; came to U.S., 1959; s. Darbar Gopaldas and Bhaktiben (Amin) D.; m. Heide S. Golitz; children: Monika, Mark, Mira. MD, Grant Med. Coll., Bombay, 1958; MA, U. Iowa, 1963. Diplomate Am. Bd. of Psychiatry and Neurology. Intern St. Francis Hosp., Honolulu, 1959-60; resident Gowanda Psychiat. Ctr., Helmuth, N.Y., 1960-61; rsch. assoc. U. Iowa, Iowa City, 1961-63; sr. psychiatrist Gowanda Psychiat. Ctr., Helmuth, 1963-67; supr. psychiatrist Rockland Psychiat. Ctr., Orangeburg, N.Y., 1968-74; unit chief Rockland Psychiat. Ctr., Orangeburg, N.J., 1974-80; clin. dir. Rockland Psychiat. Ctr., Orangeburg, 1980-83; staff psychiatrist Mental Hygiene Clinic, VA Med. Ctr., Lyons, N.J., 1986—; clin. asst. prof. NYU Med. Sch., Rutgers U. Med. Sch. Dir. United Way of Gujarat-affiliate of United Way Internat., Alexandria, Va. Lt. col. USAR, 1983—. Fellow Am. Psychiat. Assn. (del. to assembly, 1982-88, pres. West Hudson dist. branch, 1981-82). Democrat. Unitarian. Home: 312 Alexandria Way Basking Ridge NJ 07920-2794

DESAI, CAWAS JAL, metals distribution company executive; b. Bombay, Mar. 6, 1938; came to U.S. 1968; s. Jal Tehmurasp and Dina Jal (Batliwalla) D.; m. Kamal Aspy Cavina, Apr. 7, 1963; children: Darius, Adil. B in Commerce and Econs., U. Bombay, 1959, LLB, 1962. Chartered acct., India. Ptnr. Dalal, Desai & Kumana, Bombay, 1963-68; sr. acct. Arthur Young & Co., N.Y.C., 1968-69, acting mgr., 1970-71; contr. Guggenheim Internat. Corp., Jersey City, 1971-73; mgr. acctg. and audit Intsel Corp., N.Y.C., 1973-74, dir. acctg., 1975, contr., 1976-81; controller Pechiney Trading Internat., 1981-84; v.p. control Pechiney World Trade U.S.A., Inc., N.Y.C., 1985-87; exec. v.p. Gugenheim Corp., North Bergen, N.J., 1987-91; exec. v.p., chief oper. officer Guggenheim Corp., North Bergen, 1991—. Pres. Zoroastrian Assn. Pa. and N.J., 1979-81. Fellow Inst. Chartered Accts. Republican. Home: 661 Nancy Dr Morrisville PA 19067-1975 Office: Guggenheim Corp 2001 Tonnelle Ave North Bergen NJ 07047-1597

DESAI, HEMANT KISHORE, educational counselor; b. Bombay, India, Dec. 8, 1962; s. Kishore and Suman (Kishore) D. BA in Social Scis., Bombay U., 1983; MA in Sociology, Shivaji U., 1988; MPS in Human Rels., N.Y. Inst. Tech., 1992. Credit appraiser Housing Devel. Fin. Corp., Bombay, 1983; mgmt. trainee Allo Dies Inc., Bombay, 1984-86, mng. ptnr., 1986-90; columnist Debonair Pubs., Bombay, 1989-90; grad. rsch. asst. N.Y. Inst. Tech., Old Westbury, 1991-92, ednl. counselor, 1992—; adj. instr. N.Y. Inst. Tech., 1991-92, acad. tutor, 1991-92. Editor newsletter Psi-Phi, 1991-92. Spl. Grad. scholar N.Y. Inst. Tech., 1991-92; Music award Union Coll., 1990. Mem. Am. Assn. Counseling and Devel., Soc. Psychol. Study of Social Issues. Office: NY Inst Tech French Chateau 209 Old Westbury NY 11568

DE SANCTIS, VINCENT, college president; b. Paterson, N.J., July 13, 1941; s. Vincent and Helen (Ruocco) De S.; m. Francine Barone, Aug. 19,

1967; children: Gregory, Stephanie. BA in Social Studies, William Paterson Coll., 1963; MA in Social Studies, Montclair State Coll., 1966; EdD in Adminstrn. and Supervision, Rutgers U., 1970. Tchr., dept. chmn. Passaic County Tech. and Vocat. High Sch., Wayne, N.J., 1963-68; rsch. asst. Grad. Sch. Edn. Rutgers U., New Brunswick, N.J., 1968-69; asst. dir. Adult Edn. Resource Ctr. Montclair State Coll., Upper Montclair, N.J., 1969-70, dir. Adult Edn. Resource Ctr., 1970-72, dir. HEW region II adult continuing edn. staff devel. project, 1972-75; dean community edn. Williamsport (Pa.) Area Community Coll., 1975-78; asst. prof. Sch. Edn. So. Ill. U., Edwardsville, 1978-82; campus exec. officer Pa. State U.-Shenango Valley, Sharon, 1982-87; pres. Warren County Community Coll., Washington, N.J., 1988—; mem. steering com. Lifelong Learning Conf., U. Md., 1986, licensure approval adv. bd. N.J. Dept. Higher Edn.; title III reader U.S. Dept. Edn. Mem. editorial bd. Adult Literacy and Basic Edn., 1977-82, Pitman Learning Series CBTE, 1978-79, Setting the Pace, 1980-82; editorial cons. Career Edn. quarterly, 1979-80; contbr. articles to profl. jours. Chmn. Commn. Adult Basic Edn., 1974; evaluator 70 001, Inc., 1979; bd. dirs. United Way Northampton and Warren Counties, Tri-State; trustee Warren County Libr. Commn.; reader U.S. Dept. Edn. Title III Programs. Mem. Am. Assn. Community and Jr. Colls., County Community Coll. Pres.'s Assn. N.J., Coun. County Colls. N.J. (chair fin. com. 1988—), Adult Edn. Assn. (cert. leadership), Nat. Accrediting Commn. Cosmetology Arts and Scis. (evaluator 1981-83), Hackettstown C. of C. (bd. dirs.), Rotary (chair youth exch. program Belvidere chpt.). Home: 830 Lopatcong St Belvidere NJ 07823-2012 Office: Warren County Community Coll Rte 57 Box 55A Washington NJ 07882

DE SANTO, DONALD JAMES, psychologist, educational administrator; b. Bklyn., July 5, 1942; s. Vincent James and Rose Ann (Dowd) DeS. B.A. cum laude, St. Francis Coll., N.Y., 1964; M.A. in Clin./Child Psychology, St. John's U., 1966, profl. diploma, 1976; m. Loretta DePippo, Aug. 25, 1962; children: Dolores, Jennifer, Marisa. Asst. law libr. rsch. asst. Dewey, Ballantine, Bushby, Palmer & Wood, N.Y.C., 1960-64; rsch. asst. St. John's U., N.Y., 1964-65, teaching fellow, 1965-66, project dir. 2 federally funded grants, 1975-76; dir. The Rugby Sch., Freehold, N.J., 1977—. Mem. Youth Guidance Com., Freehold, 1983—, chmn. econ. devel. com., 1984-86; mem. Econ. Devel. Com., Freehold, 1983—; mem. Zoning Bd. Adjustment, Freehold, 1985-86; commr. Lake Topanemus Commn., 1990—; Rep. campaign chmn., Freehold, 1990, 91; bd. dirs. Monmouth County Transp. Assn., 1990, 91-92; mem. U.S. Selective Svc. Bd., 1991—; apptd. Selective Svc. Commn, 1992; v.p. Freehold Rep. Club, 1991—. Contbg. editor Channels jour. special educators, 1986—. Recipient Fire Prevention medal, N.Y.C., 1954; citation for outstanding contbn. to arts in edn. N.J. Commr. Edn., 1981; Title VIb Fed. grantee, 1972-78. Mem. NRA, Am. Psychol. Assn. (pub. relations com. div. 16), Nat. Assn. Pvt. Schs. Exceptional Children. Nat. Assn. for Retarded Citizens, Council for Exceptional Children, N.J. Assn. Schs. and Agys. for Handicapped (sec., conf. chmn. 1983-84, pub. relations chmn. 1984-86), Assn. for Help Retarded Children, Monmouth County Hist. Assn., Internat. Platform Assn., N.J. Assn. Children With Learning Disabilities, Nat. Assn. Pvt. Schs. for Exceptional Children, Nat. Trust for Historic Preservation, Optimists, Elks, Psi Chi, Phi Delta Kappa. Roman Catholic. Home: 222 Park Ave Freehold NJ 07728-2006 Office: PO Box 1403 Belmar NJ 07719-1403

DESANTO, MICHAEL FRANCIS, trade association administrator; b. Washington, Sept. 3, 1949; s. Renaldo and Edna Mary (Brush) DeS.; children: Christina, Katharine. BA, Frostburg State Coll., 1971; MFA, George Washington U., 1981. Cert. govt. affairs, 1985. Staff aide U.S. Senator Hubert H. Humphrey, Washington, 1976-78; tchr. Flint Hill Prep. Sch., Oakton, Va., 1979-81; lobbyist Nat. Tire Dealers Assn., Washington, 1982-83; govt. affairs dir. Washington/Md. Svc. Sta. Assn., Lanham, Md., 1984-86; state affairs mgr. Nat. Solid Wastes Mgmt. Assn., Washington, 1987-90; northeast regional mgr. Nat. Solid Waste Mgmt. Assn., Framingham, Mass., 1991-92, dir. state govt. affairs, 1992—. Publisher (newsletter) Northeast Compactor, 1990—; contbr. articles to profl. jours. Mem. Arts Coun., Sudbury, Mass., 1991—. Sgt. U.S. Army, 1971-75. Mem. Mass. Environ. Bus. Coun., N.Y. Bus. and Industry Coun., Associated Industries Mass., Metro West C. of C. Epsicopalian. Office: Nat Solid Wastes Mgmt Assn NE Region 1 Speen St # 120 Framingham MA 01701-4644

DESARNO, JUDITH MARTIN, health association administrator; b. Denver, Sept. 17, 1944; d. John Mark and Lorna (McLean) Martin; divorced; children: Michael, Mark, Martin. Student, Hood Coll., 1962-65. Adminstrv. asst. Mullin, Rhyne, Emmons & Topel, Washington, 1969-78; chief of staff Congressman Michael D. Barnes, U.S. Ho. of Reps., Washington, 1979-86; v.p. U. Md., Balt., 1987-89, Close Up Found., Washington, 1989-90; exec. dir. Nat. Family Planning and Reproductive Health Assn., Washington, 1991—; chair Md. Action, Hyattsville, 1974-77; dir. Human Rights Campaign Fund, Washington, 1989-91. Campaign dir. Michael Barnes for Congress 8th dist., Md., 1987; com. chair Friendship House, Washington, 1992. Democrat. Presbyterian. Office: Nat Family Planning and Reproductive Health Assn 122 C St NW Ste 380 Washington DC 20001

DESELLO, EUGENE TE, computer systems consultant; b. Iloilo, Panay, The Philippines, Nov. 14, 1961; came to U.S., 1978; s. Antonio Gellangarin and Natividad Lim (Te) DeS. BS in Computer Sci. summa cum laude, Poly. U., Bklyn., 1982, MS in Computer Sci., 1983. Cons. Skantek Corp., Warren, N.J., 1983-84, Siemens Data Switching Systems, Hauppauge, N.Y., 1985-88; cons. AT&T Bell Labs., Whippany, N.J., 1984-85, Middletown, N.J., 1988—. Mem. Tau Beta Pi, Eta Kappa Nu. Home: 162 Hwy 34 Ste 107 Matawan NJ 07747-9514 Office: AT&T Bell Labs Rm HR-1G-238 480 Red Hill Rd Middletown NJ 07748-3072

DESFOSSES, LOUIS ROBERT, management consultant, educator; b. Holyoke, Maine, Sept. 25, 1937; s. Robert and Stephanie Desfosses; m. Judith Ann Finn, Jan. 22, 1961; children: Julie, Louis Jr., Suzanne. BS, Villanova U., 1960; MBA, Boston Coll., 1967; PhD, U. Mass., 1970. Asst. prof. Becker Jr. Coll., Worcester, Mass., 1964-66, Nichols Coll., Dudley, Mass., 1966; instr. U. Mass., Amherst, 1967-70; assoc. prof. U. R.I., Kingston, 1970-75, 76-79; prof. mgmt. SUNY, Brockport, 1979—; prof. mgmt. Somali Inst. for Devel. and Mgmt., Mogadishu, Somalia, 1989-90; cons. R.I. Dept. Edn., Providence, 1972-78, Naval War Coll., Newport, R.I., 1975-78, Naval Air Rework Facility, North Kingston, Naval Underwater Systems Ctr., Newport, New London, Conn., 1970—. Contbr. over 50 articles to profl. jours. Mem. exec. com. Monroe County Federation of Tchrs., Rochester, 1991—. Health, Edn. and Welfare Title II grant fellow, 1989. Mem. Northeast Am. Inst. for Decision Scis. (pres. 1975-76), United Univ. Profs. (v.p. academics 1989-91, pres. 1991—). Home: 96 Lynnwood Dr Brockport NY 14420-1464 Office: SUNY at Brockport 309 Fob Brockport NY 14420

DES GACHONS, GILLES PEYROT, biotechnology company executive; b. Boulogne, Seine, France, Dec. 31, 1959; came to U.S., 1988; s. Guy Peyrot des Gachons and Eliane (Delphis) Crozat; m. Valerie Marie Cotton de Bennetot, June 21, 1986; children, Priscilla, Laurianne. PhD in Health Econs., Lariboisiere-St Louis Med Sch., Paris, 1986, MD, 1988; MPH, Harvard U., 1989. Pres. Med. Computer Lab., Paris, 1985-87; resident Salpetriere Hosp., Paris, 1985-88; rsch. asst. Harvard Sch. of Pub. Health, Boston, 1989; product mgr. Ortho Biotech, Johnson & Johnson, Raritan, N.J., 1989-91; internat. product mgr. Ortho Diagnostic Systems, Inc., Johnson & Johnson, Raritan, 1991; product dir. Otho Biotech, Raritan, 1992—; cons. St. Louis Hosp., Paris, 1984. Author: Avoiding Cholesterol in Your Gourmet Diet, 1987. Youth sect. leader Rassemblement pour la Republique, Neuilly-sur-Seine, France, 1984-86. Mem. APHA, Harvard Club Boston. Home: 9 Carroll Dr Somerville NJ 08876 Office: Ortho Biotech 700 Rte 202 S Raritan NJ 08869

DESHONG, JOHN KIRK, corporate tax lawyer; b. Phila., Oct. 29, 1953; s. Howard Cooper and Jane Herd (King) D.; m. Francine Lou Sdao, Apr. 12, 1980; children: Michael A., Alison J. BA, Swarthmore Coll., 1975; JD, Villanova U., 1979, LLM in Taxation, 1984. Bar: Pa., 1979; U.S. Dist. Ct. (ea. dist.) Pa., 1979. Tax atty. Montgomery, McCracken, Walker & Rhoads, Phila., 1979-82; assoc. tax counsel Sun Co., Inc., Radnor, Pa., 1982-89; tax counsel Arco Chem. Co., Newtown Square, Pa., 1989—; mem. Fgn. Activities of U.S. Taxpayers com. ABA Tax Sect., 1989—; chmn. bus. tax subcom. Pa. Chamber of Bus. and Industry. Committeeman Radnor Twp. Rep. Com., 1982-85, Newtown Twp. Rep. Com., 1987-90; authority mem. Newtown Twp. Mcpl. Authority, 1989-90. Recipient Labor Law award Lawyer's Co-op Pub. Co., Villanova (Pa.) Law Sch., 1977. Mem. Delta Upsilon (alumni sec. Swarthmore chpt. 1987-90). Republican. Office: Arco Chem Company 3801 W Chester Pike Newtown Square PA 19073-2387

DESILETS, BRIAN HENRY, physics educator; b. Leominster, Mass., Oct. 7, 1927; s. Henry Joseph and Mary Louise (Goguen) D.; m. Kathleen Alice Rooney, Aug. 15, 1970; children: Frances, Kathleen, Brian. BA in Math., Marist Coll., 1950; MA in Math., St. John's U., 1954; MS in Physics, NYU, 1958; PhD in Physics, Cath. U., 1964. Tchr. Dubois High Sch., N.Y.C., 1950-54; asst. prof. Marist Coll., Poughkeepsie, N.Y., 1954-60, prof. physics, 1964-74, 91—; lectr. elec. engring. dept. Cath. U., Washington, 1963-64; engr. IBM R & D Lab., East Fishkill, N.Y., 1974-81, sr. engring. mgr., 1981-91; prof. physics Marist Coll., Poughkeepsie, N.Y., 1991—; cons. IBM Rsch., Poughkeepsie, 1958-60. Contbr. articles to profl. publs.; patentee in field. Roman Catholic. Home: 6 Lake Oniad Dr Wappingers Falls NY 12590-3855

DESILETS, PIERRE ANDRE, mechanical engineer; b. New Haven, Mar. 12, 1961; s. Remi and Luce (Beauchemin) D.; m. Barbara Louise Chiappetta, May 9, 1986; 1 child, Lindsay Anne. ASME, Norwalk State Tech. Coll., 1981; BSME, Bridgeport Coll., 1988. Designer Bullard Co., Bridgeport, Conn., 1981-82, Dorr-Oliver Inc., Stamford, Conn., 1982-85; project designer Nash Engring. Co., Norwalk, Conn., 1985-88; sr. sales engr. Nash Engring. Co., 1988—. Mem. ASME. Home: 94 Soundview Dr Stamford CT 06902-7113 Office: The Nash Engring Co 310 Wilson Ave Norwalk CT 06854-4681

DE SIMONE, VIRGINIA CAREY, association executive; b. Morris, Ill., Sept. 3, 1930; d. J. Leo and Loretta Louise (Conley) Carey; m. Daniel V. De Simone, Aug. 13, 1955 (div. 1990); children: Jane Ellen, James Michael, Daniel Carey. BA, George Washington U., 1969. V.p. The Innovation Group, Arlington, Va., 1980-86; pres. League of Women Voters of Arlington, 1981-83; v.p. League of Women Voters of Va., Richmond, 1985-90; 1st v.p. League of Women Voters of U.S., Washington, 1990—. Editor: Teaching Political Science: Politics in Perspective, Heldref Corp., Washington, 1984-85; lobby corps chmn. League Women Voters of U.S., 1985-91. Exec. com. Arlington United Way, 1989—, No. Va. govt. rels. com. chmn., Fairfax, Va., 1989—; vice chmn. Arlington Com. of 100, 1989—. Home: 2743 N Wakefield St Arlington VA 22207

DESIND, PHILIP, art gallery director, author, educator, mathematical statistician; b. N.Y.C., Feb. 28, 1910; s. Max and Bertha (Gleichenhaus) D.; m. Anne Feuer (dec.); children: Barbara Harriet, Herbert Stephen. B.S., CCNY, 1934, M.S., 1938; postgrad. Columbia U., 1938-42. Works project supt. in charge of remedial reading program, Works Project Adminstrn., N.Y.C., 1936-42; statistician, ships program War Prodn. Bd., Washington, 1942-45; math. statistician U.S. Navy dept., Washington, 1945-61, U.S. Postal Service, 1962-71; dir. Capricorn Galleries, Bethesda, Md., 1964—; adj. prof. Am. U., 1956-71, Cath. U., 1961-64, Howard U., 1960-62, U. Md., 1961; statis. cons., 1971-81. Author: Jewish and Russian Revolutionaries Exiled to Siberia, 1991; contbg. author: Teaching Children to Read, 1938; author: Reading Tastes of High School Students, 1939; contbr. articles to profl. jours. Designer system for counting mail for U.S. Postal Svc. Mem. Ctr. Jewish Studies Harvard U. Recipient Meritorious award U.S. Postal Svc., 1965. Mem. Am. Statis. Assn., Am. Assn. Advancement Slavic Studies, Assn. Jewish Studies, Am. Jewish Hist. Soc., Jewish Book Coun. Office: Capricorn Galleries 4849 Rugby Ave Bethesda MD 20814-3043

DESIO, PETER JOHN, chemistry educator; b. Boston, June 29, 1938; s. Benjamin and Mary (LaRosa) D. B.S. in Chemistry, Boston Coll., 1960; Ph.D. in Organic Chemistry, U. N.H., 1964. Research assoc. MIT, Cambridge, 1964-66; from instr. to assoc. prof. U. New Haven, 1966-78, chmn. dept. chemistry, 1977-78, 76-80, prof. chemistry, 1980—. Contbr. articles to profl. jours. Advisor Chemistry Club, U. New Haven. U. N.H. teaching fellow, 1963-64. Fellow Royal Soc. Chemistry; mem. Am. Chem. Soc., Soc. Coll. Sci. Tchrs. (system membership coordinator 1982-84), AAUP, Sigma Xi. Democrat. Roman Catholic. Home: 529 Emerson Dr Branford CT 06405-5808 Office: U New Haven 300 Orange Ave West Haven CT 06516-1999

DESJARDINS, ALICE, federal judge; b. Montreal, Que., Can., Aug. 11, 1934; d. Louis and Alexandrina (Venne) D. BA, U. de Montreal, 1954, LLL, 1957; LLM, Harvard U., 1967. Lawyer Que. Bar Assn., Montreal, 1958—; asst. prof. law U. de Montreal, 1961-68, assoc. prof., 1968-69; legal counsellor Privy Coun. Office, Ottawa, Can., 1969-74; dir. adv. and adminstrv. law dept. Justice, Ottawa, 1974-81; judge Que. Superior Ct., Montreal, 1981-87; judge appeal divsn. Fed. Ct. Can., Ottawa, 1987—, ex-officio mem. trial divsn., 1987—; judge Ct. Martial Appeal Ct. Can., Ottawa, 1988—. Chair Que. Selection Com. for Rhodes Scholarship, 1989—, Inst. Pub. Adminstrn. Can., 1975-78; bd. govs. Donner Can. Found, 1974-81, Found. Internships Roncalli, 1982-87. MacKenzie King Traveling scholar, 1958-59, Ford Found. scholar, 1966. Office: Fed Ct Can Supreme Ct Can Bldg, Kent & Wellington Sts, Ottawa, ON Canada K1A 0H9

DESMARAIS, GERALD FRANCIS, college admissions director; b. Holyoke, Mass., July 20, 1952; s. Francis Xavier and Doris Ida (Gosselin) D.; m. Mary Jane Douglas, June 28, 1980; 1 child, William Francis. BSBA, North Adams State Coll., 1974, MEd in Adminstrn., 1977. Athletic trainer/coach North Adams (Mass.) State Coll., 1974-75, admissions counselor, 1975-77, asst. dir. admissions, 1977-79, assoc. dir. admissions, 1979-83, dir. admissions, 1983—; mem. Regents Adv. Commns. on Admissions Standards, 1989-90. Pres. New Eng. Transfer Articulation Assn., 1982-84; leader Boy Scouts Am., North Adams, 1986—; mem. exec. bd. Berkshire County Guidance Assn., Pittsfield, Mass., 1991; bd. dirs. North Adams Teen Commn., North Adams, 1989-90. Named one of Outstanding Young Men in Am., 1983. Mem. Nat. Assn. Coll. Admission Counselors, New Eng. Assn. Coll. Admission Counselors, Nat. Assn. Coll. Registrar & Admissions Counselors, New Eng. Assn. Coll. Registrars & Admissions Officers (chmn. 1991, profl. devel. and ethics com. 1989—), Mass. Sch. Counselors Assn., New Eng. Transfer Articulation Assn. (pres. 1982-84), Berkshire County Soccer Officials Assn. Home: 978 E Main St North Adams MA 01247

DESMARAIS, JAMES, financial consultant; b. Hartford, Conn., Oct. 26, 1956; s. Armand E. and Irene (Cesanek) D.; m. Mary L. Follert, Oct. 2, 1982; children: Christopher James, Alyssa Marie. BBA, U. Conn., 1978. Sales engr. J. H. Bertram & Co., Bloomfield, Conn., 1980-87; fin. cons. Merrill Lynch, Hartford, Conn., 1987—. Ski Patroller, Nat. Ski Patrol Assn., SK Sundown, New Hartford, 1985—. Member Hartford Stock Broker Club. Home: 65 Venice Dr Burlington CT 06013-2509 Office: Merrill Lynch City Place 185 Asylum St Hartford CT 06103

DESMARAIS, NAUREEN G(ERTRUDE), beauty salon owner; b. Newport, R.I., Oct. 19, 1944; d. Joseph Anthony and Gertrude (Farrera) Correira; divorced; children: David Joseph, Scott Christopher. Student, Angelos Sch. Cosmotology, Providence, 1964, U. R.I. Owner wig bus. for chemotherapy patients, Middletown, R.I., Naureen's Hair Studio, Middletown, 1970-90, Shaklee Co., Middletown, 1980-84, Design Ctr. 2000, Newport, 1992—. Author poetry. Founder Workaholic Anonymous Group, R.I., 1991. Home: 21 Bailey Ave Middletown RI 02840 Office: Design Ctr 2000 109 Bellvue Ave Newport RI 02840

DE SMET, LORRAINE MAY, artist; b. Passaic, N.J., May 5, 1928; d. Peter John and Mary (Lovas) Prevelige; m. Louis John de Smet, May 17, 1952; children: Mary Lizabeth, Jean Marie, Carolyn, Allise Marie. Student, Berkeley Bus. Sch., 1945, Art Students League, 1979-82. One woman show Pen and Brush Club, 1984 (Solo Show award). Recipient 1st prize Livingston (N.J.) Art Assn., 1987, 88, and others. Mem. U.S. Coast Guard Artists, Am. Artists Profl. League, Pen and Brush Club of N.Y. (bd. dirs. 1985—, v.p. 1989—, dir. brush div. 1987-89, membership dir. 1990—), Art Ctr. of N.J., Somerset Art Assn., West Essex Art Assn., Art Students League of N.Y. (life), Millburn-Short Hills Art Assn. Home: 33 Campbell Rd Fairfield NJ 07004-1735

DESMOND, WILLIAM JAMES, philosophy educator; b. Cork, Ireland, July 1, 1951; came to U.S., 1974; s. Eugene Patrick and Hanna (Hannigan) D.; m. Maria Goretti Kelly, Oct. 2, 1972; children: William, Hugh, Oisin. BA, Nat. U. Ireland, 1972, MA, 1974; PhD, Pa. State U., 1978. Asst. prof. St. Bonaventure U., Olean, N.Y., 1978-79; lectr. U. Coll., Cork, Ireland, 1979-81, St. Patrick's Coll., Maynooth, Ireland, 1981-82; asst. prof. Loyola Coll., Balt., 1982-86, assoc. prof., 1986-88, dept. chmn., 1986—, prof., 1988—. Author: Art and the Absolute, 1986, Desire Dialectic and Otherness, 1987, Hegel and His Critics, 1989, Philosophy and Its Others, 1990, Beyond Hegel and Dialectic, 1992. Mem. Am. Philosophical Assn., Metaphysical Soc. Am. (sec.-treas. 1986-91), Hegel Soc. Am. (v.p. 1984-86), Hegel Soc. (pres. 1990-92), Road Runners Am. Roman Catholic. Office: Loyola Coll Dept Philosophy 4501 N Charles St Baltimore MD 21210-2601

DE SOUSA, DAVID JAMES, safety professional; b. Cranston, R.I., Aug. 2, 1943; s. James Robert and Louise Marie (Ogden) de S.; m. Marcia Jean Mollica, Dec. 26, 1965; children: Robin Leslie, James Robert. BS, Utah State U., 1966. Civil engr. USAF, various cities, 1967-76; owner 3-de Logging Co., Center Harbor, N.H., 1976-85; chief exec. officer Energy Farms Inc., Meredith, N.H., 1980-85; owner Diamonds, Meredith, 1982-85; prodn., tng. and safety coord. Bartlett Tree Experts, Stamford, Conn., 1985—; leader time mgmt. seminars, 1986—. Author: Power Scheduling, 1991; contbr. articles to profl. mags. Mem. Rep. Nat. Com., Washington, 1984—; com. mem. N.H. Safety Coun., Concord, 1988—. Mem. Am. Soc. Safety Engrs., Am. Legion, Nat. Arborist Assn., Internat. Soc. Arborculture, N.H. Arborist Assn., Utility Arborist Assn., Kiwanis. Office: Bartlett Tree Experts PO Box 246 Meredith NH 03253-0246

DESPRES, ROBERT LEON, urban planner; b. Chgo., Aug. 15, 1940; s. Leon Mathis and Marian (Alschuler) D.; m. Louise Fay, Feb. 16, 1974; 1 child, Frederick Leon. BA in Polit. Sci., U. Wis., 1961; MS in City and Regional Planning, U. Bridgeport, 1984. Urban renewal rep. HUD, Phila., 1961-68; reporter urban affairs The Telegram, Bridgeport, Conn., 1968-78, copy editor, 1978-79; copy editor The Hour, Norwalk, Conn., 1979-81; sr. planner Action for Bridgeport Community Devel., 1982-86, assoc. dir., 1986-87; comprehensive planner Greater Bridgeport Regional Planning Agy., 1987—; cons. Weston (Conn.) Planning and Zoning Commn., 1985; alt. commr. Westport (Conn.) Planning and Zoning Commn., 1986-88; apptd. to South Western Regional Planning Agy., 1987—. V.p. Phila. Council Am. Youth Hostels, 1965-66. Named Outstanding Journalist, Hope Ctr., 1975. Mem. Am. Planning Assn., Am. Inst. Cert. Planners. Democrat. Jewish. Home: 3 Peters Ln Westport CT 06880-3937 Office: Greater Bridgeport Regional Planning Agy 525 Water St Bridgeport CT 06604-4373

DESROCHERS, GERARD CAMILLE, surgeon; b. Marlboro, Mass., June 8, 1922; s. Emery Hector and Eliane (Lemire) DesR.; m. Ellen Franklin, Sept. 27, 1959; children: Gerard, Emery, Lewis, Anthony. AB, Coll. of Holy Cross, 1944; MD, Tufts Coll., 1947. Diplomate Nat. Bd. Med. Examiners. Gen. rotating intern St. Mary's Hosp., Waterbury, Conn., 1947-48; teaching fellow in pathology Tufts Med. Sch., 1948-49; straight surg. intern Boston City Hosp., 1949-50, asst. resident surgeon, 1950-51; resident in surgery New Eng. Med. Center, Boston, 1955-57; practice medicine specializing in surgery, Manchester, N.H.; gen. surgeon staff Cath. Med. Center, Manchester; med. dir. Sea Supply Corp., Bangkok, Thailand, 1953-54; asst. chief surgery VA Hosp., Manchester, 1971-78. Contbr. articles to profl. jours. Incorporator Cath. Med. Ctr., Thomas More Found., Merrimack, N.H.; adv. bd. Lincoln Inst.; mem. N.H. Right to Life Com.; mem. bd. of policy Liberty Lobby; mem. New Eng. Med. Ethics Forum. Served as 1st lt. M.C., U.S. Army, 1970. Named Disting. Physician Am., 1989. Mem. AAAS, Manchester Med. Soc., Hillsboro County Med. Soc., Disting. Physicians Am., Internat. Coll. Physicians and Surgeons. Home: 402 Sagamore St Manchester NH 03104-3937 Office: 648 Belmont St Manchester NH 03104

DESROSIERS, MARC FREDERIC, research chemist; b. Fall River, Mass., July 17, 1956; s. Arthur Edmond and Yvette (Gagnon) D.; m. Maria Emelda Valadez, Aug. 14, 1981; 1 child, Christian. BS in Chemistry, Boston Coll., Chestnut Hill, Mass., 1978; PhD in Chemistry, U. Calif., Santa Barbara, 1983. Postdoctoral fellow Argonne (Ill.) Nat. Lab., 1984-86; rsch. assoc. prof. U. Md., Catonsville, 1986-89; rsch. chemist Nat. Inst. Standards and Tech., Gaithersburg, Md., 1989—. Cons. editor Proc. 2d Internat. Symposium on ESR Dosimetry and Applications, 1989; contbr. articles to sci. jours. Recipient bronze medal U.S. Dept. Commerce, 1991. Mem. Am. Chem. Soc., Radiation Rsch. Soc., Internat. Electron Paramagnetic Resonance Soc. Office: Nat Inst Standards and Tech Bldg 2445 Rm C229 Gaithersburg MD 20899

DESROSIERS, RONALD CHARLES, microbiology and molecular genetics educator; b. Manchester, N.H., June 16, 1948; s. Armand Joseph and Stella Anne (Rogala) D.; m. Marguerite Ann Arel, Aug. 15, 1970; children: Aimee, Jesse. BA, Boston U., 1970; PhD, Mich. State U., 1975. Instr. microbiology, molecular genetics Harvard Med. Sch., Southborough, Mass., 1977-79, asst prof. microbiology, molecular genetics, 1979-85; acting chmn. div. microbiology New Eng. Regional Primate Rsch. Ctr., Southborough, 1983-84, chmn. div. microbiology, 1984—; assoc. prof. microbiology, molecular genetics Harvard Med. Sch., Southborough, 1985-91, prof. microbiology, molecular genetics, 1991—; coord. AIDS unit New Eng. Regional Primate Rsch. Ctr., Southborough, 1988—; rsch. assoc. Yale U., 1977; lectr. in field. Editor Intervirology, 1988—, AIDS Rsch. and Human Retroviruses, 1990-93, Jour. Virology, 1991-93; contbr. numerous articles and revs. to profl. jours. NIH Postdoctoral fellow, 1975-77, Med. Found. of Boston Inc. fellow, 1979-81, Leukemia Soc. Am. Spl. fellow, 1982-84. Office: New Eng Regional Primate Rsch Ctr 1 Pine Hill Rd # 9102 Southborough MA 01772-1312

DESSAUER, JOHN PHILLIP, publisher, financial management company executive; b. Rochester, N.Y., Apr. 21, 1936; s. John H. and Margaret (Lee) D.; m. Joan Cross, June 18, 1960; children: Theresa, Karen, Christine, Mary, John. BS in Physics, Le Moyne Coll., 1959; LLB, Cornell U., 1962. Bar: N.Y. 1962. Assoc. Harris, Beach et al, Rochester, 1962-67; trust officer Security Trust Co., Rochester, 1967-73, head trust dept., 1978-80; sr. investment officer Citibank, Zurich, Switzerland, 1974-77; pub. Dessauer's Jour. Fin. Markets, Limmat Publs., Orleans, Mass., 1980—; prin. Dessauer Asset Mgmt., Orleans, 1986—; panelist Wall Street Week, Owings Mills, Md., 1989—. Author: International Strategies for American Investors, 1987, Passport to Profits,1990; columnist World Monitor mag., 1988—. Office: Box 1718 Orleans MA 02653

DESSAUER, ROLF, research chemist; b. Nuremberg, Fed. Republic Germany, Nov. 3, 1926; s. Adolphe and Lucy Lilly (Schloss) D.; widower, Oct., 1982; children: Stanley Coates, Peter Coates; m. Dec. 1991. BS, U. Chgo., 1948, MS, 1949; PhD, U. Wis., 1952. Chemist DuPont Co., Wilmington, Del., 1952-60; sr. rsch. chemist DuPont Co., 1960-68, rsch. assoc., 1969-86, sr. rsch. assoc., 1986-87; sr. rsch. assoc. DX Imaging, Lionville, Pa., 1987-91; dir. rsch. Photo Imaging Ltd. (UK), 1991—; speaker Diamond Conf., Santa Barbara, Calif., 1987, Inst. for Graphic Communication, Andover, Mass., 1984-85; cons. Imaging Tech. Co-author: Advances in Photochemistry, 1963, Neblett's Imaging Materials, 1989. With U.S. Army, 1944-46. Mem. Am. Chem. Soc. (alternate counselor 1965-67), Soc. Photographic Scientist Engrs. (lectr. Tokyo symposium 1977), Wilmington Ski Club (pres. 1964-66), DuPont Country Club. Democrat. Home: PO Box 3796 Wilmington DE 19807-0796

DESSEL, ARNOLD MARTIN, manufacturing executive; b. Boston, Aug. 5, 1921; s. H. William and Dora (Markus) D.; m. Florian Helen O'Donnell, Sept. 2, 1948; children: Joan, Elaine, Paula, Barbara, William. BA, Yale U., 1946. Sales mgr. CHR Inc, New Haven, 1950-64; bus. mgr. Hercules, Wilmington, Del., 1964-68; mktg. mgr. Ametek Inc., N.Y.C., 1968-71; mktg. rep. Hull Corp., Hatboro, Penn., 1971-79; co-owner, pres., treas. Sil-Med Corp., Taunton, Mass., 1979-90, exec., bd. dirs., 1990—; mem. Health Industry Mfrs. Assn., bd. dirs., 1982-86. Served to capt. USN, 1950-52, Korea. Mem. Metacomet Country Club (East Providence, R.I.), Yale Club (N.Y.C.), Barrington (R.I.) Yacht Club. Home: 4 Heritage Rd Barrington RI 02806-2711 Office: Sil-Med Corp 700 Warner Blvd Taunton MA 02780-4345

DESSNER, ALLAN, software manufacturer; b. N.Y.C., May 11, 1938; s. Joseph and Sally (Barasch) D.; m. Phyllis Mendelsohn, Mar. 25, 1961 (div. Feb. 1990); children: Stephanie, Leslie, David. BS, NYU, 1960. Indsl. engr. Shoe Factory Supply Corp., Bklyn., 1962-65; pres. Alpa Industries, Inc., Bklyn., 1965-69, Contrac Pac, Bklyn., 1969-73, Bayberry Assocs., Bklyn., 1973-87, Big Byte Solutions, N.Y.C., 1987—. Capt. USAR, 1960-68. Mem. Mfg. Jewelers and Silversmiths. Office: Big Byte Solutions Inc 340 E 64th St New York NY 10021-7503

DESTEFANO, JOSEPH LOUIS, physician; b. Bklyn., June 6, 1943; s. Louis and Frances (Schepis) DeS.; m. Rita Calouri, Sept. 28, 1968; children: Danielle, Lila, Joseph Jr. MD, Georgetown Med. Coll., 1969. Diplomate Am. Bd. Ob/Gyn. Intern Thomas Jefferson U. Hosp., Phila., 1969-70; resident Georgetown U., Washington, 1970-73; mem. interview com. Georgetown Coll., Washington, 1974—; prin. Drs. DeStefano and Feldman, Atlantic City, N.J., 1973—; dir. dept. ob/gyn. Atlantic City Med. Ctr., 1987—. Mem. exec. com. Atlantic City Tomorrow, 1990-92; mem. Holocaust com. Ann Frank exhibit Stockton State Coll., Pomona, N.J., 1991. Fellow Am. Coll. Ob/Gyn., Am. Coll. Surgeons; mem. AMA, Am. Coll. Ob/Gyn., (dist. II adv. coun.), Am. Fertility Soc., N.J. Med. Soc. (com. on child health and maternal care, subcom. maternal mortality), Atlantic County Med. Soc. (exec. com. 1980-84, pres. 1982). Office: Drs DeStefano and Feldman 4401 Ventnor Ave Atlantic City NJ 08401

DE SZIGETHY, JAMES RIDGWAY, public relations executive; b. N.Y.C., Nov. 20, 1953; s. Count Edmund and Ann-Elizabeth Durst (Ridgway) de S.; m. Catherine Hume Schley, Dec. 31, 1980; 1 child, Jolie Schley. BS in Edn., U. Houston, 1981; postgrad., U. So. Calif., 1981-82. Devel. officer U. So. Calif., L.A., 1981-82; dir. mktg. Aultenburg Co., L.A., 1982-87; pub. rels. cons. L.A., 1987-89, N.Y.C., 1989—. Author: Hamilton Ridgway: Victorian Architect, 1988; soc. editor Cultural Audience Bull., 1992—; social columnist Society Rag mag., 1992—; contbr. articles to profl. jours. Dir. Centennial Celebration Com., Pasadena, Calif., 1986; dir. Navy League of U.S., Pasadena, 1987-88, Internat. Sister Cities Com., Pasadena, 1987-89; cons. The English Speaking Union, L.A., N.Y.C., 1987-92. Mem. Noble Order of St. Stephen (grande master 1989—). Episcopalian. Home: 429 E 65 St # 18 New York NY 10021

DETLEFSEN, ARTHUR LOUIS, JR., safety engineer; b. N.Y.C., May 26, 1936; s. Arthur Louis and Wilma Georgenia (Schickler) D.; m. Elaine Margret Abrahamsen, Sept. 9, 1961; children: Laura, Mark, Leif. AS, S.I. Community Coll., 1964; BA, Richmond Coll., 1970. Cert. safety profl. Party chief Bd. Water Supply, S.I., N.Y., 1962-65, safety engr., 1966-70; safety engr. Bd. Water Supply, N.Y.C., 1970-78, Dept. Environ. Protection, N.Y.C., 1978—; safety engr. Richmond shaft and tunnel, N.Y.C. Water Tunnel #3, 1962—; speaker polit. and ednl. chamber tours, N.Y.C., 1975—. Contbr. articles to profl. newsletter. First aid instr. ARC, N.Y.C., 1967-74; defensive driving instr. Nat. Safety Coun., N.Y.C., 1967—. With U.S. Army, 1955-57. Mem. Am. Soc. Safety Engrs. (pres. Met. chpt. 1983-84, constrn. div. adminstr. 1984-85). Conservative. Lutheran. Home: 19 Old Brook Ln Warwick NY 10990-3311

DETMAR-PINES, GINA LOUISE, school system administrator; b. S.I., N.Y., May 3, 1949; d. Joseph and Grace Vivian (Brown) Sargente; m. Michael B. Pines, Sept. 11, 1988. BS in Edn., Wagner Coll., 1971, MA in Edn., 1972; MA in Urban Affairs and Policy Analysis, The New Sch. for Social Research, 1987; postgrad., CUNY, 1987—. Cert. adminstr. and supr., sch. dist. adminstr. Tchr. pub. schs. N.Y.C., 1971-82; coord. spl. projects, pub. affairs N.Y.C. Bd. Edn., 1982, spl. asst. to exec. dir. pupil svcs., 1983, asst. to chancellor, 1983-84, dir. Tchr. Summer Bus. Industry Program, 1984—; liaison for the Tchr. Industry Program, N.Y.C. Ptnrship., 1985—. Mem. Com. to re-elect Borough pres. Lamberti, S.I., 1985. Mayor's scholar City of N.Y., 1984—. Mem. ASPA, Fgn. Lang. Instrs. Assn., U.S. Seaplane Pilot's Assn., Internat. Orgn. for Lic. Women Pilots, Chinese-Am Soc., Am. Mgmt. Assn., Acad. Mgmt., Strategic Mgmt. Soc., Ea. Acad. Mgmt., Cambridge Flying Group Club. Episcopalian. Office: NYC Partnership 1 Battery Park Plz 4th Fl New York NY 10004

DETWEILER, DAVID KENNETH, veterinary physiologist, educator; b. Phila., Oct. 23, 1919; s. David Rieser and Pearl Irene (Overholt) D.; m. Inge E. A. Kludt, Feb. 2, 1965; children: Ellen, Diane, Judith, David, Inge, Kenneth. VMD, U. Pa., 1942, MS, 1949; ScD (hon.), Ohio State U., 1966; MVD (hon.), U. Vienna, Austria, 1968; DMV (hon.), U. Turin, Italy, 1969. Asst. instr. physiology and pharmacology Sch. Vet. Medicine, U. Pa., Phila., 1942-43; instr. Sch. Vet. Medicine, U. Pa., 1943-45, assoc. in physiology, pharmacology, 1945-47, asst. prof., 1947-51, assoc. prof., 1951-62; assoc. prof. Sch. Vet. Medicine, U. Pa. (Grad. Sch. Arts and Scis.); chmn. dept. vet. med. scis. Sch. Vet. Medicine, U. Pa. (Grad. Sch. Medicine), 1956-68, dir. comparative cardiovascular studies unit, 1960-90, prof., head lab. physiology and pharmacology, 1962-68, prof., head lab. physiology, 1968-90, prof. faculty arts and scis., 1968-90, chmn. grad. group comparative med. scis., 1971-87, prof. emeritus, 1990—; mem. Inst. Medicine, NAS, 1974—; guest USSR Acad. Sci.; cons. cardiovascular toxicology, 1950—. Contbr. numerous articles to various publs. Recipient Disting. Veterinarian award Pa. Vet. Med. Assn., 1989, Disting. Practitioner award Nat. Acads. of Practice in Vet. Medicine, 1989; D.K. Detweiler prize in cardiology established in his honor German Group of World Vet. Med. Assn., 1982; Guggenheim fellow, 1955-56. Fellow AAAS; mem. Am. Physiol. Soc., Am. Assn. Vet. Physiology and Pharmacology (pres.), N.Y. Acad. Scis., Am. Vet. Med. Assn. (Gaines award and medal 1960, Honor Roll award 1990), Coun. Basic Scis., Am. Heart Assn., Acad. Vet. Cardiology (pres.), Am. Coll. Vet. Internal Medicine (diplomate, cardiology group), Vet. Med. Alumni Soc. (Merit award U. Pa. 1981), Phi Zeta. Office: U Pa Sch Vet Medicine 3800 Spruce St Philadelphia PA 19104-6008

DETWILER, DAVID ALAN, systems engineer; b. Phoenixville, Pa., Oct. 10, 1950; s. Frank H. Jr. and Eleanor B. (Bauer) D.; m. Cynthia L. Lodge, Oct. 28, 1978; children: Laura E., Gregory L. BS, Muhlenberg Coll., 1972; MS, Carnegie-Mellon U., 1974. Systems engr. GRD, Inc., Warminster, Pa., 1975-79; sr. systems analyst Analytics, Inc., Willow Grove, Pa., 1979-84; prin. engr. GE Aerospace, Valley Forge, Pa., 1984—. Mem. Singing City Choir, Phila., 1978-83, Bucks County Choral Soc., Doylestown, Pa., 1992—; elder North & Southampton Reformed Ch., Churchville, Pa., 1982—. Mem. Soc. Am. Baseball Rsch., GE Elfun Soc., Phi Beta Kappa. Republican. Home: 1174 Davisville Rd Warminster PA 18974 Office: GE Aerospace PO Box 8048 Philadelphia PA 19101

DEUTSCH, HOWARD JAY, school psychologist, educator; b. N.Y.C., Oct. 23, 1946; s. Edwin and Evelyn (Wenig) D.; m. Eileen Sherman, June 9, 1968; children: Matthew, Eric. BS, CCNY, 1967, MA, 1970; MS, Fordham U., 1972, PhD, 1982. Cert. sch. psychologist, N.Y. Sci. tchr. N.Y.C. Bd. Edn., Bronx, 1967-89; sch. psychologist-in-tng. Com. on Spl. Edn., #7, N.Y.C. Bd. Edn., Bronx, 1989-90, sch. psychologist, 1990—; adj. assoc. prof. psychology Pace U., White Plains, N.Y., 1984—. N.Y. State Regents scholar, 1963-67; B.F. Skinner postgrad. fellow Behavior Therapy Inst., 1982-84. Mem. Nat. Assn. Sch. Psychologists, N.Y. Assn. Sch. Psychologists, Am. Psychol. Assn., Westchester County Psychol. Assn. Office: Com on Spl Edn #7 778 Forest Ave Bronx NY 10456-7899

DEUTSCH, JOHN LUDWIG, chemistry educator, researcher; b. N.Y.C., May 5, 1938; s. James Erwin and May (Pomerantz) D.; m. Edna Wishart Robertson, July 31, 1961; children: Karin Anne, Erik Robertson. BS with honors, Tulane U., 1959; DPhil, Oxford (Eng.) U., 1963. Chartered chemist, U.K. Lab. instr. Tulane U., New Orleans, 1956-59; vis. asst. prof. chemistry Pomona (Calif.) Coll., 1964-66; assoc. prof. SUNY, Geneseo, 1966-77, prof., 1977—, acting chmn. dept., 1974-75; vis. researcher Inst. Physics, U. Stockholm, 1973, Phys. Chemistry Lab., Oxford, summers 1980-81, 83; vis. scientist Herzberg Inst. AAstrophysics, Ottawa, Ont., Can., summers 1986-87; vis. prof. U. Rochester, N.Y., 1987-88. Honor scholar Tulane U., 1955-59, Rhodes scholar Rhodes Trust, Oxford, 1959-62; postdoctoral fellow NSF, Oxford, 1963-64. Fellow AAAS, Royal Soc. Chemistry, Am. Inst. Chemists; mem. Am. Chem. Soc., N.Y. Acad. Sci., Phi Beta Kappa, Sigma Xi, Sigma Pi Sigma. Office: SUNY Dept Chemistry Geneseo NY 14454

DEUTSCH, JUDITH, clergywoman; b. N.Y.C., Apr. 18, 1929; d. Charles Shepard and Sadie (Freedman) Greene; m. Marshall E. Deutsch, June 27, 1947; children: Pamina Margret, Ethan Amadeus, Freeman Sarastro. BA, Hunter Coll., 1950; MA, New Sch. Social Rsch., 1965, Boston Coll., 1980. Ordained to ministry Unitarian-Universalist Ch., 1981. Dir. Hexiad, Cambridge, Mass., 1979-80; intern First Parish, Framingham, Mass., 1981; assoc. minister Unitarian-Universalist Soc., Hartford, Conn., 1982-85; interim minister First Parish Petersham, Mass., 1985-87, First Parish Sharon, Mass., 1988-90, Unitarian Universalist Ch., Worcester, Mass., 1990-91; minister Unitarian-Universalist Ch., Rockland, Mass., 1987-88, First Parish Medfield, Mass., 1991—; bd. dirs. Internat. League Religious Socialism, Stockholm, 1989—; co-chair religion and socialism com. Dem. Socialists Am., 1989—; chmn. Religious Coalition for Abortion Rights, Boston, 1987-90; acting pres. James Luther Adams Found., Newton, Mass., 1989-91. Author curriculum materials; contbr. articles to profl. publs. Co-chair Citizens for Kennedy and Johnson, Morris County, N.J., 1960; mem. Sudbury (Mass.) Dem. Town Com., 1985—; del. Mass. Dem. Conv., 1990; lobbyist Coalition for Choice, Boston, 1988—. Mem. Unitarian Universalist Ministers Assn., Liberal Religious Education Dirs. Assn., Mass. Bay Ministers Assn. Home: 41 Concord Rd Sudbury MA 01776 Office: First Parish Medfield 26 North St Medfield MA 02052

DEUTSCH, MARSHALL E(MANUEL), medical products company executive, inventor; b. N.Y.C., Aug. 17, 1921; s. David and Madeline Lea (Roth) D.; m. Judith Greene, June 27, 1947; children: Pamina Margret, Ethan Amadeus, Freeman Sarastro. BS, CCNY, 1941; PhD, NYU, 1951. Tech. dir. NEN-Picker Radiopharms., Boston, 1966-68, Picker-Hoechst Inc., Bedford, Mass., 1968-70, Mead Diagnostics, Inc., Bedford, 1970-72, CIS Radiopharms., Bedford, 1972-74, Thyroid Diagnostics Inc., Bedford, 1972-85; chmn. Marshall Diagnostics Inc., Bedford, 1985-87; v.p. dir. R&D J&S Med. Assocs., Natick, Mass., 1988—; bd. dirs., corp. sec. Health Svcs. Internat., Washington, 1983—; contractor Joint Publs. Rsch. Svc., Arlington, Va., 1984—. Inventor self-contained technetium generator, 1971, various radiopharm. products, 1973, various clin. chem. test kits, devices, 1953-91; contbr. articles to mags. Cons. Agy. Internat. Devel., Zaire, 1979, UN Capital Devel. Fund, People's Republic of Bénin, 1977. 1st lt. U.S. Army, A.C., 1942-45, ETO. Fellow AAAS; mem. Am. Assn. Clin. Chemistry (chmn. pub. relations com. 1962), Am. Chem. Soc. (sr.), N.Y. Acad. Scis., Sci. Research Soc. Am. Unitarian. Home: 41 Concord Rd Sudbury MA 01776-2328 Office: J&S Med Assocs 19 Strathmore Rd Natick MA 01760-2418

DEUTSCH, NORMAN, physician; b. Bklyn., July 2, 1927; s. Charles and Rebecca (Pollack) D.; m. Alice Joan Leinhardt, Aug. 30, 1953; children: James Alan, Andrew Marc, Nancy Jane. AB in Biochemistry, U. Calif., Berkeley, 1950; postgrad., NYU, 1950-53; MD, SUNY, Bklyn., 1957. Intern Bklyn. Jewish Hosp., 1957-58, resident in pediatrics, 1958-60; pvt. practice Bklyn., 1960—; mem. pediatrics dept. Bklyn. Hosp. Ctr., L.I. Coll. Hosp. Mem. long range planning com. Poly Prep. Country Day Sch., Bklyn.; trustee Packer Collegiate Inst., Bklyn. Mem. Am. Acad. Pediatrics, N.Y. Med. Soc., Kings County Med. Soc., Bklyn. Acad. Pediatrics, Heights Casino. Home: 83 Remsen St Brooklyn NY 11201-3401

DEUTSCH, STANLEY, anesthesiologist, educator; b. N.Y.C., Apr. 4, 1930; s. Elias and Estelle (Press) D.; m. Margaret R. Zuanic, July 11, 1971; children: Susan, Ellen, Nina, Eva. BA, NYU, 1950; MA, Boston U., 1951, PhD, 1955, MD, 1957. Diplomate Am. Bd. Anesthesiology. Rsch. and teaching fellow in physiology Sch. Medicine Boston U., 1951-55; intern Grad. Hosp. U. Pa., 1957-58; resident in anesthesiology Hosp. U. Pa., 1958-61; asst. prof. anesthesiology U. Pa., 1963-65; asst. prof. Harvard U., 1965-69; prof. U. Chgo., 1969-71; prof., head. dept. anesthesiology U. Okla. Health Scis. Center, 1971-82; prof. anesthesiology U. Tex. Med. Sch., Houston, 1982-89, George Washington Sch. Medicine, Washington, 1989—; cons. VA Med. Center, Oklahoma City. Contbr. articles to profl. publs. Capt., M.C. USAR, 1961-63. Mem. AMA, Am. Soc. Anesthesiologists), Okla. Med. Assn., Tex. Med. Assn., Sigma Xi, Alpha Omega Alpha. Home: 1508 N Colonial Ct Arlington VA 22209 Office: George Washington U Hosp 901 23d St Washington DC 22037

DEVANAND, DAVANGERE PRAHALAD, psychiatrist, researcher; b. Bangalore, India, June 13, 1955; came to U.S., 1980; s. Davangere Krishna and Jaya P. (Rao) D. MBBS, Christian Med. Coll., Vellore, Tamil Nadu, India, 1978; MD, N.Y. State U., 1989. Diplomate Am. Bd. Psychiatry and Neurology, 1985. Resident in psychiatry SUNY Upstate Med. Ctr., Syracuse, 1980-82, Yale U. Sch. of Med., New Haven, 1982-84; rsch. fellow N.Y. State Psychiatric Inst. and Columbia U., N.Y.C., 1985-87; asst. prof. Columbia U., N.Y.C., 1987—; dir. Electroconvulsive Therapy Svc., N.Y. State Psychiat. Inst., N.Y.C., 1987—, asst. dir. Memory Disorders Clinic, 1988—. Contbr. articles to profl. jours. Rsch. grantee. Mem. Am. Psychiatirc Assn., AMA. Office: NY State Psychiat Inst 722 W 168th St New York NY 10032-2603

DEVEER, ROBERT K., JR., investment banker; b. Englewood, N.J., Apr. 22, 1946; s. Robert Kipp and Patricia Ann (Mulcare) deV.; m. Sally J. Staub, Dec. 21, 1968; children: Robert Kipp III, James Britten. BA in Econs., Yale U., 1968; MBA, Stanford U., 1973. Assoc. The First Boston Corp., N.Y.C., 1973-78, v.p., 1978-85, mng. dir., 1985—, dir. east coast investment banking, 1988-92; head natural resources group The First Boston Corp., 1992—; bd. dir. First Boston Found. Trust, N.Y.C., 1987—. Lt. USN, 1968-71. Arjay Miller scholar Stanford Bus. Sch., 1973. Mem. Canoe Brook Country Club (Summit, N.J.), Long Cove Club (Hilton Head, S.C.). Office: First Boston Corp Park Ave Plz 55 E 52d St New York NY 10055-0002

DE VELASCO, MARIA MERCEDES, educator, researcher; b. Caicedonia, Valle, Columbia, June 12, 1949; came to U.S., 1981; BA in Lit., Universidad del Valle, Cali, Columbia, 1981; M in Lit., Syracuse U., 1984, PhD in Latin Am. Lit., 1986. Asst. prof. Fitchburg State Coll., 1986-89, assoc. prof., 1990—. Author: (book, critic) Teatro Colombiano, 1986 (book) Teatro Colombiano; Politica y arte, 1991; co-author y las Mujeres:, 1991, (antology) Dramaturgas Latinoamericanas, 1991. Recipient NEH award Brown Univ., 1990. Mem. New England Modern Lang. Assn., Modern Lang. Assn., Amnesty Internat., Columbian Human Rights. Office: Fitchburg State College Fitchburg MA 01420

DEVEREUX, OWEN FRANCIS, metallurgy educator; b. Lexington, Mass., Aug. 23, 1937; s. George Francis and Mildred Anna (Gleeson) D.; m. Sally Williamson, June 15, 1957 (div. June 1969); children: Owen M., Amy L., Jonathan W., Nancy J.; m. Olivia Elaine Marin, June 13, 1969. BS, MIT, 1959, MS, 1960, PhD, 1962. Research chemist Chevron Research Co., La Habra, Calif., 1962-64, Corning (N.Y.) Glass Works, 1964-66, Chevron Oil Field Research Co., La Habra, 1966-68; assoc. prof. U. Conn., Storrs, 1968-76, prof., 1976—, head metallurgy dept., 1983—. Author: Topics in Metallurgical Thermodynamics, 1983; contbr. articles to profl. jours. Rsch. grantee NSF, 1970-76, U.S. Dept. Energy, 1976-86, NSF Industry/Univ. Corp. Rsch. Ctr. for Grinding Rsch. and Devel., 1990—. Mem. AIME, AAUP, Electrochem. Soc. (div. editor 1987-90), Nat. Assn. Corrosion Engrs. Home: PO Box 391 Storrs Mansfield CT 06268-0391 Office: Univ of Conn Box U-136 97 N Eagleville Rd Storrs CT 06268

DEVEREUX, RICHARD BLYTON, internal medicine educator; b. Phila., Oct. 23, 1945; s. Robert T. and Dorothea A. (Kern) D.; m. Corinne Keating, Oct. 3, 1970; children: Jane Helena, Robert Jed. BA, Yale U., 1967; MD, U. Pa., 1971. Diplomate Am. Bd. Internal Medicine, Sub-bd. Cardiovascular Diseases. Intern, resident in internal medicine N.Y. Hosp., N.Y.C., 1971-74; fellow in cardiology Hosp. of U. Pa., Phila., 1974-76; dir. echocardiography lab. N.Y. Hosp., N.Y.C., 1978—; asst. prof. medicine Cornell U. Med. Coll., N.Y.C., 1978-83, assoc. prof. medicine, 1983-92, prof. medicine, 1992—; mem. epidemiology study sect. NIH, Bethesda, Md., 1991-95. Mem. editorial bd. Am. Jour. Cardiology, Jour. Hypertension, Am. Jour. Hypertension, Circulation; contbr. articles to profl. jours. Recipient Physician-Scientist award Andrew Mellon Found., 1980-82, rsch. award Nat. Marfan Found., 1987. Fellow Am. Coll. Physicians, Am. Coll. Cardiology, Coun. on High Blood Pressure Rsch. Am. Heart Assn., Am. Soc. Hypertension (publs. com. 1990-93). Episcopalian.

DE VINCENZO, DORIS KREMSDORF, nursing educator; b. N.Y.C., July 21, 1923; d. Max and Hannah (Newman) K.; m. Salvatore De Vincenzo, Nov. 5, 1955. RN, Bellevue Sch. of Nursing, 1944; BS, NYU, 1948, MA, 1950, PhD, 1970. Pub. health nurse N.Y.C. (N.Y.) Health Dept., 1946-47; staff nurse Post Grad. Hosp., N.Y.C., 1948-49; head nurse, asst. psychiat. nursing Vet. Adminstrn. Hosp., Bronx, Manhattan, N.Y., 1948-58; asst. to exec. dir. N.Y. Counties RN Assn., N.Y.C., 1958-59; dir. of internat. affairs Am. Nurses Assn., N.Y.C., 1962-69; assoc. DON Bernstein Inst. Beth Israel Med. Ctr., N.Y.C., 1970-73; staff therapist Nat. Inst. for the Psychotherapies, N.Y.C., 1973-75; assoc. to full prof. Pace Univ. Lienhard Sch. of Nursing, Pleasantville, N.Y., 1974-89; prof. emerita Pace Univ. Lienhard Sch. of Nursing, Pleasantville, 1989; v.p., mem. N.Y. State Bd. Nurse Examiners, Albany, 1957-67; cons., researcher N.Y. State Dept. Corrections, Albany, 1978-83, Burke Rehab. Ctr., White Plains, N.Y., 1983-92, VA Hosp., Bronx, 1982-85; nurse cons. Harlem Valley Psychiat. Ctr., N.Y. State Dept. Mental Health, 1988-89. Contbr. articles to profl. jours., profl. program meetings, and books. Mem. coop. edn. adv. bd. for Briarcliff, Pleasantville, Pocantice Hills, 1980-81, community adv. bd. to White Plains Mental Health Ctr., 1985—; advisor Student Nurses' Assn., N.Y.C. area, 1957-64. 1st lt. U.S. Army Nurse Corps, 1944-46, ETO. U.S. Fulbright scholar to U.K./U. London/Maudsley Inst. Psychiatry, 1952-53. Mem. ANA, Am. Assn. for Nursing History, Westchester Nurses Assn. (past bd. dirs.), Westchester County Hist. Soc., Coun. Nurse Researchers, Coun. Psychiat. Mental Health Specialists, Kappa Delta Pi, Sigma Theta Tau (past chpt. v.p.). Home: 1161 Bedford Rd Pleasantville NY 10570-3910 Office: Pace Univ Bedford Rd Pleasantville NY 10570-1002

DEVINE, CHARLES ARTHUR, illustrater; b. East Springfield, Pa., Aug. 5, 1965; s. Dayton Edward Jr. and Mary (Stefanelli) D. Student, Erie County Vo-Tech, 1982-83. Artist, illustrater Devine Greetings, East Springfield, 1989-92. Home and Office: Devine Greetings 11894 E Maine St East Springfield PA 16411

DEVINE, DONN, lawyer, city official; b. South Amboy, N.J., Mar. 30, 1929; s. Frank Edward and Emily Theresa (DeRevere) D. m. Elizabeth Cecilia Baldwin, Nov. 23, 1951; children: Edward (dec.), Mary Elizabeth, Martin Joseph. BS, U. Del., 1949; JD with honors, Widener U., 1975. Bar: Del. 1975, U.S. Dist. Ct. Del. 1976; cert. genealogist, genealogy instr. Devel. chemist Allied Chem. Corp., Claymont, Del., 1950-52; newspaper writer, editor corp. publs. Atlas Powder Co., Wilmington, Del., 1952-60; mgmt. cons., 1960-68; dir. renewal planning City of Wilmington, 1968-79, dep. dir. planning, 1979-80, dir. planning, 1981-85; cons. Wilmington City Coun., 1985—; pvt. practice, 1985—; archival cons. Cath. Diocese Wilmington, 1989—; spl. counsel Del. Div. Alcoholism, Drug Abuse and Mental Health, 1990—. Author: Delaware National Guard, A Historical Sketch, 1968, DeRevere Family of Peekskill, New York, 1982; editor Del. Geneal. Soc. Jour., 1980-81; assoc. editor Del. Jour. Corp. Law, 1974-75. Past bd. dirs. Small Bus. Devel Corp., Wilmington Econ. Devel. Corp.; past officer Delmarva Ecumenical Agy.; emeritus bd. dirs., past officer Geriatric Svcs. Del.; past officer Christina Cultural Arts Ctr., Cath. Interracial Coun., Del. chpt. ACLU, St. Mary's-St. Patrick's Parish Coun. With USAR, 1950-54; 2d lt. to brig. gen. Del. Army N.G., 1954-84. Decorated Meritorious Svc. medal. Mem. ABA, Am. Planning Assn., Am. Inst. Cert. Planners, Am. Chem. Soc., Del. Soc. SAR (past pres.), Del. Geneal. Soc. (past pres.), Ft. Delaware Soc. (Recognition award), Univ. and Whist Club (Wilmington), Chemists Club of N.Y.C., Ancient Order Hibernians, Phi Kappa Phi, Delta Theta Phi. Democrat. Roman Catholic. Home: 2004 Kentmere Pky Wilmington DE 19806-2014

DEVINE, JAMES JOSEPH, chemical products manufacturing company executive; b. Bklyn., Aug. 14, 1926; s. Peter Charles and Gertrude Marie (Flanagan) D.; m. Maud Hearn, Apr. 18, 1953; children: Lynn, Jeffrey, Drew, Douglas. BSChemE, Bucknell U., 1950; MBA, Rutgers U., 1959. Supr. Merck & Co., Elkton, Va., 1950-51, Danville, Pa., 1951-53; asst. plant mgr. Clorox Co., Jersey City, 1954-59; coating supt. Natvar Corp., Rahway, N.J., 1959-66; organic plant supt. Vulcan Materials Co., Newark, 1966-69; mfg. mgr. Shulton Inc., Clifton, N.J., 1969-72; chem. mfg. mgr. Fisher Sci. Co., Fair Lawn, N.J., 1972-87; engr. Heterene Chem. Co., Paterson, N.J., 1987—. Served with USNR, 1944-46, PTO. Mem. Am. Chem. Soc., Am. Inst. Chem. Engrs., Alpha Chi Sigma, Sigma Chi. Republican. Roman Catholic. Home: 32 Terrill Rd Old Bridge NJ 08857-2144 Office: PO Box 247 Paterson NJ 07543-0247

DEVINE, SHANE, federal judge; b. Feb. 1, 1926. B.A., U. N.H., 1949; J.D., Boston Coll., 1952. Bar: N.H. 1952. Formerly ptnr. Devine, Millimet, Stahl & Branch, Manchester, N.H.; judge U.S. Dist. Ct. N.H., 1978—, now chief judge. Mem. ABA, N.H. Bar Assn. (pres. 1973-74), Manchester Bar Assn. Office: US Dist Ct NH 55 Pleasant St # 892 Concord NH 03301-3954*

DEVINE, THOMAS GERARD, education educator; b. Somerville, Mass., Jan. 18, 1928; s. Thomas J. and Anna G. D.; m. Claire T. Lawlor, Nov. 17, 1956; 1 child, Thomas James. AB, Boston U., 1950, AM, 1952, EdD, 1961. Assoc. prof. R.I. Coll., Providence, 1961-65, Boston U., 1965-80; prof. edn. U. Mass., Lowell, 1980—; cons. state dept. edn., N.H., Miss., N.Y., Conn., Md., Tex., N.J.; pres. R.I. Coun. Tchrs. English, 1965. Author: Teaching Reading Comprehension, 1986, Teaching Study Skills, 1987, Teaching Reading in Elementary School, 1989, (with others) Mastering Study Skills, 1989. Fellow Nat. Conf. Rsch. in English; mem. Nat. Coun. Tchrs. English (bd. dirs. 1961-65), Internat. Reading Assn. (pres. Merrimack Valley Coun. 1983), Mass. Coun. Tchrs. English (Outstanding Tchr. award 1983). Home: 8 Rambler Rd Jamaica Plain MA 02130-3428 Office: Univ Mass 1 University Ave Lowell MA 01854-2881

DE VISSCHER, FRANCOIS MARIE, investment banker; b. Louvain, Belgium, Sept. 24, 1953; s. Michel and Jacqueline (Velge) deV.; m. Maura Michaela Nicholson, Oct. 4, 1980; children: Patrick Michel. BA in Applied Econs., U. Louvain, 1975; MBA, Rutgers U., 1977. CPA, N.Y. Staff asst. Coopers & Lybrand, Brussels, 1975-76; staff acct. Coopers & Lybrand, N.Y.C., 1977-79, sr. acct., 1979-80, supr. audit, 1980; assoc. Smith Barney, Harris Upham & Co., Inc., N.Y.C., 1981-82, 2d v.p., 1983-84, v.p., 1985-88, mng. dir., 1988-90; pres. de Visscher & Co., Stamford, Conn., 1990—. Mem. AICPA, Nat. Assn. Securities Dealers (registered rep.), N.Y. Soc. CPAs, Belgium Am. C. of C. (bd. dirs.), Bekaert N.V. Belgium (bd. dirs.), Larchmont Yacht Club (N.Y.), Westchester Country (Rye, N.Y.), Univ. Club (N.Y.C.), Sandanona Club (Millbrook). Clubs: Larchmont Yacht (N.Y.); Westchester Country (Rye, N.Y.); Univ. (N.Y.C.); Sandanona (Millbrook). Office: de Visscher & Co 1111 Summer St Stamford CT 06905-5507

DEVITIS, JOSEPH LIBERATORE, educator; b. Balt., Apr. 24, 1945; s. Joseph L. and Mary (Romaniello) DeV.; m. Linda Haren Irwin, June 4, 1988; 1 child, Leigh Garrett Irwin. BA, Johns Hopkins U., 1967, MEd, 1969; PhD, U. Ill., 1972; MA, Bowie State U., 1985. Tchr. Balt. City Schs., 1968-69; prof. edn. U. Tenn., Martin, 1972-88; prof. edn. and human devel. SUNY, Binghamton, 1988—. Co-author: Theories of Moral Development, 1985, Helping and Intervention, 1990; co-editor: Building Bridges for Educational Reform, 1989, School Reform in the Deep South, 1991; editor: Women, Culture and Morality, 1987; mem. editorial bd. Ednl. Theory, 1990, Ednl. Studies, 1990—, Vitae Scholasticae, 1990—, Tchr. Edn. Quar., 1991—. Bd. dirs. Habit for Humanity, Oneonta, N.Y., 1988—, Jackson, Tenn., 1986-88, Crime Victims Assistance Ctr., Binghamton, 1990—; pres. Jackson Writers Group, 1985-88. Mem. Am. Ednl. Studies Assn. (pres. 1988-89), S.E. Philosophy of Edn. Soc. (pres. 1988-89), Coun. of Learned Socs. in Edn. (pres.-elect 1990-92). Democrat. Home: RR 1 Box 271B Oneonta NY 13820-9782 Office: Sch Edn and Human Devel SUNY-Binghamton Binghamton NY 13902-6000

DEVITO, ALBERT KENNETH, musician, composer, editor, publisher; b. Hartford, Conn., Jan. 17, 1919; s. Ralph and Rose (Abronze) DeV.; m. Irene Scally, May 27, 1983. student Hartford Fed. Coll., 1939-41, Columbia U., 1950-52; BS, NYU, 1948, MA, 1950; PhD, Midwestern U., 1975; MusD (hon.), East Nebr. Christian Coll., 1974; mgr., G. Schirmer, Inc., N.Y.C., 1948-52; instr. music Westbury (N.Y.) Public Schs., 1952-55; ind. composer, 1955—. Composer piano sonata, over 15 chorals, 5 organ solos, over 55 piano solos, 2 vocal solos, 2 popular songs; editor The Piano Tchr's. Art; editor, contbr. Tech. Control for the Modern Pianist; contbr. numerous articles to profl. jours.; author: Computer, MIDI, Desktop Publishing Dictionary, 1991, also numerous instruction books for chord organs, organ

methods, piano method books, 1 music terms dictionary, 2 piano arrangements; compiler many original works including collections for organ and piano; contbr. piano arrangements of sch. music instrn., book series; lectr. and cons. in field; TV performances Saturday Night Live, Guiding Light, As The World Turns, Ryan's Hope, Search for Tomorrow, All My Children, Loving, Another World, One Life To Live, many major movies. Past bd. dirs. Spiritual Frontier Fellowship, nat. chpt. Served with inf., Spl. Services, U.S. Army, 1942-46. Decorated Victory medal, Am., European, African, Middle East theatre campaign ribbons: recipient numerous prizes in music, panel awards, ASCAP, Merit award Nat. Fedn. Music Clubs, 1974. Mem. Internat. Platform Assn., Am. Choral Dirs. Assn., Am. Music Center, N.Y. State Music Tchr. Assn. (cert. emeritus), ASCAP, Music Tchrs. Assn. (cert. emeritus), Screen Actors Guild, AFTRA, Dramatists Guild, Actor's Equity Assn., Nat. Acad. TV Arts and Scis., Assn. Musicians Greater N.Y., Assn. Music Tchrs. League, Music Educators Nat. Conf., Keyboard Tchrs. Assn. Internat. (hon., pres., emeritus), Italian Actors Union, DAV (exec. com., liason officer), VFW (chaplain Westburg chpt.), Piano Tchrs. Congress N.Y.C. (past pres., hon. mem.), N.Y. State Sch. Music Assn., Nat. Geog. Soc., Phi Mu Alpha (past pres. B.E. chpt.). Home and Office: 361 Pinoak Ln Westbury NY 11590-1941

DEVITO, DONATO ENRICO, executive; b. Bklyn., Dec. 6, 1955; s. Joseph Anthony and Angelina (Lo Cascio) DeV.; m. Philomena Louise Graci, Apr. 21, 1979; children: Angelina, Donato, Nicole. Student, Bklyn. Coll., 1973-75. Stock cashier Weeden & Co., N.Y.C., 1974-75; margin clk. E.F. Hutton & Co., N.Y.C., 1975-76, Kidder Peabody & Co., N.Y.C., 1976-77; select mags. MPR, DMM, SMS, N.Y.C., 1978-83, Balt., 1978-83; mktg. mgr. Curtis Circulation Co., Balt., 1983-84; regional .gr. Penthouse Internat., Balt., 1984-86; exec. v.p. Mag. & Paperback Mktg. Inst.; v.p. mktg. A.C.I.D.A., Balt., 1986—. Republican. Roman Catholic. Office: M P M I 4000 Coolidge Ave Baltimore MD 21229-5500

DEVITO, MATHIAS JOSEPH, real estate executive; b. Trenton, N.J., Aug. 23, 1930; s. Charles P. and Margaret L. DeV.; m. Rosetta Kormuth, July 26, 1956; children: Ann Margaret, Charles Michael. B.A., U. Md., 1954, LL.B. with highest honors, 1956; L.H.D., Salisbury State Coll., 1984. Bar: Md. Asst. atty. gen. State of Md., 1963-64; ptnr. Piper & Marbury, Balt., 1965-70; sr. v.p., gen. counsel, then exec. v.p. Rouse Co., Columbia, Md., 1968-73; pres., chief exec. officer, dir. Rouse Co., 1973-84, chmn. bd., pres., chief exec. officer, 1984—; bd. dirs. 1st Md. Bancorp., U.S. Air Group, Inc., Trizec Corp.; chmn. Greater Balt. Com., 1990-92. Editor Md. Law Rev., 1955-56. Chmn. bd. trustees Md. State Colls., 1970-73; trustee Johns Hopkins U., 1983-89. Mem. Order of Coif. Roman Catholic. Clubs: Elkridge, Union League, Adirondack League. Office: Rouse Co 10275 Little Patuxent Pky Columbia MD 21044-3414

DEVITO, MICHAEL A., lawyer; b. Bklyn., June 2, 1924; s. Michael Anthony and Susan (Nmi) (Antonelli) ; widower; children: John E., Therese Pritchard. BBA, St John's U., 1950; JD, Fordham U., 1957. Bar: N.Y. 1958, Mass. 1960. Contracts dir. ITEK, RCA, RAYTHEON and others, Lexington, Mass., 1958-76, ITT, Madrid, Spain, 1976-78, Simmonds Precision Products, Tarrytown, N.Y., 1978-81, Lockheed Corp., Riyadh, Saudi Arabia, 1981-84; assoc. DeVito, Pransky & Stavros, Deham, Mass., 1984—; pres. Nat. Security Indsl. Orgn., Boston, 1975-76. With USN, PTO, 1943-46. Mem. NAt. Contract Mgmt. Assn. (pres. 1973-75), Mass. Bar Assn.

DEVITO, PAUL LEONARD, psychology educator; b. Pitts., Nov. 19, 1953; s. Albert and Bertha (Aragonese) DeV.; m. Rebecca Sue Lipner, Aug. 24, 1980; 1 child, Zachary Lipner. BS, U. Pitts., 1975, MS, 1978, PhD, 1980. Asst. prof. St. Joseph's U., Phila., 1980-86, assoc. prof., 1986—, chair dept. psychology, 1987—; presenter at profl. confs. Contbr. articles to profl. publs. Mem. Am. Psychol. Assn., Am. Psychol. Soc. (charter), Ea. Psychol. Assn., Midwestern Psychol. Assn., Psychonomic Soc., Sigma Xi. Office: Dept Psychology Saint Josephs Univ 5600 City Ave Philadelphia PA 19131-1376

DE VIVIES, PATRICE PHILIPPE, oil company executive; b. Saigon, Vietnam, Feb. 29, 1952; came to U.S., 1990; s. Pierre and Marguerite (des Moutis) de V.; m. Isabelle M. Calbiac, Oct. 2, 1976; children: Guillaume, Aude, Maylis, Gaelle. Degree in chem. enging., Ecole Nat. Superieure de Chimie de Paris, 1974; PhD, U. Paris, 1974; MBA, Ecole Superieure de Sci. de Economiques et Commerciales, Paris, 1976. Scientific attache French Embassy, Bogota, Columbia, 1976-78; economist Exploration div. Total, Paris, 1978-81, chief economist far east div., 1981-86; gas mgr. Total Indonesie, Jakarta, Indonesia, 1981; v.p. gas Total Trading Internat., Tokyo, Japan, 1986-87; exec. v.p. Total Coree Svcs., Seoul, Korea, 1987-90, Total Am. Svcs., N.Y.C., 1990—; chmn. Total Oil Inc., N.Y.C., 1990—; counsellor for internat. trade French Ministry of Trade and Industry, Paris, 1989—. Home: 16 Locust Ave Larchmont NY 10538-3825 Office: Total 527 Madison Ave New York NY 10022-4304

DE VIZIA, ANN MARIE RUTH, psychotherapist, social worker; b. Wilkes-Barre, Pa., Sept. 22, 1945; d. Joseph Francis and Ruth Mary (Miller) De V.; m. Richard Alapack, June 10, 1967 (div. Sept. 1977); 1 child, Nicole Marie. BA in Social Studies and Secondary Edn., Coll. of Misericordia, Dallas, Pa., 1967; MS in Counselor Edn., Duquesne U., 1977. Tchr. remedial reading Crestwood Sch. Dist., Mountain Top, Pa., 1978-79; psychotherapist Hazleton/Nanticoke (Pa.) Mental Health Mental Retardation, 1979-80; drug and alcohol prevention specialist Awareness Inc., Kingston, Pa., 1980-83; psychiat. therapist 1st Hosp. Wyoming Valley, Wilkes-Barre, Pa., 1983-88; dir. vols. and environ. svcs. Mercy Hosp., Wilkes-Barre, 1988-91; psychotherapist Ferrell & Assocs., Wilkes-Barre, 1988—; social worker Wyoming Valley West Sch. Dist., Kingston, 1991—. Councilman Boro of Penn Lake, Pa., 1980-82; mem. adv. bd. Helpline, Wilkes-Barre, 1989—, Vol. Action Ctr., Wilkes-Barre, 1990—, Ret. Sr. Vol. Program, Kingston, 1991—. Mem. AACD. Democrat. Roman Catholic.

DEVLIN, ELISE SEIBERT, writer, calligrapher; b. Chevy Chase, Md., Nov. 11, 1954; d. Vernon Elliott and Barbara Ruth (Mullins) Seibert; m. Robert J. Devlin, Apr. 16, 1977; children: Laura Marie, Matthew Robert. BS, U. Md., 1976. Writer, calligrapher Poetry Plus, Sadsburyville, Pa., 1981—. Recipient Gift of Time award Am. Family Inst. at Valley Forge, 1991, 92. Presbyterian. Home and Office: Route Rd # 30 Sadsburyville PA 19369-9999

DEVLIN, PAUL LEO, labor organization executive; b. Boston, Jan. 8, 1939; s. Leo G. and Mary C. (Hawkins) D.; m. Dorothy A. Terrio, Jan. 25, 1961; children: Mary C., Elizabeth J., Paul L. Jr., Peter A., Sarah A. BS, Boston Coll., 1961; MEd, Salem State Coll., 1964. Tchr., math. Salem (Mass.) Classical and High Sch., 1961-67; coord. math. Peabody (Mass.) Pub. Schs., 1967-71; staff rep. Mass. Fedn. Tchrs., Boston, 1971-75, assoc. exec. sec., 1975-80; v.p. Mass. AFL-CIO, Boston, 1975—, Am. Fedn. Tchrs., Washington, 1976—; pres. Mass. Fedn. Tchrs., 1980—; bd. dirs. Blue Cross/Blue Shield Mass., Boston, Tax Equity Alliance Mass., Boston; mem. Commn. on Conditions of Teaching, Boston, 1986-87; mem. Blueprint 2000, 1989-90. Del. Dem. Nat. Conv., N.Y.C., 1980, Atlanta, 1988, Dem. State Convs., Mass., 1980-90. Recipient Arthur R. Osborn Dedication award Mass. AFL-CIO, 1989. Democrat. Roman Catholic. Office: Mass Fedn Tchrs 216 Tremont St Boston MA 02116-4725

DEVLIN, ROBERT I ARTIN, physiologist educator; b. Albany, N.Y., Oct. 13, 1931; s. Patrick C. and Katherine (Martin) D.; m. Wanda Theresa Karandy, July 10, 1960; children: Kristin, Theresa, Michael. BS, SUNY, Albany, 1959; MA, Dartmouth Coll., 1961; PhD, U. Md., 1963. Asst. prof. N.D. State U., Fargo, 1963-65; asst. prof. U. Mass., Amherst, 1965-68, assoc. prof., 1968-74, prof., 1974—. Author: Plant Physiology, 1966; co-author: Photosynthesis, 1970, Biology of Human Concern, 1972, Exercises in Plant Physiology, 1986. Commr. Town of Barnstable, Mass., 1973-75; bd. dirs. Assn. for Preservation of Cape Cod, Mass., 1971; judge U.S. Figure Skating Assn., 1972-76. Pfc. U.S. Army, 1952-54. Recipient Disting. Mem. award Northeastern Weed Sci. Soc., 1990, Fellow award Weed Sci. Soc. of Am., 1991, Hon. degree of Dr. Honoris Causa, 1990. Fellow Weed Sci. Soc. of Am. (chmn. outstanding rsch. award com.); mem. Plant Growth Regulator Soc. of Am. (v.p. 1973-74, pres. 1974-76, 80-82), Internat. Weed Sci. Soc., Coun. for Agriculture, Sci. & Tech. (bd. dirs. 1980—), Am. Coun. on Sci. & Health (bd. sci. advisors, 1978—). Roman Catholic. Home: 157 Bristol Ave Hyannis MA 02601-2607 Office: U of Mass Glen Charlie Rd PO Box 569 East Wareham MA 02538-0569

DEVOE, JOANNE MCMAHON, public relations and communications consultant; b. Troy, N.Y., July 5, 1943; d. Thomas E. and Alice (Connors) McMahon; m. Wesley E. DeVoe III, Dec. 26, 1966; children: Ryan Thomas, Elizabeth Anne. BS, SUNY, Plattsburgh, 1965. Cert. elem. tchr., N.Y. Tchr. Mechanicville (N.Y.) Pub. Schs., 1965-70; substitute tchr. Ballston Lake, N.Y., 1970-80; pub. rels. asst. Proctor's Theatre, Schenectady, 1980-83; v.p. community rels. and spl. projects Schenectady County C. of C., 1983-89; sole propr., pres. DeVoe Assocs. Pub. Rels., Schenectady, 1989—. Grant chair League of Schenectady Symphony, 1989—; v.p. Schenectady Symphony Orch., 1990—; mem. City of Schenectady Urban Cultural Park Adv. Coun., 1988—. Named Woman of Vision, Schenectady YWCA, 1987. Mem. Women's Press Club of N.Y. State (officer), Am. Women in Radio and TV, Schenectady County C. of C. (accreditation team), Leadership Schenectady Alumni Assn. Home: 196 West Side Dr Ballston Lake NY 12109 Office: DeVoe Assocs 30 Jay St Schenectady NY 12019

DEVREOTES, PETER NICHOLAS, biochemistry educator; b. Long Branch, N.J., Apr. 22, 1948; s. Peter and Lucille (Mignon) D.; m. Aline Devreotes, Aug. 15, 1980. BS, U. Wis., 1971; PhD, Johns Hopkins U., 1977. Postdoctoral fellow U. Chgo., 1977-80; asst. prof. Sch. of Medicine, Johns Hopkins U., Balt., 1980-85, assoc. prof., 1985-87, prof. biol. chemistry, 1987—; mem. sci. rev. com. Am. Cancer Soc., Atlanta, 1990—; dir. biochemistry, cellular and molecular biology program Johns Hopkins U. Sch. Medicine, 1990—; established investigator Am. Heart Assn. Contbr. numerous articles to profl. jours. Am. Cancer Soc. grantee. Mem. Am. Soc. Biochemistry and Molecular Biology, Am. Soc. for Cell Biology. Office: Johns Hopkins U Sch of Medicine 725 N Wolfe St Baltimore MD 21205-2105

DE VRIES, JACOBUS E., investment banker; b. Jakarta, Java, Indonesia, Oct. 24, 1934; came to U.S., 1950, naturalized, 1955; s. Egbert and Tine (Berg) de V.; m. Lynne Shaw, May 10, 1969; 1 child, Margot Shaw. BA cum laude, Harvard Coll., 1961; MBA, Harvard U., 1964. V.p. Baker Weeks & Co., N.Y.C., 1974-77; mng. dir. Wm. Sword & Co., Princeton, N.J., 1977-80, Ardshiel Assocs., N.Y.C., 1980-82, J.M. Revie & Co., Morristown, N.J., 1982-83; pres., owner Morris Capital Cons., Inc., Morristown, N.J., 1983—; mgmt. cons. G.H. Besselaar, Assocs., Princeton, N.J., 1984-88. Pres. Springbrook Homes Assn., Morris Twp., N.J., 1977-87; bd. dirs. Hist. Speedwell Assn., Morristown, Iden Industries, Somerset, N.J.; trustee St. Barnabas Devel. Found., Livingston, N.J., 1983-87. With U.S. Army, 1955-57. Mem. N.Y. Soc. Security Analysts, Morris County Golf Club, Morristown Club. Republican. Episcopalian. Home: 41 Hilltop Cir Morristown NJ 07960 Office: Morris Capital Cons Inc 101 Poor Farm Rd Princeton NJ 08540-2955

DEVRIES, ROBERT CHARLES, scientist, researcher, consultant; b. Evansport, Ohio, Oct. 10, 1922; s. Charles and Rebecca (Goethe) DeV.; m. Ruth Elizabeth Wood, Oct. 30, 1943; children: David, Peter, Charles, Jonathon, Katherine. BA, DePauw U., 1948; PhD, Pa. State U., 1953. Topographer U.S. Geol. Survey, Washington, 1943-46; postdoctoral fellow Pa. State U., State College, 1953-54; staff scientist rsch. lab. GE, Schenectady, N.Y., 1954-61, staff scientist corp. R& D Ctr., 1965-88; assoc. prof. Rensselaer Poly. Inst., Troy, N.Y., 1961-65; cons. P-T-X, Burnt Hills, N.Y., 1988—; cultural exch. visitor, Japan, 1974; Coolidge fellow, 1981. Editor: The Reactivity of Solids, 1968, contbr. numerous articles to profl. jours.; patentee in field. With USAF, 1943. Rector scholar DePauw U., 1941; recipient Coolidge fellow GE R&D Ctr., 1981, Engrin. Materials Achievement award Am. Soc. Metals, 1973. Fellow Am. Ceramic Soc., Am. Mineral. Soc.; mem. AAAS, Am. Assn. Crystal Growth, Mineral. Soc. London, Sigma Xi. Home and Office: 17 Van Vorst Dr Burnt Hills NY 12027-9712

DEVYLDER, EDGAR PAUL, JR., corporate lawyer; b. Waterbury, Conn., Jan. 7, 1945; s. Edgar Paul Sr. and Lillian (Cordett) DeV.; m. Elaine Jordan, Jan. 8, 1972; children: Joseph Steven, Jordan Edgar. AB, Yale U., 1967; JD, U. Mich., 1974. Bar: Conn. 1974, Fla. 1978, U.S. Dist. Ct. Conn. 1975, U.S. Ct. Appeals (2nd cir.) 1975, U.S. Supreme Ct. 1979. Assoc. Cummings & Lockwood, Stamford, Conn., 1973-79; counsel Gen. Signal Corp., Stamford, 1979-85, sr. atty., 1985-87; v.p., gen. counsel BTR, Inc., Stamford, 1988—. Lt. USN, 1967-71.

DE WAAL, IAN C. SMITH, lawyer; b. Bklyn., June 23, 1950; s. John and Lillian (Jaffe) DeW.; m. Caroline A. Smith, Sept. 3, 1990. BA, SUNY, Buffalo, 1972, JD, 1975; BM, New Eng. Conservatory, 1989. Bar: N.Y. 1976, U.S. Dist. Ct. (we. dist.) N.Y., U.S. Ct. Appelas (2nd cir.) 1976, Mass. 1985, U.S. Dist. Ct. Mass. 1985, U.S. Ct. Appeals (1st cir.), 1985, U.S. Ct. Appeals (4th cir.) 1987, U.S. Supreme Ct. 1979. Staff attorney Monroe County Legal Assistance Corp., Rochester, N.Y., 1975-84, Nat. Consumer Law Ctr., Boston, 1985-88; asst. atty. gen. Dept of Mass. Atty. Gen., Boston, 1988-90; trial atty. U.S. Dept. Justice, criminal div., fraud sect., Washington, 1990—. Mem. Boston Bar Assn. Orchestra, MIddlesex Community Band. Mem. ABA, ACLU, Boston U. Alumni Band (assoc. mem.), 1986—. Home: 9504 Warren St Silver Spring MD 20910 Office: US Dept Justice Criminal Div 1400 New York Ave NW Washington DC 20005-2107

DEWALD, HORACE ALBERT, retired research medicinal chemist; b. Emlenton, Pa., Oct. 25, 1922; s. Arthur Gilroy and Anna Elsa (Heydenreich) DeW.; m. Sarah Mary Ireys, May 28, 1955; children: Nancy, Laura, Carolyn, David, Kenneth, Charles. BS, Allegheny Coll., 1944; PhD, U. Ill., 1950. Chemist Eastman Kodak, Rochester, N.Y., 1944-46; chemist surfactants Gen. Aniline & Film, Easton, Pa., 1950-52; fellow Mellon Inst., Pitts., 1952-57; assoc. rsch. chemist Parke Davis, Detroit, 1957-60, Ann Arbor, Mich., 1960-64; sr. rsch. chemist to sr. rsch. scientist to rsch. assoc. Warner Lambert/Parke Davis, Ann Arbor, 1964-86, ret., 1986. Patentee in field; contbr. articles to profl. jours. Mem. Am. Chem. Soc., Phi Beta Kappa. Republican. Home: 241 Woodhaven Dr Pittsburgh PA 15228-1550

DE WAN-CARLSON, ANNA THERESA, artist; b. Syracuse, N.Y., Dec. 29, 1949; d. William Martin and Sarah Theresa (Kirchhof) De Wan; m. David G. Carlson, Aug. 8, 1971 (div. 1981); 1 child, Adam Edward. AAS, Art Inst. Pitts., 1971; student, Syracuse U., 1967, 68, 87. Selected exhibits include The Space Group of Korea 6th Internat. Miniature Print Biennial, Seoul, Arts Ctr. of the Grand Prairie 5th Nat. Miniature Annual Art Exhibit, Stuttgart, Ark., Cooperstown Nat. Juried Art Exhibit, Cooperstown, N.Y., Munson-Williams-Proctor Inst. Artists of Cen. N.y. Annual Juried Exhibit, Utica, N.Y. and many others; represented in collections Print Club of Albany, Onondaga Savs. Bank, Carrier Corp., Syracuse Savs. Bank and others. Fundraiser March of Dimes, Jordan, N.Y., 1978-79. Mem. Print Club of Albany, Print Club Rochester, Print Club Phila., Associated Artists Syracuse, Manhattan Graphics Ctr., Everson Mus., Syracuse (N.Y.) Printmakers (pres. 1981, bd. mem., collection curator, exhibits curator, publicist 1989—). Home: 145 Avon Rd Syracuse NY 13206-3036

DEWEES, DONALD CHARLES, securities company executive; b. Phila., Sept. 7, 1931; s. John Coleman and Elva (Burke) DeW.; B.S. in Commerce and Finance, Bucknell U., 1953; M.B.A., U. Pa., 1954; m. Martha V. Folk, July 31, 1954; children—Donald C., Suzanne C., Gretchen F. Data processing rep. Nat. Cash Register Co., Wilmington, Del., 1954-62; account rep. Francis I. duPont Co., investments, Wilmington, 1962-67, br. mgr., Balt., 1968; br. mgr. Butcher & Singer, Wilmington, 1969-71, v.p., 1971-76, 1st v.p., 1977, sr. v.p., 1978—, resident mgr., 1969-76, ltd. ptnr., 1976-87, exec. v.p., 1987, sr. exec. v.p., 1988-89, mng. dir., 1989-91 also bd. dirs.; dir. Mgmt. Scis. Inc., Bus. Trends Inc., Computer Terminals and Tapes Ltd., Wheat Securities; underwriting mem. Lloyds of London; cons. in field. Active Wilmington YMCA; bd. dirs. Butcher & Singer, Delaware Ctr. of Contempary Arts, Ingleside Nursing Home, Ch. Home Found., Episcopal Home of Del., Del Marva Boy Scouts of Am., 1989. Served with AUS, 1952-53, 58-59, Korea. Mem. Fin. Analysts Soc., Am. Philatelic Soc., Phi Kappa Psi. Republican. Methodist. Clubs: University (Wilmington); Collectors (N.Y.). Masons, Shriners. Author sales tng. publs. Home: 4200 Pyles Ford Rd Wilmington DE 19807-1734 also: 25 Kelly Ln Bethany Beach DE 19930 Office: 300 Delaware Ave Wilmington DE 19801-1608

DEWEESE, JAMES ARVILLE, surgeon, educator; b. Apr. 5, 1925; s. Arville Otis and Vergie (Jenkins) DeW.; m. Margaret Brown, June 20, 1950 (dec. 1960); children: James Arville, Margaret Ann, Elizabeth Lynn, Joanne Spencer; m. Patricia Bidwell, May 5, 1962; children: Robert Bidwell, Jamie Susan. Student, Harvard U., 1942-43, Kent State U., 1943-44; MD, U. Rochester, 1949. Diplomate Am. Bd. Surgery (bd. dirs. 1986-91), Am. Bd. Thoracic and Cardiovascular Surgery (bd. dirs. 1987-91); cert. spl. qualifications gen. vascular surgery. Intern Strong Meml. Hosp., Rochester, N.Y., 1949-50, resident, 1950-52, 54-56; instr. surgery U. Rochester (N.Y.) Sch. Medicine and Dentistry, 1955-58, asst. prof. surgery, 1958-63, assoc. prof. surgery, 1963-69, prof. surgery, 1969-74, prof. cardiothoracic surgery, 1975—, chmn. div. cardiothoracic surgery, 1975-91, assoc. chmn. dept. surgery, 1986-90, chief sect. vascular surgery, 1987-90. Bd. dirs. Jour. Vascular Surgery, 1983—; editor: Vascular Surgery, 1985; contbr. over 200 articles to sci. jours. and over 60 chpts. to books. Mem. bd. trustees Clifton Springs (N.Y.) Hosp., 1980—. Mem. Am. Heart Assn. (bd. dirs. 1982-86, chmn. coun. cardiovascular surgery 1982-84), Ea. Vascular Soc. (pres. 1988), Internat. Soc. Cardiovascular Surgery (pres. N.Am. chpt. 1984-85), Pan Pacific Surg. Assn. (sec. gen. 1987—, pres. 1989-91), Soc. Vascular Surgery (pres. 1977-78), Oak Hill Country Club (Rochester) (bd. govs. 1978-81). Home: 121 Newcastle Rd Rochester NY 14610 Office: U Rochester Dept Surgery M&D Cardiothoracic Div 601 Elmwood Ave Rochester NY 14642-9999

DEWEY, CLARENCE FORBES, engineering educator; b. Pueblo, Colo., Mar. 27, 1935; s. Clarence F. and Elsie (Hafermalz) D.; m. Carolyn Miller, Aug. 3, 1963; 1 child, Devan Forbes. BE, Yale U., 1956; MS, Stanford U., 1957; PhD, Calif. Inst. Tech., 1963. Asst. prof. U. Colo., Boulder, 1963-68; assoc. prof. MIT, Cambridge, 1968-75, prof. engring., 1975—; vis. scientist Inst. fur Plasmaphysick, Garching, Fed. Republic of Germany, 1966-67; vis. prof. Harvard Med. Sch., 1978-79, Hefei Poly. U., Republic of China, 1986; bd. dirs. Concurrent Computer Corp., Tinton Falls, N.J., Celadon Corp., Cambridge, Mass.; cons. in field. Patentee in field; contbr. articles to profl. jours. Grantee NIH, Bethesda, Md., 1971—, Office Naval Rsch., San Diego 1970-75, 1987-89, Air Force Office Sci. Rsch., Washington, 1976-79. Mem. Am. Phys. Soc. Home: Marblehead MA 01945 Office: 77 Massachusetts Ave Cambridge MA 02139-4307

DEWEY, PAT PARKER, broadcast executive, composer; b. Berkeley, Calif., Jan. 27, 1923; d. George and Mildred (Johnston) Parker; student Sullins Jr. Coll., 1940-41; Mus.B., U. Miss., 1943; m. Grayson Headley, Dec. 30, 1946 (dec. 1961); m. 2d, M. Lee Williams, Dec. 18, 1964 (div.); 1 son, Philip Lee Williams; m. Ralph B. Dewey, Dec. 26, 1976. Woman's dir. radio sta. WNNT, Warsaw, Va., commentator daily women's program, Chat with Pat, 1952-60, now owner, pres. radio station WNNT AM-FM; partner WKWI-FM, Kilmarnock, Va.; asst. soc. editor Jackson Daily News, 1943-44. Composer: concerto for piano and orch., Rhapsody of Youth, performed by Nat. Air Force Symphony, Washington, Lisner Auditorium, 1947, guest pianist with Nat. Air Force Symphony, 1964, 75; (song) Cotton Picking Blues, featured in several musicals in Miss., Washington; (song) Maid of Cotton, used as theme song Nat. Cotton Council, 1945-51; (song) Lucky X, ofcl. song Chi Omega. Chmn., Red Cross water safety program, Lancaster County, Va., 1950-56; mem. exec. com. Jr. Assembly, Washington; jr. chmn. Home Hospitality Com., Washington, 1943-46; jr. chmn. UN Club activities, Washington, 1943-48. Mem. Am. Women in Radio and Television (dir. Va. 1962-65), Nat. Soc. Arts and Letters (music chmn. Washington chpt. 1964-65), Va. Assn. Broadcasters, Internat. Platform Assn., Nat. Assn. Am. Composers and Conductors, Women's Com. for Nat. Symphony Orch., Nat. Mus. Women in Arts (founder 1986, mem. women's com.), Chi Omega, Delta Beta Sigma, Sigma Alpha Iota, Alpha Psi Omega. Episcopalian. C-lubs: Friday Morning Music; Debutante of Miss., Women's (chmn. music div. Lancaster County, Va. 1956-60), Washington, Kenwood Garden, Congl. Golf, Indian Creek Yacht and Country. Home: 6211 Garnett Dr Bethesda MD 20815-6617

DEWIND, ADRIAN WILLIAM, JR., Latin American and Caribbean studies educator; b. Washington, Dec. 23, 1943; s. Adrian William and Joan Elizbeth (Mosenthal) DeW.; m. Dona D.S. Ratterree, Nov. 26, 1983; children: Adrian Samuel Ratterree, William Leclare Ratterree. BA, Columbia U., 1966, PhD, 1977. Researcher N.Am. Congress on Latin Am., N.Y.C., 1973-79; rsch. fellow NYU, N.Y.C., 1980; cons. Rockefeller Found., N.Y.C., 1980-81; dir. immigration rsch. program Columbia U., N.Y.C., 1981-88; assoc. prof. Hunter Coll., CUNY, N.Y.C., 1988—, dir. Latin Am. and Caribbean Studies Program, 1988—; chmn. bd. Ctr. for Immigrants Rights, N.Y.C., 1985-89; exec. com. Nat. Coalition for Haitian Refugees, N.Y.C., 1981—; mem. Nat. Immigration, Refugee, and Citizenship Forum, Washington, 1980—. Author: Aiding Migration, 1988 (Best Book award New Eng. Coun. Latin Am. Studies 1989), Peasants Become Miners, 1977. Bd. mem. Open Space Inst., N.Y.C., 1984—. Rsch. and conf. grantee Andrew W. Mellon, Ford Found., Nat. Inst. Child Health and Human Devel., Revson Found., Aaron Diamond Found., Joyce Mertz-Gilmore Found., N.Y. Community Trust. Mem. Am. Anthropol. Assn., Latin Am. Studies Assn., New Eng. Coun. Latin Am. Studies. Democrat. Office: Hunter Coll Latin Am and Caribbean Studies Program New York NY 10021

DEWIT, ROLAND, physicist, researcher; b. Amsterdam, Netherlands, Feb. 28, 1930; came to U.S., 1950; s. Louis Willem and Marianne (Carels) deW.; m. Gloria Winkel, Aug. 22, 1954; children: Bruce, Keith. BS, Ohio U., 1953; PhD, U. Ill., 1959. Asst. rsch. physicist U. Calif., Berkeley, 1959-60; physicist Nat. Bureau Standards (now Nat. Inst. Standards and Tech.), Gaithersburg, Md., 1960—. Contbr. articles to profl. jours. U. fellow U. Ill., Urbana, 1953-55, Gulf Oil fellow U. Ill., Urbana, 1957-58. Mem. ASME, ASTM, The Minerals, Metals and Materials Soc. of AIME, Am. Acad. Mechanics, Am. Phys. Soc., Soc. Exptl. Mechanics, Am. Soc. Metals Internat., Washington Acad. Scis., Md. Inst. Metals, Phi Beta Kappa, Sigma Xi, Phi Eta Sigma. Home: 11812 Tifton Dr Rockville MD 20854-3538 Office: Nat Inst Stds and Tech Gaithersburg MD 20899

DEWITT, HARRY MORTON, management consultant; b. Birmingham, Ala., Jan. 16, 1920; s. Harry Morton and Lucile (Wells) D.; m. Christine Elizabeth Rydholm, Aug. 25, 1944; children: H.M. Lee, Linda Margaret. BS in Indsl. Engring., Auburn U., 1942; MBA, George Washington U., 1952; LLB, Blackstone Coll., Chgo., 1952; Dipl., Nat. Def. U., Washington, 1956. Registered profl. engr.; registered investment advisor; lic. real estate broker, insurance broker. Indsl. engr. U.S. Steel, Birmingham, Ala., 1937-42; chief prodn. scheduling for major ships USN, 1942; project dir. USPHS, Washington, Chgo., 1942-43; spl. engring. asst. Kaiser Industries, Washington, 1943; mgmt. staff asst. to Q.M. gen., 1944; chief mgmt. control Pacific supply ops. U.S. Army, 1945; chief mgmt. engr. USPHS, Washington, 1946; prin. Dewitt & Assocs., Washington, 1947—; dir. Mgmt. Rsch. Ctr., U.S. Army, 1948-49; dir. Mgmt. Improvement Prog., Armed Forces, Washington, 1950-52; chief indsl. engr. Sylvania TV, Batavia, N.Y., 1952-53; budget/planning dir. Westinghouse Elec., Balt., 1954-64; chief Army personnel rsch. U.S. Army, 1965-67; chmn. Washington Star Newspaper Project, 1981—. Author: Comptrollership in Armed Forces, 1952, Organization for National Security, 1953, Management Service Program, 1945; contbr. articles to profl. jours. Chmn. Best Candidate Com., Washington, 1970—, Washington Star Newspaper Project, 1981—, Fedn. of World Communities, 1991—. Col. U.S. Army, 1943-80. Mem. Fedn. World Communities (chmn. 1991—), Army Navy Country Club. Presbyterian. Home: 11619 Gilsan St Silver Spring MD 20902-3122 Office: National Cons Group 1400 20th St NW # 114 Washington DC 20036-5906

DEWOODY, BARBARA MCKENNA, industrial hygienist; b. Mineral Wells, Tex., July 8, 1966; d. William Joseph McKenna and Linda Arlene (Housley) Moorhouse; m. Daniel Curtis DeWoody, June 24, 1989. BS in Safety Mgmt., Indiana U. Pa., 1987. Safety intern Contraves Goertz, Pitts., 1986-87; indsl. hygienist Three Rivers Health and Safety, Pitts., 1987-88; safety cons. Ionodi Constrn. Co., Pitts., 1988; indsl. hygiene cons. Penrun Corp., Pitts., 1988; indsl. hygienist Schneider Engrs., Bridgeville, Pa., 1988-90, SE Technologies Inc. (formerly Schneider Engrs.), Bridgeville, Pa., 1990—; cons. in field. Mem. Am. Soc. Safety Engrs., Am. Indsl. Hygiene Assn., Human Factors Soc. Republican. Methodist. Home: PO Box 178 Eighty Four PA 15330-0181

DE WYN GAERT, LAURA LANE, gifted and talented education educator; b. Boston; d. George Edward and Gertrude Marie (Connolly) Lane; m. Paul Herbert De Wyn Gaert Jr., Oct. 18, 1947; children: Mark Alan, Paul Herbert III, Jude Maria, Karl Damian. Diploma, Sch. Practical Art, Boston, 1943; BFA, Monmouth Coll., 1966, MS in Adminstrn., summa cum laude, 1969, PhD. Cert. Tchr. Artist Cronin, Whinnem & Goode Advt. Agy., Boston, 1944; film animator MIT, Cambridge, 1945-46; artist, illustrator Watson Labs., Eatontown, N.J., 1947-48; artist, co-owner Precision Color Printing Co., Newark, 1949—; prin., supr. tchr environ. art State Dep. Edn., Sandy Hook, N.J.; tchr. art St. Mary's Sch., New Monmouth, N.J.; curriculum designer and tchr. gifted and talented Middletown (N.J.) Twp. Sch. System, 1985—; curriculum designer and tchr. fine arts, various programs throughout state, N.J. Dept. Edn.; tchr. adult animation, Brookdale Community Coll., Lincroft, N.J., 1981; coord., judge art shows for bus. and community agys.. Contbr. numerous articles to profl. jours.; one-women show Middletown Town Hall, Monmouth Mus., Lincroft, N.J.; presenter in field. Mem. bicentennial com. U.S. Constn, N.J., 1986-89. Recipient numerous awards including Outstanding Educator award Middletown Jaycees, 1982, Most Outstanding Person in Arts award, 1984, others. Mem. AAUW, N.J. Art Educators, Assn. Curriculum Supervision and Devel., Monmouth County Hist. Soc., Zonta (internat. pres. 1980-82, bd. dirs. 1985-87), Bus. and Profl. Women, Women in the Arts, (charter mem. Washington chpt.), Lambda Sigma Tau, Alpha Delta Kappa (pres. 1980-82, 86, state historian 1984-86, Most Honoured Mem. award N.J. chpt.), Phi Delta Kappa. Home: 270 Sunrise Rd Belford NJ 07718-1319 Office: Thorne Sch 70 Murphy Rd Port Monmouth NJ 07758-1099

DEXTER, FREDERICK JAY, dentist; b. Bklyn., Apr. 12, 1947; s. Michael M. and Muriel Dexter; m. Deborah Rosenzweig, Aug. 12, 1972 (div. 1978); 1 child, Michael J. BS in Aerospace Engring., U. Md., 1970, DDS, 1979; BSME, Johns Hopkins U., 1974. Registered profl. engr.; cert. dentist. Mech. engr. U.S. Army, Aberdeen Proving Ground, Md., 1970-75; pvt. practice dentistry Thurmont, Md., 1980—, Reisterstown, Md., 1981—; dental cons. Ivy Hall Nursing Home, Balt., 1979—, Bent Nursing Home, Reisterstown, 1985-88. Author articles various newspapers, 1981—. Mem. Gen. Practice Orthodontics (adv. to bd. 1987—), Lions (v.p. Thurmont club 1986—), Optimists (v.p. Reisterstown club 1984), Tau Beta Pi. Home: 620 Main St Reisterstown MD 21136-1910 Office: 100 S Center St Thurmont MD 21788-1599

DEY, MARLENE MELCHIORRE, nursing educator, critical care nurse; b. L.I., N.Y., June 9, 1952; d. Ralph and Ann (Doria) Melchiorre; m. Theodore J. Dey, Jr.; children: Lauren, Michael. BSN, Fairleigh Dickenson U., 1974; MS in Nursing, Seton Hall U., 1983. RN, N.J. Clin. coord. critical cardiac unit Newark Beth Israel Med. Ctr.; instr. nursing Passaic County Community Coll., Paterson, N.J.; staff relief nurse med. ICU, Hackensack (N.J.) Med. Ctr.; asst. prof. med.-surg. nursing Essex County Coll., Newark; project dir. Karl Perkins Vocat.-Edn. Grant-Nursing Dept. Essex County Coll. Mem. ANA (cert. med.-surg. nurse), N.J. Nurses Assn., Seton Hall U. Alumni Assn. (bd. dirs.), Coll. of Nursing Alumni Assn. (sec.).

DEYSHER, PAUL EVANS, training consultant; b. Reading, Pa., Oct. 16, 1923; s. Paul Stauffer and Ida Estelle (Evans) D.; m. Myrtle Constance Stover, June 17, 1950; children: David Paul, Mark Edward. BS, Albright Coll., 1945; M in Ednl. Adminstrn., Temple U., 1949. Math. and sci. tchr. Lebanon City (Pa.) Sch. Dist., 1950-56; asst. high sch. prin. Ocean City Sch. (N.J.) Dist., 1956-57; high sch. prin. Yeadon Sch. (Pa.), Dist., 1957-60; mgr. pers. adminstrn. Philco Corp., Phila., 1960-66; tng. specialist AMP, Inc., Harrisburg, Pa., 1966-80, supr. mgmt. tng., 1980-85, mgr. mgmt. tng. and devel., 1986; cons. and lectr. in field. Co-author: Transistor Fundamentals, 1962; contbr. chpts. to books and articles to profl. jours. Pres. Albright Coll., Lebanon County Alumni chpt., 1979—; trustee Albright Coll., Reading, Pa., 1985-89. Mem. NEA (life), Am. Soc. Pers. Adminstrn. (cert., sr. prof. in human resources), ASTD (past pres.), Annville-Cleona Club, Kiwanis (bd. dirs.), Phi Delta Kappa. Republican. Lutheran. Home: 39 S Mill St Lebanon PA 17042-3124

DHARLO, RINCHEN, Tibetan representative; b. Nyanang, U-Tsang, Tibet, July 1, 1948; came to U.S., 1987; s. Ngawang and Senam (Dolma) Bhusepa; m. Sonan Gyalmo, Jan. 15, 1985; children: Tenzin Dolkar, Tenzin Choedon, Tenzin Dikyi. Student, Cen. Sch. for Tibetans, Simla, India, 1962-65, Ednl. Cum Vocat. Tng. Ctr., Pachmari, India, 1965-70. Bilingual sec. to rep. Office of H.H. Dalai Lama's, Kathmandu, Nepal, 1972-74, supr. edn. sect., 1974-78; acting rep. H.H. Dalai Lama, Kathmandu, Nepal, 1978-82, rep., 1982-86; rep. and head Office of Tibet H.H. Dalai Lama, N.Y.C., 1987—; chmn. Jawalakkel Handicraft Ctr., Kathmandu, 1982-86, Tarshi Palkhyl Handicraft Ctr., Pokhara, Nepal, 1982-86; co-chair Tibetan U.S. Resettlement Project, N.Y., 1990—. Author: A Guide to Buddhist Holy Places of Nepal, 1985. Mem. Temple of Understanding, N.Y.C., 1987—; pres. Tibet Fund, N.Y.C., 1987—; mem. adv. bd., N.Am. planning com. UN Environment Program; bd. dirs. Internat. Campaign for Tibet, Washington, 1989—; dir. Carpet Tng. Ctr., Kathmandu, 1982-86, Show Lion Found., Kathmandu, 1982-86; Tibet House, N.Y.C., 1988—; founding mem. Srongtsen Brikuti Sch., Boudha, Kathmadu, Nepal, Atisha Primary Sch., Jawalakhel, Nepal, Namgyal High Sch., Kathmandu, Nepal, Jampa Ling Day Sch., Hellitar, Nepal, Paljor Ling Primary Sch., Pokhara, Nepal. Mem. Global Forum (steering com. N.Y.C. chpt. 1987-88). Office: 241 E 32d St New York NY 10016

D'HARNONCOURT, ANNE, museum director; m. Joseph J. Rishel, June 19, 1971. B.A., Radcliffe Coll., 1965; M.A. with distinction, Courtauld Inst. Art, U. London, 1967. Curatorial asst. Phila. Mus. Art, 1967-69; asst. curator 20th Century art Art Inst. Chgo., 1969-71; curator 20th Century art Phila. Mus. Art, 1971-82, the George D. Widener dir., 1982—. Organizer: (with McShine) exhbn. Marcel Duchamp, 1973-74, (with others) Philadelphia: Three Centuries of American Art, 1976, Eight Artists, 1978, (with Percy) Violet Oakley, 1979, Futurism and the International Avant-Garde, 1980, (with Sims) John Cage: Scores and Prints, 1982; author: (with Walter Hopps) Etant Donnes. Reflections on a New Work by Marcel Duchamp, 1969, The Cubist Cockatoo: Preliminary Exploration of Joseph Cornell's Hommages to Juan Gris, 1978, also prefaces for various books. Mem. Am. Philos. Soc. Office: Phila Mus Art Benjamin Franklin Pkwy PO Box 7646 Philadelphia PA 19101-7646

DHEIN, RICHARD D., company executive; b. Wilkes-Barre, Pa., Nov. 23, 1953; s. Delmar R. and Larinice (Ballam) D.; m. Paula C.S., July 28, 1955. BS in Bus., U. N.H., 1975. Mgr. Saga Foods, Washington Crossing, Pa., 1975-76; gen. mgr. Wotten Sailing, Montvale, N.J., 1976-80; sales mgr. Howmar Boats, Edison, N.J., 1980-83; v.p. MacKissic, Parker Ford, Pa., 1983—; dir. OPEDA Assocs. Office: MacKissic PO Box 111 Parker Ford PA 19457-0111

DHINDSA, RAGWINDER KAUR, sociology educator; b. Kalka, Punjab, India, Jan. 29, 1937; came to U.S., 1962, naturalized, 1973; d. Badan Singh and Harjit (Kaur) Sekhon; m. Dharam Singh Dhindsa, Sept. 11, 1961; children: Hardeep, Harinder, Ranjit. MA in Polit. Sci., Agra (India) U., 1958; EdB, Punjab U., India, 1959; MA in Sociology, Mont. State U., 1963, MEd, 1963; PhD in Sociology, U. Ill., 1968. Prof. Guru Nanak Girls Coll., Saharanpur, India, 1959-61; rsch. asst. U. Ill., Urbana, 1964-67; lectr. Lewis and Clark Coll., Portland, Oreg., 1970-75, Portland Community Coll., 1971-75, U. Md., College Park, 1977-78; prof. Anne Arundel Community Coll., Arnold, Md., 1978—; co-dir. Ctr. for the Study of Local Issues, Anne Arundel Community Coll., Arnold, 1982-86; speaker colls., high schs., and assns., Rockville, Md., Arnold, Md., 1978—; chairperson workshops for colls., Arnold, 1978—. Mem. Nat. Inst. Against Prejudice and Violence, Am. Sociol. Assn., Groves Conf. on Marriage and the Family, Gamma Sigma Delta. Home: 2310 Glenmore Ter Rockville MD 20850-3034 Office: Anne Arundel Community Coll 101 College Pky Arnold MD 21012-1895

DHONDT, STEVEN THOMAS, marketing executive; b. Xenia, Ohio, Aug. 4, 1944; s. Maurice Bernard and Madeline (Pierson) D.; m. Elizabeth Ann Emrick, June 11, 1966 (div. June 1972); 1 child, Jennifer Elizabeth; m. Patty Ruth Bayley, Jan. 9, 1982. BA, Adrian Coll., 1966; MA, Utah State U., 1967; Phd, Bowling Green State U., 1968, SUNY, Buffalo, 1971. Instr. English SUNY, Buffalo, 1968-74; assoc. dean of faculty SUNY, 1969-74; assoc. acad. dean Salem State Coll., Salem, Mass., 1974-77; dir. publishing Am.-Scandinavian Found., N.Y.C., 1977-79; prin. Dhondt Enterprises, N.Y.C., 1978-81; mgr. corp. communications Merck & Co., Inc., Rahway, N.J., 1981-83; sr. v.p., asst. dir. creative resources Shearson Lehman Bros. Inc., N.Y.C., 1983—; trustee N.J. Coun. on Econ. Edn., Trenton, 1981-83, Borough of Manhattan Community Coll. Fund, Inc., N.Y.C., Poets House, N.Y.C.; cons. Bayley, Leighton & Ryan, Inc., N.Y.C., 1988—. Author: First Reading, 1972; mng. editor Coll. English Assn., Buffalo, 1972-74. Trustee N.J. Coun. on Econ. Edn., Trenton, 1981-83, Borough of Manhattan Community Coll. Fund, Inc., N.Y.C., 1992—, Poets House, N.Y.C., 1992—. Democrat. Methodist. Home: 175 W 93d St Apt 14C New York NY 10025

DIAISO, ROBERT JOSEPH, civil engineer; b. Jersey City, N.J., Jan. 3, 1940; s. Dominick A. and Marie M. (Sarno) DiA.; m. Elaine Ricca, June 8, 1963; 1 child, Michael. BS, U.S. Naval Acad., 1962; M in Civil Engring., NYU, 1964; M in Urban and Regional Planning, 1971, 1964, PhD, 1972. Engr. Clarke, Hartman & Dunn, 1955-57, 69; project dir. Inst. Urban Policy Analysis, 1970-71; assoc. partner Dewberry, Nealon & Davis, Annapolis, Md., 1971-81; sr. assoc. Dewberry & Davis, Annapolis, 1981-82; prin. Dewsberry & Davis, 1983-84; pres. Property Improvement Collaborative, Inc., 1984—, LandScope, 1985—; dir. LandTech Corp., 1985-88, mng. dir., 1988—; mng. dir., chief exec. officer, organizer, dir. Bay Nat. Bank; Land Tech. Corp., 1986—; bd. dirs. Scotts Seaboard Corp.; pres. Peacock Mgmt. Systems. Pres., Crofton Civic Assn., 1973; trustee Anne Arundel Community Coll., 1974—, past chmn. bd. trustees; mem. County Zoning Adv. Task Force, 1983-84; mem. county coun. adv. com. on adequate facilities, 1977-78; bd. dirs. Anne Arundel Trade Coun.; chmn. Public Works Rev. Bd.; mem. Sewer Allocation Task Force; chmn. County Exec. Transition Task Force, 1982; mem. County Exec. Transition Team, 1991; mem. Gov's. com. on Affordable Housing, 1976-78. Served with USAF, 1962-69. Named Bus. Leader of Yr., Anne Arundel Trade Coun., 1982; HEW fellow, 1970-72. Mem. ASCE, Am. Planning Assn., Am. Inst. Certified Planners, Nat. Soc. Profl. Engrs., Assn. County Engrs. Roman Catholic. Office: 147 Old Solomons Island Rd Annapolis MD 21401-0904

DIAMANTE, JOHN MATTHEW, environmental protection agency executive; b. N.Y.C., Jan. 14, 1940; s. Matthew and Elizabeth Diamante; m. Donna Davis. BA in Aero. Engring. cum laude, NYU, 1957, MS, 1963, PhD, 1969. Various positions Office Oceanic and Atmosphere Rsch., NOAA, Silver Spring, Md., 1977-90; chief sci. and emerging issues Office Internat. Activities, EPA, Washington, 1990—. Home: 1614 Sherwood Rd Silver Spring MD 20902-3961 Office: EPA Office Internat Activities Waterside Mall 401 M St SW Washington DC 20460

DIAMOND, DAVID JOSEPH, nuclear engineer, consultant; b. N.Y.C., Dec. 31, 1940; s. Harry A. and Blanche R. (Benin) D.; m. Ellen S. Schatz, Aug. 20, 1941; children: Gary, Russell, Brian. BS in Engring. Physics, Cornell U., 1962; MS in Nuclear Engring., U. Ariz., 1963; PhD in Nuclear Engring., MIT, 1968. Nuclear engr. Westinghouse Astronuclear Lab., Pitts., 1963-64, Brookhaven Nat. Lab., Upton, N.Y., 1968—; adj. prof. Polytech. Inst. N.Y., Farmingville, 1977-78; cons. Singer-Link, Silver Spring, Md., 1982-90, Electric Power Rsch. Inst., Palo Alto, Calif., 1984-88, Govt. of Ont., Can., 1987, Gen. Physics, Columbia, Md., 1990—, Atomic Energy Control Bd., Can., 1991—, Paul Scherrer Inst., Switzerland, 1991. Contbr. numerous articles to profl. jours. Recipient Spl. Fellowship award U.S. Atomic Energy Commn., 1967. Mem. Am. Nuclear Soc. (chmn. Long Island sect. 1982-83). Club: Setauket Yacht (Port Jefferson, N.Y.). Home: 4 Settlers Path Prt Jefferson NY 11777-1414 Office: Brookhaven Nat Lab BNL 130 Upton NY 11973

DIAMOND, EDWARD JAY, nuclear utility engineer; b. Gloversville, N.Y., Apr. 27, 1948; s. Bernard and Toby (Sciens) D.; m. Laura Ann Semlear, Jan. 25, 1975; 1 child, Sara Beth. AAS, RCA Inst., 1970. Cert. sr. operator Nuclear Regulatory Commn. Elec. technician Consolidated Edition, Inc., N.Y.C., 1970-72, reactor operator, 1972-77, sr. reactor operator, 1978-80; nuclear tng. specialist N.Y. Power Authority, N.Y.C., 1980-86, sr. plant engr., 1986—. Home: 17 Sycamore Dr Beacon NY 12508-3937 Office: NY Power Authority PO Box 215 Buchanan NY 10511-0215

DIAMOND, ELAYNE FERN, interior designer, small business owner; b. Newark, July 1, 1945; d. Charles Ronald and Louise Pearl (Fern) Newman; m. Stanley Diamond, Nov. 20, 1965; children: Garrett L., Robin Fern. Student, N.Y. Sch. Interior Design, 1963-67. Pres. Elayne Diamond Interiors, Union, N.J., 1964—; owner, pres. Novelty Express, Union, Springfield, Totowa, N.J., 1975-80, Personalitees, Beach Haven, N.J., 1978-84, Put Togethers, Surf City, N.J., 1979-81, Designer's View Inc., Greenbrook, N.J., 1988—; cons. in field; designer, owner Yellow Brick Rd., Inc., Springfield, Beach Haven, 1975-79; cons. to constrn. cos., window mfgs., N.J., 1969—; distbr. Energy Controls, Springfield, 1985-86; pres. Advantage Point, Woodbridge, N.J., 1990. Contbr. designs to trade and comml. mags., various home tours, newspaper articles, 1964—. Fund raiser Ctr. Sch. for the Learning Disabled, N.J., Am. Cancer Soc., others. Mem. Allied Bd. Trade.

DIAMOND, ELLIOT, secondary education educator; b. Phila., Jan. 31, 1952; s. Emanuel and Pearl Violet (Frankford) D. BS in Psychology, Pa. State U., 1973, MS in Health Edn., 1976; DPM, Pa. Coll. Podiatric Medicine, 1980. Cert. acupuncturist. Instr. Coll. Health and Phys. Edn. Pa. State U., Phila., 1973, 74, instr. dept. continuing edn., 1974—; resident Broad St. Hosp. and Med. Ctr., 1980-81, instr. podiatric surgery, 1981-85; instr. CPR ARC, 1978-79; guest lectr. CIGNA Workmen's Compensation Specialists, 1987, Ctr. for Sports Medicine and Rehab., Jefferson Med. Sch., 1985, 87, Temple Med. Sch., 1987; speaker in field. Author textbook on podiatric rehab., 1976; contbr. articles to profl. jours. Mem. Am. Podiatric Med. Assn., Traditional Chinese Medicine, Chinese Med. Assn. Democrat. Jewish. Office: Ctr Podiatric Medicine 2429 Brown St Philadelphia PA 19130-1930

DIAMOND, G. WILLIAM, secretary of state; b. West Gardiner, Maine, Feb. 19, 1945; s. Elsie (Fellows) Emery; m. Jane Estes; children: Karyn, Kris. BS, Gorham State Coll., 1968; MS, U. So. Maine, 1972. Tchr. Field-Allen Elem. Sch., Windham Center, Maine, 1968-72; prin. Manchester Sch., North Windham, Maine, 1973-76; tchr. Windham Jr./Sr. High Sch., 1976-84; owner, founder Suburban Security, Inc., Windham, 1980—, Profl. Security Tng., Windham, 1985-87, Bill Diamond Assocs., Windham, 1987—; supt. schs. Raymond (Maine) Sch. Dept., 1987-88; sec. state State of Maine, Augusta, 1989—. State rep. Maine Legislature, Augusta, 1976-82, state senator, 1982-86; gubernatorial candidate State of Maine Primary, 1986. Ford Found. fellow, 1972-73. Mem. Nat. Assn. Secs. State. Democrat. Lutheran. Home: 261 Windham Center Rd Windham ME 04062-4336 Office: State Dept Nash Bldg Sta 148 Augusta ME 04333

DIAMOND, GUSTAVE, federal judge; b. Burgettstown, Pa., Jan. 29, 1928; s. George and Margaret (Solinsky) D.; m. Emma L. Scarton, Dec. 28, 1974; 1 dau., Margaret Ann; 1 stepdau., Joanne Yoney. A.B., Duke U., 1951; J.D., Duquesne U., 1956. Bar: Pa. bar 1958, U.S. Ct. Appeals bar 1962. Law clk. to judge U.S. Dist. Ct., Pitts., 1955-61; 1st asst. U.S. atty. Western Dist. Pa., 1961-62, U.S. atty., 1963-69; partner firm Cooper, Schwartz, Diamond & Reich, Pitts., 1969-75; formerly individual practice law Washington, Pa.; former solicitor washington County, Pa.; now judge U.S. Dist. Ct. Western Dist. Pa.; chmn. Jud. Conf. Com. on Defender Svcs. Mem. ABA, Fed. Bar Assn., Pa. Bar Assn., Allegheny County Bar Assn., Washington County Bar Assn. Office: US Dist Ct 821 US Courthouse 7th & Grant Sts Pittsburgh PA 15219

DIAMOND, HERBERT S., physician; b. N.Y.C., Mar. 21, 1938; m. Carol G.; children: Stewart, Elise. BA, NYU, 1958; MD, SUNY, N.Y.C., 1962. Intern Kings County Hosp., Bklyn., 1962-63; resident Kings County Hosp., 1963-65; asst. chief gen. med. svc. Fitzsimmons Gen. Hosp., Denver, 1966-68; instr. medicine SUNY Downstate Med. Ctr., N.Y.C., 1968-70; attending physician Kings County Hosp., N.Y.C., 1968-88, SUNY Hosp., N.Y.C., 1968-88; asst. prof. SUNY-Downstate Med. Ctr., N.Y.C., 1970-73, assoc. prof., 1973-77, chief rheumatology, 1977-82; prof. medicine SUNY, Stony Brook, 1985-88; chmn. medicine L.I. Jewish Med. Ctr., New Hyde Park, N.Y., 1982-88, West Penn Hosp., Pitts., 1989—; clin. prof. medicine U. Pitts., 1989—; cons. med./rheumatism St. John's Hosp., Bklyn., 1970-81; dir. Gen. Clin. Rsch. Ctr., SUNY-Downstate Med. Ctr., 1978-82. Contbr. numerous articles and abstracts to profl. jours. Exec. com., bd. trustees Arthritis Found., 1982, v.p. rsch. and edn., 1982-85, mem. med. and sci. com., 1975-85, chmn. med. and sci. com., 1981-85. Recipient Mitchell prize, 1962, Master Tchr. award SUNY Bklyn. Alumni Assn., 1987; Ivan T. Hirschl Trust Career Scientists, 1976-81. Fellow ACP; mem. AMA, Am. Coll. Rheumatology, Assn. of Program Dirs. in Internal Medicine (com. on internat. edn. 1989—, fin. com. 1987—, long range planning com. 1991—), N.Y. Rheumatism Assn. (pres. 1982-83). Jewish. Office: West Penn Hosp 4800 Friendship Ave Pittsburgh PA 15224

DIAMOND, PAMELA SHAFFER, hospital administration consultant; b. Cin., Feb. 17, 1948; d. Vernon Raymond and Verna Merle (Larrick) Shaffer; m. Michael Keith Diamond, Apr. 27, 1945. BA in Polit. Sci., U. Cin., 1970; MPA, U. Va., 1970. Sr. planning analyst EPA, Washington, 1971-77; dir. govt. rels. Conn. Gen., Bloomfield, Conn., 1978-81; dir. govt. rels. Cigna Corp., Bloomfield, 1981-83, dir. operational planning, 1983-85; cons. St. Francis Hosp. and Med. Ctr., Hartford, Conn., 1990-91. Bd. govs. Newington Children's Hosp., Hartford, 1985-91; chair rare wine auction Conn. Pub. TV, Hartford, 1988-90; pres. Mark Twain Meml., Hartford, 1990-91. Mem. Am. Econ. Assn., N.Am. Planning Soc. Methodist. Home: 27 Tanglewood Dr Glastonbury CT 06033-2625 Office: 1000 Asylum Ave # 30 Hartford CT 06105-1703

DIAMOND, RICHARD SCOTT, lawyer; b. Newark, June 26, 1960; s. Robert and Arlene (Cohen) D.; m. Denise E. Block, Oct. 12, 1988. BA in Econs./Bus., Rutgers U., 1981; JD, Seton Hall U., 1984. Bar: N.J. 1984, Fla. 1991, U.S. Dist. Ct. N.J. 1984. Jud. clk. to judge State of N.J., Union County, N.J.; assoc. Law Firm of Robert Diamond, Springfield, N.J.; ptnr. Diamond Hodes & Diamond, Springfield, Gourvitz, Diamond, Hodes, Braun & Diamond, Springfield, Diamond & Diamond P.A., Millburn, N.J.; lectr. TV broadcasts; radio lectr., speaker state bar functions. Mem. Union County Bar Assn. (matrimonial practice, exec. com.), Essex County Bar (matrimonial practice), N.J. State Bar (matrimonial practice, lectr.). Office: Diamond & Diamond PA 225 Millburn Ave Ste 208 Millburn NJ 07041

DIAMOND, SUZANNE BARBARA, secretary, administrative assistant; b. DuBois, Pa., May 4, 1941; d. Earl E. Houck and Katherine M. Harris; m. Frank E. Kafka Jr., Feb. 12, 1963 (dec.); children: Laura, Linda. Grad., DuBois Bus. Coll., 1961. Clk., receptionist Coca-Cola Bottling of N.Y., Inc., N.Y.C., 1961-62; actress various film and stage prodns., N.Y.C., 1964-85; girl friday League of Women Voters, N.Y.C., 1982-84; sec. Office Temporary, N.Y.C., 1984-85; adminstrv. sec. Philip Morris Cos., N.Y.C., 1985-88; adminstrv. ins. analyst Chase Manhattan Bank, N.Y.C., 1988—. Leader, asst. dist. fin. coord. Girl Scouts Am., N.Y.C., 1975-80; active role in church and community. Mem. Am. Mgmt. Assn., Am. Film Soc., Am. Biog. Inst., Soka Gakkai Internat. Democrat.

DIAMONDSTONE, LAWRENCE, paper company executive; b. N.Y.C., Mar. 27, 1928; s. Harry A. and Sally (Margulies) D.; B.S., U. Ill., 1950; m. Helen O'Connor, Dec. 8, 1984; 1 child, Cynthia Ann. Founder, pres., chief exec., chmn. bd., officer Newbrook Paper Div., N.Y.C., 1958—, Cottonwood Converting Div., Memphis, 1971—, Garden State Converters Div., Bayonne, N.J., 1973—, Triangle Mktg. Corp., N.Y.C., 1975—. Home: 2 Beekman Pl New York NY 10022-8058 Office: 32 Bleecker St New York NY 10012

DIAZ, CLIFTON STANLEY, bus operator, crime prevention consultant; b. Bronx, N.Y., Mar. 25, 1949; s. David and Gwendolyn (Diaz) Stanley; m. Vivian Ann James, Sept. 18, 1976 (div.); 1 stepchild, Kendra Marlay James; m. Shirley Bonita Mc Kethan, July 10, 1988;children: Clifton Stanley Jr. and Neil Michael. AA, N.Y.C. Tech. Coll., Bklyn., 1975; student, York Coll. CUNY, 1975-77, 85-86, 92—, Community Coll. Air Force, Montgomery, Ala., 1977-82; cert. Nat. Crime Prevention Inst., U. Louisville, 1981. Coll. asst. York Coll. CUNY, Queens, 1971-76; security police officer USAF Security Police, Kelly AFB, Tex., 1977-80, Wright-Patterson AFB, Ohio, 1980-83; housing mgr. Related Mgmt. Corp., Queens, N.Y., 1983; traffic enforcement investigator N.Y.C. Dept. Traffic, Queens, 1983-84; aast. dir. security Queens Coll. CUNY, 1984-86; taxi and limousine inspector/peace officer N.Y.C. Taxi & Limousine Commn., Queens, 1986-88; police officer U.S. Dept. Vets. Affairs, Queens, 1989; bus operator N.Y.C. Transit Authority, Queens, 1989—. Chmn. bd. dirs. Rochdale Village Housing Coop., Jamaica, N.Y., 1986—; vice-chmn. Coordinating Coun. Coops., Manhattan, N.Y., 1992; mem. Mayor's Southeast Queens Anti-Drug Task Force, Jamaica, 1987-89, N.Y.C. Community Planning Bd., Queens, 1988-90. Sgt. USAF, 1977-83. Recipient Community Svc. award Rochdale Village Bd. Dirs., 1991, Robert B. Jacob award for Police Officers and Firefighters, 100 Club Dayton, Ohio, 1982, Outstanding Airman of Yr. citation Air Force Assn., 1980, Outstanding Airman of Yr. USAF, 1980, Outstanding Achievement cert. U.S. Congress, 1980. Mem. Am. Soc. Notaries, N.Y. State Sheriffs' Assn. (hon.), N.Y. State FOP. Democrat. Episcopalian. Home: 172-20 133 Ave Apt 2D Jamaica NY 11434 Office: Rochdale Village Inc 169-65 137th Ave Jamaica NY 11434

DIAZ, JEAN MICHAEL, investment banker; b. Oxnard, Calif., Oct. 26, 1949; s. Freddie B. and Katharina (Diel) D.; m. Elizabeth Scordalakis, Jan. 22, 1989. BA, Calif. State U., Fullerton, 1972, M of Pub. Adminstrn., 1981; MBA in Fin., U. Pa., 1987. Adminstrv. intern to county supr. Orange County, Santa Ana, Calif., 1972, real property agt. real estate div., 1972-77; mgr. real property City of Palo Alto, Calif., 1978-85; owner, prin. Terra Firma Assocs., Palo Alto, 1983-87; investment banker Citicorp Securities Markets, Inc., N.Y.C., 1987—; speaker in field. Author 2 manuals on real estate mgmt.; contbr. articles to profl. jours. Trip asst. canoeing and backpacking courses Avanti, San Jose and Sunnyvale, Calif., 1982-85; vol. tutor math Phila. Pub. Schs., 1986. Mem. Internat. Right of Way Assn. (sr., cert. instr., internat., regional and local chmn. 1983, Profl. of Yr. award 1983, 84), Urban Land Inst., World Affairs Council. Democrat. Roman Catholic. Office: Citicorp Securities Markets Inc 55 Water St New York NY 10043

DIAZ, MICHAEL HARLAN, federal official; b. Milw., Oct. 6, 1966; s. Robert Harlan Jr. and Alice (Mellon) D. BA cum laude, U. Vt., 1988; postgrad., Am. U., 1990—. Intern M&I Marshall & Isley Bank, Milw., 1986-87; editor Am. Appraisal Assocs., Inc., Milw., 1989-90; import compliance specialist U.S. Dept. Commerce, Washington, 1991—. Bd. dirs. Mequon-Thiensville (Wis.) Am. Field Svc. chpt., 1990. Mem. World Affairs Coun., Inst. World Affairs, Phi Beta Kappa, Phi Alpha Theta, Phi Eta Sigma. Home: 10453 N Circle Rd Thiensville WI 53092-5929

DIAZ, ORFELINA ROSA, podiatrist; b. Marianau, Cuba, Dec. 22, 1962; came to the U.S., 1968; d. Roberto Clemente and Adelfa Orlanda (Alonso) Diaz; m. Joseph Patrick Boylan, Apr. 10, 1987. AA in Biology, Key West Community Coll., 1982; BA in Biology, U. South Fla., 1984; DPM, N.Y. Coll. Podiatric Medicine, 1988. Pvt. practice Union City, N.J., 1989—; staff mem. St. Mary Hosp., Hoboken, N.J., 1990-91. Mem. N.J. Podiatric Med. Soc., Phi Theta Kappa. Office: 2008 Kennedy Blvd Union City NJ 07087-2028

DI BACCO, RICHARD DAVID, podiatric surgeon; b. Erie, Pa., Sept. 8, 1940; s. Richard William and Sophie Theresa (Jankowski) DeB.; m. Priscilla M. Herbstritt, Aug. 8, 1964; children: Cherlyn Ann, Alicia Rae, Rachele Marie, Richard David. BA in Biology, Gannon U., 1962; D Podiatric Medicine, Ohio Coll. Podiatric Medicine, 1967. Diplomate Am. Bd. Podiatric Surgery, Am. Bd. Quality Assurance and Utilization Rev., Internat. Coll. Podiatric Laser Surgery. Resident in surgery Foot Clinic of Youngstown, Ohio, 1968, clinician, 1969-72; podiatric surgeon Podiatry Assocs. of Erie Inc., 1969—; pvt. practice, 1969—; adj. clin. instr. Ohio Coll. Podiatric Medicine, Cleve., 1977—, Pa. Coll. Podiatric Medicine, Phila., 1980, Des Moines Coll. Podiatric Medicine, 1987—; dir. podiatry Martin Luther King Ctr., Erie, 1987—; chief podiatry Metro Health Ctr., Erie, 1991—; ins. reviewer various ins. cos., 1970-74; instr. podiatric accelerated program Gannon U., Erie, 1981—; chmn. seminars in field; mem. State Bd. Podiatric Medicine, Harrisburg, Pa., 1991. Contbr. articles to profl. publs. Bd. dirs. Harlin Pre-Sch., Erie, 1970-75, Ohio Coll. Podiatric Medicine, 1980-83, Union City (Pa.) Meml. Hosp., 1980-83; div. chief United Way, Erie, 1974, 86, 87. Cpl. USMC, 1962-67. Recipient Recognition award Am. Podiatric Med. Assn., 1986. Fellow Am. Coll. Foot Surgeons, Acad. Ambulatory Foot Surgery, Am. Assn. Hosp. Podiatrists, Am. Coll. Foot Orthopedists,

Am. Soc. Laser Medicine and Surgery; mem. Am. Acad. Podiatric Sports Medicine (assoc.). Democrat. Roman Catholic. Home: 5755 Schultz Rd Erie PA 16509-3745 Office: Podiatry Assocs of Erie Inc 4402 Peach St Erie PA 16509-1358

DIBENEDETTI, PAUL E. R., chemical company executive; b. Cambridge, Mass., Apr. 18, 1937; s. Nicholas and Catherine C. (Cronin) DiB.; m. Joan A. Rogers; children: Karen J., Susan J., Paul E., Lisa J. AB, Harvard Coll., 1958. Chemist UBS Chem. Co., Cambridge, 1958-60; mgr. new products A.E. Staley Mfg. Co., Decatur, Ill., 1960-64; pres. Interpolymer Corp., Canton, Mass., 1964-70; gen. mgr. Butcher Polish Co., Marlboro, Mass., 1970-73; pres. Neleco, Inc., Chestnut Hill, Mass., 1973—. Patentee, polymer composition; contbr. articles to TAPPI publs. Mem. Am. Inst. Chemists, Am. Arbitration Assn., N.Y. Acad. Sci., Chamberlain Club, Vespers Club. Republican. Roman Catholic. Office: Neleco Inc PO Box 67369 Chestnut Hill MA 02167-0004

DIBERARDINIS, LOUIS JOSEPH, industrial hygiene engineer, consultant, educator; b. Lawrence, Mass., July 2, 1947; s. Salvatore and Jane Marie (Lombari) DiB. BSChemE, Northeastern U., 1970; MS in Indsl. Hygiene, Harvard U., 1975. Diplomate Am. Acad. Indsl. Hygiene, Bd. Cert. Safety Profls. Rsch. asst. dept. environ. health scis. Harvard Sch. Pub. Health, Boston, 1966-68, staff indsl. hygienist, 1975-76, vis. lectr., 1986—, cons. dept. continuing edn., 1978—; asst. chemist div. occupational hygiene Mass. Dept. Labor and Industries, Boston, 1968-69; indsl. hygienist dept. environ. health and safety Harvard U. Health Svcs., Cambridge, Mass., 1976-86; indsl. hygiene engr. dept. health, safety-environ. affairs Polaroid Corp., Waltham, Mass., 1986-89; assoc. indsl. hygiene officer environ. med. svc. MIT, Cambridge, 1989-92, indsl. hygiene officer, 1992—; pres. DiBerardinis Assocs., Inc., indsl. hygiene cons., Wellesley, Mass., 1980—; mem. com. on safety codes for exhaust systems Am. Nat. Standards Inst., 1984—, also chmn. subcom. on lab. ventilation. Author: (with others) Guidelines for Laboratory Design: Health and Safety Considerations, 1987; contbr. articles to profl. jours., chpt. to book. Mem. sci. adv. com. City of Cambridge, 1984-86. Mem. Am. Conf. Govtl. Indsl. Hygienists, Brit. Occupational Hygiene Soc., Air Pollution Control Assn., Am. Soc. Safety Engrs., Am. Indsl. Hygiene Assn. (pres. New Eng. sect. 1985-86), Am. Acad. Indsl. Hygiene (sec.-treas. 1983-88, pres. 1992). Home: 4 Martin Rd Wellesley MA 02181-2440 Office: MIT Rm 20C-204 77 Massachusetts Ave Cambridge MA 02139-4307

DIBERARDINO, MARIE ANTOINETTE, developmental biologist, educator; b. Phila., May 2, 1926; d. Henry and Adelina (Belfi) DiB. BS in Biology, Chestnut Hill Coll., 1948, JD (hon.), 1990; PhD in Zoology, U. Pa., 1962. Rsch. asst. Inst. for Cancer Rsch., 1948-58, rsch. assoc., 1960-64, asst. mem., 1964-67; assoc. prof. anatomy Med. Coll. Pa., Phila., 1967-71, prof. anatomy, 1971-81, prof. physiology, 1981—; mem. bd. advisors Robert Chambers Lab. for Cellular Microsurgery, N.Y., 1984—. Adv. bd.: Internat. Rev. of Cytology, 1976—, Differentiation, 1981—, Series: Developmental Biology, A Comprehensive Synthesis, 1982—; assoc. editor Jour. Exptl. Zoology, 1984-86; Contbr. articles on devel., genetics and cell biology to sci. jours.; contbr. book revs. in field. Mem. NIH Fogartz Internat. Fellowship Study Group, 1984. NSF grantee; NIH grantee. Fellow AAAS; mem. Am. Soc. Cell Biology, Soc. for Devel. Biologists (treas., trustee 1975-78), Am. Soc. Zoologists, Internat. Soc. Devel. Biologists, Internat. Soc. of Differentiation (exec. com. 1978-85, 87-90, bd. dirs. 1985—), Sigma Delta Epsilon. Office: Med Coll Pa 3300 Henry Ave Philadelphia PA 19129-1191

DIBIASIO, DANIEL ANTHONY, university administrator; b. Cleve.; s. Anthony James and Julie (Garronna) DiB.; m. Christine Burns, June 25, 1976; children: Matthew, Michael. BA, Ohio Wesleyan U., Delaware, 1971; MA, Ohio State U., 1972, PhD, 1982. Residence dir. Ohio Wesleyan U., 1971-72; tchr. English Bay Village (Ohio) High Sch., 1972-74; admissions counselor Rocky Mountain Coll., Billings, Mont., 1974-75, dean of students, 1975-78; asst. dean Grad. Sch. Ohio State U., Columbus, 1981-84; exec. officer Coun. of Presidents New Eng. Land Grant Univs., Durham, N.H., 1984-87; exec. asst. to pres. U. N.H., Durham, 1987-91, interim v.p. for student affairs, 1991—. Mem. Mayor's Task Force on Edn., Dover, N.H., 1989. Reicpient Earl Anderson award Coll. Edn. Ohio State U., 1978. Mem. Nat. Assn. State Univs. and Land Grant Colls., Am. Coun. on Edn., Nat. Assn. Student Pers. Adminstrs., Phi Kappa Phi, Omicron Delta Kappa. Democrat. Congregationalist. Home: 69 Stark Ave Dover NH 03820-4225 Office: U NH Thompson Hall Durham NH 03824

DICARLO, DOMINICK L., federal judge; b. Bklyn., Mar. 11, 1928; m. Esther Hansen (dec.); children: Vincent, Carl, Robert, Barbara DiCarlo Basgaard; m. Susan L. Hauck. BA, St. John's Coll., 1950, LLB, 1953; LLM, NYU, 1957. Asst. U.S. atty. Eastern Dist. N.Y., 1959-62, chief organized crime and racketeering sect.; spl. asst. to U.S. atty., 1962; counsel to minority leader N.Y. Council, 1962-65; mem. N.Y. State assembly, 1965-81, dep. minority leader, 1975-78; vice chmn. N.Y. State Legis. Commn. Crime, 1969-70, Select Commn. Correctional Insts. and Programs, 1972-73; asst. sec. state for internat. narcotics matters Dept. State, Washington, 1981-84; rep. U.S. Commn. on narcotic drugs of econ. and social coun. UN, 1982-84; judge U.S. Ct. Internat. Trade, N.Y.C., 1984-91, chief judge, 1991—. Office: US Ct Internat Trade 1 Federal Pla New York NY 10007

DICARLO, EDWARD FRANCIS WILLIAM, marketing executive; b. Balt., Nov. 27, 1953; s. Edward Joseph and Dorothy (Koerner) DiC.; m. Valerie Joanne Lithotomos, May 27, 1983; 1 child, James E. BSEE in Technology, Capital Inst. Tech., 1975; MBA, U. Balt., 1985. Engr. Westinghouse Electric Corp., Balt., 1975-77, mktg. mgr., 1987—; engr. Gen. Dynamics, Pomona, Calif., 1977-79; sr. engr. Advanced Tech., Inc., McLean, Va., 1979-81; cons. Balt., 1981-87. Patentee in field. Mem. IEEE, AIAA, Soc. Logistics Engrs. Home: 9638 Sea Shadow Columbia MD 21046-2031

DICELLO, JOHN FRANCIS, JR., physicist, educator; b. Bradford, Pa., Dec. 18, 1938; s. John Francis and Nicolina Camille (Costello) D.; m. Shirley Ann Rodgers, Aug. 25, 1962; children: John Francis III, Paul T. BS, St. Bonaventure U., 1960; MS, U. Pitts., 1962; PhD, Tex. A&M U., 1968. Instr. St. Bonaventure U., 1962-63; Univ. grad. fellow Tex. A&M U., College Station, 1963-65; AEC-Assoc. Western Univs. grad. fellow Los Alamos Nat. Lab., 1965-67, staff scientist, 1973-84; rsch. assoc., rsch. scientist Columbia U., N.Y.C., 1967-73; faculty U. N.Mex., Los Alamos, 1980-82; faculty fellowship Northwest Coll. and Univ. Assn. for Sci., Pacific N.W. Labs., 1989; prof. physics Clarkson U., Potsdam, N.Y., 1982—. Bd. dirs. N.Mex. div. Am. Cancer Soc., 1978-82; mem. sci. com. Nat. Radiation Protection and Measurements, 1992—. Recipient Young Scientist travel award Am. Assn. Physicists in Medicine, 1972. Mem. editorial bd., assoc. editor Radiation Rsch. jour., 1992—. Mem. AAUP, IEEE (nuclear and plasma scis. div.), Am. Assn. Physicists in Medicine, Radiation Rsch. Soc. (editorial bd., assoc. editor Radiation Rsch. jour. 1992—), Am. Inst. Biol. Scis. (radiation health peer rev. panel to NASA 1990—, peer rev. panel specialized ctrs. of rsch. and tng. 1991—, ad hoc com. NIH and NASA 1991—), Am. Phys. Soc., NASA Specialized Ctrs. of Rsch. and Tng. (Am. Inst. Biol. Scis. Peer Rev. panel 1991—), Nat. Coun. Radiation Protection and Measurements (sci. com. #88), Sigma Xi (pres. Clarkson U. chpt. 1991-92), Sigma Pi Sigma. Roman Catholic. Research in field of physics, dosimetry, microdosimetry, radiation biology, cancer research, integrated circuits, accelerator and nuclear physics; cons. with Fermilab and Loma Linda U. on first clinically dedicated proton accelerator designed for cancer therapy. Office: Clarkson U Dept Physics Potsdam NY 13699

DICHTER, BARRY JOEL, lawyer; b. Brookline, Mass., Feb. 19, 1950; s. Irving Melvin and Arlene Dichter; m. Judith Rand, Oct. 22, 1972; children: Rebecca Lynn, Jason Benjamin. AB magna cum laude, Harvard U., 1972, JD cum laude, 1975. Bar: Mass. 1975, N.Y. 1976, U.S. Dist. Ct. (so. and ea. dists.) N.Y. 1976, D.C. 1980, U.S. Dist. Ct. D.C. 1980, U.S. Ct. Appeals (D.C. cir.) 1985. Assoc. Webster & Sheffield, N.Y.C., 1975-82; assoc. Cadwalader, Wickersham & Taft, N.Y.C., 1983-84, ptnr., 1984—; lectr. in field. Vice chmn. Harvard Law Sch. Fund, Cambridge, Mass., 1984-88; class agt., 1988—; bd. dirs. Childrens' Corner, Inc. Mem. ABA (task force on sect. 1110), Assn. of Bar of City of N.Y. (bankruptcy com. 1986-89, 91—), N.Y. UJA Fedn. (exec. com., bankruptcy and reorgn. group of lawyers div. of N.Y.). Office: Cadwalader Wickersham & Taft 100 Maiden Ln New York NY 10038-4818

DICHTER, MISHA, concert pianist; b. Shanghai, Peoples Republic of China, Sept. 27, 1945; came to U.S., 1947, naturalized, 1953; s. Leon and Lucy (Lhevine) D.; m. Cipa Glazman, Jan. 21, 1968; 2 children. Student, UCLA, 1963-64; B.S., Juilliard Sch., 1968. Performed world concert tours, 1966—; appeared with maj. world orchs. including Phila., Boston Symphony, Chgo. Symphony, L.A. Philharm., N.Y. Philharm., Cleve. orchs., Leningrad Symphony, Gewandhaus orchs., Leipzig, Vienna Philharm., Berlin Philharm., Israel Philharm.; rec. artist with RCA, Phillips; contbr. articles to N.Y. Times, other mags. Recipient Silver medal Moscow Tschaikovsky Competition, 1966. Office: Shuman Assocs Inc 120 W 58th St New York NY 10019-2126

DICIOCCIO, JOSEPH JOHN, product designer, purchasing agent, instructor; b. Goshen, N.Y., Aug. 18, 1955; s. Antonio Giovanni and Mary (Amodio) DiC. AAS in Archtl. Tech., Orange County Community Coll., Middletown, N.Y., 1976; BSBA, Mt. St. Mary Coll., Newburgh, N.Y., 1980. Sales mgr. ADB Fire Apparatus, Walden, N.Y., 1980-86; design draftsman Amthor, Inc., Walden, 1976-80, mgr., purchasing agt., 1986—; instr. Orange County Community Coll., Goshen, N.Y., 1989—. Mem. Maybrook (N.Y.) Fire Dist., 1973—; notary pub. N.Y. State, 1986—. Mem. Smithsonian Assocs., Mt. St. Mary Coll. Alumni Assn. (sec. 1988-91, 2d v.p. 1991-92, 1st v.p. 1992—), Orange County Community Coll. Alumni Assn., Nat. Notary Assn. Republican. Roman Catholic. Home: 608 Homestead Ave Maybrook NY 12543-1508

DICK, KATHERINE RESTAINO, college administrator; b. Bklyn., Nov. 14, 1937; d. John Joseph and Katherine Marie (Fischetti) Restaino; m. Bernard F. Dick, July 31, 1965. BA, Good Counsel Coll., White Plains, N.Y., 1960; MA, Fordham U., Bronx, 1962, PhD, 1966. Assoc. prof. English Mercy Coll., Dobbs Ferry, N.Y., 1963-70, Good Counsel Coll., White Plains, N.Y., 1970-71; acad. dean Coll. of White Plains, 1971-72, pres., 1972-75; dean and chief adminstr. St. Peter's Coll., Englewood Cliffs, N.J., 1975—, coord. grad. studies, 1991—; accreditation evaluator Middle States Assn. Colls. and Univs., 1975—; mem. N.J. Statewide Task Force on Continuing Edn., 1978-80. Contbr. articles to profl. jours. Fordham U. grad. assistantship, 1960-63; recipient Boni Consilii award for svcs., Coll. of White Plains, 1975. Mem. MLA, N.J. Coll. and Univ Coalition on Women's Edn. Roman Catholic. Home: 580 Wyndham Rd Teaneck NJ 07666-2612 Office: St Peters Coll Hudson Ter Englewood Cliffs NJ 07632-2804

DICKE, ROBERT HENRY, educator, physicist; b. St. Louis, May 6, 1916; s. Oscar H. and Flora (Peterson) D.; m. Annie Henderson Currie, June 6, 1942; children: Nancy Jean Dicke Rapoport, John Robert, James Howard. A.B., Princeton U., 1939; Ph.D., U. Rochester, 1941, D.Sc. (hon.), 1981; D.Sc. (hon.), U. Edinburgh, 1972, Ohio No. U., 1981; DSc. (hon.), Princeton U., 1989. Microwave radar devel. Radiation Lab., MIT, 1941-46; physics faculty Princeton U., 1946—, Cyrus Fogg Brackett prof. physics, 1957-75, Albert Einstein prof. sci., 1975-84, Albert Einstein prof. sci. emeritus, 1984—, chmn. physics dept., 1967-70; mem. adv. panel for physics NSF, 1959-61; chmn. adv. com. atomic physics Nat. Bur. Standards, 1961-63; mem. com. on physics NASA, 1963-70, chmn., 1963-66; chmn. physics adv. panel Com. on Internat. Exchange of Persons (Fulbright-Hays Act), 1964-66; chmn. adv. com. on radio astronomy telescopes NSF, 1967, 69; mem. Nat. Sci. Bd., 1970-76; vis. com. Nat. Bur. Standards, 1975-79, chmn., 1979; vis. prof. Harvard U., 1954-55, Inst. Advanced Study, 1970-71; Sherman Fairchild Disting. scholar Calif. Inst. Tech., 1975; Walker Ames prof. U. Wash., Seattle, 1979; Jaynes lectr. Am. Philos. Soc., 1969; Scott lectr. Cambridge U. (Eng.), 1977. Author: (with Montgomery, Purcell) Principles of Micro-wave Circuits, 1948, (with J.P. Wittke) An Introduction to Quantum Mechanics, 1960, The Theoretical Significance of Experimental Relativity, 1964, Gravitation and the Universe, 1970. Trustee Assoc. Univs. Inc., 1980-88. Recipient Nat. Medal Sci., 1970, NASA medal for exceptional sci. achievement, 1973, Cresson medal Franklin Inst., 1974, Michelson Morley award Case Western Res. U., 1987, Pioneer award IEEE Microwave Theory and Techniques Soc., 1991. Mem. NAS (Comstock prize 1973), Am. Philos. Soc., Am. Geophys. Union, Am. Phys. Soc., Am. Astron. Soc., Am. Acad. Arts and Scis. (Rumford medal 1967), Royal Astron. Soc. (assoc.).

DICKENS, DORIS LEE, psychiatrist; b. Roxboro, N.C., Oct. 12; d. Lee Edward and Delma Ernestine (Hester) Dickens; B.S. magna cum laude, Va. Union U., 1960; M.D., Howard U., 1966; m. Austin LeCount Fickling, Oct. 15, 1975. Diplomate Nat. Bd. Med. Examiners. Intern, St. Elizabeth's Hosp., Washington, 1966-67, resident, 1967-70; staff psychiatrist, dir. Mental Health Program for Deaf, St. Elizabeth's Hosp., Washington, 1970-87; clin. prof. Howard U. Coll. Medicine, 1982—. Co-founder Nat. Health Care Found. for Deaf (named now Deaf Reach); med. officer Region 4 Community Mental Health Ctr., Washington, Commn. on Mental Health, 1987—. Recipient Dorothea Lynde Dix award, 1980. Mem. Am. Psychiat. Assn. (achievement awards bd. 1988-89), Washington Psychiat. Soc., Alpha Kappa Mu, Beta Kappa Chi. Author: How and When Psychiatry Can Help You, 1972; You and Your Doctor; contbg. author: Hearing and Hearing Impairment, 1979; contbg. author Counseling Deaf People, Research and Practice. Home: 12308 Surrey Circle Dr Tantallon MD 20744

DICKER, ADAM PAUL, physician, radiation oncologist; b. Chgo., June 8, 1961. BA, Columbia U., 1984; PhD, Cornell U., 1991, MD, 1992. Pres. Biochem. Electronics, N.Y.C., 1984-91; with dept. surgery Lenox Hill Hosp., N.Y.C., 1992—; pres. Biomed. Computing. Recipient Rsch. award AMA, 1990.

DICKERMAN, DOROTHEA WILHELMINA, lawyer; b. Washington, Apr. 2, 1958; d. John Melville and Serafina Amelia (Peoria) D.; m. Richard Kevin Anthony Becker, May 24, 1986. BA summa cum laude, Amherst (Mass.) Coll., 1980; JD, U. Chgo., 1983. Bar: U.S. Ct. Appeals (D.C. cir.) 1983, Va. Supreme Ct. 1990. Salesperson Dickerman Realty, Washington, 1976-83; assoc. Shaw, Pittman, Potts & Trowbridge, Washington, 1983-86; from assoc. to ptnr. Stohlman, Beuchert, Egan & Smith, Washington, 1986—. Member endowment com. Western Presbyn. Ch., Washington, 1991—; mem. alumni bd. Amherst Coll., N.Y.C., 1983-87; sec. Amherst Club of Washington, 1987-88. Mem. DAR, Comml. Real Estate Women, Congl. Country Club. Office: Stohlman Beuchert Egan & Smith 1775 Pennsylvania Ave NW Washington DC 20006-4605

DICKERMAN, JOHN MELVIN, lawyer; b. Hope, Ark., Aug. 21, 1914; s. Charles and Dorothy W. (Schultz) D.; m. Serafina Peoria, Oct. 26, 1956; 1 child, Dorothea W. BA, U. Ill., 1938, JD, 1940. Bar: Ill. 1940, Ohio 1942, U.S. Supreme Ct. 1944, U.S. Dist. Ct. (D.C. dist.) 1964. Atty. Rep. Steel Corp., Massillon, Ohio, 1940-42, U.S. Alien Property Custodian, Chgo., 1942-43; atty., Washington rep. Airline Pilot's Assn., 1943-47; legis. dir. Nat. Assn. Home Builders, Washington, 1947-52, exec. v.p., 1952-64; pres. John Dickerman & Assocs., Inc., Washington, 1964—. Mem. Nat. Assn. Home Builders (life, bd. dirs. 1964, named to Hall of Fame 1980), Am. Soc. Assn. Execs., Chgo. Bar Assn., Bar Assn. D.C., D.C. Bar Assn., Lambda Alpha. Republican. Office: 1201 L St St NW Ste 400 Washington DC 20005

DICKERMAN, WATSON BRADLEY, historical preservation professional; b. N.Y.C., Mar. 1, 1947; s. Watson Bradley Dickerman and Mary McBurney (Philbin) Gaynor. BA, Harvard U., 1969. Sec.-treas. Internat. Fund Monuments (now World Monument Fund), N.Y.C., 1978-85; chmn. Boston chpt. Save Venice, Inc., 1986—; vice-chmn., treas. Katmandu Valley Preservation Trust, Cambridge, Mass., 1990—. Episcopalian. Home: 304 Beacon St Boston MA 02116-1455 Office: Katmandu Valley Preservation Trust 24 Quincy St Cambridge MA 02138-3804

DICKERSON, DOLORES PAWLEY, university administrator; b. Englewood, N.J.; d. James Augustus and Carmen Elizabeth (Hinton) P.; 1 child, Michael Watt Spraggins. BA, Howard U., 1966; MEd, U. Md., 1973, PhD, 1975. Elem. sch. tchr., 1966-75; grad. asst. U. Md., College Park, 1973-75; asst. prof. Howard U., Washington, 1975-78, assoc. prof., 1978—, assoc. dean sch. edn., 1989-91, dir. tchr. edn. program, 1991—; pres. D.C. Reading Coun., 1984-85; mem. affirmative action com. Internat. Reading Assn., Newark, Del., 1988-91; bus. cons. Co-author: Games As Tools for Learning, 1978; co-author: (workbooks) Real World Functional Reading Materials, 1980; contbr. articles to profl. jours. Ch. sch. tchr. St. George's Episcopal Ch., Washington. Acad. scholar Howard U., 1965-66. Mem. Phi Delta Kappa, Kappa Delta Pi, Delta Sigma Theta. Office: Howard U Sch Edn Washington DC 20059

DICKIE, BRIAN, opera director; b. July 23, 1941; s. Robert Kelso and Harriet Elizabeth (Riddell) D.; m. Victoria Teresa Price, 1968; 3 children; m. Nancy Gustafson, 1989. Student, Haileybury, Trinity Coll., Dublin. Adminstrv. asst. Glyndebourne Opera, 1962-66; adminstr. Glyndebourne Touring Opera, 1967-81; opera mgr. Glyndebourne Festival Opera, 1970-81, gen. adminstr., 1981-89; gen. dir. Can. Opera Co., Toronto, 1989—; artistic dir. Wexford Festival, 1967-73; artistic advisor Theatre Musical de Paris, 1981-87. Mem. Theatre Nat. Com. (vice chmn. 1980-85, chmn. opera com. 1976-85), Theatrical Mgmt. Assn. (v.p. 1983-85), London Choral Soc. (chmn. 1978-85), Opera Am. (bd. dirs.), Garrick Club. Office: Can Opera Co, 227 Front St E, Toronto, ON Canada M5A 1E8

DICKINSON, LINDA KNOWLES, art director; b. Winchester, Mass., Sept. 9, 1951; d. Kenneth Mason and Ruth Elinore (Schaffner) Knowles. BA, U. N.H., 1973; postgrad., Art Inst. Boston, 1975-76. Tech. artist Stone & Webster, Boston, 1973-76; advt. designer Allyn and Bacon, Newton, Mass., 1976-81; freelance advt. designer, copywriter U.K., 1981-85; art dir. Allyn & Bacon/Simon & Schuster, Needham, Mass., 1985—. Recipient awards for book cover design, Art Direction mag., Communication Arts, Print mag., Graphic Design: USA, others. Mem. Bookbuilders of Boston, Art Dirs. Club Boston. Office: Allyn & Bacon 160 Gould St Needham MA 02194-2300

DICKINSON, MALCOLM MACFARLAN, III, computer consultant, musician; b. N.Y., Sept. 27, 1967; s. Peter Kolff and Constance Page (Kaufman) D. BA, Yale U., 1991. Sales clk. Winnetka (Ill.) True Value Hardware, 1983-84; computer operator Ernie Loberg Constrn. Co., Northbrook, Ill., 1985; computing asst. Yale U. Computer Ctr., New Haven, Conn., 1985-88; computer cons., instr. Sears Mortgage Corp., Lincolnshire, Ill., 1986-87; computer cons. pvt. practice, Chgo., Ill., Conn., 1987-91; saxophone tchr. pvt. practice, New Haven, Conn., 1987—; computer pub. adminstr. GIST Inc., New Haven, 1992—; computer cons., vol. Winnetka (Ill.) Yacht Club, 1987—, U.S. Sailing Assn., Newport, R.I., 1988—. Contbr. articles on saxophone and sailing to profl. jours. Asst. scoutmaster Boy Scouts Am. Troop 20, Winnetka, 1988-90; scoutmaster Boy Scout Troop 111, New Haven, 1990—. Recipient Dr. Richard S. Fleming Pub. Svc. award St. Luke's Episcopal Ch., New Haven, Conn., 1991, Dwight Hall Humanitarian Svc. award, Yale U., 1991. Mem. N.Am. Saxophone Alliance, U.S. Sailing Assn., Order of the Arcoon Lodge, Yale U. Concert Band. Home: 1731 Yale Station New Haven CT 06520-1731

DICKLER, HOWARD BYRON, biomedical administrator, physician; b. Chgo., Jan. 2, 1942; s. Jerome Alvin and Josephine Rae (Sweet) D.; m. Leah Kayser, June 26, 1966 (div. Apr. 1986); 1 child, Joanna; m. Ana Isabel Martinez, Sept. 20, 1986; 1 child, Carl. BA, Johns Hopkins U., 1964; MD with honors, George Washington U., 1968. Diplomate Am. Bd. Internal Medicine, Nat. Bd. Med. Examiners. Lt. comdr. USPHS, 1972, advanced through grades to capt., 1985; intern in medicine N.Y. Hosp.-Cornell U. Med. Ctr., N.Y.C., 1968-69, resident, 1969-71; rsch. assoc. Rockefeller U., N.Y.C., 1971-72; clin. assoc. Nat. Cancer Inst., Bethesda, Md., 1972-74, sr. investigator, 1974-89, mem. instnl. rev. bd., 1982-84; acting dep. div. dir. Nat. Inst. Allergy and Infectious Disease, Bethesda, 1990-91, chief clin. immunology br., 1989—; com. vice chmn. WHO, Geneva, 1981-85; sci. lectr. at over 30 univs.; speaker, symposium chmn. at over 25 nat. and internat. sci. meetings. Assoc. editor Jour. Immunology, 1976-79; contbr. articles to Jour. Exptl. Medicine, Advances in Immunology. Recipient Commendation medal USPHS, 1985, Outstanding Svc. medal, 1991. Mem. Am. Assn. Immunologists, Am. Fedn. Clin. Rsch., Am. Soc. Clin. Investigation, Clin. Immunology Soc. (councilor 1991—), Alpha Omega Alpha. Democrat. Jewish. Home: 11009 Fawsett Rd Rockville MD 20854-1721 Office: NIH/NIAID Solar Bldg Rm # 4A-19 Bethesda MD 20892

DICKMAN, ROBERT LAURENCE, physicist, researcher; b. N.Y.C., May 16, 1947; s. Sidney and Eve (Goldberg) D.; m. Albertina Catharina Otter, Sept. 14, 1975; children: Joshua, Ilana. AB, Columbia U., 1969, PhD, 1976. Postdoctoral rsch. assoc. Rensselaer Poly. Inst., Troy, N.Y., 1975-77; mem. tech. staff The Aerospace Corp., L.A., 1977-80; faculty rsch. assoc. U. Mass., Amherst, 1980-85, assoc. prof., staff assoc., 1985-92; program mgr. Nat. Sci. Found., Washington, 1992—. Editor: Molecular Clouds in the Milky Way and External Galaxies, 1988; contbr. 80 articles to profl. jours. Recipient Ernest Fullam award Dudley Obs., 1986. Mem. Am. Phys. Soc., Am. Astron. Soc., Internat. Astron. Union. Office: NSF Div Astronomical Scis 1800 G St NW Washington DC 20550

DICKSON, JOHN ROBERTSON VAN, construction manager; b. Tucson, Ariz., Dec. 16, 1941; s. John Rigden Van and Betty (Hirshfeld) D.; m. Nancy O'Neil Montgomery, Dec. 31, 1988; children: Morgan Elizabeth May, Heather O'Neil Kyla. BS, U. Md., 1987, MS, 1992. Draftsman Beall and LeMay, Washington, 1964-69; draftsman, designer Internat. Engring., San francisco, 1969-72; inspector Constrn. Bechtel Assocs., Washington, 1972-73; engr. AA Mathews, Rockville, Md., 1973-77; resident engr. Ralph M. Parsons, Washington, 1977-82; resident engr., phase coord. Washington Met. Area Transit Authority, 1982-92, project mgr., 1992—, resident engr., 1982-92, gen. mgr., 1992—. With USNR, 1958-69. Mem. Am. Pub. Transit Assn., Am. Railway Engring. Assn., Soc. Am. Mil. Engrs., Washington Area Railway Engring. Soc. Democrat. Episcopalian. Home: 1840 Lamont St NW Washington DC 20010

DICKSON, JOSEPH CRAIG, JR., lawyer; b. Ashland, Pa., Feb. 1, 1935; s. Joseph C. and Bertha L. (Dickson) D.; m. Joan S. Wyman, Apr. 15, 1961; children: Jean Anne, Patricia, Mary Jane, Craig, Jennifer. BA, Washington & Lee U., 1957; LLB, Rutgers U., 1960. Bar: N.J. 1961, U.S. Dist. Ct. N.J. 1962. Assoc. Donohue & Donohue, Attys., Nutley, N.J., 1961-64; ptnr. Dickson & Dunphy, Attys., Upper Montclair, N.J., 1964-70, Harris, Dickson, Upper Montclair, 1970—; asst. town atty. City of Montclair, 1966-76, town atty., 1976—; referee juvenile conf. com. Essex County Domestic Rels. Ct., Newark, 1966-73; lectr. Bloomfield (N.J.) Coll., 1965-66; chmn. fee arbitration com. Essex County N.J. Supreme Ct., 1987-88. Vice chmn. Montclair Red Cross; elder Presbyn. ch. Named Pub. Employee of Yr. Montclair Jaycees, 1983. Mem. ABA, N.J. Bar Assn., Essex County Bar Assn., Montclair-West Essex Bar Assn. (pres. 1973). Home: 519 Highland Ave Montclair NJ 07043-1203 Office: Harris Dickson 250 Bellevue Ave Montclair NJ 07043-1394

DICKSON, RICHARD DALLAS, JR., city administrator; b. Phila., Apr. 29, 1956; s. Richard Dallas and Lillian Dolores (Pitts) D. BA, Houghton (N.Y.) Coll., 1978; MPA, Temple U., 1980. Spl. asst. U.S. Congressman, Washington, 1979-81, chief legis. asst., 1981-83; dir. regulations and pub. svc. Phila. Parking Authority, 1983—. Campaign mgr. Congl., State Legis., City Coun. and Jud. candidates, Phila., 1980-92; committeeperson 18th Ward Dem. Exec. Com., Phila., 1984-88, treas., 1986-88. Mem. Pa. Parking Assn., Instl. and Mcpl. Parking Congress. Home: 2228 Kater St Philadelphia PA 19145-1139 Office: Phila Parking Authority 344 N Broad St Philadelphia PA 19102

DICKSON, RICHARD LYALL, education educator; b. Rumford, Maine, Feb. 8, 1944; s. William Henry and Kathryn Ann (Davis) D.; m. Jean Williston Bailey, Apr. 19, 1969; children: Erica Beth, Joel Kerr. BS, U. Maine, 1966; MA, U. Conn., 1967, PhD, 1971. Tchr. Childrens Village, Hartford, Conn., 1967-69; counselor Parish High Sch., Chaplin, Conn., 1970-71; coord. spl. edn. Hartford (Conn.) Bd. Edn., 1969-70; prof. R.I. Coll., Providence, 1971—; interim assoc. dean Sch. Edn. R.I. Coll.; interim dean Sch. Edn. R.I. Coll.; assoc. dean sch. of Edn. R.I. Coll.; cons. Lakeside Treatment Ctr., Warwick, R.I., 1971-80, Harmony Hill Schs., Chepachet, R.I., 1977-82, R.I. Dept. Edn., Providence, 1989—, St. Andrew's Sch., Barrington, 1981—, Burrville Sch. Dept., 1988—, Crisis in the Classroom Spl. Edn. Programs for Students with Behavior Disorders. Author: Team Decision Making, 1991. Profl. adv. com. Harmony Hill Sch., Chepachet, 1988—. Grantee USOE, 1976-81. Mem. Am. Edn. Rsch. Assn., Coun. for Exceptional Children (pres. R.I. chpt. 1977). Home: 26 Karen Ann Dr Smithfield RI 02917-2324 Office: RI Coll 600 Mt Pleasant Ave Providence RI 02908-1924

DICKSON, THOMAS PAGE, lawyer; b. Arlington, Va., June 4, 1944; s. Raymond Page and Mary Elizabeth (Hildebrand) D. AB, Harvard U., 1966, JD, 1972. Bar: N.Y. 1973, U.S. Dist. Ct. (so. and ea. dists.) N.Y. 1975, U.S. Ct. Appeals (2d cir.) 1975. Assoc. Milbank, Tweed, Hadley & McCloy, N.Y.C., 1972-80, ptnr., 1981—. Home: 142 W 26th St #4 New York NY 10001 Office: Milbank Tweed Hadley & McCloy 1 Chase Manhattan Pla New York NY 10005

DICKSON, VIVIAN FRANCO, biomedical research consultant; b. Phila., June 2, 1937; d. Joseph Patrick and Vivian (Lange) Franco; m. James F. Dickson, III, Dec. 23, 1977. BA, U. Del., 1958; postgrad., Jefferson Med. Coll., 1959. Cert. med. technologist Am. Soc. Clin. Pathologists. Med. technologist NIH, Bethesa, Md., 1959-67, adminstr., 1968-74, 78-88; health policy analyst Office of Asst. Sec. Health, Dept. Health and Human Svcs., Washington, 1975-77; cons. in health care policy Mass., 1988—; cons. in devel. Hospice for Visiting Nurse Assn., Cape Cod, Mass., 1988—; mem. hospice profl. adv. com. Vis. Nurse Assn., Cape Cod, Mass., 1991—. Office: PO Box 343 Provincetown MA 02657-0343

DICKSTEIN, CYNTHIA DIANE, Soviet-American exchange specialist; b. Binghamton, N.Y., June 28, 1946; d. Simon and Marcella D. BA, Syracuse U., 1968; MA, Calif. State U., Los Angeles, 1973. Peripatologist Braille Inst. AM., Los Angeles, 1974-77, Perkins Sch. for the Blind, Boston, 1978, Mass. Assn. for the Blind, Boston, 1981-84; adminstr. dept. of ophthalmology Mass. Eye and Ear Infirmary Harvard Med. Sch., Boston, 1981-89. Contbr. articles to profl. jours. Mem. LWV; developer program Citizen Exchange Council, Boston, 1979-80, field advisor, 1980—; developer exchange programs Orgn. for Am.-Soviet Exchanges, Boston, 1980—, pres., 1981—; dir. Soviet program New Eng. Soc. Newspaper Editors, Boston, 1984—.

DICKSTEIN, HARVEY LEONARD, pharmaceutical company executive; b. Springfield, Mass., Jan. 19, 1936; s. David and Ruth (Stein) D.; m. Judith Marie Barton, Mar. 26, 1966; children: Jason Adam, Debra Ann. BA in Biology, Am. Internat. Coll., 1957; MD, Tufts U., 1961. Diplomate Nat. Bd. Med. Examiners. Intern then resident Bronx Mcpl. Hosp. Ctr., 1961-63; surg. resident Springfield (Mass.) Hosp., 1963-64; surg. resident, then chief resident Boston U. Med. Ctr., 1964-66; med. monitor Baxter Labs., Morton Grove, Ill., 1968-69; assoc. dir. hosp. products div. Abbott Labs., North Chgo., Ill., 1969-72, assoc. dir. exptl. therapy, 1972-73; dir. clin. rsch. Johnson & Johnson, New Brunswick, N.J., 1973-83; group leader surg. anesthetic and dental products FDA, Rockville, Md., 1983-85; dir. regulatory med. affairs E.R. Squibb, New Brunswick, 1985-87; v.p. regulatory affairs Parke-Davis Div. of Warner-Lambert, Morris Plains, N.J., 1987-89, v.p. med. rsch., 1989-91, v.p. med. affairs, 1992—. Lt. comdr. USPHS, 1966-68. New England Arthritis and Rheumatism Found. summer scholar, 1959. Office: Parke Davis/Warner Lambert 201 Tabor Rd Morris Plains NJ 07950-2693

DICKSTEIN, MORRIS, English educator; b. N.Y.C., Feb. 23, 1940; s. Abraham and Anne (Reitman) D.; m. Lore Willner, Jan. 3, 1965; children: Jeremy Elliot, Rachel Ariela. AB, Columbia U., 1961; MA, Yale U., 1963; postgrad., Cambridge U., Eng., 1963-64; PhD, Yale U., 1967. Instr. English Columbia U., N.Y.C., 1966-67, asst. prof. English, 1967-71; assoc. prof. English Queens Coll., CUNY, 1971-75, prof. English, 1976—; prof. English CUNY Grad. Ctr., 1974—; vis. prof. U. Paris VIII, 1980-81; humanities cons. Basic Books, Inc., N.Y.C., 1972-80; adv. bd. Revue Francaise d'Etudes Americaines, Paris, 1986—. Author: Keats and His Poetry, 1971, Gates of Eden, 1977, Double Agent, 1992; co-editor: Great Film Directors, 1978; contbg. editor Partisan Rev., Boston, 1972—. Fellow, J.S. Guggenheim Found., 1973-74, ACLS, 1977, Rockefeller Found., 1981-82, NEH, 1986-87, Nat. Humanities Ctr., 1989-90. Mem. MLA, Nat. Soc. of Film Critics, Am. Studies Assn., Nat. Book Critics Cir. (dir. 1983-89). Home: 230 W 105th St 11D New York NY 10025 Office: Queens Coll Dept English Flushing NY 11367

DICLAUDIO, RICHARD ALEXANDER, investment officer; b. Greensburg, Pa., Feb. 13, 1959; s. Richard Bernard and Mary (Moyer) DiC.; m. Carole Ann Quaranto, June 18, 1982; children: Alexander, Christen. BS in Fin. and Econs., St. Vincent Coll., 1981; Cert. of Grad. Studies, Duquesne U., 1986; MBA, Baldwin Wallace Coll., 1989. Corp. fin. trainee LTV Corp., Dallas, 1981-82; analyst M & A J & L Steel Corp., Pitts., 1982-83; div. controller Ga.-Pacific Packaging Group, Cleve., 1983-85, salesman, 1985-86, dir. sales, 1986-87; mgr. spl. projects The Hillman Co., Pitts., 1987-90, investment officer, 1990—; cons. Penn State Water Co., Pitts., 1991, Pasta Disc, Pitts., 1987-89, Alam Printing & Design, Pitts., 1988—; v.p. Appalachian Mtn. Spring Water Co., N.Y.C., 1989—. Dir. Three Rivers Job Tng., Pitts., 1992, Homeless Action Com., Pitts., 1989. Mem. Svc. Capital Devel. Project, Consul of Petroleum Acctg. Soc., Am. Mgrs. Assn., Rivers Club. Republican. Office: The Hillman Co 1900 Grant Bldg Pittsburgh PA 15219

DICOLO, ROBERT LOUIS, retirement and estate planning executive; b. Providence, Feb. 9, 1958; s. Robert Schiano and Grace Marie (Petteruti) DiC. BS, Providence Coll., 1980; CLU, Am. Coll., 1991. Life ins. planner Am. Coll., Bryn Mawr, Pa., 1989-90, CLU, 1989-91; v.p. Kidder, Peabody, and Co., Providence, 1991—. Co-writer, producer: (video tape) Retiring in the 1990s: From Wall Street to main Street, 1989. Incorporator Women and Infants Hosp., R.I., 1990, devel. found., Providence, 1990. Home: 850 Laten Knight Rd Cranston RI 02921 Office: GE Financial Svcs 1200 Fleet Ctr Providence RI 02903

DICOSOLA, LOIS ANN, artist, educator; b. Bklyn., Jan. 23, 1935; d. Morris and Lena (Filangeri) Bock; m. Leonard DiCosola, June 4, 1955; 1 child, Leonard. Studied with, Ella F. Jackson, 1950-53; diploma in fine arts, Mus. of Modern Art Studio Sch., Bklyn., 1953; student, New Sch., N.Y.C., 1960, Pratt Graphics Ctr., 1973; B of Profl. Studies, SUNY, 1985. Adj. prof. art Hofstra U., Hempstead, N.Y., 1990—. Exhibited works in shows at Carnegie Inst. Fine Art, Pitts., Assoc. Am. Artists Galleries, N.Y.C., Camino Gallery, N.Y.C., Aegis Gallery, N.Y.C., Hecksher Mus., Huntington, N.Y., N.Y. Worlds Fair, 1964, Finch Coll. Mus., 1964, Paula Cooper Gallery, Galerie Aldonna, N.Y.C., Pratt Graphics Ctr. Gallery, N.Y.C., Cultural Ctr., Turnhout, Belgium, Florence (Italy) U., Vered Gallery, Easthampton, N.Y., Elaine Benson Gallery, Bridgehampton, N.Y., others. Mus. Modern Art grantee, 1951-52; recipient award in printmaking Carnegie Fine Arts Inst., 1953, Augustus St. Gauden's medal for Fine Draughtsmanship, 1953, award Art Dirs. Club, N.Y.C., 1954, award for painting and drawing Guild Hall Mus., Easthampton, N.Y., 1963, curator's award for painting and drawing Guggenheim Mus., 1964, curator's award for painting, Whitney Mus., 1964. Mem. Nat. Drawing Assn. (co-chair 1989—). Home: 25 Arch Ln Hicksville NY 11801-4438

DICRESCE, GARY PETER, insurance agent; b. Amsterdam, N.Y., Dec. 30, 1946; s. G. Angelo and Florence (Sanzen) DiC.; m. Nancy Lee Karbocus, May 26, 1973. BA, Siena Coll., 1971. Sales rep. Mutual of N.Y., Albany, 1971—. Bd. dirs. Hospice, Schenectady, N.Y., 1988—. Mem. Nat. Assn. Life Underwriters, Saratoga C. of C., Million Dollar Roundtable. Republican. Roman Catholic. Office: PO Box 850 Saratoga Springs NY 12866-0850

DIDION, DALE A., social services administrator; b. Toledo, Ohio, Dec. 14, 1957; s. John and Genevieve (Fall) D.; m. Catherine J. Jay; children: Ashley, Ryan, Ian. MA, George Washington U., 1981. With office info. and regulatory affairs Office Mgmt. and Budget, Washington, 1981-83, budget analyst exec. office of pres., 1983-87; program officer U.S.-Saudi Arabian Joint Econ. Commn., Saudi Arabia, 1987-90; v.p. govt. rels. Humane Soc. U.S., Washington, 1990-91; exec. dir. Carrying Capacity Network, Washington, 1991—. Committeeman Rep. Cen. Com., Toledo, 1979; youth del. Rep. Nat. Conv., Detroit, 1980; pres. U. Toledo Young Reps., 1978. Grantee Wolcott Found., 1979-80; recipient various vol. awards Social Svcs./Resolve Crisis Svcs. Mem. ASAE, Maumee Valley High Twelve Club, Friends Assisting Nat. Symphony, Masons. Roman Catholic. Home: 1635 Cecile St McLean VA 22101 Office: Carrying Capacity Network 1325 G St Ste 1003 Washington DC 20005-3014

DIDOMIZIO, ROBERT ANTHONY, JR., mechanical engineer; b. Ft. Worth, Aug. 3, 1955; s. Robert Anthony and Mary Rose (Bethell) D.; m. Diane Kathryn Sciacca, Mar. 17, 1979; children: Robert Anthony III, Gina Luisa, Nicolas Harry. AS in Tech. Engring., Montgomery County Community Coll., Blue Bell, Pa., 1975; BS in Mech. Engring., Drexel U., 1978, MS in Materials Engring., 1985. Registered profl. engr., Pa. Sr. design engr. Honeywell, Inc., Ft. Washington, Pa., 1978-81; supr. computer aided design SKF Bearing Industries, Inc., King of Prussia, Pa., 1981-87; pres. RAD Engring., Lansdale, Pa., 1987—; cons. MRC Bearings, Jamestown, N.Y., 1987—, Precision Rebuilding Corp., Reading, Pa., 1985—, SKF Bearings, King of Prussia, 1987—, Johnson & Johnson, 1991—, Bulova Techs., 1991—. Patentee in field. Committeeman Montgomery County Rep. Com., Lansdale, 1980-82; Webolos leader Cub Scut Pack 397; asst. scoutmaster Troop 141 Boy Scouts Am.; little league mgr. Towamencin Youth Assn. Mem. Soc. Carbide and Tool Engrs. (sec. 1987-88, vice chmn. 1988-89), Pa. Soc. Profl. Engrs. (bd. dirs. 1988—, v.p., Young Engr. of Yr. 1990), North Pa. C. of C., Order Sons of Italy, Masons, Tau Beta Pi, Pi Tau Sigma. Republican. Roman Catholic. Home: 1804 Robin Dr Hatfield PA 19440-3754 Office: 135 E Hancock St Ste 200 Lansdale PA 19446-3842

DIDONATO, EDWARD JOSEPH, lawyer; b. Phila.; m. Marianne Meehan, 1977; children: Kristin, Catherine, Edward W. BA, Villanova U., 1975; JD, Widener U., 1978. Atty. U.S. Dist. Ct., Phila., 1978-79, U.S. Bankruptcy Ct., Phila., 1979-80, Clark Ladner Fortenbaugh & Young, Phila., 1980-81, Fell & Spalding, Phila., 1982-84; ptnr. Ciardi Fishbone & DiDonato, Phila., 1984—; exec. com. Eastern Dist. Bankruptcy Conf., Phila., 1989—. Author: Nuts & Bolts of Bankruptcy Law -- Automatic Stay, 1983. Dir. CORA Health Agy., Phila., 1982-89. Named Man of the Year Italian-Am. Press, 1980. Mem. Justinian Soc. (bd. dirs. 1986—), Nat. Assn. Bankruptcy Trustees, Phila. Bar Assn. (bankruptcy subcom.), Pa. Bar Assn., Sons of Italy in Am., Widener U. Sch. Law Alumni Assn. (bd. dirs. 1988—), Cen. High Sch. of Phila. Alumni Assn. (bd. dirs. 1987—). Republican. Roman Catholic. Office: Ciardi Fishbone & DiDonato 1900 Spruce St Philadelphia PA 19103-6613

DIEBOLD, FOSTER FRANK, university president; b. Orange, N.J., Oct. 24, 1932; s. Barnard A. and Gladys Lillian (Neer) D.; m. Patricia Elizabeth Gorski, Apr. 27, 1974; children: Jessica, Stacey. B.S. in Edn, Monmouth Coll., West Long Branch, N.J., 1959; M.A. in Ednl. Adminstrn, Seton Hall U., East Orange, N.J., 1964; postgrad. (Wall St. Jour. fellow 1963), Rutgers U.; postgrad. in edn., U. Pitts., 1987; LLD (hon.), U. Sindh, Pakistan, 1991, Govt. of Pakistan, Province of Sindh, 1991. Tchr. English and psychology, asst. to supt. schs. Neptune Twp. (N.J.) Public Schs., 1965-69; supr. Arthur Brisbane Child Treatment Center for Emotionally Disturbed, Farmingdale, N.J., 1957-58; dir. div. coll. devel. and planning Kean Coll. of N.J., 1969-76; exec. sec. to bd. regents, spl. asst. to pres. U. Alaska Statewide System, 1976-77, pres., 1977-79; also Regent's prof. U. Alaska Statewide System (Sch. Mgmt.); pres. Edinboro U. of Pa., 1979—; lectr. on issues of ethics in edn.; mem. adv. bd. Marine Bank, corp. bd. St. Vincent's Health Ctr., Erie, Pa. Mem. corp. bd. Hamot Med. Ctr., Erie, Pa., St. Vincent Health Ctr., Erie, Pa.; mem. adv. bd. William J. McMannis and A. Haskell McMannis Ednl. Trust Fund.; mem. scholarship rev. com. Pitts. Plate Glass, 1981—; bd. dirs. United Way Erie County, 1986—. Recipient Gold medal award U. Sindh, 1990, U. Balochistan, 1990, Shah Latif U., 1990 (all in Pakistan); named Hon. Pres., Zibo (Peoples Republic of China) Tchrs. Coll., 1987. Mem. Commn. Univ. Presidents of State System of Higher Edn. (coms. adminstrn. and fin., ednl. policies and human resources mgmt.), World Future Soc. (edn. policy com. 1983-84, charter), Am. Assn. State Colls. and Univs. (com. on purposes, policies and priorities 1991—), Pa. Assn. Colls. and Univs. (mem. govt. relations com.), Sr. Colleague Adv. Network. Office: Edinboro U Pres's Office Edinboro PA 16444

DIECK, WILLIAM WALLACE SANDFORD, chemical engineer; b. Newark, May 23, 1924; s. George Ernst and Gladys Dorothy (Sandford) D.; m. Jane Elizabeth Humphreys, Sept. 30, 1950; children: Christopher, Gretchen, David, Louisa. BChemE, Rensselaer Polytech. Inst., 1948; MS in Engring., Princeton U., 1952. Registered profl. engr., N.Y. From engr. to div. mfg. mgr. Eastman Kodak Co., Rochester, N.Y., 1949-84; cons. Rochester, 1984—. Patentee in field. V.p. William Warfield Scholarship Eastman Sch. Music, 1986—. 1st lt. USAF, 1943-46. Mem. Am. Inst. Chem. Engrs. (sect. dir. 1984—), Am. Chem. Soc., Soc. for Imaging Sci. and Tech., N.Y. Acad. Scis., Princeton Club N.Y., Phi Lambda Upsilon, Sigma Xi. Presbyterian. Home and Office: 225 Idlewood Rd Rochester NY 14618

DIEHL, ANN MARIE, assistant dean, program director; b. Teaneck, N.J., June 27, 1938; d. Arnault George and Ann Schellenberg. AS, SUNY, Farmingdale, 1979; BS, Adelphi U., 1981; MBA, L.I. U., 1985; cert., Harvard U., 1990. Coord. spl. progrsm SUNY, Farmingdale, 1978-82, dir. community edn., 1982-85, asst. dean pub. svc., 1985—. Contbr. articles to ednl. jours. Mem. Continuing Edn. Assn. N.Y. (pres. 1992—).

DIEHL, DANIEL LEE, 19th century restoration designer, historian; b. Alliance, Ohio, May 7, 1948; s. Gerald Randolph and Freda Marie (Stoller) D. Student, Kent State U., 1966-69. Pvt. practice design Alliance, Ohio, 1970-74; prin. Kaiser Bill's Night Club, Akron, Ohio, 1974-76, Victorian Interior Restoration, Pitts., 1976—; co-founder, gen. ptnr. Computer Lectern Systems, 1991—; co-chair Archtl. Review Bd., Pitts., 1986-87. Contbr. numerous articles to profl. jours.; editor Gilded Age, 1988-89. Recipient Archtl. Restoration award Nat. Trust Main St. Program, Pitts., 1986. Mem. Historical Soc., Victorian Soc. Am. (v.p. 1987-88). Home and Office: Victorian Interior 2321 Sidney St Pittsburgh PA 15203-2114

DIEMENTE, DAMON L., chemistry educator. With U. Va.; chemistry tchr. Trinity Sch., N.Y.C. Office: Trinity Sch 139 W 91st St New York NY 10024

DIENER, BETTY JANE, marketing educator, former university administrator; b. Washington, Sept. 15, 1940; d. Edward George and Minnie (Feild) D. AB, Wellesley Coll., 1962; MBA, Harvard U., 1964, DBA, 1974. Account exec. Young & Rubicam, Inc., N.Y.C., 1964-70; product mgr. Am. Cyanamid Co., Wayne, N.J., 1970-72; asst. dean, Sch. Bus. Case Western Res. U., Cleve., 1974-79; dean Sch. Bus. Adminstrn., Old Dominion U., Norfolk, Va., 1979-82; sec. commerce and resources Commonwealth of Va., Richmond, 1982-86; prof. mktg. Old Dominion U., Norfolk, Va., 1986-87; provost, vice chancellor acad. affairs U. Mass., Boston, 1987-88, prof. mktg., 1988—. Contbr. articles to profl. publs. Commr. Norfolk Indsl. Devel. Authority, 1979-82; mem. Citizens Coun. for Chesapeake Bay, 1986-87; bd. dirs. Norfolk Conv. and Visitors Bur., 1979-82, Norfolk C. of C., 1979-82, Greater Norfolk Corp., 1986-87, Va. Orch. Group, 1982-87, Va. Stage Co., 1986-87, Karamu House, 1975-79, Womenspace, 1975-79, Rapid Recovery, 1975-79, Woodruff Hosp., 1975-79, Women's City Club Cleve., 1976-79; adviser Jr. Achievement, 1963-64, Plans for Progress, 1968-70, Leadership Met. Richmond, 1980-82; adv. com. on state and local govt. programs John F. Kennedy Sch. Govt., Harvard U., 1986-88; mem. Mass. gov.'s adv. com. on sci. and tech., 1988-90; arbitrator Am. Arbitration Assn., 1991—. Named Outstanding Working Woman, Glamour Mag., 1979, one of 10 Outstanding Career Women of Decade, Glamour Mag., 1984; recipient Honor award Soil Conservation Soc., 1984. Democrat. Home: 2001 Marina Dr Apt 411W North Quincy MA 02171 Office: U Mass at Boston Harbor Campus Boston MA 02125

DIENSTAG, ELEANOR FOA, corporate communications consultant; b. Naples, Italy; d. Bruno Garibaldi and Lisa (Haimann) Foa; m. Jerome Dienstag (div. 1978); children: Joshua Foa, Jesse Paul. BA, Smith Coll., Northampton, Mass., 1959. Asst. editor Random House/Harper & Row, N.Y.C., 1959-62; editor/writer Monocle Mag., N.Y.C., 1962-65; book pub. columnist and reviewer N.Y. Herald Tribune, N.Y.C., 1965-70; cultural columnist Genesee Valley Newspapers, Rochester, N.Y., 1970-72; sr. writer/mgr. mgmt. communications Am. Express, N.Y.C., 1978-83; pvt. practice as corp. communications cons., freelance journalist N.Y.C., 1983—; lectr. in field. Author: (book) Whither Thou Goest, 1976; contbr. articles, essays, feature stories to profl. jours., including N.Y. Times, Harper's, Psychology Today, Travel & Leisure, The New Republic, McCalls's, Frequent Flyer. Recipient Award of Merit for Speechwriting N.Y Internat. Assn. Bus. Communications, 1981, 82, Award of Merit "Backgrounder" Am. Express Mgmt. Newsletter N.Y. Internat. Assn. Bus. Communications, 1981, Outstanding Mem. award Women in Communications, 1984. Mem. Am. Soc. Journalists and Authors, Nat. Writer's Union. Home and Office: 435 E 79th St New York NY 10021-1034

DIENSTAG, JULES LEONARD, physician, medical researcher; b. N.Y.C., Dec. 10, 1946; m. Judy Iris Gordon, Feb. 3, 1974; children: Josh, Jonathan. AB magna cum laude, Columbia Coll., 1968; MD, Columbia U., 1972. Diplomate Am. Bd Internal Medicine. Intern in medicine Billings Hosp., Chgo., 1972-73, resident in medicine, 1973-74; postdoctoral fellow, rsch. assoc. NIH, Bethesda, Md., 1974-76; clin. and rsch. fellow Mass. Gen. Hosp., Boston, 1976-78, clin. asst. medicine, 1978-79, asst. in medicine, 1979-82, asst. physician, 1983-87, assoc. physician, 1988—; asst. prof. of medicine Harvard Med. Sch., Boston, 1978-82, assoc. prof., 1982—; vis. scientist Lab. of Epidemiology, The Lindsley F. Kimball Rsch. Inst. of The N.Y. Blood Ctr., 1980-82; expert panelist on viral hepatitis Lister Hill Nat. Ctr. for Biomed. Communications, Nat. Libr. Medicine, 1980-82, advisor, 1982-86; mem. Merck Sharp & Dohme Hepatitis Faculty, 1982—, co-dir., 1982-84; numerous teaching appointments; lectr. in field. Mem. editorial bd. Jour. Clin. Microbiology, 1977-86, Hepatology, 1980-86, Infectious Disease Series, Marcel Dekker Med. div., 1981-85, Gastroenterology, 1981-86; editor: Gastroenterology Series, Marcel Dekker, 1983-86, Mass. Gen. Hosp. Liver-Biliary-Pancreas Ctr. Newsletter, 1990—; assoc. editor: Gastroenterology, 1986-91, Viral Hepatitis Knowledge-Base, New Eng. Jour. Medicine, 1986-89. With USPHS res., 1976-83, surgeon, 1983—. Recipient Clin. Investigator award USPHS, 1978-79. Fellow ACP; mem. AAAS, Internat. Assn. Study of the Liver, European Assn. Study of the Liver (corr.), Am. Soc. Microbiology, Am. Fedn. Clin. Rsch. Am. Assn. Immunologists, Am. Assn. Study Liver Diseases (abstract selection com. hepatitis, immunology 1979-85, 89—, tng. and edn. com. 1980-83, nominations com. 1989-90), Am. Gastroent. Assn. (abstract selection com., liver-biliary-bile 1983-84, 89—), Mass. Med. Soc., Phi Beta Kappa. Office: Mass Gen Hosp Gastrointestinal Unit Boston MA 02114

DIETEL, JAMES EDWIN, lawyer; b. Dallas, Sept. 14, 1941; married; 1 child. BSME, So. Meth. U., 1964; JD, George Washington U., 1969; LLM in Internat. Trade, Georgetown U., 1977; MBA, U. Pa. The Wharton Sch., 1992. Bar: D.C. 1971, U.S. Dist. Ct. D.C. 1971, U.S. Ct. Appeals (D.C. cir.) 1975, U.S. Supreme Ct. 1975, Va. 1990. Engr. CIA, Washington, 1964-70; program evaluation officer CIA, 1970-73, assoc. gen. counsel, 1979-80, assoc. dep. gen. counsel, 1980-83, dep. gen. counsel, 1983-91; inspector, 1991—; participant 4th ann. Jud. Conf. D.C. Cir., 1986; speaker, lectr. in field; mem. faculty numerous profl. confs. Author: Leading A Law Practice to Excellence, 1992; contbr. articles to profl. jours. Mem. ABA (chmn. govt law dept. mgrmt. com. law practice mgmt. sect., chmn. electgovt. and pub. sector lawyers div.), Pi Tau Sigma, Kappa Mu Epsilon, Kappa Alpha. Office: CIA Washington DC 20505

DIETER, RICHARD CHARLES, marketing professional; b. Northampton, Pa., Feb. 13, 1952; s. Roland George and Martha (Bierman) D.; m. Ann Elaine Urwin, May 21, 1983; children: Amara Katherine, Cary Richard. BA, Valparaiso U., 1973; MDiv, Luth. Sch. Theology, Chgo., 1974. Exec. dir. Orgn. NorthEast, Chgo., 1976-84; dir. pub. relations Green Mountain Coll., Poultney, Vt., 1986-87; pres., performing artist mgr. and rep. Dieter Assocs., Pitts., 1984—; cons. on econ. devel. North Side Innovation Ctr., Pitts.; bus. incubator cons. Editor: Neighborhood Development, 1978. Bd. dirs. People's Music Sch., Chgo., 1980-83. Mem. Am. Soc. Assn. Execs., Phi Mu Alpha Sinfonia. Home and Office: 289 W Prospect Ave Pittsburgh PA 15205

DIETERICH, DOUGLAS THOMAS, gastroenterologist, researcher; b. Queens, N.Y., Mar. 1, 1951; s. Albert Frederick and Florence Anna (Kilroy) D. BS, Yale U., 1973; M in Health Adminstrn., C.W. Post, 1974; MD, NYU, 1978. Diplomate Am. Bd. Internal Medicine and Gastroenterology. Intern, then resident Bellevue Hosp., N.Y.C., 1978-81, fellow gastroenterology, 1981-83; attending physician NYU Hosp., 1983—; cons. Rockefeller Ctr. Mgmt. Corp., N.Y.C., 1983-87, ITT World Hdqrs., N.Y.C., 1983-86; asst. dir. medicine Gouverneur Hosp., N.Y.C., 1983-85; acting med. dir. ITT World Communications, Secaucus, N.J., 1985-86; attending physician Gouverneur Hosp. Walk In Clinic, 1981-83; teaching asst. NYU, 1979-83, clin. instr. medicine, 1983-88, clin. asst. prof., 1988—; mem. AIDS Clin. Trials Group NIH, 1986-91. Contbr. articles to profl. jours. Mem. Am. Liver Found., N.J. Fellow ACP, Am. Coll. Gastroenterology; mem. AMA, Am. Gastroent. Assn., Am. Soc. Gastrointestinal Endoscopy, Am. Soc. Internal Medicine, N.Y. County Med. Soc., N.Y. State Med. Soc., N.Y. Acad. Gastroenterology, Yale Club, Cherry Valley Club. Republican. Lutheran. Home: 62 St James St S Garden City NY 11530-6344 Office: 345 E 37th St New York NY 10016-3217

DIETERT, RODNEY REYNOLDS, immunology educator; b. Ft. Lee, Va., Dec. 6, 1951; s. Ralph O. and Beverly (Reynolds) D.; m. Margaret Flowers, May 24, 1975; children: Grant C., Matthew W. BS, Duke U., 1974; PhD, U. Tex., 1977. Asst. prof. immunogenetics Cornell U., Ithaca, N.Y., 1977-83, assoc. prof., 1983-89, prof., 1989—, head grad. program in immunology, 1989-92; cons. pesticide program EPA, Washington, 1984-86; cons. Embrex, Inc., Research Triangle Park, N.C., 1991—; panelist Nat. Inst. Environ. Health Scis. (AIDS Therapeutics), Research Triangle Park, 1988; speaker at profl. confs. Jour. editor CRC Press, Inc., Boca Raton, Fla., 1986-90, editor book series, 1990—; editor jour. Elsevier Sci. Publs., Ltd., Barking, U.K., 1990—; contbr. to profl. publs. Bd. dirs. Wesley Found. Bd., Ithaca, 1979-84; chmn. Minority Edn. Com., Ithaca, 1980; mem. Ancillary Scientist Liaison Com., Champaign, Ill., 1987—. Mem. Am. Assn. Immunologists, Poultry Sci. Assn., Soc. Exptl. Biology and Medicine, Internat. Soc. Devel. and Comparative Immunology, Soc. Leukocyte Biology, Soc. Toxicology. Office: Cornell Univ Dept Microbiology 104 Rice Hall Ithaca NY 14853

DIETRICH, BRUCE LEINBACH, planetarium and museum administrator, astronomer, educator; b. Reading, Pa., Oct. 10, 1937; s. Harold Richard and Emily Jeannette (Leinbach) D.; m. Renee Carol Long, Nov. 25, 1959; children: Dodson Bruce, Katie Ellen. BS, Kutztown U., 1960; MS, SUNY, Oswego, 1969. Tchr. Reading Pub. Schs., 1960-67; curator space sci. Reading Mus., 1967-69, dir. planetarium, 1969-92, dir., 1976-92, dir. emeritus, 1992—; prof. astronomy Reading Area Community Coll., 1972—. Contbr. articles to profl. jours. Treas. Berks County Mus. Coun.; sec. Interactive Video Sci. Consortium; v.p. Reading Musical Found., 1980-88, trustee, 1987—. Named Kellogg Mus. Profl., 1987; NSF grantee, 1965-67. Fellow Internat. Planetarium Soc.; mem. AAAS, Can. Assn. Planetariums, Mid-Atlantic Planetarium Soc., Am. Assn. Mus., Pa. Soc., Torch Club (Reading) (pres. 1987), Kiwanis (pres. 1969). Home and Office: 1546 Dauphin Ave Reading PA 19610-2118

DIETRICH, RENÉE LONG, educational administrator; b. Emerald, Pa., Oct. 10, 1937; d. Emmett A. and Arlene I. (Fenstermaker) Long; m. Bruce L. Dietrich, Nov. 25, 1959; children: Dodson, Katie. BS, Kutztown (Pa.) U., 1959; MLS, Rutgers U., 1966. Cert. ednl. specialist II English, Social Studies, Libr. Tchr. history Reading (Pa.) Pub. Schs., 1959-65, libr., 1965-69; coord. coop. ed. Reading (Pa.) Area Community Coll., 1978-81, program adminstr. title III grant, 1982—, coord. community and legis. rels., 1983-91, dir. institutional advancement, 1991—; exec. dir. Foundation for Reading Area Community Coll., 1986—; cons. Pa. Power and Light Co., Allentown, 1981—, U.S. Office of Edn., Washington, 1990—; coord. Berks County Women's Coll., Reading, 1980. Editor Reading Area Community Coll. newsletter, 1983—; contbr. articles to profl. jours. Bd. dirs. Kutztown U. Found., 1981; chmn. bd. trustees Kutztown U., 1976-81; mem. LWV, host-moderator "LWV Presents..." TV talk show; mem. program com. Berks Community TV, Reading, 1989—. Recipient Disting. Alumni award, Kutztown U., 1981. Mem. Berks County Women's Coun., Coll.-Univ. Pub. Rels. Assn. Pa., Nat. Soc. Fundraising Execs., Delta Kappa Gamma (hon. edn. soc.). Mem. United Ch. of Christ. Home: 1546 Dauphin Ave Reading PA 19610-2118 Office: Reading Area Community Coll 10 S 2d St Box 1706 Reading PA 19603

DIETZ, ROBERT BARRON, lawyer; b. San Diego, May 14, 1942; s. J. Thomas and Mary Agnes (Barron) D.; m. Grace Louise Purcell, Aug. 19, 1967; children: Thomas E., Michael B., Denis P., M. Alison. AB, Coll. Holy Cross, 1964; JD, Cornell U., 1968. Bar: N.Y. 1968, U.S. Dist. Ct. (no. dist.) N.Y. 1968, U.S. Dist. Ct. (so. and ea. dists.) N.Y. 1973, U.S. Supreme Ct. 1974. Asst. dist. atty. County of Dutchess, Poughkeepsie, N.Y., 1969-70,

confidential law clk. to surrogate of Dutchess County, 1970-73; corp. counsel City of Poughkeepsie, 1973-75; assoc. Garrity & Dietz, Poughkeepsie, 1969-73, ptnr., 1973-75; assoc. Gellert & Cutler, P.C. and predecessor firms, Poughkeepsie, 1975-78, ptnr., 1978-86; pvt. practice law Poughkeepsie, 1986—; lectr. Dutchess Community Coll., Poughkeepsie, 1985—; mem. grievance com. 9th Jud. Dist., N.Y., 1987—; bd. dirs. Youth Resource Devel. Corp. Bd. dirs. Dutchess County coun. Boy Scouts Am., Mid Hudson Workshop for Disabled, Sports Mus. Dutchess County; chmn. Mid Hudson adv. bd. Salvation Army. Fellow Dist. 721 Rotary, Poughkeepsie, 1964-65. Mem. ABA, N.Y. State Bar Assn., Dutchess County Bar Assn., Internat. Assn. Basketball Ofcls., Poughkeepsie C. of C., Kiwanis (pres. Poughkeepsie club 1974-75). Republican. Roman Catholic. Office: 2 Cannon St Poughkeepsie NY 12601-3224

DIETZ, SCOTT DOUGLAS, art director; b. Ilion, N.Y., Dec. 5, 1965; s. Daryl Brian Dietz and Cheryl Ann (Morris) Casler. AAS in Advt., Mohawk Valley Community Coll., 1986; BFA in Graphic Design, U. Bridgeport, 1988. Art dir. C & D Advt., Inc., South Norwalk, Conn., 1987-90, Inside/Out Communications, Inc., Holliston, Mass., 1990—.

DIETZ, WILLIAM HARRY, pediatrician; b. Phila., Oct. 6, 1944; s. William H. and Margaret (Shoemaker) D.; m. Nancy Fenn, May 6, 1966; children: Jonathan, Sarah. BA, Wesleyan U., 1966; MD, U. Pa., 1970; PhD, MIT, 1981. Diplomate Am. bd. Pediatrics. Intern Children's Hosp. Phila., 1970-71; resident Upstate Med. Ctr., Syracuse, N.Y., 1974-76; rsch. assoc. NIH, 1971-74, MIT, Cambridge, 1976-81; assoc. prof. Tufts U. Sch. Medicine, Boston, 1986—; dir. clin. nutrition New England Med. Ctr., Boston, 1983—. Fellow Am. Acad. Pediatrics (chmn. task force on children and TV, Elk Grove Village, Ill., 1984-87); mem. Am. Soc. Clin. Nutrition (counselor). Office: New England Med Ctr Box 213 750 Washington Boston MA 02111

DI FERDINAND, ROSALIE CHILLEMI, dental hygienist; b. Phila., Sept. 28, 1955; d. Rudolph Albert and Anna Agnes (Mizii) Chillemi; m. James Anthony Di Ferdinand. Cert. in Dental Hygiene, U. Pa., 1985; BS in Dental Hygiene Edn., Thomas Jefferson U., Phila., 1987. Registered dental hygienist. Faculty dept. periodontology Sch. Dental Medicine, U. Pa., Phila., 1985—; faculty dept. dental hygiene Coll. Allied Health Sciences, Thomas Jefferson U., Phila., 1987—. Mem. ch. choir St. Mary Magdalen Ch., Media, pa., 1988—. Mem. Am. Dental Hygienist Assn., Am. Acad. Handicapped Dentistry, Am. Soc. Dentistry for Children, Sigma Phi Alpha. Roman Catholic. Home: 1295 N Providence Rd B108 Media PA 19063

DIFIORE, ALBERT ANGELO, lawyer; b. Providence, May 12, 1939; s. Gerard and Letizia (Mirando) DiF.; m. Diane Lapolla, Aug. 13, 1966; children: Debra Marie, Dina Marie. BSFS, Georgetown U., 1961, LLB, 1964. Bar: R.I. 1964. Assoc. Tillinghast, Collins & Tanner, Providence, 1964-67; ptnr. Beals, Jerue & DiFiore, Providence, 1967-76; v.p. Ted Arnold, Ltd., Providence, 1976-83; assoc. Quinn, Cuzzone & Geremia, Providence, 1983-89; ptnr. Beals & DiFiore, Providence, 1989—. Mem. Dem. Town Com., East Greenwich, R.I., 1973-78; bd. dirs. Kent County Vis. Nurses, Warwick, R.I., 1983-90, pres., 1984-86. Democrat. Roman Catholic. Home: 135 Cindy Ann Dr East Greenwich RI 02818-2426 Office: Beals & DiFiore 1345 Westminster St Providence RI 02909-1412 also: 1226 Main St West Warwick RI 02893

DI GIACOMO, THOMAS ANTHONY, financial services company executive; b. Toronto, Ont., Can., Dec. 22, 1941; s. John R. and Alice M. (Caruso) Di G. B in Comm., U. Toronto, 1964; MBA, U. Chgo., 1966. Portfolio mgr. U.S. equities Mfrs. Life Ins. Co., Toronto, 1966-68, 71-72, Andresen & Co., Montreal, Can., 1968-71; fin. v.p. U.S. securities Mfrs. Life Ins. Co., Toronto, 1972-74, fin. v.p. U.S. investments, 1974-75, fin. v.p. North Am. securities, 1975-76, fin. v.p. North Am. securities and internat. investments, 1976-77, v.p. investments, 1977-79, sr. v.p. investments, 1979-84, exec. v.p., 1984-85, pres., chief operating officer, 1985-87, pres., chief exec. officer, 1987—, chmn. bd., 1990—; chmn., pres., chief exec. officer Manulife Fin.; pres., chief exec. officer Mfrs. Life Capital Corp.; chmn. Mfrs. Life Property Corp.; bd. dirs. Cabot Devel. Corp., Simcoe Erie Investors Ltd., Mfrs. Life Ins. Co. U.K. Ltd., ManuLife Mgmt. Ltd. Office: Mfrs Life Ins Co, 200 Bloor St E, Toronto, ON Canada M4W 1E5

DIGIOVACHINO, JOHN, educator, consultant, administrator; b. Newark, Mar. 20, 1955; s. John and Mary (Trapasso) Di G. BA, William Paterson Coll., 1977, MEd, 1981. Dir. libr. skills program for mentally handicapped in East Orange (N.J.) Pub. Libr., 1978; tchr. handicapped Deron Sch., Livingston, N.J., 1978-80; tchr. handicapped Dover (N.J.) Pub. Schs., 1981-84, learning disability tchr., cons., 1984-89; dir. child study team Bedminster (N.J.) Pub. Sch., 1989—; tchr. lerning disabilities, cons. Town Dover (N.J.) Bd. Edn.; cons. to adv. bd. Bldg. Blocks Learning Child Care Svcs., Randolph, N.J., 1985—. Coord. recreation program for handicapped Friends of East Hanover, N.J., 1977-83; mem. Hanover Park Regional High Sch. Dist. Bd. Edn., East Hanover, 1983-89; mem. East Hanover Twp. Bd. Edn., 1989—, v.p. 1990-92; chmn. East Hanover Drug Awareness Coun., 1987—. Mem. N.J. Assn. Pupil Pers. Svcs., N.J. Assn. Learning Cons., N.J. Fedn. for Drug Free Communities, K.C., Pi Lambda Theta, Kappa Delta Pi. Home: 26 Goldblatt Ter East Hanover NJ 07936-1416 Office: Bedminster Elem Sch 350 Main St Bedminster NJ 07921-2602

DIGIOVANNA, LEONARD DOMINICK, nuclear medicine technologist; b. Bklyn., Sept. 16, 1955; s. Joseph and Nancy (Manno) DiG.; m. Denise Ann Segreti, June 2, 1979; children: Amanda Elizabeth, Melinda Sara. BS in Tech. Scis., Thomas Edison Coll., 1983. Cert. nuclear medicine technologist. Staff technologist North Shore U. Hosp., Manhasset, N.Y., 1978-83; dir. nuclear medicine Brookdale Hosp., Bklyn., 1983-86, St. John's Episcopal Hosp., Smithtown, N.Y., 1986-89; cardiovascular technician Cardiovascular Assocs., Mineola, N.Y., 1989—; dir., treas. A.T.F. Consolidated Inc., Deer Park, N.Y., 1989—. Patentee Emission Tomography Carousel, 1991; mng. editor N.T.R.S. Mag., 1982-84. Mem. Am. Registry of Radiologic Technologist, Soc. Nuclear Medicine, L.I. Soc. Nuclear Technologist (comml. liasion 1984, Fredrick T. Spector award 1978). Roman Catholic. Home: 307 Maple St West Hempstead NY 11552-3203 Office: Cardiovascular Assocs 166 E Jericho Tpke Mineola NY 11501-2052

DIGIOVANNI, ELEANOR ELMA, scaffold installation company executive; b. Long Island City, N.Y., May 14, 1944; d. Charles and Josephine (Laureni) DiG. Student Queensboro Coll. Collector Atlas/Re/Sun Ins. Co., N.Y.C., 1965-69; instr. Oak Manor Equitation, Weyers Cave, Va., 1970-76; dispatcher, salesperson Safway Steel Products, Long Island City, N.Y., 1977-83; ops. mgr. York Scaffold, Long Island City, 1983—; ptnr. E-Z Scholarship Data Svc., 1992—. Mem. Mus. Natural History, Nat. Assn. Female Execs., Women in Constrn., Internat. Platform Assn. Democrat. Roman Catholic. Avocations: reading, horseback riding, needlepoint. Home: 14-34 30th Rd Astoria NY 11102

DIGIOVANNI, JOAN FIMBEL, psychology educator; b. Jersey City, N.J., June 18, 1935; d. Albert Charles and Selma Caroline (Kugler) Fimbel; m. Philip DiGiovanni, June 23, 1956; children: Juliet Paula, Portia Jonquil. Student abroad, U. Miss., Europe, 1954; BA in Edn., Fla. So. Coll., 1954; MA in Psychology, Columbia U., 1955; PhD in Psychology, Baylor U., 1961. Lic. psychologist, elem. and sch. psychologist, Mass. Counselor women's residence halls, dean of women's office U. Ill., Champaign, 1955-57; teaching asst. psychology dept. Baylor U., Waco, Tex., 1958-61; asst. prof. psychology Old Dominion U. (formerly Norfolk Coll. of William and Mary), Norfolk, Va., 1961-63; coord. field work svcs. and rehab. counseling U. Mass., Amherst, 1963; asst. prof. psychology Springfield (Mass.) Coll., 1963-65; dir. counseling svc., asst. prof. psychology Western New Eng. Coll., Springfield, 1966-73, prof. psychology, 1973—, chmn. dept. human studies, 1990-92; adj. prof. psychology Westfield State Coll., 1980—; rsch. assoc. U. Mass., Amherst, 1963; instr. Am. Internat. Coll., Springfield, 1963; vis. scholar U. N.Mex., Albuquerque, 1989, NYU, 1988, Inst. Fine Arts, NYU, 1985. Presenter in field. Mem. APA (mem.-at-large div. 10 Psychology of Art 1990—), Am. Soc. Psychopathology of Expression, Am. Assn. Women Psychology, Mass. Psychol. Assn., New Eng. Psychol. Assn., Ea. Psychol. Assn., Internat. Coun. Psychologists, N.Mex. Psychoanalytic Assn., Psi Chi, Alpha Kappa Delta, Phi Theta Kappa. Unitarian Universalist. Office: Western New Eng Coll Box 2055 1215 Wilbraham Rd Springfield MA 01119

DIGIOVANNI, LARRY JOSEPH, human resources executive; b. Phila., Sept. 23, 1948; s. Salvatore and Viola (Lafen) DiG.; m. Susan Marie Pacelli, June 27, 1975. BBA, LaSalle U., Phila., 1970. Adminstrv. systems analyst Reliance Ins. Cos., Phila., 1971-74; salary analyst ICI Ams., Wilmington, Del., 1974-75; compensation and benefits specialist Mobil Chem. Co., Macedon, N.Y., 1975-77; compensation cons. NL Industries, Hightstown, N.J., 1977-79; mgr. compensation Hercules, Inc., Wilmington, 1979-82, dir. human resources, 1985-88; v.p. human resources aerospace div. Hercules, Inc., Salt Lake City, 1982-85; v.p. human resources Hercules Aerospace Co., Wilmington, Del., 1988—; mem. adv. com. Del. Gov.'s Compensation Com., Wilmington, 1980-82. Mem. adv. group Nat. Alliance of Bus., Salt Lake City, 1984-85; bd. dirs. Utah Health Cost Mgmt. Found., Salt Lake City, 1983-85. Served with USN, 1971-73. Mem. Am. Compensation Assn., Aerospace Industries Assn. (human resources coun. 1987—). Republican. Roman Catholic. Office: Hercules Aerospace Co 1313 N Market St Wilmington DE 19894-0001

DIGIOVANNI, LEONARD JEROME, educational administrator; b. Bklyn., July 8, 1928; s. Robert and Katherine DiG.; m. Erika Busch, June 22, 1952; children: Angela, Leonard, Robert, Nina, William; m. Pamela L. Day, Mar. 26, 1988. BS, Fordham U., 1950; BS in Edn., CCNY, 1951; MS in Edn., Rutgers State U., 1957; EdD, NYU, 1970. Prin. Plainedge (N.Y.) Pub. Schs., 1957-72; prin. dist. curriculum coord. Pub. Schs., South Plainfield, N.J., 1972-75; coord. elem. edn. Pub. Schs., West Orange, N.J., 1975-76; supt. schs. Plainedge (N.Y.) Pub. Schs., Fairfield, N.J., 1976-78; cons., pogram coord. N.J. State Edn. Dept., 1978-80; sec. bd. bus. adminstrn. Springfield (N.J.) Bd. Edn., 1980-85, interim supt. of schs., 1986-87; sec. bd. bus. adminstrn. Belleville (N.J.) Bd. Edn., 1987-88; sec. bd., bus. mgr. Rochelle Park (N.J.) Bd. Edn., 1989-90; lectr. Rutgers State U.; adj. prof. edn.; instr. St. John's U., Keane Coll.; instr. Command and Gen. Staff Coll., 1972-74. Bd. dirs. Pooled Ins. Programs N.J., 1984-87. With U.S. Army, 1951-53, maj. USAR. NSF grantee, 1959; recipient Founders Day award NYU, 1970. Mem. NEA, Nat. Elem. Prins. Assn., N.Y.U. Roundtable, Watchung Arts Council (co-founder), Wildwood Crest Townhouse Condo Assn. N.J. (v.p. 1983, treas. 1987, bd. dirs. 1984-87), Assn. Sch. Bus. Officials Internat., Internat. Platform Assn., Optimists Internat., Masons. Home: 27 Upper Mountain Ave Montclair NJ 07042-1906

DIGNAN, THOMAS GREGORY, JR., lawyer; b. Worcester, Mass., May 23, 1940; s. Thomas Gregory and Hester Clare (Sharkey) D.; m. Mary Anne Connor, Sept. 16, 1978; children—Kellyanne E., Maryclare E. BA, Yale U., 1961; JD, U. Mich., 1964. Bar: Mass. 1964, U.S. Supreme Ct. 1968. Assoc. firm Ropes & Gray, Boston, 1964-74; ptnr. firm Ropes & Gray, 1974—; spl. asst. atty. gen. State of Mass., 1974-76; dir. Boston Edison Co. Asst. editor: Mich. Law Rev., 1963-64; contbr. articles to profl. jours. Bd. dirs. Family Counseling and Guidance Ctrs., Inc., 1967-76, 78—, v.p., 1983-87, pres. 1987-89; bd. dirs. Gov.'s Mgmt. Task Force, 1979-81; mem. fin. com. Town of Sudbury, 1982-85; moderator Town of Sudbury, 1985—; bd. advisers Environ. Law Ctr., Vt. Law Sch., 1981—; mem. vis. com. U. Mich. Law Sch.; corporator Emerson Hosp., 1989—. Mem. ABA, Mass. Bar Assn., Boston Bar Assn., Assn. Internationale du Droit Nucleaire, Am. Nuclear Soc., Am. Law Inst., Downtown Club, Union Club, Nashawtuc Country Club, Order of the Coif, Phi Delta Phi. Republican. Roman Catholic. Home: 8 Saddle Ridge Rd Sudbury MA 01776-2772 Office: Ropes & Gray One International Pl Boston MA 02110

DILEMMO, RALPH PASQUALE, restaurant franchise official; b. Phila., May 14, 1956; s. Ralph William and Philomena (Di Battista) DiL.; m. Nora Anne Rider, Mar. 17, 1990. BEd, Temple U., postgrad., 1974-76, 83. With Marriott Corp., Phila., 1973-75, supr., 1976, asst. mgr., 1977-79, gen. mgr., 1979-90; conversion mgr. Hardee's Food Systems, Washington, Phila. and, N.Y.C., 1990—. 2d lt. CAP, USAF Aux., Phila., 1972-82; instr. in criminal law Pa. State Police, Phila., 1984-86. Mem. NRA, Aircraft Owners and Pilots Assn. Republican. Roman Catholic. Home: 1908 Cardinal Cir Norristown PA 19403-2846 Office: Hardees Food Systems # 5 Neshaminy Interplex Trevose PA 19053

DILEO, PETER GEORGE, psychotherapist; b. Hackensack, N.J., Aug. 6, 1953; s. John M. and Ann R. (Carfora) DiL.; m. Meredith Bruorton, June 3, 1986; 1 child, Indea. BA, George Washington U., 1975; MA, Fairfield U., 1982; MS, U. Bridgeport, 1989. Researcher U.S. Senate subcommittee to investigate juvenile delinquency, Washington, 1974-76; editor and publ. community newspaper, Stamford, Conn., 1978—; v.p. Petric Corp., Great Neck, N.Y., 1981-83; staff mgr. Brooks Internat., Montvale, N.J., 1984-85; pres. DiLeo Communications, Stamford, 1984—; program developer Community Action Agy., Stamford, 1988-91; clin. dir. South End Med. Ctr., Stamford, 1989—; dir. devel. Hospice Care, Inc., Stamford, 1991—; bd. dirs. Domestic Violence Svcs., Stamford, 1990—, Black Artists Theatre, 1990—. Mem. AACD, Am. Assn. Marriage and Family Therapists.

DILEONE, CARMEL MONTANO, dental hygienist; b. New Haven, Aug. 24, 1926; d. Nicholas and Martha (Ercolano) M.; m. Eugene Francis Dileone, Jan. 28, 1948; children: Gina, Richard. Dental Hygienist, Temple U., 1945; AA, Albertus Magnus Coll., 1980; BS, U. Bridgeport, 1983; MS, So. Conn. State U., 1985. Registered dental hygienist. Dental hygiene practitioner George M. Montano, DDS, New Haven, 1946-50, 59—; dental hygiene practioner Francis R. Mullen, DDS, West Haven, 1950-55, Herbert Saunders, DDS, Orange, Conn., 1958-63; instr. Huntington Inst., North Haven, Conn., 1983; adj. assoc. prof. U. Bridgeport (Conn.), Fones Sch. Dental Hygiene, 1985—. Mem. APHA, Am. Soc. Dentistry for Children, Am. Dental Hygienist Assn., Conn. Dental Hygienists Assn. (treas. 1986-88, v.p. 1988-89, pres.-elect 1989-90, pres. 1991, Mabel C. McCarthy award 1983). Roman Catholic. Home: 348 Racebrook Rd Orange CT 06477-3109 Office: George V Montano DDS 436 Whalley Ave New Haven CT 06511-3032

DILL, M. REESE, JR., business owner; b. Cleve., Aug. 14, 1937; s. M. Reese Sr. and Gladys (Frode) D. BSME, Mich. State U., 1959; MBA, Harvard U., 1961. Product mgr. Lewish Shepard Co., Watertown, Mass., 1961-64, asst. to pres., 1964-66; new bus. mgr. Ganteaune & McMiller, Inc., Boston, 1966-70, sr. assoc., 1970-80; pres., owner Dilltec, Inc., Bedford, Mass., 1981—, Dill & Co., Bedford, 1981—. Inventee inflate-a fork, spl. pallet. Treas. New Eng. Esccdrile, Manchester, N.H., 1987-88, pres., 1989-91. Mem. Soc. Mfg. Engrs., Inst. Indsl. Engrs., Internat. Material Mgmt. Soc. (regional v.p.), Inst. Mgmt. Cons., Aero Club New Eng. (bd. dirs.), Harvard Club. Home: 9 Legion Rd Weston MA 02193 Office: Dilltec Inc Civil Air Terminal Bedford MA 01730

DILL, WILLIAM ALLEN, lawyer; b. Sharon, Pa., May 18, 1918; s. Harry Armitage and Mary Rose (McCann) D.; m. Marjorie Croft, Sept. 3, 1946; children—Mary Alyson, Laurie Ann, Thomas Allen. B.S., U. Pitts., 1940, J.D., 1948. Bar: Pa. 1949. Pilot, Pan Am. Airways, North and South Atlantic, N.Y.C., 1941-42, Central and South Am., Miami, 1942-43; spl. lectr. U. Pitts. Sch. Transp., 1946-48; assoc. Fruit & Francis, Sharon, 1949-68; ptnr. Fruit Dill, Goodwin & Scholl, Sharon, 1968—; asst. dist. atty., 1952-54; solicitor City of Sharon, 1958-68; spl. dep. atty. gen., 1966-71; lectr. Pa. Bar Inst., Def. Research Inst., Pa. Def. Inst., Am. Arbitration Assn. Rep. state committeeman, 1954-78. Served to capt. USNR, 1944-70, ret. Mem. Am. Jurisprudence Soc., Pa. Bar Assn., Mercer County Bar Assn. (pres. 1969). Home: 219 Case Ave Sharon PA 16146-3427 Office: 32 Shenango Ave Sharon PA 16146

DILLABER, PHILIP ARTHUR, resource decision support specialist, economist, consultant; b. Springfield, Mass., Aug. 24, 1922; s. Ralph E. and Grace (Holman) D.; m. Jacqueline M. Bertin, July 16, 1946; children: Anne Erline (Mrs. Donald Youngblood), Katherine Marie, John Philip, Patricia Elizabeth (Mrs. Joseph Mickley). BA, Am. Internat. Coll., 1949; MBA, Ind. U., 1950; postgrad., U. Mich., Ind. U., 1950-54; PhD, Pacific Western U., 1985. Clk. rsch. and devel. div. Springfield Armory, 1946-47; rsch. asst. dept. econs. Ind. U., 1951, lectr. econs., 1955-57; orgn. and methods examiner USAF, Gulfport, Miss., 1952-53; mgmt. analyst 5th U.S. Army, Chgo., 1954-61; program progress and resources mgmt. analyst Continental Army Command, Ft. Monroe, Va., 1962-66; adminstrv. officer U.S. Army NIKE-X System Office, Alexandria, Va., 1967; program analyst Office Asst. Chief Staff Force Devel. Dept. Army, Washington, 1967-71, budget analyst Office Dep. Chief Staff Logistics, 1971-74; budget analyst Office Dep. Chief Staff Rsch., Devel. and Acquisition, Washington, 1974-80; sr. analyst Info. Spectrum, Inc., Arlington, Va., 1980-87; mem. Nat. Def. Exec. Reserve, Washington, 1985—; cons. Profl. Group, Inc., 1992—; guest lectr. econs. Purdue U., 1959-61. With AUS, 1943-46. Mem. ASPA, SAR, Am. Econ. Assn., Nat. Contract Mgmt. Assn., Am. Def. Preparedness Assn., Performance Mgmt. Assn., Am. Assn. Budget Program Analysis, Project Mgmt. Inst., Beta Gamma Sigma.

DILLARD, NANCY ROSE, naval officer; b. Rosebud, Tex., Oct. 31, 1950; d. Hilyard Blanchard and Rose Lee (Kuhn) D. BSEd, Ga So. Coll., 1973, MEd, 1974, EdS, 1990; MS, Naval Postgrad. Sch., 1990. Sch. health svcs. coord. Savannah/Chatham County Pub. Schs., Savannah, Ga., 1974-79; field agt. N.Y. Life Ins. Co., Savannah, 1979-81; commd. ensign USN, 1982, advanced through grades to lt., 1986, active duty, 1982—. Mem. Chatham County Alcoholism Adv. Bd., S.E. Ga. region Am. Lung Assn., Savannah, 1978; mem. maternal and infant health care com. United Way, Savannah, 1978; mem. combined pub. health nurses com. Chatham County Health Dept., Savannah, 1978. Decorated D.S.M. Mem. Ga. Assn. Intercollegiate Athletics for Women (chmn. ethics and eligibility com., bd. dirs. 1976-78), Ga. Assn. Health, Phys. Edn., Recreation and Dance (v.p. for health 1977), U.S. Naval Inst., Pilot Club, Delta Kappa Gamma. Roman Catholic. Home: 10103 King Edward Ct Upper Marlboro MD 20772-4832

DILLE, KENNETH LEROY, chemist; b. Caldwell, Idaho, May 9, 1925; s. Roger Gordon and Fern (McCormick) D.; m. Kathryn Kerrick, Aug. 24, 1952; children: Patricia Ann, Pamela Sue, Kenneth Joel, Nancy Jane. BA in Chemistry (magna cum laude), Coll. of Idaho, 1950; MA in Organic Chemistry, Oreg. State Coll., 1952, PhD in Organic Chemistry, 1954; 1980-88. Rsch. chemist Texaco Rsch. Ctr., Beacon, N.Y., 1954-59; acting group leader Texaco Fuels Rsch., Beacon, 1959-61; group leader Texaco Chems. Rsch., Beacon, 1961-64; group leader Texaco Fuels Rsch., Beacon, 1964-68, asst. supr., 1968-73, supr., 1973-80; coord. Environ. Affairs, Beacon, 1980-88; sr. program coord. TSCA Programs, Beacon, 1988-89, mgr., 1989—; cons. in field. Contbr. publs. to profl. jours.; patentee in field. Sgt. U.S. Army, 1944-47. Named Disting. Idahoan, 1986. Home: 9 Sherrywood Rd Wappingers Falls NY 12590-1217 Office: Texaco Inc PO Box 509 Beacon NY 12508-0509

DILLMAN, JOSEPH JOHN THOMAS, electric utility executive; b. Shenandoah, Pa., July 30, 1941; s. Joseph Bartholomew and Mary (Tomcho) D.; m. Beverly Carol Ann Holmes, Oct. 5, 1963; children: Thomas, Alan, Janice. BSME, Drexel U., 1963; MS, SUNY, Buffalo, 1969. Asst. to supt. Dunkirk (N.Y.) Steam Sta. Niagara Mohawk Power Corp., 1965-73, asst. ops. supr., 1973-74; gen. foreman mech. maintenance C.R. Huntley Sta. Niagara Mohawk Power Corp., Tonawanda, N.Y., 1974-75, supt. mech. maintenance, 1975-82, plant mgr., 1982—. Dir. Town of Tonawanda Devel. Corp., 1991—. 1st lt. U.S. Army, 1963-65. Mem. ASME, N.Y. Utility Power Generation Com. (chmn. 1986-87). Roman Catholic. Home: 24 Cree Ton Dr Buffalo NY 14228-1607 Office: Niagara Mohawk Power Corp CR Huntley Sta 3500 River Rd Tonawanda NY 14150-7781

DILLON, JAMES CHARLES, government official; b. Pitts., Sept. 14, 1951; s. John Coady and Catherine (Stehle) D.; m. Alice Marie Bridy, Apr. 28, 1979; children: John, Ann, Mary. BA, John Carroll U., Cleve., 1974; MPA, U. Okla., 1987. Data review technician U.S. Social Security Adminstrn., Arlington, Va., 1976-77; mgmt. asst. U.S. GSA, Arlington, Va., 1977-78; clk.-typist FDA, Rockfille, Md., 1978-79, mgmt. asst., 1979-80, mgmt. analyst, 1980-88, supervisory program integrity officer, 1989-90, program integrity officer, 1991—. Recipient Spl. Achievement award GSA, 1978, Commendable Svc. award FDA, 1992. Mem. Am. Soc. Pub Adminstrn., Am. Soc. for Deaf Children. Roman Catholic. Home: 19351 Frenchton Pl Gaithersburg MD 20879-2907 Office: Div Ethics and Program Integrity (HFA-20) 12420 Parklawn Dr Rockville MD 20857

DILLON, JOHN ANDREW, management consultant; b. Torrington, Conn., Jan. 28, 1954; s. Patrick Joseph and Mary Catherine (Penders) D.; m. July 11, 1981; two children. BS in Biology, U. Detroit, 1976. Cert. personnel cons. Rsch. engr. Torrington (Conn.) Co., 1976-79; sales rep. Kodak Co., Rochester, N.Y., 1979-80; dir. labs. Turner & Seymour, Inc., Torrington, 1980-81; dir. purchasing, asst. to pres. CSI, Inc., Torrington, 1981-85; acct. exec. RJS Assocs., Hartford, Conn., 1985-87; pres. Dillon & Co. Inc., Hartford, 1987—. Member, vice chmn. Torrington Human Rels. Commn., 1976-82; former chair Mayor's Adv. Coun. on Youth, 1977-81; mem., past vice chmn. Torrington Bd. of Edn., 1979—. Mem. EDP Audit Soc., Conn. Assn. Bds. Edn. (pres. 1992—, bd. dirs. 1985—, chmn. fed. lobbying com. 1988-89, v.p. govt. rels. 1990-91), Jaycees (v.p. 1978-80, dist. dir. 1980-81). Democrat. Office: Dillon & Co Canton Bus Pk 101 River Rd Collinsville CT 06022

DILLON, ROBERT SHERWOOD, non profit organization executive; b. Chgo., Jan. 7, 1929; s. Dale Crowell and Viola May (Sherwood)D.; m. Caroline Sue Burch, June 16, 1951; children: Dale, Robert Jr., John, Elizabeth, Thomas. BA, Duke U., 1951; postgrad., Princeton U., 1958-59. Fgn. svc. officer (including U.S. Amb. Lebanon, 1981-83) Dept. State, Washington, 1956-84; asst. sec. gen. UN, Vienna, Austria, 1984-88; pres. Am.-Mideast Ednl. & Tng. Svcs., Washington, 1988—. Cpl. U.S. Army, 1947-48. Recipient Presdl. Honor award, White House, 1983. Office: Am-Mideast Ednl & Tng Svcs 1100 17th St NW Washington DC 20036

DILLON, WILLIAM JOSEPH, small business owner; b. N.Y.C., Oct. 21, 1938; s. William Joseph and Irene Jenny (Boyd) D.; m. Nadine Haskins, June 19, 1965. BSBA, Syracuse (N.Y.) U., 1960. Copywriter Popular Club Plan, Passaic, N.J., 1962-65, J.C. Penney, N.Y.C., 1965-66; agy. liaison copy chief Consol. Edison, N.Y.C., 1966-73; copywriter Fletcher Walker Gessell, Ridgewood, N.J., 1973-74; owner, mgr. Boyce Travel Svc., Ridgewood, 1975—; pres. Fish of Ridgewood and vicinity, 1971, 73. Author: Moosings, 1977; playwrite, screenwriter lyrics Valhalla, 1992. Sch. dir. Upper Ridgewood Community Ch., 1973; bd. dirs. Community Chest of Ridgewood and vicinity, 1966-70, YMCA, Ridgewood, 1967-72. Capt. U.S. Army, 1960-66, ETO. Mem. Am. Soc. Travel Agys. Republican. Office: Boyce Travel Svc 216 Dayton St Ridgewood NJ 07450-4409

DILLON-MALONE, BASIL, marketing executive, electrical engineer; b. Ballina, Ireland, May 23, 1947; came to U.S., 1969; s. Hugh J.P. and Patricia Conry D.-M.; m. Janet Lindsay, June 25, 1977; 1 child, Barry. BE, Univ. Coll., Dublin, Ireland, 1969. Product planner, dist. sales mgr. GE, various locations, 1969-80; dir. mktg. Honeywell Optoelectronics, Richardson, Tex., 1980-81; gen. sales mgr. Arrow Electronics, Syracuse, N.Y., 1981-83; br. mgr. Future Electronics, Syracuse, N.Y., 1983-84; mktg. mgr. Pass & Seymour/Legrand, Syracuse, 1985—; del. Am. Nat. Standards Inst./IEEE; del. Internat. Electrotech. Commn. for Surge Protective Devices; panelist IEEE/Power Engring. Soc. Conf., N.Y.C., 1988, Electromagnetic Compatibility Symposium, Zurich, Switzerland, 1989. Contbr. articles to profl. jours. Mem. IEEE (surge protective devices subcom., task force chmn. AC varistor applications group), Internat. Conf. Electromagnetic Compatibility, Nat. Elec. Mfrs. Assn. (tech. com., low voltage transient voltage suppressor sect.). Roman Catholic. Home: 4215 Mill Run Rd Liverpool NY 13090 Office: Pass & Seymour/Legrand 50 Boyd Ave Syracuse NY 13209

DILLON-MCHUGH, CATHLEEN THERESA, librarian, consultant; b. Newark, Jan. 31, 1951; d. William David and Rose (Baker) Dillon; m. Joseph F. McHugh, Apr. 16, 1988. BA cum laude, Bloomfield (N.J.) Coll., 1973; MLS, Rutgers U., 1976. Reference-cataloging libr. Neptune (N.J.) Pub. Libr., 1976-77; indexer Popular Periodical Index, Wayne, N.J., 1979—; sch. libr. Hudson Cath. High Sch., Jersey City, 1980-81; govtl. reference libr. N.J. State Libr., Trenton, 1981-82, law reference libr., 1982-83, referral libr., 1983-87; tech. reference libr. Bell Communications Rsch., Red Bank, N.J., 1987; reference libr. Middletown Twp. Pub. Libr., N.J., 1988-89; libr./info. specialist, cons. various corps., N.J. and Maine, 1990—; cons. Quantum Enterprises, Inc., Middletown, 1985-86; dir. Edith Belle Libby Meml. Libr., Old Orchard Beach, Maine, 1991—. Mem. ALA, Maine Libr. Assn., Spl. Libr. Assn.

DILORENZO, FRANK R., mechanical engineer; b. Shirley, Mass., Nov. 1, 1965; s. Saverio F. and Maria Pia DiLorenzo. BSME, Carnegie-Mellon U.,

1988. Cert. engr.-in-tng., Pa. Mech. engr. ICF Kaiser Engrs., Pitts., 1988—; Inventor historically based game for dual educating purposes, Vacusan. Mem. ASME, ASHRAE, Ea. States Blast Furnace and Coke Oven Assn. Roman Catholic.

DI LORENZO, KRIS M., writer, editor; b. N.Y.C., Nov. 3, 1950; m. Jonathan Miles, Sept. 11, 1987. Trained, Royal Nat. Theatre, London; studied with John Barton, Royal Shakespeare Co.; studied with Patrick Tucker, Drama Studio, London. founder Not the Nat. Theatre, N.Y.C., 1991—; co-founder Creative Collective Internat. One woman show Virtual Reality, 1992; appeared with Riverside Shalespeare Co., Actors Classical Troupe, Nuyorican Poets, Cafe, Ensemble Studio Theatre, films, tv; author: (lyrics and poetry) Rumours From the Continent, 1986, (novel) Stardust Man, 1992; co-author (screenplays) Lost in the Mail, Roomates, Temping, The Real Life Comedy Show. Coord. Women Against Pornography, N.Y.C., 1980-82; mem. Met. Coun. on Housing, N.Y.C., 1985-90. Mem. SAG (mem. women's com. 1992), AFTRA, Nat. Assn. Women in Music (sec., pres. 1975-79), Nat. Writers Union, Editorial Freelancers Assn. Office: SNAP Creative Svcs 317 W 77th St Ste 2R New York NY 10024

DILUGLIO, DOMENIC RAYMOND, college administrator; b. Providence, Feb. 3, 1920; s. Ralpha nd Victoria (Rossi) DiL.; m. Dorothea Evelyn Anthony, Feb. 16, 1943; children: Charles H., Edward R., Paula J. PhB, Providence Coll., 1942; MEd, R.I. Coll., 1956; C.A.G.S., U. Conn., 1968; Dr.Pub. Edn., U. R.I., 1982. Tchr. Warwick (R.I.) Sch. Dept., 1947-55, asst. prin., 1955-56, prin., 1956-64, asst. supt. schs., 1964-69, supt. schs., 1969-82; spl. asst. to pres. N.E. Inst. of Tech., Warwick, 1980—. Trustee Kent County Meml. Hosp., Warwick, 1972—; pres. Community Coll. of R.I. Found., 1978-80; v.p. Jr. Achievement of R.I., Providence, 1976—; bd. dirs. Blue Cross Blue Shield, Providence, 1976—; mem. Naval War Coll. Found., Newport, R.I., 1985—; mem. Gove.'s Commn. of Children and Youth, 1983-87. Maj. USMC, 1942-46. Paul Harris fellow, 1981; named Man of the Yr. R.I. Coun. for Econ. Edn., 1982, Warwick Beacon, 1982; named to Hall of Fame, R.I. Gridiron Club, 1980. Mem. N.E. Assn. Schs. and Colls., N.E. Assn. Collegiate Registrars and Admissions Officers, R.I. Assn. Sch. Supts. (pres. 1975-76), N.E. Assn. Sch. Supts. (dir. 1976-82), N.E. Sch. Devel. Coun. (dir. 1975-82), Mil. Order Fgn. Wars, Univ. Club. Roman Catholic. Home: 130 Ocean Ave Mantunck Point Wakefield RI 02879 Office: New Eng Inst Tech 2500 Post Rd Warwick RI 02886-2266

DILUZIO, ADRIAN LOUIS, lawyer; b. Phila., Sept. 26, 1946; s. Frank Paul and Rose (Campagna) DiL.; m. Kim Stacey Hollander, Apr. 27, 1991; 1 child, Zachary James. BA, U. Pa., 1969, JD, 1972. Bar: Pa. 1972, N.Y. 1980. Asst. dist. atty. Dist. Atty.'s Office, Phila., 1972-78, Dist. Atty's Office Nassau Cunty, Mineola, N.Y., 1978-81; assoc. counsel Stephen P. Scaring, Mineola, N.Y., 1981-85; pvt. practice Mineola, N.Y., 1985—. Mem. Phila. Bar Assn. (exec. com. criminal justice sect. 1976-77), Nassau County Bar Assn. (chmn. criminal law and procedure com. 1986-87). Republican. Roman Catholic. Office: Adrian L DiLuzio Esq 1015 Broadway Woodmere NY 11598

DIMANT, JACOB, internist; b. Rehovot, Israel, Apr. 27, 1947; came to U.S., 1972, naturalized, 1977; s. Simcha and Ita D.; m. Rose Bea Jearolmen, Sept. 11, 1974. MD, Hebrew U., Jerusalem, 1972. Diplomate Am. Bd. Internal Medicine and Rheumatology and Geriatric Medicine, Am. Bd. Quality Assurance and Utilization Rev. Physicians. Intern Maimonides Med. Ctr., Bklyn., 1972-73; resident in medicine Maimonides Med. Ctr., 1973-75; chief resident in medicine Maimonides Med. Ctr., Bklyn., 1975-76; fellow in rheumatology Downstate Med. Ctr., Bklyn., 1976-78; practice medicine specializing in internal medicine and rheumatology Bklyn., 1975—; dir. rheumatology Maimonides Med. Ctr., Bklyn., 1978-89, assoc. dir. med. edn., 1978-80; med. dir. Clove Lakes Nursing Home, Staten Island, N.Y., 1985—; med. dir. Prospect Park Nursing Home, Bklyn., 1977-87, Crown Nursing Home, Bklyn., 1983—; pres. Crown Nursing Home Assocs., Inc., Bklyn., 1989—; asst. prof. medicine SUNY, Bklyn., 1978—. Contbr. articles to profl. jours. Named hon. police surgeon N.Y.C. Police Dept., 1982; fellow Arthritis Found. of N.Y., 1977-78. Fellow ACP, Am. Rheumatism Assn.; mem. Am. Geriatric Soc., Am. Med. Dirs. Assn., N.Y. Med. Dirs. Assn. Office: Crown Nursing Home 3457 Nostrand Ave Brooklyn NY 11229-5194

DIMARCO, ANTHONY, health care advocate; b. N.Y.C., Aug. 15, 1947; s. Antonio and Josephine (Barbera) DiM. BS in Psychology, CCNY, 1969; MPA, Baruch Coll., 1975. Analyst N.Y.C. Health & Hosp. Corp., 1975-83; adminstr. Coney Island Hosp. E. D., Brklyn., 1983-84; exec. dir. Empire Nine Regional Emergency Med. Svc., Rochester, 1984-85; health care advocacy dir. N.Y. Statewide Sr. Action Coun., Albany, 1986-88; dir. Ontario County Office for the Aging, Canandaigua, N.Y., 1988-90; coord. Coalition for a Nat. Health System, Rochester, N.Y., 1986—; adj. faculty mem. Empire State Coll., 1982; bd. dirs. Nat. Gray Panthers, Washington, 1987-90; mem. U.S. Health Care Tour, Can., 1985, Nicarauga, 1989, Cuba, 1990. Author: (slide presentations) Nicaraguan and Cuban Health Care Systems: Implications for the U.S., 1989, 90. Mem. WHEC-TV Adv. Bd., Rochester, 1987—, Long Term Care Com. and Subcom. on Universal Coverage/Congresswoman Slaughter, 1988—. Mem. Am. Pub. Health Assn. Home and Office: 49 Corwin Ave Rochester NY 14609-2129

DI MASCIO, JOHN PHILIP, lawyer; b. Bklyn., Feb. 4, 1944; s. Eugenio and Stella (Scheuermann) Di M.; m. Angela Piccininni, Apr. 2, 1967 (div. 1980); children: John Philip, Jr., Christine, Thomas. BA, C.W. Post Coll., 1975; MA, L.I. U., 1976; JD, St. John's U., 1983. Bar: N.Y. 1984, U.S. Dist. Ct. (ea. and so. dists.) N.Y. 1984, U.S. Ct. Appeals (2d cir.) 1984. Sr. ct. officer N.Y. State Supreme Ct., Mineola, N.Y., 1971-82; assoc. Joel R. Brandes, P.C., Garden City, N.Y., 1984; pvt. practice Carle Place, N.Y., 1984-87; ptnr. Di Mascio, Meisner & Koopersmith, Carle Place, 1987—. With USN, 1963-69. Recipient various acad. awards. Mem. N.Y. State Bar Assn. (family law com. 1982), Nassau County Bar Assn. (matrimonial com. 1984). Office: Di Mascio Meisner & Koopersmith 1 Old Country Rd Ste 225 Carle Place NY 11514-1817

DIMASCIO, WILLIAM MICHAEL, public relations counselor; b. Phila., Aug. 31, 1943; s. Albert L. and Marian (Quisito) D., m. Louise S. Scheerbaum, June 18, 1966; children: Michelle, Kathleen, Jennifer. BS in Communications, Temple U., 1966. Newsman Associated Press, Phila., 1969-70; corr. Associated Press, Harrisburg, Pa., 1970-73, Pitts., 1973-74; bureau chief Associated Press, Nashville, 1974-76, Columbus, Ohio, 1976-81; exec. editor Cleve. Press, 1981-82; independent communications cons. Phila., 1982-84; v.p. Paul Werth Assocs., Columbus, 1984-90; pres. DiMascio Pub. Rels., Phila., 1990—. 1st lt. U.S. Army, 1966-69, Vietnam. Mem. Counselors Acad., Pub. Rels. Soc. Am. (counselor), World Affairs Counsel, Veterans of Fgn. Wars. Office: DiMascio & Assocs 201 N Presidential Blvd Bala Cynwyd PA 19004

DIMATTEO, JOHN R., health facility administrator; b. Portland, Maine, Sept. 13, 1931; s. Rosario and Josephine (Proietti) DiM.; m. Patricia H. Huddleston, Sept. 9, 1956; children: Susan DiMatteo Keiler, Martha DiMatteo Vorlicek, Andrew. BS, Babson Coll., 1953. Acct. Arthur Anderson and Co., Boston, 1955-59; acct. Jordan and Jordan, Portland, 1959-72, ptnr., 1963-72; exec. v.p., gen. mgr. Guy Gannett Pub. Co., Portland, 1972-78, pres., 1978—, also bd. dirs., 1978-91; dir. Maine Med. Ctr., Portland, 1991—; trustee Maine Savs. Bank, Portland; bd. dirs. The One Bancorp, Portland, Utilities Inc., Standish, Maine. Past pres., trustee Westbrook Coll., Portland; trustee Maine Med. Ctr., Portland Mus. Art. With U.S. Army, 1953-55. Mem. Am. Inst. CPA's. Office: Maine Medical Center 22 Bramhall St Portland ME 04102

DIMAURO, PATRICK SAMUEL, human resources manager; b. Syracuse, N.Y., Sept. 4, 1949; s. Pasquale A. and Josephine (Pento) DiM.; m. Diane O. Canino, Aug. 22, 1970 (div. Dec. 1975); m. Beth A. Yaro, June 16, 1979; children: Nicole Beth, Michelle Patricia, Michael Patrick. BS in Edn., SUNY, Buffalo, 1971, MS in Edn., 1972. Tchr. Syracuse (N.Y.) City Sch. Dist., 1972-74; assoc. dir. SUNY Health Sci. Ctr., Syracuse, 1974-79; pers. mgr. Instruments for Cardiac Rsch., Syracuse, 1979-85; tech. employment mgr. UTC Carrier Corp., Syracuse, 1985-86; exec. human resource officer Key Bank of Cen. N.Y., Syracuse, 1986-89; mgr. tng. and spl. projects Pyramid Mgmt. Group, Inc., Syracuse, 1989—; cons. in field. Member health promotion com. CIM Hosp., Syracuse, 1985—; mem. health adv. group Congressman Walsh, Syracuse, 1990—; chmn. Syracuse Bus. Group on Health, 1986—; bd. dirs. United Way, Syracuse, 1985-88, Bus. & Industry Coun., Syracuse, 1986—. Mem. ASTD, Soc. for Human Resources Profls. Home: 7751 Bainbridge Dr Liverpool NY 13090-2577 Office: Pyramid Mgmt Group Inc 4 Clinton Sq Syracuse NY 13202-1041

DI MEO, DOMINICK, painter, sculptor; b. Niagara Falls, N.Y., Feb. 1, 1927; s. Antonio and Michelina (Sandonato) Di M.; m. Judith S. Cousins, Dec. 26, 1963. B.F.A., Sch. Art Inst., Chgo., 1952; M.F.A., State U. Iowa, 1953. vis. artist Sch. of Art Inst. Chgo., 1977; instr. Chgo. Acad. Fine Arts, 1967-69. One man shows include Lake Forest (Ill.) Coll., 1955, Bemidji (Minn.) Coll., 1963, Fairweather-Hardin Gallery, Chgo., 1964, 68, 71, Barat Coll., Lake Forest, 1966, Chgo. Public Library, 1966, Kendall Coll., Evanston, Ill., 1967, Westbroadway Gallery, N.Y.C., 1973, 75, 76, Project Studios One, Long Island City, N.Y., 1982, group exhbns. include, Albright-Knox Art Gallery, Buffalo, 1953, 54, Art Inst. Chgo, 1959, 60, 61, 63, 65, 66, 67, 68, 71, 76, 79, 89-90, Mus. Contemporary Art, Chgo., 1969, Joan Miro Internat. Drawing Prize Competition, Barcelona, Spain, 1977, 78, 79, 80, Centro Cultural/Arte Contemporaneo, Mexico City, Nov. 1986-Jan. 1987, Art Inst. Chgo., 1989-90; represented in permanent collections, Art Inst. Chgo., Whitney Mus. Am. Art, N.Y.C., U. Mass., Amherst, Nat. Collection Fine Arts, Smithsonian Instn., Elmhurst (Ill.) Coll. Fellow Guggenheim Found., 1972, sculpture fellow Nat. Endowment for Arts, 1983. Mem. Momentum (founding mem.), Participating Artists Chgo.), Artists Collaborative. Address: 429 Broome Street New York NY 10013

DIMEO, JAMES STEPHEN, sales executive; b. Providence, June 5, 1954; s. Salvatore Walter and Joan (Reynolds) DiM.; m. Bonnie Jean Ferguson, Apr. 19, 1980. BA, Providence Coll., 1977. Asst. technician E.I. DuPont de Nemours & Co., Rumford, R.I., 1977-78, technician, 1978-80; tech. rep. Mobay Corp., Rumford, R.I., 1980-82; tech. sales rep. Mobay Corp., Union, N.J., 1985-86; account exec. Mobay Corp., Pitts., 1986—. Mem. TAPPI (exec. com. 1988-90), Paper Industry Mgrs. Assn., Tyler Point Yacht Club. Roman Catholic. Home: 31 Bradford St Barrington RI 02806-2252 Office: Mobay Corp Mobay Rd Pittsburgh PA 15205-9741

DIMINNIE, CHARLES RICHARD, mathematician; b. Paterson, N.J., June 18, 1944; s. Edward and Mary (Napoleone) D.; m. Helen Carol Bruce, June 14, 1968; children: David, Jonathan, Daniel. BS in Math., St. Bonaventure U., 1966; MS in Math., Mich. State U., E. Lansing, 1967, PhD in Math., 1970. Asst. prof. math. Bowling Green (Ohio) State U., 1970-71; asst. prof. math. St. Bonaventure (N.Y.) U., 1971-75, assoc. prof. math., 1975-79, prof. math., 1979--; vis. lectr. U. Mo., St. Louis, 1980-81. Contbr. numerous articles to profl. and scholarly jours.;. Mem. Math. Assn. Am. (Seaway sect. 1st vice-chair 1988-89, chair 1989-91), Am. Math. Soc., Consortium for Math. and its Applications, Sigma Xi, Pi Mu Epsilon. Home: 58 N 3rd St Allegany NY 14706-1032 Office: St Bonaventure Univ Dept Math Saint Bonaventure NY 14778

DI MINO, ANDRÉ ANTHONY, manufacturing executive, consultant; b. Bklyn., Aug. 24, 1955; s. Alfonso and Nancy (Zarbo) DiM.; m. Jenny DiCapua, May 30, 1981. BS in Indsl. Engring., Fairleigh Dickinson U., 1978, MBA in Fin., 1981. Engr. ADMTronics Inc., Emerson, N.J., 1977-79; dir. tech. ADMTronics Inc., Emerson, 1979-82; sec./treas. ADMTronics Inc., Northvale, N.J., 1982-86; exec. v.p. and dir. ADMTronics Inc., Northvale, 1986—; founder, dir. Enviro-Pack Devel. Corp., Northvale, N.J., 1991—; ptnr., cons. Tech. Mgmt. Cons., Woodcliff Lake, N.J., 1978—; v.p., dir. Pegasus Labs., Inc., Northvale, N.J., 1989—, Sonotron Med. Systems Inc., Northvale, 1988—, VET-Sonotron Systems, Inc., Northvale, 1988—; bd. dirs. Arthronix Corp., N.Y.C. Inventor in field. Mem. coun. Borough of Woodcliff Lake, 1984, pres., 1987—; corr. sec. Office N.E. Rep. Orgn. (NERO), 1989—, treas., 1992; co-chmn. privatization subcom. Bergen County Cost Containment Rev. Team, 1991; fundraising dir. Our Lady Mother of the Ch., Woodcliff Lake; founding mem., 1st v.p. Woodcliff chpt. Unico Nat. Svcs. Orgn., 1990-92, pres., 1992—; founder, pres. Community Access TV studio WCL-TV, 1990—; founder, chmn. Woodcliff Lake Sr. Assn., 1989—. Named Vol. of Yr. Bergen County, N.J., 1991. Republican. Roman Catholic. Office: ADMTronics Inc 224S Pegasus Ave Northvale NJ 07647-1904

DIMMIG, BRUCE DAVID, architect; b. Buffalo, N.Y., Apr. 19, 1956; s. George Clayton and June (Legler) D. AAS with honors, Dutchess Community Coll., 1976; BArch cum laude, Kans. State U., 1980. Lic. architect Kans., N.J. Staff architect The Shaver Partnership, Salina, Kans., 1980-84; staff/project architect Fullerton, Carey & Oman, Kansas City, Mo., 1984-87; project architect The Ramos Group, Kansas City, 1987-88; archtl. project mgr. Toys "R" Us, Inc., Paramus, N.J., 1988-89; project mgr. Schenker, Schenker & Rabinowitz, Paterson, N.J., 1989-91; assoc. L. Michael Schenker, Architect, Paterson, 1991—; participant Govs. Task Force on Aging, New Brunswick, 1990, Monmouth Housing Alliance Competition, Marlboro, N.J., 1991, ADA video Kean Coll., 1992. Ch. treas. St. Mark's Evang. Luth. Ch., Salina, 1982; mem. ch. bd. edn. Gethsemane Evang. Luth. Ch., Kansas City, 1987, Sunday sch. tchr., 1987. Recipient Regents scholarship N.Y. State, 1974, Academic scholarship Phi Kappa Phi, Kans. State U., 1979, Neighborhood award Tenn. Town, Topeka, 1979. Mem. Nat. Coun. Archtl. Registration Bds., Bldg. Ofcls. and Code Adminstrs. Internat. Home: 193 Godwin Ave Apt 5 Wyckoff NJ 07481

DIMOND, THOMAS, investment advisory company executive; b. Scarsdale, N.Y., Jan. 24, 1916; s. George A. and Jessie (Kennedy) D. BA magna cum laude, Princeton U., 1939; MBA, Harvard U., 1941. Mem. faculty Wharton Sch. Fin., U. Pa., 1948; economist, account mgr. Lionel D. Edie & Co., 1948-50; economist, mgr. comml. rsch. Youngstown Sheet & Tube Co., Ohio, 1951-56; sr. account mgr., security analyst deVegh & Co., N.Y.C., 1956-60; pres. Humes-Schmidlapp Assocs., N.Y.C., 1960—; bd. dirs. Mercer Mgmt. Corp., co-mgr. Mercer Fund, 1963-67; bd. dirs. Scudder Spl. Fund, 1967-72, Scudder Duv-Vest, 1968-71; gen. ptnr. HS Spl. Fund. Contbr. articles to profl. pubs. Trustee, Humes Found., 1963—. Capt. USAAF, 1941-46. Mem. N.Y. Soc. Security Analysts, Racquet & Tennis Club, Down Town Assn. (N.Y.C.). Episcopalian. Home: 200 E 66th St New York NY 10021-6728 Office: 345 Park Ave New York NY 10154-0095

DINAN, JAMES GERARD, investment executive; b. Balt., May 22, 1959; s. Robert Joseph and Jeanette (Farland) D. BS in Econs., U. Pa., 1981; MBA, Harvard U., 1985. Assoc. investment banking Donaldson Lufkin & Jenrette, N.Y.C., 1981-83; gen. ptnr. Kellner DiLeo & Co., N.Y.C., 1985-91; mng. ptnr. York Capital Mgmt. LP, N.Y.C., 1991—. Office: York Capital Mgmt LP 505 Park Ave 4th Fl New York NY 10022

DINE, RICHARD, banker; b. Cin., May 12, 1958; s. Mark Saul and Esther (Rivkin) D.; m. Sarah Blank, July 9, 1984; children: Jonathan, Elliot. BS, Georgetown U., 1980; MBA, U. Pa. Wharton Sch. Bus., 1984. Asst. dir. Task Force on Rgn. Policy, Ho. Rep. Rsch. Com., Washington, 1981-82; asst. v.p. Marine Midland Bank, N.Y.C., 1984-88; v.p. Bank Austria, N.Y.C., 1988-91; investment officer Czech & Slovak Am. Enterprise Fund, Washington, 1991—; asst. sec. Fgn. Bd. Holders Protection Coun., Washington, 1986—. Home: 809 Lamberton Dr Silver Spring MD 20902 Office: Czech & Slovak Am Fund 1620 I St NW #703 Washington DC 20006

DING, CHEN, investment banker; b. Wuxi, Jiangsu, Peoples Republic of China, Feb. 10, 1919; came to U.S., 1985; s. Zugeng and Shu (Feng) D.; m. Fuzhen Tang, Sept. 30, 1950; children: Dahai, Dadi. BA, Jiaotong U., Shanghai, Peoples Republic of China, 1939; MA, U. Pa., 1943; PhD, Harvard U., 1946. Corp. sec., chief fin. officer Sung Sing Textile Corp., Shanghai, 1947-49; vice chmn. Shanghai Fedn. Industry and Commerce, 1949-85; N.Y. rep. China Internat. Trust & Investment Corp., Beijing and N.Y.C., 1985—, also bd. dirs., 1983—. Office: CITIC NY Rep Office 2 World Trade Ctr Ste 2250 New York NY 10048-0203

DINGES, RICHARD ALLEN, entrepreneur; b. Englewood, N.J., June 17, 1945; m. Kathie A. Headley; children: Kelly, Courtney. Grad., Jersey City State Coll., 1967; MEd, U. Hawaii, 1972; postgrad., William Peterson Coll., 1974-79. Cert. sch. adminstr.; cert. sch. spl. services dir., N.J., Ariz., Hawaii. Pres. Def. Industry Assocs., Sierra Vista, Ariz., 1979—, Fed. Career Cons., Sierra Vista, Ariz., 1985; dir. Nat. Scholarship Locators, Sierra Vista, 1985—. Editor: Guide to U.S. Defense Contractors, 1985, 87, 10 Step Guide to College Selection, Salary Negotiations for Military, How to Survive the Job Interview. Vice prin. Little Egg Harbor Primary Sch. Mem. Cochise County Merit Commn. (vice-chmn.), Platform Soc. Speakers' Assn. Office: 2160 E Fry Blvd Ste 400 Sierra Vista AZ 85635-2709

DINGFELDER, TAMMI LEE, mental health therapist; b. Homestead, Pa., Mar. 26, 1965; d. Charles Frederick and Bonnie Lee (Gable) D. BA in Sociology, Thiel Coll., 1987; MA in Counseling Svcs., Slippery Rock U., 1990. Resident advisor Turtle Creek Valley Mental Health/Mental Retardation, Inc., Homestead, 1987-88; grad. asst. Slippery Rock (Pa.) U., 1988-90; grad. intern Luth. Youth & Family Svcs., Zelienople, Pa., 1990; supr. community living arrangement Care Unlimited, Inc., Pitts., 1990—; resident advisor Assn. For Retarded Citizens, Pitts., 1990-91; mental health therapist Irene Stacy Community Mental Health Ctr., Butler, Pa., 1991—. Mem. AACD, Am. Mental Health Counselors Assn., Alpha Gamma Delta (recording sec. 1986, scholarship 1985). Presbyterian. Home: 5163 Willock Rd E Pittsburgh PA 15236-2238 Office: Irene Stacy Community Mental Health Ctr 112 Hillvue Dr Butler PA 16001-3498

DINGLE, PERCY ARNOLD, air force officer; b. Sumter, S.C., Dec. 16, 1962; s. Mable (Carter) D.; m. Zelander Brannon, July 11, 1987. BS in Bus. Adminstrn. and Econs., Benedict Coll., 1988; postgrad., U. S.C., 1986-89. Asst. mgr. Eckerd Drug Store, Columbia, S.C., 1988-89; commd. 2d lt. USAF, 1989, promoted to 1st lt., 1991; chief personnel programs 42 MSSQ, Loring AFB, Limestone, Maine, 1989-91, chief customer assistance, 1991—. V.p. Loring AFB Black Heritage Com., 1990-91. Mem. Co. Grade Officers Coun., Alpha Phi Alpha Frat. Inc. Baptist. Home: General Delivery Trenton NJ 08650-9999 Office: 42 Mission Support Squadron Loring AFB ME 04751-3602

DINI, JOSEPH J., aircraft leasing and special projects director; b. Somerville, Mass., Apr. 25, 1941; s. John Paul and Rose C.; m. Teresa C. Dini, Apr. 26, 1964; 1 child, Lisa M. BS in Fin., Northeastern U., 1973; MS in Mgmt., Lesley Coll., 1984. Lic. real estate broker. Br. mgr. Arlington Nat. Bank, Bedford, Mass., 1963-66; fin. and mktg. adminstr. Bankers Leasing, Inc., Boston, 1967-73; v.p. Integrated Resources, Inc., Lexington, Mass., 1973-85; pres. First NH Resources, Inc., Boston, 1985-87; v.p. Airfund Corp., Lexington, Mass., 1987-88; v.p. aircraft DPF Group, Ltd., Waltham, Mass., 1988-92; prin. United Fin. Svcs., 1992; founder Morgaid Corp., 1990; seminar dir. Integrated Resources Equity Mktg., Lexington, Mass., 1984-85; instr. mktg. mgmt., Merrimack Coll., N. Andover, Mass., 1985-87, fin. (masters level) Lesley Coll. Nat. Outreach, Cambridge, Mass., 1987-90. Author: Equipment Leasing, Encyclopedia of Investments 2nd edit., 1990, 2nd edit. update, 1991. Town meeting mem., Lexington, Mass., 1991—; master tchr. Archdiocese of Boston, 1977-86. Mem. Sigma Epsilon Rho. Roman Catholic.

DINIC, CARL JOSEPH, retired finance educator; b. N.Y.C., July 2, 1903; s. Joseph Francis and Anne (Wimmer) D.; m. Evlyn Alcox, June 20, 1931 (dec. June 1983). BS, U. Calif., Berkeley, 1926; MBA, Harvard U., 1930. Exec. asst. Ea. Gas & Fuel Assocs., Boston, 1930-38; asst. mgr. bus. rsch. U.S. Steel Corp., Pitts., 1938-44; exec. asst. to pres. Am. Locomotive Co., N.Y.C., 1944-47; exec. v.p. Gen. Steel Products, N.Y.C., 1961-62; gen. mgmt. cons. Ebasco Svcs., Inc., N.Y.C., 1951-64; asst. prof., asst. dean Adelphi U., Garden City, N.Y., 1964-68, ret., 1968. Author: (case 27766) Domestic Fuels-Atlantic Seaboard, 1939; (financial sect.) N.Y. Times, 1958. Mem. fin. com. Zion Episocpal Ch. Douglaston, N.Y.; 1st v.p. Queens County Grand Juror's Assn., Forest Hills, N.Y. Mem. Newcomen Soc. (life), Harvard Bus. Sch. Club N.Y. (former bd. dirs. and treas.), Harvard Club N.Y.C., Hofstra U. Club. Republican. Home: 262 Ridge Rd Flushing NY 11363-1309

DINKES, MARC, computer company executive, consultant; b. Bklyn., Aug. 3, 1954; s. Philip Dinkes and Natalie (Hollander) Dinkes Pinkowitz; m. Rita Milner, Oct. 27, 1991. BEE, Cooper Union, N.Y.C., 1976; ME in Computer Systems, Rensselaer Poly. Inst., 1977. Mem. tech. staff AT&T Bell Labs., Holmdel, N.J., 1977-84; supr. AT&T Bell Labs., West Long Branch, N.J., 1984-90; dir. systems engring. Laser Recording Systems, Sparta, N.J., 1990; pres. Imaging Solutions, Middletown, N.J., 1991—. Mem. Tau Beta Pi, Eta Kappa Nu. Office: Imaging Solutions 25 Davis Ln Red Bank NJ 07701-5507

DINKINS, DAVID N., mayor; b. Trenton, N.J., July 10, 1927; m. Joyce Burroughs; children: David Jr., Donna. BA in Math., Howard U.; JD, Bklyn. Law Sch. Pvt. practice atty., 1956-75; assemblyman N.Y. State, 1966; pres. Bd. Elections City of N.Y., 1972-73, city clk., 1975-85; pres. borough Manhattan, 1986-89; mayor City of N.Y., 1990—. Served with USMC. Recipient Disting. Svc. award Fedn. Negro Civil Svc. Orgns., Pioneer of Excellence award World Inst. Black Communications, Man of Yr. award Nat. Assn. Negro Bus. and Profl. Women's Clubs, Man of Yr. award Correction Guards Assn. Mem. NAACP, Urban League Greater N.Y., Black-Jewish Coalition, Coun. Black Elected Dems. N.Y. State, Nat. Conf. Black Lawyers. Office: City Hall Office of Mayor New York NY 10007

DINKLAGE, LILLIAN BRANDON, psychologist; b. Filbert, S.C., Oct. 31, 1937; d. Isaac Lonnie and Lillian Emily (Robinson) Brandon; m. Kenneth Taylor Dinklage, June 17, 1966; 1 child, Joshua Brandon. AB, Meredith Coll., Raleigh, N.C., 1960; EdM, Harvard U., 1963, EdD, 1968. Lic. psychologist, Mass., lic. ednl. psychologist, Mass. Tchr. Baldridge Reading Svc., Greenwich, Conn., 1961-62; statis. asst. Ednl. Testing Svc., Princeton, N.J., 1960-63; guidance counselor pub. schs., Newton, Mass., 1963-65; tchr., researcher Harvard U., Cambridge, Mass., 1963-68; psychologist N.H. Children's Aid Soc., Manchester, 1964-66, Mystic Valley Mental Health Assn., Lexington, Mass., 1967-70; psychotherapist Lesley Schs. for Children, Cambridge, 1970-74; psychologist Lexington Pub. Schs., 1973—; pvt. practice Belmont, Mass., 1970—; cons. Peace Corps, Washington, 1968-70. Coauthor: Career Development, 1970. Mem. adv. bd. Early Childhood Com., Lexington, 1986-92. Mem. Am. Psychol. Assn., Nat. Register Health Providers in Psychology, Mass. Psychol. Assn., Mass. Sch. Psychologists Assn. Home: 10 Ivy Rd Belmont MA 02178-3364 Office: Lexington Pub Schs Lexington MA 02173

DINNERSTEIN, LOIS, art historian; b. N.Y.C., Oct. 24, 1932; d. Paul Behrke and Fay (Isbitzer) Blank; m. Harvey Dinnerstein, May 25, 1951; children: Rachel, Michael. BA, NYU, 1953, MA, 1960; PhD, CUNY, 1979. Instr. Vassar Coll., Poughkeepsie, N.Y., 1959-61, Washington Sq. Coll./NYU, N.Y.C., 1964, Bklyn. Coll./CUNY, N.Y.C., 1964, 66-77; rsch. curator Montclair (N.J.) Art Mus., 1975-76; adj. instr. Fashion Inst. Tech.-SUNY, N.Y.C., 1978-80; adj. prof. L.I. U./Bklyn. Ctr., N.Y.C., 1982-85, Coll. New Rochelle, N.Y., 1985; adj. prof. Grad. Sch. Arts and Sci. NYU, N.Y.C., 1988; lectr. Art Students League N.Y., N.Y.C., 1990—; Contbr. essays to arts mags. Rockefeller Found. fellow in Am. art, 1977. Mem. Coll. Art Assn., Assn. Historians Am. Art. Home and Office: 933 President St Brooklyn NY 11215-1603

DINNERSTEIN, SIMON ABRAHAM, artist, educator; b. Bklyn., Feb. 16, 1943; s. Louis and Sarah (Kobilansky) D.; m. Renée Sudler, Aug. 28, 1965; 1 child, Simone. BA, CCNY, 1965; postgrad., Bklyn. Mus. Art Sch., 1964-67, Hochschule für Bildende, Kassel, Fed. Republic Germany, 1970-71. Instr. in fine arts New Sch. Social Rsch., Parson Sch. of Design, N.Y.C., 1975—; adj. lectr. N.Y.C. Tech. Coll., Bklyn., 1979—; vis. prof. Pratt Inst., Bklyn., 1986-87; vis. artist Calhoun Sch., N.Y., 1988-89; lectr. Am. Acad. Rome, 1977-78, USIS, Barcelona and Madrid, Spain, 1979, Pa. State U., 1984, Pt. Washington Pub. Libr., 1990, St. Paul's Sch., Concord, N.H., 1991. One-man shows include Staempfli Gallery, N.Y.C., 1975, 79, 88, Inst. Internat. Edn., 1976-77, 79, Am. Acad. Rome, 1977, Pratt Inst., 1987, New Sch. Social Rsch., 1981, Martin Luther King Labor Ctr., N.Y.C., 1985, St. Paul's Sch., Concord, 1991; subject ofbook The Art of Simon Dinnerstein, 1991; included in anthology Drawing from Life, 1992. Recipient Ingram Merrill Found. award for painting, 1978-79, Cannon prize NAD, 1988, Childe Hassam purchase award Am. Acad. Arts and Letters, 1976, 77, 78; recipient fellowships Fulbright Found., 1970-71, Am. Acad. in Rome, 1976-78, Louis Comfort Tiffany Found., 1976, N.Y. Found. for Arts, 1987. Mem. NAD, Soc.

Fellows Am. Acad. Rome. Democrat. Jewish. Home and Office: 415 1st St Brooklyn NY 11215-2507

DINNIMAN, ANDREW ERIC, county commissioner, history educator, academic program director; b. New Haven, Oct. 10, 1944; s. Harold and Edith (Stephson) D.; m. Margo Portnoy, June 8, 1969; 1 dau., Alexis. BA, U. Conn., 1966; MA, U. Md., 1969; EdD, Pa. State U., 1978. Student pers. worker U. Md., 1969-71, U. Denver, 1971-72; prof. history West Chester (Pa.) State U., 1972—; dir. Ctr. for Internat. Programs, 1986—; commissioner Chester County, 1992—. Chmn. Chester County Dem. Com., 1979-85; mem. Pa. Dem. State Com., 1982-89, mem. exec. com., 1984-89; chmn. Eastern Pa. Dem. County Chmn. Assn., 1982-85; mem. Dem. Nat. Com., 1984-89; pres. Pa. Coun. on Internat. Edn., 1989-91; v.p. Downington Area (Pa.) Sch. Bd., 1975-79; mem. Central Chester County Vocat.-Tech. Sch. Bd., 1978-79; mem. Chester County Conservation Dist., 1992—; mem. Pa. State Transp. Adv. Com., 1992—. Recipient Bicentennial award Pa. Sch. Bds. Assn., 1976, Outstanding Acad. Service award Commonwealth Pa., 1977, Human Rights award W. Chester State U. chpt. NAACP, 1980. Mem. Chester County Hist. Soc., Pa. Soc. Jewish. Author: Book of Human Relations Readings, 1980, Education for International Competence in Pennsylvania, 1988; also articles. Home: 467 Spruce Dr Exton PA 19341-2025 Office: Courthouse 2 N High St West Chester PA 19380

DINSMORE, ROBERTA JOAN MAIER, library director; b. Phila., Sept. 30, 1934; d. Bert Faust and Emma Baker (Keen) Maier; m. Ray W. Dinsmore Sr., Oct. 20, 1956; children: Ray Wilson Jr., Jeffrey Maier, Debra Joan, Matthew Bert. BA, Pa. State U., 1956; MLS, Clarion U. Pa., 1990. Proofreader Aluminum Co. Am., Pitts., 1957-60; office mgr. Dinsmore, Lithographer, Punxsutawney, Pa., 1969—; dir. Punxsutawney Meml. Library, 1978—; free-lance writer Greenburg (Pa.) Tribure Rev., 1980-81; adult edn. tchr. Jeff Tech., Reynoldsville, Pa., 1981-82. Head hostess Welcome Wagon Internat., Memphis, 1976-80; ch. librarian Punxsutawney Presbyn. Ch., 1985—, mem. Jefferson County Constitution Com.; tchr. adult discussion class; chairperson numerous orgns. Mem. ALA, Pa. Library Assn., Pa. Citizens for Better Libraries, Clarion Dist. Library Assn. (pres. 1984-86), AAUW (Woman of Yr. 1987), Punxsutawney Area Hist. and Geneol. Soc., Inc. (sec. bd. dirs., charter mem.), Bus. and Profl. Women, Friends of Library, Punxsutawney Area Hosp. Auxiliary, Goschenhoppen Historians. Republican. Presbyterian. Club: Garden (past pres. Punxsutawney chpt.), Irving (past pres.). Lodge: P.E.O. Home: 808 E Mahoning St Punxsutawney PA 15767-2320 Office: Punxsutawney Meml Libr 301 E Mahoning St Punxsutawney PA 15767-2122

DINSTBER, GEORGE CHARLES, construction design engineer, consultant; b. N.Y.C., Jan. 31, 1966; s. George C. and Madelen Anne (Martin) D. Grad. high sch., Brentwood, N.Y. Driller Soil Mechs. Drilling Corp., Seaford, N.Y., 1984-86, Ind. Testing Labs. Inc., College Point, N.Y., 1987-88, Warren George Inc., Jersey City, 1988-89; chief exec. officer, owner Shawnee Falcon Drilling Corp., East Islip, N.Y., 1988—; constrn. insp., engr. Constrn. Techs. Inc., Garden City Park, N.Y., 1989—. Mem. Am. Concrete Industry, Nat. Waterwell Assocs., ASTM (engring. standards com), East Islip C. of C., L.I. Small Bus. Coun. Home and Office: 10 Jefferson St East Islip NY 11730-1808

DINTENFASS, JULIUS, chiropractor; b. Bklyn., Sept. 25, 1910; s. Abraham and Mary (Amsterdam) D.; m. Ruth Keisler, Feb. 26, 1939; children: Ellen Joan Dintenfass Berger, Marylyn Sue Dintenfass, Nancy Dintenfass Gurewitz. BS, Columbia U., 1932; postgrad., U. Heidelberg, Germany, 1932-33, NYU, 1940-41; D in Chiropractic, Eastern Chiropractic Inst., 1936. Pvt. practice chiropractic N.Y.C., 1936—; mem. faculty depts. pathology and kinesiology Chiropractic Inst. N.Y., 1936-56; dir. Chiropractic Bur. Health Care Services N.Y.C. Dept. Health, 1968-76;. Author: Chiropractic - A Modern Way to Health, 1966; editor Sci. Sidelights, 1936-63. Trustee Nat. Coll. Chiropractic, Lombard, Ill.; mayor Village of Woodsburgh, N.Y., 1987-89. Fellow Internat Coll. Chiropractors; mem. Internat. Coll. Applied Nutrition, Am. Met. Dist. (pres. 1978-79), Gerontol. Soc. N.Y. State Bd. Chiropractic Examinres (charter 1963-71, chmn. 1965-66, 69-70), N.Y. State Chiropractic Assn., N.Y. County Chiropractic Assn. (pres. 1978-79), Seawane Club (Hewlett Harbor, N.Y.). Club: Seawane (Hewlett Harbor, N.Y.). Home and Office: 64 Meadow Dr Woodmere NY 11598-2259

DINWIDDIE, HEATHER LEAH, trade association research administrator; b. Wroughton, Eng., Apr. 11, 1953; d. James Fearing and Jacquelyn Ruth (Struble) D.; m. Ernst Alfred Kotzmann, June 5, 1976 (div. June 1983); m. Thomas Kennedy Hill, Mar. 31, 1990. BA, Mt. Holyoke Coll., 1975; M. Music, Acad. of Music, Vienna, Austria, 1983; MBA, SUNY, Binghamton, 1986. Freelance musician Austria, 1975-83; gen. mgr. Peninsula Symphony of Va., Newport News, 1983-84; mgmt. intern Lincoln Ctr. for Performing Arts, N.Y.C., 1986; dir. of rsch. Am. Symphony Orch. League, Washington, 1986—; cons. Binghamton Symphony, 1986; pres. bd. Devco, Inc. Mem. NAFE, Am. Fedn. Musicians, Am. Soc. Assn. Execs.

DION, ARNOLD SILVA, biochemist, educator; b. Laconia, N.H., June 26, 1939; s. Silva Emile and Alberta Aurore (Boucher) D.; m. Charlene Jean Williams, Sept. 25, 1981; children: Tina Marie, Michèle Anne, Arnold Silva II, Sarah Shoshana. BS, U. N.H., 1964, PhD, 1969. Postdoctoral fellow dept. therapeutic rsch. U. Pa., Phila., 1969-71; asst. mem. Inst. for Med. Rsch., Camden, N.J., 1971-72, assoc. mem., 1972-76, head, mem. dept. molecular biology, 1976-86; dir., mem. Inst. Molecular Genetics, Ctr. for Molecular Medicine and Immunology, Newark, 1986—; mem. exptl. immunology study sect. NIH, Bethesda, Md., 1981-84, mem. breast cancer task force Nat. Cancer Inst., 1984-88; adj. prof. dept. microbiology and Immunology N.Y. Med. Coll., Valhalla, 1989—. Rsch. grantee Nat. Cancer Inst., NIH, 1978, 80, 81, 86. Mem. Am. Chem. Soc., Am. Assn. for Cancer Rsch., N.Y. Acad. Scis., Sigma Xi. Office: Ctr Molecular Medicine and Immunology 1 Bruce St Newark NJ 07103-2709

DIONNE, JOSEPH LEWIS, publishing company executive; b. Montgomery, Ala., June 29, 1933; s. Antonio Ernest Joseph and Myrtle Mae (Armstrong) D.; m. Joan F. Durand, June 12, 1954; children: Marsha Joan Dionne Guerin, Gary Joseph, Darren Durand. B.A., Hofstra U., 1955, M.S., 1957; Ed.D., Columbia U., 1965. Guidance counselor L.I. Public Schs., 1956-61; asst. prof. Hofstra U., Hempstead, N.Y., 1962-63; dir. instrn., project dir. Ford Found. Sch. Improvement grant Brentwood (N.Y.) Pub. Schs., 1963-66; v.p. research and devel. Ednl. Developmental Labs., Huntington, N.Y., 1966-68; v.p., gen. mgr. CTB/McGraw-Hill, Monterey, Calif., 1968-73; sr. v.p. corp. planning McGraw-Hill, Inc., N.Y.C., 1973-77, exec. v.p. ops., 1979-81; pres. McGraw-Hill Info. Systems Co., N.Y.C., 1977-79; pres. McGraw Hill, Inc., N.Y.C., 1981—, chief exec. officer, 1983, chairman, 1988—; bd. dirs. Equitable Life Ins. Co. Am., Sprint., Harris Corp. Elder Presbyn. Ch. New Canaan; past pres. Soc. To Advance Retarded; past chmn. bd. trustees Hofstra U. 2d lt. U.S. Army, 1955-56. Mem. Phi Alpha Theta, Kappa Delta Pi, Phi Delta Kappa. Clubs: Woodway Country (Darien, Conn.), Blind Brook Club, Inc. (Purchase, N.Y.). Office: McGraw-Hill Inc 1221 Ave Of The Americas New York NY 10020-1001

DIORIO, MARY ANN LUCIA, writer, business owner; b. Norristown, Pa., Nov. 11, 1945; d. Augustus Joseph and Vincenza Concetta (Addevico) Genova; m. Dominic Anthony Diorio, Oct. 25, 1969; children: Lia Cristina, Gina Luciana. BA, Immaculata (Pa.) Coll., 1967; MA, Middlebury (Vt.) Coll., 1968; MPh, U. Kans., 1974, PhD, 1977. Instr. in Italian U. Kans., Lawrence, 1970-71; instr. in French and Italian Cumberland County Coll., Vineland, N.J., 1973-75; supr. in English and fgn. langs. Fairton (N.J.) Christian Ctr. Acad., 1979-83; co-owner, chmn. JDM Internat., Millville, N.J., 1979—; owner, pres. Daystar Communications, Millville, 1984—. Author: Selling Yourself on You, 1989, Dating Etiquette For Christian Teens, 1984, Balancing Your Budget God's Way, 1987. Mem. Soc. N.J. Artists, Christian Writers Guild, Christian Writers Fellowship Internat., Nat. Writers Club, Writers Info. Network, St. Davids Christian Writers Assn., N.J. Soc. Christian Writers (founder, dir.), Greater Phila. Christian Writers Fellowship. Republican. Office: Daystar Communications PO Box 748 Millville NJ 08332-0748

DI PAOLA, ROBERT ARNOLD, mathematics and computer science educator; b. N.Y.C., Nov. 28, 1933; s. Anthony and Lucy Philomena (Parente) Di P. BS, Fordham U., 1956, MA, 1959; PhD, Yeshiva U., 1964. Mathematician Grumman Aircraft Corp., Bethpage, N.Y., 1957-59; asst. prof. UCLA, 1964-66; mathematician The Rand Corp., Santa Monica, Calif., 1966-72; prof. math. and computer sci. CUNY, 1975—; vis. prof. U. Siena, 1976-77, 84, 85, 89, U. Oxford, Eng., 1989; cons. in field; mem. coun., Sch. Specialization in Math. Logic, U. Siena, Italy. Contbr. rsch. papers to math. jours. Grantee, NSF, 1982-85, 85—. Mem. Am. Math. Soc., Assn. Symbolic Logic. Republican. Roman Catholic. Office: Grad Sch Univ Ctr 33 W 42d St New York NY 10036

DI PAOLO, JOSEPH AMADEO, geneticist; b. Bridgeport, Conn., June 13, 1924; s. John Anthony and Nancy (Montagano) Di P.; m. Arleta Mae Schrieb, June 14, 1952; children: Nancy, John. BA, Wesleyan U., 1948; MS, Western Res. U., 1949; PhD, Northwestern U., 1951; MD (hon.), U. Cagliari, Italy, 1991. Instr. genetics bacteriology dept. biology Loyola U., Chgo., Il., 1951-53; instr. clin. and exptl. pathology Northwestern U. Med. Sch., Chgo., 1953-55; sr. cancer research scientist Roswell Park Meml. Inst., Buffalo, 1955-63; research pharmacologist, cell biologist biology br., div. chem. and phys. carcinogenesis program Nat. Cancer Inst., Bethesda, Md., 1963-76, chief lab. biology, div. cancer etiology, 1976—; assoc. prof. lectr. anatomy George Washington U., Washington, 1973—; chmn. U.S.-Germany Cancer Program Area for Environ. Carcinogenesis, 1979-86, U.S.-USSR Mammalian Sometic Cell Genetics Related to Neoplesic Program, 1973-76. Editor, co-author: Chemical Carcinogenesis, 1974; assoc. editor: Jour. of Nat. Cancer Inst., 1968-71, Cancer Rsch., 1970-78, Teratogenesis, Carcinogenesis, Mutagenesis, 1982-92; editorial acad. Internat. Jour. Oncology, 1992—. Served with USN, 1943-46. Fellow N.Y. Acad. Sci., AAAS; mem. Am. Assn. Cancer Rsch. (bd. dirs. 1983-86), Am. Soc. Human Genetics, Am. Soc. Exptl. Pathology, Genetics Soc. Am., Teratology Soc., Hamster Soc., Tissue Culture Assn., Am. Assn. Pathology, European Assn. for Cancer Rsch., Sigma Xi. Home: 6605 Melody Ln Bethesda MD 20817-3154 Office: Nat Cancer Inst Bldg 37-2A-19 Rockville Pike Bethesda MD 20892

DI PASQUALE, EMANUEL PAUL, poet, English language and literature educator; b. Sicily, Ragusa, Italy, Jan. 25, 1943; came to U.S., 1957; s. Serafino and Giuseppa (Scannavino) Di P.; (div. 1991); children: Paul, Laura. BA, Adelphi U., 1965; MA, NYU, 1966. Instr. Elizabeth (N.C.) City State U., 1966-68; asst. prof. English Middlesex County Coll., Edison, N.J., 1968—. Author: The Dynamics of Student Writing, 1984, Genesis, 1989. Home: 392 Ocean Ave # 1gs Long Branch NJ 07740-5753 Office: Middlesex County Coll Edison NJ 08818

DI PASQUALE, GENE, biomedical researcher; b. N.Y.C., July 17, 1932; s. Emidio and Maria (De Gennaro) Di P.; m. Anita Famiglietti, Sept. 7, 1962; children: Lora, Dean. BS, Iona Coll., 1954; MS, Long Island U., 1960; PhD, NYU, 1970. From scientist to assoc. dir. Warner Lambert Rsch. Inst., Morris Plains, N.J., 1957-77; mgr. immuno-pharmacology I.C.I. Am. Pharm., Wilmington, Del., 1977-89; dir. osteoarthritis, inflammation CIBA-GEIGY Pharm., Summit, N.J., 1989—. Contbr. numerous articles to profl. jours. With U.S. Army, 1954-56. Recipient Founders Day award, N.Y.U. Mem. Am. Soc. Eptl. Pharmacology and Therapy, Am. Physical Soc., Am. Endocrine Soc., Soc. Exptl. Biology and Medicine. Home: 39 Running Brook Rd Glen Mills PA 19342-1218

DIPERNA, KAREN ANN, insurance underwriter; b. Malden, Mass., Jan. 11, 1956; d. Roland H. Schnaitmann and Dorothy A. (Veerman) Magras; m. David C. DiPerna, July 8, 1989; stepchildren: Christine, Kathleen. AA, Fisher Jr. Coll., Boston, 1976; BA, U. Mass., 1981. CPCU. Sr. underwriting technician Peerless Ins., Woburn, Mass., 1981-84; account mgr. Sedgwick James, Boston, 1984-87; sr. underwriter Am. Internat. Co., Boston, 1987—. Mem. Phi Theta Kappa. Home: 119 Drake Rd Burlington MA 01803-1841 Office: Am Internat Co 101 Federal St Boston MA 02110-1800

DI PLACIDO, JOSEPH MARTIN, safety engineer; b. Eddystone, Pa., Mar. 10, 1957; s. Frank Paul and Elizabeth (De Maria) Di P.; m. Eileen Carr, Oct. 27, 1990; 1 child, Elizabeth Maria. AAS in Fire Protection, Del. Tech. Coll., 1979; BS in Indsl. Safety, U. Md., 1984; MS in Pub. Safety, St. Joseph's U., Phila., 1991. Cert. safety profl. Campus safety officer Widener U., Chester, Pa., 1977-79; loss control rep. Transam. Ins. Group, Pitts., 1979-82; firefighter Greenbelt (Md.) Fire Dept., 1982-85; coord. safety and tng. Del. Adminstrn. for Reg. Transit, Wilmington, 1985-87; occupational safety officer Southeastern Pa. Transp. Authority, Phila., 1987—. Editor newsletter System Safety Scene. Capt. Hanley Hose Co. 1, Chester, 1975—; mem. Fairview Vol. Fire Co., South Fayette, Pa., 1980-83; coach wrestling St. James High Sch., Chester, 1983-88. Named Greenbelt Fire Dept., 1984. Mem. Am. Soc. Safety Engrs. (profl.), Am. Indsl. Hygiene Assn. (assoc.), Am. Conf. Govt. Indsl. Hygienists (assoc.), Am. Pub. Transit Assn., Pa. Fireman's Assn., U. Md. Alumni Assn. (life). Republican. Roman Catholic. Home: 7301 Union Ct North Wales PA 19454-3764 Office: Southeastern Pa Transp Authority-System Safety Philadelphia PA 19107

DIPOLVERE, EDWARD JOHN, environmental protection administrator; b. Phila., Nov. 22, 1929; s. Michael and Philomena (DeLorenzo) DiP.; m. Lucia Spera, June 27, 1957; children: Mario, Celia. BSME, Drexel U., 1959. Component design engr. GE Space Systems, Phila., 1959-62, subsystem engr., 1965-69; chief design engr. Rockwell Mfg. Co., Hopewell, N.J., 1962-65; project supervising engr. Intertech Corp., Princeton, N.J., 1969-70; sr. environ. engr. N.J. Dept. Environ. Protection, Trenton, 1970-72, chief Office of Noise Control, 1972—; founding pres. Nat. Assn. Noise Control Ofcls., Trenton, 1978-80, adminstr./treas., 1984—, bd. dirs. Contbr. articles to profl. jours. Co-organizer West Windsor Jr. Football League, 1973-78, 81-82; chmn. West Windsor Environ. Commn., 1970-75, 88; supr., chmn. Mercer County Soil Conservation Dist., Trenton, 1979—; pres. N.J. Assn. Conservation Dist., 1991—, Assunpink Environ. Inst., 1992—. Sgt. U.S. Army, 1952-55. Recipient award of merit Goodyear Conservation, 1987, cert. of merit Nat. Environ. Health Assn., 1988, Citizens award West Windsor Twp., 1988. Mem. Acoustical Soc. Am. (pres. Del. Valley chpt. 1980), Inst. Noise Control Engrs. (assoc.), Lions (pres. West Windsor Club 1961—), Masqueraders Square Dance Club (co-pres. 1991—). Roman Catholic. Home: 53 Cubberly Ave Trenton NJ 08690-2019 Office: Nat Assn Noise Control 53 Cubberly Ave Trenton NJ 08690-2019

DIRESTA, JAMES JOHN, podiatrist, podiatric surgeon; b. Methven, Mass., Nov. 3, 1952; s. James Joseph and Michelina A. (Marino) DiR.; m. Susan Patricia Pendergast, May 24, 1974; children: Katharine, Jason, Joseph, Daniel, Paul, Nathanial. AB, Boston Coll., 1974; D of Podiatric Medicine, Pa. Coll. Podiatric Medicine, 1978. Diplomate Am. Bd. Podiatric Surgery. Resident in surgical podiatry Northlake (Ill.) Hosp., 1978-79; pvt. practice Newburyport, Mass., 1979—; mem. staff Amesbury (Mass.) Hosp., Green Leaf Nursing Home, Salesbury, Mass., Anna Jaques Hosp., Newburyport, Brigham Manor Nursing Home, Newburyport, Maplewood Manor Nursing Home, Amesbury. Mem. parish pastoral coun. St. Anne's Ch., Winewbury, Mass., 1988-91. Recipient Samitz award, Pa. Coll. Podiatry Medicine, 1978. Fellow Am. Coll. Foot Surgeons, Am. Assn. Hosp. Podiatrists; mem. Am. Podiatric Med. Assn., Mass. Podiatric Med. Soc., Merrimack Valley Watershed Coun. Republican. Roman Catholic. Office: Forrester St Newburyport MA 01950-1916

DIRIENZO, JOSEPH MICHAEL, microbiologist, researcher; b. Derby, Conn., Sept. 20, 1950; s. Joseph P. and Concetta (Ricciardi) DiR.; m. Sharon Barbara Mills, Aug. 31, 1974; children: Elizabeth Anne, Brian David. BSc, Providence (R.I.) Coll., 1972; PhD, McGill U., 1977. Rsch. assoc. SUNY, Stony Brook, 1976-79; asst. prof. U. Pa., Phila., 1980-86, assoc. prof., 1986—. Mem. editorial rev. bd. Oral Microbiology and Immunology, 1989—; author: (chpt.) Peridontal Disease: Pathogens and Host Immune Responses, 1991; article review Monoclonal Antibodies Against Bacteria, 1986; contbr. articles to profl. jours. Grantee U. Pa., Am. Cancer Soc., NIH. Mem. AAAS, Am. Soc. Microbiology, N.Y. Acad. Sci. Roman Catholic. Home: 515 Shadeland Ave Drexel Hill PA 19026-1419 Office: U Pa Sch Dental Medicine 4001 Spruce St Philadelphia PA 19104-6003

DIRMEIER, MICHAEL DENNIS, management consultant, accountant; b. San Antonio, Aug. 13, 1950; s. Melvin Dennis and Edna Dirmeier; m. Georgia Giddings, Dec. 29, 1971; children: Lisa Marie, Kristen Elizabeth. BS with high honors, Tex. A&M U., 1971; MBA, U. Chgo., 1973. Cert. mgmt. acct. Fin. analyst Bendix Corp., Southfield, Mich., 1974-76; cons. Touche, Ross & Co., N.Y.C., 1976-79; prin. Georgetown Cons. Group, Ridgefield, Conn., 1979—. Vestryman St. John's Episcopal Ch., Passaic, N.J., 1977-78, St. Mark's Episcopal Ch., Mt. Kisco, N.Y., 1983-85, treas., 1987-88. Home: Pine Bridge Rd # 2 Katonah NY 10536-9713 Office: Georgetown Cons Group 456 Main St Ridgefield CT 06877-4593

DI ROBERTO, SAMUEL JOSEPH, accounting educator; b. West Wyoming, Pa., Feb. 26, 1937; s. Alexius and Hedwig (Froncek) Di R.; m. Velma Jean Bertocci, Sept. 6, 1958; children: James, Michael, David. BS in Acctg., King's Coll., Wilkes Barre, Pa., 1958; MS in Acctg., Pa. State U., 1960; MA in Ops. Mgmt., U. Pa., Phila., 1968. CPA, Pa. Acct. H. Weller & Co., CPAs, Jenkintown; assoc. prof. acctg. Pa. State U., Abington; fin. cons. Furlong, Pa.; bd. mem. Pa. State Inst. for Accts., Abington, 1980-90; cons. Amtrack, Inc., 1991. Researcher Manpower Resources for Urban Development, Vols. I and II, 1967. Named Outstanding Educator, Pa. State U., Abington, 1978. Mem. AICPAs, Pa. Inst. CPAs. Democrat. Roman Catholic.

DIRR, PETER J., broadcasting executive, educator; b. N.Y.C., Apr. 12, 1941; s. Peter G. and Marie C. (Haggerty) D.; m. Janice L. Clark, Sept. 19, 1964 (div. Aug. 1974); children: Peter Christopher, Patrice, Matthew; m. Delores E. Finkbiner, July 19, 1980; children: Renee, Andrew. BA in Philosophy, St. Joseph's Sem., 1962; MA in Guidance and Counseling, Fairfield U., 1964; PhD in Communications, NYU, 1970. Tchr. Stepinac High Sch., White Plains, N.Y., 1963-64; edn. instr. Manhattanville Coll., Purchase, N.Y., 1964-67; utilization coord. Sta. WNET-Channel 13, N.Y.C., 1965-69; assoc. dir. rsch. and devel. complex SUNY, Buffalo, 1969-74, coord. of rsch., 1974-77; project mgr., edn. Corp. for Pub. Broadcasting, Washington, 1977-81; assoc. dir. rsch. and planning Annenberg/Corp. for Pub. Broadcasting, Washington, 1981-84, dep. dir., 1984—; rsch. assoc. Am. Ctr. for Studies in Distance Edn., Pa. State U., 1989—; mem. adv. bd. Ctr. for Learning and Telecommunications, Am. Assn. Higher Edn., Washington, 1980-83; mem. media adv. com. Niagara County Community Coll., Saunders, N.Y., 1975-78; ednl. advisor Sta. WNED-Channel 17, Buffalo, 1973-77. Contbr. numerous chpts. to books and articles to profl. jours. Mem. Families Adopting Children Everywhere (FACE), Washington, 1987—. Recipient Exemplary TV Prodn. award N.Y. State Regents, Albany, 1976. Roman Catholic. Office: Corp for Pub Broadcasting 901 E St NW Washington DC 20004-2037

DISALVO, ANTHONY JOSEPH, therapeutic recreation executive; b. N.Y.C., Oct. 1, 1950; s. Joseph and Teresa (Maglia) DiS. BA, CCNY, 1972. Leadership dir. Am. Youth Hostels, N.Y.C., 1974-79; exec. dir., founder Sprout, Inc., N.Y.C., 1979—; dir. travel/leadership Am. Youth Hostels, N.Y.C., 1979-85. Author: Working With the Disabled Outdoors, 1987; founder outdoor program for developmentally disabled, 1979, outdoor program for mentally ill, 1990. Recipient Jefferson award WNYN Fox 5, 1988. Home: 219 Park Ave Hoboken NJ 07030-3743 Office: Sprout Inc 893 Amsterdam Ave New York NY 10025-4403

DI SALVO, JACQUELINE ANNE, English educator; b. Bklyn., Feb. 26, 1943; d. Anthony and Gladys (Sica) Di S. BA, Antioch Coll., 1965; PhD, U. Wis., 1977. Asst. prof. Livingston Coll. Rutgers U., New Brunswick, N.J., 1972-84; assoc. prof. Baruch Coll. and Grad. Ctr., CUNY, N.Y.C., 1984—. Author: War of Titans: Blake's Critique of Milton & the Politics of Religion, 1984; author poetry; contbr. articles to profl. jours. Woodrow Wilson Found. fellow, 1965-66, Danforth Found. fellow, 1967-72; grantee CUNY. Mem. Modern Lang. Assn., Milton Soc., The Grail. Office: CUNY Baruch Coll 17 Lexington Ave New York NY 10010-5526

DISALVO, JOANNE P., recruitment coordinator; b. Warefield, R.I., May 30; d. Ralph F. and Mary Nancy (Feraco) DiS. BS, Northeastern U., 1978; MEd, Harvard U., 1987. Ednl. coord. Action/Vista, Somerville, Mass., 1974-75; head tchr., ednl. coord. Challenge Detention Ctr., Mattapan, Mass., 1978-79; tchr. Mass. Correctional Instn., Concord, Mass., 1979-80; recruitment coord., admissions asst. Harvard Law Sch., Cambridge, Mass., 1980—. Composer of folk songs; composer of musical including Believe in Yourself, 1987. Dir. music program for children's liturgy St. Paul's Cath. Ch., Cambridge, 1986-91; musician, vol. Children's Hosp., Boston, 1982—. Office: Harvard Law Admissions Cambridge MA 02138

DISANDRO, EDMOND A., lawyer; b. Providence, Aug. 9, 1932; s. Nicandro and Adeline (Mascio) DiS.; 2 children. A.B. magna cum laude, Providence Coll., 1955; J.D., Boston U., 1960. Bar: R.I. 1960, U.S. Dist. Ct. R.I. 1961, U.S. Ct. Appeals (1st cir.) 1980. Assoc., Goldberg & Goldberg, 1960-61; sr. assoc. Kiernan, Connors, and Kenyon, 1961-64; mng. ptnr. Coia, Hirsh and DiSandro, 1964-66, DeSimone, Sammartino and DiSandro, 1966-70; sr. assoc. DiSandro, Assocs., 1970-80; mng. ptnr. DiSandro-Smith & Assocs., P.C., Inc., Providence, 1980—; lectr. in field. Exec. dir. Smithfield (R.I.) Indsl. Devel. Commn., 1969-70; chmn. Smithfield Democratic Town Com., 1970-71; bd. dirs. R.I. Legal Services, Inc., 1971-73. Mem. ABA, Assn. Trial Lawyers Am. (treas. R.I. chpt. 1968-69), R.I. Trial Lawyers Assn. (v.p. 1979-81, bd. govs. 1991—), Am. Judicature Soc., New Eng. Bar Assn., Fed. Bar Assn.; fellow R.I. Bar Assn. (ho. dels. 1979-83). Home: 6 Birch Rd Greenville RI 02828-2602 Office: DiSandro Smith & Assocs PC Inc 155 S Main St Providence RI 02903-2963

DISHEROON, FRED RUSSELL, lawyer; b. Hot Springs, Ark., Nov. 21, 1931; s. Andrew Russell and Ruth Fayrene (Bearden) D.; m. Laurel Joan Picou, Apr. 1, 1961 (div. Dec. 1977); children: Terri Suzanne, John Frederick; m. Diane L. Donley, Apr. 8, 1989. AB, Hendrix Coll., 1953; JD, So. Meth. U., 1956; LLM in Environ. Law, George Washington U., 1976. Bar: Tex. 1956, U.S. Ct. Appeals (1st, 5th, 6th, 8th, 9th, 10th, 11th D.C. and fed. cirs.), U.S. Supreme Ct. 1964, Va. 1974. Atty. Superior Ins. Co., Dallas, 1960-64; claims atty. Sentry Ins. Co., Dallas, 1964-67; litigation counsel Stigall, Maxfield & Collier, Dallas, 1967-69; sole practice Dallas, 1969-70; asst. gen. counsel for litigation C.E. U.S. Army, Washington, 1970-75; spl. litigation counsel Dept. Justice, Washington, 1975—; instr. environ. law U. Ala.-Huntsville, 1979-82; lectr. law George Washington U., 1981-86; vis. rsch. specialist U. Calif., Davis, 1990. Editor Southwestern Law Jour., 1955-56. Col. JAGC, USAR. Recipient numerous outstanding performance awrds U.S. Army, Dept. Justice, Sr. Exec. Svc. meritorious award Dept. Justice, 1984, Outstanding Civilian Svc. medal Dept. Army. Mem. Sr. Execs. Assn., Res. Officers Assn. Home: 3508 Riverwood Rd Alexandria VA 22309-2720 Office: Dept Justice Environment and Natural Resources Div 601 Pennsylvania Ave NW Rm 5602 Washington DC 20530

DISTASO, STEPHEN ANTHONY, environmental consultant; b. Jersey City, NJ, Oct. 5, 1956; s. Anthony Leo and Rose (Monto) DiS.; m. Jacqueline Rachel Esposito, Oct. 6, 1990. BS, Rutgers U., 1978. Health inspector Woodbridge (N.J.) Twp. Health Dept., 1978-86; sr. project mgr. TRC Environ. Cons. Inc., Somerset, N.J., 1986-88; v.p. MDL Consulting Group Inc., East Windsor, N.J., 1988—. Mem. Natural Resources Defense Coun., Air & Waste Mgmt. Assn. Office: MDL Consulting Group Inc 614 US Rte 130 PO Box 1319 East Windsor NJ 08520

DITCHEK, BRIAN MICHAEL, materials scientist; b. N.Y.C., Jan. 31, 1951; s. Leon H. and Libby (Rimland) D.; m. Judith S. Licht, July 3, 1975; children: Jacob Samuel, Sharon Emily. B in Engring., SUNY, Stony Brook, 1973; PhD, Northwestern U., 1977. NRC postdoctoral fellow Nat. Bur. Standards, Gaithersburg, Md., 1977-78; rsch. scientist Martin Marietta Labs., Balt., 1978-81; mem. tech. staff GTE Labs., Inc., Waltham, Mass., 1981-88, mgr. electronic materials, 1988—; prin. investigator NASA, 1988—, Office Naval Rsch., 1986—, Office Sci. Rsch., USAF, 1985-87. Contbr. articles to profl. jours.; patentee in field. Mem. Materials Rsch. Soc., Metall. Soc., Am. Assn. Crystal Growth, Am. Ceramic Soc. Office: GTE Labs 40 Sylvan Rd Waltham MA 02154-1168

DITULLO, MICHAEL JOSEPH, economic development company executive; b. Poughkeepsie, N.Y., Aug. 23, 1952; s. Michael Salvatore and Carmela Marie (Catanzaro) DiT.; m. Joan Marie LaFalce; children: Michael, Matthew. Student, Dutchess Community Coll., Poughkeepsie, 1972, SUNY, New Paltz, 1988. Pres., chief exec. officer Main Mall Markets, Inc., Poughkeepsie, 1973-80, Bus. Cons., Inc., Poughkeepsie, 1980-84; econ. devel. specialist Dutchess County Econ. Devel. Corp., Poughkeepsie, 1984-86; pres.,

chief exec. officer Orange County Partnership, Goshen, N.Y., 1986—; bd. dirs. Mid Hudson Patterns, Newburgh, N.Y. Contbr. bus. and econ. devel. articles to profl. jours. Bd. dirs. Orange County Community Coll., Middletown, N.Y., 1988—, Hudson Valley Tech. Ctr., New Paltz, 1989—, Inst. Bus. and Industries, Middletown, 1986—; mem. exec. bd. Boy Scouts Am., Hudson-Del. coun., Middletown, 1989; mgr. Little League, Poughkeepsie, 1980-87; basketball ofcl. CYO Basketball, Poughkeepsie, 1985-87. Mem. Indsl. Brokers Assn. (dir. 1986—), Hudson Valley Econ. Devel. Assn., N.Y. State Bus. Coun. Republican. Roman Catholic. Home: 4 Crystal Rd Wallkill NY 12589-2908 Office: Orange County Partnership 55 Main St Ste 2 Goshen NY 10924-2105

DIVENUTO, JOHN PAUL, management consultant; b. Newark, Jan. 22, 1940; s. Benjamin John D. and Rita Elizabeth (Yacenda) DiV.; m. Barbara Ann Macchia, June 17, 1967; children: Donna, Gina. BA in Social Sci., Jersey City State Coll., 1965, MA in Edn., 1967. Tchr. Newark Bd. Edn., 1965-67, Union (N.J.) Township Bd. Edn., 1967-68; compensation analyst Thomas J. Lipton, Inc., Englewood Cliffs, N.J., 1968-70; mgmt. cons. Touche, Ross & Co., N.Y.C., 1970-75; dir. human resources Church & Dwight, Inc., Princeton, N.J., 1975-78; chmn., chief exec. officer Deven Internat., Inc., Verona, N.J., 1978—. Bd. dirs. Found. for Free Enterprise, Hackensack, N.J., 1988—. Named Finalist for Entrepreneur of Year, Venture Mag., 1988; recipient commendation Essex County Bd. of Freeholders, N.J., 1988. Mem. Internat. Assn. Exec. Search Cons., Internat. Assn. Corp. and Profl. Recruiters, Inst. Mgmt. Cons., Greater Newark C. of C. (bd. dirs.), Essex County Country Club. Office: Deven Internat Inc 1 Claridge Dr Verona NJ 07044-3050

DIVILIO, LOUIS THOMAS, surgeon; b. Washington, Jan. 14, 1949; s. Francis M. and Mary Sue (Brown) D.; m. Susan P. Divilio (div. Dec. 1986); children: Christopher, Daniel, Franklin. BS, U. Md., 1971; MD, U. Md., Balt., 1975; postgrad., U. Pa., 1991—. Diplomate Am. Bd. Surgery. Surg. resident Med. Coll. Ga., Augusta, 1975-80; pvt. practice Easton, Md., 1980—; chmn. dept. surgery Meml. Hosp., Easton, 1991—; dep. med. examiner Talbot County, Md., 1989—. Fellow Am. Coll. Surgeons, Southeastern Surg. Congress; mem. Am. Med. Assn., Am. Soc. Gastrointestinal Endoscopic Surgeons. Office: Gen and Vascular Surgery 404 Marvel Ct Easton MD 21601

DIWAN, JOYCE JOHNSON, biologist, educator, researcher; b. Bklyn., Dec. 25, 1940; d. John Henry and Lillian Freida (Russ) Johnson; m. Romesh Kumar Diwan, Oct. 25, 1970. AB, Mt. Holyoke Coll., 1962; PhD, U. Ill., Chgo., 1967. Postdoctoral fellow U. Pa. USPHS, Phila., 1966-69; asst. prof. Rensselaer Poly. Inst., Troy, N.Y., 1969-75, assoc. prof., 1975-91, prof., 1991—; vis. fellow U. Warwick, Eng., 1976-77. Editor: Advances In Membrane Biochemistry and Bioenergetics, 1987; mem. editorial bd. Jour. Bioenergetics and Biomembranes, 1991—; contbr. numerous articles to profl. jours. Mem. adv. com. Hudson Valley Community Coll., Troy, 1982—. Recipient rsch. grants NIH, 1974-76, 77-81, 83-87, 88—. Mem. AAAS, AAUP, Am. Soc. Biochemistry and Molecular Biology, Am. Soc. Cell Biology, Assn. Women In Sci., Biophysical Soc., N.Y. Acad. Scis. Democrat. Home: 6 Bolivar Ave Troy NY 12180-7006 Office: Rensselaer Poly Inst Sci Ctr Biology Dept Troy NY 12180-3590

DIXON, ALLEN WALTER, law enforcement officer; b. Paterson, N.J., Oct. 17, 1948; s. Walter William and Ann Katherine (Santo) D.; m. Barbara Jean Refi, Nov. 18, 1969; children: Ian Walker, Jennifer Lynn. BS, Rutgers U., 1980; MA, William Paterson Coll., 1988. Export document specialist Gen. Foods Corp., Clifton, N.J., 1970-73; police patrol officer Parsippany (N.J.)-Troy Hills Police Dept., 1973-80, police detective, 1980-82, police sgt., 1982-87, police lt., 1987-88, police capt., 1988—; emergency response team commdr. Parsippany Police Dept., 1987-89. With U.S. Army, 1966-69. Mem. Superior Officers Assn., Policemen's Benevolent Assn. (local 131 v.p. 1982). Office: Parsippany Police Dept 3339 Rte 46 Parsippany NJ 07054

DIXON, ANDREW DOUGLAS, real estate investment executive; b. Ithaca, N.Y., Nov. 18, 1958; s. Kenneth Earl and Helen Carleda (Carlson) D.; m. Debra Sue Montner, June 3, 1984, 1 child, Erik Kenneth. BS, Cornell U., 1981. Asst. contr. Houragency, Inc., Ithaca, 1979-81; asst. fin. dir. Stonehenge Capital Corp., N.Y.C., 1981-83; syndication analyst, asset mgr. The Patrician Group, Inc., N.Y.C., 1983-85; sr. investment analyst fin. and systems The ITD Group, Inc., Stamford, Conn., 1985-89; sr. investment analyst Retirement Ctrs. Network, Inc., Stamford, 1985-89; pres. A.D. Dixon & Co., Norwalk, 1988—; ptnr. DeChelly Assocs., Tenafly, N.J., 1989—; dir. of adminstrn. Weg and Myers, N.Y.C., 1990—. Contbr. articles to profl. jours. Active Small Bus. Coun. Tompkins County, Ithaca, 1980. Mem. Tompkins County C. of C., Stamford C. of C., Cornell Club of Fairfield County (v.p.). Office: Federal Plz 52 Duane St New York NY 10007-1207

DIXON, ANDREW LEE, JR., cable TV company executive, lawyer; b. Pitts., Apr. 9, 1942; s. Andrew Lee and Dorothy (McCullough) D.; B.S. in Microbiology, Howard U., 1968; M.B.A., Case Western U., 1973; J.D., Suffolk U. Law Sch., 1981; m. Jerline Shaw, Oct. 5, 1968; children—Andrew Lee, Chad Leonard. Microbiologist, lab. supr. Calgon Corp., Pitts., 1968-70; personnel mgr., mgr. adminstrn. dept. Polytech, Inc., Cleve., 1970-76, v.p. adminstrn. ECO-Labs., Inc., 1973-76; corp. compensation mgr., sr. personnel mgr. Arthur D. Little Inc., Cambridge, Mass., 1976-82; sr. v.p. human resources Continental Cablevision, Inc., Boston, 1982—; instr. minority contractors program Cleve. State U., 1963-76. Chmn. bd. dirs. SE Com. Center for Human Services, Cleve., 1968-70; bd. dirs. Program to Aid Citizens Enterprise, Pitts., 1972-76; scoutmaster Nat. Capital Area coun. Boy Scouts Am., 1968-70. Mem. Am. Compensation Assn. (dir. 1979-83, Contbn. to Mgmt. Edn. award 1978, 81; cert.), New Eng. Compensation Assn. (founder 1980-83), New Eng. Soc. Human Resources Mgmt. (v.p., dir. 1983), Nat. Cable TV Assn., Nat. Assn. Minorities in Cable, Boston Indsl. Rels. Rsch. Assn., Alpha Phi Alpha. Contbr. articles to profl. jours. Office: Continental Cablevision Pilot House Lewis Wharf Boston MA 02110

DIXON, ANTHONY, lawyer, banker; b. Hazleton, Pa., July 30, 1947; s. Leon R. and Margaret M. (DeCusatis) D.; m. Kathleen A. O'Donnell, Dec. 28, 1968; children: Amanda, Tara. BSChemE, Lehigh U., 1969; JD, Templeton U., 1974. Process engr. Sun Oil Co., Phila., 1969-71, patent agt., 1971-74, patent atty., 1974; sole practice West Hazleton, Pa., 1974-91; pres. Greater Pa. Savs. Assn., Hazleton, 1984-90; sr. v.p., chief operating officer Am. Savs. Bank, Hazleton, 1990—. Mem. ABA, Pa. Bar Assn., Luzerne County Law and Library Assn., Hazleton Rotary. Democrat. Roman Catholic. Home: 661 Irving St Hazleton PA 18201-1509 Office: 120 E Broad St Hazleton PA 18201-6531

DIXON, ARMENDIA PIERCE, education educator; b. Laurel, Miss., July 15, 1937; d. L.E. and Denothras (Pickens) Pierce; m. Harrison D. Dixon Jr., Aug. 28, 1971; 1 child, Harrison D. III. BS in Edn., Jackson (Miss.) State U., 1960; postgrad., No. Ill. State U., 1965-66; MEd, Edinboro (Pa.) U., 1978; postgrad., Kent State U., 1991. Cert. English and secondary edn., Miss. Tchr. English, libr. Laurel City Schs., 1962-67; tchr. English, dir. summer pre-sch. Erie (Pa.) Pub. Schs., 1967-72; tchr. English, drama, journalism, forensic coach Crawford Cen. Schs., Meadville, Pa., 1972-85, asst. prin., facilitator sch. improvement coun., 1985-89, coord. succesful student partnership, 1988—; adj. asst. prof. Kent State U., 1990—; exec. dir. Meadville Latch-Key Program, 1985—; coord. Urban Tchrs. Project, Kent State U., adj. asst. prof., 1989—, dir. Prospective Tchrs.' Program for Phi Delta Kappa; charter mem. Results chpt., Kent State U., 1990. Fundraiser Cystic Fibrosis Found., Pitts., 1976. 79, 81, Sickle Cell Anemia, Erie, 1978-83; pres. Martin Luther King Jr. Scholarship Fund, Inc., 1979-89. Mem. NAACP (pres. Meadville chpt. 1984—), Nat. Assn. Secondary Sch. Prins., Pa. Assn. Secondary Sch. Prins., Order Eastern Star (worthy matron), Navy Mothers, Rainbow Ill, Burres, Phi Delta Kappa, Alpha Kappa Alpha. Methodist. Home: 716 Jefferson St Meadville PA 16335-2205 Office: Crawford Cen Schs 847 N Main St Meadville PA 16335-2690

DIXON, ELIZABETH GRUSE, designer; b. Pitts., Dec. 23, 1927; d. William Arthur and Teresa (Densmore) Gruse; children: Jai, Amalya, Om. AB, U. Chgo., 1950. Free lance design Z Design Ltd., Chgo., N.Y., Washington, 1950-74; dir. publs. Woodrow Wilson Internat. Ctr. for Scholars/Smithsonian, Washington, 1974-89; free lance design Z Design Ltd., Washington, R.I., 1989—. Designer: The Wilson Quar. Mag., 1976-80, Books for Oxford U. Press and Yale Univ. Press, 1985-89. Bd. dirs. Women's Nat. Book Assn., Washington, 1978-80; mem. Washington Book Publishers, 1976—; bd. mem. Casa Del Libros, PR, 1991—. Home and Office: 90 Main St Wickford RI 02852

DIXON, KELVIN NORMAN, naval officer, mechanical engineer; b. Tampa, Fla., Jan. 6, 1959; s. Norman Roosevelt and Rosalie Register (Armwood) D.; m. Monica Ellan Lewis, Feb. 13, 1984. BSME, Prairie View A&M U., 198l. Registered profl. engr. Commd. ens. USN, 1981, advanced through grades to lt., 1985; safety magr., weapons analyst Shore Intermediate Maintenance Activity Nav. Rsc. Facility, Newport, R.I., 1986—; workplace monitor SIMI NRMF, Newport, R.I., 1987—; Laser analyst Dept. Navy, Washington, 1986-87; asbestos control analyst Harvard U. Sch. Medicine, 1989. Tutor Lit. Guild, Newport, 1987—; CPR instr. Am. Heart Assn., Providence, 1987—; EMT Newport Hosp., 1988—; mem. basic disaster com. ARC, Newport, 1989—; Desert Storm/UN ops. officer, 1991. Mem. S.E. New Eng. Field Fed. Safety and Health Coun. (vice chmn. 1988—), Newport Flight Club. Democrat. Roman Catholic. Home: 11795 Bayfield Ct PO Box 2384 Reston VA 22090-0384 Office: SIMA NRMF Bldg 68 Pier II NETC Newport RI 02841

DIXON, LAWRENCE PAUL, insurance company executive; b. N.Y.C., Oct. 23, 1938; s. Clinton DeForge and Frances Margaret (Van Deusen) D.; m. Barbara Carell, June 18, 1960; children: Laurie Jean, Gregory, Linda, Kenneth; m. Zelen Wilde, July 3, 1981. BA, Forham U., 1960. Lic. captain. Sr. underwriting officer Chubb & Son, Inc., Short Hills, N.J., 1960-73; sr. v.p. Contractors Coverage Corp., Great Neck, N.Y., 1973-76; v.p., ptnr. Global Planning Corp., Great Neck, 1976-78; pres. Dixon Brokerage, Inc., Melville, N.Y., 1978—, Ledd Co., Inc., Melville, 1987—; bd. dirs. Ebony Internat.; pres. Tiburn Svcs., Ltd., Melville. Mem. U.S. Congl. Adv. bd., mem. The Pres.'s Com., Rep. Presdl. Task Force, Rep. Nat. State Elections Com., Am. Security Council Found.; pres. Fathers Club LaSalle Mil. Acad., chmn. Beef-o-Rama, 1982; trustee U.S. Merchant Marine Acad. Mem. Profl. Ins. Agts., Ind. Ins. Agts., Am. Subcontractors Assn., Subcontractors Trade Assn., Assn. Gen. Contractors, Advancement Commerce and Industry, Old Chester Hills Civic Assn., Gen. Contractors Assn., Northport Yacht Club, Drug & Chem. Club, Huntington Yacht Club, Green Turtle Yacht Club, North Palm Beach Yacht, Club, Familiares Club (bd. dirs.), Ducks Unltd. Club. (sponsor). Home: 35 Bunker Hill Rd Huntington NY 11743-5705 Office: 150 Broadhollow Rd Melville NY 11747

DIXON, ROBERT F., telecommunications executive; b. Newport, R.I., July 5, 1948; s. Robert and Helen (Dowd) D. BFA, R.I. Sch. Design, 1970, BArch, 1971. Intern architect State of Conn., Hartford, 1971-72, engring. asst., 1972-73, mgmt. analyst I, 1973-75, mgmt. analyst II, 1975-78, mgmt. analyst assoc., 1978-80; prin. analyst telecommunications Office of the Comptroller, Hartford, 1980-83, dir. telecommunications div., 1983-89; dir. telecommunications Office of Info. and Tech., Hartford, 1989—. Trustee, mem. exec. com. R.I. Sch. Design, Providence, 1989—; dir. Rope Ferry Commons, a part of the Jordan Village Historic Dist., Waterford, 1987—. Mem. R.I. Sch. Design Alumni Assn. (pres. 1989-91), Coun. of State Govts. (orgnl. planning and coord. com. 1991—), Nat. Assn. State Telecommunications Dirs. (pres. 1991—), Conn. Telecommunications Assn. (pres. 1985-86). Office: State of Conn Info & Tech 55 Elm St Rm 215 Hartford CT 06106-1773

DIXON, ROSINA BERRY, physician, pharmaceutical development consultant; b. Columbus, Ohio, Dec. 3, 1942; d. Loren C. and Florence H. (Bateson) Berry; m. Richard W. Dixon, July 4, 1970; children: Erica H., Douglas R., Andrew D. BA in Chemistry, Radcliffe Coll., 1964; MD, Columbia U., 1968. Diplomate Am. Bd. Internal Medicine. Sr. assoc. Ciba-Geigy, Summit, N.J., 1972-74; exec. dir. Ciba Geigy Pharm. Div., Summit, 1979-81; dir. Church & Dwight Co., Inc., Princeton, N.J., 1979—; med. dir. Schering Labs., Kenilworth, N.J., 1981-84; v.p. Med. Market Spltys., Boonton, N.J., 1985-86; cons. pharm. devel. Bernardsville, N.J., 1986—; med. dir. Advanced Clin. & Epidemiol. Rsch., Union, N.J., 1990—; instr. in medicine Coll. Physicans and Surgeons, Columbia U., 1972—; preceptor in family practice Overlook Hosp., Summit, 1979—; trustee The Steps at Mendham, N.J., 1991—. Mem. Am. Coll. Clin. Pharmacology, Am. Soc. Clin. Pharmacology and Therapeutics, Nat. Assn. Corp. Dirs. Episcopalian. Home and Office: 43 Old Wood Rd Bernardsville NJ 07924

DIZARD, WILSON PAUL, III, journalist; b. Washington, May 9, 1953; s. Wilson Paul and Lynn Margaret (Wood) D.; m. Avery Spencer Johnson, Apr. 17, 1982; 1 child, Wilson Paul Dizard IV. Student, Brown U., 1970-71, Georgetown U., 1971-80; BS summa cum laude, George Washington U., 1988. Info. analyst Franklin Inst. Rsch. Labs, Washington, 1976-78; rsch. assoc. Cuban Am. Nat. Found., Washington, 1981-83; writer, cons. Washington Post Mag., Washington, 1984-86; editor Pasha Publs. Inc., Arlington, 1986-91, Coal Mag. Maclean-Hunter Press, Washington, 1990—; asst. editor McGraw-Hill Inc., Washington, 1991—. Author: Guide to Demonstrations of Solar Energy, 1976, Castro and the Bankers, 1983, Guide to Market Opportunities, 1990; contbr. articles to profl. jours. Mem. Amnesty Internat., Washington, 1989—. Mem. Nat. Press Club, The Writer's Ctr., Soc. Environ. Journalists. Democrat. Presbyterian. Home: 4225 Jenifer St NW Washington DC 20015 Office: McGraw-Hill Inc 1120 Vermont Ave NW Washington DC 20005

DJANG, ARTHUR H.K., public health administrator, physician, scientist; b. Beijing, Feb. 12, 1925; s. Wei-Fang DJang and Sujen Liu; m. Mary Helen Winston; divorced; children: Phillipp, Douglas, Lincoln, David; m. Tina Marie Barone, July 25, 1983; 1 child, Anna Claire. MD, Harbin (China) Med. U., 1944; MPH, U. Minn., 1951; PhD in Infectious Diseases, UCLA, 1955. Cert. specialist in Clin. Pathology, Anatomic Pathology, Nuclear Med. Chief state epidemiologist, dir. chronic & communicable diseases State Dept. Pub. Health, Santa Fe, 1956-58; pres., dir. Biomedical Sci. Labs., Albuquerque, 1962-74; chmn. dept. pathology & nuclear med. Jamestown (N.Y.) Gen. Hosp., 1975-85; clin. prof. of molecular biology SUNY, Fredonia, 1977-86; pres. Internat. Health Inc., Jamestown, 1987—; med. dir. Medina (N.Y.) Meml. Hosp., 1991—; cons. prof. in pathology N. Mex. State U., University Park, 1963-74; cons. physician NASA White Sands Facility, N. Mex., 1966-74, Medina Meml. Hosp., 1991—; disting. vis. prof. Grad. Sch. Health Scis. Dalian (China) U., 1988—, bd. dirs. Author monographs in field; cons. editor Jour. Gerontology, 1988—; discoverer main ingredients used in disinfectants, 1955. Bd. dirs. Am. Heart Assn., Albuquerque, 1965-75, Am. Cancer Soc., 1965-74, Chautauqua Bd. Health, Mayville, N.Y., 1976-84; coun. mem. SUNY, Fredonia, 1978-86. Named hon. chmn. Scis. Tech. Commn., hon. pres. Yantai Internat. Red Cross Hosp., hon. prof. Dalian Inst. Gerontology, 1988, Harbin Med. U., 1981. Fellow Am. Coll. Pathologists, Am. Coll. Nuclear Med. (chmn. internat. com. 1984-85), Am. Coll. Preventive Med. (mem. by-laws com. 1983-85); mem. AAAS, Am. Coll. Physician Execs., N.Y. Acad. Scis., Sigma Xi. Office: Medina Meml Hosp 200 Ohio St Medina NY 14103

DJEDDAH, RICHARD NISSIM, investment banker; s. Joseph N. and Nelly (Serper) D.; m. Rachel Ruth Baron; 1 child, Esteevered. BS in Physics, CCNY, 1971; MBA, CUNY, 1986, PhD in Fin., 1990. Notary pub., N.Y. Prin., pres. Richard N. Djeddah & Assocs., N.Y.C., 1976—. Author: The Impact of Advertising on Security Prices, 1990. Mem. N.Y. Acad. Scis., Alliance Francaise, Baron Rothschild Golf and Country Club (Caesaria). Republican. Home: 346 Heathcote Rd Scarsdale NY 10583 Office: RN Djeddah & Assocs 4 Park Ave New York NY 10016

D'LAURO, FRANK ANDREW, JR., real estate development executive; b. Phila., Nov. 11, 1940; s. Frank Andrew and Dorothy (Adams) D'L. BA, Washington and Lee U., 1962; MArch, U. Pa., 1965. Architect FKWP, Phila., 1967-68; project mgr., exec. v.p., pres. Frank A. D'Lauro Co., Phila., 1968—; pres. D'Lauro Devel. Corp., Phila., 1974—, D'Lauro Corp., Phila., 1979—. Chmn. Montgomery County Young Rep. Fedn., 1970-72; mem. Montgomery County Rep. Fin. Com., 1972—, Worcester Twp. Planning Commn., 1990—; bd. dirs. Young Reps. of Pa., 1972-74; chmn. Montgomery County Housing Authority, 1976—; bd. dirs., v.p. Big Bros. Assn. Phila., pres., 1972—; bd. dirs. Sacred Heart Hosp., 1980—. Capt. U.S. Army, 1965-67, Vietnam. Decorated Bronze Star with oak leaf cluster, Soldiers medal; recipient award of merit Big Bros. Phila., 1972. Mem. S.R., Sigma Nu. Clubs: Union League, Racquet Philadelphia Cricket (Phila.). Office: 218 E Willow Grove Ave Philadelphia PA 19118-2999

D'LOWER, DEL, manufacturing executive; s. Max and Estere (Gerlatky) D.; m. Helen Fuchs, June 5, 1937 (dec. Mar. 1980); 1 child, Esther Ann. Student, U. Tulsa, 1942-44, New Sch., N.Y.C., 1960-63, 81-82. Cosmetologist, Seligman & Latz, N.Y.C., 1936-41, Del's, Tulsa, 1941-46; beauty salon owner Delby, N.Y.C., 1946-75; greeting card mfr., 1972; diversified bus. exec., pres., chief exec. officer Delby System, N.Y.C., 1975—, personal care products mfr., 1976. Author: Ginny the Pretty White Doe, 1973; composer: High Cheek Bones, 1960, Only the Ashes Remain, The Wedding Waltz, Goodby Diane, 1990; patentee in field. Fellow ASCAP. Jewish. Avocations: creative writing, composing, poems, plays. Office: Delby System 450 7th Ave New York NY 10123-0101

DLUGOFF, MARC ALAN, lawyer; b. N.Y.C., Oct. 6, 1955; s. Arnold M. and Ruth B. (Schnall) D. AB, Colgate U., 1976; JD, Hofstra U., 1980; LLM in Taxation, NYU, 1981. Bar: N.Y. 1981, D.C. 1985, Calif. 1988. Law clk. to presiding justice U.S. Tax Ct., Washington, 1981-83; assoc. Mudge, Rose, Guthrie, Alexander & Ferdon, N.Y.C., 1983-85; assoc. Milbank, Tweed, Hadley & McCloy, N.Y.C., 1985-89, ptnr., 1989—. Fund raiser lawyers div. United Jewish Appeal, N.Y.C. chpt., 1986-88. Charles Dana scholar Colgate U., 1976. Mem. ABA, N.Y. State Bar Assn., Assn. of Bar of City of N.Y., State bar of Calif., Phi Beta Kappa. Jewish. Home: 130 Water St New York NY 10005-1637 Office: Milbank Tweed Hadley & McCloy One Chase Manhattan Plz New York NY 10005

DLUGY, ALEXANDER, engineer, consultant; b. Moscow, Mar. 28, 1941; came to U.S., 1980; s. Josef and Elena (Gorin) C.; m. Inna Lopato, July 23, 1960; children: Gary, Yana. BSME, Poly. Inst., Moscow, 1963, MSME, 1965. Dept. head, researcher, engr. Sci. Rsch. & Mfg. Enterprise of Agrl. Engring., Moscow, 1965-79; staff engr. Stone & Webster Engring., Boston, 1980-82; lead engr. United Tech. Corp., Seabrook, N.H., 1982-86; sr. test engr. Parametric Tech. Corp., Waltham, Mass., 1986-88; chief engr. N.Am. Industries, Everett, Mass., 1988-92; pres. AID Cons. Co., Peabody, Mass., 1989—. Contbr. articles to profl. jours.; patentee agrl. machinery. Republican. Home: 6 Monson Dr Peabody MA 01960-3549

DLUHY, DEBORAH HAIGH, higher education institution dean; b. Summit, N.J., Mar. 4, 1940; d. Richard Hartman Haigh and Elin Frederika Anderson Neumann; m. Robert George Dluhy, June 11, 1962; 1 child, Leonore Alexandra. BA, Wheaton Coll., 1962; postgrad., Boston U., 1962-63, U. Heidelberg, Germany, 1963-65; PhD, Harvard U., 1976. Instr. fine arts Wheaton Coll., Norton, Mass., 1975-76, Radcliffe Coll., Cambridge, Mass., 1977, Boston Coll., Newton, Mass., 1976-77, 78; devel. officer Mus. Fine Arts, Boston, 1978-84, asst. dir. devel., 1984-86; assoc. dean adminstrn. Sch. of Mus. Fine Arts, Boston, 1986-87, dean acad. programs and adminstrn., 1987—. Trustee Wheaton Coll. Norton, Mass., 1988—, Cultural Edn. Collaborative Boston, 1987—; mem. commn. on rsch. Nat. Assn. Schs. Art & Design, Reston, Va., 1990—. woodrow Wilson fellow, 1963. Home: 104 Fletcher Rd Belmont MA 02178-2018 Office: Sch Mus of Fine Arts 230 The Fenway Boston MA 02115

DOAK, KENNETH WORLEY, research consultant; b. Gallatin, Md., Jan. 27, 1916; s. Harry Alexander Doak and Sarah Tarwater; m. Mary Isabel Miller, Aug. 11, 1945; children: Kenneth Alexander, Michael Justin, Janice Anne. AB, Cen. Meth. Coll., 1938; PhD, Johns Hopkin's U., 1942. Rsch. chemist U.S. Rubber Co. (UNIROYAL), Passaic, N.J., 1942-55; rsch. assoc. Koppers Co., Inc., Pitts., 1955-60; asst. dir. plastics Dart Industries, Inc., Paramus, N.J., 1961-65, dir. cen. rsch., 1966-70; mgr. plastics rsch. Arco Polymers, Inc., Monroeville, Pa., 1971-77; tech. advisor Arco Chem. Co., Monroeville, 1978-81; freelance cons. Murrysville, Pa., 1981—. Co-editor: Crystalline Clefin Polymers, 3 vols., 1966; inventor in field; contbr. articles to profl. jours. Warner Nat. fellow Johns Hopkin's U., 1938-42. Home: 3469 Burnett Dr Murrysville PA 15668-1347

DOBBIN, EDMUND J., university administrator; b. Bklyn., 1935. BA in Philosophy, Villanova U., 1958; MA, Augustinian Coll., 1962; DST, U. Louvain, Belgium, 1971. ordained priest Episcopalian Ch., 1962;. Tchr. math. and religion, prefect of students Malvern Prep. Sch., 1962-67; tchr. systematic theology Washington Theol. Union, 1971-87, asst. prof., assoc. prof.; asst. prof., then assoc. prof., faculty mem. Villanova (Pa.) U., 1987—, pres., 1988; guest prof. systematic theology Va. Sch. Theology, Alexandria, fall 1979; vis. prof. grad. summer session course Villanova U., 1973-86. Trustee Villanova U., 1979-87, Merriment Coll., North Andover, Mass., 1971-89, chmn. bd., 1986-89; mem. provincial coun. Augustinian Province of St. Thomas of Villanova, 1982-89. Mem. Am. Acad. Religion, Cath. Theol. Soc. Am. Office: Villanova U Office of President Villanova PA 19085*

DOBBINS, ROBERT NEWTON, technical consulting company executive; b. Verona, N.J., Oct. 18, 1904; s. Justus W. and Caroline E. (Bowen) D.; m. Ruth E. Webster, Aug. 12, 1926; children: Ruth Elizabeth, Robert N. Jr. BSME, Newark Coll. Engring., 1939, postgrad., 1948-51; MEd, Rutgers U., 1947. Registered profl. engr., N.J. Shop supt. Curtiss-Wright Flying Svc., Valley Stream, N.Y., 1929-30; night foreman Am. Airlines, Newark, 1931; sr. tchr. aviation dept. Essex County Vocat. Schs., Bloomfield, N.J., 1931-39; dir. war prodn. tng. Essex County Vocat. Schs., Newark, 1939-42; commd. ensign, naval aviator USN, 1942, commd. lt., naval aviator, 1960, ret., 1964; asst. dir. tng. N.Y. Port Authority, N.Y.C., 1947-51; field cons. Rsch. Inst. Am., N.Y.C., 1951-63; supr. installation Engring. Electronics Command, Ft. Monmouth, N.J., 1963-74; pres. Robert N. Dobbins Assocs., Eatontown, N.J., 1974—; owner, mgr. Automotive & Aircraft Svcs., Verona, N.J., 1931-39; pilot, flight instr. Somerset Hills Airport, Basking Ridge, N.J., 1937-41; tng. officer CAP, Trenton, 1941-42; instr. grad. studies CCNY, 1962-72. Instr. U.S. Power Squadrons, Shrewsbury, N.J., 1960-85; comdr. flotilla 22, USCG Aux., Sandy Hook, N.J., 1965-75; mem. Eatontown Bd. Adjustment, 1968-69; chmn. site and design Eatontown Planning Bd., 1970-73. Mem. NSPE, ASME, AIAA, Soc. Automotive Engrs., Naval Inst., Family Motor Coach Assn., Masons, Shriners. Republican. Presbyterian. Home and Office: 733 Plantation Estates Dr # 412A Matthews NC 28105-6550

DOBBINS, SHARON KAY, ethics educator, lawyer; b. Akron, Ohio, Dec. 10, 1955; d. Richard Dean and Zelda Dolores (Shumate) D.; m. Ramsey Bancroft Alberson, Mar. 3, 1990. MusB summa cum laude, Kent State U., 1982; JD, U. Akron, 1985; M of Theol. Studies, Harvard U., 1987; diploma in Law, Oxford U., 1989. Bar: Ohio 1985. Vis. asst. prof. philosophy and humanities Wesleyan U., Middletown, Conn., 1991, 92; adj. prof. philosophy U. New Haven, West Haven, Conn., 1990, So. Conn. State U., New Haven, Conn., 1990—; atty. Akron, 1985—; bus. ethics cons. Haluch & Assocs., Trumbull, Conn., 1990—. Author (booklet) How to Protect the Children and Keep the Church out of Court, 1988; contbr. articles to profl. jours. Treas. Greater Bridgeport Luth. Ministry Coalition, Bridgeport, Conn., 1992. Mem. ABA, Ohio Bar Assn., Soc. of Law and Medicine. Home and Office: 342 Navajo Loop Huntington CT 02138

DOBBS, WARREN, marketing executive; b. N.Y.C., Oct. 2, 1950; s. Warren and Alice (Creighton) D.; m. Rosemarie Posillico, Aug. 19, 1972; children: Brian, Lauren. BA, Boston U., 1972. Media supr. Cunningham & Walsh, N.Y.C., 1974-76; sr. account exec. Ayer, N.Y.C., 1976-79; v.p., account supr. Foote, Cone & Belding, N.Y.C., 1980-85; exec. v.p., mktg. dir. Simmons Market Rsch. Bur., N.Y.C., 1985—; com. mem. Advt. Rsch. Found., N.Y.C., 1989—. Office: Simmons Market Rsch Bur 380 Madison Ave New York NY 10017-2513

DOBERENZ, ALEXANDER R., nutrition educator, chemist; b. Newark, Aug. 17, 1936; s. Alexander J. and Marie (Zink) D.; m. Angela Rajoppi, June 7, 1958; children: Annamarie, Judith Lynn, Hoke Jr. B.S. in Chemistry, Tusculum Coll., 1958; M.S., U. Ariz., 1960, Ph.D. in Biochemistry and Nutrition, 1963. Research assoc. dept. physics U. Ariz., Tucson, 1963-69; vis. assoc. prof. nutrition U. Hawaii, 1969; assoc. prof. nutritional scis. U. Wis., Green Bay, 1969-71; prof. U. Wis., 1971-76, assoc. dean Coll. and Sch. Profl. Studies, 1969-76, prof. growth and devel., 1975-76; prof. food sci. and human nutrition U. Del., Newark, 1976—; dean Coll. Human Resources U. Del., 1976—, coordinator home econs. research Coll. Agrl. Scis., 1978—; cons. food industry, 1976—; mem. nat. steering com.

new initiatives for home econs. U.S. Dept. Agr., 1979-81, USDA Planning com. Workshops on Improving Health Maintenance, 1984-87. Contbr. numerous articles on food chemistry and nutrition to profl. publs. Head underwater recovery unit Pima County Sheriff's Dept., 1966-68; warrant officer CAP, 1965-69; mem. Brown County Comprehensive Health Planning Council, 1973-76; bd. dirs. Pima County Sheriff's Search and Rescue, 1968. Recipient Research Career Devel. award NIH, 1966-69, Outstanding Educator Am., 1971, 72. Fellow Am. Inst. Chemists; mem. Am. Chem. Soc., Am. Home Econs. Soc., Am. Inst. Nutrition (Mead Johnson award nominating com. 1973-76), Nutrition Soc. Today, Soc. for Nutrition Edn., Nutrition Soc. London Soc. Exptl. Biology and Medicine, Am. Soc. Clin. Nutrition, AAAS, Assn. Adminstrs. of Home Econs., Del. Gerontol. Soc. (exec. com. 1978), Nat. Council Adminstrs. Home Econs. (exec. bd. 1982-83), Am. Pub. Health Assn., Del.-Panama Ptnrs. of Ams., Assn. for Devel. Computer Based Instruction, Del. Acad. Sci., Sigma Xi, Phi Lambda Upsilon., Phi Kappa Phi. Roman Catholic. Clubs: University and Whist. Office: U Del 101 Alison Hall Newark DE 19716

DOBLER, BRUCE GARSIDE, English educator; b. Chgo., June 30, 1939; s. John Martin and Dorris (Curry) D.; m. Patricia Anne Averdick, Dec. 30, 1961; children: Stephanie Anne, Lisa Caitlin. Student, U. Ill., Chgo., 1957-60; BA in English, Roosevelt U., Chgo., 1963; MFA in English, U. Iowa, 1968. Asst. prof. English, Windham Coll., Putney, Va., 1969-71, dir. pub. rels., 1971-73; publs. editor Alyeska Pipeline Svc. Co., Anchorage, 1975; asst. prof. U. Ariz., Tucson, 1976-77, U. Tex., El Paso, 1977-78; assoc. prof. U. Pitts., 1979—; Author: I Made it Myself, 1973, (novels) Icepick, 1974, The Last Rush North, 1976; contbg. editor Pa. Illustrated, 1979, Pitts. mag., 1984-85, 88-91, Pa. Traveller, 1988. Recipient Golden Quill award Pitts. Press Club, 1989; George Bennett fellow Phillips Exeter Acad., 1968-69, rsch. fellow U. Augsburg, Fed. Republic Germany, 1987; grantee Pa. Arts Coun., 1981, 87. Home: 2918 49th St N Saint Petersburg FL 33710-2724 Office: U Pitts English Dept CL-526 Pittsburgh PA 15260

DOBRINSKY, HERBERT COLMAN, university administrator; b. Montreal, Quebec, Can., Apr. 6, 1933; came to U.S., 1962; s. Victor and Lillian D.; m. Dina Loebenberg, Dec., 1954; children—Deborah Kramer, Tova Cohen, Aaron David. B.A., Yeshiva U., 1954, M.S. in Edn., 1959, D. in Edn., 1980; Semikha (rabbinic ordination), Rabbi Isaac Elchanan Theological Sem., Yeshiva U., 1957. Rabbi, Beth Israel Synagogue, Halifax, N.S., Can., 1958-62; assoc dir. div. communal services Yeshiva U., N.Y.C., 1962-73, dir. rabbinic placement, 1964-73, dir. Sephardic community activities program div. of communal service, 1964-80, exec. asst. to pres., 1973-80, v.p. univ. affairs, 1980—. Author: A Treasury of Sephardic Laws and Customs, 1986. Office: Yeshiva U Univ Affairs 500 W 185th St New York NY 10033-3201

DOBROW, HARVEY ROBERT, ophthalmologist; b. N.Y.C., Sept. 19, 1942; s. Benjamin and Eleanor (Rubin) D.; m. Diane Beth Stein, Aug. 24, 1967; children: Lawrence, Julie, Ilyse. Student, Tufts U., 1960-63; MD, SUNY, Bklyn., 1967. Diplomate Am. Bd. Ophthalmology. Intern Montefiore Hosp. Med. Ctr., Bronx, N.Y., 1967-68; resident Manhattan Eye, Ear, Nose, Throat Hosp., N.Y.C., 1968-71; pvt. practice ophthalmology Fair Lawn, N.J., 1973—; sec. Bergen/Passaic Cataract Laser Ctr., Fair Lawn, 1992—; chmn. dept. ophthalmology Barnert Meml. Hosp., Paterson, N.J., 1984-88. Maj., U.S. Army, 1971-73. Fellow ACS, Am. Acad. Ophthalmology; mem. AMA, Med. Soc. Stte N.J., N.J. Soc. Ophthalmology and Otolaryngology. Office: Elmwood Profl Bldg 1215 Broadway Fair Lawn NJ 07410

DOBROW, MARVIN PAUL, sales executive; b. Boston, Dec. 1, 1934; s. Harry Lewis and Rose (Goldman) D.; m. S. Natalie Goldstein, June 26, 1960 (div. 1972); children: Andrew, Lisa, Michael; m. Mindy Carole Lightman, Apr. 9, 1988. BS, Boston U., 1964, MSW, 1966. Advt. sales Fairchild Publication, N.Y.C., 1958-61; dir. Brookline Brighton Newton Jewish Community Ctr., Brighton, Mass., 1961-68; exec. dir. Dorchester (Mass.) House, 1968-71; area dir., planner Commonwealth of Mass. State Dept. Mental Health, Framingham, 1971-76; pres., owner Arlington (Mass.) Real Estate, 1976-79; exec. dir. Blackstone Valley Mental Health Ctr., Hopedale, Mass., 1979-85; comml. estate sales Duana Hills & Co., Boston, 1985-86; v.p. mktg. Century 21 Winnco, Worcester, Mass., 1986-88; mktg. cons. Century 21 of New England, Burlington, Mass., 1988—.

DOBROWOLSKI, KATHLEEN, data processing executive; b. Pitts., July 5, 1954; d. Benedict and Alfreda (Miaczynski) Dobrowolski; m. James R. Monk, June 10, 1974 (div. 1978);1 1 child, James R.; m. Dennis E. Beck, Sept. 1, 1990 (div. 1992). BA in Sociology, LaRoche Coll., Pitts., 1987; MA, U. Pitts., 1987. Contract/cons. computers various orgns., Pa., Tex., 1975-80; programmer Union Nat. Bank, Pitts., 1980-81; sr. programming analyst Beecham Products U.S.A., Pitts., 1981-84; computer contract/cons. Pitts., 1984-85; sr. systems analyst Blue Cross of Western Pa., Pitts., 1985-86; computer contract/cons. Pitts. Bus. Cons., 1986-89; project leader Thrift Drug Co., Pitts., 1989-90; contract cons., instr. KCS Computer Svcs., Inc., Monroeville, Pa., 1990—; owner Coll. Funds Rsch. Ctr., 1992—; adj. instr. Community Coll. Allegheny County, Pitts., 1989—, LaRoche Coll., Pitts., 1989—, Coll. of St. Francis, 1991; owner Coll. Funds Rsch. Ctr., Pitts. With U.S. Army, 1973-75. Recipient Outstanding Achievement award La Roche Coll. Alumni Assn., 1991. Mem. NEFE, Am. Anthropol. Assn. Soc. for Anthropology of Europe, E. European Soc., Nat. Geog. Soc., Nat. Student Anthropologists Soc., Nat. Assn. Practice of Anthropology, Assn. Political & Legal Anthropology, Smithsonian Instn., Nat. Audubon Soc., Nat. Trust Assn., Carnegie Mus., Allegheny County Police Assn., La Roche Coll. Alumni Assn. (Outstanding Achievement award). Democrat. Roman Catholic. Home: 509 Serpentine Dr Pittsburgh PA 15243-2057

DOBSEVAGE, ALVIN PHILIP, language educator, editor; b. N.Y.C., Nov. 29, 1922; s. Solomon Arthur and Bertha Dobsevage; m. Jane Chaney (div. 1968); children: Peter (dec.), Tina, David (dec.), Beth; m. Ruth Maidman; children: Michael, Sarah. BA, CCNY, 1942; MA, Harvard U., 1948; M in Philosophy, Columbia U., 1954; MA in Spanish, Cen. Conn. State U., 1982. Commd. 2d lt. U.S. Army, 1943, advance through grades to lt. col.; instr. philosophy Bklyn. Coll., 1951-53; vice consul U.S. Info. Service, Salisbury, Rhodesia, 1955-58; tchr. Latin Wilton (Conn.) High Sch., 1958-65; prof. French and Latin Western Conn. State U., Danbury, 1965—; estab. sects. for ann. patristic medieval and renaissance papers Augustine Inst. of Villanova U., 1979—; adj. prof. Latin NYU, 1960-68; adj. assoc. instr. philosophy Danbury State Coll., 1962—; lectr. U. Conn., Stamford, 1963-64; bd. dirs. honors program Western Conn. State U., 1989-91. Author: Cerebration, Army, 1961, Existential Values are Humanistic, Jour. of Philosophy, 1963; transl. Horace's "Maecenas Atavis", Classical Outlook, 1973, (play) Whither Education, 1989; editor, pub.: Hermes Americanus Opus Fundatum Academiae Latinae Danburiensis, 1983—, "Logic Occamensis", Soc. Internat. Philosophiae Medievalis, Helsinki, Finland, 1987; presented papers at profl. confs. Decorated Bronze Star. Mem. Am. Philos. Assn., Am. Philol. Assn., Mediaeval Acad. Am., Classical Assn. New Eng., Conn. Classical Assn. (bd. dirs. 1985-88), MLA, Townsend Harris High Sch. Alumni Assn. (bd. dirs. 1984—), CCNY Alumni Varsity Assn. (bd. dirs. 1989—). Home: PO Box 322 Bethel CT 06801-0322 Office: Western Conn State U 181 White St Danbury CT 06810-6885

DOBSON, JAMES GORDON, JR., cardiovascular physiologist, educator; b. Waterbury, Conn., Jan. 23, 1942; s. James Gordon and Mildred (Stinson) D.; m. Susan Jones, Aug. 28, 1971; 1 child, Sarah Bentley. BS, Cen. Conn. State U., 1965; MA, Wesleyan U., Middletown, Conn., 1967; PhD, U. Va., 1971. NIH postdoctoral fellow U. Calif., San Diego, 1971, asst. rsch. pharmacologist, 1971-73; from asst. prof. to assoc. prof. U. Mass., Worcester, 1974-1985, prof. physiology, 1985—, prof. medicine, 1989—; cons. NIH, 1978—; editorial referee profl. jours., 1975—. Mem. editorial bd. Am. Jour. Physiology; contbr. over 6 chpts. to books in field; contbr. over 84 articles to profl. jours. Bd. dirs. Mass. Heart Assn., Boston, 1976-82; coun. mem. Am. Heart Assn., Citizen's Adv. Group adv. bd. sch. com., Shrewsbury, Mass., 1983—; mem. adminstrv. bd. Wesley United Meth. Ch., 1975—. Recipient rsch. career devel. award NIH 1980, rsch. merit award Nat. Heart, Lung, and Blood Inst. 1987; numerous rsch. grants. Mem. Am. Physiol. Soc. (membership com. 1989—), Biophys. Soc., Internat. Soc. Heart Rsch. Office: U Mass Med Sch Dept Physiology 55 Lake Ave N Worcester MA 01655-0001

DOBY, RAYMOND, engineering consultant; b. N.Y.C., Oct. 9, 1923; s. William and Mary (Gottlieb) D.; m. Sylvia Rossi, May 11, 1968 (div. Dec. 1980); two children (both dec.). Cert. profl. competence meteorology, U. Chgo., 1944; BME, NYU, 1947, MS in Math., 1951; PhD in Engring., U. Pa., 1962. Sr. engr. Westinghouse Electric Corp., Lester, Pa., 1953-62; adv. engr. Westinghouse Astronuclear Lab., Large, Pa., 1963-66; assoc. prof. Swarthmore (Pa.) Coll., 1966-71; cons. R-D Assocs., Swarthmore, 1971-78; mgr. engring. Consolidated Rail Corp., Phila., 1978-90; adj. prof. Drexel U., Phila., 1954-62, Camden County Coll., Blackwood, N.J., 1990—. Contbr. articles to profl. jours. Mem. Rent Rev. Bd., Cherry Hill, 1991. 1st lt. USAF, 1942-46. Mem. ASME, Sigma Xi. Home: 409W Colonial Apts Cherry Hill NJ 08002

DOCKEN, EDSEL ARDEAN, SR. (DEAN DOCKEN), urban planner; b. Jasper, Minn., Mar. 7, 1928; s. Edwin Alexander and Audrey (Norton) D.; m. Helen Jane Stokes, Oct. 10, 1954; children: Edsel A. Jr., Robin J. BS, U. Md., 1963; postgrad., Boston U., 1966, George Washington U., 1972; AA in Bus. Adminstrn. with honors, Harford Community Coll., 1981, cert. Real Estate Brokerage, 1983. Cert. real estate salesman. Enlisted U.S. Army, 1951, advanced through grades to lt. col., 1967, retired, 1971; insp. Test and Evaluation Commn., Aberdeen, Md., 1969-70; payroll mgr. Bata Shoe Co. Inc., Belcamp, Md., 1971-76; urban planner Town of Bel Air, Md., 1976-90; founder, exec. dir. Ordnance Mus. Found., Inc., Aberdeen, Md., 1991—; mem. Md. Energy Office, Balt., 1977-83. Key man United Way of Cen. Md., 1978-87; chmn. tennis March of Dimes, 1978-79; bd. dirs. Rolling Green Community Assn., 1985—; life mem. nat. com. for motor fleet ops. Mich. State U. Mem. Am. Planning Assn. (charter), Am. Compensation Assn., Internat. Adminstrv. Mgmt. Soc., Mt. Ararat Lodge. Democrat. Lutheran. Home: 3109 Rolling Green Dr Churchville MD 21028-1313 Office: Ordnance Mus Found Inc 39 N Hickory Ave AberdenProvingGround MD 21005

DOCKENDORFF, ROBERT LAWRENCE, computer graphics designer; b. Bronx, N.Y., May 19, 1930; s. Lawrence Christian and Madeline (Krollmann) D.; m. Geraldine Neyens, Oct. 10, 1954 (div. Aug. 1978); m. Kathleen Rose McGlynn, July 27, 1980. Student, Pratt Inst., Bklyn., 1949-51, Cornell U., 1955-56. Tech. illustrator GE Advanced Electronics Ctr., Ithaca, N.Y., 1956-65; indsl.-graphics designer Electronics Lab. GE, Syracuse, N.Y., 1965-69; human factors designer GE Genigraphics, Syracuse, 1969-77, cons. trainer, 1975-79; pres., cons. DK: Assocs., Syracuse, 1979, Basking Ridge, N.J., 1979-80, Sparta, N.J., 1980-85; pres., chief exec. officer Computer Arts, Inc., Sparta, 1985—; cons. Aetna Ins. Co., Hartford, Conn., 1979-85; cons., trainer Digital Equipment Corp., Bedford, Mass., 1979-85, Exxon Rsch., Houston, 1979-85, Nat. Security Agy., Ft. Meade, Md., 1979-84. Author, designer: (trade periodical) Police Vehicle Concept, 1969; author: (tng. course) Genigraphics System, 1971-74, (trade periodical) History-Genigraphics Devel., 1987. Chmn. publicity com. United Fund, Ithaca, 1963-65. Staff sgt. USAF, 1951-55, Korea. Recipient Computer Graphics Pioneer award Computer Graphics Pioneers, Chatsworth, Calif., 1988. Mem. Assn. Presentation Graphics Users, Lake Mohawk County Club. Republican. Home: 3 Hillspring Rd Sparta NJ 07871-2213 Office: Computer Arts Inc Upper Lake Plaza Sparta NJ 07871-1122

DODARO, JOHN CARL, electrical contracting executive; b. N.Y.C., Apr. 27, 1951; s. Egidio and Marie (Pudano) D.; m. Jackeline Fitzgerald, Apr. 7, 1991. Grad. high sch., Ronkonkoma, N.Y., 1970. Lic. master electrician. Electrician Anlo Constrn. Co., N.Y.C., 1970-74; pres. Dodaro Constrn. Co., Medford, N.Y., 1974—. Fellow Stony Brook Yacht Club. Roman Catholic. Home: 17 Miller Woods Dr Miller Place NY 11764 Office: Dodaro Constrn Co Inc 269 Middle Island Rd Medford NY 11763

DODD, CHRISTOPHER J., senator; b. Willimantic, Conn., May 27, 1944; s. Thomas J. and Grace (Murphy) D. B.A. in English Lit., Providence Coll., 1966; J.D., U. Louisville, 1972. Bar: Conn. 1973. Vol. Peace Corps, Dominican Republic, 1966-68; mem. 94th-96th Congresses from 2d Conn. Dist., 1975-80; U.S. Senator from Conn., 1980—. Served with AUS, 1969-75. Democrat. Office: US Senate 444 Russell Senate Bldg Washington DC 20510

DODD, MORGAN CARY, fund raising executive; b. Bay Shore, N.Y., May 14, 1951; s. Daniel Cary Dodd and Jeanne (Bowlan) Zimmerman; m. Jurate Maria Grazina Victoria Koncius, Sept. 3, 1983; 1 child, Nicholas Koncius. BS in Fgn. Svc., Georgetown U., 1974. Cert. fund raising exec. Assoc. dir. alumni fund Georgetown Alumni Assn., Washington, 1976-83; ann. fund dir. Wolf Trap Found. for Performing Arts, Vienna, Va., 1985-86, Corcoran Gallery of Art, Washington, 1986—. Bd. dirs. Francis Scott Key Park Found., Washington, 1983—. Mem. Nat. Soc. Fund Raising Execs. (bd. dirs. Greater Washington D.C. area chpt. 1990, ann. meeting. com. 1987-89, co-chmn. 1990, chmn. 1991), Planned Giving Study Group Washington. Home: 3155 Jocelyn St NW Washington DC 20015-1311 Office: Corcoran Gallery Art 500 17th St NW Washington DC 20006-4899

DODD, PETER FREDERIC, transportation engineer; b. N.Y.C., May 6, 1946; s. Daniel Cary and Jeanne (Bowlan) D.; m. JoAnn Phoenix, May 2, 1971; children: Jason, Ryan, Shannon, Brendan. Student, Suffolk Community Coll., Selden, N.Y., 1968-69. Traffic technician Suffolk County Traffic Safety Dept., Hauppauge, N.Y., 1970-77; traffic engr. transp. div. Town of Brookhaven, Medford, N.Y., 1977-86; dir. traffic safety Town of Smithtown (N.Y.), 1986-87; prin. transp. engr. Cashin Assocs., Port Jefferson Station, N.Y., 1987—; exec dir. Smithtown Traffic Safety Bd., 1986-87. Asst. local troop, Boy Scouts Am., Shirley, N.Y., 1983—; em. Suffolk County Traffic Safety Bd., Hauppauge, 1987. Mem. Inst. Transportation Engrs. (assoc.). Republican. Home: 56 Washington Dr Mastic Beach NY 11951-6019 Office: Cashin Assocs 4616 Nesconset Hwy Port Jefferson Station NY 11776

DODD, SARA MAE PALMER, executive assistant; b. Cin.; d. Charles Austen and Ruth Halsey (Miller) Palmer; m. Edward Dodd, Mar. 31, 1953 (dec.); children: J. Edward, Diane Dodd Peterson. BA, Hiram Coll., 1949; postgrad., Rutgers U., 1968. Exec. dir. Camp Fire Girls, Inc., Indpls., 1949-53; regional field advisor Camp Fire Girls, Inc., N.Y.C., 1973; substitute tchr. Piscataway (N.J.) Sch. Dist., 1974-79; asst. to pres. Ctr. for Profl. Advancement, East Brunswick, N.J., 1979-89. Active LWV, Piscataway, N.J., 1957-87, pres., fin. chmn., newsletter editor, 1957-87, v.p., 1985-87, leadership com., 1987-89; adv. Piscataway Twp. Sr. Citizen Adv. Commn.; vol. tutor in ESL program Literacy Vols. of Am. Methodist.

DODGE, CALVERT RENAUL, public relations executive, author, teacher; b. Chgo., Apr. 15, 1921; s. Lawrence Frank and Anna Rose (Manke) D.; m. Mary Irene Dodge, Apr. 2, 1951; children: Lawrence Wesley, Laura Irene, Valarie Le, James Calvert. BS in Agrl. Sci., U. Wyo., 1947, MA in Sociology, 1957; cert., Air U., Montgomery Ala., 1968; PhD in Speech Communication, U. Denver, 1971. Cert. supr. edn., Calif.; masters lic. 100 ton + ships, U.S. Coast Guard. Dir. youth, ednl. activities Standard Oil Ind. AMOCO, Chgo., 1948-51, dir. employee, pub. rels., 1951-55; pres. Western Concrete Products Inc., Laramie, Wyo., 1955-62; dir. state tng. ctr. State of Colo. Youth Svcs., Denver, 1964-71; dir. rsch. Ky. Manpower Devel. Commn., Louisville, 1971-76; assoc. prof. U. D.C., Washington, 1976-82; instr. U. Md., College Park, 1976-82; exec. v.p. Human Equations, Inc., Balt., 1982-87; pres. Dodge-Marck Assocs., Balt., 1991—; pres. Seminars at Sea, Balt., 1983—; dir. pub. affairs Md. Motorcycle Safety Program., Balt., 1990-92, employee devel. officer, 1992—. Editor: A Nation without Prisons, 1975; author: A World without Prisons, 1979, Executive Communication, 1985, Profit Recovery Management (Supervisory Development Strategies), 1986, Strategic Sales Development Systems, 1986. Candidate State Treas., Wyo., 1964; sponsors com. Nat. 4H, Nat. FFA, Nat. Jr. Achievement. Maj. USAF. Grantee U.S. Dept. Justice, 1966, '69; recipient Outstanding Community Svc. award, Am. Assn. Community Resource Devel., 1990. Mem. Md. Assn. Adult Edn., Inter-Am. Assn., Dodge Family Assn., Annapolis Naval Sailing Assn., Masons, Alpha Zeta, Omicron Delta Kappa, Tau Kappa Epsilon. Buddhist. Home: 8 S Broadway Baltimore MD 21231-1713 Office: Md Transp Authority Dundalk Sparrows Point MD 21222

DODGE, DONALD WILLIAM, chemical company executive; b. Worcester, Mass., Aug. 29, 1928; s. Herbert LaForest and Florence Mabel (Hatton) D.; m. Bernice Einar Flodin, June 24, 1950; children: Gary Richard, Robin Einar. BS in ChemE, Worcester Poly. Inst., 1950, MS in ChemE, 1952; PhD in ChemE, U. Del., 1958. Chem. engr. Arthur D. Little, Inc., Cambridge, Mass., 1952-53; research engr. E.I. du Pont Co., Buffalo, 1957-60, research supr., 1960-63; research mgr. Buffalo and Circleville, Ohio, 1963-66; mfg. supt. Richmond, Va., 1966-68; product mgr. Wilmington, Del., 1968-75, profit ctr. mgr., 1975-83, tech. dir., 1983-85; pvt. practice cons. Wilmington, 1985—. Contbr. articles to profl. jours. Bd. dirs. Chesapeake Bay Council Girl Scouts U.S., Wilmington, 1970-78; vestryman St. Albans Ch., Wilmington, 1982-87, sr. warden, 1985-86. Mem. Am. Inst. Chem. Engrs., N.Y. Acad. Sci., Tau Beta Pi, Sigma Xi. Republican. Episcopalian. Home and Office: 330 Brockton Rd Wilmington DE 19803-2412

DODGE, ELLEN ELIZABETH, community college administrator; b. Harrisburg, Pa., Feb. 17, 1932; d. Karl Franklin and Olive Victoria (Stickler) D. MusB, U. Mich., 1953; BA, Cornell U., 1955; MA, Columbia U., 1959, EdD, 1979. Tchr. various sch. dists., 1959-64; instr. Schoolcraft Coll., Livonia, Mich., 1965-67; from asst. prof. to prof. Butler (Pa.) County Community Coll., 1967-88, chmn. humanities and social scis. div., 1988—; pres. faculty orgns. Butler County Community Coll., 1986-88; participant Workshop of Nat. Inst. for Leadership Devel., Portland, Oreg., 1989. Flutist Butler County Symphony Orch., 1967-80, mem., 1985-91, rec. sec., 1986-89. Mem. Am. Assn. Women in Community and Jr. Colls., Pi Kappa Lambda. Lutheran. Office: Butler County Community Coll College Dr Oak Hills Butler PA 16003-1203

DODGE, MARTIN CLARK, forester, educator; b. New Haven, Conn., Nov. 2, 1942; s. Nelson Hovey Dodge and Elizabeth (Adams) Bradley; m. Margaret Anne Mattraw, June 26, 1965; children: Rebecca Anne, Andrea Lynne. BA in Chemistry, Colby Coll., 1965; MF, Utah State U., 1972. Tchr. Thomaston (Maine) Grammer Sch., 1965-67, Finger Lakes Community Coll., Canandaigua, N.Y., 1972—; coach Woodsmens Team Finger Lakes Community Coll. (12 nat. championships), 1974—; cons. forester, Naples, N.Y., 1987—; nature trail cons. Cumming Nature Ctr., Rochester, N.Y., 1974-78, Town of Canandaigua, 1990—. Architect/builder numerous rustic log structures; contbr. articles to profl. jours. Chmn. Environ. Commn., Naples, N.Y., 1975-78; scout master Boy Scouts Am., Maine, Alaska, N.Y. Lt. USCG, 1967-70. Rochester Museum and Sci. Ctr. fellow, 1978. Mem. Soc. Am. Foresters, N. Ea. Loggers Assn. Democrat. Protestant. Home: 8912 Garlinghouse Rd Naples NY 14512 Office: Finger Lakes Community Coll Lincoln Hill Rd Canandaigua NY 14424-8321

DODGE, ROBERT EARL, educational administrator; b. Portland, Maine, Dec. 4, 1945; s. Kendrick Earl and Norma Frances (Gray) D.; m. Lucille Rita Mininni, May 23, 1970 (div. July 1991); children: Erika Lynne, Jessica Anne. B Applied Sci., Boston U., 1976; MBA, Babson Coll., 1979. Supr. performance systems group Digital Equipment Corp., Bedford, Mass., 1974-79; mgr. customer svc. Scully Data Systems, Inc., Wilmington, Mass., 1979-80; dir. info. systems Axel Johnson Inc., N.Y.C., 1980-89; dir. fin. and mgmt. info. Portland Pub. Schs., 1989—. Bd. dirs. World Affairs Coun. Maine, Portland, 1991—. With USN, 1966-74. Mem. Assn. Sch. Bus. Ofcls., Maine Assn. Sch. Bus. Ofcls. Office: Portland Pub Schs 331 Veranda St Portland ME 04103-5535

DOE, PATRICIA LOUISE, industrial engineer; b. Hazelton, Pa., Mar. 8, 1948; d. Thomas Victor and Dorothy Eleanor (Kimmel) McLaughlin; m. Lawrence Whittier Doe, Dec. 27, 1969; children: Lawrence Whittier Jr., Christopher Thomas. BA in Math., Newark State Coll., 1970; MS in Indsl. Engring., Lehigh U., 1987. Sr. tech. analyst Bell Telephone Labs, N. Andover, Mass., 1970-72; math tchr. St. Maria Goretti High Sch., Hagerstown, Md., 1976-77, 80-81; programer analyst Air Products & Chems., Inc., Allentown, Pa., 1981-83; sr. programmer analyst Air Products & Chems., Inc., Allentown, 1983-84, tech. support analyst, 1984-85, sr. tech. support analyst, 1985-88, prin. tech. analyst, 1988-91, prin. tech. assessment analyst, 1991-92, prin. info. tech. analyst applied tech., 1992—. Asst. treas. Washington County (Md.) PTA, 1980-81; fin. sec. Faith Presbyn. Ch., Emmaus, Pa., 1982-84; dir. bell choir St. Andrews Presbyn. Ch., Williamsport, Md., 1978-81. Mem. Nat. Computer Graphics Assn., Kappa Delta Pi. Republican. Home: 1816 Pine Needle Cv Fogelsville PA 18051-1529 Office: Air Products & Chemicals 7201 Hamilton Blvd Allentown PA 18195-9642

D'OENCH, RUSSELL GRACE, JR., consultant; b. N.Y.C., Feb. 16, 1927; s. Russell Grace and Dorothie (Sharp) D'O.; m. Ellen Gates, Sept. 10, 1949; children: Peter, Ellen, Russell Grace III. Reporter Berkshire Eagle, Pittsfield, Mass., 1947-52; pub., editor Sunnyvale (Calif.) Standard, 1952-56; pres. Sagamore Press, Inc., N.Y.C., 1956-58; editor, chmn. bd. dirs. Middletown (Conn.) Press, 1959-91; chmn. Dormers Corp., Middleton, 1992—; mem. Middletown adv. bd. Conn. Nat. Bank, chmn. adv. bd., 1982-86; vis. lectr. Wesleyan U., 1967-71; corporator Farmers and Mechanics Bank, Middletown; bd. dirs. Middlesex Mut. Assurance Co. Chmn. bd. dirs. Wilcox Coll. Nursing, 1991—; bd. dirs. Conn. Hosp. Assn., 1991—, Conn. Coun. on Freedom of Info., Goodspeed Opera Found., Conn. Pub. Expenditure Coun., 1965-67, 87-91; past bd. Govs. for Higher Edn., chmn., 1983-88; past bd. dirs. Conn. Student Loan Found., Conn. Humanities Coun.; pres. Middleton Found. for Arts; mem. Commn. To Study Higher Edn., Conn. Gov.'s Commn. on Higher Edn. and Economy; past chmn. Conn. Joint Com. on Ednl. Tech. With USMC, 1945-46. Mem. Am. Soc. Newspaper Editors, New Eng. Soc. Newspaper Editors (pres. 1965), Sigma Delta Chi (past sec.). Home: 147 Phedon Pky Middletown CT 06457-2450 Office: Dormers Corp 51 Warwick St Middletown CT 06457

DOEPKENS, FREDERICK HENRY, agriscience educator; b. Annapolis, Md., Dec. 2, 1958; s. William Phillip and Marjorie (Desmarais) D. BS in Agrl. Edn., U. Md., 1980. Cert. advanced profl. teaching agr. grades 7-12. Agr. tchr. Hereford High Sch., Parkton, Md., 1980-84; agrisci. tchr. Hereford Mid. Sch., Monkton, Md., 1984-86, agrisci. tchr.-in-charge, 1986-87, agrisci. dept. chmn., 1987—; workshop instr., presenter Md. Mid. Sch. Assn., Balt., 1988; workshop coord. hydrophonics pilot Baltimore County Pub. Schs., Towson, Md., 1989-91; co-coord./cons. Md. Agr. in the Classroom Conf., Annapolis, Md., 1990-91; bd. dirs. Md. Agr. Edn. Found., Inc., Balt., 1989—. Author: Hydroponics, 1989, Agriscience in the Middle School, 1990; inventor ednl. materials Portable Hydroponics Unit, 1990. Recipient Achievement in Curriculum award Md. State Dept. Edn., Balt., 1989; named Md. Agrisci. Tchr. of Yr., Nat. FFA Orgn., 1991; hydroponics grantee Tech. Edn. Assn. Md., Balt., 1989; agrl. engring. grantee Md. Agrl. Edn. Found., Inc., Balt., 1991. Mem. NEA, Nat. Vocat. Agrl. Tchrs. Assn. (outstanding young mem. 1984), Am. Vocat. Assn., Md. Agr. Tchrs. Assn. Md. Vocat. Assn., Md. Mid. Sch. Assn. Roman Catholic. Home: 3702A Mt Carmel Rd Upperco MD 21155-9569 Office: Hereford Mid Sch 712 Corbett Rd Monkton MD 21111-1500

DOERFLER, LEONARD ANTHONY, psychologist; b. Pitts., May 21, 1954; s. Edward Henry and Marian Rose (Zotter) D.; m. Diane Fay Meyers, Sept. 3, 1988; 1 child, Jessica. BS summa cum laude, U. Pitts., 1976; MA, U. Mo., 1979, PhD, 1982. Intern U. Miss. Med. Ctr., VA Med. Ctr., Jackson, 1982; Asst. prof. psychology Auburn (Ala.) U., 1982-87; asst. prof. div. preventive and behavioral medicine U. Mass. Med. Ctr., Worcester, 1987-89; asst. prof. psychology Assumption Coll., Worcester, 1989—; asst. prof. psychiatry U. Mass. Med. Ctr., 1989—; speaker in field. Contbr. articles to profl. jours. KC scholar, U. Pitts., 1972-74; Rsch. grantee Auburn U., 1984-85, 84-86, NIMH, 1984-85; recipient Grad. Teaching award U. Mo., 1979. Mem. Am. Psychol. Assn., Am. Assn. Advancement Behavior Therapy, Soc. Behavioral Medicine, Phi Beta Kappa. Home: 26 Pinedale Rd Shrewsbury MA 01545 Office: Assumption Coll Psychology Dept 500 Salisbury St Worcester MA 01615-0005

DOERFLER, THOMAS EUGENE, statistician; b. Dayton, Ohio, Feb. 16, 1937; s. Edwin Francis and Gertrude (Feldmeyer) D.; m. Norma Jean Petkwitz, Apr. 27, 1968; children: Mark, Karyn. BS, U. Dayton, 1959; MS, Iowa State U., 1962, PhD, 1965. Programmer Rsch. Inst. U. Dayton, 1955-60; project scientist Booz-Allen Applied Rsch., Chgo., 1965-70; dir. mgmt. sci. Columbia House div. CBS, N.Y.C., 1970-73; sr. cons. Arthur D. Little, Cambridge, Mass., 1973—. Mem. Am. Statis. Assn. Roman Catholic. Home: 13 Brucewood Rd Acton MA 01720-4451 Office: Arthur D Little Inc 35-321A Acorn Park Cambridge MA 02140

DOERING, ALAN NORBERT, computer company executive; b. Phila., June 19, 1940; s. Andrew Alan and Margaret Adelaide (Dempster) D.; m.

Catherine Travis Roscoe, Dec. 24, 1960 (div. 1975); children: Lynley Michelle, Michael Alan, Lauryn, Heather Elizabeth, Holly; m. Deborah Lynne Widing, Aug. 25, 1978. Grad. high sch., Bryn Athyn, Pa., 1958. Rsch. engr. Burroughs Corp., Pasadena, Calif., 1969-71, Univac Corp., St. Paul, 1971-74; software engr. Rockwell Collins, Dallas, 1974-77; sr. engr. RCA Govt. Systems, Camden, N.J., 1977-78; pres. Q.I.D. Systems, Inc., Langhorne, Pa., 1978—; mgr. engring. Delta Data Systems, Inc., Trevose, Pa., 1982-86; mgr. software devel. Multi Solutions, Inc., Lawrenceville, N.J., 1986-88; v.p. devel. SSS Technologies, Inc., Phila., 1988-90; pres. Doering Technologies, Inc., Langhorne, 1990—; staff UCLA Computer Ctr., 1969; software engr. Burroughs Corp., Paoli, Pa., 1965-69; programmer Penn Mut. Life, Phila., 1963-65. Contbr. articles to profl. jours. Treas. Neshaminy Sch. Dist. Student Loan Fund, Langhorne, 1981—; bd. dirs. Phila. Jaycees, 1964. Republican. Home and Office: 146 Windham Dr Langhorne PA 19047-1598

DOERR, VERONICA M., educator, drama critic; b. Budapest, Hungary, July 29; d. Laszlo Szalai and Anna Ringler Tauber; m. David Bergholz, July 3, 1959 (div. 1970); 1 child, Jonathan Edward; m. Edgar R. Doerr III, Sept. 13, 1979; 1 child, Damon Matthew. BS in English, Carnegie Inst. Tech.; MA in English, Carnegie Mellon U. Publicity dir., charter mem. Pitts. Poor Players, 1971-72, producer, chair bd. dirs., 1972; dir. Allegheny Campus Entertainers, Pitts., 1973-74, 76; prof. of English Community Coll. of Allegheny County, Pitts., 1970-91; cons. Pitts. Lab. Theatre, 1976. Contbg. drama critic, reviewer (author Ronald Ribman): Masterplots II: Drama Series on Cold Storage, 1990; stage appearances include The White House Murder Case, 1971, Rocco the Rolling Stone, 1972; producer (plays) The Trial of the Catonsville Nine, 1972, One Flew Over the Cuckoo's Nest, 1972; dir. (plays) The Crucible, 1973-74, A Cry of Players, 1976, Under Milk Wood, 1976. Mem. N.E. Regional Conf. English in Two-Yr. Coll. (exec. bd. 1988-89, exec. bd. and treas. 1991—, location chair), Audubon Soc., Phi Kappa Phi. Home: 6421 Bartlett St Pittsburgh PA 15217-1831 Office: Community Coll of Allegheny County 808 Ridge Ave Pittsburgh PA 15212

DOERSAM, CHARLES HENRY, JR., engineer; b. N.Y.C., Nov. 1, 1921; s. Charles Henry, Sr. and Mary Emily (Davenport) D.; m. Cynthia Ann Wick, Dec. 7, 1954 (div. dec. 1980); children: Charles Henry III, Donna Davenport, Dean Robert. BS in Engr., Columbia U., 1942, MSME, 1944; post grad., MIT, U. Mich., N.Y.U. Registered profl. engr., N.Y. Indsl. engr. Pratt & Whitney, East Hartford, Conn., 1941-42; tech. staff Bell Telephone Labs, N.Y.C., 1942-44; sr. project engr Specl. Devices Ctr., Sands Pt., N.Y., 1946-53; project mgr. Sperry Gyroscope Co., Lake Success, N.Y., 1953-60; new product planning mgr. Potter Instrument Co., Plainview, N.Y., 1960-62; dir. mktg. chief engr. Instruments for Industry, Hicksville, N.Y., 1962-64; prof. Polytech. Instit. of Bklyn., 1964-69; pres. Com Comp Inc, Hauppauge, N.Y., 1969-71; pres. DOERCO Cons., CUB Computer Co., NUTEK Corp., Princeton Automated Labs., Pedagogy Rsch. Inst.; nat. chmn. IRE Profl. Group on Space Electronics, 1950. Pantentee in field; contbr. articles to profl. jours. Bd. Advisors Waldorf Sch., Garden City, N.Y., 1964-68, Portledge Sch., Locust Valley, N.Y., 1977. Mem. North Shore Yacht Club (commn. 1968-69), Point O'Woods Club. Republican. Congregationalist. Home and Office: 67 Shore Rd PO Box 927 Old Lyme CT 06371

DOERSAM, CHARLES HENRY, III, real estate developer, marine consultant; b. Glen Cove, N.Y., Jan. 15, 1957; s. Charles Henry Jr. and Cynthia Ann (Wick) D. BA, Conn. Coll., 1979. Owner, operator, bd. dirs. Charles H. Doersam III Real Estate Devel., Fire Island, N.Y., 1979—; owner, operator Charles H. Doersam III Marine Cons., Fire Island, 1979—, Marco Polo Marine, Fire Island, 1980—, Charles H. Doersam III Photog., Fire Island, 1984—; ptnr. Davenport Real Estate Devel., Old Lyme, Conn., 1984—; directing ptnr. Charles H. Doersam III Real Estate Devel., Fire Island, N.Y., 1983—. Inventor spl. close-up photography; contbr. to 4 books of photography. Marine cons. Point O'Woods Yacht Club, Fire Island, 1979—; cons. Club at Point O'Woods, 1980—. Mem. South Bay Explorers Club (founder, bd. dirs. 1985—), Point O'Woods Rod and Gun Club (founder, pres. 1983—), Salt Lodge (pres. 1984—). Home and Office: 24 Pt Owoods Bay Shore NY 11706

DOHERTY, DANIEL EDWARD, lawyer; b. Quincy, Mass., Sept. 14, 1952; s. Edward William and Pauline Josephine (Dalessio) D. BA, U. Mass., 1978; JD, New Eng. Sch. of Law, 1982. Bar: Mass., 1982. Asst. dist. atty. Norfolk County Dist. Atty.'s Office, Dedham, Mass.; assoc. Brickley, Sears & Sorett, Boston, 1986-87; asst. dist. atty. Suffolk County Dist. Atty.'s Office, Boston, 1987-92; assoc. Swartz and Swartz, Boston, 1992—. Mem. Boston Bar Assn. Office: Swartz & Swartz 10 Marshall St Boston MA 02108

DOHERTY, EVELYN MARIE, data processing consultant; b. Phila., Sept. 26, 1941; d. James Robert and Virginia (Checkley) D. Diploma, RCA Tech. Inst., Cherry Hill, N.J., 1968. Freelance data processing programmer N.J., 1978-81; data processing cons. N.J., 1981—; cons. brokerage, banking, med., edn., transp., pub., food wholesaleing, utility systems, mfg.; reseller of PC's and software; lectr. data processing Camden County (N.J.) Coll. Contbr. articles in field. Chairwoman Collingswood (N.J.) Dems.; founder Babe Didikson Collingswood Softball Team for Women; organizer Erlton South Town Watch. Mem. Data Processing Mgmt. Assn. (chmn., mem. ednl. com., bd. dirs. N.J. chpt. 1980—). Roman Catholic. Office: PO Box 3780 Cherry Hill NJ 08034

DOHERTY, JOHN L., lawyer; b. Pitts., Dec. 17, 1934; s. John A. and Carmella G. (Conte) D.; m. Diane J. Passetti, Aug. 10, 1963; children: John F., Kathleen A. BA, Duquesne U., 1960, JD, 1966. Bar: Pa. 1966. Law clk. to chief judge U.S. Dist. Ct. Western Dist. Pa., 1966-67; asst. Livingston, Miller & Haywood, Pitts., 1967-75; city solicitor Pitts., 1969-70; law clk. to judge Allegheny County Ct. Common Pleas, Pitts., 1971-73; ptnr. Manifesto, Doherty & Donahoe, P.C., Pitts., 1975-92; chief disciplinary counsel Disciplinary Bd. of the Supreme Ct. Pa., 1992—. Served with U.S. Army, 1954-56. Fellow Am. Coll. Trial Lawyers, Acad. Trial Lawyers (past pres.); mem. Allegheny County Bar Assn., Pa. Trial Lawyers Assn. (past chmn. criminal trial sect.), Assn. Trial Lawyers Am., Pa. Criminal Def. Assn., Pa. Bar Assn. (bd. govs.), Assn. Trial Lawyers in Criminal Ct. (past pres.).

DOHERTY, KATHERINE MANN, librarian, writer; b. N.Y.C., July 11, 1951; d. Jack Howard Mann and Glenn (Ellis) Andrews; m. Craig A. Doherty, June 16, 1973; 1 child, Meghan Corinne. BA, U. N.Mex., 1973; MSLS, Simmons Coll., 1976. Cataloger Mass. Hist. Soc., Boston, 1976-79; libr. media specialist Zuni (N.Mex.) Pub. Sch.s, 1982-86; libr. dist. Zuni Pub. Schs., 1985-86; unified media specialist Nantucket (Mass.) Elem. Sch., 1986-87; dir. learning resources Fortier Libr. N.H. Tech. Coll., Berlin, 1987—. Author: (children's books) Apaches and Navajos, 1989, Iroquois, 1989, (young adult) Benazir Bhutto, 1990. Office: NH Tech Coll Coll Libr 2020 Riverside Dr Berlin NH 03570-3799

DOHERTY, PATRICIA ANN, computer systems analyst; b. Perth Amboy, N.J., Jan. 21, 1959; d. William Urban and Marion Ann (Mazola) O'Brien; m. Stephen Joseph Doherty, Feb. 12, 1983; children: Kathleen Elizabeth, Brian Stephen. BA summa cum laude, Rutgers U., 1981, MS in Math., 1987. Cert. tchr. math., N.J. Bank teller Nat. State Bank, Elizabeth, N.J., 1979; intern Merck & Co., Inc., Rahway, N.J., summer 1980, programmer technician, 1981-82, from programmer to sr. tech. assoc./project mgr., 1982—; math. workshop tutor, Rutgers U., New Brunswick, 1978-81. Adviser Saint James Youth Group, Saint James Ch., Woodbridge, N.J., 1985-86; commuter adviser, Rutgers U., pres., 1979-80. Recipient award for excellence Merck & Co., Inc., 1990. Mem. Am. Math. Soc., Phi Beta Kappa, Pi Mu Epsilon (sec. 1980-81, Jr. award in Math. 1980), Kappa Delta Pi (v.p. 1980-81). Roman Catholic. Home: 7 Old Hickory Ln Edison NJ 08820-1124

DOHERTY, ROBERT FRANCIS, JR., aerospace industry professional; b. Quincy, Mass., Aug. 7, 1954; s. Robert Francis and Rose Virginia (Wheeler) D. BS in Mgmt., So. Mass. U., 1977. Sales mgr. Jordan Marsh Co., Boston, 1977-78; ops. mgr. Cramer Electronics, Newton, Mass., 1978-79; contracts mgr. Data Gen. Corp., Westboro, Mass., 1981-84, ops. analyst, 1979-81; sales ops. mgr. Printronix, Inc., Malden, Mass., 1984-87; contract adminstrn. mgr. M/A-Com, Inc., Burlington, Mass., 1987-89; mktg. mgr. M/A-Com, Inc., Chelmsford, Mass., 1989—; bd. dirs. M/A-Com Fed. Credit Union, Burlington, also newspaper correspondent, chair various restructuring coms. Mem. Nat. Contract Mgmt. Assn., Assn. of Old Crows, M/A-Com Mgmt. Club. Roman Catholic. Home: 9 Wolcott Park Medford MA 02155

DOJKA, EDWIN SIGMUND, civil engineer; b. Niagara Falls N.Y., Dec. 20, 1924; s. Zygmunt Joseph and Felixa (Pasek) D.; BCE, Rensselaer Poly. Inst., 1951; m. Jean L. Keller, July 9, 1949; children: Paul, Gail Dojka Rutkowski, Jay. Structures engr. Bell Aircraft Corp., Wheatfield, N.Y., 1951-52; design engr. Hooker Electro Chem. Corp., Niagara Falls, N.Y., 1952-55; civil engr. City of Niagara Falls (N.Y.), 1955-58, asst. city engr., 1958-60, dep. city engr., 1960-63, city engr., 1963-79; city engr. City of North Tonawanda, 1979-85; mem. sewer commn., plumbing bd., 1963-85, mem. planning bd., 1963-66, bd. equalization rev., 1963-71; mem. Niagara County Planning Bd., 1978-91, Traffic Safety Commn., 1979-85. Mem. United Fund Community Budget Com., 1962-68; mem. Community Ambassador Gen. Com., 1958, 59; Fleet Safety adv. commr., Niagara Falls, 1960-68; bd. assocs. Mt. St. Mary's Hosp., 1969-70. With inf. AUS, World War II; ETO. Decorated Bronze Star, Purple Heart, Combat Infantryman's badge. Registered profl. engr., land surveyor, N.Y. Fellow ASCE; mem. Soc. Am. Mil. Engrs., Am. Pub. Works Assn., Am. Water Works Assn., Nat. Soc. Profl. Engrs., Water Pollution Control Fedn., Am. Planning Assn., Inst. for Engring., Am. Arbitration Assn. (comml. panelist 1978—), DAV, Am. Legion, 102d Inf. Div. Assn., AMVETS, Meml. Day Assn., Boys Club Alumni Assn., VFW, Pulaski Civic League, Polish Legion Am. Vets., Royal Canadian Legion (hon.), Mil. Order Purple Heart, 40 and 8, 2d Armored Div. Assn., 25th Bomb Group Assn., Hon. Order Ky. Cols., Kosciuszko Found., Dom Polski Club, First Friday Club, Echo Club, Sertoma Club, K.C. (hon.), Elks, Sigma Xi, Chi Epsilon, Tau Beta Pi. Roman Catholic. Home and Office: 509 80th St Niagara Falls NY 14304-2301

DOKA, KENNETH J., gerontology professor; b. N.Y.C., Feb. 12, 1948; s. Frank and Josephine (Martin) D.; 1 child, Michael. BA, Concordia Coll., Ft. Wayne, Ind., 1969; MDiv, Concordia Sem., 1973; PhD, St. Louis U., 1978. Assoc. prof. Concordia Coll., Bronxville, N.Y., 1973-81; prof. Coll. of New Rochelle, 1981—; Cons. Thomas M. Quinn and Sons, N.Y.C., 1983—, Nat. Found. of Funeral Svc., Evanston, Ill., 1983—. Author: Disenfranchised Grief, 1989, Living with Life-Threatening Illness, 1992, Death and Spirituality, 1992. Bd. dirs. Variety Boys and Girls Club of Queens (N.Y.), 1975—; editorial bd. Nat. Kidney Found., N.Y., 1990—, bd. dirs. Recipient Program award Boys' Clubs Am., 1981. Mem. Gerontol. Soc. Am., Am. Soc. on Aging, Am. Sociol. Assn., Assn. for Death Edn. and Counseling (bd. dirs. 1985-87, v.p. 1991). Republican. Lutheran. Office: Coll of New Rochelle Dept Gerontology New Rochelle NY 10805

DOKURNO, ANTHONY DAVID, lawyer; b. Gardner, Mass., Mar. 14, 1957; s. Anthony Chester and Damey Anteena (Aleson) D.; m. Andee J. Rappazzo. BA, Holy Cross Coll., 1979; JD, Vt. Law Sch., 1982. Bar: Mass. 1982, U.S. Ct. Mil. Appeals 1986, U.S. Supreme Ct. 1987. Pvt. practice law Fitchburg, Mass., 1982-86; appellate counsel Navy-Marine Corps Appellate Rev. Activity, Washington, 1986-88; atty. admiralty div. JAG, Washington, 1988-90, atty. ops. and mgmt., 1991—. Lt. USNR, 1986—. Mem. ABA, Fed. Bar Assn., Maritime Law Assn., Am. Soc. Internat. Law, Boston Computer Soc., Friends Nat. Zoo, Cousteau Soc., Sierra Club, Phi Beta Kappa. Home: 200 N Pickett St Apt 1504 Alexandria VA 22304-2127

DOLAK, TERENCE MARTIN, health care executive; b. Youngstown, Ohio, Sept. 24, 1951; s. Edward Andrew and Verona Rose (Hugoboom) D.; m. Lisa Ann Pavlick, Apr. 20, 1985. BS in Biochemistry, Ohio State U., 1973; PhD in Organic Chemistry, Univ. S. Car., 1977. Sr. scientist Bristol-Myers Co., Evansville, Ind., 1979-81, sr. research scientist, 1981-84; sect. head Ayerst Labs. Research, Princeton, N.J., 1984-86; dir. research Bausch & Lomb, Inc., Rochester, N.Y., 1986-88, v.p. R&D, 1988—; presenter at profl. seminars. Contbr. chpt. to book, articles to profl. jours.; patentee U.S. and abroad. Active in Town of Canandaigua Zoning Bd. Mem. Am. Chem. Soc., Am. Assn. for the Advancement of Sci., N.Y. Acad. of Sci., Assn. for Research in Vision and Ophthalmology. Roman Catholic. Home: PO Box 375 Canandaigua NY 14424-0806 Office: Bausch & Lomb 1400 Goodman St N Rochester NY 14609-3596

DOLAN, EDWARD CORCORAN, real estate developer and investor; b. Boston, July 8, 1952; s. Francis William and Barbara Ann (Corcoran) D.; m. Susan Pauline Knoettner, Apr. 21, 1979; children: Jared Edward, Jessica Susan. BA in Econs. and Bus., St. Anselm's Coll., 1975. Lic. real estate broker, Mass. Asst. credit mgr. The Fin. Ctr. a subsidiary of Fidelcor, Woburn, Mass., 1976-77; credit rep. Ford Motor Corp., Woburn, 1978; pres., founder, owner Franklin Realty Co., No. Reading, Mass., 1979—; trustee, Susan Realty Trust, 1982—, Union Realty Trust, 1983—, Orchard Realty Trust, 1983—, Grandover Realty Trust, 1986—, Villa Park Realty Trust, 1988—, No. Reading; pres., treas., owner, Sparhawk Devel. Corp., a Tex. Corp., No. Reading and Houston, 1988—; ltd. ptnr. Elmira Pioneers, a Boston Red Sox Affiliate, Elmira, N.Y., 1987—, Great Expectations Investment Assn., Boston, 1978—. Board dirs. Lazarus House Ministries, Lawrence, Mass., 1988—. Mem. Jaycees (Reading chpt. bd. dirs. 1986-87, sec. 1986, award of honor, 1986), Thomson Country Club (tournament com. 1989). Office: Franklin Realty Co 348 Park St Park Pl E North Reading MA 01864

DOLAN, EUGENE THOMAS, educator; b. Bklyn., Feb. 20, 1930; s. John J. and Isabelle A. (Faye) D.; m. Peggy A. Derham, June 19, 1954; children: Nancy, Kathy, Eugene Jr., Betsy, John J. II, Megan. BS in Naval Sci., Villanova (Pa.) Coll., 1952; MA in Personnel Mgmt., George Washington U., 1962, ABD, 1977. CDP, CDE. Commd. 2d lt. USMC, 1952, advanced through grades to lt. col., 1968, ret., 1972; asst. prof. George Washington U., 1967-71; assoc. prof. U. D.C., Washington, 1972—; curriculum rev. and devel. officer Dept. Def. Computer Inst., Washington, 1966-68. Mem. Data Processing Mgmt. Assn. (chpt. bd. dirs. 1968, 70-74, chpt. pres. 1980-85, Bronze award 1984, Silver award 1985, Gold award 1968, Emerald award 1990). Republican. Roman Catholic. Office: Univ DC 4200 Connecticut Ave NW Washington DC 20008-1174

DOLAN, JOHN PATRICK, psychiatrist; b. Bklyn., Jan. 23, 1935; s. James Francis and Agnes Barrett (Lane) D.; m. Mary McLaughlin, Dec. 21, 1964 (div. June 1972); children: Deborah Jean, John McLaughlin; m. Margaret Abel, Sept. 6, 1974. AB in History, Bklyn. Coll., 1958; MD, N.J. Coll. Medicine, 1962. Cert. Am. Bd. Psychiatry and Neurology. Resident Washington U., 1966-69, St. Louis U., 1970-72; intern medicine Kings County Hosp., Bklyn., 1963; resident neurology Washington U., St. Louis, 1969; resident psychiatry St. Louis U. Sch. Medicine, 1972, asst. prof. dept. psychiatry, 1972-78; chmn. dept. psychiatry Conemaugh Valley Meml. Hosp., Johnstown, Pa., 1979-83; clin. asst. prof. dept. psychiatry U. Pitts. Sch. Medicine, 1979-83; chmn. dept. psychiatry St. Vincent's Med. Ctr., Bridgeport, Conn., 1983—; clin. assoc. prof. psychiatry N.Y. Med. Coll., Valhalla, N.Y., 1987—; psychiat. cons. Pru-Care N.Y. and Conn., 1988—; past pres. Fairfield/Litchfield chpt. Conn. Psychiat. Soc., 1988-89; v.p. Alliance for Health IPA, Bridgeport, 1987—; counsellor Conn. Psychiat. Soc., 1985-89. Mem. Catchment Area Coun., Bridgeport, 1983-87, Southwest Regional Mental Health Bd., Fairfield County, Conn., 1983-87, legis. com. (Conn.) State Bd. Mental Health, 1985-86. Mem. Bridgeport Psychiat. Soc. (pres. 1987—), Am. Psychiat. Assn., Am. Acad. Med. Dirs., Am. Acad. POsychiatrists in Alcoholism and Addiction, N.Y. Acad. Scis., South Shore Music Club. Office: St Vincents Med Ctr 2800 Main St Bridgeport CT 06606-4292

DOLAN, MICHAEL JOHN, therapist; b. Ashland, Pa., June 16, 1958; s. William J. and Elizabeth A. (Bolich) D.; m. Debra Lee Sharpless, May 16, 1987; children: Jamie Elizabeth, Michael John. BA in Psychology, Penn State U., 1980; MA in Counseling Psychology, Kutztown U., 1988. Diplomate addiction counseling Pa. Chem. Abuse Cert. Bd. Counselor On Drugs Inc., State Coll., Pa., 1979-81; drug and alcohol counselor Good Samaritan Hosp., Pottsville, Pa., 1981-82; counselor, program dir. Endeavor Inc., Bethlehem, Pa., 1982-88; clin. supr. Lehigh Valley Behavioral Health Ctr., Allentown, Pa., 1988-91; therapist Community Psychol. Svcs. Consultants Inc., Allentown, 1989—; bd. dirs. Aids Svcs. Ctr., Bethlehem, 1988—. Mem. AACD. Home: 3155 Shakespeare Rd Bethlehem PA 18017-2731 Office: Community Psychol Svcs 2341 Walbert Ave Allentown PA 18104-1351

DOLE, ELIZABETH HANFORD, charitable organization administrator, former secretary of labor; b. Salisbury, N.C., July 29, 1936; d. John Van and Mary Ella (Cathey) Hanford; m. Robert Joseph Dole (U.S. Senator from Kans.), Dec. 6, 1975. B.A. with honors in Polit. Sci., Duke, 1958; postgrad., Oxford (Eng.) U., summer 1959; M.A. in Edn., Harvard U., 1960, J.D., 1965. Bar: D.C. 1966. Staff asst. to asst. sec. for edn. HEW, Washington, 1966-67; practiced law Washington, 1967-68; assoc. dir. legis. affairs, then exec. dir. Pres.'s Com. for Consumer Interests, Washington, 1968-71; dep. dir. Office Consumer Affairs, The White House, Washington, 1971-73; commr. FTC, Washington, 1973-79; chmn. Voters for Reagan-Bush, 1980; dir. Human Services Group, Office of Exec. Br. Mgmt., Office of Pres.-Elect, 1980; asst. to Pres. for pub. liaison, 1981-83; sec. U.S. Dept. Transp., 1983-87; with Robert Dole Presdl. Campaign, 1987-88; participant 1988 Presdl. and Congl. campaigns; sec. U.S. Dept. Labor, 1989-90; pres. ARC, 1991—; mem. nominating com. Am. Stock Exchange, 1972, N.C. Consumer Council, 1972. Trustee Duke U., 1974-88; mem. coun. Harvard Law Sch. Assocs.; mem. vis. com. Harvard Sch. Pub. Health, 1992—; bd. overseers Harvard U., 1989. Recipient Arthur S. Flemming award U.S. Govt., 1972, Humanitarian award Nat. Commn. Against Drunk Driving, 1988, Disting. Alumni award Duke U., 1988; named one of Am.'s 200 Young Leaders, Time mag., 1974, one of World's 10 Most Admired Women, Gallup Poll, 1988. Mem. Phi Beta Kappa, Pi Lambda Theta, Pi Sigma Alpha. Office: ARC care Michelle J Dupuis 17th & D Sts NW Washington DC 20006

DOLE, VINCENT PAUL, III, food products executive; b. N.Y.C., May 30, 1944; s. Vincent Paul Dole and Elizabeth (Strange) Paine; m. Genevieve de la Pieuse, Jan. 17, 1945; 1 child, Alexandre Paul. BA, U. Pa., 1966; MBA, NYU, 1971. Chmn. Dolefam Corp., Washington, 1979—; bd. dirs. JMC Investment Co., Washington, North Fork Group, St. Louis. Mem. Bus. Promotion Coun., U.S. Dept. Commerce, Washington, 1988—; bd. dirs. Hosp. Relief Fund, Washington. Mem. Nat. Assn. Specialty Foods (dir. 1985—), U. Club (N.Y.C.), Club des Alpes (Nice, France). Office: Dolefam Corp 2000 K St NW Washington DC 20006-1809

DOLEAC, CHARLES BARTHOLOMEW, lawyer; b. New Orleans, Sept. 20, 1947; s. Cyril Bartholomew and Emma Elizabeth (St. Clair) D.; m. Denise Kilfoyle, Feb. 2, 1972; children: Keith Gabriel, Jessa Lee. BS cum laude, U. N.H., 1968; JD, NYU, 1971. Bar: Mass. 1972, N.H. 1972, Maine 1973. Law clk. to Justice Grimes N.H. Supreme Ct., Concord, 1972-73; assoc. Boynton, Waldron, Dill & Aeschliman, Portsmouth, N.H., 1973-76; ptnr. Boynton, Waldron, Doleac, Woodman & Scott, Portsmouth, 1977—; delegation mem. to tour Chinese Legal system Chinese Ministry of Justice, 1982; del. to Peoples Rep. of China/U.S. Joint Session on trade investments and econ. law Chinese Ministry Justice/U.S. Dept. Justice, Beijing, 1987; pres. bd. trustees Strawbery Banke Inc.; prop. Portsmouth Athenaeum; incorporator Piscataqua Savs. Bank. Contbr. articles to profl. jours. Mem. citizens adv. council Portsmouth Community Devel. Program, 1976-77, Incorp. N.H. Charitable Found.; pres., bd. dirs. Seacoast United Way, 1976; chmn. Portsmouth Bd. of Bldg. Appeals, 1976-77; chmn. stewardship com. Soc. Preservation New Eng. Antiquities, 1980-84, trustee; founder, pres. Japan-Am. Soc. N.H. NEH fellow, Aspen Inst. fellow, moderator; named Portsmouth Vol. Citizen of Yr., 1991. Fellow N.H. Bar Found.; mem. Mass. Bar Assn., Maine Bar Assn., N.H. Bar Assn. , Assn. Trial Lawyers Am., N.H. Trial Lawyers Assn., Maine Trial Lawyers Assn. Home: Little Harbor Rd Portsmouth NH 03801-5575 Office: Boynton Waldron Doleac Woodman & Scott PA 82 Court St PO Box 418 Portsmouth NH 03801-0418

DOLEZAL, DALE FRANCIS, truck manufacturing company executive; b. Ronan, Mont., Apr. 9, 1936; s. Henry Lewis and Regina Marie (Nedjelski) D.; m. Patricia Louise Johnson, Aug. 27, 1960 (div. Dec. 1980); children: Craig, Kelly, Kathleen, Kari. BS in Indsl. Engring., Mont. State U., 1961; student Program for Mgmt. Devel., Bus. Sch., Harvard U., 1974. Indsl. and methods engr. Westinghouse Electric Corp., Sunnyvale, Calif., 1961-63; chief indsl. engr. Clarke Equipment Corp., Spokane, Wash., 1963-65; mgr. materials Freightliner Corp., Portland, Oreg., 1965-67; with Internat. Harvester Co., 1967—, dir. purchasing and inventory mgmt., Chgo., 1977-80, dir. materials and ops. planning, 1980-81; gen. mgr. parts and retail Indsl. Trucks div. Eaton Corp., Phila., 1981-84; pres. Modern Group, Phila., 1984-86, group v.p., gen. mgr. Holland Hitch Co., Whitehouse Sta., N.J., 1986—, Holland Atlantic Hitch Co. of Denmark, S.C.; pres. Positive Prints, Inc.; dir. Real Am. Corp.; mem. bd. bus. and indsl. advisers U. Wis., Madison; bd. dirs. Ops. Tng. Inst., Ea. Leadership Mgmt., Inc. Mem. parents adv. bd. Naperville (Ill.) Central High Sch., 1977—; mem. adv. bd. Sch. Dist. 203, Naperville, 1978—; mem. New Hope (Pa.) Solebury Sch. Bd., 1982-87 . Served with USMC, 1954-57. Registered profl. engr., Oreg. Mem. Am. Inst. Indsl. Engrs., Am. Prodn. and Inventory Control. Soc. (pres. 1968-74), Am. Soc. Indsl. Engrs., Rotary (bd. dirs. 1988—, pres. 1989-90), K.C. (pres.), Harvard Club. Republican. Contbr. articles to trade jours. Avocations: golf, hunting, fishing. Home: 3149 Landing Way Orangeburg SC 29115 Office: Holland Group Ridge Rd White House Station NJ 08889-9623

DOLIS, JOHN, English educator; b. St. Louis, Apr. 25, 1945; s. John J. Sr. and Anne Marie (Bonelle) D. BA, St. Louis U., 1967; MA, Loyola U., 1969, PhD, 1978. Teaching asst. Loyola U., Chgo., 1967-69, 70-73; instr. Notre Dame High Sch., Chgo., 1969-70; lectr. Loyola U., Chgo., 1974-75, 78-80; instr. Northeastern Ill. U., 1978-80; Fulbright lectr. U. Turin, Italy, 1980-81; instr. U. Kansas, 1981-85; assoc. prof. Pa. State U., Scranton, 1990-92; sr. Fulbright lectr. U. Bucharest, Romania, 1989-90; instr. Columbia Coll., Chgo., 1970-71. Editor: Nat. Assn. Remedial/Devel. Studies in Post-Secondary Edn. newsletter, 1979-80, Loyola U. Info. Systems newsletter, 1972; mem. editorial bd. Franciscan Sesquicentennial Poetry Contest, 1974, Ill. English Bull., 1970, 71; TV scriptwriter CBS, WTTW, 1966, 71; copywriter, music writer Neil Stewart and Assocs., Chgo., 1973-74; interviewer U.S. Info. Agy.; contbr. articles to profl. jours. Mem. Am. Philos. Assn., Internat. Assn. for Fantastic in Arts, Internat. Assn. Philosophy and Lit., Internat. Husserl and Phenomenological Rsch. Soc., Internat. Imagery Assn., Internat. Soc. for Phenomenology and Human Scis., Internat. Soc. for Phenomenology and Lit., Assn. for Applied Psychoanalysis, Ctr. for Psychoanalytic Studies, Fulbright Assn., Modern Lang. Assn., Nathaniel Hawthorne Soc., Northeast Modern Lang. Assn., North East Popular Culture Assn., Soc. for Advancement of Am. Philosophy, Soc. for Phenomenology and Existential Philosphy, Soc. for Phenomenology and Psychiatry, Thoreau Soc., World Phenomenology Inst. Home: 309 Summit Pt Scranton PA 18508-1057 Office: Pa State U Dept English Dunmore PA 18512

DOLL, CRAIG ALLEN, lawyer; b. Phila., Oct. 7, 1948; s. Carl William and Jacquelyn Lucille (Kurtz) D.; m. Kathleen Mary Verdelli, Aug. 14, 1971; 1 child, Stephen Michael. BA, Pa. State U., 1970; JD, Suffolk U., 1975. Bar: Pa. 1976, U.S. Tax Ct., U.S. Supreme Ct. Law clk. Barron & Stadfeld, Boston, 1971-75; lawyer Commonwealth of Pa. Pub. Utility Commn., Harrisburg, 1976-81, bur. dir., 1981-83; pvt. practice lawyer Harrisburg, 1983-90; sr. assoc. LeBoeuf, Lamb, Leiby & MacRae, Harrisburg, 1990—. Mem. Pa. Bar Assn., Skull and Bones Soc. Office: LeBoeuf Lamb Leiby & MacRae 320 Market St Ste E400 Harrisburg PA 17101

DOLL, JIMMIE DAVE, chemistry educator; b. San Diego, Oct. 19, 1945; s. David Dean and Margie Elizabeth (Carpenter) D.; m. Margaret Ann Schreiber, Aug. 20, 1966; 1 child, John Michael. BS in Chemistry, U. Kans., 1967; PhD, Harvard U., 1971. NSF postdoctoral fellow U. Calif., Berkeley, 1971-72; vis. asst. prof. U. Ill., Urbana, 1972-73; asst. prof. SUNY, Stony Brook, 1973-75, assoc. prof., 1975-79; lab. fellow Los Alamos (N.Mex.) Nat. Lab., 1979-89; prof. chemistry Brown U., Providence, 1989—. Co-author: Quantum Simulation of Condensed Matter Phenomena, 1990. A.P. Sloan fellow, 1974; Los Alamos Nat. Lab. fellow, 1981. Office: Dept Chemistry Brown Univ Providence RI 02912

DOLL, PATRICIA MARIE, public relations consultant; b. Bryn Mawr, Pa., Apr. 13, 1960; d. Otello Louis (dec.) and Eleanor Caroline (De Pasquale) De Grandis; m. John Russell Doll, Oct. 5, 1985. BS in Speech Communications, Millersville (Pa.) U., 1982. Lic. radio operator. Advt. asst. ELMCO Merchandising, Wayne, Pa., 1983-85; freelance writer, 1984-90; dir. communications Rouse & Assocs., Malvern, Pa., 1987-90; pres. Publicity Works, Narvon, Pa., 1990—; part time broadcaster, writer,

promoter Sta. WNAR Radio, Sta. WLAN Radio, Sta. WGAL-TV8, 1982-85. Contbr. articles to local newspapers and trade publs.; producer TV documentary, 1982. Recipient awards for articles. Mem. Gt. Valley Regional C. of C., Phila. Pub. Rels. Assn., Chester County Devel. Coun., Am. Heart Assn., Berks County C. of C. Roman Catholic.

DOLLARD, MICHAEL JOSEPH, state agency administrator; b. Jersey City, Jan. 26, 1939; s. Nicholas Henry and Zelda Emma (Brink-Seidlen) D.; m. Suzanne MacEachron, Apr. 18, 1964; children: Norín, Seán, Maryanne, Malcolm, Kieran. BA, Siena Coll., 1965; MPA, SUNY, Albany, 1972. From pers. examiner to prin. pers. examiner N.Y. State Dept. Civil Svc., Albany, 1965—. Co-author, editor: Employment Testing of Persons with Disabling Conditions, 1990. Chmn. Coalition Against Racism and Apartheid, Albany, 1981-87; gen. sec. Irish Rep. Clubs of N.Am., 1977-81. With USAF, 1956-60. Mem. Internat. Pers. Mgmt. Assn. (bd. dirs. assessment coun. 1989—, Handler award 1990), Nat. Coun. on Measurement in Edn., Mid-Atlantic Pers. Assessment Consortium (pres. 1987-88, agy. rep.), NAACP (bd. dirs. 1981-85, Social Justice award 1981), Delta Epsilon Sigma. Home: 243 Mt Hope Dr Albany NY 12202-1017 Office: NY State Dept Civil Svc Bldg 1 Harriman Campus Albany NY 12239

DOLLARD, VIRGINIA MARIE, healthcare executive; b. Milton, Mass., Nov. 30, 1952; d. William Patrick and Evelyn Clare (Quinn) Toland; m. Wayne Joseph Dollard, July 29, 1972; 1 child, Jason. Student, Trinity Coll., Washington, 1970-73; BS, Roger Williams Coll., 1976; MA, Pepperdine U., 1980. Mgr. br. office ops. Blue Cross, Washington, 1972-74; assoc. dir. enrollment R.I. Group Health, Providence, 1975-78; mgr. utilization rev. Naval Regional Med. Ctr., Okinawa, Japan, 1979-80; qualification officer Dept. Health and Human Svcs., Rockville, Md., 1980-82; dir. med. group mgmt. Group Health Assn., Washington, 1982-86; exec. dir. Network Health Plan (Jurgovan & Blair, Inc.), Fairfax, Va., 1986-87; v.p. Jurgovan & Blair, Potomac, Md., 1987-88; exec. v.p. and COO Health Plus Inc., Greenbelt, Md., 1988—; cons. U.S. Govt., Washington, 1982-86; preceptor Washington U., St. Louis, 1984-85, Duke U., Chapel Hill, N.C., 1985-86, Med. Coll. of Va., Richmond, 1989, George Washington U., Washington, 1990—. Contbr. articles to Utilization Mgmt., 1986, Health Benefits Mgmt., 1988. Lector St. John Neuman Ch., Reston, Va., 1985-88, St. Catherine of Siena Ch., Great Falls, Va., 1988—. Mem. Am. Coll. of Healthcare Execs., Group Helath Assn. Am. (mem. coms. 1985-86), Nat. Capitol Area Health Care Coalition (mem. adv. bd. 1988). Roman Catholic. Home: 1172 Robindale Dr Great Falls VA 22066-1851

DOLNY, WARREN STUART, printing company executive; b. Bronx, N.Y., June 29, 1928; s. Jack W. and Gertrude (Neiditch) D.; m. Violet Port, Nov. 19, 1949; children: David, Debra, Denyse. BBA, CCNY, 1957. Salesman Port Printed Products Co., N.Y.C., 1951-55, sales mgr., 1955-59, gen. mgr., 1959-67, pres., 1967-80, chief exec. officer, 1981—. Chmn. local bd. 13 U.S. Selective Svc., 1981—; mem. drainage commn. Town of Ramapo, N.Y., 1972-77; mem. transp. adv. com. County of Rockland, N.Y., 1975—; bd. dirs. M.T.A., N.Y.C., 1989—. Sgt. USMC, 1951-53, Korea. Mem. Stationers Assn. N.Y. (pres. 1982-83, Man of Yr. 1986), Nat. Office Products Assn. (dist. gov. 1985-86, Gov. of Yr. 1986), Jewish War Vets. U.S.A. (nat. comdr. 1992—, state comdr. 1977-78, nat. policy com. 1982—, Vet. of Yr. dept. of N.Y. 1981), N.Y. City Transit Police Gonen Soc. (hon.). Democrat. Home: 30 Jill Ln Monsey NY 10952 Office: Port Printed Products Corp 31-00 47th Ave Long Island NY 11101

DOMAGALA, RICHARD EDWARD, sales executive; b. Stamford, Conn., Aug. 16, 1947; s. Edward Melton and Adele Bellavita (Devitalis) D.; m. Susan Lewis, Jan. 1, 1972 (div. 1976); m. Andrea Blake Cerreta, Sept. 4, 1976; children: Lisa Cerreta Domagal, Scott Michael Blake. BS in Edn., The U. Conn., 1971. Asst. mgr. Household Fin. Corp., Stamford, Conn., 1973-74; mng. editor Pub. Dynamics, Inc., Stamford, 1974-76; transp. coord. Advo-System, Inc., Hartford, Conn., 1977-79; dir. corp. svc. Advo-System, Inc., Hartford, 1983-85; dir. govt. rels. Advo-System, Inc., Windsor, Conn., 1985-89; dir. sales, ops. TransAdvo, Inc., Hartford, 1979-83, v.p. sales and mktg., 1989-92; dir. Patriot Logistics Group, Meriden, Conn., 1992—; pub. rels. chmn. Postal Customer Coun., Hartford, 1988-89; treas. Advo Polit. Action Com., Windsor, 1985-89. Creator, producer: (video PSA) AIDS Don't Care, 1988 (Mercury award 1988, Pub. Svc. award 1988); writer, editor articles for mags. Campaign communications chmn. United Way/Combined Health Appeal, Hartford, 1989. With U.S. Army, 1970-73. Mem. Pub. Rels. Soc. Am. (accredited, pres. Conn. Valley Chpt. 1990, bd. dirs. N.E. dist. 1990-91, pres.-elect 1989, treas. and pub. svc. chmn. 1988, chmn. literacy sub-com. 1989, nat. com. on pub. svc. 1991, Merit award 1988, Presdl. Citation 1988). Office: Patriot Logistics Group 1550 N Colony Rd Meriden CT 06450

DOMBECK, HAROLD ARTHUR, engineering company executive; b. Bronx, N.Y., Mar. 23, 1941; s. Max J. and Rose R. (Schefren) D.; m. Peggy A. Weissman, Apr. 7, 1963 (div. Nov. 1982); children: Mark J., Glenn D.; m. Cynthia E. Kofoed, May 14, 1983; 1 child, David S. B of Civil Engring., NYU, 1962, M of Civil Engring., 1963. Profl. engr., N.Y., N.J., Conn. Instr. San Antonio Coll., San Antonio, Tex., 1964-65, SUNY, Farmingdale, 1965-68; project mgr. H2M Group, Melville, N.Y., 1965-74, dir. environ. engring., 1971-81, dir. mktg., 1982-85, exec. v.p., 1986-88, pres., 1989-91, pres., chief exec. officer, chmn., 1991—; chmn., chief exec. officer Architects and Engrs. Ins. Co., Dover, Del., 1987—; chmn. bd. dirs. Am. Cons. Engrs. Pension Trust, St. Louis; dir. Architects and Engrs. Loss Control, Inc., Northbrook, Ill., 1988—. Pres. High Woods Civic Assn., St. James, N.Y., 1971-73. 1st lt. USAF, 1963-65. Fellow ASCE; mem. Am. Acad. Environ. Engrs. (diplomate), NSPE (dir. 1982-85), N.Y. State Water Pollution Control Assn. (dir. 1980-83), Am. Cons. Engrs. Coun. (pres. L.I. 1982-84), N.Y. State Soc. Profl. Engrs. (pres. 1983-84, pres. Suff County chpt. 1978-80, Engr. of Yr. 1989, 90, Outstanding Svc. awards 1988, 89). Office: H2M Group 575 Broadhollow Rd Melville NY 11747-5023

DOMBROWSKI, DAVID, baseball team executive; b. Chgo., July 27, 1956; s. Ronald Edward and Laurie Dombrowski. B of Adminstrn., Western Mich. U., 1979. Adminstrv. asst. Chgo. White Sox, 1978-79, dir. player devel. & scouting, 1979-80, asst. gen. mgr., 1980-85, v.p. baseball ops., 1985-86; dir. player devel. Montreal Expos, 1986-87, asst. gen. mgr., 1987-88, gen. mgr., 1988—. Bd. dirs. Chgo. Baseball Cancer Charities, 1981—. Named Exec. of Yr. by UPI, 1990.

DOMBROWSKI, FRANK PAUL, JR., pharmacist; b. Nashua, N.H., May 10, 1943; s. Frank Paul and Yvonne Joan (Paris) D.; B.S., Mass. Coll. Pharmacy, 1965, M.S., 1967; m. Eleanor Cassady, June 15, 1968; children—Michael, Peter, Laura, Cheryl, Douglas. Pharmacist, Androscoggin Valley Hosp., Berlin, N.H., 1974-75, Eastern Maine Med. Center, 1975-77; dir. pharm. services and central supply Concord Hosp., N.H., 1977-82; founder, pres. Hosp. Home Health Care of N.H., 1982-92, Hosp. Home Health Care of Maine, 1986; commr. N.H. Bd. of Registration of Pharmacy; cons. nurse anesthetist sch. Concord Hosp. Served with U.S. Army, 1968-74. Decorated Combat Inf. badge, Bronze Star medal, Army Commendation medal. Fellow Am. Acad. Med. Adminstrs.; mem. Am. Pharm. Assn., Am. Soc. Hosp. Pharmacists, N.H. Pharm. Assn., N.H. Soc. Hosp. Pharmacists, Nat. Assoc. Retail Druggists. Club: Lions (chpt. pres.). Home: RRH5 Box 443 Broadcove Rd Contoocook NH 03229 Office: 835 Hanover St Ste 104 Manchester NH 03104-5401

DOMINGOS, HENRY, electrical engineering educator; b. Massena, N.Y., Sept. 17, 1934; s. Acacio and Joaquin (Rodriguez) D.; m. Huguette Marie Levesque, July 19, 1958; children: Gigi, Chantal, Scott. BEE, Clarkson Coll., 1956; MSEE, U. Southern Calif., 1958; PhD, U. Wash., 1963. Engr. Hughes Aircraft Co., Culver City, Calif., 1956-58; asst. prof. U. Nev., Reno, 1958-60; instr. U. Wash., Seattle, 1960-63; assoc. prof. Clarkson U., Potsdam, N.Y., 1963-80; prof. Clarkson U., 1980—, chmn. elec. engring dept., 1988—. Mem. IEEE, Am. Soc. Engring. Edn. Republican. Roman Catholic. Home: RR 1 Box 263 Potsdam NY 13676-9735 Office: Elec Engring Dept Clarkson U Potsdam NY 13699-5720

DOMINIQUE, PAUL A., vocational counselor; b. N.Y.C., July 8, 1947; s. Leon K. and Alera M. (George) D.; m. Jocelyn Y. Ellis, June 5, 1982; children: Paul Andre Jr., Jason Pierre, Olivia Grace. BA, Manhattan Coll., 1969; MA, NYU, 1977; postgrad. in Pub. Adminstrn., Baruch Coll., 1984-86. Nat. cert. counselor. Vocat. counselor N.Y. State Dept. of Labor, N.Y.C. Mem. NAACP (bd. dirs., labor dept. br.), Bronx Devel. Ctr. Br. of N.Y. Assn. for Mentally Retarded (bd. dirs.), Internat. Assn. Pers. in Employment Security. Home: 100 31B Elgar Pl Bronx NY 10475

DOMINO, ANTHONY JOSEPH, JR., pension consultant; b. Buffalo, July 16, 1962; s. Anthony J. Domino and Carolyn Todaro Romano; m. Meg Beth Fulton, May 20, 1989; 1 child, Nicholas Anthony. BA in Religious Studies, Brown U., 1984. Sr. pension cons. Nat. Pension Svc., White Plains, N.Y., 1984—; lectr. in field. Contbr. articles to profl. jours. Bd. dirs. Regis Devel. Coun., N.Y.C., 1991—. Named New Assoc. of the Yr. Guardian Life, 1988, named to Pres.'s Coun., 1990, 91. Mem. Life Underwriters Assn. Westchester (bd. dirs., sec. 1991-92, v.p. 1992-93), Westchester County CLU and ChFC Assn. (bd. dirs. 1991—, pres.-elect 1992-93), Brown U. Alumni Assn. (bd. dirs. 1987—). Republican. Roman Catholic. Office: Nat Pension Svc 1025 Westchester Ave White Plains NY 10604

DOMPIERRE, JUDITH EVLYN, educator; b. Morocco, Feb. 28, 1957; d. Robert Randall and Marta Selma (Liebig) B.; m. Gilles Dompierre, July 8, 1989. B. BE, Johnson State Coll., 1979; MEd, U. Vt., 1988. Cert. elem. tchr., edn. adminstrn. Tchr. math., asst. prin. Alburg Elem. Sch., Alburg, Vt., 1982-88; reading cons., grade 1 and 4 Pollard Sch., Plaistow, N.H., 1989—; com. mem. workshop, developer, presenter Network Northwest Vt. Outcomes-Based Master Network, 1985-86; participant Vt. Seminar on Edn., Tchr. Talks, 1986; vis. team mem. Vt. Pub. Sch. Approval, 1987. Troop leader, chmn. Vt. Girl Scouts U.S., 1973-75. Mem. Nat. Coun. Tchrs. Math., Assn. Tchrs. Math. New Eng., Vt. Coun. Tchrs. Math., Vt. Acad. Arts and Scis., Assn. Supervision and Curriculum Devel., Nat. Assn. Female Execs. Home: 15 R Brian Ave Derry NH 03038-4342 Office: Pollard Sch 120 Main St Plaistow NH 03865-0001

DOMZELLA, JANET, library director; b. Marquette, Mich., Mar. 22, 1935; d. Jack Carl and Alice Margaret (Blom) Messenger; m. Theodore S. Wodzinski (div. 1974); children: Christopher, Joseph, Daniel; m. Perry Landon Domzella, July 15, 1977; stepchildren: Perry, Pamela. BS, No. Mich. U., 1973; MLS, U. Buffalo, 1979. Sch. libr. media specialist Niagara Falls (N.Y.) Bd. Edn., 1974-75, Iroquois Ctrl. Sch., Elma, N.Y., 1975-77; dir. Lewiston (N.Y.) Pub. Libr., 1977—. Co-author: Lewiston: Self Guided Tour, 1986. Vol. firefighter Upper Mountain Vol. Fire Co., Lewiston, 1980-90, treas., 1984-90; mem. Town of Lewiston Bur. Fire Prevention, 1988-90; mem. adv. bd. Documentary Heritage Program. Mem. N.Y. Libr. Assn. Democrat. Roman Catholic. Office: Lewiston Pub Libr 305 S Eighth St Lewiston NY 14092

DONAGI, RON, mathematics educator; b. Tel Aviv, Mar. 9, 1956; s. Alexander Emanuel and Rachel Donagi. BS, Tel Aviv U., 1973; MS, PhD, Harvard U., 1977. Teaching fellow Harvard U., Cambridge, Mass., 1976-77; Hedrick asst. prof. UCLA, 1977-79; asst. prof. U. Utah, 1979-82; mem. Inst. for Advanced Study, Princeton, N.J., 1981-82; assoc. prof. U. Utah, 1982-84, Northeastern U., Boston, 1983-86; prof. Northeastern U., 1986-87, U. Pa., Phila., 1987—; rsch. prof. Math. Scis. Rsch. Inst., Berkeley, Calif., 1989-90. Contbr. articles to profl. jours. David P. Gardner fellow U. Utah, 1981, Alfred P. Sloan Rsch. fellow, 1982-84; Rsch. & Scholarship Devel. Fund grantee, 1985, NSF rsch. grantee, 1977. Mem. Am. Math. Soc. Office: U Pa Dept Math 33d & Walnut Sts Philadelphia PA 19104

DONAHOO, MELVIN LAWRENCE, aerospace management consultant, industrial engineer; b. Balt., Dec. 28, 1930; s. Lawrence E. and Margaret (Hartman) D.; m. Charlene B. Donahoo; children from previous marriage: Patricia Ann, Joseph, Teresa, Melvin Lawrence Jr. BS, U. Balt., 1954, MBA, 1974; postgrad., Am. Univ., 1964-67, George Washington U., 1969-71. Cons., v.p. L.E. Donahoo & Assoc., Phila., 1954-58; chief indsl. engring. Martin Marietta Corp., Balt. and Orlando, Fla., 1958-63; with program mgr. staff NASA Goddard Space Flight Ctr., Greenbelt, Md., 1963-90; dir. ops. Idea, Inc., 1990—; instr. indsl. mgmt. Author: Aircraft Learning Curves, 1959, Project Planning Handbook, 1970; also research papers. With USN. Mem. Soc. Mfg. Engrs. (sr., life, mem. coms.), Inst. Indsl. Engrs. (sr., life, mem. coms.), Am. Legion (post comdr. Md. 1983, county comdr. 1984-86), Kent Island Yacht Club, KC, Elks, Moose. Home: 2417 Pelham Ave Baltimore MD 21213-1036

DONAHUE, C. RICHARD, social worker; b. Albany, N.Y., Nov. 1, 1931; s. Clarence Joseph and Julia Loretta (Carroll) D.; m. Therese Marie Murray, Dec. 27, 1958; children: Elizabeth Anne, Michael Richard. BA, Siena Coll., 1955; MSW, NYU, 1959; MA, Columbia U., 1972. Lic. social worker, N.Y.; diplomate Am. Bd. Examiners in Social Work (N.Y. State rep. 1992—), NASW; Assn. Cert. Social Workers. Probation officer Family Ct., White Plains, N.Y., 1959-64; sr. social worker spl. edn. dept. Bd. Coop. Ednl. Svcs., Yorktown Heights, N.Y., 1964—; adj. prof. NYU, 1967—; supr. field work Grad. Sch. Social Work, N.Y.C. Mem. Adv. Com. Spl. Edn., Yorktown Heights, North Salem (N.Y.) Group Home Bd. Capt. U.S. Army, 1955-57. Fellow Soc. Clin. Social Work Psychotherapy, Am. Orthopsychiat. Assn.; mem. Internat. Assn. Pupil Pers. Workers, Internat. Fedn. Social Workers, World Fedn. forMental Health, N.Y. United Tchrs., North Salem Libr. Assn., North Salem Hist. Soc., N.Y. Sch. Social Workers (past pres., award 1978). Democrat. Roman Catholic. Home and Office: 71 Great Oaks Ln Purdys NY 10578 Office: Bd Coop Ednl Svcs Spl Edn Dept Pines Bridge Rd Yorktown Heights NY 10598

DONAHUE, CHARLOTTE MARY, lawyer; b. Columbus, Ohio, Sept. 29, 1954; d. Patrick Henry and Helen Dillon (Meany) D. AB, Holy Cross Coll., 1976; JD, U. Toledo, 1983. Bar: Pa. 1984, D.C. 1985, U.S. Dist. Ct. (ea. dist.) Pa. 1985, U.S. Ct. Appeals 3d cir.) 1985, U.S. Surpeme Ct. 1990, Mass. 1992. Jud. clk. to presiding justice Commonwealth Ct. Pa., Phila., 1983-84; spl. asst. U.S. atty. U.S. Dist. Ct. (ea. dist.) Pa., Phila., 1987-90; atty. HUD, Phila., 1984—. Mem. Fed., Pa., Phila., D.C. Bar Assns., Order of Barristers, Internat. Platform Assn., Supreme Ct. Hist. Soc. Home: PO Box 58862 Philadelphia PA 19102-8862 Office: HUD 105 S 7th St Philadelphia PA 19106-3324

DONAHUE, JOHN F., insurance executive; b. Phila., Mar. 23, 1936; s. Charles William and Marie Binigna (Carr) D.; m. Joyce A. Endt, Apr. 23, 1960; children: Cheryl, Bryan. CPCU. Underwriting dir. ITT Hartford, Hartford, Conn., 1967-69, asst. sec., 1969-73, sec., 1973-76, asst. v.p., 1976-81, v.p., 1981-89, sr. v.p., 1989—; chmn. Hartford Reins. Co., 1987, Gen. Policy Com. on U.S. Aviation Ins. Group, N.Y.C., 1990, Am. Nuclear Insurers, Farmington, Conn., 1990, Nat. Coun. on Compensation, Boca Raton, Fla., 1990; ins. svcs. ofcl. Comml. Risk Svcs., N.Y.C., 1990. Bd. dirs. ARC, Hartford, 1991, Bushnell, Hartford, 1991, Conn. Community Care, Inc., Hartford, 1991. Republican. Roman Catholic. Office: ITT Hartford Hartford Pla Hartford CT 06115

DONAHUE, JOHN F., investment company executive; b. Pitts., 1924. Grad., U.S. Mil. Acad., 1946. Pres. Federated Investors, Pitts. Office: Federated Investors Federated Investors Tower Pittsburgh PA 15222

DONAHUE, JOHN JOSEPH, ships master, shipping officer; b. Bklyn., June 9, 1931; s. Martin J. and Marie H. Donahue; m. Winifred Sullivan, Feb. 9, 1955; children: John T., Thomas J. B in Marine Sci., CCNY, 1953. Cert. master oceans unltd. USCG, C.S.P. Ships officer Farrell Lines Inc., N.Y., 1954-58; terminal mgr. Atlantic & Gulf, N.Y., 1960-61; ships officer Am. Export Lines, N.Y., 1960-66, ops. mgr., 1966-70; sr. marine cargo cons. Marsh & McLennan Inc., N.Y., 1970-72; safety dir. United Brands, N.Y., 1972-73; mgr. loss prevention U.S. Industries, N.Y., 1973-76; ship master Energy Transp. Corp., N.Y., 1976—. Honored by UN, 1984. Mem. Am. Soc. Safety Engrs. (profl.), Coun. Am. Master Marines, 7th Rgts. Vets. Assn., Masons.

DONAHUE, MARY ROSENBERG, psychologist; b. N.Y.C., Dec. 20, 1932; d. Lester and Ethel (Hyman) Rosenberg; children: Laurie, Rachel. BA, Adelphi U., 1954; MA, N.Y. U., 1958; PhD, St. John U., 1968. Tchr. Elmont, N.Y., 1954-57, sch. psychologist, 1957-63; cons. psychologist NIMH, 1964-65; sch. psychologist Mamaroneck, N.Y., 1966-67; pvt. practice psychology Bethesda, Md., 1971—; pres. Automated Psychol. Svcs.; bd. dirs. SPIFE, comprehensive testing svc.; expert witness local jurisdictions regarding domestic issues, womens issues, abuse, 1974—; speaker on custody evaluations and expert witness considerations. NIMH grantee, 1962-63, 64-65. Mem. Am. Psychol. Assn., Md. Psychol. Assn., D.C. Psychol. Assn., Am. Orthopsychiat. Assn., Assn. Pvt. Practitioners, Nat. Assn. Women Bus. Owners. Home: 12017 Edgepark Ct Rockville MD 20854-2138 Office: 5902 Hubbard Dr Rockville MD 20852-4823

DONALD, DAVID HERBERT, author, history educator; b. Goodman, Miss., Oct. 1, 1920; s. Ira Unger and Sue Ella (Belford) D.; m. Aida DiPace, 1955; 1 son, Bruce Randall. Student, Holmes Jr. Coll., 1937-39; A.B., Millsaps Coll., 1941, L.H.D., 1976; A.M., U. Ill., 1942, Ph.D., 1946, LHD (hon.), 1992; M.A. (hon.), U. Oxford, 1959, Harvard U., 1973; Litt.D. (hon.), Coll. Charleston, 1985. Teaching fellow U. N.C., 1942; research asst. history U. Ill., 1943-45, research assoc., 1946-47; fellow Social Sci. Research Council, 1945-46; instr. history Columbia U., 1947-49; assoc. prof. history Smith Coll., 1949-51; asst. prof. history Columbia U. Grad. Faculty, 1951-52, assoc. prof., 1952-57, prof. history, 1957-59; prof. history Princeton U., 1959-62; prof. Am. history Johns Hopkins U., Balt., 1962-73; Harry C. Black prof. Johns Hopkins U., 1963-73, dir. Inst. So. History,, 1966-72; Charles Warren prof. Am. history and prof. Am. civilization Harvard U., 1973-91, prof. emeritus, 1991—, chmn. grad. program in Am. civilization, 1979-85; prof. emeritus, 1991—; vis. assoc. prof. Amherst Coll., 1950; Fulbright lectr. Am. history U. Coll. North Wales, 1953-54; mem. Inst. Advanced Study, 1957-58; Harmsworth prof. Am. history Oxford U., 1959-60; John P. Young lectr. Memphis State U., 1963; Walter Lynwood Fleming lectr. La. State U., 1965; Benjamin Rush lectr. Am. Psychiat. Assn., 1972; Commonwealth lectr. Univ. Coll., London, 1975; Samuel Paley lectr. Hebrew Univ. of Jerusalem, 1991. Author: Lincoln's Herndon, 1948, Divided We Fought, A Pictorial History of the War, 1861-1865, 1952, Inside Lincoln's Cabinet: The Civil War Diaries of Salmon P. Chase, 1954, Lincoln Reconsidered: Essays on the Civil War Era, 1956, rev., 1961, A Rebel's Recollections, (G.C. Eggleston), 1959, Charles Sumner and the Coming of the Civil War, 1960 (Pulitzer Prize in biography), Why the North Won the Civil War, 1960, (with J.G. Randall) The Civil War and Reconstruction, 2d edit, 1961, rev., enlarged edit., 1969, The Divided Union, 1961, The Politics of Reconstruction, 1863-67, 1965, The Nation in Crisis, 1861-1877, 1969, Charles Sumner and the Rights of Man, 1970, (with Sidney Andrews) The South Since the War, 1970, Gone for a Soldier, 1975, (with others) The Great Republic, 1977, rev. edit., 1981, 3d edit., 1985, 4th edit., 1992, Liberty and Union, 1978, Look Homeward: A Life of Thomas Wolfe, 1987, (Pulitzer Prize 1988); editor: War Diary and Letters of Stephen Minot Weld, 1979; gen. editor: Documentary History of American Life, The Making of America Series, 6 vols.; co-editor: (with wife) Diary of Charles Francis Adams, 2 vols, 1964; contbr. articles to periodicals. Recipient C. Hugh Holman prize Modern Langs. Assn., 1988, Disting. Alumnus award U. Ill., 1988; Guggenheim fellow, 1964-65, 85-86; fellow Am. Council Learned Socs., 1969-70, Center for Advanced Study Behavioral Scis., 1969-70, George A. and Eliza G. Howard fellow, 1957-58; Nat. Endowment for Humanities sr. fellow, 1971-72. Fellow Am. Acad. Arts and Scis.; mem. Orgn. Am. Historians, Am. Hist. Assn., So. Hist. Assn. (v.p. 1968, pres. 1969), Soc. Am. Historians, Mass. Hist. Soc., Am. Antiquarian Soc., Phi Beta Kappa, Phi Kappa Phi, Pi Kappa Delta, Pi Kappa Alpha, Omicron Delta Kappa. Episcopalian. Clubs: Harvard (N.Y.C.); Cosmos, Signet, Fox. Home: 41 Lincoln Rd PO Box 158 Lincoln MA 01773

DONALD, JAMES MAITLAND, investment management executive; b. Toronto, Ont., Can., Feb. 22, 1961; s. Rodney Stewart Craik and Penelope Susan (Passant) D.; m. Sonya Pamela Rolin, May 21, 1989; 1 child, Jonathon Sebastian Reiss. BA with honors, Huron Coll., U. Western Ont., 1983. Assoc. Wood Gundy Inc., Toronto, 1983-85; portfolio mgr. Mercury Asset Mgmt. Ltd., London, 1985-88; v.p., sr. officer Warburg Investment Internat. Mgmt. Can. Ltd., Montreal, 1988-90; v.p. Warburg Internat., N.Y.C., 1990—; v.p. and treas. The United Kingdom Fund, Inc., N.Y.C., The Europe Fund, Inc., Warburg Internat. Fund. Fundraiser Liberal Party of Can., Toronto, 1984. Mem. East India Club (London), Zeta Psi (chpt. pres. 1981-82). Office: Warburg Investment 3401 780 3d Ave New York NY 10017

DONALD, ROGER THOMAS, publishing executive; b. N.Y.C., May 18, 1936; s. Harry and Yves (Powers) D.; m. Diana Van Der Vlis, June 6, 1960; children: Adrienne, Matthew. BA with honors, Yale U., 1957, Cambridge U., 1959; MA, Cambridge U., 1959. Sr. editor McGraw Hill, N.Y.C., 1960-66; editorial dir. Funk and Wagnalls, N.Y.C., 1966-68; editor in chief World Pub. Co., N.Y.C., 1968-69; from N.Y. editor to publisher Little Brown and Co., Boston and N.Y.C., 1969–. With USAR, 1959-60. Mem. PEN Club. Office: Little Brown and Co 1271 Avenue of Americas New York NY 10020

DONALDSON, FRED LEE, JR., clergyman; b. Greenville, N.C., Mar. 11, 1946; s. Fred Lee Sr. and Leather Louise (Richardson) D.; m. Patricia Faye Waller, Oct. 19, 1991; children: Worjroh, Esther, Loretta Joi, Tyrone. AAS, Bryant and Stratton Bus. Inst., 1979; student, St. John Fisher Coll., 1979-80. Recreation leader Bur. of Recreation, Rochester, N.Y., 1971-75; youth div. aide N.Y. State Div. Youth, Rochester, 1975-77, 82-85; counselor confined persons Monroe County Jail House, Rochester, 1976-80; coord. WOULF, community worker Lewis St. Ctr., Rochester, 1979-80; owner, mgr. F.D. New & Used Store, Rochester, 1985-88; counselor, pastor Attica (N.Y.) Correctional Facility, 1988—; community worker Jesus Disciples, House of Prayer, Rochester, 1988—; pastor, tchr. Jesus Disciples, House of Prayer, Rochester, 1977—; counselor Disciples Rescue Alliance, Rochester, 1985. Composer Christian gospel songs, 1991. With Signal Corps, U.S. Army, 1965-67, sgt. USAF, 1967-71. Mem. VFW (life), NAACP (housing chmn. 1991—). Republican. Mem. Apostolic Ch. Home: 25 University Ave Rochester NY 14605 Office: Jesus Disciples House of Prayer 71 Portland Ave Rochester NY 14605

DONALDSON, JAMES OSWELL, III, neurology educator; b. Butler, Pa., July 19, 1942; s. James Oswell Jr. and Estelle Mathilda (Unverzagt) D.; m. Mary Hoopingarner, Aug. 23, 1969 (div. Dec. 1983); 1 child, Andrew Robert; m. Susan McKernin, Nov. 3, 1984. BS, Haverford Coll., 1964; MD, U. Pa., 1968. Diplomate Am. Bd. Psychiatry and Neurology, Am. Bd. Internal Medicine. Intern in medicine Hosp. of U. Pa., Phila., 1968-69, resident, 1969-70, resident in neurology, 1974-76; hon. house physician Nat. Hosp. for Nervous Diseases, London, 1973-74, sr. vis. fellow, 1991; asst. prof. neurology U. Conn. Sch. Medicine, Farmington, 1977-82, assoc. prof., 1982-88, prof., 1988—. Author: Neurology of Pregnancy, 1978, 2d edit., 1989. Maj. M.C., U.S. Army, 1970-73. Fellow ACP, Am. Acad. Neurology; mem. Am. Neurol. Assn. Office: U Conn Health Ctr 263 Farmington Ave Farmington CT 06030-0001

DONALDSON, JOHN CECIL, JR., consumer products company executive; b. Bklyn., Dec. 8, 1933; s. John Cecil and Josephine (Greason) D.; m. Marilyn J. Smith, Aug. 29, 1959; children: Susan, John III. AB, Brown U., 1956; MBA, U. Pa., 1959; postgrad., Bentley Sch. Acctg., 1957, LaSalle Law Sch., 1959. Various positions Gen. Motors Corp., Flint, Mich., 1960-71; zone mgr. Gen. Motors Corp., Buffalo, 1971-76; zone mgr. Gen. Motors Corp., Newark, 1976-77, mgr. forward product planning, 1977-78; from dir. sales and mktg. to v.p. Corbin Ltd., 1979-85; exec. v.p. and gen. mgr. TMG Corp., N.Y.C., 1986—; pres. Gen. Motors Exec. Club, Newark, N.J., 1977-78. Mem. Am. Mktg. Assn. Republican. Home: 36 Nottingham Way Millington NJ 07946-1917

DONALDSON, THOMAS, ethicist, educator; b. Wichita, Kans., July 23, 1945; s. Paul J. and Louisene (Sadler) D.; m. Sally Leisure, May, 1970 (div. 1973); m. Jean Shephard, Sept. 3, 1977; children: Paul, Keith, Paige. Student, U.S. Naval Acad., 1963-65; BS, U. Kans., 1967, PhD, 1976. Asst. prof. Loyola U. Chgo., 1976-81, assoc. prof., 1981-84, Henry J. Wirtenberger prof. ethics, 1984-88; C. Stewart Sheppard vis. prof. bus. adminstrn. U. Va., Charlottesville, 1988-89; John Carroll prof. bus. ethics Georgetown U., Washington, 1989-92, John F. Connelly prof. bus. ethics, 1992—; adj. prof. dept. philosophy Georgetown U., 1989—, sr. rsch. fellow Kennedy Inst. for Ethics, 1989—. Editor: Issues in Moral Philosophy, 1986, Case Studies in Business Ethics, 1987,Ethical Issues in Business, 1979, 83, 87, 92; author: The Ethics of International Business, 1989, Corporations and Morality, 1982; contbr. articles to profl. jours.; mem. editorial bd.: Jour. Bus. Ethics, 1979—, Philosophy in Context, 1984,Bus. Ethics Quarterly, 1990—, Employee Responsibilities and Rights Jour., 1988—. Exec. bd. mem., usher 1st United Meth. Ch. Evanston, Ill., 1979-85. With USN, 1963-65. Fellow

Bus. Enterprise Trust; mem. Ctr. for Advanced Study Ethics (coun. scholars 1990—). Home: 10116 Carmelita Dr Rockville MD 20854-4236 Office: Georgetown U Washington DC 20057

DONALDSON, WILLIAM HENRY, financial executive; b. Buffalo, June 2, 1931; s. Eames and Guida (Marx) D.; m. Sept. 17, 1960; children—Kimberly, Matthew. BA, Yale U., 1953; MA (hon.), 1970; MBA, Harvard U., 1958; LLD (hon.), Webster U., 1992. Chmn., chief exec. Donaldson, Lufkin & Jenrette, Inc., N.Y.C., 1959-73; undersec. of state U.S. Dept. State, Washington, 1973-74; spl. cons., adv. to v.p. of U.S., Washington, 1974; dean, Beinecke prof. mgmt. Yale Grad. Mgmt. Sch., New Haven, 1975-80; chmn., chief exec. officer Donaldson Enterprises, Inc., N.Y.C., 1980-90; chmn., chief exec. New York Stock Exchange, N.Y.C., 1991—; bd. dirs. Aetna Life & Casualty, Honeywell Inc., Philip Morris Cos. Inc. Trustee, chmn. fin. com. Ford Found., N.Y.C., 1968-80, Yale U., New Haven, 1970-75; bd. dirs. N.Y.C. Partnership, Bus. Coun. of State of N.Y., Lincoln Ctr. for Performing Arts, N.Y.C.; trustee St. Lawrence U., Marine Corps Command and Staff Coll. Found., Carnegie Endowment Internat. Peace; chmn. Aetna Found.; gov. Foreign Policy Assn. Served to 1st lt. USMC, 1953-55. Recipient Pres's. Disting. Service award SUNY, 1976; named Businessman of Yr., AP, 1969. Mem. Inst. Chartered Fin. Analysts, N.Y. Stock Exchange (dir. 1972-73), Coun. on Fgn. Rels., Coun. for Econs. Devel. Office: NYSE Office of Chmn 11 Wall St New York NY 10005*

DONALDSON-EVANS, MARY PRUDHOMME, foreign language educator; b. Duluth, Minn., Jan. 15, 1943; d. Lawrence James and Lillian Isabelle (Hinman) Prudhomme; m. Lancelot Knox Donaldson-Evans, June 22, 1968; children: Catherine, Andrew. BA, Marquette U., 1965; MA, U. Wis., Milw., 1968; PhD, U. Pa., 1975. Teaching asst. U. Wis., Milw., 1966-67; part-time instr. Villanova (Pa.) U., 1969; instr. U. Del., Newark, 1969-76, asst. prof., 1976-82, assoc. prof., 1982-91, prof., 1991—. Author: A Woman's Revenge: The Chronology of Dispossession in Maupassant's Fiction, 1986; asst. editor: French Review; co-editor: Modernity and Revolution in Late Nineteenth-Century France; contbr. articles to profl. jours. Recipient Gen. Univ. Rsch. grant Univ. Del., 1988. Mem. AAUP, Am. Assn. Tchrs. of French, Modern Lang. Assn., L'Ordre des Palmes Academiques (Chevalier award 1989). Democrat. Episcopalian. Home: 425 W Rose Tree Rd Media PA 19063-2014 Office: U Del Dept Fgn Langs Newark DE 19716

DONATH, CLARENCE EDGAR, retired architect; b. Sedalia, Mo., Mar. 10, 1912. B.S. in Architecture, U. Ill., 1938; postgrad., Art Inst. Buffalo, 1939-40, SUNY-Buffalo, 1969-71. Registered architect, N.Y. Prin., Clarence E. Donath, Architect, East Aurora, N.Y., 1956-65; ptnr. Kideney, Smith, Fitzgerald, Laping, Buffalo, N.Y., 1965-80; now retired. Prin. archtl. works include churches, libraries, and colleges. Mem. Internat. Soc. Philos. Enquiry. Home: 91 Hillcrest Rd East Aurora NY 14052-1311

DONATO, ALFRED VIRGIL, electrical engineer, consultant; b. CN.Y.C., Feb. 8, 1917; s. Philip and Mary (Tafuri) D.; m. Josephine Louise Marsiglia, Sept. 7, 1947; 1 child, Beverly. BSEE, NYU, 1940; MS in Electric Ship Propulsion, Poly. Inst., 1943. Cert. profl. engr., Md. Elec. engr. marine Gibbs & Cox, N.Y.C., 1940-45, GE, Schenectady, N.Y., 1945-47, Bethleham Steel Ship Building, Balt., 1947-50, Gen. Svcs. Adminstrn., Washington, 1950-53; interdisciplinary supervisory elec. engr. Dept. of Army Corps of Engrs. New Dist., N.Y.C., 1953-88; ret., 1988; cons. elec., Bklyn., 1980—; cons. estimator, Bklyn., 1968—. Author: Load Shedding brochure (Significant Achievement award Corps of Engrs., 1987,88), 1982. Mem. legis. adv. com. N.Y. State Senator, 21st Dist., Albany, 1979; mem. Rep. Nat. Com., Washington; supporter St. Anselmi Cath. Ch., Bklyn. Recipient Superior Performance award Corps of Engrs., 1967, 76, Significant Achievement award Corps of Engrs., 1984, 85, Outstanding Leadership award Corps of Engrs., 1987. Mem. AIEE, Soc. Naval Architects and Marine Engrs., Naval Inst. (Washington), Am. Mil. Engrs., N.Y. Acad. Scis., Crecent Hill Club, Athletic Club.

DONAWICK, WILLIAM JOSEPH, veterinary surgeon, educator, consultant; b. Troy, N.Y., Aug. 18, 1940; s. Joseph Charles and Gladys Marion (Fields) D.; m. Bonnie Jean Martin, Feb. 1961; children—Stephanie Eileen, Melinda Jean. Student Cornell U., 1957-59, D.V.M., 1963; postgrad. U. Pa., 1966-1969, M.S. (hon.), 1973. From instr. to assoc. prof. vet. surgery U. Pa., Phila., 1966-78, prof. vet. surgery, 1978—; cons. Profl. Exam. Service, N.Y.C., 1981—, Gen. Econopak, Phila., 1985—. Recipient Norden award for Disting. Teaching, U. Pa., 1970; grantee NIH, 1973-78. Diplomate Am. Coll. Vet. Surgeons (pres. 1982-83, chmn. 1983-84); mem. Phi Zeta (pres. 1976-77). Republican. Clubs: Debonaire Flyers, Inc. (pres. 1978—); Aero Club of Pa. (adv. 1982—). Home: 1501 Brandywine Dr West Chester PA 19382-6802 Office: U Pa 382 W Street Rd New Bolton Ctr Kennett Square PA 19348

DONCASTER, HILARY LOUISE, nurse; b. Fitchburg, Mass., Dec. 9, 1960; d. Donald Dempsey and Janet Maryann (McKay) D. BS in Nursing, Fitchburg State Coll., 1982; postgrad computer programming, Cen. N.E. Coll., 1988-89; postgrad. in Mgmt. Info. Systems, Nichols Coll., 1990—. RN, Mass. Staff nurse neurosurgery USAF Med. Ctr., Lackland AFB, Tex., 1983-86; ambulatory surg. specialist Katy (Tex.) Community Hosp., 1986; community nurse Worcester (Mass.) VNA, 1986; nurse reviewer Mass. Peer Rev. Orgn., Waltham, 1986-89; utilization rev. coord. Paul Revere Ins. Co., Worcester, Mass., 1989—. Capt. USAF, 1983-86. Decorate Air Force Commendation medal. Mem. NAFE, Air Force Assn., Health Ins. Assoc., Fitchburg State Coll. Alumni Assn. Democrat. Roman Catholic. Home: 16 Duncannon Ave Apt 1 Worcester MA 01604-5128

DONDERS, JOSEPH GERARD, priest; b. Tilburg, N. Brabant, The Netherlands, Mar. 11, 1929; came to U.S., 1984; s. Jan P.J. and Riet L. (Panhuijsen) D. BA, Gregorian U., Rome, 1958, MA, 1960, PhD, 1962. Ordained priest, Roman Cath. Ch., 1957. Lectr. Tilburg U., Holland, 1962-68; vis. reader Nairobi Univ., Kenya, 1968-74, prof., chmn. dept. philosophy and religious studies, 1974-84; exec. dir. Africa Faith and Justice Network, Washington, 1984-87; prof. Mission and Cross-cultural Studies Washington Theol. Union, Washington, 1987—. Author: Non Bourgeois Theology, 1986, Jesus the Stranger, 1971 (Nat. Religious Book award 1979), Praying and Preaching the Sunday gospel, 1990 (Cath. Book Club selection 1991), over forty other books in several langs. Mem. U.S. Cath. Mission Assn. (bd. dirs. 1990—), Philos. Assn. of Kenya (founder 1972), Thomistische Vereniging, Teilhard de Chardin Assn. Roman Catholic. Home: 1624 21st St NW Washington DC 20009-1055 Office: Washington Theol Union New Hampshire Ave Silver Spring MD 20903-2401

DONDES, ROBERT JONATHAN, healthcare executive, consultant; b. Albany, N.Y., Feb. 14, 1960; s. Seymour and Gloria Hannah (From) D. BS, U. Mich., 1981, postgrad. med. sch., 1979-81; postgrad., SUNY, Albany, 1981-84. Account exec. George Washington U. Health Plan, Washington, 1984-85, dir. mem. svcs., 1985-86; assoc. mktg. dir. WellCare of N.Y., Inc., Newburgh, 1986-87; coord. mktg. ops. The WellCare Mgmt. Group, Kingston, N.Y., 1987-88, dir. planning and devel., 1988-89, dir. ops., 1989—. Author: The WellCare Perspective, 1988. Bd. dirs. Maternal Infant Svcs. Network, 1991—; asst. to co-chmn. Rep. Nat. Com., Washington, 1984. A.H. Robbins Pharm. Corp. scholar, 1979, U. Mich. scholar, 1978, Am. Heart Assn. scholar, 1978; NSF fellow, 1977. Mem. Group Health Assn. Am., U. Mich. Alumni Assn., Sigma Chi. Jewish. Office: The WellCare Mgmt Group PO Box 4059 Kingston NY 12401-0994

DONEGAN, CAROLYN MAY, artist; b. Rochester, N.Y., July 4, 1937; d. Lawrence Alexander and Madeline May (Doud) Heslip; m. William Eugene Donegan, Jan. 30, 1960; children: David Loring, Christine Ann, Bradley Lawrence. Sculptor Arts Reach, Rochester, N.Y., 1990—. Prin. works include sculptures, Coping Series at Strong Meml. Hosp., U. Rochester Med. Ctr., Pain Treatment Ctr., Cancer Action. Mem. Arts for Greater Rochester. Home: 379 Beckwith Rd West Henrietta NY 14586-9713

DONELSON, SCOTT EUGENE, aerospace engineer; b. Toledo, Aug. 3, 1968; s. Eugene Otis and Patricia Jean (Reed) D. BS in Aerospace Engring., Tri-State U., 1990. Flight test engr. Naval Air Test Ctr., Patuxent River, Md., 1990—. Mem. AIAA, Soc. Flight Test Engrs. Home: 621 Hewitt Rd Great Mills MD 20634-6305

DONELY, GEORGE ANTHONY THOMAS, III, economist, consultant; b. New Orleans, Aug. 14, 1934; s. George A.T. and Valerie Clare (Burmaster) D.; m. Lisa Suzanne Young, June 30, 1963; 1 child, Valerie Jennie Young. AB in Econs. cum laude, Williams Coll., 1956; MA in Econs., Columbia U., 1958; PhD, U. Mashad, Iran, 1967. Economist Lionel D. Edie & Co., N.Y.C., 1959-60; instr. La. State U., New Orleans, 1960-61; joined Fgn. Service, Dept. State, 1961-69; economist IMF, Washington, 1969-91; cons. Miss Lisa's Sugarless Foods, Inc., Washington, 1985—. Contbr. articles to profl. jours. Mem. steering com. Friends of Music at Smithsonian, Washington, 1972—; vol. Md. Hist. Trust, Annapolis, 1982-85. Ford Found. fellow Columbia U., 1958. Mem. Am. Econ. Assn., Econ. History Assn. Clubs: Roundtable, Metropolitan, Williams. Home: St Richard's Manor Millstone Landing Rd PO Box 773 Lexington Park MD 20653

DONG, ALVIN LIM, lawyer, law librarian; b. Seattle, Dec. 11, 1955; s. Hep Tai and Fannie (Woo) Dong. BA, U. Wash., 1978, MLS with distinction, 1981; JD, SUNY, Buffalo, 1988. Life cert. profl. libr., Wash. Law libr. Norfolk Law Libr., Dedham, Mass., 1985-86; staff atty. Criminals Appeals Bur. Legal Aid Soc., N.Y.C., 1988-89; lawyer, libr. New York Law Sch. Libr. N.Y.C., 1989-92. Student editor Law and Policy, 1987-88. Co-dir. Buffalo Pub. Interest Law Program, 1984-85. U.S. Dept. Edn. Title II-B fellow, 1979-80; recipient Cert. of Disting. Svc. Asian-Am. Student Counseling Svcs.-Community Advising Bd., 1983-84. Mem. Am. Assn. Law Librs., Nat. Asian Pacific-Am. Bar Assn., Asian-Am. Bar Assn. N.Y. Democrat.

DONLICK, DANIEL KALENA, seminary dean; b. Endicott, N.Y., Dec. 30, 1941; s. Charles and Josephine (Hrebacka) D.; m. Delores Marie Bowers, July 25, 1964; children: David, Daniel, Deborah, Thomas. Diploma orthodox theology, St. Tikhon's Theol. Sem., 1965; BA in History, Kings Coll., Wilkes-Barre, Pa., 1971; MS in Edn., Marywood Coll., Scranton, Pa., 1976. Ordained priest Eastern Orthodox Ch., 1965. Pastor St. Nicholas Ch., Olyphant, Pa., 1965-71, St. Michael's Ch., Jermyn, Pa., 1971-78; dir. admissions St. Tikhoh's Theol. Sem., South Canaan, Pa., 1972-76, registrar, 1978-88, dean students, 1978-88, acad. dean, 1988—, instr. ch. history and Russian ch. history, 1971-76; chaplain Fairview State Hosp., Waymart, Pa., 1965-80; parish administr. Holy Trinity Mission Parish, Stroudsburg, Pa., 1978-87; treas., bd. mem. Telespond, Inc. of Lackawanna County, Scranton, Pa., 1975-77; sec.-treas. Diocese of Ea. Pa., 198-90. Co-editor newsletter The Spirit of St. Tikhon's, 1987-88; advisor yearbook The Tikhonaire, 1987-90. Sec., bd. dirs. St. Tikhon's Children's Home, South Canaan, 1965—; trustee St. Tikhon's Sem., South Canaan, 1978—; treas., bd. mem. Telespond, Inc. of Lackawanna County, Scranton, 1975. Mem. AACD, Am. Coll. Pers. Assn., Nat. Assn. Acad. Affairs Adminstrs., Phi Alpha Theta, Lambda Chi Alpha. Home: Ryan Rd # 67S Lake Ariel PA 18436 Office: St Tikhons Theol Sem PO Box 34 South Canaan PA 18459-0034

DONLIN-SMITH, COLLEEN M., speech pathologist; b. East Patterson, N.J., July 20, 1961; d. William A. and Patricia L. (Teachout) Donlin; m. Thomas H. Donlin-Smith, Aug. 14, 1982. BA in Speech and Hearing Sci., Ohio State U., 1982; MA in Speech-Lang. Pathology, U. Md., 1984; cert. health systems adminstr., Rochester Inst. Tech., 1992. Lic. speech pathologist, N.Y. Clin. fellow InSpeech, Inc., Charlottesville, Va., 1984-85; supr. speech pathology Woodrow Wilson Rehab. Ctr., Fisherville, Va., 1985-87; speech-lang. pathologist U. Va. Med. Ctr., Charlottesville, 1987-88; sr. speech pathologist Specialized Rehab. Svcs., Rochester, N.Y., 1988-90; dir. speech pathology F.F. Thompson Hosp., Canandaigua, N.Y., 1988-90. Mem. Farmington (N.Y.) Libr. Adv. Bd. Mem. Am. Speech-Lang.-Hearing Assn. (spl. interest groups, neurophysiology and neurogenic communication disorders, adminstrn., and dysphagia), Wayne-Finger Lakes Speech-Lang.-Hearing Assn. Office: FF Thompson Hosp Speech Pathology Dept 350 Parrish St Canandaigua NY 14424-1793

DONLON, WILLIAM JOSEPH, utility company executive; b. Albany, N.Y., Jan. 28, 1930; s. Charles Joseph and Margaret Mary (Shanahan) D.; m. Patricia Pommer, Aug. 26, 1952; children: Deborah, William, Robert, Susan, James, Brian. BS in Econs., Siena Coll., 1962. With Niagara Mohawk Power Corp., Syracuse, N.Y., 1948—; supr. sales and services tng. Niagara Mohawk Power Corp., Albany, N.Y., 1960-62; supr. sales and services tng. Niagara Mohawk Power Corp., Buffalo, N.Y., 1962-64, sales mgr., 1964-68, comml. v.p. western div., 1968-70; v.p., gen. mgr. Eastern div. Niagara Mohawk Power Corp., Albany, N.Y., 1970-76; sr. v.p. Niagara Mohawk Power Corp., Syracuse, N.Y., 1976, pres., 1976-88, chmn. bd., CEO, 1988—; bd. dirs. Nat. Comml. Bank & Trust Co., Utilities Mut. Ins. Co. Bd. dirs. Albany area United Fund, Albany area ARC, Capital dist. Jr. Achievement, Better Albany Living; trustee Coll. St. Rose; bd. govs. Albany Med. Ctr. Hosp. Served with USN, 1952-54; ETO. Mem. Capital Dist. C. of C. (membership chmn. 1973-74). Republican. Roman Catholic. Clubs: Ft. Orange (Albany); Century (Syracuse, N.Y.). Office: Niagara Mohawk Power Corp 300 Erie Blvd W Syracuse NY 13202-4250*

DONNELL, BRUCE BOLTON, stage director; b. San Francisco, Feb. 7, 1946; s. Otto Dewey Jr. and Jean (Bolton) D. AB, Columbia Coll., 1967; MA, Columbia U., 1970. Mem. staging staff opera cos. San Francisco, Toronto, Memphis, Houston, N.Y.C., Newark, Geneva, Paris, Palermo, Tehran, Netherlands, San Diego, Buenos Aires, Santa Fe, Boston; stage dir. Met. Opera, N.Y.C., 1975—; bd. dirs. Santa Fe Opera, 1983—, Ridiculous Theatrical Co.; judge Internat. Competition for Verdian Voices, Busseto, Italy, 1981-89. Bd. dirs. Sullivan Found. Recipient Emmy for Outstanding Program Achievement in Performing Arts, 1983-84. Mem. Am. Guild Mus. Artists (bd. govs. N.Y.C. 1983—). Office: Met Opera Lincoln Ctr New York NY 10023

DONNELLY, HARRISON JAMES, infectious diseases physician, internist; b. Hiawatha, Utah, Feb. 10, 1930; s. Maurice and Mae Elizabeth (Schaut) D.; children: Andrew, Kathryn; m. Mariella Horna, 1991. BA, Northeastern Ill. U., 1974; MD, Autonomous U. of Guadalahara, Mex., 1974. Internship, residency anesthesia and internal medicine NYU Med. Ctr., St. Clare's Hosp. and Med. Ctr., 1976-81; engr. McConnell-Douglas Corp., Huntington Beach, Calif., 1952-70; physician Cath. Med. Ctr., Jamaica, N.Y., 1984—; adj. faculty mem. Meml. Sloan-Kettering Cancer Ctr., N.Y.C., 1987—. Contbr. articles to profl. publs. Sgr. USAF, 1946-49. Mem. AAAS, N.Y. Acad. Scis. Roman Catholic. Office: Cath Med Ctr 88-25 153d St Jamaica NY 11432

DONNELLY, JOHN JAMES, III, immunologist, blood banker; b. Phila., June 26, 1954; s. John James Jr. and Erma Marie (Cocci) D.; m. Betsy Ann Burkhardt, Dec. 30, 1976; children: Ann Marie, James Arthur. BA, U. Pa., Phila., 1975, PhD, 1979. Postdoctoral fellow U. Cambridge, U.K., 1979-81, Johns Hopkins U., Balt., 1982-83; asst. prof. U. Pa., Phila., 1983-88; rsch. fellow Merck & Co., Inc., West Point, Pa., 1988—; adj. asst. prof. U. Pa., Phila., 1988—; cons. WHO, Geneva, 1983—, U.S. Agy. for Internat. Devel., Washington DC, 1988—. Author: (book chpt.) Molecular and Cellular Mechanisms of Hypersensitivity, 1989, Vaccines, '91, 1991; contbr. articles to profl. jours. Dir. Blood Donor Program, 79th U.S. Army Res. Command, Pa., 1987-90. Maj. USAR, 1984—. Decorated Bronze Star; NIH predoctoral fellow, 1975, Fight for Sight, Inc. postdoctoral fellow, 1980, NIH postdoctoral fellow, 1982. Fellow Royal Soc. Tropical Medicine and Hygiene; mem. Am. Assn. Immunologists, Assn. for Rsch. in Vision and Ophthalmology, British Soc. for Immunology. Office: Merck Sharp Dohme Rsch Labs Sumneytown Pike West Point PA 19486

DONNELLY, PATRICK C., theatrical stagehand, actor; b. Olean, N.Y., Feb. 23, 1956; s. Paul Edward and Betsy Jane (Hilliard) D.; m. Wendy Roberta Maxwell, Sept. 3, 1988. BA, Tex. Tech. U., 1979. Resident tech. IATSE Local #903, Lubbock, Tex., 1977-81; asst. tech. dir. Majestic Performing Art Ctr., San Antonio, 1981-82, dir. ops., 1982-83; archtl. cons. Palace Performing Arts Ctr., New Haven, 1983, ops. mgr., 1984; prodn. mgr. Oakdale Musical Theatre, Wallingford, Conn., 1986, 87; originator Snazz-n-Guffaw Comedy, New Haven, 1989; pres., dir. Snazz Theater Projects, New Haven, 1990—; property mgr. Shubert Performing Arts Ctr., New Haven, 1990—. Playwrite: As The World Stalls, 1979; originator: (improve comedy troupe) Snazz-n-Guffaw, 1989 (named Best in Town 1989). Mem. IATSE (local #74 exec. bd. 1990—, #481), Conn. Zool. Soc., San Antonio Zool. Soc.

DONNER, WILLIAM TROUTMAN, psychiatrist; b. Sharon Pa., Jan. 8, 1921; s. Raymond H. and Edna (Troutman) D.; student U. Pa., 1939-42, M.D., 1946; m. Alice Easby Wilkinson, Apr. 12, 1946; children: William W., Marda Elisa, Mary Alice, Margot Ramona. Intern, Allegheny Gen. Hosp., Pitts., 1945-46; resident Friends Hosp., Phila., U. Pa., 1950-51; practice medicine specializing in psychiatry, Abington, Pa., 1951—; psychiatrist Neuropsychiat. Assos. of Old York Rd., Abington, 1962-64; dir. mental health clinic Abington Meml. Hosp., 1958-64, interim chmn. dept. psychiatry, 1983-85; instr. U. Pa., 1951-58, asso. psychiatry, 1958-78; clin. asst. prof. Hahnemann Med. Coll., 1978—; acting chmn. Dept. Psychiatry, Abington (Pa.)Meml. Hosp., 1988—. Pres. bd. dirs. Family Service Montgomery County, 1966-67. Served with AUS, 1946-48. Mem. Am., Pa. psychiat. assns., AMA, Pa. State, Montgomery County med. socs., Am. Group Psychotherapy Assn. Contbr. articles to tech. jours. Home: 314 Wellington Ter Jenkintown PA 19046-3832 Office: 1245 Highland Ave Ste 403 Abington PA 19001-3774

D'ONOFRIO, DOMINIC ANTHONY, police officer; b. Passaic, N.J., July 18, 1944; s. Anthony and Filomena (Manicone) D'O.; 1 child, Tara. Cert., Lincoln Tech. Inst., Newark, 1968; grad., Bergen County Policy Acad., Mahwah, N.J., 1968. Police officer Lodi (N.J.) Police Dept., 1968—, now lt., coord. Police Dept. Terminal Agy. Fireman Lodi Vol. Fire Dept, 1978—, past pres. 1982-84, sgt. at arms 1987—. With U.S. Army, 1962-65. Mem. NRA (cert. pistol, rifle and shotgun instr. N.J.), Internat. Assn. Identification, Internat. Narcotic Enforcement Officers Assn., N.J. State Honor Legion, N.J. Police Benevolent Assn., N.J. Detective Crime Clinic, N.J. Exempt Fireman's Assn., N.J. Mut. Aid Fire Assn., Bergen County Mut. Aid Soc., N.J. Vehicle Theft Investigators Assn., Internat. Auto Theft Assn. Investigators, Bergen County Rein Officers Group, Lodi Police Dept. Honor Guard, Kodak Pro Passport Profl. Network, VFW. Roman Catholic. Home: 46 Mitchell St PO Box 565 Lodi NJ 07644-0565

DONOGHUE, JOHN FRANCIS, physicist, educator; b. Roslyn, N.Y., Nov. 30, 1950; s. Francis C. and Catherine (Finley) D.; m. Elaine Janik, June 21, 1973; children: Suzanne, Kathryn, Evan. BS in Physics, U. Notre Dame, 1972; PhD in Physics, U. Mass., 1976. Postdoctoral fellow Carnegie-Mellon U., Pitts., 1976-78, MIT, Cambridge, Mass., 1978-80; asst. prof., then assoc. prof. of physics U. Mass., Amherst, 1980-88, prof., 1988—; sci. assoc. CERN, Geneva, 1989-90. Co-author: Dynamics of the Standard Model, 1992. Fellow Am. Phys. Soc. Office: U Mass Dept Physics Amherst MA 01003

DONOVAN, DONNA MAE, newspaper publisher; b. Jersey City, Mar. 14, 1952; d. William Clayton and Elizabeth Dorothy (Hanley) Hagemann; m. Jerome Francis Donovan, Nov. 6, 1982; children: Matthew James, Andrew William. BA in Journalism, Syracuse U., 1974. Pub. Burlington (Vt.) Free Press, 1986-91, Utica (N.Y.) Observer-Dispatch, 1991—; v.p. East region Gannett Co., 1986-88; bd. dirs. Health Ins. Vt. Bd. dirs. Chittenden County United Way, 1987-91, also chmn. community svcs. div.; bd. dirs. Leadership Champlain, 1987-91, United Way Greater Utica Area, 1991—, Leadership Mohawk Valley, 1992—, Sch. & Bus. Alliance, 1992—. Roman Catholic. Office: Observer-Dispatch 221 Oriskany Plz Utica NY 13501-1201

DONOVAN, JOHN FRANCIS, government official; b. Dorchester, Mass., July 13, 1946; s. Matthew Thornton and Frances Elizabeth (Currier) D.; m. Judy Ann Morono, Feb. 31, 1971; children: Patrick Anthony, Timothy Michael. BS in English Lit., U. N.H., 1969; postgrad., U. Wis., 1979. Reporter Concord (N.H.) Monitor, 1966-69; sports editor The New Hampshire, Durham, 1966-68; reporter Kansas City (Mo.)Star, 1968, 72; pub. affairs officer U.S. Army, 1969-72; pub. affairs specialist White Sands Missile Range, N.Mex., 1972-74, U.S. Army Test & Evaluation Command, Aberdeen, Md., 1974-80; pub. affairs chief Picatinny Arsenal, Dover, N.J., 1980-82; chief medial rels. U.S. Army Materiel Command, Alexandria, Va., 1982-84, assoc. chief pub. affairs, 1984-85; asst. chief pub. affairs Dept. of Army, Washington, 1985—. Author: White Sands Missile Range and History of the U.S. Rocket Program, 1971. Ch. activities dir. George Brent Coun., KC, Manassas, 1989-91; organizer Medugorie Prayer Group, 1990-91. Lt. comdr. USNR, 1973-78. Recipient Wall St. Jour. newspaper award scholar, 1968. Decorated Army Commendation medals (3). Roman Catholic. Office: Dept of Army (SAPA-ZD) Run 2E646 The Pentagon Washington DC 20310-1502

DONOVAN, JOSEPH RICHARD, JR., diplomat; b. Goshen, N.Y., June 29, 1951; s. Joseph R. and Helen (Priest) D.; m. Mei-Chou Wu, July 6, 1985; children: James, Matthew. BS in Fgn. Svc., Georgetown U. Vol. U.S. Peace Corp, Seoul, Korea, 1973-75; vice consul Am. Embassy, Doha, Qatar, 1977-79; second sec. Am. Embassy, Seoul, 1979-83; trainee AIT Chinese Lang. Sch., Taipei, Taiwan, 1983-85; polit. officer Am. Embassy, Beijing, China, 1985-87; polit., mil. officer U.S. State Dept., Washington, 1987-89; br. chief Am. Inst., Kaohsiung Br., Taiwan, 1989—. Mem. Kaohsiung Lighthouse Rotary (charter pres. 1990-91), Mercantile Club (gov. 1989—). Office: A I T Taipei Dept of State Washington DC 20521-4170

DONOVAN, MARYANN, small business owner; b. Queens, N.Y., July 28, 1960; d. Thomas Joseph and Marion Loretta (Feretti) Bonomo; m. Kevin G. Donovan, Nov. 26, 1983; children: Kathryn, John. BA in Psychology, Fairfield U., 1982. Human resources adminstr. MCI Telecommunications, Rye Brook, N.Y., 1983-84; v.p. Gambrill & Assocs., Port Chester, N.Y., 1984-89; pres., owner Impact Pers., Inc., Darien, Conn., 1989—. Mem. Nat. Assn. Pers. Cons., Conn. Assn. Pers. Cons. (region v.p.), Fairfield U. Alumni Assn. (bd. dirs. 1990—). Office: Impact Pers Inc 40 Richards Ave Norwalk CT 06854

DONOVAN, PETER MORSE, investment professional; b. Washington, Mar. 1, 1943; s. James and Abbie (Morse) D.; m. Alexandra Kujan, Nov.; children: Aaron, Sara. BA in Econs., Goddard Coll., 1965. Chartered fin. analyst. Various positions Wright Investors' Svc., Bridgeport, Conn., 1966-74, sr. v.p., treas., 1974-84, exec. v.p., 1984-87, sr. exec. v.p., 1987-88, pres., 1988—; bd. dirs. Winthrop Corp., Bridgeport; exec. com. WorldScope/Disclosure Ptnrs., Bridgeport, 1990—; pres. Wright Managed Investment Funds, Bridgeport, 1975—. Governing mem. Com. on Developing Am. Capitalism, Fairfield, Conn. Mem. Internat. Soc. Fin. Analysts, N.Y. Soc. Security Analysis, Hartford Soc. Security Analysis, Assn. Investment Mgmt. and Rsch., Army and Navy Club, Pequot Yacht Club, Pequot Runners Club. Office: Wright Investors Svc 1000 Lafayette Blvd Bridgeport CT 06604-4700

DONOVAN, RICHARD ZELL, natural resource management specialist; b. Englewood, N.J., Aug. 6, 1952; s. Lawrence Joseph and Berniece (Bailey) D.; m. Karen Anne Alfonsi, Oct. 2, 1982; children: Andrew Barden, Emily Frances. BA in History and Romance Lang., U. S.Fla., 1974; MS in Natural Resource Mgmt., Antioch New Eng. Coll., 1981. Constrn. supr. Nassau Pools Inc., Naples, Fla., 1970-74; water and sanitation advisor U.S. Peace Corps, Washington, Paraguay, 1975-77; forestry, logging advisor Antioch New Eng., Keene, N.H., 1978-80; natural resource cons. U.S. Peace Corps, various locations, 1978-81; natural resources specialist Assocs. in Rural Devel., Inc., Burlington, Vt., 1980-87; forest conservation project dir. World Wildlife Fund, Washington, Costa Rica, 1987-90; natural resource cons. World Wildlife Fund, Inter-Am. Devel. Bank, Washington, 1990—; internat. bd. dirs. Centro de Estudios Ambientales y Politicas, Neatropica Found., San Jose, Costa Rica, 1990—; sustainable devel. advisor Royal Vet. and Agrl. U., Frederiksberg, Denmark, 1991—. Fellow World Wildlife Fund; mem. Internat. Soc. Tropical Foresters, Forest Product Cert. Working Group. Home: PO Box 436 Richmond VT 05477-0436

DONOVAN, ROBERT JOSEPH, psychiatrist; b. Scranton, Pa., Mar. 30, 1923; s. William Murray and Kathryn (King) D. BS, U. Scranton, 1943; MD, U. Pa., 1947. Assoc. in psychiatry U. Pa., Phila., 1955-86; assoc. Pa. Hosp., Phila., 1955-86; mem. courtesy staff Inst. of Pa. Hosp., Phila., 1955-86; psychiatrist Family Ct. Phila., 1955-79, Hall-Mercer Mental Health Ctr., Phila., 1967-86, Ctr. Mental Health, Waltham, Mass., 1986-90, Scranton Counseling Ctr., 1991—. Pfc. U.S. Army, 1943-46. Fellow Am. Psychiatric Assn. (life); mem. AMA, Lackawanna County Med. Soc. Office: Scranton Counseling Ctr 326 Adams Ave Scranton PA 18503-1604

DOODY, AGNES G., communications educator, management and communication consultant; b. New Haven; d. Daniel M. and Carrie Mae (Goodrich) D.; m. Arthur D. Jeffrey, Dec. 22, 1962 (dec. Sept. 1985); children: Andrew N., Jill; m. Ellis H. Maris, Jr., June 28, 1991. BA, Emerson Coll., 1952; MA, Pa. State U., 1954, PhD, 1961; cert. program on negotiation, Harvard U. Prof. communications U. R.I., Kingston, 1958—; pres. Arthur Assocs.; bd. dirs. PierBank, Narragansett, R.I.; pres. Arthur Assocs., R.I. Mediation Svc. Mem. Soc. Profls. in Dispute Resolution, Internat. Communication Assn., Speech Communication Assn., Ea. Communication Assn. (pres. 1967-68), Rotary (newsletter editor Wakefield 1989-90). Home: One Post Rd Wakefield RI 02879

DOODY, DANIEL PATRICK, pediatric surgeon; b. Evergreen Park, Ill., July 19, 1952; s. Francis Xavier and Mary Therese (Neylon) D.; m. Scarlet Beverly Artruc, Nov. 28, 1981; children: Colin James, Shaylyn Claire, Evan Patrick. BS, U. Ill., Urbana, 1973; MD, U. Ill., Chgo., 1977. Intern surgery U. Ill., Chgo., 1977-78, resident surgery, 1978-79; rsch. fellow Mass. Gen. Hosp., Boston, 1979-81; resident surgery U. Ill./Cook County Hosps., Chgo., 1981-83, chief resident surgery, 1983-84; rsch. fellow Mass. Gen. Hosp., Boston, 1984-85, pediatric surgeon, 1987—; resident pediatric surgery Montreal (Que., Can.) Children's Hosp., 1985-87; instr. advanced trauma life support, Boston, 1988-92, pediatric ALS, Boston, 1990-92; asst. prof. surgery Harvard Med. Sch., 1990. Contbr. articles on basic sci., pediatric and pediatric surgery to profl. jours., chpts. to books. Recipient Golden Apple award U. Ill. Sch. Medicine, Chgo., 1984. Fellow ACS, Am. Acad. Pediatrics; mem. Am. Pediatric Surg. Assn., New Eng. Pediatric Surg. Soc., Warren Cole Soc., Karl Meyer Soc. Home: 2 Fletcher Rd Lynnfield MA 01940 Office: Mass Gen Hosp Fruit St Boston MA 02114

DOOLING, BRIAN THOMAS, sales executive; b. West Point, N.Y., Nov. 9, 1965; s. Stephen Vincent Dooling and Joan Ann (Forrest) Palmer. BA in English, Boston Coll. Sales rep. Champion Internat., Bala Cynwyd, Pa., 1988—. Alumni vol. B.C. Club of Washington, 1991, D.C. Cares. Republican. Roman Catholic. Office: Champion Internat 401 E City Ave Ste 909 Bala Cynwyd PA 19004-1122

DOON, JOHN ANTHONY, college official; b. Worcester, Mass., July 2, 1935; s. John A. and Evelyn Marie (White) D.; m. Eleanor Theresa Cronin, July 1, 1961; children: Patricia, John, Elizabeth, James. AB, Holy Cross Coll., 1957; MA in History, Polit. Sci., Clark U., 1959; EdD in Higher Edn. Adminstrn., U. Mass., 1990. History tchr. Lincoln/Sudbury Regional High, Sudbury, Mass., 1959-66; prof. history Boston State Coll., 1966-82; assoc. dean student affairs Quinsigamond Community Coll., Worcester, Mass., 1982—; Quinsigamond control profl. Am. Assn. Jr. Community and Jr. Colls./Kellogg Beacon Coll. Project, 1990-91. With USAR, 1958-64. John Hay fellow John Hay Found., 1964. Mem. Naf. Assn. Fgn. Student Advisors, C.C. Transfer Counselors, C.C. Student Activity Dirs., Consortium Student Activity Dirs., Worcester Consortium for Higher Edn. Home: 7 Chester St Worcester MA 01605-3118 Office: Quinsigamond Community Coll 670 W Boylston St Worcester MA 01606-2092

DOOREY, ANDREW, cardiologist; b. Darby, Pa., Feb. 18, 1952; s. Michael J. and Katherine (Thomas) D.; m. Nancy Ann Small, Feb. 14, 1981; children: Kelsey, Jennifer, Alicia. AB, Princeton U., 1974; MD, Harvard U., Boston, 1978. Diplomate Am. Bd. Internal Medicine. Intern/resident U. Mich. Hosp., Ann Arbor, 1978-80; fellow in cardiology Brigham & Women's Hosp. and Harvard Med. Sch., Boston, 198-83, staff cardiologist, 1984-85; fellow in invasive cardiology and angioplasty U. Heidelberg, Ger., 1983-84; cardiologist The Lankenau Hosp., Phila., 1985-87; dir. cardiac angioplasty Med. Ctr. of Del., Wilmington, 1987—; instr. medicine Harvard Med. Sch., Boston, 1980-85; asst. clin. prof. medicine Jefferson Med. Coll., Phila., 1985-91, assoc. clin. prof. medicine, 1991—. Contbr. articles to profl. jours. Cons. cardiovascular adv. com. FAA, Oklahoma City, 1986—. Rose Seegal prize, Harvard Med. Sch., 1978; Alexander Vol Humbolt fellow, 1983. Fellow ACP, Am. Coll. Cardiology, Am. Coll. Chest Physicians, Coun. on Clin. Cardiology of Am. Heart Assn., Soc. for Cardiac Angiography and Interventions; mem. Aerospace Med. Assn. Office: Cardiology Cons PA 4745 Ogletown-Stanton Rd Newark DE 19713

DORAIN, PAUL BRENDEL, chemistry educator; b. New Haven, Aug. 30, 1926; s. Hugh Alfred and Marion Edith (Burritt) D.; m. Elsie V. Ahlberg, Aug. 19, 1950; children: Melanie, Douglas Edwin. BS, Yale U., 1950; PhD, Ind. U., 1954. Teaching fellow Ind. U., Bloomington, 1953-54; postdoctoral rsch. assoc. U. Chg., Enrico Fermi Inst. for Nuclear Studies, 1954-56; physicist solid state Aero. Rsch. Lab., Wright Patterson AFB, Ohio, 1956-58; asst. prof., assoc. prof. chemistry Brandeis U., 1958-61, 61-67, prof. chmistry, 1967-81; sr. rsch. scientist applied physics dept. Yale U., 1982-85; prof. chemistry Amherst (Mass.) Coll., 1985-91; v.p. acad. affairs, dean of faculty Colby Coll., 1981-82; vis. rsch. scientist Nat. Magnet Lab., MIT, 1971-72; Tallman vis. prof. physics and chemistry Bowdoin Coll., 1974-75; vis. fellow engring. and applied sci. dept. Yale U., 1979-80. Mem. AAAS, Am. Phys. Soc., Am. Chem. Soc., Sigma Xi, Catalyst Soc. N.Y., Materials Rsch. Soc. Home: 113 Amherst Rd The Meadows South Hadley MA 01075 Office: Amherst Coll Amherst MA 01002

DORÉ, JEAN, mayor; s. Jean and Therese (Lauze) D.; m. Christiane Sauvé, 1986; children: Amélie, Magali. Student, McGill U.; JD, U. Montreal. Bar: Can. 1978. Atty. Montreal; founding mem. Montreal Citizens Movement, 1974; opposition leader City Council, Montreal, 1984-86; vice chmn. Montreal Urban Community, 1986; mayor of Montreal, 1986—. Office: Office of Mayor, 275 rue Notre-Dame Est, Montreal, PQ Canada H2Y 1C6

DOREMUS, ROBERT HEWARD, glass and ceramics processing educator; b. Denver, Sept. 16, 1928; s. Francis Heward and Elsie Marion (Segelke) D.; m. Germaine Briancon, Mar. 19, 1956; children—Marc Francis, Elaine, Carol, Natalie. B.S., U. Colo., 1950; M.S., U. Ill., 1951, Ph.D., 1953; Ph.D. (Fulbright fellow), U. Cambridge, Eng., 1956. Phys. chemist Gen. Electric Research and Devel. Ctr., Schenectady, 1956-71; N.Y. State prof. glass and ceramics Rensselaer Poly. Inst., Troy, N.Y., 1971—; cons. in field. Author: Glass Science, 1973, Rates of Phase Transformations, 1985. Co-editor: Growth and Perfection of Crystals, 1958; Contbr. articles to profl. jours. Bd. dirs. Phila. Luth. Sem., 1967-76. Fellow Am. Ceramic Soc.; mem. AAAS, Sigma Xi, Sigma Tau, Tau Beta Pi. Lutheran. Home: 1544 Keyes Ave Niskayuna NY 12309-5116 Office: Materials Dept Rensselaer Poly Inst Troy NY 12181

DOREN, HENRY JULIUS THADDEUS, artist, painter; b. N.Y.C., May 20, 1929; s, Thaddeus Karol and Rozalia (Myslicki) Dutkiewicz; m. Anna Tanska (div. 1959); 1 child, Charles Henry (dec.); m. Eleanor Joyce Carlson, Nov. 24, 1962. BS, N.Y.U., 1948; MA, Ottawa U., Can., 1959; postgrad., Art Students League N.Y., 1959-62, Frank Reilly Sch. Art, 1962-64; MFA, Instituto Allende San Miguel, de Allende, Mex., 1965. Freelance artist Labow Advt. Svcs., East Orange, N.J., 1965-69; ast. prof. Trenton (N.J.) State Coll., 1963-64; part time art instr. Fairleigh Dickinson U., Madison, N.J., 1966-68, Seton Hall U., South Orange, N.J., 1967-72; assoc. prof. art County Coll. of Morris, Randolph, N.J., 1969-83; artist, painter pvt. studio, Madison, N.J., 1983—; lectr., Art Assn. Librs., N.J., 1970—; art judge Art Orgns., N.J., 1975—; exhibits one-man, group shows, N.J., N.Y., 1970—. Author: Survey of Polish Art (slides and booklet), 1976; editor: Art Newsletter, County Coll. of Morris, 1976-83; publisher: N.J. Art mag., 1979-83; contbr. articles to profl. jours. Art works of H. Doren: Mother and Child Hosp., Lodz, Poland, 1987, Environment and 20 Century, Dom. Polonii Mus., Pultusk, Poland, 1989, Paderewski portrait, Consulate of the Polish Republic, N.Y.C., 1991, Solidarity Graphic, Collection of Gov. Burne and U.S. Senator Bradley, N.J., 1981. Exch. scholar, Polish Acad. Sci., Warsaw, 1974-75. Mem. Art Students League N.Y. (life). Home: 17 Madison Ave Apt 61 Madison NJ 07940-1466 Studio: Madison NJ 07940

DORENFELD, ALAN STEVEN, paper distributor executive; b. Balt., Nov. 30, 1945; s. Sylvan and Edith (Rosenberg) D.; m. Sharon Roslyn Heyman, July 3, 1966; children: Melissa Pam, Amy Lynn, David Jonathan. BS, U. Md., 1967; MS, George Washington U., 1971. Registered profl. engr., Md. Design engr. U.S. Coast Guard, Washington, 1966-71; project engr. Century Engring., Balt., 1971-77; exec. Monumental Paper Co., Balt., 1977—; pres. Md. Paper Trade Assn., Balt., 1986-88; adv. coun. Ga.-Pacific Corp., Atlanta, 1992—. Pres. WGN Community Swim Club, Balt., 1986-88; v.p. Beth El Congregation, Balt., 1991. Lt. (j.g.) USCG, 1968-71. Recipient Disting. Svc. award United Cerebral Palsey, 1985. Mem. ASCE, Tau Beta Pi, Chi Epsilon Civil Engr. Soc. Jewish. Home: 4706 Hawksbury Rd Baltimore MD 21208

DORF, MARTIN EDWARD, pathology educator, immunologist; b. Bound Brook, N.J., May 16, 1944; s. Paul and Hilda Hetty (Zuerendorfer) Dorf; m. Judy Shershow, Aug. 8, 1976; children: Samuel Noah, Benjamin Steven. AB, Rutgers U., 1966; MS, PhD, Duke U., 1973; MA (hon.), Harvard U., 1985. Instr. pathology Harvard U., Cambridge, Mass., 1974-75, asst. prof., 1975-77, assoc. prof., 1977-83, prof., 1984—, chmn. com. on immunology, 1988—; comdr. 419 Med. Lab., USAR, 1987—,. Editor: Role of the MHC, 1981; sect. editor Jour. Immunology, 1988—; mem. editorial bd. Cellular Immunology Jour., 1988—. Col. U.S. Army Res., 1969-91. Recipient Rsch. Career Devel. award NIH, Bethesda, 1976-81, Nat. Cancer Inst. Outstanding Investigator grant, 1985-92. Mem. Am. Assn. Immologists (trainee affairs com. 1980—), Am. Assn. Pathologists, Transplantation Soc. Democrat. Jewish. Office: Harvard Med Sch 200 Longwood Ave Boston MA 02115-5716

DORINSON, JOSEPH, education educator, civic leader; b. Jersey City; s. Peter and Rita (Mandel) D.; m. Eileen Susan Levine, Dec. 25, 1968; children: Hilary Beth, Paula Michelle, Robert Greg. BA, Columbia Coll., 1958; MPhil, Columbia U., 1976. Tchr. N.Y.C. Bd. Edn., Bklyn., 1961-63, Lehman Coll., Bronx, N.Y., 1963-65, Kean Coll., Union, N.J., 1964-66, Columbia U. sch. Gen. Studies, N.Y.C., 1965; from asst. prof. to prof., chmn. history dept. Long Island U., Bklyn., 1966—; asst. dean Long Island U. Sch. Bus.; lectr. in field. Author: The Educational Alliance: Assimilation & Identity of the Lower East Side, 1992; contbr. articles to profl. jours. Active Bklyn. Community Sch. Bd., 1988—. scholar N.Y. State, Oslo U., 1961; N.Y. State Regents Coll. Teaching fellow; NEH grantee; recipient David Newton award for Excellence in Teaching. Mem. Danforth Assocs. N.Y. (pres. 1985-88), Madison Marine Civic Assn. (pres. 1985-88). Democrat. Jewish. Home: 1851 E 26th St Brooklyn NY 11229-2437 Office: L I Univ 1 University Plz Brooklyn NY 11201-5372

DORIO, MARC ANTHONY, industrial psychologist, consultant; b. Woodbury, N.J., Oct. 8, 1944; s. Marcus Anthony and Marie Antionette (Tortella) D.; m. Patricia Mary King, Mar. 5, 1988; stepchildren: Ian, Christina. BA in Philosophy, St. Bernards Coll., 1966, ThM, 1969, MDiv, 1970; MS in Applied Psychology, Stevens Inst. Tech., 1979. Roman Cath. priest, asst. supt. schs. Diocese of Camden, N.J., 1970-77; adminstr. Stevens Inst. Tech., Hoboken, N.J., 1977-78; v.p. McCooe and Assocs., Ridgewood, N.J., 1978-90; pres. Trine Co. div. Trax Systems Inc., Princeton, N.J., 1990—; adj. prof. Bloomfield (N.J.) Coll., 1983-88. Author: Personnel Managers Desk Book, 1989; contbr. articles to profl. jours. Mem. Am. Psychological Assn. (assoc.), N.J. Psychological Assn. (assoc.), Soc. Indsl. Organizational Psychology. Home: 6 Maddock Rd Titusville NJ 08560-1309 Office: Trine Co 3 Independence Way Princeton NJ 08540-6626

DORKEY, CHARLES EDWARD, III, lawyer; b. Phila., June 23, 1948; s. Charles Edward and Peggy O'Neal D.; children: Charles Edward IV, John Hilliard, Marjorie Lyddon. AB cum laude, Dartmouth Coll., 1970; JD, Univ. Pa., 1973. Bar: Pa. 1974, N.Y. 1975, D.C. 1977. Law clk. to hon. Samuel J. Roberts Supreme Ct. of Pa., 1973-74; assoc. Sullivan & Cromwell, N.Y.C., 1975-81; ptnr. Reboul, MacMurray, Hewitt, Maynard & Kristol, N.Y.C., 1981-84, Richards & O'Neil, N.Y.C., 1984-91, Haythe & Curley, N.Y.C., 1992—; bd. dirs. Hickson (USA) Corp., Trade Indemnity (USA) Inc., Trade Indemnity (USA) Holdings Inc.; mem. coun. Alumni Dartmouth Coll., 1990—, pres. class 1970, 1991—; nat. chmn. Law Ann. Giving, 1991—. Mem. Alumni Council, Univ. Pa. Law Sch., 1989—. Mem. ABA, N.Y. State Bar Assn. (fed. litigation sect. 1986—, internat. law and practice sect. 1988—), Assn. of Bar of City of N.Y. (products liability com. 1982-86, fed. legis. com. 1990—), Heights Casino Club. Republican. Congregationalist. Home: 205 E 69th St Apt 6C New York NY 10021-5464 also: 74 Pascal Ave Rockport ME 04856 Office: Haythe & Curley 237 Park Ave New York NY 10017

DORLAND, DODGE OATWELL, registered investment advisor; b. N.Y.C., Feb. 27, 1948; s. Joseph Warner and Marion (Dodge) D.; m. Bonita Gillette Zeese, Jan. 9, 1971. Diploma, Choate Sch., 1966; BA, Colgate U., 1970; MBA, NYU, 1975. Cert. fin. analyst; chartered market tech., fin. analyst I. With Mfrs. Hanover Trust Co., N.Y.C., 1970-77, asst. sec., 1974-77; with Bank of Montreal Trust Co., N.Y.C., 1977-86, v.p., 1979-86, v.p. communications unit, 1982-86, U.S. industry coord. for communications, 1983-86; v.p. Shearson Lehman Bros., Inc., N.Y.C., 1986-88; v.p. GE Capital Corp., 1988-90; mng. gen. ptnr. Continental Cellular, 1989-90; prin. LANDOR Investment Mgmt., 1990—; bd. dirs. So. Telecom, Inc., West Ga. Cable, Inc. Author: The Communications Industry: An Informational Overview, 1983; contbr. papers in field to profl. jours. Treas. Learning for Living Inst., N.Y.C., 1977-81; chmn. bd. dirs. 325 E. 72d St. Apts., N.Y.C., 1978-81; participant NYU Grad. Sch. Bus. Mgmt. Decision Lab., 1977-79, bd. dirs.; mem. investment com. Assn. for Relief of Elderly Inc., 1984—. Mem. Internat. Soc. Fin. Analysts, Assn. for Investment Mgmt. & Rsch., Soc. Quantitative Analysts, N.Y. Soc. Security Analysts (CFA com.), Market Technicians Assn. (columnist newsletter), Soc. Quantitive Analysts, SAR, Nat. Cable TV Assn., Nat. Assn. Broadcasters, Cellular Telecommunications Industry Assn., The Elfun Soc. N.Y., Communications Tech. Analysts Assn., Drama League N.Y., Broadcast Fin. Mgmt. Assn., Telocator Network Am., Internat. Platform Assn., Media and Entertainment Analysts Assn. N.Y., Am. Film Inst., Smithsonian Inst., Vets Corp. Arty., Soc. Colonial Wars, Mil. Order Loyal Legion U.S., Knickerbocker Greys Vets. Corp., Holland Soc., World Univ. Roundtable, Yale Club (N.Y.C.), Meadow Club, Bathing Corp. Club (Southampton, N.Y.), Toastmasters (v.p. Mfrs. Hanover chpt. 1975-78). Republican. Episcopalian.

DORMAN, LYN, accountant; b. Hanover, N.H., Mar. 29, 1953; d. Robert Leroy and Lillian (Fortin) Conrad; m. D. Douglas Dorman, July 21, 1973; children: Jake D., Rebecca D. BS in Bus. Adminstrn., Youngstown State U., 1986. Bus. office mgr. Dartmouth Med. Sch., Hanover, N.H., 1978-80; business owner Mediclaims, White River Junction, Vt., 1980-81; grad. student asst. U. Pitts., 1986; bus. owner, operator Door-Opener Resumes, Sharon, Pa., 1983-86; bus. mgr. Sharon Steel Workers Fed. Credit Union, Farrell, Pa., 1987-88; acct. Advanced Motobloc, Inc., Hermitage, Pa., 1989-90, Carbis, Walker & Assocs., New Castle, Pa., 1991—. Mem. fin. com. YMCA, Hermitage. Office: Carbis Walker & Assocs 2599 Wilmington Rd New Castle PA 16105-1699

DORMANN, HENRY O., magazine publisher; b. N.Y.C., Mar. 5, 1932; s. Henry Maroni and Ivara (Soberg) D.; m. Alice Andreasen, Apr. 7, 1958; children: Kaari, Kristi. Chmn. bd. Nat. Enquirer, 1971-72, chmn. exec. com., 1987-89; chmn. Internat. Bd. Indsl. Advisors, 1964—; pres., editor-in-chief S.I.P.A. News Service, N.Y.C., 1966—; pres. U.S. Tech. Devel. Co., 1969-70; pres., editor-in-chief Holiday Mag., 1976-77; pres. editor-in-chief Leaders Mag., 1977—; Mem. adv. council Joint Legis. Com. on Met. and Regional Areas Study N.Y. State, 1969-72; chmn. N.Y. State Assembly Council on Econ. Devel., 1972-80. Founder Libr. Presdl. Papers, Inst. for Study of Presidency; trustee Am. U., Washington; bd. dirs. Inst. Edn. Affairs, Washington; trustee IATA Internat. Airline Tng. Fund, 1988—; founder, pres. Found. for Family Values, 1990—. Served with USCG. Office: 59 E 54th St New York NY 10022-4211

DORN, DAVID NORMAN, international labor affairs advisor; b. Mpls., Dec. 28, 1944; s. Earl Norman and Betty Jane (Andberg) D.; m. Diane Elizabeth Daly, Nov. 11, 1978; children: Elizabeth Brennan Dorn, David Andrew Cross Dorn. BA, Drake U., 1966; postgrad., Denver U., 1969-70. Vol. U.S. Peace Corps, Peru, 1966-68; pres. U.S. Youth Coun., N.Y.C./Washington, 1971-76; exec. dir. U.S. Youth Coun., Washington, 1976-78; cons. Internat. Labor Program of Georgetown U., Washington, 1976-78; asst. sec. gen. Internat. Fedn. Free Tchrs. Unions, Brussels, 1979-80; dir. internat. affairs Am. Fedn. Tchrs., Washington, 1981--; mem. exec. com. Social Dems. U.S.A., Washington, 1983-89; Fgn. Student Coun., Washington, 1986-87. Contbr. articles in newspapers and labor press. Democrat.

DORN, SUE BRICKER, museum director; b. Seattle, Apr. 1, 1934; d. Barney and Frances B. (Schnitzer) Bricker; m. Philip Henry Dorn, Dec. 31, 1955; children: Charles, Martha Dorn Maurer. BA, Stanford U., Palo Alto, 1955; MA, Bank St. Coll., 1973. Cert. tchr., N.Y. Dir. promotion exec. compensation svc. Am. Mgmt. Assn., N.Y.C., 1956-58; tchr. spl. edn. N.Y.C. Bd. of Edn., 1969-77; assoc. dir. Yale U., New Haven, 1977-79; v.p. Bank St. Coll. of Edn., N.Y.C., 1979-81, Aspen Inst. for Humanistic Studies, N.Y.C., 1981-82; assoc. v.p. Yale U., New Haven, 1982-87; dep. dir. devel. and pub. affairs Mus. of Modern Art, N.Y.C., 1987—; mem. maj. gifts coun. Stanford U. Member dirs. adv. bd. Yale Comprehensive Cancer Ctr., Yale U., 1990—; pres. LWV, Warren, Mich., 1962-65, Stanford Alumni Club of N.Y., N.J. and Conn., N.Y.C., 1968-70, 25 East 86th Street Corp., N.Y.C., 1989—; bd. dirs. Valida Found., N.Y., 1988—. Named Citizen of the Yr., Warren C. of C., 1962; recipient Citation, City of Warren, 1963, Gold Spike award and Cert. of Outstanding Achievement, Stanford U., 1976. Mem. Art Table, Univ. Club, Stanford Assocs. Home: 25 E 86th St New York NY 10028-0553 Office: Mus of Modern Art 11 W 53d St New York NY 10019

DORNER, BARBARA EMILIA, educator; b. Bronx, N.Y., Jan. 6, 1945; d. Helmut H. and Pierina E. (Gillio) D. BS, SUNY, New Paltz, 1967; MA, Hofstra U., 1971; AS in Bus. Adminstrn., Nassau Community Coll., 1979; postgrad., Adelphi U., 1988. Cert. fin. planner. Tchr. Merrick (N.Y.) Union Free Sch. Dist., 1967—. Vol. Internat. Games for Disabled, 1984; bd. dirs. 280 Guy Lombardo Owners' Assn., 1986-87. Mem. Am. Fedn. Tchrs., N.Y. State United Tchrs., Merrick Faculty Assn. (sec. exec. bd. 1968-69, exec. bd. 1968-78, 79-82, 91—, treas. 1991—), L.I. Soc. Inst. Cert. Fin. Planners, Phi Theta Kappa. Home: 280 Guy Lombardo Ave Freeport NY 11520-4955 Office: Lakeside Sch Merrick Rd Merrick NY 11566-3432

DOR-NER, ZVI RICHARD, television producer; b. Lvov, Poland, July 13, 1941; came to U.S., 1979; s. Karel Nathan and Johana (Barel) Dorner; m. Alexandra Dane, Dec. 31, 1968 (dec. June 1991); children: Tamar Dane, Daphne Dane. BSc, Boston U., 1967; postgrad., Harvard U., 1977. Cameraman Israeli TV, Jerusalem, 1968-69, dir., 1969-72, producer, 1972-75, sr. producer, dir., 1975-79; exec. producer Sta. WGBH-TV, Boston, 1979—. Exec. producer PBS TV series Arabs and Israelis, 1973-74 (DuPont Columbia award 1975), Enterprise, 1979-85 (Emmy award 1982), War and Peace in Nuclear Age, 1985-89 (various awards), Columbus and the Age Discovery, 1989-91 (various awards). Nieman fellow, 1977. Home: 19 Alton Brookline MA 02146 Office: Sta WGBH-TV 125 Western Ave Boston MA 02134

DORNFEST, BURTON SAUL, anatomy educator; b. N.Y.C., Oct. 31, 1930; s. Irving and Yetta (Rosengarten) D.; BA, N.Y.U., 1952, MS, 1954, PhD, 1960; m. Eveline Drucker, June 13, 1954; children: Michael, Barry. Rsch. asst. dept. biostats. Sloan-Kettering Inst. and Meml. Hosp., N.Y.C., 1952-53; rsch. asst. dept. biology N.Y.U., 1953-54, 56-58, instr. gen. sci., 1958-63; instr. anatomy N.Y. Med. Coll., 1963-64; instr. anatomy SUNY Health Sci Ctr. at Bklyn., 1964-67, asst. prof., 1967-73, assoc. prof., 1973-91; adj. prof. CCNY, 1974—; adj. prof. hematology sch. health scis. Hunter Coll., 1978-82, 90-91, anatomy Inst. Continuing Biomed. Edn., 1979-86, N.Y. Med. Coll., 1982-85, 91—, Touro Coll. Ctr. Biomed. Edn., 1983—, Einstein coll., Medicine, 1991—. NIH fellow, 1958-60, 61-63; Leukemia Soc., 1960-61; Nat. Inst. Arthritis and Metabolic Diseases grantee, 1964-71; Nat. Cancer Inst. grantee, 1973-75; Mildred Werner League for Cancer Research grantee, 1976-77; co-prin. investigator NIH Heart, Blood and Lung Inst., 1982-85. Served with U.S. Army, 1954-56. Mem. AAAS, N.Y. Acad. Scis., Reticuloendothelial Soc., Am. Soc. Hematology, Internat. Soc. for Exptl. Hematology, Am. Assn. Anatomists, Am. Assn. Clin. Anatomists, Harvey Soc., Sigma Xi. Jewish. Contbr. articles in field to profl. jours. Home and Office: 96 Everett Rd Demarest NJ 07627-1225

DORNFEST, STANLEY, creative art director; b. N.Y.C., May 3, 1939; s. Julius and Edith (Classner) D.; m. Natalie Gordon, June 4, 1961; children: Gabrielle, Joshua. BFA, Cooper Union, 1959. Graphic designer Chermayeff & Geismar, N.Y.C., 1959-60; graphic designer sales promotion Esquire mag., N.Y.C., 1960-61; group art dir. William Douglas McAdams, N.Y.C., 1961-67, 73-77, Cunningham & Walsh, N.Y.C., 1967-73; v.p. exec. art dir. Wesson & Warhaftig, N.Y.C., 1977-81; v.p. group art supr. Kallir Philips & Ross, N.Y.C., 1981-85; sr. v.p. creative dir. Sutton Communications, N.Y.C., 1985-91, Medicus Intercon, N.Y.C., 1991—; judge Max awards, N.Y.C., 1990, 91, 92. Recipient Andy award Advt. Club N.Y., 1980, 81, 83, Cert. award Rx Club, 1988, 89, Awards, Art Dirs. Club N.Y., 1975, The One Club, 1975, Best Commls. of the Yr. award Advt. Age, 1973. Office: Medicus Intercon 1675 Broadway New York NY 10019

DORNIČ, IVAN DUŠAN, priest; b. Udol, Ruthenia, Czechoslovakia, Feb. 13, 1939; came to U.S., 1957; s. Vasko and Marja (Timko) D.; m. Ann Koba, Aug. 30, 1957; children: Demetrian, Myron, Yvonne, Corina, Tania. BPF in Theology, Prague U., 1956; MA, Duquesne U., 1975; DMin, Drew U., 1983. Ordained priest Orthodox Greek Cath. Ch., 1957. pres. Lemko Housing, Balt., 1979—, Tatry Housing, Balt., 1984—. Editor Slavic Report, 1980-81. Pres. Nat. Slavic Conv., 1980-91. Mem. Nat. Cath. Mus. and Inst. Inc. (pres. 1980—). Home: 5609 Merville Ave Baltimore MD 21215-4122 Office: 16 S Patterson Park Ave Baltimore MD 21231-2106

DORNSIFE, SAMUEL JONATHAN, interior designer; b. Williamsport, Pa., Feb. 4, 1916; s. Henry Albert and Lizzie Lottie (Spatz) D. DFA (hon.). Lycoming Coll., 1976. Pvt. practice interior design, 1934-91, designer in charge restorations including Gallier House, New Orleans, 1971-79, San Francisco Plantation, Garyville, La., 1973-77, Hermann-Grima House, New Orleans, 1976-85, White House of Confederacy, Richmond, Va., 1983-91; cons. on restoration Hermitage, Nashville, Biltmore, Asheville, N.C., Gov.'s Mansion, Jefferson City, Mo., Devereaux, Salt Lake City, Genesee Village, Mumford, N.Y., Gov.'s Mansion, Columbia, S.C., Edmondston-Alston House, Charleston, S.C., Maxwell Mansion, Phila., Iolani Palace, Honolulu, 1982-91; lectr. Columbia U., Cornell U., Lycoming Coll; participant symposia Sotheby's, N.Y.C., Victorian Soc. in Am., Natchez Antiques Forum, Decorative Arts Soc. Author intro. and bibliography: Exterior Decoration, 1975, Some ources for 19th Century drapery Designs, 1975; sects. on wallpaper Engy. Victoriana, 1975, 19th Century Carpet Technology, 1981. Mem. bd. Lycoming County Hist. Soc., 1950-82, Greater Williamsport Community Arts Coun., 1970-91; advisor to Hist. Architecture Rev. Bd., Williamsport; mem. archtl. tech. adv. com. Williamsport Area Community Coll., 1983-91. With U.S. Army, 1942-46. Recipient commendation for carpet design for Iolani Palace, Resources Coun., 1983. Fellow Royal Soc. Arts (London); mem. Am. Soc. Interior Designers (preservation award 1980), Soc. Archtl. Historians, Assn. for Preservation Tech., Decorative Arts Soc., Victorian Soc. Am. (bd. dir. 1970-77), Victorian Soc. U.K., Furniture History Soc., Nat. Trust for Historic Preservation. Episcopalian. Home and Office: 830 1st Ave Williamsport PA 17701-3068

DORR, DOUGLAS DAVID, company executive; b. Lynn, Mass., Aug. 21, 1963; s. Clifford Walton and Anne Theresa (Pillsbury) D. BS, U. N.H., 1986. Assoc. dir. NYNEX Corp., Boston, 1986—. Home: 378 Sudbury St Marlborough MA 01752-1761 Office: NYNEX Corp 225 Franklin St # 1920 Boston MA 02110-2895

DORRIS, MICHAEL ANTHONY, anthropologist, writer; b. Louisville, Jan. 30, 1945; s. Jim and Mary Besy (Burkhardt) D.; m. Louise Erdrich, 1981; children: Reynold Abel (dec. 1991), Jeffrey Sava, Madeline Hannah, Persia Andromeda, Pallas Antigone, Aza Marion. B.A. magna cum laude, Georgetown U., 1967; M.Phil., Yale U., 1970. Grad. asst. Yale U., 1969-70; asst. prof. anthropology Johnston Coll., U. of Redlands, 1970-71; asst. prof. Franconia Coll., N.H., 1971-72; prof. Dartmouth Coll., Hanover, N.H., 1972—; founder, chmn. dept. native Am. studies, Dartmouth Coll., 1972-85. Author: Native Americans: 500 Years After, 1975, A Guide to Research in Native American Studies, 1984, (novel) A Yellow Raft in Blue Water, 1987, The Broken Cord, 1989 (Nat. Book Critics Cir. award), Morning Girl, 1992; co-author: (with Louise Erdrich) The Crown of Columbus, 1991, Route 2, 1991; editor Viewpoint, 1967-68, A Sourcebook for Native American Studies, 1977; mem. editorial bd. Am. Indian Culture Ctr. Jour., UCLA, 1974—; contbr. articles to profl. and lit. jours. Mem. Smithsonian Coun., Native Am. Rights Fund; bd. dirs. Save the Children, 1991—. Recipient Indian achievement award, 1985, PEN Syndicated Fiction award, 1988, Christopher award, 1990, Heartland prize, 1990, Sarah Josepha Hale award, 1991; Danforth grad. fellow, 1967, Woodrow Wilson grad. fellow, 1967; NIMH fellow, 1970, grantee, 1971; Guggenheim fellow, 1978, Woodrow Wilson

faculty fellow, 1980, Rockefeller fellow, 1985-86, Nat. Endowment for Arts creative writing fellow, 1989. Fellow Soc. Applied Anthropology, PEN Am. Ctr., Author's Guild; mem. Writer's Guild, Am. Anthrop. Assn., Nat. Congress Am. Indians. Address: care Rembar and Curtis 19 W 44th St New York NY 10036

DORSCH, RAYMOND MICHAEL, III, real estate investment banker; b. Phila., Mar. 7, 1956; s. Raymond M. Dorsch Jr. and Susan (Moore) Dahme; m. Carmen Turner, Oct. 20, 1984; 1 child, Raymond Michael Dorsch IV. BSME, Brown U., 1978; MBA, Harvard U., 1984. Sales engr. Westinghouse Electric Corp., Hartford, Conn. and Phila., 1978-80; asst. dir. Worldwide Alumina Dorr-Oliver, Inc., Stamford, Conn., 1980-82; assoc. N.V. Indivers, Woburn, Mass., 1983; v.p. Winthrop Fin. Corp., Boston, 1984-86, Milestone Properties Corp., Boston, 1986-88; pres. Back Bay Fin. Corp., Boston, 1989; mng. dir. Corp. Realty Capital, Boston, 1990—; lectr. Mass. Bar Assn., Associated Industries of Mass. Mem. Greater Boston Real Estate Bd., Urban Land Inst. Office: Corp Realty Capital One Financial Ctr Boston MA 02111

DORSEY, MAURICE WAYNE, education administrator, education consultant; b. Balt., May 10, 1947; s. James Roswell Dorsey and Zelma Virginia (Curry) D. BS in Home Econs., U. Md., 1970; M in Liberal Arts, Johns Hopkins U., 1975; M in Ednl. Mgmt. and Supervision, Loyola Coll., Balt., 1976; postgrad., N.C. State U., 1979, 80; PhD, U. Md., 1983; postgrad., Va. Poly. Inst. and State U., 1987, U. D.C., 1988. Draftsman Montgomery Ward, Balt., 1970-71; instr. Harford Community Coll., Bel Air, Md., 1971-72; tchr. pub. schs. City of Balt., 1973-76; assoc. prof. Morgan State U., Balt., 1974-76; agt. home econs. Coop. Extension Svc. U. of D.C., 1976-92, acting state program leader Coop. Extension Svc., 1992—; supervising agt. U. of D.C., 1976-92, mem. rsch. and publs. com., 1976-78, mem. univ. planning com., 1984-87, mem. exec. com. of univ. planning com., 1985-87, mem. sub-com. for ann. assessment of univ. master plan, 1985-87, ward chairperson, 1980-88, mem. pub. svc. com., 1990, chmn. strategic planning com. coop. extension svc., 1990, reservations chmn. planning com. 4-H Vol. Leader Forum, 1989. Contbr. articles to profl. jours. Project dir. Dept. Pub. and Assisted Housing, Washington, 1990—; bd. dirs. ARC 1991—, Urban Philharm. Soc., Inc., 1992—, D.C. Youth Gardens, 1990—, Met. Mental Health Assn., Balt., 1984-85; mem., co-chmn. inaugural dinner Presdl. Inaugural Planning com., 1988; Featured for Black History Month in the newspaper Aegis, Bel Air, 1990. Recipient Home Econs. award Forecast mag., 1975; Other Race fellow U. Md., 1978-83, grantee Mid-Atlantic Fisheries Found., 1985. Mem. D.C. Assn. Extension Home Economists (founder, 1st pres. 1978), Epsilon Sigma Phi, Phi Delta Kappa (life), Alpha Phi Alpha (life). Democrat. Roman Catholic. Home: 10 Slate Mills Ct Baltimore MD 21228-2542 Office: U of DC 4200 Connecticut Ave NW Washington DC 20008-1174

DORSEY, PETER COLLINS, federal judge; b. New London, Conn., Mar. 24, 1931; s. Thomas F., Jr. and Helen Mary (Collins) D.; m. Cornelia McEwen, June 26, 1954; children: Karen G., Peter C., Jennifer S., Christopher M. B.A., Yale U., 1953; J.D., Harvard U., 1959. Ptnr. Flanagan, Dorsey & Flanagan, New Haven, 1963-74; U.S. atty. Dept. Justice, New Haven, 1974-77; ptnr. Flanagan, Dorsey & Mulvey, New Haven, 1977-83; judge U.S. Dist. Ct. Conn., Hartford, 1983—. Councilman Town of Hamden, Conn., 1961-69; town atty., 1973-74; commr. Bd. of Police, Hamden, 1977-81. Served to lt. comdr., USNR, 1953-56. Fellow Am. Coll. Trial Lawyers; mem. ABA, Conn. Bar Assn. (pres. 1977-78), New Haven County Bar Assn., Conn. Def. Lawyers Assn. (pres. 1982-83). Roman Catholic. Office: US Dist Ct 450 Main St Hartford CT 06103-3001*

DORSEY, THOMAS EDWARD, pharmaceutical scientist; b. N.Y.C., June 6, 1946; s. Edward Nagel and May Henrietta (Bomhoff) D. PhD, CUNY, 1974. Sr. scientist Revlon Health Care, Tukahoe, N.Y., 1974-83; clin. scientist Am. Home Products, N.Y.C., 1984-86; project mgr. Organon Inc., S. Orange, N.J., 1986-88; sr. assoc. dir. Pfizer Pharms. Inc., N.Y.C., 1988—. Contbr. articles to profl. jours. Mem. Am. Assn. Pharm. Scientists. Lutheran. Home: 235 E 57th St New York NY 10022-2842 Office: Pfizer Inc 235 E 42nd St New York NY 10017-5703

D'ORVILLE, HANS, diplomat; b. Dinkelsbuehl, Bavaria, Germany, Oct. 9, 1949; s. Friedrich and Erika (Föll) d'O.; m. Mehri Madarshahi, Jan. 6, 1979; 1 child, Anoush André. MA in Econs., U. Konstanz, Fed. Republic of Germany, 1973, PhD, 1977. From asst. to 1st officer UN, N.Y.C., 1975-80, sec. com. on confs., 1980-82; asst. sec. governing coun., sr. exec. rels. officer UNDP, N.Y.C., 1982-8; exec. coord. InterAction Coun./African Leadership Forum, N.Y.C., 1988—. Contbr. numerous articles to profl. jours. Trustee Ctr. for Internat. Contemporary Art, 1991-92. Mem. Am. Coun. on Germany, German Fgn. Policy Assn., African Leadership Found. Inc. (pres., bd. dirs. 1988—). Home: 1255 5th Ave # 7K New York NY 10029-4417 Office: Interaction Coun 821 UN Plaza 7th Fl New York NY 10017

DORWART, HAROLD LAIRD, mathematics educator; b. Greenville, Pa., Aug. 27, 1902; s. George Wilson and Clara (Laird) D.; m. Carolyn Frances Yeisley, Jan. 2, 1933; 1 child, Roger Wilson. AB, Washington & Jefferson Coll., 1924, DSc (hon.), 1968; PhD, Yale U., 1931. Asst. to instr. math. Yale U., New Haven, Conn., 1924-28; instr. Williams Coll., Williamstown, Mass., 1928-30, 31-35; faculty mem. Washington & Jefferson Coll., Washington, Pa., 1935-49; Seabury prof. math., chmn. dept. Trinity Coll., Hartford, Conn., 1949-67, dean, 1967-68. Author: (book) The Geometry of Incidence, 1966, (book chpt.) Mathematics and Yale in the Nineteen Twenties, 1989, (learning materials kit) Configurations, 1968; co-author: (book chpt.) Chromatic Graphs, 1979; contbr. articles to profl. jours. Mem. Am. Math. Soc., Math. Assn. Am., Phi Beta Kappa, Sigma Xi. Home: 17 Cobble Rd Salisbury CT 06068-1501

DORWART, ROBERT ALAN, psychiatrist; b. Milford, Conn., Apr. 15, 1947; s. Walter George and Katherine (Kachmar) D.; m. Nancy Langman, Mar. 8, 1948; children: Kirsten, Stefan. AB, Harvard U., 1969, MS, 1983; MD, Tulane U., 1976, MPH, 1976. Intern dept. psychiatry Harvard Med. Sch., Cambridge, Mass., 1977-78, resident dept. psychiatry, 1978-81; assoc. prof. Psychiatry Harvard Med. Sch., Cambridge, 1985-91; chmn. mental health policy working group John F. Kennedy Sch. Govt., Cambridge, 1985—; panelist NIMH, 1989—. Author: Citizen Participation in Mental Health, 1981; contbr. articles to profl. publs. Recipient Barton award Am. Coll. Mental Health Adminstrn., 1987. Fellow Am. Psychiat. Assn. (chmn. com. 1988—), Mass. Psychiat. Soc. (councillor). Office: Cambridge Hosp Psychiatry Dept 1493 Cambridge St Cambridge MA 02139-1099

DOSANJH, DARSHAN S(INGH), aeronautical engineer, educator; b. Sultanwind, Punjab, India, Feb. 21, 1921; came to U.S., 1946, naturalized, 1965; s. S. Arur and Inder (Hundal) D.; B.Sc. (honours) Physics, Punjab U., India, 1944, M.S., 1945; M.S. in Aero. Engring., U. Mich., 1948; Ph.D. in Aeros., Johns Hopkins U., 1953; m. Harwant K. Gill, Mar. 18, 1957; children—Amrita K., Kiren K., Rajit S. Research assoc. U. Md. Inst. Fluid Dynamics and Applied Math., 1955-56; assoc. prof. mech. and aerospace engring. Syracuse (N.Y.) U., 1956-62, prof., 1962—; vis. prof. Coll. Aeros., Cranfield, Eng., 1961-62; Fulbright-Hayes sr. faculty research fellow and vis. prof. Southampton (Eng.) U., 1971-72. NATO fellow, 1967. Mem. AIAA (aeroacoustics tech. com.; assoc. fellow); mem. Acoustical Soc. Am., Am. Phys. Soc., ASME, Am. Soc. Engring. Edn., AAUP. Editor: Modern Optical Methods in Gas Dynamics Research, 1971; Effects of Noise on Hearing, 1976; contbr. numerous articles to sci. jours. Home: 5176 Brockway Ln Fayetteville NY 13066-1704

DOSS, MICHAEL PETER, education consultant, American Indian education advocate; b. Billings, Mont., Jan. 22, 1944; s. Peter William and Mildred Francis (Wolfe) D. BS in Secondary Edn., Ea. Mont. Coll., 1970, MS in Guidance and Counseling, 1972; postgrad., MIT, 1974-77; EdD, Harvard U., 1977. Minority guidance counselor Billings Pub. Schs., 1970-72; prin. Pryor (Mont.) Pub. Schs., 1972-74; legis. and ednl. planning cons. Plenty Coups High Sch. Project, Cambridge, Mass., 1974-75; assoc. dir. Am. Indian program Harvard U., Cambridge, 1975-76; orgnl. devel. and planning cons. Am. Indian policy rev. comm. U.S. Senate, Washington, 1976-77; orgnl. devel. and planning cons. chmn. Crow tribe Crow Agy., Mont., 1976-77; pres. Arrow Creek Assocs., Cambridge, 1977-79, Washington, 1983—; exec. dir. Nat. Adv. Coun. Indian Edn., Washington, 1979-83. Author: Plenty Coups, 1989. With U.S. Army N.G., 1965-71. Recipient Outstanding Contbn. to Am. Indians and Alaskan Natives award Nat. Indian Urban Coun., 1983-84; fellow Ford Found., 1974-77. Mem. nat. Indian Edn. Assn. (cons. 1985-86, bd. dirs. 1988-91, legis. chmn., Indian Educator of the Yr. 1983-84, Dedicated Svcs. award 1991), Crow Nation Culture Commn. Democrat. Methodist. Home and Office: Arrow Creek Assocs 2450 Virginia Ave NW Ste E-106 Washington DC 20037

DOSSIN, ERNEST JOSEPH, III, transportation company executive; b. Detroit, May 24, 1941; s. Ernest Joseph and Jean (Dickson) D.; m. Mary Jane Mortimore, July 24, 1965; children: Ernest Joseph IV, Tobias Alfred. BA in Bus., Valparaiso U., 1963; MBA in Fin., Fairleigh Dickinson U., 1978. Asst. store mgr. W.T. Grant, Norfolk, Va., 1967-68; dir. acctg. Am. Express, Trenton, N.J., 1968-72; corp. dir. credit Americana Hotels, N.Y.C., 1972-79; v.p. Myers Group, Rouses Point, N.Y., 1979—; exec. v.p. Global Collections Inc., Plattsburgh, N.Y., 1985—; guest lectr. Plattsburgh State U., 1985; leader seminars in improving credit practices, 1985-91. Author: Strictly Business, 1991. Congl. pres. Redeemer Luth. Ch., Plattsburgh, 1985-89; bd. dirs. Oratorio Soc., Plattsburgh, 1986-90; treas. Luth. Coll., Teaneck, N.J., 1975-79. Lt. USN, 1963-67. Mem. Nat. Assn. Credit Mgrs. (cited 1984, 85), Internat. Credit Assn. (exec.), Soc. Cert. Consumer Credit Execs. (cert. exec.), Plattsburgh C. of C., Soc. for Preservation Barbershop Quartet Singing (v.p. 1990—), Mgmt. Club Plattsburgh (bd. dirs. 1987-91). Republican. Lutheran. Home: 71 Hobbs Rd Plattsburgh NY 12901-9613 Office: Myers Group Myers Bldg Rouses Point NY 12979

DOSS-QUINBY, EGLAL, language professional, educator; b. Alexandria, Egypt, July 19, 1953; came to U.S., 1965; d. Raouf and Suzanne (Sabbagh) Doss; m. David Quinby, Sept. 5, 1975; 1 child, Laura. BA, SUNY, Stony Brook, 1973; MA, NYU, 1976, PhD, 1982. Instr. French NYU, 1978-80; asst. prof. The Univ. of Tex., Austin, 1982-88; assoc. prof. Smith Coll., Northampton, Mass., 1989—; cons. Harcourt Brace Jovanovich, Inc., 1986; speaker convs. in field. Author: Les refrains chex les trouvères, 1984; contbr. articles to profl. jours. Recipient Penfield Fellowship NYU, 1977-78, Jean Picker Fellowship Smith Coll., 1991-92, rsch. grantee, 1990-92, U. Tex., 1984; Regents scholar N.Y. State, 1970-74. Mem. Modern Lang. Assn. (speaker conv. 1988), Am. Assn. Tchrs. of French (speaker conv. 1982), Medieval Acad. of Am., Internat. Courtly Lit. Soc. Office: Smith Coll Dept French Northampton MA 01063

DOTO, PAUL JEROME, accountant; b. Newark, July 22, 1917; s. Anthony and Edith Margaret (Mascellaro) D. BS, NYU, 1947. CPA, N.J., N.Y.; registered mcpl. acct., N.J.; registered pub. sch. acct., N.J. Acct. John Hewitt Foundry Co., East Newark, N.J., 1941-43; acct. S.D. Leidesdorf & Co., N.Y.C., 1947-56; CPA Peat Marwick Mitchell & Co., N.Y.C., 1956-64; asst. controller Lincoln Ctr. for the Performing Arts Inc., N.Y.C. 1964-69; controller Seton Hall U., South Orange, N.J., 1969-74, Belart Products, Applied Coatings, Maddock, Inc., N.J., 1974-80, Internat. Trading Sales, Inc., Pan Atlantic Paper Co., N.Y.C., 1980; cons. Controller's Office, City N.Y., 1966. Bd. dirs. Parkway, Ltd., 1973-78. Served with AUS, 1943-46. Mem. Nat. Police Hall of Fame. Mem. N.Y. State Soc. CPA's (chmn. govtl. accounting com. 1963-64, chmn. internal control quest on aid of municipalities N.Y. State), AICPA, Cath. Accts. Guild (bd. govs. 1961-64), N.J. Soc. CPA's, Fin. Exec. Inst., Am. Acctg. Assn., N.Y. Assn. Profs., Smithsonian Assocs. (charter), Nat. Wildlife Fedn., Am. Legion, Am. Mus. Natural Hist. N.Y.C. (assoc.), Nat. Police Hall Fame. Address: PO Box 2508 Bloomfield NJ 07003

DOTY, MARLENE JOAN, learning resources center director; b. Paterson, N.J., Dec. 17, 1955; d. Kenneth J. and Mildred S. (Skinner) D. BS, William Paterson, Wayne, N.J., 1979; MA, Pratt Inst., Bklyn., 1984. Cert. profl. librarian/ ednl. media specialist. Reference libr. Clifton Pub. Libr., 1984—; libr. Manchester Regional Highschool, Haledon, N.J., 1979-89; libr. dir. Berkeley Coll., W. Paterson, N.J., 1989—. Mem. Am. Libr. Assn., Assn. of Coll. & Rsch. Libraries. Home: 106 Ridgewood Rd Clifton NJ 07012-1438 Office: Berkeley Coll Bus 44 Rifle Camp Rd West Paterson NJ 07424-3353

DOTY, MATTHEW EMERSON, engineering company executive; b. Long Beach, Calif., Sept. 10, 1959; s. Jack Emerson and Grace Edith (Westberg) D. BS, U. Calif., Berkeley, 1984. Chemist Fairchild Semiconductor, San Rafael, Calif., 1984-85, lab. supr., 1985-86; device engr. Internat. Rectifier, El Segundo, Calif., 1986-87, quality and reliability mgr., 1987-88, reliability engring. mgr., 1988-89; engring. mgr. Internat. Rectifier, 1989-90; quality and reliability engring. mgr. Telecommunications Techniques Corp., 1990—. Home: 6140 31st Pl NW Washington DC 20015-1502 Office: TTC 20410 Observation Dr Germantown MD 20876-4024

DOTY, WILLIAM D'ORVILLE, metallurgical engineering consultant; b. Rochester, N.Y., Mar. 11, 1920; s. Lawrence Pierce and Anna Katharine (Northrop) D.; m. Yvonne Laforest, May 24, 1923; children: William Sanford, Pamela Jane. B.Metall. Engring., Rensselaer Poly. Inst., Troy, N.Y., 1942, M.Metall. Engring., 1944, PhD in Metallurgy, 1946. Registered profl. engr., Pa. Welding metallurgist U.S. Steel Corp., Pitts., 1947-54; rsch. engr. welding U.S. Steel Corp., Monroeville, Pa., 1954-58, div. chief bar, plate, forged products, 1958-66, rsch. cons., 1966-72, chief staff engr. - product engr., 1972-77, sr. cons., 1977-85; pres., prin. cons. Doty & Assocs., Inc., Pitts., 1985—; chmn. pressure vessel rsch. com. Welding Rsch. Coun., N.Y.C., 1967-73, chmn. welding procedures com., 1989—; adv. com. Nat. Bd. of Boiler & Res. Vessel Inspection, Columbus, Ohio, 1978—. Co-author: Weldability of Steels, 1953, 2d edit. 1971, 3d edit. 1978; contbr. articles to profl. jours. Chmn. Zoning Hearing Bd. of Borough of Whitehall (Pa.), 1975—; mem. standing com. Episcopal Diocese of Pitts., 1984-88. Fellow ASME (main com. boiler and pressure vessel com. 1970-90, J. Hall Taylor medal 1984), Am. Soc. for Metals, Am. Welding Soc. (hon., Sparagen award 1966); mem. Metall. Soc. of AIME. Republican. Episcopalian. Home: 1276 Earlford Dr Pittsburgh PA 15227-1521 Office: Doty & Assocs Inc PO Box 98243 Pittsburgh PA 15227-0643

DOUCETTE, DAVID ROBERT, computer systems company executive; b. Pitts., Feb. 2, 1946; s. Adrian Robert and Mary Alyce (Newland) D. B.S.E.E., Poly. Inst. Bklyn., 1968, M.S.E.E., 1970, Ph.D., 1974. Asst. prof. elec. engring. Poly. Inst. N.Y. (now Poly. U.), 1973-74; assoc. prof. computer sci., 1975-82, prof., 1982—; sr. staff specialist advanced planning Grumman Data Systems Corp., Bethpage, N.Y., 1979-80, program mgr., 1979-80, mgr. graphics systems, 1980-84, from asst. dir. to dir. interactive systems support, 1984-86, dir. interactive systems, 1986—. Active Friends of Long Island Heritage, Nassau County Hist. Soc., Garden City Hist. Soc. Mem. IEEE (past sect. chmn., Centennial medal), Assn. Computing Machinery (past chpt. chmn.), L.I. Forum for Tech. (past dir.), AIAA (sect. dir.), Planetary Soc., Sigma Xi, Tau Beta Pi, Eta Kappa Nu. Club: Univ. of L.I. (dir.), Long Island Early Fliers. Home: 146 Washington Ave Garden City NY 11530-3013 Office: Grumman Data Systems Corp Bethpage NY 11714

DOUCETTE, MARY-ALYCE, computer company executive; b. Pitts., Feb. 12, 1924; d. Andrew George and Alice Jane (Sloan) Newland; m. Adrian Robert Doucette, Feb. 6, 1945 (dec. June 1983); children: David Robert, Regis Robert. BS, U. Pitts., 1945. Mgr. Newland Bros., Millvale, Pa., 1946-53; gen. mgr. Newland-Ludlo, Pitts., 1953-72; mgmt. cons. D3 Software, Garden City, N.Y., 1972-80, sec., corp. officer, 1980—. Fin. sec. Cerebral Palsy Assn., Garden City, Helen Keller Svcs. for Blind, Garden City; mem. Winthrop-U. Hosp. Aux., Mercy League, Friends of Hist. St. George Ch. of Hempstead, N.Y., Adv. Coun. for Continuing Edn., Garden City Sch. Dist., 1988—. Mem. AAUW, L.I. Panhellenic, Univ. Club, Nassau County Hist. Soc. (life), Garden City Hist. Soc., Community Club Garden City-Hempstead, Woman's Club Garden City, Alpha Delta Pi, Pi Lambda Theta. Home: 146 Washington Ave Garden City NY 11530-3013 Office: D3 Software PO Box 8051 Garden City NY 11530-8051

DOUDERA, GERARD EMIL, artist; b. Sharon, Conn., Dec. 29, 1932; s. Edward and Marion (Dennis) D.; m. Irene Roade, June 4, 1959 (div. 1975); children: Gunther, Jason. BFA, Hartford Art Sch., 1956; postgrad., U. Ill., 1957-58. Prof. art U. Conn., Storrs, 1962-87, prof. emeritus, 1987—. One man shows include Slater Meml. Mus., Norwich, Conn., 1989, Pindar Gallery, N.Y.C., 1990, William Benton Mus. Art, Conn., 1990, Kerygma Gallery, Ridgewood, N.J., 1991; represented in permanent collections at Wadsworth Atheneum, New Britain Mus. Am. Art, Butler Inst. Am. Art, Lane Found. Named Artist in Residence, Camargo Found., Cassis, France, 1987. Home: 490 Lewis Hill Rd Coventry CT 06238-1668

DOUGARD, RONALD JOSEPH, chief of police; b. Newark, N.J., May 19, 1945; s. Alphonso J. and Julia (Kuchinskas) D.; m. Mary Boland, Mar. 7, 1970; children: Ronald, Jr., Mary Elizabeth, James V. AS in Criminal Justice, Ocean Community Coll., Toms River, N.J., 1974; BA in Criminal Justice, Monmouth Coll., 1979. Motor vehicle examiner N.J. Div. Motor Vehicles, Trenton, 1967-69, inspector, hwy. patrol, 1969-72; police officer Brick Twp. Police Dept., N.J., 1972-74, police sgt., 1974-80, police lt., 1980-90, chief of police, 1990—, emergency mgmt. coord., 1990—; evaluator Nat. Commn. on Law Enforcement Accreditation, Fairfax, Va. Cpl. U.S. Army, 1965-67, Vietnam. Decorated Purple Heart, Combat Infantry badge; named Policeman of the Yr., K.C., 1974. Mem. Ocean County Police Chiefs Assn., N.J. State Chiefs Assn., Internat. Assn. Chiefs of Police, Police Benevolence Assn., 196 Light Infantry Assn., Disabled Am. Vets., Kiwanis. Home: 176 Calvin Ct Brick NJ 08724-1706 Office: Brick Township Police Dept 401 Chambersbridge Rd Brick NJ 08723-2898

DOUGHERTY, CATHY WEST, mechanical engineer; b. Balt., Feb. 5, 1956; d. Garnet Earl and Harlenna Fay (King) West; m. John Thomas Dougherty; children: Christopher, Lauren, Stephanie. Student, Carnegie-Mellon U., 1974-77; BS, Ohio State U., 1981. Cert. waste water ops. Prodn. engr. Dow Chem. Co., Ironton, Ohio, 1981-82; field service engr. Dow Chem. Co., Granville, Ohio, 1982-83, rsch. engr., 1983-85; sr. prodn. engr. lightgvard Dow Chem. Co., Gales Ferry, Conn., 1985-86, sr. prodn. engr. styrofoam, 1986-88, sr. prodn. engr. latex, 1988-89; project engr. Bostik div. Black & Decker, Middleton, Mass., 1989-91; project mgr. remediation U.S. Tech. Environ. Cons., Inc., Lexington, Mass., 1991—; tech. advisor Canoe River Aquifer Assn.; com. mem. Soc. Plastic Industry, 1984-85. Patentee in field. Troop leader Girl Scouts Am., Ironton, 1981-83; counselor Jr. Achievement, Ironton, 1981-83. Mem. Soc. Women Engrs., Ohio State Alumna Assn., Delta Gamma. Home: 88 Cocasset St Townhouse # 1 Foxboro MA 02035 Office: US Tech Environ Cons Inc 1 Forbes Rd Lexington MA 02173-7303

DOUGHERTY, JAMES, orthopedic surgeon, educator; b. Lawrence, Mass., July 31, 1926; s. James A. and Maude D. (Dillard) D.; m. Rita Buchman; children: James (dec.), Charles, Janice, Jonathan, Christopher. BS, Trinity Coll., Hartford, Conn., 1950; MD, Albany Med. Coll., N.Y., 1951. Diplomate Am. Bd. Orthopaedic Surgery. Intern U. Chgo. Clinics, 1951-52, resident, 1951-56, instr., 1955-56; chmn. div. orthopaedic surgery SUNY, Syracuse, 1958-59; prof. clin. surgery Albany Med. Coll., 1960—; trustee, chmn. med. staff Albany Med. Ctr., 1987-89; cons. Subacute Care Alternative Project, Washington. Contbr. articles to profl. jours. Mem. Bd. Edn. Ravena-Coeymans-Selkirk Central Schs., Ravena, N.Y., 1960-75; med. dir. N.Y. Sr. Games, 1986-89; trustee Schaeffer Meml. Libr., 1990—; bd. dirs. Inst. for Study Aging, 1990—. With U.S. Army, 1944-46. Fellow Am. Acad. Orthopaedic Surgeons; mem. Crawford Cambell Soc. (founder, pres. 1978-84), Northeastern Regional Assn. Sports Medicine (chmn. 1984-89), Albany Med. Coll. Alumni Assn. (trustee 1990—, pres.-elect 1992—), Internat. Platform Assn., Alpha Omega Alpha, Sigma Psi. Baptist. Home: Onesquethaw Rd Feura Bush NY 12067 Office: 1 Executive Park Dr Albany NY 12203-3717

DOUGHERTY, JUDE PATRICK, university dean; b. Chgo., July 21, 1930; s. Edward Timothy and Cecilia Anastasia (Loew) D.; m. Patricia Ann Regan, Dec. 28, 1957; children: Thomas, Michael, John, Paul. BA, Cath. U. Am., 1954, MA, 1955, PhD, 1960. Instr. Marquette U., 1957-58; instr. Bellarmine Coll., 1958-60, asst. prof., 1960-63, assoc. prof., 1963-66; assoc. prof. Cath. U. Am., 1966-76, prof., 1976—; dean Cath. U. Am. (Sch. Philosophy), 1967—; Vis. assoc. prof. Georgetown U., summer, 1965; vis. prof. Katholieke Universiteit te Leuven, Belgium, 1974-75. Author: Recent American Naturalism, 1960; co-author: Approaches to Morality, 1966; Editor: Theological Directions of the Ecumenical Movement, 1964, The Impact of Vatican II, 1966, The Good Life and Its Pursuit, 1985; editor: Rev. of Metaphysics, 1971—; gen. editor: Studies in Philosophy and the History of Philosophy, 1978—. Bd. advisers Franklin J. Matchette Found., 1971—; trustee Bellarmine Coll., 1972-75; mem. Pontifical Acad., St. Thomas, Rome, 1981—, Academia Scientiarum et Artium Europae, Salzburg, 1991—. Recipient William T. Miles award Bellarmine Coll., 1964. Mem. Am. Philos. Assn. (program chmn. ea. div. 1988, exec. com. ea. div. 1989—), Am. Cath. Philos. Assn. (pres. 1974-75), Washington Philosophy Club (pres. 1968-69), Soc. for Philosophy Religion (pres. 1978-79), Metaphys. Soc. Am. (pres. 1983-84). Home: 9036 Rouen Ln Rockville MD 20854-3130 Office: Cath U Am Sch Philosophy 620 Michigan Ave NE Washington DC 20064

DOUGHERTY, RAYMOND EDWARD, artist, educator; b. Wildwood, N.J., June 15, 1942; s. Edward Joseph and Dorothy Florance (Eckert) D.; m. Madiline Dougherty, 1969; children: Raymond Edward Jr., Micheal, Sean. Diploma, Pa. Acad. Fine Arts, 1965; BFA, U. Pa., 1970; cert. in teaching, Glassboro (N.J.) State U., 1974. Cert. art tchr., N.J. Instr. Lower Cape May Regional Sch., Lower Township, N.J., 1970-78; Ocean City (N.J.) Art Ctr., 1973-78; instr. Wildwood Cath. High Sch., North Wildwood, N.J., 1980-84, Helmbold Edn. Ctr., Corbin City, N.J., 1984-89, Atlantic County Spl. Svcs., Corbin City, 1989—. Represented in permanent collection U. Medicine and Dentistry N.J. With U.S. N.G., 1964-70. Mem. Nat. Soc. Painters in Casein and Acrylic (bd. dirs. N.Y.C. chpt. 1980-85, 89-91, v.p. 1985-88, pres. 1988-89, cert. of merit 1983), Am. Acad. Inst. Arts and Letters (Benney & Smith award 1979), Nat. Arts Club (Dr. David Soloway award 1984), Audubon Artist Painters Soc. Home and Studio: 932 Main St Erma NJ 08204-4828

DOUGLAS, CAROLYN JORY, psychiatrist; b. N.Y.C., Sept. 27, 1953. BA summa cum laude, Princeton U., 1976; MD, Harvard U., 1980. Diplomate Am. Bd. Psychiatry and Neurology. Resident Payne Whitney Clinic, N.Y.C., 1980-84; asst. clin. prof. psychiatry Presbyn. Hosp., Columbia U. Coll. Surgeons and Physicians, N.Y.C., 1984—; dir. Eye-6 inpatient psychiatric unit, Presbyn. Hosp., N.Y.C., 1986—. Contbr. articles to profl. jours. Mem. Am. Psychiatric Assn., Phi Beta Kappa. Office: 160 E 89th St Apt 1B New York NY 10128-2336

DOUGLAS, DONALD DEAN, gastroenterologist; b. Waukegan, Ill., July 30, 1944; s. Donald B. and Regina (Rovelle) D.; m. Dorothy V. Early, June 7, 1969; children: Theresa A., David B., Virginia R. BS, Creighton U., 1966; MD, U. Md., 1970. Diplomate Am. Bd. Internal Medicine, Am. Bd. Gastroenterology. Intern Henry Ford Hosp., Detroit, 1970-71; resident Mayo Clinic, Rochester, Minn., 1973-75; fellow U. Wis., Madison, 1975-77; pres. Susquehanna Gastroenterology Assocs., Williamsport, Pa., 1977-88, Donald D. Douglas, P.C., Lewisburg, Pa., 1990—; head medicine Evang. Community Hosp., Lewisburg, 1991—. Inventor tubular sheath for endoscope, 1980, temperature, volume, pressure for insuflation device. Lt. USN, 1971-73. Mem. FACP, AMA, Am. Soc. Gastrointestinal Endoscopy, Am. Soc. Gastroenterology, Am. Gastrointestinal Assn. Republican. Roman Catholic. Home: 2009 Madison Ave Lewisburg PA 17837 Office: Brookpark Office Ctr 260 Reitz Blvd Ste 1 Lewisburg PA 17837

DOUGLAS, FRED WALTER, counselor; b. Englewood, N.J., Feb. 3, 1949; s. Frank Hienman and Edna Mae (Sommers) D.; m. Nancy Ellen Feaster, June 29, 1985; 1 child, Michael Anthony Shackley. BA, Jersey City State Coll., 1970; MA, Montclair (N.J.) State Coll., 1988. Cert. pupil pers. svcs., cert. sch. social worker, cert. secondary tchr. math. Tchr. math. Parsippany (N.J.) and Parsippany Hills High Schs., 1970-89; secondary sch. counselor Parsippany (N.J.) Hills High Sch., 1989—; pvt. practice coll. counselor Morris Plains, N.J., 1991—; v.p. Peer Leaders Adv. Network, No. N.J., 1990-91; cons. Ednl. Software Svc., Ridgewood, N.J., 1990-91. Mem. Parsippany (N.J.) Alcohol/Drug Coun., 1990-91. Mem. AACD, NEA, N.J. Assn. for Counseling and Devel., N.J. Sch. Counselors Assn. (student scholarship 1991), N.J. Edn. Assn., Morris County Edn. Assn., Morris County Profl. Counselors Assn. (student scholarship 1992), Parsippany Troy Hills Edn. Assn. Home: 122 Patriots Rd Morris Plains NJ 07950-1129 Office: Parsippany Hills High Sch 20 Rita Dr Parsippany NJ 07054

DOUGLAS, JAMES HOLLEY, state official; b. Springfield, Mass., June 21, 1951; s. Robert James and Cora Elizabeth (Holley) D.; m. Dorothy Foster, May 24, 1975; children: Matthew James, Andrew Foster. A.B.,

Middlebury Coll., 1972. Gen. mgr. Credit Bur. of Middlebury, Vt., 1972-76; exec. dir. United Way of Addison County, 1976-79; exec. asst. to Gov. of Vt., 1979-80; sec. of state State of Vt., Montpelier, 1981—; mem. Vt. Ho. of Reps., 1973-79, majority leader, 1975-77, 77-79. Mem. Nat. Assn. Secs. State (pres.). Republican. Congregationalist. Lodge: Masons. Office: Sec of State 26 Terrace St Montpelier VT 05609-1101*

DOUGLAS, JAMES MERRILL, chemical engineering educator, consultant; b. Aurora, Ill., July 27, 1933; s. Merrill Harry and Carolyn (Klocke) D.; m. Mary Elizabeth Grubb, Mar. 8, 1958; children: Mary Lynn, Robert James. BE, Johns Hopkins U., 1954; PhD, U. Del., 1960. Rsch. engr. ARCO, Phila., 1960-65; assoc. prof. chem. engring. U. Rochester, N.Y., 1965-68; prof. U. Mass., Amherst, 1968—, dept. head, 1979-81; cons. duPont, Wilmington, Del., 1965—, ICI-UK, 1965—; bd. dirs. Computers and Chem. Engring. Corp., Houston, 1988-90. Author: Process Dynamics and Control VI, 1972, VII, 1972, Concept Dies of Chemical Process, 1988; contbr. articles to tech. jours. Mem. Monroe County Pure Water Agy., Rochester, 1964. Lt. U.S. Army, 1959-60. Rsch. grantee NSF, Petroleum Rsch. Fund, Dept. Energy, 1965—. Mem. AICE (program com. 1971-88, bd. editors jour. 1978-80, Cast Divsn. award 1987), Sigma Xi, Tau Beta Pi. Home: 335 Long Plain Rd Leverett MA 01054 Office: U Mass Dept Chem Engring Amherst MA 01003

DOUGLAS, JOHN HOFFMANN, foundation executive; b. Jersey City, May 25, 1920; s. Paul Hazzard and Florence (Hoffmann) D.; m. Joan Walbridge Battey, Dec. 10, 1949 (dec. July 1976); children: Parker Hazzard, Jonathan Battey, Johanna Vail, Bernard Martin III. Student, Trinity Coll., Hartford, Conn., 1939-41. Asst. sales mgr. Bourjois, Inc., N.Y.C., 1946-51; product mgr. Am. Safety Razor Corp., Bklyn., 1951-53; market devel. mgr. Shulton, Inc., N.Y.C., 1953-55, European liaison mgr., 1960-61; co-founder, gen. mgr. Shulton, N.V., Leiden, The Netherlands, 1955-60, Holland House Cosmetics, N.V., Haarlem, The Netherlands, 1961-76; sec., counselor Service Corps. Retired Execs., Stamford and Norwalk, Conn., 1978-84; co-founder, pres. English Speaking Union br., Greenwich, Conn., bd. dirs., mem. exec. com., N.Y. Trustee, sec. Greenwich Hist. Soc., 1983-88; patron Met. Opera. With USCG, 1941-46. Fellow Mcpl. Art Soc.; mem. Brothers of the Order of St. John (assoc. brother officer), Nat. Inst. Social Scis., Nat. Com. on Am. Fgn. Policy, Newcomener Soc., Forum for World Affairs, Ambs. Round Table, Pilgrims of U.S., Field Club of Greenwich, Delta Kappa Epsilon. Republican. Episcopalian. Home: 8 Weathervane Ln Cos Cob CT 06807-2732 Office: English Speaking Union Greenwich PO Box 7744 Greenwich CT 06836-7744

DOUGLAS, LAURA LYNN, international education specialist, consultant; b. Northampton, Mass., Apr. 22, 1960; d. John George Jr. and Priscilla (Delahunt) D. B of Social Welfare cum laude, U. So. Maine, 1982; M in Internat. Adminstrn., Sch. for Internat. Tng., Bratteboro, Vt., 1990. Dir. English and culture Nozomi Sch., Niigata, Japan, 1982-85; project mgr. LEX Am., Cambridge, Mass., 1986-90; internat. coord. Teikyo, Waterbury, Conn., 1990—; ednl. cons. Japan Sotoshu Relief Com., Thailand, 1986; presentor UN Ednl. div., Bangkok, 1986. Author: Cross Cultural Training Modules for LEX America, 1987, Cross Cultural Training Modules for Teikyo Post U., 1991. Community worker, Holy Innocents Home Care Svc., Portland, Maine, 1980-82; active in Internat. 4-H Youth Exchange, New Eng., 1989—. Exchange student, Youth for Understanding, 1976. Mem. Nat. Assn. Fgn. Student Affairs, Soc. Internat. Edn., Tng. and Rsch., Nat. Assn. of Internat. Educators (Conn. rep.). Democrat. Lutheran. Office: Teikyo Post U 800 Country Club Rd Waterbury CT 06708-3200

DOUGLAS, MARILYN EILEEN, library administrator; b. Troy, N.Y., May 13, 1941; d. Frank Sandholdt and Pauline (Kawka) Hansen; m. Peter Ashley Douglas, Apr. 17, 1971. BA in English, Coll. St. Rose, 1963; MS in Libr. Sci., Syracuse U., 1964. Libr., youth svcs. N.Y. Pub. Libr., N.Y.C., 1964-66; libr. Vauxhall Manor Sch., London, 1967-73, chmn., English dept., 1973-74; libr. N.Y. State Libr., Albany, 1974-85, sr. libr. humanities, 1985-87, head, state agy. svcs., 1987—. V.p. Pine Hills Neighborhood Assn., Albany, 1988—; trustee Friends of New Netherland Project, Albany, 1987—. Mem. ALA (various exec. positions), Ea. N.Y. Assn. Coll. and Rsch. Librs. Assn., N.Y. Libr. Assn. (chmn. com. profession 1989—, pres. govt. docs roundtable 1990-91), N.Y. Interagy. Info. Group (legis chmn. 1991, pres. 1988-89), Capital Dist. Libr. Coun., Spl. Librs. Assn., Beta Phi Mu. Roman Catholic. Home: 52 Ryckman Ave Albany NY 12208-2528 Office: NY State Libr Cultural Edn Ctr Albany NY 12230

DOUGLAS, MICHAEL THOMAS, controller; b. Bronx, N.Y., June 28, 1961; s. Thomas and Mary (Tormey) D.; m. Lora Reimann, Sept. 29, 1990. BA in Acctg., Iona Coll., New Rochelle, N.Y., 1985. Acct. MacMillan Inc., N.Y.C., 1980-82; mgr. acctg./reporting CBS Inc. Holt Rhinehart Winston, N.Y.C., 1983-87; pub. group contr. Maxwell Communications, N.Y.C., 1988-90; contr. Schnell Pub. Co., N.Y.C., 1990—; mem. fin. com. Am. Bus. Press, N.Y.C., 1991—. Mem. Chemist Club. Home: 777 N Macquesten Pky Mount Vernon NY 10552-1625 Office: Schnell Pub Co 80 Broad St New York NY 10004-2209

DOUGLAS, PATRICIA JEANNE, instructional systems designer; b. Coats, Kans., Sept. 27, 1939; d. Curtis Claire and Pearl L. (Haney) Coe; divorced; children: Tricia Jeanne Douglas Nash, Robert Charles Jr. Student, Willamette U., 1958-59; BA, U. Ariz., 1961, MEd, 1973; PhD, Colo. State U., 1988; postgrad., Columbia U. Cert. tchr., Ariz., Colo. Tchr. Amphitheater Sch. Dist., Tucson, 1962-83; corp. trainer IBM, Boulder, Colo., 1983-86, systems analyst Internat. Purchasing and Distbn. Ctr., 1987-88, rsch. statistician, 1988-89, instnl. system designer, 1989—; asst. expense acct. analyst Colo. State U., Ft. Collins, 1986-87, rsch. assoc., 1988-89. Mem. tchr. workshops LDS Ch., Boulder, 1988; mem. Substance Prevention Project, Boulder, 1988; election judge Boulder County, 1988; vol. in schs., Wappingers Falls, N.Y., 1991. IBM grantee, 1988. Mem. Inter-Am. Orgn. for Higher Edn., Internat. Coun. for Distance Edn., Consortium-Distance Edn. Network Orgn. U.S., Phi Delta Kappa, Omicron Tau Theta. Office: 500 Columbus Ave Thornwood NY 10594-1900

DOUGLAS, PAUL HOFMANN, housing development executive; b. Plymouth, Mass., Aug. 9, 1947; s. Paul Gehman and Clara Lillian (Hofmann) D.; m. Katherine Gilmore Procak, Aug. 14, 1971; children: Matthew Ian, Jonathan Procak. BA, U. Mass., 1973. Dir. econ. devel. Franklin County C. of C., Greenfield, Mass., 1973-75; residential loan processor Franklin County Regional Housing Authority, Greenfield, 1975-76, mgmt. dir., 1976-79, community devel. dir., 1980-82; asst. exec. dir. Franklin County Regional Housing Authority, Turners Falls, Mass., 1982-87, exec. dir., 1987—; exec. dir. Shelburne Housing Authority, Shelburne Falls, Mass., 1987—, Rural Devel., Inc., Turners Falls, 1990—; cons. Community Revitalization Tng. ctr., Bethesda, Md., 1982-87; bd. dirs. Western Mass. Mortgage Rev. Bd., 1985-90, Mass. Nonprofit Housing Assn., Boston, 1987—, Mass. Housing Fin. Agy., Boston, 1990—, Citizens Housing and Planning Assn., Boston, 1991—; mem. Franklin County Affordable Housing Task Force, 1987—. Treas. Franklin Regional Transit Authority, Greenfield, 1984-90; pres. Franklin County Home Care Corp., Montague, Mass., 1987—; bd. dirs. Commn. Vets. Affairs, Boston, 1992; mem. Legis. Rental Study Com., Boston, 1992. Sgt. U.S. Army, 1966-69, Vietnam. Decorated Bronze Star medal, 1967. Mem. Nat. Rural Housing Coalition, Nat. Assn. Housing and Redevel. Ofcls., Country Club Greenfield. Episcopalian. Home: Wilson Hill Colrain MA 01340 Office: Franklin County Regional Housing Authority PO Box 30 Turners Falls MA 01376

DOUGLASS, IRWIN BRUCE, chemistry educator; b. Des Moines, Sept. 2, 1904; s. Alonzo Cline and Mary Margaret (Findley) D.; m. Grace Fannie Fetherston, Aug. 15, 1931; children: Nancy Grace, Miriam Lois. BS, Monmouth Coll., 1926, DSc (hon.), 1958; PhD, U. Kans., 1932. Tchr. chemistry and physics Monmouth (Ill.) High Sch., 1926-28; instr. chemistry Kansas City (Mo.) Jr. Coll., 1930-31; teaching asst. U. Kans., Lawrence, 1929-32; asst. prof. chemistry N.D. Agrl. Coll., Fargo, 1932-33; asst. prof. then prof. chemistry No. Montana Coll., Havre, 1933-37, 38-40; rsch. fellow Yale U., New Haven, Conn., 1937-38; asst. then prof. chemistry U. Maine, Orono, 1940-72; ret., 1972; seasonal ranger, naturalist Nat. Park Svc., Yellowstone Nat. Park, 1936-40; cons. Maine Potato Starch Mfrs., Aroostook County, Maine, 1952-53; vis. scholar UCLA, 1962-63. Contbr. over 50 articles to chem. jours. Mem. Town of Orono (Maine) Coun., 1975-77, Bd. Environ. Protection, State of Maine, Augusta, 1974-77. Fellow AAAS; mem. Am. Chem. Soc., Sigma Xi. Democrat. Methodist. Home: 904 St George Rd Williston VT 05495-9721

DOUGLASS, JACKSON FRED, academic administrator; b. Amsterdam, N.Y., Nov. 11, 1940; s. Dayton William and Roberta (Bowerman) D.; m. Anna Mae Vianese, Oct. 5, 1963; children: David Dayton, Stephen Carl, Danise Ann, Matthew Jackson. AAS, SUNY, Morrisville, 1962; BA in Biology, SUNY, Plattsburgh, 1969. Lab. food technician Beech-Nut Nutrition Corp., Canajoharie, N.Y., 1962-65; lab. teaching asst. Fulton-Montgomery Community Coll., Johnstown, N.Y., 1965-68, instr. sci. div., 1969-73, asst. dir. continuing edn., 1973-84, acting dean student and community svcs., 1984-85, dir. non-credit programs and bus./indsl. tng., 1985—. Justice Town of Canajoharie, N.Y., 1979-85, town supr., 1986—; chmn. bd. Montgomery County, Fonda, N.Y., 1990; pres. St. Peter and Paul Ch. Coun., Canajoharie, 1985; mem. exec. com. Montgomery County Emergency Med. Svcs. Coun., 1991. Recipient Eagle and Feather award Canajoharie Cen. Sch., 1991. Mem. Continuing Edn. Assn. N.Y. (com. mem. 1989), Montgomery County C. of C. (chmn. leadership com. 1989—), Circle K-FMCC (advisor 1984—), Kiwanis (pres. Amsterdam chpt. 1980-81, lt. gov. Mohawk div. 1986-87, Disting. Pres. award 1981, Disting. Kiwanian award N.Y. Dist. 1987). Home: RD #1 Box 143 Canajoharie NY 13317 Office: Fulton Montgomery Community Coll Rte 67 Amsterdam NY 12095

DOUGLASS, MELVIN ISADORE, educator, clergyman; b. N.Y.C., July 21, 1948; s. Isadore Douglass and Esther L. Tripp. AS in Early Childhood Edn., Vincennes U., 1970; BS in Early Childhood and Elem. Edn., Tuskegee Inst., 1973; MS in Urban Elem. Edn., Morgan State U., 1975; MA in Orgn. Adminstrn. Supervision, NYU, 1977; MEd in Curriculum and Teaching, Columbia U., 1978, EdD in Family and Community Edn./Social Studies, 1981. Cert. social studies tchr., N.Y.; cert. sch. adminstr. and supr., N.Y.; cert. elem. tchr., N.Y.; ordained to ministry Bapt. Ch., 1987. Tchr., dean students Bronx Pub. Sch., N.Y., 1973-75; sch. age program dir. Amistad Child Day Care Ctr., Jamaica, N.Y., 1976-77; adminstrv. dir. Beck Meml. Day Care Ctr., Bronx, 1983-84; primary sch. dept. chair City of N.Y. Dept. Juvenile Justice, 1984-85, ombudsman, 1985-88; chmn. depts. English, reading and social studies Stimson Jr. High Sch., Huntington Station, N.Y., 1988—; coord. various edn. confs., 1986—; mem. community adv. bd. City of N.Y. Dept. of Correction, Queens House of Detention for Men, 1991—; ednl. liaison N.Y. State Senator Alton R. Waldon, Jr., 1991—. Author: Black Winners: A History of Spingarn Medalists, 1915-1983, 1984, Carter G. Woodson: A Biography, 1987; contbr. articles to profl. jours. Assisting minister Calvary Bapt. Ch., 1987—; co-chairperson edn. com. N.Y.C. Black Leadership Council, 1987-88, N.Y. State Conf. NAACP, 1986—; chmn. anti-drug com. Met. Council NAACP Brs., 1986-89; cons. Jamaica East/West Adolescent Pregnancy Consortium, 1986—; mem. area policy bd. #12 subunit 2, 1987—; mem. Queens adv. bd. N.Y. Urban League, 1988—; pres. bd. dirs. N.Y.C. Transit br. NAACP, 1984-89; bd. dirs. Queens Council on Arts, 1983-86, Black Exptl. Theatre, 1982—, United Black Men Queens County Inc., 1986—, Dance Explosion, 1987-89; ednl. liaison N.Y. State Sen. Alton R. Waldor Jr., 1991—. Recipient citation for community svc. N.Y. State Gov. Mario Cuomo, 1986, citation award N.Y.C. Mayor Edward Koch, 1986, citation of honor Queens Borough Pres. Claire Shulman, 1986, Svc. award N.Y.C. Transit br. NAACP, 1986, Jefferson award Am. Inst. for Pub. Svc. and WNYW-Fox TV, 1987, Civil Rights award N.Y.C. Transit br. NAACP, 1988, citation N.Y.C. Coun., 1988, Alumni Faculty citation Vincennes U., 1991, resolution Senator A.R. Waldon, Jr., 1991; named Nu Omicron chpt. Omega Man of Yr., 1987. Mem. Nat. Black Child Devel. Inst., NEA, St. Albans C. of C. (v.p. bd. dirs. 1987-89), L.I. Tuskegee Alumni Assn. (v.p. bd. dirs. 1987-89), Jamaica Track Club (pres., founder 1973—), Masons, Shriners, Kappa Delta Pi, Omega Psi Phi (basileus Nu Omicron chpt. 1986-89, bd. dirs. Nu Omicron chpt. Day Care Ctr. 1984—). Address: 108-38 167th St Jamaica NY 11433

DOUGLASS, ROBERT DUNCAN, lawyer; b. Bklyn., Aug. 18, 1941; s. George Wilbur Douglass and Gladys (Harding) Naffke; children: Benjamin R., Samuel H. BA, Lafayette Coll., 1963; JD, Harvard U., 1966. Bar: Pa. 1967, U.S. Dist. Ct. (we. dist.) Pa. 1984, U.S. Cir. Ct. (3d cir.) 1984. Assoc. Joseph N. Mack, Indiana, Pa., 1966-69; ptnr. Pierce & Douglass, Indiana, 1969-75; sole practice Indiana, 1975-89; ptnr. Bonya & Douglass, Indiana, 1989; Bonya and Douglass, 1989—; asst. prof. Ind. U., Pa., 1970-72, lectr. continuing edn. Ind. U., 1982-84, 90. Mem. ABA, Pa. Bar Assn., Indiana County Bar Assn. (sec. 1975-86, v.p. 1986-87, pres. 1987-88), Rivers Club (Pitts.), Indiana Country Club, DKE-Yale Club N.Y.C. Clubs: Rivers (Pitts.), Ind. Country, Yale (N.Y.C.).

DOUGLASS, ROBERT ROYAL, banker, lawyer; b. Binghamton, N.Y., Oct. 16, 1931; s. Robert R. and Frances (Behan) D.; m. Linda Ann Luria, June 2, 1962; children: Robert Royal, Alexandra Brooke, Andrew. B.A. with distinction, Dartmouth Coll., 1953; LL.B., Cornell U., 1959. Bar: N.Y. Asso. Hinman, Howard & Kattell, 1959-64; 1st asst. counsel to Gov. N.Y. State, Albany, 1964-65; counsel to gov. Gov. N.Y. State, 1965-70, sec. to gov., 1971-72; partner Milbank, Tweed, Hadley & McCloy, 1972-76; exec. v.p., gen. counsel Chase Manhattan Bank, N.Y.C., 1976-83; exec. v.p. Chase Manhattan Bank, 1983-85, vice chmn., 1985—; dir. Rockefeller Center, Inc., 1976-82; chmn. Nelson Rockefeller's Campaign for Republican Nomination for Pres., 1968; commr. Port Authority of N.Y. State and N.J., 1972-76; trustee N.Y.C. Public Library, 1972-86; bd. dirs., chmn. exec. com. Downtown-Lower Manhattan Assn., N.Y.C., 1973—; mem. vis. com. John F. Kennedy Sch. Govt., Harvard U., 1974-79; mem. N.Y. Landmarks Conservancy, 1977-80. Trustee Dartmouth Coll., 1983—, Mus. of Modern Art, 1989—. With M.C., U.S. Army, 1954-56. Recipient Wallace award Am.-Scottish Found., 1974. Mem. ABA, N.Y. State Bar Assn., Council Fgn. Relations. Roman Catholic. Clubs: Century Assn, World Trade Center, Round Hill, Harbor, Blind Brook. Office: Chase Manhattan Corp 1 Chase Manhattan Plz New York NY 10081-0001

DOUGLASS, WILLIAM JAMES, JR., architect; b. Youngstown, Ohio, May 12, 1932; s. William James and Emily Elizabeth (Best) D.; m. Ellen Peterson, June 30, 1954; children; W. Scott, Julie L., Tracy E., Perry H. BFA in Architecture, Ohio U., 1954. Registered architect, Pa., Ohio. Archtl. draftsman Walter Mallorie, AIA, Sharon, Pa., 1956-58; architect Kling & Frost, Architects, Youngstown, Ohio, 1958-61, Walter Mallorie, Sharon, Pa., 1961-63, Hunter-Heiges, Architects/Engrs., Meadville, Pa., 1963-70; architect, exec. v.p. Hunter Heiges Sabo Douglass Rogers, Meadville, Pa., 1970-91; exec. vp. Hayden Heiges Sabo Douglass Rogers, Inc. Architects/Engrs., Meadville, Pa., 1991—; bd. dirs. 1st Nat. Bank Pa., Erie. Pres. Meadville Lions Club, 1974, Meadville C. of C., 1976, Meadville Area Indsl. Devel.; asst. chmn. Crawford U. Indsl. Commn., Meadville. Pfc. U.S. Army, 1954-56. Mem. AIA, Pa. Soc. Architects, Country Club (pres. 1980-82). Republican. Presbyterian. Home: 755 Seminole Rd Meadville PA 16335 Office: Hayden Heiges Sabo Douglas Rogers Inc Architects/Engrs 210 Chestnut St Ste B Meadville PA 16335

DOUMANI, GEORGE ALEXANDER, earth and environmental scientist; b. Acre, Palestine, Apr. 16, 1929; s. Alexander A. and Victoria (Issa) D.; m. Julie Molnar, Mar. 15, 1957 (div. 1984); children: Alexandra, Victor, Aziza. BA in Geol. Scis., U. Calif., Berkeley, 1956, MA in Paleontology, 1957; PhD in Environ. Scis., Pacific Western U., 1985. Geologist, glaciologist Glaciologist Arctic Inst., Byrd Station, Antarctica, 1958-60; rsch. assoc. Inst. Polar Studies Ohio State U., Columbus, 1960-63; head cold regions bibliography sect. Sci. and Tech. div. Libr. of Congress, Washington, 1963-66; sci. adviser to U.S. Congress Sci. Policy Rsch. div. Libr. of Congress, Washington, 1966-75; pres. Adar Corp., Washington, Beirut, 1975-77, Tech. Transfer Internat. Corp., Washington, 1977-79; v.p. tech. transfer Human Resources Mgmt., Inc., Washington, 1979-85; dir. U.S. Peace Corps, Yemen Arab Republic, Yemen Arab Republic, 1985-88; dir. office tech. policy Dept. of Energy, Washington, 1988-90; dir. earth and environ. scis. program Directorate for Edn. and Human Resources, NSF, Washington, 1990-91; cons. and lectr. in field. Editorial adv. bd. Sci. Digest, 1970-81; author numerous books, papers, reports and articles; appeared on numerous radio broadcasts, domestic and overseas including UN radio, Sta. BBC, and Voice of Am.; several TV appearances, domestic and fgn. Recipeint Antarctic Svc. medal Def. Dept., 1961; decorated Knight of Nat. Order of the Cedars, Lebanese Republic, 1961; W. W. Van Arsdale meml. scholar, 1954-55; U.S. Bd. on Geographic Names named Doumani Peak 1962 and Mount Doumani in Antarctica, 1967. Fellow Geol. Soc. Am. (com. on geology and pub. policy); mem. Am. Assn. Petroleum Geologists, Am. Polar Soc., Antarctican Soc. (pres. 1970-71), Geol. Soc. Washington, Nat. Environ. Edn. Tng. Program Adv. Com., Cosmos Club, Sigma Xi (life mem.).

DOUMAR, ALBERT GEORGE, bank executive, lecturer; b. Bklyn., Feb. 3, 1935; s. George Elias and Marie (Raphael) D.; m. Evelyn Ann Owen, June 3, 1962; children: Theresa, Claire. BBA summa cum laude, St. Francis Coll., Bklyn., 1957; MBA, NYU, 1966; postgrad., Pace U., N.Y.C. Enrolled agt. IRS; cert. practitioner of taxation; cert. trust and fin. advisor. With Chase Manhattan Bank, N.A., N.Y.C., 1960—, in taxation field, 1964—, v.p., tax rsch. officer, 1983—; tax lectr. Am. Inst. Banking, N.Y.C., 1971-90, Bank Adminstrn. Inst., 1977-79, N.Y. State Bankers Assn. Tax Sch., 1974—. Co-author: Basic Fiduciary Income Taxation, 1977; contbr. articles to profl. jours. With U.S. Army, 1958-60. Mem. Banking Instns. on Taxation (com.), N.Y. State Bankers Assn., Nat. Assn. Tax Preparers. Office: Chase Manhattan Bank NA Tax Svcs 35th Fl 1211 Avenue of Americas New York NY 10036-8701

DOUSKEY, FRANZ THOMAS, humanities educator; b. New Haven, Dec. 2, 1941; s. Stanley and Wadia (Mekdeci) Douskey. BA, Goddard Coll., 1973, MA, 1975. Chmn. dept. humanities So. Cen. Community Coll., New Haven, 1977-90, prof., 1990—. Author: Rowing Across the Dark, 1981; contbr. articles to the New Yorker, Rolling Stone, The Nation, others. Pres. Mill River Preservation, Hamden, 1987—; mem. Hamden Hist. Soc. Mem. PEN Am. Ctr., Internat. Platform. Home: 50 Ives St Hamden CT 06518-2202

DOVALE, ANTONIO JOSEPH, JR., chemical engineer; b. Newark, Feb. 25, 1954; s. Antonio Joseph and Rose (Bevacqua) DoV.; m. Fern Louise Crandall, Oct. 17, 1981. BSChemE, N.J. Inst. Tech., 1975. Registered profl. engr., N.J., Mass., Conn., Fla. Sr. process engr. M.W. Kellogg Co., Hackensack, N.J., 1975-84; chief process engr. Wheelabrator Air Pollution Control, Pitts., 1984-86, mgr. flue gas desulfurization systems, 1986-90, dir. wet flue gas desulfurization ops., 1990—. Mem. Am. Inst. Chem. Engrs., Sigma Xi, Omega Chi Epsilon, Tau Beta Pi. Roman Catholic.

DOVE, BRUCE ALAN, electrical engineer; b. New Rochelle, N.Y., Apr. 6, 1958; s. Robert Alan and Charlotte (Lubeck) Yingling. BSEE, Rensselaer Poly. Inst., 1980. Elec. engr. Teradyne, Inc., Boston, 1980-90; sr. engr. Mass. Gen. Hosp., Boston, 1990—; cons. Thinking Machines, Inc., Cambridge, Mass., 1987; pres. Quadrant Engring., Natick, Mass., 1991—. Mem. IEEE, AIAA, AAAS, Audio Engring. Soc. Home: 43 Mill St Natick MA 01760-4102

DOVE, KENLEY ROYCE, philosophy educator, researcher; b. Appleton, Minn., Aug. 31, 1936; s. Thoralf Olaf and LuVerne Garnet (Bjorgan) D.; m. Christa Ruth Schlieske, Jan. 27, 1963 (div. 1982); children: Andrea Kirsten, Sonja Elizabeth; m. Jennifer Mavis Middleton, Apr. 13, 1990. BA magna cum laude, St. Olaf Coll., 1958; MA, Yale U., 1960, PhD, 1965. Lectr. Yale U., New Haven, Conn., 1962-63, instr., 1965-66, asst. prof., 1966-72; instr. Williams Coll., Williamstown, Mass., 1963-65, assoc. prof., 1972-73; assoc. prof. The New Sch., N.Y.C., 1973-76; assoc. prof. SUNY, Purchase, 1977-87, prof., chair, 1987—; editorial cons. Univ. Presses, Publishers, Jours., 1968—; pres. SUNY Purchase Faculty, 1987-89; vis. lectr. Oxford U., Oxford, Eng., 1978, 90, Heidelberg U., Tubingen U., Frankfurt U., Fed. Republic Germany, 1968-78, Internat. Hegel Confs., Stuttgart, Fed. Republic Germany, Zurich, Switzerland, 1970, 75, 86. Author: (book chpt.) Hegel and The Sciences, 1984, Hegel-Jahrbuch, 1987; co-translator: M. Heidegger, Hegel's Concept of Experience, 1970, 2d edit. 1990; contbr. articles to profl. jours. Mem. New Haven, Conn. Dem. Ward Com., 1973-82. Woodrow Wilson fellow, 1958-59, Morse fellow Yale U., 1967-68, Hadley fellow Bennington (Vt.) Coll., 1980-81; Matchette Found. lectr. Catholic U. Am., 1972, Villanova U., 1976. Fellow Soc. for Systematic Philosophy (pres. 1977-86); mem. Internat. Hegel Gesellschaft, Hegel Soc. Am. (v.p. 1974-76), Internat. Assn. for Greek Philosophy, Soc. for Ancient Greek Philosophy, Phi Beta Kappa. Home: 34 Seaman Ave Apt 4A New York NY 10034-2977 Office: SUNY Dept of Philosophy Purchase NY 10577

DOVER, CARL BELLMAN, physicist, consultant; b. Milw., Feb. 10, 1941; s. Charles B. and Flora E. (Klug) D.; m. Argyro S. Kartsonis, Dec. 21, 1969; children: Anna, Dimitri. BS, MIT, 1963, PhD, 1967. Asst. U. Heidelberg, Fed. Republic of Germany, 1967-70; charge recherche U. Paris, 1970-71; asst. physicist Brookhaven Nat. Lab., Upton, N.Y., 1971-73, assoc. physicist, 1973-75, physicist, 1975-82, sr. physicist, 1982—; adj. prof. Yale U., New Haven, 1991—; mem. nuclear sci. adv. com. U.S. Dept. of Energy/NSF, 1988-91. Mem. editorial bd. Phys. Rev. Jour., 1991—; contbr. over 170 articles to profl. jours. Humboldt Found. grantee, 1989. Fellow Am. Phys. Soc. Office: Brookhaven Nat Lab Bldg # 510A Upton NY 11973

DOW, MICHAEL MCDONALD, science administrator; b. Dundee, Scotland, Apr. 24, 1936; came to U.S., 1965; s. James Blyth D. and Florence Thomson (McDonald) De Laurent; m. Miriam Violet Wein, Apr. 24, 1962; children: Stephanie Akosua, Michael Alexander. BS with honors, Aberdeen (Scotland) U., 1957; PhD, London U., 1965. Lectr. biochemistry U. Ghana, Legon, Aelra, Accra, 1957-65; head African affairs Nat. Acad. Scis., Washington, 1966-68; assoc. dean Haile Sellassie I U., Coll. Agrl., Alemaya, Ethopia, 1968-72; assoc. dir. Nat. Acad. Scis., Washington, 1972-91, acting dir. bd. sci. and technology internat. devel., 1991—; cons. in field. Contbr. articles to profl. jours. Mem. Assn. Advancement Agrl. Scis. in Africa (founder), Am. Philatelic Soc. Office: Nat Acad Scis 2101 Constitution Ave NW Washington DC 20418

DOWBENKO, ROSTYSLAW, chemist; b. Kremianets, Ukraine, Jan. 8, 1927; came to U.S., 1950; 1 child, Uri. PhB, Northwestern U., 1954, PhD, 1957. Rsch. chemist PPG Industries Inc., Pitts., 1957-59, from rsch. assoc. to sr. scientist, 1959-82, dir. polymer rsch., 1982-86; tech. dir. PPG Industries Inc., Paris, 1986-89; corp. fellow PPG Industries Inc., Pitts., 1989—. Contbr. 30 articles to profl. jours. Mem. Am. Chem. Soc., Fed. Soc. Paint. Office: PPG Industries Inc PO Box 9 Allison Park PA 15101-0009

DOWDALL, JEAN A., academic administrator, educator; b. N.Y.C., Aug. 25, 1942; d. Karl V. and Ethel R. (Rabinowitz) Amatneek; m. Gerald M. Shapiro, June 9, 1963 (div. 1969); 1 child, Nina; m. George W. Dowdall, Dec. 20, 1970. AB, Brown U., 1963, PhD, 1972; MA, U. Rochester, 1965. From asst. to assoc. prof. sociology Buffalo State Coll., 1973-82, exec. asst. to pres., 1979-82; dean arts and scis. West Chester (Pa.) U., 1982-86; v.p. acad. affairs Beaver Coll., Glenside, Pa., 1986—. Contbr. articles to profl. jours. Woodrow Wilson Found. fellow, 1963, Am. Coun. on Edn. fellow, 1978-79. Mem. Mendelssohn Club of Phila. (pres. 1990—), Phi Beta Kappa. Office: Beaver Coll Glenside PA 19038

DOWDEN, ALBERT RICKER, corporate executive, lawyer; b. N.Y.C., Dec. 15, 1941; s. Albert Godfré and Katherine (Ricker) D.; m. Carol Nelson; children: James, Christopher, William. BA, Middlebury Coll., 1963; JD, NYU, 1966. Bar: N.Y. 1967, U.S. Dist. Ct. (so. and ea. dist.) N.Y.1967, U.S. Supreme Ct. Atty. Rogers & Wells, N.Y.C., 1967-74; v.p., gen. counsel Volvo N.Am. Corp, Rockleigh, N.J., 1974-79, sr. v.p., 1979-86; exec. v.p., dir. Volvo N.Am. Corp, N.Y.C., 1986-91; pres., chief exec. officer, dir. Volvo N.Am. Corp., N.Y.C., 1991—; dir. Assn. of Internat. Automobile Mfrs., chmn., 1987-89; dirs. The Hertz Corp., 1991—, IJ Holdings, 1991—, Highway Users Fedn., mem. exec. com., 1988—; bd. dirs. Cortland Trust. Dir. Madison Sq. Boys & Girls Club, N.Y.C., Ctr. for Internat. Leadership, 1987—. Mem. ABA, Motor Vehicle Mfrs. Assn. (bd. dirs.), Nat. Assn. Mfrs. (bd. dirs.), Univ. Club N.Y, Waccabuc Country Club.

DOWDYE, EDWARD HENRY, JR., communications engineer; b. Washington, Nov. 13, 1943; s. Edward Henry Dowdye and Rachelle Elizabeth Rue Richardson; m. Kathy Lee Graham, Aug. 12, 1972; children: Erik Sebastian, Melanee Diane. BS, Hampton U., 1967; Diplom-Physiker, Heidelberg U., Germany, 1976. Mathematician Pacific Missile Range, Point Mugu, Calif., 1967-70; engring. assoc. Western Elec. Co., Greensboro, N.C., 1970-72; technician Atomic Physics Electronic Lab., Heidelberg, 1972-76; engr. Vitro Lab., Silver Spring, Md., 1976-77; phys. scientist, analyst CIA, Washington, 1977-82; sr. engr. Singer Kearfott Div., Totowa, N.J., 1982-84;

sr. mem. tech. engring. staff ITT Avionics Div., Nutley, N.J., 1984-87; sr. communication system engr. Space System Div., M&DSO, GE, Valley Forge, Pa., 1987-91; mgr. internat. ops. Spectral Intelligence Corp., Malvern, Pa., 1991—; researcher natural laws wave propagation alternative to relativity. Author book on an alternative theory of natural laws equivalent to relativity. Democrat. Baptist. Home: 1003 General Greene Dr West Chester PA 19382

DOWIS, LENORE, lawyer; b. N.Y., Nov. 7, 1934; d. Thomas and Julianna (Csitkovits) Esteves; widow; children: Daniel, Lenore, Denise, Jonathan. AAS, Suffolk County Community Coll., 1981; BA, SUNY, Stony Brook, 1983; JD, Touro Coll., 1987. Bar: N.Y. 1988, N.J. 1988, U.S. Dist. Ct. (no. dist.) N.J. 1988. Tel. operator N.Y. Tel. Co., L.I., 1951-58; real estate sales agt. Gen. Devel. Corp., Hauppauge, N.Y, 1974-75; ptnr., owner Davis Trucking Co., Huntington, N.Y., 1957-67; student law clk. to assoc. judge appellate div. U.S. Supreme Ct. N.Y., Bklyn., 1986; staff atty. Nassau/Suffolk Law Svcs., Bay Shore, N.Y., 1988; pvt. practice, Smithtown, N.Y., 1988—. Mem. ABA, Suffolk County Bar Assn., N.Y. State Bar Assn., Phi Theta Kappa, Alpha Beta Gamma. Republican. Home and Office: 33 Beverly Rd Smithtown NY 11788

DOWLING, EDWARD THOMAS, economics educator; b. N.Y.C., Oct. 22, 1938; s. Edward Thomas and Mary Helen (Finegan) D. B.A., Berchmans Coll., Philippines, 1962, M.A. in Philosophy, 1963; M.Div., Woodstock Coll., Md., 1969; Ph.D., Cornell U., Ithaca, N.Y., 1973. Asst. prof. econs. Fordham U., Bronx, 1973-79, assoc. prof. econs., 1979-85, prof. econs., 1985—, dean, 1982-86, chmn. econs. dept., 1988—. Author: Development Economics, 1977, Mathematics for Economists, 1980, Calculus for Business, Economics, and the Social Sciences, 1990, Introduction to Mathematical Economics, 1992. Mem. Am. Econ. Assn. Home: Fordham U New York NY 10458-5198

DOWLING, JAMES HAMILTON, public relations executive; b. Chgo., Oct. 20, 1931; s. Joseph Henry D. and Margaret (Hamilton) Dowlig; m. Julie Anne Pastor, Apr. 7, 1958; children: James Hamilton, Kenneth Edward, Tracy Anne. B.J., U. Mo., 1957. Writer, editor UPI, New Orleans, 1957, Newsweek, Atlanta and N.Y.C., 1958-59, AP, Chgo., NY, 1960-63; pub. relations staff Mobil Oil Corp., N.Y.C., 1963; with Burson-Marsteller Inc., 1964—; gen. mgr. Burson-Marsteller Inc., N.Y.C., 1968-70, Chgo., 1970-75; pres. Burson-Marsteller, N.Y.C., 1975-92, chief exec., 1988-92, chmn. bd., 1992—. Mem. exec. com. Pres.'s Pvt. Sector Survey on Cost Control in Fed. Govt.; mem. devel. bd. Central Park Conservancy. Served with USMC, 1952-55. Li Found. fellow, 1957-58. Mem. Pub. Relations Soc. Am. Office: Burson-Marsteller 230 Park Ave S New York NY 10003-1513*

DOWLING, MARIE AUGUSTINE, mathematics educator; b. Balt., Aug. 19, 1924; d. Samuel Augustine D. and Helen Marie (Wallenhorst) Smith. BA, Coll. Notre Dame Md., 1945; MS, Cath. U. Am., 1958. Tchr. math. and chemistry St. Mary's High Sch., Anapolis, Md., 1946-48, Notre Dame Md. Prep. Sch., Balt., 1948-59; math. tchr. Coll. Notre Dame Md., Balt., 1959—. Contbr. articles and book revs. to profl. jourss. Mem. Math. Assn. Am., Delta Epsilon Sigma, Kappa Gamma Pi, Kappa Mu Epsilon. Democrat. Roman Catholic. Home and Office: 4701 N Charles St Baltimore MD 21210-2404

DOWNES, VICTORIA ANN, counselor; b. Augsburg, Fed. Republic Germany, June 1, 1964; came to U.S, 1966; d. James Addison Jr. and Marjorie Ann (Miller) Mounts; m. Gary Wayne Downes, Sept. 10, 1988. BA in Psychology summa cum laude, Salisburg State Coll., 1986; MA in Counseling and Pers. Svcs., U. Md., 1988. Intern Bowie (Md.) Youth Svcs., 1987-88; clin. case mgr. Cedar Creek Residential Treatment Ctr., Lincoln, Del., 1988-90; behavioral analyst Stockley Ctr., Georgetown, Del., 1990-92; adolescent treatment coord. Div. Child Mental Health, Dover, Del., 1992—. Mem. adminstrv. bd. Calvary United Meth. Ch., Milford, Del., 1989—. Grad. Merit scholar College Park, Md., 1986. Mem. AACD, Phi Kappa Phi, Phi Gamma Mu, Phi Alpha Theta, Psi Chi, Phi Eta Sigma. Home: 37 N Woodside Dr Milford DE 19963-1613 Office: Div Child Mental Health 400 Court St Dover DE 19901

DOWNEY, JOHN ALEXANDER, physician, educator; b. Sept. 16, 1930. B.Sc. (Med.), U. Man., M.D. with honors, 1954; PhD, Oxford U., 1962. Diplomate Am. Bd. Phys. Medicine and Rehab. Intern, Vancouver Gen. Hosp., B.C., Can., 1953-54; resident phys. medicine and rehab. Columbia Presbyn. Med. Ctr., N.Y.C., 1954-56, resident, 1957-58; asst. resident internal medicine Peter Bent Brigham Hosp., Boston, 1956-57; asst. to med. dir., cons. phys. medicine Blythedale Children's Hosp., Valhalla, N.Y., 1957-59; research assoc. Columbia U. and vis. fellow Presbyn. Hosp., N.Y.C., 1958-59; sr. resident internal medicine Peter Bent Brigham Hosp., 1959-60; vis. worker Med. Research Council Group for Body Temperature Control, Oxford, Eng., 1960-62; asst. prof. rehab. medicine Columbia U. Coll. Physicians and Surgeons, 1962-64, assoc. prof., 1964-67, prof., 1967-74, Simon Baruch prof., 1974-90, chair dept. rehab. medicine, 1974-90, asst. prof. medicine, 1963-64; asst. attending Presbyn. Hosp., N.Y.C., 1962-64, assoc. attending, 1964-68, attending, 1968—, dir. rehab. medicine svc., 1974-90; vis. prof. dept. human physiology and pharmacology U. Adelaide, Australia, 1969. Author: Stroke: Two to Recover, 1969; also articles. Co-editor: Physiological Basis for Rehabilitation, 1971; The Child with Disabling Illness: Principles of Rehabilitation, 1974, 2d edit., 1982; Bereavement of Physical Disability: Recommitment to Life, Health and Function, 1982; editorial bd. Brenneman's Practice of Pediatrics, 1974. Films: Rehabilitation: A Patient's Perspective, 1973; I Had a Stroke, 1978; PHysiatry: A Physician's Perspective, 1981. Diplomate Am. Bd. Phys. Medicine and Rehab. Fellow Royal Coll. Physicians (Can.); mem. Inst. Medicine of NAS, AAAS, AMA, Am. Congress Rehab. Medicine, Am. Acad. Phys. Medicine and Rehab., Assn. Acad. Physiatrists, Am. Physiol. Soc., Am. Rheumatism Assn., N.Y. Rheumatism Assn., N.Y. Acad. Scis., N.Y. Acad. Medicine, N.Y. Soc. Phys. Medicine and Rehab., Med. Soc. N.Y. State, New York County Med. Soc. Office: Dept Rehab Medicine Columbia U Coll Physicians New York NY 10032

DOWNEY, THOMAS JOSEPH, congressman; b. Queens, N.Y., Jan. 28, 1949; s. Thomas Anthony and Norma Rita (Morgillo) D.; m. Dr. Chris Milanos, Dec. 1978; children—Lauren Katherine, Theodore Jonathan. B.S., Cornell U., 1970; postgrad., St. John's U. Law Sch., 1972; J.D., Am. U., 1980. With personnel dept. Macy's, N.Y.C., 1970-71; mem. 94th-102nd Congresses from 2d N.Y. dist., 1975—; mem. ways and means com., select com. on aging, chmn. subcom. on human svcs. Congl. SALT II adv., 1978-79; observer START; del. Democratic Nat. Conv., 1972; committeeman N.Y. State Dem. Com., 1972; mem. Suffolk County (N.Y.) Legislature, 1971-74. Mem. Sons of Italy. Methodist. Office: 2232 Rayburn House Office Bldg Washington DC 20515*

DOWNIE, LEONARD, JR., newspaper editor, author; b. Cleve., May 1, 1942; s. Leonard and Pearl Martha (Evenheimer) D.; m. Barbara Lindsey, July 15, 1960 (div. 1971); children: David Leonard, Scott Leonard; m. Geraldine Rebach, Aug. 15, 1971; children: Joshua Mark, Sarah Elizabeth. B.A., Ohio State U., 1964, M.A., 1965. Reporter, editor Washington Post, 1964-74, met. editor, 1974-79, London corr., 1979-82, nat. editor, 1982-84, mng. editor, 1984-91, exec. editor, 1991—; dir. L.A. Times-Washington Post News Svc., 1992—; chmn. adv. coun. Ohio State U. Sch. Journalism, 1992—. Author: Justice Denied, 1971, Mortgage on America, 1974, The New Muckrackers, 1976. Recipient Gavel award ABA, 1967, Front Page 1st pl. award for newswriting Washington-Balt. Newspaper Guild, 1967, 68, award John Hancock Ins. Co., 1969; Alicia Patterson Found. fellow, 1971-72. Office: Washington Post Co 1150 15th St NW Washington DC 20071-0002

DOWNING, FORREST WILLIAM, insurance executive; b. Bryn Mawr, Pa., May 28, 1949; s. Wilfred R. and Ruth B. (Bates) D.; m. Sherry J. McKay, Feb. 17, 1978; 1 child, Courtney Elizabeth. BS, Pa. State U., 1971; MBA, U. Tex., Arlington, 1977. Cert. assoc. in risk mgmt. Marine underwriter INA Internat., Phila., 1974-76, Dallas, 1976-77; mgr. INA Internat., Brussels, 1078-81; marine mgr. Cigna Worldwide Inc., Boston, 1981-86; v.p. marine Cigna Worldwide Inc., Phila., 1986-88, v.p. speciality lines, 1988—; lectr. various groups. Lt. (j.g.) USN, 1971-74. Mem. Am. Inst. Marine Underwriters, Beta Gamma Sigma. Office: Cigna Worldwide Inc Two Liberty Place PO Box 7716 Philadelphia PA 19103

DOWNING, MICHAEL BERNARD, writer, educator; b. Pittsfield, Mass., May 8, 1958; s. John Frederick and Gertrude Nora (Martin) D. AB, Harvard U., 1980. Assoc. editor Oceanus mag., Woods Hole, Mass., 1983-84; sr. editor FMR mag., Milan, 1984-86; instr. Bentley Coll., Waltham, Mass., 1987-88; dir. writing Wheelock Coll., Boston, 1988—. Novelist: A Narrow Time, 1987, Mother of God, 1990; contbr. articles to various publs. Writers' com. Share Our Strength, Washington. Harvard-Shrewsbury fellow Harvard Coll., Shrewsbury, Eng., 1980-81. Mem. PEN, Authors Guild. Democrat. Roman Catholic. Home: 11 Story St Apt 27 Cambridge MA 02138-4927 Office: Wheelock Coll 200 Riverway Boston MA 02215-4176

DOWNING, ROBIN WILSON, financial analyst; b. Newton, Mass., Aug. 16, 1962; d. Robert H. and Dolores T. (Gargaro) Wilson; m. Michael F. Downing, Oct. 8, 1989. BS, Boston Coll., 1984; MBA, Babson Coll., 1990. Telemktg. rep. ADP, Waltham, Mass., 1984-85; assoc. program analyst Raytheon Co., Wayland, Mass., 1985-87; program analyst Raytheon Co., Marlboro, Mass., 1987-88; program analyst Raytheon Co., Wayland, Mass., 1988-89, sr. program analyst, 1989—. Admissions vol. Boston Coll. Alumni Assn., 1985—. Mem. Sudbury/Wayland Mgmt. Club, Raytheon Mgmt. Club. Home: 3 Nobscott Rd Medway MA 02053-2171 Office: Raytheon Co 430 Boston Post Rd Wayland MA 01778-1824

DOWNING, WILLIAM MYRON, physician; b. Glouersville, N.Y., Sept. 2, 1907; s. William Henry and Madge (Gorton) B.; m. Evelyn W. Kirshbaum, Aug. 19, 1950 (div. 1974); children: Jill, Lee, Jeff, Greg; m. Janice Marie Mulkern, 1975. BA, U. Mich., 1931; MD, Boston U., 1937. Diplomate Am. Bd. Surgery. Surgeon Sturdy Meml. Hosp., Attleboro, Mass., 1949-84; pvt. practice Attleboro, 1984—. Capt. U.S. Army, 1942-46, ETO. Mem. ACS, Boston Surg. Soc., Mass. Med. Soc., Bristol North Dist. Med. Soc. Home: 135 Rita Rd Attleboro MA 02703

DOWNS, JAMES WILLIAM, educator; b. Ft. Wayne, Ind., May 18, 1927; s. James Hamel Downs and Leona Emma (Poiry) Noble; m. Patricia Wharton, Feb. 3, 1951; children: Amanda Rohr, James William Jr., Anita Shaughnessy. BA, Harvard U., 1951; MA, NYU, 1966. Cert. tchr., Conn., N.J., N.Y. Tchr. Brunswick Sch., Greenwich, Conn., 1954-59; dean of faculty The Rockland Country Day Sch., Congers, N.Y., 1959-69; tchr. Saybrook High Sch., Old Saybrook, Conn., 1969-70; headmaster The Rockland Country Day Sch., 1970-74; tchr. Pascack Valley High Sch., Hillsdale, N.Y., 1974-89; ret., 1989—. Contbr. articles to profl. publs. Sgt. U.S. Army, 1945-47. Democrat. Episcopalian. Home: 304 Old Nyack Turnpike Spring Valley NY 10977-5842

DOWNS, STEVEN EDWARD, magazine editor; b. Saranac Lake, N.Y., Oct. 20, 1960; s. Herman L. and Gloria E. (Quirk) D. BA in English, BA in Mass Communications, Canisius Coll., Buffalo, 1982; MS Athletics Adminstrn., Western Ill. U., 1984. Publicity dir. Bio-Growth Distbrs., Kenmore, N.Y., 1984-85; proof editor Rama Printing, Buffalo, 1985-86; ptnr. Flexerco Athletic Products, North Tonawanda, N.Y., 1985-86; pres., owner Titan Athletic Club, Lockport, N.Y., 1987-89; exec. dir. Lake Plains YMCA, Medina, N.Y., 1986-89; editorial dir. Chelo Pub., Inc., N.Y.C., 1989—; chmn. World Natural Bodybuilding Fedn., N.Y.C., 1989—. Author: (novel) The Storm, 1984; editor Natural Physique, 1988-89; contbr. Jour.-Register Newspaper, Medina; contbr. articles to sports mags. Vol. Am. Diabetes Assn., Buffalo, 1985-86, Lake Plains YMCA, Medina, 1989-90, Nat. Gym Assn., 1990—; mem. Orleans County Human Svc. Coun. Recipient Program Achievement award YMCA-APD, 1988, 89, Svc. award, 1989, sr. dir. cert., 1989. Mem. Assn. Fitness in Bus., Nat. Strength and Conditioning Assn., Am. Coll. Sports Medicine, Am. Running & Fitness Assn., World Natural Bodybuilding Fedn. (chmn. 1989—), KC. Roman Catholic.

DOX, IDA, medical illustrator; b. Honduras, Central America, July 8, 1927; came to U.S. 1947; d. John and Catherine (Headman) D.; m. B. John Melloni; children: H. Paul, June L., Peter J., Roy G. BFA, Newcomb Coll., New Orleans, 1950; MS, Johns Hopkins U., 1954; PhD, U. Md., 1990. Med. illustrator Georgetown U. Med. Ctr., Washington, 1954-69; med. illustrator select com. on assassinations of J.F. Kennedy and Martin Luther King, Jr. of U.S. Ho. of Reps, Washington, 1978-79; med. illustrator/author Bethesda, Md., 1969—. Author: Melloni's Illustrated Medical Dictionary, 1979 (Best Med. Book award 1979), Melloni's Illustrated Review of Human Anatomy, 1988 (Award of Excellence 1989); contbr. articles to profl. jours. Recipient L.S. Neill prize, Newcomb Coll., 1949, E.Woodwad Meml. Prize, 1950, Indsl. Graphics Internat. awd., 1977. Address: 9308 Renshaw Dr Bethesda MD 20817

DOYLE, BRIAN BOWLES, psychiatrist; b. Boston, May 20, 1941; s. Joseph Bernard and Margaret (Kelley) D.; m. Margaret Mary Ready, Oct. 4, 1975; children: Mairin McCready, Cavan Kelley, Colin Calnan. BA magna cum laude, Harvard U., 1962; MD, McGill U., 1966. Diplomate Am. Bd. Psychiatry and Neurology. Resident in psychiatry Mass. Mental Health Ctr., Boston, 1967-70; clin. prof. psychiatry Georgetown Med. Sch., Washington, 1983—; pvt. practice, Washington, 1972—. Maj. U.S. Army, 1970-72. Fellow Am. Psychiat. Assn. Democrat. Roman Catholic. Office: 1325 18th St NW Apt 209 Washington DC 20036-6511

DOYLE, EILEEN MARIE, radiologic technology educator; b. Rochester, N.Y., Mar. 11, 1953; d. John David and Mary M. (Welch) D. AAS, Monroe Community Coll., Rochester, 1973; BS, Rochester Inst. Tech., 1986. Lic. radiologic tech., N.Y. Instr. Monroe Community Coll., Rochester, 1973-77, asst. prof., 1978-92, assoc. prof., 1992—; mem. Monroe Community Coll. faculty senate, 1989-91, exec. com. 1990-91, adminstrv. affairs com. chmn., 1990-91. Editor: (reference book) Genesee Region Health Careers Directory, 1983. Mem. Occupational Edn. Adv. Com. Wayne-Finger Lakes B.A.C.E.S., Stanley, N.Y., 1981—, chmn. 1990-91. Mem. Am. Soc. Radiologic Technologists, Assn. Educators in Radiologic Technology of N.Y. (corr. sec. 1984-86, rec. sec. 1986-88, pres. elect 1988-90, pres. 1990-92, chmn. of bd. 1992-94), Rochester Soc. Radiological Technologists. Office: Monroe Community Coll 1000 E Henrietta Rd Rochester NY 14623-5780

DOYLE, EVA CURLEE, bank officer; b. Knoxville, Tenn., Sept. 16, 1961; d. Frank Lewis and Ruth (Conley) Curlee; m. Chris L. Doyle, May 19, 1990. BA, U. Tenn., 1982; MBA, U. Md., 1989. Language analyst U.S. Dept. Def., Ft. Meade, Md., 1982-84, ops. analyst, 1985-86, contract cost analyst, 1986-89; comml. banking officer 1st Nat. Bank of Md., Columbia, 1989—; instr. Am. Inst. Banking, Balt., 1992—. Tutor Project Literacy, Howard County, Md., 1991-92. Leroy P. Graf scholar U. Tenn., 1981-82, U. Md. scholar, 1986-87. Mem. Reistertown-Owings Mills-Glyndon (Md.) C. of C., Phi Beta Kappa. Office: 1st Nat Bank of Md 6395 Dobbin Rd Ste # 106 Columbia MD 21045

DOYLE, JOHN THOMAS, financial services company executive, consultant; b. Kearny, N.J., Jan. 16, 1943; s. Thomas Francis and Margaret Gertrude (McCormack) D.; children: John Kevin, Kristina Anne. BA, Rutgers U., 1971; MBA, Fordham U., 1973; postgrad., New Sch. for Social Rsch. Cert. EDP systems and programming. Cons. First Jersey Nat. Bank, Jersey City, 1966-69; treas. Comml. Alliance Corp., N.Y.C., 1969-73; sr. v.p. Horizon Creditcorp, Morristown, N.J., 1973-83; exec. v.p., gen. mgr. Clark Equipment Credit, Cedar Knolls, N.J., 1983-86; pres., chief exec. officer Security Marine Creditcorp, Bay Head, N.J., 1986—. Contbr. articles to profl. jours. Mem. Morris County Rep. Party, 1975-90. Maj. U.S. Army, 1965-86. Mem. Nat. Assn. Marine Mfg., Nat. Marine Bankers Assn., Am. Assn. Equipment Lessors, N.Y. Yacht Club (capt. 1981—), Ocean Reef Club, U.S. Power Squadron (lt. comdr. 1977-80). Republican. Roman Catholic. Home: 339 Venice Dr Chadwick Island NJ 08735-2921 Office: Am Marine Creditcorp 571 W Lake Ave Bay Head NJ 08742

DOYLE, JOSEPH ANTHONY, lawyer; b. N.Y.C., June 13, 1920; s. Joseph A. and Jane (Donahue) D.; m. Eugenie A. Fleri, Aug. 19, 1944; children: Christopher, Stephen, Eugenie, Jane, Richard. B.S., Georgetown U., 1941; LL.B., Columbia U., 1947. Bar: N.Y. 1948, U.S. Dist. Ct. (so. and ea. dists.) N.Y. 1950, U.S. Ct. Appeals (2d cir.) 1949. Assoc. Shearman & Sterling, N.Y.C., 1947-57, ptnr., 1957-79, 81—; asst. sec. for manpower, res. affairs and logistics U.S. Navy, Washington, 1979-81; bd. dirs. The Fuji Bank & Trust Co., N.Y.C., Heller Internat. Corp., Chgo., Heller Fin. Inc., Chgo., OKI Am., Inc., Hackensack, N.J., Roxbury (Conn.) Land Trust, Inc. Bd. dirs. USO of Met. N.Y., 1982-90. Lt. USNR, 1941-45. Decorated Navy Cross, D.F.C. with 3 gold stars, Air medal with 7 gold stars; recipient Disting. Pub. Service award Sec. of Navy, 1980. Mem. ABA, Assn. Bar City N.Y., N.Y. State Bar Assn., Metropolitan Club (Washington), Downtown Athletic Club (N.Y.C.), India House. Democrat. Roman Catholic. Home: 32 Washington Sq W New York NY 10011-9156 Office: Shearman & Sterling 599 Lexington Ave at 53d St New York NY 10022

DOYLE, KEVIN JOHN, magazine editor; b. Fitzroy Harbour, Ont., Can., Feb. 6, 1943; s. John and Teresa Agnes (McHale) D.; m. Marion Helen Edmonds, June 26, 1970. BA, U. Ottawa, 1965; MSc, London Sch. Econs., 1972. Gen. reporter The Windsor (Can.) Star, 1965-67; parliamentary reporter The Can. Press, Ottawa, 1967-70, corr. London div., 1970-75, corr. Washington div., 1975-76; fgn. and nat. editor Maclean's mag., Toronto, Ont., 1976-77, mng. editor, 1977-79, dep. editor, 1981-82, editor, 1982—; mng. editor The FP News Service, 1979-80; gen. editor Newsweek mag., 1980-81. Office: MacLean's, 777 Bay St, Toronto, ON Canada M5W 1A7

DOYLE, MICHAEL FRANCIS, architect; b. N.Y.C., Sept. 14, 1951. AB, Colgate U., 1973; MArch, Harvard U., 1977. Registered architect, Tex., N.Y., Ohio, N.J., D.C. Prin. Acheson Thornton Doyle, Architects, N.Y.C., 1985—; chmn. adv. council archtl. history Harvard U., Cambridge, Mass., 1987. Exhibitor drawings Urban Design of Kathmandu Valley, hdqrs. UNESCO, Paris, 1980, Harvard U., 1982. Trustee Coll. Mt. St. Vincent, N.Y.C., 1986, Ptnrs. for Liveable Places, Washington; vice-chmn. Kathmandu Valley Preservation Trust. Nat. Endowments for Arts fellow, 1976, teaching fellow Harvard U., 1976, 77, Appleton fellow in Nepal, Harvard U., 1977. Mem. AIA (N.Y. chpt. dir.), Soc. Archtl. Historians, Asia Soc. Roman Catholic. Office: Acheson Thornton Doyle 72 Spring St New York NY 10012-4019

DOYLE, ROBERT GERARD, college administrator; b. Tarrytown, N.Y., Apr. 27, 1950; s. George A. and Elise M. (Sullivan) D.; m. Monique B. Doyle, Apr. 15, 1978; children: Sara K., Alicia C., Emily E. Student, Clark U., 1971, 72, Worcester Mus. Sch., 1972; BA, Worcester State Coll., 1973; MEd, Bridgewater State Coll., 1976; postgrad., Mass. Coll. Art, 1977, NYU, 1977; EdD, Boston U., 1986. Film tchr. Summer's World, Worcester, Mass., 1973; media technician Brockton (Mass.) High Sch., 1973-75; audio-visual media dir. Medway (Mass.) Pub. Schs., 1975-81; mass media instr. Dean Jr. Coll., Franklin, Mass., 1979; dist. mgr. Projection Inc., Boston, 1981-84; dir. instrnl. media and piano tech. svcs. Harvard U., Cambridge, Mass., 1984—; freshman acad. advisor Harvard U., Cambridge, 1988—. Legal photographer, 1978—; researcher Job Satisfaction Studies, 1985, 91—. Mentor Cambridge Partnership for Pub. Edn., 1987—; Dewitt-Wallace adv. bd. Cambridge Pub. Schs., 1991—; prin. selection com. mem. Oak St. Sch., Franklin, 1991; practice interviews com. mem. Academic Decathlon, Franklin, 1991—. Mem. Internat. Assn. Lang. Learning, Assn. for Ednl. Comm. and Tech., Mass. Assn. for Ednl. Media (conf. tri-chair 1991), Pi Lambda Theta. Office: Harvard U Grays Hall Cambridge MA 02138

D'PROVIDENCE, ROSSI, mathematician; b. Providence, Mar. 7, 1939. Student, Brown U., 1960. Tutor in math., 1960—. Maj. USAF, 1954-56. Mem. Am. Math. Soc. Home and Office: PO Box 45 Seekonk MA 02771-0045

DRAEGER, KENNETH W., high technology company executive; b. Wyandotte, Mich., July 30, 1940; s. Wilfred Draeger and Marjorie (Rapp) Draeger Fair; m. Carol Ann Ahola, Sept. 7, 1963; children: Kimberley, Tracey. BS, Western Mich. U., 1962; MBA, Wayne State U., 1967. Systems engr. IBM, Kalamazoo, 1962-64; analyst fin. staff Fort Motor Co., Dearborn, Mich., 1964-69; exec. v.p. Cyphernetics Corp., Ann Arbor, Mich., 1969-76; pres. ADP Network sVc. Div., Ann Arbor, Mich., 1976-81; group v.p. Informatics Gen. Corp., Franklin Lakes, N.J., 1981-84; chmn., chief exec. officer, pres. Compute Corp. of Am., Cambridge, Mass., 1984-86; chief exec. officer, pres. Autographix, Waltham, Mass., 1986-88; pres. Agfa Compugraphic, Wilmington, Mass., 1988-92; bd. dirs. Ctr. for Graphic Communications Mgmt. and Tech., NYU, N.Y.C., 1989-92. Home: 337 Wellesley St Weston MA 02193

DRAGO, ROBERT JOHN, psychologist; b. Queens, N.Y., Dec. 7, 1958; s. Michael Anthony and Adeline Barbara (Alberico) D. BA, St. John's U., 1980, MS, 1983, PhD, 1985; postdoctoral diploma, Adelphi U., 1991, addiction specialist cert., 1991. Lic. psychologist; cert. sch. psychologist, N.Y. Psychologist Blueberry Day Treatment Ctr., Bklyn., 1986-88; cons. Birch Early Childhood Ctr., Springfield Gardens, N.Y., 1990; sch. psychologist West Hempstead (N.Y.) Union Free Sch. Dist., 1988—, Birch Sch. for Exceptional Children, Flushing, N.Y., 1991—; pvt. practice Williston Park, N.Y., 1988—; instr., supr. psychotherapy Advanced Ctr. Psychotherapy, Jamaica Estates, N.Y., 1990-91. Office: 225 Hillside Ave Williston Park NY 11363-1318

DRAGON, ELIZABETH ALICE, research molecular biologist; b. Mineola, N.Y., June 12, 1948; d. Harry L. and Alice L. (Clayton) Oosterom; m. Frank X. Dragon, Aug. 24, 1972; 1 child, Michael. BS, U. N.H., 1970; PhD, Yeshiva U., 1980. Postdoctoral fellow Brookhaven Nat. Lab., Upton, N.Y., 1980-82; rsch. scientist CODON, Brisbane, Calif., 1982-87; sr. rsch. scientist, group leader CODON, South San Francisco, Calif., 1987-90; group leader Roche Diagnostic Systems, Nutley, N.J., 1990-91; dir. diagnostics devel. Roche Molecular Systems, Branchburg, NJ, 1992—. Research grantee NIH, 1983-86. Mem. AAAS, Am. Soc. Microbiology, Am. Soc. Parasitologists. Home: 460 Summit St Ridgewood NJ 07450-1530 Office: Roche Molecular Systems 1080 US Hwy 202 Branchburg NJ 08876-1760

DRAGONE, ALLAN R., manufacturing company executive; b. Melrose, Mass., 1926; m. Jane Brady, 1955; children: Allan Jr., Peter, Christopher, Jennifer, Alyssa. B.A., Middlebury, (Vt.) Coll., 1950; M.B.A., Harvard U., 1952. With Celanese Corp., N.Y.C., 1966-83, corp. pres., chief operating officer, 1980-83, also bd. dirs.; pres., chief exec. officer Akzo Am. Inc., N.Y.C., 1986-90; dir Arcadian Corp, N.Y.C., 1989—; dir. Arcadian Corp., N.Y.C., Gen. Waterworks Corp., Wellman, Inc., Am. Cyanamid. Chmn. bd. trustees Middlebury Coll., 1983-89. Mem. N.Y. Racing Assn. (trustee 1985—, chmn. 1990—), Harmony Landing Country Club, Harvard Club, Jockey Club, Wee Burn Country Club, Woods Hole Country Club. Office: Arcadian Corp 630 5th Ave New York NY 10111-0002

DRAGT, ALEXANDER JAMES, physicist; b. Lafayette, Ind., Apr. 7, 1936; s. Gerrit and Beulah (Westra) D.; m. Lavonne Ann Wolters, Nov. 28, 1957; children: Alison Ann, Alexander James, William David. A.B., Calvin Coll., 1958; Ph.D. in Physics (NSF fellow), U. Calif., Berkeley, 1964. Sr. scientist Lockheed Missiles & Space Corp., Palo Alto, Calif., 1961-62; staff scientist Aerospace Corp., Los Angeles, 1963; mem. Inst. Advanced Study, Princeton, N.J., 1963-65; asst. prof. physics U. Md., 1965-68, assoc. prof., 1968-74, prof., 1974—, chmn. dept. physics and astronomy, 1975-78; mem. vis. staff Los Alamos Sci. Lab., 1978-79, cons., 1979—vis. prof. Tex. A&M U., 1984; mem. vis. staff Tex Accelerator Ctr., 1984; guest scientist Lawrence Berkeley Lab., 1985, cons., 1985—. Fellow Am. Phys. Soc.; Mem. Am. Geophys. Union, AAAS, Am. Math. Soc. Mem. Christian Reformed Ch. Office: U Md Dept Physics and Astronomy College Park MD 20742

DRAPER, MARY LYTTON, writer; b. Staunton, Va.; d. Julius Sidney and Mary Ellen (Bright) Lytton; m. David W. Draper; children: David W. Jr., Darryl L. BA, Coll. of William and Mary, Williamsburg, Va.; MALS, Georgetown U., postgrad. Freelance writer; editor-in-chief Colonial Echo, Coll. William and Mary. Mem. NAFE, Washington Opera Guild, Tamarack Civic Assn., Sierra Club, World Wildlife Fund, Nat. Audubon Soc., Soc. of the Alumni Coll. William and Mary (Met. Washington area), Pi Delta Epsilon, Chi Delta Phi, Psi Chi. Home and Office: 1602 Northcrest Dr Silver Spring MD 20904-1459

DRASNER, FRED, publishing company executive. Pres. U.S. News and World Report, N.Y.C., 1984—. Office: US News & World Report 599 Lexington Ave New York NY 10022*

DRAY, VALERIE ELIZA, illustrator; b. Somerville, Mass., Oct. 22, 1945; d. Charles Fredrick and Edith Ida (Carpenter) D.; 1 child, Jason Timothy Banfield. Student, Mass. Coll. Art, Brookline, 1964-66, New Eng. Sch. Art, Boston, 1967-68, Boston Mus. Sch., 1968. Make-up designer, make-up artist Pucci Manikins Inst., N.Y.C., 1983—; illustrator Zotos Internat., Darien, Conn., 1982—, Matrix Essentials, Solon, Ohio, 1988—, Alberto Culver, Melrose Park, Ill., 1990—, Wella Internat., Englewood, N.J., 1991—. Illustrator: Christine Valmy's Skin Care and Make-Up Book, 1983, John Delaria...Changing Styles, 1984, How to Cut, Curl and Care For Your Hair, 1985, Color Your Life...With Haircolor, 1986; represented in permanent collection at Mus. Art, Portland, Oreg., 1992; patentee in field. Home: 148 Sullivan St # 6 148 Sullivan St #5 New York NY 10012

DRAYER, CALVIN SEARLE, JR., lawyer; b. Phila., Sept. 12, 1939; s. Calvin S. and Madeleine (Schellenberg) D.; m. Sandra Ellen Scott; children: Robert Scott, Mary S., Barbara L. BA, Conn. Wesleyan U., 1961; LLB, U. Pa., 1964; LLM, Temple U., 1982. Bar: Pa. 1964, U.S. Ct. Appeals (ea. dist.) Pa.1964. Law clk. to presiding judge Phila., 1964-65; assoc. White and Williams, Phila., 1966-72; ptnr. Wilson, Drayer, Morrow & Hagarty, Norristown, Pa., 1972—; lectr. law Villanova (Pa.) U., 1984-88. Co-author, editor: Practice and Procedure in Register of Wills and Orphans Court, 1981. Pres. Gladwyne (Pa.) Civic Assn., 1973-74; commr. Lower Merion Twp., Ardmore, Pa., 1986-91. Fellow Am. Coll. Trust and Estate Counsel. Republican. Presbyterian. Home: 1016 Black Rock Rd Gladwyne PA 19035-1407 Office: Wilson Drayer Morrow & Hagarty 1 E Airy St # 389 Norristown PA 19401-4802

DRAYER, JAN IGNATIUS, medical company executive, physician; b. Amsterdam, The Netherlands, Jan. 31, 1946; came to U.S., 1980; s. Roelof P. and Anna (De Swart) D.; m. Thea Van Kalmthout, June 3, 1972; children: Myke, Joris. MD, U. Nijmegen, The Netherlands, 1975. Intern St. Radboud Hosp., Nijmegen, The Netherlands, 1969-71; resident in dept. medicine U. Nijmegen (The Netherlands), 1971-75; instr. medicine N.Y. Hosp., Cornell U., N.Y.C., 1975-77; rsch. assoc. Cardiovascular Ctr., N.Y. Hosp., Cornell U., N.Y.C., 1975-77; internist Dept. Medicine, St. Radboud Hosp., Nijmegen, The Netherlands, 1977-80; assoc. prof. medicine U. Calif., Irvine, 1980-85; assoc. chief VA Med. Ctr., Long Beach, Calif., 1980-85; dir. clin. rsch. Boehringer Ingelheim Pharm., Inc., Ridgefield, Conn., 1985-88; v.p. mktg. support G. H. Besselaar Assocs., Princeton, N.J., 1988-90, sr. v.p. sci. and pub. affairs, 1990—; cons. NIH Spl. Study Sect., 1984, Am. Coll. Chest Physicians, Sect. on Hypertension, 1985, Danbury (Conn.) Hosp., 1988. Author numerous book chpts. on hypertension, over 70 clin. rsch. abstracts; editor: Practical Clinical Guide Series, 1988, Drug Therapy in Hypertension, 1986; co-editor: Clonidine in Hypertension, 1985, Ambulatory Blood Pressure Monitoring, 1984, Mineralocorticoids in Essential and Secondary Hypertension, Clinical and Experimental Hypertension Vols. 9 and 10; contbr. over 100 articles to profl. jours. Fellow Am. Coll. Clin. Pharmacology, Coun. for High Blood Pressure Rsch., Am. Coll. Chest Physicians, Am. Coll. Cardiology; mem. Internat. Soc. Hypertension, Am. Soc. for Clin. Pharmacology and Therapeutics (nominating com. 1988, co-chair CME com. 1985, chair CME com. 1992—), Internat. Soc. Chronobiology, Am. Geriatrics Soc., Am. Soc. Hypertension (charter), Am. Fedn. for Clin. Rsch. Home: 160 Bertrand Dr Princeton NJ 08540-2904 Office: G H Besselaar Assocs 103 College Rd E Princeton NJ 08540-6602

DRAZEN, JEFFREY MARK, medical educator, hospital administrator; b. St. Louis, May 19, 1946; s. Yale and Sylvia (Wainer) D.; m. Erica Coburn Drazen, July 27, 1969; children: David, Daniel. BS, Tufts U., 1968; MD, Harvard U., 1972. Diplomate Am. Bd. Internal Medicine, Am. Bd. Pulmonary Medicine. Parker B. Francis prof. Med. Sch. Harvard U., Boston, 1977—; chief pulmonary and critical care medicine div. Brigham & Women's and Beth Israel Hosps., Boston, 1985—; mem. RAP study sect. NIH, 1981-86, mem. pulmonary disease adv. coun., 1988—. NIH grantee, 1972—. Mem. Am. Soc. Clin. Investigation, Am. Thoracic Soc., Am. Physiology Soc., Am. Soc. Pharmacology and Exptl. Therapeutics, Assn. Am. Physicians. Office: Brigham & Women's Hosp 75 Francis St Boston MA 02115-6195

DREHER, MARIAM JEAN, education educator; b. Memphis; d. James Ralph and Nina M. (Wells) W.; m. Peter Dreher; 1 child, Silvia. BA, U. Calif., Riverside; MA, U. Calif., PhD. Elem. tchr. Rialto (Calif.) Unified Sch. Dist., reading tchr.; instr. U. Calif., Riverside; asst. prof. U. Md., College Park, assoc. prof. Recipient Constance McCullough Rsch. award Calif. Reading Assn., Elva Knight Rsch. grant Internat. Reading Assn. Mem. Internat. Reading Assn., Nat. Conf. Rsch. in English, Nat. Reading Conf., Phi Beta Kappa. Office: U Md Dept Curriculum and Instrn College Park MD 20742

DREIBHOLZ, FREDERICK JOHN, foodservice executive; b. Pitts., May 12, 1955; s. John Hunter Dane and Nancy (Mosebarger) Augustine; m. Catherine Marie Mueller, May 15, 1982; children: Christina, Elizabeth, Frederick. BS, Cornell U., 1977; MBA, Marquette U., 1986. CPA. Contr. Sky Chefs, various locations, 1977-87; sr. analyst Sanwa Bus. Credit, Chgo., 1987; corp. contr. Flik Internat. Corp., Mamaroneck, N.Y., 1987—. Mem. AICPA, Cornell Soc. Hotelmen, Soc. of Food Svc. Mgmt. Home: 55 Danner Ave Harrison NY 10528-3315 Office: Flik Internat Corp 910 E Boston Post Rd Mamaroneck NY 10543-4100

DREIKAUSEN, MARGRET, artist; b. Cologne, Fed. Republic Germany, Jan. 9, 1937; came to U.S., 1961; d. Wilhelm and Anna Maria (Rapp) D. AAS, Fashion Inst. Tech., 1968; BA, CUNY, 1975, MA, 1978. Asst. prof. U. Conn., Storrs, 1978-79; instr. Fashion Inst. Tech., N.Y.C., 1980, Parsons Sch. Design, N.Y.C., 1979—; dir. LIC Artists, Inc., 1987—; fashion designer IGS, Istanbul, Turkey, 1970, various mfrs., N.Y.C., 1963-78; bd. dirs. LIC Artists, 1990—. Artist numerous group and one-person exhibitions, U.S., Fed. Republic Germany; author: Aerial Perception, 1985; contbg. author: Essays on Creativity & Science, 1986. Mem. Coll. Art Assn. Home: 141 E 62nd St New York NY 10021-7606 Studio: LIC Artlofts 37-06 36th St Long Island City NY 11101

DREMAN, DAVID NASANIEL, investment counselor, security analyst; b. Winnipeg, Man., Can., May 6, 1936; came to U.S., 1965; s. Joseph and Rae (Trone) D.; m. Holly Altner, Mar. 24, 1984; children: David Nasaniel Jr., Meredith Wakefield. B of Commerce, U. Man., 1957; postgrad. in Fin., Columbia U., 1958. Security analyst Dreman & Co., Winnipeg, 1958-64; sr. editor Value Line Investment Svc., N.Y.C., 1965-67; sr. investment officer J & W Seligman, N.Y.C., 1967-75; dir. N.Y. rsch. Rauscher Pierce Refsnes, N.Y.C., 1976-78; founder, pres. Dreman Value Mgmt. L.P., N.Y.C., 1978-91; chmn., chief investment officer Dreman Value Mgmt. L.P., 1991—. Author: Psychology of the Stock Market, 1977, Contrarian Investment Strategy, 1980, The New Contrarian Investment Strategy, 1982; columnist Forbes mag., 1980—. Founder, pres. David N. Dreman Found., 1986—; bd. govs. India House. Mem. Fin. Analysts Fedn., N.Y. Soc. Security Analysts, N.Y. Stock Exch. Luncheon Club, Navesink Country Club (Middletown, N.J.), Seabright Lawn Tennis and Cricket Club (Rumson, N.J.), Monmouth Beach (N.J.) Bath and Tennis Club. Office: Dreman Value Mgmt LP 10 Exchange Pl Ste 2050 Jersey City NJ 07302-3905

DRENNAN, WILLIAM D., publishing executive, editor; b. N.Y.C., Feb. 12, 1935; s. William P. and Olga (Koch) D.; m. Christina Lavery, Mar. 18, 1978; children: Caroline, William. BA, St. John's U., 1956, postgrad., 1956-57. Copy editor Doubleday & Co., N.Y.C., 1961-67; chief copy editor L.W. Singer Co., N.Y.C., 1967-68; assoc. acquisitions and planning editor Am. Mgmt. Assn., N.Y.C., 1968-70; editor Praeger Pubs., N.Y.C., 1970-72; cons. editor N.Y.C., 1972-80; pres., editorial dir. Drennan Communications, Weston, Conn., 1980—. Mem. Nat. Assn. Book Editors (mem.-at-large 1969-70). Republican. Roman Catholic. Office: Drennan Communications 6 Valley Forge Ln Weston CT 06883-2013

DRESS, SUSAN HILDEBRANT, engineer; b. Allentown, Pa., Feb. 20, 1948; d. Harold Orwood and Frieda Gisella (Hutter) Hildebrant; m. Jeffrey William Dress, June 20, 1981; 1 child, Ashley Elizabeth. Diploma, St. Joseph's Sch. Nursing, 1968; BS in Biomed. Engring., Boston U., 1980; MBA, Northeastern U., 1986. Staff nurse St. Luke's Hosp., Bethlehem, Pa., 1968-69, Mass. Gen. Hosp., Boston, 1969-74; head nurse emergency Chelsea (Mass.) Meml. Hosp., 1974-75; RN supr. emergency Faulkner Hosp., Boston, 1975-79; con. clin. engr. Technology in Medicine, Newton, Mass., 1979-80; mgr. neonatal market Hewlett Packard, Waltham, Mass., 1980-85; engr. sales devel. Mass. Computer Corp., Westford, Mass., 1985-86; sr. copr. quality engr. Mass. Computer Corp., Westford, 1986-89; product mgr. Siemens Med. Electronics, Danvers, Mass., 1989-91, sr. product mgr., 1991—; cons. (book) Medical Products Reference, 1982. Contbr. articles to profl. jours. Mem. IEEE, Am. Soc. Quality Control (steering com. 1988-89), Emergency Dept. Nurses Assn. (founder, sec. 1970-74), Am. Nurses Assn., Emergency Med. Svcs. for Mass. (Excellence award 1977). Roman Catholic. Home: 25 Upland Rd Burlington MA 01803-1417 Office: Siemens Med Electronics 16 Electronics Ave Danvers MA 01923-1047

DRESSEL, HENRY FRANCIS, lawyer; b. Bklyn., Apr. 11, 1914; s. Henry Philip and Ernestine (Delmar) D.; AB, Washington Sq. Coll., NYU, 1943, JD, 1949; m. Rose Marie Valentine, Nov. 24, 1937; 1 child, Diana (Mrs. Anthony P. Fradella). Bar: N.Y. 1949. Assoc. corp. law firm Chadbourne, Stanchfield & Levy (and its successors), N.Y.C., 1933-43; pvt. practice law, N.Y.C., 1950-86; ptnr. Dressel & Altman, P.C.; of counsel Berger & Steingut 1986—. Lt. USNR, 1943-46. Named hon. col. Okla., 1958, Okie, 1969. Mem. ABA, N.Y. State Bar Assn., Assn. Bar City of N.Y., N.Y. County Lawyers, Am. Judicature Soc., Justinian Soc., Internat. Footprint Assn., Danish Athletic Club, Phi Delta Phi. Democrat. Episcopalian. Home: Bay Royal Tower Apt 11A 420-64th St Brooklyn NY 11220 Office: 600 Madison Ave New York NY 10022-1615

DREXLER, EDWIN SMITH, dairy farm owner; b. Norwich, N.Y., Apr. 29, 1952; s. Henry Paul and Leah (Smith) D.; m. Pauline M. Brooks, Oct. 19, 1975; childrne: Paul, Emily, Renee, Travis. BS in Animal Sci., Cornell U., 1974. Farm mgr. Sandy Acres Farm, Smyrna, N.Y., 1974-77; real estate salesman Whipple Real Estate, Altamont, N.Y., 1977-78; dairy farm owner Weathertop Farm, St. Johnsville, N.Y., 1979-81, Fabius, N.Y., 1981-85; owner Drexler's Trees, Fabius, N.Y., 1984—; pres. Farm Sitter Svc., Inc., Fabius, N.Y., 1986—; owner, operator Tree Song Dairy, New Woodstock, N.Y., 1990—. Cub scout leader Boy Scouts Am., Fabius, 1985-88, camp counselor, Oran, 1989—. Mem. N.Y. Christmas Tree Growers Assn., N.Y. State Deer Farmers Assn., Holstein Assn. Episcopalian. Home: 1806 Swamp Rd Fabius NY 13063-9756

DREXLER, JOANNE LEE, art appraiser; b. Washington, Mar. 21, 1944; d. Elias J. and Beatrice Charlotte (Goldberg) D.; m. James R. Cohen, May 31, 1965; children: Terri C. Sirotkin, Brett F. Cohen. Student, Louvre, Paris, 1963-64; BA, Tufts U., 1965; Diamond and Pearl Cert., GIA, N.Y.C., 1974. Tchr. of French Stuyvesant High Sch., N.Y.C., 1965-66; decorator, art cons. Joanne Cohen Interiors, Mamaroneck, N.Y., 1967-69; assoc. prof. Hofstra U., L.I., N.Y., 1979-80; pres. Esquire Appraisals, N.Y.C. and Larchmont, N.Y., 1969—; numerous TV appearances including CNN, Sept. 1991; cons., lectr. in field; art judge various contests. Weekly columnist Gannett chain newspapers, 1980-86. Mem. Am. Soc. Appraisers (sr., v.p. White Plains chpt. 1989, bd. dirs. 1987, pres. 1991—), Appraisers' Assn. Am. (cert.), Nat. Arts Club N.Y. Home: 10 Normandy Rd Larchmont NY 10538 Office: Esquire Appraisals Inc 45 E End Ave New York NY 10028-7953

DREXLER, MICHAEL DAVID, advertising agency executive; b. N.Y.C., Nov. 2, 1938; s. Benn and Evelyn (Goldfarb) D.; m. Nancy Karen Drexler, Apr. 5, 1981; children: Staci Ann, Denise Susan, Lauren Michele, Benjamin Alex. BS, L.I. U., 1959. Media asst. Ogilvy and Mather Inc., N.Y.C., 1960-62, media planner, buyer, 1963-66, v.p. assoc. media dir., 1967-69, sr. v.p., media dir., 1970-74; exec. v.p., media dir. Doyle Dane Bernbach, N.Y.C., 1974-86, Bozell, Jacobs, Kenyon and Eckhardt, N.Y.C., 1986—; vice-chmn. Audit Bur. Circulation, Schaumburg, Ill., 1980-86. Author: (with others) Marketing in an Electronic Age, 1985; contbr. articles to profl. pubs. Mem. Am. Assn. of Advt. Agencies (media council), Media Dirs. Council (bd. dirs., pres. 1980-81), Advt. Research Found. (co-chmn. TV Audience Measurement Com. 1980-81), Internat. Radio and TV Soc. (bd. dirs. 1980-85), Audit Bur. of Circulations (vice chmn. 1982-86).

DREYER, RANDOLPH EUGENE, research institute official; b. Anaheim, Calif., Aug. 24, 1957; s. William Frank and Lorraine Stella (Amelotte) D. Student, Cypress Coll., 1975-76. Adminstrv. asst. field sales dept. Rsch. Inst. Am., N.Y.C., 1981-83, adminstrv. mgr. field sales dept., 1983-90, mgr. meetings and exhibits, 1990—; planner meeting events freelance, N.Y.C. Democrat. Office: Rsch Inst Am 90 5th Ave New York NY 10011-7629

DREYFUS, MARC GEORGE, physicist, optical engineer, educator; b. Bklyn., Mar. 5, 1926; s. Louis and Frances (Weintraub) D.; m. Ruth Schechtman, July 25, 1954 (div. Sept. 1977); children: Katherine Ann, David Harry; m. Joan King, Dec. 16, 1978. AB magna cum laude, Harvard U., 1947, SM, 1949; postgrad., MIT, 1947-50. Rsch. physicist Am. Optical Co., Southbridge, Mass., 1950-54; head optics sect. Librascope Inc., Glendale, Calif., 1954-59; mgr. spectroscopy sect. Barnes Engring. Co., Stamford, Conn., 1959-63; chief scientist North Am. Philips Corp., Briarcliff Manor, N.Y., 1964-67, BAI Corp., Stamford, 1967-75; pres. Dreyfus-Pellman Corp., Stamford, 1975-80; sr. scientist Am. Cystoscope Makers, Inc., Stamford, 1980-86; cons. in optics various, Fairfield, Conn., 1986—; prof., head optics dept. Norwalk (Conn.) State Tech. Coll., 1987—. Patentee in field; author tech. papers. With U.S. Army, 1944-45. Fellow Optical Soc. Am.; mem. SPIE, Phi Beta Kappa. Home: 337 Eastfield Dr Fairfield CT 06432-1119 Office: Norwalk State Tech Coll 181 Richards Ave Norwalk CT 06854-1635

DREYLING, ROBERT H., controller; b. New Brunswick, N.J., July 10, 1943; s. Louis R. and Freda P. (Rogers) D.; m. Luba Myronenko, Oct. 6, 1968; children: Brenda A., Christopher M. BA in Econs., Ursinus Coll., 1965. CPA, N.J. Div. controller IPCO Hosp. Supply Corp., Piscataway, N.J., 1968-73; controller Regal Accessories, Inc., North Bergen, N.J., 1973-82; v.p. fin. Maurice Silvera, Inc., N.Y.C., 1982-87; corp. controller Spencer Industries, Inc., New Brunswick, 1987—. Mem. Cranbury (N.J.) Twp. Bd. Edn., 1979—, Cranbury Twp. Planning Bd., 1987—; active troop 52 Boy Scouts Am., Cranbury, 1988—. Presbyterian. Home: 369 Old Cranbury Rd Cranbury NJ 08512-3104 Office: Spencer Industries Inc 120 Albany St New Brunswick NJ 08901-2163

DRIELSMA, WILLEM FRANS CAREL, management consultant, retired bank executive; b. Belinjoe, Bangka, Indonesia, Sept. 29, 1919; came to U.S., 1957; s. Isidore Adam and Margaretha Louise (Meulenhoff) D.; m. Mae Johanna Keiser (dec. Aug. 1980); children: Brenda, Mae. Student, Netherlands U., 1937-42, U. The Netherlands, 1942; postgrad., Am. Inst. Banking, 1964, NYU. With Govt. of The Netherlands, 1942-46; officer Netherlands Trading Soc., 1946-57; various positions to head Far East div. Bank of Am. Internat., N.Y.C., 1957-68; exec. v.p., mgr., dir. Crocker Internat. Bank, N.Y.C., 1968-76; exec. v.p., mgr. Bayerische Hypotheken und Wechselbank, N.Y.C., 1976-86; pvt. practice mgmt. cons., 1986—. Officer Cadet 2d Rgt Royal Netherland Army, 1938-41. Mem. City Midday and Drug, N.Y., Netherlands Club N.Y., Montclair Golf Club, Valley of North N.J., Scottish Right, Salaam, Shriners, Masons, Netherland-Am. Amity Trust (dir.). Republican. Netherlands Reformed. Home: 5950 SW 37th Ter Fort Lauderdale FL 33312-6201 also: 24 Dawson Dr West Caldwell NJ 07007

DRINAN, ROBERT FREDERICK, lawyer, former congressman, educator, clergyman; b. Boston, Nov. 15, 1920; s. James Joseph and Ann Mary (Flanagan) D. A.B., Boston Coll., 1942, M.A., 1947; LL.B., Georgetown U., 1949, LL.M., 1950; Th.D., Gregorian U., Rome, 1954; study, Florence, Italy, 1954-55; LL.D. (hon.), Worcester State Coll., 1970, L.I. U., 1970, R.I. Coll., 1971, St. Joseph's Coll., Phila., 1975, Syracuse U., 1977, Villanova U., 1977, Framingham (Mass.) State Coll., 1978, U. Santa Clara, 1980, Kenyon Coll., 1981, Lowell U., 1981, U. Bridgeport, 1981, Loyola U., Chgo., 1981, Gonzaga U., 1981, Curry Coll., 1982, De Paul U., 1984, U. San Diego, 1984, Mt. St. Mary Coll., 1985, Hebrew Coll., 1987, Notre Dame Coll., Manchester, N.H., 1989, Walsh Coll., Ohio, 1990, Georgetown U., 1991. Bar: D.C. 1950, Mass. 1956, U.S. Supreme Ct. 1955; ordained priest Roman Cath. Ch., 1953. Asst. dean Boston Coll. Law Sch., 1955-56, dean, 1956-70; vis. prof. U. Tex. Law Sch., 1966-67; mem. 92d-96th Congresses from 4th Mass. dist.; mem. jud. com., govt. ops. com., house select com. on aging, chmn. subcom. on criminal justice; columnist Nat. Cath. Reporter, 1980; prof. Georgetown U. Law Ctr., Washington, 1980—; Chmn. adv. com. Mass. U.S. Commn. Civil Rights, 1962-70; mem. vis. com. Div. Sch., Harvard U., 1975-78; bd. dirs. Bread for the World; founder Nat. Interreligious Task Force on Soviet Jewry.; Mem. exec. com. Assn. Am. Law Schs. Author: Religion, the Courts and Public Policy, 1963, Democracy, Dissent and Disorder, 1969, Vietnam and Armageddon, 1970, Honor the Promise, America's Commitment to Israel, 1977, Beyond the Nuclear Freeze, 1983. Editor: The Right To Be Educated, 1968, God and Caesar on the Potomac, 1985, Cry of the Oppressed: The History and Hope of the Human Rights Revolution, 1987, Stories from the America Soul, 1990, The Fractured Dream, 1991; editor in chief Family Law Quar., 1967-70; contbr. editor: nat. Cath. weekly America, 1958-70. Contbr. articles to jours. of opinion. Pres. Ams. for Dem. Action, 1981-84. Fellow Am. Acad. Arts and Scis.; mem. ABA (chmn. sect. individual rights and responsibilities 1990-91), NCCJ (nat. trustee), Am. Law Inst., Common Cause (nat. governing bd. 1984-87), Mass. Bar Assn. (v.p. 1961), Boston Bar Assn. Office: Georgetown U Law Ctr 600 New Jersey Ave NW Washington DC 20001-2022

DRIPCHAK, DAVID ALAN, financial executive; b. Derby, Conn., Dec. 2, 1955; s. Stephen Edward and Helen Agnes (Pczonka) D.; m. Susan Elizabeth Hessenius, Aug. 25, 1984; children: Eric, Alexander. BS in Acctg., Boston Coll., 1977. CPA, Conn. Audit supr. KPMG-Peat Marwick, N.Y.C., 1977-81; asst. to v.p. ops. Fotomat Corp., Wilton, Conn., 1982; dir. budget Norelco Consumer Products Co., Stamford, Conn., 1983-86, controller, 1986-88, v.p. fin., 1988—; counselor alumni admissions Boston Coll., Chestnut Hill, Mass., 1977—. Campaign coord. United Way, Stamford. Mem. AICPA, Conn. State Soc. CPAs. Office: Norelco Consumer Products Co 3 High Ridge Pk Stamford CT 06904

DRISCOLL, CONSTANCE FITZGERALD, educator, author; b. Lawrence, Mass., Mar. 29, 1926; d. John James and Mary Anne (Leecock) Fitzgerald; A.B., Radcliffe Coll., 1946; postgrad. Harvard U., U. Hartford (Conn.), U. Bridgeport (Conn.), Worcester (Mass.) State Coll.; m. Francis George Driscoll, Aug. 21, 1948; children: Frances Mary, Martha Anne, Sara Helene, Maribeth Lee. Secondary sch. tchr., North Andover, Mass., 1946-48; book reviewer N.Y.C. and Boston pubs., 1955-64; asst. conf. edn. dir. U. Hartford, 1964-68; lectr. Pace U., N.Y.C., 1973-74; edn. commentary Radio WVOX, New Rochelle, N.Y., 1974-75; asst. ednl. adv. Nat. Girl Scouts, 1972-74; pres., owner, dir. Open Corridor Schs. Cons., Inc., Bronxville, N.Y., 1972-84, pres., dir. Open Corridor Schs., Inc., Oxford, Mass., 1984—; creator in-svc. edn. programs pub. schs., Norwalk, Conn., 1983-88; assoc. Worcester State Coll. (Mass.) 1984-85, Fitchburg State Coll., 1986-87; assoc., dir. grad. edn. programs for tchrs. Anna Maria Coll., Paxton, Mass., 1990—; tutor, cons. Worcester County sch. dists., 1989—; CEU mgr. for Conn. Dept. Edn. O.C.S., Inc., Conn., 1989—; dir. off-campus grad. credit tchr. edn. courses O.C.S., Mass., Conn., 1990—; bi-lingual instr. for Indian and Vietnamese students in grades 5-12, 1988—; freelance writer newspapers and small jours., 1991—. Author curriculum materials; contbr. poetry to newspaper and small presses. Recipient Educator award Nat. Coun. ARC, Washington, 1985, Edn. award Nipmuc Am. Indian Coun., Webster, Mass, 1985. Home: 338 Main St Oxford MA 01540-1728 Office: Box 564 Oxford MA 01540

DRISCOLL, JOHN GERARD, college president; b. N.Y.C., Apr. 17, 1933; s. John P. and Mary T. (Kennedy) D. B.S., Iona Coll., 1954; M.S., St. John's U., 1957; Ph.D., Columbia U., 1969; D.Sc., Coll. New Rochelle, 1971. Tchr. elem. schs. Rice High Sch., 1956-57, St. Joseph Sch., Antigua, 1957-61, Power Meml. Sch., 1961-65; prof. math. Iona Coll., New Rochelle, N.Y., 1965—; asst. to pres. Iona Coll., 1969-71, pres., 1971—; bd. dirs. Chase N.B.W. Bank, City Harvest, Inc., N.Y. Trustee St. Joseph's Sem. and Sch. Theology, Yonkers, N.Y.; bd. dirs. New Rochelle Hosp. Med. Ctr., Irish Am. Sports Found. Mem. World Trade Inst. Office: Iona Coll 715 North Ave New Rochelle NY 10801-1890

DRISCOLL, JOHN S., newspaper editor; b. Melrose, Mass., Aug. 31, 1934; s. James Frank and Mary Elizabeth D.; m. Dolores Driscoll, May 3, 1958; children—LeeAnne, Jennifer, Maryellen, Susan. Grad., Northeastern U., Boston, 1957. Former mem. staff Manchester Union Leader, N.H.; former mem. staff UP; mem. staff, asst. exec. editor Boston Globe, mng. editor, exec. editor, editor, 1986—; tchr. Sigma Delta Chi scholarship program Northeastern U. Contbr. articles to mags., Ency. Brit. Charles Hayden scholar; Melrose Lions Club scholar. Mem. Am. Soc. Newspaper Editors, AP Mng. Editors Assn., New Eng. AP News Execs. Assn. Roman Catholic. Office: Boston Globe 135 Morrissey Blvd Boston MA 02107*

DRISCOLL, ROBERT EUGENE, association executive; b. Billings, Mont., Mar. 10, 1949; s. James T. and Inez S. (Loendorf) D.; m. Margaret L. Cooper, Nov. 5, 1977; children: Jennifer A., Matthew T. BA, Carroll Coll., Helena, Mont., 1971; MA, U. Tex., 1973. Exec. v.p. Fund for Multinational Mgmt. Edn., N.Y.C., 1973-84; pres., exec. dir. U.S.-ASEAN Ctr. Technology Exchange, Inc., N.Y.C., Washington, 1984-89; pres. U.S.-ASEAN Coun. Bus. and Technology, Washington, 1989—; cons. Sears, Roebucj & Co., Chgo., 1976-77, Ctr. Internat. Pub. Issues, N.Y.C. and London, 1981-84, The Manchester Group, Ltd., Washington, 1987-88; bd. dirs. US Environ. Tng. Inst., US-Asian Coun., Ten Days at Princeton, N.Y.C., 1981-91; lectr. European Mgmt. Ctr., Brussels, 1982, World Trade Inst., N.Y.C., 1989; adviser Indonesian ambassador to U.S., U.S.-Indonesia Joint Investment Com., 1986—; advisor U.S. Del. to Escap, 1991; mem. adv. coun. Univ. Coll., U. Md. Author: Social and Economic Impact of MNCs, 1976; editor: National Industrial Policies, 1983; contbr. articles to bus. publs. Vice-chmn. parish coun., Great Falls, Va., 1989-90. Mem. U.S.-Philippine Bus. Com., Univ. Club N.Y., Internat. Club of D.C. Office: 1400 L St NW Washington DC 20005-3509

DRIVER, C. STEPHEN, banker; b. Chgo., Mar. 26, 1936; s. Arthur Stephen Driver and Carlisle (Osborne) Driscoll; m. Deborah Connell, Sept. 25, 1960; 1 child, Paul Stephen. BSME, U.S. Mcht. Marine Acad., Kings Point, N.Y., 1958; MBA, U. Pitts., 1965. Engr. Westinghouse Electric Co., Pitts., 1958-67; adminstr. Perkin-Elmer Corp., Norwalk, Conn., 1967-69; mgr. Heritage Village, Southbury, Conn., 1970-72; v.p. Pilgrims Harbor, Inc., Wallingford, Conn., 1972-75, Albertson Sharp Ewing, Inc., Norwalk, 1975-87, Lockwood Kessler & Bartlett, Inc., Norwalk, 1987-89; pres. Limewood Cons., 1989-91; asst. v.p. Mechanics & Farmers Savs. Bank, Bridgeport, 1991; mgr. tech. svcs. Chase Manhattan Bank, Conn., N.A., Bridgeport, 1991—; real estate broker, Conn., 1971—; U.S. marine engr., 1958-68. Mem., vice chmn. Redding (Conn.) Planning Commn., 1971-76; mem. Redding Wetland Com., 1976-78, Redding Rep. Town Com., 1975—, Fairfield (Conn.) 2000, 1986-90; pres., nat. bd. dirs. New Eng. Resource Conservation and Devel., 1984—; past pres. Kings Mark Resource Conservation and Devel., 1985-91. Mem. Am. Inst. Cert. Planners. Home: 4 Tunxis Trl West Redding CT 06896-2508

DRIVER, ELWOOD THOMAS, safety and aviation executive; b. Trenton, N.J., Aug. 20, 1921; s. Robert Thomas and Mary Susan (Morris) D.; m. Imogene V., Dec. 29, 1942 (div. 1960); 1 child, Timothy J.; m. Shirley Martin, June 29, 1960. BS, N.J. State Coll., Trenton, 1942; MA, NYU, 1948. Cert. Safety Profl.; comml. pilot. Major command pilot USAF, 1942-62; chief safety engr. North Am. Aviation, Orange County, Calif., 1962-67; dir., assoc. adminstr. Nat. Highway Traffic Safety Bd., Washington, 1967-78; vice chmn. Nat. Transp. Safety Bd., Washington, 1978-1981; pres. Elwood T. Driver & Assocs., Rockville, Md., 1981-86; dir. aircraft office NASA, Washington, 1986—; cons. Nat. Inst. for Safety Analysis, Rockville, Md., 1981-86; bd. dirs. Aviation Research & Edn. Found., Herndon, Va., Inst. of Safety & System Mgmt., Los Angeles, Embry Riddle Aviation Coll., Fla. Major USAF 1942-62 (N. Africa, Sicily, Italy, Japan, Korea) (DFC, D.S.C., Air Medal 3 clusters, commendation medal). Recipient: Commendation Cert. and Cert. Merit, N. Am. Aviation. Fellow: System Safety Soc. (pres. 1968-69; profl. mem. Am. Soc. Safety Engrs.; mem. Internat. Soc. Air Safety Investigation, Nat. Soc. Profl. Engrs., Tuskegee Airman Inc., Metro Sailors Yacht Club. Baptist. Home: 2501 Pegasus Ln Reston VA 22091-4226

DRIVER, RICHARD ELLIS, JR., publishing executive; b. Phila., Aug. 16, 1926; s. Richard Sr. and Helen (Birchett) D. Pres. R.E. Driver Assn., Phila., 1959—; editor, publisher Scoop U.S.A., Phila., 1960—. Sgt. U.S. Army, 1944-46. Recipient Community Svc. award Temple U., 1990, Pa. Legis. Black Caucus, 1991; named to Four Chaplains Legion of Honor, 1989. Mem. United Black Bus. Assn., NAACP (Disting. Svc. award). Baptist. Office: Scoop USA 1220 N Broad St Philadelphia PA 19121-5139

DRIVER, RODNEY DAVID, mathematics educator, state legislator; b. London, July 1, 1932; came to U.S., 1945; s. William T. and Marjorie E. (Carter) D.; m. Carole J. Frandsen, Sept. 4, 1955; children: David M., Karen L., Bruce K. BSEE, U. Minn., 1953, PhD in Math., 1960. Postdoctoral fellow Rsch. Inst. for Advanced Studies, Balt., 1960-61; staff mem. Math. Rsch. Ctr., Madison, Wis., 1961-62, Sandia Labs., Albuquerque, 1962-69; assoc. prof. math. U. R.I., Kingston, 1969-74, prof., 1974—; mem. R.I. Ho. of Reps., 1987—. Author: Ordinary and Delay Differential Equations, 1977, Introduction to Ordinary Differential Equations, 1978, Why Math?, 1984; contbr. articles on functional differential equations to math. jours. Del. R.I. Constl. Conv., 1986. NSF grantee, 1976-77, 80-81, Air Force Office Sci. Rsch. grantee, 1977-79. Mem. Am. Math. Soc., Amnesty Internat., Greenpeace. Democrat. Unitarian. Home: 37 Hoxsie Rd West Kingston RI 02892-1017 Office: URI Kingston RI 02881

DRIVER, SHARON HUMPHREYS, marketing executive; b. Staten Island, N.Y., Jan. 5, 1949; d. William Edward and Gloria Patra (McCrave) Humphreys; m. William Weston Driver, Jr., June 3, 1972; children: Christopher John, Andrea Nicole. BA, Manhattanville Coll., Purchase, N.Y., 1970; MA, Coll. New Rochelle (N.Y.), 1973. Lic. tchr., N.Y. Tchr. Somers (N.Y.) Cen. Sch. Dist., 1970-76, Ossining (N.Y.) Village Recreation Dept., 1983-87; media coord./bookkeeper Equation Communications, White Plains, N.Y., 1986-89; media dir. Sims Freeman O'Brien, Elmsford, N.Y., 1989-90; project dir. Rsch. Advantage, Hawthorne, N.Y., 1990-92; pres. Quality Media Cons., Briarcliff, N.Y., 1990—; cons. Merson/Greener Assocs., Tarrytown, N.Y., 1992—. Sec. tng. liason, Jr. League, Westchester-on-Hudson, 1982-88; sustainer, trainer-facilitator, Jr. League, Tarrytown, N.Y., 1988—; past pres. St. Teresa's Parish Coun., Briarcliff Manor, N.Y.; sec. bd. dirs. Ossining Open Door Health Clinic, 1985-89. Mem. Women in Communications, Sleepy Hollow Toastmasters (charter, sec. exec. com.). Roman Catholic. Home: 197 Macy Rd Briarcliff Manor NY 10510-1017

DROBASHEVSKY, VLADIMIR, exhibit and industrial designer; b. Belgrade, Yugoslavia, Mar. 27, 1929; came to U.S., 1949; s. Vitaly and Milissa (Jankovic) D.; m. Elfrieda Baumann, July 17, 1954; children: Elizabeth, Michael. BS in Industrial Design, Bridgeport U., 1959. Cert. design mgmt., CAD mgmt. Indsl. designer Jenter Bros., Mt. Vernon, N.Y., 1960-61; exhibit designer Gardner Displays, Pitts., 1961-65, G.R.S. & W. Inc., Pitts., 1965-76, Giltspur Exhibits, Pitts., 1976-78; design dir. Giltspur Exhibits, 1978—; cons. nuclear industry, 1966—, on langs. Pitts. C. of C., 1981—; designer Elizabeth Floating MSM, 1970, Seabrook Edn. Ctr., 1977, Tex. Utility Info. Ctr., 1982, Point Beech Info. Ctr., Wis., 1984. Mem. YMCA, Pitts., 1982—. Sgt. U.S. Army, 1951-53. Mem. Nat. Wildlife, Am. Translators Assn., Am. Assn. Retired Persons, Am. Legion. Republican. Russian Orthodox. Home: 1433 Burchfield Rd Allison Park PA 15101-4035

DROEGE, PETER FRIEDRICH VALENTIN, city designer; b. Munich, Apr. 6, 1952; came to U.S., 1976; s. Freidrich Erdmann Droege and Elfriede Doellein. Diploma in architecture, Tech. U. Munich, 1976; MArch in Advanced Studies, MIT, 1978. Sr. designer, mgr. Carr, Lynch Assocs., Cambridge, Mass., 1979-82; pres. Porter and Droege, Inc., Boston, 1983-86; prin. architect office of programming div. capital planning Commonwealth Mass., Boston, 1985-86; mission leader UN Devel. Program, Ghana, Oman, 1986-88; various acad. positions MIT, Cambridge, 1978-91; urban devel. and design advisor City of Amsterdam, 1991-92; endowed chair holder U. Tokyo, 1992—; acad. cons. MIT/Qinhua U., Beijing, 1985, Tokyo Inst. Tech., 1988; dir. strategic progam for Nat. Capital Planning Commn., Washington, 1988-90; strategy advisor Nat. Computer Bd. Singapore, 1991; urban form advisor Andersen Cons./Kinhill Sydney, 1988-89; assoc. ptnr. Rsch. Inst. on Built Environ., Amsterdam, 1992; overseas ops. dir. Atlantis Assocs., Tokyo, 1991—; rsch. affiliate MIT, 1992—. Guest editor Places, 1988; editor-in-chief Intelligent Environments, 1992; contbr. articles to profl. jours. Recipient 3d Prize Internat. Design Competition, Bonn, Germany, 1983, Grand Prix, Japan Assn. Planning Adminstrn., 1987, 2d award Boston Visions Com., 1988, Grand Prix, Sagami Bay Urban Alliance Japan, 1990. Mem. AIA (assoc., 3 awards photo competition 1990), Internat. Soc. City and Regional Planners. Home: 4 Harris Ave Boston MA 02130 Office: MIT Rm 10-485 Cambridge MA 02139

DROMS, WILLIAM GEORGE, finance educator; b. Schenectady, Aug. 20, 1944; s. George William and Frances (Maguire) D.; m. JoAnn Gilberti, June 17, 1967; children: Courtney, Justin. AB, Brown U., 1966; MBA, George Washington U., 1971, DBA, 1975. Prof. Georgetown U., Washington, 1973—, Powers Chair prof., 1990—, assoc. dean, faculty chair Sch. Bus. Adminstrn., 1978-81, 87-89, 92—, John T. Powers Jr. prof., 1990—; cons. various fin. instns., 1975—. Author: Finance and Accounting for Nonfinancial Managers, 1979, 83, 90, (with others) The Dow Jones Irwin Guide to Personal Financial Planning, 1982, 86, (with others) Personal Financial Management, 1982, 86, (with others) Dow Jones-Irwin No-Load Mutual Funds, 1986, (with others) The Life Insurance Investment Advisor, 1988, The Dow Jones Irwin Mutual Fund Yearbook, 1984, 85; editor: Managing a Global Investment Program, 1991; contbr. numerous articles to profl. jours. Lt. USN, 1966-70. Fellow Inst. Chartered Fin. Analysts; mem. AAUP, Am. Fin. Assn., Eastern Fin. Assn., Fin. Analysts Fedn., Fin. Mgmt. Assn., D.C. Soc. Investment Analysts. Republican. Roman Catholic. Office: Georgetown U Sch Bus Adminstrn Washington DC 20057

DROSSMAN, JAY LEWIS, aerospace executive; b. Bklyn., Dec. 30, 1932; s. Murray L. and Ruth (Cohen) D.; m. Sylvia F. Solomon, Dec. 26, 1954 (dec. July 1972); children: Bruce, Mark; m. Phyllis Cynthia Cross, July 3, 1974; stepchildren: Meri Wieder Sirkin, Drew Wieder. BA in Psychology, NYU, 1954; BSME, CCNY, 1960; MSME, CUNY, 1963. Dir. Trident programs Kearfott Guidance & Navigation Corp., Wayne, N.J., 1978-91, dir. strategic programs, 1992—; mem. Fleet Ballistic Missile Programs, Washington, 1978—. Inventor optical meads of measuring rotation. Bd. dirs. Temple Emeth, Teaneck, N.J., 1976-79. 1st lt. inf. USN, 1954-56, ETO. Mem. AIAA, IEEE, Jewish War Vets. Republican. Home: 57 Old Orchard Dr Hawthorne NJ 07506 Office: Kearfott Guidance Navigation Corp 150 Totowa Rd Wayne NJ 07474

DROTAR, BLASE THOMAS, JR., food services company executive; b. Norristown, Pa., Dec. 14, 1959; s. Blase Thomas and Joanne (Verguldi) B.; children: Adam Jonathan, Blase Tito; m. Lisa Frances Heistand, Mar. 3, 1990; 1 child, Matthieu Thomas. BS, LaSalle U., 1980. CPA, Pa. Staff acct. L.F. Tornetta, CPA, Plymouth, Pa., 1980-82; sr. acct. Clairmont, Paciello, CPA, King of Prussia, Pa., 1982-84; pvt. practice Norristown, Pa., 1984-88; sr. staff auditor ARA Svcs. Inc., Phila., 1988-89, audit mgr., 1989-90, dir. audit and controls, 1990—. Cons. Community Accts., Phila., 1990—. Mem. AICPA, Inst. Mgmt. Accts., Pa. Inst. CPAs, Cert. Fraud Examiners (assoc.). Home: 1750 Skippack Pike Apt 1906 Blue Bell PA 19422-1306

DROZDZIEL, MARION JOHN, aeronautical engineer; b. Dunkirk, N.Y., Dec. 21, 1924; s. Steven and Veronica (Wilk) D.; m. Rita L. Korwek, Aug. 30, 1952; 1 child, Eric A. BS in Aero. Engring., Tri State U., 1947, BS in Mech. Engring., 1948; postgrad., Ohio State U., 1948, Nigara U., 1949-51, U. Buffalo, 1951-52. Stress analyst Curtiss Wright Corp., Columbus, Ohio, 1948; project engr. weight analysis Bell Aerospace Textron, Buffalo, 1949-52, stress analyst, 1952-60, asst. supr. stress analysis, 1960-64, chief stress analysis propulsion, 1964-79, chief engr. stress and weights, 1979-84, staff scientist, 1984-85, cons. structures and fractures mechanics, 1985—; mem. Am. Aerospace Materials Del. to USSR, 1989, Am. Aerospace Industries Del. to People's Republic China, 1991, Am. Aerospace Materials Del. to Czechoslovakia and Commonwealth Ind. States, 1992. Del. Internat. Citizens Ambassador Prog.; active Buffalo Fin Arts Acad. With U.S. Army, 1944-47. Recipient cert. of achievement NASA-Apollo, 1972; cert. commendation U.K. NATO program, 1982. Mem. AAAS, AIAA (Membership Chmn's award 1988, 89, 90, 92), Soc. Reliability Engrs., U.S. Naval Inst., Am. Space Found., Nat. Conservancy, Nat. Audubon Soc., Am. Acad. Polit. and Social Sci., Acad. Polit. Sci., Union Concerned Scientists, Air Force Assn., Nat. Space Soc., Soc. Allied Weight Engrs., Planetary Soc., Am. Mgmt. Assn., Bibl. Archeology Soc., Archeol. Inst. Am., Cousteau Soc., Smithsonian Assocs., Buffalo Audubon Soc., Bell Mgmt. Club, Natural History Mus., Internat. Hypersonic Rsch. Republican. Roman Catholic. Home and Office: 152 Linwood Ave Tonawanda NY 14150-4020

DRUCKER, JAKOB RICHARD, chemical engineer; b. N.Y.C., June 26, 1946; s. Julius Joseph and Marion (Peltz) D.; m. Lorraine Gale Diorio, Mar. 27, 1969 (div. 1983); children: Erik Scott, David Ian, Marc Harry; m. Susan Katz, Sept. 10, 1983. BA in Sci., Montclair State Coll., Upper Montclair, N.J., 1971; postgrad., Ctr. for Continuing Edn., Brunswick, N.J., 1976,78,80, 83. Butcher Grand Union Co., East Paterson, N.J., 1971-72; chemist Airwick Ind., Inc., Teterboro, N.J., 1972-74; sr. field/chem. engr. Graver Water, Union, N.J., 1974-82; sr. chem. engr. Water Purification Sys., Inc., Keansburg, N.J., 1982-83; sr. field svc. engr. Infilco Degremont Inc., Richmond, Va., 1983-86; equip. specialist The Purolite Co., Bala Cynwyd, Pa., 1986-88; pres. J & S Tech. Svcs., Inc., Norristown, Pa., 1988; sr. process field engr. Graver Water, Union, 1988—; cons. Energy Products Enrichment, Inc., 1986—. Contbr. articles to profl. jours. With USN, 1963-67. Mem. ACS, Am. Water Works Assn., Am. Nuclear Soc., ASTM, B'nai B'rith (v.p. 1988-89). Democrat. Jewish. Home: 108 Brill St Lakewood NJ 08701-4111 Office: Graver Water 2720 Us Hwy 22 E Union NJ 07083-8595

DRUCKER, MORT, commercial artist; b. Bklyn., Mar. 22, 1929; s. Edward and Sarah (Spielvogel) D.; m. Barbara Hellerman, Aug. 28, 1948; children: Laurie Drucker Bachner, Melanie Drucker Amsterdam. Student public schs. Staff artist Nat. Periodicals, N.Y.C., 1948-50; freelance artist, 1951—. Artist for: Mad mag., 1956—; artist: covers for Time mag; also nat. advt. agencies, TV commls. and movie posters; author: (with Paul Laikin) JFK Coloring Book, 1961, (with Jerry Dumas) Benchley comic strip, 1984, (with Laikin) Ollie North Coloring Book, 1987, (David Duncan with Mort Drucker) Familiar Faces, The Art of Mort Drucker, 1988, (with Laikin) Farewell Tribute to Ronald Reagan Coloring Book, 1988. Recipient cert. merit Art Dirs. Club N.Y., Excellence award San Francisco Soc. Communicating Arts, Gold award, 1980, Andy award distinction Advt. Club N.Y., 1983, Showtime award Rochester Soc. Communicating Arts, 1983, Internat. Comic award Barcelona, Spain, 1985, Best in Spl. Features award Nat. Cartoonist Soc., 1986, 87, 88, Best Cartoonist award Nat. Cartoonist Soc., 1988. Mem. Graphic Artists Guild. Office: care Mad Mag 485 Madison Ave New York NY 10022-5803*

DRUKER, HENRY LEO, investment banker; b. Des Moines, Aug. 20, 1953; s. Boni B. Druker and Dorothy (Marks) Vogel. BA, Colo. Coll., 1975; MBA, JD, U. Pa., 1980. Bar.: Pa. 1980. Assoc. Goldman Sachs & Co., N.Y.C., 1980-82; v.p. Investors in Industry, Boston, 1982-83; mng. dir. Rothschild & Co., N.Y.C., 1983-88; ptnr. Gordon Capital Inc., N.Y.C., 1989—. Com. mem. Save Children Found., N.Y.C., 1985—. Office: Gordon Capital Inc 767 5th Ave New York NY 10153-0002

DRUM, ALICE, college administrator; b. Gettysburg, Pa., June 22, 1935; d. David Wentz and Charlotte Rebecca (Kinzey) McDannell; m. D. Richard Guise, June 15, 1957 (div. Aug. 1975); children: Gregory, Brent, Richard, Robert, Clay; m. Ray Kenneth Drum, Mar. 2, 1979; 1 child, Trevor. BA magna cum laude, Wilson Coll., 1957; PhD, Am. U., 1976. Adj. prof. gen. studies Antioch U., Columbia, Md., 1976-78; adj. asst. prof. English Gettysburg (Pa.) Coll., 1977-80; lectr. in gen. studies Georgetown U., Washington, 1980-81; lectr. in gen. honors U. Md., College Park, 1980-83; asst. prof. English Hood Coll., Frederick, Md., 1981-85, coord. writing program, 1981-83, assoc. dean acad. affairs, 1983-85; dean of frehmen Franklin and Marshall Coll., Lancaster, Pa., 1985-88, v.p., 1988—; team mem. Mid. States Accreditation Assn., 1989-91; cons. in field. Contbr. chpts. to books, articles and book revs. to profl. jours. Chair Lancaster County DA Commn., Lancaster, 1990-91; mem. Lancaster County Commn. on Youth Violence, Lancaster, 1990-91. Mellon grantee, 1979, Davison Foreman fellow, 1975-76. Mem. MLA, N.E. MLA, Am. Assn. Higher Edn., Assn. Am. Colls., Eastern Assn. Coll. Deans (pres. 1988-89), Coll. English Assn., Phi Beta Kappa (pres. chpt. 1990-91), Phi Kappa Phi. Democrat. Episcopalian. Office: Franklin and Marshall Coll Lancaster PA 17604-3003

DRUMM, GREGORY WILLIAM, industrial hygienist; b. Albany, N.Y., Mar. 13, 1965; s. Gary Glen and Frances Eileen (Montanye) D. BS, Clarkson U., 1987. Coord. safety and environ. affairs N.A. Taylor Co., Inc., Gloversville, N.Y., 1988-89; indsl. hygienist Stearns & Wheler, Cazenovia, N.Y., 1989—. Mem. Am. Indsl. Hygiene Assn., Am. Acad. Indusl. Hygienists, Am. Soc. Safety Engrs. Office: 1 Remington Park Dr Cazenovia NY 13035-9464

DRURY, LEON ARTHUR, III, athletics director; b. Fitchburg, Mass., Oct. 9, 1944; s. Leon Arthur Jr. and Helen Christina (MacDonald) D.; m. Eileen Ann Cormier, July 21, 1973; children: Michelle, Lauren, Mark. BS, Springfield Coll., 1966, MS, 1968. Tchr., coach Litchfield (Conn.) High Sch., 1967-69; tchr. Esek Hopkins Jr., Providence, 1969-71; freshman basketball coach Brown Univ., Providence, 1969-72; intramural dir., asst. athletic dir., coach Bryant Coll., Smithfield, R.I., 1972-78; head basketball coach, athletics dir. Bryant Coll., Southfield, 1978-89; athletic dir. Bryant Coll., Smithfield, 1989—. mem. Dan Mazzella scholarship meml. com., Johnston, R.I., 1988—; co-chair Kristin Kitch Meml. Road Race Com., Smithfield, 1990—. Named Coach of the Yr. in Basketball, State of R.I., 1980. Mem. NCAA, Nat. Assn. Coll. Dirs. Athletics. Episcopalian. Home: 85 Mapleville Rd Greenville RI 02828-1015 Office: Bryant College 1150 Douglas Pike Smithfield RI 02917-1220

DRUSIN, LEWIS MARTIN, physician, educator; b. N.Y.C., Sept. 25, 1939; s. David and Gladys Margaret (Apfel) D. BS, Union Coll., 1960; MD, Cornell U., 1964; MPH, Columbia U., 1974. Med. intern 2nd medicine (Cornell div.) Bellevue Hosp., N.Y.C., 1964-65; jr. asst. resident in medicine Med. Ctr. Hops. of Vermont, Vt., 1965-66; sr. asst. resident N.Y. Hosp., N.Y.C., 1968-69; fellow in medicine div. allergy and infectious diseases Cornell U. Med. Coll., N.Y.C., 1969-70; asst. prof. pub. health Cornell U., N.Y.C., 1970-77, asst. prof. medicine, 1972-79, assoc. prof. pub. health, 1977-84, assoc. prof. clin. medicine, 1979—, prof. clin. pub. health, 1984—; dir. dept. epidemiology The N.Y. Hosp., N.Y.C., 1970—, assoc. attending physician, 1979—; cons. The Rockefeller Univ. Hosp., N.Y.C., 1981—; regional dir. for N.Am. Internat. Union Agains Venereal Diseases and Treponematoses, Leeds, Eng., 1986—. Contbr. book chpts., articles. Task Force Syphilis, N.Y. State Dept. Health, 1990-91. Sr. surgeon USPHS, 1966-68. Fellow ACP, Am. Coll. Preventive Medicine, Infectious Disease Soc. Am., N.Y. Acad. Medicine, Royal Soc. Medicine, Royal Soc. Tropical Medicine and Hygiene; mem Am. Venereal Disease Assn. (pres. 1982), Soc. Hosp. Epidemiology Am., Phi Beta Kappa, Sigma Xi, Alpha Omega Alpha. Office: NY Hosp Cornell Med Ctr 520 E 68th St New York NY 10021

DRUTZ, DAVID JULES, pharmaceutical executive; b. Knoxville, Tenn., Apr. 20, 1938; s. Abe Morris and Lillian (Billig) D.; m. Lydia Anne Hall, June 28, 1962; children: Gretchen, Adam, Gregory, Jonathan. BA, U. Louisville, 1958, MD, 1962. Cert. Am. Bd. Internal Medicine. Intern Louisville Gen. Hosp., 1962-63; resident Vanderbilt U. Hosp., 1963-65; infectious disease fellow Vanderbilt U. Med. Ctr., 1965-67; chief infectious diseases San Francisco Gen. Hosp., 1969-74; asst. prof. medicine U. Calif., San Francisco, 1969-74; chief infectious diseases U. Tex. Health Sci. Ctr., San Antonio, 1974-86, prof. medicine and microbiology, 1974-86, founder, dir. Ctr. for Cell Regulation, 1984-86; v.p. SmithKline & French Labs., King of Prussia, Pa., 1986-90; v.p. Daiichi Pharm. Corp., Ft. Lee, N.J., 1990—, bd. dirs.; clin. prof. medicine Seton Hall U. Sch. Grad. Med. Edn., Newark, 1990, U. Pa. Sch. Medicine, Phila., 1986-90, adj. prof. medicine and microbiology Temple U. Med. Sch., Phila., 1986-90. Editor: Systemic Fungal Infections, 1988-89; contbr. articles and abstracts to profl. jours.; assoc. editor Jour. Infectious Diseases, 1983-88, editorial bd., 1988-91; editorial bd. Am. Rev. Respiratory Diseases, 1979-84, Am. Jour. of the Med. Scis., 1983-91. Chmn. sci. adv. bd. Leonard Wood Memnl., 1984-87. Lt. comdr. USNR, 1967-69, Taiwan. Rsch. grantee NIAID, VA, NSF, 1970-86. Fellow Am. Coll. Physicians, Infectious Diseases Soc. Am. (councillor 1986-88); mem. Am. Soc. for Clin. Investigation, Western Soc. for Clin. Investigation, So. Soc. for Clin. Rsch., Am. Soc. for Microbiology, AMA, Alpha Omega Alpha. Office: Daiichi Pharm Corp 1 Parker Plz Fort Lee NJ 07024-2937

DRYE, WILLIAM JAMES, business owner; b. Phila., Aug. 27, 1939; s. William James and Louvenia (Spearman) D.; 1 child, William Bradley. Cert. in acctg., U. Pa., 1966, BBA, 1968. Cert. energy reduction specialist. Clk. U. Pa., Phila., 1957-60, acct., 1960-63, asst. to treas., 1966-67, asst. to bus. mgr., 1967-68, acting comptroller, 1974, asst. comptroller, 1968-81, assoc. comptroller, 1981-83; pres. Delaware Valley Energy Conservation, Phila., 1983—. Mem. Springfield Twp. Town Watch, 1987. Served with U.S. Army, 1963-65. Mem. Am. Mgmt. Assn., Nat. Energy Specialist Assn. (performance award 1987). Home and Office: 1211 Meadow Dr Blue Bell PA 19422-3302

DRYER, MOIRA JANE, artist; b. Toronto, Ont., Can., Aug. 9, 1957; came to U.S., 1978; d. Douglas and Pegeen (Synge) D.; m. Victor Alzamora, Jan. 8, 1982 (dec. 1983). BFA, Sch. Visual Arts, N.Y.C., 1981. Exhibited in solo shows San Francisco Mus. Fine Arts, 1990, Mary Boone Gallery, N.Y.C., 1990, 92, Mario Diacono Gallery, Boston, 1991, Fred Hoffman Gallery, Santa Monica, Calif., 1991; exhibited in group shows at U. Fla., Tampa, 1988, Mus. Contemporary Art, L.A., 1988; represented in collections at Carnegie Mellon Inst., Pitts., Mus. Contemporary Art, L.A., Hirshhorn Mus., Washington; represented by Mary Boone Gallery. Studio: 121 Varick St 2d Fl New York NY 10000

DRYGULSKI, JOHN STANLEY, construction company executive; b. Warsaw, Poland, May 15, 1949; came to U.S., 1958; s. Casimir and Jennie (Dlugolecki) D.; m. Alicia E. Stepien, June 23, 1979. BCE, Manhattan Coll., 1972; postgrad., Bernard Baruch Coll., 1972-74. Project engr. Montrose Constrn., White Plains, N.Y., 1972-74; sr. engr. Arabian-Am. Oil Co., Saudi Arabia, 1975-79; prin. engr. Stone and Webster Engring. Co., N.Y.C., 1980-87; pres. Roadcoat Corp., N.Y.C., 1988—. Republican. Roman Catholic. Office: Roadcoat Corp 415 E 54th St New York NY 10022-5101

DRYJA-SWIERSKI, KAREN ANN, public relations director; b. Johnstown, Pa., June 28, 1954; d. James Wesley and Alberta Louise (Hoffman) Henger; 1 child, Felix S. Swierski IV. BA, U. Buffalo, 1976; postgrad., U. Coll. Buffalo. Community svcs. rep. March of Dimes, Buffalo, 1976-80; asst. dir. devel. Millard Fillmore Hosp., Buffalo, 1980-82; dir. community rels. and devel. Lafayette Gen. Hosp., Buffalo, 1982-83; dir. pub. rels. Children's Hosp of Buffalo, 1983-92; pub. rels. cons. Children's Hosp. of Buffalo, 1992—. Contbr. articles to profl. jours. Mem. Am. Soc. for Health Care Mktg. and Pub. Rels. (regional dir. 1988-90, chmn. membership com. 1988, chmn. aff. soc. com. 1992, Nat. Touchstone award 1987). Episcopalian. Home: 2836 Transit Rd Orchard Park NY 14127

DU, HONGHUA, materials researcher, educator; b. Hunan, China, July 18, 1962; came to U.S., 1983; s. Ziyun Du and Guixiang Li; m. Fang Li, Dec. 31, 1985. BS, South China U. Sic. and Tech., 1982; PhD, Pa. State U., 1988. Rsch. asst. Pa. State U., University Park, 1984-88; from rsch. assoc. to rsch. asst. prof. Stevens Inst. Tech., Hoboken, N.J., 1988-90; asst. prof. Stevens Inst. Tech., Hoboken, 1990--. Contbr. articles to profl. jours. Mem. Am. Ceramic Soc., Nat. Inst. Ceramic Engrs., Electrochem. Soc., Materials Rsch. Soc. Office: Stevens Inst Tech Dept Materials Sci Hoboken NJ 07030

DUARTE, FRANK, communications manager; b. Yonkers, N.Y., July 17, 1965; s. Jose Dias and Maria Eugenia (De Oliveira) D. BEEE, Manhattan Coll., 1988. Kitchen mgr. Sizzler, Yonkers, 1981-87; heating, ventilation and air conditioning technician Marriott Corp., Thornwood, N.Y., 1987-88; dist. mgr. U.S. Communications, Yonkers, 1988—. Republican. Roman Catholic. Home: 28 Cherrywood Rd Yonkers NY 10710-1102 Office: US Communications 1383 Seabury Ave Bronx NY 10461

DUARTE, PATRICIA, real estate and insurance broker; b. Truro, Mass., Feb. 23, 1938; d. Antone Jr. and Marjorie (Beckley) Duarte. Grad. high sch., Provincetown, Mass. Lic. ins. and real estate broker; constrn. supt. Sec. various ins. agys., Amherst, Mass., 1957-60; ins. and real estate agt. Duarte Ins. & Real Estate, Truro, 1960-66, owner, prin. agt., 1966-78; ins. risk mgr. J.L. Marshall & Sons, Inc., Pawtucket, R.I., 1979-92; owner, mgr. Patricia-Duarte Real Estate, Rockport, Maine, 1988—; restorer antique homes New Eng., Mass., 1979—. Mem., sec. Truro Planning Bd., 1965-72, chmn., 1974-78; mem. exec. com. Cape Cod Planning and Econ. Devel. Com., 1971-76; mem. Reelect Brawn for Senate Com., Camden, Maine,1988; mem. Rockport Planning Bd., 1991—, Rockport Comprehensive Planning Com., 1991-92; co-chmn. Rockport Capital Improvement Com., 1991—; bd. dirs. Cape Cod chpt. Am. Heart Assn., 1963-70; mem. Opera House Commn., 1992—. Mem. Penobscot Bay Bd. Realtors, Profl. Ins. Agts. New Eng. (bd. dirs. 1974-76), Gen. Fedn. Women's Clubs (2nd v.p. Camden chpt. 1989). Republican. Roman Catholic. Home and Office: 46 Pascal Ave Rockport ME 04856

DUAX, WILLIAM LEO, biological researcher; b. Chgo., Apr. 18, 1939; s. William Joseph and Alice B. (Joyce) D.; m. Caroline Townsend Dowell, May 6, 1966; children: Julia, Sarah, William, Stephen. BA, St. Ambrose Coll., 1961; PhD, U. Iowa, 1967. Postdoctoral research fellow Ohio U., Athens, 1967-68; research assoc. Med. Found. Buffalo, 1968-69, head crystallography dept., 1969-70, head molecular biophysics dept., 1970—, assoc. dir. research, 1983-88, research dir., 1988—, also bd. dirs.; adj. assoc. prof. Medicinal Chemistry Dept. SUNY, Buffalo, 1973—, assoc. research prof. Dept. Biochemistry, 1981—; dir. distbn. Cambridge Database in U.S., Buffalo, 1983—; lectr. various internat. confs. Editor: Atlas of Steroid Structure Vol. I, 1975, Vol. II, 1984, Molecular Structure and Biological Activity, 1982, Molecular Structure and Biological Activity of Steroids, 1992; contbr. chpts. to books. Mem. Am. Field Service, Amherst, N.Y. Served with USAR, 1961-67. Fulbright scholar Council for Internat. Exchange, 1987; grantee NIH, 1971—; recipient Spl. Merit award Inst. Arthritis and Metabolic Diseases NIH, 1987—, Disting. Alumni award, St. Ambrose Coll., 1983. Mem. AAAS, Am. Crystallographic Assn. (v.p. 1985, pres. 1986, exec. office 1988—), Am. Chem. Soc., Am. Cancer Soc., Biophys. Soc., Internat. Union Crystallography (charter mem., sec. com. on small molecules 1984—), Am. Inst. Physics (bd. govs. 1987—, exec. com. 1992), Coun. Sci. Soc. Pres. (govt. and pub. affairs com. 1987). Democrat. Roman Catholic. Club: Saturn (Buffalo). Office: Med Found of Buffalo Inc 73 High St Buffalo NY 14203-1196

DUBAI, MATTHEW MICHAEL, arts adminstrator; b. Lockport, N.Y., Apr. 24, 1953; s. Matthew M. Sr. and Helen (Blonkowski) D.; m. Maryann Zaleski, Aug. 12, 1978; children: Matthew Michael III, Thomas Michael. BS in Psychology, SUNY, Geneseo, 1975; MS in Edn., U. Buffalo, 1977. Hall coord. U. No. Iowa, Cedar Falls, 1977-80; student devel. asst. U. No. Colo., Greeley, 1980-90; assoc. dean for student affairs Alfred (N.Y.) U., 1991—; dir. presenting Clemens Ctr., Elmira, N.Y., 1991—. Asst. fire chief A.E. Crandall Hook and Ladder Co., 1989—; treas. Allegany Arts Assn., Belmont, N.Y., 1985-87, pres., 1983-85; panelist N.Y. State Coun. on Arts, N.Y.C., 1986—; mem. Chemung Valley Arts Coun., Corning, N.Y., 1986-89; panelist, mem. focus group Mid Atlantic Arts Fedn., Balt., 1989—. Roman Catholic. Home: 1357 Belmont Rd Alfred Station NY 14803 Office: Clemens Ctr PO Box 1046 Elmira NY 14902

DUBE, NOREEN MARY, real estate executive, consultant; b. Portsmouth, N.H., Oct. 29, 1941; d. William Ellis and Emily Pierce (Tilley) Kelly; m. Romeo Gilbert Dube, Sept. 17, 1960; children: Donna Marie, Mark James, Michelle Therese, Renee Annette. Grad. high sch., Portsmouth. Lic. real estate broker, mgmt. specialist. Ptnr. R & N Properties, Portsmouth, 1960—; owner, gen. mgr. Keepsakes, Portsmouth, 1970—; sales assoc. Langelier Realty, Portsmouth, 1971-73; ptnr., gen. mgr. Century 21 Ocean Realty, Portsmouth, 1979-84; owner, pub., cons. Sales and Mgmt. Techniques, Portsmouth, 1984—; cons. Century 21 New England, Burlington, Mass., 1984—; dir. sales and mgmt. devel. Century 21 New Eng., Burlington, Mass., 1987-89; independent cons. Century 21 Internat., 1989—; speaker in field. Author: They Never Come Late, 1983, Training for Success, 1983. Mem. Internat. Real Estate Trainers Assn., Nat. Assn. Realtors, N.H. Assn. Realtors (v.p., Nat. Honor Soc.), Seacoast Bd. Realtors. Club: Toastmasters (Portsmouth). Office: Sales and Mgmt Techniques 5A Riversedge Dr Salem NH 03079-3264

DUBE, RAJESH, software development manager; b. Indore, India, Dec. 11, 1952; came to U.S., 1977; s. Jayadev Prasad and Sharad Kumari (Dubey) D.; m. Veena Mehta, May 21, 1983; 1 child, Varun. BME, U. Indore, 1974; M in Tech., Indian Inst. Tech., Kanpur, India, 1977; MS, Rutgers U., 1980, PhD, 1989. Rsch. asst. Rutgers U., New Brunswick, N.J., 1977-80; assoc. systems analyst RCA Corp., Princeton, N.J., 1980-81, systems analyst, 1981-82, ops. rsch. analyst, 1982-85; mgr. telephone systems AT&T Bell Labs.,

Middletown, N.J., 1985-89, supr., dist. mgr., 1989—. Contbr. articles to profl. jours. Mem. IEEE, Am. Assn. Artificial Intelligence. Hindu. Office: AT&T Bell Labs HR2B-006 480 Red Hill Rd Middletown NJ 07748

DUBÉ, RICHARD LAWRENCE, landscape specialist, consultant; b. Portland, Maine, Mar. 25, 1950; s. Clarence Everett and Nancy Ann (Rowles) D.; m. Mary Louise Roberts, Sept. 7, 1974. AS in Forestry, Hocking Tech. Coll., 1973, AS in Recreation and Wildlife, 1975. Interpretive naturalist Ohio Dept. Natural Resources, 1975-78; asst. mgr. Treeland, Portland, 1979-83; landscape designer Lucas Tree Experts, Portland, 1983-86, mgr. landscaping, 1986-88, mgr. landscape and tree depts., 1988—; speaker Celandine Info. Svc., Buxton, Maine, 1987—. Host for TV show Backyard Maine, 1992. Vice pres. Japan-Am. Soc. of Maine, Portland, 1989-90; bd. dirs China-Am. Friendship Assn. of Maine, 1991; founder, exec. dir. A Yr. of Peace, 1990. Mem. Associated Landscape Contractor of Am., Profl. Grounds Mgmt. Soc., Am. Assn. Nurserymen, Maine Nurseryman's Assn. Office: Lucas Tree Experts 636 Riverside St # 958 Portland ME 04103-5901

DUBEY, SATYA DEVA, statistical scientist, researcher, executive; b. Sakara Bajid, Bihar, India, Feb. 10, 1930; s. Jagdish N. and Sahodara Devi (Mishra) D.; m. Joyce, June 18, 1960; children: Jay Dev, Dean Dev, Neal Narayan. BS with honors, Patna U., India, 1951; Diploma, Indian State Inst., India, 1953; PhD, Mich. State U., 1960. Researcher Indian Inst. of Tech., India, 1953-56; rsch. asst. Carnegie Inst. of Tech., 1956-57; instr. Mich. State U., 1957-60; supr. Procter & Gamble Co., 1960-66, Ford Motor Co., 1966-68; assoc. prof. NYU, 1968-73; chief Statis. Evaluation Br./Bur. of Drugs, 1973-84, Statis. Evaluation Rsch. Br./Ctr. Drugs Rsch./Biologics/Ctr. for Drug Evalution and Rsch./FDA, 1984—; acting dir. Div. of Biometrics (FDA), 1975-76, 89-90; assoc. Staff Coll. Ctr. for Drugs/Evaluation Rsch. (FDA), 1990; organizer, lectr. confs. and seminars in field; researcher on Jesus. Contbr. articles to profl. jours.; editorial bd. Jour. of Industrial Math., Jour. of Quality Tech., Jour. of Clin. Rsch. Practices and Drug Regulatory Affairs, Clin. Rsch. and Regulatory Affairs. Recipient FDA award of Merit, 1984, 87, FDA Equal Opportunity Achievement award, 1986, FDA Commn.'s Spl. citation, 1987, USPHS Superior Svc. award, 1988, USPHS Equal Opportunity Achievement award, 1991, Parklawn Asian Pacific Am. Community award, 1989, others. Fellow AAAS, Am. Statis. Assn., N.Y. Acad. Scis., Washington Acad. Scis., Royal Statis. Soc.; mem. Internat. Statis. Inst. Home: 7712 Groton Rd Bethesda MD 20817-2036 Office: Statis Evaluation/Rsch Br Ctr for Drug Evaluation/Rch FDA Parklawn Bldg Rm 18B45 Rockville MD 20857

DUBIN, ALAN, design engineer; b. N.Y.C., Nov. 24, 1954; s. Leonard and Viola Dubin; m. Mary Anne S. Weber, June 8, 1986; 1 child, Lisette Michele. BS, MIT, 1976; MEng, U. Calif., Berkeley, 1978. Sr. engring. analyst Babcock & Wilcox Computer Svcs., N.Y.C., 1979-83; sr. design engr. Allied-Signal Engineered Plastics, Morristown, N.J., 1983—. Mem. Soc. Plastics Engrs., Soc. Automotive Engrs., N.J. Entrepreneur's Soc. Home: 27 Meslar Rd Morris Plains NJ 07950 Office: Allied Signal Inc Engineered Plastics 101 Columbia Rd PO Box 2332 Morristown NJ 07962-2332

DUBIN, CHARLES LEONARD, judge; b. Hamilton, Ont., Can., Apr. 4, 1921; s. Harry and Ethel D.; m. Anne Ruth, Dec. 2, 1951. B.A., U. Toronto, Ont., 1941; LL.B., Osgoode Hall Law Sch., 1944. Bar: Ont. 1944, appointed Queen's Counsel 1952. Practiced in Toronto, 1945-73; judge Ont. Supreme Ct. Appeal, Toronto, 1973—, chief justice, 1990—; Royal Commr. to inquire into air safety in Can., 1979; Royal Commr. to inquire into use of drugs and banned practices in athletics, 1988; lectr. Osgoode Hall Law Sch., 1945-48. Mem. Univ. Club, York Club, Toronto Hunt Club, Queen's Club, Toronto Club. Home: 619 Avenue Rd, Apt 1702, Toronto, ON Canada M4V 2K6 Office: Office of Appeal, Osgoode Hall, Toronto, ON Canada M5B 2H4

DUBIN, JOSEPH WILLIAM, union representative; b. Middletown, Conn., Apr. 7, 1948; s. Emanuel Saul and Hazel (Brenner) D.; m. Brenda Charlotte Ellen Clark, June 27, 1976; children: Brian Joseph Finnegan, Darren Clark Finnegan, Evan Jared. BA, U. Conn., 1970; postgrad., U. Mass., 1970-73. Rsch. asst. U. Conn. Health Ctr., Farmington, 1973-81; organizer Am. Fedn. Tchrs., Hartford, Conn., 1981-82; field rep. Conn. State Fedn. Tchrs., Berlin, 1982—, interest arbitrator, 1990—; vice-chmn. Fedn. Nurses and Health Profls. Nat. Steering Com., Washington, 1980-81; v.p. Greater Hartford Labor Coun., AFL-CIO, 1982-84, del., 1980-92. Contbr. articles to profl. jours. Com. chmn. troop 355 Boy Scouts Am., Newington, Conn., 1980—; cubmaster Cub Scout Pack 303, 1983-85, com. mem. 1985-89. Recipient George Meany award AFL-CIO, Hartford, 1981, Eagle Scout, Middletown, 1965. Mem. ACLU, Am. Chem. Soc. (student affiliate chmn. 1969-70), Indsl. Rels. Rsch. Assn., U. Conn. Health Ctr. Profl. Employees Assn. (pres. 1980-81), Staff Union of Conn. (sec.-treas. 1982-87), Nat. Trust Hist. Preservation, Newington Hist. Soc. and Trust, Inc., Nat. Audubon Soc., Nat. Wildlife Fedn., Am. Mus. Natural History, Smithsonian Instn. Nat. Assoc., Mystic Seaport Mus., Friends of Lucy Robbins Welles Libr., Legis. Electoral Action Program, Peoples Med. Soc., Conn. Citizens Action Group. Home: 57 Kirkham Pl Newington CT 06111-2408 Office: Conn State Fedn Tchrs 1781 Wilbur Cross Hwy Kensington CT 06037-3696

DUBIN, MICHAEL, financial services executive; b. Louisville, Sept. 20, 1943; s. Samuel Sanford and Lydia Roth (Symons) D.; m. Randi Louise Thulin, June 5, 1982; children: Krista Alexandra, Erika Ashley, Karoline Hannah. BA, Yale U., 1966; D of Bus. Adminstrn., Harvard U., 1973. Asst. mgr. Brown Bros. Harriman & Co., N.Y.C., 1973-74, dep. mgr., 1974-75, mgr., 1975-82; exec. v.p. GFTA Services Corp., N.Y.C., 1983-86, pres., chief exec. officer, 1987-90; dir. mktg. Rayner & Stonington, N.Y.C., 1990-91; exec. v.p., owner Powers & Dubin Asset Allocation and Mgmt. Co., Jersey City, 1991—; pres., chmn. bd. Sectrend Holdings, Inc., Wilmington, Dec., 1988—; bd. dirs. Firecom, Inc., Queens; pres. AP, Trendanalysen, Inc., 1989—; pres. Morgan Stanley-GFTA, Nassau, The Bahamas, 1986—; lectr. in field. Author: Foreign Acquisitions and the Growth of the Multinational Firm, 1981; contbr. articles to profl. jours. Treas. Sports Village, Sherburne, Vt., 1987—; trustee The Town Sch., N.Y.C., 1992. Carnegie Endowment fellow, 1972-73; Ctr. Internat. Affairs scholar, 1972. Mem. Am. Econ. Assn., Orgn. Internat. Bus., St. Elmo Soc., Nat. Futures Assn. (registered), Managed Futures Assn., Broad St. Club/India House, Yale Club, East Hampton Yacht Club. Home: 200 E 71st St New York NY 10021-5137 Office: Powers & Dubin 30 Montgomery St # 1245 Jersey City NJ 07302-3821

DUBIN, NORMAN HAROLD, endocrinologist; b. Paterson, N.J., Feb. 13, 1942; s. Joseph L. and Madeline J. (Eglowstein) D.; m. Valerie Kresky, July 25, 1964; 1 child, Jessica M. BA, U. Rochester, 1963; PhD, Rutgers U., 1970. Asst. prof. U. Md., Balt., 1971-75; assoc. prof. Johns Hopkins U., Balt., 1975-90; vis. scientist, sr. rsch. assoc. NIH, Bethesda, Md., 1990-91; dir. ob-gyn rsch. labs. Union Meml. Hosp., Balt., 1991—; ad hoc reviewer NIH, NSF, March of Dimes, other granting agys., also for 7 profl. jours. Contbr. over 70 articles to profl. jours. Recipient award Lalor Found., 1971. Mem. Endocrine Soc., Soc. for Study of Reproduction, Soc. Gynecologic Investigations. Home: 6210 Biltmore Ave Baltimore MD 21215-3604 Office: Union Meml Hosp 201 E University Pky Baltimore MD 21218-2829

DUBLIN, FREDERICK RAYMOND, manufacturing company official; b. Pitts., July 5, 1945; s. Clarence Oliver and Myrtle Catherian (Hazen) D.; m. Barbara Jean Etter, Aug. 12, 1967; 1 child, Rebecca C. BS, U. Richmond, 1967; MBA, Drexel U., 1978. Sales rep. Am. Can Co., N.Y.C. and Phila., 1967-75; prodn. mgr. Concord Beverages, Concordville, Pa., 1975-77; sales mgr. Dubois Chems., Cin., 1977-79; supr. material planning AMP Products Corp., Valley Forge, Pa., 1979-80, mgr. material planning, 1980-82, mgr. material planning and prodn., 1982-84, mgr. warehousing and quality, 1984-85, mgr. distbn., 1985-88; dir. customer svcs. and phys. distbn. AMP Inc., Harrisburg, Pa., 1988—; cons. SBA, Phila., 1976-78. Bd. dirs. Fairview (Pa.) Acad., 1984-87. Mem. Am. Prodn. and Inventory Control Soc. (cert. in prodn. mgmt., inventory control), Warehousing Edn. and Rsch. Coun., Internat. Customer Svc. Assn. Republican. Home: 1199 Kuhn Rd Boiling Springs PA 17007 Office: AMP Inc PO Box 3608 MS 38-31 Harrisburg PA 17105

DUBNOV, WILLIAM LYLE, psychologist; b. Washington, May 1, 1951; s. Isadore Nathan and Alberta Elizabeth (Simkevitz) Dubin; m. Ellen Henderson Heath, Aug. 18, 1990. BA, Clark U., 1973; MS, U. Pa., 1978; PhD, Byrn Mawr Coll., 1982, postgrad., 1985. Testing cons. The Pass Program, Phila., 1985; testing cons., rsch. cons. Glen Mills Schs. for Boys, Concordville, Pa., 1979—; researcher Integra Inc., Radnor, Pa., 1990—; instr. Main Line Sch., Radnor, Pa., 1984—. Co-author: Without Locks and Bars, 1989; contbr. articles to profl. jours. Office: Integra Inc 320 King Of Prussia Rd Radnor PA 19087-4440

DUBOIS, ALAIN, investment banker; b. Sarrebruck, Sarr, Apr. 30, 1955; s. Jacques-Emile and Bernice Claire (Shaaker) D.; m. Ann Marie Wagenknecht, Oct. 30, 1987; children: Walter Emile, Sydney Claire. MS, Ecole des Mines, Nancy, France, 1978; MBA, The Wharton Sch. of Bus., 1980. Registered Civil Mining Engr. Assoc. Drexel Burnham Lambert, Inc., N.Y.C., 1980-83; v.p. Thompson Securities, Inc., N.Y.C., 1983-85; sr. v.p., ltd. ptnr. Oppenheimer & Co., Inc., N.Y.C., 1985-89; dir. Smith Barney, Harris Upham & Co., Inc., N.Y.C., 1989-91; pres. Home Med. Supply, Inc., Clearfield, Pa., 1991—. Bd. dirs. AIDS Resource Ctr., N.Y.C., 1989—. Mem. Univ. Club (N.Y.C.). Home: 20 W 77th St Apt 12A New York NY 10024-5127 Office: Home Med Supply Inc 300 N 2d St Clearfield PA 16830

DUBOIS, ARTHUR BROOKS, physiologist, educator; b. N.Y.C., Nov. 21, 1923; s. Eugene Floyd and Rebeckah (Rutter) DuB.; m. Roberdeau Callery, June 21, 1950; children: Anne R., Brooks, James E.F. Student, Harvard U., 1941-43; M.D., Cornell U., 1946. Intern in medicine N.Y. Hosp., 1946-47; med. research fellow U. Rochester, 1949-51; asst. resident Peter Bent Brigham Hosp., Boston, 1951-52; asst. prof. to prof. physiology and medicine U. Pa., 1952-74; prof. epidemiology and physiology Yale U., 1974—; dir. John B. Pierce Found. Lab., 1974-88. Author: The Lung, 3d ed. 1986, Body Plethysmography, 1969; contbr. articles to profl. jours. Served with USNR, 1947-49. Recipient Rsch. Career award NIH, 1963-74; Edward Livingston Trudeau medal Am. Lung Assn., 1989. Mem. Am. Physiol. Soc., Am. Soc. Clin. Investigation, Assn. Am. Physicians, Undersea Med. Soc. Democrat. Clubs: Harvard, Cosmos. Home: 370 Livingston St New Haven CT 06511-1310 Office: 290 Congress Ave New Haven CT 06519-1403

DUBOIS, JAN ELY, judge; b. Phila., Jan. 17, 1931; s. M. Norman and Syd (Stern) DuB.; m. Ruth Harberg, Aug. 19, 1956; children: Marc Norman, Jon Stuart, Peter Andrew, Pamela Sue. Student, Valley Forge Mil. Acad., Wayne, Pa., 1948; BS, U. Pa., 1952; LLB, Yale U., 1957. Law clk. civil div. U.S. Dept. of Justice, Washington, 1956; law clk. to Hon. Harry E. Kalodner Phila., 1957-58; atty. White and Williams, Phila., 1958-88; judge U.S. Dist. Ct. (ea. dist.) Pa., Phila., 1988—. Bd. dirs. Phila. Bar Found., 1981-89, pres., 1987; Reform Congregation Keneseth Israel, Elkins Park, Pa., 1985-87. Capt. USAR, 1952-54. Recipient John Currier Gallagher prize Yale U., 1957. Mem. ABA, Pa. Bar Assn., Phila. Bar Assn. (chmn. medico-legal com.), Yale Law Sch. Assn. (past treas.), Yale Law Sch. Assn. of Phila. (exec. com., past pres.), Yale Club. Office: US Dist Ct 12613 US Courthouse 601 Market St Philadelphia PA 19106-1510

DUBOV, SPENCER FLOYD, podiatrist, educator; b. Bklyn., Nov. 26, 1935; s. Simon and Ella (Goldberg) D.; children: Valerie Ellen Dubov Tantillo, Corey Scott. Student, Bklyn. Coll., 1956; D of Podiatric Medicine, N.Y. Coll. Podiatric Medicine, 1960. Diplomate Am. Bd. Ambulatory Foot Surgery. Internship Foot Clinics N.Y., 1959-60; podiatrist out-patient dept. Queens Hosp. Ctr., L.I. Jewish Hosp., 1961-76; podiatrist Queens Foot Care, Flushing, N.Y.; mem. surg. staff St. Joseph's Hosp., Cath. Med. Ctr., Massepequa Gen. Hosp., Flatbush Gen. Hosp.; mem. attending staff Clearview Nursing Home; cons. telephone panel Aetna Ins. Co.; mem. peer rev. com. N.Y. State, 1971, 86-89; mem. Workers' Compensation Bd. Panel, 1961—; bd. mem. N.Y. State Bd. Podiatry; mem. faculty foot care confs., 1963-65, 71, N.Y. Coll. Podiatric Medicine, 1978-79, Am. Podiatry Assn. Conf., 1963; chmn. N.Y. State Grad. Edn. Program, 1965. Contbr. articles to profl. jours. Fellow Assn. Ambulatory Foot Surgery; mem. Am. Podiatric Med. Assn., Queens County Div. Podiatric Med. Soc. State N.Y. (pres., chmn. medicare liason com., Podiatrist of Yr. award 1976), Aircraft Owners Pilots Assn., Am. Radio Relay League, L.I. Mobile Amateur Radio Club, Lions Club, B'nai Brith, Knights of Pythias. Office: Queens Foot Care 69-20 Main St Flushing NY 11367

DUBRO, ALEC CHARLES, writer; b. Bklyn., Nov. 4, 1944; s. Louis and Ruth (Linden) D. BA, U. Mass., 1968. Assoc. investigator, writer Ctr. for Investigative Reporting, San Francisco, 1981-86; investigator U.S. Senate Permanent Subcom. on Investigations, Washington, 1986, Nation Inst., N.Y.C., 1986-87; speechwriter Matheson Seigle, N.Y.C., 1988-89; copywriter Craver, Mathews, Smith & Co., Falls Church, Va., 1989—; writer Pres.'s Commn. on Organized Crime, Washington, 1985. Author: Yakuza, 1986; co-author (with David E. Kaplan): Investigative Reporters and Editors (Book Prize), 1986; contbr. articles to profl. jours. Mem. Nat. Writers Union (pres. 1987-90, v.p. for organizing 1985-87, regional v.p. 1984-85, labor union publicist 1990—). Home and Office: 825 W 187th St # 3A New York NY 10033-1225

DUBUC, CARROLL EDWARD, lawyer; b. Burlington, Vt., May 6, 1933; s. Jerome Joachim and Rose (Bessette) D.; m. Mary Jane Loew, Aug. 31, 1963; children: Andrew, Steven, Matthew. BS in Acctg., Cornell U., 1955; LLB, Boston Coll., 1962; postgrad. NYU, 1964-65. Bar: N.Y. 1963, D.C. 1972, U.S. Supreme Ct. 1970, U.S. Ct. Claims 1975, U.S. Ct. Appeals (2d cir.) 1965, (4th cir.) 1977, (7th cir.) 1984, (5th and 9th cirs.) 1985, (fed. cir.) 1988, (6th Cir.) 1989, U.S. Ct. Internat. Trade 1988. Assoc. Haight, Gardner, Poor & Havens, N.Y.C., 1962-70, ptnr., 1970-83, resident ptnr. D.C. office, 1975-83; sr. ptnr. Finley, Kumble, Wagner, Heine, Underberg, Manley, Myerson & Casey, Washington, 1983-87, Laxalt, Washington, Perito & Dubuc, 1988-90; sr. ptnr. Washington, Perito & Dubuc, 1990-91, Graham & James, 1991—. Capt. AC, USN, 1955-59. Mem. ABA (chmn. aviation and space law com. 1985-86, subcom. aviation ins., subcom. internat. practice 1985-87, sr. vice chmn. alternative resolution com., mktg. legal svcs. com. 1991-92, vice chmn. ins. com. 1982-84), N.Y. State Bar Assn. (past chmn. aviation law com.), D.C. Bar Assn., Fed. Bar Assn., Internat. Bar Assn., Assn. of Bar of City of N.Y. (aeros com.), Fed. Cir. Bar Assn., 5th Fed. Cir. Bar Assn., Fed. Bar Coun., Nat. Transp. Safety Bd. Bar Assn., Maritime Law Assn. U.S., Naval Aviation Command (vice comdr.), Internat. Assn. Defense Counsel (aviation law com.), Fedn. Ins. and Corp. Counsel (mem. aviation law com.), Helicopter Assn. Internat., Transp. Lawyers Assn., Assn. Trial Lawyers Am., Def. Assn. of N.Y., Assn. of Transp. Practitioners, Internat. Soc. Air Safety Investigators, Soc. Sr. Aerospace Execs., Am. Inst. Aeronautics & Astronautics, Internat. Aviation Club, Washington chpt. Aero Club, Nat. Aeronautic Assn., French-Am. Cham. Com., Sigma Chi, N.Y. Athletic Club, Cornell Club, World Trade Ctr. Club, N.Y.C. chpt. Wings Club, Univ. Club, Congrl. Country Club. Home: 2340 Inglewood Ct Falls Church VA 22043. Office: Graham & James 2000 M St NW Washington DC 20036, also Graham & James 885 Third Ave 24th Fl New York NY 10022. Home: 2430 Inglewood Ct Falls Church VA 22043-3223 Office: Graham & James 2000 M St NW Washington DC 20036 also: Graham & James 885 Third Ave 24th Fl New York NY 10022

DUCH, WILLIAM KINGSLEY, database marketing executive; b. Norwich, Conn., Nov. 23, 1947; s. Stanley Thaddeus Duch and Marion Florence Carden Taylor. BA in Math. and Econs., UCLA, 1969; MS in Statistics, U. Conn., 1971. Sr. staff analyst Reader's Digest, Pleasantville, N.Y., 1971-77; circulation mgr. Ziff Davis Pub., N.Y.C., 1977-79; v.p., gen. mgr. Printronic Corp., N.Y.C., 1979-80; pres. Response Rsch. Assocs., N.Y.C., 1980-82; v.p. sales and mktg. Compuname Inc., N.Y.C., 1982-84; dir. mktg. svcs. Rodale Press, Emmaus, Pa., 1984-88; group exec. Acxiom Corp., Conway, Ark., 1988-91; pres. William Duch Inc., Essex, Conn., 1991—; co-founder DMRS Group, Inc., 1991—; lectr. direct mktg. Sch. Continuing Edn. NYU, 1992. Contbr. articles to profl. jours. Mem. Direct Mktg. Assn. (mem. ethics policy com. 1990—, MPS/TPS task force, 1990—).

DUCKWORTH, WILLIAM CAPELL, III, safety engineer; b. Atlanta, May 9, 1953; s. William C. and Hilda (McClaren) D. BS in Biology, Rhodes Coll., Memphis, 1975; MA in European History, U. Pitts., 1980. Cert. safety profl. Trainee Crum & Forster, Pitts., 1978-79; loss control rep. Crum & Forster, Syracuse, N.Y., 1979-81; sr. loss control rep. Crum & Forster, Pitts., 1981-82, loss control mgr., 1982-91, mem. corp. task force performance appraisal system, 1985, mem. corp. task force-Bldg. a Team Centered Culture, 1990-92, mktg. mgr., 1991—. Contbr. articles to profl. jours. Mem. AAAS, Am. Soc. Safety Engrs., Nat. Safety Mgmt. Soc., Amnesty Internat., Common Cause. Democrat. Episcopalian. Home: 265 Old Clairton Rd Pittsburgh PA 15236-4301 Office: Crum & Forster 301 Grant St Ste 1200 Pittsburgh PA 15219-1409

DUDASH, CHARLES MICHAEL, illustrator, artist; b. Mankato, Minn., Jan. 12, 1952; s. Charles John and Helen Edith (Lloyd) D.; m. Valerie Elizabeth Wing, Aug. 12, 1977; children: Alison A., Elisabeth E., Micah J. Student, Macalester Coll., 1970-71, Minn. Coll. Art and Design, 1977. Staff illustrator, artist McGraw-Hill Publishing Co., Mpls., 1977-78; freelance artist, illustrator Moretown, Vt., 1978—; guest lectr. Vt. Graphics Artists Guild, Washington U., St. Louis, R.I. Sch. Design, Art Dir.'s Club, Kansas City, Mo. Represented in permanent collections Converse Inc., Boston, MGM/United Artists, Clint Eastwood, Time/Life Inc., Boca Raton Resort & Club, Philip Morris Inc., Eddie Bauer; illustrator limited edition prints Red Fox in Fall, 1984, Isaiah's Farm, 1987, Crater Lake Nat. Park, 1988, End of the Season, 1989, US Polo Centennial I&II Edition 950, 1990; designed series of stamps UN, 1987, U.S. Postal Svc., 1992; contbr. articles to profl. jours. Pianist, guitarist lay order Franciscan Ch. of Crucified One, Moretown, Vt., 1981—. Recipient 4 awards Soc. Publ. Designers, 1978, 79, Awards of Merit Soc. Illustrators, Silver medal, 1980, Awards of Excellence Communications Arts, 1983, 87, 91, 92, Award of Excellence Desi Awards, 1980, Cert. of Distinction Art Direction Mag., 1982. Home and Office: Mission House Artworks RR 1 Box 2803 Moretown VT 05660-9702

DUDEK, HENRY THOMAS, management consultant; b. Queens, N.Y., Dec. 29, 1929; s. Wojciech and Magdalena (Swiader) D.; m. Olga Waranitsky, June 14, 1953; children: Kathryn, Nancy, Linda, Andrew, Henryk. BBA, CCNY, 1955. Acctg. mgr. A.D.T. Co., N.Y.C., 1948-54; asst. controller Dancer Fitzgerald Sample, Inc., N.Y.C., 1955-60; chief fin. officer Wunderman Ricotta & Kline, Inc., N.Y.C., 1961-69, Van Brunt & Co., N.Y.C., 1970; controller, stockholder Compton Advt., Inc., N.Y.C., 1971; pres., chief exec. officer Henry T. Dudek & Assocs., Inc., Floral Park, N.Y., 1972—; frequent speaker on finance and advt. Mem. Advt. Agy. Fin. Mgmt. Assn. (bd. dirs.). Roman Catholic. Home: 90 Beech St Floral Park NY 11001-3103 Office: PO Box 478 Floral Park NY 11002-0478

DUDICK, MICHAEL JOSEPH, bishop; b. St. Clair, Pa., Feb. 24, 1917; s. John and Mary (Jurick) D. BA, Ill. Benedictine Coll., Lisle, 1943; postgrad., St. Procopius Sem., Lisle, 1943-45; HHD (hon.), Kings Coll., 1987; DD (hon.), Scranton U., 1989. Ordained priest Roman Cath. Ch., 1945. Vice chancellor Exarchate of Pitts., 1946-55; chancellor Diocese of Passaic, N.J., 1963-68; bishop Diocese of Passaic, 1968—; mem. N.J. Coalition of Religious Leaders; cons. ecumenical and interreligious com. Nat. Conf. Cath. Bishops. Bd. regents Seton Hall U., 1968—.

DUDLEY, ALFRED EDWARD, home and auto products company executive; b. Fremont, Ohio, Sept. 12, 1928; s. John Peter and Mary Elizabeth (Oaly) D.; m. Lois Delene Murphy, July 3, 1949; children: John Alan, Richard. BS, Bowling Green U., 1951. Gen. mgr. ops. Union Carbide Corp., N.Y.C., 1972-75, v.p., gen. mgr. home prodns., 1975-78; v.p. ops. Union Carbide Corp., Danbury, Conn., 1978-86; chmn., pres., chief exec. officer First Brands Corp., Danbury, 1986—, also bd. dirs. Mem. Silver Spring Club, Foxfire Club (Naples, Fla.). Republican. Roman Catholic. Office: First Brands Corp 83 Wooster Heights Rd Box 1911 Danbury CT 06813*

DUDLEY, TERRI CRAWFORD, newspaper advertising executive; b. Lebanon, N.H., Mar. 20, 1929; d. Harry W. and Pauline Lillian (Hatch) Crawford; m. Roger Lloyd Dudley, Mar. 29, 1947; children: Sharron L. Smardon, Michael R., JoAnn D. Langone. Student, Lebanon Coll., 1985—. Engring. aide State of N.H., Lebanon, 1950-52; class advt. mgr. Valley News, West Lebanon, N.H., 1957-62, promotion mgr., 1962-68, asst. advt. mgr., 1968-73, advt. mgr., 1973-78, advt. dir., 1978—. Active City of Lebanon (court diversion chmn. 1975—, fair hearing officer 1980-89, planning commn. mem. 1985-89, city coun. mem. 1989—), Dir. communications United Way Upper Valley, Lebanon, 1984—; trustee Alice Peck Day Hosp., 1989—. Mem. New Eng. Advt. Execs. (bd. dirs.), Hanover C. of C. (past pres., bd. dirs. 1986—), Lebanon C. of C. (past pres., bd. dirs. 1979—, Community Svc. award 1987), Rotary (sec., bd. dirs. local chpt. 1988—). Congregationalist. Lodge: Rotary. Home: 38 Dana St West Lebanon NH 03784-1425 Office: Valley News 7 Interchange Dr West Lebanon NH 03784-2084

DUDZICK, THOMAS FRANCIS, playwright; b. Buffalo, Apr. 20, 1950; s. Joseph Francis and Alyce (DeSeyn) D.; m. Anu Holpus, May 17, 1975 (div. Dec. 1980); m. Holly Emily Caster, Oct. 21, 1989; 1 child, Charles Caster. Assoc., Onondaga Community Coll., 1970; BA, SUNY, Fredonia, 1973. V.p. Cimasi-Dudzick Prodns., Buffalo, 1973-79; asst. producer Melic & Mime, Inc., Buffalo, 1973-79; word processor various temporary employment agys., N.Y.C., 1980-87; adminstrv. asst. Bankers Trust Co., N.Y.C., 1987—. Co-author: (off Broadway play) Me Too, Then!, 1980; author: (off Broadway play) Greetings, 1991. Winner Double Image Short Play Festival, 1980. Home: 67-25 Dartmouth St # 6A Forest Hills NY 11375

DUDZIK, KENNETH RICHARD, academic administrator; b. Hammond, Ind., May 7, 1949; s. Richard E. and Loretta (Sielski) D. BA, Wabash Coll., 1971; JD, Western N.Eng. Coll., 1981. Assoc. dir. of bequests and trusts Brown U., Providence, R.I., 1982-84; dir. of planned giving Dickinson Coll., Carlisle, Pa., 1984-89; assoc. v.p. of coll. rels., dir. devel. Western Md. Coll., Westminster, 1989-92; dir. devel. Juniata Coll., Huntingdon, Pa., 1992—. Bd. dirs. Carlisle (Pa.) Econ. Devel. Ctr., 1985-89; vice-chmn., bd. dirs. Marathon House Providence, 1982-84; vol. Big Bros., Springfield, Mass., Madison, Wis., 1970-82. Lt. U.S. Army, 1971-72. Democrat. Episcopalian. Home: 2208 Highland Ave Huntingdon PA 16652 Office: Juniata Coll Founder's Hall Huntingdon PA 16652

DUER, ELLEN ANN DAGON, anesthesiologist; b. Balt., Feb. 3, 1936; d. Emmett Paul and Annie (Sollers) Dagon; m. Lyle Jordan Millan IV, Dec. 21, 1963; children: Lyle Jordan V, Elizabeth Lyle, Ann Sheridan Worthington.; m. T. Marshall Duer, Jr., Aug. 23, 1985. A.B., George Washington U., 1959; M.D., U. Md., 1964; postgrad., Johns Hopkins U., 1965-68. Intern Union Meml. Hosp., Balt., 1964-65; resident anesthesiology Johns Hopkins Hosp., Balt., 1965-68, fellow in surgery, 1965-68; practice medicine specializing in anesthesiology Balt., 1968—; faculty Church Home and Hosp., Balt., 1969—; attending staff Union Meml. Hosp., Church Home and Hosp., Frankling Sq. Hosp., Children's Hosp., James Lawrence Kernan Hosp., Balt., 1982—; co-chief anesthesiology James Kernan Hosp., 1983—, med. dir. out-patient surgery dept., 1987—; mem. med. exec. com. Kernan Hosp., 1988—; affiliate cons. emergency room Church Home and Hosp., Balt., 1969—, mem. med. audit and utilizaions com., 1970-72, mem. emergency and ambulatory care com., 1973-74, chief emergency dept., 1973-74; cons. anesthesiologist Md. State Penitentiary, 1971; fellow in critical care medicine Md. Inst. Emergency Medicine, 1975-76; mem. infection control com. U. Md. Hosp., 1975—; instr. anesthesiology U. Md. Sch. Medicine, 1975—; staff anesthesiologist Mercy Hosp., 1978—, audit com., 1979-80, 82; asst. prof. anesthegiology U. Md. Med. Sch., 1989—; mem. med. exec. com. Kernan Hosp., 1990—, v.p. 1990, chief of staff, 1992—. Mem. AMA, Am. Coll. Emergency Physicians, Met. Emergency Dept. Heads, Am., Md. Socs. Anaesthesiologists, Balt. County Med. Soc., Med. and Chior Faculty Md., Chiurgical Soc., Internat. Congress Anaesthesiologists, Internat. Anaesthesia Research Soc., Am., L'Hirondelle Club, Annapolis Yacht Club, Chesapeake Bay Yacht Racing Assn. Episcopalian. Address: 1011 Wagner Rd Ruxton MD 21204

DUERDEN, JOHN H., sports apparel company executive; b. 1941. With Xerox Corp., 1970-88; pres., internat. dir. Reebok Internat. Ltd., from 1988, v.p., 1989-90, sr. v.p., 1990-91; pres., CEO Reebok Brands div. worldwide, Stoughton, Mass., 1991—. Office: Reebok Internat Ltd 100 Technology Dr Stoughton MA 02072*

DUERR, DIANNE MARIE, physical education educator, professional sports medicine consultant; b. Buffalo, July 14, 1945; d. Robert John and Aileen Louise (Scherer) D. BS in health and phys. edn., SUNY, Brockport, 1967; cert., SUNY, Oswego, 1982; postgrad., Canisius Coll., 1970-71. Cert.

tchr., N.Y. Tchr. North Syracuse (N.Y.) Sch. Dist., 1967—; cons. sport medicine dept. orthopedic surgery Dept. Orthopedic Surgery SUNY Health Sci. Ctr., Syracuse, 1982—; creator Inst. for Sports Medicine and Human Performance SUNY Health Sci. Ctr., Syracuse, 1988; coord. scholastic sports injury reporting system project SUNY, 1985—. Author: SSIRS Pilot Study Report, 1987, SSIRS Fall Study Report, 1988, SHASIRS Report, 1991; creator Scholastic Sports Injury Reporting System, 1985, Scholastic Head and Spine Injury Reporting System, 1989. Co-chmn. Sports Medicine USA, Amateur Athletic Union, Nat. Jr. Olympic Games, Syracuse, 1987, vol. Sports Medicine Empire State Games, Syracuse, 1987, Sports Medicine N.Y. Sr. Games, 1990-92; active Girl Scouts U.S. Mem. Am. Coll. Sports Medicine, United Univ. Profs., Am. Alliance Health, Phys. Edn., Recreation and Dance, Am. Fedn. Tchrs., N.Y. United Tchrs., North Syracuse Tchrs. Assn., N.Y. Assn. Health, Phys. Edn., Recreation and Dance. Home: 418 Buffington Rd Syracuse NY 13224-2208 Office: SUNY Dept Orthopedic Surgery 550 Harrison Ctr Syracuse NY 13202-3054

DUERR, WERNER ALBERT, vocational school educator; b. Stuttgart, Germany, Apr. 25, 1934; came to U.S., 1953; s. Otto and Klara (Schick) D.; m. Eleanor Schmid, Feb. 20, 1989 (div.); children: Erich W., Rolf A.; m. Ann Irene Dietrich, May 12, 1990. BS, Temple U., 1971; MA summa cum laude, West Chester U., 1975. Tchr. carpentry Coatesville (Pa.) Area Sch. Dist., 1961-67; tchr. carpentry, cabinet making Chester County (Pa.) IU 24, 1967-92; travel cons. Chester County Travel Agy., Exton, Pa., 1973—. Mem. Pa. State Edn. Assn., Am. Vocat. Assn., German Soc. Pa.

DUFF, JAMES HENRY, museum director, environmental administrator; b. Pitts., Oct. 11, 1943; s. James Sylvester and Virginia (Henry) D.; m. Sally Kathryn Tredwell, Sept. 14, 1963; children: Abigail Margaret, Jessica Lauren. BA, Washington and Jefferson Coll., 1965; MA, U. Mass., 1970. Teaching asst. U. Mass., Amherst, 1965-66; dir. Mus. of Hudson Highlands, Cornwall-on-Hudson, N.Y., 1966-73, Brandywine River Mus., Chadds Ford, Pa., 1973—; exec. dir. Brandywine Conservancy, Chadds Ford, 1976—; cons. N.Y. State Council on Arts, 1970-72; panel mem. Pa. Council on Arts, 1976-79, 83-85; mem. Nat. Mus. Services Bd., 1986—. Author: The Western World of N. C. Wyeth, 1980, Landscapes, Still Lifes and Portraits by N. C. Wyeth, 1982, An American Vision, 1987; contbr. articles on mus. programs to profl. jours. Trustee Wyeth Endowment for Am. Art, 1986—. With U.S. Army, 1967-69. Mem. Mid-Atlantic Assn. Museums (pres. 1983-85), Assn. Art Mus. Dirs., Am. Assn. Mus. (coun. 1983-88). Home: PO Box 297 Chadds Ford PA 19317-0297 Office: Brandywine River Mus PO Box 141 Chadds Ford PA 19317-0141

DUFFEY, DICK, nuclear engineer, educator; b. Wabash County, Ind., Aug. 26, 1917; s. Glen and Kate (Parker) D. BS, Purdue U., 1939; MS, U. Iowa, 1940; PhD, U. Md., 1956. Registered profl. engr., D.C., Md. Engr. Union Carbide, Buffalo, 1940-42, U.S. AEC, Washington, 1946-54, MIT, Cambridge, 1954; prof. engring. U. Md., College Park, 1954—. Contbr. over 100 articles to profl. jours. With U.S. Army, 1942-46. Grantee AEC. Office: U Md Dept Engring College Park MD 20742

DUFFEY, JOSEPH DANIEL, university president; b. Huntington, W.Va., July 1, 1932; s. Joseph I. and Ruth (Wilson) D.; m. Anne Wexler, 1974; children: Michael and David Duffey, Danny and David Wexler. BA, Marshall U., Huntington, 1954; STM, Yale U., 1963; BD, Andover Newton Theol. Sch., 1958; PhD, Hartford Sem. Found., 1969; LHD, CUNY, 1978, U. Cin., 1978, U. Mass., 1991; LittD, Dickinson Coll., Pa., 1978, Centre Coll., Ky., 1977, Gonzaga U., Wash., 1980, Monmouth Coll., 1980, CCNY; LLD, Amherst Coll., Bethany Coll., Austin Coll.; LittD, Alderson-Broadus Coll., Adelphi U., Central Fla. Asst. prof. Hartford (Conn.) Sem., 1960-63; assoc. prof. and dir. Center for Urban Studies, 1965-70; fellow Harvard U. Kennedy Sch. Govt., 1971; adj. prof. and fellow Calhoun Coll., Yale U., 1971-73; exec. officer AAUP, 1974-77; asst. sec. for edn. and cultural affairs Dept. State, 1977; chmn. NEH, 1978-81; chancellor U. Mass., Amherst, 1982—, pres., 1990-91; pres. Am. U., Washington, 1991—; mem. U.S. del. 20th and 21st Gen Confs., UNESCO, 1978, 80; mem. exec. com. Nat. Council on Competitiveness Govt. and Industry Univ. Panel, Nat. Acad. Scis.; bd. dirs. Bay Bank of Springfield (Mass.). Contbr. numerous articles to profl. jours. Bd. dirs. Woodrow Wilson Internat. Ctr. for Scholars, East-West Ctr., Western Mass. Area Devel. Corp., Jewish Theol. Sem. Libr., Springfield Symphony. Decorated Order of Leopold IV (Belgium); recipient Tree of Life award Nat. Jewish Fund, 1987; Rockefeller fellow, 1966-68. Mem. Council on Fgn. Relations, Century Assn. Clubs: Cosmos, Fed. City (Washington); Century (N.Y.); Colony. Office: Am U Office of Pres 4400 Massachusetts Ave NW Washington DC 20016-8001

DUFFY, KEVIN THOMAS, federal judge; b. N.Y.C., Jan. 10, 1933; s. Patrick John and Mary (McGarrell) D.; m. Irene Krumeich, Nov. 9, 1957; children: Kevin Thomas, Irene Moira, Gavin Edward, Patrick Giles. A.B., Fordham Coll., 1954, J.D., 1958. Bar: N.Y. 1958. Clk. to chief circuit judge N.Y.C., 1955-58; asst. chief criminal div. U.S. Atty.'s Office, N.Y.C., 1958-61; assoc. Whitman, Ransom & Coulson, N.Y.C., 1961-66; partner Gordon & Gordon, N.Y.C., 1966-69; regional adminstr. SEC, N.Y.C., 1969-72; judge U.S. Dist. Ct. So. Dist. N.Y., 1972—; adj. prof. securities law Bklyn. Law Sch., 1975-80; prof. trial advocacy NYU, 1982-84, Pace Law Sch., 1984-85. Author: Cross-Examination of Witnesses: The Litigator's Puzzle, 1990, Impeachment of Witnesses, 1990. Recipient Achievement in Law award Fordham Coll. Alumni Assn., 1976, Alumni Gold medal Fordham Law Sch., 1984. Mem. ABA, Am. Bar Assn.N.Y. State, Westchester County bar assns., Assn. of Bar of City of N.Y., Fed. Bar Council (trustee 1970-72), Fordham Law Sch. Alumni Assn. (trustee 1969—, v.p.). Clubs: Adventurers (N.Y.C.), Merchants (N.Y.C.). Office: US Dist Ct US Courthouse 40 Foley Sq New York NY 10007-1502*

DUFFY, MARTIN EDWARD, management consultant, economist; b. Fall River, Mass., May 24, 1940; s. Arthur Louis and Edna Marie (Cunneen) D.; m. Irene Patricia Daley, Aug. 24, 1968 (div. Jan. 1980); 1 child, Kathryn; m. Priscilla Claire Stieff, May 14, 1988; 1 child, Brianna. BS in History, BSEE, Tufts U., 1963; MBA, U. Pa., 1967, PhD (abd), 1973. Asst. dean U. Pa., 1967-71; asst. dir. Fels Ctr., U. Pa., 1971-73; exec. asst. to fin. v.p. Harvard U., Cambridge, Mass., 1973-75; v.p. Data Resources, Lexington, Mass., 1975-84; v.p., gen. mgr. MRCA Info. Svcs., Cambridge, 1984-86; pres. The Perseus Group, Boston, 1986—; planning com. White House Conf. on Aging, Washington, 1981; cons. La. in 2001, Baton Rouge, 1982; lectr. in field. Author: The Elderly in Future Economy, 1981. Lt. USN, 1963-65. Mem. Am. Econs. Assn., Cambridge Sports Union, Tufts U. Alumni Assn. (pres. 1985, exec. com. 1982-87, mem. coun. 1978—), Nat. Bus. Travelers Assn. (bd. dirs. ednl. com. 1988—). Roman Catholic.

DUFFY, ROBERT ALOYSIUS, aeronautical engineer; b. Buck Run, Pa., Sept. 9, 1921; s. Joseph Albert and Jane Veronica (Archer) D.; m. Elizabeth Reed Orr, Aug. 19, 1945 (dec.); children: Michael Gordon, Barclay Robert (dec.), Marian Orr (dec.), Judith Elizabeth, Patricia Archer. B.S. in Aero. Engring., Ga. Inst. Tech., 1951. Commd. 2d lt. U.S. Army, 1942; commd. U.S. Air Force, advanced through grades to brig. gen., 1967; service in C.Z., Morocco, Algeria, Tunisia, Sicily, Italy, Vietnam; vice comdr. USAF Space and Missile Systems Orgn., Los Angeles, 1970-71; ret., 1971; v.p., dir. Draper Lab. div. MIT, Cambridge, Mass., 1971-73; pres., chief exec. officer Charles Stark Draper Lab., Inc., 1973-87, dir., 1973-91, dir. emeritus, 1991—. Contbr. articles to profl. jours. Decorated Disting. Service medal, Legion of Merit; recipient Thomas D. White award Nat. Geog. Soc., 1970. Fellow AIAA; mem. NAE, Internat. Acad. Astronautics, Inst. Navigation (Thurlow award 1964, pres. 1976-77), Air Force Assn., Algonquin Club, Tau Beta Pi. Home: 115 Indian Pipe Ln Concord MA 01742-4719 Office: Charles Stark Draper Lab 555 Technology Sq Cambridge MA 02139-3563

DUFOUR, RENE ANDRE, chef; b. Denver, Nov. 19, 1949; s. Rene F. and Ellen (Gray) D. AOS in Culinary Arts summa cum laude, Johnson and Wales U., Providence, 1992. Cert. sanitarian Mass. Restaurant Assn., Am. Hotel and Motel Assn. Night chef L'Amitie, Longmeadow, Mass., 1983-85; sous-chef Lord Jeffrey Inn, Amherst, Mass., 1985-86; chef, owner Pastafina, Northampton, Mass., 1987; sous-chef Springfield Country Club, West Springfield, Mass., 1986-87, 88-91; intern Harvard Club, Boston, 1991—. Mem. Alpha Beta Kappa Honor Soc. Home: 666 Elm St Mansfield MA 02048

DUGAS, RENE LOUIS, SR., retired photographer; b. Taftville, Conn., Sept. 27, 1909; s. Prime Amedore and Hosanna (Lavallee) D.; m. Rosamonde Couture, July 11, 1936 (dec. June 1946); children: Elaine Rosamonde, Rene Louis; m. Mary Rita Lorenzetti, Feb. 9, 1959 (dec. Jan. 1975). Assoc., Mohegan Community Coll., 1985; student, Winona Sch. Photography, 1954, 57, 60. Owner, operator Dugas Studio, Taftville, 1935-81; knotting machine operator Ponemah Mills, Taftville, 1925-29; velvet twister J. B. Martin Co., Taftville, 1929-36; milling machine operator Pratt & Whitney Aircraft, Willimantic, Conn., 1941; sci. photographer Columbia Univ. Div. of War Rsch., New London, Conn., 1941-44; photographic engr. Templetone Radio Corp., New London, 1944-46; speaker photography Conv. Conn. N.Y., N.H. & Assns., 1940-75; speaker historian N.H. Assn. Mohegan Coll., Concord, 1985—; speaker genealogist N.H. Assn. Mohegan Coll., 1985—. Author: (books) History of the Wequonnoc Movement, 1942, Taftville Marriages and Data, 1990, (booklets) Traveling the U.S. During the Great Depression, 1988, Motoring Through Mexico in 1950, 1988; contbr. articles to jours. State rep. Conn. Gen. Assembly, Hartford, 1947-49, 57-59; mem. Republican Town Com., Norwich, 1947-75; v.p. 5th Dist. Better Govt. Com., Taftville, 1947-77; mem. Norwich (Conn.) Community Devel. Adv. Com., 1975. Recipient 12 awards N.E. Photographers Assn. Mem. Conn. Profl. Photographers, Explorer Travel Club (exec. com.), K.C., Elks. Roman Catholic. Home: 41 Hunters Ave Taftville CT 06380

DUGGAN, EDWARD JAMES, metal company executive; b. Newark, Aug. 12, 1931; s. Edward Lawrence and Monica (Hopper) D.; m. Janet Marie Dwyer, Nov. 29, 1958 (dec. 1988); children: James, Thomas, Timothy, Maureen, Kathleen, Christopher, Melissa; m. Christina Coyle, Aug. 17, 1991. BA in Philosophy, U. Notre Dame, 1953; MBA, Seton Hall U., 1970. Cons. Duggan & Duggan, Newark, 1958-66; exec. v.p. Am. Aluminum Co., Mountainside, N.J., 1966—, also bd. dirs.; bd. dirs. Seal-Spout Corp., Liberty Corner, N.J.; conductor seminars in field. Leader, mem. com. Boy Scouts Am., Berkeley Heights, N.J., 1968-80; coach baseball and softball PAL, Berkeley Heights, 1970-75; mem. Union County Employers Legis. Com., bd. dirs., 1980-88. 1st lt. USAF, 1954-56. Mem. Indsl. Mgmt. Assn. (bd. dirs. 1980-85), Union County C. of C. (bd. dirs. 1979-80), New Club (chmn. 1976-86). Roman Catholic. Home: 26 Great Hills Rd Short Hills NJ 07078 Office: Am Aluminum Co 230 Sheffield St Mountainside NJ 07092

DUGGAN, EDWARD PATRICK, director career development, economics educator; b. Washington, Dec. 31, 1945; s. Gerald Charles and Mary Teresa (Bonanno) D.; m. Sharon Anne Ryan, Aug. 5, 1967; children: Lisa Maureen, Jeffry Ryan. BA (with high honors), U. Md., 1967; MA, U. Wis., 1969, U. Wis., 1970; PhD, U. Wis., 1972. Asst. prof. econs. Thomas More Coll., Ft. Mitchell, Ky., 1971-75, Dickinson Coll., Carlisle, Pa., 1975-79; dir. career devel. Goucher Coll., Towson, Md., 1979—; adj. prof. econs. and mgmt., Goucher Coll. Author: (book) The Impact of Industrialization on an Urban Labor Market, 1972, 1985; contbr. articles to profl. jours. Trustee Md. chpt. Nat. Multiple Sclerosis Soc., Towson, 1983—; active mgmt. com. State of Md. Tech. Assistance Program, Balt., 1989—. Named Individual of Yr. Nat. Multiple Sclerosis Soc. of Md., 1986-87, Family of the Yr. 1989-90. Mem. Econ. History Assn., Mid. Atlantic Placement Assn. (com. chair 1986-89), Chesapeake Assn. Econ. Educators (past sec., v.p., pres. 1987-89), Balt. Econ. Soc. (gov., treas. 1986—), Md. C. of C., Balt. County C. of C. (com. chair 1983-84). Home: 1341 Kenton Rd Baltimore MD 21234-6012 Office: Goucher Coll Baltimore MD 21204

DUGGAN, EUGENE JOSEPH, surgeon, podiatrist; b. Mount Vernon, N.Y., Jan. 4, 1933; s. Eugene Joseph and Florence (Purcell) D.; m. Margaret McMahon, Apr. 23, 1979. BS, St. Peter's Coll., 1954; D of Surg. Chiropody, Temple U., 1961, D of Podiatric Medicine, 1961. 1st lt. U.S.A. Chem. Corps, 1955-57; podiatrist Middletown, N.J., 1962—. Police surgeon Middletown (N.J.) Police Dept., 1967-69; mem. Kiwanis, 1963-67. Recipient Community Svc. award Middletown Twp. Police, 1983, Citizen's award VFW, 1986, Community Betterment award, 1979, Svc. award Bayshore Sr. Citizens, 1987. Mem. Am. Legion, Podiatric Med. Soc., Am. Ambulatory Foot Surgeons, Royal Soc. Health, N.J. State Police Assn., Am. Fedn. Musicians, Spl. Police Assn. Monmouth County. Republican. Roman Catholic. Office: Eugene J Duggan 230 State Hwy #35 Red Bank NJ 07701

DUGGAN, ROBERT MAURICE, administrator; b. N.Y.C., Nov. 23, 1939; s. Maurice Ignatius and Alice (Whitty) D.; m. Dianne Connelly, 1968 (div. 1981); children: Blaize, Jade; m. Susan Karen Elliott, June 10, 1984. Ma in Theology, St. Joseph's Sem., 1964; MA in Edn., NYU, 1970; MA, Coll. Traditional Acupuncture, 1973. Diplomate Nat. Commn. Cert. Acupuncturists. Priest Archdiocese of N.Y., 1964-68; acupuncture practitioner Coll. Traditional Chinese Acupuncture, Oxford, England, 1972-74, Ctr. Traditional Acupuncture, Columbia, Md., 1975—; registrar Coll. Traditional Chinese Acupuncture, Leamington Spa, England, 1973-80; pres. Traditional Acupuncture Inst., Columbia, 1980—; chmn. Acupuncture Adv. Coun., Md., 1982—; officer Nat. Coun. Acupuncture Schs. and Colls., Washington, 1983-89. Contbr. articles to profl. jours. Mem. Am. Assn. Acupuncture and Oriental Medicine (bd. dirs. 1983-87, commr. nat. accreditation commn. 1988—), Md. Acupuncture Soc. Office: Traditional Acupuncture Ins Am City Bldg Ste 100 Columbia MD 21044

DUGMORE, EDWARD, painter; b. Hartford, Conn., Feb. 20, 1915; s. Walter and Ellen (Spragg) D.; m. Edith Oslund, Aug. 20, 1938; 1 child, Linda Carol. One-man shows include Stable Gallery, N.Y.C., 1953, 54, 56, Holland-Goldowsky Gallery, Chgo., 1959, Howard Wise Gallery, N.Y.C., 1960, 61, 63, Des Moines Art Center, 1972, Green Mountain Gallery, N.Y.C., 1971, 73, Carlson Gallery, San Francisco, 1990, Manny Silverman Gallery, L.A., 1991; 2-man shows Anita Shapolsky Gallery, N.Y.C., 1991; group exhbns. include Pitts. Internat. Exhbn. of Contemporary Painting, Carnegie Inst., 1955, Am. Abstract Expressionists and Imagists, Guggenheim Mus., 1961, 65th Ann, Art Inst. Chgo., 1962 (M.V. Kohnstamm award), Painting and Sculpture in Calif.-The Modern Era, San Francisco Mus. Art, 1976-77, Nat. Fine Arts Collection, Washington, 1975, 77, Kansas City Art Inst., Mo., 1982, Vintage N.Y. One Penn Plaza, 1983-84, The Ingber Gallery, 1985, Vanderwoude Tananbaum Gallery, 1989, Anita Shapolsky Gallery, N.Y.C., 1989, Carlson Gallery, San Francisco, 1990, Manny Silverman Gallery, L.A., 1991; represented in permanent collections Albright-Knox Art Gallery, Buffalo, Walker Art Center, Mpls., Des Moines Art Center, Weatherspoon Art Gallery, Greensboro, N.C., Kresge Art Center, East Lansing, Mich., Ciba-Geigy Corp., N.Y.C., Mobil Oil Corp., Arlington, Va., Hirshhorn Mus. and Sculpture Garden, Washington, 1987. Served with USMC, 1943-44. Recipient award Am. Acad. and Inst. Arts and Letters, 1980, Ingram Merrill Found. award for lifetime's work as a painter, 1992; grantee Nat. Endowment Arts, 1976, fellow, 1985-86; Guggenheim fellow, 1966-67. Address: 118 W 27th St New York NY 10001

DUGUNDJI, JOHN, aeronautical engineer; b. N.Y.C., Oct. 25, 1925; s. Basile and Rosa (Finale) D.; m. Wraye Polkey, July 25, 1965; children—Elenna Rose, Elisa Anthe. B.A.E., N.Y. U., 1944; M.S. in Aero. Engring, M.I.T., 1948, Sc.D. in Aero. Engring, 1951. Research engr. Grumman Aircraft Co., Bethpage, N.Y., 1948-49; dynamics engr. Republic Aviation Corp., Farmingdale, N.Y., 1951-56; research asso. M.I.T., 1956-57, asst. prof. aero. engring., 1957-62, asso. prof., 1962-70, prof., 1970—. Served with USN, 1944-46. Mem. AIAA, Sigma Xi, Tau Beta Pi. Greek Orthodox. Home: 39 Albert Ave Belmont MA 02178-4203 Office: MIT Dept Aeros And Astronautics Cambridge MA 02139

DUHAIME, ARTHUR JOSEPH, III, manufacturing company executive; b. Norwich, Conn., July 18, 1951; s. Arthur Joseph Jr. and Martha (Armenakas) D.; m. Susan Patry, Oct. 4, 1975; children: Jessica, Susan, Joshua Patry. BSBA, U. Conn., 1973, MBA, 1979. CPIM. Mgr. systems and procedures Simmons Precision Products, Vergennes, Vt., 1980-81; materials mgr. Gerber Systems Tech., South Windsor, Conn., 1981-85; cons. Peat Marwick, Hartford, Conn., 1985-87; gen. mgr. Turbine Components Corp., Branford, Conn., 1987—; adj. prof. ops. mgmt. Eastern Conn. State U., Willimantic, Conn., 1985-87. Mem. Am. Prodn. and Inventory Control Soc. (bd. dirs., pres. 1988, speaker 1988—). Home: 219 Briggs Rd Lebanon CT 06249-1316

DUHAMEL, RAYMOND CONRAD, biochemist, researcher; b. New Bedford, Mass., Oct. 4, 1942; s. Donat Alfred and Louise Vitaline (Saulnier) D.; m. Louise Pauline Gardner, Apr. 20, 1964; children: Marc, Michael, Matthew. BS, Stonehill Coll., North Easton, Mass., 1963; MS, Boston Coll., 1969; PhD, U. Mass., 1977. Assoc. prof. Massasoit Community Coll., Brockton, Mass., 1968-72; rsch. assoc. dept. pharmacology U. Ariz., Tucson, 1976-81, rsch. asst. prof., 1981-85, rsch. assoc. prof., 1985-86; project scientist Bard Vascular Systems div. C.R. Bard, Inc., Billerica, Mass., 1986-88, staff scientist, 1988-89, rsch. mgr., 1989—. Contbr. articles to profl. jours. and chpts. to books; patentee on vascular prosthesis. Recipient Nat. Rsch. Svc. award NIH, 1979. Mem. AAAS, Soc. for Biomaterials, Am. Soc. for Artificial Internal Organs, Am. Soc. for Biochemistry and Molecular Biology, Sigma Xi. Home: 8 Woodbine St Chelmsford MA 01824-2444 Office: CR Bard Vascular Systems 129 Concord Rd PO Box M Billerica MA 01821

DUKAKIS, MICHAEL STANLEY, former governor of Massachusetts; b. Brookline, Mass., Nov. 3, 1933; s. Panos and Euterpe (Boukis) D.; m. Katharine (Kitty) Dukakis, 1963; children: John, Andrea, Kara. BA, Swarthmore Coll., 1955; LLB, Harvard U., 1960. Bar: Mass. 1960. Mem. Hill and Barlow, Boston, 1960-74; gov. State of Mass., Boston, 1975-79, 83-91; Dem. nominee for pres. U.S., 1988; Mem. Mass. Ho. of Reps., 1962-70; moderator pub. TV program The Advocates 1970-73; lectr., dir. Intergovtl. Studies, John F. Kennedy Sch. Govt., Harvard U., 1979-82; former chmn. Indsl. and Entrepreneurial Economy Com., Policy Commn. Dem. Nat. Com.; former chmn. New Eng. Gov.'s Conf.; former chmn. econ. devel. com., former chmn. Coalition of N.E. Govs.; tchr. Fla. Atlantic U., Boca Raton, 1992; tchr. govt. Northeastern U., Boston, 1992—. With U.S. Army, 1955-57, Korea. Mem. Nat. Gov.'s Assn. (vice chmn. com. on econ. devel. and tech. innovation 1984, chmn. com. on econ. devel. and tech. innovative 1985-87, co-chair task force on jobs, growth and competitiveness, exec. com. 1987), Dem. Govs.' Assn. (chmn. 1986-87). Office: Northeastern Univ Dept Pol Sci Meserve Hall Boston MA 02115*

DUKE, CHARLES RICHARD, academic dean; b. West Stewartstown, N.H., July 6, 1940; s. George Tunicliffe and Evelyn Agnes (Murray) D.; m. Leona Ruth Hubbard, June 1, 1983. BE, Plymouth (N.H.) State Coll., 1962; MA, Middlebury (Vt.) Coll., 1968; PhD, Duke U., 1972. Tchr. English, head dept. Sunapee (N.H.) High Sch., 1962-68; prof. English Plymouth State Coll., 1968-78, Murray (Ky.) State U., 1978-84; prof., head dept. secondary edn. Utah State U., Logan, 1984-89; dean Coll. Edn. and Human Svcs. Clarion (Pa.) U., 1989—; dir. West Ky. Writing Project, 1980-84; co-dir. Utah Writing Project, 1984-89, Clarion U. Student Literacy Corps, 1990—. Author Creative Dramatics and English Teaching, 1974, Writing through Sequence, 1983, Strategies for Teaching, 1987; contbr. articles to profl. jours; editor Exercise Exchange, 1979—. Am. Studies fellow Coe Found., 1964; recipient Alumni Outstanding Svc. award Plymouth State Coll., 1977. Mem. ASCD, Internat. Reading Assn., Nat. Coun. Tchrs. English, Am. Assn. Colls. Tchr. Edn., Assn. Tchr. Educators, Phi Delta Kappa. Office: Clarion U Office Dean Clarion PA 16214

DUKE, GEORGE WESLEY, financial executive; b. Nashville, Dec. 27, 1953; s. Harold Wesley and Justine Hope (Perry) D.; 1 child, Elizabeth. BBA, Coll. William and Mary, 1976; M Taxation, Va. Commonwealth U., 1981; MBA, Darden Sch., 1983; MEd, Vanderbilt U., 1989; M of Liberal Arts, Johns Hopkins U., 1992. CPA, Va. Acct. KPMG Peat Marwick, Richmond, Va., 1976-81; v.p. Jacques-Miller, Nashville, 1983-86; sr. v.p. Alex Brown Kleinwort Benson, Balt., 1986—. Mem. AICPA, STOR, Nat. Speakers Assn. Office: Alex Brown Kleinwort Benson 2 N Charles St Baltimore MD 21201-3754

DUKE, MICHAEL CHARLES, health care facility executive; b. Chester, Pa., Apr. 11, 1956; s. Paul Robert and Cecelia Mary (McCann) D.; m. Ann DelGrippo, June 26, 1982; children: Claire Marie, Michael John, Martha Cecelia, Elizabeth Ann. BA, Georgetown U., 1978, JD, 1981. Bar: Pa. 1981. Assoc. Fronefield & de Furia, Media, Pa., 1982-85; gen. counsel Medscan, Inc., Phila., 1985-87; assoc. Sebastianelli & Tsoules, Paoli, Pa., 1987-89; v.p., gen. counsel Renal Treatment Ctrs., Inc., Berwyn, Pa., 1989—. Mem. Nat. Health Lawyers Assn., Pa. Bar Assn., Healthcare Fin. Mgmt. Assn. Office: Renal Treatment Ctrs Inc 1180 W Swedesford Rd Berwyn PA 19312-1076

DUKER, NAHUM JOHANAN, pathologist; b. N.Y.C., Oct. 27, 1942; s. Abraham and Lillian (Sandrow) D.; m. Naomi Maisel, June 13, 1972 (div.); children: Eli Avishai, Joshua Jair, Jonathan Jacob, Ezra Avishai; m. Vita Khayyat, Apr. 12, 1992. BS, U. Ill., 1962; MD, U. Ill., Chgo., 1966. Diplomate pathologic anatomy and clin. pathology Am. Bd. Pathology. Intern Bellevue Hosp., N.Y.C., 1966-67; resident NYU Med. Sch., N.Y.C., 1970-76, instr., 1976-77; asst. prof. Temple U. Med. Sch., Phila., 1977-82, assoc. prof., 1982-87, prof., pathology, 1987—. Contbr. articles to profl. jours. Capt. U.S. Army, 1967-69. Recipient Career Devel. award, Nat. Cancer Inst., 1983. Mem. Agudath Israel of Phila. (treas. 1984—). Republican. Jewish. Office: Temple U Med Sch 3400 N Broad St Philadelphia PA 19140-5196

DUKES, REBECCA WEATHERS (BECKY DUKES), musician, singer, songwriter; b. Durham, N.C., Nov. 21, 1934; d. Elmer Dewey Weathers and Martha Rebecca (Kimbrough) Weathers-Hall; m. Charles Aubrey Dukes Jr., Dec. 20, 1955; children: Aurelia Ann, Charles Weathers, David Lloyd. BA, Duke U., 1956. Lic. elem. sch. tchr. Tchr. Durham City Schs., 1956-57; sec. USMC, Arlington, Va., 1957-58; tchr. Arlington County Schs., 1958-59; office mgr. Dukes and Kooken, Landover, Md., 1976; musical performer Washington and various locations, Va., Md., 1982—; chmn. semi-finalist awards event Marian Anderson Internat. Vocal Arts Competition, 1991. Vocal student Todd Duncan; pianist, vocalist Back Alley Restaurant Lounge, 1982, also various hotels, lounges, 1982—; original program, A Life Cycle in Song, presented throughout mid-Atlantic states and Washington; full operatic solo recital, 1983; featured performer benefit for Nat. Symphony Orch.; frequent performer pvt. functions, athletic, civic, religious and cultural events including appearances at Capitol Ctr., Cole Field House, George Washington U., Smith Ctr.; operatic solo concert with pianist Glenn Sales, 1985; benefit appearance U. Md. Concert Series, 1986, 87; holds copyrights for over 90 original songs including Between the Lovin' and the Leavin', Covers of My Mind, Gentle Thoughts (lead song Nat. Capitol Area Composers Series), Headin' Home Again, I Would Like to Be Reborn, Miss You, Tears, You Played a Part in My Life; author: (poems) Pottery. Pres. Nat. Capitol Law League, Washington, 1976-77; pres. women's group, deacon Riverdale Presby. Ch., Hyattsville, Md., 1968-70; chmn. event honoring wives of Supreme Ct. justices, 1981; mem. women's com. Nat. Symphony, 1980—; chmn. awards event Marian Anderson Internat. Vocal Arts Competition, 1991. Recipient Friend of Yr. award Md. Summer Inst. for Creative & Performing Arts U. Md., 1986; named hon. trustee Prince George's (Md.) Arts Council, 1984—. Mem. Songwriter's Assn. Washington, William Preston Few Assn. of Duke U. (pres. couns., exec. bd. of ann. fund.), Internat. Platform Assn. Republican. Clubs: Founders of Duke U.; Pres.' of U. Md.; Univ. (Balt.). Home and Office: 7111 Pony Trail Ln Hyattsville MD 20782-1031

DULANSKI, GARY MICHAEL, electrical engineer, educator, consultant; b. Hornell, N.Y., Nov. 15, 1955; s. Raymond Steven and Hattie Blanch (Wonsiewicz) D.; m. Robin Lynoar Reichert, Aug. 12, 1978. AAS in Elec. tech., Erie Community Coll., Buffalo, 1975; BSEE, SUNY, Buffalo, 1978. Applications engr. Lutron Electronics Co., Coopersburg, Pa., 1978-86; sales engr. Warshaw Electric Co., Jamaica, N.Y., 1986—; prof. Parsons Sch. Design, N.Y.C., 1992—; com. mem. ednl. seminar com. Lightfair, tradeshow, 1991—. Contbr. articles to profl. publs. Lector St. Lukes Ch., Long Valley, N.J., 1990—. Mem. Illuminating Engring. Soc. (residential lighting com. 1985-92, bd. dirs. 1988—).

DULAUX, RUSSELL FREDERICK (RUSSELL FREDERICK LAUX), lawyer; b. West New York, N.J., Dec. 30, 1918; s. Frederick and Theresa A. (Noble) L.; m. Ann deFriedberg, Aug. 22, 1962 (dec.); m. Eva DeLuca, Dec. 24, 1985. Student, Pace Inst., 1938-40, Fordham U., 1946-48; LLB summa cum laude, N.Y. Law Sch., 1950; postgrad., Pace Coll., 1951, Columbia U., 1955. Bar: N.Y. 1951, U.S. Dist. (so. dist.) N.Y. 1951, U.S. Ct. Appeals (2d cir.) 1951, U.S. Ct. Claims 1952, U.S. Tax Ct. 1952, U.S. Dist. Ct. (ea. dist.) N.Y. 1953, U.S. Ct. Customs and Patent Appeals 1963, U.S. Ct. Mil. Appeals 1963, U.S. Supreme Ct. 1963. Mem. staff N.Y. State Dept. Law, Richmond County Investigations, 1951-54, N.Y. State Exec. Dept. Office of Commr. of Investigations, 1954-57; comptroller-counsel Odyssey Produc-

tions, Inc., 1957-59; ptnr. Ryan, Murray & Laux, N.Y.C., 1951-61, Ryan & Laux, N.Y.C., 1961; pvt. practice N.Y.C., 1961—. Served with AUS, 1940-46; capt. JAG, vet. corps. of arty. State of N.Y., 1975-92, maj., 1992—; spl. agt. counter intelligence corps and security intelligence corps; col. U.S. Army. Recipient Eloy Alfaro Grand Cross Republic of Panama. Mem. NATAS, Bronx County Bar Assn. (Townsend Wandell Gold medal), Met. Opera Guild, Internat. Platform Assn., VFW (adjutant Floyd Gibbons Post 500), Order of Lafayette, Sons Union Vets. Civil War, Soc. Am. Wars, Nat. Sojourners, Heroes of '76, Navy League, St. Andrews Soc. N.Y., St. George Soc. N.Y., Soc. Friendly Sons St. Patrick, English Speaking Union, Asia Soc., China Inst. Am., Army and Navy Union USA, Am. Legion (past post comdr. admen's post 209), Mid Manhattan C. of C., Res. Officers Assn. U.S. (col.), Delta Theta Phi, Lambs Club, Knights Hospitaller of St. John of Jerusalem, Grand St. Boys' Club, Soldiers' Club, Sailors' and Airmen's Club, Order Ea. Star, Masons (past comdr. N.Y. Masonic War Vets), Shriners, Knights of Malta, Knights of St. George, Sovereign Mil. Order of Temple of Jerusalem. Presbyterian. Office: 1040 First Ave Ste # 109 New York NY 10022

DULCHINOS, PETER, lawyer; b. Chicopee Falls, Mass., Feb. 2, 1935; s. George and Angeline D.; m. Thalia Verros, Aug. 28, 1960; children: Matthew George, Paul Constantine, Gregory Peter. BSEE, MIT, 1956, MSEE, 1957; MS in Engring. Mgmt., Northeastern U., 1965; JD, Suffolk U., 1984. Bar: Mass. 1984, U.S. Dist. Ct. (Mass.) 1984, U.S. Ct. Appeals (1st cir.) 1985, U.S. Supreme Ct. 1988, U.S. Patent and Trademark Office 1989, U.S. Claims Ct. 1989. With Sylvania Co., Waltham, Mass., 1957-61, Needham, Mass., 1963-66; with Tech Ops, Burlington, Mass., 1961, RCA, Burlington, 1962-63, Raytheon Co., Bedford, Mass., 1966—; computer ops. mgr. tactical software devel. facility Patriot Ground Computer System, 1977-86, intellectual property mgr., 1986—; lectr. Fitchburg State Coll., 1985—; corporator Cen. Savs. Bank, Lowell, Mass., 1980-92; sec.-treas. U. Lowell Bldg. Authority, 1974-80. Mem. human studies subcom. Bedford VA Hosp., 1987-90; pres. Chelmsford Rep. Club, 1964-70; chmn. Chelmsford Rep. Town Com., 1972-76, 80—; assoc. Town Counsel for Tyngsborough (Mass.), 1985-87; chmn. Chelmsford Bd. Health, 1972-87; mem. Nashoba Tech. High Sch. Com., 1970-71. 2d lt. Signal Corps, U.S. Army, 1957-58. Mem. IEEE, Mass. Bar Assn., Boston Patent Law Assn. Republican. Greek Orthodox. Home: 17 Spaulding Rd Chelmsford MA 01824-1021 Office: Raytheon Co Hartwell Rd Bedford MA 01730-2407

DULKA, JOSEPH JOHN, ecologist, chemist; b. Cleve., Jan. 12, 1951; s. Joseph Andrew and Elizabeth Mary (Ruska) D.; married, 1978; children: Susan Elizabeth, Joseph Michael. BS, Miami U., Oxford, Ohio, 1972; PhD, Pa. State U., 1977. Rsch. chemist DuPont Agrl. Products, Wilmington, Del., 1977-79, sect. chemist, 1979-87, sr. rsch. chemist, 1987-91, rsch. assoc., ecol. field coord., 1991—. Contbr. articles to profl. jours. Active aquatic dialog group Nat. Wildlife, Washington, 1990-91, Nat. Pyrethroid Work Group, 1990—. Mem. ASTM, Am. Chem. Soc., Soc. Environ. Toxicology and Chemistry, Nat. Agrl. Chem. Assn. (ecotoxicology group 1990—, chmn. non-target plant work group 1991—), Phi Lambda Upsilon, Sigma Phi. Office: DuPont Agrl Products DuPont Exptl Sta Wilmington DE 19880-0402

DUMAINE, DEBORAH LOUISE, business training firm founder; b. Nashua, N.H., May 12, 1948; d. Henry Edward and Claire Corrinne (Villeneuve) D. BA, Smith Coll., 1970, EdM, 1971; postgrad., U. Iowa, 1974, Boston U., 1975. Pres. Better Communications Writing Workshops, Boston, 1978—. Author: Write to the Top, 1983; contbr. World Book Ency. Active Back Bay Chorale. Mem. Am. Soc. Tng. Devel., Instructional Systems Assn. Office: Better Communications Writing Tng 401 Commonwealth Ave Boston MA 02215-2317

DUMAIS, JOHN MARTIN, trade association executive; b. Laconia, N.H., Aug. 30, 1949; s. Lionel Joseph and Wladyslawa (Surowiec) D.; m. Mary M. Murphy, July 8, 1978. BS in Bus. cum laude, N.H. Coll., 1984. Owner Surowiec's Market Inc., Franklin, N.H., 1971-74; v.p. N.H. Retail Grocers Assn. Inc., Manchester, N.H., 1974-84, pres., chief exec. officer, 1984—; treas. N.H. Food Industry Credit Union, Manchester, 1987—; adminstr. Grocers Ins. Agy., Manchester, 1989—; mem. N.H. Food Bank Adv. Bd., 1989—. Editor News and Food Report, 1985—, N.H.'s Food Industry, 1985—. Mem. N.E. Soc. Assn. Execs. (bd. dirs. 1989—), Food Industry Scholarship Fund N.H. (treas. 1990—), Mems. Only Svc. Trust (trustee 1990—), Food Mktg. Inst. (bd. dirs. 1990-91), KC (treas. 1983-85), Food Industry Assn. Execs. (chmn. bd. dirs. 1990-91). Republican. Roman Catholic. Home: 6 Gates St Concord NH 03301-5743 Office: NH Retail Grocers Assn Inc 110 Stark St Manchester NH 03101-1934

DUMBAULD, EDWARD, federal judge; b. Uniontown, Pa., Oct. 26, 1905; s. Horatio S. and Lissa Grace (MacBurney) D.; m. Mary Ellen Whelpley, Jan. 1, 1941. A.B., Princeton U., 1926; LL.B., Harvard U., 1929, LL.M., 1930; Dr. Law, U. Leyden, Netherlands, 1932; LL.D. hon., Findlay Coll., 1981. Bar: Mem. Pa., D.C., U.S. Supreme Ct. bars. Practitioner before ICC, FCC (other adminstrn. agys.); former spl. asst. to atty. gen. U.S., Washington; (charge of litigation under acts regulating transp. and communications); judge Ct. Common Pleas Fayette County, 1957-61; U.S. dist. judge Western Dist. Pa., 1961—; sec. Am. Soc. Internat. Law, 1948-78, hon. v.p., 1979-87, hon. pres., 1988-90. Author: Interim Measures of Protection in International Controversies, 1932, Thomas Jefferson, American Tourist, 1946, The Declaration of Independence and What It Means Today, 1950, The Political Writings of Thomas Jefferson, 1955, The Bill of Rights and What It Means Today, 1957, The Constitution of the United States, 1964, Sayings of Jesus, 1967, Life and Legal Writings of Hugo Grotius, 1969, Thomas Jefferson and the Law, 1978. Democratic county chmn., Fayette County, 1934-36; del. Dem. Nat. Conv., Phila., 1936. Mem. Pa. Bar Assn. (chmn. com. on lawyers referral service). Presbyn. Club: Cosmos (Washington). Lodge: Kiwanis (pres. Uniontown 1955). Office: US PO & Courthouse 7th & Grant Sts Rm 501 Pittsburgh PA 15219

DUMONT, CLARK PETER, public affairs and communications executive; b. Manchester, N.H., Nov. 18, 1955; s. Lucien Emile and Phyllis Marie (Clarkin) D.; m. Anne Lachance, Aug. 6, 1977; children: Clark Peter, Jason Patrick. BA in Communications, The Am. U., 1977. Accredited Pub. Rels. Soc. Am., 1991. News dir. Sta. WKNE AM/FM, Keene, N.H., 1977; asst. news dir Sta. WGIR AM/FM, Manchester, 1977-81; dir. pub. affairs Blue Cross & Blue Shield of N.H., Concord, 1981-88, v.p. pub. affairs and communications, 1988—. Bd. dirs. Child and Family Svcs. of N.H., 1987—, First Night N.H., 1987—, N.H. Lung Assn., 1980-85, pres. 1983-85; chair N.H. Safety Belt Task Force, 1984-85, N.H. Pub. TV Auction, 1990, Gov.'s Coun. on Phys. Fitness, 1991; vice chair N.H. Gov.'s Mgmt. Rev., 1983; active N.H. Hwy. Traffic Safety Commn., 1984—, chair, 1988-90; mem. steering com. N.H. Bus. Com. for the Arts 1984—; trustee Granite State Pub. Radio/WEVO, 1984-89, chair 1987-88; bd. govs. United Way of Merrimack County , 1989-90, mem. campaign cabinets, 1982-83, 89-90, 91; bd. dirs. Daniel Webster coun. Boy Scouts Am., 1987-91, chmn. Scouting for Food, 1988, 89; mem. congl. task force Rep. William Zeliff, 1991. Mem. Pub. Rels. Soc. of Am. (bd. dirs. 1990—), Greater Manchester C. of C. (bd. dirs.), Rotary Club Manchester. Office: Blue Cross & Blue Shield 2 Pillsbury St Concord NH 03306-0001

DUMONT, RICHARD GEORGE, academic administrator, sociology educator; b. Sanford, Maine, July 6, 1940; s. George Joseph and Elsie (McComb) D.; m. Nancy C. Hanks; children: Elizabeth, Katherine, Peter, Ashley. BA summa cum laude, U. Maine, Orono, 1963; MA in Sociology, U. Mass., 1967, PhD, 1968. Asst. prof. sociology Bates Coll., Lewiston, Maine, 1969-74; dir. instl. rsch. SUNY, Alfred, 1974-76; chmn. dept. sociology Tenn. Technol. U., Cookville, 1976-84; exec. asst. to pres. Towson State U., Balt., 1984-86; v.p. acad. affairs N.W. Mo. State U., Maryville, 1986-88; from v.p. acad. affairs to interim pres. U. Maine, Ft. Kent, 1988-90, pres., 1990—; dir. performance funding project Tenn. Higher Edn. Commn., Nashville, 1977-78; dir. student assessment and program evaluation project Tenn. State Bd. Regents, Nashville, 1979-82; external evaluator title III spl. needs program Ga. So. Coll., Statesboro, 1982-84; bd. dirs. Maine Productivity Coun., Presque Isle, 1989. Author: The American View of Death, 1972; contbr. articles to profl. jours. Active Leaders Encouraging Aroostook County (Maine) Devel., 1989, Chancellors Com. on Info. Tech., Bangor, Maine, 1990; bd. advisors Franco Am. Ctr., U. Maine, Orono, 1990. U. Mass. fellow, 1965. Mem. Am. Assn. State Coll. and U., Am. Assn. for Higher Edn., Am. Ednl. Rsch. Assn., Am. Sociol. Assn., Assn. for the Study Higher Edn., Ft. Kent Rotary, Maryville Rotary, Phi Beta Kappa, Phi Kappa Phi, Kappa Delta Pi. Home: 20 Pleasant St Fort Kent ME 04743-1240 Office: U Maine 25 Pleasant St Fort Kent ME 04743-1292

DU MONT, ROBERT JAMES, SR., valve company executive; b. Newark, Sept. 9, 1942; s. Carl Whitaker and Eleanor Mary (Reed) DuM.; m. Barbara Jean Gesek, Nov. 25, 1967 (div. July 1974); m. Patricia Marie Carroll, Mar. 6, 1975; children: Robert James Jr. Student, Rutgers U., 1960-62, Fairleigh Dickinson U., 1965-68. Asst. valve sales mgr. Strahman Valves, Inc., Florham Park, N.J., 1968-73, valve sales mgr., 1973-76, product mgr., 1976—; chmn. mgmt. adv. com. Strahman Valves, Inc., Florham Park, 1985—, mem. corp. oper. com., 1991—. Mem. adv. planning rsch. panel, Livingston Twp., N.J.; judge Miss Livingston contest, 1974. With U.S. Army, 1962-65. Mem. Parenteral Drug Assn. Inc., Rutgers U. North Jersey Scarlet R Club (exec. com. 1986-88). Home: 44 Calais Rd Randolph NJ 07869-2802 Office: Strahman Valves Inc 3 Vreeland Rd Florham Park NJ 07932-1590

DUNAGAN, JOHN CHARLES, packaging company executive; b. Monahans, Tex., May 14, 1942; s. John Conrad and Kathlyn (Cosper) D.; m. Fradessa Charlene Sumner, Nov. 5, 1970; children: Natalie Loren, John Christopher, Sarah Christina. BA, U. Tex., 1964; MBA, Harvard U., 1967. Pres. Southwest Canners, Portales, N.Mex., 1974-80, Permian Coca-Cola, Monahans, Tex., 1970-84, Western Container, Big Spring, Tex., 1980—; bd. dirs. First State Bank, Monahans, Kermit (Tex.) State Bank. Mem. Tex. Soft Drink Assn. (pres. 1978), Rotary (pres. Monahans chpt. 1979, fellowship 1968), Racquet Club (Midland, Tex.), Wade Hampton Golf Club (Cashers, N.C.), Harvard Club (N.Y.C.), Hunt Club (Fairfield, Colo.), Mashomack Fish and Game Club, Sailfish Point Golf Club. Home: 193 North Ave Westport CT 06880-2231

DUNBAR, ANNE CYNTHIA, social services administrator; b. N.Y.C., Sept. 24, 1938; d. Eric Henry Hines and Adella Costilda (Clarke) Joseph; divorced; 1 child, Christopher Dunbar. BA in Sociology/Urban Affairs, Bklyn. Coll., 1973, MS in Edn./Guidance and Counseling, 1977; cert. from Grad. Sch. Pub. and Internat. Affairs, Columbia U. Ordained Evangelist, 1991. Asst. to v.p. community affairs First Venture Corp. N.Y., N.Y.C., 1969-70; dir. fin. aid CUNY, 1970-76; dir. community rels., asst. dir. N.Y. State Dept. Correctional Svcs., N.Y.C., 1976-89; mgmt. cons. Girl Scouts U.S., N.Y.C., 1989-90; dep. adminstr. community affairs/vol. svcs. N.Y.C. Human Resources Adminstrn., 1990—; instr. CUNY. Chair adv. bd. Bronx br. N.Y. Urban League; chair special program for handicapped N.Y.C. Bd. Edn.; v.p. Bronx Boys Clubs; bd. visitors Kirby Forensic Psychiat. Ctr.; mem. adv. com. to N.Y.C. Commn. to UN, N.Y. State Cath. Conf., Criminal Justice Adv. Bd., Chancellor's Adv. Com. Special Edn., N.Y.C. Bd. Edn., Community Sch. Bd. 12; cons. sickle cell blood disease program NIH; vol. women's unit Gov.'s Office, office edn. and vol. svcs. N.Y. State Dept. Correction; Bronx tour hostess Mrs. Jimmy Carter and Mrs. George Bush; founding mem. Ford-Whitefield-Young Scholarship Fund; active Bronx Boys and Girls Club. Recipient citation U.S. Congl. Record, Merit citation Fernando Ferrer, Pres. Borough Bronx, Parent Leadership award Coun. Suprs. and Adminstrs. of N.Y.C. Bd. Edn., Outstanding Leadership award City Coun. N.Y., Dist. Community Svc. award Coun. Chs., N.Y.C., Community Svc. award Consol. Edison Co. N.Y., Inc., Cardiac Diagnostic and Gen. Med. Svcs. Humanitarian award Bronx County, Community Leadership award Bus. and Profl. Women's Clubs, Community Svc. award Black Bar Assn. Bronx County, Sojourner of Truth Meritorious Svc. award Nat. Assn. Negro Bus. and Profl. Women's Club, Inc.; named Citizen of Yr., Bronx Boys Clubs, Honoree for Internat. Women's Yr., Nat. Coun. Negro Women. Mem. NAACP (founding mem., pres. Parchester br.). Home: 1940 E Tremont Ave Bronx NY 10462 Office: NYC Human Resources Adminstrn 250 Church St Rm 500 New York NY 10013

DUNBAR, JILL H., bookseller; b. New Haven, Feb. 10, 1949; d. Carl Owen and Ann (Peck) D. BA, Boston U., 1971, MA, 1973. Staff New England Conservatory, Boston, 1973-75; gallary staff Betty Parsons Gallery, N.Y.C., 1975-78; owner Three Lives & Co. Bookshop, N.Y.C., 1978—. Mem. Am. Booksellers Assn., Sisters in Crime (nat. membership chair 1990-92). Home: 52 W 12th St New York NY 10014-1912 Office: Three Lives & Co Ltd 154 W 10th St New York NY 10014-3113

DUNBAR, JOAN MARY, registered nurse; b. Buffalo, Apr. 18, 1931; d. Joseph M. and Josephine H. (WhiteHouse) Finucane; m. Joseph E. Dunbar, Aug. 13, 1951; children: Mary Jo, William J., Madonna T., Jennifer L. AAS, Trocaire Coll., 1977; BSN, Dyouville Coll., 1980. RN. Staff nurse Buffalo Gen., 1980—. Mem. Kappa Gamma. Democrat. Roman Catholic. Home: 81 Como Ave Buffalo NY 14220-1507

DUNBOBBIN, BRIAN ROY, engineering executive; b. Warrington, Lancashire, Eng., Jan. 2, 1951; s. Roy and Frances Muriel (Watkins) D.; m. Jane Ann Riley, July 5, 1975; children: Georgina, Naomi, Richard. BSChemE, Leeds (Eng.) U., 1973, PhDChemE, 1976. Chartered engr. Rsch. engr. Union Carbide Corp., Bound Brook, N.J., 1977-79, Union Camp Corp., Princeton, N.J., 1979-80; engring. assoc. Air Products & Chems. Inc., Allentown, Pa., 1980—; dir. Fractionation Rsch. Inst., Stillwater, Okla., 1989—, Heat Transfer Rsch. Inst., Alhambra, Calif., 1986-89. Contbr. numerous articles and papers to profl. jours.; patentee. Fellow Inst. Chem. Engrs.; mem. Am. Inst. Chem. Engrs. Home: 412201 Benner Rd Allentown PA 18104-4669 Office: Air Products & Chems Inc 7201 Hamilton Blvd Allentown PA 18195-9642

DUNCAN, CAROL SPINDLER, non-profit agency administrator; b. Boston, Feb. 24, 1942; d. Herbert George and Alice Mary (Carroll) Spindler; m. George L. Duncan, Feb. 4, 1967; children: Alison C., Andrew W. AB, Brown U., 1963; MA, Boston U., 1967. Asst. buyer Jordan Marsh Co., Boston, 1963-65; tchr. Dracut (Mass.) Jr. High Sch., 1967-71; pvt. tutor Lowell, Mass., 1982-90; exec. dir. Lowell Girls Club, 1991—; mem. adv. coun. Coalition for a Better Acre, Lowell, 1991; mem. adv. bd. early learning awareness Middlesex Community Coll., Lowell, 1991. Mem. sch. improvement coun. Moody and Reilly Schs., Lowell, 1986-88; mem. exec. com. Merrimack Repertory Theatre, Lowell, 1990-91; mem. design selection com. Polland Meml. Libr., Lowell, 1990-91; chmn. Reilly Sch. PTO, Lowell, 1982-85; chmn. bd. trustees Pollard Meml. Libr., Lowell, 1989-91. Mem. Merrimack Valley Nat. Alumni Schs. Program (chmn. 1986-91), Lowell Gen Hosp. Aux. (bd. dirs. 1987-91), Florence Crittenton League (v.p. 1989-91), D'Youville (Mass.) Manor Ladies Guild (founder, sec. 1968-91), People's Club of Lowell (pres. 1987-91), Am. Mensa Ltd. Home: PO Box 4178 Vineyard Haven MA 02568-4178 Office: Lowell Girls Club 220 Worthen St Lowell MA 01852-1823

DUNCAN, CONSTANCE CATHARINE, psychologist; b. Watertown, Wis., Nov. 2, 1948; d. Howard Burton and Mary Elizabeth (Fagan) Duncan; m. Allan Franklin Mirsky, July 4, 1986. BA, Northwestern U., 1970; AM, U. Ill., 1973, PhD, 1978. Sr. rsch. analyst Adolf Meyer Mental Health Ctr., Decatur, Ill., 1971-73; rsch. and teaching asst. Dept. Psychology, U. Ill., Champaign, 1974-78; postdoctoral fellow Dept. Psychiat. and Behavioral Scis., Stanford U. Sch. Medicine, Palo Alto, 1978-81; rsch. psychologist VA Med. Ctr., Palo Alto, 1978-81; sr. staff fellow Lab. of Psychology & Psychopathology, NIMH, Bethesda, Md., 1981-88; chief unit on psychophysiology NIMH, Bethesda, Md., 1982-89, rsch. specialist, 1989—; pvt. practice psychology Bethesda, Md., 1981—; adj. assoc. prof. Johns Hopkins Sch. Hygiene and Pub. Health, Balt., 1987—. Assoc. editor Psychophysiology, 1987—; cons. editor 15 sci. jours.; contbr. articles to profl. jours., chpts. to books. Found. assoc. Nat. Women's Econ. Alliance. Recipient Nat. Rsch. Svc. award, NIH, 1978-81, Golden Anniversary Scholarship award, AAUW, 1974; USPHS fellow, 1970-74. Mem. APA (fellow 1992—), Soc. for Psychophysiol. Rsch. (dir. 1982-85, Disting. Sci. award for early career contbn. 1980, chmn. awards com. 1981-84, chmn. conv. com. 1983-87, chmn. program com. 1987, mem. Blue Ribbon panel on State of the Soc. in the Yr. 2000, 1990—), Soc. for Rsch. in Psychopathology (dir. 1986-88, membership com. 1987-88), Soc. for Neurosci., Internat. Neuropsychol. Soc., Am. Psychopathol. Assn., Mortar Bd., Shi-Ai, Sigma Xi, Phi Kappa Phi, Alpha Lambda Delta, Pi Mu Epsilon, Phi Beta Kappa. Home: 6204 Perthshire Ct Bethesda MD 20817-3348 Office: Lab Psychology & Psychopathology NIMH Bldg 10 Rm 4C110 Bethesda MD 20892

DUNCAN, ERICA JOAN, psychiatrist; b. Toronto, Ont., Can., July 3, 1953. AB, Brown U., 1975; MD, McGill U., Montreal, Que., Can., 1983. Diplomate Am. Bd. Psychiatry and Neurology. Internship Hahnemann U., Phila., 1983-84; resident in psychiatry NYU-Bellevue Hosp., N.Y.C., 1984-87; attending psychiatrist N.Y. VA Med. Ctr., N.Y.C., 1987—; asst. prof. psychiatry NYU, N.Y.C., 1987-90; asst. prof., 1990—; pvt. practice N.Y.C., 1987—; cand. N.Y. Psychoanalytic Inst., N.Y.C., 1986—. Mem. Am. Psychiat. Assn., Am. Psychoanalytic Assn., N.Y. Acad. Sci., Basal Ganglion Soc. Office: 32 W 94th St New York NY 10025-7112

DUNCAN, JACK G., lawyer; b. Horry, S.C., Dec. 8, 1939; s. Jack and Theresa (McKenzie) D. BA, Furman U., Greenville, S.C., 1960; JD, U. S.C., Columbia, 1963. Atty. U.S. Dept. State, Washington, 1964-65, U.S. Dept. HEW, Washington, 1965-68; counsel and staff dir. Subcom. on Select Edn., Edn. and Labor Com., U.S. Ho. Reps., Washington, 1968-79; owner Duncan & Assocs., Washington, 1979—; spl. counsel Am. Coun. for the Arts, 1979—; gen. counsel Coun. of State Adminstrs. of Vocat. Rehab., Washington, 1990—. Editor Update Arts newsletter, 1979—. Recipient Pres. award, Am. Acad. Phys. Medicine, 1979, Nat. Rehab. Assn., 1979. Mem. ABA, Fed. Bar Assn. (1967), S.C. Bar Assn. (1963). Home: 5126 Albemarle St NW Washington DC 20016-4306 Office: Duncan & Assocs 1213 29th St NW Washington DC 20007-3332

DUNCAN, WILLIAM MILLEN, banker; b. Toledo, Ohio, July 25, 1939; s. John and Elizabeth (Job) D.; m. Patricia Munson, Apr. 27, 1986; children: Elizabeth J., Howard P., William M. Jr., Korinne J. Munson. BA, Trinity Coll., 1962. Sr. v.p. Chem. Bank, N.Y.C., 1962-86; chmn., pres. 1st Am. Bank N.Y., N.Y.C., 1986—. Mem. Belle Haven Club (Greenwich, Conn.), Econ. Club N.Y. Home: 80 Fairfield Rd Greenwich CT 06830-4870 Office: 1st Am Bank NY 350 Park Ave New York NY 10022-6022

DUNCOMBE, RAYNOR BAILEY, lawyer; b. Washington, July 17, 1942; s. Raynor Lockwood and Avis Ethel (Bailey) D.; m. Janice Assunta Rini, Apr. 12, 1969; children: Christina Luccioni, Raynor Luccioni. AB, Franklin and Marshall Coll., 1965; JD, Syracuse U., 1968. Bar: N.Y. 1972, U.S. Dist. Ct. (no. dist.) N.Y. 1972. Staff atty. State of N.Y., Albany, 1968-70; mgmt. trainee State Bank Albany, 1970-72; staff atty. Vibbard, Donaghy & Wright, Schoharie, N.Y., 1972-73, F. Walter Bliss, Esq., Schoharie, 1973-74; pvt. practice Schoharie, 1974—; chmn. bd. dirs. Fulmont Mut. Ins. Co.; town atty. 8 towns and 1 village in Schoharie County, 1975—; adminstr. Assigned Counsel Program, 1975—; sch. atty. Middleburgh (N.Y.) Schs., 1981-85; atty. Schoharie County, 1982-87, 90-91, Schoharie County Hist. Soc., 1975—. Republican committeman Schoharie County, 1984—; dist. commr. Boy Scouts Am., 1987—, asst. scoutmaster, 1988-91, Explorer advisor, 1991—. Mem. ABA, N.Y. State Bar Assn., Schoharie County Bar Assn. (sec.-treas. 1975—), Rotary (past pres.), Masons (past master), Lions. Presbyterian. Home: RR 2 Box 320 Middleburgh NY 12122-9802 Office: 319 Main St Schoharie NY 12157

DUNDAS, PHILIP BLAIR, JR., lawyer; b. Middletown, Conn., Apr. 29, 1948; s. Philip Blair Sr. and Madolyn Margaret (Bassett) D.; m. Elizabeth Anne Adorno, Aug. 9, 1969; children: Philip B. III, Chapman P. BA, Wesleyan U., Conn., 1970; JD, Washington and Lee U., 1973. Bar: N.Y. 1974. Assoc. Shearman & Sterling, N.Y.C., 1973-81, ptnr., 1981—, ptnr. in charge of Abu Dhabi, United Arab Emirates Office, 1981—. Mem. ABA, Internat. Bar Assn., N.Y. State Bar Assn., Assn. of Bar of City of N.Y., Union Internationale des Avocats, Clinton Country Club. Office: 599 Lexington Ave New York NY 10022-6030

DUNDY, RICHARD ALAN, emergency medicine physician; b. N.Y.C., June 26, 1945; s. Harold David and Sophie (Edelstein) D.; m. Alison Kate Shore, May 30, 1982. BA, Brandeis U., 1967. Diplomate Am. Bd. Internal Medicine. Intern Detroit Gen. Hosp., 1974-75; resident in internal medicine Kings County Med. Ctr., N.Y.C., 1979-80; chmn. emergency dept. Beth Israel Hosp. North, N.Y.C., 1987—. Recipient Disting. Med. Svc. award East Manhattan C. of C., 1991. Fellow Am. Coll. Emergency Physicians. Office: Beth Israel Hosp North 170 E End Ave New York NY 10128-7603

DUNHAM, PHILIP BIGELOW, biology educator, physiologist; b. Columbus, Ohio, Apr. 26, 1937; s. T. Chadbourne and Margaret (Bigelow) D.; m. Gudrun Bjarnarson, Mar. 9, 1985. B.A., Swarthmore Coll., 1958; Ph.D., U. Chgo., 1962. USPHS postdoctoral fellow Carlsberg Found., Copenhagen, 1962-63; asst. prof. zoology Syracuse U., 1963-67, assoc. prof., 1967-71, prof., 1971—; rsch. prof. pharm. SUNY Health Sci. Ctr., Syracuse, 1990—; vis. assoc. prof. physiology Yale U. Sch. Medicine, 1968-70, vis. prof. 1986; vis. scientist physiol. lab. U. Cambridge, Eng., 1979, August Krogh Inst., Copenhagen, 1985-87; vis. honors examiner Swarthmore Coll., 1966-67, 73-74, mem. alumni council, 1971-73; mem. exec. com. bd. trustees Marine Biol. Lab., Woods Hole, Mass., 1972-76; mem. physiology study sect. NIH, 1986-89. Assoc. editor Am. Jour. Physiology, 1984-87; contbr. 95 rsch. publs. in field. Mem. Soc. Gen. Physiologists (council 1967-69), Am. Physiol. Soc., Biophys. Soc. Home: 6402 Terese Ter Jamesville NY 13078-9430 Office: Syracuse U 130 College Pl Syracuse NY 13244-1220

DUNKELBERGER, ROSEMARIE, professional society administrator; b. Reading, Pa., Oct. 1, 1926; d. Louis and Louise M. (Piccino) Farr; m. Robert E. Dunkelberger, Oct. 14, 1950 (dec. Jan. 1981); 1 child, Robin Louise Dunkelberger Tumberello. BCS, Rider Coll., 1947; BS in Edn., Temple U., 1972; MEd, Lehigh U., 1975. Med. lab. asst. Reading Hosp., 1947-48; exec. med. sec. St. Joseph's Hosp., Reading, 1948-51; med. asst. Dr. William McKinney, Reading, 1957-60; owner, operator The Rosemarie Dress Shoppe, Reading, 1960-68; tchr. Berks Vocat.-Tech. Sch., Oley, Pa., 1968-88; state facilitator Health Occupations Students Am. Dept. Edn., Harrisburg, Pa., 1988—. Contbr. articles and programs in field. Active Concerned Citizens Hampden Heights, Reading, 1992—. Mem. Health Occupations Students Am. (nat. hon., nat. chmn. bd. 1987-88, nat. bd. dirs. 1985-88, 88-91, 92—, exec. dir. Pa. chpt. 1988—, chmn. bd. Pa. chpt. 1987-88, bd. dirs. Pa. chpt. 1980—, cons. to bd. dirs. Pa. chpt. 1988—). Home: 1502 Bern St Reading PA 19604 Office: Pa Dept Edn 333 Market St 6th Fl Harrisburg PA 17126-0333

DUNKERLEY, WILLIAM, editor, publishing consultant; b. Paterson, N.J., Nov. 22, 1942; s. William Irving Sr. and Dorothy Nellie (MacNab) D.; m. Jill Diane Tompkins, Aug. 30, 1966 (div. 1980); 1 child, Lori Diane; m. Linda Johnson, Aug. 16, 1988. Student, Fairleigh Dickinson U., 1961-65, Columbia U., 1962, U. Alaska, 1962-63. Asst. sec. Am. Radio Relay League, Newington, Conn., 1966-72, mng. editor, 1972-78, publs. mgr., 1978; pres. SCELBI Publs., West Hartford, Conn., 1978-80; cons. New Britain, Conn., 1981—; editor Editors Only, New Britain, 1988—; dir. Amsat, Washington, 1970-79, Studio of Electronic Music, Simsbury, Conn., 1983-84. Communications officer, Civil Def. Coun., Elmwood Park, N.J., 1963-65; dir. Am. Cancer Soc., Plainville, Conn., 1984—. Recipient Outstanding Service award, Talcott Mountain Sci. Ctr., Avon, Conn., 1981. Mem. Fgn. Affairs Coun., Orgn. Devel. Network, Soc. Nat. Assn. Publs. (dir. 1975-80), N.Y. Bus. Press Editors Assn. Office: 275 Batterson Dr New Britain CT 06053-1005

DUNLAP, GERARD WILLARD, designer; b. Pitts., Oct. 10, 1956; s. Willard Walter D.; m. Cheryl Lyn Hopkins, Aug. 8, 1987. AA, Art Inst. of Pitts., 1977. Artist Applied Sci. Assocs. Inc., Butler, Pa., 1977-79; prodn. asst. Soc. Automotive Engrs., Warrendale, Pa., 1979-86, assoc. designer, 1986-87, prodn. mgr., 1987—; instr. Tri-County Community Edn. Agy., Butler, Pa., 1979-81. Mem. Sportsman's Assn. of Valencia (sec. 1986-92, treas. 1987-88). Office: Soc of Automotive Engrs 400 Commonwealth Dr Warrendale PA 15096-0001

DUNLAP, PHILIP GLENN, physician; b. San Diego, Feb. 20, 1940; s. Emmett E. and Mary Elizabeth (Gray) D.; m. Shelagh Heath Dewar, Nov. 11, 1973. BS, Purdue U., 1960; DO, Kirksville Coll. Osteo. Med., 1968; MPH, Harvard U., 1990, MSc, 1991. Diplomate Am. Coll. Gen. Practice. Intern Grand Rapids (Mich.) Osteo. Hosp., 1968-69; emergency rm. staff physician New Berlin (Wis.) Osteo. Hosp., 1969-71; physician Dir. Relief

Found., Kaboul, Afghanistan, 1971-73, Ulleung-Do, Republic of Korea, 1973-75; attending staff physician Physician's and Surgeon's Hosp., Alice, Tex., 1973-89; physician, owner La Hacienda Clinic, San Diego, 1973-89; med. dir. La Hacienda Nursing Home, San Diego, 1986-89; Harvard U. Frank Knox Traveling fellow dept. epidemiology and pub. health Univ. Coll., London, 1991—, Queen's U., Belfast, Northern Ireland, 1991—; med. examiner FAA, 1976-89. Mem. Am. Osteo. Assn., Tex. Osteo. Med. Assn., Am. Coll. Cryosurgery. Home: 2 Casey Cir Waltham MA 02154-2169

DUNLAP, PHILIP STANLEY, real estate appraiser, consultant; b. Manchester, N.H., Oct. 10, 1918; s. Clifton Stanley and Hazel Olive (Elliott) D.; m. Shirley Virginia Holmes, Jan. 23, 1928; children: William Holmes, Ann LeBourdais, Robert Elliott, John Philip. BS in Econs., U. N.H., 1940, LLD (hon.), 1980; DLitt (hon.), N.H. Coll., 1981. V.p. Morrill & Everett Inc., Concord, N.H., 1952-84; v.p., treas. No. R.R., Nashua, N.H., 1970-86; pres., treas. N.H. Real Estate Investment Corp., Concord, 1986—; trustee Dunlap Realty Trust, Hopkinton, N.H.; bd. dirs. Globe Mfg. Co., Pittsfield, N.H., Massaseaum Timber Corp., Bradford, N.H. Pres. N.H. Ind. Ins. Agts. Assn., Concord, 1960, N.H. Senate Pres., Lt. Gov., Concord, 1962, 63, 64; chmn. bd. trustees U. N.H., Durham, 1972-78, acting pres.-chancellor, 1978, N.H. Jud. Coun., 1985—. Recipient Meritorious Service award U. N.H., Durham, 1981. Mem. Nat. Assn. Real Estate Appraisers. Republican. Congregationalist. Club: Snowshoe (Concord). Lodge: Masons. Home: RR 1 Box 357 Contoocook NH 03229 Office: NH Real Estate Investment Corp 18 Low Ave Concord NH 03301-4940

DUNLEAVY, PATRICIA ELIZABETH, personnel director; b. Scranton, Pa., Mar. 14, 1955; d. Joseph A. and Marion (Conboy) D. BA in Music and English, Mansfield U., 1977; MA in Music, Marywood Coll., 1983, MS in Bus., 1991. Accounts payable clk. Nat. Book Co. (W.W. Norton), Dunmore, Pa., 1977-80; studio piano tchr. Home & Marywood Coll., Scranton, Pa., 1977-90; dept. asst. Marywood Coll., Scranton, 1980-82, coord. payroll, 1982-84, dir. pers., 1985—; guest speaker Keystone Jr. Coll. Career Day, LaPlume, Pa., 1990-92. Performer solo piano recitals, 1976, 81, liturgical dances, 1988, 89. Mem. Skills in Scranton Job Fair Com., 1990—. Recipient Gold and Silver medals Internat. Piano Competition, 1983. Mem. Regional Coll. Pers. Assn., Scranton Area Pers. Assn., Phi Kappa Lambda. Democrat. Roman Catholic. Office: Marywood Coll 2300 Adams Ave Scranton PA 18509-1598

DUNLOP, BRUCE ROBERT, sales executive; b. Newburgh, N.Y., Jan. 13, 1953; s. Robert Cameron and Loretta Teresa (Cennamo) D.; m. Cindy Lee Shepherd, June 12, 1976; children: Melissa Kim, Michael Christopher, Sarah Raye. Student, Bloomfield Coll., 1970-72. Sales corr. Tidland Corp., Oak Ridge, N.J., 1977-80; regional sales mgr. Emtek Corp., Denville, N.J., 1980-81; marine salesman Marotta Sci. Controls, Inc., Montville, N.J., 1981—. Composer: Wrote This Song, 1991, Modern Ode, 1991, Sezitall, 1991, No Answer, 1991, Gettin' By, 1991, Li'l Melissa, 1991, Paid the Price, 1991, Thanx for Saving Me, 1991, Pickin' With Richie, 1991, D'Based, 1991, Wasted, 1991, Never Ending Story, 1991, J'maica, 1991. Capt. Community Fie Co. # 1, Newfoundland, N.J., 1982, lt., 1980-81. Office: Marotta Sci Controls Inc 78 Boonton Ave Montville NJ 07045

DUNLOP, JAMES JOSEPH, management consultant; b. Palo Alto, Calif., May 10, 1934; s. Joseph James and Ruth (Zagor) D.; m. Nancy Felix, Mar. 10, 1957 (div. June 1959); 1 child, Debra; m. Judith Mitchell, Nov. 3, 1962; children: John, Andrew. BS in Engring., U.S. Coast Guard Acad., 1955; MBA, Harvard U., 1962. Cons. Arthur O. Little, Inc., Cambridge, Mass., 1962-83; pres. James Dunlop and Co., Inc., Marblehead, Mass., 1983—. Author: Leading the Association: Striking the Right Balance Between Staff and Volunteers, 1989. First vice chmn. Mass. chpt. Nat. Multiple Sclerosis Soc., Waltham, 1991—. Lt. USCG, 1955-60. Mem. Am. Soc. Assn. Execs. Democrat. Unitarian.

DUNLOP, JOHN THOMAS, economics educator, former secretary of labor; b. Placerville, Calif., July 5, 1914; s. John W. and Antonia (Forni) D.; m. Dorothy Webb, July 6, 1937; children: John Barrett, Beverly Claire, Thomas Frederick. AB, U. Calif., 1935, PhD, 1939; LLD, U. Chgo., 1968, U. Pa., 1976, Harvard U., 1987. Acting instr. Stanford U., 1936-37; instr. Harvard U., 1938-45, assoc. prof. econs., 1945-50, prof. econs., 1950-85, Lamont U. prof., 1970-85, dean faculty arts and scis., 1970-73; Served as vice chmn. Boston Regional War Labor Bd., 1944-45; chmn. Nat. Joint Bd. for Settlement of Jurisdictional Disputes in bldg. and constrn. industry, 1948-57; cons. Office Econ. Stabilization, 1945-47, NLRB, 1948-52, Atomic Energy Labor Panel, 1948-53; mem. bd. inquiry Bituminous Coal Industry, 1950; pub. mem. ESB, 1950-52; mem. Emergency Bds. 109, 130, 167 Presdl. R.R. Commn., 1960-62, Missile Sites Labor Commn., 1961-67, Pres.' EEOC, 1964-65; impartial chmn. constrn. Industry Joint Conf., 1959-68; dir. Cost of Living Coun., 1973-74; sec. labor, 1975-76; chmn. Pay Adv. Com., 1979-80, Social Security Coun., 1989-91. Author: Wage Determination under Trade Unions, 1944, Collective Bargaining; Principles and Cases, 1949, Industrial Relations Systems, 1958, (with D. C. Bok) Labor and the American Community, 1970, The Lessons of Wage and Price Controls, 1977, Business and Public Policy, 1980, Dispute Resolution: Negotiation and Consensus Bulding, 1984, The Management of Labor Unions, 1990; editor Wertheim Series in Industrial Relations, 1945—. Named to Nat. Housing Hall of Fame; recipient Murray, Meany, Green award AFL-CIO, 1987. Mem. Am. Acad. Arts and Scis., Am. Philos. Soc., Inst. Medicine (life), Nat. Acad. Arbritrators. Home: 509 Pleasant St Belmont MA 02178-3238 Office: Harvard U 208 Littauer Ctr Cambridge MA 02138

DUNN, ANDREW DIEDRICH, electrical contractor; b. Bryn Mawr, Pa., July 23, 1959; s. David A. and Karoline M. (Fahlenkamp) D.; m. Maria F. Lubragge, June 15, 1991. Owner Dunn Electric Co., Drexel Hill, Pa., 1981—. Republican. Episcopalian.

DUNN, CHARLES WILLIAM, educator, author; b. Arbuthnott, Scotland, Nov. 30, 1915; came to U.S., 1928, naturalized, 1961; s. Peter Alexander and Alberta Mary Margaret (Freeman) D.; m. Patricia Campbell, June 21, 1941 (dec. 1973); children: Deirdre, Peter Arthur; m. Elaine Birnbaum, Oct. 25, 1974; 1 son, Alexander Joseph. B.A. with honors, McMaster U., 1938; A.M., Harvard, 1939, Ph.D., 1948; LL.D. (hon.), St. Francis Xavier U., 1983. Asst. in English Harvard, 1939-40, tutor, 1940-41; instr. humanities Stephens Coll., 1941-42; instr. English Cornell U., 1943-46; instr. then asso. prof. English Univ. Coll., U. Toronto, 1946-56; prof. English N.Y. U., 1956-63; prof. Celtic langs. and lits., chmn. dept. Harvard U., 1963-84, emeritus prof., 1984—, master of Quincy House, 1966-81, Margaret Brooks Robinson prof. Celtic langs. and lits., 1967-84; Taft lectr. U. Cin., 1956. Author: Highland Settler: A Portrait of the Scottish Gael in Nova Scotia, 1953, corrected reprint, 1968, rev. edit., 1991, The Foundling and the Werwolf: A Study of Guillaume de Palerne, 1960 (Chgo. Folklore prize 1960), (with Morton W. Bloomfield) The Role of the Poet in Early Societies, 1989; editor: A Chaucer Reader, 1952, History of the Kings of Britain (Geoffrey of Monmouth), 1958, Chronicles (Froissart), 1961, Romance of the Rose, 1962, Lays of Courtly Love, 1963, (with Edward Byrnes) Middle English Literature, 1973, rev. edit., 1990; contbr. articles, revs. to profl. jours. Dexter fellow N.S., summer 1941; Rockefeller fellow N.S., 1942-43; Nuffield fellow Dublin, Edinburgh and Aberystwyth, 1954-55; Guggenheim fellow Scotland, Wales and Brittany, 1962-63; recipient Canada award Fedn. Gaelic Socs., 1955. Fellow Am. Acad. Arts and Sci., Soc. Antiquaries of Scotland; mem. MLA, Mediaeval Acad. Am., Early English Text Soc., Scottish Text Soc., Royal Scottish Country Dance Soc., St. Andrews Soc. N.Y., Mass. Hist. Soc. (resident), Comunn Gaidhealach (Scotland), Celtic Union Edinburgh, Scots' Charitable Soc. Boston, Commanderie de Bordeaux à Boston (Maître), Phi Beta Kappa (hon.). Clubs: Tavern, Somerset, Odd Volumes (Boston). Home: 25 Longfellow Rd Cambridge MA 02138-4737

DUNN, CHRISTOPHER LESLIE, rental company executive; b. Birmingham, U.K., Nov. 17, 1953; came to U.S., 1988; s. Leslie and Joyce (Turner) D.; m. Ticia Ulaneck, Mar. 3, 1981; 1 child, Christopher James. Sales mgr. Jones & Crossland Ltd., Birmingham, 1971-74; personal mgr. Zomba Mgmt. Ltd., London, 1982-83; studio mgr. Battery Studios-Zomba Recording Ltd., London, 1983-85; gen. mgr. Dreamhire-Zomba Recording Ltd., London, 1985-88, Dreamhire-Zomba Recording Corp., N.Y.C., 1988—. Musician City Boy, 1974-79. Mem. Performing Rights Soc. Office: Zomba Recording Corp 137-139 W 25th St New York NY 10001

DUNN, GRACE VERONICA, retired executive secretary; b. Bklyn.; d. Richard William and Grace Veronica (Mason) D. BA, Our Lady of the Lake U., 1940; postgrad., Columbia U., 1958. Sec. Hunt Oil Co., Dallas, 1947-48, Standard Oil Co. (N.J.), N.Y.C., 1955-59, Pan Am. Health Orgn., Washington, 1964-76. Mem., vol. Stephanie Roper Com., Upper Marlboro, Md., 1987—, Friends of the Kennedy Ctr., Washington, 1991—; soprano soloist Holy Trinity Cath. Ch., Dallas, 1945-47, Ch. of the Incarnation Episcopal Ch., Dallas, 1945-47; soloist White House Christmas Tree, 1988. Grad. fellow Karl Schultz Found., 1940; pvt. scholar Elisabeth Schumann, N.Y.C., 1948-52. Roman Catholic.

DUNN, JAMES ALAN, educator; b. Knoxville, Tenn., Mar. 23, 1933; s. Wade Patterson and Juanita Imogene (Carmichael) D.; m. Patricia Sheridan Moore, June 1958; children: Thomas Michael, Kevin Brian. BS, Wayne U., 1954; PhD, U. Mich., 1962; postdoctoral, Harvard U., 1967. Asst. prof. Wayne State U., Detroit, 1962-64, U. Mich., Ann Arbor, 1964-67; vis. fellow Harvard U., Cambridge, Mass., 1967-68; sr. rsch. scientist Am. Inst. for Rsch., Palo Alto, Calif., 1968-77; prof. ednl. psychology Cornell U., Ithaca, N.Y., 1977—. Author: (with J. Bergan) Psychology and Education, 1977. 1st lt. USAF, 1955-57. Recipient numerous rsch. grants. Office: Cornell U 409 Kennedy Hall Ithaca NY 14853

DUNN, JAMES MILTON, religious organization adminstrator; b. Ft. Worth, Tex., June 17, 1932; s. William Thomas and Edith (Campbell) Dunn; m. Marilyn McNeely, Dec. 19, 1958. BA, Tex. Wesleyan Coll., 1953; BD, Southwestern Bapt. Theol. Sem., 1957, ThD, 1966, PhD, 1978; LLD, Alderson-Broaddus Coll. Ordained to ministry So. Bapt. Conv. and Am. Bapt. Ch. in U.S.A., 1955. Assoc. pastor First Bapt. Ch., Weatherford, Tex., 1955-57; pastor Emmanuel Bapt. Ch., Weatherford, 1957-61; religion instr., campus minister W. Tex. State U., Canyon, 1961-66; dir. christian life commn. Bapt. Gen. Conv. Tex., Dallas, 1967-80; exec. dir. Bapt. Joint Com. on Pub. Affairs, Washington, 1981—; sec. bd. Ams. United for Separation Ch. & State, Silver Spring, Md., 1978—; bd. dirs. Bread for the World, Washington, pres., 1987; mem. ethics commn. Bapt. World Alliance, McLean, Va., 1975—. Editor, co-author: Politics a Guidebook for Christians, 1970, Endangered Species, 1976; co-author: An Approach to Christian Ethics, 1979, Teacher Renewal, 1987; author: (with others) Equal Separation, 1990, The Fundamentalist Phenomenon, 1990. Sec. Anti-Crime Coun. Tex., Dallas, 1968-80; founding mem. Dallas Dem. Forum, 1976-80; mem. Fair Campaign Practices Com., Dallas, 1972-76, Gov.'s Juvenile Coun., State of Tex., Austin, 1976-77. Recipient Disting. Svc. award Christian Life Commn. of So. Bapt. Conv., 1979, Moore-Bowman Award of Excellence, Tex. Coun. on Family Relations, 1979, Disting. Svc. award Chs. Ctr. for Theology and Pub. Policy. Mem. Soc. for the Sci. Study of Religion, Lions (pres. Canyon chpt. 1965-66). Office: Baptist Joint Com 200 Maryland Ave NE Washington DC 20002-5724

DUNN, KENNETH RALPH, insurance company executive; b. Paterson, N.J., Apr. 9, 1958; s. Ralph and Florence Louise (May) D.; m. Martha Jean Davis, Sept. 6, 1980; children: Laura Jean, Jonathan Ralph, David Allan. BS, Messiah Coll., 1980. External auditor Selective Ins. Co. Am., Branchville, N.J., 1980-82, bond underwriter, 1982-84, br. bond mgr., 1984—. Author: Messiah College Baseball Encyclopedia, 1991. Treas., deacon, softball coach, youth leader Newton (N.J.) 1st Bapt. Ch., 1980-84; deacon, recreation dir., ch. tng. dir., softball coach Calvary Bapt. Ch., Bel Air, Md., 1984-90; softball coach, recreation dir. Covenant Bapt. Ch., Charlotte, N.C., 1991; sec., pres. Sussex County Softball League, Newton, 1982-84. Mem. Mid-Atlantic Surety Assn. (by-law com. 1987, sec. 1988, treas. 1989), Messiah Coll. Baseball Assn. (founder, pres./sec. 1989, sec. 1990, newsletter editor 1989-92), Carolinas Surety Underwriters Assn. (treas. 1992). Republican. Baptist. Home: 14316 Blue Granite Rd Pineville NC 28134-8312 Office: Selective Ins Co Am Wantage Ave Branchville NJ 07890-0001

DUNN, MARK RODNEY, playwright; b. Memphis, July 12, 1956; s. Bobby Wayne and Miriam (McDaris) D.; m. Mary Weekley, May 29, 1982. BA, Memphis State U., 1978; postgrad. in screenwriting, U. Tex., 1980-81. playwright-in-residence Thirteenth St. Repertory Co., N.Y.C., 1988—. Playwright: Belles, 1990 (Margo Jones playwriting award 1986-87), Minus Some Buttons, 1991, Sandpies and Scissorlegs, 1992. Trustee Met. Duane United Meth. Ch., N.Y.C., 1992. Mem. Dramatists Guild. Home: 25 Charles St # 6E New York NY 10014

DUNN, PAUL FRANCIS, JR., bookkeeper; b. Woonsocket, R.I., Jan. 13, 1958; s. Paul F. and Claire (Girouard) D. Diploma, Internat. Corr. Schs., Scranton, Pa., 1988, Internat. Corr. Schs., Scranton, Pa., 1990. Lab. technician Wellman, Boston, 1976—. Recording artist Music, 1976 (Music award 1992). Pres. Webster House, Brookline, Mass., 1992-93. Republican. Roman Catholic. Home: 1069 Beacon St Brookline MA 02146

DUNN, RAY ALOYSIUS, III, real estate company executive; b. Miami Beach, Fla., Mar. 2, 1948; s. Ray A. Jr. and Roberta (Bryant) D.; m. Elizabeth MacDonald, June 17, 1973 (div. 1976); m. Marco S. Dunn, Aug. 8, 1981; children: Melessa, Sara. BA in Econs., Georgetown U., 1970; MBA, U. Va., 1979. Resident mgr. Marriott Hotels, Boston, 1982-84; dir. of ops. Courtyard by Marriott, Washington, 1984-86; chief oper. officer, dir. Great Inns of Am., Annapolis, Md., 1987-91; bd. dirs. South Charles Realty/Md. Nat. Corp., Balt.; v.p. hotel div. South Charles Realty/MNC, Balt., 1991—. Mem. Crofton (Md.) Civic Assn., 1987-90. Mem. Army-Navy Country Club, Crofton Country Club (bd. dirs. 1988-89). Democrat. Roman Catholic. Home: 1577 Eton Way Crofton MD 21114

DUNN, SUSAN CAROLE, apparel designer; b. Quantico, Va., Apr. 2, 1956; d. David Joseph and Marilyn Frances (Percaccia) Dunn; m. James Hutton Collins, May 23, 1981 (div. 1986). AB in Econs., Stanford U., 1978. Prin. Peprica, Inc., L.A., 1979-82; pres. Policappelli, Inc., L.A., 1983-87, Susan Dunn Intimates, Inc., N.Y.C., 1987—. Mem. Mus. Modern Art, Met. Mus. of Art. Office: Susan Dunn Intimates Inc 183 Madison Ave # 300 New York NY 10016-5113

DUNN, SUSAN RHEA, accountant; b. Minden, La., Mar. 22, 1946; d. William Duane and Martee (Davidson) Rhea; m. John Dunn, Nov. 8, 1970; children: Thomas Eugene, William Phillips, Laura Diantha. BS, La. State U., 1968. CPA, Pa. Staff acct. Arthur Andersen & Co., New Orleans, 1967-69; acct., cons. Arthur Andersen & Co., Denver, 1969-70; tax acct. Dawson, Nagle, Sherman & Howard, Denver, 1970; acct., cons. Root, Spitznas & Smiley, Erie, Pa., 1971-72, Susan R. Dunn, CPA, Erie, 1972—. Corp. sec., dir. YMCA of Greater Erie, 1978—; corporator St. Vincent's Health Ctr., Erie, 1983—; pres. Erie Philharmonic Orch., 1986-87; trustee, auditor, chmn. system rev. com. Ch. of the Covenant, Erie, 1983-84; mem. Jr. League, 1972-80. Recipient Bus. Woman of Yr. award, Bus. and Profl. Women of Denver, 1970, Woman of Yr. award YMCA of Greater Erie, 1988. Mem. Pa. Inst. CPA's (fed.tax com., continung edn. com., estate planning conf. com.), Estate Planning Coun., Nat. Soc. Tax Profls. Republican. Presbyterian.

DUNNE, DANA PHILIP C., management consultant; b. N.Y.C., July 30, 1963; s. Philip M. and Diane (Cantine) D. BA, Wesleyan U., 1985; MBA, Wharton Sch., 1990; MA in Internat. Studies, U. Pa., 1990. Asst. treas. Chase Manhattan Bank, N.Y.C., 1985-87; cons. McKinsey & Co., Inc., 1990—. Author: Financial Instability: An Empirical Analysis; editor-in-chief Wesleyan Economic Review. Mem. Meals for Homeless St. James' Ch., 1985—; mentor Underprivileged Youths in South Bronx, 1986. Named Disting. Internat. Young Leader Cambridge U. Am. Biog. Inst., Eng., 1987. Episcopalian. Home: 750 Park Ave New York NY 10021-4252

DUNNE, DIANE C., marketing executive; b. Milw.; d. Francis and Ruth Borman Cantine; 1 child, Dana Philip. BS, Marquette U., 1970; MBA, NYU, 1985. Mgr. advt. NBC, N.Y.C., 1975-77; dir. mktg. CBS, N.Y.C., 1977-80; dir. funding Bloomingdale's, N.Y.C., 1980—; dir. 750 Park Ave. Corp., N.Y.C., 1985—; dir. Women's Econ. Round Table, 1988—. Author: Guidelines to Advertising All News Radio, 1976. Author: Guidlines for Catalogue Copywriters, 1985; asst. editor Am. Cancer Soc., Gourmet Guide for Busy People by Famous People, 1985, The Internat. Directory of Disting. Leadership; contbr. articles to profl. jours. Mem. Am. Cancer Soc., N.Y.C., 1980—; chair St. James Ch. Feed the Homeless com., N.Y.C., 1984—; mem. pastoral and community ministry com. St. James Altar Guild. Mem. Fashion Group (co-chair regional com.), Women's Econ. Roundtable (bd. dirs. 1988), NYU Exec. MBA Assn. Episcopalian. Avocations: opera, jogging, skiing, squash. Home: 750 Park Ave New York NY 10021-4252 Office: Bloomingdales 770 Lexington Ave New York NY 10021-8165

DUNNIGAN, T. KEVIN, electrical and electronics manufacturing company executive; b. 1938; married. B.A. in Commerce, Loyola U., 1971. With Can. Elec. Distbg. Co., prior to 1962; with Thomas & Betts Corp., Bridgewater, N.J., 1962—, div. pres., 1974-78, corp. exec. v.p. electronics, 1978-80, pres., 1980—, chief oper. officer, 1980-85, chief exec. officer, 1985—, chmn. bd., 1992—; bd. dirs. Nat. Starch and Chem. Corp. Mem. Electronics Industry Assn. (bd. govs.). Office: Thomas & Betts Corp 1001 Frontier Rd Bridgewater NJ 08807-2902

DUNNING, RONALD RICHARD, marketing executive; b. Parsippany, N.J., Nov. 19, 1942; s. John Burlington and Helen E. (Hinterliter) D.; m. Linda Jane Woodruff, Aug. 24, 1963; children: Steven Scott, Edward Michael. Degree in bus. mgmt., Fairleigh Dickinson U., 1968. Gen. sales corr. Allied Chem., Morristown, N.J., 1965-69; gen. sales rep. Allied Chem., Atlanta, 1969-74; regional sales rep. Allied Chem., Chgo., 1974-78; mgr. sales Allied-Signal Inc., Chgo., 1978-80; mgr. sales Allied-Signal Inc., Morristown, 1980-82, dir. mktg. and sales, 1980-91, bus. dir., 1991—. Office: Allied Signal Inc PO Box 1053R Morristown NJ 07962-1053

DUNSTAN, RUSS FRANK, psychological services professional; b. Allentown, Pa., Dec. 22, 1953; s. Ralph Charles and Margaret Elizabeth (Fick) D. Student, Davis and Elkins (W.Va.) Coll., 1971-73; BS in Biology, SUNY, Syracuse, 1976; MA in Clin. Psychology, West Chester (Pa.) U., 1988. Med. technologist Hialeah (Fla.) Hosp., 1979-80, Meml. Gen. Hosp., Elkins, 1980-81, Greene County Meml. Hosp., Waynesburg, Pa., 1981-85, Brandywine Hosp., Caln Township, Pa., 1985-88; psychotherapist prison program J.J. Peters Inst., Phila., 1988-89; psychol. svcs. assoc. II State Correctional Instn. of Graterford, Pa., 1988—. With U.S. Army, 1976-79. Mem. APA (assoc.), Pa. Psychol. Assn., Psi Chi. Home: 1119 W Lincoln Hwy Coatesville PA 19320-1836 Office: SCI Graterford PO Box 246 Collegeville PA 19426-0246

DUONG, THIEU, anesthesiologist; b. Hanoi, Vietnam, June 21, 1936; came to U.S., 1975; s. Phan T. and Thao T. (Pham) D.; m. Diep T. Nguyen; children: Anh T., Vi T., Mai T. MD, Saigon Med. Sch., 1962; MPH, Tulane U. Sch. Pub. Health, 1971. Diplomate Am. Bd. Anesthesiology. Intern Framingham (Mass.) Union Hosp., 1977-78; resident, fellow in anesthesiology Brigham & Women's Hosp., Boston, 1980-83; attending physician Cen. Hosp., Hue, Vietnam, 1966-67; chief Provincial Health Dept., Dalat, Vietnam, 1967-70; chmn. dept pub. health tng. Nat. Inst. Pub. Health, Saigon, Vietnam, 1971-75; anesthesiologist The Univ. Hosp. Dept. Anesthesia, Boston, 1983—; pres. ADE Anesthesia Design and Edn. Inc., Boston. Contbr. articles to profl. jours. Mem. AMA, Am. Soc. Anesthesiologists, Soc. Cardiovascular Anesthesia, World Assn. of Cardiac, Thoracic and Vascular Anesthesia, Soc. Edn. in Anesthesia, Mass. Med. Soc. Roman Catholic. Home: 55 Westmoor Rd West Roxbury MA 02132-4709 Office: The Univ Hosp 88 E Newton St Roxbury MA 02118-2347

DUPONG, WILLIAM GREGG, physician; b. Bklyn., Aug. 31, 1911; s. David William and Bertha (Ferris) D.; B.S., Columbia U., 1935; M.D., L.I. Coll., 1939; m. Jessie MacLeman, Feb. 7, 1942. Intern, Norwegian Hosp., Bklyn., 1939-40; resident Swedish Hosp., Bklyn., 1940-41; practice medicine, specializing in occupational medicine and surgery, Bklyn., 1942—; mem. staff Lutheran Med. Center; exam. physician N.Y. Telephone Co., 1943-53, med. dir., L.I., 1953-66, L.I., Upstate N.Y. Telephone, 1966-69, Manhattan, Bklyn., Queens, 1969-75, med. dir. clin. tech., 1975-76; dir. clin. lab. N.Y.C. Dept. Health, 1965-77; cons. Workers' compensation N.Y.C. Law Dept., 1976—; lectr. dept. environ. medicine Coll. Medicine Down-State Med. Center; chmn. indsl. medicine com. Luth. Med. Center, mem. tissue rev. com., 1982-85legal def. com., 1982-85; mem. impartial specialist adv. com., mem. rehab. adv. com. N.Y. State Workers' Compensation Bd.; chmn. Council Tb and Health Assns. N.Y. Mem. Park Slope Civic Council, 1958—. Diplomate in occupational medicine Am. Bd. Preventive Medicine; diplomate Am. Bd. Family Practice (recert. 1976, 82); certified instr. cardiopulmonary resuscitation N.Y. Heart Assn. Fellow Am. Coll. Preventive Medicine, Am. Acad. Family Practice, Am. Soc. Legal and Industrial Medicine, Indsl. Med. Assn., N.Y. Indsl. Med. Assn., N.Y. Acad. Medicine, Am. Acad. Occupational Medicine, Am. Pub. Health Assn.; mem. N.Y. Pub. Health Assn., Royal Soc. Health, AMA, N.Y. State (sec. sect. occupational medicine 1975, sec. 1976, vice chmn. sect. legal medicine and workers' compensation 1977-78, chmn. 1978—), Kings County (chmn. adv. com. on indsl. medicine, chmn. indsl. health com., pub. health com. 1968—, mem. workers' compensation com. 1968—, chmn. 1976-80, peer rev. com. 1971—) med. socs., Am. Heart Assn., N.Y. Heart Assn., Bklyn. Tb and Respiratory Disease Assn. (dir., exec. com., med. adv. com., v.p. 1965-68, pres. 1968-70), Am. Lung Assn. (rep. dir. bd. dirs. 1965-80), Assn. Tchrs. Preventive Medicine, N.Y. State Acad. Gen. Practice (indsl. med. adv. com. 1969—), Nat. Council on Alcholism, Am. Soc. Legal and Indsl. Medicine (gov. 1971—). Methodist. Club: Masons. Contbr. articles to profl. jours. Home: 555 1st St Brooklyn NY 11215-2305

DUPONT, BARBARA JEAN, therapist; b. Haverhill, Mass., June 16, 1946; d. Carl Robert and Louise Elizabeth (Pickering) Stewart; m. Henry Philip Dupont, July 12, 1969; children: Mary Patricia, Valerie Lynn. AS in Human Svcs./Mental Health, N.H. Tech. Inst., Concord, 1988; BS, Springfield Coll., 1990; MA in Counseling Psychology, Lesley Coll., 1992. Tax examiner IRS, Andover, Mass., 1970-80; ednl. coord. Namaste Ctr., Manchester, N.H., 1985; inventory mgr. 1400 Motors of Nashua (N.H.), Inc., 1985-86; counselor, intern Youth Devel. Ctr., Manchester, N.H., 1987; clinician, intern Hampstead (N.H.) Hosp., 1987-88; psychiat. technician Nurses QOD, Inc., Merrimack, N.H., 1988-89, Lakeshore Hosp., Manchester, 1989; therapist, intern Home Health and Hospice Care, Nashua, 1990, Health and Edn. Svcs., Salem, Mass., 1991—; peer tutor N.H. Tech. Inst., Concord, 1987-88. Hospice vol. Home Health and Hospice Care, Nashua, 1990; hotline vol. Citizen's Against Drug Abuse Hot Line, Derry, N.H., 1982. Mem. AACD, APA (student affiliate). Home: 9 Mallard Ln Londonderry NH 03053-2262

DUPONT, EDWARD CHARLES, JR., petroleum distribution company executive, state senator; b. Dover, N.H., Mar. 10, 1950; s. Edward C. and Madeleine M. (Colell) D.; m. Andrea M. Castonguay, Oct. 19, 1979. Student, U. N.H., 1968-72. Pres., Strafford Fuels, Rochester, N.H., 1972—; senator State of N.H., Concord, 1983—, senate pres., 1990—. City councilor Rochester City Council, N.H., 1982-85. Mem. Rochester C. of C. (pres.-elect 1985). Republican. Roman Catholic. Lodge: Rotary. Avocation: private pilot. Home: 5 Westview Dr Rochester NH 03867-5010 Office: Strafford Fuels 25 Hancock St Rochester NH 03867-3528 Other: N H State Senate State Capitol Concord NH 03301

DUPRE, PATRICIA DIANNE, social services administrator; b. San Francisco, May 26, 1957; d. Albert and Edna Grace (Winston) D. AA, Community Coll. R.I., 1987; student, R.I. Coll., 1988—. Cert. chem. dependency profl. Youth counselor Channel One, Central Falls, R.I., 1985-87; counselor, adminstrv. aide Robert J. Wilson, Pawtucket, R.I., 1987-88; case manager The Providence Ctr., 1988-90; case mgr., mental health asst. Kent County Mental Health, 1990; supr. clubhouse Assocs. for Human Svcs., Attleboro, 1991; coord. resid. program Inst. for Devel. Disabilities, Attleboro, 1991—; psychiat. cons. Traveler's Aid Soc., 1989; group leader alcohol edn. group Quitting Time, 1989; coord. residential program Crystal Springs Sch., 1991—. Co-producer Visions Video; editor, producer Substance Free News. CPR instr. ARC, Providence, 1988; relief worker, leader Women's Substance Abuse Group, Pro-Cap Interim House, Providence, 1988-91; mental retardation worker State of Mass., 1991; clubhouse supr. Assocs. Human Svcs., 1991—. New Eng. Sch. Addiction Studies scholar, 1989. Mem. NASW, NOW, R.I. Assn. Alcohol and Drug Abuse Counselors, Nat. Assn. Children of Alcoholics, Shielders Club, Phi Theta Kappa. Democrat. Roman Catholic.

DUPREE, THOMAS ANDREW, forester, state official; b. Cambridge, Mass., Jan. 18, 1950; s. Glenn Stewart and Elvira (Pacifici) D.; m. Sandra Ann Becker, Aug. 31, 1975; 1 child, Steven. BS in Forestry, U. Mass., 1972. Svc. forester R.I. Div. Forest Environ., Hope Valley, 1974-76, sr. forester,

1976-78, prin. forester, 1978-86; chief R.I. Div. Forest Environ., Scituate, 1986—; past chmn. R.I. Tree Farm Com. Bd. mem. USS Mass. Meml. Com., Fall River, 1987—; vice chmn. Northea. Forest Fire Protection Commn., 1988-89, chmn., 1990—; pres. So. New England Forest Consortium, Inc., 1990—. Mem. Soc. Am. Foresters (chmn. Yankee div. 1988), Am. Forestry Assn., Nat. Assn. State Foresters, New Eng. Soc. Am. Foresters (exec. com. 1982-90), Northeast Area Assn. State Foresters (sec.-treas. 1990, v.p. 1991), R.I. Fire Chiefs Assn. Home: 7 Elmonte Dr Coventry RI 02816-7713 Office: RI Div Forest Environ 1037 Hartford Pike North Scituate RI 02857-1847

DUPUIS, SYLVIO LOUIS, optometrist, educator, administrator; b. Manchester, N.H., June 2, 1934; s. Arthur Edward Dupuis and Alma Lizotte; m. Cecile Marie Pellerin, July 14, 1956; children—Jeanne-Marie, Michelle, Marc, Mary Carol. Student, St. Anselm Coll., 1952-54; B.S., O.D., Ill. Coll. Optometry, 1957; L.H.D. (hon.), Notre Dame Coll., Manchester, N.H., 1975; D.Pub. Service (hon.), St. Anselm Coll., 1983. Sr. ptnr. Dupuis/Michaud/Collins/Noury/Allard Assocs., optometry, Manchester, N.H., 1957-71; mayor City of Manchester, 1971-75; pres., chief exec. officer Cath. Med. Ctr., Manchester, 1975-83, 89-; pres., chief exec. officer, prof. The New Eng. Coll. Optometry, Boston, 1985-89; pres., chief exec. officer Cath. Med. Ctr., Manchester, N.H., 1989—; commr. health and welfare State of N.H., Concord, 1983-85; trustee Energy North Corp., Manchester, 1982—; dir. N.E. Healthcare Assembly, 1991—. Bd. dirs. Community Concert Assn., Manchester, 1978-89, Currier Gallery Art, Manchester, 1974-88, N.H. Performing Arts Ctr., Manchester, 1976-86, N.H. Charitable Fund, 1980-87, N.H. Assn. for Blind, 1987-90; bd. visitors U.S. Mil. Acad., West Point, N.Y., 1977-81; pres. United Health Systems Agy., Concord, 1981; trustee St. Anselm Coll., 1985—, Brewster Coll., 1985-90, N.H. Vision Plan, 1989—; pres. Palace Theatre Trust, 1990—; mem. Gov.'s Commn. on N.H. in 21st Century, 1990—; dir. N.H. Bus. Com. for Arts, Bus. and Industry Assn. Decorated D.S.M. Knight of Holy Sepulchre of Jerusalem; named State Citizen of Yr. Boy Scouts Am., Citizen of Yr. Manchester C. of C., 1979; recipient Fellowship award NCCJ, 1980, Granite State award U. N.H., 1975, Man of Vision award Nat. Soc. Prevention Blindness. Fellow Am. Acad. Optometry; mem. Am. Coll. Hosp. Adminstrs., Am. Optometric Assn. (trustee 1969-71), Am. Acad. Health Adminstrs., Nat. Health Coun. (bd. dirs. 1986—), New England Coun. Optometrists (chmn. ann. congress, Disting. Svc. award 1984), N.H. Optometric Assn. (pres. 1969-70, Optometrist of Yr. award 1970), Nat. Soc. to Prevent Blindness (publs. rev. com. 1991—), Cath. Health Assn. (govt. rels. com. 1991—, bd. dirs. N.E. conf. 1991—), N.H. Bus. Com. for the Arts (bd. dirs. 1990—), Bus. and Industry Assn. N.H. (bd. dirs.), Manchester C. of C. (chmn.-elect 1990), Tomb and Key, Beta Sigma Kappa. Democrat. Roman Catholic. Home: 451 Coolidge Ave Manchester NH 03102-3214 Office: Cath Med Ctr 100 Mcgregor St Manchester NH 03102-3770

DUQUETTE, DAVID JOSEPH, materials science and engineering educator; b. Springfield, Mass., Nov. 4, 1939; s. Joseph Albert and Jeannette Marie (Bernier) D.; m. JoAnn Nazarko, July 31, 1982; children: David Joseph Jr., Peter James. BS, USCG Acad., 1961; PhD, MIT, 1968. Commd. officer USCG, 1961, advanced through grades to lt., 1965; rsch. asst. MIT, Cambridge, Mass., 1965-68; sr. rsch. assoc. Adv. Materials R&D Lab. Pratt & Whitney, Middletown, Conn., 1968-70; faculty mem. Rensselaer Poly. Inst., Troy, N.Y., 1970—; vis. prof. Imperial Coll. of Sci. & Tech., U. London, 1973; vis. sr. scientist Max Planck Institut fur Eisenforschung, Dusseldorf, 1983-84; mem. panel on material performance 5 NAS/NAE, Washington, 1980—, NASA Space Processing Rev. Com., Huntsville, Ala., 1978-83. Contbr. articles to tech. jours. Mem. North Colonie Bd. of Edn., 1974-79, Albany County Airport Adv. Com., 1976-79. Recipient Excellence award ALCOA Found., 1978, 79, Humboldt prize Alexander von Humboldt Found., 1983, Willis Rodney Whitney award Nat. Assn. of Corr. Eng., Tex., 1990, Centennial scholar Case Inst. of Tech., Cleve., 1980, fellow ASM Internat., Metals Park, Ohio, 1986. Mem. Alpha Sigma Mu (hon.). Office: Rensselaer Poly Inst Materials Engring Dept Troy NY 12180-3590

DURANT, LINDA SUE, college administrator; b. Malone, N.Y., Mar. 7, 1950; d. Arthur James and Gladys (Barnes) D.; m. Timothy M. Sullivan, July 1, 1989. BS, SUNY, Plattsburg, 1972; MS, SUNY, Cortland, 1976. Tchr. Newfield (N.Y.) Cen. Schs., 1972-76; tchr., prin. Pasadena (Tex.) Ind. Schs., 1976-80; tng. mgr. Pullman Power Products, Seabrook, N.H., 1980-85; program mgr. Portsmouth (N.H.) Naval Shipyard, 1985-86, U. N.H., Durham, 1986-88; dir. tng. ctr. Bristol Community Coll., Fall River, Mass., 1989-90, dir. devel., 1990—; cons. Nat. Assn. Ednl. Buyers, New Eng. group, 1989; profl. presenter Nat. Univ. Continuing Edn. Assn., New Eng. region, 1990, Nat. Conf. on Mgmt. and Profl. Devel. Programs, Fla., 1988, 91. Mem. ASTD (v.p. programming Bay Colonies 1989-90, pres. 1990-92), Coun. Advancement and Support of Edn., Career Connections, Inc. (exec. bd. dirs.). Office: Bristol Community Coll 777 Elsbree St Fall River MA 02720-7307

DUREK, THOMAS ANDREW, computer company executive; b. Sharpsville, Pa., July 1, 1929; s. Joseph Adam and Helen Barbara (Ondish) D.; m. Phyllis H. Norris, Aug. 1, 1987. BA, Pa. State U., University Park, 1953; MA, Baylor U., 1957; MS, Stanford U., 1959. Mgmt. scientist USAF, Pentagon, Washington, 1959-65; project engr. North Am. Rockwell Corp., Washington, 1965-68; systems engr. TRW, Inc., Washington, 1968-81, facility mgr., Patuxant, Md., 1981-82, project mgr., Washington, 1982-86; project mgr., prin. mem. tech. staff Software Productivity Consortium, Herndon, Va., 1986-89; sr. tech. staff, software technologist Systems Integration Group TRW Inc., Fairfax, Va., 1989—; professorial lectr. George Washington U., 1960-66, George Mason U., 1991—; chair software reusability conf. Nat. Inst. for Software Quality and Productivity, 1989-91, mem. adv. bd., 1991—; speaker in field. Contbr. articles to profl. jours. Mem. parish coun. Church of St. Stephen Martyr, Washington, 1970-78, pres., 1975-78, liturgical minister, 1973-87. With USAF, 1953-65; to col. USAFR, ret., 1984. Decorated Meritorious Svc. medal, 1984. Roman Catholic. Home: 7915 Quarry Ridge Way Riverhill Bethesda MD 20817

DURELL, JACK, psychiatrist; b. N.Y.C., July 5, 1928; s. Sam and Helen (Schwartzman) D.; m. Viviane M. diGioja, May 19, 1955. BA summa cum laude, Harvard U., 1949; MD cum laude, Yale U., 1953. Rsch. biochemist NIMH, Bethesda, Md., 1954-57; chief, sect. of psychiatry NIMH, 1963-67; v.p. med. affairs, clin. dir. The Psychiat. Inst., Washington, 1967-72; pres., med. dir. The Psychiat. Inst., 1972-78; assoc. dir. sci. Nat. Inst. Drug Abuse, Rockville, Md., 1979-86; med. dir. clin. affairs div. Ea. Va. Med. Authority, Norfolk, 1986-87; chmn. dept. psychiatry Mercy Cath. Med. Ctr., Phila., 1987—; prof. psychiatry U. Pa., Phila., 1987—; pres. The Psychiat. Inst. Found., Washington, 1973-78; trustee Phila. Mental Health Care Connection, 1987-89. Editor: The Changing Clinical Picture of Schizophrenia, 1977; asst. editor-in-chief Jour. Psychiat. Rsch., 1966-82, mem. editorial bd., 1982—; contbr. to numerous med. publs. With USPHS, 1953-56. Fellow Am. Psychiat. Assn.; mem. Am. Acad. Psychiatrists in Alcoholism and Addictions (sec.-treas. 1985—), Am. Psychopathological Assn., Am. Coll. Neuropsychopharmacology. Office: Mercy Cath Med Ctr 54th St at Cedar Ave Philadelphia PA 19143

DURETTE, PHILIPPE LIONEL, organic chemist; b. Manchester, N.H., Aug. 17, 1944; s. Emile P. and Marie Anne (Martin) D.; m. Anne Louise Patrizio, June 1967; children: Caroline Anne, Suzanne Louise. BS, Marquette U., 1966; PhD, Ohio State U., 1971. Fellow dept. chemistry U. London, 1971-72, U. Hamburg, Fed. Republic Germany, 1972-73; sr. rsch. chemist Merck & Co., Inc., Rahway, N.J., 1974-79, rsch. fellow, 1979-89, sr. rsch. fellow, 1989—. Mem. editorial adv. bd. Jour. Carbohydrate Chemistry, 1982-87; contbr. articles to profl. publs.; patentee in field. Mem. Am. Chem. Soc., Chem. Soc., Sigma Xi, Phi Lambda Upsilon. Roman Catholic. Home: 187 Pine Way Nw Providence NJ 07974-1824 Office: Merck & Co PO Box 2000 Rahway NJ 07065-0900

DURFEE, HERBERT ASHLEY, JR., medical educator; b. Burlington, Vt., Nov. 5, 1924; s. Herbert Ashley and Margaret Elizabeth (Spaulding) D.; m. Elizabeth Lea Dole, Sept. 18, 1947; children: Herbert Ashley III, Eleazer Lea Dole. BS, Yale U., 1948; MD, U. Vt., 1948. Diplomate Am. Bd. Ob-Gyn. Intern Lenox Hill Hosp., N.Y.C., 1948-50; fellow in pathology Free Hosp. Women, Brookline, Mass., 1950; resident in obstetrics Boston Lying-In Hosp., 1951; resident in surgery Faulkner Hosp., Jamaica Plain, Mass., 1953; resident in ob-gyn. Boston Lying-In Hosp. and Free Hosp. Women, Brookline and Boston, 1954-57; from instr. to assoc. prof. ob-gyn. U. Vt., Burlington, 1957-70, prof. ob-gyn., 1970-90, prof. emeritus ob-gyn., 1990—; assoc. chmn. Dept. Ob-Gyn., U. Vt., Burlington, 1965-90, acting chmn., 1961, 69, 76, 85; pres. med. staff Med. Ctr. Hosp. Vt., Burlington, 1985, 89, chmn. various coms. Capt. USAF, 1951-53. Mem. AMA, Am. Coll. Ob-Gyn. (Vt. sect. past vice-chmn., chmn.), N.Am. Ob-Gyn. Soc. (sec.-treas., 1980-90), Vt. State Med. Soc., N.E. Med. Assn., Baker-Channing Soc. Republican. Home: 25 Woodcrest Ln Burlington VT 05401-4151

DURGIN, SCOTT, airline executive; b. Topeka, Kans., Nov. 14, 1961; s. Stephen Byron Durgin and Faith Abbott; m. Kim Marie Slone, Feb. 10, 1990. BSBA, U. New Haven, 1983. Sta. mgr. Pilgrim Airlines, Flushing, N.Y., 1980-84; city mgr. New Air, Inc., N.Y.C., 1984-85; sta. mgr. Bus. Express, Inc., Flushing, 1985-87; regional dir. stas. Bus. Express, Inc., East Boston, Mass., 1987—. Captain U. New Haven football, 1982-83. Mem. Logan Airport Mgmt. Coun. Republican.

DURHAM, ASHLEY GREY, program analyst, instructor; b. Newbern, N.C., Feb. 4, 1959; d. Carl Hanna and Barbara Brookes (Horne) D. BA in Art History, NYU, 1981; postgrad., U. N.C., 1983-84; MBA, U. Balt., 1988; postgrad. in ops. analysis, U. Md., 1988—. Mgr. Bruce Teleky Graphics, N.Y.C., 1980-82; rsch. asst. Amman U., 1982; asst. trust ops. Equitable Bank, N.A., Balt., 1985-87; rsch. asst. U. Balt., 1987-88; instr. info. systems U. Md., Balt., 1988-90; program analyst Health Care Financing Adminstrn., Balt. HHS, 1988—. Contbr. articles to profl. bus. and info. systems jours. Vol. Big Sister, N.Y., 1978-84; mem. Dem. Nat. Com., Washington, 1987—. NYU scholar, 1978-80. Mem. AAUW, LWV, Am. Soc. Prodn. and Inventory Control (treas. 1987—), Profl. and Bus. Women's Assn., IEEE Computer Soc., Am. Assn. for Artificial Intelligence, Amnesty Internat. Democrat. Home: 656 Portland St Baltimore MD 21230 Office: Balt Dept Health Care Fin Adminstrn Security Blvd 1-B-2 Baltimore MD 21207-5187

DURHAM, GUY FLOYD, novelist, journalist; b. Petersburg, Va., July 16, 1937; s. Guy Thomas Durham and Thelma Floyd; m. Melinda Florian Papp, June 18, 1982; children: Nathan, Sarah. BSc., NYU, 1961. With Yale Coll. Spl. Student Program, New Haven, 1991—. Author: Stealth, 1989, Extreme Prejudice, 1991; contbr. articles to profl. jours. With USN, 1955-58. Mem. Internat. Crime Writers Assn., Authors' Guild, Mystery Writers Am., Mory's Assn., Univ. Club, U.S. Croquet Club, Point O'Woods Club, U.S. Treasury Pistol Club.

DURHAM, J(AMES) MICHAEL, retail executive; b. Louisville, Oct. 2, 1945; s. James Alton and Mary E. (Agustus) D.; m. Linda R. Hastings, June 5, 1965 (div. July 1983); m. Germaine Myra Judd, Jan. 25, 1987; children: Cassandra, Jason, Jamie. BA in English, U. Ky., 1968. English tchr. Clark County High Sch., Winchester, Ky., 1969-70; sales rep. Mass. Mutual Ins. Co., Lexington, Ky., 1970-71, Lorillard Tobacco Co., Lexington, 1972-79; owner/mgr. Durham Sales, Louisville, Lexington, 1979-85; owner/pres. Chesapeake Sport Shop, Balt., 1985—, Stadium Sports, Balt., 1991—. Mem. Nat. Sporting Goods Assn., Harbor Place Mchts. Assn. (v.p. 1991-92, bd. dirs. 1990-91), Balt. Tour Assn., Balt. C. of C. Office: The Sport Shop 201 E Pratt St Baltimore MD 21202

DURHAM, JEANETTE RANDALL, artist, educator; b. Plainfield, N.J., June 17, 1945; d. F. Gilbert and Alice (Petricek) Randall; m. Ormonde G. Durham III, June 26, 1971; 1 child, O. Ethan. BA in Fine Arts, Montclair State Coll., 1967; postgrad., Art Students League, 1970-72, Westchester Art Workshop, 1980-81; MS in Edn., SUNY, Oneonta, 1991. Cert. art tchr. N.Y., N.J.; cert. reading tchr. N.Y. Art instr. Mohawk Valley Ctr. Arts, Little Falls, N.Y., 1983, Owen D. Young Cen. Sch., Van Hornesville, N.Y., 1987—. One woman shows include Gallery 57, Cambridge (Mass.) Arts Coun., 1984, Gannett Gallery, SUNY Tech., Utica, N.Y., 1988, South Shore Arts, Little Falls, N.Y., 1991; exhibited in group shows at 37th Art of N.E. U.S.A., Silvermine, New Canaan, Conn., 1986, WMHT Exhbn. N.Y. State Mus., Albany, 1988, 56th Ann. Nat. Exhbn. The Cooperstown Art Assn., 1991, Coast to Coast Pleiades Gallery, N.Y.C., 1991, 56th Midyear Ann. Butler Inst. Am. Art, 1992. Named Best in Show, Mohawk Valley Ctr. Arts Invitational, 1983, People's Choice, N.Y. State Art Tchrs. Assn. Cen. Sect., 1990. Mem. Nat. Assn. Women Artists (elected artist mem., William Meyerowitz Meml. award 1991), Copley Soc. of Boston, N.Y. Artists Equity (elected artist mem.). Home: RR 1 Box 123 Jordanville NY 13361-9731

DURHAM, TINA MARIE, instructional designer, consultant; b. Billings, Mont., Jan. 3, 1953; d. Leland Keith and Shirley Mae (Pierce) Montabon; m. Scott A. Fernau (div. July 1984); m. Tom Dean Durham, Mar. 22, 1985; 1 child, Katherine. BA, U. Colo., 1975. DA operator Mountain Bell, Denver, 1975-76, analytical clk., 1976, svc. rep., 1976-78, supr., 1978-80, course developer, 1980-83; staff mgr. AT&T, Parsippany, N.J., 1984-87; project dir. DFS Internat., Phillipsburg, N.J., 1987-89; sr. ptnr. The Writer's Group, Phillipsburg, 1989—; cons. system documentation AT&T Card Ops., Kansas City, Mo., 1989-91; cons. and new product tng. U.S. Sprint, Kansas City, 1990; cons. system tng. AT&T Gen. Bus. Systems, Parsippany, 1991. Mem. ASTD, Nat. Assn. Women Bus. Owners, Nat. Soc. for Performance and Instrn., Rotary. Home: 2710 Belvidere Rd Phillipsburg NJ 08865-2160 Office: The Writers Group 2710 Belvidere Rd Phillipsburg NJ 08865-2160

DURHAM, (JOHN) WILLIAM, artist; b. Flint, Mich., Mar. 14, 1937; s. Rollie Paris Durham and Dagmar (Hotala) Korpi; m. Gloria Jean Albaugh, June 1, 1957 (dec. 1980); m. Lisa Hach Peters, June 21, 1987. BA, Mich. State U., 1960, postgrad., 1961. Painter, sculptor N.Y.C. and Amagansett, N.Y., 1966—. One-man shows include Benson Gallery, Bridgehampton, N.Y., 1967, 71, 72, 74, Art Placement Internat., 1981, Bryant Gallery, Roslyn, N.Y., 1988, Vered Gallery, Easthampton, N.Y., 1990; exhibited in group shows at AAAL, N.Y.C., 1972, Butler Inst. Am. Art, Youngstown, Ohio, Chgo. Hat Inst., Guild Hall Mus., East Hampton, N.Y., Nat. Acad Design, N.Y.C. Mem. Jimmy Ernst Artists Alliance. Home and Studio: Main St Amagansett NY 11930

DURKEE, DANIEL EDWARD, accountant; b. Dayton, Ohio, Aug. 12, 1964; s. John William and Mary Antonia (Hayden) D.; m. Lisa Anne Panico, June 17, 1989; 1 child, Andrew Ryan. BS in Acctg., Fairfield U., 1986. CPA, Conn. Acct. Coopers & Lybrand, Hartford, Conn., 1986-91, Internat. Marine Holdings, Inc., Guilford, Conn., 1991—; bd. dirs. Goodwin Tract Conservancy, Inc., Hartford, 1988-91. Mem. Conn. Soc. CPAs (speaker, discussion leader, mem. com. on cooperation with bankers 1990-91), Thrift Auditors Conn. (speaker, mem. planning com. 1988-91). Republican. Home: 50 Booth Ter Hamden CT 06518-2011

DURKIN, DOROTHY ANGELA, university dean; b. Glen Cove, N.Y., June 23, 1945; d. Frank Vincent and Rose Marie Durkin; 1 child, David Francis. BA, SUNY, Stony Brook, 1968; MA, NYU, 1974. Adminstrv. asst. SUNY, Stony Brook, 1965-67; prodn. editor Holt, Rhinehart & Winston, Inc., Stony Brook, 1967-69; editor Hill & Wang Pub., Inc., N.Y.C., 1969-70; asst. dir. pub. info. Sch. Continuing Edn. NYU, N.Y.C., 1970-72, assoc. dean pub. affairs and student svcs. Sch. Continuing Edn., 1983—; cons. N.Y.C. Ctr. for Lifelong Learning, 1974; producer TV series Continuum, Sta. WNYC, 1974; speaker, cons. coll. bd. Editor: NSF student mag., 1961. Recipient Andy Advt. award of merit, 1972; Direct Mktg. Leadership award, 1977, 80, 87; Nat. Univ. Continuing Edn. Assn. awards, bronze, silver, and gold medals, 1978, 81-88, merit award Art Dirs. Club, 1980, Merit award Soc. of Illustrators, 1980, Admissions Mktg. Report awards, 3 Gold medals, Merit award, 1986, 87, 88, 89, John Caples award 1987, 88, Catalog Age award, 1988. Mem. NUCEA (group leader learn from success), Am. Coll. Pub. Rels. Assn. (nat. award 1973), Coun. for Advancement and Support of Edn. (awards 1981, 82, 83, 84, 86, 87, 88, Grand Gold and Silver award 1989, chmn. nat. award), Women in Communications (job chmn.), N.Y. Radio Broadcasters Assn. (Big Apple award 1985), Univ. Continuing Edn. Assn. (chmn. info. svcs. div. 1980-81, chair mktg. adv. com. 1989-90), Pub. Rels. Soc., Am. Demographics (adv. bd. 1989-90), Direct Mktg. Assn. (Echo Leadership award 1987, 88), SUNY Alumni Assn. (bd. dirs., speaker, cons.), Scuba Diving Club, Community Sing Club, Parent Assn. Club. Office: NYU Sch Continuing Edn 326 Shimkin Hall New York NY 10003

DURNIN, RICHARD GERRY, education educator; b. Haverhill, Mass., Mar. 9, 1920; s. William Edward and Ethel (Millett) D. BS, Columbia U., 1947; MEd, Harvard U., 1950; postgrad. summers, U. Nottingham, 1950, U. Oxford, 1956; EdD, U. Pa., 1968. Tchr. pub. schs., N.J., Mass., 1946-49; instr. State Coll. at Fitchburg (Mass.), 1949-51; dir. Antioch Sch., Yellow Springs, Ohio, 1951-52; asst. prof. SUNY, Buffalo, 1952-58; vis. lectr. edn. Tufts U., spring 1957; dir. Smith Coll. Day Sch., 1958-59; asst. prof. edn. Rutgers U., 1959-65; prof. social and hist. founds. of edn. CCNY, 1965-90, prof. emeritus, 1990—; instr. U. Nev., U. N.H., Coll. William and Mary, Johns Hopkins U., summers 1951-68. Author: American Education: A Guide to Information Sources, 1982; contbr. articles to profl. jours. Bd. dirs. Internat. Social Svc.-WAIF; mem. nat. coun. Travelers Aid Internat. Social Svc., 1972-77, Middlesex County (N.J.) Cultural and Heritage Commn., 1976—; mem. adv. commn. Mercer County (N.J.) C.C., 1980-87; trustee Proprietary House Assn., N.J., 1977—; mem. adv. com. The Old Barracks, Trenton, N.J., 1982-88, trustee, 1992—. 1st lt. USAAF, 1942-46. Mem. SAR, History of Edn. Soc., New Brunswick (pres. 1969-71), N.Y., N.J., Nat. Ry. Hist. Socs., Soc. War of 1812, Essex Inst., Soc. Mayflower Descs., Soc. Colonial Wars, English-Speaking Union (pres. New Brunswick br. 1991—), Kappa Delta Pi, Phi Delta Kappa. Episcopalian. Home: 50 Chester Cir New Brunswick NJ 08901-1526 Office: CCNY Sch Edn New York NY 10031

DURRANI, SAJJAD HAIDAR, space communications scientist; b. Jalalpur, Pakistan, Aug. 27, 1928; came to U.S., 1959, naturalized, 1966; s. Inayat Ullah and Hameedah Khanum D.; m. Brita Katarina Yasmin Portin, May 21, 1959; children: Zarina, Amina, Arif. B.A., Govt. Coll., Lahore, Pakistan, 1946; B.Sc. in Elec. Engring. with honors, Engring. Coll. Lahore, 1949; M.Sc.Tech., Coll. Tech., Manchester, Eng., 1953; Sc.D., U. N.Mex., 1962. Lectr., asst. prof. Engring. Coll., Lahore, 1949-59; instr., research assoc. U. N.Mex., Albuquerque, 1959-62; sr. engr. Gen. Electric Co., Lynchburg, Va., 1962-64; prof., chmn. dept. elec. engring. Engring. U. Lahore, 1964-65; assoc. prof. Kans. State U., Manhattan, 1965-66; sr. engr. RCA Space Center, Hightstown, N.J., 1966-68; staff scientist, br. mgr. COMSAT Labs., Clarksburg, Md., 1968-73; sr. scientist Ops. Research, Inc., Silver Spring, Md., 1973-74; sr. engr. NASA-Goddard Space Flight Center, Greenbelt, Md., 1974-79; mgr. for system planning, tracking and data relay satellite system NASA-GSFC, 1981-84; mgr. research and planning NASA Communications Div., 1984-88; chief communications scientist NASA Hdqrs., Washington, 1979-81, mgr. programs, Advanced Systems Office, Office of Space Communications, 1988-92; consulting engr. Computer Scis. Corp., Beltsville, Md., 1992—; vis. prof. U. Md., 1972; adj. prof. George Washington U., 1980-82, 86, 87; mem. Engring. Manpower Commn., Am. Assn. Engring. Socs., 1981; bd. dirs. Nat. Telesystems Conf. Mem. editorial bd.: COMSAT Tech. Rev, 1972, IEEE Spectrum, 1975-78, IEEE Procs., 1988—. Pres. Muslim Community Ctr., Silver Spring, 1976-82, trustee, 1989—. Recipient spl. achievement award NASA, 1977, 78, 90. Fellow IEEE (gov. aerospace and electronic systems soc. 1977—), pres. 1982-83, Citation of Honor U.S. Activities Bd. 1980, Outstanding Mem. Region 2 1982, dir. Div. XI 1984, 85, mem. publs. bd. 1986, 87, 91, 92, bd. dirs. nat. telesystem conf. 1991—), Washington Acad. Scis., AIAA (assoc. fellow). Office: Computer Scis Corp 4600 Powder Mill Rd Beltsville MD 20705

DURSIN, HENRY LOUIS, opinion survey company executive, retired; b. Woonsocket, R.I., May 3, 1921; s. Henry and Mary Regina (Butler) D.; m. Margaret Alice Smith, Apr. 20, 1943 (dec.); children: Henry Peter, Philomene Louise, Margaret Elizabeth , Stefanie Marie; m. Marie Ann Novosedlik, May 22, 1982. AB with honors, Brown U., 1942; MBA, Harvard U., 1948. Supr. corp. research Gen. Electric Co., N.Y.C., 1948-63; supr. corp. research Harper-Atlantic Sales Co., N.Y.C., also dir. research and promotion, 1963-67; dir. research ORC Caravan Surveys Co., Princeton, N.J., 1968-70, pres., 1970—; v.p. Opinion Research Corp., Princeton, 1970-74, sr. v.p., 1974-91. Chmn. agy. com. United Fund No. Westchester, 1960-68, pres. 1967-68; v.p. Westchester County United Fund, co-chmn. agy. com. 1966-67. Served with USAAF, 1942-46. Mem. Am. Assn. Pub. Opinion Research. Roman Catholic. Club: Harvard (N.Y.C.). Home: 42 Bear Brook Rd Princeton NJ 08540-6216 Office: Opinion Rsch Corp PO Box 183 Princeton NJ 08544-0999

DURSO, PETER JOSEPH, systems planner, sound designer; b. Bklyn., Aug. 13, 1954; s. Ralph James and Jean (Macchia) D.; m. Karen Francis Finamore, Oct. 13, 1979; children: Lisa Marie, Danielle. Student, Bklyn. Poly., 1971-72, Bklyn. Coll., 1972-77. Systems programmer N.Y. Telephone, N.Y.C., 1978-82, methods expert, 1982-83; methods expert NYNEX Svc. Co., N.Y.C., 1984-88; exec. info. planner NYNEX Sci. and Tech., White Plains, N.Y., 1988—. Mem. Am. Mensa. Office: NYNEX Sci and Tech 1113 Westchester Ave White Plains NY 10604-3510

DURST, MICHAEL CHARLES, lawyer; b. Perth Amboy, N.J., Feb. 24, 1954; s. Wallace Julian and Alice (Berman) D.; m. Carol Emig, May 1, 1983. BA, Williams Coll., 1975; MS, MIT, 1978; JD, U. Calif., Berkeley, 1981; LLM, Harvard U., 1985. Bar: D.C. 1981. Assoc. Jones, Day, Reavis & Pogue, Washington, 1981-84; rsch. assoc. internat. tax program Law Sch., Harvard U., Cambridge, Mass., 1985-86, lectr. law, 1986, 88; assoc. prof. U. Notre Dame (Ind.) Law Sch., 1986-89; vis. assoc. prof. Law Sch., Northwestern U., Chgo., 1988-89; spl. counsel to Office of Chief Counsel IRS, Washington, 1989-90; of counsel Jones, Day, Reavis & Pogue, Washington, 1990—; adj. prof. Law Sch., Georgetown U., Washington, 1985, 90—; cons. Mass. Dept. Revenue, Boston, 1985-87. Co-author: Corporate Taxation, 1992. Mem. ABA (chmn. com. on standards of tax practice tax sect. 1990-92). Office: Jones Day Reavis & Pogue 1450 G St NW Washington DC 20005-2088

DUSEL, ROBERT GEORGE, pharmaceutical consultant; b. Bklyn., May 19, 1942; s. George and Mary (Geisen) D.; m. Marie Rose Marra, Nov. 8, 1964; children: Robert, Andrew, Kathy Ann. MS in Chemistry, C.W. Post Coll., 1974; PhD in Indsl. Pharmacy, St. Johns U., 1984. R&D chemist Endo Labs., Garden City, N.Y., 1964-74; devel. pharmacist Dupont Pharms., Garden City, 1975-84; rsch. leader Chelsea Labs., Lakeview, N.Y., 1984-85; pharm. cons. Lachman Cons. Svcs., Westbury, N.Y., 1986—. Mem. Am. Pharm. Assn., Am. Soc. Pharm. Engrs., Acad. Pharm. Scis. Home: 10440 105th St Jamaica NY 11417-2329 Office: Lachman Cons Svcs 1600 Stewart Ave Westbury NY 11590-6611

DUSENBERRY, PHILIP BERNARD, advertising executive; b. Bklyn., Apr. 28, 1936; s. Harry Augustus and Margaret Maria (Shaw) D. Student, Emory and Henry Coll., 1955. Copywriter Batten, Barton, Durstine & Osborne, Inc., N.Y.C., 1962-65, creative supr., 1965-67, v.p., 1967-69, assoc. creative dir., sr. v.p., dir., 1977-78, creative dir., 1978-80, exec. creative dir., exec. v.p., mem. exec. com., from 1980, later vice chmn., exec. creative dir.; vice chmn. BBDO Worldwide, 1986—, also bd. dirs.; chmn. bd. dirs., chief creative officer BBDO New York from 1986, now also chief exec. officer; owner Dusenberry-Ruriani-Kornhauser, N.Y.C., 1969-73, Clyne-Dusenberry, 1973-76. Author: (motion picture) (with Larry Spiegel) Hail to the Chief, 1973, (screenplay) The Natural, 1975, (with Norman Cohen) August Strangers, 1977. Served with USNG, 1960-61. Office: BBDO New York 1285 Ave Of The Americas New York NY 10019-6028*

DUSENBURY, LINDA ANNE, research psychologist, consultant; b. Florence, S.C., Aug. 5, 1959; d. Richard Green and Susan (Law) D.; m. Jeffrey Conrad Laurence, July 4, 1987. BA, U. Vt., 1980, MA, 1982, PhD, 1984. Postdoctoral rsch. assoc. Ind. U. Psychology Dept., Bloomington, 1984-85; rsch. assoc. Cornell U. Med. Coll., N.Y.C., 1985-86, asst. prof., 1986—; mem. Ind. Prevention Rsch. Ctr., Indpls., 1984-85; prevention cons. Boys Clubs Am., N.Y.C., 1986; tech. cons. Carnegie Corp., Meharry Med. Coll., Nashville, 1990-91; mem. Disability Prevention Work Group, Dept. Health, Albany, 1990. Co-editor: Readings in Primary Prevention, 1984, Prevention, Powerlessness and Politics, 1988; contbr. articles to profl. jours. Recipient Vt. Conf. on Primary Prevention award U. Vt., 1980. Mem. Am. Psychol. Assn. Democrat. Home: 3 Briar Close Rd Larchmont NY 10538-1009 Office: Cornell U Med Coll 411 E 69th St New York NY 10021-5697

DUSOLD, LAURENCE RICHARD, chemist, computer specialist; b. Chgo., Nov. 15, 1944; s. Henry E. and Colette M. Dusold; m. Karen A. Marsh, Aug. 29, 1970; children: Amy, Lauren, Patricia, Amanda. BS in Chemistry, Purdue U., 1966; MS, U. N.C., 1969; postgrad., Wayne State U., 1969-71.

Rsch. chemist, residue analysis and methods investigation br. Bur. Foods FDA, Washington, 1971-75, chemist, computer specialist, div. chemistry and physics, 1975-81, sr. chemist, computer specialist, div. of chemistry and physics, 1981-86, chief telecommunications and scientific computer support, 1986—; mem. faculty, evening div. U. Md., 1973—; mem. fed. engrng. planning group Dept. Health and Human Svcs., 1990-92. Mem. editorial bd. Scientific Computing & Automation, 1990-92; contbr. articles to profl. jours. and book chpt. Mem. AAUP, Computer Soc. of IEEE, Assn. Computing Machinery (chmn. SIGAPL, D.C. chpt. 1978-91), Greater Washington Fed. Agy. APL Users Group (co-chmn. 1977-87), Alpha Chi Sigma, Phi Lambda Upsilon. Republican. Roman Catholic. Office: FDA 200 C St SW Washington DC 20204-0002

DUSSERT, CLAUDINE V., social psychologist, consultant; b. La Mure, Isére, France, Mar. 28, 1942; d. Jules and Renée (Fribourg) Villard; m. Bernard A. Dussert, Aug. 26, 1942; 1 child, Bertrand. BA in Biochemistry, U. of Lyon, France, 1966; postgrad. in Mktg., Mgmt., Sch. of Social and Econ. Scis., Paris, 1975; MA in Sociology, Am. U., 1984, PhD in Sociology, 1992; Cert., Indsl. Mgmt. IFG, Paris, 1978. Cert. sociologist, social psychologist. Adviser, market researcher French C. of C., Tokyo, 1967-68; tchr. in French Alliance Francaise, Santiago, Chile, 1968-69; rsch. specialist CERCHAR, Paris, 1969-70; procurement rsch. officer POCLAIN (SA), Paris, 1970-72; tchr. in French Greek Sch., Bujumbura, Burundi, Africa, 1976-78; adj. faculty sociology dept. The Am. U., Washington, 1985—; social psychologist, rsch. devel. cons. Strategies for Success Inc., Silver Spring, Md., 1987—. Contbr. articles to profl. jours. Hall of Nations fellow, 1984-85. Mem. Am. Sociol. Assn., D.C. Soc. Sociol., Internat. Assn. of Sociologist of French Lang. (rep. Washington area 1986—), Alpha Kappa Delta Intern Soc. Home: 8617 Irvington Ave Bethesda MD 20817-3603 Office: Strategies for Success Inc 2815 Aquarius Ave Silver Spring MD 20906-1812

DUTKA, ANDREW JOSEPH, neurologist, military officer; b. New Haven, Conn., May 24, 1951; s. Joseph John and Mary (McGillicuddy) D.; m. Ellen Shea, Nov. 11, 1978; children: Joseph, Michael. BS, Yale U., 1973; MD, Albert Einstein Coll., 1976. Diplomate Am. Bd. Psychiatry and Neurology. Commd. ensign USN, 1976; advanced through grades to capt., 1992; neurology resident Naval Hosp., Bethesda, Md., 1976-80; staff neurologist Naval Hosp., Bethesda, 1980-81; head EEG/EMG labs. Naval Hosp., San Diego, 1981-83; head medicine div. diving medicine Dept. Naval Med. Rsch. Inst., Bethesda, 1983-91; chmn. neurology dept. NAT NAVAL MEDCEN, Bethesda, Md., 1991—; assoc. prof. Neurology Uniformed Svcs. U. of Health Scis., Bethesda, Md., 1983—. Fellow Am. Acad. Neurology; mem. Am. Soc. for Neurol. Investigation, Undersea and Hyperbaric Med. Soc. Office: Diving Medicine Dept Naval Med Rsch Inst NNMC Bethesda MD 20814-5055

DUTOIT, CHARLES, conductor; b. Lausanne, Switzerland, Oct. 7, 1936. Studied at, Conservatory of Lausanne, Acad. Music, Geneva, Academia Musicale Chigiana, Siena, Conservatory Benedetto Marcello, Venice, Italy; attended session in conducting, Berkshire Music Center, Tanglewood, Mass. Formerly violinist with Lausanne Chamber Orch.; debut as condr. with Bern Symphony Orch., Switzerland, 1963; condr. and asst. music dir., Bern Symphony Orch., 1964, later music dir.; condr. and artistic dir., Radio-Zurich Orch., Switzerland, 1967; also guest condr. Vienna Opera; mus. dir. Nat. Symphony Orch. of Mex., Orch. Nat. de France, 1991—; apptd. regular condr. Goteborg Orch., Sweden, 1975; music dir., condr., Montreal Symphony Orch., 1977—; prin. guest condr. Minn. Orch., 1982-85; prin. condr., artistic dir. Phila. Orch., 1990-91; guest condr. all major orchs, S.Am., Europe, Japan, Australia, U.S., Can. and Israel, rec., Deutsche Gramophon, Erato, CBS, Decca/London; with Bavarian Radio Symphony, Boston Symphony Orch., Gothenburg Symphony Orch., London Philharm. Orch., many others. Recipient Canadian Music Council medal, 1988. Office: Orchestre Symphonique, 85 Ste Catherine W Ste 900, Montreal, PQ Canada H2X 3P4*

DUTTA, AJIT SINGH, international management consulting company executive; b. Jamshedpur, India, Mar. 19, 1944; came to U.S., 1978; s. Rajinder Singh and Kanchan Kaur (Sabbarwal) D.; m. Bonnie Louise Galat, Sept. 29, 1985; 1 child, Danielle Nadia Kaur. BA in Econs., Psychology, Ranchi U., 1963; BCom in Acctg., Ranchi U., Jamshedpur, 1965; MBA in Procurement, George Washington U., 1982. CPA, Va. CFO TransCentury Corp., Washington, 1978-80; cons. Ajit S. Dutta, Alexandria, Va., 1980-86; assoc. exec. dir. Planned Parenthood NYC, 1983-86; pres., owner Datex, Inc., Washington, Cairo and Guttenberg, N.J., 1986—; asst. to chief exec. officer Zawawi Group, London, Muscat, Hill Samuel & Co., London, Arthur Andersen & Co., London; fin. com. Internat. Inst. Rural Reconstrn., N.Y. and Philippines, 1986—; cons. various non-profit orgns., N.E. U.S.A., 1980—. Author: Indirect Costs, 1981, (manual) A PVOs Guide to AID, 1982, (newsletter) Washington Briefs, 1981-82. Speaker Adv. Com. on Vol. Fgn. Aid, Washington, 1981-82; chmn. SCOPE, London, 1970-72. Fellow Inst. Chartered Accts. in England & Wales; mem. AICPA, Inst. Chartered Accts. India, Inst. Cost Mgmt. Accts. London, Assn. PVO Fin. Mgr. (founding), Westchester Field Hockey Club, Lions. Democrat. Sikh. Home: 7004 Blvd 329A E Guttenberg NJ 07093 Office: Datex Inc Ste 750 1400 I St NW Washington DC 20005

DUVAL, RAYMOND ALFRED, controller; b. Brunswick, Maine, July 5, 1933; s. Wilfred J. and Eva M. (Dehetre) D.; m. Georgette I. Caron, May 25, 1957; children: Monique J., Colette M., George W.R. BS in BA, Portland U., 1956. Cashier Maine Fidelity Life Ins. Co., Portland, 1957-60; controller Wright and Pierce, Engrs., Topsham, Maine, 1960-65; v.p., controller Brunswick (Maine) Pub. Co., 1965—; bd. dirs. Pubs. Corp., Brunswick. Corporator Mid Coast Health Svc., Brunswick, 1990. Mem. Maine Chess Assn. (treas. 1975—). Democrat. Roman Catholic. Home: 13 Lincoln St Brunswick ME 04011-1911 Office: The Times Record Industry Rd Brunswick ME 04011-1512

DUVALL, BERNICE BETTUM, artist; b. Washington, Mar. 17, 1948; d. William A. and Bergny (Farovig) Bettum; m. Donald Dunn Duvall, Oct. 5, 1968; children: Gregory Thomas, Peter Brian. Grad. high sch., Washington, 1966; art edn. pvt. study, 1970-74. Artist watercolor, acrylic, needlework design Chevy Chase, Md., 1972—; with pub. rels. and publicity Town Ctr. Gallery, Rockville, Md., 1986-89; banner designer St. Paul's Luth. Ch., Washington, 1985—; exhibit judge various art orgns., Md., Va. Exhibited paintings in numerous shows including Summer Sch. Mus. and Archives, Washington, 1991, 92, Springfield (Mo.) Art Mus., 1988, Fine Art Mus. of South, Mobile, Ala., 1990, Butler Inst. Am. Art, Youngstown, Ohio, 1983, Westmoreland Mus. Art, Greensburg, Pa., 1982, 87, DeLand (Fla.) Mus., 1984, others; prin. works represented in many pub. and pvt. collections, including Montgomery County Contemporary Art Acquisitions, New England Life Ins. Co., Pelavin Assocs., Inc., Capricorn Gallery; contbr. articles to Am. Artist, Watercolor, The Artist mag. Vol. artist Nat. Zoo, Washington, 1985-91; art judge Art in Schs., Parks, Pub. Places, Montgomery County, Md., 1988-90; speaker various pub. schs., Montgomery County, 1988, 92. Recipient Award of High Commendation Internat. Artists in Water Colors, 1981, Arthur Alexander award So. Water Color Soc., 1981, Award of Merit Md. Fedn. Art, 1980, Liquitex award Adirondacks Am. Watercolorists, 1989, Bendann Gallery award Balt. Water Color Soc., 1990. Mem. Art League (bd. dirs. 1982-86), Washington Water Color Assn. (bd. dirs. 1986-87), Town Ctr. Gallery (bd. dirs. 1986-89), Potomac Valley Watercolorists, Arttists Equity, Arts Coun. Montgomery County, So. Watercolor Soc., Balt. Watercolor Soc. Lutheran. Home and Studio: 3414 Taylor St Chevy Chase MD 20815

DUVALL, CHARLES PATTON, physician; b. Evanston, Ill., June 16, 1936; s. Charles Fleming and Edith (Osgood) D.; m. Nancy Ash, June 21, 1958; children: Lawrence Charles, Stephen Rogers, Douglas Patton, Lauren Lynne. AB, Cornell U., 1958; MD, U. Rochester, N.Y., 1962. Diplomate Am. Bd. Internal Medicine, Am. Bd. Med. Oncology. Intern Yale New Haven Med. Ctr., 1962-63; resident in medicine U. Rochester, 1963-64; clin. assoc. Nat. Cancer Inst., NIH, Bethesda, Md., 1964-66; resident in medicine Georgetown U. Hosp., Washington, 1966-67, USPHS spl. fellow in hematology, 1967-68; physician Foxhall Internists, Washington, 1978—; clin. prof. medicine Georgetown U. Hosp., Washington, 1968—; vice chmn. dept. medicine Sibley Hosp., Washington, 1987-90, chmn. 1990—; mem. emeritus staff Washington Hosp. Ctr., 1988—. Contbr. articles to profl. jours. Elder Bradley Hills Presbyn. Ch., Bethesda, 1974-77; mem. prof. edn. com. Am. Cancer Soc., D.C. chpt., 1978-79; chmn. bd. Blue Cross Blue Shield Nat. Capital area, Washington, 1986—, Group Hospitalization Med. Svcs., Inc., Washington, 1986—. Lt. comdr. USPHS, 1964-66. Recipient 5 Yr. Svc. award Am. Cancer Soc., 1978. Fellow ACP; mem. Am. Soc. Internal Medicine (pres. rsch. found. 1987-88, pres. elect 1988-89, pres. 1989—, Spl. Recognition award 1979), AMA (del. 1988—, coun. on legislation 1991—), D.C. Soc. Internal Medicine (pres. 1977), Specialties and Svcs. Soc. (pres. 1990-91, sect. coun. IM), Coun. Internal Medicine (chmn. sect. 1987-88), Osler Soc. D.C. (pres. 1978-79), Congl. Country Club, Bear Creek Club, Alpha Omega Alpha, Sigma Chi. Republican. Presbyterian. Home: 4 Hartman Ct Rockville MD 20854-4252 Office: Foxhall Internists 3301 New Mexico Ave NW Washington DC 20016-3622

DUVALL, LAWRENCE DELBERT, insurance company executive; b. Jacobsburg, Ohio, Mar. 5, 1942; s. Lawrence and Lillian Elizabeth (Brocklehurst) D.; m. Sandra Lee Parrish, May 16, 1970. BS, Ohio State U., 1964; MBA, Columbia U., 1976; BS in Meterology, Northwestern U., 1966. Cert. constrn. engr., N.Y. Exec. mgmt. trainee Crum & Forster, N.Y.C., 1967-69; inland marine underwriter, mgr. Am. Home Assurance Co., Constrn. Div., N.Y.C., 1969-73; Southwestern regional property mgr. Am. Home Assurance Co., Dallas, 1973-76; mgr. Ins. Co. of the State Pa., Dallas, 1976-82; atty.-in-fact A. I. Lloyds Ins. Co., Dallas, 1976-82; southwestern regional property mgr. Nat. Union Fire Ins. Co., Dallas, 1973-76; v.p. A.I. G. Energy Inc., N.Y.C., 1982-86, Starr Tech. Risk Agy., Inc., N.Y.C., 1986—. Fundraiser USMC Dependent Scholarship Fund, 1987—. With USMC, 1963-67, Vietnam. Decorated Silver Star, Purple Heart with gold star; Medal of Merit (Vietnam); named Constrn. Cons. of Yr., U. Wis., 1971. Mem. Soc. Petroleum Engrs., Conf. Spl. Risk Underwriters, Tex. Ins. Adv. Assn. Home: 171 Park Rd Parsippany NJ 07054-1731 Office: 80 Pine St Ste 300 New York NY 10005-1702

DUVIVIER, ROGER, obstetrician-gynecologist; b. Jeremie, Haiti, July 15, 1945; came to U.S., 1964; s. Max Ulrick and Lily (Hilaire) D.; m. Edna Salguero, Apr. 6, 1968; children: Jacqueline, Jean-Paul, Julie-Marie. BS in Biology, St. John's U., Jamaica, N.Y., 1968; MS in Physiology, L.I. U., 1970; MD, Albert Einstein Coll., 1974. Diplomate Am. Bd. Ob-Gyn. Instr. ob-gyn. Albert Einstein Dept. Ob/Gyn., Bronx, N.Y., 1978-79, asst. prof. in ob-gyn., 1979-83, dir. faculty practice, 1979-83; dir. faculty practice Winthrop U. Hosp., Mineola, N.Y., 1984—, dir. gynecology, 1984—, dir. ambulatory care, 1984—; asst. prof. SUNY, Stony Brook, 1984—. Author: (with others) Inferitility Surgery of Dr. Strangle, 1991; contbr. articles to profl. jours. Physician dir. Choice Care L.I., 1987-88; mem. Spl. Olympics, Bronx, 1983-84; bd. dirs. alumni bd. govs. Albert Einstein U., 1983—. Fellow Am. Coll. Ob-Gyn., Assn. of Profs. of Ob-Gyn., N.Y. Acad. of Medicine, N.Y. Acad. Scis., N.Y. Obstet. Soc.; mem. AMA (Physician Recognition 1986, 88, 90), Am. Assn. of Gyn. Laparoscopists, Am. Fertility Soc., Am. Registry of Diagnostic Med. Sonographers. Office: Winthrop U Hosp 259 First St Mineola NY 11501

DUVOISIN, ROGER CLAIR, physician, medical educator; b. Towaco, N.J., July 27, 1927; s. Roger Antoine and Louise (Fatio) D.; m. Winifred Theresa Murray, Feb. 21, 1948; children: Anne, Marc, Jacques, Jeanne. BA, Columbia U., 1950; MD, N.Y. Med. Coll., 1954. Diplomate Am. Bd. Neurology. Intern, rotating Lenox Hill Hosp., N.Y.C., 1954-55, resident in neurology, 1955-56; resident in neurology Presbyn. Hosp., N.Y.C., 1956-58; rsch. assoc. in neurology Coll. Physicians and Surgeons, Columbia U., N.Y.C., 1962-64, asst. prof. neurology, 1964-69, assoc. prof. neurology, 1969-72, prof. neurology, 1972-73; prof. neurology Mt. Sinai Sch. Medicine, N.Y.C., 1973-79; chmn., dept. neurology UMDNJ-Robert Wood Johnson Med. Sch., New Brunswick, N.J., 1979—, William Dow Lovett prof. neurology, 1990—; cons. Fed. Air Surgeon, Dept. Transp., Washington D.C., 1965-73; mem. scientific adv. bd. Parkinson Disease Found., N.Y.C., 1965-91, Ctr. for Advanced Biotech. and Medicine, Piscataway, N.J., 1987-91, Dystonia Med. Rsch. Found., L.A., 1989—; bd. dirs. Robert Wood Johnson U. Hosp., New Brunswick, N.J., 1991—. Author: Parkinson's Disease: A Guide for Patient and Family, 1978, 2d edit., 1984, 3d edit., 1990; editor: The Olivopontocerebellar Atrophies, 1989; contbr. numerous scientific articles and reviews to med. jours. With USNR, 1945-46, ETO; Maj. USAF, 1955-62. NIH grantee, 1985—; recipient Disting. Alumni award N.Y. Med. Coll., 1992, Springer award Am. Parkinson Disease Assn., 1992. Fellow Am. Acad. Neurology, Am. Coll. Physicians; mem. Am. Neurol. Assn. (sec.-treas.), Soc. for Neuroscience. Office: UMDNJ-Robert Wood Johnson Medical Sch One Robert Wood Johnson Pl New Brunswick NJ 08903

DWELLER, CLIFF, poet, reference editor; b. Providence, Feb. 9, 1953; s. Bruce Elliot and Lorraine (Proulx) Saunders; m. Linda Jean Grabner, June 1, 1985. BA in Creative Writing, Roger Williams Coll., 1975; postgrad., U. N.H., 1978-80; MFA in Creative Writing, U. Ariz., 1984. Freelance writer The NewPaper, Providence, 1980-85; assoc. faculty in writing Pima Community Coll., Tucson, 1984-85; lectr. in English Mohegan Community Coll., Norwich, Conn., 1985-87; instr. of English Roger Williams Coll., Bristol, R.I., 1987; reference editor H.W. Wilson Co., Cambridge, Mass., 1988—. Author: Windows of the Sun, 1987, The Persistence of Desire, 1991, Mapping the Asphalt Meadows, 1991. Recipient prize Acad. Am. Poets, 1983. Home: 23 Cary Ave Lexington MA 02173-7709

DWIGHT, HARVEY ALPHEUS, small business owner; b. Albany, N.Y., Apr. 21, 1928; s. Harvey Alpheus and Tessa Blanche (Gellert) D.; m. Helen Jean Fowler, Apr. 20, 1951; children: Diana, Lesley, Jessie, Harvey. Grad. high sch., Albany, N.Y., 1949. Lic. master plumber, N.Y. Owner Dwight Heating Supply Co., Rensselaer, N.Y. With Army N.G., 1949-58. Mem. Albany Lic. Plumbers (v.p. 1985-86). Office: Dwight Heating Supply Co 3d Ave Ext RD 2 Rensselaer NY 12144

DWORETZKY, MURRAY, physician, educator; b. N.Y.C., Aug. 18, 1917; s. Samuel and Frieda (Newhoff) D.; m. Barbara Ratner, June 11, 1943; children: Thomas Alan, Joan Mara. B.A., U. Pa., 1938; M.D., SUNY, Coll. Medicine, N.Y.C., 1942; M.S. in Medicine, U. Minn., 1950. Diplomate: Am. Bd. Internal Medicine (examiner allergy subbd. 1967-71), Am. Bd. Allergy and Immunology (founding mem., dir. 1971-74), Pan Am. Med. Assn. Intern City Hosp., N.Y.C., 1942-43; asst. resident pathology City Hosp., 1943, fellow in pathology, 1946-47; resident pathology U. Chgo., 1947-48; fellow in medicine Mayo Found., Rochester, Minn., 1948-50; practice medicine, specializing in internal medicine, allergy and clin. immunology N.Y.C., 1951—; asst. physician N.Y. Hosp., 1951, physician, 1951-56, asst. attending physician, 1956-61, assoc. attending, 1961-66, attending physician, 1966—, physician-in-charge Allergy Clinic, 1961-88; asst. in medicine Cornell U. Med. Coll., 1951-52, instr. medicine, 1952-56, clin. asst. prof., 1956-61, clin. asst. prof. pub. health, 1957-62, clin. assoc. prof. medicine, 1961-66, dir. tng. program div. allergy and immunology, 1961-88, clin. prof. medicine, 1966—; attending physician Manhattan Eye, Ear and Throat Hosp., 1953-62; Med. dir.-at-large Asthma-Allergy Found. Am., 1963-64, bd. dirs., 1964-78, mem. exec. com., 1964-77; founding mem. bd. dirs. Am. Bd. Allergy and Immunology, 1971-74; examiner sub-bd. allergy Am. Bd. Internal Medicine, 1967-71. Contbr. articles to profl. jours. Served to capt., M.C. AUS, 1943-46. Recipient Frank L. Babbott Meml. award Alumni Assn., Coll. Medicine, SUNY, Bklyn., 1992. Fellow Am. Acad. Allergy and Immunology (past pres. 1968; Disting. Service award 1989), N.Y. Acad. Medicine, ACP; mem. N.Y. County Med. Soc., N.Y. Allergy Soc. (past pres.), Soc. Exptl. Biology and Medicine, Harvey Soc., Am. Fedn. Clin. Research, AMA (chmn. allergy sect. council 1974-77, mem. residency rev. com. for allergy and immunology 1980-85), Am. Assn. Immunologists, Sigma Xi. Home: 21 E 87th St New York NY 10128-0506 Office: 115 E 61st St New York NY 10021-8172

DWYER, ANDREW T., utility and utility service company executive; b. Morristown, N.J., 1948. Student, Yale U., 1971; JD, NYU, 1974. Chmn. Jamaica Water Supply co., Lake Success, N.Y.; chmn., former pres. JWP Inc., Purchase, N.Y.; chmn. Welsbach Elec. Corp., Astoria, N.Y.; bd. dirs. Welsbach Corp., Welsbach Elec. Corp., JWP Inc. Office: JWP Inc 2975 Westchester Ave Purchase NY 10577-2518*

DWYER, BERNARD JAMES, congressman; b. Perth Amboy, N.J., Jan. 24, 1921; s. Daniel F. and Alice (Zehrer) D.; m. Lilyan Sudzina, 1944; 1 dau., Pamela Dwyer Stockton. Student, Rutgers U. Ins. broker, owner Fraser Brothers, Edison, N.J.; mem. 97th-100th Congresses from 15th Dist. N.J.; Mem. City Council, Edison, N.J., 1958-69; mayor City of Edison, 1969-73; mem. N.J. Senate, 1974-80, majority leader, 1979-80. Trustee John F. Kennedy Med. Center. Served with USN, 1940-45. Mem. VFW, Am. Legion, Edison C. of C. Democrat. Roman Catholic. Clubs: K.C, Elks. Office: 404 Cannon House Office Bldg Washington DC 20515*

DWYER, CHARLES BREEN, arbitrage specialist; b. Lawrence, Mass., Sept. 25, 1952; s. Joseph Justin and Gertrude Caroline (Breen) D. AB in English Lit. cum laude, Georgetown U., 1973. Cert. internat. financier. Asst. to consul Australian Consulate, Geneva, Switzerland, 1975-78; pres. Commd. Cleaning Co., Andover, Mass., 1979-84, CBD Assocs., Andover, Mass., 1985—; chmn. Major's Bay Devel. Corp., Cayman Islands, 1987—. Author: The Senator's Son, 1978. Mem. SAR, Pioneer Inst., Internat. Soc. Financiers. Roman Catholic.

DWYER, FRANCIS GERARD, chemical engineer, researcher; b. Phila., June 13, 1931; s. Francis George and Elizabeth Agnes (Foley) D.; m. Miriam Helen Hutelmyer, Jan. 8, 1961; children: Sharon, Timothy, Sean, Sheila, Colleen. B Chem. Engring., Villanova U., 1953; MSChemE, U. Pa., 1963, PhDChemE, 1966. Jr. technologist Mobil R & D Corp., Paulsboro, N.J., 1953-54; sr. rsch. engr. Mobile R & D Corp, Paulsboro, N.J., 1956-63, engrng. assoc., 1969-78, sr. rsch. assoc., 1978-81, mgr. catalytic R & D group, 1981-82, sr. scientist, 1982-85; mgr. catalytic R & D sect. Mobil R & D Corp., Paulsboro, 1985—. Author: Shape Selection Catalysis, 1989; editor: Intrazeolite Chemistry, 1983; also articles; numerous patents in field. With U.S. Army, 1954-56. Recipient Personal Achievement in Chem. Engring. award Chem. Engring. mag., 1990; fellow Mobil Oil Corp., 1963. Mem. Am. Inst. Chem. Engrs. (Achievement award in chem. engring. practice 1990), Am. Chem. Soc., Internat. Zeolite Assn. (coun. 1986-92, treas. 1989-92), Catalysis Soc. N.Am. Roman Catholic. Home: 1128 Talleyrand Rd West Chester PA 19382-7462 Office: Mobil R & D Corp PO Box 480 Paulsboro NJ 08066-0480

DWYER, HERBERT EDWARD, lay worker; b. Boston, Dec. 23, 1940; s. Herbert J. and Klara (Bill) D.; m. Linda C. Pepe, Aug. 23, 1962; children: Erin, Herbert D. Assoc. EE, Lowell (Mass.) Tech., 1963; BS in Mktg., Northeastern U., 1968; MBA, Boston Coll., 1972. Missionary My Father's House, Springbrook, N.Y., 1980-85, Elim Fellowship, Lima, N.Y., 1987—; founder Light of India Ministry, Mendon, N.Y., 1987—; Christian worker Elim Fellowship, Lima, 1988—; home group leader Elim Gospel Ch., Lima, 1990—; v.p. sales/mktg. AMTX, Inc., Canandaiqua, N.Y., 1988—; bd. dirs. Christ for India, Anaheim, Calif., 1988—. Editor (newsletter) News from India. Mem. Internat. Soc. Hybrid Mfrs. (pres. 1990—). Republican. Home: 4 Churchside Dr Mendon NY 14506-9704 Office: AMTX Inc 5450 Campus Dr Canandaigua NY 14425-9632

DWYER, JOHANNA TODD, nutrition research scientist, educator; b. Syracuse, N.Y., Oct. 20, 1938; d. M. Harold and Frances (Markey) D. BS with distinction, Cornell U., 1960; MSc, U. Wis., 1962; MS, Harvard Sch. Pub. Health, Boston, 1965, DSc, 1969. Asst. prof. Harvard Sch. Pub. Health, 1969-73; home economist Proctor & Gamble, Cin., 1962-64; rsch. asst. U. Wis., Madison, 1960-62; assoc. prof. Tufts Med. Sch., 1974, prof. nutrition, 1984—; sr. scientist human nutrition rsch. USDA, Boston, 1988—; dir. Frances Stern Nutrition Ctr., New Eng. Med. Ctr., Boston; adj. prof. Harvard Sch. Pub. Health, 1988—. Author of 3 books, 1979, 83; contbr. 300 articles to profl. jours. Mem. Mass. Nutrition Bd., Boston, 1980—; cons. Exec. Office of the Pres., Washington, 1976; mem. bd. sci. counselors Nat. Cancer Inst., 1985-89; com. mem. and nutrition work study Am. Cancer Soc., 1990—. Recipient Lenna Frances Cooper award Am. Dietetic Assn.; Robert Wood Johnson Health Policy fellow, 1980-81, John Stalker award Am. Sch. Food Svc. Assn., 1990. Fellow Soc. for Nutrition Edn. (bd. dirs. 1975-77, pres. 1976, J. Harvey Wiley award 1983); mem. APHA (program devel. bd. 1990—), Am. Soc. Parenteral and Enteral Nutrition (adv. bd. 1978—), Inst. Medicine Nat. Acad. Scis. (food and nutrition bd.), Am. Soc. Clin. Nutrition (sec. 1990—), Nutrition Screening Initiative (tech. and sci. rev. com. 1990—), Am. inst. Wine and Food (bd. dirs.). Home: 31 Lakeville Rd Apt 1 Jamaica Plain MA 02130-2010 Office: New Eng Med Ctr 750 Washington St Box 783 Boston MA 02111

DYE, CECIL MARION, digital equipment corporation executive; b. Eustis, Fla., July 9, 1940; s. Cecil Witson and Mildred S. (Milam) D.; m. Joyce Shoudy Dye, Mar. 29, 1963; children: Cecil, Debra, Donna. BSEE, The Citadel, 1962; postgrad., Babson Coll., 1981-82; MBA, Xavier U., Cin., 1983; postgrad. in mgmt. devel., Harvard U., 1987. Sales and svc. engr. Leeds & Northrup Co., 1965-70; sales rep., sales mgr. Digital Equipment Corp., Mass., 1970-84; mgr. corp. sales programs Digital Equipment Corp., Stow, Mass., 1984-85, mgr. corp. sales tng., 1985-89, mgr. corp. sales and software svcs. tng., 1988-89; dir. sales gen. internat. area Digital Equipment Corp., Mass., 1989-91; channels sales and mktg. rep. gen. internat. area Digital Equipment Corp., Acton, Mass., 1991—. Contbr. articles to profl. jours. Fund raiser Citadel Devel. Found., 1989. lst lt. USAF, 1963-65. Mem. Nat. Soc. Sales Tng. Execs., Citadel Alumni Club. Republican. Baptist. Home: 118 Graniteville Rd Chelmsford MA 01824 Office: Digital Equipment Corp 100 Nagog Park Acton MA 01720-3499

DYE, DAVID ALAN, industrial psychologist; b. Sharon, Pa., Dec. 28, 1956; s. James E. and Jane (Richmond) D.; m. Mary Jane De Sonia, Jan. 12, 1985; children: Katherine, Carol. BS, Bowling Green State U., 1979; MPhil, George Washington U., 1986, PhD, 1991. Mgmt. cons. Psychol. Svcs., Inc., L.A. and Washington, 1979-86; pers. rsch. psychologist U.S. Office of Pers. Mgmt., Washington, 1986—; cons. in field; faculty George Washington U., George Mason U., Am. U., all Washington, 1988—. Editorial bd.: Test Validity Yearbook, 1989; author: Biodata Handbook, 1991. Recipient Dirs. award U.S. Office Pers. Mgmt., 1990, 91. Mem. APA, Soc. for Indsl. and Orgnl. Psychology (sci. affairs com. 1989-91), Internat. Pers. Mgmt. Assn., Pers. Testing Coun. of Metro Washington (pres. 1985-86). Home: 5720 Lofthill Ct Alexandria VA 22303 Office: US Office of Pers Mgmt 1900 E St NW Washington DC 20415

DYE, FRANK JOHN, biology educator; b. Bronx, N.Y., Jan. 12, 1942; s. John Lester D. and Lucia Concetta (Del Pozzo) D.; m. Kathleen Susan Mauks, Aug. 5, 1967; children: John, Kathleen. B.S., Western Conn. State U., 1963; M.S., Fordham U., 1966, Ph.D., 1969. Prof. biology Western Conn. State U., Danbury, 1967—; Mellon vis. faculty fellow Yale U., New Haven, 1979-80, vis. fellow, 1981-87, 90-92. Fellow NIH, 1965-67, Nat. Inst. Dental Research, 1975-76; grantee Conn. State U., 1985-88, 91—, student-faculty collaborative grantee, 1990-91, 92—, Elias Howe Yankee ingenuity initiative high tech. grantee, 1990-91. Mem. Am. Soc. for Cell Biology, Soc. for Devel. Biology, Tissue Culture Assn., N.Y. Acad. Scis., Sigma Xi. Avocations: wildlife photography; bicycling; hiking; collecting amphibians. Office: Western Conn State U 181 White St Danbury CT 06810-6885

DYE, GLENN W., automotive executive; b. Wildwood, N.J., Aug. 21, 1921; s. Glenn A. and Grace M. (Adams) D. Degree in Refrig. Engring, Phila. Tech. Inst., 1947. Parts mgr. Fitzpatrick Chevrolet, Wildwood, 1953, Burke Motors, Wildwood, 1953-81; claims mgr. Scrivani Buick, Inc., Wildwood, 1981—; pres. Cys Hotel Corp., 1954-60, 5121 Park Corp., 1960-87; exec. dir. ann. stamp exhibit Precanex, Wildwood, N.J.; curator Davis Meml. Libr. Editor: We'll Be Brief, 1950, (periodical) Precancel Stamp Collector; developer naval postal charts. Member Rep. Nat. Com. With USN. Mem. VFW, Nat. Assn. Precancel Collectors (sec., treas. 1950—), Henry Collectors of Am., Inc., USS LCI Nat. Assn. Office: Nat Assn Precancel Collectors 5121 Park Blvd Wildwood NJ 08260-0121

DYER, ESTHER R., insurance company executive; b. Albany, N.Y., Aug. 30, 1950; d. Luther Hungerford and Ruth (Lindheimer) Dyer; m. John W. Lappin, Oct. 7, 1990. BA, SUNY, New Paltz, 1972; MLS, SUNY, Albany, 1973; PhD, Columbia U., 1976. Prof. St. John's U., Queens, N.Y., 1976-77, Rutgers U., New Brunswick, N.J., 1977-83; corp. archivist Empire Blue Cross/Blue Shield, N.Y.C., 1983-84, mgr., 1984-86, dir. govt. and community affairs, 1986—; dir. Children's Health Fund, N.Y.C., 1988—. Editor: European Library Networks, 1990, Public Schools and Academic Media, 1988, Cultural Pluralism, 1978; author: Cooperation in Library Services to Children, 1978. Named Disting. Alumna SUNY, Albany, 1989; Tangley Oakes Grad. fellow, 1976. Mem. N.Y.C. Jr. C. of C. (v.p. 1979—),

NAt. Arts Club (co-chair admissions 1985—, chair edn. com. 1991—). Office: Empire Blue Cross 3 Park Ave New York NY 10016-5902

DYER, FREDERICK CHARLES, writer, consultant; b. St. Louis, Feb. 17, 1918; s. George Leo and Katherine Mary (Dobson) D.; m. Lucrecia E. Herrera-Ibarguen, 1946; children: John R., Michael G., Lisa M. Dyer Fitzpatrick. B.A., Holy Cross Coll., 1938; M.B.A., Dartmouth Coll., 1948. Ednl. writer, editor tng. publs. Bur. Naval Personnel, 1948-58, asst. for spl. projects, leadership staff, 1958-64; spl. asst. to Undersec. Navy U.S. Navy, 1964-66; asst. for spl. projects Office Civilian Manpower Mgmt., Dept. Navy, 1966-68; dir. program analysis div. Navy Publs. and Printing Service, Washington, 1968-74; profl. lectr. George Washington U., 1956-60; adj. prof. Drexel Inst. Tech., 1962-67; profl. lectr. Am. U., 1967-73; adv. Ctr. for Applied Research in Apostolate, 1979-85. Author, co-author: Putting Yourself Over in Business, 1957, Executive's Guide to Handling People, 1958, Executive's Guide to Effective Speaking and Writing, 1962, Blueprint for Executive Success, 1964, Bureaucracy vs. Creativity, 1965, rev. edit., 1969, How to Make Decisions About People, 1966, The Petty Officer's Guide, 6 edits., 1952-66, The Enjoyment of Management, 1971, 82; contbr. more than 70 articles to profl. jours.; contbg. editor The Pope Speaks mag., 1954-64, Wall St. Rev. of Books, 1977-82. Mem. Town Council Somerset, Md., 1962-64; chmn. U.S. Civil Service Task Force on Mgmt. Edn. for Computers, 1965-66. Served with USNR, 1943-46; PTO; Navy Dept., 1948-52; ret. comdr., 1961. Mem. Authors Guild, Authors League Am., Washington Ind. Writers. Clubs: Columbia Country (Chevy Chase, Md.); Cosmos (fin. and hist. coms.), Nat. Press (library com.), Army and Navy (Washington). Home and Office: 4509 Cumberland Ave Bethesda MD 20815-5459

DYER, ROBERT FRANCIS, JR., internist; b. Washington, Nov. 18, 1926; s. Robert Francis and Sallie Antoinette (Worley) D.; AB, U. Mich., 1951; MD, George Washington U., 1955; cert. Postgrad. Med. Sch. Harvard U., 1958; m. Doris Anne Swain, June 27, 1970; children: Robert Francis, William Edward, Anne-Marie Helen Sallie, Scott Robertson McGavin. Intern, George Washington U. Hosp., 1955-56; resident in medicine D.C. Gen. Hosp., 1956-57, VA Hosp., Washington, 1957-58; chief resident physician George Washington U. Hosp., 1958-59; chief of staff Herndon (Va.) Med. Ctr., 1960-61, U.S. Army Hosp., Ft. Lewes, Del., 1963-65; chief of medicine U.S. Army Hosp., Ft. Indiantown Gap, Pa., 1962-63, dep. comdr., 1964-65; practice medicine specializing in internal medicine, Washington and Chevy Chase, Md., 1965—; chmn. dept. medicine Sibley Hosp., 1986-89—, vice-chmn. continuing edn. com., 1987—; mem. staffs George Washington U. Hosp., Washington Hosp. Center, Drs. Hosp. (all Washington); dir. Rsch. Lab. on Eosinophil Effect of Heparin, Washington, 1959-71; asst. clin. prof. medicine George Washington U., 1963—; pres. Washington Coll. Occupational Medicine, 1982-84, dean; dir. clin. rsch. Police & Fire Clinic, Washington, 1964—, acting chief of medicine, 1970, clinic adminstr., 1973-75, clinic dir., 1973-80; mem. clin. faculty Georgetown U. Sch. Medicine, 1988—; dep. med. dir. Washington Nat. Airport, 1961; nat. med. dir. Emphysema Control Com., 1967-70; med. cons. bd. ARC, 1985—; med. cons. on Occupational Safety Act and Health Act of 1983, City of Washington; sr. internist med. rev. bd., D.C. Dept. Labor, 1983—; mem. D.C. Mayor's Adv. Bd. on Emergency Med. Svc., 1974-75; bd. dirs. ECG-VCG Corp., 1989; chmn. bd. Protective Svc. Physicians, Washington, 1973-80; lectr. U.S. Park Police Acad., Alexandria, Va., 1964-76, D.C. Fire Tng. Acad., 1964—; chief med. flight surgeon Met. Police, Washington, 1968—, U.S. Park Police Helicopter Corps, 1970—; cons. in medicine D.C. Gen. Hosp., Walter Reed Army Hosp., VA, George Washington U. Hosp. Cardiology Clinic. Bd. dirs. Bd. Police and Fire Surgeons, Washington, 1963-80, sec., 1964-71, chmn., 1973-80; founder, dir. Police and Fire Surgeons Library, 1976—; chmn. bd. dirs. D.C. Bd. Police and Fire Surgeons, 1973-80. With M.C., U.S. Army, 1945-47, to col., 1956-65, Korea. Decorated Knight Order of St. Lazarus, Cross of Merit, Knight of Grand Cross Internat. Order Templare, 1985; recipient E. H. Hill award U. Mich., 1950, Citizenship award Am. Legion, 1954, Osler award George Washington U., 1954; diplomate Nat. Bd. Med. Examiners. Fellow Internat. Coll. Angiology, Am. Coll. Angiology, Am. Geriatrics Soc., Royal Soc. Health, InterAm. Coll. Physicians, Am. Occupational Med. Assn., Am. Acad. Med. Dirs.; mem. AMA, Am. Soc. Clin. Rsch., Med. Soc. of Washington (governing bd. internal medicine sect. 1991—, ho. of dels. 1992—), George Washington U. Med. Soc., D.C. Med. Soc. (pres. sect. occupational medicine 1979—, inter-splty. bd. 1975, chmn. state com. on environ. and occupational health 1980—, pres.-elect, med. editor Metro-Intercom 1977-80, com. pub. health 1989), Nat. Capital (dir., exec. sec. 1979-80, v.p. 1980—, pres. occupational medicine sect. 1979—), Am. Soc. Internal Medicine, U.S. Assn. Mil. Surgeons, So. Med. Assn., Pan Am. Med. Soc. (pres. 1981-83), Am. Coll. Occupational and Environ. Medicine, Washington Coll. Occupational Medicine (pres. 1982-84, dean 1991-92), Internat. Assn. Fire Chiefs (sec. med. sect. 1973-76), SAR (v.p. chpt. 1974-76, pres. 1976-77, state pres. 1976-78, surgeon gen. 1979—), Descs. Colonial Physicians (gov. gen. 1974—), Sons of Union Vets. (state comdr. 1980-81), Nat. Soc. Sons of Revolution (surgeon gen. 1991—), Washington Assembly, Am. Assn. Police Physicians and Surgeons (founder 1976), Washington Med. and Surg. Soc. (exec. sec. 1977-78, pres. 1978-79), Hippocrates-Galen Med. Soc. (chmn. bd. 1976-77), George Washington U. Faculty Club, Soc. Colonial Wars (gov. chpt. 1969-72, mem.2—, dep. gov. gen. 1978-81), D.C. Med. Soc. (ho. of dels. 1985—), Sovereign Mil. Order of Temple U.S.A. (nat. pres. 1984—), Delta Deuteron (pres. 1950), Phi Sigma Kappa (scholarship award 1950), Phi Chi (v.p. 1965, pres. 1977—). Clubs: Army and Navy (pres. Augustus Gardner Post Soc. 1983-84), Univ., Kenwood Golf and Country, George Washington U.; Annapolis Yacht; Royal Health (London). Med. editor Met. Intercom Jour., 1973-80; contbr. articles to profl. jours. Home: 5608 Albia Rd Westwood Bethesda MD 20816 Office: 5530 Wisconsin Ave NW Washington DC 20815

DYER, WILLIAM FREDERICK, interior design executive; b. Cliffside Park, N.J., July 23, 1949; s. Frederick Frank and Corinne (Lisi) D.; m. Patricia Catherine Albert, July 31, 1971; children: Todd, Brad. BS in Architecture, N.Y. Inst. Tech., 1971. Mgr. facilities design and planning ADP Inc., Roseland, N.J., 1971-85; dir. tenant design and planning Bellemead Devel. Corp., Roseland, 1985-90; v.p. ops. facility svcs. Brenner Bus. Interiors, Newark, 1990—. Cubmaster Boy Scouts Am., Ramsey, N.J., 1983-88, commr., 1985-87, scoutmaster, Mountain Lakes, 1989—. Office: Brenner Bus Interiors 330 Washington St Newark NJ 07102-2681

DYKSTRA, DAVID LAURIE, history educator, editor, small business owner; b. Rice Lake, Wis., Oct. 3, 1946; s. David Livingstone and Evalyn Marie (Enger) D.; m. Janet Frances Saltz, June 27, 1982; children: Jeffrey Scott, Craig Michael. AB, Bates Coll., 1968; MA, U. Va., 1969, PhD, 1973. Grad. instr. U. Va., Charlottesville, 1971-72; prof. Dean Jr. Coll., Franklin, Mass., 1974-91; lit. survey editor History Microcomputer Rev. Pittsburg (Kans.) State U., 1990—; dir. Occasional Computer Svcs., Medway, Mass., 1991—. Reviewer scholarly jour., 1991—. Capt. USAR, 1971-79. DuPont fellow U. Va., 1970, 71; Am. Hist. Assn. grantee, 1982. Mem. Am. Assn. State and Local History, Am. Hist. Assn., Orgn. Am. Historians, Soc. for Historians of Am. Fgn. Rels., Boston Computer Soc. Home and Office: 10 Priscilla Rd Medway MA 02053-2330

DYKSTRA, THOMAS KARL, photographic company executive, retired; b. Grand Rapids, Mich., May 9, 1935; s. Clarence John and Bertha Henrietta (Veen) D.; m. Lois Ruth Dykehouse, Aug. 11, 1959; children: Susan Dykstra Poel, Linda Dykstra Jonker. AB, Calvin Coll., 1957; PhD, U. Ill., 1961. Sr. chemist Eastman Kodak Co., Rochester, N.Y., 1961-66, rsch. assoc., 1966-71, lab. head, 1971-81, dir. planning and program devel., 1981-84, dir. materials devel., 1984-86, mgr. pers. rels., 1986-89, mgr. univ. rels., 1989-92; mem. govt. rels. com. Coun. for Chem. Rsch., Washington, 1990-92. Editor: Kodak Rsch. Mag., 1988-92; contbr. articles to profl. publs., chpt. to book; patentee in field. Mem., officer various sch. bds. and ch. orgns., Rochester, 1961—. Mem. Christian Reformed Ch.

DYMICKY, MICHAEL, retired chemist; b. Lwiw, Urkraine, Oct. 1, 1920; came to U.S., 1949; s. Mykola and Eva (Andrushkiw) D.; m. Olga Zhmurko, Jan. 22, 1943; children: Lida Dymicky Pakula, Oksana Dymicky Matla. Degree in chem. tech., Chem. Tech. Polytechnic, Lwiw, 1943; BS, U. Innsbruck, Austria, 1947, Doctorandum, 1949; PhD, Temple U., 1960. Chemist Am. Sugar Refining Co., Phila., 1949-52; rsch. chemist U. Pa. Med. Sch., Phila., 1952-53, Wyeth Inst. Med. Rsch., Radnor, Pa., 1953-56, 59-62; rsch. chemist Agr. Rsch. Svc. USDA, Phila., 1956-59, 66-89; assoc. prof. Kutztown (Pa.) U., 1962-65; gen. sec. Internat. Student Svcs., Innsbruck, 1947-49. Contbr. articles to profl. jours.; patentee in amino acid derivatives and anticlostridial agts. Recipient Citation of Merit DAV, 1970, Chem. Abstract Svc., 1971, USDA, 1989; Investor's award U.S. Dept. Commerce, 1987. Mem. Am. Chem. Soc. (student adviser 1963-65), Shevchenko Sci. Soc. (coun. 1968—), Sigma Xi. Home: 9653 Dungan Rd Philadelphia PA 19115-3221

EADS, DARWIN LEROY, management psychologist; b. Dodge City, Kans., July 16, 1949; s. Arthur Leroy and Rosalyn Irene (Way) E. BA in Psychology, Ottawa U., 1971; MS in Counseling, U. Kans., 1976, PhD in Counseling Psychology, 1980. Psychologist Miami County Mental Health Ctr., Louisburg, Kans., 1980, Osawatomie (Kans.) State Hosp., 1981; pers. cons. Marion Labs., Kansas City, Mo., 1981-85, dir. human resources, 1985-88; dir. orgn. devel. KV Pharm. Co., St. Louis, 1988-91; ptnr., v.p., sec. Corp. Resource Group, Inc., Balt., 1991—; cons. Vocat. Rehab. Ctr., Topeka. Bd. dirs. Kans. Bapt. Convention, Topeka, 1968-70, Transitional Living Consortium, Kansas City, 1985-88, Cen. Bapt. Theol. Sem., Kansas City, 1985-88. Mem. Am. Psychol. Assn., Am. Soc. Tng. Devel., Am. Compensation Assn., Soc. for Human Resource Mgmt., Md. Psychol. Assn., Kans. Psychol. Assn. (cert.), Mo. Psychol. Assn. (lic.), Rotary, Phi Beta Kappa. Home: 304 Glenrae Dr Baltimore MD 21228-5850 Office: Corp Resource Group 1300 York Rd Ste 150 Lutherville MD 21093

EADS, M. ADELA, state legislator; b. Brooklyn, N.Y., Mar. 2, 1920. Ed. Sweet Briar Coll. Mem. Conn. Ho. of Reps., 1976-89; mem. Conn. Senate, from 1980; senate minority leader serving on legis. mgmt. com., exec. nominations com.; mem. adv. bd. New Milford Bank & Trust Co., Glenholm Devereux Sch.; mem. task force on minority farmers. Trustee Marvelwood Sch., Cornwall, Conn.; bd. dirs. Drugs Don't Work. Republican. Mem. Conn. Bd. Edn., 1972-76., Nat. Orgn. Women Legislators. Home: 160 Macedonia Rd Kent CT 06757-1306 Office: Conn State Senate State Capitol Bldg Hartford CT 06106

EAGAN, MARIE T. (RIA EAGAN), chiropractor; b. Rockville Ctr., N.Y., June 17, 1952; d. John F. and Mary (Ebner) E. BA, Goddard Coll., 1975; D in Chiropractic Medicine, N.Y. Chiropractic Coll., 1983. Pvt. practice chiropractic medicine N.Y.C., 1983—; bd. dirs. Chalice Found., L.A., 1986. Fellow N.Y. Chiropractic Assn., Am. Chiropractic Assn., Internat. Chiropractic Assn. Democrat. Office: 231 W 21st St Apt B New York NY 10011-3119

EAGER, GEORGE SIDNEY, JR., electrical engineer, business executive; b. Balt., Sept. 5, 1915; s. George S. and Ada Elizabeth (Heinz) E.; m. Ruth Duff, Oct. 10, 1945; children: Robert W., John W., George S. III. BEE, Johns Hopkins U., 1936, PhD in Engring., 1941. Rsch. supr., asst. dir., assoc. dir. to dir. rsch. Gen. Cable Corp., Edison, N.J., 1945-80; pres. GRJ Cons. Svcs. Inc., Upper Monclair, N.J., 1980—, Cable Tech. Labs., Inc., New Brunswick, N.J., 1982—. Contbr. numerous articles to profl. jours. Author 35 patents elec. wires and cables. Lt. col. Signal Corps, U.S. Army, 1941-45, ETO. Fellow IEEE, Montclair Golf Club. Republican. Congregationalist. Home: 14 Bellegrove Dr Montclair NJ 07043-2527 Office: Cable Techs Labs Triangle Rd off Jersey Ave PO Box 707 New Brunswick NJ 08903-0707

EAGLE, JACK, commercial actor, comedian; b. N.Y.C., Jan. 15, 1926; s. Henry Eagle and Ida Mershon; children: Nikki, Jobbi, Ian; m. Susan M. Mohney, July 31, 1988. Trumpet player Muggsy Spanier, Georgie Auld, Henry Jerome, Boyd Raeburn, 1943-55; comedian Eagle & Man, 1955-65; solo comedian and comml actor., 1965—; comml. actor, goodwill ambassador Xerox, 1975—. Comml. actor for numerous cos. including Xerox's "Brother Dominic" (Clio award 1976), Fleischman Margarine's "Mr. Cholesterol", Carefree Chewing Gum's "Columbus's 1st Mate", Gillette's "The Perfect Face". Recipient Man of Yr. award Quick Print mag., Mr. Printing Week award Printing Industries. Mem. AFTRA, AGVA, Screen Actors Guild, Am. Fedn. Musicians.

EAGLES, DOUGLAS ALAN, neurophysiologist; b. New Britain, Conn., Feb. 22, 1943; s. Clyde Austin and Helen Frances (Sibley) E.; m. Joyce Pauline Juskalian, June 24, 1967; 1 child, Ross Brandon. BA, Lake Forest Coll., 1965; MA, U. Mass., 1968, PhD, 1972. Lectr. U. Mass., Amherst, 1970-71; postdoctoral fellow U. Iowa, Iowa City, 1971-73; asst. prof. biology Georgetown U., Washington, 1973—. Author: Your Weight, 1982, Nutritional Diseases, 1987, The Menace of AIDS: A Shdow on our Land, 1988; contbr. articles to profl. jours. Coach Prince William Soccer Inc., Prince William County, Va., 1980-90; judge sci. fairs Prince William County Schs. Mem. AAAS, Am. Soc. Biologists, Soc. for Neurobiology, Sigma (pres. Georgetown U. chpt. 1984-85, sec. Georgetown U. chpt. 1989—, chair mid-Atlantic region, nominating com. 1988—). Office: Georgetown U 37th & O Sts NW Washington DC 20057-1028

EAGLES, LEE NEILD, real estate company officer; b. Newark, N.J., Nov. 14, 1947; s. Eugene and Laurel (Neild) E.; m. Rosemary Mele, Nov. 28, 1985. BSBA, Fairleigh Dickinson U., 1971. Sales mgr. Lee Pharms., Calif., 1973-77; v.p. Alexander Summer Co., Bramus, N.J., 1977—; bd. dirs. Orient (N.Y.) Yacht Club, 1986—;. Sgt. USAF N.G., 1971-77. Mem. Commerce & Industry Assn., Fairleigh Dickinson U. Club (co-chairman 1990—), Fairleigh Dickinson Alumni Assn. (gov. 1988—). Office: Alexander Summer Co East 80 Rte 4 Paramus NJ 07652

EAGLET, ROBERT DANTON, electrical engineer, aerospace consultant, retired military officer; b. Cleve., Mar. 2, 1934; s. Albert Rudy and Dorothy Margaret (Beamer) E.; m. Sally Perry; children: Suzanne Carolyn, Allison Leigh, Kevin Robert. BEE, U. Ariz., 1962; MEE, U. So. Calif., 1968, PhD in Elec. Engring., 1970. Commd. 2d lt. USAF, 1956, advanced through grades to maj. gen., 1986, forward air contr. in Vietnam, 1965-66; div. chief classified program space div. USAF, L.A., 1966-68; chief strategic def. div. hdqrs. USAF, Washington, 1970-74, mil. asst. to dep. undersec. def., 1974-75; dep. gen. mgr. NATO airborne early warning program Brussels, 1975-79; dep. chief staff systems command USAF, Andrews AFB, Md., 1979-84; dep. comdr. armament div. USAF, Eglin AFB, Fla., 1984-86; dir. internat. F-16 program USAF, Wright Patterson AFB, Ohio, 1986-89; dep. asst. sec. of air force Pentagon, Washington, 1989-91; ret. USAF, 1991; pres. Eaglet International. Assocs., Vienna, Va., 1992—. Decorated Legion of Merit with oak leaf cluster, Disting. Svc. medal with oak leaf cluster, Silver star, disting. flying cross; named Outstanding Alumnus U. So. Calif. Mem. Air Force Assn., Armed Forces Communications-Electronics Assn., Assn. Old Crows. Republican.

EAKES, JOHN ASHLEY, psychologist; b. Waco, Tex., Aug. 25, 1953; s. Edward Eugene and Martha Jane (Lowry) E. AB summa cum laude, Princeton U., 1975; MPhil, George Washington U., 1981, PhD, 1985. Lic. psychologist, Pa. Intern clin. psychology Nat. Naval Med. Ctr., 1981-82; head psychology br. Naval Hosp., Jacksonville, Fla., 1982-84; head alcohol rehab. dept. Naval Hosp., Phila., 1984-86, head outpatient psychiatry clinic, 1986-88; staff psychologist Valley Forge Med Ctr., Norristown, Pa., 1988; employee assistance program adminstr. Southeastern Pa. Transp. Authority, Phila., 1988—; pvt. practice psychology Phila., 1988—. Lt. USN, 1981-88. Mem. Am. Psychol. Assn., Phila. Soc. Clin. Psychologists. Office: SE Pa Transp Authority 841 Chestnut St Philadelphia PA 19107-4427

EAKINS, WAYNE, environmental engineer; b. Indpls., Mar. 21, 1926; s. Frank and Josephine (Bohn) E.; m. Betty McDuffee (div. 1979); 1 child, Heather; m. Florence A. Moodie, 1991. Student, Purdue U., 1947-49; BSEE, Columbia U., 1952. Registered profl. engr., N.Y., N.J., Mass. Project engr. Bogert and Childs, N.Y.C., 1951-62; assoc. Clinton Bogert Assocs., Ft. Lee, N.J., 1962-74, prin. assoc., 1974-79; prin. Clinton Bogert Assocs., Englewood Cliffs, N.J., 1979—. Contbr. articles to profl. publs. With USAF, 1944-46, PTO. Mem. ASME, Water Pollution Control Fedn., Am. Water Works Assn., Am. Pub. Works Assn., N.J. Soc. Profl. Engrs., New Eng. Water Works Assn., Inst. Solid Wastes. Home: 3 Club House Rd Bloomingdale NJ 07403-1403

EANES, EDWARD DAVID, chemist; b. Rochester, N.Y., Sept. 2, 1934; s. Edward Wilbur and Harriet Lura (Briggs) E.; m. Beverly Elaine Kinsman, Aug. 19, 1961; children: Mark David, Donna Ruth. BS, Coll. of William and Mary, 1957; MA, Johns Hopkins Univ, 1959, PhD, 1961. Asst. prof. Cornell Univ. Med. Coll., N.Y.C., 1963-67; assoc. scientist Hosp. for Spl. Surgery, N.Y.C., 1963-67; chief, mineral chemistry and structure sect. Nat. Inst. Dental Rsch., Bethesda, Md., 1967—. Editorial bd.: Calcified Tissue Internat. jour., 1989—; contbr. numerous articles to profl. jours. With USPHS, 1961-63. Recipient Dir.'s award NIH, Bethesda, 1978, Biol. Mineralization award Internat. Assn. for Dental Rsch., Washington, 1983. Fellow AAAS; mem. Am. Chem. Soc., Am. Assn. Dental Rsch., Sigma Xi. Office: Nat Inst Dental Rsch Bldg 30 Rm 106 Bethesda MD 20892

EANNELLO, DOMINICK MICHAEL, academic administrator; b. N.Y.C., Mar. 1, 1932; s. Joseph Michael and Josephine Eannello; m. Michelle Scotti, June 19, 1982; 1 child, Joseph. BS, Siena Coll., 1954, MS, 1969; PhD, SUNY, Albany, 1973. Commd. 2d lt. U.S. Army, 1954, advanced through grades to col., 1984, retired, 1985; chemist City of Troy (N.Y.), 1958-60; v.p. Hudson Valley Community Coll., Troy, 1960—; cons. U.S. Army Arsenal, Watervliet, N.Y., 1981—; treas. Hudson Valley Endowment Corp., Troy, 1984—. Author: Planning Curricular Programs, 1978. Pres. Troy Livability Campaign, 1985, Schenectady (N.Y.) chpt. ROA, 1986; bd. dirs. Econ. Devel. Zone, Troy, 1990; mem. exec. bd. Boy Scouts Am., Albany, N.Y., 1988. Recipient High Merit award and medal Boys Town Italy, 1989, Svc. award Boy Scouts Am., 1988; fellow SUNY, Albany, 1972. Mem. Sons of Italy (sentiniel 1989—), Quincentenniel Commn. (com. chair 1990—), Friends of China (medal 1989), Troy Rotary Club (pres. 1966-67), Phi Delta Kappa. Roman Catholic. Home: 809 Parkside Ave Niskayuna NY 12309-6217 Office: Hudson Valley Community Coll 80 Vandenburgh Ave Troy NY 12180-6025

EARLE, NATHANIEL CABOT, board of trade executive; b. Providence, Feb. 27, 1952; s. Charles Crompton and Anne (Price) E.; m. Anne Clyde Gordon, June 28, 1975; childrren: Nathaniel Cabot Jr., Ashley Alexandra. BA in German, Middlebury Coll., 1974. Tchr. fng. langs., asst. dir. admissions Moses Brown Sch., Providence, 1974-80; credit analyst R.I. Hosp. trust Nat. Bank, 1980-81, loan officer, 1981-88, 1st v.p. precious metals group, 1988-89; pres. Jewelers Bd. Trade, East Providence, R.I., 1989—. Mem. Boston Jewelers Club, Providence Jewelers Club, Diamond Peacock Club, Agawam Hunt Club, Rolling Rock Club, Weekapaug Yacht Club. Episcopalian. Office: Jewelers Bd Trade 70 Catamore Blvd East Providence RI 02914-1206

EARLEY, ANTHONY FRANCIS, JR., utilities company executive, lawyer; b. Jamaica, N.Y., July 29, 1949; s. Anthony Francis and Jean Ann (Draffen) E.; m. Sarah Margaret Belanger, Oct. 14, 1972; children: Michael Patrick, Anthony Matthew, Daniel Cartwright, Matthew Sean. BS in Physics, U. Notre Dame, 1971, MS in Engring., 1979, JD, 1979. Bar: Va. 1980, N.Y. 1985, U.S. Ct. Appeals (6th cir.) 1981. Assoc. Hunton & Williams, Richmond, Va., 1979-85, ptnr., 1985; gen. counsel L.I. Lighting Co., Hicksville, N.Y., 1985-89, exec. v.p., 1988-89, pres., chief oper. officer, 1989—, also bd. dirs. Contbr. articles to profl. jours. Bd. dirs., vice chmn. United Way of Long Island, 1987—. Served to lt. USN, 1971-76. Mem. ABA, Nassau County Bar Assn. Roman Catholic. Office: LI Lighting Co 175 E Old Country Rd Hicksville NY 11801-4280

EARLEY, JOSEPH EMMET, chemistry educator; b. Providence, Apr. 6, 1932; s. Daniel McGlynn and Margaret Theresa (Doran) E.; m. Shirley Ann Titus, June 23, 1956; children: Thomas, David, Joseph. BS in Chemistry, Providence Coll., 1954; PhD in Phys. Chemistry, Brown U., 1957. Asst. prof. chemistry Georgetown U., Washington, 1958-63, assoc. prof., 1963-67, prof. chemistry, 1968—, chmn. dept. chemistry, 1984-90; coord. chem. rsch. evaluation USAF Office Sci. Rsch. Bolling AFB, Washington, 1961-87; vis. assoc. Calif. Inst. Tech., Pasadena, 1967-68; vis. researcher U. Libre de Brussels, 1976. Editor: Individuality and Cooperative Action, 1991; contbr. 80 articles and revs. to profl. jours. and chpts. to books. Capt. USAR, 1954-64. Recipient Rsch. Opportunity award Rsch. Corp., 1990; grantee NSF, Dept. of Energy, BEP, NASA, 1958-90; JSPS fellow Hokkaido U., Japan, 1992. Mem. AAAS (life), Am. Catholic Philosphical Assn. (life), Am. Chem. Soc., Am. Philosophical Assn. Democrat. Roman Catholic. Office: Georgetown U Dept Chemistry Washington DC 20057

EARLY, JOSEPH DANIEL, congressman; b. Worcester, Mass., Jan. 31, 1933; s. George F. and Marry V. (Lally) E.; m. Marilyn Powers, Apr. 7, 1956; 1 child, Joseph D. BSBA, Coll. of Holy Cross, 1955; LL.D., Cen. New Eng. Coll. Tech., 1975. Tchr. St. John's Prep. Sch., Shrewsbury, Mass., 1962-65; tchr., coach David Prouty High Sch., Spencer, Mass., 1959-63; mem. Mass. Ho. of Reps., 1963-74, vice-chmn. Ways and Means Com., 1973-74; mem. 94th-102d Congresses from 3d Mass. dist., 1975—, mem. House Appropriations Com., State, Justice, Commerce, Judiciary, Labor/HEW subcoms., 1975—; mem. exec. com. Dem. Nat. Congl. Com. Served as ensign USN, 1955-57. Roman Catholic. Office: 2349 Rayburn House Office Bldg Washington DC 20515 also: 34 Mechanic St Worcester MA 01608

EARLY, MARY BETH, occupational therapy educator; b. Columbus, Ohio, Oct. 7, 1949; d. James Michael and Mary Agnes (Valentine) E.; m. Robert John Dehler, July 1, 1983; 1 child, Jeffrey. BA, Manhattanville Coll., 1970; MS, Columbia U., 1974. Activities therapist Hillside Hosp., Glen Oaks, N.Y., 1974-75; occupational therapist Blueberry Sch., Bklyn., 1975-77; instr. La Guardia Community Coll., CUNY, L.I., 1977-79, asst. prof., 1979-82, assoc. prof., 1982-85, prof., 1985—. Author: Mental Health Concepts and Techniques for the Occupational Therapy Assistant, 1987. sec. 423-443 Tenants Corp., Bklyn., 1980-81, pres., 1981-83; treas. Bklyn. (N.Y.) YWCA Montessori PTA, 1991-92. Mem. World Fedn. Occupational Therapists, Am. Occupational Therapy Assn., N.Y. State Occupational Therapy Assn., Metro N.Y. Dist. Occupational Therapy Assn. (bd. dirs. 1984-86). Office: La Guardia Community Coll 31-10 Thomson Ave Long Island NY 11101

EARNER, GEORGE EDWARD, data processing analyst; b. Conshohocken, Pa., Mar. 19, 1930; s. John Henry and Edythe Lillie (Morrison) E.; m. Donna Jeanne Voss, Dec. 26, 1953; children: Timothy, Christopher, Michael. BA, Miami U., Oxford, Ohio, 1953, MA, 1958. Dir. info. services SciTek, Morristown, N.J., 1975-76; sr. cons. project leader AGS Computers, Mountainside, N.J., 1976-79; sr. tech. cons. GE Cons. Services, Piscataway, N.J., 1979-88; project mgr. CCH Legal Info. Svcs., N.Y.C., 1989—; cons. Comprehensive Health Services Plan, Newark, 1974-75, Growth & Facilities Data Base, Morristown, 1975. Precinct capt. Candidates for N.J. Assembly, Morristown, 1971, 75; election judge Sch. Bd. Election, Morris Twp., 1972; cons. Ret. Sr. Vol. Program, Morris County, 1972—; election news corr. radio/TV networks, N.Y.C., 1976, 80, 84. Served to capt. USAF, 1953-58. Presbyterian. Home: 5 John Glenn Rd Morristown NJ 07960-5611 Office: CCH Legal Info Svcs 1633 Broadway New York NY 10019-6708

EASH, MAURICE JAMES, education educator, consultant; b. Fulton County, Ind., Dec. 20, 1928; s. Edward Augustine and Gertrude Ethel (Barkman) E.; m. Edith Alma Syrjala, July 3, 1981. BSc, Manchester Coll., 1950; MA, Ohio State U., 1955; EdD, Columbia U., 1959. Tchr. Gary (Ind.) City Schs., 1953-57; asst. prof., then assoc. prof. Ball State. U., Muncie, Ind., 1959-65; assoc. prof. CUNY, 1965-69; prof. edn. U. Ill., Chgo., 1969-85, U. Mass., Boston, 1985—; cons. Nat. Dairy Coun., Chgo., 1975-86, Inst. Real Estate Mgmt., Chgo., 1976-80, ASHE, Chgo., 1978-85, Philippine Higher Edn., Manila, 1980-81. Author: Reading and Thinking, 1968; contbr. over 100 articles to profl. jours. Recipient Disting. Svc. award CAM, Chgo., 1981, Disting. Alumni award Manchester Coll., 1982. Mem. Assn. Advancement of Sci., Am. Ednl. Rsch. Assn., N.Y. Acad. Scis. Home: 35 Pierce Rd Watertown MA 02172-3032 Office: U Mass Boston Boston MA 02125

EASLEY, DAVID, economics educator; b. Lexington, Ky., Nov. 3, 1952; s. Alan Eugene and Jean (Ogden) E.; m. Maureen O'Hara, July 13, 1977; children: Megan, Casey. BA, U. Ky., 1974; PhD, Northwestern U., 1979. Asst. prof. econs. Cornell U., Ithaca, N.Y., 1979-84, assoc. prof., 1984-88, prof., chmn. econs. dept., 1988—; vis. prof. Calif. Inst. Tech., Pasadena, 1985-86. Contbr. articles to profl. jours. Recipient numerous grants NSF. Mem. Econometric Soc. Office: Cornell U Dept Econ Uris Hall Ithaca NY 14853

EASON, RICHARD ODELL, electrical engineering educator; b. Anniston, Ala., July 18, 1956; s. H. Odell and Betty Lee (Skidmore) E.; m. Mary Anne Stapleton, Apr. 8, 1978; children: Christopher Mills, Richard Parker. BSEE, U. Tenn., 1978, MSEE, 1980, PhDEE, 1988. VLSI design engr. Zilog, Inc., Cupertino, Calif., 1980-82; rsch. and teaching asst. U. Tenn., Knoxville, 1975-80, rsch. asst., 1982-88; asst. prof. elec. engring. U. Maine, Orono, 1988—; cons. Anzac Electronics, Bangor, Maine, 1989; invited researcher Kyushu Inst. Tech., Kitakyushu, Japan, 1989; vis. scholar U. Tenn., Knoxville, 1990. Author: (with others) Computers for Artificial Intelligence Processing, 1990; contbr. articles to profl. jours. Fred M. Roddy scholar U. Tenn., 1976, 77, W.O. Leffell scholar, 1984. Mem. IEEE, Computer Soc. of IEEE, Soc. Photo-Optical Instrumentation Engrs. Office: U Maine Barrows Hall Orono ME 04469

EASTMENT, THOMAS JAMES, lawyer; b. N.Y.C., Mar. 3, 1950; s. George Thomas and Grace Anne (Manning) E. BChemE, Manhattan Coll., 1972; JD, U. Mich., 1975. Bar: N.Y. 1976, D.C. 1977. Assoc. Morton, Bernard, Brown, Washington, 1975-77; assoc. Baker & Botts, Washington, 1977-84, ptnr., 1985—. Mem. D.C. Bar Assn., Fed. Energy Bar Assn. Republican. Roman Catholic. Office: Baker & Botts 555 13th St NW Ste 500 Washington DC 20004-1109

EASTON, THOMAS ATWOOD, writer, educator; b. Bangor, Maine, July 17, 1944; s. Thomas William and Alice Janet (Bartlett) E.; m. Elizabeth Susan Nelson, June 13, 1967; 1 child, Joellen. BA, Colby Coll., 1966; PhD, U. Chgo., 1971. Assoc. editor Scott, Foresman Co., Glenview, Ill., 1972-76; adj. instr. Unity (Maine) Coll., 1978-80, U. Maine, Orono, 1980-83; adj. asst. prof. Thomas Coll., Waterville, Maine, 1983-91, adj. assoc. prof., 1991—; book columnist Analog Sci. Fiction and Sci. Fact Mag., N.Y.C., 1979—. Author: How to Write a Readable Business Report, 1983, Working for Life: Careers in Biology, 1984, 2d edit., 1988, Careers in Science, 1985, 2d edit., 1990, Using Consultants: A Consumer's Guide for Managers, 1985, Cutting Loose: Making the Transition from Employee to Entrepreneur, 1985, Focus on Human Biology, 1992, others; author: (novels) Sparrowhawk, 1990, Greenhouse, 1991, Woodsman, 1992; contbr. poetry, short fiction to various publs., contbr. articles to profl. publs. Sci. cons. Conant for Congress campaign, Winslow, Maine, 1983-84, 85. NSF fellow, 1966-70. Mem. AAAS, Sci. Fiction and Fantasy Writers Am. (grievance com. 1980-84). Home: RR 2 Box 805 Belfast ME 04915-9630 Office: Thomas Coll Waterville ME 04901

EASTWOOD, DANA ALAN, consultant; b. Poughkeepsie, N.Y., June 1, 1947; s. Donald Edward and Edith Margaret (Davis) E.; m. Cynthia Carol Allen, Jan. 1, 1984; children: Athena Yvonne, Ashlee Lyn, Alysa Bryhn. Diploma, Am. Inst. Banking, Washington, 1980; Diploma with highest honors, Paralegal Inst., Phoenix, 1983. Proprietor Eastwood Studio, Hyde Park, N.Y., 1965-70; credit rep. Bankers Trust of Hudson Valley, N.A., Poughkeepsie, 1970-73; installment loan supr. Poughkeepsie Savs. Bank, 1973-75, installment loan mgr., 1975-78, consumer loan officer, 1978-79, compliance officer, 1979-87, compliance officer, data security adminstr., 1987-89; compliance, community reinvestment act and loan rev. officer, 1989-91; pres. Modern Bus. Advisors of the Mid-Hudson, 1991—; pres., chmn. bd. Consumer Credit Assn. of Mid-Hudson Valley, Poughkeepsie, 1973-75; 1st v.p. Consumer Credit Group of N.Y. State, N.Y.C., 1978-79; 1st v.p. Internat. Consumer Credit Assn., Dist. 2, N.Y. and N.J., 1978-79; mem. consumer credit com. Savs. Banks Assn. of N.Y. State, N.Y.C., 1982-85. Author: Gravity Park, 1978; editor The Right Banker, 1979-82; also painter of modern acrylic artworks. Mem. consumer edn. adv. com. Dutchess County Coop. Extension Assn., Millbrook, N.Y., 1975-77. Recipient Award for Outstanding Leadership Consumer Credit Assn. Mid-Hudson Valley, Poughkeepsie, 1974, John C. Corliss Meml. award, 1977, Dedicated Service award Consumer Credit Group N.Y. State, N.Y.C., 1979. Fellow Soc. Cert. Credit Execs.; mem. Internat. Platform Assn., World Future Soc. Home and Office: 7 Carriage House Ct Hyde Park NY 12538-1505

EATON, CANDACE JOHNSON, financial director; b. Beverly, Mass., Apr. 3, 1952; d. George Andrew and Elizabeth Louise (Feltis) Johnson; m. Robert Norman Eaton, July 2, 1983. Student, Boston Archtl. Ctr., 1975-78, Northeastern U., Boston, 1975. Bookkeeper, data processor United Engrs. & Constructors, Inc., Boston, 1970-72; adminstr. Jackson & Moreland Internat., Inc., Boston, 1972-78; fin. dir. Downeast Health Svcs., Inc., Ellsworth, Maine, 1979—; pres. Option One, Inc., Sullivan, Maine, 1982—; treas. Sullivan Woods, 1991—; cons. Hancock County Child Protection Coun., Ellsworth, 1987—. Treas. Campaign to Elect Robert Eaton, Maine, 1987-88; treas. Sullivan Bicentennial Com., 1988-89; co-chair Sullivan 2000 Comprehensive Plan, 1989-91. Mem. Maine Fedn. Bus. and Profl. Women (bd. dirs. 1985—, co-editor jour. 1990—, nominating chair 1990-91, corres. sec. 1989-90, del. to annual nat. convs. 1985, 86, 88, 90), Ellsworth Bus. and Profl. Women (bd. dirs. 1985—, del. to annual state cons. 1985—, pres. 1985-87, fin. chair 1990-91, legis. chair 1988-90, Mem. of Yr. award 1988), Ellsworth C. of C., Women's Bus. Devel. Corp. Office: Downeast Health Svcs Inc Christian Ridge Rd PO Box 1087 Ellsworth ME 04605

EATON, EDGAR PHILIP, JR., manufacturing executive; b. Milw., Jan. 17, 1923; s. Edgar P. and Dorothy (Morgenthau) E.; m. Rita Beverly Shachat, June 7, 1945 (div.); children: Richard Michael, Randall Charles; m. Helen Yansura. BS in Mech. Engring., MIT, 1944; MS in Bus. Adminstrn., Boston U., 1948. Asst. plant engr. Gen. Dynamics Corp., Groton, Conn., 1944-45; sales engr., supr. Allis Chalmers Mfg. Co., Boston, Conn., 1945-49; sales mgr., asst. to pres. Allis Chalmers Mfg. Co., Boston, 1949-51; exec. v.p. Carbone Corp., Boonton, N.J., 1951-56, pres., 1957—, also dir.; pres. Carbone-Lorraine Industries Corp., 1974-89, chmn.bd. dirs., 1989-91; prin. Brinton-Eaton Assocs., Morristown, N.J.; chmn. bd. Advance Carbon Products, Inc., San Gabriel, Helecoflex Corp., Carbone Lorraine Corp., Montreal, Que., Can., Ferraz, Rockaway, N.J., Xetron Corp., Cedar Knolls, N.J., Carbone U.S.A. Corp.; dir. N.J. Blue Shield and Blue Cross; cons. to mgmt. pers.; dir. Atlantic Health Systems, 1984—. Author: The Marketing of Heavy Power Equipment, 1948. Active Urban League; chmn. United Fund, 1959-60, 60-61; chmn. Morris County Community Chest, 1959-60, 60-61, pres., 1963-64; chmn. Morris-Sussex Regional Health Facilities Planning Coun., 1960-79; chmn. hosp. governing bds. Am. Hosp. Assn., 1968-69; bd. dirs. Morristown Mem. Hosp., Morris Mus., 1985—, Ctr. for Addictive Illness Corp.; pres. Winston Sch., 1979—, Shakespeare Festival, 1982, dir., 1984—; treas. PRO-No., N.H., 1980—. Served with AUS, 1942-43. Mem. Young Pres.'s Orgn. (chmn. 1963-64), ASME, IEEE, Am. R.R. Assn., Nat. Elec. Mfrs. Assn. (treas., dir.), Assn. Iron and Steel Engrs., Nat. Rolls-Royce Owners Club Inc. (pres.), Morristown Club, Rockaway River Golf Club. Home: 30 Colonial Dr Morristown NJ 07960-4728 Office: Brinton Eaton Assocs Inc 30 Galesi Dr Wayne NJ 07470-4840

EATON, EDMUND DENIS, JR., military officer; b. Bklyn., June 12, 1951; s. Edmund Denis and Eileen Rose (McEnerney) E.; m. Dawn Marie Sherman, Apr. 26, 1980; children: Denis Paul Xavier, Stephen Daniel. BS in Internat. Studies, U.S. Naval Acad., 1973; MA in Internat. Studies, Old Dominion U., 1987; MS in Strategic Intelligence, Def. Intelligence Coll., Washington, 1988. Commd. 2d lt. USMC, 1973, advanced through grades to lt. col.; 2d lt. to 1st lt. 3d Marine Div. III Marine Amphibious Force, Okinawa, Japan, 1974-75; 1st lt. to capt. Marine Corps Devel. & Edn. Command, Quantico, Va., 1975-79; Amphibious Warfare Sch., Quantico, 1979-80; co. officer U.S. Naval Acad., 1980-83; capt. to maj. 3d Marine Div., III Marine Amphibious Force, 1983-84; with USCINCLANT Airborne Command Post, 1984-87; maj. to lt. col. Hdqrs. USMC, Washington, 1988-91; CMC fellow Ctr. for Strategic and Intrnat. Studies, Washington, 1991—. Den leader Cub Scout Pack 1121, Boy Scouts Am., Springfield, Va., 1989—; mem. Neighborhood Watch, Springfield, 1991—. Fellow Ctr. for Strategic and Internat. Studies; mem. Naval Acad. Alumni Assn., Naval Acad. Athletic Assn., U.S. Naval Inst., Marine Corps Assn. Roman Catholic. Home: 5313 Weymouth Dr Springfield VA 22151-1503 Office: Hdqrs USMC Washington DC 20380

EATON, GEORGE BENJAMIN, army officer; b. Portland, Oreg., Sept. 12, 1958; s. Donald Barnett and Joan Carolyn (Turner) E.; m. Annette Louise Zemek, June 7, 1981; 1 child, Madelynn Jeanne Zemek. BA cum laude, Knox Coll., 1980; MA in Internat. Rels., U. So. Calif., 1987; MA in Mil. History, U. Minn., 1990; hon. grad., Command and Gen. Staff Coll., 1990. Commd. 2d lt. U.S. Army, 1980, advanced through grades to maj., 1991; material readiness officer 7th Div. Support Command, Ft. Ord, Calif., 1983-84; logistics plans officer Hdqrs. VII Corps, N.Y., 1984-86; commdr. supply and transport troop 2d Armoured Cavalry Regiment, Calif., 1986-88; asst. prof. mil. history dept. U.S. Mil. Acad., West Point, 1990-91; asst. prof. mil. history and exec. officer Dept. History U.S. Mil. Acad., West Point, 1991—; officer in charge Theatre Arts Guild, USMA, 1991—. Tech. dir. 4th St. Playhouse/Cabaret Theater, Ft. Ord, 1980-83; officer-in-charge Cadet Theatre Arts Guild, 1991—. Decorated Civic Svc. award, 1982; Meritorious Svc. medal, 1986, 88; recipient Herbert W. Alden award, 1984. Mem. Assn. U.S. Army, Soc. for Mil. History, Phi Delta Theta, Phi Alpha Theta. Republican. Episcopalian.

EAVES, JAMES EDWIN (ED EAVES), video tape editor; b. Prescott, Ark., Mar. 31, 1953; s. Andy Olsen and Helen Marie (Crain) E.; m. Ina Irl Edens, July 21, 1973; children: Lindsey Eden, James Logan. AA, United Electronic Inst., 1973. Photographer, editor KTHV TV, Little Rock, 1974-76; chief editor KATV, Little Rock, 1976-83; video tape editor ABC News, Washington, 1983—. Editor: (TV documentary) Tradegy at Tienanmen: The Untold Story, 1989 (Emmy award 1989), (TV segments) Prisoners of Care, 1989 (Emmy award 1989), Race Relations in America (Emmy nomination 1990). Named Photographer of Yr., Ark. News Photographers Assn., 1974, 75. Mem. White House News Photographer Assn. Office: ABC News Prime Time Live 1717 Desales St NW Washington DC 20036-4407

EBANKS, MARLON UDEL, health paraprofessional; b. Bklyn., Feb. 17, 1967; s. Udel Clifton and Austria Adrienne (Sanders) E. AA, Iona Coll., 1989. Seasonal office aide N.Y.C. Bd. of Edn., Bklyn., 1985, 86, provisional office aide, 1987, family assoc., 1987-90, health paraprofl., 1992—; family asst. pre-kindergarten program N.Y.C. Bd. of Edn., Bklyn., 1988. Songwriter, producer The Game, 1990, Feelings of Love, 1990. Vol. Woodhall Hosp., Bklyn., 1990; performer Kwanzaa Holiday Expo, Borough Manhattan Community Coll., 1990. Democrat. Episcopalian. Home: 964 Eastern Pkwy Brooklyn NY 11213 Office: NYC Bd of Edn IS 391 790 E New York Ave Brooklyn NY 11203

EBB, FRED, lyricist, librettist; b. N.Y.C., Apr. 8, 1936; s. Harry and Anna Evelyn (Gritz) E. B.A., NYU, 1955; M.A. in English Lit., Columbia U., 1957; Hon. Degree in Theatre Arts, Emerson U., 1975. lectr. in field. Lyricist: musicals Flora, The Red Menace, 1963, Cabaret, 1965, Zorba, 1966, The Happy Time, 1968, (also co-author book) 70, Girls, 70, 1971, (also book with Bob Fosse) Chicago, 1974, The Act, 1977, Woman of the Year, 1981, The Rink, 1983, Kiss of the Spider Woman, 1990, And The World Goes Round, 1991; TV shows Liza with a Z, 1967, Ole Blue Eyes is Back, 1972, Gypsy in My Soul, 1976, Goldie and Liza Together, 1980, Baryshnikov on Broadway, 1980; motion pictures Cabaret, 1970, Funny Lady, 1973, Lucky Lady, 1976, New York, New York, 1977, Stepping Out, 1991. Recipient Tony award League N.Y. Theatres and Producers, 1967, 81, Drama Desk award N.Y. Drama Critics Circle, 1967, 68, Outer Circle award Org. Writers on Theatre, 1968, 69, George Foster Peabody award Grady Sch. Journalism, U. Ga., 1972, Drama Critics Circle award, 1967, Image award NAACP, 1973, Achievement award B'nai B'rith, 1978, Christopher award Cath. Socs., 1976; named to Songwriters. Hall of Fame, 1983, Theatre Hall of Fame, 1991; named Winner Outer Circle Critic Circle award, 1990. Mem. Dramatists Guild, Equity, Nat. Acad. TV Arts and Scis. (Emmy award 1972, 75, 76), Am. Guild Authors and Composers, Acad. Motion Picture Arts and Scis.

EBBS, GEORGE HEBERLING, JR., management consulting company executive; b. Sewickley, Pa., Sept. 20, 1942; s. George Heberling and Mae Isabelle (Miller) E.; m. Agnes Rak, 1989; children: Stacey Kirsten, Cynthia Lynn. BS in Engring., Purdue U., 1964; MBA, U. Wash., 1966; PhD in Bus., Columbia U., 1970. Sr. engr. Boeing Co., Seattle, 1966; assoc. Booz Allen & Hamilton, N.Y.C., 1969-72, sr. v.p., 1974-86; v.p. Fry Cons., N.Y.C., 1973; chmn., pres. The Canaan Group, Greenwich, Conn., 1986—; adj. prof. Columbia U., N.Y.C., 1978-80. Bronfman fellow, Columbia U., N.Y.C., 1967; Purdue Old Master. Mem. Met. Opera Club, Wings Club, Country Club (New Canaan), Iron Key, Omicron Delta Kappa, Beta Gamma Sigma. Presbyterian. Home: 9 Glen Ct Greenwich CT 06830-4505 Office: The Canaan Group Ltd 500 W Putnam Ave Greenwich CT 06830-6096

EBENHOLTZ, SHELDON MARSHAL, psychology educator, vision consultant; b. N.Y.C., Nov. 27, 1932; s. David and Sally (Werier) E.; m. Jean Miriam Cohen, Jan. 30, 1955; 1 child, Keith. B.S., CCNY, 1955; M.A., New Sch. Social Rsch., 1958, Ph.D., 1961. Asst. prof. Conn. Coll., New London, 1961-66; assoc. prof. U. Wis.-Madison, 1966-70, prof. psychology, 1970-86; prof. vision sci. Inst. Vision Rsch., Coll. Optometry, SUNY, 1986—, assoc. dean for rsch. and grad. studies, 1988-90, dir., 1988, disting. prof., 1989. Mem. vision com. Nat. Acad. Sci./NRC, 1984-87; dir. Inst. Vision Rsch., 1988. Cons. editor Perception and Psychophysics, 1974-89; contbr. book chpts. and articles to prof. jours. Killam Sr. fellow, 1971; Spatial Orientation rsch. grantee NSF, 1984; vision rsch. grantee Nat. Eye Inst., 1984. Fellow AAAS, Am. Psychol. Assn., Am. Psychol. Soc., Am. Acad. Optometry; mem. Aerospace Med. Assn., Am. Inst. Aeronautics and Astronautics, Optical Soc. Am., Assn. Rsch. in Vision and Ophthalmology, Psychonomic Soc., Sierra Club. Avocations: hiking, backpacking. Home: 29 Heritage Dr Edison NJ 08820-1632 Office: SUNY Coll Optometry Inst Vision Rsch New York NY 10010

EBERHART, ALLAN CHARLES, finance educator; b. Kansas City, Kans., Nov. 16, 1961; s. Carl Allan and Kathleen (Hemp) E. BA, Thomas More Coll., 1983; MA, U. Cin., 1985; PhD, U. S.C., 1989. Asst. prof. Georgetown U., Washington, 1989—. Jr. Faculty fellow Georgetown U., 1992. Mem. Am. Fin. Assn., Am. Econ. Assn., Fin. Mgmt. Assn., Western Fin. Assn., So. Fin. Assn., Ea. Fin. Assn. Office: Georgetown U Sch Bus Adminstrn Washington DC 20057

EBERHART, ROBERT JAMES, retired veterinary medicine educator, researcher; b. Lock Haven, Pa., Sept. 9, 1930; s. Harry James Eberhart and Ruth (Moyer) Jackson; m. Jeannette McCall Watson, Dec. 2, 1953; children: Suzanne, Andrew, Gretchen, Peter. AB, Cornell U., 1952; VMD, U. Pa., 1959; MS, Pa. State U., 1964, PhD, 1966. Instr. vet. medicine Pa. State U., University Park, 1959-66, asst. prof., 1966-72, assoc. prof., 1972-78, prof., 1978-90; prof. emeritus Pa. State U., 5, 1990—. Contbr. articles to sci. jours. Mem. Halfmoon Twp. Planning Commn., Centre County, Pa., 1991—. Lt. (j.g.) USN, 1952-55, Korea. Grantee USDA, Pa. Dept. Agr., 1970-89. Mem. AVMA (fellow 1962-65), AAAS, Nat. Mastitis Coun. (bd. dirs. 1981-86, pres. 1985), Am. Dairy Sci. Assn. (West-Agro Inc. award 1985). Home: 104 Maholo St Port Matilda PA 16870-9553 Office: Pa State U 101 Henning Bldg University Park PA 16803

EBERLE, LAURIE ANN, screenwriter, novelist; b. Newark, Sept. 10, 1953; d. Raymond George and Janet May (Young) E.; divorced 1985; children: Michael Raymond DiPilla, Brian Ross. Student, Mercer County Coll., 1979. Author: (novels) For the Sake of Revenge, 1990, The Community, 1990, (screenplays) Scope of Terror, 1991, Tri-Sector Strike, 1991. Home: 3000 Ford Rd Apt 9C Bristol PA 19007-1474

EBERLE, WILLIAM DENMAN, business executive; b. Boise, Idaho, June 5, 1923; s. Julius Louis and Clare (Holcomb) E.; m. Jean Cilista Quick, Sept. 20, 1947; children—Jeffrey Louis, William David, Francis Quick, Cilista Clare. B.A., Stanford U., 1945; M.B.A., Harvard U., 1947, JD, 1949; LLB (hon.), Gonzagua U., 1976. Bar: Idaho 1950. Ptrn. firm Richards, Haga & Eberle, Boise, 1950-60; mem. Idaho Ho. of Reps. from Ada County, 1953-61, majority leader, 1957, minority leader, 1959, speaker, 1961; dir. Boise Cascade Corp., 1952-68, sec., 1960-65, v.p., 1961-66; pres., chmn., dir. Am. Standard, Inc., N.Y.C., 1966-71; Pres.'s spl. rep. for trade negotiations Washington, 1971-75; exec. dir. Cabinet Council on Internat. Econ. Policy, 1974-75; mem. Pres.'s Econ. Policy Bd., 1974-75; pres., chief exec. officer Motor Vehicle Mfrs. Assn., 1975-77; chmn. Holders Capital Corp., Santa Monica, Calif., 1977—, EBCO Inc., Boise, 1978—; pres. Manchester Assocs. Ltd., Washington, 1977—; bd. dirs. Mitchell Energy & Devel. Corp., Ampco-Pitts. Corp., Alexander Proudfoot Cos., Oak Industries. Chmn. Idaho Republican Finance Com., 1961-66; mem. Nat. Rep. Finance Com., 1961-66; Trustee Stanford U., 1970-80, Com. for Econ. Devel., UN Assn., Atlantic Council, trustee Overseas Devel. Coun. Population Crisis Com. Lt. USNR, 1944-46. Mem. Council Fgn. Relations, ABA, Idaho Bar Assn., Com. for Econ. Devel., UN Assn. of U.S., Internat. C. of C. on Trade and Related Issues (vice chmn. U.S. Council, chmn.), Chief Exec. Orgn. (chmn.) U.S. Japan Found., U.S. Coun. for Internal. Bus. CED (vice chmn.), Internat. Rsch. Policy Com., U.S. Can. Com., (co. chmn.) Aspen Inst. Project The U.S. and World Economy, Univ. Club (N.Y.) Met. Club (Washington) Essex Country Club, Manchester Yacht Club. Episcopalian. Office: EBCO Inc 1 Cranberry Hl Lexington MA 02173-7397

EBERLY, DAVID MICHAEL, fundraiser, development consultant, writer; b. Boston, Nov. 20, 1947; s. John Franklin and Mary Pauline (McCollum) E. Student, Brandeis U., Waltham, Mass., 1967. Libr. Boston U., Boston, 1970-81; dir. devel. rsch. Tufts U., Medford, Mass., 1982-85; dir., devel. svcs. Harvard Med. Sch., Boston, 1985—; pres., dir. New England Devel. Rsch. Assn., Boston, 1990—, 1989-90. Author: What Has Been Lost, 1982. Trustee Ellen La Forge Meml. Poetry Found., Cambridge, Mass., 1988—. Home: 187 St Botolph St Boston MA 02115-5164 Office: Harvard Med Sch 25 Shattuck St Boston MA 02115-6092

EBERSBERGER, ARTHUR DARRYL, insurance company executive, consultant; b. Balt., June 18, 1946; s. George Henry and Althea May (Watts) E.; m. Judith Simison, Nov. 18, 1982; 1 child, Leonard Darryl. BS, Susquehanna U., 1968; MBA, Loyola Coll., Balt., 1985; postgrad., Am. Coll., Bryn Mawr, Pa. CLU, CHFC. Exec. v.p. Ebersberger & Assocs., Inc., Severna Park, Md., 1968—; pres. Ebersberger Consulting Inc., Severna Park, Md., 1986—; sec. Anne Arundel Trade Coun. Pres. Sheltered Workshop of Anne Arundel County, Glen Burnie, Md., 1978; chmn., v.p. Md. Conf. on Small Bus., 1989-90. With USNR, 1969-71, Vietnam. Mem. U.S. Jaycees (adv. bd. 1982, Outstanding Young Man Am. 1980-81, pres. Severna Park br. 1976), Assoc. Bldrs. and Contrs. (pres. 1986), Anne Arundel Life Underwriters (pres. 1981, life mem.), Million Dollar Round Table, CLU's (bd. dirs. Balt. chpt. 1981-83), Md. C. of C. (sml. bus. coun. 1989—), Profl. Liability Agts. Network (pres. 1985-86, exec. com. 1986—), Chartwell Golf and Country Club (Severna Park) (bd. dirs. 1981-83). Republican. Lutheran. Home: 51 Boone Trail Severna Park MD 21146 Office: 645 Baltimore-annap Blvd Severna Park MD 21146

EBERSTADT, FREDERICK, writer, photographer; b. Huntington, N.Y., July 24, 1926; s. Ferdinand and Mary Ann Arsdale (Tongue) E.; m. Isabel Nash, Nov. 12, 1954; children: Nicholas, Fernanda. Grad., Phillips Exeter Acad., 1944; BA, NYU, 1991. Freelance photographer N.Y.C., 1958—, writer, 1985—. Photographer: (book) Dyonisis in 1969, 1971; co-author: There Did Tuffy Hide, 1955; contbr. articles to profl. jours., gen. circulation mags. With USN, 1945-47. Mem. Am. Assn. Mag. Photographers, Knickerbocker Club (N.Y.C.), Piping Rock Club (Locust Valley, N.Y.), Ausable Club (St. Huberts, N.Y.). Republican. Episcopalian. Office: Eberstadt Studio 791 Park Ave New York NY 10021-3551

EBERT, ALAN M., writer, psychotherapist; b. Bklyn., Sept. 14, 1935; s. Philip Ebert and Mollie Grosswirth. BA, CUNY, 1957; MS in Edn., Fordham U., 1974. Coord. Spl. Press Projects NBC-TV, N.Y.C., 1963-67; exec. v.p. McFadden, Strauss, Irwin, N.Y.C., 1967-71; writer, contbg. editor Good Housekeeping mag., N.Y.C., 1971—. Author: (nonfiction) The Homosexuals, 1977, Every Body Is Beautiful, 1979, Intimacies, 1980, (novels) Traditions, 1981, The Long Way Home, 1984, Marriages, 1987. Vol. friendly visitor program AIDS unit Roosevelt Hosp., N.Y.C., 1987—. Recipient volunteerism award Roosevelt Hosp., 1990. Mem. Am. Soc. Journalists and Authors, Writers Guild Am. Home and Office: 353 W 56th St Apt 11A New York NY 10019-3777

EBERT, TERRY HAROLD, management consultant; b. Bklyn., Apr. 17, 1946; s. David and Frances (Bechler) E.; m. Susan Gootzeit, June 15, 1969; 1 child, Shelby Nicole. BA, Queens Coll., 1967; MA, SUNY, Binghampton, 1971; EdD, Hofstra U., 1980. Tchr. Kings Park (N.Y.) Pub. Schs., 1970-73; tchr., asst. prin. Smithtown (N.Y.) Pub. Schs., 1973-77; prin. South Amboy (N.J.) Pub. Schs., 1977-80; mgr. Spiridellis and Assocs., N.Y.C., 1980-82, Morgan Stanley, N.Y.C., 1982-88; dir. The Tng. Group, Marlboro, N.J., 1988-89; mgr. Anderson Consulting, N.Y.C., 1989-90; v.p. The Ayres Group, N.Y.C., 1990—; cons. AT&T Network Ops., Piscataway, N.J., 1988, Sea-Land Svcs. Inc., Port Elizabeth, N.J., 1988, Bankers Trust & Co., N.Y.C., 1991—, North Am. Philips, N.Y.C., 1991—. Author: Alternative Careers, Teachers, 1988; contbr. articles to profl. jours. Bd. dirs. Temple Rodeph Torah, Marlboro, 1991—; coach Youth Soccer League, Marlboro, 1987—. Mem. Internat. Assn. Outplacement Profls., Phi Delta Kappa. Office: The Ayers Group 370 Lexington Ave New York NY 10017

EBINGER, MARY RITZMAN, pastoral counselor; b. Reading, Pa., Nov. 23, 1929; d. Michael Erwin and Daisy Mae (Shaeffer) R.; m. Warren Ralph Ebinger, Aug. 11, 1951; children: Lee, Lori, Jonathan. BA, North Cen. Coll., Naperville, Ill., 1951; MS, Loyola Coll., Balt., 1981; grad. student, Wesley Theol. Sem., 1976, Cath. U., 1977. Cert. counselor Dept. of Md. Health and Mental Hygiene, cert. nat. counselor Am. Assn. Pastoral Counselors. Elem. tchr. Naperville Washington Sch., 1952-54; dir. adult work Millian Ch., Rockville, Md.; pastoral counselor Washington Pastoral Counselors; assoc. dir. Balt. Conf. Pastoral Care and Counseling, Wheaton, Md., 1990—; pres. Wesley Guild Wesley Theol. Seminary, Washington, 1987-89; mem. adj. faculty psychology Frederick (Md.) Community Coll., 1982-87, Anne Arnold (Md.) Community Coll., 1988, 90. Author: I Was Sick and You Visited Me, 1976, Does Anybody Care, 1978. Pres. Ch. Women United, Springfield, Ill., 1969-71; chmn. Episcopacy com. United Meth. Ch., Balt., 1988-90. Recipient Disting. Alumnus award North Cen. Coll., 1990, Loyola Coll., 1991, Two Thousand Women of Achievement award Dartmouth Eng. Mus., 1969. Mem. Am. Assn. Counseling and Devel., Am. Assn. Pastoral Counseling (cert., Atlantic region chmn. theol. and social concerns 1988—). Home: 6 St Ives Dr Severna Park MD 21146-1430 Office: Balt Conf Pastoral Care and Counseling 10700 Georgia Ave Wheaton MD 20902-4799

EBLEN, JACK ERICSON, consultant; b. Cin., Sept. 20, 1936; s. Marvin Clinton and Marie Christine (Ericson) E.; m. Trudi Jennes Kramer, June 5, 1962; children: Jennifer, Thor. BS, U. Wis., 1959, MS, 1961, PhD, 1966; postgrad., U. Pa., 1970-71. Sr. fellow Sch. Hygiene and Pub. Health Johns Hopkins U., Balt., 1972-73, 74-76; program mgr. population div. UN, N.Y.C., 1976-79; task force mgr., svc. and psychosocial rsch. WHO, Geneva, 1979-86; dir., prof. N.Am. Ctr., Friends World Coll., Huntington, N.Y., 1986-88; cons. Douglaston, N.Y., 1988—; sr. rsch. fellow Nat. Inst. Child Health and Human Devel., 1972-73, 74-76; teaching asst. history U. Wis., 1960-62; instr. history No. Ill. U., 1964-65; asst. prof. history Calif. State U., Fresno, 1965-66; Fulbright-Hays prof. U. Liberia, 1968-69; asst. prof. history U. Conn., 1966-71; assoc. prof. history U. Okla., 1970-73; assoc. prof. sociology U. Chgo., 1973-74; prof. demography U. Philippines, 1973-74; cons. Econ. Commn. for Europe, Geneva, Switzerland, 1983, various govts., 1979—. Author: The First and Second United States Empires: Governors and Territorial Government, 1784-1912, 1968, World Population Trends and Policies: 1977 Monitoring Report, Volume I: Population Trends, 1979, 1979 Monitoring Report, 1980, Recent Levels and Trends in Mortality (1950 to Present), 1980. V.p. Am. Cancer Soc., Huntington, N.Y., 1986-88. Rsch. grantee U. Conn., 1967-69, Am. Philos. Soc., 1971, U. Okla., 1971-73, Nat. Inst. Child Health and Human Devel., 1970-72, 72-73, 74-76, U. Pa. postdoctoral fellow, 1970-71; recipient Fulbright-Hays lecturing award U.S. Dept. State, U. Liberia, 1968-69. Mem. AAAS, Internat. Union Sci. Study Population, Population Assn. Am., Am. Hist Assn. Home and Office: 239-53 65th Ave Flushing NY 11362

EBY, CLARE VIRGINIA, educator; b. Harrisonburg, Va., May 10, 1959; d. Cecil D. Eby and Patricia (McGuire) Aldridge. BA in English, Ind. U., 1980; MA in English, U. Mich., 1985, PhD in English, 1988. Asst. prof. English U. Conn., Hartford, 1988—. Grantee U. Conn., 1989, 90. Mem. MLA, Dreiser Soc. (charter). Home: 25 Shultas Pl Hartford CT 06114-1343 Office: U Conn at Hartford 85 Lawler Rd West Hartford CT 06117-2697

ECHERUO, MICHAEL JOSEPH CHUKWUDALU, literary critic, educator; b. Umunumo, Imo, Nigeria, Mar. 14, 1937; came to U.S., 1989; s. Joseph Michael and Martha Nwulari (Nwosu) E.; m. Rose Nkeonyere Ikwueke, June 8, 1968; children: Ike, Oke, Ijeoma, Chinedu, Ugonna. BA, U. London, Eng., 1960; MA, Cornell U., 1963, PhD, 1965; LittD (hon.), U.

Nebr., 1991. Prof. U. Nigeria, Nsukka, 1965-74; prof. U. Ibadan, Nigeria, 1974-81, dean Grad. Sch., 1979-81; pres. Imu State U., Okigwe, Nigeria, 1981-89; vis. prof. Ind. U., Bloomington, 1989-90; Safire prof. Syracuse (N.Y.) U., 1990—; adviser U. Malawi, Zomba, 1975-77. Author: Mortality, poems, 1968, Victorian Lagos, 1977, Dimensions of ORder, 1979, The Conditioned Imagination, 1978, The Novel of Africa, 1971. Dir. War Info. Bur., Rep. of Biafra, 1967-70. Mem. MLA, Phi Kappa Phi, Phi Beta Kappa. Office: Syracuse U Dept English 410 Hall of Langs Syracuse NY 13244

ECHIKSON, RICHARD, retail consultant; b. Newark, N.J., Feb. 5, 1929; s. Joseph I. and Pearl (Comando) E.; m. Lenora Greenspan, June 25, 1956 (div. Jan. 1967); children: Andrea, James; m. Florence Roberta Papov, Oct. 18, 1969; children: Pamela, Stephen. BA, Dartmouth Coll., 1950; MBA, Amos Tuck Sch., Hanover, N.H., 1951. Mdse. adminstrv. buyer, exec. training sq. R.H. Macy Inc., N.Y.C., 1951-65; pres. The Fabric Tree Inc., N.Y.C., 1965-78; exec. v.p. W.R. Grace & Co., N.Y.C., 1978-81; chmn. Retail Cons. Inc., Millburn, N.J., 1981—; dir. Met. Pres. Organs., N.Y.C., 1980—, Mgmt. Decisions Lab, NYU Grad. Sch. of Bus., 1980-84, Young Pres. Organs., 1970-80; exec. com. Darthmouth Coll. Class, Hanover, 1960—; class agent Amos Tuck Sch., 1980—. Author: (book) International Council of Shopping Centers, 1988; contbr. articles to mags. Served to 1st lt. USAF, 1951-53, Japan. Mem. Internat. Coun. Shopping Ctrs., Pension Real Estate Assn., NAt. Retail Fedn., Dartmouth Club (N.Y.C., suburban N.J.). Office: Retail Cons Inc 374 Millburn Ave Millburn NJ 07041-1343

ECHOLS, DOROTHY, academic administrator; b. Sylvester, Ga., July 22, 1955; d. John Lee and Mae Eva (Lowe) E. BA, Northwestern U., 1977; MA, Ohio State U., 1980. Rsch. asst. Ohio State Univ., Columbus, 1977-78, coord. cooperative edn., 1978-80; dir. exptl. learning Ramapo Coll., Mahwah, N.J., 1980-91; adj. faculty Ramapo Coll., Mahwah, 1987—, sr. advisor to pres. for affirmative action, 1988-91; asst. to v.p. for acad. affairs Ramapo Coll., Mahwak, 1991—; field reader Dept. Edn., Washington, 1983—. Recipient fellowship Ohio State Univ., Columbus, 1977. Mem. Am. Assn. Higher Edn., Assn. 100 Black Women. Office: Ramapo Coll 505 Ramapo Valley Rd Mahwah NJ 07430-1623

ECK, KENNETH CHRISTOPHER, safety engineer, geologist; b. Suffern, N.Y., Mar. 16, 1960; s. Henry Charles and Jean Marilyn (Campbell) E.; m. Robin Diane Hayward, Aug. 24, 1991. BA, SUNY, Geneseo, 1982. Cert. safety profl., fire protection specialist. Field technician LMS Engrs., Pearl River, N.Y., 1982-83; lab. technician Agfa Geavert, Paramus, N.J., 1983-84; asst. safety dir. Tilcon N.Y., Inc., Haverstraw, 1984-87; safety coord. Rockland County BOCES, West Nyack, N.Y., 1987—; pres., chief exec. officer Hazard Abatement Systems, Inc., Blauvelt, N.Y., 1990—; pvt. practice cons., Blauvelt, N.Y., 1987—. Tech. reviewer Nat. Safety Coun. Mem. Blauvelt Vol. Fire Co., 1983; dep. emergency med. svc. coord. Rockland County Emergency Med. Svcs., Pomona, N.Y., 1989—; bd. dirs. South Organgetown Ambulance Corps, Orangeburg, 1984; mem. Highland Falls Ambulance, 1991—, Disaster Med. Assistance Team, 1990. Recipient Rockland County Meritorious Svc. award; named EMT of the Yr., 1990; recipient Orangetown Chiefs Assn. Meritorious Svc. award, Amelia Earhart award Civil Air Patrol. Mem. AAAS, Am. Soc. Safety Engrs., Nat. Fire Protection Assn., N.Y. State Fire Marshals Assn., N.Y. State Coalition on Safety Belts. Presbyterian. Home: 2 Cooks Ln Highland Falls NY 10928-1706 Office: Rockland County BOCES 61 Parrot Rd West Nyack NY 10994-1044

ECKARDT, CARL R., chemical and building materials executive; b. 1931; married. BS, Seton Hall U., 1959. With Allied Chem. Corp., 1950-68, J.P. Stevens & Co., Inc., 1968-74; with GAF Corp., Wayne, N.J., 1974—, v.p., 1979-81, exec. v.p., 1981—, also bd. dirs. With USN, 1953-55. Office: GAF Corp 1361 Alps Rd Wayne NJ 07470-3700*

ECKARDT, MICHAEL JON, psychologist; b. Glendale, Calif., Apr. 3, 1943; s. Ralph Benjamin and Betty June (Davey) E.; m. Johneen Kennedy Pofahl, Aug. 9, 1968; children: Shea, Neil, Rory. BS, Calif. State U., Northridge, 1965; MS, U. So. Calif., 1967, U. Mich., 1970; PhD, U. Oreg. Med. Sch., 1975. Lic. psychologist Md., 1978. Rsch. psychologist VA Med. Ctr., Sepulveda, Calif., 1975, Nat. Inst. Alcohol Abuse & Alcoholism, Rockville, Md., 1977-83; clin. assoc. prof. psychiatry Oreg. Health Sci. Ctr., Portland, 1986—; staff affiliate, psychology Clin. Ctr. NIH, Bethesda, Md., 1987—; chief, sect. clin. brain rsch. Nat. Inst. Alcohol Abuse & Alcoholism, Bethesda, 1983—; chief lab. clin. studies Nat. Inst. Alcohol Abuse and Alcoholism, Bethesda, 1991—; cons. Nat. Naval Med. Ctr., Bethesda, 1987—, VA Hosp., Washington, 1989-90; exec. sec. NIAAA Human Rsch. Com., Bethesda, 1983—. Contbr. 109 scientific papers to profl. jours. Recipient Adminstrs. award, Alcohol Drug Abuse Mental Health Adminstrn., 1989, Spl. Recognition award, Pub. Health Svc., 1983. Mem. Am. Psychol. Assn., Md. Psychol. Assn., Rsch. Soc. Alcoholism (chmn. scientific program), Soc. Neurosci., Internat. Assn. Biomed. Rsch. Alcoholism. Office: Nat Inst Alcohol Abuse 9000 Rockville Pike Bethesda MD 20892

ECKART, CHRISTIAN, artist; b. Calgary, Alb., Can., Jan. 9, 1959; came to U.S., 1984; MFA, Hunter Coll., 1986. Exhibited in solo shows at Rubin Spangle Gallery, N.Y.C., Rhona Hoffman Gallery, Chgo., Galerie Tanit, Munich and Cologne, Fed. Republic Germany; represented in mus. and pub. collections throughout the U.S., Western Europe, and Japan. Home: 232 Broadway Brooklyn NY 11211-6203

ECKBRETH, KELLY ANNE, ergonomics engineer; b. Princeton, N.J., Nov. 3, 1967; d. Alan Charles and Barbara (Hocking) E. BS in Indsl. Engring., Lehigh U., 1989; MS in Indsl. and Ops. Engring., U. Mich., 1990. Jr. quality control engr. The Wiremold Co., West Hartford, Conn., 1987; indsl. engring. intern United Parcel Svc., Hartford, Conn., 1988, 89; ergonomics engr. AT&T Network Systems, North Andover, Mass., 1990—. Nat. Inst. Occupational Safety and Health scholar, U. Mich., 1989. Mem. Inst. Indsl. Engrs., Ergonomics Soc., Human Factors Soc., Am. Soc. Safety Engrs. Episcopalian. Office: AT&T Network Systems 1600 Osgood St Dept 20910 North Andover MA 01845

ECKEL, PETER DWIGHT, student affairs professional; b. Mason, Mich., Oct. 5, 1966; s. Peter J. and Janice (Vincent) E. BA in Journalism, Mich. State U., East Lansing, 1989; MA in OCunseling and Student Personnel, U. Md., College Park, 1991. Grad. asst. mktg. & PR Undergrad. Admissions U. Md., College Park, Md., 1989-91; NASPA summer intern Nat. Assn. Student Personnel Adminstrn., Washington, 1990; cons. U. Md. Greek System, College Park, 1989-91; instr. career devel. and freshman orientation course U. Md., College Park, student leadership course, Mich. State U., East Lansing, 1988-89. Coord. Mid-Mich. Spl. Olympics Track & Field Meet, Lansing, Mich., 1988. Mem. Am. Coll. Personnel Assn., Am. Assn. Counseling & Devel., Nat. Assn. Student Personnel Adminstrn., Sigma Chi Nat. Frat. Office: Office of Undergrad Admissions U Md College Park 130F Mitchell Blvd College Park MD 20742

ECKER, LEROY GORDON, pilot; b. Boyne City, Mich., July 21, 1942; s. Raymond and Venetta June (Sparks) E.; m. Sandra Mae LaBrecque, June 15, 1963; children: Jerry Lee, Jon Lane, Corey Leroy. BS in Edn., Mich. State U., 1964; MS in Edn., So. Ill. U., 1975. Commd. USAF, 1965; computer ops. officer USAF, March AFB, Calif., 1965-67; pilot USAF, 1967-85; radar ops. officer USAF, Ft. Yukon, Ala., 1972-73; personnel officer USAF, Scott AFB, Ill., 1976-78; squadron ops. officer USAF, Frankfurt, Fed. Republic of Germany, 1978-82; computer programmer USAF, Scott AFB, 1982-85; airline pilot U.S. Air, Pitts., 1985—. Author: The Chicken or the Egg, 1990; computer programmer for Flight Planning, 1985. Mil. pastor Reorganized Ch. of Jesus Christ of Latter-day Saints, Europe, 1978-82. Maj. USAF, 1965-85, Vietnam. Decorated D.F.C., 1970, Air medal, 1970. Home: 3204 Postgate Dr Bethel Park PA 15102-1426

ECKER, PAUL GERARD, physician, educator; b. Cleve., Dec. 28, 1919; s. Enrique Eduardo and Marie Josephine (van Reeth) E.; m. Henriette Juliette Dumas, Nov. 25, 1950; children: Hendrik Michel, Christian Paul. BS, Case Western Res. U., 1942, MD, 1944. Fellow Rockefeller Inst., N.Y.C., 1946-48; teaching fellow Med. Sch. Harvard U., Boston, 1948-49; instr. Columbia-Presbyn. Coll., N.Y.C., 1950-55; asst. prof. psychiatry U. Pa., Phila., 1955-60; chief functional disease svc. Hosp. U. of Pa., Phila., 1957-60; tng. analyst Inst. Phila. Assn. for Psychoanalysis, Phila., 1968—; cons. surgeon gen. USAF, USN, US Army, Washington. Mem. acquisitions com. Phila. Mus. of Art; benefactor Cleve. Mus. Art, Phila. Mus. Art., Mc Darcy Mus. Chgo. With USN, 1945-46, 52-54, capt. USNR. Decorated Legion of Merit. Fellow ACP, Am. Coll. Psychiatrists; mem. Am. Psychoanalytic Assn., Century Assn., Phila. Cricket Club, Soc. Med. Cons. to Armed Forces (past pres.), Phila. Assn. for Psychoanalysis (past pres.), Royal Navy Club London, Sigma Xi. Roman Catholic. Home and Office: 631 St Georges Rd Philadelphia PA 19119-3341

ECKERT, ARLENE GAIL, case manager; b. Euclid, Ohio, July 28, 1956; d. Robert S. and Madolyn A. (King) Lough; m. Theodore Eckert III, May 14, 1983 (div. Oct. 1985). BS in Law Enforcement, U. No. Ala., 1978. Cert. social worker. Probation, parole officer Tenn. Dept. Corrections, Columbia, 1978-83; child protection svc. specialist II Tex. Dept. Human Svcs., Killeen, 1984-86; child protective svcs. specialist IV, Tex. Dept. Human Svcs., Gatesville, 1988-90; coord. employees assistance project Associated Counseling Svcs., Harker Heights, Tex., 1986-88; case mgr. Dept. of Justice, Fed. Bur. of Prisons, Danbury, Conn., 1990—. Bd. dirs. Truancy Bd. Pulaski, Tenn., 1978-84, Truancy Bd., Lawrenceburg, Tenn., 1978-84, Multidisciplinary Child Abuse Rev. Team, Columbia, Tenn., 1979-84. Mem. Am. Correctional Assn., Tenn. State Employees Assn., NAFE. Lutheran. Office: FCI Danbury Rte 37 Danbury CT 06810

ECKERT, DAVID PAGE, psychologist; b. N.Y.C., May 6, 1957; s. Harvey and Phyllis (Kosow) E.; m. Karen Linda Werbin, Jan. 2, 1983. BA in Psychology, Amherst Coll., 1979; MA in Psychology, Yeshiva U., Bronx, 1983, PsyD in Clin. Psychology, 1986. Lic. psychologist, N.Y. Applied behavioral scis. specialist Cath. Charities, Bklyn., 1984-86; psychologist Queens Children's Psychiatric Ctr., Bellerose, N.Y., 1986-88; psychology cons. County Counseling Ctr., Bayside, N.Y., 1987-89; dir. psychology tng. and coord. spl. case rev. The Children's Village, Dobbs Ferry, N.Y., 1988—; pvt. practice psychotherapy Bayside, N.Y., 1988-91, Roslyn Heights, N.Y., 1991—; psychol. cons. Forest Hills IPA/Holliswood Hosp., N.Y., 1991—. Active Resolve of L.I., Plainview, 1987. Mem. Am. Psychol. Assn., N.Y. State Psychol. Assn., N.Y. Soc. Clin. Psychologists. Democrat. Office: The Children's Village Dobbs Ferry NY 10522

ECKERT, WILLIAM TERRY, aerospace researcher; b. Seattle, Aug. 11, 1948; s. Walter Ethelbert Jr. and Gracejean (Quintin) E.; children: Lisa Kristine, Wendy Michelle; m. Sandra Rowe Means, May 12, 1990; stepchildren: Sarah Joy Means, David Charles Means. BS in Aeronautics, U. Wash., 1970; MS in Applied Math., U. Santa Clara (Calif.), 1977; postgrad., U. Pa., 1981, San Jose State U., 1982. Rsch. aide Aerospace Rsch. Lab., U.Wash., Seattle, 1969-70; aerospace rsch. engr. U.S. Army Aeromechanics Lab., NASA Ames Rsch. Ctr., Moffett Field, Calif., 1970-79; chief rsch. support div. U.S. Army Aeroflightdymanics Dir., NASA Ames Rsch. Ctr., Moffett Field, 1979-84, 1985-90, asst. dir., 1988-90; dep. chief AH-64 Apache acquisition team U.S. Army Aviation Systems Command, St. Louis, 1984-85; program mgr. NASA Hdqrs., Washington, 1990—; speaker, lectr., tech. cons. in field; mem. steering com. NASA-Army Rotorcraft Tech. Conf., Washington, 1986-87. Contbr. articles to profl. publs.; editor: DoD Major System Procurement, 1984. Mem. Phi Eta Sigma. Office: NASA Hdqrs Code RI Washington DC 20546

ECKERT, YATES PETER, trust company executive; b. Utica, N.Y., Dec. 7, 1929; s. Adam James and Gertrude (Yates) E.; m. Mary Loudon, Sept. 25, 1953; children: Thomas, Marcie. AB, Dartmouth Coll., 1952; MBA, 1953. Chief ops. officer, treas. Mohawk Valley Investing Co., Utica, 1956-63; v.p. Marine Midland Banks, Inc., Utica and Buffalo, 1963-69; v.p., sr. investment officer Fidelity Union Trust Co., Newark, 1969-77; exec. v.p., chief ops. officer Union Capital Mgmt. Co., Cleve., 1977-80; exec. v.p., chief investment officer Horizon Trust Co., Morristown, N.J., 1981-82, Union Trust Co., New Haven, Conn., 1982—; trustee Olsen Meml. Fund, Utica, 1959-69, Whitlac Inc., Utica, 1956—. Mem. Newark Fiscal Adv. Bd., 1973-74. 1st lt. Fin. Corps, U.S. Army, 1953-56. Mem. N.Y. Soc. Security Analysts, Kuyahoora Yacht Club, Quinnipiac Club. Office: Union Trust Co Corner Ch and Elm Sts New Haven CT 06502

ECKHARDT, DONALD HENRY, geophysicist; b. Flushing, N.Y., Dec. 20, 1932; s. Henry and Freda (Kludas) E.; m. Mary Victoria Quigley, Nov. 18, 1955; children: Ronald, Raina, Randall, Rebecca. BS in Geophysics, MIT, 1955, PhD in Geophysics, 1961. Geologist Magnolia Petroleum Co., Scottsbluff, Nebr., 1955-56; seismic interpreter Mobil Oil Co., Caracas, Venezuela, 1956-58; rsch. assoc. U. Ariz., Tucson, 1961-63; rsch. physicist Air Force Cambridge Rsch. Lab., Hanscom AFB, Mass., 1963-75; chief geodesy and gravity br. Air Force Geophysics Lab., Hanscom AFB, 1975-83; dir. earth scis. Phillips Lab., Hanscom AFB, 1983—; chmn. Geophys. Monographs Bd., books Bd. Assoc. editor Moon and the Planets, Geophys. Rsch. Letters; series editor Geodynamics Book Series; contbr. articles to profl. jours. Fellow Internat. Assn. Geodesy (pres. spl. study group on gravimetric tests of Newtonian gravity law); mem. Am. Geophys. Union. Home: 3 Princess Pine Dr Bedford MA 01730-1228 Office: Phillips Lab/GP Hanscom AFB MA 01731

ECKHAUS, JAY ELLIOT, lawyer; b. N.Y.C., Apr. 16, 1944; s. Herman and Sylvia (Woolwick) E.; m. Gail Ellen Garfield, Dec. 19, 1971. BS in Bus. Adminstrn., Bowling Green (Ohio) State U., 1965; JD, Ohio State U., 1968. Bar: Ohio 1968, N.Y. 1969, U.S. Dist. Cts. (so. and ea. dist.) N.Y. 1969, U.S. Ct. Appeals (2nd cir.) 1975. Ptnr. Ehrlich & Eckhaus, N.Y., 1969-73; mktg. and cen. region counsel Burger Chef Systems, Inc. subs. Gen. Foods Corp., White Plains, N.Y., 1973-77; sr. atty. Gen. Foods Corp., White Plains, 1977, div. counsel, 1977-82, dept. counsel, 1982-84; v.p., chief counsel Entenmann's, Inc., 1984-88, counsel breakfast foods div., 1985-88; v.p., chief counsel Gen. Foods Bakery Cos., Inc., White Plains, 1988-89; v.p., gen. counsel, sec. Alfa-Laval, Inc., Ft. Lee, N.J., 1989-90; pvt. practice N.Y.C., 1990—. Fellow Am. Bar Found.; mem. ABA (antitrust sect.), N.Y. Bar Assn. (corp. counsel sect., chmn. litigation and comml. arbitration com. 1981-84, chmn. mergers and acquisitions com. 1984-86, exec. com. 1987—), N.Y.C. Bar Assn., Ohio State U. Alumni Club of Greater N.Y. (bd. govs. 1992—). Home: 445 E 86th St Apt 13G New York NY 10028-6433

ECKLER, TODD HARRISON, consultant; b. Louisville, Ky., Jan. 27, 1967; s. James Kenneth and Carol Lee (Cushing) E. Student, London Sch Econ. & Polit. Sci., 1987; AB magna cum laude, Dartmouth Coll., 1989. Cons. Monitor Co., Cambridge, Mass., 1989—. Project mgr. Dartmouth Alumni in the Schs., Boston, 1991. Mem. Phi Beta Kappa. Home: 13 Thorndike St Somerville MA 02144-2717 Office: Monitor Co 25 1st St Cambridge MA 02141-1800

ECKLIN, ROBERT LUTHER, glass company executive; b. Lancaster, Pa., Sept. 26, 1938; s. Luther Joseph and Ella Frances (Smith) E.; m. Loretta Rohrer Stoner, Sept. 3, 1960; children: Robert Luther, Jr., Suzanne Beth, Kristina Ann, Stephanie Ann. B in Archtl. Engring., Chgo. Tech. Coll., 1961; postgrad., Dartmouth U., 1983, cert., 1984. With Corning (N.Y.) Glass Works, 1961—, pres. Corning Engring., 1982-86, corp. v.p. bus. devel., chmn. Corning Engring., 1986-88, sr. v.p., 1988—; chmn. Malkin Ltd., Stoke-on-Trent, Eng., 1983-86; ptnr. Ecklin & Ecklin Investments, Lancaster, 1986—, Stoner Estates, Lancaster, 1986—; bd. dirs. Panelogic Inc., Corning, U.S. Precision Lens, Cin., Alfred U. Tech. Resources, Pitts.-Corning Corp.; chmn. bd. Cormetech Inc. Chmn. Com. of 50, Corning, 1985—; pres. Univ. Industry Pub. Partnership for Econ. Growth. Mem. Conn. Venture Group, N.Y. Assn. for Corp. Growth, Corning C. of C., Corning Country Club, Rotary. Republican. Methodist. Home: 248 Cedar St Corning NY 14830-3128 Office: Corning Inc Houghton Pk Corning NY 14831

ECKMAIR, FRANK CORNWALL, artist, educator; b. Norwich, N.Y., June 21, 1930; s. Frank Eckmair and Gladys (Cornwall) Keys; m. Leigh Chadwick, Aug. 24, 1959; children: Antoni Franz, Kelley Marie, Stephanie Ann. BA, U. Iowa, 1953; MFA, Ohio U., 1962. Tchr., dir. Bd. of Coop. Edn. Svcs., Richfield Springs, N.Y., 1953-55, 57; instr. Denison U., Granville, Ohio, 1961-62; asst. prof. Millikin U., Decatur, Ill., 1962-63; from asst. prof. to prof. Buffalo State Coll., 1963—; cons. Gallery Assn. of N.Y., Hamilton, 1976-80, Rising Paper Co., HMP Conf., Housatonic, Mass., 1980, hartwick Coll., Oneonta, N.Y., 1984-86, Jamacian Ptnrs. in Western N.Y.,1 986; exhbn. cons. N.Y. State Landscape, SUNY Gallery, Albany, 1980; instr., cons., instr. Orgn. of Am. State, Costa Rica, 1982; pres. TAROT Designing and Printing, Gilbertsville, N.Y., 1969—; juror N.Y. State Coun. of Arts, 1975. Author: (booklet) Relief Printmaking An Outline, 1969, 2d edit., 1971, Options in Printmaking, 1973, Handmade Paper and Prints, 1976; co-author: My Little Ampersand in American Wood Type, 1984; designer, printer (book) Witches of Salem, 1972, (portfolio) A Pride of Rabbis, 1970, Printmakers 1973, 1973, Bi-Centennial Prints, 1976; artist, printer represented in permanent collections Butler Inst. of Am. Art, Met. Mus. of Art, N.Y.C., Palace of Legion of Honor, San Francisco, Libr. of Congress, Smithsonian Instn., Pushkin Mus. Fine Arts, Moscow, British Mus., London, Vatican Libr., Rome, Costa Rica Nat. Mus., San Jose, Phila. Mus. Arts; works included in editions for Associated Am. Artists, N.Y., Roten Galleries, Balt., Lakeside (Mich.) Studios, Tomlinson Collection, Balt., Marsdin Galleries, Balt., Uniroyal Corp., N.Y. Member senate Buffalo State Coll., 1968-69; mem. edn. com. Burchfield Art Ctr., Buffalo, 1989-91; founding mem. United Univ. Professions, Buffalo State Coll., 1963-91, project dir. Latvian Exch. Program, Riga, Latvia, 1990-91; bd. dirs. Cooperstown (N.Y.) Art Assn., 1970-84. Capt. USAF, 1955-57, Korea. SUNY fellow, 1967, 70, 72, 75, 77, 78; N.Y. State Bicentennial Commn. grantee, 1975, NEA grantee, 1978. Mem. Coll. Art Assn. Home: 2 Green St Gilbertsville NY 13776 Office: Buffalo State Coll 1300 Elmwood Ave # 310 Buffalo NY 14222-1095

ECKMAN, GEORGE, lumber company executive; b. Manchester, N.H., Feb. 21, 1919; s. Hyman and Rose (Winnett) E.; m. Gwendolyn Sandler, May 30, 1945; children: Harold R., Gerald A., Laurence N. BSCE, U. N.H., 1941. Civil engr. TVA, Knoxville, 1941-43, E. B. Badger, Boston, 1946-48; plant engr. Waumbec Mills, Manchester, N.H., 1948-56; pres. Reeds Ferry Lumber Co., Merrimack, N.H., 1956-73, chmn., 1973—. Pres. Temple Israel Brotherhood,m Manchester, 1946, Reef Condo Assn., Palm Beach, Fla., 1988; bd. dirs. Temple Adath Yeshurhn, Manchester, 1956-62. Capt. USAF, 1943-45, Africa-Middle East Theater. Mem. N.E. Retail Lumber Assn. (pres. 1965-66, bd. dirs. 1956-70). Republican. Jewish. Office: Reeds Ferry Lumber Corp PO Box 790 Merrimack NH 03054-0790 Home: 156 Walnut Hill Ave Manchester NH 03104-2131

ECKROAT, LARRY R., biology educator; b. Bloomsburg, Pa., July 18, 1941; s. Raymond E. and Helen M. (Smeck) E.; m. Cozella E. Harvey, Aug. 14, 1971; children: Andrea M., Todd J. BS in Biology, Bloomsburg U., 1964; MS in Zoology, Pa. State U., 1966, PhD in Zoology, 1969. Assoc. prof. biology Pa. State U., Erie, 1969—. Author: (with others) The Byssus of the Zebra Mussel, 1991. Office: Pa State U Erie-The Behrend Coll Station Rd Erie PA 16563

ECKSTEIN, E(DMUND) CHARLES, dentist; b. Paterson, N.J., June 15, 1944; s. Arthur Jess and Alice (Belkin) E.; m. Susan Lynn Bressler (div. Oct. 1979); m. Michele Carol Pirone, Dec. 7, 1979; children: Karen Alyse, Lindsey Ann, Andrew Jess. BA, Rutgers Coll., 1966; D Dental Medicine, Jersey Coll. Dentistry, 1972. Staff mem. Fairleigh Dickinson Dental Sch., Hackensack, N.J., 1975-82, Bergen Community Coll., Paramus, N.J., 1975-82; dentist pvt. practice, Tenafly, 1975—; dir. Prudential Ins. Co. / No. N.J. Dental, Parsippany, 1985—; Founder, chief exec. officer MetroCare Inc., Tenafly, N.J., 1985—; co-dir. handicapped dental program Holy Name Hosp., Teaneck, N.J., 1976-79; mem. staff Englewood (N.J.) Hosp., 1975—; peer rev. expert N.J. State Bd. Dentistry, Newark, 1983—; cons. to pvt. attys., 1976—. Co-author: The Dynamics of Dental Practice, 1977; contbr. articles to profl. jours. Forensics cons. dep. Bergen County Sheriff's Dept. Hackensack, 1990. Acad. Gen. Dentistry fellow, 1979. Mem. Am. Acad. Forensic Scis., N.Y.. Soc. Forensic Dentistry, Acad. Medicine N.J. (bd. trustees). Republican. Jewish. Home: 513 Piermont Ave S Westwood NJ 07675-5713 Office: Metro Care Inc 121 County Rd Tenafly NJ 07670-1838

ECKTON, MARY LOUISE, counselor; b. Portland, Maine, May 28, 1932; d. Arthur A. and Alice (Crimmins) Small; m. Wallace H. Eckton, Aug. 22, 1959; children: Susan A., Wallace H. III, Michael A., Teresa L. BS, U. Maine, 1954, MEd, 1957. Cert. guidance counselor, Pa. Tchr., counselor Brunswick (Maine) High Sch., 1954-58, North Valley Regional High Sch., Danarest, N.J., 1958-59; counselor Schuylkill Valley High Sch., Leesport, Pa., 1978-79, Tulpehocken High Sch., Bernville, Pa., 1979—; founder, charter mem. Montessori Country Day Sch., Wyanissing, Pa., 1965-70. Chmn. various coms. Cornwall Terr. Community Assn., Spring Twp., 1963-73. Mem. AACD, NEA, AAUW (pres. 1976-78, v.p. 1972-76, Reading, Pa. chpt.), Am. Sch. Counselors Assn., Pa. Edn. Assn., Pa. Sch. Counselors Assn. (bd. dirs.), Berks Area Counselors Assn. (liaison v.p. 1986-90), Phi Delta Kappa. Home: 101 Shakespeare Dr Reading PA 19608-1721 Office: Tulpehocken High Sch RR 2 Bernville PA 19506-9802

ECONOMOPOULOS, NICHOLAS THEODORE, numismatist, consultant; b. New Brunswick, N.J., Mar. 9, 1949; s. Theodore Nicholas and Helen Constantina (Velikas) E.; m. Beverly Jean-Ann Pekitis, July 17, 1977; 1 child, Elena Nicole. BA in Classics, Rutgers Coll., 1971; MA in Classics, Pa. State U., 1973; postgrad., U. Colo., 1973-74, U. Pa., 1974-76. Aircraft dispatcher Continental Airlines, Houston, 1978-83; fin. cons. Merrill Lynch, Houston, 1983-86; v.p. Edward J. Waddell, Ltd., Bethesda, Md., 1986-89; pres., owner Economopoulos Enterprises, Holicong, Pa., 1989—. Mem. Am. Numismatic Soc., Soc. for Ancient Numismatics, Am. Numismatic Assn., Am. Inst. Archaeology, Hist. Numismatic Guild, Royal Numismatic Soc. Greek Orthodox. Office: Economopoulos Enterprises PO Box 199 Holicong PA 18928-0199

ECONOMOU-PEASE, BESSIE CARASOULAS, city planner, consultant; b. N.Y.C., Sept. 29, 1933; d. Alexander Stelianos and Maria (Trilivas) Carasoulas; m. Constantine J. Economou, Sept. 10, 1955 (div. May 1966); m. Robert Barnard Pease, Oct. 1, 1976; children: Robert W., Richard B. BA, Barnard Coll., 1955; postgrad., Columbia U., 1955-57, MS in Urban Planning, 1960. Med. researcher Coll. Physicians and Surgeons Columbia U., N.Y.C., 1955-60; planning and renewal cons. Brown & Anthony, Engrs. Planners, N.Y.C., 1960-62; dir. research, edn. ACTION Inc., N.Y.C., 1962-66; exec. asst. to adminstr. N.Y.C. Housing and Devel. Admin., N.Y.C., 1966-69; dep. dir., exec. asst. N.Y. State Urban Devel. Corp., N.Y.C., 1969-73; exec. v.p. Nat. Housing Conf., Washington, 1973-76; prin. Bessie C. Economou Assocs., Pitts., 1976—; dir. ACTION Housing, Inc., Pitts., 1982-88, Nat. Housing Conf., Washington, 1973—, also exec. v.p. 1973-76, Health Systems Agy. Western Pa., Pitts., 1984-87; adj. prof. U. Pitts, 1986—; mem. adv. com. Bur. Census Housing, 1977-81. Mem. Am. Inst. Cert. Planners (cert.), Nat. Assn. Housing and Redevel. Officials, Lamda Alpha.

EDDINGTON, THOMAS L., compensation and benefits consultant; b. Ypsilanti, Mich., Mar. 10, 1960; s. William Thomas and Janet Lorraine (Woodard) E. BA in Bus. Psychology, Adrian Coll., 1982. Employee benefits rep. Aetna Life Ins. Co., N.Y.C., 1982-84, Concord, N.H., 1984-86; account exec. Aetna Life Ins. Co., Phila., 1986-90; cons. Hewitt Assocs., Phila., 1990—. Mem. Pa. Employee Benefits Assn., World Affairs Coun., Phila. Young Reps., Racquet Club. Presbyterian. Home: 508 S 3rd St Philadelphia PA 19147-2308 Office: Hewitt Assocs The Curtis Ctr Philadelphia PA 19106

EDDISON, ELIZABETH BOLE, entrepreneur, information specialist; b. Bronxville, N.Y., June 3, 1928; d. Hamilton Biggar and Elizabeth Owsley (Boyle) Bole; m. John Corbin Eddison, Feb. 10, 1951; children: Jonathan B., Elizabeth O., Martha C. AB, Vassar Coll., 1948; MS, Simmons Coll., 1973. Pres., bd. dirs. Lahore (Pakistan)-Am. Sch., 1959-61; chmn. evaluation com. Karachi (Pakistan)-Am. Sch., 1961-63; treas. bd. dirs. La Paz Coop. Sch., Bolivia, 1963-65; v.p. Assn. Am. Fgn. Svc. Women; coord. social svcs. Urban Svc. Corps, Washington Pub. Schs., 1965-69; sec. bd. dirs. Colegio Nueva Granada, Bogota, Colombia, 1969-71; chmn., treas. Warner-Eddison Assocs., Inc., Cambridge, Mass., 1973-88, pres., 1981-88; chmn., v.p. Inmagic Inc., Cambridge, 1984—; mem. steering com. State House Conf. on Small Bus., Mass., 1986-88; mem. bd. advisors Internat. Sch. Info. Mgmt., Irvine, Calif., 1984—, adv. coun. Engring. Info., Inc., N.Y., 1988—; mem. computer applications com. Cary Meml. Libr., Lexington, Mass., 1986. Compiler: Words that Mean Business, 1981; contbr. articles to profl. jours. Mem. adv. com. on internat. and tech. devel. U.S. Dept. State, 1980-83; mem. small bus. com. Mass. Gov.'s Bus. Adv. Coun., 1985-89; co-chmn. Lexington Dem. Town Com., 1990-92; mem. Mass. Bd. Libr. Commrs., 1990-91. Recipient Alumni Achievement award Simmons Coll., 1986, Disclosure Achievement

award Libr. Mgmt. Bus. and Fin. div. Spl. Librs. Assn., 1987. Mem. Info. Industry Assn. (chmn. emeriti com. 1983-88, small bus. forum 1986-89, entrepreneur award com. 1989-90, co-chmn. publs. com. 1984-87, Entrepreneur award 1989), Assoc. Info. Mgrs. (chmn. publs. com. 1984-86, bd. dirs. 1984-86, Knox award 1988), Spl. Librs. Assn. (chmn. program com. libr. mgmt. div. 1984-85, profl. devel. com. 1987-88, chmn.-elect 1988, chmn. 1989-90, bd. dirs. 1991—), Am. Soc. Info. Scientists, Beta Phi Mu. Democrat. Office: Inmagic Inc 2067 Massachusetts Ave Cambridge MA 02140-1338

EDDISON, JOHN CORBIN, economist; b. N.Y.C., Nov. 4, 1919; s. William Barton and Mary (Corbin) E.; m. Elizabeth Owsley Bole, Feb. 10, 1951; children: Jonathan B., Elizabeth O., Martha C. Grad., St. Paul's Sch., 1938; A.B., Cornell U., 1942, M.S., 1948; Ph.D., MIT, 1955. Personnel asst. E.I. duPont de Nemours & Co., 1947-48; indsl. engr. Campbell Soup Co., 1949-51; indsl. advisor EDA, San Juan, P.R., 1955-56; asst. to rep. in Burma, Ford Found., 1956-57; econ. advisor to Govt. W. Pakistan, Harvard Adv. Group, Lahore, 1958-61, to; Pakistan Planning Commn., Karachi, 1961-63; dep. dir. AID mission to Bolivia, La Paz, 1963-65, Central Am. affairs Dept. State, Washington, 1965-68; dir. Near East affairs AID, 1968-69; econ. adviser to planning dept. Govt. Colombia, Harvard U. Devel. Adv. Service, Bogota, 1969-71; asso. dir. Harvard U. Devel. Adv. Service, Harvard Inst. for Internat. Devel., Cambridge, Mass., 1974-80; exec. v.p. and treas. Warner-Eddison Assocs., Inc., Cambridge, 1980-84; assoc. dir. Ctr. Asian Devel. Studies, Boston U., 1984-85. Author papers, reports. Selectman Town of Lexington, Mass., 1984—, chmn. bd. of selectman, 1986-88, 90. Capt. CE, AUS, 1942-46. Overseas fellow Ford Found., 1953-54. Mem. ACLU, Am. Econ. Assn., Alpha Delta Phi. Episcopalian. Home and Office: 20 Nickerson Rd Lexington MA 02173-6822

EDDS, KENNETH TIFFANY, biology educator; b. Glen Ridge, N.J., July 17, 1945; s. Mac Vincent Jr. and Louise (Tiffany) E.; m. Kathryn Ann Hendrick, May 17, 1975; children: Brian, Susan, Matthew. BS, U. R.I., 1969; PhD, SUNY, Albany, 1974. Asst. scientist Marine Biol. Lab., Woods Hole, Mass., 1976-79; asst. prof. SUNY, Buffalo, 1979-85, assoc. prof., 1985—. Contbr. articles to profl. jours. Recipient rsch. grants NIH, 1976-79, NSF, 1981-84, 91—. Mem. AAAS, Am. Soc. Cell Biology, Corp. Marine Biol. Lab. Office: SUNY/Buffalo Main St Buffalo NY 14202-4103

EDDY, ELSBETH MARIE, retired government official, statistician; b. Buffalo, Apr. 8, 1934; d. Willy and Wilhelmine (Hartman) Gnueg; m. Leonard John Eddy, Feb. 5, 1956; children: John, Bruce, Lisa. Student, schs. in Md., Va., N.C.; spl. courses, U.S. Dept. Agriculture Grad. Sch.; cert. in mgmt., Prince Georges Coll., 1976. With fgn. trade div. U.S. Bur. Census, Washington, 1967-90, chief metals and minerals, 1980-90. Recipient Cert. of Appreciation, USAF, 1973. Democrat. Home: 13000 Piscataway Dr Fort Washington MD 20744-6620

EDDY, NANCY BURNS, educational administrator; b. Wilson, Pa., Dec. 27, 1937; d. Rodney C. and Carolyn H. (Withrow) Burns; m. S. Philip Eddy, July 25, 1959; children: John, Sara. BA, Mt. Holyoke Coll., 1959; MPA, U. Mass., 1983. Rsch. assoc. Inst. for Environ. Psychophysics U. Mass., Amherst, 1960-64, staff assoc. Sch. Engring., 1973-79; asst. dean adminstrn. Holyoke (Mass.) Community Coll., 1979-83, dean adminstrn., 1983—; dir., health and welfare sec. Bd. Regents, 1985—; bd. dirs. Heritage Bank for Savs., Holyoke. Contbr. articles to profl. publs.; author monographs in field. Bd. dirs. Valley Health Plan, 1981-85; pres. Mass. Mcpl. Orgn., Boston, 1979-80; chair Local Govt. Adv. Commn. to Gov., Boston, 1977-80; chair Bd. Selectmen, Amherst, 1971-80. Named Citizen of Yr., Amherst C. of C., 1974, Outstanding Bus. Officer Nat. Coun. Community Coll. Bus. Officers, 1987. Mem. Am. Assn. Women in Community and Jr. Colls. (v.p. 1989—), Ea. Assn. Coll. and Univ. Bus. Officers (bd. dirs. 1990—, 2d v.p. 1991—), LWV (pres. Amherst chpt. 1964-66), Am. Soc. Pub. Adminstrn. (chair Western Mass. chpt. 1983-84), Mass. Am. Coun. on Edn. (bd. dirs. 1990). Democrat. Office: Holyoke Community Coll 303 Homestead Ave Holyoke MA 01040-1099

EDDY, WALLACE LESLIE, academic administrator; b. Randolph, Vt., May 14, 1964; s. David L. and Jean (Pratt) E. BS, Castleton (Vt.) Coll., 1987; MS, We. Ill. U., 1989. Coord. jud. and Greek affairs Dickinson Coll., Carlisle, Pa., 1989-90, asst. dir. student activities, 1990—. Mentor Big Bros./Big Sisters, Harrisburg, Pa., 1990—; communications com. United Way. Mem. Am. Coll. Pers. Assn., Assn. Frat. Advisors, Nat. Assn. Student Pers. Adminstrs., Delta Upsilon. Episcopalian. Office: Dickinson Coll Holland Union Bldg Carlisle PA 17013

EDEL, ABRAHAM, philosophy educator; b. Pitts., Dec. 6, 1908; s. Simon and Fannie (Malamud) E.; m. May Mandelbaum, Jan. 30, 1934 (dec. May 1964); children: Matthew (dec.), Deborah; m. Elizabeth Flower, May 11, 1973. B.A., McGill U., 1927, M.A., 1928; B.A., Oxford U., 1930; Ph.D., Columbia U., 1934. Mem. dept. philosophy Coll. City N.Y., 1931-73, prof. emeritus philosophy, 1973—; Distinguished prof. philosophy City U. N.Y. Grad. Sch., 1970-73, emeritus, 1973—; research prof. philosophy U. Pa., 1974—; vis. appointments Columbia U., U. Calif. (Berkeley), Swarthmore Coll., U. Pa., Western Res. U., SUNY Downstate Med. Ctr., others. Author: The Theory and Practice of Philosophy: Ethical Judgment, 1955, 2d edit., 1961, Science and the Structure of Ethics, 1961, Method in Ethical Theory, 1963, Aristotle, 1967, (with May Edel) Anthropology and Ethics, 1959, rev. edit., 1971, Analyzing Concepts in Social Science, 1979, Exploring Fact & Value, 1980, Aristotle and his Philosophy, 1982, Interpreting Education, 1985, (with Elizabeth Flower and Finbarr O'Connor) Morality, Philosophy, and Practice, 1988, Relating Humanities and Social Thought, 1990, The Struggle for Academic Democracy, 1990, In Search of the Ethical, 1992. Assoc. Nat. Humanities Center, 1978-79; sr. fellow Center for Dewey Studies, 1981-82. Recipient Butler Silver medal Columbia, 1959; Guggenheim fellow, 1944-45; Rockefeller Found. grantee, 1952-53; NSF grantee; 1959-60. Mem. Am. Philos. Assn. (v.p. Ea. div. 1972), Metaphys. Soc., Am. Soc. Polit. and Legal Philosophy, Am. Soc. Value Inquiry (pres. 1984), Internat. Assn. Philosophy Law and Social Philosophy (v.p. Am. sect. 1971-73, pres. 1973-75), Philosophy Edn. Soc., Soc. for Advancement Am. Philosophy. Office: U Pa Philosophy Dept 3440 Market St Fl 460 Philadelphia PA 19104-3325

EDELBAUM, PHILIP R., lawyer; b. Bklyn., June 2, 1936; s. Maurice and Selma (Samuels) E.; m. Corinne Edelbaum, May 29, 1960 (div. Mar. 1974); children: Stacey K. Boretz, Evan Mark. BA, Adelphi U., 1957; LLB, NYU, 1960. Bar: N.Y. 1961, U.S. Dist. Cts. (so. and ea. dists.) N.Y. 1962, U.S. Ct. of Appeals (2d cirs.) 1964, (3d cir.) 1977, U.S. Supreme Ct. 1965. Atty. criminal div. Legal Aid Soc., N.Y.C., 1961-63; pvt. practice N.Y.C., 1963—; faculty Nat. Inst. Trial Advocacy-N.E. Region, Nat. Inst. Trial Advocacy-N.E. Master Advocates, Hempstead, N.Y., 1985—; faculty trial techniques program Hofstra U. Sch. of Law, Hempstead, 1985—. Chmn. pool feasibility com. Town of Eastchester, N.Y., 1971-72. Mem. Assn. Bar of the City of N.Y. (com. on criminal cts. op. and budget 1988—, numerous subcoms. on criminal justice 1988—), N.Y. Criminal Bar Assn. Home: 345 E 93d St New York NY 10128 Office: 100 Church St New York NY 10128

EDELGLASS, STEPHEN MARK, physicist, educator, consultant; b. Bklyn., Dec. 28, 1935; s. Jack and Rose (Fink) E.; m. Susan Jane Schwartz, June 6, 1964 (div. July 1979); children: Alexandra, William; m. Hanna Forster, Apr. 3, 1988. SB, MIT, 1956, SM, 1958; MS, Stevens Inst. Tech., Hoboken, N.J., 1964, PhD, 1973. Registered profl. engr., N.Y. Dir. sci. Threefold Ednl. Found., Spring Valley, N.Y., 1974—; from adj. instr. to adj. prof. Cooper Union for Advancement of Sci. and Art, N.Y.C., 1958-83; from adj. asst. prof. to adj. prof. Stevens Inst. Tech., 1969-86; ind. forensic cons., Chestnut Ridge, N.Y., 1973—. Author: Engineering Materials Science, 1966 (Rossi prize 1966); co-author: Matter and Mind, 1992; contbr. chpts. to books. NSF faculty fellow, 1967-68. Mem. Am. Phys. Soc., N.Y. Acad. Scis., ASM Internat., Am. Acad. Forensic Scientists. Office: Threefold Ednl Found Hungry Hollow Rd Spring Valley NY 10977

EDELMAN, ALAN IRWIN, lawyer; b. Poughkeepsie, N.Y., June 14, 1958; s. Edwyn Herman and Shirley Frances (Kandel) E.; m. Erica Joy Schwartz, Aug. 16, 1981; children: Leah Hanit, Avram Natan. BA, Cornell U., 1980; JD, Boston U., 1983. Bar: D.C. 1983, U.S. Dist. Ct. D.C. 1985, U.S. Supreme Ct. 1991. Atty. enforcement div. SEC, Washington, 1983-86, atty. Office of Gen. Counsel, 1986-87; counsel Senate Permanent Subcom. on Investigations, Washington, 1987—. Edward F. Hennessy scholar Boston U., 1983. Mem. ABA, Fed. Bar Assn. Office: US Senate 100 Russell Senate Bldg Washington DC 20510

EDELMAN, HARRY ROLLINGS, III, engineering and construction company executive; b. Pitts., Aug. 16, 1928; s. Harry Rollings, Jr. and Marian A. (Crooks) E.; m. Nancy Jane McCune, Aug. 26, 1950; children: Lisa E. Turbeville, Harry Rollings IV, John Reed, Amy L. B.S., U. Pitts., 1950. With Heyl & Patterson, Inc., Pitts., 1950—, exec. v.p., 1960-65, pres., chmn., 1965-91, chmn. bd., chief exec. officer, 1991—, also bd. dirs.; v.p. Bridge & Crane Inspection, Inc., 1986—. Author papers in engring., constrn., religion and mgmt. Bd. dirs. Allegheny Health Edn. and Rsch. Found.; past pres. Christian Assn. S.W. Pa., St. Christopher's Hosp. for Children, Allegheny United Hosps., Inc.; chmn. Med. Coll. Pa.; chmn. bd. dirs. Presbyn. Assn. Aging; past chmn. Allegheny Neuropsychiat. Inst., Vocat. Rehab. Ctr. Allegheny County; past moderator Pitts. Presbytery. With AUS, 1952-54. Recipient Regional Ecumenism award, 1985. Mem. World Pres.'s Orgn., Chief Execs. Orgn., Duquesne Club, Pitts. Club. Field Club, The Club at Seabrook. Office: Heyl & Patterson Inc PO Box 36 Pittsburgh PA 15230-0036

EDELMAN, HARRY ROLLINGS, IV, photographer; b. Pitts., Apr. 30, 1955; s. Harry R. III and Nancy Jane (McCune) E.; m. Elaine Innes, July 29, 1978; children: Elizabeth A., Rebecca D., Harry R. V. AAS, Rochester Inst. Tech., 1977, BFA, 1977. Prin. H. Edelman Photography, Pitts., 1977—. Mem. numerous local art groups. Mem. Am. Soc. Mag. Photographers (bd. dirs.), Press Club of Pitts. Clubs: Rotary (Forest Hills, Pa.) (bd. dirs.), Press (Pitts.).

EDELMAN, MARTIN, psychologist, consultant; b. Bklyn., Aug. 15, 1939; s. Sam and Anna (Danowitz) E.; m. Joy Waller; 1 child, Steven; m. Revell J. Motin, July 18, 1981; stepchildren: Laura Mantell, Deborah Mantell. BA, Bklyn. Coll., 1963; MA, Hunter Coll., 1966; PhD, Yeshiva U., 1977. Lic. psychologist, N.Y. Staff psychologist Orange County Child and Family Clinic, Newburgh, N.Y., 1977-81, Rockland Childrens Psychiat. Ctr., Orangeburg, N.Y., 1971-77; program dir. Rockland Childrens Psychiat. Ctr., Orangeburg, 1983-85; cons. psychologist Child Protective Svcs., Westchester, N.Y., 1981-83, N.Y. State Div. for Youth, Goshen, 1985—; pvt. practice, 1978—; adj. lectr. Bklyn. Coll., 1968-73; rsch. scientist Lower Eastside Svc. Ctr., N.Y.C., 1968-71. Incentive scholar N.Y. State, 1963-64; rsch. fellow Hunter Coll., 1965-66; title IV fellow NDEA, 1966-68. Mem. APA. Home: 60 Village Green Bardonia NY 10954-2037

EDELMAN, RICHARD WINSTON, public relations executive; b. Chgo., June 15, 1954; s. Daniel J. and Ruth Ann (Rozumoff) E.; m. Rosalind Ann Walrath, May 17, 1986. B.A., Harvard U., 1976, M.B.A., 1978. Pres., chief oper. officer Daniel J. Edelman, Inc., N.Y.C.; chief exec. officer Edelman Internat. Corp., N.Y.C. Bd. dirs. Young Profls. for Gov. Jim Thompson, Chgo., 1978, Young People for Ed Koch, N.Y.C., 1985, Planned Parenthood Fedn. Am., 1980-81. Mem. Pub. Relations Soc. Am. (Silver Anvil award 1981). Jewish. Clubs: Harvard, Harmonie (N.Y.C.). Home: 277 W End Ave Apt 4B New York NY 10023-2608 Office: Edelman Internat Corp 1500 Broadway 25th Fl New York NY 10036*

EDELMAN, ROBERT, chemist; b. N.Y.C., Apr. 30, 1942; s. Irving Samuel and Ann (Birnbaum) E.; m. Diane Gail Goldman, Aug. 6, 1972. BS, Bklyn. Coll., 1963; PhD, Rutgers U., 1969. Rsch. assoc. Celanese Corp., Summit, N.J., 1969-82; tech. mgr. M&T Chems., Rahway, N.J., 1982-89; tech. mgr. Permabond div. Nat. Starch and Chem. Co., Bridgewater, N.J., 1989—. Mem. Am. Chem. Soc., Soc. Advancement of Material and Process Engring. Office: Nat Starch and Chem Co 10 Finderne Ave Bridgewater NJ 08807-3300

EDELMANN, CAROLYN FOOTE, author, poet, editor; b. Toledo, Ohio, Nov. 28, 1937; d. James Wendell and Lillian Edna (Foote) Stower; children: Diane Lydia, Catherine Lynne. BS, St. Mary of Woods Coll., 1959; pvt. studies with Theodore Weiss, Galway Kinnell, Stanley Plumly, Princeton U. Author: (poetry) Gatherings, 1987; appearances include (TV) People are Talking, Phila., (radio) Pub. Radio, Manhattan. Publicist Princeton (N.J.) Med. Ctr., N.J. Psychiat. Inst., Congressman Peter Kostmayer, Doylestown, Pa.; charter mem. Princeton Joint Commn. on Aging. Recipient William Carlos Williams prize Paterson Pub. Libr., 1977, N.J. Poetry Monthly prize, 1978. Mem. Acad. Am. Poets, Nat. League Am. Penwomen, Poetry Soc. Am., Internat. Women's Writing Guild, N.J. Penwomen, U.S. 1 Poet's Coop. (sustaining), Poets and Writers. Democrat.

EDELSON, ALAN MARTIN, medical publisher, neurophysiologist; b. N.Y.C., Mar. 17, 1937; s. H. Edward and Jean (Malsman) E.; m. Carol M. Herman, Jan. 21, 1959; children—Richard, Helena. B.S., U. Rochester, 1959; M.S., Columbia U., 1964, Ph.D., 1972. Founder, pub. Raven Press (med. pubs.), N.Y.C., 1964-90; pres., chief exec. officer J. B. Lippincott Co. (med. pubs.), Phila., 1991—; rsch. postdoctoral fellow dept. neurology Coll. Physicians and Surgeons Columbia U., 1972-73. Mem. AAAS, N.Y. Acad. Sci., Med. Libr. Assn., Am. Chem. Soc., Internat. Soc. Neurochemistry, Phi Beta Kappa, Sigma Xi. Office: J B Lippincott Co 227 E Washington Sq Philadelphia PA 19106-3780

EDELSON, EDWARD H., research chemist; b. N.Y.C., Jan. 28, 1947; s. Charles and Augusta (Benjamin) E.; m. Judith Linda Miller, Mar. 28, 1970; children: Erica, Mindy Carol. BS, CUNY, 1973; PhD, Rensselaer Poly. Inst., 1977. Rsch. assoc. Ames Rsch. Ctr. NASA, Moffet Field, Calif., 1977-79; instr., rsch. asst. U. So. Calif., L.A., 1979-80; rsch. chemist Exxon Rsch. and Engring. Co., Baytown, Tex., 1980-85; sr. rsch. chemist Mobil Rsch. and Devel. Corp., Paulsboro, N.J., 1985—. Author: (with others) COSPAR Life Sciences and Space Research, 1980, 1980 McGraw-Hill Yearbook of Science and Technology, 1980, Origin of Life, 1981; contbr. articles to profl. jours. Mem. Am. Chem. Soc. (chmn. symposium 1978, 80), Soc. Automatic Engrs. Office: Mobil Rsch and Devel Corp PO Box 480 Paulsboro NJ 08066-0480

EDELSON, PAUL JEFFREY, physician, educator, historian; b. Newport News, Va., Dec. 5, 1943; s. Harry and Ruth (Levine) E.; m. Ingrid Karen Rosner, Jan. 11, 1981; children: Jonathan, Katherine. AB in Math., U. Rochester, 1964; MD summa cum laude, SUNY, Bklyn., 1969. Diplomate Nat. Bd. Med. Examiners, Am. Bd. Pediatrics. Intern in pediatrics Yale-New Haven Hosp., 1969-70, asst. resident, 1970-71; fellow in medicine U. Calif. Med. Ctr., San Francisco, 1971-72; fellow Rockefeller U., N.Y.C., 1972-74, asst. prof., 1974-77; asst. prof. of pediatrics Harvard Med. Sch., Boston, 1977-82; assoc. prof. of pediatrics Cornell U. Med. Coll., N.Y.C., 1982—; cons. coun. on therapeutics AMA, Chgo., 1985—; mem. Gov.'s Task Force on Neonatal HIV Infection, Albany, N.Y., 1988; cons. NIH, Bethesda, Md., 1979—; reviewer various med. jours., 1982—. Editor: Methods of Studying Monoclear Phagocytes, Childhood AIDS, 1991; contbr. more than 60 articles to profl. publs., chpts. to books. Spl. fellow Leukemia Soc. Am., 1973-77; Fritz travelling fellow SUNY, 1975, Rudin fellow Columbia, 1991; recipient Rsch. Career Devel. award NIH, 1978-83. Mem. AAAS, Soc. Pediatric Rsch., N.Y. Acad. Medicine, Am. Assn. History of Medicine, Am. Hist. Assn. Jewish. Office: Cornell U Med Coll 1300 York Ave New York NY 10021-4896

EDELSTEIN, ALAN SHANE, physicist, researcher; b. St. Louis, June 27, 1936; s. Abraham and Lilian (Ginsberg) E.; m. Maravene Gram, Aug. 12, 1963; children: Rachel, Rebecca. BS in Engring. Physics, Washington U., St. Louis, 1958; MS in Physics, Stanford U., 1959, PhD in Physics, 1963. Post doctoral fellow Stanford (Calif.) U., 1963-64; NSF post doctoral fellow Leinden (Holland) U., 1964-65; tech. staff IBM, Yorktown Heights, N.Y., 1965-68; assoc. prof. U. Ill., Chgo., 1968-80; rsch. physicist Naval Rsch. Lab., Washington, 1980-88, supervisory rsch. physicist, 1988—; cons. Argonne (Ill.) Nat. Lab., 1969-78. Author: Kondo Effect, Nanostructured Materials, 1981; contbr. over 90 articles to profl. jours. Mem. Am. Phys. Soc., Materials Rsch. Soc. Jewish. Office: Naval Rsch Lab Code 6371 Washington DC 20375

EDELSTEIN, JASON ZELIG, rabbi, psychologist; b. Boston, Jan. 31, 1930; s. Abraham and Anna (Freedman) E.; m. Eva Bamberger, Aug. 3, 1952; children: Philip, Sharon, Joseph. BA in Psychology, U. N.H., 1951, MA in Clin. Psychology, 1953; BHL, Hebrew Union Coll., 1956, MAHL, 1969; DMin, Pitts. Theol. Sem., 1977; DD, Hebrew Union Coll.-Jewish Inst. Religion, 1983. Ordained rabbi, 1958. Rabbi Temple David, Monroeville, Pa., 1960—; chaplain VA Med. Ctr., Pitts., 1962-90; lectr. St. Vincent Coll., Latrobe, Pa., 1968—, Seton Hill Coll., Greensburg, Pa., 1981—; nat. coord. Hotline, Cen. Conf. Am. Rabbis, N.Y.C., 1979&; pastoral psychol. cons. Sisters of Mercy, Pitts., 1990—; mem. com. Chesky Inst. on Judaism and Psychotherapy, N.Y.C., 1990—. Contbr. articles to profl. publs. Lt. USN, 1955-60. Mem. Cen. Conf. Am. Rabbis (ex-officio mem. long range planning com. 1990—, ex-officio mem. rabbi's family com. 1989—), Am. Psychol. Assn., Religious Edn. Assn., Viktor Frankl Inst. Logotherapy, Nat. Honor Soc. in Psychology. Home: 135 Mayberry Dr Monroeville PA 15146-4721 Office: Temple David 4415 Northern Pike Monroeville PA 15146-2997

EDEN, BRUCE DOUGLAS, pension fund administrator; b. Bethlehem, Pa., Aug. 5, 1961; s. Arthur B. and Martha L. (Miller) E.; m. Maria Frant, July 8, 1989. BA, Moravian Coll., 1983; MBA, Wilkes U., 1989. Trust officer Independence Bancorp., Perkasie, Pa., 1984-87; v.p. Meridian Asset Mgmt., Allentown, Pa., 1987—; adj. faculty econs., Lehigh County Community Coll., Allentown, 1990—. Group exec. PBA Group III, Allentown, 1989—. Home: 4840 Lisa Dr Schnecksville PA 18078 Office: Meridian Asset Mgmt 7th and Hamilton Sts Allentown PA 18105

EDER, PAULA RUTH, psychotherapist; b. Cleve., Aug. 12, 1943; d. Samuel and Rose (Gross) E.; m. Christopher J. Linell, Nov. 3, 1972; 1 child, Aaron Matthew. BA in Elem. Edn., U. Mich., 1965, MA in Guidance and Counseling, 1966; PhD in Early Childhood Edn., U. Calif., Berkeley, 1971. Head tchr. Beth Israel Nursery Sch., Ann Arbor, Mich., 1965-66; tchr. Springfield (Oreg.) Pub. Schs., 1966-67, Oakland (Calif.) Pub. Schs., 1967-68; dir. presch. Jewish Community Ctr., Oakland, 1969-70; rsch. asst. U. Calif., Berkeley, 1969-70, counselor for grad. students, 1970-71; assoc. prof. edn. New Eng. Coll., Henniker, N.H., 1971-77; ednl. dir. Head Start Belknap-Merrimack (N.H.) Counties, 1973-74; pvt. practice psychotherapy Francestown, N.H., 1977—; presenter workshops in field. Contbr. articles to profl. publs. Mem. adv. bd. U. N.H. Sch. Continuing Studies, Durham, 1973. Mem. AACD, N.H. ASCD, Am. Mental Health Counseling Assn.

EDER, RICHARD GRAY, newspaper critic; b. Washington, Aug. 16, 1932; s. George Jackson and Marceline (Gray) E.; m. Esther Garcia Aguirre, Apr. 21, 1955; children: Maria, Ann, Claire, Michael, Luke, Benjamin, James. BA, Harvard U., 1954. Fgn. corr. N.Y. Times, various countries in Europe and Latin Am., 1962-77, 80-82; theater critic N.Y. Times, 1977-79; book critic L.A. Times, 1982—. Recipient Pulitzer prize for criticism, 1987. Mem. Nat. Book Critics Circle (citation for reviewing 1987). Roman Catholic. Office: Los Angeles Times 86 Charles St Boston MA 02114-4614

EDERLE, DOUGLAS RICHARD, lawyer; b. St. Louis, Aug. 10, 1962; s. Richard Joseph and Mary Ellen (Gorman) E.; m. Virginia Foss Mara, June 5, 1988; 1 child, Ryan Douglas. BS in Acctg., U. Ill., 1984; JD, Harvard U., 1987. CPA, Ill.; Bar: Tex., Mass. Assoc. Hughes & Luce, Dallas, 1987-88, Testa, Hurwitz & Thibeault, Boston, 1989—. Mem. ABA, Tex. Bar Assn., Mass. Bar Assn., Boston Bar Assn., AICPA. Roman Catholic. Home: 32 Hounds Ditch Ln Duxbury MA 02332-4421 Office: Testa Hurwitz & Thibeault 53 State St Boston MA 02109-2809

EDERMA, ARVO BRUNO, physician, medical administrator; b. Haapsalu, Estonia, May 13, 1928; came to U.S., 1949; s. Bruno Immanuel and Erika (Drake) E.; m. Miriam Maris Kikas, Sept. 25, 1954; children: Karin Erika, Tiina Inge, Erik Arvo. BA, Lenoir Rhyne Coll., 1952; M.S.P.H., U. N.C., 1953; MD, Bowman Gray Sch. Medicine, Winston-Salem, N.C., 1957. Diplomate Am. Bd. Gen. Preventive Medicine. Intern USPHS Hosp., Balt., 1957-58; med. officer in charge U.S. AEC, Germantown, Md., 1958-60; medi. cons. Fed. Employee Health Program, Washington, 1960-62; dep. chief Fed. Employee Health Program, Silver Spring, Md., 1962-65; asst. dir. Div. of Fed. Employee Health, Hyattsville, Md., 1965-75; dir. Div. of Fed. Employee Occupational Health, Hyattsville, 1975-84, Div. of Beneficiary Med. Programs, Rockville, Md., 1984-85; dep. dir. Gillis W. Long Hansen's Disease Ctr., Carville, La., 1985-90; acting dir. Regional Hansen's Disease Program, Carville, 1986-90; chmn. med. adv. bd. Estonian Am. Fund, Inc., 1990—; pub. health adv. bd. U.S. Baltic Found., 1991—; adj. assoc. prof. of preventive medicine and biometrics F. Edward Hebert Sch. Medicine, Uniformed Svcs. Univ., Bethesda, Md., 1978-87. Contbr. articles to profl. jours. Pres. PTA, Lewisdale Elem. Sch., Hyattsville, Md., 1968-69; pres., sec., council mem. St. Mark's Estonian Lutheran Ch., Washington, 1969-85. Capt. USPHS, 1957—. Recipient Disting. Alumnus award Lenoir Rhyne Coll., 1976, commendation medal USPHS, 1977, Meritorious Svc. medal USPHS, 1984, Outstanding Svc. medal USPHS, 1987, Outstanding Unit citation USPHS, 1988. Fellow Am. Occupational Med. Assn., Am. Coll. Preventive Medicine, Am. Acad. Occupational Medicine; mem. AMA, Assn. Mil. Surgeons of U.S., Commissioned Officer Assn. Republican. Lutheran. Home and Office: 10800 Kirkwall Terrace Rockville MD 20854

EDGREEN, ROBERT J., equities company executive; b. Coudersport, Pa., May 23, 1946; s. Howard J. and Lucille (Leete) E.; m. Sherian J. Campbell, Aug. 23, 1969; children: Kristen, Gregory. BS in Aerospace Engring., Pa. State U., 1968; MBA, U. Va., 1972. V.p. Merrill Lynch Capital Markets, N.Y.C., 1975-81; 1st v.p. E.F. Hutton & Co., N.Y.C., 1981-86; chmn. Rotor Tool Co., Cleve., 1986-89; pres. Integrated Resources Acquisitions, N.Y.C., 1986-89; chmn. Learjet Corp., Wichita, Kans., 1987-89; pres. K.D. Equities, N.Y.C., 1989—; dir. Childtime, Inc., Brighton, Mich., 1990—. Mem. Sky Club. Presbyterian. Office: KD Equities 40 Broad St New York NY 10004-2315

EDINGER, CHARLES B., physician; b. N.Y.C., Mar. 8, 1934; s. Isidore and Augusta (Yigdoll) E.; m. Bridgid Hilda Kerr-Baulch, Aug. 26, 1956; children: Valerie Jean, Jacqueline Gail, Paul Douglas. BA, Columbia U., 1954; MD, U. de Geneve, Switzerland, 1959. Diplomate Am. Bd. Ob-Gyn. Pvt. practice Westbury and Plainview, N.Y., 1967-76; v.p. M&E Obstetrics & Gynecology, P.C., Plainview, 1976-88, pres., 1988—; pres. med. staff Cen. Gen. Hosp., 1979. Capt. USAF, 1961-63. Fellow Am. Coll. Surgeons, Am. Coll. Ob-Gyn.; mem. AMA, Nassau Surg. Soc. Republican. Jewish. Office: 2110 Northern Blvd Manhasset NY 11030

EDLOW, JEREMY BARTH, database analyst, consultant; b. Elizabeth, N.J., Apr. 26, 1960; s. Harold Edlow and Esther Blonsky. BA, Rutgers U., 1982; MA, NYU, 1984; MLS, Rutgers U., 1989; PhD, NYU, 1990; postgrad. in Bus. Adminstrn., Rutgers U., 1992—. Asst. mgr. Marriott Corp./Svc. Systems, N.Y.C., 1978-84; grad. asst. NYU, N.Y.C., 1984-86; reference libr. Merrill Lynch Capital Markets, N.Y.C., 1988; rsch. asst. Bloomberg L.P., Princeton, N.J., 1992—; cons. Johnson & Johnson, New Brunswick, N.J., 1991. Composer, The Sailor's Port of Call, 1990, The Wonderland of Israel, 1991; asst. to editor BITZARON, 1982-91. Recipient Richard Scheuer fellowship NYU, 1983, David Rose fellowship NYU, 1984. Mem. Spl. Librs. Assn., Am. Soc. Composers, Authors and Pubs. Jewish. Home: 238 Lincoln Ave Elizabeth NJ 07208

EDMISTON, MARK MORTON, publishing company executive; b. Yonkers, N.Y., July 9, 1943; s. Marcus Morton and Josephine (Brown) E.; m. Lisa Mary Pustorino, Aug. 28, 1965; children: Ann Kathleen, Laura Mary. B.A., Wesleyan U., 1966. Circulation mgr. Life mag., N.Y.C., until 1969; circulation and mktg. dir. Life mag., Tokyo, 1969-70; circulation dir. Saturday Rev., Inc., 1971-73; circulation dir. internat. edits. Newsweek, Inc., 1973-76, pub., 1976-78, pres., 1978-79, corp. exec. v.p., 1979-81, chmn. and pres., 1981-86; pres. TVSM Inc., N.Y.C., 1987-91; exec. v.p. Times Mirror Mag., N.Y.C., 1991—. Trustee Wesleyan U., 1983—, Children's Aid Soc. Mem. Mag. Pub. Assn. (dir.). Office: TVSM Inc 475 5th Ave New York NY 10017-6220

EDMISTON, RONALD LEE, career officer; b. Altoona, Pa., Aug. 26, 1946; s. Eugene Bernard and Helen Gail (Dengate) E.; m. Rebecca Jean Clark, June 6, 1968; children: Ronald Lee Jr., Jeffery Scott. BS in Engring., USCG Acad., 1968; MA in Counseling, R.I. Coll., 1982; EdS in Human Resource Devel., George Washington U., 1991. Engring. asst. High Endurance Coast Guard Cutter, Portland, Maine, 1968-71; marine inspector

Marine Inspection Office, Seattle, 1971-74; chief engr. USCG Cutter Active, New Castle, N.H., 1974-76; marine inspector Marine Inspection Office, Sturgeon Bay, Wis., 1976-79; exec. officer Marine Safety Office, Providence, 1979-82; sch. chief Marine Safety Sch., Yorktown, Va., 1982-87; hearing officer Fifth Coast Guard Dist., Portsmouth, Va., 1987-90; commanding officer, Capt. of the Port USCG, Balt., 1990—; civil rights officer Fifth Coast Guard Dist., Portsmouth, Va., 1988-89; designed model course for Internat. Maritime Orgn., London; instr. math. and physics Tidewater Community Coll., 1988—, Community Coll. of Balt., 1988—. Coach Youth Leagues Basketball, Yorktown, Va., 1982-88; youth dir. Crooks Meml. United Meth. Ch., Yorktown, 1986. Mem. Nat. Soc. for Performance Instruction (v.p. spl. interest group armed forces chpt. 1987, named for Outstanding Mil. Tng. Orgn. 1985, 87). Office: Marine Safety Office Custom House Baltimore MD 21202

EDMONDS, ANDREA MAGDELENE, management consultant; b. Phila., May 13, 1944; d. Leroy Joseph Edmonds and Adele Ruby (Thompson) Valle; divorced; children: Michele, Leslie, Gina, Philip, Tamika. BA, Antioch U., 1983; MEd, Temple U., 1986. Caseworker, community svcs. liaison, Dept. Human Svcs. State of Pa., Phila., 1978-89; organizational devel. cons. Phila., 1989—; cons. Nynex Corp., 1991, Sch. Dist. Phila., 1989-91, Urban League Leadership Inst., Phila., 1989-91, Opportunities Industrialization Ctr., Phila., 1987—. Author: (poetry) On the Bus, 1978. Mentor Sen. Allyson Schwartz, 1991—. Winner Golden Poet award, 1989, Silver Poet award, 1990 World of Poetry; recipient Disting. Svc. award Mental Health Assn. Pa., 1989. Mem. Assn. Black Psychologists, Sisters in Spirit (founder, pres. 1990—). Home and Office: 7000 Lincoln Dr Philadelphia PA 19119

EDMONDS, WALTER, artist; b. Phila., Apr. 21, 1938; s. Faulkner and Carlene (Dickerson) E.; children: Pamel, Walter, Hope, Nicole, Zachary, Langston. Student, Pa. Acad. of Fine Arts, 1991. Art instr. Bd. Edn., Phila., 1962-63, Christina Community, Wilmington, Del., 1968-69; cons. and art instr. Brandywine Graphics Workshop, 1979-83; commns. West Phila. Regional Libr., Camden, N.J., John Glousher House, Point Breeze Area, House of Imoja, Belmont Sch., Ch. of the Advocate and others. Exhbns. Recherche, Levy Gallery, Moore Coll. Art, Phila., 1990, Art in City Hall, Arts in Commerce Gallery, Afro-Am. Hist. & Cultural Mus., Phila., Stockton State Coll., N.J., Adirondacks Nat. Exhbn. Am. Watercolor, N.Y., Cen. Mich. U., Montgomery Coll., Md., Pensacola Mus. Art, Fla., U. Minn., Krasl Art Ctr., Mich., 1988, and numerous others. Democrat. Episcopalian. Home: 1120 S 46th St Philadelphia PA 19143-3711

EDMONDSON, GEORGE BRADLEY, editor-in-chief; b. Venice, Fla., Feb. 20, 1959; s. Thomas Osborn and Meredith (Senterfit) E.; m. Katherine McAdoo, Apr. 3, 1982; children: William, Emma. Student, Deep Springs Coll., 1976-79; BA, Cornell U., 1980-81. Editor-in-chief Ithaca (N.Y.) Times, 1981-85; editor Am. Demographics, Ithaca, 1985-90, editor-in-chief, 1990—. Mem. Jon Crispen Soc. (pres.). Office: Am Demographics 127 W State St Ithaca NY 14850

EDRIS, JAMES ALAN, executive; b. Harrisburg, Pa., Nov. 2, 1944; s. Frank Harold and Violet Mae (Kelley) E.; m. Susan Jane Gruber, Feb. 28, 1964; children: Rithy, Andrew, Matthew, Timothy. BA in History, Dickinson Coll., 1966. Fgn. svc. officer U.S. Info. Agy., Washington, 1966-76; mgr., pub. info. Hershey Foods Corp., Hershey, Pa., 1976-80; mgr., fin. info. Hershey Foods Corp., 1980-86, dir., investor rels., 1986—. Chmn. Hershey Polit. Action Com., 1988-89; treas. Cen. Pa. Employment Consortium, 1988—; pres. Hershey Youth Soccer Assn., 1986-87, bd. dirs. 1978-86. Mem. Nat. Investor Rels. Inst., Pa. Pub. Rels. Soc., Cen. Pa. Corp. Rels. Soc. (pres. 1988-89). Republican. Methodist. Office: Hershey Foods Corp PO Box 810 Hershey PA 17033-0810

EDSALL, HOWARD LINN, consulting executive; b. N.Y.C., Nov. 17, 1904; s. John Linn and Alise (Stoughton) E.; m. Florence S. Small, July 5, 1930 (dec. 1986); children: Florence Linn (Mrs. Robert James Whitehouse). Student pub. schs., pvt. tutoring. Lic. radio officer at age 15, 1920. On sea tug Barwick out of Galveston and on various ships for RCA's Radiomarine div., 1920-26; advt. and sales promotion mgr. electron tube div. RCA, 1944-47; with The Public Ledger Curtis-Martin Newspapers, Inc., Phila., 1926; mktg., sales promotion exec., copy chief, plans writer R.E. Lovekin Corp., 1927-34, Bridge & King, Contr. Ed. Community Jeweler, 1934-35, E.F. Houghton Co., Phila., 1935-37; co-founder, dir. G.S. Rogers & Co., Chgo., 1937-40, Ajax Metal Co. & Affiliates; editor Metelectric Progress, 1940-44; exec. cons. Rockport Press, The Reporter, Household Fin. Corp., 1948; v.p., dir. Craven & Hedrick (AM-TV's The Big Story), 1949-52; exec. v.p. Fred Wittner Advt., N.Y.C., 1953-57; sec., dir. Plastomics Products Co., Inc., 1946; pres., founder AIMS, Inc. (counselors to profl. mgrs.), 1959-70; ptnr. Bonniview Lodge, Lake Penage, Whitefish, Ont., Can.; founder, mem. Am. Marketplace Foods, Inc., 1990, bd. dirs., 1991-92. Author: An Unexplored Musical Resource Journal of the Franklin Institute, 1944, The Ten Commandments of Salesmanship, 1946, Borrow and Prosper, 1946, Management Consultant and Reporter, 1968, The How You Can Borrow and Prosper Kit, 1972, Song of Free Man, 1985 (awarded Presdl. Order Merit 1986), Society of Wireless Pioneers, 1986; co-author: One To Ten Thousand Copies, 1963; cons. editorial bd. Jour. Mgmt. and Bus. Consulting, 1976; contbr. fiction and articles to U.S. and fgn. mags. including London Graphic, Harper's, The American, Saturday Evening Post; inventor Violute for symphony orchestras, 1939. Mem. Re-Employment Planning Assocs., 1966; charter mem. Presdl. Task Force, 1984; dir. spl. events UN Coun., 1944-45. Mem. SAR, Am. Soc. Metals (bd. editors 1944-47), Jewelry Industry Coun. (advt. dir. 1951), Soc. Profl. Mgmt. Cons. (charter 1960, v.p., dir. 1967-69), Inst. Mgmt. Cons. (founder-mem.), Poets and Writers Directory of Am. Fiction Writers, N.J. Writers Directory, U.S. Senatorial Club (preferred mem.), Pen and Pencil Club (Phila.), Morse Telegraph Club, Listentome Club (N.J.). Home: The Carriage House 39-A N Mountain Ave Montclair NJ 07042-2351

EDSALL, JOHN TILESTON, biological chemistry educator; b. Phila., Nov. 3, 1902; s. David Linn and Margaret Harding (Tileston) E.; m. Margaret Dunham, May 1, 1929 (dec. 1987); children—James Lawrence Dunham (dec.), David Tileston, Nicholas Cranford. A.B., Harvard U., 1923, M.D., 1928; postgrad., Cambridge U., Eng., 1924-26; D.Sc. (hon.), U. Chgo., Western Res. U., U. Mich., N.Y. Med. Coll.; D.Phil. (hon.), U. Göteborg, Sweden, 1972. With Harvard U., Cambridge, Mass., 1928—; asst. prof. biol. chemistry Harvard U., 1932-38, assoc. prof., 1938-51, prof., 1951-73, emeritus, 1973—; John Simon Guggenheim Meml. Found. fellow Calif. Inst. Tech., 1940-41, Harvard U., 1954-56; Fulbright lectr. U. Cambridge, 1952, U. Tokyo, 1964; vis. prof. Coll. de France, Paris, 1955; pres. 6th Internat. Congress Biochemistry, N.Y.C., 1964; vis. prof. UCLA, 1977; vis. lectr. Australian Nat. U., Canberra, 1970. Author: (with E.J. Cohn) Proteins, Amino Acids and Peptides, 1943, (with J. Wyman) Biophysical Chemistry, 1958, (with H. Gutfreund) Biothermodynamics, 1983; editor: (with F.M. Richards and C.B. Anfinsen) Advances in Protein Chemistry, Vols. 1-42, 1944-91, Jour. Biol. Chemistry, 1958-67, (with D. Bearman) Archival Sources for the History of Biochemistry and Molecular Biology, 1980; chmn. editorial bd. Procs. NAS, 1968-72; chmn. survey of sources The History of Biochemistry and Molecular Biology, 1975-80; contbr. articles to profl. jours. Recipient Passano Found. award, 1966; scholar Fogarty Internat. Ctr. NIH, Bethesda, Md., 1970-71. Mem. Am. Philos. Soc., Nat. Acad. Scis., Am. Chem. Soc. (sec. div. biol. chemistry 1946-48, chmn. 1948-49, Willard Gibbs medal Chgo. sect. 1972), Am. Soc. Biol. Chemists (pres. 1957-58), Am. Acad. Arts and Scis. (rep. on U.S. Nat. Commn. for UNESCO 1950-56), AAAS (mem. com. on sci. freedom and responsibility 1976-82, chmn. 1979-81, Philip Hauge Abelson award 1989), Deutsche Akademie der Naturforscher, European Molecular Biology Orgn. (assoc.), Royal Danish Acad. Scis., Royal Swedish Acad. Scis. Home: 985 Memorial Dr Apt 503 Cambridge MA 02138-5769 Office: Harvard U Dept Biochemistry and Molecular Biology 7 Divinity Ave Cambridge MA 02138-2092

EDSALL, THOMAS BYRNE, reporter; b. Cambridge, Mass., Aug. 22, 1941; s. Richard Linn and Katharine (Byrne) E.; m. Mary Deutsch, Aug. 22, 1965; 1 child, Alexandra Harding Tileston. BA, Boston U., 1966. Reporter Providence Jour., 1965; vol. VISTA, Balt., 1966-67; reporter Balt. Sun, 1967-81, Washington Post, 1981—. Author: The New Politics of Inequality, 1984, Power and Money, 1988, (with Mary D. Edsall) Chain Reaction: The Impact of Race, Rights and Taxes in American Politics, 1991; co-editor: The Reagan Legacy, 1988; contbr. articles to popular jours. Recipient Front Page award, Bill Pryor Meml. award Washington-Balt. Newspaper Guild, 1981. Home: 511 4th St SE Washington DC 20003-4222 Office: Washington Post 1150 15th St NW Washington DC 20071-0002

EDSON, KAY LOUISE, equity trader; b. Montpelier, Vt., Apr. 9, 1946; d. Robert Robinson and Evelyn S. (Stowell) E. Student, Northeastern U., Boston, 1964-66, Johnson State Coll., 1984-85. Engrng. aide Gen. Electric Co., Burlington, Vt., 1967-70; asst. equity trader Nat. Life Ins. Co., Montpelier, 1971-75, head equity trader, 1975-86; v.p., head equity trader Nat. Life Investment Mgmt. Co., Montpelier, 1986—. Membership chair Dist. One Altrusa Internat., East. Can., New Eng., Bermuda, 1986-88, fundraising coord., 1988-90. Mem. Vt. Women's Bowling Assn. (dir. 1985—), Twin City Women's Bowling Assn. (dir. 1967—), Altrusa Club of Barre (pres. 1986-88). Republican. Office: Nat Life Investment Mgmt Co One National Life Dr Montpelier VT 05604

EDWARDS, ALLISON REGINA, cardiologist, health facility administrator; b. Georgetown, Guyana, South Am., Apr. 7, 1955; came to U.S., 1969; d. Weinic Sydney and Agnes Vivian (Jonas) E.; (div. 1981). BS in Chemistry cum laude, Howard U., 1974, MS in Biochemistry and MD, 1981. Intern in internal medicine Howard U. Med. Svc./D.C. Gen. Hosp., Washington, 1981-82, resident in internal medicine, 1982-83, 83-84, chief resident in internal medicine, 1983; fellow in cardiology Howard U. Hosp., Washington, 1984-86; assoc. dir. stress test lab. Family Health Ctr. Prince George's Hosp. Ctr., Cheverly, Md., 1987-88; med. officer-in-charge Emergency Care Ctr. D.C. Gen. Hosp., Washington, 1988—; pvt. practice cardiologist, Washington and Md., 1987—. Fellow ACP; mem. N.Y. Acad. Sci., Am. Heart Assn., Am. Med. Women's Assn. Office: PO Box 981 Hyattsville MD 20783-0981

EDWARDS, BARRY REESE, pharmaceutical sales and marketing executive; b. Phila., Apr. 28, 1956; s. Paul Lamar Sr. and Olwen Alice (Reese) E.; m. Susan Ann, Feb. 19, 1977; 1 child, Michael Charles. Student, Columbia U, 1974-77, Drexel U, 1980-85; BA in Bus. Mgmt. cum laude, Allentown Coll., 1987. With shipping dept. Lemmon Co., Sellersville, Pa., 1977-79, quality assurance mgr., 1979-81, asst. to pres., 1981-82, dir. regulatory compliance, 1982-85, exec. devel. program, 1985-87, dir. strategic planning & corp. devel., 1987-89, dir. mktg. & corp. devel., 1989-91; exec. dir. Gate Pharms. (div. Lemmon Co.), Sellersville, Pa., 1991—. Mem. Am. Soc. Quality Control. Office: Gate Pharms 650 Cathill Rd Sellersville PA 18951

EDWARDS, BERT TVEDT, accountant; b. Washington, Aug. 23, 1937; s. Archie Campbell and Geniana (Rasmussen) E.; m. Susan Elizabeth Dye, July 18, 1964; children: Christopher Andrew, Stacey Elizabeth. BA, Wesleyan U., 1959; MBA, Stanford U., 1961. CPA, D.C., Va., N.C., La. With Arthur Andersen & Co., Washington, 1961-69, 70—, mgr., 1965-69, 70-71, ptnr., 1971—; fin. v.p. Leisure Time Industries, Inc., 1969-70. Trustee Barker Found., 1968-78, treas., 1968-71, 1st v.p., 1971-72, pres., 1972-75; trustee, treas. Population Reference Bur., Inc., 1975—; bd. dirs. Jr. Achievement Met. Washington, Inc., 1973-87, treas., 1973-74, 2d v.p., 1974-75, 1st v.p., 1975-77, pres., 1977-78, chmn., 1978-80; bd. dirs., treas. Heritage Walk Homes Corp., 1975-80; mem. Spl. Adv. Commn. for Indsl. and Comml. Devel., D.C. City Coun., 1972-74; mem. D.C. Mayor's Com. on Budget and Fiscal Priorities, 1989-91; chmn. Nat. Bus. Leadership Conf., 1978. Recipient Outstanding Achievement award Stanford U., 1982, Outstanding Publ. award Soc. Mil. Comptrollers, 1983, Bronze Leadership award Jr. Achievement, 1979, Silver Leadership award, 1981; Victor Royall fellow Stanford U., 1960-61. Mem. AICPA (govt. acctg. and auditing com. 1982—, fed. govt. audit subcom. 1981-84, ad hoc task force univ. audit 1985-87, task force on quality of govt. audits 1986-87, author, editor single audit course 1985-92, task force on quality of fed. program audits 1991—), D.C. Inst. CPAs (chmn. membership com. 1973-74, SEC com. 1974-75, govt. acctg. com. 1979-81), Va. Soc. CPAs, Inst. Mgmt. Accts., Am. Acctg. Assn., Md. Mcpl. League, Healthcare Fin. Mgmt. Assn., Assn. Sch. Bus. Ofcls., Govt. Fin. Officers Assn. (co-chmn. ann. conf. 1985), Md. Pub. Fin. Officers Assn. (bd. dirs. 1992—), Assn. Govt. Accts., Govt. Fin. Officers Assn. Met. Washington (co-founder, bd. dirs. 1984-91), Met. Bd. Trade, Wesleyan U. Alumni Club Wash. (pres. 1969-71), Univ. Club (mem. bd. admissions 1976-82, chmn. 1980-82, bd. govs. 1982-85). Methodist. Home: 10712 Stapleford Hall Dr Rockville MD 20854-4449 Office: 1666 K St NW Washington DC 20006-2893

EDWARDS, BOB (ROBERT ALAN EDWARDS), radio news anchor; b. Louisville, May 16, 1947; s. Joseph Richard and Loretta Bernardine (Fuchs) E.; m. Sharon Ann Kelly, May 14, 1979; children—Brean, Susannah, Nora. B.S. in Commerce, U. Louisville, 1969, D.Pub. Service (hon.), 1985; M.A. in Communication, Am. U., 1972; LHD (hon.), Grinnell Coll., 1991. News dir., program dir. Sta. WHEL-AM, New Albany, Ind., 1968-69; news anchor Sta. WTOP-AM, Washington, 1972; corr., night editor Mut. Broadcasting System, Washington, 1972-73; assoc. producer Nat. Pub. Radio, Washington, 1974, co-host All Things Considered, 1974-79, host Morning Edit., 1979—. Producer, anchor radio documentaries. Bd. visitors U. Ala. Sch. Communication, Tuscaloosa, 1984—; bd. advs. Am. U. Sch. Communication, Washington. Served with U.S. Army, 1969-71, Korea. Recipient Edward R. Murrow award Corp. for Pub. Broadcasting, 1984, Oral Communication award L.I. U., 1980, Fleur-de-Lis award Louisville Forum, 1985, Unity award in media Lincoln U., Jefferson, City, Mo., 1983, Gabriel award Cath. Assn. Broadcasters, 1987, 90, Alumni Recognition award Am. U., 1991, Oak award Ky. Advs. for Higher Edn., 1991; named to Esquire Register, Esquire mag., 1986. Mem. AFTRA (nat. v.p. 1988—), Radio-TV Corrs. Assn., Soc. Profl. Journalists, U. Louisville Alumni Assn., St. Xavier High Sch. Alumni Assn. Office: Nat Pub Radio 2025 M St NW Washington DC 20036-3309

EDWARDS, CARL NORMAND, management consultant; b. Norwood, Mass., Jan. 22, 1943; s. Wilfred Carl and Cecile Marie-Anne (Pepin) E.; m. Mary Louise Buyse, Jan. 22, 1982. Student Brdigewater State Coll.; MEd, Suffolk U., 1969; postgrad. Harvard U. Cons. dept. social relations Harvard, 1966-69, research fellow, 1969-71, lectr. social relations, 1971-72; cons. research psychologist Cambridge Computer Assocs., Mass., 1966—; assoc. clin. prof. psychiatry Tufts U. Sch. Medicine, 1971—, research social psychologist Tufts-New Eng. Med. Center, 1969—; dir. Four Oaks Research Inst., Norfolk, Mass., 1974—; sr. assoc. for policy planning and research Justice Resource Inst., 1971—; field faculty grad. program Goddard Coll., Plainfield, Vt., 1972-82; chmn. bd. dirs. MEDx Systems, Ltd., Dover, Mass., 1985—; chmn. bd. trustees Ctr. for Birth Defects Info. Services, Inc., Dover, 1984—; tchr. seminars; cons. to major corps., govt. agys. and pub. instns. in human dynamics and pub. policy; lectr., thesis adviser, program devel. cons. schs., colls., insts. Contbr. articles to profl. jours., monographs, revs. Mem. USNG, 1963-64. Mem. Am., Mass. psychol. Assns., Soc. for Psychol. Study Social Issues, Peace Research Soc., Nat. Pilots Assn., Nat. Trust for Hist. Preservation. Clubs: Harvard (Boston); Appalachian Mountain, Norfolk Hunt, Blue Ridge Hunt. Author: Drug Dependence: Social Regulation and Treatment Alternatives. Contbr. articles to profl. jours., monographs, revs. Home: Four Oaks Off Springdale PO Box 279 Dover MA 02030-0279

EDWARDS, CHARLES MERRIWELL, government official, pharmaceutical specialist; b. Oak Park, Ill., Mar. 16, 1941; s. Axel Sigbjorn and Grace Ellen (Dean) E.; m. V. Joanne Schrag, July 20, 1963. BS, Wheaton (Ill.) Coll., 1963. Investigator FDA, Chgo., 1963-68; sr. investigator FDA, Phila., 1968-79, nat. expert drugs, 1979—; conducted on-site quality assurance audits in 36 fgn. countries and U.S.; lectr. seven univs./fgn. and U.S.; trained fgn. nat. drug ofcls: WHO (19 countries), Kingdom of Saudi Arabia, 1991, Switzerland, 1992, Orgn. for Econ. Cooperation and Devel. toxicity lab. auditors, The Netherlands, 1992. Recipient awards of merit FDA, 1976, 89, Spl. Svc. award Fgn. Svc. Cadre, 1989. Mem. Cen. Atlantic States Assn. Food and Drug Ofcls. Methodist. Home: 224 White Marsh Way Cherry Hill NJ 08034-2941 Office: US FDA US Custom House Rm 900 2d and Chestnut Sts Philadelphia PA 19106-2973

EDWARDS, CLIFFORD MURRAY, oil company executive; b. Ft. Worth, Sept. 23, 1952; s. Charles E. and Mary Ann (Ramsey) E.; m. Carolyn Carbarrey, Jan. 18, 1989. BS in Geophysics summa cum laude, Tex. A&M U., 1973, MS in Geophysics magna cum laude, 1975; MS in Bus. Adminstrv. Sci., U. Tex., Dallas, 1979. Geophysicist exploration Mobil Corp., Dallas, 1975-79; supr. exploration Mobil Corp., New Orleans, 1979-82; supt. exploration Mobil Corp., The Hague, The Netherlands, 1982-84, Houston, 1984-85; mgr. geophysics Mobil Corp., Denver, 1985-87; sr. planning cons. Mobil Corp., N.Y.C., 1987-88; mgr. seismic processing Mobil Corp., Dallas, 1988-89, mgr. geophysics rsch., 19891; mgr. geophysics, 1991-92; chief geophysicist Mobil Corp., Fairfax, Va., 1992—. Mem. Am. Assn. Petroleum Geologists, Soc. Exploration Geophysics. Republican. Presbyterian.

EDWARDS, DAWN ANN, marketing professional; b. Valley Forge, Pa., Jan. 13, 1956; d. George Francis and Severina (Bacer) E. BS, Syracuse U., 1978, MS, 1979. Account mgmt. staff asst. Ted Bates Worldwide, Inc., N.Y.C., 1980-83; asst. account exec. Backer & Spielvogel, Inc., N.Y.C., 1983-85; asst. product mgr. Am. Home Products Corp., N.Y.C., 1985-86, Carter-Wallace, Inc., N.Y.C., 1986-89; product mgr. L&F Products Inc. subs. Eastman Kodak, Montvale, N.J., 1989-91; bus. devel. mgr. Pfizer, Inc., N.Y.C., 1991—. Mem. Healthcare Bus. Women's Assn., Am. Mgmt. Assn., Syracuse U. Alumni Assn., Delta Gamma Alumnae. Home: 1 Nevada Plz Apt 9H New York NY 10023-5017 Office: Pfizer Inc 235 E 42nd St New York NY 10017-5703

EDWARDS, DIANE ELAINE, early childhood organization executive; b. Revere, Mass., Feb. 23, 1959; d. Albert H. and Bridget (Lennon) Hovasse; m. Peter Daniel Edwards, July 12, 1986; children: Matthew Cannon, Casey Lawrence. MA, Lesley Grad. Sch., Cambridge, Mass., 1987; BA, Merrimack Coll., North Andover, Mass., 1981. State cert. Lead Tchr. Infants, Toddlers, Preschool, Dir. II. Vol. Peace Corps., Dominican Republic., 1983-84; bilingual adminstrv. asst. CAPIC Head Start, Winthrop, Mass., 1984-85, program cord., 1985-87; program dir. CAPIC Child Devel. Ctr., Winthrop, Mass., 1987-89; coll. instr. North Shore Community Coll., Lynn, Mass., 1990—; pres., co-founder Nat. Coalition for Early Childhood Profls., Inc., Boston, 1991—. Host parent, rep. Intercultural Student Exch., Lynnfield, Mass., 1990-91; vol. Office for Children. Mem. Mass. Tchrs. Assn., Nat. Assn. for Edn. of Young Children. Office: Nat Coalition for Early Childhood Professionals Inc 510 Commonwealth Ave Ste 289 Boston MA 02215-2602

EDWARDS, FRANCIS CHARLES, city manager; b. Trenton, N.J., July 11, 1947; s. Frank Layton and Jane Marie (Archer) E.; m. Gloria Theresa Gioscio, June 14, 1969; children: Elaine Elizabeth, Denise Michelle. BA in Secondary Edn., Trenton State Coll., 1965-69; MA in Geography, Rutgers U., 1972-74; M in Regional Planning, Penn. State U., 1974-76; M in Pub. Adminstrn., Old Dominion U., 1978-81. Community planner II Pasco County Fla. Planning Dept., Port Richey, 1976-77; city planner II Va. Beach Planning Dept., Va., 1977-81, devel. review coordinator, 1981-84; dir. planning and zoning Newport (R.I.) Planning Dept., 1984-87; acting city mgr. City of Newport, R.I., 1986-87, city mgr., 1987—. Served with U.S. Army, 1969-71. Mem. Am. Planning Assn., Am. Inst. Cert. Planners, Am. Soc. Pub. Adminstrn., Internat. City Mgmt. Assn., R.I. City and Town Mgmt. Assn. (pres.), Phi Kappa Phi, Pi Alpha Alpha. Office: City Newport City Hall Broadway Newport RI 02840

EDWARDS, HARRY T., federal judge; b. N.Y.C., Nov. 3, 1940; s. George H. and Arline (Ross) Lyle E.; children: Brent, Michelle. B.S., Cornell U., 1962; J.D., U. Mich., 1965. Assoc. firm Seyfarth, Shaw, Fairweather & Geraldson, Chgo., 1965-70; prof. law U. Mich., 1970-76, 77-80; vis. prof. law Harvard U., 1975-76, prof., 1976-77; now judge U.S. Ct. Appeals, Washington, 1980—; vis. prof. Free U. Brussels, 1974; dir. AMTRAK, 1977-80, chmn. bd., 1979-80; disting. lectr. law Duke U., 1983—; lectr. law Georgetown Law Ctr., 1986-87; lectr. Harvard Law Sch., 1981—, Mich. Law Sch., 1988—. Mem. Adminstrv. Conf. of U.S., 1976-80. Co-author: Labor Relations Law in the Public Sector, 1975, 79, 85, Lawyer as a Negotiator, 1977, Collective Bargaining and Labor Arbitration, 1979, Higher Education and the Law, 1979. Mem. Nat. Acad. Arbitrators (dir. 1975-80, v.p. 1978-80), Am. Arbitration Assn. (dir. 1979-80), Am. Bar Assn. (sec. sect. labor law 1976-77), Am. Law Inst., Order of Coif. Office: US Ct Appeals 3rd & Constitution Ave NW Washington DC 20001*

EDWARDS, IOLA DARLENE, publisher, writer, marketing professional; b. Buffalo; d. Johnnie Quincy Adams and Sylvia (King) E. AA, SUNY, Buffalo, 1991, BA, 1992. Owner Darliwood Pub., BMI, Buffalo, 1988—; writer Whole Truth News, Memphis, 1991—. Author: Naming the New Star, 1990, (play) Conspiracy Against Innonence, 1988; composer (album) Don't Be Afraid, 1991. Coord. Vol. Income Tax Assistance Program, Buffalo, 1989-92, Young Christian Athlete's Day, Canisius Coll., Buffalo, 1992—, Comfort My People, 1989—, Real to Reel, 1985—; researcher common coun. George K. Arthur campaign for Pres., 1991; mem. exec. bd. Masten Neighborhood Human Svc. Corp., 1988-92. Recipient Recognition award State of N.Y., 1987, Housing and Urban Devel. award. Mem. Western N.Y. Assn. for Learning Disabilities (exec. bd. 1985-88), Neighborhood Adv. Coun., Music and Composers Assn. (pub. 1988—). Mem. Ch. of God in Christ.

EDWARDS, JEAN BUTLER, health care professional; b. Clearfield, Pa., Dec. 18, 1950; d. Clair Ernest and Ann Dorothy (Johnson) Butler; m. Jeffrey Lynn Selvage (div. 1982); m. Bryan Thomas Edwards, Oct. 21, 1989. BA, Pa. State U., 1987. Edn. administr. Pa. State U., University Park, 1979-84; mktg. specialist, account exec. Bell Systems Bell Atlantic, Harrisburg, Pa., 1984; media specialist Pa. Blue Shield, Camp Hill, 1987—. Contbr. articles to profl. jours. Renaissance scholar, 1986-87. Mem. Pub. Rels. Soc. Am., Internat. Assn. Bus. Communicators. Home: 6 Blackmore Ct Camp Hill PA 17011-1749 Office: Pa Blue Shield 1800 Center St Camp Hill PA 17089-0001

EDWARDS, JOANN LOUISE, human resources executive; b. Lebanon, Pa., June 15, 1955; d. Harold Eugene and Kathryn Faye (Smith) E. AA in Human Svcs. with honors, Harrisburg Area Community Coll, 1975; BS with honors, Pa. State U., 1981. Residential program worker Pan Am. Corp., Hershey, Pa., 1975-80, residential program supr., 1981-82, intensive behavior shaping supr., 1982-83; program mgr. Devel. Resources, Inc., Harrisburg, Pa., 1983-85, dir. minimum supervision, 1985-86; dir. human resources New Directions for Progress, Inc. (formerly Devel. Resources, Inc.), Harrisburg, 1986—; faculty grad. program indsl. rels. St. Francis Coll., Harrisburg, 1991—; com. mem. New Directions for Progress Personnel Com., Harrisburg, 1988—. Com. mem. Christian Chs. United Personnel Com., Harrisburg, 1989-90. Mem. Harrisburg Area Personnel Assn., Soc. Human Resource Mgmt., Harrisburg Personnel Assn. Republican. Methodist. Home: 3022 N 3rd St Harrisburg PA 17110-2102 Office: New Directions for Progress 3544 N Progress Ave Harrisburg PA 17110-9638

EDWARDS, JOHN RALPH, chemist, educator; b. Streator, Ill., Feb. 27, 1937; s. Ralph E. and Ruth M. (Wilson) E.; m. Margaret E. Smith, July 15, 1961; children: Peter J., Sharon E., Susan D. BS, Ill. Wesleyan U., 1959; PhD, U. Ill., 1964. NIH postdoctoral fellow Tufts U., Boston, 1964-66; asst. prof. chemistry Villanova (Pa.) U., 1966-73, assoc. prof., 1973-80, prof., 1980—, chmn. dept. chemistry, 1980-90. Contbr. articles to profl. jours. Active Boy Scouts Am. NIH grantee, 1970-76. Mem. Am. Soc. Biochemistry and Molecular Biology, Am. Chem. Soc. (bd. dirs. Phila. sec.), U.S. Orienteering Fedn., NY Acad. Sci., Sigma Xi, Phi Kappa Phi. Office: Villanova U Dept Chemistry Villanova PA 19085

EDWARDS, LARRY GLENN, fund raising executive, educator; b. Balt., June 11, 1945; s. Bayne Camet and Henrietta Edna (Yearsley) E.; m. Judith Belle Burkhalter, Aug. 23, 1969; 1 child, Joshua Stant. Student, Ind. U., 1962; BA, Salem Coll., 1966; MA, Duke U., 1970. Instr. history Mercer U., Macon, Ga., 1968-72; asst. headmaster Chatham (Va.) Hall Sch., 1973-81; interim headmaster St. Anne's-Belfield Sch., Charlottesville, Va., 1981-82; headmaster Joseph T. Walker Sch., Marietta, Ga., 1982-84, Cape Henry Collegiate Sch., Virginia Beach, Va., 1984-86; dir. pub. rels. Valley Forge Mil. Acad. and Jr. Coll., Wayne, Pa., 1986-92; dir. devel. Perkiomen Sch., Pennsburg, Pa., 1992—. Contbr. articles to mags. and local newspapers. Trumpet player, trustee Va. Beach Community Orchestra, 1984-86. Mem. Del. Valley Press Club. Episcopalian. Office: Valley Forge Mil Acad and Jr Coll 1001 Eagle Rd Wayne PA 19087-3694

EDWARDS, MARC T., healthcare executive; b. Seattle, Apr. 14, 1949. BA, U. Washington, 1971; MD, U. Colo., Denver, 1975. Diplomate Am. Bd. Family Practice. Intern/resident in family medicine Thomas Jefferson U. Hosp., Phila., 1975-78; staff physician Arabian Am. Oil Co., Dhahran, Saudi Arabia, 1978-84, Cigna Healthplan Tex., Dallas, 1984-89; med. dir. Aetna Life Ins. Co., Hartford, Conn., 1989—; instr. dept. preventive medicine U. Colo., Denver, 1974-75; attending physician family practice residency program St. Paul's Hosp., Dallas, 1987-89. Contbr. articles to profl. jours. Recipient Gutherie prize U. Washington, 1969, Florence Sabin Meml. award U. Colo., 1975. Mem. Am. Coll. Physician Execs., Am. Acad. Family Physicians, Phi Beta Kappa. Home: 15 Pilgrim Rd West Hartford CT 06117-2240 Office: Aetna Life Ins Co 151 Farmington Ave MCA 3 Hartford CT 06156

EDWARDS, PHILLIP MILTON, import and export company executive; b. Borger, Tex., Feb. 24, 1933; s. Aaron Moses and Ada Elsie (Feist) E.; m. Mildred M. L. Weber, Aug. 18, 1956. BA, Okla. U., 1958. Polit. officer U.S. Embassy, Jedda, Saudi Arabia, 1961-64; vice consul U.S. Consulate Gen., Dhahran, Saudi Arabia, 1965-67; sr. advisor Dept. of Army, Vinh Long, Vietnam, 1968-70; publs. mgr. DOT Systems, Incorp., Vienna, Va., 1971-77; v.p. Transcontinental Trade Corp., Washington, 1978-81, Security Support Svcs., Washington, 1981—. Contbr. articles to profl. jours. Recipient Silver medal SAR, 1979. Presbyterian. Home: 1917 Aubrey Place Ct Vienna VA 22182-1976 Office: Security Support Svcs 403 Seward Sq SE Washington DC 20003-1113

EDWARDS, THEODORE UNALDO, deputy commissioner, educator; b. N.Y.C., Sept. 18, 1934; s. Joseph Unaldo and Mary A. (Boston) E.; m. Ione L. Dunkley; 1 child, Donna Edwards O'Bannon. BS in Econs., St. Peter's Coll., 1955; MSW, Rutgers U., 1962; cert., Baro Clinic, Bklyn., 1967. Probation officer, agt. U.S. Cts./Justice Dept., N.Y.C., 1962-69; dir. social svcs. Villa Loretta Sch. for Girls, Peekskill, N.Y., 1969-71; clin. dir. Harlem Child Guidance Clinic, N.Y.C., 1969-78; dir. res. programs Wiltwyck Sch. for Boys, Inc., Yorktown, N.Y., 1971-73; exec. dir. C.A.U.S.E., N.Y.C., 1973-76; program adminstr. Police Athletic League, N.Y.C., 1976-77; dept. commr. City of New Rochelle, N.Y., 1977—; adj. prof. Coll. of New Rochelle, 1979—; bd. dirs. Social Work Adv. Bd., New Rochelle. Editor: (newspaper column) Tomorrow Newspaper, 1987—; contbr. articles to various mags. and books. Treas. New Rochelle Coun. of Community Svc., 1987—; Commnr. Orrice of Black Ministry Archciocese N.Y., N.Y.C., emeritus 1990; bd. dirs. Cath. Big Bros., 1975-89; vice chmn. bd. dirs. Salvation Army, New Rochelle, 1980—. Recipient Spike Harris award N.Y. Counselors, 1985, numerous Service awards Coll. of New Rochelle, Iona Coll., White Plains Bd. of Edn. Mem. N.Y. Park & Recreation Assn., Lions Club of New Rochelle, Omega Psi Phi Frat. (keeper of records & seal, leadership award 1988). Roman Catholic. Home: 18 Muir Pl New Rochelle NY 10801-3104

EDWARDS, THOMAS ASHTON, lawyer; b. McKeesport, Pa., June 29, 1960; s. Thomas and Gladys (Ashton) E.; m. Jeannette Maria Valls, June 5, 1987. BSBA, Duquesne U., 1982; postgrad. in econs., U. Pitts., 1987; JD, Duquesne U., 1991. Bar: Fla. 1992. Asst. contr. 1st Home Savs. Assn., Pitts., 1983-87; contr. Concord-Liberty Savs. Bank, Monroeville, Pa., 1987-89; exec. asst. Investment Timing Svcs., Inc., Pitts., 1989-90; law clk. Welch and Gold, Evashavik and Della Vecchia, Pitts., 1990-91; assoc. Valls Enterprises, Miami, Fla., 1991—; cons., bus. mgr. Behavior Cons., Monroeville, 1986-91; legal rsch. teaching asst. Duquesne U. Sch. Law; jud. clk. U.S. Dist. Ct. (we. dist.) Pa. Mng. editor Juris mag., 1988-89. Mem. Phi Alpha Delta. Democrat. Presbyterian. Office: Valls Enterprises 700 SW 36th Ave Forbes Ave Miami FL 33135

EDWARDS, WILLIAM NEWTON, insurance claims consultant; b. Savannah, Ga., Oct. 2, 1929; s. William Newton and Alma (Rozier) E.; m. Helen Kay Howard, Feb. 18, 1955 (dec.); children: Helen Kimberly Edwards Falzarano, Laurie Edwards Haunor, Elizabeth Alison Edwards Kelly. BBA, U. Ga., 1952. CPCU. Claims mgr. Sentry Ins. Co., various locations, 1959-69; product liability specialist Sentry Ins. Co., Stevens Point, Wis., 1969-72; claims mgr. Abbott Labs., North Chicago, Ill., 1972-74; product liability specialist Am. Re-Ins. Co., N.Y.C., 1974-75, asst. sec., 1975-77, asst. v.p., 1977-83, v.p., 1983-91; ins. claims cons., Princeton, N.J., 1991—. Author: Litigation Management, 1985, Claims Management Made Simple, 1990. With U.S. Army, 1954-55. Mem. Soc. CPCU's (pres. N.Y. chpt. 1988). Republican. Home and Office: 33 Brookwood Ct Princeton NJ 08540-9405

EFAW, CARY R., manufacturing company executive; b. Waynesburg, Pa., Dec. 26, 1949; s. William C. and Julia M. (Whitfield) E.; m. Kathleen E. Dunkle, July 21, 1973; children: Dawn, Heather, Nathan. BS in Acctg./Econs., Waynesburg Coll., 1975; MBA, Youngstown State U., 1989. Sr. acct. Ernst & Whinney, Pitts., 1975-79; staff acct. Equitable Resources, Pitts., 1979-81; sr. fin. analyst Joy Mfg. Co., Pitts., 1981-82; owner, cons. Efaw Enterprise, Pitts., 1982—; mgr. gen. and cost acctg. Cooper Industries, Grove City, Pa., 1987—; bd. dirs., advisor 84 Electronics, Houston, Pa., 1980-87; cons. Hodor Assocs., Eighty-Four, Pa., 1979-85, Lindley Enterprise, Washington, Pa., 1981-85. Contbr. articles to profl. jours. Advisor, State Rep., Upper St. Clair, Pa., 1981-84; Sunday sch. tchr. Westminster Ch., Upper St. Clair, 1982-85; elder Calvin Ch., Zelienople, Pa. With USMC, 1969-71. Named Competent Toastmaster, 1980. Mem. Assn. MBA Execs., Am. Legion, VFW, DAV (life), Nat. Assn. Accts. (assoc. dir. 1977-78), Alpha Kappa Psi, Steel Town Corvettes Club (treas. 1977-80), Masons. Presbyterian. Home: 1 Zelie Dr Zelienople PA 16063-9707

EFIMOV, IGOR MARKOVICH See YEFIMOV, IGOR MARKOVICH

EFRON, SAMUEL, lawyer; b. Lansford, Pa., May 6, 1915; s. Abraham and Rose (Kaduchin) E.; m. Hope Bachrach Newman, Apr. 5, 1941; children: Marc Fred, Eric Michael. B.A., Lehigh U., 1935; LL.B., Harvard U., 1938. Bar: Pa. 1938, D.C. 1949, N.Y. 1967. Atty. forms and regulations div., also registration div. SEC, 1939-40; Office Solicitor Dept. Labor, 1940-42; asst. chief real and personal property sect. Office Alien Property Custodian, 1942-43; chief debt claims sect., also asst. chief claims br. Office Alien Property, Dept. Justice, 1946-51; asst. gen. counsel internat. affairs Dept. Def., 1951-53, cons., 1953-54; partner firm Surrey, Karasik, Gould & Efron, Washington, 1954-61; exec. v.p. Parsons & Whittemore, Inc., N.Y.C., 1961-68; now partner Arent, Fox, Kintner, Plotkin & Kahn, Washington.; Mem. internat. relations vis. com. Lehigh U.; adv. bd. Ctr. for biomedical ethics, U. Va.; vis. com. Harvard Sch. of pub. health. Author: Creditors Claims Under the Trading with the Enemy Act, 1948, Foreign Taxes on United States Expenditures, 1954, Offshore Procurement and Industrial Mobilization, 1955, The Operation of Investment Incentive Laws with Emphasis on the U.S.A. and Mexico, 1977. Served to lt. USNR, 1943-46. Decorated Order of the Lion of Finland 1st class. Mem. Am., Fed., Inter-Am. bar assns., Am. Soc. Internat. Law, Assn. Bar City N.Y., Bar Assn. D.C., Phi Beta Kappa. Clubs: Army-Navy (Washington), Cosmos (Washington), Harvard, Internat. (Washington), Fed. Bar (Washington); Harvard (N.Y.C.), Lehigh (N.Y.C., Washington), Lotos (N.Y.C.). Home: 3537 Ordway St NW Washington DC 20016-3173 Office: Arent Fox Kintner Plotkin & Kahn 1050 Connecticut Ave NW Washington DC 20036-5303

EFTHIMIADES, MICHAEL CONSTANTINE, political journalist; b. Manhattan, N.Y., Sept. 3, 1958; s. Constantine and Ellen (Voudiotes) E.; m. Theodora Skarmoutsos, Nov. 1, 1987; children: Themistocles Michael, Jason Constantine. BA cum laude, CCNY, 1980; MBA, Adelphi U., 1985. Compiler News Election Svc., N.Y.C., 1980; rsch. and tech. asst. N.Y. Pub. Libr., N.Y.C., 1981-83; contbg. editor and UN corr. Hellenic Times, N.Y.C., 1980-88; polit. reporter Western Queens Gazette, Astoria, N.Y., 1985-90; reporter N.Y.C. Tribune, 1990-91; community news editor Queens Ledger, Maspeth, N.Y., 1990—. Freelance polit. writer for numerous publs.; author: Scouting in the Eastern Orthodox Church, 1986; contbr. articles to profl. jours. Pub. relations, dir., newsletter editor Hellenic U. Club, N.Y.C., 1983-85, treas., 1984-85; scouting coord. Boy Scouts Am., N.Y.C., 1985-87. Recipient cert. Outstanding Community Journalism, Community Planning Bd. I, Astoria, 1988, Congressman Thomas Manton, 1988; Outstanding Local Journalism, State Assemblyman Denis Butler, Long Island City, 1988; Youth Commn. Sci. award, Knights of Pythias, N.Y.C., 1973. Mem. N.Y. Press Club, Nat. Writers Club, Soc. Profl. Journalists, Deadline Club, AHEPA (bd. govs. Hermes chpt. 1983-84), Sigma Delta Chi. Democrat. Greek Orthodox. Home: 22-25 77th St Apt 2B Jackson Hgts NY 11370 Office: Queens Ledger 65-17 Grand Ave Maspeth NY 11378

EFTHIMIOU, MILTON BASIL, religious organization administrator, priest; b. Boston, Jan. 20, 1935; s. Basil and Helen (Caramanlis) E.; children: Basil, Kimberley. BA, Holy Cross, 1957, BD, 1958; STM, Boston U., 1959; PhD, Miami U., 1974. Ordained priest Greek Orthodox. Priest Greek Orthodox Archdiocese of North and South Am., N.Y.C., 1958—, priest, exec. dir. dept. inter-ch. rels. Author: History of Greek Orthodox Church in America, 1983, Greeks and Latins on Cyprus, 1985; contbr. articles to profl. jours. Mem. exec. com. Nat. Coalition on Pornography, Washington. Mem. Medieval Acad. Am. Office: Archdiocese of N & S Am 10 E 79th St New York NY 10021

EGAMI, TAKESHI, materials scientist; b. Fukuoka, Japan, July 15, 1945, came to U.S., 1968; s. Tatsuro and Fujiko (Murakami) E.; m. Sayuri Matsumoto, Dec. 23, 1969; children—Tadashi, Yasushi, Kiyoshi. B of Engring., U. Tokyo, 1968; PhD, U. Pa., 1971. Postdoctoral fellow U. Sussex, Eng., 1971-72; vis. scientist Max-Planck Institut fur Metallforschung, Fed. Republic Germany, 1972-73, 79-80; asst. prof. materials sci. and engring. U. Pa., 1973-76, from assoc. prof. to prof., 1980—; vis. prof. dept. physics U. Tokyo, 1987. Recipient Metal Physics Achievement award, Japan Inst. Metals, 1988; research grantee NSF, Army Rsch. Office, Office Naval Rsch., Electric Power Rsch. Inst., IBM. Mem. Am. Phys. Soc., Metall. Soc. of AIME (Robert Lansing Hardy Gold medal 1974), Am. Soc. Metals, IEEE, Mater Rsch. Soc. Contbr. over 180 articles profl. jours. Discovered soft magnetic properties of amorphous alloys and displacive short range order in superconducting oxides; developed energy dispersive x-ray diffraction method for structural study of amorphous solids, theory on glass transitions and defects in metallic glasses; patentee in field. Home: 16 Morris Cir Wayne PA 19087-3844 Office: 3231 Walnut St Philadelphia PA 19104-6202

EGAN, EDWARD M., bishop; b. Oak Park, Ill., Apr. 2, 1932; s. Thomas J. and Genevieve (Costello) E. Ph.B., St. Mary of Lake, Mundelein, Ill., 1954; S.T.L., Gregorian U., Rome, 1958; J.C.D., Gregorian U., 1963. Ordained priest Roman Catholic Ch., 1957. Sec. to Albert Cardinal Meyer Archdiocese of Chgo., 1958-60, sec. to John Cardinal Cody, 1966-68, co-chancellor, 1969-72; faculty Pontifical N.Am. Coll., Vatican City, 1960-65; judge Sacred Roman Rota, Vatican City, 1973-85; aux. bishop, vicar for edn. Archdiocese of N.Y., N.Y.C., 1985-88; bishop of Bridgeport Conn., 1988—. Office: 238 Jewett Ave Bridgeport CT 06606-2892

EGAN, JOHN FREDERICK, electronics executive; b. Council Bluffs, Iowa, Feb. 25, 1935; s. Frederick Emerson and Ruth Pauline (Russell) E.; m. Anne B. Patterson, June 14, 1958; children: John Jr., James Michael. AB in Physics with honors, Grinnell Coll., 1957; MEE, Northwestern U., 1958, PhD in Elec. Engring., 1961. Tech. dir. computer systems, Electronics Systems div. USAF, Bedford, Mass., 1964-67; sr. staff specialist intelligence Office Dir. Def., Research and Engring., Washington, 1967-71; chief scientist command support Office Chief Naval Ops., Washington, 1971-73; group dir. fed. systems Sanders Assocs., Inc., Nashua, N.H., 1973-77; v.p. Sanders Assoc., Inc., Nashua, N.H., 1977-87; group v.p. Lockheed Corp., 1987—; mem. exec. panel Chief Naval Ops., Washington, 1971—. Chmn. alumni fund Grinnell Coll., 1972—; mem. dean's adv. com. Northeastern U. Sch. Engring., 1987—. With USAF, 1961-64. Baker scholar, 1953-57; Transp. Ctr. fellow, 1957-61. Mem. IEEE, AIAA, Assn. for Computing Machinery, NAS (naval studies bd. 1990—). Office: Lockheed Electronic Systems Group C S 2050 NHQ 1-719 Nashua NH 03061-2050

EGAN, JOSEPH J(OHN), English educator; b. N.Y.C., Feb. 2, 1940; s. Joseph A. and Charlotte M. (Flynn) E.; m. Mary Joan Girlinghouse, June 15, 1974. BA in English, St. Francis Coll., N.Y.C., 1961; MA in English, U. Notre Dame, 1962, PhD in English, 1965. Instr. English St. John's U., N.Y., 1964-66; asst. prof. Manhattan Coll., N.Y.C., 1966-69; assoc. prof. Slippery Rock (Pa.) U., 1969-72, prof., 1972—. Co-author: History of Clan Egan, 1979; contbr. numerous articles to profl. jours. Mem. Irish Nat. Caucus, Washington, 1982—. Named Baron of Carigacashel under the MacCarthy Mór, Prince of Desmond, Ireland. Mem. Assn. Pa. State Univs., Irish-Am. Cultural Inst., cAth. Acad. of Scis., A Niadh Nask, Order of St. Lazarus of Jerusalem (officer). Democrat. Roman Catholic. Home: 417 Summit St Grove City PA 16127-2313 Office: Slippery Rock U Slippery Rock PA 16057

EGAN, ROBERT WHEELER, biochemist; b. Mineola, N.Y., Apr. 15, 1943; s. Francis Joseph and Alice Louise (Kirkpatrick) E.; m. Susanne Renol Revere, Dec. 4, 1965; children: Robert Revere, Sean Kirk. BS, Brown U., 1965; PhD, McGill U., 1972; postgrad., Johns Hopkins U., 1972-74. Sr. scientist Merck & Co., Rahway, N.J., 1974-82, assoc. dir., 1982-85; sect. leader biochemistry Warner Lambert Co., Ann Arbor, Mich., 1985-86; assoc. dir. allergy rsch. dept. Schering Plough Co., Bloomfield, N.J., 1986-89, dir., 1989—; adj. prof. physiology U. Medicine and Dentistry of N.J., Newark, 1990—. Sect. editor: Annual Reports in Medicinal Chemistry, 1984-87; contbr. articles to profl. jours. Dir. Manasquan (N.J.) Recreation Commn., 1977-80. Fellow Xerox Corp., 1968-69, Nat. Rsch. Coun. Canada, 1969-72, NIH, 1972-74. Mem. Am. Chem. Soc., Am. Soc. for Biochemistry and Molecular Biology, AAAS, Elks. Roman Catholic. Office: Schering Plough Co 60 Orange St Bloomfield NJ 07003-4795

EGAN, WILLIAM JOSEPH, lawyer; b. Manhasset, N.Y., Sept. 21, 1956. BA, U. Va., 1978, JD, 1981. Bar: Pa. 1981, U.S. Dist. Ct. (we. dist.) Pa. 1981, N.Y. 1988. Assoc. Reed, Smith, Shaw and McClay, Pitts., 1981-87; assoc. LeBoeuf, Lamb, Leiby and MacRae, N.Y.C., 1987-90, ptnr., 1991—. Office: LeBoeuf Lamb Leiby & MacRae 520 Madison Ave New York NY 10022-4213

EGBUFOR, EMMANUEL MICHAEL UKADIKE, accountant, business executive, educator; b. Asaba, Nigeria, July 15, 1941; came to U.S., 1969; s. Francis Okeleke and Comfort Adaeze (Onwuegbuzia) E.; m. Patricia Omaneme Okudah, Dec. 28, 1960; children: Dorothy, Chukwudumebi, Thepiso, Charles. AS in Pub. Acctg., Southeastern U., Washington, 1973, BS in Acctg., 1974, MBPA, 1976; PhD in Acctg., Sussex (Eng.) Coll. Tech., 1979. Gen. mgr. acctg. and fin. depts. Bendix Field Engring. Corp., Columbia, Md., 1974-80; asst. prof. acctg. Rider Coll., Lawrenceville, N.J., 1980-81; assoc. prof. acctg. Trenton (N.J.) State Coll., 1981-84; auditor N.J. State Dept. Higher Edn., 1988-90; teaching fellow Catonsville (Md.) Community Coll., 1990-91; mem. acctg. faculty U. Md., Balt., 1991—; pres., chief exec. officer Emma-Pat Assocs. Ltd., Trenton, 1985—; fin. advisor internat. div. Found. for Coop. Housing, Washington, 1980; vis. prof. auditing Black Execs. Exch. Program, Nat. Urban Leage, N.Y.C., 1970. Author: Fundamentals of Practical Book-Keeping and Accounting for West Africa, 1991. Fellow Inst. Adminstrv. Acctg. and Data Processing (London); mem. Assn. Cost and Exec. Accts. (London), Brit. Assn. Accts. and Auditors, Brit. Inst. Mgmt., Nat. Assn. Accts. (state assoc. dir. 1979). Office: Emma-Pat Assocs Ltd PO Box 3812 Trenton NJ 08629-0812

EGELER, WILLIAM GEORGE, college dean, consultant; b. Amityville, N.Y., Aug. 4, 1954; s. William G. II and Mary Joan (McMurray) E.; m. Jane Louise Vanier, June 2, 1979; children: Teressa Joan, Erica Anne. BS, U. Maine, 1976; MSB, Husson Coll., Bangor, Maine, 1981. Resident dir. U. Maine, Orono, 1978-79, coord. complex, 1979-80; residential dir. No. Maine Tech. Coll., Presque Isle, 1981-84, assoc. dean students, 1984—, acting dean, 1991—; bd. dirs. Valley Investment Co., Inc., Presque Isle; mem. task force on chem. dependency Vocat. Tech. Insts., Augusta, Maine, 1982—. Grad. Leadership Presque Isle, 1988; mem. Presque Isle City Comprehensive Planning Commn., 1990—. Mem. NEA, New Eng. Assn. Coll. Admissions Counselors, Assn. Coll. and Univ. Housing Officers Internat., Maine Assn. Student Fin. Aid Adminstrs. (bd. dirs. 1988-91), Maine Tchrs. Assn., Omicron Nu. Lutheran. Office: No Maine Tech Coll 33 Edgemont Dr Presque Isle ME 04769-2099

EGER, FELIX MARTIN, physics educator; b. Lwów, Poland, May 31, 1936; came to U.S., 1947; s. Arnold and Sonja (Krutjanska) E.; m. Judith Kirshner, Oct. 15, 1971. BS, MIT, 1958; PhD in Physics, Brandeis U., 1963. Postdoctoral appointee Lawrence Livermore (Calif.) Lab., 1965-67; sr. rsch. assoc. Ctr. for History of Philosophy of Sci., Boston U., 1974-75; assoc. prof. physics Coll. S.I., CUNY, Staten Island, 1976—. Bd. editors Sci. and Edn., Vordrecht, The Netherlands, 1991—; contbr. articles to sci. publs. Mem. Am. Phys. Soc., Philosophy of Sci. Assn., Soc. Lit. and Sci., Philosophy of Edn. Soc. Office: CUNY SI Coll 130 Stuyvesant Pl Staten Island NY 10301-1953

EGGENBERGER, ANDREW JON, federal agency administrator; b. Harlowton, Mont., May 8, 1938; s. Andrew D. and Gladys E. Eggenberger. BS, Carnegie Mellon U., 1961, PhD, 1967; MS, Ohio State U., 1963. Prof. U. S.C., Columbia, 1967-72; project mgr. D'Appolonia Cons. Engrs., Pitts., 1972-84; program dir. NSF, Washington, 1984-89; vice chmn. Def. Nuclear Facilities Safety Bd., Washington, 1989—; fellow Marshall Space Flight Ctr., Huntsville, Ala., 1969, Lewis Rsch. Ctr., Cleve., 1967, 68; rsch. engr. Boeing Co., Seattle, 1961-63. Recipient Ralph R. Teetor award Soc. Automotive Engrs., 1968. Mem. AIAA, Am. Nuclear Soc., Earthquake Engring. Rsch. Inst., Sigma Alpha Epsilon. Lutheran. Office: Def Nuclear Facilities Safety Bd 625 Indiana Ave NW Ste 700 Washington DC 20004-2901

EGGERT, GERALD GORDON, American history educator; b. Berrien County, Mich., Apr. 12, 1926; s. Gordon De Witt and Marguerite (Inman) E.; m. Jean Higgins, June 20, 1953; children: Michael Leroy, Susan Diane, Christine Elizabeth. B.A., Western Mich. U., 1949; M.A., U. Mich., 1951, Ph.D., 1960. Tchr. social studies secondary pub. sch., Battle Creek, Mich., 1949-54; instr. history U. Md., College Park, 1957-60; asst. prof. history Bowling Green State U., Ohio, 1960-65; asst. prof. Am. history Pa. State U., University Park, 1965-67, assoc. prof., 1967-72, prof., 1972-91, prof. emeritus, 1991—, head dept., 1980-85. Author: Railroad Labor Disputes, 1967, Richard Olney, 1974, Steelmasters and Labor Reform, 1981. Served with U.S. Army, 1946-48. Mem. Pa. Hist. Assn. (bus. sec.). Home: 517 Nimitz Ave State College PA 16801-6414

EGGLER, DAVID HEWITT, geochemistry educator; b. Ashland, Wis., May 15, 1940; s. Willis Alexander and Dorothy (Smith) E.; m. Betsey Louise Abbey, Feb. 10, 1974; children: Aimee, Willis. AB, Oberlin Coll., 1962; PhD, U. Colo., 1967. Rsch. assoc. Pa. State U., University Park, 1967-70; asst. prof. Tex. A&M U., College Station, 1970-72; staff mem. Carnegie Inst. Washington, 1972-77; prof. Pa. State U., University Park, 1977—, assoc. dept. head, 1988—; panel cons. NSF, Washington, 1982-85, NAS, Washington, 1990-92. Contbr. articles to profl. jours. Recipient Wager prize Internat. Assn. Volcanology, 1979; NSF grantee, 1977—. Fellow Mineral. Soc. Am., Geol. Soc. Am. Home: 199 Betty Cir Reedsville PA 17084-9604 Office: Pa State U 303 Deike Bldg University Park PA 16802

EGGLESTON-WEHR, SYLVIA ELAINE JOHNSON, university administrator; b. Balt., Oct. 24, 1940; d. Ralph I. and Hazel (Ring) Johnson; m. Joseph Carr Eggleston (dec. Jan. 1989); children: ELizabeth Ridley Eggleston-Drigotas, Anne Fleming Eggleston, Elaine Price Eggleston; m. Frederick T. Wehr, Jan. 1990. BA, Goucher Coll., 1962; MAS, Johns Hopkins U., 1981. Dir. programs for women returning to coll. Goucher Coll., Balt., 1979-82, lectr. dept. bus. mgmt. and econs., 1981-84, dir. Goucher Ctr. for Ednl. Resources, 1982-84; dir. of devel. for medicine U. Md., Balt., 1984-85; dir. devel. Sch. of Hygiene and Pub. Health, Johns Hopkins U., Balt., 1985-89, assoc. dean for external affairs, 1989—. Bd. dirs. Child Care Found., Balt., 1988-90, Ctr. to Prevent Childhood Malnutrition, Washington, 1988-89; mem. Johns Hopkins Hosp. Women's Bd., 1975-80; bd. trustees Bryn Mawr Sch., Balt., 1980-90, exec. com. 1981-90; chmn. Community Adv. Bd., 1975-78; vestry Ch. of the Redeemer, 1981-84; pres. Jr. League Balt., Inc., 1977-79. Home: 500 Edgevale Rd Baltimore MD 21210-1902 Office: Johns Hopkins U Sch Hygiene & Pub Health 615 N Wolfe St # 1604 Baltimore MD 21205-2103

EGGLETON, ARTHUR C., former mayor; b. Toronto; m. Brenda Louise Clune, Dec. 1981; 1 child, Stephanie. Accountant; mem. Toronto City Coun., 1969-91, pres., 1975-76, 78-80; budget chief City of Toronto, 1973-80, vice chmn. City Exec. Com., 1980s, mayor, 1980-91; spl. advisor in planning and orgn. of World Urban Forum, UN Conf. on Environ. and Devel., 1991—. Former mem. Met. Toronto Coun., Met. Toronto Police Commn.; hon. bd. dirs. Can. Nat. Exhbn.; past bd. dirs. Fedn. Can. Municipalities; past co-chair Nat. Action Com. on Race Rels. Recipient Civic award of merit City of Toronto, 1992. Mem. Soc. Mgmt. Accts. Office: 2 Toronto St Ste 500, Toronto, ON Canada M5C 2B6

EGHBAL, MORAD, geologist, lawyer; b. Tehran, June 7, 1952; s. Mohammad Ali and Fari Eghbal; m. Niloofar Sadjadi, July 17, 1983; 1 child, Elahé. BA, George Washington U., 1975, MA, 1977, JD, Howard U., 1989, LLM, U. of the Pacific, 1991. Asst. George Washington U., Washington, 1972; asst. to dir. Smithsonian Instn., Washington, 1972-75; spl. advisor to dir. Georgetown U., 1975; cons. Leo A Daly, Washington, 1975, Kodak, Rochester, N.Y., 1976; chief exec. officer MERE Enterprises, Washington, 1976-87; fgn. assoc. Pestalozzi, Gmuer & Heiz, Zurich, Switzerland, 1989; law clk. Hon. William B. Bryant, U.S. Dist. Ct. D.C., 1990-91; trustee, chief fin. officer Riess Found., Washington, 1983—; dir. The Grail Corp., Gasco, Inc.; judge oral arguments and memls. internat. semi-finals Jessup Competition Internat. Law Students Assn. Researcher: The Divining Hand (E.P. Dutton), 1973-79. Keynote speaker symposium Dickinson Sch. Law, Carlisle, Pa., 1991. Recipient Cert. of Achievement, Pacific Energy & Mineral Resources Conf., 1978, Ga. U., 1980, 2d Place Nat. Roscoe Hogan Environ. Law Essay Contest award Assn. Trial Lawyers Am., 1988, finalist, 1989, Outstanding Student Advocate award, Met. Trial Lawyers Assn. Mem. ABA, Am. Assn. Petroleum Geologists (founding mem. energy minerals div.), Geol. Soc. Am., Soc. Econ. Paleontologists and Mineralogists, Potomac Appalachian Trails Club, Nat. Capital Area Paralegal Assn., Nat. Bar Assn., Internat. Law Soc., Nat. Lawyers Club, U.S. Japan Trade Coun., Phi Delta Phi. Address: Riess Found PO Box 9555 Washington DC 20016

EGINTON, WARREN WILLIAM, federal judge; b. Bklyn., Feb. 16, 1924. A.B., Princeton U., 1948; LL.B., Yale U., 1951. Bar: N.Y. 1952, Conn. 1954. Assoc. Davis Polk & Wardwell, N.Y.C., 1951-53; ptnr. Cummings & Lockwood, Stamford, Conn., 1954-79; judge U.S. Dist. Ct., Bridgeport, Conn., 1979—. Mem. Am. Judicature Soc., ABA, Am. Bar Found., Conn. Bar Assn., Fgn. Policy Assn. Office: US Dist Ct 915 Lafayette Blvd Bridgeport CT 06604-4706

EGLOW, MICHAEL E., podiatric surgeon; b. Newark, Apr. 26, 1956; s. Alvin Sanford and Eileen Ruth (Stacher) E. BS in Zoology, George Washington U., 1978; D of Podiatric Medicine, Pa. Coll. Podiatric Medicine, 1982. Diplomate Am. Bd. Podiatric Surgery. Surg. resident West Essex Gen. Hosp., Livingston, N.J., 1982-83; pvt. practice Maplewood, N.J., 1983—. Office: 2168 Milburn Ave Maplewood NJ 07040

EGNATINSKY, JACK, anesthesiologist, medical director; b. Bklyn., Apr. 16, 1941; s. Sidney and Sarah (Sperling) E.; m. Judith Ellen Buchert, June 14, 1964; children: Wayne Andrew, Susan Beth, Roberta Louise. BS, Queens Coll., Flushing, N.Y., 1961; MD, SUNY, Syracuse, 1965. Diplomate Am. Bd. Anesthesiology. Commd. USN, 1963, advanced through grades to lt. comdr., 1969, resigned, 1971; intern St. Joseph's Hosp., Syracuse, 1965-66; resident in anesthesiology U.S. Naval Hosp., Phila., 1966-68; chief of anesthesiology Crouse Irving Meml. Hosp., Syracuse, 1974-82, attending anesthesiologist, 1971—; attending anesthesiologist Community Gen. Hosp., Syracuse, 1990—; chief of anesthesiology, med. dir. Harrison Ctr. Outpatient Surgery, Syracuse, 1987—; clin. assoc. prof. SUNY, Syracuse, 1972—. Contbr. articles to profl. jour. Coord. Ethiopia program Anesthesia Overseas, Inc., Washington, 1987-88; bd. edn. Temple Soc. Concord, Syracuse, 1978-82, trustee, 1978-83, Jewish Family Svc., Syracuse, 1979-89. Fellow Am. Coll. Anesthesiologists; mem. AMA, Am. Soc. Anesthesiologists, N.Y. State Soc. Anesthesiologists (bd. dirs. 1991—, chmn. com. govt. and legal affairs 1988—, Testimonial award 1986), Med. Soc. State of N.Y., Onondaga County Med. Soc. (exec. coun. 1991—), Internat. Anesthesia Rsch. Soc., Undersea and Hyperbaric Med. Soc., Soc. Ambulatory Anesthesia. Office: Harrison Ctr Outpatient Surgery 550 Harrison Ctr Ste 230 Syracuse NY 13202-3054

EGNER, DONALD OTTO, physicist, consultant; b. Cleve., Apr. 18, 1928; s. Otto and Beatrice M. (Pick) E.; m. Leona J. Godack, Mar. 4, 1950; children: Laura, David, Christopher, Dennis. AB, Western Md. Coll., 1949. Physicist U.S. Dept. Def., Aberdeen Proving Ground, Md., 1949-87; tech. cons. Md., 1987—; cons., mem. steering com. ALT Project, 1987—; prof. math. Essex (Md.) C.C., 1986—; bd. dirs. Tech. Assocs. Inc., Belair, Md., 1965-68. Chmn. local ch. bd., Middle River, Md., 1983-89; chmn. Cub Scouts, Middle River, 1973-75. 1st lt. U.S. Army, 1949-51. Mem. Rotary (pres. Middle River chpt. 1971-72). Methodist. Home and Office: 5806 Pine Hill Dr White Marsh MD 21162-1902

EGO-AGUIRRE, ERNESTO, physician; b. Lima, Peru, Dec. 16, 1928; came to U.S., 1956; s. Ernesto and Benjamina (Palma) E. B in Medicine, San Marcos U., 1947, MD, 1955; postgrad. in biometrics, Cornell U., 1965-66. Diplomate Am. Bd. Surgery. Intern in surgery Barnes Hosp. Washington U., St. Louis, 1956-57, resident asst. in surgery, 1957-60; asst. and sr. resident in surgery Ellis Fischel Cancer Hosp., Columbia, Mo., 1960-62; spl. fellow plastic and reconstructive surgery Meml. Sloan Kettering Cancer Ctr., N.Y.C., 1963-64, sr. resident, fellow in surgery, 1965-69; fellow in rsch. Sloan Kettering Inst., N.Y.C., 1964-69; attending in surgery N.Y. Infirmary, 1970-78, Doctors Hosp., N.Y.C., 1978—. Contbr. articles to profl. jours. Fellowship grant Nat. Cancer Inst., 1965-68, Am. Cancer Soc., 1968-69; recipient 8 Continuous Med. Edn. award AMA, 1969—. Mem. N.Y. County Med. Soc., N.Y. State Med. Soc., N.Y. Acad. of Scis., Vet. Corps of Artillery (N.Y.), Mil. Order of the Loyal Legion, Sovereign Orthodox Order Knights Hospitallier of St. John, Seventh Regiment Rifle Club (N.Y.). Republican. Roman Catholic. Home: 209 E 56th St New York NY 10022-3705 Office: 135 William St Fl 10 New York NY 10038-3805

EHINGER, ALBERT LOUIS, JR., securities trader; b. Lansing, Mich., May 20, 1927; s. Albert Louis and Irene B. (Cavanaugh) E.; m. Anita Jean Gay, Feb. 9, 1963; 1 child, Andrew. BA, Mich. State U., 1950; MBA, U. Pa., 1954. Researcher Nat. Bur. Econ. Research, N.Y.C., 1954-55; bond portfolio mgr. Nat. City Bank, Cleve., 1955-57, Chem. Bank, N.Y.C., 1957-61; bond dept. mgr. Parabas Corp., N.Y.C., 1962-64; bond investment officer SwissRe Corp., N.Y.C., 1964-70; bond trader Wood, Struthers & Winthrop, Inc., N.Y.C., 1970-74; mng. ptnr. Albert Ehinger & Ptnrs., N.Y.C., 1974—; sr. ptnr. Fieldsend, Ehinger & Co., N.Y.C., 1986—. Pres. Albert and Anita Ehinger Found., N.Y.C., 1983—; trustee Robert R. Livingston Masonic Library, N.Y.C., 1987—. Served with USNR, 1945-46. Mem. Money Marketeers N.Y.U. (bd. dirs. 1987—), Soldiers, Sailors and Airmen's Club, Catherine Lorilard Wolfe Art Club (hon. male mem. 1986—), Union Club, St. George's Soc. N.Y., Masons. Episcopalian. Home: 444 E 82d St New York NY 10028 Office: 200 Liberty St One World Fin Ctr New York NY 10281

EHLERS, WILLIAM HENRY, ophthalmologist, educator; b. Philip, S.D., Sept. 29, 1950; s. Marvin William and Bernadette Naomi (Hanson) E. BFA, U. Nebr., 1973; MD, U. Nebr., Omaha, 1985. Diplomate Am. Bd. Ophthalmology, Am. Bd. Med. Examiners. Resident in ophthalmology Eastern Va. Grad. Sch. Medicine, Norfolk, 1985-89; fellow in cornea and external disease U. Conn., Farmington, 1989-90; assoc. physician Eye Physician Assocs. of Hartford, West Hartford, Conn., 1990—; asst. clin. prof. medicine U. Conn. Med. Sch., Farmington, 1990—; chmn. Eye Injury Registry of Conn., Hartford, 1991—. Contbr. articles to profl. jours. Vol. vision screener Conn. Soc. to Prevent Blindness, Hartford. Fison's Corp. grantee for rsch. in contact lens sci. and immunology, 1990. Mem. AMA, Am. Acad. Ophthalmology, Assn. for Rsch. in Vision and Ophthalmology, Contact Lens Assn. Ophthalmologists, Conn. Soc. Eye Physicians, Hartford County Med. Soc., Phi Chi. Home: 11 Winthrop Rd West Hartford CT 06110 Office: Eye Physician Assocs Hartford 29 N Main St West Hartford CT 06107

EHMAN, MICHAEL FREDERICK, electronics executive; b. Springfield, Ohio, Aug. 14, 1945; s. Burnell Frederick and Doris (Daugherty) E.; m. Carol Gampher; children: Heather Lyn, Matthew Frederick. BA in Mineralogy, Miami U., Oxford, Ohio, 1967; PhD in Solid State Sci., Pa. State U., 1970; MBA, So. Meth. U., 1982. With tech. staff Rockwell Internat., Anaheim, Calif., 1970-74; mgr. engring. Rockwell Internat., Chgo., 1975, Newport Beach, Calif., 1976; dir. engring. Rockwell Internat., Dallas, 1977-80; v.p. advt. tech. optoelectronics TRW, Carrolton, Tex., 1980-81; pres. Morgan Semiconductor Inc., Garland, Tex., 1982-85; gen. mgr. elect. materials Ethyl Corp., Garland, 1985-89; mktg. mgr. Alcoa Electronic Packaging, 1989-92, Splty. Metals div. Alcoa, New Kensington, Pa., 1992—; bd. dirs. ESS Technologies, San Francisco. Contbr. 22 articles to profl. jours.; patentee in field. Mem. IEEE, Am. Soc. Metals, Electrochem. Soc., Am. Assn. Crystal Growth. Republican. Methodist. Office: Alcoa Splty Metals Div 600 Freeport Rd New Kensington PA 15068

EHMER, MARJY ARDUINA NICCOLL, psychologist, educator; b. N.Y.C., Feb. 3, 1927; d. George A. and Ray (Haberman) Niccoll. B.A. cum laude, Bklyn. Coll., 1947; postgrad., NYU, 1947-49; Ph.D., U. Rochester, 1959; assoc. fellow Inst. Advanced Study in Rational Psychotherapy, N.Y.C., 1976-77; m. Richard Ehmer, Jan. 23, 1948 (div. Sept. 1965); 1 child, George; m. Jess L. Dow, Sept. 1971. Lab. asst. Bklyn. Coll., 1946-48, instr., 1947-48; rsch. asst. U. Rochester, N.Y., 1948-51, Tufts Coll., Medford, Mass., 1951-54; instr. Brandeis U., Waltham, Mass., 1952; instr. U. R.I., Kingston, 1954-58, asst. prof., 1958-60, U. Bridgeport (Conn.), 1960-61, assoc. prof., 1961-62; trainee VA Hosp., West Haven, Conn., 1962-63; assoc. prof. So. Conn. State U., New Haven, 1963-69, prof., 1969-85, prof. emeritus, 1985—, dir. mental health specialization psychology dept., 1979-85; pvt. practice psychology, 1977—. Contbr. articles to profl. jours. Dist. cons. Dept. of Rehab. Svcs., 1989—. Bd. dirs., chmn. safety svcs. com. So. Cen. Conn. chpt. ARC, 1979-84, also mem. exec. com. Mem. Am. Psychol. Assn., Eastern Psychol. Assn. (election com. 1958), New Eng. Psychol. Assn. (steering com. 1982-85, 87—, pres.-elect 1985, pres. 1986, past pres. 1987, editor NEPA Newsletter 1989—), Conn. Psychol. Assn. (co-chmn. continuing edn. com. 1977-79, editor Conn. Psychologist 1979-80), Internat. Coun. Psychologists, John Cain Golf Club, Mount Sunapee Ski Club, Sigma Xi, Psi Chi. Address: 497 Dogwood Rd Orange CT 06477

EHNTHOLT, DANIEL JAMES, chemist; b. Manchester, N.H., Sept. 19, 1945; s. Daniel James Dolores (Donohue) E.; m. Eileen Marie Dunne, Aug. 14, 1971; children: Kimberly, Amy, Christopher. BS, Fordham U., 1966; PhD, SUNY, Stony Brook, 1971. Postdoctoral fellow Brandeis U., Waltham, Mass., 1971-72; asst. prof. Boston U., 1972-77, Worcester (Mass.) State Coll., 1977-78; cons. Arthur D. Little, Inc., Cambridge, Mass., 1978-84, unit mgr., 1984-91, v.p., 1991—, also dir. Contbr. articles to profl. jours. Commr. Conservation Commn., Hudson, Mass., 1974-79; mem. bd. Health, Hudson, 1981-88, 91—. N.Y. State Regents fellow, 1962-70, German Acad. Exchange fellow Max Planck Inst., Mülheim an der Ruhr, 1974. Mem. ACS (Petroleum Research fellow 1970), Assn. Ofcl. Analytical Chemists, Am. Inst. Chemists, Nat. Sci. Tchrs. Assn., Phi Lambda Upsilon. Roman Catholic. Office: Arthur D Little Inc 15 Acorn Park Cambridge MA 02140-2301

EHRENBERG, MIRIAM COLBERT, psychologist; b. N.Y., Mar. 16, 1930; m. Otto Ehrenberg, Sept. 20,1956; children: Ingrid, Erica. BA, Queens Coll.; MA, CUNY; PhD, New Sch. Social Rsch. Psychologist pvt. practice, N.Y., 1970—; dir. psychotherapy Spence Chapin, N.Y., 1974-84. Author: The Psychotherapy Maze, 1987, Optimum Brain Power, 1985, The Intimate Circle, 1988. Office: 118 Riverside Dr New York NY 10024

EHRENFELD, JOHN ROOS, environmental policy educator; b. Chgo., May 16, 1931; s. Louis and Alice (Roos) E.; m. Myrna Goodman; children: Peter, Elizabeth, Thomas; m. Ruth R. Budd, Aug. 7, 1983. BS in Chem. Engring., MIT, 1953, ScD in Chem. Engring., 1957. Sr. engr. Arthur D. Little Inc., Cambridge, Mass., 1957-61, sr. cons., 1981-84; sr. engr. Prototech, Inc., Cambridge, 1961-62; dir. applied rsch. GCA Corp., Bedford, Mass., 1962-67; pres. Walden Rsch. Corp., Cambridge, 1967-75; v.p., tech. dir. Energy Resources Co., Cambridge, 1975-78; chmn. New England River Basins Commn., Boston, 1978-81; sr. environ. rsch. mgr. Abt Assocs., Cambridge, 1985; sr. rsch. assoc. MIT, Cambridge, 1986—; advisor H&Q Environ. Tech. Fund, Boston, 1989—; assoc. dir. EPA N.E. Hazardous Substances Rsch. Ctr., Boston, 1988—. Contbr. over 60 articles to profl. jours.; inventor electrochemical structures. Chmn. Acton (Mass.) Dem. Town Com., 1962-67, Lincoln (Mass.) Dem. Town Com., 1970-72; bd. dir. Mass. Tech. Devel. Corp., Boston, 1978-87. 1st lt. U.S. Army, 1957-59. Fellow NSF, 1953-55. Mem. AAAS, Am. Inst. Chem. Engrs., Soc. for Risk Analysis, Am. Chem. Soc. (chmn. IEC div. 1977), Air and Waste Mgmt. Assn., Sigma Xi, Tau Beta Pi. Office: MIT Rm E 40-241 Cambridge MA 02139

EHRENFELD, PHYLLIS RHODA, editor, playwright, book reviewer; b. Montreal, Quebec, Canada, Sept. 28, 1932; came to U.S., 1954; d. Carl and Thelma (Azeff) S.; m. Sylvain Ehrenfeld, May 29, 1955; children: David, Temma. BA in Psychology, Sir George Williams Coll., Montreal, 1952; BSW, McGill Sch. of Social Work, Montreal, 1953; postgrad. in lit., Columbia U., 1954-57. Social worker Jewish Family Welfare, Baron de Hirsch Inst., Montreal, 1952-54; tchr., program dir. Jack & Jill Day Care Ctr., Landing, N.J., 1956—; editor-in-chief, sr. editor Am. Anorexia Bulimia Assn. Newsletter, N.Y.C., 1980—. Playwright four plays; book reviewer No. N.J. NOW Newsletter, 1987-88, New Directions for Women, 1989—. Publicity chmn. Ethical Culture Soc. of Bergen County, Teaneck, 1987-88; drama coord. Garden State Playwrights, Teaneck, 1989—; tchr. adult edn. programs, librs., svc. groups. Recipient Arnold Gingrich award for Fiction, N.J. State Council on the Arts, 1980-81, nomination for Hodder Fellowship in the Humanities, Princeton (N.J.) U., 1981. Mem. Am. Anorexia Bulimia Assn. (bd. dirs. 1981-89, sec. 1981-87, recording sec. 1990-91), Inst. for Ethical Edn. (program com.), Ethical Culture Soc. (program chair 1992—). Home: 276 Grove St Teaneck NJ 07666-3214 Office: Am Anorexia Bulimia Assn 418 E 76th St New York NY 10021-3130

EHRENKRANTZ, DAVID, medical researcher; b. New Haven, Aug. 26, 1952; s. Harold Louis and Katherine (Russo) E. BA magna cum laude, U. Hartford, 1979; MSW, Adelphi U., 1982; MPH, N.Y. Med. Coll., 1987; ScD, U. Pitts., 1991. Cert. social worker, N.Y. Rsch. asst. U. Conn. Sch. Medicine, 1985. Contbr. articles to sci. jours. Mem. Alpha Chi.

EHRLICH, CHARLES EDWARD, media liaison; b. Phila., Aug. 20, 1969; s. George Edward and Gail E. AB cum laude, Harvard Coll., 1991; MSc in Econs., London Sch. Econs., 1992. Features editor The Exonian, Exeter, N.H., 1984-87; founder, chmn. The Argument, Exeter, N.H., 1984-87; tutor Bur. of Study Counsel, Cambridge, Mass., 1989-91; founder, dir. La Mesa Castellana, Cambridge, Mass., 1989-91; media liaison Organizing Com. of the 1992 Barcelona Olympics, Banyoles, Spain, 1991—. Researcher, writer Let's Go, Spain, 1988, 89; author travel guidebook: Let's Go, the Budget Guide, 1989, To Spain, Portugal and Morocco, 1990. Harvard Coll. Dept. History rsch. grantee, 1991, scholar, 1990. Mem. Ctr. European Studies (Iberian Group), Inst. Politics Study Group, Nottinghamshire County Rowing Assn. (Eng.). Office: One Independence Pl # 1101 241 S 6th St Philadelphia PA 19106

EHRLICH, GEORGE EDWARD, physician, international pharmaceutical consultant; b. Vienna, Austria, July 18, 1928; came to U.S., 1938, naturalized, 1944; s. Edward and Irene (Elling) E.; m. Gail S. Abrams, Mar. 30, 1968; children: Charles Edward, Steven L. Abrams, Rebecca Sayles. A.B. cum laude, Harvard U., 1948; M.B., M.D., Chgo. Med. Sch., 1952. Intern Michael Reese Hosp., Chgo., 1952; resident Francis Delafield Hosp., N.Y.C., 1955, Beth Israel Hosp., Boston, 1956, New Eng. Center Hosp., Boston, 1957; fellow rheumatology NIH, Bethesda, Md., 1958, Hosp. for Spl. Surgery, N.Y.C., 1959-61; asst. attending physician Hosp. for Spl. Surgery, 1960-64; spl. fellow Sloan Kettering Inst., 1960-61; instr. medicine Cornell U., 1960-64; dir. Arthritis Center, chief rheumatology Albert Einstein Med. Center and Moss Rehab. Hosp., Phila., 1964-80; asst. prof. medicine Temple U., 1964-67, asso. prof. medicine, 1967-72, prof. medicine, 1972-80, asso. prof. rehab. medicine, 1964-74, prof., 1974-80; vis. lectr. U. Pa., 1964-80; prof. medicine, dir. div. rheumatology Hahnemann U., Phila., 1980-83; v.p. Anti-Inflammatory/Endocrine CIBA-Geigy Pharmaceuticals, Summit, N.J., 1983-86; head med. affairs CIBA-Geigy Ltd., Switzerland, 1987-88; pres. George E. Ehrlich Assocs., pharmaceutical cons.; adj. prof. clin. medicine NYU Med. Ctr., 1984—; clin. prof. of medicine U. Pa., 1989-91, adj. prof. clin. medicine, 1992—; adviser/cons. Diabetes and Other Nocommunicable Diseases Unit WHO, 1990—; mem. arthritis adv. com. FDA, 1991—. Author: Differential Diagnosis of Rheumatoid Arthritis, 1972, Oculocutaneous Manifestations of Rheumatic Diseases, 1973, Total Management of the Arthritic Patient, 1973, Rehabilitation Management of Rheumatic Conditions, 1980, 2d edit., 1986, (with J. Fries) Prognosis, 1981, (with H.E. Paulus) Controversies in the Clinical Evaluation of Analgesic-Anti-Inflammatory-Antirheumatic Drugs, 1981; (with P. Utsinger, N. Zvaifler) Rheumatoid Arthritis, 1985, (with W. Simon) Medicolegal Consequences of Trauma, 1992; editor: Jour. Albert Einstein Med. Center, 1966-71, Arthritis and Rheumatic Diseases Abstracts, 1968-71, (with W. Simon) Consequences of Trauma, 1992; editorial bd.: Inflammation, 1974-88, Psychosomatics, 1977-83, Sexual Medicine Today, 1977-84, Jour. Rheumatology, 1982—, Immunopharmacology, 1985—, Med. Problems Performing Artists, 1985—; contbr. articles to profl. jours. Pres. Eastern Pa. chpt. Arthritis Found., 1970-72; mem. Phila. Mayor's Sci. and Tech. Adv. Council, 1972-81; chmn. ad hoc adv. com. Bur. Drugs, FDA, 1971; mem. subcom. on redefinition of disability Social Security Adminstrn., 1982-86; cons./advisor Diabetes and Other Noncommunicable Diseases unit World Health Orgn., Geneva, 1990—; mem. arthritis adv. com. U.S. FDA, 1991—. Served to comdr. M.C. USNR, 1953-55; Res. to 1975. Recipient citations City Phila., 1969, 74, Distinguished Alumnus award Chgo. Med. Sch., 1969; decorated Cavaliere Order of Star of Italian Solidarity. Fellow ACP, Phila. Coll. Physicians, Am. Coll. Rheumatology (com. for publ. Arthritis and Rheumatism 1977-79, mem. editorial bd. 1980-83); mem. Am. Soc. Clin. Pharmacology and Therapeutics, AMA (editorial bd. Jour. 1972-82), Assn. Mil. Surgeons (Philip Hench award 1971), Brit. Assn. Rheumatology and Rehab. (overseas mem., editorial bd. 1979-82), Alpha Omega Alpha. Club: Harvard (Boston, N.Y.C.). Home: 38 Holly Dr Loveladies NJ 08008 Office: 1 Independence Pla 241 S 6th St Philadelphia PA 19106-3727 also: Grellingerstrasse 9, 4020 Basel Switzerland

EHRLICH, ROBERT STARK, biochemist, environmental scientist; b. N.Y.C., Aug. 30, 1940; s. Louis Herman and Sylvia (Stark) E.; m. Marion Faith Stern, May 28, 1966; 1 child, Heather Anne. AB, Columbia U., 1962; PhD, Rutgers U., 1967. Asst. prof. Muskingum Coll., New Concord, Ohio, 1969-70; instr. CCNY, 1970-71; postdoctoral fellow Rutgers Med. Sch., Piscataway, N.J., 1971-73; rsch. assoc. U. Del., Newark, 1973-86, assoc. scientist, 1986—; mem. Peer Review Com. Del. Heart Assn., Wilmington, 1990—. Contbr. articles to profl. jours. Bd. dirs. Wilmington Del. Dem. Orgn., 1978—. Recipient N.Y. State Regent's scholarship, 1958. Mem. Am. Soc. Biochemists and Molecular Biologists, Del. Mineral. Soc. Home: 1424 Carson Rd Wilmington DE 19803-5116 Office: U Del Chemistry Dept Newark DE 19716

EHRLICHMAN, HOWARD, psychology educator, researcher; b. Bronx, N.Y., Oct. 5, 1944; s. Milton and Joy (Merwin) E.; m. Elizabeth Safferson, June 11, 1966; 1 child, Samuel Milton. BA, CUNY, 1966; PhD, New Sch. for Social Rsch., 1971. Postdoctoral fellow Ednl. Testing Svc., Princeton, N.J., 1971-73; from asst. prof. to full prof. Grad. Sch. CUNY, N.Y.C., 1973—; prof. Queens Coll., CUNY, N.Y.C., 1991—; mem. sci. adv. bd. Fragrance Rsch. Fund, N.Y.C., 1987—. Contbr. chpt. and articles to profl. jours. Home: 44-59 Kissena Blvd Flushing NY 11355 Office: Queens Coll CUNY 65-30 Kissena Blvd Flushing NY 11367

EHRLING, SIXTEN, orchestra conductor; b. Malmö, Sweden, Apr. 3, 1918; came to U.S., 1963; s. Gunnar and Emilia (Lundgren) E.; m. Gunnel Lindgren, Sept. 19, 1947; children: Elisabeth, Ann-Charlotte. Student, Royal High Sch. Music, Stockholm, 1936-40. Head conducting and orch. dept. Juilliard Sch., N.Y.C., 1973-88. Condr. Royal Opera House, Stockholm, 1940-53, 90; prin. condr., music dir., 1953-60, condr., music dir. Detroit Symphony Orch., 1963-73; mus. advisor, prin. guest condr. Denver Symphony, 1978-89, music advisor, 1989—; guest condr. Met. Opera, N.Y.C., U.S., Europe, Japan, Australia, South Am., Vienna State Opera.

EIBEL, ANDREW H., lawyer; b. N.Y.C., Sept. 3, 1950; s. A. Isadore and Cecele (Wainstein) E.; m. Nancy Roberta Stenzler Friedrich, June 22, 1987. AB, Columbia Coll., 1971; JD, Hofstra U., 1976. Bar: N.Y. 1977. Staff atty. criminal appeals bur., parole revocation def. Legal Aid Soc., N.Y.C., 1976-79; staff atty. criminal def. div. Legal Aid Soc., Bklyn., 1979-89, supervising atty. criminal def. div., 1989—. Mem. Nat. Assn. Criminal Def. Lawyers, N.Y. State Assn. Criminal Def. Attys., N.Y. State Defender Assn., Kings County Bar Assn. Democrat. Home: 140 8th Ave Apt 5A Brooklyn NY 11215 Office: Legal Aid Soc Criminal Def 175 Remsen St 4th Fl Brooklyn NY 11201

EICHELBERGER, R. TONY, education evaluator; b. Pekin, Ill., Apr. 15, 1940; s. Tony and Eva Alosia (Brown) E.; m. Sandra Shannon, 1966 (div. 1974); children: Erin Shannon, Derek Joseph; m. Rita M. Bean, May 28, 1983. BS in Edn., So. Ill. U., 1966, PhD, 1970. Cert. math. and sci. tchr., Ill. Baseball player San Francisco Giants, Springfield and El Paso, Tex., 1962-65; mgr. Medford (Oreg.) Giants, 1967; coord., rsch. design Dallas (Tex.) Ind. Sch. Dist., 1970-71; rsch. assoc. Learning Rsch. & Devel. Ctr., Pitts., 1971-79; asst. to assoc. prof. Univ. Pitts., Pa., 1972—. Author: Disciplined Inquiry, 1989; editor: Evaluation News, 1984-85; contbr. chpt. to book. Bd. mem. Generations Together, Pitts., 1989—. NDEA Doctoral fellowship So. Ill. Univ., Carbondale, 1966-69. Mem. Am. Evaluation Assn. (editor Evaluation Practice 1986-88), Am. Ednl. Rsch. Assn., Nat. Soc. for Study Edn., Rsch. on Evaluation, Multiple Linear Regression, Pa. Ednl. Rsch. Assn., Ea. Evaluation Rsch. Soc. Office: U Pitts 5P30 Forbes Quad Pittsburgh PA 15260

EICHELMAN, BURR SIMMONS, JR., psychiatrist, researcher, educator; b. Hinsdale, Ill., Mar. 20, 1943; s. Burr Simmons and Evelyn Cora (Budde) E.; children by previous marriage: Kathryn Elise, Andrew Burr; m. Anne del Carmen Gonzalez-Hartwig; 1 child, Ian David. S.B. with honors, U. Chgo., 1964, M.D., 1968, Ph.D. in Biopsychology, 1970. Diplomate Am. Bd. Psychiatry and Neurology. Pediatric intern U. Calif.-San Francisco, 1969-70; resident, then fellow in psychiatry Stanford U., Calif., 1972-75, Kennedy fellow in medicine, law and ethics, 1975-76; asst. prof. psychiatry U. Wis.-Madison, 1976-79, assoc. prof., 1979-84, prof., 1984-88; chief psychiatry service, dir. lab. behavioral neurochemistry William S. Middleton Meml. VA Hosp., Madison, 1976-87; cons. Mendota Mental Health Inst., Madison, 1984-87; clin. dir. Dorothea Dix Hosp., Raleigh, 1987-90; prof. psychiatry U. N.C., 1988-90; prof., chmn. dept. psychiatry Temple U. Sch. Medicine, 1990—. Co-editor: Terrorism and Interdisciplinary Perspectives, 1983. Contbr. chpts. to books, articles to profl. jours. Elder, Presbyn. Ch. Served to lt. comdr. USPHS, 1970-72. Recipient A.E. Bennett award Soc. Biol. Psychiatry, 1972; Westerman prize (hon. mention) Am. Fedn. Clin. Research, 1976. Fellow Am. Coll. Neuropsychopharm. (chmn. ethics com. 1985-86), Am. Psychiat. Assn. (Falk fellow 1973-75), Am. Psychol. Assn.; mem. Internat. Soc. Research on Aggression (co-chmn. ethics com. 1980-84, coun. 1988-90), Soc. Neurosci., Sigma Xi, Alpha Omega Alpha. Avocations: music (piano and voice); tennis; skiing. Office: Temple U Dept Psychiatry 3401 N Broad St Philadelphia PA 19140-5189

EICHNER, PATRICK RAMSEY, commercial real estate developer; b. Houston, Nov. 14, 1960; s. L. John and Joann (Mansfield) E.; m. Darlene Ann Vaccarello, Sept. 4, 1988; 1 child, Meghan Rose. BS in Econs., Lehigh U., 1982. Asst. v.p. Murray Constrn. Co., Inc., Springfield, N.J., 1985-88, v.p. real estate, 1988—. Legis. com. Nat. Assn. of Office and Indsl. Parks, 1983—. Mem. Union County Rugby Football Club (v.p. 1988-89, pres. 1992, MVP award 1990). Republican. Lutheran. Office: Murray Constrn Co Inc 51 Commerce St APO AE 09081-5000

EICKELBERG, W. WARREN BARBOUR, educator; b. N.Y.C., Jan. 19, 1925; s. Graham Alexander and Lillian (Hayes) E.; student Harvard U., 1942-43; BA, Hope Coll., Holland, Mich., 1949; MA (Dennison fellow), Wesleyan U. Conn., 1951; children—William, Margaret, Robert, Janet. Prof., Adelphi U., Garden City, L.I., N.Y., 1952—, dir. devel., v.p., 1958-66, dir. premed. curriculum, 1967-89; cons. devel. planning Nat. Ctr. for Disability Svcs., Albertson, N.Y., Joseph Bulova Sch., Woodside, N.Y. 1958—; mem. biomechanics cons. group Pres.'s Com. on Disabled; mem. ad hoc com. N.Y. State Joint Legis. Com. on Transp. Chmn. Nassau County Museum Council, 1966-67; mem. founding com. Adelphi Suffolk Coll.; nat. cons. Nat. Council Cath. Men, 1969. Served to 1st lt. USAAF, 1943-46. Recipient Flambeau award Adelphi U., 1956, Disting. Service award, 1981, Disting. Teaching award, 1985; L.I. Gov.'s award, 1966, Alpha Epsilon Delta award, 1989, Joseph Serio award, 1990, 91; certificate of distinction Dictionary Internat. Biography, 1968; Wisdom award, 1970. Mem. N.Y. Acad. Scis., Internat. Soc. Biomechanics (charter), Nat. Soc. Fund Raisers, Public Relations Soc. Am. (accredited, pres. L.I. chpt. 1980), L.I. Pub. Relations Assn. (past pres., dir.), L.I. Sci. Tchrs. Assn. (past pres., dir.). Sigma Xi, Kappa Eta Nu. Clubs: Lions; Wesleyan (N.Y.C.); Unqua Yacht (Amityville). Home: 38 Unqua Pl Amityville NY 11701-4231 Office: Adelphi U Garden City NY 11530

EICKHOFF, HAROLD WALTER, college president, humanities educator; b. Natoma, Kans., Apr. 2, 1928; s. William and Emma (John) E.; m. Rosa Lee Smith, Aug. 19, 1955; children: Sharon Lee, Janet Lee. BA in History, U. Kansas City, 1957, MA in History and Govt., 1958; PhD in History, U. Mo., 1964. Asst. prof. history U. Mo., St. Louis, 1961-64, assoc. prof., dean studies, 1964-69; prof. history, exec. asst. to pres., sec. to bd. visitors Old Dominion U., Norfolk, Va., 1969-74, exec. v.p., 1974-76; prof. history, acad. v.p. Ft. Hays (Kans.) State U., 1976-79; prof. humanities, pres. Trenton (N.J.) State Coll., 1980—; mem. Edn. Commn. of States com. on undergrad. edn., 1985-87; bd. dirs. Assn. Am. Colls. Mem. bd. overseers Gov.'s Sch., Trenton, 1986—; bd. dirs. Mercer Med. Ctr., Trenton, 1980—, Mercer County C. of C., Trenton, 1980—; trustee Pennington Sch., 1981—. Served with USN, 1948-52, Korea. Recipient Service Above Self award Norfolk Rotary Club, 1976, Gov.'s Albert Einstein award for service to edn., 1988, N.J. Pride award State of N.J., 1991. Mem. Am. Coun. on Edn. (sec. 1986-88), N.J. Governing Bds. Assn., N.J. Assn. Colls. and Univs., Assn. Am. Colls. Presbyterian. Home: 110 Murphy Dr Pennington NJ 08534-1914 Office: Trenton State Coll Hillwood Lakes PO Box 4700 Trenton NJ 08650-4700

EICKOFF, MARGARET KATHYRN, economic consultant executive; b. Sedalia, Mo., Apr. 11, 1939; d. Leo Edward and Magdalene (Piatt) E.; m. Alfred James Smith Jr., Mar. 9, 1973. BA, U. Mo., 1960; MA, NYU, 1971. Rsch asst. Van Alstyne Noel & Co., N.Y.C., 1961-62, Townsend-Greenspan & Co. Inc., N.Y.C., 1962-85; sr. economist, chief economist U.S. Office of Mgmt. & Budget, Washington, 1985-87; econ. cons., pres. Eickoff Economics, N.Y.C., 1987—; bd. dirs. Townsend-Greenspan Co., N.Y. Futures Exchange, Interpace Clevepac, Upjohn Co., Tenneco Inc., AT&T, National Westminister Bancorp. Truste Manhattan Inst., N.Y.C., 1987. Fellow Nat. Assn. of Bus. Economists (pres. 1981); mem. Conf. of Bus. Economists (chmn. 1991), The Econ. Club of N.Y. Office: Eickoff Economics Inc 510 LaGuardia Pl Ste # 400 New York NY 10012

EIDELHOCH, LESTER PHILIP, physician, educator, surgeon; b. N.Y.C., Jan. 7, 1932; s. Abraham David Eidelhoch and Ella (Sarah) Lovinger; m. Cecily Ruth Rosenberg, Apr. 28, 1963; children: Alison Marc, Arthur Mark, Meredith Marc. BA, Columbia U., 1952; MD, NYU, 1956. Diplomate Am. Bd. Med. Examiners. Intern Stron Meml. Hosp., Rochester, N.Y.; resident Harvard Surg. div. Boston City Hosp., 1958-62; pvt. practice New Hartford, N.Y., 1965—; med. cons. walsh Med. Ctr., Rome, N.Y., 1991—; mem. faculty SUNY. Bd. dirs. Jewish Fedn., Utica (N.Y.) Symphony, Charles T. Sitrin Home. Lt. comdr. USN, 1962-64. Recipient Lindner Surg. award NYU. Fellow ACS, Royal Coll. Medicine; mem. N.Y. Cen. Soc. Surgeons, Cen. N.Y. Acad. Medicine, Oneida County Med. Soc. Republican. Home and Office: 6 Old Willow Rd New Hartford NY 13413-2419

EIGEN, MICHAEL, psychologist; b. Passaic, N.J., Jan. 11, 1936; s. Sol and Jeanette (Brody) E.; m. Betty Gitelman, Dec. 27, 1980; children: David Joshua, Jacob Paul. AB, U. Pa., 1957; PhD, New Sch. Social Rsch., N.Y.C., 1974. Lic. psychologist and psychoanalyst, N.Y. Past. dir. tng. Inst. for Expense Analysis; supr., faculty New Hope Guild, 1972-91, past mem. faculty, supr., 1980-85; mem. faculty, control tng. analyst NYU, N.Y.C., 1990—. Author: The Psychotic Core, 1986, Coming Through The Whirlwind, 1992; co-editor: Evil: Self and Culture, 1984; contbr. numerous articles to profl. jours. Mem. Nat. Psychol. Assn. for Psychoanalysis. Office: 225 Central Park W # 101A New York NY 10024

EIGER, RICHARD WILLIAM, publisher; b. N.Y.C., May 11, 1933; s. William and Helen M. (Fetten) E.; m. Ruth B. Engelke; 1 child, Keith

R. BFA, Pratt Inst., 1955; MBA, NYU, 1960. With Western Pub. Co., N.Y.C., 1958-80, pub. dir., 1968-74, v.p. pub., 1975-80; pres. Macmillan Ednl. Co., N.Y.C., 1980-91; sr. v.p. Macmillan Pub. Co., N.Y.C., 1980-91; v.p. Funk & Wagnalls Corp., Mahwah, N.J., 1991—. Dir. Pratt Inst. Alumni Bd., N.Y.C., 1986—; trustee Pratt Inst., 1992—. Lt. U.S.Army, 1956-57. Home: 459 Franklin Ave Wyckoff NJ 07481-1306 Office: Funk & Wagnall Corp 1 International Blvd Mahwah NJ 07495

EIL, CHARLES, programs director, educator, endocrinologist; b. Mpls., Dec. 15, 1946; s. Harry Meyer and Lois Helen (Latts) E.; m. Adele Ruth Griffin, July 8, 1978; children: Andrew, Matthew, Phillip. BA, U. Rochester, N.Y., 1968; PhD in Biochemistry, U. Chgo., 1972, MD, 1974. Diplomate Am. Bd. Internal Medicine, sub-bd. Endocrinology. Intern U. Mich., Ann Arbor, 1974-75, resident, 1975-76; fellow NIH, Bethesda, Md., 1976-80; staff physician Bethesda Naval Hosp./USN, 1980-86; program dir. Clin. Rsch. Ctr. Brown U., Providence, 1986-91; clin. assoc. prof. medicine Brown U., 1991—. Contbr. numerous articles to profl. jours.; contbr. chpts. in books. Mem. Providence Singers Choral Group, 1988—. Served to capt. USNR, 1980—. Recipient Peter Forsham award Soc. Uniformed Endocrinologists, 1985. Mem. Am. Soc. Clin. Investigation, Am. Soc. Bone and Mineral Rsch., Am. Fedn. Clin. Rsch., Am. Thyroid Assn., Endocrine Soc. Home: 159 President Ave Providence RI 02906-4625 Office: Truesdale Clinic Inc 1030 President Ave Fall River MA 02720-5923

EILERS, ROBERT PAUL, psychiatric administrator; b. Jersey City, Mar. 13, 1949; s. Christian Carl and Pauline Gail (Coverne) E. BS, Ursinus Coll., 1972; MD, Thomas Jefferson U., 1976. Diplomate Am. Bd. Psychiatry and Neurology. Resident psychiatry Ea. Pa. Psychiat. Inst., 1976-79; dir., partial hosp. program VA Outpatient Clinic, Phila., 1979-87; med. dir. Ancora Psychiatric Hosp., Hammonton, N.J., 1987—. Contbr. articles to profl. jours. Mem. Am. Psychiatric Assn., Am. Pub. Health Assn., Phila. Writers Assn. Democrat. Home: 1514 Pine St Philadelphia PA 19102-4660 Office: Ancora Psychiat Hosp Hammonton NJ 08037

EIMICKE, VICTOR W(ILLIAM), publishing company executive; b. N.Y.C., Feb. 4, 1925; s. Victor H. and Anna (Gille) E.; m. Maxine Howard Thome, Aug. 6, 1955; children: Laura Eimicke Klimley, Alicia Eimicke Barbieri. A.B., NYU, 1945, M.A., 1946, Ph.D., 1951; Litt.D. (hon.), Hope Coll., 1987. Lectr. NYU, 1945-47, Bklyn. Coll., 1946-49; dir. audio visual dept. CCNY, 1947-53; asst. prof. Pace Coll., 1953-56; v.p. Inst. Human Research in Industry, N.Y.C., 1947-48; pres. V.W. Eimicke Assocs. Inc., N.Y.C., 1951—, V.W. Eimicke Ltd., Peterborough, Can., 1978—; chmn. Eimicke Assocs. Ltd., London, 1956-69; pres. Action Aids, Inc., N.Y.C., 1969-73, Laurel Office Aids, Inc., N.Y.C., 1969-73, Action List Services, Inc., Yonkers, N.Y., 1976-80, Eimicke Pub. Co., Yonkers, 1976-78, Geschäftsführer, Envelo-Formulare GmbH, Krefeld, Ger., 1978-83, Geschäftsführer, V.W. Eimicke GmbH, 1983—; dir. New England Grocer Supply Co., Worcester, Mass., 1964-68, Nathan's Famous, Inc., N.Y.C., 1974-79, 85-87, Wetson's, Inc., N.Y.C., 1975-79. Author: (with Laura Klimley) Managing Human Resources - Documenting the Personnel Function. Pres. bd. trustees Halsted Sch., Yonkers, 1969-74; bd. govs. Lawrence Hosp., Bronxville, N.Y., 1971-74, mem. corp., 1986—; bd. dirs. Japan Internat. Christian U. Found., Inc., 1972—, v.p., 1990; trustee Hope Coll., Holland, Mich., 1976-87, chmn. bd. trustees, 1978-87, hon. trustee, 1987—; bd. dirs. Community Fund of Bronxville, 1982-87, pres., 1983-86, hon. dir., 1987—. Mem. Assn. Churchill Fellows of Westminster Coll., 1986—. Mem. Am., Eastern, N.Y. State, Westchester Psychol. Assns., Nat. Inst. Social Scis., Laymen's Nat. Bible Assn. (dir., treas. 1969-70, pres. 1982—), Am. Yacht Club (Rye, N.Y.), Met. Club, Met. Opera Club, Union League, University Club (N.Y.C), Siwanoy Country Club (Bronxville), Lake Placid Club (N.Y.), Phi Beta Kappa, Kappa Delta Pi, Phi Delta Kappa. Mem. Ref. Ch. (elder, mem. consistory or gt. consistory 1968—). Home: 20 Hereford Rd Bronxville NY 10708-5408 Office: 35 E Grassy Sprain Rd Yonkers NY 10710-4611

EIMON, PERRY LEROY, psychologist; b. Superior, Wis., Dec. 3, 1933; s. Perry Arthur and Deweyetta Beatrice (Dolysh) E.; m. Marilyn Carol Linnerson, June 16, 1961. BA, U. Minn., 1958, PhD, 1970. Lic. psychologist, Mass. Chief psychologist Hastings (Minn.) State Hosp., 1961-71; staff psychologist Brockton (Mass.)/West Roxbury VA Med. Ctr., 1971—; pvt. practice cons., Hastings, 1961-71, Brockton, 1971—. Contbr. articles to profl. jours. Fellow Mass. Psychol. Assn.; mem. Am. Psychol. Assn., Internat. Neuropsychol. Soc., New Eng. Psychol. Assn., N.Y. Neuropsychol. Group. Office: Brockton/West Roxbury VA Med Ctr 940 Belmont St Brockton MA 02401-5596

EIN, DANIEL, allergist; b. Liege, Belgium, Nov. 26, 1938; came to U.S., 1941; s. Max Motel and Sabine (Toeman) E.; m. Marion Hess, June 25, 1961 (div. 1978); children: Mark David, Jon Spencer; m. Marina Wallach, Apr. 10, 1988. AB, Columbia U., 1959; MD, Albert Einstein Coll. Medicine, 1964. Diplomate Am. Bd. Internal Medicine, Am. Bd. Allergy and Immunology. Intern Bronx Mcpl. Hosp., N.Y.C., 1964-65; staff assoc. Nat. Cancer Inst., Washington, 1965-67, clin. assoc., 1967-68; asst. resident Mass. Gen. Hosp., Boston, 1968-69; sr. investigator Nat. Cancer Inst., Washington, 1969-71; pvt. practice Washington, 1971—; clin. prof. medicine George Washington U., 1982—. Contbr. articles to profl. jours. and newspapers. Fellow ACP, Am. Acad. Allergy; mem. Med. Soc. of D.C. (pres. 1991), Greater Washington Allergy Soc. (pres. 1979), Cosmos Club. Jewish.

EINHORN, DAVID ALLEN, lawyer; b. Bklyn., Dec. 11, 1961; s. Harold and Jane Ellen (Wiener) E. BA in Computer Sci. magna cum laude, Columbia U., 1983, JD, 1986. Bar: N.Y. 1987, D.C. 1988, U.S. Dist. Ct. (so. and ea. dists.) N.Y. 1989. Assoc. Kaye, Scholer, Fierman, Hays & Handler, N.Y.C., 1986-89; ptnr. Anderson Kill Olick & Oshinsky P.C., N.Y.C., 1989—; lectr. Licensing Execs. Soc., 1987, Nat. Innovation Soc., 1988; ann. judge Harlan Fiske Stone moot ct. honors competition Columbia U. Law Sch., Cardozo/BMI Entertainment and Comm. moot ct. competition. Author: Copyright and Patent Protection for Computer Software: Are They Mutually Exclusive?, appendix to Milgrim on Trade Secrets, 1990; contbr. articles to profl. jours. Capt. N.Y. Guard, 1987—. Harlan Fiske Stone scholar Columbia U., 1985; recipient nat. prize Nathan Burkan Copyright Essay Competition, 1985, Order of Merit, Les Amis du Vin, 1982. Mem. ABA (chmn. software patent subcom. 1988-91, chmn. software licensing subcom. 1991—), Am. Israel Pub. Affairs Com., Computer Law Assn., Les Amis du Vin (bd. dirs. 1982—), Am. Intellectual Property Assn. (electronic and computer law com.), N.Y. Patent, Trademark and Copyright Law Assn., U.S. Trademark Assn., D.C. Bar (computer law sect.), Columbia Soc. Law and Tech (pres. 1985-86), Phi Beta Kappa. Jewish. Democrat. Home: 235 W 102d St #16S New York NY 10025 Office: Anderson Kill Olick Oshinsky PC 666 3d Ave New York NY 10017

EINHORN, HAROLD, lawyer, writer; b. N.Y.C., Dec. 17, 1929; s. Abe and Pauline (Miller) E.; m. Jane Ellen, June 16, 1957; children: David, Edward. AB, N.Y. U., 1951, MA, 1957; JD, Columbia U., 1960. Bar: N.Y., 1961. Pat. atty. Exxon Rsch. & Engring. Co., Linden, N.J., 1960-65, sr. pat. atty., 1965-72, pat. csl., 1972-81; gen. tech. atty. Exxon Chem. Co., Linden, N.J., 1982—; v.p. Exxon Chem. Patents Inc., 1989—; lectr. Practicing Law Inst., Am. Mgmt. Assn., World Trade Inst., Franklin Pierce Law Sch., Cen. Inst., Bridgeport U., Seton Hall U., N.J. Inventor's Congress. Bd. trustees Temple B'nai Israel, Elizabeth, N.J., 1980—, pres., 1985-89. Served with CIC, U.S. Army, 1953-55. Mem. ABA (subcom. chmn. 1981, 1985, 86, 89, 91, 92), N.Y. Patent Law Assn. (assoc. editor bull. 1968-76, lectr.), Licensing Execs. Soc. (lectr.), Am. Intellectual Property Law Assn. (lectr.), Rochester Patent Law Assn. (lectr.), Assn. Corp. Patent Counsel. Author: Patent Licensing Transactions, 2 vols., rev. ann., 1970—; contbg. author: Domestic and International Licensing of Technology, 1980, Domestic and Foreign Technology Licensing, 1984, Trends in Biotechnology and Chemical Patent Practice, 1989, Antitrust Law Developments, 1991; contbr. articles to profl. jours. Home: 382 Orenda Cir Westfield NJ 07090-2927

EINSTEIN, THEODORE LEE, physics educator; b. Cleve., Jan. 20, 1947; s. Siegfried and Arlene (Landstein) E.; m. Deborah Hazel Johnson, Jan. 23, 1982; children: David, Nathan. AB summa cum laude, MA, Harvard U., 1969; PhD, U. Pa., 1973. Postdoctoral rsch. assoc. U. Pa., Phila., 1973-74; vis. asst. prof. U. Md., College Park, 1975-77, asst. prof., 1977-80, assoc. prof., 1980-87; vis. prof. U. Padua, Italy, 1987; prof. U. Md., College Park, 1987—; physicist, guest worker Nat. Inst. Standards & Tech., Gaithersburg, Md., 1986—; mem. summer univ. faculty Sandia Nat. Labs., Livermore, Calif., 1988; expert cons. Spensley, Horn, Jubas, Lubitz, L.A., 1988-89; part-time program dir. NSF, Washington, 1989-90. Contbr. numerous articles to profl. jours. Mem. Am. Phys. Soc., Am. Vacuum Soc. (exec. com. div. surface sci. 1983-85), Phys. Electronics Conf. (com. 1990—), Conf. on Phase Transitions on Surfaces (internat. program com. 1981). Home: 13709 Castle Cliff Way Silver Spring MD 20904-5473 Office: U Md Dept Physics College Park MD 20742-4111

EISCH, JOHN JOSEPH, chemist, educator; b. Milw., Nov. 5, 1930; s. Frank Joseph and Gladys (Riordan) E.; m. Joan Terese Scheuerell, Sept. 5, 1953; children: Margaret (dec.), Karla, Paula, Joseph, Amelia. B.S. summa cum laude, Marquette U., 1952; Ph.D. (Procter and Gamble fellow 1955, Union Carbide fellow 1956), Iowa State U., 1956. Postdoctoral fellow Max Planck Inst. für Kohlenforschung, Mülheim, Germany, 1956-57; research assoc. European Research Assocs., Brussels, 1957; faculty St. Louis U., 1957-59, U. Mich., 1959-63, Catholic U. Am., Washington, 1963-72; chmn. dept. chemistry State U. N.Y., Binghamton, 1972-78; prof. State U. N.Y., 1972—, disting. prof., 1983—; cons. to bus., 1957—, Tex. Alkyls, 1985—, Akzo Chem., 1988—. Author: The Chemistry of Organometallic Compounds, 1967, (with R.B. King) Organometallic Syntheses, Vol. I, 1965, Vol. II, 1981, Vol. III, 1986, Vol. IV, 1988. Mem. Am. Chem. Soc., Am. Inst. Chemists, Sigma Xi, Phi Lambda Upsilon, Phi Kappa Phi. Home: RD1 Sheedy Rd Box 387A Vestal NY 13850 Office: SUNY Dept Chemistry Binghamton NY 13901

EISEN, STUART TERRY, retail executive; b. Washington, May 18, 1952; s. Irving A. and Patricia (Lewis) E.; m. Rona Beth Rubin, June 16, 1974; children: Bradley Steven, Tracey Colleen. BS, U. Md., 1975, postgrad. Stocker Boyce & Lewis, Washington, 1965-67, salesman, 1967-68; buyer, mgr. Boyce & Lewis, Bethesda, 1968-72; mgr. Boyce & Lewis of Md., Bethesda, 1973—; owner Boyce & Lewis Inc., Bethesda, 1986—. Contbr. articles to profl. jours. Pres. Mems. Redskin Marching Band, Washington, 1983-84; coord. Jewish Coalition fo Reagan Bush Md., 1984. Mem. Am. Numismatic Soc. (assoc.), Numismatics Internat. (publicity chair 1980—), Amity, Shaare Tefila Men's Club (pres. 1989-91). Republican. Jewish. Office: Boyce & Lewis 10400 Old Georgetown Rd Bethesda MD 20814-1914

EISENBERG, ALAN DAVID, sales professional; b. Hillside, July 28, 1942; s. Max and Sylvia (Gottlieb) E.; m. Marica Ellen Seitel, Aug. 22, 1968; children: Marc Samuel, Gary Philip. Student, Union Coll., Cranford, N.J., 1960-61, 64-65, Rutgers U., 1961-62, 70-71; BA, Am. U., 1968. Writer exec. letters div. Prentice-Hall, Englewood Cliffs, N.J., 1968-70; sales promotion specialist The Prudential Ins. Co., Newark, 1971-79, mgr. audio/video tng. and mktg., 1979—. Board dirs. Franklin Twp. Bicentennial Com., N.J., 1974-75, United Community Corp., Newark, 1974-78, Anshe Emeth Meml. Temple, New Brunswick, N.J., 1991—. With U.S. Army, 1962-64. Recipient Award of Excellence, Life Communicators Assn., Des Moines, 1978, 87, 88, 89. Jewish. Home: 18 Newkirk Rd Somerset NJ 08873-1712 Office: The Prudential Ins Co 213 Washington 10th St Newark NJ 07102-2917

EISENBERG, ANNE MENDEL, educator; b. Richmond, Va., Apr. 22, 1942; d. Julius M. and Hannah (Adelanski) Mendel; 1 child, Julia Eisenberg. BA, Barnard Coll., 1963; MA, U. Iowa, 1965; PhD, NYU, 1978. Instr. N.Y. Tech. Coll., Bklyn., 1974-77, asst. prof., 1977-78; asst. prof. Polytechnic U., Bklyn., 1978-83, assoc. prof., 1983-89, prof., 1989—; cons. Am. Chem. Soc., Washington, 1980—, Merck Pharms., Rahway, N.J., 1984—. Author: Guide to Technical Editing, 1992, Writing Well for the Technical Professions, 1989, Effective Technical Communication, 1982, 2nd edit. 1992, Reading Technical Books, 1978, 2nd edit. 1989; columnist IEEE Spectrum, Technically Speaking; contbr. articles to profl. jours; script writer: (film/video) Technical Writing. Home: 95 Reade St New York NY 10013-3846 Office: Polytechnic U 333 Jay St Brooklyn NY 11201-2990

EISENBERG, BERTRAM WILLIAM, lawyer; b. Phoenix, Feb. 22, 1930; s. Louis and Mary Ethel (Fiddle) E.; m. Carlene Brown, Feb. 28, 1953; children: Stephen W., Lawrence D. AB, Syracuse U., 1948; LLB, Harvard U., 1951. Bar: N.Y. 1951, U.S. Dist. Ct. (so. dist.) N.Y. 1973. Assoc. Harrison & Coughlin, Binghamton, N.Y., 1954-60; ptnr. Appelbaum & Eisenberg, Liberty, N.Y., 1960—. Served as 1st lt. JAGC, 1951-54. Office: Appelbaum & Eisenberg 6 N Main St Liberty NY 12754-1844

EISENBERG, GEORGE HENRY GILBERT, JR., army officer; b. St. Louis, Mar. 4, 1940; s. George Henry Gilbert and Camille Fredericka (Kuhne) E.; m. Nancy Anderson, Aug. 14, 1965; children: Lani Brooke. BS, MIT, 1962; PhD, U. Md., 1971. Commd. U.S. Army, 1965, advanced through grades to lt. col., to present; microbiologist Brooke Army Med. Ctr., Ft. Sam Houston, Tex., 1971-72, Walter Reed Army Inst. of Rsch., Washington, 1972-74; chief microbiology sect. USAMRU-BELEM (Transamazon), Belem, Brazil, 1974; microbiologist Walter Reed Army Inst. Rsch., 1974-78; chief div. cutaneous hazards Letterman Army Inst. Rsch., San Francisco, 1979-82; chief microbiology div. 10th Med. Lab., Landstuhl, Germany, 1984-87; microbiologist U.S. Army Inst. Dental Rsch., Washington, 1987-91, chief microbiology br, 1991—; cons. in field. Contbr. articles to profl. jours. Mem. Assn. U.S. Army, Am. Inst. Biol. Scis., AAAS, Am. Soc. Microbiology, Phi Kappa Phi. Republican. Methodist. Office: US Army Inst Dental Rsch Walter Reed Army Med Ctr Washington DC 20307-5300

EISENBERG, HOWARD EDWARD, physician, psychotherapist, educator, consultant; b. Montreal, Que., Can., Aug. 5, 1946; s. Harold and Elsie (Goldbloom) E.; m. Nancy Roberta Jeffries, Jan. 10, 1976; children: Taryn Noelle, Jory Michael, Meredith Kate, Tessa Chloe. B.Sc. with honors in Psychology, McGill U., 1967, M.Sc., 1971, M.D.C.M., 1972. Intern Sunnybrook Med. Ctr., U. Toronto, 1973; research asst. psychology dept. McGill U., 1966-69, research asst. gerontology unit Alan Meml. Inst. Psychiatry, McGill U., 1968, clin. fellow Clarke Inst. Psychiatry, U. Toronto, 1973; lectr. Centre for Continuing Edn., York U., 1973-78, Sheridan Coll., Oakville, 1974-76; supr. individual directed study Faculty Environ. Studies, York U., 1975; lectr. dept. interdisciplinary studies U. Toronto, 1975; instr. ind. studies program, Innis Coll., U. Toronto, 1975-78, lectr. 1976-81, spl. conf. coordinator, 1977-79, 88-89, lectr. Sch. Continuing Studies, 1977-89; lectr. continuing edn. U. Vt., 1990—; assoc. dir. edn. and growth opportunities program York U., 1975-76, dir. E.G.O. program, 1976-78; lectr. Sch. Adult Edn., McMaster U., 1980-89; instr. profl. and mgmt. devel. Humber Coll., 1982-85; pvt. practice psychotherapy, Toronto, Ont., 1973-91, Stowe, Vt., 1991—; pres. Synectia Cons., Inc., Toronto, 1980-84, Syntrek, Inc., Stowe, Vt., 1989—, Synectia Prodns., Inc., Toronto, 1974—. Author: Inner Spaces, 1977, The Tranquility Experience, 1987, Stress Mastery for the Real World, 1991; contbr. articles to profl. jours. McGill scholar, 1966-67; Quebec scholar, 1967-68; Earle C. Anthony fellow, 1967-68; Ont. Arts Council grantee, 1977. Mem. Can. Med. Assn., Ont. Med. Assn. (former chmn. sect. ind. physicians), Can. Psychiat. Assn., Orgnl. Devel. Network, Assn. for Humanistic Psychology, Vt. State Med. Soc. Address: Syntrek Inc PO Box 1393 Stowe VT 05672

EISENBERG, JOSEPH MARTIN, psychologist; b. Bklyn., June 19, 1944; s. David and Dora (Levine) E.; B.A. in Psychology magna cum laude, C. W. Post Coll., 1966; M.A. in Psychology, U. Alta., 1969, Ph.D. in Psychology, 1971; m. Susan Joan Kahn, Aug. 16, 1980; children: Ian, Lara, Jason, Davida. Psychol. diagnostician, counselor dept. psychology U. Alta. (Can.), 1969-70; field researcher Dept. youth Alta., 1967-69; assoc. dir. Toronto (Ont.) YMCA Centre for Counseling and Human Relations, 1970-71; counselor, cons. York Regional Sch. Nursing, Toronto, 1970-71; chief psychologist Salvation Army House of Concord, Toronto, 1971-72; dir. outpatient service St. Vincent Hosp. Community Mental Health Center, Erie, Pa., 1972-73; dir. Erie County Center for Learning Disabilities, 1973-74; pvt. practice psychology, Erie and Balt., 1972—; v.p. in charge personnel and communications Bridge Energy Corp., Balt., 1981—; pres. Reason House, Balt., 1981—; spl. cons. Md. Children and Family Services, Inc.; mem. profl. adv. bds. Balt. Assn. Children with Learning Disabilities, Feingold Assn.; cons. Mormac Ltd., 1979—; forensic cons. Howard County/Balt. County/Carroll County, Office of Public Defenders and Balt. City Solicitor's Office, 1977—. Chmn., Carroll County Child Abuse Consultation Com., 1978-80; dir. Psychol. Services for the Metabolic Nutrition Program, 1986-89; mem. profl. adv. bd. Catonsville Group Home, 1980-81. Recipient Richard P. Runyon award, 1966; cert., lic., Md.; cert. clin. hypnotherapist, Negotiation Inst. Mem. Am. Psychol. Assn., Md. Psychol. Assn., Assn. Advancement of Psychology, Balt. Psychol. Assn., Am. Bd. Profl. Disability Cons., Balt. County C. of C. (exec. dialogue program), Psi Chi, Phi Theta. Co-author computer software; contbr. articles to profl. jours. Office: Penthouse 204 E Joppa Rd Ph 10 Baltimore MD 21204-3145

EISENBERG, LEE B., publishing executive; b. Phila., July 22, 1946; s. George M. and Eve (Blonsky) E.; m. Linda Reville, June 7, 1986; children: Edmund George, Katherine Eve. AB, U. Pa., 1968; MA, Annenberg Sch. Communications, 1970. Assoc. editor Esquire Mag., N.Y.C., 1970-72, sr. editor, 1972-74, mng. editor, 1974-75, editor, 1976-77, 84-87, v.p. devel., 1980-84, editor-in-chief, 1987-90; founding editor-in-chief Esquire, U.K., London, 1990-91; mem. core team The Edison Project, Knoxville, Tenn., 1992—; cons. N.Y. Times Co., 1977-78, Warner Bros., Los Angeles, 1978-79; founder Eisenberg, McCall & Okrent, N.Y.C., 1978-81. Author: Sneaky Feats, 1974, Atlantic City, 1978, Ultimate Fishing Book, 1981. Founder Rotisserie League Baseball, N.Y.C., 1980—. Recipient One Show award Art Dirs. Club, 1976, Gold Cindy award Assn. Visual Communications, 1984. Mem. Am. Soc. Mag. Editors. Office: care The Edison Project 333 Main St Knoxville TN 37902

EISENBERG, MURRAY, mathematics educator; b. Phila., May 23, 1939; s. Samuel William and Bluma (Levin) E.; m. Phyllis Paula Fine, June 11, 1961; children: Jon Kenneth, Michael Edward. AB, U. Pa., Phila., 1960; MA, U. Pa., 1962; PhD, Wesleyan U., 1965. Asst. prof. to prof. math. U. Mass., Amherst, 1965—. Author: Axiomatic Theory of Sets and Classes, 1970, Topology, 1974; contbr. articles to profl. jours. NSF grantee, 1981-84. Mem. Am. Math. Soc., Math. Assn. Am., Assn. for Computing Machinery (apl spl. interest group), Sigma Xi, Phi Beta Kappa. Office: U Mass Dept Math & Statis LGRT Amherst MA 01003

EISENBERG, R. NEAL, restoration company executive; b. Newark, July 15, 1936; s. William C. and Elsie G. (Greenfield) E.; m. Barbara J. Mayer, Dec. 18, 1966; children: Michael S., Elissa P. Student, Stevens Inst. of Tech., 1954-55; postgrad., N.Y.U. Coll. of Engring., 1955-57; BS in Acctg., NYU, 1960. Sr. acct. Puder & Puder (now Deloitte Touche), Newark, 1958-60, J.H. Cohn & Co., Roseland, N.J., 1960-63; ptnr. Universal Engring. and Waterproofing Svc., Newark, 1963-69; pres. Universal Restoration and Waterproofing Svc., Inc., Cranford, N.J., 1970—; v.p. Universal Restoration, Inc., Washington, 1967-69, pres., chief exec. officer, 1991—; v.p. Restoration Svcs., Inc., Washington, 1967-69; pres. Vitrifix of N.Am., Inc., Washington, 1986-87, Universal Waterproofing Svc. Inc., Cranford, N.J., 1969—; chmn. Universal Family Group, Cranford, N.J., 1987—; cons. and expert in structural restoration. Co-inventor Dekosit/Permo-Bond Restoration Method. Recipient Second Biennial Design award Gen. Svcs. Administrn., 1967. Mem. Constrn. Specifications Inst., Nat. Assn. Waterproofing Contractors, Nat. Trust Hist. Preservation, N.J. Bus. and Industry Assn., Masons. Office: Universal Waterproofing Svc 70 Jackson Dr Cranford NJ 07016-3510

EISENBERGER, MARIO ALFREDO, medical oncology educator, physician; b. Rio de Janeiro, Mar. 16, 1949; came to U.S., 1973; s. Fritz Herbert and Anneliese (Lewin) E.; m. Johanna Jacomina Magdalena Hazenoot, Dec. 18, 1976. BS, Brazil-Am. Coll., 1966; MD, Fed. U. Rio de Janeiro, 1972. Diplomate Am. Bd. Internal Medicine, Am. Bd. Med. Oncology. Intern in medicine Michael Reese Hosp., Chgo., 1973-74, resident, 1974-75, fellow in hematology, 1975-76; fellow in oncology U. Miami (Fla.), 1976-78, asst. prof. hematology and oncology, 1980-82; pvt. practice Lauderdale Lakes, Fla., 1978-80; sr. investigator Nat. Cancer Inst., NIH, Bethesda, Md., 1982-84; asst. prof. medicine and oncology U. Md. Cancer Ctr., Balt., 1984-88, assoc. prof., 1988—; chief oncology sect. Balt. VA Hosp., 1984-87; participant nat. and internat. meetings; lectr. and researcher in field. Contbr. articles and abstracts to med. jours., chpts. to books. Mem. Am. Soc. Clin. Oncology (several grants/contracts), Am. Fedn. Clin. Rsch., S.W. Oncology Group (chairperson advanced prostate cancer com. 1988—, vice-chmn. genito-urinary com. 1990—). Jewish. Home: 4407 Bedford Pl Baltimore MD 21218-1002 Office: U Md Cancer Ctr 22 S Greene St Baltimore MD 21201-1544

EISENBUD, DAVID, mathematics educator; b. N.Y.C., Apr. 8, 1947; s. Leonard and Ruth-Jean (Rubinstein) E.; m. Monika Margarte Schwabe, June 3, 1970; children: Daniel, Alina. BS, U. Chgo., 1966, MS, 1967, PhD, 1970. Lectr. Brandeis U., Waltham, Mass., 1970-72, asst. prof., 1972-76, assoc. prof., 1976-80, prof., 1980—, chmn. dept. of math., 1982-84; vis. prof. U. Bonn, Fed. Republic of Germany, 1979-80, MSRI, Berkeley, 1986-87, Harvard U., 1987-88; mem. adv. panel in maths. NSF, 1978-81; mem. vis. com. Brigham Young U., 1989. Editor; Proceedings of Am. Math. Soc., 1978-82, Asterisque, 1983-88, (book series) Wadsworth Advanced, 1985—; contbr. numerous articles to profl. jours. Alfred P. Sloan Found. fellow, 1973-75; NSF grantee, 1970—. Mem. Am. Math. Soc. (coun.). Office: Brandeis U Dept Math South St Brighton MA 02135-5108

EISENSTADT, RAYMOND, mechanical engineer, educator; b. Bklyn., May 13, 1921; s. Morris and Bertha (Chaiken) E.; m. Beverly Stein; children: Neil J., Janice A. Cove, Lowell P., Marcy R. Freeman. B in Mech. Engring., CCNY, 1941; MS in Mech. Engring., Columbia U., 1943, PhD, 1953. Asst. prof. engring. mechanics Lehigh U., 1953-54; prof. mech. engring. Schenectady (N.Y.) Coll., 1954—; cons. Gen. Electric Co., Schenectady, Watervliet Arsenal, Troy, N.Y., 1981—, Am. Locomotive Co., Schenectady, 1941—, Wright Aircraft, Patterson, N.J., 1942, Corbett-Tinghir Cons. Engrs., N.Y.C., 1946-49, P.M. Gussow, Cons. Engr., N.Y.C., 1946-49, U.S. War Dept., 1946-49. William Petit Trowbridge fellow, 1950-52, NSF fellow, 1960-61; grantee Gen. Electric Co., NASA, ASTM. Mem. ASME, Am. Soc. Engring. Edn., ASM, Soc. for Experimental Stress Analysis, ASTM (com. on crack growth and fatigue), Welding Rsch. Coun. (plastic fatigue strength subcom., elevated temperature design pressure vessel rsch. com.), Sigma Xi. Office: Union Coll Dept Mech Engring Schenectady NY 12308

EISENSTEIN, THEODORE DONALD, pediatrician; b. N.Y.C., July 4, 1930; s. Harry and Myra (Drexler) E.; m. Ellen Roob, Dec. 9, 1956; children: Janet, Stephen. Student, NYU, 1948-49; A.B., Johns Hopkins U., 1952; M.D., Albany Med. Coll., 1956. Diplomate Am. Bd. Pediatrics. Pediatric intern Kings County Med. Ctr., Bklyn., 1956-57; resident in pediatrics N.Y. Hosp., N.Y.C., 1957-59; NIH vis. fellow in pediatric endocrinology Columbia-Presbyn. Med. Ctr., N.Y.C., 1961-62; practice medicine specializing in pediatrics West Caldwell, N.J., 1962—; full attending staff St. Barnabas Med. Ctr.; v.p. Pediatric Assos. West Essex, P.A.; asst. clin. prof. pediatrics Columbia U. Coll. Phys. and Surg., 1970—; clin. asst. prof. pediatrics N.J. Coll. Medicine and Dentistry, Rutgers U., 1970—. Research on pediatric endocrinology, human growth hormone. Mem. alumni coun. N.Y. Hosp.-Cornell Med. Ctr. Served with M.C., USAF, 1959-61. Fellow Am. Acad. Pediatrics; mem. AMA, Acad. Medicine N.J., Am. Diabetes Assn., AAAS, Soc. Practitioners Columbia-Presbyn. Med. Ctr., Albany Med. Coll. Alumni Assn., Am. Physicians Fellowship, N.J. Med. Sch. Faculty Orgn. Jewish. Home: 7 Byron Rd Caldwell NJ 07006-4203 Office: 700 Passaic Ave W Caldwell NJ 07006

EISERER, LEONARD ALBERT CARL, publishing executive; b. Polar, Wis., June 3, 1916; s. Herman Frederick and Anna Elizabeth (Schnieder) E.; m. Lorraine Elizabeth Hickey, June 28, 1941; children: Carol Jean, Elaine Roberta, Leonard Arnold, Beverly Arlene. B.A., Roosevelt U., Chgo., 1937; M.S. in Journalism, Northwestern U., 1939. Editor Am. Aviation Publs., Inc., Washington, 1939-51, v.p., gen. mgr., 1952-57, exec. v.p., sec., 1958-62; pres., pub. Sports Age, Inc., Washington, 1962-63; chmn., pres., pub. Bus. Pubs., Inc., Silver Spring, Md., 1963—. Chmn. Carol Jean Cancer Found., Inc.; bd. dirs. U. N.C. at Greensboro Excellence Found.; dir. Eiserer-Hickey Found., Inc. Served to lt. USN, 1942-46. Mem. Air and Waste Mgmt. Assn., Water Pollution Control Fedn., Soc. Profl. Journalists, Newsletter Pubs. Assn., Nat. Press Club, Univ. Club. Home: 9101 Sligo Creek Pky Silver Spring MD 20901-3360 Office: Bus Pubs Inc 951 Pershing Dr Silver Spring MD 20910-4432

EISINGER, ROBERT PETER, nephrologist, educator; b. N.Y.C., Oct. 29, 1929; s. Jacob Samuel and Rose (Sapir) E.; m. Miriam Blumberg, Sept. 4,

1956; children: Ari, Dina. AB, Swarthmore Coll., 1951; MD, Columbia U., 1955. Diplomate Am. Bd. Internal Medicine, Am. Bd. Nephrology. From instr. to assoc. prof. NYU Sch. Medicine, N.Y.C., 1963-73; prof. medicine, chief nephrology U. Medicine & Dentistry N.J., Robert Wood Johnson Med. Sch., New Brunswick, 1973—. Capt. USAF, 1959-61. Office: U Medicine & Dentistry NJ Robert Wood Johnson Med Sch 1 RW Johnson Pl CN-19 New Brunswick NJ 08903

EISLER, RONALD, biologist; b. N.Y.C., Feb. 23, 1932; s. Harry A. and Ann (Brand) E.; m. Jeannette Lustig, Aug. 29, 1963; children: David, Charles. BA, NYU, 1952; MS, U. Wash., 1957, PhD, 1961. Radiochemist U. Wash. Lab. Radiation Ecology, Seattle, 1958-61; fishery rsch. biologist U.S. Fish and Wildlife Svc., Highlands, N.J., 1961-66; bioscience advisor U.S. Fish and Wildlife Svc., Washington, 1979-84; sr. rsch. biologist U.S. Fish and Wildlife Svc., Laurel, Md., 1984—; rsch. aquatic toxicologist U.S. EPA, Narragansett, R.I., 1966-79; adj. prof. George Mason U., 1989—, Am. Univ., 1980-89, U. R.I., 1970-79; vis. prof. Hebrew U. of Jerusalem, 1972-73. Editorial advisor Marine Ecology Progress series, 1980—; assoc. editor: Transactions of the American Fisheries Soc., 1973-77; author: Trace Metal Concentrations in Marine Organisms, 1981; contbr. articles to profl. jours., chpts. to books in field. Cpl. AMEDS, 1953-55. Office: US Fish and Wildlife Svc Patuxent Wildlife Rsch Ctr Laurel MD 20708

EISMAN, WAYNE BROOK, otolaryngologist; b. Springfield, Mass., Apr. 12, 1948; s. Sidney and Evelyn Pearl (Berger) E.; m. Susan Ellen Jaffe, May 22, 1977; children: Matthew, Jesse, Evan. BA, U. Mass., 1971; MD, Baylor U., 1975. Intern NYU, 1976-77; resident in otolaryngology Mt. Sinai Sch. Medicine, N.Y.C., 1977-80; pvt. practice Westchester Otolaryngology, White Plains, N.Y., 1983—; chmn. dept. otolaryngology White Plains Hosp., 1992—. Trustee, treas. Windlard Sch., White Plains, 1987—. Mem. N.Y. State Med. Soc., Westchester County Med. Soc. (chmn. div. otolaryngology 1991—). Office: 28 Popham Rd Scarsdale NY 10583

EISNER, ALAN S., newspaper editor; b. Boston, May 12, 1948; s. Robert Harold and Margaret Ruth (Levangie) E.; m. Arlene Etta Fox, June 22, 1975; 1 child, Morgan. BA, U. Mass., 1971; MEd, Suffolk U. Editorial asst. Boston Herald, 1973, reporter, 1974-81, asst. city editor, 1981-82, city editor, 1982-83, exec. city editor, 1983, dep. mng. editor, 1983-84, mng. editor, 1984—. Dir. New Eng. Holocaust Meml. Com. 1988—. Office: Boston Herald 1 Herald Sq Boston MA 02106-2096

EISNER, ALFRED, career officer; b. Teplice Shanov, Czechoslovakia, Apr. 5, 1932; came to U.S., 1949.; s. Joseph and Maria (Lederer) E.; m. Toshiko Yorita Eisner, Aug. 4, 1958; children: Robert Hiroshi Eisner, Diana Akemi Eisner. AA in Criminal Justice/Law Enforcement, Montgomery Coll., 1986. With U.S. Army Worldwide Svc. retired, 1951-79; career fevel. officer Bendix-Syianco Corp., Riyadh, Saudi Arabia, 1980; adminstrv. officer Saudi Arabia Nat. Guard Modernization Program, Riyadh, 1981-84; military personnel officer U.S. Army, 1985-89; adminstrv. officer Military Dist. of Washington, 1989—; adjutant minuteman Md. State Guard, Pikesville, 1986—; chaplain VFW, 1985-87. Capt. Md. State Guard, 1986—. Decorated Bronze Star Medal, Meritorious Svc. Medal, Army Commendation Medal, Commanders Award Medal, U.S. Army, 1968-88, Md. State Commendation, Md. Nat. Guard, Pikesville, 1990; recipient Army Achievement award Dept. of Army, 1991. Fellow mem. Assn. of U.S. Army. Republican. Methodist. Home: 12609 Farnell Dr Wheaton MD 20906-3873 Office: Office of Deputy Chief of Staff for Resource Mgmt Fort McNair Washington DC 20319-5050

EISNER, CAROLE SWID, artist; b. N.Y.C., Oct. 30, 1937; d. David and Selma (Claar) Swid; m. Richard Alan Eisner, May 7, 1961; children: Joseph, Susan, Michael, Douglas, Hallie. AB, Syracuse U., 1958; studies with Schwabacher, N.Y.C., 1963; studies with Marge Walzer, Westport, Conn., 1969-78; postgrad., Internat. Sch. Photography, 1976-78. Solo shows include Silvermine (Conn.) Ctr. for Arts, 1977, 84, Lubin House Gallery, N.Y.C., 1979, 82, Segal Gallery, N.Y.C., 1984-85, 86, Jill Youngblood Gallery, L.A., 1985, Jack Gallery, N.Y.C., 1987, 88, First Women's Bank, N.Y.C., 1988, New Inst. of Contemporary Art, London, 1988, David Findlay Galleries, N.Y.C., 1990; group shows include SEgal Gallery, N.Y.C., 1985, 86, Guggenheim Mus., N.Y.C., 1986, Images Gallery, Norwalk, Conn., 1986, Jack Gallery, N.Y.C., 1987, Inst. of Contemporary Art, London, 1988, Gallery Sagau, Tokyo, 1992, Gallery Paniahisa, Tokyo, 1992, many others; represented in permanent collections at Guggenheim Mus., Syracuse U., Nat. Assocs., Inc., S.E. Banking Corp., Northstar Reinsurance Co., Knoll Internat., FMC Corp., Skadden, Arps, Meager & Flom, Orion Bank, Ltd., Goldmark Ptnrs., Inc., MBS Multi Mode, Inc., Bill Silver Assocs.; created stage design for four Off-Broadway plays at Theater XII, 1978. Recipient Award for Sculpture Merchants Bank and Trust Co., 1975, Champion Internat. Corp., 1980, Rosenthal Award for Outdoor Sculpture, 1978; named among ten outstanding young women Mademoiselle Mag., 1962; finalist Nat. Sculpture Competition, 1980. Home and Office: 1107 5th Ave New York NY 10128-0145

EISNER, HOWARD, engineering educator; b. N.Y.C., Aug. 8, 1935; s. Samuel Eisner and Mary (Isser) Wegodner; m. Joan Arlene Knopfer, Feb. 9, 1957; children: Seth Eric, Susan Rachel, Oren David. BEE, CCNY, 1957; MS, Columbia U., 1958; DSc, George Washington U., 1966. Teaching asst. Columbia U., 1957; lectr. dept. physics Bklyn. Coll., 1957-59; lectr., asst. professorial lectr. George Washington U., 1961-67; prof. U. Maryland, 1987-89; various engring. positions ORI, Inc., Rockville, Md., 1959-68, v.p., 1968-71, exec. v.p., 1971-84, corp. exec. v.p., 1984-85, also dir.; pres. Intercon Systems Corp. subs. ORI, Group, Inc., Rockville, 1985-89, Atlantic Research Services Corp., Alexandria, Va., 1987-89; Disting. rsch. prof. George Washington U., Washington, 1989—. Author: Advanced Algebra, 1960, Computer-Aided Systems Engineering, 1988; contbr. articles in field. Fellow IEEE, N.Y. Acad. Scis.; mem. AIAA, Ops. Rsch. Soc. Am., Inst. Mgmt. Sci., Sigma Xi, Tau Beta Pi, Eta Kappa Nu, Omega Rho. Office: George Washington U Gelman Libr Washington DC 20052

EISNER, JOSEPH, librarian; b. N.Y.C., May 14, 1929; s. Harry R. and Clara (Holzer) E.; B.A. cum laude, Syracuse (N.Y.) U., 1950, postgrad., 1950-51; M.S. in Library Sci., Columbia U., 1954; m. Naomi Leff, May 6, 1951; children—Carol, Barry, Andrew. Dir. Plainview-Old Bethpage (N.Y.) Public Library, 1955-68, Assn. N.Y. Libraries Tech. Services, 1968-72, Plainedge (N.Y.) Public Library, 1972—; del. Gov. N.Y. Conf. Libraries, 1965, 78; mem. Commr. of Edn.'s Com. Library Devel., 1968-71; exec. bd. Nassau Library System, 1975-80, chmn., 1976-77, mem. budget and services com., 1983-86, fin. com., 1992—; adj. prof. C.W. Post Coll. Library Sch., 1968—; lectr. Rutgers U., 1985-88; cons. in field. Bd. dirs. Plainedge Community Blood Bank, 1973—, Camp Apollo, Plainview, N.Y., 1969—, Vis. Nurses Assn. Oyster Bay and Glen Cove, 1977—, Diocese Rockville Center Ednl. TV Council, 1979-82, Youth Environ. Services, Massapequa, N.Y., 1977-91, Vis. Nurse Assn. L.I., 1984—; mem. Town of Oyster Bay Adv. Com. Arts, 1976-87, chmn., 1976-81; mem. Nassau County Cultural Devel. Bd., 1980—; mem. adv. com. Nassau County Coop. Extension Assn. Home Econs., 1980-91; mem. quality assurance com. Massapequa Gen. Hosp., 1988—; coord. Nassau County chpt. Medicare-Medicaid Assistance Program Am. Assn. Retired Persons, 1988—; trustee Plainview Old Bethpage Public Library, 1981—, chmn., 1988-91. Served to lt. (j.g.) USNR, 1951-52. Life mem. N.Y. State PTA. Mem. N.Y. Library Assn. (chmn. legis. com. 1964-69, 70-71), N.Y. State Library Trustees Found. (sec. 1961-66), Nassau County Library Assn. (pres. 1959-61). Author, editor in field. Home: 54 Nassau Ave Plainview NY 11803-3538 Office: 1060 Hicksville Rd Massapequa NY 11758

EITEL, ERIC VAUGHN, academic administrator; b. Miami, Fla., Apr. 6, 1964; s. Douglas Ray and Raquel (Moczo) E. BA in English Lit., Siena Coll., 1987. Mktg. assoc. Lake George (N.Y.) Opera Festival, summer 1987; dir. devel. Northeastern Assn. of the Blind, Albany, N.Y., 1987-89; dir. found. and corp. support Phillips Acad., Andover, Mass., 1989—. Home and Office: Phillips Acad Andover MA 01810

EIZENBERG, MICHAEL, educational society executive; b. Brockton, Mass., June 21, 1947; s. David Joseph and Lisa (Egler) E.; m. Suzanne Murcia, June 13, 1970; 1 child, Leda. BA, Clark U., 1969; MA, Tufts U., 1972. Assoc. dir. Am. Leadership Study Groups, Worcester, Mass., 1970-78; pres., co-founder Am. Coun. for Internat. Studies, Boston, 1978—. Dir. AIFS, Inc., San Francisco, 1987—, Coun. for Standards Internat. Ednl. Travel, Washington, 1988-90; trustee Richmond Coll., London, 1987—. Office: ACIS 19 Bay State Rd Boston MA 02181

EK, BRIAN ROY, computer software retail executive; b. Brockton, Mass., Oct. 11, 1952; s. Roy R. and Pearl L. (Olson) E.; m. Lyle J. Cervenka, Sept. 6, 1976; children: Robert, Jessica. BA in English, Upsala Coll., 1974; MA in Journalism, Pa. State U., 1976. Reporter, night editor Gannett Pub. Co., Bridgewater, N.J., 1976-79; communicatins specialist BorgWarner, Parsippany, N.J., 1979-85; mgr. communicatins Prodigy subs. IBM/Sears, White Plains, N.Y., 1985—; cons., writer Electro-Nucleonics Inc., Fairfield, N.J., 1981-84. Mem. N.Am. Ski Writers, Eastern Ski Writers. Home: 5 Pine St Brookfield CT 06804-2314 Office: Prodigy Svcs Co 445 Hamilton Ave White Plains NY 10601-1814

EKELAND, BRIAN J., computer company executive; b. College Park, Md., Oct. 9, 1959; s. William Conrad and Marion Gertrude (Myers) E. BS, U. Md., 1981, MA in MIS, 1992. Account rep. IBM, Greenbelt, Md., 1982-83; distbn. specialist IBM, Washington, 1983-85; sr. adminstrv. specialist IBM, Bethesda, Md., 1985-86, account adminstr., 1986-89, account rep., 1989—. Fundraiser Seva Found., Alexandria, Va., 1987-88, Hunger Project, Alexandria, 1986; tutor D.C. Pub. Schs., 1984.

EKONG, ETIM SAMUEL, mechanical and industrial engineer, consultant; b. Calabar, Nigeria, Nov. 11, 1953; s. Johah Udoh and Eyeyen Gloria (Ukpabio) E.; 1 adopted child, Marion Atim. BSMechE, U. Washington, 1980; MS in Indusl. Engring., Ga. Inst. of Tech., 1983. Registered profl. engr., N.Y. Indsl. engr. Genuine Hardware Corp., Atlanta, 1983-84; systems engr. EDS/Gen. Motors Corp., Troy, Mich., 1984-86; mfg. engr. Unisys Corp., Great Neck, N.Y., 1986—; cons. Z-Mar Industries, Hempstead, N.Y.; pres. Simba Investment Club of N.Y., N.Y.C. Author: thesis, Agr. Modesl, 1984; tech. papers, Design For Automation, 1987 (SAE Trans. award 1988), Automation 1982 (SAE Prod. award 1982), Systems Integration, 1987 (IPC Prod. award 1987), Ekong, S.E., In Total Control of the Factory Floor: A Systems Approach, 1990, Pacific Conference on Mfg, 1990. Big Brother vol. Big Brother/Big Sister of USA, N.Y., 1987-89; orgn. Democratic Party of N.Y., 1988-89. Named MVP USA Soccer Fedn., Chgo., 1982, session chmn. Cars & Fact of Future, Detroit, 1988; recipient Gov.'s Vol. Svc. award N.Y. State. Mem. Inst. Indsl. Engrs. (sr.), Engring. Soc. Detroit, Soc. Mfg. Engrs. (com. chmn. 1985-86), Toastmasters Internat., Simba F.C. (Seattle; mgr. 1978-81). Home: 100 Washington St Apt 3T Hempstead NY 11550-3102

EL-ACHKAR, ISSAM, mathematics educator; b. Halba, Lebanon, Apr. 6, 1962; came to U.S. 1981; s. Wadih and Souad (Sabbagh) El-A. BS, N.Y. Inst. Tech., 1985; MS in Applied Stats., Poly. U. Bklyn., 1988, MS in System Engring., 1989, PhD in Stats., 1990. Teaching fellow Poly. U., Bklyn., 1986-89, instr. math., 1989-91; asst. prof. math. New Jersey City State Coll., 1991—. Office: Poly U Dept Math 333 Jay St Brooklyn NY 11201-2990

ELAM, LESLIE ALBERT, association executive; b. Balt., May 12, 1938; s. Albert and Mary (Walker) E.; m. Judith Anne Clark, Apr. 4, 1964; children—Jennifer Helen, Jeffrey Walker. B.A., Lehman Coll., City U. N.Y., 1973. Editor J.J. Augustin, Inc. Pub., Locust Valley, N.Y., 1958-61; editorial asst. Am. Numis. Soc., N.Y.C., 1963-66; editor Am. Numis. Soc., 1966-89, adminstrv. officer, 1966-69, sec., 1969—, dir., 1972—. Editor: Am. Numis. Soc. Museum Notes, 1966-89. Served with AUS 1961-63. Mem. Phi Beta Kappa. Home: Old Post Rd Rte 35 South Salem NY 10590 Office: Broadway at 155th St New York NY 10032

ELBLING, IRVING NELSON, chemist; b. Salem, Mass., July 30, 1920; s. Alexander and Ida Belle (Shushelsky) E.; m. Gloria Raffle, June 30, 1946; children: Julian Alan, Howard Burton. BS in Chemistry, Northeastern U., Boston, 1943. Engr. plastics sect. dept. chemistry Westinghouse R&D, Pitts., 1943-52, group leader insulation dept., 1952-61, mgr. splty. coatings, 1961-78, ops. mgr. chem. scis. div., 1978-85. Patentee in field. Mem. Soc. for Paint Tech. (Roon award 1959), B'nai B'rith (dist. pres. 1970-71). Jewish. Home: 1437 Severn St Pittsburgh PA 15217-1303

ELBOW, PETER, educator, writer; b. Apr. 14, 1935; m. Caroline Campbell Pelz; 2 children. BA in English Lit., Williams Coll., 1957; BA, Oxford U., 1959, MA, 1964; PhD, Brandeis U., 1970. Instr. lit. sect. MIT, 1960-63, asst. prof. lit. sect., 1968-72; faculty, chmn. interdisciplinary core curriculum Franconia (N.H.) Coll., 1963-65, assoc. dean of faculty, 1964-65; faculty Evergreen State Coll., Olympia, Wash., 1972-81; Kent postdoctoral fellow Wesleyan U., Middletown, Conn., 1981-82; prof. English, dir. writing project SUNY, Stony Brook, 1982-86; prof. English U. Mass., Amherst, 1986—. Author: Writing Without Teachers, 1973, Oppositions in Chaucer, 1975, (with others) On Competence: A Critical Analysis of Competence-Based Reforms in Higher Education, 1979, Writing with Power: Techniques for Mastering the Writing Process, 1981, Embracing Contraries: Explorations in Learning and Teaching, 1986, (with P. Belanoff) A Community of Writers: A Workshop Course in Writing, 1989, Sharing and Responding, 1989, What Is English?, 1991; contbr. articles to profl. jours. Moody fellowship, Exeter Coll., Oxford, 1957, Woodrow Wilson Hon. fellowship, 1957, Danforth fellowship, 1957, Old Dominion fellowship MIT, 1971. Mem. MLA. Home: 47 Pokeberry Rdg Amherst MA 01002-1514 Office: U Mass English Dept Amherst MA 01003

ELDEIRY, BAHIG RIAD P.E., mechanical engineer; b. Cairo, Jan. 23, 1944; came to U.S., 1978; s. Maurice Riad and Rawhia Iskander (Abou El Saad) E.; m. Magda William Elkholy, July 14, 1970; children: Maged, Laura. BSME, Cairo U., 1968; MSME, SUNY, Stony Brook, 1983. Registered profl. engr., N.Y. Mech. engr. Egyptian Army Forces, 1960-70; prin. engr. SNS Ennaba, Algeirs, Algeria, 1970-77; chief engr. Aliep Alger, Algeirs, 1977-78; design engr. Wiebel Tool Co., Port Jefferson, N.Y., 1979-84; computer aided design mgr., sr. hydraulic design engr. Arkwin Industries, Westbury, N.Y., 1984-89; pres. Ho. of Engrs. P.C., 1989—. Office: House of Engrs PC 506 Old Post Rd Port Jefferson NY 11777

ELDER, MARK PHILIP, conductor; b. Hexham, Eng., June 2, 1947; s. John and Helen E.; m. Amanda Jane Stein, 1980; 1 child, Katherine Olivia. BA with honors, Cambridge U., MA; hon. degree, Royal Acad. Music, 1984. Music staff Wexford Festival, 1969-70; chorus master and asst. condr. Glyndebourne, 1970-71; music staff Covent Garden, Royal Opera House, London, 1970-72; staff condr. Australian Opera, 1972-74; staff condr. English Nat. Opera, London, 1974-77, assoc. condr., 1977-79, music dir., 1979—; music dir. Rochester (N.Y.) Philhar. Orch.; prin. guest condr. BBC Symphony Orch., London, 1982-85, London Mozart Players, 1980-83; music dir. Rochester Philharm., 1989. Comdr. Brit. Empire. Address: Rochester Philharm Orch Inc 108 East Ave Rochester NY 14604

ELDON, ETHAN CAWTHORNE, environmental company executive; b. N.Y.C., Oct. 7, 1938; s. Rene Cawthorne and Natalie (Norris) E.; div.; children: Kim, Michele, Douglas; m. Carol Hattie Plaquet, May 12, 1977; children: William Towers Jr., Laura. BA, SUNY, 1976. Exec. asst. Office of U.S. Congressman J. H. Schever, Washington, N.Y.C., 1968-70; dir. Office of Corp. Hdqrs., City of N.Y., 1970-73; commr. N.Y.C. Dept. Air Resources, 1974-77; chief exec. officer, pres. Eldon Environ. Mgmt. Corp., Westbury, N.Y., 1977—; chmn. bd. N.Y. State Facilities Devel. Corp., Albany, 1984-88; adj. faculty Grad. Sch. Pub. Adminstrn. NYU, 1976-78. Contbr. articles to N.Y. Times, Newsday, others. Bd. dirs. Daytop Found., Inc., N.Y.C. Recipient cert. commendation Planning Coun. N.Y. Westchester and L.I., 1975, Meritorious Svc. award N.Y. EPA, N.Y.C., 1976, Lung Assn., N.Y.C., 1977. Mem. Air and Waste Mgmt. Assn., Assn. Environ. Profls. (pres. 1973, 78), Assn. Local Air Pollution Control Officers (v.p. 1975-77). Episcopalian. Home: 289 Vineyard Rd Huntington NY 11743-1258 Office: Eldon Environ Mgmt Corp 900 Ellison Ave Westbury NY 11590-5114

ELDRIDGE, RICHARD CLEMENT, vintager, educator; b. Balt., Jan. 22, 1937; s. Arthur Clement and Bertha Jean (Klitch) E.; m. Valerie De Bourmont, Aug. 29, 1964; children: Robert, Cecile. BA, Harvard U., 1959; MD, PhD, New Sch., 1979. Owner, founder Brimstone Hill Vineyard, Pine Bush, N.Y., 1979—. Mem. Hudson River Region Wine Coun. (pres. 1990-92). Office: Brimstone Hill Vineyard 51 Brimstone Hill Rd Pine Bush NY 12566

EL-EID, GHASSAN EZZAT, political science educator, researcher; b. Ain Zhalta, Lebanon, May 17, 1952; came to U.S., 1976; s. Ezzat Salim and Anissah (Halaby) El-Eid; m. Ahlam Jurdi, Aug. 19, 1979; children: Baha, Jason, Natalie, Nadene. BA, Am. Univ. of Beirut, 1978, U. Nebr., 1979; MA, U. Nebr., 1981, PhD, 1988. Rsch. asst. U. Nebr., Lincoln, 1983-84; instr. Creighton U., Omaha, Nebr., 1984-85; asst. prof. Westminster Coll., Fulton, Mo., 1986-87, Kearney (Nebr.) State Coll., 1987-88; vis. prof. Butler U., Indpls., 1988-89; asst. prof. Cen. Conn. State U., New Britain, Conn., 1989—; cons. Am.-Arab Anti-discrimination Com., Meriden, Conn., 1990—. Pres. Am. Druze Soc., N.Y.C., 1990—. Recipient rsch. grant. AAUP, 1990. Mem. Am. Polit. Sci. Assn., Internat. Studies Assn., Third World Studies Assn., Am. Coun. for Studies of Islamic Societies, Middle East Inst. Office: Cen Conn State U 1615 Stanley St New Britain CT 06053-2439

ELEON, PATRICIA ANASTASIA, human geneticist, educator; b. Port Maria, Jamaica, W.I., July 13, 1944; came to U.S., 1976, naturalized citizen, 1991; d. Leonard Percival and Louise Monica (Green) Martin; m. Winston Emanuel DeLeon, Dec. 16, 1971; children: Ruth, Jeffrey. BSc, U. W.I., Kingston, 1967, MSc in Med. Genetics, 1969; PhD in Microscopic Anatomy, U. Western Ont., 1972. Postdoctoral fellow McGill U., Montreal, Que., Can., 1972-75, sessional lectr., 1975-76; asst. prof. sch. life scis. U. Del., 1976-81; assoc. prof. biology dept., U. Del., Newark, 1981-91, prof., 1991—; vis. scientist Sch. Medicine, Johns Hopkins U., Balt., 1983-84; vis. scientist, speaker Franklin Inst., Phila., 1990—; mem. Recombinant DNA Adv. Com. NIH, 1992—. Contbr. chpts. to books, articles to sci. jours. Bd. dirs. local chpt. March of Dimes. Jamaica Tchrs. scholar, 1964-67; NIH rsch. grantee, 1980-88. Mem. Am. Soc. Human Genetics, Del. Tchrs. Sci., Sigma Xi (sec. Del. chpt. 1981-82, v.p. 1982-83, 85). Presbyterian. Avocations: cooking, gardening, theatre. Office: U Del Sch Life and Health Scis Newark DE 19716

ELEY, THOMAS WENDELL, media executive; b. Washington, Mar. 6, 1953; s. Lynn W. Eley and Elizabeth (Hill) Youngblood; m. Katharine Haskell, Aug. 11, 1973 (div. 1983); m. Susan Margaret Davis, June 7, 1985. Student, Amherst Coll., 1970-72; BA, U. Wis., 1974; diploma in acting, Juilliard Sch., 1976; MBA, Columbia U., 1979. Account exec. Compton Advt., N.Y.C., 1979-82; dir. account handling Adel-Compton, Athens, Greece, 1983; v.p. account supr. Saatchi and Saatchi Compton, N.Y.C., 1983-84; v.p. SSC&B Lintas Worldwide, N.Y.C., 1984, v.p. mgmt. supr., 1985-86; with bus. devel. dept. Gannett Outdoor Network USA, N.Y.C., 1986—. Coun. mem. St. Mary's Hosp. for Children. Mem. The Glenburnie Club (bd. dirs.), Madison Square Boys and Girls Club (council mem.), Phi Kappa Phi. Office: Gannett Outdoor Network 535 Madison Ave New York NY 10022-4212

ELFIN, MEL, magazine editor; b. Bklyn., July 18, 1929; s. Joseph and Bess (Margolis) E.; m. Margery Lesser, June 21, 1953; children—David, Dana. A.B., Syracuse U., 1951; M.A., Harvard U., 1952; postgrad., New Sch. Social Research, 1955-58. Copywriter Marvin and Leonard, Boston, advt. staff, 1953-54; successively reporter, travel editor, asst. city editor L.I. Daily Press, Jamaica, N.Y., 1954-58; mem. staff Newsweek mag., 1958—, gen. editor, 1964-65; chief Washington bur., 1965-85, sr. editor, 1985-86; editor spl. projects U.S. News and World Report, 1986—; TV panelist; cons. Ednl. Facilities Lab., N.Y.C. Author: (with others) Bricks and Mortarboards, 1963; editor America's Best Colleges, 1987—, Triumph Without Victory, 1992; contbr. articles to various publs. Served as officer SAC, USAF, 1952-53. Recipient George Polk Meml. award reporting, 1957, N.Y. Newspaper Guild Page One award, 1957; award Edn. Writers Assn., 1966. Mem. White House Corr. Assn., Phi Beta Kappa. Home: 4515 30th St NW Washington DC 20008-2126 Office: 2400 N St NW Washington DC 20037-1153

ELFMAN, ERIC MICHAEL, lawyer; b. Phila., Oct. 24, 1954; s. Isaac Selig and Mae (Kline) E.; m. Barbara Cecile Feldstein, Oct. 9, 1982; children: Elizabeth, Bradley. BS in Econs., U. Pa., 1975, MS in Acctg., 1976; JD, George Washington U., 1980. Bar: Calif. 1980, U.S. Tax Ct. 1981, Mass. 1986; CPA, Pa. Acct. Peat, Marwick, Mitchell and Co., Phila., 1976-77; assoc. Pettit & Martin, San Francisco, 1980-83; assoc. office of tax legis. counsel U.S. Dept. of Treas., Washington, 1983-85; ptnr. Ropes & Gray, Boston, 1985—. Mem. ABA (taxation sect.), Mass. Bar Assn., Boston Bar Assn., AICPA, Mass. Soc. CPAs. Home: 49 Willis Rd Sudbury MA 01776-1614 Office: Ropes & Gray One International Pl Boston MA 02110-2624

ELGIN, JOHN TOM, construction company executive; b. Oneonta, Ala., Dec. 15, 1940; s. John Bannister and Zella Lucille (Morton) E.; m. Linda Kay Meeks, Oct. 5, 1947; children: Sandie Kay, John Scott, Elizabeth, Jason Bannister, Grant Monroe. BS in Mech. Engring., U. Ala., 1965. Foreman TCI div. U.S. Steel, Birmingham, 1965, gen. foreman r.r. shop, 1966; regional sales engr. Butler Mfg. Co., Birmingham, 1967; pres. Killearn Properties Constrn. Div., Tallahassee, 1972; exec. v.p., bd. dirs. Killearn Properties Corp., Tallahassee; mgr. Southeastern constrn. Butler Mfg. Co., Birmingham, 1980; nat. sales mgr. Vulcan Metal Products, Birmingham, 1985, v.p. internat. sales, 1985—; cons. Design/Build Contractors, Birmingham, 1980—. Bd. dirs. United Cerebral Palsy, Birmingham, 1980—. Mem. Constrn. Specifications Inst., Assn. Builders and Contractors, Assn. Gen. Contractors, Sigma Chi. Republican. Methodist. Lodge: Rotary, Sertoma (v.p. 1973). Home: 259 Washington St Sherborn MA 01770-1019 Office: Essex Builders Co Inc Point West Office Ctr 3 Speen St Framingham MA 01701-4658

ELIAS, DONALD FRANCIS, environmental consultant; b. Cleve., Aug. 8, 1949; s. Richard Joseph and Marie Terese (Sievers) E. BS in Chemistry, U. S.C., 1971; cert. in meteorology, St. Louis U., 1972; MS in Environ. Engring., Wash. State U., 1977. Chemist S.C. Dept. of Health and Environ. Control, Columbia, 1974-75; rsch. asst. Wash. State U., Pullman, 1975-77; sr. assoc. scientist I.I.T. Rsch. Inst., Chgo., 1977-78; mgr. Northrop Svcs., Research Triangle Park, N.C., 1978-80; prin. Dames & Moore, Houston and Bethesda, Md., 1980-83; mgr. Camp, Dresser & McKee, Denver and Edison, N.J., 1982-86; prin. Research Triangle Park Environ. Assoc., Green Brook, N.J., 1978-86, pres., prin., 1986—. Contbr. articles to profl. jours. Lt. Martinsville (N.J) Rescue Squad, 1984—; Eucharistic min., lectr. Blessed Sacrament, Martinsville, 1986—; mem. Green Brook Rescue Squad, 1988—. Lt. USAF, 1971-74; pres. Matinsville Rescue Squad. Mem. Am. Chem. Soc., Natural Resources Def. Coun., Assn. Energy Engrs. (sr.), Air and Waste Mgmt. Assn. (vice chmn. waste source group 1989—), Environ. Def. Fund, Amnesty Internat., Sierra Club (life). Office: RTP Environmental Assoc Inc 239 Us Route 22 E Green Brook NJ 08812

ELIAS, PETER, electrical engineering educator; b. New Brunswick, N.J., Nov. 26, 1923; s. Nathaniel Mandel and Ann (Wahrhaftig) E.; m. Marjorie Forbes, July 8, 1950; children—Ellen, Paul, Daniel. Student, Swarthmore Coll., Pa., 1940-42; S.B., MIT, 1944; M.A., Harvard U., 1948, M.Engring. Sci., 1949, Ph.D., 1950. Jr. fellow Harvard U., 1950-53; asst. prof. MIT, Cambridge, 1953-56, assoc. prof., 1956-60, prof., head dept. elec. engring., 1960-66, Edwin S. Webster prof., 1974—; vis. prof. U. Calif.-Berkeley, 1958, Harvard U., Cambridge, Mass., 1967-68, 83-84, Imperial Coll., London, 1975-76. Editor, mem. editorial bd. Info. and Control jour., 1957—. Contbr. numerous articles on info. theory and communications to profl. jours. Served with USN, 1944-46. Fellow Am. Acad. Arts and Scis., IEEE (chmn. info. theory group 1965; Shannon lectr. 1977), AAAS (mem. council 1983—, chmn. engring. sect. 1986); mem. Nat. Acad. Scis., Nat. Acad. Engring., Assn. Computing Machinery, Inst. Math. Stats. Democrat. Office: MIT Dept Elec Engring 77 Massachusetts Ave Cambridge MA 02139-4307

ELIASON, ROBERT GORDON, career counselor; b. Chestertown, Md., Sept. 9, 1959; s. John Cree and Margot (Foose) E. BA in Human Rels., High Point U., 1980; MS in Human Resource Mgmt., Wilmington Coll., 1988; cert. in counseling and career devel., Johns Hopkins U., 1991. Exec. East Carolina Coun. Boys Scouts Am., Kinston, N.C., 1981-84; exec. Del-Mar-Va Coun. Boys Scouts Am., Wilmington, Del., 1984-86; dir. Easter Seal Soc. of Del-Mar, Chestertown, Md., 1986-90; counselor Frank Everett and Assocs., Dover, Del., 1990—, Del. Tech. and Community Coll., Dover, 1991—. Mem. AACD, Nat. Career Devel. Assn. Republican. Home: 103 Mill Creek Dr Dover DE 19901-1050 Office: Del Tech and Community Coll 1832 N duPont Pkwy Dover DE 19901

ELIASOPH, PHILIP, art historian, gallery director. BA, Adelphi U., 1972; MA, SUNY, Binghamton, 1975; PhD, SUNY, 1979; studied with, Kenneth C. Lindsay. From instr. to prof. art histry and art criticism Fairfield (Conn.) U., 1975-77, chmn. fine arts dept., 1984—, dir. Thomas J. Walsh Art Gallery, 1990—; editor Art New Eng., Conn., 1984-87; alt. mem., mem. advt. com. Stamford (Conn.) Pub. Arts. 1986—; ednl. cons. TV series Art of the Western World, PBS, 1987—; judge at numerous art exhibitions. Author numerous art reviews and catalogues; arranger collections U. Miami, 1981, Fairfield U., 1984, New Britain Mus. Art, 1985, Kennedy Galleries, 1988, Nat. Sculpture Soc., 1991, Thomas J. Walsh Art Gallery, 1991—, others. Bd. dirs. Parents and Friends of Retarded, Kennedy Ctr., 1989—. Recipient Golden Eagle award CINE, 1986. Mem. Coll. Art Assn. Am., Internat. Assn. Art Critics. Office: Thomas J Walsh Art N Benson Rd Fairfield CT 06430-5152

ELIASTAM, MICHAEL, physician; b. Springs, Republic of South Africa, Jan. 3, 1944; came to U.S., 1967; s. Theodore and Isa Eliastam; m. Suzanne Maynard, Dec. 31, 1983; children: Taylor, Jordan, Monet. MB B.Ch., U. Witwatersrand, Johannesburg, Republic of South Africa, 1966; MPA, Harvard U., 1972, MPP, 1973. Diplomate Am. Bd. Emergency Medicine, Am. Bd. Internal Medicine. Intern Rush Presbyn. St. Lukes Hosp., Chgo., 1967-68, resident, 1968-71; asst. prof. Stanford U., Stanford, Calif., 1974-83; dir. emergency svcs. Stanford U. Hosp., Palo Alto, Calif., 1974-90; assoc. prof. emergency medicine Stanford U., Palo Alto, 1983-90; deputy commr. for med. affairs, med. dir. Dept. of Health & Hosps. City of Boston, 1991—. Editor: Manual of Emergency Medicine, 1989; contbr. articles to profl. jours. Fellow Am. Coll. Emergency Physicians, Am. Coll. Physicians; mem. Univ. Assn. for Emergency Medicine. Jewish. Office: Dept Health and Hosps Admin 5 818 Harrison Ave Roxbury MA 02118-2999

ELIN, RONALD JOHN, pathologist; b. Mpls., Apr. 14, 1939; s. John Matthew and Helen Sophia (Lind) E.; m. Susan May Krogh, June 14, 1969; children: Derek, Justin. BA, U. Minn., 1960, BS, 1962, MD, 1966, PhD, 1969. Diplomate Am. Bd. Pathology, Am. Bd. Clin. Chemistry. Intern U. Hosp. Calif., San Diego, 1969-70; commd. med. officer USPHS, 1970, advanced through grades to med. dir., 1975; staff assoc. Nat. Inst. Allergy and Infectious Diseases NIH, Bethesda, Md., 1970-73, resident clin. pathology dept., 1973-74, chief clin. pathology dept., 1975—, chief chemistry svc., 1977—; clin. prof. Uniformed Svcs. Univ. of Health Scis., Bethesda, 1978—; intiator, first chmn. Gordon Rsch. Conf. on Magnesium in Biomed. Processes in Medicine, 1978. Contbr. over 140 articles to profl. jours. Decorated Commendation medal USPHS, 1980, Meritorious Svc. medal USPHS, 1984. Fellow Am. Coll. Nutrition, Coll. Am. Pathologists, Am. Soc. Clin. Pathologists; mem. Am. Assn. Pathologists, Am. Assn. Clin. Chemisty, Acad. Clin. Lab. Physicians and Scientists (sec./treas. 1985-87, pres. 1990-91). Lutheran. Home: 11401 Marcliff Rd Rockville MD 20852-3635 Office: NIH Clin Pathology Dept Rm 2C-306 9000 Rockville Pike Bethesda MD 20892-0001

ELIOT, JOHN, psychologist educator; b. Washington, Oct. 28, 1933; s. Charles William and Regina (Dodge) E.; m. Sylvia Hewitt, July 3, 1959; children: John Cooper (dec.), Mary Ashley, Catherine Hewitt. AB, Harvard U., 1956, M of Art in Teaching, 1958; EdD, Stanford U., 1966. Asst. prof. Northwestern U., Evanston, Ill., 1967-69; assoc. prof. U. Md., College Park, 1969-77, prof., 1977—. Author: (with I. Smith) Spatial Tests, 1983, Models of Psychological Space, 1987; contbr. articles to profl. jours. Trustee Reservations, Milton, Mass., 1960—. Mem. Am. Psychol. Assn., Soc. Research Child Devel., Brit. Psychol. Soc., Soc. Internat. Psychologists. Democrat. Episcopalian. Home: 2705 Silverdale Dr Silver Spring MD 20906-5322 Office: Inst Child Study U Md College Park MD 20742

ELIOT, LUCY CARTER, artist; b. N.Y.C., May 8, 1913; d. Ellsworth and Lucy Carter (Byrd) E. B.A., Vassar Coll., 1935; postgrad., Art Students League, 1935-40. tchr. painting and drawing Red Cross Bronx Vets. Hosp., N.Y.C., 1950, 51. Exhibited one-woman shows, Rochester Meml. Art Gallery, 1946, Cazenovia Coll., 1942, 47, 62, Syracuse Mus. Fine Arts, 1947, Wells Coll., 1953, Ft. Schuyler Club, Utica, N.Y., 1971, Nat. Shows, Pa. Acad. Fine Arts, Phila., 1946, 48, 49, 50, 52, 54, Corcoran Biennial, Washington, 1947, 51, Va. Biennial, Richmond, 1948, NAD, N.Y.C., 1971, 78, 90, Butler Inst. Am. Art, 1965, 67, 69, 70, 72, 74, 81, Cooperstown Art Assn. ann. exhbn., 1978, 80, 90; represented in permanent collections: Rochester Meml. Art Gallery, Munson-Williams-Proctor Inst., also pvt. collections. Bd. dirs. Artists Tech. Research Inst., 1975-79. Recipient First prize Rochester Meml. Art Gallery, 1946, Purchase prize Munson-Williams-Proctor Inst., 1949, Painting of Industry award Silvermine Guild, 1957, 1st prize in oils Cooperstown Art Assn., 1978, Elaine and James Hewitt award Audubon Artists, 1991. Mem. Nat. Assn. Women Artists, N.Y. Soc. Women Artists, N.Y. Artists Equity, Audubon Artists (bd. dirs. oil 1983-85, chmn. awards 1986-88), Am. Soc. Contemporary Artists, Pen and Brush Club N.Y.C. (Liquitex Art award spring oil exhbn. 1989, 90, Cecilia Cardman Meml. award 1991), Cazenovia Club, Cosmopolitan Club. Episcopalian. Home: Apt 11G 131 E 66th St New York NY 10021-6129 also: 70 Sullivan St Cazenovia NY 13035

ELIZONDO, EDUARDO LUIS, electronics engineer; b. Cienfuegos, Las Villas, Cuba, Nov. 12, 1935; came to U.S., 1959; s. Gonzalo Pastor and Ana (Silva) E.; m. Marion H. Goldberg, Dec. 13, 1987. BSEE, MIT, 1955; EE, U. Habana, Cuba, 1959; MSEE, Polytech. U., 1964; MS in Computer Sci., N.J. Inst. Tech., 1984. Design engr. Blonder-Tongue Labs., Newark, 1958-62, sr. project engr., 1962-64, project mgr., 1964-67; with RCA Astro Electronics, Princeton, N.J., 1967-87, mgr. integration and testing, 1980-81, payload mgr., 1981-87; mgr. communication systems GE Astro Space Div., Princeton, 1987-89, mgr. advanced systems, 1989-90, div. fellow, 1990—; Participant in UN sponsored Space Conf. of the Ams., Costa Rica, 1991. Contbr. articles to profl. jours. Recipient NASA Order of the Big Dipper TIROS and Dynamics Explorer Pub. Svc. Group Achievements awards. Fellow AIAA (assoc. fellow); mem. IEEE (sr. mem.), Assn. for Computing Machinery, MIT Alumni Assn. Princeton (v.p. membership com. 1978-81, 90—, bd. of govs. 1982—), Amateur Computer Groups, MENSA. Office: GE Astro Space Div PO Box 800 Princeton NJ 08543-0800

ELK, SEYMOUR BENJAMIN, mathematics and chemistry educator, researcher; b. Passaic, N.J., Sept. 4, 1932; s. Benjamin Raymond and Janet Ruth (Cohen) E.; m. Rosalind Rosen, Aug. 30, 1959; children: Marilyn Elk Jacob, Janet Elk Davis. BS, Yale U., 1954; MS, Purdue U., 1957, Washington U., St. Louis, 1970; DSc, Eurotechnical Rsch. U., 1989. Missile engr. McDonnell Aircraft Corp., St. Louis, 1954-55; design data coord. Raytheon Corp., Bedford, Waltham, Mass., 1957-59; engring. rsch. specialist Lockheed Missile & Space Co., Sunnyvale, Calif. and Huntsville, Ala., 1962-65; chmn., dept. gen. sci. Parks Coll. Aero Tech. St. Louis U., Cahokia, Ill., 1965-68; lehrer, math. Albrecht Thaer Gymnasium, Hamburg, Fed. Republic Germany, 1971-73; spl. lectr., math. N.J. Inst. Tech., Newark, 1977-81; cons. and writer Elk Tech. Assoc., New Milford, N.J., 1984—; prof. chemistry and math. U. Bridgeport, Conn., 1990—; vis. assoc. prof. Jersey City State Coll., 1986-87; referee Jour. Chem. Info. and Computer Sci., 1987—, Royal Soc. Chemistry, London, 1989—; chpt. reviewer Internat. Union Pure and Applied Chemistry, 1988. Author 3 math. textbooks; contbr. articles to profl. jours. Mem. Am. Chem. Soc. (various nomenclature coms. 1984—), Internat. Soc. Math. Chemists, Hudson-Bergen Chem. Soc. (bd. dirs. 1986—, pres. 1989), Toastmasters (sec. 1989, competent toastmaster 1984, able toastmaster 1988). Home and Office: 321 Harris Pl New Milford NJ 07646-1203

ELKAN-MOORE, BROOKE, marketing consultant; b. Summit, N.J., May 16, 1951; d. George and Barbara (Moore) Koechlein; m. Lawrence J. Moore, Oct. 22, 1988. BA in Art/English, Hiram (Ohio) Coll., 1973; MS in Edn., Bank St. Coll., N.Y.C., 1976. Mem. staff Park as Sch. Prog. Central Park Task Force, N.Y.C., 1978-79; coordintor pub. progs. Internat. Ctr. for Photography, N.Y.C., 1979-81; dir. pub. info./edn. S.I. Hist. Soc., 1983-84; cons. Brooke Elkan Cons., N.Y.C., 1979—; dir. Mus. Village in Orange County, Monroe, N.Y., 1985—; mktg. cons. New Windsor; reviewer IMS GOS Awards, Washington, 1988, 89. Contbr. articles to profl. jours., slide/video tapes. Chmn. Cultural Arts Network, Middletown, N.Y., 1988—, Hudson River Valley Assn. Group Tour Com., Cold Spring, N.Y., 1988—; bd. dirs. Arts Coun. Orange County, 1988—. Mem. Mid-Atlantic Assn. Mus., Am. Assn. Mus., Hudson River Valley Assn., N.Y.C. Mus. Educators Roundtable (steering com. 1980-83), Rotary (v.p. 1989—).

ELKIND, MORT WILLIAM, creative and business consultant; b. N.Y.C., Sept. 10, 1925; s. Samuel William and Leah Fannie (meschen) E.; m. Mary Johanna Ruggiero, June 10, 1972; children: Lori Ann, Susan Marie, Edward William. BS in Chemistry, U. S.W. La., 1949; MS in Analytical Chemistry, La. State U., 1951; postgrad., Geogetown U. Inst. Lang., 1952, UCLA, 1954-55. Intelligence officer CIA, Washington, 1952-53; head waiter Scaroon Manor Hotel, Schroon Lake, N.Y., 1956-57; copywriter J. B. Rundle; Sanders & Lowen; Cayton, Inc., N.Y.C., 1959-65; dir. profl. rels. Kings County Rsch. Labs., Bklyn., 1965-67; copywriter L. W. Frohlich, N.Y.C., 1967-74; sr. copywriter William Douglas McAdams, N.Y.C., 1974-76; copy supr. Kallir, Philips, Ross, Inc., N.Y.C., 1976-85; cons. Chestnut Ridge, N.Y., 1965—; co-founder Photocell Corp. of Am., 1965, Screen Features, Inc., 1966; founder, prin. MWE Assocs. Advt., 1970; co-founder Quadrisec, Inc., 1980, Modular Experts, Inc., 1988; v.p. mktg. Am. Investor Note Paper Corp., N.Y.C., 1985-86; dir. mktg. Air Baby, Inc., Blauvelt, N.Y., 1990-91. Author: Internecine, 1957; editor: MeNeil Psychiatric Calendar, 1978-83; writer, producer TV series Billy Bang-Bang, 1966-68; creater (film) The Internecine Project, 1974; creator TV series Bringing Up Kids, 1989. Polit. cons. N.Y. State Senator, Rockland County and Albany, N.Y., 1978-80. Sgt. C.E., U.S. Army, 1943-46, ETO. Named to U. S.W. La. Hall of Fame, 1978; recipient Andy award N.Y. Advt. Club, 1979. Mem. Blue Key, Phi Kappa Phi, Phi Lambda Upsilon. Home: 27 Eastbourne Dr Spring Valley NY 10977-6402 Office: MWE Assocs 27 Eastbourne Dr Spring Valley NY 10977-6402

ELKINS, ROBERT N., health association administrator; b. N.Y.C., June 5, 1943; s. Jacob B. and Lee (Marcus) E.; m. Mary Beth Ackerley (div. 1991). BA, U. Pa., 1965; MD, SUNY, N.Y.C., 1975. Gen. ptnr. Hampstead (N.H.) Hosp. Physician Group, 1976-79; pres. Cen. Md. Health Systems, Inc., 1978-80; gen. ptnr., co-founder Continental Care Group, Md., 1980-86; chmn., chief exec. officer Integrated Health Svcs., Inc., Hunt Valley, Md., 1986—. Active Associated Jewish Charities, Balt. Recipient Entrepreneur of Yr. award Ernst & Young Inc. Mag., Merrill Lynch, 1991. Mem. Caves Valley Club. Office: Integrated Health Svcs Inc 11011 Mccormick Rd Cockeysville Hunt Valley MD 21031-1422

ELKINS, WILSON HOMER, academic administrator; b. Medina, Tex., July 9, 1908; s. Willie and May (Stevens) E.; m. Dorothy Blackburn, June 1938 (dec. 1971); children: Carole, Margaret; m. Vivian Helen Noh, Aug. 4, 1972. BA, U. Tex., 1932, MA, 1932; BLitt, Oxford U., Eng., 1936; DPhil., Oxford U., 1936. Instr. U. Tex., Austin, 1936-38; pres. San Angelo Jr. Coll., Tex., 1938-48, U. Tex., El Paso, 1949-54, U. Md., College Park, 1954-78; pres. emeritus U. Md., 1978—; cons. in field. Author: Forty Years as a College President, Memoirs of Wilson Elkins, 1981. Vice chmn. So. Reg. Edn. Bd., 1959-61; bd. visitors U.S. Naval Acad., 1967-70, Air U. of Maxwell AFB, 1958-61, others. Rhodes scholar, 1933-36; named Disting. Alumnus, Schreiner Coll., 1979, U. Tex., 1972. Mem. Nat. Assn. Land Grant Colls. and State U. (pres. 1970-71), Middle States Assn. of Schs. and Colls. (pres. 1966-67), So. Univ. Conf. (pres. 1971). Democrat. Episcopalian. Home: 7104 Eversfield Dr Hyattsville MD 20782-1049

EL KODSI, BAROUKH, gastroenterologist; b. Cairo, Aug. 24, 1923; s. Moussa and Zohra (Aslan Cohen) El K.; came to U.S., 1957, naturalized, 1963; M.D., Cairo U., 1945; m. Marie Menasha, Mar. 26, 1960; children—Sylvia, Robert, Karen. Intern, Univ. Hosp. Cairo Sch. Medicine, 1946; resident in gen. medicine Jewish Hosp., Cairo, 1947-50, attending physician, 1950-57; intern, Miriam Hosp., Providence, 1958; resident in internal medicine, Boston City Hosp., 1959-61, chief resident, 1961-62, fellow in gastroenterology, 1962-64; asst. dir. medicine Union Hosp., Framingham, Mass., 1964-65; asso. dir. medicine Maimonides Med. Center, Bklyn., 1965-67, dir. gastroenterology, 1968—; chief gastroenterology Coney Island Hosp., N.Y.C., 1967-68; instr. Boston City Hosp., 1962-65; instr. Downstate Med. Center, SUNY, Bklyn., 1965-69, asst. prof. medicine, 1969-76, asso. prof., 1976—. Chmn. Bklyn. physicians com. United Jewish Appeal. Fellow Am. Coll. Gastroenterology, ACP; mem. Am. Fedn. Clin. Research, Am. Gastroent. Assn., Am. Soc. Gastrointestinal Endoscopy, Am. Soc. Study of Liver Disease, AMA, N.Y. Gastroenterologic Assn. (pres. 1985-86), Ostomy Club (mem. exec. council). Contbr. articles to profl. jours. Home: 118 Girard St Brooklyn NY 11235-3010 Office: 925 48th St Brooklyn NY 11219-2919

ELKOWITZ, LLOYD KENT, dental anesthesiologist, dentist, pharmacist; b. Bklyn., Jan. 26, 1936; s. Paul and Lillian (Applebaum) E.; m. Deanna A. Weinger; children: Sheryl, Andrew, Marc. BS in Pharmacy, Columbia U., 1956; DDS, Case Western Res. U., 1960, postgrad., 1961. Resident in anesthesiology U. Ctr. Hosp, Pitts., 1961, fellow in anesthesiology, 1966; anesthesiologist Walson Army Hosp., Fort Dix, N.J., 1962-64; pvt. practice Queens, N.Y., 1964—; dir. div. dental anesthesiology dept. dentistry Nassau County Med. Ctr., East Meadow, L.I., 1975—; pres. dental adv. coun. Adelphi U., Tufts U., Garden City, N.Y., 1986—; adj. prof. dept. biology Adelphi U., 1982—; chmn. dept. dental anesthesiology Flushing (N.Y.) Hosp. Med. Ctr., 1989—. Trustee Kings Point (N.Y.) Civic Assn., 1978—. Capt. U.S. Army, 1962-64. Recipient Callahan Meml. award Ohio State Dental Assn., 1960. Fellow Am. Dental Soc. Anesthesiology, Acad. Gen. Dentistry, Am. Soc. for Advancement Anesthesia in Dentistry; mem. ADA, Am. Pharm. Assn., N.Y. State Dental Assn., Queens Dental Assn., Internat. Anesthesia Rsch. Soc., Am. Soc. Dentistry for Children, Queens Inst. for Continuing Dental Edn. (charter) Alpha Zeta Omega, Alpha Omega, Alpha Epsilon Delta. Office: 42-60 Main St Flushing NY 11355

ELLEFSEN, EARLE REGINALD, technology company executive; b. Hempstead, N.Y., Apr. 18, 1944; s. Earl R. Ellefsen and Mary Avis (Jacobsen) Richmond; m. Barbara Lomuscio, Mar. 9, 1974; 1 child, Jill. BS, Rensselaer Poly. Inst., 1966. Prodn. mgr. Materials Rsch. Corp., Orangeburg, N.Y., 1966-73; dir. ceramic R & D Materials Rsch. Corp., Pearl River, N.Y., 1973-74; plant mgr. Sintercast div. Chromalloy, West Nyack, N.Y., 1974-81; v.p. Internat. Advanced Materials, Suffern, N.Y., 1981-83; pres., chief exec. officer Pure Tech Inc., Carmel, N.Y., 1983—. Bd. dirs. Ossining (N.Y.) Vol. Ambulance Corps, 1978-83, lt., 1979-82, capt., 1982-83. Mem. Am. Ceramic Soc., Am. Vacuum Soc., Am. Inst. Physics. Home: 5 Cunningham Ln Pawling NY 12564 Office: Pure Tech Inc PO Box 1319 Carmel NY 10512-8319

ELLER, EVELYN (ROSENBAUM), artist; b. N.Y.C., Apr. 17, 1933; d. Charles and Beatrice (Horowitz) E.; m. Robert Lee Rosenbaum, June 14, 1959; children: Paul B. Rosenbaum, Jennifer Rosenbaum. Student, Art Students League, N.Y.C., 1951-54, Acad. Belle Arte, Rome, 1954-55, Sch. Visual Arts, N.Y.C., 1988-89. Adminstrv. asst. Mus. Modern Art, N.Y.C., 1958-59; lectr., tchr. Alliance Queens (N.Y.) Artists, 1989—. Solo exhbns. include Mus. Modern ARt, Miami, Fla., 1959, Columbia U., N.Y.C., 1979, Inst. Internat. Edn., N.Y.C., 1978, 80, Queensborough Pub. Libr., N.Y.C., 1985, Lowenstein Libr. Gallery, Fordham U., N.Y., Plandome Gallery, L.I., N.Y., 1988, Manhasset (N.Y.) Libr. Gallery, 1991; group shows include Whitney Mus., N.Y.C., 1958, DADA Mus., Einhop, Israel, 1985, King Stephens Mus., Hungary, 1986, others Queens Mus., N.Y., 1974, 75, 89, Nat. Mus. Women in Arts, Washington, 1991; represented in pvt. and corp. collections including Bristol-Myers, Indpls. Mus. Fine Arts, others. Mem. N.Y. Artist Equity, Ctr. Book Arts, Women's Caucus for Art, Alliance Queens Artists, Orgn. Ind. Artists. Democrat. Jewish. Home: 71-49 Harrow St Forest Hills NY 11375

ELLER, WILLIAM, educator, writer; b. Janesville, Wis., Apr. 11, 1921; s. Benjamin Louis and Winifred Ruby (Macmillan) E.; m. Betty Jean Sanders, Oct. 20, 1944; 1 son, Charles B. B.S. in Edn., Wis. State U. 1942; M.A., U. Iowa, 1949; Ph.D., 1950. Tchr. math. New Lisbon High Sch. (Wis.), 1942-43; asst. prof. Eastern Ill. State U., Charleston, 1950-5l; dir. reading lab. U. Okla., Norman, 1951-54; dir. reading clinic U. Iowa, Iowa City, 1954-62; prof. edn. SUNY-Buffalo, 1962—, chmn. dept. learning and instrn., 1981-87. Co-author: Introduction to Literature, 1964, 70; Study of Literature, 1964-70; sr. author Laidlaw Reading Program, 1976, 80; mem. editorial bd. Reading Research Quar., 1968-79, Early Yrs. Mag., 1978—. Served to capt. USAAF, 1943-47. Mem. Nat. Reading Conf. (pres. 1960-61), Internat. Reading Assn. (pres. 1977-78, dir. 1971-74), Nat. Conf. on Research in English (sec.-treas. 1964-67), Reading Hall of Fame (pres. 1991). Home: 89 Stonecroft Ln Buffalo NY 14226-4129 Office: SUNY Dept Learning and Instrn 593 Baldy Hall Amherst NY 14260

ELLETT, JOHN DAVID, II, producer; b. Morristown, N.J., Apr. 5, 1966; s. John David and Irma Sacorro (Cruz) E. AS in Bus. Adminstrn., County Coll. Morris, Randolph, N.J., 1989; student, Kean Coll., 1989-90. Program dir. A to Z Music Video, Dover, N.J., 1989-90; exec. producer Octavision, Inc., Dover, N.J., 1990, sec., treas., 1990—; pres. Z Vision, Dover, N.J., 1991—. Writer: (TV series) A to Z Music Video, 1989-90; exec. producer: (film) Patricia List Story, 1990. Mem. Nat. Arbor Day Found., 1991—, Ctr. for Sci. in the Pub. Interest, 1989—, Wilson Ctr. Assocs., 1989—. Republican. Methodist.

ELLIG, BRUCE ROBERT, personnel executive; b. Manitowoc, Wis., Oct. 15, 1936; s. Robert Louis and Lucille Marie (Westphal) E.; 1 child, Brett Robert. B.B.A., U. Wis., 1959, M.B.A., 1960. With Pfizer, Inc., N.Y.C., 1960—, mgr. compensation and pers. rsch., 1968-70, corp. dir. compensation and benefits, 1970-78, v.p. compensation and benefits, 1978-83, v.p. employee rels., 1983-85, v.p. pers., 1985—; speaker at workshops, seminars and confs.; assoc. adv. council Commerce Clearing House, mem. pfizer standing coms. corp. contributions Employee Compensation and Mgmt. Devel., Employee Stock Ownership, Retirement Plan, Retirement Plan Assets, Savs. and Investment. Author: Compensation and Benefits: Analytical Strategies, 1978; Executive Compensation: A Total Pay Perspective, 1982; Compensation and Benefits: Design and Analysis, 1985; contbg. author: Encyclopedia of Professional Management, 1978; Handbook of Business Administration, 1984; cons. editor Compensation and Benefits Rev.; mem. editorial bd., pers. adv. bd. Jour. Compensation and Benefits; contbr. articles to profl. jours. Mem. Mayor's Adv. Pay Commn., N.Y.C., 1977-78, chmn., 1980; mem. bus. sector staff Council on Wage and Price Stability, 1979-80; mem. Ctr. for Advanced Human Resource Studies Cornell U., Human Resource Roundtable, Presdl. Quadrennial Pay Commn., 1976, U.S. Civil Svc. Commn. Merit Pay Task Force, 1979; mem. adv. bd. Ky. Ednl. TV, 1987—. Mem. Am. Compensation Assn. (editorial bd. jour.), Am. Soc. Pers. Adminstrs., N.Y. Assn. Compensation Adminstrs., Nat. Assn. Mfrs., Am. Mgmt. Assn., N.Y. Pers. Mgmt. Assn., N.E. Sr. Human Resources Exec. Mtg. Group, Bus. Roundtable, Conf. Bd. Coun. Human Resources Rsch., Human Resources Roundtable Group, N.Y. Indsl. Rels. Assn., Pharm. Mfrs. Assn., Sr. Execs. Forum, U. So. Calif. Ctr. for Effective Orgns., U. Wis. Bus. Sch. Alumni Assn., Phi Beta Kappa, Beta Gamma Sigma, Phi Eta Sigma,, others. Republican. Roman Catholic. Office: Pfizer Inc 235 E 42d St New York NY 10017

ELLIOT, JOE OLIVER, computer science educator, research physicist; b. Ames, Iowa, Feb. 8, 1923; s. Jay Franz and Rose Valere (Johnson) E.; m. Lois Helen Torok, July 8, 1950; children: Stephen Charles, Louise Ann. BS, Iowa State U., 1943; AM, Columbia U., 1947; PhD, U. Md., 1955. Rsch. physicist dept. war rsch. Iowa State U., Ames, 1944; rsch. physicist dept. terrestrial magnetism Carnegie Inst., Washington, 1945; lectr. Columbia U., N.Y.C., 1946-49; rsch. nuclear physicist Naval Rsch. Lab., Washington, 1949-65, phys. sci. adminstr., 1965-82; assoc. prof. computer tech. Prince George's Community Coll., Largo, Md., 1983—; sabbatical fellow Inst. of Oceanography, U. B.C., Vancouver, Can., 1968-69. Contbr. articles to profl. jours. Mem. Am. Phys. Soc., Am. Geophys. Union. Home: 5123 Temple Hill Rd Temple Hills MD 20748-4845 Office: Prince Georges Community Coll 301 Largo Rd Upper Marlboro MD 20772

ELLIOT, RALPH GREGORY, lawyer; b. Hartford, Conn., Oct. 20, 1936; s. K. Gregory and Zarou (Manoukian) E. BA, Yale U., 1958, LLB, 1961. Bar: Conn. 1961, U.S. Dist. Ct. Conn. 1963, U.S. Ct. Appeals (2d cir.) 1966, U.S. Supreme Ct. 1967. Law clk. to assoc. justice Conn. Supreme Ct., Hartford, 1961-62; assoc. Alcorn, Bakewell & Smith, Hartford, 1962-67, ptnr., 1967-83; ptnr. Tyler, Cooper & Alcorn, Hartford, 1983—; adj. prof. law U. Conn., Hartford, 1973—; sec. Superior Ct. Legal Internship Com., Conn., 1971—; chmn. Superior Ct. Legal Specialization Screening Com., Conn., 1981—, U.S. Dist. Ct. Panel Spl. Masters, Hartford, 1983-88. Chmn. bd. editors Conn. Law Tribune, 1986-87. Chmn. U.S. Constn. Bicentennial Commn. Conn., 1986-91, Criminal Justice Commn. Conn. Fellow Am. Bar Found.; mem. ABA (standing com. on ethics and profl. responsibility 1989—, ho. of dels. 1983-87), Conn. Bar Assn., (officer, bd. govs. 1971-79, 83-87, pres. 1985-86), Am. Law Inst., Yale Law Sch. Assn. (pres. 1988-90, chmn. exec. com. 1990—), Yale Club (pres. 1977-79, Nathan Hale award 1984), Hartford Grad. Club (New Haven), Phi Beta Kappa. Republican. Episcopalian. Office: Tyler Cooper & Alcorn City Pl 35th Fl Hartford CT 06103-3488

ELLIOTT, BYRON KAUFFMAN, lawyer, business executive; b. Indpls., May 5, 1899; s. William Frederick and Effie (Marquardt) E.; m. Helen Alice Heissler, July 15, 1938 (dec. 1973); children: Barbara (Mrs. John D. Niles), Kent, David. A.B. cum laude, Ind. U., 1920, LL.D., 1955; LL.B., Harvard, 1923; L.H.D., Northeastern U., 1971. Bar: Ind. 1921. Began practice in Indpls.; asst. atty. gen. Ind., 1925; elected judge Superior Ct., Indpls., 1926-29; pres. Curtiss Flying Service of Ind., 1927-29; mgr., gen. counsel Am. Life Conv., 1929-34; pres. Am. Service Bur., 1929-33, chmn. bd., 1933-34; with John Hancock Mut. Life Ins. Co., 1934-69, gen. counsel, 1936, v.p., gen. counsel, 1937-47, exec. v.p., 1947-57, pres., 1957-65, chmn. fin. com., 1961-69, chmn. bd., 1963-69; trustee Provident Instn. Savs., 1950-70; dir. Arthur D. Little Co., 1949-69, Pullman Co., 1950-64, Am. Research and Devel. Co., 1952-70, 1st Nat. Bank of Boston, 1960-69, Boston Edison Co., 1961-69. Author booklets, articles ins. law. Resident mem. Mass. Hist. Soc.; mem. Nat. Commn. Coop. Edn.; trustee Wellesley Coll., 1951-69, Ind. Coll. Funds Am., Boston Mus. Sci., 1952-70, Fed. City Council, Washington, Tufts Civic Edn. Center, French Library in Boston, Hosp. Research and Edn. Trust Am. Hosp. Assn., 1960-69; bd. overseers Boston Symphony Orch.; chmn. bd. trustees, chmn. corp. Northeastern U., 1960-72; bd. dirs. Ind. U. Found., World Wildlife Fund, 1964-70, Boston Opera Assn., World Affairs Council Boston, 1950-68; nat. chmn. Ind. U. Sesquicentenniel Fund, 1970; gen. chmn. United Fund Greater Boston, 1960; bd. advisers Nat. Fund for Med. Edn.; chmn. devel. fund Cape Cod Conservatory of Music and Art, 1975-79; mem. corp. Peter Bent Brigham Hosp. Served as 2d lt. CAC, World War I. Recipient Disting. Alumni Service award Ind. U., 1981, Lifetime Achievement award Northeastern U., 1987. Fellow Am. Acad. Arts and Scis.; mem. ABA, Am. Law Inst. (life), Am. Judicature Soc., Council Fgn. Relations, Assn. Life Ins. Counsel (pres. 1949-50), Mass. Charitable Fire Soc., Mass. Com. Catholics, Protestants and Jews (exec. com. 1957-60), Inst. Life Ins. (dir., chmn. 1965-66), Am. Legion, Mil. Order Loyal Legion, Pilgrims, S.A.R., Soc. Colonial Wars, Bostonian Soc., U.S. C. of C. (mem. task force on econ. growth), Ind. Pioneers, Scribes, Comml. Club (pres. 1950-52), Harvard Club, Brookline Country Club, Algonquin Club, St. Botolph Club (Boston), Tavern Club (Chgo.), Dramatic Club (Indpls.), Masons (33 degree), Beta Theta Pi, Sigma Delta Chi, Sigma Delta Kappa. Republican. Presbyterian. Home: 780 Boylston St Apt 23I Boston MA 02199-7827 Office: 200 Berkeley St PO Box 111 Boston MA 02117-0111

ELLIOTT, CANDICE K., interior designer; b. Cedar Rapids, Iowa, Aug. 29, 1949; d. Charles H. and Eunice A. (Long) Goodrich; m. John William Jr. Elliott, Jan. 27, 1973; 1 child, Brandon Christian; 1 stepchild, John William III. BA, U. Iowa, 1971. Interior designer Dayton's, Mpls., 1971-76, Candice Interior Space Planning and Design, Guilford, Conn., 1981-87; owner, interior designer Sofa Works, King of Prussia, Pa., 1987-90; interior designer Jerrehians's Home Furnishings, West Chester, Pa., 1990-92; dir. sales and visual merchandising Sheffield Furniture, Malvern, Pa., 1992—. Bd. dirs. The Old Capitol Restoration Com., Iowa City, 1970-76; curator Guilford Keeping Soc., 1983-88; cons. Zion Episcopal Ch., North Branford, Conn., 1985-88. Mem. Am. Soc. Interior Designers (bd. dirs. Conn. chpt., profl. mem.). Republican. Home: 13 Windsor Ct Wayne PA 19087-5724

ELLIOTT, DENI, philosophy educator; b. Nanticoke, Pa., Nov. 16, 1953; d. Francis J. and Lottie (Peitrovich) Nitkowski; m. James P. Cramer; 1 child, James Wesley. BA, U. Md., 1974; MA, Wayne State U., 1982; DEd, Harvard U., 1984. Cert. secondary tchr., Mich. Journalism and English tchr. Plymouth (Mich.) Canton High Sch., 1979-81; assoc. prof. dept. communications Utah State U., Logan, 1985-88; rsch. assoc. prof. dept. edn. Dartmouth Coll., 1988—; dir. Ethics Inst., Dartmouth, Hanover, N.H., 1988—; adj. assoc. prof. dept. philosophy Dartmouth Coll., 1988—; reporter, ethics coach Sta. WCSH-TV, Portland, 1988, Louisville Courier-Jour., 1987,

Phila. Inquirer, Phila., 1985. Producer video documentary A Case of Need, 1989 (Silver Apple 1991), Buying Time, 1991; columnist FineLine Mag., Louisville, 1989-91; contbr. articles to profl. jours. and book chpts. Recipient Bronze Plaque Columbus Internat. Film Festival, 1990; Marion and Jasper Whiting Found. fellow Harvard U., 1983, Rockefeller fellow Dartmouth Coll., 1987. Mem. Investigative Reporters and Editors, Soc. of Profl. Journalists, Am. Philosophical Assn., Philosophy of Edn. Soc., Assn. for Edn. in Journalism and Mass Communication, Assn. for Practical and Profl. Ethics (governing bd.). Home: 10 Austin Ave Hanover NH 03755-2242 Office: Ethics Inst Dartmouth Coll Hanover NH 03755

ELLIOTT, DENNIS DAWSON, communications executive; b. Evansville, Ind., Jan. 30, 1945; s. Thomas Ira Elliott and Mary Pauline (Dawson) Schultheis; m. Rebecca Lynn Robinett, Jan. 28, 1967 (div. Oct. 1987); children: Jodi Suzanne, Dawn Denise. AB in Journalism, Ind. U., 1969. Bus. intern Mead Johnson & Co., Evansville, 1967-68, pub. rels. assoc., 1968-69, coord. product pub. rels., 1969-70, advt. mgr., 1970-75, assoc. dir., advt. and promotion, 1973-75, advt. mgr. Pharm. div., 1975-80, dir., devel. affairs Pharm. div., 1980-85; advt. dir. Bristol-Myers U.S.P. & G., Evansville, 1985-89; exec. v.p. Campus Group Cos., Tuckahoe, N.Y., 1989-92; pres. Interactive Edn., N.Y.C., 1992—. Publicity chmn. Operation City Beautiful, Evansville, 1970s, Easter Seals Campaign, Evansville, 1970s, Cystic Fibrosis Assn., Evansville, 1970s; bd. dirs. So. Ind. Region Sports Car Club of Am., Evansville, 1970s. Recipient news photography award AP, 1967, Ernie Pyle scholarship Ind. U. Sch. Journalism, Bloomington, 1967. Mem. Ind. U. Alumni Assn. (life, pres. 1969-79, sec./treas., bd. dirs. Vanderburgh County), Pharm. Advt. Coun., Sigma Delta Chi. Methodist. Home: 2A Olde Willow Way Briarcliff Manor NY 10510-1452

ELLIOTT, JOAN ELIZABETH, engineering company professional; b. Pottstown, Pa., Sept. 29, 1945; d. John and Sophia (Kobza) Dimon; divorced; children: Michael, Matthew. Student, Pierce Bus. Sch., Phila., Reading Area Community Coll., 1982-84. Dept. sec. Sanders & Thomas Engrng. Co., Pottstown, 1979-83; adminstrv. asst. to pres. Imperial Distbrs., Auburn, Mass., 1986-87; exec. sec. to pres. Cullinan Engrng. Inc., Auburn, 1987-89; exec. sec. to gen. mgr. Worcester (Mass.) Marriott, 1990—; freelance artist, 1970—; soloist, flutist Elliott & Boucher Dinner Music. Music therapist Luth. Home for Elderly, Worcester, mass., 1985-86; flutist Pottstown Symphony,1969-71; cantor/soloist St. Joseph's Ch., Auburn, 1986—; mem. Salisbury Singers, 1985—. Mem. Pottstown Hist. Soc., Worcester Cultural Assn., Cen. Mass. Tennis Assn., Rotary, Doe Club. Republican. Roman Catholic. Home: 36 Paul St Auburn MA 01501-2833.

ELLIOTT, STUART JAY, editor, journalist; b. Bklyn., July 20, 1952; s. Eli and Sylvia (Perlo) E. BS of Journalism, Northwestern U., 1973, MS of Journalism, 1974. Reporter, copy editor, columnist The Times-Union, Rochester, N.Y., 1974-79; reporter, columnist Detroit Free Press, 1979-82; reporter, dep. N.Y. bur. chief Advt. Age, 1982-87; exec. editor Investment Dealers Digest, N.Y.C., 1987; bus. reporter Gannett News Service, Washington, 1988; advt. and mktg. reporter USA Today, N.Y.C., 1988-91; advt. columnist The N.Y. Times, N.Y.C., 1991—. Mem. Soc. Profl. Journalists, Sigma Delta Chi. Home: 340 E 93d St #15-L New York NY 10128 Office: The NY Times 229 W 43d St New York NY 10036

ELLIOTT, THOMAS MICHAEL, professional association executive, educator, consultant; b. Evansville, Ind., Aug. 4, 1942; s. Thomas Ira and Pauline (Dawson) E.; m. Susan M. Spiers, July 8, 1967 (div. Aug. 1975); 1 son, Christopher Michael; m. Loretta S. Glaze, Jan. 28, 1976. AB in Zoology, Ind. U., 1965, MS in Higher Edn., 1967, EdD, 1970. Asst. to pres. Purdue U., West Lafayette, Ind., 1972-73, asst. provost, 1973-74; exec. dir. Nat. Commn. United Methodist Higher Edn., Nashville, 1974-77; dep. commr. Mo. Dept. Higher Edn., Jefferson City, 1977-79; exec. dir. Ark. Dept. Higher Edn., Little Rock, 1979-82, IEEE Computer Soc., Washington, 1982—; ptnr. Planning Mgmt. Services Group, Washington, 1976-82; cons. numerous colls. and univs. Author: Computer Simulation System, 1975; contbr. articles to profl. jours. Bd. dirs., mem. exec. com. So. Regional Edn. Bd., Atlanta, 1980-82; mem. Cabinet of Gov. Bill Clinton and Gov. Frank White, State of Ark., 1979-82. Mem. IEEE (sr.), IEEE Computer Soc., State Higher Edn. Exec. Officers Assn., Am. Soc. Assn. Execs., Am. Mgmt. Assn. Home: 1735 Q St NW Washington DC 20009-2407 Office: IEEE Computer Soc 1730 Massachusetts Ave NW Washington DC 20036-1992

ELLIOTT, WILLIAM DITTO, biology educator; b. Hagerstown, Md., Dec. 19, 1930; s. Dwight Zillus and Vida Jenette (Barnhart) E.; m. Juanita Gale Carr, May 28, 1976; children: Beth Elliot, David Bittle, Beth Bittle, Amy Bittle. BS in Biology, Shippensburg U., Pa., 1957; MEd, Johns Hopkins U., Balt., 1963; M in Biology, Coll. William and Mary, Williamsburg, Va., 1965; EdD, Am. U., Washington, 1972. Tchr. Balt. County Bd. Edn., Balt., 1958-66, Hagerstown Jr. Coll., Hagerstown, Md., 1966—; team mem. Middle States Assn. Coll. and Schs. of the Commn. on Higher Edn., Phila., 1986—. Co-author: Investigations In Biology, D.C. Heath Montgomery and Elliott, 1991. Recipient Md. Community Coll. Excellence award, Md.State Bd. for Community Coll., 1990. Mem. Assn. for Biology Lab. Edn., Nat. Edn. Assn. Democrat. Episcopalian. Home: 7542 Overlook Dr Boonsboro MD 21713-2520 Office: Hagerstown Jr Coll Robinwood Dr Hagerstown MD 21742-4468

ELLIOTT, WILLIAM PAUL, climatologist; b. Geneva, Ill., June 16, 1928; s. William and Freda Emert (Umbreit) E.; m. Marie Gross, June 21, 1952; children: Erica, Paul. BA, St. John's Coll., Annapolis, Md., 1947; MS, U. Chgo., 1952; PhD, Tex. A&M U., 1958. From instr. to asst. prof. dept. oceanography Tex. A&M U., College Station, 1955-57; rsch. physicist Air Force Cambridge Rsch. Lab., Bedford, Mass., 1957-68; assoc. prof. rsch. sch. oceanography Oreg. State U., Corvallis, 1968-74; rsch. meteorologist Nat. Oceanic & Atmospheric Adminstrn., Silver Spring, Md., 1974-90, supervisory meteorologist, 1990—; chmn. rapporteurs on CO2 World Meterol. Orgn., Geneva, 1983-87. Contbr. articles to profl. jours. Mem. Am. Meteorol. Soc. (radiation com. 1962-64, editor 1983-87), Am. Geophys. Union (editor 1984-89), AAAS, Audubon Soc. Corvallis (pres. 1973-74). Office: Air Resources Lab Nat Oceanic Atmosphere 1325 E West Hwy Silver Spring MD 20910-3233

ELLIS, ANNE ELIZABETH, fundraiser; b. Ornegstad, Aruba, Aug. 21, 1945; d. Thomas Albert and Anne Elizabeth (Belis) Wolfe; m. Earl Edward Ellis, Feb. 14, 1970. BS, La. State U., 1967. Fashion coord. Baton Rouge, 1962-67; textile researcher La. State U., Baton Rouge, 1965-67; buyer I.H. Rubensteins., Baton Rouge, 1967-68; fashion distbr. J.C. Penney, Inc., Arlington, Tex., 1969-70; asst. buyer J.C. Penney, Inc., Dallas, 1970-73; exec. dir. Nassau County Mus. Fine Art Assn., Roslyn, N.Y., 1985-88; speaker C.W. Post U., Greenvale, N.Y., 1988—; cons. in field. Chmn., editor: (cookbook) Specialities of the House, 1981-83. Bd. dirs., com. chmn. Congregational Ch., Manhasset, N.Y., 1975—; exec. vp., bd. dirs., com. chmn. Jr. League L.I., Roslyn, 1977—, Area I Coun. Jr. League Internat.; benefit gala chmn., com. chmn. Grenville Baker Boys & Girls Club, Locust Valley, N.Y., 1983—; pres. bd., vice-chmn. community outreach, benefit gala chmn. Tilles Performing Art Ctr. L.I. U., Greenvale, N.Y., 1985—; bd. dirs., benefit co-chmn. Nassau County Family Assn. Svcs., Hempstead, 1988—; benefit vice-chmn. Glen Cove/North Shore Community Hosp., 1989—; mem. exec. bd., trustee WLIW, L.I. Pub. TV, 1990—; trustee Community Found. of Oyster Bay, 1991—. Recipient Vol. of Yr. award Jr. League L.I., 1984, 85, Sustainer Excellence award, J. League L.I., 1992, Outstanding Vol. Svs. and Commitment, County of Nassau, 1989, Juliette Low award Nassau County Girl Scouts, L.I., 1991, Disting. Leadership award, L.I., 1991. Mem. P.E.O. (pres. 1985-87), The Creek Inc., Meadowbrook Club Inc., Lost Tree Club, Kappa Kappa Gamma (alumna pres. 1971-72). Republican. Congregationalist.

ELLIS, BERNARD J., management consultant; b. N.Y.C., Sept. 1, 1926; s. Harry and Bess (Hinden) E.; m. Evelyn Ellis, Feb. 2, 1947; children: Karen, Barbara. BBA, CCNY, 1948; MBA, NYU, 1952. Sr. bus. analyst U.S. Dept. Commerce, Washington, 1960-65; comptr. Am. Bankers Assn., N.Y.C., 1965-70; sr. v.p. Mastercard Internat., N.Y.C., 1970-80; pres. B.J. Ellis Assocs. Inc., Hillsdale, N.J., 1980—; mem. various bus. coms. concerning credit cards. With USAAF, 1945. Office: BJ Ellis Assocs Inc 93 Standish Rd Hillsdale NJ 07642-1110

ELLIS, BERNICE, financial planning company executive, investment advisor; b. Bklyn.; d. Samuel and Clara (Schrier) H.; m. Seymour Scott Ellis; children: Michele, Wayne. BA, Bklyn. Coll.; MS, Queens Coll., 1970. Cert. fin. planner, N.Y. 1987, elem. educator, N.Y.C. Elementary tchr. L.I. Sch. Dists., Merrick, N.Y., 1956-60; tchr. reading N.Y.C. Bd. of Edn., Bklyn., 1972-73; coordinator Reading is Fundamental, Lawrence, N.Y., 1973-75; pres., founder N.Y. State Assn. for the Gifted and Talented, Valley Stream, N.Y., 1974-87; pres. Ellis Planning, Valley Stream, N.Y., 1984—; cons. Nassau County Bd. Coop. Ednl. Svcs., Westbury, N.Y., 1973-74; adminstrv. intern region II U.S. Office Edn., 1977-78; adj. asst. prof. Nassau Community Coll., Garden City, N.Y., 1975-91, adj. assoc. prof., 1991—; fin. commentator Money Talk radio program WHPC FM. Contbr. articles to profl. jours and fin. newsletters. Recipient Ednl. Professions Devel. Act fellow CUNY Inst. for Remediations Skills for Coll. Personnel, Queensborough Community Coll., 1970-73. Mem. AAUW (North Shore bd., chmn. Money Talk 1991—), Inst. for Cert. Fin. Planners, Inst. for Cert. Fin. Planners L.I. (bd. dirs.), Internat. Assn. Fin. Planners (legis. com. L.I. chpt. 1986-87), N.Y. State Reading Assn., Adj. Faculty Assn. Nassau Community Coll., Sales Exec. Club N.Y., L.I. C. of C. Office: Ellis Planning Inc 628 Golf Dr Valley Stream NY 11581-3594

ELLIS, CHARLES RICHARD, publishing executive; b. N.Y.C., July 20, 1935; s. Charles and Ruth Frances (Allen) E.; m. Nathalie Likwas, Sept. 15, 1957 (div. 1963); 1 child, Kenneth; m. Jeanne Marie Laurent, May 28, 1963; stepchildren: Christopher, Patrick, Shannon, Nicholas Moore. AB, Princeton U., 1957; MA, Columbia U., 1961. Tchr. Barnard Sch., N.Y.C., 1958-63; mgr. Sci. Rsch. Assocs., Chgo., 1963-68; exec. editor D.C. Heath, Boston, 1968-70; chmn., mng. dir. D.C. Heath Ltd., U.K., 1970-75; co-mng. dir. Pergamon Press, U.K., 1975-78; internat. mktg. dir. Elsevier Pub., Amsterdam, 1978-81; pres. Elsevier Sci. Pub. Co., N.Y.C., 1981-88; exec. v.p. John Wiley & Sons, N.Y.C., 1988-90, pres., chief exec. officer, 1990—; pres. bd. trustees Princeton Univ. Press, 1987—; vice chmn. Copyright Clearance Ctr., Salem, Mass., 1987-88. Contbr. articles to profl. jours. Mem. Assn. Am. Pubrs. (vice chmn. 1986-87, 91, chmn. 1991—), Princeton Club of N.Y. Democrat. Home: 630 1st Ave New York NY 10016-3700 Office: John Wiley & Sons 605 3rd Ave New York NY 10158-0180

ELLIS, CHARLES WARREN, former manufacturing executive, educator; b. Randolph, Vt., Oct. 8, 1927; s. Charles Warren and Edna (Moore) E.; m. Madaleen Jacobs Ellis, June 30, 1950; children: Kathleen A., Stephen C., John R. B.S. in Aero. Engrng., MIT, 1951, M.S., 1952. Chief test engr. Kaman Aircraft, Bloomfield, Conn., 1952-63, chief devel. engr., 1963-65; dir. tech. Boeing Vertol Co., Phila., 1965-68, dir. engrng., 1968-72, v.p., 1972-90; adj. prof. Rensselaer Poly. Inst., 1990—; mem. sci. adv. bd. U.S. Army, Washington, 1970-76; mem. aeronautics and space engrng. bd. Nat. Rsch. Coun., 1989—. Patentee in field. Contbr. articles to profl. jours. Chmn. Park Commn., Windsor Locks, Conn., 1959; mem. Joint Airport Zoning Bd., Phila. Internat. Airport, 1972-80; dir. Greater Phila. C. of C., 1981-85. Served with USN, 1945-48. Fellow AIAA, Am. Helicopter Soc. (hon.). Republican. Presbyterian. Avocations: skiing; woodworking; computing.

ELLIS, DANIEL SUMNER, physician; b. Bluefield, W.Va., Mar. 28, 1913; s. William Daniel and Emily (Jones) E.; m. Eloise Goodman, June 24, 1939; children: Daniel S. Jr., Carolyn H. Student, Duke U., 1930-33; MD, Harvard U., 1939. Diplomate Am. Bd. Internal Medicine, Am. Bd. Gastroenterology. House officer Mass. Gen. Hosp., Boston, 1939-41, sr. physician, instr. medicine, 1942—; resident medicine Wis. Gen. Hosp., Madison, 1941-42; assoc. clin. prof. medicine Harvard Med. Sch., Boston, 1946-83; mem. bd. commrs. Joint Commn. of Accreditation of Hosps., Chgo., 1975-82, chmn. bd., 1981-82. Maj., M.C., AUS, 1942-45. Decorated Bronze Star. Fellow ACP (gov., regent, mastership, Alfred Stengle award), Am. Gastroent. Soc.; mem. AMA, Mass. Med. Soc. Republican. Home: Fox Hill Village 10 Longwood Dr Westwood MA 02090 Office: Mass Gen Hosp Fruit St Boston MA 02114

ELLIS, DAVID WERTZ, museum director; b. Huntingdon, Pa., Feb. 8, 1936; s. Calvert Nice and Elizabeth Oller (Wertz) E.; m. Marion Elizabeth Schmitt, June 24, 1961; children: Kathryn Dana, Lorna Beth, Audrey Heather. B.A. with honors in Chemistry, Haverford Coll., 1958; Ph.D. in Chemistry, MIT, 1962; LL.D. (hon.), Lehigh U., 1979; D.Sc. (hon.), Susquehanna U., 1982, Ursinus Coll., 1985; LHD (hon.), Juniata Coll., 1990. Asst. prof. chemistry U. N.H., 1962-67, asso. prof., 1967-78, acting asst. dean Grad. Sch., 1967, asst. dean Coll. of Tech., 1968, asso. acad. v.p., 1968-71, vice provost, v.p. acad. affairs, 1971-78; pres. Lafayette Coll., Easton, Pa., 1978-90; pres., dir. Mus. of Sci., Boston, 1990—. Author: (with others) Calculations of Analytical Chemistry, 7th edit., 1971; contbr. articles to profl. jours. Mem. long-range planning com. Oyster River Coop. Sch. Dist., 1966-68; bd. dirs. Elderhostel, 1983-87, 89—, chmn. 1990—, Sta. WGBH Pub. Broadcasting, 1990—. Dupont fellow, 1960-61. Mem. AAAS, Am. Chem. Soc., Am. Assn. Mus., Space Theater Consortium, Assn. Sci. Mus. Dirs., Nat. Assn. Ind. Colls. and Univs. (bd. dirs. 1986-90, vice chair 1987-88, chair 1988-89), Harvard Club (Boston). Mem. United Ch. of Christ. Home: Thomas Graves' Landing # 710 6 Canal Park Cambridge MA 02141 Office: Mus of Sci Science Park Boston MA 02114

ELLIS, EDWARD STEVEN, insurance company executive; b. Bklyn., Aug. 9, 1950; s. Alfred and Pearl (Lazar) E.; m. Ann Lucille Reilly, Mar. 9, 1976; children: Michael, Brian. BA, Bowling Green State U., 1971; postgrad., Case Western U., 1975. Cert. chartered property casualty underwriters, sr. claim law assoc. Claims adjuster Hartford Ins. Co., L.I., N.Y., 1975-85, Atlantic Cos., L.I., 1985-88; claims adjuster Chubb Group, N.Y.C., 1988—, asst. v.p., 1992—. Author: Insurance in the Workplace, 1987. Lt. U.S. Army, 1971-72. Republican. Office: Chubb Group 100 William St New York NY 10038-4568

ELLIS, ELLEN WILKINS, public relations specialist; b. Oxford, Miss., Aug. 11, 1962; d. William Thomas and Martha Ann (Huddleston) Wilkins; m. Joseph John Ellis, Dec. 17, 1989; 1 child, Michael Alexander. AB cum laude, Mt. Holyoke Coll., 1984; MA, Ind. U., 1986; postgrad., Princeton U., 1987. Assoc. instr. Ind. U., Bloomington, 1984-86; dir. communications Mass. Rep. Party, Boston, 1987, Joe Malone for U.S. Senate, Boston, 1988; assoc. dir. govt. rels. Mass. Mut., Springfield, 1989, dir. govt. rels., 1990—; Mem. Corp. Profl. Devel. Bd., Springfield, 1990. Vol. cons. pub. rels. Children's Mus., Holyoke, Mass., 1988-89; active Planned Parenthood League Mass., Boston, 1989-90. Grad. fellow Princeton U., 1986-87. Mem. Mass. Insights, Pub. Affairs Coun. Presbyterian. Office: Mass Mut 1295 State St Springfield MA 01111-0001

ELLIS, HERBERT LEE, historian; b. Long Beach, Calif., Aug. 30, 1912; s. James Otis and Ethel Florence (Warner) E.; m. Lucy Elvira Burleigh, Dec. 23, 1938; children—Lucy Lee, Mary Margaret. B.A., Duke U., 1933; M.A., Columbia U., 1943, Ph.D. (Doherty Found. fellow), 1956. Substitute tchr., 1933-35; agt. N.Y. Life Ins. Co., 1935-37; tchr. history Rutherford (N.J.) High Sch., 1937-47; mem. faculty dept. history William Paterson Coll., Wayne, N.J., 1947—, prof. history, 1955-82, prof. emeritus, 1982—, chmn. dept. social scis., 1949-68. Co-author: New Jersey Citizen, Rights and Responsibilities, 1954; New Jersey, the Garden State, 1957; sr. author: New Jersey, The State and Its Government, 1962. Mem. Bd. Edn., Wayne, 1962-64; chmn. N.J. Public Coll. Salary Com., 1959-66. Recipient Honor Key, Kappa Delta Pi. Mem. Am. Acad. Polit. and Social Sci., Am. Hist. Assn., N.J. Hist. Assn., NEA, N.J. Edn. Assn., N.J. State Coll. Faculty Assn. (past pres.). Home: 56 Sunset Terr Wayne NJ 07470

ELLIS, JOHN, school system administrator; b. Amherst, Ohio, Sept. 15, 1929; s. Edward Pierson and Jean (Scott) E.; m. Carolyn Elizabeth Collier, Dec. 29, 1951; children: Linda Ellis Wieand, Jeanine Ellis Klausing, Jeanette Ellis Hale, John Edward. BS, Bowling Green State U., 1953; MA, Case Western Res. U., Cleve., 1958; EdD, Harvard U., 1964. Tchr. pub. schs., Lorain, Ohio, 1953-54, prin., 1957-61, asst. supt. schs., Massillon, Ohio, 1963-64, supt. schs., 1964-66, Lakewood, Ohio, 1966-71, Columbus, Ohio, 1971-77; adj. prof. ednl. adminstrn. Ohio State U., Columbus, 1971-77; exec. dep. commr. edn. U.S. Office Edn., Washington, 1977-80; supt. schs., Austin, Tex., 1980-90; commr. N.J. Dept. Edn., 1990—. Elder local Presbyn. Ch. Served with USAF, 1947-49, 54-57. Recipient Massillon Young Man of Yr. award, 1965; named to Saturday Rev. Honor Roll, 1977. Mem. Phi Delta Kappa, Pi Kappa Alpha, Phi Alpha Theta, Kappa Delta Pi, Gamma Theta Upsilon. Lodge: Rotary. Home: 8 Benjamin Trail Pennington NJ 08534-9747 Office: Dept Edn 225 W State St Trenton NJ 08608-1001

ELLIS, JOHN TAYLOR, pathologist, educator; b. Lufkin, Tex., Dec. 27, 1920; s. John Taylor and Rowena (McCurdy) E.; m. Marian A. Caldwell, Dec. 26, 1942; children: Evelyn Floy, George Caldwell, John Taylor. BA, U. Tex., 1942; MD, Northwestern U., 1946. Diplomate Nat. Bd. Med. Examiners, Am. Bd. Pathology. Rotating intern St. Luke's Hosp., Chgo., 1945-46, asst. resident in pathology, 1946; rsch. asst. William Buchanan Blood Ctr., Baylor Hosp., Dallas, 1984; resident in pathology N.Y. Hosp., N.Y.C., 1948-49; asst. in pathology Cornell U. Med. Coll., N.Y.C., 1948-49, instr. in pathology, 1949-50, asst. prof., 1950-56, assoc. prof., 1956-62; prof., chmn. dept. pathology Med. Coll., Emory U., N.Y.C., 1962-67, Med. Coll., Cornell U., N.Y.C., 1968—; attending pathologist, pathologist in chief N.Y. Hosp., 1968—; attending pathologist Meml. Sloan-Kettering Cancer Ctr., N.Y.C., 1973—; acting dir. dept. pathology N.Y. Infirmary-Beekman Downtown Hosp., N.Y.C., 1991—; mem. adv. bd. Office Chief Med. Examiner, N.Y.C., 1988. Capt. USMC, 1946-48. Recipient Milton Helpern Meml. award. Milton Helpern Libr. Legal Medicine, 1989. Mem. AMA, Am. Assn. Pathologists, Coll. Am. Pathology, Assn. Pathology Chmns., Internat. Acad. Pathology, Arthur Purdy Stout Soc., Harvey Soc., N.Y. Path. Soc. Democrat. Home: 180 E End Ave New York NY 10128-7763 Office: NY Hosp-Cornell Med Ctr 525 E 68th St New York NY 10021-4873

ELLIS, LOREN ELIZABETH, artist, educator; b. Binghamton, N.Y., Dec. 12, 1953; d. William Thomas and Ann (Dyshuk) E. BA, U. South Fla., 1974; MFA, Fla. State U., 1977. Instr. Fla. State U., Tallahassee, 1976-77, U. South Fla., Tampa, 1978-81, Columbia Preparatory Sch., N.Y.C., 1989—, Parsons Sch. Design, N.Y.C., 1990—. Solo exhibits at Lotos Club, N.Y.C., A.G. Ludwick Gallery, Tampa, M. Ingbar Gallery, N.Y.C., Sands Hotel, Atlantic City, Gallery Saireido, N.Y.C.; author: Photographs and Thoughts, 1977. Fellow Fla. State U., 1977, Fla. Arts Coun., 1977, Tampa/Hillsborough Arts Coun., 1991. Home: 7120 Wrenwood Cir Tampa FL 33617-8435 Office: 2350 Broadway New York NY 10024-3202

ELLIS, BROTHER PATRICK (H. J. ELLIS), academic administrator; b. Balt., Nov. 17, 1928; s. Harry James and Elizabeth Alida (Evert) E. AB, Cath. U. Am., Washington, 1951; AM, U. Pa., 1954, PhD, 1960; postgrad., Barry Coll., 1963-64, Inst. Catholique, Paris, 1958; LHD (hon.), Assumption Coll., 1982; HHD (hon.), King's Coll., 1987; LLD (hon.), U. Scranton, 1988, C.C. Phila., 1992. Joined Bros. of Christian Schs., Roman Cath. Ch., 1946. Tchr. English dept. West Cath. High Sch. for Boys, Phila., 1951-60; chmn. English dept. West Cath. High Sch. for Boys, 1956-58, guidance dir., 1959-60; dir. practice teaching, sch. prin. St. Gabriel's Hall, Phoenixville, Pa., summers 1960-61, 65-66; asst. prof. English La Salle U., Phila., 1960-62; assoc. prof. La Salle U., 1968-73, prof., 1973—, dir. housing, 1961-62, dir. honors program, 1964-69, dir. devel., v.p., 1969-76, pres., 1977-92; pres. Cath. U. Am., Washington, 1992—; prin. La Salle High Sch., Miami, Fla., 1962-64. Condr.: series for How To Read Gt. Books, U. of the Air, WFIL-TV, Phila., 1961, 65; Contbr. articles to profl. publs. Trustee Manhattan Coll., N.Y.C., St. John's High Sch., Washington, St. Mary's Coll., Calif., St. Mary's Coll., Minn., 1981-84; bd. dirs. Phila. Cath. Charities, 1986-92, Greater Phila. Urban Coalition, Police Athletic League, Phila., Free Libr. Phila., 1990-92, Delaware Valley Citizens' Crime Commn.; former trustee Community Leadership Seminars, Better Bus. Bur. Recipient Lindback award for disting. teaching LaSalle Coll., Phila., 1965. Mem. Pa. Bar Assn. (com. on professionalism), Coun. on Fgn. Rels., Pa. Assn. Colls. and Univs. (past chmn.), Am. Coun. on Edn., Assn. Cath. Colls. and Univs. (past chmn.), Archdiocesan Adv. Com. on Renewal, Phi Beta Kappa. Clubs: Union League, Sunday Breakfast (Phila.), Phila., Univ. (D.C.). Home and Office: Catholic U of Am Washington DC 20064

ELLIS, RAYMOND CLINTON, JR., association executive; b. Chgo., May 11, 1921; s. Raymond Clinton and Frances Geraldine (Hersma) E. PhB, U. Chgo., 1950, MBA, 1953. Lic. ins. broker and agt., D.C. Various positions Marshall Field & Co., Chgo., 1938-52, safety dir., 1953-55; staff rep., dir. small bus. program Nat. Safety Coun., Chgo., 1955-61; dir. mem. rels. Variety Stores Assocs., N.Y.C., 1961-64; fleet safety coord. Am. Ins. Assn., N.Y.C., 1964-67; group adminstr. Hotel Safety Group, N.Y.C., 1967-77; dir. risk mgmt. and ops. Am. Hotel and Motel Assn., N.Y.C., 1977—; exec. v.p. Am. Hotel and Motel Assn. Gen. Agy., Inc., N.Y.C., 1977—; sec., project dir. Am. Hotel and Motel Assn. Rsch. Found., N.Y.C., 1977—; sec. bd. trustees Hotel Assn. Group Trust, 1977—; mem. occupational safety/health com. Bus. Rsch. Adv. Coun., B.L.S., U.S. Dept. Labor, 1979-92. Author: Security and Loss Prevention Management for the Lodging Industry, 1985; editor: Student Manual-Security Course, 1978; contbr. articles to profl. jours. Elder N.Y. Ave. Presbyn. Ch. Served with USAAF, 1943-46, ATO. Named to Hospitality Tech. Hall of Fame, Internat. Assn. Hospitality Accts., 1989. Mem. Am. Soc. Safety Engrs., Vets. of Safety, Nat. Fire Protection Assn., Nat. Safety Coun. (Disting. Svc. to Safety award 1986, mem. exec. com. indsl. div.), Bldg. Ofcls. and Code Adminstrs. Internat., So. Bldg. Code Congress Internat., Internat. Coun. Bldg. Ofcls., Western Fire Chiefs Assn. Republican. Home: Apt 1020 1221 Massachusetts Ave NW Washington DC 20005-5302 Office: Am Hotel and Motel Assn 1201 New York Ave NW Washington DC 20005-3931

ELLIS, RICHARD EMANUEL, historian, educator; b. N.Y.C., Sept. 7, 1937; s. Daniel and Marion E.; m. Sharon J. Waldfogel, Feb. 8, 1939; children: Jonathan, Daniel, Rebekah, Deborah. BA, U. Wis., 1960; MA, U. Calif., Berkeley, 1961, PhD, 1969. Teaching asst. dept. history U. Calif., Berkeley, 1961-63, 64-65; instr. dept. history U. Chgo., 1965-68; asst. prof. dept. history U. Va., Charlottesville, 1968-71, assoc. prof., 1971-74; prof. of history SUNY, Buffalo, 1974—; vis. assoc. prof. history, Harvard U. Summer Sch., 1973; lectr. in field. Author: The Jeffersonian Crisis, 1971 (Nat. History Soc. prize 1972), The Union at Risk, 1987; contbr. articles/essays to profl. publs. Recipient John Simmon Guggenheim Found. fellowship, N.Y.C., 1972-73, summer fellowship NEH, 1987, SUNY Rsch. Found. fellowship, 1983, Canadian Embassy Faculty Enrichment award, 1982; fellow Am. Enterprise Inst./NEH, Washington, 1978-79, Charles Warren Ctr. for Studies in Am. History/Harvard U., 1972-73, Harvard Law Sch., 1972-73, others. Mem. Am. Hist. Assn., Orgn. of Am. History, Inst. of Early Am. History, So. Hist. Assn., Soc. for Histories of the Early Republic. Home: 4399 Main St Buffalo NY 14226-3506 Office: Dept History/SUNY Park Hall Buffalo NY 14261

ELLIS, W. FRANK, psychologist; b. Peabody, Mass., Oct. 14, 1952; s. William Henry and Mary Ann (O'Rourke) E.; m. Emily Martha Bufferd, June 22, 1980; children: Robert William, Matthew Joseph. BA, Merrimack Coll., 1974; PhD, U. S.C., 1983. Instr., adminstr. U. S.C., Columbia, 1981-83; dir. licensing, evaluation Maine Dept. Mental Health and Mental Retardation, Augusta, 1983-86; pvt. practice Auburn, 1985—; adj. assoc. prof. U. Maine, Augusta, 1984—. Mem. Nat. Assn. Sch. Psychologists, Am. Psychol. Assn., Maine Psychol. Assn. Democrat. Home: 111 Pond Rd Lewiston ME 04240-1608 Office: One Auburn Ctr Ste 207 Auburn ME 04210

ELLISON, CRAIG WILLIAM, psychology and urban studies educator, administrator, counselor; b. Springfield, Mass., Aug. 21, 1944; s. William Craig and Marilyn A. (Otto) E.; m. Sharon Roberta Andre, Sept. 20, 1969; children—Scott, Timothy, Jonathan. B.A., The King's Coll., 1966; M.A., Wayne State U., 1969, Ph.D. in Social Devel. Psychology, 1972. Program coordinator MacGregor Meml., Conf. Ctr., Wayne State U., Detroit, 1969-70; asst. prof. Westmont Coll. (Calif.), 1971-76, assoc. prof. psychology, 1977-78, dir. summer sessions, 1977, 78, dir. interterm, 1977-78; vis. prof. SUNY-Binghamton, 1973; prof. psychology and urban studies, chmn. dept. psychology, dir. summer inst. urban missions, adminstr. Simpson Community Counseling Ctr., Simpson Coll., San Francisco, 1978-83; prof. urban studies and psychology Alliance Theol. Sem.-Nyack (N.Y.) Coll., 1983—; bd. dirs., founder, mem. adv. council Family Research Council of Am., 1981—; western regional dir. Christian Assn. Psychol. Studies, 1973-83; cons. in urbanology Christian and Missionary Alliance, 1979-86, World Vision, 1982-84, Intervarsity, 1982-83, Evang. Presbyn. Ch., 1986. Author: The Urban Mission, 1974, 2d edit., 1983, Self-Esteem, 1976, Modifying Man: Implications and Ethics, 1978, Your Better Self, 1983, Saying Goodbye to Loneliness and Finding Intimacy, 1983, Healing for the City: Counseling for the Urban Context, 1992; host Perspective on Personal Living, nationwide

radio broadcast, 1981—; series editor Urban Ministry Resource Series, Zondervan, 1990—; developer Spiritual Well-Being Scale; contbg. editor Jour. Psychology and Theology, 1989—; contbr. articles to profl. jours. Active Common Cause, 1972—, Fairmede Alliance Ch., 1978-83. Mem. Simpson Meml. Ch., 1983—. Mem. Am. Psychol. Assn., Am. Sci. Affiliation, Christian Assn. Psychol. Studies (Disting. Mem. award 1986), Soc. Psychol. Study Social Issues. Office: Alliance Theol Sem Nyack Coll Nyack NY 10960

ELLISON, KATHERINE RUFFNER WHITE, psychologist, educator; b. Charleston, W.Va., Jan. 17, 1941; d. Christian Streit and Katherine Ruffner (Hughey) White. BA, Agnes Scott Coll., 1962; PhD, CUNY, 1976. Prof. Montclair State Coll., Upper Montclair, N.J., 1977—; cons. various law enforcement agys., 1973—. Author: Psychology & Criminal Justice, 1981, Stress & The Police Officer, 1983; contbr. articles to profl. jours. Ruling elder Maywood (N.J.) Presbyn. Ch., 1987—. Mem. Am. Psychol. Assn. (sec., treas. police psychology sect. 1977—), Internat. Assn. Chiefs of Police, Phi Beta Kappa. Democrat. Office: Montclair State Coll Psychology Dept Upper Montclair NJ 07043

ELLISON, SARAH HIGBIE, retired educator; b. Newark, Nov. 22, 1915; d. Daniel Lee and Florence Marie (Rosch) Higbie; m. Vernon Alton Ellison, Apr. 20, 1940; children: Verna Marie, Alice Marie, Ellis Woolley. BA, Kean Coll. N.J., 1973; student, New Sch. Fine Art, 1935-37. Tchr. art Bd. Edn., Matawan, N.J., 1959-79. Mem. Monmouth Arts Found., Shrewsbury, N.J., 1979—, Art Alliance, Red Bank, N.J., 1980—; mem. Ret. Sr. Vol. Program Com., Long Branch, N.J., 1989—; mcpl. rep. Office of Aging, Monmouth County, N.J., 1986—; mem. Monmouth County Sr. Coul, Ocean Twp., N.J., 1988—; mem. Monmouth County Heritage Commn. Freehold, 1987—; sec. Hist. Sites Commn., 1975-91; chief docent Burrowes Mansion, Matawan; mem. Matawan Aux. to Bayshore Hosp., 1989—. Mem. Matawan Hist. Soc. (pres. 1990-92, In Appreciation award 1988), Nat. Trust for Hist. Preservation, Trinity Episc. Ch. Women (pres. 1986-91). Republican. Episcopalian. Home: 24 Monroe St Matawan NJ 07747-3218 Office: Matawan Hist Soc PO Box 41 Matawan NJ 07747-0041

ELMAN, ROBERT, writer, editor; b. N.Y.C., Nov. 14, 1930; s. Dave and Pauline (Reffe) E.; m. Loris Harrington, Mar. 4, 1957 (div. 1975); children—Natalie Harrington, Thomas Harrington; m. Ellen Catherine Schwartz, Sept. 18, 1976; children—Daniel Walter, Catherine Elaine. B.S., Columbia U., 1953. Mng. editor, editor-in-chief Maco Pub. Co., N.Y.C., 1960-69; outdoors editor Ridge Press, N.Y.C., 1969-72; assoc. editor, editor-in-chief Winchester Press, N.Y.C., 1973-75; writer-in-residence Ridge Press, N.Y.C., 1975-77; editor-in-chief Winchester Press, Tulsa and Piscataway, N.J., 1979-84; writer, cons. editor, 1984—; editorial and pub. cons. Amwell Press, Clinton, N.J., also other mag. and book pubs. Author: The Great American Shooting Prints, 1972, The Hiker's Bible, 1974, 2d edit., 1981, The Living World of Audubon Mammals, 1976, America's Pioneering Naturalists, 1981, Bears, 1992, others. With inf. U.S. Army, 1953-55. Mem. Authors League, Authors Guild, Explorers Club, Wilderness Soc. Home: Rte 1 Box 582 Stewartsville NJ 08886

ELMONT, MAXINE, behavioral science educator; b. Bklyn.; d. Saul and Rose (Morse) Seinfeld; widowed; 1 child, Stephen. BA, Suffolk U., 1966; MEd, Boston U., 1968; EdD, U. Mass., 1986. Lic. social worker, rehab. counselor, Mass. Program supr. Jewish Community Ctr., Boston, 1953-63; program dir. Margaret Fuller House, Cambridge, Mass., 1963-65; dir. Neighborhood Youth Corps, Chelsea, Mass., 1967-68; prof. Mass. Bay Community Coll., Wellesley, Mass., 1968—; workshop leader, speaker various community orgns. Contbr. articles to profl. jours. Vol. AIDS Action Com., Boston, 1988—; career counselor Project Integration, Temple Israel, Boston, 1990—; bd. dirs. Brookline (Mass.) Vis. Nurse Svcs., 1990—. Mem. AACD, Am. Rehab. Counselors. Assn., Nat. Assn. Devel. Edn. (Outstanding Dissertation award 1991), Learning Assistance Assn. New Eng. (exec. bd. 1983—, pres. 1987-89). Home: 80 Toxteth St Brookline MA 02146-6910 Office: Mass Bay Community Coll 50 Oakland St Wellesley MA 02181-5359

ELMORE, ANDREW MONTEVERDE, psychologist; b. Seattle, Feb. 1, 1952; s. Robert Graham and Jane Charlotte (Monteverde) E.; m. Gail Eleanor Miers, Aug. 22, 1981; 1 child, Austen Chance. BA, Ill. Wesleyan U., 1974; PhD, SUNY, Stony Brook, 1979. Lic. psychologist, N.Y.; cert. biofeedback therapist, cognitive therapist. Psychologist pvt. practice N.Y.C., 1979—; asst. clin. prof. psychiatry Mount Sinai Sch. Medicine, N.Y.C., 1981—; staff psychologist Found. for Rsch. on Manic Depression, N.Y.C., 1981-91; psychol. dir. Tim. J. and Dental Phobia Clinic Mt. Sinai Hosp., N.Y.C., 1981—; staff psychologist L.I. Jewish/Hillside Med. Ctr., New Hyde Pk., N.Y., 1975—; dir. biofeedback clinic N.Y.C., 1979-88; chairperson Mount Sinai Hosp. Psychologists, N.Y.C., 1984-87; cons. psychologist Gracie Sq. Hosp., N.Y.C., 1984—. Author: (screenplay) The Master and Margarita, 1982; author: Introduction to Natural Psychology, 1992. Recipient NIMH Predoctoral fellowship, 1976, Biomed. Rsch. fellowship SUNY at Stony Brook, 1978. Mem. APA, N.Y. Acad. Scis., Am. Assn. for Applied Psychophysiology and Biofeedback, Am. Assn. for Study of Headaches. Office: Andrew Elmore PhD 401 E 80th St New York NY 10021

ELROD, EUGENE RICHARD, lawyer; b. Roanoke, Ala., May 14, 1949; s. James Woodrow and Selma Fromer (Steinbach) E. AB, Dartmouth Coll., 1971; JD, Emory U., 1974. Bar: Ga. 1974, D.C. 1976, U.S. Ct. Appeals (D.C. cir.) 1985, U.S. Ct. Appeals (5th cir.) 1987, U.S. Dist. Ct. D.C. 1987, U.S. Supreme Ct. 1987. Trial atty. Fed. Power Com., Washington, 1974-76; atty.-advisor Fed. Energy Adminstrn., Washington, 1977; assoc. Sidley & Austin, Washington, 1977-80, ptnr., 1981—; mem. adv. bd. The Keplinger Cos., Houston. Mem. selection com. for Woodruff scholars Emory U. Law Sch., Dartmouth '71 Exec. Com. Mem. ABA, D.C. Bar Assn., Ga. Bar Assn., Fed. Energy Bar Assn. (chmn. oil pipeline com. 1982-83, tax com. 1980-81, liaison with adminstrv. law judges 1986-87), Dartmouth Club (exec. com. Class of 1971), Mt. Vernon Swimming and Tennis Club (Washington). Clubs: Dartmouth, Mt. Vernon Swimming and Tennis (Washington). Home: 4300 Hawthorne St NW Washington DC 20016-3571 Office: Sidley & Austin 1722 I St NW Washington DC 20006-3705

ELSEN, SHELDON HOWARD, lawyer; b. Pitts., May 12, 1928; m. Gerri Sharfman, 1952; children: Susan Rachel, Jonathan Charles. AB, Princeton U., 1950; AM, Harvard U., 1952, JD, 1958. Bar: N.Y. 1959, U.S. Supreme Ct. 1971. Ptnr. Orans, Elsen & Lupert, N.Y.C., 1965—; adj. prof. law Columbia U. Law Sch., 1969—; chief counsel N.Y. Moreland Act Commn., 1975-76; asst. U.S. atty. So. Dist. N.Y., 1960-64; cons. Pres.'s Commn. Law Enforcement Adminstrn. Justice, 1967; mem. faculty Nat. Inst. Trial Advocacy, 1973; mem. First Dept. Disciplinary Com., 1990—. Contbr. articles to legal jours. Fellow Am. Coll. Trial Lawyers, Am. Bar Found.; mem. Assn. of Bar of City of N.Y. (v.p. 1988-89, chmn. com. on fed. legislation 1969-72, mem. com. on judiciary 1972-75, chmn. com. on fed. courts 1983-86, chmn. nominating com. 1986-87), Am. Law Inst., Phi Beta Kappa. Home: 50 Fenimore Rd Scarsdale NY 10583-2251 Office: 1 Rockefeller Pla New York NY 10020

ELSER, JOHN ROBERT, retired insurance company executive; b. Harrisburg, Pa., Sept. 4, 1912; s. Aaron Hackman and Edna (Cooper) E.; m. Mary Duncan Wirt, Sept. 21, 1940; children: Robert Cooper, Mary Duncan, Jo Anne. Student, U. Pa., 1935-38. Successively office mgr., asst. sec., corp. sec., pres., chief exec. officer Mchts. and Businessmen's Mut. Ins. Co., Harrisburg, 1937-1978, chmn. bd. dirs., 1970-85, now bd. dirs. Chmn. Mechanicsburg (Pa.) Sch. Dist. Authority, 1953; mem. Mechanicsburg Area Joint Sch. Bd., 1953-65, pres., 1960, sec., 1965-73; pres. Mechanicsburg Area Pub. Libr. Bd., 1976-78; chmn. bd. dirs. West Shore YMCA, Camp Hill, Pa., 1974-76, mem. bd. dirs. 1984-89; bd. dirs. Area YMCA, Harrisburg, 1978-84, vice chmn., 1980-82. 1st lt. U.S. Army, 1944-47, PTO. Mem. Rotary.

ELSTER, ROBERT JAMES, JR., publisher; b. Detroit, Jan. 11, 1952; s. Robert James and Jeanne Marie (Ruane) E. BA in English Lit., Wayne State U., 1976, MS Libr. Sci., 1981. Rsch. coord. Gale Rsch. Inc., Detroit, 1980-84, sr. editor, 1985-89; pub. The Taft Group, Washington, 1989—. Mem. Newsletter Assn., Washington Directory Assn., Am. Prospect Rsch. Assn., Nat. Assn. of Fund Raising Execs., Spl. Librs. Assn., New England Donor Rsch. Assn. Home: 3701 Connecticut Ave NW Washington DC 20008

ELSWORTH, DEREK, geological engineer; b. Glasgow, Scotland, May 3, 1958; came to the U.S., 1982; s. Jack and Rosalind Sinclair (Learmonth) E.; m. Susan Jane Wheeler, Mar. 6, 1986; children: Geneviève Wheeler, Cooper Wheeler. BS in Engring. Geology, Portsmouth Poly., United Kingdom, 1979; MS in Engring. Rock Mechanics, Imperial Coll., London, 1980; PhD in Engring., U. Calif., Berkeley, 1984. Registered profl. engr. Engr. Komex Cons. Ltd., Calgary, Canada, 1980-82; asst. prof. U. Toronto, Ontario, Canada, 1984-85; asst. prof. Pa. State U., University Park, 1985-88, assoc. prof., 1991—; rsch. assoc. prof. U. Waterloo, Canada, 1988-89, adj. prof., 1989—; cons. numerous state, fed. and pvt. orgns., 1984—, cons. to local twps. and spl. interest groups, 1985—. Author: Laminar and Turbulent Flow in Rock Fissures and Fissure Networks, 1987. Mem. Soc. Mining Engrs. (chmn. environ. sect. and publs. com. 1985—), Am. Acad. Mechanics, ASCE, Internat. Soc. for Rock Mechanics (Manuel Rocha medal 1987), Am. Geophys. Union. Office: Pa State U Dept Mineral Engring University Park PA 16802

ELTON, WILLIAM R., English literature educator, poet; b. N.Y.C., Aug. 15, 1921; s. William and Mollie E. AB, Bklyn. Coll., 1941; MA, U. Cin., 1942; PhD, Ohio State U., 1957. Asst. Ohio State U., 1942-45, instr., 1945-46; instr. Brown U., Providence, 1946-50, NYU, 1950-51; vis. asst. prof. English U. Conn., 1952-53; asst. prof. Ohio State U., 1953-55; asst. prof. to prof. U. Calif., Riverside, 1955-69; vis. prof. Columbia U., 1969; prof. English lit. CUNY, 1969—; 1st vis. Mellon prof. Inst. for Advanced Study, Princeton, 1984-85; bd. dirs. Shakespeare Inst. of N.Y.; lectr. Lincoln Coll., Oxford, Eng., 1951, U. Paris VIi, Ecole Normale Supérieure, 1990; Fulbright lectr., India, 1960, New Coll., Oxford, 1990; cons. in field. Author: Guide to the New Criticism, 5th edit. 1953, King Lear and the Gods, 1966, 2nd edit. 1968, 3rd. edit., 1988, Shakespeare's Ulysses und die Frage des Wertes, 1968, Wittgenstein's Trousers: Poems, 1991, others; contbr. numerous artices to profl. jours., chpts. to books; editor Shakespearean Research and Opportunities, 1965—; co-editor, Poetry New York, 1985—; adv. editor Shakespeare Studies, 1965—; cons. editor Jour. of the History of Ideas, 1981—. Recipient numerous fellowships, grants from various orgns. including CUNY Research Found., 1984-85, 85-86, Huntington Library, 1988. Mem. MLA, Renaissance Soc. Am., Malone Soc., Internat. Soc. for Neoplatonic Studies, Shakespeare Assn. Am., Soc. for Renaissance Studies (Eng.), PEN Club, English Inst., Am. Philol. Assn., Soc. for Ancient Greek Philosophy, Internat. Assn. Profs. of English. Home: 788 Columbus Ave # 100 New York NY 10025-5951 Office: 33 W 42nd St New York NY 10036-8003

ELVIN, PETER WAYNE, healthcare executive, consultant; b. Augusta, Maine, Mar. 10, 1955; s. Grahame Dennis and Clemence Marie (Poulin) E.; m. Suzanne Piché. Student, U. Maine, 1973-74, U. Cin., 1974-75; AA, Cin. Tech. Coll., 1977; MS in Mgmt., Lesley Coll., 1985. Physicians asst. Monson Devel. Ctr., Palmer, Mass., 1977-86; rep. Blue Cross and Blue Shield of Maine, Portland, 1986—; dir. physician practices TVM, Inc./Miles Health Care, Damariscotta, Maine, 1990—; pvt. practice cons., 1989—; health care analyst Mass. Dept. Health, Boston, 1984-86; cons. Med. Care Devel., Augusta, 1985-86, Rural Health Ctrs., Maine, 1985-86; adminstr. Harrington (Maine) Family Health Ctr. Mem. Maine Rep. Party, Rep. Nat. Com. mem. Am. Acad. Physicians Assts., Assn. MBA Execs., Inc., Lesley Coll. Alumni Assn., Rental Housing Assn. Greater Springfield, Bath/Brunswick Rental Housing Assn., Maine Hosp. Assn., U.S. C. of C., Nat. Fedn. Ind. Bus., Boston Computer Soc., Profl. Cons. of Maine. Republican. Episcopalian. Club: Springfield Sportsmans. Home: RR 1 Box 4215 Dresden ME 04342-9729 Office: Dresden Cons Group RR 1 Box 4215 Dresden ME 04342-9729

ELWOOD, PATRICIA, educator, political consultant; b. Haverhill, Mass., Oct. 22, 1941; d. Raymond Bernard and Florence Eva (Cowan) Kupsov; children: Robert Michael, Douglas Matthew. BS, Tufts U., 1963; MEd, Boston U., 1965; PhD, U. Md., 1978. Tchr./trainer Boston Pub. Schs., 1964-67; dir. Head Start Prog., various cities, Mass., 1968; adminstrv. asst. Dept. Child Study Tufts U., Medford, Mass., 1967-68; diagnostician, tchr./counselor Program for Hearing Impaired Richmond (Calif.) Pub. Schs., 1968-69, supr., 1970-73; asst. to dir. Berkeley (Calif.) Profl. Studies Abroad Program, New Delhi, 1969-70; curriculum writer Prince Georges County Pub. Schs., Upper Marlboro, Md., 1974; learning problems and hearing specialist Prince Georges County Pub. Schs., 1976-80, hearing therapist, 1980—; mktg. researcher, 1990—; lectr. Trinity Coll., Washington, 1980-84; cons. Pan Am. Health Orgn., Caribbean, 1978-80; coord. state conf. early childhood edn., 1978. Co-author: Social and Emotional Development of Young Children, 1968, Alameda County California Public Schools Health Curriculum, 1969, Piaget's Theory as It Relates to Early Childhood Curricula, 1979; co-editor: Parent-Centered Programs for Young Hearing Impaired Students, 1976; contbr. articles to profl. jours. Mem. fin. com. Sidwell Friends Sch., 1985-90; mem. Dem. State Com., Washington, 1985—, fin. chmn., 1988-90; 1st vice chmn. Ward III Dem. Com., Washington, 1988-91, treas., 1986-88; past mem. fin. and policy coms. presdl., senate, ho. reps., gubernatorial campaigns; campaign co-chmn., ward chmn. steering com. D.C. and Greater Washington area polit. candidate campaigns, 1980—; bd. dirs. Little League and Boys and Girls Club, 1986-91, Nat. Child Rsch. Ctr., 1977-82, Washington Hearing and Speech Ctr., 1984-87, Washington Tufts Alliance, co-chairperson, 1984-86, vice chairperson, 1985-88, treas., 1988—; appointed Coun. Govts. Task Force Com. on Growth and Transp., 1990—; commr. Mayoral Appointee, Nat. Capital Planning Commn., 1987—; mem. nominating com., trustee U. D.C., 1988—; presdl. appointee Selective Svc. Bd., 1988-91; bd. dirs. Ft. Myer Swim Team, 1983-85, 89-90; elected mem. alumni coun. Tufts U., 1988—. Named Outstanding Young Woman in Am., 1966. Mem. Nat. Assn. for Edn. Young Children, World Affairs Coun., Nat. Trust for Historic Preservation, Tufts U. Alumnae Assn. Democrat. Home: 2740 34th St NW Washington DC 20008-2714 Office: Prince Georges County Bd Edn Upper Marlboro MD 20008

ELWOOD, WILLIAM EDWARD, tax and corporate lawyer; b. Woodbury, N.J., Apr. 17, 1943; s. Glenn Edward and Evelyn Marguerite (Lehner) E.; m. Anne Stacy Bitner, June 24, 1967; children: William Edward Jr., Stacy Anne. BS, Pa. State U., 1965; JD, U. Pa., 1968; LLM, Georgetown U., 1975. Bar: Pa. 1969, D.C. 1971, U.S. Supreme Ct. 1973, Mich. 1990. Tech. atty. Chief Counsel's Office, IRS, Washington, 1970-74; assoc. firm Lee, Toomey & Kent, Washington, 1974-77; asst. gen. counsel Communications Satellite Corp., Washington, 1977-85; v.p., tax counsel Primark Corp., McLean, Va., 1985-86; ptnr. Dickinson, Wright, Moon, Van Dusen & Freeman, Washington, 1985—; mem. adv. bd. Tax Found., Inc., 1986, program com., 1991—. Author: Employee Fringe Benefits, 1983, revised edit., 1992; editor U. Pa. Law Rev., 1966-68; articles editor Tax Lawyer, 1976-80; dept. editor The Tax Times, 1986-87; contbr. articles and revs. to profl. jours. Parliamentarian Alexandria Rep. City Com., Va., 1974-78; mem. Alexandria Traffic and Parking Bd., 1975-77; bd. dirs. Leadership Action, Cabin John, Md., 1983-85. Capt. U.S. Army, 1968-70. Mem. ABA (co-chmn. tax sect. subcom. 1982-84), Tax Execs. Inst. (chmn. nat. fed. tax com. 1984-85), Internat. Fiscal Assn., Washington Tax Group, Belle Haven Country Club, Alpha Pi Mu, Omicron Delta Kappa, Phi Eta Sigma (pres.). Republican. Episcopalian. Home: 2016 Glen Dr Alexandria VA 22307-1137 Office: 1901 L St NW Ste 800 Washington DC 20036-3506

ELWORK, AMIRAM, graduate program director; b. Tel Aviv, Israel, Aug. 4, 1949; came to U.S., 1959; s. Grigori and Fania (Nemenof) E.; m. Andrea Block, Aug. 4, 1974; children: Rachael F., Rebecca G. BA in Psychology, Temple U., 1971; PhD in Psychology, U. Nebr., 1977, post-doctorate, 1977-80; intern, U. Pa., 1981-82. Lic. psychologist, Pa. Asst. prof., rsch. Univ. Nebr., Lincoln, 1977-80; assoc. prof., dir. law psychology Hahnemann U., Phila., 1981-89; dir. law and psychology program Widener Univ., Chester, Pa., 1989—; pvt. practice psychologist, part time Gwynedd, Pa., 1983—; cons. Adminstrv. Office of Cts., Trenton, N.J., 1984-86; dir. forensic psychology Introspect, Lansdale, Pa., 1990—. Author: (book) Making Jury Instructions Understandable, 1982; editor: (spl. issue jour.) Psycholegal Testimony, 1984; assoc. editor: (jour.) Computers In Human Behavior, 1984-87; co-author: (computer program) Manuscript Manager, 1988; contbr. articles to profl. jours. and chpts. to books. Recipient Rsch. grants NSF, 1976, Law Enforcement Assistance Adminstrn., 1978, NIMH, 1978, State of N.J., 1984. Mem. Am. Psychol. Assn. (chair annual conv. div. 41, Washington, 1983), Am. Psychology-Law Soc., Pa. Psychol. Assn. Home: PO Box 447 Gwynedd PA 19436-0447 Office: Inst Grad Clin Psychology Widener U Chester PA 19013

ELY, DONALD JEAN, clergyman, educator; b. Frederick, Md., July 15, 1935; s. George Kline and Jennie Mabel (Boyer) E. m. Lois Jean Kirkpatrick, Aug. 27, 1967; children: Kathleen Rose, Stephen David, Yvonne Elaine. AB, Gettysburg Coll., 1955; BD, Lancaster Sem., 1958; MEd, Bloomsburg State U., 1972. Ordained to ministry Evang. and Reformed Ch., 1958. Pastor St. John Evang. and Reformed Ch., Riegelsville, Pa., 1958-61, Zion's Reformed Ch., Ashland, Pa., 1961-64, Augusta Reformed Parish, Sunbury, Pa., 1964-74, Salem United Meth. Ch., Middleburg, Pa., 1974-79, Salem Ind. Brethren Ch., Middleburg, Pa., 1979-83; tchr. social studies Shikellamy High Sch., Sunbury, Pa., 1966—. Bd. dirs. Sunbury Area YMCA, 1966—, sec., 1973-80, 88—; bd. dirs. Northumberland County unit Am. Cancer Soc., 1971-74, Snyder County unit, 1974-84; rep. candidate state legis., 1982; vice chmn. Govt. Study Commn. of City of Sunbury, 1989-91; mem. Northumberland County Rep. com., 1989—, state committeeman, 1992—. Mem. SAR (chaplain 1971—, chpt. pres. 1981-86), Pa. Coun. Social Studies, Snyder County Hist. Soc. (pres. 1980-83, life mem.), Northumberland County Hist. Soc. (trustee 1972-83, life mem.), Union County Hist. Soc., Hist. Soc. Evang. and Reformed Ch., Hereditary Register of U.S., Ams. for Constl. Action, Am. Conservative Union, Masons. Home: PO Box 765 Sunbury PA 17801-0765 Office: 1149 Market St Sunbury PA 17801

ELY, DONALD PAUL, education educator, consultant; b. Buffalo, Sept. 3, 1930; s. Paul Bernard and Florence Mae (Fuller) E.; m. Martha Louise Spencer, Sept. 6, 1952; children: Mark, Scott, Christopher. BA, SUNY, Albany, 1951; MA, Syracuse U., 1953, PhD, 1961. Asst.prof. SUNY, New Paltz, 1952-55; dir. audiovisual edn. Hicksville (N.Y.) Pub. Schs., 1955-56; asst. prof. to prof. ednl. tech. Syracuse (N.Y.) U., 1956—; adj. prof. U. Twente, Enschede, Netherlands, 1980—, Coll. Environ. Sci. and Forestry, SUNY, Syracuse, 1982—. Author: Media Personnel in Education, 1976, Teaching and Media, 1981; editor: Educational Media and Technology Yearbook, 1988. Trustee Onondaga County Pub. Libr., Syracuse, 1986—. With USAR, 1951-54. Named Disting. Alumnus SUNY-Albany, 1974. Mem. Assn. Ednl. Communications and Tech. (pres. 1964-65, Internat. Contbn. award 1986, Disting. Svc. award 1987). Presbyterian. Home: 704 Hamilton Pky Syracuse NY 13214-2338 Office: Syracuse U 333 Huntington Hall Syracuse NY 13244

ELY, TIMOTHY CLYDE, book artist, educator; b. Snohomish, Wash., Feb. 9, 1949; s. Everett Charles and Frances Lois (Tuengel) E.; m. Ruth Averil Antrich, June 21, 1984. BA in Drawing and Printmaking, Western Wash. U., 1972; MFA in Design, U. Wash., 1975. Instr. Oreg. Sch. Arts & Crafts, Portland, 1980-85; instr., artistic dir. Ctr. for Book Arts, N.Y.C., 1985—; workshop instr. Pratt Graphics Inst., N.Y.C., 1985, Arrowmont, Gatlinburg, Tenn, 1987, Penland (N.C.) Sch., 1988, Minn. Ctr. for Book Arts, Mpls., 1989, Pyramid Atlantic, Washington, 1987, 88, 91. Solo exhbns. include Eaton/Shoen Gallery, San Francisco, 1984, N.Y. Acad. Scis., N.Y.C., 1987, Contemporary Crafts Gallery, Portland, Oreg., 1988, Victoria & Albert Mus., London, 1989, Minn. Ctr. Book Arts, Mpls., 1989, Granary Books, N.Y.C., 1989, 91, 92; group shows include Ctr. Book Arts, 1984, 85, 86, 88, 89, 90, N.Y.C. Pub. Libr., 1984, Met. Mus. Art, N.Y.C., 1986, Maison Livre l'Image du Son, France, 1988, Bibliotheque de l'Arsenal, Paris, 1990, Anchorage Hist. Fine Arts Mus., 1991, others. Recipient awards Pollock-Krasner Found., 1985, Art Matters, Inc., 1988, 90, Temari Jurors award 1985, Rutgers Purchase award, 1981; Nat. Endowment for Arts fellow, 1982. Home and Office: 255 W 84th St New York NY 10024-4321

EMA, YASUO, communications executive; b. Hagi, Yamaguchi, Japan, Jan. 4, 1945. BA in Drama, Waseda U., 1968. Asst. dir. Nippon TV Network Corp., Tokyo, 1968-71, dir., 1971-73, producer, 1973-86; sr. v.p. NTV Internat. Corp., N.Y.C., 1986—. Dir. (TV) Comedy Series, 1968, producer (TV) Orchestra Theater, 1972. Mem. Nat. Assn. TV Program Execs., Nat. Acad. TV Arts and Scis. Home: 236 E 47th St New York NY 10017-2130 Office: NTV Internat Corp 50 Rockefeller Plz New York NY 10020

EMAD, JAMAL, psychiatrist; b. Iran, Aug. 6, 1931; came to U.S., 1957; s. Habib and Alieh Karbor; m. Jean A. Cognetto, July 23, 1982; children: Linda, Paul, Jeffery. MD, Tehran Med. Sch., 1957. Intern Mercy Hosp., Hamilton, Ohio, 1958; resident in psychiatry Marcy (N.Y.) Psychiat. Ctr., 1959-62; psychiatrist N.Y. State Office Mental Health, Utica, N.Y., 1959—; pvt. practice psychiatry N.Y., 1965—; psychiatrist, unit chief Mohawk Valley Psychiat. Ctr., Utica, 1973-90; cons. psychiatrist Lewis County Community Mental Health Ctr., Lowville, N.Y., 1990—, McPike Alcoholism Treatment Unit, Utica, 1991—; staff psychiatrist St. Elizabeth, Utica, St. Lukes Meml. Hosp., Utica, Faxton Hosp., Utica, Rome City Hosp. Fellow Am. Orthopsychiat. Assn.; mem. Am. Psychiat. Assn., Med. Soc. N.Y., Oneida County Med. Soc. Home: RD Box 249 RR 2 Box 20 Barneveld NY 13304-9723 Office: 1627 Genesee St Utica NY 13501-4792

EMANUEL, JAMES STEVEN, financial consultant; b. Turtle Creek, Pa., Oct. 12, 1949; s. James Luther and Dorothea A. (Voltz) E.; m. Pamela Breniser, Jan. 2, 1971; children: Joshua James, Sarah L. BA, Mich. State U., 1971; MA, U. So. Calif., 1973. ChFC, CLU. Agt. Minn. Mut. Life, Pitts., 1974-76; brokerage mgr. Union Mut., Pitts., 1976-80; sales mgr. Home Life Ins., Pitts., 1980-84; sr. cons. fin. planning The Advisor Group, Pitts., 1984-87; owner Emanuel Fin. Cons., Mt. Lebanon, Pa., 1987—; instr. bus. ins. Pitts. Life Underwriters, 1981-82; instr., investment advisor, speaker various ins. and investment cos., 1976—. Scoutmaster Boy Scouts Am., Mt. Lebanon, 1980-85; coach Mt. Lebanon Girls Soccer Assn., 1985-87; vol. cons. Benedictine Ctr., Pitts., 1986—; vol. Special Olympics; instr. religious edn., fin. com. Unitarian Universalist Ch. South Hills. Mem. Mt. Lebanon Girls Softball Assn. (coach 1987—), Lincoln Nat. Life Pres.'s Club/Cabinet. Democrat. Home: 405 Parker Dr Pittsburgh PA 15216 Office: Emanuel Fin Cons 345 Mt Lebanon Blvd Pittsburgh PA 15234

EMANUELSON, RICHARD GILSEY, oncologist, hematologist; b. Buffalo, Dec. 5, 1954; s. Harold LeRoy and Carol Ruth (Gilsey) E.; m. Kathleen Jo Niezgoda, Mar. 14, 1981; children: Kristin Alysse, Steven Anthony, Karin Ruth. BS in Biology, Denison U., 1976; MD, SUNY, Buffalo, 1980. Diplomate Am. Bd. Internal Medicine in med. oncology and hematology. Physician Home-One Assocs. of N.E. Pa., Inc., Scranton; mem. dir. Scranton Regional Career and Imaging Ctr., Clarks Summit, Pa., 1989—; sect. chief hematology-oncology Community Med. Ctr., Scranton, 1986—; med. dir. VNA Hospice, Scranton, 1989—. Mem. ACP, AMA, Pa. Med. Soc., Pa. Soc. Home-One, Lackawanna County Med. Soc. (pub. rels. com.). Office: Home-One Assocs NE Pa Inc 611 Morgan Hwy Clarks Summit PA 18411

EMBER, CAROL R., anthropology educator, author; b. Bklyn., July 7, 1943; d. Hy and Elsie (Kardonsky) Ruchlis; m. Lawrence Baldwin, 1963 (div. 1969); m. Melvin Ember, Mar. 21, 1970; children: Katherine Ann, Julie Beth. BA, Antioch Coll., 1965; postgrad., Cornell U., 1965-66; PhD, Harvard, 1971. Lectr. Hunter Coll. CUNY, 1970-71; from asst. prof. to assoc. prof. CUNY, 1971-80, prof., 1981—. Author: (with Melvin Ember) Marriage, Family and Kinship: Comparative Studies of Social Organization, 1983, Anthropology, 7th edit., 1993, Cultural Anthropology, 7th edit., 1993, Anthropology: A Brief Introduction, 1991. Woodrow Wilson fellow, 1965-66, predoctoral fellow NIMH, 1969-70; rsch. grantee NSF, 1983-84, 86-88, 89-93, 90-92, USIP, 1990-92. Mem. Am. Anthrop. Assn., Soc. for Cross-Cultural Rsch. (pres. 1985), Soc. for Psychol. Anthropology. Office: Hunter Coll. CUNY 695 Park Ave New York NY 06524

EMBODY, DANIEL ROBERT, biometrician; b. Ithaca, N.Y., July 10, 1914; s. George Charles and Mary Madeline (Riceman) E.; m. Margaret Constance Gran, Mar. 21, 1946 (dec. Mar. 1961); children: James Michael, Daniel Robert, David Richard. BS, Cornell U., 1938, M.S., 1939, postgrad., 1939-42; postgrad., N.C. State Coll., summer 1940. Instr. limnology Cornell U., Ithaca, N.Y., 1940-42; sr. math. analyst Arnold Bernard & Co., N.Y.C., 1947-48; statistician Wash. Water Power Co., Spokane, 1949-53; head statistics sect. E.R. Squibb & Sons-Olin, New Brunswick, N.J., 1953-57, mgr. electronic data processing svc. ctr., 1958-63, coord. sci. computations, 1964-65; math. statistician Bur. Ships, Navy Dept., Washington, 1965-67; biometrician Dept. Agr., Beltsville, Md., 1967-72; staff biometrician animal and plant health inspection svc. Dept. Agr., Hyattsville, Md., 1972-87; sr.

ptnr. EIC Assocs., Hyattsville, 1981—; cons. Idaho Fish and Game Dept., 1950-60, U.S. Geol. Survey, 1953-58, N.J. Dept. Fish and Game, 1953-60. Contbr. articles to profl. jours. Lt. comdr. USNR, 1942-46, ETO. Mem. NRA, Am. Statis. Assn., Biometric Soc., Entomol. Soc. Am. (cert., emeritus), N.Y. Acad. Scis., Am. Legion, Am. Fisheries Soc., Sigma Xi, Gamma Alpha. Home: 5025 Edgewood Rd College Park MD 20740-4603

EMBRY, STEPHEN CRESTON, lawyer; b. Key West, Fla., Feb. 13, 1949; s. Jewell Creston and Julia Martine (Taylor) E.; m. Priscilla Mary Brown, Aug. 21, 1971; children: Nathaniel, Julia, Jessamyn. BA, Am. U., 1971; JD, U. Conn., 1976. Bar: Conn. 1976, U.S. Dist. Ct. Conn., 1976, U.S. Ct. Appeals (2d, 5th and 9th cirs.). Staff aide to Pres. The White House, Washington, 1969-72; assoc. Turner & Hensley, Great Bend, Kans., 1976, O'Brien, Shafner, Bartinik, & Stuart, Groton, Conn., 1976-85, Embry and Neusner, Groton, Conn., 1985—. Mem. Groton Rep. com., 1976-83, North Stonington Rep. com., 1984-88; chmn. Groton Housing Authority, 1979-80. Mem. Am. Trial Lawyers Assn. (chair workers compensation sect. 1984-85), Maritime Claimants Attys. Assn. (bd. dirs. 1980—), Conn. Trial Lawyers, Conn. Bar Assn. (mem. exec. bd.). Republican. Lodge: Grange.

EMERICK, ROBERT TWITE, computer information scientist; b. Harrisburg, Pa., June 6, 1950; s. Twite Shoop and Nancy Jane (Wehrenberg) E.; m. Carol Jean Weaver, Aug. 24, 1974 (div. Oct. 1980). BS in Edn., Millersville (Pa.) State Coll., 1972; BS in Computer Sci., Millersville U., 1991. Cert. tchr. Pa. Tchr. Harrisburg Middle Sch., 1972-75, Susquehanna Twp. High Sch., Harrisburg, 1975-77; property mgr. DelBrook Manor Apts., Mechanicsburg, Pa., 1978; commercial property mgr. Am. Realty & Mortgage, Harrisburg, 1978; instr. Central Pa. Bus. Sch., Summerdale, 1978-83; print and pub. mgr. Tng. Resource Corp., Harrisburg, 1983-85; estimator, coord. BSC Litho, Harrisburg, 1985-86; coord. support svcs. Tng. Resource Corp., Harrisburg, 1986-88; application programmer, project librarian Millersville U., 1989-90, programmer/analyst, 1990—. Mem. Central Pa. Printing House Craftsmen (v.p. 1982-83), Susquehanna Twp. Edn. Assn. (pres. elect 1976-77). Home: 17B Mary St Millersville PA 17551-1916

EMERSON, ALICE FREY, political scientist, educator emeritus; b. Durham, N.C., Oct. 26, 1931; d. Alexander Hamilton and Alice (Hubbard) Frey; divorced; children: Rebecca, Peter. A.B., Vassar Coll., 1953; Ph.D., Bryn Mawr Coll., 1964; LLD (hon.), Wheaton Coll., 1986; DHL (hon.), Trinity Coll., 1992. Tchr., Newton (Mass.) High Sch., 1956-58; mem. faculty Bryn Mawr (Pa.) Coll., 1961-64; mem. faculty U. Pa., Phila., 1966-75, asst. prof. polit. sci., 1966-75, dean of women, 1966-69, dean of students, 1969-75; pres. Wheaton Coll., Norton, Mass., 1975-91, pres. emerita, 1991—; sr. fellow Andrew Mellon Found., N.Y.C., 1992—; bd. dirs. Bank of Boston Corp., First Nat. Bank of Boston, Eastman Kodak Co.; trustee Penn Mut. Life Ins. Co., 1977-92; adv. bd. HERS Mid-Am. Past mem. adv. bd. Com. for Nat. Security, Nat. Corp., Legal Def. and Edn.; bd. dirs. Corp. for Public and Pvt. Ventures, 1978-82, 86—, World Resources Inst., 1987—; mem. adv. bd. Great Woods Ednl. Forum, 1987—. Sr. fellow Andrew W. Mellen Found. Mem. Coun. on Fgn. Rels. Home: 353 E 72d St #24C New York NY 10021 Office: Andrew W Mellen Found 140 E 62d St New York NY 10021

EMERSON, ANDI (MRS. ANDI EMERSON WEEKS), sales and advertising executive; b. N.Y.C., Nov. 1, 1932; d. Willard Ingham and Ethel (Mole) E.; m. George G. Fawcett, Jr. (div.); children—Ann Emerson II, George Gifford III, Christopher Babcock; m. Kenneth E. Weeks (div.); 1 child, Electra Ingham. Student, Barnard Coll. Successively v.p. Eugene Stevens, Inc., N.Y.C.; pres., dir. Emerson Mktg. Agy., Inc., N.Y.C., 1960—; pres., dir. Mail Order Operating Co. Ltd., N.Y.C. and London, 1976-88, Ingham Hall, Ltd., 1977-83; chmn. bd. dirs. Sonal World Mktg. Ltd., N.Y.C. and Delhi, India, 1983-87; instr. NYU, 1960-65, 87—. Vol. children's ward Meml. Hosp., 1964-66, Hosp. for Spl. Surgery, 1967; mem. adv. com. African Students League, 1965-67; bd. dirs. Violet Oakley Meml. Found., Phila., 1964-81; founder, pres., chmn. John Caples Internat. Awards, 1977—; elected N.Y. State Del. to White House Conf. on Small Bus., 1986. Inducted into Silver Apple Hall of Fame, 1985. Mem. Nat. Assn. Women Bus. Owners, Direct Mktg. Assn. (Hall of Fame selection com. 1989-91), Soc. Profl. Writers, Direct Mktg. Creative Guild (Andi Emerson award 1991, pres. 1975-81, bd. dirs. 1975—), Direct Mktg. Club of N.Y. (treas. 1960-61). Home: 16 E 96th St New York NY 10128-0753 Office: Emerson Mktg Agy Inc 17 Battery Pl New York NY 10004-1101

EMERSON, STEVEN A., journalist, author; b. N.Y.C., June 6, 1954; s. Michael Kenneth and Elaine Emerson. BA, Brown U., 1976, MA, 1977. Investigator, speech writer U.S. Senate Fgn. Relations Com., Washington, 1977-80; exec. asst. to Senator Frank Church Washington, 1981; writer New Republic mag., Washington, 1982; assoc. editor U.S. News and World Report, Washington, 1985-87, sr. editor, nat. security corr., 1987-89; freelance journalist and author, 1990—; spl. corr. CNN, 1991. Author: The American House of Saud, 1985, Secret Warriors: Inside the Covert Military Operations of the Reagan Era, 1988, Terrorist: The Inside Story of the Highest Ranking Iraqi Terrorist Ever to Defect to the West, 1991; co-author: The Fall of Pan Am 103: Inside the Lockerbie Investigation, 1990; contbr. articles to newspapers and mags. Recipient Investigative Reporters and Editors award, 1982, 89, 90; Laurel for disting. reporting Columbia Journalism Rev., 1982. Mem. Council on Fgn. Relations. Office: 3930 Connecticut Ave NW Ste 202 Washington DC 20008

EMERSON, WILLIAM KEITH, zoologist; b. San Diego, May 1, 1925; s. Horace P. and Vera (Vaught) E. A.B., Calif. State U.-San Diego, 1948; M.S., U. So. Calif., 1950; Ph.D., U. Calif.-Berkeley, 1956. Paleontologist U. Calif. Mus. Paleontology, Berkeley, 1951-55; asst. curator invertebrates Am. Mus. Natural History, 1955-61, asso. curator, 1961-66, curator, 1966—, chmn. dept. living invertebrates, 1960-74; research asso. San Diego Natural History Mus., 1962-82; rsch. assoc. Santa Barbara Mus. Natural History, 1991—; Leader, Puritan expdn. to Western Mexico Am. Mus. Natural History, 1957; mem. Belvedere Expdn. to Gulf of Calif., 1962. Author: (with M.K. Jacobson) Shells of the New York City Area, 1961, Wonders of the World of Shells: Sea, Land and Fresh-Water, 1971, American Museum of Natural History Guide to Shells, 1976, Wonders of Starfish, 1977, (with Andreas Feininger) Shells, 1972, (with Arnold Ross) Wonders of Barnacles, 1974; Contbr. papers to profl. jours. Bd. trustees Del. Mus. Natural History, Wilmington, 1989—. Fellow AAAS, Calif. Acad. Scis. (hon.); mem. Am. Malacological Union (pres. 1961-62, mem. coun. 1963-65, 87-89, hon. life 1989—), Western Soc. Malacologists (pres. 1968-69, mem. coun. 1970-72), Paleontology Soc., Soc. Systematic Zoology (coun. 1960-63, 70-72), Coun. Systematic Malacologists (pres. 1988-91), Paleontol. Rsch. Instn., San Diego Soc. Nat. History, Calif. Malacozool. Soc., Blue Key, Sigma Xi, Sigma Phi Epsilon. Home: 10 E End Ave New York NY 10021-1106 Office: Am Mus Natural History Central Park St W New York NY 10026-4355

EMERSON, WILLIAM R., retired library executive, historian; b. Little Rock; student Hendrix Coll., U. Mo.; B.A. in History, Yale; Ph.D. (Rhodes scholar), Oxford (Eng.) U., 1952; m. Barbara Clogher Woodriff. Formerly mem. history faculty Yale U., King prof. history U.S. Naval War Coll., asst. to pres. Hollins Coll.; dir. research grants Nat. Endowment for Humanities, Washington, 1969-74; dir. Franklin D. Roosevelt Library, Hyde Park, N.Y., 1974-91. Served with USAAF, World War II; MTO. Home: 155 Fox Run Poughkeepsie NY 12603-3520

EMERY, HOWARD IVAN, JR., management consultant, telecommunications specialist; b. N.Y.C., June 21, 1932; s. Howard I. and Margaret E. (Kayser) E.; m. Jean L. Winters, Sept. 24, 1955; children: David P., Donald P. BCE, Cornell U., 1955; MS in Advanced Mgmt., Pace U., 1979; M of Engring. (hon.), Cornell U., 1988. Registered profl. engr., N.Y. Various line and staff N.Y. Telephone, N.Y.C., 1957-77; div. mgr. regulatory strategy AT&T, N.Y.C., 1977-79; div. mgr. exec. edn. N.Y. Telephone, N.Y.C., 1979-82; corp. dir. strategic planning Nynex Corp., White Plains, N.Y., 1982-85; v.p. internat. Nynex Internat. Co., White Plains, 1985-90; mgmt. cons. Huntington, N.Y., 1990—; bd. dirs. PTT Telecom Netherlands US, N.Y.C., Internat Computers and Communications, Washington; chmn. civil engr. adv. coun. Cornell U., Ithaca, N.Y., 1991—, guest lectr. in internat. strategy, 1986—. Bd. edn. Harborfields Pub. Schs., Greenlawn, N.Y., 1966-73; active admissions and alumni groups Cornell U., Ithaca, 1960—. 1st lt. U.S. Army, 1955-57. Mem. Internat. Computers and Communications (bd. dirs. 1990—), Internat. Telecom Soc. Home and Office: 119 Huntington Bay Rd Huntington NY 11743

EMERY, ROBERT FIRESTONE, economist, educator; b. Kenton, Ohio, Jan. 18, 1927; s. Clayton Sprague and Sarah Webster (Firestone) E.; m. Phyllis Eileen Swanson, June 29, 1957; children: Ross David, Ann Elaine, Hope Roberta. BA, Oberlin (Ohio) Coll., 1951; MA, U. Mich., 1952, PhD, 1956. Fellow U. Mich., 1954-55; economist Fed. Res. Bd., Washington, 1955-92; adj. prof. econs. Southeastern U., Washington, 1960-88, chmn. dept. fin. adminstrn., 1963-65, dean sr. div., 1965-68, prof. emeritus, 1988. Author: The Financial Institutions of Southeast Asia, 1971, The Japanese Money Market, 1983, The Money Markets of Developing East Asia, 1991. Mem. admstrv. bd. Chevy Chase (Md.) United Meth. Ch., 1978-80. Served as midshipman U.S. Mcht. Marine Cadet Corps, 1945-47. Horace H. Rackham Grad. fellow U. Mich., 1952-53; Fulbright Grad. Research student U. Rangoon, Burma, 1953-54. Mem. Am. Econ. Assn., Soc. Govt. Economists (treas. 1976-78), Internat. Economists' Club (pres. 1977-92). Republican. Methodist. Home: 3421 Shepherd St Chevy Chase MD 20815-3223

EMINI, EMILIO ANTHONY, research scientist; b. N.Y.C., Dec. 9, 1953; s. Emilio and Maria (Pescione) E.; m. Jacquelynn Ruby Cunliffe, Dec. 27, 1980; children: Emilia C., Alessandra J. BS, Manhattan Coll., 1975; PhD, Cornell U., 1980. Research fellow SUNY, Stony Brook, 1980-83; sr. scientist Merck, Sharp and Dohme Research Labs., West Point, Pa., 1983-86, research fellow, 1986-89, assoc. dir., 1989-90, dir., 1990-92, sr. dir., 1992—. Contbr. articles to profl. jours.; patentee in field. Fellow NSF, 1976, Am. Cancer Soc., 1980, NIH, 1981-82. Mem. AAAS, Am. Soc. Microbiology, N.Y. Acad. Sci., Phi Beta Kappa. Democrat. Roman Catholic. Avocation: ancient history. Office: Merck Sharp and Dohme Research Labs West Point PA 19486

EMMERICH, JOHN PATRICK, computer infosystems company executive; b. N.Y.C., Feb. 15, 1950; s. Clifford L. and Anna V. E.; BS, Fla. State U., 1970, JD, 1974; MBA, Syracuse U., 1976. V.p., treas. Applied Devices Corp., Hauppage, N.Y., 1968-76; exec. v.p. Ontel Corp., Woodbury, N.Y., 1976-82; sr. v.p. Visual Tech. Inc., 1983-89; pres. Ontech Corp., Nashua, N.H., 1989—; bd. dirs. Ontel Corp., Lowell, Mass, Visual Tech. Internat. Inc., Lowell. V.p. N. Creek Property Owners Assn. (N.Y.), 1980. Recipient commendation U.S. Army. Mem. U.S. Naval Inst., Am. Mgmt. Assn., Nat. Microfilm Assn., Am. Def. Preparedness Assn., Pres. Club, L.I. Assn. Bus. Commerce. Roman Catholic. Contbr. articles to profl. jours. Home: 89 Cox St Nashua NH 03060-1525

EMMETT, MARTIN FREDERICK CHEERE, investment banker; b. Johannesburg, South Africa, Aug. 30, 1934; s. Cecil Frederick Cheere and Thelma Marie (Ford) E.; m. Alice Ellen Lavers, Aug. 18, 1956; children: Karen Ann, Robert Martin Cheere, Susan Marie. BSME, U. Witwatersrand, Johannesburg, 1957; MBA, Queens U., Kingston, Ont., Can., 1962. V.p. consumer products Alcan Aluminum Co., Montreal, Que., Can., 1962-72; pres., chief exec. officer Standard Brands Ltd., Montreal, 1972-76, N.Y.C., 1980-81; pres. Internat. Standard Brands Ltd., N.Y.C., 1976-79; sr. exec. v.p., bd. dirs. Nabisco Brands, Inc., N.Y.C., 1981-83; chmn., chief exec. officer Internat. Nabisco Brands, 1981-83; vice chmn. Nabisco Brands, Ltd., Toronto, Ont., Can., 1985—; vice chmn. Burns, Fry and Timmins, Inc., N.Y.C., 1983-85, chmn., 1985—; chief exec. officer Tambrands Inc., 1989—; bd. dirs. Fry Ltd., Toronto. Mem. Assn. Profl. Engrs. Ont. Clubs: Econ.; Brook. Home: Frost Rd Greenwich CT 06830-3825 Office: Burns Fry & Timmins Inc Wall Street Pla New York NY 10005 also: Tambrands Inc 1 Marcus Ave Lake Success NY 11042*

EMOND, LEONARD DAVID, orthopaedist; b. Greenville, N.H., Aug. 20, 1928; s. David Charles and Albina (Boulay) E.; m. Julienne M. Bolduc, June 19, 1955; children: Marc D., James A., Christopher J. BS, U. N.H., 1950; post grad., Laval U., 1956, U. Pa., 1957. Diplomate Am. Bd. Neurol. and Orthopedic Surgery. Intern Laval Univ. Hosp., Quebec City, Quebec, Can., 1956; resident gen. surgery Bradford (Pa.) Hosp., 1956-57; resident orthopaedic surgery Akron Gen. Hosp., Akron Children's Hosp., 1957-60; orthopedic surgeon Med. Assocs., Dubuque, Iowa, 1960-63, pvt. practice, Manchester, N.H., 1963—; cons. N.H. Retirement System, Concord, 1991—; pres. New Eng. Disability Evaluations, Manchester, 1991—; staff mem. Cath. Med. Ctr., Manchester, N.H., 1965—. Assoc. editor: Jour. of Disability, 1990, 91, 92; contbr. articles to profl. jours. Fellow Am. Acad. Neurol. and Othopaedic Surgery, Am. Acad. Disability Evaluations (lectr. 1987—, bd. dirs. 1989—, chmn. clin. tng. program 1989-91); mem. Nat. Opera Co. Quebec (tenor 1954-55), N.H. Med. Soc., Hillsboro County Med. Soc., Souhegan Valley Choral Soc. (tenor 1992—), Applalachin Mountain Club (mem. 4000 footer club). Republican. Roman Catholic. Home: 110 Crestview Rd Manchester NH 03104 Office: New Eng Disability Evals 20 Webster St Manchester NH 03104

EMOND, LIONEL JOSEPH, management consulting firm executive; b. Winnipeg, Man., Can., May 31, 1932; s. Henri R. and Anastasia E.; m. Elizabeth Boelen, Sept. 9, 1957; children: Catherine, Pierre, Marise, Robert. B in Commerce, McGill U., 1953, MBA, 1957. Chartered acct., Can. Pvt. practice auditing, 1953-55; with Shell Oil Co. of Can., Montreal, 1955-58; mgr. fiscal dept. Can. Chem. & Cellulose Co., 1958-60; asst. corp. controller Kruger Pulp & Paper Co., 1960-62, controller, 1962-65; mgr. fin. Dominion Bridge Co., Montreal, 1965-68; asst. gen. mgr. Churchill Falls Project, 1968-70; sr. fin. cons. Acres Internat., 1970-71; v.p. fin. Can. Gen. Ins. Co., 1971-75; v.p., treas. United Coops. of Ont., Toronto, 1976-80; v.p. fin. services The S.N.C. Group, Montreal, 1980-83; ptnr. Guerra Emond Internat. Mgmt. Cons., 1983—; pres., L.J. Emond Cons., Inc., 1986—; lectr. fin. Concordia U. Mem. editorial bd. Cost and Mgmt., 1965—; contbr. articles to profl. jours. Pres. Etobicoke Rate Payers Assn., 1978-80; mem. bd. mgmt. Etobicoke Olympium, 1977-80; mem. exec. com. Canadian Coop. Credit Soc., 1977-80. Recipient citation Canadian Coop. Credit Soc., 1980. Mem. Fin. Exec. Inst. (pres. 1986-87), Inst. Chartered Accts., Soc. Mgmt. Accts., Am. Assn. Cost Engrs., Montreal Amateur Athletic Assn., Les Artisanats Centre-Ville Montreal (pres. 1984—). Roman Catholic. Home and Office: 203 Outremont Ave, Outremont, PQ Canada H2V 3L9

EMORY, ALAN STEUER, journalist; b. N.Y.C., May 7, 1922; s. Henry and Ethel (Steuer) Epstein; m. Nancy Carol Goodman, Oct. 15, 1950; children: Marc Douglas, John Alan, Katharine Blair. Grad., Phillips Exeter (N.H.) Acad., 1939; AB, Harvard U., 1943; MS, Columbia U., 1947. State editor Watertown (N.Y.) Daily Times, 1948-49, legis. corr., 1949-51, Washington corr., 1951—; Washington corr. Empire State Report, N.Y.C., 1986—, Schenectady (N.Y.) Gazette, 1954-83, Oswego (N.Y.) Palladium-Times, 1952-80; corr. Batavia News, 1990—, Malone Telegram, 1991—, Catskill Daily Mail, 1991—. Author: So You Want to Go to Washington, Series on Alaska, 1958, Series on Soviet Union, 1977. Bd. dirs. Lake Barcroft Community Assn., Fairfax County, Va. S/Sgt. U.S. Army, 1943-46, ETO. Mem. Soc. Profl. Journalists (treas. Washington chpt. 1973-74, v.p. 1974-75, pres. 1975-76, chmn. Washington Hall of Fame 1982—, Named to Hall of Fame 1979), White Ho. Corrs. Assn., State Dept. Corrs. Assn., Overseas Writers, Regional Reporters Assn., Gridiron Club (exec. com. 1982, music chmn. 1982, 88), Sigma Delta Found. of Washington (treas. 1979—). Home: 6302 Crosswoods Cir Falls Church VA 22044-1302 Office: Johnson Newspaper Corp 1001 National Press Bldg Washington DC 20045-2001

ENBERG, HENRY WINFIELD, legal editor; b. Bethlehem, Pa., Oct. 4, 1940; s. Henry Winfield and Mildred Elizabeth (Jordan) E. BS, U. Denver, 1962; LLB, NYU, 1965. Bar: N.Y. 1967. Digester, Winthrop, Stimson, Putnam & Roberts, N.Y.C., 1965-69; sr. legal editor Practising Law Inst., N.Y.C., 1969—. Contbr. articles. to profl. jours. Mem. Baker St. Irregulars, Wolfe Pack Club, Priory Scholars Club. Republican. Episcopalian. Home: 250 W 27th St New York NY 10001-5908 Office: Practising Law Inst 810 7th Ave New York NY 10019-5818

ENCINAS, JAIME FERNANDO, international executive; b. Santiago, Chile, Feb. 20, 1948; came to U.S., 1970; s. Raul T. and Elena (Montalban) E.; m. Elena Chirani, Apr. 6, 1971; children: Raoul N., Katerina, Alexandra. BSBA, U. Chile, Santiago, 1970; MBA, U. Detroit, 1973. Corp. auditor Chrysler Corp., Highland Park, Mich., 1973-75; internat. auditor Merck & Co., Rahway, N.J., 1975-77, fin. mgr. Ecuador div., 1977-80; fin. mgr. Latin Am. div. Parker Pen Co., Janesville, Wis., 1980-82, gen. mgr. Mex. div., 1982-86; corp. controller Roburn Internat. Corp., Elmwood Park, N.J., 1986-89; dir. Latin Am. div. Potters Industries, Inc., Parsippany, N.J., 1989—. Member Mex.-U.S. C.of C., Mex., 1982-85, Kiwanis Internat., Randolph, 1989-90; mem. adv. com. Twp. Mgmt., Randolph, 1990—. Mem. Writing Instruments Mfg. Assn. (chmn. Mexico City chpt. 1985), Beta Gamma Sigma.

ENCK, HENRY SYNDER, history educator, university official; b. Cleve., Apr. 29, 1942; s. Henry Samuel and Elanor Pauline (Brown) E.; m. Judith Eleanor Johnson, July 17, 1964; children: Mary Allyson, Adrienne Eleanor. BA, U. Richmond, 1964; MA, U. Cin., 1965, PhD, 1970. Instr. history Cen. Conn. State U., New Britain, 1968-70, asst. prof., 1970-76, assoc. prof., 1976-81, prof., 1981—, asst. to v.p. for academics, 1982-84, acting dean instrnl. svcs., 1984-85, faculty athletics rep., 1982-91, exec. asst. to pres., 1987—, coord. devel. initiatives in Beijing, 1990—; coord. initiatives Cen. Conn. State U., Wroclaw, Poland, 1990—. Contbr. articles to hist. jour. Office: Cen Conn State U 1615 Stanley St New Britain CT 06053-2439

ENDERS, ELIZABETH MCGUIRE, artist; b. New London, Conn., Feb. 18, 1939; d. Francis Foran and Helen Cuseck (Connolly) McGuire; m. Anthony Talcott Enders, June 9, 1962; children: Charles Talcott, Alexandra Eustis, Camilla, Ostrom II. BA, Conn. Coll., 1962; MA, NYU, 1987. Trustee Artists Space, N.Y.C., 1986—, Conn. Coll., New London, 1988—. One woman shows include Paul Schuster Gallery, Cambridge, Mass., 1966, Ulysses Gallery, N.Y.C., 1992; exhibited in group shows at Boston Symphony Orch., 1982, NYU, 1983, Conn. Conn., 1988, Bronx Coun. on Arts, 1990-91; represented in permanent collections at Addison Gallery of Am. Art, Andover, Mass., 1981, Graham Gund, Cambridge, 1982, Daimler Benz Holding Co., 1990. Mem. nat. fin. coun. Dem. Nat. Com., Washington, 1988—. Recipient Citation of Appreciation, Conn. Coll., 1990. Mem. The Drawing Soc., The Bklyn. Mus., Williams Coll. Mus. of Art, Whitney Mus. Am. Art, Williams Club. Democrat. Roman Catholic. Home: 530 E 86th St New York NY 10028-7535

ENDIEVERI, ANTHONY FRANK, lawyer; b. Syracuse, N.Y., May 21, 1939; s. Santo and Anne Rose (Zeolla) E.; m. Arlene Rita McDonald, May 20, 1967; children: Anne C., Steven A. BA, Syracuse U., 1961, JD, 1965. Bar: N.Y. 1967, U.S. Dist. Ct. (no. dist.) N.Y. 1967, U.S. Ct. Appeals (2d cir.) 1969, U.S. Supreme Ct. 1970. Assoc. Ronald Crowley, Atty., North Syracuse, N.Y., 1965-67, Love, Balducci & Scacciz, Syracuse, 1967; pvt. practice law, Camillus, N.Y., 1968-70; appellate counsel Hiscock Legal Aid, Syracuse, 1968-70; asst. corp. counsel, prosecutor City of Syracuse, 1970-74; participant Nat. Coll. Advocacy, 1981-83, 86; lectr. Melvin Belli seminar, San Francisco, 1987, Kansas City, Mo., 1988, Boston, 1989; speaker Melvin Belli Seminar, San Diego, 1990. Mem. ministry program Syracuse Diocese Pre-Deacon Study, 1980-82. Served to maj. USMCR, 1972-88. Mem. ABA, N.Y. Bar Assn., Onondaga County Bar Assn., N.Y. Trial Lawyers Assn., Assn. Trial Lawyers Am. (speaker nat. conv. 1990, seminar 1990, ultimate trial advocacy course 1991). Democrat. Roman Catholic. Home: 205 Emann Dr Camillus NY 13031-2009

ENDRIES, JOHN MICHAEL, utility executive; b. New Berlin, N.Y., Sept. 10, 1942; s. Norton Leo and Alice (Simons) E.; m. Anne Jones, Sept. 9, 1967; children—Carrie Anne, John Michael. B.B.A. in Acctg, U. Notre Dame, 1964. CPA, N.Y. Audit mgr. Price Waterhouse & Co. (CPA's), Syracuse, N.Y., 1964-73; asst. to v.p. fin., then v.p., controller Niagara Mohawk Power Corp., Syracuse, 1973-80, sr. v.p., 1980-87, exec. v.p., 1987-88, pres., 1988—, also bd. dirs.; bd. dirs. Niagara Mohawk Power Corp., Marine Midland Banks Inc., Utilities Mutual Ins. Co., Hydra-Co Enterprises, Inc., Marine Midland Bank, N.A., Opinac Inc. Bd. regents Le Moyne Coll.; bd. dirs. Child and Family Svc., Sta. WCNY-TV/FM, Cornell Coop. Extension, Boy Scouts Am., United Way, Crouse-Irving Meml. Hosp. Found. Mem. AICPA, N.Y. State Soc. CPAs, Edison Electric Inst., Fin. Execs. Inst. Home: 8518 Equestrian Rdg Manlius NY 13104-9777 Office: Niagara Mohawk Power Corp 300 Erie Blvd W Syracuse NY 13202-4250

ENDYKE, MARY LOUISE, communications executive; b. Andover, Mass., Apr. 17, 1960; d. Walter Francis and Mary Ellen (Brosnan) E. BS in BA, Northeastern U., Boston, 1984; postgrad., Babson Coll., 1991—. Pub. svc. campaign dir. WBZ-TV, Boston, 1983-84; pres. Boston Media Group, 1984-88; regional mgr. Bus. Wire, Boston, 1988—. Creator Spl. Event Trademark, "Monster Dash", 1981. Vol. Mass. Spl. Olympics, Wakefield, 1986—, Mass. Easter Seal Soc., Boston, 1989—. Mem. Nat. Investor Rels. Inst., Pub. Rels. Soc. Am., MIT Enterprise Forum. Office: Bus Wire 101 Federal St Boston MA 02110-1800

ENG, KENNETH Y., physician; b. Glen Ridge, N.J., Dec. 31, 1950; m. Gladys Eng. BA, Rutgers Coll., 1972; MD, UMD N.J., 1977. Fellow in retinal surgery Mass. Eye and Ear Infirmary, Boston, 1981-82; fellow in diabetic retinopathy Joslin Diabetes Ctr., Boston, 1982—; trustee U. Medicine and Dentistry N.J. Med. Sch. Alumni. Fellow Am. Acad. Ophthalmology; mem. Union County Med. Soc., Rsch. to Prevent Blindness. Office: 210 W Saint George Ave Linden NJ 07036

ENGBRETSON, PETER CURTIS, public administrator; b. Pasco, Wash., May 11, 1939; s. Paul Leonard and Betty (Cooper) E.; m. Susan Pacheco, 1962 (div. 1972); children: Elisa Ann, Jon Peter; m. Jean Marie McMahon, 1981; 1 child, Caitlin Maria. BA, San Francisco State Coll., 1966; MS, U. Oreg., 1969, postgrad., 1969-71. Underwriter Safeco Ins. Co., Burlingame, Calif., 1962-66; instr. U. Oreg., Eugene, 1969-72; asst. prof. U. Portland, Oreg., 1972-73; exec. dir. Burnside Projects, Inc., Portland, 1973-75; program coord., then commr.'s asst. City of Portland, 1975-84; dep. dir. Austin (Tex.) Parks and Recreation Dept., 1984-87; exec. dir. Phila. Ranger Corps, 1987—; pres., chief exec. officer Corps Group, Inc., Phila., 1991—. Active Pa. Environ. Coun., Phila. Com. on City Policy; trustee Cliveden of the Nat. Trust; gov. PhilaPride Amb. Corps.; del. Citizens Assembly for a Greater Phila.; grad. Leadership, Inc. Mem. Am. Soc. Pub. Adminstrn. (pres. Phila. region chpt. 1991—), Nat. Soc. Fund Raising Execs., Internat. City Mgrs. Assn., Nat. Recreation and Pk. Assn., Nat. Trust for Hist. Preservation, Nat. Civic League, World Futures Soc. Home: 411 E Allens Ln Philadelphia PA 19119-1104 Office: Corps Group Inc Belmont Ave at States Dr Philadelphia PA 19131-3712

ENGEBRECHT, PATRICIA ANN, construction company executive, owner; b. L.A., Dec. 19, 1935; m. Ronald Henry Engebrecht, Dec. 19, 1954; children: Jeffrey, Kurt. Grad. high sch., Milwakie, Oreg., 1954. Sec. Oreg. State U., 1955-56, Bendix Aviation, Mich., 1959-60; freelance writer Oreg., N.Y., 1964-75; pres., owner L & L Developers Inc., Victor, N.Y., 1983—. Author: Under the Hay Stack, 1970. Mem. Rochester Home Builders Assn. (bd. dirs. 1988—)., Home and Office: 7271 Hertfordshire Way Victor NY 14564-1101

ENGEL, ELIOT L., congressman; b. N.Y.C., Feb. 18, 1947; s. Philip and Sylvia (Bleend) E. BA, CUNY, 1969, MS, 1973. Counselor, advisor N.Y. Urban Corps, 1968; tchr., dept. chmn. N.Y. Bd. Edn., 1969-76; guidance counselor N.Y. Pub. Schs., 1973-75; mem. N.Y. State Assembly from 81st dist., 1977-89, 101st-102nd Congresses from 19th N.Y. dist., 1989—. Columnist Co-op City News, 1972. V.p. Park-East Ind. Dem. Club, N.Y., 1970-71; del. Bronx Com. for Dem. Voters, 1971-76, v.p., 1975-76; del., mem. steering com. Youth Caucus, Dem. Nat. Conv., 172; v.p. Ind. Dems. of Co-op City, 1972-73, pres., 1974-75; committeeman Bronx County Dem. Com., N.Y., 1972—; mem. exec. coun. N.Y. State New Dem. Coalition, 1973-75; founder New Dem. Club Co-op City, 1975, pres., 1975-76; jud. del. N.Y. Supreme Ct. Conv., 1st Jud. Dist., 1975-76, dist. leader, 1976—. Recipient Man of Yr. award FDR Ind. Dem. Club, 1976. Mem. United Fund Tchrs., Ams. for Dem. Action (bd. dirs. N.Y. 1974—), Zionist Orgn. Am., K.P. Jewish. Office: US Ho of Reps Office House Mems Washington DC 20510*

ENGEL, JAMES MARC, financial planner; b. N.Y.C., Oct. 12, 1956; s. Leroy and Bonnie (Badler) E.; m. Peggy Barnett, July 9, 1988. BA in Math. and Physics with honors, Clarkson U., 1979; MBA in Fin., NYU, 1984; CFP, Colo. Coll., 1990. Media planner Benton & Bowles Advt., N.Y.C.,

1979-82; sr. rsch. analyst Gen. Foods, White Plains, N.Y., 1982-85; product mgr. J.E. Seagram & Sons, N.Y.C., 1985-89; asst. v.p. Kidder Peabody/GE Capital, N.Y.C., 1989—. Mem. ANA. Office: Kidder Peabody 200 Park Ave New York NY 10166

ENGEL, JOHN JACOB, communications executive; b. N.Y.C., June 9, 1936; s. Stewart I. and Beatrice (Schapiro) E.; m. Miriam Jarman, Aug. 17, 1986; children by previous marriage: Susan Lisa, Mark Alan; stepchildren: Alan Brett, Amy Ruth. BA, Adelphi U., Garden City, N.Y., 1957; MS, Boston U., 1959. Program dir. Sta. WLAD FM, DAnbury, Conn., 1954-57; account exec. Sta. WBRY AM, Waterbury, Conn., 1959-62, Sta. WNHC AM, New Haven, 1962-63; account exec. N.Am. Precis Syndicate, Inc., N.Y.C., 1963-68, exec. v.p., prin., 1968—; guest lectr. Publicity Club of N.Y., 1971. Mem. Manalapan-Englishtown Bd. Edn., N.J., 1971-77, pres., 1975-77; treas. Rosegate Condominium Assn., Old Bridge, N.J., 1986-87. Mem. Pub. Relations Soc. Am. Club: Publicity of N.Y. Lodge: B'nai B'rith (pres. 1967-69). Home: 13 Lindsey Cir Old Bridge NJ 08857-2678

ENGEL, LEONARD W., English educator; b. Phila., Jan. 11, 1936; s. L.W. and Madeline (Malone) E.; m. July 11, 1950 (div. Apr. 1980); children: Lenny, Tom, Kristin, Melissa; m. Moira McCloskey, Aug. 20, 1988; 1 child, Tessa Ariana. BA, Rutgers U., 1958; MA, Fordham U., 1961, PhD, 1977. Cert. tchr., Conn. English prof. Quinnipiac Coll., Hamden, Conn., 1964—, chmn. English dept., 1978-88; cons. and lectr. in field. Contbr. articles to profl. jours. Mem. MLA, Western Lit. Assn., Popular Culture Assn. N.E. MLA. Democrat. Roman Catholic.

ENGELBERG, EDWARD, comparative literature educator; b. Chemnitz, Germany, Jan. 21, 1929; s. Jakob and Paula (Weber) E.; m. Elaine A. Rosen, July 27, 1950; children: Stephen Paul, Michael Joseph, Elizabeth Joyce. BA, Bklyn. Coll., 1951; MA, U. Oreg., 1952; PhD in English, U. Wis., 1957. Assoc. prof. English U. Mich., Ann Arbor, 1957-65; prof. comparative lit. and European cultural studies dept. Romance and comparative lit. Brandeis U., Waltham, Mass., 1965—. Author: The Vast Design: Patterns in W.B. Yeats Aesthetic, 1964, 2d edit., 1989, The Unknown Distance: From Conscience to Consciousness, Goethe to Camus, 1972, Elegiac Fictions: The Motif of the Unlived Life, 1989; author, editor: The Symbolist Poem: The Development of the English Tradition, 1967; mem. editorial bd. South Atlantic Quar., 1987-90, Yeats: 1 of An Annual of Critical and Textual Studies, 1990—. Fulbright scholar Cambridge U., Eng., 1955-57. Mem. MLA, Am. Comparative Lit. Assn. (adv. com. 1988-91), Phi Beta Kappa. Jewish. Home: 58 Turning Mill Rd Lexington MA 02173-1010 Office: Brandeis U Dept Romance and Comparative Lit Waltham MA 02254-9110

ENGELL, JAMES THEODORE, English educator; b. Danville, Pa., Sept. 6, 1951; s. Frederick Jacob and Ruth Louise (Mumaw) E.; m. Ainslie Sheridan Brennan, June 2, 1984; children: Marleny Brennan, Alexander E. BA, Harvard Coll., 1973; PhD, Harvard U., 1978. Asst. prof. Harvard U., Cambridge, Mass., 1978-80, assoc. prof., 1980-83, prof. English and Comparative Lit., 1983—, chair degree program in history and lit., 1988—. Author: The Creative Imagination, 1981 (Thomas Wilson prize 1982), Forming the Critical Mind, 1989; editor, contbr.: Johnson and His Age, 1984, Teaching Literature: What is Needed Now, 1988; editor: Coleridge's Biographia Literaria, 1983; editorial advisor: Jour. History of Ideas, 1986—, Coll. Lit., 1990—. Corporator Emerson Hosp. and Health System, Concord, Mass., 1989—. Ford Found. grantee, 1978. Mem. Am. Soc. 18th Century Studies, MLA, Johnsonians (chair 1990-91). Office: Harvard U Dept English Warren St # 11 Cambridge MA 02141-1015

ENGELMAIER, WERNER, executive; b. Vienna, Austria, Feb. 7, 1939; came to U.S., 1962; s. Karl Maria and Henriette Kornelia (Unger) E.; m. Dolores Osie Halouska, May 16, 1935; children: Heide Marie, Peter Werner. Ingenieur degree, Tech. Gewerbe-Museum, Vienna, Austria, 1958; BSME, U. S.C., 1965; SMME, MIT, 1966. Engr. Kolben Kraus, Vienna, 1958-60, MAN, Augsburg, Germany, 1960-62; mem. rsch. staff AT&T Bell Labs., Whippany, N.J., 1966-90; pres., tech. dir. Engelmaier Assocs. Inc., Mendham, N.J., 1990—; sr. rsch. scientist U. Md., College Park, 1991—; sr. assoc. PPM Assocs. Inc., San Jose, Calif., 1990—. Inventor in field; contbr. articles to profl. jours. Mem. Bd. Adjustment, Mendham, 1969-73; mem., treas. Mendham Twonship First Aid Squad, 1972-90; mem. Nat. Ski Patrol, Denver, 1972-90. Recipient Rsch. and Devel. 100 award, Rsch. and Devel. Mag., 1978, 81. Mem. ASME, Internat. Electronics Packaging Soc. (Electronics Packaging Achievement award 1987), Inst. Interconnecting and Packaging Electronics Circuits (com. chmn. 1984—, Pres. award 1988). Home and Office: 23 Gunther St Mendham NJ 07945

ENGELMAN, ARTHUR, software engineer; b. N.Y.C., Mar. 17, 1930; s. Max and Julia (Shaoul) E.; m. Claire Esa Ludlow, June 18, 1955; children: Robert Eric, Alan Neal, Eileen Beth. BS, CCNY, 1950; MS, NYU, 1951, postgrad., 1951-52, 54-55; postgrad., Syracuse U., 1955-57. Rsch. asst. rsch. div. NYU, N.Y.C., 1950-52, 54-55; rsch. meteorologist Rome (N.Y.) Air Devel. Ctr., 1955-57; sr. engr. Raytheon Co., Bedford, Mass., 1957-59; v.p., tech. dir. GCA Corp., Bedford, 1959-86; pres. Engelman Cons., Framingham, Mass., 1986-87; program mgr. CTA Inc., Bedford, 1987—. 1st lt. U.S. Army, 1952-54. Home: 15 Woodward Rd Framingham MA 01701-7824

ENGER, EDWARD HENRY, JR., editor, writer; b. Mpls., Mar. 16, 1930; s. Edward Henry Sr. and Anastasia (Barber) E.; m. Carolyn Sue Bush, June 1, 1964. BS in Edn., U. Minn., 1952; cert. in teaching, U. Calif., Berkeley, 1953. Tchr. Downers Grove (Ill.) Pub. Sch., 1956-58; editor Harper & Row, Evanston, Ill., 1958-62; author Harper & Row, N.Y.C., 1975-78; editor Silver Burdett Co., Morristown, N.J., 1962-68, Dell Pub. Co., N.Y.C., 1968-75; author Nat. Textbook Co., Chgo., 1979-81; editorial dir. Amsco Sch. Publs., N.Y.C., 1982—. Author: Writing by Doing, 1981, (textbook series) Language Basics, 1975-78. Served to cpl. U.S. Army, 1954-56, Korea. Mem. Nat. Council Tchrs. English. Democrat.

ENGERMAN, STANLEY LEWIS, economist, educator, historian; b. Bklyn., Mar. 14, 1936; s. Irving and Edith (Kaplan) E.; m. Judith Rader, June 21, 1963; children—David, Mark, Jeffrey. B.S. cum laude, N.Y. U., 1956, M.B.A., 1958; Ph.D., Johns Hopkins, 1962. Asst. prof. econs. Yale, 1962-63; asst. prof., then asso. prof. U. Rochester, N.Y., 1963-71, prof. econs. and history, 1971—. Co-author: Time on the Cross: The Economics of American Negro Slavery, 1974; Co-editor: The Reinterpretation of American Economic History, 1971, Race and Slavery in the Western Hemisphere: Quantitative Studies, 1975, Between Slavery and Free Labor: The Spanish Speaking Caribbean in the Nineteenth Century, 1985, Long-Term Factors in American Economic Growth, 1986, British Capitalism and Caribbean Slavery: The Legacy of Eric Williams, 1987. Mem. AAAS, Econ. History Assn., Am. Econ. Assn., Am. Hist. Assn., Social Sci. History Assn., Assn. Caribbean Historians, Orgn. Am. Historians, Econ. Hist. Soc., Southern Hist. Assn., Cliometrics Soc. Home: 181 Warrington Dr Rochester NY 14618-1122 Office: U Rochester Dept Econs Rochester NY 14627

ENGESSER, DONALD GILBERT, consultant; b. Westfield, N.J., May 5, 1927; s. August and Anna (Gray) E.; m. Sylvia Stewart, Apr. 16, 1955; children: Curtis, Ruth, Stewart. BS in Adminstrn., Engring., Lafayette Coll., 1951; MS in Mech. Engring., N.J. Inst. Tech., 1954. Project dir. Creole Petroleum Co., Venezuela, 1968; engr. Esso R&D Co., Linden, N.J., 1951; mgr. tanker dept. Exxon Internat., N.Y.C., 1974; mgr. tech. dept. Exxon Rsch. & Engring., Florham Park, N.J., 1972; gen. mgr. engring. Exxon Rsch. & Engring., Florham Park, 1982; pres. Pmex. Inc., Chatham, N.J., 1982—; mem. adv. bd. N.J. Inst. Tech., 1980-89. With U.S. Navy, 1945-46. Mem. AICHE (project mgmt. sect.). Republican. Presbyterian. Home and Office: Pmex Inc. 707 Fairmount Ave Chatham NJ 07928-1157

ENGLAND, RICHARD, building materials company executive; b. 1920; married. Grad., Harvard U., 1942. With Hechinger Co. Inc., Landover, Md., 1946—, co.-chmn., co-chief exec. officer, now chmn. emeritus, also dir. Office: Hechinger Co 1616 McCormick Dr Landover MD 20785*

ENGLE, RICHARD MALLORY, college administrator, civil engineer; b. Chgo., Jan. 5, 1933; s. Robert Henry Sr. and Faerie Josephine (Mallory) E.; m. Claudia Standish White, June 7, 1958 (div. Sept. 1990); children: Jennifer K. Radl, Diana T., Adele S.Schneider, Richard H.W. BArch, U. Ill., 1956, MS in Architecture Engring., 1957. Registered profl. engr. Commd. C.E. Corps. U.S. Navy, Washington, many areas, 1957; advanced through grades to commdr. U.S. Navy, retired, 1978; physical plant dir. Miami Univ., Oxford, Ohio, 1978-86; assoc. v.p. for facilities Rutgers U., New Brunswick, N.J., 1986—. Contbr. various tech. articles to profl. pubs.; presentor Software Ownership, Nat. Bur. of Standards, 1983. 1st V.P. United Fed. Credit Union, Japan, 1970-75; vol. Boy Scouts Am., 1957—; vestry Episc. Ch., various locations, 1965-66, 80-86, 88—. Decorated Navy Achievement medal; Navy Commendation medal; recipient Thanks badge, Far East Coun. Girl Scouts Am., Atsugi, Japan, 1975. Mem. NSPE, Nat. Eagle Scout Assn., Assn. of Phys. Plant Adminstrs. (Midwest v.p.1984-86). Protestant. Home: 15 Silver Hollow New Brunswick NJ 08902 Office: Rutgers U Bldg 4115 Livingston Campus PO Box 5075 New Brunswick NJ 08903

ENGLISH, CURTIS RIEGEL, university administrator; b. Montoursville, Pa., Aug. 9, 1934; s. Curtis Albert and Ruth L. (Roberts) E.; m. Janet Laura Emery, June 16, 1956; children: Curtis Riegel III, Gary E., Scott T. BS, Bloomsburg U., 1956; MA, U. Okla., 1971; EdD, Vanderbilt U., 1985. Commd. ensign USN, 1956, advanced through grades to capt., 1978; staff officer Office of Chief of Naval Ops., Washington, 1968-72, 74-76; exec. asst. to chief of naval edn. and tng. USN, Pensacola, Fla., 1972-74; comdg. officer Naval and Marine Corps Res. Ctr., Washington, 1980-82; spl. asst. to dir. of Office of Space Flight NASA, Washington, 1982-83; comdg. officer Naval Res. Pers. Ctr., New Orleans, 1983-85; exec. dir. Pres.'s Commn. on Mcht. Marine and Def., Washington, 1985-86; mgr. corp. planning VSE Corp., Alexandria, Va., 1986-87; v.p. fin. and adminstrn. East Stroudsburg (Pa.) U., 1987—. Decorated Legion of Merit, Meritorious Svc. medals. Mem. Am. Assn. Higher Edn., Assn. Naval Aviation, Bloomsburg Alumni Assn., Kiwanis Internat. (pres. 1988-89, Disting. Pres. 1989). Methodist. Office: East Stroudsburg U East Stroudsburg PA 18301

ENGLISH, DAVID FLOYD, lawyer; b. Corning, N.Y., Feb. 21, 1948; s. Floyd W. English Jr. and Carolyn C. E.; m. Marcia Lynn Allen, Sept. 5, 1970; children: Eric Allen, Lynne Marie. BS, U. Rochester, 1970; JD, U. Miami, 1977. Bar: Fla. 1977, N.Y. 1978, U.S. Dist. Ct. (mid. dist.) Fla. 1978, U.S. Dist. Ct. (we. dist.) N.Y. 1978. Ptnr. English and English, Corning, 1978-80, Yorio, Tunney and English, Painted Post, N.Y., 1980-87, Yorio and English, Painted Post, 1988-90, Yorio, English and Roche, Painted Post, 1990—; atty. Town of Erwin, N.Y., 1988; chief counsel, Three Rivers Devel. Found., Inc., Corning, 1982—. Den leader Boy Scouts Am. Steuben Area Coun., Bath, N.Y., 1986-89; committeeman Steuben County Rep. Com., Bath, 1980-85. With USN, 1970-74; commdr. USNR, 1974—. Named to Corning Sports Hall of Fame, 1987. Mem. ABA, N.Y. Bar Assn., Fla. Bar Assn., Steuben County Bar Assn., Corning Bar Assn. (treas. 1980-87). Presbyterian. Home: 215 Watauga Ave Corning NY 14830-3233 Office: Yorio English & Roche 145 W High St Painted Post NY 14870-1298

ENGLISH, JAMES HILTON, JR., real estate and insurance company executive; b. Vineland, N.J., Apr. 3, 1919; s. James H. and Alice (Kling) E.; m. Kathryn S. Jones, Feb. 14, 1939; children: James H. III, J. Kent, Philip, Christopher. Grad. high sch., Salisbury, Md. Pres. The English Co., Salisbury, 1934-65; v.p., bd. dirs. Fairlanes Inc., Balt., 1962-65; v.p. Pocomoke Realty Inc., Salisbury, 1955—; pres., v.p. English Realty Inc., Ocean City, Md., 1965—; pres. English Ins. Co., Salisbury, 1968—. Mem. Salisbury C. of C., Masons, Lions. Office: English Ins Co 1319 Mt Hermon Rd Ste 4C Salisbury MD 21801-5219

ENGLISH, JOHN WINFIELD, foundation administrator; b. Canton, Ill., Mar. 27, 1933; s. Donald Ernest and Helen Marquis (Krout) E.; m. Ann Raster, Sept. 5, 1954; children: John R., Sarah Mellon, Laura Zmijeski. BA, U. Iowa, 1955. Various mgmt. jobs in the Bell System, 1955-81; dir. investment mgmt. AT&T, N.Y.C., 1975-81; v.p., chief investment officer The Ford Found., N.Y.C., 1981—; bd. dirs. Parabus Concord Trust Ltd., Mainstream Inc.; adv. com. pension mgrs. N.Y. Stock Exch. Investment com. Howard Hughes Med. Inst.; adv. com. N.Y. State Common Retirement System, Gen. Bd. Pensions United Meth. Ch., Smithsonian Inst.; trustee Itech/Parabus Trust for Insts., ARC of Greater N.Y.; chmn. bd. trustees ARC Endowment Fund; active Am. Coun. UN U., Tokyo; bd. dirs. U. Iowa Found., chmn. investment com. Mem. Phi Beta Kappa. Republican. Methodist. Home: PO Box 640 Summit NJ 07902-0640 Office: The Ford Found 320 E 43rd St New York NY 10017-4816

ENNEKING, RONALD LEO, data processing company executive; b. Batesville, Ind., Apr. 7, 1953; s. Alphonse Arthur and Edna Marie (Flaspohler) E.; m. Sandra K. Forsgren, Dec. 30, 1978; 1 child, Jason Michael. BS in Acctg. with distinction, Ind. U., 1975; MBA, Xavier U., 1984. CPA, Ind. Staff acct. Crowe Chizek & Co., CPAs, Elkhart, Ind., 1975-77; contr. Elkhart Motor Car Co., Inc., 1977-78, Batesville Casket Co., Inc., Nashua, N.H., 1985-87; fin. exec. Batesville (Ind.) Casket Co., Inc., 1978-85; dir. fin. Courier Corp., Westford, Mass., 1987-89; dir. mfg. Courier Corp., Lowell, Mass., 1989-91; sr. mgr. U.S. ops. Phoenix Techs. Ltd., Norwood, Mass., 1991—. Pres. St. Louis Parish Bd. Edn., Batesville, 1983-84. Mem. Nat. Assn. Accts., Ind. CPA Soc., New England Book Builders, Software Pubs. Assn., Merrimack Valley Rotary Club. Roman Catholic. Home: 19 Cimmarron Dr Nashua NH 03062 Office: Phoenix Techs Ltd 846 University Ave Norwood MA 02062

ENNIS, HERBERT LEO, research biochemist; b. N.Y.C., Jan. 6, 1932; s. Rudolph and Fannie (Stringer) E.; m. Judith Wolper, June 5, 1960; children: Ronald D., Ethan W. BS, Bklyn. Coll., 1953; MS, Northwestern U., 1954, PhD, 1957. Instr. Harvard U. Med. Sch., Boston, 1960-64; mem. staff St. Jude Children's Rsch. Hosp., Memphis, 1964-69, Roche Inst. Molecular Biology, Nutley, N.J., 1969—; mem. adv. com. Am. Cancer Soc., Atlanta, 1990—. Mem. editorial bd. Antimicrobial Agts. and Chemotherapy, 1972-77, editor, 1977-87; contbr. numerous articles to sci. jours. Mem. AAAS, Am. Soc. Biochemistry and Molecular Biology, Am. Soc. for Microbiology, N.Y. Acad. Scis., Sigma Xi. Office: Roche Inst Molecular Biol 340 Kingsland St Nutley NJ 07110-1199

ENNIS, LOUIS JOSEPH, university executive, educator; b. Boston, Mar. 21, 1929; s. Lewis and Veronica (Pittman) E.; m. Roberta M. Aymie, Aug. 31, 1958; children: Louis C., Jeanmarie, Mark T., Sean J., Caroline. MA in Econs., Boston Coll., 1960, MBA, 1970. Adminstr. Smithsonian Astrophys. Obs., Cambridge, Mass., 1959-60; asst. dir. employee rels. High Voltage Engring. Corp., Burlington, Mass., 1960-65; v.p. employee rels. Brandeis U., Waltham, Mass., 1965—; sr. lectr. Northeastern U., Boston, 1973—. Mem. pers. com. Toward Bedford, Mass., 1965. With USCG, 1951-54. Mem. Lexington Club. Home: 29 Wildwood Dr Bedford MA 01730-1124 Office: Brandeis U 415 South St Waltham MA 02154-2700

ENO, PAUL FREDERICK, editor; b. Hartford, Conn., Mar. 30, 1953; s. Earl Bryan and Bernice Sarah (Landers) E.; m. Jaclyn Ann Blackmon, June 7, 1981; children: Jonathan David, Benjamin Thomas. AA, St. Thomas Sem., Bloomfield, Conn., 1973; BA in Philosophy, Wadhams Hall Coll., Ogdensburg, N.Y., 1975; postgrad., Trinity Coll., Hartford, Conn., 1976-78. Book series editor Warbrooke Pub. Ltd., Montreal, Que., Can., 1974-76; staff writer Pawtuxet Valley Daily Times, West Warwick, R.I., 1979-80; mng. editor Observer Publs., Smithfield, R.I., 1980-83; copy editor Providence Jour., 1985-91; freelance editor and writer, 1976—; instr. writing R.I. Coll., Providence, 1982-83; instr. editing Brown U., Providence, 1990-91; editorial cons. R.I. Hist. Soc., Providence, 1986—. Editor John Brown's Adirondack Empire, 1988, Flexography: Principles and Practices, 1990; contbr. articles to mags. Vice chmn. Cumberland Hist. Dist. Commn., 1987-92. With USCGR, 1983-89. Recipient medal R.I. Hist. Soc., 1987. Mem. R.I. Press. Assn. (bd. dirs., treas. 1982-89, Best Editorial of Yr. 1981, 82), New Eng. Press Assn., Blackstone Valley Hist. Soc., Cumberland Beagle Club. Home: PO Box 211 Manville RI 02838-0211

ENOS, CHRIS, artist, educator; b. Burbank, Calif., Aug. 21, 1944; d. George Sydney and Wanda Ingrid (Thorsen) Schlatter. BA in Sculpture, San Francisco State U., 1969, MFA in Photography, 1970. Instr. photography San Francisco Acad. Art, 1972-73, U. Calif., San Francisco, 1972-73, Boston U., 1975, Harvard U., Cambridge, Mass., 1977, 80; asst. prof. Windham Coll., Putney, Vt., 1974, Hampshire Coll., Amherst, Mass., 1974-75; instr., dir. gallery, coord. lecture series New Eng. Sch. Photography, Boston, 1977-78; asst. prof. U. N.H., Durham, 1986—; artist-in-residence Internat. Ctr. Photography, N.Y.C., 1980, coord. advanced studies, 1982; vis. artist U. Colo., Boulder, 1982, Smith Coll., Northampton, Mass., 1982-83; vis. lectr. UCLA, 1984-85, RISD, Providence, 1985; lectr. numerous colls. and univs., 1975—. One-woman shows, 1974—, latest being Zoe Gallery, Boston, 1987, 89, DeCordova Mus., Lincoln, Mass., 1987, Spaces Gallery, Cleve., 1988; exhibited in numerous group shows in U.S. and fgn. countries, 1975—, latest being Internat. Ctr. Photography, 1987, Brockton (Mass.) Art Mus., 1987, Grand Rapids (Mich.) Art Mus., 1988, Fogg Mus., Harvard U., 1989; represented in numerous collections, including San Francisco Mus. Modern Art, Portland (Maine) Mus. Art, Mus. Fine Arts, Boston. Recipient award Artists Found., Inc., 1983, Silver award Art Dirs. Club New Eng., 1987, Englehard award Inst. Contemporary Art, Boston, 1988; photography fellow Artists Found., 1975, 80, Nat. Endowment Arts, 1981; grantee Mass. Coun. on Arts and Humanities, 1985, 86, Nynex faculty grantee U. N.H., 1987. Home: 1 Fitchburg St Apt 420C Somerville MA 02143-2129 Office: U NH Paul Arts Ctr Durham NH 03824

ENOS, GREGORY JOSEPH, professional development and technical training executive. BS, Rochester Inst. Tech., 1972; MS in Edn., U. So. Calif., 1979. Sports info. dir. Rochester (N.Y.) Inst. Tech., 1971-72; mgr. employee communications, communications editor Data Systems div. Raytheon Co., Norwood, Mass., 1980-82; sr. tng. specialist Submarine Signal div. Raytheon Co., Portsmouth, R.I., 1982-85; mgr. tech. tng. Raytheon Co., Lexington, Mass., 1985—; speaker nat. and regional confs. on organizational devel., training, and listening. With U.S. Army, 1973-79. Mem. ASTD, Internat. Listening Assn., Am. Humor Assn. Office: Raytheon Co 141 Spring St Lexington MA 02173-7899

ENQUIST, LYNN WILLIAM, molecular biologist; b. Denver, Oct. 23, 1945; s. Clarence Andrew and Doris Alice (Hajenga) E.; m. Kathleen Marie Siverson, Aug. 10, 1968; 1 child, Brian Joseph. BS, S.D. State U., 1967; PhD, Va. Commonwealth U., 1971. Postdoctoral fellow Roche Inst. of Molecular Biology, Nutley, N.J., 1971-73; staff fellow NIH, Bethesda, Md., 1973-77; staff scientist NIH, Bethesda, 1977-81; rsch. dir. Molecular Genetics Inc., Minnetonka, Minn., 1981-84; rsch. leader DuPont Cen. Rsch., Wilmington, Del., 1984-90; sr. rsch. fellow DuPont Merck Pharm. Co., Wilmington, 1991—; adj. assoc. prof. U. Pa. Dept. Microbiology, 1988-93. Mem. editorial bd. Jour. of Virology, 1979-81, 89-91; contbr. numerous articles to profl. jours.; patentee in field; author: Experiments with Gene Fusions, 1984. Named Disting. Alumnus, Va. Commonwealth U., 1983, S.D. State U., 1984. Mem. Am. Soc. for Microbiology, AAAS, Am. Soc. for Virology. Office: DuPont Merck Pharm Co Exptl Stn E328 B31 Wilmington DE 19880-0328

ENRICO, FERORELLI, photographer; b. Lubiana, Italy, Aug. 29, 1941; came to U.S., 1971; s. Medoro and Laura (Lolli) F.; m. Martha Saxton, July 11, 1977; children: Francesco, Josephine. LLD, U. Naples, 1965. Pres. Ferorelli Enterprises Inc., N.Y.C., 1983—; photographer N.Y.C., 1968—. Mem. Am. Soc. Mag. Photographers (bd. mem. 1990), Soaring Soc. Am., Theodore Gordon Fly Fishing Club, The Doolittle Club (Norfolk, Conn.).

ENRIGHT, ARTHUR JOSEPH, business management educator; b. N.Y.C., Oct. 9, 1932; s. Francis A. and Theresa M. (Tax) E.; m. Joan M. Conway, July 18, 1959 (dec. 1985); children: Marie, Patrick, Thomas. BS in Physics, Manhattan Coll., 1959; MS in Indsl. Mgmt., Poly. Inst. N.Y., 1966; D in Profl. Studies, Info. Systems, Pace U., 1992. Physicist, accelerator engr. various NASA Labs., 1959-68; mgr. computer ctr. Gen. Electric Co., N.Y.C., 1968-71; cons., owner Enright Assocs., L.I., 1971-82, cons., pres., 1982—; dir. computer svcs., assoc. prof. bus. adminstrn. Dowling Coll., Sayville, N.Y., 1977-82; asst. prof. bus. sch. C.W. Post Coll. L.I. U., Brookville, N.Y., 1989—; cons. in field. dir. radiol. svcs. civil emergency Dept., Brookhaven Twp., N.Y., 1962-69. With USN, 1951-55. Mem. Assn. Computing Machinery, Soc. for Info. Mgmt., Acad. Mgmt., Am. Phys. Soc., KC, Delta Phi Alpha, Sigma Pi Sigma. Home: 26 Carlson Rd Ronkonkoma NY 11779-4124 Office: LI U CW Post Campus Brookville NY 11548

ENSMINGER, RONALD JAY, computer company executive; b. Darby, Pa., Nov. 4, 1943; s. William Alfred and Wava Marie (Swenk) E.; m. Carole Kay Koch, Nov. 27, 1965; children: Stacey N., W. Todd. BS in Computer Engring., Pa. Mil. Coll., Chester, 1965; MBA, Widener U., 1977. Nat. account mgr. data processing div. IBM Corp., Phila., 1965-66, 69-72; v.p. mktg. Pinkerton Computer Cons., Warminster, Pa., 1972-75; co-founder, v.p. Infomark, Frazer, Pa., 1975-78, dir., exec. v.p., 1978-82; v.p. mktg. Jonathans Computer Ctrs., Marlton, N.J., 1982-86; v.p., gen. mgr. Camera Shop Inc., Visual Sound Co., Broomall, Pa., 1986—; adv. bd. Control Data Corp. Mem. alumni bd. Widener U. Capt. USN, 1966-69. Recipient Maj. F.L. Martin award Pa. Mil. Coll., 1965; Atlantic Richfield grantee, 1961-65. Mem. Fellowship Christian Athletes, Navy League, Res. Officers Assn., Naval Res. Assn. Republican. Home: 37 Barr Rd Berwyn PA 19312 Office: Camera Shop Inc 485 Parkway S Broomall PA 19008

ENSOR, RICHARD JOSEPH, athletic conference commissioner, lawyer; b. Jersey City, Mar. 1, 1953; s. Melvin Francis and Mary Elizabeth (Short) E.; m. Deirdre Anne Byrnes, Aug. 8, 1986; children: Kaitlin, Brendan, Kiernan. BA, St. Peter's Coll., Jersey City, 1975; MS, U. Mass., 1983; JD, Seton Hall U., 1987. Bar: N.J. Asst. athletic dir. Seton Hall U., South Orange, N.J., 1985-86; asst. prof. U. Mass., Amherst, 1986-88; commr. Metro Atlantic Athletic Conf., Lyndhurst, N.J., 1988—. Co-author: (with others) (text) Sport Marketing, Promotion and Public Relations; contbr. chpts. to books, articles to law jours. and reviews and articles to athletic trade mags. and popular jours. Mem. NACDA (various positions), ABA, N.J. Bar Assn., Sports Lawyers Assn. Democrat. Roman Catholic. Home: 503 Lakeside Dr N Forked River NJ 08731 Office: Metro Atlantic Athletic Conf 1099 Wall St W Ste 242 Lyndhurst NJ 07071-3617

ENSTINE, RAYMOND WILTON, JR., propane gas company executive; b. Southampton, N.Y., Aug. 28, 1946; s. Raymond Wilton and Ruth Carolyn (Pulver) E.; m. Gwendolyn Louise Gehman, June 12, 1971; 1 child, Scott Raymond. BA in Bus. Adminstrn., Lycoming Coll., 1968. Mgr. CW Pulver, Inc., Bridgehamtpon, N.Y., 1970-76; pres. CW Pulver, Inc., 1976—. Author poems. Past treas. Water Mill Village (N.Y.) Improvement Assn.; treas. bd. deacons 1st Presbyn. Ch., Southampton, 1981-84; mem. Southampton Village Vets. Meml. Hall. Com., Suffolk County Vietnam Vets. Meml. Commn., 1987-91, War Meml. Scholarship Com., 1988—, L.I. R.R. Shippers Adv. Bd., 1987-89, Southampton Hosp. Quarter Backers Steering Com., 1991—. Sgt. AUS, 1969-70. Decorated Bronze Star. Mem. Nat. Propane Gas Assn. (edn. com., chmn. maintenance and oversight subcom. 1989—), N.Y. LP Gas Assn. (pres. 1986-88, Vol. of Yr. award 1985), L.I. LP Gas Assn. (pres. 1979-80, Meritorious Svc. award 1982), Nat. LP Gas Assn. (chmn. dist. 9 edn. com. 1985-88), East Hampton C. of C. (treas. 1979), Cotillion Club (bd. dirs. 1985-86), Southampton Golf Club, Rotary (pres. Southampton club 1988-89, area 1 rep. for dist. gov. 1989). Home: Cobb Rd Water Mill NY 11976 Office: CW Pulver Inc Montawk Hwy Bridgehampton NY 11932-9999

ENTES, JUDITH, reading educator; b. N.Y.C., Feb. 18, 1951; d. Jack and Beatrice (Shapiro) E. BS, SUNY, Stony Brook, 1972; MS, CCNY, 1974; PhD, Fordham U., 1989. Grad. fellow CCNY, 1973-74; adj. lectr. Fordham U., N.Y.C., 1987; lectr. Baruch Coll., N.Y.C., 1974-88, asst. prof., 1988—. Author: Protocol Analysis, 1990; producer (video) Cultural Enrichment, 1991; co-author: On Publishing in the Academy, 1990. Recipient Aaron Diamond Found. grant, 1990-91, PSC-CUNY Rsch. award, 1989-90. Mem. Nat. Reading Conf. (field coun. 1989—), MLA, Nat. Coun. Tchrs. English, Internat. Reading Assn., N.Y. Met. Assn. for Devel. Edn. (chair profl. devel. 1990—), N.Y. Coll. Learning Skills (rsch. com. 1990—), Kappa Delta Pi (v.p. Lambda Xi chpt. 1989—). Home: 601 Kappock St Bronx NY 10463-7717 Office: Baruch Coll 17 Lexington Ave New York NY 10010-5526

ENTINE, JOSEPH HOWARD, surgeon; b. Phila., Nov. 6, 1927; s. Louis Entine and Lena Sewell; m. Betti Granitz, 1950 (div. Sept. 1979); children: Elizabeth Debra, Susan Lee. MD, Hahnemann Med. Coll., 1949. Resident surgery Hahnemann Hosp., Phila., 1950-54; chmn. dept. surgery Community Hosp., Phila., 1958-64, Kensington Hosp., Phila., 1964-70, Rolling Hill Hosp., Elkins Park, Pa., 1970-72, Lawndale Community Hosp., Phila., 1988-90; assoc. prof. surgery Hahnemann Med. Coll. and Hosp., Phila., 1958-65,

Med. Coll. Pa., Phila., 1988—; pres. Surg. Svcs. Ltd., Phila., 1971-92. Contbr. articles to surg. jours. Capt. USAF, 1954-56. Fellow ACS, Am. Soc. Abdominal Surgeons, Internat. Coll. Surgeons, Am. Bd. Surgery; mem. Alpha Omega Alpha. Home: 1715 Cary Rd Huntingdon Valley PA 19006 Office: Surg Svcs Ltd 9892 Bustleton Ave Philadelphia PA 19115

ENYEART, JAMES L., museum director; b. Auburn, Wash., Jan. 13, 1943; s. Lyle F. and Emma A. (Ham) E.; m. Roxanne Enyeart Malone, Sept. 7, 1964; children: Mara, Sascha, Megan. BFA, Kansas City Art Inst., 1965; MFA, U. Kans., 1972. Dir. Albrecht Gallery Art, St. Joseph, Mo., 1967-68; curator photography, assoc. prof. Spencer Mus. Art, U. Kans., 1968-76; exec. dir. Friends of Photography, Carmel, Calif., 1976-77; dir., adj. prof. art Ctr. for Creative Photography, U. Ariz., 1977-89; dir. Internat. Mus. Photography at George Eastman House, Rochester, N.Y., 1989—; cons. Polaroid Corp., 1983-89, design and constrn. Archives addition Internat. Mus. Photog. at George Eastman House, 1988; cons. visual arts Nat. Endowment Arts, 1986, panel mem. Design Excellence Project, L.A., 1984, Challenge Grants/Special Projects, Washington, 1986, grants panel Special Exhbns. Category, Washington, 1985; advisor Ctr. Am. & Commonwealth Arts and Studies, U. Exeter, Eng.; mem. Univ. Survey Photog. Resources Com., U. Calif., Riverside, 1984-86; lectr. various colls. and univs. Author: Creative Camera, 1976, Francis Bruguiere, 1977, Jerry Uelsmann: Twenty-Five Years, A Retrospective, 1982, Edward Weston's California Landscapes, 1984 (Am. Inst. Graphic Arts award), (with R.D. Monroe, Philip Stokes) Three Classic American Photographs: Texts and Contexts, 1982; contbr. Edward Weston Omnibus, 1984, Contemporary Photographers, 1983, 2d rev. edit., 1986-87; editor: Decade by Decade: A Survey of Twentieth Century American Photography, 1989; co-editor: Henry Holmes Smith: Collected Writings 1935-1985, 1986; contbr. introductions to Andreas Feininger: A Retrospective, 1986, Aaron Siskind: Terrors and Pleasures, 1931-1980, 1982, W. Eugene Smith: Master of the Photographic Essay, 1981, Landscapes 1975-1979, 1981, Photography of the Fifties: An American Perspective, 1980, George Fiske, Yosemite Photographer, 1980, Peekamoose, 1973; editor Kans. Album, 1977, Heinecken, 1980, The Archive, 1988, Image, 1989—; designer print study rm. Spencer Mus. Art, U. Kans., 1976, Ctr. Creative Photography, U. Ariz., 1989; author, curator exhbn. Judy Dater: Twenty Years; represented in collections Albrecht Gallery, St. Joseph, Mo., Mus. Art, U. Kans., Bibliotheque Nationale, Paris, Internat. Mus. Photography at George Eastman House, Rochester, Sheldon Meml. Gallery, Lincoln, Nebr., Nat. Mus. Am. Art. Commr. Kans. Arts Commn., 1973-74; selection com. Ariz. Gov's. Arts Awards, 1984; creative arts award com. Brandeis U., Waltham, Mass., 1990—; adv. bd. Aaron Siskind Found., 1981—, W. Eugene Smith Meml. Fund, Inc., 1983—; nom. com. MacArthur Found., 1982; rev. panel Bush Found. Fellowships, St. Paul, 1980. Recipient Josef Sudek medal Ministry Culture, Union Visual Arts, Czechoslovakia, 1989, Photokina Obelisk award, Fed. Republic Germany, 1982; grantee NEA, 1973, 74, 75; Hon. Rsch. fellow U. Exeter, 1974; OAS fellow, 1966-67, John Simon Guggenheim Meml. fellow, 1987. Mem. Am. Assn. Art Mus. Dirs., Am. Assn. Art Mus., Am. Photography Inst. (adv. bd. 1991—), Am. Photog. Hist. Soc. (hon. life), Oracle (co-founder). Office: Internat Mus Photography 900 East Ave Rochester NY 14607

ENZ, CATHY ANN, organizational management educator, consultant; b. Prescott, Ariz., June 19, 1956; d. Richard William and Betty Jean (Waples) E.; m. James C. McKee, Apr. 26, 1987; children: Benjamin, Elizabeth. BS, Ariz. State U., 1977; PhD, Ohio State U., 1985. Ops. mgr. Am. Hosp. Supply Corp., Chgo. and Columbus, Ill., Ohio, 1977-79; rsch. assoc. Ohio State Univ., Columbus, 1979-84; rsch. analyst Nationwide Ins. Co., Columbus, 1984; asst. prof. Ind. Univ., Bloomington, 1985-90; assoc. prof. Cornell Univ., Ithaca, N.Y., 1990—. Assoc. editor: Jour. Mgmt. Edn.; author: Power and Shared Values in Corporate Cultures, 1986; contbr. chpts. to books and articles to profl. jours. Recipient Anna Dice Rsch. fellowship, 1983, Ameritech Rsch. scholar Ameritech Found., 1988-89, 90. Mem. Acad. Mgmt. (mem., officer Midwest div.), Coun. on Hotel, Restaurant and Instnl. Edn. (rep. at large 1988-89), Acad. Internat. Bus., Orgnl. Behavior Teaching Soc. (bd. dirs. 1989-91). Office: Statler Hall Cornell U Ithaca NY 14853

EPALE, PRISO HORACE, microbiologist; b. London, Apr. 23, 1959; came to U.S., 1979; s. Simon Joseph and Tessa Eunice (Davis) E. BS in Biology, U. Minn., 1982; MS in Microbiology, Wagner Coll., N.Y.C., 1987. Microbiologist Hartz Mountain Corp., Harrison, N.J., 1987-89; assoc. scientist Hoffmann-La Roche, Nutley, N.J., 1989—. Mem. Am. Soc. for Microbiology, Minn. Alumni Assn. Home: 11 W 94th St # 2A New York NY 10025 Office: Hoffmann-La Roche Inc 340 Kingsland St Nutley NJ 07110

EPHRON, NORA, author; b. N.Y.C., May 19, 1941; d. Henry and Phoebe (Wolkind) E.; m. Dan Greenburg (div.); m. Carl Bernstein (div.); children: Jacob, Max; m. Nicholas Pileggi. BA, Wellesley Coll., 1962. Reporter N.Y. Post, 1963-68; free-lance writer, 1968—; contbg. editor, columnist Esquire mag., 1972-73, sr. editor, columnist, 1974-78; contbg. editor N.Y. mag., 1973-74. Author: Wallflower at the Orgy, 1970, Crazy Salad, 1975, Scribble Scribble, 1978, Heartburn, 1983, Nora Ephron Collected, 1991; screenwriter: (with Alice Arlen) Silkwood (nominated Acad. award for best original screenplay), 1983, Heartburn, 1986, When Harry Met Sally (nominated Acad. award, Brit. Oscar for screenplay), 1989, My Blue Heaven, 1990; screenwriter (with Delia Ephron), dir.: This Is My Life, 1992; co-exec. producer, co-screenwriter Cookie, 1989. Mem. Writers Guild Am., Authors Guild, Acad. Motion Picture Arts and Scis. Office: care Sam Cohn ICM 40 W 57th St New York NY 10019-4001

EPP, ARTHUR JACOB, minister energy, mines and resources; b. St. Boniface, Man., Can., 1939; m. Lydia Martens, 1961; 1 child, Lisa. BA in History, U. Man., 1961, BE, 1965; LLD (hon.), Trinity Western U., Langley, B.C., Can., 1987. High sch. tchr.; M.P. from Provencher (Man.) dist. Ho. of Commons, 1972—; apptd. min. Indian and no. affairs, 1979-80, min. nat. health and welfare, 1984-88, min. energy, mines and resources, 1988—; mem. coms.: priorities and planning, planning and priorities Can. unity, constl. negotiations, econ. and trade policy, environment, fgn. and def. poli cy. Mem. Community Fellowship Ch., Steinbach, Man. Progressive Conservative. Home: PO Box 2800, 313 Main St, Steinbach, MB Canada R0A 1A0 Office: House of Commons, Parliament Bldgs, Ottawa, ON Canada K1A 0A6

EPPIG, AILEEN, stockbroker, financial advisor; b. N.Y.C., May 9, 1951; d. Edwin H. and Annette (Bohan) E. BA, Albertus Magnus Coll., New Haven, 1973; MA, Dowling Coll., Oakdale, N.Y., 1976. Stockbroker, fin. advisor Prudential Securities, Bay Shore, N.Y., 1978—. Mem. Zonta Club of Suffolk Area (pres. 1990-92, area dir. Dist. 3 1992—), South Bay Cruising Club, The Corinthians, The Babylon Yacht Club, U.S Sailing Assn. (del. 1992—). Roman Catholic. Home: 153 Eaton Ln West Islip NY 11795-4503 Office: Prudential Securities 1701 Sunrise Hwy Bay Shore NY 11706

EPPLER, LAURA SHARON, community relations and publications director; b. Syracuse, N.Y., Oct. 30, 1961; d. Al Uriel and Jane (Thurman) Sharon; m. Edward Craig Eppler, Oct. 20, 1984; 1 child, Craig Phillip. BSBA, Bucknell U., 1983; MBA, Wilkes U., 1990. Customer svc. rep. Automatic Bus. Ctrs., Moorestown, N.J., 1983-84; dir. mktg. Trukman's/D&W Repographics, Morristown, N.J., 1984-85; account exec. Musselman Advt., Inc., Allentown, Pa., 1985-87; dir. community rels. and publs. Lehigh County Community Coll., Schnecksville, Pa., 1987—; adj. mem. bus. faculty Lehigh County Community Coll., 1991—; cons. in field. Member mktg. com. Mayfair, Allentown, 1987, Musikfest, Bethlehem, Pa., 1987, mem. ball com., 1988. Mem. Internat. Assn. Bus. Communicators (parliamentarian, historian 1989-90), Nat. Coun. Mktg. and Pub. Rels. (Bronze, Silver and Gold awards 1989-91), Nat. Coun. on Resource Devel. Presbyterian. Office: Lehigh County Community Coll 4525 Education Park Dr Schnecksville PA 18078-9372

EPPLER, RICHARD ANDREW, chemical engineer, educator, consultant; b. Lynn, Mass., Apr. 30, 1934; s. Walter T. and Faith E. (Marden) E.; m. Ruth Marilyn Coon, June 20, 1959; children: Katherine R., Rebecca E., Walter R., Douglas R., Bruce A. BS, Carnegie-Mellon U., 1956; MS, U. Ill., 1958, PhD, 1960. Registered profl. engr., N.Y. Research chemist Corning (N.Y.) Glass Works, 1959-65; research scientist Mobay Chem. Corp., Balt., 1965-84; supr. ceramics Olin Corp., New Haven, 1984-86; cons. Eppler Assocs., Cheshire, Conn., 1986—; assoc. prof. chem. engring. U. Lowell, Mass., 1986-89. Over 20 patents in field; contbr. articles to profl. jours. Served with USAR, 1960. Fellow Am. Ceramic Soc. (v.p. 1984-85, John Marquis award 1974), ASTM (chmn. com. 1980-85, merit award 1984); mem. Am. Chem. Soc., Electrochem. Soc., Sigma Xi. Republican. Congregationalist. Home and Office: Eppler Assocs 400 Cedar Ln Cheshire CT 06410-2222

EPPLEY, JENNIFER ANN, health facility specialist; b. Reading, Pa., June 27, 1967; d. Paul David and Catherine May (Seidel) Liesman; m. Vance H. Eppley III, May 20, 1989. BS, Albright Coll., 1989; MEd, Temple U., 1990. Student aide Albright Coll. Continuing Edn., Reading, 1985-88; vol. Planned Parenthood N.E. Pa., Reading, 1986, health care asst., 1986-89; ctr. asst., counselor Planned Parenthood, Phila., 1989-90; asst. ctr. dir. Planned Parenthood Md., Balt., 1990-91; healthcare asst. Planned Parenthood Cent. Pa., York, 1991—. Mem. Am. Assn. Counseling and Devel., Assn. Humanistic Edn. and Devel. Lutheran. Home: 216 W Walnut St Dallastown PA 17313-1024 Office: Planned Parenthood Cent Pa 728 S Beaver St York PA 17403

EPPLEY, ROLAND RAYMOND, JR., retired financial services executive; b. Balt., Apr. 1, 1932; s. Roland and Verna (Garrettson) E.; m. LeVerne Pittman, June 20, 1953; children: Kimberly, Kent, Todd. B.A., Johns Hopkins U., 1952, M.A., 1953; D.C.S. (hon.), St. John's U., 1984. Pres., chief exec. officr Comm. Credit Computer, Balt., 1962-68; pres., chief exec. officer CIPC, Balt., 1968-71; vice chmn. Eastern States Monetary, Lake Success, N.Y., 1982-88; pres., chief exec. officer, dir. Affiliated Financial, Wilmington, Del., 1983-85, Eastern States Bankcard, Lake Success, N.Y., 1971-88; ret., 1988; chmn. bd. Eppley-Tongue Assocs., Inc.; adj. prof. St. John's U., 1973-88; bd. dirs. Eastern States Monetary, Veritas Inc., Hanover Funds, chmn., 1989—; chmn. bd. Eppley-Longue Assocs., Inc., 1992—. Chmn. bd. dirs. Eppley-Tongue Assocs., 1992—; chmn. bd. trustees Calgary Bapt. Ch., Balt., 1969-71; chmn. investment com. Community Ch., Manhasset, N.Y., 1983-88; bd. advisors St. John's U., 1973-88; mem. Trinity Meth. Ch., Palm Beach Gardens, Fla. Recipient Disting. Service award St. John's U., 1981, 84 Laucheimer grantee, 1952-53. Mem. Am. Bankers Assn., Data Processing Mgmt. Assn., Am. Mgmt. Assn. Pres. Assn., Electronic Funds Transfer Assn., Mensa, Phi Beta kappa, Omicron Delta Epsilon, Beta Gamma Sigma, Sigma Phi. Epsilon (citation). Republican. Clubs: Madison Square Garden, Meadowbrook, Plandome Country (dir. 1977-86), Hillendale Country, PGA Country. Lodges: Masons, Shrine. Home: 105 Coventry Pl West Palm Beach FL 33418-8001

EPPS, KURT EMIL, educator, consultant; b. Perth Amboy, N.J., Mar. 21, 1948; s. Lamar Jon and Ethel Marie (Kurowsky) E.; m. Donna Marie Barreto, July 18, 1984; children: Brett, Kacy. BA in English, Montclair State Coll., Upper Montclair, N.J., 1969; MA in Student Personnel Svcs., Kean Coll. of N.J., 1976. Cert. tchr., N.J. Tchr. English Passaic (N.J.) Pub. Sch., 1969-71, Arthur L. Johnson Regional High Sch., Clark, N.J., 1971—; football announcer Arthur L. Johnson Regional High Sch., 1977—, advisor student coun., 1980—, dir. pageant, 1981—, advisor sch. newspaper, 1990—. Chmn. Perth Amboy Port Authority, 1988—, Olde Aboy Civic Assn., 1990—; mem. Perth Amboy Bd. Edn., 1989—; capt. Mayor's Econ. Devel. Com., Perth Amboy, 1990—; trustee Proprietary House Assn., Perth Amboy, 1989—, Simpson United Meth. Ch., 1991—. Home: 163 Water St Perth Amboy NJ 08861-4702 Office: Arthur Johnson Reg High Sch 365 Westfield Ave Clark NJ 07066-1792

EPSTEIN, JEFFREY MARK, neurosurgeon; b. Newark, Apr. 7, 1951; s. Herbert Joseph and Roberta Laura (Sank) E.; m. Ronit Adler. BA, Johns Hopkins U., 1973; MD, Autonomous U. Guadalajara, Mex., 1979. Diplomate Am. Bd. Neurol. and Orthopedic Surgery, Am. Bd. Pain Mgmt. 5th channel clerkship Newark Beth-Israel Med. Ctr., 1979-80; intern in surgery Muhlenberg Hosp., Plainfield, N.J., 1980-81; resident in neurosurgery SUNY-Downstate and Kings County Hosp. Ctr., Bklyn., 1981-85, chief resident neurosurgery, 1985-86; instr. neurosurgery SUNY-Downstate, 1986-87, asst. prof. neurosurgery, 1987-88; pvt. practice West Islip, N.Y., 1988—. Contbr. articles to Anesthesia Jour., 1985. Mem. N.Y. State Neurosurgery Soc., Med. Soc. State N.Y., Suffolk County Med. Soc., Magoun Landing Yacht Club, Alpha Epsilon Delta (v.p. 1973). Jewish. Office: 735 Montauk Hwy Ste A West Islip NY 11795

EPSTEIN, JOSEPH, philosophy educator; b. N.Y.C., Jan. 19, 1917; s. Isador and Ida (Snofsky) E.; m. Lucille Goldberger, June 22, 1940; children—Joshua Morris, Samuel David. B.S., CCNY, 1939; Ph.D., Columbia U., 1951; M.A. (hon.), Amherst Coll., 1961. Physicist research and devel. U.S. Army Signal Corps. Labs., 1942-44; physicist research and devel. Fed. Telephone & Radio Corp., Newark, 1944-46; from lectr. to asst. prof. Columbia U., 1946-51; faculty Amherst Coll., Mass., 1952-71; prof. philosophy Amherst Coll., 1961-71, Crosby prof. philosophy, 1976—; vis. prof. philosophy Yale U., 1966-67; mem. consulente aggregato Centro Superiore di Logica e Scienze Comparate, Bologna, Italy, 1972—. Editor: Alexandrian Editions, 1960, Rene Descartes: A Discourse on Method and Other Works, 1965, (with Gail Kennedy) The Process of Philosophy, 1967; contbr. articles to profl. jours. Rockefeller Found. grantee, 1958; Ford Humanities grantee, 1972. Mem. AAUP, Am. Philos. Assn., Am. Assn. Physics Tchrs., Mind Assn. N.Y. Acad. Scis., Sigma Xi. Home: 148 Lincoln Ave Amherst MA 01002-2011

EPSTEIN, MICHAEL FRANK, retirement plan service company owner; b. N.Y.C., Apr. 28, 1941; s. Emanuel and Anne June (Blum) E.; m. Carole Louise Steves, Apr. 9, 1983; 1 child, Laura Ann. BA in Econs., Hunter Coll., 1967. Ops. auditor Union Svc. Group, N.Y.C., 1967-73; asst. v.p. Bradford Trust Co., N.Y.C., 1973-77; v.p. Citibank, N.A., N.Y.C., 1977-85; dir. benefit systems Martin E. Segal Co., N.Y.C., 1985-87; v.p. Merrill Lynch, N.Y.C., 1987-89; exec. v.p. Electronic Pension Systems, Hazlet, N.J., 1989—; pres. Pro-Ben Svcs., Hazlet, 1990—. Author: The 401(k) Guide, 1990; contbr. articles to profl. jours. Office: 3 Tralee Rd Hazlet NJ 07730-1123

EPSTEIN, MIKHAIL NAUMOVICH, philosopher, scholar; b. Moscow, Apr. 21, 1950; came to U.S., 1990; s. Nallm Moiseevich and Mariia Samuilovna (Lifshits) E.; m. Elena Georgievna Ioukina, May 17, 1975; children: Olga, Dmitrii, Peter, Eugene. MA in Philology summa cum laude, Moscow State U., 1972; postgrad., Inst. Slavic/Balkan Studies, Moscow, 1990. Lectr. Moscow Power Inst., 1973-76; researcher World Lit. Inst./Acad. Scis. USSR, Moscow, 1973-78; chmn. Assn. Image and Thought, Moscow, 1986-88, Lab. Modern Culture, Exptl. Creative Ctr., Moscow, 1988-90; asst. prof. dept. Russian Emory U., Atlanta, 1990—; fellow Woodrow Wilson Internat. Ctr. for Scholars, Washington, 1990-91; faculty Dept. Russian Studies, Emory U., Atlanta, 1991—; vis. prof. gorky Lit. Inst., 1988-89, Wesleyan U., Middletown, Conn., 1990; lectr. Union of Writers, Zhanie Soc., Moscow, 1979-89; organizer, conf. chmn. Cen. House Art Workers, Moscow, 1980-84; chmn. Club Essayists, Moscow, 1982-87. Author: Paradoksy Novizny, 1988, Priroda, Mir, Tainik Vselennoi, 1990, Tagebuch fur Olga Chronikeiner Vaterschaft, 1990; contbr. to lit. publs.; editorial bd. Common Knowledge jour. Recipient Golden medal Moscow Coun. People's Edn., 1967. Mem. Writers' Union USSR, Internat PEN, Russian-Am. Inst., Profl. Com. Writers Moscow. Office: Emory U Dept Russian Study 501 Humanities Bldg 1000 Jefferson Dr SW Atlanta GA 30318-8008

EPSTEIN, PAUL MARK, biomedical researcher; b. Bklyn., June 24, 1946; s. Markus and Hilda (Winner) E.; m. Grace Carita Herkimer, May 25, 1975; children: Naomi, Serena, Alisa. AB in Chemistry, Columbia Coll., 1967; PhD in Molecular Biology, Albert Einstein Coll. Medicine, 1975. Rsch. assoc. U. Tex. Med. Sch., Houston, 1975-78, instr., 1978-79; asst. prof. U. Conn. Health Ctr., Farmington, 1979-85, assoc. prof., 1985—; dir. Grad. Program in Pharmacology and Cell and Molecular Toxicology, U. Conn. Health Ctr., Farmington, 1988-91. Contbr. over 38 articles to sci. publs. Grantee Nat. Inst. Dental Rsch., 1988—, NIH, 1988—, Leukemia Rsch. Found., 1981-84, Am. Cancer Soc., 1983-84, Am. Heart Assn., 1981-82. Mem. AAAS, N.Y. Acad. Sci., Soc. for Neurosci., Am. Soc. for Pharmacology and Exptl. Therapeutics, AAUP (pres. 1986—), Sigma Xi. Office: U Conn Health Ctr 263 Farmington Ave Farmington CT 06030-0001

EPSTEIN, RALPH ALAN, anesthesiologist, educator; b. N.Y.C., Apr. 3, 1939; m. Mary Anne Farrell. BA, Columbia U., 1969; MD, Harvard U., 1963. Diplomate Am. Bd. Anesthesiology. Intern U. Calif., San Francisco, 1963-64; clin. assoc. NIH, Bethesda, Md., 1967-69; resident in anesthesiology Columbia U., N.Y.C., 1964-66, postdoctoral fellow in pharmacology, 1966-67, asst. prof. anesthesiology, 1969-75, assoc. prof., 1975-81; dir. respiratory therapy svc. Columbia-Presbyn. Med. Ctr., N.Y.C., 1969-81; prof., chmn. dept. anesthesiology U. Conn., Farmington, 1981—, assoc. dean clin. program planning and coordination, 1989-91. Office: U Conn Sch Medicine Farmington CT 06030

EPSTEIN, SANDRA GAIL, psychologist; b. Boston, July 19, 1939; d. Mischa and Frances (Greenfield) Schneiderman; 1 child, Suanne Charyl. AB, Boston U., 1962; MA, U. Conn., 1969, diploma, 1978, PhD, 1979. Sch. psychol. examiner various pub. schs., Conn., 1970-73, sch. psychologist, 1973—; staff psychologist Day Kimball Hosp. Mental Health Clinic, Putnam, Conn., 1971-74; psychologist Thompson (Conn.) Med. Ctr., 1973-80; pvt. practice Woodstock, Farmington, Conn., 1982-85, Putnam, Farmington, 1985—; instr. Annhurst Coll., Woodstock, Conn., 1971-76; cons. N.E. Area Regional Ednl. Svc., Wauregan, Conn., 1978-79, Capitol Region Ednl. Coun., West Hartford, Conn., 1980—, Ctr. for Interpersonal Rels., Putnam, 1985-88, Hebrew Acad. Greater Hartford, Bloomfield, Conn., 1983-89. Mem. Am. Psychol. Assn., Internat. Soc. Hypnosis, Internat. Psychosomatics Inst., N.Y. Acad. Sci., Conn. Psychol. Assn., Am. Soc. Clin. Hypnosis, Am. Acad. Pain Mgmt., N.Y. Acad. Sci. Office: 365 Woodstock Ave Putnam CT 06260-1015

EPTON, RONDA (ARLI) LYNN, fund-raiser; b. Bklyn., Sept. 28, 1951; d. Irving and Ida Sarah (Gesson) E. BA, Bard Coll., 1973; MA, New Sch. for Social Rsch., 1985. Editorial, publicity and promotion asst. Avon Books, N.Y.C., 1971-74; editorial asst. Basic Books, N.Y.C., 1974-76; publications assoc. Theatre Communications Group, N.Y.C., 1976-78; editor Kraus-Thomson Orgn., Millwood, N.Y., 1978-81; assoc. editor H. W. Wilson Co., Bronx, N.Y., 1982-84; devel. assoc. The Hebrew Arts Sch., Merkin Concert Hall, N.Y.C., 1987-88, Catalyst for Women, N.Y.C., 1988-89; asst. mgr. devel./rsch. N.Y. Zool. Soc., Bronx, N.Y., 1989—. Vol. No. Westchester Ctr. for the Arts, Goldens Bridge, N.Y., 1986-87. Mem. Am. Prospect Rsch. Assn., Westchester Assn. Devel. Officers, Women in Fin. Devel. Office: NY Zool Soc Bronx Zoo Bronx NY 10460

ERAKLIS, ANGELO JOHN, surgeon; b. Portland, Maine, Jan. 11, 1933; s. George and Georgia E.; m. Katherine Sferes, Sept. 13, 1959; children: Elaine, Marianna. AB, Bowdoin Coll., Brunswick, Maine, 1954; MD, Harvard U., 1958. Diplomate Am. Bd. Surgery, Am. Bd. Thoracic Surgery, Am. Bd. Pediatric Surgery. Intern in surgery Peter Bent Brigham Hosp., 1958-59, jr. resident in surgery, 1959-60; jr. resident in surgery Children's Hosp. Med. Ctr., 1960-61; chief resident in pediatric surgery Boston City Hosp., 1961-62; sr. resident in surgery Peter Bent Brigham Hosp., 1962-64; chief resident in surgery Children's Hosp. Med. Ctr., 1964-65; pvt. practice specializing in pediatric surgery Boston, 1965—; instr. in surgery to asst. prof. surgery Harvard Med. Sch., Boston, 1968-76; assoc. prof. surgery Harvard Med. Sch., 1976—; sr. surgeon Children's Hosp. Med. Ctr., 1968-92, dir. ambulatory surg. svcs., 1968-87, mem. staff Mt. Auburn Hosp., Newton-Wellesley Hosp.; vis. surgeon George Washington U., 1975, Northwestern U., 1975, St. Louis U., 1977, U. S.D., 1979; cons. in field, lectr. in field; founder, co-chmn. Health Care Internat. Ltd., Clydebank, Scotland; co-chmn. Ctr. Advanced Health Care. Contbr. articles to profl. jours. Mem. Boston Surg. Soc., Am. Pediatric Surg. Assn., Assn. Acad. Surgery, ACS (fellow), Am. Acad. Pediatrics, New Eng. Pediatric Soc., Mass. Med. Soc., Norfolk County Med. Soc., Phi Beta Kappa. Greek Orthodox. Home: 400 Brookline Ave Boston MA 02215 Office: Children's Hosp Med Ctr 300 Longwood Ave Boston MA 02115-5737

ERATH, SALLY (GRACE MARIE), small business owner; b. Beaver Falls, Pa., Oct. 26, 1927; d. James Clyde and Marie (Krabill) Twinem; m. Edwin P. Earth; children: James Andrew, Peter Brian. BS, BA, Geneva Coll., 1949. Tchr., music supr. Wellsville (Ohio) Pub. Schs., 1949-50; tchr. Eng. and speech East Palestine (Ohio) Pub. Schs., 1950-57; tchr. Geneva Coll., Beaver, Pa., 1967-76, dir. alumni rels., 1976-91; field dir. Beaver-Castle Girl Scouts U.S., Beaver Falls, Pa., 1976-91; owner, pres. Agenda by Sally Erath & Assocs., Beaver Falls, 1991—. V.p. allocations, chmn. small bus. solicitor, United Way of Beaver County, Monaca, Pa., 1989-91; sec. of bd. United Way of S.W. Pa., 1989-91. Named Woman of Distinction Beaver-Castle Girl Scouts U.S., Beaver, 1991; recipient Disting. Svc. award Geneva Coll., 1991. Mem. AAUW (newsletter pub.), Nat. Soc. Fundraising Execs., Geneva Coll. Women's Aux. (pres. 1990-92), Exec. Women's Club (pres. 1991—), Chippewa Women's Club (pres. 1965). Republican. Methodist. Home and Office: 616 Shenango Rd Beaver Falls PA 15010-1661

ERB, DENNIS JOSEPH, chemistry educator; b. Phila., Apr. 19, 1952; s. Earl J. and Elaine E. (Stemple) E.; m. Ellen L. Kerstetter, Aug. 6, 1982; children: Christopher, Jonathan, Meredith, Elizabeth. BA, East Stroudsburg U., 1973; PhD, SUNY, Buffalo, 1978. Rsch. asst prof. dept. chemistry Kalamazoo (Mich.) Coll., 1973-79; asst. prof. dept. chemistry East Stroudsburg (Pa.) U., 1979-84, assoc. prof. dept. chemistry, 1984-90, prof., chmn. dept. chemistry, 1990—; vice chmn. Monroe County LEPC, Stroudsburg, 1983—, Monroe County Health Systems Coun., East Stroudsburg, 1980-85, NESHA, Inc., Stroudsburg, 1987—. Mem. Am. Chem. Soc., N.Y. Acad. Sci., Pa. Acad. Sci., Sigma Xi. Office: East Stroudsburg U Dept Chemistry 208 Gessner Sci East Stroudsburg PA 18301

ERBE, GARY THOMAS, artist; b. Union City, N.J., Sept. 2, 1944; s. Herman Charles and Florance (Bertone) E.; children: Kim, Chantell. student public schs., Union City. One man shows: Pace Gallery, Houston, 1970. Veldman Gallery, Milw., 1971, New Britain Mus. Am. Art, 1976, Summit (N.J.) Art Center, 1976, Bergen Community Mus., Paramus, N.J., 1979, Alexander Gallery, N.Y.C., 1982, 85, N.J. State Mus., Trenton, 1983, Butler Inst. Am. Art, Youngstown, Ohio, 1985, Sordon; Art Gallery, Wilkes Barre, Pa., 1985, Montclair Art Mus., N.J., 1988, Westmoreland (Pa.) Mus. Art, 1988, Canton (Ohio) Art Inst., 1988, Woodmere Art Mus., Phila., 1988; exhibited in group shows: Newark Mus., 1971, Rutgers U., 1971, Heritage Gallery, N.Y.C., 1972, N.J. State Mus., 1972, 75, The Baseball Hall of Fame, Cooperstown, N.Y., 1991; represented in permanent collections: Butler Inst. Am. Art, N.J. State Mus., New Britain Mus. Am. Art, Montclair Art Mus., Woodmere Art Mus., Archives of Am. Art. Recipient Julius Hallgarten award NAD, 1975, 1st award Salmagundi Club, 1975, Noyes Mus., N.J., 1992. Mem. Allied Artists Am. (Gold medal of Honor 1975, 84, 91, John Young-Hunter Meml. award 1982, 85, Emily Lowe award 1989), Conn. Acad. Fine Arts, Assoc. Artists N.J., Audubon Artists (Emily Lowe award 1991, Beatrice Jackson Humphreys Meml. award, 1992). Developed contemporary approach to Am. Trompe l'oeil called Levitational Realism, and extended this sch. to 3 dimensional compositions, oil on bronze. Office: 539 42D St Union City NJ 07087

ERBE, JOAN, artist; b. Balt., Nov. 1, 1926; m. Conrad Hamp Edwards, 1945 (div. 1956); children: Joan Randolph Edwards, Constance Carver Edwards; m. George Udel, May 22, 1956; 1 child, Jacob. Student, Md. Inst. Coll. Art, 1937-55. Numerous one-woman shows including Balt. Mus. Art, 1966, Nat. Acad. Arts & Letters, N.Y.C., 1980, Nye Gomez Gallery, Balt., 1991; represented in permanent collections Samuel & Helen Greenbaum, David Lloyd Kreegar, Balt. Mus. Art, Corcoran Gallery of Art, U. Md., Mcpl. Ct. D.C., Morgan State U. Recipient over 25 best of show and purchase awards. Home and Studio: 103 Woodlawn Rd Baltimore MD 21210

ERBE, JONATHAN RICHARD, software company executive; b. Bethesda, Md., Apr. 18, 1968; s. Richard Wesley Erbe and Elsbeth T. (Von Wimmersperg) Magnarelli. BA, NYU, 1990. Mktg. publicity dir. Aspex Inc., N.Y.C., 1988-90; pres. Pro-Rec, Inc., N.Y.C., 1990. Home: 106 W 13th St Apt 13 New York NY 10011-7824 Office: Pro-rec Inc 106 W 135th St Ste 13 536 Broadway New York NY 10011

ERCOLE, JOSEPH R., mortgage finance officer; b. Ridgewood, N.Y., July 13, 1965; s. Abramo Ercole and Josephine (Abbate) Tutolo. BA, St. John's U., 1987. Retail sales rep. R.H. Macy's and Co., Garden City, N.Y., 1986-87; cons. Romano-Gatland, Lindenhurst, N.Y., 1987-89; program aide

N.Y.S. Mortgage Loan Corp., N.Y.C., 1989—; assoc. real estate broker ERA Realty, Huntington, N.Y., 1990—. Author: Wonder, 1987, Allegation, 1989, Carbon Body, 1990; contbr. poems; inventor in field. Lic. referee L.I. Jr. Soccer League, Plainview, N.Y., 1991-92. Mem. Fedn. Internat. of Football Assn., Smithsonian Inst. Office: NYS Mortgage Loan Corp 11 W 42nd St New York NY 10036-8002

ERDEL, BERT PAUL, manufacturing executive; b. Duesseldorf, Germany, Nov. 9, 1943; came to U.S., 1974; s. Felix and Gertrud (Schornstein) E.; 1 child, Christoph Felix Paul. M in Engring., Duesseldorf U., Fed. Republic of Germany, 1970; BA, Cologne U., Fed. Republic of Germany, 1972. Nat. sales mgr. DEUTZ Corp., Atlanta, 1973-80; pres. Scharmann Machine Tool Corp., Carol Stream, Ill., 1980-83, MAPAL, Inc., Piscataway, N.J., 1983—; instr. Rutgers U., New Brunswick, N.J., 1989—. Mem. Soc. Automotive Engrs. (sr.), Soc. Mfg. Engrs. (sr.), Soc. Aviation and Aeronautics. Republican. Roman Catholic. Home: 99 Adams Dr Belle Mead NJ 08502-4618 Office: MAPAL Inc 81 Suttons Ln Piscataway NJ 08854-5755

ERDHEIM, ALLEN, financial and computer consultant; b. New Orleans, Aug. 31, 1943; s. Morris and Leora (Edelman) E. BS in Econs., U. Pa., 1965; MBA, Columbia U., 1967. Fin. analyst Springs Mills, N.Y.C., 1971-73; dir. investor rels. Norlin Corp., White Plains, N.Y., 1973-82; pvt. practice fin. and computer cons. N.Y.C., 1982—. Dir. 360 East 72nd St. Coop, N.Y.C., 1988—. Lt. USN, 1968-71. Mem. Nat. Coun. for Geocosmic Rsch., N.Y. PC User Group. Jewish. Home: 360 E 72nd St Apt B-905 New York NY 10021

ERDMAN, DAVID VORSE, English educator, author, editor; b. Omaha, Nov. 4, 1911; s. Carl Morris and Myrtle (Vorse) E.; m. Virginia Bohan: children: Wendy Erdman Surlea, Heidi Erdman Van Someren. BA, Carleton Coll., 1933; PhD, Princeton U., 1936. Editor edn. dept. United Auto Workers-CIO, Detroit, 1943-46; editor libr. publs. N.Y. Pub. Libr., N.Y.C., 1956-68; prof. English Ark. A&M Coll., Monticello, 1936-37, U. Wis., Madison, 1937-38, Olivet (Mich.) Coll., 1939-40, The Citadel, Charleston, S.C., 1940-43, U. Minn., Mpls., 1948-52, Duke U., Durham, N.C., 1952-53, SUNY, Stony Brook, 1968—; editor Ammunition United Auto Workers-CIO, 1943-45; editor Bull. N.Y. Pub. Libr., 1974-87; archivist English Inst., 1941-92; mem. adv. bd. Bernard Shaw Soc., N.Y.C. Author: Blake: Prophet Against Empire, 1954, The Poetry and Prose of William Blake, 1965, The Notebook of William Blake, 1973; author: (with others) Collected Works of Samuel Taylor Coleridge, 1978; editor: Blake's Designs for Young's Night Thoughts, 1982, Commerce des Lumiéres: John Oswald and the British in Paris, 1790-1793, 1986, Romantic Movement Bibliography, 1952—; co-editor: Blake's The Four Zoas, 1987; contbr. numerous articles to profl. jours. Guggenheim fellow Guggenheim Found., 1947, 54. Mem. AAUP, ACLU, Assn. Princeton Grad. Alumni, Amnesty Internat., Am. Soc. for 18th Century Studies, Am. Byron Soc., N.Am. Conf. on Brit. Studies. Home: 58 Crane Neck Rd East Setauket NY 11733-1632

ERDRICH, KAREN LOUISE, fiction writer, poet; b. Little Falls, Minn., June 7, 1954; d. Ralph Louis and Rita Joanne (Gourneau) E.; m. Michael Anthony Dorris, Oct. 10, 1981; children: Abel (dec.), Sava, Madeline, Persia, Pallas, Aza. BA, Dartmouth Coll., 1976; MA, Johns Hopkins U., 1979. Vis. poet, tchr. N.D. State Arts Council, 1977-78; tchr. writing Johns Hopkins U., Balt., 1978-79; communications dir., editor Circle-Boston Indian Council, 1979-80; textbook writer Charles Merrill Co., 1980. Author: (textbook) Imagination, 1981, (poems) Jacklight, 1984, Baptism of Desire, 1989, (novels) Love Medicine, 1984 (fgn. edits. in over 18 langs., numerous awards including Nat. Book Critics Circle award for best work of fiction 1984), The Beet Queen, 1986, Tracks, 1988, (with Michael Dorris) The Crown of Columbus, 1991, (with Michael Dorris) Route 2, 1991; contbr. numerous short stories, essays and poems to profl. jours. and popular mags. Johns Hopkins U. teaching fellow, 1979; Macdowell Colony fellow, 1980; Yaddo Colony fellow, 1981; vis. fellow Dartmouth Coll., 1981; Guggenheim fellow, 1985-86; recipient numerous awards for profl. excellence including Nelson Algren award, 1982, Pushcart prize, 1983, Nat. Mag. Fiction award, 1983, 87, First prize O. Henry awards, 1987. Mem. PEN (exec. bd. 1985-90), Authors Guild. Address: PO Box 70 Cornish Flat NH 03746

ERENRICH, EVELYN SCHWARTZ, chemist, educator; b. N.Y.C., Dec. 16, 1946; d. Werner W. and Gladys (Weil) S.; m. Eric H. Erenrich, June 25, 1967; children: Amy, Jordan. BS, Cornell U., 1967, MS, 1969, PhD, 1971. Lectr. in chemistry Cornell U., Ithaca, N.Y., 1971-72; scientist Leeds & Northrup Co., North Wales, Pa., 1972-74, sr. scientist, 1974-76, prin. scientist, 1976-79, cons., 1979—; lectr. in chemistry Rutgers U., New Brunswick, N.J., 1990—. Home: 9 Constitution Ct East Brunswick NJ 08816-3437

ERFANI, SHERVIN, electrical engineer; b. Tehran, Iran, Mar. 28, 1948; came to U.S. 1982; s. Ibrahim and Rashedeh (Naraghi) Erfani; mem. Janet E. Kovar, Dec. 30, 1982. MSEE, U. Tehran, Iran, 1971; MS, So. Meth. U., 1974, PhD in EE, 1976. Asst. prof. Nat. U. Iran, Eveen, 1978-82; research assoc. So. Meth. U., Dallas, 1982-83; asst. prof. U. Mich., Dearborn, 1983-85; mem. tech. staff AT&T Bell Labs., Holmdel, N.J., 1985—. Translator: Elec. Engring. textbook, Circuit Design & Synthesis, 1985; assoc. editor Computers and Elec. Engring.: An Internat. Jour., Jour. of Network and System Mgmt., Jour. Network and Systems Management; contbr. articles to profl. jours. 2nd lt. Signal Corps Iran Army, 1972-73. Mem. IEEE (sr. mem., v.p. S.E. Mich. chpt. 1985), N.Y. Acad. Scis., Tau Beta Pi, Eta Kappa Nu. Islam. Home: 82 Statesir Pl Red Bank NJ 07701-6128 Office: AT&T Bell Labs Crawfords Corner Rd Holmdel NJ 07733-1908

ERICKSON, CHARLES EDWARD, insurance company executive; b. Omaha, July 29, 1947; s. Eric Gerald and Genevieve Verona (Johnson) E.; m. Judith Carol Capazo, Feb. 3, 1973; children: Alicia Genevieve, Christopher Charles. BA, U. Nebr., 1970. Claims adjuster State Farm Ins. Co., Lincoln, Nebr., 1970-73, supr., 1973-77; mgr. ops. Signet Reins. Co., Omaha, 1977-80; asst. v.p. Signet Reins. Co., Morristown, N.J., 1980-82, v.p., 1982-84, exec. v.p., 1984-91, pres., chief exec. officer, 1991—; lectr. Grad. Sch. Bus., Fla. State U., Tallahassee, 1988—, disting. lectr. Sch. Risk Mgmt. and Ins., 1988—; lectr. R. W. Strain Seminars, Wingdale, N.Y., 1987-90; bd. dirs. Merrill Mgmt. Corp., Reinserco Inc., Morristown, Signet Reins. Co.; mem. N.J. Adv. Commn. on Reins., 1989-90. Contbr. articles to profl. jours. Loan exec. United Way Lincoln, 1973-74; advisor Jr. Achievement, Lincoln, 1974-75; chmn. Saunders County (Nebr.) Rep. party, 1971-72; coach Soccer Club Mendham, 1986, Mendham Patriots Midget Football, 1989—; league rep. Morris County Midget Football League, 1992—. Named Advisor of Yr., Jr. Achievement, 1974. Mem. Ind. Reins. Underwriters Assn. Inc. (treas. 1985-86, sec. 1986-88, pres. 1988-90, chmn. bd. trustees 1991—, George D. Young Meml. award for Profl. Excellence 1991), Ins. Inst. Am. (adv. com. 1990—), Nat. Risk Retention Assn., Masons. Congregationalist. Office: Signet Reins Co 175 Morristown Rd Basking Ridge NJ 07920-1675

ERICKSON, EDWARD LEONARD, medical diagnostic systems company executive; b. Chgo., Dec. 7, 1946; s. Leonard Gerald and Eleanore Antoinette (Picek) E.; m. Helen Leonora Masten, Dec. 29, 1979. BS in Math. and Physics, Ill. Inst. Tech., 1968, MS in Math., 1970; MBA in Gen. Mgmt., Harvard U., 1980. Mktg. rep. IBM, Miami, Fla., 1975-76; sr. systems engr. Advanced Tech., Inc., McLean, Va., 1976-78; cons. Bain & Co., Boston, 1979-80; sr. assoc. Resource Planning Assocs., Washington, 1980-82; mgmt. con Resource Planning Assocs., London, 198397; dir. corp. devel. Amersham Internat. plc., Little Chalfont, Eng., 1983-86, gen. mgr. internat. ops., 1986-88; v.p. fin. ops. The Ares-Serono Group, Boston, 1988-90; pres. Serono-Baker Diagnostics (The Ares-Serono Group), Allentown, Pa., 1990-91; pres., chief exec. officer Cholestech Corp., Hayward, Calif., 1991—. Contbr. articles to profl. jours. Mem. Rep. Nat. Com., Washington, 1990—, The 1991 Presdl. Trust, Washington, 1991; charter mem. Rep. Campaign Coun., Washington, 1991; precinct chmn. Va. Rep. Party, Aldie, 1977. Lt. USN, 1970-75. John L. Loeb fellow Harvard U., 1979, George F. Baker scholar, 1980, NASA fellow, 1968-70. Mem. Am. Mgmt. Assn., Harvard Club of Boston, Sigma Pi Sigma. Republican. Home: 6887 Tohickon Hill Rd Pipersville PA 18947-1524

ERICKSON, INGRID GEIJER, advertising agency executive; b. Washington, Oct. 26, 1967; d. Carl Forrest and Astrid Marie (Geijer) E. BA summa cum laude, Mary Baldwin Coll., 1989. Acct. coord. Scali, McCabe, Sloves, Inc., N.Y.C., 1989-90, asst. account exec., 1990-91; account exec. Messner, Vetere, Berger, Carey, Schmetterer Advtg., N.Y.C., 1991; press vol. Challenger Ctr. for Space Sci. Edn., Alexandria, Va., 1992. Mem. Am. Diabetes Assn., Juvenile Diabetes Assn.; vol. advance rep. The White House Advance Office of Pres. of U.S., Washington, 1988. Mem. Omicron Delta Kappa. Presbyterian. Home: 11802 Coldstream Dr Potomac MD 20854

ERICKSON, JULIA ANN, city manager; b. Warren, Minn., Aug. 19, 1958; d. John David and Nancy Ann (Olson) E. BA, Smith Coll., 1980; postgrad., U. Wis., 1980-81. Teaching asst. Women's Studies program U. Wis., Madison, 1980-81; devel. officer Bronx (N.Y.) Frontier Devel. Corp., 1981-84; fundraising cons. Washburn & Assocs., N.Y.C., 1984; asst. dir., dept. community supports Community Svc. Soc., N.Y.C., 1984-90; assoc. commr. pub./pvt. initiatives N.Y.C. Dept. Employment, 1990—; exec. dir. Workforce Devel. Corp., 1992—. Bd. dirs. N.Y. AIDS Coalition, N.Y.C., 1988—. Mem. Sierra Club. Democrat. Office: NYC Dept Employment 220 Church St New York NY 10013-3843

ERICKSON, KAREN LOUISE, chemist, educator; b. Covington, Mich., Aug. 4, 1939; d. Godfrid and Loretta (Wakeford) E.; BS, Siena Heights Coll., 1960, hon. degree, 1981; Ph.D., Purdue U., 1965. Postdoctoral NIH fellow Cornell U., 1964-65; asst. prof. Clark U., Worcester, Mass., 1965-69, assoc. prof., 1969-79, prof. chemistry, 1979—; NIH spl. fellow U. Hawaii, 1972-73; vis. lectr. U. Canterbury, Christchurch, N.Z., 1975; vis. rsch. prof. Ariz. State U., Tempe, 1986-87; prof. chemistry Clark U., Worcester, Mass., 1979—. Contbr. articles to profl. jours. Rsch. fellow Roche Rsch. Inst., Sydney, Australia, 1979-80. Mem. Am. Chem. Soc., Sigma Xi. Office: Clark U Dept Chemistry 950 Main St Worcester MA 01610-1473

ERICKSON, NANCY JOAN, health care consultant; b. Summit, N.J., Apr. 20, 1947; d. Benjamin R. and Margaret A. (Indico) Nigro; m. John Erickson, May 20, 1978 (div. 1986); m. Philip Rubin, Mar. 3, 1990. BA, Drew U., 1969; MSW, Rutgers U., 1979. Social svc. worker Essex County Welfare Bd., Newark, 1969-78; sr. planning analyst Regional Health Planning Coun., Newark, 1978-81; v.p. Network, Inc., Randolph, N.J., 1981-84; prin. New Solutions, Inc., Hackensack, N.J., 1984—; bd. dirs. Health Care Planning and Mktg. Soc. N.J., Princeton; editorial staff Health Care Fin. Mgmt. Assn., N.J. chpt., 1989—. Mem. Am. Hosp. Assn., N.J. Hosp. Assn., Soc. for Health Care Planning and Mktg. and Physician Svcs. Sect. Office: New Solutions Inc 340 W Passaic St Rochelle Park NJ 07662-3018

ERICKSON, RAYMOND LEROY, university dean, psychologist; b. Jamestown, N.Y., Feb. 11, 1925; s. Raymond J. E. and Grace (Myers) E.; m. Barbara Joan Golden, Apr. 29, 1956; children: Leslie Ann, Laurel Meredith, Douglas Alan. BA magna cum laude, SUNY, Buffalo, 1951; MA, UCLA, 1954, PhD, 1962. Psychol. intern Calif. Dept. Corrections, 1954; lectr. U. Md. Overseas Program, 1956-58; instr., then asst. prof. Whittier Coll., 1958-63; mem. faculty U. N.H., 1963-92, prof. psychology, 1967-92, chmn. dept., 1965-71, dean Grad. Sch., 1974-92, dir. research, 1974-81, assoc. v.p. acad. affairs, 1981-83, interim v.p. acad. affairs, 1983-85, spl. asst. to pres., 1985-90. Served with AUS, 1943-46. Mem. Am. Psychol. Assn., N.H. Psychol. Assn. (pres. 1967-68), Phi Beta Kappa. Home: 4 Lantern Ln Exeter NH 03833-2212

ERICKSON, ROBERT ANDREW, tax law specialist, autograph dealer; b. Chisholm, Minn., Oct. 13, 1953; s. Emil and Ruth Genevieve Erickson. BS in Bus. with distinction, U. Minn., 1979. Revenue agt. IRS, Mpls., 1979-87; tax law specialist IRS, Washington, 1987—; autograph dealer pvt. practice, Mpls., 1984-87, Washington, 1987—. Editor The Pen and Quill, 1990—. Mem. Universal Autograph Collectors Club (ethics bd. 1986-87, sec. 1987-90, pres. 1990—), Manuscript Soc. Democrat. Home: 1313 Vermont Ave NW Apt 14 Washington DC 20005-3634

ERICKSON, RONALD KENT electric company owner; b. St. Paul, June 29, 1938; s. Axel Eugene and Evelyn Mary (Schario) E.; m. Jane Marie Darrow, July 6, 1966 (dec. July 1987); m. Dorothy Ann Melley, Sept. 3, 1988; children: Kevin, Kathleen, Maureen, Laura, Alicia, Christopher, Ellen. Drafter Balowin-Stewart Electric Co., Hartford, Conn., 1960-66; estimator Delta Electric, White Plains, N.Y., 1966-73; owner Sovereign Electric Co., Old Saybrook, Conn., 1973—. Author: Fire Safety in Buildings, 1978. Sgt. U.S. Army, 1956-59. Republican. Roman Catholic. Home: 52 Forest Hills Dr Madison CT 06443-3348 Office: Sovereign Electric Co 1752 Elm St Old Saybrook CT 06475-1120

ERICSON, ALVIN CHARLES, marketing professional, consultant; b. Pittsfield, Mass., June 25, 1955; s. Alvin Justin and Bernice Martha (Bence) E. BS, MIT, 1977; MBA, Northeastern U., 1985. Draftsman Unistress Corp., Pittsfield, Mass., 1977-79; sales rep. San-Vel Concrete Corp., Littleton, Mass., 1979-82; mktg. dir. New Eng. region Prestressed Concrete Inst., Chgo., 1982-88; ind. cons. tech. mktg., 1988—. Mem. Mass. Soc. Profl. Engrs. (treas. Met. chpt. 1984-87, pres. 1988-89), Boston Soc. Civil Engrs. (chmn. structural group 1990-91), Am. Concrete Inst. (bd. dirs. 1983-91, pres. New Eng. chpt. 1989-90), Soc. Am. Mil. Engrs., Prestressed Concrete Inst. (mktg. com. 1987—, bridge producers com. 1989—, mem. seismic com. 1991—, erectors com. 1990—). Republican. Lutheran. Home and Office: 18 Scott Rd Harvard MA 01451-1642

ERIKSEN, GARY L., sculptor, author; b. Jackson, Mich., Sept. 11, 1943; 1 child, Grant. BA, Oberlin Coll., 1966; MA, Kent State U., 1968; postgrad., U. Chgo., 1971-73, Accademia Delle Belle Arti, Italy, 1973-77; diploma, Scuola dell Arte Della Medaglia, Italy, 1977. Instr. econs. U. Akron, Ohio, 1969-71; lectr. econs. U. Ill.-Chgo., 1971-73; free-lance sculptor N.Y.C., 1977—. Commn. include: Bishop O. M. Kelly, Ch. of God in Christ, N.Y.C. and Memphis, 1980, Thirty Bas Reliefs, Nat. Basketball Hall of Fame, Springfield, Mass., 1985, Erasmus Hall High Sch. Seal, Bklyn., 1987; cons. Sculpture House, Inc., N.Y.C., 1980-81; author: This Book Is Long Past Due, 1973, 2d edit. 1989. Vol. Deaf Contact-Helpline, Marble Collegiate Ch., N.Y.C., 1981-86. Recipient N.Y. State Council on Arts grantee 1983; 1st prize Salmagundi Club, 1983. Mem. Am. Medallic Sculpture Assn. (co-founder, pres. 1982-83, bd. dirs. 1983-87). Home: PO Box 7222 New York NY 10163-7222

ERLA, KAREN, artist, painter, collagist, printmaker; b. Pitts., Nov. 17, 1942; d. Jack and Lenore (Kamons) Franklin; children: Stephanie, Joan. BFA, George Washington U., 1965; postgrad., Parsons Sch. Design, 1979-81, Carnegie Inst., 1958-59, Boston U., 1960-62, Pratt Inst., 1980-82, NYU, 1982. Solo exhbns. include Phoenix Gallery, N.Y.C., 1985, E.L. Stark Gallery, N.Y.C., 1988, Bertha Urdang Gallery, N.Y.C., 1986, Bennett and Siegel Gallery, 1989, 90, U. of South, Sewanee, Tenn., Manhattanville Coll., Purchase, N.Y., 1982, Printmaking Council of N.J., 1982, Bennet Siegel Gallery, N.Y.C., 1990, Bryant Gallery, N.Y.C., 1990, Queens Coll., N.Y.C., 1991; group shows include Herbert Johnson Mus. Art, Atlanta Coll. Art, Van Straaten Gallery, Chgo., Greene Gallery, Guilford, Conn., Nat. Mus. of Am. Art, Washington, D.C., Fine Arts Museum of L.I., N.Y., Zimmerli Mus., New Brunswick, N.J., Printmaking Council of N.J., Somerstown Studios and Gallery, Somers, N.Y., Cork Exhbn. in Lincoln Ctr., Fay Gold Gallery, Atlanta, 1984, Boston Printmakers 37th Nat. Exhbn., 1985, The Print Club's 61st Internat. Juried Exhbn., Phila., Schering-Plough Corp. Gallery, Madison, N.J., New Brunswick, N.J., Australian Nat. Gallery, 1989, E.L. Stark Exhbn., 1990, Am. Embassy, 1990, others; represented in permanent collections at Balt. Mus. of Art, Herbert F. Johnson Mus., Cornell U., Bklyn. Mus. Art, Huntsville Mus. Art, Ala., L.A. County Mus. Art, Met. Mus. Art, N.Y., Nat. Museum Am. Art, Australian Nat. Gallery, Smithsonian Inst., New Orleans Mus. Art, Phila. Mus. Art, Tampa Mus., Fla.; featured in Monograph of Karen Erla (text by Ronnie Cohen) 1988, Monoprints Karen Erla (text by Dr. Mary Lee Thompson), Paintings: Karen Erla (text by Bertha Urdang and E.L. Stark); featured in Newsday as New Yorker mag.; solo exhibitions E.L. Stark Gallery, Bertha Urdang Gallery, N.Y.C. Harrison Library, Harrison, N.Y. Manhattanville Coll., Purchase, N.Y., Sound Shore Gallery, N.Y.C., The Print Club 62d Internat., Phila. Recipient Nat. Art award, Pa., 1959, Herbert F. Johnson Mus., Cornell U.; Mamroneck Artists Guild award, 1983. Mem. World Print Council, Printmaking Council N.J., Artists Equity, Pratt Graphic Ctr., L.A. Printmaking Soc. Address: Old Orchard St North White Plains NY 10604

ERLENMEYER-KIMLING, L., psychiatric and behavior genetics researcher, educator; b. Princeton, N.J.; d. Floyd M. and Dorothy F. (Dirst) Erlenmeyer; m. Carl F. E. Kimling. B.S. magna cum laude, Columbia U., 1957, Ph.D., 1961. Sr. research scientist N.Y. State Psychiat. Inst., N.Y.C., 1960-69; assoc. research scientist N.Y. State Psychiat. Inst., 1969-75, prin. research scientist, 1975-78, dir. div. devel. behavioral studies, 1978—, acting chief med. genetics, 1991—; asst. in psychiatry Columbia U., 1962-66, rsch. assoc., 1966-70, asst. prof., 1970-74, assoc. prof., psychiatry and human genetics, 1974-78, prof., 1978—; vis. prof. psychology New Sch. Social Research, 1971—; mem. peer rev. group NIH, 1976-80; mem. work group on guidance and counseling Congl. Commn. on Huntington's Disease, 1976-77; mem. task force on intervention Pres.'s Commn. on Mental Health, 1977-78; mem. initial rev. group NIMH, 1981-85; adv. bd. Crotian Inst. Brain Rsch., 1991—. Editor: Life-Span Research in Psychopathology, 1986; issue editor: Differential Reproduction, Social Biology, 1971, Genetics and Mental Disorders, Internat. Jour. Mental Health, 1972; mem. editorial bd. Social Biology, 1970-79, Schizophrenia Bull., 1978—, Jour. Preventive Psychiatry, 1980—, Croatian Med. Jour., 1991—. Recipient Merit award NIMH, 1989; NIMH grantee, 1966-69, 71—, Scottish Rite Com. on Schizophrenia grantee, 1970-74, 84-87, 89-91, W.T. Grant Found. grantee, 1978-86, MacArthur Found. grantee 1981. Fellow AAAS, APA, Am. Psychopath. Assn., Am. Psychol. Soc.; mem. Am. Soc. Human Genetics, World Psychiat. Assn. (com. epidemiology and community psychiatry), Behavior Genetics Assn. (mem.-at-large 1972-74, Theodosius Dobzhansky award 1985), Soc. Study Social Biology (dir. 1969-84, 92—, sec. 1972-75, pres. 1975-78), Scientists Ctr. for Animal Welfare, Phi Beta Kappa, Sigma Xi.

ERNENWEIN, RAYMOND JOSEPH, agriculture educator; b. Rome, N.Y., Mar. 19, 1941; s. Raymond Lyle and Stella Jane (Luczynski) E.; m. Judy Jurhs, Nov. 22, 1966; children: Raymond Albert, Brett Alan, Neil James. BS, Cornell U., 1964, MA in Teaching, 1969. Tchr. agr. Monroe BOCES, Hitson-Kendall, N.Y., 1965-67, Kendall Cen. Sch., 1967—; curriculum cons. State Edn., Albany, 1967—; item writer Ednl. Testing Svcs., Atlanta, 1986. Co-author: Basic Agriculture Skill Curriculum Guide, 1988; co-author instrnl. modules, 1985-87; editor Assn. of Tchrs. of Agr. of N.Y. Newsletter, 1989-90. Mem., chmn. Town of Kendall Planning Bd., 1967—; contest chmn. FFA State Fair Com., N.Y.C., 1971—; coach Kendall Youth Soccer, 1969-89; contest chmn. County Jr. Fair, Knowlesville, 1967—. Named Outstanding Young Mem., N.Y. Agr. Assn., 1970, Hon. Empire FFA Degree, N.Y. Assn. FFA, 1972, Hon. Am. FFA Degree, Nat. FFA Orgn., 1984, Agrisci. Tchr. of Yr., N.Y. Agrl. Tchr. Assn., 1990, Outstanding Educator, Nat. Vocat. Agrl. Tchrs. Assn., 1991. Mem. N.Y. State FFA (pres. bd. trustees 1982-83), Assn. Tchrs. Agr. N.Y. (pres. 1990-91), Genesee/Orleans Cornell Alumni (pres. 1988-90), Kendall Lions (charter pres., treas. 1981-84, Melvin Jones fellow 1990). Home: 2106 Kendall Rd Kendall NY 14476

ERNST, KATHRYN FITZGERALD, management, marketing consulting firm executive, author; b. N.Y.C., Nov. 12, 1942; d. Joseph Michael and Helen Ann (Dougherty) Fitzgerald; m. John Lyman Ernst, Dec. 7, 1971 (div. Apr. 1977). BA in Econs., Wells Coll., Aurora, N.Y., 1963; postgrad N.Y. U., 1964. Portiolio analyst Donaldson, Lufkin & Jenrette, N.Y.C., 1966-68; asst. v.p. Prentice-Hall, Englewood Cliffs, N.J., 1968-74; v.p. Franklin Watts/Grolier, N.Y.C., 1975-77; mktg. mgr. ITT, N.Y.C., 1977-80: mng. dir. Warburg, Paribas Becker, N.Y.C., 1980-82; pres., owner Ernst Assocs., Inc., N.Y.C., 1982—. Author: Danny and His Thumb, 1972, Mr. Tamerin's Trees, 1978 (Nat. Sci. Tcrh.s award 1979), Owl's New Cards, 1979 (ALA-Children's Choice award 1980), Charlie's Pets, 1980, Indians: The First Americans, 1981, ESP McGee & The Mysterious Magician, 1984, The Complete Calorie and Carbohydrate Counters for Dining Out, 1987. Recipient Outstanding Achievement award Fed. Govt., 1966, Pub. Achievement award Christopher Soc., 1973, Acad. Women Achievers YWCA, 1979. Mem. Direct Mktg. Assn. (Echo award 1985), Nat. Adv. Coun. for Artss for Am., Williams Club. Avocations: bridge, chess, golf, modern art, jazz. Office: Ernst Assocs Inc 59 E 54th St Rm 64 New York NY 10022-4262

ERNST, LAURA WATERS, chiropractic college official, chiropractor; b. Mt. Holly, N.J., Dec. 20, 1953; d. Russell M. Jr. and Marjorie L. (Means) Waters; m. Peter J. Ernst, Mar. 13, 1982. BA in Psychology, Montclair State Coll., 1975, post BA cert. in music therapy, 1978; D Chiropractic, Sherman Coll., Spartanburg, S.C., 1986. With social svcs. dept. Essex County Corrections Ctr., Caldwell, N.J., 1976-78; music therapist Essex County Hosp. Ctr., Cedar Grove, 1980-81, Greystone Park (N.J.) Psychiat. Hosp., 1981-82; chiropractor Piedmont Chiropractic Ctr., Greenville, S.C., 1986-88; dir. R & D, Pa. Coll. Straight Chiropractic, Horsham, 1990—. Mem. Piedmont Peace Resource Ctr., Greenville, 1986-88; bd. dirs. Internat. Arts and Entertainment Sch., Camden, N.J., 1991—. Mem. Pa. Chiropractic Fellowship, Nat. Assn. for Music Therapy (registered). Office: Pa Coll Straight Chiropractic 200 Tournament Dr Ste 100 Horsham PA 19044-3689

ERNST, RICARDO, business administration educator; b. Caracas, Venezuela, Jan. 9, 1959; came to U.S. 1983; s. Erwin Ernst and Mina Hamersfeld Weiss; m. Isabel de la Cruz, June 2, 1989; children: Carolina, Felipe. Civil Engr., U. Catolica Andres Bello, Caracas, 1981; MBA, Instituto Estudios Superiores, Caracas, 1983; MA, U. Pa., 1986, PhD, 1987. Asst. prof. prodn. and ops. mgmt. Georgetown U., Washington, 1987—; cons. Cohen & Lee Assocs., Phila., 1985—, Arthur D. Little, Caracas, 1988-89. Contbr. articles to profl. jours. Recipient Joseph M. LeMoine award for undergrad. and grad. teaching excellence Georgetown U., 1991, Faculty Rsch. award Georgetown U., 1992. Mem. Inst. Mgmt. Sci., Ops. Rsch. Soc. Am., Assn. of Prodn. and Inventory Control, Decision Scis. Inst., Prodn. and Ops. Mgmt. Soc. Office: Georgetown Univ SBA Washington DC 20057

ERRERA, SAMUEL JOSEPH, civil engineer, consultant; b. Hammonton, N.J., Jan. 7, 1926; s. Peter and Grace (Ruggeri) E.; m. Jeannette Calise, Aug. 6, 1949 (dec. Apr. 1984); children: Carol Ann Errera McCandless, Mary Catherine Errera Shanahan; m. Jane Henninger, Feb. 9, 1986. BCE, Rutgers U., 1949; MS in Structural Engring., U. Ill., 1951; PhD in Structural Engring., Cornell U., 1965. Reg. profl. engr. Assoc. prof. Lehigh U., Bethlehem, Pa., 1951-62; mgr. structural rsch. Cornell U., Ithaca, N.Y., 1962-70; tech. cons. Bethlehem Steel Co., 1970-91; cons. Bethlehem, 1991—; vis. prof. U. Fla., Gainesvile, 1981-82. Author: (with others) Structual Design-Materials, 1972, author: Automotive Structural Components, 1980; contbr. articles to profl. jours. Sgt. U.S. Army, 1944-46. Fellow ASCE (sect. pres. 1973-74); mem. Structural Stability Rsch. Coun. (chmn. 1986-89), Am. Iron and Steel Inst. (chmn. 1984-90, mem. specification com.). Home: 1730 Maple St Bethlehem PA 18017-5129

ERSTLING, CHRISTOPHER MICHAEL, psychoanalyst; b. N.Y.C., Nov. 1, 1947; s. George Everett and Margaret (Foy) E.; m. Susan Marie Schilling, May 27, 1979; children: Emily Caroline, Katherine Marie. AB, Seton Hall U., 1969; MD, N.J. Coll. Medicine, 1973; grad., Pitts. Psychoanalytic Inst., 1991. Diplomate Am. Bd. Psychiatry and Neurology. Intern Pitts. Med. Ctr., 1973-74; resident Western Psychiat. Inst., 1973-76; asst. prof. psychiatry U. Pitts., 1976-79, clin. asst. prof. psychiatry, 1979—; pvt. practice Pitts., 1979—; faculty family practice Shadyside Hosp., Pitts., 1976—, chief psychiatry, 1984—; faculty Washington (Pa.) Hosp., 1977—, St. Margaret Hosp., Pitts., 1985—; cons. psychiatrist Chatham Coll., Pitts., 1983—. Mem. Am. Psychiat. Assn., Am. Psychoanalytic Assn., Am. Psychosomatic Soc., Pitts. Psychiat. Soc. (pres. 1991-92), Pitts. Golf Club, Univ. Club. Home: 712 St James St Pittsburgh PA 15232-1437 Office: 401 Shady Ave Pittsburgh PA 15206-4409

ERUMSELE, ANDREW AKHIGBE, development policy analyst; b. Auchi, Nigeria, Nov. 18, 1944; came to U.S., 1966, naturalized, 1971; s. Erumsele Bello and Itete (Isadoh) Iyoke; m. Mary Catherine Wimbley, Dec. 6, 1969 (div. 1975); 1 child, Uwadia Alexis, ; m. Laura Ann Stepanski, Jan. 21, 1987; children: Ashley Idiagbon, Tristan Iyoke. BA magna cum laude, Loyola U., L.A., 1969; MPA (Univ. scholar, Nigerian Govt. scholar), UCLA, 1971; MA, Am. U., 1974, PhD, 1977. Leadership fellow Los Angeles County Planning Commn., 1969-70; research fellow UN Inst. for Tng. and Research, 1970; mem. staff U.S. Congressional Commn. on Reorgn. of D.C. Govt., 1972-73; mgmt. and policy analyst U. D.C., Washington, 1973—, also asst. to dean Coll. Life Scis.; founder, pres. Devel. Analytics, Inc., 1983—; exec. dir. Inst. Nigerian Affairs, 1992—; cons. Internat. City Mgmt. Assn., Orgn.

of African Unity, Inst. for Public Adminstrn. Recipient Hall of Nations award Am. U., Washington, 1972. Mem. Am. Soc. for Public Adminstrn., Acad. Polit. Sci., Soc. for Internat. Devel., Am. Soc. for Internat. Law, Pi Gamma Mu. Democrat. Moslem. Spl. corr. for various African newspapers. Office: PO Box 39067 Washington DC 20016-9067

ERVIN, BILLY MAXWELL, aerospace company executive; b. Dante, Va., July 29, 1933; s. Willie Beldon and Ollie Lowel (Biggs) E.; m. Barbara Frances Walsh, June 27, 1971; children: Honore McDonough, Kerry Thompson. BS, U.S. Naval Acad., 1955; M in Marine Affairs, U. R.I., 1971; postgrad., U. Mass., 1985—. Commd. ensign USN, 1955, advanced through grades to capt., 1975; chief engr. aircraft carrier USN, Pacific, 1969-70; destroyer capt. USN, Atlantic/Pacific, 1971-73; project mgr. USN, Washington, 1973-78, head logistics br., 1978-80, head rsch. and devel. br., 1980-82; insp. gen. Europe USN, London, 1982-85; ret. USN, 1985; adminstr. Baystate Eye Care, P.C., Springfield, Mass., 1986-88; mgr. engring. adminstrn. and planning Kaman Aerospace Corp., Bloomfield, Conn., 1990—. Decorated Bronze Star; recipient Meritorious Svc. Medal award Pres. of the U.S., 1985. Mem. Naval War Coll. Found., Navy League, St. Andrew's Soc., Clan Irwin Assn. Home: 20 Magnolia Ter Springfield MA 01108-2512 Office: Kaman Aerospace Old Windsor Rd PO Box 2 Stratford CT 06497-0001

ERWIN, DELL COATS, educational administrator; b. Demopolis, Ala., June 13, 1936; d. Edric Herschner and Earline Mae (Glass) Coats; m. John Robert Erwin, June 13, 1956; children: Vance, Gregg, Gayle. Cert., Emmaus Bible Coll., 1956. Freelance writer, editor, cons., 1977—; asst. to judge Va. Ct. Appeals, McLean, 1984-87; dir. tng. Prison Fellowship, Washington, 1987-89, dir. program and tng. devel., 1989—; presenter workshops in field. Editor Serendipity, 1990-91; author: The Man Who Keeps Going to Jail, 1978, (series) Free for Sure, 1982, also newspaper feature series (1st Place Best Feature of Yr. award), tng. manuals and videos. Chgo. Tract Soc. grantee, 1979. Mem. ASTD, Nat. Soc. Performance and Inst., Am. Correctional Assn., Correctional Edn. Assn. Office: Prison Fellowship PO Box 17500 Washington DC 20041-0500

ERWIN, FREDERICK JOSEPH, broadcast executive; b. Waterbury, Conn., Feb. 23, 1925; s. Frederick J. and Gertrude (O'Connell) E.; m. Patricia Deeley, Nov. 27, 1955; children: David, Steven, Dana, Judith, Joseph. BS, Bryant Coll., 1949. With sales dept. IBM, Bridgeport, Conn., 1953-55; salesman Sta. WATR, Waterbury, 1955-68; gen. mgr. Stas. WATR, WWYZ-FM, Waterbury, 1968—. Served to 1st sgt. U.S. Army, 1943-46, 50-52. Democrat. Roman Catholic. Office: Stas WATR/WWYZ-FM 1 Broadcast Ln Waterbury CT 06706-1819

ESAKI, HOWARD YUJI, economist; b. Monterey, Calif., Oct. 20, 1953; s. George T. and Jean M. (Oishi) E. AB, Princeton U., 1975; MA, Yale U., 1977, PhD, 1981. Economist Fed. Res. Bank N.Y., N.Y.C., 1980-87; v.p. Shearson/Lehman/Hutton, N.Y.C., 1987-88; assoc. dir. Moody's Investors Svc., N.Y.C., 1988—. Mem. Am. Econ. Assn. Office: Moodys Investors Svc 99 Church St New York NY 10007-2701

ESAKI, LEO, physicist; b. Osaka, Japan, Mar. 12, 1925; came to U.S., 1960; s. Soichiro and Niyoko (Ito) E.; m. Masako Kondo, May, 31, 1986; children from previous marriage: Nina Yvonne, Anna Eileen, Eugene Leo. B.S., U. Tokyo, 1947, Ph.D., 1959. With Sony Corp., Japan, 1956-60; with Thomas J. Watson Research Center, IBM, Yorktown Heights, N.Y., 1960-92; IBM fellow Thomas J. Watson Research Center, IBM, 1967-92, mgr. device research, 1965-92; dir. IBM-Japan, 1975-92; pres. U. Tsukuba, Ibaraki, Japan, 1992—. Recipient Stuart Ballantine medal Franklin Inst., 1961, Japan Acad. award, 1965, Nobel prize in physics, 1973; decorated Order of Culture Govt. of Japan, 1974. Fellow Am. Phys. Soc. (Internat. prize for new materials 1985, councillor-at-large 1971-74), IEEE (Morris N. Liebman Meml. prize 1961, Medal of Honor 1991), Japan Phys. Soc., Am. Vacuum Soc. (dir. 1973-74); mem. Am. Acad. Arts and Scis., NAS (fgn. assoc.), NAE (fgn. assoc.), Academia Nacional de Ingenieria Mex. (corr.), Japan Acad. Home: Takezono 3-772, Tsukuba Ibaraki 305, Japan Office: U Tsukuba, Tsukuba Ibaraki 305, Japan

ESCALANTE, JUDSON ROBERT, business consultant; b. Schenectady, N.Y., Jan. 31, 1930; s. James S. and Katherine H. (Judson) E.; m. Charlotte D. Carpenter, June 7, 1958; children: David J., Katherine Anne. BA, Union Coll., 1953. Asst. estate planning officer Nat. Comml. Bank, Albany, N.Y., 1955-65; founder, v.p., sec., dir. Fidelity Bank of Colonie, Latham, N.Y, 1966-69; area dir. Gen. Bus. Svcs., Latham, 1969-81, Micro Bus. Svcs., 1981—; bd. dir. Mfr.'s Hanover Trust Co. Capital Region, 1970-88; v.p. fin. Gad Cruise Lines, Inc., 1987-88; instr. in field. Bd. dirs., treas. Capital Artists Opera Co., 1970-74, 79; mem. fund dr. com. Union Coll., 1979-80; vestryman, treas. Episcopal Ch.; treas., chief fin. officer; Chatham Vis. Nurse Assn., 1983-89; trustee Chatham Vis. Nurse Assn. Profit Trust, 1985—; auditor Chatham Conservation Found., 1985—. With U.S. Army, 1953-55. Mem. Colonie C. of C. (treas., bd. dir. 1972-76), Union Coll. Alumni Soc. (pres. 1971-73, Alumni Gold medal 1978), Dutch Settlers Soc. of Albany, Boston Computer Soc. Republican. Home: 400 Old Comers Rd Chatham MA 02633-1315

ESCALET, FRANK DIAZ, artist, educator; b. Ponce, P.R., Mar. 16, 1930; s. Frank Thillet and Concepcion Rodriguez (Diaz) E.; m. Shirley Leslie Fanner, Sept. 29, 1953 (div. Aug. 1955); children: Judith Alicia, Susan Edith; m. Marjorie Janet Gaydash-Huebner, July 19, 1964; 1 child, Frank Daniel (dec.). Owner, operator Talent Shop, N.Y.C., 1955-58, House of Escalet, N.Y.C., 1958-71, Pandora's Box, Eastport, Maine, 1971-73, Cobbler's Bench Art Gallery, Pembroke, Maine, 1973-82, House of Escalet Gallery, Kennebunkport, Maine, 1982-84, House of Escalet Studios, Kennebunkport, 1984—; tchr. leathercraft Pasamaquoddy Reservation, Perry, Maine, 1971-72, Vocat. Sch. for Retarded Children, Calais, Maine, 1972-73. Works included in solo traveling exhibit Czechoslovakia, Russia, Poland, Yugoslavia, Hungary, Ukraine, 1991—; represented in permanent collections including Naprstkovo Mus., Prague, Czechoslovakia, Union of Artists, Moscow. Recipient numerous internat. and U.S. awards. Home and Office: House of Escalet Studios 13 Fletcher St Kennebunk ME 04043-1901

ESCH, KAREN EILEEN, public relations consultant, marketing consultant; b. Pitts., Aug. 10, 1943; d. William Ross and Veronica Elizabeth (Heffernan) E. BA, Duquesne U., 1965; MEd, U. Pitts., 1966. Acct. exec. Fourth Allegheny Corp., Pitts., 1967-73; account exec. Ketchum Pub. Rels., Pitts., 1973-75; supr. pub. rels J&L Steel Corp. (LTV), Pitts., 1975-78, assoc. dir. advt., 1978-79; mgr. mktg. communications Copperweld Corp., Pitts., 1979-84, dir. corp. communications, 1984-86; dir. pub. rels. Dravo Corp., Pitts., 1986-88; prin. Karen Esch Assocs., Pitts., 1988—. Dir., adv. bd. Three Rivers Shakespeare Festival, Pitts., 1987—; assoc. Pitts. Dance Coun., 1990—. Mem. Pub. Rels. Soc. Am. (v.p. Pitts. chpt. 1992), Bus./Profl. Advt. Assn., Pitts. Advt. Club, Edgewood Racquet Club. Office: Karen Esch Assocs 4140 Saline St Pittsburgh PA 15217-2716

ESCHWEILER, PETER QUINTUS, planning consultant; b. Milw., Nov. 2, 1932; s. Alexander Chadbourne Jr. and Dorothy Quincy (Adams) E. m. Mickie Pauline Symonds, Aug. 13, 1955; children Susan Marie, Steven Adams. BA, Cornell U., 1955, M of Regional Planning, 1957. Assoc. planner Frederick P. Clark & Assocs., Rye, N.Y., 1960-66; chief planner Westchester County, White Plains, N.Y., 1967, dep. commr. of planning, 1968-69, commr. of planning, 1969-91. Served to 1st lt. USAF, 1957-60. Mem. Am. Inst. Cert. Planners, Nat. Assn. County Planning Dirs. (pres. 1984-85), N.Y. State Assn. of Counties (pres. 1980-81, recognition award 1991), N.Y. Assn. of County Planning Dirs. (pres. 1970, bd. dirs. 1969-91), Nat. Assn. of Counties (bd. dirs. 1987-89), Nat. Assn. Regional Couns. (bd. dirs. 1988-89), Am. Soc. for Photogrammetry and Remote Sensing (bd. dirs. North Atlantic region 1987—, sec.-treas. 1988—), Cornell Club (N.Y.C.), Rotary (pres. White Plains, N.Y. 1985-86). Presbyterian. Home and Office: 36 Wilton Rd Pleasantville NY 10570-2000

ESECSON, ROBERT M., business executive, investment advisor, financial ad management consultant; b. Malden, Mass., Dec. 28, 1950; s. Bernard and Sylvia Esecson; m. Renee Schur, Aug. 21, 1986; children: Lauren Deandra, Jacob Channing. BS in Mgmt. and Acctg., Bentley Coll., Waltham, Mass., 1972; JD, N.E. Sch. Law, Boston, 1981. Asst. v.p. ops. Nat. Hardgoods Distbrs., Newton, Mass., 1972-75; pres. R&G Assocs., Inc., Lexington, Mass., 1972-81; exec. v.p., prin. Esecson Assocs., Waltham, 1975-81; co-mgr. dir. corp. fin. Cheverie & Co., Boston, 1981-85; mng. dir., pres. Esmarox Corp., Acton, Mass., 1985—; cons. in fin. mgmt., ad mergers and acquisitions, mktg. retirement, investment and estate planning to various pub. and pvt. corps., law and acctg. firms and internat. clients. Mem. Masons. Office: Esmarox Corp 3 Ashley St Acton MA 01720-5829

ESHLEMAN, SILAS KENDRICK, III, psychiatrist; b. Gainesville, Fla., June 28, 1928; s. Silas Kendrick Jr. and Aileen Hope (McClamroch) E.; m. Judith Cooper, July 3, 1954; 1 child, Diane Eshleman Olson. BS, U. Fla., 1949; MD, U. Pa., 1953. Diplomate Nat. Bd. Med. Examiners, Am. Bd. Psychiatry and Neurology, Am. Bd. med. Psychotherapists. Chmn. dept. psychiatry St. Joseph Hosp., Lancaster, Pa., 1968-88; pvt. practice Lancaster, 1959—; cons. in psychiatry VA Med. Ctr., Lebanon, Pa., 1961—. Capt. M.C., U.S. Army, 1955-57. Fellow Am. Psychiat. Assn., Am. Orthopsychiat. Assn., Coll. Physicians of Phila.; mem. AMA, Cliosophic Soc. (program chmn. Lancaster chpt. 1983-84), Torch Club. Episcopalian. Home: PO Box 306 Paradise PA 17562-0306 Office: 317 N Duke St Lancaster PA 17602-4915

ESHOO, BARBARA ANNE RUDOLPH, academic official; b. Worcester, Mass., Sept. 27, 1946; d. Charles Leighton and Irene Isabella (Wheeler) Rudolph; divorced: 1 child, Melissa Clinton; m. Robert Pius Eshoo, July ll, 1981. Student, Morehead State U., 1964-66, U. N.H., 1974, 75; BA, New Eng. Coll., 1976. Asst. to dir. Currier Gallery Art, Manchester, N.H., 1976-78, coord. pub. rels., 1979-82; dir. pub. rels. Daniel Webster Coll., Nashua, N.H., 1982-88, chief advancement officer, 1988—; mem. faculty Currier Art Ctr., Manchester, 1977-79; bd. advisers New Eng. Coll. Art Gallery, Henniker, N.H., 1989-91. Adviser on planned giving United Way, Nashua, 1989-90; com. mem. Manchester Mayor's Task Force on Youth Affairs, 1986-88, Manchester Bd. of Sch. Commn., 1986-90; del. N.H. Sch. Bds. Assn., 1988-90; trustee Manchester Historic Assn., 1989—; mem. Mayor's Com. on Leadership, Manchester, 1988-91; bd. dirs. Swiftwater coun. Girl Scouts U.S.; chair parents com. Bennington Coll. Mem. Nat. Soc. Fund Raising Execs. (bd. dirs., v.p. pub. affairs N.H./Vt. chpt.), Advt. Club N.H. (bd. dirs., v.p. 1980-82), Nashua Rotary West. Democrat. Home: 47 Amoskeag Pl Manchester NH 03101-1237 Office: Daniel Webster Coll 20 University Dr Nashua NH 03063-1300

ESHOO, ROBERT PIUS, artist, educator; b. New Britain, Conn., Apr. 27, 1926; s. Pius and Alice (Lazar) E.; m. Barbara Rudolph Eshoo, July 11, 1981; children: Martha, Amy, Nina. Diploma, Sch. Mus. Fine Arts, Boston, 1950-55; BFA, Syracuse U., 1956, MFA, 1957. Grad. asst. Syracuse (N.Y.) U., 1956-57; instr. Fitchburg (Mass.) Art Mus., 1957-58; painting instr. Phillips Andover (Mass.) Acad., 1963-64; art instr. Derry Field Sch., Manchester, N.H., 1965-80; supr., dir. Currier Art Ctr., Manchester, 1958—; pres., owner Hatfield Gallery, Manchester, 1977—. Exhibited in one-man and group shows including The Currier Gallery, 1975, 81, 85, Pucker/Safrai Gallery, 1975, 79, Mus. of Fine Arts, 1977, Mobile Art Gallery, 1975, New Britain Mus. Am. Art, 1974, Fuller Meml. Art Mus., 1970, Lenox Hill Hosp. and Showhegan Ann. Art Exhbn. and Sale, 1967, Inst. Contemporary Art, 1965, 66, 67, Corcoran Gallery, 1963. Bd. dirs. Manchester (N.H.) Boys Club, 1968-74, Fed. Arts of Manchester; mem. adv. com. Manchester Hist. Commn., 1980—. With USN, 1944-46. Recipient 2d Place Painting award Boston Arts Festival, 1952, scholarship Skowhegan Sch. Painting, 1954, fellowship MacDowell Colony, 1957-58. Home: 47 Amoskeag Pl Manchester NH 03101-1237 Office: Hatfield Gallery 34 Hanover St Manchester NH 03101-2212

ESKANDARIAN, EDWARD, advertising agency executive; b. Telford, Pa., Nov. 20, 1936; s. Michael and Katherine (Arslanian) E.; m. Nancy Rose Boujicanian, June 20, 1965; children—Wendy, Kristin, Jill. B.S., Villanova U., 1958; M.B.A., Harvard, 1965. Engr. Pitman Dunn Labs., Phila., 1958-60; project engr. GE, Phila., 1961-63; v.p., account supr. Compton Advt., Inc., N.Y.C., 1965-71; chmn., chief exec. officer HBM/Creamer Inc., Boston, 1971-88; chmn. Della Femina McNamee, Boston, 1988-89; chmn., chief exec. officer Arnold Fortuna Lane, Boston, 1989—. Overseer Boston Symphony, 1987—, Boston Mus. Sci. 1987—. With USAF, 1959-60. Mem. Am. Assn. Advt. Agys. (sec.-treas. 1988-89, ea. region gov.-at-large 1989-91), New Eng. Broadcasters Assn. (pres. 1982-83), Advt. Club Boston (pres. 1977-78, trustee 1980—), Harvard Bus. Sch. Assn. Boston (pres. 1984-85). Clubs: Harvard, Algonquin, Weston Golf. Home: 21 Decatur Ln Wayland MA 01778-2106 Office: Arnold Fortuna Lane 420 Boylston St Boston MA 02116

ESKELL, CAMILLE A., visual artist, curator; b. Queens, N.Y., Oct. 18, 1954; d. Joseph and Florrie (Ezra) E.; m. Frank Raymond Bernardo, Aug. 9, 1987. BA, Queens Coll., 1976, MFA, 1979. Visual artist Eskell Lace Co., N.Y.C., 1979—. One-woman shows include Kirkland Art Ctr., 1992, Bryant Libr., 1991, Jagendorf-Bacchi Gallery, 1990, AAH Galleries, 1990, First St. Gallery, 1989, Grace Gallery, N.Y.C., 1989, Winfisky Gallery, Salem, Mass., 1989, Doshi Ctr. for Contemporary Art, Harrisburg, Pa.,1 988, Gallery 410, U. of Lowell, 1987, Armory Art Gallery, 1987, Moravian Coll., Bethlehem, Pa., 1986; exhibited in group shows including Museo de Art Moderno, Bogata, 1991, Mexico City, 1990, Rio, 1990, Santiago, 1990 and others. Recipient Artist fellowship grant Found. for the Arts, 1986, Artist grant Artist Space, 1986. Mem. Women's Caucus for Art, Silvermine Guild for the Arts, Artist Equity. Office: Eskell Lace Co 79 Madison Ave New York NY 10016

ESKEW, RON WAYNE, psychologist; b. Cordell, Okla., May 17, 1951; s. Travis J. and Vivian L. (Selle) E.; m. Kathryn Regan, July 27, 1985; children: Travis Joseph, Edward Logan. BS, Okla. State U., 1973; MS, Purdue U., 1975, PhD, 1978. Postdoctoral fellow Tex. Rsch. Inst. of Mental Scis., Houston, 1978-79; assoc. psychologist Hutchings Psychiat. Ctr., Syracuse, N.Y., 1979-85; program dir., geriatrics Hutchings Psychiat. Ctr., Syracuse, 1980-85; chief psychologist Buffalo (N.Y.) Psychiat. Ctr., 1985—, assoc. clin. dir., 1989—. Contbr. chpt. to book and articles to profl. jours. Mem. Am. Psychol. Assn., Gerontol. Soc. Am., Psychol. Assn. Western N.Y. (pres. 1989-90), Assn. Upstate N.Y. Dirs. of Psychology (pres. 1989-90), Nat. Register of Health Svc. Providers Psychology, Coalition of Hosp. and Instnl. Psychologists. Office: Buffalo Psychiat Ctr 400 Forest Ave Buffalo NY 14213-1207

ESKOWITZ, LEONARD IRVING, English and American literature educator; b. Boston, June 28, 1948; s. William and Bertha (Lipkind) E.; m. Evelyn Josephine Dorosz, June 2, 1978; 1 child, Michael Morris. MA, U. Wis., 1973, ABD, 1973-75. Cert. secondary English, history and social studies tchr., Mass., Maine. Tchr. mid. sch. Westbrook (Mass.) Pub. Schs., 1979-80; coord. exch. student program E.F. Inst., Portland, Maine, 1980; tchr. high sch. Somerville (Mass.) Pub. Schs., 1980-81; survey processor, editor ABT Assocs., Cambridge, Mass., 1985-90; acad. support tutor Middlesex Community Coll., Lowell, Mass., 1990-91; instr. Mt. Washuttes Community Coll., Gardens, Mass., 1992—; participant Seeing New Eng. Conf., U. So. Maine, Portland, 1980; vol. tchr. Eastern Mass. Literacy Coun., Lexington, 1990-91. Author: (monograph) The Shaping of Typee, 1986; author poetry. Travel fellow Clark U., 1968-71. Mem. MLA, Am. Acad. Poetry, Worcester (Mass.) County Poetry Assn. (awards 1984, 90), Ind. Scholars in Lang. and Lit., New Eng. Poetry Club. Home: 59 Faraday St 40 Milton St Boston MA 02136

ESMAN, ROSA MENCHER, art gallery executive; b. N.Y.C., Nov. 29, 1927; d. Maurice and Edith (Goldstein) Mencher; m. Aaron H. Esman, June 14, 1951; children: Susanna Singer, Marjorie, Abigail. BA, Smith Coll., 1948. Adminstrv. asst. to dir. Mus. Modern Art, N.Y.C., 1951-52; pres. Tanglewood Press, Inc., N.Y.C., 1964—; dir. original edits. Harry N. Abrams, Inc., N.Y.C., 1970-72; pres. Rosa Esman Gallery, N.Y.C., 1972—; bd. dirs. Artable, N.Y.C., 1987-88. Pub. original prints and multiples by maj. internat. artists. Mem. Art Dealers Assn. Am. Office: Rosa Esman Gallery 575 Broadway New York NY 10012-3230

ESOLDI, VINCENT CARMINE, special events producer; b. Summit, N.J., Apr. 9, 1947; s. Vincent F. and Mary A. (Pepe) E. BA in History cum laude, St. Thomas of Villanova, 1969; MA in Theatre, Villanova (Pa.) U., 1973; AAS in Fashion Design, Fashion Inst. Tech., 1975; student, Daytona Sch. Cosmetology, 1977. Coord. summer festival N.J. Div. Parks and Forestry, 1982-90; producer ann. Night of a Thousand Gypsies Award Ceremonies, 1985-86. Mem. wardrobe staff (Broadway plays) Harrigan and Hart, Longacre Theatre, 1984, Grind, mark Hellinger Theatre, 1985, Song and Dance, Plymouth Theatre, 1985-86, Meet in St. Louis, Gershwin Theatre, 1990, Oliver, Mark Hellinger Theatre, 1984, Dream Girls, Imperial Theatre, 1982-84; mem. wardrobe staff, dresser and hair stylist (Broadway plays) Is There Life After High School?, Barrymore Theatre, 1982, You Can't Take It WithYou, Plymouth Theatre, 1983; hair stylist Barnum, St. James Theatre, 1980-8. Recipient N.J. Gov.'s Art in Edn. award, 1985. Mem. Theatrical Wardrobe Attendants, Hairstylists and Make-up Artists. Home: 37 Stonehenge Rd Morristown NJ 07960

ESPE, DAVID RONALD, computer and management consultant; b. Portland, Oreg., Feb. 7, 1955; s. Ronald Kenneth and Elizabeth Ann (Lokken) E. BS in Secondary Edn. and Math., Bloomsburg U., 1977; postgrad., Drexel U., 1977-78. Programmer Sperry Univac, Norristown, Pa., 1977-78; assoc. specialist Digital Equipment Corp., Blue Bell, Pa., 1978-79, specialist, 1979-81; sr. specialist Digital Equipment Corp., Cherry Hill, N.J., 1981-82, prin. specialist, 1982-83, cons., 1983-85; sr. cons. Digital Equipment Corp., Landover, Md., 1985-87; sr. cons. Digital Equipment Corp., Cherry Hill, 1987, tech. mgr. project ctr., 1987-89; mgr. Price Waterhouse, Phila., 1989-90; dir. systems devel. F. W. Dodge div. McGraw-Hill, Hightstown, N.J., 1990—; instr. project mgmt. Digital Equipment Corp. Software Services, Landover, 1985-87. Author: Mid-Atlantic Area Guide to Professional Services, 1986. Active ch. coun., chmn. congl. resources com. Luth. Ch. of Our Savior, Haddenfield, N.J. Recipient Software Excellence awards 1981-83, 1985. Mem. Kappa Mu Epsilon. Republican. Home: 121 Deerfield Dr Cherry Hill NJ 08034-3033

ESPER, WILLIAM JOSEPH, dramatic arts educator; b. Pittsburgh, Aug. 2, 1932; s. James V. and Daisy May (Perram) E.; B.A., Western Res. U., 1954; grad. Neighborhood Playhouse Sch. Theater, 1958; m. Suzanne Marie Oberjat, Nov. 23, 1973; children—Michael James, Shannon Lucia. Tchr. acting Am. Mus. and Dramatic Acad., N.Y.C., 1963-65; tchr. Neighborhood Playhouse Sch. Theater, N.Y.C., 1965-74, asso. dir. acting dept., 1974-77; dir. William Esper Studio for Actors, Inc., N.Y.C., 1965—; dir. company workshop Circle Repertory Co., N.Y.C., 1975-76; prof., head MFA and BFAprofl.tng. programs, BFA Mason Gross Sch. of Arts, Rutgers U., New Brunswick, N.J., 1977—; chmn. theater arts dept., 1986—; guest instr. Banff Festival Arts (Can.), 1977; cons. St. Nicholas Theater Co. Sch., Chgo., 1976-80; guest artist Nat. Theater Sch. of Can., Montreal, 1990, Workships for Profl. Artists Van Coueve, B.C., Can., 1988, 90, Nat. Theater Ctr., Tannersville, N.Y., 1989, 90; artistic dir. Summer Shakespeare Fest Levin Theater Co., 1989—. Interviewee New Generation of Acting Tchrs. in Am., 1989. Served with AUS, 1954-56. Mem. Univ. Resident Theatre Assn. (nat. bd. dirs. 1984-87, v.p. 1987-90), Nat. Assn. Schs. of Theatre (mem. nat. bd. 1988—). Democrat. Club: Players. Dir. plays Circle Repertory Co., WPA Theater, N.Y.C., Rutgers Theater Co., St. Nicholas Theater Co., off Broadway. Office: Rutgers U Mason Gross Sch Arts New Brunswick NJ 08903

ESPOSITO, BRUCE JOHN, history educator; b. N.Y.C., Feb. 9, 1941; s. John Salvatore and Frances (Frazin) E.; m. Virginia Ann Jackson, Sept. 11, 1965 (dec. 1970); 1 child, Joan Elizabeth. BA in History and Econs., Bklyn. Coll., 1961; MA in Internat. Rels., Am. U., 1965, PhD in East Asian Area Studies, 1968. Part time rsch. analyst Rsch. Analysis Corp., McLean, Va., 1966-68; part time rsch. cons. U.S. Dept. of State, Washington, 1968-69; asst. prof. Asian history U. Hartford, Conn., 1968-76, assoc. prof., 1976—; sr. Asian cons. Eastern Rsch. Analysis Corp., Farmington, Conn., 1975—; cons. Asian bus. Eng, Lau & Lee Fin. Svcs., N.Y.C., 1988—; mem. inner Asia seminar Harvard U., 1983—, China seminar, 1976—. Editor newsletter China Energy, 1975-88; contbr. articles to profl. publs. Bd. dirs. World Affairs Coun., Hartford, 1970—, Mott Inst., Inc., N.Y.C., 1988—; program cons. Hebrew Home and Hosp., Hartford, 1970—. Lilly Found. fellow, 1975-76; grantee Freidrich-Ebert Found., 1976, John C. Lincoln Found., 1971-77, Coffin grantee U. Hartford, 1973. Mem. New Eng. Conf. Assn. for Asian Studies (various offices 1975—), Japan Soc. Conn., New Eng. Hist. Assn., N.Y. Oriental Club. Home: 7 Carrington Ln Farmington CT 06032-2322 Office: U Hartford Dept History 200 Bloomfield Ave West Hartford CT 06117-1500

ESPOSITO, CHARLES JOSEPH, electronics distributor; b. Phila., Apr. 22, 1964; s. Charles Joseph and Gertrude (Dudkiewicz) E. BS, Temple U., 1986. Evening mgr. Eagle Lodge Conf. Ctr., Lafayette Hill, Pa., 1981-86; sales rep. Arrow Electronics, Inc., Marlton, N.J., 1986—. Mem. Sons of Italy. Republican. Roman Catholic. Home: 7305 Union Ct North Wales PA 19454-3764

ESPOSITO, CHERYL LYNNE, lawyer; b. Cleve., Dec. 13, 1964; d. John J. and Patricia A. (Manilla) E.; m. John J. Nebel III, Oct. 20, 1990; 1 child, Deanna Teresa. BA in Polit. Sci., U. Pitts., 1986, JD, 1989. Bar: Pa. 1989, U.S. Dist. Ct. Pa. 1989. Assoc. Riley & DeFalice, P.C., Pitts., 1989—. Soprano U. Pitts. Choral Soc., 1986-91; cantor St. James Ch., Wilkinsburg, Pa., 1991—; mem. steering com. Tribute to First 100 Women Lawyers in Allegheny County, 1992. Mem. ABA (tort and ins. div.), Pa. Bar Assn., Allegheny County Bar Assn. Roman Catholic. Office: Riley & DeFalice PC 1001 Liberty Ave Pittsburgh PA 15222

ESPOSITO, JOHN CHARLES, physician; b. Phila., Jan. 1, 1926; s. Charles and Anna Sylvia (Primiano) E.; m. Janice C. Jerostic, Oct. 4, 1952; children: Suzanne, Nancy, Patrica. Student, Temple; MD, Georgetown U., 1951. Intern Phila. Gen., 1951-52, resident, 1952, 55-57; pvt. practice Springfield, Pa., 1958—; instr. Hahnemann Hosp., 1976—, Jefferson Hosp., 1981—; med. advisor Del. County Community Coll., Media, Pa., 1983—. Past comdr. Am. Legion. Capt. USAF, 1955-58. Mem. Am. Coll. Allergy and Immunology, Pa. Allergy Soc., Phila. Allergy Soc. Republican. Roman Catholic. Office: 226 E Springfield Rd Media PA 19064-3221

ESPOSITO, JOSEPH JOHN, publishing company executive; b. Englewood, N.J., June 19, 1951; s. Ross and Ann (Tamborinno) E.; m. Kim Ann Loretucci. AB, Rutgers U., 1973, MA, 1977, M in Philosophy, 1978. Editor Rutgers U. Press, New Brunswick, N.J., 1978-81, Dover Publs., N.Y.C., 1981-82; v.p. spl. projects New Am. Libr., N.Y.C., 1982-85; pres. reference div. Simon & Schuster, N.Y.C., 1985-88; v.p. reference, pres. Fodor's Travel Publs. Random House Pub. Co., N.Y.C., 1988-90; pres. Merriam-Webster, Springfield, Mass., 1990—. Mem. ACLU, Dictionary Soc. N.Am. Office: Merriam-Webster 47 Federal St Springfield MA 01105-1194*

ESPOSITO, MICHAEL PATRICK, JR., banker; b. Hackensack, N.J., Oct. 6, 1939; s. Michael Peter and Maria Carmela Esposito; m. Ellen Lyons, Sept. 2, 1962; children: Michael, John, James. B.B.A., Notre Dame U., 1961; M.B.A., N.Y.U., 1967. Supr. Chase Manhattan Bank, N.Y.C., 1965-66; acctg. officer Chase Manhattan Bank, 1967-68, 2d v.p., 1968-70, v.p., 1970-74, sr. v.p., 1975-83, exec. v.p., controller, 1983-86, exec. v.p., chief fin. officer, 1986—. Served with USMCR, 1961-63. Mem. Bank Adminstrn. Inst. (chmn. acctg. and fin. commn. 1981-83, chmn. bd. 1988-89), Nat. Assn. Accts., Fin. Execs. Inst. Republican. Roman Catholic. Office: Chase Manhattan Corp 1 Chase Manhattan Plz New York NY 10081-0001

ESPOSITO, VINCENT, human development trainer, writer, therapist; b. Rome, Feb. 25, 1957; s. John and Elizabeth (Foster) E.; m. Beba Yale Bissell, Aug. 23, 1987. Student, IBM Sales & Mktg. Inst., 1974-75, NYU, 1977-79, McKinley Inst., 1980-83. Sales mgr. Avon, 1974-76; regional sales mgr. IBM, 1974-77; mktg. analyst Hisae's Restaurant chain, 1979-82; mktg. cons. Essential Resources, Inc., 1979-84; pres., chief exec. officer Kedara Cons. and Mktg., N.Y.C.; writer, trainer, corp. productivity seminars, 1989—; pres., chief exec. officer, trainer The Prosperity Network of America, Inc., N.Y.C., 1989—. Co-chmn. bd. dirs. Friends of Clinton South (N.Y.), bd. dirs. West Side Lofts, Ltd. Mem. Nat. Assn. Real Estate Investors, Am. Mgmt. Assn., Creative Investors Am., Profl. Fin. Assocs., McKinley Inst., Decus, NAJ, NAJE, KS, MENC The Gray Film Atlier (L.A.). Democrat. Office: The Prosperity Network of Am Inc 530 W 23d St Ste 407 New York NY 10011-1101

ESPY, HERBERT HASTINGS, chemist, consultant; b. Rochester, N.Y., June 4, 1931; s. Herbert Graham and Blanche (Eastwood) E.; m. Sarah Davis, Sept. 5, 1953; children: Ruth, Margaret. AB, Harvard Coll., 1952; PhD, U. Wis., Madison, 1956. Rsch. chemist Hercules, Inc., Wilmington, Del., 1956-69, sr. rsch. chemist, 1969-78, rsch. scientist, 1978-83, 85-90, mgr. tech. info., 1983-84, rsch. assoc., 1990-91; ret., 1992; bd. dirs. New Castle County Coun. Chs., 1963-66, sec., 1964-66, mem. coun. Episcopal Diocese of Del., 1974-79, treas., 1976-79, standing com., 1979-83, commn. on ministry, 1979-83, dep. to gen. conv., 1979-85, alt., 1988. Author: (book chpt.) Wet Strength Resins; contbr. articles to TAPPI Jour., Jour. Am. Chem. Soc. Mem. Am. Chem. Soc., Tech. Assn. Pulp and Paper Industry. Home: 35 Marsh Woods Ln Wilmington DE 19810-3942

ESSER, ARISTIDE HENRI, psychiatrist; b. Padalarang, Java, Indonesia, May 11, 1930; came to U.S., 1961; s. Samuel Jonathan and Anganita (Tawalujan) E.; m. Ada Reif; children: Jonathan Hendrik, Jessica. MD, U. Amsterdam, The Netherlands, 1955. Diplomate Am. Bd. Psychiatry and Neurology. Med. dir. N.S. Kline Inst., Orangeburg, N.Y., 1962-69; dir. research Letchworth Village, Thiells, N.Y., 1969-71; dir. Cen. Bergen Community Mental Health Ctr., Paramus, N.J., 1971-77; med. dir. Mission for Immaculate Virgin, S.I., N.Y., 1977-80; dir. quality assurance Bronx (N.Y.) Psychiat. Ctr., 1980-85; unit chief for supportive rehab. Rockland Psychiat. Ctr., Orangeburg, 1985-88, chief geriatrics div., 1988-90; psychiatrist St. Dominic's Home, Orangeburg, 1990—; rsch. prof. NYU Med. Ctr., N.Y.C., 1985—. Co-author: Mental Illness: A Homecare Guide, 1989, Chi Gong: The Ancient Chinese Way to Health, 1990; co-editor: Behavior and Environment, 1971, Design for Communality and Privacy, 1978; editor Jour. Man-Environment Systems, 1969— (Internat. Design award 1973). Recipient travel grant City of Leyden, The Netherlands, 1960; Lederle Labs. fellow Yale U., 1961. Fellow AAAS, Am. Psychiat. Assn.; mem. Soc. for Biol. Psychiatry, Soc. for Gen. Systems Research, Am. Acad. Acupuncture (founding), Assn. for Study Man-Environment Relations (founding). Home: 435 S Mountain Rd New City NY 10956-5731 Office: 21 N Broadway Nyack NY 10960-2621

ESSEX, MYRON ELMER, microbiology educator; b. Coventry, R.I., Aug. 17, 1939; s. Myron Elmer and Ruth Hazel (Knight) E.; m. Elizabeth Katherine Jordan, June 19, 1966; children—Holly Anne, Carrie Lisa. B.S., U. R.I., Kingston, 1962; D.V.M., Mich. State U., East Lansing, 1967; M.S., Mich. State U., 1967; Ph.D., U. Calif.-Davis, 1970; M.A. (hon.), Harvard U., 1979; DSc (hon.), U. R.I., 1987, Mich. State U., 1988, U. Madrid, 1989. Research fellow Karolinska Inst., Stockholm, 1970-72; asst. prof. Harvard U., Cambridge, Mass., 1972-76, assoc. prof., 1976-78, prof., chmn. dept. microbiology, 1978-81, chmn. dept. cancer biology, 1981—, assoc. dir. Ctr. Infectious Diseases, 1981-88, Mary Woodard Lasker prof. health scis., 1989—, chmn. AIDS Inst., 1988—; mem. sci. adv. bd. Cambridge Biosci. Corp., ARC, Virus Rsch. Inst. Editor: Viruses in Cancer, 1980. Co-editor: Human T-cell Leukemia Viruses, 1984. Contbr. articles to profl. jours. Patentee test for human T leukemia virus infection and AIDS blood tests and vaccines. Bd. sci. counselors Nat. Cancer Inst., 1982—; mem. Lasker award jury Albert & Mary Lasker Found., 1982-84, 87—; sci. adv. bd. ARC, 1985-89. Leukemia Soc. Am. scholar, 1972; Am. Cancer Soc. Nat. Cancer Inst. grantee, 1973—; recipient Bronze medal Am. Cancer Soc., 1978, Ralston-Purina rsch. award, 1985, Outstanding Investigator award Nat. Cancer Inst., 1985, Disting. Alumnus award Mich. State U., Lasker award, 1986, Carnation Rsch. award, 1987, Disting. Alumnus award U. Calif., Davis, 1987, Presdl. medal of honor Govt. of Senegal, 1991; Mary Woodward Lasker prof. health scis., 1989. Mem. Inst. Medicine of NAS, AVMA, AAAS, Am. Assn. Cancer Research, Am. Soc. Microbiology, Am. Assn. Immunologists, Internat. Assn. Research in Leukemia, Infectious Disease Soc. Am., Am. Soc. Virology, Nat. Acad. Practitioners, Reticuloendothelial Soc., Soc. Gen. Microbiology, Am. Cancer Soc. (research com. Mass. br. 1975-86), Leukemia Soc. Am. (adv. bd. 1978-83, 85—). Office: Harvard Sch Pub Health Dept Cancer Biology 665 Huntington Ave Boston MA 02115-6021

ESSLINGER, JOHN THOMAS, lawyer; b. Ephrata, Pa., Aug. 11, 1943; s. Doster Alvin and Lucy Mildred (Ream) E.; m. Patricia Lynn Smith, Aug. 15, 1970; 1 child, John David. BA, Yale U., 1965; JD, Georgetown U., 1973. Bar: D.C. 1973, U.S. Dist. Ct. D.C. 1974, U.S. Supreme Ct. 1974, U.S. Ct. Appeals (D.C. cir.) 1974. Assoc. Morgan, Lewis & Bockius, Washington, 1973-76; ptnr. Schmeltzer, Aptaker & Shepard, P.C., Washington, 1976—. Capt. USMC, 1966-70, Vietnam. Decorated Purple Heart, Bronze Star, Gold Star. Mem. ABA, Bar Assn. D.C., D.C. Bar Assn., Maritime Adminstrv. Bar Assn. Episcopalian. Home: 9102 Brierly Rd Chevy Chase MD 20815 Office: Schmeltzer Aptaker & Shepard PC 2600 Virginia Ave NW Ste # 1000 Washington DC 20037

ESSMAN, ROBERT NORVEL, small business owner, graphics designer; b. St. Louis, Feb. 6, 1937; s. Paul M. and Rose (Solinsky) E. BFA, State U. of Iowa, 1959. Artist Simplicity Pattern Co., N.Y.C., 1961-62; artist Life Mag., N.Y.C., 1962-68, art dir., 1969; art dir. Show Mag., N.Y.C., 1969-70, Bus. Week Mag., N.Y.C., 1970-74; logo designer, creative dir. N.Y.C. Bicentennial Commn., N.Y.C., 1974-76; art dir. People Weekly Mag., N.Y.C., 1974-82; art dir., pres. Bob Essman: Design, The Cricket Press, N.Y.C., 1982—. Pubr./design dir.: Revival: Theatrical History Revisited, 1992. Bd. dirs. N.Y. League for Hard of Hearing, 1977—, recording sec., 1987—. Recipient Vol. of Yr. award N.Y. League for Hard of Hearing, 1990, Excellence of Design award, Advt. Club of N.Y., 1977, Art Dirs. Club of N.Y., 1978, Gen. Excellence Nat. Mag. award Am. Soc. Mag. Editors, 1973. Mem. Am. Inst. Graphic Arts (Excellence of Design award 1980), Soc. Pub. Designers (bd. dirs. 1972-79, pres. 1976-79, Excellence of Design award 1972, 73, 75, 76, 78), Overseas Press Club (Designer Dateline 1991-92), The Players Club (bd. dirs. 1979-85), Dutch Treat Club (medal 1989, 90, 91, 92). Home and Office: The Cricket Press 63 E 9th St New York NY 10003-6302

ESSWEIN, ARTHUR JOSEPH, internist; b. Apr. 15, 1947; m. Vivian E. Esswein; children: Karen, Christine, Arthur, Carolyn, Katherine. BS, Fordham U., 1968; MD, Downstate Med. Ctr., 1972. Diplomate Nat. Bd. Med. Examiners, Am. Bd. Internal Medicine, Am. Bd. Gastroenterology; lic. physician, N.Y., Mass. Intern Nassau County Med. Ctr., East Meadow, N.Y., 1972-73, resident, 1973-75, fellow, 1975-76; fellow gastroenterology U. Mass., Worcester, 1983-85; assoc. attending physician Rochester (Mass.) Gen. Hosp., 1976-81, attending physician, 1981-83; assoc. attending physician Park Ridge Hosp., 1979-81, attending physician, 1981-83; instr. medicine U. Mass. Med. Ctr., 1984—, assoc. attending physician, 1985—; clin. instr. SUNY, Stony Brook, 1975-76; mem. provisional staff Falmouth Hosp., 1985, mem. active staff, 1986—, mem. libr. com., 1987-89, tissue and transfusion com., 1989-91, chmn., 1991—; treas. Falmouth Physicians, Inc., 1987—; bd. mem. Falmouth Health Resources, 1987—. Mem. fin. com. St. Ambrose Ch., 1981-83. Recipient Physicians Recognition award AMA, 1978, 82. Mem. Am. Soc. Internal Medicine, Am. Gastroent. Assn., Am. Soc. Gastrointestinal Endoscopy. Home: 105 Two Ponds Rd Falmouth MA 02540

ESTEBAN, MARIANO, microbiologist, biochemist; b. Villalon, Valladolid, Spain, July 26, 1944; came to U.S., 1974; s. Victorino and Victoria (Rodriguez) E.; m. Victoria Jimenez, De. 27, 1979; children: Julia, Jorge. MS, Sch. of Pharmacy, Santiago, Spain, 1967, PhD, 1970; MS, Sch. of Biol. Scis., Santiago, Spain, 1972. Rsch. assoc. Nat. Inst. Med. Rsch., Mill Hill, London, 1970-74; instr. Rutgers Med. Sch., Piscataway, N.J., 1974-77; asst. prof. SUNY Downstate Med. Ctr., Bklyn., 1979-82; assoc. prof. SUNY Health Sci. Ctr., Bklyn., 1982-85, prof., 1985—; vis. prof. Molecular Biology Inst., U. Gent, Belgium, 1978; co-dir. molecular genetics course SUNY, Bklyn., 1980-86, chmn. recombinant biohazards com., 1990-92, group leader AIDS rsch., 1990—; prof. rsch. Consejo Superior de Investigaciones Cientificas, Madrid, 1987—. Contbr. articles to profl. jours. Pres. Spanish Profls. Am., ALDEEU, N.Y., 1990. Fellow British Coun., 1970-71; grantee SUNY, 1980-81, NIH, 1980-85, NSF, 1987-91. Mem. AAAS, Am. Soc. Microbiology, British Soc. Microbiology, Harvey Soc., N.Y. Acad. Scis., Sigma Xi. Office: SUNY Health Sci Ctr 450 Clarkson Ave Brooklyn NY 11203

ESTEP, SARAH VIRGINIA, association executive; b. Altoona, Pa., Mar. 1, 1926; d. Benner Marshal and Helen Rebecca (Sellers) Wilson; m. Charles Sheldon Estep, Apr. 12, 1952; children: Cynthia Jane, Rebecca Anne, Robert Wilson. BA, Mary Washington U., Fredericksburg, Va., 1947. Social worker Blair County Childrens's Aid Soc., Altoona, Pa., 1947-52; tchr. Anne Arundel Bd. Edn., Annapolis, Md., 1952-75; pvt. camp dir. Hartford County, Md., summer 1963; camp dir. Girl Scouts of Cen. Md., Balt., summer 1964; dir. camping Camp Fire Girls Md., Balt., 1966-67; founder, dir. Am. Assn. Electronic Voice Phenomena, Severna Park, Md., 1982—; cons. in field; lectr. in field; conductor workshops in field. Author: Voices of Eternity, 1988; editor/pub. quar. newsletter, AA-EVP News, 1982; contbr. articles to profl. jours. Office: Am Assn Electronic Voice PO Box 668 Severna Park MD 21146-0668

ESTERMAN, BENJAMIN, ophthalmologist; b. Vilna, Lithuania, May 6, 1906; came to U.S., 1908; s. Marcus and Bella (Shirling) E.; m. Sophie Milgram, Sept. 5, 1935 (dec. Oct. 1968); children: Mark, Daniel, Laura; m. Cinnabelle Morris, Dec. 3, 1972; 1 stepchild, Errol Morris. AB, Columbia U., 1927; MD, Cornell U., 1931. Diplomate Am. Bd. Ophthalmology. Resident in ophthalmology N.Y. Post-Grad. Hosp., N.Y.C., 1931-32; resident in ophthalmologic surgery Knapp Meml. Eye Hosp., N.Y.C., 1933-35, ophthalmic surgeon, 1935-40; ophthalmic surgeon Manhattan Eye & Ear Hosp., N.Y.C., 1940-80, cons. opthalmology surgeon, 1980—; dir. ophthalmology Peninsula Hosp., L.I., 1940-80, St. John's Episcopal Hosp., L.I., 1940-80, L.I. Jewish Hosp., 1940-80; pres. med. bd. Peninsula Hosp., 1961, St. John's Episc. Hosp., 1961. Author: The Eye Book, 1977; contbr. articles to profl. jours. Trustee Temple Israel, Lawrence, N.Y., 1945—; founding mem. Aircraft-Noise Abatement Nassau County, L.I., 1961. Fellow ACS, Am. Acad. Ophthalmology, Internat. Coll. Surgeons, N.Y. Acad. Medicine; mem. N.Y. Acad. Sci., N.Y. Soc. for Clin. Ophthalmology (pres. 1955), Manhattan Ophthal. Soc. (pres. 1976), Alpha Omega Alpha.

ESTEROW, MILTON, magazine editor, publisher; b. Bklyn., July 28, 1928; s. Bernard and Yetta (Barash) E.; m. Jacqueline Levine, Jan. 6, 1951; children: Judith, Deborah. Student, Bklyn. Coll., 1946-49. Reporter N.Y. Times, N.Y.C., 1948-63, asst. to cultural news dir., 1963-68; assoc. dir. Kennedy Galleries, N.Y.C., 1968-72; editor, pub. ARTnews, N.Y.C., 1972—, The ART newsletter, 1975—; chmn. ARTnews Books, 1980—, Corporate ARTnews, 1984—, Esterow Communications Corp., 1981, Annellen Publs., 1982; lectr. numerous colls., univs., museums. Author: The Art Stealers, 1966. Office: ARTnews Assoc 48 W 38th St New York NY 10018-6211

ESTERS, DONALD J., audio and video company executive; b. 1939. With Ernst & Whinney, 1962-74, Harman Dardon, Inc., 1974-79, James H. Rodes & Co., Inc., 1979-80; with Harman Internat. Industries, Inc., Washington, 1980—, now pres., COO. Office: Harman Internat Industries 1120 Pennsylvania Ave NW Washington DC 20004*

ESTERSOHN, HAROLD SYDNEY, retired podiatrist, educator; b. Trenton, N.J., Jan. 3, 1927; s. Mathew and Celia (Olitsky) E.; m. Mildred Evins, Dec. 25, 1949; children: Eileen Lisa, Michele Beth, Laura Rene. D of Podiatric Medicine, Dr. William M. Scholl Coll., Chgo., 1952. Diplomate Am. Bd. Podiatric Surgery. Resident Dr. William M. Scholl Coll. Podiatric Medicine, Chgo., 1952-53; dir. podiatry staff Daus. Israel Home for the Aged, Newark and West Orange, N.J., 1953-73; dir. podiatry residency programs and podiatry externship program St. Michael's Med. Ctr., Newark, 1974-86, established fellowship in lower extremity infectious diseases, 1984-86, dir. podiatric med. edn., 1986-88; assoc. dean podiatry div. Seton Hall U., South Orange, N.J., 1987-88; cons. Schering Corp., Union, N.J., 1964, Stryker Corp., Kalamazoo, 1972; adj. clin. instr. N.Y. Coll. Podiatric Medicine, 1974-86, Pa. Coll. Podiatric Medicine, Ohio Coll. Podiatric Medicine, Ill. Coll. Podiatric Medicine, Calif. Coll. Podiatric Medicine; podiatry staff South Amboy Meml. Hosp., West Essex Gen. Hosp., St. Vincent's Hosp.; dir. podiatry residency program Hadassah U. Hosp., Ein Karem, Israel, 1987-88; dir. podiatry staff St. Michaels Med. Ctr., 1972-86; staff Doctor's Hosp., Newark, 1958-68, West Essex Gen. Hosp., 1962-80, Newark Beth Israel Med. Ctr., 1963-73, Columbus Hosp. Newark, 1968-76, St. Michael's Med. Ctr., 1972-86, South Amboy Meml. Hosp., 1982-84, St. Vincent Hosp., 1974-80; lectr. in field. Co-author: Current Therapy in Podiatric Surgery, 1989; contbr. articles to profl. jours. Chmn. youth activities Young Israel Synagogue, Newark, 1961-63; podiatry adv. com. N.J. Dept. Instns. and Agys., Trenton, 1969-72; bd. dirs. N.J. affiliate Am. Diabetic Assn., 1975-83, lectr. on diabetic foot, 1974-82. Grantee Schering Corp., 1964, 66, Stryker Corp., 1972; recipient Astra award Astra Pharm. Products, Hershey, Pa., 1985. Fellow Am. Coll. Foot Surgeons (pres. ea. div. 1969-71); mem. Am. Podiatry Assn. (25 Yr. award 1977), N.J. Podiatry Assn. (pres. 1967-68), N.J. Podiatry Soc. (ea. div. pres. 1959-60), B'nai Brith (Svc. award 1956). Home: 210 Olive St Port Saint Lucie FL 34952

ESTERSON, LARRY L., stock broker; b. Norfolk, Va., Jan. 23, 1916; s. Albert A. and Mollie (Beskin) E.; m. Sallye Josephs, Dec. 1, 1946; children: Michael J., Perry S., Scott G. BS in Econs., Pa. State U., 1937. V.p. Cat's Paw Rubber Co., Balto Md., Drumonondville, Quebec, Can., 1937-68, Holtite Mfg. Co., Balto Md., Drumondville, 1937-68, Foster Rubber Co., Balto Md., Drumonondville, 1937-68; assoc. v.p. Prudential Securities, Balto, 1968—. With U.S. mil., 1942-45. Mem. Baltimore Bond Club. Republican. Jewish. Home: 7121 Park Heights Ave Baltimore MD 21515 Office: Prudential Securities Inc 250 W Pratt St Fl 21 Baltimore MD 21201

ESTES, JOSEPH WORTH, physician, medical history educator; b. Lexington, Ky., May 10, 1934; s. Joseph Alvie and Betsy (Worth) E.; m. Cynthia Waggoner, June 20, 1959. AB, Harvard U., 1955; MA, Boston U., 1963, MD, 1964. Intern Mass. Gen. Hosp., Boston, 1964-65; fellow Univ. Hosp., Boston, 1965-66, Hosp. for Sick Children, London, 1966-67; asst. prof. Sch. of Medicine Boston U., 1967-72, assoc. prof. Sch. of Medicine, 1972-81, prof. history of pharmacology Sch. of Medicine, 1981—. Author: Hall Jackson & The Purple Foxglove, 1979, The Medical Skills of Ancient Egypt, 1989, Dictionary of Protopharmacology, 1990, (with others) The Changing Humors of Portsmouth, 1986; co-editor: Medicine in Colonial Massachusetts, 1620-1820, 1980. Pres. Mass. Libr. Trustees Assn., 1973-77; vice chair Mass. Gov.'s Conf. on Librs., 1973-81. With U.S. Army, 1955-57, CBI. Mem. Am. Assn. for the History of Medicine (sec., treas. 1989—). Office: Boston U Sch Medicine 80 E Concord St Roxbury MA 02118-2394

ESTRADA, MIKE, JR., production manager; b. Ala., Feb. 9, 1959; s. Mike Sr. and Martha (Amado) E.; m. Michele McCarthy, July 18, 1981; children: Gina Noel, Elisabeth Michele, Anthony Michael. BA, Humboldt U., 1981; postgrad., Bentley Coll., 1990—. Plant mgr. Letica Corp., Fremont, Ind., 1987-89; prodn. mgr. Dennison Mfg., Fitchburg, Mass., 1989—. Forum mem. coun. on diversity of North Worcester County, Mt. Wachusett Community Coll., Gardner, Mass., 1991—. Capt. USMC, 1981-87. Mem. United Divers Cen. Mass. Republican. Office: Avery Dennison 224 Industrial Rd Fitchburg MA 01420-4634

ESTRIN, NORMAN FREDERICK, consulting company executive; b. Bklyn., Apr. 1, 1939; s. Sam and Anne (Ashkenazi) E.; m. Marlene Goldshore; children: Laura, Melissa, Eric. BS, Bklyn. Coll., 1959; MS, NYU, 1962; PhD, Fla. State U., 1968. Tchr. chemistry Jane Addams, Vocat. High Sch., Bronx, 1961-62; chemist Clairol, Inc., Stamford, Conn., 1962-63; rsch. asst. Fla. State U., Tallahassee, 1964-68; asst. scientific dir. The Cosmetic, Toiletry and Fragrance Assn., Washington, 1968, dir. sci., 1968-71, v.p. sci., 1971-81, sr. v.p. sci., 1981-85; v.p. sci. and tech. The Health Industry Mfrs. Assn., Washington, 1985-90; pres. Estrin Cons. Group, Inc., Potomac, Md., 1991—; bd. dirs. Discovery Pharms., Inc., Instr. for Advancement Med. Comm., Phila., Nat. Com. for Clin. Lab. Standards, Phila., 1988-91; bd. advisors mid-Atlantic region Fed. Lab. Consortium, Washington, 1989-91; pres. Health Edn. Tech. Assocs.; mem. editorial adv. bd. Med. Devices and Diagnostic Industry, 1988-91; participant in establishing cosmetic ingredient rev. program and Johns Hopkins Ctr. for Alternatives to Animal Testing. Editor: The Cosmetic Industry: Scientific and Regulatory Foundations, 1984, The Medical Device Industry: Science, Technology and Regulation in a Competitive Environment, 1990, The Cosmetic Ingredient Dictionary, 1973, 77, 82, and others; contbr. articles to profl. jours. Bd. trustees Nat. Mus. for Health and Medicine Found., 1990—; tech. advisor Girl Scouts Coun. of the Nations Capital, 1989. Recipient Outstanding Sci. Contbn. and Svc. award Cosmetic Industry Buyers and Suppliers, 1986, Maison G. deNavarre medal Soc. of Cosmetic Chemists, 1985, Chemists award Chemists Club, 1982. Mem. Regulatory Affairs Profl. Soc., Am. Soc. Assn. Execs., Food and Drug Law Inst. Montgomery County High Tech. Coun., Soc. Cosmetic Chemists, Tech. Transfer Soc. Home and Office: Estrin Cons Group Inc 9109 Copenhaver Dr Potomac MD 20854-3014

ESTUS, BOYD, film director, cinematographer, film and television producer; b. Pitts., June 18, 1941. Student, MIT, 1959-62; BSBA magna cum laude, Boston U., 1965, postgrad., 1967. Dir., cinematographer Film Dept. Sta. WGBH-TV, Boston, 1967-79; pres., dir., cinematographer Boyd Estus Prodns., Boston, 1976-84; pres., co-owner, dir., cinematographer Heliotrope Studios, Ltd., Cambridge, Mass., 1984—. Dir. photography (TV series) Nova, 1973— (Red Ribbon award Am. Film Festival for segment Will the Fishing Have to Stop?, Yellow Ribbon award Am. Film Festival for segment First Signs of Washoe, also Media award of Yr. Am. Psychiat. Assn.), Poetry for People Who Hate Poetry, 1980, What Every Baby Knows, 1984-85, The Ring of Truth, 1987-88, Unsolved Mysteries, 1987—, (features) Songwriter--Making the Music, 1984, Quest for the Killers, 1984, Tender Places, 1985 (Peabody award 1986, Emmy award 1986), Secrets, 1986 (Emmy award 1987), A Jumpin' Night in the Garden of Eden, 1988; (PBS series) Eyes on the Prize, 1989, Astronomers, 1990, Pacific Century, 1990; dir. photography, dir., producer, (TV series) High Risk, 1988, Where the Galaxies Are, 1990 (Cindy award, U.S. Indsl. Film and Video Festival award), Mapping the Universe, 1991; dir., dir. solar photography Nova: Eclipse of the Century, 1991; dir. photography, creative cons. (documentary) How to Prevent a Nuclear War, 1987 (Blue Ribbon award Am. Film Festival 1988); dir. photography, dir. Fire Power, 1986 (Blue Ribbon award Am. Film Festival, Silver Hugo award Chgo. Internat. Film FestivalWorldfest Houston Gold award, Silver Quester, Bronze Apple), Vt. Pub. Health Nurses Program pub. svc. announcements, 1989 (Telly award); dir. photography, producer, dir., writer (film) The Southwest, 1983; dir. photography, dir., assoc. producer (film) The Navigators: Pathfinder of the Pacific, 1982; dir. photography, co-dir., co-producer (documentary) Eight Minutes to Midnight, 1979-80 (nominated for Acad. award 1981); dir. photography, dir., co-producer (films) Tahlia: Fresh Water from the Sea, 1978-79, Tahlia: Water Unlimited, 1978-79; dir. photography, co-dir., editor (feature) Arthur Fiedler: Just Call Me Maestro, 1978 (Emmy nomination, Cine Golden Eagle award 1979); dir. photography, assoc. producer, co-editor (documentary) Flight of the Gossamer Condor, 1976-77 (Acad. award 1978, Gold Cindy award, Blue Ribbon Am. Film Festival, CINE Golden Eagle award, numerous others); dir., cinematographer (series ZOOM, (Emmy award); dir., cinematographer, editor (series) Evening at Pops (Emmy award; cinematographer (feature) Mr. Speaker: A Portrait of Tip O'Neill, also numerous PBS films; camera operator (series) Spenser: For Hire, 1984-88; lighting cameraman many BBC prodn.; other prodn. credits include for 20/20, Lucasfilm Ltd., Frontline, many others. Mem. NATAS, Soc. Motion Picture and TV Engrs., Audio Engring. Soc., Assn. Visual Communicators, IATSE (local 644 photographers, local 771 editors). Office: Heliotrope Studios Ltd 21 Erie st Cambridge MA 02139

ESWEIN, BRUCE JAMES, II, human resources executive; b. San Mateo, Calif., Oct. 26, 1951; s. Bruce James and Janet Gordon (Copeland) E.; m. Sarah Anne Shames, Feb. 7, 1981 (div.); children: Thomas Jonathan, Elizabeth Anne. Student, U. Wash., 1969-71; A.B., U. Calif.-Berkeley, 1973, M.B.A., 1977. Brand asst. Clorox Co., Oakland, Calif., 1977-79, coll. rels. mgr., 1979-83; mgr. exec. recruitment and devel. BBDO Worldwide, N.Y.C., 1983-84, v.p., 1984-87, v.p. personnel adminstrn., 1987-88, v.p. human resources, mgr. worldwide tng. and devel., 1988-89, v.p. human resources internat., 1989-90, v.p., dir. human resources internat., 1990—. Mem. Soc. for Human Resources Mgmt., U. Calif. at Berkeley Bus. Sch. Alumni Assn. (bd. dirs. 1980-83), Phi Beta Kappa, Chi Psi (v.p. 1972-73, bd. dirs. 1979-82, trustee ednl. trust 1983-84, trustee emeritus 1984—). Episcopalian. Home: 27 N Scenic Dr Croton On Hudson NY 10520-1853 Office: BBDO Worldwide 1285 Avenue of the Americas New York NY 10019-6028

ESWORTHY, HELEN FEAGA, reading specialist; b. Frederick, Md., Oct. 21, 1950; d. R. Monroe and Catherine (Stauffer) Feaga; m. Artie R. Esworthy, Jr., July 31, 1976; children: Artie R. III, Conner H. BA, Towson State Coll., 1972; MA, Hood Coll., 1975. Tchr. 1st grade Waverley Elem. Sch., Frederick, 1972-75; reading specialist Middletown (Md.) Elem. Sch., 1975—; master clinician, parent advisor Reading Clinic, Hood Coll., Frederick, 1975-81, reading instr. Grad. Sch., 1977-80. Mem. Fredericktowne Players, Frederick, 1976—; mem. Elephant Club of Frederick County, 1976—, Hist. Soc., Frederick City, 1977—. Mem. Internat. Reading Assn., State of Md. Reading Assn. (Outstanding Tchr. Educator award 1990), Frederick Reading Assn., Phi Delta Kappa, Delta Kappa Gamma, Kappa Kappa Iota. Republican. Lutheran. Home: 16 Clarke Pl Frederick MD 21701-6528

ETHERTON, BUD, botanist, educator, researcher; b. Wardner, Idaho, Nov. 16, 1930; s. Lewis Washington and Hannah (Sutton) E.; m. Alison Elliott Mann, Sept. 14, 1957; children: Kirk, Laura. BS in Psychology, Wash. State Coll., 1956; PhD in Botany, Washington State U., 1962. Rsch. assoc. biophysics dept. U. Edinburgh, Scotland, 1962-63; lectr. plant sci. dept. Vassar Coll., Poughkeepsie, N.Y., 1963-64, asst. prof. biology dept., 1964-67; vis. scientist biology div. Argonne (Ill.) Nat. Lab., 1967-68; assoc. prof. botany dept. U. Vt., Burlington, 1968-80, prof. botany dept., 1980—. Mem. editorial bd. Plant Physiology jour., 1979—; contbr. articles to Sci. and Plant Physiology. Mem. Nat. Resource Commn., South Burlington, Vt., 1973-75. Postdoctoral fellow NSF, 1962-63, rsch. grantee, 1965-67, 73-75, 79-81. Mem. Am. Soc. Plant Physiology (mem. exec. com. N.E. sect. 1991). Democrat. Unitarian. Home: 42 Elsom Pky S Burlington VT 05403-6609 Office: Marsh Life Sci Bldg U Vt Burlington VT 05405-0086

ETLINGER, JOSEPH D., biology educator; b. Albany, N.Y., Feb. 23, 1946; s. Murry and Rosaline (Spiegel) E.; m. Susan Ellen Neschis, July 12, 1970; children, Ari, Benjamin, Matthew. BS in Physics, Rensselaer Poly. Inst., 1968; PhD in Biophysics, U. Chgo., 1974. Rsch. fellow Harvard Med. Sch., Boston, 1974-77; asst. prof. anatomy and cell biology SUNY Downstate Med. Ctr., Bklyn., 1977-80, assoc. prof., 1980-85, dir. molecular and cellular biology, 1984-88, prof., 1985-87, prof., vice chmn., 1987-88; prof., chmn. cell biology and anatomy N.Y. Med. Coll., Valhalla, N.Y., 1988—; cons. Merck, Sharp and Dohme, Rahway, N.J., 1984-87, NIH, 1981-85, NASA, Ames, Calif., 1978-81. Author 70 jour. articles and chpts. in textbooks. Grantee NIH, NASA, Muscular Dystrophy Assn. Mem. AAAS, N.Y. Acad. Sci., Am. Heart Assn. (established investigator 1980-85), Am. Physiol. Soc., Am. Soc. Cell Biology. Office: NY Med Coll Dept Cell Biology and Anatomy Valhalla NY 10595

ETSKOVITZ, FREDRIC JON, accountant; b. Phila., Aug. 23, 1954; s. Jack I. and Joan H. (Wenger) E.; m. Amy Gray, June 4, 1977; children: Natalie, Julie. BS, Pa. State U., 1976; MBA, U. Pa., 1980. CPA, Pa. Sr. acct. Laventhol & Horwath, Phila., 1976-78; supr. corp. acctg. E.I. DuPont, Wilmington, Del., 1980-86; ptnr. Heller Etskovitz & Casterline, Norristown, Pa., 1987—. Bd. mem. Am. Cancer Soc., Plymouth Whitemarsh, Pa., 1991; bd. mem., treas. Resource for Children's Health, Phila., 1991; vol. Community Accts., Phila., 1991; coach Whitemarsh Youth Basketball, Whitemarsh Twp., Pa., 1989-91. Mem. AICPAs, Pa. Inst. CPAs. Office: Heller Etskovitz & Casterline 801 E Germantown Pike Ste 1H Norristown PA 19401-2480

ETTER, HOWARD LEE, artist; b. Moberly, Mo., Jan. 22, 1931; s. John Harmon and Mildred Lee (Elsea) E.; m. Martha Lou Klepfer, Jan. 20, 1952; 1 child, Cynthia Lou. Student, Art League of Calif., San Francisco, 1954-55, Acad. of Art, San Francisco, 1955-57. Illustrator various studios, San Francisco, 1957-60, New Ctr. Studios, Detroit, 1960-61, Kolyer Studios, Detroit, 1961-62; illustrator, art dir. Wagner Advt. Agy., Detroit, 1962-67; artist, cons. self-employed, Oak Park, Mich., 1967-77; art instr. Lawrence Inst. Tech., Southfield, Mich., 1967-77; artist self-employed, Albuquerque, 1977-80, Camden, Maine, 1980—. Author: Perspective for Painters, 1990. With USNR, 1948-52. Recipient Purchase award Friends of Am. Art, 1975. Home and Office: PO Box 740 Camden ME 04843-0740

ETTER, PAUL COURTNEY, oceanographer; b. Phila., Oct. 27, 1947; s. Richard T. and Ellen M. (Cunliffe) E.; m. Alice D. Eblighatian, June 21, 1969; children: Gregory M., Andrew D. BS in Physics, Tex. A&M U., 1969, MS in Oceanography, 1975. Quality control technician Technitrol, Inc., Phila., 1969; rsch. asst. Tex. A&M U., College Station, 1973-76; sr. engr. MAR, Inc., Rockville, Md., 1976-82; sr. tech. dir. ODSI Def. Systems, Inc.,

Rockville, Md., 1982-89; sr. scientist Radix Systems, Inc., Rockville, Md., 1989—; instr. Tech. Svc. Corp., Silver Spring, Md., 1982—. Author: Underwater Acoustic Modeling, 1991; contbr. articles to Jour. of Physical Oceanography, Shock and Vibration Digest, Continental Shelf Rsch., Sea Tech. Del. Montgomery County Coun. PTA, Rockville, 1987-90; judge Montgomery County Sci. Fair, Gaithersburg, Md., 1982—. Lt. USN, 1969-73. Fellow Wash. Acad. Scis.; mem. Am. Geophysical Union, Am. Meteorol. Soc., Acoustical Soc. Am. Democrat. Lutheran. Home: 16609 Bethayres Rd Rockville MD 20855-2043 Office: Radix Systems Inc 201 Perry Pkwy Gaithersburg MD 20877-2140

ETTER, THOMAS CLIFTON, JR., lawyer; b. Phila., Apr. 7, 1938; s. Thomas Clifton and Mildred Evelyn (Phillips) E.; B.A. in History, U. Pa., 1961; M.B.A. in Fin., Temple U., 1972; J.D. cum laude, Del. Law Sch., 1975; LL.M. in Securities Law, Georgetown U., 1981; m. Susan M.F. Atkins, Jan. 19, 1980. Stockbroker Bioren & Co., Phila., 1962-66; admitted to Pa. bar, 1975, U.S. Supreme Ct. bar, 1979, D.C. bar, 1980; atty. SEC, Washington, 1975—; adj. prof. fin. Southeastern U., 1977-78; adj. prof. bus. law Benjamin Franklin U., 1977-78. Served with U.S. Army, 1961-62, 1st lt. USAR. Mem. Fin. Analysts Fedn., Washington Soc. Investment Analysts, Am. Legion (comdr. Augustus P. Gardner post Washington 1987-88), Soc. Colonial Wars (gov. D.C. soc. 1984-86), SAR (pres. Washington soc. 1983-84), Soc. War 1812 (treas. gen. 1990—), SR (gen. sec. 1988—), Sons Union Vets., Hereditary Order of Descendants of Loyalists and Patriots of Am. Revolution, 1st Troop Phila. City Cavalry. Republican. Episcopalian. Clubs: Met., Rittenhouse, Racquet (Phila.); Merion Cricket (Haverford, Pa.); Met. (Washington). Home: 2904 S Buchanan St Arlington VA 22206-1504 Office: SEC 450 5th St NW Washington DC 20549

ETTLINGER, STEPHEN RALPH, book producer, author; b. Highland Park, Ill., Feb. 7, 1949; s. Ralph Jr. and Margery (Helm) E.; m. Gusty Lange, Oct. 9, 1983; 1 child, Dylan Alexanger Lange. BA in Polit. Sci., Tufts U., 1971. Comml. attaché Cidelcem Industries, Paris, 1971-72; European mgr. S.A.R.L., Paris, 1972-74; asst. bur. chief Magnum Photos, Paris, 1974-76; prodn. mgr. Avant Industries, Wheeling, Ill., 1976-78; assoc. picture editor Geo Mag., N.Y.C., 1978-85; pres. Stephen R. Ettlinger Editorial Projects, N.Y.C., 1985—. Author: The Complete Illustrated Guide to Everything Sold in Hardware Stores, 1988, The Complete Illustrated Guide to Everything Sold in Garden Centers, 1992, The Kitchenware Book, 1992. Mem. Am. Book Producers Assn. (pres. 1990—). Office: Ettlinger Edit Projects 225 E 28th St Ste 1 New York NY 10016

ETTRICK, MARCO ANTONIO, theoretical physicist; b. Panama City, Panama, July 17, 1945; came to U.S., 1963; s. Clemente Adolfo and Olga Rosa (Birmingham) E.; m. Adys Marie Hippolyte, Oct. 22, 1966 (div. Mar. 1977); children: Rudolphe Antoine, Marc Edouard. BS in Math., Poly. Tech. U., Bklyn., 1968; MS in Math., Poly. Tech. U., 1986, doctoral study. Programmer analyst Citibank, N.Y.C., 1969-71; lic. bacteriologist Lincoln Hosp., N.Y.C., 1975-76; lectr. in math. Queens (N.Y.) Coll., 1980-81, L.I. U., Bklyn., 1981-82, N.Y. Tech. Coll., Bklyn., 1982-84, Houston Community Coll., Bklyn., 1984—, Medgar Evers Coll., Bklyn., 1986—; mem. staff Poly. U., 1990—; mem. NASA Langley Ctr. and Washington Hdqrs. Contbr. articles to sci. jours. Mem. AAAS, Am. Fedn. Scientists, Am. Phys. Soc., N.Y. Acad. Scis., Math. Assn. Am., Pi Mu Epsilon. Roman Catholic. Home: 79 Sterling St Brooklyn NY 11225-3318

ETZEL, KATHLEEN BYRON, research analyst; b. Manhasset, N.Y., Dec. 6, 1960; d. Allister Adrian and Joan (Miklesen) E. BA in English, Pine Manor Coll., 1982; M in Urban Affairs, Boston U., 1988. Staff asst. Boston U., 1982-84; adminstrv. asst. Harvard Med. Sch., Boston, 1984-85; fin. aid officer Wentworth Inst. of Tech., Boston, 1986-88, asst. dir. fin. aid, 1988-89; rsch. asst. NYU, 1989; rsch. analyst CUNY, 1990—; rsch. cons. Wentworth Inst. Tech., Boston, 1989-90, Fordham U., N.Y.C., 1990—. Contbr. poetry to mags. Named Golden Poet World of Poetry Press, 1990-91. Mem. N.Y. Sports Club. Office: CUNY 555 W 57th St New York NY 10019-2925

EUDENBACH, GRACE CAINE, registered nurse; b. Fall River, Mass., Aug. 27, 1936; d. Raymond William and Emma Grace (Gardella) Caine; m. Peter Timothy Eudenbach, Feb. 22, 1962; children: Elizabeth, Harry J., Peter T. Jr., Michael R. Diploma RN, St. Anne's Hosp. Sch. Nursing, Fall River, 1957; student, Salve Regina Coll., 1980-81. Mem. RN staff Newport (R.I.) Hosp., 1957-60, head nurse, 1960-62; sch. nurse Newport Sch. for Girls, 1966-69; pvt. duty nurse Margaret van Beuren, Newport, 1976-87; office mgr. Dr. Peter T. Eudenbach, Middletown, R.I., 1987-90; RN vol. Haitian Health Found., Jeremie, Haiti, 1991. Pres. New Eng. Coun. Optometry Aux., Boston, 1991-92. Mem. Seaside Garden Club Newport (pres. 1990-92). Democrat. Roman Catholic. Home: 416 Gibbs Ave Newport RI 02840-3327

EUILLE, WILLIAM DARNELL, construction contracting company executive; b. Alexandria, Va., May 3, 1950; s. William O. and Doris (Simons) E. BS, Quinnipiac U., 1972. V.p., controller A.A. Beiro Constrn. Co., Inc., Alexandria, 1972-87; pres., owner Wm. D. Euille & Assocs., Inc., Constrn. Contractors, Washington, 1987—. Campaign treas. Va. House of Del. Candidate, Alexandria, 1983; bd. dirs. Alexandria City Sch. Bd., 1974-84, Washington Urban League, Alexandria, 1974—, United Way Am., Alexandria, 1984—. Named Outstanding Young Men of Am., Jaycees, 1974; recipient Disting. Svc. award Alexandria Jaycees, 1975. Mem. Alexandria Bus. Industry Assn., Associated Builders Contractors, D.C. Contractor's Assn., Alexandria Jaycees (v.p., treas. 1974-78). Baptist. Home: 1721 Price St Alexandria VA 22301-1731 Office: 733 15th St NW Ste 1100 Washington DC 20005-2128

EULER, ALINE, environmental center executive, naturalist; b. N.Y.C.; d. Henry and Alice (Revaz) E. BA, Queens Coll., 1960, MS, 1966, 77; EdD, St. John's U., 1988. Cert. permanent tchr., N.Y. Play street dir. Police Athletic League, Bklyn., 1960; elem. tchr. Bellew Pub. Sch., West Islip, N.Y., 1960-78; dir. edn. Alley Pond Environ. Ctr., Douglaston, N.Y., 1978—; instr. elem. edn. Adelphi U. Grad. Sch., Garden City, N.Y., 1981; instr. elem. sci. Queens Coll., Flushing, N.Y., 1982, 91, 92; instr. continuing edn. Queensborough Community Coll., Bayside, N.Y., 1988—. Contbr. articles to various publs. Sec. Orgn. Gen. Slocum Survivors, Queens Village, N.Y., 1984—; v.p. Bayside Hist. Soc., 1985-87; chmn. Oakland Lake and Ravine Conservation Commn., Bayside, 1986—. Recipient Environ. Quality award U.S. EPA Region 2, 1970, 90. Mem. Nat. Assn. for Rsch. in Sci. Teaching, N.Am. Assn. Environ. Edn., Elem. Sch. Sci. Assn. (presnter), Environ. Ednl. Adv. Coun., Nat. Sci. Tchr. Assn., Queens County Bird Club (Flushing), Phi Delta Kappa. Home: 204-05 43d Ave Bayside NY 11361 Office: Alley Pond Environ Ctr 22806 Northern Blvd Flushing NY 11362-1096

EVANGELISTA, JESUS SORIANO, physician; b. Manila, Philippines, Apr. 19, 1946; came to U.S., 1972; s. Feliciano Coronel and Cristina (Soriano) E.; m. Mary Ann Stancoven, May 6, 1978; children: Nicole Maria, Nathan Jess. BS in Zoology, U. Santo Tomas, Manila, 1966, MD, 1971. Diplomate Am. Acad. Family Physicians. Rotating intern St. Peter's Hosp., Albany, N.Y., 1972-73; family practice resident Washington Hosp., 1973-75; assoc. mem. staff Cohoes (N.Y.) Meml. Hosp., 1975-76; mem. active staff Washington (Pa.) Hosp., 1975—; mem. courtesy staff Canonsburg (Pa.) Gen. Hosp., 1985—; chmn. dept. family practice Washington Hosp., 1981-83. Chmn. exec. com. Washington Hosp., 1986-87. Fellow Am. Acad. Family Physicians, Am. Geriatrics Soc.; mem. AMA, Pa. Acad. Family Physicians, Washington County Med. Soc. (pres. 1989), Pa. Med. Soc., Cert. Am. Med. Dirs. Democrat. Roman Catholic. Home: 109 Trenton Cir Canonsburg PA 15317-3657 Office: 50 E Wylie Ave Washington PA 15301-6299

EVANGELISTA, THOMAS ANTHONY, distributing company executive; b. N.Y.C., Jan. 17, 1951; s. Thomas Joseph and Dora (Caggiano) E.; m. Marie Fazio, Aug. 11, 1974; children: Gregory, Cara, Perry. BA in Biology, Rutgers U., 1973. From sales trainee to sales mgr. Fisher Sci., Springfield, N.J., 1973-84; from mktg. mgr. to v.p. corp. accts. Fisher Sci., Pitts., 1984—. Republican. Roman Catholic. Home: 1503 King Charles Dr Pittsburgh PA 15237-1527 Office: Fisher Scientific 711 Forbes Ave Pittsburgh PA 13219

EVANS, ABIGAIL RIAN, academic administrator, educator; b. Phila., Oct. 26, 1937; d. Edwin H. and Marian (Schall) Rian; m. Robert Maxwell Evans, Dec. 12, 1959 (div. 1976); children: Stephen Edwin, Nathanael Cameron, Matthew M.S., Thomas Evan, Rachel; m. John Richard Powers, June 25, 1988. BA, Jamestown Coll., 1958; diploma in Brazailian lang. and culture, Escola Linguas e Orientacao, Campinas, Brazil, 1960; MDiv, Princeton Sem., 1968; PhD, Georgetown U., 1984. Ordained to ministry Presbyn. Ch., 1969. Missionary United Presbyn. Ch., Santa Catarina, Brazil, 1959-64; instr. liturgy and ch. history Campinas (Brazil) Theol. Sem., 1966-67; pastor, community organizer Ebenezer Presbytery, Ky., 1968-70; dir. Broadway U. Ministries, N.Y.C., 1971-76; assoc. pastor Broadway Presbyn. Ch., N.Y.C., 1971-76; Presbyn. chaplain Columbia U., N.Y.C., 1971-76; staff assoc. in med. edn. and ethics rsch. dept. Coll. Physicians and Surgeons Columbia U., N.Y.C., 1976-79; assoc. synod exec. Synod of Vas., Presbyn. Ch. U.S., Roanoke, 1976-79; rsch. and teaching asst. Kennedy Inst. Ethics Georgetown U., Washington, 1981-84, dir. new programs, sr. staff assoc., 1984-88; founder, dir. NCP Health Ministries, sr. cons. Kennedy Inst. Ethics, Georgetown U., Washington, 1984—; assoc. prof. practical theology, dir. field edn. Princeton (N.J.) Theol. Sem., 1991—; mem. Nat Capital Presbytery, Washington, 1976—; instr. Wesley Theol. Sem., 1984; vis. prof. Theol. Consortium, Washington, 1986, Howard U., Washington, 1987, Presbyn. Sch. Christian Edn., 1988; speaker, lectr. in field; preached in over 100 chs. throughout U.S., 1983—; cons. fin field, 1983—; bioethics cons. NIH, 1983-89; cons. Office Substance Abuse Prevention, U.S. govt., 1990—; del. World Coun. Chs., Bangkok, 1973, Switzerland, 1988. Editor: Human Resources Catalog, 1977, Reflections, 1976-78; mng. editor Jour. Medicine and Philosophy, 1984; assoc. editor Jour. Clin. Ethics; contbr. articles to profl. publs. Mem. commn. on values D.C. Bd. Edn., 1987—; bd. govs. Washington Ecumenical Inst., 1985—; bd. dirs., chmn. mission com. Coun. Chs. Greater Washington, 1984—; mem. ethics com. S.W. Organ Procurement Found., 1988—; mem. George Washington U. Animal Rsch. Commn., 1988-92, Human Genome Working Group, 1991—. Grad. fellow United Presbyn. Ch., 1982-84. Mem. Soc. for Health and Human Values.

EVANS, ALFRED SPRING, physician, educator; b. Buffalo, Aug. 21, 1917; s. John H. and Ellen (Spring) E.; m. Brigitte Kluge, July 26, 1952 (dec. Oct. 1985); children: John Kluge, Barbara Spring Evans Paganelli, Christopher Paul. AB, U. Mich., 1939, MPH, 1960; MD, U. Buffalo, 1943; MA (hon.), Yale U., 1966. Diplomate Am. Bd. Internal Medicine. Intern U. Pitts. Hosps., 1943-44; resident Goldwater Hosp., N.Y.C., 1944; USPHS postdoctoral research fellow Yale Med. Sch., 1947-48, from instr. to asst. prof. medicine, 1949-50, prof. epidemiology, dir. WHO serum reference bank, dept. epidemiology and pub. health, 1966-89, John Rodman Paul prof. epidemiology, 1982-88, emeritus prof., 1988—, dir. div. infectious disease, 1982-85; resident Buffalo Gen. Hosp., 1948-49; assoc. prof. preventive medicine and med. microbiology U. Wis. Sch. Medicine, 1952-59; prof., chmn. dept. preventive medicine, also dir. Wis. State Lab. Hygiene, 1959-66; mem. microbiology fellowship panel NIH, 1960-64; mem. microbiol. panel space flight NRC/NASA; cons. Philippine Health Dept., WHO, 1962, 1964, cons. tropical diseases, 1977-82; cons. epidemiology Surgeon Gen. U.S. Army, 1969-85, USN Bur. Medicine, 1973-76, viral epidemiology sect. Nat. Cancer Inst. NIH, 1988, 92. Author: (with M.J. Kelsey and D. Thompson) Observational Methods in Epidemiology, 1985; editor: Yale Jour. Biology and Medicine, 1971-73; editor-in-chief, 1973-76; editor: Viral Infections of Humans, 1976, 82, 89; (with H.A. Feldman) Bacterial Infection of Humans, 1982; (with P.A. Brachman) 2d edit., 1991; contbr. articles on med. history, infectious diseases and epidemiology to profl. jours. Served to capt. M.C. AUS, 1944-46, 50-52. Recipient Best Book for Physicians award Am. Med. Writers Assn., 1977, Thomas Frances Jr. lectureship and award Sch. Pub. Health, U. Mich., 1986, Harrington lectureship and award U. Buffalo, 1988, Disting. Med. Alumnus award U. Buffalo, 1992. Fellow Am. Pub. Health Assn. (Abraham Lilienfeld award for teaching excellence 1990), Am. Coll. Epidemiology (bd. dirs., pres. 19889-90, Abraham Lilienfeld Disting. award 1986); mem. Soc. Epidemiol. Research, Am. Epidemiol. Soc. (sec.-treas. 1968-73, pres. 1973-74), Infectious Disease Soc. Am., Internat. Epidemiol. Assn., Am. Assn. History of Medicine, Soc. Med. Cons. to Armed Forces (chmn. preventive medicine 1973-76, council 1976-84, v.p. 1979-80, pres. 1980-81, John R. Seal award 1987), Delta Omega. Home: 88 Notch Hill Rd Apt 317 North Branford CT 06471-1852 Office: 60 College St Box 3333 New Haven CT 06510

EVANS, CHARLIE ANDERSON, chemist; b. Columbus, Ga., Dec. 29, 1945; s. James William and Mollie Ree (Carter) E.; m. Phyllis Angela Roberts, Dec. 16, 1967 (div. 1992); children: Timothy Anderson, Laurin Stephen, Paul Thomas. BS, Ga. Inst. Tech., 1968; PhD, U. Ga., 1974. Postdoctoral fellow Centre d'Etudes Nucleaire, Grenoble, France, 1973-74, U. Western Ont., London, 1974-76; applications chemist Varian Assocs., Florham Park, N.J., 1976-80; applications chemist JEOL, Cranford, N.J., 1980-81, mgr. applications lab., 1981-84; scientist Berlex Labs., Cedar Knolls, N.J., 1984-87; sr. prin. scientist Schering-Plough Corp., Bloomfield, N.J., 1987-90, devel. fellow, 1990—; part-time insr. Ga. Inst. Tech., Atlanta, 1967-68; adj. asst. prof. Drew U., Madison, N.J., 1978; adj. prof. Fairleigh Dickinson U., 1988—. Contbr. articles to profl. jours. With U.S. Army, 1969-71. Muscogee Found. scholar, 1964-68; NSF summer fellow, 1967; NDEA Title IV fellow, 1971-73; Fulbright-Hays fellow, 1973-74. Mem. AAAS, Am. Chem. Soc. (chmn. NMR disc. group 1988), N.Y. Acad. Sci., Internat. Soc. Magnetic Resonance. Democrat. Presbyterian. Office: Schering-Plough Corp 2015 Galloping Hill Rd Kenilworth NJ 07033

EVANS, CRAIG, association executive; b. Klamath Falls, Oreg., Apr. 14, 1949; s. Joseph Fuller Evans and Toni Opel (Hooper) Johnson; m. Susan Jean Murphy, Dec. 27, 1980. BA in English, Calif. State U., San Jose, 1971. Reporter San Jose (Calif.) Mercury News, 1968-71; adventurer 1st person to walk end-to-end through the Alps North Face, Berkeley, Calif., 1972-73; freelance writer Los Gatos, Calif., 1973-75; editor Backpacker Mag., N.Y.C., 1975-77; author William Morrow & Co., N.Y.C., 1977-81; exec. dir. Am. Hiking Soc., Washington, 1979-81; owner, chief exec. officer Syntax, Mktg. Communications, Falls Church, Va., 1981-84; assoc. exec. dir. Population-Environment Balance, Washington, 1984-86; pres. The WalkWays Ctr., Washington, 1986-90; environ. and mktg. cons. Craig Evans, Inc., Washington, 1989-90; cons. environ. programs and publs. Am. Soc. Landscape Architects and Am. Farmland Trust, Washington, 1990—; mountain tour leader Better Camping Mag., French & Swiss Alps, 1972-73; trails cons. U.S. Dept. of the Interior, Washington, 1979-81; lobbyist Am. Hiking Soc., Washington, 1979-81; U.S. Rep. European Rambler's Assn., 1977-84. Author: (7 book series) On Foot Through Europe, 1982; (pub. law) National Trails System Act Amendments of 1983; project editor: (book) Backpacking Equipment Buyer's Guide, 1977; creator, author (travel mag.) Tripping, 1973; contbr. articles to profl. jours. Treas. Am. Trails Network, Washington, 1988-89. Recipient One Show Merit award The Art Dirs. Club, Inc., N.Y.C., The Copy Club of N.Y., 1974. Mem. Am. Soc. of Assn. Execs., Natural Resources Coun. of Am., Author's Guild, Internat. Platform Assn. Democrat. Club: Appalachian Mountain (Boston) (chair internat. com. 1983-84). Home: 404 Kentucky Ave SE Washington DC 20003-3009 Office: Am Farmland Trust 1920 N St NW # 400 Washington DC 20036-1601

EVANS, DANIEL ARTHUR, librarian; b. Pen Argyl, Pa., July 6, 1948; s. Arthur George and Virginia May (Miller) E.; m. Donna Lee Stratton, Oct. 16, 1971; 1 child, Jeffrey Scott. BA in History, Elizabethtown Coll., 1970; MLS, Drexel U., 1971. Reference libr. Lafayette Coll., Easton, Pa., 1971-86, head acquisitions dept., 1986—. Mem. Classic Thunderbird Club Internat., Am. Friends of Lafayette. Office: Lafayette Coll Acquisitions Dept Easton PA 18042

EVANS, DAVID ANDREOFF, linguistics and computer science educator; b. St. Louis, Mar. 2, 1948; s. Joseph Steven and Eleanor Marie (Andreoff) E.; m. Jean Lynnae Richter, Mar. 21, 1969; children: Brynn Marie, Erinn Lynnae. AB, Stanford U., 1971, BS, 1975, PhD, 1982. Rsch. assoc. Ctr. for Advanced Study in Behavioral Scis., Stanford, Calif., 1982, Cognitive Sci. Program, U. Calif., Berkeley, 1982-83; asst. prof. English Carnegie Mellon U., Pitts., 1983-85, asst. prof. depts. philosophy and computer sci., 1985-88, dir. computational linguistics program, 1986—, dir. lab. for computational linguistics, 1987—, assoc. prof. philosophy and computer sci., 1988—. Author: Situations and Speech Acts, 1985; editor: Cognitive Science in Medicine, 1989; contbr. articles to profl. jours. Mem. ACM, Cognitive Sci. Soc., Linguistics Soc. Am., Assn. for Computational Linguistics, Am. Soc. for Info. Sci., Am. Med. Informatics Assn., Am. Ednl. Rsch. Assn., Am. Assn. for Artificial Intelligence. Office: Carnegie Mellon U Schenley Park Pittsburgh PA 15213-3830

EVANS, DONALD FRANK, computer systems analyst; b. Lawton, Okla., Apr. 16, 1952; s. Elden Earnest and Isabelle Nora (Jones) E.; m. Sharon Bernice Edge, June 4, 1972 (div. 1982); chldren: Carson Christian Edge-Evans, Jennifer Mari Grace Edge-Evans; m. Pamela Jo Uesley, July 6, 1984. B Univ. Studies, Okla. State U., 1976. Exec. v.p. Prince Petroleum Inc., Tulsa, 1978-84; contr. Penland (N.C.) Sch. Crafts, 1984-86; systems analyst NASA, Bethesda, Md., 1986-87; dept. dir. info. mgmt. div. Nat. Endowment for Arts, Washington, 1987-92, dept. dir. exec. secretariat, 1992—. Author software Flisim, Flisim II, Security, Quick Code; inventor hardware QRQ Keyer. Fellow Nat. Endowment for Arts, 1987, grantee, 1988. Mem. Washington Area Data Ease Users Group (host 1987—), Mil. Affiliate Radio System. Democrat. Roman Catholic. Office: Nat Endowment for Arts 1100 Pennsylvania Ave NW Washington DC 20506-0005

EVANS, DONNA IRENE, journalist; b. Vancouver, B.C., Can., Sept. 21, 1951; came to U.S. 1979.; d. Donald John and Thelma Irene (Rock) Ashby; m. James Nelson Evans, Feb. 27, 1971; children: Nathalie Jeanne, Blythe Alicia, Seth Alexander. BA, SUNY, Buffalo, 1983. Model Covergirl Agy., Edmonton, Alta., 1976-79, June II/Volkert Agy., Buffalo, 1979-83; instr. Erie Community Coll., Buffalo, 1983-85; reporter Buffalo Bus. Jour., 1985-86, assoc. editor, 1986-87; staff writer Erie County Legis., 1986-87; pub. rels. cons. The Buffalo Found., Buffalo/Rochester, 1990—, Health Care Plan, 1991—. Freelance writer/editor handling journalism, mktg. and tech. assignments; tech. writing cons. Computer Task Group, Buffalo, 1989-90. Campaign staff writer County Dem. Legis. Candidate Leonard Lenihan, 1983. Mem. Women for Downtown (newsletter editor 1987-89). Home: 6 Saville Dr Orchard Park NY 14127-1919

EVANS, ELIZABETH CARPENTER, retired social worker and family counselor; b. Glens Falls, N.Y., Jan. 3, 1911; d. William Morton and Beulah (Mason) Carpenter; m. John E. Evans, Jr., Aug. 28, 1933 (dec. Oct. 1982); children: John Edgar III, Claire Louise. AB, Radcliffe Coll., 1932; MSW, U. Pitts., 1964. Dir. family counseling Cath. Social Svc., Pitts., 1964-76; ret., 1976. Sec. Southwestern Pa. coun. Girl Scouts U.S.A., 1975-76, v.p. 1976-82, bd. dirs., 1982-85. Mem. Nat. Assn. Social Workers, Zonta (pres. Pitts. 1975-76), Pitts. Coll. Club (bd. dirs.). Republican. Methodist. Home: 100 Whitehampton Ln Apt 322 Pittsburgh PA 15236

EVANS, ERNEST PIPKIN, JR., municipal official; b. St. Petersburg, Fla., Mar. 6, 1944; s. Ernest Pipkin and Carrie (McLeod) E. BS, U. Md., 1972. Chief investigator U.S. Senate Com. on Small Bus., Washington, 1967-74; asst. dir. Com. on Fed. Paperwork, Washington, 1975-77; spl. asst. Dept. Justice Immigration and Naturalization Svc., Washington, 1977-80; sr. ptnr. Ernest Evans & Assocs., Washington, 1980-90; pres. Stonewall Broadcasting Co., Elkton, Va., 1986—; spl. asst. Office of the Mayor, Washington, 1991—; bd. dirs. Am. Internat. Mgmt. Co., Washington, Alternative Investments, Washington. Producer: (radio series) Our Community, Our World, 1989; (radio advt. campaign) Small Market Broadcasters, 1989 (hon. mention). Mem. Dem. Com., Page County, Va., 1990, Gertrude Stein Dem. Club, Washington, 1991. Recipient Reader's Digest cert. of merit, 1965. Mem. Assn. Former Senate Aides, Congl. Correspondents Club, Human Rights Campaign Fund., Lambda Legal Defense Fund. Episcopalian. Home: 318 10th St SE Washington DC 20003-2129 Office: Exec Office of the Mayor 1350 Pennsylvania Ave NW Washington DC 20004-3001

EVANS, ESSI H., research scientist; b. Bad-Schwalbach, W.Ger., Jan. 12, 1950; came to U.S., 1951, naturalized, 1957; d. John H. (b. Horst H. Jahn) and Jean E. (von Schwerin); m. Everett M. Turner, Jr., Aug. 16, 1974. BS in Agr. (James Harris scholar), U. Md., 1972; MS in Animal Sci., U. Guelph, 1974, PhD in Animal Sci., 1976. Polymer chemist Monarch Rubber Co., Balt., 1972; rsch. asst., teaching asst. U. Guelph (Ont., Can.), 1972-76; project dir. animal nutrition Can. Packers Inc., Toronto, Ont., 1976-85; tech. mgr. animal nutrition and animal health Can. Packers, Inc., Toronto, 1986-89, rsch. mgr., 1989-90, gen. rsch. and nutrition mgr. shur-gain div., 1990—; farm cons.; guest lectr. Hubbard Farms fellow, 1975-76; NRC Indsl. postdoctoral fellow, 1976-79; recipient Hamilton Milk Producers award, 1973, 74; Ont. Ministry of Agr. and Foods Provincial Lottery grantee, 1980-83. Mem. Am. Soc. Animal Sci., Am. Dairy Sci. Assn., Ont. Comml. Rabbit Growers Assn., Am. Assn. Vet. Nutritionists, Coun. for Agrl. Sci. and Tech., Nat. Feed Industry Assn., Can. Feed Industry Assn. Republican. Contbr. to sci. publs. and confs. Home: 64 Scugog St, Bowmanville, ON Canada L1C 3J1 Office: Rsch Ctr Can Packers Inc, Shur-Gain Div, 2700 Matheson Blvd Ste 600 East, Mississauga, ON Canada L4W 4V9

EVANS, GEORGE EDWARD CHARLES, psychiatrist; b. Cleve., June 14, 1930; s. Fred Charles and Laura Margaret (Knoll) E.; m. Kathleen Renata Grube, June 6, 1954; children: George E.C. II, Claudia Sue Evans Zale, Christie Lynn Evans Sturges, Stephanie Michelle Evans Hemdal. BS, Case Western Res. U., 1951; postgrad., Ohio State U., 1951-52; DO, Coll. Osteo. Medicine, Des Moines, Iowa, 1956. Diplomate Am. Bd. Psychiatry. Intern Okla. Osteo. Hosp., Tulsa, 1956-57; gen. practice medicine Norwalk, Ohio, 1957-63; resident psychiatry Embreeville State Hosp., Coatesville, Pa., 1963-65; fellow in psychiatry Phila. Mental Health Clinic, 1965-67; pvt. practice psychiatry, 1967-79; supervisory psychiatrist Wernersville (Pa.) State Hosp., 1986—. Capt. USN, 1979-84. NIMH grantee, 1965-67. Mem. Am. Coll. Neuropsychiatrists (sr.), Am. Psychiat. Assn., Psychiat. Physicians Pa., Assn. Mil. Surgeons U.S., Pennsy. Republican. Unitarian. Home: 1915 Meadow Ln Reading PA 19610-2706 Office: Wernersville State Hosp Dept Psychiatry Bldg 19 2 Wernersville PA 19565-0300

EVANS, JOEL RAYMOND, marketing educator; b. N.Y.C., Sept. 17, 1948; s. Joseph and Betty Erna (Loonstein) E.; m. Linda Ruth Lieber, Dec. 19, 1970; children: Jennifer Faith, Stacey Beth. BA, Queens Coll., 1970; MBA, Bernard M. Baruch Coll., 1974; PhD, CUNY, 1975. MBA dir. Hofstra U., Hempstead, N.Y., 1975-77, asst. prof., 1975-79, assoc. prof., 1979-84, prof. mktg., 1984—, assoc. dean, 1981-82; chmn. Dept. Mktg. Hofstra U., Hempstead, N.Y., 1978-85; retail mgmt. inst. disting. prof. bus. Hofstra U., Hempstead, N.Y., 1989—; cons. N.Y. Telephone, 1978, Pepsico, 1979, ARA/Slater Food Svcs., 1981-82, McCrory, 1989, Fortunoff, 1990, other orgns. Co-author: Readings in Marketing Management, 1984, Principles of Marketing, 2d edit., 1988, Retail Management, 5th edit., 1992, Marketing, 5th edit., 1992. Recipient Disting. Service award, Hofstra U., 1982, Hofstra U. Sch. Bus. Dean's award, 1979, 81; named One of Outstanding Young Men of Am., 1979. Mem. Am. Mktg. Assn., So. Mktg. Assn., Acad. Mktg. Sci., Product Devel. & Mgmt. Assn., Am. Collegiate Retailing Assn., Southwestern Mktg. Assn., Beta Gamma Sigma. Home: 14 Melrose Ln Commack NY 11725-1615 Office: Hofstra U Dept Mktg 135 Weller Hall Hempstead NY 11550

EVANS, JOHN MILLARD, retired industrial engineer; b. Washington, July 17, 1918; s. William Lewis and Sadie F. (White) E.; m. Beatrice Baldwin, June 12, 1943 (dec. Apr. 1983); children: Gail, Robert, Sandra, James; m. Rae E Sedgwick, July 28, 1984. BS in Indsl. Engr., Syracuse U., 1942; MS in Indsl. Engr., U. Pitts., 1950. Registered profl. engr., Pa. Ind. engr. Armstrong World Industries, Lancaster, Pa., 1946-80; dir. to pres. Heritage Savs. Assn., Lancaster, 1967-82, bd. dirs. emeritus. Author: (manual) How to Help Hospitals, 1979. Pres., negotiator Warwick Sch. Bd., Lititz, Pa., 1967-82; advisor budget Lancaster Coun. Chs., 1972—; treas. Manheim Twp. Ambulance Assn., Lancaster, 1984-88; arbitrator Better Bus. Bur., Lancaster, 1987-89, Lt. USNR, 1943-46, 51-52. Republican. Methodist. Home: 255 Primrose Ave Lancaster PA 17601-3820

EVANS, JUDITH M., social services administrator; b. Atlantic City, N.J., Sept. 7, 1962; d. Richard Amandus Miller and Patricia Loretta (McGovern) Abbott; m. Thomas Michael Evans, Oct. 18, 1986. BS in Bus. Studies, Stockton State Coll., 1984. Cashier, bookkeeper Supermarkets Gen. Corp./Pathmark, Pleasantville, N.J., 1979-84, customer svc. mgr., 1984-85, bakery mgr., 1985-87, store trainer, 1987-88; devel. dir. Assn. for Retarded Citizens, Pleasantville, 1988—. Coach, mem. adv. com. N.J. Spl. Olympics Area 8, Atlantic, Cumberland and Cape May Counties, 1989-91; bd. dirs., coach Pleasantwoods Recreation Assn., Egg Harbor Twp., N.J., 1980-91. Mem. Nat. Soc. Fundraising Execs. (ethics com.), Assn. for Retarded Citizens. Democrat. Roman Catholic. Home: 929 Oak Grove Ave Linwood NJ 08221-1846 Office: Assn for Retarded Citizens 1033 N Main St Pleasantville NJ 08232-1146

EVANS, MARK DAVID, engineering educator; b. Holyoke, Mass., May 26, 1958; s. John B. and Joan M. (Provost) E.; m. Denise Marie Beaumont, June 27, 1981; children: Carolyn Rose, Margaret Catherine, Rosemary Lauren. BS, Northeastern U., 1981; MS, U. Calif., Berkeley, 1984, M Engring., 1985, PhD, 1987. Registered profl. engr., Calif., Mass., Ga., Md. Geotech. engr. CH2M Hill, Inc., Atlanta, 1987-88; project engr. Geosvcs., Inc., Atlanta, 1988-90; asst. prof. engring. Northeastern U., Boston, 1990—. NSF initiation grantee, 1991. Mem. ASCE (mem. editorial bd. Geotech. Engring. Jour. 1990—, soil properties com. geotech. engring. group 1988—), ASTM. Office: Northeastern U 420 Snell Engring Ctr Boston MA 02115

EVANS, MICHELLE, advertising copywriter; b. Glen Ridge, N.J., Aug. 17, 1963; d. Edward Evans and Julie Deane Lochridge. BA, U. N.H., Durham, 1985. Account exec. Greene Inc., N.Y.C., 1986-87, Gerald Freeman Inc., Clifton, N.J., 1987; copywriter Bloomingdale's By Mail, Ltd., N.Y.C., 1987-90; sr. copywriter Bozell Rydge Pty. Ltd., Sydney, Australia, 1990-91; freelance copywriter N.Y.C., 1991—. Communications specialist Women's Health Action and Mobilization, N.Y.C., 1991-92, NOW, N.Y.C., 1992; treas. Amnesty Internat., N.Y.C., 1988-90. Democrat. Home: 322 W 57th St 48V New York NY 10019

EVANS, PATRICK JAMES, physicist; b. New Haven, July 7, 1950; s. Francis Edward and Ermenia (Mizii) E.; m. Kathleen Marie King, June 17, 1972; children: Gregory, Daniel. BS in Math. and Physics, Boston Coll., 1972; MS, Purdue U., 1974, PhD in Physics, 1978. Sr. staff physicist Applied Physics Lab., Johns Hopkins U., Laurel, Md., 1978-80; mem. tech. staff Analytic Sci. Corp., Reading, Mass., 1980-84, dept. staff analyst, 1984-86; mem. tech. staff AT&T Bell Labs., Whippany, N.J., 1986-90, disting. mem. tech. staff, 1990—. Contbr. numerous govt. reports. Alumni admission counselor Boston Coll., Balt., 1979. Mem. Am. Phys. Soc., N.Y. Acad. Sci. Roman Catholic. Home: 34 Claude Ave Denville NJ 07834-2408 Office: AT&T Bell Labs 67 Whippany Rd Whippany NJ 07981-1508

EVANS, PAUL, osteopath; b. Nutley, N.J., May 23, 1950; m. Roxanne Romack. BS cum laude in Biology, U. Miami, 1972; DO, Phila. Coll. Osteopathic Med., 1979. Diplomate Am. Bd. Family Practice, Nat. Bd. Osteo. Examiners, Am. Acad. Pain Mgmt.; cert. Am. Osteo. Bd. Gen. Practice. Commd. 2d lt. U.S. Army, 1972, advanced through grades to lt. col., 1989; asst. chief mil. pers. U.S. Army Med. Svc. Corps, Frankfurt, Fed. Republic Germany, 1972-75; intern Letterman Army Med. Ctr., San Francisco, 1979-80; resident in family practice Womack Army Community Hosp., Ft. Bragg, N.C., 1980-82; dir. family practice quality assurance Tripler Army Med. Ctr., Hawaii, 1984-86, dir. residency tng. dept. family practice, 1984-86; asst. prof. family practice, physician Uniformed Svcs. U. Health Scis., F. Edward Hebert Sch. Med., Bethesda, Md., 1986-91, clerkship dir., 1986-88, dir. continuing med. edn., 1987—, field tng. exercise surgeon, 1991—, asst. prof. mil. medicine and family practice, 1991—; presenter, lectr., cons. in field; part-time clin. faculty mem., family practice resident DeWitt Army Hosp., Ft. Belvoir, Va., 1986-89, 91—, Malcolm Grow USAF Med. Ctr., Andrews AFB, Md., 1989-91; reviewer Patient Care jour., 1988—;. Contbr. articles to profl. publs. Asst. med. dir. Old Dominion 100 mile run, Front Royal, Va., 1990, med. dir., 1991—; asst. med. dir. Am. Diabetes Assn. Youth, Honolulu, 1984, med. dir., 1985. USUHS grantee. Fellow Am. Acad. Family Practice; mem. Am. Acad. Family Physicians, Uniformed Svcs. Acad. Family Physicians (mem. edn. com. 1988—), Soc. Tchrs. Family Medicine (mem. genogram rsch. com. 1989—), Am. Acad. Pain Mgmt., Assn. Mil. Surgeons, Am. Osteo. Acad. Sports Medicine, Phila. Coll. Osteo Medicine Alumni Assn. (life), Omicron Delta Kappa, Alpha Epsilon Delta. Home: 11669 Newbridge Ct Reston VA 22091 Office: 4301 Jones Bridge Rd Bethesda MD 20814-4799

EVANS, PETER YOSHIO, ophthalmologist, educator; b. Tokyo, Dec. 19, 1925; came to the U.S., 1957; s. Paul Yuzuru Kawai and Vicki (Wichgraf) Evans; m. Helga Kemp, Sept. 19, 1953; children: Johannes, Marina, Michael, Andre, Thomas, Ursula, Christiane. MD, Innsbruck U., 1951. Resident Innsbruck & Frankfurt (Germany) Univs., 1951-55; intern Sisters Charity Hosp., Buffalo, N.Y., 1957-58; fellow Georgetown U., Washington, 1958-59, program dir. div. ophthalmology, 1963-69, chmn., 1969-83, prof., 1973—; chief dept. ophthalmology D.C. Gen. Hosp., 1958-63; cons. D.C. Columbia Lighthouse for the Blind, 1959-63; sr. cons. D.C. Child and Maternal Welfare Dept., 1961-74; exec. v.p. Joint Commn. Allied Health Personnel in Ophthalmology, St. Paul, 1983—. Author, producer scientific films; contbr. articles to profl. jours.; editor numerous jours. Fellow Am. Acad. Ophthalmology (Disting. Svc. award 1982), Austrian Ophthalm. Soc. (Ernst Fuchs Meml. Lectr. 1975), German Ophthalm. Soc., Am.-Austrian Soc. (pres. 1989-91), Cosmos Club D.C. Lutheran. Home: 3113 Lewis Pl Falls Church VA 22042 Office: Georgetown U Ctr for Sight 3800 Reservoir Rd NW Washington DC 20007

EVANS, R. DANIEL, educator; b. Newark, N.J., Jan. 26, 1944; s. William Samuel and Mary Mildred (Cranston) E. BA, Adelphi U., 1967; MA, Columbia U., 1968; cert., Pa. Acad. Fine Arts, 1984. Assoc. prof. Community Coll. of Phila., 1971—. Co-editor-in-chief Painted Bride Quar., 1975-82; exhibited paintings at 20th Century Gallery, 1984—; exhibited in one-man shows at Gianetta Gallery, 1987, 88. Kleinbard award Pa. Acad. Fine Arts, 1983. Mem. Am. Cultural Assn. (speaker).

EVANS, RICHARD JOHN, management; b. Bristol, Avon, England, Oct. 3, 1956; came to U.S., 1989; s. John Brereton and Muriel Eileen (Strawford) E.; m. Jacqueline Anne Howell, July 14, 1979; children: Judith Rebecca, Jenifer Lowri, Benedict Owen John. BA with honors, Trinity Coll., Cambridge, England, 1977, MA with honors, 1979. Gen. mgr. Wessex Opera, Bristol, England, 1979-82; chief exec. officer Bath (England) Internat. Festival of Music and Arts, 1982-88; exec. dir. The Found. for Bath Festival, 1988-89; v.p. Nat. Arts Stabilization Fund, N.Y.C., 1989-90; sr. ptnr. The Icarus Partnership, N.Y.C., 1990—; cons. in field. Recipient Arts award Assn. Bus. Sponsorship of Arts, London, 1986, Internat. Vis. award U.S. Info. Agy., Washington, 1989. Mem. Soc. Promotion of New Music.

EVANS, ROBERT, JR., economics educator; b. Sterling, Colo., Mar. 20, 1932; s. Robert and Mary Louise (Paradise) E.; m. Lois Ellen Herr, Nov. 6, 1955; children: Karen E., Robert, Janet K., Thomas W., L. Midori, Laura E., Katherine Joan. S.B., MIT, 1954; Ph.D. (Hillman fellow), U. Chgo., 1959. Asst. prof. indsl. relations MIT, 1959-65; assoc. prof. Brandeis U., Waltham, Mass., 1965-71, prof., 1971—, Atran prof. labor econs., 1975—, chmn. dept. econs., 1970-72, 73-75, 84-87, dean Coll. Arts and Scis., 1975-81; vis. prof. Keio U., Tokyo, 1966-67, 72-73, 82-83, 88-89; Fulbright Rsch. scholar, Japan, 1982-83, 88-89; research dir. study on prison industries Can. Corrections Assn., 1968-69. Author: Public Policy Toward Labor, 1965, The Labor Economics of Japan and the United States, 1971, Developing Policies for Public Security and Criminal Justice, 1973. Mem. Acton (Mass.) and Acton Boxborough Regional Sch. Com., 1971-72, 74-82, 84-88, regional chmn., 1972, 79-80, 85-86, town chmn., 1975-77. With U.S. Army, 1955-57. Mem. Am. Econ. Assn., Indsl. Relations Assn., Assn. Asian Studies. Home: 43 High St Acton MA 01720-4213 Office: Brandeis U Dept Econs Waltham MA 02254

EVANS, ROBERT CAREY, travel industry executive; b. Bklyn., Oct. 24, 1955; s. Andrew Joseph and Mary Louise (Schnelly) E.; m. Brett Alison Martin, Aug. 13, 1989. BS, Hofstra U., 1977; AAS, Nassau Community Coll., 1975. Lic. guide N.Y. State Dept. Environ. Conservation. Programmer, cons. Automated Concepts, Inc., N.Y.C., 1977-79; sr. programmer analyst various banks, N.Y.C., 1979-81; implementations mgr. Chase Manhattan Bank, N.Y.C., 1981-83; sr. cons. Telecommunications Bus. Systems, Bagota, N.J., 1983-85; project mgr. Empire Blue Cross and Blue Shield, N.Y.C., 1985-86; ind. cons. Oceanside, N.Y., 1986-87; mgr. data processing direct mktg. Am. Express Co., N.Y.C., 1987-91; chief exec. officer, chmn. bd. dirs. Outback Adventures Ltd., Oceanside, 1988—; v.p., cons., DCR, Inc., Valley Stream, N.Y., 1983-88. Scoutmaster Nassau County area Boy Scouts Am., 1986-88, chmn. troop com., 1988-91, mem. coun. tng. staff, 1988—, dist. roundtable commr., 1986-88, asst. dist. commr., 1990—; tng. advisor Nat. Order of the Arrow, 1992—. Recipient Dist. Award of Merit, Boy Scouts Am., 1990. Mem. N.Y. State Guides Assn., Data Processing Soc., U.S. Snowshoe Assn. Republican. Roman Catholic. Home: 320 E Waukena Ave Oceanside NY 11572-4338 Office: Outback Adventures Ltd Church Street Sta PO Box 2482 New York NY 10008-2482

EVANS, ROBERT SHELDON, corporate executive; b. Pitts., 1944. BA in History, U. Pa., 1966; MBA in Fin., Columbia U., 1968. V.p. Evans & Co. Inc., 1971-74; v.p. internat. ops. Crane Co., N.Y.C., 1974-78, sr. v.p., 1978-79, exec. v.p., dir., 1979-84, chmn., chief exec. officer, 1984—, pres., chief ops. officer, 1986-91; chmn., chief exec. officer, bd. dirs. Medusa Corp.; bd. dirs. HBD Industries Inc. Mem. dean's adv. coun. Columbia Grad. Sch. Bus.; trustee Allen Stevenson Sch., Eaglebrook Sch. Office: Crane Co 711 5th Ave New York NY 10022-3109

EVANS, ROBERT STACY, electrical engineer; b. Jacksonville, Fla., Aug. 11, 1946; s. Robert Herron and Anne Mary (Butler) E.; m. Nellie Webb Arrington, Jan. 3, 1981; children: Elyse Anne, Meredith Jeanne. BS, U.S. Naval Acad., 1968; MSEE, Naval Postgrad. Sch., 1974; M in Adminstrv. Sci., Johns Hopkins U., 1980. Engr. in tng., Md. Commd. ensign USN, 1968, advanced through grades to lt. comdr., 1977, resigned, 1981; sr. engr. Westinghouse Electric Corp., Balt., 1981—; lectr. G.W.C. Whiting Sch. Engring. Johns Hopkins U., Balt., 1986—. Decorated with Bronze Star medal with Combat V. Mem. U.S. Naval Acad. Alumni Assn. (life), U.S. Naval Acad. Athletic Assn. Episcopalian.

EVANS, TERRI LYNNE, local area network analyst; b. Cleve., July 27, 1963; d. Elmer Caroll and Barbara Jean (Washington) E. BS, Miami U., 1985; MA, Columbia U., 1991. Cert. network engr. User support cons. Barnard Coll., N.Y.C., 1987-89; field engr. Local Area Network Systems, N.Y.C., 1989-90; local area network analyst Johnson and Higgins, N.Y.C., 1990-92; network cons. Charles River Computers, N.Y.C., 1992—. Recipient Disting. Svc. medal, Miami U., 1985, cert. of Merit, 1985. Mem. NAt. Soc. Black Engrs., NAFE.

EVANS, THOMAS CHIVES NEWTON, communications executive; b. Corpus Christi, Tex., Apr. 20, 1947; s. Lynn Augustus and Tena Vivian (Wimbish) E.; m. Sandra Louise McKee, Sept. 1, 1985; 1 child, Thomas Chives Newton II. BA, Austin Coll., 1969; MDiv, Harvard U., 1972, postgrad., 1973; MA, Syracuse U., 1981, PhD, 1986; postgrad., Columbia U., 1983-84. Teaching asst. Syracuse (N.Y.) U., 1976-77; rsch. assoc. U. Nairobi, Kenya, 1977-79; editorial asst. African Studies Rev., Syracuse, 1979-80; rsch. analyst NBC, N.Y.C., 1981-82, adminstr. rsch. and sales devel., 1982-85, dir. rsch., 1985-86; dir. rsch. Mut. Broadcasting System, N.Y.C., 1986, dir. rsch. Westwood One Radio Network div., 1986-87; v.p. rsch. Westwood One, Inc., N.Y.C., 1987—; mem. adv. com. Ossining (N.Y.) Cable TV, 1987; judge broadcast grants program Nat. Assn. Broadcasters, 1991, 92. Bd. dirs. Immedia Found.; mem. Ossining Police Community Rels. Bd., Central Park Precinct Community Coun., N.Y.C., 1981—; chmn. 20th Precinct Community Coun., N.Y.C., 1984-85; judge NAB Rsch. Grants in Broadcasting Program, 1991, 92—; clk. session Scarborough Presbyn. Ch. Recipient cert. of appreciation Mayor Office, City of N.Y., 1985; named Eagle Scout, Boy Scouts Am., 1959; Syracuse U. Faculty Senate research grantee, 1975; Shell Found. Internat. fellow, 1978-79. Mem. Am. Statis. Assn., Ossining Hist. Soc., U.S. Power Squadron, N.Y. Radio and TV Rsch. Coun., Radio Advt. Bur. (GOALS com.), Advt. Rsch. Found. (radio coun.), Austin Coll. Alumni Assn. (bd. dirs.), Electronic Media Rating Coun. (bd. dirs., chairperson radio com.). Democrat. Home: 19 Ferris Pl Ossining NY 10562-3509 Office: Westwood One Inc 1700 Broadway New York NY 10019-5905

EVANS, TODD ROBERT, molecular biologist; b. Gary, Ind., Aug. 17, 1960; s. James Arthur and Karen Eunice (Emmett) E.; m. Anne Clare Gordon, July 3, 1961. BA, Northwestern U., 1982; PhD, Columbia U., 1987. Grad. fellow Columbia U., N.Y.C., 1982-87; staff fellow NIH, Bethesda, Md., 1987-90; asst. prof. Univ. Pitts., 1990—; prin. investigator/ rsch. group U. Pitts., 1990—. Contbr. articles to profl. jours. Grantee NIH, 1991; Searle scholar Chgo. Community Trust, 1991, March of Dimes, 1991.

EVANS, WILLIAM DAVIDSON, JR., lawyer; b. Memphis, Jan. 20, 1943; s. William D. and Maxey (Carter) E.; m. Eileen McKenna, June 19, 1971; children: William D., Carter M., Alexander B. BA, Vanderbilt U., 1965; JD, U. Tenn., 1968; LLM, Georgetown U., 1985. Bar: Tenn. 1968, D.C. 1988. Spl. agt. FBI, N.Y.C., 1968-72; ptnr. Glankler, Brown, Gilliland, Chase, Robinson & Raines, Memphis, 1972-82; trial atty. environ. enforcement sect. U.S. Dept. of Justice, Washington, 1982-86; of counsel Washington, Perito & Dubuc, Washington, 1986-91, Graham & James, Washington, 1991—. Editor Digest Environ. Law of Real Property, 1986-90, Environ. Hazards, 1989-90. Mem. environ. issues group George Bush for pres. campaign, Washington, 1987-88. Mem. ABA, D.C. Bar Assn., Tenn. Bar Assn., Memphis Bar Assn., Def. Rsch. Inst., Environ. Law Inst. Republican. Roman Catholic. Home: 4949 Hillbrook Ln NW Washington DC 20016-3208 Office: Graham & James 2000 M St NW Washington DC 20036-3307

EVARTS, CAREN GOODIN, music educator; b. Indpls., May 6, 1942; d. John Dee and Catherine (Johnson) Goodin; m. Steven Lane Evarts, Nov. 28, 1969; children: Jennifer Lynne, Johnathan Scott. MusB, Ind. U., 1965; MusM, Butler U., 1968; student, Oberlin Conservatory, 1960-61, 63. Mem. teaching faculty spl. instrn. div. Butler U., Indpls., 1966-68; teaching assoc. Hartt Coll. U. Hartford, West Hartford, Conn., 1968-76; mem. piano faculty Miss Porter's Sch., Farmington, Conn., 1968—; pvt. tchr. Bristol, Conn., 1972—; composer sacred and classical music for chs., performance; performer (with students) benefit concerts for hosps., convalescent homes, AIDS rsch., and the homeless. Recordings inlude Moszkowski Concerto IPL #1001, N.Y., performed 1967; cassette tapes of Candlelight Classics performed 1969-76, produced 1990, Opus 1 Reflections, Opus 2 Con Spirito. Recipient Sterling Achievement award Mu Phi Epsilon, Ind. U., 1964-65, scholarship for Aspen study Butler U., 1966, cert. of participation Busoni Internat. Piano competition, Bolzano, Italy, 1967. Mem. Musical Club of Hartford, Pi Kappa Llambda, Mu Phi Epsilon. Republican. Congregationalist. Home: 290 Sonstrom Rd Bristol CT 06010 Office: Music Dept Miss Porters Sch Farmington CT 06032

EVELAND, GEORGETTE ANNE, artist; b. Trenton, N.J., Feb. 15, 1945; d. James Andrew and Anna Rose (Reber) Westerman; m. Walter Edward Eveland Jr., Feb. 13, 1965 (div. Sept. 1987); children: James Edward, Scott Douglas. Grad. high sch., Trenton. Teller Commonwealth Nat. Bank, York, Pa., 1978-83; teller York Bank and Trust Co., 1983-85, customer svc. rep., 1985-88; customer svc. rep. First Capitol Bank, York, 1988-91; owner, artist Kiosk Studio, York, 1989—; freelance artist York, 1985—; advisor The Arts Discovery Ctr. of United Arts Coun., York, 1988-91, artist-in-residence, 1991—, dir., 1992—. Author series of pen and ink hist. sketches, 1985—(purchase awards 1985—); guest designer logo York County Bar Assn., 1989; editor York Daily Record, 1991—. Commr. York City Planning Commn., 1989. N.J. State scholar, 1962. Mem. Women's Network of York, Inc. (corp. sec. 1990-92). Home: 341 E Locust St York PA 17403 Studio: The Arts Discovery Ctr 236 N George St York PA 17401

EVENCHIK, LYNN ROBIN, sales professional; b. Lorain, Ohio, Feb. 5, 1956; d. Harvey Burton and Cyvia Marilyn (Baer) E. BA in Edn., U. Ariz., 1977. Gen. mgr. Chateau Travel, Tucson, 1973-82; customer svc. agt. Trans World Airlines, Tucson, 1978-79; instr. Pima Jr. Coll., Tucson, 1981-82; installation specialist Am. Airlines, Ft. Worth, 1983-84; sales specialist Am. Airlines, 1984-86, regional mgr., 1986-87, div. mgr., 1988; sales mgr. Unisys Corp. Airlines & Communications, Blue Bell, Pa., 1988—; cons. in field. Youth group advisor Temple Emanuel, Tucson, 1973-77; chmn. U. Ariz. chpt. March of Dimes, 1975-76; vol. feed the needy Salvation Army, 1987; mem. Mus. of Art., World Wildlife Ogrn. Mem. NAFE, Am. Jewish Com., Am. Israel Pub. Affairs Com., U. Ariz. Alumni Assn.., Texpac Club, Alpha Epsilon Phi. Republican. Home: 216 Copper Beech Dr Blue Bell PA 19422-2836

EVERETT, DANIEL CHARLES, public television programming executive; b. Presque Isle, Maine, Aug. 5, 1942; s. Charles Edwin and Hilda Mae (Aucoin) E.; m. Laurie Ann Toth, May 25, 1987; children by previous marriage: Jon J., Andrew C., Adam D. BA, U. Maine, 1971. Staff announcer, asst. news dir. WLBZ Radio, Bangor, Maine, 1964-69; exec. producer, pub. affairs Maine Pub. Broadcasting Network, Orono, 1970-72, dir. community svcs., 1972-73, dir. TV programming, 1973-74, program mgr. for radio and TV, 1974-77; program mgr. KAID-TV, Boise, Idaho, 1977-79; dir. programming KRMA-TV, Denver, 1979-80; program dir. for broadcast WGBH Ednl. Found., Boston, 1980-82, dir. broadcasting, 1982—; mem. editorial adv. com. Am. Documentary Consortium, N.Y.C., 1986-89; judge Awards for Cable Excellence, Washington, 1985-89; mem. adv. com. Inter-Regional Program Svc., Boston, 1980-83; cons., faculty assoc. U. Maine, Orono, 1973-77, 80. Vice pres. Literacy Vols. of Maine, Waterville, 1972-76. Recipient Tom Phillips award UPI, 1972, pub. awareness award Corp. for Pub. Broadcasting, 1975. Mem. Am. Mgmt. Assn. Office: WGBH Ednl Found 125 Western Ave Allston MA 02134-1098

EVERETT, GRAHAM, English language educator, poet, publisher; b. Oceanside, N.Y., Dec. 23, 1947; s. James H. and Jacqueline (Vaughn) E.; m. Elyse Arnow, Dec. 27, 1980; 1 child, Logan James. BA in English, Canisius Coll., 1970; MA in English, SUNY, Stony Brook, 1987, PhD in English, 1992. Pub., editor Street Press, Port Jefferson, N.Y., 1972-92; dir. Backstreet Editions, Inc., Port Jefferson, 1980-86; asst. dir. Taproots, Inc., Stony Brook, N.Y., 1986-88; asst. dir. Poetry Ctr. SUNY, Stony Brook, 1988-91; adj. prof. Suffolk Community Coll., Selden, N.Y., 1987—; writer in residence N.Y. State Poets in Sch. Program, L.I., 1973-86. Author: (poetry) Strange Coast, 1979, Sunlit Sidewalk, 1985, Minus Green, 1992; co-editor: Paumanok Rising, 1980. Sec.-treas. bd. dirs. Taproots, Inc., 1985. Mem. Assoc. Writing Programs, Modern Lang. Assn., Nat. Coun. Tchrs. English, N.Y. State Tchrs. Union. Office: Street Press PO Box 772 Sound Beach NY 11789-0772

EVERETT, JAMES WILLIAM, JR., lawyer; b. Buffalo, Oct. 26, 1957; s. James William and Esther (Kratzer) E. BA in Polit. Sci., Coll. Wooster (Ohio), 1979; JD, SUNY, Buffalo, 1984; LLM in Banking Law with honor, Boston U., 1985. Bar: N.Y. 1985, U.S. Dist. Ct. (we. dist.) N.Y. 1989, U.S. Dist. Ct. (no. dist.) N.Y. 1990, U.S. Supreme Ct. 1991. Officer Emil A. Kratzer Co., Inc., Buffalo, 1980—; assoc. John C. Peters, P.C., Hartford, Conn., 1986-87; counsel coms. on banking, corps., ins. and sml. bus. N.Y. Assembly, Albany, 1987-88; asst. counsel to N.Y. Senate Majority on Banks, Commerce, Real Property Tax Laws, Uniform Comml. Codes and Consumer Affairs, 1988—; speechwriter for chair policy com. for nat. adv. counsel on women's edn. programs. Contbr. polit. commentaries Buffalo News. Active Erie County (N.Y.) Rep. Com., 1979—. Recipient Cummings-Rumbaugh prize Coll. of Wooster. Mem. ABA (forum com. on affordable housing), N.Y. State Bar Assn. (banking law com.), Erie County Bar Assn., Albany C. of C. Republican. Presbyterian. Home: 38 Exeter Rd Buffalo NY 14221-3399 Office: Office Senate Majority Counsel Capitol 433 Albany NY 12247

EVERETT, MELINDA BROWN, public relations executive; b. Humboldt, Tenn., June 29, 1946; d. Carl Atherton and Margaret (Booker) Brown; m. Wayne H. Everett, Aug. 15, 1970 (div. 1992); children: Philip Atherton, Jeffrey Stanwood. AB in English with distinction, Sweet Briar Coll., 1968; MS in Journalism, Boston U., 1970. Sr. pub. info. specialist N.Y. State Narcotic Addiction Control Commn., Albany, 1970; pub. rels. specialist Laplante Assocs., Auburn, Mass., 1975-79; assoc. editor Landmark Newspaper, Holden, Mass., 1979-83; writer pub. rels. Worcester (Mass.) Meml. Hosp., 1983-86, mgr. pub. rels., 1986-88; dir. pub. rels. Med. Ctr. Cen. Mass., Worcester, 1988—. Mem. adv. bd. Sweet Briar Coll. Alumnae Mag., 1990—. Bd. dirs. Am. Cancer Soc., Worcester, 1987—; co-chair task force Worcester Fights Back!, 1990—; mem. pub. rels. com. YWCA Greater Worcester, 1990—. Recipient Gold Key award Mass. chpt. Am. Coll. Emergency Physicians, 1990. Top 10 Nat. Consumer Edn. Publs. award FDA and Nat. Consumer Edn. Coalition, 1989, Publ. of Yr. award Worcester County Editor's Coun., 1991; named Communicator of Yr., 1991. Mem. Am. Soc. for Health Care Mktg. and Pub. Rels. (cert. in pub. rels., leader roundtable discussion 1990, 91, nat. coms. 1990, 91), Pub. Rels. Soc. Am. (accredited), New Eng. Hosp. Pub. Rels. and Mktg. Assn. (assoc. editor jour. 1990—). Office: Med Ctr Cen Mass Hahnemann Campus 281 Lincoln St Worcester MA 01605-2192

EVERETT, PATRICIA ROBERTSON, clinical psychologist; b. Tokyo, Japan, Nov. 2, 1957; came to U.S., 1959; d. William Henry Everett and Jean (Matthews) Halverson; m. Theodore Jacob Ellenhorn, Aug. 4, 1990. BA, Williams Coll., 1979; MA in Art History, Columbia U., 1982; MA in Psychology, NYU, 1985; MA, PhD in Clin./Sch. Psychology, Adelphi U., 1989. Dir. Barbara Mathes Gallery, N.Y.C., 1982-86; instr. Adelphi U., Garden City, N.J., 1987-89; asst. psychologist Jewish Bd. Family & Children's Svcs., N.Y.C., 1989-90; pvt. practice Amherst, Mass., 1990—; psychotherapist Inst. fo Contemporary Psychotherapy, N.Y.C., 1989-90; clin. psychologist Hampden Dist. Mental Health Clinic, Springfield, Mass., 1990-92; group practice, Keene, N.H., 1991—; adj. instr. U. Mass., Amherst, 1991—. Contbr. articles to profl. jour. Grantee Am. Coun. of Learned Socs., 1990. Mem. APA. Office: 664 Main St Amherst MA 01002-2428

EVERETT, WALTER HOWELL, minister; b. Asbury Park, N.J., Sept. 13, 1934; s. Arthur Reighton and Marion (Height) E.; m. Nancy Bellmeyer Nogan, May 9, 1992. AB, Drew U., 1956, MDiv, 1960. Ordained to Meth. Ch., 1960. Pastor various chs., N.J., 1956-62, Woodrow and Wesley Meth. Chs., S.I., N.Y., 1962-66, Woodrow United Meth. Ch., S.I., 1966-71, Stamford (N.Y.) and Harpersfield United Meth. Chs., 1971-77, Jesse Lee United Meth. Ch., Easton, Conn., 1977—; v.p. Coun. Chs. N.Y.C., 1970; bd. dirs. United Meth. Homes Conn., Shelton, 1982—. Active Commn. on Aging, Easton, 1984-91. Mem. Kiwanis (pres. Bridgeport ch. 1980-81). Home: 26 Flat Rock Rd Easton CT 06612 Office: Jesse Lee United Meth Ch 25 Flat Rock Rd Easton CT 06612

EVERETT, WENDY ANN, toy designer; b. East Lansing, Mich., May 6, 1950; d. Donald Franklin and Mary Margaret (Marshall) E. BA in Edn., Fine Arts, Mich. State U., 1972; M in Early Childhood Devel., Fairfield (Conn.) U., 1989. Elem. sch. tchr. Fraser (Mich.) Pub. Schs., 1973-77; creative dir. WFR Ribbon Corp., N.Y.C., 1977-79; pres. Wendy Everett Creations, Westport, Conn., 1979—; fashion model, N.Y.C., 1977-90. Author: The Great Gift Book, 1986, Active Bulletin Boards, 1979; composer (children's musical) The Vegetable Garden, 1973 (children's TV show) The Dream Makers, 1990; contbr. articles to mags.; designer Barbie Doll Fashions, 1983—, Care Bears, Strawberry Shortcake, Cabbage Patch Doll Clothes, Americana Crafts, ET Quilt, ET Wallhanging, 1983, Stenciling Hunt Mfg. Co. Kits, 1979—, Pastime Industries Crafts, 1990—, Bath Buddies toy line, 1989—. Mem. Cooper Hewitt Mus., Fifth Ave. Presbyn. Ch., Meml. Sloan Kettering Pediatric Craft Program. Mem. Am. Craft Assn., Phi Beta Kappa. Home: 1123 Sasco Hill Rd Fairfield CT 06430 Office: 333 W 57th St Ste 5-H New York NY 10019

EVERHARD, MARTIN E., surgeon; b. Pitts., Jan. 28, 1933; s. Martin and Anna (Golaki) E.; m. Donna Ann Holden, July 30, 1988. BS, William & Mary Coll., 1953; PhD, U. Va., 1959; MD, NYU, 1967. mem. med. bd. Phelps Meml. Hosp., Tarrytown, 1989—, dir., 1991. Contbr. articles to profl. jours. Bd. dirs., trustee Phelps Meml. Hosp. Lt. USN, 1953-59. Merit scholar NYU, 1963-67, Rubin scholar, 1963-67. Fellow ACS, Internat. Coll. Surgeons; mem. Westchester Surg. Soc. Office: Westchester Surg Group 308 Chappaqua Rd Briarcliff Manor NY 10510-1300

EVERHART, SALLY MARIE, vocational school educator; b. Pa., Sept. 17, 1952; d. Dean Baker and Muriel Rebecca (Heckler) E. BS in Home Econs. Edn., Messiah Coll., 1974; MEd in Vocat. Edn., Pa. State U., 1986. Cert. vocat. supr. York County (Pa.) Area Vocat. Tech. Sch. York (Pa.) Country Area Vocat. Tech. Sch., 1974-75; food mgmt., prodn., svc. tchr. and adult edn. Franklin County Area Vocat. Tech. Sch., Chambersburg, Pa., 1975—. Mem. Am. Vocat. Assn. (life), Pa. Vocat. Assn. (pres. cen. region 1990-92), Am. Home Econs. Assn., Pa. Home Econs. Assn. (sec.-treas. south cen. region 1987-91, treas. 1991—), Future Homemakers Am. (hon., Advisor of Yr. award 1986), Iota Lambda Sigma, Delta Kappa Gamma, Phi Delta Kappa. Home: 549 Highland Ave Chambersburg PA 17201-3764

EVERLY, WILLIAM, college official; b. Glens Falls, N.Y., Aug. 4, 1967; s. H. Luther and Lillian (Marchese) E. BS, Castleton State Coll., 1989; postgrad., Manhattanville Coll. Residential counselor Expt. with Travel, Springfield, 1989-91; grad. asst. Springfield Coll., 1989-91; asst. dir. student activities Manhattanville Coll., Purchase, N.Y., 1991—. Mem. Cambridge Valley Rescue Squad, 1991, Harrison Vol. Ambulance Corps, 1991; com.

mem. troop 62 Boy Scouts Am., Cambridge, 1990-91. Mem. AACD, Am. Coll. Pers. Assn., Assn. Coll. Unions Internat., Psi Chi. Roman Catholic. Home: 125 Purchase St Purchase NY 10577-2400

EVERS, MARTIN LOUIS, internist; b. Newark, Dec. 17, 1957; s. George and Eva (Auslander) E. BA in Biochemistry, Rutgers U., 1979; MD, U. Medicine and Dentistry N.J., 1985. Diplomate Am. Bd. Internal Medicine. Emergency medicine resident Hershey (Pa.) Med. Ctr., 1985-86; internal medicine resident Raritan Bay Med. Ctr., Perth Amboy, N.J., 1986-89; critical care fellow Presbyn. Hosp., Pitts., 1989; emergency room physician Shadyside Hosp., Pitts., 1989-90; assoc. program dir. St. Francis Med. Ctr., Trenton, N.J., 1990—; ACLS instr. Ctr. for Emergency Medicine, Pitts., 1990, St. Francis Med. Ctr., Trenton, 1991—. Fellow Acad. Medicine N.J.; mem. AMA, ACP, Soc. Critical Care Medicine. Jewish. Office: St Francis Med Ctr 601 Hamilton Ave Trenton NJ 08629-1986

EVERS, SEAN ROBERT, clinical psychologist; b. Jersey City, Apr. 18, 1949; s. John Robert and Katherine (Pilerci) E.; m. Anne Ellman, May 3, 198l; 1 child, Erin. BA in English, Marietta Coll., 1971; MA in Psychology, New Sch. for Social Rsch., 1977; PhD in Clin. Psychology, Fla. Inst. Tech., 1981. Lic. psychologist, N.J.; diplomate Am. Bd. Med. Psychotherapists, Am. Acad. Behavioral Medicine, Am. Acad. Pain Mgmt.; cert. addiction specialist. Tchr. Bricktown (N.J.) Bd. Edn., 1971-79; therapist/intern Bayshore Youth Svcs. Bur., Keyport, N.J., 1979-81; pvt. practice Brielle, N.J., 1981—; cons. N.J. Div. Mil. and Veterans Affairs, Trenton, N.J., 1989—. Fellow Am. Ortho Assn., Am. Bd. Vocat. Experts; mem. APA, Am. Orthopsychiat. Assn., N.J. Psychol. Assn., N.J. Acad. Psychology, Assn. Advancement of Psychology. Office: Brielle Hills Office Pk 2640 Hwy 70 Bldg 7 Ste 301 Manasquan NJ 08736

EVERT, TERESA DIANE, communications company executive; b. Albuquerque, Mar. 2, 1957; d. Jack Kenneth Evert and Eleanor Diane (Ports) Valdez; 1 child, Dana Nicole Parise. BA, U.S. Internat. U., 1979; MS, Georgetown U., 1981. Internat. telecommunications U.S. Coun. for Internat. Bus., N.Y.C., 1981-84; internat. bus. and govt. rels. mgr. AT&T Communications Internat., Morris Plains, N.J., 1984-85; internat. pub. affairs AT&T Internat., Basking Ridge, N.J., 1985-88; internat. govt. rels. mgr. AT&T Network Systems, Berkeley Heights, N.J., 1988—. Mem. Women in Internat. Trade. Office: Internat Strategic Planning and Bus Devel One Oak Way Berkeley Heights NJ 07922

EVERTS, TODD, investment executive; b. Brockport, N.Y., July 16, 1966; s. Clifford and Betty (Gilmer) E. Student, Brockport State U. Regional mgr. First Investors, Pittsford, N.Y., 1986—. Republican. Methodist. Home: 35 Covington Rd Rochester NY 14617-4527

EVEY, LOIS REED, psychiatric nurse; b. Burgettstown, Pa., Aug. 23, 1925; d. Harry Lemoyne and Willa Blanche (Miller) Reed; diploma Presbyn. Hosp. Sch. Nursing, Pitts., 1946; B.Nursing Edn., U. Pitts., 1959, M.Nursing Edn., 1963, postgrad., 1978; m. Raymond Cuervo, Sept. 1946; 1 son, Craig Dale; m. 2d, Kenneth George Evey, Aug. 20, 1959. Successively staff nurse, relief head nurse Women's Hosp., Pitts., 1946-53; staff nurse, then head nurse, asst. bldg. supr. Woodville (Pa.) State Hosp., 1953-59; med.-surg. nursing instr. St. Margaret Meml. Hosp., Pitts., 1959-61; psychiat. staff nurse Council House, Inc., Pitts., 1962-66, acting exec. dir., 1966, exec. dir., 1966-80; exec. dir. VA Med. Center, Pitts., 1982—, coordinator in-patient psychosocial rehab. program, 1984-85; lectr. community mental health workshops; mem. nurse adv. bd. Pitts. Planned Parenthood; mem. Task Force to Establish Domiciliary Care, Community Human Service Center, Pitts.; mem. Greater Pitts. Rehab. Council; mem. Pitts. chpt. Gov.'s Com. Employment of Handicapped; mem. citizens council bd. St. Francis Gen. Hosp., Western Psychiat. Inst. and Clinics; bd. dirs. continuing edn. for nurses U. Pitts., Indiana U. of Pa., Carlow Coll. Author: (with others) Rehabilitating the Mentally Ill in the Community. Served with Cadet Nurse Corps, U.S. Army, 1943-46. USPHS grantee, 1961-63. Mem. Am. Orthopsychiat. Assn., Internat. Assn. Psycho-Social Rehab. Services (co-founder, dir.), Pa. Assn. Mental Health and Mental Retardation Service Providers, Nat. Council Therapy and Rehab. Through Horticulture, Am. Nurses Assn. (legis. com.), Pa. Nurses Assn., Nat. Assn. Mental Health Adminstrs., Pa. Assn. Mental Health Adminstrs., Am. Public Health Assn., Pa. Public Health Assn., United Mental Health, Nat. Assn. Retarded Citizens, Pa. Assn. Retarded Citizens, Western Pa. Aftercare Assn., Health and Welfare Planning Assn., Pitts. Exec. Women's Council (charter), U. Pitts. Alumni Assn., Presbyn. U. Hosp. Alumni Assn. (past pres.; life), Sigma Theta Tau, Alpha Tau Delta. Republican. Mem. United Ch. of Christ. Club: East Hills (life) (Pitts.). Home: 305 Lougeay Rd Pittsburgh PA 15235-4502

EVILSIZOR, WILLIAM (CHRIS), marketing professional; b. Mansfield, Ohio, Jan. 29, 1960; s. Richard William and Laura Mae (Shipley) E. BA in Microbiology, Miami U., Oxford, Ohio, 1983; MBA. Ter. rep. Roche Labs., Lima, Ohio, 1984-88; med. ctr. rep. Roche Labs., Columbus, Ohio, 1986-88; div. sales mgr. Roche Labs., Greenbrae, Calif., 1988-90; product mgr. Roche Labs., Nutley, N.J., 1990—. Office: 340 Kingsland St Nutley NJ 07110-1199

EWALD, ELIN LAKE, fine arts damage-loss appraisal company executive, writer; b. Raleigh, N.C., July 7, 1940; d. John Marshall and S. Jane (Palmer) Lake; children: Augusta, Patrick; m. Lewis P. Johnson, Mar. 17, 198l. Student, Art Inst. Chgo., 1960-63; MA, NYU, 1987, postgrad., 1987—. Writer, editor various mags., N.Y.C., 1969-74; assoc. O'Toole-Ewald Art Assocs. Inc., N.Y.C., 1974-79, v.p., 1979-82, pres., 1982—; expert witness in art, civil and fed. criminal cts. Contbr. articles to Personal Property Jour., 1989—, also other profl. publs. Mem. Am. Soc. Appraisers (bd. dirs. N.Y.C. 1980—, editor N.Y. chpt. newsletter, Outstanding Contbn. N.Y. chpt. 1985-88), Nat. Assn. Rev. Appraisers, Am. Assn. Mus., Claims Prevention and Procedure Coun., Am. Bankruptcy Inst., Nat. Forensic Ctr., Am. Arbitration Assn. (panelist 1988—), Kappa Delta Pi. Office: O'Toole-Ewald Art Assocs 1l33 Broadway New York NY 10010

EWALD, PAUL WILLIAM, biologist, educator; b. Evanston, Ill., Sept. 18, 1953; s. Arno Wilfred and Sara Jeanne (Hauke) E.; m. Christine Edith Bayer, Apr. 11, 1981; children: Sarah Elisabeth, Samuel Bennet. BS, U. Calif., Irvine, 1975; PhD, U. Wash., Seattle, 1980. Vis. asst. prof. dept. biol. scis., jr. fellow U. Mich., Ann Arbor, 1980-83; postdoctoral scholar NATO/NSF & Imperial Coll., U. London, 1984-85; asst. prof. biology Amherst (Mass.) Coll., 1983-89, assoc. prof. biology, 1989—; adj. asst. and assoc. prof. U. Mass., Amherst, 1985—; grant reviewer Am. Philos. Soc., Nat. Geog. Soc., H.F. Guggenheim Found., U.S.-Israel Binat. Found., NSF.; sci. publ. reviewer Am. Naturalist, Animal Behavior, Am. Ornithologists' Union, Behavioral Ecology & Sociobiology, Condor, Ecology and others. Contbr. articles to profl. jours. Recipient Amherst Coll. Faculty Rsch. award, 1988-89, 89-91, 91-92; grantee Audubon Soc., 1977-78, Frank M. Chapman Fund, 1977-78, NSF, 1977-79, 80, 84-85, 89-91, H.F. Guggenheim Found., 1980-82, NIH, 1983-85, 86-87, Wellcome Trust, 1985, Miner D. Crary fellowship, 1986-87, Amherst Coll. Trustees Faculty fellowship, 1987-88, Max and Etta Lazerowitz lectureship, 1989-90, George E. Burch fellow, 1991-93. Mem. AAAS, Am. Ornithologists' Union, Animal Behavior Soc., Cooper Ornithol. Soc., Diarrheal Diseases Info. Svcs. Ctr., Wilson Ornithol. Soc. Office: Amherst Coll Biology Dept PO Box 2237 Amherst MA 01002-2237

EWELL, ERIC RICHARD, public relations executive; b. Syracuse, N.Y., Mar. 27, 1962; s. Richard E. and Marilyn (Andrews) E. Student, Colgate U., 1980-84. Ptnr., pres. Spencer Communications Group, N.Y.C., 1986—. Supr. Alliance Capital, 1992, Seagrams, 1992, Summagraphics, 1992, Time Warner (Paragon), 1992. Republican. Episcopalian. Office: Spencer Communications Group 1114 Avenue of the Americas New York NY 10036

EWERS, PATRICIA O'DONNELL, university administrator; b. Chgo., July 22, 1935; d. Patrick Brenden and Johanna Marie (Galvin) O'D.; m. John Leonard Ewers, July 26, 1958; children: John P., Michele M. Ewers DeCesare. BA in English summa cum laude, Mundelein Coll., 1957; MA in English, Loyola U., Chgo., 1958, PhD in English, 1966. Instr. English Mundelein Coll., Chgo., 1964-66; asst. prof. English DePaul U., Chgo., 1966-69, dir. humanities div. gen. edn. program, assoc. prof. English, 1969-73, chair dept. English, assoc. prof. English, 1973-76, dean Coll. Liberal Arts and Scis., prof. English, 1976-80, v.p., dean faculties, prof. English, 1980-90; pres. Pace U., N.Y.C., 1990—; ptnr. N.Y.C. Partnership, 1990—; chmn., mem. North Cen. Assn. Accreditation Teams, 1977-90; mem. Ill. State Com. for Am. Coun. on Edn. Nat. Identification Program for Women in Higher Edn., 1983-86; commr. at large North Cen. Assn. Colls. and Schs., 1984-87; mem. com. on study of undergrad. edn. State of Ill. Bd. Higher Edn., 1985-86, 1989-90; mem. Commn. on Minorities in Higher Edn., Am. Coun. on Edn., 1990. Trustee Riverside (Ill.) Pub. Libr., 1980-86, N.Y. Downtown Hosp., 1991, Coun. Adult and Experiential Learning, 1992; bd. dirs. Cath. Charities, Com. on Social Svc., 1986-90, subcom. on employer assistance programs, 1986-88; trustee Cath. Theol. Union, Chgo., 1985-90, sec., 1986-90; mem. Chgo. Network, 1986—, fair campaign practices com. Westchester County Fair LWV, 1991—; bd. mem. Women's News, Harrison, N.Y., 1990—; bd. dirs. Am. Brands, 1991, Women's Forum, Inc., 1991; trustee Commn. on Ind. Colls. & Univs./N.Y. State Commn. on Ind. Colls. & Univs., 1992—, Coun. for Adult and Experiential Learning, 1992—. Recipient Outstanding Alumna award Loyola U., Chgo., 1984. Mem. Regional Plan Assn. (coun. for the region tomorrow 1990—), Downtown Lower Manhattan Assn., Inc. (bd. dirs. 1991—), Women's Forum, Inc. (bd. dirs. 1991—), Econ. Club. of N.Y., Univ. Club, Met. Club, Pi Gamma Mu, Beta Gamma Sigma, Alpha Lambda Delta, Delta Epsilon Sigma. Roman Catholic. Office: Pace U Office of Pres Pace Pla New York NY 10038

EWING, ANDREW GRAHAM, chemistry educator; b. Huntington, N.Y., Jan. 19, 1957; s. Robert Edward and Virginia (Harwood) E.; m. Lena Suzanne Karlsson, July 22, 1977; children: Michael Andrew, Anna-Lena Kristine, Christopher Steijmer, Stefan Robert. BS, St. Lawrence U., 1979; PhD, Ind. U., 1983. Teaching asst. St. Lawrence U., Canton, N.Y., 1977-79; assoc. instr. Ind. U., Bloomington, 1979-82; rsch. asst. Ind. U., 1980-83; rsch. assoc. U. N.C., Chapel Hill, 1983-84; asst. prof. Pa. State U., University Park, 1984-89; assoc. prof. Pa. State U., 1989—, asst. dept. head for grad. student recruiting, selection, 1990—. NSF Presdl. Young Invest scholar, 1987, Alfred P. Sloan Found. rsch. fellow, 1989, Camille and Henry Dreyfuss Rsch. Found. teacher-scholar, 1989, Swedish Med. Coun. Vis. Scientist fellow, 1990-91. Mem. AAAS, Am. Chem. Soc., Soc. for Electroanalytical Chemistry, N.Y. Acad. Scis., Soc. Analytical Chemists of Pitts., Soc. for Neuroscience, Sigma Xi. Office: Pa State U 152 Davey Lab University Park PA 16802

EWING, BLAIR GORDON, federal official; b. Kansas City, Mo., Dec. 3, 1933; s. Lynn Moore and Margaret (Blair) E.; m. Barbara F. Thompson, Jan. 3, 1959; children: Blair Gordon, Chatham Boyd. AB, U. Mo., 1954; postgrad. (Rotary Found. fellow), U. Bonn (Germany), 1957-58; AM, U. Chgo., 1960. Reporter Chgo. City News Bur., 1958-59, UPI, 1959-60, Traffic World Mag., 1960-61; instr. polit. sci. Chgo. City Jr. Coll., 1961-62, SUNY, Binghamton, 1962-67; planning and mgmt. cons. Harold Wise and Assocs., Washington, 1967-69; program analyst Office of Asst. Sec. HEW, Washington, 1969-70; dir. criminal justice planning D.C. Govt., 1970-72; dir. dept. pub. safety Met. Washington Coun. of Govts., 1972-74; dir. planning and evaluation div. U.S. Dept. Justice, Washington, 1974-78; dep. dir. Nat. Inst. Law Enforcement and Criminal Justice, Dept. Justice, 1976—; acting dir., 1977-79; asst. dir. U.S. Office Pers. Mgmt., Washington, 1979-81, dep. dir., 1981-83; sr. exec. U.S. Office Mgmt. and Budget, 1983-86; dir. Directorate for Mgmt. Improvement, Dept. Def., 1986—; adj. prof. Law Ctr. Georgetown U., 1971-74. Author: Peace Through Negotiation:The Austrian State Treaty, 1966; contbr. articles to profl. jours. Mem. Montgomery County (Md.) Human Rels. Commn., 1975-76; mem. Montgomery County Bd. Edn., 1976—, pres., 1982-83, 90-91. With U.S. Army, 1954-56. Woodrow Wilson fellow, 1956-57; recipient disting. Svc. award Office Pers. Mgmt., 1981, U.S. Dept. Def. Disting. Civilian Svc. award, 1990, Presdl. Rank award Meritorious Sr. Exec., 1990. Office . Mem. Am. Soc. Pub. Adminstrn., Phi Beta Kappa. Democrat. Unitarian. Home: 8536 Manchester Rd Silver Spring MD 20901-4347 Office: The Pentagon Office Sec Def Office Compt Washington DC 20000

EWING, DAVID LEON, radiation biologist; b. Shreveport, La., Aug. 20, 1941; s. Arlington B. and Mary Lenore (Bryant) E.; m. Mary Dessagene Crawford, Feb. 6, 1965; children: Kelly Michelle, Scott Emlyn. BS in Physics, Centenary Coll., Shreveport, La., 1963; MS in Radiol. Health, U. Calif., Berkeley, 1965; PhD in Zoology, U. Tex., 1969. Radiobiologist NASA, Houston, 1965; rsch. scientist U. Tex., Austin, 1972-74, asst. prof., 1974-76; assoc. prof. Grad. Sch. and Med. Coll. Hahnemann U., Phila., 1976-82, prof., 1982—. Contbr. over 50 articles to profl. jours. Recipient Bell Telephone Sci. award 1959, Radiation Rsch. Soc. Travel awards, 1974, 79, Nat. Cancer Inst. Travel award, 1977; Centenary Coll. Freshman scholar, 1959-60, The Magale Found. fellow, 1960-63, AEC Health Physics fellow, 1963-64, USPHS grantee, 1964-65, Genetics Tng. grantee, 1965-69, NIH postdoctoral fellow, 1970-72. Mem. AAAS, The Radiation Rsch. Soc., Tex. Assn. Radiation Rsch., N.Y. Acad. Scis., Environ. Mutagen Soc., Soc. for Free Radical Rsch., Assn. for Radiation Rsch., Phila. Cancer Club, The Oxygen Soc., Alpha Sigma Pi. Home: 88 S Spring Ln Phoenixville PA 19460-2706 Office: Hahnemann U Broad and Vine Sts Philadelphia PA 19102

EWING, DESSA CRAWFORD, educator; b. Houston, July 28, 1941; d. William J. and Odessa (Barnes) Crawford; divorced 1992; children: Kelly Michelle, Scott Emlyn. BA, Centenary Coll., 1963; MA, Tex. Christian U., 1965; PhD, U. Tex., 1970. Tech. writer NASA Manned Spacecraft Ctr., Houston, 1965; rsch. assoc. History of Sci. Rarebooks Libr., Austin, 1966-68; instr. Univ. Tex., Austin, 1972-74, Drexel Univ., Phila., 1976-77; assoc. prof. to prof. English and humanities Delaware County Community Coll., Media, Pa., 1977—; cons. Communication Assocs., Phila., 1978—. Contbr. articles to profl. jours. Mem. Am. Assn. Women in Community and Jr. Colls., Community Colls. Humanities Assn., Modern Lang. Assn. Office: Dept Humanities DCCC Media Line Rd Media PA 19063-1028

EWING, FRANK CROCKETT, marketing entrepreneur, photographer; b. N.Y.C., July 17, 1951; s. William Milne and Emma Mai (Thompson) E. Honor cert. comml. photography, Germain Sch. of Photography, 1972; cert. in fundamental econs., Henry George Sch. of Social Sci., 1983. Photographer Bachrach Inc., N.Y.C., 1969-70, Genelli Studios, Sioux City, Iowa, 1971-72; photographer, owner Ewing Photography, Whitehouse and Bernardsville, N.J., 1972-77; model/photographer Modell Gruppen, Stockholm, 1978-79; freelance photographer N.Y.C., 1980-81, mktg. cons., 1982-85; pvt. practice mktg. dir. N.Y.C. and Stockholm, 1985—; mktg. assocs. Gatto Internat., Stockholm, 1986-87; mktg. cons. Dyna Corp., Osaka, Japan, 1987-89, EMEA Concepts Mktg., Inc., N.Y.C., 1987-89, Hard Rock Cafe, N.Y.C., Dallas, London, Tokyo, 1986—; freelance photographer N.Y. Times; prodr. ofcl. jackets for movie Platoon, Orion Pictures, Hard Rock Cafe; marketer environ. info. products and svcs., 1989—; speaker NYU, 1991, Columbia U., 1991. Mem. Rock Found. Reclaim Our City's Kids Partnership, N.Y.C., 1990-91. Mem. Profl. Photographers of Am., Better World Soc., The Wilderness Soc., Soc. for Theatre Arts Resources, Christian Appalachian Project, Handgun Control Inc., Masons. Presbyterian. Home: 431 E 20th St Ste 10F New York NY 10010 Office: 235 W 48th St Ste 6G New York NY 10036-1404

EWING, KENNETH PATRICK KY, lawyer; b. Washington, Nov. 3, 1964; s. Ky P. and Almuth (Rott) E. BA, Yale U., 1987; LLB, U. Mich., 1991. Bar: Md. 1991, U.S. Dist. Ct. Md. 1992, U.S. Ct. Appeals (4th cir.) Md. 1992. Law clk to honorable Paul V. Niemeyer U.S. Ct. Appeals (4th cir.), Balt., 1991—. Assoc. editor Mich. Law Rev., 1989-90, contbg. editor, 1990-91. Home: 8317 Comanche Ct Bethesda MD 20817

EWING, MARTIN S., astronomer, electrical engineer; b. Albany, N.Y., May 4, 1945; s. Galen Wood and Alice (Sipple) E.; m. Eva Reissner, June 11, 1966; children: Margaret, Robert, Eric. BA, Swarthmore Coll., 1966; PhD, MIT, 1971. Mem. prof. staff Calif. Inst. Tech., Pasadena, 1971-89; vis. assoc. CSIRO Div. Radiophysics, Sydney, Australia, 1985-86; dir. sci. and engring. computing facility Yale U., New Haven, 1989—. Author: Forth Manuel D'Application, 1984; contbr. articles to profl. jours. Mem. IEEE, AAAS, Internat. Astronomical Union, Assn. Computing Machinery. Office: Yale U PO Box 1968 New Haven CT 06520-1968

EWING, ROBERT, lawyer; b. Little Rock, July 18, 1922; s. Esmond and Frances (Howell) E.; m. Elizabeth Smith, May 24, 1947; 1 child, Elizabeth Milbrey. BA, Washington and Lee U., 1943; LLB, Yale U., 1945. Bar: Conn. 1945. Assoc. Shipman & Goodwin, Hartford, Conn., 1945-50; partner Shipman & Goodwin, 1950—; asst. pros. atty. West Hartford, Conn., 1953-55; dir., asst. sec. H.W. Steame Co. Inc., Rocktide Inc.; dir., pres. Still Pasture Corp. Mem. U.S. Constitution Bicentennial Commn. of Conn., 1986-91; incorporator Hartford Hosp., Hartford Camerata Conservatory; bd. dirs. Travelers Aid Soc. Hartford, 1951-57, treas., 1954-57; bd. dirs. Greater Hartford chpt. ARC, 1974—, chmn., 1977-79, mem. exec. and coord. coms., 1977—, blood svcs. com., 1986-91; chmn. ARC Blood Svcs. Conn. region, 1989-92; mem. Ea. Ops. Adv. Coun., 1988-91; bd. dirs. Family Svc. Soc., 1961-65, Conn. Pub. Expenditure Coun., 1986-91, Old State House, 1991—; trustee Watkinson Libr. Trinity Coll., Hartford, 1989—; spl. Master U.S. Dist. Ct. Conn. Fellow Am. Bar Found.; mem. ABA, Conn. Bar Assn. (chmn. fed. practice com. 1976-79, exec. com. corp. sect. 1981-85), Hartford County Bar Assn., Am. Law Inst., Conn. Hist. Soc. (standing com. 1954-77, trustee 1978—, chmn. adminstrv. com. 1980-88, v.p. 1982-89, chmn. pers. com. 1987-89, pres. 1989—), Newcomen Soc. N.Am. Congregationalist. (sr. deacon 1972-75). Clubs: Twentieth Century (pres. 1975-76), Hartford (counsel 1975-90, bd. govs. 1991—), Mory's Assn., Dauntless, Rotary (pres. Hartford 1966-67, Paul Harris fellow 1988). Home: 28 Birch Rd West Hartford CT 06119-1007 Office: Shipman & Goodwin One Amercian Row Hartford CT 06103-2819

EWING, WILLIAM HENSZEY, lawyer; b. Phila., Apr. 13, 1939; s. Joseph Neff and Anne Henszey (Ashton) E.; m. Anne Constant, Aug. 25, 1962; children; Susannah Constant, Rebecca Henszey. BA, Princeton U., 1961; JD, U. Pa., 1965. Bar: D.C. 1966, Pa. 1970, U.S. Supreme Ct. 1987. Law clk. Hon. Warren E. Burger, U.S. Ct. Appeals, Washington, 1965-66; lectr. Haile Sellassie U., Faculty of Law, Addis Ababa, Ethiopia, 1966-69; asst. prof. Haile Sellassie U., Faculty of Law, Addis Ababa, 1969-70; lawyer Hangley Connolly Epstein Chicco Foxman & Ewing, Phila., 1970—; bd. dirs. Pub. Interest Law Ctr. of Phila., 1985—, vice chair, 1990-92, chair, 1992—; del. Third Cir. Jud. Conf., 1991; mem. Zoning Bd. of Adjustment of City of Phila., 1986-89. Editor: Consolidated Laws of Ethiopia, 1972, Consolidated Legislation of Addis Ababa, 1970; also articles on Ethiopian law. Bd. dirs. Greater Phila. Urban Affairs Coalition, 1983—, Com. for Dignity and Fairness Homeless Shelter, Inc., 1985-90; pres. Cen. Germantown Community Devel. Corp., Phila., 1982-84, 88-92; chmn. Phila. Com. on City Policy, 1978-82; pres. Energy Coop. Assn., Phila., 1985-90; pres. bd. trustees First United Meth. Ch., Germantown, 1983-84; co-chair Pa.'s Campaign for Choice, 1991—. Recipient Edgar Baker award, East Mt. Airy Neighbors, Inc., Phila., 1980, Com. Service award, Greater West Oak Ln. Coordinating Council, 1974, Com. Service award, United Polit. Action Com. of Chester County, Penna., 1980, William Penn Human Rights award, Phila., 1980. Mem. ABA, Phila. Bar Assn., Fed. Bar Assn. Office: Hangley Connolly Epstein Chicco Foxman & Ewing 1515 Market St Fl 9 Philadelphia PA 19102-1901

EYDGAHI, ALI MOHAMMADZADEH, engineering educator; b. Tehran, Iran, May 17, 1957; s. Mohammad and Zahra Eydgahi; m. Maryam Taabodi, Sept. 3, 1983; children: Hoda, Mahdi. BS, Detroit Inst. Tech., 1979; MS, Wayne State U., 1981, PhD, 1986. Vis. prof. Rensselaer Polytech. Inst., Troy, N.Y., 1985-86; prof. SUNY, New Paltz, 1986—; presiding chair Third Nat. Conf. EUREKA, San Antonio, 1989. Expert reviewer Dept. Edn., Washington, 1989-90; contbr. articles to profl. jours. Recipient rsch. grant IBM, 1988, ASEE Dow Outstanding Young Faculty award, 1990. Mem. IEEE (sr., reviewer N.J. 1987—, edn. chmn. Mid-Hudson sect. 1988-89, program chmn. 1990—), Am. Soc. Engring. Edn. (Dow Outstanding Young Faculty award 1990), Soc. Mfg. Engrs. (chpt. 74 1990-92, vice chmn., edn. avd.), Sigma Xi. Islam. Office: SUNY Dept Elec Engring New Paltz NY 12561

EYERER, DAPHNE MARGARET BERTA, sales executive; b. Beverly, Mass., Aug. 17, 1953; d. Rudolf Emil and Joan (Cox) E. BA in History, U. Maine, 1975, MBA, 1983. Adminstrv. asst. Ropes & Gray, Boston, 1976-78; banking assoc. HypoBank, Munich, Germany, 1978-80; asst. auditor Arthur Young & Co., GmbH, Munich, 1980-81; asst. treas. Chase Manhattan Bank, N.A., N.Y.C., 1984-88; fin. mgr. Shea & Gould, N.Y.C., 1988-89; staff acct. Dysart's Transp. Inc., Bangor, Maine, 1990; campaign staff Cohen for Senator Campaign, Portland, Maine, 1990; staff asst. U.S. Senator William S. Cohen, Bangor, Maine, 1991-92; internat. salesperson Spirometrics, Inc., Auburn, Maine, 1992—. Mem. Maine Humanities Coun., World Affairs Coun. Maine, Maine Audubon Soc., Bangor Hist. Soc., Nature Conservancy. Republican. Roman Catholic. Home: 393 Center St # 115E Auburn ME 04210

EYO, CLEMENT I.B., lottery market analyst; b. Oron, Akwa Ibom, Nigeria, Dec. 31, 1944; came to U.S., 1970; s. Henry Bieto and Nkoyo (Anwana) E.; m. Fannie Plain, Oct. 8, 1979; children: Koehen I.B., Honesty I.B. BA, Tex. Tech. U., 1974; MA, Iowa State U., 1977; PhD in Pub. Adminstrn., Howard U., 1989. Mgmt. cons. Nigerian Fed. Govt., Lagos, 1977-80; asst. prof. Prince George's Community Coll., Largo, Md., 1986-89; mktg. analyst D.C. Lottery and Charitable Games Control Bd., Washington, 1988—; pres. Clemfan Mktg. Cons. Internat., Washington, 1989—. Author: Public Policy and Development of Small Scale Industry in Nigeria: A Policy Analysis, 1989, Using Cost-Benefit Analysis to Determine Government Investment in Public Programs, 1976. Recipient Lottery Excellence award Pub. Gaming Internat., 1990. Mem. Soc. for Internat. Devel., Advt. Club Washington Met. Area, Oron Devel. Union Washington (pres.). Roman Catholic. Home: 3801 Blaine St NE Washington DC 20019-3356

EZELL, EDWARD CLINTON, museum curator; b. Indpls., Nov. 7, 1939; s. Eugene Bryan and Katherine Naomi (Krause) E.; m. Holly Everding, Aug. 12, 1968 (dec. 1971); m. Linda Neuman, Oct. 13, 1973 (div. 1983); m. Virginia Hart Sahm, Mar. 13, 1987. BA, Butler U., 1961; MA, U. Del., 1963; PhD, Case Inst. Tech., 1969. Asst. prof. N.C. State U., Raleigh, 1966-70, Sangamon State U., Springfield, Ill., 1970-72; v.p. Interarms Pte. Ltd., Singapore, 1972-74; historian NASA, Houston, 1974-80; ctr. historian Johnson Space Ctr., NASA, Houston, 1980-82; supervisory curator Nat. Mus. of Am. History, Washington, 1982—; dir. Inst. for Rsch. on Small Arms in Internat. Security, Washington, 1989—; chair Colt Adv. Bd., Hartford, Conn., 1990. Author: The Partnership: ASTP, 1977, On Mars, 1984, Great Rifle Controversy, 1984, Small Arms Today, 1984, 2d edit. 1986; contbr. articles to profl. jours. Mem. AIAA, Co. of Mil. Historians, Soc. for History of Technology (exec. coun.), Interuniv. Seminar on Armed Forces and Soc. Office: Nat Mus of Am History Smithsonian Instn Washington DC 20560-0002

EZELL, WILLIAM BRUCE, JR., college dean, entomological consultant; b. Atlanta, Oct. 1, 1941; s. William Bruce and Floride (Patterson) E.; m. Nancy Johnson, Sept. 1, 1963; children: Nancy Summer, William Bruce III, Gretchen Edna, H. Elizabeth J. BS in Biology, Lander Coll., Greenwood, S.C., 1963; DLitt (hon.), Lander Coll., 1988; MS in Zoology, Clemson U., 1965, PhD in Entomology, 1971; postgrad., Colo. State U., 1975, Oxford U., Eng., 1986. Listed in Am. Registry of Profl. Entomologists. Bank teller Banker's Trust of S.C., Ninety Six, 1969-60; grad. rsch. asst. Clemson (S.C.) U., 1963-65, instr., 1968; instr. biology Winthrop Coll., Rock Hill, S.C., 1965-67; from asst. prof. to prof. biology The Citadel, Charleston, S.C., 1970-80; prof., head dept. biology Ga. So. U., Statesboro, 1980-81; pres., prof. Erskine Coll. and Sem., Due West, S.C., 1981-89; exec. asst. to pres. U. Maine, Orono, 1989-91; dean Coll. Grad. Studies and Extended Learning Kutztown (Pa.) U., 1990—; pres.'s rep. Maine Community Leadership Forum, Augusta, 1989-90; inst. rep. Faculty Devel. Coun. for Pa. System of Higher Edn., Harrisburg, 1990—. Contbr. articles to sci. jours. Bd. dis. S.C. Found. for Ind. Colls., Greenville, 1981-89, S.C. Wildlife Fedn., Columbia, 1977-79; mem. bd. visitors Med. U. S.C., Charleston, 1981-82, trustee, 1981-89. Named Conservation Educator of Yr., S.C. Wildlife Fedn., 1975; recipient Outstanding Leadership award Rotary, Greenville, 1986. Mem. S.C. Entomol. Soc. (pres. 1975-76), S.C. Mosquito Control Assn. (pres. 1977), S.C. Assn. Colls. and Univs. (pres. 1985-86), St. Andrew's Soc. Upper S.C., Sigma Xi, Gamma Sigma Delta. Democrat. Presbyterian. Home: 202 Independence Ct Blandon PA 19510-9676 Office: Kutztown U Kutztown PA 19530

EZERSKY, LAUREN ELISE, journalist; b. N.Y.C., May 14, 1954; d. Robert and Gloria E.; m. Jordan Plittleris, May 14, 1988. Student,

Northeastern U., 1972-74, Garland Coll., 1974-75. TV anchor and hostess Behind the Velvet Ropes, N.Y.C., 1989-92; journalist Paper Mag., N.Y.C., 1992—. Author Lunch With Lauren Column, 1992. Organizer First Ann. Cable TV awards, N.Y.C., 1992. Office: Paper Mag 1065 Lexington 529 Broadway New York NY 10012

EZHAYA, JOSEPH BERNARD, brokerage house executive; b. Waterville, Maine, July 17, 1943; s. Bernard Joseph and Isabelle (Karter) E.; m. Carol Ann Jurdak, May 28, 1978; children: Paul Bernard, Amy Carol. BA, Boston Coll., 1965; JD, U. Maine, Portland, 1968; diploma, Judge Advocate Gens. Sch., 1988, Command & Gen. Staff Coll., 1991. Bar: Maine 1971. Dir. human resources Maine Mcpl. Assn., Augusta, 1972-74; atty. Law Office Joseph B. Ezhaya, Waterville, 1974-81; stockbroker Advest, Inc., Waterville, 1981-86; br. mgr. A.G. Edwards & Sons, Inc., Waterville, 1986—; adj. faculty Thomas Coll., Waterville, 1991—. Editor pamphlet; author essay (1st prize 1972). Mem. Waterville Bd. Edn., 1975-79; mem. Waterville City Coun., 1980-81; chair Waterville Area YMCA, 1986—; dir. Maine C. of C. and Industry, Augusta, 1988— (Elias A. Joseph award 1986); vice chmn. Maine Bus. Polit. Action Com., Augusta, 1988—; mem. govt. rels. com. Securities Industry Assn., Washington, 1989—; commr. Govt. Ethics and Election Practices, Augusta, 1990—; treas. Maine Securities Assn., 1992—. Capt. U.S. Army, 1969-72, Vietnam, maj. Maine Army Nat. Guard, 1983—. Decorated Oak Leaf Cluster, Bronze Star. Mem. Maine Bar Assn., Waterville Bar Assn., Maine Mil. Hist. Soc. (chair of publs. 1988—), Waterville Rotary (dir. 1989-91), Boston Coll. Club (pres. 1986-91). Democrat. Roman Catholic. Home: 125 Silver St Waterville ME 04901 Office: AG Edwards & Sons Inc 193 Main St Waterville ME 04901

FABBRI, WILLIAM PAUL, emergency physician; b. N.Y.C., Feb. 19, 1955; s. William and Y. Marie (Bufano) F.; m. Monica Rothe, Sept. 9, 1989; 1 child, Molly Elisabeth. AB cum laude, Clark U., 1977; MD, N.Y. Med. Coll., 1981. Diplomate Am. Bd. Emergency Medicine. Intern in surgery Boston U., Boston, 1981-82, resident in surgery, 1981-83; resident in emergency medicine Johns Hopkins Hosp., Balt., 1983-85; mem. staff Francis Scott Key Med. Ctr., Balt., 1985—; asst. prof. Emergency Medicine Johns Hopkins Hosp., Balt., 1987—; cons. in emergency medicine, Balt., 1987—, cons. in paramedic edn. Md. State Police, Balt., 1989—; instr. in paramedic edn. Essex Coll., Balt., 1987—; sr. aviation med. examiner Fed. Aviation Adminstrn., Balt., 1988—. Mem. Balt. City Amb. Adv. Com., 1985-90, Md. Emergency Med. Svcs. Adv. Com., 1990—. Fellow Am. Coll. Emergency Physicians; mem. AMA, Aerospace Med. Assn., Nat. Flight Paramedics Assn., Md. Med. Chirurg. Soc., Phi Beta Kappa. Episcopalian. Office: dept Emergency Medicine Francis Scott Key Med Ctr Baltimore MD 21224

FABER, SUSAN GAIL, music educator; b. Bethpage, N.Y., Dec. 10, 1960; d. Alwin Albert and Louise C. (Di Franco) F. BS in Music, Hofstra U., 1982; MBA, Adelphi U., 1991. Prof. Five Towns Coll., Dix Hills, N.Y., 1984—; songwriter/producer A.D. Prodns., Seaford, 1982-86; studio mgr. Star Mix Studios, Ltd., Massapequa, N.Y., 1986-89; songwriter/producer Second Story Records, Inc., Massapequa, 1986-89; pres., songwriter/ producer En Revanche Prodns., Massapequa, 1990—; pres., cons. Music Bus. Assocs., Inc., Massapequa, 1990—; mem. host com. for Grammy awards Nat. Acad. of Recording Arts and Scis., N.Y.C., 1991. Mem. Broadcast Music Inc., Nat. Guild of Piano Tchrs., Nat. Bus. Educators Assn., ASCD, NAFE, Songwriters Guild, Phi Sigma Eta (hon.). Office: Five Towns Coll N Service Rd Dix Hills NY 11747

FABERT, JACQUES, artist, educator; b. Paris, Apr. 24, 1925; came to U.S., 1957; m. Bonnie MacLean, Aug. 19, 1981; 1 child, David Wolodia Graham. Student Ecole Nat. Superieure des Beaux-Arts, Paris, 1943-47. Prof. fine arts San Francisco Art Acad., 1963-70, Calif. Coll. Arts and Crafts, Oakland, 1963-72, Princeton Art Assn., N.J., 1978—; designer tapestries Beverly Godfrey Weaving Studios, 1992—. One man shows at Nordness Gallery, N.Y.C., 1969, E.B. Crocker Mus. Art, Sacramento, 1969, Gilman Gallery, Chgo., 1970, Carroll Reece Mus., E. Tenn. State U., 1974, Genest Gallery, Lambertville, Pa., 1991, others; exhibited in group shows at: Calif. Palace Legion of Honor, San Francisco, 1963-65-67; Am. Fedn. of Art, N.Y.C., 1968; San Francisco Mus. Art, 1968-69-70; Nat. Inst. Arts and Letters, N.Y.C., 1970; Expo '70, Osaka, Japan, 1970; Stedman Gallery, Rutgers U., 1977-79; N.J. State Mus., Trenton, N.J., 1978-79; represented in permanent collections at Butler Inst. Am. Art, Youngstown, Ohio, City of San Francisco Art Commn., Norfolk Mus. Art, Va., City of Phila. Free Library, others. Address: 2682 Rt 413 PO Box 103 Buckingham PA 18912

FABIAN, JEROME FRANCIS, tile distributing company executive; b. Kingston, Pa., Jan. 4, 1943; s. Frank E. and Mary (Ridzon) F.; m. Carol J. Hischak, Feb. 8, 1964; children: Michelle, Jonelle. Grad. high sch., Plymouth, Pa. Installer Fabian Tile, Plymouth, 1961-70; mgr. Tile Distbrs. Wilkes-Barre, Pa., 1971-81; pres., owner Tile Distbrs. Am., Wilkes-Barre, 1981—. Chmn. Heart Fund, Jackson Twp.; mem. Jackson Twp. Vol. Fire Dept. Mem. Ceramic Tile Distbrs. Assn. (bd. dirs. 1990), Fraternal Order Police, Tatra Club Wyoming Valley, K.C. (3 degree). Republican. Roman Catholic. Office: Tile Distbrs Am 300 Mundy St Wilkes Barre PA 18702-6819

FABIAN, LOUIS JAMES, university program director; b. Tustin, Calif., July 27, 1955; s. James Marshall and Marlene H. (Albrecht) F.; m. Gillian Barrie Greenhill, June 30, 1979 (div. 1988); m. Amy Lynn Bohl, June 18, 1988; children: Anna Elizabeth, Noel Patrice. BS, U. Ill., 1977; MPA, Pa. State U., 1984. Announcer Key Broadcasting Co., Lexington Park, Md., 1978-80; staff asst. Pa. State U., University Park, Pa., 1980-84; asst. planning analyst Pa. State U., University Park, 1984-87, planning analyst, 1987-88, cons., 1988; dir. planning and evaluation Lock Haven (Pa.) U., 1988—, instr., 1989; speaker State System of Higher Edn., Harrisburg, Pa., 1990, Assn. Instnl. Rsch., Louisville, Ky., 1990, Soc. Coll. and U. Planners, Seattle, 1991. Independent. Home: 420 W Walnut St Lock Haven PA 17745-2842 Office: Lock Haven U N Fairview St Lock Haven PA 17745-2454

FABIAN, MICHAEL WILLIAM, physiology educator; b. Mercer, Pa., Sept. 27, 1931; s. Steve and Mary (Matanin) F.; m. Dec. 20, 1952; children: Bruce, Nancy. MS, Mich. State U., 1954; PhD, Ohio State U., 1964. Instr. Cleve. Pub. Schs., 1954-56, Ariz. State U., Tempe, 1957-58; asst. prof. Geneva Coll., Beaver Falls, Pa., 1958-61; assoc. prof. Westminster Coll., New Wilmington, Pa., 1961-64; chmn. and prof. biology Grove City (Pa.) Coll., 1964—. Bd. dirs. Mercer County Hist. Soc.; chmn. Mercer County Conservation Bd.; bd. dirs. Meth. Ch. NSF fellow, 1960-61. Mem. AAAS, Am. Inst. Biol. Sci., Masons. Home: 510 Oakland Ave Grove City PA 16127-1813 Office: Grove City Coll Dept Biology Grove City PA 16127

FABIANO, ROBERTA MARY, musician; b. Carle Place, N.Y.; d. Anthony Albert and Eleanor (Digiacinti) F. BA in Composition and Arrangement, Berklee Coll. Music. Guitarist, vocalist, composer Lester Lanin Orch., Peter Duchin Orch., Ray Bloch Prodns., Jerry Kravat Entertainment, Birdie, N.Y.C., 1983-84, Am. Invasion, N.Y.C., 1984, T.M. Stevens and the Pump, N.Y.C., 1984-85, Doc Pomus, N.Y.C., 1984—; musician with Warner Bros. artist Al B. Sure!, 1988. Songwriter: Medicine Man (N.Y. Songwriters Showcase award, 1984, N.Y. State Senate Achievement award, 1984), Walls in my Room (Am. Song Festival award 1982).; writer for Count Basie Band; performed for Queen Elizabeth and Royal Family, 1985, 86, 150th anniversary of Cunard Cross-Atlantic Celebration, also with Cleo Laine, Buster Poindexter, Milton Berle, Julie Budd, Gloria Loring, Steve Allen, Debbie Gibson, Nell Carter, Frank Gorshin, Carol Channing, Melissa Manchester, Jerry Vale, Al Martino, and others; appeared on (radio program) Don K. Reed Show, (TV soap opera) Loving, (film) Working Girl; rec. artist for CBS and TK Records; endorsee for Steinberger Guitars; art exhibit Gracie Sq. Art Show, N.Y.C. Mem. Am. Fedn. Musicians, Songwriters Guild, AFTRA.

FABIETTI, VICTOR ARMANDO, accountant; b. Roccamorice, Abruzzi, Italy, June 18, 1920; came to U.S., 1930; s. Agostino and Maria C. (Pietrangelo) F.; m. Alda Lorraine Santini, Sept. 13, 1952; twin daughters, 1 son. Student, Camden Comml. Coll., N.J., 1947-49. CPA, N.J. Owner V.A. Fabietti & Co. CPAs, Atlantic City, N.J., 1958-90; chmn. Premium Fed. Savs. Bank, Gibbsboro, N.J., 1987—, also bd. dirs., 1987—; pres., adminstrv. ptnr. Fabietti & Assocs. Pub. Accts., Pleasantville, N.J., 1990—; bd. dirs. Atlantic Nat. Bank, Atlantic City, 1970-82. Mem. congl. staff Thomas C. McGrath, 1978; comdr. Richard S. Somers Soc., Atlantic City, 1988. Sgt. maj. U.S. Army, 1942-46, ETO. Decorated Bronze Medals, Croix de Guerre (France). Fellow N.J. Soc. of CPAs; mem. AICPA, AICPA Div. for CPA Firms. Republican. Roman Catholic. Home: 106 S Quincy Ave Margate City NJ 08402-2540 Office: Fabietti & Assocs Pub Accts 600 S Fire Rd Pleasantville NJ 08232-9640

FABISH, THOMAS JOHN, materials scientist; b. Youngstown, Ohio, Feb. 27, 1938; s. Joseph and Ann (Yavorsky) F.; widowed; children: James, Peter, Thomas. B in Aero. Engring., Ohio State U., 1960, M in Physics, 1966; PhD in Material Sci., U. Rochester, 1975. Rsch. engr. N.Am. Aviation, Columbus, 1961-62; staff cyclotron lab. Ohio State U., Columbus, 1962-66; rsch. engr. Battele Meml. Inst., Columbus, 1966-69; scientist Xerox Corp., Webster, N.Y., 1969-80; sr. rsch. chemist Ashland Chem. Co., Dublin, Ohio, 1980-83; prin. material scientist Am. Cyanamid Co., Stanford, Conn., 1983-85; tech. specialist Alcon Tech. Ctr., Alcon Center, Pa., 1985—. Editor: Photon, Electron, Ion Probes of Polymer Structure Properties, 1981; contbr. articles to profl. jours. Mem. Am. Chem. Soc., Am. Phys. Soc., Sigma Xi. Home: 4917 Simmons Dr Export PA 15632-9330 Office: Alcoa Tech Ctr Alcoa Center PA 15069

FABRICANT, CATHERINE GRENCI, microbiologist; b. Davoli, Calabria, Italy, Sept. 24, 1919; came to U.S., 1920; d. Francesco Sabato and Maria Antonia (Sinopoli) Grenci; m. Julius Fabricant, Dec. 8, 1945; children: Barbara Louise, Daniel Grenci. BS, Cornell U., 1942, MS, 1948. Head med. technician infirmary Cornell U., Ithaca, N.Y., 1942-44; grad. asst. N.Y. State Coll. Vet. Medicine Cornell U., Ithaca, 1945-48, rsch. assoc., 1959-62, acting asst. prof., 1963, rsch. assoc., 1965-73, sr. rsch. assoc., 1973-85, vis. fellow, 1986—; vis. rsch. assoc. U. Aarhus (Denmark) Med. Sch., 1964-65, vis. sr. rsch. assoc., 1973. Author rsch. studies on viral inducted urinary obstruction and viral induced atherosclerosis. Vol. Ithaca area Am. Heart Assn., 1980, 84, Birth Defects Soc., 1990. Grantee Morris Animal Found., 1973-74, Ralston Purina Co., 1975-82, NIH, 1976-83. Mem. Morris Animal Found.; mem. Am. Soc. Pathologists, Am. Soc. Virologists, Fedn. Am. Socs. Exptl. Biology, Sigma Xi, Sigma Delta Epsilon. Office: Cornell U NY State Coll Vet Medicine Schurman Hall 802 Hanshaw Rd Ithaca NY 14853

FABRICIUS, RICHARD NEIL, orthopedic surgeon; b. Albany, N.Y., Aug. 14, 1928; s. John and Janet Muir (Meekin) F.; m. Janet Carrie Pitcher, Oct. 27, 1957. BS, Springfield (Mass.) Coll., 1949; MD, Vt. Coll. Medicine, 1953. Diplomate Am. Bd. Orthopedic Surgery, Nat. Bd. Med. Examiners. Intern Albany (N.Y.) Med. Ctr., 1953-54, surg. resident, 1956-57; orthopedic resident Ochsner Clinic, New Orleans, 1957-60, staff orthopedist, 1960-61; mem. med. staff Putnam Meml. Hosp., Bennington, Vt., 1961—, pres. med. staff, 1969-70, chief surgery, 1970-76; orthopedic surgeon Orthopedic & Hand Surgery P.C., Bennington; guest speaker Fla. Orthopedic, West Palm, Fla., 1976. Lt. comdr. USN, 1954-56. Mem. Am. Acad. Orthopedic Surgeons (Vt. councilor), New Eng. Orthopedic Soc. (sec. 1990—). Home: 12 Fairview Rd 17 Fairview Rd Old Bennington VT 05201 Office: Orthopedic & Hand Surgery 332 Dewey St Bennington VT 05201

FABRIZIO, TUULA IRJA, physician, writer; b. Helsinki, Finland, May 13, 1931; d. Aine Valfria Joniken and Jenny Lydia Johansson; m. John A. Fabrizio, Aug. 4, 1962. MD, U. Helsinki, 1958. Orthopedist cen. hosp. U. Helsinki, 1960-62; attending physician emergency medicine dept. Park City Hosp., Bridgeport, Conn., 1964, Norwalk (Conn.) Hosp., 1966-69, Milford (Conn.) Hosp., 1973-77, St. Vincent's Med. Ctr., Birdgeport, 1977-1979; practice medicine specializing in occupational medicine Bridgeport, 1979—. Columnist Finnish Med. Jour., Nordisk Medicin mag., Health 2000; contbr. articles to profl. jours. Coordinator local state rep. campaigns, Norwalk, 1968-74. Recipient Medal award Finnish Med. Assn., 1980. Fellow Am. Coll. Preventive Med., Am. Acad. Family Physicians (charter); mem. AMA, Fairfield County Med. Assn., Conn. State Med. Soc., Am. Coll. Emergency Physicians, Am. Pub. Health Assn., Am. Assn. for Automobile Med., Internat. Coll. Pediatrics, Acad. Polit. Sci., Am. Med. Writers Assn., World Acad. N.Z. Home and Office: 42 Stevens St Norwalk CT 06850-3525

FABROS, ROBERTO TANCINCO, private equity investment administrator; b. Manila, Nov. 17, 1950; came to U.S., 1973; s. Mario D. and Sol (Tancinco) F.; m. Kathleen White, Oct. 13, 1979; children: Christian Taylor, Mark Sebastian, Marissa Nicole. BA, Ateneo de Manila, Quezon City, Philippines, 1972; MBA, Harvard U., 1976. Investment banker Chase Manhattan, N.Y.C., 1976-83; treas. Pepsico Internat., Purchase, N.Y., 1983-85; investment banker First Chgo. Corp., N.Y.C., 1985-88; head Latin Am. mergers and acquisitions Bankers Trust Co., N.Y.C., 1988-91; mng. gen. ptnr. Am. Capital Ptnrs., N.Y.C., 1991—. Roman Catholic. Home: 245 E 87th St Apt 18A New York NY 10012-8000 Office: Americas Capital Ptnrs 152 W 57th St Fl 25 New York NY 10019-3301

FABRY, THOMAS LESTER, gastroenterologist, educator; b. Budapest, May 30, 1937. BSc, St. Andrews Coll., Scotland, 1961; PhD, Yale U., 1963; postgrad., Albert Einstein Coll. Medicine, 1973-74. Instr. Yale U., New Haven, 1963-65; asst. prof. Columbia U., N.Y.C., 1965-69; intern and resident Mt. Sinai Hosp., N.Y.C., 1973-76, fellow in gastroenterology, 1976-78, asst. clin. prof., 1979, assoc. clin. prof., 1990—, assoc. attending, 1990—; cons. interactive edn. Am. Soc. Gastrointestinal Endoscopy. Editor: Guide to Liver Transplantation. Fellow Am. Coll. Gastroenterology; mem. Am. Gastroent. Assn., Am. Soc. Gastrointestinal Endoscopy, N.Y. Soc. Gastrointestinal Endoscopy. Office: 853 Fifth Ave New York NY 10021

FABYAN, SCOTT SPOONER, portfolio manager, consultant; b. Boston, Aug. 2, 1962; s. John Davis and Susan (Farnsworth) Spooner; m. Holly Helliwell, June 1, 1991. BS, Babson Coll., 1986. Personal investment banker Boston Co., 1986-87; portfolio mgr., fin. cons. Shearson Lehman Bros., Boston, 1987—. Mem. fin. com. to elect Geoff May, Brookline, Mass., 1991-92. Mem. Country Club of Brookline (Mass.), Stone House Yacht Club, Boston Racquet Club, Ducks Unltd., New Eng. Aquarium, Mass. Beach Buggy Assn., U.S. Boardsailing Assn. Republican. Home: 7 Old Neck Rd Manchester MA 01944 Office: Shearson Lehman Bros 53 State St 39th Fl Boston MA 02109

FACE, WAYNE BRUCE, retail professional; b. Everett, Mass., June 20, 1942; s. Ward Jr. and Margaret Irene (Keil) F.; m. Sharon Lucille Blythe, Mar. 25, 1967; children: Jonathan Jacob, Joseph Matthew. ASA, Bentley Coll., 1962, BSA, 1967; MBA, Pepperdine U., 1975; EdD, Vanderbilt U., 1986. Div. analyst Varian Assocs., Palo Alto, Calif., 1969-71, sr. fin. analyst, 1972-75; acctg. mgr. Veeco Instruments, Sunnyvale, Calif., 1971-72; product line controller Nat. Semiconductor, Santa Clara, Calif., 1975-76; assoc. prof. Hawthorne Coll. of Bus., Antrim, N.H., 1976-86, dept. chmn., 1983-86; owner Learn to Live, Warner, N.H., 1986-88; acctg. mgr. N.H. Correctional Industries, Concord, 1988-91; owner Sharway Gifts, Warner, 1991—. Advisor Jr. Achievement, Palo Alto, 1971-73; den leader Cub Scouts, Warner, 1990-91; coach Kearsarge Youth Basketball, New London, N.H., 1991—; bd. dirs. Kearsarge Children's Ctr., Warner, 1987-88. With U.S. Army, 1964-67, Korea. Democrat. Home and Office: RR# 2 Box 1838 Main St Warner NH 03278

FACHADA, EDERITO PAUL, podiatrist; b. Cumberland, R.I., Apr. 6, 1929; s. Ernesto J. and Julia Augusta (Loucas) F.; m. Vera Phillips; children: Paul, Peter, Mark. BS, Providence Coll., 1950; D Podiatric Medicine, Temple U., 1955. Instr. surgery R.I. Hosp., Providence, 1953-54, Temple U., Phila., 1954-55; intern, resident Phila. Gen. Hosp. and Temple U. Hosp., Phila., 1955-56; chmn. bd. Examiners, Concord, N.H., 1983—; staff mem. Chesire Med. Ctr., Maplewood Hosp. and Nursing Home; state del. Nat. Bd. Examiners, 1988. Mem. Keene (N.H.) Bd. Health; chmn. bd. dirs. Keene Sr. Ctr.; state chmn. Columbia Squires, Keene; staff mem. Cheshire Med. Ctr., Maplewood Hosp. and Nursing Home, Prospect Hill Home. Mem. Am. Podiatric Med. Assn., N.H. Podiatric Med. Assn. (pres. 1961-62). Home: 24A Stonehouse Ln Keene NH 03431-5241 Office: 112 Washington St Keene NH 03431-3104

FACHNIE, H(UGH) DOUGLAS, film manufacturing company official; b. Windsor, Ont., Can., Sept. 8, 1952; came to U.S., 1957; s. Harold Lennox Fachnie and Mary Jane (Schultz) MacKenzie. B Gen. Studies, U. Mich., 1973. Salesman Quarry, Inc., Ann Arbor, Mich., 1974; store mgr. Quarry, Inc., Ann Arbor and Saginaw, Mich., 1974-77; dist. mgr. Fotomat Corp., San Diego, 1977-80; dir. ops. Fotomat Corp., Wilton, Conn., 1980-81, dir. merchandising, 1981-83; mgr. optical products Fuji Photo Film U.S.A., Inc., N.Y.C., 1983-84; product mgr. consumer film Fuji Photo Film U.S.A., Inc., Elmsford, N.Y., 1984-89, sr. product and packaging mgr. consumer film, 1989—. Mem. Photog. Mktg. Assn., Am. Mgmt. Assn. Republican. Home: 30 Fleetwood Dr Danbury CT 06810-7010 Office: Fuji Photo Film USA Inc 555 Taxter Rd Elmsford NY 10523-2314

FADER, SEYMOUR JEREMIAH, management and engineering consulting company executive; b. N.Y.C., Feb. 9, 1923; s. Louis and Bertha (Stachel) F.; m. Shirley Ruth Sloan, June 26, 1951; children: Susan Deborah, Steven Micah. Student, CCNY, 1938-42; BSEE, U. Pa., 1949, MBA in Indsl. Mgmt., 1950. Mgr. prodn. Bogue Electric Mfg. Co., Paterson, N.J., 1950-56; mgr. planning and control Rowe Mfg. Co., Whippany, N.J., 1956-58; cons., engr. Koor Crafts & Industries, Ltd., Tel Aviv, 1958-59; dir. mfg. ops. ESC Electronics Corp., Palisades Park, N.J., 1959-62; mgr. mfg. Artistic Mfg., Sun Chem. Corp., Carlstadt, N.J., 1962-66; mgr. ops. Fairchild Instrumentation, Fairchild Camera & Instrument Corp., Clifton, N.J., 1966-67; v.p. Graphic Products, Inc., Hackensack, N.J., 1967-69; gen. mgr., v.p. Berkey Tech., Berkey Photo, Inc., Woodside, N.Y., 1969-72; pres. Susste Assocs., Paramus, N.J., 1972—; asst. prof. mgmt. Ramapo Coll., Mahwah, N.J., 1972-75, assoc. prof., 1975-80, prof. mgmt. and indsl. relations, 1980—, bd. dir. Study Abroad programs, 1983—; adj. prof. mgmt. Grad. Sch. Bus., Fordham U., 1982—; arbitration panelist Better Bus. Bur. of Bergen, Passaic and Rockland Counties, 1983—. Author: Fundamentals of Management for First-Line Supervisors, 1974, The Manufacturing Manager, 1975; co-author: Jobmanship, 1979; contbr. articles to profl. jours.; patentee coreless reeler, desk-top copier, photo-copier. Mem. pub. health study N.J. State Assembly Commn. on Conservation, Natural Resources, Air and Water Pollution, 1972-73; commr. Paramus Environ. Commn., 1973-78, vice chmn., 1977-78, chmn. inventory and land use com., 1974-78. With U.S. Army, 1942-45. Mem. Am. Mgmt. Assn. (cert. of achievement 1974), Am. Arbitration Assn. (panelist), Am. Inst. Indsl. Engrs., Soc. Advancement of Mgmt., Nat. Panel Consumer Arbitrators, Am. Prodn. and Inventory Control Soc. Home and Office: 377 Mckinley Blvd Paramus NJ 07652-4725

FADER, SHIRLEY SLOAN, writer; b. Paterson, N.J.; d. Samuel Louis and Miriam (Marcus) Sloan; m. Seymour J. Fader; children: Susan Deborah, Steven Micah Kimchi. B.S., M.S., U. Pa. Writer, journalist, author Paramus, N.J., 1956—; chmn., coord. ann. writers seminar Bergen Community Coll., 1973-76. Author columns Jobmanship, People and You, Family Weekly mag., 1971-82, How to Get More From Your Job, Glamour mag., 1978-81, Start Here, Working Woman mag., 1980-88, Work Strategies, Working Mother mag., 1987-88, Women Getting Ahead, Ladies Home Jour., 1980-90, How Would You Handle It, New Idea mag., 1984—, Moving Up, Woman mag., 1989—, Career Expert, Woman's World mag., 1992—; contbg. editor Family Weekly, 1971-82, Glamour mag., 1978-81, Working Woman mag., 1980-88, Working Mother mag., 1987-88, Ladies Home Jour., 1980-90, Woman mag., 1989-90; contbr. articles to mags., worldwide, 1956—; author: The Princess Who Grew Down, 1968, From Kitchen to Career, 1977, Jobmanship, 1978, Successfully Ever After, 1982, Brit. edit., 1985, Wait a Minute: You Can Have It All, 1992. Mem. Authors Guild, Am. Soc. Journalists and Authors (chmn.-moderator ann. writes conf. 1971-92, nat. v.p. 1976-77, mem.-at-large nat. exec. coun. 1976-78, 83-86), Nat. Press Club . Address: 377 McKinley Blvd Paramus NJ 07652

FAGAN, JULIE MIRIAM, animal sciences educator; b. N.Y.C., Dec. 9, 1953; d. Harold B. and Eleanor (Winer) F.; m. Lloyd H. Waxman, Aug. 30, 1986; 1 child, Jordan Michael. AA, Colby-Sawyer Coll., 1973; BS, Syracuse U., 1975; MS, U. Mass., 1977; PhD, U. Ariz., 1983. Postdoctoral fellow Harvard Med. Sch., Boston, 1983-86; asst. prof. animal scis. Rutgers U., New Brunswick, N.J., 1986-90, assoc. prof., 1990—, researcher, 1986—. Contbr. articles to profl. jours. Recipient 1st award NIH, 1988-93, Established Investigator award Am. Heart Assn., 1989—; grantee USDA, 1989—. Mem. AAAS, Am. Physiol. Soc., Am. Soc. for Biochemistry and Molecular Biology, Soc. for Exptl. Biology and Medicine, Am. Soc. for Animal Sci., Biochem. Soc., Am. Coll. Sports Medicine. Office: Rutgers U Dept Animal Scis PO Box 231 New Brunswick NJ 08903-0231

FAGAN, KEVIN JOSEPH, administrative assistant; b. Corning, N.Y., Apr. 24, 1954; s. Bernard John and Sarah Louise (Cooper) F. BA, Alfred (N.Y.) U., 1976. With pub. rels. dept. Taylor Wine Co., Hammondsport, N.Y., 1972-78; asst. reservations mgr. Breakers Hotel, Palm Beach, Fla., 1978-79; asst. rsch. mgr. Fagan's Inc., Bath, N.Y., 1979-87; adminstrv. asst. Chief Exec.'s Orgn., Bethesda, Md., 1987—; pastry chef Pleasant Valley Manor, N.Y., 1980. Instr. Literacy Vols. Am., 1987—; vol. Washington Nat. Cathedral, 1988—; sr. organist St. Mary's Ch., Bath, N.Y., 1966-75; assoc. organist St. Thomas Ch., Bath, N.Y., 1980-87. Mem. Am. Guild of Organists. Republican. Roman Catholic. Home: Apt 516 1255 New Hampshire Ave NW Washington DC 20036-2352

FAGAN, WILLIAM THOMAS, JR., urologist; b. Rutland, Vt., Sept. 21, 1923; s. William T. Sr. and Irene (Hevey) F.; m. Joy A. Lipman; children from previous marriage: Susan A. Barry, William T. III. BS, U. Vt., 1945, MD, 1948. Diplomate Am. Bd. Urology. Intern Mary Fletcher Hosp., 1948-49; resident Med. Ctr. Hosp. Vt., Burlington, 1952-86, attending physician urology, 1952—; assoc. prof. U. Vt., Burlington, 1954; chief urology dept. Fanny Allen Hosp., Winooski, Vt., 1956-86; cons. in urology Littleton Hosp., N.H., 1961—, Cottage Hosp., Woodsville, N.H., 1981—. Contbr. articles to profl. jours. Fellow ACS; mem. N.Y. Acad. Scis., Am. Urol. Assn., Am. Geriatric Soc., AMA, Royal Soc. Medicine. Home and Office: PO Box 1508 Stowe VT 05672-1508

FAGBEMI, STEPHEN FOLA, psychologist; b. Abeokuta, Ogun, Nigeria, Aug. 16, 1953; came to U.S., 1982; s. James Olaniyan and Fanny Wuraola (Okuyiga) F.; m. Antonia Javier, May 20, 1989. BS, U. Nigeria, 1979; MS, U. Lagos (Nigeria), 1981; PhD, U. Tex., Dallas, 1987. Lectr. U. Lagos (Nigeria), 1980-82; teaching asst. U. Tex., Dallas, 1983-87; asst. prof. Greater Hartford (Conn.) Community Coll., 1987—; adj. prof. psychology U. Hartford, West Hartford, Conn., 1988—; cons. psychologist Career Cons. Svcs., Bristol, Conn., 1988—. Mem. APA, AACD. Democrat. Baptist. Home: 308 W Washington St Bristol CT 06010-5369

FAGG, LAWRENCE WELLBURN, nuclear physicist, researcher, educator; b. East Orange, N.J., Oct. 10, 1923; s. Lawrence Wellburn Fagg and Doris Virginia Shea Fagg Gedney; m. Simone Fastres, May 5, 1950 (div. 1956); m. Patricia Menendez, Dec. 14, 1958 (div. 1962). MS in Physics, U. Md., 1947; MA in Physics, U. Ill., 1948; PhD in Physics, Johns Hopkins U., 1953; MA in Religion, George Washington U., 1981. Physicist Naval Rsch. Lab., Washington, 1953-58; sr. physicist Atlantic Rsch. Corp., Alexandria, Va., 1958-63; physicist Naval Rsch. Lab., Washington, 1963-76; rsch. prof. physics Cath. U. Am., Washington, 1977—. Author: Two Faces of Time, 1985; co-author: Electric and Magnetic Giant Resonances in Nuclei, 1991; contbr. articles to profl. publs. With AUS, 1942-45. Recipient Meritorious Civilian Svc. award Naval Rsch. Lab., 1975. Fellow Am. Phys. Soc.; mem. Inst. on Religion in Age of Sci. (v.p. 1981-86), Internat. Soc. for Study Time. Office: Cath U Am 4th St NEand Michigan Ave Washington DC 20064-0001

FAGG, WILLIAM HARRISON, systems analyst, state government official; b. Indpls., Mar. 28, 1924; s. Lloyd Ralph and Jeannette (Marker) F.; B.S., Purdue U., 1951; postgrad. Butler U., 1948-49, SUNY, Albany, 1970-71; m. Marie Aurora Schecton, Aug. 24, 1952; children—William H., Anthony Scott, Michael Lloyd. Engr., Gen. Electric Co., 1951-53, value analyst, 1953-56; sr. systems analyst Sperry Rand Univac, Indpls., 1956-63; application engr. Gen. Electric, Schenectady, 1963-65; supr. data processing N.Y. State Dept. Mental Hygiene, 1968-69; asst. dir. R/T systems N.Y. State Dept. Motor Vehicles, Albany, 1968-69; asso. EDP cons. N.Y. State Div. Budget, 1969-70; dir. adminstrv. and organizational analysis N.Y. State Dept. Motor Vehicles, 1970-74, dir. R/T systems, 1974-77, dir. systems coordination and control, 1977-81, dir. div. systems planning, 1981-85, dir. electronic data processing and adminstrv, analysis, 1985-86, dir. records mgmt. ops., 1986-89, dir. office records mgmt., 1989-90, ret., 1990. Active Boy Scouts Am. Served with USMC, 1943-46. Mem. Assn. Records Mgrs. and Adminstrn. Internat., Soc. Advancement Mgmt., IEEE, Adminstrv. Mgmt. Soc., Am.

Ordnance Soc. Methodist. Clubs: Masons, Scottish Rite, York Rite, Shriners, Royal Order of Jesters, Elks. Home: 34 Crestwood Dr Schenectady NY 12306-3325

FAHERTY, KEVIN M., insurance company executive; b. Bklyn., Dec. 10, 1943; s. Thomas F. and Alice (Mannion) F.; m. Suzanne Cantwell, Sept. 19, 1969; children: Michael, Stephen, James. Underwriting clk. U.S. Life, N.Y.C., 1962-64; underwriter Union Labor Life, N.Y.C., 1964-67; group adminstr. Frenkel & Co., N.Y.C., 1967-69; underwriting mgr. CNA Ins., N.Y.C., 1969-78, sr. mktg. exec., 1978-86; greater N.Y. regional mgr. Mutual of Omaha, Morristown, N.J., 1986—. Corp. U.S. Army N.G., 1964-70. Mem. Group Ins. Assn. of N.Y. (pres. 1984-86), Friends of Columbus Coun. (bd. dirs., chmn. 1973-74), KC (Grand Knight 1972). Republican. Roman Catholic. Office: Mutual of Omaha 10 Madison Ave PO Box 2149 Morristown NJ 07962-2149

FAHEY, JAMES EDWARD, financial executive; b. N.Y.C., May 4, 1953; s. John Michael and Kathleen Rose (Brady) F. BBA, Iona Coll., New Rochelle, N.Y., 1975, MBA, 1977. Territory asst. European Am. Bank, N.Y.C., 1978-80; internat. analyst Texaco, Inc., White Plains, N.Y., 1981-83; mgr. internat. treasury Am. Standard Inc., N.Y.C., 1984-88; asst. treas. Perkin Elmer Internat., Inc., 1988—; sr. mgr. internat. treasury Perkin Elmer Corp., Norwalk, Conn., 1988—. Active Friends of Am. Cancer Soc., N.Y.C., 1986-90. Mem. Soc. Internat. Treas., N.Y. Corp. Treasury Assn. Home: 178 E 80th St New York NY 10021-0450 Office: Perkin Elmer Corp 761 Main Ave Norwalk CT 06859-0001

FAHEY, PATRICIA ANNE, editor; b. Methuen, Mass., Aug. 6, 1957; d. Edward James and Evelyn Fay (Benedix) Howard; m. Thomas Francis Fahey, Jr., Mar. 5, 1982; children: Ryan Thomas, Caitlin Elizabeth (dec.), Emily Catherine. AA in Liberal Arts with highest honors, No. Essex Community Coll., Haverhill, Mass., 1977; BA in English magna cum laude, Notre Dame Coll., Manchester, N.H., 1987. News reporter Salem (N.H.) Observer, 1975-77, news editor, 1977-78; news corr. Union Leader Corp., Manchester, N.H., 1978-80; lifestyle reporter Union Leader Corp., Manchester, 1980-82, news reporter, 1982-86, copy editor, 1986—. Mem. Future Planning Commn., Town of Auburn, N.H., 1983-84; mem. adv. bd. Manchester Assn. Retarded Citizens, 1984-85. Recipient Community Service award Am. Cancer Soc., 1985. Mem. The Newspaper Guild. Congregationalist. Home: 2 Timmins Rd Bow NH 03304-4207 Office: Union Leader Corp PO Box 9555 Manchester NH 03108-9555

FAHLUND, MICHAEL JAY, museum administrator, consultant; b. Grand Rapids, Mich., May 17, 1949; s. George T.R. and Angeline C. (VanDenberg) F.; m. Pamela A. Stuart, Dec. 23, 1972. BA, Vassar Coll., 1972; MA, U. Calif., Berkeley, 1975, MS, 1976. Fellow Nat. Endowment for the Arts, Washington, 1976; project coord. Office Acad. V.P. U. Calif., Berkeley, 1977-79; exec. asst. to dir. The Detroit Inst. Arts, 1979-83, assoc. dir. devel., 1983-85; dir. devel. Plimoth Plantation, Plymouth, Mass., 1985-89; asst. dir. The Carnegie Mus. of Art, Pitts., 1989—. Alfred E. Hertz fellow U. Calif., 1973-74, 74-75, W.K. Rose fellow Vassar Coll., 1976, Fulbright-Hays fellow to Rome, 1976. Mem. Detroit Econ. Club, Planned Giving of New Eng., Am. Assn. Mus. Office: The Carnegie Mus of Art 4400 Forbes Ave Pittsburgh PA 15213-4080

FAHMY, IBRAHIM MOUNIR, hotel executive; b. Alexandria, Egypt, July 4, 1943; came to U.S., 1986; s. Ambassador Mounir Ibrahim and Aziza (Kelada) F.; m. Brenda Lee Chenier, Sept. 18, 1970 (div. Jan. 1991); children: Susun Lee, Christine Lynn. Certs., St. Mark's Coll., Alexandria, 1949-62; student, U. Alexandria, 1962-62. V.p., gen. mgr. King Edward Hotel, Toronto, Can., 1982-86; sr. v.p. Can. Forte Hotels Inc., N.Y.C., 1986—; exec. v.p. Forte Hotels Inc., San Diego, Calif., 1986—; dir. Hotel Assn. Met. Toronto, Ont. Hostelry Inst.; mem. adv. com. Humber Coll. Vol. Kidney Found., Muscular Dystrophy, The Can. Children's Found. Mem. Internat. Wine & Food Soc. Home and Office: Watergate Hotel 2650 Virginia Ave NW Washington DC 20037

FAIR, CHARLES MAITLAND, neuroscientist, author; b. N.Y.C., Sept. 18, 1916; s. Charles Maitland Fair and Gertrude Modora (Bryan) Knapp; m. Mary Katherine Ruddy, Feb. 2, 1952 (div. 1980); children: Ellen, Katherine, Charles (dec.); m. Louise Sadler Kiessling, May 5, 1980. Guggenheim fellow Brain Rsch. Inst., UCLA, 1963-64; resident scientist MIT Neuroscis. Rsch. Program, 1964; lab. scientist Mass. Gen. Hosp., Boston, 1966-67, MIT, 1967; officer Synax, Somerville, Mass., 1970-72. Author: The Physical Foundations of the Psyche, 1963, The Dying Self, 1969, From the Jaws of Victory, 1971, The New Nonsense, 1974, Memory and Central Nervous Organization, 1988, Cortical Memory Functions, 1992; contbr. articles and revs. to profl. jours. With USNR, 1938. Am. Acad. Arts. and Scis. grantee, 1961. Mem. AAAS, N.Y. Acad. Sci. Democrat. Home: Jerry Brown Farm 110 Firelane # 1 Wakefield RI 02879-9802

FAIRBAIRN, BARBARA JEAN, program director; b. N.Y.C., May 31, 1950; d. Desmond Noble and Anne Elizabeth (Fisher) F. BA, Stetson U., 1972; MS, W.Va. U., 1976. Vol. counselor Roslyn (N.Y.) Walk-In Crisis Ctr., 1972-74; customer svc. corr. Pubs. Clearing House, Port Washington, N.Y., 1973-75; coord. svcs. for students with disabilities Binghamton (N.Y.) U., 1977—; actress Leonard Melfi Repertory Co.; producer Rainbow-Time Children's Theater Co. Bd. dirs. Sheltered Workshop for Disabled, Inc., Rehab. Svcs. Inc., Binghamton; past bd. dirs. So. Tier Independence Ctr.; active Peace Making Task Force Susquehanna Valley Presbytery, Binghamton; ruling elder Conklin Presbyn. Ch. Named Woman of Achievement, Soroptimists at Broome County Status of Women Coun., 1985. Mem. ACA, Assn. Handicapped Student Svcs. Programs Post-Secondary Edn. Office: SUNY Binghamton PO Box 6000 Binghamton NY 13902-6000

FAIRBANKS, DOUGLAS ELTON, JR., actor, producer, writer, corporation director; b. N.Y.C., Dec. 9, 1909; s. Douglas Elton and Anna Beth (Sully) F.; m. Lucille LeSueur (Joan Crawford), June 1929 (div. 1933); m. Mary Lee Epling, Apr. 22, 1939 (dec. Sept. 1988); children: Daphne Fairbanks-Weston, Victoria Van Gerbig, Melissa Morant; m. Vera Shelton, May 30, 1991. Student, Bovée and Collegiate Schs., N.Y.; cadet, Knickerbocker Greys, N.Y., Harvard Mil. Sch., L.A.; student, Pasadena (Calif.) Poly.; pvt. tutoring, London, Paris, L.A.; DFA (hon.), Westminster Coll., 1966, Sr. Churchill fellow; vis. fellow, St. Cross Coll., Oxford U.; M.A., Oxford U., 1971; LLD (hon.), Denver U., 1974; fellow, Boston U. Libraries, 1978. Chmn. Dougfair Corp. and subsidiaries, The Fairbanks Co., Calif., 1946, Fairtel Corp., N.Y., 1969, Douglas Fairbanks Ltd., Eng., 1952—, (and asso. cos.), 1952-58; past pres. Boltons Trading Co., Inc.; also past dir. or cons. several internat. bus. corps., U.S., Europe, Asia; gov. Am. Mus. in Britain; trustee Edwina Mountbatten Trust; mem. exec. com., bd. govs. Royal Shakespeare Theatre, Stratford-on-Avon, Eng.; bd. govs. Ditchley Found., U.K., U.S.; mem. adv. com. Denver Ctr. for Performing Arts; chmn. Internat. Cultural Ctr. for Youth, Jerusalem; lectr. attached Joint Chiefs Staff, Washington, 1971-81. Author (autobiographies) The Fairbanks Album (with Richard Schickel), 1975, Salad Days, 1988, A Hell of a War, 1992, also screen plays, articles, polit. essays, short stories; exhibitor paintings and sculpture; began film career, 1923, stage career, 1927; acted in more than 75 films including 3 in French (produced or co-produced 15 in U.S. and U.K.), and about 20 plays U.S., Can., Australia, and U.K.; produced 160 1-act TV plays, 1953-58; films include Stella Dallas, A Woman of Affairs, The Barker, Chances, Union Depot, Little Caesar, Dawn Patrol, Catherine the Great, The Little Accident, The Amateur Gentleman, Accused, Outward Bound, Morning Glory, The Narrow Corner, The Young in Heart, Having Wonderful Time, The Joy of Living, The Prisoner of Zenda, Gunga Din, The Rage of Paris, The Corsican Brothers, Angels Over Broadway, Lady in Ermine, Sinbad the Sailor, The Exile, The Fighting O'Flynn, State Secret, Ghost Story, others; plays include The Dummy, Toward the Light, Romeo and Juliet, Young Woodley, The Jest, Man in Possession, Saturday's Children, The Winding Stairway, Moonlight Is Silver, My Fair Lady, The Pleasure of His Company, The Secretary Bird, Present Laughter, Out on a Limb; numerous TV and radio plays for CBS, NBC, ABC, CBC, BBC, TV narrations for symphony orchs. throughout U.S. and Europe, various song recordings for Columbia, Caedman, others; organized own prodn. co., Criterion Films Corp., U.K., 1934; subject of biography Knight Errant (by Brian Connell), 1955. Nat. vice-chmn. Com. Defend America by Aiding Allies, 1940-41, Franco-British War Relief Assn., 1939-41; Presdl. envoy for spl. S.Am. mission, 1941; spl. advisor to comdr. 6th Fleet, NATO, 1969-70; U.S. naval del. SEATO Conf., London, 1971; Nat. v.p. Am. Assn. For UN, 1946-63; nat. chmn. Com. for CARE, 1946-50; chmn. Am. Relief for Korea, 1950-53. Served to capt. USNR, 1941-52, ETO. Decorated Silver Star, Combat Legion of Merit with valor attachment U.S.; knight comdr. Order Brit. Empire; knight Order St. John of Jerusalem; D.S.C. (U.K.); officer Legion of Honor (mil. and civil); Croix de Guerre with palm (France); knight comdr. Order George I (Greece); comdr. Order Orange-Nassau (Netherlands); War Cross for Mil. Valor; comdr. Order of Merit; Star of Italian Solidarity (Italy); knight comdr. Order of Merit (Chile); officer Order So. Cross (Brazil); officer Order of the Crown (Belgium); Comdr. Cross Order of Merit (Fed. Rep. Germany); Nat. medal of Korea; Med. for Svc. Murmansk Naval Escort of Convoys (USSR); Hon. Citizen of Korea; others; recipient Gold Medal of Honor VFW, 1966; Armed Forces award, 1972; Am. Image award, 1976; award for contbn. to arts U. Notre Dame, 1971; award for contbn. to world understanding and peace World Affairs Council, Phila., 1978; Spl. award for internat. artistic achievements New Sch. for Social Research, 1978; Nat. Humanitarian award NCCJ, 1979; Nat. Brotherhood award Salvation Army, 1980; Ann. Nat. Vet.'s Day award, 1981; Illustrious Moderns award, 1981; St. Nicholas Soc. Medal of Merit, 1986; Apptd. spl. post-war missions State Dept. Mem. Council Fgn. Rels. (councilor), Brit-Am. Alumni Assn. (pres. 1950-57), Am. Soc. Order St. John Jerusalem (gov. 1970—, dep. vice chancellor), Groupe Navale d'Assaut (hon.), Battalion de Choc (hon.), Assn. des Anciens Combatants (France), Pilgrim's Soc. U.S. (bd. dirs.), Racquet Club (Chgo.), Brook Club, Century Club, Knickerbocker Club (N.Y.C.), Myopia Hunt Club (hon.), Met. Club (Washington), Reading Room (Newport, R.I.), White's Club, Beefsteak Club, Garrick Club, Mil. Club, R.A.C. (London), Traveller's Club (Paris). Episcopalian. Home: The Beekman 575 Park Ave New York NY 10021 Office: Inverness Corp 545 Madison Ave New York NY 10022-4219

FAIRCHILD, SAMUEL WILSON, professional services company executive, former federal agency administrator; b. Ft. Eustis, Va., July 16, 1954; s. Henry Howell and Ruby Mae (Love) F.; m. Linda Elizabeth Doremus, May 17, 1986; 1 child, Elizabeth Christine. BS, BA, Coll. of William and Mary, 1977. Cons. ITT, Inc., Smithfield, Va., 1977; v.p., gen. mgr. P.A., Inc., Hampton, Va., 1977-83; sr. policy advisor Exec. Office of the Pres., Washington, 1983-89; dep. asst. sec. U.S. Dept. Transp., Washington, 1989-91; v.p., sr. fellow Ctr. for Tech. and Pub. Policy Rsch. BDM Internat., Inc., McLean, Va., 1991—. Author, editor: Moving America, 1989. Active Boy Scouts Am., Irving, Tex., 1972—, mem. World Scout Bur., Geneva, 1972-80, Coun. for Excellence in Govt.; co-chmn. ARC, Alexandria, Va., 1988-90. Recipient Disting. Alumni award Christopher Newport Coll., 1990; Usry Garland scholar Coll. William and Mary/Christopher Newport Coll., 1975. Mem. NDTA, NAA, Coun. for Excellence in Government, Aero Club. Republican. Presbyterian. Home: 7402 Colshire Dr Mc Lean VA 22102 Office: BDM Internat Inc 7915 Jones Branch Dr Mc Lean VA 22102-3396

FAIRFIELD-SONN, JAMES WILLED, management educator and consultant; b. Nashua, N.H., Aug. 21, 1948; s. David Alexander and Christine Mary (Fairfield) Sonn; m. Lynn Groark, July 3, 1982; 1 child, Anne Madeline. MS, Cornell U., 1979; MA, Yale U., 1980, MPhil, 1982, PhD, 1985. Mgr. office adminstrn. Hartford Ins. Group, Indpls., 1972-76; asst. prof. mgmt. U. Hartford, West Hartford, Conn., 1982-88, assoc. prof., 1988—, chmn. mgmt. dept., 1987-90; pres. Fairfield-Sonn Assocs., Old Lyme, Conn., 1981—. Contbr. articles and revs. to profl. jours. Cornell U. indsl. and labor rels. fellow, 1977-78, Yale U. fellow, 1978-82, Olin fellow, 1981. Mem. Acad. Mgmt., Am. Psychol. Assn., Internat. Personnel Mgmt. Assn., Internat. Coun. for Small Bus., Ea. Acad. Mgmt., Assn. Yale Alumni (chmn. grad. and profl. schs. com. 1982-83). Republican. Congregationalist. Home and Office: PO Box 1047 Old Lyme CT 06371

FAIRLEY, RICHARD L., university administrator; b. Washington, July 16, 1933; s. Richmond Alvin and Gladys (Wilkinson) F.; m. Wilma King Holmes, Aug. 25, 1955 (div. Jan. 1980); children: Ricki Louise, Sharon Renee; m. Charlestine Dawson. BA, Dartmouth Coll., 1935; MA, Stanford U., 1969; EdD, U. Mass., 1974; DHL, Rust Coll., Holly Springs, Miss., 1988, St. Pauls Coll., Laurenceville, Va., 1989. Tchr. D.C. Pub. Sch. Systems, Washington, 1955-61; mem. faculty Eastern Tng. Ctr., Dept. Def. Staff Coll., Bklyn., 1961-64; ednl. specialist U.S. Office of Edn., Washington, 1964-65, regional dir., 1965-68, chief so. br., 1968-70, dep. commr., 1970-80, dpe. asst. sec., dir., 1980-90; exec. v.p. U. D.C., Washington, 1990—; mem. faculty Nova U., Ft. Lauderdale, Fla., 1987—, Nat. Coll. Edn., McLean, Va., 1989—. Author numerous articles and govt. publs. U.s. Office of Edn. fellow, 1966, Nat. Inst. Pub. Affairs fellow, 1968. Mem. NEA, NAACP, Am. Coun. on Edn., Nat. Urban League, NAFEO, Kappa Phi Kappa. Home: 608 Cloverfield Pl Silver Spring MD 20910-4305 Office: US Dept Edn 400 Maryland Ave SW Washington DC 20202-0002

FAIRWEATHER, WILLIAM ROSS, small business owner; b. San Francisco, Nov. 21, 1943. AB, U. Calif., Berkeley, 1964; MS, Cornell U., 1966; PhD, U. Wash., 1973. From sr. assoc. to ptnr. Electronic Filing Svcs., Silver Spring, Md., 1987—. Office: Electronic Filing Svcs 1320 Downs Dr Silver Spring MD 20904-2035

FAISON, LINDA KAY GAINEY, association professional; b. Petersburg, Va., Aug. 11, 1952; d. Ellis Cleon and Lillian Earle (Clark) Gainey; m. Marvin Lee Faison, Sept. 28, 1974. BS in Edn. summa cum laude, Longwood Coll., Farmville, Va., 1974. Tchr. Prince George County (Va.) Schs., 1976-82; sec. Tams Witmark Music Pub., N.Y.C., 1982-83; mktg. asst. Coty, div. Pfizer, N.Y.C., 1983-86; exec. asst. Avon Books div. Hearst Corp., N.Y.C., 1986-90, Am. Pharm. Assn., Washington, 1990—. Home: 3102 Southgate Dr #204 Alexandria VA 22306 Office: Am Pharm Assn 2215 Constitution Ave NW Washington DC 20037

FAIZ, ASIF, banker; b. Muzaffarabad Azad Kashmir, Pakistan, Jan. 29, 1947; came to U.S., 1969; s. Faiz Mohammed and Zohra (Sher Ali) Piracha; m. Surraya Noor Mohammed, Aug. 10, 1971; children: Lalarukh, Maryam, Aysha. BSCE with honors, Peshawar U., Pakistan, 1968; MSCE, Purdue U., 1971, PhD in Transp. Engring., 1975; postgrad., Mid. East Tech. U., Turkey, 1968-69, Va. Poly. Inst., Blackburg, 1988-89. Profl. engr., Pakistan. Rsch./teaching asst. Purdue U., West Lafayette, Ind., 1969-71, grad. instr., 1971-75; young profl. World Bank, Washington, 1975-76, economist, 1976-81, sr. economist, 1981, asst. to dir., West Africa Projects Dept., 1981-85, sr. transport. econ., East Asia and Pacific Region, 1985-86, advisor, Transp. Dept., 1986-89, hwys. advisor, Infrastructure Dept., 1989-92; div. chief infrastructure ops. World Bank, Brazil, Peru, Venezuela, 1992—; keynote speaker/chair several internat. confs. in U.S. and abroad. Co-author: Road Deterioration in Developing Countries-World Bank Policy Study, 1988; contbr. over 30 articles to profl. jours. Mem. transp. com. Little Hunting Creek Citizens Assn., Inc., Fairfax County, Va., 1978-79. Recipient Recognition cert. Internat. Road Fedn., Washington, 1989, Best Instr. award Purdue U., 1974. Mem. ASCE (Daniel Mead prize for Zone II 1974), Transp. Rsch. Bd., U.S. Nat. Rsch. Coun., Nat. Cooperative Hwy. Rsch. Program, Engring. Assn. Asia and Australasia, Permanent Internat. Assn. of Road Congresses, UN Environ. Program, Orgn. for Econ. Cooperation and Devel. Home: 8615 Camden St Alexandria VA 22308-2316 Office: World Bank 1818 H St NW Washington DC 20433-0002

FAKUNDINY, ROBERT HARRY, geologist, educator, consultant; b. Manitowoc, Wis., Feb. 11, 1940; s. Walter P. and Ann (Kakes) F.; m. Anne J. Finch, Jan. 28, 1978. BA in Geology, U. Calif., Riverside, 1962; MA in Geology, U. Tex., 1967, PhD in Geology, 1970. Vol. U.S. Peace Corps., Ghana, West Africa, 1963-65; assoc. scientist and sr. scientist N.Y. State Geol. Survey, Albany, 1970-78, state geologist and chief, 1978—; consulting geologist, Albany, 1967—, adj. asst. prof. SUNY, Albany, 1975-87; cons. to profl. groups, industries and govt. agys. Contbr. articles to profl. jours. Bd. trustees Esquatak Town Hist. Soc., 1983-86; bd. dirs. N.E. Sci. Found., 1988-91; advisor New England River Basins Commn., 1973-75; mem. site selection com. CoCorp, 1978—; mem. com. on energy resources IOCC, 1978-89, mem. com. on oil and gas info. and data base mgmt., 1989—. Hogg fellow U. Tex., 1969; recipient numerous scholarships and grants; chmn. N.Am. Com. on Stratigraphic Nomenclature, 1988. Fellow Geol. Soc. Am. (engring. geology div. mgmt. bd., 1987), Geol. Assn. Can.; mem. Am. Assn. Petroleum Geologists, Am. Geophysical Union, AAAS, Assn. Am. State Geologists (v.p. 1989-90, pres.-elect 1990-91, pres. 1991-92, chmn. low-level radioactive waste com 1980-86, liaison to COCORP/EDGE 1978—, chmn. radon com. 1990-91), Am. Inst. Profl. Geologists (cert., nat. selection com. 1991—, del. to Soviet Union 1990), Nat. Assn. Geology Tchrs., N.Y. Acad. Sci., Assn. Earth Sci. Editors, Soc. Exploration Pateontologists and Mineralogists, Assn. Engring. Geologists, Assn. Women Geoscientists, Assn. Geoscientists for Internat. Devel., Multi Agy. Group for Neotechnics in Eatern Can., Buffalo Assn. Profl. Geologists, Sigma Xi, Sigma Gamma Epsilon. Achievements include research in seismic hazard determination, application of glacial studies to environmental issues, geology of low-level radioactive waste disposal, geologic structure of Adirondack Mountains. Home: River Rd #9J Rensselaer NY 12144-5112 Office: NY State Geol Survey CEC 3136 ESP Albany NY 12230

FALBER, HAROLD JULIUS, food service executive; b. Mt. Vernon, N.Y., Apr. 14, 1946; s. Max William and Cora (Leff) F.; m. Susan Levine, Sept. 14, 1986; 1 child, Aaron. Student, Hartwick Coll., 1963-65, C.W. Post Coll., 1965-67, MIT, 1981-82. Acct. exec. Scali, McCabe, Sloves, N.Y.C., 1967-71; advt. mgr. Volvo of N. Am., Rockleigh, N.J., 1972; acct. exec. Della Femina, Travisano & Ptnrs., N.Y.C., 1973-75; advt. mgr. Polaroid, Cambridge, Mass., 1976-82; dir. mktg. RJR Nabisco, N.Y.C., 1983-87; pres. Trade Area Restaurant Group, Inc., Stamford, Conn., 1987—, AOMAC Realty Group, Bridgeport, Conn., 1986—; cons. in field. Home: 26 Revere Ln Trumbull CT 06611 Office: Trade Area Restaurant Group 934 Hope St Stamford CT 06907-2201

FALCO, LOUIS, dancer, choreographer, dance company director; b. N.Y.C., Aug. 2, 1942. Studied with, Jose Limon, Charles Weidman, Martha Graham, Am. Ballet Theatre Sch. Participant Nat. Endowment Dance Touring Program; artist-in-residence numerous colls. and univs. throughout U.S. Prin. dancer Jose Limon Dance Co., 1960-70, toured Cen. and S.Am., N.Am., Europe and Far East, formed The Louis Falco Dance Co. Inc., 1967, since toured with co. throughout U.S., Can., Mexico and Europe, 10th tour, 1975; presents ann. seasons, N.Y.C.; works include Argot, 1967, Huescape, 1968, Timewright, 1969, Caviar, 1970, Ibid, 1970, Sleepers, 1971, Soap Opera, 1972, Avenue, 1973, Twopenny Portrait, 1973, Storeroom, 1974, Eclipse, 1974, Caterpillar, 1975, Pulp, 1975, Champagne, 1976, Hero, 1977, Tiger Rag, 1977, Escargot, 1978, Saltimbocca, 1979, Early Sunday Morning, 1979, Kate's Rag, 1980, Service Compris, 1980, Black & Blue, Little Boy; revived with Rudolph Nureyev Moor's Pavane, 1974, filmed for Dutch and German TV, choreographer: La Scala Opera Ballet, Alvin Ailey Dance Theatre, Boston Ballet, Washington Opera Soc., Caramoor Festival, Australian Ballet, Les Ballets Jazz de Montreal, Ballet Rambert and the, Netherlands Dance Theatre, Paris Opera Ballet Co.; choreographer: films Fame, 1979, Angel Heart, Leonard Part 6, (TV) Collisions, Photo Finish, Superfalco, Mixed Media Special, The Sleepers, Hero; choreographer, performer 6 episodes of TV series for RAI-TV of Italy, 1981; The Louis Falco Dance Co. Inc. is a non-profit corp. supported in part by Nat. Endowment for Arts, N.Y. State Coun. on Arts, many works are collaborations with prominent artists including Robert Indiana, Stanley Landsman, William Katz, Marisol; incorporates spoken dialogue in works. Recipient Harkness award, 1979. Address: 131 W 24th St New York NY 10011*

FALCON, RAYMOND JESUS, JR., lawyer; b. N.Y.C., Nov. 17, 1953; s. Raymond J. and Lolin (Lopez) F.; m. Debra Mary Bomeisl, June 4, 1977; children: Victoria Marie, Mark Daniel. BA, Columbia U., 1975; JD, Yale U., 1978. Bar: N.Y. 1979, U.S. Dist. Ct. (so. and ea. dist.) N.Y. 1979, U.S. Ct. Appeals (D.C. and 2d cirs.) 1983, Fla. 1987, N.J. 1988, U.S. Dist. Ct. N.J. 1988. Assoc. Webster and Sheffield, N.Y.C., 1978-82; ptnr. Falcon and Hom, N.Y.C., 1982-85; sr. atty. Degussa Corp., Ridgefield Park, N.J., 1985-88, v.p., sec., gen. counsel, 1989—. Contbr. articles to profl. jours. Dem. candidate Town Justice, Town of Rye, N.Y., 1983; Dem. jud. del., Westchester, N.Y., 1984—. Mem. ABA, N.Y. State Bar Assn., Assn. of Bar of City of N.Y., N.J. State Bar Assn., Fed. Bar Coun., Assn. Trial Lawyers Am., Columbia Alumni of Westchester County (v.p., dir. 1983—). Home: 582 Colonial Rd River Vale NJ 07675-6107 Office: Degussa Corp 65 Challenger Rd Ridgefield Park NJ 07660-2104

FALCONE, DAVID JOHN, psychology educator; b. Harrisburg, Pa., Dec. 10, 1950; s. Marino and Carrie Falcone; m. Connie Elaine Lehman, Apr. 11, 1972; children: Jessica, Dylan. BS, U. Dayton, 1972; MS, We. Ill. U., 1974; PhD, U. Ky., 1981. Instr. Acad. Health Scis., San Antonio, 1974-76, U. Ky., Lexington, 1978-79; asst. prof. psychology LaSalle U., Phila., 1981-86, assoc. prof., 1986—, chmn. dept., 1987—; rsch. appointment Dayton (Ohio) Bd. Edn., 1972-73; rsch. assoc. Addiction Rsch. Ctr., Nat. Inst. Drug Addiction, Lexington, 1976-77; rsch. cons. Grow, Inc., Lexington, 1978-80; statis. cons., 1985—. Author (monograph) Cooperatives, 1982; co-contbr. articles to profl. jours. 1st lt. U.S. Army, 1972-76. Fellow Lilly Co., 1981-82, PEW Found., 1984-85; faculty grantee LaSalle U., 1980, 84, 87. Mem. APA, Ea. Psychol. Assn., Jean Pioget Soc., Soc. Computers in Psychology. Democrat. Home: 6900 Henley St Philadelphia PA 19119-3414 Office: LaSalle U Dept Psychology Philadelphia PA 19141

FALCONE, SEBASTIAN ANTHONY, priest, academic administrator, educator; b. Rochester, N.Y., Oct. 15, 1927; s. Augustus Michael and Rose (Lanteri) F. Licentiate in Sacred Theology, Cath. U., 1961, postgrad., 1978—. Joined Capuchin-Franciscan Order, Roman Cath. Ch., 1943, ordained priest, 1951. Prof., dean St. Lawrence Sem., Beacon, N.Y., 1951-58; prof., rector Immaculate Heart Sem., Geneva, N.Y., 1961-67; prof. St. Bernard's Sem., Rochester, 1967—, acad. dean, 1972-78; acad. dean St. Bernards's Inst., Rochester, N.Y., 1981-88; pres., chief exec. officer St. Bernard's Inst., Rochester, N.Y., 1981—; regional councilor Capuchin-Franciscan Order, N.Y.C., 1955-65, vice-provincial, Newton, N.J., 1958-61; pres. Capuchin Ednl. Conf., N.Y.C., 1959-61, Franciscan Commitment Conf., Newton, 1963-72; mem. Rochester Ctr. for Theol. Studies, 1972—, co-chair, 1981—; cons. continuing edn. Diocese of Rochester. Author poetry, ency. articles, editorials; editor, contbr. various newsletters. Organizer House of Concern, Geneva, N.Y., 1966, Seneca Falls, N.Y., 1967. Mem. Am. Acad. Religion, Soc. Bibl. Lit. Office: St Bernard's Inst 1125 Park Ave Rochester NY 14610-1738

FALES, GREGG BOOTH, trade newsletter and magazine editor; b. N.Y.C., Dec. 18, 1945; s. Henry Whitman and Dorothy (Booth) F.; m. Mary Agatha Kohlberger; children: Hilary Alison, Elizabeth Rose. BA in Journalism, Lehigh U., 1969. Reporter Call-Chronicle Newspapers, Bethlehem, Pa., 1969-76; staff writer Sunday Call-Chronicle, Allentown, Pa., 1976-78; pres. Fourwinds Publishing Co., Allentown, 1978-79; news editor Wilkes-Barre Publishing Co., Wilkes-Barre, Pa., 1979-81; editor, co-founder Boca Raton Mag., Boca Raton, Fla., 1981-86; editor PaperAge, Westwood, N.J., 1986-89, Walden-Mott Corp., Oradell, N.J., 1989—; pres. 3-G Publishing, Westwood, 1986—. Post founder Explorers, Boy Scouts Am., Allentown, 1977; coach Youth Soccer Assn., Boca Raton, 1981. Mem. TAPPI. Republican. Presbyterian. Home: 342 Skyline Lakes Dr Ringwood NJ 07456-1921 Office: Walden Mott Corp 225 N Franklin Tpke Ramsey NJ 07446-1600

FALES, HENRY MARSHALL, chemist; b. N.Y.C., Feb. 12, 1927; s. Henry Marshall and Cecile Marie (Vatet) F.; m. Caroline Eleanor McCullagh, Dec. 20, 1947; children: Marsha Kent Fales Mazz, Suzanne Kent Fales Palmer, Henry Richard. BSc in Chemistry, Rutgers U., 1948, PhD in Organic Chemistry, 1953. Instr. Rutgers U., New Brunswick, N.J., 1953; rsch. chemist, lab. chief Nat. Heart, Lung and Blood Inst., NIH, Bethesda, Md., 1953—. With USN, 1944-46. Recipient Meritorious Svc. award U.S. Govt., 1987. Mem. Am. Chem. Soc., Am. Soc. Mass Spectrometry (sec., v.p. programs, pres.-elect). Home: 63 Orchard Way N Rockville MD 20854-6127 Office: NIH Rm 7N318 Bethesda MD 20892

FALK, CHARLES DAVID, chemical company executive; b. Chgo., July 18, 1939; s. Leo Maurice Falk and Mildred Francine (Bloom) Fellin; m. Diane Sena Miller, July 16, 1965 (div. Oct. 1980); 1 child, David Andrew; m. Margaret Elizabeth Pearce, Aug. 8, 1981. Student, Wright Jr. Coll., 1957-59; SB, U. Chgo., 1959-61, PhD, 1961-66; postgrad., U. Sussex, Brighton, England, 1966-67. Research chemist E.I. DuPont De Nemours, Wilmington, Del., 1967-70; plant mgr. Riverton Labs., Newark, 1970-74; research and devel. mgr. Engelhard Corp., Menlo Park, N.J., 1974-84; v.p. research and devel. Lopat Enterprises, Inc., Wanamassa, N.J., 1985—. Inventor, contbr. articles. Fellow NASA, 1962-65, postdoctoral Nat. Inst. Health, 1966-67. Mem. Am. Chem. Soc., Royal Soc. of Chemistry, Catalysis Club of N.Y.

Home: 3 Jacata Rd Marlboro NJ 07746-1524 Office: Lopat Enterprises Inc 1750 Bloomsbury Ave Asbury Park NJ 07712-3941

FALK, ELLIOTT GEORGE, college administrator; b. Balt., May 1, 1927; s. Harry Solomon and Ada (Levy) F.; m. Esther Kristman, June 28, 1959; children: Joshua Martin, David Alan. BA, Johns Hopkins U., 1948; cert. in pub. adminstrn., U. Ala., Tuscaloosa, 1949, U. Tenn., 1949, U. Ky., 1949. Fiscal analyst Ky. Dept. Revenue, Frankfort, 1949-52, asst. dir., dir. accounts and controls, 1952-55; field cons. Ky. Dept. Fin., Chgo., 1955-57; dir. accounts Pa. Gov.'s Office of Adminstrn., Harrisburg, 1957-61; exec. dir. Pa. State Pub. Sch. Bldg. Authority, Harrisburg, 1961-67; dep. exec. dir. Pa. Gen. State Authority, Harrisburg, 1967-68; v.p. for fin. affairs Robert Morris Coll., Pitts., 1968—. Loaned exec. Allegheny County Bd. Commrs., Pitts., 1980; chmn. Pa. Legis. Audit Adv. Com., 1970-72; mem., chmn. Allegheny County Hosp. Devel. Authority, Pitts., 1975-86; bd. dirs. Poale Zedeck Congregation, 1974—, pres., 1987-89. Recipient Award of Merit, Allegheny County Bd. Commrs., 1980; named Couple of Yr., Poale Zedeck Congregation, Pitts., 1991. Mem. Nat. Assn. Coll. & Univ. Bus. Officers (Cost Reduction award 1st place 1990), Ea. Assn. Coll. & Univ. Bus. Officers, Pitts. Coun. Higher Edn. (bus. officers com.), Hillel Acad. Pitts. (bd. dirs., pres. 1977-79). Democrat. Jewish. Home: 223 Anita Ave Pittsburgh PA 15217-3120 Office: Robert Morris Coll 600 5th Ave Pittsburgh PA 15219 also: Robert Morris Coll Narrows Run Rd Coraopolis PA 15108

FALK, GERHARD, education educator; came to U.S., 1931; s. Leonard and Hedwig (Cibulski) Falck; m. Ursula Adler, Jan. 8, 1949; children: Cynthia, Daniel, Clifford. BA, Western Res. U., 1953, MA, 1954; EdD, SUNY, Buffalo, 1969. Prof. SUNY, Buffalo, 1957—. Author: Jews in Christian Theology, 1992, The Academic Professional, 1991, Murder, 1990, Aging in America, 1987; contbr. articles to profl. publs. Home: 109 Louvaine Dr Buffalo NY 14223-2743 Office: State Coll NY 1300 Elmwood Ave Buffalo NY 14222-1095

FALK, GLENN EDWARD, electrical engineer; b. Buffalo, June 15, 1965; s. Frank and Marlene Falk. BS in Elec. Engring., GMI Engring. & Mgmt. Inst., Detroit, 1988. Coop student CPC div. Gen. Motors, Linden, N.J., 1983-87, paint process engr. CPC div., 1987—. Mem. IEEE, Tau Beta Pi, Eta Kappa Nu. Home: 2 Quail Ct Shelton CT 06484-4820

FALK, HARVEY L., apparel company executive; b. 1934. Grad., NYU, 1955. With Clarence Rainess & Co., N.Y.C., 1955-64, Man Mfg., Inc., 1964-77, BTK Industries, Inc., 1977-82; with Liz Claiborne, Inc., N.Y.C., 1982—, successively sr. v.p. fin., sr. v.p. and treas., exec. v.p. fin., now pres., also bd. dirs. Office: Liz Claiborne Inc 1441 Broadway New York NY 10018-2002*

FALK, JOAN FRANCES, public relations executive; b. Flushing, N.Y., Jan. 15, 1936; d. Leo Carl Hjalmar and Frances Louise (Masin) F. Cert., Parsons Sch. Design, N.Y.C., 1955; BS, NYU, 1956, MBA, 1958. Assoc. editor Fairchild's Fin. Manual, N.Y.C., 1956-58; editor, costs mgr. Western Printing & Lithography, N.Y.C., 1958-61; dir. rsch. and costs Grolier, Inc., N.Y.C., 1961-64; budget supr. Ted Bates & Co., N.Y.C., 1965-82; bus. mgr. N.W. Ayer Pub. Rels. (Div. of N.W. Ayer, Inc.), N.Y.C., 1982—, Diamond Info. Ctr. (Div. of N.W. Ayer, Inc.), N.Y.C., 1992—. Contbr. photographs to Grolier Internat., 1964, Encyclopedia Brittanica, 1970. Active Broadway Flushing Homeowners; vol. fundraiser pub. broadcast TV, WNET, N.Y.C., WLIW, L.I. Mem. Daus. of Nile (queen of Al Kanbay Temple #22 1970, supreme temple officer 1980), Order Ea. Star (matron of Bayside Pleiades #737 1962, dist. dep. grand matron 1987), Orgn. Triangles (past queen of Rising Star #69, Capital award Nat. Leadership Coun. 1991), Bayside High Sch. Alumni Assn. Republican. Lutheran. Home: 164-16 32d Ave Flushing NY 11358 Office: NW Ayer 825 8th Ave New York NY 10019-7416

FALK, KATHERINE, physician, psychiatrist; b. N.Y.C., June 17, 1944; d. Joseph G. and Hilda (Bronberg) F. AB, Barnard Coll., 1966; MD, Mt. Sinai Sch. of Medicine, 1970. Diplomate Am. Bd. Psychiatry and Neurology. Intern St. Luke's Hosp., N.Y.C., 1970-71, asst. resident, 1971-72, resident in psychiatry, 1972-75; pvt. practice N.Y.C., 1975—; asst. unit chief Payne Whitney Clinic, N.Y. Hosp., Cornell Med. Ctr., N.Y.C., 1975-76, acting unit chief, 1976-77; psychiatrist Day Hosp., N.Y. Hosp., N.Y.C., 1975-81; founder, pres. Project for Psychiat. Outreach to the Homeless, Inc., N.Y.C., 1991—; psychiatric cons. Inst. for Crippled and Disabled, N.Y.C., 1977-78, Student Health Svc., Columbia Presbyn. Med. Ctr., 1977-78; chmn. task force on vol. svcs. tothe homeless, N.Y. Dist. Branch of Am. Psychiatric Assn., 1985—; asst. prof. psychiatry, Columbia U. Coll. of Physicians and Surgeons, Columbia Presbyn. Med. Ctr., 1981—. Recipient Disting. Alumnae award, The Birch Wathen Sch., N.Y.C., 1989. Fellow Am. Psychiat. Assn., Am. Women's Med. Assn., Physicians for Social Responsibility, Project for Psychiat. Outreach to the Homeless (founder, pres.). Office: 141 E 88th St New York NY 10128-2248

FALK, LLOYD LEOPOLD, water pollution control consultant; b. Ocean Grove, N.J., Nov. 6, 1919; s. Leroy and Della (Blum) F.; m. Eleanor Ruth McCoy, Sept. 9, 1945; children: David Lawrence, Laurie Ann, Gary Lee. BS in Chemistry, Rutgers U., 1941, PhD in Sanitation, 1949. Rsch. assoc. Rutgers U., New Brunswick, N.J., 1945-49; cns. E.I. duPont de Nemours & Co., Wilmington, Del., 1949-76, prin. cons., 1977-81; cons. Wilmington, Del., 1982—. Contbr. articles to profl. jours. Mem. water resources adv. com. Water Resources Agy. for New Castle County, Del., 1974-91. 1st lt. USAF, 1943-45, ETO. Fellow Delmarva Ornithol. Soc. (pres. 1969-71); mem. Am. Chem. Soc., Water Environment Fedn. (life), Am. Birding Assn., Cape May Bird Observatory, N.J. Audubon Soc., Md. Ornithol. Soc., Am. Recorder Soc., Phi Beta Kappa, Phi Lambda Upsilon, Sigma Xi. Home: 123 Bette Rd Wilmington DE 19803-3430

FALK, PATRICK GEORGE ALEXANDER, information sciences professional; b. Geneva, June 18, 1944; s. Jean-Louis Camille and Janie (Uhlmann) F.; m. Helen T. Bielinski, Dec. 22, 1973. BS in Aero. and Astronautics Engring., NYU, 1972; MS in Ops. Rsch., MIT, 1974. Cert. airline transp. pilot. Logistic cons. F. Uhlmann-Eyraud S.A., Geneva, 1965-68; cons. Procter & Gamble Co., Cin., 1974-76, Am. Can Co., Greenwich, Conn., 1976-77; project mgr. Internat. Paper Co., Purchase, N.Y., 1977-82; mng. ptnr. InfoTech, Norwalk, Conn., 1982—; founder Resource Mgmt. Systems, Cambridge, Mass., PSA/InfoTech, Norwalk, Fairfield County (Conn.) Small Bus. Sch.; pres. Fairfield County Bus. Roundtable, 1982-85; chmn. MIT Enterprise Forum, Fairfield County, 1985-87. Contbr. articles to profl. jours. Capt. CAP, USAF Aux. Unit, 1992—. Recipient Alexander Klemin award Daniel Guggenheim Sch., N.Y.C., 1973, George Granger award George Granger Found., N.Y.C., 1973, Founders Day award NYU, 1973. Mem. MIT Alumni Ctr. of N.Y., Wings Club, Soc. Nautique de Geneve, Sigma Xi, Tau Beta Pi. Office: InfoTech 24 Grey Hollow Rd Norwalk CT 06850-1305

FALK, ROBERT BARCLAY, JR., anesthesiologist, educator; b. Lancaster, Pa., July 1, 1945; s. Robert Barclay and Miriam (Neff) F.; BA, Franklin and Marshall Coll., 1967; MD, Jefferson Med. Coll., 1971; m. Carol Anne Gundel, May 30, 1970; 1 child, Juliana Gundel. Intern, Conemaugh Valley Meml. Hosp., Johnstown, Pa., 1971-72; resident in anesthesiology M.H. Hershey Med. Sch. Hosp., 1974-77; partner Anesthesia Assos., Lancaster, 1977—; staff anesthesiologist Lancaster Gen. Hosp., 1977—; clin. asst. prof. dept. anesthesiology Hershey (Pa.) Med. Sch., 1977—, vice chmn. dept. anesthesiology, 1984-85, chmn., 1985. Participant alumni phonathon Franklin and Marshall Coll., 1978-81, vice chmn., 1981, chmn., 1983, mem. alumni admissions com., 1977-79, chmn., 1980-87, chmn. 20th reunion gift com.; mem. Lancaster Regional Alumni Council, 1987-91, trustee athletic com., 1988—; mem. Lancester Area Arts Coun., 1989-91; Sunday sch. tchr. Trinity Lutheran Ch., Lancaster, 1977-80; bd. dirs. Lancaster Summer Arts Festival, 1981—, v.p., 1982-84, pres., 1985-90; bd. dirs. Pa. Acad. Music, 1991—, vice-chmn., 1991—. Lt. M.C., USNR, 1972-74. Diplomate Am. Bd. Anesthesiology. Mem. AMA, Am. Soc. Anesthesiologists, Pa. Soc. Anesthesiologists, Internat. Anesthesia Rsch. Soc., Pa. Med. Soc., Lancaster Country Club, Hamilton Club, Masons, Shriners. Republican. Contbr. articles in field to profl. jours. Home: 1025 Marietta Ave Lancaster PA 17603-3106 Office: Anesthesia Assocs 133 E Frederick St Lancaster PA 17602-2294

FALKIE, THOMAS VICTOR, mining engineer, natural resources company executive; b. Mount Carmel, Pa., Sept. 5, 1934; s. Victor J. and Aldona M. Falkie; m. Jean C. Broscius, Nov. 27, 1957; children: Ann, Thomas, Lawrence, Michael, Christine. BS in Mining Engring., Pa. State U., 1956, MS in Mining Engring., 1958, PhD in Mining Engring., 1961. Fellow, research asst. Pa. State U., University Park, 1956-61; various staff and managerial positions Internat. Minerals and Chem. Corp., Skokie, Ill., 1961-69, Bartow, Fla., 1961-69; prof., head mineral engring. dept. Pa. State U., 1969-73; dir. U.S. Bur. Mines Dept. Interior, Washington, 1974-77; pres. Berwind Natural Resources Corp., Phila., 1977; bd. dir. Berwind Natural Resources Co.; bd. dir. Cyprus Minerals Co.; adj. prof. indsl. engring. U. Fla./U. So. Fla., 1966; cons. UN, 1971-73; chmn. coal task force project ind. study U.S. Govt., 1974; chmn. interagy. task force Fed. Council on Sci. and Tech., 1975-76; nat. arbitrator of joint industry health and safety com. of United Mine Workers and Bituminous Coal Operators Assn., 1973; mem. bd. mineral and energy resources NRC, 1982-88; mem. adv. com. mining and mineral resources rsch. Dept. Interior, 1988—. Contbr. articles to profl. jours. Mem. Soc. Mining Engrs. of AIME (disting. mem., v.p. 1977-79, bd. dirs. 1976-79, 84-87, bd. dirs. 1971-75, 84-87, pres. 1985, Henry Kumb lectr. 1977-78), AIME (chmn. Phila. sect.. bd. dirs. 1980-81, pres. 1988, Erskine Ramsay medal 1991), Pa. Coal Assn. (bd. dirs. 1980-84), Nat. Coal Assn. (bd. dirs. 1980—), Nat. Acad. of Engring., Mining and Metall. Soc. Am., Sigma Gamma Epsilon, Tau Beta Pi, Union League Club (Phila.). Republican. Roman Catholic. Home: 347 Echo Valley Ln Newtown Square PA 19073-1619 Office: 3000 Centre Sq W 1500 Market St Philadelphia PA 19102

FALKOWITZ, DANIEL, clothing manufacturing company executive; b. Wilkes-Barre, Pa., Oct. 2, 1936; s. Joseph and Esther (Wolzinger) F.; m. Sharon Freed, July 10, 1960; children: Lisa Joan, Kenneth Jay, Steven James. BS in Commerce and Fin., Wilkes Coll., 1958. CPA, Pa. With Laventhol, Krekstein, Horwath & Horwath, CPAs, Wilkes-Barre, 1958-65; asst. contr., then contr., asst. treas. Leslie Fay Inc. (name now Leslie Fay Cos., Inc.), Wilkes-Barre, 1965-78; corp. treas. Leslie Fay Inc., Wilkes-Barre, 1978—. Chmn. sch. bd. Temple Israel, Wilkes-Barre, 1976-77, trustee Temple, 1976-79; treas. Jewish Community Ctr., 1982-86, v.p., 1986-88, pres., 1988-90; bd. dirs. Jewish Family Svc. Greater Wilkes-Barre, 1991—. Mem. AICPA, Pa. Inst. CPAs, Jewish War Vets., B'nai B'rith (lodge pres. 1969-70,bd. dirs. housing found. 1969-70, trustee 1970—). Office: The Leslie Fay Cos Inc Rt 325 PO Box D Wilkes Barre PA 18773

FALKOWITZ, ED, corporate executive, treasurer; b. Phila., Oct. 15, 1946; s. Louis and Sylvia (Sidewater) F. BS in Acctg., Calif. State U., Long Beach, 1969; MBA, Fordham U., 1972. CMA, CPA. Acctg. mgr. Butler Aviation Internat., Paramus, N.J., 1973-76; controller Roberts Consol. Industries, City of Industry, Calif., 1976-82; chief fin. officer Landmark Edn., San Francisco, 1982-83; chief operating officer Action Techs., San Francisco, 1983-84; owner Fin. Freedom Group, San Francisco, 1984-88; v.p., chief fin. officer Laticorp, San Francisco, 1988-89; v.p., treas. Thorn EMI, Boston, 1989—. Mem. ASTD, Nat. Assn. Accts., Fin. Execs. Inst., U.S./U.K. Treas.'s Assn. Home: PO Box 620264 Newton Lower Falls MA 02162

FALLAW, WALTER ROBERT, JR., college educator; b. Durham, N.C., Mar. 19, 1935; s. Walter Robert and Amy Wilson (Childs) F.; m. Margaret Ruth Quoos, June 25, 1964; children: Stephen, Peter, Michael, Timothy. AB, Duke U., 1957; MA, Princeton U., 1959, PhD, 1966. Asst. history prof. U. N.C., 1960-70; history prof., history dept. chair Washington Coll., Chestertown, Md., 1970—. Contbr. articles to profl. books. Mem. Am. Hist. Assoc., Soc. for Historians, Am. Republic. Home: 530 N Kent St Chestertown MD 21620-1661 Office: Washington College Washington Ave Chestertown MD 21620-1616

FALLER, JACK W., chemistry educator; b. Louisville, Jan. 7, 1942; s. John William and Anna Mae (Ratterman) F.; m. Eleanor Warren, Nov. 24, 1979. BS, U. Louisville, 1963, MS, 1964; PhD, MIT, 1967; MA (hon.), Yale U., 1975. Prof. chemistry Yale U., New Haven. Home: 14 Turtle Bay Dr Branford CT 06405 Office: Yale U PO Box 6666 New Haven CT 06491-8118

FALLESEN, GARY DAVID, journalist; b. Rochester, N.Y., July 24, 1959; s. Karl David and Mary Lou (Putnam) F.; m. Elaine Gertrude Busse, July 3, 1982; 1 child, Jesse Dane. BA, St. John Fisher Coll., Rochester, 1981. Sports clk. Democrat & Chronicle, Rochester, 1979-82, sports writer, 1982-88, sports columnist, 1988—. Contbr. articles to Soccer Am., Soccer World, Sporting News, other sports pubs. Named Sports Writer of the Yr., N.Y. State Wrestling Coaches Assn., 1984, Rochester Press-Radio Club, 1986, Hon. Mention, N.Y. State AP Writers Contest, 1989. Mem. Profl. Football Writers Am. (2d place columns 1990, 1st place columns 1991), Golf Writers Assn. Am. Lutheran. Office: Dem & Chronicle 55 Exchange Blvd Rochester NY 14614-2001

FALLOWS, JAMES MACKENZIE, magazine editor; b. Phila., Aug. 2, 1949; s. James Albert and Jean (Mackenzie) F.; m. Deborah Jean Zerad, June 22, 1971; children: Thomas Mackenzie, Tad Andrew. B.A. magna cum laude, Harvard U., 1970; diploma in econ. devel. (Rhodes scholar), Oxford U., 1972. Staff editor Washington Monthly, 1972-74; free-lance mag. writer, 1972-76; assoc. editor Tex. Monthly, 1974-76; chief speech-writer Pres. U.S., Washington, 1977-79; Washington editor Atlantic Monthly, 1979—; nat. commentator Pub. Radio, 1987—. Author: National Defense, 1981, More Like Us, 1989; contbr. articles to numerous mags. and jours. Office: Atlantic Monthly 745 Boylston St Boston MA 02116-2636

FALOTICO, RAYMOND, recording studio owner and producer, arranger; b. L.I., N.Y., Jan. 25, 1951; s. Frank Anthony and Frances (Leporace) F.; m. Dona Stavrevich, Nov. 29, 1991; 1 child, Casey Rae. BA in Music Edn., U. Pitts., 1973. Cert. tchr., Pa. Gen. ptnr., leader Opus, Travelling Music Show Band, Pitts., 1974-84; gen. ptnr. Falotico Prodns., Pitts., 1984—; pres. Magnificat, Inc., Pitts., 1989—; choir dir. spl. ch. functions Ellwood City, Pa. Composer music including Pitts. Pirates Theme Song. Mem. Pitts. Radio and TV Club, Pitts. Ad Club. Democrat. Roman Catholic. Office: Falotico Prodns 209 9th St Ste 100B Pittsburgh PA 15222-3501

FALSO, STEVEN MICHAEL, food products executive; b. Johnson City, N.Y., Sept. 15, 1960; s. Rolando Harry and Jacquelyn Sue (Casterline) F.; m. Diane Elizabeth Nisbet, Sept. 11, 1982; children: Michael Anthony, Nicole Marie. AAS, Hudson Valley Community Coll., 1980; BS cum laude, Siena Coll., 1982. Asst. grocery mgr. Albany Pub. Market, Latham, N.Y., 1981-82; ter. sales mgr. Carnation Co., Clifton Park, N.Y., 1982-84; group mgr. Carnation Co., Boston, 1984-86; sr. group mgr. Carnation Co., Balt., 1986-87; asst. regional mgr. Carnation Co., Boston, 1987-89; regional bus. mgr. Nestlé/Carnation Food Co., Buffalo, 1989—. Chief YMCA Indian Guides, Amherst, N.Y., 1990—; mgr. Lou Gehring Instructional T-Ball, Amherst, 1991—. Recipient scholarship Weis Markets, 1978. Mem. Food Industry Sales Execs. of Western N.Y. (sec. 1989, trade banquet chmn. 1990). Republican. Office: Nestlé/Carnation Food Co 346 S Harris Hill Rd Buffalo NY 14221-7407

FALUDI, SUSAN C., journalist. Formerly with West Mag., San Jose, Calif., Mercury News; with San Francisco Bur., Wall St. Jour. Author: Backlash: The Undeclared War Against American Women, 1991; contbr. articles to mags. Recipient Pulitzer Prize for Explanatory Journalism, 1991, Gen. Non-fiction award Nat. Critics Cir., 1992. Office: care Crown Pubs 201 E 50th St Author's Mail New York NY 10022*

FALZONE, JOSEPH SAM, retired airlines company executive; b. Passaic, N.J., June 20, 1917; s. Ross and Concetta (Miada) F.; m. Anna Rand, June 21, 1947; children: Michael Joseph, Connie R. AAD, Western Air Coll., 1941. Lead field insp. Transworld Airlines, N.Y.C., 1946-83; ret. Author: The Atoms' Constant of Motion I, 1987, Vol. II, 1988, Volume I and Volume II Revised to Conform with Model of the Atom, 1991; patentee in field. With USN, 1941-43. Recipient Aviation Mechanic citation FAA, 1975. Mem. AAAS, N.Y. Acad. Sci. Roman Catholic.

FAMA, DONALD FRANCIS, mathematics educator, computer scientist; b. Ilion, N.Y., Oct. 12, 1938; s. Frank Anthony and Claire Elizabeth (Lyons) F.; m. Barbara Joyne, Mar. 21, 1964; children: Christopher Donald, Jeffrey Robert. BA, Utica Coll., 1961; MS, Syracuse U., 1965; M Engring. Tech., U. Ill., 1969; M Adminstrn., SUNY, Brock Port, 1976. Design, draftsman Sperry Rand Corp., Utica, N.Y., 1961-62; math. instr. Manlius (N.Y.) Mil. Acad., 1962-64; prof. math. and computer sci. Cayuga Community Coll., Auburn, N.Y., 1965—; advisor Omicron-Gamma chpt. Phi Theta Kappa, Auburn, 1976—. Recipient Chancellor's award SUNY, 1973. Home: 75 Steel St Auburn NY 13021-4825

FAMIGHETTI, ROBERT JOSEPH, editor; b. N.Y.C., Apr. 26, 1947; s. Joseph John and Marion (Bulfair) F.; m. Jerilyn June Seife, Nov. 1, 1969; 1 child, Karen Beth. BBA, CCNY, 1967; postgrad., Yale U., 1967-68, NYU, 1968. Aide N.Y.C. Council on Consumer Affairs, 1967; tchr. N.Y.C. Bd. Edn., N.Y.C., 1968-69; various editorial positions Macmillan/P.F. Collier, N.Y.C., 1970-75; mng. editor Macmillan Ednl. Co., N.Y.C., 1975-82, exec. editor, 1982-91; editor-in-chief yearbook dept. P.F. Collier, Inc., N.Y.C., 1991—; editor Collier's Encyclopedia Yr. Book, 1975—, Health & Med. Horizons, 1982—; editorial assoc. The Wharton Mag., Phila., 1980-81. Contbr. articles to profl. jours. Office: PF Collier 866 3d Ave 11th Fl New York NY 10022

FAMIGLIETTI, NANCY ZIMA, computer executive; b. Hartford, Conn., Nov. 10, 1956; d. Jospeh and Angeline (Morello) Zima; m. Arthur R. Famiglietti Jr., May 23, 1981. BA in Math., Computer Sci., Eastern Conn. State Coll., Willimantic, 1978. Sr. programmer analyst Hamilton Standard, Windsor Locks, Conn., 1978-82; system analyst Cigna Corp., Hartford, 1982-83, system designer, 1983-86, lead system designer, 1986-89; system advisor Aetna Life & Casualty Co., Hartford, 1989—. Active Conn. Trolley Mus., East Windsor, Conn. Fire Mus., East Windsor, Bushnell Carousel Soc., Hartford, Conn. Pub. TV., Hartford, Channel 57, Springfield, Mass. Mem. Kappa Mu Epsilon. Home: 81 Mcgrath Rd South Windsor CT 06074-1123

FANCHER, ROBERT TRENOR, psychotherapist; b. Reno, Nev., Jan. 14, 1954; s. James Parkes and Margret Ewilda (Trenor) F.; m. Nan Bagwell, Dec. 21, 1974 (div. 1983); m. Janet K. Acker, Aug. 2, 1986. BA, Miss. Coll., 1975; MA, So. Ill. U., 1977; PhD, Vanderbilt U., 1980; cert. in psychotherapy, Blanton-Peale Grad. Inst., 1990. Project mgr. Vanderbilt Inst. Pub. Policy Studies, Nashville, 1982-84; program officer Twentieth Century Fund, N.Y.C., 1984-85; psychotherapist Blanton-Peale Counseling Ctr., N.Y.C., 1985-88, Washington Sq. Inst., N.Y.C., 1990—; pvt. practice psychotherapy N.Y.C., 1988—; cons. TriSource Group, N.Y.C., 1988—; adj. asst. prof. NYU, 1991—. Co-author, co-editor: Against Mediocrity: The Humanities in America's High Schools, 1984; editorial bd. Jour. Mental Health Counseling, 1991—; contbr. articles, papers to profl. pubis. Henry Luce Found. scholar, 1980-81. Mem. AACD, Am. Mental Health Counselors Assn., Am. Philosophy Assn. Democrat.

FANDREYER, ERNEST EGON, mathematician, educator; b. Bonn, Fed. Republic of Germany, Oct. 30, 1926; came to U.S., 1958; s. Emil and Bertha (Schulz) F.; m. Heide Hildebrand, Oct. 28, 1959. Diploma in math., U. Bonn, 1956; MS, Marquette U., 1971; EdD, Boston U., 1984. Sec. and high sch. math. tchr., 1956-68; prof. dept. math. Fitchburg (Mass.) State Coll., 1968—. Mem. Math. Assn. Am. Office: Fitchburg State Coll Dept Math Fitchburg MA 01420

FANE, LAWRENCE, sculptor, educator; b. Kansas City, Mo., Sept. 10, 1933; s. Irvin and Bernice (Smith) F.; m. Diana Gilmore, Nov. 22, 1963; children: Dimitri, Anthea. BA, Harvard U., 1955; student, Boston Mus. Sch., 1956, Demetrios Sch., Gloucester, Mass., 1956-59. Instr. R.I. Sch. Design, 1963-66; instr. sculpture Queens Coll., CUNY, 1966—; One person shows at Zabriskie Gallery, N.Y.C., 1969, Marilyn Pearl Gallery, N.Y.C., 1976, 78, 82, 85, Duke U., 1977, Bard Coll., Annandale-on-Hudson, N.Y., 1977, Spazio Oolp, Turin, Italy, 1980, Washington (Conn.) Art Assn., 1983, Bill Bace Gallery, N.Y.C., 1991; public collections include De Cordova Mus., Lincoln, Mass., Corcoran Gallery of Art, Washington, Mus. Contemporary Am. Art, Udine, italy, Mus. U. of Mass., William Benton Mus., U. Conn., Secker & Warburg, Ltd., London, others. Group exhibits include The Nina Owen Gallery, Chgo., 1991, Phila. Art Alliance, 1990, Hudson River Mus., Yonkers, 1988, de Cordova Mus., Lincoln, Mass., 1987, Schulman Sculpture Park, White Plains, N.Y., 1987, Marilyn Pearl Gallery, N.Y.C., 1985, Nat. Acad. of Design, N.Y.C., 1984, Colby Coll. Mus. Art, Watertown, Maine, 1983, Coll. Mus. of Art, Watertown, 1983, Greater Hartford Arts Coun., Conn., 1980, Galleria Il Mercato del Sale, Milan, Italy, 1979, Zabriskie Gallery, N.Y.C., 1971, many other. Grantee Rsch. Found. of CUNY, 1986, 82, U.S. Dept. HUD, 1973; Ingram Merrill Found. fellow, 1972-73, 84. Fellow Am. Acad. in Rome (exec. bd. 1977-81), Phi Beta Kappa. Home: 355 Riverside Dr New York NY 10025-2747 Office: 10 Beach St New York NY 10013-2425

FANELLI, JOSEPH JAMES, public affairs executive; b. Hartford, Conn., Mar. 22, 1924; s. George A.M. and Nicoletta (Lamarra) F.; m. Pirkko Annikki Saarinen, Aug. 30, 1958; children: George Tauno, John Timo, Christina Colette. BS, Syracuse U., 1949; cert. mgmt., Mich. State U., 1969. Stockbroker G.H. Walker & Co., N.Y.C. and Hartford, Conn., 1949-51; broker, br. mgr. Schibo Corp., Jersey City and Boston, 1952-55; asst. dir. devel. U. Hartford, 1955-56; spl. asst. U.S. Rep. Edwin H. May Jr., Washington, 1957-58, U.S. Senator Prescott Bush, Washington, 1959-62; asst. mgr., then mgr. U.S. C. of C., Washington, 1963-75; pres. Bus.-Industry Polit. Action Com., Washington, 1975—. Editor: Enhancing the Image of Business, 1972. Mem. Md. Rep. State Cen. Com., Montgomery County, 1970; vol. Community Chest, ARC, Conn. and Md.; active numerous polit. campaigns at local, regional, and state levels, 1956—. Staff Sgt. USAF, 1943-46, PTO. Recipient Legion of Hon. award Chapel of the Four Chaplains, 1980, Scholastic Hon. award Alpha Kappa Psi, 1949. Mem. U.S. C. of C., Nat. Assn. Mfrs. (pub. affairs steering com. 1976—), D.C. Lions Club (pres. 1984-85, Lion of Yr. 1987, 92), Internat. Club (Washington), Greater Washington Sigma Chi Aulmni Assn. (community amb. to France, designee Experiment in Internat. Living, Significant Sig award 1991). Republican. Roman Catholic. Home: 11602 Monticello Ave Silver Spring MD 20902 Office: Bus Industry Polit Action Com 1747 Pennsylvania Ave NW Washington DC 20006

FANELLI, LESLIE ELLEN, artistic director, educator; b. Cin., May 27, 1957; d. Elmer Allen and Rose Elizabeth (Zimmerman) Reuter; m. Anthony Angelo Fanelli, Aug. 16, 1986; 1 child, Hannah Rose. BS in Theatre/Urban Affairs, CUNY, 1986. Writer, actress, singer Floating Hosp. Ednl. Theatre, N.Y.C., 1981-86; project supr., workshop leader Found. for the Creative Community, N.Y.C., 1986; creative educator Cen. Pk. Conservancy, N.Y.C., 1985-88; workshop leader Adelphi Univ., N.Y.C., 1988, Fordham Univ., N.Y.C., 1988; v.p., program mgr. Enact, Inc., N.Y.C., 1987-90; instr. ESL 92 Street Y, N.Y.C., 1990—; adj. prof. Baruch Coll., N.Y.C., 1988—; exec. artistic dir., founder Theatre in Motion, Inc., N.Y.C., 1990—; dir. spl. edn. Festival of Music, Inc., 1991—; guest speaker Julliard Sch. at Lincoln Ctr., 1991. Democrat. Office: Festival of Music Inc 12125 6th Ave College Point NY 11356-1104

FANG, PEN JENG, engineering executive and consultant; b. Tainan, Taiwan, Republic of China, July 13, 1931; came to U.S., 1958; s. Den Chuang and Wu Tien (Su) F.; m. Elizabeth Meiling Yang, Aug. 4, 1962; children: Kenneth, Terry, Shona. BS, Nat. Taiwan U., 1955; MS, Okla. State U., 1960; PhD, Cornell U., 1966. Registered profl. engr., R.I.; registered structural engr., Ill. Sr. engr. Inar D. Hillman & Assocs., Chgo., 1960-63; sr. rsch. engr. Applied Rsch. Lab., U.S. Steel Corp., Monroeville, Pa., 1965-68; asst. prof. engring. Concordia U. (formerly Sir George Williams U.), Montreal, Que., Can., 1968-70; asst. to assoc. prof. U. R.I., Kingston, 1970-81; mgr. engring. analysis ITT-Grinnell Corp., Providence, 1981-84; pres. EngiTek, Inc. and CadMetrix, Inc., Cranston, R.I., 1983—; head div. engring. and tech. Roger Williams Coll., Bristol, R.I., 1987-90; engr. Town of West Warwick, R.I., 1989—; exec. cons. Promon Engring. Co., Rio de Janeiro, 1975-78, Natron Engring. Co., Rio de Janeiro, 1978-81. Contbr. tech. articles to profl. jours. Vice chmn. bd. dirs. R.I. Assn. Chinese-Ams., Providence, 1978-86; commr. State Fire Safety Bd. Appeal and Rev., North Providence, R.I., 1988—; mem. R.I. Heritage Commn., Providence, 1988—; mem. Zoning Bd. Rev., North Kingstown, R.I., 1991—. Mem. ASCE (structural div., Collingwood prize 1967), Assn. Energy Engrs., Nat. Fire Protection Assn., Am. Concrete Inst., Rotary. Home: 95 Sedgefield Rd

North Kingstown RI 02852-3838 Office: EngiTek Inc/CadMetrix Inc 1370 Plainfield St Johnston RI 02919-6891

FANGER, MARK, psychologist, psychotherapist, consultant; b. Boston, Dec. 6, 1943. AB in Polit. Sci., Syracuse U., 1965; EdM in Psychology, Boston State Coll., 1972; EdD in Counseling Psychology, Boston U., 1977; grad. Clin. Consultation Program, Boston Inst. for Psychotherapy, 1984. Lic. psychologist, Mass.; cert. social studies tchr., guidance counselor and dir., Mass.; diplomate Am. Bd. Family Psychology, Am. Acad. Behavioral Medicine. Clin. dir. Milford Assistance Program Community Mental Health Ctr., Milford, Mass., 1971-74; clin. cons. drug treatment program Boston City Hosp., 1975-77; staff psychologist Bay Area Psychiat. Assocs., Burlington, Mass., 1977-80, Suburban Counseling Assocs., Weston, Mass., 1977-80; clin. supr. Whiteman House, Survival, Inc., Quincy, Mass., 1982-84; pvt. practice psychotherapy, Newton Highlands, Mass., 1979—; mem. adj. faculty dept. counseling psychology Boston U., 1976-77, dept. psychology Boston State Coll., 1977-79; mem. adj. faculty Antioch's Inst. Open Edn., Cambridge, Mass., 1979-80; mem. adj. faculty, supr. family therapy Mass. Sch. Profl. Psychology, Newton, 1982-83; group psychotherapy cons. People for People, Inc., Framingham, Mass., 1990-92; mem. faculty group psychotherapy tng. program Northeastern Soc. for Group Psychotherapy, 1991—; presenter in field; condr. workshops. Recipient Svc. of Self award Rotary Club, Franklin, Mass., 1974; grantee Mass. Gen. Hosp., 1975. Fellow Mass. Psychol. Assn.; mem. APA, Am. Group Psychotherapy Assn. (clin. mem.), Am. Assn. Marriage and Family Therapy (clin. mem.), Internat. Acad. Behavioral Medicine, Counseling and Psychotherapy (diplomate in profl. psychotherapy and behavioral medicine), Psychologists for Social Responsibility, Soc. for Family Therapy and Rsch. (edn. com. 1984-87), Mass. Assn. Marriage and Family Therapy (clin.), N.E. Soc. Study of Multiple Personality and Dissociation, Northeastern Soc. Group Psychotherapy (membership com. 1986-88, program chmn. 1988—), Pi Lambda Theta, Phi Delta Kappa. Office: 72 Floral St Ste 2 Newton MA 02161-1523

FANNIN, LEON FRANCIS, sociologist, educator; b. Sibley, Ill., Feb. 24, 1926; s. Paul Clark and Agnes Marie (Wurzberger) F.; m. Renee Kaprelian, Aug. 15, 1959; children: Helen, Laura, Jane, Jennifer. BA, U. Wis., 1953, MA, 1957, PhD, 1962. Instr. U. Wis., Sheboygan, 1957-58, Beloit (Ill.) Coll., 1958-59; instr., asst. prof. Ohio U., Athens, 1959-62; asst. prof. to full prof. U. Hartford (Conn.), 1962-73, Clemson (S.C.) U., 1973-74; prof. sociology Mercy Coll., Dobbs Ferry, N.Y., 1974—; cons. on juvenile delinquency, State of Conn., 1969-72. Contbr. articles to profl. jours. With U.S. Army, 1944-46. Fulbright grantee, 1954-55; Ford Found. grantee, 1963. Mem. Am. Sociol. Assn., Phi Kappa Phi. Office: Mercy Coll 555 Broadway Dobbs Ferry NY 10522-1189

FANNING, JAMES JEFFERY, accountant; b. Bronx, Aug. 5, 1948; s. James John and Dorothy Mary (Kern) F.; m. Carol Ann Cardarelli, June 12, 1971; children: Marlene, Brian. BS in Acctg., Le Moyne Coll., 1970. CPA, N.Y. Staff acct. Ernst & Young, N.Y.C., 1970-75, mgr., 1976-79, prin., 1979-82, mem. nbat. banking com., 1980-88, ptnr., 1982—, dir. internat. banking, 1989—; mgr. Ernst & Young, Frankfurt, Germany, 1975-76; mem. internat. banking and fin. svcs. com. Ernst & Young Internat., 1984—. Contbr. articles to profl. jours. Capt. USAR, 1970-78. Mem. AICPAs, N.Y. State Soc. CPAs (com. on rels. with bankers 1978-81, com. on rels. with comml. credit grantors 1981-82, others), Inst. Internat. Bankers (profl liaison com. 1986—), Le Moyne Coll. Alumni Assn. (bd. govs. 1978—), Nisseguogue Golf Club. Home: 122 Washington Blvd Commack NY 11725 Office: Ernst & Young 277 Park Ave New York NY 10172

FANTON, JONATHAN FOSTER, university president; b. Mobile, Ala., Apr. 29, 1943; s. Dwight F. F. and Marion (Foster) Fanton Bemer; m. Cynthia Greenleaf, Aug. 2, 1986. B.A., Yale U., 1965, M.Phil., 1977, PhD, 1978. Carnegie teaching fellow in history Yale U., 1965-66, lectr. history, 1966-78, spl. asst. to pres., 1970-73, exec. dir. Summer Plans, 1973-76, assoc. provost, 1976-78; v.p. planning U. Chgo., 1978-82; pres., prof. history New Sch. Social Rsch., N.Y.C., 1982—. Trustee N.Y. State Commn. Ind. Coll.s and Univs., 1988—, Nat. Assn. Ind. Colls. and Univs.; bd. dirs. Am. Ditchley Found., United Way, N.Y., Charter 77 Foun.; chm. Helsinki Watch Com.; co-chair 14th St.-Union Sq. Local Devel. Corp. Mem. Am. Hist. Assn., Coun. on Fgn. Rels., Econ. Club. Home: 939 Black Rock Tpke Easton CT 06612-1154 Office: New Sch for Social Rsch Office of Pres 66 W 12th St New York NY 10011-8693

FANUELE, MICHAEL ANTHONY, research engineer; b. Bronx, N.Y., Feb. 24, 1938; s. Joseph A. and R. Fanny (Rubino) F.; m. Joyce L. Cassidy, May 23, 1964; children: Gina M., Peter A. BEE, NYU, 1959; MSEE, Rutgers U., 1968. Electronics engr. U.S. Army Combat Surveillance & Target Acquisition Lab., Fort Monmouth, N.J., 1960-72, sr. electronics engr., 1972-80, project officer, 1980-81, dir. ISTA systems div., 1981-85; chief systems and signals analysis div. U.S. Army Electronic Warfare, Reconnaissance Surveillance and Target Acquisition Ctr., Fort Monmouth, N.J., 1985-88; sr. rsch. engr. Ga. Tech. Rsch. Inst., Ga. Inst. Tech., 1988—; cons. in field; chmn. dept. electromagnetic engring. U.S. Army Internal Tng. Program, Ft. Monmouth, 1968-78, advisor, 1978-88; Army chmn. Tri-Service Radar Symposium Steering Group, Ft. Monmouth, 1973-88; Army mem. Internat. Tech. Group, 1977-81, Internat. Radar panel, 1984-88. Patentee in field; contbr. articles to profl. jours. Served to 2d lt. U.S. Army, 1959-60. Mem. IEEE (sr.), Assn. Old Crows. Roman Catholic. Lodge: KC (treas. Brickton, N.J. 1968-70). Home: 440 Colleen Ct Toms River NJ 08755-7376

FANUS, PAULINE RIFE, librarian; b. New Oxford, Pa., Feb. 14, 1925; d. Maurice Diehl and Bernice Edna (Gable) Rife; m. William Edward Fanus, June 20, 1944; children: Irene Weaver, Larry William, Daniel Diehl. BS, Pa. State U., 1945; MLS, Villanova U., 1961; postgrad., Temple U., 1986—. Periodical librarian Tex. Coll. Arts Industries, Kingville, 1945; tchr. nursery sch. Studio Sch., Wayne, Pa., 1953-55; librarian circulation, reference Franklin Inst., Phila., 1963-66; asst. librarian Ursinus Coll., Collegeville, Pa., 1966; catalog librarian, instr. Eastern Coll., St. Davids, Pa., 1967-71; head librarian Agnes Irwin Sch., Rosemont, Pa., 1971—. Book reviewer The Book Report. Mem. AAUP (chpt. sec. Eastern Coll. 1970-71), Pa. Library Assn. Home: Country Club Rd Phoenixville PA 19460-2783 Office: Agnes Irwin Sch Ithan Ave Bryn Mawr PA 19010-1041

FARAGHAN, GEORGE TELFORD, photographer; b. Phila., July 8, 1926; s. Joseph Telford and Sarah (Earnest) F.; m. Ida Jane Hanley, Dec. 8, 1948; children: Karen, Kurt, Kim, Kyle, Ken. Student, Pa. State U., 1947; grad. comml. photography magna cum laude, Yawn Sch. Photography, Phila., 1949. Printer Thomas Melvin Studio, Phila., 1949-50; printer, asst. Willand Steward Studio, Wilmington, Del., 1950-51; freelance photographer Phila., 1951-52; owner George Faraghan Studio, Phila., 1953—. Inventor spl. camera unit used in pharm. rsch. With USN, 1944-46, PTO. Recipient 3 George Berry awards, Profl. Photographers Assn. Del. Valley, Phila. Art Dirs. Shows awards, N.Y Art Dirs. Show Neographics award; photographer 50 Best of Ads of Yr., 1960. Mem. Phila. Art Dir.'s Club (over 100 awards). Republican. Office: 940 N Delaware Ave Philadelphia PA 19123-3111

FARAONE, STEPHEN VINCENT, psychologist, behavioral scientist, educator; b. Babylon, N.Y., July 27, 1956; s. Vincent Donato and Maria (Bampoucis) F.; m. Kathleen Anne Borah, June 3, 1978; children: Michael, Zachary, Dylan. BA, SUNY, Stony Brook, 1978; MA, U. Iowa, 1980, PhD, 1982. Lic. psychologist, Mass., R.I. Clin. psychology intern Brown U., Providence, 1982-83, rsch. fellow dept. psychiatry and human behavior, 1983-84, asst. instr., 1984-85; health statistician Brockton/West Roxbury (Mass.) VA Med. Ctr., 1985—; prof., staff appointment in psychology, psychol. svcs. Mass. Gen. Hosp., Boston, 1989—; instr. in psychiatry Harvard Med. Sch., Boston, 1985—, asst. prof. psychology, 1989—; psychol. cons. Mass. Disability Determination Svc., 1986-88, R.I. Disability Determination Svc., 1986-88; with allied health personnel privileges in clin. psychology Woonsocket (R.I.) Hosp., 1986-89; cons. for psychol. evaluation and therapy Blackstone Valley Psychol. Inst., Woonsocket, 1985—. Author: (with others) The Genetics of Mood Disorders, 1990; contbr. articles to profl. jours. and chpts. to books. Mem. AAAS, APA, Am. Psychol. Soc., N.Y. Acad. Scis., Behavior Genetics Assn. Office: Brockton VAMC Dept Psychiatry 116A 940 Belmont St Brockton MA 02401-5596

FARAONE, TED, public relations executive, consultant; b. Providence, Feb. 21, 1956; s. Raffaele Pietro and Jennie (Landi) F.; m. Teri Dickstein, June 1, 1988. BA, Columbia U., 1978. Accredited by Public Relations Soc. Am., 1988. Publicity dir. Sta. WNYC Radio-TV, N.Y.C., 1979-81; press rep. Sta. WNBC-TV, N.Y.C., 1981-82, Sta. WCBS-TV, N.Y.C., 1982-83; dir. press relations Sta. WCAU-TV, Phila., 1983-86, Sta. WBBM-TV, Chgo., 1986-87; pres. Faraone Communications, N.Y.C., 1987—. Editor: mag. Sta. WNYC Program Guide, 1979-81. Mem. Nat. Acad. TV Arts and Scis., Internat. Radio and TV Soc., Publicity Club of N.Y., Pub. Relations Soc. Am. (accredited 1988), Writers and Artists for Peace in the Middle East, Phi Beta Kappa. Club: Columbia of N.Y. Office: Faraone Communications Inc 123 W 44th St New York NY 10036-4000

FARB, THOMAS FOREST, financial executive; b. N.Y.C., Oct. 28, 1956; s. Peter and Oriole (Horch) F.; m. Stacy Siana Valhouli, Apr. 29, 1961; children: Peter Forest Valhouli-Farb, Siana Louisa Valhouli-Farb. AB, Harvard U., 1980. Research assoc. Mass. House Ways and Means Com., Boston, 1976-78; asst v.p. Bank of Boston, 1980-83; v.p., chief fin. officer and gen. mgr. ea. ops. Symbolics, Inc., Burlington, Mass., 1983-89; sr. v.p., chief fin. officer & controller Airfund Corp., Lexington, Mass., 1989—; bd. dirs. Hecht-Nielsen Neurocomputer, Inc., San Diego, Airfund Corp., Lexington. Editorial bd. Auerbach Pubs., N.Y.C. Mem. Fin. Execs. Inst., Bus. Assocs. Club, Treas. Club Boston, Newcomen Soc. Home: 167 North Shore Rd Hampton NH 03842 Office: Airfund Corp 2 Militia Dr Lexington MA 02173-4704

FARBER, JERRY S., orthopedic surgeon; b. Chgo., Oct. 16, 1932; s. Albert H. and Cecelia (Shallat) F.; m. Sharon Iris Weisbach, Apr. 23, 1961; children: K. Allen, Lori, Daniel. BS, U. Ill., 1954; MD, U. Ill., Chgo., 1958. Internship Cook County Hosp., Chgo., 1958-59; residency Hines VA Hosp., Maywood, Ill., 1959-62, Shriners Hosp., 1962-63; pres. MOST, Silver Spring, Md., 1991—. Author clin. paper. Capt. USAF, 1964-66. Fellow Am. Acad. Orthopedic Surgeons, ACS. Jewish. Office: MOST 8630 Fenton Silver Spring MD 20910

FARBER, PHILLIP ANDREW, biological and allied health sciences educator; b. Wilkes-Barre, Pa., Sept. 19, 1934; s. Phillip Henry and Josephine Mary (Penkala) F.; m. Larice M. Krebs; children: Michael, Steven, Phillip, Matthew. BS, King's Coll., Wilkes-Barre, 1956; MS, Boston Coll., 1958; PhD, Cath. U. Am., 1963. Asst. instr. biology dept. Georgetown U., Washington, 1962-63; rsch. biologist perinatal physiology lab. Nat. Inst. Neurol. Diseases and Blindness, NIH, Bethesda, Md., 1963-64; rsch. instr. dept. phys. medicine and rehab. NYU Med. Ctr., N.Y.C., 1964-66; prof. Bloomsburg (Pa.) U., 1966—; cytogenetics cons. dept. lab. medicine and pathology Geisinger Med. Ctr., Danville, Pa., 1967—; commd. officer U.S. Pub. Health Svcs., jr. asst. officer, 1960; mem. Lab. Parasite Chemotherapy, Nat. Inst. Allergy and Infectious Diseases, NIH, Bethesda. Contbr. articles to profl. jours. Summer rsch. fellow NSF, Cath. U. Am., 1962, Oak Ridge Associated Univs., 1969; USPHS rsch. grantee NYU Med. Ctr., 1965. Mem. AAAS, Am. Soc. Clin. Pathologists, Am. Soc. Human Genetics, Assn. Cytogenetic Technologists, Teratology Soc., Pa. Acad. Sci., Commonwealth of Pa. Univ. Biologists, Assn. Pa. State Coll. and Univ. Facilities, Sigma Xi. Republican. Roman Catholic. Home: PO Box 92 Mifflinville PA 18631-0092 Office: Bloomsburg U Dept Biol & Allied Health Scis Bloomsburg PA 17815

FARBSTEIN, MARVIN, college official; b. Phila., Mar. 24, 1931; s. Norman and Reba (Smith) F.; m. Rochelle Bishow, Sept. 9, 1956; children: Lisa M., Heidi E., Amy L. BS, Temple U., 1951, MEd, 1952; EdD, Rutgers U., 1960; LittD (hon.), Exptl. Coll. Inst. for, Behavioral Rsch., Rockville, Md., 1975. Tchr., counselor Parsippany (N.J.)-Troy Hills Schs., 1956-61; asst. prof. assoc. prof. Paterson State Coll., Wayne, N.J., 1961-66; prof. Morgan State U., Balt., 1966-70; dir. div. higher edn. Md. Dept. Edn., Balt., 1979-76; dean Grad. Sch., Hood Coll., Frederick, Md., 1976-89; v.p. Touro Coll., N.Y.C., 1989—; accreditator Commn. on Higher Edn., MSA, Phila., 1976—, Edn. Licensure Commn., Washington, 1980—. Author 4 books; contbr. over 75 articles to profl. jours. Capt. U.S. Army, 1953-56, Korea. Grantee U. Va., 1970, U. Fla., 1971, Oxford (Eng.) U., 1975. Mem. Am. Assn. Univ. Adminstrs. B'nai B'rith (pres. Balt. 1975), Phi Delta Kappa. Home: 8 Highridge Dr Huntington NY 11743-3645 Office: Touro Coll 350 5th Ave Ste 5122 New York NY 10118-5198

FARHI, EDWARD, physicist; b. N.Y.C., June 26, 1952; s. Raphael and Helen (Bressler) F. BA, Brandeis U., 1973, MS, 1973; PhD, Harvard U., 1978. Rsch. assoc. Stanford Linear Accelerator Ctr., Palo Alto, Calif., 1978-80; sci. assoc. CERN, Geneva, 1980-81; postdoctoral MIT, Cambridge, 1981-82, asst. prof., 1982-86, assoc. prof., 1986—. Fellow Alfred P. Sloan Found. 1984. Mem. Am. Phys. Soc. Office: MIT Ctr Theoretical Physics Cambridge MA 02139

FARIDI, HAMED, food research and development executive; b. Arak, Iran, June 29, 1947; came to U.S., 1971; s. Allaedin and Ejlal (Rafii) F.; m. Afsaneh Behroon, May 17, 1979; 1 child, Michael. BS in Agriculture, Shiraz U., Iran, 1969; MS in Food Sci., Kansas State U., 1973, PhD in Cereal Chemistry, 1975; MBA, Fairleigh Dickinson U., 1989. Food scientist USDA-ARS Western Wheat Quality Lab, Pullman, Wash., 1979-83; dir. biophys. sci. Nabisco Foods Group, East Hanover, N.J., 1983—; adv. bd. mem. Swiss House of Wheat and Bread, Echallens, Switzerland, 1988—. Editor, author 6 books on rheology, cereals; patentee in field; contbr. over 36 papers to profl. publs. Recipient scholarship Nabisco Brands, 1972-75; grantee Pacific N.W. Wheat Commns., 1979-83. Mem. Am. Assn. Cereal Chemists, Inst. Food Technologists, Am. Chem. Soc., Am. Soc. Quality Control. Home: 17 Rhoda Ter Parsippany NJ 07054 Office: Nabisco Foods Group 200 DeForest Ave East Hanover NJ 07936

FARINA, PETER R., biochemist; b. N.Y.C., Apr. 30, 1946; s. Peter J. and Angela M. (Spinello) F.; m. Linda J. Peterman, Sept. 1, 1968; children: Diana, Gregory. BS, Hofstra U., 1967; PhD, SUNY, Buffalo, 1972. Rsch. scientist Union Carbide Corp., Tarrytown, N.Y., 1974-77, project leader, 1977-78, group leader, 1978-79; sr. prin. biochemist Boehringer Ingelheim Pharms. Inc., Ridgefield, Conn., 1980-83, sect. leader, 1983-89, dir., 1990—. Contbr.: Modern Drug Research-Paths to Better and Safer Drugs 1989. Allied Chem. Corp. pre-doctoral fellow 1970, NIH postdoctoral fellow 1972-73. Mem. Am. Chem. Soc. Home: Sunset Dr North Salem NY 10560 Office: Boehringer Ingelheim Pharm 900 Ridgebury Rd Ridgefield CT 06877-4623

FARKAS, CHARLES MICHAEL, management consultant; b. Miami, Fla., May 8, 1951; s. Daniel and Ruth (Morison) F.; m. Lora Elizabeth Sperber, Aug. 6, 1983; children: Alexander James, Cameron Elizabeth. AB, Princeton (N.J.) U., 1973; MA, Brandeis U., 1977; MBA, Harvard U., 1980. Asst. to the provost Princeton U., 1973-74; instr. Brandeis U., Waltham, Mass., 1975-76; gen. mgr. Philippine Ventures, Manila, 1976-78; cons. Bain and Co., Boston, 1979-82, mgr., 1982-85, ptnr., 1985—, dir., 1990—; bd. dirs. Internat. Mgmt. and Devel. Inst., Washington, Dart Group Corp., Landover, Md.; trustee Brigham Med. Ctr., Boston, 1989—. Inst. for Internat. Edn./Fulbright Com. fellow, 1977. Mem. Siasconset Casino Assn., Princeton Club of N.J., Harvard Club of Boston, Algonquin Club. Office: Bain and Co 2 Copley Pl Boston MA 02116

FARKAS, EDWARD BARRISTER, airport administrator, electrical engineer; b. Bklyn., Jan. 17, 1954; s. Willhelm and Esther (Davidovic) F.; m. Marianna Safarian, Feb. 16, 1989. AA, LaGuardia Coll., 1973; AS, CUNY, 1985; BS, Inst. Tech., 1990; PhD. (hon.), U. Calif., Modesto, 1991. Dir. campus activities CUNY, Queens, 1970-72; asst. dir. fin. aid CUNY, L.I., 1972-73; prodn. mgr. LAGZ Ltd., Cali, Colombia, 1974-85; dir. engring. North Techtronics, Queens, 1980-85; dir. project mgmt. Port Authority of N.J.-N.J., Queens, 1985—; utility liaison Port Authority of N.J.-N.J., N.Y.C., 1985-86; test engr. Port Authority of N.J.-N.J., Jersey City, 1986-87; airport adminstr. Port Authority of N.J.-N.J., Queens, 1987—; bd. dirs. Briarwood (N.Y.) Engring. Group. Editor NewsNet Jour., 1987-91; author, researcher: Power Engineering Review, Ground Faults, 1984; inventor various patents electrochem. oxidation inhibitor, thermal electrolyte, etc.; editor (newsletter) Monitor, 1980-87. Fellow Elec. Engring. Tech. Assn., Electrotech. Engring. Soc. (Engring. Rsch. award 1987); mem. IEEE (chmn. gov. act. com. 1987-90, Engring. Professionalism award 1985, Profl. leadership award 1990), AIAA, N.Y. Acad. Sci., Am. Assn. Airport Execs., Nat. Elec. Testing Assn., Am. Inst. Corrosion Control (bd. dirs. N.Y.C. chpt. 1989—). Office: Port Authority of NY-NJ LaGuardia Airport Sta # H7C Queens NY 11371

FARKAS, JAMES PAUL, educator, researcher, preservationist; b. Buffalo, Mar. 21, 1947; s. Paul Edward and Marie Edith (Weigel) F. BS in Edn., SUNY, Buffalo, 1968, MA in Am. History, 1971; MS in Ednl. Adminstrn., Niagara U., 1976, Specialist in Ednl. Adminstrn., 1976; EdD in Ednl. Adminstrn., SUNY, Buffalo, 1983; grad. with honors, U.S. Army Command and Gen. Staff Coll., 1985. Educator Buffalo Pub. Schs., 1968-70, Amherst Cen. Schs., 1970—; dir. Fed. Sect. Chpt. I programs, 1976-79; guest lectr. SUNY, Buffalo, 1984-85, project cons. office dean faculty of ednl. studies, 1985. Contbr. numerous articles on mgmt., leadership and occupational stress to profl. jours.; manuscript reviewer Issues in Edn., 1984-89. Active devel. coun., adv. coun. Studio Arena Theatre. Lt. col. C.E. U.S. Army. Decorated Army Commendation medal, Humanitarian Svc. medal, Meritorious Svc. medal. Mem. numerous profl. socs. Home: 165 Chapin Pky Buffalo NY 14209-1040 Office: 55 Kings Hwy Buffalo NY 14226-4398

FARKAS, LISA JEAN KOVACS, psychologist; b. Bethlehem, Pa., Dec. 31, 1962; d. Richard Blase Kovacs and Jean Katherine (Szabo) Edraney; m. Mark William Farkas, June 11, 1988. BS, Pa. State U., 1985; PsyD, Wright State U., 1989. Lic. psychologist, Pa. Psychology intern CPC Mental Health Svcs., Eatontown, N.J., 1988-89; psychologist Villanova (Pa.) U. Counseling Ctrs., 1989—. Mem. Am. Psychol. Assn. Democrat. Office: Villanova U Counseling Ctr 106 Corr Hall Villanova PA 19085

FARKAS, PAUL STEPHEN, gastroenterologist; b. N.Y.C., 1952; s. Benjamin J. and Ellen (Tanner) F.; m. Esta Miriam Cantor, June 24, 1973; children: Melanie Sharon, Joshua David. AB magna cum laude with distinction in psychology, Brandeis U., 1972; MD, Tufts U., 1976. Diplomate Am. Bd. Internal Medicine, Am. Bd. Gastroenterology. Intern Baystate Med. Ctr., Sprinfield, Mass., 1976-77, resident in internal medicine, 1977-79; fellow in gastroenterology Albert Einstein Coll. Medicine, Bronx, N.Y., 1979-81; asst. clin. prof. medicine Tufts U., Boston, 1985—; med. advisor Med. Assist Program Springfield Tech. C.C., 1989—; adj. asst. prof. clin. pharmacology Mass. Coll. Pharmacy, Boston, 1982—. Author: Diagnostic Diagrams Gastroenterology, 1985; contbr. book chpts., articles and revs. in field. Co-dir. med. edn. Mercy Hosp., Springfield, 1990—, dir. libr., 1988—; med. adv. bd. VNA, Springfield, 1984-88; bd. dirs. B'nai Jacob Synogogue, Springfield, 1987-88, Com. for Longmeadow, Mass., 1989. Fellow ACP; mem. AMA, Am. Coll. Gastroenterology, Am. Gastroent. Assn., Am. Soc. Gastrointestinal Endoscopy, New England Soc. Gastrointestinal Endoscopy. Office: 299 Carew St Springfield MA 01104

FARLEY, DONAL EYMARD, university administrator; b. N.Y.C., Nov. 23, 1935; s. John Thomas and Margaret (Ryan) F.; m. Maureen Margaret Ferguson, June 3, 1961; children: Kevin, Thomas, Brian, Patrick, John. BCE, Manhattan Coll., 1957. Registered profl. engr., N.Y. Various positions to sr. budget examiner N.Y.C. Mayor's Office of Mgmt. and Budget, 1957-67; exec. asst. to vice chancellor CUNY, N.Y.C., 1967-71, univ. asst. dean, 1971-73, univ. assoc. adminstr., 1973-78, univ. adminstr., 1978-81, vice chancellor, 1981-86, sr. vice chancellor, 1986—. Mem. Bd. Edn. Capital Task Force, N.Y.C., 1987-88; mem. capital planning com. Manhattan Coll., Bronx, N.Y., 1988—; mem. facility adv. com. Greater N.Y. YMCA, N.Y.C., 1984. Roman Catholic. Office: CUNY 535 E 80th St New York NY 10021-0767

FARLEY, DONALD, newspaper executive; b. Towanda, Pa., Aug. 23, 1960; s. Robert and Mary Louise (Maloney) F.; m. Margaret Mary Moseley, Mar. 20, 1991. BA in Communications, California (Pa.) State Coll., 1982. Sales rep. Towanda Printing Co., 1983; mgr. Pocono Shopper, East Stroudsburg, Pa., 1984-87; v.p., gen. mgr. Times/Shamrock Free Paper Div., Owego, N.Y., 1988, Balt. City Paper, 1989—. Bd. dirs. Times/Shamrock Communications, Scranton, Pa., 1992; fundraiser Multiple Sclerosis Soc. Md., 1989—. Mem. Balt. Film Forum (v.p. 1991—), Towanda Jaycees, Delta Chi (alumni bd. 1992). Republican. Roman Catholic. Home: 1102 S Clinton St Baltimore MD 21224

FARLEY, EUGENE JOSEPH, accountant; b. N.Y.C., Jan. 3, 1950; s. John Joseph and Rita Sara (Johnston) F.; m. Rosaleen Therese Scully, Jan. 10, 1981; children: Sarah, Laura, Patrick. BBA in Acctg., Siena Coll., 1977; MBA in Fin., Russell Sage Coll., 1985. CPA, N.Y. Cost acct. Callanan Industries, S. Bethlehem, N.Y., 1972-75; tax auditor N.Y. State Dept. Taxation and Fin., Albany, 1977-83, EDP auditor, 1983-85, assoc. acct., 1985-89; prin. acct. N.Y. Dept. Taxation & Fin., Albany, 1989—. Fund raiser Siena Coll. Alumni Fund; vol. Albany's Tri-Centennial Com., 1986. Mem. AICPA, N.Y. State Soc. CPAs, Assn. Govt. Accts. (fin. mgmt. standards com. 1988-91, Capital chpt. bd. dirs. 1989—). Democrat. Roman Catholic. Home: 9 Middlesex Dr Slingerlands NY 12159-9661 Office: NY Dept Taxation & Fin State Office Campus Albany NY 12227

FARLEY, HUGH T., state senator, law educator; b. Watertown, N.Y.; s. Edward A. and Laura Eleanor (Burns) F.; m. Sharon L. Rose, July 3, 1958; children: Susan, Robert, Margaret. BS cum laude, SUNY, 1958; JD, Am. U., 1964. Law prof., head law dept. SUNY, Albany, 1965—; mem. N.Y. Senate, 1977—, chmn. com. on aging, 1979-84, com. on environ. conservation, 1985-88, com. on banks, 1989—, select com. on interstate coop., sub-com. on librs.; nat. vice chmn. Coun. State Govts., 1985-86, chmn. ea. region, 1984, chmn. orgn. and planning com., mem. bd. govs., chmn. publs. subcom.; chmn. resources com. Nat. Conf. State Legislatures, mem. spl. com. on health care cost containment, mem. exec. com. state fed. assembly; vice chmn. Interstate Legis. Com. on Lake Erie; del. White House Conf. on Librs., White House Conf. on Aging; chmn. Senate Com. on Aging, Environ. Conservation, Com. on Banks; alt. del. Rep. Nat. Conv., 1980. Recipient Nat. Comdrs. award DAV, Cert. of Merit Statewide Sr. Action Coun., Velma K. Moore award for dist. svc. to librs., Most Disting. Alumni award Mohawk Valley Community Coll., 1974. Mem. Nat. Rep. Legislators Assn. (pres. 1985-86), Northeastern Bus. Law Assn. (past pres.). Office: NY State Senate State Capitol Albany NY 12247

FARLEY, JAMES DUNCAN, retired banker; b. Chgo., June 24, 1926; s. Donald Stephen and Alice (Duncan) F.; m. Mary Kay Tracy, Feb. 27, 1960; children—Frances, James Duncan, Kathryn, Andrew. B.S., Georgetown U., 1949. Trainee, mgr. First Nat. City Bank, Buenos Aires, Argentina, 1950-64; v.p. overseas div. First Nat. City Bank, N.Y.C., 1964-67; exec. v.p., gen. mgr. Merc. Bank of Can., 1967-68; sr. v.p. personal banking group First Nat. City Bank (now Citibank N.A.), N.Y.C., 1968, exec. v.p., from 1969, exec. v.p. mcht. banking group, 1975; exec. v.p. Caribbean (Central Am. and S. Am. banking group), from 1980; vice chmn., dir. Citicorp and Citibank N.A., 1984-91; ret., 1991; bd. dir. Moore Corp. Chmn. John A. Hartford Found. Ensign USNR, 1945-46, lt., 1951-52. Mem. Round Hill Club (Greenwich, Conn.), Wequetonsing (Mich.) Golf Club, Cypress Point Club (Pebble Beach, Calif.), Birnam Wood Golf Club (Santa Barbara, Calif.), The Valley (Montecito, Calif.), L.A. Country Club, Loblolly Pines Golf Club (Hobe Sound, Fla.). Office: Citibank 399 Park Ave New York NY 10043-0001

FARLEY, PEGGY ANN, finance company executive; b. Phila., Mar. 12, 1947; d. Harry E. and Ruth (Lloyd) F.; m. Reid McIntyre, Dec. 31, 1985 (div.); 1 child, Margaret Ruth Farley. AB, Barnard Coll., 1970; MA with high honors, Columbia U., 1972. Admissions officer Barnard Coll., N.Y.C., 1973-76; adminstr. Citibank NA, Athens, Greece, 1976-77; cons. Orgn. Resources Counselors, N.Y.C., 1977-78; sr. assoc. Morgan Stanley and Co. Inc., N.Y.C., 1978-84; mng. dir., chief exec. officer AMAS Securities Inc., N.Y.C., 1984—; also bd. dirs. AMAS Securities, Inc., N.Y.C.; bd. dirs. AMAS Group, London. Author: The Place Of The Yankee And Euro Bond Markets In A Financing Program For The People's Republic of China, 1982. Mem. Columbia U. Seminar on China-U.S. Bus., Rep. Senatorial Inner Circle, Fgn. Policy Assn. Mem. Asia Soc., China Inst., Met. Club, Econ. Club of N.Y. Republican. Presbyterian. Home: 64 E 86th St Apt 10B New York NY 10028 also: Box 819 RD 8 Newton NJ 07860 Office: AMAS Securities Inc 520 Madison Ave New York NY 10022-4213

FARLEY, ROBERT JAMES, chemistry educator; b. Upper Darby, Pa., Aug. 11, 1932; s. James Aloysius and Margaret Ellen (Brewster) F.; m. Irene Anne Halász, Mar. 17, 1966; children: Erin Elizabeth, Robin Margaret. AB, Villanova U., 1956; MS, U. Pa., 1966, MA, 1970, PhD, 1973. Cert. sci. and English tchr., Pa., N.J. Tchr., coach Archdiocese of Phila. Sch. System, 1956-59, Devon (Pa.) Preparatory Sch., 1959-61, Malvern (Pa.) Preparatory Sch., 1961-65; asst. prof. LaSalle U., Phila., 1970-71; asst.prof. Jersey City (N.J.) State Coll., 1971-72; fellow U. Pa., Phila., 1972-73, lectr., 1973-74; continuing edn. dean Chestnut Hill Coll., Phila., 1974-75; educator Sch. Dist. Phila., 1976-84; chemistry prof. Cen. High Sch., Phila., 1984—; coach Franklin Learning Ctr., Phila., 1976-82, Cen. High Sch., Phila., 1985—. Author: Concepts of Discipline in Education, 1973. Ofcl. Pa. Relay Carnival, 1965—, Millrose Games, N.Y.C., 1982—, Olympics, L.A., 1984, The Athletics Congress, 1976—. With U.S. Army, 1957-58. Named Legion of Honor Chapel of Four Chaplains, 1989; recipient Presdl. scholarship, 1953-56, Nat. Def. Edn. Act fellowship Dept. Health, Edn. and Welfare, 1966-69, Univ. fellowship U. Pa., 1969-70. Mem. Nat. Right to Life Com., Pa. Sheriff's Assn. (hon.), Pa. Interscholastic Athletic Assn. (ofcl. 1973—), Schoolmen's Club Phila., The Irish Soc., Emerald Soc. (mem. edn. com. 1980—), U. Pa. Edn. Alumni Assn. (bd. dirs. 1988—), Phi Delta Kappa, Delta Epsilon Sigma. Republican. Roman Catholic. Home: 189 Gypsy Ln King Of Prussia PA 19406-3720 Office: Ctrl High Sch Ogontz and Olney Aves Philadelphia PA 19141

FARLEY, ROSEMARY CARROLL, mathematics and computer science educator; b. N.Y.C., Apr. 7, 1952; d. Joseph William and Nancy (Flaherty) C.; m. Dennis Michael Farley, Oct. 10, 1976; children: Christopher, Mary Ann, Brian, Nancy. BS, Coll. Mt. St. Vincent, 1974; MS, NYU, 1976, PhD, 1991. Instr. Fordham U., Bronx, N.Y., 1976-79; instr. Manhattan Coll., Bronx, N.Y., 1979-82, asst. prof., 1989—; asst. prof. Coll. Mt. St. Vincent, Bronx, N.Y., 1982-88. Mem. Math. Assn. Am., Am. Math. Soc., Am. Statis. Assn. Democrat. Roman Catholic. Home: 120 Bennett Ave Yonkers NY 10701-6310 Office: Manhattan Coll Manhattan College Pky Bronx NY 10471-3913

FARLOW, STANLEY JERRY, mathematician, educator; b. Emmetsburg, Iowa, Mar. 7, 1937; s. Stanley Wier and Dorothy (Bohn) F.; m. Susan Takach, June 22, 1968. BS, Iowa State U., 1959; MS, U. Iowa, 1962; PhD, Oreg. State U., 1967. Computer scientist NIH, Bethesda, Md., 1964-69; prof. math. U. Maine, Orono, 1969—. Author: Partial Differential Equations, 1983, Finite Mathematics, 1988, Differential Equations, 1990, Applied Mathematics, 1990. Home: 104 Forest Ave Orono ME 04473-1416 Office: U Maine Orono ME 04473

FARMANFARMAIAN, A. VERDI, physiology educator; b. Teheran, Iran, June 10, 1929; came to U.S., 1948; s. Abdol Hossein and Hamdam (Talai) F.; m. Parvin Saidi, May 27, 1958; children: Dellara, Kimya. BA, Reed Coll., 1952; MA, Stanford U., 1955, PhD, 1959; postdoctoral cert., U. Calif., Berkeley, 1961. Prof. physiology Rutgers U., Piscataway, N.J., 1967—, chmn. dept. physiology, 1979-82, dir. grad. program in physiology, 1979-82; instr. Marine Biol. Lab., Woods Hole, Mass., 1960, 64, 65, investigator, 1966-83; vis. prof. Stanford (Calif.) U., 1972, ARC Inst. Animal Physiology, Cambridge, Eng., 1976, Princeton (N.J.) U., 1982; cons. in aquaculture and environ. Ctr. Coastal Environ. Sci., Rutgers U., 1970—. Contbr. numerous articles to sci. jours., chpts. to books. Mem. Soc. Gen. Physiologists, Am. Physiol. Soc., N.Y. Acad. Scis., World Aquaculture Soc. Office: Rutgers U Dept Biol Scis Piscataway NJ 08855

FARMER, JAMES A., II, trial attorney; b. N.Y.C., May 23, 1956. BA, Rutgers U., New Brunswick, 1978; JD, Rutgers U., Camden, 1981. Bar: N.J., Pa. Sr. trial attorney Office of Pub. Defender, Camden, N.J., 1983—. Vol. Phila. Com. for Homeless, 1989; big brother Big Brothers/Big Sisters Assn., Phila., 1983—; mem. Chapel of 4 Chaplains Legion Honor, 1986. Recipient Cert. of Appreciation for Outstanding Efforts Big Brother/Big Sister Assn., 1988. Mem. Rutgers Alumni Assn., Rutgers Camden Sch. Law Alumni Assn., Phi Beta Kappa, Phi Sigma Iota. Democrat. Home: 4929 Warrington Ave Philadelphia PA 19143 Office: Office of Pub Defender 101 Haddon Ave Ste 8 Camden NJ 08103

FARMER, JOHN MARTIN, state senator; b. St. Johnsbury, Vt., Mar. 25, 1934; s. Edward Baldwin and Clara (Martin) F.; m. Judith Stook Farmer, June 15, 1956; children: Scott Martin, Tamara Farmer Hathaway. BS in Engring. and Bus. Adminstrn., MIT, 1956. Mfg. trainee Gen. Electric, Lynn, Mass., Schenectady, N.Y., 1956-58; v.p. Farmer Electric Products Co. Inc., Natick, Mass., 1958-73; commr. econ. devel. State of Vt., Montpelier, 1973-76, sec. agy. devel. community affairs, 1976; mem. Vt. Ho. of Reps., Montpelier, 1981-86; state senator Vt. Senate, Montpelier, 1989—. Trustee St. Johnsbury Acad., 1976-89, Copley Hosp., 1982—, Vt. State Colls., 1990—. Lt. USAR, 1956-63. Mem. Rotary (pres. 1972-73). Office: Vt State Senate State Capitol Montpelier VT 05602

FARMER, SUSAN LAWSON, broadcasting executive, former secretary of state; b. Boston, May 29, 1942; d. Ralph and Margaret (Tyng) Lawson; m. Malcolm Farmer, III, Apr. 6, 1968; children: Heidi Benson, Stephanie Lawson. Student, Garland Jr. Coll., 1960-61, Brown U., 1961-62. Mem. Providence Home Rule Charter Commn., 1979-80; sec. of state State of R.I., Providence, 1983-87; chief exec. officer, gen. mgr. Sta. WSBE-TV, Providence, 1987—; spl. adv. R.I. Family Ct., 1978-83; mem. nat. voting standards panel Fed. Election Commn. co-chmn. Nat. Voter Edn. Project; mem. electoral coll., 1984; chmn. Gov.'s Com. on Ethics in Govt., 1985-86; mem. teaching facility and adv. panel Internat. Ctr. on Election Law and Adminstrn.; mem. natl. edn. adv. com. Pub. Broadcasting System, 1987—; trustee Eastern Ednl. TV Network, 1987—. Bd. dirs. Justice Resources Corp., Marathon House, Inc., R.I. Council Alcoholism, R.I. Hist. Soc.; mem. Mayor's Task Force on Child Abuse, R.I. Film Commn.; v.p. Miriam Hosp. Found.; mem. adv. com. Women in Polit. and Govtl. Careers Program, U. R.I., 1985—; mem. adv. bd. Com. for Study of Am. Electorate-Ford Found. Project-Efficacy in State Voting Laws, 1986; mem. Commn. to Study Length of Election Process, 1985—; steering com. Nat. Fund for America's Future, Project Vote R.I.; bd. dirs. Dawn for Children Tng. Thru Placement; pres. Channel 36 Found.; bd. dirs. R.I. Anti-Drug Coalition Exec. Com. Named Woman of Yr., Nat. Women's Polit. Caucus, 1980. Mem. R.I. Women's Polit. Caucus (Woman of Yr. award 1980), Bus. and Profl. Women (Woman of Yr. award 1984), LWV, Common Cause, Save the Bay, Women for Non-nuclear Future, Providence Preservation Soc., Orgn. State Broadcasting Execs., Agawam Hunt Club (Providence), Mill Reef Club (Antigua, West Indies). Home: 147 Lloyd Ave Providence RI 02906-1552 Office: Sta WSBE-TV 50 Park Ln Providence RI 02907-3145

FARMER, WILLIAM SILAS, JR., government research administrator, nuclear engineer; b. Waterville, Maine, Apr. 16, 1922; s. William Silas and Genevieve Elizabeth (Fye) F.; m. Hazel Roberta Vernon, Feb. 8, 1947; children: Pamela, Martha, Ann, William Silas III. BSChemE magna cum laude, Tufts U., 1944; MSChemE, U. Tenn., 1950, postgrad., 1950-51. Lic. profl. engr., Md. Rsch. engr. Oak Ridge Nat. Lab., 1946-53; project mgr. Pratt & Whitney, Hartford, Conn., 1953-57; mgr. tech. planning Allis Chalmers, Washington, 1957-62; tech. dir., Bethesda, Md., 1962-70; staff cons. AEC, Bethesda, 1970; mgr. nuclear projects Potomic Electric Power Co., Washington, 1971-73; rsch. program mgr. Nuclear Regulatory Commn., Rockville, Md., 1973—. Active, Boy Scouts Am., 1962-68; bd. dirs. Hillandale Swim and Tennis Assn., Silver Spring, Md., 1964-66, 79-80; trustee Christ Congl. Ch., Silver Spring, 1974-78. Recipient Merit award Nuclear Regulatory Commn., 1978, 80, 89; Tufts nat. scholar Tufts U., Medford, Mass., 1940-44; DuPont grad. fellow U. Tenn., Knoxville, 1949-50. Mem. IEEE, Nuclear Power Engring. Com.Sub Com. 4, Am. Inst. Chem. Engrs., Am. Chem. Soc., Am. Nuclear Soc., Sigma Xi, Tau Beta Pi. Republican. Avocations: golf; tennis; sailing. Home: 10115 Green Forest Dr Silver Spring MD 20903-1535 Office: Nuclear Regulatory Commn 5650 Nicholson Ln Washington DC 20555

FARMERIE, SAMUEL ALBERT, academic administrator, educator; b. Pitts., Aug. 24, 1931; s. Harold S. and Mae (Wolpert) F.; m. Janice C. Norman, Apr. 1, 1961; children: Randy Lynn, Todd Alan, Wendy Kaye. BS in Edn., Clarion State U., 1954; MS, Westminster Coll., 1960; EdD, Pa. State U., 1964. Cert. secondary prin., asst. supt., Pa. Tchr. SRU Joint Sch. Dist., East Smithfield, Pa., 1956-61; grad. asst. Pa. State U., University Park, 1961-63; registrar Lebanon Valley Coll., Annville, Pa., 1963-66; prof. Westminster Coll., New Wilmington, Pa., 1966—, adminstr., 1980—; cons. various sch. dists., colls. in Pa., W.Va., 1980—. Author: History of Clarion State U., 1967, A History of Volant College, 1990. Active Boy Scouts Am., Lawrence County, Pa., 1970. Named Disting. Faculty lectr. Westminster Coll., 1983, Educator of Yr. Phi Delta Kappa, New Wilmington, 1986. Mem. Pa. Assn. Grad. Schs. (pres. 1988-89), Pa. Coun. Ednl. Adminstrn. (exec. bd. 1982-90), Pa. Hist. Assn., Nat. Orgn. Legal Problems in Edn., Pa. Assn. Colls. and Tchr. Educators (exec. bd. 1975-81, 86-88). Presbyterian. Office: Westminster Coll New Wilmington PA 16172

FARNAN, JOSEPH JAMES, JR., judge; b. Phila., June 15, 1945; s. Joseph James and Philomena (DeLaurentis) F.; m. Patricia Candice Winner, June 28, 1969; children: Joseph James III, Brian, Kelly, Tracie, Michael. BA, King's Coll., (Pa.), 1967; JD, U. Toledo Coll. Law, 1970. Bar: N.J. 1970, Del. 1972. Dir. crime justice program Wilmington Coll., New Castle, Del., 1970-73; pvt. practice law Wilmington, 1973-76; asst. pub. defender State Del., Wilmington, 1973-75; county atty. New Castle County, Wilmington, 1976-79; chief dep. atty. gen. Del. Dept. Justice, Wilmington, 1979-81; U.S. atty. U.S. Dept. Justice, Wilmington, 1981-85; judge U.S. Dist. Ct. Del., Wilmington, 1985—. Mem. ABA, Del. State Bar Assn., N.J. State Bar Assn., Am. Trail Lawyers Assn., Fed. Bar Assn. Republican. Roman Catholic. Home: 7 Crenshaw Dr Wilmington DE 19810-3620 Office: US Dist Ct 844 N King St # 27 Wilmington DE 19801-3519*

FARNHAM, THOMAS JAVERY, historian; b. Bennington, Vt., May 7, 1938; s. Harold Frederick and Marjorie Lucille (Javery) F.; children: Jonathan, Christopher, Julia; m. Gwen Davis, Mar. 19, 1983; stepchildren: Andrew Davis, Jennifer Davis. BA, Ohio Wesleyan U., 1959; MA, U. N.C., 1961, PhD, 1964. Asst. prof. Moorhead (Minn.) State Coll., 1964-66; mem. faculty dept. history So. Conn. State U., New Haven, 1966—, prof., 1971—; pres. TLI Assocs., Inc., 1987—. NEA fellow, 1969-70, Early Am. Industries fellow, 1982, Robert Newman fellow, 1991-92. Mem. Assn. Study Conn. History, New Haven Colony Hist. Soc. (dir., v.p.), Orgn. Am. Historians. Author: Regulators of North Carolina, 1971; A Child I Set Much By, 1976; Weston: The Forging of a Connecticut Community, 1979; Upper State Street: Our History, 1982, Fairfield: The Biography of a Community, 1989; co-author: New Haven: An Illustrated History, 1981. Home: 189 3d Ave Milford CT 06460-5243 Office: So Conn State U Seabury Hall New Haven CT 06515

FARNKART, JAMES EDWARD, industrial psychologist; b. Fostoria, Ohio, Jan. 21, 1946; s. Marion Michael and Agnes Mary (Rheinhart) F.; m. Judy B. Frankart, May 10, 1074; children: Amy Lynn, Andrew James. A in Electronics, U. Toledo, 1970, BA in Psychology, 1978; M in Indsl. Psychology, U. Akron, 1980. Laborer Roppe Rubber Corp., Fostoria, 1964-65; shipper Union Carbide Corp., Fostoria, 1965-66; machinist Excello Corp., Fostoria, 1967-69; press operator Chrysler Corp., Toledo, 1969-78; test specialist City of Akron, Ohio, 1980-81; pers. analyst Pa. Civil Svc. Commn., Harrisburg, 1981—. Mem. APA, Mid Atlantic Pers. Assessment Consortium, Internat. Pers. Mgmt. Assn., Harrisburg Pers. Mgmt. Assn. Democrat. Presbyterian. Home: 21 Houston Dr Mechanicsburg PA 17055-1612 Office: Pa Civil Svc Commn PO Box 569 Harrisburg PA 17108-0569

FAROUK, BAKHTIER, mechanical engineer, educator; b. Dhaka, Bangladesh, Dec. 5, 1951; came to U.S., 1976; s. Abdullah and Sophia (Sarwar) F.; m. Nadira Begum, Aug. 22, 1982; 1 child, Samira. BS, Bangladesh Engring. U., 1975; MS, U. Del., 1978, PhD, 1981. Lectr. Bangladesh Engring. U., Dhaka, 1975-76; rsch. asst. U. Houston, 1976-77; rsch., teaching asst. U. Del., Newark, 1977-81; asst. prof. Drexel U., Phila., 1981-86, assoc. prof., 1986-89, prof. mech. engring., 1989—; faculty rsch. assoc. Naval Rsch. Lab., Washington, summer 1988. Recipient Teetor award Soc. Automotive Engrs., Warrendale, Pa., 1986, Henry Marion Howe medal Am. Soc. Metals, Ohio, 1988. Mem. Am. Soc. Mech. Engrs., Am. Inst. Aeronautics & Astronautics, Iron and Steel Soc., Combustion Inst. Office: Drexel U Dept Mech Engring Philadelphia PA 19104

FARQUHARSON, GORDON MACKAY, lawyer; b. Charlottetown, P.E.I., Can., July 12, 1928; s. Percy Alfred and Rachel Lillian (MacKay) F.; m. Judy Lynne Bridges, Oct. 10, 1980; children: Trevor, Jordan; children by previous marriage: Douglas, Tanyss, Robbie, Karen. B.A., U. Toronto, 1950; LL.B., Osgoode Hall Law Sch., 1954. Bar: Called to Ont. bar 1954; Queen's Counsel 1965. Pvt. practice Toronto, 1954—; ptnr. Lang Michener, 1964—; dir. GSW Ltd., Camco Inc., Valleydene Corp. Ltd., Showerlux Can. Ltd., NN Life Ins. Co. Can., Shaw Industries Ltd., Doverhold Investments Ltd., Tambrands Can., Inc. Mem. Friends of L'Arche, Univ. Club (Toronto), Craigleigh Ski Club, Founders Club (Toronto), Phi Gamma Delta (pres. 1954). Clubs: University (Toronto), Craigleigh Ski. Home: 419 Brunswick Ave, Toronto, ON Canada Office: BCE Pl, 181 Bay St Ste 250D PO Box 747, Toronto, ON Canada M5J 2T7

FARQUHARSON, WALTER HENRY, minister, church official; b. Zealandia, Sask., Can., May 30, 1936; s. James and Jessie Ann (Muirhead) F.; m. Patricia Joan Casswell, Sept. 16, 1958; children: Scott, Michael, Catherine, Stephen. BA, U. Sask., Saskatoon, 1957, Diploma in Edn., 1969; BD, St. Andrew's Coll., Saskatoon, 1961, DD (hon.), 1975. Ordained to ministry United Ch. of Can., 1961. Min. Saltcoats-Bredenbury-Churchbridge Pastoral Charge, Sask., 1961—; moderator United Ch. of Can., 1990—; exec. gen. coun., pres. Sask. Conf. Contbr. numerous hymns and religious songs. Home: PO Box 126, Saltcoats, SK Canada S0A 3R0 Office: United Ch of Can, PO Box 58, Saltcoats, SK Canada S0A 3R0 also: United Ch of Can, 85 St Clair Ave E, Toronto, ON Canada M4T 1M8

FARR, CHARLES SIMS, lawyer; b. Hewlett, N.Y., June 29, 1920; s. John Farr and Hazel (Zealy) Sims; m. Mary Randolph Rue, Dec. 21, 1946 (dec. Dec. 1980); children: Charles Sims, Virginia Farr Ramsey, Randolph Rue, John II; m. Muriel Tobin Byrnes, Oct. 13, 1990. Student, Princeton U., 1938-40; LLB, Columbia U., 1948. Bar: N.Y. 1949, Fla. 1984. Assoc. White & Case, N.Y.C., 1948-58, ptnr., 1959-88, of counsel, 1989-92, ret.; mem. bd. visitors Columbia U. Sch. Law. Contbr. articles to profl. publs. Chmn. Commonwealth Fund, N.Y.C.; trustee St. Luke's-Roosevelt Hosp. Ctr., 1972-92, Gen. Theol. Sem., 1968-77, N.Y. Zool. Soc., Kent Sch., Children's Storefront; mem. bd. fgn. parishes Protestant Episc. Ch., 1954-78, pres., 1977; chancellor to pres. bishop Protestant Episc. Ch. in U.S.A., 1977-85; mem. vestry St. James' Ch., N.Y.C., 1966-76, sr. warden, 1973-76, jr. warden, 1984-86; mem. coun. Rockefeller U. Lt. comdr. USN, 1941-45, ETO, MTO, PTO. Decorated Atlantic Campaign ribbon, European Campaign ribbon with 4 battle stars, Pacific Campaign ribbon, Sec. Navy Commendation ribbon; recipient Alumni Assn. medal Columbia U., 1977. Fellow Am. Coll. Probate Counsel (regent 1960-75), Am. Bar Found.; mem. ABA, N.Y. State Bar Assn., Assn. of Bar of City of N.Y., Am. Law Inst., Century Club (trustee), Links Club, River Club, Pilgrims Club, Yeamen's Hall (S.C.). Republican. Home: 200 E 66th St New York NY 10021-6728 also: Avery Rd Garrison NY 10524 also: 81 King St Charleston SC 29401 Office: White & Case 1155 Ave of the Americas New York NY 10036-2711

FARR, JAMES FRANCIS, lawyer; b. Ludlow, Mass., Mar. 17, 1911; s. Charles H. and Stella (Greene) F.; AB, Harvard U., 1933, LLB, 1936. Bar: Mass. 1937. Pvt. practice Boston, 1937—; sr. ptnr. Haussermann, Davison & Shattuck, 1948-89, Peabody & Arnold, 1989—; bd. dirs., clk. Durkee-Mower, Inc., Cape Cod Candle & Gift Shops, Inc.; bd. dirs. H F G Co., Chgo., Cape Cod Mgmt. Inc., Babson Bros. Co., Blumberg Co., Inc., Robert McF. Brown & Sons, Inc., Currier Cons., Inc. Former bd. dirs., clk. Scottish Rite Mus. and Libr., Inc.; former pres. Cambridge YMCA; former chmn. bd. dirs. New Eng. Deaconess Hosp.; treas., bd. dirs. New Eng. Edn. Soc. Served to lt. USCGR, World War II. Methodist (trustee), Mason (33 deg., Shriner, dir. grand lodge). Clubs: Cambridge Economy (past pres.), Cambridge, Harvard (Boston). Author: (with Mayo A. Shattuck) An Estate Planner's Handbook, 1953; Loring, A Trustee's Handbook Farr Revision, 1961; An Estate Planner's Handbook, 1966, co-author 1979 edit., supplement, 1982, 85, 87, 88, 89, 90, 91, 92. Home: 51 Martin St Cambridge MA 02138-1616 Office: 50 Rowes Wharf Boston MA 02110-3328

FARR, JAMES WOODHULL, biologist; b. N.Y.C., Mar. 18, 1952; s. Hollon and Anne (Mathews) F. BA, Dowling Coll., 1978; BS in Biology, C.W. Post Coll., 1981; MS in Biology, Fordham U., 1985. Field worker Suffolk County Mosquito Control, Yaphank, N.Y., 1978-79; rsch. biologist Westchester County Dept. Health, White Plains, N.Y., 1985; rsch. biologist, sanitarian Nassau County Dept. Health, Mineola, N.Y., 1986-89; self employed Bellport, N.Y., 1989—. Contbr. to Marine Biota of Long Island, 1984; contbr. articles to profl. jours. Pres. steering com. Greater Opportunity Program, Lakeville, Conn., 1970; mem. open space com. Brookhaven Village, 1987—. Mem. N.Y. Water Pollution Control Fedn., Audubon Soc., L.I. Marine Biology Assn., L.I. Green Party, Alpha Club, Sigma Xi. Presbyterian.

FARR, JO-ANN HUNTER, psychologist; b. Brackenridge, Pa., Apr. 29, 1936; d. Francis Lytle and Dorothy (Colin) Hunter; m. William R. Hughes (div.); children: Cynthia Jo O'Hora, William Hunter, Christopher Eric, Michael Patrick, Amy Elizabeth; m. John E. Farr (div.); 1 child, John Herschel; m. James K. Medeiros, June 10, 1984. BS in Psychology and Physiology, Pa. State U., 1970, MS in Psychology, 1971, PhD in Psychology, 1974. Diplomate Am. Bd. Sexology, Am. Acad. Clin. Sexologists (founding clin. fellow 1991). Dir., therapist Devel. Vision Ctr., State College, Pa., 1969-71; cons. Pk. Forest Nursery Sch., State College, Pa., 1970-71; in-take supr. psychol. clin. Pa. State U., University Park, 1972-73; cons. Centre County Youth Svc. Bur., State College, 1972-78, Juniata Tri-County Mental Health/Mental Retardation Adminstrn., Lewistown, Pa., 1974-76; asst. prof. of psychology Pa. State U., 1975-77; pvt. practice State College, 1977—; sponsored NIMH guest lectr. Kinsey Inst., Bloomington, Ind. Contbr. articles to profl. jours. Mem. Govs. Counsel for Sexual Minorities, Pa.; bd. dirs. Pa. Assoc. of Families, State Coll., Parents Without Ptnrs., State Coll. John W. White fellow Pa. State U., 1970-71, U.S. Pub. Health Svc. fellow Pa. State U., 1970-74; nominated Outstanding Pennsylvanian State Dept. of Health adn Welfare, 1986. Fellow Am. Acad. Clin. Sexologists (clin.); mem. APA, Sex Info. and Edn. Coun. U.S. (assoc.),. Assn. for Advancement of Behavior Therapy, Soc. for Sci. Study of Sex, Am. Soc. Sex Educators, Counselors and Therapists, Assn. Behavior Analysts, Pa. Psychol. Assn., Nat. Register Health Svc. Providers, Mental Health Profls. of Cen. Pa., Am. Soc. Clin. Hypnosis. Office: Jo-Ann Hunter Farr & Assocs 3490 W College Ave State College PA 16801-2505

FARR, JUDITH BANZER, literature educator; b. N.Y.C., Mar. 13, 1937; d. Russell John and Frances Anna (Wissell) Banzer; m. George F. Farr, Jr., June 30, 1962; 1 child, Alec Winfield. BA, Marymount Manhattan Coll., 1957; MA, Yale U., 1959, PhD, 1965. Instr. in English Vassar Coll., Poughkeepsie, N.Y., 1961-63; asst. prof. St. Mary's Coll., Moraga, Calif., 1964-68; assoc. prof. SUNY, New Paltz, 1968-77; assoc. prof. Georgetown U., Washington, 1978-90, prof. of English, 1990—; vis. assoc. prof. Georgetown U., 1977-78. Author: The Life and Art of Elinor Wylie, 1983, The Passion of Emily Dickinson, 1992; editor: Twentieth Century Interpretations of Sons and Lovers, 1970; contbr. articles, poems, short stories to profl. publs. Recipient Alumnae award for Distinction in Arts and Letters, Marymount Manhattan Coll., N.Y.C., 1976, fellowship Am. Philos. Soc., 1983, Morgan-Porter fellowship, Yale U., 1960-61; grantee Am. Coun. Learned Socs., 1986. Mem. Modern Lang. Assn., AAUP. Office: Georgetown U 330 New North Hall 37th St and O Washington DC 20057

FARR, LONA MAE, fund-raising executive; b. Phila., June 4, 1941; d. Alonzo Schroeder and Lillyan (Nickels) F.; m. Malcolm J. Gross, Aug. 24, 1963 (div. Mar. 1976); children: Andrea Lillyan, Stacey Jane, John Farr; m. David V. Voellinger, Sept. 27, 1981. AB in History and English, Muhlenberg Coll., 1962; MS in Edn., Temple U., 1968. Tchr. Swain Sch., Allentown, Pa., 1962-63, St. Monica's Sch., Berwyn, Pa., 1963-65, Hebrew Day Sch., Scranton, Pa., 1965-66; pub. rels. assoc. Muhlenberg Coll., Allentown, 1973-75, dir. alumni affairs, 1975-77; dir. devel. and pub. rels. Allentown Coll. St. Frances de Sales, Allentown, 1977-81; dir. pub. rels. Good Shepherd Home, Allentown, 1981-84, dir. devel., 1984-87, group exec., v.p. instnl. devel., 1987—. Producer (films) More Than a Name, 1983 (Golden Eagle award 1984), Venture of Faith, 1984 (silver medal N.Y. Film Festival 1985), Spirit of Good Shepherd Day, 1987, (video) The Best You Can Be, 1988. Bd. dirs. Muhlenberg Coll., 1982—, Wiley House, Allentown, 1986—; bd. dirs. Allentown Symphony, 1987—, pres., 1990—; bd. dirs. Baum Sch. Art, Allentown, 1987—, United Way Lehigh County, 1990-93; founding bd. dirs. Vol. Action Ctr., Lehigh Valley, Pa., 1984-89, Lehigh Valley Interfaith TV, 1988—; adviser Lehigh County Human Svcs., Allentown, 1986-91. Recipient Disting. Sales award Sals and Mktg. Execs. Lehigh Valley, 1984. Mem. Pub. Rels. Soc. Am., Nat. Soc. Hosp. Devel., Nat. Soc. Fund Raising Execs. (cert., rep. nat. bd. dirs. 1987—, founding pres. Greater N.E. Pa. chpt. 1986-88, Outstanding Exec. award 1988, Fund Raising Exec. of Yr. 1988), Nat. Certification Bd., Appalachian Health Care Pub. Rels. and Mktg. Assn. (pres. 1987), Muhlenberg Coll. Alumni Assn. (pres. 1981-85), Rotary (bd. dirs. Allentown 1988—, pres. elect 1992—), Quota Club (pres. Allentown 1986-88). Home: 2238 W Chew St Allentown PA 18104-5548 Office: Good Shepherd Home 6th St Allentown PA 18101-2102

FARRA, CHUCRI RONALD, retail executive; b. Beirut, Oct. 18, 1948; came to the U.S., 1986; s. Anwar Chucri and Marguerite (Fata) F.; m. Monique Finan, Apr. 21, 1979 (div. Mar. 1989); 1 child, Philip Ronald; m. Maggy Chreim, July 1, 1989; children: Marc Anwar, Alain Carl. BBA, Am. U. Beirut, 1970. Asst. mgr. Anwar Farra Co., Beirut, 1966-73, mgr., 1974-81, gen. mgr., 1982-85; pres., chief exec. officer Domus Design Ctr. Inc., Fairfield, N.J., 1985—; cons. Ballabio Export, Mariano Comense, Italy, 1982—, Venier Mobilificio SpA Treviso, Italy, 1983—; Lebanese-Am. C. of C. (officer 1988-90). Mem. Lebanese Red Cross Active Team, Beirut, 1968, Intercommunity Rels. Armenian Caths., Beirut, 1974-75, Khalil Gibran Centennial Found. (N.Y.) Com., 1989; off icer Lebanese Am. C. of C. (N.Y.), 1988-90. Mem. Coun. Lebanese Am. Orgns. (exec. vice-chmn. 1990-91), Scouts of Lebanon (commr. 1968-75), Am. Lebanese League, Com. for Free and Sovereign Lebanon, Rotary. Armenian Catholic. Home: 5 Concord Way Morris Plains NJ 07950-1271 Office: Domus Design Ctr Inc 2 Main Ave Passaic NJ 07055-4417

FARRALL, GEORGE WILLIAM, marketing executive; b. Beverly, Mass., Feb. 16, 1959; s. Robert Arthur and Nancy Mary (Georgi) F.; m. JoAnn Steigler. BS in Mgmt, Fairfield U., 1981. Ops. mgr. Interstate Yacht Maintenance, Rye, N.Y., 1978-81; div. mgr. Amerco, Phoenix, 1981-82, ops. mgr., 1982-83; product mktg. mgr., specialist Clairex Electronics, Mt. Vernon, N.Y., 1983-88, mgr. product mktg., 1988-90; sales mgr. Tyco Backplanes, Stafford Springs, Conn., 1990-91; pres. LDC Communications, Stamford, Conn., 1991—; cons. Lowall Distbg. Corp., Rye, 1988—, also bd. dirs. Active Rye Pub. Sch. System, N.Y., 1980. Mem. Nat. Desktop Pub. Assn., Am. Mgmt. Assn., Am. Mktg. Assn., Am. Yacht Club, Mystic Seaport. Democrat. Home: 180 Glenbrook Rd Unit 8 Stamford CT 06902-3025 Office: Two Stamford Landing Southfield Ave Ste 100 Stamford CT 06902-7217

FARRAND, DONALD GEORGE, agricultural instructor; b. Corning, N.Y., Feb. 28, 1939; s. Raymond Grover and May (Risley) F.; m. Anna Mae Houghtaling Van Zile, Oct. 26, 1962; 1 child, Donise Ann Farrand Leonard; stepchildren: Vernon I. Van Zile, Steven J. Van Zile. AAS in Agr., Alfred (N.Y.) Agrl. Tech, 1959; BS in Agr., U. Ga., 1969; MS in Edn., Elmira Coll., 1974; cert. of advanced study, SUNY, Brockport, 1987. Cert. in agr. edn.; cert. work study program coord., sch. dist. adminstr. Dairy farmhand Cameron, N.Y., 1952-63; acting wildlife tech. Bur. Wildlife N.Y. State Dept. Environ. Conservation, Avon, N.Y., 1963-71; agrl. and conservation instr. Schuyler, Chemung, Tioga Bd. Coop. Ednl. Svcs., Elmira, 1971—, youth advisor Future Farmers Am., 1971—, dir. Youth Conservation Corps., 1974-80, dir. N.Y. State Conservation Corp., 1988-90; supervising tchr. Cornell U., Ithaca, N.Y., 1974-92; specialty contest coord. N.Y. State Future Farmers Am., Albany, N.Y., 1991—. Author: (transparencies) Chainsaw Safety and Maintenance, 1981; (slides) Woodlot Mgmt. for Multipurpose, 1983; film tech. advisor Backhoe and Bulldozer Safety and Operation, 1978, Loading and Unloading Heavy Equipment, 1979. Com. person Republican Orgn., Erwin, N.Y., 1985—; active Zoning Bd. Appeals, Erwin, 1991—, 4H Youth Com./Chemung County, Elmira, 1991—, v.p., 1992. Recipient Hon. State degree N.Y. State Future Farmers Am., 1981, Hon Am. degree Nat. Future Farmers Am., 1990, Soil and Water Conservation award Chemung County, 1991, Region 8 Outstanding Contbn. award N.Y. State Coun. Vocat. Edn., 1991. Mem. NRA (N.Y. chpt.), Nat. Vocat. Agrl. Tchrs. Assn., N.Y. State Conservation Coun., Assn. Tchrs. Agr., Hunter Edn. Assn. (instr.

U.S. and Can. chpts. 1971—), N.Y. State Hunter Safety (instr.), Masons (32d degree, sr. warden Robinson Lodge 895 1963, 25 yr. pin 1985). Republican. Methodist. Home: 139 Main St Box 45 Coopers Plains NY 14827 Office: Schuyler Chemung Tioga Bd Coop Ednl Svcs 431 Philo Rd Elmira NY 14903

FARRAND, GEORGE NIXON, JR., marketing professional; b. N.Y.C., Apr. 1, 1936; s. George Nixon and Pauline (Merchant) F.; m. Elyn Marie Hallberg, Aug. 26, 1961; 1 child, Kathryn Elyn (dec. 1985). BSBA, Lehigh U., 1958; postgrad. in bus. adminstrn., NYU, 1962. Advt. and promotions writer Union Carbide Corp., N.Y.C., 1959-62; account exec. McCann-Erickson, Inc., N.Y.C., 1962-63, Vick Chem. Co., N.Y.C., 1963-64; sr. account exec., supr. Grey Advt., Inc., N.Y.C., 1964-65; products mktg. mgr. Hoffmann-LaRoche, Inc., Clifton, N.J., 1965-67; dir. new markets Inmont Corp., N.Y.C., 1967-69; sr. v.p. Bliss/Grunewald, Inc., N.Y.C., 1969-73; pres., chief exec. officer Farrand Mktg. Assoc., Inc., Saddle River, N.J., 1973—, Farrand Enterprises, Saddle River, 1983—. Sgt. U.S. Army, 1959. Mem. Sales Execs. Club N.Y.C., Lehigh U. Alumni Club (past treas. and pres.), Saddle River Swim and Tennis Club. Republican. Presbyterian. Home: 70 Ripplewood Dr Saddle River NJ 07458-1422 Office: Farrand Mktg Assocs Inc Saddle River NJ 07458

FARRAR, JAMES MARTIN, chemist, educator; b. Pitts., June 15, 1948; s. Martin and Lorraine (Williams) F.; m. Kathy Meyer, Mar. 20, 1971; children: Stacey, Andrew. AB, Washington U., 1970; MS, U. Chgo., 1972, PhD, 1974. Rsch. assoc. Lawrence Berkeley (Calif.) Lab., 1974-76; asst. chemistry prof. U. Roschester (N.Y.), 1976-82, assoc. prof., 1982-86, prof., 1986—; vis. fellow Joint Inst. for Lab. Astrophysics, Boulder, Colo. Author and Editor: Techniques of Chemistry, 1988; contbr. articles to profl. jours. Recipient Marc Perry Galler award U. Chgo., 1975, Edward Peck Curtis award U. Rochester, 1985; NSF fellowship, 1970; Alfred P. Sloan Found. fellow, 1981. Mem. Am. Chem. Soc., Am. Physical Soc. (fellow). Home: 122 Chelmsford Rd Rochester NY 14618-1710 Office: U Rochester Dept of Chemistry Rochester NY 14627

FARRELL, DUNCAN GRAHAM STUART, professional society administrator; b. Evanston, Ill., Apr. 29, 1935; s. Lawrence Stewart and Katherine Ellen (Wiggins) F.; m. Emily Moore Mahan, Aug. 3, 1957 (div. 1970); children: Laura Emily, Grace Moore III, Anne Stuart; m. June Martinick, July 31, 1971. BA in Econs., Wesleyan U., 1957; MBA in Econs., U. Chgo., 1959. Cert. meeting profl. Assoc. McKinsey and Co., Chgo., 1962; mgr. Interstate Vending Co., Chgo., 1962-64, Lippincott and Margulies, N.Y.C., 1964-67, Batten, Barton, Durstine and Osborn, N.Y.C., 1967-69, Ea. Airlines, Miami, Fla., 1969-74; v.p. Travel Industry Assn. Am., Washington, 1974-80; sr. v.p. Nat. Tour Assn., Lexington, Ky., 1980-82; pres. Am. Mgmt. Svcs., Inc., Chevy Chase, Md., 1982—; gen. mgr. Soc. Travel Agts. in Govt., Washington, 1984—. Mem. Meeting Planners Internat., Am. Soc. Assn. Execs. Republican. Episcopalian.. Office: 6935 Wisconsin Ave Chevy Chase MD 20815

FARRELL, EDGAR HENRY, lawyer, building components manufacturing executive; b. N.Y.C., Aug. 31, 1924; s. Edgar Henry and Lillian Sarah (Lancaster) F.; student Tex. A&M U., 1943, Stanford U., 1943-45, George Washington U. Law Sch., 1948-49; J.D., U. Md., 1950; postgrad., Harvard U. Bus. Sch., 1965; m. Mary Louise Whelan, May 3, 1952; children: Brooke Larkin Cragan, Elizabeth Lancaster, Kimberley Hopkins. Exec. sales asst. A.C. Gilbert Co., N.Y.C., 1950; asst. legal counsel U.S. Senate Crime Com., 1951; zone mgr. Life Mag., N.Y.C., 1951-52; account exec. Time Mag., N.Y.C., 1952-55, Phila., 1955-59, Detroit, 1959-62; nat. automotive sales mgr. Worldwide Automotive Products, Detroit, 1962-64, div. sales mgr., 1964-68, sales mgr., 1968; regional mgr. Communications/Research Machines, Inc., Mich., Ohio, 1968; central advt. dir. Petersen Pub. Co., Detroit, 1969; chief exec., officer Internat. Concrete Bldg. Group, London, 1972-79; asst. to pres. Dillon Co., Akron, Ohio, 1979-80; pres. and chief exec. officer Bldg. Components Group, Akron, 1980—; pres. Motorhome Holidays Internat., Camp Can. Inc., BEK Press, Camp Am., Inc.; housing cons. Saudi Arabia, Nigeria, Sri Lanka. Publicity chmn. Youth for Eisenhower Com., N.Y.C., 1952; trustee Baldwin Library, Birmingham, Mich., 1962-65. Served to lt. U.S. Army, 1945-46; PTO. Recipient Low Cost Housing award Ministry of Housing, Sri Lanka, 1979. Mem. Am. Mktg. Assn., Nat. Assn. Home Builders, Phi Delta Theta, Gamma Eta Gamma, Phi Alpha Sigma. Republican. Episcopalian. Author: Computer Center Construction, 1984. Home and Office: 1 Woodbury Hills Woodbury CT 06798-2937

FARRELL, HAROLD MARON, JR., chemist; b. Pottsville, Pa., Sept. 5, 1940; s. Harold M. and Marie G. (Daley) F.; m. Susan Gares, June 15, 1963; children: Judith A., Jonathan K. BS in Chemistry, Mt. St. Mary's Coll., 1962; MS in Biochemistry, Pa. State U., 1965, PhD, 1968. Postdoctoral fellow USDA Eastern Regional Rsch. Ctr., Phila., 1967-69, rsch. chemist, 1969-75, supervisory rsch. chemist, 1975—. Contbr. articles to profl. jours. and chpts. to books. Pres. Old York Rd. Community Concerts, Abington, Pa., 1991—, Glenside (Pa.) United Ch. of Christ, 1987-91; active troop 354 Boy Scouts Am., Willow Grove, Pa., 1980-90, cubmaster pack 336, 1978-80. Fellow Sigma Xi; mem. Am. Chem. Soc., Am. Dairy Sci. Assn. (com. chair 1976-80, Borden award 1985), Am. Soc. for Biochemistry and Molecular Biology, Phila. Biochemists Club (treas.-sec. 1978-80). Home: 500 Innam Ter Willow Grove PA 19090-3614 Office: USDA 600 E Mermaid Ln Philadelphia PA 19118-2598

FARRELL, RAYMOND MAURICE, JR., art gallery director; b. Bridgeport, Conn., Aug. 9, 1940; s. Raymond Maurice Sr. and Freida Margarethe (Swanson) F.; m. Linda Gale Wheeler, July 17, 1965 (div. Oct. 1977); 1 child, Sarah Elizabeth; m. Marilyn Agnes Havlen, July 30, 1980. AA, Mitchell Coll., 1967; BS in Art Edn., Southern Conn. State U., 1968, MS in Art Edn., 1974, postgrad. degree in adminstrn., 1980; postgrad., Columbia U., 1979. Cert. art tchr., prin., adminstr., Conn. Art tchr. Danbury (Conn.) Pub. Schs., 1969-84, adult edn. tchr. in Art, 1971-79; dir. O'Farrell Gallery, Brunswick, Maine, 1985—; adj. prof. of Art Southern Conn. State U., New Haven, 1978-82; supr. student teaching Southern Conn. State U., 1978-82; evaluator Conn. State Bd. Edn. Evaluating Team, Hartford, 1979, 84. Filmmaker Lumia Theatre, 1974 (hon. mention Tokyo 1974); contbr. articles to profl. jours.; tchr., artist ceramic mural Conn. Edn. Assn., Hartford, Conn., 1975. Bd. dirs. Mid-Coast Econ. Devel. Found., Bath, Maine, 1989; civilian co-chmn. Mil. Community Coun. Recipient Excellence in Communication award Conn. Bds. Edn., 1982; internat. study grantee Danbury Cultural Commn., 1981. Mem. Maine Art Dealers Assn. (pres. 1987-92), Brunswick C. of C. (chmn. bd. dirs. 1989), Rotary (sec. Brunswick 1988-89), Phi Delta Kappa. Office: 58 Maine St Brunswick ME 04011-2016

FARRELL, RONALD WILLIAM, private investigator; b. N.Y.C., Mar. 2, 1951; s. George J. and Joan G. (Schweers) F.; B.A., Cathedral Coll. of Immaculate Conception, Douglaston, N.Y., 1973. Br. mgr. Guardsmark, Inc., N.Y.C., 1972-75; v.p. Centurion Investigations, Inc., N.Y.C., 1975-86; v.p. Cavalier Security Services, Inc., N.Y.C., 1986—; pistol instr. Nat. Rifle Assn.; polygraph examiner; security cons.; alarm expert. Lic. locksmith, N.Y.C.; notary pub., N.Y. Mem. Am. Soc. Indsl. Security (affiliate). Democrat. Roman Catholic. Club: K.C. Contbr. articles on security subjects to trade publs. Office: Cavalier Security Svcs Inc 304 Park Ave S New York NY 10010-5312

FARRELL-LOGAN, VIVIAN, actress; b. N.Y.C.; m. Harvey Lewis, Aug. 5, 1979 (dec. Aug. 1980); m. Tracy Harrison Logan, June 3, 1984. BS in Edn., Syracuse U.; MA in Theatre, NYU. Tchr. elem. sch. Levittown (N.Y.) Schs., 1965-75; tchr. workshops Coll. of Cape Breton, N.S., Can., 1977-79. Actress: (stage) Gateway Playhouse, Bellport, N.Y., Playhouse 3200, Richmond, Va., Bartke's Dinner Theatre, Tampa, Fla., (film) Impulse; narrator for Nutcracker, Eglevsky Ballet Co. with L.I. Symphony Orch., Nassau Coliseum, Uniondale, N.Y., 1978-79; appeared as The Musical Storyteller, Lincoln Ctr., N.Y.C., Carnegie Recital Hall, N.Y.C., various libraries and schs., N.Y. area; performer, writer (album) The Musical Storyteller, 1978; author: (children's book) Robert's Tall Friend: A Story of the Fire Island Lighthouse, Island-Metro Publs., Inc., 1987; appeared in numerous schs., librs. in Author Narrates Her Book Robert's Tall Friend, 1989-92. Nassau County (N.Y.) Office Cultural Devel. grantee, 1986-92, N.Y. State Coun. on the Arts grantee, 1988-92. Mem. Actors Equity Assn., Screen Actors Guild, AFTRA, Twelfth Night Club, Ninety-Nines, Alpha Psi Omega, Zeta Phi Eta. Office: PO Box 734 Lindenhurst NY 11757-0734

FARRINGTON, HELEN AGNES, personnel director; b. Queens, N.Y., Dec. 1, 1945; d. Joseph Christopher and Therese Marie (Breazzano) F. AS, Interboro Inst., N.Y.C., 1965; AA, Ohio State U., 1983, BS in Human Resource Mgmt., 1987. Mgmt. cert. U. Mich., 1980. Supr. human resources Ohio Power div. Am. Electric Power Co., Newark, Ohio, 1979-87; mgr. human resources Citizens Utilities Co., Stamford, Conn., 1987-88; mgr., exec. search firm Arthur Lyle Assocs., Norwalk, Conn., 1988-89; dir. human resources CaroLee Designs, Inc., Greenwich, Conn., 1990—. Mem. NAFE, Am. Mgmt. Assn., Am. Soc. of Personnel Adminstrn., Am. Soc. Profl. Female Execs. Home: 97 Richards Ave Apt 4B Norwalk CT 06854-1652

FARRINGTON, HUGH G., wholesale food and retail drug company executive; b. 1945; married. BA, Dartmouth Coll., 1968. With Hannaford Bros., Scarborough, Maine, 1968—, exec. v.p., 1981-84, pres., 1984—, chief operating officer, from 1984, dir. Office: Hannaford Bros Co PO Box 1000 Portland ME 04104-5005*

FARRIS, JEFFREY IAN, controller; b. Lexington, Mass., Mar. 17, 1969; s. Uriel (Kip) Duncan and Donnalee Anne (Comlin) F. BS with honors, Babson Coll., 1991. Mktg. asst. I.D.S./Am. Express, Boston, 1990; mem. collections dept., customer svc. rep. Nationwide Cellular Svcs., Newton, Mass., 1990; internat. income contr. State Street Bank & Trust, Quincy, Mass., 1991—. Mem. Omicon Delta Epsilon (v.p. 1991). Home: 158 Maple St Lexington MA 02173 Office: State Street Bank & Trust One Enterprise Dr Quincy MA 02170

FARRIS, SUSAN ELIZABETH, economist; b. Cambridge, Mass., Mar. 21, 1966; d. Kip Duncan and Donnalee Anne (Comlin) F. BA in Econs. magna cum laude, Cornell U., 1988. Fin. rsch. asst. Beth Israel Hosp., Boston, summer 1986; bus. intern W.R. Grace & Co., Cambridge, Mass., summer 1987; bus analyst W.R. Grace & Co., 1989; student mgr. Noyes Ctr. Browsing Library, Ithaca, N.Y., 1984-88; European internal auditor Cargill U.K. Ltd., London, Eng., Eng., 1989-90; economist Cahners Econ. Forecasting, Newton, Mass., 1991—. Cornell fellow, 1985-88, Cornell Women's Fedn. scholar, 1985-88, Hayden Recreation Ctr. scholar, 1984-88; recipient Disting. & Outstanding Svc. award, Cornell Dept. Unions and Activities, 1985-88. Mem. Cornell Club of Boston, Kappa Delta (chpt. edn. officer 1986-87). Democrat. Home: 158 Maple St Lexington MA 02173-2520

FARRON, ROBERT, family physician; b. N.Y.C., May 17, 1947; s. Irving and Anne (Zavoznick) F.; m. Lorraine Herzberg, May 27, 1972; children: Cory, Eric, Jeffrey. BS, CCNY, 1968; DO, Kansas City Coll. Osteopathy, 1972. Diplomate Am. Bd. Family Practice, Am. Osteopathic Bd. Gen. Practice. Intern Interboro Gen. Hosp., Bklyn., 1972-73; practice medicine specializing in family practice Far Rockaway, N.Y., 1973—, Franklin Sq., N.Y., 1978—; attending physician Peninsula Hosp. Ctr., Far Rockaway, N.Y., 1985—; mem. physician adv. panel Med. World News. Recipient Physicians Recognition award AMA, 1983, 86, 89. Mem. Am. Osteopathic Assn., Am. Acad. Family Physicians, N.Y. Osteopathic Soc., Am. Osteopathic Coll. of Gen. Practice, L.I. Soc. Osteopathic Physicians, Mensa. Office: 2240 Mott Ave Far Rockaway NY 11691-3070 also: 725 Franklin Ave Franklin Square NY 11010

FARROW, MIA VILLIERS, actress; b. Los Angeles, Feb. 9, 1945; d. John Villiers and Maureen Paula (O'Sullivan) F.; m. Andre Previn, Sept. 10, 1970 (div. Feb. 1979); children: Matthew Phineas and Sascha Villiers (twins), Lark Song, Fletcher Farrow, Summer Song, Gigi Soon Mi, Misha, Satchel. Student pub., pvt. schs. Actress appearing in TV and films. Debut in The Importance of Being Earnest, N.Y.C., 1964; starred in TV series Peyton Place; films include Hurricane, Rosemary's Baby, 1968, See No Evil, 1971, The Public Eye, 1972, The Great Gatsby, Peter Pan, A Wedding, 1978, Death on the Nile, A Midsummer Night's Sex Comedy, Zelig, The Purple Rose of Cairo, 1985, Broadway Danny Rose, Hannah and Her Sisters, 1986, September, 1987, Radio Days, 1987, Another Woman, 1988, Oedipus Wrecks, 1989, Alice, 1990, Shadows and Fog, 1992, Husbands and Wives, 1992; appeared in stage plays Romantic Comedy, Mary Rose, The Three Sisters, The House of Bernarda Alba, Ivanov; joined Royal Shakespeare Co., London, 1974. Recipient Golden Globe award, 1967; Best Actress award French Acad., 1969; Rio de Janeiro Film Festival award, 1969; Italian Academy award, 1970; D. W. Griffith award for best actress, 1990. Address: ICM care Sam Cohn 40 W 57th St New York NY 10019*

FARROW, ROBERT SCOTT, economist, educator; b. L.A., Dec. 5, 1952; s. Robert Bruce and Eleanor (Dietrich) F.; m. Elaine A. King, July 3, 1988. BA, Whitman Coll., Walla Walla, Wash., 1974; MA, Wash. State U., 1980, PhD, 1983. Researcher Frank LeRoux Inc., Walla Walla, Wash., 1975-77; economist Coun. on Wage and Price Stability, Exec. Office of the Pres., Washington, 1979, Minerals Mgmt. Svc., U.S. Dept. Interior, Washington, 1985-86; ptnr. West Ten Organic Farm, Walla Walla, Wash., 1975-90; asst. prof. Carnegie Mellon U., Pitts., 1982-89, assoc. prof., 1989—; sr. economist, assoc. dir. Coun. on Environ. Quality, Exec. Office of Pres., 1990—; cons. Office of Tech. Assessment, Coun. on Wage and Price Stability; speaker on offshore oil and gas devel.; mem. sci. com. of the outer continental shelf adv. bd. U.S. Dept. Interior. Author: Managing The Outer Continental Shelf Lands, 1990; contbg. author, researcher: The Myth of U.S. Agricultural Prosperity, 1976; reviewer, contbr. articles to profl. jours. Mem. rev. com. for the aged and disadvantaged United Way, Pitts., 1988-89. Lindbergh grantee Charles A. Lindbergh Fund, Mpls., 1984; Marine Policy fellow Woods Hole Oceanographic Inst., 1988-89. Mem. Am. Econs. Assn., Assn. Environ. and Resource Econs. (editorial coun., nominating com. 1989-92), Pitts. Athletic Assn., Phi Kappa Phi. Office: Coun on Environ Quality 722 Jackson Pl NW Washington DC 20503-0001

FARTHING, CHARLES FRANK, medical educator, AIDS researcher; b. Christchurch, New Zealand, Apr. 22, 1953; came to U.S., 1989; s. Jack Raymond and Ngaire Emily (Green) F. MB, ChB, Otago Med. Sch., Dunedin, New Zealand, 1976. Intern, resident Christchurch Hosp., 1977-81; fellow in renal medicine Riyadh (Saudi Arabia) Mil. Hosp., 1981-82; registrar in genitourinary medicine St. Thomas' Hosp., London, 1982-83; resident in dermatology, AIDS rsch. fellow St. Stephen's Hosp., Westminster Hosp., London, 1983-89; clin. instr. div. infectious diseases dept. medicine NYU Med. Ctr., N.Y.C., 1989—; bd. dirs. Found. for AIDS Counselling and Treatment, London, 1988—. Author: Colour Atlas of AIDS, 1986, AIDS Treatment, 1988; also articles. Mem. All Party Parliamentary Com. on AIDS, London, 1986-89; patron London Lighthouse, 1988—. Recipient award for svcs. to AIDS, Terence Higgins Trust, London, 1986; fellow Winston Churchill Meml. Trust, 1988. Fellow Royal Australasian Coll. Physicians, Royal Soc. Medicine; mem. ACP, AMA, Royal Coll. Physicians, Brit. Med. Assn. Episcopalian. Home: 20 Waterside Plz Apt 7E New York NY 10010-2619 Office: NYU Med Ctr 550 1st Ave New York NY 10016-6402

FARWELL, NANCY LARRAINE, public relations executive; b. Sellersville, Pa., May 2, 1944; d. Warren Gregory and Mary Rita (Zaniboni) F. BA, Pa. State U., 1966. Asst. TV rep. H.R. TV Reps., Phila., 1966-68; various positions Hawthorne Advt. Inc., Phila., 1968-73; dir. employee rels. Colonial Penn Group, Inc., Phila., 1973-75, mgr. press rels., 1976-78, mgr. pub. rels., 1978-82; dir. communications Provident Mutual Life Ins. Co., Phila., 1982-83, asst. v.p., communications, 1983-87; pres. Nancy Farwell Assocs., Phila., 1987-90; v.p. Anne Klein & Assocs., Inc., Mt. Laurel, N.J., 1990-92, sr. v.p., 1992—; Adv. bd. City of Phila. Century IV Tall Ships, 1982. Author: (photo essay) Philadelphia, 1976. Founder, co-chair Portico Row Reighborhood Assn., Phila., 1989-92; bd. dirs. Washington Square West Project Area Com., Phila., 1990-92, Boys and Girls Clubs of Metro Phila., 1991—; adv. com. Phila. 6th Police Dist., 1990—. Recipient 2 Gold Quill Phila. chpt. Internat. Assn. Bus. Communicators, 5 Awards of Excellence Life Communicators Assn., Art Dirs. Club of Phila.; named Super Communicator of the 80's Women in Communications, Phila. chpt. Mem. PRSA (5 Pepperpot awards, Award of Excellence), Phila. Pub. Rels. Assn. Office: Anne Klein & Assocs Inc 533 Fellowship Rd # 250 Mount Laurel NJ 08054-3447

FARWELL, RUSS, professional hockey team executive; b. Apr. 20, 1956; m. Brenda Farwell. Gen. mgr. Medicine Hat, Can., Tigers, Seattle Thunderbirds, 1988-90, Phila. Flyers NHL, 1990—. Recipient Lloyd Saunders Trophy Western Hockey League, 1990. Office: Phila Flyers The Spectrum Philadelphia PA 19148*

FASANO, ANTHONY, aeronautical engineer; b. N.Y.C., Oct. 28, 1934; s. Gaetano and Helen (Santucci) F.; m. Norma Frasca, Apr. 30, 1960; children: Karen, Laura, Stephen, Susan. MS in Engring. Sci., Rensselaer Poly. Inst., 1961, MS in Mgmt., 1978. Test engr. United Techs. Rsch. Ctr., Hartford, Conn., 1956-66, supr. wind tunnel project, 1966-91, chief test facilities, 1991—; chmn. Subsonic Aerodynamic Testing Assn., 1974-76. Pres. Exch. Club South Windsor, Conn., 1975. Mem. AIAA. Republican. Roman Catholic. Home: 44 Old Musket Rd Glastonbury CT 06033-3332 Office: United Techs Rsch Ctr Silver Ln East Hartford CT 06118-1010

FASCETTA, SALVATORE CHARLES, pharmaceutical company executive; b. N.Y.C., Oct. 14, 1940; s. Nicholas and Anne (Piedevillano) F.; m. Debra Parks; children: Christopher, Kevin, Timothy. BS in Pharmacy, St. John's U., 1963; MS in Pharmacy, U. Pitts., 1966. Devel. pharmacist Wallace Labs., Cranbury, N.J., 1967, group leader pharm. devel., 1968-70, mgr. pharm. devel., 1970-74; dir. pharm. devel. Knoll Pharm. Co., Whippany, N.J., 1974-77, prodn. mgr., 1978-79, plant mgr., 1979-84, v.p. plant ops., 1984-92; v.p. plant ops. Lohmann Therapy Systems Corp., West Caldwell, N.J., 1992—. Pres. East Windsor Rescue Squad. 1969-70. Mem. Am. Pharm. Assn. (Lunson Richardson Pharm. award, 1963), Am. Soc. Hosp. Pharmacist, Acad. Pharm. Scis., Pharm. Mfrs. Assn., Soc. Mfg. Engrs., Soc. Chem. Engrs., Parenteral Drug Assn., Nat. Assn. Retail Druggists, Internat. Soc. Pharm. Engrs., Am. Prodn. and Invetory Control Soc., Am. Soc. Quality Control, Am. Assn. Pharm. Scis. Office: LTS Corp West Caldwell NJ 07981

FASMACHT, ANNETTE ZELDER, marketing executive; b. Pitts., Sept. 15, 1950; d. John George and Margaret Ann (Watral) zelder; m. Roger A. Fasnacht, July 22, 1972; 1 child, Annika Nicole. BA, Thiel Coll., 1972; MBA, DePaul U., 1979. V.p. mktg. Abiomed Inc., Danvers, Mass., 1992—. Office: Datascope Corp 14 Philips Pky Montvale NJ 07645

FASMAN, GERALD DAVID, biochemistry educator; b. Drumheller, Alta., Can., May 28, 1925; came to U.S., 1955, naturalized, 1964; s. Morris and Sarah (Stauffer) F.; m. Jean Schalit, Dec. 27, 1953; children—Michael, Daniel, Jonathan. B.S., U. Alta., 1948; Ph.D., Calif. Inst. Tech., 1952; postgrad., Cambridge (Eng.) U., 1951-53, Eidg. Technische Hochschule, Zurich, Switzerland, 1953-54, Weizmann Inst. Sci., Rehovoth, Israel, 1954-55. Research asst. Children's Cancer Research Found., Children's Med. Center, Boston, 1955-56; research asso. pathology Children's Med. Center and Children's Cancer Research Found., Boston, 1957-61; asst. in pathology Harvard U. Med. Sch., 1957-58, research asso. pathology, 1958-60, research asso. biol. chemistry, 1960-61; lectr. protein chemistry Boston U., 1958-59; asst. head biophys. chemistry lab. Children's Cancer Research Found., Boston, 1959-61; tutor in biochem. sci. Harvard, 1960-62; established investigator Am. Heart Assn., 1961-66; asst. prof. biochemistry Brandeis U., Waltham, Mass., 1961-63, assoc. prof., 1963-67, prof., 1967—, Rosenfield prof. biochemistry, 1971—; cons. African Primary Sci. Program, Ednl. Services, Inc., Dar es Salam, Tanzania, 1966, mem. program steering com., Accra, Ghana, 1967, mem. adv. group, 1968-69; mem. sci. adv. com. Am. Cancer Soc., 1979-83; mem. molecular biology adv. panel NSF, 1980-82. Editor: CRC Critical Revs. in Biochemistry, 1972—, Chemtracts, Biochemistry and Molecular Biology, 1990—; adv. bd.: Biopolymers, 1975—; editorial bd.: Internat. Jour. Peptide and Protein Research, 1976-82, Biophys. Jour., 1976-79, Cell Biophysics, 1982—, Jour. Protein Chemistry, 1982—, CRC Critical Revs. in Eukaryotic Gene Expression, 1987—. NSF sr. postdoctoral fellow Protein Inst., Osaka (Japan) U. and Weizmann Inst. Sci., 1967-68; Guggenheim fellow, 1974-75, 88-89; research fellow Japan Soc. for Promotion of Sci., 1979. Fellow AAAS, Am. Inst. Chemists; mem. Am. Chem. Soc., Biophys. Soc., Am. Soc. Biochemistry and Molecular Biology, Chemists, Royal Soc. Chemistry (London), N.Y. Acad. Sci., Sigma Xi. Home: 69 Kingswood Rd Newton MA 02166-1013 Office: Brandeis U Waltham MA 02254

FASSOULIS, SATIRIS GALAHAD, communications company executive; b. Syracuse, Aug. 19, 1922; s. Peter George and Anastasia P. (Limpert) F. B.A., Syracuse U., 1945. Vice pres. Commerce Internat. Corp., N.Y.C., 1945-48; pres. Commerce Internat. Corp., 1949-75; chmn. Global Communications Co., N.Y.C., 1976—, Global Def. Products Inc., N.Y.C., 1976—; dir Comml. Exports (Overseas) Ltd., U.K., CIC Internat. Ltd., N.Y.C. Mem. U.S. Congl. Adv. Bd.; bd. dirs. Better Life Enterprises for the Blind, Inc.; mem. Rep. Presdl. Task Force. Served to 1st lt., USAAF, 1941-45. Decorated Purple Heart, Air medal with 3 oak leaf clusters. Mem. N.Y. C. of C., Am. Def. Preparedness Assn., Navy League U.S., Armed Forces Communications and Electronics Assn., U.S. Naval Inst., Air Force Assn., Assn. of U.S. Army, Internat. Platform Assn. Republican. Episcopalian. Clubs: N.Y. Athletic, Order of Ahepa. Home: 20 Waterside Plz New York NY 10010-2612 Office: 10 Waterside Plz New York NY 10010-2602

FAST, HOWARD MELVIN, author; b. N.Y.C., Nov. 11, 1914; s. Barney and Ida (Miller) F.; m. Betty Cohen, June 6, 1937; children: Rachel Ann, Jonathan. Student, NAD, 1933. Began writing, 1932, Army film project, 1944; European corr. Esquire and Coronet mags., 1945; mem. staff Office of War Info., 1942-44, chief newswriter, originator Voice of Am., 1982-83. Emmy award for The Ambassador, Benjamin Franklin 1974; author: (novels) Two Valleys, 1932, Strange Yesterday, 1933, The Children, 1936, Place in the City, 1937, Conceived in Liberty, 1939; biography Haym Salomon, 1941; (novel) The Last Frontier, 1941; (biography) Baden Powell, 1941; (novel) Tail Hunter, 1942, The Unvanquished, 1942; (biography) Goethals and the Panama Canal, 1942; (novel) Citizen Tom Paine, 1943, Freedom Road, 1944; Peekskill, U.S.A, 1951; (novel) Spartacus, 1952; The Naked God, 1957; Moses, Prince of Egypt, 1958, Tony and the Wonderful Door, 1968, The Crossing, 1971; General Zapped an Angel, 1971, Last Frontier, 1971; The Hessian, 1972; My Glorious Brothers, 1972, A Touch of Infinity, 1973, (under name E.V. Cunningham) Sylvia, 1960, Phyllis, 1962, Alice, 1963, Helen, 1966, Margie, 1966, Sally, 1967, Samantha, 1967, Cynthia, 1968, Millie, 1973, The Case of the One Penny Orange, 1977, The Case of the Russian Diplomat, 1978, The Case of the Poisoned Eclairs, 1979, The Case of the Sliding Pool, 1981, The Case of the Kidnapped Angel, 1982, The Case of the Murdered Mackenzie, 1984; Editor: Selected Works of Paine, 1945, Collection of Short Stories: Patrick Henry and the Frigate's Keel, 1945, Under the Name of Howard Fast, The American (biography of Peter Altgeld, former gov. of Ill.), 1946, Carkton, 1947, My Glorious Brothers, 1948, Departure, 1949, Literature and Reality, 1949, The Proud and the Free, 1950, The Passion of Sacco and Vanzetti, 1953, Silas Timberman, 1954, The Story of Lola Gregg: The Winston Affair, 1959, April Morning, 1961, Power, 1962, The Crossing; (play) Agrippa's Daughter, 1964, The Hill; (drama), 1963, Torquemada, 1966, The Hunter and the Trap, 1967, The Jews, 1968, The Hessians, 1970, The Immigrants, 1977, Second Generation, 1978, The Establishment, 1979, The Legacy, 1981, Max, 1982, The Outsider, The Novelist, 1986; 1984, The Immigrant's Daughter; (novel), 1985, Citizen Tom Paine, (play), 1986; (novel) Dinner Party, 1987, The Pledge, 1988, (newspaper column), Greenwich Time, 1981, The Confession of Joe Cullen, 1989, (autobiography) Being Red, 1990; columnist N.Y. Observer, 1989—. Mem. World Peace Council, 1950-55; Am. Labor Party Congl. candidate 23d Dist., N.Y., 1952. Recipient Schumburg award for race relations, 1944, Newspaper Guild racial equality award, 1944, Lion award N.Y. Pub. Library, 1945, Peace Prize USSR, 1954, Secondary Sch. award, 1961, Emmy award Nat. Acad. TV Arts and Scis., 1976. Jewish. Office: care Sterling Lord One Madison Ave New York NY 10010

FASTOOK, MARY ANN, school counselor; b. Bklyn., Sept. 29, 1944; d. Theodore Elias and Josephine Mildred (Mardany) F. BA in English, St. John's U., Bklyn., 1966; MA in English, St. John's U., Jamaica, 1968; MS in Reading, MS in Counseling, Fordham U., 1980, 84; PD in Counseling, 1988. Lic. sch. counselor N.Y.; nat. cert. counselor. English tchr. All Saints High Sch., Bklyn., 1970-71, St. Andrew's Sch., Queens, N.Y., 1972-73, Boys High Sch., Bklyn., 1973-74, Jr. High Sch. 113, Bklyn., 1974-75, Prospect Hts. High Sch., Bklyn., 1974-75; English content specialist Hightstown (N.J.) High Sch., 1976-77; English tchr. Boys and Girls High Sch., Bklyn., 1977-83,

Samuel Tilden High Sch., Bklyn., 1983-85; sch. counselor Seward Park High Sch., N.Y.C., 1985—. Driver Bklyn. Hts. Civilian Patrol, 1990—. Mem. N.Y.C. Assn. for Counseling and Devel., N.Y. State Assn. For Counseling and Devel., Nat. Assn. for Counseling and Devel., Toastmasters (v.p. 1989). Home: 225 Adams St Apt 15F Brooklyn NY 11201-2805 Office: Seward Pk High Sch 350 Grand St New York NY 10002-4693

FATIĆ, VUK MARKO, electrical engineer, educator, researcher; b. Pancevo, Serbia, Yugoslavia, Mar. 22, 1932; came to U.S., 1970; s. Marko V. and Nelka (Vuletic) F.; m. Nada A. Dragic, Aug. 10, 1970. Diploma in electrical engring., Belgrade U., 1960; MS, Va. Poly. Inst. and State U., 1973, PhD, 1976. Rsch. engr. Vojno Tehnicki Inst., Beograd, Yugoslavia, 1961-68; asst. Novi Sad (Yugoslavia) U., 1968-70; instr. Va. Polytechnic Inst. and State U., 1973-75; asst. prof. Union Coll., Schenectady, N.Y., 1975-76, assoc. prof., 1985—; from asst. prof. to assoc. prof. Tri-State U., Angola, Ind., 1976-85; assoc. prof. Rose Hulman Inst. Tech., Terre Haute, Ind., 1985. Contbr. over 55 articles on variational principles for dissipative systems of profl jours. Rsch. grantee Internat. Rsch. & Exch. Bd., N.Y.C., 1970-71, NSF & NEH, Washington, 1980. Mem. IEEE (sr.), Sigma Xi, Phi Kappa Phi, Eta Kappa Nu, Tau Beta Pi. Home: 1377 Tracy Ave Niskayuna NY 12309-3712 Office: Union Coll Dept Elec Engring and Computer Sci Schenectady NY 12308

FATOVIC, JOHN, electrical engineer, consultant; b. Sestrunj, Croatia; s. Ciril and Stosija (Svorinic) F. B.E.S., Stevens Tech. U., 1960, M.S.E.E., 1964. Engr. XLO, Englewood, N.J., 1969-72; engring. cons. Bendix Corp., Teterboro, N.J., 1973-76; engr. Conrac Corp., West Caldwell, N.J., 1976-79, Exxon Enterprises, Florham Park, N.J., 1979-81; engring. cons. Bendix, Conrac Corp., Teterboro, N.J., 1981—; pres. CDF Industries Inc., Teterboro, N.J., 1972—. Patentee in field. Served with U.S. Army, 1954-56; Korea. Mem. IEEE. Home: 94 Passaic Valley Rd Montville NJ 07045-9675

FAUE, JEFFREY LAWRENCE, health and human resources consultant; b. Mpls., Mar. 16, 1946; s. Vincent Clyde and Yvonne (Skrade) F.; m. Alice F. Kelly, June 9, 1985. BA, Augsburg Coll., 1968; MDiv, Princeton Theol. Sem., 1972; MSW, Rutgers U., 1972, PHD, 1985. Dir. Urban Data Bank, Upsala Coll., NSF, East Orange, N.J., 1972-73; exec. dir. Nat. Assn. Social Workers N.J., Trenton, 1973-84; pres. Fauecast Cons., New Brunswick, 1984—; dir. pub. affairs Human Resource Assoc., Highland Park, N.J., 1984—; sec., treas. Supreme Coffee Svc. Corp., New Brunswick, 1987—, Allied Maintenance Corp., South Amboy, N.J., 1990—; adj. prof. Rutgers U., New Brunswick, 1991—. Mem. Employee Assistance Profls. Assn. Office: PO Box 756 New Brunswick NJ 08903

FAUGHNAN, JAMES PATRICK, JR., risk management consultant; b. Albany, N.Y., July 18, 1933; s. James P. and Frances (Held) F.; m. M. Gayle Johnson, Jan. 25, 1958; children: James P. III, R. Thomas, Michael A., Suzanne E. Student, Manhattan Coll., 1951-52, Siena Coll., 1952-53, 55-57. Asst. loan mgr. Upstate Loan Co., Delmar, N.Y., 1957-59; asst. treas. West End Savs. & Loan, Albany, 1959-62; field rep. Aetna Casualty & Surety, Albany, 1962-65; exec. v.p. Austin & Co., Inc., Albany, 1965-89; pres. Confirm, Inc., Albany, 1989—; pres. The Cons. Alliance, Albany, 1990—; bd. dirs. The Eddy, Troy, N.Y., Sr. Care Connection, Troy, LaSalle Sch., Albany, 1991—. Cpl. U.S. Army, 1953-55. Mem. Soc. Risk Mgmt. Cons. Republican. Roman Catholic. Home: 22 Springwood Manor Dr Loudonville NY 12211 Office: Confirm Inc 111B Green St Albany NY 12202

FAUL, JAN WALKLEY, photographer; b. Port Chester, N.Y., 1945; d. Henry and Dorothy Day (Walkley) F. BA, George Washington U., 1969. Owner Jan Faul Studios, Washington, 1970-79, 89—, Rainbow Studio, Copenhagen, 1979-89. One-man shows at Montgomery (Ala.) Mus. Fine Arts, 1976, Gallery Blomsten, Copenhagen, 1984, Wohlfarth Galleries, Washington, 1991, also Smithsonian Nat. Mus., Photo Impressions Gallery; exhibited in group shows at Space Sci. Exposition Ctr., Tokyo, 1980, Clarence Kennedy Gallery, Cambridge, Mass., 1985, Photokina, Cologne, Germany, 1988, Internat. Mus. Photography at George Eastman House, 1989; represented in permanent collections at Smithsonian Instn., Montgomery Mus. Fine Arts, Corcoran Gallery Art, Nat. Gallery Art, Houston Mus. Art, San Francisco Mus. Modern Art, Royal Mus. Art, Denmark, Aperture Found., Va. Mus., Cath. U., Internat. Mus. Photography at George Eastman House, Ilford/Ciba-Geigy Collection, Polaroid Internat. Collection, Moderna Museet, Sweden, Joseph A. Hirschhorn Collection, U. Wis., George Washington U., Kuhn Libr. & Gallery, U. Md., also pvt. collections. Recipient Bronze medal Pictures of the Yr., 1974, awards Art Dirs. Club Met. Washington, 1975, 77, 78, 91, Silver medal AIA, 1977, Bronze medals Corcoran Gallery Art, 1978, The Washington Post, 1979, awards Am. Soc. Mag. Photographers, 1988, others. Studio: 903 Girard St NE Washington DC 20017-3425

FAULKENBERRY, RICHARD ERNEST, mathematics educator; b. Lancaster, S.C., Oct. 20, 1962; s. Alfred Elmore and Carol Jean (Cauthen) F.; m. Susan Marie McCourt, June 7, 1986; 1 child, Daniel Andrew. AB, Duke U., 1983; PhD, U. Md., 1990. Asst. prof. math. U. Mass., Dartmouth, 1990—. Asst. dir. ATLAST project NSF, 1992—. Mem. Internat. Linear Algebra Soc., Am. Math. Soc., Math. Assn. Am., Soc. Indsl. and Applied Math. Episcopalian. Office: U Mass Dept Math North Dartmouth MA 02747

FAULKNER, JOHN CHARLES, management consultant, marketing professional; b. Keene, N.H., June 30, 1922; s. John C. Jr. and Hazel Helen (Ford) F.; m. Susan Ellen Ott, July 17, 1954; children: Sarah Ford, Cynthia Hahn, John Barrett. BS, Harvard, 1944, MBA, 1948. Cert. mgmt. cons., N.Y. Officer/pres. Faulkner & Colony Mfg. Co., Keene, N.H., 1948-54; cons. George H. Elliott & Assoc., N.Y.C., 1954-55; assoc. Stewart Dougall Assoc., N.Y.C., 1955-58; prin. Cresap, McCormick & Paget, N.Y.C., 1958-73; v.p. Case & Co., N.Y.C., 1973-83; pvt. practice Darien, Conn., 1983—; pres., bd. mem. Inst. Mgmt. Cons., N.Y. chpt., 1980-87. Contbr. articles to profl. pubs. 1st lt. USAF, 1943-45, ETO. Mem. Harvard Bus. Sch. Club of N.Y. (career counseling v.p. 1974—), Darien Audubon Soc. (past pres., bd. dirs.), Noroton Yacht Club (past fleet capt.). Home & Office: 27 Nearwater Ln Darien CT 06820-5614

FAULKNER, MARILYN HAUCH, consumer products company executive; b. St. Joseph, Mich., May 9, 1942; d. Ernest and Doris Esther (Obendorfer) Hauch; B.A., Northwestern U., 1964; M.A., U. Mich., 1965; m. Bert L. Rondelli, Dec. 27, 1966 (div.); 1 son, Michael Louis; m. David Faulkner. Reference librarian Chgo. Public Library, 1965, J. Walter Thompson Co., Chgo., 1965-67; asso. librarian Schering Corp., Bloomfield, N.J., 1967-70; info. scientist Ortho Pharm. Corp., Raritan, N.J., 1974-75; librarian Ortho Diagnostics, Inc., Raritan, 1975-80; mgr. bus. and tech. info. Johnson & Johnson Baby Products, Skillman, N.J., 1980—; mgr. bus. and tech. info. ctr. Johnson & Johnson Consumer Products, Inc., 1989—; cons. Schering Corp., 1972-73. Active United Way. Mem. Spl. Libraries Assn., Gamma Phi Beta. Office: Johnson & Johnson Consumer Products Co Grandview Rd Skillman NJ 08558-1308

FAUNCE, ROBERT ALAN, secondary education educator; b. Abington, Pa., Nov. 22, 1956; s. Grant George and Lois Florence (Doak) F. MusB in Edn., Temple U., 1979, MusM in Choral Conducting, 1985, cert. in supervision, 1989. Cert. music educator, N.J.; registered music educator. Dir. instrumental activities Jenkintown (Pa.) High Sch., 1981-83; dir. choral activities West Deptford High Sch., Westville, N.J., 1985—, fine arts dept. chair, 1990—; condr. Haddonfield (N.J.) Symphony Chorus, 1986-88, South Jersey Jr. High Chorus, Penns Grove, N.J., 1989, Salem County Chorus, N.J., 1991. Mem. Am. Choral Dirs. Assn., N.J. Edn. Assn., N.J. Music Educators Assn. (exec. bd. regional pres. 1991-93), N.J. Choral Procedures Com., South Jersey Choral Dirs. Assn. (pres. 1991-93), Phila. Orch. Edn. (adv. coun. 1990—), Music Educators Nat. Conf. Office: West Deptford High Sch 1600 Old Crown Point Rd Westville NJ 08093

FAUQUIER, MICHELLE RUTH, psychotherapist; b. Teaneck, N.J., Feb. 14, 1951; d. Kenneth Gordon and Ruth Margaret (Albers) F.; 1 child, Tracey. AA, Bergen Community Coll., 1985; BA, Ramapo Coll., 1987; MA, L.I. U., 1989; postgrad., Internat. Sem. Program supr. Loeb House Community Residence for Emotionally Disturbed, Wesley Hills, N.Y., 1988-90; psychotherapist N.Y. Ctr. Eclectic Psychotherapy, Nanuet, N.Y., 1990—; clin. cons. St. Anne's Sch., Nyack, N.Y., 1991—. Mem. Am. Psychol. Assn. Office: Ctr Eclectic Psychotherapy 168 N Middletown Rd Nanuet NY 10954-1813

FAUST, MARCUS G., lawyer; b. Salt Lake City, Feb. 23, 1953; s. James E. and Ruth (Wright) F.; m. Susan Jone Hadley, June 23, 1971; children: Nicole, John, Ryan, Justin, Elise. BA cum laude, U. Utah, 1974; JD cum laude, Brigham Young U., 1976. Bar: Utah 1977, D.C. 1980. Staff asst. U.S. Sen. Frank E. Moss, Salt Lake City, 1975-77; legis. counsel U.S. Rep. Gunn McKay, Washington, 1977-80; subcom. counsel Com. on Interior and Insular Affairs, U.S. Ho. Reps., Washington, 1980-81; pvt. practice Washington, 1981—. Polit. adv. U.S. Sen. Frank E. Moss, Salt Lake City, 1976, U.S. Rep. Gunn McKay, Washington, 1978, '80; nat. fundraiser U.S. Rep. Jim Santini, Washington, 1982;vol. coach Fairfax (Va.) Police Youth Club, 1981—; scoutmaster, troop com. mem. Boy Scouts Am., Oakton, Va., 1986—. Recipient Honor award Nat. Water Resources Assn., Washington, 1982; named one of Capitol's Top 25 Lobbyists, Washington Bus. Jour. Mem. Utah State Bar Assn., D.C. Bar. Democrat. Mormon. Home: 10232 Martinhoe Dr Vienna VA 22181-5367 Office: 332 Constitution Ave NE Washington DC 20002-5922

FAUST, NAOMI FLOWE, educator, poet; b. Salisbury, N.C.; d. Christopher Leroy and Ada Luella (Graham) Flowe; AB, Bennett Coll.; MA, U. Mich., 1945; PhD, N.Y. U., 1963; m. Roy Malcolm Faust, Aug. 16, 1948. Elem. tchr. Pub. Schs. Gaffney (S.C.); tchr. English, French, phys. edn. Atkins High Sch., Winston-Salem; instr. English, Bennett Coll. and So. U., Scotlandville, La., 1944-46; prof. English, Morgan State Coll., Balt., 1946-48; tchr. English, Greensboro (N.C.) Pub. Schs., 1948-51, N.Y.C. Pub. Schs., 1954-63; prof. edn. Queens Coll. of City U. N.Y., Flushing, 1964-82; lectr. in field; writer, lectr., poetry readings, 1982—. Named Tchr.-Author of 1979, Tchr.-Writer; cert. of Merit for poem Cooper Hill Writers Conf., 1970; Achievement award L.I. br. AAUW, 1985. Mem. AAUP, Nat. Coun. Tchrs. English, Nat. Women's Book Assn., Nat. Assn. Univ. Women (L.I. br.), World Poetry Soc. Intercontinental, N.Y. Poetry Forum, NAACP, United Negro Coll. Fund, Alpha Kappa Alpha, Alpha Kappa Mu, Alpha Epsilon. Author: Discipline and the Classroom Teacher, 1977; (poetry) Speaking in Verse, 1974, All Beautiful Things, 1983, And I Travel by Rhythms and Words, 1990; contbr. poetry to jours. Home: 11201 175th St Jamaica NY 11433-4135

FAVA, DONALD ANTHONY, clinical psychologist; b. Paterson, N.J., Sept. 20, 1948; s. Michael A. and Josephine (Fusilli) F.; 1 child, Joshua. BA, Monmouth (Ill.) Coll., 1970; PhD, New Sch. Social Rsch., N.Y.C., 1978. Lic. psychologist N.Y., N.J. Rsch. asst. Calif. State U., Arcata, 1970-71; psychol. intern Dept. Spl. Svcs., Bd. Edn., Paterson, N.J., 1971-72; clin. psychol. trainee Kingsbrook Jewish Med. Ctr., Bklyn., 1972-73; grad. clin. supr. New Sch. Social Rsch., N.Y.C., 1972-76; clin. psychologist Passaic County Diagnostic Ctr., Paterson, N.J., 1973-78, sr. clin. psychologist, 1978-80; adj. instr. psychology LaGuardia Coll., CUNY, N.Y.C., 1975-82, Seton Hall U., S. Orange, N.J., 1981-82; clin. dir. St. Francis Acad., Inc., Lake Placid, N.Y., 1984—; founder, dir. Adirondack Inst. Mental Health, Lake Placid, 1984—; dir. No. N.Y. and Vt. Region, Inst. Forensic Psychology, Lake Placid, 1986—. Co-author monograph: Understanding Visual Metaphor, 1980. Bd. dirs. Community Svc. Bd., Elizbethtown, N.Y., Mental Health Bd. Essex County; chmn. Mental Health Com., Elizabethtown; mem. Profl. Adv. Bd. Greater Patterson Community Mental Health Ctr., 1975-77. New Sch. for Social Rsch. trustees scholar, 1972-76, teaching fellow, 1973-76. Mem. Am. Psychol. Assn., N.Y. Psychol. Assn., N.J. Psychol. Assn., N.Y. Soc. Clin. Psychologists, Southeastern Psychol. Assn. Home: Fawn Ridge Estates Lake Placid NY 12946 Office: Adirondack Inst Crestview Plz # 1108 Lake Placid NY 12946

FAVIN, DAVID LEONARD, electrical engineer; b. Phila., Feb. 14, 1926; s. Louis and Jennie (Green) F.; m. Marion Favin; children: Carol S., Jean L. BSEE, U. Pa., 1950; MSEE, MIT, 1952. Mem. tech. staff AT&T Bell Labs., Holmdel, N.J., 1952—; chmn. Tech. Oriented/Telephone Pioneers, Holmdel, 1968—. 25 patents in field. With USAAF, 1944-45. Mem. IEEE. Home: 221 Queens Dr S Little Silver NJ 07739-1630 Office: AT&T Bell Labs Holmdel NJ 07733

FAVREAU, SUSAN DEBRA, management consultant; b. Cleve., Dec. 15, 1955; d. Donald Francis and Helen Patricia (Rafferty) F. Cert., N.Y. State Police Acad., 1974; student, Cornell U., 1984, SUNY, 1986. Communications specialist N.Y. State Police, Loudonville, 1974-87; communications specialist div. hdqrs., 1987—; mgmt. cons., sec.-treas., dir. Don Favreau Assocs., Inc., Clifton Park, N.Y., 1983-86, v.p., 1986—; adj. faculty Internat. Assn. Chiefs of Police; NYSPIN coord. FBI/Nat. Crime Info. Ctr. cert. program, 1986—. Author: Teamwork in the Telecommunication Center, 1986, One More Time: How to be a Mature and Successful Telcommunications Manager, 1987, Law Enforcement Terminal Security, 1991; also NYSPIN cert. manuals. Recipient Dirs. commendation N.Y. State Police Acad., 1977, commendation N.Y. State Police, 1978, Supt.'s commendation, 1986. Mem. NAFE, N.Y. State Civil Svc. Assn., Emergency Communicators Profl. Assn. (adv. bd.), Colonie Police Benevolent Assn. (hon.), Am. Soc. Law Enforcement Trainers, Assoc. Pub. Safety Communications Officers (planning commn. Atlantic chpt. 1991, registration chair ann. NE conf. 1991), N.Y. State Troopers Police Benevolent Assn. (hon.), Nat. Bus. Women Am., Internat. Assn. Chiefs Police, Am. Horse Shows Assn., Am. Soc. Law Enforcement Trainers, Capital Dist. Hunter/Jumper Coun. Republican. Roman Catholic. Home: 4D Hollandale Ln Clifton Park NY 12065-5240 Office: Hdqrs NY State Police State Office Bldg Campus Bldg #22 Albany NY 12226

FAWCETT, HOWARD HOY, chemical health and safety consultant; b. McKeesport, Pa., May 31, 1916; s. Harry Garfield and Ada (Deetz) F.; m. Ruth Allen Bogan, Apr. 7, 1942 (dec. Oct. 1986); children: Ralph Willard, Harry Allen. BS in Indsl. Chemistry, U. Md., 1940; postgrad. U. Del., 1945-47. Registered profl. engr., Calif. Rsch. chemist Manhattan project E.I. DuPont de Nemours & Co., Inc., Chgo., Hanford, Wash., 1944-45, rsch. and devel. chemist organic chemistry div., Deepwater, N.J., 1945-48; cons. engr. GE, Schenectady, N.Y., 1948-64; tech. sec. com. on hazardous materials Nat. Acad. Scis.-NRC, Washington, 1964-75; staff scientist, project mgr. Tracor Jitco, Inc., Rockville, Md., 1975-78; sr. chem. engr. Equitable Environ. Health, 1978-81; pres., sr. engr. Fawcett Consultations, Inc., 1981—; mem. adv. com. study on socio-behavioral preparations for, responses to and recovery from chem. disasters NSF, 1977-82; adj. prof. Fed. Emergency Mgmt. Agency Acad., 1983—; cons. to industry and govt. agys. Author Am.-Can. supplement Hazards in Chemical Lab., 1983, Hazardous and Toxic Materials, Safe Handling and Disposal, 1984, 2d edit., 1988; co-editor: Safety and Accident Prevention in Chemical Operations, 1965, 2d edit., 1982; mem. editorial adv. bd. Jour. Safety Rsch., 1968—, Transp. Planning and Tech., 1972—; N.Am. regional editor Jour. Hazardous Materials, 1975—; also book chpt. Chief radiol. sect. Schenectady County CD, 1953-63; bd. dirs. Safety sect. Schenectady C. of C., 1957-64; tech. advisor Hazmat Emergency Response Team, Montgomery County, Md., 1988—. Deacon Warner Meml. Presbyn. Ch., Kensington, Md., 1990—. Recipient Disting. Svc. to Safety citation Nat. Safety Coun., 1966, Cameron award, 1962, 69. Fellow Am. Inst. Chemists; mem. Am. Chem. Soc. (sec. com. chem. safety, chmn. council com. on chem. safety 1974-77, chmn. div. chem. health and safety 1977-79, 91, vice-chair, 1990-91, chair, 1991—, councilor 1980-82, archivist, 1984—, author audio course on hazards of materials 1977)., ASTM (membership sec. 1972—, sub-chmn. D-34 com.), Am. Inst. Chem. Engrs. (com. on occupational health and safety 1977—, editor newsletter 1988-89), Internat. Platform Assn., Am. Indsl. Hygiene Assn. (dir. Balt.-Washington chpt. 1975-77), Alpha Chi Sigma. Home and Office: PO Box 9444 12920 Matey Rd Wheaton MD 20916

FAWCETT, MARIE ANN FORMANEK (MRS. ROSCOE KENT FAWCETT), civic leader; b. Mpls., Mar. 6, 1914; d. Peter Paul and Mary (Stepanek) Formanek; m. Roscoe Kent Fawcett, Mar. 16, 1935; children: Roscoe Kent, Peter Formanek, Roger Knowlton II, Stephen Hart. Grad. high sch., Mpls.; cert. Harvard U., 1976, 77, 78, 79, 80, 81, 82, 83. Chmn. of vols. Merry Go Round, Greenwich, Conn., 1948-92, v.p., chmn. recreation, bd. dirs.; bd. dirs., vol. chmn., corr. sec. Nathaniel Witherell Hosp., Greenwich, 1952-92, chmn. vols., 1956-89; chmn. vols. Greenwich Hosp., 1953-54; dist. chmn. ARC, Community Chest, Mental Health, 1946-50; vol. mentally retarded children Milbank Sch., Greenwich, 1958-92. Bd. dirs. Cerebral Palsy, Greenwich Symphony, 1958-90, Putnam Indianfield Sch., Greenwich Merry Go Round, for Sr. Citizens, Multiple Sclerosis Soc., 1948—, v.p., 1970, corr. sec., 1958—; bd. dirs. Nathaniel Witherell Hosp. Aux., 1954-90, corr. sec., 1952-90; trustee Greenwich Merry Go Round News for Elderly, 1948-90, chmn. entertainment, 1970-90, bd. dirs., 1948-91; v.p., corr. sec., trustee Merry Go Round Club House and News. 1948-90; bd. dirs. Nathaniel Witherell Aux., 1952-91, Greenwich Symphony, 1956-92; active drives for ARC, Community Chest, Leukemia, Muscular Dystrophy, Mental Health, Mentally Retarded Children Milbank Sch.; participating mem. Huxley Inst. Biosocial Rsch.; mem. polo com. Susan Cancer Fund, Pegasus Therapeutic Riding and Rusk Inst. Re ab. Medicine. Named Woman of Year, Soroptomist Club, 1967; recipient Community Svc. award United Cerebral Palsy Assn. Fairfield County, 1972, Fund Drive award Cerebral Palsey, 1970, citations for 36 yrs. outstanding vol. svcs. Nathaniel Witherell Hosp. Aux., Conn. Dept. Health, 1977. Mem. Internat. Platform Assn., The Woman's Club of Greenwich, Travel Club of Greenwich (corr. sec., bd. dirs. 1981-92). Address: 515 E Putnam Ave Greenwich CT 06830

FAY, BARRY GEORGE, configuration manager; b. Balt., Oct. 1, 1951; s. Joseph George and Lita (Phillips) F.; m. Melanie Jane; 1 child, Michelle. BA in history, U. Md., 1973. Configuration mgmt. staff Westinghouse Electric Corp. Elec. Systems Group, Balt., 1973-85, mgr. configuration mgmt., 1986—. Democrat. Jewish. Home: 2413 Taney Rd Baltimore MD 21209

FAY, DAVID B., sports association executive; b. N.Y.C., Oct. 12, 1950; s. Peter Donald and Sarah (McGrath) F.; m. Joan Margaret Mcananey, June 2, 1979; children: Katherine, Mary Elizabeth. BA, Colgate U., 1972. Communications dir. Met. Golf. Assn., N.Y.C., 1975-78; tournament rels. mgr. U.S. Golf Assn., Far Hills, N.J., 1978-81, dir. rules and program devel., 1981-87, asst. exec. dir., 1987-89, exec. dir., 1989—; joint sec. World Amateur Golf Coun., 1991—. Office: USGA Golf House Far Hills NJ 07931

FAY, ROWAN H., minister; b. Wells, N.Y., Apr. 10, 1943; s. Orrin Lewis and Dorothy Francis (Posson) F.; m. Judith Ann Smith, Sept. 8, 1962; children: Scott, Yolanda, Vicki, Ramona. Assoc. Constrn. Engring., Hudson Valley Community Coll., 1961-62, 62-63. Draftsman Parker Dodge Assn., Renselaer, N.Y., 1961-62; trainee Niagara Mohawk Power, Albany, N.Y., 1962-63; salesman Albany (N.Y.) Lumber, 1963-65, Abele Tractor & Equipment, Albany, 1965-71; sales mgr. Vermeer of N.Y., Castleton, 1971-73, Contractor Sales, Albany, 1970-73; owner Spectra Physics of N.Y., Averill Park, 1972-73; pastor Pilgrim Holiness Ch., East Worcester, N.Y., 1973-79, Marcy, N.Y., 1979—. Bd. mem. Appalachian Youth Camp, Roxbury, Pa., 1986-92, Love Inc., Utica, N.Y., 1991-92; chmn. Inter-Ch. Bus. Convs., Marcy, 1988-92. Mem. Internat. Pin Collectors Club (pres. 1980—, publ. newsletter 1980-92). Home: PO Box 227 Marcy NY 13403 Office: Pilgrim Holiness Ch 6079 Cavanaugh Rd Marcy NY 13403

FAZZINA, FREDERICK B., educator; b. Fall River, Mass., July 22, 1944; s. Frederick B. and Anna L. (Cloutier) F.; m. Kadeshia Ablaham, July 7, 1973; children: Arianna, Jenna. ABS, Johnson/Whales U., 1966; BS, Hysson Coll., 1969; MEd, Bridgewater State Coll., 1976. Educator City oif Fall River (Mass.) Pub. Schs., 1969—; facilitator Student Drug Free Am., Fall River, 1980—; substance abuse team Mid. Sch. Children in Crisis, Fall River, 1989—. Fellow NEA, Mass. Tchrs. Assn., Fall River Educators Assn. (pres. 1976-78, v.p. 1975-76, exec. bd. 1970—). Democrat. Roman Catholic. Office: Henry Lord Mid Sch Tucker St Fall River MA 02720

FEASTER, DOROTHEA VIVIEENE, parks and recreation talent director; b. N.Y.C., Mar. 22, 1954; d. Claude Walter and Marion Henrietta (Stoney) F.; 1 child, Taiysha Mone Brown. Student, CCNY, 1971-73, Coll. New Rochelle and Coll. Laguardia, 1978-90. Dir. Bronx (N.Y.) Fiscal Pks. and Recreation, 1983-90, Bronx (N.Y.) Pks. and Recreations Talent Network, 1990—; treas. women's com. Pks. and Recreation, 1989—. Office: Dept Pks and Recreation 1 Bronx River Pky Bronx NY 10462

FEATHERMAN, BERNARD, steel company executive; b. Phila., May 3, 1929; s. Jacob H. and Eva (Feldman) F.; m. Sandra Green, May 29, 1958; children: Andrew C., John James. B.S., Temple U., 1951, postgrad. Grad. Bus. Sch., 1951-52, Law Sch., 1952-54; postgrad. Wharton Sch., U. Pa., 1965-66. Pres. Bernard Franklin Co., Phila., 1958—, Western Steel Co., Phila., 1961—; chmn. bd. Western Metal Bed Co., Phila., 1978—, JBM Equipment Group, Inc., Phila., 1987—; chmn. bd. dirs. Automated Techs., Phila., 1988-92; dir. Pa. Steel and Aluminum Corp., Huntingdon Valley, Pa.; chmn. bd. JBM Equipment Group, Phila. 1986—; bd. dirs. Material Handling Inst., Pitts., 1978-79. Contbr. articles to profl. jours. Inventor electronics locking locker. Mem. exec. bd. Southeast chpt. Nat. Found. March of Dimes, 1969-82, vice chmn., 1978-80; pres. Phila. Assn. for Retarded Citizens, 1975-77, trustee, 1983—; trustee Phila. Devel. Disabilities Corp., 1991—, Equity 591 F8AM, 1990—; chmn. Mayor's Adv. Com. on Mental Health-Mental Retardation, Phila., 1979—; mem. tax policy and budget rev. com. City of Phila., fiscal adv. com., 1990; mem. bd. Costar, Inc., 1989-92; co-chmn. Mayor's Small Bus. Adv. Com., Phila., 1979—; del. White House Conf. on Small Bus., 1980, Pa. del., vice chmn., 1986; chmn. small bus. council Democratic Nat. Com., 1982-84; fin. chmn. Pa. Dem. Orgn., 1985-86; mem. adv. bd. Coll. Liberal Arts and Scis., Temple U., 1982-91, chmn. incubator program, 1989-91, chmn. Entrepreneurial Inst., 1990; adv. bd. West Chester (Pa.) State U. Bus. Sch., 1986-87, Frankford Hosp., 1983—; steering com. entrepreneurial forum Drexel U. Bus. Sch., 1988—; chmn. 3d Congl. Small Bus. Council, Phila., 1984-88; bd. dirs. Phila. Citywide Devel. Corp., 1984—; bd. dirs. Phila. Loan Fund, Inc., 1987-88. Recipient award of appreciation Small Bus. Council, Dem. Nat. Com., 1983; Gold medal of Honor Adult Trainees Found., Phila., 1976; citation White House Conf. on Small Bus., 1980; named Entrepreneur of Yr. Mid Atlantic Region Supporter of Entrepreneurship, 1990, Ea. Pa. Small Bus. Adv. of Yr. SBA, 1991. Mem. Assn. of Steel Distbrs. (nat. pres. 1975-76, 86-87, named Steel Distbr. of Yr. 1976), Inst. Am. Entrepreneurs (life), Shelving Mfrs. Assn. (nat. chmn. 1977-78), Pa. Soc., Assn. Steel Distbrs. (nat. pres. 1975-76, 86-87, Hunting Park West Bus. Assn. (pres. 1986—), Rotary, Masons (trustee), B'nai Brith (pres. 1980-82, Nat. Youth Services award Quaker City lodge 1985). Home: 2100 Spruce St Philadelphia PA 19103-6504

FECHTMEYER, GARY KEVIN, investment banker; b. Balt., May 22, 1963; s. Gary Paul Fechtmeyer and Elizabeth Stuart Potof; m. Holly Delight Goodsell, June 9, 1990. BS, U. Ariz., 1985; MBA, Columbia U., 1989. CPA, N.Y.; reg. rep. N.Y. Audit semi-sr. Touche Ross & Co., N.Y.C., 1985-87; assoc. First Boston Corp., N.Y.C., summer 1988, Merrill Lynch Capital Mkts., N.Y.C., 1989-90, Kidder, Peabody & Co., Inc., N.Y.C., 1990—. Author mktg. manual: The Lead Factory, 1984; sr. editor Columbia Jour. World Bus. Mem. N.Y. Soc. CPAs. Office: Kidder Peabody & Co Inc 10 Hanover Sq New York NY 10005-3516

FECZKO, WILLIAM ALBERT, radiologist; b. Homestead, Pa., May 27, 1937; s. Albert George and Rosalia Melania (Toth) F.; m. Margaret Ann Cloonan, July 8, 1961; children: Margaret Christine, William Martin. AB, St. Vincent Coll., Latrobe, Pa., 1959; MD, U. Pitts., 1963. Diplomate Am. Bd. Radiology. V.p. Almar Radiologists, Inc., Pitts., 1975—; assoc. dir. St. Francis Med. Ctr., Dept. Diagnostic Radiology, Pitts., 1978-86; dir. radiology residence prog. St. Francis Med. Ctr., Pitts., 1980-86; med. dir. Imaging Ctr., Pitts., 1986—; v.p. med. staff St. Francis Med. Ctr., 1988, pres., 1989, bd. dirs., chmn. exec. com., 1990-91. Contbr. articles to profl. jours. Capt. USAF, 1965-67. Fellow Am. Coll. Radiology; mem. Pitts. Roentgen Soc. (treas. 1984-85), Pa. Radiologic Soc. (bd. dirs. 1985-88), AMA, Allegheny County Med. Soc., Pa. Med. Soc., Radiol. Soc. N.Am., Am. Inst. Ultrasound in Medicine, Am. Roentgen Ray Soc. Republican. Roman Catholic. Home: 217 Highland Rd Pittsburgh PA 15238-2136 Office: Imaging Ctr 4221 Penn Ave # 102G Pittsburgh PA 15224-1389

FEDDECK, MICHAEL BRENDAN, accountant; b. Bronx, N.Y., July 8, 1944; s. Fred Frank and Mary (Trainor) F.; m. Mary Theresa Nagle, Mar. 22, 1975. BA in History, Marist Coll., Poughkeepsie, N.Y., 1966; cert. Electronic Data Processing, Fordham U., 1972; MS in Mgmt., Manhattan Coll., 1979; MBA, Iona Coll., 1982. IRS enrolled agt. Revenue officer IRS, N.Y.C., 1972-83; pvt. practice acctg. Bronxville, N.Y., 1983—; auditor U.S.

Customs Svc., N.Y.C., 1988—; adj. instr. Iona Coll., Yonkers, N.Y., 1985—, Monroe Bus. Inst., New Rochelle, N.Y., 1983-84, Mercy Coll., Dobbs Ferry, N.Y., 1981-84. mem. Nat. Soc. Pub. Accts., N.Y. Soc. Ind. Accts., KC, Delta Psi Omega. Home: 14 Parkview Dr Bronxville NY 10708-4608 Office: 6 World Trade Ctr New York NY 10048-0206

FEDDOES, SADIE CLOTHIL, bank executive; b. Saint Vincent and Grenadines, Sept. 30, 1931; came to U.S., 1952; d. Jane (Crick) F. B in Profl. Studies, Pace U., 1977. Bookkeeper to Platform Ofcl. Citibank, Bklyn., 1955-77, v.p. community and govt. rels., 1977—. Columnist N.Y. Amsterdam News; frequent TV appearances. Bd. dirs., chmn. Bedford-Stuyvesant Restoration Corp., Bklyn., Bklyn. Econ. Deve. Corp.; chmn. Billie Holiday Theater Restoration Bd.; adtive N.Y. Regional Panel Pres.'s Commn. White House Fellowships, 1984-85. Recipient Outstanding Performance award Citibank, 1970, Journalism award ARC, 1980; named Woman of Yr., Bd. Mgrs. Bklyn. Home for Aged People, 1982, NAACP Bklyn. chpt., 1984; numerous other awards. Mem. Coalition of 100 Black Women, Nat. Womens' Coalition, Nat. Women in Communications, N.Y. Women in Communications (Outstanding Mem. award 1984). Republican. Episcopalian. Office: Citibank NA 885 Flatbush Ave Brooklyn NY 11226-4017

FEDELE, CHARLES ROBERT, dermatologist; b. Somerville, N.J., June 8, 1942; s. Vincent Francis and Mary Lucille (Sanchini) F.; B.S. in Biology, Villanova U., 1964; M.D., Bologna (Italy) U., 1970; m. Kathleen Ann Fox, June 23, 1972; children—Charles Robert, Kerry Ann, David Vincent. Intern, No. Westchester Hosp., Mt. Kisco, N.Y., 1971-72; resident Univ. Hosps. of Cleve., Case Western Res. Med. Sch., 1972-75; dermatologist asso. Guthrie Clinic, Sayre, Pa., 1977-81, chief dermatology sect., 1981—; mem. staff Robert Packer Hosp., Sayre; asst. clin. prof. dermatology SUNY, Syracuse. Served to maj. U.S. Army, 1975-77. Diplomate Am. Bd. Dermatology. Fellow Am. Acad. Dermatology; mem. Dermatology Found., AMA, Pa., Bradford County med. socs., Pa. Acad. Dermatology. Roman Catholic. Home: 114 S Pennsylvania Ave Sayre PA 18840-1014 Office: Guthrie Clinic Guthrie Sq Sayre PA 18840-1606

FEDELE, MICHAEL CHRISTIAN, computer company executive; b. Minturno, Italy, Mar. 30, 1955; came to U.S., 1957, naturalized, 1965; s. Antonio and Filomenia (Corrente) F.; A.S., Norwalk State Tech. Coll., 1975; B.S., Fairfield U., 1977; m. Carol Ann Zezima, Oct. 17, 1976; children—Michael Christian, Briana Lyn, Alesandra. Computer operator Bristol Myers Co., Stamford, Conn., 1973-75, systems programmer, 1975-79; sr. systems programmer Duracell Internat., Bethel, Conn., 1979-80, mgr. systems and ops., 1980-81, asst. dir. info. systems, 1981-86, dir. info. systems, 1986-88; pres. Dana Mktg. Inc., Stamford, 1988-91; pres., owner Pinnacle Techs. Corp., 1991—. Constable, Stamford, Conn., 1983-87, town bd. reps., 1987-91; mem. Stamford Republican Town Com., 1985—. Mem. Data Processing Mgrs. Assn., Am. Mgmt. Assn. Roman Catholic. Home: 64 Huckleberry Hollw Stamford CT 06903-3940 Office: Pinnacle Techs Corp Ste 18 192 Richmond Hill Ave Stamford CT 06902-5629

FEDER, DANIEL SETH, lawyer; b. N.Y.C., Aug. 28, 1962; s. Charles and Ora Feder. BA, NYU, 1988; JD magna cum laude, Benjamin N. Cardozo Sch. Law, 1990. Bar: N.Y. 1991. Law clk. to Hon. Glenn E. Mencer U.S. Dist. Ct., Pitts., 1990-91; assoc., litigation Shearman & Sterling, N.Y.C., 1991—. Mem. N.Y. State Bar Assn., N.Y. County Lawyers Assn., Federalist Soc., Mensa. Democrat. Office: 153 E 53d St New York NY 10022

FEDER, HARRY SIMON, bank executive; b. N.Y.C., Aug. 20, 1953; s. Morris Louis and Lucy (Kraus) F.; m. Gilli Bortman, Mar. 1, 1977; children: Jean Ella, Laura Ann. BA in Econs., NYU, 1974; MBA in Internat. Fin., Syracuse U., 1976. Credit analyst Israel Discount Bank of N.Y., N.Y.C., 1977-78, with domestic lending, 1978-79, with internat. lending, 1979-81, asst. v.p. corr. banking, 1981-85, v.p. treasury, 1986—. Home: 66 Dora Ln New Rochelle NY 10804-1006 Office: Israel Discount Bank NY 511 5th Ave New York NY 10017-4903

FEDER, KENNETH L., archaeologist, writer; b. N.Y.C., Aug. 1, 1952; s. Murray H. and Grace (Tattenbaum) F.; m. Melissa Jean Kalogeros, Aug. 30, 1981; 1 child, Joshua Max. BA, SUNY, Stonybrook, 1973; MA, U. Conn., 1977, PhD, 1982. Teaching asst. Univ. Conn., Storrs, 1974-77; instr. Cen. Conn. State Univ., New Britain, 1977-82; asst. prof. Cen. Conn. State Univ., 1982-84, assoc. prof., 1984-90, prof., 1990—; regional editor Man in the Northeast (jour.), Albany, N.Y., 1982—; cons. editor The Skeptical Inquirer, Buffalo, 1986—. Co-author: (book) Human Antiquity, 1989; author (book) Frauds, Myths, and Mysteries, 1990; contbr. articles to profl. jours. Recipient Archaeology grants Nat. Park Service, 1986, 87, Found. for Field Rsch., 1990, Conn. State Univ. Found., 1990, 91. Mem. Soc. for Am. Archaeology, Soc. for Hist. Archaeology, Com. for the Sci. Investigation of Claims of the Paranormal (cons.), Archaeological Soc. of Conn. (v.p. 1980-82, pres. 1982-84), Ea. States Archaeological Fedn. Home: 150 Firetown Rd Simsbury CT 06070-1901 Office: Anthropology Dept CCSU 1615 Stanley St New Britain CT 06050

FEDER, LEWIS MORRIS MONTGOMERY, dermatologist, cosmetic plastic surgeon; b. N.Y.C., Feb. 11, 1943; s. Abraham Al and Geraldine (Roselli) F. BA, Hobart Coll., 1964; MD, N.Y. Med. Coll., 1968. Cert. Am. Bd. Dermatology. Intern U.S. Pub. Health Svc. Hosp., S.I., N.Y.; resident USPHS, S.I., N.Y.; dermatologist N.Y. Hosp., Cornell Med. Ctr., 1970-72, chief resident, 1972-73; pvt. practice N.Y.C. Author: About Face, 1989, The Fifth Avenue Doctors Video Guide to Dermatology and Cosmetic Surgery, 1989. Hon. N.Y.C. Commr. for Youth, 1977-85. Lt. USPHS, 1968-70. Fellow Am. Acad. Cosmetic Surgery, Am. Acad. Dermatology, Am. Soc. Dermatologic Surgery, Am. Bd. Dermatology; mem. Nat. Bd. Med. Examiners (diplomate), Internat. Soc. Aesthetic Surgery (Tokyo). Republican. Universalist. Home: 965 Fifth Ave New York NY 10021

FEDER, ROBERT, lawyer; b. N.Y.C., Nov. 29, 1930; s. Benjamin and Bertha (Bloodstein) F.; m. Marjorie Feder, Dec. 3, 1950; children: Susan E., Judith D., Benjamin D., Jessica R., Abigail M. BA cum laude, CCNY, 1953; LLB, Columbia U., 1953. Bar: N.Y. 1953, U.S. Tax Ct. 1956, U.S. Dist. Ct. (so. dist.) N.Y. 1973. V.p., gen. counsel Presdl. Realty Corp., White Plains, N.Y., 1953-71; ptnr. Cuddy & Feder, White Plains, 1971—; bd. dirs. Westchester County (N.Y.) Legal Aid Soc., 1972—, pres., 1974-78; adj. prof. sch. bus. Columbia U., 1988-89. Pres., White Plains Community Action Program, 1967-69; chmn. bd. dirs. White Plains Hosp. Ctr., 1992—, also sec., treas., vice chmn. 1980-92—; commr. White Plains Housing Authority, 1984—; trustee SUNY-Purchase Coll. Found., 1988—; adj. prof. Pace U. Law Sch., 1985-87. Mem. ABA, N.Y. State Bar Assn., Westchester County Bar Assn., White Plains Bar Assn., Am. Coll. Real Estate Lawyers. Home: 9 Oxford Rd White Plains NY 10605-3602 Office: Cuddy & Feder 90 Maple Ave White Plains NY 10601-5105

FEDER, ROBERT ELLIOT, psychiatrist; b. Detroit, July 8, 1951; s. Norman W. and Helen (Kadushin) F.; m. Marsha Susan Cooper; children: Daniel, Elana. BS with high honors, U. Mich., 1972; MD, U. Wash., 1977. Diplomate Am. Bd. Med. Examiners, Am. Bd. Psychiatry and Neurology. Resident in psychiatry Yale U., New Haven, 1981; assoc. psychiatrist Elmcrest Psychiat. Inst., Portland, Conn., 1980-81; med. dir. inpatient psychiatry Beverly (Mass.) Hosp., 1981-83; chief psychiatrist Matthew Thornton Health Plan, Nashua, N.H., 1983-86; attending staff Nashua Meml. Hosp., 1983—; courtesy staff St. Joseph's Hosp., Nashua, 1984—, Cath. Med. Ctr., Manchester, N.H., 1988—; dir. outpatient svcs. Brookside Hosp., Nashua, 1986—, N.E. Psychiat. Assocs., Nashua, 1986—; chmn. dept. psychiatry Nashua Meml. Hosp., 1988—, chmn. credentials com., 1991—. Contbr. articles in psychiatry to profl. jours. Recipient Exemplary Psychiatrist award Nat. Alliance for Mentally Ill, 1992. Mem. AMA, Am. Psychiat. Assn., Am. Assn. Gen. Hosp. Psychiatrists, Physicians for Social Responsibility, N.H. Psychiat. Soc. (chmn. pub. affairs, mem. exec. com. 1985—), Am. Psychiat. Assn. Arts Assn. (sec.-treas. 1985-87), Phi Beta Kappa, Phi Eta Sigma. Democrat. Office: NE Psychiat Assocs 11 Northwest Blvd Nashua NH 03063-4068

FEDERING, ERIC K., press secretary, motion picture preservationist; b. Bronx, N.Y., Feb. 10, 1960; s. Abraham M. and Eileen (Katz) F. BA with Distinction, George Washington U., 1982. Aide U.S. Dept. State, Washington, 1979-81; founder, dir. motion picture restoration effort MAD WORLD Campaign, Washington, 1982-91; press sec., speechwriter for mem. of congress Rep. Norman Y. Mineta, Washington, 1987—; freelance writer, 1982-87; contract writer Larsen-Pomada Lit. Agts, San Francisco, 1984—; advisor media and motion pictures The Lincoln Theatre Found., Washington, 1989-90. Press sec. to nat. co-chair Dukakis-Bentsen Presdl. Campaign, Washington, 1988. Recipient Commendation for Outstanding Achievement by Sec. of State, 1981. Mem. Phi Beta Kappa. Democrat.

FEDOR, GEORGE MATTHEW, III, industrial engineer; b. Bridgeport, Conn., Nov. 17, 1967; s. George Matthew and Joan Patricia (Hammond) F. AS in Mech. Engring., Waterbury State Tech. Coll., 1987; BS in Indsl. Engring., Western New Eng. Coll., 1991. Engr. Avco Lycoming Textron, Stratford, Conn., 1987; advanced devel. engr. Black & Decker (U.S.) Inc., Shelton, Conn., 1988—. Mem. ASME, Inst. Indsl. Engrs., Am. Soc. Quality Control, Am. Prodn. and Inventory Control Soc., Tau Beta Pi, Sigma Beta Tau. Home: 51 Applewood Dr Shelton CT 06484

FEDOR, KATHERINE WUSYLKO, accountant, tax consultant; b. Pitts., Dec. 1, 1956; d. Michael and Nancy (Tuskevich) Wusylko; m. Maxim Andrew Fedor, July 6, 1980. BA cum laude, Duquesne U., 1978; MBA in Acctg., U. Pitts., 1985; postgrad. Taxation, Robert Morris Coll., 1988—. CPA, Pa. Adminstrv. asst. Allegheny County Chmn. Bd. Commrs., Pitts., 1978-80; rsch. analyst Allegheny County Dept. Devel., Pitts., 1980-85; tax mgr. Deloitte, Haskins & Sells, Pitts., 1985—; cons. U.S. Taxes, Deloitte, Haskins & Sells, Caracas, Venezuela, 1988. Treas. St. Alexander Nevsky Orthodox Cathedral, Pitts., 1988—; bd. dirs. Make-a-Wish Found., Pitts., 1989—; violinist Pitts. Internat. Folk Theatre and McKeesport Symphony; del. candidate President Carter campaign, 1979; mem. Young Dems. Allegheny County. Recipient 4 year scholarship Duquesne U., Tamburitzans, Pitts., 1974-78. Mem. Pa. Real Estate License Bd., Am. Inst. CPA's, Pa. Inst. CPA's, Federated Russian Orthodox Clubs (treas. Nat. Conv. 1988-89). Home: 113 Sycamore Dr Pittsburgh PA 15237-3912

FEDRICK, JAMES LOVE, retired chemist; b. Lordsburg, N.Mex., Apr. 17, 1930; s. Julian Richard and Cecilia Elizabeth (Jones) F.; m. Carolyn Susan Hartmann, Feb. 1, 1964; children: Michael, Maria, Thomas, Monica. BS, U. Ariz., 1953, MS, 1955; PhD, U. Ill., 1958. Rsch. chemist Lederle Labs., Pearl River, N.Y., 1958-61, rsch. group leader, 1961-64, tech. dir. fine chems., 1964-65, dir. med. product and process devel., 1966-74, dir. pharm. devel., 1975-76, mem. toxicology task force, 1976-77; mem. staff patent law div. Am. Cyanamid, Stamford, Conn., 1977-90; ret., 1990. Contbr. articles to profl. publs. Roman Catholic. Home: 51 Sparrowbush Rd Mahwah NJ 07430-1524

FEELEY, EDMUND JOHN, management consultant; b. Oak Park, Ill., Apr. 25, 1960; s. Robert Jerome and Patricia Claudette (Czechanski) F.; m. Maryellen Farmer, May 24, 1987. BS in Engring., U. Mich., 1982; MBA, Coll. William and Mary, Williamsburg, Va., 1985. Engr. Newport News Shipbuilding, 1982-83, lead project engr., 1983-84; assoc. Booz Allen & Hamilton, Inc., Bethesda, Md., 1985-87; sr. assoc. Booz Allen & Hamilton, Inc., N.Y.C., 1988-91, prin., 1991—. Adminstrv. asst. Rep. Nat. Conv. Com., Detroit, 1980; dir. Cath. Big Bros. N.Y., 1990—. Mem. Coun. of Logistics Mgmt., Manchester Bath & Tennis Club. Republican. Roman Catholic. Office: Booz Allen & Hamilton 101 Park Ave New York NY 10178-0002

FEELY, HERBERT WILLIAM, research geochemist; b. Bklyn., Apr. 29, 1928; s. John Bernard and Jessie Adelaide (Rounds) F.; m. Marjorie Elizabeth Vosqian, Aug. 23, 1952 (dec. 1967); m. Ethel Hilda Widman, June 15, 1967; children: Wayne, Roger, Barbara, Timothy. BS, CCNY, 1950; AM, Columbia U., 1952, PhD, 1956. Instr. Upsala Coll., East Orange, N.J., 1955-57; sr. rsch. scientist Teledyne Isotopes, Westwood, N.J., 1957-67; assoc. prof. Queens Coll. of CUNY, Flushing, N.Y., 1967-76; sr. rsch. assoc. Lamont-Doherty Geol. Obs., Palisades, N.Y., 1967-76; rsch. chemist U.S. Dept. Energy, Environ. Measurements Lab., N.Y.C., 1976—. Contbr. articles to profl. jours. Mem. Am. Geophys. Union, Am. Meteorol. Soc., Air and Waste Mgmt. Assn., Nat. Atmospheric Deposition Program. Lutheran. Office: US DOE/EML 376 Hudson St New York NY 10014

FEELY, MATTHEW STEPHEN ANTHONY, naval career officer; b. Boston, Oct. 14, 1960; s. Richard John and Constance Virginia (Lynch) F. BS, U.S. Naval Acad., 1983; MBA, U. Pa., 1992, postgrad., 1992—. Commd. lt., asst. supply officer U.S.S. Austin (LPD-4) USN, 1984-85; submarine officer student U.S. Submarine Officer's Sch. USN, Groton, Conn., 1985-86; supply officer U.S.S. Providence (SSN-719) USN, 1986-88; logistics office Adminstrv. Support Unit, Bahrain, 1988-89. Roman Catholic. Home and office: 120 Mt Vernon St Dedham MA 02026-3102

FEENEY, RICHARD JOSEPH, trade association executive, journalist; b. Scranton, Pa., Dec. 3, 1944; s. Joseph Gerald and Eileen Mary (O'Toole) F.; m. Annemarie Donohoe, June 10, 1978; 1 child, Mary Elizabeth. AB in Internat. Rels., Cath. U. Am., 1972. Co-owner World Wide Wines, Inc., Washington, 1971-74; spl. asst. U.S. Rep. Thomas N. Downing, Washington, 1974-76; asst. dir. Select Com. on Assassinations, Washington, 1976-77; dir. pub. affairs Nat. Meat Assn., Washington, 1977-79; dir. office of govtl. affairs Commodity Futures Trading Commn., Washington, 1979-81; legis. and pub. affairs specialist Dept. of Def., Washington, 1981-88; exec. dir. Nat. Vintners Assn., Washington, 1988—; legis. corres. Coin World, Sidney, Ohio, 1991—; bd. dirs. v.p. Am. Against Drugs, Inc., Washington, 1990—. Contbr. articles to profl. jours. Lt. comdr. USNR, 1981-87. Mem. Army and Navy Club Washington, Touchdown Club Washington. Roman Catholic. Home: 4845 Glenbrook Rd NW Washington DC 20016 Office: Nat Vintners Assn 1629 K St NW Ste 1100 Washington DC 20006

FEFFERMAN, HILBERT, lawyer, government official; b. N.Y.C., June 5, 1913; s. Jacob and Sarah F.; m. Helen Libby Relkin, June 16, 1940. BS, NYU, 1934; LLB, Harvard U., 1937. Bar: N.Y. 1938, U.S. Supreme Ct. 1953. Pvt. practice N.Y.C., 1938-41; atty. U.S. Housing and Home Fin. Agy., Washington, 1941-59, asst. gen. counsel for legislation, 1960-62, assoc. gen. counsel for ops., 1962-67; chief legislative counsel HUD, Washington, 1967-72; cons. Housing and Devel. Legislation, Bethesda, Md., 1973—; lectr., vis. prof. city planning MIT, Cambridge, Mass., 1973-76. Contbr. articles to profl. jours. Recipient Disting. Svc. award HUD, 1968. Home and Office: 5661 Bent Branch Rd Bethesda MD 20816-1049

FEIFFER, JULES, cartoonist, writer, playwright; b. N.Y.C., Jan. 26, 1929; s. David and Rhoda (Davis) F.; m. Judith Sheftel, Sept. 17, 1961 (div. 1983); 1 child, Kate; m. Jennifer Allen, Sept. 11, 1983; 1 child, Halley. Student, Art Students League, N.Y.C., 1946, Pratt Inst., N.Y.C., 1947-48, 49-51. Asst. to syndicated cartoonist Will Eisner, 1946-51; co-chmn. maj. funds com. Yaddo Corp. Cartoonist, author: syndicated Sunday page Clifford, 1949-51; engaged in various art jobs, 1953-56; contbg. cartoonist: Village Voice, N.Y.C., 1956—; cartoons pub. weekly in London (Eng.) Observer, 1958-66, 72-82; regularly in Playboy mag, 1959—; cartoons nationally syndicated U.S., 1959—; author: books Sick, Sick, Sick, 1958, Passionella and other stories, 1959, The Explainers, 1961, Boy, Girl, Boy, Girl, 1962, Hold Me, 1962; mus. revue The Explainers, 1961; one act play Crawling Arnold, 1961; novel Harry, The Rat with Women, 1963; Feiffer's Album, 1963, The Unexpurgated Memoirs of Bernard Mergendeiler, 1965, The Great Comic Book Heroes, 1965, Feiffer's Marriage Manual, 1967; (plays) Little Murders, 1967 (voted best fgn. play of yr. by London critics, Obie award, Outer Circle Drama Critics award), Feiffer on Civil Rights, 1967, God Bless, 1968, O Calcutta, 1969 (contbr. revue) The White House Murder Case, 1970; screenplays Little Murders, 1971, Carnal Knowledge, 1971; books Pictures at a Prosecution, 1971, Feiffer on Nixon: The Cartoon Presidency, 1974; play Knock-Knock, 1976; revue Hold Me!, 1977; novel Ackroyd, 1977; cartoon novel Tantrum, 1979; screenplay Popeye, 1980; play Grownups, 1981, A Think Piece, 1982; book Jules Feiffer's America: From Eisenhower to Reagan, 1982, Marriage is An Invasion of Privacy, 1984, Feiffer's Children, 1986, Ronald Reagan In Movie-America, 1988; TV scripts Hold Me!, 1981, Grown Ups, 1985, play Carnal Knowledge, 1988, screenplay I Want to Go Home, 1989 (Best Screenplay Venice Film Festival 1989), Urban Blight, 1989 (contbr. revue), plays Anthony Rose, 1989, Elliot Loves, 1990. Served with AUS, 1951-53. Recipient Acad. award for animated cartoon, Munro 1961, spl. George Polk Meml. award 1962, Obie award, 1969, Outer Circle Drama Critics award 1969, 70; Pulitzer prize for editorial cartooning, 1986. Mem. Authors Guild, Dramatists Guild (council, pres. found. 1982-83), P.E.N., Writers Guild of Am.

FEIGEN, IRENE, artist, educator; b. Bklyn., Aug. 13, 1944; d. Max and Jean (Weingarten) Marder; m. Daniel Feigen, Mar. 29, 1963; children: Erik, Nicole, Ross. BFA, Bklyn. Coll., 1964; MFA, CCNY, 1965; cert. Printmaking, NYU, 1985. Lic. tchr., N.Y.; cert. printmaker, N.Y. Tchr. fine arts N.Y.C. Bd. Edn., 1962-65; prof. fine arts Fairleigh Dickinson U., Madison, N.J., 1980-87; freelance artist, art educator Art Expo N.Y., 1980-90; artist in residence, Livingston Home and Sch. Assn., 1980—, Riker Hill Art Park, Livingston, N.J., B'nai Abraham, Livingston, 1987. Exhibitions include Robert Ward Galleries, N.Y.C., Korby Gallery, Cedar Grove, N.J., Bergen Mus., Paramus, N.J., Morris Mus., Morristown, N.J., Montclair Mus., Hebrew Home for Aged, Riverdale, N.Y., The Nese Gallery, Irvine, Calif., Newark Mus., Papermill Playhouse Gallery, Millburn, N.J., Straleys Gallery, Livingston, N.J., Whichcraft Studio, South Orange, Long Beach Island, N.J., The Key Gallery, N.Y.C., Art 3 Assocs., Livingston, Art 3 of Ft. Lee, N.J., MCI, SONY, Lewis Internat., Clifton Radiology Ctr., among others. Mem. Allied Bd. Trade; bd. dirs. Arts Coun. Livingston, 1990, 92. Recipient numerous artistic awards. Mem. Internat. Soc. Arts, West Essex Watercolor Soc., Essex County Arts Soc. (bd. dirs. 1980-85), Livingston Arts Assn. (v.p. 1977-85, bd. dirs. 1970-85), The Printmakers Coun., Mus. Contemporary Crafts, Artists Equity. Home and Studio: 48 Blackstone Dr Livingston NJ 07039

FEIGENBAUM, ABRAHAM SAMUEL, nutritional biochemist; b. N.Y.C., Mar. 11, 1929; s. Benjamin and Pearl Feigenbaum; m. Hannah Devries, Aug. 17, 1952; children: Benjamin, Josef, Miriam. BS, Rutgers U., 1951, MS, 1959, PhD, 1962. Chemist E.R. Squibb, New Brunswick, N.J., 1954-57; rsch. asst. Rutgers U., New Brunswick, N.J., 1957-61; rsch. scientist, chief neuroendocrinology N.J. Bur. Rsch. in Neurology and Psychiatry, Skillman, 1961-73; dir. clin. nutrition, dir. clin. coordination Warren-Teed Pharm./Adria Labs., Inc., Columbus, Ohio, 1973-81; clin. project dir., dir. rsch. Pharm. Rsch. Inst., sub. Akzo, Columbus, Ohio, 1981—; dir. clin. devel. Organon, Inc., West Orange, N.J., 1981—; guest lectr. in nutrition Hahnemann Med. Coll., Phila., 1977-80. Mem. Bd. Edn., Highland Park, N.J., 1969-73, pres., 1970-72, v.p., 1972-73. NSF fellow, 1961. Mem. Am. Inst. Nutrition, Am. Chem. Soc., Soc. Exptl. Biology and Medicine. Home: 22 Berkshire Rd Maplewood NJ 07040-1428 Office: Organon Inc 375 Mt Pleasant Ave West Orange NJ 07052-2798

FEIGENBAUM, JOAN, computer scientist, mathematician; b. Bklyn., Sept. 19, 1958; d. Harry and Joyce Leslie (Gildersleeve) F.; m. Jeffrey Nussbaum. BA magna cum laude, Harvard U., 1981; PhD, Stanford U., 1986. Mem. tech. staff AT&T Bell Labs., Murray Hill, N.J., 1986—; adj. prof. computer sci. Columbia U., N.Y.C., 1988—; program chair CRYPTO-91, Santa Barbara, Calif., 1991; mem. program com. STOC-91, New Orleans, 1991, co-chair DIMACS Workshops, 1989, 90; speaker various colls., univs. and confs. Editorial bd. mem. Jour. of Cryptology, 1991—, Jour. of Algorithms, 1992—; area editor Communication of Assn. for Computing Machinery, 1988-89; guest editor: Jour. of Computer and System Scis., 1991-92; contbr. articles to profl. jours. Mem. computing rsch. assn. com. Status of Women. Math. Scis. Postdoctoral fellow NSF, 1986, Xerox Corp. Grad. fellow, 1984. Mem. Am. Math. Soc., Assn. for Computing Machinery, Assn. for Women in Math., Internat. Assn. for Cryptologic Rsch. (program com. CRYPTO89 conf. 1989, Eurocrypt92 conf. 1992), N.Y. Acad. Scis., Radcliffe Club N.Y. (sec. bd. dirs. 1988-90), Phi Beta Kappa. Democrat. Jewish. Home: 148 W 23d St Apt 2A New York NY 10011-2447 Office: AT&T Bell Labs 600 Mountain Ave Rm 2C473 Murray Hill NJ 07974-0636

FEIGENBAUM, RUTH I., mathematics educator; b. Paterson, N.J., May 4, 1944; d. Paul S. and Celia (Neumann) Schulmann; children: Adam, Tobie, Heidi, Ellen. BA in Math., Rutgers U., 1966; MA in Math. Edn., Columbia U., 1967; PhD in Math., U. S.C., 1975; MS in Computer Sci., Fairleigh Dickinson U., Teaneck, N.J., 1986. Math/Spanish tchr. Ridge St. Sch., Port Chester, N.Y., 1967-69; math tchr. Columbia (S.C.) High Sch., 1969-70; vis. lectr. N.C. Cen. U., Durham, 1974; asst. prof. Kean Coll. of N.J., Union, 1976-81; asst. prof. math. Fairleigh Dickinson U., 1982-86, Bergen Community Coll., Paramus, N.J., 1986—; coordinator developmental math prog. Kean Coll. of N.J., 1978-81. Mem. Spl. Edn. Adv. Coun., Franklin Lakes, N.J., 1987-91. Mem. Nat. Council Tchrs. Math., Am. Math. Soc., Math. Assn. of Two-Yr. Colls. of N.J. (campus rep. 1988—), Phi Beta Kappa, Pi Mu Epsilon. Jewish. Office: Bergen Community Coll 400 Paramus Rd Paramus NJ 07652-1508

FEIL, RICHARD NORMAN, psychology, educator; b. Chgo., Sept. 12, 1936; s. Lawrence William and Harriet Elizabeth (Reitz) F.; m. Judith Jacques, Aug. 13, 1964 (div. Feb. 1989); children: Mark, Mary, Thomas, Matthew; m. Jennifer Hutchinson, Aug. 5, 1989. BA, Loyola U., Chgo., 1961; MA, Cath. U. of Am., 1963, PhD, 1968. Cert. psychologist. Rsch. psychologist U.S. Army Behavioral Rsch. Office, Washington, 1965-68; prof. Mansfield (Pa.) Univ., 1968—; rsch. assoc. Rural Svcs. Inst., Mansfield (Pa.) Univ., 1989—. Author: Computer-Assisted Psychological Evaluations, 1988, The Public Mind, 1989, 90, 91, 92; contbr. articles to profl. jours. Recipient several univ. and state grants. Mem. Am. Psychol. Assn., Freedom From Religion Found. Office: Mansfield U Psychology Dept Mansfield PA 16933

FEIN, ADAM RICHARD, public relations executive; b. N.Y.C., Mar. 21, 1957; s. Bernard and Elaine (Schneir) F.; m. Linda Keithan, Aug. 22, 1981; 1 child, Cassidy. BS, Syracuse U., 1979; MS, Johns Hopkins U., 1984. Promotion specialist United Bus. Publs., N.Y.C., 1979-80; corp. communications dir. AAI Corp., Hunt Valley, Md., 1980-91; pres. ARF Prodns., Phoenix, Md., 1991—. Screenwriter numerous teleplays, 1987—. Mem. Pub. Relations Soc. Am., Writers Guild Am., Aviation and Space Writers Assn., Internat. TV Assn., Beta Gamma Sigma. Office: ARF Prodns Phoenix MD 21131

FEIN, PAUL STOCKSER, writer; b. Springfield, Mass.; s. Irving and Lillian (Stockser) F. Student, Cornell U. Media dir. Ford & Mayotte Mgmt. Cons., Ellicott City, Md., 1982-90; owner, mgr. Internat. Sports Clipping Svc., Agawam, Mass., 1985—; tennis expert/cons.; TV tennis commentator Continental Cablevision, 1985—. Writer for more than 20 fgn. and more than 20 U.S. sports and tennis mags. including Tennis, Tennis Wk., World Tennis, Tennis USA, Inside Tennis, Advantage, Internat. Tennis Weekly, Inside Women's Tennis, Women's Sports and Fitness, Match Ball (Italy), Tennis Mag. (Ger.), Smash (Japan), others;tennis writer Springfield Daily News, 1981-90. Recipient great Am. Tennis Writing award, Tennis Wk., 1991, New Eng. Lawn Tennis Assn. Media award, 1988, Springfield Tennis Opportunity Program Community Svc. award, 1987, U.S. Profl. Tennis Assn. Svc. award, 1984. Mem. U.S. Tennis Writers Assn., U.S. Tennis Assn. (tournament cons.), U.S. Profl. Tennis Registry, Internat. Assn. Sports Press, Nat. Assn. Sports Writers and Sportscasters, Nat. Writers Union, U.S. Profl. Tennis Assn., Lawn Tennis Assn. (U.K.), Springfield Tennis Club (pres. 1988-91), Springfield Tennis Coun. (pres. 1992). Democrat. Jewish. Home: 39 Beekman Dr Agawam MA 01001-2608

FEINBAUM, GEORGE, internist; b. Samarkand, USSR, July 31, 1945; came to U.S., 1965, naturalized, 1972; s. Joseph and Cyrla (Szoken) F.; student Med. Acad. Wroclaw, Poland, 1963-65, Queens Coll., 1966-70; M.D., Albert Einstein Coll. Medicine, 1973; m. Dec. 17, 1964; m. Yoanna Sobocinska-Feinbaum; 1 son, Livius. Diplomate Am. Bd. Internal Medicine. Intern, Met. Hosp. Ctr., N.Y.C., 1973-74, resident in internal medicine, 1974-76, fellow in endocrinology and metabolism, 1976-77; practice medicine, specializing in internal medicine, Bklyn., 1977—; asst. in medicine Brookdale Hosp. Med. Ctr., Bklyn., 1977—. Mem. ACP, Kings County Med. Soc., N.Y. Acad. Scis., Mensa. Office: 934 Manhattan Ave Brooklyn NY 11222 also: 3245 Nostrand Ave Brooklyn NY 11229

FEINBERG, EUGENE ALEXANDER, mathematics educator; b. Moscow, Apr. 28, 1954; came to U.S., 1988; s. Alexander Z. and Julia S. (Subbotnik) F.; m. Irene Feinberg, Oct. 1, 1977; 1 child, David. MS, Moscow Inst. Transport Engring, USSR, 1976; PhD, Vilnius U., Lithuania, 1979. Research scientist Moscow Inst. of Transport Engring., 1976-79, assoc. prof., 1979-88; vis. assoc. prof. Yale U., New Haven, 1988-89; prof. SUNY, Stony

Brook, 1989—. Contbr. articles to profl. jours. Mem. Am. Math. Soc., Ops. Research Soc. of Am., Inst. of Mgmt. Sci. Office: SUNY W Averall Harriman Sch for Mgmt and Policy Stony Brook NY 11794-3775

FEINBERG, GLORIA GRANDITER, psychologist; b. N.Y.C., Dec. 18, 1923; d. David and Ray (Davis) Granditer; B.A., U. Pa., 1944; M.A., N.Y. U., 1947; m. Mortimer R. Feinberg, June 22, 1947; children—Stuart Andrew, Todd E. Asst. psychologist Grasslands Hosp., Valhalla, N.Y., 1948-51; cons. BFS Psychol. Assos., N.Y.C., 1960-77, pres., 1977—. Mem. Am. Psychol. Assn., Phi Beta Kappa, Pi Gamma Mu. Author: Leavetaking, 1978. Home: 34 Brook Ln Cortlandt Mnr NY 10566-6502 Office: 666 Fifth Ave New York NY 10103

FEINBERG, HARVEY MICHAEL, history educator; b. Hartford, Conn., Apr. 17, 1938; s. Jacob M. and Mildred (Berman) F.; m. Susan Beth Elconin, June 17, 1962; children: Victor, Paul. BA, Yale U., 1960; MA, Am. U., 1963; postgrad., UCLA, 1965-66; PhD, Boston U., 1969. Manuscripts asst. Libr. of Congress, Washington, 1961-62; from asst. to prof. Southern Conn. State U., New Haven, 1969—; evaluator grant proposals NEH, Washington, 1989, 90; manuscript evaluator Internat. Jour. African Hist. Studies, Boston, 1970—. Author: Africans and Europeans in West Africa, 1989; contbr. articles to profl. jours. Member Regional Planning Authority of South Cen. Conn., 1984-86; commr. Capital Projects Com., New Haven, 1986-90. NDEA fellow UCLA, 1965-66, Social Sci. Rsch. Coun. fellow, 1966-68, Am. Philos. Soc. fellow, 1972, '77, '85, '92, Yale U. fellow, 1990-91, Fulbright scholar U.S. Dept. Edn., 1991. Mem. Conn. Acad. Arts and Scis. (v.p. 1990—), New Eng. Hist. Assn., African Studies Assn. Home: 189 Westwood Rd New Haven CT 06515-2244 Office: So Conn State U New Haven CT 06515

FEINBERG, MILTON, entrepreneur; b. N.Y.C., Jan. 26, 1926; s. Julius and Gussie Feinberg. Exec. textile and toy industries, 1940-80; exec. pub. internat. mktg. mag., 1980-84; project developer WORLD SHIP, 1985—. Home: 344B Heritage Vlg Southbury CT 06488-1707

FEINBERG, NORMAN MAURICE, real estate executive; b. Bklyn., Nov. 28, 1934; s. Harry and Beatrice (Soroca) F.; m. Arline S. Itzkoff, Nov. 26, 1960; children: Mitchell, David. BS, NYU, 1956. Exec. Columbia Pictures Corp., N.Y.C., 1956-62; pres. Gateside Corp., Rye, N.Y., 1965—; owner, gen. ptnr. 27 companies, Rye. Arbitrator Am. Arbitration Assn., N.Y.C.; trustee, vice-chmn. Bklyn. Museum; bd. dirs. Assn. for Mentally Ill Children, Scarborough, N.Y. Mem. World Pres. Orgn., Young Pres. Orgn. (chmn.), Chief Execs. Officers. Home: 791 Park Ave New York NY 10021-3551 Office: Gateside Corp 555 Theodore Fremd Ave Rye NY 10580-1437

FEINBERG, RICHARD BURT, brokerage house executive; b. Bklyn., May 22, 1945; s. Jack and Rebecca (Koenigsberg) F.; m. Carolyn Joan Leifer, June 3, 1972; children: Russell, Michael, Andrew, Matthew. BS in Acctg., CUNY, Bklyn., 1967. Ops. prin. Russell & Saxe, Jersey City, 1964-71; mng. ptnr. Richardt-Alyn & Co., Phila., 1971—; Bd. govs. Phila. Stock Exch., Inc., from 1981, formerly vice chmn. Mem. Nat. Security Traders Assn., Masons (master 1983). Office: Richardt-Alyn & Co 114 S 20th St Philadelphia PA 19103-4451*

FEINBERG, ROBERT EDWARD, advertising agency executive, writer; b. N.Y.C., May 16, 1935; s. Alfred and Esther (Krutick) F.; m. Frances Greenfield, Sept. 1962 (div. 1980); children: Bradford, Karen; m. Jane Laurie Scheckter, Apr. 1980. AB, Hunter Coll., 1956. Publicist Bernstein Kornzweig, N.Y.C., 1956-59; pub. dir. William Morris Agy., N.Y.C., 1959-64; v.p., creative dir. Kameny Assocs., N.Y.C., 1964-68; copy group head J. Walter Thompson, N.Y.C., 1968-72; v.p., creative dir. William Esty Co., N.Y.C., 1972-77; exec. v.p. creative dir. Bozell and Jacobs, Los Angeles, 1977-82; exec. v.p., creative dir. Bozell, Jacobs, Kenyon & Eckhardt, N.Y.C., 1982-89; exec. v.p., exec. creative dir. Grey Direct Mktg. Group, N.Y.C., 1989—. Author: (motion pictures) The American Way, 1962, Caribbean Celebration, 1980, (play) Everybody Else, 1976; writer (TV series) Mork & Mindy, 1978, Adventures of Sheriff Lobo, 1979, Out of the Blue, 1978, Working Stiffs, 1980, Blitz, 1986; contbr. articles Playboy mag., 1958. Recipient Internat. Broadcast award Hollywood Radio and TV Soc., 1966, 86, 87, Belding award Los Angeles Advt. Club, 1978, Clio awards, 1979, 80, 85, 86, 87, 88, 89, 90, Mobius award Chgo. Internat. Film Festival, 1986, Internat. Film and TV Festival award N.Y. Market Radio Advertisers, 1986 87, Creativity '87 award Art Direction mag., 1987, Andy award N.Y. Advt. Club, 1987, Effie award Am. Mktg. Assn., 1986, 88, 90. Mem. Writers Guild of Am. Office: Grey Direct Internat 875 3d Ave New York NY 10022-6225

FEINBERG, ROBERT I(RA), lawyer; b. Boston, Jan. 6, 1956; s. Philip I. and Evelyn Helene (Hurvitz) F.; m. Lisa Michelle Palmer, Aug. 18, 1991. BA magna cum laude, Brown U., 1978; JD, U. Pa., 1981. Bar: Mass. 1982, Fla. 1985. Assoc. Parker, Coulter, Daley & White, Boston, 1981-83; ptnr. Feinberg and Alban, P.C., Brookline, Mass., 1984—; v.p. MVP Assocs., Brookline, 1980-87. Author: Jewish Voting Patterns in America, 1978. Active Anti-Defamation League, Boston, 1987—. Mem. Mass. Acad. Trial Attys. (lectr.), Mass. Bar Assn., Boston Bar Assn., Nat. Polit. Action Com. (Washington). Jewish. Home: 685 Centre St Newton MA 02158-2342 Office: Feinberg & Alban PC 1051 Beacon St Brookline MA 02146-5622

FEINBERG, ROBERT MARK, economics educator; b. Newark, Apr. 11, 1951; s. Julius A. and Sylvia (Weinberg) F.; m. Katherine V. Kelley, Oct. 10, 1982; children: Nina Kelley, Rose Kelley. BA, U. Pa., 1972; PhD, U. Va., 1976. Asst. prof. Pa. State U., University Park, 1976-79, assoc. prof., 1980-87; economist anti-trust div. Dept. Justice, Washington, 1979-80; economist U.S. Internat. Trade Commn., Washington, 1987-89; assoc. prof. econs. Am. U., Washington, 1989-91, prof., 1991—; vis. prof. U. Louvain, Belgium, 1984. Author: The Job Search Theory, 1984; contbr. articles to profl. jours. Recipient Spl. Merit award AMEX Bank Rev. Internat. Essay Competition, 1989; Rsch. fellow Internat. Inst. Mgmt., West Berlin, 1983; grantee European Integration, 1983. Mem. Am. Econ. Assn., So. Econ. Assn., Indsl. Orgn. Soc., European Assn. Rsch. Indsl. Econs. Office: Am U Dept Econs 4400 Massachusetts Ave NW Washington DC 20016-8029

FEINBERG, ROBERT S., plastics manufacturing company executive, marketing consultant; b. Newark, May 14, 1934; s. Clarence Jacob and Sabina (Zorn) F.; BA in English, BS in Chemistry, Trinity Coll., Hartford, Conn., 1955; MBA in Mktg., Fairleigh Dickinson U., 1966; advt. diploma Assn. Indsl. Advt., 1967, advt. diploma N.Y. Inst. Advt., 1967; Pres., Trebor Assocs. and Trebor Plastics Co., Teaneck, N.J., 1961—; mktg. cons. computer software Zettler Softwear Co., Burroughs Corp.; sr. council Yankelovich, Skelly and White, Inc.; cons. Greenwich Assocs.; co-chmn., ptnr. Edgeroy Co., Inc., Ridgefield and Palisades Park, N.J., 1973—; co-chmn., ptnr. LeMont Sales Co., Teaneck, 1973—; cons. plastic formulations W.R. Grace, Endicott Johnson, Brown Shoe Co., U.S. Shoe Co., Ciba, Uniroyal. Mem. Soc. Plastics Engrs. (sr.), Sporting Goods Mfrs. Assn., Sell Overseas Am., U.S. Profl. Tennis Assn., Bergen County Tennis League (v.p.). Club: Ahdeek Tennis. Author: Olympia Shoe Co., 1966; co-inventor Edgeroy Ball Press (Internat. Tennis Hall of Fame, Newport, R.I.); patentee in polymer and mech. engring. fields. Home: 81 Edgemont Pl Teaneck NJ 07666-4605

FEINBERG, SAMUEL, newspaper columnist; b. N.Y.C., Sept. 22, 1908; s. Louis and Dora (Garfinkel) F.; m. Nettie Weissman, Feb. 23, 1939; children: Lawrence, Richard, Alice Batson. LHD (hon.), Lab. Inst. Merchandising. Gen. asst. Garment Trade Rev., N.Y.C., 1925-32, mng. editor, 1933-37; spl. features reporter Women's Wear Daily, N.Y.C., 1937-46, store ops. editor, 1946-50, columnist, 1950—. Author: How Do You Manage?, 1965, Management's Challenge, 1976. Recipient Bus. Achievement award, Black Retail Action Group, 1977, The Atrium award, Henry W. Grady Sch. Journalism, 1981, Silver Plaque award, Nat. Retail Merchants Assn., 1982. Home: 300 Mercer St New York NY 10003-6724 Office: Women's Wear Daily 7 W 34th St New York NY 10001

FEINBERG, WILFRED, federal judge; b. N.Y.C., June 22, 1920; s. Jac and Eva (Wolin) F.; m. Shirley Marcus, June 23, 1946; children: Susan, Jack, Jessica. BA, Columbia U., 1940, LLB, 1946, LLD (hon.), 1985; LLD (hon.), Syracuse U., 1985. Bar: N.Y. 1947. Law clk. U.S. dist. judge U.S. Dist. Ct. (ea. dist.) Pa., 1947-49; assoc. Kaye, Scholer, Fierman & Hays, N.Y.C., 1949-53; ptnr. McGoldrick, Dannett, Horowitz & Golub, N.Y.C., 1953-61; dep. supt. N.Y. State Banking Dept., 1958; U.S. judge So. Dist. N.Y., 1961-66; U.S. judge Ct. Appeals 2d Cir., 1966—, chief judge, 1980-88; sr. judge U.S. Ct. Appeals 2d Cir., 1991—; mem. U.S. Jud. Conf. U.S., 1980-88, chmn. exec. com., 1987-88, mem. long range planning com. , 1991—; Madison lectr. NYU Law Sch., 1983; Sonnett lectr. Fordham U. Law Sch., 1984. Editor-in-chief Columbia Law Rev, 1946. With AUS, 1942-45. Recipient Learned Hand medal for excellence in fed. jurisprudence, 1982, Gold medal N.Y. State Bar Assn., 1990, Medal for excellence Columbia Law Alumni Assn., 1990. Mem. ABA, Assn. of Bar of City of N.Y., N.Y. County Lawyers Assn., Am. Judicature Soc., Am. Law Inst., Phi Beta Kappa. Office: US Courthouse Foley Sq New York NY 10007-1501

FEINBLUM, DAVID ALAN, research and development company executive; b. Bronx, N.Y., May 20, 1946; s. Jacob A. and Ida G. Feinblum; m. Vicki N. Ackerman, June 21, 1964 (dec. Dec. 1985); children: Miriam Rivka, Ruth Naomi; m. Phyllis Orgel, Aug. 30, 1987. B Mech. Engring., Cooper Union, 1960; PhD in Physics, Rensselaer Poly. Inst., 1966. Asst. prof. physics SUNY, Albany, 1964-71; sr. mathematician Univac, Whippany, N.J., 1971-73; prin. mathematician Sperry/Univac, Whippany, 1973-75; sr. scientist Xybion Corp., Cedar Knolls, N.J., 1975-77, prin. scientist, 1977-82, tech. dir., 1983—, v.p. def. systems, 1991—. Contbr. articles to sci. jours. Fellow NSF, 1965, Princeton U., 1967, Weitzmann Inst. Sci., Rehovot, Israel, 1969. Mem. Sigma Xi, Sigma Pi Sigma, Pi Tau Sigma. Office: Xybion Corp 240 Cedar Knolls Rd Cedar Knolls NJ 07927-1604

FEINER, AVA SOPHIA, public affairs/management consultant, economist; b. Bklyn., Feb. 13, 1950; d. Ignace and Lola (Pasternak) F.; m. Clifford Douglas Stromberg, June 25, 1972; children: Kimberly Greta, Eric George. BA summa cum laude, Yale U., 1971; MA, Harvard U., 1974, PhD in Govt., 1978. Legis. asst. to U.S. Senator Bill Bradley, Washington, 1979-82; dir. internat. trade policy U.S. C. of C., Washington, 1982-83, mgr. internat. policy dept., 1983-85; corp. program dir. IBM, Washington, 1985-87, corp. dir. pub. affairs, trade and investment, 1987; pres. Feiner Pub. Affairs Cons., Washington, 1988—; co-founder, dir. Washington Alive! Inc., 1989-90; pres. Washington Networks, 1990—; teaching fellow Harvard U., Cambridge, Mass., 1972-74; lectr. nat. and internat. politics and econs., 1978—; bd. dirs., World Trade Forum, Washington, 1987-89. Co-author: American Excellence in A World Economy, 1987; contbr. articles on econs., trade, fgn. policy to various publs. Del. to Atlantic Coun. Young Leadership Program, Wis. and Can., 1978, 80, Aspen Inst. Exec. Seminar, 1982, Germany-U.S. Young Leadership Conf., San Francisco, 1982. Fgn. Policy fellow Brookings Instn., 1975-76, guest scholar, 1976-77; Carnegie Endowment for Internat. Peace fellow, 1975-76. Mem. Coun. Fgn. Rels. (task force on women 1988-91, term membership com. 1988-91, internat. affairs fellows com. 1991—), Trade Policy Forum, Phi Beta Kappa.

FEINERMAN, LEON JUDAH, insurance agent, small business owner; b. Harrisburg, Pa., June 4, 1945; s. Aaron Samuel and Sara Gertrude (Silberman) F.; m. Francine Miriam Greenberg, May 12, 1969; children: Judd, Jessica. AB, U. Pitts., 1967. V.p. Feinerman Ins. Agy., Harrisburg, Pa., 1967-84; pres. Feinerman Ins. Agy., Harrisburg, 1984—; bd. dirs. Holy Spirit Hosp. Pres. Harrisburg (Pa.) City Coun., 1976-77, Yeshiva Acad., Harrisburg, 1980-84, United Way of Capital Area, Harrisburg, 1987-88; chmn. Dauphin County Social Svc. for Children & Youth, Harrisburg, 1974-80, Harrisburg Housing Authority, 1983—; pres. Beth El Temple, Harrisburg, 1991-92. 2nd lt. U.S. Army, 1969-73. Mem. Nat. Assn. Ind. Ins. Agts., Pa. Assn. Ind. Ins. Agts., Harrisburg Assn. Ind. Ins. Agts. (pres. 1975-76), Profl. Ins. Agts. Assn., Nat. Assn. Life Underwriters, Nat. Adv. Coun. St. Paul (Minn.) Ins. Co., Nat. Adv. Coun. Aetna Casualty & Surety, Nat. Adv. Coun. Millers Mutual Ins. Co., Harrisburg. Democrat. Jewish. Home: 2941 Green St Harrisburg PA 17110-1233 Office: The Feinerman Group 2745 N Front St Harrisburg PA 17110-1221

FEINSOD, ARTHUR BENNETT, theatre arts educator; b. N.Y.C., June 4, 1951; s. Robert Lewis and Kalma Jewel (Shapiro) F.; m. Mary Elizabeth Kramer; children: Lincoln Peterson, Simon Peterson. BA magna cum laude, Harvard U., 1973; MA, U. Calif., Berkeley, 1978; PhD, NYU, 1986. Artistic dir. Berkeley Lights Theater Ensemble, 1976-80; tchr. drama The Branson Sch., Ross, Calif., 1976-80; instr. in theater and speech N.Y. Inst. Tech., N.Y.C., 1983-85; asst. prof. Trinity Coll., Hartford, Conn., 1985-92; assoc. prof. Trinity Coll., Hartford, 1992—; chmn. theater and dance dept. Trinity Coll., Hartford, Conn., 1986-89, 91-93; prof. Elder Hostel, Verona, Padua and Lake Garda, Italy, summers, 1990, 92. Author: The Simple Stage, 1992; playwright: (plays) Play for Keeps, 1983, The Lost City of Cibola, 1991, (adaptation) Everyman, 1989. Pearl Hickman fellow U. Calif., 1973-75; NEH grantee, 1987; recipient Arthur Hughes award Trinity Coll., 1991. Mem. Phi Beta Kappa. Office: Trinity Coll Austin Arts Ctr Hartford CT 06106

FEINSTEIN, ALVAN RICHARD, physician; b. Phila., Dec. 4, 1925; s. Joel B. and Bella (Ukasz) F. B.S., U. Chgo., 1947, M.S. in Math, 1948, M.D., 1952; M.A. (hon.), Yale U., 1969. Intern, then resident Yale-New Haven Hosp., 1952-54; research fellow Rockefeller Inst., 1954-55; resident Columbia-Presbyn. Med. Center, N.Y.C., 1955-56; clin. dir. Irvington House, N.Y.C., 1956-62; instr., then asst. prof. N.Y. U. Sch. Medicine, 1956-62; chief clin. pharmacology VA Hosp., West Haven, Conn., 1962-64; chief clin. biostatistics VA Hosp., 1964-74; mem. faculty Sch. Medicine, Yale U., 1962—, prof. medicine and epidemiology, 1969—, dir. clin. scholar program, 1974—, Sterling prof., 1991—; chief Eastern Research Support Ctr. VA, 1967-74; pres. New Haven area chpt. Assn. Computing Machinery, 1968-69. Author: Clinical Judgment, 1967, Clinical Biostatistics, 1977, Clinical Epidemiology, 1985, Clinimetrics, 1987; editor Jour. Clinical Epidemiology; also articles. Served with AUS, 1944-46. Recipient Francis G. Blake award for outstanding teaching Yale Med. Sch., J. Allyn Taylor Internat. prize, awards Soc. for Gen. Internal Medicine, U. Chgo., Ludwig Heilmyer Soc. (Europe). Mem. ACP (award), AMA, Assn. Am. Physicians, Am. Soc. Clin. Investigation, Am. Epidemiol. Soc., Inst. Medicine, Am. Bd. Internal Medicine, Am. Fedn. Clin. Research, Am. Soc. Clin. Pharmacology Therapeutics, Am. Statis. Assn., Assn. Computing Machinery, Biometric Soc., Am. Assn. History Medicine, Alpha Omega Alpha. Home: 164 Linden St New Haven CT 06511-2400 Office: Yale U Sch Medicine 333 Cedar St New Haven CT 06510-0825

FEINSTEIN, JONATHAN EDWARD, coffee company executive, consultant; b. New Bedford, Mass., Oct. 11, 1953; s. Elliott and Pauline (Liss) F. BA, Case Western Res. U., 1975; MA, U. Miss., 1980. Salesman Tropical Tea & Coffee, Co., Marion, Mass., 1975-81; v.p. Tropical Tea & Coffee, Inc., Marion, 1981-88; plant mgr., gourmet coffee cons. Autocrat, Inc., Marion, 1988-90; freelance writer, 1990—. Author, editor: Pre-Dawn Leftist, 1973—. Mem. Splty. Coffee Assn. Am., Soc. for Creative Anachronism (arms 1975, baron 1978, regional arts and scis. officer 1981-83, corp. dir. rsch. 1983-89, dep. corp. dir. rsch. 1989—), Master of Pelican award 1983). Jewish.

FEINSTEIN, MYRON ELLIOT, chemist, technical consultant; b. N.Y.C., Jan. 7, 1943; s. Gerald and Esther (Levine) F.; m. Barbara Ann Shuff, Dec. 27, 1964; children: Christopher, Eric. BS, CCNY, 1963, MA in Chemistry, 1965, PhD in Phys. Chemistry, 1967; MBA, Chapman U., Orange, Calif., 1984. Tech. mgr. Unilever Europe, various locations, 1968-77; mfg. mgr. Lever Bros. Co., Hammond, Ind., 1977-81; plant mgr. Lever Bros. Co., L.A., 1981-87; dir. tech. and facilities planning Lever Bros. Co., N.Y.C., 1987—. Editor Ency.: World Book, sections on Soap, Detergents, 1989; contbr. articles to profl. jours. Pres. bd. dirs. Indsl. Coun. of the City of Commerce (Calif.), 1986; bd. advisors Ind. U. N.W., Gary, 1979-81. Mem. AAAS. Republican. Office: Lever Bros Co 818 Sylvan Ave Englewood Cliffs NJ 07632-3298

FEINSTEIN, PETER ALAN, orthopedic surgeon; b. N.Y.C., July 7, 1950; s. Gilbert Jean and Barbara (Cohen) F.; m. Jane Benovitz, June 7, 1977; children: Andrew, Eric, Ross. BA, Brown U., 1972, M Med. Sci., 1974, MD, 1975. Diplomate Am. Bd. Orthopedic Surgery, Arthroscopy Bd. N.Am. Surg. resident Albert Einstein Coll. Medicine, Montefiore Hosp., Bronx, N.Y., 1975-77; orthopedic resident Columbia Presbyn. Hosp. Coll. Physicians and Surgeons, Bronx, 1977-80; pvt. practice orthopedic surgery Wilkes Barre (Pa.) Gen. Hosp., 1980—, Mercy Hosp., Wilkes-Barre, 1980—, Nesbitt Meml. Hosp., Wilkes-Barre, 1980—; chmn. Orthopedic Rsch. and Edn. Found., Northeastern Pa., 1991-92; mem. test devel. com. Arthroscopy Bd. N.Am., 1990. Contbr. articles to profl. jours. Bd. dirs. N.E. Pa. Philharmonic, Wilkes Barre, 1982-90, Jewish Community Ctr., Wilkes Barre, 1982-90; bd. dirs. United Jewish Appeal, Wilkes Barre, 1982-92, mem. Nat. Young Leadership Cabinet, 1986-91, chmn. campaign, 1992. Mem. ACS, AMA, Am. Acad. Orthopedic Surgeons, Arthroscopy Assn. N.Am., Ea. Orthopedic Assn., Pa. Med. Soc., Luzerne County Med. Soc. Office: Bone & Joint Assocs 35 W Linden St Wilkes Barre PA 18702

FEINSTEIN, SHELDON ISRAEL, molecular biologist, educator; b. Bklyn., Sept. 17, 1950; s. Harry George and Naomi T. (Weingarten) F.; m. Martha Louise Logan, May 15, 1983; children: Brian Isaac, Sarah Anne, Joseph Abraham, Elizabeth Gail. BA, Yeshiva U., 1971; MPhil, Yale U., 1974, PhD, 1977. Postdoctoral fellow Yale U., New Haven, 1977-80; vis. scientist Weizmann Inst., Rehovot, Israel, 1980-82; staff assoc. Columbia U., N.Y.C., 1983-84; asst. prof. Rockefeller U., N.Y.C., 1984-87, U. Pa., Phila., 1987—. Patentee in field; contbr. articles to profl. jours. Grantee Am. Lung Assn., 1988-89, Life and Health Ins. Fund, 1988-91, Nat. Heart, Lung and Blood Inst., 1991—. Mem. Am. Heart Assn. (arteriosclerosis coun.; grantee 1988, 89, 88-91). Home: 7661 Brookhaven Rd Philadelphia PA 19151-2023 Office: U Pa Sch of Medicine 1 John Morgan Bldg 36th St and Hamilton Walk Philadelphia PA 19104-6068

FEINSTEIN, STEVEN P., economics educator; b. Newark, Nov. 7, 1958; s. Burton Joseph and Hermina (Schwartz) F. BA, Pomona Coll., 1981; MA, Yale U., 1983, MPhil, 1986, PhD, 1989. Economist Fed. Res. Bank, Atlanta, 1987-90; asst. prof. Boston U., 1990—. Contbr. articles to profl. jours. Mem. Am. Fin. Assn., Am. Econs. Assn., Finl. Mgmt. Assn. Home: 1514 Beacon St Apt 45 Brookline MA 02146-2621

FEIST, STANLEY CHARLES, psychology educator, psychotherapist; b. Bklyn., June 20, 1924; s. Nathan and Leah (Meltzer) F.; children: Lynn Lerner, Arnold, William; m. Margaret Helen Newerla, Dec. 19, 1982. BS, Bklyn., 1965, MS, 1969; PhD, NYU, 1983. Tchr. Newfield High Sch., Selden, N.Y., 1966-67; prof. Coll. Tech. SUNY, Farmingdale, N.Y., 1967—; chmn. conf. on Teaching Undergrad. Psychology Northeastern U.S., 1985—, Am. Mental Health Counselor Assn. Marriage and Family Network, 1992—; presenter in field. Editor: conf. proceedings Teaching of Psychology, 1988-91; contbr. articles to profl. jours. Recipient award Farmingdale Found., 1989, Chancellor's award State of N.Y., 1990, Excellence award United U. Profs., 1990. Mem. ACD, Am. Assn. Marriage & Family Therapy, Am. Mental Health Counselor Assn., N.Y. State Mental Health Counselors Assn., N.Y. State Counselors Assn., N.Y. State Assn. Marriage & Family Therapist. Home: 10 Rochelle Ct Amityville NY 11701-3509 Office: SUNY Coll Tech Dept Psychology Knapp Hall Farmingdale NY 11735

FEIT, GLENN M., lawyer; b. Elizabeth, N.J., Oct. 16, 1929; s. Charles Theodore and Beatrice (Esther) F.; m. Rona F. Gottlieb, June 14, 1953 (div. 1974); children: Glenn M., John Paul, Adam Gibbs (dec.); m. Barberi Platt Paull. BS in Econ., U. Pa., 1951; JD, Harvard U., 1957. Bar: N.Y. 1958, U.S. Dist. Ct. (2d dist.) 1959). Assoc. Cravath, Swaine & Moore, N.Y.C., 1957-64; ptnr. London, Buttenwieser & Chalif, N.Y.C., 1965-70, Feit & Ahrens, N.Y.C., 1970-88, Feit & Shor, N.Y.C., 1988-89, Proskauer Rose Goetz & Mendelsohn, N.Y.C., 1989—; bd. dirs. Charter Power Systems, Inc., Wundies Industries, Inc., N.Y.C., Blair Industries, Inc., Scott City, Mo., Ea. Aviation Svcs., Inc., Montgomery, N.Y.; sec. Charterhouse Group Internat., Inc., N.Y.C. Mem. editorial bd. Harvard Law Rev., 1955-57. Mem. Friends of the IDF, N.Y.C. Lt. USN, 1951-54. Mem. ABA, Assn. of Bar of City of N.Y., Aircraft Owners & Pilots Assn., Harvard Club , East Hampton Yacht Club, Seaplane Pilots Assn., Exptl. Aircraft Assn. Office: Proskauer Rose Goetz & Mendelsohn 1585 Broadway New York NY 10036-8200

FEIT, RICHARD H., ophthalmologist; b. N.Y.C., Sept. 20, 1952; s. Herbert H. and Toube (Frisch) F.; m. Jo-Ann Charak, Apr. 1, 1992; 1 child, Benjamin. AB, U. Chgo., 1974, MD, 1978. Diplomate Am. Bd. Ophthalmology. Intern in medicine Hosp. of the Good Samaritan, L.A., 1978-79; resident Tufts-New Eng. Med. Ctr., Boston, 1979-82; fellow Univ. Hosp. of Cleve., 1983-84; ophthalmologist Harvard Community Health Plan, Boston, 1984—. Fellow Am. Acad. Ophthalmology. Jewish. Office: Harvard Community Health Plan 2 Fenway Plaza Boston MA 02215

FEITELBERG, SUSAN FRANCIS, financial consultant; b. Fall River, Mass., Jan. 1, 1962; d. Joseph Henry and Sheila (Dunne) F. BA in Econs., Coll. of the Holy Cross, Worcester, Mass., 1984; MBA, Northeastern U., Boston, 1990. Asst. mktg. mgr. Heim Internat., Nagoya, Japan, 1984-86; pension portfolio acct. State St. Bank, Boston, 1986-88; fin. cons. Cowan Fin. Group, N.Y.C., 1990—. Contbr. articles to profl. jours. Northeastern Acad. assistantship, 1989. Mem. Import/Export Assn., Am. Women in Econ. Devel., Japan Soc. (bd. dirs. 1986-90), Holy Cross Club of N.Y. (bd. dirs. 1991—), N.Y. Rd. Runners Club. Roman Catholic. Home: 324 E 61st St Apt 2FE New York NY 10021 Office: Cowan Fin Group 14th Fl 530 Fifth Ave New York NY 10036

FELD, ELIOT, dancer, choreographer; b. Bklyn., July 5, 1942; s. Benjamin Noah and Alice (Posner) F. Student, High Sch. Performing Arts, N.Y.C., 1954-58; DFA (hon.), Juilliard Sch., 1991. Debut as child prince in: The Nutcracker, (N.Y.C. Ballet, 1954; mem. cast: West Side Story, 1958; danced with cos. of Donald McKayle, Sophie Maslow, Pearl Lang, Mary Anthony, 1954-59; with co.: I Can Get It for You Wholesale, 1962; began dancing with Am. Ballet Theatre, 1963, later resident choreographer; solo dance appearances in: Les Noces, Wind in the Mountains, Dark Elegies, Fancy Free, Billy the Kid, Helen of Troy, Giselle; founder Am. Ballet Co., 1968, subsequently prin. dancer, mgr., chief choreographer, 1969-71; with Bklyn. Acad. Music two seasons, guest choreographer, N. Am. and Europe, 1971-73; founder, artistic dir., chief choreographer Feld Ballets/N.Y., 1974; founder New Ballet Sch., 1978; choreographed: Harbinger, 1967, At Midnight, 1967, Meadowlark, 1968, Intermezzo, 1969, Cortege Burlesque, 1969, Pagan Spring, 1969, Early Songs, 1970, Cortege Parisien, 1970, Consort, 1970, A Poem Forgotten, 1970, Romance, 1971, Theatre, 1971, The Gods Amused, 1971, A Soldier's Tale, 1971, Eccentrique, 1971, Winters Court, 1972, Jive, 1973, Sephardic Song, 1974, Tzaddik, 1974, The Real McCoy, 1974, Mazurka, 1975, Excursions, 1975, Impromptu, 1976, Variations on 'America', 1977, A Footstep of Air, 1977, Santa Fe Saga, 1978, La Vida, 1978, Danzon Cubano, 1978, Half-Time, 1978, Papillon, 1979, Circa, 1980, Anatomic Balm, 1980, Scenes, 1980, Play Bach, 1981, Song of Norway, 1981, Over the Pavement, 1982, Straw Hearts, 1983, Summer's Lease, 1983, Three Dances, 1983, Adieu, 1984, The Jig Is Up, 1984, Moon Skate, 1984, Intermezzo No. 2, 1985, Against the Sky, 1985, The Grand Canon, 1985, Aurora I, 1985, Aurora II, 1985, Medium: Rare, 1985, Echo, 1986, Bent Planes, 1986, Skara Brae, 1986, Embraced Waltzes, 1987, A Dance for Two, 1987, Shadow's Breath, 1987, Petipa Notwithstanding, 1988, Kore, 1988, The Unanswered Question, 1988, Asia, 1988, Love Song Waltzes, 1988, Ah Scarlatti, 1989, Mother Nature, 1989, Contra Pose, 1990, Charmed Lives, 1990, Ion, 1990, Fauna, 1990, Common Ground, 1991, Savage Glance, 1991, Clave, 1991, Evoe, 1991, Endsong, 1991, Wolfgang Strategies, 1992, To the Naked Eye, 1992, Hello Fancy, 1992. Recipient Dance Mag. award, 1990. Office: Feld Ballets/NY 890 Broadway 8th Fl New York NY 10003

FELD, JOSEPH, construction executive; b. N.Y.C., June 25, 1919; s. Morris David and Gussie (London) F.; m. Doris Rabinor, Apr. 10, 1948; 1 child, Elaine Susan. Student, CCNY, 1946-47. Builder housing, apt. projects L.I., N.Y.C., N.J., 1948-54; pres. Kohl and Feld, Inc., builder housing devels., Rockland County, N.Y., 1955-57, Feld Constrn. Corp., New City, N.Y., 1957—, Birchland Constrn. Corp., 1957-70, Ramapo Towers, Inc., 1963-83; bd. dirs. Rockland County Citizen Pub. Corp., 1959-60; bd. dirs., past vice chmn. People's Nat. Bank Rockland County, Monsey, N.Y., 1974-85. Mem. Clarkstown Bldg. Code Com., 1959; mem. indsl. devel. adv. com. Rockland County Bd. Suprs., 1969-71; chmn. housing adv. coun. Rockland County Legislature, 1976—; chmn. Housing Task Force, 1979-80; mem., past v.p. New City Jewish Ctr.; past pres. Men's Club; mem. Rockland County coun. Jewish War Vets., past comdr. New City post. Staff sgt. AUS, 1941-45. Mem. Rockland County Assn., Inc. (former bd. dir.), Rock-

land County Home Builders Assn. (past pres., bd. dir., chmn. rental housing com.), Nat. Assn. Home Builders (past bd. dir., mem. rental housing com.), N.Y. State Assn. Home Builders (past dir., mem. rental housing com.), Rockland County Apt. Owners Assn. (pres., bd. dir. 1971—), Rockland County Bd. Realtors, N.Y. State Assn. Realtors (past dir.), New City C. of C., Masons, Lions (local pres. 1959-60, zone chmn. 1961-62), B'nai B'rith. Home: PO Box 366 New City NY 10956-0366 also: 3821 Environ Blvd Lauderhill FL 33319 Office: 20 S Main St PO Box 366 New City NY 10956

FELD, JOSEPH, SR., accountant; b. Bronx, N.Y., Dec. 21, 1933; s. Joseph Solomon and Florence (Stewart) F.; m. Paralee Farrison (div. Jan. 1971); children: Joseph, Pamela, Naomi, Tyrone, Bryant, Joann, Angela, Sharon. Student, LaSalle Inst., 1956; A in Bus. Adminstrn., McNeese State U., 1954. CPA, N.J. Ptnr. RM White Cons., Camden, N.J., 1992—; treas., bd. dirs. Camden Investment Group, 1991-92; asst. contr. Litton Industries, N.Y.C. Author: (computer program) Autoval, 1992. Vice-chmn., bd. trustees Camden City Youth Assn., 1989—, exec. dir. 1988—; city chmn. Camden City Rep. Com., 1990-91; active Cherry St. Civic Assn., 1992. With USAF, 1952-56, Korea. Recipient Cert. Recognition Coord. Com. for Drug Free Life, Camden, 1989, Outstanding Participation award Am. Radio Coun., Garland, Tex., 1987. Fellow Masons, Elks. Home: PO Box 328 Camden NJ 08101-0328 Office: RM White Consultants 2900 Federal St Camden NJ 08105

FELD, KAREN IRMA, columnist, journalist, public speaker; b. Washington, Aug. 23, 1947; d. Irvin and Adele Ruth (Schwartz) F. Student, U. Pitts., 1965-67; BA, Am. U., 1969. Columnist, reporter Roll Call Newspaper, Washington, 1969-74; nat. pub. relations coordinator Ringling Bros./Barnum & Bailey Circus, Washington, 1971-74; publicist Twentieth Century Fox, Los Angeles, 1974-75; pub. relations account exec. Harshe, Rotman & Druck, Los Angeles, 1975; freelance writer, broadcaster, 1970—; corr. People mag., Washington, 1980-85; broadcaster Voice of Am., 1984; columnist, contributing editor Capitol Hill mag., Washington, 1980-89; columnist Washington Times, 1986-87, Universal Press Syndicate, 1988-89, Creators Syndicate, 1989-90; syndicated columnist Capital Connections, 1990—; Prodigy polit. columnist, 1990—; adj. instr. Kent State U. Pol. Campaign Mgmt. Inst., 1981. Contbr. articles to People mag., Money mag., Time mag., Vogue mag., Los Angeles Times Syndicate, others. Mem. AFTRA, NAt. Fedn. Press Women (Excellence in Journalism awards 1984-91), Women in Communications, Capital Press Women (v.p. 1985-91, Excellence in Journalism awards 1984-92), Am. Soc. Journalists and Authors, Nat. Press. Club, Capitol Hill Club, Woodmont Country Club (Rockville, Md.), U.S. Senate Press Gallery White House Corr. Assn., Am. Newswomen's Club, Sigma Delta Chi. Jewish. Home and Office: 1698 32d St NW Washington DC 20007

FELD, MYRON JACOB, management consultant; b. New Bedford, Mass., Feb. 2, 1948; s. Harry and Sadie (Benlifa) F.; m. sara Mitzenmacher, Dec. 25, 1977; children: Michael, Susanne. BS in Math., MIT, 1970; MBA, Harvard Bus. Sch., 1982. Mgr. software devel. Kurzweil Computer Products, Cambridge, Mass., 1978-80; cons. Boston Cons. Group, 1982-86, mgr., 1986-90, v.p., 1990—. Home: 64 Rollingwood Ln Concord MA 01742-4302 Office: Boston Cons Group 53 State St Boston MA 02109-2809

FELDBERG, STEPHEN WILLIAM, chemist; b. N.Y.C., July 22, 1937. AB, Princeton U., 1958, PhD, 1961. Sr. scientist Brookhaven Nat. Lab., Upton, N.Y., 1961—. Contbr. over 70 articles to sci. jours. Mem. Am. Chem. Soc., Electrochem. Soc. Office: Brookhaven Nat Lab Bldg 815 Upton NY 11973

FELDBERG, SUMNER LEE, retail company executive; b. Boston, June 19, 1924; s. Morris and Anna (Marnoy) F.; married; children: Michael S., Ellen R.; stepchildren: Mollye S., Beth, James. B.A., Harvard, 1947, M.B.A., 1949. With New Eng. Trading Corp., 1949-56; treas. Zayre Corp., 1956-73, sr. v.p., 1965-68, exec. v.p., 1969-73, chmn. bd., 1973-87; chmn. exec. com. Zayre Corp. (name now TJX Cos., Inc.), 1987-89; chmn. bd. Waban Corp., 1989—, TJX Cos., Inc., Framingham, Mass., 1989—; trustee Mass. Mut. Corp. Investors, Mass. Mut. Participation Investors. Trustee Beth Israel Hosp., Combined Jewish Philanthropies of Greater Boston. Served to 1st lt. USAAF, 1943-46. Office: TJX Cos Inc 770 Cochituate Rd PO Box 9175 Framingham MA 01701 also: Waban Corp 1 Mercer Rd Natick MA 01760

FELDER, LAWRENCE JAY, artist; b. Newark, Sept. 9, 1958; s. Arthur Edgar and Beatrice (Addis) F. BA, Montclair State, 1980. Represented in permanent collections at Township of Union, N.J., The Smithsonian Inst., The CTA Goup, Bruce Springsteen, Steve Martin, Douglas Salthouse. Active polit. campaigns, N.J., 1976, 80, 84. Discovered reptile fossil over 180 million yrs. old. Mem. Soc. Vertebrate Paleontology. Home and Office: 4308 Hana Rd Edison NJ 08817-2569

FELDER, RAOUL LIONEL, lawyer; b. N.Y.C., May 13, 1934; s. Morris and Millie (Goldstein) F.; m. Myrna, May 26, 1963; children: Rachel, James. BA, NYU, 1955, JD, 1959; postgrad. U. Bern (Switzerland), 1955-56. Bar: N.Y., 1959, U.S. Dist. Ct. (so. and ea. dists.) N.Y., 1962, U.S. Ct. Appeals (2d cir.), 1962, U.S. Supreme Ct., 1970. Pvt. practice, N.Y.C., 1959-61, 1964—; asst. U.S. atty., N.Y.C., 1961-64; mem. faculty, Practicing Law Inst., 1979, Marymount Coll., 1982—, Ethical Culture Sch., 1981, 82; moderator Nat. Conf. on Child Abuse, 1989. Author: Divorce: The Way Things Are, Not the Way Things Should Be, 1971, Lawyers Practical Handbook to the New Divorce Law, 1981, Raoul Felder's Encyclopedia of Matrimonial Clauses, 1990; columnist Fame mag., 1988-92; contbr. articles on law to profl. jours. and N.Y. Times, editorials to Newsweek mag., Harper's Bazaar mag., Newsday newspaper, N.Y. Post, Penthouse mag.; commentator Cable News Network, 1989. Chmn. Nat. Kidney Found. Auction, also N.Y. fund; chmn. Dinner Jerusalem Reclamation Project. Named Man of Yr. Bklyn. Sch. for Spl. Children, Met. Geriatric Ctr.; Grand Marshall U.S.A.Day Washington, Israel Day Parade N.Y.C.; recipient Defender of Jerusalem medal, 1990. Mem. Assn. of Bar of City of N.Y. (spl. com. matrimonial law 1975-77), ABA (judge nat. finals client counseling competition), N.Y. State Bar Assn., N.Y. State Dist. Attys. Assn., N.Y. State Trial Lawyers Assn. (past chmn. matrimonial law 1974-75), Nat. Criminal Def. Lawyers Assn., N.Y. State Soc. Med. Jurisprudence, Am. Judicature Soc., Am. Arbitration Assn., Nat. Coun. on Family Rels., N.Y. Women's Bar Assn., Minion of the Stars (chmn. bd.). Home: 985 5th Ave New York NY 10021-0160 Office: 437 Madison Ave New York NY 10022

FELDMAN, BRUCE ALLEN, otolaryngologist; b. Washington, Mar. 22, 1941; s. Irvin and Miriam Thelma (Rothstein) F.; m. Sharon Lee Pearlman, Dec. 25, 1966; children: Kathryn Ellen, Michael Aaron. AB, Dartmouth Coll., 1962, B Med. Sci., 1963; MD, Harvard U., 1965. Diplomate Am. Bd. Otolaryngology. Intern Hosp. of U. Pa., Phila., 1965-66, resident in surgery, 1966-67; resident in otolaryngology Mass. Eye and Ear Infirmary-Harvard U., Boston, 1967-70; pvt. practice Washington, 1972—; presenter at med. meetings, 1981, 87; pres. elect med. staff Children's Hosp., Washington, 1992—. Contbr. articles to med. jours., chpt. to book. Lt. comdr. M.C., USNR, 1970-72. Mosby scholar, 1963; recipient Physician's Recognition award Children's Hosp. Washington, 1991. Fellow ACS, Am. Laryngol., Rhinol. and Otol. Soc. (Mosher award 1981); mem. AMA, Med. Soc. D.C., Jacobi Med. Soc. (pres. 1986-87), Washington Met. Ear, Nose and Throat Soc. (pres. 1978-79), Woodmont Country Club (Rockville, Md.), Phi Beta Kappa, Alpha Omega Alpha, Phi Delta Epsilon (pres. grad. club 1979-80). Jewish. Office: 1145 19th St Washington DC 20036

FELDMAN, GARY MARC, nutritionist, consultant; b. Bklyn., Dec. 3, 1953; m. Debra Lynn Bieler, Sept. 21, 1984. Diploma in Sci. of Nutritional Cons., Am. Nutrition Cons. Assn., 1986. Pres. Steps In Health, Ltd., Douglaston, N.Y., 1986-88, Margate, Fla., 1988-90, Nesconset, N.Y., 1990—; educator for children in sci. of food and nutritional supplementation; ind. tester household products for lead content. Vol. listen to children program Mental Health Assn. and Vol. Program Broward County (Fla.) Pub. Schs., 1989; mem. Ctr. for Sci. in the Pub. Interest, Washington. Mem. Am. Nutrition Cons. Assn., Life Extension Found., Pub. Citizen Health Rsch. Group, People for Ethical Treatment of Animals, Doris Day Animal League, Humane Soc. Broward County, Ctr. for Sci. in the Pub. Interest, Internat. Platform Assn., Tri-City Jaycees, Better Bus. Bur. South Fla. (arbitration participant 1989-90), L.I. Assn., Inc. Office: PO Box 83 Nesconset NY 11767-0083

FELDMAN, HAROLD SAMUEL, neuropsychiatrist, forensic psychiatry consultant; b. Boston, May 18, 1917; s. Hyman and Ethel (Gitstein) F.; m. Judith Gloria Nelson, June 10, 1945; children: David Joseph, Edward Lee, Robert Charles, Carol Ann. BS in Pharmacy, Mass. Coll. Pharmacy, 1939, MSc in Pharmacy, 1942; PhD in Clin. Pharmacology, Boston U., 1945, MD, 1949. Diplomate Am. Bd. Med. Examiners. Intern in medicine and surgery Boston Marine Hosp./USPHS, 1949-50; resident in internal medicine USPHS, Staten Island, N.Y., 1949-52; resident in psychiatry and neurology Essex County Hosp./U.S. Vet. Hosp., East Orange, N.J., 1961-64; pvt. practice psychiatry and neurology, 1975—; nat. formulary fellow Mass. Coll. Phrmacy, Boston, 1939-42; asst. in pharmacology Boston U. Sch. Medicine, 1942-49; med. dir. Maltbie Labs., Newark, 1953-55; family practice U. Medicine and Dentistry N.J., Livingston, N.J., 1952-61; pvt. practice, cons. Livingston, N.J., 1978—; asst. in pharmacology Harvard U. Sch. Medicine, Boston, 1943-45; state police chemist State of Mass., Boston, 1943-45; prof. pharmacology Northeastern U., Boston, 1945-47; pharmacist Macy Drug Co., Boston, 1939-40; biochemist New Eng. Med. Ctr., Boston, 1943-44; dir. Quinn Drug Rehab. Program Essex County, Caldwell, N.J., 1964-66; adj. prof. Seton Hall U. Law Sch., Newark, 1973-75; asst. prof. dept. psychiatry UMDNJ, 1963-66, assoc. prof. dept. psychiatry, 1967-89. Contbr. articles to med. jours. Chief sch. physician Livingston Pub. Schs., 1960-65; trustee Short Hills (N.J.) Millburn Rep. Club, 1984-89. Sr. asst. surgeon USPHS, 1949-53, Korea. Charles Hayden scholar, 1938-42. Fellow Am. Psychiat. Assn. (life), Am. Acad. Forensic Scis., Am. Coll. Clin. Pharmacology, Am. Geriatric Soc., Begg Med. Soc. Home and Office: 12 E 30th St PO Box # 8 Barnegat Light NJ 08006 Home (winter): 3476 Mistletoe Ln Longboat Key FL 34228

FELDMAN, HARRY H., stockbroker; b. Linz, Austria, Apr. 19, 1949; came to U.S., 1950; s. Israel Feldman and Hena Glanz; m. Kathleen Feldman (div. 1983);l children: Jarrett, Matthew. BS, Hunter Coll., 1973. Sales mgr. Gen. Devel., Boston, 1973-75; account exec. Merrill Lynch, N.Y.C., 1975-77; pres. Harry H. Feldman Assocs., N.Y.C., 1977-90; v.p. Aspen Trading Co., 1990—. Fundraiser HIAS, N.Y.C., 1980-85; patron Aspen (Colo.) Ballet Co., 1987; fundraiser United Jewish Appeal, N.Y.C. Mem. Am. Stock Exch. Democrat. Jewish. Office: 86 Trinity Pl New York NY 10006-1818

FELDMAN, JEFFREY MARC, podiatrist; b. N.Y.C., Oct. 14, 1949; s. Abraham D. and Lilo (Mendelssohn) F.; m. Melanie Lewin, Oct. 21, 1985. BA in Psychology, Fairleigh Dickinson U., 1971; D of Podiatric Medicine, Ohio Coll. Podiatric Medicine, 1976. Pvt. practice Great Barrington, Mass., 1981—, Pittsfield, Mass., 1985—; mem. staff dept. surgery Fairview Hosp., Great Barrington; mem. courtesy staff dept. orthopedics Hillcrest Hosp., Pittsfield; mem. cons. staff dept. orthopedics Berkshire Med. Ctr., Pittsfield; chief podiatry svcs. Dalton (Mass.) Nursing Home, Camp Eisner, Great Barrington, Camp Kingsmont, West Stockbridge, Mass.; cons., lectr. in field. Editor Current Podiatric Medicine jour., 1984; editorial cons. Physicians & Computers jours., 1987; contbr. articles to profl. publs. Fellow Am. Soc. Podiatric Medicine (bd. cert., asst. sec. 1984-85, chmn. sci. seminar 1984-85, constitution com. 1985-86), Am. Coll. Podopediatrics (bd. cert.), Am. Acad. Ambulatory Foot Surgery (bd. cert.); mem. Am. Acad. Podiatric Sports Medicine (assoc.), Am. Running and Fitness Assn., Mass. Podiatric Med. Soc., Am. Podiatric Med. Assn. Office: 777 S Main St Great Barrington MA 01230-2005 also: Shipton Bldg 152 North St Pittsfield MA 01201

FELDMAN, LARRY JOHN, rehabilitation counselor; b. Portland, Oreg., Sept. 20, 1931; s. Harry Theodore and Margaret Rose (Mueller) F.; m. Kathryn Shoppel, Feb. 20, 1959 (div. 1978); 1 child, Jeffery Lee. BA, San Francisco State U., 1960; MA, U. Conn., 1962; PhD, Kennedy Western U., 1991. Cert. rehab. counselor, counselor. Vocat. rehab. counselor Jewish Employment and Vocat. Svc., Phila., 1963-64, Occupational Ctr. Essex County, Orange, N.J., 1964-65; exec. dir. Ocean County Sheltered Workshop, Lakewood, N.J., 1965-75; pvt. practice Meditation Ctr., Howell, N.J., 1975-82, Humanist Psychiat. Ctr., Red Bank, N.J., 1976-80; rehab. specialist Intercorp, Inc., Wilmington, Del., 1982-84; pain and stress therapist Pain & Stress Ctr., Newport, Del., 1985—; pub. speaker Pain and Stress Ctr.; cons. Whole Health Ctr. Author: Feeling Better, 1984, Impact of Psychological Factors on Human Immune Response, 1992, Feeling Good Again, 1992. Mem. AACD, Inst. for Advancement of Health, Inst. for Noetic Sci., N.Y. Acad. Sci., Ctr. for Frontier Scis., Nat. Assn. for Preservation and Perpetuation of Storytelling. Roman Catholic. Home: 9-92 Colonial Village N New Castle DE 19720 Office: Pain and Stress Ctr 240 N James St Ste # 110 Newport DE 19804

FELDMAN, LEONARD CECIL, physicist; b. N.Y.C., June 8, 1939; s. Milton and Minnie (Schulman) F.; m. Elizabeth Gecsey, July 5, 1964; children: Gregory, Dana. MS, Rutgers U., 1963, PhD, 1967. Mem. tech. staff radiation physics rsch. dept. AT&T Bell Labs., Murray Hill, N.J., 1967-83, supr. materials interfaces, 1983-84, dept. head materials interfaces and ceramics, 1984-87, dept. head thin film semicondr. rsch., 1987-90, dept. head silicon device rsch., 1990—; guest scientist Aarhus (Denmark) U., 1970-71; vis. prof. Cornell U., Ithaca, N.Y., 1981, 82, 88; cons. Livermore (Calif.) Nat. Lab., 1989—; chmn. Gordon Conf. on Particle Solid Interactions, 1978; chmn. internat. adv. com. Danish Microelectronics Ctr.; mem. adv. com. N.J. Inst. Tech., Colo. Sch. Mines. Co-author: Materials Analysis by Ion Channeling, 1982, Fundamentals of Surface and Thin Film Analysis, 1986 (transl. into Japanese 1988, Russian 1989), Electronic Thin Film Science, 1991; editor Applied Surface Sci., 1985—; contbr. over 200 articles on semiconductor interface sci. to sci. jours. Recipient Disting. Merit award in material sci. and engring. U. Ill., 1989. Fellow Am. Phys. Soc.; mem. IEEE, Materials Rsch. Soc., Am. Ceramic Soc. Home: 200 Lorraine Dr Berkeley Heights NJ 07922-2362 Office: AT&T Bell Labs 600 Mountain Ave New Providence NJ 07974-2010

FELDMAN, MARTIN ROBERT, chemist, educator; b. N.Y.C., Apr. 23, 1938; s. Michael Ira and Ruth Dorothy (Levitt) F.; m. Janet Steinfeld, Dec. 20, 1959; children: Jonathan, Lisa. BA, Columbia U., 1958; PhD, UCLA, 1963. Prof. Howard U., Washington, 1971—, asst. prof., 1963-68, assoc. prof., 1968-71; vis. scientist Kings Coll. U. London, 1977-78. V.p. Hands-on Sci. Outreach, Rockville, Md., 1980—. NSF fellow, 1969-70, Smithsonian Instn. fellow, 1987. Mem. Am. Chem. Soc., History of Sci. Soc., Soc. for History Tech. Home: 116 Hamilton Ave Silver Spring MD 20901-3415 Office: Howard U Dept Chemistry Washington DC 20059

FELDMAN, MARVIN, college president; b. Rochester, N.Y., May 24, 1927; s. Max and Blanche F.; m. Dorothy Owens, July 29, 1954; children—Brian, Michael. Student, U.S. Mil. Acad., 1948-51; A.B., San Francisco State U., 1953; Ph.D. in Edn, Northeastern U., 1973. Tchr. math. public schs. San Francisco, 1952-57; v.p. Cogswell Coll., 1958-64; program officer Ford Found., N.Y.C., 1964-69; asst. to spl. com. office edn. HEW, Washington, 1969-71; asst. dir. OEO, 1969-71; pres. Fashion Inst. Tech., 1971—; dir. Gerber Garmet Tech. Corp.; mem. Pres.'s Nat. Adv. Council on Vocat. Edn., 1968-79. Contbr. articles to profl. jours. Bd. dirs. 34th St. Midtown Assn., N.Y.C., DeVry Inst., Shankar Coll. Served with USN, 1944-46; Served with U.S. Army, 1948-53, PTO. Recipient Meritorious award Nat. Adv. Council on Vocat. Edn., 1972, 75, 78. Mem. Orgn. Rehab. through Tng., Pres.'s Assn., West Point Soc. Home and Office: 210 W 27th St New York NY 10001-5901

FELDMAN, MAX, insurance executive; b. Newark, Jan. 24, 1935; s. Daniel J. and E. Ruth (Fast) F.; m. Bernita Braha, June 14, 1959; children: Alan, Renee. BBA cum laude, U. Miami, Coral Gables, Fla., 1956; MA, Western Mich. U., 1958. Ins. agt. The Feldman Agy., Clifton, N.J., 1958—. Owner Rotisserie baseball team. Sec. Congregation Ahawas Achim B'nai Jacob and David, West Orange, N.J., 1963—, pres. Men's Club, 1970-80; chmn. Israel Bond Campaign, West Orange, 1971-80; committeeman West Orange Dem. Com., 1974-82. Master sgt. USAR, 1952-59, Korea. Mem. Profl. Ins. Agts., Ind. Ins. Agts., N.J. Ins. Brokers Assn., N.J. U. Miami Alumni Assn. (pres. 1972-74), West Orange Current Affairs Club, Huntington Lakes Tennis Club, B'nai B'rith. Home: 10 Wessman Dr West Orange NJ 07052-2809 Office: The Feldman Agy Inc PO Box 1069 1246 Broad St Bloomfield NJ 07003

FELDMAN, ROBERT C., public relations executive; b. N.Y.C., Oct. 22, 1956. BA, Syracuse U., 1978. Gen. mgr. Sta. WPNR-FM Utica Coll. Syracuse U., 1976-78; from asst. acct. exec. to sr. v.p., group mgr. Burson-Marsteller, 1978-88; exec. v.p. Ketchum Pub. Rels., N.Y.C., 1988—. Office: Ketchum Pub Rels 1133 Ave of the Americas New York NY 10036*

FELDMAN, ROGER DAVID, lawyer; b. N.Y.C., Apr. 7, 1943; s. Louis and Dora (Goldsmith) F.; m. Gail Steg, May 31, 1969; children: Rebecca, Seth. A.B., Brown U., 1962; LL.B., Yale U.; M.B.A., Harvard U. Bar: N.Y. 1966, D.C. 1977. Ops. research analyst Office Asst. Sec. Def., Washington, 1967-68; staff asst. Office of Pres. U. S., Washington, 1968-69; assoc. LeBoeuf Lamb Leiby & MacRae, 1969-75; dep. asst. adminstr. FEA, Washington, 1975-77; ptnr. Le Boeuf Lamb Leiby & MacRae, 1977-83; mng. ptnr. project fin. group Nixon Hargrave Devans & Doyle, Washington, 1983-89; head ptnr. project fin. group McDermott Will & Emery, Washington, 1989—; mem. faculty Inst. Gas Tech., 1988, 91—, Practicing Law Inst., 1986-88; mem. fin. adv. bd. EPA, 1989—; bd. dirs. R.J. Rudden & Assocs. Inc., Cogeneration Inst., Assn. Energy Engrs., Competitive Power Policy Forum, Nat. Ind. Energy Producers, 1988-91, Environ. Engrs. and Mgrs. Inst., pub.-pvt. venture divsn. Am. Road and Transp. Builders; vice chmn. bd. dirs., pres. Privatization Coun., 1983—; mem. bd. advisors Exnet, Inc. Author: (with others), mem. editiorial bd. Infrastructure Finance, 1988, Public-Private Ventures in Transportation, 1990; mem. bd. editors Yale Law Jour., 1964-65, Cogeneration Jour., 1988—, Environ. Fin.; Washington editor Cogeneration Letter, 1987—, Environ. News, 1990—; contbr. articles to profl. jours. including JOur. of Commerce. Mem. ABA (chmn. energy law com. 1980-83, alt. energy sources com. 1981-84, 86-90, chmn. environ. values com. 1983-89, com. on privatization 1985-90, chmn. energy fin. 1990-91, privatization and energy fin. 1991-92, electric power 1992—), Fed. Energy Bar Assn. (chmn. cogeneration com. 1981-82), Internat. Cogeneration Soc. (bd. dirs. 1982-85), N.Y. Bar Assn., D.C. Bar Assn., Assn. Energy Engrs. (Cogeneration Profl. of Yr. 1990), Phi Beta Kappa. Office: McDermott Will & Emery 1850 K St NW Washington DC 20006-2213

FELDMAN, SAMUEL, writer, direct marketing consultant; b. N.Y.C., Aug. 24, 1936; s. Aaron R. and Marcia (Popick) F.; m. Dorothy L. Resnick, Mar. 25, 1973. BS in Bus., Econs., N.Y.U., 1959, MA in History, Edn., 1961. Educator N.Y.C. Sch. System, 1961-71; pres. Target Mailing Lists, N.Y.C., 1972-75; prin. Sam Feldman Assocs., N.Y.C., 1975—. Author: The Home Health Record Book, 1984, The Big Book of Business Information, 1987; co-author 999 Ways to Make Money at Home, 1982, How to Operate a Mail Order Business, 1982. Jewish. Home and Office: Sam Feldman Assocs 165 W End Ave New York NY 10023-5503

FELDMAN, STEPHEN, university president; b. N.Y.C., Sept. 11, 1944; s. Harry and Mae (Morris) F.; m. Constance M. Lerudis, June 1, 1969; children—Jennifer Dawn, Timothy Richard. BBA, CCNY, 1966, MBA, 1968, PhD (fellow), 1971. Chmn. dept. banking, fin. and investments Hofstra U., Hempstead, N.Y., 1969-77, assoc. prof., 1974-77; dean Ancell Sch. of bus. Western Conn. State U., Danbury, 1977-81, univ. pres., 1981-92; pres. Nova U., Ft. Lauderdale, Fla., 1992—; bd. dirs. Ethan Allen Inc., Kane Inc., Alfred Industries Inc., Sci. Horizons Inc; cons. IBM, N.Y. Telephone Co. Editor: Credit Unions, 1974, Handbook of Wealth Management, 1977, Smarter Money, 1985; contbr. articles to profl. publs. Trustee Danbury Hosp., United Way. Mem. Am. Assn. State Colls. and Univs. (chmn. corp. coll. rels.). Office: Nova U 3301 College Ave Fort Lauderdale FL 33314

FELDMAN, SUSAN ELEANOR, information consultant; b. N.Y.C., Feb. 14, 1947; d. Bernard and Ruth (Gold) G.; m. Robert Larry Feldman, June 25, 1967; children: David, Elana. BA, Cornell U., 1967; AM in Libr. Sci., U. Mich., 1968. Lic. libr., Calif., N.Y. Tech. info. specialist Nat. Tech. Info. Svc., Springfield, Va., 1968-70; audio-visual coord. South Cen. Rsch. Libr. Coun., Ithaca, N.Y., 1970-71; young adult svcs. libr. Tompkins County Pub. Libr., Ithaca, 1972-75; adj. prof. Syracuse U. Sch. Info. Studies, Ithaca, 1975; reference libr. Cuesta Community Coll., San Luis Obispo, Calif., 1976-79, instr., 1977-78, mgmt. intern, 1978-79; asst. to dir. Ithaca Coll. Libr., 1980-81; prin. assoc. Datasearch, Ithaca, 1981—; pres. LAMP, San Luis Obispo, 1978-79; mem. reference com. South Cen. Rsch. Libr. Coun., 1984-89. Violist San Luis Obispo Orch., 1976-79, Beaux Eaux Quartet, Ithaca, 1981—, Cornell U. Orch., Ithaca, 1989—; instr. Gifted and Talented Program, 1983-90. Mem. Assn. Ind. Info. Profls. (ethics com. 1986-87, pres. elect 1992). Office: Datasearch 170 Lexington Dr Ithaca NY 14850-1719

FELDMANN, SHIRLEY CLARK, psychology educator; b. Niagara Falls, N.Y., Apr. 14, 1929; d. Franklin T. and Mildred L. (Payne) Clark; m. Robert Feldmann, June, 1952 (dec.); m. Horace S. Bush. B.A., Barnard Coll., 1951; M.A., Columbia U., 1952, Ph.D., 1961. Asst. prof. edn. SUNY-Fredonia, 1958-60; asst. research prof. psychiatry N.Y. Med. Coll., N.Y.C., 1960-63; prof. sch. edn. City Coll., CUNY, N.Y.C., 1963—; prof., Ph.D. program in ednl. psychology CUNY Grad. Sch., 1974—, exec. officer, 1976-85. Contbr. articles to prof. jours. Mem. Am. Psychol. Assn., Internat. Reading Assn., Am. Ednl. Research Assn. Home: 11 Cedar Lake Rd Chester CT 06412-1009 Office: CUNY Grad Sch 33 W 42d St New York NY 10036

FELDSTEIN, KATHLEEN FOLEY, economist, consultant; b. Boston, Feb. 3, 1941; d. Charles Joseph and Eleanor (Croxon) Foley; m. Martin Feldstein, June 19, 1965; children: Margaret, Janet. BA, Radcliffe Coll., 1962; PhD, MIT, 1977. Pres. Econs. Studies, Inc., Belmont, Mass., 1987—; bd. dirs. Bank Am. Corp., San Francisco, Kleinwort Benson Australian Income Fund, N.Y.C.; mem. corp. Sherrill House, Inc., 1989—. Contbr. articles to nat. and internat. newspapers. Corp. mem. Winsor Sch., Boston, 1985—, Simmons Coll., Boston, 1986—; mem. bd. overseers Mus. of Fine Arts, Boston, 1990—; trustee Com. for Econ. Devel., 1990—. Home: 147 Clifton St Belmont MA 02178-2603 Office: Econs Studies Inc 147 Clifton St Belmont MA 02178-2603

FELGRAN, STEVEN DAVID, economist, educator; b. N.Y.C., July 1, 1953; s. Howard H. and Ilse H. (Sturm) F.; m. Kathy Lynne Jackowitz, Aug. 21, 1983; 1 child, Eric. BA, U. Pa., 1975; MA in Econs., Yale U., 1978, MPhil in Econs., 1978, PhD in Econs., 1982. Intern World Bank, Washington, 1977; researcher, teaching asst. Yale U., New Haven, 1978-79; cons. Arthur D. Little, Inc., Cambridge, Mass., 1981-83; economist Fed. Res. Bank of Boston, 1983-89; prof. Coll. Bus. Adminstrn. Northeastern U., Boston, 1989—; analyst Congl. Budget Office, Washington, 1975-76; numerous presentations to profl. orgns. Contbr. numerous articles to profl. jours., mags. and newspapers. Mem. Am. Econ. Assn., Fin. Mgmt. Assn., Ea. Fin. Assn., Soc. Govt. Economists, Phi Beta Kappa. Office: Northeastern U Coll Bus Adminstrn 413 Hayden Hall Boston MA 02115

FELICIO, DIANE MARIE, social psychologist, educator; b. Queens, N.Y., Apr. 26, 1962; d. George Joseph and Florence Elizabeth (Jordan) F. BA, Adelphi U., Garden City, N.Y., 1984; MA, U. Vt., 1986, PhD, 1990. Core vaculty mem. social psychology Goddard Coll., Plainfield, Vt., 1989—. Guest editor Hawthorne Press, 1987, 91; contbr. articles to profl. jours. Vol. adminstr. Outright Vt., Burlington, 1991—; mem. Burlington Women's Coun., 1988-89. U. Vt. Grad. Teaching fellow, 1987, travel grantee, 1988, 90, rsch. grantee, 1989. Mem. Am. Psychol. Assn. (reviewer Div. 35), nat. Women's Studies Assn., Soc. for Personality and Social Psychology, Vt. Psychol. Assn. (co-chair com. on women and minorities), Assn. for Women in Psychology (reviewer 1988). Home: RR 2 Box 392 Jericho VT 05465-9449 Office: Goddard Coll Plainfield VT 05667

FELINSKI, WILLIAM WALTER, regional engineering coordinator; b. Phila., June 19, 1953; s. William Jr. and Elizabeth Miriam (Hare) F.; m. Christina R. Bleistine, Sept. 30, 1989. BA, La Salle U., 1976; MBA, LaSalle U., 1991. Registered chemist. Patent rsch. chemist ARSYNCO, Inc., Carlstadt, N.J., 1976-78; chem. engr. Indsl. Risk Insurers, Hartford, Conn., 1978-81; cons. Alexander & Alexander, Inc., N.Y.C., 1981-83; sr. cons. Alexander & Alexander, Inc., Phila., 1983-85; regional cons. HSB I&I Co., Phila., 1985-86; regional mgr. HSB I&I Co., Atlanta, 1986-87; sr. corp. cons. HSB I&I Co., Hartford, Conn., 1987-89; regional coord. HSB I&I Co.,

Phila., 1989—. Patentee in field. Mem. Am. Chem. Soc., Nat. Fire Protection Assn., Am. Mgmt. Assn., La Salle U. Alumni Assn. Republican. Roman Catholic. Home: 7206 Valley Ave Philadelphia PA 19128-3220 Office: Hartford Steam Boiler Inspection & Ins Co 610 Freedom Bus Ctr Dr #300 King Of Prussia PA 19406

FELITTO, BRYAN JOSEPH, college administrator; b. Utica, N.Y., May 18, 1943; s. Joseph A. and Margaret (Baker) F.; m. Johann M. Tarnowski, Aug. 14, 1965; children: Kristen, Erik. BA in Econs., King's Coll., 1965; MEd in Ednl. Adminstrn., St. Lawrence U., 1982; postgrad., U. Buffalo, 1984-85. Purchasing agt. SUNY Coll. of Tech., Canton, N.Y., 1965-67, asst. dir. facilities planning, 1967-72, dir. sponsored rsch., 1972-76, asst. to v.p., dir. continuing edn., 1976-79, co-exec. asst. to pres., 1979—, dir. Leadership Inst., 1985-92; interim pres. Mater Dei Coll., Ogdensburg, N.Y., 1992—. Author/co-author technical studies in field. Active St. Lawrence County Pvt. Industry Coun., Canton, 1976—, Gov.'s Balance of State Manpower Planning Coun., Albany, N.Y., 1976-79, Gov.'s Balance of State Youth Planning Coun., Albany, N.Y., 1976-79; No. Tech. Coun., Potsdam, N.Y., 1987—. Phi Delta Kappa. Roman Catholic. Office: Mater Dei Coll Ogdensburg NY 13669

FELIX, DAVID, history educator; b. New Britain, Conn., Dec. 26, 1921; s. Benjamin and Mollie (Leibowitz) F.; m. Georgette Byk, Aug. 12, 1966. BA, Trinity Coll., Hartford, Conn., 1943; MA, U. Chgo., 1947; PhD, Columbia U., 1970; Cert., Law Faculty Paris, 1955. Reporter Pitts. Sun-Telegraph, 1947-50; info. officer U.S. Econ. Mission to Austria, Vienna, 1950-54; corres. Internat. News Svc., Paris, 1955-56; mng. editor Challenge, Mag'e Econ. Affairs, N.Y.C., 1957-59; fin. writer Baron Pub. Rels., N.Y.C., 1960-64; instr. to prof. history CUNY, 1965—; cons.-panelist NEH, Washington, 1975-80; cons. N.Y.C. Bd. Edn., 1980-81, Lehrman Inst., N.Y.C., 1982-85. Author: Protest: Sacco-Vanzetti and the Intellectuals, 1965, Walther Rathenau and the Weimer Republic, 1971, Marx as Politician, 1983. With U.S. Army, 1943-45. Mem. Am. Hist. Assn., Am. Econ. Assn. Home: 49 E 86th St New York NY 10028-1060

FELIX, TED MARK, accountant; b. Bklyn., Apr. 23, 1947; s. Jack and Shirley (Starr) F.; m. Vicki Jane Robin, Dec. 23, 1967; children: Randi Sue, Jennifer Lynn. BS in Acctg., L.I. U., 1968, MBA in Fin., 1976. CPA, N.J., N.Y. Sr. auditor KPMG Peat Marwick, N.Y.C., 1968-71, 75-80; mgr. tech. standards Clarence Rainess & Co., N.Y.C., 1971-75; ptnr. Trien, Rosenberg, Felix, Rosenberg, Barr & Weinberg, N.Y.C. and Morristown, N.J., 1980—; adj. prof. acctg. Ocean County Coll., Toms River, N.J., 1976-79, Rutgers U., New Brunswick, N.J., 1981-83; bd. dirs. Internat. Group Acctg. Firm, N.Y.C., London, Hong Kong. Contbr. articles to profl. jours. Bd. dirs. JCC of Metrowest, Whippany, N.J., 1989—, v.p., 1992—. Mem. AICPA (dir. quality control rev. div. 1975-80, numerous coms.), N.Y. Soc. CPA's (numerous coms.), N.J. Soc. CPA's (trustee 1989-90, numerous coms.), B'nai B'rith (pres. West Morris 1987-89, bd. govs. dist. 3, 1988—, treas. No. N.J. coun. 1989-90, v.p. 1990—). Republican. Home: 10 Springhill Rd Randolph NJ 07869 Office: Trien Rosenberg Felix Rosenberg Barr & Weinberg 177 Madison Ave Morristown NJ 07960-7331

FELL, DEREK JOHN, photographer; b. Morecambe, Lancashire, Eng.; s. Albert J. and Mary (McCafferty) F.; children: Christina, Derek Jr., Victoria. Newspaper reporter Shrewsbury Chronicle, Eng., 1956-58; account exec. O.D. Gallagher Ltd., London, 1958-64; catalog mgr. Burpee Seeds, Phila., 1964-71; dir. All Am. Selections and Nat. Garden Bur., Gardenville, Pa., 1971-74; freelance photographer Gardenville, 1974—. Author: Deerfield-An American Garden Through Four Seasons, 1985 (Best Book 1986), A Kid's First Book of Gardening, 1989 (Best Book 1990), 550 Home Landscaping Ideas, 1991, Renoir's Garden, 1991, The Impressionist Garden, 1992; (ann. calendar) Great Gardens, 1988—. Fellow Garden Writers Assn. Am. (bd. dirs. 1986-90, numerous awards); mem. Soc. Am. Travel Writers. Office: Derek Fell Co PO Box 1 Gardenville PA 18926-0001

FELLBAUM, CHRISTIANE DOROTHEA, psychology researcher; b. Braunschweig, Germany, Dec. 18, 1950; came to U.S., 1969; d. Hubert E. and Hanna E. (Hausser) F.; m. Elliott H. Lieb, Dec. 18, 1975. BA, Northeastern U., 1974; PhD, Princeton U., 1980. Assoc. prof. Westminster Choir Coll., Princeton, N.J., 1987—; rsch. staff psychology dept. Princeton U., 1987—; cons. Ednl. Testing Svc., Princeton, 1980-82; vis. scholar LADL, U. Paris 7, 1986. Contbr. articles to profl. jours. Mem. Linguistic Soc. Am. Office: Princeton U Psychology Dept Princeton NJ 08540

FELLER, BENJAMIN E., actuary; b. Bronx, Mar. 4, 1947; s. Morris and Beatrice (Wolff) F.; m. Debra May Morane, June 1973 (div. 1983); children: Amy; m. Sue Ann Kaufman, Sept. 23, 1984; children: Meredith; stepchildren: Stefanie McCoy, Alison McCoy. BS in Math., Clarkson U., Potsdam, N.Y., 1968; MA in Math., Ind. U., 1971. Enrolled actuary. Actuarial asst. U.S. Life Ins. Co., N.Y.C., 1971-75; assoc. actuary The Wyatt Co., Washington, 1975-76; cons. actuary Buck Cons., N.Y.C., 1976-85; ptnr. Chernoff Diamond & Co., Williston Park, N.Y., 1985—. Fellow Soc. Actuaries; mem. Am. Soc. Pension Actuaries, Am. Acad. Actuaries. Republican. Jewish. Home: 10 Allison Dr Old Bethpage NY 11804-1602 Office: Chernoff Diamond & Co 11 Hillside Ave Williston Park NY 11596-2344

FELLER, SIEGFRIED, retired librarian; b. Essen, Germany, Jan. 15, 1926; came to U.S. 1927; s. Hermann Otto Feller and Rose Marie Vahle Krause; m. Karen Wynell Bartok, Apr. 15, 1961; children: Geoffrey Alan, Bart Kendall. BA in English Lit., U. Mich., 1950, MA in English, German, 1951; MS in Libr. Sci., U. Ill., 1960. Mgr. Bob Marshall's Book Shop, Ann Arbor, Mich., 1951-55; ptnr., mgr. Creative Bookmen, Riverside, Calif., 1955-57; traveling rep. A.A. Lampl Art Books, Costa Mesa, Calif., 1958-59; asst. acquisitions libr. So. Ill. U., Carbondale, 1960-61; chief acquisitions librarian U. Okla., Norman, 1961-63, U. Minn., Mpls., 1964-67; chief bibliographer, assoc. dir. librs. collection devel. U. Mass. Libr., Amherst, 1967-91; cons. and lectr. in field. Editor, pubr. Cartomania newsletter, 1986—; contbr. numerous articles to profl. jours. With U.S. Army, 1944-46. Mem. ALA, Assn. Coll. and Rsch. Librs. (Western European specialists sect. Internat. Rels. Round Table), Ctr. for Rsch. Librs. (collection devel. officers adv. panel), Verein Deutsche Bibliothekare. Home: 8 Amherst Rd Pelham MA 01002-9746 Office: U Mass Amherst MA 01003

FELLER, WILLIAM FRANK, surgery educator; b. St. Paul, Nov. 2, 1925; s. William and Eva Caroline (Nordstrom) F.; children: William Frank III, Elizabeth Susan. BA magna cum laude, U. Minn., 1948, BS, 1952, MD, 1954, PhD, 1962. Diplomate Am. Bd. Surgery. Intern U. Minn., Mpls., 1954-55; asst. prof. Georgetown U., Washington, 1964-69, assoc. prof., 1969—. Contbr. articles to profl. jours. Warden St. John's Episc. Ch., Chevy Chase, Md., 1975-76. Mem. AAAS, ACS, Am. Assn. Cancer Rsch., Am. Scandinavian Found. (chpt. pres. 1969-71), Med. Soc. D.C., Am. Cancer Soc. (D.C. div. pres. 1984-85), Washington Acad. Medicine, Southeastern Surg. Congress, N.Y. Acad. Sci. Office: Georgetown U 3800 Reservoir Rd NW Washington DC 20007-2196

FELLOWS, JOHN ROGER, marketing professional; b. Lewiston, Maine, Dec. 13, 1953; s. Leslie Charles and Yvonne Lucy (Gibbs) F.; married Oct. 18, 1986 (div.); 1 child, Kaley Rae. BS, N.H. Coll., 1980. Cert. radio mktg. cons. Owner, gen. mgr. Jeraf Mktg., Portsmouth, N.H., 1986—. Author: Nuts 'n' Bolts: Time-Tested Street-Level Selling Tips That Work!, 1992; contbr. articles to profl. publs. Recipient Pres.'s Club award Barnstable Broadcasting, Waltham, Mass., 1990, Sr. Mktg. Cons. award Fuller-Jeffrey Broadcasting, Sacramento, Calif., 1988. Mem. Seacoast Communication Network (bd. dirs. 1990-91), Appalachian Mountain Club (registered trip leader 1984-91), N.H. Ad Club (bd. dirs. 1990-91). Baptist. Office: Jeraf Mktg 49 Underwood Falmouth ME 04105

FELSENTHAL, GERALD, physiatrist, educator; b. N.Y.C., Aug. 27, 1941; s. Richard and Fay (Braunspiegel) F.; m. Diane Shretter, June 6, 1964; children: David, Steven, Suzann. BA, NYU, 1963; MD, Albany Med. Coll., 1967. Diplomate Am. Bd. Phys. Medicine and Rehab., Am. Bd. Electrodiagnostic Medicine (residency rev. com. 1990—). Rotating intern USPHS Hosp., Seattle, 1967-68; resident in phys. medicine and rehab. Bronx Mcpl. Hosp. Ctr., Albert Einstein Coll. Medicine, 1970-73; assoc. physiatrist Sinai Hosp., Balt., 1973-76, assoc. chief, 1976-86, chief dept. rehab. medicine, 1986—; head div. rehab. medicine Levindale Hebrew Geriatric Ctr. and Hosp., Balt., 1983—; dir. residency tng. prog. in phys. medicine and rehab. Sinai Hosp.-Johns Hopkins U., 1986—; assoc. prof. U. Md. Coll. Medicine, Balt., 1987-92, prof., 1992—; assoc. prof. Johns Hopkins U. Sch. Medicine, 1989—. Contbr. over 50 articles and abstracts to med. jours., chpts. to books. Surgeon USPHS, 1967-70. Fellow Am. Acad. Phys. Medicine and Rehab., Am. Assn. Electrodiagnostic Medicine (bd. dirs. 1990—); mem. AMA, Am. Geriatric Soc., Am. Congress Rehab. Medicine, Assn. Acad. Physicatrists, Am. Coll. Physician Execs., Md. Geriatric Soc., Med. and Chirurg. Faculty Md. Office: Sinai Hosp Dept Rehab Med Belvedere at Greenspring Baltimore MD 21215

FELSENTHAL, NORMAN ALLAN, communications educator; b. Lafayette, Ind., Nov. 14, 1934; s. Monroe Bernhard and Mary Ann Ruth (Levy) F.; m. Helen Martha Potts, Mar. 30, 1957; children: David, Kim Ellen. BS, Miami U., Oxford, Ohio, 1956; MA, San Diego State U., 1962; PhD, U. Iowa, 1969. Tchr. San Diego County Schs., Poway, Calif., 1959-63, San Diego, 1963-66; asst. prof. communications Purdue U., West Lafayette, Ind., 1969-73; prof. communications Temple U., Phila., 1973—. Author: Mass Communication, 1981; co-author: (textbook) English/Grade 7, 1983; contbr. articles to profl. jours. Chmn. Lower Merion Twp. Cable TV Com., Ardmore, Pa., 1985—. Lt. (j.g.) USN, 1956-59. Faculty Fellow, Nat. Assn. TV Programming Execs., 1983; recipient Best Tchr. award Purdue U., 1973. Mem. NATAS (trustee 1988-92, gov. Phila. chpt. 1986-92), Speech Communication Assn. (div. chmn. 1979-80), Broadcast Edn. Assn., Internat. Radio and TV Soc. (Frank Stanton fellow 1992). Jewish. Home: 103 Merbrook Ln Merion Station PA 19066-1619 Office: Temple U Dept of Radio/TV/Film Philadelphia PA 19122

FELTCH, CYNTHIA ANNE, freelance photographer; b. Medford, Mass., July 31, 1955; d. Chester William and Rose Joanne (McPhee) F. BSBA, Suffolk U., 1978; cert. tng., Am. Grad. U., L.A., 1984. Bus. mgr. Suffolk Jour., Boston, 1975-77; advt. saleswoman Denver Dispatch Newspapers, Wheatridge, Colo., 1978-79; customer svc., pub. relations rep. Purolator Courier, Boston, 1979-81; new product planner Data Gen. Corp., Westboro, Mass., 1980-81; product mgr. Data Gen. Corp., Westboro, 1981-84; program mgr. I Prime Computer, Inc., Farmingham, Mass., 1984-86; program mgr. II Prime Computer, Inc., Farmingham, 1985-86, sr. mgr., 1986-88; owner, operator Attitash Valley Motor Inn, Glen, N.H., 1988-90; skii instr. Attitash Mountain, Bartlett, N.H., 1990—; head chef Grammy MacIntosh Restaurant, Conway, N.H., 1990—; photographer Newport Doctrine, 1988—. Mem. NAFE, NOW, Appalachin Mt. Club (Boston), Phi Chi Theta.

FELTHAM, ALAN ERIC, marketing professional; b. Providence, Oct. 3, 1949; s. Eric L. and Phyllis (Hurst) F.; m. Bernadette Heeran, Oct. 24, 1980; 1 child, Eric M. BS, Wentworth Inst., 1973; MBA, Anna Maria Coll., 1978. Sales proposal engr. Cin. Milacron, Worcester, Mass., 1973-84, export sales coord., 1984-86, account product engr., 1986-88, sr. sales product engr., 1988-90, mgr. market rsch., 1990—; adj. prof. Anna Maria Coll., Paxton, Mass., 1988—, Cen. N.E. Coll. of Tech. Engring. Econs., Worcester, 1979-88; indsl. adv. bd. Wentworth Inst., Boston. Home: 36 Kenilworth Rd Shrewsbury MA 01545-5920 Office: Cin Milacron 10 New Bond St Worcester MA 01606-2699

FELZER, STANTON BERNARD, consulting psychologist; b. Phila., Nov. 6, 1928; s. Philip and Esther (Willig) F.; m. Stephanie Levick, Nov. 17, 1956; children: Andrea, Susan, Sharon. AB, Temple U., 1950, MA, 1951, PhD, 1954. Lic. psychologist, Pa. Sr. clin. psychologist Ea. Pa. Psychiat. Inst., Phila., 1956-59; assoc. prof. dept. psychiatry Sch. Medicine Temple U., Phila., 1961-69, asst. dir. Community Mental Health Ctr. Sch. Medicine, 1965-69, assoc. v.p. for planning Health Scis. Ctr., 1973-86; v.p. Woehr Assocs., Phila., 1959-61, 69-73; exec. v.p. Woehr Assocs., Haddonfield, N.J., 1986-91; pres. Felzer Assocs., Phila., 1991—; cons. NIMH, Rockville, Md., 1965-69. Pres. Abington (Pa.) Schs. Parent Coun., 1973-75; sec. bd. govs. Temple Hosp., 1975-86; cons. Phila. Mayor's Commn. on Health in 80's, 1982. With U.S. Army, 1954-56. NIMH grantee, 1965-69. Fellow Am. Psychol. Assn., Pa. Psychol. Assn. (pres. 1967-68); mem. Phila. Soc. Clin. Psychology (pres. 1963-64). Jewish. Home: 296 Ironwood Cir Elkins Park PA 19117 Office: 234 N Delaware Ave Philadelphia PA 19106

FEMMINELLA, CHARLES J., JR., real estate appraiser, tax assessor; b. Bklyn., Aug. 10, 1938; s. Charles J. and Rose (Lanza) F.; m. Mary Ann DeCaro, Sept. 11, 1965; children: Cindy L., Christy J. BS, Fairleigh Dickinson U., 1966. Cert. gen. real estate appraiser, tax assessor, N.J. Pres. Cert. Valuations, Inc., Randolph, N.J., 1986—; instr. real estate, Rutgers U.; expert witness in real estate affairs. Author: Real Property Appraisal, 1974 (Presdl. Citation 1978). Pres. Randolph Rep. Club, 1980, Pla. 447 Condominium Assn., 1986—, also bd. dirs. Cpl. USMC, 1958-61. Mem. Soc. Profl. Assessors, Randolph C. of C. (v.p., dir. 1972). Lodge: Kiwanis, KC. Office: Cert Valuations 447 Rt 10 St 6 Randolph NJ 07869

FENCHEL, GERD H(ERMAN), psychoanalyst; b. Berlin, Mar. 29, 1926; arrived in U.S., 1940; s. Eric Otto and Rosa (Goldschmidt) F.; children: Karen Fenchel Spiler, Erich; m. Leslie Spitz, June 30, 1991. BSS, CCNY, 1949, MS in Edn., 1950; PhD, NYU, 1959; cert., Washington Sq. Inst., 1970. Cert. psychologist, N.Y., Pa. Pvt. practice psychoanalysis N.Y.C., 1949—; asst. dean Alfred Adler Inst., N.Y.C., 1955-73; psychotherapist, supr. and dir. group psychotherapy L.I. Cons. Ctr., Forest Hills, N.Y., 1953-60; mem. faculty Inst. for Analytic Psychotherapy, N.J., 1960-71; exec. dir., dean Washington Sq. Inst., N.Y.C., 1960—. Co-author: Development of Ego and Emergence of the Self in Group Psychotherapy, 1979; contbg. editor jour. Group, 1984—; contbr. articles to profl. jours. Fellow Coun. Psychoanalysts and Psychotherapists (pres. 1966-67); mem. Am. Psychol. Assn., Internat. Group Psychotherapy Assn. Office: Washington Sq Inst 41-51 E 11th St New York NY 10003

FENERTY, PAUL JOSEPH, professional land surveyor; b. Allentown, Pa., Oct. 12, 1953; s. Joseph F.X. and Lois (Oswald) F.; m. Karen Marie French, July 17, 1976; children: Stephen, Brian, Katherine. B of Mgmt., La Salle Coll., 1974. Profl. land surveyor. Surveyor Guy F. Atkinson Co., Long Beach, Calif., 1977-83, Penoni Assoc. Inc., Phila., 1984-86; survey mgr. Burkett Assoc., Ocean City, N.J., 1986-90; dir. ops. La Terre & Assocs., Millville, N.J., 1990-91; county surveyor Atlantic County (N.J.), 1991—. Coach Mays (N.J.) Landing Athletics Assn., 1988—. Mem. N.J. Soc. Profl. Land Surveyors, South Jersey Profl. Land Surveyors, Cumberland-Salem Surveyors Assn. Republican. Roman Catholic. Home: 4506 Concord Pl Mays Landing NJ 08330

FENGER, MANFRED, manufacturing executive, retired; b. Mt. Vernon, N.Y., Aug. 2, 1928; s. Friedrich Ludwig and Ingeberg (Horn) F. m. Emily Martha Fenger, Apr. 1948 (div. Apr. 1976); children: Laura Anne, Ronald Emil; m. Elizabeth Wanda Melvin, Nov. 1976. BEE, NYU, 1953, Newark Coll., 1962. Registered profl. elec. engr., R.I. Indsl. engr. Kollsman Instrum Co., Elmhurst, N.Y., 1960-62; production mgr. Wilcolator Co., Elizabeth, N.J., 1962-64; design engr. Leviton Mfg. Co., Bklyn., 1948-53; indsl. engr. Warwick, R.I., 1953-60, chief indsl. engr., 1964-74; internal cons. Leviton Mfg. Co., Warwick, R.I., 1974-79; dir. ops. planning Leviton Mfg. Co., Little Neck, N.Y., 1979-90, v.p. ops. planning, 1990; retired, 1990. Mem. Soc. for Advancement of Mgmt. (pres. 1959-60, Hamilton award 1960). Republican. Lutheran.

FENIAK, JUAN NICOLAS, electronics service company executive, financial consultant; b. Avellaneda, Buenos Aires, Argentina, Dec. 24, 1939; came to U.S., 1964; s. Wladimiro and Anna (Drobot) F.; m. Irena Anna Nakoneczny, June 7, 1974; children: Olena, Emilia, Cristina, Monica. Assoc. degree Electronics Engring., U. Buenos Aires, 1960; student, Inst. of Electronics, Buenos Aires, 1962, RCA Inst., Cherry Hill, N.J., 1967. Mgr. electronics Pregon Electronics, Villa Dominco, Argentina, 1958-62, Ducilo (DuPont), Berazategui, Argentina, 1962-64; electronic technician Cert. Performace Svc., Horsham, Pa., 1964-67; owner, pres. Geloso Electronics, Abington, Pa., 1968—; with life-health ins. Primerica, Southampton, Pa., 1987—, account exec. investments, fin. cons., 1987—; real estate agt., 1991—; pres. electronics svcs. Geloso Electronics, Abington, 1968—. Recipient Appreciation award RCA Consumer Electronics, 1975. Mem. TV Svc. Assn. Delaware Valley (pres. Phila. chpt. 1974-75, 76, Man of the Yr. 1975, Merit award 1974-76). Roman Catholic. Office: Geloso Electronics Corp 1769 York Rd Abington PA 19001-1801

FENICHEL, DOUGLAS MORGAN, publishing executive, consultant; b. Hartford, Conn., Dec. 27, 1953; s. Norman Stuart and Talma F. (Tonkin) F.; m. Karen Ellen Kolko, Jan. 4, 1975; children: Eli, Ethan. B of Journalism, U. Mo., 1975; postgrad., Webster U., 1984-85. Registered paramedic. Suburban editor New Haven (Conn.) Register & Jour. Courier, 1978-83; news editor Columbia (Mo.) Tribune, 1983; staff supr. pub. rels. AT&T, Basking Ridge, N.J., 1983-88; group supr. Coleman & Pellet Pub. Rels. Inc., Union, N.J., 1988-89; pres. Pulse Communications Inc., Flanders, N.J., 1989—. Publ. Emergency Products Update; contbr. articles to profl. jours. Paramedic various hosps. Mem. Soc. Profl. Journalists, Nat. Assn. EMTs. Office: Pulse Communications Inc PO Box 240 Linden NJ 07036-0301

FENN, DEBORAH HORTON, public relations professional; b. Portland, Maine, Mar. 3, 1951; d. Roger Plant and Frances (Davies) Horton; m. Peter Hartness Fenn, Dec. 12, 1981; children: Kyle, Brian. BA, Boston U., 1973; MS, Syracuse U., 1975. Pub. rels. assoc. Morton D. Wax and Assocs., N.Y.C., 1975-76, Peter Levinson Communications, N.Y.C., 1976-80; creative dir. Tauco Mktg. and Media, Buffalo, 1980-81; media specialist Buffalo Area Coun. Churches, 1985-87; mgr., dir. pub. rels. Millard Fillmore Hosps., Buffalo, 1988-90; corp. communications dir. Community Gen. Hosp., Syracuse, N.Y., 1990—. Health columnist Amherst Bee, 1989-90; contbr. articles to profl. publs. Tchr. Project Head Start, Cambridge, Mass., 1973; pub. rels. asst. Syracuse Stage Regional Profl. Theatre, 1975; pub. rels. coord. Antorama-Buffalo, 1981, 82, 83; spl. events coord. Boys and Girls Clubs Buffalo and Erie County, 1988; tchr. Literacy Vols., Buffalo, 1986; exec. com., bd. dirs. Buffalo Area Coun. Churches, 1989-90; deacon, elder United Ch. Fayetteville, N.Y., 1991. Mem. Pub. Rels. Soc. Am., Women in Communications. Democrat. Office: Community Gen Hosp Broad Rd Syracuse NY 13215-2402

FENNELL, MICHAEL DANIEL, aerospace engineer; b. Cheverly, Md., Apr. 5, 1968; s. Edward Ray and June Jeanette (Bentz) F.; m. Jackie Leigh Fritz, Oct. 12, 1991. BS in Aerospace Engring., Va. Poly. Inst. and State U., 1990. Aerospace engr. NASA Goddard Space Flight Ctr., Greenbelt, Md., 1990—. Mem. AIAA. Republican. Roman Catholic. Home: 14808 Ashford Pl Laurel MD 20707-3770 Office: NASA Goddard Space Flight Ctr Code 745.1 Laurel MD 20771

FENNESSY, MARSHA BEACH STEWART, sales executive, entertainment executive; b. Memphis, Jan. 17, 1952; d. Bruce Charles and Marjorie Hudson (Campbell) Stewart; m. Sean Francis Fennessy, Aug. 28, 1977. BBA in Internat. Bus., U. Tex., 1982; MFA in Arts Adminstrn./Dance Mgmt., Yale U., 1985. Mng. dir. Yale Cabaret, New Haven, 1984-85; agt. Columbia Artists Mgmt., Inc., N.Y.C., 1985-90; v.p., dir. sales SATRA Arts Internat. (formerly Classical Artists), N.Y.C., 1990—; dancer with Louisville (Ky.) Ballet (formerly Civic), 1967-70, Actor's Theatre of Louisville, 1972, Arena Stage, Washington, 1972, Disney on Parade, NBC, S.Am., Europe, Africa, 1974, 75, 76, Geneva (Switzerland) Ballet Co., 1975, 76; dance chairwoman cultural entertainment com. U. Tex., Austin, 1981-82. NEA fellow, 1983, assoc., 1984. Mem. NAFE, Yale U. Alumni Assn., Yale Club of N.Y.C., Scottish Heritage Soc., N.Y. Caledonian Club, Texas Exes. Office: SATRA Arts Internat 599 W Putnam Ave Greenwich CT 06830

FENNEY, NICHOLAS WILLIAM, retired pharmaceutical educator, consultant; b. New Haven, July 18, 1906; s. William Nicholas and Jennie Mary (Genovese) F.; m. Annamae Evangeline Dwyer, June 10, 1930 (dec. 1974); children: Nicholas William Jr., Barbara Jane; m. Anne Mary Manduck, Oct. 1, 1977; children: Nancy, Karen. Grad. in pharmacy, Columbia U., 1925; PhC, Conn. Coll. Pharmacy, 1930; BS in Pharmacy, U. Conn., 1942; MPH, Yale U., 1946. Lic. pharmacist, Conn. Instr. pharmacy Conn. Coll. Pharmacy, New Haven, 1925-35; asst. prof. U. Conn., Storrs, 1935-46, assoc. prof., 1946-50, prof., 1950-68, prof. emeritus, 1968—; pharm. and drug info. cons. Blue Cross and Blue Shield Conn., North Haven, 1968—. Author: Prescription Writing; also numerous articles. Recipient Sidney R. Rome award Conn. chpt. Alpha Zeta Omega, 1964, Disting. Faculty award from students U. Conn., 1965, Alumni award for disting. svc. in pharmacy to Conn. and nation, 1974, Bowl of Hygeia award A.H. Robins Co., 1969, Nat. Assn. Retail Druggists-Lederle Nat. Interprofl. Svc. award, 1969. Mem. Conn. Pharm. Assn. (hon.), New Haven Pharm. Assn. (hon.), Hartford County Pharm. Soc. (hon.), Mortar and Pestle (hon.), Kappa Psi (grand regent 1953-55, editor Mask 1955-68). Roman Catholic. Home: 62 Broadfield Rd Hamden CT 06517-1503 Office: Blue Cross-Blue Shield Conn 370 Bassett Rd North Haven CT 06473-4201

FENNO, JOHN BROOKS, management consultant; b. Boston, July 25, 1934; s. John Brooks Fenno and Virginia (Chapman) Hopkins; married, Dec. 5, 1964 (div. June 1984); children: Edward T., Arthur C. AB, Princeton U., 1956; MBA, Harvard U., 1962. Pers. adminstr. Sylvania Electronics, Needham, Mass., 1954-60; brand mgr. Procter & Gamble, Cin., 1962-63; v.p. Europe, bus. products div. Itek, Rochester, N.Y., 1963-70; prin. Salesmark, Wellesley, Mass., 1970—; adj. prof. Babson Coll., Wellesley, 1986-90. Author: Helping Your Business Grow, 101 Dynamic Ideas in Marketing, 1983; co-author: Air Cushion Vehicles Transportation of the Future, 1962. 1st lt. U.S. Army, 1956-58. Mem. Inst. Mgmt. Cons. (bd. dirs. 1991—), Harvard Bus. Sch. Assn. Boston (bd. dirs. 1990—), Princeton Assn. New Eng. (past pres. 1986-88), Princeton U. Alumni Assn. (trustee 1986-88). Home and Office: Salesmark Five Linden Sq Wellesley MA 02181-4717

FENSTER, CRAIG MICHAEL, actuary; b. N.Y.C., Jan. 5, 1964; s. Harvey Leonard and Edy Lou (Gelfand) F. AB, Columbia U., 1986. Actuarial trainee Am. Internat. Group, N.Y.C., 1986, actuarial assoc., 1986-91, sr. actuarial analyst, 1991—. Mem. exec. com. Varsity C Club of Columbia U., track chmn., 1988—; asst. scoutmaster Troop 1 Roseland (N.J.) Boy Scouts Am., 1982-86. James P. Gorman Meml. scholar West Essex Regional High Sch., 1982. Mem. Nat. Eagle Scout Assn., Old Guard of Camp Glen Gray, Phi Epsilon Pi (v.p. 1986). Office: Am Internat Group 70 Pine St New York NY 10270-0199

FENSTERHEIM, HERBERT, psychologist, writer; b. Bklyn., July 22, 1921; s. Harry and Mollie (Feder) F.; m. Jean Baer, June 20, 1968. BA, NYU, 1941, PhD, 1958; MA, Columbia U., 1942. Diplomate Am. Bd. Behavioral Psychology. Pvt. practice N.Y.C., 1952—; clin. assoc. prof. N.Y. Med. Coll., 1964-72; clin. assoc. prof. Med. Coll. Cornell U., N.Y.C., 1972-85, clin. prof. Med. Coll., 1985—; attending psychologist The N.Y. Hosp., 1985—; sports psychologist U.S. Olympic Fencing Team, 1981-85. Author: (with others) Don't Say Yes When You Want to Say No, 1975 (APA Media award), Behavioral Psychotherapy, 1983, Advances in Behavior Therapy, 1971, 72, Help Without Psychoanalysis, 1971, Stop Running Scared, 1977, Making Life Right When It Feels All Wrong, 1988; contbr. articles to profl. jours. Staff sgt. U.S. Army, 1942-45. Jewish. Home and Office: 151 E 37th St New York NY 10016-3157

FENSTERMACHER, ROBERT LANE, physics educator; b. Scranton, Pa., May 30, 1941; s. John Walter and Romayne Elizabeth (Lane) F.; m. Nancy G. Howe, June 13, 1964 (div. 1977); 1 child, Robert Lane Jr.; m. Anne H. Jacobson, July 8, 1983; 1 child, Sara Jacobson. BA in Physics, Drew U., 1963; PhD in Physics, Pa. State U., 1968. NASA doctoral trainee Pa. State U., State College, 1965-68; asst. prof. physics Drew U., Madison, N.J., 1968-73, assoc. prof. physics, 1973-80, prof. physics, 1980—, chair dept. physics, 1975—; dir. N.J. Gov.'s Sch. in Scis., Madison, 1983-87, assoc. dir., 1988-90. NASA Faculty fellow, Jet Propulsion Lab., Pasadena, Calif., 1979, 86. Mem. Am. Phys. Soc., Am. Assn. Physics Tchrs., Soc. Physics Students (councillor 1985, 92), AAUP. Office: Drew U 36 Madison Ave Madison NJ 07940-1493

FENSTER-NUNEZ, RITA GAIL, family therapist; b. Queens, N.Y., Dec. 15, 1960; d. Robert Jacob and Iris Diane (Schoenberg) Fenster; m. Raul Emilio Nunez, June 29, 1991. BS cum laude, Queens Coll., 1981, MS in Edn., 1983; postgrad., Canterbury Family Inst., Great Neck, N.Y., 1986. Family cons. Queensboro Soc. for Prevention of Cruelty to Children, Far Rockaway, N.Y., 1983-86; family counselor N.Y. Foundling Hosp.-Family Svcs. for Deaf Children & Adults, N.Y.C., 1986—; family therapist Italian

Bd. Guardians, Bklyn., 1987—. Mem. Am. Assn. Marriage and Family Therapy (assoc.), Am. Assn. for Counseling & Devel., Ortho.

FENTI, DANIEL JOSEPH, sales engineer; b. Hornell, N.Y., June 21, 1945; s. Lundy Valentine and Theresa (Constantino) F.; m. Ivanna Cathleen Fenti, Dec. 20, 1967; 1 child, Daniel. AAAS, Tompkins Cortland Commty Coll., 1970; BS, Cornell U., 1972. Tchr. Ithaca (N.Y.) City Schs., 1972-75; salesman R. L. Kistler, Rochester, 1975-76; mgr. R.L. Kistler, Syracuse, 1976-85, v.p., 1985—. With U.S. Army, 1967-69, Vietnam. Mem. ASHRAE (pres. Syracuse chpt. 1985-86). Office: RL Kistler Inc 5615 Business Ave North Syracuse NY 13212-0374

FENTON, DOUGLAS JOHN, community relations director; b. Buffalo, June 15, 1956; s. Robert Simpson and Ruth Esther (Woods) F.; children: Christopher, Katherine. AAS in Bus., Niagara Community Coll., Sanborn, N.Y., 1976; BA in Journalism, Fredonia State Coll., 1978. Reporter Evening Observer, Dunkirk, N.Y., 1978-85; mktg., pub. rels. dir. Lake Shore Hosp., Irving, N.Y., 1985-86; mng. editor Buffalo Bus. Jour., 1986-87; mktg., pub. rels. dir. Brooks Meml. Hosp., Dunkirk, N.Y., 1987—. Mem. adv. bd. Ctr. for Bus. and Industry, Fredonia, 1986—; chmn. United Way Communications Com., Dunkirk, N.Y., team leader allocation com., 1989-90; v.p. Lakeshore chpt. Parents without Ptnrs.; vestry mem. Trinity Epsic. Ch., Fredonia, 1992—. Nominee Golden Apple award, N.Y. State Tchrs. Assn., 1984. Mem. Empire Communicators (pres. 1990-91), Am. Hosp. Assn., North County Jaycees (v.p. pub. rels. Dunkirk chpt.). Home: 624 Main St Dunkirk NY 14048 Office: Brooks Meml Hosp 529 Central Ave Dunkirk NY 14048-2599

FENTON, JILL RUBINSON, English educator; b. Phila., Aug. 17, 1943; d. Harold Rubinson and Louise (Lowenthal) Sernoff; m. David Fenton, Aug. 16, 1981; children: Andrew, Joshua, Anny. AB in English cum laude, Cornell U., 1965; AM, Harvard U., 1966, PhD, 1983. Instr. English Emmanuel Coll., Boston, 1967-69; teaching fellow Harvard U., Cambridge, Mass., 1969-71; evaluation specialist Cambridge Model Cities, Cambridge, 1970-71; dir. Community Learning Ctr. for Adults, Cambridge, 1971-75; dir. spl. svcs. U. Maine at Augusta, 1978-84, spl. asst. to pres. (part time), 1986-91, assoc. prof. English, 1984—; cons. Adult Literacy Scheme, Dorset, Eng., 1975-76, Cambridge Pub. Schs., 1977-78, New Bedford (Mass.) Pub. Schs., 1978; project evaluator U. Maine at Machias, 1985-86. Author: (with others) From Page to Screen: Women Writers, 1990. Bd. dirs. New Eng. Assn. Ednl. Opportunity Program Personnel, Boston, 1982-84; mem. Reaccreditation Team New Eng. Assn. Schs. and Colls., Boston, 1990. Recipient Univ. fellowship Harvard U., Cambridge, 1967-69. Mem. Modern Lang. Assn., Phi Beta Kapp, Phi Kappa Phi. Office: U Maine University Heights Augusta ME 04330

FENVESSY, STANLEY JOHN, management consultant; b. Rochester, N.Y., Oct. 30, 1918; s. John H.W. and Bessie Ruth (Weber) F.; m. Doris Goodman, July 10, 1943; children: Alice Fenvessy Healy, Barbara Fenvessy Kahlow. BS in Econs., U. Pa., 1940; LLB, Georgetown U., 1943. Bar: Ill. 1947. With Aldens, Inc. Chgo., 1945-50; prin. Cresap, McCormick and Paget, N.Y.C., 1950-55; exec. v.p. Am. Merchandising div. Rapid Am. Corp., N.Y.C., 1955-60; adminstrv. v.p. Ethan Allen, Inc., Danbury, Conn., 1960-65; pres. Fenvessy Assocs., Inc., Mgmt. Cons., N.Y.C., 1965-82; chmn. Fenvessy & Schwab, Inc., N.Y.C., 1982-86, Fenvessy & Silbert, Inc., N.Y.C., 1987-88, Fenvessy Consulting, N.Y.C., 1988—; bd. dirs. The Sharper Image, The Lighthouse, Inc. Author: Keep Your Customers and Keep Them Happy, 1976, Fenvessy On Fulfillment, 1988; contbr. to Graphic Arts Manual, Mag. Public Mgmt., Direct Mail Advt., Selling for Retailers, Direct Mktg. Handbook, also bus. publs.; patentee addressing methods. Served to lt. (s.g.) Intelligence Corps, USNR, 1941-45. Named to Hall of Fame Fulfillment Mgmt. Assn. Mem. Chgo. Bar Assn., Inst. Mgmt. Cons., Direct Mktg. Assn. (dir.), Am. Arbitration Assn., Univ. Club (N.Y.C.), Govs. Club (Palm Beach, Fla.). Republican. Home: 167 E 61st St New York NY 10021-8128 Office: 110 E 59th St New York NY 10022-1304

FENWICK, MILLICENT HAMMOND, retired diplomat, former congresswoman; b. N.Y.C., Feb. 25, 1910; d. Ogden Haggerty and Mary Picton (Stevens) Hammond; children: Mary Fenwick Reckford, Hugh. Student, Columbia Extension Sch., New Sch. for Social Research. Assoc. editor Conde Nast Publs., N.Y.C., 1938-50; mem. N.J. Gen. Assembly, 1938-52; dir. div. consumer affairs N.J. Dept. Law and Pub. Safety, 1973-74; mem. 94th-97th Congresses from N.J. 5th Dist., 1975-83; U.S. amb. UN Food and Agr. Orgn., 1983-87. Author: Vogue's Book of Etiquette, 1948, Speaking Up, 1982. Vice chmn. N.J. advisory com. to U.S. Commn. on Civil Rights, 1958-72; mem. Bernardsville (N.J.) Bd. Edn., 1938-41; mem Bernardsville Borough Council, 1958-64. Republican. Home: Mendham Rd Bernardsville NJ 07924-1604. Died Sept. 16, 1992.

FERARES, KENNETH, automobile executive; b. Bklyn., Jan. 29, 1957; s. William Harry and Elsie Marion (Millard) F.; m. Rosanne Misiti, Oct. 11, 1981; children: Jessica Lee, Michael Kenneth, Gina Michelle. Grad. high sch., Bayside, N.Y. Parts salesman Ed DiBenedetto Imports, Great Neck, N.Y., 1981-82, Penn Toyota, Roslyn, N.Y., 1982-83; mgr. Wantagh (N.Y.) Mitsubishi, 1983-88, Hassett Lincoln Mercury, Wantagh, 1988-91, Manhasset (N.Y.) Mitsubishi, 1991—. Recipient Parts Excellence award Mitsubishi Motor Sales Am., 1986, 87, 88, 91. Mem. Mitsubishi Motors Excellence Soc., Metro N.Y. Parts and Svc. Mgrs. Guild (treas. 1991). Republican. Office: Manhasset Mitsubishi 1225 Northern Blvd Manhasset NY 11030

FERDERBER-HERSONSKI, BORIS CONSTANTIN, process engineer; b. Craiova, Romania, May 17, 1943; came to U.S., 1980; s. Boris Modest and Anetta (Mihail) F.; m. Alexandra Ionescu; children: Boris Constantin Jr., Alexandru Vlad. MS in Process Engring., Poly. Inst., Bucharest, Romania, 1968; diploma fgn. trade, Romanian U., Bucharest, 1975. Registered profl. engr., Romania; engr.-in-tng., N.J. Plant engr. Pham. Complex, Bucharest, 1968-69, plant mgr., 1969-73; prin. engr. Indsl. Export Import, Bucharest, 1973-75, fgn. trade diplomate, 1975-80; sr. process engr. Foster Wheeler Corp., Livingston, N.J., 1980-85; projects mgr. CPC Internat./Best Foods, Fairfield, N.J., 1985-91; sr. process engr. Allied Signal Aquatech div., Morristown, N.J., 1991—; founder, pres. B.F.H. Design Corp., 1984—. Inventor in field. Mem. Rep. Nat. Com., Washington, 1981. Mem. Am. Inst. Chem. Engrs., Instrument Soc. Am., Am. Rowing Assn. Office: PO Box 376 Hopatcong NJ 07843-0376

FERENS, MARCELLA, educator, business executive; b. Pitts.; d. Ignatius and Marcella (Buzas) Slevinskas; student Greensburg Bus. Coll., 1934-35, Maison Frederic Cosmetology, 1936, Kree Inst. Electrolysis, N.Y., 1952; B.S., U. Pitts., 1957; postgrad. Mid-Western U., 1962; M.Ed., Duquesne U., 1964; m. Joseph J. Ferens, Nov. 27, 1937; children—Joseph Ferens, James. Cosmetologist and electrologist, Manor and Darragh, Pa., 1937—; research in hair regrowth, Darragh, 1954—; tchr. cosmetology Uniontown (Pa.) Vocat. High, 1954-55; tchr. algebra, reading and drama dir. Harold Jr. High Sch., Greensburg, Pa., 1958—; pres. Marcella Ferens Inc.; treas. Schumacher Labs. Inc., Darragh. Insp., Chem. Corps, Dept. Army, N.Y., 1951. Mem. Nat. Coun. Tchrs. Math., Nat. Edn. Assns., Pa. Edn. Assns. Patentee in field. Home: PO Box 84 Darragh PA 15625-0084

FERET, ADAM EDWARD, JR., dentist; b. Newark, Mar. 5, 1942; s. Adam Edward and Bronislawa Anne (Szorc) F. BA (athletic scholar), Seton Hall U., 1963; DMD, U. Medicine & Dentistry of N.J., 1967. Pvt. practice Westfield, N.J., 1972—. With USNR, 1967-70. Fellow Am. Acad. Gen. Dentistry; mem. ADA, N.J. Dental Assn., L.D. Pankey Study Club, Soc. Oral Physiology and Occlusion, Quest Study Club, Internat. Coll. Oral Implantologists, Am. Soc. Oral Implantology, Central Dental Soc., Balloon Fedn. Am., Polish-Am. Guardian Soc., Polish Falcons of Am., Copernicus Soc. Am., Toastmasters, Psi Omega. Roman Catholic. Home and Office: 440 E Broad St Westfield NJ 07090-2124

FERGUSON, ANDREW ROBERT, environment investment banker; b. Cleve., May 12, 1954; s. Stanley Andrew and Margaret (Wragg) F.; m. Lisa Joan Limont, Aug. 8, 1987. BA in History, Oberlin Coll., 1975; student, Purdue U., 1977, Caja Laboral Popular, Mondragon, Spain, 1988. Natural beef herdsman Meadowfork Farm, Given, W.Va., 1975-76; dairy herdsman Derry-Grove Farm, Cochranville, Pa., 1977; pub. New Roots Mag., Greenfield, Mass., 1978-80; exec. dir. Northeast Appropriate Tech. Network, Greenfield, 1978-80; gen. mgr., treas., ptnr. New Eng. Country Dairy, Greenfield, 1980-88; ptnr., mng. dir. The Catalyst Group, Brattleboro, Vt., 1988-90; pres. New Equity Ptnrs., Colrain, Mass., 1991—; dir. N.E. Coop., Brattleboro, Mass. National Fertilizer Co., Westminster, Cherry Hill Cannery, Barre, Vt.; leader, organizer civic tour Vist to the Mondragon Coops. with Western Mass. Community Leaders, 1988. Editor New Roots, 1980. Mem. adv. bd. Greenseal, Washington, 1989—; dir. Twin Pines Found., San Francisco, 1990—; founding bd. mem. Seabrook Emergency Com., Amesbury, Mass., 1989—; mem. major gifts com. New Eng. Learning Ctr. for Women in Transition, Greenfield, 1991—; del. Mass. Dem. Conv., 1990. Mem. Organic Foods Prodn. Assn. N.Am. (vice chair internat. rels. coun. 1991—), Mass. Assn. Dairy Farmers (vice chair legis. coun. 1989—). Office: New Equity Ptnrs Box 144 Colrain MA 01340

FERGUSON, DONALD GUFFEY, radiologist; b. W. Newton, Pa., July 19, 1923; s. Rutherford Hayes and Beulah Cristabel (Guffey) F.; B.S., U. Pitts., 1944, M.D., 1946; m. Anne Benedict Gallagher, Mar. 4, 1961. Intern, S. Side Hosp., Pitts., 1946-47; resident in radiology and radiation therapy Meml. Sloan-Kettering, N.Y.C., 1950-52; Am. Cancer Soc. fellow, staff radiologist Thomas Jefferson U. Hosp., Phila., 1952-55; attending radiologist Mercy Hosp., Pitts., 1955-57; sr. staff S. Side Hosp., Pitts., 1957—, St. Clair Meml. Hosp., Pitts., 1957—; clin. asst. prof. radiology U. Pitts., 1956—. Served with M.C., U.S. Army, 1948-50. Diplomate Am. Bd. Radiology, Am. Bd. Nuclear Medicine. Fellow Am. Coll. Radiology (dist. councilor 1972-78, pres. Pa. chpt. 1979-80); mem. Soc. Nuclear Medicine (chpt. pres. 1957-58), Pitts. Roentgen Soc. (pres. 1967-68), Am. Med. Assn. (ho. of del. 1987—), Pa. Med. Soc. (ho. of del. 1986-90, v.p. 1990-91, pres.-elect 1991-92, pres. 1992—), Radiol. Soc. N. Am., Am. Roentgen Ray Soc., Allegheny County Med. Soc., Pitts. Athletic Assn. Presbyterian. Club: Masons (Shriner). Home: Hidden Valley Rd Canonsburg PA 15317-2604 Office: 1000 Bower Hill Rd Pittsburgh PA 15243

FERGUSON, DOUGLAS EDWARD, financial executive; b. Bronx, N.Y., Apr. 21, 1940; s. Lawrence and Claire (Billingheimer) F.; m. Cynthia L. Kords, Jan. 29, 1966; children: Elisabeth, Keith, Jonathan. AB, Columbia Coll., 1962. Chartered fin. analyst. Security analyst Heritage Securities/Nat. Securities and Rsch. Corp., N.Y.C., 1963-68; asst. v.p. John W. Bristol & Co., Inc., N.Y.C., 1968-74; v.p. Van Cleef, Jordan & Wood, Inc., N.Y.C., 1974-75; portfolio mgr. Trustees of Columbia U., N.Y.C., 1975-76; mgr. investment svcs. Trascott, Alyson, Craig, Inc., Teaneck, N.J., 1977-84; v.p. portfolio mgmt. Swiss Bank Corp., N.Y.C., 1984-88; pres. Ferguson Investment Cons., Inc., North Tarrytown, N.Y., 1988—. Contbr. articles to profl. jours. and newspaper. Pres. Westchester County chpt. N.Y. State Assn. Retarded Citizens; mem. Estate Planning Coun., Westchester County. Mem. N.Y. Soc. Security Analysts. Home and Office: Ferguson Investment Cons 528 Bellwood Ave North Tarrytown NY 10591-1336

FERGUSON, EARL WILSON, cardiologist, air force medical officer; b. Lebanon, Pa., Aug. 29, 1943; s. Warren Earl and Norma Laura (Wilson) F.; m. Bonnie Rose Harrington, May 29, 1965; children: Steven Mark, Matthew Earl, Erin Lee. BA in Chemistry, Baylor U., 1965; MD, PhD in Physiology, U. Tex., Galveston, 1970. Diplomate Am. Bd. Internal Medicine, Am. Bd. Cardiovascular Disease, Am. Bd. Preventive Medicine, Am. Bd. Med. Mgmt. Grad. teaching asst. dept. physiology U. Tex. Med. Br., Galveston, 1967-70, intern medicine, 1970-71; resident medicine, then fellow cardiology Duke U. Med. Ctr., Durham, N.C., 1971-75, mem. assoc. faculty dept. medicine, 1974-75; research assoc. cardiology VA Hosp., Durham, 1974-75; commd. lt. USAF, 1966, advanced through grades to col.; staff cardiologist, dir. coronary care Wilford Hall USAF Med. Ctr., Lackland AFB, Tex., 1975-76, chief cardiology, dir. cardiology tng. program, 1983-84; asst. prof. biochemistry, medicine and mil. medicine Uniformed Services U. Health Scis., Bethesda, Md., 1976-80, assoc. prof. physiology, medicine and mil. medicine, 1980-84, asst. comdt., 1977-82, mem. faculty senate, 1979-80, adj. prof. physiology, 1984—; dir. hosp. services USAF Med. Ctr., Scott AFB, Ill., 1984-86; comdr. USAF Hosp., Little Rock AFB, Ark., 1986-88; dep. command surgeon Mil. Airlift Command, Scott AFB, 1988-90; comdr. USAF Med. Ctr., Wiesbaden, Fed. Republic of Germany, 1990—; cons. to surgeon gen. of Air Force for cardiology, medicine and physiology, 1980—; cons. N.J. State Police, 1984-88, Ind. Atty. Gen.'s Office, 1985-87; mem. life scis. adv. subcom. NASA, 1989—. Contbr. numerous articles to sci. jours. Research grantee VA, 1974-75, Dept. Def., 1976-82, NASA, 1982-84. Fellow Am. Coll. Cardiology (bd. govs. 1985-88), ACP, SOc. Air Force Physicians (bd. govs. 1982-85, v.p. 1987-88), Am. Coll. Preventive Medicine; mem. Am. Physiol. Soc., Am. Coll. Execs. Medicine, Am. Heart Assn. Unitarian Universalist. Office: USAF Med Ctr Weisbaden PSC 18 Box 152 APO AE 09220-5300

FERGUSON, HELAMAN ROLFE PRATT, mathematician, sculptor; b. Salt Lake City, Aug. 11, 1940; s. Helaman and Jeanne (Reinhardt) Pratt; adopted Samuel and Dora (Call) Ferguson; m. Claire Eising, Apr. 16, 1963; children: David, Sam, Ben, Noelle, Jonathan, Alexander, Michael Paul. AB, Hamilton Coll., 1962; MS, Brigham Young U., 1966, U. Wash., 1968; PhD, U. Wash., 1971. Prof. math. Brigham Young U., Provo, Utah, 1971-91; rsch. scientist Supercomputing Rsch. Ctr., Bowie, Md., 1988—; vis. fellow Princeton (N.J.) U., 1983-84; sr. scientist Geomath, Orem, Utah, 1981-82; cons. algorithms, supercomputers, vector-parallel processors, applied logic, geophysics, geometric design, computer-aided manufacture, biomed. modeling. Contbr. articles to profl. jours.; commd. for numerous sculptures with math. themes; patentee in field. Research grantee Brigham Young U., 1971-85. Mem. Am. Math. Soc., Math. Assn. Am., Internat. Jugglers Assn., Internat. Sculpture Ctr. Home and Studio: 10512 Pilla Terra Ct Warfield's Range Laurel MD 20723-5728 Office: Supercomputer Rsch Ctr/IDA 17100 Science Dr Bowie MD 20715-4300

FERGUSON, ROBERT, financial services executive, writer; b. N.Y.C., Nov. 24, 1937; s. Lawrence and Claire (Billingheimer) F.; m. Catherine Latil, July 7, 1961 (div. Dec. 1982); children: Anne, Alice); m. Magali Vigo, Apr. 26, 1991. BA, Columbia U., 1959; M of Philosophy, NYU, 1983, PhD, 1987. V.p. Bradford Trust Co., N.Y.C., 1977-78, Coll. Retirement Equities Fund, N.Y.C., 1978-82; exec. v.p. Leland O'Brien Rubinstein Assocs., L.A., 1982-91; pres. Axiomatic Systems, N.Y.C., 1986—; vice chmn. SuperShare Svcs., L.A., 1989-91; assoc. prof. fin. Fordham U. Sch. Bus., N.Y.C., 1991—; bd. dirs. SuperShare Svcs. Corp.; assoc. editor Fin. Analysts Jour., 1974—; adj. assoc. prof. fin. Columbia U. Sch. Bus., 1987—. Contbr. articles to profl. jours. With USAR. Mem. Fin. Analysts Fedn. (Graham & Dodd award 1961, 78, 80), Investment Tech. Assn. (chmn. bd. 1975), Inst. for Quantitative Research in Fin. (chmn. 1974-75). Avocations: bicycling, aviation.

FERGUSON, THOMAS H., newspaper executive. Pres., gen. mgr. Washington Post Newspaper. Office: Washington Post Co 1150 15th St NW Washington DC 20071-0002*

FERGUSON, WILLIAM ROTCH, foreign language educator, writer; b. Fall River, Mass., Feb. 14, 1943; s. William III and Helen Gilman (Rotch) F.; m. Nancy King, Nov. 26, 1983. BA, Harvard U., 1965, MA, 1970, PhD, 1975. Asst. prof. Spanish Boston U., 1971-77; asst. prof. Spanish Clark U., Worcester, Mass., 1977-84, assoc. prof. Spanish, 1984—, chair fng. langs. and lits., 1990—; Author: Freedom and Other Fictions, 1984, (scholarly) La versificacion imitativa en Fernando de Herrera, 1981; author poems. Mem. Modern Lang. Assn. Democrat. Home: 1 Tahanto Rd Worcester MA 01602-2523 Office: Clark U Dept Fgn Langs Worcester MA 01610

FERGUSON-PELL, MARGARET ALICE, health science facility press and public relations officer; b. New Haven, Aug. 14, 1951; d. Franklin Eldridge and Virginia Boardman (Porter) F.; m. Martin William Ferguson-Pell, Dec. 1973; 1 child, Grace. BA in English summa cum laude, Wheaton Coll., 1973. Antiquarian book specialist John Smith & Son, Glasgow, Scotland, 1974-76; book editor Heatherbank Press, Milngavie, Scotland, 1977-78; press officer Scottish Opera Theatre Royal, Glasgow, 1978-82; pub. relations and devel. officer Helen Hayes Hosp., West Haverstraw, N.Y., 1982—. Pub. info. officer Rockland County Disaster Preparedness Team, Rockland, N.Y., 1983—; bd. dirs. Westchester Ind. Living Ctr., White Plains, N.Y., 1988—, Arthritis Found. Mem. N.Y. State Head Injury Assn. (bd. dirs. Southern region, Recognition award 1986), Nat. Union Journalists, Rockland Devel. Group, Phi Beta Kappa. Office: Helen Hayes Hosp RR 9 West Haverstraw NY 10993

FERGUSSON, FRANCES DALY, college president, educator; b. Boston, Oct. 3, 1944; d. Francis Joseph and Alice (Storrow) Daly. BA, Wellesley Coll., 1965; MA, Harvard U., 1966, PhD, 1973. Asst. prof. Newton Coll., Mass., 1969-75; assoc. prof. U. Mass., Boston, 1974-82, asst. chancellor, 1980-82; provost, prof. Bucknell U., Lewisburg, Pa., 1982-86; pres. Vassar Coll., Poughkeepsie, N.Y., 1986—; bd. dirs. Marine Midland Bank. Trustee Mayo Found., 1988—, Ford Found., 1989—, Historic Hudson, 1990—; bd. dirs. Marine Midland Bank, 1990—. Recipient Founder's award Soc. Archtl. Historians, 1973. Office: Vassar Coll Office of the Pres Raymond Ave Poughkeepsie NY 12603-2312

FERGUSSON, WILLIAM BLAKE, civil engineering educator, researcher; b. Boston, Apr. 24, 1924; s. Stanley Major and Ruth Mehitabel (Blake) F.; m. Jean Elizabeth Hathaway, Apr. 24, 1948; children: Nancy Jean, Jane H., William Blake Jr., Elizabeth D., Stanley M., Katherine M. AB in Geology, Boston U., 1951, MA in Geology, 1953; PhD in Geology, U. Ariz., 1965. Exploration geologist AEC, Grand Junction, Colo., 1953-54; exploration geologist, cons. to small mining cos., Grand Junction, 1954-56; teaching fellow geology dept. U. Ariz., Tucson, 1956-59; geologist Pa. R.R. Co., Phila., 1959-67; assoc. dept. civil engring. Villanova (Pa.) U., 1967—; geotech. cons. various engring. cos., Phila., 1967—. Contbr. articles to profl. jours. Sgt. AUS, 1942-46, PTO. Fulbright sr. scholar, Korea, 1982-83. Fellow Geol. Soc. Am.; mem. Assn. Engring. Geologists, Internat. Assn. Engring. and Environ. Geologists, Sigma Xi, Tau Beta Pi, Chi Epsilon. Democrat. Episcopalian. Office: Villanova U Civil Engring Dept Villanova PA 19085

FERMAN, IRVING, lawyer, educator; b. N.Y.C., July 4, 1919; s. Joseph and Sadie (Stein) F.; m. Bertha Paglin, June 12, 1946; children: James Paglin, Susan Paglin. B.S., N.Y.U., 1941; J.D., Harvard, 1948. Bar: La. 1948, D.C. 1974. Partner Provensal, Faris & Ferman, New Orleans, 1948-52; dir. Am. Civil Liberties Union, Washington, 1952-59, Am. Civil Liberties Clearing House, 1952-54; exec. vice chmn. Pres.'s Com. Govt. Contracts, 1959-60; v.p. Internat. Latex Corp., 1960-66; pres. Piedmont Theaters Corp., 1966-69; adj. asso. prof. mgmt. NYU Grad. Sch. Bus., 1964-68; adj. prof. law Howard U., 1968-69, prof. law, 1969-86, prof. emeritus, 1986—; dir. Project for Legal Policy, 1976—; vis. prof. law Am. U., 1971-72; mem. Am. Com. Cultural Freedom, 1954; mem. Com. of Arts and Scis. for Eisenhower, 1956; mem. citizens adv. com. U.S. Commn. on Govt. Security, 1957; chmn. Police Complaint Rev. Bd., 1965-73; mem. Dept. HEW Reviewing Authority, 1969-79; chmn. Interdisco Ltd., London, 1986—; bd. dirs. Control Fluidics, Inc., Greenwich Conn., D.C. Housing fin. Agy. Contbr. to books and revs. Mem. bd. dirs. New Orleans Acad. Art, 1948-51. Served from cadet to 1st lt. USAAF, 1942-46. Mem. ABA, La. Bar Assn., D.C. Bar Assn., New Orleans Bar Assns., Internat. Club (Washington), Army-Navy Country Club (Arlington, Va.), Army-Navy Club (Washington), Harvard Club (N.Y.C.), Caterpillar Club (N.Y.C.). Jewish. Home: 3818 Huntington St NW Washington DC 20015-1928 also: Rt 1 Sullivan Harbor ME 04689 Office: 2935 Upton St NW Washington DC 20008-1194

FERN, ALAN MAXWELL, art historian, museum director; b. Detroit, Oct. 19, 1930; s. Martin and Rose (Coral) F.; m. Lois Ann Karbel, Mar. 17, 1957. A.B., U. Chgo., 1950, M.A., 1954, Ph.D., 1960; Fulbright scholar, Courtauld Inst., U. London, 1954-55. Asst., instr., asst. prof. humanities The Coll., U. Chgo., 1952-61; asst. curator prints and photographs div. Library of Congress, Washington, 1961; curator fine prints Library of Congress, 1962-64, asst. chief, 1964-73, chief, 1973-76, dir. research dept., 1976-78, dir. spl. collections, 1978-82; dir. Nat. Portrait Gallery, 1982—. Author: A Note on the Eragny Press, 1957, (with others) Art Nouveau, 1960, (with M. Constantine) Word and Image, 1968, Leonard Baskin, 1970, (with M. Constantine) Revolutionary Soviet Film Posters, 1974; introductory essay Lasansky: Printmaker, 1975, Eichenberg, The Wood and the Graver, 1977, People and Power, 1985; contbr. articles to profl. jours. Bd. dirs. Phillips Coll., Swann Found., Herman Miller, Inc. Decorated chevalier Ordre de la Couronne (Belgium); Ordre des Arts et Lettres (France); comdr. Royal Order of Polar Star (Sweden). Mem. Print Coun. Am. (past pres.), Coll. Art Assn. Am., Am. Antiquarian Soc., AIA (hon.), Double Crown Club (hon.), Cosmos Club (Washington), Grolier Club (N.Y.C.). Home: 3605 Raymond St Chevy Chase MD 20815 Office: Nat Portrait Gallery F St at 8th St NW Washington DC 20560

FERNALD, JAMES MICHAEL, engineer; b. Portsmouth, N.H., Oct. 12, 1964; s. R. Alden and Ruth Ann (Conlon) F. BS in Aerospace Engring., Syracuse U., 1986; BSME, U. N.H., 1992. Engring. technician Aquidneck Mgmt. Assn., Middleton, R.I., 1988; engr. Life Cycle Engring., Inc., Portsmouth, 1988—. Treas. troop 164 Boy Scouts Am., Portsmouth, 1989-91. Mem. AIAA, ASHRAE (assoc.), Syracuse U. Alumni Assn., Golden Key, Tau Beta Pi (pres. 1991-92), Theta Chi. Roman Catholic. Office: Life Cycle Engring Inc 500 Spaulding Tpke Ste 120N Portsmouth NH 03801-3162

FERNANDES, JEANNE MARY, human resource administrator; b. Nairobi, Kenya, May 21, 1948; came to U.S., 1984; d. John Joseph and Joan Bertha (Correya) Athaide; m. Leonard Maurice Fernandes, Oct. 17, 1970; children: Donna Michelle, Nigel Leonard. Royal Soc. arts Diploma, Kenya Poly., 1965. Sec. East African Community, Nairobi, Kenya, 1966-67; exec. sec. East African Airways, Nairobi, 1968-69; adminstrv. asst. to M.D. Cadbury Schweppes, Nairobi, 1969-73; exec. sec. Pfizer Africa Middle East M.C., Nairobi, 1973-79, pers. adminstr., 1979-84; internat. pers. specialist Pfizer, Inc., N.Y.C., 1984-87, sr. pers. assoc., 1987-91, assoc. pers. mgr., 1991—. Mem. NAFE, Am. Fedn. Police, Am. Mgmt. Assn., N.Y. Personnel Mgmt. Assn., Nat. Fgn. Trade Coun. (immigration com.). Roman Catholic. Home: 27 Ballaro Dr Shelton CT 06484-2424 Office: Pfizer Internat Inc 42nd St New York NY 10017

FERNÁNDEZ, INÉS TERESA, educator; b. Cardiff, Wales, Sept. 26, 1952; came to U.S. 1955; d. Emilio and Saturnina (Ostolozaga) F.; m. Stephen Robert Fadarishan, June 25, 1988. AA, Keystone Jr. Coll., LaPlume, Pa., 1973; BS in Edn. (Spanish), Bloomsburg (Pa.) U., 1975; MS in Sec. Edn./Eng., U. Scranton (Pa.), 1984. Mgr. Kiosks Inc., Allentown, Pa., 1976; dist. mgr. Kiosks Inc., 1976-79; tchr. Spanish and English, Elk Lake Sch. Dist., Dimock, Pa., 1979-90; tchr. Spanish and reading Wilde Lake Mid. Sch., Howard County Sch. Dist., Columbia, Mo., 1991—. Mem. ASCD, Am. Assn. Tchrs. Spanish and Portuguese, Am. Coun. on Teaching Fgn. Langs., Nat. Coun. Tchrs. English, Md. Coun. Tchrs. of English Lang. Arts, Md. Fgn. Lang. Assn. Republican. Roman Catholic.

FERNANDEZ, JOSEPH A., educational administrator; b. 1935. BA in Edn., U. Miami, 1963; MEd, Fla. Atlantic U., 1970; EdD, Nova U., 1985; HHD (hon.), Marymount Manhattan Coll., N.Y.C., 1990, Bank St. Coll. Edn., N.Y.C., 1990, CUNY, 1990; LHD, CUNY, 1990, Bank Street Coll. Edn., 1990. Former tchr. math., former supt. Dade County Pub. Schs., Miami; chancellor N.Y.C. Pub. Schs., 1990—. Office: NYC Pub Schs 110 Livingston St Brooklyn NY 11201-5065

FERNANDEZ-OBREGON, ADOLFO CARLOS, dermatologist, dermatologic surgeon; b. Havana, Cuba, Nov. 29, 1951; came to U.S., 1961; s. Adolfo Rogelio and Maria Antonia (Obergon) F.; m. Dorys Josefina Barban, Dec. 21, 1974; children: Michelle-Ana, Gabriel Carlos. BA, Columbia Coll., 1974; MD, N.Y. Med. Coll., 1978. Diplomate Am. Bd. Dermatology, Am. Bd. Med. Examiners. Attending Naval Hosp., Dept. Dermatology, Portsmouth, Va., 1985-87; chief surg. tng. Bayley Seton Hosp., S.I., N.Y., 1987—; asst. prof. dermatology N.Y. Med. Coll., Valhalla, 1978—; prin. clinician Hudson Dermatology and Skin Cancer Ctr., Hoboken, N.J., 1987—. Mem. planning com. Oper. Medication Awareness, Hudson County, 1991. With USN, 1979-87. Fellow Am. Acad. Dermatology, Am. Soc. Dermatologic Surgery, Assn. Acad. Dermatologic Surgeons; mem. ACP, AMA, Spanish-Am. Med. Assn. (treas. 1988—, v.p. 1992), Hudson County Med. Soc. (bd. censors, exec. com. 1987—). Office: Hudson Dermatology Ctr 10 Church Tower Hoboken NJ 07030

FERNANDEZ-POL, BLANCA DORA, psychiatrist, researcher; b. Buenos Aires, Mar. 5, 1932; came to U.S., 1967; d. Balbino Fernandez and Maria

Remedios van Pol. MD, U. Buenos Aires, 1958. Diplomate Am. Bd. Psychiatry and Neurology. Intern N.Y. Polyclinic Med. Sch., 1967-68; resident in psychiatry UCLA/Brentwood Hosp., 1968-69, NYU/Bellevue Hosp., 1969-71; gen. practitioner Hosp. Espanol, Buenos Aires, 1959-62; forensic psychiatrist Criminoloy Inst., Buenos Aires, 1963-65; clin. attending psychiatrist Bellevue Psychiat. Hosp., N.Y.C., 1971-75; pvt. practice St. Petersburg, Fla., 1976-78; chief psychiat. svcs. USAF Hosp. Yokota, Tokyo, 1980, USAF Hosp., Homestead, Fla., 1981; chief continuing treatment program dept. psychiatry Bronx-Lebanon Hosp., Bronx, 1983—; prof. psychology U. Moran, Buenos Aires, 1962-67; asst. prof. psychiatry N.Y. Med. Coll., N.Y.C., 1972-74; clin. asst. prof. psychiatry Albert Einstein Coll. Medicine, Bronx, 1982—. Contbr. articles to profl. jours. Maj. USAF, 1978-81. Mem. Am. Psychiat. Assn., N.Y. Acad. Scis., Am. Acad. Psychiatrists in Alcoholism and Addictions, Am. Soc. Addiction Medicine, Assn. Mil. Surgeons of U.S. Home: PO Box 21644 Brooklyn NY 11202-0036 Office: Bronx Lebanon Hosp 1285 Fulton Ave Bronx NY 10456-3401

FERNENDES, JOHN HENRY, mechanical engineer; b. Tiverton, R.I., Aug. 21, 1924; s. Joseph Francis and Margaret Angela (Moran) F.; m. Ann Frances Lopes, June 9, 1947; children: Ann Marie, John Edward, Mary Lou, Judy C., Mark J., Carolyn J. BSME, U. R.I., 1949; MSME, Lehigh U., 1953; SCd, Calvin Coolidge Coll., 1960. Registered profl. engr., Pa., N.J., N.Y., Conn., R.I., Mass., Hawaii, Kans., Mich. Combustion engr., serviceman Combustion Engring. Inc., N.Y.C., 1949-50; dir. tech. transfer Combustion Engring. Inc., Windsor, Conn., 1963-84; assoc. prof., dir. evening div. Lafayette Coll., Easton, Pa., 1950-60; prof., head dept. Manhattan Coll., N.Y.C., 1960-63; v.p. energy div. Maguire Group Inc., Foxborough, Mass., 1984-90; pvt. cons. Fernandes & Assoc., Tiverton, R.I., 1990—; cons. Maguire Group, 1990—, Dravo Corp., Pitts., 1990—, Worldwater Inc., Hopewell, N.J., 1990—, IPEC, Kingston, R.I., 1990-91. Contbr. articles to profl. publs., chpt. to book. Head air and water abatement com. Otn of Windsor, Conn., 1973-84; cons. Profl. Hiring Commn., Easton, 1958-60. Fellow ASME (sr. v.p., chmn. coun. on codes and standards, coun. on engring. com. on tech. planning, bd. pub. info., v.p. bd. performance test codes, chmn. performance test code com. on incinerators, now bd. govs., Centennial award, Performance Test Codes medal, Code and Standards medal); mem. AAAS, Nat. Soc. Profl. Engrs., Air and Waste Mgmt. Assn., Am. Acad. Environ. Engrs. (diplomate), Pi Tau Sigma, Mu Epsilon. Republican. Roman Catholic. Home and Office: Fernandes & Assocs 294 Riverside Dr Tiverton RI 02878-4206

FERRAGAMO, MICHAEL CHARLES, senior project engineer; b. Boston, Oct. 2, 1952; s. Michael Angelo and Mildred Vincenta (Altimar) F.; m. Cynthia Ann Horan, Jan. 31, 1981; children: Michael Frederick, Theresa Anna. BS in Biology, Suffolk U., 1975. Rsch. techician B-D Life Support Systems, Sharon, Mass., 1976-78; quality control mgr. Cott Beverages, Millis, Mass., 1978-80; rsch. assoc. Mansfield (Mass.) Sci. Inc., 1981-83; project engr. Delmed Inc., Canton, Mass., 1983-85, Pharmacia Deltec Inc., Walpole, Mass., 1985-89; sr. project engr. Bard Cardiopulmonary Div., Tewksbury, Mass., 1989-90, Acufex Microsurgical, Mansfield, 1990—. Coauthor 2 patents in field of catheters. Mem. Soc. Plastics Engrs. (sr.), N.Y. Acad. Scis. Democrat. Roman Catholic. Home: 2355 Old Wellington St North Dighton MA 02764 Office: Acufex Microsurgical 130 Forbes Blvd Mansfield MA 02048

FERRAIO, NICHOLAS L., rehabilitation services professional; b. Rochester, N.Y., Sept. 9, 1946; s. Laverne Leslie and Blanche Rose (Yates) F.; m. Carroll Ann Doolittle, June 4, 1971; children: Amy Lynn, Shannon Alicia. BS in Psychology, Sociology, U. Rochester, 1976, MS in Individual Treatment, 1980; MPA, SUNY, Brockport, 1990. Cert. alcoholism counslor, N.Y.; nat. cert. addiction counselor. Rsch. tech. U. Rochester, N.Y., 1965-79; psychotherapy counselor Joseph A. DiPoala, M.D., Rochester, 1977-81, 81-86; intake coord. Daybreak Alcoholism Treatment Facility, Rochester, 1986-89; dir. inpatient svcs. program Daybreak Alcoholism Treatment Facility, 1989-91; mgr. chem. dependency and mental health svcs. unit Preferred Care, Rochester, 1991—; adj. faculty lectr., SUNY Health Scis. Chem. Dependence Svcs. Program, Brockport, N.Y., 1988—, cons., 1979-84. Mem. APA, N.Y. State Fedn. Alcoholism Counselors, Employee Assistance Profls. Assn. Republican. Roman Catholic. Home: 225 Greenway Blvd Churchville NY 14428-9217 Office: Preferred Care 259 Monroe Ave Rochester NY 14607

FERRAND, CAROLE THELMA, speech scientist, educator; b. Johannesburg, South Africa, July 30, 1949; came to U.S., 1977; d. Isadore and Anne (Axelrod) Friedman; m. Edward Chester Ferrand, Dec. 12, 1975; 1 child, Matthew Ian. BA in Liberal Arts, U. Witwatersrand, South Africa, 1971; MS, Pa. State U., 1981, PhD, 1989. Speech pathologist Kern County Sch. Dist., Bakersfield, Calif., 1981-83; instr., PhD candidate Pa. State U., University Park, 1984-88; asst. prof., dir. Speech Sci. Lab. Hofstra U., Hempstead, N.Y., 1989—. Contbr. articles to profl. jours.; presents papers at nat. and internat. confs. Mem. Am. Speech-Lang.-Hearing Assn., Internat. Fluency Assn., N.Y. State Speech-Lang.-Hearing Assn., Am. Assn. Phonetic Scis. Office: Hofstra U Hempstead Tpke West Hempstead NY 11552-2123

FERRANTE, ROBERT LOUIS, marketing and public affairs executive, consultant; b. N.Y.C., Feb. 2, 1937; s. Victor Francis and Margaret Ann (Krausch) F.; m. Michelina Ann Giudice, Jan. 17, 1959; children: Robert Jude, Lisa Marie, Laura Ann, Matthew Charles. BA, U. Notre Dame, 1958. Editor Western Electric Co., N.Y.C., 1960-64; account exec. Doremus & Co., N.Y.C., 1964-67; mgr. N.Y.C. office PR Counselors, Inc., 1967-69; sr. v.p. Hill and Knowlton, Inc., N.Y.C., 1969-77; dir. corp. communications Combustion Engring., Inc., Stamford, Conn., 1977-81; sr. v.p. Stone Hallinan Assocs., N.Y.C., 1981-83; ptnr. Chester Burger & Co., N.Y.C., 1983-87; pres. R.L. Ferrante & Co., Inc., N.Y.C., 1987—. Author: (with others) Inside Public Relations, 1987; contbr. articles to profl. jours. Lt. (j.g.) USN, 1958-60. Recipient George Washington medal Freedom Found., 1959, N.Y. Urban Coalition citation, 1972. Mem. Pub. Rels. Soc. Am. (mgmt. com. Counselors Acad. 1985-87, citation 1991). Home: 992 S Pine Creek Rd Fairfield CT 06430-6553 Office: R L Ferrante & Co Inc 122 E 42nd St New York NY 10168

FERRARA, BERNADETTE MARY, computer graphic designer; b. N.Y.C., May 30, 1955; d. Norman E. and Doris (Farago) Moore. Student, Fashion Inst. Tech., 1973-78, Parsons Sch. Design, 1978-82. Chartist McCall Pattern Co., N.Y.C., 1976, mech. artist, 1976-79; art dir. Parklane Hosiery, New Hyde Park, N.Y., 1979-80; freelance artist N.Y.C., 1980-81; computer illustrator Medicus Intercom/B&B, N.Y.C., 1981-82, studio mgr., asst. advt. dir., 1982-83; pres. Ferrara Advt. & Design, N.Y.C., 1983—, computer graphic designer, 1990—; gymnastic coach YMCA, YWCA, pvt. clubs, The Door, YM-HA, N.Y.C., 1981—. Mem. The One Club, NYMUG. Home: 139 E 12th St 2B New York NY 10003 Studio: Ste 1314 1133 Broadway New York NY 10010

FERRARA, LAWRENCE, pianist, music educator, author; b. N.Y.C., May 16, 1949; s. Jerrold Ferrara and Nancy Coscia; m. Kathryn Evans, June 30, 1974; children: Lawrence, Elissa. BA, Montclair State Coll., Upper Montclair, N.J., 1971; MM, Manhattan Sch. Music, N.Y.C., 1973; PhD, NYU, 1978. Instr. Union Coll., Cranford, N.J.; prof. music, dir. doctoral studies dept. music NYU, N.Y.C., 1979—; editor-in-chief Excelsior Music Pubrs., N.Y.C., 1990—. Author: Keyboard Harmony and Improvisation, 1986, Philosophy and Music Analysis, 1991; contbr. articles to profl. jours.; appeared as pianist on ABC TV, BBC, Eng., Cable Network TV, numerous radio stas. Yale U. fellow, 1972, Presdl. fellow, 1985; Fed. grantee for rsch. in Performing Arts Medicine, 1988. Mem. Sinfonia, N.Y. Musicians Club, Pi Kappa Lambda, Phi Delta Kappa. Office: NYU Rm 777 35 W 4th St New York NY 10003

FERRARA, THOMAS CHARLES, market research firm executive; b. N.Y.C., Feb. 26, 1951; s. Charles Thomas and Caroline (Puchalski) R.; m. Frances Palo, Dec. 18, 1982; 1 child, Alexandra. BS in Acctg., St. John's U., Jamaica, N.Y., 1973, MBA in Exec. Mgmt. and Operational Rsch., 1978. Data processing mgr. Shenandoal Foods Corp., Harrisonburg, Va., 1973-76, corp. mgr., 1976-78, pres., chief exec. officer, 1978-85; pres. Mortgage Fin. Corp., Chantilly, Va., 1985-88; pvt. practice cons. Washington, 1988-90; pres., chief exec. officer ICC Corp., Owings Mills, Md., 1990—. Contbr. articles to indsl. jours. Vol. St. Mark's Roman Cath. Ch., Vienna, Va., 1986—. Republican. Roman Catholic. Home: 10816 Melanie Ct Oakton VA 22124 Office: ICC Corp 11419 Cronridge Dr Ste # 1 Owings Mills MD 21117-0629

FERRARI, JOSEPH RICHARD, psychologist, educator, researcher; b. Bklyn., July 23, 1956; s. Clemente and Rose Ferrari; m. Sharon M. Ferrari. BA, St. Francis Coll., Bklyn., 1978; MS, SUNY, Cortland, 1981; MA, Adelphi U., 1985, PhD, 1989. Instr. psychology and sociology Elizabeth Seton Coll., Yonkers, N.Y., 1980-83; asst. prof. Mohawk Valley Community Coll., Utica, N.Y., 1985-88; vis. asst. prof. CUNY, 1989-90; asst. prof., coord. psychology Cazenovia (N.Y.) Coll., 1990—. Office: Cazenovia Coll Ctr for Life Studies Cazenovia NY 13035

FERRARI, RICHARD HAROLD, bank executive, educator; b. Suffern, N.Y., Dec. 5, 1956; s. Harold John and Marie Rose (Ferretti) F.; m. June 11, 1988. BA and MS in Edn., Oneonta (N.Y.) State U., 1979; MA, Columbia U., N.Y.C., 1981; MBA, Iona Coll., 1988; diploma in commercial lending, Am. Inst. Banking, 1984, diploma in bank mgmt., 1987. Asst. store mgr. Marty's Sporting Ctr., Nanuet, N.Y., 1973-79; substitute tchr. Clarkstown Cen. Sch. Dist., West Nyack, N.Y., 1979-81; from mgmt. trainee to asst. v.p. and comml. lender Bank of N.Y., Nanuet, 1981—; prof. Am. Inst. Banking, New City, N.Y., 1983—, pres., 1985-89; bd. dirs., state com. rep. Am. Inst. Banking, Rockland County, 1986—; lectr. CPA continuing edn. program Rockland Community Coll., 1990—; lectr. bus. adminstrn. Dominican Coll., Blauvelt, N.Y., 1991. Contbr. articles to profl. jours. Mem. Rockland County Assn., West Nyack, 1988—, Rockland County United Way, New City, 1989—; mem. team Rockland County Amateur Softball Assn. N.Y. State Regents scholar, 1975; Paul Harris fellow Rotary Internat., 1988; recipient Outstanding Svc. award Rockland County United Way, 1989. Mem. Rockland County Bankers Assn. (v.p.), Nyacks C. of C. (bd. dirs. 1984-85), West Nyack Rotary, South Orangetown Rotary, Kappa Delta Pi. Office: Bank of NY 250 S Middletown Rd Nanuet NY 10954-3395

FERRARO, GERALDINE ANNE, lawyer, former congresswoman; b. Newburgh, N.Y., Aug. 26, 1935; d. Dominick and Antonetta L. (Corrieri) F.; m. John Zaccaro, 1960; children: Donna, John, Laura. B.A., Marymount Manhattan Coll., 1956, hon. degree, 1982; J.D., Fordham U., 1960; postgrad., N.Y. U. Law Sch., 1978, hon. degree, 1984; hon. degree, Hunter Coll., 1985, Plattsburgh Coll., 1985, Coll. Boca Raton, 1989, Va. State U., 1989, Muhlenberg Coll., 1990, Briarcliffe Coll. for Bus., 1990, Potsdam Coll., 1991. Bar: N.Y. 1961, U.S. Supreme Ct. 1978. Pvt. practice, N.Y.C., 1961-74; asst. dist. atty. Queens County, N.Y., 1974-78; chief spl. victims bur., 1977-78; mem. 96th-98th Congresses from 9th N.Y. Dist.; sec. House Democratic Caucus; first woman vice presdl. nominee on Democratic ticket, 1984; fellow Harvard Inst. of Politics, Cambridge, Mass., 1988. Author: Ferraro, My Story, 1985. Chmn. Dem. Platform Com., 1984; bd. dirs. N.Y. Easter Seal Soc.; Dem. candidate U.S. Senate, 1992. Mem. Queens County Bar Assn., Queens County Women's Bar Assn. (past pres.), Nat. Dem. Inst. for Internat. Affairs (bd. dirs.), Coun. Fgn. Rels., Internat. Inst. Women's Polit. Leadership (former pres.). Roman Catholic. Office: 218 Lafayette St New York NY 10012-4021

FERREIRA, KENNETH ROY, small business owner, engineer; b. New Bedford, Mass., June 4, 1950; s. Edward and Tillie (Roderick) F.; m. Elizabeth Jorge Ferreira, Apr. 17, 1971; children: Kimberly Ann, Kelly Lynn and Kristen Joy (triplets). BS in Engring., U. Mass., 1972, MBA, 1985. Registered profl. engr., Mass., registered profl. land surveyor, Mass. Land surveyor GHR Engring. Corp., New Bedford, 1970-78; office mgr. Hayward Bonyton & Williams Corp., Taunton, Mass., 1978-82; co-founder, chief exec. officer Olde Boston Land Survey Co. Inc., New Bedford, 1983—; chmn. Wareham (Mass.) Zoning Bd. of Appeals, 1983-91. Eucharistic minister St. Patrick's Roman Cath. Ch., Wareham, 1986—. Fellow ACSM (surveyor gen. 101 Club New Eng. chpt. 1985); mem. Nat. Soc. Profl. Engrs., Am. Congress on Surveying and Mapping, Mass. Assn. Surveyors and Engrs., Mass. Fedn. Planners Bds., Prince Henry Soc. Mass. (pres. 1990-91, pilot 1989), St. Vincent de Paul Soc., New Bedford C. of C. (bd. dirs. 1990-91). Democrat. Office: Olde Boston Land Survey Co Inc 172 William St New Bedford MA 02740-6022

FERRELL, SONJA DENISE, claims examiner; b. Balt., Mar. 26, 1951; d. Chester Hopes and Josephine (Alston) Wortham; m. James Nimie Lawson, June 14, 1969 (wid. Feb. 1971); m. Marion Antonio Ferrell, Nov. 24, 1979 (separated Nov. 1983); children: Melissa, Dexter, Dante, Antoine, Aaron. Student, Am. Tng. Svc., 1977-78. Telephone operator C&P Telphone Co., Balt., 1969-70; carry out asst. mgr. Durant's Carryout, Balt., 1972-78; cashier Food-A-Rama Supermarket, Balt., 1977-78; claims examiner Blue Cross Blue Shield, Owings Mills, Md., 1978—. Author: (poetry collection) Remember This, 1990, others. Mem. Internat. Soc. Poets. Democrat. Apostolic. Home: 6734 Windsor Mill Rd Baltimore MD 21207-4332 Office: Blue Cross Blue Shield Md 11455 Mill Run Cir Owings Mills MD 21117-4212

FERRELLI, CYNTHIA SUSAN, podiatrist; b. Buffalo, Dec. 19, 1962; d. Remo Peter and Lorraine Marie (Drzewiecki) F. BA in Biology, Canisius Coll., 1985; D Podiatric Medicine, Ohio Coll. Podiatric Medicine, 1989. Podiatrist Snyder, N.Y., 1989—. Mem. Am. Podiatric Med. Assn. (assoc.), Am. Podiatric Med. Postgrad. Assn. (sec., parliamentarian 1989—). Home: 28 Hillsboro Dr Orchard Park NY 14127-3411

FERREN, ANN SPEIDEL, university official, education educator; b. Iowa City, Dec. 4, 1939; d. Thomas Dennis and Edna Dorothy (Warweg) Speidel; m. John Maxwell Ferren, Sept. 4, 1961 (div. 1984); children: Andrew John, Peter Maxwell. AB, Radcliffe Coll., 1961; MA in Teaching, Harvard U., 1962; EdD, Boston U., 1971. Tchr. Deerfield (Ill.) High Sch., 1962-64; assoc. dean Am. U. Coll. Arts and Sci., Washington, 1980-85, assoc. prof. edn., 1985—, assoc. dean faculties, 1985-89, dir. gen. edn., 1987—, asst. provost, 1989—; faculty mem. Nat. Humanities Faculty, Atlanta, 1978-84; trainer cons. D.C. Pub. Schs., Washington, 1976-83. Author: (manual) Improving Instruction through Supervision, 1981; contbr. articles to profl. jours. Named Washington Educator of Yr. Phi Delta Kappa, 1989, Outstanding Freshman Advocate Ctr. for Study of Freshman Yr. Experience, 1990. Mem. Assn. for Gen. and Liberal Studies (exec. coun. 1988-91). Democrat. Roman Catholic. Office: Am U 4400 Massachusetts Ave NW Washington DC 20016-8001

FERRERI, NICHOLAS RAYMOND, immunologist, educator, scientist; b. N.Y.C., May 1, 1956; s. Rosario and Grace Elaine (Palazzo) F.;m. Nancy Angela Gentile, Nov. 4, 1983; 1 child, Nicholas Roy. BA, Case Western Res. U., 1978; PhD, N.Y. Med. Coll., 1984. Postdoctoral fellow Scripps Clinic and Rsch. Found., LaJolla, Calif., 1984-87; assoc. rsch. scientist Yale U. Sch. Medicine, New Haven, 1987-90; asst. prof. pharmacology N.Y. Med. Coll., Valhalla, 1990—. Contbr. articles to profl. jours. Rsch. Starter grantee Pharm. Mfrs. Assn., 1990-92. Mem. AAAS, Am. Assn. Immunologists, Internat. Soc. Immunopharmacology. Roman Catholic. Home: 202 Stanley Rd Hamden CT 06514 Office: NY Med Coll Dept Pharmacology Valhalla NY 10595

FERRERI, VITO RICHARD, lawyer; b. Phila., Feb. 17, 1949; s. Vito and Lucrecia (Poleo) F.; 1 child, Michelle Lee. BA, U. Pitts., 1970; JD, Rutgers U., 1973; postgrad. Nat. Coll. Advocacy, 1976. Bar: N.J. 1973, U.S. Dist. Ct. N.J. 1973, U.S. Supreme Ct. 1977, U.S. Ct. Appeals (3d cir.) 1978. Ptnr., Moss, Thatcher, Moss, McNeill & Ferreri, Runnemede, N.J., 1972-86, Ferreri & Wood, 1986—; arbitrator Am. Arbitration Assn., Somerset, N.J., 1980—, adv. bd., 1985—; prosecutor Voorhees Twp., 1973-75, Washington Twp., 1973-75, Mantua Twp., 1975-79, Berlin Borough, 1979-82; spl. investigating prosecutor Washington Twp., 1986; pub. defender Voorhees Twp., 1989; judge Voorhess Twp. Mcpl. Ct., 1989-91, Barrington Borough Mcpl. Ct., 1990—. Trustee St. Andrew the Apostle Roman Cath. Ch., 1987-89; mem. Camden County Rep. Exec. Com. Named One of Outstanding Young Men of Am. 1981-84. Mem. Camden County Bar Assn., Assn. Trial Lawyers Am. Office: Ferreri & Wood PC 1000 White Horse Rd Ste 402 Voorhees NJ 08043

FERRI, EVERETT LOUIS, JR., university official; b. Tampa, Fla., Apr. 12, 1945; s. Everett L. and Henrietta (Ferretti) F.; m. Suzanne Durand, Feb. 14, 1988. Postgrad., Columbia U., 1968, Ohio State U., 1969, Temple U., 1973, U. Mich., 1977, U. Pa., 1992—. Indsl. engr. USAF Advanced Logistics Systems Ctr., Wright-Patterson AFB, Ohio, 1968-70; mgr. programs Am. Medicorp Inc., Bala Cynwyd, Pa., 1970-73; sr. mgmt. analyst Hosp. of U. Pa., Phila., 1976-78; prin. E.L. Ferri-Health Facilities Planning, Phila., 1978-80; v.p. Health Facilities Design Inc., Phila., 1978-80; planning coord. Hahnemann U., Phila., 1973-76, asst. v.p. materials/facilities mgmt., 1980—; chmn. Built-Rite Constrn. Program, Phila., 1985—; dir. Phila. Area Labor Mgmt. Com., 1986—; bd. dirs. Cen. Phila. Devel. Corp., 1990—. Bd. dirs. Programs for Exceptional People, 1989—; mem. bldg. com. United Way of Phila., 1990—. Recipient Gov.'s Labor-Mgmt. Cooperation award State of Pa., 1988, Vol. Recognition awrd Emergency Aid of Pa., 1991. Mem. Am. Coll. Healthcare Execs., Assn. Phys. Plant Adminstrs., Soc. Coll. and Univ. Planners, Internat. Dacilities Mgmt. Assn. Office: Hahnemann U Broad & Vine Sts Philadelphia PA 19102

FERRIGNO, THOMAS HOWARD, chemical consultant, researcher; b. Newark, Dec. 3, 1925; s. Thomas Anthony and Rosa Martha (Haase) F.; m. Hilda M. Adams, July 5, 1947; children: Melody, Heidi. BS in Chemistry, Seton Hall U., 1951. Rsch. supr. for minerals and chems. Philipp Corp., Menlo Park, N.J., 1955-63; asst. tech. dir. United Sierra, Trenton, N.J., 1963-67; rsch. supr. plastics div. Tenneco, Flemington, N.J., 1967-70; cons. Improde, Trenton, 1971—. Author: Rigid Plastics Foams, 1963, rev. edit., 1967; contbr. numerous articles to profl. jours., chpts. to books including prin. chpt. in Handbook of Fillers for Plastics, 1987. Sgt. AUS, 1943-46, ETO. Fellow Am. Inst. Chemists; mem. Soc. Plastics Industry, Soc. Plastics Engrs., N.Y. Rubber Group. Republican. Office: Improde 29 Clover Hill Cir Trenton NJ 08638-1305

FERRIS, FREDERICK JOSEPH, gerontologist, social worker; b. Troy, N.Y., June 2, 1920; s. John and Amelia (Deeb) F.; m. Ellen J. Walsh, June 12, 1965. BA cum laude, SUNY, Albany, 1942; MS, Columbia U., 1949, DSW, 1968. Head social studies dept. Heatly High Sch., Green Island, N.Y., 1946-47; sec. info. svc. Greater N.Y. Fund, N.Y.C., 1949-51; exec. sec. N. Met. div. United Community Svcs., Boston, 1951-53, mem. rsch. div. com., 1953-57; dir. community orgn., asst. prof. Boston Coll. Sch. Social Work, 1953-57; dean, prof. Nat. Cath. Sch. Social Svc., Cath. U. Am., Washington, 1960-69; with AARP-Nat. Ret. Tchrs. Assn., Washington, coord. White House Conf. on Aging, 1970-72; dir. planning and rsch. dept. and adminstr. Andrus Found., 1970-86; adv. assoc. prof. Fordham U. Sch. Social Svc., 1957-60; lectr. Adelphi U., Rutgers U., 1959-60; social planning cons. Am. Found. for Blind, 1958-59; proposal reviewer NSF; cons. Inst. Community Studies, United Way Am., 1970, Psychiat. Inst. Found.; del. White House Conf. on Aging, 1971, resource person, 1981; tech. rev. panel Nat. Coun. on Aging; mem. commn. on svcs. to aging Archdiocese of Washington, 1971-76; vice chmn. Joint Legis. Com., Boston, 1954-57. Mem. editorial bd. Jour. Applied Gerontology; book reviewer Social Thought. Mem. exec. com. Nat. Vol. Orgns. for Ind. Living for the Aging, 1972-74, 77-82; mem. commn. on aging Nat. Conf. Cath. Charities, 1972—, chmn., 1978-84; bd. dirs. Social Svc. Exch., Boston, 1955-57, Child Welfare League Am., 1966-70, Cath. Internat. Union Social Svc., 1967-72, Christ Child Soc. Washington, 1967-73; treas., bd. dirs. Nat. Conf. Cath. Charities, 1971-74; bd. dirs. Associated Cath. Charities, Archdiocese of Washington, 1976-83; chmn. Washington com. 13th Internat. Conf. Schs. Social Work, 1965-66; active Montgomery County Commn. on Aging, 1987—, 1st vice chmn., 1988—, mem. exec. com., pub. policy com., planning com., nominating com., chmn. econ. security com., 1988-90; mem. Am. Task force for Lebanon. Capt. U.S. Army, 1942-46, maj. Res. Recipient Lasker Doctoral fellowship Columbia U., 1957-58, Pres.'s Centennial medal Cath. U. of Am., 1988. Mem. Nat. Assn. Social Workers (chpt. treas., 1956-57, task force on svcs.to aging 1973-75), Nat. Ret. Tchrs. Assn., Am. Assn. Ret. Persons, Mass. Conf. Social Work (dir., chmn. nominating com. 1956-57), Alumni Assn. Columbia U. Sch. Social Work (chpt. chmn. 1954-55, dir. 1956-59), United Community Funds and Councils Am. (nat. adv. com. health and welfare services 1955-57, council planning execs. 1957-59), Nat. Assn. Hearing and Speech Agy. (nat. tng. adv. com. 1963-70), Acad. Cert. Social Workers, Council Social Work Edn. (deans adv. com. fed. welfare agys. 1962-64, 66-68; ho. of dels. 1977-86), So. Gerontol. Soc. (dir. 1981-89—), Am. Soc. on Aging, Assn. Gerontology in Higher Edn. (com. interorganizational relations, program com.), Gerontol. Soc., John Carroll Soc., Internat. Club Washington. Home: 5101 River Rd Bethesda MD 20816-1512

FERRIS, GARY WILLIAM, university administrator; b. White Plains, N.Y., Dec. 14, 1957; s. Herbert Elmer and Lorraine Isabel (Fischer) F.; children: Jillian Lena, Kimberly Victoria. Student, Boston U., 1980-87; AA, Niagara U., 1989, BA in English, 1990. Head of distbn. Alron Ltd., White Plains, N.Y., 1978-80; editor Drum Corps News, Boston, 1980; media rels. coord. Boston U., 1980-85, rsch. asst., 1985-87, devel. rsch. officer, 1987, asst. dir. rsch., 1987; coord. rsch. & grants Niagara U., Niagara Falls, N.Y., 1987-91; asst. dir. corp. rels. Case Western Res. U., Cleve., 1991; rsch. officer U. Buffalo, N.Y., 1991—; pres. The Ferris Co., Olcott Beach, N.Y., 1988—; music adjudicator Performing Arts Cons., Short Hills, N.J., 1989—; coord. model libr. Am. Prospect Rsch. Assn. Conf., 1989. Editor, pub. (directory) Western N.Y. Media Directory, 1988, '90; editor Boston U. Media Guide Book, 1984. Dir. Niagara U. Band, Niagara Falls, 1988-91; citizens adv. com. Newfane Cen. Sch. Dist., 1989—; mem. ad hoc com. on revenue enhancement Sch. Dist. City Niagara Falls, 1989-90, Van Horn Restoration Com. Newfane Hist. Soc., 1990—. Mem. Nat. Soc. Fund Raising Execs., Am. Prospect Rsch. Assn., New Eng. Devel. Rsch. Assn., Soc. for Comml. Archaeology, Great Lakes United, Masons, Delta Epsilon Sigma. Democrat. Presbyterian. Home: 243 Washburn St Lockport NY 14094-4534 Office: U Buffalo Found PO Box 590 Buffalo NY 14231-0590

FERRIS, HENRY D., JR., veterinarian; b. Bklyn., Mar. 30, 1949; s. Henry D. and Iva (Brooker) F.; m. Deborah Burke, June 23, 1973; children: Marc H., Melissa A. BS in Animal Sci., Pa. State U., 1971; VMD, U. Pa., 1974. Staff vet. Maple Hills Vet. Hosp., Wescosville, Pa., 1974-75, Monmouth Animal Hosp., Little Silver, N.J., 1975-80; ptnr. Little Silver (N.J.) Animal Hosp., 1980-82; owner, dir. Middletown (N.J.) Animal Hosp., 1982—; vet. adv. Middletown (N.J.) Police Canine Corps, 1985-88; ptnr., pres. Monmouth County Vet. Emergency Svc., Middletown, 1986-89; vet. mem. Monmouth County Rabies Task Force, Monmouth County, 1990—. Mem. Am. Vet. Med. Assn., N.Y. Acad. Sci., Met. Vet. Med. Assn. Republican. Episcopalian. Office: Middletown Animal Hosp 1330 Hwy 35 Holmdel NJ 07733-1031

FERRIS, PETER GERARD, mutual fund manager; b. Beverly, Mass., Aug. 7, 1956; s. Joseph Thomas and Elizabeth (Fallon) F.; m. Gail Ann Murray, June 11, 1983; 1 child, Carol Ann Constance. BSBA, Salem State Coll., 1978. CPA, Mass. Sr. auditor dept. state Commonwealth of Mass., Boston, 1979-81; mgr. Coopers and Lybrand, Boston, 1981-89, Fidelity Investments, Boston, 1989—. Mem. AICPA, Mass. Soc. CPAs, Investment Co. Inst.

FERRIS, PETER SIMON, JR., contractor; b. Utica, N.Y., Nov. 16, 1929; s. Peter Simon and Helen (Dickson) F.; m. Josephine Carino, June 28, 1952 (div. 1971); 1 child, Peter III; m. Diane Serour, July 6, 1985. Grad. high sch., Utica. Carpenter Utica Drop Forge & Tool, Yorkville, N.Y., 1954-64; ptnr. FerMarc Millwork, Utica, 1964-67; owner, contractor Ferris Constrn., Old Forge, N.Y., 1967—. Bd. dirs. Arts Guild, Inc., Old Forge, 1969-79, pres., 1979-80; mem. Webb (N.Y.) Planning Bd., 1978—, chmn., 1988—. Sgt. U.S. Army, 1948-53. Mem. Am. Legion, KC. Republican. Roman Catholic. Office: Ferris Constrn PO Box 509 Old Forge NY 13420-0509

FERRIS, THEODORE VINCENT, chemical engineer, consulting technologist; b. Rochester, N.Y., Apr. 26, 1919; s. Theodore Clodoveo and Lucille T. (Pucci) F.; m. Doris Donaghue, June 26, 1943; children: William, Donald, Jean, Peter, Kathleen. BSChemE, MIT, 1941, MS in Chem. Engring. Practice, 1942. Registered profl. engr., Mass. Process engr. Allied Chem. Corp., Buffalo, 1942; devel. engr. GE Plastics, Pittsfield, Mass., 1943-44; process engr. Aspinook Corp., Lawrence, Mass., 1946-48; chief engr. Dehydrating Process Co., Boston, 1949-54; project engr., cons. Monsanto Co., Springfield, Mass., 1954-85; adj. prof. mech. engring. Western New England Coll., Springfield, 1986; cons. Ferris Tech. Svcs., Longmeadow, Mass., 1985—. Contbr. articles to profl. jours. Coach Little League,

Longmeadow, 1955-65; cubmaster Boy Scouts Am., Longmeadow, 1955-65; co-author, mem. Bldg. Code Com., Longmeadow, 1955-56; chmn. Regional MIT Ednl. Coun., 1987—. Lt. USN Ordnance, 1944-46. Mem. Am. Inst. Chem. Engrs. (chmn. west Mass. sect. 1958), Assn. Cons. Chemists and Chem. Engrs., MIT Club of Conn. Valley (treas. 1987—). Roman Catholic. Home and Office: 58 Clairmont St Longmeadow MA 01106-1002

FERRO, DAVID NEWTON, entomology educator; b. San Bernardino, Calif., Sept. 26, 1946; s. Richard B. Ferro and Arlene (Mitchell) Horton; m. Margaret Alice Staneer (div. 1984); m. Leonne Merritt Every, Oct. 15, 1989; children: Amanda, Richard. BA, San Jose (Calif.) State U., 1969; MS, Wash. State U., 1973, PhD, 1975. Lectr. Lincoln (New Zealand) Coll., 1975-77; prof. U. Mass., Amherst, 1977—. Editor: New Zealand Insect Pests, 1976; editor 3 books; contbr. numerous articles to profl. jours. Mem. Entomol. Soc. Am. (Disting. Achievement award 1989), Potato Assn. Am., Sigma Xi. Office: U Mass Dept Entomology Amherst MA 01607

FERRUCCI, JEANNE SMITH, reading specialist educator; b. Newark, Feb. 3, 1940; d. Joseph Charles and Marie Bernice (Hagan) Smith; m. Louis Ferrucci; 1 child, Katherine. BA, Newark State Coll., 1961; MA, Seton Hall U., 1968. Cert. elem. tchr. Elem. tchr. Irvington Pub. Schs., Irvington, N.J., 1961-67; reading specialist Irvington Pub. Schs., Irvington, 1968—; coord. Ptnrs. in Learning-Union Ave. Schs., Irvington, 1988-89; train the trainer, N.J. Principals and Suprs. Assn. Urban Schs. Instructional Leadership Proj., Princeton, N.J., 1987-89; assoc. chair Reading is Fundamental Com., Irvington, 1978; mem. speaker's cadre for dropout prevention Nat. Found. for Improvement of Edn., 1991. Contbr. articles to profl. jours. Treas., bd. dirs. Hunterdon Adult Literacy Program, 1991. Recipient N.J. Outreach grant Nat. Found. for Improvement of Edn., Washington, 1988, Gov.'s grant award N.J. Dept. Edn., 1988, A For Kids Disseminator grant award, 1992-93. Mem. Internat. Reading Assn., N.J. Edn. Assn., Essex Co. Edn. Assn., Irvington Edn. Assn. (sec. 1963-68). Roman Catholic. Home: 56 Circle Dr Hampton NJ 08827-9753 Office: Union Ave Sch 427 Union Ave Irvington NJ 07111-2811

FERRY, JOAN EVANS, school counselor; b. Summit, N.J., Aug. 20, 1941; d. John Stiger and Margaret Darling (Evans) F. BS, U. Pa., 1964; EdM, Temple U., 1967; postgrad., Villanova U., 1981. Cert. elem. sch. tchr., elem. sch. counselor. Indsl. photographer Bucksco Mfg. Co., Inc., Quakertown, Pa., 1958-59; math. and German tutor St. Lawrence U., Canton, N.Y., 1959-61; research asst. U. Pa., Phila., 1963; tchr. elem. sch. Pennridge Schs., Perkasie, Pa., 1964-74, 75-77, elem. sch. counselor, 1981—; pvt. practice counselor, real estate partnership Perkasie, 1981—; tutor math., German, St. Lawrence U., Canton, N.Y., 1959-61; supervisory tchr. East Stroudsburg U., Pennridge Schs., 1971-74; research asst. U. Pa., Phila., 1963; mem. acad. coms. for Pennridge Schs.; adj. faculty Bucks County Community Coll., 1983—; instr. Am. Inst. Banking, 1982—; notary pub., 1986—; mcpl. auditor, sec. bd. auditors, 1984-90, mcpl. auditor 1990—, chmn. bd. auditors 1990—; cons. in field. Author (with others) Life-Time Sports for the College Student: A Behavioral Objective Approach, 1971, 3d rev. edit. 1978, Elementary Social Studies as a Learning System, 1976. Vol. elem. sch. counselor Perkasie, 1979-81; mem. Hilltown Civic Assn., 1965-70; exec. com. chairperson Hilltown Parent Tchr. Orgn., 1965-73; mem., soloist Good Shepherd Episcop. Ch. Choir, Hilltown, 1964-77; mem., steering com. Perkasie Sch., 1989—. NSF grantee, Washington, 1972-73, Philanthropic Edn. Orgn. grantee, Doylestown, Pa., 1982; recipient Judith Netzky Meml. Fellowship award B'nai B'rith, Phila., 1979, World Decoration of Excellence Medallion, 1989, Statesman's award, 1989; Durning scholar Delta Delta Delta, Arlington, Tex., 1981, Am. Mgmt. Assns. scholar, N.Y.C., 1982, Statesman's award World Inst. Achievement, 1989, Internat. Cultural Diploma of Honor, 1989, Achievement award Women's Inner Circle, 1990, Commemorative Medal of Honor, 1990, Internat. Order of Merit, 1990, Woman of Yr. award, 1990, Golden Acad. award for Lifetime Achievement, 1991, Personality of Yr. award, 1991, silver Shield of Valor, 1992; named to Internat. Tennis Hall of Fame, to 2000 Notable Am. Women Hall of Fame, 1989, Community Leaders of Am. Hall of Fame, 1990, Internat. Book of Honor Hall of Fame, 1990, Most Admired Woman of Decade, 1992. Fellow Internat. Biog. Assn.; mem. AAUW, NEA, NAFE, World Inst. Achievement, Pa. State Edn. Assn. (polit. action com. for edn., chair Pennridge Schs. 1986—, del. leadership conf. 1987, 89), Pennridge Edn. Assn. (faculty rep 1986-88, exec. council 1986—, negotiations resource com. 1987-89, 91—, steering com. Perkasie Sch. 1989—), Am. Inst. Banking (chairperson 1987), U.S. Tennis Assn. (hon. life), Pa. and Middle States Tennis Assn. (hon. life), U.S. Profl. Tennis Registry, Mid. States Profl. Tennis Registry, Women's Internat. Tennis Assn., Nat. Ski Patrol System, Pa. Elected Women's Assn., Bucks County Assn. of Twp. Ofcls., Pa. Sch. Counselors Assn., Pa. Assn. Notaries, Am. Soc. Notaries, Internat. Fedn. of Univ. Women, Internat. Platform Assn., Am. Biog. Inst. Rsch. Assn., (rsch. bd. advisors, bd. govs. 1989—), World Inst. Achievement, Shawnee-at-Highpoint Racquet Club, Pennridge Community Rep. Club (recording sec. 1986-91, publicity chmn. 1991-92, Pen care chmn. 1992—), Mediterranean Club, Nockamixon Boat Club, Peace Valley Yacht Club, Highpoint Racquet Club, Kappa Delta Pi. Episcopalian. Clubs: Mediterranean, Nockamixon Boat, Peace Valley Yacht, Highpoint Racquet. Home: 834 Rickert Rd Perkasie PA 18944-2661 Office: Pennridge Schs 601 N 7th St Perkasie PA 18944-1599

FERSTANDIG, LOUIS LLOYD, chemicals executive; b. N.Y.C., Apr. 26, 1924; s. Jacob and Anne (Berger) F.; m. Elaine Bernstein, Aug. 31, 1946; children: Russell, Richard, Gail. BS, U. Ill., 1945; PhD, Cornell U., 1949. Rsch. assoc. Chevron Rsch., Richmond, Calif., 1950-64; rsch. dir. Halocarbon Products Corp., River Edge, N.J., 1964-70, tech. dir., 1970-77, v.p., tech. dir., 1977—. Contbr. chpts. to books and articles to profl. jours.; patentee in field. Sgt. USAF, 1944-46. Office: Halocarbon Products Corp 887 Kinderkamack Rd River Edge NJ 07661-2307

FESSLER, ANN HELENE, artist, photography educator; b. Toledo, Oct. 2, 1949; d. Clifford Manum and Hazel Rose (Grove) F. BA in Art, Ohio State U., 1971; MA in Media Studies, Webster Coll., 1975; MFA in Photography, U. Ariz., 1981. Faculty Webster Coll., St. Louis, 1975-79; vis. artist Tyler Sch. Art, Phila., 1981-82; prof. Md. Inst., Coll. Art, Balt., 1982—; artist in residence Derbyshire (Eng.) Coll. Higher Edn., 1987, Visual Studies Workshop, Rochester, N.Y., 1989, Glasgow (Scotland) Sch. Art, 1990, 91; bd. dirs. Mus. for Contemporary Arts, 1990—; artist, bd. dirs. Md. Art Place, Balt., 1985-87, artist adv. com., 1983-85; panelist, site visitor Md. State Arts Coun., 1989—. Author: (artists' book) Guide to Coloring Hair, 1982, First Aid for the Wounded, 1987, Water Safety, 1989, Art History Lesson, 1991, Genetics Lesson, 1992. Md. State Arts Coun. fellow, 1985, 88, 92, Nat. Endowment for the Arts fellow, 1989; Art Matters, Inc. grantee, 1990. Office: Md Inst Coll Art 1300 W Mt Royal Ave Baltimore MD 21217-4134

FETCHKO, PETER J., museum administrator; b. Yonkers, N.Y., July 3, 1943; m. Francoise Fetchko, Nov. 16, 1968; children: Nicolas, Sebastien. B.A., Westminster Coll., 1965; M.A., George Washington U., U. Paris, Sorbonne, 1972. Curatorial asst. Peabody Mus., Salem, Mass., 1968-70, asst. curator ethnology, 1970-71, curator ethnology, 1975-77, asst. dir., 1977-80, acting dir., 1980, dir., 1980—. Bd. dirs. Japan Soc. Boston; mem. Salem Redevel. Authority, Salm Hosp. Corp. Mem. Mass. Hist. Soc., Club of Odd Volumes, Colonial Soc. Boston, Am. Assn. Museums, New Eng. Museums Assn., Pacific Arts Assn., Tattoo Club Japan, Mass. Hist. Soc., Salem Hosp. Corp., Marine Soc. at Salem, Am. Ceramic Circle. Home and Office: Peabody Mus Salem E India Sq Salem MA 01970-3783

FETNER, GERALD LAWRENCE, university administrator, consultant; b. N.Y.C., Feb. 7, 1945; s. Nathan and Betty (Abowitz) F.; m. Leslee Siegel, July 2, 1970; children: Jennifer, Geoffrey. BA, Queens Coll., 1966, MA, 1968; PhD, Brown U., Providence, 1973. Program officer Nat. Endowment for Humanities, Washington, 1973-75; from asst. dir. to staff dir. ABA, Chgo., 1975-81; dir. found. rels. U. Chgo., 1981-86, Columbia U., N.Y.C., 1986—; instr. Queens Coll., N.Y.C., 1966-68, R.I. Coll., Providence, 1971-73, Salve Regina Coll., Newport, R.I., 1970-72, Brown U., Providence, 1969-72, New Sch. Social Rsch., N.Y.C., 1988, Columbia U., N.Y.C., 1988; panelist Nat. Endowment for Humanities, Washington, 1987; cons. WBEZ Pub. Radio, Chgo., 1980-81, Ill. Humanities Coun., Chgo., 1982-83, Mars Hill, Alexandria, Va., 1989—, N.Y.C. Partnership, 1989, WTVS Pub. TV, Detroit, 1991. Author Ordered Liberty, 1983. Mem. Coun. Support Advancement Edn. Office: Columbia Univ PO Box 400 New York NY 10027-0400

FETSCHER, PAUL GEORGE WILLIAM, commercial real estate corporation executive; b. Bklyn., Dec. 21, 1945; s. William Paul Albert and Marion Beatrice (Darragh) F. BS in CE, The Citadel, 1967. Owner/operator The Waterwheel Resort, Summerville, S.C., 1968; civil engr. Raymond Internat., N.Y.C., 1968-69; real estate rep. Fotomat Corp., LaJolla, Calif., 1969-70; real estate broker Newmark & Co., N.Y.C., 1970-71; v.p. Cushman & Wakefield, N.Y.C., 1971-80; pres. Great Am. Brokerage, N.Y.C., 1981--; bd. dirs. Protel Communications; pub. speaker Internat. Coun. Shopping Ctrs.; guest lectr. NYU, Adelphi U.; instr. The Learning Annex, N.Y.C. Contbr. articles to various publs.; guest columnist for Nation's Restaurant News. Vol. Games for the Disabled Spl. Olympics, Nassau County, N.Y., 1986-89; bd. dirs. Vanderbilt YMCA. Holds record running time from Providence to Boston. Competitor in over 220 marathons; number of races run exceeds 1,300; 1st American to run a marathon in USSR, 1982, East Germany, 1990; Nat. Champion 50km run. Mem. Internat. Coun. Shopping Ctrs., Real Estate Bd. of N.Y., Southwest Conn. Comml. and Investment Coun. (v.p. 1973-89), Nat. Bd. of Realtors, Nat. Assn. Real Estate Bds. (cert. comml. investment mem.). Home: 183 Maxine Ct West Hempstead NY 11552-2652 Office: Gt Am Brokerage 405 Lexington Ave The Chrysler Bldg-37th Fl New York NY 10174

FETTEROLF, DONALD EDWARD, physician, consultant; b. Scranton, Pa., Apr. 26, 1953; s. Donald James and Louise Ann (Pedrick) F.; m. Vicki Lynne Cochran. BA in Chemistry and Biochemistry, U. Pa., 1975, MD, 1979; MBA, U. Pitts., 1991. Diplomate Am. Bd. Internal Medicine, Nat. Bd. Med. Examiners, Am. Bd. Quality Assurance and Utilization Rev. Physicians. Intern and resident in internal medicine Hosp. U. Health Ctr. of Pitts., Presbyn. U. Hosp., 1979-82, fellow in occupational/environ. medicine, 1982-83; pvt. practice Pitts., 1982-88; pres., chmn. Allegheny Intermed, Ltd., Pitts., 1988—, St. Clair Hosp. LCO, Inc., Pitts., 1987—; chmn. med. dir. Alpha Health Network, Pitts., 1990—; dir. data chmn. Buy Right Coun. S.W. Pa., Pitts., 1988—; mem. staff Canonsburg (Pa.) Gen. Hosp., 1982—, West Allegheny Hosp., Oakdale, Pa., 1985-86; bd. dirs. Lifecare Health Svcs., Inc., Allegheny Medcare; emergency room physician Suburban Gen. Hosp., Pitts., 1981-82; house physician St. Clair Meml. Hosp., Pitts., 1981-82. Contbr. articles to profl. jours. Fellow Am. Coll. Utilization Rev. Physicians; mem. AMA, Pa. Med. Soc., Am. Coll. Physician Execs., Allegheny County Med. Soc. (mem. patient rels. com. 1986-88, chmn., 1988), Mensa. Home: RR 5 Box 1 Mc Donald PA 15057-9735 Office: Allegheny Intermed 1050 Bower Hill Profl Office Bldg Ste 202 Pittsburgh PA 15243

FETTEROLL, EUGENE CARL, JR., human resources professional; b. Hartford, Conn., Mar. 8, 1935; s. Eugene Carl and Gladys Marion (Crilley) F.; m. Barbara Ann Meeker, June 15, 1957; children: Eugene Carl III, Douglas Alan, Steven Joseph, Gary Michael. BA, U. Conn., 1957; MEd, Suffolk U., 1973. Supt. cumstomer svc., mgr. personnel svcs., dir. tng. Boston Gas Co., 1957-76; dir. Ea. Enterprises, Boston, 1977-81; dir. Associated Industries of Mass., Boston, 1981-87, v.p. human resources, 1987-89; pres. Fetteroll Assocs., Medfield, Mass., 1989—; bd. dirs. GOAL/QPC, Methuen, Mass., 1990—. Editor: Trainer's Resource, 1989. Vol. United Way, Mass. and R.I., 1965—; vice chmn. bd. trustees Medfield (Mass.) Pub. Libr., 1966-70; chmn. Sch. Land Acquisition Com., Medfield, 1963-65; bd. dirs. GOAL/QPC, Methuen, Mass. Mem. Am. Soc. Tng. and Devel. (pres. Mass. chpt. 1972-73, R.I. chpt. 1981-82, mem. nat. ethics com. 1985—, Torch award 1979), Mass. Assn. Adult and Continuing Edn., Mass. Arms Collectors, Medfield Hist. Soc. Republican. Roman Catholic. Home and Office: Fetteroll Assocs 18 Pound St Medfield MA 02052

FETTWEIS, YVONNE CACHÉ, archivist; b. L.A., Nov. 28, 1935; d. Boyd Eugene and Georgette Louisa (Tilmann) Adams; m. Rolland Phillip Fettweis, July 22, 1967; children: Maurice C.B. II, Michele-Yvonne (Mrs. Paul E. Cenzer); m. Maurice Lee Caché, Jan. 8, 1955 (div. 1962). BA, Wagner Coll., 1954; postgrad, Am. U., 1973, Bentley Coll., 1981. Legal sec., asst. Judge, Davis, Stern, Orfinger & Tindall, Daytona Beach, Fla., 1961-66; head rec. sect., bd. dirs. 1st Ch. Christ Scientist, Boston, 1969-71, rsch. assoc., 1971-72, adminstrv. archivist, 1972-78, sr. assoc. archivist, 1979-84, records adminstr., 1984-91, div. mgr. records mgmt./orgnl. archives, 1991-92, div. mgr. ch. history, 1992—. Exec. sec. Volusia County Goldwater campaign, Daytona Beach, 1964. Mem. Soc. Am. Archivists (editor The Archival Spirit), Automated Records and Techniques Task Force, Am. Mgmt. Assn., Orgn. Am. Historians, Ctr. for Study of Presidency, New Eng. Archivists, Assn. Records Mgrs. and Adminstrs. (bd. dirs. 1983—), Assn. Coll. and Rsch. Librs., Bay State Hist. League, Order Ea. Star, Order Rainbow (bd. dirs. 1972-77). Republican. Christian Scientist. Home: 42 Edgell Dr Framingham MA 01701-3181 Office: 1st Ch Christian Sci 175 Huntington Ave # 143A Boston MA 02115-3187

FEUER, CY, motion picture and theatrical producer, director; b. N.Y.C., Jan. 15, 1911; s. Herman and Ann (Abrams) F.; m. Posy Greenberg, Jan. 20, 1945; children—Robert, Jed. Student, Inst. Mus. Art Julliard Found., 1928-32. Head music dept. Republic Pictures, 1938-42, 45-47; partner Feuer and Martin Prodns., N.Y.C., 1947—; mgr.-dir. San Francisco Civic Light Opera Assn., 1975-80; Pres. The League of Am. Theatres and Producers, 1989—. Theatrical prodns. include Where's Charley, 1948, Guys and Dolls, 1950, Can-Can, 1953, The Boy Friend, 1954, Silk Stockings, 1955, Whoop-Up, 1958, How To Succeed in Business Without Really Trying, 1961 (Pulitzer prize for drama), Little Me, 1962, Skyscraper, 1965, Walking Happy, 1966, The Goodbye People, 1968, The Act, 1977; producer: motion pictures Cabaret, 1972 (winner 8 Acad. awards), Piaf, 1975, Chorus Line, 1985. Office: Feuer and Martin 630 Park Ave New York NY 10021-6544

FEUER, ROBERT CHARLES, environmental biologist; b. N.Y.C., Feb. 23, 1936; s. Harry and Sara Gertrude (Bender) F.; m. Joan F. Colton, Mar. 29, 1969. B.S., Cornell U., 1956; M.S., Tulane U., 1958; Ph.D., U. Utah, 1966. Instr. Purdue U., Hammond, Ind., 1963-64; asst. prof. Phila. Coll. Pharmacy and Sci., 1964-74; sr. environ. analyst McCormick Taylor Assocs., Phila., 1975-76; sr. ecologist Louis Berger Assocs., East Orange, N.J., 1978; herpetologist LGL Environ. Research Assocs., Muscatine, Iowa, 1980; cons. in environ. biology, Broomall, Pa., 1977—; columnist The Beachcomber, Ship Bottom, N.J., 1964—. Contbr. articles to profl. jours. Editor Bull. of Phila. Herpetological Soc., 1969-84, Phila. Grotto Digest, 1967-72. Chmn. Environ. Adv. Bd., Marple Twp., Pa., 1971-73, 84-89; flotilla comdr. U.S. Coast Guard Aux., Media, Pa., 1977. NSF fellow, 1960-61; Sigma Xi grantee, 1959-60; Karl P. Schmidt Meml. Fund grantee, 1960. Fellow Herpetologists League; mem. Am. Soc. Ichthyologists and Herpetologists, Soc. for Study Amphibians and Reptiles, Phila. Herpetol. Soc. (editor 1969-84, pres. 1991—), Nat. Speleological Soc., Sigma Xi. Avocations: fishing; boating; reading; horticulture. Address: 102 S New Ardmore Ave Broomall PA 19008

FEUERBERG, MARK STANLEY, financial services company executive; b. N.Y.C., June 4, 1942; s. Benjamin H. and Rose (Wattenberg) F.; m. Marlise J. Rockey; children: Jacqueline, Gillian. AAS, Staten Island Community Coll., 1961; BS, CCNY, 1964. CLU, chartered financial cons. Field underwriter John Hancock Mutual Life Ins. Co., Woodside, N.Y., 1964-66; mktg. mgr. Chesebrough-Pond's Inc., Greenwich, Conn., 1966-73, Cooper Labs, Inc., Bedford Hills, N.Y., 1973-74; mdse. mgr. Plough, Inc., Memphis, 1974-75; mktg. mgr. Nylon Net Co., Inc., Memphis, 1975-77; premium dir. Lever Bros. Co., N.Y.C., 1977-81; dir. sales Shaw Creations, Inc., N.Y.C., 1981-83; sr. ptnr. The Benefits Assocs., N.Y.C., 1987--; dist. mgr. The Equitable Cos., N.Y.C., 1983--. Author: (chpt.) LUTC: Basic Life Insurance, 1987; contbr. articles to profl. jours. Mem. town council of Monroe, Conn., 1974, econ. devel. commnr., 1973. Recipient National Quality awards Life Ins. Mktg. and Rsch. Assn., 1985-92. Fellow Life Underwriter Training Coun. (course moderator 1985-89); mem. Nat. Assn. Life Underwriters (Nat. Sales Achievement awards 1986-89), Nat. Assn. Chartered Life Underwriters and Chartered Fin. Cons., Premium Msde. Club N.Y. (pres. 1981-82, exec. v.p. 1980-81, bd. dirs. 1978-84), Million Dollar Round Table. Republican. Jewish. Home: 11241 72d Rd Forest Hills NY 11375-4659 Office: The Equitable Cos 2 Penn Plz Ste 1600 New York NY 10121

FEUERBURGH, JOSEPH, psychologist; b. Bronx, N.Y., Aug. 4, 1908; s. Nathan and Regina Rose (Frischer) F.; m. Sophie Empel, Dec. 25, 1941. BA, L.I. U., 1931; MA, NYU, 1936, PhD, 1954. Psychologist Bur. Child Guidance Spl. Project, N.Y.C., 1934-35, Adult Guidance Service, N.Y.C., 1935-38, Spl. Sessions Ct. Probation Bur., N.Y.C., 1938-42; clin. psychologist VA, 1946, USPHS Hosps., Ellis Island, N.Y., 1946-51, S.I., 1951-75; pvt. practice psychology, N.Y.C., 1955-69, 73-78, 81—; inst. psychology dept. Bklyn. Coll., evenings 1947-48; cons. psychologist Am. Tech. Tng. Ctrs., N.K.C., 1968; lectr. 1981—. Chmn. speakers com. Ind. Dem. Assn., Bronx, 1933. Served to capt. Adj. Gen. Dept. AUS, 1942-46. Mem. APA, N.Y. State Psychol. Assn., Am. Group Psychotherapy Assn. (assoc.), N.Y. Soc. Clin. Psychologists, N.Y. Acad. Scis. Jewish. Address: 15 Stuyvesant Oval New York NY 10009

FEUERMAN, CAROL JEANNE, artist; b. Hartford, Conn., Sept. 21, 1945; d. Milton and Doris Sue Ackerman; m. Richard Feuerman (div.); children: Lauren, Craig, Sari. Student, Hofstra U., 1963, Temple U., 1964; cert. of art, Sch. Visual Arts, 1967. Pres. Feuerman Studios, Mineola, N.Y., 1967—; mem. learning through the arts program Solomon R. Guggenheim Mus.; active various workshops in field. One-person shows include Gallerie Ninety-Nine, Bay Harbor Islands, Fla., 1982, 84, 86, 87, Sindin Gallery, N.Y.C., 1982, OK Harris West, Arz., 1982, RVS Fine Arts, Southampton, N.Y., 1986, Queens Mus., Flushing, N.Y., 1987, Ann Jaffe Gallery, Bay Harbor Islands, 1989, Gallery Henoch, N.Y.C., 1989, 92, Espace Quasar, Paris, 1990, Laura Larkin Gallery, Del Mar, Calif., 1990, Arnesen Gallery, Vail, Colo., 1990, Jaffe Baker Gallery, Boca Raton, Fla., 1991, Hokin Gallery, Palm Beach, Fla., 1992, others, also exhibited in numerous group shows, pvt. collections. Recipient Betty Parsons Sculpture award 1970, Charles D. Murphy Sculpture award 1981, Amelia Peabody award for sculpture 1982, 1st prize U.S. Nat. Fine Arts Competition 1984. Mem. Internat. Assn. Art-UNESCO, Nat. Assn. Women Artists, Internat. Sculpture Ctr., Am. Assn. Mus., Orgn. Ind. Artists. Home: 200 Mercer St Apt 1F New York NY 10012-1510 Studio: Feuerman Studios 371 Sagamore Ave Mineola NY 11501

FEULNER, EDWIN JOHN, JR., research foundation executive; b. Chgo., Aug. 12, 1941; s. Edwin John and Helen J. (Franzen) F.; m. Linda C. Leventhal, Mar. 8, 1969; children: Edwin John III, Emily V. BS, Regis Coll., 1963; MBA, U. Pa., 1964; PhD, U. Edinburgh, 1981; hon. degree, Nichols Coll., 1981, Universidad Francisco Marroquin, Guatemala City, 1982, Hanyang U., Seoul, Korea, 1982, Bellevue Coll., Nebr., 1987, Gonzaga U., 1992. Richard Weaver fellow London Sch. Econs., 1965; pub. affairs fellow Hoover Instn., 1965-67; confidential asst. to sec. def. Melvin Laird, 1969-70; adminstrv. asst. to U.S. Congressman Philip M. Crane, 1970-74; exec. dir. Rep. Study Com., Ho. of Reps., 1974-77; pres. Heritage Found., Washington, 1977—; chmn. Inst. European Def. and Strategic Studies, 1977—; mem. U.S. adv. com. pub. diplomacy USIA, 1982-92, chmn., 1982-91; vice chmn. bd. dirs. Fed. Capital Bank, N.A.; mem. nat. adv. bd. Ctr. for Edn. and Rsch. in Free Enterprise, Tex. A&M U.; disting. fellow Mobilization Concepts, Devel. Ctr. Nat. Def. U., 1983-89; mem. Pres.'s Commn. on White House Fellows, 1981-83; mem. Carlucci Commn. on Fgn. Assistance, 1983; pub. del. UN 2d Spl. Session on Disarmament, 1982; White House cons. domestic policy, 1987. Author: Congress and the New International Economic Order, 1976, Looking Back, 1981, Conservatives Stalk the House, 1983; contbr. articles to profl. jours., chpts. to books. Trustee Lehrman Inst., Am. Coun. on Germany, Sarah Scaife Found., Regis U., 1991—, St. James Sch., 1990—; vice chmn. bd. Aequus Inst.; chmn. bd. Intercollegiate Studies Inst.; vice chmn. bd. dirs. Roe Found.; bd. govs., mem. exec. com. Coun. Nat. Policy, Found. Francisco Marroquin, St. James Sch., Regis U.; chmn. Citizens for Am. Edn. Found.; mem. coun. acad. advisors Bryce Harlow Found. Recipient Disting. Alumni award Regis Coll., 1985, Superior Pub. Svc. award Dept. of Navy, 1987, Presdl. Citizens medal, 1989; named Free Enterprise Man of Yr., Tex. A&M U., 1985. Mem. Am. Econs. Assn., Am. Polit. Sci. Assn., Internat. Inst. Strategic Studies, U.S. Strategies Inst., Inst. d'Etudes Politiques, Phila. Soc. (treas. 1964-79, pres. 1982-83), Mont Pelerin Soc. (treas.), G.K. Chesterton Soc. (chmn. internat. com. 1989-92), Belle Haven Country Club (Alexandria, Va.), Union League (N.Y.C.), Met. Club (Washington), Reform Club (London), Bohemian Club (San Francisco), Knights of Malta, Alpha Kappa Psi. Republican. Roman Catholic. Office: The Heritage Found 214 Massachusetts Ave NE Washington DC 20002-4958

FEWELL, CHARLES KENNETH, JR., lawyer; b. Washington, Jan. 26, 1943; s. Charles Kenneth and Mary Amanda (Hunt) F.; m. Christine Baker Huff, Jan. 23, 1971; children: Anna Catherine, John Maenner. BA magna cum laude, Dartmouth Coll., 1964; JD, Harvard U., 1967. Bar: N.Y. 1968, U.S. Dist. Ct. (so. dist.) N.Y. 1970, U.S. Ct. Appeals (2d cir.) 1975. Law clk. U.S. Dist. Ct. (so. dist.) N.Y., N.Y.C., 1967-68; assoc. White & Case, N.Y.C., 1968-75; v.p., counsel Nat. Westminster Bank, N.Y.C., 1975-80; sr. counsel, sr. v.p. Deutsche Bank AG, N.Y.C., 1980—; v.p., sec., gen. counsel Deutsche Bank Fin., Inc., N.Y.C., 1986—; arbitrator Am. Arbitration Assn., N.Y.C., 1980—. Mem. ABA (banking com. 1980—), Inst. Internat. Bankers (legis. and regulatory com. 1988—), German Am. Law Assn. (dir. 1982—), N.Y. State Bar Assn. (internat. banking and securities markets 1987—), Phi Beta Kappa. Office: Deutsche Bank AG 31 W 52d St New York NY 10019-3001

FEY, CURT F., financial analyst, investment manager; b. St. Gallen, Switzerland; came to U.S., 1950; s. Felix N. M. and Irma (Stein) F.; m. Marion Harris, June 16, 1962; 1 child, Carl Felix. BS with honors, Haverford Coll., 1954; PhD, U. Pa., 1960; MBA, U. Rochester, 1975. Chartered financial analyst. Staff scientist Rsch. Labs. Gen. Dynamics, Rochester, N.Y., 1960-61; adv. scientist IBM, Bethesda, Md., 1961-65; prof. Am. U., Washington, 1963-65; mem. corp. staff Tex. Instruments, Dallas, 1965-70; prof. North Tex. State U., Denton, 1969-70; prin. scientist Xerox Corp., Rochester, N.Y., 1970-84, El Segundo, Calif., 1984-87, Rochester, 1987—. Author (with others): VLSI Handbook, 1989; contbr. articles to profl. jours; patentee in field. Mem. IEEE (exec. com. 1968-72), Computer Soc. IEEE, Systems Sci., Man and Cybernetics Soc. of IEEE (exec. com. 1974-76), Assn. for Investment Mgmt. and Rsch. Home: PO Box 22853 Rochester NY 14692-2853 Office: Xerox Corp Wilson Ctr for Tech 800 Phillips Rd Webster NY 14580-9791

FIACCO, NORENE PFAUTZ, English language educator. BA in English, SUNY, Potsdam, 1965; MEd in English, U. Miss., 1971; EdS, Appalachian State U., 1990. Tchr. English Norwood (N.Y.)-Norfolk Cen. Sch., 1965-67, Belpre (Ohio) High Sch., 1967-68; supr. of tchrs., dir. ednl. svc. ctr. Prentis County Bd. Edn., Booneville, Miss., 1968-70; tchr. English, dept. chmn. Corinth (Miss.) High Sch., 1971-73; faculty, reading specialist, staff devel. chmn. Paducah (Ky.) City Schs., 1973-83; asst. prof. English Ea. Nazarene Coll., Quincy, Mass., 1983-89, assoc. prof. English, 1990—; faculty English dept. Paducah Community Coll., 1980-83; tech. writing cons. Hygienetics, Inc., Boston, 1985-88; elected Mass. state coord. Coll. Devel. Edn. Programs, 1987—; presenter papers and workshops various ednl. devel. confs. Office: Ea Nazarene Coll 23 E Elm Ave Quincy MA 02170-2999

FIALKOW, STEVEN, accountant; b. Bklyn., July 24, 1943; s. Irving and Ida (Berglass) F. m. Arlene Michele Klein, Oct. 19, 1963 (div. Oct. 1985); children: Cheri Ann, Laura Beth; m. Frances Theresa Miller, Apr. 15, 1986. BBA, CUNY, 1965, MBA, 1970. CPA, N.Y. Profl. staff Price Waterhouse & Co., N.Y.C., 1965-69; asst. treas., contr. Anglo Am. Corp., N.Y.C., 1969-72; treas., contr. Video Playbacks, Inc., N.Y.C., 1972-75; adminstrv. mgr. Kenneth Leventhal & Co., N.Y.C., 1975-77; instr. N.Y. Inst. Tech., N.Y.C., 1975-79; ptnr. Herzig, Blumenfeld & Fialkow, CPAs, N.Y.C., 1979-81; assoc. dir. nat. acctg. and audit profl. edn. Touche Ross & Co., N.Y.C., 1981-83; mng. ptnr. Steven Fialkow & Co., CPAs, Coram, N.Y., El Paso, Tex., 1983—; cons. Banis Securities Corps. N.Y.; chmn. fin. com. CCHOA, U.S. Virgin Islands, St. Croix. Bd. dirs. outreach program YMCA, L.I., N.Y. Mem. AICPA, N.Y. State Soc. CPAs, Mensa, Masons. Republican. Home: 368 Woodland Ct Coram NY 11727-3657 Office: Fialkow Bldg 976 Skyline Dr Coram NY 11727-3670 also: Ste 48 4800 N Stanton El Paso TX 79902

FICA, JUAN, endocrinologist; b. Santiago, Chile, Jan. 18, 1949; came to U.S., 1974, naturalized, 1977; s. Moises and Olga (Cisternas) F.; B.S., U. Chile, 1971, M.D., 1974; m. Margarita Martinez, Dec. 30, 1971; children—Michelle, Pamela, Vanessa Olga, Kristina Margarita. Intern, Booth Meml. Hosp., NYU, N.Y.C., 1974-75, resident, 1975-76; sr. resident Wellesley Hosp., U. Toronto (Ont., Can.), 1976-77; fellow in endocrinology U. Conn., Farmington, 1977-79; clin. instr., 1979—; practice medicine special-

izing in endocrinology, Waterbury, Conn., 1979—; endocrine cons. Bristol (Conn.) Hosp., 1979—; founder, dir. Diabetes Ctr. Bd. dirs. Watertown (Conn.) Pub. Nurses Assn. Am. Field Service Internat. scholar, 1965. Diplomate Am. Bd. Internal Medicine, Am. Bd. Endocrinology and Metabolism. Mem. AMA, New Haven County Med. Soc., Waterbury Med. Soc., Conn. Endocrine Soc., Am. Diabetes Assn., N.Y. Acad. Scis., Assn. Insulin Pump Therapists, Met. Opera Assn. Lodge: Rotary. Home: PO Box 1102 159 Northridge Dr Middlebury CT 06762-1420 Office: 171 Grandview Ave Waterbury CT 06708-2517

FICARRA, BERNARD JOSEPH, retired surgeon, legal medicine and bioethics consultant; b. N.Y.C., Jan. 1, 1914; s. Humphrey and Rose Marie (D'Ambra) F.; B.A. magna cum laude, St. Francis Coll., 1935, Sc.B., 1936; M.D., Georgetown U., 1939; Sc.D., U. Steubenville, 1950; LL.D., St. Francis Coll., N.Y.; Ph.D., Minerva U., Milan, Italy, 1960; m. Jean Alice Augustine, Aug. 31, 1967; 1 son, Bernard Thaddeus. Diplomate Am. Bd. Surgery. Surg. intern Kings County Hosp. Med. Center, Bklyn., 1939-41, resident pathology, 1941-42, resident surgery, 1942-44; fellow surgery Lahey Clinic Found., Boston, 1946-48; practice medicine specializing in surgery, N.Y.C., 1948-60, Greenvale, N.Y., 1953-70; mem. vis. surg. staffs Kings County, St. Peters, Holy Family, St. Mary's hosps.; dir. surg. research Ficarra Found., Inc., 1949-69; prof. physiology St. Francis Coll., 1948-51; prof. research physiology St. John's U. Postgrad. Sch., 1951-61; professorial research asso. L.I. U., Postgrad. Sch., 1961-73; dir. Somerset Enterprises, Ltd., Doric Corp. Trustee L.I. Ednl. TV Council Inc., Sta. WLIW; pres. Cath. Acad. Scis. U.S.A. Fellow Am. Coll. Gastroenterology (com. for legal matters), Am. Coll. Legal Medicine (edn. com.), Am. Coll. Angiology (achievement honor award 1964-65); mem. AMA, N.Y. State Med. Soc., N.Y. Acad. Medicine, N.Y. Soc. Med Jurisprudence, Acad. Templars (Bologna, Italy), Greenvale C. of C., Lahey Clinic Alumni Assn. (mem. council), Cath. Acad. Scis. (U.S.)(pres.), Alpha Omega Alpha, Pi Alpha, Phi Chi. Lodges: Lions (honors: Knight of Malta, Knight Cmdr. of St. Gregory the Great), Equestrian Order of the Holy Sepulchre of Jerusalem (sect. rep. southeastern lieutenancy Washington, So. Md., No. Va., Knight Grand Cross). Author: Diagnostic Synopsis of Acute Surgical Abdomen, 1950; Emergency Surgery, 1953; Thyroid and Parathyroid Diseases, 1958; Surgical and Allied Malpractice, 1968; Medicolegal Handbook, 1983; Medicolegal Examination Evaluation and Report, 1986, Abortion Analyzed, 1989, Feudal Chateau, 1990, Church on The Hill, 1990; mem. adv. bd. jour. Med. Malpractice Prevention; mem. editorial bd. Jour. Contemporary Health Law and Policy; contbr. 250 articles to profl. jours. Named to Alumni Hall of Fame St. Francis Preparatory Sch., N.Y., 1990; received Silver Palm of Jerusalem, His Beatitude Archbishop Michele Sabbah, Latin Patriarch of Jerusalem, 1988 Office: PO Box 9611 Washington DC 20016

FICCO, DANE PATRICK, medical practice administrator; b. Greensburg, Pa., Oct. 27, 1961; s. James Vincent and Dorothy Elizabeth (Benson) F.; divorced; children: Ryan Patrick, Daniel Martin, Geoffrey Christian. BS in Econs., St. Vincent Coll., 1983; MBA, U. Pitts., 1991. Adminstr. Martin A. Murcek, M.D., Ltd., Greensburg, Pa., 1984—; Cons., pvt. practice, Greensburg, Pa., 1987—. Republican. Roman Catholic. Home: 1624 Mountain Way Ln Monroeville PA 15146-1766 Office: Martin A Murcek MD Ltd 562 Shearer St Ste 1012 Greensburg PA 15601-2746

FICHENBERG, ROBERT GORDON, newspaper editor, consultant; b. Phila., Jan. 1, 1920; s. Samuel Harrison and Katherine (Gordon) F.; m. Ruth Pollard, Sept. 14, 1947; children: Ruth Ann, Kathryn Leigh. B.S., Syracuse U., 1940. City editor Adirondack Daily Enterprise, Saranac Lake, N.Y., 1940-42; reporter, copy editor, asst. city editor Binghamton (N.Y.) Press, 1942-57; mng. editor Knickerbocker News, Albany, N.Y., 1957-66; exec. editor Knickerbocker News, 1966-78; chief Washington bur. Newhouse Newspapers, editor Newhouse News Svc., 1979-91; writer, cons. Nat. Assn. Dist. Attys., Washington, 1991—; bd. dirs. Nat. Press Found. Served to 1st lt. Signal Corps AUS, 1942-46; to capt. U.S. Army, 1951-52. Mem. Am. Soc. Newspaper Editors, N.Y. State Soc. Newspaper Editors (pres.), AP Mng. Editors Assn., White House Corr. Assn., N.Y. State AP Assn. (past pres.), Nat. Press Club, Army and Navy Club, Soc. Prof. Journalists. Clubs: Fed. City, Internat., Gridiron (Washington), Army and Navy of Washington. Home: 1605 Mason Hill Dr Alexandria VA 22307-1930 Office: Nat Dist Attys Assn 99 Canal Center Plz Alexandria VA 22314

FICKIES, ROBERT HOWARD, geologist; b. Bklyn., Mar. 23, 1944; s. Howard T. and Kathryn (Franklin) F.; m. Elaine C. Manna, July 5, 1969; children: Jonathan, Loren. BS, CUNY, 1966, MS, 1969. Cert. profl. geologist, Ga. Lectr. CUNY, Bklyn., 1966-69; engring. geologist Gerard Engring., Jersey City, 1969-70, Tippetts-Abbett-McCarthy & Stratten, N.Y.C., 1970; geologist J.R. Dunn & Assocs., Averill Park, N.Y., 1970-74; mgr., geotech. group Dunn Geosci. Corp., Latham, N.Y., 1974-78; assoc. geologist N.Y. State Geol. Survey, Albany, 1978-86, asst. chief, 1986—; hearing officer Am. Arbitration Assn., Syracuse, N.Y., 1982—; cons. in field. Contbr. articles to profl. jours. Pres. Averill Park and Sand Lake Fire Co., 1983; scoutmaster Boy Scouts Am., Averill Park, 1984-87; sci. adviser N.Y. State Disaster Preparedness Commn., Albany, 1987-91. Grantee U.S. Geol. Survey, 1980-83. Fellow Geol. Soc. Am. (editor 1979-85); mem. ASCE, Assn. Engring. Geologists, Am. Inst. Profl. Geologists, Hendrick Hudson Fish and Game, Masons, Sigma Xi. Home: RR 3 Box 52 Averill Park NY 12018-9507 Office: NY State Geol Survey Rm 3136 CEC Albany NY 12230

FICKS, F. LAWRENCE, communications executive; b. Denver, Apr. 4, 1930; s. Herman and Roselee (Pearl) F.; m. Carlyn Scheff, Sept. 9, 1939 (div. 1970); m. Shola Lewis, Nov. 10, 1979; children: Robin, Georgia, Randi. BS, Pa. State U., 1951, MS, 1952. Commd. 2d lt. U.S. Army, 1953, advanced through grades to capt., 1963; col. USAR, 1963-83, ret., 1983; with Bell Labs and AT&T, various locations, 1970-83; dir. Bellcore, Livingston, N.J., 1984—; sr. engr. Avco, Lawrence, Mass., 1983-85; project mgr., sr. engr. McDonnald, St. Louis, 1985-86; adj. prof. U. Md., Franfurt, Fed. Republic of Germany, 1958-60, Newark (N.J.) Coll. Engring., 1968-75. Contbr. articles to profl. jours. Decorated Legion of Merit. Home: 100 Stone Hill Rd # 11A Springfield NJ 07081-2115 Office: Bellcore 290 W Mt Pleasant Ave Livingston NJ 07039-2747

FIDDLER, BARBARA DILLOW, administrator; b. Decatur, Ill., Sept. 2, 1940; s. N. Eugene and Ruth (Kirchhoff) Dillow; children: John Eugene, Thomas Crawford. BA, U. Vt., 1963. Grad. registrar Troy State U., European div., Wiesbaden, W. Ger., 1977-79; adminstrv. asst. Mt. Mansfield Co. Mktg. Dept., Stowe, Vt., 1980-84; asst. dir. promotions and advt. Rossignol Ski Co., Tennis div., Williston, Vt., 1984-85; project mgr. Birch Hill Devel. Co., Stowe, 1985-86; asst. to dir. of devel. Johnson State Coll., Johnson, Vt., 1986-89; asst. dir. devel. The Trustees of Reservations, Beverly, Mass., 1989-91; adminstr. Epsilon Inc., Burlington, Mass., 1991—; bd. dirs. Robert Alden Ellsworth Trust, Johnson, Vt., 1991—. Bd. dirs. United Way of Lamoille County, Hyde Park, 1988—; mem. Stowe Planning Commn., 1985-87; bd. dirs. chmn. fin. and fundraising com. Johnson Friends of the Arts, 1986-88. Mem. Women in Devel. in Greater Boston, Lamoille Valley C. of C. (bd. dirs.). Republican. Episcopalian. Home: Upper Baird Rd Stowe VT 05672 Office: Epsilon Inc 50 Cambridge St Burlington MA 01803-4606

FIDOTEN, ROBERT EARL, consultant, information and communication educator; b. N.Y.C., Oct. 21, 1927; s. Herman and Martha (Pomerantz) F.; m. Marsha A. Fidoten, Apr. 21, 1948; children: Douglas Sinclair, Eric Bradford. BA, NYU, 1949; BLS, Pratt Inst., 1950; PhD, U. Pitts., 1970. Chief libr. Republic Avaiation Corp., Farmingdale, N.Y., 1956-64; mgr. rsch. and staff svcs. PPG Industries Glass Rsch., Pitts., 1964-71; dir. info. systems PPG Industries Glass Group, Pitts., 1971-89; assoc. prof. Slippery Rock (Pa.) U., 1989—; pres., founder REF Assocs., Pitts., 1989—; project mgr. Digital Magic, Inc., Pitts., 1992—; cons. Vernate Piennitalia SPA, Genoa, Italy, 1985-88, Boussois, S.A., Paris, 1985-88; mem. bd. visitors Slippery Rock U. Coll. of Info., Sci & Bus. Adminstrn., 1988-91. Pres. sch. bd. Plainview-Old Bethpage, N.Y., 1962-64; civil svc. commr. O'Hara Township, Pa., 1979-82; com. mem. Sierra Club Allegheny County, Pitts., 1991. Recipient Presidential citation Am. Ceramic Soc., 1980; named Disting. Alumnus U. Pitt. Sch. Libr. & Info. Sci., 1981. Mem. Am. Soc. for Info. Sci. (pres. Pitts. chpt. 1991-92), Office Systems Rsch. Assn. (pres. 1988-89, v.p. membership com. 1991-92), Internat. Commn. on Glass (chmn. congress 1980). Office: 118 Greyfriar Dr Pittsburgh PA 15215-1110

FIDRYCH, MARIELLEN JOHANNA, association administrator; b. Salem, Mass., Nov. 26, 1958; d. Richard Dunstan and Rosalie Marie (Collette) Higgins; m. Gary Peter Fidrych, May 14, 1983; 1 child, Collette Marie. BA in Sociology, Assumption Coll., 1980; MA in Criminal Justice, U. Lowell, 1990. Exec. asst. Mass. Dept. Correction, Boston, 1980-81, spl. projects coord., 1981-83; dir. treatment Longwood Treatment Ctr., Boston, 1983-85; dir. programs MCI Shirley (Mass.) Prison, 1985-87; dep. dir. Mass. Com. on Criminal Justice, Boston, 1987-90; exec. dir. Mass. Sheriff's Assn., Boston, 1990—; instr. criminal justice Boston U., 1990-91. Mem. Dem. City Com., Peabody, Mass., 1980-83. Mem. Nat. Sheriffs' Assn., Am. Jail Assn., Am. Correctional Assn., Greater Salem Jaycees. Democrat. Roman Catholic. Office: Mass Sheriffs Assn 200 Nashua St Boston MA 02114-1102

FIEGEL, JOHN LELAND, scientific organization administrator; b. Rochester, Minn., Jan. 8, 1944; s. Leland Gordon Fiegel and Anna Mae (Towey) Terry; m. Sheryl Dekour Ameen, Apr. 17, 1988; children: Leland Joseph, Andrea Elizabeth. BA in Mgmt., Tex. A&M U., 1965; MS in Internat. Affairs, Troy State U., 1977. Commd. 2d lt. USAF, 1965, advanced through grades to lt. col.; dep. dir. planning and requirements Office of Sec. of Def., Washington, 1985-87; ret. USAF, 1987; exec. dir. Assn. for Unmanned Vehicle Systems, Washington, 1988-91, Soc. Environ. Toxicology and Chemistry, Washington, 1990-91, Internat. Dist. Heating and Cooling Assn., Washington, 1992—. Bd. dirs. Washington Concert Opera, 1986-90, coun. mem. Bravo!, 1984—. Mem. Nat. Assn. Execs. Club, Am. Soc. Assn. Execs. (cert.), Greater Washington Soc. Assn. Execs. (com. mem. 1990—). Home: 8005 Spring Rd Cabin John MD 20818-1218 Office: Internat Dist Heating & Cooling Assn Ste 700 1101 Connecticut Ave NW Washington DC 20036

FIEKERS, JEROME FRANCIS, anatomy-neurobiology educator; b. Cambridge, Mass., Nov. 14, 1946; m. Andrea J. Hughes; children: Lauren, Mark, Bryan, Katherine. BS in Pharmacy cum laude, Mass. Coll. Pharmacy, 1970, MS in Pharmacology, 1973; PhD in Pharmacology, U. Conn., Farmington, 1978. Lab. technician Dewey and Almy Chem. div. W.R. Grace Corp., Sommerville, Mass., 1965-69; NIH postdoctoral fellow dept. physiology and biophysics U. Vt. Coll. Medicine, Burlington, 1978-80, rsch. asst. prof. dept. anatomy and neurobiology, 1979-81, asst. prof. dept. anatomy and neurobiology, 1981-87, assoc. prof. dept. anatomy and neurobiology, 1987—; vis. scientist Sandoz Inst. for Med. Rsch., London, 1988-89; co-prin. investigator NSF, 1981-83; prin. investigator Muscular Dystrophy Assn., 1980-81, 84-86, U.S. Army Med. Def. Command, 1985-88, 88-89, NIH, 1989-92. Gillette fellow in biol. scis., 1971-73, Internat. Brain Rsch. Orgn./UNESCO Internat. fellow; recipient ASPET Internat. Travel award; Internat. Brain Rsch. Orgn.-MacArthur scholar in neurosci., 1988-89; NIH rsch. grantee, 1989-92; NIH Small Instrumentation grantee, 1990, Rsch. Adv. Coun. Equipment grantee, 1990; NATO co-grantee, 1981-83, Biomed. Rsch. Support grantee U. Vt., 1985. Mem. Soc. for Neurosci., Am. Soc. for Pharmacology and Exptl. Therapeutics, AAAS, Internat. Brain Rsch. Orgn., N.Y. Acad. Scis., Vt. Chpt. for Neurosci. (treas. 1981-83), Rho Chi. Office: U Vt Coll Medicine Dept Anatomy & Neurobiology Given Med Bldg Rm D-401 Burlington VT 05405

FIEL, DAVID HY, marketing professional, product developer; b. N.Y.C.; s. Max and Ida (Miller) F.; m. Maxine Lucille Stempel; children: Meredith, Lisa. Student, CCNY, 1935-37, Lowry Sch. Tech., 1941-42, U.S. Army Sch. Elec. Engring., Calcutta, India, 1943-44. Designer, cons. Canvas Industries, Inc., N.Y.C., 1946-77; cons. Tohka Madison Mail Order Co., Tokyo, 1978-81; dir. mktg. rsch., purchasing agt. Imperial Enterprises, Inc., N.Y.C., Tokyo, London, 1981—; also bd. dirs. Imperial Enterprises, Inc.; mktg. cons. Fiel "5" Enterprises Ltd., Great Neck, N.Y.; pres. Internat. Shopping Network, N.Y.C., 1990—, The Inst. for Better Vision, N.Y.C., 1990—. Contbg. editor Japanese Overseas Press-Mktg. News; inventor revolving shoe rack; designed and invented the eye muscle exerciser; designer combination carrying bag and roll. Fund raiser Dem. Nat. Party, Alden Manor, N.Y., 1960-75; Temple B'Nai Israel, Alden Manor, 1952-60. With USAF, 1942-45. Mem. Periwinkle Nat. Repertory on Drug Abuse (bd. dirs. 1980—), East End Yacht Club (commodore 1968-74), Lotos Club. Home: 26933G Grand Central Pky Floral Park NY 11005-1200

FIELD, EDWIN MARTIN, public relations executive, writer; b. Bklyn., Nov. 14, 1924; s. Richard Michael and Frances M.F.; m. Selma G. Kreisberg, Apr. 3, 1947; children: Jessica Lynn Cohen, Shelly Irene, Deborah Lynn. BPS, SUNY, N.Y., 1983, MA, 1985. Mgr. Kreisberg Heating Svc., Monticello, N.Y., 1957-60; assoc. editor Fuel Oil News, Bayonne, N.J., 1959-62; pres. Field Assocs., Monticello, N.Y., 1960-89. Author: (books) Oil Burners, 1979, rev. 1984, (tng. manual) A Complete Heating Course, 1978, Successful Fund Raising Dinners, 1980, Tiling for the Professional, 1992, Marketing for the Craftsperson, 1992. Bd. dirs. Mid-Hudson Patterns for Progress, Newburgh, N.Y., 1976-82; mem. Sullivan County Publicity Commn., Monticello, N.Y., 1980—; bd. dirs. Ethebert B. Crawford Pub. Libr., Sullivan County Charter Commn., Ulster-Sullivan Mediation, Inc., 1987—, Nat. Ctr. for Homeopathy, 1992—. Sgt. U.S. Army, 1942-45, ETO, PTO. Mem. Pub. Relations Soc. Am. (accredited). Home and Office: 25 Landfield Ave Monticello NY 12701-1396

FIELD, MICHAEL STANLEY, information services company executive; b. London, Sept. 28, 1940; came to U.S., 1966; s. Stanley Frank Owen and Violet May (Collins) F.; m. Jenny Callen Chitwood, May 27, 1972; children: Shelley Callen, Heather Collins, Michael Randolph. B of Tech. Electrical Engring., U. Loughborough, 1962. Grad. engr. British Aerospace Corp., Luton, England, 1962; systems mgr. IBM (UK) Ltd., London, 1963-66; systems designer IBM Rsch. Ctr., Cambridge, Mass., 1966-68; dir., mgr. Nat. CSS, Wilton, Conn., 1969-74, v.p. data systems, 1974-80; v.p. applied tech. The Dun & Bradstreet Corp., N.Y.C., Conn., 1981-83; mng. dir. Dun & Bradstreet European Bus. Info. Ctr., Harefield, England, 1983-85; group exec. v.p. Dun & Bradstreet Info. Svcs., Murray Hill, N.J., 1989—; corp. v.p. The Dun & Bradstreet Corp., N.Y.C., 1981—. contbr. articles to profl. jours. and mags. Mem. Engring Coun. (charter mem.), British Computer Soc., Inst. Electrical Engrs., Lake Club. Republican. Episcopalian. Home: 73 Turning Mill Ln New Canaan CT 06840-3832 Office: Dun & Bradstreet Corp 299 Park Ave New York NY 10171

FIELD, STEVEN PHILIP, medical educator; b. Newark, Feb. 21, 1951; s. Irving and Florence (Engel) F. BA, Yale U., 1973; MD, NYU, 1977. Diplomate Am. Bd. Internal Medicine, Am. Bd. Gastroenterology. Intern in internal medicine Bellevue Hosp., N.Y.C., 1977-78, resident in internal medicine, 1978-81; instr. in medicine Mt. Sinai Hosp., N.Y.C., 1981-83; instr. in medicine NYU Sch. of Medicine, N.Y.C., 1983—, clin. asst. prof. medicine, 1991—. Contbr. articles to profl. jours. Recipient John Addison Porter Prize Yale U., 1973. Mem. Am. Gastroenterological Assn., N.Y. Acad. of Gastroenterology, N.Y. Soc. for Gastrointestinal Endoscopy (mem. exec. coun. 1991—), Yale Club of Cen. N.J. Office: 245 E 35th St New York NY 10016

FIELD, TED WAYNE, company executive; b. Rochester, Minn., Feb. 7, 1948; s. Max Wayne Field and Phyllis Lorraine (Pesch) Bump; m. Virginia Baverly, Apr. 24, 1980 (div. 1983); m. Karen Kimball, Nov. 25, 1987. BA, U. Minn., 1974. Cert. fund raising exec. Pres. Rembrandt Enterprises Inc., Edina, Minn., 1974-85; dir. March of Dimes Birth Defects Found., White Plains, N.Y., 1985-88, Cystic Fibrosis Found., Bethesda, Md., 1988-89; pres. Footprints Unltd., Inc., Bethesda, 1989—. Dir. Brookmont Civic League, Bethesda, 1989—, Combined Urban Ministries Ctr., Washington, 1991. With U.S. Army, 1969-70, Vietnam. Mem. Nat. Soc. Fund Raising Execs. (found. liaison officer 1991—), Exch. Club Capitol Hill (dir. 1990—). Home: 6424 Broad St Bethesda MD 20816-2608

FIELDER, DOUGLAS STRATTON, physicist, educator; b. Washington, July 22, 1940; s. Albert Green and Kathryn Marie (Welch) F.; m. Dorothy Scott Davis, July 13, 1968; 1 child, William. BS, Va. Mil. Inst., 1962; MS, U. Va., 1964, PhD, 1987. Asst. to full prof., physics SUNY, Oneonta, 1969—. Contbr. articles to profl. jours. Mem. bd. edn. Schenevus Cen. Sch., 1988—, pres., 1989—. Capt. U.S. Army Corps of Engrs., 1967-69. Mem. Schenevus Rotary (v.p. 1988-89, pres. 1989-90). Methodist. Home: RR 1 Box 1038 Maryland NY 12116-9801 Office: SUNY Dept Physics and Astronomy Oneonta NY 13820

FIELDING, STUART, psychopharmacologist; b. Bronx, N.Y., Oct. 31, 1939; s. Harry and Ethel (Weisberg) Feinblatt; m. Maralyn J. Lowy, Aug. 26, 1962; children: Kimberly Ellen, Bradford Scott. BA, Monmouth Coll., 1962; MS, Howard U., 1964; PhD, U. Del., 1968. Mgr. psychopharmacology rsch. Ciba-Geigy Corp., Summit, N.J., 1967-75; assoc. dir. pharmacology Hoechst-Roussel Pharms., Inc., Somerville, N.J., 1975-76, assoc. dir. biol. sci., mgr. pharmacology, 1977-84, dir. pharmacology, 1984-86, dir. biol. rsch., 1987-89; v.p. R & D Interneuron Pharms., Inc., Lexington, Mass., 1989—. Editor: (book) Psychopharmacology of Clonidine, 1981, (book series) Industrial Pharmacology: A Monograph Series, 1974-79, (jour.) Drug Devel. Rsch., 1980—; contbr. articles to profl. publs. Fellow Am. Psychol. Assn.; mem. Am. Chem. Soc., Am. Soc. Pharmacology and Exptl. Therapeutics, Soc. Neurosci. Home: 6 Canal Park Apt 407 Cambridge MA 02141-2212 Office: Interneuron Pharms Inc 99 Hayden Ave Lexington MA 02173-7966

FIELDS, EDWARD, management consultant; b. N.Y.C., Sept. 11, 1945; children: Barry, Lisa. BBA in Econs., CCNY, 1967; MBA in Fin., NYU, 1968. Pres. The Cons. Firm, Inc., Old Bridge, N.J., 1976—; adviser in field; asst. prof. fin. Rider Coll., 1976-80; lectr. Grad. Sch. Bus., Fairleigh Dickinson U., 1977-80; course leader, lectr. Am. Mgmt. Assn.; guest lectr. NYU, Boston U., U. Mass., U. Hartford, Conn. Mem. Am. Mgmt. Assn. Home and Office: The Cons Firm Inc 4 Belaire Ct Old Bridge NJ 08857

FIELDS, STUART HOWARD, employee relations specialist; b. Chgo., Dec. 15, 1943; s. Albert B. and Cecelia (Kessler) F.; m. Birgit Willeke, Dec. 5, 1971; children: Jessica N., Jascha D. BS, UCLA, 1965; MS, U. Calif., Northridge, 1968. Cert. tchr. and instr., Calif. Labor relations specialist Hughes Tool Co., Culver City, Calif., 1970, Dept. of the Navy, Point Mugu, Calif., 1971-76, Pub. Health Svc., Rockville, Md., 1985-86; employee relations specialist Agricl. Rsch. Svc., Hyattsville, Md., 1976-81; labor relations specialist Agricl. Rsch. Svc., 1981-84; cons. Potomac, Md., 1984-85; employee relations specialist Def. Nuclear Agy., Bethesda, Md., 1986-88, Consumer Product Safety Commn., Bethesda, 1988-89, U.S. Dept. Commerce, Washington, 1989—; presdl. classroom instr.; cons. in field. Author: Requirements for Top Positions in Personnel Administration, 1968. Lt. U.S. Army, 1968-70. Mem. Soc. Fed. Labor Relations Profls., Jewish Community Ctr., Mensa. Democrat. Jewish. Home: 9949 Reach Rd Potomac MD 20854-2866 Office: US Dept Commerce Rm 5108 14th St & Constitution Ave NW Washington DC 20230

FIELO, MURIEL BRYANT, space engineer, interior designer; b. Bklyn., Dec. 11, 1921; d. Harry and Minnie (Dick) Bryant; m. Julius Fielo, June 17; 1 child, Michael Kenneth. Student, CCNY, 1938-41, Rutgers U., 1965-69; cert. N.Y. Sch. Interior Design, 1970. Gen. mgr. Fidelity Discount Corp., Irvington, N.J., adv. supr. Lincoln Loan Co., Essex County, N.J., 1941-49; interior designer Alex Fielo Interior Decorators, Newark, 1942-49, prin., 1949-69, owner, 1969—; designer, cons. space engr. MUDGE Interior Design Studios, East Orange, N.J., 1969—. Mem. adv. panel Interior Design Mag, 1977—. Essex County freeholder clk. Bd. Freeholders, 1972-76; commr. East Orange Bus. Devel. Authority, 1977-86; mem. U.S. adv. coun. SBA-Region II, 1980-81; active LWV, 1950-55; organizer, 1st pres. South Orange chpt. Women's Am. ORT, 1952-54, mem. nat. speakers bur., 1952-65, parliamentarian No. N.J. coun., 1955-65; pres. Amity chpt. B'nai B'rith, Newark, 1946-48, v.p. No. N.J. coun., 1948-49, various nat. and state positions, 1948-80; mem. nat. com. on sect. fund raising Nat. Coun. Jewish Women, 1979-81, nat. tour. chmn., 1979-81; trustee community svcs. coun. Oranges and Maplewood, United Way of Essex and West Hudson, 1981-83; bd. dirs. East Orange Central Ave. Mall Assn., 1979-83, chmn. new voter registration drive East Orange 2d Ward, 1955—, entire city, 1969; pres. East Orange Dem. Club, 1957-58, campaign coord. for Dem. mayoral candidate, 1969, calendar coord. Essex County Dem. Party, 1970-76; mem. N.J. Bipartisan Coalition for Women's Appts., 1981—. Named Outstanding Entrepreneur of 1984 N.J. Gov., Outstanding Orgn. Pres. Kean Coll. Profl. Women's Assn., 1985, Wonder Woman of 1986, Bus. Jour. of N.J., One of 8 Women to Watch in 1987 Jersey Woman Mag., 1987; also recipient various awards for civic svc.; named Bus. Person of Yr. East Orange C. of C., 1988. Mem. Internat. Soc. Interior Designers (bd. dir. 1981-85), Nat. Home Fashions League (N.J. membership chmn. N.Y. chpt. 1981-82), Interior Design Soc., N.J. Assn. Women Bus. Owners (state bd. 1979-82), Women Entrepreneurs N.J. (pres. 1981-85, chief exec. officer 1987—), N.J. Home Furnishings Assn. (bd. dirs. 1981-84, 86—), Constrn. Specifications Inst., N.J. Soc. AIA (profl. affiliate), Guild Designer Woodworkers, Women Bus. Ownership Ednl. Coalition (N.J. State pres. 1985-87, chief exec. officer 1987—, mem. steering com. interior designers for licensing in N.Y. 1985—), East Orange C. of C. (bd. dir. 1977—, v.p. 1981-85), Bus. and Profl. Women's Club of Oranges (bd. dir. 1958-66). Jewish. Home and Office: MUDGE Interior Design Studio 185 S Clinton St East Orange NJ 07018-3039

FIERHELLER, GEORGE ALFRED, communications company executive; b. Toronto, Ont., Can., Apr. 26, 1933; s. Harold Parsons and Ruth Hathaway (Bauld) F.; m. Glenna E. Fletcher, Apr. 17, 1957; children—Vicki Elaine, Lori Ann. B.A., U. Toronto, 1955; LL.D., Concordia U. With IBM, Toronto, 1955-58, account mgr., 1962-65, mktg. mgr., 1966-68; founder, pres. Systems Dimensions Ltd., Ottawa, Ont., 1968-79; pres., chief exec. officer Rogers Cable TV Broadcasting Co. Ltd., Vancouver, B.C., Can., 1979-85, Cantel Inc., Toronto, 1985-90; chmn., chief exec. officer Roger Cantel Mobile, Inc., 1990—; bd. dirs. Crownx Inc., Rogers Communications Inc., GBC N.Am. Fund Inc., Norr., Telestat Mobile Inc., Teleglobe Inc., Pacific Telecomm., Inc., Toronto Bd. of Trade. Contbr. articles to profl. jours. Gen. chmn. United Appeal Campaign, Ottawa, 1972; chmn. campaign Carleton U., 1975-77, also chmn. bd. govs., 1977-79; mem. adv. com. Norman Paterson Sch. Internat. Affairs; bd. dirs., v.p. United Way Ottawa, 1975-79; Opera Ottawa, 1970-71; trustee, mem. exec. com. Nat. Arts Ctr., 1973-79; trustee Royal Ottawa Hosp., 1978-79, Vancouver Gen. Hosp. Found., 1981-85; mem. Vancouver Centennial Commn., 1983-84; bd. govs. Simon Fraser U., Vancouver, 1981-84; chmn. United Way Vancouver, 1981; chmn. B.C. Council of 80's, 1980-83; trustee United Way Met. Toronto, chmn. gen. campaign, 1991; vice chmn. Vision 2000. Mem. Can. Info. Processing Soc. (pres. 1970-71), Information Tech. Assn. Can. (vice-chmn.), World Pres. Orgn., Chief Execs. Orgn. (sec.-treas., dir. 1971-73), Can. Assn. Data Processing Svc. Orgns., Assn. Cert. Computer Profls. (founding com.), Can. Ctr. for Philanthropy (bd. dirs. 1987—), Bus. Coun. on Nat. Issues, Cellular Telecommunications Industry Assn. (bd. dirs.). Clubs: Shaughnessy Golf and Country, Vancouver Lawn Tennis, Vancouver, Rideau, Granite, Nat. Ontario, Rosedale Golf. Home: 24 Pearwood Crescent, Don Mills, ON Canada M3B 2C2 Office: York Mills Centre, 10 York Mills Rd E, North York, ON Canada M2P 2C9

FIERMAN, GERALD SHEA, electrical distribution company executive; b. Wilkes-Barre, Pa., Dec. 14, 1924; s. Abe and Mary (Jacobs) F.; A.B. in Liberal Arts, Pa. State U. 1948; m. Bernice Perloff, June 12, 1949; children: Robert Alan, Lawrence David, Daniel Jon. Pres. Shea Realty Corp., Wilkes-Barre, 1959—, Barre Realty Corp., Wilkes-Barre, 1955—, Chase Wholesale Elec. Supply, Stroudsburg, Pa. 1960—, Tomberg Elec. Supply Co., Wilkes-Barre 1954—, ANESCO, Kingston, Pa. 1949—; v.p. L&R Elec. Supply Co., Scranton, Pa., Effco Inc., Scranton. Chmn. United Jewish Campaign, Wilkes-Barre, 1963; pres. Jewish Fed. of Wyoming Valley (Pa.), 1971-74. Served with 82d Airborne Div., AUS, 1942-46. Decorated Purple Heart. Mem. Temple Israel of Wilkes-Barre. Clubs: Westmoreland of Wilkes-Barre, Jockey of Miami, Valley Tennis, Mason, Keystone Consistory. Home: 76 James St Wilkes Barre PA 18704-4730 Office: 517 Pierce St Kingston PA 18704

FIERO, PATRICK, physician; b. Bklyn., May 10, 1954; s. Phillip and Concetta (Amato) F.; m. Rose Passalacqua, Jan. 24, 1976; children: Jared, Jenna, Patrick Jr. BA, NYU, 1976; MD, U. Northeast, Tampico, Mex., 1980. Resident physician Bklyn. (N.Y.) Jewish Hosp., 1980-81, St. Vincent's Med. Ctr. of Richmond, Staten Island, N.Y., 1981-86; attending physician Staten Island Ob-Gyn. Assocs., 1986-91; pvt. practice Staten Island, N.Y., 1991—. Mem. Richmond County Med. Soc., N.Y. State Med. Soc. Republican. Roman Catholic. Office: Patrick Fiero MD 4345 Hylan Blvd Staten Island NY 10312-6501

FIERSTEIN, HARVEY FORBES, playwright, actor; b. Bklyn., June 6, 1954; s. Irving and Jacqueline Harriet (Gilbert) F. Acting debut in Andy

Warhol's Pork, N.Y.C., 1971; tv appearances include In The Shadow of Love, 1991; writing debut In Search of the Cobra Jewels, N.Y.C., 1973; playwright: Freaky Pussy, 1975, Flatbush Tosca, 1976, book for La Cage Aux Folles, 1983 (Tony award for Best Book of a Musical), Spookhouse, 1984, (with Peter Allen and Charles Suppon) Legs Diamond, 1989; playwright and star: The International Stud, part 1 of Torch Song Trilogy, 1978, Fugue in a Nursery, part 2 of Torch Song Trilogy, 1979, Widows and Children First!, part 3 of Torch Song Trilogy, 1979, Torch Song Trilogy debut as a whole, 1981 (Obie award 1982), Broadway debut of Torch Song Trilogy, 1982 (Tony awards for Best Play and Best Actor in a Play, Drama Desk awards for Best Play and Best Actor in a Play, L.A. Critics Circle award, Newsday Playwrighting award, Hull/Warriner award Dramatists Guild, Theatre World award, Dramalogue award), (London debut) Torch Song, 1985 (nominated Oliver award 1985), Safe Sex, 1987; author screenplay and star: Torch Song Trilogy, 1988, HBO Showcase film Tidy Endings, 1988 (Best Dramatic Special award, Best Screenplay for Dramatic Special award Acad. Cable Excellence); actor off-Broadway play The Haunted Host, 1991; appeared in films Garbo Talks, 1984, The Harvest, 1992; guest star appearances (TV) The Simpsons, Cheers, 1992; actor spl. project Am. Film Inst. TV or Not TV; narrator film: The Times of Harvey Milk. Office: care William Morris Agy 1350 Ave of the Americas New York NY 10019-4701

FIEST, DAVID L., sales manager; b. Allentown, Pa., July 3, 1952; s. Arthur L. and Alice M. (Trexler) F.; m. Greta Dawson Wagner, June 3, 1977; children: Erika, Gregory. AB in Geology, Princeton (N.J.) U., 1974; MS in Oceanography, U. Del., 1977. Lab. mgr. Energy Resources Co., Cambridge, Mass., 1977-85; lab. dir. Cambridge Analytical Assocs., Boston, 1983-85; sales rep. Hewlett Packard Co., Andover, Mass., 1985-89; sales mgr. Hewlett Packard Co., Valley Forge, Pa., 1989—. Contbr. articles to profl. jours. Presbyterian. Office: Hewlett Packard Co 2750 Monroe Blvd Valley Forge PA 19482

FIFER, KENNETH, humanities educator; b. N.Y.C., Oct. 6, 1947; s. William and Shirley (Zlatkin) F.; m. Elizabeth Nusbaum, Dec. 26, 1971; 1 child, Benjamin. BA, CCNY, 1968; MA, U. Mich., 1969, PhD, 1971. Chmn. dept. of humanities Allentown Coll., Center Valley, Pa., 1981—; poetry cons. Pa. Dept. Edn., N.J. Dept. Edn., Pa. Coun. on the Arts; dir. honors coun., Allentown Coll., 1990—. Author: Falling Man, 1979; editor: Big Numbers, 1980, Staring At the Word Mexico, 1978, Frog Theory, 1979; contbr. poetry to more than 200 mags. Jewish. Home: 5525 Spring Dr Center Valley PA 18034-9312 Office: Allentown Coll Center Valley PA 18034

FIGLER, MICHAEL HOWARD, psychology educator, researcher; b. Madison, Wis., Mar. 2, 1944; s. Harry Herschel and Ida Edith (Pover) F.; m. Paula Rene Zimbro, Jan. 3, 1981; children: Seth Evan, Sabrina Elena. B.S., U. Wis.-Madison, 1966; M.A., Mich. State U., 1968; Ph.D. in Psychology, 1970. Asst. prof. Earlham Coll., Richmond, Ind., 1970-71; prof. psychology Towson (Md.) State U., 1971—, dir. grad. program in exptl. psychology, 1976—; vis. prof. U. Calif., San Francisco, 1978-79; del. NATO Advanced Study Inst, France, 1980; grant reviewer NSF, 1972—. Manuscript reviewer internat. sci. jours., 1970—; author: Travel Stress Management, 1990; contbr. articles to profl. jours. Grantee NSF, 1971; fellow USPHS, 1966; postgrad. fellow NIMH, 1974. Fellow Internat. Soc. Research Aggression; mem. Am. Psychol. Assn., Animal Behavior Soc., Psychonomic Soc., Internat. Soc. Human Ethology. Am. Men and Women of Sci., Phi Eta Sigma, Phi Kappa Phi, Sigma Xi. Democrat. Jewish. Avocations: travel, reading, bicycling, fishing. Home: 1015 Trickling Brook Rd Cockeysville MD 21030-3120 Office: Towson State U Dept Psychology Towson MD 21204

FIGUEROA, ANTONIO, architect; b. N.Y.C., Mar. 23, 1947; s. Antonio Figueroa and Francisca (Martinez) Dominguez; m. Olga Lugo, June 10, 1967 (div. July 1969); m. Andrea Lisa Fooner, Mar. 2, 1980; children: Sara Elena, Ariel Antonio. BArch, Cooper Union U., 1969; MS in Urban Planning, Columbia U., 1973. Lic. architect, N.Y., Conn. Designer Castro-Blanco, Piscioneri & Assocs., N.Y.C., 1969-71; program developer Aspira of Am., N.Y.C., 1971-72; coord. architect N.Y. State Urban Devel. Corp., N.Y.C., 1972-73; dir. planning Fernando Higueras-Diaz Architect, Madrid, 1973-75; project architect Patricio Sanchez-Camus Architect, N.Y.C., 1975-77; prin. architect Sanchez & Figueroa Architects, N.Y.C., 1977-92; dep. commr. Dept. of Corrections, N.Y.C., 1992—; tchr. Bronx Coun. on the Arts, N.Y.C., 1990—; bd. dirs. Citizens Housing and Planning Coun., N.Y.C., 1991—. Treas. Hostos Community Coll. Coun., N.Y.C., 1982—; trustee Community Svc. Soc., N.Y.C., 1988—. William F. Kinney fellow Columbia U., 1973. Mem. Soc. Spanish Engrs., Planners and Architects (chmn. 1977—). Democrat. Roman Catholic. Office: NYC Dept Corrections 60 Hudson St New York NY 10001

FILEPP, GEORGE EDWARD, public accountant, financial services professional; b. Bklyn., Jan. 31, 1949; s. George and Josephine (Emanuel) F. BS in Acctg., Rutgers U., 1976; postgrad., St. John's U., S.I., N.Y., 1978-80. Lic. pub. acct., cert. tax profl. Auditor Suplee, Clooney & Co., CPAs, Elizabeth, N.J., 1976-77, Bennett, Kielson & Co., CPAs, New Rochelle, N.Y., 1978; pvt. practice Bridgewater, N.J., 1973—. With USAR, 1969-75. Mem. Am. Soc. Notaries, Inst. Mgmt. Accts., Nat. Assn. Tax Practitioners, Nat. Soc. Tax Profls., Nat. Soc. Pub. Accts., Inst. Bus. Appraisers, Inc., Nat. Notary Assn., N.J. Assn. Pub. Accts., Inst. Cert. Fin. Planners, Somerset County C. of C. Office: 15 King Arthurs Ct Bridgewater NJ 08807-2823

FILIPPIDES, GEORGE JOHN, insurance company analyst; b. New Britain, Conn., July 19, 1966; s. John Emmanuel and Calliope (Lambros) F. BS in Math. Edn., U. Conn. Sales assoc. The Gap Stores Inc., Meriden, Conn., 1983-84; foreman constrn. crew Changebridge of Montville (N.J.) Assocs., 1984; mus. guard William Benton Mus. of Art, Storrs, Conn., 1986-87; guitarist, songwriter, mgr. Melrose Angel, Middletown, Conn., 1988—; underwriter The Traveler's Ins. Cos., Hartford, Conn., 1988-89, rating analyst, 1989-90, acct. analyst, 1990—. Patentee in field. Voted as Hartford, Conn.'s #1 Rock Band, 1991, Area #1 Hard Rock Band, 1992, #1 Requested Song at WSAM Radio Sta., 1989. Home: 233 Ridgefield Dr Middletown CT 06457 Office: Travelers Ins Co One Tower Sq Hartford CT 06183

FILIPPINI, CHRISTINE MARIE, counselor; b. Norristown, Pa., Aug. 1, 1957; d. Nicholas John Caramenico and Christine (Dougherty) Stayton; m. Anthony John Filippini, May 26, 1989; 1 child, Anthony. AB, Muhlenberg Coll., 1979; MEd, Millersville (Pa.) U., 1980. Sch. counselor West Perry Sr. High Sch., Elliottsburg, Pa., 1980-84, READS Inc., Levittown, Pa., 1984-87; sch. counselor, coord. teen/parent program Methacton Sch. Dist., Fairview Village, Pa., 1987—; co-chair Montgomery County Teen/Parent Task Force, Norristown, 1991—. Presentor Chester County (Pa.) Intermediate Unit, 1989, March of Dimes Conf., Phila., 1990, Pa. Dept. of Edn., State College, 1991—. Mem. AACD (del. 1990), Pa. Sch. Counselors Assn., Pa. Counseling Assn. (exec. coun. and com.), Pa. Edn. Assn., Methacton Edn. Assn., Montgomery County Counselors Assn. (senator 1989-92), Pa. Counselors Assn. (exec. bd. 1989-92). Office: Methacton Sch Dist Kreible Mill Rd Fairview Village PA 19403

FILLER, RONALD, public defender; b. Passaic, N.J., May 17, 1957; s. Michael and Josephine (Kulka) F. BS, Rider Coll., 1979. Sales mgr. Pinebrook (N.J.) Tire Co., 1980; sales person Allied Stores of N.Y., Inc., Paramus, N.J., 1981; inventory person Automobile Bumpers, Inc., Clifton, N.J., 1981-82; svc. sta. attendant Amerada Hess Corp., Maywood, N.J., 1982; counter worker Harry M. Stevens, Inc., East Rutherford, N.J., 1982; constrn. worker Longo Enterprises, White Plains, N.Y., 1982; sales rep. Nat. Wholesalers, Inc., Garfield, N.J., 1983; stock clerk Sam Goody, Inc., Paramus, 1983-84; atty. Bergen County Ceta, Inc., Hackensack, N.J., 1983—; atty. Dept. Environ. Protection, Trenton, N.J., 1990; pub. defender Bur. of A.T.F., Springfield, Va., 1989—; esquire Nat. Crime Prevention Coun., Washington, 1989. Author: Letter Tray, 1989. Donor Salvation Army, Paterson, N.J., 1983, Vietnam Vets. of Am., Oxnard, Calif., 1989, Humane Soc. of Bergen County, Hasbrouck Hgts., N.J., 1988; attendee Visual Comm. Congress, N.Y.C., 1984; mem. N.J. Rep. State Com., 1985—. Mem. ACLU, Community Assns. Inst., Am. Numismatic Assn., Medic Alert Internat. Found., Student Entertainment Coun. (coord. 1976), Mktg. Club, Theta Chi Frat. Roman Catholic. Home: 60 Garwood Ct N Garfield NJ 07026

FILLINGHAM, PETER J., metallurgical engineer; b. Rochester, N.Y.; s. Frederick O. and Hertha (Hos) F.; m. Patricia Child; children: Michael, David, Lydia. AB, Cornell U., 1948; BME, Rensselaer Poly. Inst., 1953; MSc, N.J. Inst. Tech., 1967; PhD, Stevens Inst. Tech., 1972. Mem. tech. staff Bell Telephone Labs., Murray Hill, N.J., 1953-67; asst. prof. Stevens Inst. Tech., Hoboken, N.J., 1967-73; sr. engr. The Singer Co., Fairfield, N.J., 1973-86; mem. tech. staff AT&T Bell Labs, Whippany, N.J., 1986—; cons. P.S.E.A.G., Newark, 1983. Mem. Am. Soc. Metals, The Metall. Soc., Internat. Metall. Soc. Home: 29 S Valley Rd West Orange NJ 07052

FILLMAN, JAMES, psychotherapist; b. Norristown, Pa., Jan. 29, 1951; s. James M. Sr. and Margaret Mary (Furey) F.; m. Sharon L. Klink, Aug. 30, 1969 (div. Jan. 1988); children: Shannon D., Joshua C. AS, Peirce Jr. Coll., Phila., 1971; student, Villanova U., 1972-75; BA, Allentown Coll. of St. Francis de Sales, 1988; MA, Rider Coll., 1991. Contr., acct. Pileggi & Sons, Inc., North Wales, Pa., 1973-88; psychotherapist Ctr. for Family Psychology, Newtown, Pa., 1990—; guest speaker Rider Coll., Lawrenceville, N.J., 1990—, Trenton (N.J.) State Coll., 1990, Recovery Ctr., Wilmington, Del., 1991; owner Options in Treatment: Serving the Gay and Lesbian Community, Yardley, Pa., 1992. Speaker Gay and Lesbian Growth Orgns., Phila., 1990—; participant AIDS Walk, Phila., 1991. Mem. Forum for Psychotherapists, Northwestern Inst., Alpha Sigma Lamda, Delta Delta. Democrat. Episcopalian. Home: 105 N Main St Yardley PA 19067 Office: Ctr for Family Psychology The Stocking Works 301 S State St Ste S-102 Newtown PA 18940

FILOR, ANNA MAY, educator; b. N.Y.C., Apr. 12, 1941; d. Hugo and Ann Theresa (Humbros) Mileo; m. Stephen Wilson Filor, Dec. 20, 1969; children: Daniel Post, John-Hugo. BS, NYU, 1963; MS, SUNY, New Paltz, 1968, cert. for advanced study, 1989. Cert. sch. adminstr. and supr., sch. dist. adminstr., N.Y. Tchr. Dover Jr.-Sr. High Sch., Dover Plains, N.Y., 1963-68; tchr. Poughkeepsie (N.Y.) High Sch., 1968—, dept. chmn., 1975-84; adj. lectr. Dutchess Community Coll., 1973-85. Author: jour. articles and newletters. Sr. warden, vestry woman, lay reader St. Paul'd Ch. Poughkeepsie. Grantee NDEA, NSF, NEH. Mem. ASCD, N.Y. State Social Studies Supervisory Assn. (bd. dirs. 1985-91, sec. 1986-88), Nat. Coun. for Social Studies, Mid. States Coun. Social Studies (bd. dirs. 1987-91), Hudson Valley Coun. Econ. Edn. (chmn. 1975-85), N.Y. State Coun. Social Studies (bd. dirs. 1985-87), Mid. Huston Social Studies Coun. (pres. 1983-87), N.Y. State Coun. Edn. Assns., Delta Kappa Gamma (v.p. 1986-88), Phi Delta Kappa. Democrat. Episcopalian. Home: 46 Durocher Ter Poughkeepsie NY 12603-6407

FILYAW, LISTON NATHANIEL, counselor; b. New Haven, Conn., Oct. 31, 1949; s. Macceo Nathaniel and Katheryn Dorothy (Bryant) F. AA in Liberal Arts, South Ctrl. C.C., New Haven, 1970; BA in Sociology, U. Conn., 1972, MA in Rehab. Counseling, 1978; MS in Elem. Edn., Ea. Conn. State U., 1976. Coord. programs, employment Hartford (Conn.) Housing Authority, 1979-81; asst. dir. Afro-Am. Cultural Ctr. U. Conn., Storrs, 1983-86, counselor Ctr. for Acad. Programs, 1986—; pvt. cons. various orgns., Conn., 1981-83. Author several plays. Chartered mem., pres. Vital Elements of the Arts. Mem. New Eng. Assn. Ednl. Opportunity Program Pers., Conn. Coun. Black Students and Profls., Conn. Assn. Ednl. Opportunity Programs, U. Conn. Profl. Employees Assn., Conn. State Fedn. Tchrs., Am. Fedn. Tchrs., AFL/CIO (union rep.), U. Conn. Black Alumni Assn., U. Conn. Black Employees Assn. (charter, co-chair). Democrat. Home: PO Box 583 Storrs CT 06268 Office: U Conn 341 Mansfield Rd U-170 Storrs CT 06269

FINBERG, BARBARA DENNING, foundation executive; b. Pueblo, Colo., Feb. 26, 1929; d. Rufus Raymond and Velma Aileen (Hopper) Denning; m. Alan R. Finberg, June 21, 1953. B.A., Stanford U., 1949; M.A., Am. U. of Beirut, Lebanon, 1951. Intern U.S. Dept. State, Washington, 1949-50, fgn. affairs officer, Tech Coop. Adminstrn., 1952-53; program specialist, area chief Inst. Internat. Edn., N.Y.C., 1953-59; editorial assoc., program officer Carnegie Corp. N.Y., N.Y.C., 1959-80, v.p. program, 1980-88, exec. v.p., 1988—; program advisor A.L. Mailman Family Found. Trustee Stanford U., 1976-86, v.p. bd. dirs. 1982-85; trustee N.Y. Found., 1979-91, vice chmn. bd. dirs., 1983-85, chmn., 1985-89; mem. accreditation com. Assn. Am. Law Schs., 1986-88; adv. com. The Henry A. Murray Rsch. Ctr. for the Study of Lives, Radcliffe Coll., 1986—; bd. dirs. The Hole in the Wall Gang Fund, Inc., 1987—, Investor Responsibility Rsch. Ctr. Inc., 1989—, Ind. Sector, 1990—, Consortium for the Advancement of Pvt. Higher Edn., 1992—. Rotary Found. fellow, 1950-51. Mem. Am. Ednl. Research Assn., Soc. for Research in Child Devel., Council on Fgn. Relations. Club: Cosmopolitan of N.Y. Home: 165 E 72d St Apt 19L New York NY 10021-4351 Office: Carnegie Corp NY 437 Madison Ave New York NY 10022-7001

FINCH, CHARLES BAKER, utilities company executive; b. N.Y.C., Mar. 1, 1920; s. Henry LeRoy and Mary (Baker) F.; m. Angela Cobb Sessions, Oct. 22, 1943; children: Charles Baker, William P. A.B., Yale U., 1941, LL.B., 1943. Bar: N.Y. 1943. With Milbank Tweed & Hope (and successor firms), N.Y.C., 1943-54; v.p. Allegheny Power System Inc., N.Y.C., 1954-72; pres., chief exec. officer Allegheny Power System Inc., 1972-85, chmn., 1981-92; retired, 1992. Bd. dirs. Josiah Macy Jr. Found.; trustee Cooper Union. Mem. St. Nicholas Soc. City N.Y., Phi Beta Kappa, Phi Delta Phi, Delta Kappa Epsilon. Club: Union.

FINCH, EDWARD RIDLEY, JR., lawyer, former diplomat, author, lecturer; b. Westhampton Beach, N.Y., Aug. 31, 1919. AB with Atwater honors, Princeton U., 1941; JD, NYU, 1947; LLD (hon.), Mo. Valley Coll., 1963; DSc (hon.), Cumberland Coll., 1985. Bar: N.Y. 1948, U.S. Supreme Ct. 1953, D.C. 1978, Fla. 1980, Pa. 1992. Ptnr. Finch & Schaefler, N.Y.C., 1950-85; ptnr. Le Boeuf, Lamb, Leiby & MacRae, N.Y.C., 1986-88; commr. City of N.Y., 1955-58; gen. counsel St. Giles Found.; U.S. del. 4th UN Congress, Geneva, 1970, 5th UN Congress, Japan, 1975; U.S. spl. ambassador to Panama, 1972; legal advisor, mem. U.S. Del. Unispace, Vienna, 1982; lectr. in field. Author: Hands In Your Pockets, Astro Business-A Guide to Commerce and Law of Outer Space, Judicial Politics; contbr. articles to legal and sci.jours. Commr. City of N.Y., 1955-59; pres., dir. St. Nicholas Soc. N.Y., 1948—, N.Y. Inst. Spl. Edn., 1950—; bd. dirs., counsel St. Giles Found., 1974—; bd. dirs. Fluegge Found., 1981—; mem. faculty adv. com. dept. politics Princeton U.; pres. N.Y. Inst. for Spl. Edn., 1969; treas. Jessie Ridley Found., N.Y.C.; pres. Crippled Children's Friendly Aid Assn. Inc., Finch Trusts, Adams Meml. Fund Inc; trustee St. Andrew's Dune Ch., Southampton, Cathedral of St. John the Divine, 1989-92, others. Col. USAFR, 1941-72. Decorated U.S. Legion of Merit with oak leaf cluster, Order of Brit. Empire, Knight Order of St. John, Legion of Honor (France). Fellow Am. Bar Found. (chmn. aerospace coun. sect. sci. and tech 1986-92); mem. ABA (ho. of dels. 1971-72, chmn. aerospace law div. internat. law sect.1973-79), Fed. Bar Assn., Inter-Am. Bar Assn. (Hallgarter award 1991), N.Y. State Bar Assn., Pa. Bar Assn., Fla. Bar Assn., Internat. Bar Assn., Judge Advs. Assn. U.S. (past pres.), Am. Law Inst., Am. Judicature Soc., AIAA, Internat. Astronautical Acad. (full elected mem.), Am. Arbitration Assn. (panelist), Univ. Clubs of Wash. and N.Y., Union League Club, Union Club, Princeton Club (bd. govs. 1982—), L.I. Club, Bathing Corp. of Southampton. Office: Dir and Gen Counsel Am Internat Peroleum Corp 640 Fifth Ave No 18 New York NY 10019

FINCH, ELEANOR HARRISON, retired editor; b. Washington, Mar. 9, 1908; d. George Augustus and Mae (Wright) Finch. AB cum laude, Trinity Coll., Washington, 1929; LLB, George Washington U., 1932. Bar: D.C.1933. Editorial asst. Am. Soc. Internat. Law, Washington, 1929-40; exec. sec. Am. Soc. Internat. Law, 1948-61; sec. bd. editors Am. Jour. Internat. Law, Washington, 1948-68; asst. editor Am. Jour. Internat. Law, 1968-72, asst. editor emerita, 1972—; research asst. Office Air Transport Info., Civil Aeronautics Adminstrn., Washington, 1942-43; div. asst. Office of Advisor on Air Law, Aviation div. Dept. State, Washington, 1943-48; sec. U.S. sect. Internat. Tech. Com. of Aerial Legal Experts, 1946-47; advisor U.S. Delegation to 1st Ann. Assembly, Provisional Civil Aviation Orgn., Montreal, 1946. Contbr. articles to profl. jours. Mem. Am. Soc. Internat. Law (life), George Washington U. Law Assn., DAR (chpt. regent 1973-75, state recording sec. 1976-78), Kappa Beta Pi. Republican. Roman Catholic. Home: 5703 Wyngate Dr Bethesda MD 20817-2554

FINCH, JAMES NELLIS, school superintendent; b. St. Johnsville, N.Y., Sept. 13, 1932; s. Fred Nellis and Edna Kinnum (Mang) F.; m. Jean Elizabeth Mullen, Aug. 25, 1956; children—Sally Jean, Douglas James. B.S., SUNY-Oneonta, 1954; M.A., Columbia U., 1957, Ed.D., 1967. Tchr. East Williston Pub. Sch., N.Y., 1957-58; tchr., prin. East Greenbush Pub. Sch., N.Y., 1958-61; dist. prin. Menands Pub. Schs., N.Y., 1961-64; asst. supt. schs. Piscataway Pub. Schs., N.J., 1965-69; supt. schs. Fitchburg Pub. Schs., Mass., 1969-72, Sweet Home Pub. Schs., Amherst, N.Y., 1972-91, ret., 1991; pres. community adv. council U. Buffalo, 1985-87; dir. Niagara Frontier Industry Ednl. Council, Buffalo, 1980—. Contbr. articles to profl. jours. Active Erie County Drug Abuse Task Force. Recipient Disting. Alumnus award SUNY-Oneonta, 1982. Mem. Suburban Sch. Supts., Am. Assn. Sch. Adminstrs., N.Y. Council Sch. Supts., Nat. Secondary Sch. Prins.; Erie/Niagara Sch. Supts.

FINCH, RUTH W., photographer, civic volunteer; b. Rochester, N.Y., Feb. 27, 1916; d. Orator Frank and Persis Earle (Davis) Woodward; m. E.C. Kip Finch, Nov. 24, 1951 (dec. Dec. 1988); children: Ruth Persis Simons, Earle Kip Finch. BA, Bryn Mawr (Pa.) Coll., 1937. Asst. editor Gold World, 1948-50; photographer Am. Indians. Treas. Conn. Conservation Assn., Bridgeport, Conn., 1988—; bd. dirs. Nat. Mus. of Art, Indpls., 1980-90. Mem. U.S. Golf Assn. (com. mem. 1953-62), Colonial Dames (N.Y.C.), New Canaan (Conn.) Counatry Club, New Canaan Garden Club. Republican. Episcopalian.

FINCK, WILLIAM HARRY, medical services executive, accountant; b. Phila., Sept. 12, 1945; s. Alton Harry and Elmina Anna (Bratton) F.; m. June Ann Hyde, May 20, 1972 (div. Nov. 1978); m. Mary Margaret Mihaich, May 31, 1980; 1 child, Bernadette Mary. BS, LaSalle Coll., 1972; MBA, Temple U., 1978. CPA, N.J. Staff acct. Harry K. Cohen & Co., Phila., 1969-70, Miller, Cohen & Co., Trenton, N.J., 1970-71; asst. controller Our Lady of Lourdes Hosp., Camden, N.J., 1971-75, asst. adminstr., 1975-77; acctg. mgr. Underwood Meml. Hosp., Woodbury, N.J., 1977-81; controller Meml. Hosp. of Burlington County, Mt. Holly, N.J., 1981-82, dir. of fin., 1982-83; v.p., treas. Home-Medic Lifeline Inc., Pennsauken, N.J., 1983-89, pres., 1989—. Member Good Neighbors of Collingswood, N.J., 1983. Sgt. U.S. Army, 1965-67, maj. N.J. Army N.G., 1973—. Fellow Healthcare Fin. Mgmt. Assn. (bd. dirs. Princeton, N.J. chpt. 1982-83, v.p. 1984-85, William G. Fulmer Merit award 1983, Reeves Silver merit award 1988); mem. Am. Coll. Healthcare Execs. Democrat. Episcopalian. Office: Homemedic Life Line Inc 721 Hylton Rd Pennsauken NJ 08110-1364

FINE, BENJAMIN, mathematician, educator, consultant, researcher; b. N.Y.C., Oct. 12, 1948; s. Reuben Fine and Sonya Lebeaux; m. Linda Smith, June 22, 1969; children: Carolyn, David. BS, Bklyn. Coll., 1969; MS, N.Y. U., 1971, PhD, 1973. Prof. math. Fairfield (Conn.) U., 1974—; vis. researcher Yale U., New Haven, Conn., 1977-78; vis. prof. U. Calif., Santa Barbara, Calif., 1984-85, N.Y. U.-Courant Inst., N.Y.C., 1987-88; cons. QED Assocs., Stamford, Conn., 1977—. Author: Algebraic Theory of the Bianchi Groups, 1989; contbr. articles to profl. jours. With U.S. Army, 1970-71. Sloan fellow N.Y. U., 1971, Lilly fellow Yale U., 1977; scholar-in-residence grantee, 1987. Mem. Am. Math. Soc., Math. Assn. Am., Am. Soc. Quality Control. Democrat. Jewish. Office: Fairfield U Fairfield CT 06430

FINE, JANE MADELINE, visual artist; b. N.Y.C., Sept. 25, 1958; d. Arnold and Cecile (Glassen) F. BA, Harvard U., 1980; MA, Tufts U., 1982; postgrad., Skowhegan Sch. Painting, 1989. Exhibited in group shows at Bard Coll., 1991, Marymount Coll., 1990, PS 122 Gallery, 1989, The Drawing Ctr., 1988, Soho Ctr. for Visual Artists, 1988, White Columns, N.Y., 1992. Fellow Millay Colony for the Arts, 1990, Yaddo, 1990, NEA, 1989.

FINE, JO RENÉE, training consultant; b. Norfolk, Va., June 19, 1943; d. Ruby Arthur and Tillie Fern (Goldman) F.; BA, Smith Coll., 1965; MA, NYU, 1968, PhD, 1973; m. Edward Trieber, Apr. 12, 1981; 1 child, Jessica Fine Trieber. Probation officer N.Y.C. Office Probation, 1966; res. asst. N.Y.U., N.Y.C., 1966-68, assoc. res. scientist Inst. Devel. Studies, 1968-73, res. scientist, 1973-77, adj. asst. prof. dept. ednl. psychology, 1973-76; program analyst N.Y. State Dept. Mental Hygiene, N.Y.C., 1977-78; pvt. practice psychotherapy, N.Y.C., 1978-81; pres. CVM Prodns., Inc., N.Y.C., 1978—; adj. asst. prof. ednl. communication and tech. NYU, 1988—; cons. to bds. edn., N.Y.C., also greater met. area, 1973—, tng. cons., 1990—. Mem. APA, ASTD, Am. Jewish Com. (v.p.). Co-author: The Synagogues of New York's Lower East Side, 1978. Home and Office: 55 W 16th St New York NY 10011-6305

FINE, MARLENE GAIL, communications educator; b. Long Branch, N.J., Jan. 7, 1949; d. Frederick and Lillian (Gelblat) F.; children: William, Julius. BA in Speech cum laude, U. Mass., 1970; MA in Speech Communication, U. Minn., 1972; PhD in Communication Studies, U. Mass., 1980, MBA in Fin., 1984. Teaching assoc. U. Minn., Mpls., 1970-72; instr. Clarion (Pa.) State Coll., 1972-74; lectr. and teaching assoc. U. Mass., Amherst, 1974-79; acting dir. writing Clark U., 1980; sr. ptnr. Communication Edn. Assocs., 1978-83; fin. analyst Capital Formation Svc., Sml. Bus. Devel. Ctr., U. Mass., Amherst, 1983; assoc. dean Coll. of Mgmt., U. Mass., Boston, 1984-85; dir. MBA program Coll. of Mgmt., U. Mass., Amherst, 1985-89; asst. prof. analysis and communication Coll. of Mgmt., U. Mass., Boston, 1985-91, assoc. prof. analysis and communication, 1991—; lectr. and cons. in field. Contbr. numerous articles to profl. jours.; editorial bd. Communication Monographs, 1992; assoc. editor Women's Studies in Communication, 1986—. Grantee U. Mass. ub. Svc., 1990, Dept. Edn. Title III, 1986-89, EPA, 1986, Clearinghouse Ctr. Community Based Free-Standing Ednl. Instns., 1979, Ford Found., 1978; recipient Prof. of the Yr. award MBA Assn., U. Mass., Boston, 1989, Schaeffer Eaton award, U. Mass., Amherst, 1984. Mem. NAFE, Speech Communication Assn. (2d vice chair feminist and women studies div. 1991—, newsletter editor Women's Caucus 1987-88), Internat. Communication Assn., Eastern Communication Assn., Acad. of Mgmt., Assn. for Bus. Communication, Mortar Bd., Pi Kappa Delta, Beta Gamma Sigma, Delta Sigma Rho-Tau Kappa Alpha. Office: U Mass/Boston Coll Dept Mktg and Communication Boston MA 02125-3393

FINE, MICHAEL JOSEPH, publishing and communications company executive; b. N.Y.C., Jan. 30, 1937; s. William and Rosa F.; m. Marlene Rosen, Apr. 4, 1959; children: Antony Adeus, Kaethe Elizabeth. Student, U. Fla., 1953-54; BA, Bklyn. Coll., 1957; postgrad., State U. Iowa, 1959-60. Propr. Paper Place Bookstore, Iowa City, 1960-63; v.p. Paperback Affiliates, Inc., N.Y.C., 1963-74; mgr., co-owner The Paperback Forum Bookstore, N.Y.C.; mgr. The Manhattanville Book Forum, Manhattanville Coll., Purchase, N.Y.; asst. to pres. Simon & Schuster, Inc., N.Y.C., 1964-65; v.p. Assoc. Ednl. Svcs., N.Y.C., 1966; assoc. dir. Washington Square Press Simon & Schuster, Inc., N.Y.C., 1967-69, mem. editorial bd., 1968; founder, pub. trade paperback div. Simon & Schuster Clarion Books, N.Y.C., 1967-69; founder, exec. v.p. Bookthrift, Inc., 1971-78; pres. Bookthrift, Inc. div. Simon & Schuster, 1978-81; sr. v.p., exec. com. mem. Ingram Book Co., Nashville, 1981-83; pres., chief exec. officer Ingram Ventures, Inc., N.Y.C., 1981-83; chief exec. officer Feeling Fine Programs, Inc., 1984-86; co-founder, pres. Lynx Communications, Inc., N.Y.C., 1987-90; founder, pres. Fine Creative Media, Inc., N.Y.C., 1991—. Contbr. articles to profl. jours. Past chmn. bd. dirs. St. Michaels Montessori Sch., N.Y.C.; bd. dirs. Morningside Area Alliance, Inc., 1974-83. Mem. N.Y. Acad. Scis. (mem. publs. com. 1984-88), The Reality Club (N.Y.C.).

FINE, MIRIAM BROWN, artist, educator, poet, writer; b. Vineland, N.J., Mar. 8, 1913; d. Abraham and Katie (Walidarsky) Brown; m. Irvin Fine, Nov. 3, 1935; children: Ruth Eileen Fine, Adele Aviva Fine Gross. BFA, The U. the Arts (formerly Indsl. Sch. Arts) and U. Pa., 1935; postgrad., Cheltenham (Pa.) Art Sch., 1968-77, Temple U., 1977—. Tchr. art and watercolor painting Phila. Pub. Schs., 1953-60; lectr., watercolor tchr. Assn. Retired Profls. Temple U., 1976—; pvt. tchr. art, Phila., 1952-77; tchr., vis. artist Abington Friends Com., 1989-90; tchr. watercolor N.E. Cultural Art Coun. Phila.1, 1987-90; tchr. watercolor, speaker poetry forum David G. Neuman Sr. Ctr., Jewish Community Ctr. Phila., 1991—. Executed 7 murals at Spruance Elem. Sch., Phila., 1951; Holocost, oils and watercolors displayed in Temple Sholom Synagogue, Oxford Cir. Synagogue, UN Women's Conf., Nairobi, Kenya, 1985—; 15 one-person exhbns. 1975-88; 27 group exhbns.; author: (poetry and illustrations) Word and Drawings, 1984, Mom I

Didn't Know It Was Like That Family History, 1984, The Full Moon Energises My Creativity, 1988, You Are In My Galaxy, 1990, That's Life, 1992. Did benefit for St. Christopher's Children's Hosp., Phila., 1984-87; mem. City of Hope, Phila., 1935—. Recipient Chapel of Four Chaplains award City of Hope, 1964, 50 Yr. Svc. award, 1981, 60 Yr. svc. award, 1991; scholar Nat. Conf. Art in Pub. Places, Phila. Fairmont Park Commn., 1987. Mem. NOW, Artists Equity Inc., Phila. Watercolor Club, Women's Caucus for Art, Univ. Arts Alumni Assn., Acad. Am. Poets, Nat. Fedn. State Poetry Socs., Writers Cadence Crafters, Poets Study Group, Nat. Mus. of Women in Arts, Temple U. Assn. Ret. Profls. (pres. emeritus, award), Pa. State Poetry Socs. Republican. Jewish. Home and Studio: 1438 Devereaux Ave Philadelphia PA 19149

FINE, STANLEY SIDNEY, pharmaceuticals and chemicals executive; b. N.Y.C., Sept. 26, 1927; s. Morris and Sophie (Brajer) F.; m. Eleanor D. Baker, July 21, 1955 (dec. 1972); children: Lauren Allison, Stephen Sidney (dec.); m. Astrid E. Merget, June 8, 1984 (div. Apr. 1987); m. Li L. Yang, July 31, 1991. Student, NYU, 1944-45; B.S., U.S. Naval Acad., 1949; postgrad., Coll. William and Mary, 1955-56, U. Va., 1956-57; MBA, Am. U., 1959; postgrad., Harvard U., 1963-65. Commd. ensign U.S. Navy, 1948, advanced through grades to rear adm., 1972; comdg. officer USS Hawk, 1954-56, Polaris Program, 1956-59, USS Lowe, 1961-63; comdr. Escort Div. 33, 1963; comdg. officer USS Ingraham, 1965-67; br. head Navy Material Command, Washington, 1967-68; exec. asst., naval aide to asst. sec. Navy, 1968-70; study dir. Center for Naval Analysis Navy Dept., Washington, 1970; dep. dir. Navy Program Info. Center, 1970-71; br. head OPNAV, 1971; spl. asst. to dir. Navy Program Planning, Washington, 1971-72; dep. chief Programs and Fin. Mgmt.; comptr. Naval Ship Systems Command, Washington, 1972-73; dir. fiscal mgmt. div. Office Chief Naval Ops., Washington, 1973-78; dir. budget and reports Navy Dept., 1975-78; ret., 1978; sr. v.p. United-Guardian, Inc. (AMEX), Hauppauge, N.Y., 1979—, also bd. dirs.; v.p., bd. dirs. New Energy Leasing Corp., McLean, Va.; bd. dirs. Micron Products Inc.; cons. GAO. Co-author: The Federal Budget: Cost Based in the 1980's, 1979, The Military Budget on a New Plateau: Strategic Choices for the 1990's; contbr. articles to profl. jours. and other publs.; lectr., TV commentator on def. and fed. budget issues. Mem. Presdl. transition team Dept. Commerce, 1980-81; bd. dirs. Bronx High Sch. of Sci. Found., N.Y.C.; dir. Com. for Nat. Security, 1987—, Montgomery County Fiscal Affairs Com., 1987-88; sr. fellow Bus. Execs. for Nat. Security. Decorated D.S.M., Navy Commendation medal, Legion of Merit with gold star; recipient Outstanding Mgmt. Analyst award Am. Soc. Mil. Comptrollers, 1971. Mem. Naval Inst., World Affairs Coun. D.C., Naval Acad. Alumni Assn., Harvard U. Bus. Sch. Alumni Assn., Harvard Club Washington. Democrat. Jewish. Office: United-Guardian Inc 230 Marcus Blvd Hauppauge NY 11788-3751

FINELLI, FREDERICK CHRISTOPHER, general surgeon, attorney; b. Rochester, N.Y., Apr. 14, 1954; s. Joseph Frederick and Rose Mary (Fallico) F. BA, U. Colo., 1976; MD, SUNY, Buffalo, 1979; JD, Georgetown U., 1989. Bar: Pa. 1991; diplomate Am. Bd. Surgery. Trauma surgeon MedStar, Washington, 1985-88; pvt. practice in gen. surgery Washington, 1989—, pvt. practice in law, 1991—. Contbr. articles to profl. jours. Mem. ABA, AMA. Roman Catholic. Home: 2921 Olive St NW Washington DC 20007 Office: 106 Irving St NW #120 Washington DC 20010

FINELLI, GERARD PETER, educational administrator; b. N.Y.C., Apr. 11, 1947; s. Gerard J. and Juanita Ruth (Behan) F.; m. Charlotte Noel Drysdale, Aug. 23, 1969; children: Danielle, Justine, Elizabeth. BA in Polit. Sci., Fordham U., 1969; MS in Edn., St. John's U., 1973; postgrad., N.Y.U., 1973-77. Cert. sch. adminstr., supr., elem. sch. prin., N.Y. 5th and 6th grade tchr. Pub. Sch. 29, Bronx, N.Y., 1969-76, phys. edn. tchr., 1979; 6th grade and phys. edn. tchr. Pub. Sch. 55, Bronx, 1976-78; coordinator of staff devel., chpt. 53 dist. adminstr. Community Sch. Dist. 7, Bronx, 1979-88; asst. prin. George W. Miller Sch., Nanuet, N.Y., 1988-90; prin. Kent Elem. Sch., Carmel, N.Y., 1990—; seminar presentation Internat. Reading Assn., Atlant, 1984, N.Y. State Reading Assn., N.Y.C., 1983. Community chmn. United Way of Westchester, Thornwood, N.Y., 1986-87; planning bd. mem. Town of Mount Pleasant, N.Y., 1985; councilman Town of Mount Pleasant, 1988-91. Recipient Bronze award, United Way of Westchester, 1986-87, Congl. Cert. Appreciation, Rep. Joseph Dioguardi, U.S. Congress, 1986. Mem. ASCD, Nat. Assn. Elem. Sch. Prins., KC, Lions. Home: 660 Warren Ave Thornwood NY 10594-1519 Office: Kent Elem Sch Rt 52 Carmel NY 10512

FINER, MICHAEL SCOTT, accountant; b. Boston, Dec. 17, 1964; s. Philip Finer and Lorna Leslie (Milich) Kerner. BS, Babson Coll., 1987. Sales assoc. ERA/VIP Real Estate, Inc., Sharon, Mass., 1985-87; sr. tax acct. Ernst & Young, Boston, 1987-91; acct. Ernst and Young, Boston, 1992—; chmn. bd. dirs. Finer Industries, Sharon; bd. dirs. Empire Properties, Inc., Apollo Investments, Ltd.; notary pub., Mass. Contbr. articles to Army mag., Quar. Jur. Mil. History. Mem. Sharon Rep. Town Com.; vol. Am. Cancer Soc.; mem. accts. team Am. Diabetes Soc., Combined Jewish Philanthropies, com. Gen. Douglas MacArthur. Decorated Army Commendation medal; recipient Army Res. Components Achievement medal. Mem. Assn. U.S. Army (assoc.), Res. Officers Assn. (v.p. chpt. 22 audit com., v.p. Mass. dept. budget com., Outstanding Achievement award, 1st prize in Essay Contest, jr. v.p.), U.S. Combat Martial Arts Assn., Internat. Martial Arts League (instr.), Armed Forces Martial Arts Assn. (instr., sta. mgr.). Home: PO Box 411 Sharon MA 02067-0411 Office: Ernst and Young 200 Clarendon Ave Boston MA 02116

FINESTONE, ALBERT JUSTIN, medical educator, dean; b. May 12, 1921; m. Alma Perch, 1951; children: Toby Gail Grubman, Jay David, Audrey Kanoff. AB, Temple U., 1942, MD, 1945, MSc in Internal Medicine, 1951. Diplomate Am. Bd. Internal Medicine. Intern Temple U. Hosp., Phila., 1945-46, resident in medicine, 1959-51, co-chmn. utilization com., 1964-74; fellow in pathology Georgetown U. Hosp., Washington, 1948-49; head metabolic svc. Episcopal Hosp. of Phila., 1954-72; asst. dean continuing med. edn. Sch. of Medicine, Temple U., Phila., 1972-79, chmn. biomed. scis. rev. com., 1973-81, prof., 1979, assoc. dean continuing med. edn., 1979—; physician rep. for radiation protection Temple U., Phila., 1984; mem. athletic coun. Temple U., 1989, assoc. dean emeritus continuing med. edn., 1991, geriatrics coord. Sch. Medicine, 1991; dir. Inst. on Aging, Temple U. Sch. Medicine, 1991—; geriatrics cons. Pa. Blue Shield, 1989—, mem. corp., 1988—. Mem. bd. editorial cons. Clin. Therapeutics, 1983, specialist reviewer, 1987; cons. editor Hospita. Medicine, Geriatrics, 1990; contbr. numerous articles to profl. jours. Capt. M.C., U.S. Army, 1946-48. Fellow ACP, Coll. Physicians of Phila.; mem. AMA (rep. med. schs. sect. 1988—), Am. Psychosomatic Soc., Am. Geriatrics Soc., Pa. Med. Soc. (commn. on accreditation 1984-90), Phila. County Med. Soc. (bd. dirs. 1978-84, 91—, chmn. med. edn. com. 1978-84, 91—, del. Pa. Med. Soc. 1980—, sec. 1987-88, exec. com. 1987-88, chmn. student affairs com. 1987-88, bd. dirs. Pfahler Found. 1987-88, field liaison credentials com. 1987-91, chmn. subcom. on reaccreditation 1988-89, membership com. 1988-90, resident med. student affairs com. 1988-90, liaison com. with Blue Cross/Blue Shield), Pa. Med. Soc. (commn. on accreditation), Med. Alumni Assn. Temple U. Sch. Medicine (bd. dirs., chmn. awards com., Man of Yr. 1976), Soc. Med. Coll. Dirs. Continuing Med. Edn., Alliance for Continuing Med. Edn., Assn. Dir. Acad. Geriatric Medicine Programs, Alpha Omicron Alpha. Home: 606 Webb Rd Philadelphia PA 19117-2538 Office: Temple U Hosp Parkinson Pavilion Broad & Tioga Sts Philadelphia PA 19140

FINGER, JOEL DAVID, graphic design professional; b. Hackensack, N.J., May 6, 1956; s. Edwin Warner and Florence (Evelyn) F.; m. Ellen Teresa Richards Nov. 19, 1982 (div. Mar. 1991). AS, Rochester Inst., 1976; BFA, Sch. Visual Arts, N.Y.C., 1978. Graphic designer Mercedes-Benz of N.A., Montvale, N.J., 1978-84; art dir. Einson Freeman, Paramus N.J., 1984-86; creative dir. Graphic Innovations, Pompton Lakes, N.J., 1986—. Mem. N.J. Art Dirs. Club (Cert. of Excellence), Assn. of Graphic Artists (Cert. of Spl. Merits). Episcopalian. Home and Office: Graphic Innovations 1129 Ringwood Ave Pompton Lakes NJ 07442

FINGER, LOUIS JUDAH, lawyer; b. Wilmington, Del., Dec. 9, 1920; s. Aaron and Anna Ethel (Breskman) F.; m. Dorothy Kraushar, Mar. 8, 1953; children: Jonathan R., David L., Susan J. BA, Haverford (Pa.) Coll., 1941; LLB, Yale U., 1947. Bar: Del. 1947, U.S. Dist. Ct. Del. 1948, U.S. Ct. Appeals (3d cir.) 1955, U.S. Supreme Ct. 1952. Assoc. Richards, Layton & Finger, Wilmington, Del., 1949-53; mem. firm Richards, Layton & Finger, 1954-91, ret., of counsel, 1991—; dep. atty. gen. State of Del., 1951-52; mem. Bd. Profl. Responsibility of the Del. Supreme Ct., 1970-82; spl. dep. atty. gen. State of Del., 1953-54; mem. Del. Supreme Ct. Adv. Com. for Code of Evidence, 1978—. Bd. dirs., v.p., Jewish Fedn. Del., 1960-68; bd. dirs. Wilmington Music Sch.; vice chmn. Com. on Drafting Del. Uniform Comml. Code, pres., 1992—. 1st lt. USAAF, 1943-45. Jewish. Office: Richards Layton & Finger 1 Rodney Sq # 551 Wilmington DE 19801-3305

FINGER, PHYLLIS THOMAS, language arts educator; b. Jacksonville, Fla., June 25, 1947; d. Charles Joseph and Avis Mary (Tacke) Thomas; m. Homer Ellis Finger III, Aug. 15, 1970; 1 child, Geoffrey Thomas. BA, Fla. So. Coll., 1969; MA, Syracuse U., 1970; EdD, Lehigh U., 1985. Cert. English tchr. Tchr. gifted program Easton (Pa.) Area Sch. Dist., 1974—; tchr. English Lawrence Township Sch. Dist., Trenton, N.J., 1970-73; asst. to the dean Lehigh U. Sch. Edn., Bethlehem, Pa., 1979-81; del. Pa. Tchr. Exch. to Omiya, Japan, 1989; judge Odyssey of the Mind, Southeastern Pa. Vice chmn. Northampton County Bicentennial Constitution Commn. and Solid Waste Adv. Com.; elder 1st Presbyn. Ch., Easton, 1990—, chair Christian Edn. and Mission Com. Mem. AAUW, ASCD, LWV (pres. Easton 1987-89), Nat. Coun. Tchrs. English, Lehigh U. Alumni Assn. (pres. 1991—), Historic Easton, N.Y. Marathon, Phi Delta Kappa (pres. 1985). Democrat. Home: 118 E Wayne Ave Easton PA 18042-1644 Office: Easton Area Sch Dist 12th & Northampton Sts Easton PA 18042

FINGON, JOAN CARROLL, education educator; b. Milford, Conn., Oct. 6, 1951; d. Edward and Claire Carroll; m. Robert J. Fingon, Apr. 23, 1977; children: Shallon, Collin. BS in Edn., So. Conn. U., 1973; MS, Castleton State Coll., 1980, CAGS, 1987; EdD in Higher Edn. Adminstrn., Vanderbilt U., 1990. Cert. tchr. elem. and secondary phys. edn., reading, secondary sci., Vt. Asst. prof. edn. Green Mountain Coll., Poultney, Vt., 1989—; adj. instr. Castleton (Ct.) State Coll., 1981-89; exec. bd. dirs., AIDS chair PTA Vt. State, Rutland, 1989—. Editor Vt. PTA Newsletter, 1990—. Mem. sch. bd. Rutland Twon Sch., 1988-90, PTA. Mem. Vt. Coun. on Reading (chair parents and reading 1989-91, treas. 1990-91, v.p. 1991-92, pres.-elect 1992-93, dir. student membership 1992—). Office: Green Mountain Coll 16 College St Poultney VT 05764-1199

FINK, ABEL KING, psychologist, educator; b. N.Y.C., Aug. 5, 1927; s. Max and Esther (Levy) F.; m. Billey Levinson, 1959 (div. 1990); children: Elias, Mira, Micah. BA, Bklyn. Coll.-CUNY, 1949; MA, Columbia U., 1950, EdD, 1956. Elem. tchr. Roosevelt Sch., Stamford, Conn., 1952-54; vis. prof. U. P.R., Rio Piedras, 1964-65; ednl. cons. N.Y.C., Buffalo, 1955—; asst. prof. to prof. ednl. founds. Buffalo State U., 1956—. Author films: Warm-up to Psychodrama, Generation Gap; author tv programs: The Importance of Feedback, Finding One's Place In a Group; contbr. articles to profl. jours. Co-dir. Citizens Coun. on Human Rels., Buffalo. SUNY Rsch. Found. grantee. Fellow Am. Soc. for Group Psychotherapy and Psychodrama; mem. Am. Psychol. Assn., Inter-Am. Soc. of Psychology, Soc. for Psychol. Study of Social Issues, Psychol. Assn. of Western N.Y. (pres. 1971, archivist), Torch Internat., Phi Delta Kappa. Democrat. Jewish. Office: Buffalo State U Coll 1300 Elmwood Ave Buffalo NY 14222-1095

FINK, DAVID LEONARD, surgeon; b. St. Louis, June 6, 1936; s. Sidney Fink and Estelle Esses Goldstein; m. Frances Carole Bower, June 13, 1965; children: Dana Lynne, Denise Lysette. BA, Columbia Coll., 1957; MD, Cornell U., N.Y.C., 1961. Diplomate Am. Bd. Surgery. Resident in surgery St. Luke's Hosp. Med. Ctr., N.Y.C., 1961-64, U. Wis. Med. Ctr., Madison, 1964-66; pvt. practice, Paterson, N.J., 1970—; chief exec. officer Gen. Surgeons North Jersey, P.A., Paterson, 1970—; chief surgery Barnert Meml. Hosp., Paterson, 1982-86, pres. med. staff, 1988. Maj. U.S. Army, 1966-70. Decorated Army Commendation medal. Fellow ACS, Soc. of Surgeons of N.J.; mem. Vascular Soc. N.J., Ea. Vascular Soc., Southeastern Surg. Soc., Cornell U. Med. Alumni Assn. (bd. dirs. 1986-89), Stuyvesant Yacht Club. Office: Gen Surgeons North Jersey 707 Broadway Paterson NJ 07514-1488

FINK, DAVID WARREN, chemist; b. Bklyn., Mar. 30, 1944; s. George and Celia (Gottfried) F.; m. Sharon Betci Goldberg, June 22, 1967; children: Stephen, Laurie. BS in Chemistry, CUNY, 1964; PhD in Chemistry, Lehigh U., 1969. Rsch. chemist Lever Bros. R & D, Edgewater, N.Y., 1969-71; sr. rsch. chemist Merck Sharp & Dohme Rsch. Labs., Rahway, N.J., 1971-72, rsch. fellow, 1972-73, sect. leader, 1973-77, asst. dir., 1977-84, assoc. dir., 1984—; presenter in field. Contbr. over 50 articles to profl. jours., chpts. to books. Fellow Assn. Ofcl. Analytical Chemists (assoc. referee 1984—, Associate Referee of Yr. award 1980); mem. Am. Chem. Soc. Home: 31 Ethan Allen Rd Freehold NJ 07728-3356 Office: Merck Sharp & Dohme Rsch Labs PO Box 2000 Rahway NJ 07065-0900

FINK, EUGENE RICHARD, security company executive, lawyer; b. N.Y.C., Feb. 27, 1944; s. William and Anne (Kimsorofsky) F.; m. Sheila Barbara Boodish, Jan. 14, 1968; children: Zachary Evan, Jason Alexander. BS, NYU, 1966; JD, U. Tulsa, 1969. Bar: N.Y., 1970. Assoc. Booth, Lipton & Lipton, N.Y.C., 1970-72; exec. Nat. Kinney Corp., N.Y.C., 1972-75; v.p. Holmes Protection, Inc., 1974-75; pres. Winfield Security Corp., N.Y.C., 1975—; guest lectr. John Jay Coll. of Criminal Justice. Treas. So. Riverdale (N.Y.) Baseball League, 1983-89; chmn. Spuyten-Duyvil Inf., Riverdale, 1985-91. Mem. Am. Soc. Indsl. Security, Com. Nat. Securities Co. (sec. 1988-90, dir. 1988—), Assn. Lic. Detectives of N.Y. State (sec. 1991), Ridgeway Country Club (White Plains, N.Y.). Office: Winfield Security Corp 35 W 35th St New York NY 10001-2205

FINK, JOANNA ELIZABETH, art dealer; b. Boston, Aug. 8, 1958; d. Alan Donald and Barbara Emma (Swan) F. Student, Wellesley Coll., 1976-78; BA, NYU, 1980; MA, NYU, Inst. Fine Arts, 1983. Asst. dir. Nardin Gallery, N.Y.C., 1979-80; photographer, adminstrv. asst. NYU, Dept. Fine Arts, N.Y.C., 1980-82, instr. art history, 1982; registrar Estate of Milton Avery, N.Y.C., 1982; rsch. cons. Chase Manhattan Bank, N.Y.C., 1983; dir. Alpha Gallery, Boston, 1983—; hon. bd. mem. Artcetera Auction/Aids Action Commn., Boston, 1990. Author: Georg Baselitz, 1985, The Books of Anselm Kiefer, 1992; editor: Goya & British Satirical Prints, 1991. Mem. Boston Art Dealers Assn. Office: Alpha Gallery Inc 14 Newbury St Boston MA 02116-2902

FINK, MARTIN RONALD, engineering consultant; b. N.Y.C., Apr. 27, 1931; s. David Peter and Etta Alice (Checker) F.; m. Jacqueline Fay Klein, Aug. 24, 1952; children: Howard Jeffrey, Andrew Charles, Douglas Reuben. BS in Aero. Engring., MIT, 1952, MS in Aero. Engring., 1953. Rsch. asst. MIT, Cambridge, Mass., 1952-53; rsch. engr. United Techs. Rsch. Ctr., East Hartford, Conn., 1953-58, supr. missile aeronautics, 1959-63, supr. aero. group, 1964-67, sr. cons. engr., 1967-80; chief aerodynamics Norden Systems, Norwalk, Conn., 1980-89; pvt. practice cons. Fairfield, Conn., 1989—. Fellow AIAA (assoc.); mem. Tau Beta Pi, Sigma Xi (pres. Hartford chpt. 1980-81). Jewish. Home: 183 Woody Ln Fairfield CT 06432-2039

FINK, SHELDON EDWIN, painter, etcher, lithographer; b. Bklyn., Sept. 10, 1925; s. Leo Bernard and Sally (Mehrstein) F.; m. Christina Willebeek-Le Mair, (div. 1975); children: Jennie Aafje, Timothy Pip, Nellie Wren. Grad. music and art high sch., 1943. Art dir. Irving Serwer Advt., N.Y.C., 1938-42; draftsman Anaconda Copper Mining Co., N.Y.C., 1943; art dir. George Elliot Advt., N.Y.C., 1946-47, Silberstein Goldsmith Advt., N.Y.C., 1947-49, Weintraub Advt., N.Y.C., 1949-50; various positions for other firms, 1950-53; freelance illustrator and fine art painter Bklyn., 1953-62; fine artist, portrait painter, master carpenter Mass., 1962—; pres. Shelly's Jentimnel Corp., Great Barrington, Mass., 1982—. One-man shows include Albany (N.Y.) Art Inst., Berkshire Art Mus., Pittsfield, Mass., Lenox (Mass.) Libr., F.A.R. Gallery, N.Y.C., Michelson Galleries, Washington, Gallery 52, S. Orange, N.J., Tyringham Galleries, Lee, Mass.; exhibited in group shows at Davis Galleries, N.Y.C., Nat. Arts Club, N.Y.C., Sarasota Sch. Art, Fla., Internat. UNICEF Show, 1976, Internat. Graphic Arts Soc., N.Y.C., Pratt Graphic Art Ctr., Internat. Miniature Exhbn., Cartoonists & Illustrators Sch.; illustrator Sports Illstrated, Jewish history, books and others, 1954-59. Chmn. group to restore and preserve Bklyn. Heights (N.Y.) Assn., 1959-62; chmn. Planning Bd., Alford, Mass., 1966-67; union organizer longshoremen Bklyn. Docks, Red Hook, 1953-54; mem. Com. for Nuclear Disarmament, Great Barrington, Mass., 1985—. With USN, 1943-46. Recipient 1st prize gold medal John Wanawaker award, 1930, 32, 35; grantee Tiffany Found., 1957, 63. Democrat. Jewish. Office: Shellys Art Supplies 940 S Main St Great Barrington MA 01230-2013

FINKBEINER, HERMAN LAWRENCE, research laboratory administrator; b. Syracuse, N.Y., July 20, 1931; s. Herman and Agnes (Vollmer) F.; m. Frances Marie Gerstner, June 2, 1954. AB, Park Coll., 1952; MS, U. Mich., 1958, PhD, 1959. Rsch. chemist Spencer Chem. Co., Pittsburg, Kans., 1953-56; staff scientist GE Rsch. Lab., Schenectady, N.Y., 1959-68, mgr. chem. synthesis br., 1968-76, mgr. employee rels. ops., 1976-78, mgr. planning and resources, 1978-82, mgr. biol. scis. lab., 1982-91, mgr. chem.-biol. reactions lab., 1991—. Author: Polymerization Processes, 1977; contbr. articles to profl. jours.; inventor, patentee in field. Bd. dirs. Saratoga County Planning Bd., Ballston Spa, N.Y., 1980-87, Town of Clifton Park (N.Y.) Planning Bd., 1972-88; bd. dirs., treas. Schenectady Mus., 1981-83. E.C. Britton fellow U. Mich., 1957, IBM fellow U. Mich., 1958; recipient IR-100 award Indsl. Rsch. Assn., 1963. Fellow AAAS; mem. Am. Chem. Soc. (nat. bd. com. on pub. affairs). Home: 492 Riverview Rd Rexford NY 12148 Office: GE Corp R&D PO Box 8 Schenectady NY 12301-0008

FINKE, HANS-JOACHIM, cultural organization administrator; b. Königsberg, Prussia, Germany, Nov. 23, 1939; came to U.S., 1954; s. Karl Josef Erich Finke and Renate Gertrud (Montzka) Novak; m. Leslie Chree O'Malley, Oct. 22, 1966; 1 child, Rupert. BA and AM, Temple U., 1962; PhD, U. Del., 1970. Asst. prof. Temple U., Phila., 1969-72; adj. asst. prof. Lehigh U., Bethlehem, Pa., 1972-74; adj. assoc. prof. Moravian Coll., Bethlehem, 1974-76; program dir. Regional Coun. of Hist. Agys., Syracuse, N.Y., 1976-86; exec. dir. Western N.Y. Assn. of Hist. Agys., Avon, 1986-91; dept. head, records mgmt. officer Ontario County, Canandaigua, N.Y., 1991—; coord. capital fund drive Moravian Coll., 1976; freelance history cons. and German translator. Co-author: The Bethlehem Oil Mill, 1984; contbr. numerous articles to profl. jours. Board trustees Schweinfurth Art Ctr., Auburn, N.Y., 1987-89. With U.S. Army, 1956-59. U. Del. fellow, 1966. Mem. Am.Assn. State and Local History, Am. Assn. Mus., Mid-Atlantic Mus. Assn., Phi Alpha Theta. Lutheran. Home: 1126 Cunningham Dr Victor NY 14564-9503 Office: Archives Info Mgmt Svcs Dept Records 3869 County Rd # 6 Canandaigua NY 14424

FINKEL, GILBERT, food scientist, researcher; b. Bklyn., Dec. 12, 1935; s. Reuben and Sarah (Shadovitz) F.; m. Millicent Heft, Sept. 7, 1958; children: Richard Howard, Lynn Finkel Lutz. BSc, Delaware Valley Coll., Doylestown, Pa., 1957; MBA, Fairleigh Dickinson U., 1973. Rsch. chemist Standard Brands, Inc., Stamford, Conn., 1957-59; group leader DCA Food Industries, Inc., N.Y.C., 1959-67; sr. scientist Lever Bros. Co., Edgewater, N.J., 1967-68; mgr. product devel. M & M/Mars, Hackettstown, N.J., 1968-72; pres. Food-Tek, Inc., Morris Plains, N.J., 1972—. Contbr. articles to profl. jours.; patentee in field. With U.S. Army, 1959. Office: Food-Tek Inc 28 E Hanover Ave Morris Plains NJ 07950-2431

FINKEL, JANET PEARL, real estate broker and executive; b. Manhasset, N.Y., Feb. 24, 1961; d. Sidney and Dorothy (Mendlow) F. BA, NYU, 1984. Lic. real estate broker, N.Y. Rsch. asst. Peter Wolf Inc., Land Planning and Land Investment Mgmt., N.Y.C., 1984-85; assoc. broker J.I. Sopher & Co. Inc., N.Y.C., 1985-88; chief exec. officer Luxury Habitat, Inc., N.Y.C., 1989—. Mem. NAFE. Jewish. Office: Luxury Habitat Inc 155 E 55th St Ste # 302-B New York NY 10017-2416

FINKEL, SANFORD NORMAN, lawyer; b. Troy, N.Y., Oct. 19, 1946; s. Max and Mildred (Fares) F.; m. Amy Lynn Gordon, Oct. 13, 1974 (div. July 1994); children: Marcy Jennifer, Melanie Gordon. BA, SUNY, Buffalo, 1968; JD, Union U., 1974. Bar: N.Y 1975, U.S. Dist. Ct. (no. dist.) N.Y. 1975. Sci. tchr. Enlarged City Sch. Dist. of Troy, N.Y., 1968-71; pvt. practice Troy, 1976—; counsel to the dem. study group N.Y. State Assembly, Albany, 1977-78; instr. in para-legal studies Jr. Coll. Albany div. Russell Sage Coll., 1977-81; dep. corp. counsel City of Troy, 1990—. Mem. Rensselaer County Bar Assn. Home: 19 Capitol Place Rensselaer NY 12144-9658 Office: 68 Second St Troy NY 12180-3932

FINKELSTEIN, ALLEN LEWIS, lawyer; b. N.Y.C., Mar. 19, 1943; s. David and Ella (Miller) F.; m. Judith Elaine Stutman, June 20, 1964 (div. Mar. 1980); children: Jill, Jennifer; m. Shelley Gail Barone, June 15, 1980; 1 child, Amanda. BS, NYU, 1964; JD, Bklyn. Law Sch., 1967; MBA, Long Island U., 1969. Bar: N.Y. 1968, U.S. Dist. Ct. (ea. and so. dists.) N.Y. 1973, U.S. Ct. Appeals (2d cir.) 1973, U.S. Supreme Ct. 1976, U.S. Tax Ct. 1979. Sr. ptnr. Finkelstein, Bruckman, Wohl, Most & Rothman and predecessor firms, N.Y.C., 1974—; asst. prof. L.I. U., N.Y.C., 1969-73, adj. assoc. prof., 1973-74; bd. dirs. Amotrophic Laterial Sclerosis Assn., Myser Found. Fund. Mem. dem. adv. com. N.Y. State Senate, N.Y.C., 1985—. Mem. ABA (family law sect.), N.Y. State Bar Assn., Assn. of Bar of City of N.Y., Queens County Bar Assn. Jewish. Lodge: Masons. Home: 425 E 63d St New York NY 10021 Office: Finkelstein Bruckman Wohl Most & Rothman 575 Lexington Ave New York NY 10022-6102

FINKELSTEIN, EDWARD SYDNEY, department store executive; b. New Rochelle, N.Y., Mar. 30, 1925; s. Maurice and Eva (Levine) F.; m. Myra Schuss, Aug. 13, 1950; children: Mitchell, Daniel, Robert. B.A., Harvard U., 1946, M.B.A., 1948; DCS (hon.), N.Y.U., 1988. Successively trainee, buyer mdse. adminstr. Macy's, N.Y.C., 1948-62; sr. v.p., dir. merchandising Macy's, N.J., 1962-67, exec. v.p., merchandising and sales promotion, 1967-69; pres. Macy's, Calif., 1969-74; pres., chmn., chief exec. officer Macy's, New York, 1974-80; chmn., chief exec. officer R.H. Macy & Co. Inc., 1980-92; dir. R.H. Macy, Inc., 1971-92; cons. R.H. Macy & Co.; dir. Chase Manhattan Bank, Chase Manhattan Corp., Time Warner, Inc.; mem. adv. bd. Yale Sch., 1984-89. Mem. nat. adv. council Cystic Fibrosis, 1975-80; trustee Cystic Fibrosis Found., 1977-80, hon. trustee, 1980—; bd. dirs. adv. bd. Harvard Bus. Sch., 1983-91. Served with USN, 1943-46. Mem. Harvard Club. Jewish. Office: R H Macy & Co Inc 151 W 34th St New York NY 10001-2124

FINKELSTEIN, GARY STAN, surgeon; b. Phila., Dec. 5, 1948; s. Albert and Ann B. (Chasens) F.; m. Phyllis Malissa, June 26, 1971; children: Joanne, Lauren. BS, Albright Coll., 1970; MD, Temple U., 1974. Intern, then resident in surgery Abington (Pa.) Meml. Hosp., 1974-79; attending surgeon Grand View Hosp., Sellersville, Pa., 1979—. Bd. dirs. Bux Mont United Jewish Appeal, Ft. Washington, Pa., 1989-92; mem. missions com. United Jewish Appeal, Phila., 1991-92; dist. gov. Key Club Internat., Pa., 1965. Fellow ACS; mem. AMA, Pa. Med. Soc.

FINKELSTEIN, JACOB, chemist; b. N.Y.C., Oct. 27, 1910. BS, CCNY, 1933; MA, Columbia U., 1934, PhD, 1939. Organic chemist The Rsch. Corp., N.Y.C., 1935; rsch. chemist Merck & Co., Rahway, N.J., 1935-43, Hoffmann-LaRoche, Inc., Nutley, N.J., 1943-75; prof. organic chemistry St. Peter's Coll., Jersey City, N.J., 1976-77; chem. cons. Teaneck, N.J., 1977—. Patentee in field; contbr. articles to profl. publs. Fellow Am. Inst. of Chemists; mem. Am. Chem. Soc. (Eminent Chemist of N.J., 1981, exec. com. North Jersey sect., chmn. organic chemistry discussion group), Sci. Rsch. Soc. of Am., Phi Lambda Upsilon, Sigma Xi. Home and Office: 648 Sunderland Rd Teaneck NJ 07666-2017

FINKELSTEIN, JAMES DAVID, physician; b. N.Y.C., Oct. 16, 1933; s. Harry and Sylvia Z. (Bernstein) F.; m. Barbara Joan Eisenberg, Dec. 12, 1959; children—Donna Ilene, Laura Helene. A.B., Harvard U., 1954; M.D., Columbia U., 1958. Diplomate Am. Bd. Internal Medicine. Intern, resident in medicine Presbyn. Hosp., N.Y.C., 1958-61; fellow in gastroenterology Columbia U., N.Y.C., 1961-63. Chief med. service VA Med. Ctr., Washington, 1979—, chief gastroenterology, 1970-79, assoc. chief staff for research, 1975-79, med. investigator, 1970-75, clin. investigator, 1965-68, chief biochemistry research lab., 1965—; cons. Children's Hosp., Washington, 1968-85; prof. medicine George Washington U., 1969—; clin. prof. medicine Georgetown U., 1981—; prof. medicine Howard U., Washington, 1983—; mem. Nutrition Study sect. NIH, 1972-78. Contbr. articles biochemistry and nutrition of methionine to profl. jours. Served as surgeon USPHS, 1963-65. Recipient F.P. Gay Research award Columbia U., N.Y.C., 1956; Arthur S. Fleming award Jr. C. of C., Washington, 1971; NIH grantee, 1966—. Mem. Am. Soc. for Clin. Investigation, Am. Gastroent. Assn., Assn.

of Am. Physicians, Am. Inst. Nutrition, Am. Soc. Clin. Nutrition, Am. Fedn. Clin. Research. Club: Harvard. Office: VA Med Ctr 50 Irving St NW Washington DC 20422-0002

FINKELSTEIN, JAY LAURENCE, aerospace engineer; b. Bklyn., Mar. 26, 1938; s. Martin Mark and Sally (Heimer) F.; m. Honora Ellen Moore, Mar. 15, 1980; children: Aileen, Kathleen, Bridget, Michael. BA, Rice Inst., 1960, BS, 1961; MS, Calif. Inst. Tech., 1965. Project engr. Naval Missile Ctr., Point Mugu, Calif., 1962-66; sr. analyst Navy Space Systems Activity, L.A., 1966-68, sr. systems engr., 1968-76; head systems utility div. Naval Electronic Systems Command, Washington, 1976-88; head. space survey div. Space and Naval Warfare Systems Command, Washington, 1988-90, asst. program mgr. environ. satellite acquisition, 1990—; dir., pres. Systems Analysis, Inc., Ojai, Calif., 1974-76; computer cons. Communications, Ink, Reston, Va., 1980—. Author: Tactical Meteorological Systems; co-patentee missile launcher; contbr. articles to profl. jours. Fellow AAAS; mem. Am. Men and Women of Sci. Home: 12202 Nutmeg Ln Reston VA 22091-1207 Office: Space and Naval Warfare Systems Command PMW 165-4 Washington DC 20363

FINKELSTEIN, ROBERT, robotics scientist; b. N.Y.C., Oct. 13, 1942; s. Sam. and Rose (Herschkopf) F.; m. Beverly Karen Sokol, Dec. 5, 1964; children: Marni, Michael, Lori. BA in Physics, Temple U., 1964; MS in Physics, U. Lowell, 1966; MS in Optics Rsch., George Washington U., 1974, Applied Scientist, 1977, postgrad., 1991—. Antisatellite systems officer U.S. Army Missile Intelligence Agy., Redstone Arsenal, Ala., 1966-68; mem. tech. staff MIT, Cambridge, 1968-70; task leader Computer Scis. Corp., Silver Spring, Md., 1970-72; project mgr. Atlantic Rsch. Corp., Alexandria, Va., 1972-75; sr. analyst Ketran, Inc., Rosslyn, Va., 1975-76; project mgr. Mantech Corp., Rockville, Md., 1976-77; systems scientist MITRE Corp., McLean, Va., 1977-85; pres. Robotic Tech. Inc., Potomac, Md., 1985—; adj. prof. U. Ala., Huntsville, 1966-68, Cen. Mich. U., Washington, 1974-77, George Mason U., Fairfax, Va., 1977-78, George Washington U., Washington, 1982. Co-editor Unmanned Systems Jour., 1983-91; contbr. articles to profl. jours. 1st lt. U.S. Army, 1966-68. Mem. AAAS, Am. Phys. Soc., Ops. Rsch. Soc. Am., Am. Assn. for Artificial Intelligence, Am. Cybernetics Soc., Internat. Neural Network Soc., Assn. for Unmanned Vehicle Systems (trustee 1981—, 7 awards 1982-88). Home and Office: 10001 Crestleigh Ln Rockville MD 20854-1821

FINKLE, BEVERLY ARTHUR, retired army officer, educator; b. Faribault, Minn., Oct. 11, 1915; s. Beverly A. and Edna C. (Whalen) F.; m. Edith A. Kneeland, June 25, 1949; 1 child, Ann B.F. Pierce. A.B., U. Nebr., 1938, M.A., 1946, postgrad., 1946-48; postgrad Boston U., 1949-50, U.S. Army Arty. Sch., 1942, 58, U.S. Army Intelligence Sch., 1950, U.S. Army Counterintelligence Sch., 1949, U.S. Army Mgmt. Sch., 1961, U.S. Army Command and Gen. Staff Coll., 1959. Commd. 2d lt. U.S. Army, 1942; advanced through grades to col., 1967; service with 45th Inf. Div., Africa and Europe, World War II; service in Japan, Korea, Korean War; service in Alaska, 1955-58, Pacific, 1964-67, Vietnam War, ret., 1968; mem. faculty U.S. Army Command and Gen. Staff Coll., Ft. Leavenworth, Kans., 1959-61, 62-64, grad. honors faculty, 1962-64, ret., 1968; assoc. prof. LaSalle Coll., Phila., 1952-55; with Robert Morris Coll., Pitts., 1969-81, assoc. prof. polit. sci., 1975-81, emeritus, 1981—, chmn. dept. social scis., 1970-74, chmn. dept. econs., 1973-74; mem. N.H. Hist. Soc., Bridgewater (N.H.) Hist. Soc., Bridgewater Planning Bd., Newfound Aera Sch. Bd. Decorated French Croix de Guerre with palm and star, Legion of Merit, Purple Heart, Bronze Star with Clusters, Army Commendation medal with clusters. Mem. AAUP, Am. Polit. Sci. Assn., Am. Acad. Polit. and Social Sci., Acad. Polit. Sci., Northeastern Polit. Sci. Assn., , Nat. Hist. Soc., Calvin Coolidge Found., Am. Econs. Assn., Internat. Platform Assn., Constitution Mus., Center Study Democratic Instns., Center Study of Presidency, Truman Library, J.F. Kennedy Library, 1st Inf. Div. Assn., 2d Inf. Div. Assn., 45th Inf. Assn., Anzio Beachhead Assn., Ret. Officers Assn., Res. Officers Assn., Assn. U.S. Army, Mil. Order World Wars, 157th Inf. Regt. Assn., VFW, Amvets. Am. Legion, Republican. Roman Catholic. Clubs: Army-Navy of Washington, Univ. of Lincoln, White Mountain Country (N.H.). Lodge: Elks. Contbr. articles and revs. to profl. and mil. jours. Home: Masquebec Newfound Lake Bridgewater NH 03222

FINKLE, JEFFREY ALAN, professional association executive; b. Newark, Ohio, Apr. 22, 1954; s. Richard James and Margery (Orr) F.; m. Diane Elizabeth Letchford, Aug. 20, 1983 (div. July 1989). BSc cum laude, Ohio U., 1976; postgrad., Ohio State U., 1978-80. Legis. dir. Ohio Rep. Party, Columbus, 1976-78; legis. liason Ohio Dept. Mental Health, Columbus, 1978-80; mktg. dir. Systems 80, Bethesda, Md., 1980-81; exec. asst. HUD, Washington, 1981-83, dep. asst. sec., 1983-86; exec. dir. Nat. Council for Urban Econ. Devel., Washington, 1986—; mem. adv. com., Ohio U. Inst. for Local Govt. Adminstrn. and Rural Devel., 1986—. Bd. dirs., pres. Bollinger Found., 1989—; mem. advv. bd. Bush for Pres. Urban Policy Task Force, 1988; mem. exec. com. Greater Washington Open, 1988, 89. Mem. Housing Rehab. Assn. (bd. dirs. 1986-90), Nat. Assn. Ind. Living Ctrs. (nat. adv. bd. 1987-89), Sr. Living Choices (bd. dirs. 1991—), Ohio U. Alumni Assn. (past pres., past bd. dirs.). Republican. Roman Catholic. Office: Nat Coun for Urban Econ Devel 1730 St NW Ste 915 Washington DC 20006

FINLEY, DAVID ALLEN, education consultancy specialist; b. Munhall, Pa., Oct. 6, 1943; s. Samuel Albert and Martha Eleanor (Wycoff) F.; m. Anna Marie Balint, Nov. 7, 1964; 1 child, Nathan Allen. ABA in Bus. Adminstrn., Pa. State U., Dubois, 1979; BS in Communicaton, Clarion U. of Pa., 1982, MS, 1984. Cert. in mgmt. Supr. printing and mail svcs. The Stackpole Corp., St. Marys, Pa., 1965-80; grad. teaching asst. Clarion U. of Pa., 1982-84; edn. technologist Burroughs Corp., King of Prussia, Pa., 1984-85; sr. edn. technologist Unisys Corp., King of Prussia, 1985-87; prin. edn. technologist Unisys Corp., Princeton, N.J., 1987-89; edn. consultancy specialist Unisys Corp., Blue Bell, Pa., 1989—. Author: Development Standards, 1988; designer software. With USAF, 1966-72. Mem. Nat. Soc. for Performance and Instrn., Clarion U. Pa. Alumni Assn., Pa. State U. Alumni Assn. Republican. Methodist. Home: 55 Netherwood Dr Coatesville PA 19320-1469 Office: Internal Edn and Devel PO Box 500 MS C1NW12 Blue Bell PA 19424

FINLEY, SKIP, broadcast executive; b. Ann Arbor, Mich., July 23, 1948; s. Ewell W. and Mildred Virginia (Johnson) F.; m. Karen Michele Woolard, May 6, 1971; children: Kharma I., R. Kristin. Student, Northeastern U., 1966-71. Owner Skifin Gallery, Boston, 1970-71; floor dir. WHDH-TV, Boston, 1971; floor mgr., asst. dir., producer WSBK TV, Boston, 1971-72; account exec. WRKO-AM, Boston, 1972-73; account mgr. Humphrey, Browning, MacDougall Advt., Boston, 1973-74; sales mgr. for WAMO-AM/FM Sheridan Broadcasting Corp., Boston, 1974-75, gen. mgr. WAMO-AM/FM, 1975-76, v.p. radio div., 1976-77; dir. of sales Sheridan Broadcasting Network, 1977-79, exec. v.p., gen. mgr., 1979-81, pres., 1981-82; gen. ptnr. KEZO AM/FM, Omaha, 1983-88, KDAB-FM, Salt Lake City and Ogden, Utah, 1985-90; pres., gen. mgr. WKYS-FM, Washington, 1988—; pres., chief exec. officer Albimar Communications, Washington, 1982—. Contbr. numerous articles on media-related subjects to various publs. Testimony to House subcom. on Communications, 1977, Congl. Black Caucus, 1990; mem. bd. overseers, trustee Vineyard Open Land Found. Recipient Excellence in Media award Nat. Assn. Media Women, 1981, Communicator of Yr. award Washington area Media Orgn., 1982, New Horizons award D.C. Gen. Hosp., Washington, 1990, Advocacy in Edn. award D.C. Pub. Schs., Washington, 1990. Mem. Nat. Assn Black Owned Broadcasters (bd. dirs.), Radio Advt. Bur. (bd. dirs.), Nat. Assn. Broadcasters (bd. dirs.), Washington Area Broadcasters Assn. (bd. dirs.), Nat. Thespian Soc., Martha's Vineyard Rod and Gun Club. Office: Sta WKYS-FM 4001 Nebraska Ave NW Washington DC 20016-2795

FINN, DAVID, public relations company executive, artist; b. N.Y.C., Aug. 30, 1921; s. Jonathan and Sadie (Borgenicht) F.; m. Laura Zeisler, Oct. 20, 1945; children: Kathy, Dena, Peter, Amy. BS, CCNY, 1943. Co-founder Ruder Finn, Inc., N.Y.C., 1948, pres., 1956-68, chmn. bd., chief exec. officer, 1968—, also bd. dirs.; adj. assoc. prof. NYU. One-man show New Sch. for Social Research, N.Y.C.; exhibited in group shows at Nat. Acad., Washington, Met. Mus. Art, N.Y.C., Boston Mus. Art, L'Orangerie, Paris, Andrew Crispo Gallery, N.Y.C., Westchester County Ctr., others; author Public Relations and Management, 1956, The Corporate Oligarch, 1969; photographer: (books) Embrace of Life, 1969, As the Eye Moves, 1970, Donatello: Prophet of Modern Vision, 1973, Henry Moore Sculpture and Environment, 1976, Michelangelo's Three Pietas, 1975, Oceanic Images, 1978, The Florence Baptistry Doors, 1980, Sculpture at Storm King, 1980, Busch-Reisinger Museum, 1980, Canova, Giambologna, Donatello, Cellini, David by the Hand of Michelangelo, In the Mountains of Japan, others; contbr. articles and chpts. to profl. jours. and art publs. Mem. adv. bd. Council for Study Mankind; mem. adv. council advanced mgmt. programs Internat. Bus. Inst., Baruch Coll., N.Y.C.; bd. visitors CCNY; bd. dirs. New Hope Found., Ctr. for Research in Bus. and Social Policy, Victor Gruen Ctr. for Environ. Planning, Inst. Advanced Studies in Humanities, MacDowell Colony, Inst. for Future, Artists for Environment Found., Internat. Ctr. Photography, Am. Coll. Switzerland, Jewish Theol. Sem. Am.; bd. overseers Parsons Sch. Design, N.Y.C. Served to 1st lt. A.C. AUS, 1944. Mem. Am. Fedn. Arts, Am. Inst. Graphic Arts (past dir.), Internat. Pub. Relations Assn., Kappa Tau Alpha (hon.). Office: Ruder Finn Inc 165 W End Ave Apt 14F New York NY 10023-5520*

FINN, DAVID THURMAN, artist, sculptor; b. Urbana, Ill., July 7, 1952; s. Robert Kaul and Lucille (Rassmussen) F. BS, Cornell U., 1975; MFA, Mass. Coll. Art, 1982. vis. asst. prof. Wake Forest U., Winston-Salem, N.C., 1988-91. One man-shows include Salvatore Ala Gallery, N.Y.C., 1984, 87, Milan, Italy, 1985, Anders Tornberg Gallery, Lund, Sweden, 1985, Third Eye Ctr., Glasgow, Scotland, 1988, City Contemporary Gallery, CCDC, Hong Kong, 1989, Atrium Gallery, U. Conn., Storrs, 1991, Watermans Art Ctr., West London, Eng., 1991, Leeds (Eng.) City Gallery, 1992. Artist fellow NEA, 1990, N.Y. Found. for the Arts, 1988, Residence fellow Bemis Found., Omaha, 1987; New Works grantee Pub. Art Fund, Inc., N.Y.C., 1985-86. Home: PO Box 539 Jeffersonville NY 12748-0539 Office: Salvatore Ala Gallery 560 Broadway New York NY 10012-3938

FINN, DOUGLAS GEORGE, otolaryngologist; b. Newark, Apr. 11, 1951; s. Alfred Ernest and Magdalena (Adams) F.; m. Christina McClellan, June 2, 1985. BA, Wesleyan U., 1972; MD, N.Y. Med. Coll., 1975. Intern St. Vincent's Hosp., N.Y.C.; resident Duke U. Med. Ctr. Mem. AAAS, ACS (Bklyn.-L.I. chpt.), Am. Acad. Otolaryngology, N.Y. Head and Neck Soc., Kings County Med. Soc. (sec., treas. otolaryngology sect. 1991—), Bay Ridge Lions Club, Masons.

FINN, FRANCES MARY, biochemistry educator; b. Pitts., May 6, 1937; d. Stephen B. and Geraldine H. (Weber) F.; m. Klaus Hofmann, Feb. 26, 1965. BS in Chemistry, U. Pitts., 1959, MS in Biochemistry, 1961, PhD in Biochemistry, 1964. Asst. rsch. prof. biochemistry U. Pitts., 1969-73, assoc. rsch. prof., 1973-80, assoc. prof. medicine, 1980-88, prof., 1988—. Mem. Am. Chem. Soc., Endocrine Soc., Am. Soc. for Biochemistry and Molecular Biology. Home: 1467 Mohican Dr Pittsburgh PA 15228-1613 Office: U Pitts Protein Rsch Lab 3550 Terrace St Pittsburgh PA 15261-0001

FINN, GILBERT, lieutenant governor; b. Inkerman Ferry, N.B., Can., Sept. 3, 1920; s. Ephrem and Felicite (Finn) F.; m. Jeannine Boudreau, Sept. 8, 1948; children: Louise, Marthe, Yvette, Suzanne, Thérése, Pierre, Céline, Jacques, Jean. Student, Sacred Heart Sem., Halifax, N.S., 1944-46; BA, Laval U., Que., Can., 1947; hon. doctorate, St. Anne U., N.S., 1977, St. Thomas U., Fredricton, N.B., 1981, U. Moncton, N.B., 1987. CLU. With Acadian Coop. Movement, 1948-63, v.p. Caisse populaire de St. Anselme, 1961-63; with Assumption Mut. Life Assurance Co., 1950-87, pres., chief exec. officer, chmn. exec. com., 1969-80, chmn. bd., chief exec. officer, 1975-80, chmn. bd., 1980-87; pres. U. Moncton, N.B., 1980-85; lt. gov. New Brunswick Fredricton, 1987—; pres. Union des Mutuelles-Vie françaises, 1963-64; mem. N.B. Research and Productivity Council, 1966-72; mem. N.B. Higher Edn. Commn., 1971-74, Econ. Council Can., 1973-76, Lebel Commn., 1974-75, Maritimes Provinces Higher Edn. Commn., 1974-77, Econ. Study Com. Fedn. des francophones Hors-Que., 1979-81, N.B. Devel. Inst., 1979-82; dir. Inst. Acadian Coop. Movement, 1978-80; mem. retirement plan com. Provincial Bank Can., 1980-86; bd. dirs., mem. retirement plan com. Nat. Bank Can., 1980-86, auditing com., 1986-87; founding chmn. Econ. Council N.B., 1980-82; pres. Atlantic Enterprise Program, 1986-87; adv. com. Fondation Donatien Frémont, Inc., 1986-87. Chmn. bd. trustees St. Anselme Sch., 1958-64; bd. govs. U. Moncton, 1965-71, mem. exec. and fin. coms., 1965-71; chmn. bd. Dr. Georges L. Dumont Hosp., 1971-87; bd. dirs. Villa Providence, Shediac, N.B., 1972-87, Villa Heritage, Moncton, 1972-87; chmn. bd. Assumption Pl. Ltd., 1972-80, 85-87; hon. pres. Atlantic Boy Scouts Assn., 1975-85; mem. com. to establish tng. inst. for N.B. francophones, 1977-78; co-chmn. Task Force on Amateur Sport in N.B., 1979-81; pres. organizing com. Le Matin, 1982-85; trustee Les Presses francophones N.B., 1984-87; diocesan pres. Ligue du Sacré-Coeur, 1958-60. Decorated Order of Can. Office: Office of Lt Gov, 736 King St, Fredericton, NB Canada E3B 1G2

FINN, JOHN MCMASTER, research physicist; b. Washington, Jan. 8, 1947; s. John Louis and Frances (Jones) F.; m. Agnes Schickel, Oct. 22, 1977; children: Pauline, John, Ryan, Madeline, William. BS in Physics, Ga. Inst. of Tech., 1969; MS in Math, U. Houston, 1971; PhD in Physics, U. Md., 1974. Postdoctoral rsch. fellow Princeton (N.J.) U., 1974-76; rsch. assoc. Cornell U., Ithaca, N.Y., 1976-79, Sci. Applications, Inc., McLean, Va., 1979-81; rsch. scientist Naval Rsch. Lab., Washington, 1981-83; rsch. assoc. Lab. for Plasma Rsch., U. Md., College Park, 1982-85, assoc. rsch. scientist, 1985-88, sr. rsch. scientist, 1988—; cons. plasma physics lab. Princeton U., 1982—, Naval Rsch. Lab., 1983—, Sci. Applications, Inc., McLean, 1983—; collaborator Los Alamos (N.Mex.) Lab.; workshop presenter in field. Contbr. numerous articles to profl. jours.; patentee in field. Fellow Am. Phys. Soc. (div. plasma physics), Am. Geophys. Union, Phi Kappa Phi, Pi Mu Epsilon. Home: 5321 Thayer Ave Alexandria VA 22304-2741 Office: U Md Lab for Plasma Rsch College Park MD 20742

FINN, PATRICK MATTHEW, academic program director, coach; b. Richmond, Va., Dec. 3, 1959; s. Raymond Eugene and Doris Finn; m. Regina Thomas Bahr, Aug. 6, 1988; 1 child, Emily Killoran. BA, U. Va., 1982; MS in Exercise and Sport Sci., Pa. State U., 1992. Asst. Lacrosse Coach Pa. State U., State Coll., Pa., 1984-85; internship, ticket office U. Va., Charlottesville, Va., 1985-86; asst. Lacrosse Coach U. Va., Charlottesville, 1985-86; asst. dir. of devel. Canterbury Sch., New Milford, Conn., 1986-87; dir. of admissions Canterbury Sch., New Milford, 1987—. Mem. Alumni Mag., Pallium (author 1977); bd. dirs. Internat. Alliance of Children, New Milford, 1987—; founder, coach New Milford Youth Lacrosse League, 1990—. Named All Am. Team Sec. Schs., U.S. Lacrosse Coaches Assn., 1977, Most Valuable Player, Conn. Valley Lacrosse Club, Hartford, Conn., 1987. Mem. Western Conn. Boarding Sch. Assn. (bd. dirs. 1988—), Zeta Psi (v.p. 1981), Charlottesville Lacrosse Club (mgr. 1986). Home: 6 Elkington Farm Rd New Milford CT 06776-2929 Office: Canterbury Rd Aspetuck Ave Caller Box 5000 New Milford CT 06776

FINN, PETER, public relations executive; b. N.Y.C., Mar. 31, 1954; s. David and Laura (Zeisler) F.; m. Sarah Duncan; children: Noah J., Emily M. BA, Brown U., 1976; MA, Columbia U., 1977. Researcher Research & Forecasts Inc., N.Y.C., 1977-79, dir. ops., 1979-81, chmn., 1981-84; chmn. fin. com. Ruder-Finn, Inc. (formerly Ruder, Finn & Rotman, Inc.), N.Y.C., 1984—, chief fin. officer, 1985—, exec. v.p., 1986-87, chmn. exec. com., 1988—. Office: Ruder-Finn Inc 165 W End Ave Apt 14F New York NY 10023-5520

FINNEFROCK, CRAIG ALAN, cruise line executive; b. Pitts., Oct. 7, 1942; s. Robert F. and Anna Marie (Horst) F.; m. L. Jo Parrish, Aug. 31, 1963; children: Adam, Jessica, Kate. Student, U.S. Naval Acad., 1960-63; BA, Calif. State U., Long Beach, 1970. Div. materials mgr. Hubbell Lighting, Christiansburg, Va., 1971-81; mng. dir. Intercontinental Purchasing Svcs. Co. div. Intercontinental Hotels Corp., N.Y.C., 1981-85; pres. Hotel Source/Unifood div. Sheraton Corp., Boston, 1985-88; exec. v.p. Minibar A.G., Zurich, Switzerland, 1988-90; v.p. purchasing Cunard Line, N.Y.C., 1990—; speaker in field. Mem. fin. bd. Representative Town Meeting, Darien, Conn., 1982-85. Mem. Marine Hotel Catering and Duty Free Assn. (bd. dirs. 1990—). Republican. Office: Cunard Line PO Box 1291 New York NY 10163-1291

FINNEGAN, HUGH PATRICK, lawyer; b. N.Y.C., May 7, 1958; s. Philip Joseph and Nora Mary (Kilkenny) F.; m. Peggy Donlon, Dec. 27, 1981; children: Philip James, Mary Kate, Conor John. AB, Fordham U., 1980, JD, 1983. Bar: N.Y. 1984. Assoc. Sage, Gray, Todd & Sims, N.Y.C., 1983-86, DeForest & Duer, N.Y.C., 1986-87, Siller, Wilk, Mencher & Simkin, N.Y.C., 1987-90; spl. counsel Siller, Wilk & Mencher, N.Y.C., 1991—; ptnr. Siller, Silk & Mencher, N.Y.C., 1992—. Mem. N.Y. State Bar Assn., Com. on Comml. Leasing and Litigation (real property law sect., environ. law sect.), Ireland C. of C. U.S. Office: Siller Wilk & Mencher 747 3d Ave New York NY 10017-2803

FINNEGAN, RICHARD BRENDAN, political science educator; b. Boston, July 2, 1942; s. Neal Francis and Mary Theresa (McNeill) F.; m. Joanne Carmela Scotti, Apr. 24, 1988; children: Scott, Jesse, Richard. AB, Stonehill Coll., 1964; AM, Boston Coll., 1966; PhD, Fla. State U., 1971; EdM, Harvard U., 1989. Prof. polit. sci., dir. Irish and internat. studies Stonehill Coll., Easton, Mass., 1968—; vis. prof. Boston (Mass.) U., 1980-81; pres. internat. law sect. Internat. Studies Assn., 1974-75, New England Internat. Studies Assn., 1979-80, New England Conf. for Irish Studies, 1984-85. Author: Ireland, 1983 (Outstanding Academic Book 1984), The U.S. and Ireland, 1992; co-author: Law and Politics in International System, 1979, Aspirations and Realities, 1992; contbr. articles to profl. jours. Pres., founder Norwell Charitable Chowder and Dancing Soc., Norwell, Mass., 1985-90. Recipient summer stipend NSF, 1971, Dept. of the Army, U.S. Mil. Acad., 1982, NEH, U. Conn., 1983, NEH, Yale U., 1987, Fulbright, People's Republic China, 1989, NEH, UCLA, 1990. Mem. Pi Sigma Alpha, Phi Delta Kappa, Alpha Sigma Lambda. Office: Stonehill Coll Martin Inst Easton MA 02357

FINNEGAN, SHARYN MARIE, art educator; b. N.Y.C., Aug. 16, 1946; d. James P. and Margaret P. (Connell) F.; m. George P. Prans, Oct. 26, 1974; 1 child, Kate Finnegan-Prans. BFA, Marymount Coll., Tarrytown, N.Y., 1967; MA, NYU, 1971. Instr. art Marymount Manhattan Coll., N.Y.C., 1978-79, Mt. St. Vincent's Coll., Bronx, N.Y., 1979-82, Parsons Sch. Design, N.Y.C., 1987—; dir. Prince Street Gallery, N.Y.C., 1974-75, 77-79; artist-in-residence Roswell Mus. Fine Arts, 1976, Palisades Park, N.Y., 1979. One-man shows include Prince Street Gallery, 1974-89, Roswell (N.Mex.) Mus. Fine Arts, 1977. MacDowell Colony fellow, Peterborough, N.H., 1979. Office: Prince St Gallery 14 E 4th St Apt 1104 New York NY 10012-1143

FINNELL, ALFRED WAYNE, data processing executive; b. Scottsbluff, Nebr., Feb. 12, 1936; s. Wayne Russell and Natalie (Butherus) F.; m. Joyce Ann Estes, Dec. 30, 1982; 1 child, Lee Alfred. BS, Oreg. State U., 1961. Computer specialist U.S. Air Force, Denver, 1971-84; computer specialist Bur. Indian Affairs, Washington, 1984-85, communications mgr., 1985-89, MIS coord., 1989—. With U.S. Army, 1955-56. Home: 5812 Lane Dr Alexandria VA 22310 Office: BIA/OTED/MIB-4513 18th and C Sts Washington DC 20245

FINNELL, LEONARD WILLIAM, electrical engineer; b. Spokane, Wash., Apr. 25, 1928; s. William Leonard and Jean Hamilton (Simpson) F.; m. Nancy Faith Rau, Oct. 19, 1957; children: Douglas William, Joy Elizabeth. BSEE, Wash. State U., 1950. Profl. engr. Svc. technician Sears Roebuck and Co., Spokane, 1944-50; engr. Westinghouse Electric Corp., East Pittsburgh, Pa., 1950-60, sr. engr., 1960-70, supervising engr. large rotating apparatus div., 1970-74, mgr. advanced engring. large motor dept., 1974-77, mgr. elec. design, large motor and medium turbine generator dept., 1977-78, fellow engr. advanced programs, 1978-84; adv. engr. machinery tech. div. Westinghouse Electric Corp., Large, Pa., 1984-90; engring. cons. Finnell Svcs., Pitts., 1990—; assoc. Electro Mechanical Engring. Assocs., Pitts., 1990—. Patentee in field. Mem. exec. bd. east Valley Area Coun. Boy Scouts Am., Forest Hills, Pa., 1986—. 2d lt. USAR, 1950-55. Mem. IEEE (sr. mem.). Republican. Presbyterian. Home and office: 312 Sharon Dr Pittsburgh PA 15221

FINNELL, RONNIE WARD, human resource executive, organizational researcher, management consultant, educator, author; b. Indpls.; s. Joseph Henry and Bessie Ida (Walton) F.; 1 child, Brian Lamont. BS, U. Md.; MA, Antioch Sch. Law, Washington; MPA, U. So. Calif., DPA. Dir. human resources Washington Fire Dept., 1970-74; mgr. human resources U.S. Dept. Health and Human Svcs., Washington, 1974-80 81-87, dir. fellows program, 1980-81; sr. rsch. analyst U.S. Merit Systems Protection Bd., Washington, 1987-91; sr. rsch. assoc. Inst. for Workplace Learning, Alexandria, Va., 1991—; sr. assoc. Econ. Devel. Alternatives, Washington, 1984—; mem. faculty USDA Grad. Sch., Washington, 1990—, Prince Georges Community Coll., Largo, Md., 1985-88, Nat.-Louis U., McLean, Va., 1992—; cons. Ednl. Testing Svc., Princeton, N.J., 1991—. Contbr. articles to profl. jours. Athletic coach Boys Clubs Am., Prince Georges County, 1975-80. Mem. Conf. Minority Pub. Adminstrs. (exec. bd., Chairman's award 1990), Am. Soc. Pub. Adminstrn., Am. Psychol. Assn., Nat. Forum for Black Pub. Adminstrs., Internat. Personnel Mgmt. Assn., Nat. Assn. for Equal Edn. Opportunity, NAACP, Big Bros Am., Urban League. Home: 14817 Whitegate Rd Silver Spring MD 20905-5710

FINNERTY, PETER JOSEPH, water transportation executive; b. Petersburg, Va., Sept. 9, 1942; s. Peter Francis and Alice P.F.; m. Tory Boone, Aug. 23, 1969; children: Peter, Will, Kate, Michael. BS, N.Y. Maritime Coll., 1964; MBA, U. Pa., 1966; JD, Georgetown U., 1972. Bar. D.C. 1973. Asst. to pres. Am. Merchant Marine Inst., N.Y.C., 1966-68; dep. dir. Am. Assn. Port Author, Washington, 1968-69; mgr. adminstrn. Sea-Land Svc., Washington, 1970-71, dir. govt. sales, 1971-73; v.p. CSX Corp., Washington, 1987—; dir. regulatory affairs Sea-Land Svc., Edison, N.J., 1974; v.p. pub. affairs Sea-Land Svc., Edison, 1977-87; mgr. fed. affairs R.J. Reynolds Industries, Washington, 1974-76; chmn. Maritime Inst. for Rsch. and Ind. Devel., Washington, 1988-91; cons., bd. ENO Found., Washington, 1990-91; trustee U.S. Coun. on Internat. Bus., N.Y.C., 1985-88, 91. Bd. dirs., chmn. exec. com., v.p. USCG Found., Stonington, Conn., 1991; bd. dirs. Seamen's Ch. Inst., N.Y.C., 1991. Lt. (j.g.) USNR, 1964-70. Mem. Maritime Adminstrn. Bar Assn., India House, Georgetown Club, City Club, Nat. Press Club, 116 Club, Propeller Club of U.S. (v.p. 1990-91). Roman Catholic. Home: 1423 36th St NW Washington DC 20007-2606 Office: 5530 Wisconsin Ave Ste 533 Bethesda MD 20815-4430

FINNERTY, THOMAS CONAN, rail transportation executive; b. Scranton, Pa., Jan. 16, 1954; s. Pau. Gerald and Ann Marie (Gordon) F.; m. Josephine Ann M. Marianelli, Sept. 17, 1983; 1 child, Brianna Marie. BS in Acctg., Wilkes Coll., 1982. Lead accounting technician Nat. Credit Union Adminstrn., Washington, 1979-81; acct. Dept. HEW, Hyattsville, Md., 1979; various postions Conrail/Erie Lackawan R.R., various, 1975-81; analyst Conrail, Newark, N.J., 1981-82; sr. ops. planning and control analyst N.J. Transit Rail/Conrail, Newark, 1982-84; mgr. engring. fin. planning and control N.J. Transit Rail, Newark, 1984-91, mgr. ops. control, 1991—. Democrat. Roman Catholic. Home: 3269 Oak Ave Scranton PA 18505 Office: NJ Transit 1 Penn Plz E Newark NJ 07105-2246

FINOCCHIARO, ALFONSO G., bank executive; b. Catania, Italy, Aug. 20, 1932; came to U.S., 1960; s. Giovanni and Giuseppina (Cavalieri) F.; m. Diana Louise Cavagnolo, May 14, 1960; children: John Paul, Carol Anne. D in Polit. Sci., U. Catania, 1958; MBA in Internat. Fin., Pace U., 1967. V.p. Chem. Bank, N.Y.C., 1966-77; pres., gen. mgr. Conn. Bank Internat., N.Y.C., 1977-78; exec. v.p., regional dir. Banco Portugues do Atlantico, N.Y.C., 1978—; dir. BPA Futures Cayman, 1989—, Internat. Strategy Svcs., 1990—. Comdr., Order Infante D. Henrique, Republic Portugal. Fellow Internat. Mgmt. and Devel. Inst. (Leadership award); mem. Portugal C. of C. (bd. dirs., past pres.), Am. Portuguese Soc. (bd. dirs. 1979—), Luso-Am. Bus. Coun., Global Econ. Action Inst. (bd. dirs. 1991—), Internat. Mgmt. and Devel. Inst., European-Am. C. of C. in the U.S. (bd. dirs. 1991—), Pace U. Lubin Grad. Sch. Bus. Alumni Assn. (bd. dirs.). Republican. Roman Catholic. Lodge: Rotary. Office: Banco Portugues do Atlantico 2 Wall St New York NY 10005-2001

FINSER, SIEGFRIED ERNEST, management consultant, counselor; b. Heilbronn, West Germany, Apr. 2, 1932; came to U.S., 1935; s. Hans and Frieda (Eberlein) Just; m. Ruth E.M. Alexander, Aug. 21, 1955; children: Torin M., Mark A, Angela M. BA, Rutgers U., 1954; CRT, Das Goetheanum, Dornach, Switzerland, 1961; MA, NYU, 1968. From tchr. to adminstr. Rudolf Steiner Sch., N.Y.C., 1955-61; sr. cons. Barrington & Co., N.Y.C., 1961-65; unit mgr. Xerox Corp., N.Y.C., 1965-68; mgr. mgmt. devel.

ITT World Hdqrs., N.Y.C., 1968-70, dir. human resource devel., 1972-76; dir. mgmt. devel. ITT Europe, Africa, Brussels, Belgium, Belgium, 1970-72; pres. Threefold Ednl. Found., Spring Valley, N.Y., 1976-81; pvt. practice cons. Chatham, N.Y., 1981—; trustee Rudolf Steiner Found., Harlemville, N.Y., 1972-80, pres., 1980—. Contbr. articles to profl. jours. Mem. Anthroposophical Soc. Am. (treas.). Home and Office: RR 1 Box 147A Chatham NY 12037-9730

FINZI, HILDA (GOLDENHORN), psychologist, educator; b. N.Y.C., Jan. 9, 1925; d. Seidel and Rose (Goldman) Goldenhorn; m. Alfons Finzi, Aug. 1, 1950; children: Rima Finzi-Strauss, Eric. BA, Hunter Coll., 1945; PhD, NYU, 1961; cert., Advanced Inst. Analytic Psychotherapy, 1969. Lic. psychologist, N.Y. Social investigator N.Y.C. Dept. Welfare, 1949-52; psychology intern Neurol. Inst. Columbia-Presbyn. Hosp., N.Y.C., 1952; lectr. Queens Coll., N.Y.C., 1962; asst. prof. Queensborough Community Coll., N.Y.C., 1965-77; dean Advanced Inst. for Analytic Psychotherapy, N.Y.C., 1970-86; chief youth svcs. Advanced Ctr. for Psychotherapy, N.Y.C., 1970-86; pvt. practice psychotherapist N.Y.C., 1970—; asst. prof. St. John's U., N.Y.C., 1990—. Mem. APA, AAUP, Am. Acad. Psychotherapists. Office: St Johns U Utopia & Grand Ctrl Pky Jamaica NY 11439

FIORATO, HUGO, conductor; b. N.Y.C., Aug. 28, 1914; s. Noe and Anna (Kress) F.; m. Beverly Cohen, May 1, 1948 (div. 1974); m. Joelyn Scott, June 23, 1975; children: James, Jan Fiorato O'Connor (dec.). Student, Damroche Sch. Mus. Prin. conductor N.Y. City Ballet, 1950—; instr. chamber music Sarah Lawrence Coll., N.Y.C., 1960-69, conducting Columbia U., N.Y.C., 1960-69; music dir., conductor Boston Ballet, 1962-70; conductor Hartford Ballet, Conn., 1968-70, Houston Ballet, 1972-74. Mem. Pequot Yacht Club (Southport, Conn.), Fairfield Country Hunt Club (Westport, Conn.), Fairfield Beach Club. Office: NYC Ballet NY State Theater Lincoln Ctr Plz New York NY 10023

FIORE, NICHOLAS FRANCIS, specialty metals and materials company executive; b. Pitts., Sept. 24, 1939; s. William H. and Margaret (Scinto) F.; m. Sylvia M. Chinque, Aug. 13, 1960; children: Maria L., Nicholas F., Kristin M., Anthony T. B.S., Carnegie-Mellon U., 1960, M.S., 1963, Ph.D., 1964. Asst. prof. metall. engring. and materials sci. U. Notre Dame (Ind.), 1966-69, prof., 1969-81, chmn. dept., 1969-72, 80-81; v.p. Cabot Corp., Boston, 1982-89; mng. dir. materials and applied physics Arthur D. Little Inc., Cambridge, Mass., 1989-90; v.p. Carpenter Technology Corp.; vis. scientist Argonne Nat. Labs. (Ill.), 1974-75. Co-author: Binding of Solute to Dislocations, 1967; Hydrogen Related Embrittlement of High Temperature Materials, 1975. Editor: (with B.J. Berkowitz) Advanced Techniques for Characterizing Hydrogen in Metals, 1982. Contbr. articles to profl. jours. Chmn. adv. bd. Primary Day Sch. Inc.; mem. sci. and tech. edn. com. New Eng. Council. Served to capt. U.S. Army, 1964-66. Fellow Am. Soc. Metals; mem. AIME, Alpha Sigma Mu. Office: Carpenter Tech PO Box 14662 Reading PA 19612-4662

FIORE, PAUL DAVID, credit union executive; b. Queens, N.Y., Dec. 31, 1964; s. Anthony John and Madeline Nellie (Hein) F. BS, NYU, 1992, postgrad., 1992—. Acct. GHQ Fed. Credit Union, 1983-85; mgr. Continental Bank, Garden City, N.Y., 1985-87; fin. analyst Shearson Lehman Hutton, N.Y.C., 1987-89; v.p., chief fin. officer AT&T Employees Fed. Credit Union, New Providence, N.J., 1989—; PSG adv. com. NJCU League, Hightstown, 1992—; product rev. com. Credit Union Svcs., Cambell, Calif., 1991—. Sec. Local Christian Assembly, Forest Hills, N.Y., 1987. Mem. Assn. for Image and Info. Mgmt., Electronic Banking Econs. Soc., Credit Union Execs. Soc. Office: AT&T Employees Fed C U 560 Central Ave Murray Hill NJ 07974

FIORELLA-RUSSO, D. CHRISTINE, elementary school educator, university English instructor; b. N.Y.C., July 24, 1931; d. Anthony Joseph and Assunta Mary (Moroni) Fiorella; m. Victor Donald Russo, Jr., Apr. 30, 1960. BA, Marymount Manhattan Coll.; MS, Fordham U., 1959; diploma in reading, Hofstra U., 1978, postgrad., 1987; cert. in litigation, Adelphi U. and Nat. Ctr. for Paralegal Tng., 1980. Cert. elem. and secondary English tchr., N.Y., reading specialist, N.Y. Tchr. St. Margaret's Sch., Bronx, N.Y., 1955-56, Sacred Heart, Manhattan, N.Y., 1956-57, Bd. Edn., N.Y.C., 1957-60, Harborfields Dist. 6, L.I., 1960—; instr. Marymount Manhattan Coll., N.Y. Bd. dirs. Marymount Alumnae Adv. Coun., N.Y., 1985—, Fordham U. Pres.'s Coun., Bronx, 1985-87, Fordham U. Recruitment Program, Bronx, 1983-87; campaign worker Dem. Party, N.Y.C., 1990, 92; Marymount rep. N.Y. State Bundy/Affairs Fund, 1982-83; L.I. rep. Marymount Recruitment Program, 1992; chmn. Ft. Salonga Assn., L.I., 1979-83. Recipient Disting. Leadership in Edn. award Marymount Coll., 1986, Outstanding Recruitment award Fordham U., 1985, Tchr.-Student Participation award Suffolk Reading Coun., 1991-92. Mem. APA, Internat. Soc. Intelligence Edn. (v.p. 1991, bd. dirs. 1990—), N.Y. Acad. Scis., N.Y. Orton Dyslexia Soc., Nat. Dyslexia Rsch. Found., Coun. for Exceptional Children, World Coun. for Gifted and Talented Children, Am. Assn. Higher Edn. Roman Catholic. Home: 7 Bonnie Dr Northport NY 11768-1448

FIORENTINO, THOMAS MARTIN, transportation executive, lawyer; b. Washington, Aug. 4, 1959; s. Thomas Martin Sr. and Julia (Bray) F.; m. Mary Ann Hammer, June 12, 1983; children: Sara Elizabeth, Caroline McKay. BA, U. Fla., 1980; JD, Mercer U., 1983. Bar: Fla. 1984. Claims rep. Seaboard System R.R., Evansville, Ind., 1983-84; claims atty. Seaboard System R.R., Jacksonville, Fla., 1984-86; dir. risk mgmt. CSX Corp., Jacksonville, 1986-87; asst. to pres. CSX Tech., Jacksonville, 1987-89; chief of staff Fed. R.R. Adminstrn., 1989-90; counselor dep. sec. of transp. Office of the Sec., Dept. Transp., Washington, 1990-91; asst. v.p. pub. affairs CSX Transp., Jacksonville, 1991—. Mem. bd. visitors The Bolles Sch., 1990—; bd. dirs. Jacksonville Community Coun., Inc., 1991—, Bapt. Hosp. Found. for Healthcare, Inc., 1992—. Mem. ABA, Fla. Bar Assn., Jacksonville Bar Assn., Jacksonville C. of C. (govt. affairs com.), First Coast Mfrs. Assn. (bd. dirs.), Fla. Yacht Club, Univ. Club, Tournament Players Club, Jacksonville Kappa Alpha Alumni Assn. (bd. dirs. 1987-88), Phi Delta Phi. Republican. Methodist. Home: 2815 Grand Ave Jacksonville FL 32210-4324

FIORI, MICHAEL J., pharmacist; b. Brunswick, Maine, Nov. 25, 1951; s. Columbus H. and Marie Alice (Pelletier) F.; m. Anna Marie Robinson, Dec. 25, 1980; 1 child, Michela. BA in Biology, Bowdoin Coll., 1974; BS in Pharmacy, Mass. Coll. Pharmacy, 1977; MBA, U. Maine, 1987; PhD in Bus. Adminstr., LaSalle U., 1992. Rsch. student Rsch. Inst. Gulf Maine, 1974-75; pharmacy intern Newton-Wellesley (Mass.) Hosp., 1977; pharmacist Allen Drug Store, Brunswick, 1977-78; cons. pharmacist Allen Drug Store, Bangor, Maine, 1977-84; pres., chief operating officer Downeast Pharmacy, Inc.; pres., cons. Pharmacists of New Eng. Downeast Pharmacy, Inc., various cities, Maine, 1984—; pres. Guardian Healthcare Downeast Pharmacy, Inc., 1990—; commr. Maine Commn. Pharmacy, 1985-90; pres. and chief exec. officer Vector Assocs., Inc. dba ODV, Inc. commr. Maine Commn. Pharmacy, 1985-90; pres., chief exec. officer Vector Assocs., Inc. dba ODV, Inc. Earle S. Thompson scholar, 1971-73, Charles Lowery scholar, 1974; named one of Outstanding Young Men Am., 1986. Fellow Am. Soc. Cons. Pharmacists; mem. Am. Soc. for Pharmacy Law, Narcotic Enforcement Officers Assn., Internat. Assn. for Identification, Internat. Assn. of Chiefs of Police, Nat. Assn. of Bds. of Pharmacy, Maine Pharmacy Assn., Health Care Providers, Inc., Nat. Assn. Retail Druggists, Mass. Coll. Pharmacy Alumni Assn., Bowdoin Coll. Alumni Assn., U. Maine Alumni Assn., Italian Heritage Soc., Gyro Internat., Maine Health Care Assn., NRA (life), KC, Elks, Beta Theta Pi (chpt. pres. 1972-73, ho. corp. pres. 1985—, ho. corp. dir. 1975—, dist. chief 1979-84, 87-90). Democrat. Roman Catholic. Home: 2079 Essex St Bangor ME 04401-2112 Office: Downeast Pharmacy Inc 185 Harlow St Bangor ME 04401-4933

FIORITO, FRANK ANTHONY, English educator; b. Newark, Oct. 21, 1927; s. Donald Anthony and Mary Ann (Carlomusto) F.; m. Mary Agliozzo, Aug. 21, 1965; 1 child, Frank A. Jr. BA, Columbia Coll., 1947, MA, 1951. Cert. tchr., N.J. Tchr. English Newark Bd. Edn., 1959—. Author: The Anatomy of a Strike, 1970,. Del. Dem. Nat. Convention, N.Y.C., 1976. Cpl. U.S. Army, 1951-53. Mem. Am. Fedn. Tchrs. (exec. v.p. Newark tchrs.' union 1965-70), N.J. State Fedn. Tchrs. (pres. 1970-73), Maplewood Unico (pres. 1985-88). Roman Catholic. Home: 130 Oakland Rd Maplewood NJ 07040

FIRCHOW, THOMAS MARK, sales executive; b. Washington, Apr. 10, 1955; s. Kenneth Glenn and Ingrid Selma (Geppert) F.; m. Marilyn Marie Heinerichs, July 10, 1982; children: April, Ashley. AAS, Del. County Community Coll., Media, Pa., 1977; BS, Villanova (Pa.) U., 1981. Dist. mgr. The Gittelman Co., Ft. Washington, Pa., 1982-86; account exec. Ctr. City Film & Video, Phila., 1986-91; v.p. sales Videosmith Inc., Phila., 1991—.

FIREMAN, JACK MERVIN, osteopathic physician; b. Pitts., May 16, 1926; s. Nathan and Anna (Caplan) F.; 1 child, Marjorie; m. Barbara Jean Sim, Dec. 17, 1977. BS in Pharmacy, U. Pitts., 1950, postgrad., 1950-52; DO, Phila. Coll. Osteopathic Medicine, 1970. Lic. physician, R.I. Owner Fireman's Pharmacy, Pitts., 1952-66; ptnr. Post Rd. Med. Assocs., Warwick, R.I., 1971-75; pvt. practice Warwick, 1975-80; pres. Post Rd. Med. Group, Ltd., Warwick, 1980—; cons. R.I. Dept. Health, Providence,1972—; chmn. gen. practice dept. Cranston (R.I.) Gen. Hosp., 1980-82; physician mem. R.I. Bd. Med. Licensure and Discipline, 1987—. Chmn. pub. edn. com. Kent County Cancer Soc., Warwick, 1974-76, pres., 1976-78; mem. R.I. Formulary Commn., Providence, 1978-82; trustee Cranston Gen. Hosp., 1980-81. With U.S. Army, 1944-46, PTO. Decorated Bronze Star. Mem. Am. Osteopathic Assn., Am. Coll. Osteopathic Gen. Practitioners, R.I. Soc. Osteopathic Physicians and Surgeons (pres. 1984-86, Man of Yr. 1976). Home: 27 Cottrell Rd Saunderstown RI 02874-3413 Office: Post Rd Med Group Ltd 857 Post Rd Warwick RI 02888-3397

FIRESTIEN, ROGER LEE, creativity educator, consultant, author; b. Greeley, Colo., Nov. 27, 1955; s. Wilbert W. and Ruth (Brug) F,. BA, U. No. Colo., 1977; MS, Buffalo State Coll., 1979; PhD., SUNY, Buffalo, 1987. Sr. ptnr. Multiple Resources Assocs., Buffalo, 1982-84; asst. prof. Ctr. for Studies in Creativity, Buffalo, 1984-91, asst. dir., 1991—; cons., speaker various corps. and orgns., 1987—. Author/narrator: (audio tape) Power Think, 1987, From Basics to Breakthroughs, 1988; author: Why Didn't I Think of That?, 1989. Mem. ASTD. Office: Ctr for Studies in Creativity Buffalo State Coll 1300 Elmwood Ave Buffalo NY 14222

FIRESTONE, CHARLES MORTON, lawyer, educator; b. St. Louis, Oct. 16, 1944; s. Victor and Betty (Solomon) F.; m. Pattie Winston Porter, Apr. 19, 1975; children: Laurel, Asa. BA, Amherst Coll., 1966; JD, Duke U., 1969. Bar: D.C. 1969, U.S. Ct. Appeals (D.C. cir.) 1970, U.S. Ct. Appeals (5th cir.) 1972, U.S. Ct. Appeals (9th cir.) 1973, U.S. Ct. Appeals (2d cir.) 1975, U.S. Ct. Appeals (3d cir.) 1976, U.S. Ct. Appeals (8th cir.) 1977, U.S. Supreme Ct. 1977, Calif. 1983. Litigation atty. FCC, Washington, 1969-73; dir. litigation Citizens Communications Ctr., Washington, 1973-77; adj. prof. law, dir. communications law program, UCLA, 1977-86; counsel firm Mitchell, Silberberg & Knupp, L.A., 1983-90; vis. lectr. UCLA Sch. Law, 1986-90; dir. program on communications and soc. Aspen Inst., 1989—; faculty adviser Fed. Communications Law Jour., L.A., 1977-86; cons. FTC, Washington, Pub. Agenda Found., N.Y.C., 1978; counsel statewide TV debates LWV, Calif. 1978-90, counsel Calif. media Dukakis/Bentsen Com.; co-chmn. LWV, Calif., Adv. com. Speak Out 1988, Election Project; pres. Bd. Telecommunications Commrs., City of L.A., 1984-86. Editor case materials, symposia resource manuals on communications; contbr. articles to profl. jours. Bd. dirs. Corp. for Disabilities and Telecommunications, L.A., 1980-82, KCRW Found., Santa Monica, Calif., 1982-90 (vice chmn. 1987-90); trustee Ctr. for Law in Pub. Interest, 1988-89, adv. com. campaign Mondale for Pres., Los Angeles, 1984. Recipient Am. Jurisprudence award, 1968, 69; Cert. Commendation award Mayor L.A., 1986; Resolution Commendation award City Council L.A., 1986; Recognition award NOW, Nat. Black Media Coalition, Nat. Latino Media Coalition, Nat. Citizens Com. for Broadcasting, Washington, 1977; Luther Ely Smith scholar and Andrew Laurie scholar Amherst Coll., 1965-66. Mem. ABA (chmn. broadcast and spectrum use com., sect. sci. and tech. 1981-83, chmn. electronic campaigning com. 1984-86), Fed. Communications Bar Assn., Soc. Satellite Profls. (sec. bd. dirs. So. Calif. chpt. 1984-87), So. Calif. Cable Assn. Jewish. Office: 1250 Connecticut Ave NW Ste 700 Washington DC 20036-2613

FIRESTONE, RAYMOND ARMAND, chemist; b. N.Y.C., Jan. 20, 1931; s. Tibor Aaron and Pearl (Liebovits) F.; m. Beatrice Carolyn Rapp, Mar. 9, 1952 (dec. Aug. 1983); children: Albert, David, Rebecca; m. Jean Hamerman Prebluda, June 28, 1987. AB, Cornell U., 1951; PhD, Columbia U., 1954. Sr. chemist Merck & Co., Rahway, N.J., 1956-71, rsch. fellow, 1971-76, sr. rsch. fellow, 1976-80, sr. investigator, 1980-87; dist. rsch. fellow Bristol-Myers, Wallingford, Conn., 1987—. Patentee in field; contbr. articles to profl. jours. With U.S. Army Chem. Corps, 1954-56. Fellow Royal Soc. Chemistry. Home: 387 Temple St New Haven CT 06511-6801 Office: Bristol-Myers Squibb PRI PO Box 5100 Wallingford CT 06492-7660

FIRETOG, THEODORE WARREN, lawyer; b. Bklyn., Sept. 18, 1950; s. Max E. and Ilene (Volk) F.; m. Kathleen Ann Neudecker, Feb. 21, 1980; children: Heather, Philip. BS in Natural Resources, U. Mich., 1974, MS in Natural Resources, 1976; JD, SUNY, Buffalo, 1979. Bar: N.Y. 1980, U.S. Dist. Ct. (ea. dist.) N.Y. 1986, U.S. Dist. Ct. (so. dist.) N.Y. 1986. Dir. nature and conservation Nassau County coun. Boy Scouts Am., N.Y., 1967-73; teaching fellow dept. natural resources U. Mich., Ann Arbor, 1975-76; staff atty. Environ. Law Inst., Washington, 1979-80; atty., advisor EPA, Washington, 1980-85; sr. assoc. Rivkin, Radler, Dunne & Bayh, Uniondale, N.Y., 1985-87; environ. counsel Shea & Gould, N.Y.C., 1987—; lectr. various environ. seminars. Contbr. articles to profl. jours. Mem. com. Nassau County Dem. Com., 1987—. Sea Grant Law fellow U. Buffalo, 1977; recipient Cert. of award EPA, 1985. Mem. ABA (natural resources div.), Environ. Law Inst. (assoc.), N.Y. Bar Assn. Jewish. Home: 111 Thomas Powell Blvd Farmingdale NY 11735-2251 Office: Shea & Gould 1251 Ave of the Americas New York NY 10020-1104

FIRST, WESLEY, publishing company executive; b. Erie, Pa., Feb. 18, 1920; s. Orson John and Pearle (Unger) F.; m. Margaret Elizabeth Whittlesey, Apr. 3, 1943 (div. June 1967); children: Karen Lee, Michael; m. Dianne Jones, Dec. 1975 (div. Sept. 1981); m. Suzanne Lavenas, Jan. 9, 1982. Student, U. Mich., 1937-40; BS, Columbia U., 1958; MA, New Sch. for Social Research, 1963. Reporter Erie Dispatch, 1943-47, asst. city editor, 1947-48, asst. to editor, 1948-50; with N.Y. World-Telegram and Sun, N.Y.C., 1950-63; successively copyreader, night news editor N.Y. World-Telegram and Sun, 1950-57, asst. mng. editor, 1957-60, mng. editor, 1960-63; prof. journalism Ohio State U., 1963-65; dir. univ. relations Columbia, N.Y.C., 1965-67; asst. to pres. Sarah Lawrence Coll., 1967-68, Juilliard School, N.Y.C., 1968-69; editor Travel Weekly, 1969-76; editor-in-chief Psychology Today, 1976-77; staff v.p. editorial Ziff-Davis Pub. Co., 1977-82, cons., 1982—; guest lectr. newspaper design and makeup Fordham U.; instr. journalism Finch Coll., N.Y.C.; Rep. to newspaper design and makeup seminar Am. Press Inst., 1957. Editor: Columbia Remembered, University on the Heights. With USAAF, 1944-46. Woodrow Wilson Fellow, 1959. Mem. U. Mich. Alumni Assn., Columbia U. Alumni Assn., Phi Beta Kappa, Kappa Tau Alpha, Sigma Delta Chi. Clubs: Overseas Press, Silurians. Home: Montauk Manor Edgemere St Rd 2 Box 226C Apt 413 Montauk NY 11954

FISCHER, DAVID EUGENE, financial planner, stockbroker; b. Albany, N.Y., Feb. 25, 1961; s. Robert E. and Grace M. (Critchlow) F.; m. Leslie J. Busch, Nov. 26, 1983. AAS in Mktg., Hudson Valley Community Coll., Troy, N.Y., 1985; BSBA, Regents Coll., Albany, N.Y., 1990. Cert. fin. planner; registered investment advisor. Payroll adminstr. Key Bank N.A., Albany, 1982-85; mgr. fin. planning dept. 1st Albany corp., 1985—. Mem. Internat. Assn. for Fin. Planning (treas. 1988—). Republican. Home: 32 Tryon Ct Albany NY 12203 Office: 1st Albany Corp 41 State St Albany NY 12207

FISCHER, ERIC ROBERT, lawyer, educator; b. N.Y.C., Aug. 22, 1945; s. Maurice and Pauline (Pilcer) F.; m. Anita Ellen Cohen, July 31, 1977; children: Joshua, Lauren. BA, U. Pa., 1967; MBA, JD, Stanford U., 1971; LLM in Taxation, Boston U., 1982. Bar: N.Y. 1975, Mass. 1977. Assoc. Fried, Frank, Harris, Shriver & Jacobson, N.Y.C., 1971-76; v.p., asst. gen. counsel, asst. sec. First Nat. Bank of Boston, 1976-86; sr. v.p., gen. counsel, corp. sec. UST Corp., Boston, 1986—; lectr. on law Boston U. Law Sch., 1984—. Trustee Boston Lyric Opera, Inc., 1989—; bd. dirs. Boston Area Youth Soccer, 1989-90, Spirit of Mass. Boys Soccer Club, 1991—. Mem. ABA (banking law com.), Bank Capital Markets Assn. (chmn. banking law subcom. 1984-90), UN Assn. Boston (treas. 1978-91), New Eng. Legal Found. (bd. dirs. 1990—). Jewish. Home: 205 Waban Ave Newton MA 02168-2101 Office: UST Corp 40 Court St Boston MA 02108-2202

FISCHER, HENRY GEORGE, Egyptologist; b. Phila., May 10, 1923; s. Henry G. and Agnes Beatrice (Hurdman) F.; m. Eleanor Armstrong Teel, Dec. 15, 1951; 1 dau., Katherine Fraser (Mrs. Woodman Taylor). B.A., Princeton U., 1945; Ph.D., U. Pa., 1955. Instr. English Am. U. Beirut, 1945-48; asst. Egyptian sect. U. Pa. Mus., 1949-56; mem. univ. expdn. to Mit Rahineh, Egypt, 1955, 56; asst. prof. Egyptology Yale Grad. Sch., 1956-58; asst. curator Egyptian art Met. Mus. Art, 1958-63, assoc. curator, 1963-64, curator, 1964-70, Lila Acheson Wallace curator in Egyptology, 1970-79, rsch. curator, 1979-91, curator emeritus, 1992—; adj. asst. prof. fine arts Inst. Fine Arts, N.Y. U., 1962-64, adj. assoc. prof., 1964-66, adj. prof., 1966-80; vis. lectr. art history and archaeology Columbia U., 1960-61; sec.-treas. Am. Com. to Preserve Abu Simbel, 1964-70. Author: Inscriptions from the Coptite Nome: Dynasties VI-XI, 1964, Ancient Egyptian Representations of Turtles, 1968, Dendera in the Third Millennium B.C, 1969, Egyptian Studies I: Varia, 1976, II: The Orientation of Hieroglyphs, Part 1: Reversals, 1977, Ancient Egyptian Calligraphy, 1979, The Renaissance Sackbut and Its Use Today, 1984, L'écriture et l'art de l'Egypte ancienne, 1986. Trustee Am. Research Center in Egypt, 1955-66; bd. dirs. Ams. for Middle East Understanding, 1967—, v.p., 1971—. Guggenheim fellow, 1956-57. Mem. Egypt Exploration Soc. (London), Société Française d'Egyptologie , German Archaeol. Inst., Phi Beta Kappa. Home: 29 Mauweehoo Hl Sherman CT 06784-2312

FISCHER, JUDITH HUMMEL, educator, consultant; b. Phillipsburg, Pa., Nov. 23, 1937; d. Joseph Ormand Pattee and Ruth Ann (Whitmore) Hummel; m. David Hackett Fischer, Nov. 23, 1960; children: Susan Frederick, Anne Whitmore. BA, Carleton Coll., 1959; MAT, Johns Hopkins U., 1960; EdD, U. Mass., Amherst, 1991. Cert. tchr. in biology, gen. sci. and art, Mass. Tchr. Kenwood High Sch., Essex, Mass., 1960-61; adj. asst. prof. Simmons Coll., Boston, 1965—; instr. Boston U., 1986-90; cons. Phillips Exeter Acad., Exeter, N.H., 1989—, Jamaica Plain High Sch./Simmons Coll. Collaborative, 1977-85, NSF Tchr. Insts., Simmons Coll., 1986-90; regional coord. Wis. Fast Plants-U. Wis., Madison, 1988—. Enrichment Insts. in Math and Sci. grantee, Title II/Eisenhower, 1987—. Mem. Nat. Assn. Biology Tchrs., Nat. Sci. Tchrs. Assn. Home: 36 Rich Valley Rd Wayland MA 01778-2428 Office: Simmons Coll 300 The Fenway Boston MA 02115

FISCHER, KURT WALTER, education educator; b. Balt., June 9, 1943; s. Kurt Wilhelm and Irmgaard-Louise (Funke) F.; m. Sandra Pipp (div.); 1 child, Seth; m. Jane Haltiwanger, Dec. 7, 1986; 1 child, Johanna. BA in Psychology summa cum laude, Yale U., 1965; MA in Soc. Rels., Harvard U., 1968, PhD in Soc. Rels., 1971. Asst. prof. Univ. Denver, 1972-78, assoc. prof., 1978-85, prof., 1985-87; prof. edn. Harvard U., Cambridge, Mass., 1986—; vis. scholar Univ. Geneva, 1978-79; vis. prof. U. Pa., Phila., 1985-86. Co-author: (with P. Shaver and A. Lazerson) Psychology Today: An Introduction, 2d and 3rd edits., 1972, 75; co-author: Human Development From Conception to Adolescence, 1984; author: Cognitive Development, 1981, Levels and Transitions in Cognitive Development, 1983; others; contbr. articles to profl. jours. Recipient fellowships James McKeen Cattell Fund, 1985-86, Ctr. for Advanced Study, Palo Alto, Calif., 1984; grantee Carnegie Found., Spencer Found., MacArthur Found., Sloan Found., 1973-91. Mem. Jean Piaget Soc. (pres. 1988-91), Phi Beta Kappa, Sigma Xi. Home: 29 Vincent Ave Belmont MA 02178-4418 Office: Harvard Grad Sch Edn Appian Way/Larsen Hall 7th Fl Cambridge MA 02138

FISCHER, ROBERT LEIGH, environmental chemist, consultant; b. Chgo., July 29, 1926; s. George and Ida (Genin) F.; Carmel Along, July 5, 1954; children: Maryl L., Carmel L., Robert L. BS, No. Ill. U., 1950; MS, U. Ill., 1951, PhD, 1954. Chemist E. I. DuPont, Wilmington, Del., 1954-55; asst. prof. Univ. Tenn., Memphis, 1955-61; head protein rsch. Campbell Soup Co., Camden, N.J., 1961-66; chief clin. chemist Phila. (Pa.) Gen. Hosp., 1966-78; dir. police lab. Phila. (Pa.) Police Dept., 1978-80; rsch. scientist N.J. Dept. Environ. Protection, Trenton, N.J., 1980—. Sgt. U.S. Army, 1945-46. Fellow Am. Inst. Chemists; mem. Am. Chem. Soc. Democrat. Roman Catholic. Home: 714 Hilltop Rd Riverton NJ 08077-3343 Office: NJ Dept Environ Protection CN027 Trenton NJ 08625

FISCHER, RONALD LEE, physician, anesthesiologist, educator; b. Levittown, N.Y.; s. Emery and Mae (Bressloer) F. BSChemE, Cornell U., 1977; MD, SUNY, Syracuse, 1981. Diplomate Am. Bd. Anesthesiology, Am. Bd. Pain Mgmt. Resident in anesthesiology Harvard U., Boston, 1984; asst. prof. Rush U., Chgo., 1986, Brown U., Providence, 1989; chief anesthesiologist Meml. Hosp./Brown U., Providence, 1989, dir. Sch. Anesthesia, 1989—; pres. Atlantic Anesthesia Cons., Inc., Providence, 1989—. Author: (with others) Arrythmias, 1991; contbr. articles to profl. jours. Rsch. grantee Roche Labs., 1991. Fellow Am. Coll. Chest Physicians; mem. Am. Soc. Anesthesiologists, R.I. Med. Soc. Office: Atlantic Anesthesiology Cons Inc 301 Westminster St Providence RI 02903

FISCHER, TERENCE JOSEPH, engineer, researcher; b. Dayton, Ohio, Nov. 9, 1959; s. Robert Charles and Patricia Louise (McFarland) F.; m. Jamie Sheryl Aaranson, July 25, 1987; 1 child, Alyssa Hope. BS in Engring., Wright State U., 1985; MS in Indsl. Systems Engring., Va. Poly Inst. & State U., 1991. Indsl. engr. USAF, Wright-Patterson AFB, Ohio, 1982-85; human factors engr. SRL Inc., Dayton, 1985-86; researcher Va. Poly Inst. & State U., Blacksburg, 1986-87; human factors engr. Ketron Inc., Warminster, Pa., 1988-89; sr. engr. CTA Inc., McKee City, N.J., 1989—; forensic engr. George Widas Assn., Voorhees, N.J., 1988. Contbr. articles to profl. jours. Mem. Human Factors Soc. (pres. student chpt. 1983-84), Soc. Automotive Engrs., Am. Soc. Safety Engrs. Home: 904 Scarborough Dr Pleasantville NJ 08232-4838 Office: CTA Inc 2500 English Ave Ste 1000 McKee City NJ 08232

FISCHMAN, BURTON LLOYD, communications educator, management consultant; b. Newark, Nov. 19, 1930; s. Harry and Anna (Blackstone) F.; m. Rhoda Chorney, June 7, 1959; children: Gail, Helene. BS, Curry Coll., 1958; MA, Seton Hall U., 1960; PhD, U. Conn., 1971. Prof. communications Bryant Coll., Smithfield, R.I., 1966—; cons. to more than 100 different businesses, govtl. agys. and profl. assns., 1970—. Author: New Directions in Public Speaking, 1972, Business Report Writing, 1975, Developing Leadership, 1976. With U.S. Army, 1951-53, Korea. Recipient Disting. Faculty award Alumni of Bryant Coll., 1984, Youth Svcs. award B'nai B'rith, 1990. Office: Bryant Coll 1850 Douglas Ave Providence RI 02904-3869

FISCHMAN, GARY JOSEPH, podiatrist, educator; b. N.Y.C.; s. Isidore and Sally (Gold) F.; m. Elaine Sue Dworkin, July 12, 1981; 1 child, Isadora Sydnie. BA, Hunter Coll., 1963; Dr, Pa. Coll. Podiatric Medicine, 1972; PhD in Pathology, Thomas Jefferson U., 1980. Technician dept. microbiology Dalhousei U., Halifax, N.S., Can., 1964-67; rsch. scientist Pa. Coll. Podiatric Medicine, Phila., 1968-72, instr. histology and anatomy, 1972-75; pvt. practice podiatry, Phila., 1972-75, Long Island City, 1976-85, Bklyn., 1985—; fellow community health and adminstrn. N.Y. Coll. Podiatric Medicine, N.Y.C., 1977-78, asst. prof. pathology, 1978-84, rsch. cons., 1984—; podiatry cons. Rockland Psychiat. Ctr., 1985—. Recipient Am. Podiatry Assn. fellow, 1972-75. Fellow Am. Soc. Podiatric Medicine; mem. AAAS, N.Y. Acad. Scis., Am. Podiatry Assn., Tissue Culture Assn., Am. Soc. Microbiology, Am. Pub. Health Assn., Can. Soc. Microbiologists, Can. Soc. Cell Biology, Micros. Soc. Can., Am. Acad. of Pain Mgmt. (diplomate). Office: 530 Montgomery St # F Jersey City NJ 07302-3128

FISCHMAN, LEONARD LIPMAN, economist; b. Bklyn., Jan. 23, 1919; s. Murray M. and Sadie G. (Link) F.; m. Evelyn R. Kay, Apr. 18, 1958. AB, NYU, 1937; MA, Am. U., 1939. Asst. operation head U.S. Bur. Census, Washington, 1940-41; chief stats. and spl. studies br. program coordination div. UNRRA, Rome, 1946-47; acting chief Mediterranean sect. Office Internat. Trade, U.S. Dept. Commerce, Washington, 1948-50; internat. economist, editor Minerals Yearbook U.S. Bur. Mines, Washington, 1950-53; cons. P.R. Econ. Devel. Adminstrn., San Juan, 1953-58; econ. cons. and dir. Econ. Assocs. Inc., Washington, 1958-63, pres., 1963-74, 80-91; sr. rsch. assoc., fellow and sr. fellow Resources for Future, Washington, 1973-79; econ. cons. Washington, 1992—. Author: (with Landsberg and Fisher) Resources in America's Future, 1963, World Mineral Trends and U.S. Supply Problems, 1980. Served with U.S. Army, 1941-46. Fellow AAAS;

mem. Am. Econ. Assn., Nat. Assn. Bus. Economists, Soc. Internat. Devel., Internat. Club (Washington), Nat. Economists Club. Home: 700 New Hampshire Ave NW Washington DC 20037-2406 Office: 2025 Pennsylvania Ave NW Washington DC 20006-1813

FISCHMAN, MYRNA LEAH, accountant, educator; b. N.Y.C.; d. Isidore and Sally (Goldstein) F. BS, Coll. City N.Y., 1960, MS, 1964; PhD, NYU 1976; CPA, N.Y. Asst. to contr. Sam Goody, Inc., N.Y.C.; tchr. accounting Ctr. Comml. High Sch., N.Y.C., 1960-63, William Cullen Bryant High Sch., Queens, N.Y., 1963-66, vocat. adviser, 1963-66; instr. acctg. Borough of Manhattan Community Coll., N.Y.C., 1966-69; self employed acct., N.Y.C., 1960—; chief acct. investigator rackets, Office Queens Dist. Atty., 1969-70, community rels. coord., 1970-71; adj. prof. L.I. U., 1970-79, prof. acctg. taxation and law, 1979—, coord. grad. capstone courses, 1982-86, dir. Sch. Profl. Accountancy Bklyn. campus, 1984—, dir. Ctr. Acctg. and Tax Edn., 1986—; dir. Faculty Acctg. Taxation and Law Bklyn. campus, 1986—. Editor Ea. Bus. Educators Jour., 1988. Rsch. cons. pre-tech. program Bd. Edn., City N.Y.; acct.-adviser Inst. for Advancement of Criminal Justice; acct.-cons. Coalition Devel. Corp., Interracial Coun. for Bus. Opportunities; treas. Breakfree Inc., Lower East Side Prep. Sch.; mem. edn. task force Am. Jewish Com., 1972—; mem. steering com., youth div. N.Y. Dem. County Com., 1967-68, del. to Nat. Conv., Young Dems. Am., 1967, rep. assigned to women's activities com., 1967; mem. Chanceller Com. Against Discrimination in Edn., 1976—; chmn. supervisory com. Fed. Credit Union #1532, N.Y.C., 1983—; mem. legis. adv. bd. N.Y. State Assemblyman Denis Butler, 1979—; chmn. consumer coun. Astoria Med. Ctr., 1980—; mem. subcom. on bus. edn. to the econ. devel. and mktg. com. Bklyn. C. of C., 1984—. Recipient award for meritorious service Community Svc. Soc., 1969; C.P.A., N.Y. Mem. Jewish Guild for Blind, Jewish Braille Inst., Friends Am. Ballet Theatre, Friends Met. Mus. Art, Community Welfare Com. Assn., Govt. Accts. (pres. 1990-91, bd. dirs. N.Y. chpt. 1984—, dir. rsch. and manuscripts 1985—, pres. elect N.Y. chpt. 1989-90), Am. Acctg. Assn., AICPAs, Nat., Eastern (co-chmn. ann. meeting 1967, bus. edn. assns.), Nat., Eastern (chmn. ann. meeting, 1968, bus. tchrs. assns.), Internat. Soc. Bus. Edn., Grad. Students Orgn. NYU (treas. 1971-73, v.p. 1973-74), Inst. Mgmt. Accts. (dir. N.Y. chpt. 1983—, dir. manuscripts 1991-92), Assn. Govt. Accts. (dir. N.Y. chpt. 1983—, pres. elect N.Y. chpt. 1989-90, pres. N.Y. chpt. 90-91), NEA, AAUP, Doctorate Assn. N.Y. Educators (v.p. 1975—), Am. Assn. Jr. Colls., Young Alumni Assn., Fed. Credit Union (chmn. supervisory com. #1532, N.Y.C., 1983—), Emanu-El League Congregation Emanu-El, N.Y. (chmn. community svcs. com. 1967-68), N.Y. State Soc. CPAs (mem. com. on recruitment for CPA careers 1981—, auditing com. 1991—, gen. com. on edn. in colls. and univs. 1991—), Nat. Assn. Accts. (bd. dirs. N.Y. chpt. 1985—, dir. profl. devel. 1986-87, dir. pub. rels. 1987-88), Tax Inst. L.I. U. (dir. Bklyn. chpt. 1984—), Women's City Club (N.Y.C.), Delta Pi Epsilon (treas. 1976). Jewish. Democrat. Developed new bus. machine course and curriculum Borough Manhattan Bus. Community Coll. Office: LI U Zeckendorf Campus Brooklyn NY 11201

FISCHMAN, STUART LEE, oral medicine educator, dentist; b. Buffalo, Nov. 29, 1935; s. Ben and Lillian (Friedland) F.; m. Jane Ann Vogel, June 25, 1960; 1 child, Lisa. Student, Cornell U., 1953-56; DMD, Harvard U., 1960. Diplomate Am. Bd. Oral Pathology, Am. Bd. Oral Medicine. Resident Boston VA Hosp., 1960-61; prof. SUNY, Buffalo, 1961—; vis. prof. U. P.R., San Juan, 1974, Hebrew U., Jerusalem, 1981, 89; cons. Cheseborough Ponds, Trumbull, Conn., 1965—, ADA, Chgo., 1975—, Unilever Rsch., Eng., 1985—; hon. prof. Nat. U., Paraguay, 1976; dir. dentistry Erie County Med. Ctr., Buffalo, 1973—. Contbr. numerous articles to profl. jours.; contbr. 3 textbooks. Named Disting. Alumnus, Harvard U., 1988. Fellow Am. Acad. Oral Pathology, Am. Coll. Dentists, Internat. Coll. Dentists. Jewish. Home: 255 Louvaine Dr Buffalo NY 14223-2757 Office: SUNY 315 Squire Hall Buffalo NY 14214

FISCHOFF, GARY CHARLES, lawyer; b. Manhasset, N.Y., Nov. 23, 1954; s. Harold and Ann (Yablon) F.; m. Linda Lee Sacca, Nov. 22, 1985; 1 child, Lisa Frances. BA, U. Buffalo, 1976; JD, St. John's U., Jamaica, N.Y., 1983. Bar: N.J. 1983, U.S. Dist. Ct. N.J. 1983, N.Y. 1984, U.S. Dist. Ct. (s. and e. dists.) N.Y. 1985, U.S. Dist. Ct. (n. and w. dist.) N.Y., U.S. Ct. Appeals (2d cir.) 1988. Asst. treas. IAP, Inc., Lyndhurst, N.J., 1980-82; assoc. Hannoch Weisman, Roseland, N.J., 1983-85; ptnr. Fischoff & Gelberg, Garden City, N.Y., 1985—; lectr. seminar Nat. Bus. Inst., Westbury, N.Y., 1990, 91. Rep. Greentree Homeowners Assn., Northport, N.Y., 1988-89. Mem. ABA (litigation sect.), Bankruptcy Lawyers Bar Assn., N.Y. State Bar Assn. (real property sect.), Nassau County Bar Assn. (mem. bankruptcy com., jud. liaison 1988—). Jewish. Office: Fischoff & Gelberg 600 Old Country Rd Garden City NY 11530-2001

FISH, DAVID EARL, insurance company executive; b. Port Jervis, N.Y., Sept. 22, 1936; s. William Earl and Elizabeth Dorthea (Schleer) F.; m. Patricia Ann Reilly, June 14, 1958; children: Nancy S., Susan L., Brian D. BSBA, Muhlenberg Coll., 1958. With Liberty Mut. Ins., 1961—; claims adjuster East Orange, N.J., 1961-65; claims supr. Pitts., 1966-68; claims examiner Boston, 1969-70; claims mgr. Buffalo, Syracuse, Balt., Phila., 1971-80; asst. div. claims mgr. Phila., 1980-81; asst. v.p. Chgo., 1981-86, div. claims mgr., asst. v.p., 1986-87; v.p. Boston, 1988—; bd. dirs. Cert. Automotive Parts Assn., Washington. Home: 13 Chandler Dr East Sandwich MA 02537-1729 Office: Liberty Mut Ins Co 175 Berkeley St Boston MA 02117

FISH, GORDON EDWARD, physicist, magnetics researcher; b. Dayton, Tenn., Jan. 4, 1951; s. Lloyd Edward and Mary Lois (Hodges) F.; m. Patricia Balsam, Jan. 10, 1981. BS, Wheaton Coll., 1972; MS, U. Ill., 1973, PhD, 1977. Teaching asst. U. Ill, Urbana, 1972-73, rsch. asst., 1973-77; postdoctoral rsch. fellow Nat. Bur. Standards, Gaithersburg, Md., 1977-79; rsch. physicist Rsch. and Tech. Allied Signal, Inc., Morristown, N.J., 1979-83, sr. rsch. physicist, 1983-88, rsch. assoc., 1988—; treas. Conf. on Magnetism and Magnetic Materials, Houston, 1987-90, gen. chmn. 1992. Contbr. articles to profl. jours.; patentee in field. Fellow U. Ill., 1972. Mem. IEEE (sr.), Magnetics Soc. of IEEE (adminstrv. com. 1988—), Am. Sci. Affiliation, Am. Phys. Soc., Sigma Pi Sigma, Sigma Xi. Office: Allied Signal Inc Box 1021 Morristown NJ 07962

FISH, HAMILTON, public interest executive; b. Washington, Sept. 5, 1951; s. Hamilton and Julia (Mackenzie) F.; m. Sandra Harper; 1 child, Eliza Mackenzie Fish. BA, Harvard U., 1973. Mng. dir. Human Rights Watch, N.Y.C.; dir. Wolfson Ctr. for Nat. Affairs The New Sch., N.Y.C., 1989-90. Co-producer films Memory of Justice, 1975-76, Hotel Terminus, 1985-88; pub. Nation mag., N.Y.C., 1977-87; producer Broadway play Asinamali, 1987. Candidate for U.S. Ho. of Reps., 1988. Recipient Acad. award for the film Hotel Terminus, 1989. Office: Human Rights Watch 485 5th Ave New York NY 10017-6104

FISH, HAMILTON, JR., congressman; b. Washington, June 3, 1926; s. Hamilton and Grace (Chapin) F.; m. Julia Mackenzie (dec. Mar. 1969); children: Hamilton III, Julia Alexandra, Nicholas S., Peter L.; m. Billy Laster Cline, Apr. 3, 1971 (dec. May 1985); m. Mary Ann Knauss, Dec. 31, 1988. AB, Harvard U., 1949; LLB, NYU, 1957; postgrad., John F. Kennedy Sch. Pub. Adminstrn.; LLD (hon.), Mercy Coll., 1989, Marist Coll., 1978, St. Thomas Acquinas Coll., 1981; LHD (hon.), Mt. St. Mary Coll., 1989. Bar: N.Y. Vice consul to Ireland, 1951-53; with firm Alexander and Green, N.Y.C., 1957-64; practice law Poughkeepsie and Millbrook, N.Y., 1964—; mem. 91st-102d Congresses from N.Y. State 21st dist., 1969—; vice chmn. judiciary com.; mem. numerous sub-coms.; mem. House/Senate Joint Econ. Com., Washington. Mem. Franklin Delano Roosevelt Meml. Commn., Environ. and Energy Study Conf.; co-chmn. ad hoc Congl. Com. for Irish Affairs, mem. Congl. Caucus for Women's Issues, exec. com. Congl. Human Rights Caucus; mem. N.E.-Midwest Coalition; asst. sec. N.Y. State Congl. del., adv. com. of Clearinghouse on the Future. Recipient Disting. Pub. Servant award NYU Sch. Law, 1974, Walter White award NAACP, 1989, Congl. Civil Liberties award ACLU, 1990, Eleanor Roosevelt Valkill medal, 1990, Ea. Paralyzed Vets. Assn. award, 1990, Pub. Policy award Computer and Bus. Mfrs. Assn., 1990. Mem. N.Y. State Bar Assn., Dutches County Bar Assn., Soc. Cin., Jewish Fedn. Greater Orange County, Am. Legion, VFW, S.R., Soc. of Friendly Sons of St. Patrick of Putnam County, Order of Red Men, Masons, Elks. Republican. Office: US Ho of Reps 2269 Rayburn Washington DC 20515

FISH, JAMES EDMOND, medicine educator; b. Ann Arbor, Mich., Nov. 29, 1945; s. Robert Gerard and Jeanne Elizabeth (Kenney) F.; m. Pamela Stecker, Apr. 26, 1985; children; James E., Cory O. BS, U. Notre Dame, 1967; MD, Northwestern U., 1971. Diplomate Am. Bd. Internal Medicine, Nat. Bd. Med. Examiners. Resident Duke U. Med. Ctr., Durham, N.C., 1971-73; rsch. assoc. in pulmonary disease Johns Hopkins Med. Insts., Balt., 1973-75; fellow in pulmonary diseases Northwestern U. Med. Sch., Chgo., 1975-76, assoc. in medicine, 1976-77, asst. prof. medicine, 1977-79; asst. prof. medicine Johns Hopkins U. Sch. Medicine, Balt., 1979-83; assoc. prof. medicine and environ. health sci. Johns Hopkins U., Balt., 1983-85; prof. medicine, dir. pulmonary medicine and critical care Jefferson Med. Coll., Phila., 1985—, acting chmn. medicine, 1990—; bd. dirs. Meth. Hosp., Phila. Editorial bd. Am. Rev. of Respiratory Disease, 1981-86, Respiratory Medicine, 1990—, Postgraduate Medicine, 1991—; contbr. numerous articles to profl. jours. Bd. dirs. Am. Lung Assn. Phila., 1990-93. Comdr. USPHS, 1973-75. Walsh-Hudson-Cavanaugh scholarship, 1966-67; Am. Lung Assn. fellowship, 1975-76, Owen L. Coon Found. fellowship, 1975-76, Edward L. Trudeau fellowship, 1976-78; grantee NIH, 1976-78. Fellow ACP, Am. Coll. Chest Physicians, Phila. Coll. Physicians; mem. AAAS, AMA, N.Y. Acad. Sci., Am. Physiol. Soc., Am. Fedn. Clin. Rsch., Am. Thoracic Soc., Am. Thoracic Assn. Pulmonary Program Dirs. (pres. Eastern sect. 1989-92, trustee 1989-92), Am. Acad. of Allergy and Clin. Immunology, Pa. Thoracic Soc., Pa. Soc. for Pulmonay Physicians, Am. Sleep Disorders Assn., Pa. Med. Soc., Phila. County Med. Assn., Alpha Epsilon Delta, Alpha Omega Alpha. Home: 1526 Monticello Dr Gladwyne PA 19035-1246 Office: Jefferson Med Coll 1025 Walnut St Philadelphia PA 19107-5083

FISH, JANET ISOBEL, artist; b. Boston, May 18, 1938; d. Peter and Florence (Voorhees) F. B.A., Smith Coll., 1960; postgrad., Skowhegan (Maine) Art Sch., summer 1961; B.F.A., M.F.A., Yale U., 1963. Represented in permanent collections Whitney Mus. Am. Art, N.Y.C., Met. Mus. Art, N.Y.C., Cleve. Mus. Art, Dallas Mus. Fine Arts, Am. Airlines, Am. Fedn. Arts, Am. Acad. Inst. Arts and Letters, Art Inst. Chgo., Nat. Gallery, Kansas City (Mo.) Art Inst., Albright-Knox Gallery, Buffalo, N.Y., Robert Miller Gallery, N.Y., 1978—, Newark Mus., Mpls. Mus. of Art, Nat. Gallery of Victoria, Melbourne, Australia, Okla. Art Ctr., Port Authority of N.Y. and N.J., Colby Coll., Waterville, Maine, Chase Manhattan Bank, N.Y. Mus. of Fine Arts, Houston Art Ctr., Paine Webber Group, Inc., N.Y.C., R.I. Sch. Design, Providence, Mus. Art, Providence, Va. Mus. Fine Arts, Richmond, Yale U., New Haven. Bd. govs. Skowhegan Sch. Painting and Sculpture, Marie Walsh Sharp Art Found. Recipient Harris award Chgo. Bienale award, 1974, Hubbard Mus. award, 1991; MacDowell fellow, 1968, 69, 72, Yale scholar; Australian Coun. for Arts grantee, 1975. Mem. Am. Acad. and Inst. of Arts and Letters (assoc.).

FISH, JOHN PERRY, oceanographic company executive, historian; b. Boston, Jan. 13, 1949; s. Robert Story and Sylvia Colby (Draper) F.; m. Marjorie Ann Moore, May 15, 1982; children: Madelyn Moore, Colby Draper. AS, Boston U., 1970; BA in Biology, Windham Coll., 1972. Mktg. assoc. Benthos, Inc., N. Falmouth, Mass., 1975-81; ops. dir. Hydrolab Project/NOAA-FDU, St Croix, V.I., 1981-82; pres. Oceanstar Systems, Inc., Cataumet, Mass., 1983—; v.p. Am. Underwater Search and Survey, Ltd., Cataumet, 1986—; bd. dirs. Hist. Maritime Group New Eng., Cataumet, Draper Bros. Co., Canton, Mass.; archael. cons. Debraak Recovery Project, Lewes, Del., 1984; ambassador Nat. Assn. Underwater Instrs., Colton, Calif., 1983. Author: Unfinished Voyages, 1989, Sound Underwater Images: Guide to Generation of Side Scan Sonar Data, 1990, Discrete Object Recognition in Side Scan Sonar Data, 1992; contbr. articles to profl. jours. Recipient Recognition award Nat. Oceanic and Atmospheric Adminstrn., 1986. Mem. Marine Tech. Soc., Soc. Colonial Wars, U.S. Naval Inst., Woods Hole Oceanographic Inst.

FISH, STEPHEN RICHARD, real estate development and construction executive; b. Phila., Jan. 4, 1953; s. John Richard and Ann Marie (Shoemaker) F.; m. Irene E. Applebaum, Sept. 1, 1984. BA, U. Mich., 1975. Architect Shipley Bulfinch, Boston, 1978-81; proj. mgr. Jackson Constrn., Dedham, Mass., 1981-84, Brett Constrn., Attleboro, Mass., 1985-86; prin. Springfield Assocs., Easton, Mass., 1979—. Bd. dirs. Clairmont Neighborhood Assn., Boston, 1980-82. Fellow Nat. Trust for Hist. Preservation; mem. Citizens Housing and Planning Assn. Office: Springfield Assocs Inc PO Box 938 South Easton MA 02375-0129

FISH, VIRGINIA DART, banker; b. Buffalo, Apr. 28, 1954; d. Warren Hugh and Joan Sewell Dart; m. Ronald Alan Fish, Apr. 30, 1988. BA, Allegheny Coll., 1976; MBA, Va. Tech., 1982; grad., Nat. Sch. Banking, 1990. Mgr. investor rels. Verdix Corp., Chantilly, Va., 1985-86; v.p. Loyola Fed. Savs. Bank, Balt., 1986—. Co-chmn. Loyola United Way Campaign, Balt., 1990. Recipient merit scholar, Allegheny Coll., Meadville, Pa., 1972. Republican. Office: Loyola Capital Corp 1300 N Charles St Baltimore MD 21201-5705

FISHBEIN, BARBARA TCATH, psychotherapist; b. Providence, Aug. 11, 1929; d. Benjamin David and Lillian Beatrice (Schein) Tcath; m. Irwin H. Fishbein, June 15, 1952; children: Jonathan S., Linda F. Altman, David J., Robert A. BA Psychology, Sociology magna cum laude, Fairleigh-Dickinson U., 1978; MS Social Work, Columbia U., 1980; postgrad., The Fielding Inst., Santa Barbara, Calif., 1984—. Cert. hypnotherapist N.Y. Milton H. Erickson Soc. for Psychotherapy and Hypnosis, cert. social worker, N.Y., cert. Nat. Registry of Health Care Providers, Acad. Cert. Social Workers; bd. cert. diplomate in clin. social work; lic. marriage and family therapist, N.J. Psychotherapist Rabbinic Ctr. for Rsch. and Counseling, Westfield, N.J., 1978—. Licensure chairperson N.J. Soc. for Clin. Social Work, 1982-84. Fellow Am. Orthopsychiat. Assn.; mem. Am. Soc. Clin. Hypnosis (student), Am. Group Psychotherapy Assn. (student), N.J. Psychol. Assn. (student), Am. Assn. for Marriage and Family Therapy (clin.), Acad. Clin. Social Workers, N.Y. Soc. for Clin. Social Work, N.J. Assn. Women Therapists (peer supervision covener 1982—, mem.-at-large governing bd. 1984-86), NASW (N.J. chpt., com. on inquiry 1987—, com. for the Social Worker as Psychotherapist Inst. 1980-85). Office: Rabbinic Ctr for Rsch & Counseling 128 E Dudley Ave Westfield NJ 07090-3138

FISHBEIN, DIANA HANNA, criminology educator, researcher; b. Washington, June 22, 1954; d. Meyer Harry and Evelyn Rose (Centner) F.; m. Howard Steven Shapiro, May 2, 1981; children; Daniel Shapiro, Alana Shapiro. BS, U. Md., 1976; MS in Criminology, Fla. State U., 1978, PhD of Psychobiol. Criminology, 1981. Rsch. asst. Univ. Rsch. Corp., Washington, 1979-80; survey researcher Leon County (Fla.) Courthouse, Dept. of Def., 1980; postdoctoral fellow U. Md. Med. Sch., Balt., 1982-85; prof. criminology U. Balt., 1981—; staff scientist Addiction Rsch. Ctr., Nat. Inst. Drug Abuse, Balt., 1985—; cons. Forensic Habilitation, Inc., Fairfax, Va., 1981-82, Lorton (Va.) Task Force on Prison Reform, 1982, Va. State Dept. Corrections, 1982-85, Fed. Bur. Prisons, 1982-83, Montgomery County Pre-release Ctr., Rockville, Md., 1984—, NAS, 1989—; numerous presentations to profl. orgns. Author: (with others) Evolution, The Brain and Criminal Behavior, 1990, Neuropsychology and the Law, 1990; mem. editorial bd. Criminology: An Interdisciplinary Jour., 1990—, Criminology and Criminal Law, 1991—; contbr. articles to Jour. Criminology, Jour. Behavioral Scis. and the Law, Biol. Psychiatry, Am. Jour. Drug and Alcohol Abuse, Addictive Behaviors, Jour. Learning Disabilities, Jour. Studies on Alcohol, and others. Dir. Baby Talk, Silver Spring, Md., 1990—; community activist. Named among 83 people to watch in 1983, Baltimore Mag., Balt. Mem. AAAS, APA, AAUW (fellow 1979), Am. Soc. Criminology, Am. Acad. Criminal Justice Scis., Am. Inst. Biosocial Rsch., Am. Correctional Assn. Office: U Balt 1420 N Charles St Baltimore MD 21201-5720

FISHCO, ROBERT MELVIN, dean business technologies; b. Bayonne, N.J., July 29, 1939; s. William and Fannie (Sweet) F.; m. Carol Ann Spincola, June 30, 1963; children: Wendy M., Sandra M. BA, Trenton State Coll., 1962; MA, NYU, 1966; EdD, Temple U., 1976. Tchr. North Bergen (N.J.) High Sch., 1962-68; faculty mem. Middlesex County Coll., Edison, N.J., 1968-74, chmn. dept. bus. adminstrn., 1974-85, dean div. bus. techs., 1985—; cons. sales training, 1978-85. Text reviewer various pubs., 1974-85. Mem. Am. Vocat. Assn., N.J. Assn. Mktg. Edn. Tchrs., Nat. Assn. Mktg. Edn. Tchrs., Cen. N.J. Assn. Mktg. Edn. Tchrs. Office: Middlesex County Coll PO Box 3050 155 Mill Rd Edison NJ 08818-3050

FISHEL, CAROL THOMAS, counselor; b. West Jefferson, N.C., Jan. 12, 1949; d. Edison McCauley and Agnes Louise (Osborne) Thomas; m. James Leroy Fishel, June 8, 1968; children: Rebecca, Jonathan, Mary Beth. BA summa cum laude, U. Md., 1973; MA, W.Va. U., 1981; PhD, Pa. State U., 1983; MA, Liberty U., Lynchburg, Va., 1991. Tchr. Arlington Bapt. Sch., Balt., 1973-74, Elk Valley Sch., Elkview, W.Va., 1979-80; grad. asst. Pa. State U., University Park, 1980-83; adminstrv. asst. to pres. Arlington Bible Coll., Balt., 1983-84; tchr. and vice prin. Arlington Bapt. Schs., Balt., 1984-87; tchr. Liberty Christian Sch., Owings Mills, Md., 1987-88; adj. faculty U. Md., Catonsville, 1985-90; counselor Christian Counseling Ctr. Annapolis, Md., 1990—; cons. Chesapeake Theol. Sem., Balt., 1988-89. Contbr. articles to profl. jours., chpts. to books. Founders scholar Presbyn. Coll., 1969. Mem. Am. Assn. Counseling and Devel., Am. Assn. Mental Health Counselors, Phi Kappa Phi, Phi Delta Kappa, Pi Lambda Theta. Republican. Presbyterian. Home: 4269 Mary Ridge Dr Randallstown MD 21133-4316

FISHER, ALLAN CAMPBELL, railway executive; b. Westerly, R.I., Aug. 9, 1943; s. Arthur Chester and Norma Jean (Campbell) F.; m. Ellen Tryon Roop, June 14, 1969; children: Bradford Booth, Katherine Thayer. BA in Econs., St. Lawrence U., 1965; MS in Transp., Northwestern U., 1970. Rsch. economist Gen. Motors Rsch. Labs., Warren, Mich., 1969; mgmt. trainee Penn Cen., 1970, asst. trainmaster, Chgo., 1970-71, trainmaster, Toledo, 1971-72, terminal trainmaster, Elkhart, Ind., 1972, trainmaster, Cleve., 1972-74, asst. terminal supt., Cleve., 1974, terminal supt., Balt., 1974-75, asst. div. supt. Chesapeake div., Balt., 1975-76, terminal supt. Conrail, Conway, Pa., 1976, div. supt. N.J. div., Elizabethport, 1977, Lehigh div., Bethlehem, Pa., 1978, regional supt. ops. improvement Cen. region, Pitts., 1978-80, dir. budget control, 1980-82, regional supt. indsl. engring. So. region, Indpls., 1982-83, system dir. operating rules, Phila., 1983—. Served with U.S. Army, 1966-67, Vietnam. Decorated Bronze Star medal; Urban Transp. fellow, 1969. Mem. Internat. Assn. Oper. Officers, Am. Inst. Indsl. Engrs. (sr.), Assn. Am. R.R.'s (oper. rules com., chmn. transport nuclear waste com.), Oper. Rules Assn. (vice chmn.), Norac Rules Adv. Com. (chmn.), Mayflower Descendents (life), Phila. Boys Choir and Men's Chorale (bd. dirs., Man of Yr. 1987, 89, 90, 91), Masons, Sigma Chi (life). Unitarian-Universalist. Home: 215 Poplar Ave Wayne PA 19087-3503 Office: 2001 Market St 2 Commerce Sq Philadelphia PA 19101-1414

FISHER, ARON BAER, physiology and medicine educator; b. Phila., Apr. 20, 1936; m. Joan C. Fisher, 1957; children: Marc L., Steven A., Eric R., Mara E. BS in Chemistry summa cum laude, Dickinson Coll., 1956; MD, U. Pa., 1960. Diplomate Am. Bd. Internal Medicine; diplomate Nat. Bd. Med. Examiners. Intern and resident in medicine U. Hosps., Cleve., 1960-61, 64-65; resident in pulmonary medicine Hosp. U. Pa., 1965-66; fellow dept. physiology U. Pa., 1966-68, assoc. in medicine, assoc. in physiology, 1968-70, from asst. prof. to assoc. prof. medicine, 1970-80, prof. medicine, 1980—, from asst. prof. to assoc. prof. physiology, 1970-1980, prof. physiology, 1980—, prof. environmental medicine, 1986—; staff physician VA Hosp., Phila., 1968-73, clin. investigator, 1973-76, cons. in pulmonary medicine, 1976-82; mem. med. staff Hosp. U. Pa., 1976—, dir. hyperbaric medicine clin. practice, 1985—; dir. Inst. Environ. Medicine U. Pa., 1985—; mem. Am. Heart Assn. student rsch. fellowship adv. com. U. Pa., 1983—, mem. diabetes ctr. adv. com., 1985—, mem. teaching awards com., 1989—, chmn. animal care com. 1982-84, 87-89, chmn. com. for animal facility planning, 1985-86, chmn. transgenic mouse facility com., 1989, chmn. instnl. animal care and use com., 1989—, mem. bioengring. grad. group, 1988—, chmn. biochemistry grad. group rev. com., 1989-90, others, supr. grad. students; fellow dept. biophysics and phys. chemistry U. Pa., 1971-72; mem. study sect. Pa. Coal Worker's Respiratory Disease Program, 1976-78; mem. cardiovascular study sect. A NIH, 1979-81, mem. respiratory and applied physiology sect., 1981-83; mem. adv. panel U.S. Army Med. R&D Command, 1980-85. Editor: (with others) Handbook of Physiology: The Respiratory System (Section 3), vol. 1, 1980-85; mem. editorial bd. Exptl. Lung Rsch. 1979-88, Am. Rev. Respiratory Diseases, 1981-87, Jour. Applied Physiology, 1984-87, Am. Jour. Physiology, 1988—; guest editor Symposium on Lung Surfactant Apoproteins, 1984; contbr. numerous articles and revs. to profl. jours., chpts. to books. With USPHS, 1958, 59-61; capt. MC USAR, 1961-65. Grantee NIH, 1986-91, 1988—; recipient Clin. Investigator award VA Res. Svc., 1973-76, Established Investigator award Am. Heart Assn., 1977-82, Christian R. and Mary F. Lindback Found. award for Disting. Teaching, 1984. Mem. AAAS, ACP, Am. Physiol. Soc. (chmn. respiration dinner 1991, councillor respiratory sect. 1991—), Am. Thoracic Soc. (sec. assembly on structure, function and metabolism 1973-74, chmn. 1981, sec. sect. on pulmonary circulation 1979, councillor ea. sect. 1973-77, chmn. ann. meeting program com. 1976, pres. 1983), Am. Fedn. Clin. Rsch., Am. Soc. Clin. Investigation, Am. Heart Assn. (cardiopulmonary coun.), Am. Soc. Cell Biology, Undersea and Hyperbaric Med. Soc., Oxygen Soc., Aerospace Med. Assn., John Morgan Soc. U. Pa., Laennec Soc. Phila., Pa. Thoracic Soc. (chmn. rsch. com. 1985-87), Phi Beta Kappa, Alpha Omega Alpha. Home: 239 E Gowen Ave Philadelphia PA 19119-1021 Office: U Pa Inst Environ Medicine One John Morgan Bldg 36th St and Hamilton Walk Philadelphia PA 19104-6068

FISHER, BART STEVEN, lawyer, lecturer; b. St. Louis, Feb. 16, 1943; s. Irvin and Orene (Moskow) F.; m. Margaret Cottony, Mar. 1, 1969; 1 child, Ross Alan. AB, Washington U., 1963; MA, Johns Hopkins Sch. Advanced Internat. Studies, 1967, PhD, 1970; JD, Harvard U., 1972. Bar: D.C. 1972. Assoc. Patton, Boggs & Blow, Washington, 1972-78, ptnr., 1978—; adj. prof. internat. rels. Geogetown U. Sch. Fgn. Svc., Washington, 1974-82; profl. lectr. internat. rels. Johns Hopkins U. Sch. Advanced Internat. Studies, 1983—, George Mason U., 1991. Author: The International Coffee Agreement, 1972; (with John H. Barton) International Trade and Investment: Regulating International Business, 1986; editor: Regulating the Multinational Enterprise, 1983; Barter in the World Economy, 1985. Pres. Aplastic Anemia Found. Am. Inc., Balt., 1983—; bd. dirs. Literacy Coun. No. Va., Nat. Marrow Donor Program; program com. Georgetown Leadership Seminar, Washington, 1981—; mem. adv. bd. No. Va. Youth Svcs. Coalition; pres. Intertrade, Ltd., Capital Baseball, Inc.; ex-officio, bd. govs. Internat. Practice sect. Bar of Va.; v.p. Prince William Cannons, Inc. Recipient Dean's Cert. Appreciation Georgetown U. Sch. Fgn. Svc., Washington, 1984. Mem. ABA, Internat. Bar Assn., Am. Soc. Internat. Law (rapporteur, panel trade policy and insts. 1974-77), Va. State Bar (bd. govs. internat. law sect.), Wash. Fgn. Law Soc., Parkville Post Am. Legion, Great Falls Swim and Tennis Club Va. Jewish. Home: 9009 Potomac Forest Dr Great Falls VA 22066-2801 Office: Patton Boggs & Blow 2550 M St NW Washington DC 20037-1301

FISHER, D. MICHAEL, state senator; b. Pitts., Nov. 7, 1944; s. C. Francis and Dolores (Darby) F.; m. Carol Hudak, Aug. 9, 1973; children: Michelle Lynn, Brett Michael. AB, Georgetown U., 1966; JD, Georgetown Law Ctr., 1969. Bar: Pa. 1970. Asst. dist. atty. Allegheny County, Pitts., 1970-74; rep. Pa. Ho. of Reps., Harrisburg, 1974-80; mem. Pa. Senate, Harrisburg, 1980—; ptnr. Houston Harbaugh, Pitts., 1984—; chmn. House Subcom. on Crime and Corrections, 1979-80, Senate Environ. Resources & Energy, 1981-90, Senate Majority Policy Com., 1988-90; vice-chmn. Senate Jud. Com., 1981-90; elected Majority Whip, 1990—. Author numerous reports. Rep. candidate for lt. gov. Pa., 1986; mem. Pa. Gov.'s Energy Coun., 1981-86, Pa. Energy Devel. Authority, 1984-86, Environ. Quality Bd., 1980-90, Pa. Commn. on Crime and Delinquency, 1979—; del. Rep. Nat. Conv., 1988. Named Man of Yr. Upper St. Clair Rep. Club, 1980, Outstanding Young Man Am., 1977-79, Man of Yr. Vector's Law & Govt., 1991. Mem. Pa. Bar Assn., Elks, Am. Legion, Bethel Park Chamber, Rotary. Roman Catholic. Office: Pa State Senate State Capitol Harrisburg PA 17120

FISHER, DALE DUNBAR, animal scientist, dairy nutritionist; b. Lewisburg, Pa., Feb. 13, 1945; s. Glenn Murray and Elsie May (Bryson) F.; divorced; children: Elsie Maria, Maria Vanessa. BS in Animal Sci., Pa. State U., 1967, MS in Animal Industry, 1978, PhD in Animal Industry, 1980. Vol. animal husbandry Peace Corps, Ciudad Quesada, Costa Rica, 1967-71; area animal husbandry-pasture specialist Costa Rican Ministry of Agr., Ciudad Quesada, 1971-73; vis. scientist Internat. Ctr. for Tropical Agr., Cali, Colombia, 1973-75; animal nutritionist Co-op. Feed Dealers, Inc., Chenango Bridge, N.Y., 1981—. Contbr. articles to profl. jours. Eva B. and G. Weidman Groff Meml. scholar Pa. State U., 1979. Mem. Am. Soc. Animal Sci., Am. Dairy Sci. Assn., Am. Soc. Agronomy, N.Y. Acad. Scis., Sigma Xi, Phi Kappa Phi, Gamma Sigma Delta. Democrat. Home: 578 Chenango St

Binghamton NY 13901-2134 Office: Coop Feed Dealers Inc PO Box 670 Chenango Bridge NY 13745-9998

FISHER, DAVID BRUCE, development executive; b. Glen Cove, N.Y., Oct. 22, 1954; s. David James and Margaret Virginia (Peters) F.; m. Janice Katherine Patterson, Oct. 25, 1980; children: Courtney Elizabeth, David Robert. BA in Geology, Susquehanna U., 1976; M in Community Planning, U. Cin., 1979. Lic. profl. planner, N.J. Dir. environ. affairs and planning N.J. Builders Assn., Plainsboro, 1979-81, 83-87; project planner Ernst, Ernst & Lissenden, Toms River, N.J., 1981-83; v.p. forward planning N.J. div. Leisure Tech., Inc., Lakewood, N.J., 1987-91; dir. regulatory affairs, prin. planner Ernst, Ernst & Lissenden, Toms River, 1991-92; v.p. devel. Sammis Co./Gale & Wentworth, Florham Park, N.J., 1992—. Chmn. N.J. Clean Water Coun., Trenton, 1985-89; mem. Citizen Com. on Permit Coordination, Trenton, 1986—; mem. N.J. Dept. Wetlands Adv. Com., Trenton, 1987—; coach Toms River Youth Soccer Club, 1989—; mem. vestry St. Raphaels Episcopal Ch., Brick, N.J., 1989—. Recipient Bus. Watch award Bus. Jour. N.J., Vol. 5, No. 5, 1988. Mem. Am. Planning Assn. (chartered), Am. Inst. Cert. Planners, Internat. Platform Assn. Office: Sammis Co/Gale & Wentworth 100 Campus Dr Ste 300 Florham Park NJ 07932

FISHER, EUGENE JOSEPH, religious organization administrator; b. Grosse Pointe, Mich., Sept. 10, 1943; s. Eugene Joseph and Caroline Marie (Damm) F.; m. Catherine Ambrosiano, Dec. 31, 1970; 1 child, Sarah Ambrosiano Fisher. BA, Sacred Heart Sem., 1965; MA in Cath. Theology, U. Detroit, 1968; MA in Hebrew Studies, NYU, 1971, PhD in Hebrew Culture, Edn., 1976. Adj. prof. U. Detroit, 1969-77; dir. tchr. tng. Archdiocese of Detroit, 1971-77; dir. Cath.-Jewish rels. Nat. Conf. Cath. Bishops, Washington, 1977—; adv. bd. Nat. Inst. Against Prejudice and Violence, 1986—, Ctr. Jewish-Christian Studies and Rels., N.Y.C., 1987—, Nat. Cath. Inst. Holocaust Edn., Seton Hill Coll., Pa., 1986—, Inst. Jewish-Christian Understanding, Muhlenberg Coll., 1990—; cons. Vatican Commn. on Religious Rels. with Jews, 1981—, Internat. Conf. Christians and Jews, Heppenheim, Germany, 1983, 85, 87, Nat. Assn. Diocesan Ecumenical Officers, 1983—, others; presenter workshops in field. Author: Faith Without Prejudice: Rebuilding Christian Attitudes Toward Judaism, 1977, The Formation of Social Policy in the Catholic and Jewish Traditions, 1980, Homework for Christians Preparing for Christian-Jewish Dialogue, 1982, rev. edit., 1986, Seminary Education and Christian-Jewish Relations, 1988, John Paul II on the Holocaust, 1988, The Jewish Roots of Christian Liturgy, 1990, In Our Time: The Flowering of Jewish-Catholic Dialogue (with L. Klenicki), 1990, others. Mem. U.S. Holocaust meml. Coun., Washington, 1987—. Recipient Disting. Alumnus award Sacred Heart Coll., 1981, Edith Stein Guild award for contbns. to Cath.-Jewish rels., 1983, Spl. Excellence award Nat. Workshop on Christian-Jewish Rels., Mpls., 1987. Mem. NCCJ, Soc. Bibl. Lit. (pres. Chesapeake Bay region 1980-81), Cath. Bibl. Assn., Nat. Assn. Profs. Hebrew, Bibl. Archaeology Soc., Svc. Internat. de Documentation Judeo-Chretienne, Am. Acad. Religion, Fellowship of Reconciliation, Christian Study Group on Judaism and Jewish People, Nat. Inst. on Holocaust, Ctr. Holocaust Studies, Nat. Assn. Ecumenical Officers, Nat. Coun. Churches Christian-Jewish Rels. Office (exec. com. 1982—). Office: Nat Conf Cath Bishops 3211 4th St NE Washington DC 20017

FISHER, GARY EDWIN, computer scientist, researcher; b. Washington, Jan. 16, 1948; s. Benjamin Franklin and Vivian Arlene (Funkhouser) F.; m. Gabriele Louise Combes, Sept. 7, 1972; children: Susanne Helen, Michele Louise, Thomas Benjamin. B.S. in Physics, Math., Edn., Coll. William and Mary, 1970; diploma in data processing, Blue Ridge Community Coll., Weyers Cave, Va., 1976. Computer programmer U. Va., Charlottesville, 1976-77; systems analyst Control Data Corp., Rockville, Md., 1977-83; computer systems programmer Gen. Svcs. Adminstrn., Falls Church, Va., 1983-85; computer scientist Nat. Inst. Standards and Tech., Gaithersburg, Md., 1985--. Author: A Functional Model for Fourth Generation Languages, 1986, Application Software Prototyping and Fourth Generation Languages, 1987, (with others) Functional Benchmarks for Fourth Generation Languages, 1991; editor: Application Portability Profile, 1991. V.p. Community Assn., Gaithersburg, 1986-87, pres. 1988. 1st lt. U.S. Army, 1970-74. Office: Nat Inst Stds and Tech Technology Bldg Rm B266 Gaithersburg MD 20899

FISHER, H. JOSEPH, labor union officer; b. Lawnside, N.J., Feb. 7, 1933; s. Horace J. and Vera Ann (Arthur) F.; m. Barbara, June 1952; children: Joseph, Jr., Darlene, Barbara, James. Student, Temple U., 1955. Regional dir. Ladies Garment Union, Phila., 1958—. Democrat. Methodist. Office: ILGWU 35 S 4th St Philadelphia PA 19106

FISHER, HANS, nutritional biochemistry educator; b. Breslau, Silesia, Fed. Republic Germany, Mar. 4, 1928; s. George and Johanna (Gottheiner) F.; m. Ruth Hirschberg, July 24, 1950; children: Deborah M. Joseph, David E. Fisher, Daniel Z. Fisher. MS, U. Conn., 1952; PhD, U. Ill., 1954. Cert. Am. Bd. Nutrition. Asst. prof. Rutgers U., New Brunswick, N.J., 1954-57, assoc. prof., 1957-62, prof., 1962-72, dept. chair, 1966-88, assoc. provost, 1988-90, disting. prof., 1972—; cons. food and pharm. industries, 1955—. Author: Rutgers Guide to Lowering Your Cholesterol, 1986; contbr. articles to profl. jours. Pres. Highland Park (N.J.) Temple Ctr., 1975-77; v.p. YMHA, Highland Park, 1958-70. Fellow AAAS, N.Y. Acad. Sci.; mem. Am. Inst. Nutrition, Am. Chem. Soc. Jewish. Home: 216 N 3d Ave Highland Park NJ 08904 Office: Rutgers U PO Box 231 New Brunswick NJ 08903-0231

FISHER, IRVING SANBORN, retired geology educator; b. Augusta, Maine, May 21, 1920; s. Franklin and Marion Rae (Sanborn) F.; m. Virginia Stockman, June 16, 1945; children: Lawrence, Beth, Charles. AB, Bates Coll., 1941; MA, Harvard U., 1949, PhD, 1952. Asst. prof. U. Ky., Lexington, 1949-53, assoc. prof., 1953-85, former asst. to dean arts and scis. Treas. Diamond Island Assn., Portland, Maine, 1985—; sec. Ricker Park Assn., Portland, 1987—; mem. Portland Planning Bd., 1989—. Lt. USNR, 1942-45, PTO. Decorated Bronze Star. Fellow AAAS. Republican.

FISHER, JACK (STUART), scientific recruitment company executive, consultant; b. Newark, 1949; s. Donald Harold and Rae Fisher. BA in Art History with high distinction, Rutgers Coll.; MA in Am. Cultural/Intellectual History, Rutgers U. Asst. v.p. loan packaging div. United Fin. Svcs., L.A., 1977-79; various positions, 1979-81; assoc. search cons. Howard Fischer Assocs., Phila., 1981-83; exec. recruiter Jack Stuart Fisher Assocs., Phila., 1983—; co-adjutant mem. faculty and adv. bd. Tng. Inst. for Sex Desegregation; rsch. asst. Women's Studies Inst. Vol. My Bro.'s House, Phila., 1988-90; publicity chmn. Westampton (N.J.) Sr. Citizens Club, 1977; sec. No. Liberties Zoning Commn., chmn. by-laws com. State of N.J. fellow, 1977. Mem. Mensa, Phi Sigma Kappa. Republican. Jewish.

FISHER, JAY MCKEAN, museum curator; b. Portland, Oreg., June 3, 1949; s. Frederick Richard and Suzanne (Cunningham) F. AB, Occidential Coll., 1971; MA, Williams Coll., 1975. Curatorial asst. Sterling and Francine Clark Art Inst., Williamstown, 1973-75; asst. curator Balt. Mus. Art, 1975-79, assoc. curator, 1979-85, curator, 1985—; instr. Md. Inst. Coll. Art, Balt., 1979—. Author: Theodore Chasseriau Ithello Illustrations, 1979, Edouard Manet: Prints, 1985. Clark Art Inst. fellow, 1973, Samuel H. Kress Found. fellow, 1975. Mem. Print Coun. Am. (v.p. 1986-56, pres. 1989—), Grolier Club. Office: Balt Mus Art Art Museum Dr Baltimore MD 21218-3898

FISHER, JERID MARTIN, psychologist, neuropsychologist; b. Houston, July 12, 1953; s. Seymour and Rhoda (Feinberg) F. BS magna cum laude, Duke U., 1975; MS in Psychology, U. Rochester, 1981, PhD in Clin. Psychology, 1981. Lic. psychologist. Clin. dir. neuropsychiatry lab. U. Rochester, Rochester, N.Y., 1982-83; asst. dir. neuropsychiatry unit U. Rochester, Rochester, 1982-83, sr. instr. psychiatry and neurology, 1981-83; dir. Head Injury Ctr. at Highgate, Troy, N.Y., 1984; dir./developer Neurologic Ctr. at Highgate, Cortland, N.Y., 1985; pres., chief exec. officer Neurorehab Assocs., Inc., Rochester, N.Y., 1985—; pres. Comprehensive Rehab Network, Inc., Rochester, N.Y., 1987—; adj. asst. prof. SUNY, Albany, 1984—; clin. asst. prof. neurology U. Rochester Med. Sch., 1988—; developer brain injury rehab. program St. Mary's Hosp., Rochester, 1987-91, Our Lady of Victory Hosp., Buffalo, 1986-91. Contbr. articles to profl. jours. Adv. Compeer, Rochester, 1978--. Mem. APA, Internat. Neuropsychol. Soc., Nat. Acad. Neuropsychology, Am. Bd. of Profl. Disability Cons., Am. Congress Rehab. Medicine, Brain Injury Rehab. Network (v.p. 1989-91), Phi Beta Kappa. Republican. Jewish. Office: Neurorehab Assocs Inc 919 Westfall Rd Bldg B Rochester NY 14618-2670

FISHER, JOEL ANTHONY, sculptor; b. Salem, Ohio, June 6, 1947; s. J. Richard and Marye (Giffin) F.; m. Pamela Robertson-Pearce, Dec. 2, 1977; 1 child, G. Noah. AB magna cum laude, Kenyon Coll., 1969. Educator Shiller Coll., Berlin, 1973-74, Goldsmiths Coll., London (Eng.) U., 1979, Bath Acad. Art, Corsham, 1980-81, 81-82, RISD, Providence, 1985, 90, Vt. Studio Sch., Johnson, 1988—, SVA, N.Y., 1988—, Parsons Sch. Design, 1990, Boston (Mass.) Mus. Sch., 1990; guest prof. Ecole des Beaux-Arts, Paris, 1991; lectr. in field. One-man shows include Diane Brown Gallery, 1992, Farideh Cadot Gallery, Paris, 1991, Gallery Hubert Winter, Wien, Austria, 1991, Galeria Comicos/Luis Serpa, Lisbon, Portugal, 1991, many others; exhibited in group shows at The Bklyn. Mus., Crown Point Press, N.Y.C., 1991, Blum Helman Gallery, N.Y.C., 1988, Albright Knox Gallery, Buffalo, 1987, others; represented in pub. collections Mus. Modern Art, N.Y.C., Tate Gallery, London, Stadfisches Mus. Monchengladback, Germany, Ctr. Georges Pompidou, Paris, Stedlijk Mus., Amsterdam, Kunstmuseum, Bern, Switzerland, many others. Recipient Kress Found. awards in art history, 1967, 68, Thomas J. Watson Traveling fellowship, 1969, 1971-72, Gast der Berliner Kunstlerprogram des DAAD, 1973-74, prize Wroclaw Drawing Triennale, 1978, Nat. Endowment fellowship in sculpture, 1984, George A. and Eliza Gardner Howard Found., 1986-87. Mem. Phi Beta Kappa. Home: Box 348 River Rd North Troy VT 05859 Office: 99 Commercial St Brooklyn NY 11222

FISHER, JOHANNA MARIE, real estate legal representative, teacher; b. Breitengussbach, Fed. Republic Germany; came to U.S., 1972; d. Manning June and Kunigunda (Fürsel) Kunigunda June; m. Herman Fisher, June 5, 1981; children: Johann, Ursula, Sabine, Herman III (stepson). B in Legal Studies cum laude, SUNY, Buffalo, 1982. Cert. legal asst., N.Y. Adminstrv. asst. def. dept. Seiman's Electronics, Fed. Republic Germany, 1976-78; credit counselor Goldome Savs. Bank, Buffalo, 1983-85; with Pack, Hartman, Ball & Huckabone, Buffalo, 1985-86; tchr. Calasanctius Sch. for Gifted Children, Buffalo, 1988-91, St. Joseph's Sch., Buffalo, 1991—; tchr. Calasanctius Prep Sch. for Gifted Children, 1988-89; cons. in field. Writer poetry, short stories. Mem. NAFE, Order Eastern Star.

FISHER, JOHN CHRISTIAN, television production executive; b. Balt., Nov. 15, 1954; s. William Hess and Jean (Reifschneider) F.; m. Maureen P. Frankola, Apr. 7, 1979; children: James, Michael, Elizabeth. Student, Miami U., 1972-74; BS in Mass Communications, Towson State U., 1976; MS, Syracuse U., 1978. Asst. to chief engr. Sta. WNET, N.Y.C., 1978-80; prodn. mgr. MTV and Nickelodeon, N.Y.C., 1980-83; dir. prodn. MTV Networks, N.Y.C., 1983-87; ind. producer TV shows Montclair, N.J., 1987-89; v.p. prodn. Comedy Channel HBO Time Warner, N.Y.C., 1989-91; v.p. prodn. HBO Downtown Prodns., N.Y.C., 1991—. Mem. NATAS. Office: HBO Downtown Prodns 120 E 23d St New York NY 10010-4519

FISHER, JOHN PHILIP, retired printing and publishing company executive; b. Knowlton, Que., Canada, June 9, 1927; s. Philip Sydney and Margaret (Southam) F.; m. Jean V. MacKay, 1978; 6 children: Amanda, Elizabeth, Julia, Robert, Adam, Simon. B.E., McGill U., 1951. With Dominion Engring. Works, Montreal, 1951-75, mgr. mktg. pulp and paper, 1971-75; sr. v.p. Fraser Inc., Edmundston, N.B., Can., 1975, exec. v.p., 1975-76, pres., 1976—, chmn., chief exec. officer, 1982—; pres., chief exec. officer Southam Inc., 1985-92, ret., 1992. Gov. McGill U., Montreal, Que.; chmn. Coun. for Bus. and the Arts in Can.; Can. co-chmn. Can./Am. Com.; chmn. Nat. Tree Found. of Can.

FISHER, JULES EDWARD, producer, lighting designer, theatre consultant; b. Norristown, Pa., Nov. 12, 1937; s. Abraham and Ann (Davidson) F. Student, Pa. State U.; BFA, Carnegie Inst. Tech., 1960. Pres. Jules Fisher Assocs. Inc. Theatre Cons., N.Y.C., 1963—, Jules Fisher & Paul Marantz Inc. Archtl. Lighting Design, N.Y.C., 1971—, Jules Fisher Enterprises Inc. Lighting Design and Theatrical Prodn., N.Y.C., 1973—; bd. dirs. Am. Conservatory Theatre. Lighting designer for over 100 Broadway prodns. including Jesus Christ Superstar, Pippin' 1973 (Tony award), Ulysses in Nightown, 1974 (Tony award), Chicago, Beatlemania, Dancin', 1978 (Tony award), La Cage aux Folles, Song & Dance, Grand Hotel, 1990 (Tony award), Will Roger Follies, 1991 (Tony award); producer: Lenny, The Rink, Dancin', Rock n' Roll- The 1st 5,000 Yrs., Elvis-An Am. Musical, Dangerous Games; exec. producer: Big Deal, 1986; prodn. supr., lighting designer: various rock tours including Tommy, Simon & Garfunkel Concert, Central Park, N.Y.C., 1981, Linda Ronstadt's Canciones de mi Padre Tour, 1988, Crosby, Stills & Nash Tour, 1990, The Teenage Mutant Ninja Turtles, 1990; lighting designer film: A Star is Born, 1976. Recipient: Antoinette Perry award (Tony), 1973, 74, 78, 90, 91, 92. Mem. United Scenic Artists, Illuminating Engring. Soc., U.S. Inst. Theatre Tech., Internat. Assn. Lighting Designer, Soc. British Lighting Designers, League Am. Theatres and Producers. Office: Jules Fisher Enterprises Inc 126 Fifth Ave New York NY 10011-5606

FISHER, JULIAN HART, media company executive, physician; b. Buffalo, June 10, 1947; s. Wilbur Jerome and Janet Adler (Hart) F.; m. Barbara Wallraff, Apr. 25, 1992. BA, Yale U., 1969; MD, Johns Hopkins U., 1973. Resident in pediatrics Children's Hosp. of Phila., 1973-75; vis. fellow in pediatrics Nutrition Rsch. Inst., Lima, Peru, 1975-76; resident in pediatrics and neurology Hosp. for Sick Children, Toronto, 1976-77; resident in neurology Strong Meml. Hosp./U. Rochester Med. Ctr., 1977-79; instr. neurology Med. Sch. Harvard U., Boston, 1979—; asst. neurology Children's Hosp., Boston, 1979-88; exec. v.p. Computers in Medicine, Inc., Cambridge, Mass., 1983-85; pres., chief exec. officer Med. Strategies, Inc., Cambridge, 1986—; sr. assoc. neurology Beth Israel Hosp., Boston, 1981—. Mem. Am. Acad. Neurology, Eastern Assn. Electroencephalography. Office: Med Strategies Inc 65 Bent St Cambridge MA 02141-2101

FISHER, JULIAN POTTER, II, group health insurance executive; b. Glen Cove, N.Y., Mar. 7, 1960; s. Peter Rowe and Cary Randolph (Fox) F.; m. Fay Satterfield Roosevelt, Aug. 24, 1985; children: Julia S., Elizabeth Cary. BA in Fgn. Affairs, U. Va., 1982. Agt. Phoenix Mut. Life, N.Y.C., 1982-86; account exec. WJ Nolan & Co., N.Y.C., 1986-87; dir. group sales Am. Resource Group, N.Y.C., 1987-88; vendor rels. coord. Guardian Life Ins. Co., N.Y.C., 1988—. Mem. Internat. Laser Class Assn., Internat. J24 Class Assn., U.S. Yacht Racing Union, Yacht Racing Assn. Long Island, Seawanhaka Corinthian Yacht Club (race com. 1991—). Republican. Episcopalian. Home: 38 Horse Hollow Ct Locust Valley NY 11560-1900 Office: Guardian Life Ins Co 201 Park Ave S New York NY 10003-1605

FISHER, KENNETH DEANE, life science association administrator; b. Lowell, Mass., Mar. 3, 1932; s. Herman Parker and Margaret (Holgate) F.; m. Lee Hoilman, June 8, 1956; children: Sarah Anne, Elizabeth Lee, Herbert Andrew. Student, Oberlin Coll., 1949-51; BS, U. Vt., 1953, MS, 1955; PhD, N.C. State U., 1960. Asst. prof. plant pathology S.D. State U., Brookings, 1960-63; plant pathologist U. Vt., Burlington, 1963-68; rsch. assoc. Am. Soc. Exptl. Biology, Bethesda, Md., 1968-72; assoc. dir. Life Scis. Rsch. Office Fedn. Am. Soc. Exptl. Biology, Bethesda, Md., 1973-77, dir. Life Scis. Rsch. Office, 1977—. Editor, author (with others): The Science of Life, 1973; contbr. over 80 sci. reports and articles to profl. jours. Mem. Montgomery County (Md.) Foster Care Rev. Bd., 1979—; pres. Gaithersburg (Md.) Washington Grove Fire Dept., 1985—. With U.S. Army, 1955-57. Washburn scholar U. Vt., 1952; recipient Sandison award Gaithersburg-Washington Grove Fire Dept., 1990. Mem. Cosmos Club, Elks. Office: Fedn Am Soc Exptl Biology Life Scis Rsch Office 9650 Rockville Pike Bethesda MD 20814-3998

FISHER, NICHOLAS SETH, marine science educator; b. N.Y.C., Apr. 29, 1949; s. Richard Arnold and Lillian (Wexler) F.; m. Irene Judith Hodes, June 23, 1974; children: Chloe Elise, Claire Calista. BA, Brandeis U., 1970; PhD, SUNY, Stony Brook, 1974. Postdoctoral investigator Woods Hole (Mass.) Oceanographic Inst., 1974-77; sr. researcher Marine Sci. Labs., Australian Ministry for Conservation, Melbourne, 1977-80; rsch. scientist Internat. Lab. Marine Radioactivity, IAEA, Monaco, 1980-85; oceanographer Brookhaven Nat. Lab., Upton, N.Y., 1986-87; prof. Marine Scis. Rsch. Ctr., SUNY, 1988—; cons. IAEA, 1987—; editorial advisor Marine Ecology Progress Series, 1984—. Contbr. over 60 articles to sci. jours. Rsch. grantee NSF, 1988-92, N.Y. Sea Grant Inst., 1989-94, Hudson River Found., 1989-90, EPA, 1990-95. Mem. Am. Soc. Limnology and Oceanography, Am. Phycological Soc. Office: SUNY Marine Scis Rsch Ctr Stony Brook NY 11794-5000

FISHER, RHODA LEE, psychologist, researcher, consultant; b. Chgo., Oct. 10, 1924; d. Isadore Mordecai and Mary (Margolis) Feinberg; m. Seymour Fisher, Mar. 22, 1947; children: Jerid Martin, Eve Phyllis. B of Music Edn., DePaul U., Chgo., 1947; MA, U. Chgo., 1948, PhD, 1956. Lic. psychologist, N.Y. Intern Elgin (Ill.) State Hosp., 1948-50; with Jewish Vocat. Svc., Houston, 1950-52; psychologist Baylor Med. Coll., Houston, 1952-54; pvt. practice Houston, 1952-61; instr. Syracuse (N.Y.) U., 1962-68; from rsch. asst. to rsch. assoc. SUNY Upstate Med. Sch., Syracuse, 1961-64; rsch. psychologist Syracuse Pub. Schs., 1963-68; pvt. practice Syracuse, 1968—. Author: Pretend the World Is Funny & Forever, 1981 (Psychology Today award 1981), What We Really Know About Childrearing, 1976, 2d edit., 1986). Mem. Am. Psychol. Assn. (chair 1989—). Home: 7484 Armstrong Rd Manlius NY 13104-1421 Office: 8116 Cazenovia Rd # 7 Manlius NY 13104-9780

FISHER, ROBERT DALE, stockbroker, retired naval officer; b. Memphis, July 30, 1924; s. Hollis Welton and Anna Sue (Parrish) F.; m. Joy Lee Chandler, Mar. 30, 1946. B.S., Am. U., 1957. Commd. ensign U.S. Navy, 1944, advanced through grades to comdr., 1963; tng. officer Polaris Missile program, 1955-58; comdr. destroyer, 1959-61, ret., 1963; stockbroker, 1963—; v.p. investments Smith, Barney, Harris, Upham, Washington, 1979—. Mem. Mil. Order of Carabao. Republican. Methodist. Clubs: Kiwanis (pres. Falls Church, Va. 1969, McLean, Va. 1979-80), Nat. Capital Economists, Army-Navy, Army Navy Country. Lodge: Masons, Shriners, Jesters. Home: 6033 Chesterbrook Rd Mc Lean VA 22101-3213 Office: 1776 I St NW Ste 900 Washington DC 20006

FISHER, ROBERT JOSEPH, marketing and corporate executive; b. Belleforte, Pa., Apr. 29, 1940; s. Donald J. and Gladys C. (Bish) F.; m. Judy C. Lucas, June 6, 1944; children: Timothy D., Daniel R., Ruth S. BS, Pa. State U., 1962; degree, Moody Bible Inst., 1965; MS, SUNY, Brockport, 1975. Asst. dept. head Eastman Kodak Co., Rochester, N.Y., 1965-67; stock broker Mayflower Securities, Rochester, 1967-70; regional sales mgr. Bapt. Life Assocs., Buffalo, 1970-75; pvt. money mgr., investment advisor Faithful Stewards, Inc., Rochester, 1975-79; fin. planner F., H. and Z., Rochester, 1979-82; pres. Rochester Fund Distbr., Inc., 1982-88; v.p. Monitrend Investment Mgmt. Inc., Rochester, 1988—; conductor nat. seminars; bd. dirs., officer Monitrend Invesment Mgmt., Inc., Ft. Lee, N.J. Author: Private Pilot Flight Curriculum, 1973, Commercial Flight Curriculum, 1974, Instrument Flight Curriculum, 1975. Mem. Internat. Assn. Fin. Planners (bd. dirs. 1984-86), Monroe County Bee Keepers Assn. (pres. 1979-83), Aircraft and Pilot's Assn. Republican. Baptist. Home: 467 Euler Rd Brockport NY 14420-9701 Office: Fisher Fin Svcs 141 E Buffalo St 41 E Buffalo St Churchville NY 14420

FISHER, SEYMOUR, psychologist, educator; b. Balt., May 13, 1922; s. Sam and Jean (Miller) F.; married; children: Jerid, Eve. MA, U. Chgo., 1943, PhD, 1948. Chief psychologist Elgin (Ill.) State Hosp., 1949-51; rsch. psychologist VA Hosp., Houston, 1952-56; assoc. prof. Baylor Coll. Medicine, Houston, 1957-61; prof. SUNY Health Sci. Ctr., Syracuse, 1961—. Author: The Female Orgasm, 1973, Development and Structure of the Body Image (vols.1 and 2), 1986, Sexual Images of the Self, 1989; co-author (with Roger Greenberg): The Scientific Credibility of Freud's Theory and Therapy, 1977, The Limits of Biological Treatments for Psychological Distress, 1989. Mem. APA. Home: 7484 Armstrong Rd Manlius NY 13104-1421 Office: SUNY Health Sci Ctr 750 E Adams St Syracuse NY 13210-2306

FISHER, TOM LYONS, chemistry educator; b. Cin., Aug. 13, 1942; s. Robert Clifford and Dixie Lou (Lyons) F.; m. Ruth Elizabeth Reed, Dec. 14, 1972. BS in Chemistry, Old Dominion, 1964; PhD in Biochemistry, Iowa State U., 1971. Post-doctoral Va. Tech., Blacksburg, Va., 1970-72; asst. prof. St. Mary's Coll. of Md., St. Mary's City, Md., 1972-76; prof. Juniata Coll., Huntingdon, Pa., 1976—; adj. prof. Va. Tech., Reston, Va., 1973. Contbr. articles to profl. jours. Mem. Am. Chem. Soc. Home: 2507 Shadyside Ave Huntingdon PA 16652-2933 Office: Juniata Coll Chemistry Dept Huntingdon PA 16652

FISHER, WESLEY ANDREW, research administrator, Soviet studies specialist; b. N.Y.C., Oct. 23, 1944; s. Mitchell Salem and Esther (Oshiver) F.; m. Regine Rayevsky, Sept. 15, 1979; children: Maxim, Katya. BA, Harvard U., 1966; M Phil. in Sociology, Columbia U., 1976, PhD with distinction, 1976, cert. Russian Inst., 1976. Instr. Dept. Sociology, W. Averell Harriman Inst., Columbia U., N.Y.C., 1972-76, asst. prof., 1976-80, adj. assoc. prof., 1981-87; assoc. chmn. Dept. Sociology, Columbia U., N.Y.C., 1980-81; sec. Am. Council Learned Socs. Commns. with USSR Internat. Rsch. & Exch. Bd., N.Y.C. and Princeton, N.J., 1981-89; asst. dir. and dir. Soviet programs N.Y.C. and Princeton, N.J., 1989—; guest lectr. Foreign Svc. Inst. U.S. Dept. of State, 1976-83; visiting lectr. New Sch. for Social Rsch., 1978-79; rsch. fellow philosophy faculty Moscow (USSR) State Univ., 1970-71, Ctr. for the Study of Population, Moscow State Univ., 1976-86; liaison Soviet Union, Am. Sociological Assn., 1976-86. Author: The Moscow Gourmet: Dining Out in the Capital of the USSR, 1974, The Soviet Marriage Market: Mate Selection in Russia and the USSR, 1980, Social Stratification and Mobility in the USSR, 1973, A Scholar's Guide to the Humanities and Social Sciences in the Baltics and the Soviet Union, 1992; contbr. articles, revs., guidebooks to acad. and profl. jours. Advisor Program for Soviet Emigre Scholars, Nat. Jewish Welfare Bd., Hebrew Immigrant Aid Soc.; bd. dirs. N.Y. Assn. for New Americans. Recipient Herbert H. Lehman fellowship in Pub. and Internat. Affairs,1966, Foreign Area fellowship Ford Found., 1970, two Fulbright-Hays fellowships, 1970-71, 76-77. Mem. Am. Assn. for the Advancement of Slavic Studies, Am. Sociological Assn., Harvard Club of N.Y.C., Phi Beta Kappa. Jewish. Home: 81 Harris Rd Princeton NJ 08540-7510 Office: Internat Rsch & Exch Bd 126 Alexander St Princeton NJ 08540-7102 also: ul Gubkina 14 Ste 55, 117312 Moscow USSR

FISHKIND, LAWRENCE, marketing consultant; b. N.Y.C., May 9, 1936; s. Samual and Fanny (Linkoff) F.; m. Lorraine Bernice Diamond, June 19, 1961; 1 child, Paul Leslie. BA in Econs., Bklyn. Coll., 1959. V.p., gen. mgr. Mort N. Marton Corp., Ossining, N.Y., 1964-70; pres. Lawrence Fishkind Assocs., N.Y.C., 1970-77; v.p., gen. mgr. Italglass USA, N.Y.C., 1977-82; v.p. mktg. Crystal Clear Industries, Ridgefield Pk, N.J., 1982-84; pres., chief exec. officer Spl. Mkts., Yorktown Hts., N.Y., 1984—; cons. in mktg. China, S.E. Asia. Contbr. articles to profl. jours. With USMCR, 1958-74. Mem. Am. Mgmt. Assn., N.Y. Housewares Club, Alpha Mu Sigma. Jewish. Home: 3163 Wharton Dr Yorktown Heights NY 10598-2524 Office: Spl Markets 3163 Wharton Dr Yorktown Heights NY 10598-2524

FISHMAN, JACOB ROBERT, psychiatrist, educator, corporate executive, investor; b. N.Y.C., Aug. 6, 1930; s. Samuel and Francis (Goldin) F.; A.B., Columbia U., 1952; M.D., Boston U., 1956; m. Tamar Hendel, June 1, 1958; children: Marc Judah, Risa Esther, Zalman Schneur, Rebecca Anne. Intern in medicine Einstein Coll. Medicine, Bronx, N.Y., 1956-57, resident psychiatry, 1957-59; research psychiatrist NIMH, Washington, 1959-62; prof. psychiatry Howard U. Coll. Medicine, Washington, 1962-71; dir. Howard-D.C. Comprehensive Mental Health Center, 1966-68; chmn. bd., pres. Univ. Research Corp., Washington, 1968-78, Am. Health Services, Inc., 1971-78; pres. Ctr. for Human Services, 1968-74, Human Service Group, 1971-78, Horizon Mental Health Group, Inc., 1981-84, Cumberland Psychiat. Hosp., 1979-84; chmn. bd. dirs. Am. Mental Health Group, Inc., Am. Health Group Inc.; chmn. psychiatry So. Md. Hosp. Ctr., 1978-81; cons. fed. agys., U.S. Congress, numerous pvt. corps.; bd. dirs. Create Inc., Entertainment Concepts Inc., First Grafton Corp., Med. Services Corp., Inc., Am. Health Group, Inc., Md. Treatment Ctrs., Inc. Bd. dirs. Webster Coll., Washington, 1971-75, Ctr. for Human Services, 1967-75, DePaul Hosp., New Orleans, 1973-78, St. Elizabeth's Hosp., Richmond, Va., 1971-78, Cin. Mental Health Inst., 1971-78, Nat. Capital Day Care Assn., 1966-68; mem. D.C. Public Health Adv. Council, 1966-68; attending psychiatrist Freedman's Hosp., Washington Vets. Hosp., D.C. Gen. Hosp., 1962-68; dir. Potomac Psychiat.

Assocs., 1978—, Am. Health Group, 1985—. Served with USPHS, 1959-61. Recipient Gold medal award Phi Lambda Kappa Med. Soc. Fellow Am. Public Health Assn., Am. Assn. Social Psychiatry; mem. Am. Psychiat. Assn., D.C. Psychiat. Soc., Potomac Psychiat. Assocs. (pres. 1978—), AAAS, D.C. Public Health Assn. (Disting. Service award), Am. Med. Soc. on Alcoholism and Other Addictive Drugs, Am. Council on Alcoholism, Nat. Assn. for New Careers in Human Svcs. (vice chmn. 1965-70), various others. Author numerous profl. articles and books. Bd. editors Nat. Jour. Research on Crime and Delinquency, 1965-71. Home: 1717 Poplar Ln NW Washington DC 20012-1135 Office: Am Health Group 3800 Frederick Ave Baltimore MD 21229-3618

FISHMAN, JAMES H., magazine executive; b. Rochester, N.Y., Apr. 24, 1940; s. Lester and Florence Fishman; m. Ardean Cavalli, July 4, 1976. BA, Columbia U., N.Y.C., 1962. V.p., pub. Yankee Mag. div. Yankee Pub., Inc., Dublin, N.H., 1989—. Home: 330 W 72d St New York NY 10023-2641 Office: Yankee Mag 303 E 43d St New York NY 10017 also: Yankee Main St Dublin NH 03444

FISHMAN, MARSHALL LEWIS, chemist; b. Phila., July 2, 1937; s. Harvey Abraham and Rose (Needleman) F.; m. Nanette Doris Hoffman, July 3, 1966; children: Harvey Abraham, Amy Lisa. AB, Temple U., 1959; MS, Villanova U., 1961; PhD, Poly. Inst. Bklyn., 1968. Postdoctoral fellow Poly. Inst. Bklyn., 1968-69; NRC/NAS postdoctoral fellow USDA, Phila., 1969-71; rsch. chemist R.B. Russel Ctr. USDA, Athens, Ga., 1971-80, USDA, Phila., 1980—. Editor: Chemistry and Function of Pectins, 1986; contbr. 45 articles to profl. jours. Mem. Am. Chem. Soc. (sec. Phila. sect. 1980, chmn. nutrition and food biochem. 1990-91, div. fellow 1991), Chromatography Forum Del. Valley (pres. 1985-86, exec. bd. 1983—). Office: East Regional Rsch Ctr USDA 600 E Mermaid Ln Philadelphia PA 19118-2598

FISHMAN, SIDNEY, retired prosthetics and orthotics educator; b. Union City, N.J., May 28, 1919; s. Abraham and Rose (Levine) F.; m. Adassa Whitman, June, 1949; children: Anne, Adam. BS, CCNY, 1939; MA, Columbia U., 1940, PhD, 1949. Prof., sr. rsch. scientist NYU Med. Sch., N.Y.C., 1947-91, dept. coord. and chmn., 1963-91; retired, 1991; chmn. Univ. Coun. on Prosthetics-Orthotics, Washington, 1960-89; cons. Social Security Adminstrn., Washington, 1970-90, World Rehab. Fund, N.Y.C., 1986—. Editor of 10 books; contbr. articles to profl. jours.; inventor in field. Chmn. local sch. bd., Dist. 6, N.Y.C., 1964-67. Capt. U.S. Army, 1943-45. Recipient citations Ministry of Health, India, Portugal, Israel, Rehab. Socs., Peru, Japan, U.S., Argentina, Egypt. Mem. Am. Acad. Orthopedic Surgeons, APA, Internat. Soc. for Prosthetics and Orthotics (v.p. 1983-86). Home: 200 Cabrini Blvd New York NY 10033-1100

FISHMAN, THEODORE DAVID, psychiatrist; b. Waltham, Mass., May 3, 1953; s. Ernest Martin and Adele (Goldstein) F.; m. Christine Kolodziej, Sept. 3, 1984. BA, Beloit Coll., 1975; MD, Universidad Del Noreste, Tampico Tam, Mex., 1981. Diplomate Am. Bd. Psychiatry. Rsch. asst. U. Conn., Farmington, 1975; resident in psychiatry U. Conn., 1983-86; intern Hartford (Conn.) Hosp., 1982-83; attending physician Hartford Hosp./Inst. of Living, 1986—. Mem. Am. Psychiat. Assn., Hartford Psychiat. Soc. (sec. 1989). Democrat. Jewish. Office: 85 Seymour St Hartford CT 06106-5501

FISK, TREVOR ANTHONY, university officer; b. Ammanford, Wales, U.K., May 8, 1943; came to U.S., 1978; s. Sidney Harold and Eira (Davies) F.; m. Pamela Mary Cherry, Aug. 3, 1968; children: Eliot, Lloyd, Sloan, Amanda. BS in Econs., London Sch. of Econs., 1964; SM in Mgmt., MIT, 1976. Dir. mktg. Nat. Extension Coll., Cambridge, U.K., 1964-66; asst. to gen. sec. Nat. Union of Tchrs., London, 1965-66; sec., v.p. Nat. Union of Students, London, 1966-68, pres., 1968-69; various positions Brit. Steel Corp., London, 1969-78; v.p. mktg. and planning Cooper Hosp. U. Med. Ctr., Camden, N.J., 1978-85; assoc. v.p. mktg. and planning Thomas Jefferson U., Phila., 1985-90, v.p. external rels., 1990—; cons. Am. Coll. of Radiology, Reston, Va., 1987—, O.E.C.D., Paris, 1968-69, Mobil Oil, London and N.Y.C., 1968-69; lectr. Wharton Sch. of Bus. Adminstrn. U. of Pa., 1984—; adj. asst. prof. Robert Wood Johnson Med. Sch., 1983—; mem. editorial bd. Jour. of Health Care Mktg., 1989—, Jour. of Strategic Healthcare Mgmt., 1983—. Co-author: Marketing and Nursing, 1989; author: Advertising Health Services, 1986; contbr. more than 20 articles to profl. jours. Mktg. com. mem. Am. Cancer Soc., Phila., 1985-86; dir. S.J. C. of C., 1979-85; trustee various colls.; councilior London Borough of Hounslow, London, 1971-75. Mem. Acad. Health Svcs. Mktg. (treas. 1991—, bd. dirs. 1990—). Office: Thomas Jefferson U 1020 Walnut St Philadelphia PA 19107

FISKE, JORDAN JAY, lawyer; b. Bklyn., Apr. 4, 1943; s. George Vlatofe and Pearl (Kalker) F.; m. Sandra Joyce Rappaport, June 22, 1974. BA, Brandeis U., 1963; JD, Fordham U., 1966. Bar: N.Y. 1967. Spl. agt. USAF Office of Spl. Investigations, Washington, 1966-71; trial atty. Dept. of Justice, N.Y.C., 1971-73; spl. asst. atty. gen. N.Y. State Office of the Spl. Prosecutor, N.Y.C., 1973-76; chief asst. dist. atty. Onondaga County Dist. Attys. Office, Syracuse, N.Y., 1976—; adviser Dist. Attys. Adv. Coun., Syracuse, 1976—; cross designee, Office of U.S. Atty., Syracuse, 1989—; mem. Criminal Justice Adv. Bd., Syracuse, 1991. Capt. USAF, 1970-71, Vietnam. Decorated Bronze Star. Mem. Jewish War Vets., Assn. Former Intelligence Officers, Disabled War Vets., Vietnam Vets. Am. Republican. Jewish. Office: Onondaga County Dist Attys Office Civic Ctr 12th Fl Syracuse NY 13202

FISKE, SANDRA RAPPAPORT, psychologist, educator; b. Syracuse, N.Y., Sept. 25, 1946; d. Sidney Saul and Helen (Lapides) Rappaport; B.S., Cornell U., 1968; M.Ed., Tufts U., 1969; M.A., Columbia U., 1971, Ph.D., 1974; m. Jordan J. Fiske, June 22, 1974. Supervising sch. psychologist St. Elizabeth's Sch., N.Y.C., 1971-76; instr. clin. psychology Tchrs. Coll., Columbia, N.Y.C., 1973, clin. asst. dept. psychology, 1975-76; adj. prof. Syracuse U., 1976; sch. psychologist Syracuse Bd. Edn., 1976-77; asso. prof. Onondaga Community Coll., Syracuse, 1976-87, prof. 1988—; pvt. practice psychology, Syracuse, 1976—. NIMH fellow, 1969-72. Mem. Am. Psychol. Assn., Psychologists of Central N.Y., Am. Orthopsychiat. Assn., Sigma Xi, Psi Chi. Home: 2 Signal Hill Rd Fayetteville NY 13066-9674 Office: Onondaga Community Coll Syracuse NY 13215

FISS, HARRY, psychologist; b. Vienna, Apr. 15, 1926; came to U.S., 1939; s. Emil and Gertrude (Roemer) F.; m. Gerda May, Oct. 20, 1962; children: Karen, Naomi. BA, NYU, 1949, PhD, 1961. Diplomate in Clin. Psychology. Instr. Albert Einstein Med. Coll., Bronx, N.Y., 1960-63, dir. of tng., 1969-71; asst. prof. NYU, N.Y.C., 1963-69; prof. L.I. U., Bklyn., 1971-73; prof., chief psychologist Univ. of Conn. Health Ctr., Farmington, 1973—. Contbr. chpts. in books and over 40 articles to profl. jours. Bd. advisors Whiting Forensic Inst., Middletown, Conn., 1982-87. Corp. U.S. Army, 1944-46, ETO. Recipient Founders Day award NYU, 1961, rsch. grant NIH, Washington, 1967. Fellow Soc. for Personality Assessment; mem. Am. Acad. of Psychoanalysis (scientific assoc.), Assn. for the Study of Dreams (bd. dirs. 1986-90). Home: 75 Westmont St West Hartford CT 06117-2929 Office: U Conn Health Ctr Dept Psychiatry Farmington CT 06030

FISSELL, WILLIAM HENRY, investment advisor; b. Newark, N.J., Nov. 29, 1931; s. William H. and Mary A. (Dalton) F.; m. Frederica Kane, Sept. 27, 1958; children: Mary, Kate, Frederica, William IV. BS in Econ., U. Pa., 1953; MS in Bus., Columbia U., 1958. Asst. Brown Brothers Harriman, N.Y.C., 1958-65; portfolio mgr. Dominick & Dominick, N.Y.C., 1965-66, A.W. Jones & Co., N.Y.C., 1966-70; sr. v.p., dir. Bessemer Trust, N.Y.C., 1970-76; portfolio mgr. F. Eberstadt & Co., N.Y.C., 1976-82; pres. Houghton Assest Mgmt., N.Y.C., 1982-85; chmn. Fissell, Laidlaw & Co., Inc., N.Y.C., 1985—. Hon. Usher St. Patrick's Cathedral, N.Y.C., 1964-71. Lt. USNR, 1954-57. Mem. N.Y. Soc. Security Analysts, Univ. Bd. Room, Bedford Golf and Tennis. Home: Rt 22 Bedford Hills NY 10507 Office: Fissell Laidlaw & Co Inc 42 Main St Bedford Hills NY 10507

FISZEL, GEOFFREY LYNN, investment banker; b. N.Y.C., Aug. 9, 1942; s. John Henry and Rebecca (Wexman) F.; m. Barbara Ann Foohey, Jan. 30, 1970; children: Sharon Lynn, Morgan Bernard, Austin Tyler, Alexander William. B.S. in Mgmt. and Ops. Research, NYU, 1974; M.S. in Acctg. and Tax (Seminar award), U. Hartford, 1976; grad. scholar program econs. of fin. Trinity Coll., 1980; m. Barbara Ann Foohey, Jan. 30, 1970; children—Sharon Lynn, Morgan Bernard, Austin Tyler, Alexander William. Cost acct. O'Malley Cos., Phoenix, 1974; regional acct., asst. regional controller Sanitas Service Corp., Hartford, Conn., 1974-75; asst. to corp. controller Bristol (Conn.) Brass Corp., 1975-76; asst. controller Security Ins. Co. of Hartford, 1976-80; controller Chase Enterprises, 1980-81, v.p., controller, 1981, sr. v.p., controller, 1985, sr. v.p. corp. and real estate devel., mergers and acquisitions, 1988-89; chief exec. officer, pres., chmn. Equity Investors Holding Co., Glastonbury, Conn., 1989—; tax and fin. cons. U. Conn.; cons. to minority small bus.; lectr. various tax insts. and seminars. Served with USMC, 1959-63. Mem. Ctr. for Study of Profl. Acctg., Real Estate Bd. of N.Y., Fin. Execs. Inst., mem. corp. fin. and taxation coms.; bd. govs. U. Hartford Tax Inst. Author: various real estate, tax and acctg. articles. Home and Office: 519 E Chimney Sweep Hill Rd Glastonbury CT 06033-3927

FITCH, VAL LOGSDON, physics educator; b. Merriman, Nebr., Mar. 10, 1923; s. Fred B. and Frances Marion (Logsdon) F.; m. Elise Cunningham, June 11, 1949 (dec. 1972); children: John Craig (dec. 1987), Alan Peter; m. Daisy Harper Sharp, Aug. 14, 1976. B. of Engring., McGill U., 1948; Ph.D., Columbia U., 1954. Instr. Columbia, 1953; instr. physics Princeton, 1954-56, asst. prof., 1956-59, 1959-60, prof., 1960—, Class 1909 prof. physics, 1968-76, Cyrus Fogg Bracket prof. physics, 1976-84, James S. McDonnel Distinguished Univ. prof. physics, 1984—; Mem. Pres.'s Sci. Adv. Com., 1970-73. Trustee Asso. Univ., Inc., 1961-67. Served with AUS, 1943-46. Recipient Research Corp. award, 1967; E.O. Lawrence award, 1968; Wetherill medal Franklin Inst., 1976; Nobel prize in physics, 1980; Sloan fellow, 1960. Fellow Am. Phys. Soc. (pres. 1987-88); mem. Am. Acad. Arts and Scis., Nat. Acad. Sci. Office: Princeton U Dept Physics PO Box 708 Princeton NJ 08544-0708

FITCHETT, KIRSTEN GLORIA, information management professional; b. Heidelberg, Germany, July 30, 1963; d. Delbert Arthur and Carmen Gloria (de la Flor) F. BA, Coll. of Notre Dame, 1985; MA, George Washington U., 1987. Info. officer Internat. Monetary Fund, Washington, 1988—. Mem. Friends of Peru, Bethesda, Md., 1989—. Roman Catholic.

FITILIS, THEODORE N., financial analyst; b. N.Y.C., July 6, 1937; s. Theris and Katherine (Barbara) F.; married, Sept. 1991; children from previous marriage: Jennifer, Hillary. BA in Econs., NYU, 1959, MBA, 1965. Cert. fin. analyst, 1969. Fin. analyst Moody's Investment Service, N.Y.C., 1960-70; fin. analyst Alliance Capital Mgmt., L.P., N.Y.C., 1970—, v.p., 1973-86, sr. v.p., 1986—; v.p. Printing and Pub. Analyst Group, N.Y.C., 1973-74. Served with U.S. Army, 1960-61. Mem. N.Y. Soc. Security Analysts, Media and Entertainment Analysts Assn. N.Y. Greek Orthodox. Home: 146 W 57th St Apt 72B New York NY 10019-3323 Office: Alliance Capital Mgmt LP 1345 Ave Of The Americas New York NY 10105-0099

FITTI, CHARLES JOHN, retired government official; b. Bryn Mawr, Pa., Sept. 9, 1929; s. Nicholas S. and Mary L. (Vassallo) F. Student, U. Pa., 1948-52, Temple U., 1957-58, Dumbarton Coll., Washington, 1966-69, George Washington U., 1968. Lab. asst. physics dept. Atomic Physics Lab., U. Pa., Phila., 1947-54; solid state physics technician Franklin Inst. Labs., Phila., 1954-56; health physicist, supr. Budd Co., Phila., 1956-63; exec. sec. adv. coms. for tech. and legal mems. of atomic safety and licensing bd. panel U.S. Nuclear Regulatory Commn., Washington, 1963-91; ret.; ret., 1990; exec. adminstr. Ad Hoc Davis Besse Rev. Group; vol. manuscript processor 20th century scientists Am. Philos. Soc., Phila., 1990—. Author: A Philosophy of Creation, 1963, A Poetry Series, 1973, Between God and Man, 1978, Death Comes to Fernwood, 1990; author poetry. Lector St. Jane Frances of Chantal Ch., Bethesda, Md. Recipient Disting. Svc. award U.S. Nuclear Regulatory Commn., 1987. Mem. Am. Nuclear Soc. (membership chmn. Phila. chpt. 1961), Health Physics Soc., Am. Mgmt. Assn., 20th Century Scientist (vol. manuscript processor), Am. Philos. Soc., Peerless Rockville Club (bd. dirs. 1985), Undine Barge Club (Phila.), Union League of Phila. Republican. Roman Catholic. Home: 160 E Kenilworth Ct Newtown Square PA 19073

FITTI, REGINA MARY, psychiatrist; b. Bryn Mawr, Pa., June 22, 1925; d. Nicholas Saverio and Mary Louise (Vassallo) F. BS, Ursinus Coll., 1945; MD, Hahnemann Med. Coll., 1949, D Homeopathic Medicine, 1949. Intern Meml. Hosp., Wilmington, Del., 1940-50; resident St. Joseph's Infirmary, Louisville, 1950-51, Hahneman Hosp., Phila., 1951-52; fellow Hedgecroft Hosp., Houston, 1952; pvt. practice Ardmore, Pa., 1953-60; gen. psychiatry Norristown (Pa.) State Hosp., 1960-62; child psychiatrt fellow Phila. Child Guidance Clinic, 1962-64, staff psychiatrist, 1964-66; staff psychiatrist Media (Pa.) Child Guidance Clinic, 1966—, clin. dir., 1977-80, child psychiatrist, 1980—. Mem. Am. Psychiat Assn., Am. Orthopsychiat. Assn., Pa. Psychiatric Soc., Phila. Psychiatric Soc., Regional Coun. Child Psychiatry. Roman Catholic.

FITTING, MELVIN CHRIS, computer science educator; b. Troy, N.Y., Jan. 24, 1942; s. Chris Philip and Helen Gertrude (Van Denburgh) F.; m. Greer Aladar Russell, Jan. 17, 1971 (div. July 1983); children: Miriam Amy, Rebecca Jo. BS, Rensselaer Polytechnic Inst., 1963; MA, Yeshiva U., 1968, PhD, 1968. Prof. computer sci., philosophy, math. CUNY, 1969—. Author: First-Order Logic and Automated Theorem Proving, 1990, Computability Theory, Semantics and Logic Programming, 1989, Proof Methods for Modal and Intuitionistic Logics, 1983, Fundamentals of Generalized Recursion Theory, 1981, Intuitionistic Logic Model Theory and Forcing, 1969; (with others) In Praise of Simple Things, 1975. Grantee NSF, 1987, 89, 91. Democrat. Home: 11 Kings Ln Montrose NY 10548-1307 Office: Lehman Coll Math Dept Bedford Park Blvd W Bronx NY 10468-1539

FITTIPALDI, THOMAS HENRY, music educator; b. Buffalo, Feb. 1, 1945; s. Alfred Richard and Mary Veronica (Brady) F.; m. Margaret Jeannette Hoffman, Nov. 9, 1969; children: Michael Preston, Marc Thomas, Erin Lynn. B in Music Edn., Westminster Choir Coll., 1971; MusM, Montclair (N.J.) State Coll., 1977. Tchr. Rahway (N.J.) Jr. High Sch., 1971-74; asst. music dir. First Meth. Ch., Westfield, N.J., 1971-77; from instr. to assoc. prof. Monroe Community Coll., Rochester, N.Y., 1978—; freelance musician, N.Y. and N.Y., 1962-77; singer, guitarist Don Sherman Group, Rochester, N.Y., 1979—. Composer (comml.) Rainey Day Umbrella, 1972, (choral arrangements) World Libr. Pub. Coach Little League of Pittsford, N.Y., 1982. With U.S. Army, 1966-68, Vietnam. Mem. Am. Fedn. of Musicians, Am. Dirs. Assn., Nat. Assn. Jazz Educators, Guitar Soc. Am., Early Music of Am. Home: 42 E Park Rd Pittsford NY 14534-1108 Office: Monroe Community Coll 1000 E Henrietta Rd Rochester NY 14623-5780

FITTS, C. AUSTIN, investment banker, former federal agency administrator; b. Phila., Dec. 24, 1950; d. William Thomas Jr. and Barbara Kinsey (Willits) F. AA, Bennett Coll., 1970; student, Chinese U., Hong Kong, 1971; BA, U. Pa., 1974, MBA, 1978. With Dillon, Read & Co., Inc., N.Y.C., 1978-89, sr. v.p., 1984-86, mng. dir., mem. bd. dirs., 1986-89; asst. sec. for housing, urban devel. and fed. housing commr. HUD, Washington, 1989-90; pres. The Hamilton Securities Group, Inc., Washington, 1990—; bd. dirs. Student Loan Mktg. Assn. Sallie Mae; active adv. bd. Fed. Nat. Mortgage Assn. Fannie Mae; mem. emerging markets adv. com. SEC, 1990—. Mem. bd. overseers Sch. Arts & Scis., U. Pa., Phila., 1986-89; mem. N.Y. Rep. Sate Fin. Com., 1986-89, N.Y.C. Food Bank, 1987-89; bd. trustees Bank St. Coll. Edn., 1988-89; graduate adv. bd. Wharton Sch., 1986—. Recipient award Women's Bond Club N.Y., 1986. Mem. Fin. Women's Assn. N.Y., Urban Land Inst., Housing Roundtable Inc. (bd. dirs. 1991—), Nat. Found. for Affordable Housing Solutions, (bd. dirs. 1991—), coun. for Excellence in Govt. (prin. 1991—), Econ. Club. N.Y., Wharton Sch. Club Washington (adv. bd. 1991—). Office: The Hamilton Securities Group 1410Q St NW Washington DC 20009

FITZ, HAROLD CARLTON, JR., research company executive; b. Charleston, S.C., Aug. 30, 1926; s. Harold Carlton and Lois Middleton (Hazlehurst) F.; m. Virginia Kate White, Dec. 27, 1949; children: Virginia L., Elizabeth A., Harold Carlton III. BS, U.S. Mil. Aca, 1949; MS, U. Ala., 1955; PhD, U. Va., 1962. Commd. 2d lt. U.S. Army, 1949, advanced through grades to lt. col., 1965; ret., 1970; rsch. scientist Gen. Rsch. Corp., Arlington, Va., 1970; div. chief Def. Nuclear Agy., Washington, Va., 1970-85; v.p. Phys. Rsch. Inc., Annapolis, Md., 1985-92; sr. v.p. Visidyne, Inc., Shadyside, Md., 1992—. Pres. Chesapeake Bay Action Program, Shady Side, Md., 1984. Recipient Disting. Civilian Svc. medal Def. Nuclear Agy., 1974, Meritorious Civilian Svc. medal Sec. Def., 1985. Mem. AIAA, Am. Phys. Soc., Am. Geophys. Union, Annapolis Yacht Club, West River Sailing Club (rear commodore), Carolina Yacht Club, Sigma Xi. Episcopalian. Home: PO Box 503 Shady Side MD 20764-0503 Office: Visadyne Inc PO Box 330 Shady Side MD 20764-0330

FITZALAN-HOWARD, BENNETT-THOMAS HENRY ROBERT, consultant, public administration and policy analyst, political theorist; b. Geneva, Oct. 10, 1955; came to U.S., 1966; s. S. and A. (Argyle-Campbel) FitzA.-H. AA, Jr. Coll. Albany, N.Y., 1973; BA, Union Coll., 1973; MS, Rutgers U., 1980; MA, Russell Sage Coll., 1987. Cert. fin. analyst, broker. Adminstrv. analyst Todd Logistics, Inc., N.J. and Saudi Arabia, 1980; owner, cons. Fitz Co., Internat., Albany, 1981—; mem. N.Y. Merc. Exchange. Author: Expropriation Predictability and Politics, 1979, The Politics of the U.S. Budget, 1987, The Courts in a Democratic System, 1987, White House-Wall Street: The October 87 Crash and the Post Regan Persidency, 1987, The Politics of Deficits, 1988, Enemyless: Can We Survive?, 1989, Responsibility and Accountability: The Forgotten Cornerstones of Democracy, 1990: contbg. author: Toward a Global Government, 1972, Conservetism: New World Order?, 1990, Tory vs. Labour: Tory: The New English Order, 1992, Hyperinflation, 1992, Eschatology Now, 1992, Eschatology and Current Events, 1992. Active local ARC, RP Found. Served with U.S. Army, 1973-77, Fed. Republic Germany. Mem. AAAS, Acad. Polit. Sci. (life), Am. Philatelic Soc. (life, gideons), Am. Psychol. Assn., Am. Vietnam Vets. Assn., Audubon Soc., Am. Numismatic Assn. (life), Fin. Analysts Fedn. (at large), Fin. Execs. Inst. (at large), Nat. Assn. Securities Dealers (at large), N.Y. Mercantile Exchange, Am. Enterprise Inst., Brookings Inst., Am. Legion, Mensa, Am. Soc. Internat. Law, Am. Bach Found., Am. Soc. Info. Sci., Am. Conservative Union, Nat. Press Club, Equestrian Club, Gideons. Office: Fitz Co Internat PO Box 1744 Albany NY 12201-1744

FITZGERALD, ASTRID MARTHA, artist; b. Wil, St. Gall, Switzerland, July 28, 1938; came to U.S. 1961; d. Ernst and Martha (Greuter) Hurlimann; m. Daniel R. Fitzgerald, July 21, 1962 (dec. 1965); 1 child, Kent; m. Richard Gordon Geldard, Oct. 15, 1983. Diplome de Commerce, Coll. St. Agnes, Fribourg, Switzerland, 1955; postgrad., Poly. Sch., London, 1958-59, Art Students League, N.Y.C., 1962. Solo exhbns. include Pietrasanta Fine Arts, N.Y.C., 1986, Atlantic Gallery, 1981, 80, Galerie Steinfeld, Zurich, 1981, Collegiate Sch., 1975, Off-Broadway Gallery, N.Y.C., 1974; group shows include Credit Suisse, N.Y.C., 1990, Swiss Inst., 1986, 87, Nohra Haime Gallery, N.Y.C., 1985, Heidi Jones Gallery, N.Y.C., 1984, 85, Jayne Baum Gallery, N.Y.C., 1982, 83, Atlantic Gallery, 1981, Aldrich Mus., Ridgefield, 1978, L.I. U., 1977, Nat. Acad. Galleries, 1977, M. Knoedler Gallery, 1975, others. Works in permanent collections at Aldrich Mus. Contemporary Art, Wellesley Coll., Marymount Coll., Rockefeller Ctr. Collection, Chase Manhattan Collection, Chem. Bank Collection, IBM Collections, Citibank, Reynolds Tobacco Co., Washington Hotel, Osaka, Japan, Loews Hotel, Monaco, many corporations; author: Platonic Solids Workbook, 1991; illustrator: The Travellers Key to Greece, 1989; inventor toys. Recipient Juror's award 4th Ann. Small Wks. Group, NYU, 1980, Levitt Award, 1978, Michael Engel award, 19th Assn. NSPCA, 1973. Home and Office: 650 W End Ave New York NY 10025-7355

FITZGERALD, CYNTHIA LEE, apparel company executive, designer; b. L.A., Mar. 13, 1946; d. Charles Williams and Jessa Lee (McCarty) Walensky. Student, U. Tex., 1964-70. Founder, designer fashion co. for plus size woman Caberra, Inc., N.Y.C., 1986—; founding mem. Plus Designers Coun., N.Y.C., 1989—. Home: 512 7th Ave Apt 3205 New York NY 10018-4603 Office: Caberra Inc PO Box 431 New York NY 10028-0004

FITZGERALD, DANIEL LOUIS, securities dealer; b. Salem, Mass., Sept. 27, 1955; s. Richard Wallace and Lucy Marie (Verza) F. BS, Providence Coll., 1977; M in Internat. Mgmt., Am. Grad. Sch. Internat. Mgmt., 1979; postgrad., U. Oxford, Eng., 1979. CFA. Ind. polit. cons., 1982-84; account exec. Smith Barney, Harris Upham & Co., Boston, 1984-87, sr. account exec., 1987—. Mem. Marblehead (Mass.) Rep. Town Com., 1984-92, fin. chmn. 1985, 91-92; del. Mass. State Rep. Conv., Boston, 1990; field coord. Reagan-Bush 1984 campaign, Peabody, Mass. Mem. Assn. Investment Mgmt. and Rsch. (Cert. of Achievement 1990-91), Peabody Historical Soc., U.S. Naval Inst. Roman Catholic. Office: Smith Barney Harris Upham & Co 53 State St Boston MA 02109

FITZGERALD, FRANK THOMAS, sociology educator; b. Chgo., Aug. 25, 1942; s. Ted and Alice Gertrude (Lockley) F.; m. Lana Metz, Apr. 22, 1963 (div. 1973); children: Sean Ted, Laurie Anne; m. Pamela Marian Robert, July 19, 1991. BS in Philosophy, Loyola U., Chgo., 1966; Ma in Sociology, New Sch. Social Rsch., 1971; PhD in Sociology, SUNY, Binghamton, 1985. Rsch. assoc. Heller Sch. Brandies U., Waltham, Mass., 1968-71; instr. Hudson Valley Community Coll., Troy, N.Y., 1972-74; assoc. prof. Coll. St. Rose, Albany, N.Y., 1974—; adj. prof. Empire State Coll., Albany, 1975, 77; vis. prof. SUNY, Albany, 1990; mem. editorial bd. Sci. & Soc., N.Y.C., 1990—; guest rschr. Inst. Argentino Para El Desarrollo Economico, Buenos Aires, 1989; lectr. in field. Author: Managing Socialism: From Old Cadres to New Professionals in Revolutionary Cuba, 1990; contbr. articles to profl. jours. Host, producer Peace Radio, WRPI, Troy, 1984-89. Mem. Am. Sociological Assn., Latin Am. Studies Assn., Ctr. Cuban Studies, Berkshire Forum (bd. cons. 1975-89). Office: Coll St Rose 432 Western Ave Albany NY 12203-1490

FITZGERALD, HAROLD KENNETH, social work educator, consultant; b. Lakewood, Ohio, Apr. 28, 1921; s. Edward James and Julia Florence (Klell) F.; m. Caroline Lee Graham, May 31, 1951; children: Mark, Matthew, Mary, Maura, Kristin. AB, John Carroll U., 1942; MSSW, Cath. U. of Am., 1948, DSW, 1953. Social worker ARC, Cin., 1950-53; exec. dir. Cath. Social Svcs., Atlanta, 1953-56; dir. social services Muscular Dystrophy Assn. of Am., N.Y.C., 1957-58; regional cons., survey dirs. Am. Found. for the Blind, N.Y.C., 1958-66; assoc. dir. Commn. on Standards and Accreditation for the Blind, N.Y.C., 1963-66; prof. social work Syracuse (N.Y.) U., 1966-88, prof. emeritus, 1988—; dir. internat. projects Coun. on Social Work Edn., N.Y.C., 1956-67; bd. dirs. Lighthouse, Syracuse, 1967-90, Cen. N.Y. Assn. for Hearing Impaired, Syracuse, 1976-90, Support, 1990—, Aurora, 1991—; cons. Nat. Conf. Cath. Charities, Washington, 1966-80, UN, Teheran, Iran, 1975-76. Contbr. articles to profl. jours. Mem. Commn. on Peace and Social Justice, Diocese of Syracuse, 1989-91. Lt. USN, 1943-46. Mem. NASW, AAUP, N.Y. State Assn. Human Svcs. (bd. dirs. 1980—), Internat. Assn. Schs. Social Work, Inter Univ. Consortium Internat. Social Devel. Roman Catholic. Home and Office: 301 Greenwood Rd Syracuse NY 13214-2327

FITZGERALD, JAMES RAYMOND, JR., cinema executive; b. Cambridge, Mass., Nov. 25, 1944; s. James R. and Katherine P. (Hickey) F.; m. Janet Joan Sienczyk, Nov. 15, 1970. BA in Econs., Northeastern U., 1968, MBA, 1970; cert. in corp. fin. mgmt., Harvard U., 1990. CPA, Mass. Audit mgr. Price Waterhouse, Boston, 1972-80; v.p., chief fin. officer Amicon Corp., Lexington, Mass., 1980-84, Amicon Corp. subs. W.R. Grace, Lexington, 1984-85, Medi Vision, Inc., Boston, 1985-87; chief fin. officer Hoyts Cinemas Corp., Boston, 1988—, also bd. dirs.; bd. dirs. Hoyts Entertainment Ltd., Wilmington, Del., Hoyts Corp. U.S. Holdings, Inc., Wilmington. Capt. U.S. Army, 1970-72. Fellow Mass. Soc. CPA; mem. Fin. Exec. Inst., Newcomer Soc., Boston C. of C. Home: 44 Blueberry Hill Ln Sudbury MA 01776 Office: Hoyts Cinemas Corp One Exeter Plz Boston MA 02116

FITZGERALD, JOHN PAUL, service executive; b. Dublin, Ireland, Jan. 19, 1951; came to U.S., 1989; s. John M. and Mary (Molloy) F.; m. Angela Condon, June 11, 1982; children: Shane, Jill, Kim. B Bus. Studies, Trinity Coll., Dublin, 1973. Pvt. practice Lang. Ctr., Dublin, 1973-80; regional officer Indsl. Devel. Authority, Limerick, Ireland, 1980; varied TMG Group, Dublin and U.S., 1981-83; gen. mgr. GKN CHEP Ireland, Dublin, 1983-86; comml. mgr. GKN CHEP, London, 1986-89; v.p. svc. CHEP USA, Park Ridge, N.J., 1989—. Roman Catholic. Home: 159 Martha Rd Harrington Park NJ 07640-1842 Office: CHEP USA One Maynard Dr Park Ridge NJ 07640

FITZGERALD, MICHAEL ANTHONY, insurance company executive; b. Boston, Mar. 18, 1944; s. John George and Margaret (McAllister) F.; m. Jeanne Zembiski, June 2, 1973; children: Sean Patrick, Laura Margaret. BA, Boston Coll., 1971; postgrad., Boston U., 1974-75. Underwriter Aetna Ins., Boston, 1964-68; v.p., chmn. nat. utility com. Alexander & Alexander, Boston, 1968-84; v.p., dep. regional mgr. utility com. Jardine Emett and Chandler, Boston, 1984-89; v.p., energy specialist Frank B. Hall & Co., Boston, 1989-91; pres. Energy div. Internat. Risk Specialist, Boston, 1991—. Served with USCG, 1964-70. Democrat. Roman Catholic. Club: Andover (Mass.) Country. Home: 8 Worthen Pl Andover MA 01810-2846

FITZGERALD, MICHAEL WILLIAM, marketing professional; b. Cleve., Aug. 20, 1954; s. Robert James and June Barbara (Gilbert) F.; m. Kathleen M. McGuire, Apr. 20, 1985. BA in Engring., Dartmouth Coll., 1976; MBA in Mktg., Cleve. State U., 1981. Quality engr. Eveready Battery Co., Fremont, Ohio, 1976-80, Cleve., 1980-83; mgr. applic. planning Eveready Battery Co., Danbury, Conn., 1983-86, product mgr., 1986-87; dir. mktg. L.R. Smith, Inc., Hartford, Conn., 1987-88, Nice-Pak Products, Inc., Orangeburg, N.Y., 1988—. Pres. Danbury Westside Homeowners, 1990. Mem. Am. Mktg. Assn. Roman Catholic. Office: Nice-Pak Products Two Nice-Pak Pk Orangeburg NY 10962

FITZGERALD, PAULA MARIE DEAN, research x-ray crystallographer; b. L.A., Nov. 28, 1949; d. Maurice John and Catharine Alice (Jones) Dean; m. Kevin Michael Fitzgerald, Oct. 10, 1975 (div. June 1980). BS in Physics, BA in History, Stanford U., 1972; PhD in Biophysics, Johns Hopkins U., 1977; postgrad., Marine Biol. Lab., Woods Hole, Mass., 1973. Postdoctoral fellow dept. biochemistry Pa. State U. Hershey Med. Sch., 1977-79; postdoctoral rsch. fellow Med. Found. Buffalo, 1979-81, rsch. scientist I, 1980-84; rsch. assoc. dept. biochemistry U. Alta., Edmonton, Can., 1984-87; rsch. fellow dept. biophys. chemistry Merck Sharp & Dohme Rsch. Labs., Rahway, N.J., 1988-91, sr. rsch. fellow, 1991—; co-chmn. diffraction methods in molecular biology Gordon Conf., N.H., 1986; mem. Commn. on Biol. Macromolecules, Internat. Union Crystallography, 1990-93; mem. U.S. Nat. Com. on Crystallography, 1991-93. Contbr. articles to sci. jours., chpts. to books. Calif. State scholar, 1967-71, scholar Stanford U., 1971-72; fellow NIH, 1972-77, 78-81. Mem. AAAS, Am. Soc. Molecular Biology and Biochemistry, Am. Crystallographic Assn. (chmn. biol. macromolecules spl. interest group 1987, nominating com. 1988-99). Office: Merck Sharp & Dohme Rsch Labs PO Box 2000 Rahway NJ 07065-0900

FITZGERALD, WALTER GEORGE, marketing executive; b. N.Y.C., Aug. 5, 1936; s. George Harold and Florence Mary (Rank) F.; m. Gwen Ann, Aug. 27, 1957 (div. May 1984); children: Pamela, Drew. BS, NYU, 1963. Mktg. research analyst Ted Bates & Co., N.Y.C., 1956-59; sr. consumer analyst Lennen and Newell, Inc., N.Y.C., 1959-63; mgr. mktg. research Nestle Co., White Plains, N.Y., 1963-67; mktg. dir. Y&S Candies div. Hershey (Pa.) Foods, 1967-79; gen. mgr. Ward Candies Fund Raising div. Terson, Inc., Chgo., 1979-82; v.p. mktg. John Middleton, Inc., King of Prussia, Pa., 1982; cons. Boyer Bros., Altoona, Pa., 1982. Contbr. numerous articles to profl. jours., 1967-79; patentee in field, 1986. Fellow Am. Mktg. Assn.; mem. Am. Mgmt. Assn. Republican. Uniterian. Office: John Middleton Inc Church and Hillside Rds King of Prussia PA 19406

FITZ-HUGH, GLASSELL SLAUGHTER, JR., bank executive; b. Charlottesville, Va., May 2, 1939; s. Glassell Slaughter and Dorothea (Meredith) Fitz-H.; m. Susan Harrison, May 11, 1963; children: G.S. III, Meredith H. BA in Sociology, U. Va., 1962; grad., Stonier Grad. Sch. Banking, 1970. Asst. v.p. Va. Nat. Bank, Martinsville, 1964-67, v.p., 1967-73; regional exec. Va. Nat. Bank, Richmond, 1981-84; pres. Va. Nat. Bank of Henry County, Martinsville, 1973-76, Va. Trust Co., Richmond, 1976-81; regional exec. Sovran Bank, Richmond, 1984-89; exec. v.p. Sovran Bank/ Nations Bank, Bethesda, Md., 1989—. Mem. Martinsville City Coun., 1974-76; mayor City of Martinsville, 1976; pres. Westminster Canterberry, Richmond, 1978-79; chmn. United Way, Richmond, 1988. Mem. U. Va. Alumni Assn. (pres. Richmond chpt. 1985), Farmington Country Club, Country Club of Va., Commonwealth Club, Rotary (pres. Martinsville chpt. 1975). Episcopalian. Home: 7608 Arrowood Rd Bethesda MD 20817 Office: Nations Bank 6610 Rockledge Dr Bethesda MD 20817

FITZHUGH, LYNNE DENNISON, nonprofit organization administrator; b. N.Y.C., Mar. 18, 1942; d. Roger Bennett and Anna Josephine (Nasvik) Dennison; m. William Wyvill Fitzhugh IV; children: J. Benjamin, Joshua D. BA, Wheaton Coll., 1964; MA, Am. U., 1983. Researcher Harvard U., Cambridge, Mass., 1967-69; editor Conservation Found., N.Y.C., 1964-65, United Ch. Press, Boston, 1969-70, Smithsonian Press, Washington, 1974-75, Today Publs., Washington, 1976-78; dir. pub. rels. and devel. Fairfax County Coun. of the Arts, Annandale, Va., 1978-82; dir., editor, founder No. Va. Arts Quarterly, Annandale, 1980-82; mng. dir. Nat. Choral Found., Washington, 1982-84; dep. dir. devel. Folger Shakespeare Library, Washington, 1984—. Democrat. Office: Folger Shakespeare Libr 201 E Capitol St SE Washington DC 20003-1004

FITZMAURICE, LAURENCE DORSET, banking executive; b. Worcester, Mass., Aug. 7, 1938; s. John Vincent and Alice (Earle) F.; m. Ann McQuaid, Apr. 15, 1961; children: Laura, Peter, Meghan. BS in Mgmt., Babson Coll., 1959; postgrad. in law, Boston Coll., 1961. Prodn. control Sylvania, Needham, Mass., 1959-61; div. controller EG&G, Inc., Bedford, Mass., 1961-69; asst. corp. controller Tyco Labs., Waltham, Mass., 1970; corp. controller Analog Devices, Norwood, Mass., 1971-73; v.p. fin. Balco, Inc., Newton, Mass., 1974-75; comptroller Commonwealth of Mass., Boston, 1976-78, commr. of revenue, 1978; sr. cons. Am. Mgmt. Systems, Arlington, Va., 1979; prin. cons. Boston, 1980-81; v.p. State St. Bank & Trust Co., Boston, 1982—, State St. Bank & Trust Co. Calif. N.A., Los Angeles, 1986—; adj. prof. Northeastern U. Grad. Sch. Polit. Sci., Boston, 1977-78; mem. Bd. Bank Incorp., Boston, 1978. Commr. Mass. State Lottery, Braintree, Mass., 1976-78; sec. Mass. Housing Fin. Agy., Boston, 1978; pres. Human Rels. Svc., trustee, 1988, 89, Wellesley, Mass., 1986—; bd. dirs. Social Policy Rsch. Group, Boston, 1981-92, Boston Mcpl. Rsch. Bur., 1985—, exec. com., 1992. Cpl. USMCR, 1957-63. Democrat. Roman Catholic. Club: Union of Boston.

FITZPATRICK, CAROLYN HENLEY, English educator; b. New Orleans, Feb. 3, 1952; d. Ira Burford and Virginia Daniels (Broadway) Henley; m. Vincent DePaul Fitzpatrick III, Aug. 8, 1981. BA in English, U. N.C., Chapel Hill, 1973; MA in English, SUNY, Stony Brook, 1974. Instr. English Kingsborough Community Coll., Bklyn., 1974-75, Rio Hondo Coll., Whittier, Calif., 1975-76, C.W. Post Coll., Greenvale, N.Y., 1977-78, Bloomfield Coll., Bloomfield, N.J., 1978-80; asst. prof. English Cumberland County Coll., Vineland, N.J., 1980-81; instr. dept. English U. Md. Baltimore County, Catonsville, 1981—, assoc. dir. Writing Program, 1988—. Co-author: The Complete Sentence Workout Book, 1985, 2d edit., 1988, 2d alt. edit., 1991, The Complete Writer's Workout Book, 1988, The Complete Paragraph Workout Book, 1989, 2d edit., 1992, Reading Pathways, 1991, Reading Thresholds, 1992; contbr. travel articles to Balt. Sunday Sun. Mem. MLA, Nat. Coun. Tchrs. English, Coll. Reading Assn., Mencken Soc. Office: U Md Baltimore County Dept English 5401 Wilkens Ave Baltimore MD 21228-5329

FITZPATRICK, FRANCIS JAMES, lawyer; b. N.Y.C., Apr. 29, 1916; s. Francis James and Susan Clemens (Tompkins) FitzP.; m. Ethel Marie Peters, Mar. 2, 1956. AB, Duke U., 1938; postgrad., Harvard U., 1939-40; JD, Cornell U., 1947. Bar: Iowa 1951, N.J. 1954. Exec. trainee U.S. Fidelity & Guaranty Co., N.Y., 1940-41; counsellor Western Electric Co., Kearny, N.J., 1942-45; pvt. practice Orange, N.J., 1954—. With M.C., U.S. Army, 1941-42. Mem. ABA, N.J. State Bar Assn., Essex County Bar Assn., Am. Judicature Soc., Cornell Law Student Assn. (sec.-treas.), Cornell U. Law Assn., Duke U. Met. Alumni Assn., Delta Theta Phi (pres.), Am. Legion (former judge adv. Orange), Sigma Alpha Epsilon. Home: 5 Ledgewood Ct Warren NJ 07059-6751

FITZPATRICK, HAROLD FRANCIS, lawyer; b. Jersey City, Oct. 16, 1947; s. Harold G. and Anne Marie F.; m. Joanne M. Merry, Sept. 22, 1973; children: Elizabeth, Kevin, Matthew, Christopher. AB, Boston Coll., 1969; MBA, NYU, 1971; JD, Harvard U., 1974. Bar: N.J. 1974, U.S. Dist. Ct. N.J. 1974, U.S. Ct. Internat. Trade, 1986. Securities analyst Chase Manhattan Bank, N.Y.C., 1970-71, Brown Bros., Harriman & Co., N.Y.C., 1971; staff asst. U.S. Senate, Washington, 1972; law clk. to assoc. justice N.J. Supreme Ct., Trenton, 1974-75; assoc. Cleary, Gottlieb, Steen & Hamilton, N.Y.C., 1975-78; mng. ptnr. Fitzpatrick & Israels, Secaucus and Bayonne, N.J., 1978—; gen. counsel Housing Authority City of Bayonne, 1976—, Dry Color Mfrs. Assn., Alexandria, Va., 1978—, N.J. Assn. Housing & Redevel. Authorities, Bayonne, 1979—, Housing Authority Town of Secaucus, N.J., 1980-88, Rahway Geriatrics Ctr. Inc., N.J., 1981—, Housing Authority City of Englewood, N.J., 1985-91, Housing Authority City of Rahway, 1986—, Edgewater Mcpl. Utilities Authority, 1986—, Housing Authority City of Woodbridge, N.J., 1988—. Mem. ABA, N.J. Bar Assn., Hudson County Bar Assn. (trustee 1984-87, officer 1987—), Nat. Assn. Bond Lawyers, Nat. Health Lawyers Assn., Am Soc. Assn. Execs. (legal sect.), Beta Gamma Sigma. Office: Fitzpatrick & Israels 400 Plaza Dr Secaucus NJ 07094-3605

FITZPATRICK, KEVIN PAUL, real estate company executive; b. Hackensack, N.J., June 7, 1954; s. Vincent F. and Gertrude L. (Young) F.; m. Mary McEwen, Aug. 9, 1980; children: Kelly Cameron, Megan Ann. BS, Cornell U., 1976; MBA, Fordham U., 1983. Cert. hotel adminstr. Asst. contr. Caneel Bay, Inc., St. John, V.I., 1976-78; comptr. Little Dix Bay Hotel Corp., Virgin Goda, V.I., 1978-80; asst. v.p. Met. Life Ins. Co., Washington, 1980-87; pres. AIG Real Estate Investment & Mgmt. Co., Inc., N.Y.C., 1987—. Mem. nominating com. Cornell U. Alumni Trustee, 1990—. Recipient Food And Wine Mag. award Cornell U., Ithaca, N.Y., 1990. Mem. Urban Land Inst., Internat. Coun. Shopping Ctrs., Cornell Real Estate Coun., Cornell U. Coun. Office: AIG Real Estate Investment & Mgmt Co Inc 70 Pine St 27th Fl New York NY 10270-0199

FITZSIMMONS, SOPHIE SONIA, interior designer; b. Paris, July 6, 1943; came to U.S., 1947; d. Oleg and Sophie (Ovsianico-Koulikovsky) Yadoff; m. J. Heath Fitzsimmons, Sept. 8, 1962; children: Gregory James, Raymond Heath, Douglas Paul. AAS with honors, Fashion Inst. Tech., N.Y.C., 1964. Design intern Euster Assocs., Inc., Armonk, N.Y., 1964; prin. Sophie Y. Fitzsimmons Interior Design, N.Y.C., Conn, 1964-77; co-owner Avon (Conn.), Interiors, Inc., 1977-89; prin. Sophie Fitzsimmons Interior Design, N.Y.C., 1989—; guest exhibitor Fashion Inst. Tech. Symposium, 1984. Mem. Nat. Soc. Interior Designers (adv. panel 1967), Hartford Stage Co. Stagehands, World Affairs Coun. (exec. forum), Mark Twain Meml. Wadsworth Atheneum, Bushnell Meml., Simsbury Farms Golf Assn. (bd. dirs. 1989), Bamm Hollow Women's Golf Assn. (bd. dirs. 1992). Office: Sophie Fitzsimmons Interior 55 Liberty St New York NY 10005-1015

FITZWATER, (MAX) MARLIN, government official, press secretary; b. Salina, Kans., Nov. 24, 1942; s. Max Malcolm and Phyllis Ethel (Seaton) F.; children: Bradley Charles, Courtney Lynn. BA, Kans. State U., 1965. Writer-editor Appalachian Regulatory Commn., Washington, 1966-68; sec., speechwriter Dept. Transp., Washington, 1970-72; with dept. press relations and pub. affairs EPA, Washington, 1972-74, dir. press office, 1974-81; dep. asst. sec. pub. affairs U.S. Dept. Treasury, Washington, 1981-83; dep. press sec. to Pres. U.S., 1983-85, press sec. to Vice Pres. U.S., 1985-87; prin. dep. press sec. to Pres. U.S. The White House, Washington, 1987-89, counselor to Pres., press sec., 1989—. Served with USAF, 1968-70. Recipient Presdl. Merit award, 1982. Home: 2001 Swan Ter Alexandria VA 22307-1361 Office: The White House 1600 Pennsylvania Ave NW Washington DC 20220-0001*

FIX, JOHN ROBERT, artist, educator; b. Pitts., Oct. 31, 1934; s. Earl Lester and Tydfil (Jones) F.; m. Marcia Elaine Nelson, Dec. 28, 1957; children: Anne Bennett, Peter Douglas. BFA, Rochester Inst. Tech., 1957; MAT, Conn. Coll., 1968; student, Allegheny Coll., Meadville, Pa., 1952-54. Cert. in edn. Conn. Art instr. D.B. Oliver High Sch., Pitts., 1957-60; art instr. Norwich (Conn.) Free Acad., 1960—, art dept. coord., 1989—; instr. sculpture and art history Upward Bound, Conn. Coll., 1969; dir. young peoples art program Lyman Allyn Art Mus., New London, 1974-82; conducted jewelry workshops Guilford Handcraft Ctr. Exhibits include Assoc. Artists Pitts. Ann., Carnegie Mus., 1957-80, New Eng. Invitational, De Cordova Mus., Lincoln, Mass., 1962, R.I. Arts Festival, Providence, 1964, Soc. Conn. Craftsmen Traveling Show, 1966, Three Rivers Art Festival, Pitts., 1971, 73, 74; metalsmithing demonstration N.Y. World's Fair, 1964; one man show retrospective Metal Works, Lyman Allyn Art Mus., New London, 1990; commns. include Host box, Glenwood Luth. Ch., Minn., 1957, chalice St. Andrew's Episc. Ch., New Kensington, Pa., 1962, altar set St. Paul's Episc. Ch., Westbrook, Conn., 1979, others. Chmn. Groton Long Point (Conn.) Conservation Com., 1976; bd. dirs. Lyman Allyn Art Mus.; elder Presbyn. Ch. USA. Recipient First Prize in Crafts, 1958, Mrs. Roy A. Hunt award 1961, Assoc. Artists Pitts. Ann., 1968, Award for Excellence in Silver, Katheryn Forrest Trust Crafts Invitational, Slater Mus., 1986, Award in Sculpture Mystic Art Assn., 1986, Purchase prize Katheryn Forrest Trust, 1989. Mem. NEA, Conn. Edn. Assn., Mystic Art Assn. (pres. 1974-75), Nat. Art Edn. Assn., Conn. Art Edn. Assn. Presbyterian. Home: Nine Cross St Box 3313 Groton Long Point CT 06340 Office: Norwich Free Acad 108 Crescent St Norwich CT 06360-3556

FIX, MEYER, lawyer; b. Manchester, Eng., July 29, 1906; came to U.S., 1910, naturalized, 1917; s. Morris and Leah (Katz) F.; m. Elizabeth Goldsmith, July 27, 1937; children: Terry E., Brian D. AB, U. Rochester, 1928; JD, Harvard U., 1931. Bar: N.Y. 1932, U.S. Supreme Ct. 1950. Assoc. John Van Voorhis' Sons, Rochester, N.Y., 1936-43; ptnr. Fix & MacCameron, Rochester, 1943-55, Meyer, Fix, Rochester, 1955-61, Fix & Spindelman, Rochester, 1961-74, Fix, Spindelman, Turk & Himelein, Rochester, 1974-77; sr. ptnr. Fix, Spindelman, Turk, Himelein & Schwartz, Rochester, 1977-83, Fix, Spindelman, Turk, Himelein & Shukoff, Rochester, 1983-91, Fix, Spindelman, Brovitz, Turk, Himelein & Shukoff, Rochester, 1991—; lectr. Cornell Law Sch., 1958-68. Contbr. articles to Scribes. Mem. ABA, N.Y. State Bar Assn., Monroe County Bar Assn., Am. Law Inst., Internat. Assn. Ins. Counsel, Fedn. Ins. Counsel, Assn. Ins. Attys., N.Y. State Trial Lawyers Assn. Club: Irondequoit Country. Lodges: Masons, Shriners. Home: 2500 East Ave Apt 30 Rochester NY 14610-3109 Office: 500 Crossroads Bldg 2 State St Rochester NY 14614-1305

FLACCO, ELAINE GERMANO, computer programmer; b. Phila., June 20, 1959; d. William Joseph and Rose Angela (Ranelli) Germano; m. Dominick Albert Flacco, Oct. 27, 1984; 1 child, Dominick William. Assoc. in Computer Sci., Peirce Jr. Coll., 1985. Asst. supr. foreclosure Fidelity Bond & Mortgage Co., Phila., 1977-79; adminstrn. asst. multi family U.S. Dept HUD, Phila., 1980-81; computer programmer, analyst Reed & Stambaugh Co., Phila., 1982-86; computer programmer, residential coordinator Linpro Co., Phila., 1986—. Democrat. Roman Catholic. Home: 28 Briar Creek Rd Sicklerville NJ 08081-1304 Office: Linpro Co 555 Lincoln Dr W Marlton NJ 08053-3421

FLACH, FREDERIC FRANCIS, psychiatrist; b. N.Y.C., Jan. 25, 1927; s. George Raymond and Margaret (Donovan) F.; m. Patricia Anne Kane, June 23, 1951 (div. 1966); children: Frederica, Christopher, Geraldine, Andrew, Winifred; m. Joyce Elizabeth Rasmussen, Sept. 9, 1971. BA summa cum laude, St. Peter's Coll., Jersey City, 1947; MD, Cornell U., 1951. Diplomate Am. Bd. Psychiatry and Neurology. Intern second med. div. Bellevue Hosp., N.Y.C., 1951-52; from resident to chief resident psychiatry Payne Whitney Clinic, N.Y.C., 1953-58; pvt. practice N.Y.C., 1958—; attending psychiatrist Payne Whitney Clinic, N.Y. Hosp., N.Y.C., 1962—, St. Vincent's Hosp., N.Y.C., 1974—; adj. assoc. prof. psychiatry Cornell U. Med. Coll., N.Y.C., 1962—; program dir. Directions in Psychiatry, N.Y.C., 1981—. Author: The Secret Strength of Depression, 1974, Choices, 1976, Fridericus, 1980, Resilience, 1988, Rickie, 1990, also others. Lt. (j.g.) USNR, 1945-46. Fellow Am. Psychiat. Assn. (life). Roman Catholic. Office: 420 E 51st St New York NY 10022-8014

FLAD, HARVEY KEYES, geography educator; b. N.Y.C., Nov. 10, 1938; s. Harold Kamp and Arlyne Francis (Keyes) F.; m. Mary Margaret Fogarty, May 27, 1966; children: Ethan Daniel, Krista Katarina, Yolanda Margareta, Rowan Kimon. BA, U. Colo., 1962; MA, Syracuse U., 1972, PhD, 1973. Tchr. Peace Corps, Nigeria, 1962-64; asst. map curator Am. Geog. Soc., N.Y.C., 1965-68; instr. geography Vassar Coll., Poughkeepsie, N.Y., 1972-73, asst. prof., 1973-79, assoc. prof., 1980-89, chmn. geography dept., 1983—, chmn. geology and geography depts., 1988—, prof. geography, 1989—; exec. dir. Hudson River Shorelands Task Force, Red Hook, N.Y., 1980-81; rsch. fellow Inst. on Man and Sci., Rensselaerville, N.Y., 1977-78; dir. Am. culture program Vassar Coll., Poughkeepsie, 1979, dir. urban studies program, 1983, dir. affirmative action, 1991—. Author book chpts.; contbr. articles to profl. jours.; researcher, interviewer film Hyde Park, 1977 (1st Prize Nat. Trust 1977). Bd. dirs. Hudson River Heritage, Inc., Rhinebeck, N.Y., 1980-86, Mohonk Preserve, Inc., Mohonk Lake, New Paltz, N.Y., 1982—, Springside Landscape Restoration, Poughkeepsie, 1986—; commr. Waterfront Adv. Commn., Poughkeepsie, 1986—. Recipient County award Dutchess County Coop. Extension, 1977; fellow Ford Found., 1971-72; rsch. grantee N.Y. State Coun. on Arts, 1978, 86. Mem. N.Am. Culture Soc. (editorial bd. 1989—), Nat. Coun. Geog. Edn., Am. Geog. Soc., Assn. Am. Geographers. Democrat. Episcopalian. Home: 115 Academy St Poughkeepsie NY 12601-4311 Office: Vassar Coll Geology and Geography Dept Poughkeepsie NY 12601

FLAHERTY, SHARON MARIE, psychologist; b. Bethesda, Md., Jan. 31, 1953; d. Anthony Joseph Flaherty and Mary (Maleckar) Parrillo. BA, Kean Coll. of N.J., 1976; MA, New Sch. for Social Rsch., 1979; PhD, U. Tenn., Knoxville, 1984. Lic. psychologist, N.J., N.Y. Psychology intern Nassau County Med. Ctr., East Meadow, N.Y., 1982-83; intake coord., staff psychotherapist Mid-Bergen Community Mental Health Ctr., Paramus, N.J., 1983-85; sr. clinician St. Clare's Hosp. Mental Health Ctr., Denville, N.J., 1985-86; cons. psychologist Essex County Hosp. Ctr., Cedar Grove, N.J., 1988-91; pvt. practice Randolph, N.J., 1986—. NIMH grantee, 1979-82. Mem. Am. Psychol. Assn., N.J. Psychol. Assn., Morris County Psychologists. Office: 2 W Hanover Ave Ste 203 Randolph NJ 07869-4212

FLAHERTY, WILLIAM E., chemicals and metals company executive; b. 1933. Formerly with GM Overseas Corp., Reynolds Metals Co.; with Gulf & Western, 1974-81, past chief operating officer zinc and chems. div.; now chmn. bd., chief exec. officer Horsehead Industries, N.Y.C. Office: Horsehead Industries 110 E 59th St New York NY 10022-1304*

FLAKE, FLOYD HAROLD, congressman; b. L.A., Jan. 30, 1945; m. M. Elaine McCollins; children: Aliya, Nailah, Rasheed, Hasan. BA in Psychology, Wilberforce U., 1967; postgrad., United Theol. Sem., Dayton, Ohio, 1990—, Northeastern U. Social worker, 1968-69; sales rep. Reynolds Tobacco Co., 1969; mktg. analyst Xerox Corp., 1969-70; assoc. dean students, dir. student activities Lincoln U., Pa., 1970-73; dean students, univ. chaplain, dir.Martin Luther King Jr. Afro-Am. Ctr. Boston U., 1973-76; mem. 101st-102nd Congresses from 6th N.Y. dist., 1987—; mem. banking, fin. and urban affairs com., small bus. com. and select com. on hunger, mem. subcoms. on housing and community devel. 101st Congress from 6th N.Y. dist., 1987—; fin. insts. supr. internat. devel., fin., trade, monetary policy, regulation, bus. opportunities and energy; gen. oversight and investigations 101st Congress from 6th N.Y. dist. Pastor Allen A.M.E. Ch., Jamaica, N.Y., past chmn. affiliate corps. including Allen Sr. Citizen Complex, Allen Christian Sch. and Multi-Purpose Ctr., Allen Home Care Agy., Allen Housing Corp., So. Jamaica Multi-Svc. Ctr. Alfred Sloan fellow Northeastern U., Danforth fellow Payne Theol. Sem.; Gilbert H. Jones scholar Wilberforce U. Office: Ho of Reps 1034 Longworth Bldg Washington DC 20515-3206

FLAMM, DONALD, retired broadcast executive, writer, real estate investor, theatrical producer; b. Pitts., Dec. 11, 1899; s. Louis and Elizabeth (Jason) F.; m. Elayne Knee, Dec. 9, 1979. Ed. pub. schs. N.Y., extension courses NYU. Pub. mags. and books, 1921-30; owner, operator radio sta. WMCA, N.Y., 1925-41, WPCH, N.Y., 1927-32; pres. and operator Intercity Radio Network, 1927-41; co-owner/founder WPAT, WPAT FM, Paterson, N.J., 1942-48; former owner, operator Alpine (N.J.) Country Club, 1946-65, Sta. WMMM-AM, WDJF-FM, Westport, Conn., 1959-87; now engaged in theatre, real estate and social welfare activities; theatrical producer, N.Y.C., London, Eng.; pres. Flamm Realty Corp., N.Y.; dir. Oscar Lewestein Plays, Ltd., London, 1959-76. Contbr. articles on theatre, radio and TV to trade publs. Former mem. N.Y. exec. com. Anti-Defamation League, mem. N.Y. regional bd., hon. life mem. nat. commn.; past chmn. N.J. Civil War Centennial Commn., apptd. by N.J. Gov.; charter founder Eleanor Roosevelt Inst. Cancer Rsch., Denver; bd. dirs., v.p. Hebrew Free Loan Soc. N.Y.; past pres., trustee Mt. Neboh Temple, N.Y.C.; trustee, former officer Manfred Sakel Inst. Served as spl. liaison officer OWI, World War II; formulated plans for Am. Broadcasting Sta. in Eng. and Voice of Am. Mem. Royal TV Soc. (London), Internat. Radio and TV Soc. U.S.A., Drama Desk, United Hunts Racing Assn., Pa. Soc., Friars Club Found. (bd. dirs. N.Y. chpt.). Clubs: Rockefeller Ctr., Cath. Actors Guild, Friars, Dutch Treat, Alpine Country Club (former owner-operator 1946-65) Le Club (N.Y.C.), Annabel's (London). Office: 25 Central Pk W New York NY 10023-7253

FLANAGAN, ANITA MARIE, public relations professional, environmentalist; b. South Charleston, W.Va., Sept. 25, 1940; d. Henry August and Mary Margaret (Hodge) Thormahlen; m. Shaun Michael Flanagan; children: Michael Lawrance, Sheilah Mary Catherine. AB, Northeastern U., 1963; BS, Southeastern Mass. U., 1977; MS in Environ. Health Mgmt., Harvard U., 1983. Planning cons. Town of Duxbury (Mass.), 1983; mgr. Pub. Participation Program Mass. Dept. Environ. Mgmt., Boston, 1984-86; community relations dir. Clean Harbors Inc., Braintree, Mass., 1986-88, Flanagan-Thompson Assocs., Plymouth, 1988-89; sr. pub. info. rep. Boston Edison Co., Plymouth, Mass., 1989-92, acting dist. mgr., 1992—; hazardous waste coord., mem. oil spill response team Town of Duxbury, 1980-85; presenter pub. info. mgrs.' conf. European Nuclear Soc., Annecy, France, 1992. Mem. APHA, AAAS, Soc. for Risk Analysis, Am. Nuclear Soc., Nat. Assn. Environ. Profls., Assn. for Women in Sci. (presenter USCEA Info '91, European Nuclear Soc. Pime '92).

FLANAGAN, FREDERICK JAMES, water systems engineer; b. Poughkeepsie, N.Y., Sept. 2, 1941; s. Frederick and Jane (Poplawska) F.; m. Sandra Dianni, July 5, 1969; 1 chld, Kathleen. Student, Rensselaer Poly. Inst., Troy, N.Y., 1959-60; BA, SUNY, Oneonta, 1967; MA, SUNY, New Paltz, 1974. Tchr. math., sci. various pub. schs., N.Y., 1967-73; gen.mgr. WKIP Radio, Poughkeepsie, N.Y., 1969-72; pubr. Hudson Valley Mag., Poughkeepsie, N.Y., 1972-74; pres., owner Aqua King Internat., Poughkeepsie, N.Y., 1974—; reg. dir. R.E.T.A., Chgo., 1985-89. Author: Hexameron, 1975, Reflections, 1981, The Nature of Water, 1989. Sec. Arlington Relays, Poughkeepsie, 1973—, Sports Mus. of Dutchess County, 1972—. With U.S. Army, 1960-63. Mem. Hall of Fame, Sports Mus. of Dutchess County, 1982, Dutchess County Slow Pitch Softball, 1986. Mem. New Eng. Ice Assn., Mid-Atlantic Ice Assn., Packaged Ice Assn. (stds. com. 1985-86), Cooling Tower Inst., Refrigerating Engrs., Am. Water Wks. Assn., Apple Valley Softball League (pres. 1973—), Bridge City Bowling League (pres. 1972—), Elks. Roman Catholic. Home: 48 Mandalay Dr Poughkeepsie NY 12603-2633 Office: Aqua King Internat 22 Freedom Plains Rd Poughkeepsie NY 12603-2600

FLANAGAN, ROSEMARY, psychologist, educator; b. Bklyn., Jan. 13, 1956; d. Patrick W. and Angela (Lauro) F. BS, St. Francis Coll., Bklyn., 1976; MA, New Sch. for Social Rsch., 1980, Hofstra U., 1982; PhD, Hofstra U., 1986; cert. advanced study, Queens Coll., 1989. Lic. psychologist, N.Y. Supr. labs. St. Francis Coll., Bklyn., 1977-81; psychologist West Hempstead (N.Y.) Union Free Sch. Dist., 1984-85, East Williston (N.Y.) Union Free Sch. Dist., 1985-86, Copiague (N.Y.) Union Free Sch. Dist., 1986-87, Baldwin (N.Y.) Union Free Sch. Dist., 1987—; asst. prof. Hofstra U., Hempstead, N.Y., 1989-91, St. John's U., Jamaica, N.Y., 1991—; pvt. practice, Hempstead, 1988—. Mem. ASCD, APA, Assn. Advancement of Behavior Therapy, N.Y. State Psychol. Assn. (pres. sch. psychology div. 1992-93), Nassau County Psychol. Assn., Nassau County Psychol. Svcs. Inst. (trustee), Queens Psychol. Assn., N.Y. Assn. Sch. Psychologists, Sch. Psychology Educators Coun. of N.Y. State. Office: 230 Hilton Ave # 1 Hempstead NY 11550-8116

FLANAGAN, WILLIAM WATKINS, III, journalist; b. Wilmington, Del., July 21, 1955; s. William Watkins and Jean Montgomery (Carr) F.; m. Ann Devlin Flanagan, Apr. 10, 1988. BS in Speech, Northwestern U., 1977; MA in Journalism, U. Mo., 1980. Reporter WDOV-AM, WDSD-FM, Dover, Del., summer 1974-78; reporter, producer CATV-4, Dover, Del., 1979; anchor, reporter KOMV-TV, Columbia, Mo., 1979-80, WNEP-TV, Avoca, Pa., 1980-82; reporter KDKA-TV, Pitts., 1982-88, money editor, 1988—. Contbr. articles to profl. jours. Bd. mem. Vocat. Rehab. Ctr., Pitts., 1991,

U. Mo. Alumni Assn., 1991; adv. com. Steel Industry Heritage Task Force, Pitts., 1991; co-chmn. Sale in the Park Magee Womens Hosp., Pitts., 1989—. Named Region III Media advocate U.S. Small Bus. Adminstrn., Pitts., 1990; recipient Dist. Dir. award IRS, Pitts., 1989, Freedom of Info. award Freedom of Info. Ctr. U. Mo., Columbia, 1980. Mem. Soc. Profl. Journalists, Soc. Am. Bus. Editors and Writers. Presbyterian. Office: Sta KDKA-TV One Gateway Ctr Pittsburgh PA 15218

FLANIGAN, JAMES CONRAD, editor, consultant; b. Wallace, Idaho, Jan. 20, 1938; s. Albert Jack and Olive Ruth (Thornhill) F.; m. Roxanne Jo Nevers, May 1961 (div. 1977); children: Carmon Merle Flanigan Friedrich, Karen Ruth Flanigan Tissue; m. Patricia Jean Hume, Dec. 10, 1977. BA in Journalism, U. Idaho, 1960. Newsman UPI, Seattle, 1960; statehouse reporter UPI, Boise, Idaho, 1960-61; newscaster Sta. KBAR, Burley, Idaho, 1961-62; news editor Burley Herald-Bull., 1961-62; reporter, editor Salem (Oreg.) Capital jour., 1962-73; N.W. news editor Oreg. Jour., Portland, Oreg., 1973-81; Washington corr. Oreg. Jour., Washington, 1981-82, The Oregonian, Portland, 1982-87; press officer U.S. Peace Corps, Washington, 1987-90, editor Peace Corps Times, 1990—; cons. Nat. Assn. Community and Jr. Colls., Washington, 1986-87, Nat. 4-H Coun., Washington, 1986-87; vis. prof. journalism Oreg. Coll. Edn., Monmouth, 1967-69. Contbr. articles to profl. jours. Mem. Nat. Press Club, Nat. Assn. Govt. Communicators (Blue Pencil award 1989), Sigma Delta Chi. Home: 821 6th St SW Washington DC 20024-3803

FLANIGAN, MICHAEL PAUL, publications editor; b. English, Ind., June 22, 1934; s. Maurice Melton and Mary Margaret (Thornbury) F.; m. Wilma Carol Schulz, Sept. 15, 1955 (div.); children: Karen Elaine, Linda Gale, Amanda Lee, Michael Paul Jr. Student, Ind. U., 1958. Proofreader U.S. Govt. Printing Office, Washington, 1966-87; pub. editor U.S. Ho. Reps., Washington, 1987—. Home: 7483 Little River Tpke # 203 Annandale VA 22003

FLANIGAN, RICHARD JOSEPH, career officer; b. Bangor, Maine, Oct. 5, 1948; s. Thomas Edmund and Mildred Marion (Myshrall) F.; m. Natalie Jean Rogers, Dec. 27, 1971; children: Nathan, Isaac, Bridget, Patrick. BSME, U. Maine, 1970; MS in Aeronautical Engring., Naval Postgrad. Sch., 1978. Registered profl. engr., Va., Pa. Commd. ensign USN, 1972, advanced through grades to lt. commdr., 1981. Twp. activist Day Care Home Assn., Newtown, Pa., 1989; meeting sponsor Suprs. Election Com., Newtown, 1988; coach Upper Makefield (Pa.) Soccer Assn., 1986-89; troop leader Bucks County Chpt. Boy Scouts Am., Upper Makefield, 1986-87. Mem. Am. Inst. Aeronautics and Astronautics, Tau Kappa Epsilon. Office: Naval Air Devel Ctr Jacksonville Rd Warminster PA 18974-1514

FLANK, SANDRA GLASSMAN, education educator; b. N.Y.C., July 2, 1935; d. Adolph and Rebecca Glassman; m. William H. Flank, Aug. 12, 1956; children: Sharon, Steven. BA in Chemistry, Temple U., MEd; PhD, Fordham U. Cert. tchr., chemistry, sci. Sci. coord. Media (Pa.) Friends Sch., 1965-71; prof., chmn. dept. tchr. edn. Pace U., White Plains, N.Y., 1972—. Contbr. articles to profl. jours. Mem. ednl. adv. com. for sci. mus., Westchester, 1991. Dwight D. Eisenhower grantee N.Y. State Edn. Dept., 1982, 83, 90, 91, Prewsvc. Sci. Edn., NSF, 1981. Mem. Assn. Edn. of Tchrs. of Sci., Nat. Sci. Tchrs. Assn., Am. Ednl. Rsch. Assn., Phi Delta Kappa (rsch. rep. 1985-90, Outstanding Leadership award 1991), Pi Lambda Theta (v.p. 1990-91). Office: Pace U Edn Dept 78 N Broadway White Plains NY 10603-3796

FLANNAGAN, BENJAMIN COLLINS, IV, lawyer; b. Richmond, Va., Sept. 7, 1927; s. Benjamin Collins and Virginia Carolyn (Gay) F.; B.A., U. Va., 1947, M.A. in Econs., 1948, J.D., 1951; LL.M., Georgetown U., 1956. Admitted to Va. bar, 1951; trial atty. Justice Dept., Washington, 1955—, chief civil litigation unit, appellate and civil litigation sect., internal security div., 1971-73, spl. asst. internal security sect. criminal div., 1973-74, sr. trial atty. spl. litigation sect., 1974-79, sr. legal adv. gen. litigation and legal advice sect., 1979—. Mem. editorial bd. Va. Law Rev., 1949-50, book rev. editor, 1950-51. Served to 1st lt. U.S. Army, 1952-55. Recipient Sustained Superior Service award Justice Dept., 1964, 74, 82, Spl. Commendation for Outstanding Service award criminal div., 1976, 84. Mem. Va. Bar Assn., Beta Gamma Sigma. Episcopalian. Clubs: Country of Va., Deep Run Hunt (Richmond). Home: 4000 Massachusetts Ave NW Washington DC 20016-5105 also: 210 Nottingham Rd Richmond VA 23221 Office: Dept of Justice 1001 G St NW Washington DC 20530

FLANNELLY, WILLIAM GEORGE, engineer; b. Scranton, Pa., May 15, 1931; s. George John and Kathryn (Cannon) F.; m. Eileen Constance Muldoon, Oct. 8, 1955; children: Mary, Shawn. BS, Rensselaer Poly. Inst., 1954. Engr. Consolidated Molded Products Corp., Scranton, Pa., 1955; engr. design Sylvania Elec. Products, Towanda, Pa., 1955-56, Hamilton Standard Div. United Techs. Corp., Windsor Locks, Conn., 1956-57; engr. Kaman Aerospace Corp., Bloomfield, Conn., 1957—. Author articles to profl. jours.; inventor, patentee 30 patents in field. Mem. Sigma Xi. Roman Catholic. Home: 108 Hilton Dr South Windsor CT 06074-3417

FLANNERY, FRANK TRAVERS, physician, lawyer, military officer; b. Elizabeth, N.J., Oct. 11, 1947; s. Eugene Leo and Mary Bernadette (Travers) F.; m. Christine Krentar, July 21, 1973; children: Frank Travers, John Eugene, Amy Elizabeth, Erin Patricia. BA, Seton Hall U., 1969, JD cum laude, 1972; M Forensic Sci., George Washington U., 1975; MD, Uniformed Svcs. U. Health Sci., 1981. Bar: N.J. 1972, Ct. Mil. Appeals 1973, U.S. Supreme Ct. 1979. Staff atty. Bar Inst. N.J., Trenton, 1972-73; commd. officer U.S. Army, 1969, advanced through grades to lt. col., 1988; forensic medicine fellow JAGC, Washington, 1974-75; med. malpractice atty. claims svc. JAGC, Ft. Meade, Md., 1975-77; cons. in legal medicine Armed Forces Inst. Pathology, Washington, 1981-85, asst. chmn. dept. legal medicine, 1985-91, chmn. dept., 1991—; chief U.S. Army Health Clinic, Ft. Detrick, Md., 1982-83; lectr. to numerous govt. and civilian local, state and regional orgns. on law and medicine. Editor Seton Hall Law Rev., 1971; contbr. articles to med. and legal jours. Instr. advanced cardiac life support Am. Heart Assn., Washington, 1985—; staff physician Carroll House, homeless shelter, Forest Glen, Md., 1985—. Decorated Meritorious Svc. medal, Army Commendation medal (with oak leaf cluster); Robert Wood Johnson Found. rsch. grantee, 1987—. Fellow Am. Acad. Family Physicians, Am. Coll. Legal Medicine; mem. Assn. Mil. Surgeons U.S. (chmn. medico-legal matters com. 1988—), N.J. Bar Assn. Democrat. Roman Catholic. Home: 15108 Emory Ln Rockville MD 20853 Office: Armed Forces Inst Pathology Dept Legal Medicine Washington DC 20306

FLANNERY, THOMAS AQUINAS, federal judge; b. Washington, May 10, 1918; s. John J. and Mary (Sullivan) C.; m. Rita Sullivan, Mar. 3, 1951; children: Thomas Aquinas, Irene M. LL.B., Cath. U., 1940. Bar: D.C. 1940. Practice in Washington, 1940-42, 45-48; trial atty. Dept. Justice, Washington, 1948-50; asst. U.S. Atty. Washington, 1950-62; partner Hamilton and Hamilton Washington, 1962-69; U.S. atty for D.C. Washington, 1969-71; U.S. dist. judge for D.C., 1971—. Served as combat intelligence officer USAF, 1942-45, ETO. Fellow Am. Coll. Trial Lawyers; Mem. Am., D.C. bar assns. Home: 5607 Jordan Rd Bethesda MD 20816-1363

FLANNERY, THOMAS LUKE, journalist; b. Mercer, Pa., Aug. 21, 1947; s. Luke and Martha Elizabeth (Peffer) F. Grad., Naval Sch. Health Scis., San Diego, 1971; BS in Cardiovascular Physiology, Columbia Pacific U., 1983, PhD, MS, 1984; MS in Journalism and Sci. Communication, Boston U., 1987. Registered securities trader. Stockbroker Hornblower, Weeks, Hemphill & Noyes Inc., N.Y.C., 1977-78; sr. staff technologist Cardiac Labs. Lancaster (Pa.) Gen. Hosp., 1978-80; adminstrv. dir. cardiac catherization & clin. electrophys. Geisinger Med. Ctr., Danville, Pa., 1980-82; dir. clin. product devel. Trinity Computing Systems Inc., Houston, 1982-84; adminstv. dir. cardiac catherization & clin. electrophys. Charlotte (N.C.) Meml. Hosp. and Med. Ctr., 1985-86; substitute high sch. tchr. Charlotte-Mecklenberg Sch. Dist., 1985-86; staff writer, intern The Intelligencer Jour., Lancaster, 1987; staff writer, chief investigative reporter The Intelligencer Jour., 1988—; grad. teaching asst. to dir. Grad. Sch. Journalism Coll. Communication, Boston U., 1986-88; staff writer The Pocono Record, Stroudsburg, Pa., 1988; lectr. Hugh O'Brien Youth Found., Pa. chpt., 1989—; mem. faculty govt. and media Leadership Lancaster, Lancaster C. of C. and Industry, 1989—; guest lectr. Elizabethtown (Pa.) Coll., 1990; instr. writing to publish Lancaster Community Coll., 1989—; contbg. cons. Thames TV PLC, London, 1989—, BBC TV and Radio PLC, London, 1989—, ABC News Nightline, 1991—; spl. cons. NBC Network News Expose, The Iraqi Network, Washington, 1991—. Contbr. writer Fin. Times London, 1989—, Reuters News Svc., 1989—, London Observer, 1991—, Health Jour., 1988. Mem. Boston U. Alumni Schs. Com. With USN, 1966-75. Recipient 1st pl. awards Pa. AP Mng. Editors, 1991, Pa. Women in Communication Inc., 1989, 90, 91, 92. Mem. N.Am. Soc. Pacing and Clin. Electrophysiology, New Eng. Sci. Writers Assn., N.Y. Acad. Sci., Boston U. Alumni Assn., Elks, Sigma Delta Chi. Democrat. Presbyterian. Home: 1011 Elm Ave Lancaster PA 17603-4812 Office: Intelligencer Jour 8 W King St Lancaster PA 17603-3809

FLANNERY, WILBUR EUGENE, health science association administrator, internist; b. New Castle, Pa., June 19, 1907; s. Charles Francis and Mary Catherine (McGrath) F.; m. Ruth Iva Donaldson, June 27, 1929; children: Charles, John, Richard, Harry. BA, Dartmouth Coll., 1929; MA, Oberlin Coll., 1930; MD, Harvard U., 1935. Diplomate Nat. Bd. Medical Examiners. Minister Meth. Ch., New Castle, 1930-31; intern Cleve. City Hosp., 1935-36; resident physician Jameson Meml. Hosp., New Castle, 1936-37; fellowship Cleve. Clinic Found., 1937-40; practice medicine specializing in internal medicine New Castle, 1940—; med. dir. Hospice of St. Francis Hosp., New Castle, 1987—; chmn. bd. Pa. Blue Shield, Harrisburg, Pa., 1975-80. Contbr. numerous articles to med. jours. Pres. Bd. of Edn., New Castle, 1947-53; former trustee Knoville (Tenn.) Coll.; former pres. or chmn. Lawrence County chpt. ARC, Lawrence County chpt. Pa. Assn. for Blind, Lawrence County Mental Health Clinic, New Castle Exec. Club, Greater New Castle C. of C. Recipient Disting. Citizens award Optimists Club, 1974; named Boss of Yr., Am. Bus. Women's Assoc., 1987. Mem. AMA (del. 1953-63), Pa. Med. Soc. (pres. 1963-64), Lawrence County Med. Soc. (sec. 1954-55, pres. 1955-56), Am. Soc. Internal Medicine, Am. Med. Writers Assn., Acad. Hospice Physicians (pres. 1990), Internat. Platform Assn., Pa. Soc., New Castle Country Club, Univ. Club (Pitts.), Lawrence Club, Youngstown (Ohio) Club, Elks, Lions (pres. New Castle 1943-44, Disting. Svc. award). Republican. Presbyterian. Home: 106 E Hazelcroft Ave New Castle PA 16105-2133 Office: Hospice St Francis 1000 S Mercer St New Castle PA 16101-4673

FLANSBURGH, EARL ROBERT, architect; b. Ithaca, N.Y., Apr. 28, 1931; s. Earl Alvah and Elizabeth (Evans) F.; m. Louise Hospital, Aug. 27, 1955; children: Earl Schuyler, John Conant. B.Arch., Cornell U., 1954; M.Arch., MIT, 1957; S.C.M.P., Harvard U. Sch. Bus., 1982. Job capt., designer The Architects Collaborative, Cambridge, Mass., 1958-62; partner Freeman, Flansburgh & Assos., Cambridge, 1961-63; prin. Earl R. Flansburgh & Assocs., Cambridge, 1963-69, pres., dir. design, 1969—; bd. dirs. Daka, Inc.; exec. v.p. Environment Systems Internat., Inc.; vis. prof. archtl. design Mass. Inst. Tech., 1965-66; instr. art Wellesley Coll., 1962-65, lectr. art, 1965-69; cons. Arthur D. Little, Inc., Cambridge, 1964-70. Archtl. works include Weston (Mass.) High Sch. Addition, 1965-67, Cornell U. Campus Store, 1967-70, Cumnock Hall, Harvard U. Bus. Sch, 1973-75, Acton (Mass.) Elementary schs, 1966-68, 69-71, Wilton (Conn.) High Sch, 1968-71, 14 Story St. Bldg, 1970, Boston Design Ctr., 1985-86, Glenwood Sch., Dallas, 1985-88, New Univ. No. B.C., Prince George, Can., 1991—; exhibited works Light Machine I, IBM Gallery, N.Y.C., 1958, Light Machine II, Carpenter Center, Harvard, 1965, 5 Cambridge Architects, Wellesley Coll., 1969, Work of Earl R. Flansburgh and Assos, Wellesley Coll., 1969, New Architecture in New Eng, DeCordova Mus., 1974-75, Residential Architecture, Mead Art Gallery, Amherst Coll., 1976, works represented in, 50 Ville del Nostro Tempo, 1970, Nuove Ville, New Villas, 1970, Vacation Houses, 1970, Vacation Houses, 2d edit., 1977, Interior Design, 1970, Drawings by American Architects, 1973, Interior Spaces Designed by Architects, 1974, New Architecture in New England, 1974, Great Houses, 1976, Architecture Boston, 1976, Presentation Drawings by American Architects, 1977, Architecture, 1970-1980, A Decade of Change, 1980, Old and New Architecture, A Design Relationship, 1980, 25 Years of Record Houses, 1981; Author: (with others) Techniques of Successful Practice, 1975. Chmn. architecture com. Boston Arts Festival, 1964, Downtown Boston Design adv. com.; bd. dirs. Cambridge Ctr. Adult Edn.; trustee Cornell U., 1972—; chmn. bldgs. and properties com., 1976-87; mem. exec. com. academic affairs com.; class sec. SCMP VII Harvard Bus. Sch., 1982-89. Served to 1st lt. USAF, 1954-56. Recipient design awards Progressive Architecture, design awards Record Houses, design awards AIA, design awards City of Boston, design awards Mass. Masonry Inst., spl. design citations Am. Assn. Sch. Adminstrs., spl. 1st prize Buffalo-Western N.Y. chpt. AIA Competition., Walter Taylor award Am. Assn. Sch. Adminstrs., 1986; Fulbright research grantee Bldg. Research Sta., Eng., 1957-58. Fellow AIA; mem. Royal Inst. Brit. Architects, Boston Soc. Architects (chmn. program com., 1969-71, commr. pub. affairs 1971-73, commr. design 1973-74, dir. 1971-74, pres. 1980-81), Boston Found. Architecture (treas. 1984-89), Cornell U. Coun., Quill and Dagger Soc., Tau Beta Pi. Home: 225 Old County Rd Lincoln MA 01773-4601 Office: 77 N Washington St Boston MA 02114-1908

FLANZER, ROBERT STEPHEN, dentist; b. Bklyn., Oct. 15, 1934; s. Abraham and Edith (Rosenzweig) F. BS, Bklyn. Coll., 1955; DDS, NYU, 1959; postgrad., Bklyn. Law Sch., 1972-73, Dartmouth Coll., 1984. Pvt. practice Bklyn., 1962—. Candidate compt. Libertarian Party, N.Y. State., 1974, N.Y.C., 1977, 8l, chmn., Bklyn., 1975; Presdl. elector, 1976, 80, 84, 88. Capt. USAF, 1959-6l. Mem. ADA, Jewish War Vets. Office: 126 W End Ave Brooklyn NY 11235-4813

FLASCHEN, EVAN DANIEL, lawyer; b. Summit, N.J., July 26, 1957; s. Steward Samuel and Joyce (Davies) F.; m. Cynthia Anne Cromwell, May 24, 1981; children: Reed Cromwell, Joan Steward, Thomas Bevan. BA, Wesleyan U., 1979; JD, U. Conn., 1982. Bar: Conn. 1982. Ptnr. Hebb & Gitlin, Hartford, Conn., 1982—; lectr. in field. Co-editor: International Loan Workouts and Bankruptcies, 1989; contbg. editor: Norton Bankruptcy Law and Practice, 1989—; mem. editorial bd. INSOL Internat. Jour., 1990—, Annual Survey of Bankruptcy Law, 1989—, Commercial Insolvency Reporter Can., 1989—; contbr. articles to profl. jours. Mem. ABA (bus. bankruptcy com. sect. of bus. law 1984—, vice-chmn. Chpt. 11 subcom. 1989—, vice-chmn. secured creditors subcom. 1988-89, internat. bankruptcy subcom. 1986—), Internat. Bar Assn. (com. creditor's rights and insolvency 1986—), INSOL Internat. (co-chmn. cross-border insolvency project 1989—), Am. Bankruptcy Inst. (chmn. INSOL sect. 1988—). Home: 43 Riverview Dr Glastonbury CT 06033-3137 Office: Hebb & Gitlin One State St Hartford CT 06103

FLATAU, CARL R., electronics executive; b. Berlin, June 21, 1924; came to U.S., 1952; s. Ralph and Anne-Marie (Kuerle) F.; m. Joanne Patricia Mastropolo; children: Ralph, Arthur, Irene, Claudia. BS in Mech. Engring., Poly. Inst., Bklyn., 1958. Sr. staff engr. Brookhaven Nat. Lab., Upton, N.Y., 1958-67; pres. Telerobotics, Inc., Bohemia, N.Y., 1976-90. Patentee in field; contbr. Teleoperated Robotics, 1985, Encyclopedia Robotics, 1988, articles to sci. jours., 1959-88. Mem. ASME, Soc. Mfg. Engrs. Office: Telerobotics Inc PO Box 43 Mattituck NY 11952-0043

FLATTO, ADAM R., real estate investment executive; b. N.Y.C., Apr. 2, 1963; s. Frederick and Gail (Slauson) F.; m. Olivia E. Tournay, Oct. 26, 1991. BA magna cum laude, Brown U., 1985; MBA, U. Pa., 1989. Assoc. Georgetown Co., N.Y.C., 1985-87, ptnr., 1989—; assoc. Richard I. Rubin, Inc., Phila., 1987-88. Mem. Harmonie Club, Omicron Delta Epsilon. Home: 400 E 71st St New York NY 10021 Office: Georgetown Co 667 Madison Ave New York NY 10021

FLAVIN, JOHN JOSEPH, JR., sales executive; b. Cohoes, N.Y., Feb. 21, 1956; s. John Joseph Sr. and Mary Joan (Brennan) F.; m. Jill Lenore Sabey. BS in Bus. Adminstrn., SUNY, 1978; MBA, U. Bridgeport, 1989. Assoc. acct. mgr. Burroughs Corp., Albany, N.Y., 1978-81; acct. mgr. Burroughs Corp., 1981; br. mgr. Gen. Electric Info. Services Corp., Stamford, Conn., 1982-83; Ea. dist. mgr. Gen. Electric Info. Services Corp., 1983-84; Ea. region mgr. U.S. Design Corp., 1984-85; nat. sales mgr. U.S. Design Corp., Lanham, Md., 1985-86; sr. acct. rep. Burroughs Corp. (now Unisys), Darien, Conn., 1986-87; br. sales mgr. Unisys, Shelton, Conn., 1987-89; br. mgr. Keane, Inc., Stamford, 1989—. Republican. Home: 26 Devils Gardens Rd Norwalk CT 06854-3315

FLAX, RICHARD L., surgeon; b. Washington, June 4, 1940; s. Emil and Bess (Gurevitz) F.; (div.); children: Valerie, Meredith; m. Katherine Alley, June 25, 1978; 1 child, Jennifer. BS, U. Md., 1962; MD, Md. Med. Sch., 1966. Diplomate Am. Bd. Surgery. Intern Univ. Hosps. of Cleve., 1966-67; resident George Washington U. Med. Ctr., Wahington, 1967-72, Malcolm Grow USAF Hosp., 1968-70; chief of surgery Columbia Hosp. for Women, Washington, 1990—. Office: 2440 M St NW Washington DC 20037-1404

FLECK, GEORGE MORRISON, chemistry educator; b. Warren, Ind., May 13, 1934; s. Ford Bloom and Deloris Magdalene (Morrison) F.; m. Margaret Dyer Reynolds, June 27, 1959; children: Margaret Morrison, Louise Elizabeth. B.S., Yale U., 1956; Ph.D., U. Wis., 1961. Asst. prof. Smith Coll., Northampton, Mass., 1961-67, assoc. prof., 1967-76, prof. chemistry, 1976—. Author: Equilibria in Solution, 1966, Chemical Reaction Mechanisms, 1971, Carboxylic Acid Equilibria, 1973, Chemistry: Molecules That Matter, 1974, Patterns of Symmetry, 1977, Shaping Space: A Polyhedral Approach, 1987. Fellow Danforth Found., 1956-61; Dupont fellow, 1960; Danforth assoc., 1982—; grantee NSF, NIH, U.S. Office Edn., Am. Philos. Soc. Mem. Am. Chem. Soc., Mass. Assn. Sci. Tchrs., New Eng. Assn. Chemistry Tchrs., Sigma Xi. Office: Smith Coll Clark Sci Ctr Northampton MA 01063

FLEEGER, RON, image consultant; b. Miami, Fla., July 5, 1955; s. Donald Raymond and Flora Mae (McDermott) F. BFA cum laude, Fla. State U., 1976. Display mgr. Bloomingdales, N.Y.C., 1981-82; visual dir. Members Only Sportswear, Inc., N.Y.C., 1982-86; owner Fleeger, Inc./Imagemakers, N.Y.C., 1986—, designer furniture, home and fashion accessories, N.Y.C., 1986—; customs rugs, fixturing, decorative hardware Fleeger Inc./Lifestyles, Products, N.Y.C., 1986—. Exhibited in group shows at MIT, 1988-89, Design Gallery 91, Soho, N.Y., 1988, 90, 91, 92; designs included in Ryuko Tsushsin, 1989, Flatiron, 1990, DNR, 1991, Flooring, 1991, Home Furnishing Daily, 1991, 'W', 1992. Home and Office: 131 E 23rd St New York NY 10010-4510

FLEETWOOD, REX ALLEN, insurance company executive; b. Newton, Kans., Aug. 17, 1951; s. Milburn William and Edna Milton (Hughes) F.; m. Donna Kay Kurr, June 3, 1972. BS, Kans. Wesleyan U., 1973. Programmer First Nat. Bank, Salina, Kans., 1971-73, State of Kans., Topeka, 1973-74; project leader Blue Cross/Blue Shield, Topeka, 1974-77; asst. v.p. data systems Great Central Ins., Peoria, Ill., 1977-81; v.p. data systems Am. Universal Inc., Providence, 1981-84, Pa. Nat. Ins., Harrisburg, 1984—; cons. Computer Systems, Boston, 1983-84. Mem. Diamond Club, United Way, Harrisburg, 1988-92. Named Speaker of Yr., Data Processing Auditors Assn., Harrisburg, 1988. Mem. Pa. Assn. Mut. Ins. Cos. (chmn. data processing com. 1987-90). Republican. Baptist. Home: 276 Ridge Hill Rd Mechanicsburg PA 17055-1748 Office: Pa Nat Ins Group 1900 Derry St Harrisburg PA 17104-2312

FLEGEAL-KIPP, SONIA R(UTH), medical services executive; b. Ft. Bragg, N.C., Apr. 14, 1949; d. Foster Franklin and Helene Virginia (Eyler) F.; m. Bruce George Kipp III. BA, Schiller Coll., Heidelberg, Germany, 1971; teaching cert., Shippensburg (Pa.) U., 1973; BS, Pa. State U., 1983; MHA, Coll. of St. Francis, 1990. Translator Def. Attaches Office, US Embassy, Bad Godesberg, Fed. Republic Germany, 1971; substitute tchr. Carlisle, Pa., 1973-74; surg. and anesthesia asst. Charles L. Stoup, Jr., DDS, Carlisle, 1974-75; tri-lingual sec. Dickinson Coll., Carlisle, 1975-81; staff acct. P.R. Hoffman Co., Materials Processing, Carlisle, 1981-83; adminstr. Belvedere Med. Corp., Carlisle, 1983—. Home: 112 Horners Rd Carlisle PA 17013-8508 Office: Belvedere Med Corp 850 Walnut Bottom Rd Carlisle PA 17013-3698

FLEISCHER, ALBERT GEORG, health facility administrator; b. Mineral Wells, Tex., Sept. 26, 1940; s. Albert Georg and Lilith Martesia (Boyd) F. AB, Austin Coll., 1962; MD, U. Tex., 1966. Fellow in spinal cord injuries Rusk Inst., N.Y.C., 1968; asst. prof. Rush Inst., N.Y.C., 1968-80; dir. rehab. medicine S.I. (N.Y.) Hosp., 1980-89; chair rehab. medicine S.I. U. Hosp., 1989—; asst. prof. Downstate Med. Ctr., Bklyn., N.Y., 1985—; assoc. clin. prof. phys. therapy div. Coll. S.I., 1991—; dir. rehab. medicine Luth. Med. Ctr., Bklyn., 1985—. Mem. Mayor's Com. for Disabled, N.Y.C., 1980—, chairperson, 1990—; chair Borough Pres. Com. for Disabled, S.I., 1989—; med. dir. United Cerebral Palsy, N.Y.C., 1991—. Paul Harris fellow, 1989. Mem. AMA, Am. Congress Rehab. Medicine, N.Y. Assn. Physical Medicine and Rehab., Am. Assn. Physical Medicine and Rehab. Republican. Presbyterian. Office: SIU Hosp 475 Sea View Ave Staten Island NY 10305

FLEISCHMAN, CHARLES ARTHUR, assistant principal; b. Allentown, Pa., Oct. 4, 1945; s. William Robert and Mary Elizabeth (Moyer) F.; m. Margaret Mary Marr; children: Keith Charles, John William. BA, Glassboro State Coll., 1967, MA, 1973, 80. Tchr. history, govt. No. Burlington County Regional High Sch., Columbus, N.J., 1967-69; tchr. history Cherry Hill High Sch. East, N.J., 1968-77; history dept. chmn. Cherry Hill High Sch. East, 1977-87, asst. prin., 1987—; econ. dist. coord. Cherry Hill Sch. Dist., 1984-91; textbook cons. McGraw Hill, N.Y.C., 1980. Contbr. articles to profl. jours. Eucharistic minister St. Joan of Arc Ch., Marlton, N.J., 1989—; recreation coach Marlton Recreation Athletics, 1984—. PEW Trust Found. fellow, 1989, 90; recipient award for outstanding contbn. to econ. edn. N.J. Coun. for Econ. Edn., 1985. Mem. NEA, ASCD, N.J. Coun. Econ. Edn., Prins. and Suprs. Assn., KC, Phi Delta Kappa. Roman Catholic. Office: Cherry Hill High Sch E Kresson Rd Cherry Hill NJ 08003

FLEISCHMAN, HERMAN ISRAEL, lawyer; b. Bklyn., Aug. 30, 1950; s. Boris and Bella (Weisbrot) F.; m. Francine Moskowitz, Feb. 3, 1973; children: Meredith, Brandon, Gary. BA, Bklyn. Coll., 1972; JD, Bklyn. Sch. Law, 1976; MPA, NYU, 1974. Bar: N.Y. 1977, U.S. Dist. Ct. (ea., so., we. and no. dists.) N.Y. 1977, U.S. Ct. Appeals (D.C. cir.) 1979, U.S. Tax Ct. 1982. Asst. counsel Amalgamated Ins. Co., N.Y.C., 1976; asst. spl. atty. gen. State of N.Y., N.Y.C., 1977-79; asst. counsel N.Y. State Dept. Mental Hygiene, Staten Island, N.Y., 1979; assoc. Ackerman, Salwen & Glass, N.Y.C., 1979-80; sole practice N.Y.C., 1980—. Mem. Thomas Jefferson Dem. Club, Bklyn., 1983-85; chmn. B'nai Brith Youth Orgn., 1980-82; bd. dirs. Big Apple Region, vice chmn., 1986-88, bd. dirs. Nassau and Suffolk Counties, N.Y. Recipient Citation, Town of Hempstead, 1986, Dist. Key award, B'nai B'rith Youth Org., 1979, Man of Yr. award, B'nai B'rith Youth Org., 1980. Mem. ABA, N.Y. State Bar Assn., Bklyn. Bar Assn., Assn. Trial Lawyers Am.

FLEISCHNER, ALOIS LEONARD, ophthalmologist, retired; b. N.Y.C., Sept. 4, 1913; s. Otto and Frances (Goodman) F.; m. Jean Sokiran, May 1, 1938 (dec. Oct. 1978); children: Mark, Richard. BS, NYU, 1932, MD, 1935. Diplomate Am. Bd. Ophthalmology. Intern, houseship eye-ear, nose and throat N.Y.C. Hosp., 1935-39; resident Queens Gen. Hosp., N.Y.C., 1939-40; pvt. practice N.Y.C., 1940-42, pvt. practice ophthalmology, 1946-88; ophthalmologist Bronx (N.Y.) Eye Infirmary, 1946-73, Montefiore Hosp. & Med. Ctr., Bronx, 1973—; cons. ophthalmologist Bronx-Lebanon Med. Ctr., 1946—. Capt. U.S. Army, 1942-46, ETO. Fellow ACS (pres. Bronx chpt. 1963); mem. Am. Acad. Ophthalmology, N.Y. Soc. Clin. Ophthalmology, N.Y. Acad. Medicine. Home: 3333 Henry Hudson Pkwy Bronx NY 10463

FLEISHER, ERIC WILFRID, retired foreign service officer; b. Washington, Jan. 31, 1926; s. Wilfrid and Greta Agda (Sundberg) F.; m. Elizabeth Fredrikson, Dec. 22, 1948 (div. 1974); children: Susanne Jane, Eric Torsten; m. Thale Gunneng, Aug. 5, 1974; 1 child, Arne Ericsson. Cert., U. Stockholm, 1948; BA, George Washington U., 1950; PhD, U. Lund, Sweden, 1953. Orientation officer U.S. Displaced Persons Commn., French Zone, Germany, 1950-51; program and ops. officer Refugee Relief Dept. State, Washington, 1954-55, intelligence rsch. analyst, 1955-58; polit. officer Am. Embassy Dept. State, Copenhagen and Consul Faroe Islands, 1959-63; polit. counselor Am. Embassy Dept. State, Helsinki, Finland, 1964-69; dep. dir., then dir. Nordic countries Dept. State, Washington, 1969-73; press attache Am. Embassy Dept. State, Stockholm, 1974-76; spl. asst. human rights and refugee affairs Dept. State, Washington, 1977-80, cons. freedom of info., 1980—. Author: Viking Times to Modern, 1953; translator, editor: Scandinavia in Great Power Politics, 1905-1908, 1958; contbr. articles to various publs. 1st lt. U.S. Army, 1944-47, Tokyo. Mem. Am. Fgn. Svc. Assn., Diplomatic and Consular Officers Ret., Am. Scandinavian Found.

Home: 5917 Woodacres Dr Bethesda MD 20816-3430 Office: Dept State Rm 1434NS Washington DC 20520

FLEISHER, GARY MITCHELL, employment industry and management consulting executive; b. Bklyn., July 10, 1941; s. Irving and Ceil F.; m. Grace M. Reynolds; children: Nina, Gwen Megan. Student Ogelthorpe U., 1959, U. Miami, 1960-61. N at. ops. mgr. Staff Builders, Inc., N.Y.C., 1967-70; v.p., gen. mgr. Career Tempforce, East Meadow, N.Y., 1970-76; exec. v.p. Uniforce Temporary Services, New Hyde Park, N.Y., 1976-83; pres. G.M. Fleisher & Assocs., Inc., 1984—, pres., dir. GMF Mgmt. Group., 1984—; pres., dir. GMF Staffing Inc.; pres. Promax Staffing, 1990-92, ProMax Pers. Systems, 1991-92. Mem. ASTD, Soc. Human Resource Mgmt., Am. Mgmt. Assn., Am. Soc. Pers. Adminstrn., Adminstrv. Mgmt. Soc., Internat. Franchise Assn., Internat. Platform Assn, Masons.

FLEISHMAN, PHILIP ROBERT, internist; b. Hartford, Conn., Apr. 17, 1935; s. Morris and Anna Lillian (Farber) F.; B.S., Trinity Coll., Harford, 1957; M.D., SUNY, Bklyn., 1961; m. Anita Rose Coopersmith, Oct. 18, 1964; children—David, Beth, Rachael. Practice medicine specializing in internal medicine, East Islip, N.Y., 1967—; attending physician, asst. dir. medicine Southside Hosp., Bay Shore, N.Y.; attending physician Good Samaritan Hosp., W. Islip, Central Islip State Hosp.; v.p. med. bd. Southside Hosp., 1986-89, pres. 1989—; clin. asst. prof. SUNY Med. Sch., Stony Brook, 1967—, asst. dir. medicine, 1988—; founder, co-dir. diabetic clinic Southside Hosp. Co-author, chmn. constn. and bylaws Pro-Arts Group Islips, 1979; asst. basketball coach Police Athletic League, 1979; v.p., pres., trustee Bay Shore Jewish Center, 1979—; pres.-elect, 1986-88, pres. 1988-90; coach CVO, 1980; active Bayshore Jewish Center Theatre Group. Served to capt. M.C., U.S. Army, 1965-67. Diplomate Am. Bd. Internal Medicine. Fellow ACP; mem. AMA, Am. Diabetes Assn., N.Y. State Med. Soc., N.Y. State Soc. Internal Medicine (past chpt. pres.), Suffolk County Med. Soc. Contbr. articles med. jours. Office: 45 E Main St East Islip NY 11730

FLEISIG, NORBERT, surgeon; b. Providence, Sept. 15, 1935; m. Jeanne C. Fleisig. BA magna cum laude, Brown U., 1957; MD, Yale U., 1961. Diplomate Am. Bd. Surgery. Intern surgery Yale Med. Ctr., New Haven, 1961-65; resident Univ. Hosp., Balt., 1965-67; assoc. prof. surgery R.I. Hosp., 1967, Brown Med. Ctr., Providence, 1968—; staff surgeon Roger Williams Hosp., Providence, 1968—; cons. surgery R.I. Med. Ctr., State R.I. U.S. Govt., Cranston, 1968—. Mem. ACS, AMA, Am. Soc. Bariatric Surgeons, Providence Surg., Providence Med. Soc., Sigma Xi, Phi Beta Kappa. Office: 1 Randall Sq Providence RI 02904

FLEISS, JOSEPH LEON, biostatistics educator; b. Bklyn., Nov. 13, 1937; s. Nathan and Esther M. (Roman) F.; m. Isabel Susan Bogorad, June 3, 1960; children: Arthur, Elizabeth, Deborah. AB, Columbia U., 1959, MS, 1961, PhD, 1967. Biostatistician N.Y. State Psychiat. Inst., N.Y.C., 1961-75; prof. biostats. Columbia U., N.Y.C., 1975—. Author: Statistical Methods for Rates and Proportions, 1981, Design and Analysis of Clinical Experiments, 1986. Recipient Spiegelman gold medal APHA, 1976. Office: Columbia U Sch Pub Health 600 W 168th St New York NY 10032-3702

FLEMING, BARTLETT SAYLES, trade association executive; b. Coshocton, Ohio, Nov. 16, 1942; s. James Frasier and Betty (Sayles) F.; m. Bethany Walker, June 5, 1965; children: Tricia Lyn, Bartlett S.F. BA, U. Ariz., 1966. Sales rep. E.F. Hutton, Tucson, Ariz., 1969-70; chief dep. treas., then treas. State of Ariz., Phoenix, 1971-78; pres. Fiscal Policy Coun., Washington, 1979-83; assoc. adminstr. Health Care Financing Adminstrn., Washington, 1983-87, exec. assoc. adminstr., 1987-88; pres. Assn. High Medicare Hosps., Washington, 1988—. Mem. vestry Truro Episc. Ch., Fairfax, Va., 1983-87; chmn. bd. dirs. Christian Stewardship Ministries, Fairfax, 1990-91. Republican. Office: Assn High Medicare Hosps 1620 I St NW Ste 202 Washington DC 20006

FLEMING, EDWARD J., priest; b. Montclair, N.J., Mar. 29, 1920; s. Timothy Joseph and Agnes (Gannon) F. Student, Seton Hall Prep. Sch., South Orange, N.J., 1932-36; A.B., Seton Hall U., 1940, M.A., 1948, LL.D., 1970; student, Immaculate Conception Sem., Ramsey, N.J., 1936-40; S.T.L., Cath. U. Am., 1944; Ph.D., St. John's U., Bklyn., 1955; grad., Inst. Advanced Studies, N.Am. Coll., Rome, 1977; postgrad., Harvard Divinity Sch., 1986. Ordained priest Roman Catholic Ch., 1944, elevated to papal chamberlain, 1963, elevated to prelate to Pope John Paul II, 1983; priest St. Teresa's Ch., Summit, N.J., 1944-49; prof. ednl. psychology and religion Seton Hall U., 1949-51, dean student affairs, 1951-53, dean coll., 1953-59, exec. v.p., 1959-69, pres., 1969-70; pastor Our Lady of Blessed Sacrament Ch., Roseland, N.J., 1970—; dean Archdiocese of Newark, 1975-77, mem. bd. of consultors; vis. scholar Oxford (Eng.) U., 1987-88; dir. devel. Seton Hall U. Seminary, South Orange, N.J., 1987—; dir. Newman studies Univ. Coll., 1987—; dir. devel. Sch. Theology Seton Hall U., South Orange, 1987—; mem. exam. bd. Archdiocesan Clergy and Seminary, 1954-64; mem. Archdiocesan Commn. Parish Visitation, 1969—; Episcopal vicar Essex County Archdiocese; coordinating dean Essex County, 1975—; pres. Roseland Council Chs.; mem. ethics com. N.J. Supreme Ct., 1979—; mem. Senate of Priests, Archdiocese of Newark, 1980—, Archdiocesan Sch. Bd., 1980. Contbr. articles on higher edn. to ednl. periodicals and jours. Mem. Army Adv. Panel ROTC Affairs, 1961-70; mem. Edn. Commn. U.S.; mem. pres.'s council Caldwell Coll., N.J.; trustee Assumption Coll., Mendham, N.J., Greater Newark Black and White Opera Co., Tri-Hosp. Ecumenical Chaplaincy Council No. N.J., 1979. Recipient Alpha Epsilon Mu award, 1956; Sapientiae Christianae Humanitarian award, 1958; John J. Crecca Found. Humanitarian award, 1967; Irishman of Year award Friends of Brian Boru, Inc., 1967; Zionist Brotherhood award, 1979; named to Athletic Hall of Fame, Seton Hall U., 1986; N.Am. Coll. fellow, Rome, 1971—, fellow Weston Theol. Ctr., Cambridge, Eng., 1986-87. Mem. Eastern Assn. Coll. Deans and Advisers of Men, Nat. Cath. Edn. Assn. (pres. Eastern unit 1965-66), Middle States Accreditation Assn., N.J. Hist. Soc. (com. of 125), Cath. Theol. Soc. Am. Office: Seton Hall U Mooney Hall South Orange NJ 07079

FLEMING, JAMES STUART, JR., pharmaceutical company manager; b. Buffalo, Sept. 1, 1936; s. James Stuart and Pauline (McClurg) F.; m. Marilyn Joyce Bartsch, June 7, 1960; children: Lois Vernette, James Stuart III. BA, Northwestern U., 1958; MS, U. Buffalo, 1962; PhD, Ohio State U., 1965; MBA, Syracuse U., 1983. Rsch. asst. Ohio State U., Columbus, 1962-65; rsch. scientist Bristol-Myers Co., Syracuse, N.Y., 1965-74, sr. rsch. scientist, 1974-82, mgr., 1982-85; assoc. dir. cardiovascular biology Bristol-Myers Co., Syracuse and Wallingford, Conn., 1985-90; assoc. dir. project planning Bristol-Myers Squibb Co., Wallingford, Conn., 1990—. Author: (with others) Platelet Aggregation Inhibitors, 1974-82; editor: Drugs and the Delivery of Oxygen to Tissues, 1989. Cons., tchr. Jr. Achievement, Wallingford, 1988-90. Mem. Am. Soc. Pharmacology and Exptl. Therapeutics, Am. Heart Assn. (coun. on thrombosis), Microcirculatory Soc., Internat. Soc. Oxygen Transport to Tissue, Am. Coll. Clin. Pharmacology, Beta Gamma Sigma. Office: Bristol-Myers Squibb Co 5 Research Pky Wallingford CT 06492-1996

FLEMING, PATRICIA JEAN, small business owner; b. Glen Ridge, N.J., Dec. 4, 1942; d. Charles M. and Eleanor (Beighley) F. PhD, Boston U., 1974; MEd, Boston State Coll., 1977. Lic. cert. social worker. Founder Women in New Growth Situations, Arlington, Mass., 1976-77; asst. dir. counseling Graham Jr. Coll., Boston, 1977-78; psychotherapist Beyond Coping Pvt. Practice, Cambridge, Mass., 1977-88; owner Personal Growth Techs., Cambridge, 1982—; vocat. program developer Conn. Assn. Retarded Citizens, Hartford, 1979-80; psychomotor therapy cons. pain unit Spaulding Rehab. Hosp. and Mass. Gen. Hosp., Boston, 1975—. Author: Software and Sympathy, 1990, Beyond Coping: How to Form a Vocational Achievement Support Group; illustrator: The Greyhound Who Wanted a Greyhound Friend. Vol. Friends of Boston Harbor Islands, 1986-90. Mem. AACD, Assn. Adult Devel. and Aging. Home and Office: Personal Growth Techs 12 Tufts St Cambridge MA 02139-4720

FLEMING, SAMUEL CROZIER, JR., publishing and consulting firm executive, management consultant; b. Phila., Sept. 30, 1940; s. Samuel Crozier Sr. and Josephine Coverdale (Plowman) F.; m. Nancy Elizabeth McAdam, Sept. 7, 1963; children: David McAdam, Timothy Crozier. BChemE, Cornell U., 1963; MBA, Harvard U., 1967. Rsch. engr. DuPont Co., 1963; mgmt. cons. Arthur D. Little, Inc., Cambridge, Mass., 1967-90, v.p., 1977-83, sr. v.p., 1983-90; pres., chief exec. officer ADL Impact Svcs., Cambridge, 1976-79; pres., chief exec. officer Arthur D. Little Decision Resources, Cambridge, 1979-83, chmn. bd. dirs., 1983-90; chief exec. officer Decision Resources, Inc., Burlington, Mass., 1990—, also bd. dirs., chmn., 1990—; mem. Cornell Chem. Engring. Adv. Coun., Ithaca, N.Y., 1986—, Cornell U. Coun., 1989—; trustee Standish Ayer & Wood Investment Trust, Boston, 1986—; corporator Cambridgeport Bank, 1989—; bd. dirs. Mastery Edn. Corp., Watertown, Mass., Cambridge; chmn. bd. dirs. Opinion Rsch. Corp., Princeton, N.J., 1984-88. Vestryman Trinity Ch., Boston, 1980-84; chmn. bd. dirs. New England Bapt. Health Care Corp., 1985—, New England Bapt. Hosp., Boston, 1985-90. 1st lt. U.S. Army, 1963-65. Mem. The Country Club (Brookline, Mass.), Harvard Club of Boston, Lake Sunapee Yacht Club, Cornell Club N.Y. Episcopalian. Home: 61 Meadowbrook Rd Weston MA 02193-2407 Office: Decision Resources Inc 17 New England Executive Park Burlington MA 01803-5223

FLEMING, STEVEN ROBERT, minister; b. San Bernardino, Calif., Apr. 30, 1951; s. Robert Ellsworth and Marie Claire (Kitzmiller) F.; m. Brenda Kay Cross, June 9, 1973. BA with honors, U. Md., 1972; D. Ministry, Union Theol. Sem., Richmond, Va., 1976. Ordained to ministry Presbyn. Ch. U.S.A., 1976. Assoc. pastor 1st Presbyn. Ch., Ft. Smith, Ark., 1976-79; pastor Shippensburg (Pa.) Presbyn. Ch., 1979-85; interim assoc. pastor Paxton Presbyn. Ch., Harrisburg, Pa., 1986-87; pastor 1st United Presbyn. Ch., Westminster, Md., 1987—; mem. Balt. Presbytery; seminar leader; mem. bd. pensions Presbyn. Ch. in U.S.A. Contbr. articles to profl. jours. Bd. dirs. Shippensburg U. Campus Ministry, 1979-85. Recipient Common Ground award Shippensburg U., 1983. Mem. Alban Inst. Republican. Office: 1st Presbyn Ch 65 Washington Rd Westminster MD 21157-5626

FLEMING, WILLIAM SLOAN, energy, environmental and technology company executive; b. Long Beach, Calif., Aug. 13, 1937; s. William Sloan and Helen Jean (Disler) F.; m. Jacquline M. Carrio, Mar. 9, 1960; children: Katherine A., Kimberly A. BSME, Calif. Maritime Acad., 1958; MBA, Syracuse U., 1970. Commd. ensign USN, 1958, advanced through grades to lt., 1967, attack pilot, 1958-67, disabled in the line of duty, ret., 1967; mech. engr. Carrier Corp., Syracuse, N.Y., 1967-70; regional sales mgr. Rheem Mfg., Atlanta, 1970-71; market devel. supr. Owens Corning Fiberglas, Toledo, 1971-73; pres. W.S. Fleming & Assocs., Inc., Syracuse, 1975-86; pres. The Fleming Group, Syracuse, 1986-87, chief exec. officer, chmn. bd., 1987—; pres. Enterlog Systems, Inc., Syracuse, 1985—; chmn. bd. Assn. Intelligent System Tech., Inc., Syracuse, 1986-90. Contbr. articles to profl. jours.; author singer energy simulation computer program (SEE), 1975-80. Recipient Energy awards Cen. N.Y., 1981. Fellow ASHRAE (chmn. tech. com. 6.7, solar energy utilization 1984-86, chmn. tech. com. 9.6, system energy utilization 1981-83, chmn. ad hoc com. 90, energy standards 1983-84, chmn. nat. program com. 1985-86, mem. edn. coun. 1989-90, rsch. and tech. com. 1991—); mem. Assn. Energy Engrs. (charter), DAV, Am. Legion, Ret. Officers Assn. Roman Catholic. Home: 4571 E Lake Rd Cazenovia NY 13035-9350 Office: The Fleming Group 6308 Fly Rd East Syracuse NY 13057-9370

FLEMMING, BRIAN, lawyer, industrialist; b. Halifax, N.S., Can., Feb. 19, 1939; s. Everett F.J. and Margaret (Meagher) F.; m. Janice Jenifer Merritt; children: Mark Alexander, Ann Louise. BS, St. Mary's U., Halifax, 1959; LLB, Dalhousie U., 1962; LLM in Pub. Internat. Law, U. London, 1964; DCL (hon.), U. King's Coll., Halifax, 1991. Bar: N.S. 1963, Ont. 1981; appointed Queen's Counsel, 1978. Assoc. Stewart, MacKeen & Covert, 1964-70, ptnr., 1971-76, 1979—; asst. prin. sec., policy adv. Prime Minister of Can., Ottawa, Ont., 1976-79; chmn., chief exec. officer VGM Capital Corp., CanEast Capital Corp.; bd. dirs. Noranda Inc., Brunswick Mining and Smelting Corp. Contbr. numerous articles to profl. pubs. Past pres. Symphony N.S. Soc., Halifax; gov. Dahousie U., Halifax. Decorated Order of Can. Mem. Can. Bar Assn., Internat. Bar Assn., Can. Council Internat. Law, Can. Inst. Internat. Affairs, Brit. Inst. Internat., Comparative Law, Am. Soc. Internat. Law, Internat. Law Assn., Assn. Can. Law Tchrs., Can. Inst. Resources Law, Law Inst. Pacific Rim, U. London Convocation. Clubs: Halifax, Royal, N.S. Yacht Squad., The Waegwoltic. Home: 2003-1470 Summer St, Halifax, NS Canada B3H 3A3

FLESCHER, IRWIN, psychologist; b. N.Y.C., June 12, 1926; s. Max and Gussie (Spiegel) F.; m. Adele Kransdorf, Dec. 20, 1953; children: Jonathan, Mark, Judy. BS cum laude, Long Island U., 1949; MA, NYU, 1950; PhD, Columbia U., 1960. Diplomate Am. Bd. Profl. Psychology, Internat. Acad. Behavioral Medicine, Counseling and Psychotherapy. Welfare worker N.Y.C. Dept. Welfare, 1951-52; placement counselor N.Y. State Employment Svc., N.Y.C., 1952-55; psychologist N.Y.C. Bur. Child Guidance, 1955-58; psychotherapist Hempstead (N.Y.) consultation Svc., 1962-63; supervising psychologist Adelphi U., Garden City, N.Y., 1967-68; supr. psychotherapy L.I. Jewish-Hillside Med. Ctr., New Hyde Park, N.Y., 1977-78; sch. and rsch. psychologist East Williston (N.Y.) Schs., 1960-86; pvt. practice clin. psychology Roslyn Heights, N.Y., 1959—; adj. assoc. prof. C.W. Post Grad. Sch. Edn., Greenvale, N.Y., 1971-74. Author: children in the Learning Factory: The Search for a Humanizing Teacher, 1973, Ocular-Manual Laterality & Perceptual rotation of Literal Symbols, 1962; contbr. articles to Jour. of Psychology. With USAAF, 1944-46, PTO. Mem. Nassau County Psychol. Assn. (pres. 1972-73), Nassau Psychol. Svcs. Inst. (trustee, chmn. bd. trustees 1975—), N.Y. State Psychol. Assn. (coun. reps. 1975-77), N.Y. Acad. Sci., Am. Psychol. Assn., N.Y. Soc. Clin. Psychologists. Home: 33 Canterbury Ln Roslyn Heights NY 11577-1442 Office: 225 Locust Ln Roslyn Heights NY 11577-1451

FLETCHER, BARBARA ELIZABETH, guidance counselor; b. Worcester, Mass., Sept. 13, 1936; d. Norman and Mary Ursula (Swanson) F. BS Edn., State Coll. Worcester, 1959, MEd, 1962; cert. advanced grad. study, Boston U., 1973. Lic. elem. tchr., elem. sch. prin., guidance counselor, sch. libr., audio visual media specialist. Tchr. Worcester Pub. Schs., 1959-70, media specialist, 1970-72, asst. prin., 1972-78, guidance counselor, 1978—. Mem. AAUW (nominating com. chair 1988-89, found. chair 1990-92), AACD, ASCD, NEA, Mass. Tchrs. Assn., Ednl. Assn. Worcester, Mass. Assn. Ednl. Media, Mass. Sch. Counselors Assn., Mechanics Hall Travelogue Series, Worcester Cunty Pers. and Guidance Assn. Methodist. Home: 4 Dixon Ave Worcester MA 01605-3606 Office: Worcester Pub Sch Pupil Pers 20 Irving St Worcester MA 01609-2493

FLETCHER, DIANE MILES, oncology nurse educator, clinician; b. Pitts., May 12, 1956; d. Eugene John and Florence Ann (Pavlakovic) Miles; m. Keith Richard Fletcher, Aug. 19, 1978; children: Gregory Robert, Michelle Marie. BSN, Ind. U. of Pa., 1978, MA in Counselor Edn., 1991. RN, Pa.; oncology cert. nurse. Med.-surg. RN Forbes Health System, Monroeville, Pa., 1978-79, oncology nurse clinician/educator, 1982—; office RN, supr. East Suburban Med. Assoc., Pitts., 1979-81; oncology educator Pitts. Cancer Inst., 1990—. Contbr. articles to profl. jours. Vol. speaker Am. Cancer Soc., Pitts. Recipient Am. Cancer Soc. nursing edn. scholarship, 1989. Mem. ACA, Oncology Nursing Soc., Sigma Theta Tau. Home: 3802 Edinburg Dr Murrysville PA 15668-1012 Office: Pittsburgh Cancer Inst 405 Iroquois Bldg 3600 Forbes Ave Pittsburgh PA 15213

FLETCHER, JEFFREY EDWARD, biochemist, researcher; b. Toledo, Mar. 11, 1948; s. John Harper and Eleanore (Jackson) F.; m. Marcia Ruth Miller, Mar. 21, 1970 (div. Mar. 1977); m. Jeanne Claire Untied, Aug. 22, 1981; children: Katherine Ann, Lindsay Nicole, Sarah Jeanne. AA, Mohegan Community Coll., 1974; BA, Conn. Coll., 1976; PhD, U. Conn., 1981. Resident rsch. assoc. NRC, Washington, 1981-83; sr. instr. dept. anesthesia Hahnemann U., Phila., 1983-85, asst. prof. dept. anesthesia, 1985-90, assoc. prof. dept. anesthesia, 1990—; mem. editorial coun. sci. jour. Toxicon, 1991—. Contbr. articles to profl. jours. With USN, 1967-73, Vietnam. Conn. Coll. scholar, 1974-76. Mem. Am. soc. for Pharmacology and Exptl. Therapeutics, Internat. Soc. Toxinology, Am. Soc. Anesthesiologists, Soc. for Exptl. Biology and Medicine, Soc. for Neurosci., Biophys. Soc., Sigma Xi, Rho Chi. Episcopalian. Office: Hahnemann U Dept Anesthesia Broad and Vine Sts Philadelphia PA 19102-1192

FLETCHER, MARY BETH, reading specialist, educator; b. Miami, Fla., Oct. 12, 1949; d. James Richard and Elmira (Neal) Brooks; m. Howard Martin Fletcher, Jr., Sept. 5, 1971; 1 child, Sarah Lindsey. BA, U. Fla., 1971; MA, U. So. Fla., 1976; EdM, Harvard U., 1985, EdD, 1990. Cert. reading specialist, elem. tchr., early childhood educator. Tchr. Pinellas County Schs., 1971-72; tchr. Lake Trafford Elem., Immokalee, Fla., 1976-78, reading tchr., 1978-80; teaching fellow Harvard U., Grad. Sch. of Edn., Cambridge, Mass., 1984-85, instr. edn., 1988-90; lectr., reading supr. and cons. Lesley Coll. Grad. Sch., Cambridge, 1986, instr. in reading, 1987; special needs tchr. Buckingham, Browne & Nichols Sch., Cambridge, 1989—. Vol. Peace Corps, Afghanistan, 1972-74; sponsor for Afghan refugee family, 1982. Mem. Internat. Reading Assn., Mass. Reading Assn. (chmn. parents and reading com. 1988-90, chmn. scholarship com. 1991—), Fla. Reading Assn., Phi Kappa Phi, Phi Delta Kappa. Office: 10 Buckingham St Cambridge MA 02138-2227

FLEUR, MARY LOUISE, legal administrator; b. Rochester, N.Y., Dec. 30, 1951; d. John James and Mary (Cisterna) Schwartz; m. Jeffrey P. Guinan, Dec. 20, 1975 (div. Dec. 1977); m. Edward R. Fleur, May 25, 1991. BA with honors, Manhattanville Coll., 1973. Legal asst. Milbank Tweed Hadley & McCloy, N.Y.C., 1975-77, managerial asst., 1978-80; office adminstr. Burlingham Underwood & Lord, N.Y.C., 1980-84; dir. adminstrn. Demov Morris & Hammerling, N.Y.C., 1984-87; dir. fin. and adminstrn. Spengler, Carlson, Gubar, Brodsky & Frischling, N.Y.C., 1987—. Contbr. articles to profl. jours. Mem. ABA (assoc., advisor com. on legal assts. 1978-80), Assn. Legal Adminstrs., N.Y.C. Paralegal Assn. (dir. 1977-79). Office: Spengler Carlson et al 520 Madison Ave New York NY 10022-4213

FLEURANT, DAVID PAUL, commercial photographer; b. Pawtucket, R.I., Aug. 24, 1948; s. Leo Francis and Lucy Ann (Nunes) F.; m. Patica C. Roy, June 1, 1968 (div.); 1child, Tonya M. Studied painting with, Hermon Itzkowitz, 1964-67; grad., R.I. Sch. Photography, 1976. Freelance photographer Observer Publs., Smithfield, R.I., 1976-79, 1979-85; ptnr., comml. photographer W.F. Assocs., Woonsocket, R.I., 1985-89; owner, pres., comml. photographer Light Impressions, Smithfield, 1989—. With USN, 1967-71. Recipient Blue Ribbon award New Eng. Profl. Photographers Am., 1987. Mem. No. R.I. C. of C. (amb. 1991—). Office: Light Impressions 10 Industrial Dr Smithfield RI 02917-1502

FLEURANT, ROBERT W., graphic designer, educator; b. Elmhurst, N.Y., Nov. 12, 1939; s. Wilfred George and Frances (Colombo) F.; m. Doris Carol Anselmetti (div. Feb. 1990); children: Cristine Groenenwegen, Suzanne Stabile. AS in Advt. and Design with honors, N.Y. Tech., 1965. Asst. package designer Bauer Studio, 1957-59; mech. and layout artist Royer & Roger, Inc., 1961-63; designer Sandgren & Murtha, Inc., 1965-66; mgr., exec. art dir. Norman Levit Studio, Inc., 1966-69; pres. Csoka Benato Fleurant, Inc., N.Y.C., 1969—; adj. prof. Fashion Inst. of Tech., N.Y.C., 1976—; mem. Advt. Design Industry Adv. Com., 1975-77. With U.S. Army, 1959-61. Recipient Creativity award Art Direction Mag., 1971, 72, 75, 83, 87, Clio award, 1977, Printing Industrieof N.Y., 1974-80. Mem. N.Y.C. C. of C. Roman Catholic. Home: 9-10 157th St Beechhurst NY 11357 Office: Csoka/Benato/Fleurant 134 W 26th St, Rm 903 New York NY 10001

FLEURY, JOACHIM, lawyer; b. Amsterdam, The Netherlands, Jan. 14, 1962; came to U.S., 1990; s. Paul and Yvonne Caroline (Eekman) F.-Eekman. M Netherlands Law, U. Amsterdam, 1984. Bar: The Netherlands, 1984. Rsch. asst. U. Amsterdam, 1983-84; fgn. assoc. Clifford-Turner, London, 1984-85; assoc. Clifford Chance, Amsterdam, 1985-90; resident ptnr. Clifford Chance, N.Y.C., 1990—. Contbr. articles to profl. jours. Mem. ABA, Internat. Bar Assn., N.Y. State Bar Assn., Assn. of the Bar of the City of N.Y., Computer Law Assn., Netherlands Assn. for Informatics and Law. Dutch Democrat. Office: Clifford Chance 10 E 50th St New York NY 10022-6812

FLICS, DAVID HAROLD, clinical psychologist, consultant; b. N.Y.C., Feb. 25, 1952; s. Seymour Aaron and Helen Rita (Lipner) F.; m. Susan Rose Sciscenti, Nov. 6, 1982. BA in Psychology magna cum laude with honors, CUNY, 1974; MA in Guidance and Counseling, NYU, 1977; PhD in Clin. Psychology, St. John's U., 1986. Lic. psychologist, N.Y. Counselor, therapist The Lowell Sch., Flushing, N.Y., 1974-83; psychotherapist L.I. Consultation Ctr., Rego Park, N.Y., 1984-87; psychologist dept. for handicapped Bklyn. Bur. Community Svc., 1985-88; pvt. practice N.Y.C., 1987—; cons. to various mental health clinics and social svc. agys.; lectr. in field to various community and acad. groups. Mem. APA, Div. of Psychotherapy of APA, Assn. for Advancement of Psychology, Psychologists in Ind. Practice, N.Y. State Psychol. Assn., Psi Chi. Office: 412 Ave of the Americas Ste 704 New York NY 10011-8416

FLINK, STANLEY EDGAR, writer, public affairs consultant; b. Newark, May 28, 1924; s. Julius Edward and Frances (Heyman) F.; m. Mary Hilson, 1949 (div. 1961); children: Wendy, Steven; m. Joy Reynolds, May 24, 1975. BA, Yale U., 1945; postgrad., Oxfor (Eng.) U., 1947. Corr. Time Inc., L.A., 1949-58; assoc. producer NBC-TV, N.Y.C., 1958-61; producer, writer CBS-TV, N.Y.C., 1961-63; chief exec. officer, cons. pub. affairs London, 1963-72; first dir. Office of Pub. Info. and Alumni Communications Yale U., New Haven, Conn., 1972-80; pres. Stanley Flink Assocs., Hamden, Conn., 1981—; dir. Nat. Theater of the Deaf, Chester, Conn., 1985—; ptnr. Benton and Flink Prodns., N.Y.C., 1987—; asst. prof. NYU Sch. Journalism and Mass Communication, 1985—. Author: But Will They Get it in Des Moines, 1960; editor: (book) Wildlife Crisis, 1968, Yale Alumni Mag., 1976-79. 2d lt. U.S. Army, 1943-47, PTO. Mem. Yale Club of N.Y.C. (bd. dirs.), New Haven Yale Club. Home and Office: 49 Deepwood Dr Hamden CT 06517-3414

FLINKSTROM, HENRY ALLAN, sales executive; b. Ashby, Mass., Feb. 19, 1933; s. William Elias and Selma Catherine (Aho) F.; m. Marian June Linnus, May 14, 1950; children: Leonard A., Eric A., Carl E. Grad. high sch., Ashby, 1951; diploma in constrn., Fitchburg (Mass.) High, 1953. Ind. carpenter Fitchburg, 1950-54; salesman Webber Lumber, Fitchburg, 1954-64; v.p. Morgan-Price Constrn., Ashburnham, Mass., 1964-66; contractor, sales mgr. Webber Lumber, Fitchburg, 1966-80; sales rep. Sawyer Lumber, Worcester, Mass., 1981-82, Webber Lumber (merger Sawyer Lumber and Webber Lumber), Worcester and Fitchburg, 1982—; home designer HAF Design, Fitchburg; dealer Sun Room Co., Leola, Pa., real estate broker Flinkstroms. Designer of over 2000 homes built in New Eng. area. Charter mem. Rep. Presdl. Task Force, Rep. Nat. Com., 1984—, Mass. Chiefs of Police Assoc., Fitchburg Art Mus. Mem. Profl. Fin. Assocs. (registered assoc.), Am. Plywood Assn. Club: Finnish-Am., Club of Saima-Fitchburg, U.S. Senatorial. Lodge: Masons. Home: HAF Design 19 Ashburnham State Rd Fitchburg MA 01420

FLIPPO, RONA FLEIG, reading educator, author, editor; b. Bklyn., Mar. 28, 1945; d. Theodore G. and Molly (Rosenfeld) F.; children: Todd G., Tara R. BS summa cum laude, Fla. Atlantic U., 1965; MEd, U. North Fla., 1975; EdS, U. Fla., 1977, EdD, 1979. Cert. reading specialist, Fla., Cert. elem. tchr., Fla., cert. early childhood tchr., Fla. Elem. instr. P.K. Yonge Lab Sch. U. Fla., Gainesville, 1975-76; reading instr. Fla. Jr. Coll., Jacksonville, 1976-77; master reading instr. Duval Pub. Schs., Jacksonville, 1977-78; dir. devel. ctr. U. S.C., Columbia, 1978-80; asst. prof. Ga. State U., Atlanta, 1980-82; ednl. staff specialist Ga. Dept. Edn., Atlanta, 1982-83; asst. prof. U. Wis.-Parkside, Kenosha, 1983-86; assoc. prof. Fitchburg (Mass.) State Coll., 1986—; vis. prof. U. Wollongong, Australia, 1988; cons. Ednl. Testing Svc., Atlanta, 1982-83, Evanston, Ill., 1985-86. Author: Testwise, 1988, Reading for Success in Elementary Schools, 1989; editor: College Reading and Study Strategy Programs, 1991, Teaching Reading and Study Strategies at the College Level, 1991, (jour.) Forum for Reading, 1982—. Undergrad. rsch. fellow Fitchburg State Coll., 1990-91. Mem. Am. Ednl. Rsch. Assn., Nat. Reading Conf., Internat. Reading Assn., Mass. Reading Assn. (Sylvia D. Brown rsch. scholar 1991), Phi Kappa Phi, Phi Delta Kappa. Office: Fitchburg State Coll 160 Pearl St Fitchburg MA 01420-2697

FLOOD, (HULDA) GAY, editor, consultant; b. Plainfield, N.J., Aug. 14, 1935; d. William Edward and Lucy (Dycker) F.; BA, Smith Coll., 1957. Picture dept. Sports Illustrated, Time Inc., N.Y.C. 1957-58, letters dept., 1958-59, reporter, 1959-60, writer-reporter, 1960-71, assoc. editor, 1971-85, sr. editor, 1985-90; editor, cons., 1990—. Mem. Alumnae Assn. Smith Coll. (life), Smith Coll. Students Aid Soc., Smith Coll. Club N.Y. Mem. consistory, chair fin. com. 1st Reformed Ch., Nyack, N.Y. Home and Office: 103 Gedney St Apt 3C Nyack NY 10960-2228

FLOOD, JOAN MOORE, corporate librarian; b. Hampton, Va., Oct. 10, 1941; d. Harold W. and Estalena (Fancher) M.; 1 child by former marriage, Angelique. B.Mus., North Tex. State U., 1963, postgrad., 1977; postgrad. So. Meth. U., 1967-68, Tex. Women's U., 1978-79, U. Dallas, 1985-86. Bar: Tex. 1982. Clk. Criminal Dist. Ct. Number 2, Dallas County, Tex., 1972-75; reins. libr. Scor Reins. Co., Dallas, 1975-80, Assocs. Ins. Group, 1980-83; corp./securities legal asst. Akin, Gump, Strauss, Hauer & Feld, 1983-89; asst. sec. Knoll Internat. Holdings Inc., Saddle Brook, N.J., 1989-90, 21 Internat. Holdings, Inc., N.Y.C., 1990—. Mem. ABA. Republican. Episcopalian. Home: Apt 2 12 E 92d St New York NY 10128

FLORA, GARY STAMLER, civil engineer; b. Myers, Ky., Jan. 28, 1934; s. Raymond Edward and Helen Stamler (Barton) F.; m. Sylva Joy Owens, June 15, 1958. BS, U.S. Naval Acad., 1958; MSCE, U. Pitts., 1965; MBA, Auburn U., 1972. Registered profl. civil engr. Commd. 2nd lt. USAF, 1958, advanced through grades to lt. col., retired, 1978; prin. engr. U.S. Labor Dept., Washington, 1978-80; tech. dir. USAF, Norton AFB, Calif., 1980-85; assoc. dir. USAF, Washington, 1985—. Mem. ASCE, Soc. Am. Mil. Engrs. (nat. dir. 1990—). Home: 8220 Labbe Ln Vienna VA 22182-5244

FLORA, JAMES ROYER, artist, writer; b. Bellefontaine, Ohio, Jan. 25, 1914; s. James Bernard and Laura (Royer) F.; m. Jane Sue Sinnickson, Mar. 1, 1941 (dec. Nov. 1985); children: Roussie, James J., Caroline, Robert, Julia; m. Patricia Lee Larsen, Mar. 12, 1988. Cert., Urbana (Ohio) U., 1933; cert., Art Acad., Cin., 1939. Sucessively art dir., advt. mgr., sales promotion mgr. Columbia Records, Bridgeport, Conn. and N.Y.C., 1942-50; art dir. Park East Mag., N.Y.C., 1951-53; freelance illustrator N.Y.C., 1952-82; art dir. Computer Design, Boston, 1961-80; painter Conn., 1980—. Author: The fabulous Fireworks Family, 1955, The Day the Cow Sneezed, 1957, Charlie Yup & Snip Snap Boys, 1959, Leopold, the See-Through Crumbpicker, 1961, Kangaroo for Christmas, 1962, My Friend Charlie, 1964, Granpa's Farm, 1965, Sherwood Walks Home, 1966, Fishing with Dad, 1967, The Joking Man, 1968, Little Hatchy Hen, 1969, Pishtosh, Bullwash & Wimple, 1972, Stewed Goose, 1973, The Great Green Turkey Creek Monster, 1976, Grandpa's Ghost Stories, 1978, Wanda and the Bumbly Wizard, 1980, Grandpa's Witched Up Christmas, 1982; marine painter, 1982—; numerous group and one man shows. Mem. Fairfield Watercolor Group, Mystic Maritime Gallery 100 Artists, Andrea Ruoff Art Assoc. Ltd. Democrat. Home and Office: 7 St James Pl Norwalk CT 06853-1827

FLORAKIS, GEORGE JAMES, ophthalmologist; b. Yonkers, N.Y., May 26, 1958; s. James G. and Helen (Psaros) F.; m. Catherine Tsoucalas, May 6, 1990. BA, Columbia U., 1979; MD, Columbia U. Coll. Physicians, 1983. Internship Overlook Hosp., Summit, N.J., 1983-84; residency in ophthalmology Harkness Eye Inst. Columbia Presbyn. Med. Ctr., N.Y.C., 1984-87; fellowship in cornea and external eye disease U. Iowa, Iowa City, 1987-88; instr. in clin. ophthalmology Harkness Eye Inst. Columbia U., N.Y.C., 1988-91; assoc. in clin. ophthalmology Columbia U., N.Y.C., 1991—; assoc. ophthalmologist The Presbyn. Hosp., N.Y.C., 1991—; cornea attending Harkness Eye Inst., N.Y.C., 1988—; med. student adviser Columbia Coll. Physicians and Surgeons, N.Y.C., 1989—; course coord. clin. sci. Harkness Eye Inst., N.Y.C., 1989—; ophthalmic cons. Olympic Airways, N.Y.C., 1991—. Author: Lyme Disease; contbr. articles to profl. jours. Mem. Ch. choir, Am. Hellenic Edn. Progressive Assn. Recipient Hellenic Med. Soc. N.Y. scholarship, 1982, Rudin Found. Scholarship, 1983, Alvin Behrens award Columbia U., 1983. Fellow Am. Acad. Ophthalmology; mem. Northeast Corner Soc., Cornea and External Disease Academic Soc., Eyebank Assn. Am., Assn. for Rsch. in Vision and Ophthalmology, Ocular Microbiology and Immunology Group, AMA. Office: Columbia Presbyn Med Ctr 635 W 165th St Box 31 New York NY 10032 also: 75 Brook St Scarsdale NY 10583

FLOREA, ROBERT WILLIAM, real estate investment executive; b. N.Y.C., June 6, 1947; s. Stanley Robert and Mildred Barbara (Schneider) F.; m. Barbara Jordan, June 22, 1974; children: Chloe, Dylan. Student, New Sch. for Social Research, 1970-71, Lee Strasberg Inst., 1970-72, L.I. U., 1968-74. v.p., gen. mgr. Pen-Mart, Inc., N.Y.C., 1969-71; dir., writer, actor various prodn. cos., Los Angeles, 1971-77; comml. real estate sales agt. Stan Brumer Co., Inc., Los Angeles, 1977-82; sales mgr. investment dept. Schacker Realty, Melville, N.Y., 1982-85; pres., owner Robert Florea Investment Realty, Melville, 1985—; lectr. Real Estate Tng. Ctr. Author: (novel) Manhattan and Me, 1979; assoc. dir. (movie) Jigsaw Puzzle, 1968, Lord of the Dragon, 1974; stage mgr. dir.'s unit Actors Studio, Los Angeles, 1973-74. Campaign rep. Suffolk County (N.Y.) Dems., 1982—. mng. coach Huntington (N.Y.) Little League, 1986—; basketball coach St. Patrick's Girls League, Huntington. Mem. L.I. Advancement Commerce Industry (mem. tennis, golf coms., Bay (Huntington) (co-chair paddle tennis com.), Pine Hollow Club. Office: Robert Florea Investment Realty Inc 510 Broadhollow Rd Melville NY 11747-3606

FLORINI, JAMES RALPH, biology researcher, educator; b. Gillespie, Ill., Sept. 22, 1931; s. Lino and Alta (Hamilton) F.; m. Barbara May Ullrich, Oct. 13, 1955; children: Karen Lee, Ann Margaret. BA in Chemistry, Blackburn Coll., 1953; PhD in Biochemistry, U. Ill., 1956. Rsch. scientist Lederle Labs., Pearl River, N.Y., 1956-60, group leader, 1960-66; assoc. prof. biology Syracuse (N.Y.) U., 1966-69, prof., 1969—; chmn. bd. trustees Gordon Rsch. Conf., various locations, 1990-91. Contbr. over 100 articles to sci. jours. and books, 1957—. Mem. Am. Soc. Biol. Chemistry, Am. Soc. Cell Biology, Endocrine Soc. (program chair 1990-91), Gerontology Soc. of Am., Cen. N.Y. Pilots Assn., Syracuse (pres. 1979), Syracuse Flying Club (pres. 1975-77). Office: Syracuse U Biology Dept 130 College Pl Syracuse NY 13244-0001

FLORIO, JIM, governor of New Jersey; b. Bklyn., Aug. 29, 1937. BA magna cum laude, Trenton State Coll., 1962; postgrad., Columbia U., 1962-63; JD, Rutgers U., 1967. Mem. law firm Florio and Maloney, 1967-74; mem. 94th-100th Congresses from 1st N.J. Dist., 1975-90, Energy and Commerce Com., Permanent Select Com. on Aging, Vets.' Affairs Com.; chmn. Subcom. on Commerce, Consumer Protection and Competitiveness; now gov. State of N.J. Mem. Camden City Council on Econ. Opportunity, 1966-67, Camden Civil Rights Commn., 1966-67, Camden County Council on Aging, 1968; chmn. East Camden Heart Fund Drive, 1967; v.p. bd. advisors Camden County Legal Service Program, 1968, borough solicitor for towns of, Runnemede, N.J., 1969-74, Woodlynne, 1970-74, Somerdale, 1972-74; mem. N.J. Gen. Assembly, 1969-74, Democratic nominee for gov. N.J., 1981. With USN, 1955-58; lt. comdr. USNR, 1958-75. Office: State House Office of Governor Trenton NJ 08625

FLORIO, THOMAS, magazine publisher. Formerly advt. dir. Conde Nast Traveler, N.Y.C., pub., 1990—. Office: Conde Nast Traveler 360 Madison Ave New York NY 10017-3124*

FLORY, THOMAS REHERD, nuclear physicist; b. Roanoke, Va., Apr. 17, 1946; s. Walter S. and Nellie Maude (Thomas) F. BS in Physics, Wake Forest U., 1967; MS in Physics, U. Va., 1971. Teaching fellow in physics U. Va., Charlottesville, 1967-69; electronic engr. Missile Command, Huntsville, Ala., 1968; mem. tech. staff TRW, Washington, 1969-70; rsch. physicist Mobility Equipment Rsch. and Devel. Ctr., Ft. Belvoir, Va., 1971; physicist Harry Diamond Labs, Woodbridge, Va., 1971-77; physicist Nuclear Effects Support Team, Adelphi, Md., 1977-89, team leader, 1989—; cons. U.S. Army Communications Electronics Command, Ft. Monmouth, N.J., 1977—, U.S. Army Armament Command, Dover, N.J., 1979—, U.S. Army Aviation Command, St. Louis, 1977—. Contbr. articles to profl. jours. Mem. Lake Ridge (Va.) Civic Assn., 1972—. Recipient Creative Exploration award Inter-Am. Coordinating Com., 1983. Mem. Am. Phys. Soc., Potomac Speleological Club, Martha Washington Investment Club (treas. 1978-81, pres. 1982-83), Sigma Xi (chpt. pres. 1983-84, soc. bd. dirs. 1988-89, 92—). Home: 12515 Colby Dr Lakeridge VA 22192-2106 Office: Army Rsch Lab 2800 Powder Mill Rd Adelphi MD 20783-1197

FLOYD, JOHN TAYLOR, electronics executive; b. Quincy, Mass., Jan. 17, 1942; s. John Taylor and Virginia Marie (Watts) F.; m. Denise Angela Dufault, Oct. 4, 1969; children: Jennifer, Aimee. BA, Northeastern U., 1965; MBA in Fin., Boston Coll., 1972. Product group controller Tex. Instruments, Attleboro, Mass., 1972-75; asst. to v.p. fin. Waters Assocs., Milford, Mass., 1975-76; group fin. mgr. Digital Equipment Corp., Maynard, Mass., 1976-82; v.p. mfg. Computer Devices, Burlington, Mass., 1982-83; dir. fin. and adminstrn. Wang Labs., Lowell, Mass., 1984-85; v.p. ops. Charleswater Products, Newton, Mass., 1985-90; v.p. Devon Group, Waltham, Mass., 1991—, also bd. dirs. Served to capt. U.S. Army, 1965-70, Vietnam. Mem. Fin. Execs. Inst., Am. Electronics Assn., Treas.' Club of Boston, Am. Legion. Republican. Home: 68 Longfellow Rd Sudbury MA 01776-1256 Office: Devon Group 800 South St Waltham MA 02154-1439

FLUHR, FREDERICK ROBERT, electronics engineer; b. Omaha, Jan. 7, 1922; s. Frederick R. and Ruby (Wright) F.; student U. Omaha, 1946-47; B.S., Iowa State U., 1949, M.S., 1950; m. Mary Annie Rosser, June 7, 1952; 1 dau., Glynis Ann. Elec. engr., head high energy laser staff U.S Naval Research Lab., Washington, 1951-81; sr. research engr. Sachs/Freeman Assocs., Landover, Md., 1981—. Served with USAAF, 1940-45. Recipient Profl. Achievement citation in Engring., Iowa State U., 1983. Mem. IEEE, VFW, AAAS. Patentee in field. Home: 8716 E Ft Foote Ter Fort Washington MD 20744-6727 Office: 1401 Mccormick Dr Hyattsville MD 20785-5322

FLY, RICHARD NELSON, electronics executive; b. Parkersburg, W.Va., Sept. 13, 1938; s. Thomas Jesse and Girtha Gladys (Young) F.; m. Joyce Wing Graves, July 1, 1961; children: Timothy Scott, Tammy Ann. Student, Mil. Electronic Schs., 1956-60. Field svc. engr. Raytheon Co., Burlington, Mass., 1960-65; assoc. indls. engr. Raytheon Co., Portsmouth, R.I., 1965-72, indsl. engr., 1972-89, mgr. 2d shift ops., 1989—, supt., 1990—. With USN, 1956-60. Republican. Baptist. Home: 7 Namquid Dr Middletown RI 02840-4570 Office: Raytheon Co W Main Rd Portsmouth RI 02871

FLYNN, BRIAN CHARLES, JR., investment fund executive; b. Elmira, N.Y., Aug. 29, 1961; s. Brian Charles and Joan Ford (Lofgren) F. BA, Williams Coll., Williamstown, Mass., 1983; postgrad., London Sch. Econs., 1981-82; MBA, Columbia U., 1987. Fin. analyst GE Capital Corp., Stanford, Conn., 1983-85; assoc. corp. fin. Donaldson, Lufkin & Jenrette, N.Y.C., 1986; cons. Bain & Co., Boston, 1987-91; pres. The Young Challengers, Boston, 1991—; ops. dir. Bachow & Assocs., Phila., 1991—. Mem. Delaware Valley Turnaround Mgmt. Assn. (bd. dirs. 1992—). Republican. Roman Catholic. Office: Bachow & Assocs 1600 Market St Fl 2020 Philadelphia PA 19103-7220

FLYNN, DENNIS MICHAEL, health facility administrator; b. Norwood, Mass., Mar. 29, 1956; s. John Edward and Alice Margaret (Long) F.; m. Cynthia Grace Strickland, May 5, 1979; children: Kathleen Marie, David Michael. Cert. computer tech., Sylvania Tech. Sch., Waltham, Mass., 1977; BS Mgmt., Johnson & Wales Coll., 1986; postgrad., Northeastern U., 1989—. Stock clk. Foxboro (Mass.) Co., 1974-81; supr. environ. Sturdy Meml. Hosp., Attleboro, Mass., 1982-83; mgr. housekeeping & laundry svc. John E. Fogarty Meml. Hosp., North Smithfield, R.I., 1983-86; dir. housekeeping & laundry North Hill Living Care Villages of Mass., Needham, 1986—. Contbr. articles to profl. jours. Mem. Nat. Exec. Housekeepers Assn. (cert. 1988, pres. 1989-91, mem. chmn. 1987-89, v.p. 1987-89, sec. 1984-87, bd. dirs. 1984), Nat. Assn. Instl. Linen Mgmt. Home: 49 South St Plainville MA 02762-2633 Office: North Hill Living Care Villages Mass 865 Central Ave Needham MA 02192-1316

FLYNN, JAMES PETER, marketing executive; b. Yonkers, N.Y., Feb. 12, 1961; s. James Edward and Ann Patricia (Adams) F. BS, Manhattan Coll., 1983; MBA, NYU, 1989. Programmer analyst AT&T, White Plains, N.Y., 1983-86, project leader, 1986-87; systems cons. AT&T, N.Y.C., 1987-88, nat. data sales exec., 1988-90; dir. mktg. Internat. Fin. Systems Ltd., N.Y.C., 1990—. Democrat. Roman Catholic. Office: Internat Fin Systems Ltd 150 E 55th St New York NY 10022-4514

FLYNN, JOHN THOMAS, physiologist, researcher; b. Chester, Pa., Mar. 14, 1948; s. Deward Belmont and Pauline (Dolski) F.; m. Harriet Yvonne Medwid, July 18, 1970; children: Susan Michelle, Mark Brian. BS, Widener U., Chester, 1970; PhD, Hahnemann U., 1974. Asst. prof. physiology Thomas Jefferson U., Phila., 1976-82, assoc. prof., 1982-87, prof., 1987—. Contbr. more than 85 articles to profl. jours. NIH grantee, 1981—. Mem. Am. Physiol. Soc., N.Y. Acad. Scis., Am. Fedn. for Clin. Rsch., The Shock Soc. (treas. 1988-92), Internat. Endotoxin Soc., Physiol. Soc. Phila. (coun. mem. 1984). Office: Thomas Jefferson U 1020 Locust St Philadelphia PA 19107-6799

FLYNN, MARIE COSGROVE, portfolio manager; b. Honolulu, Jan. 1, 1945; d. John Aloysius and Emeline Frances (Cael) Cosgrove; m. John Thomas Flynn, Jr., June 3, 1968; children: Jamie Marie, Jacqueline Elizabeth. BA., Trinity Coll., 1966. Analyst U.S. Govt., Washington, 1967-70; coord. nat. reading coun. F.X. Doherty Assocs., N.Y.C., 1970-71; security analyst Corinthian Capital Co., N.Y.C., 1971-73; portfolio mgr. Clark Mgmt. Co., Inc., N.Y.C., 1973-78; v.p., sr. portfolio mgr. Lexington Mgmt. Corp., Saddle Brook, N.J., 1978—. Mem. Fin. Analysts Fedn., Inst. Chartered Fin. Analysts, Fin. Women's Assn., N.Y. Soc. Security Analysts, Bus. and Profl. Women's Club. Home: 50 Pickle Brook Rd Bernardsville NJ 07924-1909 Office: Park 80 W Pla II PO Box 1515 Rochelle Park NJ 07662-1515

FLYNN, MICHAEL JAMES, small business owner; b. Atlanta, Dec. 11, 1920; s. Leo Gilbert and Iola (Brozitsky) F.; student Hemphill Diesel Sch., 1938-39; m. Dorothy C. Daria, Apr. 6, 1947; children—Michael G., Patricia Ann, Kevin Charles. Asst. supt. constrn. Pan Am, 1942-44; with Amer-Ind Inc., N.Y.C., 1946-47; area sales rep. John Reiner & Co., L.I. City, N.Y., 1947-49, Deere & Co., Syracuse, 1949-55; rep. in Africa, 1955-58, Australia, 1958-60; owner, pres. M.J. Flynn, Inc., East Syracuse, N.Y., 1962—; pres., chief exec. officer Outdoor Power Products, Inc.; introduced farm tractors from USSR to U.S. markets, 1974, from People's Republic China, 1992. Mem. N.Y. State Farm Equipment Club, Internat. Platform Assn. Republican. Roman Catholic. Office: M J Flynn Inc 6408 Collamer Rd East Syracuse NY 13057-1032

FLYNN, PATRICIA MARIE, economics educator; b. Lynn, Mass.; d. Thomas Peter and Angela Marie (Keane) F. BA in Econs., Emmanuel Coll., 1972; MA in Econs., Boston U., 1973, PhD in Econs., 1980. Rsch. assoc. Inst. for Employment Policy, Boston U., 1975-83; prof. econs. Bentley Coll., Waltham, Mass., 1976—; sr. rsch. fellow New Eng. Bd. Higher Edn., Boston, 1980-82; vis. sch. Fed. Res. Bd., Boston, 1983-84; exec. dir. Inst. for Rsch. & Faculty Devel., Bentley Coll., Waltham, 1986-90; assoc. dean faculty Bentley Coll., Waltham, Mass., 1991-92, dean grad. sch., 1992—; faculty mem. Intst. in Employment & Tng. Adminstrn., Harvard U., Cambridge, Mass., summers 1979-81; cons. U. Mo., Columbia, 1983-84, First Security Svcs. Corp., Boston, 1985, Devel. Alternatives, Inc., Jakarta, Indonesia, summer 1987, ABT Assocs., Cambridge, 1987-89. Author: Facilitating Technological Change, 1988; co-author: Turbulence in the American Workplace, 1991; contbr. articles to profl. jours. Adv. panel mem. Office Tech. Assessment, U.S. Congress, Washington, 1989-91; accreditation team mem. New Eng. Assn. Schs. and Colls., Wellesley, Mass., 1985—; exec. bd. mem. Nat. Identification Program Am. Coun. Edn., Boston, 1983-87; mem. Newton (Mass.) Econ. Devel. Commn., 1984-87. Grantee U.S. Dept. Labor, 1982-84, 88-89, Nat. Inst. Edn., 1982-83, NSF, 1990—; recipient Gregory H. Adamian award for teaching excellence Bentley Coll., 1986, Scholar of Yr. award, 1991. Mem. Am. Econ. Assn., Am. Vocat. Assn., Indsl. Relations Rsch. Assn., Internat. Indsl. Relations Assn., Com. on the Status Women in the Econs. Profession. Democrat. Home: 35 Pulsifer St Newton MA 02160-2220 Office: Bentley Coll 175 Forest St Waltham MA 02154-4705

FLYNN, RAYMOND LEO, mayor; b. Boston, July 22, 1939; m. Catherine Coyne; children: Raymond L. Jr., Edward, Julie, Nancy, Kathleen, Maureen. BA, Providence Coll., 1963, DPA (hon.); MEd, Harvard U., 1981; LLD (hon.), Suffolk U., Emmanuel Coll.; PhD (hon.), Northeastern U., 1986. Mem. Mass. Ho. of Reps., 1971-78, chmn. Boston Harbor Pollution Com., 3 yrs.; mem. Boston City Council, 1978-83; mayor City Boston, 1983—; chmn. U.S. Conf. of Mayors' Task Force on Hunger and Homelessness; chmn. Conf. of Mayor's Com. on Community Devel., Housing and Econ. Devel. Vice chmn. Democratic Nat. Platform Com., 1984, mem. 1988; mem. Nat. League Cities Election '88 Task Force. Recipient John Boyle O'Reilly award New Eng. and Irish Am. Labor Coalition, Pub. Service award NAACP-Boston, 1985, Youth award U.S. Conf. Mayors, 1985, Silver Ann. award NCAA, 1988, All Am. Silver Ann. award Nat. Assn. Basketball Coaches, 1988, Athletic Alumnus of Yr. award NCAA, 1988. Office: 1 City Hall Plz Boston MA 02201-1001*

FLYNN, ROBERT WARREN, environmental, land use and transportation planner, consultant; b. N.Y.C., Oct. 29, 1943; s. Edwin Vincent and Marcella (Drexler) F.; m. Evelyn Holzhauer, Mar. 20, 1976; children: Sean Michael, Mark Townley. BS, Pratt Inst., 1969; cert., LaGuardia Community Coll., 1975; postgrad., New Sch. Social Research, 1980. Cert. planner, safety profl., N.Y. Adminstrv. asst., project dir. Wilbur Smith and Assocs., N.Y.C., 1963-68; dir. transp. planning Staunton & Freeman, N.Y.C., 1968-70, dir. planning, sr. assoc., 1978-81; assoc. Tippetts-Abbett-McCarthy-Stratton, N.Y.C., 1970-78; pres. Robert W. Flynn Assocs., N.Y.C. and Kerhonkson, N.Y., 1981—; bd. dirs. OBSTACorp, Elmhurst, N.Y.; cons. Ronald A. Freeman Assocs., Mt. Kisco, N.Y., 1981—. Contbr. articles to profl. jours. Planning com. Chimney Hill Owners Assn., Wilmington, Vt., 1985—; v.p. Elmhurst Home Owners Assn., 1972-74; mem. Queens County Planning Bd. 4, 1970-73, Rochester Planning Bd., 1985-87, Rondout Valley Cen. Sch. Dist., Accord, N.Y., 1986-88. Mem. Aircraft Owners and Pilots Assn., Inst. Transp. Engrs., Am. Planning Assn., Am. Inst. Cert. Planners, World Safety Orgn. (hon. mem. 1987), U.S. Power Squadron, U.S. Sailing Assn., Commodore-Kingston Sailing Club, Yacht Racing Assn. L.I. Sound. Lodge: Elks. Office: 1133 Broadway Ste 1223 New York NY 10010-7903 also: 446 Lower Cherrytown Rd Kerhonkson NY 12446

FOCKLER, HERBERT HILL, foundation executive; b. Summersville, W.Va., Feb. 18, 1922; s. William Okey and Annie Lee (Fitzwater) F.; m. Mary Hildegarde Ziegler, May 15, 1950; 1 child, Herbert. BA, W.Va. U., 1946, MA, 1947; cert., Oxford (Eng.) U., 1948, Harvard U., 1949. Adminstr. library Princeton (N.J.) U., 1952-54, Library of Congress, Washington, 1956-58; advisor White House Confs., Washington, 1959-60; exec. NIH, Bethesda, Md., 1961-69; chmn. Sci. and Tech. Coms., Washington, 1969-70; exec. dir. Sci. Founds., Washington, 1971-72; trustee, chmn. Am. Arts Internat. Found., Washington, pres., 1984—, also bd. dirs.; trustee Nat. Mus. of Health and Medicine Found., 1989—; chmn., trustee World Tech. Found., Washington, 1988-89; advisor NSF, 1975, White House Conf. on Bus., 1975, 78, Montgomery Coll., Rockville, Md., 1978, World Bank, 1986, Winston Churchill Found., 1988, various pub. socs., 1980—, various tech. industries, 1986—, Internat. Monetary Fund, 1991—; mem. adv. coun. Coolfont Found., Berkeley Springs, W. Va., 1980-87; dir. Info. Svcs. Co., 1978-79; mem. Presdl. Rsch. Group; assoc. Woodrow Wilson Internat. Ctr., 1988; advisor IMF, 1991—. Editor: Contemporary South, 1968, also conf. records and newsletters; author sci. research reports and bibliographies. Trustee Threshold Environ. Found., Washington, 1969-75, Nat. Mus. Health and Medicine Found., 1989-90, adv. coun., 1991—; mem. pres.'s coun. Shenandoah Coll., Winchester, Va., 1982-87; mem. Found. Advancement Edn. in Scis., 1980—, Joint Bd. Edn. in Sci. and Engring., 1991—. Served as staff sgt. U.S. Army, 1941-45. Mem. Acad. Polit. Sci., Am. Polit. Sci. Assn., AAAS, Washington Acad. Sci., Fgn. Policy Inst., World Affairs Coun., Policy Studies Orgn., Found. for Advancement of Edn. in Sci., Bd. on Sci. Edn. Clubs: Harvard U., Princeton U., W.Va. (Washington). Home and Office: 10710 Lorain Ave Silver Spring MD 20901-1512

FOEGE, ROSE ANN SCUDIERO, human resources professional; b. Bklyn., Aug. 22, 1941; d. Thomas Edward and Catherine Mary (Demarsico) Scudiero; m. William Henry Foege, Apr. 19, 1975. BA, Queens Coll., 1973; MS cum laude, Iona Coll., 1981. Cert. Am. Registry Radiologic Technologists. X-ray technician St. Clare's Hosp., N.Y.C., 196-61; supr. x-ray N.Y. Internat. Longshoremen's Assn. Med. Ctr., N.Y.C., 1960-67, Life Extension Inst., N.Y.C., 1967-73; radiologic technologist Exxon Corp., N.Y.C., 1973-81, coordinator systems and records, 1981-86; staff human resources specialist Exxon Rsch. & Engrs., Linden, N.J., 1986—. Mem. exec. bd. Wykagyl Neighborhood Assn., New Rochelle, N.Y. Mem. Am. Soc. Personnel Adminstrs., Am. Mgmt. Assn., Am. Acad. Med. Adminstrs., Am. Soc. Radiologic Technologists, Nat. Assn. Female Execs., Mensa, Iona Coll. Alumni Assn. Home: 149 Wykagyl Ter New Rochelle NY 10804-3124 Office: Exxon Rsch and Engring 1900 E Linden Ave Linden NJ 07036

FOERSTER, KARL HEINRICH, chemical company executive; b. Kassel, Germany, May 10, 1959; came to U.S., 1988; m. Vicky Lagadianou, June 18, 1988. BA, Wuerzburg (Germany) U., 1982; MBA, U. R.I., 1984. Mgmt. trainee BASF AG, Ludwigshafen, Germany, 1984-85, Ludwigshafen, 1985-86; asst. to mgr. BASF Ireland, Dublin, 1986; gen. mgr. Ultra Polymers BASF U.K., Manchester, 1987-88; product mktg. mgr. BASF Corp., Parsippany, N.J., 1988-91; corp. accounts mgr. BASF Corp., Parsippany, 1991—; adv. bd. Inst. Internat. Bus., U. R.I., Kingston, 1991—. Office: BASF Corp 100 Cherry Hill Rd Parsippany NJ 07054

FOGARTY, CHARLES JOSEPH, senator; b. Providence, Sept. 15, 1955; s. Charles Joseph and Marha Jane (Hague) F. BA, Providence Coll., 1977; MPA, U. R.I., 1980. Policy assoc. Office Gov., Providence, 1978-84; spl. asst. to commr. R.I. Dept. Edn., Providence, 1985; town councilman Glocester, R.I., 1985-91; sr. policy analyst Office Gen. Treas., Providence, 1985-88; dir. policy Office Lt. Gov., Providence, 1989-91; state senator R.I., Providence, 1991—. Chmn. Glocester Dem. Town Com., 1979-85, N.W. Nurses Fundraising Com., 1991—; del. Dem. Nat. Conv., N.Y.C., 1980. Mem. Lions (pres. Glocester chpt. 1991—). Roman Catholic. Home: 230 Paris Irons Rd Harmony RI 02829 Office: Senate House State House Providence RI 02903

FOGARTY, EDWARD MICHAEL, lawyer; b. Woonsocket, R.I., Feb. 25, 1948; s. Raymond Henry and Mary (Hogan) F.; m. Gail Higgins, Jan. 8, 1977. BA, Providence Coll., 1969; JD, Georgetown U., 1972. Bar: R.I. 1972, D.C. 1973, U.S. Supreme Ct. 1977. Law clk. U.S. Dist. Ct. R.I., Providence, 1972-73; assoc. Wilkinson, Cragun & Barker, Washington, 1973-79, ptnr., 1979-82; ptnr. Baenen, Timme, De Reitzes & Middleton, Washington, 1982-83; counsel Spriggs & Hollingsworth, Washington, 1983—; legal counsel to speaker R.I. Ho. of Reps., Providence, 1987—; arbitrator R.I. Superior Ct., 1989—. Mem. ABA, R.I. Bar Assn., Am. Arbitration Assn. (nat. panel of arbitrators 1985—), Univ. Club (Washington). Democrat. Roman Catholic. Home: 488 Lloyd Ave Providence RI 02906-4550 Office: 302 State House Providence RI 02903

FOGARTY, HARRY, psychoanalyst; b. Sioux City, Iowa, Oct. 29, 1945; s. Charles Franklin and Wilma (Wells) F.; m. Aileen Koger, May 30, 1982; 1 child, Mairin. BA in Philosophy, Fordham U., 1968; MA in Econs., U. Wash., 1971; MDiv, STM with high distinction, Woodstock Coll., 1974; PhD, Union Theol. Sem., 1987. Ordained priest Roman Cath. Ch. Assoc. counselor Cath. Campus Ministry, Columbia U., N.Y.C., 1974-80; clin. assoc., tutor in psychiatry and religion Union Theol. Sem., N.Y.C., 1975-80; pvt. practice Jungian analysis N.Y.C.; instr. C.G. Jung Found. for Analytical Psychology, 1987—; coord., mem. adv. bd. C.J. Jung Referral Svc.; bd. dirs., mem. faculty C.J. Jung Inst. N.Y., 1992—; lectr. in field; mem. faculty Inst. of Religion and Health, 1991—; lectr. in psychiatry and religion Union Theol. Sem., N.Y.C., 1991—. Author: An Index of Concern: The United States Senate and Global Perspective, 1972; contbr. articles, book revs. to profl. publs. Mem. AACD, Nat. Assn. for Advancement of Psychoanalysis (bd. dirs., sec.), N.Y. Assn. Analytical Psychology, Internat. Assn. Analytical Psychology (cert. Jungian analyst). Office: 7 W 96th St Apt 1E New York NY 10025-6514

FOGARTY, KATRINA SIBLEY PARK, small business owner; b. Littleton, Mass., Sept. 13, 1920; d. John Baker and Marion (Prouty) Sibley; m. Wisner I. Park Jr., Feb. 2, 1946 (dec. May 1970); children: David Sibley, Charles Wisner, Jonathan Prouty; m. William Edward Fogarty, Dec. 10, 1983. Student, Colby Jr. Coll., 1940, Bishop-Lee Sch. Theatre, 1941. Pres. Snugbug Ltd., Wolfeboro, N.H., 1988—, Snugbug Studio, Wolfeboro, 1989—. Author: Randolph Rat, 1989, Cynthia Chicken Series, 1991. Bd. dirs. Wolfeboro Area Children's Ctr., 1990—. Mem. DAR, Nat. Rep. Club, Wolfeboro Hist. Soc., Littleton Hist. Soc., St. Augustine Fla. Hist. Soc., St. Augustine Geneol. Soc. Home and Office: 58 Pleasant St Wolfeboro NH 03894

FOGARTY, PAUL CHRISTOPHER, conference planner; b. Bryn Mawr, Pa., Dec. 30, 1956; s. Robert Henry and Phyllis Marie (Jacques) F. BSBA, Appalachian State U., 1979. Asst. buyer Hochschild Kohn, Balt., 1979-81; dept. mgr. Ivey's, Greensboro, N.C., 1981-84; buyer Hutzler's, Balt., 1984-86; mdse. mgr. Saks Fifth Ave., Balt., 1986; gen. mgr. Soc. Hill Hotel, Balt., 1986-88; gen. ops. facilitator N.J. Dept. Edn., Trenton, 1988—. Vol. March of Dimes, 1975—; bd. dirs. Miss State Capitol Scholarship Pageant; judge Miss Pa., Miss Md., Miss Mass. Scholarship Programs; rep. Mountaineer Vol. Program, Pa. and N.J. Mem. Meeting Planners Internat., Am. Vocat. Assn., Future Bus. Leaders Am.-Phi Beta Lambda (N.C. profl. div. pres. 1983-84, Disting. Alumnus award 1984), N.J. Vocat. Edn. Assn. Republican. Roman Catholic. Home: 1506 Society Pl Newtown PA 18940-3224 Office: NJ Dept Edn 225 W State St Trenton NJ 08608-1001

FOGEL, IRVING MARTIN, consulting engineer; b. Gloucester, Mass., Apr. 15, 1929; s. Jacob and Ethel (David) F.; children: Ethan, Ronit. BS, Ind. Inst. Tech., 1954, D of Engring. (hon.), 1982. Registered profl. engr., 22 states, D.C., Israel. Civil engr. Ill. Hwy. Dept., Peoria, 1954-55; field engr. Peter Kiewit Sons Co., East Gary, Ind., 1955, field engr., progress engr., cost engr., Ogdensburg, N.Y., 1955-56; supt. grading and paving Merritt, Chapman & Scott, Binghamton, N.Y., 1956; cost engr. Drake-Merritt, Goose Bay, Labrador, 1956-57; constrn. mgmt. engr. Mil. Estimating Corp., Madrid, Spain, also P.I., 1957-58; project mgr. Ministry of Def., State of Israel, 1958-59, Frederic R. Harris (Holland) N.V., The Hague, also Tehran, Iran, 1959-61; project mgr. Solel Boneh & Assocs., Addis Ababa, Ethiopia, 1961-63; asst. to tech. dir. Frederic R. Harris, Madrid, 1963-64; chief engr. McKee-Berger-Mansueto, Inc., N.Y.C., 1964-65, v.p. constrn. mgmt., 1965-69; pres. Fogel & Assocs., Inc., N.Y.C. and Ft. Lauderdale, Fla., 1969—; lectr. Fellow ASCE, Nat. Acad. Forensic Engrs.; mem. NSPE, Am. Arbitration Assn., Am. Assn. Cost Engrs., Am. Inst. Constructors, Constrn. Specifications Inst., Nat. Contract Mgmt. Assn., N.Y. Bldg. Congress, Project Mgmt. Inst., Soc. Am. Mil. Engrs. Author guides and handbooks on constrn. bus., latest being Construction Owner's Handbook of Property Development, 1992; contbr. articles to profl. jours. Home: 525 E 86th St New York NY 10028-7512 Office: 15 E 26th St Ste 1700 New York NY 10010-1505

FOGELMAN, HAROLD HUGO, child and adult psychiatrist; b. Bronx, N.Y., May 12, 1943; s. Benjamin and Ruth (Nachman) F.; m. Sandra Helene Millman, Mar. 16, 1968; children: Joshua Philip, Benjamin Gabriel. BA, NYU, 1965; MD, Albert Einstein Coll. Medicine, 1969. Diplomate Am. Bd. Psychiatry and Neurology. Med. intern Maimonides Med. Ctr., Bklyn., 1969-70; resident in psychiatry Montefiore Hosp. and Med. Ctr., Bronx, 1972-75; fellow in child psychiatry St. Luke's Hosp. Ctr., N.Y.C., 1975-77; pvt. practice Suffern, N.Y., 1977—; chief psychiatrist Child Devel. Ctr., Pomona, N.Y., 1980—; instr. in psychiatry, Columbia U., N.Y.C., 1977—; clin. supr. and assoc. attending, St. Luke's Roosevelt Hosp. Ctr., N.Y.C., 1977—. Editor: Task Force on Arteriosclerosis, 1972. Pres., trustee Nanuet (N.Y.) Union Free Sch. Dist., 1988—. Lt. comdr. USPHS, 1970-72. Mem. Am. Psychiat. Assn., Am. Acad. Child and Adolescent Psychiatry, N.Y. Coun. on Child Psychiatry, N.Y. Acad. Scis. Jewish. Office: 222 Rt 59 Suffern NY 10901-5204

FOGELSONGER, NED RAYMOND, insurance agency executive; b. Chambersburg, Pa., Jan. 24, 1947; s. Ned Martin Fogelsonger and Barbara Elizabeth (Stermer) Mummert; divorced; children: Lisa Marie, Bryan Andrew. BSBA, Shippensburg U., 1971. CLU. Agt. G. Leonard Fogelsonger Agy., Shippensburg, 1969-75, ptnr., 1975-82; prin. Fogelsonger Agy., Inc., Shippensburg, 1983—; bd. dirs. Orrstown (Pa.) Bank. Bd. dirs. Shippensburg U. Found., 1984—; pres. Shippensburg United Way, 1979, bd. dirs. 1977-82; vol. Cansurmount counselor Am. Cancer Soc., 1987—. Mem. NRA, Soc. CLU, Ind. Ins. Agts. Am., Ind. Ins. Agts. Pa. (bd. dirs. 1982-88, co-chmn. edn. com. 1984-88), Profl. Ins. Agts. Am., Profl. Ins. Agts. Pa. (edn. com. 1989—), Nat. Life Underwriters Assn. (bd. dirs. 1973-75, nat. quality award 1975-76), Nat. Coalition for Cancer Surivorship (membership com.), Soc. Cert. Ins. Counselors, Aetna's Agts. Adv. Coun. (chmn. 1986-87), Shippensburg C. of C. (bd. dirs. 1979-81, pres. 1981), Clowns Am. Internat., Shippensburg Fish and Game Club, Sons Am. Legion, Masons, Shriners (clown unit). Republican. Roman Catholic. Home: 264 Hostetter Ave Shippensburg PA 17257-9224 Office: Fogelsonger Agy Inc 66 E King St Shippensburg PA 17257-1345

FOGGIE, CHARLES HERBERT, bishop; b. Sumter, S.C., Aug. 4, 1912; s. James L. and Mamie Foggie; m. Madeline Sharpe Swan; 1 child, Charlene Marietta. AB, Livingstone Coll., 1936, DD (hon.), 1949, LLD (hon.), 1989; AM, Boston U., 1938, MDiv, 1939, MST, 1942. Ordained to ministry AME Zion Ch., 1936; elected bishop, 1968. Pastor Wadsworth St. AME Zion Ch., Providence, 1936-39, Rush AME Zion Ch., Cambridge, Mass., 1939-44, Wesley Ctr. AME Zion Ch., Pitts., 1944-68; bishop 12th dist., Ark., North Ark., Ga., South Ga., Okla., Tex., 1968-72, 5th dist., Allegheny, Phila.-Balt., Va. Confs., 1972-76, 3d dist., 1972-80, 3d dist., Allegheny, Phila.-Balt., Ohio, Guyana, Barbados Confs., 1980-88; pres. bd. bishops AME Zion Ch.; sec., trustee Livingstone Coll., Salisbury, N.C.; mem. World Coun. Chs., Nat. Coun. Chs. Past pres. Pitts. br. NAAC, Housing Authority, City of Pitts.; mem. Leadership Conf. on Civil Rights. Recipient Congl. Record citation, 50 yrs. in pastoral ministry, 1986, 1st Ann. Svc. award Pitts. br. NAACP; fellow U. Pitts. Democrat. Home: 1200 Windermere Dr Pittsburgh PA 15218-1146 Office: AME Zion Ch 1200 Windermere Dr Pittsburgh PA 15218-1146

FOGIEL, MAX, publishing executive; b. Magdeburg, Germany, Aug. 29, 1929; came to U.S., 1940; s. Abram and Sara (Pergericht) F. BME, Cooper Union U., N.Y.C., 1952; MME, Poly. Inst., Bklyn., 1954; PhD in Elec. Engring., Tech. U., Munich, Germany, 1965. Profl. Engring. Lic. Sr. engr. Ford Instrument, Long Island City, N.Y., 1952-56, Control Instrument, Bklyn., 1956-59; rsch. engr. Loral Electronics, Bronx, N.Y., 1959-61; project engr. RCA, N.Y.C., 1961-64; pres., CEO Rsch. & Edn. Assn., Piscataway, N.J., 1964—. Author: Microelectronics, 1968, 73, Life Insurance, 1972; editor: Problem Solvers, 1973—; pub. high sch. and coll. study guides and handbooks in sci. and tech.; inventor in field. Home: 44 Maple Ct Highland Park NJ 08904-1922 Office: Rsch & Edn Assn 61 Ethel Rd W Piscataway NJ 08854-5963

FOGLE, HAROLD WARMAN, retired horticulturist, researcher; b. Morgantown, W.Va., Apr. 23, 1918; s. Homer Bruce and Winnie (Warman) F.; m. Shirley Page Miller, Nov. 14, 1947; children: Linda Page Fogle Blair, David Mark. BS in Agr., W.Va. U., 1940, MS, 1941; PhD, U. Minn., 1949. Asst. county supr. FSA, USDA, Charlestown, W.Va., 1941-42; county supr. FSA, USDA, West Union, W.Va., 1942-46, Buckhannon, W.Va., 1946; rsch. asst. U. Minn., St. Paul, 1946-49; horticulturist USDA, Wash. State U., Prosser, 1949-63; investigations leader USDA, Beltsville, Md., 1963-72, rsch. horticulturist, 1972-80; co-chmn. Symposium on Plum Genetics, Cacak, Yugoslavia, 1977; chmn. Cumberland-Shenandoah Fruit Workers Conf., Beltsville, 1970. Author: (with others) Advances in Fruit Breeding, 1975, Methods in Fruit Breeding, 1980; co-editor: Germplasm Resources Inventory, 1976, North American and European Fruit and Tree Nut Germplasm Resources Inventory, 1981. Sgt. USAF, 1943-46. Mem. Am. Soc. for Horticultural Sci., Am. Pomological Soc. (pres. 1973-74, Wilder medal 1978), Sigma Xi, Alpha Zeta. Methodist. Home: 2014 Forest Dale Dr Silver Spring MD 20903-1529

FOGLE, RICK ALAN, student life director; b. Beloit, Wis., Aug. 7, 1956; s. Arnold Leroy and Betty Mae (Burchfield) F.; m. Amy Wilson Smith, May 26, 1984. EdB in Soc. Sci., U. Wis., Whitewater, 1980; MEd, U. Wis., Lacrosse, 1982. Program coord. U. Pitts., Pitts., 1983-85; dir. student life U. Pitts., Greensburg, Pa., 1985—; education session presenter Nat. Assn. Campus Activities, Columbia, S.C., 1984-87, regional conf. com. 1984-85. Chair film program Westmoreland County (Pa.) Arts & Heritage Fair, 1986. Mem. Nat. Assn. Student Pers. Adminstrs., Am. Coll. Pers. Assn., Assn. Coll. Unions Internat.

FOGLEMAN, RALPH WILLIAM, toxicologist; b. McDonald, Kans., Mar. 18, 1926; s. Ernest M. and Sue E. (Duckworth) F.; m. Betty A. Stroud, Aug. 12, 1948; children: Laurence D., Gregory S., Kevin M. DVM, Kans. State U., 1947. Lic. veterinarian, Nebr. Gen. mgr. western div. Hazleton Labs. Inc., Palo Alto, Calif., 1958-60; v.p. Hazleton Nuclear Sci. Corp., Palo Alto, 1960-62, AME Assocs. Inc., Princeton, N.J., 1962-65; pres. Biographics Inc., Princeton, 1965-66; registration's supr. CIBA Agrochem Inc., Vero Beach, Fla., 1966-69; sr. v.p. dir. Affiliated Med. Rsch. Inc., Princeton, 1969-75; prin. RW Fogleman & Assocs., Upper Black Eddy, Pa., 1975—; partner Stewart Pesticide Registration Assoc., Inc., Arlington, Va., 1988—; toxicologist N.J. Pesticide Control Coun., 1976-80; mem. N.J. Pesticides Rev. Com., 1987—; presenter in field. Mem. N.J. Agt. Orange Commn., 1980—; chmn. East Amwell Twp. Bd. Of Health, 1975-80. Capt. U.S. Army, 1950-53. Fellow AAAS, Am. Coll. Vet. Toxicologists (charter); mem. Am. Soc. Agrl. Consultants (cert.), Coun. for Agrl. Sci. & Tech. (pres. 1980, bd. dirs. 1978-81, 90—, task force 1976-90), Internat. Soc. Regulatory Pharmacology & Toxicology (coun. 1990—), Soc. Toxicology, Am. Coll. Toxicology, Masons. Republican. Home and Office: RW Fogleman & Assocs 1175 River Rd Upper Black Eddy PA 18972-9101

FOGLESONG, MARILEE ANN, librarian; b. Peoria, Ill., Nov. 13, 1936; d. Charles Wesley and Edna Ella (Kilpatrick) F. BS, Ill. State U., 1958; MSLS, U. Ill., 1962. Young adult librarian Free Library of Phila., 1962-65; reader devel. prog., community librarian, 1967, adult/young adult area specialist, to 1983; young adult head Madison (Wis.) Pub. Library, 1965-67; young adult librarian Warner Library, Tarrytown, N.Y., 1983-85; dir. South Salem Library, N.Y., 1985-87; coord. young adult svcs. The N.Y. Pub. Library, N.Y.C., 1987—; tchr. C.W. Post, L.I. U., 1986-87, Pratt Inst., Bklyn., 1988. Mem. Westchester Library Assn. (v.p. 1986-87), N.Y. Library Assn. (pres. youth svcs. sect. 1986-87), ALA (young adult svcs. div. pres. 1973-74). Office: NY Pub Libr Office of Young Adults 455 5th Ave New York NY 10016-0109

FOGLESONG, PAUL DAVID, molecular biology educator; b. Marion, Va., June 24, 1949; s. Everett Paul and Thelma Brachelle (Conner) F.; m. Clare Maria Wright, July 1, 1978 (div. Jan. 1985). BS, Va. Poly. Inst. & State U., 1971; PhD, SUNY, Stony Brook, 1980. Rsch. asst. SUNY, Stony Brook, 1973-80; postdoctoral fellow Albert Einstein Coll. of Medicine, Bronx, N.Y., 1980-82, rsch. fellow, 1982; rsch. asst. St. Jude Children's Rsch. Hosp., Memphis, 1982-86; dir. biochemistry Biotherapeutics Inc., Memphis, 1986-88; asst. prof. Memphis State U., 1988-89, Rutgers U., Camden, N.J., 1989—; cons. So. Rsch. Inst., Birmingham, Ala., 1989—. Contbr. articles to Jour. Virol., Cancer Immunol. Immunother., Anal. Biochem. Treas. Am. Guild Organists, Memphis, 1988-89, St. Mark's Ch., Phila., 1991; asst. organist St. Mary's Cathedral, Memphis, 1984-89. Gov. Westmoreland Davis scholar, 1967-71. Mem. AAAS, Am. Soc. Microbiology, Am. Soc. Virology, Am. Assn. Cancer Rsch., Phi Kappa Phi. Office: Rutgers U Biology Dept Camden NJ 08102-1401

FOGLIETTA, THOMAS MICHAEL, congressman; b. Phila., Dec. 3, 1928; s. Michael and Rose (Buttari) F. B.A., St. Joseph's Coll.; student, Temple U. Bar: Pa., U.S. Supreme Ct. Pvt. practice law Phila.; mem. 97th-102nd Congresses from 1st Dist. Pa., 1981—, Phila. City Coun. Chmn. South Philadelphia chpt. ARC, Phila. chpt. Am. Cancer Soc.; mem. Phila. Mayor's Complete Count Com. Fed. Census; bd. dirs. St. Luke's Hosp., Guiffre Med. Center, Phila. Easter Seal Soc. Mem. Sons of Italy, Justinian Soc. Democrat. Roman Catholic. Office: Dist Office William J Green Bldg 6th & Arch Sts Philadelphia PA 19106 also: 1217 Longworth Office Bldg Washington DC 20006*

FOLDI, ANDREW PETER, chemist, consultant; b. Budapest, Hungary, Feb. 24, 1931; came to U.S., 1957; s. Zoltán Kálmán and Leonóra (Lehotzky) Földi. MS in Chem. Engring., Budapest Poly. Inst., 1953; PhD in Organic Chemistry, U. Del., 1963. Lab technician Vegyészeti Kutató Laboratórium, Budapest, 1947-53; chem. engr. Tiszavidéki Vegyi Kombinát, Budapest, 1953-56; chem. engr. E.I. Du Pont, Wilmington, Del., 1957-60, sr. rsch. chemist, 1962-85; owner, cons. C. & C. Cons., Wilmington, 1985—. Adv. bd. Jour. Elastomers and Plastics, 1990—; contbr. articles to profl. jours.; presenter in field. Mem. Del. Sci. Alliance, Am. Chem. Soc. (rubber div.), Sigma Xi. Office: C & C Cons 2833 W Oakland Dr Wilmington DE 19808-2422

FOLEY, BERNARD JAMES, education specialist; b. Fitchburg, Mass., Sept. 7, 1933; s. John Patrick and Gertrude Alice (Moran) F.; m. Martha Jane Hazel, May 31, 1958; children: Martha Jane, Bernard James Jr., Ann Kristen, Thomas Patrick. BS in Edn., Fitchburg State Coll., 1955; MEd, Boston U., 1958; postgrad., Boston U./Boston Coll., 1960-78; diploma with distinction, Armed Forces Staff Coll., 1974. Cert. tchr., Mass. Tchr. Fitchburg (Mass.) Pub. Schs., 1955-57; instr., tng. shc. supr., then instr. prin. elem. tng. sch. Fitchburg State Coll., 1957-60; edn. specialist, test psychologist U.S. Army Security Agy. Sch., Ft. Devens, Mass., 1960-65; chief eval. and testing div. U.S. Army Security Agy. Sch., Ft. Devens, 1965-70, dir. instrnl. support dept., 1970-75, chief tng. analysis and design div., 1975-80; dep. dir. tng. devel. U.S. Army Intelligence Sch., Ft. Devens, 1980-83, dep. dir., dir. tng. devel., 1983-90, dir., 1990—; assoc. prof. Fitchburg State Coll., 1965-75; intelligence sch. rep. to Ednl. Testing Svc. Invitational Conf., N.Y.C.; mem. bd. trustees Fitchburg State Coll., 1984—. Contbr. to human resources handbook. Bd. dirs. Greater Fitchburg Youth Hockey Assn., 1975-78; mem. Fitchburg Dem. City Com.; vice-chmn., now chmn. bd. overseers, St. Bernard Cen. Cath. High Sch., Fitchburg, 1985-90; chair bd. trustees Fitch State Coll., 1989—; councillor-at-large, City of Fitchburg, 1982—. Mem. Mass. Mcpl. Assn. (policy com. transp., utilities, 1987—, bd. dirs. 1990—, counsellor), Mass. Mcpl. Councillors Assn. (pres. 1992—), Am. Mgmt. Assn., Soc. Applied Learning Tech., Fitchburg State Coll. Alumni, Irish Am. Club, K.C., Am. Philatelic Soc. Home: 43 Forest St Ayer MA 01432-1615 Office: USAISD ATSI ETD Fort Devens MA 01433-6301

FOLEY, EDWARD FRANCIS, financial executive, commercial lender; b. Asheville, N.C., Oct. 13, 1954; s. Edward F. and Marguerite (Guilka) F.; m. Janet Bouton, Oct. 23, 1976; children: Michael, David, Ryan. Student, U. Notre Dame, 1972-74; BS, U. Md., 1976, MBA, Loyola U., Balt., 1992. Notary public, Md. Credit mgr. Gen. Electric Capital, Plainview, N.Y., 1976-85; region mgr. Caterpillar, Columbia, Md., 1985—; dir., v.p. fin. First Fin. Svcs., Columbia, 1985—. Office: Caterpillar 100 Century Plz Columbia MD 21044

FOLEY, JAMES EDWARD, pharmaceutical company executive; b. Newburyport, Mass., Jan. 4, 1950; s. Everett James Foley and Jean Elizbeth (Wade) Doyle; m. Rosemary Ragozzine, June 3, 1972; children: Annarose, Ryan Seamus. BA in Biology, Merrimack Coll., 1972; PhD in Physiology, Dartmouth Med. Sch., 1976. Rsch. assoc. physiology and medicine Dartmouth Med. Sch., Hanover, N.H., 1976-77, postdoctoral fellow, 1977-79; guest scientist Panum Inst., Copenhagen, Denmark, 1979; lectr. physiology U. Århus, Denmark, 1979-80; rsch. asst., prof. medicine U. Tex., Phoenix, 1979-81; sr. staff fellow NIH/NIADDK, Phoenix, 1981-85; sr. scientist NIH, Phoenix, 1985-86; diabetes group leader Sandoz Rsch. Inst., E. Hanover, N.J., 1985-86, dir. diabetes, 1986—. Contbr. articles to profl. jours. Mem. AAAS, Am. Diabetes Assn., N.Am. Assn. Study of Obesity, Am. Fedn. Clin. Rsch., Am. Jour. Physiology, European Assn. Study Diabetes, N.Y. Acad. Scis. Democrat. Roman Catholic. Home: 73 Seneca Lake Rd Sparta NJ 07871 Office: Sandoz Pharms Corp Rte # 10 East Hanover NJ 07936

FOLEY, JOHN BLISS, insurance brokerage executive; b. Muskegon, Mich., Aug. 26, 1948; s. John Joseph and Grace (Bliss) F.; m. Karen Grace Bellus; children: Kathleen Anne, Megan Marie, Laura Marie, Christian Thomas. BA, St. Johns U., Collegeville, Minn.; MBA, Wharton Sch. of U. Pa. Cen. div. sales mgr. MGIC Indemnity Corp., Milw., 1978-79, asst. product dir., 1979-80; v.p. ea. region MGIC Indemnity Corp., Phila., 1980-81; v.p. sales MGIC Indemnity Corp., Milw., 1981-82; sr. mgr. specialty lines mktg. fin. instn. underwriting CNA Ins. Co., Chgo., 1982-85; sr. v.p., dir. fin. products group Alexander & Alexander, N.Y.C., 1985-90, sr. v.p., dep. dir. nat. mktg., 1990-91, corp. planning officer, dir., 1991—. Contbr. articles to profl. jours. Capt. U.S. Army, 1970-73. Mem. Nat. Assn. Corp. Dirs. (chmn. blue ribbon panel on liability of corp. dirs. 1985-86), Am. Soc. Assn. Execs. (chmn. assoc. mem. adv. com. 1987). Office: Alexander & Alexander 1211 Ave of the Americas New York NY 10036-8701

FOLEY, JOSEPH PATRICK, government relations company executive; b. Tulsa, June 5, 1949; s. Joseph Leo and Helen Virginia (Lepley) F.; m. Adrienne Marie Giebel, Mar. 18, 1977; children: Brendan Patrick, Corey Joseph. BA in History and Edn., Elon Coll., 1971; MA in Internat. Affairs, Am. U., 1980. Social worker Fla. Dept. Health, Orlando, 1971-73; House floor aide U.S. Rep. Bill Chappell, Washington, 1973-79; Congl. liaison Carter White House, Washington, 1980; spl. asst. to agy. dir. Selective Svc. System, Washington, 1980-82; Congl. rels. specialist Fed. Emergency Mgmt. Agy., Washington, 1983-86; pres., sr. legis. assoc. Foley & Co., Inc., Potomac, Md., 1986—; mktg. rep. PolyPhaser Corp., Minden, Nev., 1986—; lobbyist Unified Industries, Inc., Springfield, Va., 1991—; exec. dir. Coalition Against Non-effective Lightning Protection Technologies, 1987-89; govt. rels. cons. Media Software, Inc., Augusta, Ga., 1990—. Contbr. articles to profl. jours. County co-chair Rep. Bev Byron Re-election Com., 1989—; precinct ofcl. Montgomery County Dem. Party, Dist. 15, 1989—; sec. Dist. 15 Dem. Caucus, Montgomery County, Md., 1991—; steering com. U.S. Rep. Martin Sabo, 1987—; uncommitted Dem. conv. del. Clinton for Pres., 1992. Recipient Outstanding Legis. Staff Asst. award U.S. Rep. Bill Chappell, 1980, Silver Medal of Merit, Selective Svc. System, 1982. Mem. Am. League of Lobbyists (job bank dir. 1988), Md. Coalition on Non-Coal Surface Mining (state lobbyist), Washington Internat. Trade Assn. Democrat. Roman Catholic. Office: Foley & Co Inc PO Box 61303 Potomac MD 20859-1303

FOLEY, MICHAEL A., philosophy educator; b. Decatur, Ill., Sept. 1, 1946; s. Marion B. and Reba C (Henley) F.; children: Aaron M., Christopher A. BA, Eastern Ill. U., 1969; MA, Southern Ill. U., 1971, PhD, 1973; MPA, NYU, 1982. Asst. prof. Marywood Coll., Scranton, Pa., 1974-76, Coll. Misericordia, Dallas, Pa., 1976-80; asst. prof. Marywood Coll., Scranton, Pa., 1980-82, full prof., 1986—, honors dir., 1987—; reviewer Choice, Conn., 1985—, Arba Librs. Unlimited, Inc., Colo., 1991—; attendee NEH Summer Seminar, U. Va., 1978, 85. Co-author: Philosophical Inquiry, 1987; conbr. articles to profl. jours. Mem. Am. Philos. Assn., Nat. Collegiate Honors Coun. Home: 608 Meadow Ln Clarks Summit PA 18411 Office: Marywood Coll Scranton PA 18509

FOLEY, THOMAS LOUIS, software project manager; b. Trenton, N.J., Sept. 1, 1961; s. Edward Paul and Yolanda Mary (Lorentangeli) F.; m. Cheryl Ann Moeller, Nov. 8, 1986; 1 child, Nicole Alysa. Cert. computer programming, Taylor Bus. Inst., 1983; student in bus. adminstrn., Mercer County Community Coll., 1984-85, 91—. Computer technician N.J. Dept. Law and Pub. Safety, Trenton, 1984-86; jr. system programmer United Parcel Svc., Paramus, N.J., 1986-87, intermediate system programmer, 1988-89, sr. system programmer, 1989-90; project mgr. network software United Parcel Svc., Mahwah, N.J., 1990—. Founder, coach Bordentown Midget Wrestling Team, Grapevine Wrestling League, 1980-85; mem. Millstone Twp. Homeowners' Assn., 1990—. Mem. Am. Mgmt. Assn. (assoc.), Internat. Tandem Users' Group, No. Telecomm User's Group, N.J. Wrestling Ofcl. Assn. Roman Catholic. Home: 11 Compton Ct Perrineville NJ 08535-1001 Office: United Parcel Svc 340 Macarthur Blvd Mahwah NJ 07430-2323

FOLEY, WILLIAM E(DWARD), JR., priest, counselor; b. Washington, Oct. 8, 1952; s. William Edward Sr. and Marguerite Mary (Pratt) F. BA, St. John's U., Collegeville, Minn., 1974; MA, Christ the King Sem., 1979; MS, Loyola Coll., 1988, cert. in advanced study, 1990. Ordained priest Roman Cath. Ch. 1979. Assoc. pastor Our Lady of Lourdes Cath. Ch., Bethesda, Md., 1979-83, St. John Evangelist Cath. Ch., Silver Spring, Md., 1983-90, St. Peter Cath. Ch., Olney, Md., 1990-91; pastor Our Lady of Victory Ch., Washington, 1991—. Mem. Am. Assn. for Counseling and Devel. Roman Catholic. Home: 4835 Macarthur Blvd NW Washington DC 20007-1592 Office: Our Lady of Victory Cath Ch 4835 Macarthur Blvd NW Washington DC 20007-1592 also: Our Lady of Victory Rectory Washington DC 20007

FOLIO, CYNTHIA JO, music theory educator; b. Ft. Belvoir, Va., Dec. 24, 1954; d. Joseph Roger and Martha (Pollard) F.; m. Larry Robert Thompson, June 18, 1990. BM in Performance, West Chester U., 1976; Performers cert., Eastman Sch. Music, 1977, MA in Music Theory, 1979, PhD in Music Theory, 1985. From asst. to assoc. prof. Tex. Christian U., Ft. Worth, 1980-90; 2d flute, piccolo performer Ft. Worth Symphony Orch., 1981-90; assoc. prof. Temple U., Phila., 1990—; guest composer Contemporary Music Festival, Sam Houston State U., Tex., 1989, Symposium XV for New Band Music, Radford U., Va., 1990; presented numerous papers for music orgns. Composer, producer and performer Portfolio jazz compact disc, 1990; composer Developing Hues, 1989, One for Four, 1985; mem. editorial bd. Ex-Tempore, 1987—; contbr. articles to profl. jours. Recipient Disting. Alumni award West Chester U., 1990; grantee NEH, 1985, Yaddo Artist Colony, 1989. Mem. ASCAP, Am. Women Composers, Nat. Flute Assn., Internat. league of Women Composers, Soc. for Music Theory, Coll. Music Soc., Soc. for Composers, Inc. Office: Temple U Coll Music Philadelphia PA 19122

FOLSE, BART THOMAS, musician, conductor, educator; b. Raceland, La., Feb. 21, 1956; s. Donald Joseph and Mary Louise (Kraemer) F. B in Music Edn. summa cum laude, Loyola U., 1979; MusM, New England Conservatory, Boston, 1982. Asst. condr. New Amsterdam Singers, N.Y.C., 1982-85; founder, music dir. I Cantori di N.Y., 1984-90; chorusmaster Fest in Hellbrunn, Salzburg, Austria, 1986-89; music dir. Pro Arte Chorale, Paramus, N.J., 1987—; condr. Ch. of St. Paul the Apostle, N.Y.C., 1989—; music dir. Opera Quotannis, N.Y.C., 1990—; instr. Eugene Lang Coll. New Sch. Social Rsch., N.Y.C., 1988—. Am. premiere performance of Gluck's opera Telemaco named 1 of 10 Best Concerts of Yr., N.Y. Times, 1989. Mem. Am. Symphony Orchestra League, Am. Choral Dirs. Assn. Democrat. Roman Catholic. Office: Pro Arte Chorale 368 Paramus Rd # C Paramus NJ 07652-1598

FOLTER, ROLAND, rare books company director; b. Fulda, Fed. Republic of Germany, May 27, 1943; s. Heinz and Annemie (Bennewitz) F.; m. Siegrun Heinecke, Aug. 28, 1967 (dec. 1988); m. Mary Ann Kraus, Apr. 29, 1989; 1 child, Elizabeth. MA, Brown U., 1967, PhD, 1969. Rare books cataloger Yale U., New Haven, Conn., 1966-68; prof. U. Ill., Urbana, 1969-77; dir. H.P. Kraus Rare Books, N.Y.C., 1977—. Author: Deutsche Dichterbibliotheken, 1975; co-author: Bibliography: Its History, 1984; contbr. to ency. and articles to profl. jours. Violinist Frankfurt (Fed. Republic of Germany) Youth Symphony Orch., 1960-65. Fellow Brown U., 1968; faculty fellow U. Ill., 1970-75. Mem. Bibliog. Soc. Am. (coun. 1982-90), N.Y. Philharmonic Soc (affiliate), Assn. Internat. de Bibliophilie, Maximilian-Gesellschaft, Gesellschaft des Bibliophilen, Antiquarian Booksellers Assn. Am., Old Book Table, Princeton Club. Office: H P Kraus Rare Books 16 E 46th St New York NY 10017

FOLTZ, DAVID ALLEN, foreign language educator; b. Detroit, July 10, 1937; children: Kristen, Kimberly, Greg. BA, Principia Coll., Elsah, Ill., 1960; MA, Middlebury (Vt.) Coll., 1963; PhD, U. Ariz., 1974. Cert. rater of oral proficiency in Spanish. Prof. Spanish Principia Coll., 1960-88, dean of faculty, 1975-78, dir. adult edn., summer, 1980-84; assoc. prof. Spanish Indiana U. Pa., 1988—; acting chmn. dept. Spanish and classical langs., summer 1990; translator Joint Publ. Rsch. Svc., 1985-88; reviewer Holt, Rinehart, Winston, Harper Collins, 1991—. Editor Hispanic Jour., 1991—. Bd. dirs. River Bend United Way, Alton, Ill., 1978-88; trustee Elsah Village Bd., 1979-88. Recipient rsch. grant Univ. Senate of Ind. U. of Pa., 1990. Mem. Am. Coun. Tchrs. Fgn. Langs. (oral proficiency tng. award 1985), Am. Assn. Tchrs. Spanish and Portuguese (pres. Western Pa. chpt. 1989-91), Rotary (pres. Jerseyville, Ill. 1986-87). Christian Scientist. Home: 138 N 9th St Indiana PA 15701-1713 Office: Ind U Pa 468 Sutton Hall Indiana PA 15701

FOMBERSTEIN, BARRY JOSEPH, internist; b. N.Y.C., June 1, 1951; s. Louis and Golde (Freiner) F.; m. Deborah Sue Chayet, Oct. 12, 1980; 1 child, Kenneth Marc. BA, CUNY, 1973; MD, Albert Einstein Coll. Medicine, Bronx, 1976. Diplomate Am. Bd. Internal Medicine. Intern L.I. Jewish, 1976-77, resident, 1977-79, fellowship in rheumatology, 1979-81; chief Div. Rheumatology Dept. Medicine, St. John's Episcopal Hosp., Far Rockaway, N.Y., 1983—. Fellow ACP, Am. Coll. Rheumatology; mem. Phi Beta Kappa. Office: St Johns Episcopal Hosp 327 Beach 19th St Far Rockaway NY 11691

FONCELLO, MARTIN JOHN, JR., business and intelligence analyst, consultant; b. Bridgeport, Conn., Nov. 22, 1952; s. Martin John Sr. and Geraldine Mary (Parrella) F.; m. Mary Ann Catherine Grandieri, June 23, 1974; 1 child, Martin John III. BS, Boston Coll., 1974, MBA, 1982. Cert.

sch. bus. adminstr. Gen. mgr. Grand Mfg. Corp., Danbury, Conn., 1981-83; EDP auditor Aetna Life & Casualty, Hartford, Conn., 1983-87; EDP audit officer People's Bank, Bridgeport, 1987-90; pres. Candlewood Mktg. & Cons., 1983—; adj. prof. Western Conn. State U., Danbury, 1983—. Pres. Greenridge Tax Dist., Brookfield, Conn., 1986—; mem. Brookfield Econ. Devel. Commn., 1992—. Capt. U.S. Army, 1974-79, maj. Mass. Army N.G. Mem. N.G. Assn., Res. Officers Assn., Assn. Former Intelligence Officers, First Corps of Cadets, Order Sons of Italy. Republican. Roman Catholic. Home: 11 Drover Rd Brookfield CT 06804-3508

FONDILLER, SHIRLEY HOPE ALPERIN, nurse, journalist, educator, historian; b. Holyoke, Mass.; d. Samuel and Rose (Sobiloff) Alperin; m. Harvey V. Fondiller, Dec. 27, 1957 (div. June 1984); 1 child, David Stewart. BS, Columbia U., 1962, MA, 1963, MEd, 1971, EdD, 1980. Dir. ednl. adminstrs., cons. and tchrs. sect. Am. Nurses Assn., N.Y.C., 1964-66, coord. careers program, 1967-70, coord. clin. sessions, 1971-72; editor Am. Nurse, Kansas City, Mo., 1975-78; assoc. prof., asst. to dean for spl. projects Rush-Presbyn.-St. Luke's Med. Ctr., 1979-86; exec. dir. Mid-Atlantic Regional Nursing Assn., N.Y.C., 1986-89; adj. assoc. prof. Columbia U., 1986—; founder, prin. Pub. for Health Dimensions, phd, 1990—. Author of books; contbr. articles to profl. jours. Mem. Kappa Delta Pi, Sigma Theta Tau.

FONG, JAMES TSE-MING, mechanical engineer, consultant; b. Shanghai, China, Aug. 27, 1927; came to U.S., 1947; s. Yue Sing and Zimmei (Fong) F.; m. Solvseg Senta Zajicek, July 23, 1964; children: Tanja, Michael, Ilan. BS, MIT, 1948; MS, Columbia U., N.Y.C., 1951. Devel. engr. Griscom-Russell Co., N.Y.C., 1948-51; design engr. Burns & Roe, Inc., N.Y.C., 1951-54; rsch. engr. Foster Wheeler Corp., N.Y.C., 1955-57; project and activity mgr., cons. Westinghouse Bettis Lab., Pitts., 1957—; Patentee in field; contbr. articles to profl. jours. Mem. ASME. Office: Westinghouse Bettis Lab PO Box 79 West Mifflin PA 15122-0079

FONO, ANDREW, chemical company executive; b. Budapest, Hungary, Apr. 24, 1923; came to U.S., 1947; s. Albert and Nina (Szilasi) F.; m. Edna May Snyder, Mar. 15, 1958; children: Penelope Anne, Nicholas Albert; m. Ingeborg Majda Waizenegger, Dec. 26, 1984. PhD, Pazamany U., Budapest, 1946. Rsch. fellow U. Stockholm, 1946-47, U. Chgo., 1948-51; rsch. dir. Otto B. May, Newark, 1951; exec. v.p., tech. dir. Royce Assocs., East Rutherford, N.J., 1975—. Contbr. articles to profl. jours. Home: 29 Erwin Park Rd Montclair NJ 07042-3019 Office: Royce Assocs 207 Avenue L Newark NJ 07105-3830

FONSECA, ANTHONY GUTIERRE, coal researcher; b. Chattanooga, Tenn., Mar. 31, 1940; s. David and Esther (haven) F.; m. Carolyn Hughey, Aug. 14, 1965; children: Audrey, Carlton. BA, U. Tenn., 1962; MS, U. Ga., 1966, PhD, 1968. Rsch. scientist Conoco Inc., Ponca City, Okla., 1968-75; sr. rsch. scientist Conoco Inc., Oklahoma City, 1975-76, rsch. group leader, 1976-81, dir., 1981-82; asst. mgr., acting dir. Consol Inc. (formerly Consolidation Coal Co.), Libray, Pa., 1982-86, dir., 1986—. Patentee in field. Mem. AIME, Am. Chem. Soc. Roman Catholic. Office: Consol Inc 4000 Brownsville Rd Library PA 15129-9545

FONTAINE, BERNARD LEO, JR., small business owner, chief executive officer; b. Holyoke, Mass., Nov. 18, 1956; s. Bernard Leo and Claire Doris (Mathey) F.; m. Susan Eileen Scalia, Apr. 7, 1962. BS, Northeastern U., Boston, 1979; MS, U. Okla., 1983-84. Cert. Am. Bd. Indsl. Hygiene, Bd. Cert. Safety Profls. Indsl. hygiene tech. U.S. Dept. Labor, OSHA, Springfield, Mass., 1976-79; indsl. hygienist U.S. Dept. Labor, OSHA, Hartford, Conn., 1979-83; reg. indsl. hygienist U.S. Dept. Navy, Portsmouth, N.H., 1984-85; health and safety supr. Internat. Tech. Corp., Edison, N.J., 1985-87; corp. indsl. hygienist Atlantic Mut. Cos., Madison, N.J., 1987-90, 1987—; founder, chief exec. officer The Windsor Group, Inc., Spotswood, N.J., 1990—. Contbr. articles to profl. jours. Mem. Am. Indsl. Hygiene Assn., Am. Soc. Safety Engrs., Am. Conf. Govt. Indsl. Hygienists, Am. Acad. Indsl. Hygiene, Council on Occupational Hearing Conservation. Republican. Roman Catholic. Office: The Windsor Group Inc 243 Old Stage Rd Spotswood NJ 08884-1142

FONTAINE, EUDORE JOSEPH, JR., artist, art historian; b. Springfield, Mass., Aug. 5, 1929; s. Eudore Joseph and Antoinette Marie (Desautels) F.; m. Rose J. Brigada, June 28, 1952; children: Catherine, Christopher, Carolyn, Stephen, Thomas. BA magna cum laude, Tufts U., 1951; LLB, Harvard U., 1958. One-man shows include MIT, 1985, Crane Gallery, 1986, Babson Coll., 1987, Lily Pad Gallery, 1989, The Copley Soc. of Boston, 1989, David Findlay Gallery, N.Y.C., 1990, Mus. Fine Arts, Springfield, Mass., 1991, Elms Coll., 1991; exhibited in numerous galleries in New Eng. Lt. USN, 1951-55. Roman Catholic. Home: 73 Greylock Rd Wellesley MA 02181-1301 Office: 101 Tremont St Boston MA 02108-5004

FONTAINE, SUE (JEANE FONTAINE), public relations professional; b. Rolfe, Iowa, June 28, 1928; d. Vernette M. and Dorothy (Messinger) Gaskins m. Henry A. Fontaine, Jr., July 1, 1948 (div. 1970); children: Eva Joel, Jeffrey David. BA in Journalism, U. Iowa, 1947; MLS, U. Mo., 1977. Radio and TV dir. Swigart Advt., Inc., New Orleans, 1948-54, 62-65; producer Sta. WDSU-TV, New Orleans, 1954-60; dir. pub. rels. La. State Libr., Baton Rouge, 1960-62, Tulsa City-County Libr., 1965-67, 70-76; spl. projects asst. U. Mo. Sch. Libr., Info. Sci., Columbia, 1976-77; pub. info. officer Wash. State Libr., Olympia, 1977-81; assoc. mgr. pub. rels. N.Y. Pub. Libr., N.Y.C., 1981-85; pub. rels./mktg. dir. Queens Borough Pub. Libr., Jamaica, N.Y., 1985-91; owner SF PR/Mktg., N.Y.C., 1991—; mktg., pub. rels. cons. to various libraries and comml. clients, 1960—. Editor: (with Susan Phelps) Communications for the Humanities, 1975; Public Relations: Tick/Click, 1975; Best of Library Literature, 1981; contbr. articles to profl. jours. Recipient 5 John Cotton Dana Pub. Rels. awards, 1965-75. Mem. ALA (past sect. chmn., bd. dirs., com. chair 1990—), Pub. Rels. Soc., Women in Communications (past chpt. pres.), N.Y. Libr. Assn. (chmn. pub. rels. round table, legis. com.), Libr. Pub. Rels. Coun. (mem. exec. bd., past pres.), Alpha Xi Delta. Episcopalian. Office: SF PR/Mktg 207 E 21st St New York NY 10010-6428

FONTANESE, RICHARD A., portable spectrometer, imaging executive; b. McKeesport, Pa., Oct. 12, 1952; s. David John and Irene (Popovich) F.; m. Kathleen M. Taylor, Aug. 25, 1984; children: John Dominic, Bradley Taylor, Olivia Jane. Student, GAnnon U., 1970-72. Quality assurance insp. Westinghouse Electric, Bettis Atomic Power Div., West Mifflin, Pa., 1972-76, Astrophysics Rsch. Inc., Harbor City, Calif., 1976-77; quality assurance mgr. Am. Magnetics Inc., Carson, Calif., 1977-79, Comsip Inc., Whittear, Calif., 1979-80; dist. sales mgr. McBain Instruments, Chattsworth, Calif., 1980-85; sales. rep. Wild Leitz Inc., Rockleigh, N.J., 1985-88; area mgr. Leica USA (formerly Wild Leitz), Rockleigh, 1989-92; sales dir. Analytical Spectral Devices, Inc., 1992—. Rep. delegate, Boulder, Colo., 1988. Roman Catholic. Home: 1540 Sumac Ave Boulder CO 80304-0810 Office: 4760 Walnut St Ste 105 24 Link Dr Boulder CO 80301

FONTES, PATRICIA J., educational psychologist; b. Providence, Dec. 10, 1936; d. Manuel William and Conceicao Elizabeth (Sousa) F. BS in Edn., Boston U., 1957; MEd, Boston Coll., 1965, PhD, 1968. Tchr. Warwick (R.I.) pub. schs., 1957-59; religious sister/superior Sisters of Our Lady of Providence, 1959-65; asst. prof. U. R.I., Kingston, 1968-69; asst./assoc. prof. Salve Regina Coll., Newport, R.I., 1969-72; cons. psychologist Girl Scouts of R.I., Inc., Providence, 1972-73; research fellow Ednl. Research Ctr., St. Patrick's Coll., Dublin, Ireland, 1973-88; cons. psychologist Girl Scouts R.I., Providence, 1989—; lectr. in field. Author: Equality in Primary Teaching 1985; contbr. articles to profl. jours. Boston U. scholar, 1953-57; Boston Coll. fellow, 1965-68; Inst. for Portuguese Lang. and Culture grantee, 1982. Mem. APA, Am. Ednl. Rsch. Assn., Nat. Coun. on Measurement in Edn., Internat. Coun. Psychologists (sec.-gen. 1991—), Internat. Assn. Applied Psychology. Roman Catholic. Home: 57 Lawton Foster Rd S Hopkinton RI 02833-0062

FONTHEIM, CLAUDE G.B., lawyer, banker; b. Bethlehem, Pa., Aug. 24, 1955; s. Ernest G. and Margot (Hass) F.; m. Orit Frenkel, Dec. 7, 1985. BA in Polit. Sci. & Near East Studies with high distinction and high honors, U. Mich., M in Pub. Policy, 1981, JD, 1981. Bar: D.C. 1981. Assoc. Ginsburg, Feldman & Bress, Washington, 1981-83, Akin, Gump, Strauss, Hauer & Feld, Washington, 1983-87; ptnr. Crowell & Moring, Washington, 1988-90; mng. dir. IBECS, Inc., Washington, 1990—; prin. Fontheim & O'Rourke, Washington, 1990—; lectr. internat. trade & investment law; gen. counsel Internat. Bus. & Econs. Cons. Svcs., Inc., 1985-88, Export Coun. Renewable Energy, Washington, 1985-87; mem. adv. bd. internat. law study Renewable Energy Inst. Mng. editor Mich. Yearbook Internat. Legal Studies, 1980-81; contbr. articles to legal jours. Policy advisor nat. polit. candidates. Mem. ABA (sec. com. internat. trade 1981-83, steering com. 1983-85, former exec. dir. study internat. trade laws), Phi Beta Kappa. Democrat. Jewish. Home: 3737 Military Rd NW Washington DC 20015-1767

FONTS, H. ANTHONY, computer software sales executive; b. Havana, Cuba, Feb. 10, 1960; came to U.S., 1960; s. Humberto Gregory and Marta (Perez-Stable) F. BS, Drexel U., 1983; MBA, Villanova U., 1986. Mgmt. trainee First Pa. Bank, Phila., 1983-84; comml. lender Fidelity Bank, Phila., 1984-85; dist. mgr. A.D.P., Ft. Washington, Pa., 1985-88; sr. mktg. rep. Lotus Devel., Cambridge, Mass., 1988-91; account exec. Am. Software, Atlanta, 1991; mktg. rep. SSA-Mid Atlantic, Rochelle Park, N.J., 1991—. Republican. Roman Catholic. Home: 45 Saddlebrook Dr Sewell NJ Office: SSA - Mid Atlantic One E Uwchlan Ave Exton PA 19341

FOO, HONG TATT, artist; b. Bayan Lepas, Malaysia, Apr. 9, 1940; s. Soon Guan and Eng-Lian Ong; m. Sally Siew-Kian Foo, Aug. 14, 1967; children: Phaik Shu, Kean Foong. BFA, U. Ill., 1964, MA, 1967. Teaching Cert., N.Y. Tchr. Commack (N.Y.) High Sch., 1967-75, lead tchr., 1978—; cons. Boces Gifted and Talented Art Program. 1985-89; lectr. demo Art Orgn. in L.I., 1980—. One-man shows include Painting 1985, Farmingville 1975, Penang, Malaysia, Nat. Art Gallery 1991, Malaysia 1975, 89, Singapore 1991, Beijing, China, Art Tchr. Conv. 1985. Chmn. Brookhaven Bahai's, 1982-84, 91—; pres. Chinese-Am. Assn. Suffolk, L.I., 1985, 91—. Recipient Inst. Internat. Edn. award, 1960, 1st pl. award Acrylic Painting, West Hampston Beach, N.Y., 1972. Mem. N.Y. State Art Tchrs., Nat. Art Educators Assn. Home: 1 Link Ln Centereach NY 11720 Office: Commack High Sch Scholar Ln Commack NY 11725

FOODEN, MYRA, psychologist, consultant, educator; b. N.Y.C., June 20, 1926; d. Max and Bess (Cohen) Samit; m. Richard Fooden, Apr. 16, 1950; children: Madeleine, Bart, Melissa. BA, Hunter Coll., 1947; MS, Adelphi U., 1967; PhD, Yeshiva U., 1974. Lic. psychologist, N.Y. Asst. prof. St. John's U., Jamaica, N.Y., 1969-70; asst. prof. Lehman Coll. CUNY, Bronx, 1970-74; asst. prof. Empire State Coll. SUNY, Old Westbury, N.Y., 1974-81; pvt. practice Great Neck, N.Y., 1975—; assoc. prof. L.I. U., Bklyn., 1980-86. Editor: Second X + Womens Health, 1974; contbr. articles to profl. jours. NDEA fellow, 1971-73. Fellow Inst. Rational Living; mem. APA, Eastern Psychol. Assn.

FOOR, W. EUGENE, academic administrator; b. Wood, Pa., Feb. 7, 1936; s. Fred Franklin and Edna May (Buseck) F.; m. Juanita Ann Brumbaugh, Dec. 21, 1958; children: Wesley Eugene, Wynn Erica. BS in Edn., Shippensburg State Coll., 1958; PhD in Zoology, Univ. of Mass., 1966. Sci. tchr. Dillsburg (Pa.) Jr. High Sch., 1958-59; biology tchr. Chambersburg (Pa.) Area Sr. High Sch., 1959-62; rsch. asst. Univ. Mass., Amherst, 1962-65, predoctoral trainee, 1965-66; postdoctoral fellow Tulane Med. Sch., New Orleans, 1966-67, asst. prof. parasitology, 1967-70; assoc. prof. biology Wayne State U., Detroit, 1970-75, prof. biology, 1975-88; chmn., Div. Nat. Sci. U. Pitts., Johnstown, Pa., 1988—; vis. prof. biology, U. Port Harcourt, Nigeria, 1981-82. Contbg. author: Reproductive Biology of Inverts, 1983, 1988; author: Reproduction of Nematodes, 1976-86. Named Disting. Alumnus Shippensburg (Pa.) State Coll., 1970; grantee NIH, Bethesda, Md., 1971-80. Mem. AAAS, Am. Soc. Parasitology, Pa. Acad. Sci., Sigma Xi. Office: U Pitts Johnstown PA 15904

FOOTE, KEVIN RAFAEL, strategy consultant; b. Chicoutimi, Can., Dec. 1, 1964; came to U.S., 1965; s. John and Norma (Rivera) F. BSME, MIT, 1988. Analyst Braxton Assocs. (subs. Deloitte & Touche), Boston, 1980-90, sr. rsch. assoc., 1990-91; assoc. Braxton Assocs., Boston, 1992—; internat. field engr. GE, Schenectady, N.Y., 1991-92. Composer musical works, 1986. Vol. Big Brother Assn. Boston, 1984-85. Recipient Gold Medal of Achievement Swedish Touring Bd., Göteborg, 1990. Mem. ASME, Am. Mgmt. Assn. Office: Braxton Assocs 200 State St Boston MA 02109

FOOTE, WARREN EDGAR, neuro-scientist, psychologist, educator; b. Boston, Nov. 5, 1935; s. Warren Edgar and Edith Irene (Landry) F.; B.A., Hamilton Coll., 1958; M.A., Boston U., 1960; Ph.D., Tufts U., 1965; m. Cynthia Sue Hall, July 21, 1973; children: Pamela Fowler, Sarah Canby, Julia Landry, Christopher Warren. Research assoc. Harvard U. Med. Sch., 1966-67, vis. asst. prof. psychology, 1970-73, asst. prof., 1974-83, assoc. prof., 1983—; USPHS postdoctoral fellow Yale, 1967-69; research scientist Norwich (Conn.) State Hosp., 1969-70; sr. Fulbright scholar Max-Planck Inst., Munich, Germany, 1973-74; assoc. psychologist Mass. Gen. Hosp., Boston, 1974—, psychologist, 1984—; cons. Gen. Foods Corp., 1970-74, Neurotech Corp., 1987-88. Served with M.C., AUS, 1959-60. Recipient McCurdy prize Mass. Soc. Research in Psychiatry, 1962; sr. Fulbright fellow, 1973-74; Nat. Inst. Neurol. Disease and Stroke grantee, 1974-77; NIMH grantee, 1970-73; Nat. Eye Inst. grantee, 1979—; Wayland Pub. Sch. Found. advisor, 1982—; Nat. Inst. Communicative Disorders and Stroke grantee, 1983—. Mem. AAAS, N.Y. Acad. Scis., Soc. Neuroscis., Am. Psychol. Assn., Sigma Xi. Club: Harvard (Boston). Contbr. articles, revs. to profl. jours. Home: 5 Hilltop Pk Wilbraham MA 01095-1753 Office: Mass Gen Hosp PO Box 70 Boston MA 02114

FORASTE, ROLAND, psychiatrist; b. N.Y.C., Mar. 1, 1938; s. Paul Foraste and Anita Schonbachler. AB honors cum laude, Coll. Holy Cross, 1960; cert. neurology, U. London, 1965; MD, SUNY, Downstate, 1965. clin. instr. psychiatry Cornell Med. Coll., 1967-73, clin. asst. prof., 1973-86; attending physician Gracie Sqq. Hosp., N.Y.C., 1969—, Rye (N.Y.) Psychiat. Ctr., 1969—. Med. intern Jefferson Hosp., Phila., 1965-66; resident in psychiatry N.Y. Hosp., 1966-69, resident in child psychiatry, 1968-71, chief resident in adolescent psychiatry, 1970-71, asst. attending psychiatrist, 1973-86; med. dir. psychiatry U.S. Healthcare and Total Health, N.Y.C., 1986-90, cons., 1990—; clin. instr. psychiatry Cornell Med. Coll., 1967-73, clin. asst. prof. psychiatry, 1973-86; attending physician Gracie Sq. Hosp., N.Y.C., 1969—, Rye (N.Y.) Psychiat. Ctr. Co-author: (audiotext) The Drug Syndrome and the Teacher, 1971; co-editor, contbr. Biology Jour. of Coll. of Holy Cross, 1957-58. Benefit chmn. Hosp. Audiences, Inc., N.Y.C., 1984; chmn. Big Apple Circus benefit com. Cultural Coun. Found., N.Y.C., 1984-86, Five Guys Named Moe benefit com., 1991-92; mem. Met. Mus. Art, Modern Mus. Art. Recipient Physicians Recognition award AMA. Mem. Am. Acad. Child and Adolescent Psychiatry. N.Y. Coun. Child Psychiatry, Am. Soc. for Adolescent Psychiatry (asst. continuing med. edn. officer 1989-90, continuing med. edn. officer 1990—), N.Y. Soc. for Adolescent Psychiatry (bd. dirs. 1987-88, sec. 1988-90, pres-elect 1990-91, pres. 1992-92), Am. Psychiat. Assn. (N.Y. dist. br.), Flying Physicians Assn. (instrumentrated), N.Y. Hosp.-Cornell Med. Ctr. Alumni Assn., Aircraft Owners and Pilots Assn., Greenwich Boat and Yacht Club, Holy Cross Club N.Y., Player's Club, Westchester Flying Club, Porsche Club Am., Westxhester Country Club (mem. nominating com. 1987-88, membership com. 1987-88, 90-91, entertainment com. 1987-88, 90—), U.S. Ski Assn., Wintergreen Club (dir.-trustee 1990—, chmn. entertainment com. 1990—), KC. Republican. Roman Catholic. Home and Office: 623 Steamboat Rd Greenwich CT 06830-7140 Home and Office: 420 E 51st St New York NY 10022-8014

FORAUER, ROBERT RICHARD, educator; b. New Britain, Conn., May 14, 1946; s. Joseph Philip and Marion Margaret (Zotter) F.; m. Linda Ann Pelletier, Feb. 17, 1973; children: Jason Alan, Melissa Lynn. BS, Cen. Conn. State Coll., 1968; MA, Castleton State Coll., 1975. Tchr. Meriden Sch. Dist., Meriden, Conn., 1968-72; tchr. Wallingford Sch. Dist., Wallingford, Vt., 1972—; machinist Bryant Grinder Corp., Springfield, Vt., 1980-81. Mem. NEA, ALA, ASCD, Wallingford Tchrs.' Assn. (pres. 1981-92), Jaycees (historian Berlin, Conn. chpt. 1968-72), Vt. Fish and Game (hunter safety instr. 1976—). Home: PO Box 45 Tarbell Hill Rd Cavendish VT 05142 Office: Wallingford Elem Sch PO Box 309 School St Wallingford VT 05773

FORBES, DAVID LOWRY, management consulting firm executive, psychologist; b. Santa Monica, Calif., Mar. 2, 1950; s. David Lowry Sr. and Alma Lucille (Schuchardt) F.; m. Virginia Sherwood, May 24, 1980; children: Emma Elizabeth, Duncan August. BA, U. Calif., Riverside, 1971; MEd, Harvard U., 1973; MA, Clark U., Worcester, Mass., 1976, PhD, 1980. Lic. clin. psychologist, Mass. Clin. fellow Harvard Med. Sch., Cambridge, Mass., 1978-79; rsch. assoc. faculty Harvard Grad. Sch. of Edn., Cambridge, 1979-86; clin. cons. Judge Baker Guidance Ctr., Boston, 1979-84; rsch. cons. Kennan Rsch. and Cons., N.Y.C., 1980-84; pres., founder The Forbes Cons. Group, Newton, Mass., 1985—; cons. Bank St. Sch., N.Y., 1983-84; exec., bd. trustees Ctr. for Applied Linguistics, Washington, 1990—. Author, editor: Children's Social Reasoning, 1983. Cons. Com. to Elect Mel King, Cambridge, 1989; sponsor Boston Mus. of Sci., Cambridge, 1989-91, Boston Ballet, 1988-91. Rsch. grantee NSF, 1979, NIMH, 1981. Mem. APA, Am. Mktg. Rsch. Assn. Office: The Forbes Cons Group 432 Cherry St Newton MA 02165-2016

FORBES, IAN SCOTT, marketing executive; b. Homestead, Pa., June 21, 1930; s. John Couts and Elsie May (Maust) F.; m. Carol Kay Fasnacht, Feb. 4, 1956; children: Mary Carol Forbes Hitchell, Robert Scott, Andrew James, John Myron. BS in Econs., Thiel Coll., Greenville, Pa., 1956. Sales rep. Zimmer Mfg. Co., Buffalo, 1956-57; reporter New Castle (Pa.) News, 1957-58; reporter/county editor The Record-Argus, Greenville, Pa., 1958-62; reporter The Vindicator, Youngstown, Ohio, 1962-64, Steel Valley News, Youngstown, Ohio, 1964-65; news writer WBBW Radio, Youngstown, Ohio, 1964-65, Beacon Jour., Akron, Ohio, 1965-66; city editor The Record-Argus, Greenville, Pa., 1966-70; asst. dir. to pub. rels., dir. media svcs. Thiel Coll., Greenville, Pa., 1970-91, dir. communications, 1991—. Tech. coord. book: The History of Thiel Coll. 1866-1974, 1974, Heritage of Strength, 1991; writer/photographer coll. pubs.; contbr. articles to profl. pubs. Mktg. action team mem. Midwestern IU IV, Grove City, Pa., 1990-91; publicity com. Greenville Sesquicentennial, 1988; mem. Greenville Area Sch. Bd., 1975—, v.p., 1981-89; mem. Midwestern Intermediate Unit IV, 1984—, v.p., 1991—; chmn. Greenville Shade Tree Commn., 1970—; mem. Pa. Sch. Bds. Assn., Greenville Symphony Orch. Bd., 1966-69. Named Man of the Yr. award, Phi Theta Phi, 1983, Gilbert Love award, 1988; recipient Service award Soc. for Collegiate Journalism, 1986. Mem. Coll. and Univ. Pub. Rels. Assn. Pa., Soc. for Collegiate Journalism, Alpha Psi Omega. Republican. Presbyterian. Office: Thiel Coll 75 College Ave Greenville PA 16125-2186

FORBES, JOHN FRANCIS, federal government executive; b. Ossining, N.Y., Aug. 19, 1946; s. Frank Joseph and Sara A. (Howell) F. BA, Marist Coll., 1968; MBPA, Southeastern U., Washington, 1981; MA, Boston U., 1986. Spl. agt. U.S. Customs Svc., Rouses Point, N.Y., 1972-73; spl. agt. enforcement U.S. Customs Svc., Buffalo, 1974-78; sr. spl. agt. U.S. Customs Svc., Reston, Va., 1978-82; customs rep. U.S. Customs Svc., Bonn, Fed. Republic Germany, 1982-87; program mgr. U.S. Customs Svc., Washington, 1987-88, chief gen. smuggling sect., 1988, chief gen. smuggling br. fin. investigations divsn., 1988-91, investigator senate permanant subcom. on investigations, fin. investigation div., 1992—; spl. agt. Drug Enforcement Agy., Rouses Point, 1973-74; investigator Senate Permanent Subcom. on Investigations. Contbr. articles to profl. mag. Mem. Nat. Trust for Hist. Preservation, Washington, Friends of Kennedy Ctr., Washington. 1st lt. U.S. Army, 1968-71, Vietnam. Mem. Internat. Police Assn., Fraternal Order of Police, World Affairs Coun. Washington, Fed. Law Enforcement Officers Assn., Wilson Ctr. Assocs., Lincoln Soc., Cousteau Soc., World Future Soc., The Acad. of Polit. Sci., ASPA, Fed. Planning Network. Roman Catholic. Office: US Customs Svc 1301 Constitution Ave NW Washington DC 20229-9999

FORBES, MALCOLM STEVENSON, JR., publisher; b. Morristown, N.J., July 18, 1947; s. Malcolm and Roberta (Laidlaw) F.; m. Sabina Beekman, June 19, 1971. BA, Princeton U., 1970; LHD, Lycoming Coll., Jacksonville U.; LLD (hon.), Lock Haven U.; LittD, Heidelberg Coll. With Forbes Inc., N.Y.C., 1970—, pres., chief oper. officer, 1980-90, dep. editor in chief, 1982-90, editor in chief, chief exec. officer, 1990—; mem. adv. council econs. dept. Princeton U., 1985—; bd. dirs. Princeton U. Investment Co., 1987—; chmn. Forbes Newspapers, 1989—. Author: (filmscript) Some Call It Greed, 1977; editor: Fact and Comment, 1974. Pres. Somerset County Park Commn., N.J., 1981-91; mem. Bd. for Internat. Broadcasting, 1983—, chmn., 1985—; trustee Brooks Sch., North Andover, Mass., 1978—, pres. bd. trustees, 1987—; trustee Found. Student Communication, Ronald Reagan Presdl. Found.; bd. overseers Meml. Sloan-Kettering Cancer Ctr. Republican. Office: Forbes Inc 60 5th Ave New York NY 10011-8865

FORBES, PETER, architect; b. Berkeley, Calif., May 22, 1942; s. John Douglas and Margaret (Funkhouser) F.; m. Patricia Ann Marsh, Aug. 27, 1966 (div. 1982); children: Alexander John, Anne deMarken; m. Erica Longfellow deBerry, July 21, 1990. BArch, U. Mich., 1966; MArch, Yale U., 1967; Dr. Engring. Tech. (hon.), Wentworth Inst. Tech., 1991. Registered architect, Mass., Va., Calif., Maine, R.I., N.Y., Mich., Conn., D.C.; cert. Nat. Council Archtl. Registration Bds. Project designer Skidmore, Owings & Merrill, Chgo., 1965-66; assoc. ptnr. PARD Team, Inc., Boston, 1967-71; pres. Forbes Hailey Jeas Erneman, Inc., Boston, 1972-80, Peter Forbes and Assoc., Inc., Boston, 1980—; mem. Commonwealth of Mass. Designer Selection Bd., 1986-89, spl. commn. concerning state and county bldgs., 1978-81; bd. dir. continuing edn. Boston Archtl. Ctr., vis. critic U. Mich., 1980-82, Cath. U. Am., Rome, 1982; lectr., vis. critic Va. Poly. Inst. and State U., 1980-82, Columbia U., 1985; Thomas S. Mongaghan Disting. vis. prof., U. Mich., 1987; vis. prof. Harvard U., 1989, 91. Exhbns. include Cath. U. Am., 1982, U. Mich., 1982, 87, Va. Poly Inst. and State U., 1983, Boston Athenaeum, 1986, Harvard U., 1986; contbr. articles to profl. jours. Recipient Record House award, 1983, 86, 87, 89, New Eng. Design award, 1986, 87, 89, 91, Archtl. Excellence award Am. Inst. Steel Constrn., 1987, Tucker award Bldg. Stone Inst., 1987, 90, Honor award Am. Wood Inst., 1989, Nat. Housing Design award, 1990. Fellow AIA (nat. jud. coun. 1987—, Nat. Honor award 1986, New Eng. regional coun./design award, 1986, 87, 89, 91); mem. Mass. State Assn. Architects (pres. 1983-84), Boston Soc. Architects (bd. dirs. commr. pub. affairs, chmn. ethics com., v.p., pres. 1988-89, Excellence in Architecture award 1988, 89, 91, 92), Soc. Archtl. Historians (life), Century Club, Newport Reading Rm., Racquet and Tennis Club, Nat. Tennis Club, Yale Club, Boston Athenaeum. Home: Greenings Island Southwest Harbor ME 04679 Office: Peter Forbes and Assocs 241 A St Boston MA 02210-1302

FORBES, PETER WILLIAM, environmental project manager; b. Caribou, Maine, Dec. 1, 1955; s. William H. and Warrena D. (Bugbee) F.; m. Susan Elaine Brown, Jan. 2, 1953; children: Lucas P., Alexander B., Rosalyn C. BA, Bowdoin Coll., Brunswick, Maine, 1978; BSME, Columbia U., 1979; MSME, Ga. Inst. Tech., 1981. Project engr. Carrier Corp., Syracuse, N.Y., 1981-85; project mgr. Serve, Peshawar, Pakistan, 1986-89; v.p. engring. Regent Assocs., Presque Isle, Maine, 1989-90; owner, pres. Forbes Engring. Svcs., Presque Isle, Maine, 1990-91; IRP remedial project mgr. USAF, Loring AFB, Maine, 1991—; solar cons. Maine Rsch. & Productivity Ctr., Presque Isle, 1991. Sec. United Ostomy Assn., Presque Isle, 1990—; deacon Trinity Bapt. Ch., Camillus, N.Y.,1 983-85. Ga. Inst. Tech. Pres.'s scholar, 1980. Mem. Tau Beta Pi, Pi Tau Sigma. Advent Christian. Home: 32 Barton St Presque Isle ME 04769-2607 Office: USAF 42 CES/DEVP PO Box 1294 Loring AFB ME 04751-5000

FORBES, WILLIAM, II, information company executive; b. Columbus, Ga., Nov. 11, 1924; s. Albert Marion and Frances Bell (Weaver) F.; m. Mary Jane Colton, Nov. 6, 1976. Grad., U.S. Army Command and Gen. Staff Coll., Ft. Leavenworth, Kans., 1961; BS, U. Md., 1965; MS, George Washington U., 1969. Commd. 2d lt. U.S. Army, 1943, advanced through grades to lt. col., 1963; mem. Army Gen. Staff, Washington, 1961-63; mem. staff to Sec. of Def. Dept. Defense, Washington, 1963-66; ret. U.S. Army, 1966; program dir. Computer Scis. Corp., Washington, 1966-73; dir. ctr. SYSCON Corp., Washington, 1973-79; v.p. ops. J.J. Davis Assocs., Inc., Washington, 1979-80; mktg. researcher CACI, Inc., Washington, 1980-85; pres. Forbes Info. Services, Chevy Chase, Md., 1985—. Author: Forbes Ancestry, 1984, Hauling Brass, 1986; contbr. articles to hist. jours. Decorated Bronze Star; named Scottish Nobleman, 1988. Mem. St. Andrew's Soc. Washington (pres. 1988), Clan Forbes Soc. (v.p. 1979—, bd. dirs. 1986), Soc. Colonial Wars (bd. dirs. 1987), Nat. Hugenot Soc., Son of Confederate Vets., Soc.

War of 1812 (v.p. 1990). Home and Office: 4108 Blackthorn St Chevy Chase MD 20815-5054

FORCE, HERMAN EDGAR, psychologist; b. Passaic, N.J.. BA in Psychology, Fairleigh Dickinson U., 1956, MA in Sch. Psychology, 1962. Cert. psychologist, N.J., N.Y.; cert. tchr., N.J.; cert. sch. social worker, N.J.; cert. paralegal. Correction officer East Jersey State Prison, Rahway, N.J., 1947-54; probation officer Bergen County Probation Dept., Hackensack, N.J., 1956-63, prin. probation officer II Juvenile div., 1963-72, prin. probation officer I Family unit, 1972-79; sch. pscychologist Bd. Edn., Lodi, N.J., 1981-83; pvt. practice Lodi, N.J., 1984—. Trustee Bergen County probation officers chpt. local 1970 AFL-CIO, 1972-74; comdr. Passaic City post # 504 VFW, 1972-74; publicity chmn. Passaic Vets. Alliance, Inc. Maj. U.S. Army and Res., 1941-69, WWII, Korea, Vietnam. Deocrated Bronze Star with valor award and oak leaf cluster. Mem. APA, Nat. Assn. Sch. Psychologists. Home: 35 Pasadena Ave Apt D Lodi NJ 07644-3330

FORCE, ROLAND WYNFIELD, anthropologist, museum executive; b. Omaha, Dec. 30, 1924; s. Richard Erwin and Edna Fern (Collins) F.; m. Maryanne Tefft, Sept. 16, 1949. B.A., Stanford U., 1950, M.A. in Edn., 1951, M.A. in Anthropology, 1952, Ph.D. in Anthropology, 1958; D.Sci. (hon.), Hawaii Loa Coll., 1973. Acting instr. Stanford U., 1954; assoc. in ethnology Bernice P. Bishop Mus., Honolulu, 1954-56, dir., 1962-76, dir. emeritus, 1976—, holder C.R. Bishop Disting. chair in Pacific studies, 1976-77; dir. Mus. Am. Indian, Heye Found., N.Y.C., 1977-86, pres., dir., 1986-90, pres., dir. emeritus, 1990—; curator oceanic archeology, ethnology Field Mus. of Natural History, Chgo., 1956-61. Served with C.E. AUS, 1943-46. Fellow Am. Anthrop. Assn., AAAS, Pacific Sci. Assn. (hon. life, mem. council 1966-77); mem. Sigma Xi. Home: 161 Kalaiopua Pl Honolulu HI 96822-5005

FORD, BYRON MILTON, computer consultant; b. Hayden, Colo., Feb. 24, 1939; s. William Howard and Myrtle Oretta (Chistian) F.; B.S., U. Colo., 1964; M.S. in Mgmt. Sci., Johns Hopkins U., 1971; m. Shirley Ann Edwards, Sept. 4, 1958; children—Gregory Scott, Barry Matthew. Sr. mathematician Applied Physics Lab., Johns Hopkins U., Laurel, Md., 1964-79; computer cons., Laurel, 1979—. Mem. Ops. Research Soc. Am., Nat. Assn. Self-Employed. Address: 6909 Redmiles Rd Laurel MD 20707

FORD, DANIEL (FRANCIS), author; b. Arlington, Mass., Nov. 2, 1931; s. Patrick Joseph and Anne Theresa (Crowley) F.; B.A., U. N.H., 1954; Fulbright fellow, U. Manchester (Eng.), 1954-55; m. Sarah Lansing Paine, July 28, 1967; 1 child, Katharine Serena. Reporter, Overseas Weekly, Frankfurt, Germany, 1958; asst. editor N.H. Profiles mag., Portsmouth, 1959-60; publs. editor U. N.H., 1961-68; corr. The Nation, South Vietnam, 1964; contbg. editor Skiing mag., 1973-89. Stern Found. Mag. Writers grantee, 1964; Verville fellow Nat. Air & Space Mus., 1989-90. With AUS, 1956-57. Mem. Phi Beta Kappa, Phi Kappa Phi. Author: Now Comes Theodora, 1965, Incident at Muc Wa (filmed as Go Tell the Spartans), 1967, The High Country Illuminator, 1971, The Country Northward, 1976, Flying Tigers: Claire Chennault and the American Volunteer Group, 1991. Office: 433 Bay Rd Durham NH 03824-3407

FORD, DONALD HERBERT, psychologist, educator; b. Sioux City, Iowa, Aug. 15, 1926; s. Herbert Owen and Esther (Sanow) F.; m. Carol Clark, May 30, 1948; children—Russell, Martin, Douglas, Cameron. B.S., Kans. State U., 1948; M.S., 1951; Ph.D., Pa. State U., 1955. Counselor Kans. State U., 1948-52; asst. prof. psychology Pa. State U., University Park, 1955-64, assoc. prof., 1964-67, assoc. prof. human devel., 1967-72, prof. human. devel., 1972—; asst. dir. div. counseling, 1956-59, dir., 1959-67; dean Coll. Human Devel., 1967-77, head dept. Communications Disorders, 1988-89, head biobehavioral health, 1992. Author: Systems of Psychotherapy; A Comparative Study, 1963, Humans as Self-Constructing Living Systems, 1987, Developmental Systems Theory, 1992. Served with USAAF, 1944-45. Mem. AAAS, Am. Psychol. Assn., Am. Psychol. Soc., Ea. Psychol. Assn. Home: 130 Slab Cabin Rd State College PA 16801-6971 Office: Pa State U Coll Health and Human Devel University Park PA 16802

FORD, (ARTHUR) DOUGLAS, swimming pool and spa company executive; b. Ft. Meade, Mo., Nov. 4, 1928; s. Miles Ernest Ford and Margaret Anna (Heiner) Ford Gelie; m. Dorothy Jane Spenser, Jan. 16, 1950 (div. 1978); children: Douglas Randall, Janet Mae, Bryan Spencer, Jeffrey Charles, Todd Owen; m. Tomoko Shimizo, Jan. 11, 1980. Grad. high sch., Westminster, Mo. Surveyor Md. Hwy. Adminstrn., Balt., 1949-51; estimator, product mgr. Allied Contractors, Inc., Balt., 1951-53; projects mgr., estimator Ruth Engring. Co., Balt., 1953-58; owner, pres. Exso Constrn. Co., Inc., Balt., 1958-84, Freestate Pools, Inc., Balt., 1963-66, Freestate Sales, Inc., Fallston, Md., 1980—. Chmn. bd. dirs. YMCA of Balt., 1960-76. Mem. Nat. Spa and Pool Inst. Office: Freestate Sales Inc 2105 Bel Air Rd Fallston MD 21047

FORD, JOHN CHARLES, communications executive; b. Washington, Oct. 8, 1942; s. Edgar Martin and Mary (Crowley) F. BA, U. Md., 1964, postgrad., 1964-65, NYU, 1966; postgrad. N.Y. Inst. Finance, 1967-68, New Sch. for Social Research, 1969, Crowell-Collier Inst., 1969, Friesen-Kaye Inst., 1971, Sterling Inst., 1975, U. Wis., 1977, Colgate-Darden Sch. Bus., U. Va., 1978, Harvard U., 1982. TV prodn. asst. USIA, Washington, 1963-65; instr. U. Md., 1965; acct. exec. Ruder & Finn Inc., N.Y.C., 1965-66; asst. to exec. v.p., mgr. ednl. services Am. Stock Exchange, N.Y.C., 1966-70; mgr. communications and audio visual tng. Merrill Lynch, Pierce, Fenner & Smith Inc., N.Y.C., 1970-74; dir. edn. and tng. CBS Inc., 1974-77, dir. employee devel. and edn., 1977-79; pres. Travel U., v.p. Travel Network Corp. subs. ABC, N.Y.C., 1979-81; dir. human resources Home Box Office, Inc., 1981-84; communications cons., pres. John C. Ford Assocs., 1984—; mem. faculty N.Y. Inst. Fin., 1971-73, Katherine Gibbs Sch., 1972-74. Bd. dirs., treas. Archeus Found.; trustee U. Md. Found., 1984—; mem. chancellors adv. coun. system U. Md., 1989—; mem. U. Md. Pres.'s Club, bd. dirs., 1984—; chmn. Carnegie Hall concert U. Md. Piano Festival; bd. overseers Emerson Coll., Boston, 1978—; mem. bd. advisors cable and corp. communications program Manhattan Community Coll., CUNY; mem. devel. council Neumann Coll., Aston, Pa.; bd. dirs., v.p. 15 W 81st St. Tenants Corp., 1978-80, pres., 1979-81; mem. Council of West Side Coops., 20th Precinct Community Council, N.Y. Police Dept.; guest speaker Iowa Assn. for Life Long Learning; established John Charles Ford Professorship and Scholarship in Dramatic Arts U. Md., 1990. Mem. Nat. Acad. TV Arts and Scis. (bd. govs., trustee 1969—, sec. 1971—, trustee 1973—), Am. Soc. Tng. and Devel. (award 1978), Fin. Industry Tng. Assn. (pres. 1969-71), AAUP, Speech Communications Assn., Eastern Communication Assn. (area chmn. 1975), N.Y. State Communication Assn. (speaker), West 70th St. Assn., Fedn. West Side Block Assns., W. 82d St. Block Assn., Internat. Radio & TV Soc., Nat. Soc. Programmed Instrn., Nat. Audio-Visual Assn., Wall Street Tng. Dirs.'s Assn., Presidents Assn. of Am. Mgmt. Assns. (seminar leader), U. Md. Alumni Assn. Greater N.Y. (dir. 1966—), N.Y. Personnel Mgrs. Assns., Organizational Devel. Network, Group for Strategic Organizational Effectiveness, N.Y. Human Resource Planners, Internat. Platform Assn., Omicron Delta Kappa, Phi Delta Theta. Home and Office: 15 W 81st St New York NY 10024-6022

FORD, JOHN THOMAS, theology educator; b. Dallas, Nov. 21, 1932; s. Thomas E. and Lenora Ann (Senn) F. AB, U. Notre Dame, 1955; MA, Holy Cross Coll., 1959; STL, Gregorian U., 1960, STD, 1962. Lectr. U. Notre Dame, Ind., 1962; prof. Holy Cross Coll., Washington, 1962-68; from asst. to assoc. prof. Cath. U. Am., 1968—; cons. United Meth. Roman Cath. Dialogue, 1971-75, Consultation on Ch. Union, 1974-88, Reformed Roman Cath. Internat. Consultation, 1987-88; mem. Faith and Order Commn., Nat. Coun. of Chs., 1981—. Mem. AAUP, N. Am. Acad. Ecumenists (pres. 1974-76), Cath. Theol. Soc. Am., Cath. Hist. Assn., Am. Acad. Religion. Office: Cath U Am PO Box 236 Washington DC 20064-0001

FORD, LAWRENCE HOWARD, physicist, educator; b. Logan, Utah, Feb. 14, 1948; s. Glenn E. and Poppy F. Ford; m. Victoria Marguerite Potter, Aug. 30, 1991. BS, Mich. State U., 1970; PhD, Princeton U., 1974. Rsch. assoc. U. Wis., Milw., 1974-77, Kings Coll., London, 1977-79; asst. prof. Tufts U., Medford, Mass., 1980-85, assoc. prof., 1985—; vis. asst. prof. U. N.C., Chapel Hill, 1979-80. Contbr. articles to profl. jours. Woodrow Wilson fellow, 1969, NSF predoctoral fellow, Princeton U., 1970-73, Charlotte Elizabeth predoctoral fellow Princeton U., 1973; NSF rsch. grantee, Tufts U., 1981—. Mem. AAUP, Am. Phys. Soc., Internat. Soc. Gen. Relativity and Gravitation, N.Y. Acad. Scis. Office: Tufts U Dept Physics & Astronomy Medford MA 02155

FORD, MICHAEL ALTON, sales executive; b. Alexandria, Va., Oct. 28, 1963; s. Alton Forrestor and Katherine (McGee) F. BS in BA, Old Dominion U., 1986. Sales rep. Cable & Wireless Communications, Norfolk, Va., 1986-87; nat. account exec. Motorola Communications, Hanover, Md., 1987-91; sr. account exec. Comm-Tronic Communications, Glen Burnie, Md., 1991—. Republican. Home: 14040 Chestnut Ct Laurel MD 20707 Office: Comm-Tronics 120 Roesler Rd Glen Burnie MD 21060

FORD, RICHARD BRICE, history educator, director; b. Youngstown, Ohio, Aug. 27, 1935; s. Robert Taylor and Katherine (McMillen) F.; m. Nancy Becker, Aug. 17, 1957; children: Andrew, Linda, Jonathan, Sarah, Daniel. BA in Econs., Denison U., 1957; MAT in History, Yale U., 1959; PhD in African History, U. Denver, 1966. Asst. prof. Carnegie-Mellon U., Pitts., 1964-68; from asst. to assoc. to prof. Clark U., Worcester, Mass., 1968—, dir. internat. devel. rsch., 1980—; regional coord. Evniron. Tng. in Africa, Nairobi, Kenya, 1981-82; advisor Ministry of Environment, Nairobi, 1987-88. Author: Tradition and Change in 4 Societies, 1968, 2d edit., 1974; co-author: People, Places and Change, 1975, Participatory Rural Appraisal Handbook, 1989. Board dirs. Oxfam-Am., Boston, 1976-84, Aid-to-Artisans, 1986—; chmn. Internat. Film Found., N.Y.C., 1975—. Ford Found. grantee World Resources Inst. Mem. AAUP (chpt. pres. 1982—), African Studies Assn. Home: 3901 Knightsbridge Close Worcester MA 01609-1162 Office: Clark U Worcester MA 01610

FORD, RICHARD THOMAS, personnel manager, consultant; b. Medford, Mass., Feb. 1, 1935; s. Vernon Xavier and Myrtle Gertrude (Naugler) F.; m. Carol Ruth Herskind, Oct. 25, 1958; children: Richard T. II, Steven Eric, Douglas Ronald. BS in Edn., Boston U., 1956; MS in Edn., So. Ill. U., 1964; MBA, Syracuse U., 1966. Commd. 2d lt. USAF, 1957, advanced through grades to col., retired, 1977; personnel mgr. Digital Equipment Corp., Maynard, Mass., 1977-81; personnel dir. Softech Inc., Waltham, Mass., 1981-90; pres. High-Tech Assocs., Waltham, 1990—. Author: Building a Successful Training Program In a Small Company, 1986. Member com. Troop 60 Boy Scouts Am., Sudbury, Mass., 1987-88; chmn. worship music com. Sudbury Meth. Ch., 1982-86; choir dir. Ch. of Redeemer, Bowie, Md., 1966-70. Mem. Am. Soc. Personnel Adminstrn., Beta Gamma Sigma. Republican. Methodist. Home: 270 Sunderland Rd Apt 99 Worcester MA 01604-2556 Office: High-Tech Assocs 4001 Totten Pond Rd Waltham MA 02154-2016

FORD, THOMAS HERBERT, mental health care administrator; b. Balt., May 6, 1953; s. William Webster and Frances (Jordan) F.; m. Tracey Lynn Henson, June 7, 1986; 1 child, Thomas Henson. BS, Towson State U., 1975; MA, Duquesne U., 1976; MBA, Loyola Coll., Balt., 1990. Clin. psychologist Balt. City Jail, 1976-78, Balt. City Hosp., 1978-84; coord. psychiat. emergency svcs. Francis Scott Key Med. Ctr., Balt., 1984-89; program dir. Sheppard & Enoch Pratt Hosp., Towson, Md., 1989—; pvt. practice psychotherapy Towson, 1987—. Chair budget com. Balt. County Mental Health Adv. Counsel, Towson, 1990-92; pres. Southwestern Community Mental Health Adv. Coun., Catonsville, Md., 1990-92. Mem. AACD, Am. Assn. Mental Health Counselors. Office: Sheppard Pratt Hosps Community Programs 10151 York Rd Ste 106 Cockeysville Hunt Valley MD 21030-3314

FORDYCE, JAMES CLARENCE, beverage products executive; b. Collingwood, N.J., Oct. 13, 1937; s. James Kennedy and Henrietta (Bunker) F.; m. Barbara Ann Faux, Nov. 20, 1971; children: Susan Lynne, Debra Ann. A, Temple U., 1971; degree, Dale Carnegie, 1988. Dairy mgr. A & P Tea Co., Haddonlt, N.J., 1955-63; sales engr. Fed. Pacific Electric, Phila., 1963-69; owner Joseph Lounge & Liquor, Inc., Gloucester, N.J., 1971—; pres. N.J. Lic. Beverage Assn., Edison, 1990—. Bd. dirs. Balck Horse C. of C., Runnemede, N.J., 1986-90 (Disting. Svc. award 1990), pres., founder Gloucester City C. of C., 1987-89 (recipient disting. svc. award 1990). Warrant officer U.S. Army, 1956-59. Recipient Disting. Svc. award Retarded Citizens, Camden County, 1989; Disting. Svc. award Camden County Tavern Owners, 1992. Mem. NRA, Beer Drinkers Am. (bd. dirs. 1991—), N.J. Lic. Beverage Assn. (pres. 1990-92), Camden County Lic. Beverage Assn. (pres.), Am. Legion. Roman Catholic. Office: Joseph Lounge & Liquor Inc 308 Orlando Ave Gloucester NJ 08030

FORDYCE, SAMUEL WESLEY, electrical engineer, communications company executive; b. Jackson, Miss., Feb. 28, 1927; s. Samuel Wesley and Polly Adams (White) F.; S.B., Harvard U., 1949; M.S., Washington U., St. Louis, 1953; m. Sally Gillespie, Apr. 9, 1970; children—Katherine Peake, Debbie Fordyce, Wesley, Polly. Project engr. Emerson Electric Co., St. Louis, 1949-58; mem. tech. staff Ramo Wooldridge, Los Angeles, 1958-60, Gen. Electric Tempo, Santa Barbara, Calif., 1960-62; chief engr. communications div. NASA, Washington, 1962-84; chief oper. officer Advanced Bus. Communications, Inc., McLean Va., 1986-88, cons. Cape York Space Agy., Brisbane, Australia, 1988—; pres. Riparian Research Corp., 1984—. Served with USN, 1944-46. Registered profl. engr., Mo. Assoc. fellow AIAA; sr. mem. IEEE. Clubs: St. Louis Country; Met. of Washington; Chevy Chase. Achievements include participation in design and development of radio communications systems used on Apollo (manned lunar landing) Program. Home: 6716 Selkirk Ct Bethesda MD 20817-4936

FOREMAN, JOHN DANIEL, financial executive; b. Wheeling, W.Va., Aug. 24, 1940; s. William Carroll and Mary Katheryn (Leese) F.; m. Helen Virginia Donato, Sept. 2, 1967; children: Sean, Christopher. BA, Wheeling (W.Va.) Coll., 1962; MA, W.Va. U., 1965. Banking officer Wheeling Dollar Bank, 1964-67; prof., dept. chair Seton Hill Coll., Greensburg, Pa., 1967-81; mem. faculty, adminstr. Westmoreland County Community Coll., Youngwood, Pa., 1971-81; dir. continuing edn. St. Vincent Coll., Latrobe, Pa., 1981-84, dean enrollment and planning, 1984-87; chief fin. officer The Eye and Ear Inst., Pitts., 1987—; pres. Aquillian Corp., Greensburg, Pa., 1981—. Contbr. articles to profl. jours. Treas. bd. dirs. Westmoreland Symphony Orch., Greensburg, 1989—; bd. dirs. SUC Small Bus. Devel. Ctr., Latrobe, 1983-90, Westmoreland Trust, 1992—. Mem. Pitts. Athletic Assn. Office: The Eye and Ear Inst 203 Lothrop St Pittsburgh PA 15213

FOREMAN, KENNETH MARTIN, aerospace engineer; b. N.Y.C., , July 30, 1925; s. Louis and Jennie (Gordon) F.; m. Shirley E. Teiger, June 24, 1954; children: Elissa, Michael. B.Aero.Engr., NYU, 1950, M.Aero.Engr., 1953; MS in Mgmt., Poly. U. Bklyn., 1981, Cert. Energy Policy & Engring., 1976. Rsch. engr. Bendix Aviation Corp., Teterboro, N.J., 1951-52; project engr. Wright Aero Div., Curtiss-Wright Corp., Wood Ridge, N.J., 1952-56; rsch. engr. Fairchild Engine div. Fairchild Corp., Deer Park, N.Y., 1956-59; sci. rsch. engr. Republic Aviation Corp., Farmingdale, N.Y., 1959-65; chief project engr. EDO Corp., College Point, N.Y., 1965-66; lab. head and sr. staff scientist Grumman Aerospace Corp., Bethpage, N.Y., 1966—; chmn. Guggenheim medal award bd., N.Y.C., 1975-76. Contbr. over 90 tech. papers, articles to profl. jours., chpts. to books. Exec. v.p. and historian Hist. Soc. of the Bellmores, 1987—. Fellow AIAA (assoc.; atmospheric environ. tech. com. 1974-76, L.I. sect. chair 1979-80; Basil Staros award 1981); mem. AAAS, ASME (aerospace div. chmn. 1972-73, energy rsch. needs com. 1973-79), Am. Hist. Soc., Tau Beta Pi. Jewish. Home: 32 Stratford Ct Bellmore NY 11710-2043

FOREMAN, THOMAS ALEXANDER, dentist; b. Tionesta, Pa., Oct. 24, 1930; s. James Aura and May (Lanson) F.; student Grove City Coll., 1948-50; BS, Allegheny Coll., 1952; DDS cum laude, U. Pitts., 1957, DMD, 1970; m. Dorothy Jean Wolf, June 12, 1953; children: Bonnie Jean, Julie Marie, Mary Aleta, Lloyd George. Gen. practice dentistry, Clarion, Pa., 1961—. Mem. Clarion Hosp. Assn., 1965—; mem. exec. bd. Colonel Drake Council Boy Scouts Am., 1969-72, mem.-at-large French Creek council, 1972-73, vice chmn. Indian Trails dist., 1971-73; mem. governing council Alpha Christian Acad. Sch., 1977-81. Served with Dental Corps, USAF, 1957-61. Fellow Pierre Fauchard Acad. Fellow Acad. Dentistry Internat., Am. Coll. Dentists, Internat. Coll. Dentists, Royal Soc. Health; mem. Am. Dental Assn., Pa. Dental Assn. (dir. 8th dist. 1964-87, 91—, pres. 1974-76, trustee 1987-91), Acad. Gen. Dentistry (mem. 1977, fellow 1984, master 1988), AMA (affiliate), Clarion County Dental Soc. (pres. 1983-87), S.A.R., (pres. Capt. Samuel Brady chpt. 1970-71, 77-80), Soc. Mayflower Descs., Pilgrim Edward Doty Soc., Fedn. Dentaire Internationale, Pa. Soc., Western Pa. Conservancy, Cook Forest Ctr. for Arts, Clarion County Hist. Soc., Phi Beta Phi, Omicron Kappa Upsilon, Delta Sigma Delta, Theta Chi. Presbyn. (pres. bd. trustees 1966-67, supt. Sunday sch. 1966-67, chmn. endowment trust fund dirs. 1980-84). Mason (Shriner). Home: 147 S 7th Ave Clarion PA 16214-2006 Office: 832 Main St Clarion PA 16214

FORESTER, ERICA SIMMS, decorative arts historian, consultant, educator; b. N.Y.C., Feb. 13, 1942; d. Leon Marcus and Selma (Rosen) Simms; m. Bruce Michael Forester, Dec. 21, 1962; children: Brent Peter, Robin Ann, Russell Charles. BA, Cornell U., 1963; MA, Columbia U., 1964; cert., N.Y. Sch. Interior Design, 1973; AAS in Interior Design, Parsons Sch. Design, 1982. Owner Erica Forester, Interiors, Bronxville, N.Y., 1973—; mem. faculty Parsons Sch. Design, N.Y.C., 1982—; cons. in field, 1980—; lectr. Hudson River Mus., 1984; guest curator Scarsdale Hist. Soc., 1987. Author (with others): At Home in Westchester; Style and Design 1836-1886. Mem. adv. bd. Am. Field Svc. Rye Country Day Sch., 1984-88; bd. advisors Scarsdale Hist. Soc. Mem. Allied Bd. Trade, Decorative Arts Trust, Assn. Ind. Historians of Art. Home and Office: 55 Northway Bronxville NY 10708

FORGACS, GABOR, physics educator, researcher; b. Budapest, Hungary, June 13, 1949; came to U.S., 1986.; s. Egon and Dora (Rosenbaum) F.; m. Marta Szoke, Apr. 22, 1972; children: Andrea, Andras. BS, MS, Eötvös Roland U., Budapest, 1973, PhD, 1978. Postdoctoral fellow Dept. Chemistry SUNY, Albany, 1978-79, Dept. Physics U. Ill., Urbana, 1979-81; staff researcher Cen. Rsch. Inst. Physics, Budapest, 1981-84; sr. staff scientist French Atomic Energy Agy., Saclay, France, 1984-86; assoc. prof. dept. physics Clarkson U., Potsdam, N.Y., 1986—; vis. prof. Brookhaven Nat. Lab., Upton, N.Y., 1986, U. Paris, Orsay, 1987; cons. French Atomic Energy Agy., Saclay, 1986—, Los Alamos (N.Mex.) Nat. Lab., 1991—. Author: Phase Transitions and Critical Phenomena, 1991. Mem. Am. Phys. Soc., European Phys. Soc., French Phys. Soc., Hungarian Phys. Soc. Office: Clarkson U Dept Physics Potsdam NY 13699

FORGER, ROBERT DURKIN, professional association administrator; b. Norwalk, Conn., May 24, 1928; s. Alois John and Elsie Marie (Durkin) F.; m. Eleanor Marie Goddard, May 14, 1951; children: Gary Robert, Jeffrey Alois. B.S., Norwich U., Northfield, Vt., 1949; grad., U.S. Army Command and Gen. Staff Coll., 1970. Research and devel. engr., mgr. tech. publicity Dorr-Oliver Inc., Stamford, Conn., 1949-59; conf. mgr., pub., exec. dir. Soc. Plastics Engrs., Brookfield, Conn., 1959—. Chmn. Westport (Conn.) Public Housing Authority, 1959-64; treas. Plastics Edn. Found., 1971-75; bd. dirs. Norwich U. Alumni Assn., 1981-86, pres., 1984-86; trustee Norwich U., 1987—, Nat. Plastics Mus., 1983—. Served to lt. col. USAR. Named Conn. Assn. Exec. of Yr., 1983. Mem. Am. Inst. Chem. Engrs., Soc. Plastics Engrs. (elected disting. mem. 1984), Am. Soc. Assn. Execs., Council Engring. and Sci. Soc. Execs. (dir. 1983-85, sec. 1985-86, v.p. 1986-87, pres. 1987-88), Chemists Club N.Y.C. Home: 42 Deforest Rd Wilton CT 06897-1909 Office: 14 Fairfield Dr Brookfield CT 06804-3997

FORM, FREDRIC ALLAN, accountant; b. Bklyn., Mar. 2, 1942; s. Milton and Tedde (Bilus) F.; m. Jo Ann August, Aug. 29, 1964; 1 child, Andrew. BBA, Pace U., 1970. Sr. acct. S.P. Cooper & Co., N.Y.C., 1963-69; pvt. practice pub. acctg., Levittown, N.Y., 1969—. Bd. dirs. Wantagh Community Arts Program, Inc., 1980-84; bd. dirs., treas. Cen. Nassau County React, Inc., 1979-82; treas. Your, Ours, Mine Community Ctr., Levittown, 1987-91; v.p. Reli React, Inc., 1983-91, treas., 1983—. Mem. Nat. Soc. Pub. Accts., N.Y. Soc. Ind. Accts. (2d v.p. 1983-85, v.p. 1985-86, pres. 1986-87, bd. dirs. Nassau-Suffolk chpt. 1986-92, pres. 1992—), Kiwanis (treas. Levittown club 1988-89). Office: 2950 Hempstead Tpke Levittown NY 11756-1398

FORMAN, EDGAR ROSS, mechanical engineer; b. Camden, N.J., Oct 5, 1923; s. Edgar Charles and Annie (Baragwanath) F.; BSME, Drexel Inst., 1950, MBA, 1953; m. Alma Kuppinger, Sept. 26, 1953; children: Bruce, Dianne. Project engr. Penn Instrument div. Burgess Manning Co., Phila., 1950-55; application engr. Moore Products Co., Phila., 1955-59; chief instrument engr. Catalytic Co., Phila., 1959-67, mgr. mgmt. systems dept., 1967-71; supervising instrument engr. United Engrs. & Constructors, Inc. Phila., 1971-78; mgr. instrument and controls dept. Day & Zimmermann, Inc., Phila., 1978-89; dir. Automation Tech., 1989—; guest lectr. U.S. Naval Acad., Sun Oil Co., U. Del. Active Boy Scouts Am.; mem. president's coun. Spring Garden Coll., 1979-83, chmn. indsl. adv. com., 1984-89; past pres. Erdenheim Civic Assn. Served with AUS, 1944-46. Fellow Instrument Soc. Am. (past chmn. edn. commn., v.p. Dist. 2 1982-84, chmn. food and pharm. div., 1986-87, nat. v.p. 1989—, Man of the Yr., 1987, Eckman award, Golden Achievement award 1989, Outstanding Svc. award 1990), mem. ASME (past chmn. dynamic systems and controls div.) NSPE (pres. 1982-83), Machine Vision Soc. (charter mem.); mem. AIEEE (Man of Yr. Delaware Valley Engrs. 1990), Alpha Phi Omega (pres.), Pi Tau Sigma, Pi Nu Epsilon. Contbr. articles in field to tech. jours. Home: 702 Avondale Rd Philadelphia PA 19118-1337 Office: Day & Zimmermann Inc 1818 Market St Philadelphia PA 19103-3717

FORMAN, KENNETH HOWARD, school superintendent; b. Bklyn., July 17, 1947; s. Louis and Ethel Forman; m. Susan Levy, May 16, 1981; children: Andrew, Brett. BA, Queens Coll., 1969; MA, Bklyn. Coll., 1972; PhD, NYU, 1988. With N.Y.C. Sch. Dist. 27, 1969-84; communications coord. Ozone Pk. (N.Y.) Sch. Dist. 27, 1977-79, dir. reimbursable programs, 1980-84; dir. curriculum and instruction N.Y.C. Sch. Dist. 2, 1984-87, exec. asst. supt., 1987-91; prin. Roosevelt Island Schs., 1991—. Mem. Assn. for Supervision and Curriculum Devel., Phi Delta Kappa. Democrat. Jewish.

FORMAN, PHYLLIS WACHS, speech communication educator; b. N.Y.C., Mar. 14, 1935; 1 child, Erik. BS, NYU, 1956, MA, 1958. Asst. prof. speech communication Mercy Coll., Dobbs Ferry, N.Y., 1982—. Mem. Speech Communication Assn., Actors Equity Assn.

FORMAN, RICHARD LOREN, association executive; b. Appleton, Wis., Nov. 26, 1943; s. Loren Verne and Miriam Baily (Richardson) F.; m. Cheri Lynn Herdman, Jan. 29, 1972 (div. Sept. 1980); children: Andrew Loren, Jay William; m. Sandra Stella Hubbard, June 19, 1986. BA, Cornell U., 1966; MEd, U. Houston, 1969. Vol. VISTA program Office Econ. Opportunity, Atlanta, 1966-67; instr. U.S. Tchr. Corps, Houston, 1967-69, South Kitsap High Sch., Port Orchard, Wash., 1970-72; dir. edn. Safety, Edn. Tng. Trust Fund, Newark, N.J., 1972-78; sales and office mgr. Herdman Real Estate Co., Port Orchard, 1978-80; asst. exec. dir. Associated Gen. Contracters of N.J., Cranbury, 1980-83, exec. dir., 1983—; advisor Constrn. Industry Advancement Fund, N.J., 1983—. Mem. N.J. Soc. Assn. Execs., Am. Soc. Assn. Execs., Soc. Econ. Environ. Devel. (bd. dirs. 1990—), Phila. and Vicinity Ironworker Funds (trustee 1988—), No. N.J. Teamster Funds (trustee 1988—), Pub.-Pvt. Ptnrship. Coun. N.J. (chmn. 1991—), Kappa Sigma. Presbyterian. Office: Associated Gen Contracters 101 Interchange Plz Cranbury NJ 08512-9581

FORMAN, STUART IRVING, healthcare executive; b. Boston, Nov. 20, 1947; s. Isaac and Jeanette (Levin) F.; m. Deborah Jean Tomchik, Jan. 6, 1973; children: Adam Michael, Seth Gabriel, Matthew Reuben. BS, U. Mass., 1968; MEd, Springfield Coll., 1971; PhD, Columbia Pacific U., San Rafael, Calif., 1979. Lic. psychologist Mass. Psychiat. social worker Northampton (Mass.) State Hosp., 1968; mental health cons. Lakes Region Mental Health Ctr., Laconia, N.H., 1969-70; dir. office intergroup rels. City of Springfield, 1971-74; asst. dir. for alcohol rehab. Rutland (Mass.) Hts. Hosp., 1975-76, dir. ctr. for alcohol and substance abuse disorders, 1976-86, dir. dept. social rehab., 1986-89; asst. prof. family and community medicine U. Mass. Med. Sch., Worcester, 1986—; owner, operator, psychologist Stuart I. Forman Assocs., Worcester, 1979-90; assoc. dir. human svcs. Hubbard Regional Hosp., 1989-90; chief exec. officer Greater New Bedford Community Health Ctr., 1991—. Contbr. articles to profl. jours. Vice pres. Worcester Pub. Inebriate Program, 1979; chmn. addictions com. Mass. Hosp. Assn., Burlington, 1980-86. With USAFR, 1965-67. Recipient Manual Carballo award Gov. of Mass., 1987. Mem. Am. Assn. Counseling and Devel., Am. Coll. Healthcare Execs., Am. Pub. Health Assn., Psi Chi.

Jewish. Office: Greater New Bedford Health 1204 Purchase St New Bedford MA 02740-6637

FORMICA, PETER FRANCIS, family physician, internist, psychiatrist; b. N.Y.C., Oct. 24, 1942; s. Philip and Carmela (Donato) F.; m. Elda Felicia Montanaro, Oct. 14, 1978; children: Philip, Peter, Marisa. BA, CUNY, 1964, MA, 1967; MD, U. Milan, 1974. Diplomate Am. Bd. Psychiatry and Neurology, Am. Bd. Family Practice. Intern Brookdale Hosp. and Med. Ctr., Bklyn., 1974-75, resident in Psychiatry, 1975-78; resident in family practice Downstate Med. Ctr., Bklyn., 1980-82; chief resident in psychiatry Brookdale Hosp. and Med. Ctr., Bklyn., 1977-78; fellow in psychosomatic medicine Downstate Med. Ctr, Bklyn., 1978-80, chief resident in family practice, 1981-82; pvt. practice medicine and psychiatry, Queens, 1982—; dir. psychiat. emergency room Woodhull Hosp. and Med. Ctr., Bklyn., 1985-87; med. dir. acute care South Beach Psychiat. Ctr., S.I., N.Y., 1987-88; chief psychiatrist Creedmore Psychiat. Ctr., Queens, N.Y., 1988—; founder, med. dir. Queens Counseling Ctr., Ridgewood, N.Y., 1989—. Author: The Immunology of Tumors, 1974. Fellow Am. Acad. Family Practice. Republican. Roman Catholic. Home: 200 Ridge Rd Flushing NY 11363-1309 Office: Queens Counseling Ctr 60-83 Myrtle Ave Ridgewood NY 11385

FORMICOLA, JOHN JOSEPH, artist; b. Phila., Dec. 27, 1941; s. Girardo Charles and Theresa A. (DeCarlo) F.; m. Loretta Fortuna, Nov. 2, 1963; 1 child, Gigliola Tina Maria. CFA, Pa. Acad. Fine Arts, 1962. Owner Gallery Pane i Vino, Phila., 1965-68; 1st dir. Marion Locks Gallery, Phila., 1968-73; drawing instr. Phila. (Pa.) Coll. of Art, 1973-74; instr. painting Community Coll. of Phila., Phila., 1973-75; color instr. Moore Coll., Phila., 1974-75; design instr. Rosemont Coll., Phila., 1976-86; drawing instr. Drexel Univ., Phila., 1969-87; instr. Cleve. (Ohio) Inst. of Art, 1979-80; owner, ptnr. Chew & Formicola Fine Art, Phila., 1983—; designer, cons. Danhart-Heim Architects, Phila., 1976; painting instr. Penna Acad. Fine Arts, 1981. Exhibited in pub. collections Phila. Mus. Art, Cleve. (Ohio) Mus. Art, Carnegie Inst. Mus. of Art, Pitts., Pa. Acad. of the Fine Arts, Miami (Fla.) Mus. of Modern Art, Noyes Mus., N.J. Recipient Cresson Traveling grant Pa. Acad. Fine Art, 1962, First J. Hallgartin prize Nat. Acad. Design, 1965, Award of merit Univ. Del., Brett Taylor award Cheltenham Annual, 1991. Home: 725 Carpenter St Philadelphia PA 19147-3933

FORMOSA, DANIEL JOHN, industrial designer, ergonomics consultant; b. Jersey City, July 16, 1953; s. Daniel Joseph and Claire (Ettore) F. B in Indsl. Design, Syracuse U., 1976; MA in Ergonomics and Biomechanics, NYU, 1986. Designer Eliot Noyes Assocs., New Canaan, Conn., 1976-77, Mauro Assocs., N.Y.C., 1977-80; founding ptnr. Smart Design Inc., N.Y.C., 1980-89; pvt. practice cons. Montvale, N.J., 1989—; design specialist U.S. Info. Agy., Moscow, 1989; lectr. NYU, N.Y.C., 1987—; juror Annual Designers' Choice awards Internat. Design mag., 1991; mem. Design for the Elderly Interdesign Team, Norway, 1989. Featured in TV program segment N.J. Network State of the Arts Program, 1990; contbr. articles to N.J. Bell Jour., Art Librs. Jour. N.J. State Coun. of Arts, fellow, 1990; recipient Designers' Choice award Internat. Design mag., 1990, 91, Design award Timex Corp., 1989. Mem. Indsl. Designers Soc. Am. (Kudos award 1990, lectr. N.Y. chpt. 1989, 90, editor N.Y. chpt. newsletter Design in the USSR 1990), Human Factors Soc. Office: 280 Chestnut Ridge Rd Montvale NJ 07645-1126

FORNARI, VICTOR MASLIAH, psychiatrist; b. N.Y.C., June 20; s. Ermanno and Alice (Notrica) F.; m. Alice Johnson, Mar. 27, 1977; children: Eric, Amy, Marci. BS in Biology, Cornell U., 1974; MS in Human Nutrition, Columbia U., 1975; MD, SUNY-Downstate Med. Ctr., Bklyn., 1979. Diplomate Am. Bd. Psychiatry and Neurology, Am. Bd. Child and Adolescent Psychiatry and Neurology. Intern L.I. Coll. Hosp., Bklyn., 1979-80; resident in psychiatry Hosp. U. Pa., Phila., 1980-82; fellow in child and adolescent psychiatry L.I. Jewish Med. Ctr., New Hyde Park, N.Y., 1982-84; staff child psychiatrist Schneider's Children's Hosp./L.I. Jewish Med. Ctr., New Hyde Park, 1984-85; physician-in-charge Child Psychiatry Inpatient Unit/L.I. Jewish Med. Ctr., New Hyde Park, 1985-86; physician-in-charge, child psychiatry cons. liaison svc., eating disorders program North Shore-Cornell U. Hosp., Manhasset, N.Y., 1986-91, dir. tng./clin. svcs. div. child and adolescent psychiatry, 1991—; assoc. prof. psychiatry, pediatrics, Cornell U. Med. Coll., N.Y.C., 1991—. Bd. dirs., Children's Living After Sch. Program., Great Neck, N.Y. Mem. Am. Psychiat. Assn., Am. Acad. Child and Adolescent Psychiatry, Nassau Psychiat. Assn. (bd. dirs.), Am. Assn. of Dirs. of Psychiat. Residency Tng.

FORNAROTTO, FELICIA AGNES, controller; b. Newark, Feb. 24, 1957; d. Nicholas A. and Nancy A. (Cicalese) F.; m. Harry V. Douglas Jr.; 1 child, Harry III. Student, Middlesex County Coll., 1975-77; BS, Rutgers U., 1980. CPA. Office mgr. N.J. Shade Tree Fedn., New Brunswick, 1980; mortgage acct. First Savs. and Loan Assn., New Brunswick, 1978-81; plant/affiliation acct. Robert Wood Johnson Med. Ctr., New Brunswick, 1981-83; sr. acct. Elizabeth (N.J.) Gen. Med. Ctr., 1983-86, asst. contr., 1986-87, dir. budget/reimbursement, 1987-88, contr., 1988—; mgr. unrestricted funds Rutgers U., Piscataway, N.J., 1988. Recipient Gold Key award Nat. Assn. Accts., 1975. Mem. AICPA, Healthcare Fin. Mgmt., N.J. Soc. CPAs. Office: Elizabeth Gen Med Ctr 925 E Jersey St Elizabeth NJ 07201-2789

FORNAY, ALFRED RICHARD, publishing executive, editor; b. Cin.; s. Alfred H. Sr. and Marguertie (Weatherford) F. AAS, SUNY, 1971. Asst. ethnic mktg. mgr. Clariol Inc., N.Y.C., 1971-72; assoc. beauty editor Essence Mag., N.Y.C., 1973-74; tng. dir. Fashion Fair Cosmetics, Chgo., 1975-76, nat. beauty dir., 1977; internat. beauty dir. Fashion Fair Cosmetics, 1980-83; creative dir. polished amber collection Revlon Inc., 1978-80; beauty editor Ebony mag., N.Y.C., 1978-83; editor EM: Ebony Man mag., N.Y.C., 1984-87; contbg. fashion and beauty editor Bus. Week Careers Mag., N.Y.C., 1988—; cons. Highbeam Bus. Systems, East Orange, N.J., 1987—, Beauty Fashion Mag, N.Y.C., 1989, Fashion Fair Cosmetics, Chgo., 1974—. Author: Fornay's Skin Care and Makeup Guide for Women of Color, 1989; fashion writer Bus. Week Career Mag. 1987. Bd. dirs. Boy's Choir of Harlem, N.Y.C., 1980-85, com. mem., 1986-88; mem. The Author's Guild, Inc. Mem. N.Y. Assn. of Black Journalists, Nat. Assn. of Black Journalists, Nat. Assn. of Mag. Editors, Author's Guild. Home: PO Box 1321 New York NY 10163

FORNES, TIM MICHAEL, student assistance program coordinator; b. Rochester, N.Y., Jan. 19, 1966. BA, Glassboro (N.J.) State U., 1988; postgrad., Temple U., 1990, Rutgers U., 1991—. Youth counselor Together, Inc., Glassboro, 1986-88; health educator, drug abuse coord. Family Planning Svcs., Bridgeton, N.J., 1988-90; student assistance coord. Bridgeton Pub. Schs., 1990—; drug and alcohol coord. Bridgeton Pub. Schs., 1990—; cons. Family Planning Svcs.Bridgeton, N.J., 1990—, Youth to Youth, Columbus, Ohio, 1990—. Contbr. articles to newspapers, 1989—. Exemplary award Office of Substance Abuse Prevention, Washington, 1990. Mem. Am. Assn. Counseling and Devel. Home: 81 Lincoln Dr Clementon NJ 08021-2853

FORNEY, G(EORGE) DAVID, JR., electronics company executive; b. N.Y.C., Mar. 6, 1940; s. George David Forney and Priscilla (Brush) Forney McDonnell; m. Harriett A. Bascom, June 9, 1962 (div. 1989); children—Mark Hamilton, Priscilla Jean, William McDonnell. B.S.E., Princeton U., 1961; M.Sc., MIT, 1963, Sc.D., 1965. Mem. tech. staff Codex Corp., Watertown, Mass., 1965-70; v.p. research Codex Corp., Newton, Mass., 1970-75; v.p. research and devel. Codex Corp., 1975-78; v.p. research Codex Corp., Mansfield, Mass., 1978-82, v.p., 1986-89; v.p., dir. tech. and planning Motorola Info. Systems Group, Mansfield, 1982-86; v.p. tech. staff Motorola, Inc., Mansfield, 1980—; vis. scientist Stanford U., Calif., 1971-72; adj. prof. MIT, Cambridge, 1980-82, mem. adv. coun., 1980—, vis. prof., 1991; vis. prof. Stanford U., 1990; mem. adv. coun. elec. engrs. dept. Princeton U., N.J., 1977—; mem. adv. coun. Columbia U., 1986—, Stanford U., 1990—. Author: Concatenated Codes, 1966. Contbr. articles to profl. jours. Patentee in field. Bd. dirs. Am. Field Service, N.Y.C., 1971-74; trustee Lehrman Inst., N.Y.C., 1973-80, Mt. Auburn Hosp., Cambridge, Mass., 1986—; overseer Shady Hill Sch., Cambridge, 1980-86. Fellow IEEE (editor jour. 1970-73, info. theory group award 1970, Browder J. Thompson prize paper award 1972, Centennial medal 1984, Donald G. Fink prize paper award 1990, Edison medal, 1992); mem. NAE, IEEE Info. Theory Soc. (pres. 1992). Home: 6 Coolidge Hill Rd Cambridge MA 02138-5510 Office: Motorola Codex 20 Cabot Blvd Mansfield MA 02048-1193

FORNOFF, FRANK, JR., chemistry educator, consultant; b. Mt. Carmel, Ill., Mar. 29, 1914; s. Frank and Ada (Arnold) F. A.B., U. Ill., 1936; M.S., Ohio State U., 1937, Ph.D., 1939. Asst. prof. Lehigh U., Bethlehem, Pa., 1942-44; chem. engr. Western Electric Co., N.Y.C., 1944-45; asst. prof. chemistry Lehigh U., 1945-47, assoc. prof., 1947-53; assoc. prof. Kans. State U., Manhattan, 1953-56; lectr. Rutgers U., New Brunswick, N.J., 1956-84; sr. examiner Ednl. Testing Svc., Princeton, N.J., 1956—, group head, 1956-83. Editor AP Chemistry newsletter, 1976-90; contbr. articles to profl. jours. Active Boy Scouts Am., Princeton, 1957—. NRC fellow U. Calif., Berkeley, 1939-40; Proctor and Gamble fellow Ohio State U., 1939. Mem. AAAS, Am. Chem. Soc. (chmn. local sect. assn. publs. 1960-70), Am. Soc. Engring. Edn., Nat. Sci. Tchrs. Assn., Nat. Council Measurements in Edn., N.J. Acad. Sci., N.Y. Acad. Sci. Methodist. Home: 338 Franklin Ave Princeton NJ 08540-3929 Office: Ednl Testing Svc Princeton NJ 08541

FORREST, DAVID VICKERS, psychiatrist, educator; b. N.Y.C., July 8, 1938; s. Melbourne Arthur and Cleo Florence (Garello); m. Lynne Putnam Stetson; children: Daniel Stetson, Susannah Nissly. AB summa cum laude, Princeton U., 1960; MD, Columbia U., 1964, cert. in psychoanalysis, 1974. Cert. in psychiatry Am. Bd. Psychiatry and Neurology. Intern in medicine St. Luke's Hosp., N.Y.C., 1964-65; resident psychiatry N.Y. State Psychiat. Inst., Columbia Presbyn. Med. Ctr., N.Y.C., 1965-68; chief psychiatric clinic 935th Med. Det. (KO) 93d Evacuation Hosp., Long Binh, Vietnam, 1968-69; chief psychiatric consultation Letterman Army Med. Ctr., San Francisco, 1969-70; pvt. practice psychiatry N.Y.C., 1970—; mem. psychiatry faculty Columbia U., N.Y.C., 1970—; dir. edn. ednl. rsch. dept. N.Y. State Psychiat. Inst., 1970-77; assoc. prof. clin. psychiatry Columbia U., Coll. Physicians and Surgeons, N.Y.C., 1984—; faculty psychoanalytic ctr. Columbia U., Coll. Physicians and Surgeons, 1974—, liaison psychiatrist neurology, 1977—; lectr. psychiatry U. Saigon Med. Sch., Vietnam, 1968-69; lectr. abnormal psychology Far East div. U. Md., Long Binh, Vietnam, 1969. Author: Selected American Expressions, 1974, 76, 82; co-author: Treating Schizophrenic Patients, 1983, (video cassette series) Electronic Textbook of Psychiatry, 1972-77; editor, pub. Spring: The Jour. of the E. E. Cummings Soc., N.Y.C., 1980—; editor: Neural Net News, N.Y. State Psychiat. Inst., 1989—; contbr. articles to profl. jours., textbooks. Psychiat. cons. N.Y.C. Ballet Co., 1973; first aid instr. Boy Scouts Am., 1983—; NASA Outreach participant, 1991. Capt. USAF, 1968-70, Vietnam. Decorated Bronze Star; Gen. Motors nat. scholar. Fellow Am. Psychiat. Assn., Am. Coll. Psychiatrists, Am. Acad. Psychoanalysis (program chair), Am. Coll. Psychoanalysts (program chair 1987-89, bd. regents 1989—), Explorers Club; mem. Am. Acad. Neurology (assoc.), N.Y. Clin. Soc., Med. Strollers. Episcopalian. Office: 88 Central Pk W Ste 1W New York NY 10023-5209

FORREST, DOUGLAS WILLIAM, banker; b. Hackensack, N.J., Feb. 16, 1945; s. Harvey Sinclair and Marjorie Elizabeth (Stagg) F.; m. Marie M. Rakowsky, Oct. 1, 1967 (div. Oct. 1984); children: Chad Douglas, Kimberly Marie; m. Janet Valerie Dearborn, May 27, 1989. BS, Ithaca Coll., 1967. Capt. Eastern Airlines Inc., Boston, 1972-91; mgmt. Fleet Bank, Nashua, N.H., 1991—. Coach, hockey, baseball Recreation Dept., Exeter, N.H., 1978-83; mem. Sounding Bd., Exeter, 1979; mem. Congl. Ch., 1973—, diaconate chmn., 1982. Capt. USAF, 1967-72. Mem. Airline Pilots Assn. (Hat in the Ring 1986), Ea. Pilots Assn. Republican. Home: 9 Little Pine Ln Exeter NH 03833-3109 Office: Fleet Bank 1 Indian Head Plz Nashua NH 03060-3467

FORREST, HERBERT EMERSON, lawyer; b. N.Y.C., Sept. 20, 1923; s. Jacob K. and Rose (Fried) F.; m. Marilyn Lefsky, Jan. 12, 1952; children: Glenn Clifford, Andrew Matthew. B.A. with distinction, George Washington U., 1948; J.D. with highest honors, 1952; student, CCNY, 1941, Ohio U., 1943-44. Bar: Va. 1952, D.C. 1952, U.S. Supreme Ct. 1956, Md. 1959. Plate printer Bur. Engraving and Printing, Washington, 1942-43, 1946-52; law clk. to chief judge Bolitha J. Laws U.S. Dist. Ct., Washington, 1952-55; practice in Washington, 1952—; mem. firm Welch & Morgan, 1955-65; mem. firm Steptoe & Johnson, 1965-85, of counsel, 1986-87; trial atty. Fed. Programs Br. Civil div. U.S. Dept. Justice, Washington, 1987—; chmn. adv. bd. D.C. Criminal Justice Act, 1971-74; sec. com. admissions and grievances U.S. Ct. Appeals, D.C., 1973-79; mem. Title-1 audit hearing bd. U.S. Office Edn. HEW, 1976-79; mem. edn. appeals bd. U.S. Dept. Edn., 1979-82; mem. Lawyer's Support Com. for Visitors Service Center, 1975-87. Contbr. articles to legal jours.; advisory bd.: Duke Law Jour, 1969-75. Pres. Whittier Woods PTA, 1970-71. Served with F.A., Signal Corps U.S. Army, 1943-46. Recipient Walsh award in Irish history, 1952, Goddard award in commerce, 1952. Fellow Am. Bar Found.; mem. George Washington Law Assn., Am. Judicature Soc., ABA (council 1972-75, 1981-84, budget officer 1985-86, vice chmn. task force on sect. devel. 1987-89, chmn. com. on agy. rule making 1968-72, 1976-81, chmn. membership com. 1984-85, editor ann. reports 1973-88, adminstrv. law sect., mem. communications com. public utilities law sect., vice chmn. industry regulation com. 1985-86, chmn. communications subcom. 1983-85, antitrust law sect., internat. law sect., sec. judicial adminstrn., sect. sci. and tech., communications forum), Va. State Bar Assn., Fed. Bar Assn. (chmn. jud. rev. com. 1981-85, vice chmn. adminstrv. law sect. 1985-87), Fed. Communications Bar Assn. (del. to ABA Ho. Dels. 1979-81, exec. com. 1967-71, 76-84, v.p. 1981-82, pres. 1982-83, chmn. telecommunications com. 1983-87), D.C. Bar Assn. (past sec., exec. com.), NAM, Nat. Assn. Bar Pres., Washington Council Lawyers, Legal Aid and Pub. Defender Assn., Am. Arbitration Assn. (comml. panel 1976-87), D.C. Unified Bar (bd. govs. 1976-79, chmn. com. on employment discrimination complaint service 1973-79, chmn. task force on services to public 1974-78, chmn. com. on appointment counsel in criminal cases 1978-88, co-chmn. com. on participation govt. employees in pro bono activities 1977-79), Broadcast Pioneers, Order of Coif, Phi Beta Kappa, Pi Gamma Mu., Artus, Phi Eta Sigma, Phi Delta Phi. Democrat. Lodge: B'nai Brith. Home: 8706 Bellwood Rd Bethesda MD 20817-3033 Office: US Dept Justice 10th St & Pennsylvania Ave NW Rm 3326 Main Bldg Washington DC 20530

FORRESTER, DONALD DEAN, principal; b. Laporte, Ind., Feb. 8, 1945; s. Grady Wesley and Margaret Elizabeth (Meadows) F.; m. Anne Gaskill, June 17, 1967; 1 child, Shannon Anne. BS in Edn., Frostburg State U., 1967; MEd in Edn., Bowie State U., 1972; EdD in Edn., Nova U., 1978; MA in Theology, St. Mary's Sem. and U., 1990. Tchr. Montpelier Elem. Sch., Laurel, Md., 1967-73, ESAA Floating Faculty,, Suitland, Md., 1973-74; vice prin. Rogers Heights Elem. Sch., Bladensburg, Md., 1974-76; prin. Somerset Elem. Sch., Bowie, Md., 1976-77, Montpelier Elem. Sch., Laurel, 1977-92, Yorktown Elem. Sch., Bowie, 1992—; v.p. Montpelier Elem. Sch. PTA, Laurel, 1972-73, pres., 1973-74. Lay reader Trinity Episcopal Ch., Waterloo, Elkridge, Md., 1980-86, lay minister, 1986—; sr. warden Trinity Episcopal Ch. Vestry, Waterloo, Elkridge, 1986-90; dir. Woodbridge Crossing Homeowners Assn., Laurel, 1990—. Mem. ASCD, Am. Assn. Sch. Adminstrs., Nat. Assn. Elem. Sch. Prins., Assn. Sch. Based Adminstrs. and Suprs., Md. Assn. Elem. Sch. Adminstrs., So. Md. Reading Coun., Birmingham Lodge Ancient Free and Accepted Masons, Ancient and Accepted Lodge Scottish Rite Free Masons. Republican. Home: 8806 Ashcroft Dr Laurel MD 20708-3507 Office: Yorktown Elem Sch 7301 Race Track Rd Bowie MD 20715-1437

FORSE, ROBERT ARMOUR, surgeon; b. Montreal, Dec. 25, 1950; came to U.S., 1989; s. Raymond Armour and Arlene Mabel (Burns) F.; m. Lynda Gail Kabbash, June 21, 1975; children: Alexander, Emily. BSc, McGill U., 1972, MD, 1976, PhD, 1982. Straight intern in surgery Royal Victoria Hosp., Montreal, 1976-77, jr. resident surgery, 1977-78, sr. resident in surgery, Surg. Nutrition Svc., 1978-80, sr. resident in surgery, Gen. Surg. Svcs., 1980-81, chief resident in surgery, 1981-82, asst. attending surgeon, attending surgeon surg. ICU, 1983-89, surg. program dir., 1986-89; attending surgeon, attending surgeon surg. ICU New England Deaconess Hosp., Boston, 1989—, chief surg. metabolism lab., 1989—, surg. dir. Deaconess Nutritional Mgmt. Ctrs., dir. program for surg. mgmt. of obesity, chief div. gen. surgery., 1991—; asst. prof. surgery Harvard Med. Sch., 1989-92, assoc. prof., 1992—; rsch. fellow McGill U., Montreal, 1972-73, 78-81; rsch. fellow med. rsch. Coun. Can., Coll. Physicians and Surgeons, Columbia U., N.Y., 1982-83; demonstrator dept. anatomy McGill U., Montreal, 1978-79, asst. prof. surgery, 1983-89, dir. surg. undergrad. edn., 1987-89; asst. prof. surgery Harvard Med. Sch., Boston, 1989—; asst. surgeon Reddy Meml. Hosp., Montreal, 1984-89; assoc. mem. McGill Nutrition and Food Sci. Ctr., McGill U., Montreal, 1984-89; attending surgeon Faulkner Hosp., Jamaica Plain, N.Y.; cons. staff in surg. oncology Dana Farber Cancer Inst., Boston, 1989—; mem. numerous coms. Royal Victoria Hosp., McGill U., New Eng. Deaconess Hosp., others; tchr., presenter in field. Contbr. chpts. to books and articles to profl. jours. Recipient Equipment grant Rsch. Inst., Royal Victoria Hosp., 1984, Operating grant, 1984-85, Equipment grant Med. Rsch. Coun. Can., 1985, Cedar Cancer Found., 1985, Operating grant Med. Rsch. Coun. Can., 1985-87, Med. Rsch. Coun. Can., 1987-89, 1989-91, NIH, 1990—, others. Fellow Royal Coll. Surgeons Can., Am. Coll. Surgeons, Am. Coll. Critical Care Medicine; mem. AAAS, Am. Soc. Parenteral and Enteral Nutrition, Assn. for Acad. Surgery, Can. Assn. Gen. Surgeons, Surg. Infection Soc., European Soc. for Parenteral and Enteral Nutrition, Can. Soc. for Clin. Investigation, Can. Soc. for Critical Care, Soc. Critical Care Medicine, Am. Soc. Bariatric Physicians, Can. Assn. for Med. Edn., N.Y. Acad. Scis., Assn. for Surg. Edn., Mass. Med. Soc., Cen. Surg. Assn., others. Office: Harvard Med Sch 110 Francis St #3A Boston MA 02215

FORSH, KENNETH ALLAN, international student adviser, urban sociologist; b. Bklyn., Feb. 8, 1949; s. Levi G. and Florence Lois (Perry) F.; m. Ramona H. Hannah, Nov. 21, 1970; children: Yomi, Kyra. BA, Hunter Coll., 1971; MA, Bklyn. Coll., 1984; postgrad., CUNY, 1986. Planner's asst. Architect's Renewal Com. (ARCH), N.Y.C., 1971; program coord., edn. counselor Afro-Am. East Multisvc. Ctr., N.Y.C., 1972-74; project dir. N.Y. Community Action Programs, N.Y.C., 1974-79; dir. S.I. Br. Urban League, 1979-83; project dir. N.Y. Urban League/IBM Tng. Ctr., Queens, 1985; career program coord. CUNY, Bklyn., 1985-87, internat. student adviser, 1987—; faculty adviser Nat. Assn. Black Accts., Bklyn., 1989—. Recipient Outstanding Svc. award Nat. Black Sci. Students Orgn., Bklyn. Coll., 1990, 91, Honorable Recognition award Nat. Assn. Black Accts., Bklyn. Coll., 1990, 91, Pub. Svc. Citation Northeastern States Social Action Commn. of Delta Sigma Theta, 1978. Office: CUNY Bklyn Coll Bedford Ave Brooklyn NY 11222-3102

FORSHEY, WILLIAM OSMOND, III, data processing executive, entrepreneur; b. New London, Conn., Sept. 20, 1945; s. William Osmond Jr. and Doris (McCann) F.; m. Linda Guenthoer, Feb. 28, 1970 (div. Sept. 1977); 1 child, William Osmond IV; m. Suzanne Alice Long, Oct. 31, 1980; 1 child, Jennifer. BBA, U. Pa., 1989. Programmer, analyst DuPont, Wilmington, Del., 1969-79; asst. systems dir. Day and Zimmerman, Phila., 1979-80; bus. analyst Arabian Am. Oil Co., Dhahran, Saudi Arabia, 1980-83; asst. v.p. Anacomp, Cherry Hill, N.J., 1983; v.p., data processing mgr. Core States Fin. Corp., Phila., 1983—. Mem. Sigma Kappa Phi, Theta Xi. Home: 4 Westbrooke Ct Voorhees NJ 08043-2916 Office: Core States Fin Corp PO Box 7618 Philadelphia PA 19101-7618

FORSYTHE, DONALD JOHN, art educator, artist; b. Pitts., July 2, 1955; s. John M. and Jane M. (Morrow) F.; m. Christine A. Tickle, Mar. 4, 1978; 1 child, Christopher Michael. BS in Edn., Indiana U. Pa., 1977; MFA, Rochester Inst. Tech., 1979. Graphic designer Roberts Wesleyan Coll., Rochester, N.Y., 1979-80, instr. art, 1979-81; instr. art Grad. Sch., Rochester Inst. Tech., 1979; assoc. prof. art Messiah Coll., Grantham, Pa., 1982—; artist Dolan/Maxwell Gallery, Phila., 1983-88; dir. M. Louise Aughinbaugh Gallery, Grantham, 1984-89. Exhibited in group shows Carnegie Mellon U., Pa., 1989, Laguna Gloria Mus., Austin, Tex., 1989 (jurors award), U. Pa. Mus., Harrisburg, 1990 (art works award), Graham Ctr. Mus., Wheaton, Ill., 1990 (Best of Show award). Mem. Christians in Visual Arts (bd. dirs. 1985—, pres. 1991—). Democrat. Episcopalian.

FORT, JOHN FRANKLIN, III, manufacturing company executive; b. N.Y.C., Oct. 12, 1941; s. John Franklin and Florence (Baumrucker) F.; m. Nancy Barnett, Feb. 18, 1967; children: John Franklin, Alexandra S., Tucker H., Elizabeth B. BS, Princeton U., 1963; MS, MIT, 1966. V.p., gen. mgr. Simplex Wire & Cable Co., Newington, N.H., 1970-74, pres., 1974-79; v.p. ops. Tyco Labs., Inc., Exeter, N.H., 1979-82, sr. v.p. ops., 1982, pres., chmn. bd., chief exec. officer, 1983—; bd. dirs. Dover Corp. Trustee Berwick Acad. Recipient Corp. Leadership award MIT, 1984. Office: Tyco Labs Inc 1 Tyco Pk Exeter NH 03833

FORT, PAVEL, physician; b. Prague, Czechoslovakia, Jan. 23, 1945; s. Miloš Fořt and Miloslava (Pivrncová) Fořtová; m. Susana Dutkov'--, Dec. 13, 1970; children: Andrea, Pavel, Philip. MD, Charles U., Prague, 1969. Pediatric intern North Shore U. Hosp., Manhasset, N.Y., 1971-72, pediatric resident, 1972-74, pediatric fellow, 1974-75, pediatrician, 1975—; endocrinologist Hosp. Cornell U. Med. Coll., N.Y.C., 1975—; from instr. to assoc. prof. clin. pediatrics Cornell U. Med. Coll., N.Y.C., 1975—. Contbr. chpts. to books, articles to profl. jours.; numerous nat. orgn. meeting presentations. Med. dir. Long Island chpt. N.Y. Diabetes Assn., 1981-84, patients' svcs. com. mem. 1981—, profl. svcs. com. mem., 1984—; Long Island chpt. mem. Human Growth Found., 1978—; specialist in med. assistance program Children's Program of N.Y., 1986—. Named Outstanding Vol. Long Island chpt. Am. Diabetes Assn., N.Y., 1987, '92; Mineral Deficiencies During Growth grantee Kevin Kenny Found.; Coop Core Lab. and Clin. Nutrition Rsch. grantee NIH, Biomed Rsch. Support grantee NIH. Fellow Am. Acad. Pediatrics, Am. Coll. Nutrition; mem. AAAS, AMA, Am. Diabetes Assn., Am. Soc. Magnesium Rsch., Am. Inst. Nutrition, Am. Soc. Experimental Nutrition, Am. Soc. Clin. Nutrition, Internat. Diabetes Fedn., European Assn. Study of Diabetes, Eastern Soc. Pediatric Rsch., Nassau County Med. Soc., Nassau Pediatric Soc., N.Y. Acad. Scis., Lawson Wilkins Pediatric Endocrine Soc., Endocrine Soc., Soc. for Experimental Biology and Medicine.

FORTÉ-DOBSON, ROSITA YEVETTE, non-profit organization executive; b. Youngsville, N.C., June 5, 1954; d. Clarence Forté and Cleora (Floyd) Chavis; m. Robert Dobson, Dec. 28, 1991; children: Robert Dobson, James Dobson, Michelle Dobson, Charmion Forté. BA in History, Govt. cum laude, St. Augustine's Coll., 1976; JD, Temple U., 1987. Corp. trust officer Core States/First Pa. Bank, Phila., 1984-87, asst. v.p., 1987-90; prof. Pan African Studies Edn. Program Temple U., Phila., 1990—; exec. dir. North Phila. Partnership, 1990—. Bd. dirs. Fellowship Commn., Phila., 1988—, S&R Non-Profit Corp., Phila, 1989—, CHOICE, Phila., 1989—, chmn. Emanuel Instl. Housing Corp., Phila., 1988—; community organizer Com. to Elect Judge Ida Chen to Ct. Common Pleas, Phila., 1988, Com. to Elect Judge Nitza Quinones to Ct. Common Pleas, Phila., 1991, Com. to Elect State Rep. Curtis Thomas State Legislator, Phila., 1990. Named for Community Svc., Black Caucus/Commonwealth of Pa., 1991, Emmanuel Institutional Bapt. Ch., Phila., 1991. Mem. Internat. Tng. and Communication, Black Women's Leadership Conf., Delta Sigma Theta. Democrat. Baptist. Home: 925 W Oxford St Philadelphia PA 19122 Office: North Phila Partnership 1800 N 9th St PGW Bldg Philadelphia PA 19122

FORTENBAUGH, SAMUEL BYROD, III, lawyer; b. Phila., Nov. 6, 1933; s. Samuel Byrod Jr. and Katherine Francisca (Wall) F.; m. Patricia Lee Dooley, June 7, 1975; children: Samuel Byrod IV, Cristina Carlson, Katherine Dooley, Francesca Cowden. BA, Williams Coll., 1955; LLB, Harvard U., 1960. Bar: N.Y. 1961, U.S. Dist. Ct. (so. dist.) N.Y. 1961. Assoc. Kelley Drye & Warren, N.Y.C., 1960-69, ptnr., 1970-79; ptnr. Morgan, Lewis & Bockius, N.Y.C., 1980—; bd. dirs. Western Pub. Group, Inc., N.Y.C., Baldwin Tech. Co., Inc., Rowayton, Conn., Goodman Equipment Corp., Chgo.; bd. dirs., sec. Furgueson Capital Mgmt. Inc., N.Y.C.; chmn. bd. dirs., sec. Wall Industries, Inc., Granite Quarry, N.C.; chmn. bd. dirs. Knight Textile Corp, Saluda, S.C.; gen. ptnr. Palmetto Restoration Assocs., Columbia, S.C., 1981—; trustee Patroni Scholastici, New Brunswick, N.J., 1978—, sec. 1985—. Contbr. articles to profl. jours. Bd. dirs. The Greenwich Coun. on Youth & Drugs, Inc., 1992—. Mem. ABA, Assn. of the Bar of City of N.Y. (mem. Young Lawyers com. 1962-65, corp. law com. 1976-79, com. on securities regulation 1982-85, chmn. com. on issue an distbn. of securities 1984-85), Phi Beta Kappa. Clubs: Racquet & Tennis, Univ. (N.Y.C.); Bay Head (N.J.) Yacht. Office: Morgan Lewis & Bockius 101 Park Ave New York NY 10178-0002

FORTIN, SUSAN MARIE, risk management executive; b. Central Falls, R.I., Jan. 13, 1958; d. Rene J. and Aline A. (Ratte) F. BA in Liberal Studies cum laude, Providence Coll., 1990. Risk reduction specialist ALMACS Supermarkets, East Providence, R.I., 1980-86; dir. risk mgr. Shaw's Supermarkets, Inc., East Bridgewater, Mass., 1986—. Mem. NAFE, Risk &

Ins. Mgmt. Soc., Am. Soc. for Safety Engrs., R.I. Safety Assn. (pres. 1990-91), Providence Engring. Soc. (membership chairperson), The Food Mktg. Inst. (risk mgmt. com. 1989—).

FORTINSKY, JEROME STEVEN, political advisor, lawyer; b. Bklyn., May 9, 1962; s. Albert David and Marjorie (Morton) F. AB, Harvard U., 1983; JD, Yale U., 1987. Bar: N.Y. Asst. issues dir. Cranston-for-President Com., Washington, 1983-84; asst. to fin. dir. Dem. Nat. Com., Washington, 1984; law clk. Chambers of Hon. E.R. Korman, Albany, N.Y., 1987-88; asst. to sr. dep. sec. to the gov. Gov.'s Office, Albany, 1988-90, asst. to gov. for regional affairs, 1990-91; atty. Shearman & Sterling, N.Y.C., 1991—. Mem. Jewish Polit. Caucus; mem. exec. com. Greater N.Y. Conf. Soviet Jewry. Nahum Goldmann fellow, 1991; recipient Harlan Fiske Stone prize Yale U., 1986, Potter Stewart prize, 1986, Charles G. Albom prize, 1987; Martin Buskin scholar Newsday Mag., 1979, scholar L.I. Savs. Bank, 1979, Nat. Merit scholar, 1979. Mem. Am. Dialect Soc. Home: 400 E 71st St Apt 14Q New York NY 10021-4808 Office: Shearman & Sterling 153 E 53d St New York NY 10022

FORTUNA, FRANK ANTHONY, JR., chemical company executive; b. Elizabeth, N.J., July 2, 1946; s. Frank A. Sr. and Anna M. (Golas) F.; m. Patricia A. Nitko, May 27, 1972; children: Laura A., Frank A. III. BBA, St. Bonaventure U., 1968; MBA, Fairleigh Dickinson U., 1985. Credit analyst Amerada Hess Corp., Woodbridge, N.J., 1971-72; from credit account mgr. to western region credit mgr. BASF Wyandotte Corp., Parsippany, N.J., 1972-84; from contract adminstrn. mgr. to fin. svcs. mgr. BASF Corp., Parsippany, 1984-91; western credit sector head BASF Corp., Clifton, N.J., 1992—. Lt. U.S. Army, 1968-70, Vietnam. Mem. Nat. Corp. Cash Mgrs. Assn., Nat. Chem. Credit Assn., Am. Div. Vets. Assn., Mil. Order Purple Heart, Am. Legion. Republican. Roman Catholic. Home: 52 Clover Hill Dr Flanders NJ 07836 Office: BASF Corp 1255 Broad St Clifton NJ 07015

FORTUNE, STEPHEN JAMES, investment company executive; b. Watertown, N.Y., Oct. 26, 1951; s. Philip Robert and Margaret Mary (Burns) F.; m. Georgia E. Angel, Oct. 18, 1980; 1 child, Stephanie D. BA in English, Boston Coll., 1973; MS in Transp., MIT, 1981. Market rsch. analyst Lockheed Ga. Co., Marietta, 1981-84; assoc. gen. mgr. Fed. Express Aviation Svc., Memphis, 1984-87; dir. aircraft mtkg. Saab Aircraft of Am., Inc., Sterling, Va., 1987-90; v.p. planning Potomac Capital Investment Corp., Washington, 1990—; bd. dirs. Engine Lease Fin., Shannon, Ireland; pres. Internat. Soc. Transport Aircraft Trading, Washington, 1991—. Editor: (book) Commercial Jet Fleets, 1986-87. Lt. comdr. USN, 1973-80.

FORZLEY, PAUL EDWARD, anesthesiologist; b. Worcester, Mass., Nov. 20, 1953; s. Edward Fida and Dolores Ruth (Vigliatura) F. BS, Georgetown U., 1975, MD, 1981. Commd. 2d lt. U.S. Army, 1978, advanced through grades to maj., 1987; intern Tripler Army Med. Ctr., Honolulu, 1981-82; preventive medicine officer 2d Infantry Div., Tong DuChon, Republic of Korea, 1982-83; gen. med. officer 5th Spl. Forces Group, U.S. Army, Fort Bragg, N.C., 1984-87; resident in anesthesia Brigham and Women's Hosp., Boston, 1987-90; staff anesthesiologist Brigham and Women's Hosp., 1990—. Mem. AMA (cert.), Am. Soc. Anesthesiologists. Home: 20 Chapel St # 302A Brookline MA 02146-5458 Office: Brigham & Women's Hosp 75 Francis St Boston MA 02115-6195

FOSTER, ALLEN JAY, musician, educator; b. Phila., Nov. 24, 1962; s. Louis Franklin and Joan Marie (Kelsall) F.; m. Karen Ann Baselice, July 1, 1989; 1 child, Jeffrey Allen. Assoc. Fine Arts, Bucks County Community Coll., 1983; student, Phila. Coll. Performing Arts, 1983-85; pvt. study with, Andrew Rudin, Phila., 1983. Music tchr. Lower Bucks County, Pa., 1987—; Freelance author, Pa., 1989—; freelance performer, Pa., 1980—; freelance composer, Pa., 1978—. Co-author: Souvenirs, Volume I 1991; author: Souvenirs Volume II, 1991; author, performer (song) Look What's Happened to Jamie, 1988; editor Songwriter's Monthly, 1992; author various columns, 1989—. Mem. ASCAP, Small Press Writers and Artist Orgn., N.J. and Pa. Songwriters Assn., Penn Sounds, Bucks County Assn. Piano Tchrs. Home: 332 Eastwood Ave Feasterville PA 19053

FOSTER, ANDREA MARY, dental hygienist; b. Harrisburg, Pa., Nov. 27, 1958; d. Cornelius Louis and Veronica Louise (Stewart) Beaden; m. Eric Clifton Foster, Aug. 29, 1987; 1 child, Arrington Jamal. BS, U. Md., 1987; AA, Howard U., 1982. Registered dental hygienist; lic. minsiter. Dental technotherapist Community Dental Assocs., Harrisburg, Pa., 1977-84; dental hygienist Dr. Abraham Katz, Washington, 1984-85, Dr. Leonard Bers, Upper Marlberg, Md., 1985-87, Dr. Stephen Eisenberg, Forestville, Md., 1985-89, Dr. Jean Judy, Washington, 1989-90, Dr. Felicia Nesbit, Waldorf, Md., 1991—. Interviewee and actress TV documentary for dental hygiene: Caring for America, 1992. Elder, mentor Ebenezer AME Ch., Ft. Washington, Md., 1992—. Capt. Army N.G., 1979—. Recipient Leadership award U. Md., 1986, award Howard U., 1992; named first chaplain candidate in history D.C. Army Nat. Guard, 1992. Mem. Nat. Dental Hygientist Assn. (trustee 1984-88, pres. 1990-91, immediate past pres. 1992-93, bd. dirs., Disting. Svc. award 1991), Bay-Tri States Dental Hygienist Assn., Howard U. Dental Hygiene Alumni Assn., Nat. Dental Assn. Found. (bd. dirs.), N.G. Assn., Nat. Assn. Quartermaster Officers. Democrat. Home: 2927 Sunset Ln Suitland MD 20746

FOSTER, BARBARA MELANIE, microscopist, consultant; b. Los Alamos, N.Mex., Apr. 21, 1945; d. Lawrence Marvin and Evelyne Marilyn (Caro) Litz; m. John Michael Foster, Sept. 4, 1966 (div. Mar. 1984); m. Kenneth Martin Piel, Nov. 30, 1991. BSc in Edn., Ohio U., 1967; MS in Chemistry, U. Mass., 1979; postgrad., Brunel U., Uxbridge, Eng., 1979-81. Tchr. sci. Athens (Ohio) High Sch., 1967-68, West Springfield (Mass.) High Sch., 1968-81; cons., owner Microscopy/Microscopy Edn., Springfield, Mass., 1981-84; dir. tech. applications group Unitron, Inc., Plainville, N.Y., 1984; field product specialist, adj. mem. mktg. mgmt. group Carl Zeiss, Inc., Thornwood, N.Y., 1984-86; applications mgr. rsch. microscopy Cambridge Instruments, Buffalo, 1986-87, mgr. product devel., 1988, mgr. ednl. mktg., 1988-89; mgr. tech. mktg. Sarastro, Inc., Phila. and Bethel, Conn., 1989-91; cons., owner Microscopy/Mktg. & Edn., Springfield, 1991—; coord., prin. lectr. short courses ACS, 1983—. Author: Use & Care of the Microscope, 1986; editor The Quarterly newsletter, 1984; contbr. articles to profl. jours. Bldg. rep. West Springfield Edn. Assn., 1970, salary rep., negotiations com., 1971, chair com. 1972, 73, cons. com. 1974; founder, pres. N.E. Assn. Microscopists, 1981-85. Fellow Royal Microscopical Soc.; mem. Am. Soc. Materials, Electron Soc. Am.

FOSTER, CATHERINE RIERSON, manufacturing company executive; b. Balt., Mar. 14, 1935; d. William Harman and Ella Fredericka (Magsamen) Rierson; m. Morgan Lawrence Foster, Nov. 17, 1957 (dec. Jan. 1990); children: Diana Kay, Susan Ann, Morgan Lawrence, Heather Lynne. Student, Balt. City Coll., 1955, Johns Hopkins U., 1956-57, Glendale Coll., 1962-63. Sec. Martin Co., Balt., 1956-57, adminstrv. sec., 1957-58; v.p., corp. sec. Fostermation, Inc., Meadville, Pa., 1971-90, pres., chmn. bd., 1990—, also bd. dirs.; mem. adv. com. Vocat./Tech. Sch., Meadville, 1982-86. Pres. La Crescents, La Crescenta, Calif., 1962; active City Hosp. Aux., Meadville, 1969-86, Rep. Women's Workshop, Glendale, Calif., 1966-68, Com. to Elect Ronald Reagan, Glendale, 1967; bd. dirs. YWCA, Meadville, 1988-89, also chmn. fin. com., 1988-89. Mem. DAR (chpt. regent 1989-92), NAFE, Rotary, Order Eastern Star. Lutheran. Home: 1121 Lakemont Dr Meadville PA 16335-2826 Office: Fostermation Inc 200 Valleyview Dr Meadville PA 16335

FOSTER, DAVID VOLNEY, concert manager; b. N.Y.C., Aug. 30, 1946; s. Volney William and Ellen Adair (Orr) F.; m. Judith Naomi Kurz, Oct. 28, 1979; children: Julia Kurz Foster, Lily Augusta Foster. BA, Harvard U., 1968. Asst. account exec. Ted Bates & Co., N.Y.C., 1968-70; dir. pub. rels. New Orleans Philharm. Symphony Orch., 1970-72; rep. Columbia Artists Mgmt., Inc., N.Y.C., 1972-76, managerial assoc., 1976-81, v.p., 1980—, mgr., 1981—, also bd. dirs. Episcopalian. Office: Columbia Artists Mgmt Inc 165 W 57th St New York NY 10019

FOSTER, EDWARD PAUL (TED FOSTER), process industries executive; b. Pawtucket, R.I., Aug. 23, 1945; s. Edward Francis and Vivian Adrienne (Davagne) F.; m. Barbara Philomena Cook, Dec. 17, 1965 (div. Apr. 1978); children: Edward Robert, Gwendolyn Lucy; m. Johanna Helena Klaassen, June, 1985 (div. 1988); 2 children. BSChemE with distinction, U. R.I., 1967; MSChemE, Worcester Poly. Inst., 1970; MBA, Lehigh U., 1981. Mfg. melting engr. Corning Glass Works, Central Falls, R.I., 1966-67; group leader rsch. and devel. The Babcock & Wilcox Co., Alliance, Ohio, 1968-71; mgr. tampella process The Babcock & Wilcox Co., Barberton, Ohio, 1972-74; from commercial devel. engr. to dir. commercial devel. in gases, metallurgy, coal, chems. and polymers, and environ. areas Air Products and Chem., Inc., Allentown, Pa., 1974—; cons. U.S. Army Natick (Mass.) Lab., 1966-67. Contbr. articles to profl. jours.; patentee in field. Chmn. fin. Unitarian Ch., Bethlehem, Pa., 1985, chmn. social, 1983-84. NDEA fellow U.S. Dept. Health, Edn. and Welfare, 1967-69; ROTC scholar U.S. Army, 1965, Nat. Merit scholar, 1963. Mem. Commercial Devel. Assn., Am. Inst. Chem. Engrs., Am. Chem. Soc., Phi Kappa Phi, Tau Beta Pi. Home: 6023 Fairway Ln Allentown PA 18106-9610 Office: Air Products and Chems 7201 Hamilton Blvd Allentown PA 18195-9642

FOSTER, ERIC H., JR., retail executive; b. Nov. 8, 1943; s. Eric H. Sr. and Dorothy (Schwarz) F.; married; children: Dawn, Eric III, Kimberly, Meredith. BS in Mgmt., Rutger's U., 1969; student grad. sch. acctg. and taxation, Farleigh Dickinson U., 1973-74. Computer and peripheral equipment operator N.J. Bell Telephone Co., 1965-66; mem. prodn. planning and scheduling 3M Co., St. Paul, 1966-68, data analyst, 1968-69; supr. customer and geographic info. ctr. McGraw-Hill Book Co., Hightstown, N.J., 1969-71, staff asst. to gen. mgr. distbn. ctr., 1971-75, 78, mgr. retail accounts receivable credit and collection dept., 1975-78, 79, responsible McGraw-Hill club and retail customer svc. depts., 1979, mgr., 1979-80, mgr. spl. svcs. and returns, 1980-82, gen. mgr. profl. pub. svcs., 1982-88. Councilman Borough of Freehold, pres., chmn. water and sewer dept., mem. planning bd., finance and econ. devel. com.; bd. dirs. Freehold Presbyn. Nursery Sch.; chmn. bd. The Rugby Sch.; vice chmn. Freehold Borough Zoning Bd.; mem. vestry, bus. and personnel com., maintenance and repair com. St. Peter Episc. Ch., chmn. finance com.; advisor Youth Group; charter mem., 1st pres., mem. founding group East Freehold Fire Co.; coord. troop 151 Boy Scouts Am. Recipient Bronze Palm award Eagle Scouts Am., 1960. Mem. Direct Mktg. Assn., Direct Mktg. & Credit Assn. (bd. dirs.), Internat. Consumer Credit Assn. (bd. dirs. region II N.Y./N.J. chpts.), N.J. Assn. Schs. & Agys. for the Handicapped, Internat. Credit Assn. (cert. consumer credit exec.). Episcopalian. Home: 35 Broadway Freehold NJ 07728-1864

FOSTER, LANNY GORDON, writer, publisher; b. Harrisburg, Pa., Sept. 27, 1948; s. Gordon Eugene and Georgina Lillian (Kramer) F.; m. Carol Prescot McCoy, Nov. 29, 1975 (div. 1987); m. Denise Joy Freiman, Sept. 10, 1988. BA, Rutgers U., 1970, PhD, 1976. Postdoctoral fellow Bellevue and N.Y.U., N.Y.C., 1975-79; prodn. analyst, mgr. ops. Irving Trust Co., N.Y.C., 1979-82; med. writer Am. Home Prods., N.Y.C., 1982-83; writer various corps., N.Y.C., 1983-88; writer, owner Beta Books, Cragsmoor, N.Y., 1988—; mem. Mgmt. of HIV Disease Delegation to People's Republic of China, Citizen Ambassador Program, 1990. Author: The ABC of AIDS, 1990, The Third Epidemic, 1990; contbr. articles to Immunology Jour., 1973-79. Edn. vol. Gay Men's Health Crisis, N.Y.C., 1986-87; speaker on AIDS various radio and TV talk shows, 1987. Mem. N.Y. Acad. Scis., Am. Med. Writer's Assn., Com. Small Mag. Editors and Pubs., Internat. Platform Assn., The Harvey Soc., Writers Guild of Am. East. Office: Beta Books PO Box 40 Cragsmoor NY 12420-0040

FOSTER, LLOYD ARTHUR, principal; b. Stamford, Conn., June 11, 1933; s. Lloyd Allister and Ruth Celeste (Olmstead) F.; m. Virginia Grace Wood, June 5, 1959; children: Heidi, Leigh, Lance, Jonathan, Barry, Daniel, Victoria, Rikio. BA, Gordon Coll., Beverly, Mass., 1960; MA, U. Hartford, 1964; EdD, Nova U., 1987. Cert. elem. and secondary edn. adminstr. Sales rep. Conn. Blue Cross Ins. Co., 1960-63; tchr. Ellington (Conn.) Bd. Edn., 1963-66, prin., 1966-68; prin. Hartford (Conn.) Bd. Edn., 1968—, Annie Fisher Sch., 1971—. Co-founder program to reduce racial isolation Across the Lines, program to assist mainstream tchrs. meet the neads of students with spl. learning needs, Target; co-founder program to prepare high risk students for world of work, Annie Fisher Work Readiness; portfolio assessment program tp monitor and motivate at-risk-students, AFPAP. With USAF, 1951-55. Mem. Assn. Suprs. and Curriculum Devel., Hartford Prins. and Suprs. Assn. (v.p. 1980—), Phi Delta Kappa. Republican. Baptist. Home: 133 Dunn Rd Coventry CT 06238-1113 Office: Annie Fisher Sch 280 Plainfield St Hartford CT 06112-1798

FOSTER, VINCENT STEPHEN, fundraising executive; b. San Francisco, Sept. 15, 1943; s. Emery Vincent and Jessica Rebecca (Shahan) F.; m. Maria Elena Videtti, Dec. 18, 1965 (div. Jan. 1975); 1 child, Scott. BA, Monmouth Coll., 1966. Staff writer Asbury Park (N.J.) Press, 1963-66; dist. credit mgr. Chevron Oil Co., Perth Amboy, N.J., 1966-68; dir. personnel and pub. relations Community Meml. Hosp., Toms River, N.J., 1968-71; dir. community relations Point Pleasant (N.J.) Hosp., 1971-77; pres. Riverview Med. Ctr. Found., Red Bank, N.J., 1977-83; v.p. devel. Med. Ctr. Ocean County, Point Pleasant, 1983—; chmn. ad hoc com. on press relations N.J. Hosp. Assn., Princeton, 1975-76. Author, designer (direct mail brochure) Pathways to Progress, 1979 (Jasper award); contbr. articles to profl. jours. Mem. Nat. Soc. Fund Raising Execs. (cert.), Nat. Assn. Hosp. Devel. (accredited). Lodge: Kiwanis (sec. Point Pleasant club 1976-77). Office: Med Ctr Ocean County 2121 Edgewater Pl Point Pleasant Beach NJ 08742-2212

FOSTER, WALTER HERBERT, JR., real estate company executive; b. Belmont, Mass., Nov. 2, 1919; s. Walter Herbert and Gertrude (Sullivan) F.; m. Hazel Campbell, Aug. 7, 1942 (div. July 1979); children: Katherine D., Walter H. III, Stephen C., Banton T.; m. Nedra Ann Thompson, July 3, 1981; 1 child, Timothy John. Student, Harvard U., 1937-38; BS, U. Maine, 1947; grad. in real estate, Tri-State Inst., 1968-70. Cert. gen. appraiser, Maine. Owner, mgr. Foster Bros., Lyndeborough, N.H., 1947-56; ter. sales mgr. Beacon Milling Co., Oakland, Maine, 1956-64; v.p. Sherwood & Foster, Inc., Old Town, Maine, 1964-67; sales rep. Bangor (Maine) Real Estate, 1967-73; chief appraiser James W. Sewall Co., Old Town, 1970-73; mgr. J.F. Singleton Co., Bangor, 1973-80; pres. Coldwell Banker Am. Heritage, Bangor, 1980—; dean Tri-State Inst., 1981; mem. Maine Real Estate Commn., 1987. Mem. Rep. Nat. Com., Washington, 1980, Assessment Bd. Appeals, Old Town, Maine; bd. dirs. Penobscot Theatre, 1987—, treas., 1989. Capt. USAF, 1941-46. Mem. Nat. Assn. Realtors (bd. dirs. 1980-81), Maine Assn. Realtors (bd. dirs. 1976-80, pres. 1980, Realtor of Yr. 1976, 84), Maine Real Estate Commn. (chmn. 1991-92), Commn. to Study Real Estate Appraiser Cert. and Licensing, Bangor Bd. Realtors (bd. dirs. 1973-74, pres. 1976, Realtor of Yr. 1984), Nat. Assn. Rev. Appraisers, Am. Assn. Cert. Appraisers, Res. Officers Assn., Soc. Real Estate Appraisers (assoc.), Tarratine Club, Harvard Club (treas.), Rotary (dir. local club). Episcopalian. Home: Mistover Dole Hill Rd RFD 2 Box 692 East Holden ME 04429 Office: Coldwell Banker Am Heritage 510 Broadway Bangor ME 04401-3468

FOSTER, WILLIS ROY, physician; b. New Orleans, Dec. 8, 1928; s. Horace Frank and Callie Opal (Norman) F.; m. Delilah Stokes, July 1, 1957; children: Gregory Mark, Stuart David, Douglas Andrew. BA, La. State U., 1950, MS, 1957, MD, 1957. Rsch. assoc. George Washington U., Washington, 1957-58; postdoctoral fellow Johns Hopkins U., Balt., 1958-59; profl. assoc. Smithsonian Inst., Washington, 1959-63; assoc. dir. Smithsonian Sci. Info Exch., Washington, 1964-71; v.p. Smithsonian Sci. Info. Exch., Washington, 1972-76; tech. dir. Kappa Systems Inc., Arlington, Va., 1976-78; pres. Adv. Concepts Dev., Bethesda, 1978-83; expert cons. NIH, Bethesda, 1983-85, sr. staff physician, 1985—; cons. Metametrics, Inc., Washington, 1978-80, Pan Am. Health Orgn., Washington, 1976-78. Co-author: Human Nutrition, 1990; contbr. articles to profl. jours. Vol. ch. activities Cedar Lane Unitarian Ch., Bethesda. Mem. Washington Acad. Medicine. Home: 6117 Greentree Rd Bethesda MD 20817-3359

FOUGERE, PAUL FRANCIS, physicist, consultant; b. Cambridge, Mass., Feb. 29, 1932; s. Louis Napoleon and Helen Valerian (Weissbach) F.; m. Marguerite Marie Burwell, Dec. 27, 1952; children: Paul J., Peter L., Mark J., Gregory J., Daniel E., Gabrielle. BS in Physics cum laude, Boston Coll., Chestnut Hill, Mass., 1952, MS in Physics, 1953; PhD in Physics, Boston U., 1965. Physicist Naval Rsch. Lab., Washington, 1951-54; tech. engr. GE, Lynn, Mass., 1954-55; physicist Air Force Cambridge (Mass.) Rsch. Ctr., 1956-60, Air Force Cambridge Rsch. Lab., Air Force Geophysics Lab., 1960-76, Geophysics Lab., 1976-89; Geophysics Directorate Phillips Lab., Bedford, Mass., 1989—; pres., math. cons. FERN Cons., Bedford, 1985—. Editor: Maximum Entropy and Bayesian Methods, 1989; also articles. Recipient sci. achievement award Air Force Geophysics Lab., 1970, 77, basic rsch. award USAF, 1987, award of merit Fed. Lab. Consortium, 1990; fellow MIT Ctr. for Advanced Engring. Study, 1989-90. Mem. IEEE (sr., chmn. signal processing chpt. Boston sect.), Signal Processing Soc. (spectral estimation and modelling com.), Am. Geophys. Union, Internat. Soc. for Entropic Rsch. (bd. dirs.), Internat. Sci. Radio Union (U.S. nat. com.), Boston Computer Soc. Democrat. Roman Catholic. Office: Phillips Lab/GPIM Hanscom AFB MA 01731-5000

FOULKE, EDWIN GERHART, JR., lawyer; b. Perkasie, Pa., Oct. 30, 1952; s. Edwin G. and Mary Claire (Keller) F. BA, N.C. State U., 1974; JD, Loyola U., New Orleans, 1978. Bar: S.C. 1979, U.S. Dist. Ct. S.C. 1979, U.S. Ct. Appeals (4th cir.) 1979, Ga. 1986, U.S. Ct. Appeals (11th cir.) 1986, D.C. 1989, U.S. Ct. Appeals (D.C. cir.) 1989, U.S. Supreme Ct. 1990. Assoc. Thompson, Mann & Hutson, Greenville, S.C., 1978-83, Rainey, Britton, Gibbes & Clarkson, Greenville, 1983-85, Constangy, Brooks & Smith, Columbia, S.C., 1985-90; chmn. Occupational Safety and Health Rev. Commn., Washington, 1990—; instr. St. Mary's Dominican Coll., New Orleans, 1977-78. Field rep. Reagan/Bush Campaign, Columbia, 1980, S.C. state coordinator, 1984; sec., treas. Employment Labor Law Sect., Columbia, 1981-82. Mem. ABA, S.C. Bar Assn., Ga. Bar Assn., Richland County Bar Assn. (chmn. pub. relations com. 1984-85), Am. Inst. Parlimentarians, SAR. Roman Catholic. Lodge: Rotary. Home: 807 N Howard St Apt 120 Alexandria VA 22304-5471 Office: 1825 K St NW Ste 409 Washington DC 20006-1202

FOULKES, FRED KLEE, business management educator; b. Bklyn., July 27, 1941; s. Clarence R. and Constance (Klee) F. AB, Princeton U., 1963; MBA, Harvard U., 1965, DBA, 1968. Asst. prof. bus. sch. Harvard U., Boston, 1970-75, assoc. prof., 1975-80; prof. sch. mgmt. Boston U., 1980—, dir. Human Rsch. Policy Inst., 1980—. Author: Personnel Policy in Large Companies, 1980, Human Resources Management, 1989; editor: Executive Compensation, 1991. Recipient Award for Achievement Employment Mgmt. Assn., 1978, Five Star Achievement award NE Human Resources Assn., 1992. Mem. Am. Compensation Assn., Indsl. Rels. Rsch. Assn., Soc. for Human Resource Mgmt., Phi Beta Kappa. Republican. Methodist. Office: Boston U 621 Commonwealth Ave Boston MA 02211-0001

FOUNTAIN, EUGENIA FERRIS, library director; b. 1959. BA, U. Conn., Storrs, 1981; MLS, Simmons Coll., 1985. Ref. libr. Essex Inst., Salem, Mass., 1985-88; dir. libr. svcs. Marian Ct. Jr. Coll., Swampscott, Mass., 1988—. Office: Marian Ct Jr Coll 35 Littles Point Rd Swampscott MA 01907-2896

FOUNTAIN, KAREN SCHUELER, physician; b. Aberdeen, S.D., Oct. 14, 1947. BA, No. State Coll., Aberdeen, S.D., 1968; MD, U. Md., Balt., 1972. Diplomate Nat. Bd. Med. Examiners, Am. Bd. Radiology in Therapeutic Radiology. Intern Md. Gen. Hosp., Balt., 1972-73, resident in radiation oncology, 1973-74; fellow in radiation oncology Mayo Clinic, Rochester, Minn., 1974-76, cons. in oncology, 1976-81; clin. asst. prof. Columbia U., N.Y.C., 1981-83, residency program dir. dept. radiation oncology, 1981—, clin. assoc. prof., 1983—; mem. med. bd. Presbyn. Hosp., N.Y.C., 1983-86; faculty coun. mem. Columbia U., 1982-89; del. N.Y. State Radiological Soc., N.Y.C., 1987—. Fellow N.Y. Acad. Medicine; mem. Am. Coll. Radiology, Am. Soc. Therapeutic Radiology and Oncology, N.Y. Roentgen Soc. (sect. chair 1989-90), Am. Radium Soc., Am. Soc. Clinical Oncology. Office: Columbia-Presbyn Med C 622 W 168th St New York NY 10032-3702

FOURROUX, MELVIN ROSS, computer engineering services company executive; b. Ottumwa, Iowa, Nov. 14, 1944; s. Melvin Millet Fourroux and Donna Corene (Ross) Donaho; m. Margarita Garcia, June 5, 1978; children: Elida Josephine, Francis Matthew. BS, Tex. A&M U., 1970, MS, 1973; MBA, Fontbonne Coll., St. Louis, 1987. Commd. 2d lt. USAF, 1974, advanced through grades to maj., 1982; chief ops. evaluation USAF, Hickam AFB, Hawaii, 1978-81; ops. officer USAF Recruiting Svc., L.A., 1981-82, squadron comdr., 1982-83; course officer Air Command and Staff Coll., Maxwell AFB, Ala., 1983-84; program mgr. USAF, Scott AFB, Ill., 1984-87; ret. USAF, 1987; program mgr. Vitro Corp., Silver Spring, Md., 1987-88; v.p. systems engring. Diversified Internat. Scis. Corp., Lanham, Md., 1988—. Vol. Spl. Olympics, Montgomery, Ala., 1984; mem. Air force Hist. Found. Decorated Meritorious Svc. medal with two oak leaf clusters. Mem. Am. Mktg. Assn., Am. Meteorol. Soc., Assn. MBA Execs., Ret. Officers Assn., Armed Forces Communications & Elec. Assn. Democrat. Roman Catholic. Home: 13132 Country Ridge Dr Germantown MD 20874-1123 Office: Diversified Internat Scis Corp 9901 Business Pky Lanham Seabrook MD 20706-1840

FOUST, RUSSEL EUGENE, plastics company executive; b. Columbus, Ohio, May 15, 1947; s. Russell Sheridan and Margaret (Cook) F.; m. Donna Raye Lishka, Nov. 24, 1972; children: Eric James, Adam Troy. BSEE, U. Pitts., 1972. Quality control mgr. Lamp Group Gen. Electric Co., Pitts., 1972-74; sr. plant engr. Gen. Electric Co., Somerset, Ky., 1974-76; engring. mgr. Gen. Electric Co., Youngstown, Ohio, 1976-78; engring. mgr. Exxon Chem., Pottsville, Pa., 1978-81, mfg. mgr. films div., 1981-84; bus. mgr. polypropylene Exxon Chem., Houston, 1984-87; product mgr. Edison Plastics Co., South Plainfield, N.J., 1987-89, quality coun. dir., quality assurance mgr., 1990-91, mgr. total quality mgmt., 1991—; instr. engring. U. Ky., Somerset, 1974-76, U. Pa., Pottsville, 1979-81. Head basketball coach North Parkland; bd. dirs. Parkland Soccer Club. With USN, 1966-69. Mem. Schnecksville Playground Assn. (pres.). Republican. Lutheran. Home: 4957 Ancinetta Dr Schnecksville PA 18078-9660 Office: Edison Plastics Co 4103 New Brunswick Ave South Plainfield NJ 07080-1305

FOWLER, BRUCE ANDREW, toxicologist; b. Seattle, Dec. 28, 1945; s. Andrew and Dolores Yvonne F.; m. Mary Glenn Oler, June 9, 1968; children: Glenn Andrew, Randall Bruce. BS in Fisheries, U. Wash., 1968; PhD in Pathology, U. Oreg., 1972. Staff fellow Nat. Inst. Environ. Health Scis., Research Triangle Park, N.C., 1972-74, sr. staff fellow, 1974-77, research biologist, 1977-87, sr. scientist, 1978-86, head Metal Toxicology, 1986-87; dir. U. Md. Toxicology program, 1987; prof. pathology U. Md. Med. Sch., 1987—; dir. office collaborative studies on adaptive responses estuarine species U. Md., 1988; Meyer Bodansky lectr. Dept. of Pathology, U. Tex med. br., Galveston; adj. assoc. prof. pathology and toxicology curriculum U. N.C.; temporary adv. WHO; mem. work group Internat. Agy. Research Against Cancer; mem. Internat. Commn. on Occupational Health, Sci. Com. on Toxicology of Metals (sec.); mem. Md. Gov.'s Coun. on Toxic Substances, 1988—, chmn., 1990—; chmn. Dahlem Workshop on Mechanisms of Cell Injury: Implications for Human Health, Berlin, 1985; mem. toxicology info. program com., com. on toxicology, chmn. com. on measuring lead in critical populations, com. on women in sci. and engring., com. on biologic markers in urologic toxicology NAS/NRC, 1989; co-chmn. N.Y. Acad. of Scis. Conf. on Mechanisms of Chem.-Induced Porphyrinopathies, Rye, N.Y. Editor: Biological and Environmental Effects of Arsenic, 1983; Mechanisms of Cell Injury: Implications for Human Health; (with E.K. Silbergeld) Mechanisms of Chemical Induced Porphyrinopathies; mem. editorial bd. Chemico-Biol. Interactions, 1980-85, Environ. Health Perspectives, 1981, Toxicology and Applied Pharmacology, 1985, Jour. Toxicology and Environ. Health, 1986, Internat. Archives Environ. Health, 1986-91, Renal Failure, 1988; contbr. articles to profl. jours. and chpts. to books. Rsch. fellow Japanese Soc. for Promotion of Sci., 1990. Mem. AAAS, Am. Soc. Pharmacology and Exptl. Therapeutics, Am. Assn. Pathologists, Soc. Toxicology (councilor mechanisms of toxicity sect.), Am. Pub. Health Assn., Soc. for Occupational and Environ. Health (councilor 1988), N.Y. Acad. Sci., Sigma Xi. Office: U Md Program in Toxicology 660 W Redwood St Baltimore MD 21201-1596

FOWLER, CECILE ANN, nurse, professional soloist; b. Paterson, N.J., Feb. 14, 1920; m. Chester A. Fowler, Mar. 9, 1942. Grad., Passaic (N.J.) Gen. Hosp. Nursing Program, 1941. Nurse Beth Israel Hosp., Newark, 1941-42, Orange (N.J.) Meml. Hosp., 1942-50; asst. receptionist Dr. Stokes, Urologist, East Orange, N.J., 1943-44; nurse Mountainside Hosp., Montclair, N.J., 1960-69, head nurse, premature and newborns, 1966-67; profl. soloist,

1952-69; part-time nurse Upper Three Hosps., 1950-60; co-founder The Oratorio Soc. of N.J., Montclair, 1952; mem. quartet First Baptist Ch., Montclair. Active various coms. PTA, 1951-62; co-counder CD, Little Falls, N.J., 1967; sponsor Met. Opera Guild N.Y., 1977—; child sponsor World Vision, 1983—; mem. Rep. Presdl. Task Force, 1987; founder Challenger Ctr. for Math., Space and Sci. Edn., 1990—, Ptnrs. in Hope: St. Jude's Rsch. Ctr., 1991—. Recipient Vocal Accomplishment award Griffith Music Found., 1944, 45, medal of Merit, Pres. Reagan, 1988, Pres. Bush, 1990, Rep. Presdl. Legion of Merit. Mem. Lincoln Ctr. for the Performing Arts, Friends of Carnegie Hall, Am. Biog. Inst. Am. (rsch. bd. advs. 1989—, dep. gov., life mem., fellowship, Commemorative medal of Honor 1991), Heritage Found. (U.S. English mem. 1986—), U.S. Senatorial Club (preferred mem. 1988—), Little Falls Woman's Club (edn. chmn.), Montclair (gov. 1979-81), Montclair Operetta (various chmnships 1943—, gov. 1990—). Republican. Roman Catholic. Home: 9 Lotz Hill Rd Clifton NJ 07013-2312

FOWLER, DOLORES ELEANOR, programmer, analyst; b. Phila., Nov. 20, 1936; d. Frank and Mary Genevieve (Mains) Fraustro y Garcia; m. Harry Fowler, Sept. 13, 1956; children: Gregory Kenneth, Gary Keith, Geoffrey Kent. BS in Computer Sci., U. Pitts., 1980, postgrad., 1983-86. Rsch. technician U. Ctr. for Social Urban Rsch., U. Pitts., 1975-77, programmer, 1977-79, programmer, analyst, sampling coord., 1979—; cons. in field. Contbr. articles to profl. jours. Named Univ. scholar U. Pitts., 1979, 80; recipient scholarship U. Pa., 1955. Mem. Am. Assn. Pub. Opinion Researchers, Kappa Delta Sorority. Office: U Pitts 121 University Pl Pittsburgh PA 15260-0001

FOWLER, DONA SYLVIA B., trade union executive; b. Paducah, Ky.; d. Charles Andrew Fowler and Helen Frances Sherrill; m. Howard Kaminsky, 1965 (div. 1967). BA in English, U. Calif., Berkeley; postgrad. medieval history, Christ Ch., Oxford, 1992. Copy editor ASHRAE, N.Y.C.; contr. Columbia U., 1966; from asst. editor to assoc. editor, prodn. editor Scholastic Mags., N.Y.C., 1967-75; editor-in-chief Frontpage, bus. agt. Newspaper Guild N.Y., AFL-CIO, Can. Labor Conf., 1975—. U. Calif. Alumni scholar, Genevieve McEnerney scholar, Students Coop. Assn. scholar, pres. Hoyt Hall. Mem. Internat. Labor Communications Assn. (best headline award 1978, 1st award for unique performance 1986), Labor Press Coun. Met. N.Y. (award of merit for best news writing 1977, 80, best writing 1987, a 1st award best writing, 1992, 1st award for best single article 1992, 1st award unique performance 1992), Newspaper Guild N.Y. (chmn. scholastic unit 1967-75, chmn. rep. assembly, exec. com. 1971-75), Tower and Flame, Mask and Dagger, Thalia. Democrat. Office: Newspaper Guild NY 133 W 44th St New York NY 10036-4012

FOWLER, EMIL EUGENE, nuclear technology consultant; b. Morgantown, W.Va., Sept. 15, 1923; s. Jesse Lash and Lillian May (Everly) F.; m. Jo Ann Vigor, July 9, 1949; children: Joycelyn Elizabeth Fowler Sharp, Christopher Lash, David Vigor. BS, W.Va. U., 1945, MS, 1947. Chief licensing then dep. dir. isotopes div. U.S. Atomic Energy Commn., Oak Ridge, Tenn., 1950-56; dept asst., dir. div. civilian applications U.S. Atomic Energy Commn., Washington, 1957-60, dep. dir isotopes devel. div., 1961-65, dir. isotopes div., 1966-74; head chemistry and indsl. applications Internat. Atomic Energy Agy., Vienna, Austria, 1975-79, coord. regional coop. Asia-Pacific area, 1980-82; dir. and chief tech. adviser Office Indsl. Tech. Transfer U.N., Tokyo, 1982-85; sr. adviser Mitsubishi Kasei, Tokyo, 1986—; sr. sci. tech. adviser Asian Rare Earth Co., Ipoh, Malaysi, 1986-90; founder and chief exec. officer Kakihana & Fowler Assocs., various countries, 1987—; offical U.S. rep. UN Internat. Confs. 2d-4th on Uses of Atomic Energy, Geneva; offical U.S. rep. 5th-13th Japan Conf. on Radioisotopes. Contbr. articles to profl. jours. Oak Ridge (Tenn.) Nat. Lab. fellow, 1950, 51. Fellow Am. Inst. Chemists; mem. APHA, AAAS, Royal Soc. Health, Am. Nuclear Soc., Washington Acad. Sci., N.Y. Acad. Sci., Am. Chem. Soc., Soc. Nuclear Medicine, Am. Heart Assn., Kenwood Golf and Country Club. Republican. Episcopalian. Home: 5124 Westpath Way Bethesda MD 20816-2318

FOWLER, KEITH THOMAS, systems consultant; b. Pitts., Dec. 26, 1950; s. Robert Thomas Fowler and Grace Leah (Tuckley) Bucholtz; m. Heidi Louise Beucker, Dec. 12, 1987. BA in Polit. Sci., Tex. A&M U., 1972; postgrad., Point Park Coll., Pitts. Systems mktg. rep. Control Data Corp., Pitts., 1977-79; cons., assoc. Office of the Future, Inc., Guttenberg, N.J., 1979-80; systems analyst Westinghouse Electric Corp., Pitts., 1980-85, pres. enhanced bldg. svcs., 1985-87, systems cons. energy systems, 1987—. Mem. Polish Hill Civic Assn., Pitts., 1983-84; vol. tutor Pitts. Pub. Schs., 1987—; chmn. Brighton Heights Luth. Ch. (cemetery com. 1988-90). 1st lt. USMC, 1972-77. Republican. Roman Catholic. Home: 1020 Applejack Dr Gibsonia PA 15044-9575 Office: Westinghouse Energy Systems PO Box 355 Pittsburgh PA 15230-0355

FOWLER, MOLLY RULON-MILLER, artist; b. N.Y.C., Mar. 26, 1935; s. John and Polly Hoge (Norris) Rulon-Miller; m. Gordon Blackford, June 24, 1957; children: Gordon B. Jr., Douglas B. BA magna cum laude, Smith Coll., 1957. Intern Met. Mus. Cloisters, N.Y.C., 1955-56; mem. edn. Wadsworth Atheneum, Hartford, Conn., 1957-58; trustee Noah Webster Found., West HArtford, Conn. One-woman shows include New Birtain Mus., 1982, Smith Coll. Mus., 1982, Gallery 24 CPTV. Mem. Soc. Conn. Craftsman, Phi Beta Kappa. Episcopalian. Home: 21 Cliffmore Rd West Hartford CT 06107

FOWLER, ROBERT ARCHIBALD, infosystems company executive; b. Lewistown, Pa., May 29, 1931; s. Harry K. Fowler and Margaret (Elder) Mann; m. Gail Brewer; children: R. Wendell, Ann, Allen. BS in Econs., Franklin and Marshall Coll., 1953; MBA, Cornell U., 1958. Auditor Gen. Motors Corp., Rochester, N.Y., 1953-54; exec. trainee Mfr.'s Hanover Bank, N.Y.C., 1958-60; credit rep. Cen. Trust Corp., Rochester, 1960-61; mktg. exec. Voplex Corp., Rochester, 1961-70; chmn. 5 W Info. Services, Rochester, 1970—; treas. Clover Investment Group, Rochester, 1960—. Author: Careerism, 1970, Buyerism, 1971, Creative Winemaking, 1973; contbr. articles to profl. jours. Served with U.S. Army, 1954-56. Mem. Am. Legion. Republican. Presbyterian. Club: Penfield Golf. Office: 5W Info Svcs Inc 1475 Winton Rd N Rochester NY 14609-5803

FOWLER, RUSSELL MARCUS, economic developer; b. Butler, N.Y., Dec. 29, 1915; s. Clarence Mansfield and Ethel Irene (Walker) F.; m. Jane Olive Wandell, Apr. 21, 1945 (dec. Dec. 1984); children: John Russell, Linda Jane Fowler Van Gorder. BS, Syracuse U., 1936, MS, 1937; LLB, Fordham Law Sch., 1942. Bar: N.Y. Asst. mgr. lumber dept. Am. Sugar Refining Co., N.Y.C., 1937-42; v.p. Collister Corp., N.Y.C., 1946-63; owner, administrator Fowler Equipment Co., Syracuse, N.Y., 1963-68; econ. developer Wayne County, Lyons, N.Y., 1968-86, ret., 1986; bd. dirs. The Inst. Community Coll. of the Finger Lakes, Canadaigua, N.Y., 1986-90; cons. Sodus (N.Y.) Youth Venture, 1988-90. Contbr. Beyond Our Means (Alfred L. Malabre, Jr.), 1987. Mem. local planning com. environ. safety Wayne County, N.Y., 1987-90. 1st lt. U.S. Army, 1942-46. Recipient Letter of Commendation, Comdg. Gen. Bklyn. Port of Embarkation, 1945; named Man of Yr., Soundscriber Corp., 1958, N.Y. State Econ. Devel. Coun., 1983, Citizen of Yr., Newark (N.Y.) C. of C., 1985; Paul Harris fellow Rotary Internat., 1991. Republican. Presbyterian. Home: 168 Concord Dr North East PA 16428-1408

FOX, ANDREW MARK, small business owner; b. Lancaster, Pa., Mar. 12, 1957; s. Carl F. and Isabel (Hauser) F.; m. Pamela Joy Wallick, Oct. 13, 1979; 1 child, Alexander Mark. Mgr. Household Fin., Altoona, Pa., 1979-83; owner Dauphin Kirby, Harrisburg, Pa., 1984—. Mem. Rep. Nat. Com. 500 Club. Lutheran. Home: 830 3d St Lancaster PA 17603-5021

FOX, SISTER CECELIA MARY, registrar; b. Paterson, N.J., Aug. 15, 1954; d. Charles Bernard and Cecelia Rita (Kinney) F. AAS in Bus. Adminstrn., Ocean County Coll., 1974; BA in Elem. Edn., Georgian Ct. Coll., 1976, MA in Edn., 1990. Cert. elem. tchr., N.J. Elem. tchr. St. Mary Sch., Perth Amboy, N.J., 1977-78, St. Philip and St. James Sch., Phillipsburg, N.J., 1978, St. Elizabeth Sch., Bernardsville, N.J., 1980-84; asst. to treas. Georgian Ct. Coll., Lakewood, N.J., 1984-86, asst. registrar, 1986-89, registrar, 1989—. Mem. Mercy Higher Edn. Colloquium N.Y., N.J. Assn. Collegiate Registrars and Admissions Officers, Middle State Assn. Collegiate Registrars and Admissions Officers, Am. Assn. Collegiate Registrars and Admissions Officers, Notary Pub. Assn. Roman Catholic. Home and Office: Georgian Ct Coll 900 Lakewood Ave Lakewood NJ 08701-2697

FOX, DAVID LOUIS, press secretary; b. Waterloo, Iowa, Feb. 15, 1949; s. Richard and Goldie (Warschoff) F.; m. Carol Rinehart, Dec. 27, 1969; 1 child, Elizabeth. BA in Speech and English, U. No. Iowa, 1971. Reporter/anchor KWWL TV, Waterloo, Iowa, 1970-72; news dir. KLEU Radio, Waterloo, Iowa, 1972-73, KWPC Radio, Muscatine, Iowa, 1973-74; reporter, weatherman WHBF TV, Rock Island, Ill., 1974-75; field dir. Frank M. Magid Assocs., Marion, Iowa, 1975-76; news dir. KTHI TV, Fargo, N.D., 1976-79; reporter, corres. AP, Detroit, Centralia, 1979-87; reporter AP, Washington, 1987-89; press sec. U.S. Rep. Lynn Martin R-Ill., Washington, 1989-91, U.S. Rep. Harold Rogers R-Ky., Washington, 1991—; cons. Fox Rhinehart Assocs., Silver Spring, Md., 1990—; promotion cons. Free Flight Balloons, Cedar Rapids, Iowa and Fargo, N.D., 1974-79. Co. comdr. Md. Def. Force, Gaithersburg, 1988—. Mem. Mil. Police Regimental Assn., Md. State Guard Assn., Kings Point Maritime Assn., State Def. Force Assn. of U.S., U.S. Merchant Marine Acad. Mid-Atlantic Parents Assn. (chmn. 1991—), Nat. Assn. for Sport Divers (pres. 1987-90), Masons.

FOX, DAWNE MARIE, safety scientist; b. West Lafayette, Ind., Aug. 3, 1948; d. Gerhard P. and Betty M. (Norris) F.; m. Gerald C. Newmeyer, Oct. 4, 1969 (div. 1981); children: Mimie, Jerry. Grad. magna cum laude, Lord Fairfax, Middletown, Va., 1979; student, Casper (Wyo.) Coll., 1985. Regional safety coord. Milchem Inc., Casper, 1979-83; safety dir. Energy Insulation Inc., Casper, 1983-85; safety mgr. Western States Constrn., Loveland, Colo., 1985-86; safety officer Govt. of D.C., 1987-89; dir. safety, health svcs. Denver and Rio Grande R.R., Denver, 1989-90; safety mgr. Browning-Ferris Inc., Hyattsville, 1990-91; sr. safety scientist Gen. Physics Corp., Columbia, Md., 1991—; cons., Casper, 1983-85. Instr. ARC, Casper, 1981-85, Am. Heart Assn., Casper, 1982-85; spl. aide to Spl. Olympics, Casper, 1983-85. Mem. Nat. Safety Coun. Am. Soc. Safety Engrs. (v.p. 1982-83, pres. 1983-84, Safety Profl. award 1982). Republican. Roman Catholic. Home: 11410 Edmonston Rd Beltsville MD 20705-1731

FOX, HAROLD EDWARD, obstetrician, gynecologist, educator, researcher; b. East Orange, N.J., Feb. 19, 1945; s. Willis Edward and Elizabeth (Strathearn) F.; m. Rhea Keller, June 18, 1966; children: Harold Hamilton, Andrhea Alicia. BA, U. Rochester, 1967, MS, MD with honors, 1972. Diplomate Am. Bd. Ob-Gyn., Am. Bd. Maternal-Fetal Medicine. Intern, resident St. Reme Meml. Hosp., Rochester, N.Y., 1972-75; dir. Regional Perinatal Program, Rochester, N.Y., 1975-79; dir. obstetrics and maternal fetal medicine U. Rochester, 1977-79; dir. maternal fetal medicine Columbia U., N.Y.C., 1979—, dir. obstetrics, 1985-88, vice chmn. ob-gyn., 1988-91, chmn. protem dept. ob-gyn., 1991—; chmn. women and infant transmission study NIH, 1988—, mem. pediatric com. AIDS clin. trials group, 1989—, organizing mem. women's com.; mem. obstet. adv. com. N.Y.C. Dept. Health. Editor Pediatric AIDS, 1991—; contbr. articles to profl. jours. Grantee NIH, 1988—, USPHS, 1991—, March of Dimes. Fellow Soc. Gynecologic Investigation, Am. Coll. Ob-Gyn.; mem. Internat. AIDS Soc., Am. Inst. Ultrasound in Medicine, Perinatal Rsch. Soc. Home: 6 Whippoorwill Lake Rd Chappaqua NY 10514-2314 Office: PH-1628 CPMC 622 W 168th St New York NY 10032-3702

FOX, HARVEY MICHAEL, state official; b. N.Y.C., Nov. 11, 1942; s. Sidney and Evelyn (Berinsky) F.; m. Natalie Glassoff, July 11, 1965; children: Alyson, Darren. BA in Acctg., CUNY, 1975. Acct. S&L Taxi and Limousine Corp., N.Y.C., 1975-79, Agy. for Child Devel., N.Y.C., 1979-81; profl. fin. tests developer N.J. Dept. Civil Svc., Trenton, 1981-84; supervising pers. mgmt. analyst N.J. Dept. Pers., Trenton, 1984-89; pers. mgr. N.J. Dept. Environ. Protection and Energy, Trenton, 1989—. Mem. Internat. Pers. Adv. Assn., Cert. Pub. Mgrs. Soc. N.J. (cert. pub. mgr., cert. in supervisory mgmt.), Inst. for Aerobics Rsch. (cert. aerobics tester), KP. Home: J 101 Tenbytowne Delran NJ 08075 Office: NJ Dept Environ Protection and Energy 436 E State St Trenton NJ 08608-1503

FOX, HERBERT, educational administrator, management consultant; b. N.Y.C., May 27, 1939; s. Abraham and Pearl (Grabel) F.; S.B., M.I.T., 1960, M.S., Poly. Inst. Bklyn., 1962, Ph.D., 1964; m. Dorothy Aig, Jan. 27, 1962; children: Paul, Seth, Jeffrey. Research asst., then research assoc. aerodynamics lab. Poly. Inst. Bklyn., 1959-63, asst. prof., 1964-68; assoc. prof. aeros. and astronautics NYU, 1968-70, chmn. dept. mech. engring. tech., 1970-71; dean div. sci. and tech. N.Y. Inst. Tech., Old Westbury, 1971-77, v.p., 1982-86, sr. v.p. acad. affairs, 1986—; pres. Inst. for Advanced Technology, Inc., 1982—; project mgr., dept. head, v.p. Pope, Evans & Robbins, N.Y.C., 1978-82; cons. to industry. Chmn. bd. edn. Solomon Schechter Sch., Westchester, N.Y., 1972-73, 80-87; trustee, sec. Beth El Synagogue Center, New Rochelle, N.Y., 1971-73. Recipient Nat. Undergrad. award Inst. Aerospace Scis., 1960; Sigma Xi research award N.Y. U., 1966, Lindback Found. award excellence teaching, 1968. Fellow AIAA (assoc.; dir. 1971-74, v.p. edn. 1976-80). Author: Urban Technology: A Primer on Problems, 1973, Urban Technology: A Second Primer on Problems, 1975; also articles. Home: 35 Trenor Dr New Rochelle NY 10804-3731 Office: PO Box 170 Old Westbury NY 11568

FOX, IRA MARTIN, podiatrist; b. Lancaster, Pa., Mar. 9, 1953; s. Leonard P. and Janice (Osipow) F.; m. Helen E. Yannelli, May 10, 1980; children: Julian P., Dara A., Dylan B. BA, Johns Hopkins U., 1975; D Podiatric Medicinee, Pa. Coll. Podiatric Medicine, 1980. Asst. prof. Pa. Coll. Podiatric Medicine, Phila., 1982-91; head sect. podiatric surgery Cooper Hosp., Univ. Med. Ctr., Camden, N.J., 1984—; mem. recommendations com. N.J. Bd. Med. Examiners. Contbr. articles to med. jours. Fellow Am. Coll. Foot Surgeons (com. on trauma 1992—). Office: Cooper Hosp-Univ Med Ctr Dept Surg 3 Cooper Plz Ste 411 Camden NJ 08103

FOX, JAMES FREDERICK, public relations counsel; b. Cedar Rapids, Iowa, Feb. 5, 1917; s. Samuel James and Anna L. (Pietz) F.; m. Sylvia Porter Collins, 1979. B.A., U. Iowa, 1940; LL.D., World U., San Juan, 1975. Copywriter Kohler Co., Wis., 1940-41; partner James W. Irwin Assos., N.Y.C., 1945-48; mgr. editorial services Prudential Ins. Co., Newark, 1949-52; dir. pub. relations Congoleum-Nairn, Inc., Kearney, N.J., 1953; mgr. pub. relations chem. divs. Olin Mathieson Chem. Corp., N.Y.C., 1954-56; dir. pub. relations Chase Manhattan Bank, N.Y.C., 1957-61; v.p. Chase Manhattan Bank, 1959-61, indsl. pub. relations counsel, 1961—; cons. editor, 1982—; v.p., dir. The Sylvia Porter Orgn., Inc., 1987-90. Contbr. articles to profl. jours. Served to lt. USNR, 1942-45. Fellow Pub. Rels. Soc. Am. (chmn. counselors sect. 1970, pres. 1974, Gold Anvil award 1978); mem. Met. Opera Club (N.Y.C.), Sigma Delta Chi, Phi Delta Theta, Kappa Tau Alpha. Republican. Episcopalian. Home: Rt 5 Box 197 Pound Ridge NY 10576

FOX, JEAN, piano educator; b. Madison, Wis., Mar. 1, 1941; d. Robert Lewis and Virginia Leonie (Burnier) Meriwether; m. Virgil Grant Fox, Mar. 3, 1962; children: Linda, Frederick, Steven, Barbara. BA, Kans. State U., 1965. Pvt. piano tchr. Manhattan, Kans., 1963-66, Denver, 1966-74, Allentown, Pa., 1974—; founder Community Music Sch., Allentown, 1981, mem. faculty, 1981-86; speaker Del. Music Tchr.'s Conv., 1987-88, Music Tchrs. Nat. Conv., Wichita, Kans., 1989; lectr., workshop clinician on pvt. music teaching, Del., Md., Kans., Fla., N.Y., Pa., N.J., Calgary, B.C. Author: Performance with Pleasure, 1987 Piano Guild Notes; contbr. articles to profl. jours. Music del. People to People Program, Southeast Asia, 1989. Named to Hall of Fame Am. Coll. Musicians, Austin, Tex., 1986; selected PA Disting. Tchr. of 1988 PA Music Tchrs. Assn. Mem. AAUW, Nat. Guild Piano Tchrs. (adjudicator 1980—), Nat. Music Tchrs. Assn. (chair ind. music tchrs. com. eastern div. 1985—), Pa. Music Tchrs. Assn. (sec. 1987089, 1st v.p., pres.-elect. 1989-91, pres. 1991—), Lehigh Valley Music Tchrs. Assn. (pres. 1987-89), Ind. Music Tchrs. (chair 1985-90), Music Tchrs. Nat. Assn. (1st v.p. eastern div. 1990-92), Toastmasters. Home: 4102 Kilmer Ave Allentown PA 18104-3310

FOX, JOAN MARIE, educator; b. Flint, Mich., July 8, 1948; d. Elmer William and Elizabeth (Fisher) Skolnik; m. Richard Charles Fox, Dec. 19, 1970; children: Elizabeth Grace, Julie Anne. BA in Edn., Mich. State U., 1970; postgrad., Ind. U., 1982-83; MEd, U. Md., 1988; postgrad., Loyola Coll., 1989—. Tchr. math. Dayton (Ohio) Pub. Schs., 1970-71; tchr. 5th grade Mt. Orab (Ohio) Elem., 1971-75; docent Indpls. Mus. of Art, 1979-81; substitute instrional aide Washington Twp. Schs., Indpls., 1981-83; ednl. cons. Mastery Edn. Corp., Watertown, Mass., 1983-85; tchr. Howard County Pub. Schs., Ellicott City, Md., 1985—; bd. dirs. Mt. Hebron Nursery Sch., Ellicott City, 1984—; employee recognition com. Howard County Pub. Schs., 1988—. Mem. Md Com. for Children, Balt., 1983—, Smithsonian, Washington, 1983—, ARC, Balt. Mem. NEA, Nat. Coun. Tchrs. of Math., Phi Delta Kappa (sec. 1985-86, v.p. 1986-87, pres. 1987-88). Democrat. Episcopalian. Home: 9990 Old Annapolis Rd Ellicott City MD 21042-5602 Office: Howard County Pub Schs 5370 Oldstone Ct Columbia MD 21045-2499

FOX, JOHN JOSEPH, JR., historian; b. Pittsfield, Mass., Dec. 20, 1931; s. John J. and Blanche Julia (Pellerin) F.; BS, North Adams State Coll., 1959; MA in History, Lehigh U., 1964; postgrad. Boston U., 1968; m. Marilyn Ann Volin, Feb. 23, 1957; 1 son, John Charles. Tchr., Pittsfield (Mass.) Pub. Sch. System, 1959-61; teaching asst. Lehigh U., Bethlehem, Pa., 1961-64; prof. dept. history Salem (Mass.) State Coll., 1964—; pres. Oral History Research Assos.; cons. in oral, local history. Del. Democratic State Conv., Mass., 1970, 72; mem. Danvers Democratic Town Com., 1967-85; trustee Peabody Inst. Library, Danvers, Mass., 1976-85; mem. council Essex Inst., Salem, 1979-87. Served with inf. U.S. Army, 1952-54. Mem. Am. Hist. Assn., Orgn. Am. Historians, Social Sci. History Assn., Essex Inst. (council, 1979-87), Oral History Assn. (exec. bd. 1984-87), New Eng. Assn. of Oral History (pres. 1974-77, exec. sec. 1985—, Harvey A. Kantor award, 1982), Am. Soc. for Legal History. Democrat. Roman Catholic. Author: Oral History: Window to the Past, 1977, Parker Pride: Memories of Working Days At Parker Brothers, 1987; Window on the Past: A Guide to Oral History, 1980; Voices From the Past: Oral History in Massachusetts, in a Guide to the History of Massachusetts, 1988; Massachusetts and the Creation of the Federal Union in The Constitution and The States; compiler of bibliography Up-Date in The Oral History, Rev., 1977; book review editor Oral History Rev., 1980-87; editor The England of Oral History Annual, The New England Assn. Oral Hist. Annual; mem. editorial bd. Jour. of Nursing History, 1985-89, Locus, 1987. Home: 134 Burley St Danvers MA 01923-2366 Office: Salem State Coll Dept History Salem MA 01970

FOX, JOHN NICHOLAS, physics educator; b. Utica, N.Y., June 20, 1937; s. Albert Nicholas and Marion C. (Cole) F.; m. Joan Denise O'Connor, Sept. 12, 1959; children: James N., Jason N. BS in Physics, Lemoyne U., 1959; MS in Physics, Cath. U. Am., 1961; PhD in Physics, Wesleyan U., 1971. Instr. physics Utica (N.Y.) Coll. of Syracuse, 1961-67; assoc. prof. physics Indiana (Pa.) Univ. of Pa., 1971-74, prof. physics, 1974—, dean's assoc., 1991—; dir. Project Excels, NSF, Indiana, 1985—. Author: Interfacing the High School Laboratory to the Computer, 1990. Named Extraordinary Tchr. Am. Assn. HIgher Edn., Chgo., 1989, Univ. Disting. Prof. Indiana U. of Pa., 1990. Mem. Am. Assn. Physics Tchrs., Am. Phys. Soc., Nat. Sci. Tchrs. Assn. Office: Indiana Univ of Pa 305 Weyandt Hall Indiana PA 15701

FOX, JUNE T., education educator; b. Chgo., June 1, 1924; d. Samuel I. and Mollie (Fox) Trachtenberg; m. Marvin Fox, Feb. 20, 1944; children: Avrom, Daniel, Sheryl. BS, Northwestern U., 1945; MA, Ohio State U., 1950, PhD, 1967. Statistician USAAF, Dayton, Ohio, 1945-46, Coun. Social Agys., Chgo., 1946-48; asst. prof., project adminstr. Ohio State U., Columbus, 1967-74; mem. faculty, adminstr. Lesley Coll., Cambridge, Mass., 1975-82, dean edn. and spl. edn. grad. sch., 1982—; cons. Turning Points project, Carnegie Found., Cambridge, 1989—; site dir. Lesley Coll. Ctr. Reading Recovery, 1990—. Contbr. articles on ednl. philosophy to profl. publs. Mem. gov.'s adv. commn. Lucretia Crocker Selection Com., Christa McAuliffe Tchr. Awards, Mass., 1985—. Mem. Phi Beta Kappa. Jewish. Home: 11 Ellison Rd Newton MA 02159-1434 Office: Lesley Coll 29 Everett St Cambridge MA 02138-2790

FOX, KELLY DIANE, assistant buyer; b. Brockton, Mass., Sept. 9, 1959; d. James H. and Betty Jane (Calloway) F.; m. Alan David Goldberg, July 6, 1985; 1 child, Andrew Jason. B.A., Allegheny Coll., 1980; postgrad. in Bus. Adminstrn., Suffolk U., 1983-84; student Temple U., London, 1978, Syracuse U., London, 1979. Asst. mgr. Casual Male, Braintree, Mass., 1980, Hit or Miss, Braintree, 1981-82; merchandiser Foxmoor, West Bridgewater, Mass., 1982; distbr. Hill's Dept. Stores, Canton, Mass., 1982-85; asst. buyer BJ's Wholesale Club, Natick, Mass., 1985—; cheerleading coach Avon High Sch., Mass., 1982-83. Mem. Nat. Assn. Female Execs. Methodist. Avocations: dance, exercise, cooking, art galleries.

FOX, MARCIA ROSE, management education consultant, writer; b. Dover, N.H., May 29, 1942; d. Robert L. and Leah (Rosenberg) F.; divorced; 1 child, Lauren Rosenberg. BA, Boston U., 1963; MA, U. Pa., 1964; PhD, CUNY, 1975. Lectr. English Hunter Coll., N.Y.C., 1967-72; spl. asst. to dean Coll. of Law Ohio State U., Columbus, 1973-75; asst. dean grad. sch. pub. adminstrn. NYU, N.Y.C., 1975-80; mgmt. edn. cons. Mobil Oil Co., N.Y.C., 1981-85; sr. v.p. Drake Beam Morin, Inc., N.Y.C., 1986—. Author: Put Your Degree to Work, 1979, 2nd rev. edit., 1988. Chmn. program com. Internat. Soc. Pre-Retirement Planners, 1989-90; bd. mem.-at-large Weiner Ctr. Edn. com. United Jewish Appeal, N.Y.C., 1991—; chmn. Met. div. Jewish Guild for the Blind, N.Y.C., 1990—, bd. mem. ex-officio, 1990—. NDEA and Univ. fellow CUNY, 1972. Office: Drake Beam Morin Inc 100 Park Ave New York NY 10017-5516

FOX, MARGARET BLAIR, retail broker, real estate agent; b. Dover, Del., Nov. 5, 1951; d. William Robert Fox and Penelope Rodney (Layton) Henrickson. AD, Colby Jr. Coll., N.H., 1972; BA in Art History and Am. Studies, Colby Coll., Maine, 1974; postgrad., Katherine Gibbs Sch., Boston, 1974; postgrad. in real estate sales, NYU, 1987. Lic. real estate agent, fine jewelry broker. Founder Personal Assistance Plus, N.Y.C. and Houston, 1982-87; pub. Focus Pubs., N.Y.C., 1982-86; real estate salesperson Helen Downey Co., N.Y.C., 1986-87; retail broker Ladenburg, Thalmann & Co. Inc., N.Y.C., 1987—. Vol. numerous civic and social orgns. Mem. DAR, Descendants of Signers of Declaration of Independence, Le Club, Women Investment Brokers, Tennisport. Office: Ladenburg Thalmann & Co 540 Madison Ave New York NY 10022-3213

FOX, MARIAN, social worker, psychotherapist; b. Queens, N.Y., Nov. 25, 1950; d. Julius and Mae (Gross) Wagner. BA, Boston U., 1973; MSW, Columbia U., 1977. Supr. social svcs. Dept. Pub. Health, Boston, 1977-80; clin. social worker in pvt. practice Cambridge, Mass., 1979—; clin. assoc. Assn. for Human Resources, Concord, Mass., 1982-83; instr. Boston Ctr. for Adult Edn., 1979, Boston Hotline, 1980; educator, supr. Tapestry, Inc., Cambridge, 1980-86. Mem. Nat. Registry Clin. Social Work (diplomate), Assn. Transpersonal Psychology, Nat. Assn. Social Workers, Nature Conservancy, Humane Soc. U.S., NOW, Internat. Imagery Assn., Inst. Visualization Rsch. Democrat. Home: 76 Garfield St Cambridge MA 02138-1818

FOX, MARVIN, philosophy educator, rabbi; b. Chgo., Oct. 17, 1922; s. Norman and Sophie (Gershengorn) F.; m. June Elaine Trachtenberg, Feb. 20, 1944; children: Avrom Baruch, Daniel Jonathan, Sheryl Deena. BA, Northwestern U., 1942, MA, 1946; PhD, U. Chgo., 1950. Ordained rabbi, 1942. Faculty Ohio State U., Columbus, 1948-74, instr., 1948-52, asst. prof., 1952-56, assoc. prof., 1956-61, prof. philosophy, 1961-73, Leo Yassenoff prof. philosophy and Jewish studies, 1973-74; Philip W. Lown prof. Jewish philosophy, dir. Lown Sch. Nr. Ea. and Judaic Studies Brandeis U., Waltham, Mass., 1974—; vis. prof. Hebrew Theol. Coll. Chgo., 1955, Hebrew U., Jerusalem, 1970-71, Bar-Ilan U., Ramat-Gan, Israel, 1970-71; Shoolman Disting. vis. prof. Hebrew Coll., Brookline, Mass., 1990-92; mem. exec. com. Conf. Jewish Philosophy, 1963-69, Inst. for Judaism and Contemporary Thought, Israel, 1971—; mem. acad. bd. Melton Rsch. Ctr., Jewish Theol. Sem. Am., 1972—; mem. Internat. Coun. of Yad Yashem, Jerusalem, 1983—. Author: Modern Jewish Ethics—Theory and Practice, 1975, Interpreting Maimonides: Studies in Methodology, Metaphysics and Moral Philosophy, 1990; editor: Kant's Fundamental Principles of the Metaphysic of Morals, 1949; cons. editor jour. History of Philosophy, 1970-76; mem. editorial bd. Libr. of Living Philosophers, 1946—, Judaism, 1953—, Tradition, 1956-89, AJS Rev., 1976-84, Daat, 1978—, Jewish Edn. Yearbook, 1979—; bd. editors Studies in Judaism, 1986—; contbr. articles to profl. jours. With USAAF, 1942-46. Elizabeth Clay Howald Found. fellow, 1956-57, Am. Coun. Learned Socs. fellow, 1962-63, NEH fellow, 1980-81. Mem. AAUP, Am. Philos. Assn., World Union Jewish Studies (governing

coun.), Assn. Jewish Studies (bd. dirs. 1970—, v.p. 1973-75, pres. 1975-78), Nat. Commn. B'nai Brith Hillel Founds. (exec. com.), Medieval Acad. Am., Metaphys. Soc. Am., Am. Acad. Jewish Rsch., Conf. Jewish Philosophy. Home: 11 Ellison Rd Newton MA 02159-1434 Office: Brandeis U Dept Nr Ea and Judaic Studies Waltham MA 02254

FOX, MARY ANN WILLIAMS, librarian; b. Savannah, Ga., Jan. 16, 1939; d. Alton F. and Arthur (Colquitt) Williams; m. William Francis Fox, Dec. 26, 1960 (div. 1984); children: Katherine Frances, William Francis Jr. BA, U. Ga., 1960; MLS, Rutgers U., 1984. Libr. Metuchen (N.J.) Pub. Libr., 1983-85, Mable Smith Douglas Libr. Rutgers U., New Brunswick, N.J., 1984, Firestone Libr. Princeton (N.J.) U., 1985, The Hun Sch. of Princeton, 1985—; bd. dirs. Region 5 Libr. Coop., N.J., 1985—. Trustee East Brunswick (N.J.) Pub. Library, 1979—; bd. dirs., Cen. Jersey YWCA, New Brunswick, 1985-88, Cen. Atlantic Conf. United Ch. of Christ, 1985-88. Mem. ALA, N.J. Libr. Assn., N.J. Ind. Sch. Assn. (chair libr. sect. 1988—), Edn. Media Assn. N.J. (bd. dirs. 1987—), Librs. of Middlesex (pres.). Democrat. Mem. United Ch. of Christ. Home: 10 Redcoat Dr East Brunswick NJ 08816-2759 Office: Hun Sch Princeton Edgerstone Rd Princeton NJ 08540

FOX, MIRIAM ANNETTE, state legislative tax revenue analyst; b. Cuba, N.Y., May 27, 1959; m. Frederick S. Fox, Jan., 1991. BA in Polit. Sci., Idaho State U., 1984; MS in Pub. Mgmt. & Policy, Carnegie-Mellon, 1986. Semiconductor line technician Gould/AMI, Pocatello, Idaho, 1978-84; legal rsch. analyst Manning, Holmes And Winmill Law Firm, Pocatello, 1983-84; market rsch. intern Internat. Trade Adminstrn., Pitts., 1985; rsch. intern Health & Welfare Planning Assn., Pitts., 1985-86; acctg. clk. Carnegie Mellon U., Pitts., 1986; tax revenue analyst Pa. House Appropriations Com., Harrisburg, 1987-91, sr. tax revenue analyst, 1991—. Mem. Nat. Tax. Assn. (taxation fin. inst. 1988—), Capitol Hill Dem. Women's Club, Phi Kappa Phi. Office: Pa House Appropriation Com 512 E9 Main Capitol Bldg PO Box 54 Harrisburg PA 17108-0054

FOX, PAUL G., management training company executive; b. Boston, May 21, 1949; s. Paul Fitzpatrick and Harriott (Cole) F.; m. Cynthia Marie Callari, Oct. 2, 1973. BA in History, Union Coll., Schenectady, 1971; MS in Orgnl. Behavior, U. Hartford, 1979. Adminstr. pension plan CIGNA Corp., Bloomfield, Conn., 1971-74, sr. tng. cons., 1975-79; mgr. mgmt. devel. Conn. Bank and Trust, Hartford, Conn., 1979-86; pres. Fox Performance Group, West Granby, Conn., 1986—. Contbr. articles to profl. jours. Mem. alumni admissions com. Union Coll., 1990—; bd. dirs. Granby (Conn.) Community TV, 1991. Mem. ASTD (bd. dirs. Conn. chpt. 1982-91, chmn. region 1 conf. 1982, pres., Outstanding Contbn. award 1984), Nat. Speakers Assn., Greater Hartford C. of C. (bus. coun.). Office: 44 Day St S West Granby CT 06090-1413

FOX, RICHARD KEITH, educational association administrator, consultant; b. Flushing, N.Y., July 19, 1938; s. Frederick and Mae Averyl (Pysher) F.; m. Jane Lynn Hornby, Oct. 25, 1959; children: Richard, Carie, Robb. AB, Brown U., 1960; MEd, Antioch Coll., 1971. Cert. secondary sch. principal. Mem. faculty Vermont Acad., Saxtons River, Vt., 1961-64; acct. exec. Campbell Films, Saxtons River, Vt., 1964-66; asst. dean devel. and exec. officer William Jewett Tucker Found. at Dartmouth Coll., Hanover, N.H., 1967-74; dir. devel. Dartmouth Coll. Med. Sch., Hanover, N.H., 1974-76; v.p. Kenyon Coll., Gambier, Ohio, 1976-77; assoc. dir. devel. Brown U., Providence, R.I., 1977-78; dir. alumni affairs and devel. Groton (Mass.) Sch., 1978—; cons. schs. and not for profit orgns., 1986—. Contbr. articles to profl. jours. Mayor & 1st trustee Village of Saxtons River, Vt., 1964; selectman Town of Rockingham, Bellows Falls, Vt., 1967; 1st pres. United Way of the Upper Valley, Lebanon, N.H., 1974. Named Hon. Alumnus, Dartmouth Coll., 1963, Groton Sch., 1985. Mem. World Wildlife Fund, The Conservation Found. (nat. coun. mem. 1990—), Planned Giving Group of New England. Home: Garland Rd Lancaster NH 03584-2400 Office: Groton Sch Farmers Row # 991 Groton MA 01450-1802

FOX, RICHARD KENNETH, international exchange company executive; b. Cin., Oct. 22, 1925; s. Richard Kenneth Sr. and Kathryn Lucille (Lynch) F.; m. Jeanne Jones Fox, Sept. 2, 1950 (dec. 1991); children: Jeanne Fox Alston, Jane E., Helen K. AB, Ind. U., 1950; LLD (hon.), Valparaiso U., 1983. Assoc. dir. Minn. Fair Employment Practices Comm., St. Paul, Minn., 1955-60; spl. asst. Dept. of State, Washington, 1960-65, dep. asst. sec. Bur. Edn. & Cultural Affairs, 1970-74, dep. dir. pers., 1974-76; counselor for adminstrn. Am. Embassy Madrid, Spain, 1965-70; mem. Sr. Seminar in Fgn. Policy, Washington, 1976-77; U.S. amb. to Republic of Trinidad and Tobago, 1977-80; sr. dep. inspector gen. Dept. and Fgn. Svc., 1980-84, ret., 1984; sr. v.p. Meridian House Internat., 1984—; bd. dirs. Vesper Internat., San Leandro, Calif., 1987—. Pres. Lutheran Human Rels. Assn., Valparaiso, Ind., 1970-74; trustee U. D.C., Washington, 1972-77; pres., bd. dirs. Wheat Ridge Found., Chgo., 1979-89; treas., bd. dirs. Big Bros. Nat. Capital Area, Washington, 1985—; mem. pres.'s adv. coun. Valparaiso U., 1986—. With USN, 1944-46, PTO. Mem. Am. Fgn. Svc. Protective Assn. (pres. bd. 1979—), Washington Inst. Fgn. Affairs. Democrat. Lutheran. Home: 1936 Tulip St NW Washington DC 20012 Office: Meridian House Internat 1624 Crescent St NW Washington DC 20009

FOXMAN, ABRAHAM H., advocacy organization administrator; came to U.S., 1950; s. Joseph Foxman. BA in Polit. Sci., CCNY; JD, NYU; postgrad., Jewish Theol. Sem., New Sch. Social Rsch. Asst. dir. law dept. Anti-Defamation League of B'nai B'rith, N.Y.C., 1965-68, head middle ea. affairs dept., 1968-73, head leadership div., 1973-78, assoc. nat. dir., 1978-87, nat. dir., 1987—. Office: Anti-Defamation League of B'nai B'rith 823 UN Plz New York NY 10017*

FOXWELL, ELIZABETH MARIE, editor, writer; b. Somerville, N.J., Aug. 30, 1963; d. James Adolph and Rita Ann (Drohan) F. BS in Journalism, U. Md., 1985; MA in Liberal Studies with distinction, Georgetown U., 1990. Editorial asst. Nat. Assn. Fgn. Student Affairs, Washington, 1985-87; coord. publs. internat. student exch. program Georgetown U., Washington, 1987-91; editor Am. Assn. Colls. for Tchr. Edn., Washington, 1992—; bd. dirs. Malice Domestic, Bethesda, Md., publicity liaison, 1988—; freelance editor Editorial Experts, Inc., Alexandria, Va., 1991—; presenter Soc. Biblical Lit. Conf., Washington, 1992. Contbr. articles to profl. jours. Recipient 2d prize in play contest N.J. Ctr. for the Performing Arts, 1981, honorable mention in writing contest Interlochen Arts Acad., 1981. Home: 5513 Trent Ct # 210 Alexandria VA 22311

FOY, CHARLES DALEY, research soil scientist; b. Buena Vista, Ky., Aug. 19, 1923; s. Charles Clinton and Zylphia Gertrude (Binkley) F.; m. Doris Blanche Hornbaker, June 4, 1950; 1 child, David Alden. BS in Agriculture, U. Tenn., 1949; MS in Soil Sci., Purdue U., 1953, PhD in Soil Fertility, 1955. Tchr. Vets. Inst. on Farm Tng. Program, Connersville, Ind., 1949-51; rsch. fellow Purdue U., West Lafayette, Ind., 1951-55; asst. prof. agronomy Purdue U., West Lafayette, 1955-57; rsch. soil scientist, dept. agronomy USDA U. Ark., Fayetteville, 1957-61; rsch. soil scientist, climate stress lab. USDA Agrl. Rsch. Sta., Beltsville, Md., 1961—; cons. and lectr. in U.S. and abroad. Contbr. articles to profl. jours. With U.S. Army, 1943-46, PTO. Grad. rsch. fellow Purdue U., 1953-55; recipient Environ. Quality award Am. Soc. Hort. Sci., 1974. Fellow Am. Soc. Agronomy, Soil Sci. Soc. Am., Crop Sci. Soc. Am. Office: USDA ARS Climate Stress Lab Barc West Beltsville MD 20705

FOY, LOUIS ANDRE, journalist; b. France, June 15, 1912; came to U.S., 1938; s. Georges Albert and Suzanne (Gabriel) F.; m. Katharine Bubb Schaefer, May 15, 1943; children: Georges, Louis-Eric. Doctorate, U. Paris Law Sch., 1938; MA in Polit. Sci., U. Calif., Berkeley, 1942. Officer Compagnie Gen. Transatlantique, Le Havre-Paris, 1936-38; asst. mgr. French Pavilion, N.Y. World Fair, 1939-40; U.S. corr. Paris Presse, Paris, 1945-57; UN corr. Agence France Presse, 1957-71, White House corr., 1967-78; U.S. corr. Europe Un, Washington-N.Y.C., 1960-92, France Soir, Washington-N.Y.C., 1971-92, Radio Vatican, Washington-N.Y.C., 1988-92; pres. UN Corrs. Assn., 1971. Author: The Fifth Republic, 1942. Capt. French Mil. Svc., 1942-45. Recipient Black Star of Benin, French Govt., 1960, Order of Henry the Navigator, Portuguese Govt., 1969, Legion of Honor, French Govt., 1971. Roman Catholic. Home: 333 E 68th St New York NY 10021 Office: UN Ste C-314 UN Secretariat Bldg New York NY 10017

FOYE, PATRICK JOSEPH, lawyer; b. N.Y.C., Jan. 31, 1957; s. Luke Armstrong Jr. and Nancy (Gorman) F.; m. Suzanne Alexandra Matthews, June 25, 1983; 1 child, Caitlin Suzanne. BA, Fordham Coll., 1978, JD, 1981. Bar: N.Y. 1982, U.S. Dist. Ct. (so. dist.) N.Y. 1982. Assoc. Skadden, Arps, Slate, Meagher, & Flom, N.Y.C., 1981-89; ptnr. Skadden, Arps, Slate, Meagher, & Flom, 1989—. Author: Piercing the Corporate Veil, 1989; co-author: Defensive Recapitalizations, 1988. Counsel Matthews for Nassau County Exec. Campaign, Long Beach, N.Y., 1984-85. Mem. ABA, N.Y. State Bar Assn., Assn. of Bar of City of N.Y. Roman Catholic. Office: Skadden Arps Slate Meagher & Flom 919 3d Ave New York NY 10022

FOYES, BETTY J., government information officer, human relations coordinator; b. Delmont, Pa., Oct. 30, 1926; d. Dewey Marcus and Anna Magdaline (Durisko) Cupps; m. James W. Foyes, Dec. 24, 1948; children: William Michael, Robert Alan. Student U. Va.-Falls Church Regional Ctr., 1951-52, Jr. Cert. Bus. and Commerce, 1972, Sr. Cert. Bus. and Commerce, 1975. Lic. realtor, Va. Stenographer, sr. clk. B.F. Goodrich Co., Akron, Ohio, 1944-49; sec. U.S. Dept. Interior, Div. Investigation, Washington, 1949-62, investigations report reviewer, 1962-76, spl. agt., Div. investigation and Office of Inspector Gen., 1976-82, info. officer Office Inspector Gen., FOIA officer, Privacy Act Officer, Human Relations Coordinator, 1982—. Active Nat. Capital Area council Boy Scouts Am., 1974-75. Mem. Assn. Fed. Investigators, Am. Soc. Access Profls., Nat. Trust for Hist. Preservation, Smithsonian Assocs. Episcopalian. Avocations: fishing, boating, reading. Home: 924 N Irving St Arlington VA 22201-2202 Office: Dept Interior Office Inspector Gen 18th and C St NW Washington DC 20240

FRACKMAN, NOEL, art critic; b. N.Y.C., May 27, 1930; d. Walter David and Celeste (Barman) Stern; m. Richard Benoit Frackman, July 2, 1950; 1 child, Noel Dru Pyne. Student Mt. Holyoke Coll., 1948-50; BA, Sarah Lawrence Coll., 1952, MA, 1953; postgrad. Columbia U., 1964-67; MA, Inst. Fine Arts, NYU, 1976, PhD, 1987. Art critic Scarsdale Inquirer (N.Y.), 1962-67, Patent Trader, Mt. Kisco, N.Y., 1962-71; assoc. Arts Mag., N.Y.C., 1968—; lectr. Aldrich Mus. Contemporary Art, Ridgefield, Conn., 1967-75, Gallery Passport Ltd., N.Y.C., 1968—; curator of edn. Storm King Art Ctr., Mountainville, N.Y., 1973-75; instr. continuing edn. div. SUNYm Purchase, 1988—. Author (catalogue) John Storrs, Whitney Mus. of Am. Art, 1986; contbr. articles and/or revs. to various mags. including: Arts Mag., Harper's Bazaar, Feminist Art Jour., Art Voices. Sarah Williston scholar, 1948-50; recipient 1st prize, coll. publs. contest Mademoiselle mag., 1961. Mem. Internat. Assn. Art Critics, Art Table Inc., Coll. Art Assn. Home: 3 Hadden Rd Scarsdale NY 10583-3327

FRAIBERG, LAWRENCE PHILLIP, broadcasting company executive; b. Pitts., Oct. 12, 1921; s. Samuel S. and Molly (Silverman) F. BA in Econs., UCLA, 1949; Dr. (hon.), St. John's U., N.Y.C., 1978. Account exec. Sta. KPIX, San Francisco, 1949-53, local sales mgr., 1953-58, gen. sales mgr., 1958-59; metro TV sales Metromedia, N.Y.C., 1959-63; v.p., gen. mgr. Sta. WTTG, Washington, 1963-65, Sta. WNEW-TV, N.Y.C., 1965-69, 71-77; pres. Parallel Prodns., N.Y.C., 1969-71, Metromedia TV, N.Y.C., 1977-79, Group W TV, N.Y.C., 1980-86, MCA Broadcasting, N.Y.C., 1986-90; chmn., chief exec. officer Pinelands Inc., N.Y.C., 1991—. Mem. exec. com. Nat. Com. for Am. Fgn. Policy, N.Y.C., 1984—; trustee Outward Bound U.S.A., Greenwich, Conn., 1986—; bd. dirs. Muscular Dystrophy Assn., N.Y.C., 1977—, Fund for Dance, N.Y.C., 1982—, Vis. Nurse Svc., N.Y.C., 1991—. 1st lt. U.S. Army, 1942-46, PTO. Recipient Peabody award for lifetime achievement in the broadcasting industry, 1986, Trustees award NATAS, 1990. Mem. Theatre Devel. Fund (bd. dirs.), Vis. Nurse Svc. of N.Y. (mem. bd.), The Tony Mgmt. Com., The Dramatists Guild. Club: Univ. (N.Y.C.). Office: Pinelands Inc 445 Park Ave New York NY 10022-2606

FRAIR, ELIZABETH EVANS, public relations officer, educator; b. Bklyn., May 28, 1927; d. Anthony J. and Elizabeth (Balzer) Bollback; m. C. Hans Evans, June 10, 1961 (dec. July 1977); m. Wayne Frair, May 2, 1987. BRE, Nyack Coll., 1949; MA, NYU, 1951; postgrad. Northwestern U., 1953, Columbia U., 1952-57. Audiologist Manhattan Eye, Ear, Nose and Throat Hosp., N.Y.C., 1949-54; tchr. Lexington Sch. for Deaf, N.Y.C., 1954-59; supervising Deaf, Phila., 1960-68; prin. Middle Sch., Pa. Sch. for Deaf, 1968-71; asst. prof. spl. edn. Pa. State U., University Park, 1962-71; specialist in deaf edn. Chester County Child Devel. Ctr., Coatesville, 1971-78; assoc. dean students King's Coll., Briarcliff Manor, N.Y., 1978-86, instr. speech, 1978-79, dir. dept. continuing edn., 1980-86, cons. study skills ctr., 1982-86, dir. pub relations, 1986—; cons. Nat. Com. Library Standards for Schs. for Deaf, N.Y., 1965-66; lectr., speaker civic, religious and profl. groups. Social dir. Word of Life Summer Confs., N.Y., 1955-60; corp. mem. Lancaster Sch. of Bible, 1973; v.p. Living Word Radio Ministry Internat., 1974-77; summer seminar coordinator Camp of Woods, Speculator, N.Y., 1978—; hon. mem. program agy. United Presbyn. Ch. U.S.A., 1977—. Recipient Outstanding Service award Coatesville Area Council PTA. Mem. Presbyn. Women's Assn. (pres. 1976-77). Republican. Address: Kings Coll Briarcliff Manor NY 10510

FRAME, RAYMOND C., medical products manufacturing company executive; b. Pitts., Dec. 15, 1946; s. Raymond H. and Dorothy M. (Love) F.; m. Arlene A. Jachens, Dec. 23, 1967; children: Raymond A., Ashley A. BS in Edn., U. Tenn., 1968; MS in Adminstrn. and Supervision, Rollins Coll., 1973. Tchr., football coach Orange County Schs., Orlando, Fla., 1969-74, asst. prin., 1974-76; owner, mgr. mfg. rep. co., Orlando, 1976-80; regional mgr. for Fla. U.S. Surg. Corp., Norwalk, Conn., 1982-88, product specialist, 1988-89, key hosp. mgr., 1989—. Home: 8618 Larwin Ln Orlando FL 32817-1341 Office: US Surg Corp 150 Glover Ave Norwalk CT 06850-1346

FRAMPTON, GEORGE THOMAS, JR., conservation organization executive; b. Washington, Aug. 24, 1944; s. George Thomas Sr. and Margaret Ann (Raup) F.; m. Betsy Kimmelman, Apr. 3, 1971; children: Adam, Thomas. BA, Yale U., 1965; MS in Econs., London Sch. Econs., 1966; JD, Harvard U., 1969. Law clk. to Hon. Harry A. Blackmun U.S. Supreme Ct., Washington, 1971-72; fellow Ctr. for Law and Social Policy, Washington, 1972-73; asst. pros. Watergate Spl. Prosecution Force, Washington, 1973-75; ptnr. Rogovin, Huge & Lenzner, Washington, 1976-85; counsel Ennis, Friedman, Bersoff & Ewing, Washington, 1985-86; pres. The Wilderness Soc., Washington, 1986—; dept. dir. Three Mile Island Spl. Inquiry NRC, Washington, 1978-79; dep. ind. counsel Edwin Meese Investigation, Washington, 1984; spl. counsel State of Alaska, Juneau, 1985. Co-author: Stonewall: The Real Story of the Watergate Prosecution, 1976. Home: 3411 36th St NW Washington DC 20016-3147 Office: Wilderness Soc 900 17th St NW Washington DC 20006-2501

FRANCE, JOSEPH DAVID, securities analyst; b. Smithville, Mo., July 24, 1953; s. Raymond Hughes France and Bonnie Lee (Cavin) Vinzant; m. Judith Ann Tehel, May 29, 1976; 1 child, Lucille Terrell. BS in Pharmacy, U. Kans., 1977, MBA, 1980. Registered pharmacist; chartered fin. analyst. Staff pharmacist U. Kans. Med. Ctr., Kansas City, 1977-80; securities analyst First Nat. Bank Chgo., 1980-82; securities analyst Smith Barney, Harris Upham & Co., Inc., N.Y.C., 1982-86, mng. dir., 1986—. Mem. Am. Soc. Hosp. Pharmacists, N.Y. Soc. Securities Analysts, Fin. Analysts Fedn., Inst. Chartered Fin. Analysis. Democrat. Roman Catholic. Office: Smith Barney Harris Upham & Co 1345 Ave Of The Americas New York NY 10105-0099

FRANCESCO, ANNE MARIE CAROL-THERESA, psychology management educator; b. Worcester, Mass., Oct. 12, 1952; d. Henry Paul and Jennie Teresa (Cesary) F.; m. Hua Lee, Apr. 16, 1986; children: Anthony Heng Francesco Lee, Giancarlo Chen Francesco Lee. BA, NYU, 1973; MA, Ohio State U., 1975, PhD, 1977. Office mgr. Alert Typesetters, N.Y.C., 1972-73; grad. teaching assoc. Ohio State U., Columbus, 1974-77; vis. asst. prof. U. Tenn., Knoxville, 1977-78; owner Psychology in Action, Hong Kong, 1979-82; mng. dir. A.M. Francesco & Assocs. Ltd., Hong Kong, 1982-87; assoc. prof. U. Alaska, Fairbanks, 1987-90, Pace U., N.Y.C., 1990—; vis. lectr. Bank of Am., The Chinese U. of Hong Kong, 1978-82; adj. assoc. prof. NYU, 1986-87; cons. Pei Hua Ednl. Found., Hong Kong, 1985-86; vis. prof., cons. Guangdong Provincial Mgmt. Cadre Inst., People's Republic of China, 1982-86. Columnist South China Morning Post, Hong Kong, 1983; contbr. articles to profl. jours. Grantee U.S. Dept. Edn., 1991, Law Sch. Admission Coun., 1974; William Green Meml. fellow Ohio State U., 1973. Mem. APA, Acad. of Mgmt., Soc. for Indsl. and Orgnl. Psychology Inc. Office: Pace U Dept Mgmt Pace Pla New York NY 10038

FRANCIS, EULALIE MARIE, psychologist; b. Holmdel, N.J.; d. Richard Erickson and Cora Mina (Patterson) F. BS, Newark State, N.J., 1945; EDM, Rutgers U., New Brunswick, 1957, MA, 1961; PhD, Rutgers U, Harvard U., N.J, Mass., 1971, 1973. Cert. Edn. Psychology. Tchr. Elem. Edn. Pub. Schs., Middletown, N.J., 1945-51; Elem. supr. Pub. Schs., Red Bank, N.J., 1951-63; dir. learning disability and psychologist Pub. Schs., East Brunswick, N.J., 1984; Cons. Nat. Assn. Mental Health N.Y.C., Family and childrens Sorriccs Natigna, N.Y.C., Lincoln Sch. Tchrs. Coll., Columbia U. 1981-89; Dir. Rsch. Div. NEA Assn. Trenton N.J. 1988-89. Author, editor: Kinesthetic Method of Reading, Theory and Techniques of Auditory Perception in Reading 1964-68. Adv. State Hist. Site Coun. Trenton N.J. 1986, Cultural and Heritage Com. Holmdel N.J. 1987-89. Mem. Arts Counc. of Princeton, Monmouth Mus. Lincroft, N.J., AAUW, Adv. Com. on Status of Women, Dir. Youth and Family Svcs., Princeton Child Devel. Inst., Rumson Country Club, Springlake Golf. Republican. Presbyterian. Home: PO Box 43 Holmdel NJ 07733-0043

FRANCIS, FREDERICK JOHN, food science educator; b. Ottawa, Ont., Can., Oct. 9, 1921; came to U.S., 1954; s. Roland and Mary (Dyble) F.; m. Jean Dalton Burrows, Mar. 15, 1952; children: Margaret A. Clayton, John B., Laurie J. BA, U. Toronto, 1946, MA, 1948; PhD, U. Mass., 1954. Instr. dept. food chemistry U. Toronto, 1946-50; asst. prof. dept. horticulture U. Guelph, Ont., Can., 1950-54; prof. dept. food sci. U. Mass., Amherst, 1954—. Author 7 books; contbr. over 300 articles to profl. jours. With RCAF, 1944-45. Recipient 10 nat. and internat. sci. awards. Fellow AAAS; mem. Am. Coun. of Sci. Health (chmn. bd. dirs. 1992—), Coun. Agr. Sci. Tech. (bd. dirs. 1990—). Republican. Congregationalist. Home: 123 Pine St Amherst MA 01002-1125 Office: U Mass Dept Food Sci Amherst MA 01003

FRANCIS, GERALD PETER, mechanical engineer, educator; b. Seattle, Feb. 15, 1936; s. Perry Lucas and F. Geraldine (Arntz) F.; m. Anne V. Stewart, Aug. 29, 1964; children: Timothy, Michael, Peter. BME, U. Dayton, 1958; MME, Cornell U., 1960, PhD, 1965. Registered profl. engr., Ohio; chartered engr., Eng. Chair dept. mech. engring. SUNY, Buffalo, 1970-76; head engring. U.S. Merchant Marine Acad., Kings Point, N.Y., 1977-80; dean Engring. and Math. Coll. U. Vt., Burlington, 1980-81, prof. mech. engring., 1980—, dean div. engring., math., and bus. asminstrn., 1981-85, interim v.p. academic affairs, 1985-87, vice provost, 1987-89, interim provost, 1989-91. Co-contbr. articles to Jour. Biomech. Engring., Fluids Engring., Fluid Dynamics Measurments, Basic Engring. Mem. Vt. Indsl. Energy Conservation, Montpelier, 1982, Mt. Mansfield Colocation Assn., Burlington, 1987. Recipient Silver medal U.S. Dept. Commerce, 1979; named Engr. of Yr., State of Vt., 1989. Fellow Inst. Marine Engrs.; mem. ASME, NSPE, Am. Soc. Engring. Edn. (Excellence in Engring. award 1970). Home: 30 Oakhill Rd Shelburne VT 05482-7279 Office: U Vt Dept Mech Engring Burlington VT 05405

FRANCIS, JANE MARSHALL, artist; b. Mt. Holly, N.J., Jan. 13, 1961; d. Marshall James and Margaret Jane (Williams) F. BA, Bob Jones U., 1982. Graphic technician Microcircuit Engring. Corp., Mt. Holly, 1982-84, graphic dept. supr., 1984-86; owner Artstudio, Mt. Holly, 1986—. Artist (photography) Slanted Light, 1986, (collograph) Sanctuary, 1987, (painting) Autumn Anthem, 1989; exhibited in juried shows. Officer Zoe Aletha Literary Soc., Greenville, S.C., 1979-80. Guild S.C. Artists scholar, 1981. Mem. Southern N.J. Advs. for the Arts, Guild of S.C. Artists. Presbyterian. Office: Artstudio 810 Holly Ln Mount Holly NJ 08060-2371

FRANCIS, MRS. LEE See **LYBARGER, ADRIENNE REYNOLDS**

FRANCIS, NORMAN CHARLES, physicist; b. Rochester, N.Y., Nov. 27, 1922; s. Morris Jacob and Jennie Pearl (Levy) F.; m. Beverly Ruth Cohen, May 31, 1947; children: Cynthia Lynn Gensheimer, Karen Ann Maher, Martha Joan Fisher. BA in Physics, U. Rochester, 1947, PhD in Physics, 1952. Rsch. asst. physics dept. Ind. U., Bloomington, 1952-55; rsch. scientist GE, Schenectady, N.Y., 1955—; guest lectr. MIT, Cambridge, 1960-61; cons. in field. With USN, 1944-46. Fellow Am. Nuclear Soc. (chmn. reactor physics div. 1972, chmn. northeastern N.Y. sect. 1968); mem. Am. Phys. Soc. Democrat. Jewish. Home: 2311 Plum St Niskayuna NY 12309-5905 Office: GE KAPL Schenectady NY 12301

FRANCIS, PATRICIA LYNN, consultant; b. Balt., Nov. 19, 1952; d. Earl William Lowe and Donna Mae (Hanson) Cummins; m. Raymond C. Francis, Aug. 30, 1975; children: Monica Lynn, Alyssa Danielle. AA, Howard Community Coll., 1982; BS, U. Md., 1987. Ops. mgr. Tng. Resources, NSS, Inc., Columbia, Md., 1979-83; cons. gen. mgr. Historic Ellicott City (Md.), Inc., 1983-86; treas., chief fin. officer Corfield Enterprises, Inc., Columbia, 1986—, v.p. fin. and adminstrn., 1991—; cons. Antique Dealers of Md., Olney, 1985, various small bus., Columbia; treas. Hazmat Tng. Info. and Svcs., Inc., Columbia, 1988—, dir., 1989—; treas., dir. systematic Success Inst., Inc., 1989—. Mem. NAFE, Howard County C. of C. (rouse tribute planning com.). Office: Corfield Enterprises Inc 6480 Dobbin Rd Columbia MD 21045-5825

FRANCIS, PAUL WILBUR, JR., association executive; b. Middletown, Conn., Mar. 20, 1929; s. Paul W. and Ruth (Miller) F.; m. Barbara Ann Ingram, Aug. 1, 1953; children: David, Ann, Susan. BA, Wesleyan U., Middletown, Conn., 1950. Tchr., coach St. James (Md.) Sch., 1951-54; tchr., coach Kingswood Sch., West Hartford, Conn., 1954-66, dir. athletics, 1957-66; devel. dir. Kingswood-Oxford Sch., West Hartford, 1966-72, treas., 1972-79; exec. dir. Internat. Assn. Approved Basketball Ofcls., Inc., West Hartford, 1979—; supr. basketball ofcls. Ea. Coll. Athletic Conf., Centerville, Mass., 1986—, Ivy League, Princeton, N.J., 1988—. Mem. Collegiate Basketball Ofcls. Assn. (life), Cen. Conn. Bd. Approved Basketball Ofcls. (life), Hartford Golf Club (asst. sec., asst. treas. 1975-76). Home: 22 Castlewood Rd West Hartford CT 06107-2903 Office: Internat Assn Approved Basketball Ofcls 61 S Main St Ste 200 PO Box 661 Hartford CT 06107-2403

FRANCK, STEPHEN A., management consultant; b. Budapest, Hungary, Oct. 29, 1933; came to U.S. 1961; s. Nicholas Franck; m. Elvira Farago, Sept. 8, 1957; 1 child, John Christopher. MS in Chemistry, U. Budapest, 1956; MSChemE, Sorbonne, 1957; MBA, CUNY, 1965. Mkt. rsch. engr. Phillips Petroleum, N.Y.C., 1967-68; dir. strategy Phillips Petroleum, Brussels, Belgium, 1968-81; internat. planner Phillips Petroleum, Bartlesville, Okla., 1981-84; exec. v.p. strategy, planning and internat. bus. devel. Enichem of the ENI Group, Milan, Italy, 1984-87, cons., 1987-89; mgmt. cons. Franck & Assocs., Cranford, N.J., 1990—; adv. bd. Velco Ent., Elmsford, N.Y., 1990; cons. Enichem Am., Inc., 1990. Mem. Am. chem. Soc., Chem. Mktg. and Econs. Assn. Home and Office: 738 Willow St Cranford NJ 07016

FRANCO, CAROLE ANN, film company executive, consultant; b. Hartford, Conn., Dec. 21, 1948; d. Nicholas Lawrence and Mary Elizabeth (LaRosa) F. BA in Spanish, Duke U., 1970; grad. cert. in edn., Trinity Coll., Hartford, 1971; postgrad. in French, Sorbonne, Paris, 1980; M.Internat. Relations, Cambridge U., 1981. Tchr. West Hartford (Conn.) Pub. Schs., 1970-76; researcher on biography of Sumner Welles Washington, 1976-77; adminstr. Ctr. for Strategic and Internat. Studies, Washington, 1978-79; broker, mgr. Parks Capital Mgmt., N.Y.C., 1981-83; assoc., cons. Burgess Mgmt. Assocs., N.Y.C., 1984-88; producer, owner Kingdom Prodns., New Paltz, N.Y., 1988—; polit. advisor N.Am. Petroleum Corp., Curacao, Netherlands Antilles, 1987—; cons. Dorchester Capital Group, London, 1988—. Advisor Sangre de Cristo Found., Sussex, Eng., 1987—. Mem. Duke U. Alumni Assn. N.Y., Cambridge U. Alumni Assn. N.Y. (founder, bd. dirs. 1987-88), United Oxford-Cambridge U. Club (London). Republican. Roman Catholic. Home: PO Box 36 New Paltz NY 12561-0036

FRANCO, ROBERT, economist, consultant, professor; b. Cairo, Aug. 11, 1941; came to U.S., 1960; s. Edgard and Speranza Franco; m. Martine Pastor, June 9, 1978; children: Erik, Arnaud. BA, U. Calif., 1963, PhD, 1970; MA, San Diego State U., 1965. Economist Transp. Inst., Washington,

1970-72; mgr. CACI, Arlington, Va., 1972-74; asst. div. chief IMF, Washington, 1974—; resident rep. IMF, Senegal, 1984-87; cons. OECD, Paris, 1970-74; prof. U. Md., College Park, 1970-80. Mem. Am. Econ. Assn., AAUP, Omicron Delta Epsilon. Home: 700 19th St NW # 8206 Washington DC 20431-0001 Office: IMF 700 19th St NW Washington DC 20431-0002

FRANCOIS, FRANCIS BERNARD, association executive, lawyer; b. Barnum, Iowa, Jan. 21, 1934; s. Rudolph John and Irene Frances (McDonough) F.; m. Eileen M. Schmelzer, Feb. 6, 1960; children: Joseph, Marie, Michael, Monica, Susan. B.S., Iowa State U.; LL.B., George Washington U. Bar: Md. 1960, U.S. Patent and Trademark Office. Chief judge Orphan's Ct. Prince George's County, Upper Marlboro, Md., 1962-66; commr. Prince George's County, Upper Marlboro, Md., 1966-71, councilman, 1971-80; exec. dir. Am. Assn. State Hwy. and Transp. Ofcls., Washington, 1980—; adv. com. Ctr. Transp. Studies, MIT, 1983—; mem. adv. panel White House Intergovtl. Sci. and Engring. Tech., 1976-80; mem. Washington Suburban Transit Commn., 1978-80, chmn., 1979; dir. Washington Met. Area Transit Autority, 1978-80; exec. com. Transp. Rsch. Bd., 1980—, Strategic Hwy. Rsch. Program, 1986—; mem. permanent internat. commn. Permanent Internat. Assn. Rd. Congresses, 1990—; bd. dirs. Internat. Rd. Fedn., 1991, Nat. Ctr. for Asphalt Tech., 1991—, Intelligent Vehicle Hwy. Soc. Am., 1991—, chmn., 1992—; lectr. in field. Contbr. articles to profl. jours. Mem. adv. council Nat. Community Energy Mgmt. Ctr., 1981-82; mem. local govt. energy policy adv. com. Dept. of Energy, 1979-80; vice chmn. Md. Potomac Water Authority, 1970-80; air quality control adv. council State of Md., 1975-80; chmn. Water Resources Planning Bd., 1975-77; mem. Gov.'s Interstate Water Quality Planning Com., 1973-74; v.p. Md. Com. for Fair Representation, 1962; counselor Washington Career Inst., 1963; bd. dirs. Bowie Jaycees, Bowie Fine Arts Soc., Bowie YMCA; trustee Md. Easter Seal Soc., Prince George's United Way, Md. Soc. Crippled Children and Adults; bd. dirs. Nat. Ctr. for Asphalt Tech., 1991—. Recipient Community Service award Nat. Capital chpt. ASCE, 1980, Community Service award Bowie Jaycees, 1980, Community Service award Cedar Heights Civic Assn., 1978, Profl. Achievement on Engring. award Iowa State U., 1984, W.N. Carey Jr. Disting. Svc. award Transp. Rsch. Bd., 1990; named Washingtonian of Yr. Washingtonian Mag., 1973. Mem. Nat. Assn. Counties (pres. 1979-80), Nat. Assn. Regional Councils (pres. 1972-73), Washington Met. Council Govts. (dir. 1966-80, pres. 1971), Internat. Rd. Fedn. (bd. dirs. 1991—), Community Assns. Inst. (dir. 1975-80, pres. 1979-80). Democrat. Roman Catholic. Lodge: K.C. Home: 12421 Seabury Ln Bowie MD 20715-3113 Office: Am Assn State Hwy and Transp Ofcls Ste 249 444 N Capitol St NW Washington DC 20001-1512

FRANGER, ROBERT RICH, podiatrist; b. Buffalo, Feb. 17, 1954; s. Robert James and Lorraine (Rich) F.; m. Kristin Elizabeth Thompson, Aug. 18, 1990. BA, Hiram Coll., 1976; BS in Basic Sci., Calif.Coll. Podiatric Medicine, 1978, D Podiatric Medicine, 1980. Resident Doctors Hosp, Worcester, Mass., 1980-81; pvt. practice Shrewsbury, Mass., 1982—. Mem. Am. Podiatric Med. Assn., Mass. Podiatric Med. Assn. (div. treas. 1986—). Republican. Mem. United Ch. of Christ. Office: Shrewsbury Med Ctr 25 Oak Ave Worcester MA 01605-2751

FRANGOS, JAMES MASON, banker; b. Phila., Apr. 11, 1947; s. James John and Shirley (Mason) F.; m. Sarah Jane Aker, Sept. 19, 1982; children: Thaedra, James A., Katherine S. Student, Rider Coll., 1964-67; BA, Boston Conservatory, 1974; MA, Boston U., 1975. Dir. of rev. N.J. State Coun. on the Arts, Trenton, 1976-78; mgr. community affairs Prudential Ins., Co., Newark, 1978-88; corp. v.p. community rels. UJB Fin. Corp., Princeton, N.J., 1988—; vice chmn. Local Initiatives Managed Asset Corp., N.Y.C., 1986-88; trustee, pres. Newark Bus. Devel. Corp., Newark, 1986-88; mem. loan com. N.J. Urban Housing Program, Trenton, 1989—. With U.S. Army, 1968-70, Vietnam. Mem. N.J. Bankers Assn. (community reinvestment com. 1990—). Office: UJB Fin Corp 301 Carnegie Ctr Princeton NJ 08540-6291

FRANK, ALLAN DANIEL, communication educator; b. Sheboygan, Wis., June 16, 1930; s. Clarence Harold and Ella Marie (Strysick) F.; m. Mary Louise Andre, Apr. 7, 1956; children: David Allan, Mary Leigh, Steven George, Beth Andrea. BS, U. Wis., 1953, MS, 1954, PhD, 1967. Tchr. Oconomowoc (Wis.) High Sch., 1957-63; prof. U. Md., College Park, 1963-68, SUNY, Brockport, 1968—; cons. Communiskil, Rochester, N.Y., 1983—. author: Communicating on the Job, 1982, Organizational Communication and Behavior, 1989; contbr. articles to profl. jours. Mem. Greece (N.Y.) Dem. Com., 1982-84. With U.S. Army, 1954-56. Mem. N.Y. State Speech Communication Assn. (pres. 1978-79), Speech Communication Assn., Eastern Communication Assn., United Univ. Profls. (chmn. legislation com. 1985-87, v.p. polit. action com. 1980-84). Democrat. Home: 243 Autumn Dr N Rochester NY 14626-1339 Office: SUNY Dept Communication Dept Communications Brockport NY 14420

FRANK, ARTHUR, physician; b. N.Y.C., Dec. 25, 1934; s. Henry and Kitty (Sternberg) F.; m. Kathleen Maxa, Dec. 31, 1988. BS, MIT, 1956; MS, U. Pa., 1958; MD, NYU, 1962. Intern Stanford (Calif.) Med. Ctr., 1962-63, resident in internal medicine, 1963-66; rsch. fellow Nat. Heart Inst., NIH, 1966-68; med. dir. food and nutrition program OEO, 1968-71; med. dir. Community Health program Georgetown U. Sch. Medicine, Washington, 1971-74, asst. prof. dept. community medicine, 1971-74; med. cons. Office of Asst. Sec. for Health, Dept. HEW, Washington, 1975-76; pvt. practice internal medicine Washington, 1976—; clin. asst. prof. dept. medicine George Washington U. Sch. Medicine, Washington, 1976—, med. dir. Obesity Mgmt. program, 1991—; attending physician dept. medicine George Washington U. Hosp., 1976—; cons. physician Psychiat. Inst., 1976—. Author: The People's Handbook of Medical Care, 1973; contbr. articles to profl. jours. Mem. Am. Inst. Nutrition, N.Am. Assn. for Study of Obesity, Cosmos Club. Office: 3 Washington Cir NW Washington DC 20037-2356

FRANK, BARNEY, congressman; b. Bayonne, N.J., Mar. 31, 1940; s. Samuel and Elsie (Golush) F. AB, Harvard U., 1962, JD, 1977. Exec. asst. to mayor of Boston, 1968-71; adminstrv. asst. to U.S. congressman, 1971-72; mem. Mass. Ho. of Reps. from Boston, 1972-80, 97th-102nd Congresses from 4th Dist. Mass., 1981—; teaching fellow govt. Harvard U., 1963-67, asst. to dir. Inst. Politics John F. Kennedy Sch. Govt., 1966-67, fellow Inst. Politics, 1971. Democrat. Office: US Ho of Reps Washington DC 20515*

FRANK, CELESTE MARY, psychologist, writer; b. Detroit, Jan. 27, 1949; d. Richard S. and Joyce E. (Le Boeuf) Watts; m. Thomas Frank, Feb. 28, 1971 (div. Jan. 1974); 1 child, Justin; m. Richard Pangborn, June 6, 1992. BA with honors, U. N.Mex., 1976; MA, U. Tex., 1983, PhD, 1987. Lic. psychologist, Pa. Mktg. rep. IBM, Albuquerque and Austin, Tex., 1976-81; pvt. practice computer cons. Austin, 1981-83; doctoral practicum student Career Svcs. Ctr. U. Tex., Austin, spring 1984; doctoral practicum student for orgn. Austin, spring 1985; doctoral practicum student Counseling-Psychol. Svcs. Ctr. U. Tex., Austin, 1984, 85; doctoral practicum student Renaissance Unit for Drug Abuse Shoal Creek Hosp., Austin, fall 1985; wellness progam coor. City of Austin Electric Utilities, 1985; program counselor psychiat. hosps., Austin, 1985-86; psychology intern Inst. of Pa. Hosp., Phila., 1986-87; staff psychologist Eagleville (Pa.) Hosp., 1987-89; pvt. practice Phila. and King of Prussia, Pa., 1987—; cons. psychologist Horsham Hosp., Ambler, Pa., 1987—, Pa. Hosp., Phila., 1987—, Inst. Pa. Hosp., Phila., 1987—. Author fiction, poem, short story; contbr. articles to profl. jours. and popular mags. Active Act for Peace, Phila., 1991. Recipient Mensa scholarship, 1983. Mem. APA, NAFE, Nat. Register Health Care Providers, Pa. Psychol. Assn., Phila. Soc. Clin. Psychologists, Phila. Soc. Psychoanalytic Psychologists. Democrat. Office: 1150 1st Ave Ste 640 King Of Prussia PA 19406

FRANK, CHARLES RAPHAEL, JR., investment banker; b. Pitts., May 15, 1937; s. Charles Raphael and Lucille (Briscoe) M.; m. Susan Patricia Backman, Mar. 9, 1963 (div. June 1976); children: Elizabeth Grace, Stephen Raphael; m. Eleanor Sebastian, July 19, 1976; children: Paul Sebastian, Philip Sebastian. BS in Math., Rensselaer Poly. Inst., 1959; MA in Econs., Princeton U., 1961, PhD in Econs., 1963. Sr. rsch. fellow East African Inst. Social Rsch. Makerere U. Coll., Kampala, Uganda, 1963-65; asst. prof. econs. Yale U., New Haven, 1965-67; assoc. prof. econs. and internat. affairs Princeton (N.J.) U., 1967-70, prof., 1970-74; assoc. dir. rsch. program econ. devel. Woodrow Wilson Sch., 1967-70, dir., 1970-74; sr. fellow Brookings Inst., 1972-74; mem. policy planning staff U.S. Dept. State, 1974-77, dep. asst. sec. state for econ. and social affairs, 1977-78; v.p. Salomon Bros. Inc., 1978-87; pres. Frank & Co. Inc., 1987-88; project v.p. energy and fin. GE Capital Corp., Stamford, Conn., 1988—; ops. rsch. analyst U.S. Steel, summers 1960, 61; cons. Govt. Uganda, 1964, UN Econ. Commn. for Asia and Far East, 1969, IBRD, 1969-72, Korea Devel. Inst., 1973-74, Mathematica, 1967-68, Nat. Conf. Bd., 1969-70, Nat. Bur. Econ. Rsch., 1970-75, Brookings Instn., 1969; mem. rsch. adv. com. AID, 1971-75, cons., Washington, 1966-68, Korea, 1971-73. Author: Production Theory and Indivisible Commodities, 1969, The Sugar Industry in East Africa, 1965, (with Brian Van Arkadie) Economic Accounting and Development Planning, 2d edit., 1969, Debt and the Terms of Aid, 1970, Statistics and Econometrics, 1971, American Jobs and Trade with the Developing Countries, 1973, Foreign Exchange Regimes and Economic Development, The Case of South Korea, 1975, Foreign Trade and Domestic Adjustment, 1976, Income Distribution and Economic Growth in the Less Developed Countries, 1977. Mem. Council Fgn. Relations. Home: 25 E 86th St Apt 10A New York NY 10028 Office: GE Capital Corp 1600 Summer St Stamford CT 06905-5125

FRANK, FREDERICK, investment banker; b. Salt Lake City, May 31, 1932; s. Simon and Suzanne (Seller) F.; m. Mary Ann Nahum (div. 1979); children: Jenny Ann, Laura Kim; m. Mary Catherine Tanner. BA, Yale U., 1954; MBA, Stanford U., 1958. Chartered fin. analyst. Mng. dir. Smith Barney & Co., N.Y.C., 1958-69; mng. dir. Lehman Bros., N.Y.C., 1969-85, sr. mng. dir., 1985—; bd. dirs. R.P. Scherer, Troy, Mich., Molecular Design Ltd., San Leandro, Calif., Applied Biosci. Internat., East Millstone, N.J., Physicians Computer Network, Optical Tech. Resources. Chmn. Nat. Genetics Found., N.Y.C., 1985—; trustee Hotchkiss Sch., Lakeville, Conn.; adv. dir. Yale U. Sch. Mgmt. With U.S. Army, 1954-56. Mem. Chartered Fin. Analysts, N.Y. Soc. Security Analysts. Home: 109 E 91st St New York NY 10128-1601 Office: Lehman Bros Am Express Tower World Fin Ctr New York NY 10285

FRANK, HERBERT LAWRENCE, anesthesiologist, educator; b. Bklyn., Sept. 22, 1932; m. Starr E. Reganthal, July 10, 1970; children: Stephanie, Lisa, Erika, Erik, David. BS, Coll. of Gt. Falls, 1956; MD, U. Utrecht (The Netherlands), 1962. Diplomate Am. Bd. Anesthesiology. Intern Pittsfield (Mass.) Affiliated Hosps., 1963-64; resident in anesthesiology Montefiore Hosp. and Med. Ctr., Bronx, N.Y., 1964-66, fellow, 1966-67; fellow in anesthesiology Albert Einstein Coll. Medicine, Yeshiva U., Bronx, 1967-68, instr., assoc., asst. prof., 1967-1973; clin. fellow anesthesiology Bronx Mcpl. Hosp. Ctr., 1966-68; pvt. practice Harrisburg, Pa., 1973—; dir. anesthesiology Harrisburg Hosp., 1973-75; sr. staff anesthesiologist, 1975—; med. dirs. Harrisburg Area Sch. Anesthesia, 1973-75; assoc. clin. prof. anesthesiology Hershey Med. Ctr., Pa. State U., 1974—; presenter in field. Contbr. articles to med. jours. With USAF, 1952-55. Mem. Am. Soc. Anesthesiologists, AMA, Internat. Anesthesia Rsch. Soc., Netherlands-Am. Med. Soc., Pa. Med. Soc., Pa. Soc. Anesthesiologists, Dauphin County Med. Soc. Home: 2230 Mockingbird Rd Harrisburg PA 17112-9615 Office: Harrisburg Hosp Dept Anesthesiology Harrisburg PA 17100

FRANK, JEROME DAVID, psychiatrist, educator; b. N.Y.C., May 30, 1909; s. Jerome W. and Bess (Rosenbaum) F.; m. Elizabeth Kleeman, Jan. 4, 1948; children—Deborah, David, Julia, Emily. A.B. summa cum laude, Harvard, 1930, A.M., 1932, Ph.D. in Psychology, 1934, M.D. cum laude, 1939; LHD honoris causa, SUNY, Binghampton, 1991. Research asso. group psychotherapy research project VA, 1946-49; instr. Washington Sch. Psychiatry, 1947-49; clin. asso. prof. Howard U., 1948-49; instr. Johns Hopkins Med. Sch., 1942-46, faculty, 1949—, prof. psychiatry, 1959-74, prof. emeritus psychiatry, 1974—; psychiatrist-in-charge psychiat. out-patient dept. Johns Hopkins Hosp., 1951-64; dir. clin. services Henry Phipps Psychiat. Clinic, 1961-63, acting chief dept. psychiatry, 1960-61; staff mem. Center Study Dem. Instns., 1966; adv. bd. Patuxent Instn., 1954-78; mem. adv. coms. NIMH, 1951-55, 57-58, 59-61, 68-69, 74-78, mem. task force on homosexuality, 1967-69; mem. social sci. adv. bd. ACDA, 1970-73; mem. adv. com. psychiatry and neurology service Dept. Medicine and Surgery, VA Central Office, 1960-64; bd. dirs. Met. Balt. Assn. Mental Health, 1952—; bd. dirs. SANE, 1974-81, nat. bd. sponsors, 1983—; bd. dirs. Council for a Livable World, 1963—; mem. nat. adv. bd. Physicians for Social Responsibility, 1980—, mem. nat. adv. bd. Psychologists for Social Responsibility, 1985—. Author: Persuasion and Healing; A Comparative Study of Psychotherapy, 1961, (with J.B. Frank), 3rd rev. edit., 1991, (with Florence Powdermaker) Group Psychotherapy: Studies in Methodology of Research and Therapy, 1953, Sanity and Survival: Psychological Aspects of War and Peace, 1967 (reissued as Sanity and Survival in the Nuclear Age, 1973), (with others) Effective Ingredients of Successful Psychotherapy, 1978, Psychotherapy and the Human Predicament: A Psychosocial Approach, 1978, also articles. Served to maj. AUS, 1943-46. Fellow Ctr. Advanced Study Behavioral Scis., Palo Alto, Calif., 1958-59; praelector in psychiatry Faculty Medicine, U. St. Andrews, Dundee, Scotland, 1967; H.B. Williams travelling prof. psychiatry Australia and N.Z., 1971; Litchfield lectr. Oxford U., 1977; Recipient Emil A. Gutheil award Assn. Advancement Psychotherapy, 1970, Kurt Lewin Meml. award Soc. for Psychol. Study Social Issues, 1972, Blanche Ittleson award Am. Orthopsychiat. Assn., 1979, Spl. Research award Soc. for Psychotherapy Research, 1981, McAlpin Research Achievement award Nat. Mental Health Assn., 1981, Oskar Pfister award Am. Psychiat. Assn., 1983, award for disting. contbn. to psychology in the pub. interest Am. Psychol. Assn., 1985, Salmon medal N.Y. Acad. Medicine, 1986, Harold D. Lasswell award Internat. Soc. Polit. Psychology, 1987, others. Fellow Am. Psychiat. Assn., Am. Psychol. Assn., Soc. for Psychol. Study of Social Issues (pres. 1965-66), Am. Coll. Psychiatrists, Am. Group Psychotherapy Assn., Am. Assn. for Social Psychiatry (v.p. 1974), World Acad. Art and Sci., Royal Coll. Psychiatrists (hon.), Polish Psychiat. Soc. (hon.); mem. Am. Psychopath. Assn. (pres. 1963), Fedn. Am. Scientists (vice chmn. 1976-79, chmn. 1979), AAUP, Phi Beta Kappa, Sigma Xi, Alpha Omega Alpha. Home: 603 W University Pkwy Baltimore MD 21210 Office: Johns Hopkins Hosp. Meyer 3-181e Baltimore MD 21205

FRANK, JOE LEE, III, naval officer; b. Norfolk, Va., Feb. 11, 1947; s. Joe Lee Jr. and Barbara Olive (Bloxam) F.; m. Nancy Ellen Bruce, May 4, 1974; children: Joe Lee IV, Brian Wallace. B.S., U. S. Naval Acad., 1964, M.S. in Physics, 1975. Commd. U.S. Navy, 1968, advanced through grades to capt., 1989; asst. combat info. officer USS Mahan, 1969-70, U.S. liaison officer Fed. German Navy Destroyer Rommel, 1970-71, weapons officer USS Cook, 1971-73, ops. officer USS Sacramento, 1976-78; staff chief of naval ops., 1978-80, exec. officer USS Scott, 1981-83, ops. officer USS Iowa, 1983-85; commanding officer USS Ingersoll DD-990, Honolulu, 1986-89; exec. officer USS Mo. BB-63, Long Beach, Calif., 1989-91; dir. fin. ops. Aegis Project Office, Washington, 1991—. Pub. speaker on role of USN. Mem. Internat. Planetarium Soc., Am. Astron. Soc., U.S. Naval Inst., Surface Navy Assn., Sigma Xi. Contbr. articles to profl. jours. Moravian. Home: NSWC Qtrs M 10901 New Hampshire Ave Silver Spring MD 20903-5000 Office: Aegis Project (400E) Navsea NC-2/10W80 Washington DC 20362-5102

FRANK, LAURA JEAN, computer scientist; b. New Rochelle, N.Y., May 21, 1945; d. James Florian and Erma (Guttag) F. BA, U. Vt., 1967; MBA, Iona Coll., New Rochelle, 1971; postgrad. China Inst., N.Y.C., Polytechnic Inst., White Plains, N.Y. With Equitable Life Assurance Soc., N.Y.C., 1967-79, project leader, 1978-79; sr. planning specialist PHH Relocation, Wilton, Conn., 1979-80, project mgr., 1980-83, system mgr., 1983-88, mgr. office tech., 1988-91, system's mktg. cons., 1991—; founding prof. Homequity U., 1985-91. Editor Stamford First Nighter, bd. dirs. Tri-State Trainers; contbr. articles and featured in profl. jours. Mem. Stamford Hist. Soc., Friends of Stamford Symphony. N.Y. State Regents scholar, 1963. Mem. NAFE, WIM, Corp. Computing Mgmt. Assn. (bd. dirs.), Assn. Info. Systems Profls., B'nai B'rith, Delta Mu Delta, Alpha Epsilon Phi. Republican. Jewish. Home: 20250 Soundview Ave Stamford CT 06902-7123

FRANK, LLOYD, lawyer, chemical company executive; b. N.Y.C., Aug. 9, 1925; s. Herman and Selma (Lowenstein) F.; m. Beatrice Silverstein, Dec. 26, 1954; children: Margaret Lois, Frederick. B.A., Oberlin Coll., 1947; J.D., Cornell U., 1950. Bar: N.Y. 1950, U.S. Supreme Ct. 1973. Practice law N.Y.C., 1950—; sr. ptnr. Parker Chapin Flattau & Klimpl; sec., dir. Grow Group, Inc., N.Y.C., 1964—, also dir.; bd. dirs. Madison Industries, Inc., N.Y.C., Metro-Tel Corp., Hicksville, N.Y., Ketcham & McDougall, Inc., Roseland, N.J., Pub. Art Fund, Inc., N.Y.C., Park Electrochem. Corp., Lake Success, N.Y.; sec. Esquire Radio & Electronics, Inc., Bklyn.; lectr. Am. Mgmt. Assn., 1967-77, Probe Internat., Inc., 1975-77, Corp. Seminars, Inc., 1968-71. Mem. ABA (com. negotiated acquisitions), Assn. Bar City N.Y. (com. on environ., com. on product liability), New York County Lawyers Assn. (com. on corps., com. on corp. law). Home: 25 Central Park W New York NY 10023-7253 Office: Parker Chapin Flattau & Klimpl 1211 Ave Of The Americas New York NY 10036-8701

FRANK, RICHARD ALLAN, geographer, educator; b. Rochester, N.Y., Sept. 15, 1943; s. Louis Arthur and Bertha (Allan) F.; m. Judith Homokay, June 24, 1967; children: Richard Louis, Rebecca Louise. BS, SUNY, Geneseo, 1971; MA, SUNY, Brockport, 1976. Prof. geography Monroe Community Coll., Rochester, 1971—. Bd. dirs. Sodus Bay Heights Golf Course, Sodus Point, N.Y., 1985-91, pres., 1987-89. With USAF, 1962-66, Vietnam. Mem. Rochester Dist. Golf Assn. (asst. chmn. 1991—). Home: 252 Rogers Pky Rochester NY 14617-4206 Office: Monroe Community Coll 1000 E Henrietta Rd Rochester NY 14623-5780

FRANK, ROBERT ALLEN, advertising executive; b. Albany, N.Y., Sept. 26, 1932; s. Edward and Marian (Kostelanetz) F.; m. Cynthia Tull, Aug., 1984; children: David, Chelsea, Alison. B.A., Colby Coll., 1954; MBA, Amos Tuck Sch. Bus. Adminstrn., Dartmouth Coll., 1958. Cost control adminstr. ABC-TV, N.Y.C., 1958-59; corp. auditor CBS, Inc., N.Y.C., 1959-60, TV sales svc. account exec., 1961, account exec. radio network sales, 1962-69; exec. v.p., co-founder SFM Media Corp., N.Y.C., 1969—, pres. Media Svc. div., 1981. Radio-TV cons. Nat. Kidney Fund., 1974; active radio TV for various polit. campaigns including Robert Kennedy for Senator, 1964, Richard Nixon for Pres., 1972, Ford for Pres., 1976, Bush for Pres., 1980, Reagan for Pres., 1980, Du Pont for Pres., 1988; mem. Leadership Coun. Nat Rep. Congl. Com., Rep. Nat. Com., 1980—, Pres.' Club, 1984—, Rep. Nat. Senatorial Com. Inner Circle, 1985—, Citizens for Rep. Pres. Com., 1984—; trustee Nat. Child Labor Com., Myasthenia Gravis Found., 1984—. Served to capt. USAF, 1954-56. Mem. Internat. Radio-TV Soc., Amos Tuck Alumni Assn. N.Y. (pres. 1976-77, dir. 1979), Internat. Platform Assn., Dartmouth Club (N.Y.C.), Pi Gamma Mu. Home: 35 Lounsbury Rd Ridgefield CT 06877-4710 Office: SFM Media Corp 1180 Ave Of The Americas New York NY 10036-8401

FRANK, ROBERT STEVEN, international banker; b. N.Y.C., Feb. 10, 1954; s. Arthur Jerome and Marilyn (Goldberg) F.; m. Robin Jaffee, Nov. 11, 1978; 1 child, Jared Daniel. Student, Hebrew U., Jerusalem, 1973, London Sch. Econs., London, 1975; BA, Brandeis U., 1976; MA in Law and Diplomacy, Fletcher Sch., 1978. Intelligence analyst CIA, Washington, 1976-77; internat. credit analyst Shawmut Bank, Boston, 1978-81; asst. v.p. Bank Hapoalim, Boston, 1981-83; v.p. ABN, N.Y.C., 1983-86; v.p.-trade fin. Westpac Bank, N.Y.C., 1986-90, DG Bank, N.Y.C., 1990—. Co-author: Measures Against International Terrorism, 1976. Mem. Fletcher Club N.Y., Harvard Club Boston. Home: 5 Comstock Hill Norwalk CT 06850 Office: DG Bank 609 Fifth Ave New York NY 10017

FRANK, SAM HAGER, college president; b. King City, Mo., July 23, 1932; s. Edward Lloyd and Elmira Louise (Hager) F.; m. Ellen Wilson Snow, June 3, 1955; 1 dau., Marian Elizabeth. B.A., Fla. State U., 1953, M.A., 1957; Ph.D., U. Fla., 1961. Prof. history, chmn. div. social scis. Tift Coll., Forsyth, Ga., 1961-65; assoc. prof. history Augusta (Ga.) Coll., 1966-67; assoc. prof. history Jacksonville (Fla.) U., 1967-72, prof. history, 1972-78, dean Coll. Arts and Scis., 1972-78; chancellor La. State U., Alexandria, 1979-81; pres. Wagner Coll., Staten Island, N.Y., 1981-88, Coll. Aero. La Guardia Airport, N.Y.C., 1990—; cons. Research Studies Inst., USAF U. (Maxwell AFB), Ala., 1957-58; Fulbright prof. Osmania U., India, 1965-66; participant Conf. Acad. Deans of So. States, 1973. Author: (with M. Maurer) Air Force Combat Units of World War II, 1960, American Air Service Observation in World War I, 1961; conrbr. articles on aviation, the mil. and Asia to profl. jours. Bd. dirs. Bailey Seton Hosp., Staten Island, 1981—; active Snug Harbor Cultural Ctr., Staten Island, 1981—; v.p. Staten Island Symphony, 1981—. Served with U.S. Army, 1954-56, Korea. Mem. Am. Hist. Assn., Orgn. Am. Historians, AAUP (exec. com. Ga. sect. 1962-65), Soc. Hist. Assn., Assn. Colls. and Univs. N.Y. (bd. dirs. 1981—), Council Ind. Colls. N.Y. (bd. dirs. 1981—), N.Y.C. C of C. and Industry, Torch Club, Wings Club, Mensheviki Club, Phi Mu Alpha Sinfonia, Phi Kappa Phi, Phi Alpha Theta, Pi Sigma Alpha, Phi Delta Kappa, Omicron Delta Kappa. Home: 36-24 Corporal Kennedy St Flushing NY 11361 Office: Coll Aero La Guardia Airport Office of the Pres Flushing NY 11371

FRANK, WILLIAM FIELDING, computer systems design executive, consultant; b. N.Y.C., Oct. 27, 1944; s. Karl Frederick and Margaret Ruth (Denisson) F.; m. Linda Carol Hainfield, Dec. 20, 1965 (div. 1972); children: Aaron, Tobin. BA, Middlebury Coll., 1966; MA, U. Chgo., 1969; PhD, U. Pa., 1976. Assoc. prof. Oreg. State U., Corvallis, 1969-79; mem. tech. staff Bell Labs., Whippany, N.J., 1979-81; pres. Integrated Info. Systems Assocs., Warren, Vt., 1982—; vis. scholar MIT, Cambridge, 1981-85; cons. Citibank, 1982—, Digital Equipment Corp., 1987—, AT&T, 1984, N.Y. Times, 1985, Bank of Am., 1985, State of Calif., 1986—, Soviet Ministry of Trade, 1990, Bankers Trust, 1991. Contbr. articles to profl. jours. Research grantee NSF, 1971, 77, NEH, 1976, 81. Mem. Assn. for Computing Machinery, Computer Soc. IEEE. Republican. Congregationalist. Home: Lincoln Gap Rd # 146 Warren VT 05674 Office: Integrated Info Systems Assocs 225 Rector Pl Apt 23G New York NY 10280-1127

FRANKE, ANN HARRIET, lawyer; b. Bethesda, Md., Feb. 17, 1952; d. Charles Frederick and Mary (St. John) F. BA, MA, U. Pa., Phila., 1974, JD, 1977; LLM, Georgetown U., 1978. Bar: Pa. 1977, D.C. 1978, U.S. Ct. Appeals (D.C. cir.) 1978. Assoc. Sobol & Trister, Washington, 1978-81; asst. corp. counsel Dist. of Columbia, Washington, 1981-82; asst., assoc., counsel Am. Assn. U. Profs., Washington, 1982—; editorial advisor West Edn. Law Reporter, Mpls., 1990—. Speaker various confs. and univs., 1982—. Fulbright grantee Coun. for Internat. Exchange of Scholars, Australia, 1990. Mem. Chamber Music Conf. (bd. dirs. 1986—), D.C. Bar Assn. (steering com., labor law div.).

FRANKEL, ANDREW VANCE, international consultant; b. Albuquerque, Mar. 5, 1957; s. Alan Louis and Carolyn (Katz) F. BA, U. Calif., Santa Cruz, 1980; MIA, Columbia U., 1986. Staff asst. to Congressman Peter W. Rodino, Jr., U.S. Ho. of Reps., Washington, 1984; asst. N.Am. dir. Trilateral Commn., N.Y.C., 1986-91, sec., 1988-91; bd. dirs. PowerByte, Inc., N.Y.C., 1991—; pres. East-West Strategies, N.Y.C., 1991—. Author: Das Karlsteinhaus, 1983. Ensign USNR. Mem. Coun. on Fgn. Rels., Mid-Atlantic Club N.Y., Am. Coun. on Germany, Internat. Platform Assn.

FRANKEL, GLENN, journalist; b. N.Y.C., Oct. 2, 1949; s. Herbert A. and Betty Beck; m. Betsyellen Yeager; children: Abra, Margo, Paul. BA, Columbia U., 1971. Staff reporter Richmond Mercury, 1973-75; staff writer The Record, Hackensack, N.J., 1975-79; Richmond bur. chief The Washington Post, 1979-82, So. Africa bur. chief, 1983-86, Jerusalem bur. chief, 1986-89, London bur. chief, 1989—. Recipient Pulitzer prize internat. reporting, 1989; Stanford U. fellow, 1982-83.

FRANKEL, JUDITH LEIBHOLZ, bank executive; b. Phila., Oct. 18, 1961; d. Stephen Wolfgang and Ann Ester (Greenberg) Leibholz; m. Oliver Lincoln Frankel, Oct. 6, 1990. BA in Econs., Trinity Coll., 1983; M of Internat. Mgmt., Am. Grad. Sch. Internat. Mgmt., 1985. With customer svc. Merrill Lynch, N.Y.C., 1983-84; pres. Kinko's Word Processing, Phoenix, 1984-85; head of ops. Analytics Inc., Dayton, Ohio, 1985; credit analyst, loan officer NCNB Tex., Dallas, 1985-87; syndicate mgr. Banque Indosvez, N.Y.C., 1987-90; v.p., syndicate mgr. The Indsl. Bank of Japan, N.Y.C., 1990—; bd. dirs. Analytics Inc., Phila., 1989-91; career advisor Am. Grad. Sch. Internat. Mgmt., 1988-91. Bd. dirs., big sister Jewish Bd. Child and Family Svcs. Big Bros/Big Sisters, N.Y.C., 1987-91. Office: The Indsl Bank of Japan 245 Park Ave New York NY 10167-0002

FRANKEL, KENNETH MARK, thoracic surgeon; b. Bklyn., July 29, 1940; s. Clarence Bernard and Ruth (Rutes) F.; m. Felice Cala Oringel, Dec. 10, 1967; children: Matthew David, Michael Jacob. B.A., Cornell U., 1961; M.D., SUNY, Bkyln., 1965. Diplomate Am. Bd. Surgery, Am. Bd. Thoracic

Surgery. Intern in surgery Yale New Haven Hosp., 1965-66; resident in surgery Kings County-SUNY Med. Ctr., Bklyn., 1966-67, 69-71, chief resident in gen. surgery, 1971-72, resident in thoracic surgery, 1972-73, chief resident thoracic and cardiovascular surgery, 1973-74; attending thoracic surgeon Mercy Hosp., Springfield, Mass., 1974—, Holyoke (Mass.) Hosp., 1974—, Providence Hosp., Holyoke, 1974—; practice medicine specializing in thoracic surgery Springfield, 1974—; chief thoracic surgery Baystate Med. Ctr., Springfield, 1977—; assoc. clin. prof. cardiothoracic surgery Tufts U. Sch. Medicine, 1978—; cons. in thoracic surgery Ludlow (Mass.) Hosp., Noble Hosp., Westfield, Mass., 1976—; cons. Shriners Hosp. for Crippled Children. Contbr. articles to profl. jours. Corporator Springfield (Mass.) Symphony Orch., Stage West, Springfield. Served to capt. U.S. Army, 1967-69. Decorated Bronze Star, Gallantry Cross (Republic of Vietnam). Fellow ACS, Am. Coll. Chest Physicians; mem. AMA, ACLU, Soc. Thoracic Surgeons, Am. Thoracic Soc., Springfield Acad. Medicine (past pres), Mass. Med. Soc. (councilor 1981-83), Hampden Dist. Med. Soc. (exec. com. 1990—), Physicians for Social Responsibility, Amnesty Internat., Internat. Physicians for Prevention Nuclear War, Union Concerned Scientists. , Cornell Club of Western Mass., Porsche Club of Am., Maimonides Med. Club (past pres.). Democrat. Jewish. Home: 202 Ellington Rd East Longmeadow MA 01106-1510 Office: Baystate Med Ctr 2 Medical Center Dr Springfield MA 01107-1272

FRANKEL, LAWRENCE STEPHEN, chemist; b. N.Y.C., July 26, 1941; s. Ben and Florence (Hammer) F.; m. Joan Estel Ratner; children: David, Leslie. BA, Hofstra U., 1963; PhD in Chemistry, U. Mass., 1967. Chemist, mgr. Rohm & Hass Co., Spring House, Pa., 1969—. Contbr. articles to profl. jours.; patentee in field. Capt. U.S. Army, 1967-69. Mem. Am. Chem. Soc. Home: 1110 Delene Rd Jenkintown PA 19046-3019

FRANKEL, MARTIN RICHARD, statistician, educator, consultant; b. Washington, June 16, 1943; s. Lester R. and Vera B. Frankel; m. Jean L. Kaiser, Mar. 24, 1970; children: Jennifer, Margaux. AB, U. N.C., 1965; MA, U. Mich., 1967, PhD, 1971. Asst. prof. stats. U. Chgo., 1971-73, assoc. prof., 1974-76; prof. stats. and computer info. systems Baruch Coll., CUNY, 1977—; tech. dir. Nat. Opinion Research Ctr., U. Chgo., 1972—; chnm. Quality Research Council, Advtg. Research Found., 1988—; cons. statis. methods and quality control, 1965—; mem. panel on occupational and health stats., com. on nat. stats. Nat. Rsch. Coun., NAS, 1985-87. Author: Inference from Survey Samples: An Empirical Investigation, 1971; (co-author) SEPP: Sampling Error Program Package, 1972, Total Survey Error: Applications to Improve Health Surveys, 1979; also articles; mem. editorial bd. Pub. Opinion Quar., Ency. Statis. Scis., Sociol. Research and Methods. Fellow Am. Statis. Assn. (chmn. census adv. com. 1981, chmn. sect. survey research methods 1975-76, editorial bd. jour.), Royal Statis. Soc., Internat. Statis. Inst.; mem. Am. Assn. Pub. Opinion Research (chmn. standards com.), Market Rsch. Coun. Home: 14 Patricia Ln Cos Cob CT 06807-1734 Office: Baruch Coll 17 Lexington Ave New York NY 10010-5526

FRANKEL, MAX, journalist, newspaper editor; b. Gera, Germany, Apr. 3, 1930; came to U.S., 1940, naturalized, 1948; s. Jacob A. and Mary (Katz) F.; m. Tobia Brown, June 19, 1956 (dec. Mar. 1987); children: David M., Margot S., Jonathan M.; m. Joyce Purnick, Dec. 11, 1988. A.B., Columbia, 1952, M.A. in Polit. Sci, 1953. Mem. staff N.Y. Times, 1952—, chief Washington corr., 1968-73, Sunday editor, 1973-76, editorial pages editor, 1977-86, exec. editor, 1986—. Served with AUS, 1953-55. Recipient Pulitzer prize for internat. reporting, 1973. Office: NY Times Co 229 W 43rd St New York NY 10036-3913

FRANKEL, S. LEE, JR., electric power industry executive; b. Wilmington, Del., Oct. 17, 1948; s. Samuel L. Sr. and Marjorie (Bailey) F.; m. Sandra Nowland, Oct. 29, 1965; children: Steven, Tara, Seth. Student, U. Del., 1966-70; BSBA, Columbiá Pacific U., 1986. With dept. pub. safety State Del., Dover, 1970-72, 1977-79, aide to gov., 1972-77; supr. credit and collection Del. Power and Light Co., Newark, 1979-81; gen. supr. customer svcs. Del. Power and Light Co., Wilmington, 1981-83, mgr. corp. acct., 1983-85; dist. mgr. Del. Power and Light Co., Rehoboth Beach, 1985—. Bd. dirs. Del. Inland Bays Estuary Program, Rehoboth Beach, 1989—; co-chmn. fin. com. Carper '92, Georgetown, Del., 1991. Mem. Employee Responsible Govt. Assn. (chair 1988—), Rehoboth Bay Sailing Assn., Rehoboth Beach C. of C. (dir. 1986-91). Democrat. Episcopalian. Home: Black Duck Reach Rehoboth Beach DE 19971 Office: Del Power and Light Co PO Box 459 Rehoboth Beach DE 19971-0459

FRANKENBERG, ROBERT EDWARD, sales executive, import specialist, consultant; b. N.Y.C., Oct. 21, 1944; s. Jack M. and Muriel (Gladstone) F.; m. Barbara Reif, Nov. 14, 1965; children: Mitchell Charles, Brett David. BS, NYU, 1967. Sales rep. Paintset Fashions, N.Y.C., 1967-72; sales rep. Halmode Apparel, N.Y.C., 1972-75, sales mgr., 1975-77; owner, v.p. Mi-Brett Fashions, Inc., N.Y.C., 1978-81; sales exec. Young Gare, Inc., N.Y.C., 1981-84; owner, entrepreneur Franken Sales, N.Y.C., 1984—; field judge Long Island Assn. Football Officials, Westbury, N.Y., 1969-76. Bd. dirs. Temple Avodah, Oceanside, N.Y., 1977-86, Oceanside Theatre Guild, 1984-90, Free Sons Israel, 1973-90, pres., 1977-79. Democrat. Jewish. Office: Franken Sales 990 6th Ave Ste 10K New York NY 10018-5401

FRANKFORT, HOWARD MARK, patent agent; b. Bklyn., July 19, 1952; s. Milton and Faye (Dank) F. BS, CCNY, 1974; MS, NYU, 1978, phD, 1981. Registered patent agt. Postdoctoral assoc. Rockefeller U., N.Y.C., 1981-85; patent agt. Darby and Darby P.C., N.Y.C., 1985—. Mem. AAAS, N.Y. Acad. Sci. Home: 360 E 72nd St Apt B1002 New York NY 10021 Office: Darby and Darby PC 805 3rd Ave New York NY 10022

FRANKFORTER, A(LBERTUS) DANIEL, European history educator; b. Waynesboro, Pa., May 17, 1939; s. A. Daniel and Louise R. (Flickinger) F.; m. Karen Keene, May 26, 1973. BA, Franklin and Marshall Coll., 1961; MDiv, Drew U., 1965; MA, Pa. State U., 1969, PhD, 1971. Asst. prof. Pa. State U.-Behrend Coll., Erie, 1970-78, assoc. prof., 1979-88, prof., 1989—. Author: A History of the Christian Movement, 1978, Civilization and Survival, 1987, The Shakespeare Name Dictionary, 1991; translator, editor: Equality of Two Sexes, 1989. Home: 521 Rankine Ave Erie PA 16511-2046 Office: Pa State U Behrend Coll Station Rd Erie PA 16563

FRANKL, DANIEL RICHARD, educator, physicist; b. N.Y.C., Sept. 6, 1922; s. William and Frances (Lerner) F.; m. Estelle Marder, Aug. 26, 1951; children—Joseph Frederick, Phyllis Gail. B.Chem.Engring., Cooper Union, 1943; Ph.D., Columbia, 1953. With U.S. Rubber Co., Detroit, 1943-50; with Gen. Telephone & Electronics Labs., Inc., Bayside, N.Y., 1953-63; vis. prof. phys. metallurgy U. Ill., Urbana; (on leave Gen. Telephone & Electronics Labs.), 1962-63; prof. physics Pa. State U., University Park, 1963-88, emeritus, 1988—; Vis. sr. research assoc. U. Sussex, 1969-70; vis. research physicist U. Calif., San Diego, 1978-79; vis. fellow Fitzwilliam Coll. U. Cambridge, 1986. Author: Electrical Properties of Semiconductor Surfaces, 1967; Electromagnetic Theory, 1986. Fellow Am. Phys. Soc. Home: 438 Sierra Ln State College PA 16803-1409 Office: Pa State Univ Dept Physics University Park PA 16801

FRANKL, RAZELLE, management educator. BA in English, Temple U., 1955; MA in Polit. Sci., Bryn Mawr Coll., 1966; MBA in Organizational Devel., Drexel U., 1973; PhD, Bryn Mawr Coll., 1984. Chair codes and ordinance com. Exec Com. Neighborhood Improvement Program, Lower Merion Twp., 1967-68; pres. LWV Lower Merion Twp., 1967-68; v.p. for organizational affairs LWV, Springfield, Mass., 1968-70; chair environ. quality com. LWV Radnor Twp., 1970-71; instr. applied behavioral sci. Drexel U. Sch. Bus., 1972-73; planner office of mental health/mental retardation Dept. Pub. Health, City of Phila., 1971-73, planner office of health planning, 1971-73; coord. for health programs Phila. '76 Inc. (Official Bicentennial Corp.), 1972-74; asst. prof. Glassboro (N.J.) State Coll., 1982-88, assoc. prof. dept. mgmt., 1988—; adj. faculty Dept. mgmt. adminstrv. studies div. Glassboro State Coll., 1974-77, 81-82; presenter in field. Author: Televangelism: The Marketing of Popular Religion, 1987, Popular Religion and the Imperatives of Television: A Study of the Electric Church, 1984; author: (with others) Religious Television: Controversies and Conclusions, 1990, Teleministries as Family Businesses, 1990; New Christian Politics, 1984; contbr. articles to profl. jours. Rsch. grantee Glassboro State Coll., 1986-87, 1990-91, All-Coll. Rsch. grantee Glassboro State Coll., 1987-88. Mem. Am. Acad. Mgmt. (chair media rels. com., divsn. women in mgmt.), Soc. for Human Resource Mgmt., Am. Sociol. Assn., Ea. Sociol. Soc., Assn. for Sociology of Religion, Religious Rsch. Assn., Soc. for the Sci. Study of Religion, Internat. Sociol. Assn., Popular Culture Assn. Home: 536 Moreno Rd Wynnewood PA 19096-1121

FRANKL, WILLIAM STEWART, cardiologist, educator; b. Phila., July 15, 1928; s. Louis and Vera (Simkin) F.; m. Razelle Sherr, June 17, 1951; children: Victor S. (dec.), Brian A. B.A. in Biology, Temple U., 1951, M.D., 1955, M.S. in Medicine, 1961. Diplomate: Am. Bd. Internal Medicine, Am. Bd. Cardiovascular Disease. Intern Buffalo Gen. Hosp., 1955-56; resident in medicine Temple U., Phila., 1956-57, 59-61; mem. faculty Temple U. (Sch. Medicine), 1962-68, dir. EKG sect. dept. cardiology, 1966-68, dir. cardiac care unit, 1967-68; research fellow U. Pa., Phila., 1961-62; prof. medicine, dir. div. cardiology Med. Coll. Pa., Phila., 1970-79; prof. medicine, assoc. dir. cardiology div. Thomas Jefferson U., Phila., 1979-84; physician-in-chief Springfield (Mass.) Hosp., 1968-70; practice medicine specializing in cardiology Phila., 1962-68, 70—; prof. medicine, co-dir. William Likoff Cardiovascular Inst. Hahnemann U., Phila., 1984-86, dir. William Likoff Cardiovascular Inst., dir. div. cardiology, 1986-92, Thomas J. Vischer Prof. medicine, chmn. dept. medicine, 1987-92; prof. medicine, dir. cardiovascular programs for the Med. Coll. Hosps. and the Med. Coll. Pa., 1992—; cons. cardiology Phila. Va Hosp., 1970-79; Fogarty Sr. Internat. fellow Cardiothoracic Inst., U. London, 1978-79; pres. Pa. affiliate Am. Heart Assn., 1985-86. Contbr. articles to profl. jours. Capt. Med. Corps, U.S. Army, 1957-59. Recipient Golden Apple award Temple U. Sch. Medicine, 1967; award Med. Coll. Pa., 1972; Lindback award for distinguished teaching, 1975. Fellow A.C.P., Am. Coll. Cardiology (gov. Eastern Pa. 1986-89), Phila. Coll. Physicians, Am. Coll. Clin. Pharmacology (regent 1980-85), Council Clin. Cardiology, Am. Heart Assn. (council on arteriosclerosis); mem. N.Y. Acad. Scis., Am. Fedn. Clin. Research, AAUP, AAAS, Assn. Am. Med. Colls., Am. Heart Assn. (bd. govs. S.E. Pa. chpt. 1972—, pres. 1976), Am. Soc. Clin. Pharmacology and Therapeutic Therapeutics. Home: 536 Moreno Rd Wynnewood PA 19096-1121 Office: Med Coll Pa Main Clin Campus 3300 Henry Ave Philadelphia PA 19102

FRANKLIN, ALAN DOUGLAS, physical chemist; b. Glenside, Pa., Dec. 10, 1922; s. Benjamin Jr. and Adrienne (Kenyon) F.; m. Phoebe Taylor, 1943 (div.); children: Adrienne Parker, Christopher; m. Katherine Ann McMurdie, Apr. 16, 1960; 1 child, Mary Louise. BA in Chemistry, Princeton U., 1945, PhD in Chemistry, 1950. Vis. scientist United Kingdom Atomic Energy Authority, Harwell, 1963-64, 82; asst. inst. dir. Nat. Bur. Standards, Gaithersburg, Md., 1964-66, rsch. scientist, 1967-81; dep. dir. materials, adv. rsch. project agy. U.S. Dept. Def., Washington, 1966-67; vis. prof. dept. physics U. Md., College Park, 1983—; professorial lectr. George Washington U., 1983-86; vis. scientist Flinders U., Adelaide, Australia, 1983, 1980-81; chmn. solid state studies in ceramics Gordon Rsch. Confs., 1969; chmn. panel solid state sci. com. Nat. Rsch. Coun., 1978-79; internat. sec. tech. com. 58 Internat. Electrotech. Commn., 1965-67. Editor eight books; contbr. articles to profl. jours. Bd. dirs., pres. Columbia Heights Youth Club, Washington, 1958-81; pres. Civic Assn., Brookmont, Md., 1961-63; bd. dirs., pres. Shepherdstown Men's Club, 1983-89. 1st lt. USAF, 1942-45. Grantee NSF, 1991—. Fellow Am. Phys. Soc., Am. Ceramic Soc.; mem. Am. Chem. Soc., Soc. for Archaeol. Scis. Democrat. Home: PO Box 39 Shepherdstown WV 25443-0039 Office: U Md Dept Physics College Park MD 20742

FRANKLIN, BARBARA HACKMAN, federal agency administrator; b. Lancaster, Pa., Mar. 19, 1940; d. Arthur A. and Mayme M. (Haller) Hackman; m. Wallace Barnes, Nov. 29, 1986. BA with distinction, Pa. State U., 1962; MBA, Harvard U., 1964; D of Bus. Adminstrn. (hon.), Bryant Coll., 1973; D of Commerce (hon.), Drexel U., 1990. Mgr. environ. analysis Singer Co., N.Y.C., 1964-68; asst. v.p. Citibank, N.Y.C., 1969-71; mem. White House staff, Washington, 1971-73; commr., vice chmn. U.S. Consumer Product Safety Commn., Washington, 1973-79; sr. fellow, dir. govt. and bus. programs Wharton Sch., U. Pa., Phila. and Washington, 1979-89; pres., chief exec. officer Franklin Assocs., Washington, 1984-92; Sec. of Commerce Dept. of Commerce, Washington, 1992—; former adviser to comptroller gen. U.S., 1984—; bd. dirs. Aetna Life and Casualty Co., Dow Chem. Co., Westinghouse Electric Corp., Black & Decker Corp., Automatic Data Processing, Inc., Nordstrom, Inc., Armstrong World Industries; trustee, Pa. State U.; pub. mem. Auditing Standards Bd. Planning Com., 1989. Contbr. numerous articles to profl. jours. Apptd. by Pres. Reagan then Bush to Pres.'s Adv. Com. Trade Negotiations, 1982-86, 89—, chmn. task force on tax reform, 1985-86; co-chmn. Nat. Fin. Com. George Bush for Pres., 1985-88; bd. visitors Def. Systems Mgmt. Coll., Dept. Def., 1986-89; svcs. policy adv. Com. of U.S. Trade Representatives; apptd. by Pres. Bush and confirmed by senate as alt. rep. and pub. del. 44th Session of UN Gen. Assembly, 1989; apptd. by Gov. Thornburgh to State Bd. Edn., Commonwealth Pa., 1980-81; bd. regents U. Hartford, 1986-88. Recipient Disting. Alumni award Pa. State U., 1972, Disting. Woman award Northwood Inst., 1972, Catalyst Award for Corp. Leadership, 1981, Excellence in Mgmt. award Simmons Coll., 1981, ann. award Am. Assn. Poison Control Ctrs., 1979, cert. appreciation, Am. Acad. Pediatrics, 1978, 79, Dirs. Choice award Nat. Women's Econ. Alliance, 1987, Award for Corp. Social Responsibility, CUNY, 1988; Kappa Alpha Theta Graduate fellow, 1962, Edith Gratia Stedman, Harvard U., fellow, 1962. Fellow Nat. Assn. Corp. Dirs.; mem. Women's Forum Washington, Nat. Women's Econ. Alliance Found. (bd. govs., Dir.'s Choice award 1987), Internat. Women's Forum (founding mem.), Nat. Women's Party, Exec. Women in Govt. (founding mem., vice chmn. 1973—), Bretton Woods Com., Washington Forum, Women's Rep. Club of Lancaster County, Alumni Coun. Pa. State U., Penn State Club of Greater Washington, 1925 F Street Club, Washington, Women's Nat. Rep. Club (bd. govs. 1969-71), Econ. Club N.Y. Congregational. Avocations: exercise, skiing, sailing, reading. Office: Dept of Commerce Office of Sec 14th & Constitution Ave NW Washington DC 20230

FRANKLIN, CHURCHILL GIBSON, investment management executive; b. N.Y.C., Oct. 31, 1948; s. John Weed and Elizabeth Lloyd (Gibson) F.; m. Janet Ellen Halstead, Oct. 7, 1972; children: Churchill Halstead, Katherine Disbrow, Lindsey Weed. BA, Middlebury Coll., 197l. Comml. loan officer Bank of Boston, 1973-81; asst. treas. Thermo Electron Corp., Waltham, Mass., 1981-86; sr. v.p. Acadian Asset Mgmt., Inc., Boston, 1986—; chmn. bd. dirs. Winchester (Mass.) Healthcare Investments, Inc., 1985—; bd. dirs. Winchester Healthcare Mgmt., Inc., Winchester Healthcare Enterprises, Inc. Bd. dirs. New Eng. Wind Hotline Inc., Cambridge, Mass., 1987—; trustee Middlebury Coll., 1989—. Democrat. Congregationalist. Home: 106 Oak St Reading MA 01867 Office: Acadian Asset Mgmt Inc 260 Franklin St Boston MA 02110-3112

FRANKLIN, DONALD EVAN, treasurer; b. Newark, May 19, 1962; s. Alan Herbert and Carol (Gittlin) F.; m. Kristen J. Babahshak, May 29, 1989. Degree in Internat. Bus., U. Copenhagen, 1983; BA in Acctg., Franklin and Marshall Coll., 1984. CPA, Va. Cost acct. MCI Telecommunications, Washington, 1984-85; supervising sr. acct. KPMG Peat Marwick, Washington, 1985-89; treas., v.p. fin. Com-Site Internat., Inc., Beltsville, Md., 1989—; fin. cons. The Bankshot Orgn., Bethesda, 1989—. Mem. Bethesda Jewish Congregation, 1989, Blessed Sacrament Cath. Community, Alexandria, Va., 1989. Mem. AICPA, Va. Soc. CPAs. Home: 2830 Linden Ln Falls Church VA 22042-2312 Office: Comsite Internat Inc 12050 Baltimore Ave Beltsville MD 20705-4219

FRANKLIN, HARDY R., library director; b. Rome, Ga., May 9, 1929; B.A. in Sociology, Morehouse Coll., 1950; M.L.S., Atlanta U., 1956; Ph.D. (Higher Edn. Act fellow), Rutgers U., 1971; m. Barbara Washington; children: Petey, Regan Hayes. Tchr., librarian Rockdale County Bd. Edn., Conyers, Ga., 1950-53; various positions Bklyn. Pub. Library, 1956-64, sr. community coordinator, 1964-68; asst. prof. library sci. dept. Queens Coll. City U. N.Y., Flushing, 1971-74; dir. D.C. Pub. Library, Washington, 1974—; cons., guest lectr. in field. Pres., Middle Schs. PTA, Hempstead, N.Y., 1973-74; mem. advisory council to supt. schs., Hempstead, 1973-74; mem. advisory bd. D.C. Citizens for Better Edn., 1975—; mem. advisory bd. Streets for People, 1975—; co-chmn. One Fund campaign, 1975, 76. Served with U.S. Army, 1953-55. Recipient Bklyn. Friends of Library award, 1963, Community Leader award Freedom Nat. Bank, 1968, Disting. Svc. award Rutgers U., 1992; Council on Library Resources grantee, 1970-71; Nat. Endowment for the Humanities grantee, 1970-71; named Washingtonian of Yr., 1987. Mem. ALA (candidate pres. 1992, Allie Beth Martin award 1983), D.C. Libr. Assn. (v.p., pres. elect. 1991-92, bd. trustees Disting. Svc. award 1990), Am. Film Inst., Assn. Study of Afro-Am. Life and History, Urban League, NAACP, Sigma Pi Phi, Alpha Phi Alpha. Contbr. articles to profl. jours. Office: DC Pub Libr M Luther King Meml Libr 901 G St NW Washington DC 20001-4599

FRANKLIN, HERBERT MENDELL, government administrator; b. Milw., May 16, 1933; s. Nathan Mendel and Bessie (Ozonoff) F.; m. Barbara Braemer, Apr. 10, 1960; children: Marcia, Jonathan, David. AB cum laude, Harvard U., 1955, LLB, 1958. Bar: Wis. 1958, U.S. Supreme Ct. 1964, D.C. 1973. Assoc. firm Charne and Tehan, Milw., 1958-61; atty. Office of Chief Counsel U.S. Urban Renewal Adminstrn., Housing and Home Fin. Agy., Washington, 1961-65; dir. Urban Am., Inc., Bus. and Devel. Ctr., Washington, 1965-67; planning and devel. adminstr. Office of Mayor, City of Middletown, Conn., 1967-68; v.p. for housing and urban growth Nat. Urban Coalition, Washington, 1968-72; mem. firm Lane and Edson, P.C., Washington, 1973-89; counsel to firm Kelley Drye & Warren, Washington, 1989; exec. officer Architect of the Capitol, Washington, 1989—; adj. prof. Am. U. Sch. Govt. and Pub. Adminstrn., Washington, 1974-78; guest lectr. on land use controls, housing and community devel. Co-chair editorial adv. bd. Real Estate Taxation, 1985-89; contbr. articles to profl. jours. Founder, chmn. bd. trustees Nat. Bldg. Mus., Washington, 1987-89, bd. trustees mem. exec. com., 1989—; founder, bd. dirs., sec. Chevy Chase Found., 1977-87; bd. dirs. Nat. Housing Conf., 1967-80, mem. exec. com., 1975-80, chmn. nominations con., 1976-79; bd. dirs. Met. Washington Planning and Housing Assn., 1977-78, Potomac Inst., Inc., 1984—; pub. mem., vice. chmn. D.C. Rental Accommodations Commn., 1976-77; co-chair D.C. Mayor's Transition Com. on Housing and Community Devel., 1979. Mem. ABA (adv. commn. on housing and urban, 1977-78), Cosmos Club (garden com. 1989—, vice chmn. 1991). Office: Architect of the Capitol US Capitol SB-15 Washington DC 20515

FRANKLIN, JEFFREY ALAN, lawyer; b. Iowa City, Iowa, Dec. 24, 1964; s. Stephen Harold and Mary Sue (Brownlee) F. AB, Bucknell U., Lewisburg, Pa., 1987; JD, U. Pitts., 1990. Assoc. Ryan, Russell & McConaghy, Reading, Pa., 1990—. Exec. editor Jour. Law and Commerce, Pitts. 1989-90, assoc. editor, 1988-89. Mem. ABA, Computer Law Assn., Phila. Bar Assn., Brks County Bar Assn., Pa. Bar Assn., Bar of the Commonwealth of Pa., Phi Alpha Delta, Mortar Bd. Office: Ryan Russell & McConaghy 530 Penn Square Ctr Reading PA 19608-1112

FRANKLIN, KAREN SPIEGEL, museum director; b. Phila., Dec. 26, 1954; d. Walter F. and Jeanne (Sundheim) S.; m. Stephen D. Franklin, Oct. 29, 1978; children: Ross, Andrew, Joshua. BA, Wellesley (Mass.) Coll., 1976; MA, Temple U., 1979. Coord. edn. Judaica Mus., Riverdale, N.Y., 1985-87, adminstr., 1987-88, dir., 1988—; cons. Haus der Bayerischen Geschichte, Munich, 1989-91. Author: Eleven Generations of the Gerstle Family, 1982; contbr. articles to mags. Acting co-chmn. bd. Kingsdale Vol. Ambulance Corp., Bronx, N.Y., 1991; co-pres. Hadassah Elsie Kolinsky chpt., Bronx, 1983-85; bd. dirs. Ludlow Pk. Homeowners Assn., Yonkers, N.Y., 1986-91. Recipient Silver medal award Pres. of the German State of Schwaben, Fed. Republic of Germany, 1989. Mem. Jewish Geneal. Soc. N.Y. (mem. exec. bd. 1987-90, co-editor jour. 1987-88, Nat. Geneal. Soc. award), Coun. Am. Jewish Mus. (chmn. steering bd. 1992—, mem. steering bd. 1990-92), Wellesley Coll. Class of '76 (sec. 1986-91). Home: 104 Franklin Ave Yonkers NY 10705-2808

FRANKLIN, KENNETH WILLIAM, cardiologist; b. Wantagh, N.Y., Jan. 8, 1952; s. Harold and Eleanor (Suess) F.; m. Carol Lee Schroeder, July 12, 1975. BA magna cum laude, Amherst Coll., 1974; MD, Harvard U., 1978. Med. intern, resident N.Y. Hosp.-Cornell Med. Ctr., N.Y.C., 1978-81; fellow cardiology Hosp. U. Pa., Phila., 1981-83, fellow cardiac catharization, 1983-84; attending physician, cardiologist Stamford (Conn.) Hosp., 1984-91; clin. instr. N.Y. Med. Coll., Valhilla, N.Y., 1987-91; clin. instr. Cornell U. Med. Sch., N.Y.C., 1986-91, clin. asst. prof. medicine, 1991—; clin. affiliate N.Y. Hosp.-Cornell Med. Ctr., N.Y.C., 1986-91, attending physician, cardiologist, 1991—; bd. dirs. Tandet Ctr. Continuing Care, Stamford, 1989—; cons. cardiologist Olin Corp., Stamford, 1989—; acting med. dir., physician GTE Corp., sTamford, 1989. Contbr. articles to profl. jours. Woodruff Simpson fellow Harvard Med. Sch., 1978-79; recipient cardiac rsch. fellowship, grant Am. Heart Assn., Pa. chpt., 1982-83. Fellow Am. Coll. Cardiology; mem. ACP, Am. Heart Assn. (coun. clin. cardiology). Office: 260 E 66th St New York NY 06902

FRANKLIN, LINDA LAWRENCE, theatre company manager; b. Margaretville, N.Y., Sept. 6, 1950; d. Harvey C. and Ruth (Donovan) Lawrence; m. Ronald A. Franklin, Nov. 18, 1972; children: Jason L., Meghan E. BA, SUNY, Albany, 1972. Owner, designer Period Designs and Restoration, Middletown, R.I., 1983—; mng. dir. Newport (R.I.) Children's Theatre. Bd. dirs. Newport Players Guild, 1979—, Island Moving Co., Newport, 1985—. Mem. Costume Soc. Am. (membership com. 1988—), New Eng. Theatre Conf. Home: 14 North Dr Middletown RI 02840 Office: Newport Children's Theatre PO Box 144 Newport RI 02840-0002

FRANKS, CYRIL MAURICE, psychology educator; b. Neath, Wales, U.K., July 26, 1923; came to U.S., 1957; s. Harry and Cecelia (Zeiler) F.; m. Violet Greenberg, Mar. 29, 1952; children: Steven, Sharon. BSc, U. Wales, Swansea, 1943; MA, U. Minn., 1952; PhD, U. London, 1954. Lic. psychologist, N.J. Lectr. in sci. London Nautical Sch., 1947-50; lectr. in clin. psychology Inst. of Psychiatry U. London, 1954-57; dir. psychology Neuropsychiat. Inst. Princeton (N.J.) U., 1957-70; prof. Rutgers U., New Brunswick, N.J., 1970-74, disting. prof. Grad. Sch. Applied and Profl. Psychology, 1974—; prof. emeritus, 1992—; cons. clin. psychology Carrier Found., Belle Mead, N.J., 1957—. Author: Review of Behavior Therapy, 1973; founding editor Behavior Therapy, 1966-73, Child and Family Behavior Therapy, 1979—. Fellow APA (pres. div. 12 sect. III 1972-73), Brit. Psychol. Soc.; mem. Assn. for Advancement of Behavior Therapy (founder, 1st pres. 1966), Pavlovian Soc. N.Am. Jewish. Home: 315 Prospect Ave Princeton NJ 08540-5330 Office: Rutgers U Grad Sch Applied Profl Psychology Piscataway NJ 08855-0819

FRANKS, DAVID A., computer engineer; b. Washington, June 24, 1929; s. David Ransom and Lela Becton (Duncan) F.; m. Erta Mae Williford, June 20, 1953; children: David Bryan, Kathleen Elva. BS in Math., Howard U., 1951, MS in Math., 1952; postgrad., U. Ill., 1953-54. 1st lt. U.S. Army, 1953-57; various engring. positions Westinghouse Electric Corp., Balt., 1957—, mgr. applications software, 1968—. Mem. Am. Math. Soc., Assn. for Computing Machinery, Soc. for Indsl. & Applied Math., Data Processing Mgmt. Assn., Balt. Computer Users Group, Capital Computer Users Group. Home: 8505 Moon Glass Ct Columbia MD 21045-5630

FRANKS, GARY ALVIN, congressman, real estate professional; b. Waterbury, Conn., Feb. 9, 1953; s. Richard Dobbs and Jenary Minnie (Petteway) F.; m. Donna Williams, Mar. 10, 1990; 1 child, Jessica Lynn; 1 stepdau., Azia Forrest. BA, Yale U., 1975. Indsl./labor rels. profl. Continental Can, Conn., 1976-78, Chesebrough-Ponds, Conn., 1978-82, Cadbury Schweppes, Conn., 1982-86; pres., founder GAF Realty, Waterbury, Conn., 1986-90; mem. 102d Congress from 5th Conn. Dist, 1990—, mem. policy com., armed svc. com., aging com., small bus. com., 1990—. Alderman City of Waterbury, 1986-90, pres. pro tempore, 1986-87; vice chmn. Waterbury Zoning Com., 1986-87; mem. Environ. Control Commn., Waterbury, 1988-90; dir. ARC, Naugatuck, Conn., 1984-87, Waterbury C. of C., 1987-90; mem. Waterbury Found., 1989-90; mem. Waterbury Fire Bd., 1986-87, Waterbury Housing Assistance Program Commn., 1986-90; bd. dirs. Waterbury Opportunities Industrialization Ctr., 1985-90, Waterbury Boys Club, 1984-89, YMCA, 1988-90. Named Outstanding Young Man Waterbury Boys Club, 1971, Man of Yr. Negro Profl. Women's Club. Mem. Congl. Black Caucus, Conservative Opportunities Soc. Republican. Baptist. Office: US Ho of Reps 1609 Longworth House Office Bldg Washington DC 20515

FRANKS, GEORGE VINCENT, ceramic engineer; b. Orange, N.J., Feb. 10, 1963; s. George Vincent and Janet Louise (Graham) F. BS in Materials Engring., MIT, 1985. Devel. engr. Norton Co. High Performance Ceramics,

Worcester, Mass., 1985-88, Ceramics Process Systems, Milford, Mass., 1988—. Recipient R & D 100 award Rsch. and Devel. Mag., 1991. Home: 947 Boylston St Newton MA 02161 Office: Ceramics Process Systems 155 Fortune Blvd Milford MA 01757

FRANKS, MARTIN DAVIS, broadcast executive; b. Michigan City, Ind., Sept. 27, 1950; s. R. Wendell and Alice (Barnard) F.; m. Mari J. Schleuning. BA in Politics, Princeton U., 1972. Staff asst. Dem. Senatorial Campaign Com., Washington, 1972-74; dep. chief staff U.S. Senator John Tunney, Washington and L.A., 1975-77; chief staff U.S. Senator Patrick Leahy, Washington, 1977-79; nat. rsch. and issues dir. Carter/Mondale Prsdl. Com., Washington, 1979-80; exec. office of pres. The White House, Washington, 1980-81; exec. dir. Dem. Congl. Campaign Com., Washington, 1981-87; v.p. Charls Walker Assocs., Washington, 1987-88; v.p. Washington CBS Inc., Washington, 1988—; lectr. U. So. Calif., L.A., 1982—. Mem. Nat. Assn. Broadcasters (bd. dirs. 1988—). Office: CBS Inc 1634 I St NW # 1000 Washington DC 20006

FRANZ, DONALD EUGENE, JR., merchant banker; b. Mineral Wells, Tex., Oct. 12, 1944; s. Donald E. and Ruth M. (Eichelman) F.; m. Caroline Jones, Dec. 1, 1973. BA, Villanova U., 1966; MBA, Columbia U., 1969. Cert. N.Y. Stock Exchange supervisory analyst. Investment analyst Middendorf, Colgate & Co., N.Y.C., 1969-73, U.S. Trust Co., N.Y.C., 1969, G.H. Walker & Co., N.Y.C., 1973; dir. research Shelby Cullom Davis & Co., N.Y.C., 1973-74; asst. v.p. Smith Barney Harris Upham & Co. Inc., N.Y.C., 1974-76, v.p., 1977, 1st v.p., 1978-82, 83-84; sr. v.p., mng. dir. Smith Barney Harris Upham & Co. Inc., 1985-87; mng. dir. Fin. Security Advisers, Inc., 1987-90, pres., 1989-90; pres. Moorgate Holdings, Ltd., N.Y.C., 1991—; cons. Gulf United Corp., Jacksonville, Fla., 1982-83, Avemco Corp., Frederick, Md., 1987; pres. Gold Coast Air Taxi, Inc., 1981-90; mem. internat. adv. bd. Am. Acad. Overseas Studies, 1986—; bd. dirs. Fin. Securities Fund., 1987-90, Pres. Com. of 100, Rutland, Vt., 1981-90. Named to Investor All Star Team, Instl. Investor Mag., 1978-86. Fellow Assn. Ins. and Fin. Analysts (exec. com. 1982), N.Y. Athletic Club, Doubles Club Internat., Knickerbocker Club, Coral Beach and Tennis Club (Paget, Bermuda), Md. Club. Republican. Roman Catholic. Office: 341 Madison Ave Ste 1700 New York NY 10017-3705

FRANZ, FREDERICK WILLIAM, religious organization official; b. Covington, Ky., Sept. 12, 1893; s. Frederick Edward and Ida Louise (Krueger) F. Student, U. Cin., 1911-14. Ordained to ministry Jehovah's Witnesses, 1914, mem. internat. hdqrs. staff, 1920—; bd. dirs. Watchtower Bible and Tract Soc. N.Y., 1932—, v.p., 1949-77, pres., 1977—; bd. dirs. Watch Tower Bible and Tract Soc. Pa., 1943—, v.p., 1945-77, pres., 1977—. Address: Jehovah's Witnesses 25 Columbia Heights Brooklyn NY 11201

FRANZETTI, CARLOS ALBERTO, composer; b. Buenos Aires, June 3, 1948; came to U.S., 1970; s. Carlos Osvaldo and Beatrice (D'Giacómo) F.; m. Maria B. Lagos, Jan. 16, 1971; 1 child, Carlos Jr. BA, Salvador Conservatorio, Buenos Aires, 1965; M Composition, Nacional Musics, Buenos Aires, 1969; postgrad., Julliard Sch., N.Y.C., 1990-91. Music dir. Fermata Internat., Mexico City, 1971-73, Blank Prodns., N.Y.C., 1974-80, Sorin Films, Buenos Aires, 1983-85, Havana-N.Y. Music, N.Y.C., 1985-90, Sunday Prodns., N.Y.C., 1990—; Condr., composer Orch. Nova Chamber Group, 1991. Composer film scores Misunderstood, 1984 (Gold record 1985), Q&A, 1989, The Mambo Kings, 1991, Le Film du Roi, 1991. Recipient Trofeu Laus award D'adgfad, Barcelona, Spain, 1988, 1st prize Competition award Promusica/Yamaha, Argentina, Billboard award, U.S.A., Clio award, 1990. Mem. NARAS, SAG, AFTRA, BMI, Local 802 Musicians Union. Roman Catholic. Home: 395 S End Ave New York NY 10280-1034

FRAPPAOLO, CARL JOSEPH, computer software executive; b. Glen Cove, N.Y., Mar. 27, 1956; s. Genari Ernest and Theresa Antionette (Villani) F.; m. Ann Madeline Finnerty, Aug. 13, 1989. BA, SUNY, Buffalo, 1978. Litigation support specialist U.S. Dept. Justice, Washington, 1978-80; sr. software cons. Henco Software, Waltham, Mass., 1983-86; product mgr. Honeywell Bull, Waltham, 1986-87, PSDI, Cambridge, Mass., 1987-88; exec. v.p. Delphi Cons. Group, Boston, 1988—; co-founder Delphi Cons. Group, Boston, 1988—; product engr. Conversion Technologies, Boston, 1988. Co-author: (seminar coursebook) Information Management: The Next Generation; mng. editor EDMS Jour.; contbr. articles to profl. jours. Office: Delphi Cons Group 50 Staniford St Ste 800 Boston MA 02114-2594

FRASCONI, ANTONIO, artist, educator; b. Buenos Aires, Apr. 28, 1919; came to U.S., 1945; s. Franco and Armida (Carbonai) F.; m. Leona Pierce, July 18, 1951; children: Pablo, Miquel. Student, Circulo Bellas Artes, Montevideo, Uruguay, 1944-46, New Sch. Social Rsch., 1947-48. Polit. cartoonist Marcha and La Linea Maginot, Montevideo, 1940; tchr. The New Sch., N.Y.C., 1951; prof. visual arts SUNY, Purchase, 1980. Author: 12 Fables of Aesop, 1954 (chosen 1 of 50 books of yr. Am. Inst. Graphic Arts 1954), See and Say, 1955, Frasconi Woodcuts, 1957, The House That Jack Built, 1958, Birds from My Homeland, 1958, The Face of Edgar Allen Poe, 1959, W. Whitman Portrait, 1960, Known Fables, 1964 (chosen 1 of 50 books of yr. Am. Inst. Graphic Arts), The Cantilever Rainbow, 1965 (chosen 1 of 50 books of yr. Am. Inst. Graphic Arts), Unstill Life, 1969, Overhead the Sun, 1969, Elijah the Slave, 1970, On the Slain Collegians, 1971, Frasconi Against the Grain, 1975 ; films include: The Neighboring Shore, 1960 (Grand Prix award Venice Film Festival 1960), Antonio Frasconi--Graphic Artist, 1975; one man shows include Montevideo, Mex., Bklyn Mus., Pasadena Art Inst., Pan Am. Union, Va. Mus. Fine Arts, Balt. Mus. Art, many others; exhibited in group shows at Ateneo Montevideo, 1939, AIAPE, Montevideo, 1944, Santa Barbara Mus. Art, Calif., 1946, Bklyn. Mus., 1946, Weyhe Gallery, N.Y.C., 1948, Cleve. Mus. Art, 1952, Smithsonian Inst. Traveling Exhbn. Svc., 1953, Balt. Mus. Art, 1963, Bklyn. Mus., 1964, 34th Biennale Internat. d'Arte, Venice, 1967, Cooper-Hewitt Mus., N.Y., 1980, Am. Inst. Graphic Arts, N.Y., 1980; represented in permanent collections including Mus. Modern Art, N.Y.C. Pub. Libr., Art Inst. Chgo., numerous others. Guggenheim fellow, 1952-53; Art Students League scholar, 1944-46, Yaddo scholar, 1952; grantee Xerox Corp., 1978, Tamarind Lithography, 1962; named Nat. Academician Nat. Acad. Design, 1969; recipient Grand Prix award Venice Film Festival, 1960, purchase prize Bklyn. Mus., 1946, U. Nebr., 1951, Erickson award Soc. Am. Graphic Arts, 1952, prize Pa. Acad. Fine Arts, Nat. Inst. Arts and Letters award, 1954, Joseph H. Hirshorn Found. prize Soc. Am. Graphic Artists, 1963, W.H. Walker prize Print Club Phila., 1964, prize 2nd Biennale d'Art Graphique, 1966, Salon Nat. de Bellas Artes, Grand Premio Exposition de la Habana, 1968, others.

FRASER, DAVID ALLEN, sociologist, educator; b. Tucson, Ariz., Mar. 16, 1943; s. Thomas Henry and Edith (Johnston) F.; m. Elouise Marie Renich, Sept. 11, 1965; children: Scott Edward, Sherry Louise. AB, Stanford U., 1965; MA, Harvard U., 1969; MDiv, Fuller Theol. Seminary, Pasadena, Calif., 1975; MA, PhD, Vanderbilt U., 1986. Asst. prof. Columbia (S.C.) Bible Coll. and Seminary, 1969-73; rsch. assoc. World Vision, Internat., Monrovia, Calif., 1975-79; rsch. cons. Mission Tng. and Rsch. Ctr., Pasadena, 1979-82; interim pastor Hermitage (Tenn.) Presbyn. Ch., Harpeth Presbyn. Ch., Brentwood, Tenn., 1983, Norristown (Pa.) Schwenkfelder Ch., 1983-85; parish assoc. 1st Presbyn. Ch., Haddonfield, N.J., 1986-88; assoc. prof. Eastern Coll., St. Davids, Pa., 1986-92, prof., 1992—. Co-author: Plaanning Strategies for World Evangelization, 1980, 91; collaborator: The Primary Group, 1975; editor: The Evangelical Round Table, 1986, 87; contbr. articles to profl. jours. Harold S. Vanderbilt fellow, 1979-82. Mem. Am. Sociol. Assn., Am. Missiological Soc., Am. Anthropol. Soc., Soc. for Bibl. Lit., Soc. for Scientific Study of Religion, Phi Beta Kappa. Democrat. Home: 230 Conshohocken State Rd Gladwyne PA 19035-1332 Office: Eastern Coll Saint Davids PA 19087

FRASER, DIANE LYNCH, education educator; d. James P. and Mary C. (Joyce) L.; children: Skye, Jared. EdD, Columbia U., 1989. Asst. dir. Sch. for Lang. and Communication Devel., North Bellmore, N.Y., 1985—; asst. prof. St. John's U., Jamaica, N.Y., 1990—; coord. early childhood program St. John's U., Jamaica, 1990—. Author: Danceplay, 1982, The Complete Postpartum Guide, 1983, Getting Ready to Read, 1985, Babysignals, 1987 (Lit. Guild Selection), Playdancing, 1990, Life's Little Miseries, 1992.

FRASER, DONALD C., federal official; b. N.Y.C., Apr. 20, 1941; s. Donald Fraser and Anna Thurston; children: Lynn, Eric. S.B., MIT, Cambridge, 1962, M.S., 1963, Sc.D., 1967. Tech. staff MIT Instrumentation Lab., Cambridge, Mass., 1967-69; div. leader C.S. Draper Lab., Inc., Cambridge, 1969-81, v.p. tech. ops., 1981-88, exec. v.p., 1988-90; dep. dir. operational test and evaluation Office Sec. Def., Washington, 1990-91; dep. under-sec. of def. for acquisition Office Sec. of Def., Washington, 1991—; vis. prof. Stanford U., Calif., 1970-71; lectr. MIT Aero/Astro Dept., Cambridge, 1972—; dep. dir. operational test and evaluation Office of Sec. of Def., Washington, 1990-91, dep. under sec. of def. acquisition, 1991—; active Air Force Studies Bd. Com. Advanced Avionics, 1979-83; chmn. Air Force Studies Bd. Com. Fault Isolation, 1982-85; active U.S. Air Force Aeor. Systems Div. Adv. Group, 1984-90; mem. NASA Adv. Coun. Space Systems and Tech. Adv. Com., 1982-91, U.S. Army Sci. Bd., 1987-90. Assoc. editor AIAA Jour. Spacecraft and Rockets, 1970-72, editor-in-chief, 1974-78; editor-in-chief AIAA Jour. Guidance, Control and Dynamics, 1977-91. Fellow AAAS, AIAA (bd. dirs. New Eng. sect. 1973-75, publs. com. 1973-74); mem. NAE, Tau Beta Pi, Sigma Xi, Sigma Gamma Tau.

FRASER, JEANNETTE LYNN, university dean; b. Gary, Ind., Sept. 28, 1951; d. Adelbert Rhodes and Margaret M. (Willis) F. BA, Ohio State U., 1973, MA, 1977, PhD, 1985. Rsch. asst. Ctr. for Human Resource Rsch., Ohio State U., Columbus, 1975-80; program assoc. Nat. Ctr. for Rsch. in Vocat. Edn., Ohio State U., Columbus, 1980-85; dean ednl. rsch., planning and evaluation Williamsport (Pa.) Community Coll., 1985-87; assoc. acad. dean Pa. Coll. of Tech., Pa. State U., Williamsport, 1987—. Contbr. articles to profl. jours. Mem. exec. com. Lycoming Dem. Party, Williamsport, 1986-88; bd. dirs. Lycoming unit Am. Cancer Soc., 2d v.p., 1987-89; bd. dirs., 2d v.p. Lycoming United Way, 1990—, chair community problem solving, 1987-90; bd. dirs. United Way of Pa., 1992—. Recpient Dean Farmer award Nat. Ctr. for Rsch. in Vocat. Edn., 1987. Democrat. Office: Pa Coll Tech 1 College Ave Williamsport PA 17701

FRASER, JULIA ANN (JULIE PINGRY), industry analyst, technical writer, editor; b. Hammond, Ind., July 31, 1957; d. William Leon and Mary Catherine (Hartman) Pingry; married. BA magna cum laude, Lawrence U., 1980. Editor Fiber Optics Communications publ. Info. Gatekeepers Inc., Brookline, Mass., 1981-82, mng. editor Internat. Fiber Optics Communications publ., 1982-83; sr. editor Digital Design publ. Morgan-Grampian Co., Boston, 1983-85, editor Computer Compatible Directory, 1983-84; editor CIM (computer-integrated mfg.) Strategies newsletter Cutter Info. Corp., Arlington, Mass., 1985-91; sr. industry analyst mfg. integration Advanced Mfg. Rsch., Cambridge, Mass., 1991—; frequent speaker on advanced mfg. technologies and methodologies. Author: Practical Machine Vision, 1987, Manufacturing Cost Management, 1989; author, editor: Local Area Networks, 1986; co-author: Expert Systems in Manufacturing, 1988; translator: (play) Anatol, 1979. Mem. Soc. Mfg. Engrs. (chmn. Boston chpt. 1989-91), Phi Beta Kappa. Democrat. Home: PO Box 292 Cummaquid MA 02637-0292 Office: Advanced Mfg Rsch 101 Rogers St Ste 205 Cambridge MA 02142-1049

FRASER, RAYMOND FRANCIS, accountant; b. Norristown, Pa., June 7, 1965; s. William Calder and Martha Alwilda (ManHerz) F. AAS Mgmt., Montgomery County Community, Blue Bell, Pa., 1985. Food attendant Roy Rogers Family Restaurants, Norristown, Pa., 1982=84; staff acct., desk clk. McIntosh Motor Inns, King of Prussia, Pa., 1984-86; convention svcs. supr. Stouffers valley Forge Hotel, King of Prussia, Pa., 1986-87; regional audit cons., desk supr. Courtyard by Marriott, Rockville, Md., 1987-91; staff acct. Phila. Marriott West, West Conshohocken, Pa., 1991—. Author: The Vengenance Hammer, 1991. Republican. Presbyterian. Home: 1860 W Marshall St Norristown PA 19403

FRASER, ROBERT CARSON, business consultant; b. Port Washington, N.Y., Apr. 11, 1925; s. Irving Thomas and Elizabeth Armstrong (Kennedy) F.; m. Constance Anne Morell, May 25, 1957; 1 child, Robert Carson Jr. BA in Econs., William and Mary Coll., 1951. Pub. relations mgr. Martin Marietta Corp., Washington, 1966-69; mkt. mgr. RCA, Washington, 1969-73, Lockheed Aircraft Co., Washington, 1973-75; exec. asst. to treas. U.S. Treasury Dept., Washington, 1975-79; sr. mgr. NASA Hdqrs., Washington, 1979-88; pvt. practice cons., 1988—. Mem. Nat. Space Club (v.p.), Capitol Hill Exch. Club (pres. Washington chpt. 1986-87). Episcopalian. Home: 543 Lakeview Cir Severna Park MD 21146-2312

FRASER-HOWZE, DEBRA YOLANDA, foundation administrator; b. N.Y.C., Nov. 11, 1952; d. Herbert Nathaniel and Millicent Maude (Reid) F.; m. John Haywood Wright, Sept. 25, 1969 (div. 1985); children: Tanya, Sheena Wright Jones, Barron J.N.; m. Clinton Howze III, Oct. 24, 1987; 1 child, Clinton IV. BA, Hunter Coll., 1978; MPA, Baruch Coll., 1984. Sr. program mgr. N.Y.C. Dept. Employment, 1977-83; legis. asst. Congressman Charles B. Rangel, Washington, 1983-84; dir. teenage svcs., specialist teen pregnancy and prevention N.Y. Urban League, N.Y.C., 1985-87; founding exec. dir., CEO Black Leadership Commn. on AIDS, Inc., N.Y.C., 1988—; cons. AIDS clin. trial group NIH, Bethesda, Md., 1990—, Keystone (Colo.) Policy Group Expanded Access to Life-Saving Drugs, 1991—, NFL, N.Y.C., 1992—, N.Y. State AIDS Inst., Albany, 1989—, U.S. AID, Washington, 1986; keynote speaker NAACP-Martin Luther King Keynote Address, N.Y.C., 1992, Ednl. Alliance, various sch. bds., TV appearances. Mem. N.Y. Urban League, 1987—; vice chairperson Mayor's HIV Planning Coun., 1991—; bd. dirs. Manhattan Teen Pregnancy Program, 1986—; bd. dirs. Albert G. Oliver Scholarship Program, 1987—. Recipient Martin Luther King Humanitarian Svc. award, 1992. Mem. NAACP, Black Agy. Execs. (bd. dirs. 1989—). Democrat.

FRATER, HAL, artist; b. N.Y.C., Mar. 3, 1909; s. Jacob and Ernestine (Steiner) F.; m. Pearl Newman, 1932; 1 child, Anthony. Freelance illustrator, painter N.Y.C., 1926—. Numerous one-man shows and group exhbns.; represented in permanent colelction Thundering Seas Inst., Oreg. State U., also numerous pvt. collections in U.S. and Europe. Home: 215 Park Row New York NY 10038-1149

FRATI, WILLIAM, experimental physicist; b. N.Y.C., Sept. 14, 1931; s. Rocco William and Marie Louise (Grimaldi) F.; m. Laura M. Cacace, May 26, 1963; children: William, Marie, Joanna. BS, Bklyn. Poly., 1952; MS, Columbia U., 1955, PhD, 1961. Rsch. assoc. U. Pa., Phila., 1961-65, rsch. specialist, 1966-81, rsch. assoc. prof. physics, 1982-87, rsch. prof., 1987—. Office: U Pa Dept Physics 33d and Walnut Sts Philadelphia PA 19104

FRATZ, DONALD DOUGLAS, scientist, editor and literary critic; b. Oakland, Md., Nov. 18, 1952; s. Donald Henry and Anna Mary Blanche (Savage) F.; m. Naomi Richfield, Feb. 3, 1979; children: Alexander Paul, Erica Jean. BS in Chemistry, U. Md., 1974; MS in Environ. Sci., George Washington U., 1983. Rsch. asst. NIH, Bethesda, Md., 1972-74; chemist FDA, Washington, 1974-80; assoc. dir. sci. affairs Chem. Specialties Mfrs. Assn., Washington, 1980-87, dir. sci. affairs, 1987—; pub., editor Thrust Publs., Gaithersburg, Md., 1977—. Editor lit. rev. Thrust, 1973-89, Quantum, 1981-92; contbr. articles to profl. jours., chpts. to books. Hugo award nominee World Sci. Fiction Soc., 1980, 87, 88, 89, 90. Mem. ASTM, Am. Chem. Soc., Assn. Ofcl. Analytical Chemists, Nat. Fire Protection Assn., Sci. Fiction Writers Am., Small Press Writers and Artists Assn. Home: 8217 Langport Terr Gaithersburg MD 21520-1134 Office: Chem Specialties Mfrs Assn 1913 Eye St NW Washington DC 20006

FRAWLEY, DANIEL SEYMOUR, mayor; b. Fulton, N.Y., Nov. 9, 1943; s. John F. and Margaret (Seymour) F.; m. Bonita Buchele, Aug. 29, 1970; children: Marcus, Matthew, Marjorie. BS in Chemistry, LeMoyne Coll., Syracuse, N.Y., 1965; JD, U. Toledo, 1969; MBA, U. Pa., 1972. Bar: Ohio 1969, Pa. 1970. Atty. E.I. DuPont de Nemours & Co., Wilmington, Del., 1972-84; mayor City of Wilmington, 1985—. Active Big Bros./Big Sisters of Del., 1970—, Wilmington Sch. Bd., 1975-78, Wilmington Design Commn., 1979-80, Wilmington City Coun., 1980-84, YMCA of Del., Boy Scouts Am.; founder Housing Renovation 1st Urban Homesteader Program, 1975. Recipient Disting. Alumnus award LeMoyne Coll., 1984; N.Y. State Regents scholar, 1961. Mem. NAACP, Wilmington Rugby Club (co-founder 1974). Democrat. Office: 800 N French St Wilmington DE 19801-3590

FRAWLEY, SEAN PAUL, publishing executive; b. Doolin, County Clare, Ireland, June 24, 1940; came to U.S., 1958; s. Michael and Ellen (Scales) F.; m. Frances Mary Kelly, June 10, 1967; children: Sean, Mary, David. Student, Pace U., 1963-66. Acct. Grolier Inc., N.Y.C., 1958-74; contr. Howell Book House, N.Y.C., 1974-78, v.p., 1978-80, exec. v.p., 1981-86, pres., 1986—. Sgt. USNG, 1961-66. Mem. Miltown Malbay Club (named Man of Yr. 1990). Roman Catholic. Home: 25 Cleveland Dr Croton On Hudson NY 10520-3039 Office: Macmillan Publishing Co 866 3rd Ave New York NY 10022-6221

FRAZIER, HOWARD THOMAS, association executive; b. Etowah, Tenn., Nov. 20, 1911; s. Arthur Frank and Beulah Vesta (French) F.; m. Kate Douglas Green, Sept. 14, 1940 (dec. Feb. 1965); children: Katherine, Frances Sue; m. Alice Ellen Zeigler, May 25, 1974. BA, U. Tenn., 1934. Tchr. Clinton (Tenn.) Grammar Sch., 1934-35; rsch. aide, pers. asst. Tenn. Valley Authority, Knoxville, 1935-39, inspector, supr. inspector, 1939-42; supervising inspector U.S. Dept. Labor, Nashville, Tenn., 1946, San Francisco, 1947-58; cons. U.S. Dept. Labor, San Francisco, Washington, 1958-65; field ops. dir. Pres.' Com. on Consumer Interests, Washington, 1965-68; asst. dir. Dept. Health, Edn. and Welfare, Consumer Office, Washington, 1968-69; exec. dir. Promoting Enduring Peace, Woodmont, Conn., 1974—; pres. Consumer Fedn. Am., Washington, 1970-72, Consumer Edn. and Protective Assn., Phila., 1972-74. Editor: Uncloaking the CIA, 1978. Major USAF, 1942-46. Recipient Willard Uphaus Peace & Justice award Peace Ctr. of New Haven, Conn., 1986, Fighter for Peace award Soviet Peace Com., Moscow, 1988, Adin Ballou Peace award Unitarian-Universalist Peace Fellowship, New Haven, 1989, Citizen Diplomacy award Ctr. for Am.-Soviet Dialogue, Moscow, 1990. Mem. Am. Fedn. Govt. Employees, Am. Friends Svc. Com., Women's Internat. League for Peace and Freedom (life mem., Alice Hamilton Peace and Freedom award 1987), Fellowship of Reconciliation, Mobilization for Survival. Democrat. Home and Office: Promoting Enduring Peace 112 Beach Ave PO Box 5103 Woodmont CT 06460

FRAZIER, MARJORIE DERENE, school system administrator, consultant; b. Bklyn., Nov. 29; d. Rufus Adolphus and Ismay (Harris) Larrier; m. Nathaniel Fred Jackson, 1953 (div.); children: Juanita Bradshaw, Nathaniel, Donna; m. Julius Frazier, Sept. 21, 1972. BA, CUNY, Hunter, 1957; postgrad., CUNY, 1961; MS, Bklyn. Coll., 1968; cert. in advanced studies, CCNY, 1972. Cert. tchr., N.Y.; cert. counselor, N.Y.; cert. adminstrv. supervision, N.Y. Tchr. N.Y.C. Bd. of Edn., Bklyn., 1958-66, tchr., counselor, 1966-67; area assoc. N.Y.C. Cen. Bd. of Edn., Bklyn., 1967-69; guidance counselor N.Y.C. Bd. Edn., N.Y.C., 1978-80; ret. Bd. of Global Ministries of United Meth. Ch., N.Y.C., 1989; dir. fed. progams N.Y.C. Bd. of Edn. Dist. 16, Bklyn., 1969-72; dist. guidance coord., supr. of guidance Bd. Edn., N.Y.C., 1980-89; regional dir. ABC A Better Chance Program, N.Y.C., 1972-73; coord. coll. discovery program Queenborough Community Coll., Bayside, N.Y., 1973-75; coord. field itineration Bd. of Global Ministries of United Meth. Ch., N.Y.C., 1976-78; travel cons. Caribbean Am. Travel, Bklyn., 1980-91; dir. cruises Wol & Rose Travel, 1991—; counseling cons. Edwin Gould Found., Bklyn., 1990—. College advisor Stuyford Action Coun., Bklyn., 1964-70; reading coord. First Presbyn. Ch., Queens, N.Y., 1965-68; youth dir. Warren Street United Meth. Ch., Bklyn., 1966-68. Recipient Community Svc. award Stuyford Action Coun., 1968. Mem. AACD, Nat. Bd. for Cert. Counselors, Internat. Platform Assn., Am. Soc. Notaries, Ret. Sch. Suprs. and Adminstrs., N.Y. State Assn. Counseling and Devel., N.Y.C. Assn. Counseling and Devel. Democrat. Home: 1773 Union St Brooklyn NY 11213-5012

FRÉCHET, JEAN MARIE JOSEPH, educator; b. Chalon, France, Aug. 18, 1944; came to U.S., 1967; s. Victor H. and Renée (Mollard) F.; m. Janet R. Manning, Nov. 25, 1967; children: Jacques Christopher, Marc Alexander. MSc, SUNY, Syracuse, 1969, PhD, 1971; PhD, Syracuse U., 1971. Asst. prof. chemistry U. of Ottawa, Can., 1973-78, assoc. prof. chemistry, 1978-82, prof. chemistry, 1982-87; IBM prof. chemistry Cornell U., Ithaca, N.Y., 1987—; vis. scientist IBM Rsch. Lab., San Jose, Calif., 1979, 83; vice dean grad. studies and rsch. U. Ottawa, 1983-87; cons. Allied Signal Corp., Morristown, 1986—, Exxon Corp., Linden, N.J., 1988—, E.I. DuPont de Nemours, Wilmington, 1990—; bd. dirs. Ont. Ctr. for Materials Rsch., Toronto, Can. Contbr. numerous articles to profl. jours.; patentee in field. Recipient Award Internat. Union Pure and Applied Chemistry, 1983, Polymer Soc. of Japan, 1986, A.K. Doolittle award Am. Chem. Soc.; numerous grants for rsch. Office: Cornell U Baker Lab Ithaca NY 14853-1301

FRECKELTON, SONDRA, artist; b. Dearborn, Mich., June 23, 1936; d. William and Elizabeth (Zimmerman) F.; m. W.H. Jack Beal, Sept. 3, 1955. Student, Sch. of Art Inst. of Chgo., 1954-56, U. Chgo., 1954-56. Artist self-employed, 1956—, Tibor de Nagy Gallery, N.Y.C., 1959-64, B.C. Holland Gallery, Chgo., 1964-67, Lo Giudice Gallery, Chgo., 1968-71, Brooke Alexander Gallery, N.Y.C., 1975-85, 91, Robert Schoelkopf Gallery, N.Y.C., 1986-91, Alice Simsar Gallery, Ann Arbor, Mich., 1987—, Maxwell Davidson Gallery, Ann Arbor, 1991—. Co-author: Dynamic Still-Lifes in Watercolor, 1983; one-person exhbns. include Robert Schoelkopf Gallery, 1986, 88, 90, John Berggruen Gallery, 1982, Brooke Alexander, Inc., 1976, 79, 80, 81, Fendrick Gallery, 1980, Allan Frumkin Gallery, Chgo., 1977, Lo Giudice Gallery, 1970, B.C. Holland Gallery, 1965, Tibor de Nagy Gallery, 1961, 63; exhibited group shows at Mt. Holyoke Coll., Yale U. Art Gallery, Art Mus. of Santa Barbara, Va. Mus. Fine Arts, 1987-88, and others. Recipient Grant Ingram-Merrill Found., 1960, Print award Bradford Mus., 1979. Home and Office: 83A Delhi Stage # 64hc Oneonta NY 13820

FREDE, JONATHAN H., brokerage firm executive, educator; b. Torrington, Conn., June 26, 1950; s. Joel and Helen (Rocketto) F.; m. Lori Ellen Feintuch, Jan. 18, 1976; children: Jodi Suzanne, Cori Staci. BS in Bus. Adminstrn., Bryant Coll., 1972; postgrad., N.Y. Inst. Fin., 1976, 80, 86. Reporter Paterson (N.J.) Evening News, 1973-75; sr. instr. Securities Tng. Corp., N.Y.C., 1983—; v.p., br. office mgr. Mabon Securities Corp., N.Y.C., 1975—; arbitrator Nat. Assn. Securities Dealers, N.Y.C., 1988—. County committeman Nassau County Dem. Party, N.Y., 1982-86. Mem. Internat. Brotherhood Magicians (ring pres. 1975-76), Soc. Am. Magicians (compeer). Jewish. Home: 1527 Sylvia Ln East Meadow NY 11544 Office: Mabon Securities Corp 1 Liberty Plaza New York NY 10006

FREDENTHAL, RUTH ANN, artist; b. Detroit, Aug. 20, 1938; d. David and Miriam (Kellogg) F. Student, Phila. Mus. Coll. Art, 1957, Yale-Norfolk Sch. Art, 1959; BA, Bennington Coll., 1960; postgrad., CUNY, 1963. Art tchr. Halsey Jr. High Sch., Bklyn., 1963-72, St. Ann's Sch., Bklyn., 1972-74; adviser Willette Corp., New Brunswick, N.J., 1985—; asst. dir. Painting Space 122, Inc., N.Y.C., 1983—. One-woman shows and group exhbns. include Aldrich Mus. Contemporary Art, Ridgefield, onn., 1973, Bykert Downtown, N.Y.C., 1974-75, SUNY, Stony Brook, 1978, Susan Caldwell Gallery, N.Y.C., 1978, The Clocktower, N.Y.C., 1980, Buecker and Harpsichords, N.Y.C., 1981, Andre Zarre Gallery, N.Y.C., 1982, John Good gallery, N.Y.C., 1987, Leubsdorf Gallery, Hunter Coll., CUNY, 1988, Vera Engelhorn Gallery, N.Y.C., 1989, 90, Eric Stark Gallery, N.Y.C., 1992. Fulbright fellow, Florence, Italy, 1960-61. Democrat. Studio: 150 1st Ave Ste 501 New York NY 10009

FREDERICK, WILLIAM GEORGE DEMOTT, federal agency administrator; b. Toledo, June 23, 1936; s. Rolland Leslie Frederick and Ruth Matilda (Collins) Gates; m. Nancy Lee Spalding, June 14, 1958 (div. July 1981); m. Geralyn Goldman Middleton, Aug. 14, 1981; children: William G.D. Frederick, Frank G. Goldman, Rebecca A. Goldman. BS in Engring. Physics, U. Toledo, 1958; MS in Physics, U. Dayton, 1968; PhD in Materials Sci., U. Cin., 1973; MS in Mgmt., MIT, 1980. Solid state physicist Air Force Materials Lab., WPAFB, Ohio, 1958-73, br. chief, 1973-80, chief, plans office, 1980-83; staff specialist, surveillance Dept. of Def./Office Sec. of Def., Washington, 1983-85, asst. dir. senor tech., 1985—. Contbr. articles to profl. jours. Recipient Arthur S. Flemming award Jaycees, Washington, 1976, Henry Levinstein award Infrared Info. Symposia, Ann Arbor, Mich., 1989, Presdl. Meritorious Exec. award Sr. Exec. Svc., Washington, 1991. Mem. AAAS, Am. Phys. Soc. Home: 11511 Stonewood Ln Rockville MD 20852-4309 Office: Strategic Def Initiative The Pentagon Washington DC 20301

FREDERICKS, BARRY IRWIN, lawyer; b. Bklyn., Oct. 3, 1936; m. Beverly Sharon Cohen, June 21, 1987; children from a previous marriage: Elizabeth, Jessica, Amanda, Alexander. AB, Ohio State U., 1958; JD, U.

Mich., 1961. Bar: D.C. 1961, U.S. Dist. Ct. D.C. 1961, U.S. Ct. Appeals (D.C. cir.) 1961, U.S. Ct. Mil. Appeals, 1961, N.Y. 1965, U.S. Dist. Ct. (ea. and so. dists.) N.Y. 1965, U.S. Dist. Ct. (no. dist.) N.Y. 1985, U.S. Dist. Ct. (we. dist.) N.Y. 1991, U.S. Ct. Appeals (2d. cir.) 1965, (3rd cir.) 1978, U.S. Supreme Ct. 1965, N.J. 1972, U.S. Dist. Ct. N.J. 1972, U.S. Tax Ct. 1974, U.S. Dist. Ct. (ea. dist.) Wis. 1985, U.S. Ct. Internat. Trade 1985, Colo. 1992, U.S. Dist. Ct. Ariz. 1992. Asst. chief counsel div. corp. fin. Securities & Exchange Commn., Washington, 1961; trial atty. div. civil rights Dept. Justice, Washington, 1962, asst. U.S. atty., 1962-65, U.S. commr. for D.C., 1965-66; assoc. Robinson, Silverman, Pearce, et al, N.Y.C., 1967-71; ptnr. Harris, Fredericks, et al, N.Y.C., L.A., 1971-77, Goldschmidt, Fredericks & Oshatz, N.Y.C., 1977-85, Wolfsey, Certilman, et al, N.Y.C., 1985-87; sr. ptnr. Law Office Barry I. Fredericks, N.Y.C., Englewood Cliffs, N.Y., N.J., 1987—; govs. adv. com. N.J. Criminal Justice Standards and Goals, 1975-77; mem. bd. govs. N.J. State Law Enforcement Agy., 1977-79; pres., chief operating officer Operation Raleigh USA, 1983-87; lectr. on trial advocacy Practicing Law Inst., 1984—, Victorian Bar Coun., Melbourne, Australia, 1990; faculty Univ. Va. Sch. Law Trial Advocacy Inst., 1986—, Univ. Mich. Sch. Law Inst. Continuing Legal Edn., 1988—, Nat. INst. for Trial Advocacy, 1992—. Councilman, Ridgewood, N.J., 1980-84; mem. planning bd., Ridgewood, 1980-81. Mem. ABA, Assn. Trial Lawyers Am., N.Y. County Lawyer's Assn., N.Y. State Trial Lawyers Assn., Fed. Bar Assn. N.Y., N.J. Fed. Bar (v.p. 1981—), N.J. State Bar Assn., D.C. Bar Assn. Office: 550 Sylvan Ave Englewood Cliffs NJ 07632-3118

FREDERICKS, ROBERT JOSEPH, company executive; b. N.Y.C., Dec. 26, 1934; s. Harold D. and Mary E. (McCarthy) F.; m. Jeanette C. Kubin, July 7, 1984. BS in Chemistry, Villanova U., 1957; MS in Chemistry, St. Joseph's Coll., Phila., 1959; PhD in Chemistry, Lehigh U., 1965. Rsch. chemist GAF Corp., Easton, Pa., 1960-67; rsch. supr. Allied Chem. Corp., Morristown, N.J., 1968-72; mgr. analytical chemistry Ethicon, Inc., Somerville, N.J., 1972-74; dir. rsch. svcs. Ethicon, Inc., Somerville, 1974-76, assoc. dir. rsch., 1976-78; v.p. rsch. and devel. Surgikos, Piscataway, N.J., 1978-79, Johnson & Johnson Dental Products Co., East Windsor, N.J., 1980-82; sr. v.p. and gen. mgr. Biosci. Med. Products, Somerville, N.J., 1982-85; pres. Allen Transl. Svc., Morristown, N.J., 1985—. Author: X-Ray Diffraction for the Industrial Chemist, 1971; contbr. articles to profl. jours. Pres. Morris County Hist. Soc., Morristown, 1982-86, Wash. Assn. N.J., Morristown, 1988-92; mem. adv. bd. New Philharm. N.J., 1992—. Lt. (j.g.) USN, 1957-60. Mem. AAAS, Am. Chem. Soc., N.Y. Acad. Scis., Morristown Field Club, Morristown Club, Morristown Rotary Club, Sigma Xi. Republican. Roman Catholic. Home: 16 Butterworth Dr Morristown NJ 07960-2625

FREDERICKS, WALTER OTTO, medical technology executive; b. Newark, Nov. 14, 1939; s. Otto F. and Marion M. (Marvin) F.; m. Yvonne Beglinger, Aug. 4, 1962; children: Robert J., Carole M., Kristin L. BSBA, Clarkson U., 1961. Dir. bus. devel. Johnson & Johnson (Ortho), Raritan, N.J., 1963-74; v.p., gen. mgr. internat. Becton Dickinson Lab. Systems, Paramus, N.J., 1975-83; pres., chief exec. officer Cistron Biotechnology, Pineback, N.J., 1984-87, Life Codes Corp., Valhalla, N.Y., 1988—; bd. dirs. Environ. Diagnostics, Burlington, N.C., Dianon Systems, Inc., Stratford, Conn. Mem. Indsl. Biotech. Assn. Office: Life Codes Corp 55 West Ave Stamford CT 06902

FREDERICKS, WESLEY CHARLES, JR., businessman, lawyer; b. N.Y.C., Mar. 31, 1948; s. Wesley Charles and Dionysia W. (Bitsanis) F.; m. Jeanne Maria Judson, May 19, 1973; children: Carolyn Anne, Wesley C. III. BA Johns Hopkins U., 1970; JD, Columbia U., 1973. Bar: N.Y. 1974, Conn. 1976, U.S. Supreme Ct. 1979. Assoc. Shearman & Sterling, N.Y.C., 1973-76, 76-83, Cummings & Lockwood, Stamford, Conn., 1976; dir. Automobile Importers Am., Inc., Washington, 1983-87, British Performance Car Imports, Inc., Norwood, N.J., 1982-86, Carbodies N. Am., Inc., Dover, Del., 1983-84; chmn. bd. Lotus Performance Cars, L.P., Norwood, 1983-86, chief exec. officer, 1986-87; group exec. cons. Group Lotus PLC, 1987; automotive industry cons., 1988-90; pres, chief exec. officer Mfrs. Products Co., 1990—. Honors judge Columbia U. Law Sch. Stone Moot Ct. Honors Program, 1980—; mem. Johns Hopkins U. Alumni Schs. Com.; trustee Wilton Hist. Soc., 1986-91. With USMC, 1968-69. Mem. Blue Key Soc., India House Club (N.Y.C.), Steering Wheel Club (London), Mashomack Fish and Game Preserve, Campfire Am. Club (N.Y.), Weston Gun Club (Conn.), Detroit Athletic Club, Econ. Club Detroit, Sigma Phi Epsilon. Republican. Congregationalist. Home: 221 Benedict Hill Rd New Canaan CT 06840-2913 Office: 26020 Sherwood Ave Warren MI 48091-1297

FREDERIKSEN, ROSEMARY ANN, practical nurse; b. Rochester, N.Y., Nov. 8, 1956; d. William Charles and Mary Rose (Albers) Hastings; m. Davis Elmer Frederiksen, Aug. 5, 1978; 1 child, Bard Michael. Diploma, Rochester Sch. Practical Nurse, 1976. Lic. practical nursing. Practical nurse Portamedic, Rochester, 1990—.

FREDRICK, BETH M., health administrator; b. Elkhorn, Wis., Aug. 4, 1959; d. Gerald and Carol (Frank) F.; m. Edward Abrahams, Feb. 16, 1985. BA in English, U. Wis., 1981; postgrad., New Sch. Social Rsch., 1984-86, Pratt Inst., 1986, NYU, 1987. Program dir. Wis. Union Directorate, Madison, 1981; asst. program dir. Coun. for Arts of Greater Lima (Ohio), 1981-82; store mgr. Abrahams Bros., Freeport and Richmond, Ill., Ind., 1982-83; product mgr. W. Kotkes & Son, Inc./Diane Von Furstenberg, N.Y.C., 1983-84; asst. to dir. communications and devel. The Alan Guttmacher Inst., N.Y.C., 1985, asst. dir. communications and devel., 1986, dep. dir. communications and devel., 1986-87, dir. communications and devel., 1987—. English tutor The Internat. Ctr. N.Y., N.Y.C., 1983-87. Mem. Women in Fin. Devel. (treas. 1989-91, sec. 1992), Direct Mail Fundraisers Assn., Am. Mktg. Assn., Am. Pub. Health Assn. Office: Alan Guttmacher Inst 111 5th Ave New York NY 10003-1005

FREDRICKSON, BRUCE DONALD, elementary educator; b. Salamanca, N.Y., May 22, 1940; s. Paul Selden and Margaret Ally (Rogers) F.; m. Madelynn MArie Parks, Dec. 26, 1966; children: Lynn Andrea, Jan Nicole, Jon Bruce. BS, SUNY, 1965, MS, 1970. Cert. elem. sci., reading tchr., N.Y. Educator, elem. sch. Starpoint Cen. Sch., Lockport, N.Y., 1965—; del. Niagara-Orleans Labor Coun., Lockport, 1989-92; mem. policy bd. Orleans-Niagara Tchr. Ctr., Lockport, 1989-93; mem. Dist. Leadership Team, Lockport, 1988—; cons. in elem. econs., 1982-92. Author short stories: Discover Niagara, 1988, ElmLeaves, 1960-68. Mem. Lewiston Trail Coun. Scholar Com., Niagara County, 1986—, trainer, 1991—; vice chmn. Niagara County Boy Scouts Am., 1989— (award of Merit 1990, Wood Badge, 1988); pres., chair Univ. Scouting, Greater Niagara Frontier Coun. Boy Scouts Am., 1992—; loaned exec. United Way, Niagara County, 1991—. Mem. Starpoint Tchrs. Assn. (v.p. 1988—), Niagara County Tchrs. Pres. (del. 1988—), Ishua Valley Hist. Soc. Home: 18 Spruce St Lockport NY 14094-4922 Office: Starpoint Cen Sch 4363 Mapleton Dr Lockport NY 14094

FREDYMA, JAMES PAUL, state official; b. Hanover, N.H., Nov. 4, 1950; s. Paul Joseph and Marie-Louise (Friedman) F.; m. Judith Mae Allard, Nov. 22, 1975; children: Christian Arthur Nardi, Jessica Allard Fredyma, Molly Elizabeth Fredyma. BA in Econs., Hawthorne Coll., 1972; MS in Orgn. and Mgmt., Antioch U., 1985. Bus. mgr. Gov.'s Office, Concord, N.H., 1972-76; bus. adminstr. contracts N.H. Dept. Health and Human Svcs., Concord, 1976-79, chief, fin. planning, 1979-81, chief, prog. rev., 1981-84, adminstr. support ops., 1984-88, adminstr. fiscal svcs., 1988—; alt. rep. N.E. Regional Comm., Boston, 1974-76; owner Liberty Silver/Mail Order Antique Sales, Contoocook, N.H., 1979—. Author: Directory of Maine Silversmiths, 1972. Bd. dirs. Hopkinton (N.H.) Sch. Bd., 1985—; chmn. Sch. Adminstrn./Unit No. 24, Henniker, N.H., 1989-91. Republican. Home: 10 Carriage Ln Rt 2 Box 46 Contoocook NH 03229-9203 Office: NH Dept Health/Human Svcs 6 Hazen Dr Concord NH 03301-6501

FREE, ANN COTTRELL, writer; b. Richmond, Va.; d. Emmett Drewry and Emily (Blake) Cottrell; grad. Collegiate Sch. for Girls, Richmond, 1934; student Richmond div. Coll. William and Mary, 1934-36; m. James Stillman Free, Feb. 24, 1950; 1 child, Elissa. AB, Barnard Coll., Columbia, 1938. Reporter Richmond Times Dispatch, 1938-40; Washington corr., Newsweek, 1940-41, Chgo. Sun, 1941-43, N.Y. Herald Tribune, 1943-46; pub. information dir. UNRRA China Mission, Shanghai, 1946-47; corr. Middle and Nr. East and Europe, 1947-48; writer-photographer Marshall Plan, Washington and Western Europe, 1949-50; Washington corr. N.Am. Newspaper Alliance, 1955-80; contbg. editor Between the Species; contbr. newspapers and mags., including Washington Star and Washington Post; Washington editor EnviroSouth Quar., 1977-82; pres. Flying Fox Press. Mem. Friends of the Rachel Carson Nat. Wildlife Refuge (hon. founding mem.); chmn. Mrs. Roosevelt's Press Conf. Assn., 1943; cons. expert Rachel Carson Coun.; v.p. Vieques (P.R.) Humane Soc.; coord. Albert Schweitzer Summer Fellows Program; bd. dirs. Albert Schweitzer Fellowship; pres. Albert Schweitzer Coun. on Animals and Environment. Recipient Dodd Mead-Boys' Life Writing award, 1963, Albert Schweitzer medal, Animal Welfare Inst., 1963, Jr. Book award certificate Boys Clubs of Am., 1964; Humanitarian of Yr. awards Washington Animal Rescue League, 1971, Montgomery County Humane Soc., 1971, Washington Humane Soc., 1983, News Writing award Dog Writers Assn. Am., 1975, 78, Rachel Carson Legacy award, 1987, Disting. Alumni award The Collegiate Schs., 1992; recognition Dept. Interior, 1970. Mem. Soc. Woman Geographers, Nat. Press Club, Am. News Women's Club. Author: Forever the Wild Mare, 1963, Animals, Nature and Albert Schweitzer, 1982, No Room, Save in the Heart, 1987. Home: 4700 Jamestown Rd Bethesda MD 20816-2923 also: Lantz Mill Edinburg VA 22824

FREE, CHARLES ALFRED, biochemist; b. Cleve., Apr. 19, 1936; s. Alfred Henry and Dorothy (Hoffmeister) F.; m. Thora Claire Meade, Oct. 21, 1961; children: Charles M., Maia E. BS in Chemistry, Purdue U., 1957; PhD in Physiol. Chemistry, UCLA, 1962. Postdoctoral fellow Sloan-Kettering Inst. for Cancer Rsch., N.Y.C., 1962-65; rsch. investigator Squibb Inst. for Med. Rsch., New Brunswick, N.J., 1965-69; sr. rsch. investigator Squibb Inst. for Med. Rsch., New Brunswick, Princeton, N.J., 1969-82; rsch. leader Bristol-Myers Squibb Pharm. Rsch. Inst., Princeton, 1982—; adj. assoc. prof. chemistry Rider Coll., Lawrenceville, N.J., 1980. Contbr. 50 articles to profl. jours. Mem. AAAS, Am. Chem. Soc., Am. Soc. for Pharmacology and Exptl. Therapeutics, Am. Peptide Soc., Sigma Xi. Office: Bristol-Myers Squibb Pharm Rsch Inst PO Box 4000 Princeton NJ 08543-4000

FREE, STEPHEN J., genetics educator, researcher; b. Salt Lake City, Sept. 4, 1948. BS, Purdue U., 1972; PhD, Stanford U., 1977. Rsch. assoc. U. Wis., Madison, 1977-79; asst. prof. genetics SUNY, Buffalo, 1979-85, assoc. prof., 1985—. Office: SUNY Dept Biol Scis Cooke Hall Rm 370 Buffalo NY 14260

FREED, BARBARA FAYE, foreign language professional, educator; b. Phila., Aug. 2, 1941; d. Maurice and Lillian (Greenstein) F.; m. Sheldon Tabb, July 4, 1979. BA, U. Pa., 1963; MA, Temple U., 1971; PhD, U. Pa., 1978; cert. European Studies, Inst. for Am. Univs., Aix-en-Provence, France, 1961. French tchr. Cherry Hill Pub. Schs., Phila., 1963-67; foreign language text editor Ctr. for Curriculum Devel., Phila., 1967-69; rsch. assoc., curriculum writer Rsch. for Better Schs., Phila., 1971-72; foreign language coord., lectr., supr. U. Pa., Phila., 1972-77, program dir. summer study in France, 1979-81, asst. dean lang. instrn., 1979-83, dir. Regional Ctr. for Lang. Proficiency, 1983-86, vice dean language instruction, 1984-90, adj. assoc. prof. Romance langs., 1988, dir. lang. programs & instrn., 1988-90; prof. and chmn. modern langs. program Carnegie Mellon U., Pitts., 1990—; bd. dirs. Inst. Am. Univs., Aix-en-Provence, France, 1990—; mem. NRC Commn. on Behavioral and Social Scis. and Edn., 1991; presenter numerous lectures, 1976—. Author: From the Community to the Classroom: Gathering Second Language Speech Samples, 1978, The Loss of Language Skills, 1982, Contextos: Spanish for Communication, 1988, Contextes: French for Communication, 1988, Foreign Language Acquisition Research and the Classroom, 1991; editor: Foreign Language Acquisition Research and Instruction, 1989—, Polylingua, 1989—; contbr. numerous articles to profl. jours. Bd. dirs. Alliance Francaise De Phila., 1980—, chmn. edn. com., 1980—; bd. dirs. Friends of Settlement Music Sch., Phila., 1979-83. Consortium for Language Teaching and Learning rsch. grantee, 1988-90, Faculty Exchange fellow U.S. Info. Agency, U. Mohamed V. Rabat, Morocco, 1986. Mem. Am. Assn. Univ. Supr. and Coords., Am. Assn. Applied Liguistics, Am. Assn. Tchrs. of French (dir. commn. on testing 1983-84, commn. on proficiency 1991—), Am. Coun. Teaching of Fgn. Langs. (oral proficiency interview exec. com. 1988-91, tester & trainer 1983—), Linguistic Soc. Am., Modern Language Assn. (chmn. div. teaching 1984, del. pedagocial concerns 1983-85, 91—), Tchrs. of English to Speakers of Second Languages. Office: Carnegie Mellon U Program in Modern Languages Baker Hall 160 Pittsburgh PA 15213

FREED, CLARENCE LANDIS, plastic surgeon; b. Morwood, Pa., Oct. 13, 1945; s. John Hackman and Lizzie (Landis) F.; m. Charlotte Paula Freed, May 26, 1973; children: Bart Paul, Rachel Elizabeth Natali. AS, Phila. Community Coll., 1967; student, Temple U., MD, 1972. Intern in gen. surgery Albert Einstein Hosp., Phila., 1972-73, resident in gen. surgery, 1973-75, chief resident in surgery, 1975-76; resident in plastic surgery Lehigh Valley Hosp., Allentown, Pa., 1976-77, chief resident in plastic surgery, 1977-78; pvt. practice Sellersville, Pa., 1978—; mem. med. ethics com. Grand View Hosp., Sellersville, 1977-91. Author: A Sigh A Tear, 1976; author poetry. Mem. AMA, Pa. Med. Assn., Am. Cleft, Lip and Palate Assn. Office: 670 Lawn Ave Sellersville PA 18960-1571

FREED, EDMOND LEE, podiatrist; b. Phila., Sept. 7, 1935; s. Frank and Jean D. (Schultz) F.; m. Judith Hope Falk (div. 1982); children: David Scott, Eric Corey. D of Podiatric Medicine, Temple U., 1960. Diplomate Am. Bd. Podiatric Surgery, Am. Bd. Podiatric Orthopedics. Pvt. practice Phila., 1960—; chmn. dept. podiatric surgery Met. Hosp., Phila., 1988-89, dir. podiatric residency program, 1983-89, co-chmn. limb salvage team, 1983—; mem. clin. faculty Pa. Coll. Podiatric Medicine, Phila., 1968—. Co-author booklets: Limb Salvage Concepts, 1984, Lower Extremity Ulcerations, 1985, Neurological Manifestations of Diabetes Mellitus, 1986. Fellow Am. Coll. Foot Surgeons (Ea. div. pres. 1985-88), Am. Coll. Foot Orthopedics, Am. Assn. Hosp. Podiatrists; mem. Am. Acad. Podiatric Sports Medicine, Phila. County Podiatry Soc., Am. Podiatric Med. Assn. Office: Franklin Square Hosp 201 N 8th St Ste 502 Philadelphia PA 19106-1005

FREEDMAN, AARON DAVID, medical educator, consultant, dean; b. Albany, N.Y., Jan. 4, 1922; s. Jacob Abraham and Pauline Rebecca (Hoffman) F.; m. Alice Maurer, Sept. 10, 1948; children: Abigail, Jonathan, Jeremy. AB, Cornell U., 1942; MD, Albany Med. Coll., 1945; PhD, Columbia U., 1958; MA, U. Pa., 1972. Diplomate Am. Bd. Internal Medicine. Asst. prof. medicine and biochemistry Columbia U., N.Y.C., 1958-65; clin. prof. U. Kans., Kansas City, 1965-69, chmn. dept. medicine Menorah Med. Ctr., 1965-69; prof., assoc. dean U. Pa., Phila., 1969-75, exec. dir. Grad. Hosp., 1972-75; prof. medicine Med. Sch. CUNY, 1975—, acting dean, 1978-79, dep. dean acad. affairs, 1990—; examiner N.Y. State Bd. Med. Examiners, Albany, 1962-65; cons. Touro Coll., N.Y.C., 1980; career investigator N.Y. Pub. Health Rsch. Coun., 1963-65; dir. Danciger Med. Inst., Kansas City, Mo., 1966-69. Mem. Ardsley (N.Y.) Bd. of Edn., 1962-65. Libman Fund fellow, 1951-54, USPHS fellow, 1958-60. Mem. Am. Soc. for Cell Biology, Am. Soc. Biochemistry and Molecular Biology. Jewish. Office: CUNY Med Sch 136th St & Convent Ave New York NY 10036

FREEDMAN, ALAN REINALD, pediatrician; b. Phila., July 22, 1935; m. Arlene Barbara Chertkoff, June 17, 1962; children: Naomi Beth, Rachel Ann, David Benjamin. BA, U. Pa., 1957; MD, Thomas Jefferson U., Phila., 1962. Diplomate Am. Bd. Pediatrics. Intern Presbyn. Hosp., Phila., 1962-63; resident Children's Hosp. of Phila., 1963-65; practice medicine specializing in pediatrics Phila., 1967-74; pediatrician Phila. Health Assocs., 1974—; pediatric sect. leader, 1987-90; assoc. pediatrician Children's Hosp. of Phila., 1967—; assoc. physician Pa. Hosp., Phila., 1974—; clin. assoc. prof. pediatrics Hahnemann U., Phila., 1981—. Author: Clinical Pediatrics Handbook, 1965-74, Changes: Handbook for Parents, 1978; asst. editor: Clin. Pediatrics Jour., 1965-74. Served to capt. USAF, 1965-67. Recipient Legion of Honor Chapel of the Four Chaplains, Phila., 1981. Mem. Am. Acad. Pediatrics, Phi Beta Kappa. Jewish. Home: 57 Levering Cir Bala Cynwyd PA 19004-2609 Office: The Bourse 5th and Chestnut Philadelphia PA 19106

FREEDMAN, ALFRED MORDECAI, pscyhiatrist, educator; b. Albany, N.Y., Jan. 7, 1917; s. Jacob Abraham and Pauline Rebecca (Hoffman) F.; m. Marcia Irene Kohl, Mar. 24, 1943; children: Paul Harris, Daniel Sholom. AB, Cornell U., 1937; MD, U. Minn., 1941. Diplomate Am. Bd. Psychiatry and Neurology. Intern Harlem Hosp., N.Y.C., 1941-42; resident and fellow Bellevue Hosp., N.Y.C., 1948-51, sr. psychiatrist, 1951-54; asst. pediatrician Babies Hosp.-Columbia, N.Y.C., 1953-60; assoc. prof. psychiatry SUNY Downstate Med. Sch., Bklyn., 1955-60; prof. and chair psychiatry N.Y. Med. Coll., Valhalla, 1960-89, prof. psychiatry emeritus, 1989—; vis. prof. Harvard Med. Sch., Boston, 1988—; dir. psychiatry Westchester Med. Ctr., Valhalla, 1979-89; cons. WHO, Geneva, 1984, 89—; S.Y. Mak vis. prof. U. Hong Kong, 1989; mem. awards jury Anna Monika Stiftung, Dortmund, Ger., 1983—. Sr. editor textbook: Comprehensive Psychiatry, 1967-80; sr. editor book: Issues in Psychiatric Classification, 1986; editor-in-chief Polit. Psychology, 1981-90, Integrative Psychiatry, 1981—; contbr. articles to profl. jours. Mem. N.Y. State Commn. to Evaluate Drug Laws, Albany, 1970-73; founding trustee Ctr. for Urban Edn., N.Y.C., 1965-70; dir. Upper Park Ave. Boys Club of Am., N.Y.C., 1970-80; NGO rep. UN for World Psychiat. Assn., 1985-90. Maj. USAF, 1942-46. Recipient Henry Wismer Miller award Manhattan Soc. Mental Health, 1964; Terence Cardinal Cooke medal N.Y. Med. Coll., 1985, Lapinlahti medal, U. Helsinki, 1990, Wyeth Ayerst award World Psychiat. Assn., Copenhagen, 1989, A.M. Freedman Ann. award Internat. Soc. for Polit. Psychology, 1990. Fellow Am. Psychiat. Assn. (pres. 1973-74, Rush medal 1974), Am. Psychopathol. Assn. (pres. 1971-72, Hamilton medal 1972), Am. Coll. Neuropsychopharmacology (pres. 1972-73), Am. orthopsychiat. Assn. (dir. 1962-64), Academia Medicinae et Psychiatricae (founding fellow, pres. 1990—); mem. N.Y. Psychiat. Soc. (pres. 1986-87), Nat. Com. on Confidentiality of health Records (pres. 1976—). Home and Office: 1148 5th Ave New York NY 10128-0807

FREEDMAN, FRANK HARLAN, federal judge; b. Springfield, Mass., Dec. 15, 1924; s. Alvin Samuel and Ida Hilda (Rosenberg) F.; m. Eleanor Labinger, July 26, 1953; children: Joan Robin Goodman, Wendy Beth Greedman Mackler, Barry Alan. LL.B., Boston U., 1949, LL.M., 1950; Ph.D. (hon.), Western New Eng. Coll., Springfield, 1970. Pvt. practice law, 1950-68; mayor City of Springfield, 1968-72; judge U.S. Dist. Ct. Mass., Springfield, 1972-86, chief judge, 1986—. Chmn. fund raising drs. Muscular Dystrophy, Leukemia Soc.; mem. Susan Auchter Kidney Fund Raising Com.; mem. Springfield City Council, 1960-67, pres., 1962; del. Republican Nat. Conv., 1964, 68; mem. Springfield Rep. Com., 1959-72. Served with USNR, 1943-46. Greenaway Drive Elem. Sch. rededicated as Frank H. Freedman Sch., 1974; recipient Silver Shingle award for disting. service Boston U., 1984. Mem. Hampden County (Mass.) Bar Assn., Lewis Marshall Club on Jurisprudence (pres.). Jewish. Office: US Dist Ct 1550 Main St Rm 525 Springfield MA 01103-1422

FREEDMAN, GEORGE, metallurgist, physicist, consultant, inventor; b. Boston, Dec. 11, 1921; s. Max and Esther (Lerner) F.; m. Ruth Irene Golden, Feb. 14, 1943; children: Judith E., Deborah A. SB, MIT, 1943; AM, Boston U., 1952. Metallurgist Raytheon Co., Newton, Mass., 1943-50, mgr. advanced devel., 1950-60; pres. Tyco Semicondr. Co., Waltham, Mass., 1960-62; dir. New Products Ctr. Raytheon Co., Burlington, Mass., 1962-87; cons., inventor Wayland, Mass., 1987—; bd. dirs. Cober Electronics, Stamford, Conn.; v.p. planning Swedtech Co., Newton, 1990—. Author: Technical Editor's Handbook, 1985, The Pursuit of Innovation, 1987; editor Jour. Microwave Power, 1988-90; patentee. Mem. pers. bd. Town of Wayland, 1987—. With U.S. Navy, 1944-46, Pacific. Internat. Microwave Power Inst. fellow, Clifton, Va., 1988. Mem. IEEE. Democrat. Home and Office: 5 Brook Trail Rd Wayland MA 01778-3705

FREEDMAN, HELEN ROSENGREN, publisher, editor; b. Melbourne, Australia, Oct. 24, 1952; came to U.S., 1975; d. James Francis and Mary Elizabeth (Hogan) Rosengren; m. Howard S. Freedman, Apr. 12, 1980; 1 child, Lauren Charlotte. News reporter The Melbourne (Australia) Herald, 1970-73, feature writer, 1973-75; N.Y. corr. Melbourne (Australia) Herald Group, N.Y.C., 1976-79; assoc. editor Accent Mag., N.Y.C., 1978-80; free-lance writer N.Y.C., 1980-85; editor, publisher The Big Apple Parents' Paper, N.Y.C., 1985—; cons. bd. Natural Child Care Co., N.Y.C., 1992—. Author: The Writer's Guide to Magazine Markets: Fiction, 1983, The Writer's Guide to Magazine Markets: Non-Fiction, 1983, Big Apple Baby, 1985, 89. Mem. Parenting Pubs. of Am. (sec. 1989—). Democrat. Roman Catholic. Office: The Big Apple Parents Paper 36th E 12th St New York NY 10003

FREEDMAN, HOWARD MARTIN, financial planner; b. Bronx, N.Y., Mar. 5, 1953; s. Ralph and Jean (Hoffman) F.; m. Ann Beth Roberts, Aug. 20, 1978; children: Richard, Andrew, Tania. BA, Bradley U., Peoria, Ill., 1974; MBA in Fin. Mgmt., Pace U., 1977; postgrad., NYU, 1978. Registered investment advisor. Fin. planner personal fin. planning div. E.F. Hutton Group, N.Y.C., 1978-83; account supr. E.F. Hutton Group, Providence, 1983-86; sr. fin. advisor E.F. Hutton Group-Shearson Lehman Hutton, Stamford, Conn., 1987-89; prin. Freedman Planning & Mgmt., Norwalk, Conn., 1989—; advisor planned giving com. Pace U., N.Y.C., 1983-86. Advisor gifting program Temple Shalom, Norwalk, 1990. Republican. Office: 49 Locust Ave Ste 104 New Canaan CT 06840-4764

FREEDMAN, IRVING H., educational administrator; b. Albany, N.Y., Nov. 6, 1935; s. Max and Anna (Erlich) F.; m. Jacqueline P. Sheer, Aug. 28, 1960; children: Michele, Elaine, Amy. BA, SUNY, Albany, 1961; MPA, Syracuse U., 1962; EdD, SUNY, Albany, 1967. Budget analyst Polaris Missile Project, Washington, 1962-63; edn. fin. analyst N.Y. State Edn. Dept., Albany, 1963-68; legis. budget analyst N.Y. State Assembly, Albany, 1968-73; spl. asst. legis. rels. SUNY, 1973-75, univ. asst. vice chancellor, 1975-79; dep. sec. for edn. N.Y. Gov.'s Office, Albany, 1979-82; vice chancellor capital facilities, gen. mgr. constrn. fund SUNY System, 1983—. With U.S. Army, 1954-57. Office: State Univ Constrn Fund University Pla Albany NY 12201-1946

FREEDMAN, JAMES OLIVER, lawyer, university president; b. Manchester, N.H., Sept. 21, 1935; s. Louis A. and Sophie (Gottesman) F. AB, Harvard U., 1957; LLB, Yale U., 1962; LLD (hon.), Cornell Coll., 1982, So. Meth. U., 1988, Mt. Holyoke Coll., 1988; LHD (hon.), St. Ambrose U., 1984; postgrad., Vt. Law Sch., 1992, U. N.H., 1992. Bar: N.H. 1962, Pa. 1971, Iowa 1982. Prof. law U. Pa., 1964-82, assoc. provost, 1978, dean, 1979-82, also univ. ombudsman, 1973-76; pres., disting. prof. law and polit. sci. U. Iowa, 1982-87; pres. Dartmouth Coll., Hanover, 1987—; 8th ann. Roy R. Ray lectr. So. Meth. U. Sch. Law, 1985; bd. dirs. Houghton Mifflin Co. Author: Crisis and Legitimacy: The Administrative Process and American Government, 1978; editorial bd.: U. Pa. Press, 1974-81; chmn., 1979-82; contbr. articles to profl. jours. Mem. Phila. Bd. Ethics, 1981-82; chmn. Pa. Legis. Reapportionment Commn., 1981; chmn. Iowa Gov.'s Task Force on Fgn. Lang. Studies and Internat. Edn., 1982-83; trustee Jewish Pub. Soc., 1979—; bd. dirs. Salzburg Seminar Am. Studies, 1988-92, Am. Coun. on Edn., 1986-89. Recipient scholarship award Pa. chpt. Order of Coif, 1981, William O. Douglas First Amendment Freedom award Anti-Defamation League, 1991; fellow NEH, 1976-77. Mem. Am. Law Inst. Office: Dartmouth Coll 207 Parkhurst Hall Hanover NH 03755-3529

FREEDMAN, JUDITH GREENBERG, state senator, importer; b. Bridgeport, Conn., Mar. 11, 1939; d. Samuel Howard and Dorothy (Hoffman) G.; m. Samuel Sumner, Dec. 24, 1964; 1 child, Martha Ann. Student, Boston U., 1957-58, U. Mich., 1958-59; BS, So. Conn. State U., 1961, MS, 1972. Tchr. Hollywood (Fla.) Pub. Schs., 1961-62, White Plains (N.Y.) Pub. Schs., 1962-64, Wilton (Conn.) Pub. Schs., 1964-66; tchr. Weston (Conn.) Pub. Schs., 1966-72, tutor, 1977-80, tchr., 1982-84; owner Judith's Fancy, Wesport, Conn., 1984—; state senator from Conn., 1987—; ranking mem. human svcs. com., 1987-88, ins. com., 1987-88, appropriations com., 1989—. Pres., v.p. Rep. Women's Assn., 1976-80; pres. Rep. Women of Westport, 1976-79; mem. Bd. Edn., Westport, 1983-87, 89—, ranking mem. appropriations com. to date; chmn. Task Force on Purchase of Svcs. Commn. to Effect State Govt. Re-orgn. Mem. Order of Women Legislators (treas.). Jewish. Home: 17 Crawford Rd Westport CT 06880-1823

FREEDMAN, LEWIS S., research administrator; b. Boston, Mar. 21. 1936; s. Samuel M. and Frieda (Simon) F.; m. J. Cynthia Weber; 1 child, Samuel Frederic. BA, Harvard Coll., 1958; MA, Boston U., 1960; PhD, Cornell U., 1970. Asst. rsch. prof. NYU Med. Ctr., N.Y.C., 1972-76, assoc. rsch. prof., 1976-83; rsch. programs dir. Meml. Sloan Kettering Cancer Ctr., N.Y.C., 1981—. Pres. Town and Village Conservative Synagogue, N.Y.C., 1986-88, chmn. bd. dirs. 1988-90. Jewish. Office: Meml Sloan Kettering Cancer Ctr 1275 York Ave New York NY 10021-6094

FREEDMAN, MARVIN IRVING, mathematics educator; b. Boston, Oct. 4, 1939; s. Maurice and Rose (Kane) F.; m. Corey E. Langberg, Apr. 24, 1966; children: Emily M., Nicole L. BS, MIT, 1960; MA, Brandeis U., 1962, PhD, 1964. Instr. math. U. Calif., Berkeley, 1964-66; scientist NASA, Cambridge, Mass., 1967-70; assoc. prof. math. then prof. Boston U., 1970—, chmn. dept. math., 1991—; vis. prof. math. Brown U., Providence, R.I., 1968-69. Mem. Am. Math. Soc., Math. Assn. Am., Soc. Indsl. and Applied Math. Democrat. Jewish. Office: Boston U Dept of Math 111 Cummington St Boston MA 02215-2411

FREEDMAN, MICHAEL ALAN, investment banker; b. Worcester, Mass., June 2, 1960; s. Richard Ira and Joan Ruth (Levine) F. AB in East Asian Studies cum laude, Harvard Coll., 1983. Analyst First Boston Corp., N.Y.C., 1983-85; assoc. First Boston Corp., Tokyo, 1985-86, assoc., chief oper. officer, 1987-88; v.p., chief oper. officer 1st Boston Corp., Tokyo, 1988-89; exec. v.p. Pacific Media Holdings, Tokyo and N.Y.C., 1989—; v.p. Wasserstein Perella & Co., N.Y.C., 1989—, Nomura Wasserstein Perella, Tokyo, 1989—; bd. dirs. Pacific Media Corp., Bermuda, Pacific Media K. K., Tokyo, Frontier Booking Internat. Japan, Tokyo. Author: Zaitech, 1988. Mem. Am. Club (Japan), Tokyo Lawn Tennis Club, Fly Club, Harvard Club (N.Y.C.). Jewish. Office: Wasserstein Perella & Co 31 W 52d St New York NY 10019

FREEH, CHERI HUTCHINSON, accountant; b. Greensburg, Pa., June 2, 1961; d. Douglas Edward and Dee Ann (Davis) Hutchinson; m. Ronald L. Freeh, Nov. 27, 1981; children: Rebecca Davis, Krista Benner. AAS in Acctg., Northampton Community Coll., Bethlehem, Pa., 1982; BSBA, Thomas Edison State Coll., 1990. Cert. in fed. taxation, tax adv., Pa. Acct. DE Hutchinson Pub. Acctg., Quakertown, Pa., 1979—. Treas. Trinity United Ch. of Christ, Pleasant Valley, Pa., 1987—, stewardship com., 1987—, dir. Trinity Day Camp, Applebachsville, Pa., 1989—; leader Brownie Troop Pleasant Valley, 1990-91. Mem. Community Hosp. Assn. of Upper Bucks County (mem. fiscal integrity com. 1990—). Republican. Office: DE Hutchinson Pub Acctg 338 W Broad St Quakertown PA 18951-1234

FREELAND, WILLIAM LEE, artist; b. Pitts., June 16, 1929; s. Fitzhugh Lee Freeland and Margret (Horner) Gerner; m. Melora Korninsky, May 30,1 955 (div. Oct. 1983); 1 child, Erik Baylor. Diploma, Phila. Coll. of Art, 1955; student, Hans Hofmann Sch., Provincetown, Mass., 1957. Prof. Moore Coll. of Art, Phila., 1969-90, prof. emeritus, 1990—. One-man shows include Dolan/Maxwell, N.Y., 1989, Oscarsson Siegeltuch Gallery, N.Y., 1986, Morris Gallery, Pa. Acad. Fine Arts, 1985, Phila. Art Alliance, 1981, Touchstone Gallery, N.Y., 1980, 78, Del. Art Mus., 1972, Immaculata Coll., 1970, Swarthmore Coll., 1964, Little Gallery, Princeton, N.J., 1961, 59 and others; exhibited in group shows at Dolan/Maxwell, N.Y., 1989, Ctr. for Contemporary Art, Chgo., 1989, Siegeltuch Gallery, N.Y., 1987, Vanguard Gallery, Phila., 1986, Max Hutchinson Gallery, 1984, 82. Recipient Pollock-Krasner Found. grant, 1989, Moore Coll. Art Faculty Devel. Rsch. grant, 1988, Pa. Coun. on the Arts Fellowship award, 1987, South St. Devel. Co. Commn., 1986, Univ. Del. Purchase prize, 1984, Moore Coll. of Art Faculty Devel. Rsch. grant, 1981, Hereward Lester Cooke Found. grant, 1978, Del. Art Mus. Multiple Edit. Sculpture Commn., 1973. Home and Office: Box 67 D E Valley Hill Rd Malvern PA 19355

FREEMAN, BRUCE GEORGE, fund-raising consultant; b. Perth Amboy, N.J., Feb. 17, 1929; s. Benjamin George and Beatrice (Wright) F.; children: David B., Judith Ann Demott, Mark D; m. Marjorie V. Kler, Dec. 1983. BA, Rutgers U., 1952; MDiv, New Brunswick Theol. Sem., 1955; postgrad., Albany Med. Ctr., Andover Newton Sem., 1955-58. Minister Presbyn. Ch., various locations, N.Y., 1955-64; asst. to pres. Buena Vista Coll., Storm Lake, Iowa, 1964-66; area dir. United Presbyn. Ch. U.S.A., 1966-67; campaign mgr. Marts & Lundy, N.Y.C., 1967-75, bd. dirs., 1975—, v.p., 1979-80, treas., 1980-82; founder electron. screening div. Marts & Lundy, Lyndhurst, N.J., 1984, pres., 1982-91, chmn. and chief exec. officer, 1991—. Inventor Electron. Screening. Moderator, bd. trustees New Brunswick Theol. Sem., 1990—; trustee East Jersey Olde Towne, Inc., Piscataway, 1980—, Internat. Pain Found., Seattle, 1982—; bd. dirs. Nat. Orgn. on Disability, Washington, 1990. 1st lt. USAR, 1952-62. Auburn Sem. scholar 1958, 62. Mem. Raritan Valley Country Club, Union League N.Y.C. Republican. Home: 6 Mimosa Ct Princeton NJ 08502 Office: Marts & Lundy 1280 Wall St W Lyndhurst NJ 07071-3517

FREEMAN, DAVID HAINES, chemist, educator; b. Rochester, N.Y., June 24, 1931; married; 4 children. BS, U. Rochester, 1952; MS, Carnegie Inst. Tech., 1954; PhD in Chemistry, Mass. Inst. Tech., 1957. Rsch. assoc. phys. chemist Mass. Inst. Tech., 1957-60; asst. chemistry prof. Wash. State U., 1960-65; rsch. chemist Analytical Chem. Div. Anal. Chem. Div. Nat. Bur. Stand, Washington D.C., 1965; chief separation & purification sect. Analytical Chem. Div. Anal. Chem. Div. Nat. Bur. Stand, 1965-74; chemistry prof. U. Md., 1974—; chmn. Gordon Rsch. Conf. Ion Exch., 1973; lectr. Am. Chem. Soc., 1973-83; vis. researcher Geophys. Lab., Carnegie Inst. Wash., 1981, 89; researcher in field. Mem. adv. bd. Energy and Fuels, jour. Am. Chem. Soc., 1992—; patentee in field. Recipient Silver medal, Dept. Com., 1969. Mem. Am. Chem. Soc. Office: Dept Chem University of Maryland College Park MD 20742

FREEMAN, JOHN PAUL, chemist; b. Washington, Aug. 30, 1937; s. John Elmer and Mary Paul (Barclift) F. BS in Chemistry, Washington and Lee U., 1959; MS in Organic Chemistry, U. Wash., 1964; PhD in Organic Chemistry, Ohio State U., 1970. Index editor Chem. Abstracts Svc., Columbus, Ohio, 1962-64; lectr. Washington and Lee U., Lexington, Va., 1965-66; rsch. and supervisory chemist Eastman Kodak Co., Rochester, N.Y., 1971-85, Eastman Gelatine Corp. subs. Eastman Kodak Co., Peabody, Mass., 1985—. Mem. Am. Chem. Soc., Soc. for Imaging Sci. and Tech. Episcopalian. Office: Eastman Gelatine Corp 227 Washington St PO Box 473 Peabody MA 01960

FREEMAN, LARRAMOUR EARL, accountant; b. Erie, Pa., Sept. 16, 1931; s. Van Lloyd Herman and Margaret M. (Anderson) Freeman; m. Jane Land (div. Aug., 1979); children: Julie, Laurie, Mark. Cryptography student, Southeastern Signal Sch., Augusta, Ga., 1950; BS in Acctg., Pa. State U., 1959; student, LaSalle U., Chgo., 1963-65. CPA, Pa. Yard clk. Pa. R.R., Erie, 1953-55; acct. various cos., 1959-79; acctg. instr. Hamilton Coll., Charlotte, N.C., 1977-81; acct., pvt. practice Erie, Pa., 1981—; dept. head acctg. Hamilton Coll., Charlotte, 1977-81. With U.S. Army, 1950-53, Korea.

FREEMAN, LOUIS BARTON, nuclear engineer; b. N.Y.C., May 12, 1935; m. Toby Lee Freeman; 2 children. AB, Colgate U., 1955; AM, Harvard U., 1957; PhD, U. Pitts., 1965. Scientist, mgr., adv. scientist Westinghouse Bettis Atomic Power Lab., West Mifflin, Pa., 1958—. Contbr. articles to Nuclear Sci. and Engring., Nuclear Tech., Nuclear News, Trans. Am. Nuclear Soc., Chem. Engring. Sci. Mem. Am. Nuclear Soc. Office: Westinghouse Bettis Atomic Power Lab PO Box 79 West Mifflin PA 15122-0079

FREEMAN, MARJORIE KLER, interior designer; b. Phila., June 30, 1929; d. Joseph H. and Elizabeth VanHoesen (Vaughan) Kler; m. John Martin Hale, Dec. 26, 1953 (div. 1974); children: John Marshall, David Maclain; m. Bruce George Freeman, Dec. 17, 1983. Cert. Interior Design, Pratt Inst., 1951, BFA, 1952; MA, U. Mich., 1954. Dir. design studio Handicraft Furniture Co., Ann Arbor, Mich., 1953-63; design cons. dorms U. Mich., Ann Arbor, 1955-62; design cons. U. Del., Newark, 1963-67; bldg. and maint. designer and studio mgr. Vallery Miller Interiors, Woodland Hills, Calif., 1969-74; office mgr. Joseph H. Kler, M.D., New Brunswick, N.J., 1974-83; pres. Marjorie Kler Interiors Inc., Bound Brook, N.J., 1980—; v.p. Jewel Box of Princeton, Inc., N.J., 1988—; design cons. East Jersey Olde Towne, Inc., Piscataway, 1974—; buyer EJOT Gift Shop, 1977—; buyer creamery Meadows Found., Somerset, N.J., 1990. Author/editor cookbooks: Educated Palate, 1969, Grand Slam, 1990, Indian Queen Tavern, 1991. Pres. Bucceleuch Mansion Found., New Brunswick, 1983—; past pres., v.p. East Jersey Olde Towne, Inc., 1983-90, 91—; dir. Meadows Found., Somerset, 1989—. Mem. DAR (Jersey Blue chpt.), N.J. Assn. Bus. Women Owners, Princeton C. of C., Penn Hall Alumnae Assn. (v.p., dir. 1989—), The Trowel Club of New Brunswick (pres.-elect 1991). Republican. Presbyterian. Home and Office: 6 Mimosa Ct Princeton NJ 08540

FREEMAN, MILTON VICTOR, lawyer; b. N.Y.C., Nov. 16, 1911; s. Samuel and Celia (Gelfand) F.; m. Phyllis Young, Dec. 19, 1937; children: Nancy Lois (Mrs. Gans), Daniel Martin, Andrew Samuel, Amy Martha (Mrs. Malone). AB, CCNY, 1931; LLB, Columbia U., 1934. Bar: N.Y. 1934, D.C. 1946, U.S. Supreme Ct. 1943. With gen. counsel's office SEC, 1934-42, asst. solicitor, 1942-46; staff securities div. FTC, 1934; with Arnold & Porter (and predecessor firms), Washington, 1946—; adj. prof. Yale U., 1947, Georgetown U. Law Sch., 1952; vis. scholar various univs., 1978-79; mem. adv. bd. Bur. Nat. Affairs, Securities Regulation and Law Report, Washington, Internat. Fin. Law Rev., London. Contbr. articles to profl. jours.; bd. editors Columbia Law Rev., 1933-34 (Ordronaux prize 1934). Mem. adv. bd. Securities Regulation Inst., U. Calif., San Diego. Mem. ABA (chmn. subcom. SEC practice and enforcement 1972-83, exec. com. fed. regulatoion of securities com. 1983—, ad hoc com. on corp. governance project, ad hoc com. on insider trading), Fed. Bar Assn., D.C. Bar Assn., Internat. Law Inst. (hon. chmn. 1977-81, trustee 1955-86), Anxiety Disorders Assn. Am. (bd. dirs.), Am. Law Inst. (adviser, corp. governance project). Home: 3405 Woolsey Dr Bethesda MD 20815-3924 Office: 1200 New Hampshire Ave NW Washington DC 20036-6802

FREEMAN, RICHARD MARK, banker; b. Flushing, N.Y., Sept. 19, 1958; s. Julian Edward and Fay (Gorlin) F. BS, Adelphi U., 1979; MBA, Fordham U., 1981; postgrad., Stonier Grad. Sch. of Banking, 1987. Credit analyst Mchts. Bank of N.Y., 1981-83, platform officer, 1983-85, loan officer, 1985-88; asst. v.p. new bus. devel. Heller Fin., Inc., N.Y.C., 1988-91; asst. v.p. comml. lending Israel Discount Bank N.Y., N.Y.C., 1991—. Office: Israel Discount Bank NY 511 5th Ave New York NY 10017-4903

FREEMAN, THOMAS FRENCH, electonics engineer; b. Newport, R.I., June 27, 1956; s. Henry and Catherine (Thompson) F.; m. Tommilyn Bennet, Oct. 31, 1987. AS, Wentworth Inst., Boston, 1978; BS in Elect. Engring., N.C. A&T State U., 1982. Electronics engr. Naval Underwater Systems Ctr, Newport, R.I., 1979. Author: (song) Summer Delight, 1978, (tech. report) Impact of Task 57 on the AN BSY-2 Combat System. Math. tutor Martin Luther King Ctr., Newport, R.I., 1988; speaker Time 2 Inc., R.I. Coll., Providence, 1989; vol. photographer Naval Underwater Systems Ctr., 1991; vol. Newport Clean Green, 1990; asst. scoutmaster Boy Scouts Am.; youth advisor NAACP. Mem. IEEE, NAACP (sustaining), NRA, Nat. Speldological Soc., Profl. Assn. Diving Instrs., Audio Engring. Soc., Tiverton Gun and Rod Club (rifle chmn.). Democrat. Baptist. Home: 55 Chapel St Newport RI 02840-3255 Office: Naval Underwater Systems Ctr Newport RI 02840

FREEMAN, WILLIAM A., manufacturing company executive; b. 1943. BSBA, Pitts. State U., 1965. Acct. Price Waterhouse; ptnr. Evans & Freeman; with Zurn Industries, Inc., 1969—, v.p., contr. Vinylplex div., 1973-81, pres. Vinylplex div., 1981-86, sr. v.p. fin. adminstrn., 1986-91, pres., 1991—, also bd. dirs. Office: Zurn Industries Inc 1 Zurn Pl Erie PA 16505*

FREGOSI, JAMES LOUIS, professional baseball team manager; b. San Francisco, Apr. 4, 1942; m. Joni Fregosi; children: Jim Jr., Jennifer. Student, Menlo Coll. Profl. baseball player L.A. Dodgers, 1961-64, Calif. Angels, 1965-71, N.Y. Mets, 1972-73, Tex. Rangers, 1973-77, Pitts. Pirates, 1977-78; mgr. Calif. Angels, 1978-81, Louisville Redbirds, 1983-86, Chgo. White Sox, 1986-88; spl. assignment scout, coach Phila. Phillies, 1989-90, minor league pitching instr., spl. assignment scout, 1990, mgr., 1991—. Named to All-Star team, 1964, 66-70; recipient Gold Glove award, 1967. Office: care Phila Phillies PO Box 7575 Philadelphia PA 19101-7575*

FREIBERG, KAREN LOUISE, psychology educator, writer; b. Oneonta, N. Y., Apr. 17, 1944; d. Peter and Helen Margarethe (Nordberg) Hansen; children: Kenneth, Signelise. BS, SUNY, Plattsburgh, 1966; MS, Cornell U., Ithaca, 1968; Ph.D., Syracuse U., N.Y., 1974. Teaching asst. Cornell U., Ithaca, N.Y., 1966-67; rsch. asst. Cornell U., Ithaca, 1967-68; charge nurse Reconstruction Home, Ithaca, 1967-68; field health nurse Navajo Indian Reservation, Gallup, N.Mex.; assoc. project dir. U. of Tex. Med. Br., Galveston, Tex., 1969-70; lectr. Syracuse U., 1970-75; rsch. specialist Cornell U., Ithaca, 1976-78; asst. prof. Le Moyne Coll., Syracuse, 1978-79; assoc. prof. U. Md. Baltimore County, Catonsville, Md., 1979--. Author: Human Development, 1979, 2d edit., 1983, 3rd edit., 1987, 4th edit., 1992, Educating Exceptional Children, 1987, 89, 91. Mem. APA, Internat. Confron Infant Studies, Soc. for Rsch. in Child Devel., Soc. for Rsch. in Adolescence. Methodist. Home: 111 Rosewood Ave Catonsville MD 21228 Office: UMBC Psychology Dept 5401 Wilkens Ave Baltimore MD 21228-5329

FREIDBERG, STEPHEN ROY, neurosurgeon; b. Bklyn., Oct. 16, 1934; s. Lesly Max and Bess Bernblum; m. Helen Deorsay, May 1, 1964; children: Michael, Jonathan. AB, U. Pa., Phila., 1956; MD, Albert Einstein Coll., 1960. Intern U. Okla. Hosp., 1960-61; resident King's County Hosp., Bklyn., 1964-68; fellow Nat. Hosp. Queen's Sq., London, 1965; staff physician Lahey Clinic Med. Ctr., Burlington, Mass., 1969—, chmn. dept. neurosurgery, 1985—, bd. govs., 1970—. Contbr. articles to profl. jours. Capt. U.S. Army, 1962-64. Mem. AMA, Am. Assn. Neurol. Surgeons, Congress Neurol. Surgeons, New Eng. Neurosurg. Soc. (pres. 1981-83), Mass. Med. Soc. Jewish. Office: Lahey Clinic Med Ctr 41 Mall Rd Burlington MA 01805

FREIDENBERGS, INGRID, psychologist; b. Latvia, Aug. 6, 1944; came to U.S, 1951; d. Olgerts and Marta (Purvins) F.; m. Jack Feder, June 21, 1980; 1 child, Paul. BA, CCNY, 1966, MS, 1970; MA, L.I. U., 1973, PhD, 1975; cert. in psychoanalysis, NYU, 1983. Lic. psychologist, N.Y. Sch. psychologist Bur. of Guidance N.Y.C. Bd. Edn., 1971-73; intern in clin. psychology Bellevue Psychiat. Hosp., N.Y.C., 1973-74; with Inst. Rehab. Medicine NYU, N.Y.C., 1974—, dir. psychology intern program Inst. Rehab. Medicine, 1983-85, dir. psychol. svcs. Cancer Rehab. Svc., 1979—; adj. asst. prof. dept. counselor edn. NYU, 1978-82, clin. instr. dept. psychiatry NYU Med. Ctr., 1981—; presenter in field. Contbr. numerous articles to profl. jours. Mem. med. adv. bd. Skin Cancer Found. NSF fellow Yeshiva U., 1966, L.I. U. fellow, 1971-72. Mem. Am. Psychol. Assn., N.Y. State Psychol. Assn., Psychoanalytic Soc. of NYU, Assn. for the Advancement of Psychology. Office: 29 W 9th St New York NY 10011-8942

FREIDINGER, ROGER MERLIN, chemist, researcher; b. Pekin, Ill., July 26, 1947; s. Merlin Paul and Emily Mary (Olt) F.; m. Carol Ann Dunkel, June 28, 1969; children: Kathryn Elaine, Elizabeth Emily. BS in Chemistry, U. Ill., 1969; PhD, MIT, 1975. Sr. rsch. chemist dept. of chemistry Merck Rsch. Labs., West Point, Pa., 1975-80, asst. dir., 1985-87, assoc. dir., 1987-89, sr. scientist, 1989—; ad hoc reviewer NIH, 1984, 86, 90; mem. NIH biorganic and natural products chemistry study sect. 1990—. Editorial adv. bd. Jour. Organic Chemistry, 1988-92; contbr. articles to profl. jours.; patentee in field. With U.S. Army, 1970-72. Recipient Vincent duVigneaud award Peptide Gordon Conf., 1986. Mem. ACS, AAAS, Am. Peptide Soc. Mem. United Ch. of Christ. Office: Merck Rsch Labs Sunneytown Pike West Point PA 19486

FREIFELD, STANLEY, actuary; b. N.Y.C., Mar. 5, 1954; s. Bernard and Lee (Proshinsky) F.; m. Helen A. Goldman, June 14, 1981; 1 child, David. BS, SUNY, Stony Brook, 1974. Student actuary N.Y. Life Ins. Co., N.Y.C., 1974-77; cons. William M. Mercer, Inc., N.Y.C., 1977-81; prin. Noble Lowndes, Roseland, N.J., 1981—; enrolled actuary Dept. Treasury, Washington, 1976—. Mem. Am. Acad. Actuaries, Am. Benefits Conf., Soc. Actuaries (assoc.), Actuarial Club Greater N.Y. Republican. Jewish. Home: 10 Sisco St Wayne NJ 07470 Office: Noble Lowndes 3 Becker Farm Rd Roseland NJ 07068

FREIMAN, HAL JEFFREY, gastroenterologist; b. Bronx, N.Y.C., May 23, 1954; s. Herbert Seymour and Irene Paula (Cheiken) F.; m. Ellen Louise Babin, Aug. 3, 1980; children: Marc, Rachel. BS cum laude, Rensselaer Poly. Inst., 1978; MD, Albany Med. Coll., 1978. Diplomate Am. Bd. Internal Medicine in internal medicine and gastroenterology. Resident internal medicine St. Vincent's Hosp. & Med. Ctr. N.Y., N.Y.C., 1978-81, attending physician, 1983—; fellow gastroenterology N.Y. Med. Coll., Valhalla, 1981-83; cons. physician Village Nursing Home, N.Y.C., 1990—. Fellow Am. Coll. Gastroenterology; mem. ACP, Am. Gastroent. Assn., Am. Soc. Gastrointestinal Endocscopy, N.Y. Acad. Gastroenterology. Home: 11 Magnolia Rd Scarsdale NY 10583 Office: 59 W 12th St New York NY 10011

FREIMARCK, GEORGE STEPHEN ALFRED, educator; b. N.Y.C., May 3, 1917; s. George William and Irene Susanne (Fabricius) F.; BA, Columbia Coll., 1938; MA, Columbia U., 1942; PhD (hon.), Wentworth Inst. Tech., 1991; m. Mary Elisabeth McAvoy, Nov. 11, 1950; children: George Geoffrey, Mary Elisabeth, Catherine Carey. Grad. asst. Columbia U., 1941-42; consul, sec. diplomatic service Fgn. Service, U.S. Govt., 1945-66; with Wentworth Inst. Tech., Boston, 1966—, prof. humanities and social scis., 1967—, dean gen. studies, 1968-74, editor Context, quar. publ. Coll. Arts and Scis.; emeritus prof. humanities and social sci., 1988. Mem. parish council Our Lady Star of the Sea Ch., Marblehead, Mass., 1979-80; vol., docent in maritime history Peabody Mus. Salem (Mass.), 1988—; pres. Friends of the Abbot Pub. Libr., Marblehead, 1990-92. Served with U.S. Army, 1942-45; ETO. NEH fellow, 1979. Mem. Mass. Fedn. Tchrs. (v.p. 1982-88), Am. Fgn. Service Assn., Fgn. Service Retirees of New Eng., Acad. Polit. Sci. Clubs: John Jay Assocs. of Columbia Coll., Columbia U. Club of New Eng. (bd. dirs.), Friends of Switzerland (bd. dirs. Boston chpt.), Civic League (Marblehead), Wentworth Retirees Club (sec., treas. 1991). Author: USA, A Pictorial Survey, 1957. Home: 67 Overlook Rd Marblehead MA 01945-1445 Office: 550 Huntington Ave Boston MA 02115

FREITAS, JEFFREY ANTHONY, textile design agency executive; b. Fall River, Mass., Sept. 29, 1946; s. Antone and Belmira (Souza) F.; m. Karyn Louise Hilly, Feb. 14, 1981. AS, Franklin Inst., 1967; BS, Roger Williams Coll., 1972; student, S.E. Mass. U., 1972-73. Mech. designer Raytheon Submarine Div., Portsmouth, R.I., 1967-70; contractor mgr. Garland Corp., Brockton, Mass., 1973-77; sweater div. mgr. Health-Tex, Inc., Central Falls, R.I., 1977-80; v.p. Karyn Jeffries, Inc., Fall River, Mass., 1980-84; pres. Kartex, Inc., Pembroke, Mass., 1984—. bd. dirs. Pembroke (Mass.) C. of C., 1987-91, pres., 1988-89; v.p. Pembroke Com. Kid's Fair, 1990—; chmn. Drug Awareness & Child Luring, Prevention, Pembroke, 1989—. Mem. Masons (chmn. masonic awareness 1989—). Roman Catholic. Office: Kartex Inc 39 Farnum Rd Pembroke MA 02359-3602

FREIZER, LOUIS A., radio news producer; b. N.Y.C., Oct. 10, 1931; s. Morris and Celia (Lassersohn) F.; m. Michèle Suzanne Orban, July 6, 1968; children: Sabine, Eric. BS, U. Wis., 1953; postgrad., U. Heidelberg, Germany, 1956; MA, Columbia U., 1964, postgrad., 1966—. Corr. UPI, Madison, Wis., 1953-54; desk asst. CBS News, N.Y.C., 1956-59, newswriter, 1959-60; newswriter Sta. WCBS, N.Y.C., 1960-62, news editor, 1963-68, sr. news producer, 1968-73, sr. exec. news producer, 1973—; adj. prof. communications Fordham U.; lectr., cons. journalism and internat. relations. Producer: (pub. affairs series) Let's Find Out, 1966, International Briefing series, 1968-72. Served to 1st lt. U.S. Army, 1954-56; capt. USAR. Recipient Am. Legion medal; Radio Journalism award AMA, Radio Journalism award Nat. Headliners Club, Radio Journalism Nat. award for Outstanding Newscast UPI, 1st place award for Best Regularly Scheduled Local News Program N.Y. State AP Broadcasters Assn., spl. mention for Best One Day News Effort N.Y. State AP Broadcasters Assn.; fellow CBS News Found. Mem. Am. Polit. Sci. Assn., Acad. Polit. Sci., Am. Acad. Polit. and Social Scis., Radio-TV News Dirs. Assn., Broadcast Pioneers, Sigma Delta Chi. Home: 1619 3d Ave New York NY 10128 Office: Sta WCBS 51 W 52d St New York NY 10019

FREMON, RICHARD C., retired infosystems specialist; b. St. Louis, May 28, 1918; s. Richard Horatio and Hazel Pauline (Rhea) F.; m. Virginia Isabelle Moore, Sept. 7, 1940; children—Carolyn E. Fremon Maycher, Richard L., James N., Nancy I. Fremon Fullem. A.B., Columbia U., 1939; BEE, 1940, MEE, 1944. With personnel Bell Telephones, N.Y.C., 1941-54, dir. salary adminstrn., Murray Hill, N.J., 1954-73, dir. adminstrv. systems, 1973-81; dir. computer ctr. Centenary Coll., Hackettstown, N.J., 1981-89. Contbr. chpt. to book. Trustee Sea Cliff Sch. Bd., N.Y., 1950-52; past chmn. Engring. Manpower Commn., N.Y.C., 1965. Mem. Data Processing Mgmt. Assn., Inst. Indsl. Engrs. (sr.), Panther Valley Club. Democrat. Presbyterian. Home: 32 Barn Owl Dr Hackettstown NJ 07840-3205

FREMONT-SMITH, RICHARD, federal health care executive; b. Boston, Mar. 11, 1935; s. Maurice and Mary Dixon (Thayer) F.-S. Student, Harvard U., 1954-56; MBA, Columbia U., 1969; grad. cert., George Washington U., 1971; cert., Yale U., 1986. Enlisted USCG, 1956, advanced through grades to lt., 1966, served in Vietnam, 1965-66, resigned from active duty, 1966; advanced from lt. comdr. to capt USCGR, 1966-82; recalled to active duty USCG, 1982, dir. special projects Washington hdqrs., 1982-84, released from active duty, 1984, asst. chief med. adminstrn. Washington hdqrs., 1985-87, liaison officer to Asst. Sec. Defense, 1987—; liaison officer to asst. sec. def. Xerox Corp., N.Y.C., 1966-69; fed. account rep. Xerox Corp., Boston, 1970-71; stockbroker Paine, Webber, Jackson & Curtis, Boston, 1969-70; asst. dir. Peter Bent Brigham Hosp., Boston, 1972-75; assoc. dir. Bay State Profl. Svcs. Rev. Orgn., Boston, 1975-78; v.p. Qualicare Inc., Boston, 1978-80, R.A. Wiegand and Co. Inc., Boston, 1980-81. Contbr. articles to profl. jours. Mem., bd. dirs. ARC, Boston, Los Angeles, nat. staff, 1952—; chmn. ops. Boston chpt. 1980, vice chmn. disaster services 1978-82, mem. exec. com. 1978-82, bd. dirs. 1972-82, chief asst. med. disaster officer, chmn. emergency med. services transp. com. 1973-78. Decorated Bronze Star medal; fellow Kings Fund Coll., London, 1972. Mem. ARC Disaster Res., Fed. Mgrs. Assn., Mil. Order Loyal Legion (hon.). Home: 705 6th St SW Washington DC 20024-2721 Office: Asst Sec of Def The Pentagon Washington DC 20301

FREMUND, ZDENEK ANTHONY, manufacturing company executive; b. Prague, Czechoslovakia, Oct. 6, 1946; came to U.S., 1969; s. Karl and Francis (Davidek) F.; div.; children: Brian Daivd, Michelle Jean. Elec. Engring. degree, Czechoslovakia Inst. Tech., 1969; BSME, Newark Coll. Engring., 1976. Profl. engr., N.J. Design engr. Computer Tech. Corp., Prague, 1965-68; machinist R.G. Laurence Co., Inc., Tenafly, N.Y., 1969-71, designer, 1971-74, prodn. mgr., 1974-79, v.p. mfg., chief engr., 1979-81; v.p. ops. Kleiner Metal Specialties, Inc., South Plainfield, N.J., 1981-86, pres., 1986-89; pres. Sava Industries, Inc., Riverdale, N.J., 1989—; owner Inter-Flow Co., Special Product Cons. and Mfg., Montvale, N.J., 1977—. Mem. ASME, Am. Prodn. and Inventory Control Soc. Republican. Roman Catholic. Home: 4 Surrey Ln Montvale NJ 07645-1517 Office: Sava Industries Inc PO Box 30 4 N Corporate Dr Riverdale NJ 07457-0030

FRENCH, BEVAN MEREDITH, geologist; b. East Orange, N.J., Mar. 8, 1937; s. John Sprout and Lois Angelina (Meredith) F.; m. Mary-Hill Kueffner Childs, Dec. 23, 1967; children: James Allan Childs, William Tappan Childs, Sharon Childs Tappan. A.B., Dartmouth Coll., 1958; M.S., Calif. Inst. Tech., 1960; Ph.D., Johns Hopkins U., 1964. Aerospace technologist NASA Goddard Space Flight Center, Greenbelt, Md., 1964-72; program dir. geochemistry NSF, Washington, 1972-75; discipline scientist planetary materials NASA, Washington, 1975-84, advanced programs scientist solar systems exploration, 1984-90, discipline scientist spl. projects, 1990—; vis. prof. Dartmouth Coll., 1968; vis. research geologist U. Pretoria, Republic of South Africa, 1981-82. Author: What's New on the Moon?, 1976, Mars: The Viking Discoveries, 1977, The Moon Book, 1977, others; editor: Shock Metamorphism of Natural Materials, 1968, Meeting with the Universe, 1982, Planetary Exploration Through Year 2000: An Augmented Program, 1986, The Lunar Sourcebook: A User's Guide to the Moon, 1991. NSF fellow, 1958-61. Fellow AAAS, Meteoritical Soc.; mem. Geol. Soc. Washington, Explorers Club, Cosmos Club, Phi Beta Kappa, Sigma Xi. Home: 7408 Wyndale Ln Chevy Chase MD 20815 Office: NASA Hdqrs Code SLC Washington DC 20546

FRENCH, DAVID NICHOLS, metallurgical consultant; b. Newton, Mass., Jan. 24, 1936; s. Sydney Perkins and Donalda (Roy) F.; m. Louise Aldrich Murray, June 25, 1960; children: Katherine, Andrew, Stephen, Jonathan. BS, MIT, 1958, MS, 1959, ScD, 1962. Metallurgist Linde Div., Union Carbide, Indpls., 1962-63; mem. tech. staff Ingersoll-Rand R & D Ctr., Princeton, N.J., 1963-68; phys. metallurgist Abex Corp., Mahwah, N.J., 1968-72; mem. tech. staff P. R. Mallory R & D Ctr., Burlington, Mass., 1972-73; dir. corp. quality assurance Riley Stoker Corp., Worcester, Mass., 1973-82; v.p. quality assurance Leighton Ind. Inc., Phoenixville, Pa., 1982-83; metallurgist D G Peterson & Assocs., Greenfield, Mass., 1983-84; pres. David N. French, Inc., Metallurgists, Northborough, Mass., 1984—. Author: Metallurgical Failures in Fossil Fired Boilers, 1983. Mem. ASME,

Metall. Soc. of AIME, Am. Soc. Metals Internat., Nat. Assn. Corrosion Engrs. Boiler and Pressure Vessel Code Com. (sect. I power to boilers). Episcopalian. Home and Office: 1 Lancaster Rd Northborough MA 01532-1325

FRENCH, HAROLD STANLEY, food company executive; b. Bklyn., Oct. 2, 1921; s. Morris and Fay (Kaufman) F.; m. Claire E. Weingart, Oct. 3, 1943 (dec. Mar. 1983); children: Madelaine Diane, Janet Gail. BA, L.I. U., 1942; postgrad., NYU, 1950, Columbia U., 1960. Asst. buyer R.H. Macy Co., N.Y.C., 1949-52; group mgr. Abraham & Straus Co., Hempstead, N.Y., 1952-54; mdse. mgr. Popular Club Plan, Passaic, N.J., 1954-60, Nat. Silver Co., N.Y.C., 1964-69; mktg. dir. Waverly Products Co., Phila., 1970-74; pres. Pet Food Industries, Inc., N.Y.C., 1974—, Harold French & Co., Inc., N.Y.C., 1974—; chmn. Rosario Homes, Inc., P.R.; pres. King Agro-Indsl. Corp., 1986, Globe King Agro-Indsl. Co. Ltd. (Nigeria), 1988—, King Agro-Cattle Ranching (Nigeria) Ltd., 1988—; trade agt. to Nigerian Govt., 1992—. Patentee in field. Chmn., pres. The Nigeria Fund, Inc., 1989—; contbg. patron N.Y. Met. Opera. With M.I., U.S. Army, 1943-45. Decorated Bronze Star. Home: 60 E 8th St New York NY 10003-6514

FRENCH, HENRY PIERSON, JR., historian, educator; b. Rochester, N.Y., Nov. 21, 1934; s. Henry Pierson and Genevieve Lynn (Johnson) F.; m. Beverly Anne Bauernschmidt, Aug. 22, 1959; children: Henry Pierson III, Donna Lynn (dec.), William Dean, Susan Gayle, John Douglas. AB, U. Del., 1960; MA, U. Rochester, 1961, MA in Edn., 1962, EdD, 1968. Tchr. Pittsford (N.Y.) Cen. High Sch., 1962-66; field svc. assoc. U. Rochester, N.Y., 1962-66, assoc. lectr., 1967-68, vis. asst. prof. Coll. Edn. and E. Asian Ctr., 1968-69, asst. prof. edn., 1969-70, assoc. prof. Ctr. Spl. Degree Programs, 1970-72, lectr. East Asian studies, 1972-74, sr. lectr., 1974—, vis. prof. History, 1988-89; adj. asst. prof. history SUNY-Monroe Community Coll., 1964-67, asst. prof. history, 1967-70, assoc. prof., 1970-74, prof., 1974—, chmn. dept. history and polit. sci., 1979-85, chmn. tenure, promotion com., 1985—, sabbatical leave, 1986; vis. prof. history, 1988-89; prof. Canisius Coll., 1968, 69, 71, 73, 89, Dunlop Tire Corp. Japan Inst. faculty, 1989, Rochester Inst. Tech., 1969-70, spring 1977, SUNY, Brockport, 1971; adj. mentor State U. N.Y.-Empire State Coll., 1976, 88, 89; bd. dirs. polit. insts. Robert A. Taft Inst. Govt., 1962-65; co-dir., adminstr. NDEA insts., 1965-69; bd. dirs. Rochester Assn. UN, 1972-83, 85—, chmn. policy com., 1972-74, v.p., 1975-77, pres., 1977-78, chmn. bd., 1978-79, chmn. nominating com., 1983-84; panelist 10th conf. Internat. Assn. Historians of Asia, 1986, 12th conf., 1991. Contbr. articles to profl. jours. Vestryman St. Thomas Episcopal Ch., Rochester, 1965-68; vestryman Christ Episc. Ch., Pittsford, 1976-79, jr. warden, 1979-80, sr. warden, 1980-81, chmn. rector selection com., 1982; del. to diocesan Conv., 1989-91; 1st provisional lay dep. Gen. Conv. Episc. Ch., U.S.A., 1991; mem. commn. on Ordained Ministry, Episc. Diocese of Rochester (N.Y.), 1987—, chmn., 1992—, warden Monroe dist., 1992—; advisor Shanghai-Rochester Bishops' Visitation in U.S. and China, 1989-90, co-leader lay delegation to Shanghai and China Christian Couns., China, 1992; trustee Reynolds Libr. Bd., 1991—, Rundel Rochester Pub. Libr., 1992—; trustee Friends of Rochester Pub. Libr., 1983—, v.p., 1986-88, pres., 1988-91; chmn., presenter Rochester Literary Award to James Baldwin, 1986; mem. Edn. Adv. Bd., 1988—, Preferred Care HMO, 1988—; mem. N.Y. State Citizens' Com. for the Bicentennial of the French Revolution, 1988-90. With AUS, 1955-57, Ctr. for Internat; moderator, permanent panelist Fgn. Policy Assn. and Rochester Assn. for UN Great Decisions-1973, 77, 78 series Channel 21 Ednl. TV, Rochester; cons., panelist Gt. Decisions TV series, 1982, 84; moderator, host Disciplines Within the Social Sciences series, 1968. Programs and Comparative Studies grantee, 1970. Mem. Assn. Asian Studies, Am. Acad. Polit. and Social Scis., Chinese Lang. Tchrs. Assn., Rochester Com. on Fgn. Rels., Torch (bd. dirs. Rochester chpt. 1973-76, pres. 1974-75), Univ. Club (v.p. 1975-76, sec. 1988-90, pres.-elect 1991-92, pres. 1992-93), Delta Tau Delta. Episcopalian. Home: 78 Smith Rd Pittsford NY 14534-9727 Office: U Rochester Asian Studies Faculty Ctr Spl Degree Programs Rochester NY 14627 also: SUNY-Monroe CC Rochester NY 14623

FRENCH, JAMES EDWARD, trade association administrator; b. Center, Colo., Dec. 17, 1937; s. Donald Edward and Floy Pearl (Sharpless) F.; m. Maxine Agnes Lowndes, Apr. 25, 1964; children: Jonathan Lloyd, Jennifer Kathleen. BA, Vanderbilt U., 1959. Engring. mgr. Instrument Soc. Am., Pitts., 1963-68; tech. dir. Sci. Apparatus Makers Assn., Washington, 1968-77; asst. to pres. ETL Testing Labs. Inc., Cortland, N.Y., 1977-79; mgr. of standards Bur. of Standards U.S. Dept. Commerce, Washington, 1979-81; instr. Frederick (Md.) Community Coll., 1982-87; cons. Tech. & Mktg. Reps., Frederick, 1982-89; dir. of standards AIAA, Washington, 1989—; cons. ASTM, Phila., 1980, ACIL, Washington, 1979; dir. NCCLS, Phila., 1972-74. Author: (chpt.) Standards Management, 1989. Chair supt.'s adv. com. Frederick Bd. of Edn., 1981-82; sec., dir. Frederick Arts Coun., 1981-84. Named one of five Outstanding Young Men of Am., Md. Jaycees, 1972. Mem. Standards Engring. Soc. Democrat. Methodist. Home: 589 Pumphouse Rd Frederick MD 21702-6033 Office: AIAA 370 L'Enfant Promenade SW Washington DC 20024

FRENCH, JEFFREY STUART, architect; b. Arlington, Va., Sept. 18, 1954; s. Orville Sidney and Doris G. French; m. Anne Harvey Hollibaugh, Sept. 26, 1981; children: Courtney Allen, Kyle Stuart, Allison Calvert. BA, Princeton U., 1976; MArch, U. Va., 1978. Registered architect, Pa., N.J., Mich., Ala., S.C., Ga., Del. V.p., dir. R&D facilities The Ballinger Co., Architects/Engrs., Phila., 1978—; instr. U. Wis., Madison, 1986; lectr. in rsch. facility design; grant rev. panel NSF, 1990. Mem. AIA (cert.), Nat. Coun. of Archtl. Registration Bds., Soc. Coll. and Univ. Planning. Office: The Ballinger Co The Curtis Ctr Independence Sq W Philadelphia PA 19106

FRENCH, WILLIAM DECKER, small business owner, entrepreneur; b. Davenport, Iowa, May 2, 1946; s. George Thanet and Nancy Ann (Rendleman) F.; m. Susan Logan, Feb. 14, 1984. BA, Stanford U., 1968; MBA, Harvard U., 1970. Assoc. corp. fin. div. Dean Witter & Co., N.Y.C , 1970-73; asst. v.p. corp. fin. Paine Webber, N.Y.C , 1973-75; pres. Securities Data Co., N.Y.C , 1975-88; owner, pres. Frenchco Data Systems, N.Y.C , 1988—.

FRENI, D. RICHARD, general and thoracic surgeon, consultant, retired; b. Boston, Jan. 12, 1914; s. Louis and Pauline (Patti) F.; m. Dorothy A. Hannon, June 20, 1943; children: Richard Hannon, Donna Ann, Edward Christopher, Dorothy Hannon Freni Parker. AB, Harvard Coll., 1936; MD, Tufts U., 1942. Diplomate Am. Bd. Surgery, Nat. Bd. Med. Examiners. Intern dept. surgery Kings County Hosp., Bklyn., 1942-43; resident dept. surgery VA Hosp., West Roxbury, Mass., 1948-50, asst. chief of surgery, 1948-50; gen. surgery Lynn and Lynnfield, Mass., 1950-77; physician GE Dispensary, Lynn, Mass., 1939-42, 50-51; surg. cons. Raytheon, West Andover, Mass., 1974-76; surg. asst. West Roxbury VA Hosp. and affiliation with Mass. Gen. Hosp., Boston, 1946-48; asst. chief surgery West Roxbury VA Hosp., 1948-50; visiting surgeon Lynn (Mass.) Hosp., 1950, Union Hosp., Lynn, 1950; cons. surgeon Mary Alley Hosp., Marblehead, Mass., 1950, Danvers (Mass.) State Hosp., 1952; courtesy surgeon North Shore Children's Hosp., Salem, Mass., 1950; asst. surgeon in hand surgery VA Hosp., West Roxbury, 1950-56, VA Hosp., Jamaica Plain, Mass., 1950-62. Contbr. articles to profl. jours. Lt. USN Med. Corps, 1943. Fellow Am. Coll. Surgeons (trauma com.), Am. Geriatric Soc., Harvard Engring. Soc.; mem. AMA, Mass. Med. Soc. (coun. 1958-60), Boston Surg. Soc., Mass. Soc. Examining Physicians and Surgeons, New Eng. Surg. Soc., Essex Surg. Soc. (pres. 1968, 69), Govs. Island Club, Sr. Physicians Assn., Salem Country Club, Harvard Club Boston, Laconia Country Club. Roman Catholic. Home and Office: 136 Edgewater Dr Gilford NH 03246

FRENKEL, NAMA RACHEL, producer, marketing consultant; b. Binghamton, N.Y., Nov. 26, 1951; d. George and Viola Joyce (Darrow) Ksenics. BA, Touro Coll., N.Y.C., 1980; postgrad., NYU, 1980-81. Asst. editor Idan Studios, Jerusalem, 1976-77; film distrbn. and rights cons. Jewish Media Svcs./JWB, N.Y.C., 1979-82; assoc. producer Gesher Found., N.Y.C., 1982-85; devel. copywriter Falk & Co. Image Cons., Denver, 1985-86; creative dir. Thayer Media, Inc., Denver, 1986-88; pres. Frenkel & Thayer, Denver and Balt., 1988—; representing Milner Fenwich, Penguin USA, Epic Records, Henry Holt & Co., Behaman House, Tri-Sulom. Producer (TV shows) Jewish Mothers, 1982, Time to Read Hebrew, 1989, (exhibit) Master of Light, 1988; assoc. producer Lights: A Chanuka Story, 1984. V.P. T.R.I. Sulom, Denver, 1982-89; bd. dirs. Am. Jewish Com., Denver, 1984-86, 87-88, Hillel Coun. of B'nai B'rith, Denver, 1984-87. Youth grantee NEH, 1980. Mem. Am. Mktg. Assn. Democrat. Jewish. Office: 6200 Wallis Ave Baltimore MD 21215-3734

FRENSILLI, FREDERICK JOHN, surgeon, urologist; b. Boston, Jan. 28, 1936; s. John Anthony and Teresa (Nardi) F.; m. Patricia Ann Parrott, Nov. 20, 1960 (div. 1984); children: Carol, Susan, Janet; m. Esme Maureen Dwyer, June 3, 1988. AB cum laude, Holy Cross Coll., 1957; MD, Georgetown U., 1961. Diplomate Am. Bd. Urology. Chief of urology Naval Hosp., Charleston, S.C., 1967-70; clin. assoc. U. S.C., Charleston, 1967-70; assoc. prof. urology George Washington Med. Sch., Washington, 1971-75, clin. prof. urology, 1975—; vice chmn. dept. urology Sibley Meml. Hosp., Washington, 1991—; pres. Georgetown Clin. Soc., Washington, 1980-81. Author: Georgetown Medical Center's Introduction to Medical Terminology, 1978; contbr. numerous articles to profl. jours. Cmmdr. U.S.N., 1960-71. Fellow Am. Coll. Surgeons (pres. Washington chpt. 1986-87), Internat. Coll. Surgeons; mem. AMA, Am. Urology Soc., Soc. Univ. Urologists, Am. Fertility Soc. Republican. Roman Catholic. Office: Frederick Frensilli MD 5530 Wisconsin Ave Chevy Chase MD 20815

FRENZ, DOROTHY ANN, cell biologist; b. New Rochelle, N.Y., Jan. 17, 1954; d. Anthony Joseph and Angelina Marie (Guida) Chiodo; m. Michael Richard Frenz, Sept. 15, 1974; children: Christopher, Elizabeth. BA, Iona Coll., 1978; MS, N.Y. Med. Coll., 1986, PhD, 1988. Postdoctoral fellow Albert Einstein Coll. Medicine, Bronx, N.Y., 1988-91; asst. prof. dept. otolaryngology Albert Einstein Coll. Medicine, Bronx, 1991—, anatomy instr., 1991—. Contbr. chpts. in books and articles to profl. jours. Bd. dirs. New Rochelle YMCA; pres. Isaac E. Young Mid. Sch. PTA, New Rochelle, 1988-90; rec. sec. New Rochelle PTA Coun., 1992—; tchr., lector Blessed Sacrament Ch., New Rochelle, 1986—, parish bull. editor 1988—, parish coun. rec. sec. 1990—. Mem. Am. Assn. Anatomists, Cell Biology Soc., Assn. for Rsch. in Otolarycology, N.Y. Acad. Scis. Roman Catholic. Office: A Einstein Coll Medicine 1300 Morris Park Ave Bronx NY 10461

FRESCHI, BRUNO BASILIO, architect, educator; b. Trail, B.C., Can., Apr. 18, 1937; s. Giovanni and Irma (Pagotto) F.; m. Vaune Ainsworth, Dec. 13, 1986; children from previous marriage: Dea Rachelle, Anna Nadine, Aaron Basilio, Reuben Alessandro. BArch with honors, U. B.C., 1961; Cert. Royal Can. Acad. Art, 1973. Assoc. Erickson Massey Architects, Vancouver, B.C., 1964-70; prin. Keith, King, Freschi, Vancouver, 1970-74; prin., owner Bruno Freschi, Architects, Vancouver, 1974—, Urbanisma Designs Ltd., Vancouver, 1975—, Bruno Freschi Architect, Inc., 1986; prof. architecture U. B.C., Vancouver, 1969-79; prof., dean profl. Sch. of Architecture and Planning SUNY, Buffalo, 1988—; lectr. in field; chief architect Expo '86. Prin. works include: Jamatkhana Mosque, Expo '86 Master Plan, Expo Centre, Burnaby Mcpl. Hall, Cathedral Sq. and Ga. Place; cons. Teleport, Van, B.C. Chmn., Italian Heritage Pla., Vancouver, 1985; past mem. numerous civic and cultural orgns. Recipient Man of Yr. award Confratellanza Italo-Canadese, 1983, Gov. Gen. medal, 1984, First prize Wheel-Expo Symbol Competition, 1984, Sweney award CKVU-Vancouver, 1985. Fellow Royal Archtl. Inst. Can. (medal 1961); mem. Archtl. Inst. B.C., Royal Can. Acad. Arts (academician), Order of Can. (officer 1987). Lodge: Christopher Columbus. Avocations: painting, hiking; bike riding. Home: 166 Cleveland Ave Buffalo NY 14222-1613 Office: SUNY Sch of Architecture & Planning Buffalo NY 14214 also: 520-601 W Broadway, Vancouver, BC Canada V5Z 4C2

FRETWELL, LYMAN JEFFERSON, JR., engineer; b. Rockford, Ill., Oct. 8, 1934; s. Lyman Jefferson and Grace (Wallace) F.; m. Lenore Larson, 1963 (div. 1972); 1 child, John; m. Georgianna Quimby, Aug. 18, 1972; children: Holly, Kevin, Karen, David. BS in Physics, Calif. Inst. Tech., 1956, PhD in Physics, 1967. Mem. tech. staff AT&T Bell Labs., Whippany, N.J., 1966-68, supr., 1968-88, disting. mem. tech. staff, 1988—. Republican. Baptist. Home: 59 Mile Dr Chester NJ 07930-9633 Office: AT&T Bell Labs 67 Whippany Rd PO Box 903 Whippany NJ 07981-0903

FREUDENTHAL, ROSLYN ROTH, statistical consultant in medical research; b. N.Y.C., Dec. 10, 1909; d. Herman and Phoebe (Schweitzer) Roth; m. Bruno B. Freudenthal, Feb. 9, 1939; 1 child, Judy Bly. BS, NYU, 1931, MS, 1933, PhD, 1940; postgrad., U. Graz, Austria, 1933. Microanalyst NYU Grad. Sch., N.Y.C., 1931-35; rsch. chemist Air Pollution Survey, N.Y.C., 1936-37, N.Y. Psychiat. Inst., N.Y.C., 1937-40; dir. rsch. Killian Rsch. Lab., N.Y.C., 1940-43; biometrist, dir. rsch. Food and Drug Rsch., Long Island City, N.Y., 1943-47; statis. cons. N.Y.C., 1947—; guest lectr. Coll. Phys. and Surg., Columbia U., N.Y.C., 1969-72, ofcl. rsch. advisor, 1970-77. Contbr. numerous articles to profl. jours. Mem. N.Y. Acad. Scis., Am. Statis. Assns., Biometric Soc., Am. Med. Writers Assn., Sigma Xi. Home: 30-16 85th St Jackson Heights NY 11370

FREUND, MITCHELL DAVID, cable television executive, producer, director; b. N.Y.C., Sept. 9, 1953; s. Herbert Milton and Faye (Carpman) F.; m. Leslie Eileen Stern, June 15, 1980; children: Samuel Michael, Matthew William. BS cum laude, Boston U., 1974; MA, U. Mass., 1977. Instr. TV prodn. U. Mass., Amherst, 1975-77; prodn. mgr. Teleprompter Manhattan CATV, N.Y.C., 1977-79; dir. progamming Teleprompter Cable TV, Worcester, Mass., 1979-81; dir. affiliate rels. PRISM/New Eng., Woburn, Mass., 1981-83; regional mgr. Rainbow Programming Svcs., Woodbury, N.Y., 1983-85; asst. gen. mgr. SportsChannel New Eng., Woburn, 1985-87, v.p., gen. mgr., 1987-90; group v.p. SportsChannel Regional Networks, 1990—. Mem. Dem. Senatorial Campaign Com., Washington, 1982—, Dem. Nat. Com., 1987—. Mem. Cable TV Adminstrv. and Mktg. Soc. (grand prize mktg. award 1987), Nat. Acad. Cable Programming, New Eng. Cable TV Assn. Office: SportsChannel New Eng 10 Tower Office Park Woburn MA 01801-2120

FREUND, ROLAND PAUL, farm management extension agent; b. Finschhafen, Papua New Guinea, June 16, 1939; came to U.S., 1976; s. August Paul Harold and Dorothea Martha (Ey) F.; m. Josephine Lenola Bailey, July 7, 1971; 1 child, Ernest Andreas. Diploma of agrl., Roseworthy Agrl. Coll., 1959; student, U. New England, 1964; MS, Mich. State U., 1971. Mission agriculturalist New Guinea Luth. Mission, Wabag, Papua New Guinea, 1959-71; rural devel. officer Dept. Primary Industries, Wabag, 1972-73; lectr. agrl. econs. Vudal Agrl. Coll., Mt. Hagen, Papua New Guinea, 1974-76; county agrl. agy. Pa. State Extension, Carlisle, 1976-80; regional farm mgmt. agt. Pa. State Extension, York, 1980-82, 84—; agrl. econ. Pa. State/USAID, Swaziland, Africa, 1982-84. Feature article writer Pa. Farmer Mag., 1980—; farm mgmt. columnist Lancaster Farming, 1985—; contbr. articles to profl. jours. Mem. Nat. Assn. County Agrl. Agts. (North-east regional winner farm fin. mgmt. 1991, Disting. Svc. award 1992), Pa. Assn. County Agrl. Agts. (regional dir. 1992—, Search for Excellence Farm Income State winner 1982), Epsilon Sigma Phi. Lutheran. Home: 382 Petersburg Rd Carlisle PA 17013-9219 Office: Pa State Extension 112 Pleasant Acres Rd York PA 17402-9041

FREUND, SAMUEL J., lawyer; b. Forenwald, Germany, Jan. 3, 1949; came to U.S., 1949; s. Abraham and Syma (Skop) F.; m. Barbara Susan Sasmor, July 1, 1979; children: Alexandra, Stefanie. BS in Acctg., Bklyn. Coll., 1971; JD, Bklyn. Law Sch., 1974; LLM in Taxation, NYU, 1980. Bar: N.Y. 1975, U.S. Dist. Ct. (so. and ea. dists.) N.Y. 1978, U.S. Tax Ct. 1981, Fla. 1981, N.J. 1988. Tax acct. Oppenheim, Appel and Dixon, N.Y.C., 1974-75; assoc. Gallin & Josephson, N.Y.C., 1975; atty./advisor Bur. Hearing and Appeals, Dept. HEW, Johnstown, Pa., 1976-77; asst. counsel Goldman & DiLorenzo, N.Y.C., 1977; atty. Tax Dept. N.Y. State, N.Y.C., 1977-82; assoc. tax counsel CBS Inc., N.Y.C., 1982-84; sr. tax assoc. Am. Brands, Inc., N.Y.C., 1984-86, assoc. Friedman & Shaftan, P.C., 1986-89, Hugh Janow, P.C., Pearl River, N.Y., 1990-91; pvt. practice, Montclair, N.J., 1989-90, 91—. Mem. ABA, Fla. Bar Assn., N.J. Bar Assn. Avocations: computers, gardening, philately, wood working. Home: 1 Wendover Rd Montclair NJ 07042

FREW, ROBERT SIMPSON, architect, computer scientist, educator; b. Chapelton, Scotland, Mar. 2, 1940; emigrated to Can., 1963, naturalized, 1969; naturalized U.S. citizen, 1982; s. James Gilchrist and Hannah Morrow (Simpson) F.; m. Susan Hatch, Feb. 1988; 1 child, Susannah. Cert. in architecture, Mackintosh Sch. Architecture, Glasgow, Scotland, 1963; BArch, Man. Sch. Architecture, 1965; MASc in Systems Design, U. Waterloo, 1967, PhD in Engring., 1973. Lectr. U. Waterloo, Ont., Can., 1965-69; asst. prof. Sch. Architecture, Yale U., 1969-74, assoc. prof., 1974-79, vis. prof., 1979—; assoc. prof. computer sci. So. Conn. State U., 1979-84, prof. computer sci., 1984—, dept. chmn., 1982-84; prin. Design Research Practice, New Haven, 1978—; pvt. practice architecture, Waterloo, 1965-73; chmn. environ. design program Yale U., 1971-72; chmn. admissions Yale Sch. Architecture, 1971-78; vice chmn. ops. com. Yale Computer Ctr., 1976-79; invited lectr. profl. confs. Architect bldgs. including Kaleidoscope, Expo '67, 1965; contbr. to research and design publs. in field. V.p. State St. Assn., 1978, pres., 1981, chmn. design com.; sr. tchr. New Haven br. Royal Scottish Country Dance Soc. Mem. Ont. Assn. Architects, Royal Archtl. Inst. Can., Design Methods Group (founding dir., Can. editor), Environ. Design Research Assn. (founding dir.). Home: 204 Bishop St New Haven CT 06511-3718

FREY, FREDERICK AUGUST, geochemistry researcher, educator; b. Milw., Apr. 1, 1938; s. Frederick August and Evelyn Dorothy (Lange) F.; m. Julie Ann Golden; 1 child, Oren. BSCE, U. Wis., 1960, PhD in Chemistry, 1967. Prof. dept. earth, atmospheric and planetary scis. Mass. Inst. Tech., Cambridge, 1966—; Assoc. editor: Geochimica et Cosmochimica Acta; contbr. over 100 articles to profl. jours. Mem. Geochem. Soc., Am. Geophys. Union (VGP Bowen award 1986), Geol. Soc. Am. Office: Dept Earth Atmospheric & Planetary Scis MIT 54-1220 Cambridge MA 02139

FREY, LORI ANN, physical education educator, athletic director; b. Bloomsburg, Pa., Apr. 4, 1963; d. Dale Franklin and Joan Marie (Flick) F. BS, Pa. State U., 1985; MEd, Slippery Rock U., 1990. Asst. softball coach Slippery Rock (Pa.) U., 1986-87; instr. Wilson Coll., Chambersburg, Pa., 1988-90, athletic dir., coach field hockey and softball, 1988—, asst. prof. phys. edn., 1991—; asst. field hocky coach, Chambersburg High Sch., 1991—. Home: 3146 White Church Rd Chambersburg PA 12201 Office: Wilson Coll Philadelphia Ave Chambersburg PA 17201-1652

FREY, NANCY, investment advisor; b. Bklyn., Feb. 15, 1946; m. Edward Frey, July 8, 1967 (div. 1974); m. Errol Normandin, Sept. 12, 1985. BA, U. Mich., 1966; MA, New Sch. Social Research, N.Y.C., 1974. Investment assoc. Sanford C. Bernstein & Co., Inc., N.Y.C., 1974-77; adminstr. VSL Corp., N.Y.C., 1977-82; investment advisor Capital Devel. Assocs., N.Y.C., 1982—. Pres. Robbins Rest Homeowners Assn., Fire Island, N.Y., 1988—; bd. dirs. Fire Island Assn., 1989—. Office: Capital Devel Assocs 600 Madison Ave New York NY 10022-1615

FREY, SUZAN ANN, safety and environmental engineer; b. Pitts., Oct. 21, 1952; d. William Louis and Alice Mae (Schmale) F.; m. Victor Ronald Prybutok, Aug. 22, 1978 (div. Apr. 1985). BS in Biology and Psychology, Drexel U., 1974, MS in Environ. Sci., 1977. Cert. safety profl. Specialist in ops. svcs. Allied Chem. Co., Conshohocken, Pa., 1977-79; supr. safety, health and environ. Air Products & Chems., Paulsboro, N.J., 1979-84; mgr. safety and health Millipore Corp., Bedford, Pa., 1984-87; mgr. safety and ecology BASF Corp., Bedford, 1987—; mem. Bedford Emergency Planning Com., 1989—. Mem. Wayland (Mass.) Bd. Health, 1989-92. Mem. Am. Soc. Safety Engrs. Republican. Office: BASF Corp 35 Crosby Dr Bedford MA 01730-1471

FREY, THOMAS JOSEPH, mechanical engineer; b. Monesson, Pa., Sept. 10, 1962; s. James D. and Ardis Mae (Barnes) F.; m. Kathleen Marie Nowak, May 5, 1990. B in Mech. Engring., U. Del., 1984, M in Mech. Engring., 1990. Registered profl. engr., Del. Engr. Thiokol Corp., Elkton, Md., 1984-88, sr. engr., 1989—. Mem. AIAA, Am. Soc. for Quality Control, Soc. Material and Process Engrs., Del. Assn. Profl. Engrs.

FREY, THOMAS JOSEPH, JR., military officer; b. Takoma Park, Md., Mar. 7; s. Thomas Joseph and Velma Bertha (Cogar) F.; m. Hollis Ann Schaeffer, May 14, 1983; children: Thomas Joseph III, Elizabeth Ann. BS, U.S. Naval Acad., 1977; MEE, Naval Postgrad. Sch., 1986. Commd. ensign USN, 1977, advanced through grades to comdr., 1992; with flight tng. tng. squadrons 10 & 86 USN, Pensacola, Fla., 1978-79; nuclear safety officer attack squadron 176 USN, Oceana, Va., 1979-82; aide, flag lt. carrier group 8 USN, Norfolk, Va., 1982-83; avionics/armament div. officer attack squadron 75 USN, Oceana, 1986-87; strike ops. officer Carrier Air Wing Carrier Air Wing 3, Oceana, 1987-88; maintenance officer attack squadron 75 USN, Oceana, 1988-89; space surveillance coord. USN, Washington, 1990-91, asst. super high frequency satellite comm. Def. Satellite Systems, 1991—. Inventor solid state data recorder for NASA shuttle. Decorated Navy Commendation medals; recipient U.S. Space Program Achievement award Nat. Space Club, 1992. Mem. Armed Forces Communications and Electronics Assn. (Meritorious Svc. award 1992), AIAA, IEEE, U.S. Naval Inst., Assn. Naval Aviation, Tailhook Assn. Republican. Roman Catholic. Home: 1205 Banister Ct Virginia Beach VA 23454 Office: Navy Space Systems Div OP-943 C Rm 4C668 Pentagon Washington DC 20350-2000

FREYD, PETER JOHN, mathematician, computer scientist; b. Evanston, Ill., Feb. 5, 1936; s. Paul Robert and Pauline Margaret (Pattinson) F.; m. Pamela Parker, Jan. 1, 1957; children: Jennifer Joy, Gwendolyn Ann. AB magna cum laude, Brown U., 1958; MA (Woodrow Wilson fellow), Princeton U., 1959, PhD, 1960. J.F. Ritt instr. math. Columbia U., N.Y.C., 1960-62; faculty U. Pa., Phila., 1962—; prof. math. U. Pa., 1968—, chmn. grad. group math., 1982-87, prof. computer info. sci., 1987—; Adviser Pahlavi U., Shiraz, Iran, 1968; lectr. Canadian Nat. Rsch. Seminar, 1974; vis. researcher U. Mex., 1975, U. Sydney, 1985, U. Milan, 1986, U. Parma, 1990; vis. prof. U. Chgo., 1980, U. Louvain, Belgium, 1981; vis. prof. in computer sci. Carnegie Mellon U., 1988-89. Author: Abelian Categories, 1964; (with Andre Scedrov) Categories, Allegories, 1990; founder Jour. Pure and Applied Algebra, 1970; editor Theoretical Computer Sci., 1988—, Math. Structures in Computer Sci., 1989—, Internat. Jour. Algebra and Computation, 1990—, Jour. Knot Theory and its Ramifications, 1991—. Fulbright scholar Australia, 1971; fellow St. John's Coll., Cambridge U., Eng., 1980-81. Mem. Phi Beta Kappa, Sigma Xi. Home: 2020 1/2 Addison St Philadelphia PA 19146

FREYD, WILLIAM PATTINSON, fund raising executive, consultant; b. Chgo., Apr. 1, 1933; s. Paul Robert Freyd and Pauline Margaret (Pattinson) Gardiner; m. Diane Marie Carlson, May 19, 1984. BS in Foreign Svc., Georgetown U., 1960. Field rep. Georgetown U., Washington, 1965-67; campaign dir. Tamblyn and Brown, N.Y.C., 1967-70; dir. devel. St. George's Ch., N.Y.C., 1971; assoc. Browning Assocs., Newark, 1972-73; regional v.p. C.W. Shaver Co., N.Y.C., 1973-74; founder, chmn. IDC, Bloomfield, N.J., 1974—. Board dirs. N.J. Symphony Orch. Mem. Nat. Soc. Fund Raising Execs. (nat. treas. 1980-81, N.Y. chpt. pres. 1974-76, cert. 1982), Am. Assn. Fund Raising Counsel (sec. 1984-86), N.Y. Yacht Club, Union League Club of N.Y., Masons, Nassau Club, Circumnavigators Club. Home: 17 Thackeray Dr Short Hills NJ 07078-2920 Office: IDC 1260 Broad St Bloomfield NJ 07003-3031

FREYMANN, JOHN GORDON, physician, educator; b. Omaha, Apr. 9, 1922; s. John Joseph and Marion (Wicks) F.; m. Ruth Ellen King, Dec. 16, 1950; children: Amanda, Martha, Sarah, Vance. BS, Yale U., 1944; MD, Harvard U., 1946; DSc, U. Nebr., 1982. Diplomate Am. Bd. Internal Medicine and Oncology. Asst. in medicine Mass. Gen. Hosp., Boston, 1954-59; dir. med. edn. Meml. Hosp., Worcester, Mass., 1959-65; gen dir. Boston Hosp. for Women, 1965-69; dir. edn. Hartford (Conn.) Hosp., 1969-75; pres. Nat. Fund for Med. Edn., Hartford, 1975-87; prof. dept. family medicine Sch. of Medicine U. Conn., Farmington, 1987—; pres. Ednl. Commn. for Fgn. Med. Grads., Phila., 1968-77; cons. div. manpower intelligence HEW, Washington, 1973-75; advisor nat. health ins. House Ways & Means Com., U.S. Congress, Washington, 1975. Author: American Health Care System, 1974 (Welch award 1975); author chpts. in books; contbr. numerous articles to profl. jours. Mem. Wayland (Mass.) Bd. of Health, 1957-69; treas. Farmington Land Trust Inc., 1978-91. Lt. USPHS, 1947-49, ETO. Commonwealth Fund grantee, 1970; recipient Welch Meml. award Nat. Assn. Blue Shield Plans, 1975, John E. Leonard award Assn. for Hosp. Med. Edn., 1981. Fellow ACP; mem. AMA (adv. com. grad. med. edn. 1969-75), Assn. Am. Med. Colls., Soc. Med. Adminstrs., Am. Assn. for History of Medicine, Alpha Omega Alpha, Phi Beta Kappa. Home: 2 Catalpa Ct Avon CT 06001-4510

FREZZA, CHRISTINE ANNE, theater music composer; b. Rochdale, Eng., May 22, 1942; d. James Gaymond and Fanny (Leach) Chester; m. Daniel August Frezza, Sept. 29, 1973. MusB, U. Victoria, B.C., Can., 1967, MFA in Theatre, 1970; PhD in Theatre, U. Pitts., 1982. Guest artist U. Pitts. Theatre, 1981-85; resident composer Three Rivers Shakespeare Festival, Pitts., 1980—; lectr. U. Pitts. Theatre Arts, 1986—; planning adminstr. Three Rivers Shakespeare Festival, Pitts., 1986—; resident composer Utah Shakespearean Festival, Cedar City, Utah, 1985—; composer in field. Composer: Two Gentlemen of Verona, 1987, Cloud Nine, 1985, Twelfth Night, 1985, Hearts and Diamonds, 1980. Grantee Pa. Coun. on Arts, 1983, 81. Home: 241 S Pacific Ave Pittsburgh PA 15224-1719 Office: U Pitts Theatre Arts CL1617 Pittsburgh PA 15260

FRIARY, DONALD RICHARD, museum administrator; b. Boston, Aug. 27, 1940; s. William Harold and Anne Therese (Sullivan) F.; m. Grace Therese Gayzur, June 7, 1969; children: Donald Richard, Elizabeth Grace McCullough. AB in Am. Civilization, Brown U., 1962; AM, U. Pa., 1963, PhD, 1971. Manuscript catalogue Boston Pub. Libr., 1962-64; head tutor Historic Deerfield, Inc., Deerfield, Mass., 1965-71, dir. edn., 1971-75, asst. dir., 1973-75, exec. dir., sec., 1975—; asst. prof. history SUNY, New Paltz, 1966-71. Trustee, v.p. Dublin (N.H.) Seminar for New Eng. Folklife, 1976-85; bd. dirs. Mass. Found. for Humanities, South Hadley, 1983-89; mem. acad. affairs com. Henry Francis du Pont Winterthur Mus., Del., 1986—; trustee Williamstown (Mass.) Regional Art Conservation Lab., 1991—. Mem. Am. Antiquarian Soc., Colonial Soc. Mass., Franklin County C. of C. (bd. dirs. 1980-86), St. Botolph Club. Democrat. Roman Catholic. Home: David Dickinson House Deerfield MA 01342 Office: Historic Deerfield Inc The Street PO Box 321 Deerfield MA 01342-0321

FRICANO, JOHN CHARLES, lawyer; b. Rochester, N.Y., Oct. 10, 1930; s. Anthony J. and Lena (O'Geen) F.; m. Mary Elizabeth Fricano nee Kelly, Sept. 11, 1954; children: Lisa C., Christopher A. BS cum laude, Mt. St. Mary's Coll., Emmitsburg, Md., 1953; JD, Fordham U., 1956. Bar: D.C. 1977, N.Y. 1956, U.S. Supreme Ct. 1961, U.S. Ct. Appeals (D.C. and 2d cirs.) 1978, U.S. Ct. Appeals (3d cir.) 1985, U.S. Ct. Appeals (4th cir.) 1958, U.S. Ct. Appeals (8th and 9th cirs.) 1981, U.S. Dist. Ct. D.C. 1977, U.S. Dist. Ct. Md. 1957, U.S. Dist. Ct. (we. dist.) Pa. 1974, U.S. Dist. Ct. (so. dist.) N.Y. 1976, U.S. Dist. Ct. (ea. dist.) N.Y. 1986. Trial atty. antitrust div. Dept. Justice, Washington, 1956-73; chief trial sect. antitrust div. Dept. Justice, 1973-76; ptnr. Skadden, Arps, Slate, Meagher & Flom, Washington, 1976—; mem. antitrust and trade adv. bd. Bur. Nat. Affairs, Washington, 1979—, corp. practice series adv. bd., 1986—, civil editor Racketeer Influenced and Corrupt Orgns. Act Law Reporter, 1984—, chmn. civil adv. bd. Racketter Influenced and Corrupt Orgn. Report, Bur. of Nat. Affairs, 1985—; faculty trial practice programs for lawyers Columbia Law Sch., 1978-81. Editor: RICO Strategies, 1986; editor Fordham Law Rev., 1956; contbr. articles to profl. jours. Mem. ABA, City Club. Republican. Roman Catholic. Office: Skadden Arps Slate Meagher & Flom 1440 New York Ave NW Washington DC 20005-2111

FRICKE, RICHARD JOHN, lawyer; b. Ithaca, N.Y., Apr. 17, 1945; s. Richard I. and Jeanne L. (Hines) F.; m. Carol A. Borelli, June 17, 1967 (div. 1990); children—Laura, Richard, Amanda; m. Penny Yrizarry, Dec. 29, 1990; 1 child: Stephanie. B.A., Cornell U., 1967, J.D., 1970. Bar: Conn. 1970. Assoc., Gregory & Adams, Wilton, Conn., 1970-73; ptnr. Crehan & Fricke, Ridgefield, Conn., 1973-90; corp. counsel Safe Alternatives Corp. of Am., Inc., T.F.I. Industries, Inc.; dir. Village Bank & Trust Co.; town atty. Town of Ridgefield, 1973-81. Bd. dirs. Ridgefield Community Ctr., Ridgefield Montessori, Ridgefield Community Kindergarten; founder, pres. Ridgefield Lacrosse League; mem. Conn. Bar Commn. on Women, 1976. Mem. ABA, Conn. Bar Assn., Danbury Bar Assn. Democrat. Roman Catholic. Co-patentee low reactive pressure foam, polyurethane foam for cellulostic products. Home: 25 Buckingham Ridge Rd Wilton CT 06897

FRICKE, ROGER ALAN, equestrian products manufacturing executive; b. Blantyre, Nyasaland, British Central Africa, Mar. 9, 1942 (parents Am. citizens); s. Charles Henry and Helen Josephine (Holzhauer) F.; m. Sarah Benton, Feb. 10, 1967; 1 child, Gretchen Melinda. BBA, Baylor U., 1963. Ter. mgr. indsl. tape Polyken div. Kendall Corp., 1965-70; dist. sales mgr., bus. mgr., asst. zone mgr. Chrysler Corp., Phila., 1970-76; dist. sales mgr. Mid-Atlantic states Winnebago Corp., Phila., 1976-78; regional sales mgr. Gulf & Western, North & Judd, 1978-82, nat. sales mgr., 1982; nat. sales and mktg. mgr. Prentice Corp., Laconia, N.H., 1982-83, v.p. mktg., 1983-85; pres. Buckle Down Ltd., 1985—. Served with Intelligence Corps, USN, 1963-65. Mem. Am. Mfrs. Assn. Home: 17 Chetwynd Rd Paoli PA 19301-1817

FRIDAY, DONALD CONRAD, academic administrator; b. Glens Falls, N.Y., July 19, 1947; s. Erwin J. and Vivian H. (Bishop) F.; m. Mary Elizabeth Barrett, Aug. 28, 1971; children: Kristopher Conrad, Kathryn Corrigan. BA, SUNY, Brockport, 1969, MA, 1971. Dir. info. svcs. Finger Lakes C.C., Canandaigua, N.Y., 1981-83, dir., 1983-88, asst. dean, 1988—; chmn. Rochester (N.Y.) Area Coll. Continuing Edn., 1987-88. Mem. Continuing Edn. Assn. of N.Y. (treas. 1989, pres. 1990—), State Coun. on Vocat. Edn., Rotary. Home: 136 Washington St Geneva NY 14456-2890 Office: Finger Lake CC 4355 Lakeshore Dr Canandaigua NY 14424-8395

FRIDAY, ELBERT WALTER, JR., federal agency administrator, meteorologist; b. DeQueen, Ark., July 13, 1939; s. Elbert Walter and Mary Elizabeth (Ward) F.; m. Karen Ann Hauschild, Nov. 14, 1959; children: Kristine Ann, Kelly Sue. BS in Engring. Physics, U. Okla., Norman, 1961, MS in Meteorology, 1967, PhD in Meteorology, 1969. Commd. 2d lt. USAF, 1961, advanced through grades to col., weather officer, 1961-81, dir. environ. and life scis., Dept. Def., 1978-81, ret., 1981; dep. dir. Nat. Weather Svc., Silver Spring, Md., 1981-87, dir., 1987—; mem. com. on low level wind shear NAS, Washington, 1985-86. Contbr. articles to prof. jours. Elder Calvary Christian Ch., Burke, Va., 1985-89, trustee, 1989—. Decorated Bronze Star; recipient Def. Superior Svc. medal Dept. Def., 1981, Presdl. Rank award, 1988. Fellow Am. Meteorol. Soc. (councilor 1988-90); mem. Nat. Weather Assn., Sigma Xi. Office: Dept Commerce Nat Weather Svc 1325 East West Hwy Silver Spring MD 20910

FRIDAY, GILBERT ANTHONY, JR., pediatrician; b. Pitts., Apr. 16, 1930; s. Gilbert Anthony and Susan Dorothy (Kumer) F.; m. Christina Cecilia McShane, Sept. 12, 1959; children: Martin, Peter, Martha, Timothy, Amy, Anne, Robert. BS, Bucknell U., 1952; MD, Temple U., 1956. Diplomate Nat. Bd. Med. Examiners. Rotating intern Phila. Gen. Hosp., 1956-57; pediatric resident Children's Hosp. of Phila., 1960-62; pediatric resident Children's Hosp. of Pitts., 1962-63, asst. med. dir. ops., 1963-66, preceptorship in allergy/immunology, 1962-67; clin. instr. to asst. prof. U. Pitts., 1963-87, clin. assoc. prof., 1987, prof. pediatrics, 1987—; bd. dirs. Pa. Blue Shield, Camp Hill, 1979—, chmn. bd. dirs., 1992. Contbr. articles to profl. jours., chpts. to books. Lt. comdr. USN MC, 1956-66. Wyeth Pediatric scholar. Fellow Am. Coll. Allergy Immunology, Am. Acad. Allergy and Immunology, Am. Acad. Pediatrics; mem. AMA, Allegheny County Med. Soc. (pres. 1987), Pa. Med. Soc., Pa. Allergy Soc. (pres. 1975), Alpha Omega Alpha. Republican. Roman Catholic. Home: 1901 Highgate Rd Pittsburgh PA 15241-2210 Office: Children's Hosp of Pitts 3705 Fifth Ave Pittsburgh PA 15213

FRIDSON, MARTIN STEVEN, finance executive; b. Highland Park, Mich., Sept. 4, 1952; s. Harry Yale and Mariann (Rodd) F.; m. Elaine Rochelle Sisman, June 14, 1981; children: Arielle Amanda, Daniel Wolfe. BA cum laude in History, Harvard U., 1974; MBA, Harvard U., Boston, 1976. Chartered fin. analyst. Trader Mitchell, Hutchins Inc., N.Y.C., 1976-77; asst. v.p. Scandinavian Securities Corp., N.Y.C., 1977-79; v.p. Paine Webber Jackson & Curtis, Inc., N.Y.C., 1980-81, Salomon Bros., Inc., N.Y.C., 1981-84; prin. Morgan Stanley & Co., Inc., N.Y.C., 1984-89; mng. dir. Merrill Lynch & Co., Inc., N.Y.C., 1989—. Author: High Yield Bonds, 1989, Financial Statement Analysis, 1991; editorial bd. Fin. Analysts Jour., N.Y.C., 1989—, CFA Digest, Charlottesville, Va., 1991—; contbr. articles to profl. jours.; author light verse pub. in Playbill, N.Y. Times, Wall St. Jour. Participation chmn. Harvard Coll. Fund, Class of 1974, 1991—; benefit concert com. The InterSch. Orch. of N.Y., N.Y.C., 1991—; v.p. Jane St. Block Assn., N.Y.C., 1979; bd. dirs. Candlewood Landing Condominium Assn., 1991—; mem. adv. coun. Salomon Ctr., NYU, 1991—. Mem. Fixed Income Analysts Soc. (pres. 1984-85), Harvard Bus. Sch. Club (v.p. 1983-84), Assn. for Investment Mgmt. and Rsch., N.Y. Soc. Security Analysts, Fin. Mgmt. Assn., Harvard Club of N.Y., New Milford Racquet and Swim Club. Democrat. Jewish. Home: 250 W 94th St Apt 3G New York NY 10025-6954 Office: Merrill Lynch & Co Inc 250 Vesey St Fl 19 New York NY 10281-1012

FRIED, JEFFREY MICHAEL, health care administrator; b. Kansas City, Mo., Apr. 9, 1953; s. Harvey J. and SuEllen (Weissman) F.; m. Rosalyn Sue Matz. Student, Drake U., 1971-73; BGS, U. Kans., 1975; MHA, Washington U., St. Louis, 1979. Adminstrv. asst. Rsch. Med. Ctr., Kansas City, Mo., 1979-80; asst. to pres. Rsch. Health Svcs., Kansas City, 1980-81; asst. v.p. Sinai Hosp. Balt., 1981-83, Lancaster (Pa.) Gen. Hosp., 1983-85; v.p., chief oper. officer Lancaster (Pa.) Gen. Svcs. Corp., 1985-86, pres., 1986-88; sr. v.p. Lancaster Gen. Hosp., 1989-91, chief operating officer, 1992—; pres., bd. dirs. Lancaster Med. Equipment, Barge Ganse Vena Care; sec., bd. dirs. Preferred Health Care, Lancaster; bd. dirs. Lancaster Diagnostic Imaging, Inc.; v.p., bd. dirs., pres. Welsh Mountain Med. and Dental Ctr., Lancaster, 1989—; mng. ptnr. Rohrerstown Imaging Assocs., Lancaster, 1986—; part-time mem. faculty dept. health adminstrn. and devel. Pa. State U., 1988—, Coll. St Francis, 1988—; bus. adv. coun. Goodwill Industries, 1989—. Mem. Leadership Lancaster, 1987-88; pres., bd. dirs. Lancaster Chpt. Nat. Commn. for Prevention of Child Abuse, 1986—; treas., bd. dirs. Lancaster Jewish Fedn., 1986-91; bd. dirs. Lancaster Jewish Community Ctr., 1989-91, Clinic for Spl. Children, 1991—. Mem. Leadership Lancaster, 1987-88; pres. bd. dirs. Welsh Mt. Med. and Dental Ctr., 1989—; pres. bd. dirs. Lancaster chpt. Nat. Commn. for Prevention of Child Abuse, 1986-89; treas., bd. dirs. Lancaster Jewish Fedn., 1986-89; bd. dirs. Lancaster Jewish Community Ctr., 1989—, Temple Shaarai Shomayim, bd. dirs. Clinic for Spl. Children, 1991—. Fellow Am. Coll. Healthcare Execs. (com. on ethics 1991—); mem. Cen. Pa. Health Care Adminstrs. Jewish. Home: 423 Wetherburn Dr Lancaster PA 17601-2941 Office: Lancaster Gen Hosp 555 N Duke St Lancaster PA 17602-2223

FRIED, LAWRENCE KENNETH, computer systems engineer; b. Rego Park, N.Y., Nov. 6, 1952; s. Jack and Barbara Phyllis (Richner) F.; m. Sandra Rae Mayer, June 10, 1979; children: David Aaron, Rebecca Lainie. BA in Math., Queens Coll., 1973; MS in Computer Sci., Rensselaer Polytech Inst., 1975; MS in Statistics, Rutgers U., 1981. Teaching asst. Rensselaer Polytech. Inst., Troy, N.Y., 1973-75; analyst Loral Electronic Systems, Yonkers, N.Y., 1975-77; mem. tech. staff Bell Telephone Labs., Holmdel, N.J., 1977-81; sr. programmer analyst Morgan Guarantu Trust, N.Y.C., 1981-83; mem. tech. staff AT&T Bell Labs., Holmdel, 1983—; Speaker in field. Jewish. Home: 207 Alden Ct Aberdeen NJ 07747

FRIED, MARTIN L., law educator; b. N.Y.C., Feb. 11, 1934; s. Henry and Martha (Levine) F.; m. Suzanne Patricia Rollins, Jan. 20, 1963 (div. 1975); children: Linda, Marjorie; m. Daisy Streifler, May 28, 1978. BA, Antioch Coll, 1955; LLB, Columbia U., 1958; LLM, NYU, 1968. Bar: N.Y. 1959, U.S. Dist. Ct. (ea. and so. dists.) N.Y. 1959, U.S. Ct. Appeals (2d cir.) 1962, U.S. Tax Ct. 1967. Pvt. practice N.Y.C., 1959-68; assoc. prof. law Syracuse (N.Y.) U., 1968-72, prof., 1972-90, Crandall Melvin Prof. Wills and Trusts, 1990—; assoc. dean coll. law Syracuse U., 1981-83; vis. assoc. prof. U. Iowa, Iowa City, 1971-72; vis. prof. U. Cin., 1974, Washington U., St. Louis, 1978; counsel Weitzner, Levine & Hamburg, N.Y.C., 1986—. Author: Taxation of Securities Transactions, 1971; contbr. articles to profl. jours. Fellow Am. Bar Found.; mem. ABA, N.Y. State Bar Assn., Onondaga County Bar Assn., Soc. Am. Law Tchrs., Am. Law Inst. Jewish. Home: 6110 Royal Birkdale Jamesville NY 13078-9700 Office: Syracuse U Coll Law Ernest I White Hall Syracuse NY 13244-1030

FRIED, RACHEL SHIFRA, accountant; b. Queens, N.Y., Jan. 31, 1968; d. Eli and Gloria W. (Strassheim) Freundlich; m. Daniel Aaron Fried, May 23, 1989; children: Miriam, Sarah. BA, SUNY, Saratoga Springs, 1987. CPA, Ohio. Tax specialist Peat, Marwick, Main & Co., Chgo., 1988; sr. tax specialist Deloitte & Touche, N.Y.C., 1989—.

FRIEDBERG, SIMEON ADLOW, physicist, educator; b. Pitts., July 7, 1925; s. Emanuel B. and Lillian (Adlow) F.; m. Joan Brest, Sept. 4, 1950; children: Elizabeth B., Aaron L., Susan A. A.B., Harvard, 1947; M.S., Carnegie Inst. Tech., 1948, D.Sc., 1951. Fulbright grantee U. Leiden, Netherlands, 1951-52; research physicist Carnegie Inst. Tech., Pitts., 1952-53; mem. faculty Carnegie Inst. Tech., 1953-67, prof. dept. physics, 1962-67; prof. physics Carnegie-Mellon U., Pitts., 1967—; chmn. dept. physics Carnegie-Mellon U., 1973-80. Westinghouse fellow, 1950-51; Alfred P. Sloan Found. research fellow, 1957-61; Guggenheim fellow Imperial Coll., London, Eng., 1965-66. Fellow Am. Phys. Soc., AAAS; mem. Sigma Xi, Tau Beta Pi, Phi Kappa Phi, Pi Mu Epsilon. Home: 1220 S Negley Ave Pittsburgh PA 15217-1219

FRIEDENBERG, DANIEL MEYER, financial investor; b. Mt. Vernon, N.Y., Feb. 24, 1923; s. Samuel and Rose Abravanel (Klein) F.; BS, U. Pa., 1943; m. Maria del Carmen Joy, May 1, 1956 (div. June 1964); children: Samuel Clark, Danielle Joy; m. June Meredith Daniels, Apr. 12, 1965 (div. May 1986); children: Jay Daniels, Bertrand Russell. With John-Platt Enterprises, Inc., N.Y.C., 1947—, pres., 1957—; curator coins and medals Jewish Mus., N.Y.C., 1962-82; emeritus, 1982—; guest lectr. Columbia U., Yale U., Swarthmore Coll., Hebrew U., Jerusalem. Sec. Young Democrats N.Y.C., 1952; exec. dir. N.Y. County Liberal Party, 1945. Served with AUS, 1943-44. Recipient Spl. Achievement award Loeb mag., 1962, Spl. Achievement award Loeb Newspaper, 1965; Heath Literary award distinguished numismatic achievement, 1969; Nat. Jewish Book award, 1988. Fellow Am. Numismatic Soc.; mem. Am. Numismatic Assn. Author: Great Jewish Portraits in Metal, 1963; Jewish Medals from the Renaissance to the Fall of Napoleon, 1970, Jewish Mint Masters & Medalists, 1976, Medieval Jewish Seals from Europe, 1987, Life, Liberty and the Pursuit of Land, 1992; contbr. articles to newspapers and mags. Home: 79 Byram Shore Rd Greenwich CT 06830-6906 Office: 45 Beekman St New York NY 10038

FRIEDLAENDER, JONATHAN SCOTT, anthropology educator; b. New Orleans, La., Aug. 24, 1940; s. Marc and Clara May (Beer) F.; m. Bilge Civelekoglu, Apr. 3, 1971 (div. 1984); 1 child, Mira Asli; m. Rebecca Elizabeth Lewis, June 5, 1986; 1 child, Benjamin Lewis. BA, Harvard Coll., 1962; MA, Harvard U., 1964, PhD, 1969. Postdoctoral fellow U. Wis., Madison, 1969-70, asst. prof., 1970-71; asst. prof. Harvard U., Cambridge, 1971-74, assoc. prof., 1974-76; assoc. prof. Temple U., Phila., 1976-81, prof. of anthropology, 1981—, chmn. anthropology dept., 1988—; cons. VA, Boston, 1973-76; panelist Nat. Acad. Scis., Washington, 1972-74; mem. adv. bd. to trustees Wenner-Gren Found., N.Y.C., 1990—. Author: Patterns of Human Variation, 1975, The Solomon Islands Project, 1985; editor Yearbook of Physical Anthropology, 1991—; contbr. articles to profl. jours. Pres. Phila. Anthropol. Soc., 1990—; mem. Center City Residents Assn., Phila., 1990—. Postdoctoral rsch. grant NSF, 1976, 85; writing grant Commonwealth Book Fund, 1975. Fellow AAAS; mem. Am. Assn. of Phys. Anthropologists (exec. com.), Am. Assn. Human Biologists, Assn. of Social Anthropologists in Oceania. Home: 2114 Delancey Pl Philadelphia PA 19103-6512 Office: Anthropology Dept Temple U Broad and Berks Philadelphia PA 19122

FRIEDLAND, CLAIRE BERTHA, publishing company executive; b. N.Y.C., July 20, 1915; d. Isidore and Annie (Thomashefsky) Edelstein; m. Lester M. Friedland, Sept. 2, 1939; children: Michael, Peter. Student, Hunter Coll., 1937-40, Queens Coll., 1949-52. Asst. prodn. mgr. Book Club Guild, Manhasset, N.Y., 1958-64, Seabury Press, N.Y.C., 1964-68; prodn. mgr. Meredith Corp., N.Y.C., 1968-78; owner Friedland Enterprises, N.Y.C., 1978—. Mem. Nat. Coun. Women (pres. 1989-91), Women's Nat. Book Assn. (Disting. Bookwoman award 1987). Home: 36 East 36th St PHB New York NY 10016

FRIEDLAND, EDWARD CHARLES, orthopedic surgeon; b. N.Y.C., June 23, 1937; s. Solomon and Frances (Goldenberg) F.; m. Kathryn Amy Stern, Sept. 6, 1970; children: Steven Mark, Elizabeth Ann. AB, NYU, 1957; MD, SUNY, N.Y.C., 1961. Diplomate Am. Bd. Orthopedic Surgery. Pvt. practice Fair Lawn, N.J.; clin. asst. prof. Univ. of Medicine and Dentistry of N.J., Newark, 1970—; chmn. dept. orthopedic surgery Bamert Meml. Hosp., Paterson, N.J., 1974-75; attending orthopedic surgeon, Valley Hosp., Ridgewood, N.J., 1976—. Pres. Temple Beth Rishen, Wyckoff, N.J., 1991-93. Capt. USAF, 1963-654. Fellow Am. Coll. Surgeons, Am. Acad. Orthopedic Surgeons; mem. Ea. Orthopedic Assn., N.J. Orthopedic Soc., Bergen County Med. Soc., Zeta Beta Tau, AF&AM. Republican. Jewish. Office: 25-15 Fair Lawn Ave Fair Lawn NJ 07410

FRIEDLAND, HARVEY KARRON, lawyer, investment researcher; b. Bronx, N.Y.C., N.Y., Sept. 17, 1933. BEE, CUNY, 1957; LLB, Bklyn. Law Sch., 1963, JD, 1967. Bar: N.Y. 1964, U.S. Dist. Ct. 1969, U.S. Supreme Ct. 1970; registered profl. engr., N.J.; registered investment advisor. Lawyer, engr. self-employed Princeton Jct., N.J., investment adv. pres., rschr. Author: The Secrets of Successful Stock Picking from Seedlings, 1990, Stock Picking Flash Cards, 1990. Pres. S.I. Dem. Club, Transport Engrs., & Architects. 2d lt. U.S. Army. Mem. Guild Engrs. and Architects.

FRIEDLAND, PAUL JAY, sales executive; b. Ft. Belvoir, Va., Oct. 17, 1961; s. Irvin John and Arlene (Landy) F. BS in Bus., U. Md., 1985. Customer svc. rep. W. Bell & Co., White Oak, Md., 1982-84; sales rep. NCR Corp., Rockville, Md., 1984—. Jewish.

FRIEDLAND, RICHARD STEWART, electronics company executive; b. Pittsfield, Mass., Nov. 27, 1950; s. Armand and Frieda (Sugarman) F.; m. Shelley Mador, Aug. 29, 1971; children: Jason Michael, Nikki Gayle. BS in Acctg., Ohio State U., 1972; MBA in Fin., Seton Hall U., 1985. CPA, N.Y., N.J. Auditor Price Waterhouse & Co., Morristown, N.J., 1972-78; mgr. acctg. policies Gen. Instrument Corp., Clifton, N.J., 1978-80, mgr. fin. reporting, 1980-81, dir. fin. reporting, 1981-83, dir. fin. analysis, 1983-85, dir. treasury ops., 1985-86; v.p., treas. Gen. Instrument Corp., Lyndhurst, N.J., 1987-88, v.p., contr., 1988-90; v.p. fin., contr. Gen. Instrument Corp., N.Y.C., Chgo., 1991-92; v.p. fin., contr., CFO, Gen. Instrument Corp., Chgo., 1992—. Treas., trustee Rehab. Ctr. for Handicapped Children and Adults, Morris Plains, N.J., 1977-86. Mem. N.Y. Soc. CPA's, N.J. Soc. CPA's, Nat. Corp. Treas. Assn. Jewish. Office: Gen Instrument Corp 181 W Madison St Chicago IL 60602

FRIEDLANDER, DONALD, professional engineer; b. Bklyn., Oct. 21, 1940; s. Samuel and Bertha (Levy) F.; m. Charlotte Bernstein, July 2, 1967; children: Sara, Rebecca, Brian, Daniel. B of Mech. Engring., CCNY, 1963; M of Indsl. Mgmt., Polytechnic Inst. Bklyn., 1975. Staff engr. Grumman Aircraft Engring. Corp., Bethpage, N.Y., 1963-65; project engr. Singer Co., Elizabeth, N.J., 1965-66; supervising mech. engr. Schaefer Brewer, Bklyn., 1966-72; cons. engr. Staten Island, N.Y., 1973—; pres. Donald Friedlander, P.E., P.C., Staten Island, 1986—. Bd. dirs. Young Israel of Staten Island, 1988-89, pres. 1987-88, v.p. 1986-87. Mem. N.Y. Soc. Profl. Engrs., IEEE. Office: 1091 Willowbrook Rd Staten Island NY 10314-6514

FRIEDLANDER, HENRY Z., patent lawyer, polymer chemist; b. N.Y.C., May 18, 1925; s. Joseph and Estelle Barr (Zuckert) F.; divorced; children: Jeffrey Dean, Joel Edan. AB, Oberlin Coll., 1948; MS, U. Ill., 1949, PhD, 1952; JD, Fordham U., 1974. Bar: Conn. 1979, N.Y. 1985; U.S. Patent Office, 1975, U.S. Ct. Appeals (fed. cir.), 1979. Rsch. chemist Am. Cyanamid Co., Stamford, Conn., 1952-57; group leader AMF, Stamford, Conn., 1958-65; asst. to corp. dir. rsch. Union Carbide Corp., Tarrytown, N.Y., 1966-78; patent atty. Stauffer Chem. Co., Ardsley, N.Y., 1978-83; sr. patent atty. Lackenbach Siegel Marzullo & Aronson, Scarsdale, N.Y., 1985—; v.p., bd. dirs. 65 Main St. Corp., White Plains, N.Y., 1955-65. Author book chpts.; contbr. rsch. and review articles to profl. jours. Lay leader Stamford (Conn.) Unitarian Ch. With USN, 1944-46, PTO. Mem. Chemists Club N.Y.C. (mem. libr. com.), The Landmark Club, Am. Chem. Soc. (nat. councilor 1982-86), Am. Intellectual Property Soc., River Hills Ski Club. Republican. Unitarian. Home: 85 Riverside Ave Stamford CT 06905-4433 Office: Lackenbach Siegel Marzullo & Aronson 1 Chase Road Scarsdale NY 10583

FRIEDLANDER, JUDITH NAOMI, university dean, anthropology educator; b. N.Y.C., Apr. 10, 1944; d. Martin Friedlander and Silvia Berman Paulson. MA, Harvard U., 1967; BA, U. Chgo., 1966, MA, 1969, PhD, 1973. Asst. prof. SUNY, Purchase, 1972-79, assoc. prof., 1979-80, acting dean and chair, 1980-83, assoc. prof. anthropology, 1983-90; dean social scis., prof. anthropology Hunter Coll., CUNY, 1990—; vis. prof. U. Paris VII, 1976; cons. UNESCO, Paris, 1984-85, N.Y. Coun. for Humanities, 1987, Rockefeller Found., 1988, 89. Author: Being Indian in Hueyapan, 1975, Vilna on the Seine, 1990; co-eidotr: Women in Culture and Politics, 1986; contbr. articles to profl. jours. Organizer Tribunal on Crimes Against Women, N.Y., 1976; one of organizers Internat. Women's Studies Conf., 1979-82. Woodrow Wilson fellow, 1966-67; NDEA Title IV rsch. fellow, U. Chgo., 1968-71; Wenner-Gren Found. rsch. fellow, 1971, 79, 85; NEH rsch. fellow, 1985; Rockefeller Found. grantee, 1982. Fellow Am. Anthropol. Assn.; mem. Jewish Am. Studies Assn., The Yivo Inst., Columbia U. Seminar on Women and Soc. (chairperson 1981-82). Democrat Jewish. Office: Hunter Coll CUNY 695 Park Ave New York NY 10021

FRIEDMAN, ABIGAIL SARAH, diplomat; b. Washington, July 9, 1956; d. Abraham S. and Diana (Scott) F.; m. Eric Martin Passaglia, Sept. 4, 1983; children: Abraham, Martha. BA, Harvard U., 1977; JD, Georgetown U., 1982. Law clk. U.S. Senate Office of Legal Counsel, Washington, 1982-83; staff atty. AYUDA Legal Aid, Washington, 1984-86; diplomat U.S. Dept. of State, Washington, 1988—; polit. officer U.S. Dept. of State, U.S. Embassy, Tokyo, 1992-94.

FRIEDMAN, ABRAHAM S(OLOMON), chemist, consultant; b. N.Y.C., Oct. 25, 1921; s. Israel H. and Sarah G. (Cohen) F.; m. Diana Elena Scott, July 4, 1952; children: Danielle, Rebecca, Abigail, Michelle. AB, CUNY, 1943; PhD, Ohio State U., 1950. Rsch. assoc., dept. chemistry Ohio State U., Columbus, 1950-51; rsch. prof. U. Amsterdam, Netherlands, 1951-52; phys. chemist Nat. Bur. Standards, Washington, 1952-56; sr. chemist U.S. Atomic Energy Commn., Washington, 1956-62; European Sci. Rep. U.S. Atomic Energy Commn., Paris, 1962-65; from dep. dir. to dir. div. internat. affairs AEC, Washington, 1965-75; asst. adminstr. acctg. ERDA, Washington, 1975; sci. counselor U.S. Dept. State, various cities, various countries, 1975-83; cons. Washington, 1984—; sr. advisor U.S. Del. to IAEA, Vienna, Austria, 1969-73; alt. U.S. rep. IAEA Gen. Conf., Vienna, 1974; rsch. prof. dept. physics Cath. U., Washington, 1984-86; vis. prof. office sci. policy, George Washington U., Washington, 1990. Co-author: Ideal Gas Thermo. Functions, 1961; contbr. articles to profl. jours. Sgt. Manhattan Project, AUS, 1943-46. Decorated Order of Merit (France); recipient Disting. Alumnus award Bklyn. Coll., CUNY, 1969. Mem. Cosmos Club. Home and Office: 6305 Phyllis Ln Bethesda MD 20817-5809

FRIEDMAN, ALAN HERBERT, ophthalmologist; b. N.Y.C., 1937; B.A. in Chemistry with honors, Cornell U., 1959; M.D. (summer fellow NIH 1960, 62-63), N.Y.U., 1963; m. Sandra Yasser, 1960; children: David, Jonathan, Lisa, Jennifer. Intern in medicine Bellevue Hosp., N.Y.C., 1963-64; resident in ophthalmology N.Y.U. Med. Ctr., 1966-69, fellow ophthalmic pathology, 1969-70; research fellow histochemistry Royal Postgrad. Med. Sch., London, 1972; practice medicine specializing in ophthalmology, N.Y.C., 1970—; attending ophthalmologist and pathologist Mt. Sinai Hosp.; attending ophthalmologist Israel Med. Ctr.; clin. prof. ophthalmology and pathology, dir. eye pathology lab. Mt. Sinai Sch. Medicine; assoc. examiner Am. Bd. Ophthalmology; cons. in field. Contbr. numerous articles to profl. pubs. With M.C., USAR, 1964-66. Diplomate Am. Bd. Ophthalmology. Fellow ACS, Coll. Ophthalmologists London, Am. Acad. Ophthalmology (Sr. Honor award 1991), N.Y. Acad. Medicine, N.Y. Acad. Scis., Royal Soc. Medicine; mem. AMA, Am. Ophthal. Soc., French Ophthal. Soc., Assn. Research Vision and Ophthalmology, Am. Assn. Ophthalmic Pathologists, N.Y. County Med. Soc., Med. Soc. State N.Y., Eastern Ophthalmic Pathology Soc., Pan Am. Assn. Ophthalmology. Address: Mt Sinai Sch Medicine 1 Gustave Levy Pl Box 1183 New York NY 10029-6574 also: 888 Park Ave New York NY 10021

FRIEDMAN, ALAN JACOB, museum director; b. Bklyn., Nov. 15, 1942; s. George and Eleanor (Goldberger) F.; m. Mickey Thompson, Dec. 26, 1966. BS in Physics, Ga. Inst. Tech., 1964; PhD in Physics, Fla. State U., 1970. Research asst. Ga. Inst. Tech., Atlanta, 1960-64, Fla. State U., Tallahassee, 1964-69; asst. prof. Hiram (Ohio) Coll., 1969-74; dir. astronomy

and physics Lawrence Hall of Sci. U. Calif., Berkeley, 1973-84; conseiller scientifique Cite des Scis. et de l'Industrie, Paris, 1982-84; dir. N.Y. Hall of Sci., Corona, 1984—; vis. asst. prof. Am. studies and English Temple U., Phila, 1975; research fellow English dept. U. Calif., Berkeley, 1972-73; vis. lectr. English dept. San Franicsco State U., 1974-75. Co-author: Planetarium Educator's Workshop Guide, 1980, Einstein as Myth and Muse, 1985, Planetarium Activities for Student Success (8 vols.), 1990; mem. editorial bd. Jour. Modern Lit. Younger Humanist fellow NEH, 1972-73; recipient Disting. Service award Mid-Atlantic Planetarium Soc., 1982, Merit award Astron. Assn. No. Calif., 1983. Fellow Internat. Planetarium Soc. (Svc. award 1990); mem. Am. Assn. Physics Tchrs., Am. Assn. Mus., N.Y. State Assn. Mus. (councillor), Internat. Planetarium Soc. (pres. 1985-86), Assn. Sci.-Tech. Ctrs. (bd. dirs.), Phi Beta Kappa. Office: NY Hall Sci 47-01 111th St Flushing NY 11368

FRIEDMAN, ARNOLD CARL, diagnostic radiologist; b. Bronx, N.Y., Nov. 17, 1951; s. Isidore and Helen and (Lowenthal) F.; m. Wendy Sue Corn, June 8, 1975; children: Jeffrey Jonathan. BA in Chemistry, Cornell U., 1972; MD, Albert Einstein Coll., 1975. Intern Mt. Sinai Hosp., Hartford, Conn., 1975-76; resident Montefiore Hosp., Bronx, N.Y., 1976-79; asst. prof. Uniformed Svcs. U., Bethesda, Md., 1979-83; assoc. prof. George Washington U., Washington, 1983-84; assoc. prof. Temple U., Phila., 1984-88, prof. radiology, 1989—. Editor: Radiology of Liver, Spleen, Pancreas, Biliary Tract, 1987, Clinical Pelvic Imaging, 1990. Mem. Radiologic Soc. N.Am., Am. Roentgen Ray Soc., Assn. Univ. Radiologists, Assn. Ultrasound in Medicine, Soc. Gastrointestinal Radiology. Home: 524 Hoffman Dr Bryn Mawr PA 19010-1745

FRIEDMAN, ARNOLD S., newspaper editor; b. N.Y.C., Dec. 17, 1929; s. Milton and Edith (Ramer) F.; m. Bette M. Harris, Dec. 10, 1950; children—David Alan, Marc Harris. B.S., Syracuse U., 1950. Reporter, editor L.I. Press, Jamaica, N.Y., 1950-70, assoc. editor, 1970-75; editor Springfield Union-News/Sunday Republican, Springfield, Mass., 1975—; exec. com. Spirit of Springfield, Inc., 1989—; bd. dirs. Mass. Children's Trust Fund, 1991—. Pres. Community Music Sch. of Springfield, Mass. 1983-89, treas., 1991—; v.p. Upper State St. Community Devel. Corp., Springfield, 1980-86; trustee Baystate Med. Ctr., Springfield, 1979-88; mem. exec. com. United Way of Pioneer Valley, Springfield, 1980-91; mem. Mass. Bd. Regents of Higher Edn., 1980-82; chmn. child abuse focus com. Community Health Edn. Council for Children & Adolescents, Springfield, 1983-84; mem. New Eng. Regional Bd. Anti-Defamation League of B'nai B'rith, 1976—; mem. exec. com. World Affairs Council Western Mass., 1984-87; bd. dirs. Springfield Adult Edn. Council, 1978-91, Westfield State Coll. Found., 1982—, Temple Beth El, Springfield, Mass.; sec. Western Mass. Profl. Standards Rev. Orgn., 1980-85; bd. dirs. United Cerebral Palsy Western Mass., 1987-90, Ct. Appointed Spl. Advocates; clk. Spirit Springfield Inc. Mem. Am. Soc. Newspaper Editors, New Eng. Soc. Newspaper Editors, New Eng. AP News Execs. Assn., AP Mng. Editors Assn., Mass. Bar Assn. (press bench bar com.), Greater Springfield C. of C. (exec. com. 1977-83). Jewish. Office: Springfield Union News 1860 Main St Springfield MA 01103-1073

FRIEDMAN, BARBARA MARIE, university administrator; b. N.Y.C., Aug. 13, 1949. BA in English, Monmouth Coll., 1971; MS in Edn., Ind. U., 1973. Cert. counselor; cert. career counselor. Asst. dean women Shippensburg (Pa.) State U., 1973-77; community affairs advisor off campus coll. SUNY, Binghamton, N.Y., 1977-78, asst. dir. career devel. lab., 1978-84; dir. SUNY, Binghamton, 1984—. Mem. Mid. Atlantic Placement Assn., SUNY Career Devel. Orgn. Office: SUNY Career Devel Ctr PO Box 6013 Binghamton NY 13902-6013

FRIEDMAN, DANIEL MARK, sales executive; b. N.Y.C., Apr. 4, 1958; s. Enid Ansell and Mortimor Geisler; s. Lawrence Friedman; m. Holly Cooperstein, Dec. 8, 1984; children: Lindsay, Amanda. BS in Mktg., Am. U., 1980. Exec. in tng. Bloomingdales, N.Y.C., 1980-81, asst. buyer, dept. mgr., 1981-82; exec. v.p. sales Rayman-Ridless Product Group, N.Y.C., 1982-87; pres. Crown Pacific U.S.A., Inc., N.Y.C., 1987—. Republican. Home: 6 Kristi Ln Woodbury NY 11797-2210 Office: Crown Pacific 16 W 32d St New York NY 10001

FRIEDMAN, DIAN DEBRA, educator; b. Balt., June 12, 1943; d. Bernard Maurice and Sondra Seletta (Dolgoff) Jacobs; m. Irving Joel Friedman, June 24, 1965; children: Benjamin Aaron, Joshua Jason. AA, Miami (Fla.)-Dade Jr. Coll., 1963; BS in Elem. Edn., Fla. State U., 1965. With contracts and grants Fla. State U., Tallahassee, 1965-66; substitute tchr. Chicopee (Mass.) Sch. Systems, 1965-66; elem. tchr. City of Springfield, Mass., 1966-76; real estate salesperson Gene Kelly Real Estate, Suffield, Conn., 1985-87; ednl. tutor Suffield (Conn.) Sch. System, 1987—; curriculum coun. Suffield Sch. System, 1986-90. Bd. dirs. Child and Family Svcs., Inc., Hartford, Conn., 1986—, fin. resources com., 1988—; bd. dirs. Child and Family Charities, Inc., Hartford; chairperson Suffield Aux. Child and Family Svcs., 1978-80, mem. 1973—; mem. Citizens for Suffield, 1990—, Friends of Suffield Libr., 1973—. Mem. Fla. State Alumni Club. Democrat. Jewish. Home: 119 Marbern Dr Suffield CT 06078-1542

FRIEDMAN, DOROTHY FOSTER, education educator; b. Bridgeport, Conn., Apr. 12, 1940; d. John Wesley Reedy and Dorothy Elizabeth (Hardy) Johnson; m. Charles Ray Foster, Nov. 22, 1962 (div. June 1974); 1 child, Alison Elizabeth; m. Robin Allan Friedman, June 4, 1978; 1 child, Rebecca Claire. BA, Fla. State U., 1961; MA, U. Del., 1967; PhD, U. Okla., 1971. Tchr., ninth grade Ribault Sr. High Sch., Jacksonville, Fla., 1962-63, Alfred I. duPont High Sch., Jacksonville, 1964-65; spl. instr. U. Okla., Norman, 1965-69; asst. prof. Mo. Western Coll., St. Joseph, 1969-72, Fed. City Coll. (now Univ. D.C.), Washington, 1972-78, 82—; tutorial coord. U. Md., College Park, 1978-80; consulting editor Grad. Studies Jour., Washington, 1983-84; text reviewer Wadsworth Pubs., Belmont, Calif., 1983-85, Houghton-Mifflin Pubs., N.Y.C., 1991.; panelist convs. in field. Chmn. com., instr. Saul Bendit Adult Inst., Congregation Beth El, Bethesda, Md., 1977-91; com. chmn. Hebrew Acad. PTA, Silver Springs, Md., 1988-90; bd. dirs. Opera Americana, Alexandria, Va., 1991. Recipient poetry prize Acad. Am. Poets, U. Del., 1962, 2nd prize poetry, Jacksonville Arts Festival, 1964. Mem. Modern Langs. Assn., Southeastern Modern Langs. Assn., Coll. English Assn., Nat. Coun. Tchrs. of English, NEA, Girl Scouts Am. Democrat. Jewish. Office: Univ of DC 4200 Connecticut Ave NW Washington DC 20008-1174

FRIEDMAN, EDGAR, actuary; b. N.Y.C., Oct. 8, 1964; s. Gabriel and Eva (Merritt) F.; m. Joyce Lynn Fisher, Aug. 7, 1988. BA in Math., Johns Hopkins U., 1985. Enrolled actuary. Asst. actuary William M. Mercer, Inc., N.Y.C., 1987—. Vol. Village Vis. Neighbors, Forest Hills, N.Y., 1989. Mem. Soc. Actuaries (assoc.). Office: William M Mercer Inc 1166 Ave Of The Americas New York NY 10036-2708

FRIEDMAN, ESTELLE RAPPORT, psychologist; b. N.Y.C., Aug. 4, 1926; d. Nathan and Leah (Rosensweig) Rapport; widowed; children: Howard, Michael, Daniel, Leona, Gerald. BA, Queens Coll., 1945; MS, Columbia U., 1946; PhD, Queens Coll., 1975. Diplomate Am. Bd. Med. Psychotherapists, fellow; lic. psychologists, Conn. Clin. psychologists Utica (N.Y.) State Hosp., 1948-49; rsch. assoc. Greystone project Columbia U., N.Y., N.J., 1949; clin. psychologist Southbury (Conn.) Tng. Sch., 1957-64, Conn. Dept. Health, Hartford, 1964-82, Norwich (Conn.) Hosp., 1982-89; rsch. assoc. dept. psychiatry Yale U., New Haven, 1989—; adj. prof. Quinnipac Coll., Hamden, Conn., 1989—. Book reviewer Psychiat. Quar., Utica, 1948-68, Am. Jour. Mental Deficiency, N.Y., 1975-82. Mem. adv. bd. New Haven Assn. for Retarded Citizens, 1980-81. Mem. Conn. Psychol. Assn. (program chair, sec. 1981-85), Am. Psychol. Assn., Am. Psychol. Soc. (charter), Ea. Psychol. Assn. Home: 419 Norton Pky New Haven CT 06511-2828 Office: Quinnipiac Coll Mt Carmel Ave Hamden CT 06518-1904

FRIEDMAN, GENE, information systems specialist; b. N.Y.C., July 26, 1958; s. Isaac and Regina (Schifflinger) F. AS in Acctg., Westchester Coll., 1980; MS in Mgmt. Info. Systems, Mercy Coll., 1983; MS in Computer Sci., Pace U., 1985. Programmer Computer Scis. Internat., N.Y.C., 1983-84; programmer/analyst Mutual Benefit Life Ins., N.Y.C., 1985-86; mgr. mgmt. info. systems Citibank, N.Y.C., 1986—; cons. Best Systems Co., Bronx, N.Y., 1986—. Home: 237 W 259th St Bronx NY 10471-1922 Office: Citibank 850 3d Ave 3/1 New York NY 10043

FRIEDMAN, GERALD MANFRED, geologist, educator; b. Berlin, July 23, 1921; came to U.S., 1946, naturalized, 1950; s. Martin and Frieda (Cohn) F.; m. Sue Tyler Theilheimer, June 27, 1948; children: Judith Fay Friedman Rosen, Sharon Mira Friedman Azaria, Devorah Paula Friedman Zweibach, Eva Jane Friedman Scholle, Wendy Tamar Friedman Spanier. Student, U. Cambridge, Eng., 1938-39; BSc, U. London, Eng., 1945, DSc, 1977; MA, Columbia U., 1950, PhD, 1952; Dr rer nat (hon.), U. Heidelberg, Fed. Republic Germany, 1986. Lectr. Chelsea Coll., London, 1944-45; analytical chemist E.R. Squibb & Sons, New Brunswick, N.J., also J. Lyons & Co., London, 1945-48; asst. geology Columbia U., 1950; temporary geologist N.Y. State Geol. Survey, 1950; instr., then asst. prof. geology U. Cin., 1950-54; cons. geologist Sault Ste. Marie, Ont., Can., 1954-56; mem. rsch. dept. Pan Am. Petroleum Corp. (Amoco), Tulsa, 1956-64; sr. rsch. scientist Pan Am. Petroleum Corp. (Amoco), 1956-60, rsch. assoc., 1960-62, supr. sedimentary geology rsch., 1962-64; Fulbright vis. prof. geology Hebrew U., Jerusalem, Israel, 1964; prof. geology Rensselaer Poly. Inst., 1964-84, prof. emeritus, 1984—; prof. geology Bklyn. Coll., 1985-88, Disting. prof. geology, 1988—; prof. earth and environ. scis. Grad. Sch. CUNY, 1985-88, disting. prof. earth and environ. scis., 1988—; pres. Gerry Exploration Inc., 1982—; rsch. scientist Hudson Labs., Columbia, 1965, 66-69, rsch. assoc. dept. geology, 1968-73; vis. prof. U. Heidelberg, 1967; cons. scientist Inst. Petroleum Rsch. and Geophysics, Israel, 1967-71; lectr. Oil & Gas Cons. Internat., 1968—; pres. Northeastern Sci. Found. Inc., 1979—; vis. scientist Geol. Survey of Israel, 1970-73, 78; mem. Com. Sci. Soc. Pres., 1974-76; Gerald M. Friedman post-doctoral fellowship, Inst. Earth Scis., Hebrew U., Israel, 1990. Co-author: Principles of Sedimentology (Outstanding Acad. Books, Choice, 1979), 1978, Exploration for Carbonate Petroleum Reservoirs, 1982, Exercises in Sedimentology, 1982, Principles of Sedimentary Deposits: Stratigraphy and Sedimentology, 1992; pub. Northeastern Environ. Sci., 1982-90; editor: Jour. Sedimentary Petrology, 1964-70 (Best Paper award 1961, hon. mention 1964, 66), Northeastern Geology, 1979—, Earth Scis. History, 1982—, Carbonates and Evaporites, 1986—, 10th Internat. Congress on Sedimentology, 1978; sect. co-editor: Chem. Abstracts, 1962-69, abstractor, 1952-69; editorial bd. Jour. Geol. Edn., 1951-55, Sedimentary Geology, 1967—, Israel Jour. Earth Scis, 1971-76, Coral Reef Newsletter, 1973-75, Jour. Geology, 1977—, GeoJour., 1977-83, Facies, 1987—; contbg. co-editor: Carbonate Sedimentology in Central Europe, 1968, Hypersaline Ecosystems: The Gavish Sabkha, 1985; editor, contbr.: Depositional Environments in Carbonate Rocks, 1969; co-editor: Modern Carbonate Environments, 1983, Lecture Notes in Earth Scis., 1985—; contbr. articles to profl. jours. Mem. phys. edn. com., judo instr. Tulsa YMCA, 1958-63; adviser, instr. Judo Club, Rensselaer Poly. Inst., 1964-84; bd. dirs. Troy Jewish Community Coun., 1966-72, 74-77; v.p. Temple Beth El, 1986-89, pres., 1989-91, bd. dirs., 1965-76; bd. dirs. Leo Baeck Inst., N.Y.C., 1986—. Named hon. alumnus dept. geology Bklyn. Coll., 1989; grantee Office Naval Rsch., AEC, Dept. Energy, Petroleum Rsch. Fund, N.Y. Gas Assn. Fellow AAAS (chmn. geology and geography 1978-79, councillor 1979-80), Mineral. Soc. Am. (mem. nominating com. for fellows 1967-69, awards com. 1977-78), Geol. Soc. Am. (sr., chmn. sect. program com. 1969, candidate sect. chmn. 1969, publs. com. 1980-82), Geol. Soc. London (life, chartered geologist), Geol. Assn. Can., Soc. Econ. Geologists (sr.); mem. Am. Inst. Profl. Geologists (cert.), Am. Chem. Soc. (group leader 1962-63), Mineral. Soc. of Gt. Brit. (abstractor mineralogical abstracts 1963-64), Am. Assn. Petroleum Geologists (nat. hon. mem. 1990, Nat. Disting. Svc. award 1988, chmn. carbonate rock com. 1965-69, mem. rsch. com. 1965-71, 76-82, lectr. continuing 967—, adv. coun. 1974-75, Disting. lectr. 1972-73, mem. disting. lectr. com. 1975-78, membership com. 1982-86, ho. of dels. 1977-80, 83-87, 91—, alt. del. 1987-90, sect. sec. 1979-80, sect. treas. 1980-81, sect. v.p. 1981-82, sect. pres 1982-83, div. profl. affairs rep. from Eastern sect. 1983-84, nat. v.p. 1984-85, cert. petroleum geologist, hon. mem. Eastern sect. 1984, chmn. sect. awards com., 1989—), Soc. for Sedimentary Geology (nat. v.p. 1970-71, pres. 1974-75, sect. pres. 1967-68, Best Paper award Gulf Coast sect. 1974, hon. mention to Outstanding Paper award Jour. Paleontology 1971, hon. mem. 1984), Capital Dist. Geologists Assn. (chmn. program 1966-73), New Eng. Intercollegiate Geol. Conf. (program chmn. 1979), Am. Geol. Inst. (governing bd. 1971-72, 74-75), Geologists' Assn. (life), Internat. Assn. Sedimentologists (v.p. 1971-75, pres. 1975-78, nat. corr. U.S.A. 1971-73, hon. mem. 1982), Geol. Soc. Israel (hon.), Indian Assn. Sedimentologists (mem. governing coun. 1978-82), Geol. Vereinigung, Soc. Venezolana Historia Geociencias (internat. corr. mem.), Nat. Assn. Geology Tchrs. (nat. treas. 1951-55, pres. Okla. 1962-63, pres. Ea. sect. 1983-84), Assn. Earth Sci. Editors (v.p. 1970-71, pres. 1971-72, chairperson 1991), N.Y. State Geol. Assn. (pres. 1978-79), Cin. Mineral Soc. (v.p. 1953-54), U.S. Judo Fedn. (San Dan), Okla. Judo Fedn. (pres. 1959-60, v.p. 1961-64), Empire State Judo Assn. (v.p. 1975-77, dir. coll. devel. 1972-82), Kodokan (Japan), Sigma Gamma Epsilon (nat. v.p. 1978-82, nat. pres 1982-86, nat. hon. mem. 1986), Sigma Xi (v.p. Rensselaer chpt. 1969-70). Home: 32 24th St Troy NY 12180-1915

FRIEDMAN, HOWARD SAMUEL, cardiologist educator; b. N.Y.C., Dec. 27, 1940; s. Harry and Bella Esther (Israel) F.; m. Maud Tanowitz, June 18, 1961; children: Shawn Marcus, Saroya Danielle, Heather Eve. BA, Bklyn. Coll., 1962; MD, SUNY, Buffalo, 1966. Intern St. Louis City Hosp., 1966-67; asst. resident Barnes Hosp., St. Louis, 1967-68; asst. resident Mt. Sinai Hosp., N.Y., 1968-69, resident cardiology, 1969-70, 72-73; acting chief cardiology VA Hosp., Bronx, N.Y., 1974-76; chief cardiology Bklyn. Hosp. Ctr., 1977-90; chmn. dept. medicine L.I. Coll. Hosp., Bklyn., 1990—; prof. medicine SUNY Health Sci. Ctr. at Bklyn., 1987—. Contbr. articles to profl. jours. Dir. AMA N.Y.C. Affiliate Bd., 1985-88; chmn. Coronary Care Com., 1982-88. Fellow Am. Coll. Physicians, Am. Heart Assn., Am. Coll. Cardiology; mem. Am. Physiology Soc., Soc. for Exptl. Biology and Medicine. Democrat. Jewish. Home: 401 E 84th St New York NY 10028-6268 Office: L I Coll Hosp 340 Henry St Brooklyn NY 11201-5525

FRIEDMAN, JAY, sexuality educator, author; b. Smithtown, N.Y., Nov. 27, 1963; s. David Harry and Gloria (Larkin) F. BA, Cornell U., 1984; postgrad. in edn., U. Vt., 1992—. Cert. sexuality educator. Legal asst. Cohn and Marks, Washington, 1984-85; sexuality educator Planned Parenthood of Tompkins County, Ithaca, N.Y., 1985-88; dir. edn. Planned Parenthood of No. New England, Burlington, Vt., 1988—; dir. Inst. on Relationships, Intimacy and Sexuality, South Burlington, Vt., 1988—; cons. in field. Contbr. articles to profl. jours. Rsch. asst. Coun. Hemispheric Affairs, Washington, 1983. Recipient Editor Press award Jour. Am. Coll. Health, 1992. Mem. Sex Info. and Edn. Coun. U.S., Am. Assn. Sex Educators, Counselors and Therapists, Soc. for Sci. Study of Sex. Office: Inst Relationships Intimacy and Sexuality 125 Kennedy Dr #36 Georgetown South Burlington VT 05403-6716

FRIEDMAN, JEROME ISAAC, physics educator, researcher; b. Chgo., Mar. 28, 1930; married, 1956; 4 children. A.B., U. Chgo., 1950, M.S., 1953, Ph.D. in Physics, 1956. Research assoc. in physics U. Chgo., 1956-57; research assoc. in physics Stanford U., Calif., 1957-60; from asst. prof. to assoc. prof. MIT, Cambridge, 1960-67, prof. physics, 1967—, dir. lab. nuclear sci., 1980-83, head dept. physics, 1983-88. Recipient Nobel prize in physics, 1990. Fellow Am. Phys. Soc., Am. Acad. Arts and Scis. (co-recipient W.H.K. Panofsky prize 1989); mem. NAS. Office: MIT Dept Physics Cambridge MA 02139

FRIEDMAN, JOEL MATTHEW, oral and maxillofacial surgeon, educator; b. Chelsea, Mass., Sept. 20, 1942; s. Abraham and Theda (Epstein) F.; m. Gail Fishman, Dec. 18, 1965 (div. 1981); 1 child, Alison Beth; m. Carole Nadan, May 31, 1981 (dec.); m. Susan K. Shavin, Dec., 1991. B.A., Hofstra U., 1964; D.D.S., Columbia U., 1968. Diplomate Am. Bd. Oral and Maxillofacial Surgery. Intern, Bronx Mcpl. Hosp.-Albert Einstein Coll. Medicine, 1968-69, resident in oral and maxillofacial surgery, 1969-71; practice dentistry specializing in oral surgery, Bronx, N.Y., 1971—; dir. oral and maxillofacial surgery Bronx Mcpl. Hosp., 1971-78, dir. house-staff edn., 1971-78, dir. oral and maxillofacial surgery, 1978—; assoc. clin. prof. denistry Albert Einstein Coll. of Medicine, 1976—; asst. dir. oral and maxillofacial surgery Albert Einstein Coll. Medicine-Montefiore Med. Ctr., 1983—; dir. oral & maxillofacial surgery Yonkers Gen. Hosp., 1988; vice-chmn. oral and maxillofacial surgery St. Johns Riverside Hosp., Yonkers. Contbr. articles to profl. jours. Chmn. Bronx Health Systems Agy. Bd., 1977-78, Montefiore Community Adv. Bd., 1977—; pres. MMC-CAB, 1981-84. Fellow Am. Coll. Dentists, Am. Coll. Oral and Maxillofacial Surgeons, Interant. Coll. Dentists; mem. Bronx County Dental Soc. (treas. 1988-90, v.p. 1991-92), ADA, Am. Soc. Oral and Maxillofacial Surgeons, N.Y. State Dental Soc. Anesthesiology (pres. 1981), Am. Dental Soc. Anesthesiology, Riverdale Dental Study Group, Jarvie Soc., Riverdale Mental Health Assn. (bd. dirs. 1979—, asst. treas. 1987), Nat. Young Judaea Alumni Assn. (pres. 1990-91). Democrat. Jewish. Avocation: skiing. Home: 440 W End Ave # 15 New York NY 10024-5358 Office: 3333 Henry Hudson Pkwy Bronx NY 10463

FRIEDMAN, JON GEORGE, lawyer; b. N.Y.C., Sept. 2, 1951; s. George Alexander and Viola Elizabeth (Elson) F. BBA, Adelphi U., 1972; MBA, Golden Gate U., 1972; MPA, NYU, 1974; JD, Hofstra U., 1977; MA, NYU, 1978. Bar: N.Y. 1978, U.S. Dist. Ct. (ea. and so. dists.) N.Y. 1978, U.S. Ct. Appeals (2d cir.) 1981, U.S. Supreme Ct. 1984, U.S. Dist. Ct. P.R. 1982. V.p., gen. counsel Allou Distbrs., Inc., Brentwood, N.Y., 1978-82; bus. cons. internat. trade, fin. Long Island, N.Y., 1982—; v.p., bus. editor Caribbean Bus., San Juan, P.R., 1983-84; sole practice Long Island, P.R., 1984—. Contbr. articles to profl. jours. Mem. ABA, N.Y. State Bar Assn., Assn. of Bar of City of N.Y. Home and Office: 81-39 255th St Floral Park NY 11004

FRIEDMAN, LAWRENCE SAMUEL, gastroenterologist, educator; b. Newark, May 11, 1953; s. Maurice and Esther (Slansky) F.; m. Mary Jo Cappuccilli, Apr. 12, 1981; 1 child, Matthew Jacob. Student, Princeton U., 1971-73; BA, Johns Hopkins U., 1975, MD, 1978. Intern dept. medicine Johns Hopkins Hosp., Balt., 1978-79, resident dept. medicine, 1979-81; fellow Mass. Gen. Hosp. & Harvard Med. Sch., Boston, 1981-84; asst. prof. Jefferson Med. Coll., Phila., 1984-87, assoc. prof., vice chmn., 1987—. Editor: Gastrointesinal Disorders in the Elderly, 1990; contbr. articles to profl. jours. Med. adv. com. mem. (Phila. chpt.) Crohn's & Colitis Found. Am., 1985; nat. mem. Am. Liver Found., 1986. Fellow ACP, Am. Coll. Gastroenterology, Coll. Physicians of Phila.; mem. Am. Assn. for Study of Liver Diseases, Am. Fedn. for Clin. Rsch., Am. Soc. Gastrointestinal Endoscopy, Am. Gastroent. Assn. Jewish. Office: Thomas Jefferson Univ 465 Main Bldg 132 S 10th St Philadelphia PA 19107-5083

FRIEDMAN, LEONARD, biochemist; b. N.Y.C., Jan. 27, 1929; s. Henry and Selma (Kornreich) F.; m. Diana Ruth Barsky, July 19, 1991. BS, NYU, 1951; MS, Rutgers U., 1953, PhD, 1960. Postdoctoral fellow biochemistry dept. U. Iowa, Iowa City, 1959-61; biochemist Inst. Infectious Disease and Allergy, NIH, Bethesda, Md., 1961-62; rsch. chemist div. nutrition FDA, Washington, 1962-71; supervisory rsch. chemist div. toxicology FDA, Beltsville, Md., 1971—; acting chief metabolism br. Div. Toxicological Studies, Beltsville, 1992—. Contbr. articles to profl. publs., chpts. to books. Mem. AAAS, Am. Chem. Soc., Am. Soc. Pharmacology and Exptl. Therapeutics, Soc. Toxicology, Soc. Exptl. Biol. Medicine (treas. D.C. chpt. 1991—), Sigma Xi (FDA chpt. pres.-elect 1992, sci. fair coord. 1989—). Home: 14805 Waterway Dr Rockville MD 20853-3616 Office: FDA HFF-169 8501 Muirkirk Rd Laurel MD 20708-2843

FRIEDMAN, LEWIS, chemist; b. Spring Lake, N.J., Aug. 8, 1922; s. Joseph Henry and Tillie (Wainer) F.; m. Dorothy Kaplan, Aug. 24, 1948; children: Robert S., Beth B., Jan R. BA, Lehigh U., 1943; MA, Princeton U., 1945, PhD, 1947. Fellow Fermi Nat. Inst. U. Chgo., 1947-48; assoc. chemist Brookhaven Nat. Lab., Upton, N.Y., 1948-50, chemist, 1950-57, sr. chemist, 1957—; vis. scientist FOM Lab. Amsterdam, The Netherlands, 1960; cons. IAEC, Soreq, Israel, 1968. Author: (with others) Ion Molecule Reactions, 1970; assoc. editor: Jour. Chem. Physics, 1960-63; contbr. articles to profl. jours. Cpl. U.S. Army, 1943. Mem. Phi Beta Kappa, Sigma Xi. Office: Brookhaven Lab Chemistry Dept Upton NY 11973

FRIEDMAN, LIONEL ROBERT, physics educator, researcher; b. Phila.; s. Herman David Friedman and Rose Goodman; m. Pearl Scharfman, Sept. 2, 1956; children: Mark K., Philip C., Stephen H.D. BS, Swarthmore Coll., 1955; PhD, U. Pitts., 1961. Researcher RCA Labs., Princeton, N.J., 1963-70; sr. fellow Cavendish Labs., U. Cambridge (Eng.), 1970-72, U. East Anglia, Norwich, Eng., 1972-73; lectr. U. St. Andrews (Scotland), 1973-74, reader, 1974-80; researcher GTE Labs., Waltham, Mass., 1980-86; prof. physics Worcester (Mass.) Poly. Inst., 1986—; adj. prof. Boston Coll., Chestnut Hill, Mass., 1983-84, Tufts U., Medford, Mass., 1985-86; cons. Rome Lab., Hanscom AFB, Mass., 1986, Nat. Rsch. Coun. Associateship, 1992. Contbr. numerous articles to sci. jours. Home: 49 Winfield Rd Holden MA 01520-2442

FRIEDMAN, MALCOLM, dean; b. N.Y.C., Sept. 29, 1928; s. Martin and Anna (Schoen) F.; m. Elaine Nancy Hunt; children: Marci, Carestia. BA, NYU, 1949; MA, Bklyn. Coll., 1952; PhD, Yeshiva U., 1957. Cert. ednl. adminstr., N.Y. Dir. team teaching N.Y.C. Bd. Edn., 1962-66, dir. reading, 1977-79, dir. spl. programs, 1980-84; prin. Pub. Sch. #14, S.I., N.Y., 1966-77; prof. Hunter Coll., N.Y.C., 1966-73; assoc. dean L.I. U., Bklyn., N.Y., 1984—; adj. prof. St. John's U., N.Y.C., 1975-76; asst. examiner Bd. Examiners, N.Y.C., 1966-84. Mem. Am. Assn. Colls. for Tchr. Edn., N.Y. Acad. Pub. Edn., Internat. Reading Assn., Phi Delta Kappa. Home: 131 74th St Brooklyn NY 11209-2247 Office: LI Univ Office of Dean 1 University Plz Brooklyn NY 11201-5372

FRIEDMAN, MARIA ANDRE, public relations executive; b. Jackson, Mich., June 12, 1950; d. Robert Andre and Mary MacLean (Thompson) Hoving; m. Stanley N. Friedman, July 22, 1973; children: Alexandra, Adam. BA cum laude, U. Md., 1972, MA, 1979; DBA, Nova U., 1992. Writer, U.S. Bur. Mines, Washington, 1973-78; head writer Nat. Ctr. for Health Svc. Rsch. and Health Care Tech. Assessment, DHHS, Rockville, Md., 1978-85, chief publs. and info. br. Agy for Health Care Policy and Rsch., 1986-89; dir. Office Pub. Affairs Health Care Fin. Adminstrn., Washington, 1990—; pres. Medi-Systems, Inc., Silver Spring, Md., 1980—; v.p. Metro Med. Assocs., Silver Spring, 1982—, MediSystems Fin. Services, 1984—. Mem. Nat. Assn. Govt. Communicators, Acad. of Mgmt. Home: 12535 Heurich Rd Silver Spring MD 20902-1441 Office: Health Care Fin Adminstrn 200 Independence Ave SW Humphrey Bldg Rm 425-H Washington DC 20201

FRIEDMAN, MARK, physician, consultant; b. Bklyn., Mar. 25, 1932; s. Samuel and Ann (Sapan) F.; m. Myrna Cohen, Nov. 1, 1959; children: Suzanne, Melanie, Barbra. BA in Physics, Adelphi U., 1953; MD, Wake Forest U., 1958. Diplomate Am. Bd. Phys. Medicine and Rehab. Rotating intern Mamimodes Hosp., Bklyn., 1959-61; resident VA Hosp., Coral Gables, Fla., 1961-62, East Orange, N.J., 1962-64; attending physician John F. Kennedy Hosp., Edison, N.J., 1973—; cons. physician VA Hosp., Lyons, N.J., 1978-82; med. dir., pres. Middlesex Rehab. Hosp., North Brunswick, N.J., 1965-73; med. dir. phys. medicine Muhlenberg Hosp., Plainfield, N.J., 1965-88; cons. physician South Amboy (N.J.) Hosp., 1978—. Capt. USAF, 1959-61, CBI. Fellow Am. Acad. Phys. Medicine and Rehab., Am. Coll. Sports Medicine, Am. Acad. Disability Evaluating Physicians; mem. Am. Holistic Med. Assn. (founder), Am. Assn. Orthopedic Medicine. Office: 2509 Park Ave South Plainfield NJ 07080-5370

FRIEDMAN, MARVIN HAROLD, physicist, educator; b. N.Y.C., July 20, 1923; s. Abraham and Anna (Post) F.; m. Laura Rosalind Held, July 11, 1965; 1 child, Adam David. MS, U. Ill., 1948, PhD, 1952. NSF postdoctoral fellow Cornell U., Ithaca, N.Y., 1952-53; rsch. assoc. Columbia U., N.Y.C., 1953-55; instr. MIT, Cambridge, 1955-56, asst. prof., 1956-61; assoc. prof. Northeastern U., Boston, 1961-65, prof., 1965—; vis. scientist MIT, 1982-83, 89-90; cons. Allied Rsch. Corp., Boston, 1962-64. Contbr. articles to profl. publs. Fellow Am. Phys. Soc.; mem. N.Y. Acad. Sci., Sigma Xi, Phi Kappa Phi. Home: 32 Windemere Rd Wellesley MA 02181-4821 Office: Physics Dept Northeastern Univ 360 Huntington Ave Boston MA 02115-5096

FRIEDMAN, MICHAEL BELAIS, mental health administrator; b. N.Y.C., Mar. 21, 1943; s. Alfred Henry and Sylvia (Sclar) F.; m. Harriet Mauer, Oct. 22, 1976; 1 child, Danielle. AB cum laude, Columbia U., 1964, MA, 1970; MSW, CUNY, 1976. Cert. social worker, N.Y. Asst. prof. philosophy William Paterson Coll., Wayne, N.J., 1970-72; program dir. The Bridge, Inc., N.Y.C., 1973-77; caseworker, therapist Linden Hill Sch., Hawthorne, N.Y., 1977-78; exec. asst. Jewish Bd. Family and Children's Svcs., N.Y.C., 1978-80, dir. ops., 1980-86; exec. dir. Mental Health Assn. Westchester County, Inc., White Plains, N.Y., 1987—; mem. adv. coms. N.Y. State Coun. on

Children and Families, N.Y. State Office Health Systems Mgmt.; com. state standards of payment N.Y. State Coun. Vol. Family and Children's Svcs.; mem. Mayor's Task Force on Child Abuse, N.Y.C., 1984-86; vice-chair N.Y.C. Pub. Fatality Rev. Com., 1985-86; coord. Coalition Residential Treatment Facilities, 1984-86; mem. Advocacy Group Child Mental Health, 1980-87; mem. Hudson River regional planning adv. com. N.Y. State Office Mental Health, 1992—; com. mem., chmn. Community Coun. Greater N.Y., 1978-89; bd. dirs. Coalition Homeless Westchester. Contbr. articles to profl. publs. Mem. mgmt. assistance grants com. Greater N.Y. Fund/United Way, 1981-82, pers. devel. com., 1982-83, mgmt. assistance com., 1983-86; chmn. sub-coms. Fedn. Jewish Philanthropies, N.Y.C., 1979-84, chmn. task force family violence, 1983-85, mem. govt. rels. com., 1978-86, v.p. Commn. Synagogue Rels., 1985-86; bd. dirs. St. Bernard's Learning Ctr., 1990—; mem. mgmt. assistance program United Way Westchester, 1987-90, nominating com., 1989, task force distbn., 1990, govt. rels. com., 1990—. Mem. NASW, Assn. Mental Health Adminstrs., Nat. Mental Health Assn. (pub. policy com. 1989-90), Mental Health Assn. N.Y. State (govt. rels. com.). Jewish. Home: 12 Old Mamaroneck Rd White Plains NY 10605-2010 Office: Mental Health Assn Westchester County 29 Sterling Ave White Plains NY 10606-3099

FRIEDMAN, MILES, trade association executive, financial services company executive, university lecturer; b. N.Y.C., Apr. 18, 1950; s. Sol and Rose (Schenkerman) F.; m. Susan Liles, Apr. 26, 1975; children: David Andrew, Diana Leigh. BA in Pub. Affairs, George Washington U., 1971, MA in Polit. Sci., 1972, PhD candidate in Polit. Sci., 1976. Dep. commr. pub. works Town of Ramapo, Suffern, N.Y., 1971; grad. teaching fellow George Washington U., Washington, 1972-75; sr. assoc. Lazar Mgmt. Group, Washington, 1976-77; dir. legis. and policy Nat. Council Urban Econ. Devel., Washington, 1977-80; exec. dir. Nat. Assn. State Devel. Agys., Washington, 1980—; founder, instr. trade specialist tng. program, Phoenix, 1980—, founder, instr. fgn. investment tng. program, 1988—; instr. Fgn. Svc. Inst., U.S. and Fgn. Comml. Svc. Inst., Georgetown U., Washington, 1991, U. N.C. Basic Econ. Devel. Inst., Chapel Hill, 1984-85; cons. Pres.' Drug Abuse Prevention Office, Washington, 1972; lectr. George Washington U., Washington, 1975-77. Mem. editorial bd. Econ. Devel. Rev., 1991—; contbg. author to several books, directory; contbr. articles to profl. jours. including Wall St. Jour, Area Devel. mag., Export Today mag., others; contbg. editor Econ. Devel. Rev., 1983-84. Mem bd. dirs., sec./treas. Pub. Sector Devel. Found., Washington, 1983—; pres. Am. Devel. Fin., Inc., 1986—, also bd. dirs.; liaison subcom. Pres.'s Export Council, Washington, 1981-82; Pinewood Forest Council Owners, 1977-78; chmn. Washington Symposium Higher Edn., 1970-71. S. C. of C., Am. Soc. Assn. Execs., Nat. Assn. Execs., Tau Kappa Epsilon, Delta Phi Epsilon, Lambda Alpha. Office: Nat Assn State Devel Agys 750 1st St NE Ste 710 Washington DC 20002

FRIEDMAN, NEAL JOEL, lawyer; b. Balt., Dec. 20, 1940; s. Samuel Joseph and Beatrice Mildred (Schapiro) F.; m. Judith Ellen Friedman, June 10, 1962; children: Jane, Jay. BA, Pa. State U., 1961; JD, Am. U., 1984. Bar: D.C. 1985, Md. 1985. News reporter KTIV-TV, Sioux City, Iowa, 1962-64, WBAL-TV, Balt., 1964-76, WJLA-TV, Washington, 1976-81; dep. dir. pub. affairs Fed. Trade Commn., Washington, 1981-86; atty. Bechtel & Cole, Washington, 1985-86, Pepper & Corazzini, Washington, 1987—; bd. dirs. Sch. Communications Alumni Soc., Pa. State U., University Park. Mem. ABA, Fed. Commnications Bar Assn. Office: Pepper & Corazzini 1776 K St NW Washington DC 20006

FRIEDMAN, NORMAN, psychotherapist, writer, poet; b. Boston, Apr. 10, 1925; s. Samuel and Eva (Nathanson) F.; m. Zelda Nathanson, June 7, 1945; children: Michael, Janet. AB, Harvard U., 1948, AM, 1949, PhD in English, 1952; MSW, Adelphi U., 1978; grad., Gesalt Ctr. for Psychotherapy, 1978. Diplomate Am. Bd. Examiners in Clin. Social Work; cert. social worker, N.Y. From instr. to assoc. prof. U. Conn., Storrs, 1952-63; from assoc. prof. to prof. Queens Coll., CUNY, Flushing, 1963-88; pvt. practice Flushing, 1978—; dir. Gestalt Therapy Ctr. Queens, Flushing, 1984—; lectr. Fulbright Found., U. Nantes and Nice, France, 1966-67. Author: E.E. Cummings: The Art of His Poetry, 1960, E.E. Cummings: The Growth of a Writer, 1964, Form and Meaning in Fiction, 1975, The Magic Badge: Poems, 1953-84, 1984, The Intrusions of Love: Poems, 1992. Lt. (j.g.) USNR, 1943-46, 48. Recipient Bowdoin Essay prize, Harvard U., 1948, Northwest Rev. Annual Poetry prize, 1963, Borestone Mountain Poetry awards, 1964, 67; grantee Am. Coun. Learned Socs., 1959, 60. Fellow N.Y. State Soc. Clin. Social Work Psychotherapists, Internat. Conf. for Advancement of Pvt. Practice in Social Work; mem. NASW, MLA, Phi Beta Kappa. Democrat. Jewish. Home and Office: Gestalt Therapy Ctr Queens 33-54 164 St Flushing NY 11358-1442

FRIEDMAN, RODGER, librarian, research consultant; b. Detroit, Nov. 10, 1951; s. Stanley B. and Miriam Elizabeth (Levin) F.; m. Kiki Nelson, July 1, 1983. BA, Kalamazoo Coll., 1973; MA, U. N.Mex., Albuquerque, 1979, CUNY, 1987; PhD, CUNY, 1989. Librarian Century Assn., N.Y.C., 1982-88, Union League Club, N.Y.C., 1989—. Contbr. articles to profl. jours.; editorial staff: (jour.) Ballet Rev., 1983—. Recipient Frederick II medal U. Naples, 1991. Mem. MLA, Renaissance Soc. Am., Am. Comparative Lit. Assn. (advisor, exec. com. 1987-89), Am. Assn. Italian Studies, Assn. Internat. Studi di Lingua Letteratura Italiana, Internat. Assn. for Neo-Latin Studies. Home: 116 Pinehurst Ave New York NY 10033-1755

FRIEDMAN, SAMUEL SELIG, lawyer; b. N.Y.C., July 25, 1935; s. Nathan and Anne M. (Sobel) F.; m. Maxine E. Goldfarb, Jan. 7, 1961; 1 child, Alison J. BS, MIT, 1956; MBA, U. Pa., 1959; LLB, Columbia U., 1965. Bar: N.Y. 1965, U.S. Dist. Ct. (so. and ea. dists.) N.Y. 1967, U.S. Supreme Ct. 1984. Assoc. Lord, Day & Lord, N.Y.C., 1965-72; ptnr., mem. exec. com. Lord Day & Lord, Barrett Smith and predecessor firm, N.Y.C., 1972—. Dir. Times Square Bus. Improvement Dist. 1st lt. U.S. Army, 1959-62. Mem. ABA, N.Y. State Bar Assn., Assn. of Bar of City of N.Y., India House, MIT Club N.Y., Phi Delta Phi. Office: Lord Day & Lord Barrett Smith 1675 Broadway New York NY 10019-5874

FRIEDMAN, SARAH LANDAU, psychologist, health scientist, administrator; b. Tel Aviv, Nov. 18, 1943; d. Faivel and Ester (Vloska) Landau; m. Moshe Freidman, June 11, 1967; 1 child, Daphne. BA in English Lit. and Polit. Sci., Hebrew U., Jerusalem, 1969; MA in Ednl. Psychology, Cornell U., 1971; PhD in Devel. psychology, George Washington U., 1975. Rsch. fellow lab. devel. psychology NIMH, 1974-76, rsch. psychologist lab devel. psychology, 1976-79; neonatal rsch. psychologist dept. perinatal-neonatal pediatrics Washington Hosp. Ctr., 1977-79; rsch. asst. prof. psychiatry and behavioral sci. George Washington U. Sch. Medicine, 1979-80; rsch. assoc. Children's Hosp. Nat. Med. Ctr., Washington, 1979-80; assoc. Nat. Inst. Edn., 1980-83; rsch. psychologist lab. devel. psychology, 1983-86; grants assoc. NIH, 1986-87; health scientist adminstr. human learning and behavior br. Nat. Inst. Child Health and Human Devel., Bethesda, Md., 1987—, coord., mem. steering com. NICHD study early child care, 1989—. Editor, mem. editorial bds. various jours.; contbr. articles to profl. jours. Mem. John D. and Catherine T. MacArthur Found. Network, 1983-86. Fellow Am. Psychol. Soc.; mem. Am. Psychol. Assn., N.Y. Acad. Scis., Soc. Rsch. Child Devel., Ea. Psychol. Assn., Internat. Soc. Study Behavioral Devel., Jean Paiget Soc., Sigma Xi, Phi Kappa Phi, Phi Lambda Theta, Psi Chi. Home: 4511 Yuma St NW Washington DC 20016-2043

FRIEDMAN, SELWYN MARVIN, biology educator; b. N.Y.C., May 17, 1929; s. Louis and Leah (Weinstein) F.; m. Rivka Teitelbaum, May 28, 1972. BS, U. Mich., 1951; MS, Purdue U., 1953, PhD, 1961. Postdoctoral fellow Case-Western Res. U., Cleve., 1961-62, Albert Einstein Coll. Medicine, N.Y.C., 1962-63; rsch. fellow Columbia U. Coll. Physics and Surgery, N.Y.C., 1963-66; asst. prof. Hunter Coll. of CUNY, N.Y.C., 1966-69, assoc. prof., 1969-91, full prof. biology, 1991—; vis. scientist dept. chemistry Columbia U., N.Y.C., 1973, Pub. Health Rsch. Inst., N.Y.C., 1991; U.S. coord. Japan Coop. Sci. Program, NSF, 1977; referee NSF and AEC Grant Proposals, 1976-87. Author: (with others) Thermophilic Microorganisms, 1992; editor: Biochemistry of Thermophily, 1978; contbr. articles to profl. jours. With U.S. Army, 1954-56. Rsch. grantee NIH, 1967-70, 75-78, CUNY Rsch. Award Program, 1971-89. Mem. Am. Soc. Microbiology, N.Y. Acad. Scis. (chair microbiology sect.), Sigma Xi. Democrat. Hebrew. Home: 340 E 64th St Apt 14L New York NY 10021 Office: Hunter Coll CUNY 695 Park Ave New York NY 10021

FRIEDMAN, STEVEN, psychologist, consultant; b. Bklyn., Sept. 20, 1945; s. Isidore and Estelle (Jacobson) F.; m. Donna Haig, Mar. 23, 1973; 1 child, Sarah. BA, L.I. U., 1967, MA, 1969; PhD, Boston U., 1971. Rsch. scientist John F. Kennedy Ctr. for Rsch. on Edn. and Human Devel., Nashville, 1971-77; from asst. to assoc. prof. George Peabody Coll. Vanderbilt U., Nashville, 1971-77; postdoctoral fellow South Shore Mental Health Ctr., Quincy, Mass., 1977-78; chief psychologist Newton (Mass.) Guidance Ctr., 1978-82; assoc. prof. grad. sch. Lesley Coll., Cambridge, Mass., 1984-85; coord. child/family mental health Harvard Community Health Plan, Braintree, Mass., 1985—. Author: Infancy, 1978, Expanding Therapeutic Possibilities, 1991; contbr. over 50 articles to profl. jours. Mem. Am. Psychol. Assn., Am. Family Therapy Assn., Am. Orthopsychiatric Assn., Mass. Psychol. Assn. Home: 22 Bradley Woods Dr Hingham MA 02043-1731 Office: Harvard Community Health Plan 111 Grossman Dr Braintree MA 02184-4998

FRIEDMAN, STEVEN J., health care administrator; b. N.Y.C., Jan. 5, 1947; s. Samuel Martin and Mildred Joyce (Arschin) F.; m. Barbara Ann Gottlieb, Apr. 24, 1971; children: Joshua, Daniel. BA, CCNY, 1968; MS in Adminstrv. Medicine, Columbia U., 1970. Asst. dir. Beth Israel Med. Ctr., N.Y.C., 1970-73; program adminstr. Westchester County Dept. Mental Health, White Plains, N.Y., 1973-74, deputy dir. mental health and hosp. svcs., 1974-77, deputy dir., 1977-80, deputy commnr., 1980-88, commnr., 1988—; clin. assoc. prof. psychiatry N.Y. Med. Coll., Valhalla, N.Y., 1991; mem. Strategic Planning Advisory Com. N.Y. Office of Mental Health, Albany, 1990—, Hudson River Regional Planning Advisory Coun., 1989—, Info. Systems Office Com., 1988—, Child Protective Svcs. Advisory Com., 1988—, N.Y. Conf. Local Mental Hygiene Dirs., 1988—, Westchester County Interagency Advisory Group on Homeless, 1990—, Westchester County Employee Assistance Advisory Bd., 1990, Westchester County Oversight Com. for Emergency Housing Plan, 1990—, Westchester County Drug War Cabinet, 1990—. Contbr. articles to profl. jours. Mem. United Way of Westchester Funders Network, White Plains, 1991, New Programs and Svcs. Com., White Plains, 1985—. Mem. Columbia U. Alumni Club (Westchester chptr. bd. dirs. 1984-86). Jewish. Home: 1360 Carters Grv Yorktown Heights NY 10598 Office: Westchester County Dept Community Mental Healt 112 E Post Rd White Plains NY 10601-5113

FRIEDMAN, SUE TYLER, technical publications executive; b. Nürnberg, Germany, Feb. 28, 1925; came to U.S., 1938; d. William and Ann (Federlein) Tyler (Theilheimer); m. Gerald Manfred Friedman, June 27, 1948; children: Judith Fay Friedman Rosen, Sharon Mira Friedman Azaria, Devora Paula Friedman Zweibach, Eva Jane Friedman Scholle, Wendy Tamar Friedman Spanier. Student, Beth Israel Sch. Nursing, 1941-43. Exec. dir. Ventures and Publs. of Gerald M. Friedman, 1964—; owner Tyler Publs., Watervliet and Troy, N.Y., 1978-86; treas., dir. Northeastern Sci. Found., Inc., Troy, 1979—; treas. Gerry Exploration, Inc., Troy, 1982—; office mgr. Rensselaer Ctr. Applied Geology, Troy, 1983—. Pres. Pioneer Women/Na'amat, Tulsa, 1961-64, treas., Jerusalem, Israel, 1964, pres., Albany, N.Y., 1968-70; bd. dirs. Temple Beth-El, 1965—, dir. Hebrew Sch., 1965-80. Named hon. alumna Dept. Geology, Bklyn. Coll. at CUNY, 1989; Sue Tyler Friedman medal for distinction in history of geology created in her honor, Geol. Soc. London, 1988; recipient Disting. Svc. award Temple Beth-El, 1991. Mem. Geology Alumni Assn. (hon.). Jewish. Home: 32 24th St Troy NY 12180-1915 Office: Northeastern Sci Found Inc Rensselaer Ctr Applied Geology 15 3d St Box 746 Troy NY 12181-0746

FRIEDMAN, THOMAS LOREN, foreign correspondent; b. Mpls., July 20, 1953; s. Harold Abraham and Margaret (Phillips) F.; m. Ann Louise Bucksbaum, Nov. 23, 1978. B.A., Brandeis U., 1975; M.Phil., St. Anthony's Coll., Oxford U., 1978. Staff corr. UPI, London, 1978-79; Middle East corr. UPI, Beirut, 1979-81; reporter Bus. Day. sect. N.Y. Times, N.Y.C., 1981-82; Beirut bur. chief N.Y. Times, 1982-84, Jerusalem bur. chief, 1984-89; chief diplomatic corr. N.Y. Times, Washington, 1989—. Recipient Pulitzer prize, 1983, 1988, George Polk award L.I. U., 1982, Livingston award Livingston Found., 1983, Overseas Press Club award, 1980, Robert D. Heinl Jr. Meml. award Marine Corps History, 1985, Page 1 award N.Y. Newspaper Guild, 1984, Nat. Book award 1989 for "From Beirut to Jerusalem". Jewish.

FRIEDMAN, WILBUR HARVEY, lawyer; b. N.Y.C., May 2, 1907; s. Isador Peter and Zara (Sloat) F.; m. Frances Margolis, May 21, 1943. A.B., Columbia, 1927; LL.B., Columbia U., 1930. Bar: N.Y. 1931. Law sec. U.S. Supreme Ct. Justice Harlan F. Stone, 1930-31; atty. office U.S. solicitor gen., 1931-32; mem. firm Proskauer, Rose, Goetz, & Mendelsohn, N.Y.C., 1932-40, ptnr., 1940—; lectr. NYU Inst. on Fed. Taxation, 1943-65, Sch. Gen. Edn., 1955-60; bd. dirs., sec. Lawrence M. Gelb Found.; chmn. exec. com. bd. visitors Columbia U. Law Sch., 1977-91; mem. dean's adv. bd. NYU Coll. Dentistry. Contbr. articles to profl. jours. Chmn. bd. overseers Edith C. Blum Art Inst. at Bard Coll., 1985—; mem. Rockefeller U. Council, 1986—; mem. med. ctr. adv. bd. N.Y. Hosp.-Cornell Med. Ctr., 1986—. Mem. N.Y. County Lawyers Assn. (chmn. com. on taxation 1948-54, pres. 1975-77, exec. com. 1977-79, chmn. com. on group ins. 1960-74, chmn. spl. com. on consumers agreements 1977-83), ABA. (ho. of dels. 1978-87), N.Y. Bar Assn. (exec. com. sect. taxation 1968-76), N.Y.C. Bar Assn. (chmn. com. on mgmt. and operation profl. practice 1981-85), Phi Beta Kappa, Phi Beta Kappa Assocs., Tau Delta Phi. Clubs: Lotos, Princeton U. (N.Y.C.). Home: 1016 5th Ave New York NY 10028-0132 Office: Proskauer Rose Goetz 1585 Broadway New York NY 10036-8200

FRIEDMANN, ERIKA, health science educator; b. Boston, Oct. 2, 1952; d. Jacob Bernard Friedmann and Frances Mae (Payes) Neiman; m. Michael A. Barry, June 26, 1977; children: Miriam, Samuel. BA, U. Pa., 1973, PhD, 1978; Bklyn. Coll., CUNY, Bklyn. Coll., CUNY. Asst. prof. Chestnut Hill Coll., Phila., 1978-79; asst. prof. Bklyn. Coll., 1979-83, assoc. prof., 1984-88, prof., 1989—; lectr. Sch. of Vet. Medicine, U. Pa., Phila., 1979-85; co-dir. Ctr. of Health Promotion, Bklyn., 1985—; rsch. dir. Ctr. for Human Psychopsychology, Balt., 1982-88; cons. Life Care Health Found., Towson, Md., 1989—; bd. dirs. Am. Inst. of Stress, Yonkers, N.Y. Mem. editorial bd. Focus on Critical Care, 1986-87; contbr. numerous articles to profl. jours. Met. Life Found. grantee, 1982-84, CUNY grantee, 1982-83, 84-91, Am. Cancer Soc., 1986, Delta Soc. grantee, 1988—. Mem. APHA, Internat. Soc. for Anthrozoology (pres. 1991—), Sigma Xi. Office: Bklyn Coll Health & Nutrition Scis Bedford Ave and Ave H Brooklyn NY 11222-3102

FRIEDMANN, PAUL, surgeon, educator; b. Vienna, Austria, Dec. 2, 1933; came to U.S., 1938; s. Erich and Rochelle (Behar) F.; m. Janee Armstrong, Apr. 24, 1962; children: Pamela, Cynthia. BA, U. Pa., 1955; MD, Harvard U., 1959. Diplomate Am. Bd. Surgery, Am. Bd. Vascular Surgery. Chmn. dept. surgery Baystate Med. Ctr., Springfield, Mass., 1971—; prof. surgery Tufts U. Sch. Medicine, Boston, 1978—; mem. residency rev. com., 1985-91, chmn., 1989-91; chmn. RRC Coun., Accreditation Coun. for Grad. Med. Edn., 1989-91. Contbr. articles to profl. jours. Served to capt. USAF, 1961-63. Fellow ACS (bd. govs. 1978-84, pres. Mass. chpt. 1987); mem. Am. Surg. Assn., Assn. Program Dirs. in Surgery (sec. 1985-87, pres. 1987-89), New Eng. Soc. Vascular Surgery (recorder 1988-91, pres.-elect 1991-92, pres. 1992—), New Eng. Surg. Soc. (treas. 1991—, Harvard Club (Boston), Colony Club (Springfield, Mass.). Office: Baystate Med Ctr 759 Chestnut St Springfield MA 01199-0001

FRIEDMUTTER, MARTIN, psychologist; b. Bklyn., Jan. 14, 1947; s. David and Golda Friedmutter; m. Rena Ginsburg, Aug. 10, 1982; children: Jason, Rebecca. MA in Edn., NYU, 1981; MS in Edn., CUNY, 1982, Adv. Cert. in Edn., 1984; PhD, Yeshiva U., N.Y.C., 1987. Tchr. N.Y.C. Bd. Edn., 1981-88, sch. psychologist, 1988-90; pvt. practice, N.Y.C., 1989—; dir. Comprehensive Counseling Ctr., Queens, 1989—. With U.S. Army, 1968-70. Mem. Am. Psychol. Assn. Home: 68-37 18 St Forest Hills NY 11375 Office: 21615 Northern Blvd Flushing NY 11361-3458

FRIEDRICH, ALLEN JOHN, vocational rehabilitation counselor; b. Phila., Oct. 16, 1948; s. William Robert and Frances Elizabeth (Wagner) F.; m. Arleen Marie Ziegler, Aug. 5, 1970; children: Christopher, Teresa, Diane. BS in Psychology, Ill. Inst. Tech., 1972, MS in Counseling and Guidance, 1973. Cert. ins. rehab. specialist, rehab. counselor U.S. Dept. Labor. Vocat. evaluator Goodwill Industries, Chgo., 1973-75, Purple Heart Vet. Rehab., Long Beach, Calif., 1975-76; supr., rehab. specialist Intracor, Pasadena, Calif., 1976-78; regional vocat. svc. dir. Intracor, Dallas, 1978-79; mgr. Emeritus Rehab., L.A., 1979, Eclectics Rehab., Long Beach, Calif., 1979-81; vocat. rehab. counselor Paladin Rehab. Svcs., Garden Groves, Calif., 1981-89; rehab. specialist Jordan Rehab. Svcs., Cherry Hill, N.J., 1989-90, Harleysville (Pa.) Ins. Co., 1991—. Bd. dirs. YMCA of Camden County. Mem. Phila. Workers Compensation Claims Assn., South Jersey Workers Compensation Claims Assn., Y's Mens Club of Haddonfield. Home: 114 Pearlcroft Rd Cherry Hill NJ 08034-3334 Office: Harleysville Ins 355 Maple Ave Harleysville PA 19438-2200

FRIEDRICH, BENJAMIN CHARLES, geoscientist, educator; b. Fond du Lac, Wis., Feb. 2, 1929; s. Benjamin E. and Anna (Bloede) F.; m. Jean Loosli, Mar. 28, 1964 (div. 1978); children: Valerie, Kirsten. BS, St. Cloud State U., 1954; MS, Ind. U., 1957; EdD, Pa. State U., 1961. Instr. chemistry Luther Jr. Coll., Wahoo, Nebr., 1953-56; instr. sci. Ind. U., Bloomington, 1957-59; asst. prof. sci. edn. Northeastern U., Boston, 1961-66; prof. geosci. Jersey City (N.J.) State Coll., 1966—, chair dept. geosci., 1969-74. With USNR, 1950-52. Democrat. Unitarian. Office: Jersey City State Coll Dept Geosci Jersey City NJ 07305

FRIEDRICH, CRAIG WILLIAM, lawyer; b. Oshkosh, Wis., Oct. 25, 1946; s. William Harold and Lorraine June (Pugh) F. AB, U. Wis., Madison, 1968; JD cum laude, Harvard U., 1972. Bar: N.Y. 1973, U.S. Tax Ct. 1973, U.S. Dist. Ct. (so., ea. dists.) N.Y. 1979, U.S. Ct. Internat. Trade 1980, Maine 1986. Atty., advisor Office Tax Legis. Counsel U.S. Treasury Dept., Washington, 1974-76; assoc. Weil, Gotshal and Manges, N.Y.C., 1972-74, 1976-77, Debevoise and Plimpton, N.Y.C., 1977-81; assoc. prof. N.Y. Law Sch., N.Y.C., 1981-83; counsel Schoeman, Marsh, Updike and Welt, N.Y.C., 1982-83, ptnr., 1983-86; ptnr. Bernstein, Shur, Sawyer & Nelson, Portland, Maine, 1986—; cons. Bank Tax Inst., 1981-83; subject specialist Council Non Collegiate Continuing Edn., 1982. Mem. bd. contbg. editors, advisors Jour. Corp. Taxation, 1980—, author column, 1980—; contbr. articles to profl. jours. Mem. N.Y. State Bar Assn., Maine Bar Assn., Am. Soc. Internat. Law, N.Y.C. Bar Assn., Cumberland Club, Purpoodock Club, Phi Beta Kappa, Phi Kappa Phi, Phi Eta Sigma. Republican. Congregationalist. Home: 1 Ellie Ave Scarborough ME 04074-8549 Office: Bernstein Shur Sawyer & Nelson PO Box 9729 Portland ME 04104-5029

FRIEDRICH, MARGRET COHEN, guidance and student assistance counselor; b. Balt., June 4, 1947; d. Joseph Cohen and Judith (Kline) Cohen Roisman; m. Jay Joseph Friedrich, May 16, 1971; children: David Benjamin, Marc Adam, Samantha Lauren. BEd, U. Miami, Fla., 1969, MEd, 1970. Cert. alcoholism and addiction counselor, alcoholism and drug counselor. Grad. asst. U. Miami, Coral Gables, Fla., 1969-70; tchr. Balt. Bd. Edn., 1970; guidance counselor Ridgewood Bd. Edn., N.J., 1970—; student asst. coord., 1986—, chmn. student assistance com., 1986—; alcoholism counselor Bergen County Dept. Health, Paramus, N.J., 1981-82; in-service tchr. Ridgewood Bd. Edn., 1983, supr., coordinator peer counseling program high sch., 1979—; with Assn. Mental Health and Counseling of No. N.J., 1985—; pres. BFH, 1987—, Maggie Assoc.; exec. officer BFPK; cons. N.J. Student Assistance Program, student asst. cons. N.J. Dept. Edn., chmn. student asst. com.; presenter Coll. Bd. Conf., 1992, CEEB Conf., Phila, 1992. Author tech. papers. Exec. bd. Hadassah, Ridgewood-Glen Rock, N.J., 1971—; youth leadership com. United Jewish Appeal, Bergen County, 1974-75; sec. Bergen County Youth Com. Substance Abuse, Paramus, 1980—, conf. coord. com., 1983; treas. Ridgewood Coalition Substance Use and Abuse, 1983-84, Ridgewood Substance Abuse Prevention Commn., 1989—; participant Pres.'s Drug-Free Am.; facilitator Gov.'s N.J. Drug-Free TeleConf.; co-chmn. fundraiser, treas. United Parents/Safe Homes, Ridgewood, 1984; mem. core com. Ridgewood Agaisnt Drugs; lectr./educator Passaic County Juvenile Conf. Com., Paterson, N.J., 1984. Reisman scholar, 1969; U. Miami teaching asst., 1970, recipient Recognition award, 1968, disting. Leadership award N.J. Assn. St. Asst. Profls. Mem. N.J. Assn. Alcoholism and Drug Counselors, Nat. Assn. Suicidology, N.J. Edn. Assn., Ridgewood Edn. Assn., Bergen County Edn. Assn., N.J. Task Force on Women and Alcohol, Nat. Assn. Coll. Adminstr. Counselors, N.J. Personnel and Guidance Assn., Women of Accomplishment, Sigma Delta Tau. (exec. bd. 1965-69). Democrat. Jewish. Office: Ridgewood High Sch Ridgewood NJ 07451

FRIEDRICH, PAULA JEAN, computer programmer; b. Sharon, Pa., June 14, 1965; d. Kevin and Mary (Siwiecki) F. BA, St. Vincent Coll., 1987; MA, U. Pitts., 1989. Sci. programmer Westinghouse Elec. Co., Pitts., 1989-91; scientific programmer Westinghouse, West Mifflin, Pa., 1991—. Democrat. Roman Catholic. Home: 402 Brierly Ln West Mifflin PA 15122

FRIEDRICH, PHILIP J(OSEPH), strategic and operational management consultant; b. Massillon, Ohio, June 27, 1947; s. Paul Vincent and Thelma Diane (Doroslov) F.; m. Cheryl Ann Nick, Apr. 28, 1975; 1 child, Sarah Yung. BS in Sociology, Villanova (Pa.) U., 1969. Caseworker, casework supr., mgr. income maintenance Philadelphia County Bd. Assistance, Phila., 1972-82; rep. regional family assistance, mem. staff mgmt. devel. program Pa. Dept. Pub. Welfare, Harrisburg, 1982-84, dir. mgmt. and supervisory devel., 1984-87; dir. human resources devel. Pa. Dept. Human Services, Harrisburg, 1987-88; dir. human resource and orgnl. devel. Pa. Dept. Human Svcs., Harrisburg, Pa., 1988-89; cons. Kepner-Tregoe Inc., Princeton, N.J., 1989—. Active YMCA, Engletown Assn., Three Mile Island Alert, Harrisburg, 1983. With U.S. Army, 1969-71. Mem. Am. Soc. Tng. and Devel., Greenpeace, ACLU. Democrat. Home: 203 Harris St Harrisburg PA 17102-2426 Office: Kepner-Tregoe Inc Research Rd PO Box 704 Princeton NJ 08542-0704

FRIEDRICH, ROBERT JAMES, educator; b. Denver, Nov. 15, 1946; s. Julius Miller and Lorraine Ruth (Koch) F.; m. Elaine Robin Ader, Nov. 2, 1974 (div. 1979); m. Rebecca Ann Barton, Oct. 24, 1982; children: Philip, Elizabeth. BA magna cum laude, U. Colo., 1968; MA, U. Mich., 1970, PhD, 1977. Asst. prof. govt. Franklin & Marshall Coll., Lancaster, Pa., 1976-82, assoc. prof. govt., 1982-83, 91—, dir. acad. computing, 1984-91. Co-author: American Government, 1988, rev. edit., 1992; contbr. articles to profl. jours. Mem. Am. Polit. Sci. Assn., Midwest Polit. Sci. Assn., Phi Beta Kappa. Democrat. Home: 510 State St Lancaster PA 17603-2608 Office: Franklin & Marshall Coll PO Box 3003 Lancaster PA 17604-3003

FRIEDRICH, WAYNE HURFF, manufacturing consultant, industrial engineer; b. Bridgeton, N.J., Apr. 25, 1928; s. Charles P. and Joanna C. (Hurff) F.; m. Christine K. Erickson, Oct. 23, 1954; children: Paul E., Charles R., Karen C. BS in Adminstrv. Engring., Cornell U., 1950; MBA, Drexel U., 1957. Profl. engr., Pa. Prodn. and inventory planning mgr. John J. Nesbitt, Inc., Phila., 1953-60; plant mgr. Talbot Co., Reading, Pa., 1960-62; chief engr. Van Heusen Co., Pottsville, Pa., 1963-65; mgr. mfg. Leeds Travelwear, Inc., Clayton, Del., 1966-67; mgr. mfg. svcs. Warners, Bridgeport, Conn., 1967-69; corp. dir. indsl. engring. Warnaco, Inc., Bridgeport, 1970-71; mgr. ops. A.C. Mfg. Co., Inc., Cherry Hill, N.J., 1972-73, Liskey Architects Ural System, Linthicum, Md., 1974-75; v.p. Artic Roofing, Inc., Edgemoor, Del., 1976-78; v.p., sec., bd. dirs. K.W. Tunnell Co., Inc., King of Prussia, Pa., 1979—. Col. field artillery USAR, 1949-79, ret. Mem. Inst. Indsl. Engrs. (sr.). Home: 42 Red Oak Trl Medford NJ 08055-8826

FRIEL, DANIEL DENWOOD, SR., manufacturing executive; b. Queenstown, Md., Aug. 11, 1920; s. Samuel Edward Whiting and Martha Washington (Reynolds) F.; m. Helen June Hennessy, May 1, 1943; children: Barbara Friel Holme, Martha Friel Wilson, Patricia Friel Tully, Daniel D. Jr. BChemE, Johns Hopkins U., 1942. Supr. optical instruments Manhattan Project, U. Chgo., 1943-45; dir. applied physics E.I. du Pont, Wilmington, Del., 1945-61, mgr. investments, 1961-69, dir. electronic products, 1974-77, dir. instrument products, 1977-82; pres. Holotron Corp., Wilmington, 1969-71; pres., chmn. Edgecraft Corp., Wilmington, 1983-91; chmn. bd., chief exec. officer Edgecraft Corp., Avondale, Pa., 1991—; trustee Mt. Cuba Astron. Obs., Wilmington, 1960—. Co-author: Process Instruments and Control, 1960; contbr. articles to profl. jours. Trustee Tatnall Sch., Wilmington, 1967-74. Mem. Phys. Soc. Am., Optical Soc. Am., Instrument Soc. Am., Ams. for Competitive Enterprise System (bd. dirs.), Greenville Country Club, Tau Beta Pi. Office: Edgecraft Corp PO Box 3000 Avondale PA 19311-0915

FRIES, DEBORAH FAY, association executive; b. Allentown, Pa., Nov. 15, 1958; d. Douglas Warren Fries and Beverley Fay Fritch Antonik. BS, Kutztown (Pa.) U., 1980, MPA, 1987. Tchr. 5th grade Allentown (Pa.) Sch.

Dist., 1980-81, tchr. 6th grade, 1981-82; tchr. 7th grade Pocono Mt. Sch. Dist., Swiftwater, Pa., 1982-83; asst. dir. programs Girls' Club of Allentown, 1983-84, dir. programs, 1984-87, exec. dir., 1987—. Mem. Delta Zeta (chpt. dir. 1989—, Outstanding Alumnae in Pa. 1987). Office: Girls' Club of Allentown 1302 Turner St Allentown PA 18102

FRIES, DONALD OWEN, historian, educator; b. Jan. 22, 1939; s. Roy O. and Pearl (Paulson) F.; m. Grace E. Kvarnberg, June 23, 1962 (div. 1982);l children: Ingrid G., Kiersten S.; m. Deborah M. Weisberg, Oct. 7, 1984. BA, U. Mich., 1961, MA, 1963; PhD, Mich. State U., 1969. Assoc. prof. history Coll. Misericordia, Dallas, Pa., 1969-89, chmn. humanities, 1986—, prof. history, 1990—. Named Outstanding Tchr. Coll. Misercordia, 1979, 85, 92. Mem. Am. Hist. Assn. Office: Coll Misericordia Lake St Dallas PA 18612-1023

FRIES, JOCHEN WU, pathologist, researcher; b. Wiesbaden, Hessen, Fed. Republic of Germany, Jan. 16, 1954; came to U.S., 1984; s. Werner Adolf and Erika Liselotte (Steinheimer) F. MD, Johannes Gutenberg U., Mainz, Rheinland-Pfalz, Fed. Republic of Germany, 1978, D in Medicine, 1980. Rsch. fellow Brigham & Women's Hosp., Boston, 1984-87, 89-91, instr., 1991—; rsch. fellow Harvard Sch. Pub. Health, Boston, 1987-89. Lt. col., Navy, Fed. Republic of Germany, 1979-80. Mem. Am. Soc. Microbiology, Am. Soc. Pathology. Lutheran. Office: Brigham & Women's Hosp Pathology Dept 75 Francis St Boston MA 02115-6195

FRINK, PETER HILL, architect; b. Altoona, Pa., Feb. 20, 1939; s. Orrin and Aline (Huke) F.; m. Patti Roomet, Feb. 15, 1992. B.Arch., Pa. State U., 1962; M.S. in Arch., Columbia U., 1963; M.F.A., Yale U., 1967. Registered architect, Pa., Del., N.J., Va., N.Y., Fla. Theatre designer George C. Izenour Assos., Inc., New Haven, 1965-67; resident cons. theatre architect Geddes Brecher Qualls Cunningham, Architects, Phila., 1967-75; prin., ptnr. Frink & Beuchat, Architects, Phila., 1975—, Assembly Places Internat., Phila., 1983—; commr. theatre arch. U.S. Inst. Theatre Tech.; guest lectr. U. Pa., Temple U., Drexel U., Moore Coll. Art, U. Md. Pres., chmn. bd. dirs. Bryn Mawr Chamber Orch. William Kinne Fellows traveling fellow, 1964.Prin. works include theaters and opera houses, concert halls. Editor: Theatre Design '75, 1975; contbr. to Architectural Graphic Standards, 7th and 8th editions, Encyclopedia of Architecture, 1987-89. Fellow U.S. Inst. Theatre Tech.; mem. AIA. Home: PO Box 15740 Philadelphia PA 19103-0740 Office: Assembly Places Internat 1519 Walnut St Philadelphia PA 19102-3070

FRISCH, HARRY DAVID, lawyer, consultant; b. N.Y.C., June 5, 1954; s. Isaac and Regina (Rottenberg) F. BS, CCNY, 1976; postgrad., Rutgers U., 1976-77; JD, Pace U., 1980. Bar: N.Y 1981, U.S. Dist. Ct. (so. and ea. dists.) N.Y. 1981, U.S. Ct. Appeals (2d cir.) 1984, U.S. Supreme Ct. 1986, U.S. Ct. Appeals (5th cir.) 1987. Law clk. Shearson Hayden Stone, Inc., N.Y.C., 1977-80; assoc. gen. counsel Shearson Loeb Rhoades, Inc., N.Y.C., 1980-82; asst. v.p., asst. corp. sec., assoc. gen. counsel Shearson/Am. Express, Inc., N.Y.C., 1982-85; v.p., sr. litigator, assoc. gen. counsel Shearson Lehman Bros., Inc., N.Y.C., 1985-88; 1st v.p., sr. litigator, assoc. gen. counsel Shearson Lehman Hutton, Inc., N.Y.C., 1988-90, Shearson Lehman Bros., Inc., N.Y.C., 1990—. Contbr. articles to profl. jours. Mem. ABA, N.Y. State Bar Assn., Assn. of Bar of City of N.Y., N.Y. County Lawyers Assn., Fed. Bar Council. Democrat. Jewish. Home: 49 Hudson Watch Dr Ossining NY 10562-2442

FRISCH, HARRY LLOYD, chemist, educator; b. Vienna, Austria, Nov. 13, 1928; s. Jacob J. and Clara F. (Spondre) F.; children—Benjamin, Michael. B.A., Williams Coll., 1947; Ph.D., Poly. Inst. Bklyn., 1952. Research asso. physics Syracuse U., 1952-54; instr. U. So. Calif., 1954-55, asst. prof., 1955-56; mem. tech. staff Bell Telephone Labs., Inc., Murray Hill, N.J., 1956-67; prof. chemistry SUNY, Albany, 1967-78, disting. prof. chemistry, 1978—; assoc. dean Coll. Arts and Sci., 1969-71; vis. assoc. prof. physics Yeshiva U., 1963-65, Inst. Study Metals, U. Chgo., 1960; asst. to dean Belfer Grad. Sch. Yeshiva U., 1963-65; cons. in field. Editor: (with J. Lebowitz) The Equilibrium Theory of Classical Fluids, 1964, (with Z. Salsburg) Simple Dense Fluids, 1968; assoc. editor: Jour. Chem. Physics, 1964-66, Jour. Statis. Physics, 1970-75; mem. editorial bd.: Jour. Phys. Chemistry, 1976-80, Jour. Polymer Sci. (Physics edit.), 1976—, Jour. Membrane Sci, 1976-80, Jour. Colloid and Interface Sci., 1978-81, Jour. Adhesion, 1970-75; contbr. articles to profl. jours. NSF grantee, 1968—; recipient Sr. U.S. Scientist Humboldt award, 1987-89. Fellow Am. Phys. Soc.; mem. Am. Chem. Soc., Cosmos Club, Williams Club, Sigma Xi. Democrat. Jewish. Office: 1400 Washington Ave Albany NY 12222-0001

FRISCH, ROBERT MYRON, JR., company executive; b. New Brunswick, N.J., Nov. 26, 1956; s. Robert Myron Sr. and Lyllian Gray (Boyle) F.; m. Elizabeth Anne Clarke, Sept. 11, 1982. BA, Rutgers U., 1978. Purchasing agt. H.W. Brown Hardware, Inc, New Brunswick, 1977-81; br. mgr. Middlesex Welding Sales, Co., Inc., North Brunswick, N.J., 1981-84; mfg. supr. DelMonte Corp, Dayton, N.J., 1984-85; plant supr. warehouse ops. Myron Mfg., Maywood, N.J., 1985-86; purchasing svcs. mgr. Hanover Ins. Co., Piscataway, N.J., 1986-91; mgr. corp. purchasing Am. Internat. Group, Inc., Livingston, N.J., 1991—. Mem. North Brunswick Vol. Fire Dept., 1976—; class agt. Rutgers Prep. Sch. Alumni Assn., Somerset, N.J., 1984—. Flotilla comdr. USCG Aux., 1986—. Mem. Nat. Assn. Purchasing Mgrs., Am. Purchasing Soc., Clan Stewart Soc. Am. (state commr. 1986—), Rutgers U. Alumni Assn. (bd. dirs. 1988—), Union Club New Brunswick, Keyport Yacht Club, Greater Princeton Jaycees. Republican. Presbyterian. Home: 33 Mohawk Ave Middlesex NJ 08846 Office: Am Internat Group Inc 2 Peach Tree Hill Rd Livingston NJ 07039-5701

FRISCH, ROSE EPSTEIN, population sciences researcher; b. N.Y.C., July 7, 1918; m. David H. Frisch; children: Henry J., Ruth Frisch Dealy. BA, Smith Coll., 1939; MA, Columbia U., 1940; PhD, U. Wis., 1943. Assoc. prof. population studies Harvard U., Cambridge, Mass., 1984—. Contbr. articles to profl. jours. John Simon Guggenheim Meml. fellow, 1975-76. Mem. AAAS, Endocine Soc. Am., Population Soc. Am., Sigma Xi (nat. lectr. 1989-90). Office: Harvard U Ctr Population Studies 9 Bow St Cambridge MA 02138-5189

FRISHBERG, AARON DAVID, lawyer; b. N.Y.C.; s. Ezra and Mildred (Grodinsky) F.; m. Nancy Ellen Buckley. BS, CCNY, 1978; JD, N.Y. Law Sch., 1981. Bar: N.J. 1987, N.Y. 1987. Staff atty., mng. atty. Stevens, Hinds & White, P.C., N.Y.C., 1987-89; staff atty. MFY Legal Svcs., Inc., N.Y.C., 1989—; pres. N.Y. Lyric Circus, N.Y.C., 1987—; bd. dirs. Toussaint Inst., N.Y.C., 1988-91, Project Release, N.Y.C.; del. Legal Svcs. Staff Assn., N.Y.C., 1989-91. Contbr. articles to profl. jours. Mem. N.Y. State Bar Assn. (mem. com. phys. and mental disabilities). Home: 282 Cabrini Blvd New York NY 10040

FRISINA, ROBERT DANA, sensory neuroscientist; b. Evanston, Ill., Sept. 11, 1955; s. D. Robert and Louise (Boaz) F.; m. Susan Taylor Frisina, July 31, 1982; children: Laurin Taylor, Taylor Robert. AB in Exptl. Psychology summa cum laude, Hamilton Coll., 1977; PhD in Neurosci., Syracuse U., 1983. Rsch. asst. Hamilton Coll., Clinton, 1977; Root fellow in sci. Inst. Sensory Rsch., Syracuse, N.Y., 1977-78; NSF grad. fellow Inst. Sensory Rsch., Syracuse, 1978-81, grad. rsch. assoc., 1981-83; NIH rsch. fellow Ctr. Brain Rsch. U. Rochester, 1983-85, asst. prof. physiology and otolaryngology Ctr. Brain Rsch., 1985-91, assoc. prof. surgery and physiology, 1991—, dir. rsch. otolaryngology, 1988-92, assoc. chmn. otolaryngology, 1992—; mem. staff Nat. Tech. Inst. for Deaf, Rochester, 1975; charter mem. adv. bd. Internat. Ctr. for Hearing and Speech Rsch., 1988—; assoc. chmn. otolarynology, 1992—. Author: Hearing, 1989; contbr. articles to profl. jours. Dir. Vols. Hamilton Coll. Aspect of Marcy (N.Y.) Psychiat. Ctr., 1974-77. Recipient 1st Award in Communicative Disorders, NIH, 1988—. Fellow Am. Acad. Otolaryngology-Head and Neck Surgery; mem. Acoustical Soc. Am.,Assn. Rsch. in Otolaryngology, Soc. Neurosci., Am. Speech-Hearing-Lang. Assn., Animal Behavior Soc., Phi Beta Kappa, Sigma Xi. Roman Catholic. Office: U Rochester Med Ctr Otolaryngology Div Rochester NY 14642-8629

FRITZ, DOUGLAS PARTRIDGE, research chemist; b. Erie, Pa., Aug. 19, 1940; s. Joseph Merrick and Ruth (Conway) F.; married, Sept. 16, 1961; children: Serenna Gibson, Jennifer Fritz. BS, Pa. State U., 1962. Chemist Nabisco Corp., Fair Lawn, N.J., 1962-67; mgr. R&D Topps Chewing Gum, Inc., Duryea, Pa., 1967-80; dir. R&D Cafosa Gum, S.A. Barcelona, Spain, 1980-84; pres. Douglas Fritz Consultants, Manshawkin, N.J., 1984—. Inventor, patentee low density chewing gum. Bd. dirs. Wyoming Valley Red Cross, Wilkes Barre, Pa., 1978. Home: 196 Antioch Rd Barnegat Light NJ 08006-9999 Office: Douglas P Fritz Cons 15 Letts Ave Manahawkin NJ 08050-3140

FRITZ, JAMES EDWARD, foundation administrator; b. Cheyenne, Wyo., May 20, 1938; s. Virgil Delbert and Clara Louella (Howarter) F.; m. Diane Delp Gordon, June 3, 1967 (dec. Jan. 1971); 1 child, Ann; m. Dorothy Dale Dugan, Mar. 24, 1979. BS, U. Wyo., 1960; MBA, U. Ala., 1968. Commd. 2d lt. U.S. Army, 1960, advanced through grades to col., 1979; exec. Ind. State Bar Assn., Indpls., 1981-89; pres. Newcomen Soc. of U.S., Exton, Pa., 1990—; pres. JEF Assn. Cons., Carmel, Ind., 1989-90. Decorated Legion of Merit, Bronze Star (with 3 oak leaf clusters), Air Medal. Mem. Am. Soc. Assn. Execs., Pa. Soc. Assn. Execs., Assn. U.S. Army (bd. dirs. Washington chpt. 1985-81, Commendation 1991), U.S. Army Adj. Gen. Corps. Assn. (v.p.), Ret. Officers Assn., Am. Legion, VFW, Ind. Assn. U.S. Army (pres. Indpls. chpt. 1985-87). Republican. Presbyterian. Home: 111 Brookhollow Dr Downingtown PA 19335-4710 Office: Newcomen Soc of US 412 Newcomen Rd Exton PA 19341-1999

FRITZ, LANCE HINE, company specialist; b. Turner Falls, Mass., Aug. 20, 1947; s. William C. and Ursula (Hine) F.; m. Kathleen Yvette Fritz, Feb. 17, 1968; children: Denise E., Dianne Y., Joshua J., Erin L., Bethany A. BS, N.Y. Regents, 1985. Aux. oper. Yankee Atomic Electric, Rowe, Mass., 1973-75, reactor oper., 1975-79; supr. nuclear sta. N.H. Yankee, Seabrook, 1975-85, supt., 1985—. Mem. town meeting Town of Amesbury, 1981—; sec. Rep. Town Com., 1992—, vice chmn. fin. com., 1987—; pres. New Engl. Alliance Men, 1990-92; Deacon Haverhill Alliance Ch., 1992—, trustee, mem. governing bd.; chmn. bd. dirs. Noah's Ark Day Care Ctr.; past pres. Amesbury Girls Softball League; coach, umpire Little League. With USN, 1965-73. Mem. Masons. Republican. Home: 169 Main St Amesbury MA 01913

FRITZ, MICHAEL CHARLES, export management consultant executive, musician; b. Williamsport, Pa., Aug. 19, 1964; s. Charles Wales and Margarette Mae (Hummel) F. Grad., Miller Sch. Audio/Visual Arts, 1984. Rec. engr. John Miller Prodn. Studios, Bath, Pa., 1984-87; applicator Acoustical Spray Insulators Inc., Breinigsville, Pa., 1984-86; telephone technician Tramsco Inc., Bethlehem, Pa., 1986-88, Maverick Communications Inc., Bethlehem, 1988; dock worker Sears Roebuck Inc., Allentown, Pa., 1988-90; shipping mgr. John Pearse Guitar Strings Ltd., Center Valley, Pa., 1989-90; pres. LLF America, Inc., Lehigh Valley, Pa., 1990—; studio and live musician, Lehigh Valley, 1981—. Composer songs. Mem. Lehigh Valley World Trade Club, Hellertown Sportsmans Assn. Libertarian. Office: LLF America Inc PO Box 20166 Lehigh Valley PA 18002-0166

FRITZ, SIGMUND, meteorologist; b. Bklyn., June 9, 1914; s. Morris and Celia (Berger) F.; m. Ann Robinson, June 30, 1946; children: Maurene N., Lawrence C. BS, Bklyn. Coll., 1934; MS, MIT, 1941, ScD, 1953. Chief solar radiation U.S. Weather Bur., Washington, 1946-58, chief satellite sect., 1958-61, dir. meteorol. satellite lab., 1961-70; chief space scientist Nat Environ. Satellite Svc., Washington, 1970-75; vis. prof. and sr. assoc. U. Md., College Park, 1975-90; chief space scientist Mentor Tech. Inc., Rockville, Md., 1990—. Contbr. articles to profl. jours. Lt. comdr. USN, 1942-46. Recipient Gold Medal U.S. Dept. Commerce, 1965. Fellow Am. Meteorol. Soc., Am. Geophys. Union. Office: Mentor Tech Inc 12750 Twinbrook Pky Rockville MD 20852-1700

FRITZ, SUZANNE, university administrator; b. Torrance, Calif., Dec. 19, 1961; d. Alfred Herman and Diane (Lockhart) F. BS, U. Calif., Davis, 1985; MEd, U. Vt., 1987; postgrad., U. Mass., 1988-90. Hall advisor U. Vt., Burlington, 1985-87; residence dir. U. Mass., Amherst, 1987-90; housing coord. SUNY, Binghamton, 1990—; cons. various univs. and colls., 1989—. Vol. Planned Parenthood, Burlington, Vt., 1987; active with NOW, 1988—. Mem. Am. Coll. Pers. Assn., Am. Coll. and Univ. Housing Assn.

FRITZ, WAYNE RICHARD, aerospace marketing executive; b. South Haven, Mich., Nov. 3, 1934; s. Clarence Theodore and Mary Elizabeth (Shanley) F.; m. Joan May Thomas, Apr. 30, 1960; children: Michael, Scott, William. BS in Engring., U.S. Naval Acad., 1957; BS in Physics, U.S. Naval Postgrad. Sch., Monterey, Calif., 1964. Commd. ensign USN, 1957, advanced through grades to capt., 1980; contract adminstrv. specialist Undersea Dept. GE, Syracuse, N.Y., 1969-71, sales, mktg. rep., 1971-77; field mktg. rep. Aerospace Dept. GE, Washington, 1977-84, submarine warfare programs mgr., 1984—. Vestry St. Matthews Episcopal Ch., Liverpool, N.Y., 1974-76; Naval Acad. info. officer USN Alumni & Naval ROTC, Syracuse and Annapolis, 1972-85. Mem. Naval Submarine League (adv. coun. 1991—), Navy League of U.S., Naval Res. Assn. (life), U.S. Naval Acad. Alumni (life, pres. Washington chpt. 1991-92), Shriners. Republican. Home: 1014 Old Bay Ridge Rd Annapolis MD 21403-4255

FROCK, J. DANIEL, manufacturing company executive; b. Hanover, Pa., Mar. 10, 1940; s. Edmond Burnell and Rebecca Martha (Black) F.; m. Joanne Marie Klunk, Oct. 3, 1939; children: Carole A. Baublitz, John D. Frock, Julie M. Crapster. Student, York Coll., 1958-59. Machine operator Hanover (Pa.) Wire Cloth Co., 1957-62, supt., 1962-65, plant mgr., 1965-70, gen. supt., 1970-72, v.p. mfg., 1972-89, v.p., gen. mgr., 1989-91, v.p. ops. Hanover and Walterboro, S.C. plants, 1991—; Bd. dirs., charter mem. Hanover Area YMCA, 1972; deacon Emmanuel United Ch. Christ, Hanover, 1973; mem. reading mentorship program for elem. grade schs. Board dirs., charter mem. Hanover Area YMCA, 1972; deacon Emmanuel United Ch. Christ, Hanover, 1973. Mem. Wire Assn. Internat. (25-yr. plaque 1992), Hanover Area C. of C., Hanover Area Indsl. Mgmt. Club (past officer), Elks. Republican. Home: 309 Clearview Rd Hanover PA 17331-1313 Office: Hanover Wire Cloth E Middle St Hanover PA 17331-3115

FROEBEL, CARLTON ALFRED, JR., computer software executive; b. Elizabeth, N.J., May 23, 1938; s. Carlton Alfred and Mae Louise (Palmer) F.; m. Judy Poznik, Apr. 16, 1981; children: Shane, Tamara. BA, Coe Coll., 1960; MBA, U. Pitts., 1965. Systems engr. IBM Corp., Pitts., 1961-65; systems mgr. Scudder, Stevens & Clark, N.Y.C., 1965-69; pres. Systems Dynamics Corp., N.Y.C., 1969-72; exec. v.p. Bradford Trust Co., N.Y.C., 1972-75; v.p. Automatic Data Processing, N.Y.C., 1976-78; pres. Nat. Investor Data Svcs., Southampton, N.Y., 1978—; dir. trustee Professionally Managed Portfolios, Southampton, 1991—. Home: 1100 Meadow Ln Southampton NY 11968-4524 Office: Nat Investor Data Svcs Inc 33 Flying Point Rd Southampton NY 11968-5248

FROEHLICH, DEAN KENNETH, psychologist; b. Detroit, May 12, 1931; s. Earl Frederick and Lois Virginia (Clear) F. AB with honors, U. Mich., 1953; PhD, U. Ill., 1961. Instr. Dartmouth Coll., Hanover, N.H., 1958-61; rsch. scientist Human Resources Rsch. Office George Washington U., Washington, 1961-66, sr. scientist, 1966-70; sr. staff scientist Human Resources Rsch. Office, Alexandria, Va., 1970—. Contbr. articles to profl. jours.; compiler 4 genealogies, 1979-83. Mem. Am. Psychol. Assn. Home: 1314 Goler House Rochester NY 14620-4010

FROEHLICH, FRITZ EDGAR, telecommunications educator and scientist; b. Worms am Rhine, Hesse, Fed. Republic Germany, Nov. 12, 1925; came to U.S., 1938; s. Julius and Ida (Heilborn) F.; m. Eileen Karch, Dec. 25, 1949; children: Laurence Alan, Georgine K. Froehlich Scharff, Philip Marc. BS in Physics magna cum laude, Syracuse U., 1950, MS in Physics, 1952, PhD in Physics, 1955. Rsch. asst. Syracuse (N.Y.) U., 1950-54; asst. instr. Utica (N.Y.) Coll., 1952-54; with AT&T Bell Labs., 1954-87; tech. staff Whippany, N.J., 1954-56; supr. data transmission div. Murray Hill, N.J., 1956-63; head data theory dept. Holmdel, N.J., 1963-68, head telecommunications and data systems dept., 1968-83; head univ. relations AT&T Info Systems and Communications, Lincroft, N.J., 1983-87; ret. AT&T, Holmdel, 1987; prof. telecommunications U. Pitts., 1987—; mem. adv. bd. Ctr. for Info. and Communication Scis. Ball State U., Muncie, Ind., 1987—; nat. telecommunications adv. coun. U. Pitts., 1992—. Editor in chief Ency. of Telecommunications, 1988—; sr. editor IEEE Trans. on Communications, 1988-92; contbr. articles to profl. jours.; holder 7 patents. Trustee Cong. B'nai Israel, Rumson, N.J., 1970-84, v.p. cong., 1974-76. With U.S. Army, 1944-46. Recipient Hon. Alumnus award Pitts. U., 1992; Amer. Fritz Froehlich Award established in his honor Pitts. U. Sch. Libr. and Info. Sci., 1992. Fellow IEEE (Data Transmission and New Telephone Svcs. award), Communication Soc. IEEE (mem. data com., trans. system com. 1960—, chmn. communications terminal com. 1981-84), Phi Beta Kappa, Sigma Xi, Sigma Pi Sigma (pres. Syracuse U. chpt. 1949), Pi Mu Epsilon. Home: 10621 NW 71st Ct Tamarac FL 33321 Office: U Pitts 135 N Bellefield St 743 SLIS Bldg Pittsburgh PA 15260

FROHLICH, JACK T., labor union official; b. Bklyn., Feb. 18, 1950; s. Arthur Joseph and Florence Helen (Toppel) F.; m. Gladys Yvette Bravo, Nov. 25, 1971 (div. 1980): m. Susan Anna Christiano, Jan. 17, 1989. BA, SUNY, Stony Brook, 1973; cert. labor rels., New Sch. Social Rsch., 1986; postgrad. in law, N.Y. Law Sch., 1989—. Class B counterman Pudlin Auto Supply, Bronx, N.Y., 1973-74; trackman N.Y.C. Transit Authority, 1974-80, 82-84, track inspector, 1984-86, safety insp., 1980-81, 86—; shop steward Internat. Brotherhood Teamsters Local 239, N.Y.C., 1973, Transport Workers Union Local 100, N.Y.C., 1978-80, 81-86, vice chmn. track div., 1980-81, 86—, dir. ops. 1986-90, rec. sec., 1990—. Exec. bd. Community Free Dems., N.Y.C., 1989-90; commr. deeds office city clk. City of N.Y., 1989—; v.p. Student Bar Assn., N.Y. Law Sch., 1990-92. Mem. ABA, ACLU, Nat. Lawyers Guild, Am. Trial Lawyers Assn. Jewish. Home: 151 W 74th St Apt 5C New York NY 10023-2204

FROHLINGER, JOEL LARRY, elevator company executive; b. N.Y.C., July 9, 1949; s. Eugene and Etta (Rodman) F.; m. Linda Schlanger, Jan. 30, 1976; children: Melissa Regina, Jordan Ignatz. BBA, U. Okla., 1971. Asst. mgr. May Co., L.A., 1972-74; pres. Able Elevator & Door Repair Co. Inc., Long Island City, N.Y., 1974—; mem. Nat. Labor Com., Atlanta, 1986-87; chmn. Membership Devel., Atlanta, 1988-89; panelist N.Y. Bus. Forum, 1987. Cub master Pack 590, Boy Scouts Am., Massapequa, N.Y., 1990-91, also asst. scoutmaster Troop 90; mem. Brotherhood, Temple Judea, Massapequa, 1983—; asst. coach Massapequa Internat. Little League, 1988. Mem. Nat. Assn. Elevator Safety Authority, Nat. Assn. Elevator Contractors (bd. dirs. 1987-89, sec. 1989-90), Joint Safety Commn. on Elevator Industry (employer rep. 1988-92), Joint Apprentice Tng. Com., N.Y. Elevator Industries Assn. Democrat. Jewish. Office: Able Elevator & Door Repair 37-02 27th St Long Island City NY 11101

FROMAGEOT, HENRI PIERRE-MARCEL, chemist; b. Paris, France, Jan. 25, 1937; came to U.S., 1966; s. Antoine Pierre Arthur and Denise Marie-Andree (Hennequin) F.; m. Juana Zayas, June 19, 1963; children: Paul Yves-Maries, Xavier Pierre-Marie, Robert Francis. Chem. Engr., Ecole Nat. Superieure Chimie, Paris, 1959; BS, U. Paris, 1960; PhD in Chemistry, U. Cambridge, 1966. Rsch. engr. Ctr. D'Etudes Nucleaires de Saclay, Dept. Biochemistry, Gif-Sur-Yvette, France, 1963; rsch. assoc. Rockefeller U., N.Y.C., 1966-69; staff mem. GE, Corp. R&D Ctr., Schenectady, N.Y., 1969-78; sr. rsch. assoc. Corp. Rsch. Ctr. Internat. Paper, Tuxedo, N.Y., 1978-81; sr. R&D assoc. Corp. Rsch. Ctr. Internat. Paper, Tuxedo, 1981—. Mem. Am. Chem. Soc., TAPPI. Roman Catholic. Office: Internat Paper Long Meadow Rd Tuxedo Park NY 10987

FROMBOLUTI, SIDEO, artist; b. Hershey, Pa., Oct. 3, 1920; s. Omero and Marina (Formiconi) F.; m. Nora Speyer. BFA, Tyler Coll. Fine Art, MFA. One-man shows include 37 exhibitions in U.S. and 6 in Europe; represented in permanent collections in 8 museums.

FROME, DAVID HERMAN, dentist; b. Richmond, Va., Jan. 22, 1945; married; 3 children. Student, U. Md., 1962-64, 68; DDS, Georgetown U., 1968; MPH, Johns Hopkins U., 1973. Lic. dentist, Md., D.C. Pvt. practice Gaithersburg and Wheaton, Md., 1970—; clin. instr. dental materials Georgetown Sch. Dentistry, 1970-72; clin. instr. pediatric dentistry U. Md., 1970-73; dental dir. Group Health Assn., 1982-86, Md. State Dental Svc. Corp., 1980-81; cons. in field. Contbr. articles to profl. jours. Past pres. Layhill Village East Citizens Assn.; bd. dirs., trustee Hebrew Day Inst., pres., 1986-88; mem. adv. group FDA, 1985, 89-91. Capt. AUS, 1968-70, Vietnam. Nat. Inst. Dentistry Rsch. grantee, 1967; Pub. Health fellow; decorated Purple Heart, Bronze Star, Vietnam Svc. Ribbon, Nat. Def. Svc. Ribbon. Fellow Acad. Gen. Dentistry; mem. ADA, Md. Dental Assn., So. Med. Dental Soc., D.C. Dental Soc. (assoc.), Acad. Gen. Dentistry, Am. Pub. Health Assn. Home: 8808 Wooden Bridge Rd Rockville MD 20854-2445 Office: 431 N Frederick Ave Gaithersburg MD 20877-2419 also: 2017 Queensguard Rd Wheaton MD 20906

FROMKNECHT, THOMAS GERARD, mechanical engineer; b. Erie, Pa., Nov. 19, 1961; s. Raymond Joseph and Rita Ann (Stumpf) F.; m. Kathleen Marie Becker, Oct. 5, 1991. BSME, Gannon U., 1983, MSME, 1988; postgrad., Pa. State U., 1990—. Rsch. and devel. engr. mech. drives div. Zurn Industries, Inc., Erie, Pa., 1983-87; product engr. cen. clutch div. Zurn Industries, Inc., Woodbridge, N.J., 1986-88; mgr. project engring. Zurn Industries Inc., Erie, Pa., 1987-88, mgr. engring. tech. svcs. mech. drives div., 1988-90, mgr. engring./high performance products and systems, 1990—. Patentee torque overload protection device. Mem. ASME (treas. Erie sect. 1987—), Soc. Advancement of Material and Process Engring., Am. Soc. Materials, Am. Gear Mfgs. Assn. (mem. tech. com. 1988—), Lakeside Bicycling Assn. Home: 1032 E 35th St Erie PA 16504-1830 Office: Zurn Industries Inc 1801 Pittsburgh Ave Erie PA 16502-1916

FROMM, ELI, engineering educator; b. Niedaltdorf, Germany, May 7, 1939; s. Siegfried and Helen (Lucas) F.; m. Dorothy Mildred Gold, Dec. 23, 1962; children: Stephen Arthur, Larry Brian, Richard Michael. BSEE, Drexel U., 1962, MSE, 1964; PhD, Jefferson Med. Coll., 1967. Engr. missile and space div. GE Co., Phila., 1962; engr. Applied Physics Lab. E.I. DuPont Co., Wilmington, Del., 1963; from asst. prof. to prof. biomed. sci. Drexel U., Phila., 1967-80, prof. elec. and computer engring., 1980—, acting head dept. biol. sci., 1984-85, asst. head dept. elec. and computer engring., 1987-89, assoc. dean. Coll. Engring., 1988-89, interim dean, 1989-90, vice provost for rsch. and grad. studies, 1990—; mem. staff, congl. fellow com. sci. and tech. U.S. Ho. of Reps., 1980-81; program dir. NSF, Washington, 1983-84; vis. scientist Legis. Rsch. Office Pa. Ho. Reps., Harrisburg, 1986-87. Contbr. over 50 articles to profl. jours. Recipient Centennial medal Drexel U.; Spl. fellow NIH, 1964-67; grantee NIH, 1969-78, NSF, 1969-71, 79, 84, 88—. Fellow IEEE (bd. dirs. 1983-84, mem. coms., Centennial medal 1984), Am. Inst. of Med. and Biologic Engring.; mem. Am. Soc. Engring. Edn., Sigma Xi. Jewish. Home: 2604 Selwyn Dr Broomall PA 19008-1632 Office: Drexel U Vice Provost for Rsch Philadelphia PA 19104

FROMM, HANS, gastroenterologist, educator, researcher; b. Hagenow, Germany, Aug. 1, 1939; s. Johannes C. and Irene (Biermann) F.; m. Sharon A. Kleiv, June 8, 1968; children: H. Chris, Martin T. MD, Albert Ludwig U., Freiburg, Fed. Republic Germany, 1964. Intern Meml. Hosp., Worcester, Mass., 1966-67; resident Lemuel Shattuck Hosp., Boston, 1967-68, Albany (N.Y.) Med. Ctr., 1968-69; fellow, 1969-71; privat-dozent Medizinische Hochschule Hannover, Fed. Republic Germany, 1974-75; asst. prof. medicine U. Pitts., 1975-80, assoc. prof. medicine, 1980-84, prof. medicine, 1984; prof. medicine George Washington U., Washington, 1984—; dir. divsn. gastroenterology & nutrition George Washington Med. Ctr., Washington, 1984—; Mem. numerous grant review coms. including NIH, Med. Review Bd. Gastroenterology Med. Rsch. Svc. VA, Washington, 1984-87. Contbr. articles to profl. jours., chpts. to books; mem. editorial bds. Hepatogastroenterology, 1981-88, Hepatology, 1985-88, 1991—. Mem. Am. Soc. Clin. Investigators, Am. Gastroent. Soc. (chmn. com. on admissions 1990-91), Am. Assn. Study of Liver Diseases (chmn. pubs. com. 1988-90). Lutheran. Office: George Washington U Med Ctr 2150 Pennsylvania Ave NW Washington DC 20037-2396

FROMM, ROGER WILLIAM, archivist, librarian; b. Buffalo, Feb. 12, 1933; s. Harold William and Evelyn Sophia (Wilcox) F.; m. Mary Carolyn Willisford, June 28, 1958 (div. Aug. 1982); children: Kyle Lincoln, Kris Andrew; m. Marie Rose Badaracco, Mar. 9, 1985. BA, Ohio Wesleyan U., 1955; MEd, U. Vt., 1966; MLS, Rutgers U., 1970; MA, U. Scranton, 1979. Cert. archivist. Salesman Colgate-Palmolive Co., Buffalo, Wheeling, W.Va., 1957-60; tchr. C.P. Smith Sch., Burlington, Vt., 1960-64; prin., tchr. Sekolah Lincoln, Lirik, Sumatra, Indonesia, 1964-66; tchr. Copper Beech Mid. Sch.,

Shrub Oak, N.Y., 1966-67, Escola Inglesa de Luanda (Angola), 1967-68; prin. Am. Community Sch., Benghazi, Libya, 1968-69; assoc. libr. N.Y. State Hist. Assn., Cooperstown, N.Y., 1970-74; archivist, libr., assoc. prof. Bloomsburg (Pa.) U., 1974—. Photographic editor new series of manuals Soc. Am. Archivists, 1989—; state and local news editor Mid-Atlantic Regional Archives Conf., 1990—; author: (with others) Directions for the Decade: Libray Instruction in the 1980's, 1981. With U.S. Army, 1955-57. U.S. Govt. Title II B fellow Rutgers U., 1969-70. Mem. Soc. Am. Archivists, Mid-Atlantic Regional Archives Conf., Am. Assn. for State & Local History, Acad. Cert. Archivists, Beta Phi Mu, Phi Alpha Theta. Lutheran. Home: 14 Shawnee Rd Bloomsburg PA 17815-9439

FROMMER, HENRY, financial executive; b. N.Y.C., July 30, 1943; s. Barney and Eleanor Jeanette (Peller) F.; B.S. in Econs., U. Pa., 1964; M.B.A., Columbia U., 1966; J.D. magna cum laude, Bklyn. Law Sch., 1976; m. Barbara Gay Hymson, Feb. 3, 1980; children—David P., Katharine B. Fin. analyst N.Y. Central System, N.Y.C., 1964; asst. sec. Irving Trust Co., N.Y.C., 1968-71; asst. cashier Franklin Nat. Bank, N.Y.C., 1971-72; exec. v.p., sr. credit officer Comml. Funding, Inc., N.Y.C., 1972-85; pres., chief exec. officer Charter Fin. Inc., N.Y.C., 1985—. Served with U.S. Army, 1966-68. Decorated Army Commendation medal. Mem. N.Y. State Bar Assn. Clubs: Columbia Golf and Country (Claverack, N.Y.); Princeton (N.Y.C.). Home: PO Box 532 Claverack NY 12513-0532 Office: 444 Madison Ave New York NY 10022-6903

FROMOWITZ, ALLEN, banker; b. N.Y.C., Sept. 4, 1948; s. Irving and Pauline (Roskin) F.; m. Carol Ann Westcoatt; children: Daniel Bret, Lori Allison. BA, CUNY, 1970; Diploma in Systems Analysis, NYU, 1977; MBA in fin., Pace U., 1982. V.p. Citicorp/Citibank, N.Y.C., 1977-87; asst. v.p., dept. head money mgmt. Participants Trust Co., N.Y.C., 1987—. Mem. Treasury Mgmt. Assn. Office: Participants Trust Co 40 Rector St New York NY 10006-1705

FROMSON, ANTOINETTE DUVAL, civic worker; b. Chgo., May 22, 1925; d. Ralph A. and Yvonne (Duval) Brown; Barnard Coll., 1947; m. Howard A. Fromson, Oct. 12, 1946; children—Michele Yvonne, Michael Erik, Timothy Arthur, Brett Duval. Plaintiff, Women vs. Conn., legal action about the right of women to control their bodies, 1969; convenor, 1st chmn. Conn. Women's Polit. Caucus, 1970; organizer Westport-Weston (Conn.) chpt. NOW, 1972, organizer, convenor, pres. Southwestern conn. chpt., 1974-78; del. Conn. Democratic Conv., 1974; mem. Weston Town Dem. Com., 1972-74; bd. dirs. Westport YMCA, bd. trustess; bd. dirs. Conn. Planned Parenthood, Five Town Found., Greater Norwalk Community Coun.; lifetime mem. Nature Conservancys, Arlington, Va., Weston (Conn.) Hist. Soc. Mem. Unitarian-Universalists Women's Fedn., Barnard Alumni Assn., Nature Conservancy Arlington (life), Weston Hist. Soc. (life), Cedar Point Yacht Club, Aspetuck Valley Country Club, Fairfield Organic Gardening Club. Democrat. Unitarian. Home: PO Box 1151 Weston CT 06883-0151

FRONCZAK, THOMAS ALLAN, financial executive; b. Buffalo, Jan. 16, 1946; s. Frank Bernard and Eleanor Mary (Tills) F. BS in BA, SUNY, Buffalo, 1968. Sr. acct. Buffalo Gen. Hosp., 1968-73, chief acct., 1973-86; dir. acctg. Buffalo Columbus Hosp., 1986-87, asst. controller, 1987-88, controller, 1988-89, asst. v.p. fin., v.p. fin., chief fin. officer, 1990—; asst. treas. Buffalo Gen. Hosp. Emplyees Credit Union, 1974-85; bd. dirs. Water Front Svcs., 1991—. Republican. Roman Catholic. Office: Buffalo Columbus Hosp 300 Niagara St Buffalo NY 14201-2197

FROOM, SHARON JUNE, accountant; b. Takoma Park, Md., Feb. 3, 1958; d. Harold Lloyd and Gloria June (Smith) Campbell; m. LeRoy E. Froom, Aug. 6, 1978; 1 child, Andrew J. AA, Columbia Union Coll., Takoma Park, Md., 1978; BS, Univ. Coll., Adelphi, Md., 1985. CPA, Md. Staff acct. B.F. Saul REIT, Chevy Chase, Md., 1978-79, Ward Corp., Rockville, Md., 1979-80; staff acct. to asst. contr. Willowick Mgmt., Rockville, 1980-82; contr. Rosebeth Realty Corp., Bethesda, Md., 1982-86; pvt. practice Silver Spring, Md., 1986—. Treas. Beltsville Seventh Day Adventist Ch., 1987-89. Mem. Md. Assn. of CPAs.

FROSCH, JAMES PETER, psychiatrist; b. N.Y.C., Apr. 19, 1949; s. John and Annette (Godsick) F.; m. Amy Koel, July 5, 1982; children: Zachary Adam, Ari Benjamin. BA, Harvard U., 1971; MD, U. Pa., 1976. Diplomate Am. Bd. Psychiatry and Neurology. Asst. psychiatrist McLean Hosp., Belmont, Mass., 1980-82, attending psychiatrist, 1982-86; instr. psychiatry Med. Sch. Harvard U., Boston, 1980—; sr. assoc. in psychiatry Beth Israel Hosp., Boston, 1986—; mem. faculty Boston Psychoanalytic Soc. & Inst., Boston, 1987—. Editor: Personality Disorder, 1982; contbr. articles to profl. jours. Mem. Am. Psychiat. Assn., Am. Psychoanalytic Assn. Democrat. Office: 875 Massachusetts Ave # 54 Cambridge MA 02139-3067

FROST, A. CORWIN, architect, consultant; b. Bronxville, N.Y., Nov. 18, 1934; s. Frederick George Jr. and Gwendolyn Belle (Corwin) F.; m. Rosalie Randolph Halsey, Sept. 26, 1959; children: Frederick Halsey, Anne Randolph. AB, Princeton U., 1956; BS, R.I. Sch. Design, 1959. Registered architect, N.Y., other states. Designer, draftsman Harrison & Abramovitz, N.Y.C., 1959-60; project architect Frederick G. Frost Jr. and Assocs., N.Y.C., 1960-63, assoc., 1963-68; ptnr. Frost Assocs., N.Y.C., 1968-78; assoc. dir. archtl. and engring. services CBS Inc., N.Y.C., 1978-80, dir. planning and design, 1980-86, dir. facilities engring., 1986-88; prin. Frost Assocs. Cons., Bronxville, N.Y., 1988-92; dep. dir. dept. design, cons. and mgmt. CUNY, 1992—; trustee R.I. Sch. Design, 1989—; trustee, mem. exec. com. Westchester Preservation League, 1989—. Chmn. Bronxville Planning Bd., 1990—; trustee Coun. for Arts in Westchester, White Plains, N.Y., 1972-81 (pres. 1974-75); mem. Bronxville Adult Sch., 1982-88, Bronxville Planning Comm., 1977-80. Mem. AIA (exec. com. N.Y. chpt. 1974-76, ethics com. 1978-80, corp. architects com. 1980-82, fin. com. 1981-87). Clubs: Princeton (N.Y.C.); Bronxville Field. Home: 11 Sunset Ave Bronxville NY 10708-2208 Office: CUNY 1555 3d Ave New York NY 10128

FROST, DAVID, consultant editor; b. Bklyn., Dec. 19, 1925; s. Charles and Regina (Sad) Feivlowitz; m. Ruthann Steinberg, Dec. 24, 1946; children: Michael Joseph, Jane Alice. BS, CCNY, 1945, MED, 1949; MS, NYU, 1952, PhD, 1960. Instr. in biology CCNY, 1946-49; instr. in sci. Rhodes Sch., N.Y.C., 1949-52; asst. prof. biology Rutgers U., Newark, N.J., 1952-59; adj. prof. biology Rutgers U., New Brunswick, N.J., 1960-78; sci. editor Squibb Inst. for Med. Rsch., Princeton, N.J., 1959-75; pvt. practice, Plainfield, N.J., Olmstedville, N.Y., 1975—. Pres. N.J. SANE, Montclair, 1964-65; co-chmn. Plainfield Joint Def. Com., 1970-85; newsletter editor Cen. Jersey/Masaya, Nicaragua Friendship Cities Project, Plainfield, 1985—. Mem. Coun. Biology Editors (pres. 1982-83). Office: 1229 E 7th St Plainfield NJ 07062-1907 also: Box 41B RD 1 Olmstedville NY 12857-0041

FROST, ELIZABETH ANN MCARTHUR, physician; b. Glasgow, Scotland, Oct. 29, 1938; came to U.S., 1963; d. Robert Thomas and Annie M. (Ross) F.; m. Wallace Capobianco, Sept. 4, 1965 (dec. May 1988); children: Garrett, Ross, Christopher, Neil. MBChB, U. Glasgow, 1961. Diplomate Am. Bd. Anesthesiology, Royal Coll. Ob-Gyn., London. Intern in surgery Royal Infirmary, Glasgow, 1961-62; intern in medicine Victoria Infirmary, Glasgow, 1962; intern in obstetrics Royal Maternity Hosp., Glasgow, 1962-63; resident in internal medicine Englewood (N.J.) Hosp., 1963-64; resident in anesthesiology N.Y. Hosp., N.Y.C., 1964-66; instr. in anesthesiology Albert Einstein Coll. Medicine, Bronx, N.Y., 1966-68, asst. prof. to assoc. prof., 1968-81, prof. anesthesiology, 1981—, mem. dept. history of medicine, 1973—; prof., chmn. dept. anesthesiology N.Y. Med. Coll., Valhalla, N.Y., 1992—; dir. div. neuroanesthesia Albert Einstein Coll. Medicine and Affiliated Hosps. Book reviewer New Eng. Jour. of Medicine, 1983—; editor Preanesthetic Assessment, Anesthesiology News, 1984—, Gen. Surgery News, 1991; author/contbr. books; contbr. articles to profl. jours. Mem. N.Y. State Soc. Anesthesiologists, Am. Soc. of Anesthesiologists, Assn. of Univ. Anesthesiologists, Soc. of Neurosurg. Anesthesia and Neurologic Supportive Care, Am. Assn. of Neurol. Surgeons, Anesthesia History Assn., Internat. Trauma Anesthesia and Critical Care Soc. Office: NY Medical Coll Valhalla NY 10595

FROST, JACQUELINE FORD, museum administrator; b. Elkton, Md., Aug. 19, 1963; d. Walter Delbert and Janet (Patchell) Ford; m. Samuel Robert Frost, Feb. 22, 1986; 1 child, Samuel Ryan. BA in Communications, Western Md. Coll., 1985. Mus. coord. Steppingstone Mus., Havre de Grace, Md., 1987—. Youth advisors Churchville (Md.) Presbyn. Ch., 1988-89; co-moderator Presbyn. Women, Churchville, 1987-89; mem. Discover Harford County Tourism Coun., 1987. Mem. Balt. Tourism Assn., Vol. Coords. N.E. Md. (vice-chmn. 1988—). Republican. Presbyterian. Office: 461 Quaker Bottom Rd Havre De Grace MD 21078-1329

FROST, JOHN ELDRIDGE, librarian emeritus; b. Eliot, Maine, Jan. 13, 1917; s. Martin and A. M. (Eldridge) F.; B.A., U. Maine, 1938; S.T. B., Berkeley Divinity Sch., 1941; B.S., Columbia, 1948; M.A., U. N.H., 1948; Ph.D., N.Y.U., 1953. Asst. minister, Worcester, Mass., 1941-42; asso. rector, Westbury, L.I., N.Y., vicar, Carle Place, L.I., 1943-44; asst. librarian Drew U., 1949; asst. librarian N.Y.U. Library, N.Y.C., 1950, librarian, 1955-82, emeritus, 1982. Served with USNR, 1945-46. Mem. ALA, Bibliog. Soc. Am., Newcomen Soc. Eng. Author: Nicholas Frost Family, 1943; Colonial Village, 1948; Sarah Orne Jewett, 1953; Maine Genealogy, 1976, Maine Probate Abstracts, 2d vol., 1991. Editor: Maine Probate Abstracts, 1991; Soc. for the Libs Bull., 1958-82. Contbr. articles to profl. publs. Home: PO Box 473 York ME 03909-0473

FROST-TUCKER, VONTELL DELORES, federal agency administrator; b. Charleston, S.C., June 9, 1951; d. Henry Ball and Sallie (Davis) F.; m. Lloyd Tucker Sr., Apr. 7, 1990. B Gen. Studies, Ind. U., 1989. With Maritime Adminstrn. U.S. Dept. Transp., Washington, 1969—; info. asst. U.S. Dept. Transp., 1977-78, writer-editor trainee, 1978-79, writer-editor, 1979-84, pub. affairs specialist, 1984—. Asst. troop leader Girl Scouts U.S., Alexandria, Va., 1983. Mem. Nat. Assn. Female Execs. Democrat. Methodist. Office: Dept Transp 400 7th St SW Washington DC 20590-0002

FRUCHTMAN, STEVEN MARTIN, physician; b. N.Y.C., Apr. 7, 1951; s. Harry and Anna (Rechstman) F.; m. Miriam Baker, Aug. 18, 1985; 1 child, Genna. BA, Cornell U., 1973; MD, N.Y. Med. Coll., 1977. Intern, then resident Downstate Med. Ctr., Bklyn., 1977-81; dir. sickle cell program Mt. Sinai Hosp., N.Y.C., 1986-90, asst. prof. medicine, 1986—, dir. bone marrow transplantation, 1990—. Author: Polychythemia Vera, 1991. Mem. ACP, Am. Coll. Hematology. Home: 68 E 86th St Apt 4B New York NY 10028-1000 Office: Mount Sinai Hosp 1 Gustave Levy Pl New York NY 10029

FRUHMAN, HARRY, hospital administrator, consultant; b. Passaic, N.J., Dec. 31, 1956; s. Joseph and Sarah Adele (Lachner) F. BA, Yeshiva U., 1977; MBA, Rutgers U., 1978. CPA, N.Y., N.J. Sales rep. Equitable Assurance Soc., N.Y.C., 1979-80; sr. auditor Loeb and Troper CPAs, N.Y.C., 1980-82, sr. healthcare cons., 1991—; sr. auditor Ernst & Whinney, Newark, 1983-84; contr. Hackensack (N.J.) Med. Ctr., 1984-85, Bellevue Hosp. Ctr., N.Y.C., 1985-91; adj. prof. Baruch Coll., N.Y.C. Bd. dirs., trustee Tifereth Israel Synagogue, 1985—; bd. dirs. Hillel Acad., 1987—. Mem. AICPA, N.J. Soc. CPAs, N.Y. State Soc. CPAs, Health Care Fin. Mgmt. Assn. Home: 28 Belmont Pl Passaic NJ 07055-4502

FRUITT, PAUL N., manufacturing executive; b. Boston, Oct. 3, 1931; s. William L. and Betty (Podolsky) F.; m. Myrna L. Shufro, Nov. 13, 1955; 1 child, Lisa J. BA, Harvard U., 1953. Various mktg. and research positions safety razor div. The Gillette Co., Boston, 1954-63, mktg. research dir., 1963-65, v.p. planning and adminstrn., 1966-69; v.p. corp. planning The Gillette Co., Boston, 1969—; trustee Mktg. Sci. Inst., Cambridge, 1970-87. Home: 60 Mary Ellen Rd Newton MA 02168-1027 Office: The Gillette Co Prudential Tower Bldg Boston MA 02199

FRUMERMAN, MARCIA, management consultant; b. Sharon, Pa., Jan. 17, 1933; d. Philip and Miriam (Gross) Ellovich; m. Robert Frumerman, May 22, 1955; children: Bruce, Julie. BS, Carnegie Mellon U., 1954; MEd, U. Pitts., 1975. Mgmt. cons. M C Cons., Pitts., 1977-83; v.p. Frumerman Assocs., Inc., Pitts., 1984—; orgn. cons. Multiple Social Svc. and Ednl. Orgns., Pitts., 1973—; lectr. U. Pitts., Carnegie Mellon U., Chatham Coll., Point Park Coll., Allegheny Community Coll., Pitts., 1972—. Exec. editor By Myself I'm a Book, 1972, My Voice Was Heard, 1981, Partners in Creation, 1985; producer, co-author: (documentary film) Bridges to History, 1980. Active Nat. Coun. Jewish Women, 1964—, nat. bd. dirs., 1973-75, pres. Pitts. sect., 1970-72, advisor oral history project, 1977—; mem. adv. bd. Pa. Dept. Edn. Competency-Based Edn. Project, 1977-81; chmn. bd. dirs. ret. sr. vol. program Allegheny County, 1973-75; bd. mem. Pitts. Coun. Pub. Edn., 1970-92, Generations Together, 1984-89, Am. Jewish Com./Communal Affairs, 1980-84, Pa. Commn. on Crime and Delinquency, Select Adv. Com., 1986, Western Pa. Jewish Archives/Hist. Soc. Western Pa., 1991—, Pitts. Index Judaica and Jewish Art, 1991—, Emma Kaufman Camp, 1972-84; hon. bd. mem. Ednl. Alliance/Nat. Centennial Com., N.Y.C., 1988-89. Funding grantee Pa. Endowment for Humanities, 1981, Pa. Hist. and Mus. Commn., 1991. Mem. Exec. Women's Coun. Greater Pitts., Oral History Assn. Home: 5423 Darlington Rd Pittsburgh PA 15217-1505 Office: Frumerman Assocs Inc 218 S Trenton Ave Pittsburgh PA 15221-2793

FRUMERMAN, ROBERT, consulting engineering firm executive; b. Rochester, Pa., Aug. 14, 1924; s. Nathaniel and Goldy (Saskill) F.; m. Marcia Lynn Ellovich, May 27, 1955; children: Bruce Jeffrey, Julie Diane. BSChemE, U. Pitts., 1947; MSChemE, Carnegie Mellon U., 1955. Registered profl. engr. Pa., N.J., N.Y., Fla. Process engr. Elliott Co., Jeannette, Pa., 1947-50, process/devel. mgr., 1953-56; process/project mgr. Blaw-Knox Chem Plants, Pitts., 1950-53; project engr. mgr. Engring. and Constrn. div. Koppers Co. Inc., Pitts., 1956-59; mgr. chem. products Nuclear Materials and Equipment Corp., Apollo, Pa., 1959-62; pres., chief cons. engr. Frumerman Assocs., Inc., Pitts., 1962—. Contbr. articles to profl. jours.; patentee in field. With U.S. Army, 1944-46. Fellow Am. Inst. Chem. Engrs. (Pitts. sect. chmn. 1971-72). Office: Frumerman Assocs Inc 218 S Trenton Ave Pittsburgh PA 15221-2793

FRUNZI, GEORGE LOUIS, vocational school administrator, educator; b. Phila., Nov. 13, 1944; s. George L. Sr. and Frances T. (Bobbin) F.; m. Sandra F. Ferguson, July 5, 1980. BS, LaSalle U., 1966; MA, Villanova U., 1970; EdD, Temple U., 1976. Human resource specialist Mobile Oil Corp., Phila., 1966-68; employment mgr. TRW, Inc., Phila., 1968-69; human resource mgr. N.Am. Rockwell Corp., Norristown, Pa., 1969-71; prof. bus. adm. Wesley Coll., Dover, Del., 1971-81; prof., dir. Wilmington Coll., New Castle, Del., 1981-85; asst. supt. Sussex County Vocat. Tech. Sch. Dist., Georgetown, Del., 1985-88, supt., 1988—; mem. exec. steering com. Del. Adv. Coun. on Career and Vocat. Edn., 1976—; cons. supervisory ednl. seminars, 1977—. Author: (textbooks) Supervision: The Art of Management, Human Relations-Leadership in Organization. Recipient Outstanding Svc. award Vocat. Indsl. Clubs Am., 1988. Mem. AASPA, Am. Vocat. Assn., Del. Vocat. Assn., Del. Distributive Edn. Clubs Am. (hon. life, Great Distbr. award 1985), Del. Chief Sch. Officers Assn., Del. Consortium-Tech. Edn. (bd. dirs.), Kent-Sussex County Chief Sch. Officer Assn. (chmn.). Home: 20 Victoria Dr Milford DE 19963-9661 Office: Sussex County Vocat-Tech Sch Dist Rt 9 PO Box 351 Georgetown DE 19947

FRUTKOFF, PETER HAROLD, music educator; b. Mineola, N.Y., Nov. 20, 1953; s. Harold and Melanie Ann (Feist) F.; m. Lori Ann Hensen, June 28, 1984; 1 child, Casey; 1 stepchild, Shannon Rush. AAS, Nassau Community Coll., 1973; MusB, SUNY, Potsdam, 1975; MS, L.I. U., 1977. Cert. tchr., N.Y. Music therapist Bd. Coop. Ednl. Svcs., Patchoge, N.Y., 1975-77; elem. band dir. Franklin Square (N.Y.) Sch. Dist., 1977—; adj. prof. music C.W. Post Coll., L.I. U., Greenvale, 1975-90; freelance woodwind player, N.Y.C., 1975—; woodwind adjudicator N.Y. State Sch. Music Assn., 1989—. Musician Huntington (N.Y.) Community Band, 1970—, Oyster Bay (N.Y.) Community Band, 1985—. Mem. N.Y. State Sch. Music Assn., Nassau Music Educators Assn. (treas. 1989—, elem. band chair 1986, elem. jazz chair 1988, 89), Associated Fedn. Musicians. Home: 7 Woodbury Way Syosset NY 11791-2719 Office: Franklin Square Sch Dist Washington St Franklin Square NY 11010-4434

FRY, MARY BETH, librarian; b. McKeesport, Pa., June 17, 1961; d. Charles Theodore and Olga (Maha) F. BS in Libr. Sci., Edinboro (Pa.) U., 1984; MLS, U. Md., 1989. Acquisitions asst. Am. U., Washington, 1985-90; acquisitions librarian The Brookings Instn., Washington, 1990—. Mem. ALA, D.C. Libr. Assn. Office: The Brookings Instn Libr 1775 Massachusetts Ave NW Washington DC 20036-2188

FRY, SAMUEL EDWIN, JR., retired foreign service officer, historian; b. N.Y.C., Dec. 1, 1934; s. S. Edwin and Katharine Lucille (Zink) F.; m. Polly Wing Gann, July 25, 1965 (div. Jan. 1976). BA, Dartmouth Coll., 1956; MA, U. Edinburgh, Scotland, 1957, U. Mass., 1965. Vice consul U.S. Consulate, Trieste, Italy, 1961-63; econ. dir. office USSR affairs U.S. Dept. State, Washington, 1964-66; consul U.S. embassy Moscow, 1967-69; econ. officer U.S. embassy Oslo, 1969-72; dir. ops. ctr. U.S. Dept. State, Washington, 1972-74; dep. ambassador Helsinki, Finland, 1976-81, Bucharest, Romania, 1981-84; dir. pub. programs U.S. Dept. State, Washington, 1985-88; mem. U.S. delegation 43d UN Gen. Assembly, 1988-89; office of hist. U.S. Dept. State, Washington, 1990-91; lectr. U. Alaska, Fairbanks, 1992—. Co-author: (with others) Arctic Research of the United States, 1990. Mem. 50th Anniversary coun. Battle of Normandy Found. With U.S. Army, 1957-60. Mem. Arctic Inst. N.Am., Am. Assn. Indian Affairs, Phi Beta Kappa (pres. Washington chpt. 1989-90), Phi Kappa Phi. Congregationalist. Club: DACOR (Washington). Home: 312 C St SE Washington DC 20003-2001 Office: US Dept State C and 22d St NW Washington DC 20520

FRY, SHANTI ADDISON, banker; b. L.A., June 25, 1951; d. Edward Bernard Fry and Carol Mary (Addison) Adams; m. Jeffrey Woods Zinsmeyer, May 9, 1981. Student, London Sch. Econs., 1971-72; BA, Radcliffe Coll., 1973; MBA, Harvard U., 1985. Community developer Harvard Africa Vol. Project, Mombasa, Kenya, 1973-74; mgr. Cambridge (Mass.) Coop., 1975-77; spl. asst. to dir. Action, Washington, 1978-79; dir. mktg. and devel. div. Nat. Coop. Bank, Washington, 1980-83; summer assoc. Kidder, Peabody, N.Y.C., 1984; v.p. Bank of Boston, 1984—; mem., v.p. bd. dirs. Cambridge Coop. Corp., 1976-77. Co-chmn. fin. com. Councilor Salerno Campaign, Boston, 1988—; bd. dirs. Women's Statewide Legis. Network, Boston. Mem. Nat. Assn. Banking Women, Harvard Club. Democrat. Roman Catholic. Home: 8 Berkeley St Cambridge MA 02138-3464 Office: Bank of Boston 100 Federal St Boston MA 02110

FRYE, ROBERT DEAN, foreign language educator, consultant; b. Urbana, Ill., Nov. 1, 1948; s. Charles D. and Margaret (Dorsey) F.; m. Norma Anne Tanguay, June 3, 1978; children: Margaret, Brian. Student, U. Rouen, France, 1968-69; AB, U. Ill., 1970, MA, 1972, PhD, 1980. Instr. MIT, Cambridge, Mass., 1977-78; asst. prof. Wellesley (Mass.) Coll., 1978-87; mem. faculty Harvard U. Extension Program, Cambridge, 1978—; assoc. prof., chair dept. French Regis Coll., Weston, Mass., 1987—. Contbr. article to profl. jours. Nat. Def. Edn. Act fellow U. Ill., 1972-73. Mem. AAUP, MLA, Am. Assn. Tchrs. French, Mass. Fgn. Lang. Assn. Office: Regis Coll 235 Wellesley St Weston MA 02193-1505

FRYE, ROLAND MUSHAT, literary historian, theologian; b. Birmingham, Ala., July 3, 1921; s. John and Helen Elizabeth (Mushat) F.; m. Jean Elbert Steiner, Jan. 11, 1947; 1 child, Roland Mushat. A.B., Princeton U., 1943, M.A., 1950, Ph.D., 1952; student, Princeton Theol. Sem., 1950-52. Instr. English, Samford U., 1947-48; asst. prof. to prof. Emory U., 1952-61; research prof. Folger Shakespeare Library, Washington, 1961-65; L.P. Stone Found. lectr. Princeton Theol. Sem., 1959, vis. prof., 1963; prof. U. Pa., Phila., 1965-83; emeritus prof. U. Pa., 1983—; trustee, vice chmn., mem. adv. com. Ctr. Theol. Inquiry, 1979—, chmn., 1989—. Author: God, Man and Satan: Patterns of Christian Thought and Life in "Paradise Lost," "Pilgrim's Progress" and the Great Theologians, 1960, Perspective on Man: Literature and the Christian Tradition, 1961, Shakespeare and Christian Doctrine, 1963, Shakespeare's Life and Times: A Pictorial Record, 1967, Shakespeare: The Art of the Dramatist, 1970, Milton's Imagery and the Visual Arts: Iconographic Tradition in the Epic Poems, 1978, Is God a Creationist?: The Religious Case Against Creation-Science, 1983, The Renaissance Hamlet: Issues and Responses in 1600, 1984, Language for God and Feminist Language: Problems and Principles, 1988; editor: The Reader's Bible A Narrative: Selections from the King James Version, 1978; contbr. articles to profl. jours. Served to maj. AUS, 1943-46. Decorated Bronze Star.; Guggenheim fellow, 1956-57, 73-74; mem. Inst. Advanced Study Princeton, N.J., 1973-74, 79; grantee NEH, 1973-74, Am. Council Learned Socs., 1966, 71, 78; Am. Philos. Soc., 1968, 71, 78; vis. scholar Am. Acad. in Rome, 1971; NEH-Huntington Library fellow, 1980-81. Mem. Am. Acad. Arts and Scis., Milton Soc. Am. (pres. 1977-78, James Holly Hanford award 1979), Am. Philos. Soc. (sec. 1978-81, John Frederick Lewis prize 1979, Henry Allen Moe prize 1988), Rannaissance Soc. Am. (pres. 1984-85). Presbyterian. Clubs: Rittenhouse (Phila.); Cosmos (Washington). Home: 226 W Valley Rd Wayne PA 19087-2451 Office: U Pa English Dept D1 Philadelphia PA 19104

FRYER, DEBORAH TYLER, painter, designer; b. Utica, N.Y., Dec. 29, 1932; d. Harry Leslie and Harriet Tyler (Wheelock) Williams; m. Rodney Ian Fryer, Aug. 27, 1954; children: Allison, Wenda, Caryl, Ian. BA, UCLA, 1954. Artist Honolulu Advertiser, 1954-55; researcher U. Manchester, Eng., 1957-58; free-lance artist North Caldwell, N.J., 1972-78; decorative painter North Caldwell, 1978—. Designer showhouse rms., Montclair, N.J., 1987, 90, Bernardville, N.J., 1991 (3d Pl.). Mem. AAUW (pres. and founder local br. 1970-71, Named Scholarship award 1985). Republican. Episcopalian. Home: 5 Eton Dr Caldwell NJ 07006-4209

FRYSHMAN, BERNARD, physicist, educator; b. Montreal, Can., May 30, 1938; m. Adele Karash, Nov. 5, 1963; children: Chani, Devorah, Rivkah, Aharon, Shaindel, Sholom. BSc in Math., McGill U., 1960; PhD in Physics, NYU, 1971. Instr. physics Bklyn. Coll., 1962-68; prof. physics N.Y. Inst. Tech., N.Y.C.; exec. v.p. Accreditation Commn., AARTS, N.Y.C. Contbr. articles to profl. jours. Mem. New Eng. Interstate Water Pollution Control Commn.; mem. Nat. Adv. Com. on Accreditation and Institutional Eligibility; mem. secretariat Nat. Assn. Ind. Colls. and Univs.; bd. dirs. Coun. Postsecondary Accreditation. Mem. Am. Assn. Physics Tchrs., Am. Phys. Soc. Home: 1016 E 2d St Brooklyn NY 11230

FTHENAKIS, VASILIS, chemical engineer, consultant; b. Chania, Crete, Greece, July 21, 1951; came to U.S., 1976; naturalized, 1986; s. Menelaos and Antonia Korkidis; m. Christina Georgakopoulos, Feb. 6, 1982; 1 child, Antonia. Diploma in Chemistry, U. Athens, 1975; MS in Chem. Engring., Columbia U., 1978; PhD in Fluid Dynamics & Atmospheric Sci., NYU, 1990. Rsch. analyst Columbia U., N.Y.C., project engr.; rsch. engr. Brookhaven Nat. Lab., Upton, N.Y., 1980—; cons. in chem. engring., 1986—, semiconductor and photovoltaic cons., 1987—, petroleum and petrochemical cons., 1989—; founder, pres. Environ Inc., Upton, N.Y., 1991; chmn. confs.; adj. prof. environ. engring. CCNY, 1992—. Contbr. articles to sci. jours., chpts. to books. Mem. Am. Inst. Chem. Engrs., Semiconductor Safety Assn., Internat. Soc. Solar Energy. Home: 88 Ledgewood Dr Smithtown NY 11787-4247 Office: Brookhaven Nat Lab Bldg 475 Upton NY 11973

FUCCILLO, ARTHUR NICHOLAS, lawyer, real estate professional; b. Patchogue, N.Y., Sept. 21, 1953; s. Arthur Nicholas and Connie Fuccillo; m. Cill Kessler, Nov. 13, 1982; children: Dominick, Joseph, Angela, Maria. BA magna cum laude, Villanova U., 1975; JD, Cath. U. Am., 1978; LLM, Georgetown U., 1980. Bar: Va. 1978, Md. 1984. Assoc. Wickwire & Gavin, McLean, Va., 1978-80; gen. counsel Beltway Developers, Greenbelt, Md., 1980-81; gen. counsel acquisitions and devel. real estate div. Lerner Corp. and Lerner Enterprises, Rockville, Md., 1981—; pres. The Loudoun Partnership, Loudoun County, Va., 1991-92. Contbr. article to profl. jour. Mem. Loudoun Econ. Devel. Com., Loudoun County, 1991-92; exec. mem. Manor Country Club Community Assn., Rockville, 1991. Mem. Va. Bar Assn., Md. Bar Assn., Manor Country Club, Phi Kappa Phi. Democrat. Roman Catholic. Home: 14709 Chesterfield Rd Rockville MD 20853 Office: Lerner Corp 11501 Huff Ct North Bethesda MD 20895

FUCHS, ALFRED HERMAN, psychologist, college dean, educator; b. Englewood, N.J., Nov. 29, 1932; s. Herman and Wilhemine Katharine (Dieling) F.; m. Phyllis Elizabeth Rocke, Aug. 27, 1955; children: Christopher Frederick, Jeffrey Alfred, Lisa Marie, Eric William. AB, Rutgers U., 1954; MA, Ohio U., 1958; PhD, Ohio State U., 1960. Psychologist, scientist Gen. Dynamics/Electric Boat Co., 1961-62; asst. prof. psychology Bowdoin Coll., Brunswick, Maine, 1962-66, assoc. prof., 1966-72, prof., 1972—, chmn. dept. psychology, 1965-75, dean faculty, 1975-91; summer research participant NSF, 1963, 64. Contbr. articles to profl. jours. NSF grantee, 1963-64, 64-

65. Mem. AAAS, Am. Psychol. Assn., Ea. Psychol. Assn., Internat. Soc. History Behavioral Scis., Sigma Xi. Democrat. Home: 5 Longfellow Ave Brunswick ME 04011-2535 Office: Bowdoin Coll Dept Psychology Brunswick ME 04011

FUCHS, HELMUTH HANS, chemist, educator; b. Chgo., Aug. 25, 1931; s. Hans and Alycia F.; BS, Loyola U., 1962; MS, N.Mex. State U., 1966; PhD, Fordham U., 1974; Copy boy Chgo. Daily News, 1954-55; rsch. asst. Great Lakes Naval Tng. Center, 1960-62; sci. tchr. Franklin High Sch., Somerset, N.J., 1965-67; assoc. prof. chemistry State U. N.Y., Farmingdale, 1970-91. Bd. dirs. Germaine Pinault Sch. Music and Performing Arts, N.Y. Served with USN, 1952-54. Mem. Am. Chem. Soc., N.Y. Acad. Scis., Sigma Xi, Phi Lambda Upsilon. Composer: Ein Stueck Fuer Susanne, 1976; Lieblichkeit, 1977; Schlummerlied, 1977; Sonata for piano, 1980, 10 Fantases for piano, five impromptus for piano. Contbr. articles to sci. publs. Home: 804 Front St Dunellen NJ 08812-1016

FUCHS, JOHN MICHAEL, librarian; b. Pitts., July 4, 1945; s. John Joseph and Dolores Marie (Miskinis) F.; m. Kathryn Jeanne Bosworthick, June 17, 1967; 1 child, Linda. BS in Econs., John Carroll U., 1967; MLS, U. Pitts., 1977. Mgmt. trainee Chem. Bank, N.Y.C., 1972; asst. buyer J.C. Penney Co., Inc., N.Y.C., 1973-75; libr. Pikes Peak Libr. Dist., Colorado Springs, Colo., 1977-81; libr. dir. Pikes Peak Community Coll., Colorado Springs, 1981-84; dir. Berkshire Athenaeum, Pittsfield, Mass., 1984-91, Carmel Clay Pub. Libr., Carmel, Ind., 1991—; bd. dirs., treas. Pittsfield Community TV, 1986-91; bd. dirs. Literacy Vols. Berkshire County, Pittsfield, 1984-91. Contbr. book revs. to libr. jours. and articles to newsletter. Mem. Pittsfield Cable Comm., 1985-91. Mem. ALA, Pub. Libr. Assn., Ind. Libr. Fedn. Roman Catholic. Home: 13735 Roswell Dr Carmel IN 46032-5229 Office: Carmel Clay Pub Libr 515 E Main St Carmel IN 46032-2258

FUCHS, MARCIA GAIL, librarian; b. Dansville, N.Y., May 9, 1950; d. H. William and Norma (Burg) F. Student, Ill. Inst. Tech., 1966; BA in English magna cum claude, SUNY, Buffalo, 1972; MS in Libr. Sci., Drexel U., 1974; postgrad. liberal study program, Wesleyan U., Middletown, Conn.; postgrad., Conn. Coll., 1988—. Libr. Free Libr. Phila., 1974-81; libr. dir. Phoebe Griffin Noyes Libr., Old Lyme, Conn., 1981-82; libr. Guilford (Conn.) Free Libr., 1982—; freelance, cataloguer Dushkin Pub. Group, Guilford, Conn., 1982—; mem. adv. bd. Greenwood Press, Westport, Conn., 1991—. Contbr. critical essays to profl. jours. and books. Recipient Blue Ribbons for Baking, Chester (Conn.) Fair, 1984, 85, 89. Mem. ALA, MLA, Mus. Am. Folk Art, Lyme Hist. Soc./Florence Griswold Mus., Conn. Libr. Assn. (Pub. Rels. award 1990). Office: Guilford Free Libr 67 Park St Guilford CT 06437-2693

FUCHS, MICHAEL, computer executive; b. Havana, Cuba, Mar. 3, 1949; came to U.S., 1956; s. Carlos and Berta (Ejbszyc) F.; m. Margaret Ann Goldthwaite, May 30, 1982; 1 child, Jonathan. BS, MIT, 1970; diplomate, NYU, 1983. Software devel. mgr. Coefficient Systems Corp., N.Y.C., 1983-86; asst. v.p. E.F. Hutton & Co., Inc., N.Y.C., 1986-88; v.p. Citibank, N.A., N.Y.C., 1988—; cons. in field. Contbr. articles to profl. jours. Mem. Assn. for Computing Machinery, Data Processing Mgmt. Assn., Computer Soc. of the IEEE, Am. Mgmt. Assn., Mensa, MIT Club. Democrat. Home: 51 Drake Rd Scarsdale NY 10583-6466

FUCHS, MICHAEL J., television executive; b. N.Y.C., Mar. 9, 1946; s. Charles and Sue (Wile) F. BA in Polit. Sci., Union Coll., 1967; JD, NYU, 1971. Assoc. Marshall, Bratter, Greene, Allison & Tucker, N.Y.C., 1971-74; assoc. Bomser & Oppenheim, N.Y.C., 1974-75; dir. bus. affairs William Morris Agy., N.Y.C., 1975-76; dir. spl. programming Home Box Office, N.Y.C., 1976-77, v.p. spls. & sports, 1977-79, v.p. programming, 1979-80, sr. v.p. programming, 1980-82, exec. v.p. programming, 1982-83, pres. entertainment group, 1983-84, pres., chmn. bd., chief exec. officer, chief operating officer, 1984—; exec. v.p. Time Inc., N.Y.C., 1987—; dir. exec. com. Tri-Star Pictures, N.Y.C., from 1983; dir. Cable Satellite Pub. Affairs Network, Washington; v.p. Time Inc., N.Y.C., 1982-87, exec. v.p., 1987; dir. Electronic Techs. Inc., N.Y.C.; mem. exec. com. bd. govs. Nat. Cable Acad., Washington, 1985—; dir. Time-Life Books, Alexandria, Va. Mem. Am. Film Inst. (trustee 1982—), Vietnam Vets Ensemble Theatre Co. (chmn.), N.Y. State Motion Picture and TV Adv. Bd. (bd. dirs. 1984—), Bklyn. Acad. Music (trustee 1983—), Acad. Motion Picture Arts & Scis. (mem. execs. br. 1984—), Nat. Cable TV Assn. (exec. com. Satellite Network Com., Washington 1985—, bd. dirs. 1986). Democrat. Jewish. Office: Time Inc Time & Life Bldg New York NY 10020*

FUCHS-GIOIA, JOYCE K., marketing and sales professional; b. New Orleans, Feb. 6, 1947; d. Murrel Herman and Louise May (Goldman) Kaplan; m. Stanley Fuchs, June 20, 1970 (div. July 1981); children: Belinda Louise, Melissa Eleanor; m. Joseph Neil Gioia, Mar. 17, 1985; 1 child, Samantha Merill. BA, U. Denver, 1967; MBA, Fordham U., 1976; M in Spiritual Counseling, The New Sem., N.Y.C., 1985, M in Spiritual Theology, 1987. Asst. to corp. counsel The Raymond Lee Orgn., N.Y.C., 1970; sales cons. Modern Bride Mag., Ziff-Davis Pub., N.Y.C., 1971-75; account exec. Playgirl Mag., N.Y.C., 1974; pub. Complete Buyer's Guide to Stereo/Hi-Fi Svc. Communications, N.Y.C., 1975-81; dir. mktg. Telesel Div., The Direct Mktg. Group, N.Y.C., 1982, ACM/Burnett, N.Y.C., 1983; pres. The Great Taste Soc., New Rochelle, N.Y., 1987-89, J.K. Fuchs & Assocs., New Rochelle, N.Y., 1984—; mem. ednl. com. Direct Mktg. Day in N.Y., 1984-85, 89—, program com., 1983-84, 88-89. Bd. dirs. The Renaissance Project Found., New Rochelle, 1989—, vice chmn., 1990—; v.p. B'nai B'rith Communications Unit, N.Y.C., 1984-85, 89—, bd. dirs., 1984—. Recipient Silver award and Honorable Mention Folio Mag. Circulation awards, N.Y.C., 1985. Mem. Direct Mktg. Assn. (Semi-finalist Echo award 1990), Hudson Valley Direct Mktg. Assn., Westchester Assn. Women Bus. Owners. Office: JK Fuchs & Assocs 43 Gladstone Rd New Rochelle NY 10804-1212

FUENTEVILLA, MANUEL EDWARD, chemical engineer; b. Havana, Cuba, Feb. 17, 1923; s. Fernando and Edith Agnes (Pira) F.; B.Ch.E., Poly. Inst. Bklyn., 1947; M.S., Drexel U., 1954; m. May Belle Tutwiler, Oct. 18, 1945; children—William F., Diane G., Austin D., Eve J., Inez M. Sr. engr. Catalyic Inc., Phila., 1951-60; chief engr. Stokes Equipment div. Pennwalt Corp., 1960-67; asst. mgr. mfg. Esso Eastern, Tokyo, 1967-69, tech. supt., Okinawa, Japan, 1969-72; project mgr. Jacobs Engring. Co., Cherry Hill, N.J., 1972-75; project mgr. Stauffer Japan Ltd., Tokyo, 1975-77; dir. process devel. Alfa Laval Process, Mt. Laurel, N.J., 1977-79; tech. dir., sr. project mgr. Synergo Inc., Phila., 1979-82; chief mech. engring. Kling/Lindquist Inc., Phila., 1982—; pres. Cerus, Inc., Cherry Hill, N.J., 1986—. Served with USNR, 1943-46. Mem. Am. Inst. Chem. Engrs., Soc. History of Tech., Phi Lambda Upsilon. Club: Cooper River Yacht (Collingswood). Patentee in indsl. processes. Home: 314 Tearose Ln Cherry Hill NJ 08003-3524

FUERST, ADOLPH, consultant; b. Linz, Austria, Sept. 11, 1925; came to U.S., 1939; s. Siegfried and Anna (Strassberger) F.; m. Shirley Rita Miller, July 6, 1951; children: David Jonathan, Ellen Laura. BS in Chemistry, CCNY, 1949; MA in Chemistry, Bklyn. Coll., 1957. Chem. lab. technician Mt. Sinai Hosp., N.Y.C., 1949-50; asst. prodn. chemist U.S. Vitamin Corp., N.Y.C., 1950-52; pigment chemist Ansbacher-Siegle Corp., Rosebank, N.Y., 1952-55; pigment and dyestuff chemist Gen. Aniline & Film Corp., Linden, N.J., 1955-58; from group leader to R&D mgr. Sinclair & Valentine Co., N.Y.C. and Elmsford, N.Y., 1958-74; mgr. spl. svcs. Graphic Arts Labs. Sun Chem. Corp., Carlstadt, N.J., 1974-86; cons. Adolph Fuerst Cons., Bklyn., 1986—; mem. Nat. Assn. Printing Ink Mfrs. gloss project steering com., N.Y. and N.J., 1984-85; chmn. adv. bd. PCI Ink Complaint Handbook System, N.Y., N.J. and Pa., 1986-87. Co-author: Fountain Solution Composition & Its Effect on Printing Ink and Paper, 1986; co-reviser: The Printing Ink Handbook, 1988; co-developer: The Printing Ink Complaint Handbook System, 1988. V.p. Friends of the Libr., Cortelyou Rd. Br., Bklyn. Pub. Libr., 1984; garden guide Bklyn. Botanic Garden, 1990-92; judge Sci. Fair, Am. Inst. City of N.Y., Bklyn., 1967-92, chairperson garden guide com., 1990-92. With U.S. Army, 1944-45; ETO. Fellow Am. Inst. Chemists; mem. Am. Chem. Soc., N.Y. Microscopical Soc. (rec. sec. 1989-91, pres. 1992—), N.Y. Pigment Club (pres. 1965-66, Gavel 1966). Home: 266 Marlborough Rd Brooklyn NY 11226-4512

FUESS, BILLINGS SIBLEY, JR., advertising executive; b. N.Y.C., Mar. 11, 1928; s. Billings Sibley and Lucile (MacNeill) F.; m. Doris Vannoy, July 19, 1952; children: Billings III, Doris Jr., Frederick, Lucile. AB in Journalism, U. N.C., 1949. Analyst Gallup & Robinson, Princeton, N.J., 1952-53; writer Kenyon & Eckhardt, N.Y.C., 1953-59, Batten, Barton, Durstine & Osborn, N.Y.C., 1959-65; creative dir. Ogilvy & Mather, N.Y.C., 1965-89; pres. Billings S. Fuess Advt., Summit, N.J., 1989—; mem. selection com. N.C. Advt. Hall of Fame award. Author, editor: How to Use the Power of the Printed Word, 1985. Mem. coun. N.Y. Philharmonic, 1976—. Recipient Grand award Internat. Film and Television Festival N.Y., 1984, Stephen E. Kelly award Mag. Pubs. Assn., N.Y.C., 1983, Gold award Art Dirs. Club N.J., numerous top industry awards. Home: 19 Highland Dr Summit NJ 07901-3108

FUGGI, GRETCHEN MILLER, education educator; b. Westerly, R.I., Aug. 26, 1938; d. John Louis and Harriet (Scheid) M.; m. William Joseph Fuggi, Aug. 15, 1960; children: Gretchen, Juliann, John, Kristen. BS, So. Conn. State U., 1960, MS, 1969, 6th yr. diploma, 1991. Reading cons. Washington Magnet Sch., West Haven, Conn., 1974—; adj. prof. So. Conn. State U., New Haven, 1988—. Pres. Cath. Charity League of Greater New Haven, 1989-90. Mem. Internat. Reading Assn., Conn. Reading Assn., AAUP, Delta Kappa Gamma Soc. Internat. Roman Catholic. Home: 19 Westview Rd North Haven CT 06473-2013

FUHRER, ARTHUR K., lawyer, theatrical agency executive; b. N.Y.C., Oct. 19, 1926; s. Isadore and Toby (Schorr) Fuhrer; m. Lenore R. Lewis; children—Laura A., Robert A., David A. LL.B., Bklyn. Law Sch., 1949; postgrad. NYU Sch. Law, 1951, 52. Bar: N.Y. 1950, U.S. Dist Ct. (so. dist.) N.Y. 1951, U.S. Supreme Ct. 1977. Assoc. firm Sargoy and Stein, N.Y.C., 1951-52, firm Andrew D. Weinberger, N.Y.C., 1952-54; lawyer William Morris Agy., Inc., N.Y.C., 1954-75, v.p., 1975—; co-chmn. Television and Motion Picture Seminar Practicing Law Inst., 1973. Contbr.: Lindey on Entertainment and the Law. Office: William Morris Agy Inc 1350 Ave Of The Americas New York NY 10019-4701

FUHRMANN, AMOS ENO, marketing professional; b. Buffalo, Oct. 29, 1944; s. Phillip Louis and Grace Vachee (Ballou) F.; m. Judy Diane Stewart, Oct. 20, 1973; children: Todd Lawrence, Traci Machelle. BA, Calif. Western U., 1966; MBA, U. Del., 1969. Mkt. devel. pers. Stauffer-Hoechst Polymer Corp., Delaware City, Del., 1967-68; new product devel. pers. Rohm and Haas Corp., Phila., 1968-72; pres. Fuhrmann Enterprieses, Inc., Millsboro, Del., 1972-81; product mgr. Texaco Chem. Co., Houston, 1981-89; mgr. market rsch. W.R. Grace, Columbia, Md., 1989—. Mem. Chem. Mgmt. and Resource Assn., Comml. Devel. Assn. Office: WR Grace Washington Rsch Ctr 7379 State Route 32 Columbia MD 21044-4098

FUHRMANN, CHARLES J., II, investment and finance consultant; b. Seattle, Feb. 21, 1945; s. Carl I. and Darlene (Reynolds) F.; m. Eugenie A. Livanos, June 24, 1967 (div. 1982); children: Katharine Reynolds, Alexandra Livanos; m. Martha M. Harris, Oct. 17, 1987; children: Arianna Taylor, Charles J. III. AB summa cum laude, Harvard Coll., 1967, MBA with honors, 1969. Sr. v.p. White Weld & Co., Inc., N.Y.C., 1969-78; mng. dir. Merrill Lynch Capital Markets, N.Y.C., 1978-91. Vestry, St. James' Episcopal Ch., N.Y.C., 1979-84, treas. 1981-84. Clubs: River (N.Y.C.); Delphic (Cambridge, Mass.). Home and Office: One W 64th St New York NY 10023-6739 also: 550 Ivy Ln San Antonio TX 78209

FUJISHIRO, KATAKAZU KENNETH, urban/regional planner, engineer; b. Cambridge, Mass., Sept. 25, 1932; s. Shinji F. and Yasu (Matsudaira) F.; m. Jane Foster Eubanks, Nov. 22, 1973 (dec. 1991) 1 child, Joni. BSCE, U. S.C., 1964; postgrad., Rensselaer Poly. Inst., 1969, Ga. Inst. Tech., 1970, Mich. Tech. Inst., 1972. Casualty underwriter Am. Internat. Underwriters Corp., Tokyo and N.Y.C., 1948-57; engr./expeditor Charles J. Craig Constrn. Co., Columbia, S.C., 1958-65; planner/engr. Lyles Bissett Carlisle and Wolff, Columbia, 1965-73; environ. planner, dir. Berkeley-Charleston (S.C.)-Dorchester Regional Planning Coun. and Charleston County Planning Bd., 1973-76; chief water pollution control, prin. planner Met. Washington Coun. Govts., 1976-79; sr. program engr. Advanced Tech., Inc., McLean, Va., 1979-83; gen. engr. region 3 Fed. Emergency Mgmt. Agy., Phila., 1983-84; supr. civil engr. USCG Hdqrs., Washington, 1984—; course dir. architects and engrs. profl. devel. program Def. Civil Preparedness Agy., 1967-73; evening div. instr. Midlands Tech. Coll., Columbia, 1965, 66. Contbr. articles to profl. jours. Served with Adj. Gen. Corps. U.S. Army, 1954-56. Recipient ASCE award U. S.C., 1963; Mich. Tech. U. fellow, 1972. Mem. Am. Planning Assn. (svc. award Nat. Capitol area chpt. 1979), Am. Inst. Cert. Planners. Home: 5300 Holmes Run Pkwy # 516 Alexandria VA 22304-2839 Office: USCG Office of Engring Civil Engring Div 2100 2d St SW Washington DC 20593

FUKS, ZVI Y., medical educator; b. Tel Aviv, Apr. 7, 1936; came to U.S, 1984; married; children: Yaron, Tamar. MD, Hebrew U., Jerusalem, 1960. Am. Bd. Radiology-Radiation Therapy. Intern Hadassah U. Hosp., Jerusalem, Israel, 1961; resident in radiation therapy and med. oncology Hadassah Hosp., Tel Aviv U. Sch. Medicine, Israel, 1964-69; asst. prof. radiology Stanford (Calif.) U., 1969-76; prof., head radiation oncology Hadassah U. Hosp., Jerusalem, 1976-78, prof., chmn. dept. radiation oncology, 1978-84; chmn. dept. radiation oncology Meml. Sloan-Kettering Cancer Ctr., N.Y.C., 1984—. Mem. Am. Coll. Radiology, Am. Soc. Clin. Oncology, Am. Soc. Therapeutic Radiologists, European Soc. Therapeutic Radiol. Oncologists, Nat. Rsch. Coun., Calif. Med. Assn., European Cancer Assn., N.Y. Cancer Soc., N.Y. Roetgen Soc., Radiation Rsch. Soc. Office: Meml Sloan-Kettering Ctr 1275 York Ave New York NY 10021-6094

FULBRIGHT, HARRIET MAYOR, foundation administrator; b. N.Y.C., Dec. 13, 1933; d. Brantz and Evelyn (Griswold) M.; m. William Watts, Aug. 4, 1954 (div. 1975); children: Evelyn G. Ward, Shelby S. Watts, Heidi H. Watts; m. J. William Fulbright, Mar. 10, 1990. BA, Radcliffe Coll., Cambridge, Mass., 1955; MFA, George Wash. U., 1975. Chair art dept. Maret Sch., Washington, 1975-80; asst. dir. Congl. Arts Caucus, Washington, 1980-82, Alliance of Ind. Coll. Art, Washington, 1982-84; exec. sec. Internat. Congress Art History, Washington, 1984-87; exec. dir. Fulbright Assn., Washington, 1987-91; pres. The Ctr. for Arts in the Basic Curriculum, Washington, 1991—; bd. dirs. Coun. for Basic Edn., 1991—, Internat. Srudent House, 1991—. Author: How To Get Your Own Pre-School Play Group; editor: Fulbrighters Newsletter. Pres. Maret Sch. Bd. Office: Ctr for Arts in Basic Curriculum 725 15th St NW # 801 Washington DC 20005

FULKERSON, CONWARD GUARD, contractor; b. Curwensville, Pa., Mar. 21, 1933; s. Cecil and Twylet Fulkerson; m. Ida Gagliano, June 20, 1953; children: Kathleen, Conward Jr., John, Sheldon, Patricia, Patrick. BArch, Rochester Inst. Tech., 1957. Supt. Genesee Bldg., Rochester, N.Y., 1964-70; bldg. contractor Rochester, 1970—. Author: (genealogy) The Gagliano Family in America, 1984, (children's book) Wink and the Baby Buggy, 1985; numerous other family genealogies. Vol. Friends in Service Here (FISH), Henrietta, N.Y., 1979—, Monroe County Food Surplus, Henrietta, 1984—. Democrat. Methodist. Home and Office: 36 Gawaine Ln Rochester NY 14623-5536

FULKS, ROBERT GRADY, computer executive; b. Kansas City, Mo., Apr. 8, 1936; s. Hilburne Grady and Dora Elouise (Johnson) F.; children—Stephanie, Scott Grady. BSEE, MIT., 1958, MSEE, 1959. Engr., chief engr. v.p. engring. and product mktg. GenRad, Inc. (formerly Gen. Radio Co.), Concord, Mass., 1959-73; pres. Mirco Systems, Inc., 1973-75, Omnicomp, Inc., Phoenix, 1975-80, gen. mgr. advanced tech div. (formerly Omnicomp, Inc.) GenRad, Inc., Phoenix, 1980-86, also v.p. parent co.; v.p. engring. Telesis Systems Corp., Chelmsford, Mass., 1986-87; v.p., gen. mgr. Valid Logic Systems PCB CAD div., 1987-89, group v.p. product divs., 1989-91; v.p. Cadence Design Systems, 1992—; bd. dirs. Cirrus Sigma Ltd., Fareham, Eng., Texcon Corp., Phoenix, Custom Data Mgmt. Inc., Phoenix, Markwood, Inc., Phoenix, Office Tech. Ltd., Boston. Mem. IEEE, Assn. Computing Machinery, Concord C. of C. (former bd. dirs., chmn. fin. com.), Sigma Xi. Contbr. articles tech. jours. Patentee in field. Office: 2 Omni Way Chelmsford MA 01824-4179

FULLAN, RICHARD KENNETH, administrator; b. Toronto, Ont., Can., Dec. 26, 1946; s. Gerard McKenna and Mary Gertrude (Coffey) F.; m. JoAnne Gleasey, Dec. 20, 1970; m. Judy Anne Blank, Sept. 12, 1981; children: Sean Vincent, Shannon Jeanne. BS, Cornell U., 1971; MSW, Syracuse U., 1976. Lic. social worker. Houseparent George Jr. Republic, Freeville, N.Y., 1971-76; adult probation officer Bucks County Probation Dept., Doylestown, Pa., 1976-78; dir. social work Montgomery County Emergency Svc., Norristown, Pa., 1978-80; oncology social worker Temple U. Hosp., Phila., 1980; oncology social worker Abington (Pa.) Meml. Hosp., 1980-83, dir. social work, 1983-86, adminstrv. dir. social work, geriatric svcs., 1986—; pres. Ea. Pa. Soc. Hosp. Social Work Dirs., Abington, 1988-90. Recipient Social Work Dir. of Yr., Hosp. Assn. Pa., 1988, Ea. Pa. Soc. Hosp. S.W. Dirs., 1988, Better Life award, Pa. Health Care Assn., 1988. Mem. Ea. Montgomery County Long Care Consortium (chmn. 1984-89), Soc. Hosp. Social Work Dirs. (pres. 1991-92). Lutheran. Office: Abington Meml Hosp 1200 Old York Rd Abington PA 19001-3788

FULLER, JEFFREY P., art dealer; b. Chgo., May 14, 1950; s. Robert G. and Eleanor (Jenco) F.; m. Martha Madigan, Oct. 13, 1979; children: Daniel, Claire, Grace. Student, U. Vienna, Austria, 1970-71; BA, Coll. of Holy Cross, 1972. Asst. Hokin Gallery, Chgo., 1974-78, dir., 1978-79; pres. Jeffrey Fuller Fine Art, Ltd., Phila., 1979—. Mem. Am. Soc. Appraisers (cert., sr.), Phila. Art Dealers Assn. (treas. 1982-83, 88-89, pres. 1987-88), Phila. Art Alliance (bd. dirs. 1982-85), PHila. Vol. Lawyers for Arts (bd. dirs. 1985—). Office: 132 S 17th St Philadelphia PA 19103-5205

FULLER, LAWRENCE BENEDICT, English educator; b. Orange, N.J., July 27, 1936; s. Lawrence Augustus and Priscilla Alden (Benedict) F.; m. Christine Joann Bailey, June 19, 1971; children: Sarah Grace, Jonathan Eli. BA, Dartmouth Coll., 1958; MA, Columbia U., 1963; PhD, Johns Hopkins U., 1974; MA, Pa. State U., 1983. Community rels. Port of N.Y. Authority, N.Y.C., 1958-61; English master Blair Acad., Blairstown, N.J., 1962-66, St. Albans Sch., Washington, 1966-68; English prof. Bloomsburg (Pa.) U., 1971—; fellow Pa. Acad. for Profession of Teaching, Harrisburg, 1988—; assoc. Inst. Edn., U. London, 1986. Contbr. articles to profl. jours. Elder, deacon First Presbyn. Ch. of Bloomsburg. Recipient NEH fellowship, 1976, 84. Mem. Nat. Coun. Tchrs. of English (commn. on media 1991—), Phi Beta Kappa, Phi Kappa Phi. Republican. Office: Bloomsburg U Dept English Bloomsburg PA 17815

FULLER, MARK ADIN, JR., forest products company executive; b. Cin., Jan. 1, 1933; s. Mark Adin and Ellen Dudley (Webb) F.; m. Julia Dula Van Patten, June 9, 1956; children: Mark Adin, Ellen McClain, Mallory McKnight. BA, Princeton U., 1954. With Champion Internat. Corp., Stamford, Conn., 1957—; v.p. sales Champion Internat. Corp., 1971-79, v.p., gen. mgr., 1979-80, exec. v.p., 1980—. Trustee, immediate past pres. Xavier U. La., New Orleans; trustee New Canaan (Conn.) Nature Ctr. With USN, 1954-57. Mem. Am. Paper Inst., Muirfield Village Golf Club, Country Club of New Canaan. Office: Champion Internat Corp 1 Champion Plz Stamford CT 06921-6000

FULLER, MOZELLE JAMES, clergywoman, retired nurse; b. Greer, S.C., Aug. 10, 1909; d. William and Julia (Lipscomb) James; m. James Henry Fuller, Mar. 12, 1928; 1 child, Shirley Lindsey Berkley. Diploma, Nat. Inst. Nursing; 2d semester cert., Howard U. Sch. Religion, 1968; DD (hon.), Universal Life Ch., Christ Mission, 1980, Christ's Instn. Inc., 1980. Ordained to ministry Pentecostal Bapt. Ch., 1967; Mut. Bapt. Missionary Assn., 1967. Personality Sta. WOL and Sta. WMMJ-FM, Washington; bd. dirs. Internat. Found. for the Performing Arts; v.p. D.C. Sr. Citizens Clearinghouse Com., Inc., chaplain emeritus; chaplain Hair Expressions Beauty Salon, Acad. Sch. of Cosmetology by Hair Expressions. Mem. D.C. Commn. on Aging; co-founder Ch. of What's Happening Now; missionary Peace Bapt. Ch., 1949—; founder Sr. Citizens United To Serve Humanity. Recieved Nat. Black Monitor Hall of Fame Community Bldg. award, plaque ANC, 1990, cert. recognition Internat. Found. Performing & Creative Arts, 1991, Govt. of D.C. cert. Sr. Citizens Com., 1991; named Mother of Bus. Mothers Day 1989, BOTH Inc. Mem. Women Ministers Greater Washington, Ministers in Partnership, Am. Legion Aux. Democrat. Baptist. Home: 624 17th St NE Washington DC 20002-4682

FULLER, RICHARD ALLEN, automotive executive, real estate executive; b. Worcester, Mass., Feb. 22, 1941; s. Freeman Allen and Eleanor E. (Perks) F.; m. Carol Lee Streeter, Aug. 22, 1963 (div. 1972); children: Jeffrey, Kerri; m. Marilyn Jane Stelmok, July 24, 1974; children: Christopher, Joshua. BBA, Marietta (Ohio) Coll., 1963. Mechanic Fuller Automotive, Auburn, Mass., 1963-75; mgr. Fuller Automotive, Auburn, 1975-85, pres., 1985—; owner, pres. Northeast Auto Products Corp., Auburn, 1974-84, Dealer Mktg. Services, Auburn, 1981-85; owner, v.p. Cranberry Chevrolet-Olds, Wareham, Mass., 1984-87; owner, pres. MICORP, Auburn, 1986—; with MFA Realty Trust, Auburn, 1986—; owner, treas. Trinity Devel., Auburn, 1987—; v.p. Ragsdale-Fuller Pontiac, Cadillac, Auburn, 1991—; speaker Automotive Service Council, 1966-70; bd. dirs. Consumers Bank, Auburn. Designer various automobile anti-theft systems, 1986—. Chmn. Auburn Ambulance Commn., 1978; rep. Auburn Town Meeting, 1988—; active Auburn Pub. Works Commn., 1988—, Auburn Vehicle Purchasing Commn., 1987—. Mem. Mass. Ind. Garage Owners (v.p. 1975-76), Worcester Ind. Garage Owners (pres. 1974-75), Auburn C. of C. Home: 11 Westview St Auburn MA 01501-2323 Office: MICORP 505 Washington St Auburn MA 01501-2710

FULLER, RICHARD KENNETH, alcohol/drug abuse services professional; b. Chgo., Apr. 2, 1935; s. Marc Cornelius and Edna Jane (Gibson) F.; m. Kathleen Julia Brain, Oct. 22, 1960; children: Julia, Douglas. BA, Monmouth Coll., 1957; MD, Western Res. U., 1962; MS, Case Western Res. U., 1971. From staff physician to asst. chief GI sect. VA Hosp., Cleve., 1971-90; dir. div. of clin. and prevention rsch. Nat. Inst. on Alcohol Abuse and Alcoholism, Rockville, Md., 1990—; asst. prof., assoc. prof. medicine Case-Western Res. U., Cleve., 1974-90, asst. prof. biometry, 1972-90. Contbr. chpts. in books and articles to profl. jours. Capt. USAF, 1964-66. Office: Nat Inst Alcohol Abuse 5600 Fishers Ln Rockville MD 20857

FULLER, TIMOTHY RICHARD, college administrator; b. Syracuse, N.Y., May 20, 1957; s. Richard Harlow and Lillian Edith (Petzinger) F.; m. Carol Jay Zimmerman, Sept. 22, 1979; children: Rebecca, Daniel. BA, Houghton Coll., 1979; MBA, SUNY, Buffalo, 1989. Loan adjuster Merchants Nat. Bank, Syracuse, 1979-80; admissions counselor Houghton (N.Y.) Coll., 1980-83, asst. dir. admissions, 1983-86, dir. admissions and retention, 1986-91, exec. dir. alumni and admissions, 1991—; cons. Ont. Bible Coll., Toronto, Can., 1990, Ind. Wesleyan U., Marion, 1988, 89, Huntington (Ind.) Coll., 1989, Cen. Wesleyan Coll., 1988. Editor: Becoming an Admissions Professional, 1989, 90. Mem. Nat. Assn. Christian Coll. Admissions Pers. (v.p. 1983-85, pres. 1985-88, Admissions Officer of Yr. 1990). Republican. Wesleyan. Office: Houghton Coll 1 Willard Ave Houghton NY 14744

FULLERTON, ALBERT LOUIS, JR., bookstore owner; b. Boston, Aug. 25, 1921; s. Albert Louis and Marjorie Hubbard (Durling) F.; m. Mary Siteman, Dec. 27, 1944; children: Albert III, George, Gilbert, Lincoln. AB, Harvard U., 1947; MS, U. Colo., 1951. Sect. head Lincoln Lab. MIT, Lexington, Mass., 1952-54; project leader Melpar Inc., Boston, 1954-59; sect. head GTE Sylvania, Needham, Mass., 1959-61; tech. staff mem. Inst. Naval Studies, Cambridge, Mass., 1961-66; dept. head Sanders Assocs., Nashua, N.H., 1966-78; tech. staff mem. Mitre Corp., Bedford, Mass., 1978-87; proprietor Bernardston (Mass.) Books, 1986—. With AUS, 1942-46, PTO, ETO. Mem. Mass. and R.I. Antiquarian Booksellers, Harvard Club of Boston. Democrat. Home and Office: 219 South St Bernardston MA 01337-9452

FULLERTON, MOLLIE HAYS, psychotherapist; b. Homer City, Pa.; d. Ray Atkins and Elizabeth (Nicely) Pulliam; m. James Daniel, Feb. 23, 1963 (div. 1978); children: Jeffery, Ashley, Amanda, Jonathan. MEd, Cambridge Coll., 1988. Moderator Armed Forces Radio & TV, Reykjavik, Iceland, 1970; counselor Planned Parenthood, Colorado Springs, 1978; dir. mktg., sales Sea Watch Assoc., Bourne, Mass., 1980-84; pres. Hays Holmes, Sandwich, Mass., 1984-87; intern Independence House, Hyannis, Mass., 1987-88; pvt. practice psychotherapy Sandwich, Mass., 1988—. Republican. Episcopalian. Home: 15 Pond View Dr East Sandwich MA 02537-1718

FULLERTON, TERRENCE DAVID, psychologist, career officer; b. Camp Kilmer, N.J., Sept. 24, 1949; s. LeRoy Robert and Eleanor Alice (McDonnell) F.; m. Joan Louise Arnold; children: Matthew, Taryn. BS, U.S. Mil. Acad., 1971; MA, Mich. State U., 1978, PhD, 1979. Lic. psychologist, Md. Commd. 2d lt. U.S. Army, 1971, advanced through grades to lt. col., 1989, ops. officer Company B/75th Infantry, 1973, company comdr., 1974; ops./security officer 2nd Ranger Bn./75th Infantry U.S. Army, Ft. Lewis, Wash., 1975, company comdr. Company A 2/60 Infantry, 1976; rsch. psychologist Counseling Ctr./U.S. Mil. Acad., West Point, N.Y., 1979-82, dir., 1986-89; rsch. psychologist Walter Reed Rsch. Inst., Washington, 1982-86, dir. of tng./clin. psychology internship, 1989—; presenter in field. Contbr. articles to profl. jours. Mem. Am. Psychol. Assn., Phi Kappa Phi. Home: 9108 16th St Silver Spring MD 20910-2145 Office: Psychology Svc Walter Reed Army Med Ctr Washington DC 20307-5000

FULLWOOD, RALPH ROY, nuclear engineer; b. Hereford, Tex., Sept. 16, 1928; s. Robert Alanzo and Allie Mae Fullwood; m. Janet Adams Johnson, July 3, 1954; children: Robert, Edward, Mary. BS, Tex. Tech. U., 1952; MA, Harvard U., 1954; PhD, Rensselaer Poly. Inst., 1965. Registered nuclear engr., Calif. Physicist Gen. Electric, Schenectady, N.Y., 1956-57; rsch. assoc. U. Pa., Phila., 1957-60; assoc. prof. Rensselaer Poly. Inst., Troy, N.Y., 1960-66; staff mem. Los Alamos (N.Mex.) Sci. Lab., 1966-72; asst. v.p. Sc. Applied Internat. Corp., Palo Alto, Calif., 1972-85; tech. advisor Brookhaven Nat. Lab., Upton, N.Y., 1985—. Author: PRA in Nuclear Power, 1988; contbr. articles to profl. jours. and chpts. to books. Cpl. U.S. Army, 1954-56. Mem. IEEE, Am. Nuclear Soc., Am. Phys. Soc. Home: 70 Head Of The Neck Rd Bellport NY 11713-2032 Office: Brookhaven Nat Lab Bldg 130 Upton NY 11973

FULRATH, IRENE, corporate marketing executive; b. N.Y.C., Nov. 15, 1945; d. Logan and Grace (Sheehy) F. B.A., Wheaton Coll., Ill., 1967. Media exec. Doyle Dane Bernbach, N.Y.C., 1967-72; account exec., retail sales mgr. Sta. WABC, N.Y.C., 1972-84; account exec. Sta. WABC-TV, N.Y.C., 1984-86; corp. sales mgr., Am. Express Co., 1987—. Mem. Fin. Advt. and Mktg. Assn. (bd. dirs. 1981-84, sec. 1984-85, v.p. 1985-86, pres 1986-87). Republican. Presbyterian. Avocation: travel. Home: 150 E 56th St New York NY 10022-3631 Office: Am Express Co 100 Church St New York NY 10007-2601

FULTON, ELEANOR MARIE, music educator; b. Morristown, Tenn., Aug. 9, 1939; d. Nyanza and Myrtle (Dockery) F. BA, Bennett Coll., 1961; grad., Manhatten Sch. of Music, 1969; postgrad., Haydn Conservatory, Eisenstadt, Austria, 1980. Music specialist New Haven Pub. Schs., 1965—; piano instr. Dixwell Children's Creative Art Ctr., New Haven, 1974-81; Orff instr. Neighborhood Sch. of Music, New Haven, 1980—; choir dir. children's chorus Yale U., New Haven, 1983-84; dir. Christian edn. Battell Chapel, Yale U., New Haven, 1984-85, asst. organist, 1991—; interim organist-choir dir. Ctr. Church on the Green, New Haven, 1986-87; cons. M. L. King Concert, New Haven Symphony Orch., 1979-83, narrator Young People's Concert, 1990-91; choir dir. All City Chorus, New Haven, 1979. Co-author Let's Slice the Ice, 1979; contbr. to Music for Children, 1977. Cons. United Cerebral Palsy, Conn., 1986-91. Mem. Am. Guild Organists, Orff Schulwerk, Am. Fedn. Tchrs. Congregationalist.

FULTZ, KATHARINE RUTH, university development administrator; b. Chgo., June 24, 1960; d. Dave and Jean Laura (McEldowney) F. AB, U. Chgo., 1982; postgrad., Harvard U., 1989; CSS. Faculty asst. U. Chgo. Hosp. and Clinics, 1981-83; grant adminstr. Brigham and Women's Hosp., Boston, 1983-85; devel. researcher Harvard Med. Sch., Boston, 1986—. Poetry prize Grinnell (Iowa) Coll., 1979. Mem. New Eng. Devel. Rsch. Assn. (founder, v.p. 1987—), Women in Devel., French Club of Boston, U. Chgo. Alumni Assn. (alumni agt.). Office: Harvard Med Sch 25 Shattuck St Boston MA 02115-6092

FULWEILER, PATRICIA PLATT, civic worker; b. N.Y.C., Mar. 19, 1923; d. Haviland Hull and Marie-Louise (Fearey) Platt; m. Spencer Biddle Fulweiler, Oct. 5, 1946; children: Marie-Louise Fulweiler Allen, Pamela Spencer, Hull Platt, Spencer Biddle. AB cum laude, Bryn Mawr Coll., 1945; MBA, Columbia U., 1950. Jr. copywriter, asst. account exec. Dorland Internat. Pettingell & Fenton, N.Y.C., 1945-46; statistician, fin. staff treas.'s office GM, N.Y.C., 1950-52; asst. account mgr. investment dept. Fiduciary Trust Co., N.Y.C., 1953-61; bd. dirs. Chapin Brearley Exchange, Inc., 1964-74, treas., 1966-71, pres., 1971-73. Bd. dirs. Knickerbocker Greys, 1965—, treas., 1970-75; bd. dirs., treas. City Gardens Club, N.Y.C., 1974-79, chmn. ways and means com., 1974-81; bd. dirs. Nat. Soc. Colonial Dames State N.Y., 1973-82, asst. treas., 1973-82; mem. fin. com. Alumnae Assn. Bryn Mawr Coll., 1970-76; bd. dirs. Daus. of Cin., 1974-81, scholarship adminstr., 1976-81; pres. Ladies Christian Union, 1982-87, chmn. fin. com., 1987—; rec. sec. Women's Assn. St. James Ch., N.Y.C., 1972-75, co-chmn. Spring Festival, 1974-75, chmn., 1975-76, treas., 1976-81, mem. Altar Guild, 1975—; treas. Churchwomen's League for Patriotic Svc., 1982-86; mem. scholarship com. Youth Found., 1981—, pres., 1990—; membership chmn. Huguenot Soc. Am., registrar, 1986—. Mem. Soc. Sponsors of USN, Alumnae Coun. Spence Sch., Colonial Dames Am. (bd. dirs. 1987—), Nat. Soc. Colonial Dames, Colony Club, Thursday Evening Club, Wilson Point Beach Assn. Club. Republican. Home: 158 E 83d St New York NY 10028

FULWEILER, SPENCER BIDDLE, retired business executive; b. West Chester, Pa., Aug. 26, 1913; s. Walter Herbert and Lydia (Baird) F.; B.S. in Chemistry, Harvard U., 1937; m. Patricia Louise Platt, Oct. 5, 1946; children—Marie-Louise, Pamela Spencer, Hull Platt, Spencer Biddle. Owner, Color Photolab., Phila., 1938-42; technician Product Service Lab. and Film Quality-Control, Ansco, Binghamton, N.Y., 1946-48; dir. research Photo-Finishing Inst., N.Y.C., 1948-54; dir. process control Berkey Photo Service, N.Y.C., 1954-79. Tchr., St. James Ch. Sch., N.Y.C., 1958-69. Served to lt. comdr. USNR, 1942-46; CBI. Mem. Am. Chem. Soc., Soc. Imagins Sci. and Tech. Republican. Episcopalian. Clubs: Norwalk Yacht, N.Y. Yacht, St. Nicholas Soc. Patentee silver recovery from photog. solutions. Home: 158 E 83d St New York NY 10028

FULWILER, TOBY EDWARD, English educator; b. Milw., Dec. 6, 1942; s. Harold Edward and Mary Elizabeth (Wood) F.; m. Laura Seaman, June 14, 1966; children: Megan, Anna. BS, U. Wis., 1965, MS, 1967, PhD, 1973. Instr. english U. Wisconsin, Stevens Point, 1967-69; lectr. U. Wisconsin, Madison, 1973-76; asst. prof. Mich. Technol. U., Houghton, 1976-83; full prof. U. Vt., Burlington, 1983—; writing workshop cons., 1979—. Author: Teaching With Writing, 1986, College Writing, 1991; editor: The Journal Book, 1987; co-editor: Reading, Writing and the Study of Literature, 1989. Home: 8 School St Essex Junction VT 05452-3607 Office: Univ Vermont English Dept 304 Old Mill Burlington VT 05405

FUMO, VINCENT JOSEPH, state senator, bank executive, real estate developer, lawyer; b. Phila., May 8, 1943; s. Vincent E. and Helen (Rodgers) F.; children: Vincent E. II, Nicole S.; m. Jane Feola Scalletti, Apr. 16, 1989; 1 child, Allison. BS, Villanova U., 1964; JD, Temple U., 1972; MBA, U. Pa., 1984; LHD (hon.), Pa. Coll. Pediatric Medicine, 1989. Commnr. Bur. Profl. and Occupational Affairs, Harrisburg, Pa., 1971-73; real estate broker and developer Phila., 1973—; pres., trustee Pa. Savings Bank, Phila., 1975—; senator State Senate of Pa., Harrisburg, 1977—; chmn. Senate Dem. Appropriations Com., Harrisburg, 1984—; commnr. Del. River Port Authority, Phila.; bd. dir. Hist. Ship Preservation Guild, Phila., Independence Blue Cross, Phila.; mem. Bd. City Trust, Phila. Pres. Phila. Young Dems., 1968; ward leader Dem. City Com., Phila., 1973-80. Recipient Profl. Award of Merit, Italian Am. Press Assn., Democracy award Soc. Cavalieri d'Italia, 1989, Citation for Outstanding Svc., Gov. Pa., 1972; named to Legion of Honor, Chapel of Four Chaplins. Mem. ACLU, USCG Aux., Nat. Italian Am. Found., Pa. Soc., Phila. Justinian Soc., Irish Soc., Sons Italy. Roman Catholic. Home: 1208 Tasker St Philadelphia PA 19148 Office: Pa Senate Main Capitol Rm 545 Harrisburg PA 17120

FUNDERBURK-GALVÁN, JANET REBECCA, conductor, music educator; b. Eden, N.C., Sept. 19, 1951; d. Albert Otto and Willie Ruth (Williams) Funderburk; m. Michael Joseph Galvan, Jan. 10, 1987; 1 child, Elena Maria. MusB, U. N.C., Greensboro, 1973, MusM, 1974, EdD in Music, 1987. Music tchr. Moore County Pub. Schs., Pinehurst, N.C., 1974-79; teaching asst. Univ. N.C., Greensboro, 1981-82; asst. prof. Kearney (Nebr.) State Coll., 1982-83; assoc. prof. Ithaca (N.Y.) Coll., 1983—; mem. artistic staff Choral Music Experience, 1991—; condr. all state and regional choral festivals, nationwide, 1983—; clinician Am. Choral Dirs. Assn. Nat. and Regional Conf., 1983—, Boosey & Hawkes, 1988—, Music Educators Nat. Conf. Nat. and Regional Convs., 1988—; condr. Ithaca (N.Y.) Children's Choir, 1986—, Cayuga Chamber Orch. Chorus, Ithaca, 1989—; mem. Robert Shaw Festival Chorus, 1992. Asst. editor: (jour.) Choral Cues, 1986-90. Music dir. Choral Peace Child, Ithaca, 1988-90; mem. Carnegie Hall Centennial Chorus, 1990. Mem. Am. Choral Dirs. Assn. (chair eastern div. children's choirs 1988—). Methodist. Office: Ithaca College Scholl of Music Ithaca NY 14850

FUNER, ROLF EDWARD, chemist; b. Chgo., July 23, 1940; s. George Ernest and Anna Elizabeth (Mottel) F.; m. Elizabeth Ann Ryder, Nov. 7, 1965; children: Karl Andrew, Daniel George. BS in Chemistry, Loyola U., Chgo., 1961; PhD in Chemistry, U. Wis., 1965. Rsch. supr. E.I. duPont de Nemours & Co., Wilmington, Del., 1980-84; tech. dir. ICI Americas, Wilmington, 1984-89, AMP-Akzo Corp., Newark, 1990—. Author: (with others) Plastics in Electronics, 1988, 91; contbr. articles to profl. jours.; patentee new plastics. Pres. Civic Assn., Cardiff, 1974-75. Mem. Am. Chem. Soc., Inst. for Printed Circuitry, Internat. Soc. for Hybrid Microelectronics, Rotary. Office: AMP-Akzo Corp 710 Dawson Dr Newark DE 19713

FUNK, CYRIL REED, JR., agronomist, educator; b. Richmond, Utah, Sept. 20, 1928; s. Cyril Reed and Hazel Marie (Jensen) F.; m. Donna Gwen Buttars, Feb. 2, 1951; children: Bonnie Arlene, David Christopher, Carol Jean. B.S. (Scholarship A 1955), Utah State U., 1952, M.S., 1955; Ph.D., Rutgers U., 1961. Mem. faculty Rutgers U., New Brunswick, N.J., 1956—; rsch. prof. turfgrass breeding crop sci. dept. Rutgers U., 1969—, also instr. grad. faculty. Author, patentee in field. Served to 1st lt. AUS, 1952-54. Recipient Green Sect. award U.S. Golf Assn., 1980, Achievement award Lawn Inst., 1977. Fellow Crop Sci. Soc. Am., Am. Soc. Agronomy (research award N.E. sect. 1979); mem. AAAS (fellow 1992), Am. Genetic Assn., Am. Sod Producers Assn. (hon.), Golf Course Supts. Assn. (hon. mem.; Disting. Service award 1979), Internat. Turfgrass Soc., N.J. Turfgrass Assn. (Achievement award 1976, Hall of Fame award 1984), N.J. Golf Course Supts. Assn. (hon.), N.J. Acad. Scis., Sigma Xi, Phi Kappa Phi. Mem. LDS Ch. Home: 4 Delaware Dr East Brunswick NJ 08816-3255 Office: Rutgers U Cook Coll New Brunswick NJ 08903

FUNK, JOEL DAVID, educator; b. New Brunswick, N.J., May 25, 1946; s. Julius Jacob and Pearl (Wiseman) F.; m. Melody Rusomanis, Sept. 3, 1972; children: Rachel, Jeremy, Shoshana. BA, Rutgers U., 1967; MA, Clark U., 1974, PhD, 1977. Instr. to prof. Plymouth (N.H.) State Coll., 1975—. Contbr. articles to profl. jours.; editor/reviewer articles and books. Fin. sec. Temple B'nai Israel, Laconia, N.H., 1987—. Mem. Assn. for Transpersonal Psychology, New Eng. Psychol. Assn., Internat. Assn. for Near-Death Studies, Soc. Rsch. Adult Devel., Phi Kappa Phi. Jewish. Home: RR 1 Box 116 Rumney NH 03266-9707 Office: Plymouth State Coll Psychology Dept Plymouth NH 03264

FUNK, PATRICIA ANN, health facility administrative assistant; b. Coatesville, Pa., Dec. 14, 1934; d. Daniel Jsoeph and Mary Helen (Wolownik) Burns. AN, Coatesville Sch. Nursing, 1955; BS, West Chester (Pa.) State Coll., 1975; MEd, West Chester U., 1979. Staff nurse Coatesville Hosp., 1955-56, head nurse emergency rm., 1956-57, student nurse recruiter, 1957-59, adminstrv. asst., 1959-75, in-svc. educator, 1975-79; in-svc. coord. Pottstown (Pa.) Med. Ctr., 1979-81, dir. ednl. svcs., 1981—. Editor newsleter Sepashet, 1986. Bd. dirs. Am. Heart Assn., 1989—, Am. Cancer Soc., 1981—. Recipient Outstanding Vol. award Am. Cancer Soc., 1985. Mem. Hosp. Assn., Pa. Soc. Health Mgrs. (sec., bd. dirs. 1991—), Berks-Pottstown Arthritis Assn. (bd. dirs. 1982—), Soc. Health Edn. Trainers (bd. dirs. Southeastern Pa. chpt. 1984—), Tri-County Bus. and Edn. Coun. (bd. dirs. 1984—). Republican. Home: 459 Clearview St Pottstown PA 19464-5126 Office: Pottstown Hosp. Med Ctr 1600 E High St Pottstown PA 19464-5093

FUNKE, PHYLLIS ELLEN, freelance writer, photographer; b. N.Y.C., Jan. 4, 1941; d. Lewis Bernard and Blanche (Bier) F. BA, Smith Coll., 1961; MS, Columbia U., 1964. Women's editor Daily Argus, Mt. Vernon, N.Y., 1961-62; arts critic, reporter Courier-Jour., Louisville, 1964-66; arts critic, columnist Suffolk Sun, Deer Park, N.Y., 1966-69; contbg. editor arts Ingenue Mag., N.Y.C., 1969-71; contbg. critic Morning Telegraph, N.Y.C., 1969-72; freelance travel and arts writer various cities, 1972—. Author: (with others) The Jewish Traveler, 1987. Mem. Am. Theater Critics Assn. Home and Office: 484 W 43d St Apt 35Q New York NY 10036

FUQUA, MARY M., academic dean; b. Brattleboro, Vt., Aug. 10, 1937; d. Victor L. and Ruth J. (Reed) Morse; m. Charles Fuqua, Aug. 26, 1961; children—Andrew M., David R., Gillian O. B.A., Swarthmore (Pa.) Coll., 1959; M.A., Cornell U., 1960, Ph.D., 1965. Instr., Ithaca Coll. (N.Y.), 1963-65; instr. Williams Coll., Williamstown, Mass., 1969-71; lectr., asst. prof. North Adams State Coll. (Mass.), 1971-75, dir. continuing edn., 1975-78, dean grad. and continuing edn., 1978—; corporator No. Berkshire Health Systems, 1991—. Mem. Gov.'s Task Force on Econ. Devel. for No. Berkshire, Williamstown Planning Bd., 1989—; del. Berkshire County Regional Planning Commn., 1990—. Mem. No. Berkshire C. of C. (dir. 1983—), Phi Kappa Phi. Home: 96 Grandview Dr Williamstown MA 01267-2528 Office: North Adams State Coll North Adams MA 01247

FURBECK, PATRICIA ANN, artist. BA in Early Childhood Edn., Glassboro State Coll., 1979-83; postgrad., Middlesex County Coll., 1992—. Cert. tchr. early childhood and elem. edn. Tchr. vol. Bozorth Devel. Ctr., Glassboro (N.J.) State Coll., 1980-82, tchr. toddlers, 1982; student teaching program developer Mantua Twp. Schs., Pitman, N.J., 1982; substitute tchr. Tuckerton, Egg Harbor and Manahawkin, N.J., 1983; tutor 2d grade Edison, N.J., 1982, 84; tchr. day care New Brunswick, N.J., 1984-86; tutor 4th grade Edison, 1986; tutor 1st grade North Brunswick, N.J., 1987; owner, artist Mystical Fantasies Customized Artwork, Edison, 1990—; instr. devel. acad. and classroom program, 1985. Mem. NAFE, Inst. Shamanic Studies, Order Eastern Star. Office: Mystical Fantasies Customized Artwork PO Box 1136 Edison NJ 08817

FURBUSH, STEVEN DEAN, economist; b. Seattle, Nov. 18, 1958; s. Erving Ainsworth and Dorothy (Ranns) F.; m. Helen Rae Holcomb, Sept. 13, 1980; children: Julie Rae, Jamie Lynne, Lauren Dean. BA, U. Wash., 1981; MA, U. Md., 1988, PhD, 1990. Jr. economist exec. office of pres. Council Econ. Advisers, Washington, 1985-87; rsch. economist SEC, Washington, 1987-89; econ. advisor to the chmn. Commodity Futures Trading Comm., Washington, 1989-90; spl. cons. Economists Inc., 1990—; adj. prof. econs. Va. Polytech. Inst. and State U., 1990—; rsch. assoc. Ctr. Naval Analysis, Alexadria, Va., 1982-85. Mem. Am. Econ. Assn. Christian Scientist. Home: 13120 Buccaneer Rd Silver Spring MD 20904-3243 Office: Economists Inc 1233 20th St NW Ste 600 Washington DC 20036

FÜRER, MARTIN PIUS, computer scientist, mathematician; b. Waldkirch, St. Gallen, Switzerland, June 2, 1947; s. Pius Martin and Pia Maria (Eicher) F.; m. Dorigna Monsch, Aug. 6, 1971; children—Daniela, Andrea, Markus. Diploma Math., Swiss Fed. Inst. Tech., Zurich, 1972. Dr.sci.math., 1978. Asst., Swiss Fed. Inst. Tech., Zürich, 1972-78; research assoc. U. Wash., Seattle, 1978-79, U. Edinburgh, Scotland, 1979-81; researcher U. Tübingen, Fed. Republic Germany, 1981-82; Oberassistent U. Zurich, 1982-87; assoc. prof. Computer Sci. Dept. Pa. State U., 1987—. Contbr. articles to math. and computer sci. jours. Mem. Am. Math. Soc., Assn. Computing Machinery, Assn. Symbolic Logic, European Assn. Theoretical Computer Sci., Swiss Math. Assn. Office: Pa State U Computer Sci Dept University Park PA 16802-6100

FURGOL, EDWARD MACKIE, museum curator, historian; b. Utica, N.Y., June 4, 1955; s. Theodore Joseph and Jean Lind (Mackie) F.; m. Mary Theresa Gibbons, Sept. 10, 1981; children: Malcolm John, Katherine Elizabeth, James Philip. BA, Coll. Wooster, 1977; DPhil, U. Oxford, Eng., 1983. Supr., historian Pendle Heritage Centre, Barrowford, Eng., 1982-84; historian Hist. Scotland (formerly Hist. Bldgs. and Monuments Directorate), Edinburgh, Scotland, 1984-86; mus. curator Navy Mus., Washington, 1987—; vol. cataloguer Nat. Register Archives, Edinburgh, 1984-85; chmn. com. Scottish History Postgrad. Conf., Edinburgh, 1980-81; mem. com. Nat. Covenant Conf., Edinburgh, 1986-88. Author: A Regimental History of the Covenanting Armies, 1639-51, 1990; contbr. articles to profl. jours. Scottish Arts Coun. grantee, 1981, Twenty-Seven Found. grantee, 1986. Fellow Soc. Antiquaries of Scotland; mem. Am. Hist. Assn., Scottish History Soc. Presbyterian. Office: Navy Mus Washington Navy Yard Washington DC 20374

FURIE, BRUCE, hematologist, educator, health administrator; b. Coral Gables, Fla., Apr. 17, 1944; s. J. Leon and Bernice (Wolfe) F.; m. Barbara Cantor, May 5, 1966; children: Eric, Gregg. AB, Princeton (N.J.) U., 1966; MD, U. Pa., 1970. Diplomate Am. Bd. Hematology, Am. Bd. Internal Medicine, Nat. Bd. Med. Examiners. Intern Hosp. of U. of Pa., Phila., 1970-71, resident, 1971-72; rsch. assoc. NIH, Bethesda, Md., 1972-74; chief coagulation unit New Eng. Med. Ctr., Boston, 1975—, chief div. of hematology and oncology, 1990—; from asst. to full prof. Sch. of Medicine Tufts U., Boston, 1975—; chmn. clin. scis. study sect. NIH, Bethesda, Md., 1981-85; mem. adv. bd. Nat. Heart, Lung & Blood Inst., Bethesda, 1988—; established investigator Am. Heart Assn., 1976. Co-editor: Hematology: Basic Principles and Practice, 1991; contbr. more than 130 articles to Jour. Biol. Chemistry, Cell, Biochemistry, New Eng. Jour. Medicine, Blood, others. Surgeon USPHS, 1972-74. Grantee NIH; recipient William Dameshek prize Am. Soc. Hematology, 1984. Fellow ACP; mem. Assn. Am. Physicians, Am. Soc. for Clin. Investigation, Am. Soc. Biochemistry and Molecular Biology. Office: New Eng Med Ctr 750 Washington St Boston MA 02111-1533

FURIGAY, RODOLFO LAZO, surgeon; b. Bayom Bong, Nueva Vizcaya, Philippines, Aug. 24, 1938; came to U.S., 1963; s. Paulino Feril Furigay and Iluminada Mario Lazo; m. Margaret Josephine Reardon, Aug. 26, 1944; children: Paul Joseph, Tara Ann, Marc Damian. AA in Pre-Med. Studies, U. Santo Tomas, Manila, 1956, MD, 1961. Diplomate Am. Bd. Surgery; lic. in med. edn., Pa. Rotating intern Quincy (Mass.) City Hosp., 1963, resident in pathology, 1964, resident in gen. surgery, 1964-68; resident in cancer surgery Memorial Sloan-Kettering Hosp., N.Y.C., 1968-69; fellow gen. surgery Crouse-Irving Meml. Hosp., Syracuse, N.Y., 1969-70; mem. staff Windber (Pa.) Hosp., 1970—, chief of surgery, 1975—; Pres. Windber Hosp. Med. Staff, 1978. Fellow ACS, Am. Soc. Abdominal Surgeons, Soc. Philippine Surgeons in Am.; mem. AMA, Cambria County Med. Soc. (bd. dirs. 1982-84, pres. 1984), Pa. Med. Soc. (del. 1985—). Roman Catholic. Office: Windber Hosp 609 Somerset Ave Windber PA 15963-1399

FURLONG, JOHN WILLIAM, reinsurance company executive; b. London, Jan. 8, 1932; came to U.S., 1958; s. John and Edith Caroline (Phillips) F.; m. Barbara F. Gage, Sept. 1, 1956; children: Jennifer, Peter. Grad. pvt. sch., London. Reins. broker LLoyd's of London, Eng., 1947-50; underwriter LLoyd's of London, 1950-58; reins. broker Palmer Whitehead, Boston, 1958-70; v.p. Marsh & McLennan, Boston, 1970-78; pres. RGI, Inc. subs. Willis Corroon, Boston, 1978—. Sgt. British Army, 1950-52. Office: RGI Inc 1 Exeter Pla Boston MA 02116

FURLONG, SUZANNE T., controller; b. Albany, N.Y., Jan. 15, 1964; d. James M. and Carmella A. (Macri) F. BS, SUNY, Oneonta, 1986. Receptionist Quarad Ltd., Albany, 1986-87; adminstrv. asst. D.J. Contractors Inc., Albany, 1987-91; controller Barn Raisers Inc., Albany, 1991—. Mem. Com. to Elect Betty Barnette for treas., Albany, 1991. Mem. Northeastern Subcontractors Assn. (membership com. 1988—). Home: 99 Adams Pl Delmar NY 12054 Office: Barn Raisers Inc 76 Exchange St Albany NY 12205

FURMAN, SAMUEL ELLIOTT, dentist; b. Jersey City, Dec. 13, 1932; s. Sol T. and Cecilia (Berman) F.; m. Margaret Ann Gilardi, Feb. 27, 1971; children: Laurie, Jill, Sean, Ashley. AB, U. Pa., 1953, DDS, 1957. Diplomate Am. Bd. Quality Assurance and Utilization Rev. Physicians. Pvt. practice dentistry Tinton Falls, N.J., 1959—; sr. attending Monmouth Med. Ctr.; mem., pres. N.J. Bd. Dentistry; mem. N.E. Regional Bd. Dental Examiners. Capt. USAF, 1957-59. Fellow Acad. Gen. Dentistry, Internat. Coll. Dentists, Am. Coll. Dentists, Acad. Dentistry Internat.; mem. N.J. Soc. Dentistry for Children, Am. Prosthodontic Soc., Am. Assn. Dental Examiners, Acad. Osseointegration, Pierre Fauchard Acad., ADA, N.J. Dental Assn. (past trustee), Monmouth-Ocean County Dental Soc. (past pres.), B'nai B'rith, Omicron Kappa Upsilon, Alpha Omega. Home: 8 Woods End Rd Rumson NJ 07760-1040 Office: 1029 Sycamore Ave Tinton Falls NJ 07724

FURMANSKI, PHILIP, cancer research scientist; b. Germany, July 26, 1946; came to U.S., 1947, naturalized, 1954; s. Ed and Rose (Warsawski) F.; children: Lisa Anne, Jonathan David. BA, Temple U., 1966, PhD, 1969. Research assoc. Albert Einstein Med. Ctr., Phila., 1970; research assoc., instr. Dartmouth Coll. Med. Sch., Hanover, N.H., 1970-72; chmn., asst. dir. Mich. Cancer Found., Detroit, 1974-81; asst. prof., then assoc. prof. Wayne State U. Sch. Med., Detroit, 1974-81; assoc. dir., sci. dir. AMC Cancer Research Ctr., Denver, 1981-90; prof., chmn. dept. biology NYU, 1990—; mem. virus working group WHO/Food and Agriculture Orgn., 1977-80; mem. rev. com. Nat. Cancer Inst., Bethesda, Md., 1981—; cons. numerous indsl. and acad. concerns, 1975—; adj. prof., full mem. Cancer Ctr. U. Colo., 1988-90. Editor: Biological Carcinogenesis, 1982, Understanding Breast Cancer, 1983, RNA Tumor Viruses, Oncogenes, Human Cancer, and AIDS, 1985; mem. editorial bd. In Vivo, 1987—, Cancer Rsch., 1990—; also articles. Damon Runyon Meml. fellow NIH, 1967-72; Nat. Cancer Inst. grantee, 1969—. Mem. Internat. Soc. Exptl. Hematology, Internat. Assn. Breast Cancer Research, Am. Soc. Cell. Biology, AAAS, Am. Assn. Cancer Research. Office: NYU Dept Biology Main Bldg Rm 1009 New York NY 10003

FURST, JOHN FREDERICK, electric utility executive; b. Hagerstown, Md., Oct. 11, 1946. BS in Elec. Engring., U. Pitts., 1968. Jr. engr. Pa. Electric Co., Johnstown, 1968, dir. tech. svcs., 1977, consumer svcs. mgr., 1979, div. dir., 1981, v.p. customer svcs., 1984, v.p. customer svcs. and communications, 1990—; chmn. indsl. task force Electric Power Rsch. Inst., Palo Alto, Calif. Trustee Lee Hosp., Johnstown; mem. fund drives Talus Rock coun. Girl Scouts U.S., Johnstown; mem. coll. bus. adv. coun. Indiana U. of Pa.; mem. elec. engring. tech. indsl. adv. com. U. Pitts., Johnstown; mem. bldg. energy conservation com., chmn. weatherization and energy conservation policy coun. State of Pa. Named Young Engr. of Yr., Profl. Engrs., Johnstown chpt., 1979, Outstanding Young Man, Greater Johnstown Jaycees; recipient Community Svc. award Talus Rock Girl Scout Coun., 1989. Mem. ASHRAE, IEEE, Mktg. Execs.' Conf. (exec. com.), Nat. Soc. Profl. Engrs., Pa. Soc. Profl. Engrs. Office: Pa Electric Co 1001 Broad St Johnstown PA 15906-2498

FURST, NORMA FIELDS, academic administrator; b. N.Y.C., Feb. 26, 1931; d. Nathan B. Fields and Anne (Cooper) Platzer; m. M. Lawrence Furst, Sept. 9, 1951; children: Merrick Lee, Laura Furst Jacobs. BA cum laude, Bklyn. U., 1951; MEd, Temple U., 1963, EdD, 1967; LHD (hon.), Combs Coll. of Music, 1986. Registrar Pakistan Mission to the United Nations, N.Y.C., 1952-55; tchr., guidance counselor Harcum Jr. Coll., Bryn Mawr, Pa., 1962-63; instr., Coll. Edn. Temple Univ., Phila., 1963-65; project assoc., Joint Ednl. Psychology USOE Rsch., Temple Univ., Phila., 1965-67; asst. div. dir., Coll. of Edn. Temple Univ., Phila., 1966-68, coord., Coll. of Edn., 1967-70, assoc. prof., 1969-73, dir., Coll. Rels. and Student Devel., 1970-74, prof., Coll. Edn., 1973-83, dean student affairs, 1974-83; pres. Harcum Jr. Coll., Bryn Mawr, 1983-92; interim pres. Balt. Hebrew U., 1992—; cons. to over 25 sch. dists., univs., community colls. and ednl. consortia; lectr. in field; bd. dirs. Nat. Assn. State Univs. and Land Grant Colls. (past sec./senator, exec. com. of urban affairs div.), Nat. Assn. Ind. Jr. Colls. (v.p.), Am. Assn. of Jr., Tech. and Community Colls. (commn. on ind. colls.), Higher Edn. Referral Svc./Mid-Am. (founding dir.), Internat. B'nai B'rith/Hillel Commn. (past sec. and v.p.), Jewish PUb. Soc. (past. v.p. and sec.), Coun. Jewish Fed. & Welfare Funds. Editor: Review of Educational Research, Am. Educational Research; reviewer, editor for six pub. books; contbr. chpt. to book and articles to profl. jours. Mem. Mayor's Commn. on Literacy, Mayor's Task Force on Transit Safety, Ch. and World Instn., Jewish Campus Activities Bd. (past pres.), United Way, Nat. Coun. of Christians and Jews, Police Athletic League, Flag Day Assn., Chapel of Four Chaplains; exec. com. Cen. Agy. for Jewish Edn.; trustee Fedn. of Jewish Agys. (chmn. com. on Jewish edn., vice-chmn. com. on allocations and

planning, exec. com., long range planning com.). Recipient Lindback award for Disting. Coll. Teaching, 1969, Netsky award B'nai B'rith Career and Counseling Svcs. for Dedication to Students' Ednl. and Career Needs, 1976, Humanitarian award B'nai B'rith Educators Chpt., Phila., 1983, Disting. Svc. to Counseling and Guidance, Guidance Assn. of Pa., 1987, Rosh Pina award for disting. svcs. to edn. Am. Jewish Congress, 1989, Pacesetter award Nat. Coun. for Mktg. and Pub. Rels. Dist. I, 1990, and others. Mem. Am. Edn. Rsch. Assn., Am. Psychol. Assn., Nat. Assn. for Student Pers. Adminstrs., Pa. Assn. for Student Pers. Adminstrs., Am. Assn. for Higher Edn., Nat. Assn. Ind. Colls. and Univs. Jewish. Home: 610 Wynnewood Plz 346 E Lancaster Ave Wynnewood PA 19096 Office: Balt Hebrew U 5800 Park Heights Ave Baltimore MD 21215

FURST, SIDNEY CARL, social psychologist; b. N.Y.C., Dec. 11, 1925; s. Nathan and Anna (Levy) F.; student Princeton U., 1943; B.A., U. Chgo., 1948; M.A., Columbia U., 1950, postgrad. Bur. Applied Social Research, 1954; m. Vincenza DiMaggio, Apr. 9, 1972; children-Anne Betsy, Carl Nathaniel. Project dir. market research Batten, Barton, Durstine & Osborn Inc., N.Y.C., 1952-58; sales presentation writer ABC, N.Y.C., 1958-59; pres. Furst Survey Research Center, also Furst Analytic Center, 1959—; instr. Fairleigh-Dickinson Coll. Served with AUS, 1944-46. Author: Business Decisions That Changed Our Lives, 1964; Strategy of Change for Business Success, 1969. Home: 3 Washington Square Vlg New York NY 10012-1836

FURTADO, STEPHEN EUGENE, musician; b. Bridgeport, Conn., Aug. 3, 1942; m. Sarah Williams, Apr. 4, 1964; 1 child, Stephen Eugene Jr. Student, Berklee Sch. Music, Boston, 1960-62, Boston Conservatory, 1960-62. Appeared with numerous bands and orchestras, including Lloyd Price Orchestra, 1965, Ray Charles and Larry Elgart Orchestras, 1967, Dizzy Gillespie, Clark Terry and Lionel Hampton Orchestras, 1968, Apollo Theatre Houseband, 1969, Sy Oliver Orchestra, 1971, Thad Jones-Mel Lewis Orchestra, 1972-75, Count Basie Orchestra, 1972, 73, 83, Ellington Orchestra, 1982, Cab Calloway Orchestra, 1985, Johnny Richards Orch., Andy Kirk Orch., Howard McGee Orch., James Brown Orch., Chuck Jackson, Hines, Hines and Dad, Apollo House Band, 1969, Broadway co. Two Gentlemen of Verona, 1972, The Wiz, 1974-79, Aint Misbehavin, 1984, Black and Blue, 1989—, Sophisticated Ladies bus and truck co., 1987, Gypsy, 1974, So Nice To Be Civilized, 1980, Amen Corner, 1983, and others, (films) Cotton Club, 1983. Home and Office: 18704 Dunkirk Dr Jamaica NY 11412-3044

FURTH, JOHN JACOB, molecular biologist, pathologist, educator; b. Phila., Jan. 25, 1929; s. Jacob and Olga (Berthauer) F.; m. Mary Autry, June 24, 1959; children: Karen, Susan, Robin. BA, Cornell U., 1950; student, Yale Law Sch., 1950-51; MD, Duke U., 1958; MA (hon.), U. Pa., 1972. Intern Bellevue Hosp., N.Y.C., 1958-59; resident in pathology NYU Sch. Medicine, N.Y.C., 1959-60, postdoctoral fellow dept. microbiology, 1960-62; mem. faculty dept. pathology U. Pa. Med. Sch., Phila., 1962—, prof., 1978—. Contbr. articles to profl. jours. Bd. dirs., chmn. hist. sites com. Darby Creek Valley Assn., 1984—; bd. dirs., founder Friends of the Swedish Cabin (constructed circa 1654), Upper Darby, Pa., 1987. 2d lt. Q.M.C., U.S. Army, 1951-53. Recipient Hoffman LaRoche award, 1958; Eleanor Roosevelt fellow, 1977-78. Mem. AAAS, Am. Soc. Biol. Chemists and Molecular Biologists, Am. Assn. Cancer Rsch., Am. Assn. Pathologists. Democrat. Mem. Soc. of Friends. Home: 43 Roselawn Ave Lansdowne PA 19050-2317 Office: U Pa Sch Medicine Dept Pathology and Lab Med Philadelphia PA 19104-6082

FURTH, PETER DAVID, food products executive; b. N.Y.C., Nov. 11, 1954; s. Frank and Valerie (Jakober) F.; children: Michael, Edward, Melanie. BA in Econs., U. Rochester, 1976; MBA, NYU, 1979. Asst. to pres. Louis Furth, Inc., Maspeth, N.Y., 1976-77, v.p., 1977-86, chief exec. officer, 1986-88, pres., 1988-90, vice-chmn., 1990-91; exec. v.p. Am. Spice Trade Assn., Inc., Englewood Cliffs, N.J., 1991—. Mem. trustees' coun. U. Rochester, 1981-87, vis. com. Sch. Nursing, 1984—, mem. vis. com. Grad. Sch. Bus. Adminstrn., 1982-88. Mem. Am. Spice Trade Assn. (bd. dirs. 1986-91), Jamaican-Am. C. of C. (bd. dirs. 1989—), Nat. Coalition Food Import Assn. (chmn. legis. subcom. 1991—). Jewish. Home: 1371 Riverbank Rd Stamford CT 06903-2026 Office: Am Spice Trade Assn Inc 580 Sylvan Ave PO Box 1267 Englewood Cliffs NJ 07632

FURZE, EDWARD WILLIAM, foundation administrator; b. Syracuse, N.Y., Jan. 7, 1938; s. John T. and Marion Joy (Gieselman) F.; m. Joanne M. Sojewicz, Aug. 4, 1962; children: David John, Jeffrey Paul, Daniel Edward. BS in History, LeMoyne Coll., 1961. Exec. dir. agy. ops. United Way Cen. N.Y., Syracuse, 1965-70; exec. dir. Community Found., Syracuse, 1968-70; dir. devel. and community rels. LeMoyne Coll., Syracuse, 1970-83; v.p. Mt. St. Mary's Coll., Emmitsburg, Md., 1983-85; sr. devel. officer Pa. State U., Harrisburg, 1985-87, Fairleigh Dickinson U., Rutherford, N.J., 1987-90; exec. dir. for found., asst. v.p. devel. Gen. Hosp. Ctr., Passaic, N.J., 1990—; cons. Cyo-Brighton Family Ctr., Syracuse, 1972-73, Christ the King Retreat House, Syracuse, 1972—, Vol. Ctr., Newark, 1990-91, Ketchum, Inc., Pitts., 1989-90; trustee St. Camillus Extended Care, Syracuse, 1972-83. Alt. del. Rep. Nat. Conv., Detroit, 1980. Mem. Pub. Rels. Soc. Am., nat. Soc. Fundraising Execs., Rotary (pres. 1991). Roman Catholic. Home: 140 Hepburn Rd # 12G Clifton NJ 07012-2231 Office: Gen Hosp Ctr Found 350 Boulevard Passaic NJ 07055-2800

FUSARO, JOSEPH A., educator; b. Poughkeepsie, N.Y., Feb. 18, 1940; s. Anthony Francis and Anna Maria (Valentino) F.; m. Sandra Ann Brown, June 28, 1969; children: Marc, Scott. BA in English, Rider coll., 1962; MEd in Reading, U. Vt., 1969; EdD, SUNY, Albany, 1974; postdoctoral, U. Scranton. Cert. reading specialist and supr. of reading, tchr., Pa. Tchr. Waterbury (Vt.) High Sch., 1965-66, Harwood Union High Sch., Moretown, Vt., 1966-69, Richmond (Vt.) Elem. Sch., 1969-70, Milton (Vt.) Intermediate Sch., 1970-71; asst. prof. edn. U. Scranton, 1974-78, assoc. prof., 1978-83; prof. U. Scranton, Pa., 1983—, acting dean grad. sch., 1984-85, acting dean Coll. Health, Edn., and Human Resources, chair dept. edn., 1990-91; cons. various sch. dists., 1974—, N.Y. State Dept. Edn., 1972; investigator pers. U.S. Civil Svc. Commn., Washington, 1962-63, 65. Contbr. rsch. articles to profl. jours. Substitute driver Meals on Wheels, 1986-90; player agt. North Scranton Little League, 1986, coach, 1985; treas. Day Nursery Assn. Scranton, 1984, bd. dirs. 1979-84. With U.S. Army, 1963-65. Grantee Pa. Dept. Edn., 1980-82; fellow Nat. Def. Edn. Act., 1971. Mem. Internat. Reading Assn., Am. Ednl. Rsch. Assn. Roman Catholic. Home: 1315 Myrtle St Scranton PA 18510-1321 Office: U Scranton O'Hara Hall Rm 613 Scranton PA 18510-4603

FUSCO, RAYMOND ARTHUR, government analyst; b. South Amboy, N.J., Dec. 14, 1959; s. Albert A. and Anna (Politi) F.; m. Debra Lynn Gadsby, Mar. 4, 1989. BSBA, Monmouth Coll., 1982. CPA, N.J. Acct. 3 N.J. Div. of Pensions, Trenton, 1983-86; acct. 2 N.J. Div. Econ. Assistance, Trenton, 1986-87, acct. 1, 1987-88, adminstrv. analyst II, 1988. Fellow AICPA; mem. N.J. Soc. CPAs. Republican. Episcopalian. Office: NJ Div Econ Assistance CN 716 Trenton NJ 08625

FUSCO, VICTOR, lawyer; b. Bklyn., Dec. 2, 1949; s. Rudolph J. Fusco and Claire (Valluzzi) Stein; children: Caprice, Tiffany. BA, Hofstra U., 1972; JD, Bklyn. Law Sch., 1975. Bar: N.Y. 1976, U.S. Dist. Ct. (so. and ea. dists.) N.Y. 1977, U.S. Ct. Appeals (2d cir.) 1983, U.S. Supreme Ct. 1982. Assoc. Reisman Milberg Abramson & Magro, N.Y.C., 1975-78; ptnr. Scheine Fusco Brandenstein & Rada, Commack, N.Y., 1978—. Bd. dirs. L.I. chpt. Arthritis Found.; bd. dirs. Middle Earth Crisis Hotline, Bellmore, N.Y.; counsel to Nassau County Police Benevolent Assn., 1988—, Fraternal Order of Police Lodge 69, 1991—. Mem. ABA, N.Y. State Bar Assn., N.Y. Workers Compensation Bar Assn., N.Y. Social Security Bar Assn. (pres. 1982-84), Nassau County Bar Assn., Columbia Lawyers Assn., Suffolk County Bar Assn., Nat. Orgn. Social Security Claimants Reps. (exec. bd.). Office: Scheine Fusco Brandenstein & Rada 358 Veterans Memorial Hwy Commack NY 11725-4316

FUSILLO, THOMAS VICTOR, environmental engineer; b. Bklyn., Feb. 17, 1953; s. Pat and Catherine (Notarnicola) F.; m. Michele Fran Lipman, June 24, 1979; children: Jennifer Lynn, Steven Joseph. BS in Environ. Sci., Rutgers U., 1975, MS in Agrl. Engring., 1977. Cert. groundwater profl. Rsch. intern Rutgers U., New Brunswick, N.J., 1975-77, adj. instr., 1976-77; hydrologist U.S. Geol. Survey, Trenton, 1977-87, dist. geochemistry specialist, 1983-87; sr. assoc. Environ. Corp., Princeton, N.J., 1987-89, project mgr., 1989-91, mgr., 1991—. Mem. Am. Geophys. Union, Assn. Ground Water Scientists and Engrs., Sigma Xi, Alpha Zeta. Contbr. tech. articles on geochemistry and ground-water contamination to profl. jours.; author tech. water resources reports. Home: 1289 Fountain Rd Newtown PA 18940-3722 Office: 210 Carnegie Ctr Ste 201 Princeton NJ 08540-6233

FUSS, JOHN M., shoe company financial executive; b. Emmitsburg, Md., Sept. 26, 1930; s. John M. and Helen V. (Ohler) F.; m. Sarah C. Rice, Sept. 1, 1962; children: Susan, Diane, Carolyn. BA, Gettysburg (Pa.) Coll., 1956. CPA, Pa. Sr. auditor Arthur Andersen & Co., Phila., 1956-61; with Hanover (Pa.) Shoe, Inc., 1961—, controller, asst. treas., 1977-81, controller, v.p., asst. sec., treas., 1981-84; dir. corp. fin. svcs. C. & J. Clark Am., Inc. (parent co. of Hanover Shoe Co.), Hanover, 1984-86, controller, 1986-90, treas., 1990-91, chief fin. officer, sec., treas., v.p., contr., 1991—; dir., v.p., sec., treas. C. & J. Clark Retail, Inc.; bd. dirs. C. & J. Clark Fin. Co., Bostonian Shoe Co., N.Y.; asst. treas. C. & J. Clark, Inc., C. & J. Clark North Am. Ltd.,. Bd. dirs. South Western Sch. Dist., Hanover, 1981-89, York County (Pa.), Rep. Com., 1972—. Cpl. U.S. Army, 1951-53. Mem. AICPA, Pa. Inst. CPA's, Nat. Assn. Accts. Mem. Ch. of Christ. Office: C & J Clark Am Inc 440 Madison St Hanover PA 17331-4700

FUTEY, BOHDAN A., judge; b. 1939. BA, Case Western Reserve U., 1962, MA, 1964; JD, Cleve. State U., 1968. Ptnr. Futey & Rakowsky, Cleve., 1968-72; chief asst. police prosecutor Cleve., 1972-74; exec. asst. Mayor of Cleve., 1974-75; ptnr. Bazarko, Futey and Oryshkewych, Cleve., 1975-84; chmn. U.S. Foreign Claims Settlement Commn., 1984-87; judge U.S. Claims Ct., Washington, 1987—. Mem. ABA, Parma Bar Assn., Ukrainian Am. Bar Assn., Cleve. Bar Assn., D.C. Bar Assn. Office: US Claims Ct 717 Madison Pl NW Ste 603 Washington DC 20005-1011*

FUTRELL, BASIL LEE, association executive; b. Pendleton, N.C., Aug. 23, 1937; s. Claude K. and Lucy V. (Aycock) F.; BCS, Strayer Coll., 1959, BS, 1973; MPA, Am. U., 1980; m. Mary Allen Futrell, June 19, 1965; 1 child, Anne Marie. With FBI, Washington, 1956-61, 63-64; with Nat. Food Processors Assn., Washington, 1964—, group v.p./fin. sec., 1981—, v.p., treas. subs. cos., 1973—, including NFL, Inc., Triple S, Inc., Food Processors Assurance Ltd., also dir. Deacon Broadview Bapt. Ch., Tempel Hills, Md., 1980—, tchr., 1978—. With U.S. Army, 1961-63. Mem. Am. Mgmt. Assn., Greater Washington Soc. Assn. Execs., Washington Pers. Assn., Data Processing Mgmt. Assn., Food Processors Risk Retention Group, Food Processors Adminstrn. Assn. Avocations: fishing, gardening. Office: 1401 New York Ave NW Ste 400 Washington DC 20005-2120

FUTTER, JOAN BABETTE, school librarian; b. N.Y.C., Nov. 15, 1921; d. Samuel S. and Helen (Mosher) Feinberg; m. Victor Futter, Jan. 26, 1943; children: Jeffrey Leesam, Ellen Victoria Futter Shutkin, Deborah Gail Futter Cohan. AB, NYU, 1941; MS, L.I. U., 1966. Sch. libr. Carrie Palmer Weber Jr. High Sch., Port Washington, N.Y., 1966-91. Mem. LWV, AAUW, L.I. Sch. Media Assn., C.W. Post Libr. Assn., Cold Spring Harbor Beach Club, Manhasset Bay Yacht Club. Home: 17 Sunnyvale Rd Port Washington NY 11050-4519

FUTTERMAN, JACK, supermarket chain executive; b. 1933. Grad., Bklyn. Coll. Pharmacy, 1958; postgrad., Harvard U. Registered pharmacist. With Whelan Drugs, pres.; v.p. Supermarkets Gen. Corp., 1973-83, sr. v.p., 1983-84, pres., CEO drug store merchandising div., 1984-87, vice chmn., 1987-89; pres., CEO Supermarkets Gen. Corp., Woodbridge, N.J., 1989—, now also chmn. bd. Office: Supermarkets Gen Corp 301 Blair Rd Woodbridge NJ 07095*

FUZO, FRANK JOHN, insurance executive; b. Bklyn., Oct. 8, 1951; s. Victor J. and Mathilda (Gogel) F.; m. Deborah Landes, Jan. 18, 1952; 1 child, Amanda. Student, Somerset County Coll., 1971-72. Mgr. Slack Rack, Flemington, N.J., 1974-76; owner Quality Interiors, Whitehouse, N.J., 1976-79; agt. Prudential Ins. Co., Flemington, 1979—. Councilman City of Lambertville, N.J., 1988, mayor, 1989-92, coord. emergency emergency mgmt. coun., 1988-91; freeholder County of Hunterdon, N.J., 1991—; v.p., coach Lambertville Ramblers, 1982—; vice chmn., mcpl. chmn. Hunt County Rep. Com., 1988—; first aid instr. ARC, 1971-83; pres., capt. Whitehouse Rescue Squad, 1970-83; trustee Hunterdon Drug Awareness. Mem. Nat. Assn. Life Underwriters, West Jersey Assn. Life Underwriters (pres. 1985-86), League of Municipalities (trustee Huntersdon Drug Awareness Coun.), Elks. Republican. Presbyterian. Home and Office: 74 Douglas St Lambertville NJ 08530-1023

GABA, BARBARA BLASSINGAME, educational psychologist; b. N.Y.C., May 29, 1947; d. Samuel Timothy and Johnnie Mae (Thomas) Blassingame; m. Peter A. Gaba, May 24, 1946; children: Lanre, Ayorkor. BA, SUNY-Stonybrook, 1969; MEd, Rutgers U., 1972; PhD, Bayero U., Kano, Nigeria, 1986. Psychol. cons. N.Y. Human Resources Adminstrn., N.Y.C., 1971-74; asst. higher edn. officer Hunter Coll. of CUNY, 1974-76; lectr. Bayero U., Kano, Nigeria, 1976-85; protocol asst. to U.S. ambassador Am. Embassy, Lagos, Nigeria, 1986-87; assoc. dir. N.J. Dept. Higher Edn., Trenton, 1988—. Contbr. articles to profl. jours. Mem. Am. Community Liaison Network, Lagos, 1986-87. Mem. Am. Assn. for Higher Edn., Nat. Assn. Women Deans, Adminstrs., Counselors, Profl. and Organizational Devel. Network in Higher Edn., African Am. Inst. (ann. awards dinner com. 1987—). Office: NJ Dept Higher Edn 20 W State St # 542cn Trenton NJ 08608-1206

GABBARD, GLENN PATRICK, community college administrator, literacy educator; b. Chicopee Falls, Mass., Mar. 1, 1954; s. Benjamin Harrison and Anges (Yandall) G.; m. Ruth-Ann Rasbold, June 19, 1982; children: Megan Aliitasi, Maximillian Vaatausili. BA, Sonoma State U., Rohnert Park, Calif., 1976; MA, Am. U., 1982. Chmn. dept. English Am. Samoa Community Coll., Pago Pago, 1977-79, prof. English and English as 2d lang., 1982-84; dir. cultural programs Conacyt Project Am. U., Washington, 1980-81; coord. intercultural programs Internat. Student Office Northeastern U., Boston, 1984-85; coord. learning ctr. Mass. Bay Community Coll., Wellesley Hills, 1985-87, assoc. dean alternative instrn./basic disciplines, 1987—, dir. coll. integration project, 1989—; cons. Am. Samoa Vocat. Rehab. Coun., Pago Pago, Hawaii Early Intervention Coordinating Coun., Honolulu, 1990; mem. task force Nat. Inst. on Disability and Rehab. Rsch., Washington, 1991. Am. Samoa Govt. grad. scholar, 1979; Am. Coun. on Edn. fellow, Washington, 1991; recipient Nat. Leadership award Nat. Coun. on Disability, 1989, Teaching Excellence award Nat. Int. Student and Orgnl. Devel., 1989. Mem. Coun. Acad. Div. Adminstrs., Tchrs. of English to Speakers of Other Langs., Nat. Assn. for Fgn. Student Affairs, Nat. Assn. Asian and Pacific Am. Educators, Internat. Reading Assn., Assn. for Persons with Severe Handicaps, Assn. for Handicapped Student Svc. Programs in Post-Secondary Edn., Phi Theta Kappa. Democrat. Office: Mass Bay Community Coll 50 Oakland St Wellesley MA 02181-5359

GABEL, ELI, disability analyst; b. Bklyn., Aug. 12, 1939; s. Israel and Bertha (Orenbuch) G.; m. Leslie Ellin Heit, Mar. 22, 1964; children: Marc Matthew, Melissa Rachel. BA, Hunter Coll., 1962; M of Profl. Studies, NYU, 1984. Sales and ops. coord. Global Tours, Inc., N.Y.C., 1965-69; staff mgr. Japan Air Lines, N.Y.C., 1969-74; pub. rels. cons. Internat. Tourism and Commerce, N.Y.C., 1974-77; disability analyst N.Y. State Office of Disability Determinations, N.Y.C., 1977—; rep. Gov.'s Com. on Paperwork and Forms Reduction, Albany, N.Y., 1984-86; travel mktg. instr. Adelphi U., Garden City, N.Y., 1973, Sobelsohn Sch., N.Y.C., 1970-73. Exec. v.p. New Springville Jewish Ctr., S.I., 1990, 91; mem. parent adv. bd. On Your Mark, S.I., 1990. Mem. Nat. Assn. Disability Analysis (nat. conf. publicist 1981-83, mem. svcs. chmn. 1981-82). Jewish. Home: 23 Vassar St Staten Island NY 10314-6003

GABEL, JON ROBERT, economist; b. San Diego, Dec. 12, 1944; s. Richard and Louise Gabel; m. Judith N. Gabel, Apr. 1, 1978; children: Josh, Brad, Karen. AB, Coll. of William and Mary, 1966; MS, Ariz. State U., 1974. Vista vol. Office Econ. Opportunity, Glide, Oreg., 1968-70; rsch. assoc. Nat. Planning Assn., Washington, 1970-72, Inst. Medicine, Washington, 1974-76; econ. Health Care Fin. Adminstrn., Washington, 1976-80; sr. econ. Nat. Ctr. for Health Svcs. Rsch., Rockville, Md., 1980-85; assoc. dir. rsch. Health Ins. Assn. Am., Washington, 1986-90; dir. employee benefits rsch. KPMG Peat Marwick, Washington, 1991—; com. mem. employee benefits Nat. Assn. Mfrs., Washington, 1991—. Contbr. articles to profl. jours.; reviewer numerous jours. Basketball coach Bradock Rd. Youth Club, Fairfax, Va., 1987-91. Named one of Health Care 50 Faulkner and Gray, 1990, 91. Mem. Assn. for Health Svcs. Rsch., Am. Pub. Health Assn., Ea. Econ. Assn., Western Econ. Assn. Jewish. Home: 4912 N Centaurs Ct Annandale VA 20036 Office: KPMG Peat Marwick 2100 M St Washington DC 20036

GABEL, RONALD GLEN, telecommunications executive; b. Allentown, Pa., Nov. 22, 1937; s. Glen Harry and Mary (Oberlin) G.; m. Claire A. Hollern (div.); children: Debra K., Jeffrey A., Stacy L.; m. Elaine M. Petro, Sept. 29, 1988. Student, Pa. State U., 1957-58. Design draftsman Mack Trucks Inc., Allentown, 1958-62, Bell Telephone Labs., Allentown, 1962-66; indsl. engr. Western Electric, Allentown, 1966-84; sr. engr. AT&T, Allentown, 1984-87; adminstr. Telephone Pioneers Am., Allentown, 1987—; cons. expert Man at Arms Mag. Advisor Lehigh County Dept. Human Svcs., 1990—; solicitor United Way, 1974, 82, 89, 90; active Lehigh County Hist. Soc., Jacobsburg Hist. Soc., Lehigh County Mus. Commn., 1979-81; sec. devel. and prodn. com. Lehigh County Becentennial Commn., 1977; pres. Indian Guides Allentown YMCA, 1972, v.p., 1971; sec. ch. coun. St. James Luth. Ch., 1964-67; advisor St. James Luther League, 1964-67. Mem. U.S. Power Squadrons (dist. lt. D-5 1991—), Delhigh Power Squadron (comdr. 1990-91), Nat. Soc. Pershing Rifles, Pa. Antiques Appraisers Assn., Internat. Inst. Indsl. Engrs., Am. Inst. Indsl. Engrs. (dir. Lehigh Valley chpt. 1983, pres. 1976-77, editor nat. mfg. systems div. newsletter 1979-80, Outstanding Svc. award 1978, 5 nat. awards for profl. soc. newsletters 1971-75), NRA, Ky. Rifle Assn. (newsletter editor 1974—, pres. 1972-73, Disting. Svc. award 1979), Am. Soc. Arms Collectors (bd. dirs. 1988-91, v.p. 1991—), Tex. Gun Collectors Assn., Forks of Del. Weapons Assn., Pa. Antique Gun Collectors Assn., Ducks Unltd., Internat. Order DeMolay, Rajah Temple Upper Lehigh, Lions (pres. 1987), Knights Templar, Shriners. Republican. Office: Telephone Pioneers Am ATT 555 Union Blvd Allentown PA 18103

GABELMAN, IRVING JACOB, consulting engineer, retired government official; b. Bklyn., Nov. 12, 1918; s. William and Mary (Blumenfeld) G.; m. Leah Levitt, Feb. 13, 1949; children: Alan, Philip. B.A. in Physics, Bklyn. Coll., 1938; B.E.E., Coll. City N.Y., 1945; M.E.E., Poly. Inst. Bklyn., 1948; Ph.D. in Elec. Engring, Syracuse U., 1961. Radio engr. U.S. Army Engr. Office, N.Y.C., 1941-45; electronics engr. Watson Labs., USAF, Eatontown, N.J., 1945-51; electronic scientist Rome Air Devel. Center, Griffiss AFB, N.Y., 1951-59; dir. advanced studies Rome Air Devel. Center, Griffiss AFB, 1959-69, chief plans, 1969-71, chief scientist, 1971-75; pres. Tech. Assocs., 1975—; Chmn. avionics panel, adv. group electronic research and devel. NATO, 1971-76, U.S. nat. coordinator, 1971-76; mem. council Upper Div. Coll. Utica/Rome State U. N.Y., 1974—; adviser Div. Adv. Group Electronic Systems Div. Air Force Systems Command, 1974-76. Editor: Displays for Command and Control Centers, 1969, Techniques for Data Handling in Tactical Systems, 1969, Storage and Retrieval of Information—A User-Supplier Dialogue, 1969, Data Handling Devices, 1970; Contbr. articles tech. jours. Recipient Air Force Exceptional Civilian Service award, 1974. Fellow IEEE (chmn. systems com. nat. group on computers 1966), AAAS. Address: 225 Dale Rd Rome NY 13440

GABER, ROBERT, psychologist; b. N.Y.C., Nov. 5, 1923; s. William and Freda (Harris) G.; m. Heidi Walters, Apr. 3, 1967 (div. Jan. 5, 1976); 1 child, Nathan. BA, NYU, 1949, MA, 1951; PhD, Columbia Pacific U., San Rafael, Calif., 1982. Psychotherapist Nat. Hosp. for Speech Disorders, N.Y.C., 1954-57; psychologist Indsl. Home for the Blind, N.Y.C., 1957-58; sch. psychologist Roosevelt Sch., Stamford, Conn., 1958-60; sr. clin. psychologist N.Y. State Dept. Mental Hygiene, Thiells, 1960-64; staff psychologist N.Y. Med. Coll., N.Y.C., 1965-66; cons. psychologist The Salvation Army, Phila., 1971-72; psychologist Md. Dept. Mental Hygiene, Owings Mills, Md., 1975-76, Dept. Corrections, Balt., 1979-80; chief exec. officer Axxiom De-Stress Ctrs., Balt., 1980—; cons. Family Crisis Ctr. of Balt., 1973-74, Gov., Pa. Dept. Corrections, 1971; dir. mental health, nursery div. Dept. Welfare, N.Y.C., 1953-56. Author: Federal Prisoners' Attitudes Toward Crime and Confinement, 1982, The Experience of Enlightenment, 1980; author booklet: Comprehensive Therapy Questionnaire, 1978; author articles, pamphlets on crime, human behavior and higher states of consciousness. With USAAF, 1942-46; PTO. Mem. Am. Psychol. Assn. Democrat. Office: Axxiom De-Stress Ctrs PO Box 22115 Baltimore MD 21203-4115

GABIG, ROBERT LOUIS, JR., interior design subcontractor, musician; b. Pitts., Nov. 15, 1953; s. Robert Louis and Margaret Ruth (Fitzpatrick) G. Student, Robert Morris Coll., 1971-74, Allegheny Community Coll., 1975-76, U. Pitts., 1982. Stockboy, clk. Sherwin Williams Co., Carnegie, Pa., 1965-75; painter, paperhanger numerous cos., 1976-82; freelance paperhanger Pitts., 1983—; band leader The Blues Orphans, Pitts., 1979—. Composer numerous songs. Democrat. Roman Catholic. Home and Office: 851 Ohio River Blvd Pittsburgh PA 15202

GABLE, JOHN ALLEN, historian, association executive, educator; b. Rockford, Ill., Nov. 14, 1943; s. Allen Herman and Mary Jane (Kirkpatrick) G. AB, Kenyon Coll., 1965; PhD in History, Brown U., 1972. Asst. prof. history Briarcliff Coll., Briarcliff Manor, N.Y., 1974-77; exec. dir. Theodore Roosevelt Assn., Oyster Bay, N.Y., 1974—; adj. assoc. prof. C.W. Post L.I. U., Greenvale, N.Y., 1977-89; adj. prof. New Coll. Hofstra U., Hempstead, N.Y., 1989—. Editor, founder Theodore Roosevelt Assn. Jour., 1975—; author, editor 4 books in field; contbr. articles to profl. jours. Vestry Christ Ch., Oyster Bay, 1979—. Mem. Orgn. Am. Historians. Episcopalian. Home: 211 Glen Cove Ave Sea Cliff NY 11579 Office: Theodore Roosevelt Assn PO Box 719 Oyster Bay NY 11771

GABLE, JOHN OGLESBY, III, artist; b. Frankfort, Ky., Mar. 7, 1944; s. John Oglesby and Dorothy Lindsay (Coblin) G.; m. Anne Marie Tudor, Nov. 30, 1968; children: Thomas Lindsay, Christopher Coblin, Katharine Tudor. Student, U. Ky., 1962; BS in Indsl. Design, Art Ctr. Coll. Design, L.A., 1966. Automotive designer GM, Detroit, 1968-79. One-man shows include Payson-Weisburg Gallery, N.Y.C., Barridoff Galleries, Portland, Maine, Francesca Anderson Gallery, Boston; group exhbns. include NAD, Forum Gallery, Coe Kerr Gallery, Am. Watercolor Soc. (all N.Y.C.), Butler Inst. Am. Art, Youngstown, Ohio, Portland (Maine) Mus. Art, Rothman Gallery, Barnegat Light, N.J.; numerous commns. including commemoration of Am.'s Cup, Harvard U., Boston Classical Orch., Senator William Hathaway of Maine. With U.S. Army, 1966-68, Korea, Vietnam. Recipient William A Patton prize NAD, 1986, Artist's award Am. Watercolor Soc., 1989. Mem. Nat. Watercolor Soc. (Wurdemann prize). Home and Studio: RR 3 Box 835 Wiscasset ME 04578

GABLE, MICHAEL, biologist, educator; b. Lancaster, Pa., June 1, 1945; s. Harold Walker and Mary Catharine (Liebeck) G. BS, U. Fla., 1967; MS in Zoology, U. N.H., 1969, PhD in Zoology, 1972. Prof. Ea. Conn. State U., Willimantic, 1972—; cons. Normandeau Assocs., Bedford, N.H., 1972-82; curatorial affiliate Peabody Mus. Yale U., New Haven, Conn., 1987—. Contbr. articles to profl. jours. Mem. Am. Soc. Zoologists, Am. Soc. Parasitologists, Estuarine Rsch. Soc., Biol. Soc. Washington, Crustacean Soc., Conn. Acad. Arts and Scis., Sigma Xi. Office: Ea Conn State U Willimantic CT 06226

GABRIEL, ANTHONY PATRICK, electronic engineering executive; b. Staten Island, N.Y., Feb. 8, 1944; s. Anthony P. Gabriel and Mary V. (Niesgoda) Miller; m. Andrea Lee Hunt, Sept. 28, 1985; children: Kurt, Christian, Erik. AAS in Elec. Tech., S.I. Community Coll., 1964; BSEE, CUNY, 1972; MBA in Engring. and Tech. Mgmt., Fairleigh Dickinson U., 1983. Electronic technician N.Y. Telephone Co., Bklyn., 1964-66; system design engr. Western Electric Co., Inc., Newark, 1966-67; rsch. engr. R & D Ctr. Gen. Cable Corp., Union, N.J., 1967-78; dir. engring. Alpha wire Corp., Elizabeth, N.J., 1978-87; chief engr. electronic div. Carol Cable Co., Inc., Pawtucket, R.I., 1987-91, tech. dir. electronic div., 1991—. Patentee, internal shield design, advanced screen design, end seals for telephone cable; contbr. articles to tech. publs. Mem. Nat. Elec. Mfrs. Assn. Republican.

Lutheran. Home: 178 Lauren Dr Seekonk MA 02771-5037 Office: Carol Cable Co Inc 249 Roosevelt Ave Pawtucket RI 02860-2121

GABRIEL, EDWARD PAUL, commercial printing company executive; b. Vineland, N.J., Apr. 24, 1945; s. Joseph Peter and Rose (Gallucci) G.; m. Rosalie Gail Petrillo, July 26, 1969; children: Marisa, Peter, Michael. BS in Acctg., Pa. State U., 1967; postgrad., Lehigh U., 1967-68. Cert. mgmt. acct. Internal auditor Owens Ill., Vineland, 1968-69, cost and budget supr., 1969-71; acctg. mgr. KSM div. Omark Industries, Moorestown, N.J., 1971-74, div. contr., 1974-77, div. pres., 1977-83; pres. KSM Fastening Systems, Inc., Moorestown, 1983-85; v.p., gen. mgr. ERICO Internat., Moorestown, 1985-86; pres. Rainbow Reprodns., Inc., Moorestown, 1986—; mem. study mission to Japan, Inst. Indsl. Engrs., 1982. Vice chmn. Moorestown Planning Bd., 1983-91; bd. dirs. South Jersey Jr. Achievement, 1980-83; mem. Recreation Adv. Com., Moorestown. Sgt. U.S. Army, 1968-69. Athletic grantee Pa. State U., 1963-67. Mem. Inst. Mgmt. Accts., Inst. Cert. Mgmt. Accts., South Jersey C. of C. Republican. Roman Catholic. Home: 9 Pepperbush Ln Moorestown NJ 08057 Office: Rainbow Reprodns Inc 285 S Church St Moorestown NJ 08057

GABRIEL, EDWIN ZENITH, consulting engineer; b. Union City, N.J., Aug. 26, 1913; s. Enoch H. and Louise Beatrice (Seraydarian) G. BSME, N.J. Inst. Tech., 1936, ME, 1939, MSEE, 1952; postgrad., MIT, 1949-50. Registered profl. engr. N.J.; lic. Am. Bd. Profl. Engrs. and Land Surveyors. Heating systems engr. Webster-Talmadge Co., N.Y.C., 1938-39; efficiency engr. Prudential Ins. Co. of Am., Newark, 1939-41; mech. and elec. engr. U.S. Govt., 1941-52; project engr. Wright Aeronautical Corp., Caldwell, N.J., 1952-53, Kearfott (Singer Corp.), Clifton, N.J., 1953-55; asst. prof. elec. engring. Lehigh U., Bethlehem, Pa., 1955-56, Villanova (Pa.) U., 1956-60, Fairleigh Dickinson U., Teaneck, N.J., 1960-62; assoc. prof. weapons and engring. dept. U.S. Naval Acad., Annapolis, Md., 1962-64; electronic engr. Avionics Lab, Fort Monmouth, N.J., 1965-73. Author: Automatic Control Systems, 1965, Computer Cookbook Approach to Digital Circuits and Computers, 1984, Cookbook Approach to Analog Circuits, 1985; numerous patents on computers and handling equipment in U.S., Can., Australia. Cubmaster, asst. scoutmaster Boy Scouts Am., Eatontown, N.J., 1946-48; sec. men's club Community Ch., Eatontown, 1946-48; founder, leader Search for Truth by Youth, Ocean Grove, N.J., 1985-87; Bible study tchr., Asbury Park, 1987-89; Bible tchr. Drop-in-Ctr., Thornley Chapel, Ocean Grove, 1989-90. With AUS, 1943-45. Recipient cert. of merit Internat. Inventor's Expn., 1965; grantee NSF, Stevens Inst. Tech., 1962, U. Notre Dame, 1963. Mem. IEEE (life), ASME (acting sec. materials handling div. 1939-42), Am. Helicopter Soc., N.J. Inst. Tech. Alumni Assn. Republican. Baptist. Home and Office: 91 Mt Tabor Way Ocean Grove NJ 07756-1437

GABRIEL, OTHMAR, biochemistry educator; b. Vienna, Austria, Jan. 10, 1925; came to U.S., 1958; s. Othmar Sr. and Rosa (Fellner) G.; m. Elisabeth Rehurek, May 28, 1949 (div. 1962); children: Anna Maria, Harriet; m. Rachelle Rothenberg, Aug. 5, 1965. PhD, U. Vienna, 1954. Asst. prof. U. Vienna, 1954-58; rsch. assoc. Med. Sch. Columbia U., N.Y.C., 1958-60; rsch. chemist NIH, Bethesda, Md., 1960-65; assoc. prof. Med. Sch. Georgetown U., Washington, 1965-70, prof. Med. Sch., 1970-90; prof. emeritus Georgetown U. Med. Ctr., Rockville, Md., 1990—; vis. prof. Harvard U. Med. Sch., Boston, 1973; exec. editor Analytical Biochemistry, San Diego, 1983—. Contbr. numerous articles to profl. jours. Mem. AAUP, Am. Soc. Biol. Chemists, Sigma Xi. Office: Georgetown U Med Ctr 4 Research Ct Rockville MD 20850-3236

GACHOT, CHARLES ARTUR JACQUES, food products industry executive; b. N.Y.C., June 25, 1931; s. Charles A.J. and Jeanne Tallmadge (Sloper) G.; m. Laila Burke Bradley, Apr. 3, 1954 (div. 1974); children: Charles A.J., R. Bradley, Christopher B., W. Sanford, Laila Anne; m. Barbara Ann Cross, June 22, 1991. BS in Econs., U. Pa., 1954. Dir. sales Charles Gachot, Inc., N.Y.C., 1957-59, pres., 1976-79; resident mgr. Spear, Leeds & Kellogg, Ardmore, Pa., 1960-61; ptnr. Woodcock, Moyer, Fricke & French, Ardmore, 1961-70, Suplee Moseley, Phila., 1970-76; chmn. Gachot & Roethel, Inc., N.Y.C., 1979-88; pres., chmn. Gachot & Gachot, Inc., N.Y.C., 1988—; mem. Am. Stock Exch., 1966-70. Bd. dirs. Mental Health Assn. N.J., 1989—. 1st lt. USAF, 1955-57. Recipient diploma of honor Vatel Club, N.Y.C., 1984. Mem. Nat. Assn. Meat Purveyors, Meat Purveyors Assn. N.Y. (pres. 1985—), Chefs de Cuisine Am., Soc. Culinaire Philanthropique, Les Amis d'Escoffier Soc., Union League Club, St. Croix Yacht Club, Normandy Beach Yacht Club, Montclair Golf Club. Republican. Episcopalian. Home: 316 Highland Ave Upper Montclair NJ 07043 Office: Gachot & Gachot Inc 440 W 14th St New York NY 10014

GADE, DANIEL WAYNE, geography educator; b. Niagara Falls, N.Y., Sept. 28, 1936; s. Hugo William and Evelyn Henrietta (Jagow) G.; m. Mary Scott Killgore, Aug. 28, 1965; 1 child, Christopher. BA, Valparaiso (Ind.) U., 1959; MA, U. Ill., 1960; MS, U. Wis., 1961, PhD, 1967. Prof. geography U. Vt., Burlington, 1966—; U.S. corres. Bibliographie Geographique Internationale, Paris, 1987—. Contbg. editor: Handbook of Latin American Studies, 1988—; author: Plants, Man and the Land, 1975; contbr. articles to profl. jours. Rsch. grantee Fulbright Found., Argentina-Brazil-Uruguay, Madagascar, 1983, U.S. Spanish Joint Com., Madrid, 1988-89, Nat. Geog. Soc., 1978, Social Sci. Rsch. Found., 1970. Fellow Am. Geog. Soc.; mem. Assn. Am. Geographers, Soc. Econ. Botany, Soc. for Ethnobiology, Internat. Mtn. Soc., Conf. Latin Am. Geographers (bd. dirs. 1985-88). Home: 30 Harrington Ter Burlington VT 05401-3932 Office: Univ of Vt Dept Geography Burlington VT 05405

GADICKE, ANSBERT SCHNEIDER, health care investment manager; b. Frankfurt, Hessen, Germany, Feb. 9, 1958; came to U.S., 1987; s. Karl Herbert and Brigitte (Gadicke) Schneider-Gadicke. MD/PhD, J.W. Goethe U., Frankfurt, 1983. Postdoctoral fellow German Cancer Rsch. Ctr., Heidelberg, 1984-86, Harvard U., Cambridge, Mass., 1987-88, MIT, Cambridge, 1988-89; cons. Boston Consulting Group, 1989-92; mng. ptnr. Med. Portfolio Mgmt., Boston, 1992—. Contbr. articles to profl. jours. Col. Germany Army, 1983-84. Fellow DFG 1984, European Molecular Biology Orgn. 1987; recipient Wilsede award Deutsche Krebshilfe 1986. Home: 46 Shepard Cambridge MA 02138 Office: Med Portfolio Mgmt Inc 101 Federal St Boston MA 02110

GAETA, ROSEMARIE, social worker; b. Bklyn., Apr. 15, 1947; d. James and Rose (Scorcia) G. BS, Fordham U., 1968, MSW, 1970. Diplomate NASW; lic. social worker, N.Y. Pvt. practice S.I. and N.Y.C., 1973—. Mem. N.Y. State Soc. Clin. Social Work Psychotherapists (diplomate, chair state com. on psychoanalysis 1987-91), Nat. Fedn. Socs. Clin. Social Work (chair nat. com. on psychoanalysis 1991—), Inst. Psychoanalytic Tng. and Rsch. Office: 92 Eltingville Blvd Staten Island NY 10312-3807 Office: 31 E 12th St Apt 1E New York NY 10003-4624

GAFFIGAN, CATHERINE, actress, educator, director; b. N.Y.C.; d. James Joseph and Catherine Marie (Murphy) G.; m. Christopher Nelson, May 4, 1981 (div. 1991). BA in English, St. John's U., 1959; MFA in Speech and Drama, Cath. U. Am., 1962. Tchr. acting N.Y.C., 1972—, theatre dir., 1977—; cons. women's career issues U.S. C. of C., Washington, 1981-85; tchr. master classes in acting for profls. N.Y. studio, 1971—. Contbg. author Image Impact I, 1980, Image Impact II, 1983; editor: By Actors for Actors, 1991; N.Y. debut Journey of the Fifth Horse, Am. Pl. Theatre; actress appearing in plays including Cabaret, Once Upon a Mattress, Company, The Milky Way, Last of the Red Hot Lovers, on-Broadway in Whose Life Is It Anyway, soap operas and classics; procuder Scene Nights; dir. Restaurant Romances, Deals and Deceptions, An Evening of Hilarity and Hidden Agendas, Dance Me to the End of Love; producer/dir. The J.A.R., (off-Broadway) Lady Susan. Cons. N.Y.C. Dept. Human Resources - Welfare Office, N.Y.C., 1987-88. Mem. AFTRA, AAUW, SAG, Actors Equity Assn.

GAFFIN, GERALD ELIOT, lawyer; b. Worcester, Mass., Apr. 28, 1932; m. Joan Rockoff; children: Lisa M. Brown, David M. JD, Boston U., 1956. Bar: Mass. 1956. Assoc. Wasserman & Salter, Boston, 1956-58; pvt. practice Boston, 1958-59; ptnr. Cohen & Gaffin, Framingham, Mass., 1959—; gen. counsel/bd. dirs. Metrowest C. of C., Framingham, 1976—; counsel/bd. dirs. Metrowest United Way, 1980—; counsel Danforth Art Mus., Framingham, 1988—. Mem. Middlesex County Bar Assn. (pres. 1991-92), South Middlesex County Bar Assn. (pres. 1974-75). Office: Cohen & Gaffin 615 Concord St Framingham MA 01701-8001

GAFFNEY, DONNA MARY, children-families psychotherapist, consultant, educator; b. Irvington, N.J., Nov. 21, 1946; d. Harold Joseph and Madelon Ann (Reynolds) Aman; m. John Thomas Gaffney, Jr., Mar. 21, 1970; children: Ryan Thomas, Brendan Joseph, Lauren Anne. BSN, Hunter Coll., 1970; MA in Child Psychology, Tchrs. Coll., N.Y.C., 1972; MS in Psychiat. Nursing, Rutgers U., 1977; DNSc. in Nursing, U. Pa., 1986. Cert. clin. specialist in advanced psychiatric nursing. Dir. child life program Montefiore Med. Ctr., N.Y.C., 1971-72; patient care coord. Overlook Hosp., Summit, N.J., 1972-73; asst. prof. Rutgers U., New Brunswick, N.J., 1976-80; clin. specialist Fair Oaks Hosp., Summit, 1980-81; rsch. fellow U. Pa., Phila., 1982-83; asst. prof., grad. psychiat. nursing Columbia U. Sch. Nursing, N.Y.C., 1986-92; guest speaker Today Show, NBC TV, N.Y.C., 1986—; cons., speaker Sta. WWOR, Universal 9 TV, N.Y.C., 1991. Author: The Seasons of Grief Helping Children Grow Through Loss, 1988; author (simulation game) Pediatrix, 1977; contbr. articles to profl. jours. Bd. dirs. Helping Kids in Death, Divorce, Separation (K.I.D.D.S.), Wilmington, Del., 1990—, Community Leukemia Fund, N.J., 1985; mem. N.J. chpt. Soc. of Prevention of Youth Suicide, 1988—; speaker, mem. nat. com. for Prevention of Child Abuse, 1980. Fellow Am. Acad. Nursing, 1990, Rudin Rsch. fellow Rudin Found., 1989; named Woman of Yr.-N.J., Woman of Yr. Program,1 983. Mem. ANA, Am. Orthopsychiat. Assn., Advocates for Child Psychiat. Nursing, Assn. for Care of Children's Health, Sigma Theta Tau (grantee 1984). Home: 57 Winchip Rd Summit NJ 07901-4142 Office: Columbia U Sch Nursing 617 W 168th St New York NY 10032-3703

GAFFNEY, JOHN FRANCIS, chamber of commerce executive; b. Atlantic City, Mar. 23, 1934; s. John Fasio and Marie Bernadet (Cooney) G.; m. Judith Ann Brangenberg, Sept. 19, 1957 (div. Aug. 1985); children: Lynn, Patricia, Virginia, Kathleen; m. Carol Laura Crane, Sept. 21, 1985; children: Laurie, Amy. Land surveyor Atlantic Electric, Pleasantville, N.J., 1959-68, asst. engr., 1968-82, svc. rep., 1982-89; exec. dir. Greater Mainland C. of C., Pleasantville, 1990—. Councilman, City of Linwood, N.J., 1974-75, mayor, 1975-79; freeholder Atlantic County, N.J., 1979—; pres. South Jersey Freeholders Assn., Northfield, 1988-89. Sgt. U.S. Army, 1957-59. Mem. Nat. Assn. Counties (vice chmn. airport subcom. 1985—), Friendly Sons of St. Patrick. Republican. Roman Catholic. Office: Greater Mainland C of C 1 New York Rd Smithville NJ 08021

GAGE, CLARKE LYMAN, retired chemistry educator; b. Mason City, Iowa, Apr. 20, 1921; s. Edgar Stockbridge and Ada Fredricka (Anderson) G.; m. Jane Eaton, Dec. 16, 1944 (div. Jan. 1979); children: Michael, Timothy, Barnard. BS, Antioch Coll., 1944; PhD, Ohio State U., 1951. Chemist Monsanto Chem. Co., Dayton, Ohio, 1943-44; asst. prof. St. Lawrence U., Canton, N.Y., 1952-58, assoc. prof., 1958-66, prof., 1966-86, emeritus prof., 1986—; faculty del., bd. trustees St. Lawrence U., Canton, 1974-77. Chpt. pres. AAUP, Canton, 1963-64; bd. dirs., sec. Adirondack Mountain Club, Lake George, N.Y., 1986-91; bd. dirs. St. Lawrence County Hist. Assn., Canton, 1990—. With USN, 1944-46, PTO. Kettering scholar Charles F. Kettering Found., 1946-48; Kettering fellow Charles F. Kettering Found., 1948-51. Mem. Am. Chem. Soc. (chmn. No. N.Y. sect. 1957, 65, 82), History of Sci. Soc., Brit. History of Sci. Soc., Sigma Xi (chmn. Clarkson-St. Lawrence club 1956-57). Home: 6 Elm St Canton NY 13617-1461

GAGE, WILLIAM JAMES, film producer; b. Westfield, Wis., Aug. 30, 1932; s. Donald John and Catherine (Frye) G.; m. Nancy Lee Chaillet, Jan 1, 1955 (div. 1975); children: William Jay, Carlton Lee, Kevin Emory, Amanda Chaillett Catherine; m. Margaret Winslow Burks, May 7, 1977; stepchildren: James M. Gillispie, Jacquelyn V. Gillispie. Cert. screenwriter, video producer. Cinematographer USN, Japan, 1952-56; cameraman/dir. Creative Arts Studios, Inc., Washington, s1956-59; pres. Filmedia Studios, Inc., Washington, 1959-71; prodn. mgr. WLVA-TV, Lynchburg, Va., 1971-73; exec. producer Communications Corps, Inc., Washington, 1973-78; freelance writer/dir., Washington, 1978-79; mgr. AV programs U.S. Bur. Mines, Washington, 1979—; AV cons., Nat. Cath. News Svc. Washington 1969-71; guest speaker Internat. Quorum, San Francisco, 1983; visiting judge, MacDougall Creative Writing Contest, Gallaudet Coll. Washington 1985. Writer/dir. numerous films most recently: Bangladesh: A Beginning or An End 1976 (Cine Golden Eagle Council on Internat. Nontheatrical Events, TSE TSE 1977 (Cine Golden Eagle Award, The Only Thing I Can't Do Is Hear 1978 (Cine Golden Eagle Award, Red Ribbon Am. Film Festival, Gold Camera Award (lst place) U.S. Indsl. Film Festival,, Spl. Achievement Award Council for the Advancement & Support of Edn., Award of Merit XIV Internat. Festival of Ednl. Films Teheran, Iran), Copper, 1983 (Grand prize, Bronze medal, 1st place award). Pub. relations chmn. Young Reublicans Temple Hills, Md. 1963-64. With USN 1952-56. Mem. Internat. Quorum Film & Video Producers, Interdepartmental Com. on AV Materials for Distribution Abroad, Washington Film Coun. Republican. Home: 12624 Fantasia Dr Herndon VA 22070-2901 Office: US Bur Mines 810 7th St NW Washington DC 20241-0001

GAGLIARDI, UGO OSCAR, systems software architect, educator; b. Naples, Italy, July 23, 1931; came to U.S., 1956; s. Edgardo and Lina (Valenzuela) G.; m. Anna Josephine Italiano, July 7, 1954 (div. May 1972); children: Oscar Marco, Alex Piero. Diploma in Math. and Physics, U. Naples, Italy, 1951; DEng in Elec. Engring., U. Naples, 1954. Chief scientist U.S. Air Force, Hanscom AFB, Mass., 1966-67; v.p. tech. ops. Interactive Scis., Inc., Braintree, Mass., 1968-70; dir. engring. Honeywell Info. Systems, Waltham, Mass., 1970-75; lectr. Harvard U., Cambridge, Mass., 1967-74, prof. practice computer engring., 1974-83, Gordon McKay prof. practice computer engring., 1983—; pres. Gen. Systems Group, Inc., Salem, N.H., 1975—; chmn. Ctr. for Software Tech., Inc.; mem. NAS rsch. coun. panel Nat. Computer Systems Lab. (formerly Inst. Computer Scis. and Tech.) for Nat. Inst. Standards and Tech. (formerly Nat. Bur. Standards), 1985-91, chmn., 1988-91. Fulbright scholar, 1955-56. Home: 5 Manor Pky Salem NH 03079-2842 Office: Harvard U 33 Oxford St Cambridge MA 02138-2901

GAGNE, FAITH ELIZABETH, artist; b. Waltham, Mass., Oct. 16, 1934; d. Donald Voss Holt and Mary Louise (Linehan) Snowp; m. Edward Gagne (div.); 1 child, James Edward. AA with honors, Cape Cod Community Coll., Barnstable, Mass., 1989. Prin. art works include Morning in West Yarmouth, 1991, ltd. reprodn. print Sioux Dancer, 1991. Home: 71 Swan Lake Rd West Yarmouth MA 02673

GAGNE, KIMBERLY ANN, student personnel administrator; b. Springfield, Mass., Sept. 28, 1964; d. Richard Arnold and Joann Louise (Burnett) G. BA, North Adams State Coll., Mass., 1986; MA, Ohio State U., Columbus, 1989. Statistics peer tutor North Adams State Coll., North Adams, Mass., 1984-86, resident asst., 1984-86, administrv. asst., 1986-87; asst. residence dir. Ohio State U., Columbus, Ohio, 1987-88, counselor, 1988-89; women's resource ctr. Keene State Coll., Keene, N.H., 1989—, residence dir., 1989—; teaching asst., North Adams State Coll., Mass., 1985-86; crisis intervention worker, Women's Crisis Svcs., Keene, N.H., 1991—. Presenter: Development and Preliminary Validation of a New Measure of Children's Coping, 1987, Focus Area Programming, 1991. Mem. Am. Coll. Personnel Assn., Nat. Assn. Student Personnel Assts., Nat. Women's Studies Assn., Am. Assn. Univ. Women, Assn. Coll. and Housing Univ. Officers. Home and Office: 48 Butler Ct Keene NH 03431-4607

GAGNE, LAURA LEE, law librarian; b. Old Town, Maine, Aug. 6, 1959; d. George Howard and Jacqueline (Waugh) Jamison; m. Brian Edward Gagne. Student, Nasson Coll., 1975-80; BA in English, U. Maine, 1983; MLS, No. Tex. State U., 1985. Asst. librarian Rangeley (Maine) Pub. Library, summers 1978-83; catalog asst. Portland (Maine) Pub. Library, 1983-84; retrospective conversion asst. AMIGOS, Denton, Tex., 1985; data entry clk. U.S. Dept. Agr., Westbrook, Maine, 1985-86; loan file librarian Sun Savs. & Loan Assn., Portland, 1986; law librarian Drummond Woodsum Plimpton & MacMahon, Portland, 1986—. Editor: Sandy River Rev., 1983. Recipient fellowship, U.S. Govt., 1984-85. Mem. Law Librarian's of New Eng., Law Librarians of Portland. Office: Drummond Woodsum Plimpton & MacMahon 245 Commercial St Portland ME 04101-1117

GAGNE, ROGER OWEN, engineering executive, mechanical engineer; b. Laconia, N.H., Nov. 8, 1931; s. Napoleon Joseph and Marguerite (Richards) G.; m. Theresa Geralda Decelles, Nov. 21, 1959; children: Marc, Jean-Pierre, Martin, Eric. BSME, Okla. State U., 1959. Mgr. machine devel. Internat. Packings Corp., Bristol, N.H., 1959-75, mgr. product design, 1976-79, mgr. corp. tool, 1979-85, dir. engring., 1986-87, v.p. engr., 1987—; v.p. engr. Freudenberg-Nok, Manchester, N.H., 1987—. Patentee 3 high-pressure seals. Chmn. N.H. Adv. Coun. Vocat.-Tech. Edn., Concord, 1974-75, exec. com., 1975-77; active 20 Ctr. Vocat.-Tech. Concept, Concord, 1978, Selective Svc. Bd. Cen. N.H., 1991—; corporator Lakes Region Hosp., Laconia, N.H. Staff sgt. USAF, 1951-55. Mem. Soc. Automotive Engrs., Humane Soc., KC. Roman Catholic. Home: 115 Morrill St Gilford NH 03246 Office: Freudenberg-Nok Grenier Industrial Pk Manchester NH 03103

GAGNE, WILLIAM RODERICK, lawyer; b. Phila., Jan. 6, 1955; s. William Richard G. and Mary Elizabeth (Bast) Brennan; m. Pamela Jean Bashore, Aug. 26, 1978; children: Roderick Bashore, Evan Rhodes. BA, Ithaca Coll., 1976; JD, Dickinson Sch. Law, 1980; LLM, Georgetown U., 1983. Bar: Pa. 1980, U.S. Dist. Ct. (we. dist.) Pa. 1980, Fla. 1982, U.S. Tax Ct. 1982, U.S. Dist. Ct. (ea. dist.) Pa. 1985. Assoc. Wayman, Irvin & McAuley, Pitts., 1980-81, McClure & Watkins, P.C., Pitts., 1981-83, Pelino & Lentz, Phila., 1985-89; assoc. Clark, Ladner, Fortenbaugh and Young, Phila., 1989-90, ptnr., 1991—; bd. dirs. Edwin L. Heim Co., Harrisburg, Pa., Friends of Wistar Inst., Phila. Mem. ABA (sec. com. on S corps. sect. taxation 1988-90, chmn. subcom. on 589 publs. 1986-90, subcom. on publs. 1990-92, subcom. on newly enacted legis. 1992—, chmn. subcom. on legis. devels. 1992—), Pa. Bar Assn., Phila. Bar Assn., Phila. Cricket Club, Rittenhouse Club, Phi Alpha Delta. Republican. Episcopalian. Home: 515 Cresheim Valley Rd Philadelphia PA 19118-2408 Office: Clark Ladner Fortenbaugh & Young 1 Commerce Sq 22d Fl 2005 Market St Philadelphia PA 19103

GAGNER, THOMAS ALBERT, chemical company executive; b. Quantico, Va., Aug. 10, 1946; s. Harvey William and Grace Eileen (Dwyer) G.; m. Mary Elaine Eutsler; children: Bryan Matthew. BS in Conservation, U. Md., 1969. Prodn. supr. Union Carbide Corp., Alsip, Ill., 1974-75; project engr. Union Carbide Corp., Wayne, N.J., 1975-76; dept. head prodn. Union Carbide Corp., Freehold, N.J., 1976-80; mgr. safety, health and environ. affairs Union Carbide Corp., East Hartford, Conn., 1980-85; dir. safety, health and environ. affairs Union Carbide Corp., Danbury, Conn., 1985—. Commr. Inland Wetlands Commn., Brookfield, Conn., 1989. Capt. USMC, 1969-74. Recipient Chmn.'s award for safety, health and environ. excellence, Union Carbide Corp., 1989; Intercollegiate Amateur Athletic Assn. Am. pole vault champion, 1966. Mem. Compressed Gas Assn., Nat. Safety Council, Orgn. Resources Counselors, Am. Soc. Safety Engrs., Nat. Fire Protection Assn. Democrat. Roman Catholic.

GAGNER, WAYNE P., research facility executive; b. Worcester, Mass., Feb. 25, 1938; s. Anna (Wales) G.; m. Sue Frix; 1 child, David Wayne. AB in Econs., Boston U., 1961. Lic. comml. multi-engine pilot, FAA. Mem. air test crew Fairchild Corp., Germantown, Md., 1966-67; new bus. mgr. Singer div. Gen. Precision Corp., Rockville, Md., 1967-79; cons. Washington Aerospace Cos., 1969-71; dir. spl. systems Computer Scis. Corp., Falls Church, Va., 1971-75; cons. Cornel Aero. Systems, Washington, 1975-76; mgr. bus. devel. SYSCON Corp., Washington, 1976-81; pres. S&W Assocs., Bethesda, Md., 1981—; cons. Lockheed Electronics, 1981-89, Whittaker Electronics Systems, 1987-88, Hazeltine, 1987—, Resdel Industries, 1987-88, Kaman Aerospace, 1986-87. Inventor in electro-optics field, 1968; author numerous bus. and tech. books, 1980-89. Active many community and citizens' orgns., Bethesda, 1967—. With USAF, 1961-65. Fellow Washington D.C. Study Group; mem. USAF Assn., Old Crows, Am. Legion, Bethesda Country Club. Democrat. Roman Catholic. Home: 9104 Charred Oak Dr Bethesda MD 20817-1926

GAGNON, JOHN HARVEY, psychotherapist, educator; b. Derby, Conn., Dec. 16, 1946; s. Ernest John and Pauline Stella (Dziedulonis) G.; m. Carolyn Ingersoll, Oct. 4, 1980; 1 child, Isabelle Eleanor. BS, Fairfield U., 1969; MS, Western Conn. State Coll., 1976; PhD, Union Inst., 1982. Diplomate Am. Bd. Med. Psychotherapy; cert. marriage and family therapist, Conn., 1983—. Counselor in tng. Conn. Valley Hosp., 1972-73; counselor Whiting Forensic Inst., 1973; coord., dir. Danbury Hosp. Day Treatment Program, 1973-77; pvt. practice, 1977-80; psychotherapy intern Counseling Ctr. and N.Y. Inst. for Gestalt Therapy, 1981-83; pvt. practice, 1983—; rsch. cons. Newtown Counseling Ctr., 1987-89; instr. N.Y. Inst. for Gestalt Therapy, 1983-89; lectr. Yale U., 1983; adj. prof. Western Conn. State U., 1983-86, U. Bridgeport, 1988-90; adj. lectr. U. Conn., Torrington, 1990—. Author: Gagnon's Directory, 1986; contbr. articles to profl. jours. Adult program chmn. Unitarian-Universalist Soc. of North Fairfield County, West Redding, Conn., 1990-91, rel. edn. tchr., 1984-86; vol. cert. EMT, State Conn., 1982—. Mem. AACD, AAUP, Assn. for Counselor Edn. and Supervision, Am. Soc. for Group Psychotherapy and Psychodrama, Am. Acad. Psychotherapists, Am. Assn. for Marriage and Family Therapy, Assn. for Humanistic Psychology, Internat. Assn. for Marriage and Family Counselors, Internat. Coun. for Sex Edn. and Parenthood, Nat. Coun. on Family Relations, Phi Delta Kappa. Democrat. Home: 99 Stadley Rough Rd Danbury CT 06811-3230

GAGOSIAN, LARRY, art dealer. Owner Gagosian Gallery, N.Y.C. Office: care Gagosian Gallery Inc 980 Madison Ave New York NY 10021-1848*

GAIDEMAK, JOEL, physician, pharmacist; b. Jersey City, May 23, 1931; s. Samuel William and Rose (Ginsberg) G.; m. Elaine M. Beizer, July 14, 1961 (div. 1981); 1 child, Samuel Robert; m. Melinda Sue Meyer, Aug. 19, 1984; children: Jacob Louis, Cole Gregory. BS, Rutgers U., 1954; MD, U. Bologna, Italy, 1969. Diplomate Am. Bd. Family Practice. Intern Beth Israel Med. Ctr., Newark, N.J., 1970-71; resident in internal medicine St. Barnabas Med. Ctr., Livingston, N.J., 1971-72; med. dir. Merck Sharp & Dohme, Rahway, N.J., 1976-79; attending physician Mary Imogene Bassett Hosp., Cooperstown, N.Y., 1989—; pvt. practice Delhi, N.Y., 1972-76, 79-86. With U.S. Army Med. Corps, 1956-58. Fellow Am. Acad. Family Physicians. Home: 12 Franklin St Delhi NY 13753-1126 Office: Riverside/Bassett Rt 23 Harper St Stamford NY 13753-1126

GAILEY, FRANCES HARRIETT, home economics educator; b. Watertown, N.Y., June 26, 1932; d. Charles G. and Flossie F. (Eiss) G. BS, Syracuse U., 1953; MS, Cornell U., 1959; PhD, Ohio State U., 1973. Cert. home economist. Home econs. tchr. Munderse Acad., Seneca Falls, N.Y., 1953-57; teaching asst. Cornell U., Ithaca, N.Y., 1957-59; dietitian Wheaton (Ill.) Coll., 1959-60; tchr. home econs. Homer (N.Y.) Cen. Sch., 1960-61; from asst. prof. to prof. SUNY, Oneonta, 1961—; cons. Nat. Kitchen and Bath Assn., Hackettstown, N.J., 1987—; foodsvc. mgr. InterVarsity Christian Fellowship Cedar Campus, Madison, Wis. and Cedarville, Mich., summers 1953-77. Corp. mem. InterVarsity Christian Fellowship, Madison, Wis., 1971-81; cons. Child Care Kitchen Design, N.Y. State, Oneonta, 1988—. Recipient scholarship Elec. Women's Roundtable, Cox Assocs., Nashville, 1968-69. Mem. ASTM (various coms. 1986—), Am. Home Econs. Assn. (state nomination chair, dist. pres. 1987-89), Am. Mgmt. Assn., Coll. Educators in Home Equipment (pres. 1976-78), Am. Nat. Standards Inst. (Z21 com. gas standards 1986—), Phi Upsilon Omicron (nat. fin. chair 1984—), Kappa Omicron Nu. Methodist. Office: Home Econs Dept SUNY-Oneonta Oneonta NY 13820

GAINES, ANNE PRESTON, publication executive; b. Charleston, W.Va., July 25, 1950; d. William Thomas and Elizabeth (Tupper) Griffiths; m. William Maxwell Gaines, Feb. 21, 1987 (dec.). BFA, U. Colo., 1972. Sec. N.Y. Bailliage Confrerie de la Chaine des Rotisseurs, N.Y.C, 1976-81; asst. to pub. Mad Mag.-E.C. Publs., N.Y.C, 1980-92, gen. mgr., 1992—. Mem. Wine and Food Soc. N.Y., John More Assn. (bd. dirs. 1980-86), Ison Soc. (charter mem.). Office: Mad Mag 485 Madison Ave New York NY 10022-5803

GAINES, FRANK, JR., management consultant; b. Lansing, Mich., Feb. 9, 1918; s. Frank and Ida (Strauer) G.; m. Devonna Frances Collins, Dec. 22, 1945; children: Jerry Lee, Bonnie Lou, Stephen Frank. BS in Chem. Engring., Mich. State U., 1938; postgrad., Harvard U., 1962. Petroleum engr. Carter Oil Co., Seminole, Okla., 1938-41; asst. mgr. employee relations

Carter Oil Co., Tulsa, 1953-58; div. prodn. mgr. Carter Oil Co., Maltoon, Ill., 1958-60; petroleum engr. Creole Petroleum Corp., Caracas, Venezuela, 1946-52; asst. dist. supr. Creole Petroleum Corp., Cabimas, Venezuela, 1952-53; mgr. orgn. and exec. devel. Humble Oil Co., Houston, 1960-66; mgr. compensation and exec. devel. Exxon Corp., N.Y.C., 1966-81; pres. Gaines and Assocs., Greenwich, Conn., 1981—; mem. adv. bd. Corp. Edn. Resources, Inc., Fairfield, Iowa. Author: Succession Planning in Leading Companies, 1984. Served to lt. col. C.E., U.S. Army, 1941-46. Named Silver Anniversary Football All-Am., Sports Illustrated mag., 1962. Republican. Presbyterian. Club: Burning Tree Country (Greenwich) (pres. 1968). Home and Office: Gaines & Assocs 18 Stepping Stone Ln Greenwich CT 06830-4031

GAINES, JAMES RUSSELL, magazine editor, publisher, author; b. Dayton, Ohio, Aug. 11, 1947; s. Robert William and Harriet Elizabeth (Fenner) G.; m. Leslie Friedman, May 23,1971 (div. 1978); 1 child, Allison Gaines; m. Pamela Butler, July 9, 1983 (div. 1989); m. Karen Lipton, Feb. 9, 1992. B in Gen. Studies, U. Mich., 1970. Editor The Herald, N.Y.C., 1971-72; assoc. editor Saturday Rev., N.Y.C. and San Francisco, 1972-73, Sta. WNET/13—The 51st State, N.Y.C., 1973-74, Newsweek, N.Y.C., 1974-76; assoc. editor People Mag., N.Y.C., 1977-78, sr. editor, 1979-82, asst. mng. editor, 1982-86, exec. editor, 1986-87, mng. editor, 1987-89; mng. editor and publisher Life, N.Y.C., 1989—. Author: Wit's End: Days and Nights of the Algonquin Round Table, 1977; author, editor: The Lives of the Piano, 1981. Office: Life Mag Time and Life Bldg Rockefeller Ctr New York NY 10020

GAJDA, ANTHONY JAMES, employee benefits and compensation consulting firm executive; b. Butler, Pa., Oct. 2, 1943; s. K.S. and Mary (Kamitzky) G.; m. Alma Perlmutter, Nov. 5, 1966 (div. 1985); children: Felice Beth, Robin Michele. BA, Queens Coll., Flushing, N.Y., 1970; MA, Hunter Coll., N.Y.C., 1973. Exec. v.p. Program Planners, Inc., N.Y.C., 1967-83; prin. William M. Mercer, Inc., N.Y.C., 1983—. Editor newsletter The Mercer Bull.; contbr. articles to profl. jours. With USAF, 1961-65. Office: William M Mercer Inc 1166 Ave Of The Americas New York NY 10036-2708

GAJEWSKI, PATRICIA LOUISE, management executive; b. Erie, Pa., Feb. 18, 1959; d. Conrad and Margaret (Hyman) G. Accounts payable freight clk. Hammermill Paper Co., Erie, Pa., 1979-80, acctg. clk., 1980-81, div. sec., 1981-85, payroll specialist and human resources coord., 1985, Nortim coord., 1985-88; v.p. NORTIM Corp., Erie, 1988—; mem. Kane Area Logging Safety Com., 1985—. Bd. dirs. Foodbank of Erie, 1988. Recipient Special Recognition award Greater Erie Area Safety Coun., 1988, award Erie Engring. Soc. Coun., 1989. Mem. Am. Soc. Safety Engrs. (treas. 1988-90, Mem. of Yr. 1989), Pa. Forestry Assn. (logging and sawmill safety com., co-chmn. Kane area logging safety com. 1985—, Warren area logging safety com. 1988—), Pa. Forest Industry Assn. Republican. Roman Catholic. Home: 1691 Granada Dr Apt 14 Erie PA 16509-6810 Office: NORTIM Corp 1705 W 26th St Erie PA 16508-1233

GALANTE, JOE, recording industry executive. Pres. RCA Record Labels U.S., N.Y.C. Office: Bertelsmann Music Group 1133 Ave Of The Americas New York NY 10036-6710*

GALANTE, NICHOLAS THOMAS, III, paper manufacturing company executive; b. Albany, N.Y., Nov. 11, 1955; s. Nicholas Thomas and Violet (Broccoli) G.; m. Mary Therese Dunvar, June 10, 1978; children: Elizabeth Nolan, Nicholas Thomas, Katharine Carey, James Davis, Christina Dunvar, Alexandria Rutledge. BSBA, Georgetown U., 1977. V.p. sales and mktg. Tagson's Papers, Inc., Albany, 1977-85, exec. v.p., 1985—. Treas. N.Y. State chpt. Am. Diabetes Assn., Syracuse, 1986-89, chmn. Albany chpt., 1988-89; trustee St. Gregory's Sch., 1992—. Mem. Am. Paper Inst. (bd. dirs. 1979—, govt. adv. com. 1979-83, indsl. product com. 1983-85), Am. Paper Distbn. Coun., Albany Acad. Alumni Assn. (bd. dirs. 1990-92), Sons of Italy (trustee 1985-89). Democrat. Roman Catholic. Home: 10 Loudon Hts N Albany NY 12211-2012 Office: Tagsons Papers Inc PO Box 1999 Albany NY 12201-1999

GALANTER, EUGENE, psychologist, educator; b. Phila., Oct. 27, 1924; s. Max and Sarah (Honigman) G.; m. Patricia Anderson, Dec. 22, 1962; children: Alicia, Gabrielle, Michelle. A.B., Swarthmore Coll., 1950; A.M., U. Pa., 1951, Ph.D., 1953. From instr. to prof. psychology U. Pa., 1952-62; research fellow Harvard U., 1955-56, Center Advanced Study Behavioral Scis., 1958-59; chmn. dept. psychology U. Wash., 1962-64, prof., 1964-66; Joseph Klingenstein vis. prof. social psychology Columbia U., N.Y.C., 1966-67; prof. psychology Columbia U., 1967—; Cons. NIH, NSF, also to industry; mem. Council for Biology in Human Affairs; chmn. commn. on biology, learning and behavior Salk Inst. Author: Plans and Structure of Behavior, 1960, 2nd. edit., 1986, New Directions in Psychology, 1962, Textbook of Elementary Psychology, 1966, Kids & Computers: The Parents' Microcomputer Handbook, 1983, Kids & Computers: Elementary Programming for Kids in BASIC, 1983, Kids & Computers: Advanced Programming Handbook, 1984; Editor: Handbook of Mathematical Psychology, 3 vols., 1963-64, Readings in Mathematical Psychology, 2 vols., 1963-65, Psych Tech Notes, 1988. Served with AUS, 1942-46. Fellow AAAS; mem. APA, Eastern Psychol. Assn., Acoustical Soc. Am., N.Y. Acad. Scis., Assn. Aviation Psychologists (pres. 1970-71), Human Factors Soc., Internat. Soc. for Psychophysics, Sigma Xi. Office: 324 Schermerhorn Hall Columbia U New York NY 10027

GALDES, ALPHONSE, pharmaceutical research and development manager; b. May 10, 1952; came to U.S., 1979; s. George and Anne (Cachia) G.; m. Bridget Agius, July 20, 1976; children: Annelise, Andrew. BS with honors, U. Malta, 1973, MS in Biochemistry, 1975; DPhil in Chemistry, U. Oxford, Eng., 1979. Rsch. fellow Harvard Med. Sch., Boston, 1979-81, rsch. assoc., 1981-84; sr. scientist Boc Group Tech. Ctr., Murray Hill, N.J., 1984-87, mgr., 1987-90, sect. mgr. health care R&D, 1990—. Contbr. articles to profl. jours. Recipient Rhodes scholarship, 1975. Mem. AAAS, Am. Chem. Soc., Am. Soc. Biochemists and Molecular Biologists, N.Y. Acad. Sci., Drug Info. Assn. Office: Boc Group Tech Ctr 100 Mountain Ave Murray Hill NJ 07974

GALDIERI, ANTHONY AUGUST, psychologist; b. Scranton, Pa., June 17, 1943; s. Christopher and Ann (Bocchino) G.; m. Judith Baldin, Oct. 2, 1960 (div. Feb. 1974); m. Mary Ellen Jordan, May 26, 1978; 1 child, Anthony. BS, U. Scranton, 1965, MS, 1966; PhD, Ohio U., 1971. Lic. psychologist, Pa. Cons. Scranton (Pa.) Sch. Dist., 1973-90, Friendship House Children's Ctr., Scranton, 1972—; pvt. practice psychology Scranton, 1972—; med. advisor Fed. Dept. Human and Health Svcs., Wilkes-Barre, Pa., 1986—. Fellow Pa. Psychol. Assn.; mem. APA, Nat. Register Mental Health Providers, Ea. Psychol. Assn. Home: 110 Gentilly Dr Clarks Summit PA 18411-1032 Office: Bank Towers 4th Fl 321 Spruce St Scranton PA 18503

GALEOTTI, STEVEN, insurance executive; b. Bklyn., Feb. 1, 1952; s. Aristide Angelo and Grace (Lupo) G.; m. Rose Anne Safina; children: Alycia Dawn, Jonathan Paul. B.Chem. Engring., Pratt Inst., Bklyn., 1974; MA Occupational Safety, NYU, 1982; A in Risk Mgmt., Ins. Inst. Am. Field rep. Factory Ins. Assocs., N.Y.C., 1974-76; cons. Fred S. James & Co., Inc., N.Y.C., 1976-80; mgr. Fred S. James & Co., Inc., 1980-86; dir. Fred S. James & Co., Inc., Short Hills, N.J., 1986-89; mgr. Sedgwick James, Inc., Short Hills, 1989-90; sr. risk engr. Zurich-Am. Ins. Group, 1991—. Editor newsletter Risk Control Insights, 1988-90. Mgr. Tri-boro Little League, Bloomingdale, N.J., 1988-90; mem. Bloomingdale Zoning Bd. of Adjustment, 1990—, elected chmn., 1992; mem. Bloomingdale Bd. Edn., 1992—, v.p., 1992-83; treas. Bloomingdale Rep. Campaign, 1991. Mem. Am. Soc. Safety Engrs., Nat. Fire Protection Assn., Soc. Fire Protection Engrs., Am. Inst. Chem. Engrs. Roman Catholic. Office: Zurich Am Ins Group 1 Liberty Pla 165 Broadway New York NY 10006

GALEY, GEORGE GREGORY, food products executive, marketing professional; b. Upland, Pa., May 29, 1948. BS, Villanova (Pa.) U., 1970; MBA, Pa. State U., 1971. Mktg. devel. mgr. AMAX, Inc., Denver, 1977-84; wine supr. Nat. Wine & Spirits, Indpls., 1984-85; pres. Am. Estates Wines, Summit, N.J., 1985—. Office: Am Estates Wines 19 Hillside Ave Summit NJ 07901-1904

GALIBER, JOSEPH LIONEL, state senator; b. N.Y.C., Oct. 26, 1924; s. Joseph F. and Ethel (Bowser) G.; B.S., CCNY, 1950; J.D., N.Y. Law Sch., 1962; m. Emma Evangeline Shade, 1946; children—Pamela Susan, Ruby Dianne Wint. Bar: N.Y. 1965. practice law, Bronx, N.Y., 1965—; mem. N.Y. State Senate, 1969—; chmn. Democratic Task Force on Econ. Devel. for Bronx; mem. Black and P.R. Legis. Caucus; mem. State Commn. on Social Service and Prison Reform. Mem., chmn. Bronx County Dem. Com., 1969-79; del., asst. majority leader N.Y. State Constl. Conv., 1967; del. Dem. Nat. Conv., 1968. Served with AUS, 1943-45. Recipient Outstanding Service Human Relations CUNY, 1970; Amerigo Vespucci award, 1972; named Outstanding Legislator of Yr., Morrisania Edn. Council, 1975; named Citizen of Yr., Bronx Boys Club, 1975. Mem. ABA, Bronx Bar Assn., N.Y. Trial Lawyers Assn., Am. Legion, NAACP. Democrat. Presbyterian. Office: NY State Senate State Capitol Albany NY 12247 also: 840 Grand Concourse Bronx NY 10451

GALIE, LOUIS MICHAEL, electronics company executive; b. Phila., Aug. 10, 1945; s. Adam Michael and Phyllis Anne (Bowers) G.; m. Elizabeth D. Viviano, June 23, 1969 (div. 1980); 1 child, Kathryn Louise; m. Charlene Mary Gates, Aug. 27, 1983 (div. 1988); m. Martha Bancroft Campbell, May, 1990; 1 child, Grace F. BS, U. Chgo., 1967, MS, 1968. Prin. researcher System Devel. Corp., Santa Monica, Calif., 1975-80; dir. devel. Burroughs Corp., Danbury, Conn., 1980-82; dir. engring. Timex Corp., Waterbury, Conn., 1982-86, v.p. research and devel., 1986—. Author: Means for Database Search, 1980, Electronic Spelling Correction, 1981; patentee in field. Warden Trinity Episcopal Ch., Newtown, Conn., 1985-89. Comdr. USN, 1969-75. Mem. IEEE, Soc. for the History of Tech. Republican. Home: 141 Brushy Hill Rd Newtown CT 06470-2514 Office: Timex Corp Waterbury CT 06720

GALIMI, DOMINICK JOSEPH, urban planner, educator; b. N.Y.C., Dec. 9, 1945; s. Dominick Vincent and Edith Mary (Falciani) G.; m. Phyllis Joy Fier, Mar. 28, 1967 (div. 1985); children: Grant, Gavin, Garrett; m. Eileen Victoria Cassidy, Apr. 11, 1987; children: Craig, Christopher. BS, CUNY, 1967, MS, 1970, advanced cert., 1975. Resource tchr. to curriculum specialist Bd. Edn. N.Y.C., 1967—; pres. Package Enterprises N.Y. State, 1980-87, GGG Ins. Brokerage, Yonkers, N.Y., 1987—, Yonkers 2000 Com., Inc., 1988-90; bd. dirs. Nat. Found. for Safety, Inc., Yonkers. Chmn. Brotherhood Task Force, Yonkers, 1988—, Westchester County Commn. Commemorating Christopher Columbus 500 Yrs., 1988—. Mem. Sons of Italy. Roman Catholic. Office: GGG Brokerage Inc 155 Fisher Ave Tuckahoe NY 10707-2616

GALIVAN, JOHN HENRY, biochemist, educator; b. Albany, N.Y., June 19, 1939; s. John Henry and Mary Hortense (Sullivan) G.; m. Nancy Lynn Stiehler, Jan. 24, 1982; children: Amanda, Brendan, Julie, Kate. BS, Albany Coll. Pharmacy, 1960; MS, SUNY, Albany, 1963; PhD, Albany Med. Coll., 1967. Postdoctoral fellow Scripps Clinic and Rsch. Found., La Jolla, Calif., 1967-70; rsch. scientist Wadsworth Labs., N.Y. State Dept. Health, Albany, 1970-90, dir. pathology lab., 1990-92, dir. Div. Clin. Scis., 1992—; prof. SUNY, Albany, 1985—; assoc. prof. of biochemistry Albany Med. Coll., 1978-85; mem. exptl. therapeutics study sect. Nat. Cancer Inst., Bethesda, Md., 1985-89. Assoc. editor Jour. Cellular Pharmacology, 1992—; contbr. over 100 articles to profl. publs., chpt. to book. Mem. State Legis. Com. N.Y., 1992—. Mem. AAAS, Am. Assn. Cancer Rsch., Fedn. Am. Soc. Exptl. Biology, N.Y. Acad. Scis. Home: 162 Chestnut St Albany NY 12210-1906 Office: NY State Dept Health Wadsworth Labs Empire State Plz Albany NY 12223-0001

GALKIN, SAMUEL BERNARD, orthodontist; b. Newark, Feb. 9, 1933; s. Saul J. and Mollie (Kleinberg) G.; children from previous marriage: Jamie Michelle, Richard Stewart; m. Gail Beth Elkin, Feb. 26, 1972; children: Scott David, Seth Paul. Student, U. Conn., 1951-54; DDS, Temple U., 1958; MS in Histology, U. Ill., 1963, cert. grad. orthodontics, 1963; cert. in craniomandibular disorders, U. Medicine and Dentistry of N.J., 1989. Diplomate Am. Bd. Orthodontics. Group practice orthodontics Woodbridge, N.J., 1963—; staff orthodontist J.F.K. Community Hosp., Edison, N.J., 1966—, with cleft palate com., 1971—, dir. dental dept., 1979—; staff Woodbridge Health Ctr., 1967—, with dental adv. com., 1971—; dir. dept. dentistry John F. Kennedy Med. Ctr., Edison, 1979-81; staff orthodontist Perth Amboy (N.J.) Gen. Hosp., 1986—, dir. dept. dentistry, 1990—; staff orthodontist Rahway Hosp., N.J., 1986—; asst. prof. orthodontics N.J. Coll. Medicine and Dentistry, Jersey City, 1963-73; mem. panel physicians N.J. Crippled Children Program, 1971—; dentist Woodbridge Twp. Sch., 1989—. Chmn., Woodbridge Twp. Debutante Ball, 1970; bd. dirs. Woodbridge Twp. YMCA. Lt. Dental Corps, USN, 1958-61. Mem. ADA, Middle Atlantic Soc. Orthodontists (chmn. clinics 1969, 72), N.J. Dental Soc., Middlesex County Dental Soc., Am. Soc. Dentistry for Children, Am. Assn. Orthodontists, Am. Lingual Orthodontic Assn. (charter), Am. Assn. Dental Schs., Am. Acad. Head, Neck, Facial Pain and TMJ Orthopedics, N.E. Craniomandibular Soc., N.J. Craniomandibular Soc. (charter), Am. Acad. Oral Medicine, Alpha Omega (chpt. v.p. 1969—), Omicron Kappa Upsilon. Home: 3 Dorset Rd Colonia NJ 07067-3101 Office: 711 Amboy Ave Woodbridge NJ 07095-3193 also: 233 Madison Ave Perth Amboy NJ 08861-4306

GALL, LENORE ROSALIE, educational administrator; b. Bklyn., Aug. 9, 1943; d. George W. Gall and Olive Rosalie (Weekes) Gall Bryant. AAS, NYU, 1970, cert. tng. and devel., 1975, BS in Mgmt., 1973, MA in Counselor Edn., 1977; EdM and EdD, Columbia U., 1988. Various positions Ford Found., N.Y.C., 1967-75; dep. dir. career devel. Grad. Sch. Bus., NYU, N.Y.C., 1976-79; dir. career devel. Pace Lubin Sch. Bus., N.Y.C., 1979-82; dir. career devel. Sch. Mgmt., Yale U., New Haven, 1982-85; asst. to assoc. provost Bklyn. Coll., 1985-88, asst. to provost, 1988-91; asst. to v.p. acad. affairs Fashion Inst. Tech., 1991—; adj. asst. prof. LaGuardia Community Coll., L.I. City, N.Y., 1981—, Sch. Continuing Edn. NYU, 1983-84; dir., sec. devel. workshop Coll. Placement Services, Bethlehem, Pa., 1978-81. Bd. dirs. Langston Hughes Community Library, Corona, N.Y., 1975-83, 86-92, chair, 1975-79, 82-83, 89—, 2d v.p., 1986, 1st v.p., 1987-88, chair awards com. Dollars for Scholars, Corona, 1976—. Mem. AAUW, Assn. Black Women in Higher Edn. (exec. bd., membership chair, pres.-elect 1988, pres. 1989-93), Am. Assn. Univ. Adminstrs., Nat. Assn. Univ. Women (chaplain 1987-88, 2d v.p. 1988, 1st v.p. 1988-92), Nat. Assn. Women Deans and Adminstrs., Nat. Assn. Women in Edn., Black Faculty and Staff Assn. Bklyn. Coll (1st vice-chair 1986-87, chair 1987-88), New Haven C. of C. (chmn. women bus. and industry conf. 1984), Nat. Coun. Negro Women Inc. (life, 1st v.p. North Queens sect. 1986-89, pres. 1989-92), Nat. Assn. Negro Bus. & Profl. Women's Club (Sojourner Truth award 1991), Phi Delta Kappa, Kappa Delta Pi. Mem. A.M.E. Ch. Office: Fashion Inst Tech Office VP Acad Affairs 227 W 27th St # 913C New York NY 10001-5902

GALL, SALLY MOORE, librettist, poet, scholar; b. N.Y.C., July 28, 1941; d. John Alexander and Betty (Clark) Moore; m. John Knox Marshall, 1961 (div. 1965); m. W. Einar Gall, Dec. 8, 1967. BA in English cum laude, Harvard U., 1963; postgrad., Columbia U., 1963-65; MA in English, NYU, 1971, PhD, 1976. vis. prof. English Drew U. Grad. Program, Madison, N.J., 1978; adj. asst. prof. English NYU, 1978-81. Opera libretti include The Singers of Lesbos, David and Jonathan and In Time of Plague; collaborator with composer Robert Convery (one-act family opera) The Little Thieves of Bethlehem, with composer Dave Conner (full-length family musical) Pinocchio; author: (books) Ramon Guthrie's Maximum Security Ward: An American Classic, 1984, The Modern Poetic Sequence: The Genius of Modern Poetry (with M. L. Rosenthal), 1983, 2d edit. 1986; editor: Maximum Security Ward and Other Poems, 1984 (Explicator Lit. Found. award 1984); versification editor: Poetry in English: An Anthology, 1987; translator Chopin's songs; contbr. articles to profl. jours., poetry to literary jours. Penfield fellow, 1973-74; recipient Key Pin and Scroll award, NYU, 1976. Mem. Nat. Opera Assn., MLA, Opera for Youth, Poets and Writers, Lyrica, Dramatists Guild, Morning Music Club of Nyack (pres. 1989-91). Democrat. Home and Office: 29 Bayard Ln Suffern NY 10901-3409

GALLAGHER, CAROLE L., photographer, writer; b. N.Y.C., July 16, 1950; fosterparents Walter George and Caroline (Small) Hooke. Student, New Sch., N.Y.C., 1973; MA in Art, CUNY, 1977. Freelance photographer N.Y.C., 1973-91; instr., lectr. Kingsborough Coll.-CUNY, 1977-79, Coll. New Rochelle, N.Y., 1977, U. Utah, Salt Lake City, 1988-90; stringer UPI, Portland, Maine, 1982; dir. Nuclear Towns Documentary project Utah State Hist. Soc., Salt Lake City, 1985-90. Illustrator: Punch!, 1983, Muscles!, 1983, American Ground Zero: The Secret Nuclear War, 1993; group exhbns. include State Mus. Motovun, Yugoslavia, 1977, Galleria del Cavallino, Venice, Italy, 1977, Van Abbemuseum, Eindhoven, Netherlands, 1977, shows in USSR, Germany, Czechoslovakia, Netherlands, Poland, Sweden, Norway, Austria; solo exhbns. include Leo Castelli Gallery, 1979, 81, Mus. Contemporary Photography, Chgo., 1989, Internat. Ctr. Photography, 1993, others. Grantee Charles Stewart Mott Found., 1992, Deer Creek Found., 1987, Columbia Found., 1986, 87, 91, Ruth Mott Fund, 1988, 89, MacArthur Found., 1988, Fund Investigative Journalism, 1991, Nev. Humanities Com., 1992; art fellow Utah Arts Coun., 1989. Home and Studio: 79 Mercer St New York NY 10012-4430

GALLAGHER, EDWARD PETER, arts association administrator; b. San Francisco, Mar. 23, 1951; s. Edward Owen and Virginia Anne (Scully) G. BA, U. Calif., 1976; MBA, Columbia U., 1982. Dir. communications Wolf Trap Farm Pk. for Performing Arts, Vienna, Va., 1977; asst. program mgr. Smithsonian Inst., Washington, 1977-79, sr. program mgr., 1979-81; dir. membership Mus. Modern Art, N.Y.C., 1983-90, acting dir. devel., 1986-87; dir. NAD, N.Y.C., 1990—; cons. Cooper Hewitt Mus., N.Y.C., 1982-83; bd. dirs. Ireland Am. Arts Exch., Madison, Wis., 1988—. Mem. Internat Commn. Mus., Am. Assn. Mus. Home: 666 W End Ave # 21 New York NY 10025-7357 Office: NAD 1083 5th Ave New York NY 10128-0114

GALLAGHER, ELEANOR, university official; b. Bklyn., Jan. 2, 1939; d. Eustace and Christine (Breitenberger) Proebstl; m. William J. Gallagher, Aug. 20, 1960 (now separated); children: William E., Kathleen, Michael. BA magna cum laude, CUNY, 1960; MBA, Syracuse U., 1985; postgrad., Harvard U., 1988. Tchr. N.Y.C. Sch. System, 1960-76; grad. recorder Syracuse U. Coll. for Human Devel., 1978-80; adminstrv. asst. to the chancellor Syracuse U., 1980-85, exec. asst. to the chancellor, 1985—, sec. to bd. trustees, 1991—. Mem. Onondaga War Meml. Conv. Ctr. Commn., Syracuse, 1988-90; mem. Onondage Country Partnership for the Arts, Syracuse, 1990-92; bd. dirs. University Neighborhood Preservation Assn., Syracuse, 1990—, University Hill Corp., Syracuse, 1991—. Mem. Phi Beta Kappa, Beta Gamma Sigma. Roman Catholic. Office: Syracuse U 300 Tolley Adminstrn Bldg Syracuse NY 13244-1100

GALLAGHER, KATHLEEN E., artist, educator; b. N.Y.C., Dec. 18, 1949; d. Patrick Joseph and Sarah Ann Gallagher. BA, Marymount Manhattan Coll., 1971; MA, Lehman Coll., 1975. Permanent cert. art tchr., N.Y. Adj. instr. Mercy Coll., Dobbs Ferry, N.Y., 1983-88, Elizabeth Seton Coll., Yonkers, N.Y., 1984-88, Coll. of New Rochelle, N.Y., 1986—; tchr. Pelham (N.Y.) Art Ctr., 1983—; vis. artist Coun. for Arts in Westchester, White Plains, N.Y., 1987—. Exhibited in group shows Pratt Graphics Ctr., N.Y.C., Mus. of the City of N.Y., 1981, Associated Am. Artists, N.Y.C., 1985, Hudson River Mus., Yonkers, 1989, John Szoke Gallery, N.Y.C., 1988, Lynd Ward Traveling Exhibit, 1990-92; represent in permanent collections DeCordova Mus., Mass., Pratt Graphic Ctr., N.Y., Phila. Mus., Mus. of the City of N.Y., Portland (Oreg.) Mus. and numerous other corp. collections. Recipient award Print Club, Phila., 1980, purchase award Pratt Graphics Ctr., 1982. Mem. Soc. Am. Graphic Artists (coun.), Nat. Artists Equity, Coll. Art Assn. Home: 255 Drake Ave New Rochelle NY 10805-1609

GALLAGHER, LINDY ALLYN, banker, financial consultant; b. Kalamazoo, Sept. 27, 1954; d. Karl P. Joslow and Audrey S. Phillips; m. Thomas J. Gallagher, Nov. 29, 1975; children: James Allyn Buckley, Phillip Graham. BS, U. Pa., 1975; MBA, Columbia U., 1982. Faculty, researcher U. Pa., Phila., 1976-80; corp. banking officer Bank of Montreal, N.Y.C., 1982-84; v.p. Citibank NA, N.Y.C., 1984-89; v.p. manager Chase Manhattan Bank, N.Y.C., 1989-90; pres. The Allyn Co., New Canaan, Conn., 1990—; treas., dir. 957 Lexington Corp., 1981-87. Editor Columbia Jour. World Bus., 1980-82. Active Women's Nat. Rep. Club, 1986—; commr. Town of New Canaan; treas. Young Women's League of New Canaan, Inc. Mem. Stanwich Club. Republican. Episcopalian.

GALLAGHER, SEAN, research physiologist; b. Urbana, Ill., Oct. 18, 1955; s. James John and Rani (Cunningham) G.; m. Nancie J. Samars, June 20, 1988; 1 child, Andrew Sebastian. BA, U. N.C., 1978; MS, Pa. State U., 1984. Rsch. physiologist U.S. Bur. Mines, Pitts., 1984—. Author (circular) Reducing Back Injuries in Low Coal Mines, 1990; contbr. articles to profl. jours. Mem. Am. Indsl. Hygiene Assn. (chair ergonomics 1988-89), Am. Soc. Biomechanics (com. mem. 1989—), Human Factors Soc., Internat. Found. for Indsl. Ergonomics and Safety Rsch. Office: US Bur of Mines PO Box 18070 Cochrans Mill Rd Pittsburgh PA 15236-0070

GALLAGHER, THOMAS FRENCH, career officer, strategist; b. Centralia, Ill., July 23, 1939; s. Edgar French and Mary Maxine (Holmes) G.; m. Rebecca Agnes Belle Isle, June 6, 1963; children: Cheryl Ann Gallagher Lobb, Thomas French Jr. BS, U.S. Mil. Acad., 1963; MA, U. S.C., 1978. Commissioned U.S. Army, 1963, advanced through grades to col., 1985; facility engr. and readiness officer Safeguard Ballistic Missile Def. Complex, Nakoma, N.D., 1975-76; analyst Def. Intelligence Agy., Washington, 1978-81; sr. air def. advisor U.S. Mil. Tng. Mission to Saudi Arabia, Riyadh, 1981-82; staff officer Strategic Plans and Policy Div. U.S. Army, The Pentagon, Washington, 1982-85; dep. dir. Inst. for Nat. Strategic Studies Nat. Def. Univ., Washington, 1985-86, 88-90; dep. chief U.S. Mil. Tng. Mission to Saudi Arabia, Riyadh, 1986-88; acting dir. Inst. for Nat. Stragetic Studies Nat. Def. Univ., Washington, 1990; exec. dir. Nat. Def. Univ. Found., Washington, 1990—. Author: The Structure of Foreign Policy and Trade Relationships within North Africa, 1978; contbr. articles to profl. jours. Den leader Boy Scouts Am., Riyadh, 1986-87. Decorated two Legions of Merit, Bronze Star, two Def. Meritorious Svc. medals, two Air medals, Joint Svcs. Commendation medal, Army Commendation Valor medal, Gallantry Cross, Social Welfare Svc. medal, Def. Superior Svc. nedal. Mem. Internat. Inst. for Strategic Studies, Internat. Studies Assn., Soc. of Gulf Arab Studies, Mid. East Studies Assn., Assn. of U.S. Mil. Acad. Grads. Republican. Methodist. Home: 4201 Mayport Ln Fairfax VA 22033-3233 Office: Nat Def Univ Found Studies/Nat Def Univ Ft McNair Washington DC 20319-6000

GALLAGHER, THOMAS JOSEPH, banker; b. Elizabeth, N.J., Jan. 21, 1949; s. T. Stanley and Madeline (Buckley) G.; m. Lindy Allyn Joslow, Nov. 29, 1975; children: James Allyn Buckley, Philip Graham. BA magna cum laude, U. Pa., 1973, MBA, 1975. V.p. PNC Fin. Corp., Phila., 1975-79, Bank of Am. Nat. Trust & Savs. Assocs., San Francisco, 1979-83; v.p. fin., chief fin. officer Page Am. Group, Inc., N.Y.C., 1984-85; v.p. investment banking dept. Bankers Trust Co., N.Y.C., 1983-88; sr. v.p., group exec. The Chase Manhattan Bank N.A., N.Y.C., 1988—; dir. Corp. Officers & Dirs. Assurance Ltd. Advisor Jour. of European Bus. Trustee Internat. Ctr. Photography, N.Y.C.; commr. utilities Town of New Canaan, chmn. 1991—. Mem. Soc. Broadcast Engrs., Soc. Cable TV Engrs., Soc. Motion Picture and TV Engring., The Blue Hill Troupe, Stanwich Club, Phi Beta Kappa. Republican. Episcopalian. Home: 103 Salem Rd New Canaan CT 06840-4318 Office: The Chase Manhattan Bank NA 1 Chase Manhattan Plz New York NY 10081

GALLAND, LEO, internist, researcher; b. Bombay, Mar. 7, 1943; came to U.S., 1948; s. H. William and Rachel (Zakkai) G.; m. Christine Oelz, Sept. 29, 1974; children: Nicole, Jefferson, Jonathan, Christopher, Jordan. AB, Harvard U., 1964; MD, NYU, 1968. Diplomate Am. Bd. Internal Medicine. Resident in medicine NYU-Bellevue Med. Ctr., N.Y.C., 1968-72; instr. Albert Einstein Coll. Medicine, Yeshiva U., N.Y.C., 1972-73; asst. prof. SUNY Med. Ctr., Stony Brook, 1973-77; pvt. practice Winsted (Conn.) Hosp., 1977-82; dir. rsch. Gesell Inst., New Haven, 1982-85; pvt. practice, N.Y.C., 1985—; asst. prof. U. Conn. Health Ctr., Farmington, 1977-85; sr. rsch. cons. Gt. Smokies Diagnostic Lab., Asheville, N.C., 1990—. Author: Superimmunity for Kids, 1988; also numerous articles on nutrition and infectious diseases. Recipient Harold Harper award Am. Coll. Advancement in Medicine, 1989. Fellow ACP, Am. Coll. Nutrition; mem. Soc. for Microbial Ecology and Disease, Internat. Soc. for Neuroimmunomodulta-

tion, Soc. for Behavioral Medicine, Acad. Environ. Medicine. Home: 142 5th Ave New York NY 10011-4312 Office: 133 E 73d St New York NY 10021

GALLANT, BRIAN J., technical training administrator; b. Somerville, Mass., Jan. 18, 1955; s. Richard S. and Helen K. (Galleghar) G.; m. Lisa Ann Gooding, Sept. 12, 1981 (div. Mar. 1987). AS in Fire Sci., Safety, Cape Cod Community Coll., 1985; BS in Mgmt., Lesley Coll., 1990. Dir. training Nat. Fire & Med. Svcs., Inc., Sandwich, Mass., 1985-87; dir. fire training County of Barnstable, Mass., 1983-86; fire lt. Sandwich Fire Dept., 1977-87; training supr. Boston Edison, 1987—; cons. Nat. Loss Prevention Inst., Sandwich, 1985—, Mass. Criminal Justice Training Coun., 1982-89, Barnstable County Police Acad., 1982-88. Civil defense dir., Sandwich, 1987—; chmn. Emergency Planning Com., Sandwich, 1987—. Recipient Pres.'s award Internat. Assn. Firefighters, 1986. Mem. Nat. Assn. Fire Investigators, Soc. Fire Protection Engrs. Democrat. Roman Catholic. Home: Rural Route 6A Box 269186A Sandwich MA 02563-9805 Office: Boston Edison Co 800 Boylston St Boston MA 02199-8001

GALLANT, GEORGE WILLIAM, political scientist; b. Boston, Nov. 14, 1931; s. George William and Gladys Mary (Dalby) G.; m. Joan Cornelia Crimmins, Nov. 6, 1954; children: Judith Cornelia, Nicole Marie. AB cum laude, Boston Coll., 1952; MA, Georgetown U., 1965; PhD, Fordham U., 1971; grad., various specialized mil. schs. Commd. 2d lt. U.S. Army, 1952, advanced through grades to col., 1975; svc. in Eng., Fed. Republic Germany and Vietnam; asst. prof. U.S. Mil. Acad., West Point, N.Y., 1967-70; head Soviet and Asian communist rsch. sects. and divs. Dept. Def., 1970-75; Soviet cons. and translator, 1975—; adj. faculty mem. polit. sci. Stonehill Coll., North Easton, Mass., 1977-85, asst. prof., 1985—. Contbr. articles to profl. jours.; creator TV programs. Rep. Stoughton Town Meeting, 1975—, vice chmn. mcpl. ops. com. Decorated Legion of Merit (2), Bronze Star. Mem. Am. Assn. for the Advancement Slavic Studies, Am. Polit. Sci. Assn., New Eng. Polit. Sci. Assn., Assn. U.S. Army, Ret. Officers Assn., Phi Beta Kappa, Alpha Lambda Sigma (hon. mem. Beta Xi chpt.), Boston Coll. Alumni Club, South Shore Ret. Officers Assn. Club. Address: 303 Morton St Stoughton MA 02072

GALLANT, JAMES JEROME, English educator; b. Worcester, Mass., Oct. 23, 1950; s. George Jerome and Rita Mary (Downey) G. BA in English, Assumption Coll., 1972; MA in English, Clark U., 1975; PhD in English, U. Conn., 1988. Instr. English Assumption Coll., Worcester, Mass., 1975-77; lectr. U. Conn., Storrs, 1980-86; instr. Mt. Wachusett Community Coll., Gardner, Mass., 1986-88; lectr. Worcester State Coll., 1986-88; asst. prof., chmn. dept. English Elms Coll., Chicopee, Mass., 1988—. Editor Ouroboros mag., 1985-87; contbr. articles to profl. jours. Mem. MLA, New Chaucer Soc., Nat. Coun. Tchrs. English, Internat. Ctr. Medieval Art, Medieval Acad. Democrat. Roman Catholic. Home: 10 Lyndale Rd Worcester MA 01606-2418 Office: Elms Coll Dept English Springfield St Chicopee MA 01013-2603

GALLENO, ANTHONY MASSIMO, bank executive; b. N.Y.C., Feb. 18, 1942; m. Frances Urban, Nov. 8, 1969; children: Anthony J., Lynn Ann. BBA, Baruch Coll., 1970; MBA, Pace U., 1980; cert., Nat. Compliance Sch., U. Okla., 1988. With Bowery Div. Home Savs. of Am., N.Y.C., 1960—, v.p., contr., 1981-83, sr. v.p., fin. div., 1983-87, corp. sec., 1987—, security officer, 1991—, sr. v.p., compliance officer, security officer, 1990—, also bd .dirs., 1992—; chmn. Home's and Bowery's Contbn. Com.; bd. dirs. Bowery Advisors, Inc., 110 E 42d Operating Co., Inc., Oriental Ave., Inc.; mem. Soviet-Am. Banking Law Working Group, 1991. Treas. Bowery Polit. Action Com., N.Y.C., 1983-91; bd. mgrs. Bowery Hdqrs. Condominium, N.Y.C., 1981—; bd. dirs., fin. com., grievance com. Aetna N.Y. Health Plan, Inc.; co-chmn. luncheon for banks Greater N.Y. Boy Scouts Am., 1989—, mem. nominating com. Good Scout award, 1990. With U.S. Army, 1964-66. Recipient Good Guy award Geis Men's Assn., 1985; named Coach of Yr., Jefferson Valley, N.Y., 1987-88, Sportsman of Yr., Thurmen Assn., 1992. Mem. Fin. Mgrs. Assn., Am. Mgmt. Assn., Savs. Banks Assn. Group IV/V, Soc. of Corp. Secs., SBLI Fund (strategic planning com. 1989-91, coun. rep. exec. com. 1992). Home: 1312 Lydia Ct Mohegan Lake NY 10547-1907 Office: Bowery Savs Bank 110 E 42d St New York NY 10017

GALLENTI, VINCENT JAMES, human resources director; b. N.Y.C., July 13, 1948; s. Daniel and Phyliss Gallenti; m. Donna Lee Drummond, Oct. 13, 1973; children: Daniel Howard, James Michael. BS, Fairleigh Dickinson U., 1971; MBA, St. John's U., 1978; MS, Rutgers U., 1985. Cert. sr. profl. human resources Soc. Human Resources Mgmt. Mgr. Burrough Corp., Plainfield, N.J., 1979-80, div. mgr. human resources, 1980-84; group mgr. human resources Burrough Corp., Flemington, N.J., 1984-86; group dir. human resources, dir. integration/merger Unisys Corp., Blue Bell, Pa., 1986-87, group dir. human resources, 1987—. Mem. Nat. Soc. for Human Resource Mgmt., Am. Mgmt. Assn. Office: Unisys Corp PO Box 500 Township Lines & Jolly Rds Blue Bell PA 19424

GALLETTA, NUNZIO, engineering executive; b. Bessemer, Pa., May 23, 1927; s. John and Grace (Galletta) G.; m. Angeline Nancy Carrino, Oct. 24, 1952; children: Rosanne, Gerard Thomas, Paul Joseph, Laurel Anne. BS in Civil Engring., U. Pitts., 1949; MS in Civil Engring., 1959. Registered profl. engr., Pa., Ohio. Civil engr. Bur. of Reclamation, Coulee Dam, Wash., 1950-51, Loftus Engring. Corp., Pitts., 1951-55; cons. engr. Pitts., 1955-56; cons. engr., ptnr. Galletta & Assocs., Pitts., 1956-65; cons. engr., pres. Galletta Engring. Corp., Pitts., 1965—, bd. dirs. Mem. Zoning Bd. Appeals, Adams Twp.-Butler Count, Pa., 1980. With U.S. Army. Decorated World War II Victory medal. Fellow ASCE; mem. Am. Concrete Inst., Assn. Iron & Steel Engrs. Roman Catholic. Office: Galletta Engring Corp 610 Smithfield St Pittsburgh PA 15222-2512

GALLETTI, PIERRE MARIE, artificial organ scientist, medical science educator; b. Monthey, Switzerland, June 11, 1927; s. Henri and Yvonne (Chamorel) G.; m. Sonia Aidan, Dec. 31, 1959; 1 son, Marc-Henri. BA in Classics, St. Maurice Coll., Switzerland, 1945; MD, U. Lausanne, Switzerland, 1951; PhD in Physiology and Biophysics, U. Lausanne, 1954; ScD (hon.), Roger Williams Coll., U. Nancy, France, U. Ghent, Belgium. Asst. prof. physiology Emory U., 1958-62, assoc. prof., 1962-66, prof., 1966-67, vis. prof., 1967-68; prof. med. sci. Brown U., 1967—, Univ. prof., 1991—, chmn. div. biol. sci., 1968-72, v.p. biology and medicine, 1972-91; pres. Found. for Biotech., Turin, 1991—; mem. sci. adv. com. I-Stat, Princeton, N.J., 1984-90, Sorin Biomedica S.P.A., Turin, Italy, 1985—, Cardiopulmonics, Salt Lake City, 1988—, Cytotherapeutics, Inc., Providence, 1989-92; bd. dirs. Sorin Biomedica s.p.a., Turin, chmn. bd., 1987-90; chmn. Consensus Devel. Conf. NIH, chmn. devices and tech. br. task force; Hastings lectr. NIH, 1979; plenary lectr. World Biomaterials Conf., 1980, 88; McNeil Pharm. Spring Sci. lectr., 1982; lectr. German Surg. Soc., 1987, Japan Soc. Artificial Organs, 1987, 92, Soc. Cardiac Anesthiologists, 1992, Bio-engineering Soc., 1992; trustee Morehouse Sch. Medicine, 1982—; overseer Tufts U. Sch. Medicine, 1984—. Author: Heart-Lung Bypass: Principles and Techniques of Extracorporeal Circulation, 1962; contbr. chpts. to books, articles, abstracts to profl. jours. Trustee Morehouse Sch. Medicine, 1982—, R.I. Philharmonic, 1988—; overseer Tufts U. Sch. Medine, 1984—. Recipient John H. Gibbon award Am. Soc. Extracorporeal Technology, 1980, R.I. Gov.'s Sci. and Tech. award, 1987, Runzi prize, Switzerland, 1988, R.I. Commodore award, 1987; grantee NIH, 1962-91. Fellow Am. Coll. Cardiology, Am. Inst. Med. Biol. Engring.; mem. AAAS, Am. Physiol. Soc., Swiss Physiol. Soc., Royal Acad. Medicine (Brussels, fgn. corr.). Office: Box G B-393 Providence RI 02912

GALLEY, VIOLET URSULA, textile designer; b. Sale, Cheshire, Eng.; came to U.S., 1971, naturalized 1976; d. Herbert and Violet Hudson (Allen) Proctor; m. Charles Maurice Galley, Apr. 28, 1970 (dec. July 1979). Student, Manchester Coll. Art. Textile designer The Calico Printers Assn., Manchester, Eng., 1944-67, Fields & Currie Co Ltd., Montreal, Que., Can., 1968-71, Cohn Hall Marx Ameritex, N.Y.C., 1972-76, Aquarius Fabrics Inc., N.Y.C., 1973-76, Dae Woo Internat., N.Y.C., 1973-81, Qualfab Inc., N.Y.C., 1984, Qualitex Inc., N.Y.C., 1985-86, Reflections Inc, N.Y.C., 1988-89, Andre Charles Ltd. (now Bombay Industries), N.Y.C., 1982—. Contbr. poems to books. Mem. World of Poetry (Golden Poet 1989-91), Internat. Soc. Poets (Internat. Pen award 1991). Office: Cranston Print Works Inc 469 7th Ave New York NY 10018-7603

GALLICCHIO, DAVID MICHAEL, principal; b. Hartford, Conn., Mar. 27, 1943; s. Michael Paul and Blanche Emily (Martino) G.; m. Judith Ann Specht, Feb. 19, 1972. AS, U. New HAven, 1965; BS, Johnson State Coll., 1967; MS, So. Conn. State U., 1971, postgrad., 1979. Cert. profl. educator, Conn. Tchr. Conn. Dept. Correction, Conn. Correctional Inst. Niantic, 1967-73; prin. Unified Sch. Dist. # 1, Niantic, 1973—; chief hostage negotiator Conn. Dept. Correction, Niantic, 1980—; instr. Conn. Justice Acad., Storrs, 1980—; assessor new tchrs. Conn. State Dept. Edn., Hartford, 1991—. Contbr. articles to profl. jours. Commr. Old Saybrook (Conn.) Police Dept., 1990—; mem., chmn. Old Saybrook Youth and Family Svcs. Commn., 1984-90. Mem. Essex Corinthian Yacht Club. Home: 12 Pheasant Hill Ln Old Saybrook CT 06475-1133 Office: Conn Correctional Inst 199 W Main St Niantic CT 06357

GALLO, DEAN ANDERSON, congressman; b. Hackensack, N.J., Nov. 23, 1935; s. Dean and Selma (Anderson) G.; children—Susan, Robert. Ptnr. Gallo-DeCroce Real Estate, Parsippany, N.J., 1956—; v.p. Parsippany-Troy Hills Twp. Council, 1968-69, pres., 1970; dep. Morris County Bd. Chosen Freeholders, 1971-72, dir., 1973-75; mem. N.J. Gen. Assembly 26th Dist., 1976-84, minority leader, 1982-84; mem. Congress U.S. House of Reps., Washington, 1985—, mem. pub. works and transp. com., 1985-88, mem. small bus. com., 1985-88, regional whip, mid-Atlantic, New England states, 1985—, mem. appropriation com., 1989—, mem. budget com., 1989-90. Chmn. heart fund N.J. chpt. Am. Heart Assn. of Northwest, Parsippany, 1985—; vol. Cystic Fibrosis Walk-a-Thon, March of Dimes. Named Legislator of Yr., Nat. Republican Legislators Assn., 1982, N.J. Assn. Counties, 1978. Mem. Morris County Bd. Realtors, Parsippany C. of C. Lodge: Elks (charter mem.). Office: US Ho of Reps 1318 Longworth House Office Bldg Washington DC 20515

GALLO, FRANCIS CARL, educator; b. Bklyn., Sept. 27, 1943; s. Francis Pierini and Gertrude Elizabeth (Giordano) G.; m. Frances Carol Wallach; children: Kathryn Ann, Carolyn Elizabeth. BA, St. Bonaventure U., 1965; MA, Hofstra U., 1969. Cert. ednl. adminstr., N.Y. Secondary English tchr. Commack (N.Y.) Sch. Dist., 1965-78, asst. prin., 1987-88, acting prin., 1988, supr. English, 1978—; cons. N.Y. State Edn. Dept., 1968-70, Huntington (N.Y.) Performing Arts Found., 1969-73; conf. presenter N.Y. Inst. Tech., Huntington, 1986-87; summer sch. prin. Commack Sch. Dist., 1985—. Mem. Selden Civic Assn. (v.p., exec. bd. 1986—), Centereach Selden Youth Assn. (cons., advisor 1984—), Nat. Coun. Tchr. English, Assn. for Supervision and Curriculum Devel., Coun. at Adminstr. (supervisors exec. bd. 1986—), N.Y. State English Coun. Democrat. Roman Catholic. Home: 11 Monterey Ln Centereach NY 11720-1402

GALLO, JOSEPH, JR., safety and training administrator; b. Cambridge, Mass., Apr. 14, 1944; s. Joseph and Angela (Reale) G.; m. Doris Elnora Humston, Apr. 3, 1964; children: Joseph III, Bryan Gregory, Jeffrey Scott. AS in Instrumentation Tech., Polk Community Coll., Winter Haven, Fla., 1975, AS in Computer Tech., 1975; BS in Bus. Mgmt., Franklin Pierce Coll., 1988. Owner, mgr. Gallo Bus. Equipment, Winter Haven, 1974-84; customer svc. technician Union Carbide Corp., Billerica, Mass., 1984-88; safety and tng. engr. Union Carbide Corp., Balt., 1988-90, supt. safety and tng., 1990—. Mem. Solley Civic Assn., Balt., 1988—, South Balt. Indosl. Mut. Aid Plan, 1988—, Safety Coun. Maryland, Balt., 1988—. Sgt. USAF, 1963-67, Vietnam. Mem. Am. Soc. Safety Engrs., Am. Radio Relay League. Republican. Roman Catholic. Office: Union Carbide Corp 7350 Carbide Rd Baltimore MD 21226-1799

GALLO, SEBASTIAN JOHN, pathologist; b. Hartford, Conn., Aug. 26, 1932; m. Constance Amato, Aug. 26, 1961; children: Laura A., David S., Stephen J., Douglas J. AB, Johns Hopkins U., 1953; MD, U. Md., 1957. Diplomate Am. Bd. Anatomical, Clin. and Radioisotopic Pathology. Assoc. pathologist Middlesex Hosp., Middletown, Conn., 1962-74; sr. pathologist Middlesex Hosp., 1976—; dir. labs. Middlesex Meml. Hosp., 1977—; cons. in pathology various hosps. and labs. Fellow Coll. Am. Pathologists, Am. Soc. Clin. Pathologists; mem. Conn. Med. Soc., Middlesex County Med. Soc., Rotary. Office: Middlesex Hosp 28 Crescent St Middletown CT 06457

GALLOWAY, EILENE MARIE, national, international outerspace consultant; b. Kansas City, Mo., May 4, 1906; d. Joseph Locke and Lottie Rose (Harris) Slack; student Washington U., St. Louis, 1923-25; AB, Swarthmore Coll., 1928; postgrad. Am. U., 1937-38, 43; LLD (hon.), Lake Forest Coll., 1990, Swarthmore Coll., 1992; m. George Barnes Galloway, Dec. 23, 1924; children: David Barnes, Jonathan Fuller. Tchr. polit. sci. Swarthmore Coll., 1928-30; editor Student Svc., Washington, 1931; staff mem., edn. div. Fed. Emergency Relief Adminstrn., 1934-35; asst. chief info. sect., div. spl. info. Library of Congress, 1941-43, editor abstracts Legis. Reference Svc., 1943-51, nat. def. analyst, 1951-57; specialist in nat. def., 1957-66; sr. specialist internat. rels. (nat. security) Congl. Rsch. Svc., 1966-75; cons. internat. space activities, 1975—. Staff mem. Senate Fgn. Rels. Com., 1947; profl. staff mem. U.S. group Interparliamentary Union, 1958-66; cons. Senate Armed Svcs. Com., 1953-74, Ford Found., 1958; spl. cons. spl. Senate Com. on Space and Astronautics, 1958; spl. cons. to Senate Com. on Aero. and Space Sci., 1958-77; cons. to Senate Com. on Commerce, Sci. and Transp., 1977-82; chmn. com. edn. and recreation Washington, 1937-38; forum leader 1976-79; guest Soviet Acad. Sci., 1982, adult edn. U.S. Office Edn., 1938; mem. Internat. Inst. Space Law of Internat. Astronautical Fedn., 1958—, U.S. mem. bd. dirs., v.p., 1967-79, hon. dir., 1979—, Fedn. ofcl. observer at sessions UN Com. on Peaceful Uses Outer Space, 1981-90, 92, mem. com. for rels. with internat. orgns., 1979—; mem. Am. Rocket Soc.'s Space Law and Sociology Com., 1959-62; mem. adv. panel Office Gen. Counsel, NASA, 1971; adviser outer space del. U.S. Mission to UN Working Group on Direct Broadcast Satellites, 1973-75, legal subcom., 1976; observer UN Conf. Exploration and Peaceful Uses of Outer Space, Vienna, 1982; lectr. Nat. Acad. Sci., 1973, U.S. CSC, Exec. Seminar Center, Oak Ridge, 1973, 74, 75, 76, 78; ednl. counselor Purdue U., 1974; lectr. Inst. Air and Space Law McGill U., 1975, Inter Am. Def. Coll., 1977, 78, U. Akron, 1984, 91; mem. panel on solar power for satellites and U.S. space policy Office Tech. Assessment, 1979-80, 82-86, cons., 1982; cons. COMSAT, 1983, FCC Commn. on U.S. Telecommunications Policy, 1983-87. Pres., Theodore Von Karman Meml. Found., 1973-84; mem. alumni council Swarthmore Coll., 1976-79; mem. organizing com., author symposium on Conditions Essential For Maintaining Outer Space for Peaceful Uses, Peace Palace, Netherlands, 1984; bd. advisers Students for Exploration and Devel. of Space, 1984—. Rockefeller Found. scholar-in-residence, Bellagio, Italy, 1976; elected to Coun. of Advanced Internat. Studies, Argentina, 1985, Uruguyan Centro de Investigacion y Difusion Aeronautica-Expacial, 1985. Recipient Andrew G. Haley gold medal Internat. Inst. Space Law, 1968; NASA Gold Medal for Pub. Svc., 1984, USAF Space Command plaque, 1984; Internat. Acad. Astronautics' Theodore Von Karman award, 1986, Women in Aerospace Lifetime Achievement award, 1987, Lifetime Achievement award Internat. Inst. Space Law, 1989; Wilton Park fellow, Eng., 1968. Fellow Am. Astronautical Soc.; mem. LWV (chmn. study groups housing, welfare in D.C., 1937-38, mem. tech. com. on law and sociology task force on legal aspects 1979—), AIAA (tech. com. on legal aspects of aeros. and astronautics 1980-84, internat. activities com. 1985—), World Peace Through Law Ctr., Am. Soc. Internat. Law, Am. Astronautical Soc., Lamar Soc. Internat. Law, Internat. Acad. Astronautics (scis. sect. 1982-89), Internat. Law Assn., Phi Beta Kappa, Delta Sigma Rho, Kappa Alpha Theta. Episcopalian. Author: Atomic Power: Issues Before Congress, 1946; (with Bernard Brodie) The Atomic Bomb and the Armed Services, 1947; History of United States Military Policy on Reserve Forces, 1775-1957, 1957; Guided Missiles in Foreign Countries, 1957; The Community of Law and Science, 1958; United Nations Ad hoc Committee on Peaceful Outer Space, 1959; Satellites: A Force for World Peace, World (Security and the Peaceful Uses of Outer Space, 1960; International Cooperation and Organization for Outer Space, 1965; Space Treaty Proposals by the United States and U.S.S.R., 1966; Treaty on Principles Governing the Activities of States in the Exploration and Use of Outer Space, Including the Moon and Other Celestial Bodies: Analysis and Background Data, 1967; Remote Sensing of the Earth by Satellites: Satellites: Legal Problems and Issues, 1973, 75; The Future of Space Law, 1976; Consensus as a Basis for International Space Cooperation, 1977; The Role of the United Nations in Earth Resources Satellites, 1972; Settlement of Space Law Disputes, 1980; Agreement Governing the Activities of State on the Moon and Other Celestial Bodies, 1980, Perspectives of Space Law, 1981; Conditions for Success of International Space Institutions, 1982; Space Manufacturing, 1981; U.S. Space Policy and Programs, 1982; Space Station, 1986; U.S. National Space Legislation and Peaceful Uses Of Outer Space, 1987; Expanding Article IV of 1967 Space Treaty, 1982; History and Development of Space Law, 1982, Definition of Space Law, 1989, Law, Science and Technology for the Moon/Mars Missions, 1990, Legal and Regulatory Framework for Solar Power Satellites, 1992; editor: Space Law Symposium, 1958; The Legal Problems of Space Exploration, 1961; United States International Space Programs, 1965; International Cooperation in Outer Space: A Symposium, 1972, Use of the Geostationary Orbit, 1988; assoc. editor Advances in Earth Oriented Applications of Space Tech., 1978-82, Acta Astronautica Jour., Space Technology: Industrial and Commercial Applications; mem. editorial adv. bd. Jour. Space Law, U. Miss. Law Sch., Space Communication and Broadcasting, 1984-89. Home: 4612 29th Pl NW Washington DC 20008-2105

GALLUCCI, KATHRYN MCCLANAHAN, software engineer; b. Ankara, Turkey, Mar. 31, 1963; came to U.S., 1964; d. Roy Preston and Marie Ann (Micalizzi) McClanahan; m. John Mario Gallucci, Oct. 14, 1990. BS in Mgmt., U. Lowell, 1986. Computer analyst Data Gen., Southboro, Mass., 1986-87; software engr. DSD Laboratories, Inc., Sudbury, Mass., 1987—. Pres.-elect Greater Lowell (Mass.) YWCA, 1988—. Mem. U. Lowell Alumni Assn. (sec., bd. dirs. 1987—). Office: DSD Laboratories Inc 75 Union Ave Sudbury MA 01776

GALLUP, HOWARD FREDERICK, psychology educator; b. New London, Conn., Nov. 17, 1927; s. Wallace Lester and Edna Eudora (Ketcham) G.; m. Frances Webster Platt, June 4, 1949; children: Joshua, Sharrene, Bradford. BA, Rutgers U., 1950; MA, U. Pa., 1953, PhD, 1957. Instr. U. Pa., Phila., 1951-56; asst. prof. Hobart Coll., Geneva, N.Y., 1956-58; asst. prof., assoc. prof., prof., dept. head psychology Lafayette Coll., Easton, Pa., 1958—; vis. prof. Hampshire Coll., Amherst, Mass., 1972, Evergreen State Coll., Olympia, Wash., 1973. Author: An Invitation to Modern Psychology, 1969. Founding mem. Project of Easton, 1968—. Fellow APA, Am. Psychol. Soc., Eastern Psychol. Assn., Midwestern Psychol. Assn., Southeastern Psychol. Assn.; mem. AAAS, Sigma Xi. Democrat. Mem. Soc. of Friends. Home: 304 Frost Hollow Rd Easton PA 18042 Office: Lafayette Coll Psychology Dept Easton PA 18042

GALLUP, JOHN YOUNG, II, dental surgeon; b. Phila., Nov. 4, 1955; s. Andrew Young and Margaret (Allendorfer) G. BS, Allegheny Coll., 1978; DDS, U. Md., 1984. Researcher Wilmer Eye Clinic, Johns Hopkins Hosp., Balt., 1978-80; dental surgeon Drs. Grambow, Lilley, and Abramson, Balt., 1984—. Contbr. articles to profl. jours. Recipient Leona McNamara award for outstanding leadership qualities Orchard Park, N.Y., 1972, award Colgate Dental Health Edn. Adv. Bd., 1990; winner Regional Sci. Fair in Lectr., Demonstration Div.; Alden scholar, 1978. Mem. AMA (affiliate), Md. Dental Soc., Balt. City Dental Soc., The Key Club (pres. 1974), The Varsity Club (sec. 1974), Phi Delta Theta. Republican. Roman Catholic. Home: 1133 Oakwood Ln Bel Air MD 21015 Office: Drs Grambow Lilley et al 458 S Elrino St Baltimore MD 21224

GALOTTI, DONNA, publishing executive; b. Mountainside, N.J., Feb. 8, 1955; d. Jack and Analid Kalajian; m. Ron Galotti, Oct. 14, 1981. BS, Penn State U., 1975. Internat. credit analyst Irving Trust Co., N.Y.C., 1976-77; ad sales rep. BMT Pub., N.Y.C., 1977-79; ad sales rep. Woman's Day Mag., N.Y.C., 1979-81, cosmetics mgr., 1981-83, ea. mgr., 1984-87; v.p., ad dir. Ladies' Home Jour., N.Y.C., 1987-89, v.p., pub., 1989—. Home: 100 Park Ave New York NY 10017-5516 Office: Ladies' Home Jour 100 Park Ave New York NY 10017-5516*

GALTERIO, LOUIS, healthcare information executive; b. N.Y.C., Apr. 20, 1951; s. Elio and Angelina (Mattina) G.; m. Elizabeth Anne Coddington, May 2, 1971; children: Jason, Heather. Student, CCNY, 1969-70, Baruch Coll., 1970-75; BS in Mgmt. summa cum laude, Mercy Coll., 1978; MBA in Fin., L.I. U., 1980. Asst. mgr. Mfrs. Hanover Trust, N.Y.C., 1971-82; v.p. Bankers Trust Co., N.Y.C., 1982-87; dir., tech. mgr. Mortgage Backed Securities Clearing Corp., N.Y.C., 1987-88; mgr. capital markets and mktg. Digital Equipment Corp., N.Y.C., 1988-90, integration exec., 1990-91; chief info. officer healthcare Health and Hosps. Corp. NYC, 1991—; pres., mgmt. cons. Galterio Cons., N.Y.C., 1987—. Mem., sect. capt. Throgs Neck (N.Y.) Estates, 1988. Mem. IEEE (assoc.), Bankers Trust Alumni Orgn., Electronic mail and Messaging Assn., Am. Hosp. Assn., Coll. Healthcare Info. Mgmt. Execs., Healthcare Info. & Mgmt. Systems Soc., Alpha Chi. Republican. Home: 1417 Shore Dr Bronx NY 10465-1560

GALTERIO, ROBERT JOHN, race track manager; b. New Rochelle, N.Y., Feb. 16, 1957; s. Vincent Andrew and Josephine (Paino) G.; m. Margaret Rooney, May 29, 1983; children: Erin, Clare, Molly, Cara. BS, Boston Coll., 1979. Asst. gen. mgr. Yonkers (N.Y.) Racing Corp., 1983-85; gen. mgr. Westchester County Fair, Yonkers, 1981-86, Yonkers Racing Corp., 1985—; dir. U.S. Trotting Assn., Columbus, Ohio, 1987—; com. mem. Harness Tracks Am., Morristown, N.J., 1986—. Bd. dirs. Police Athletic League, Yonkers, 1984—. Mem. Yonkers C. of C. (1st vice chair). Office: Yonkers Racing Corp Yonkers Ave Yonkers NY 10704

GALTON, PETER MALCOLM, vertebrate biology educator; b. London, Eng., Mar. 14, 1942; came to U.S., 1967; s. Sidney Charles and Ena Victoria (Childs) G. BSc in Zoology, King's Coll., London, 1964; PhD in Zoology, U. London, 1967, DSc in Zoology, 1983. Curatorial assoc. Peabody Mus. of Natural History Yale U., New Haven, Conn., 1967-70, mem. rsch. staff geology, 1967-70; asst. prof. biology U. Bridgeport, 1970-74, assoc. prof. biology, 1974-78, prof. biology, 1978—. Contbr. over 90 articles to profl. jours. Grantee NSF, 1976-78, 78-81, 81-84, 85-90. Fellow Linnean Soc. London; mem. Soc. Vertebrate Paleontology, Sigma Xi (pres. chpt. 1983-84, 89-90), Phi Kappa Phi (pres. chpt. 1990-91). Office: U Bridgeport Coll Chiropractic Bridgeport CT 06601

GALTON, VALERIE ANNE, endocrinology educator; b. Louth, Eng., May 6, 1934; came to U.S., 1959; d. Wilfrid and Eileen (Watson) Hamilton; m. Michael Galton, Aug. 26, 1956 (dec. 1968); children—Ian Andrew, Kenneth Anthony; m. Reed Detar, Dec. 28, 1976; stepchildren—James, Elizabeth, Stephen, Susan. B.Sc. with honors, U. London, 1955, Ph.D., 1958. Research assoc. Nat. Inst. Med. Research, Mill Hill, London, 1955-58; research assoc. Med. Sch., Harvard U., Boston, 1959-61; instr., then asst. prof. Dartmouth Med. Sch., Hanover, N.H., 1961-66, assoc. prof., 1968-75, prof., 1975—; cons. NIH, Bethesda, Md., 1973—. Mem. editorial bd. Endocrinology, 1982-85, Am. Jour. Physiology, 1982-85; contbr. articles to profl. jours. NIH grantee, 1962—. Mem. Am. Thyroid Assn., Endocrine Soc. Home: Hardy Hill Lebanon NH 03766 Office: Dartmouth Med Sch Lebanon NH 03756

GALVIN, AARON ABRAHAM, electrical engineering consultant; b. Bklyn., Apr. 13, 1932; s. Max and Minnie Galvin; m. Frayda Goldman, Aug. 26, 1956; children: Jeffrey, Mark, Laurie. BS, MIT, 1955, MS, 1955. Group leader Lincoln Lab. MIT, Lexington, Mass., 1955-68; v.p. Aerospace Rsch., Inc., Allston, Mass., 1968-75, Am. Dist. Telephone Corp., N.Y.C., 1975-88; dir. New Eng. Rsch. Lab., Cambridge, Mass., 1988—; bd. dirs. Primary Rate, Inc., Salem, Mass. Patentee in field. Pilot vol. med. transport svc. Airlifeline, Boston, 1989—. Fellow IEEE; mem. Sigma Xi, Eta Kappa Nu. Home: 130 Mt Auburn St Apt 105 Cambridge MA 02138-5777 Office: New Eng Rsch Lab 124 Mt Auburn St PO Box 2823 Cambridge MA 02238

GALVIN, B(RIAN) CHRISTOPHER, secondary education educator; b. Newport, R.I., June 3, 1950; s. John Joseph and Lucille (Ryan) G.; m. Mary Jane Dorrian, June 19, 1976; children: Dorrian, Brendan, Timothy. BA, Fairfield U., 1972; MA, U. Conn., 1978. Cert. secondary English tchr., sch. libr. media specialist, Conn. Tchr. English, Waterford (Conn.) Pub. Schs., 1978—, media specialist, 1990—; cons. Project LEARN, East Lyme, Conn., 1989—; advisor Waterford Video Prodn. Club, 1989—. Producer video documentaries Harmony for the Homeless, 1989 (Conn. Gov.'s Youth Action award 1990), Forever Young, 1989, Classrooms to Careers, 1991, TV program Peace in El Salvador: Is There Hope?, 1990. Vol. Frontier Housing, Inc., Morehead, Ky., 1972-75; bd. dirs. Bert and Mary Meyer Found., Orlando, Fla., 1989—; mem. Guilford (Conn.) Peace Alliance, 1989—. Named to Athletic Hall of Fame, Fairfield U., 1991. Mem. Am. Fedn. Tchrs., Boston Film and Video Found., Coun. on Founds. Democrat. Roman

Catholic. Home: 650 Durham Rd Guilford CT 06437-2006 Office: Waterford High Sch 20 Rope Ferry Rd Waterford CT 06385-2894

GALVIN, LOUISE LEONARD, human resources executive; b. New Haven, Oct. 12, 1947; d. Thomas Francis and Christine (Finn) Leonard; m. James Justin Galvin, Aug. 3, 1985. BA in Sociology, St. Joseph Coll., 1969. Admissions counselor St. Joseph Coll., West Hartford, Conn., 1969-71; mgr. Sch. Vol. Program, Hartford, 1971-73; exec. dir. Vol. Action Ctr., Hartford, 1973-75; exec. dir. Govs. Coun. on Vol. Action, Hartford, 1975-80, mgr. employee rels., 1980-83; mgr. employment Conn. Nat. Bank, Hartford, 1983-85; dir. human resources The Hartford (Conn.) Courant, 1985—. Bd. mem. Urban League of Greater Hartford, 1986-91, chair pers. com., 1987-91; bd. mem. Inst. for Non-Profit Tng. and Devel., Hartford, 1990—. Mem. New Eng. Newspaper Assn. (chair human resources and labor rels. com. 1988—), Infoline North Cen. Conn. (adv. com. 1988—), Greater Hartford C. of C. (women execs. task force 1989—, chair women's exec. com. 1992—). Office: The Hartford Courant 285 Broad St Hartford CT 06115-2510

GALVIN, MARYANNE, psychologist, educator; b. Worcester, Mass., Mar. 6, 1954; d. Stephen F. and Bernadette M. (McGinn) Galvin; BS, Wheelock Coll., 1976; MEd U. Mass., Amherst, 1978, EdD, 1980. Psychologist, Wellesley (Mass.) Pub. Sch., 1980-81, U. Mass. Med. Sch., Worcester, 1980-81; asst. prof. U. N.H., Durham, 1981-82; pvt. practice psychology, Durham, 1981-83, Boston, 1984—; clin. dir. sch. consultation program Tufts New Eng. Med. Ctr., Boston, 1982—; rsch. psychologist Tufts Sch. Medicine, 1986—; asst. prof. Harvard Med. Sch., 1988—; psychologist McLean Hosp., Boston, 1988—; cons. McBer and Co., Boston, Dept. Youth Svcs. Mass., 1987—; dir. Counseling Ctr. Lasell Coll., 1991—; pvt. practice, Boston. Recipient of commendation UN, 1975; NSF grantee, 1985. Fellow Fedn. of Women's Clubs; mem. Internat. Council Psychologists, Am. Bd. Profl. Psychologists, Am. Psychol. Assn., Mass. Assn. for the Advancement of Individual Potential, Mass. Psychol. Assn., Physicians for Social Responsibility. Roman Catholic. Club: New Eng. Masters Competitive Swim. Contbr. articles on psychology to profl. jours. Office: 89 Massachusetts Ave # 163 Boston MA 02155-1668

GAMAR, REGINALD WILLIAM, broadcasting educator; b. Bklyn., Mar. 22, 1936; s. Reginald William and Esther Marie (Johnsen) G.; children: Nicole Suzanne, Danielle Esther, Rebecca Elisabeth. BS in Dramatic Arts, NYU, 1957; MS in Speech and Theatre (broadcasting), CUNY, 1967; postgrad., NYU, 1968-79. Adj. instr. NYU, 1961-69; prof. N.Y. Inst. Tech., 1964-67, Bklyn. Coll., CUNY, 1967—; freelance lighting cons.; announcer Sta. KCHT-AM Radio, 1957. Produced numerous TV shows including Wines of the World, As Caesar Sees It, 1962-63, Play It With Music, 1964, Window Shopping, 1957-62, Masquerade Party, 1959-62; stage mgr.: (plays) Shakespeare Repertory, 1953-57. Chmn. bd. trustees Gt. Kills Moravian Ch., S.I., N.Y., 1986—; cen. trustee United Brethren's Ch. S.I.; mem. synod Moravian Ch. Mem. Nat. Broadcasting Soc., Masons, Alpha Epsilon Rho (dir. East Region 1990—, Faculty Advisor of Yr. 1990, Regional Dir. of Yr. 1991). Republican. Home: 165A Colon Ave Staten Island NY 10308-1426 Office: Bklyn Coll CUNY TV/Radio Dept Brooklyn NY 11210

GAMBILL, MALCOLM W., metal products company executive; b. Crumpler, NC; married. B.S., Yale U. With Harsco Corp., 1955—; v.p. Heckett div., 1967-69, div. v.p. internat. ops., 1969-73, div. sr. v.p. ops., 1973-85, div. pres., 1975—, corp. exec. v.p., 1984-85, corp. pres., 1987-91,chief exec. officer, 1987—, also dir., chmn., 1991—. Served to 1st lt. USMC. Office: Harsco Corp PO Box 8888 Camp Hill PA 17001-8888

GAMBLE, (GEORGE) ALVAN, retired marketing consultant, former Canadian government official; b. Guelph, Ont., Can., Jan. 10, 1916; s. Hugh Miskelly and Margaret (Quarrell) G.; m. Jean Christeen Melrose, Aug. 3, 1940; children: Stephen John, Timothy Clifford (dec.), Lois Rebekah. Mgr., cons., co./union negotiations conciliator, Toronto, Ont., 1945-52; dir. merit employment project Am. Friends Service Com., Indps., 1952-55; exec. asst. to gen. dir., dir. info. Can. Mental Health Assn., Toronto, 1955-62; dir. health services Smith Kline & French (Can.), 1962-68; mktg. analyst Paul Maney Labs. (Can.) Ltd., Toronto, 1968-71; chief market research and immigration fgn. service info. adviser Govt. of Can. Employment and Immigration Commn., Ottawa, Ont., 1971-81; cons. mktg. and public relations, 1981-90, ret., 1990. Mem. Markham Twp. (Ont.) Planning Bd., 1959; provincial health minister's rep. Bd. of Health Regional Municipality of York, 1965-7k; bd. dirs. Union Villa Sr. Citizens Residence, Markham, 1965-71; vol. feature writer columnist Can. evang. chs. periodicals. Served with RCAF, 1940-45. Decorated Order of Can.; recipient Silver Jubilee medal, 1977, Assoc. Ch. Press award Atlantic Bapt., Canadian Ch. Press awards (2). Fellow Am. Public Health Assn.; mem. Profl. Mktg. Research Soc. (life). Baptist. Clubs: Albany (Toronto), Nat. Press (Ottawa). Home: 1097 Bronson Pl, Ottawa, ON Canada K1S 4H2

GAMBLE, (WILLIAM) PAUL, English educator, college historian, curator; b. Sharon, Pa., Jan. 16, 1911; s. William Dickey and Mabel (McMichael) G.; m. Anna Mary Shaffer, Aug. 2, 1938; children: Richard Hugh, Inalee, Robert Paul. BA, Westminster Coll., 1932, MEd, 1965, LHD (hon.)., 1991; MA, U. Pitts., 1968. Supr. recreation F.H. Buhl Club, Sharon, 1932-37; writer, announcer, pianist Sta. WKBN, Youngstown, Ohio, 1937-38; program dir. Stas. WPIC and WPIC-FM, Sharon, 1938-46; instr. radio, speech Westminster Coll., New Wilmington, Pa., 1946-49, exec. sec. alumni, 1949-60, exec. asst. to pres., 1960-65, from asst. to assoc. prof. English, 1965-77, coll. historian, curator coll. archives, 1977—. Author: Westminster's 1st Century, 1952, History of Westminster Coll. 1852-1977, 1977; playwright hist. dramas. Choir dir. United Presbyn. Ch., Mercer, Pa., 1948-49, Highland United Presbyn. Ch., New Castle, Pa., 1952-55; dir. music Covenant United Presbyn. Ch., Sharon, 1955-60. Mem. AAUP. Democrat. Home: 5865 Castle Ln Norcross GA 30093-3802 Office: Westminster Coll New Wilmington PA 16172

GAMBLE, THEODORE ROBERT, JR., investment banker; b. St. Louis, Sept. 18, 1953; s. Theodore Robert and Rispah Adele (Dowse) G.; m. Susan Lee Stupin, Mar. 3, 1984. AB, Princeton U., 1975; MArch, Harvard U., 1977, MBA, 1979. Assoc. Morgan Stanley & Co., Inc., N.Y.C., 1979-84, v.p., 1984-86, prin., 1986-87; pres. The Prescott Group Inc., N.Y.C., 1987—. Bd. dirs., exec. v.p. greater N.Y. Hist. Soc.; co-chmn. adv. com. real estate devel.; vis. com. Grad. Sch. Design, Harvard U., bus. com. Met. Mus. Art; mem. vestry St. Thomas Ch., N.Y.C.; active Boy Scouts Am.; mem. Bd. Trustees N.Y. Mem. Internat. Coun. Shopping Ctrs., Urban Land Inst. (comml. and retail devel. coun., internat. com.), Order St. John Jerusalem, Real Estate Bd. N.Y., Young Mortgage Bankers Assn., River Club, Racquet and Tennis Club, Univ. Club, Knickerbocker Club, Links Club, Brook Club, Doubles Club, Met. Opera Club, Princeton Club (bd. govs., exec. com., v.p. fin.), Harvard Club (N.Y.C. and Boston), City Club (Miami). Republican. Episcopalian. Home: 860 UN Pla New York NY 10017 Office: The Prescott Group Inc 666 5th Ave New York NY 10103-0001

GAMBUTO, ELIZABETH ANNE, mathematics educator; b. Providence, Mar. 22, 1966; d. Robert James and Marguerite Teresa (Petrone) G. BA in Math. & English, Providence Coll., 1988; M in math., U. R.I., 1991. Tutor Providence Coll., 1986-88; teaching asst. in math. U. R.I., Kingston, 1988-91, instr./tutor talent devel. program, summer, 1989-92, part-time instr., 1991, 92; part-time instr. Providence Coll., 1990, 92. Mem. Am. Math. Soc., Assn. for Women in Math., Pi Mu Epsilon. Home: 199 Garden City Dr Cranston RI 02920-5706

GAMMIE, ANTHONY PETRIE, pulp and paper manufacturing company executive; b. London, Dec. 17, 1934; married. With Bowater U.K., from 1955, mgr., 1970-75, chmn. bd., mng. dir., from 1975; with Bowater, Inc., Darien, Conn., 1978—, formerly chmn., pres., chief exec. officer, now chmn., CEO, also bd. dirs. Office: Bowater Inc 1 Parklands Dr Box 4012 Darien CT 06820*

GAMSON, ANITA GORDON, mental health counselor; b. Ely, Minn., Feb. 17, 1917; d. Louis and Sarah Ursula (Albert) Gordon; m. Arthur L. Gamson, Jan. 21, 1945; children: Neil, Leland. BS, U. Minn., 1938; cert., NIMH Pilot Project, Bethesda, Md., 1962. Cert. mental health counselor. Tchr. Aurora (Minn.) High Sch., 1939-42, Am. Sch., Buenos Aires, 1947-49, 57-59, Centro Escolar, Manila, 1950; mental health counselor Community Psychiat. Clinic, Bethesda, 1963-86, Affiliated Community Counselors, Inc., Rockville, Md., 1987—; pvt. practice Chevy Chase, Md., 1987—. V.p. Woman's Suburban Dem. Club, Montgomery County Md., 1991. Mem. AACD.

GAMWELL, LYNN, museum curator; b. Chgo., June 24, 1943; d. William and Winifred Wissing; m. Charles Michael Brown, 1989. BA, U. Ill., Chgo., 1967; MFA, Claremont Grad. Sch., 1970; MA, UCLA, 1972, PhD, 1977. Guest curator Newport Harbor Art Mus., Newport Beach, Calif., 1980-81; curator Laguna Art Mus., Laguna Beach, Calif., 1981-87; dir. SUNY Art Mus., Binghamton, 1987—. Author: Sigmund Freud and Art, 1989, The Real Thing, 1983, Inside Out/Self Beyond Likeness, 1981, Cubist Criticism: 1905-1925, 1980. Mem. Coll. Art Assn., Art Table. Home: 101 W 80th St New York NY 10024-7102 Office: SUNY Art Mus Binghamton NY 13902

GANCHROW, MANDELL I., surgeon; b. Bklyn., Feb. 6, 1937; s. Morris S. and Kate (Wallach) G.; m. Sheila Weinreb, Dec. 29, 1940; children: Marcia, Ari, Elliot. BA, Yeshiva U., 1958; MD, Chgo. Med. Sch., 1962. Intern Beth-el Hosp., Bklyn., 1962-63; surg. resident Montefiore Hosp., Bronx, N.Y., 1963-64, Brookdale Hosp., Bklyn., 1964-67; colon-rectal resident Ferguson Clinic, Grand Rapids, Mich., 1969-70; surgeon Good Samaritan Hosp., Suffern, N.Y., 1970—; cons. NYack (N.Y.) Hosp., 1970—; clin. assoc. prof. surgery N.Y. Med. Sch., 1984—. Contbr. articles to profl. jours. Pres. Hudson Valley Polit. Action Commn., Spring Valley, N.Y., 1982—, Adolph Schreiber Hebrew Acad., Monsey, N.Y., 1982-83, Community Synagogue of Monsey, 1979-80; bd. dirs. Am. Israel Pub. Affairs Commn., Washington, 1985-90; sr. v.p. Union Orthodox Jewish Congregations of Am., chmn. Inst. for Pub. Affairs. Fellow Am. Coll. Surgeons, Am. Soc. Colon and Rectal Surgeons, Am. Coll. Gastroenterology, N.Y. Colon and Rectal Surgeons, N.J. Colon and Rectal Surgeons, Soc. Am. Gastroenterologic Endoscopic Surgeons. Democrat. Home: 100 Route 59 Suffern NY 10901-4910 Office: Hudson Valley PAC 100A Schoolhouse Rd Spring Valley NY 10977

GANG, MARK JAY, psychologist, educator; b. Bklyn., Aug. 2, 1947; s. Arthur and Rita (Levy) G.; m. Marilyn Dimenstein, July 4, 1971; children: Rachel, Bonnie, Scott. BA in Psychology cum laude, U. Bridgeport, 1969, MS in Psychology, 1972; postgrad., U. Md., 1969-71; PhD in Psychology, U. Tenn., 1977. Lic. psychologist, Conn.; diplomate Am. Bd. Profl. Disability Cons. Substitute tchr. Spl. Programs Reach Each Dist., Wilton, Conn, 1971-72; asst. adminstr. in behavior rsch. Riverbend program Ea. State Psychiat. Hosp., Knoxville, Tenn., 1972-73; group practice psychotherapy, Fairfield, Conn., 1974-77; psychologist Stamford (Conn.) Pub. Schs., 1974-77; pvt. practice psychotherapy Mark Jay Gang, PhD & Assocs., Fairfield, 1976—; instr. Fairfield U., U. Bridgeport (Conn.), 1974—, 1975-79; cons. psychologist Goodwill Industries, Bridgeport, 1978-81; guest host Radio Town Meeting, Sta. WICC, 1989; producer, host U. Bridgeport Cable TV, 1984-91, Fairfield U. Cable TV, 1991; presenter, lectr. in field. Contbr. articles to profl. jours. Bd. dirs. Family Svcs.-Woodfield, Bridgeport, 1981-82, Goodwill Industries, Bridgeport, 1988—; mem. Fairfield Commn. on Aging, 1979-85; mem. interdisciplinary adv. bd. Children with Attention Deficit Disorders, 1990—; mem. adv. bd. Hispanic unit Greater Bridgeport Community Mental Health Ctr., 1982-83. Scholar U. Bridgeport, 1967-68, Dana scholar, 1968-69, NIMH, 1969-71; fellow U. Tenn., 1973-74. Mem. APA, NASP, Anxiety Disorders Assn. Am., Conn. Psychol. Assn., Conn. Assn. Children with Learning Disabilities, Phi Kappa Phi. Office: Stillson Pla Ste 308 2228 Black Rock Tpke Fairfield CT 06430-3219

GANG, STEPHEN R., motion picture executive, consultant; b. Newark, Nov. 23, 1951; s. I. Lloyd and Ruth (Jacoby) G.; m. Robin Tartaglia, Oct. 13, 1973 (div. Dec. 1984); children: Catherine Ruth, Melissa Lauren; m. Gail Graves, June 20, 1986; children: Christopher Ware, Jeffrey Stevens. AB, Amherst Coll., 1972; JD, Harvard U., 1976, MBA, 1977. Bar: Mass. 1977. Asst. dean of admission Amherst (Mass.) Coll., 1972-73; cons. Boston Consulting Group, 1977-80, mgr., 1980-84; v.p. Boston Consulting Group, L.A., 1984-86; pres., chief exec. officer Original Cinema, Inc., N.Y.C., 1986—; v.p. Telesis-Towers Perrin, N.Y.C., 1989—. Bd. dirs. African Food & Peace Found., Boston, 1985—. Mem. Harvard Club, Shelter Island Yacht Club. Home: 117 Valley St Beverly MA 01915-2223 Office: Original Cinema Inc 419 Park Ave S New York NY 10016-8410

GANGLOFF, LINDA LEE, educator, underwater photographer, writer; b. Tarentum, Pa., Aug. 8, 1942; d. Albert Carl and Mary Donna (Stennett) G. BS, Bucknell U., 1964; MA, Montclair State Coll., 1975. Cert. secondary biol. sci. and English tchr., N.J. High sch. tchr. biology Morris Sch. Dist., Morristown, N.J., 1964—, staff asst. sci. dept., 1974-78; biology text critic reader Silver Burdett Pub. Co., Morristown, 1979; presenter N.J. Sci. Conv., 1986. Author, photographer (slide-cassette program) Underwater Photography, 1988-89. Vol. N.Y. Aquarium, Bklyn., 1985-87. Recipient J. Burton Wiley Scholar award Morris Sch. Dist., 1988; Geraldine R. Dodge Found. grantee, 1988. Mem. NEA, Nat. Assn. Biology Tchrs., Nat. Marine Educators Assn., Am. Littoral Soc., Underwater Soc. Am., Internat. Oceanographic Found., N.J. Assn. Biology Tchrs., AAUW, Alpha Phi. Lutheran. Home: 17 Clairview Rd Denville NJ 07834 Office: Morristown High Sch 50 Early St Morristown NJ 07960-3898

GANGONE, LYNN M., vice president, dean of students; b. Bklyn., Sept. 10, 1957; d. Anthony Joseph and Rose Marie (Palmieri) G. BA, Coll. of New Rochelle, NY, 1979; MS, SUNY Albany, 1980, cert. advanced study, 1981; postgrad., Columbia U., NYC, 1991—. Residence dir. SUNY Albany, NY, 1979-81; counselor Coll. of St. Rose, Albany, 1979-80; placement officer Hudson Valley Community Coll., Troy, NY, 1980-81; dir. Hudson Valley Community Coll., 1981-82; staff devel. coord. NY State Edn. Dept., Albany, 1982-86; dir. Rutgers U., New Brunswick, NJ, 1986-87; v.p./dean of students Centenary Coll. N.J., Hackettstown, 1987—; conf. chairperson Nat. Assn. Student Pers. Adminstrs., Region 2, 1992; vice chairperson/cons. N.J. Coll. and Univ. Coalition for Women's Edn., 1990—. Author, project dir. Mythbusters, 1987; primary researcher Staying Poor: How the JTPA Affects Women, 1987; contbr. to articles in profl. jours. Recipient Achievement award N.Y. State Sex Equity Ctr., 1986, Cardinals award Coll. New Rochelle, 1979, NASEDIO award, 1988. Mem. Nat. Assn. of Student Pers. Adminstrs., N.J. Coll. and Univ. Coalition for Women's Edn., Independent Colleges Dean's Assn., Nat. Assn. Women in Edn. Home: 27 S 9th Ave Manville NJ 08835-1719 Office: Centenary College 400 Jefferson St Hackettstown NJ 07840-2184

GANGULY, ASHIT KUMAR, organic chemist; b. New Delhi, Aug. 9, 1934; came to U.S., 1967; s. Apurba Kumar and Protiva (Chatterji) G.; m. Jean Currie Gowans, Sept. 10, 1966; 1 child, Nomita. PhD, U. Delhi (India), 1959, Imperial Coll., London, 1962. Sr. scientist Schering-Plough Corp., Bloomfield, N.J., rsch. fellow, dir., presdl. fellow, v.p.; permanent mem. medicinal chemistry study sect. NIH, Bethesda, Md., 1986—; Khaira Disting. profl. Indian Assn. Cultivation Scis., Calcutta, 1975; Charles Sabat lectr. Rutgers U., N.J., 1987. Contbr. articles to profl. jours. Recipient Seshadri Meml. award Delhi U., 1982, Outstanding Scientist award Assn. Scientists Indian Origins in Am., 1991. Fellow Royal Soc. Chemistry; mem. ACS, N.Y. Acad. Scis. Office: Schering Plough Rsch Inst 60 Orange St Bloomfield NJ 07003-4795

GANIM, JOSEPH P., mayor of Bridgeport; b. Bridgeport, Conn., Oct. 21, 1959; s. George W. and Josephine (Tarick DeBarnardi) G. BA, U. Conn., 1981; JD, U. Bridgeport, 1983. Bar: Conn. 1983. Mem. Ganim, Ganim, Ganim & Ganim, P.C., Bridgeport, 1983—; mayor City of Bridgeport, 1991—; mem. Conn. and Fed. Spl. Pub. Defender Svcs. Mem. Conn. Bar Assn., Bridgeport Bar Assn., Assn. Trial Lawyers Am., Nat. Assn. Criminal Def. Lawyers, Soc. Internat. Law, Toastmasters, Elks. Home: 436 Gilman St Bridgeport CT 06605 Office: Office of Mayor 45 Lyon Ter # B Bridgeport CT 06604-4023

GANLEY, SUSAN ANASTASIA, insurance company executive; b. Northampton, Mass., Feb. 10, 1957; d. Stephen Joseph Sr. and Sophia (Wnukoski) Murawski; m. John Patrick Ganley, June 21, 1980. B, Hood Coll., 1979. Claims supr. Mutual of Omaha, Rockville, Md., 1979-86; div. coord. March of Dimes, Frederick, Md., 1986-87; dir. claims Group Ins. Svcs., Inc., Frederick, 1987—. Sunday sch. tchr. St. Johns Cath. Ch., Frederick, 1978-90; sec. Sheriff's Citizen Adv. Commn., 1991—. Mem. Hodd Coll. Alumnae Assn. (reunion chairperson 1990—, 2d v.p. 1991), Fredericktowne Sertoma (dri. 1991-93). Home: 227 Sandstone Dr Walkersville MD 21793-9147 Office: Group Ins Svcs Inc 636 Solarex Ct Frederick MD 21701-8624

GANN, RICHARD GEORGE, research manager; b. Hartford, Conn., Sept. 20, 1944; s. Samuel and Freda (Solomon) G.; children: Eric, Michael. BS in Chemistry, Trinity Coll., Hartford, Conn., 1965; PhD in Phys. Chemistry, MIT, 1970. Postdoctoral rsch. assoc. Space Rsch. Coord. Ctr., U. Pitts., 1970-72; rsch. chemist Naval Rsch. Lab., Washington, 1972-76; head exploratory fire rsch. Nat. Inst. Standards and Tech., Gaithersburg, Md., 1976-80, chief fire measurement and rsch. div., 1981—; program analyst Nat. Inst. Standards and Tech., 1980; chmn. Halon Alternatives Rsch. Corp. Tech. Com., Washington, 1989-90, Tech. Adv. Group, Less Fire-Prone Cigarettes, Washington, 1984-87, 91-92; coord. U.S.-Japan Panel on Fire Rsch., 1981—. Author, editor: Halogenated Fire Suppressants, 1975; contbr. tech. articles to profl. jours. Sr. Exec. fellow, J. F. Kennedy Sch. Govt., Harvard U., 1984. Mem. Am. Chem. Soc., Combustion Inst. (program chair 1989-90, ea. sect. treas. 1988-91), ASTM. Home: 9409 Eagleton Ln Gaithersburg MD 20879-1242 Office: Building and Fire Rsch Lab Nat Inst Standards & Tech Gaithersburg MD 20899

GANNON, HAROLD JOSEPH, insurance executive; b. County Clare, Ireland, Apr. 1, 1957; came to U.S., 1960; s. harold F. and Edna May (Noonan) G.; m. Ana Teresa Savio, Jan. 7, 1984; children: Heather Anne, Joseph Brendan, Robert Michael. AS, Nassau Community Coll., 1977; BS, U. San Francisco, 1979; MBA, Hofstra U., 1981; JD, Touro Coll. Sch. Law, 1986. Bar: N.J. Strategic planning cons. Met. Life Ins. Co., N.Y.C., 1979-84; tax mgr. Am. Internat. Group Inc., N.Y.C., 1984-88; v.p., asst. contr. Mut of Am. Life Ins. Co., N.Y.C., 1988—. Mem. ABA, N.J. Bar Assn. Republican. Roman Catholic. Office: Mut Am Life Ins Co 666 Fifth Ave 4th Fl New York NY 10103

GANS, EUGENE HOWARD, cosmetic and pharmaceutical company executive; b. N.Y.C., Dec. 17, 1929; m. 1953; 2 children. BS, Columbia U., 1951, MS, 1953; PhD, U. Wis., 1956. Lab. asst. Columbia U., 1951-53; sr. scientist group leader Hoffman-LaRouche, Inc., N.J., 1956-60; head new product devel. sect. Vick Div. Research and Devel. Labs. Richardson-Merrell, N.Y., 1960-64, asst. dir. devel., 1964-67, dir., 1967-71; assoc. dir. Alza Inst. Pharm. Chemistry, 1971-72; dir. research Vicks Personal Care div. Richardson-Vicks div. Proctor-Gamble, Shelton, Conn., 1972-76, v.p., dir. research and devel., 1976-87; pres. Hastings Assocs., Westport, Conn., 1987—, Lincoln Techs., Westport, Conn., 1989—; chmn. proprietary drug task group FDA, 1976-81; chmn. sci. adv. com. Cosmetic, Toiletry and Fragrance Assn., Washington, 1984—. Mem. Am. Pharm. Assn., Am. Chem. Soc., N.Y. Acad. Sci., Soc. Investigative Dermatology, Sigma Xi. Home: 5 Fairview Dr Westport CT 06880-1702 Office: Hastings Assocs 5 Fairview Dr Westport CT 06880-1702

GANS, SAMUEL MYER, temporary employment service executive; b. Phila., June 10, 1925; s. Arthur and Goldie (Goldhirsh) G.; grad. in acctg. Peirce Jr. Coll., 1946-49; m. Ada S. Zuckerman, Aug. 1, 1948; children: Gary M., Jeffrey R. Public acct., 1949-55; sales exec., 1955-58; franchise owner, pres., chief exec. officer Manpower, Inc. Delaware Valley, Pennsauken, N.J., 1958-86; owner Micrographic Services Inc., Pennsauken, 1986-72; with Allstate Services Inc., County Maintenance Corp., Affiliated Personnel Service; owner Antique & Classic Cars Storage Garage Inc., Voorhees, N.J. ; franchise cons.; instr. motivation courses. v.p., exec. bd. United Fund Camden County; v.p., bd. dirs. So. N.J. Devel. Council, ARC Camden County, Nat. Conf. of Christian and Jews; bd. mgrs. Am. Cancer Soc. Camden County; active Boy Scouts Am., Employer Legis. Com., Camden County Bicentennial Com., Score and Ace programs, Camden, YMCA, Allied Jewish Appeal, World Affairs Council; mem. N.J. Gov.'s Mgmt. Commn., 1971; trustee Camden County Heart Assn., Camden County Mental Health Assn.; exec. bd., founder Big Bros. Assn. Camden County; public relations com. U.S. Savs. Bonds, Camden and Trenton. Served with USNR, 1943-46. Mem. Nat. Assn. Temp. Services (chpt. relations com. 1973), Nat. Soc. Public Accts., Camden County C. of C., S. Jersey Public Relations Assn. (pres. 1967), S. Jersey Mfg. Assn. (exec. bd., treas.), S. Jersey Personnel Assn. (treas.), Cherry Hill C. of C. (bd. dirs., v.p.), Better Bus. Bur. Camden County, Adminstrv. Mgmt. Soc., N.J. Assn. Temp. Services (pres. 1970-72, bd. dirs.), South Jersey Purchasing Agts. Assn., Assn. of Manpower Franchise Owners, Jewish War Veterans; Jewish (exec. bd. dirs. congregation). Club: Dolphin Beach Condo. Lodges: Masons, Lions (pres. Camden 1972-73, Lion of Year 1977), Shriners, B'Nai B'Rith, Home: 4 N Derby Ave Ventnor City NJ 08406-2356 Office: 3801 Marlton Pike Camden NJ 08105-3312

GANT, DUPLAIN RHODES, retired social service administrator, government official; b. Washington, June 24, 1924; s. Wallace Porter and Carrie (Rhodes) G.; A.B., Dillard U., 1948; M.S.W., Howard U., 1951; D.S.W., Cath. U., 1958; m. Lois Alva Williams, July 24, 1949; children: Adrienne Cecelia, Duplain Rhodes. Supervisory social worker Public Assistance Div., D.C. Dept. Public Welfare, Washington, 1958-62, chief research sect. planning and research div., 1964-67, chief Bur. Spl. Ops., 1979-80, ret. 1980; research analyst Children's Bur., HEW, 1962-64; v.p. Computer Tech. Services, 1983-86; mng. ptnr. Creative Investments, 1987—; pres. Creative Maintenance Services, Inc., 1987—. Spl. cons. Pres.'s Commn. on Crime in D.C. Chmn. Foundry-Met. Community Council, Inc., 1968-69; pres. Bread for the City, 1981-82; dir. celestial choir Met. A.M.E. Ch., 1970—, chmn. student loan com., 1969—. trustee United Planning Orgn., 1969-79; adv. bd. dirs. Allen Chapel Outreach Center, 1984—. Served with U.S. Army, 1943-46. Mem. Nat. Assn. Social Workers, D.C. Public Health Assn., Acad. Cert. Social Workers, Am. Mgmt. Assn., Am. Public Welfare Assn., Am. Public Health Assn. Home: 6308 16th St NW Washington DC 20011-8010

GANZ, AURA, engineering educator; b. Bucarest, Romania, Aug. 20, 1957; came to U.S., 1987; d. Rubin and Marieta (Leibovici) Lazar; m. Zvi Ganz; children: Adi, Michal. BSc, Technion-Israel Inst. Tech., 1980, MSc, 1983, PhD, 1987. Software engr. Armament Devel. Authority, Haifa, Israel, 1980-81; teaching and rsch. asst. Technion-Israel Inst. Tech., Haifa, 1981-86; asst. prof. computer sci. Technion-Israel Inst. Tech., 1986-87; asst. prof. elec. and computer engring. U. Mass., Amherst, 1987—; cons., Motorola Semiconductor, Israel,1982-83. Contbr. articles, papers to tech. and profl. publs. Mem. IEEE (sr.). Office: U Mass Dept Elec/Computing Engring Amherst MA 01003

GANZ, CARY H., dentist; b. Bklyn., Apr. 17, 1946; s. Sol and Shari (Fischer) G.; m. Susan Rita Schneider, June 9, 1968; children: Jason, Stephanie, Jacqueline. BS, Bklyn. Coll., 1966; DDS, NYU, 1970. Cert. prosthodontics, N.Y. Div. chief of implantology and advanced prosthodontics Northshore Univ./Cornell Med. Ctr., Manhasset, N.Y., 1978-91; pvt. practice Rockville Center, N.Y., 1991—. Contbr. articles to profl. pubs. Pres. Census Area 9 Civic Assn., Dix Hills, N.Y., 1982. Fellow Am. Coll. of Dentists; mem. Am. Prosthodontic Soc., Fedn. of Prosthodontic Orgns., Acad. of Osseointegration, Am. Acad. of Implant Prosthodontics, Am. Acad. of Cosmetic Dentistry, Am. Coll. of Oral Implatology. Office: Cary Ganz DDS PC 119 N Park Ave Rockville Centre NY 11570-4113

GANZ, DAVID L., lawyer; b. N.Y.C., July 28, 1951; s. Daniel M. and Beverlee (Kaufman) G.; m. Barbara Bondanza, Nov. 3, 1974 (div. 1978); m. Sharon Ruth Lamnin, Oct. 30, 1981; children: Scott Harry, Elyse Toby, Pamela Rebecca. B.S. in Fgn. Service, Georgetown U., 1973; J.D., St. John's U., 1976. Bar: N.Y. 1977, D.C. 1980, N.J. 1985. Assoc. firm Regan, Dorsey & DeRiso, Flushing, N.Y., 1977-79; ptnr. firm Durst & Ganz, P.C., N.Y.C., 1979-80; mng. ptnr. firm Ganz, Hollinger & Towe, N.Y.C., 1981—; cons. FAO, Money Office, Rome, 1975—; cons. to sub-com. on historic preservation and coinage House Banking Com., 94th and 95th Congresses; bd. dirs. Industry Council Tangible Assets, Washington, 1983—. Author: A Critical Guide to the Anthologies of African Literature, 1973, A Legal and Legislative History of 31 USC Sec 324d-324i, 1976, The World of Coins and Coin Collecting, 1980, 2d edit., 1985; corr., Numis. News Weekly, 1969-73, asst. editor, 1973-74, spl. corr., 1974-75; contbg. editor, columnist COINage Mag., 1974—; columnist Coin World, 1974—, COINS Mag., 1973-83; contbr. articles to legal publs. Mem. U.S. Assay Commn., 1974; bd. dirs.

Georgetown Library Assocs., Washington, 1982—; mem. N.Y. County Draft Bd., 1984, Bergen County, N.J., 1985—; sec., mem. Zoning and Adjustment Bd., Fair Lawn, N.J., 1988—; elected Dem. County Com. Bergen County, 1988, 89-92. Fellow Am. Numis. Soc.; mem. Am. Numis. Assn. (legis. counsel 1978-81, 83—, elected bd. govs. 1985—, v.p. 1991—), Assn. of Bar of City of N.Y. (com. on state legis. 1987-90), N.Y. State Bar Assn. (mem. civil practice com., chmn. subcom. 1978-84), Profl. Numismatists Guild Inc. (affiliated mem. 1989, gen. counsel 1981—), Am. Soc. Internat. Law, Nat. Assn. Coin and Precious Metals Dealers (assoc. mem., gen. counsel 1981-85), Flushing Lawyers Club (pres. 1982-83). Democrat. Jewish. Avocation: numismatic. Office: Ganz Hollinger & Towe 1394 3rd Ave New York NY 10021-0404

GARA, MICHAEL ANTHONY, psychologist, researcher; b. Albany, N.Y., Aug. 4, 1953; s. Philip Joseph and Mildred Mary (Murphy) G.; m. Ellen Rachel Ball, Mar. 28, 1982; 1 child, Lauren Rose. BA summa cum laude, SUNY, Albany, 1975; MS, Rutgers U., 1978, PhD in Psychology, 1980. Rsch. psychologist Community Mental Health, Piscataway, N.J., 1980-86; rsch. dir. Community Mental Health, Piscataway, 1986—; faculty mem. Rutgers U., New Brunswick, N.J., 1986—, rsch. cons., 1981-89; reviewer jours. in field, 1983—. Contbr. articles to profl. jours. Grantee NIMH, 1989—. Mem. APA, Soc. for Rsch. Psychopathology, Highland Park Conservative Temple, Phi Beta Kappa. Office: Community Mental Health 671 Hoes Ln Piscataway NJ 08854-5633

GARAFALO, ANTHONY JOSEPH, podiatric surgeon; b. Staten Island, N.Y., Dec. 18, 1954; s. Joseph and Ann (Capriotti) G.; m. Sharon A. Lennon, Mar. 27, 1982; 1 child, Nicholas Joseph. BS in Biology, Wagner Coll., 1977; cert. physician asst., Touro Coll., 1980; D Podiatric Medicine, N.Y. Coll. Podiatric Medicine, 1987. Surg. physician asst. Kingsbrook Jewish Med. Ctr., Bklyn., 1980-83; asst. prof. phys. diagnosis physician asst. program Touro Coll., N.Y.C., 1980-89; pvt. practice podiatric surgery Staten Island, 1988—; asst. dir. diabetic foot clinics Bayley Seton Hosp., Staten Island, 1991—. Mem. N.Y. State Podiatric Med. Assn. (sci. chmn. 1989—, mem. exec. com.), Italian Club of Staten Island. Home: 81 Stone Ln Staten Island NY 10314-5944 Office: Todt Hill Med Ctr 71 Todt Hill Rd Staten Island NY 10314-4535

GARASKY, STEVEN BRIAN, economist; b. Youngstown, Ohio, Mar. 28, 1958. BA, Wittenberg U., 1980; MA, Ohio State U., 1984, PhD, 1987. Economist U.S. Dept. HHS, Washington, 1987—. Mem. Am. Econs. Assn. Home: 1729 Douglas Ave Ames IA 50010-5317

GARBAN, DOUGLAS S., investment representative; b. Bellefonte, Pa., June 13, 1964; s. Steven A. and Penny (Atkinson) G. BA, Pa. State U., 1986. Fin. cons. Merrill Lynch, Washington, 1987-90; investment rep. Alek Brown and Sons, Washington, 1990—. Office: Alex Brown and Sons 1440 New York Ave NW Ste 500 Washington DC 20805

GARBER, CHARLES ALLEN, research company executive, consultant; b. Rock Island, Ill., May 23, 1941; s. Morris and Evelyn Garber; m. Bette Garber, June 23, 1964 (div. June 1978); m. Violet Markus, Dec. 29, 1980. BS, U. Ill., 1963; MS, Case Inst. Tech., 1965, PhD, 1967. Engr.-in-tng., Del. Rsch. physicist E.I. Du Pont de Nemours & Co., Inc., Wilmington, Del., 1967-70; pres., chief exec. officer Structure Probe, Inc., West Chester, Pa., 1970—; bd. dirs. Ind. Labs. Assurance Co., Ltd., Hamilton, Bermuda. Del. White House Conf. on Small Bus., Washington, 1980, 86. Fellow Ford Found., 1963-67. Mem. Am. Chem. Soc., Electron Microscope Soc. Am., Microbeam Analysis Soc., Am. Soc. for Metals, Assn. Cons. Chemists and Chem. Engrs., Soc. Cosmetic Chemists. Home: 60 Harrison Rd E West Chester PA 19380-6749 Office: Structure Probe Inc PO Box 656 West Chester PA 19381-0656

GARBER, JANET, university official; b. N.Y.C.. BA in English and French, CUNY, 1968; MA in English, U. Rochester, 1972. Pers. specialist Schieffelin & Co., N.Y.C., 1981-85; office and pers. mgr. DeFrancisci Machine Corp., N.Y.C., 1985-87; dir. human resources Am. Mortgage Banking Ltd., N.Y.C., 1987-88; mgr. employment and employee rels. Cornell U. Med. Coll., N.Y.C., 1988—. Contbr. articles to various pubs. Vol. alumni network U. Rochester, 1988. N.Y. State Regents scholar, 1964-68, U. Rochester scholar, 1971-73. Mem. Soc. for Human Resource Mgmt. Office: Cornell U Med Coll 445 E 69th St New York NY 10021-5665

GARBIS, MARVIN JOSEPH, federal judge; b. Balt., June 14, 1936; s. Samuel and Adele E. (Warshaw) G.; m. Phyllis Lorraine Zaroff, Aug. 27, 1961; children: Kendall Rose, Jason Anders, Kerri Jill. B.E.S., Johns Hopkins U., 1958; J.D., Harvard U., 1961; LL.M., Georgetown U., 1962. Bar: D.C. 1961, Md. 1962. Trial atty. Tax Div., Dept. Justice, Washington, 1962-67; sole practice Balt., 1967-71; ptnr. Garbis, Marvel & Junghans, Balt., 1971-86, Melnicove, Kaufman, Weiner, Smouse & Garbis, Balt., 1986-88, Johnson & Gibbs, Washington, 1988-89; judge U.S. Dist. Ct. Md., 1989—; lectr. U. Md. Law Sch., 1970-85, NYU Fed. Tax Inst., 1970, 74, 79, 87-88; adj. prof. Georgetown U. Law Sch., 1978-80, U. Balt. Law Sch., 1982—; adviser on tax procedure study, judiciary com. U.S. Senate, 1969-70; mem. adv. commr. to commr. internal revenue, 1982; mem. adv. council U.S. Claims Ct., 1982—; mem. Md. Inst. for Continuing Profl. Edn. for Lawyers, 1978-80, pres., 1980—. Author: (with Frome) Procedures in Federal Tax Controversy, 1968, (with Schwait) Tax Refund Litigation, 1971, Tax Court Practice, 1974, (with Struntz) Cases and Materials on Federal Tax Procedure, Civil and Criminal, 1981, (with Junghans and Struntz) Federal Tax Litigation, 1985, (with Struntz and Rubin) Cases and Materials on Tax Procedure and Tax Fraud, 2d edit., 1987, (with Rubin and Morgan) Cases and Material on Tax Procedure and Tax Fraud, 3d edit., 1991; contbr. articles to profl. jours. E. Barrett Prettyman fellow Georgetown Law Sch., 1961-62. Mem. Fed. Bar Assn. (pres. Balt. chpt. 1972-73, nat. vice chmn. tax com. 1974-76), Md. Bar Assn. (chmn. tax sect. 1970-71, chmn. continuing legal edn. 1973-80), ABA (chmn. ct. procedure com., tax sect. 1975—), Balt. Bar Assn. (bd. govs. 1974-79), Fed. Cir. Bar Assn. (bd. dirs. 1985—). Am. Law Inst., Md. Inst. Continuing Profl. Education Lawyers (pres. 1981-82). Office: US Dist Ct 101 W Lombard St Baltimore MD 21201

GARCIA, ALBERT DANIEL, beauty consultant; b. N.Y.C., Nov. 19, 1943; s. Albert Jamison and Celia (Salazar) G. Owner Garcia Cosmetics, N.Y.C., Garcia Make Up for Success, N.Y.C.; co-owner Charles Howard Antiques, N.Y.C.; cons. in field. Home and Office: 240 E 27th St New York NY 10016 also: 110 Margate Cir Southampton NY 11968

GARCIA, GEORGE EDWARD, ophthalmologist; b. Mendocino, Calif., May 2, 1930; s. Antonio J. and Zelmeda M. Garcia; m. Lois Ann O;Connor, Jan. 2, 1955; children: Suzanne Zell, Paul Anthony. BS, U. Calif., Berkeley, 1952, M of Ophthalmology, 1953; MD, Boston U., 1961. Diplomate Am. Bd. Ophthalmology. Intern Mass. Meml. Hosp., Boston, 1961-62; fellow Howe Lab. of Ophthalmology Mass. Eye & Ear Infirmary, Boston, 1962-63, resident, 1963-66; asst. prof. Ophthalmology Boston U. Sch. Medicine, Boston, 1966-72, asst. clin. prof. Ophthalmology, 1972-79; asst. clin. prof. Ophthalmology Harvard Med. Sch., 1979—; assoc. chief Ophthalmology Mass. Eye & Ear Infirmary, Boston, 1984—, assoc. chief vis. staff, 1990—. Contbr. articles to profl. jours. Mem. AMA, New Eng. Ophthalmological Soc., Am. Assn. Ophthalmology (pres.-elect 1980, pres. 1981, mem. pub. info. com. 1980-83), Am. Acad. Opthalmology (bd. dirs. 1981-91, pres. 1990). Office: 636 Beacon St Boston MA 02193

GARCIA, JOSEPH, general surgeon, educator; b. Ponterrada, Leon, Spain, July 27, 1947; came to U.S., 1953; s. Damaso and Guadalupe (Diez) G.; m. Loretta Ann Harrop, Sept. 24, 1983; children: Jennifer, Lisa, Matthew Steven. MD, N.Y. Med. Coll., 1977. Diplomate Am. Bd. Surgery. Clin. instr. surgery NYU Sch. Medicine, N.Y.C., 1981-82; attending surgeon St. Joseph Hosp., Paterson, N.J., 1982—; also dir. surg. edn., 1982-90, also chief trauma, 1990; asst. prof. surgery St. George's U. Sch. Medicine, Grenada, Wis., 1987-89, prof., chmn. dept. surgery, 1989—; pres. bd. dirs. No. N.J. Med. Provider Orgn., Parsippany. Staff sgt. USAF, 1967-71. Mem. Prosaic County Med. Soc., N.J. Med. Soc. Roman Catholic. Home: 210 Hilltop Rd Kinnelon NJ 07450 Office: Joseph L Garcia MD PA 502 Hamburg Tpke Wayne NJ 07470

GARCIA, JOSEPH CHARLES, communications consultant, retired educator; b. Buffalo, Oct. 24, 1931; s. Joseph and Carmen (Renaibles) G.; m. Ruth Esther Toellner, Oct. 11, 1967; children: Joseph III, Karen S. Garcia Frain. BS magna cum laude, SUNY, Buffalo, 1958; MA in English, cert. adminstrn. edn., Canisius Coll., 1962. Tchr. English, Kenmore (N.Y.) Jr. High Sch., 1958-59, North Tonawanda (N.Y.) Sr. High Sch., 1961-62; tchr. English, chmn. dept. Clarence (N.Y.) Sr. High Sch., 1959-61; reporter Buffalo Evening News, 1962-63; tchr. English, Spanish and mass media communications East Aurora (N.Y.) High Sch., 1963-87; internat. liaison and communication cons. East Aurora, 1987—; chief exec. officer, pres. ILC; past columnist East Aurora Advertiser; spl. dep. sheriff Erie County; writer tech. manuals, photographer Summa Graphics, Buffalo, 1978, 1982-83; spl. fgn. corr., photographer Buffalo Evening News, Spain, 1978-79; cons., interpreter New Departure Hyatt div. GM, Cadiz, Spain, 1989-91. Author: Atoms to Ashes, 1965. Cert. N.Y. State Ombudsman for the Aging/ARC, 1991-92. With USAF, 1951-54, Korea. Mem. East Aurora Faculty Assn. (exec. bd. 1984-85, editor The Edge 1984-87), Lions (chmn. edn. scholarship com. 1965-86, 2d v.p. 1985-86, 1st v.p. 1986-87, pres. 1987-89). Home and Office: PO Box 241 East Aurora NY 14052-0241

GARCIA, JOY PARONDA, counselor coordinator; b. Manila, The Philippines, Mar. 3, 1965; came to U.S., 1986; d. Armando Lazaro Garcia and Miriam (Paronda) Rorabaugh. BS in Math., Philippine Normal Coll., Manila, 1985; MEd in Math., Millersville U., 1989, MEd in Guidance and Counseling, 1991. Instr. Bethel High Sch., Manila, 1985-86; grad. admissions asst. Millersville (Pa.) U., 1987-91, instr., tutorial coord. Upward Bound Program, 1991—, counselor coord., 1991—. Recipient Eugene K. Robb scholarship, 1991, James C. Atty scholarship, 1991, Nat. Sci. and Tech. Assn. scholarship, 1981-85. Mem. AACD, ASCD, Assn. for Multicultural Counseling and Devel., Am. Coll. Pers. Assn., Am. Sch. Counselor Assn., Assn. Religious and Value Issues in Counseling, Lancaster County Counselors Assn., Assn. Pa. State Coll. and Univs. Faculties. Home: 19 Circle Rd Millersville PA 17551-1511

GARCIA, OSCAR NICOLAS, computer science educator; b. Havana, Cuba, Sept. 10, 1936; s. Oscar Vicente and Leonor (Hernandez) G.; m. Diane Ford Journigan, Sept. 9, 1962; children—Flora, Virginia. B.S.E.E., N.C. State U., 1961, M.S.E.E., 1964; Ph.D. in Elec. Engring., U. Md., 1969. Engr. IBM Corp., Endicott, N.Y., 1962-63; asst. prof. Old Dominion U., 1963-66, assoc. prof., 1969-70; research asst., instr. U. Md., 1966-69; assoc. prof. U. South Fla., Tampa, 1970-75; prof. computer sci., chmn. dept. U. South Fla., 1975-85; prof. dept. elec. engring. and computer sci. George Washington U., Washington, 1985—; cons. and lectr. in field. Author: (with Y.T. Chien) Knowledge-Based Systems: Fundamentals and Tools, 1991. Recipient Richard E. Merwin Disting. Service award IEEE Computer Soc., 1988, Meritorious Svc. award, 1991. Fellow IEEE (pres. Computer Soc. 1981-83, bd. dirs. 1984-85, mem. U.S. activities bd. 1984, Profl. Leadership award 1991), AAAS; mem. Assn. Computing Machinery, Am. Soc. Engring. Edn., Am. Assn. Artificial Intelligence, Sigma Xi, Eta Kappa Nu, Phi Kappa Phi, Tau Beta Pi. Home: 6308 Redwing Rd Bethesda MD 20817-5918 Office: George Washington U Dept Elec Engring/Computer Sci 801 22nd St NW Washington DC 20052-0001

GARCIA, ROBERTO SIOSON, anesthesiologist, surgeon; b. Manila, Dec. 9, 1933; came to U.S., 1956; s. Vicente S. and Librada (Sioson) G.; m. Evelyn Colonna, Apr. 6, 1958; children: Robert C., Rebecca E., Melissa J. MD, U. Philippines, 1956. Diplomate Am. Bd. Anesthesiologists. Intern Ch. Home & Hosp., Balt., 1956-57, surg. resident, 1957-58; surg. resident South Balt. Gen. Hosp., 1958-61; anesthesia resident Johns Hopkins Hosp., Balt., 1961-63; instr. anesthesia Johns Hopkins Sch. Medicine, Balt., 1963-64; chief anesthesia dept. Balt. County Gen. Hosp., Randallstown, Md., 1964-89, cons. anesthesiologist, 1989—. Office: County Anesthesia Assocs 5401 Old Court Rd Randallstown MD 21133

GARCIA-GRANADOS, SERGIO EDUARDO, brokerage house executive; b. Mexico, June 11, 1942; s. Jorge and Miriam Garcia-Granados; m. Elizabeth Bentley, Apr. 3, 1973; children: Tatiana, Sybil. Law degree with honors (scholar 1960-66), U. San Carlos, Guatemala, 1966; postgrad. U. Paris, Inst. Scis. Politiques, Paris, 1966-68. Bar: 1966. Rsch. assoc. The Hague Acad. Internat. Law, 1969, Internat. Bur. Fiscal Documentation, Amsterdam, 1969-70; ptnr. law firm Saravia y Muñoz, Guatemala City, 1970-77; v.p. sales mgr. Merrill Lynch Capital Market Internat., N.Y.C., 1982-88, v.p. resident mgr. internat. div. Shearson Lehman Hutton, N.Y., 1988-89, Miami, 1989—; lectr. tax problems in Central Am. Common Market, U. San Carlos, bus. orgns., U. Landivar, Globalization of Capital Markets, Guatemalan Mgmt. Assn., 1991;Bd. dirs. Patronato de Bellas Artes, 1977-84 , Guatemala Nat. Theatre Directorate, 1979-80, Cuban Mus. Art, Miami, Fla., 1991—. Mem. Colegio de Abogados, Internat. Bar Assn., Internat. Fiscal Assn. (gen. council 1972--84), Am. Soc. Internat. Law. Contbr. articles to profl. jours. Organizer, 1st editor loose-leaf corporate taxation in Latin Am., 1970.

GARDE, DANIEL FREDERICK, safety engineer; b. Bklyn., June 17, 1940; s. Daniel Frederick and Mary A. G.; children—Kim Marie, Daniel, Michael. B.S., Fordham, U., 1962; M.A. in Safety and Health, NYU, 1977. Commd. 2d lt. U.S. Army, 1962, advanced through grades to capt., 1965; served as comdr. 426th Supply and Service Co., 101st Airborne Div., Vietnam, 1969, comdr. 577th Q.M. Co., Aerial Delivery, Germany, 1971-73, ret., 1973; safety dir. Metro Containers, Carteret, N.J., 1973-75; safety and tng. dir. LCP Chems., Linden, N.J., 1975-79; sr. safety engr. Lederle Labs., Pearl River, N.Y., 1979-81; dir. safety and security Exxon Bayway Refinery, Linden, 1981-92; mgr. safety, health, fire protection Hess Oil Virgin Islands Corp., St. Croix, 1992—; faculty Middlesex Coll., 1978, 79, Mercy Coll., 1980-81, NYU, 1983—; programchmn. Nat. Safety Coun.; mem. petroleum exec. com.; vice-chmn. Linden, N.J. local emergency planning com. Contbr. articles to profl. publs. Decorated Bronze Star, Air Medal, Vietnamese medal of honor. Mem. Am. Soc. Safety Engrs., Am. Indsl. Hygiene Assn., Nat. Fire Protection Assn. Roman Catholic. Home: 43 Wilson Ave Iselin NJ 08830-1414 Office: HOVIC Dept 31 PO Box 127 Kings Hill VI 00851

GARDE, MICHAEL JAMES, business executive; b. N.Y.C., Apr. 12, 1937; s. James Vincent Garde and Ruth Ann (Loar) Shearer; m. Evelyn Therese Simpson, Sept. 9, 1961; children: Mary Beth, Thomas, Michael F., James. AA, St. Joseph Sem., 1957; AB, Seton Hall U., 1961. Route salesman Coca-Cola Bottling Co. of N.Y., Paterson, N.J., 1961-62; regional mgr. Yoo-Hoo Beverage Co., Carlstadt, N.J., 1963-65; marine sales rep. Johns-Manville Corp., N.Y.C., 1965-71; regional mgr. Sunday Pubs., Caldwell, N.J., 1972-76; pres. Bon Venture Svcs. Inc., Flanders, N.J., 1976—. Bd. dirs. Am. Cancer Soc., Monroe County, Pa., 1985—; patron Market St. Railway Co., San Francisco, 1983—. Mem. Boston St. Railway Assn., Pa. Trolley Mus., Washington Theol. Union (bd. trustees, devel. com.), Lions (bd. dirs. 1977-90). Roman Catholic. Home: RR 6 Box 6208 East Stroudsburg PA 18301-9104 Office: Bon Venture Svcs Inc 34 Ironia Rd Flanders NJ 07836-9111

GARDENIER, JOHN STARK, II, statistician, management scientist; b. Portland, Maine, Apr. 10, 1937; s. John Stark and Lucia Esther (Christensen) G.; m. Margaret Elizabeth Mann, Jan. 26, 1962 (dec. 1976); children: Brenda Anne Marshall, Patricia Suzanne Depew, Linda Marie Sievering, Pamela Lee; m. Turkan Emine Kumbaraci, June 18, 1977; children: George Bonneval, Jason Stark. BA, Yale U., 1959; MS, George Washington U., 1968, DBA, 1973. Mem. tech. staff Computer Scis. Corp., Falls Church, Va., 1968-69; sr. analyst CONSULTEC, Rockville, Md., 1969-71; ops. rsch. analyst USCG, Washington, 1971-90; survey statistician Nat. Ctr. Health Stats., Hyattsville, Md., 1990—; cons. in field, Washington, 1971-90; adj. assoc. prof. George Washington U., 1980-81; prof. lectr. Am. U., Washington, 1982-84. Commdr. USNR, 1960-86. Recipient Silver medal U.S. Dept. Transp., 1983. Mem. AAAS, IEEE Computer Soc., Am. Statis. Assn., Soc. for Computer Simulatiuon (bd. dirs. 1978-82, sr.), Profl. Soc. Ethics Group, Naval Res. Assn. Home: 1000 Salt Meadow Ln Mc Lean VA 22101-2027

GARDINER, LINDA JANE, surgeon. BS magna cum laude, Fordham U., 1968; MS in Chemistry, Princeton U., 1969; MPhil in Chemistry, Yale U., 1972, MD, 1978. Diplomate Am. Bd. Otolaryngology, Nat. Bd. Examiners. Intern in surgery St. Vincent's Hosp. and Med. Ctr., N.Y.C., 1978-79; resident in otolaryngology Yale U. Sch. Medicine, New Haven, 1979-82; chief Otolaryngology West Haven (Conn.) VA Hosp., 1982-85; asst. prof. Surg. sect. of Otolaryngology Yale U., New Haven, 1982-85, asst. clin. prof., 1985—; mem. staff Lawrence Hosp., Meml. Hosp., New London, Conn., 1985—; cons. West Haven VA Hosp., 1985—. Contbr. articles to profl. jours. NIH rsch. fellow, 1969-72, GM scholar, 1965-68. Fellow ACS, Am. Acad. Facial Plastic & Reconstructive Surgery, Am. Acad. Otolaryngological Head & Neck Surgery; mem. Southeastern Conn. C. of C., New Eng. Otolaryngological Soc., Com. on Endocrine Surgery, Am. Cancer Soc., New London County Med. Assn., Conn. State Med. Soc., Sigma Xi, Phi Beta Kappa. Office: 471 Montauk Ave New London CT 06320

GARDINER-SCOTT, TANYA JANE, English educator; b. Tiberias, Israel, July 10, 1958; came to U.S., 1986; d. William and Darinka Milo (Glogovac) G. BA in English with honors, U. Stirling, Scotland, 1979; MA in Medieval Studies, U. York, Eng., 1980; PhD in English, U. Toronto, Can., 1986. Lectr. dept. English and Am. lit. Brandeis U., Waltham, Mass., 1987-88, instr. summer sch., 1988—; vis. asst. prof. English, Hamilton Coll., Clinton, N.Y., 1988-89; vis. asst. prof. dept. gen. edn. Berklee Coll. Music, Boston, 1989-90; assoc. prof. English Mt. Ida Coll., Newton Center, Mass., 1990—; cons. Writing Ctr., MIT, Cambridge, 1990; reviewer jours. Holocaust and Genocide Studies, Can. Lit. Author: Mervyn Peake: The Evolution of a Dark Romantic, 1989, (with others) Science Fiction and Fantasy Book Review Annual, 1988; contbr. articles to profl. jours. Open fellow U. Toronto, 1986, 87, grad. travel grantee, 1986. Mem. MLA, Nat. Coun. Tchrs. English, Mervyn Peake Soc., Internat. Assn. for Fantastic in Arts. Office: Mt Ida Coll 777 Dedham St Newton Center MA 02159-3310

GARDINO, VINCENT ANTHONY, broadcasting executive; b. N.Y.C., Sept. 19, 1953; s. Anthony John and Carmelina Mary (Boglia) G. BA magna cum laude in History, St. Francis Coll. V.p. N.Y. sales mgr., dir. spl. programming and sales Metro Radio Sales, N.Y.C., 1976-79; acct. exec. WABC Radio, N.Y.C., 1979-81; dir. ABC Radio Network, N.Y.C., 1981-85, ABC Direction and Entertainment Radio Networks, 1981-85; pres., chief ops. officer Selcom Radio, N.Y.C., 1985—; v.p., gen. sales mgr. Sta. WOR-AM, N.Y.C., 1985—. Mem. Internat. Radio and TV Soc., Mus. Broadcasting, St. Francis Coll. Alumni Assn. (bd. dirs.). Roman Catholic. Avocations: tennis, jogging, racquetball, hist. autograph collecting, bicycling. Office: WOR Radio 1440 Broadway New York NY 10018-2301

GARDNER, ALBERT HENDERSON, psychology and elementary education educator; b. Gouverneur, N.Y., Jan. 8, 1932; s. Joseph Irvon Gardner and Alice Mulvina (McDougall) Chilton; children: Scott Andrew, John Albert, Alsion Gardner Jordan; m. Ginny Fu, Feb. 20, 1987; 1 child, Emily Fu. BS, SUNY, Cortland, 1958; MA, Syracuse U., 1964, PhD, 1967. Instr. U. Vt., Burlington, 1962-66; assoc. prof. U. Md., College Park, 1966—. Sgt. U.S. Army, 1952-54. Mem. Assn. Asian Studies, Am. Ednl. Rsch. Assn., Nat. Social Scis. Assn., Eastern Ednl. Rsch. Assn. Office: U Md Human Devel Dept 3304 Benjamin College Park MD 20742

GARDNER, DAVID CHAMBERS, educator, psychologist, business executive, author; b. Charlotte, N.C., Mar. 22, 1934; s. James Raymond and Jessica Mary (Chambers) Bumgardner m. Grace Joely Beatty, 1984; children: Joshua Avery, Jessica Sarah. BA, Northeastern U., 1960; MEd (U.S. Office Edn. fellow), Boston U., 1970, Ed.D. (U.S. Office Edn.-univ. rsch. fellow), 1974; PhD, Columbia Pacific U., 1984. Diplomate Am. Bd. Med. Psychotherapists. Mgr. market devel. N.J. Zinc Co., N.Y.C., 1961-66, COMINCO, Ltd., Montreal, Que., Can., 1966-68; dir. Alumni Ann. Giving Program, Northeastern U., Boston, 1968-69; dir. career and spl. edn. Stoneham (Mass.) Pub. Schs., Boston, 1970-72; assoc. prof. div. instructional devel. and adminstrn Boston U., 1974—; coord. program career vocat. tng. for handicapped, 1974-82, chmn. dept. career and bus. edn., 1974-79, also dir. fed. grants, 1975-77, 77-79; co-founder Am. Tng. and Rsch. Assocs., Inc., chmn. bd., 1979-83, pres., chief exec. officer, 1984—; dir. La Costa Inst. Lifestyle Mgmt., 1986-87. Author: Careers and Disabilities: A Career Approach, 1978; co-author: (with Grace Joely Beatty) Dissertation Proposal Guidebook: How to Prepare a Research Proposal and Get It Accepted, 1980, Career and Vocational Education for the Mildly Learning Handicapped and Disadvantaged, 1984, Stop Stress and Aging Now, 1985, Never Be Tired Again, 1990, Windows 3.1: A Visual Learning Guide, 1992, 1-2-3 for Windows-The Visual Learning Guide, 1992, Excel for Windows-The Visual Learning Guide, 1992, Word for Windows-The Visual Learning Guide, 1992, WordPerfect for Windows-The Visual Learning Guide, 1992; editor Career Edn. Quar., 1975-81; contbr. articles to profl. jours. Served with AUS, 1954-56. Recipient Ann. Profl. Teaching and Rsch. award Region X, Am. Assn. Mental Deficiency, 1979. Fellow Am. Assn. Mental Deficiency (nat. ethics com); mem. Nat. Assn. Career Edn. (dir., past pres.), Coun. Exceptional Children, Eastern Ednl. Rsch. Assn. (founding dir.), Am. Vocat. Assn., Phi Delta Kappa, Delta Pi Epsilon. Home: 2111 Escenico Ter Carlsbad CA 92009-7912 Office: Boston U Sch Edn 605 Commonwealth Ave Boston MA 02215-1605

GARDNER, DAVID LANCE, psychiatrist, educator; b. Norfolk, Va., Dec. 11, 1950; s. Daniel McCoy and Virgie Mae Belle (Riddle) G. BA in Psychology with distinction, U. Va., 1973; MD, Med. Coll. Va., 1977. Diplomate Am. Bd. Psychiatry and Neurology, 1983. Resident in psychiatry Georgetown U. Hosp., Washington, 1977-8l; pvt. practice Washington, l98l—; staff psychiatrist, researcher NIMH, Bethesda, Md., l98l—; clin. asst. prof. psychiatry Georgetown U. Med. Sch., l98l—. Contbr. articles on pharmacotherapy of borderline personality disorders to med. jours., chpts. to books. Mem. Am. Psychiat. Assn., Washington Psychiat. Soc. Democrat. Home: 1959 39th St NW Washington DC 20007 Office: 2829 Connecticut Ave NW Washington DC 20008-1586

GARDNER, GARY ALAN, sales and marketing executive; b. Tulare, Calif., Apr. 27, 1945; s. Edgar Woodrow and Velma B. (Stadden) G.; m. Gaye Dittes, Feb. 8, 1969; children: Kristi, Heather. AA, Coll. of Sequoias, 1967; BA, Mich. State U., 1982. Regional nat. account mgr. Pitney Bowes, Dallas, 1985-87, dir. prodn. mailing systems, 1987-88; dir. nat. account mktg. Pitney Bowes, Stamford, Calif., 1988-90; v.p. sales and mktg. Internat. Mailing Systems mem. AscomGroup, Shelton, Conn., 1990—. With U.S. Army, 1965-67. Home: 46 The Blvd Newtown CT 06470-1116 Office: Ascom Hasler Mailing System 19 Forest Pkwy Shelton CT 06484-6140

GARDNER, HOWARD EARL, psychologist, author; b. Scranton, Pa., July 11, 1943; s. Ralph and Hilde (Weilheimer) G.; m. Ellen Winner; children: Kerith, Jay, Andrew, Benjamin. AB summa cum laude, Harvard U., 1965, PhD, 1971; EdD (hon.), Curry Coll., 1992. Lectr. edn. Harvard U., 1971-86, co-dir. Project Zero, 1972—, prof. edn., 1986—, affiliated prof. psychology, 1987—; prof. neurology Boston U. Sch. Medicine, 1984-87, adj. prof. neurology, 1987—; rsch. psychologist Boston VA Med. Ctr., 1978—. Author: The Shattered Mind, 1975, Art, Mind and Brain, 1982, Frames of Mind, 1983 (Am. Psychol. Assn. Best Book award 1984), The Mind's New Science, 1985 (William James award 1988), To Open Minds, 1989, The Unschooled Mind, 1991. MacArthur Prize fellow, 1981, Grawemeyer award in edn., 1990; rsch. grantee numerous govtl. and pvt. founds. Fellow AAAS; mem. Nat. Acad. Edn., Phi Beta Kappa. Office: Harvard U Grad Sch Edn Project Zero Cambridge MA 02138

GARDNER, JAMES RICHARD, pharmaceutical company executive; b. Wellsville, N.Y., Nov. 18, 1944; s. James Myers and Adelaide (Stockman) G.; m. Linda Marie Cuomo, Oct. 14, 1967; children: Alexandra K., Mindy M. BS in Engring., U.S. Mil. Acad., 1966; M in Pub. Adminstrn., Princeton U., 1968, PhD, 1977; MBA, L.I. U., 1977; grad., U.S. Army War Coll. Commd. 2d lt. U.S. Army, 1966, advanced through grades to maj., 1976, resigned,, 1977; staff asst. Office of U.S. Atty. Gen., 1973; asst. prof. U.S. Mil. Acad., West Point, N.Y., 1974-77; dir. agrl. planning Pfizer, Inc., N.Y.C., 1977-81, dir. corp. strategic planning, 1981-89, sr. dir. corp. strategic planning, 1989-92, v.p. corp. strategic planning, 1992—; v.p. Pfizer Found., N.Y.C., 1985—; mem. faculty U.S. Army Command Gen. Staff Coll., 1986—, U.S. Army War Coll., 1989; mem. adv. coun. Ctr. Internat. Studies, Princeton U., 1987—; mem. adv. com. Dept. Astrophysical Scis. Princeton U., 1992—; head USAR polit. and mil. affairs div. Dept. Army, 1989-92. Author: (with others) American National Security, 1981, Business Competitor Intelligence, 1984; editor: Handbook of Strategic Planning, 1986; contbr. articles to profl. jours. Strategic planning com. United Way of Tri-

State, N.Y.C., 1984-87; dir. adminstrn. Pfizer Inc. United Way campaign, N.Y.C., 1985-87; bd. dirs. Greater N.Y. couns. Boy Scouts Am., 1988—; N.Y.C. chmn. Nat. Eagle Scout Assn., 1989-92. Col. USAR, 1988—. Decorated Bronze Stars (3), Air medals, Rep. Vietnam Gallantry Cross with Silver Star; recipient George Washington medal The Freedoms Found., Valley Forge, Pa., 1970; recipient Silver Beaver award Boy Scouts Am., 1991, Disting. Eagle award, 1992. Mem. Planning Forum (pres. N.Y.C. chpt. 1985-86), N.Am. Soc. Corp. Planning (nat. v.p. 1984-85), West Point Soc. N.Y. (bd. dirs. 1984—, v.p. 1986-88, pres. 1988-90), USMA Assn. Grads. (strategic planning com. 1992—), Phi Kappa Phi. Republican. Roman Catholic. Home: 250 Mamaroneck Rd Scarsdale NY 10583-7242 Office: Pfizer Inc 235 E 42d St New York NY 10017

GARDNER, JOEL ROBERT, writer, historian, arts consultant; b. N.Y.C., May 12, 1942; s. Stephen H. and Diana (Schneider) G.; m. Holly Alpine Phelps, July 7, 1980. BA, Tulane U., 1962; MA, UCLA, 1966. Pres. Gardner Assocs., Cherry Hill, N.J., 1987—; cons. N.J. State Coun. on Arts, Trenton, 1987—, Oral History Rsch. Office Columbia U., N.Y.C., 1987—. Author: Oral History for Louisiana, 1980, (with others) Watercolor: Let's Think About It, 1985—, 75 Years of Good Taste: A History of the Tasty Baking Company, 1990, A History of the Pew Charitable Trusts, 1991, (with others) In the Company of Writers, 1991; editor: Built in Louisiana, 1985, Oral History and the Law, 1985. Bd. dirs. N.J. Com. for the Humanities, 1991—. Mem. Oral History Assn. (bd. dirs. 1982-83, publs. com. 1983-86, chair endowment com. 1990—), Oral History for Middle Atlantic Region (v.p. 1991—). Jewish.

GARDNER, JOHN FENTRESS, retired education educator, writer; b. San Acacio, Colo., July 3, 1912; s. Ora Fletcher and Ethel (Fentress) G.; m. Carol Hemingway, Mar. 21, 1933; children: Elizabeth Linda, Hilary Paul, Mark Andrew. Cert. d'études, U. Grenoble, France, 1929; student, Princeton U., 1929-31, Rollins Coll., 1931-32, U. Chgo., 1933-34; LittD (hon.), Adelphi U., 1974. Sr. supr. adult edn. N.Y. State Dept. Edn., 1947-49; faculty chmn. Waldorf Sch., Adelphi U., Garden City, N.Y., 1949-74; founder, chmn. Coun. for Ednl. Freedom in Am., 1974-78; pres. Waldorf Press, Inc., Garden City, 1974-78; dir. Waldorf Inst. for Liberal Edn., Garden City, 1964-78; adj. prof. edn. Adelphi U., Garden City, 1968-78; pres. Myrin Inst. for Adult Edn., N.Y.C., 1972-75, chm., 1975-78. Author: The Experience of Knowledge, 1975, Two Paths to the Spirit, 1990, American Heralds of the Spirit, 1992; contbr. articles to profl. jours. With USNR, 1942-45. Mem. Anthroposophic Soc. Home: 135 North St Shelburne Falls MA 01370

GARDNER, JOHN UNDERHILL, hospital administrator; b. Long Branch, N.J., Dec. 17, 1924; s. John Henry and Mercedee (Crum) G.; widowed; children: Sarah, John, Eve, Thomas. AB, Princeton (N.J.) U., 1949; MD, N.Y. Med. Coll., 1953; MS in Medicine, U. Minn., 1957. Diplomate Am. Bd. Internal Medicine. Pvt. practice in internal medicine New Bedford, Mass., 1958-86; v.p. med. affairs, med. dir. St. Lukes Hosp., New Bedford, 1986—; corporator Compass Savs. Bank, New Bedford, 1965—. Pres. bd. dirs. Salvation Army, New Bedford, 1965-66; med. advisor Boy Scouts Am., New Bedford, 1963-68. 2d lt. U.S. Army, 1943-46. Fellow ACP; mem. Masons. Office: Saint Lukes Hosp 101 Page St New Bedford MA 02740-3400

GARDNER, LIZ See WEDDINGTON, LIZ GARDNER

GARDNER, MARSHALL CLOSSON, foundation administrator, lawyer; b. Logansport, Ind., June 11, 1918; s. Harry Marshall and Alice Jane (Closson) G.; m. June Archer Haller, Jan. 5, 1946; children: David Marshall, Debra June. BS, George Washington U., 1943, MS, 1950, JD with honors, 1955. Bar: D.C. 1955, U.S. Supreme Ct. 1958. Biologist U.S. Fish and Wildlife Svc., Washington, 1942-55; trial atty. Antitrust Divsn. Dept. Justice, Washington, 1955-74; adminstrv. appeals judge Appeals Coun. Social Security Adminstrn., Arlington, Va., 1974-84; pvt. practice Washington, 1984-91; pres. Found. of the Fed. Bar Assn., Washington, 1991—; treas., dir. Fed. Bar Bldg. Corp., Washington, 1960—. Editor Fed. Bar Jour., 1956-71; editorial notes editor, sec. George Washington U. Law Sch. Jour., 1954-55. Pres. North Four Corners Citizens Assn., Silver Spring, Md., 1954-55. Lt. USNR, 1943-46, PTO, 1950-53, Korea. Mem. Fed. Bar Assn. (nat. pres. 1965, Pres.'s award 1989), George Washington U. Law Assn. (nat. pres. 1981), Washington Acad. Scis., Nat. Press Club, Washington Biologists and Field Club, Nat. Lawyer's Club (treas. 1975—), Am. Legion (state comdr. D.C. 1968-69, nat. legis. commn. Indpls. 1988—), Order of Coif, Sigma Xi. Home: 12118 Long Ridge Ln Bowie MD 20715 Office: Fed Bar Found 1815 H St NW Washington DC 20006

GARDNER, MARVIN ALLEN, JR., pastoral counselor; b. Washington, Mar. 15, 1943; s. Marvin Allen and Lillian Gertrude (McCracken) G.; m. Donna Frances Craven, Mar. 16, 1962 (div. 1987); children: Stephen Gregory, Sarah Elizabeth; m. Laura Churchill Mink, May 21, 1988; children: Charles Treadway, Laura Faith. BA with honors, U. Md., 1964; MDiv cum laude, Va. Theol. Sem., 1967; DMin, Wesley Theol. Sem., Washington, 1979; PhD, The Union Inst., Cin., 1991. Lic. profl. counselor; ordained priest, Episcopal Ch. Curate Ascension Epsicopal Ch., Mt. Vernon, N.Y., 1967-69; rector St. Paul's Episcopal Ch., Waldorf, Md., 1969-76; pastoral counselor Pastoral Counseling and Cons. Ctrs. of Greater Washington, Oakton, Va., 1976-81; co-dir. Marriage and Family Inst., Washington, 1981-84; dir. Family & Marriage Assocs., La Plata, Md., 1984-86; pastoral counselor Pastoral Counseling & Cons. Ctrs., Oakton, 1986—; faculty and supr. Inst. for Pastoral Psychotherapy, Oakton, 1986—; oral examiner Bd. Examiners of Profl. Counselors, Richmond, Va., 1990—. Author: Pastoral Excellence in Pastoral Counselor Education and Training, 1991; contbr. articles to profl. jours. Fellow Am. Assn. Pastoral Counselors (chair bd. govs. rsch. com. 1992—, writing and rsch. award 1991); mem. APA, Am. Assn. for Marriage and Family Therapy, Am. Counseling Assn., Coll. Pastoral Supervision and Psychotherapy. Episcopalian. Home: 4426 Windom Pl NW Washington DC 20016-2410 Office: Pastoral Counseling Ctrs PO Box 39 Oakton VA 22124-0039

GARDNER, MICHAEL JOSPEH, professional tennis coach, camp director; b. Boston, Feb. 6, 1954; s. Joseph Edgar and Rose Ann (Onelli) G.; m. Elaine Kay Small, Aug. 31, 1991. B in Biology, Curry Coll., 1975. Level 1 Profl., U.S. Profl. Tennis Assn., 1987. Tennis pro Tennis/Now Inc., Watertown, Mass., 1975-79; dir. The Club at Elm Plaza, Waterville, Maine, 1979-81, The Thoreau Club, Concord, Mass., 1981—, Adidas/Dartmouth Tennis Camp, Hanover, N.H., 1989—; mem. nat. adv. saff Dunlop Sports, Greeneville, S.C., 1986—, Nike Internat., Beaverton, Oreg., 1987—; coach U.S. Tennis Assn., N.Y.C. Named Boston's Most Eligible Bachelor, Boston Herald, 1984. Mem. U.S. Tennis Assn. (coach, N.Y.C.). Home: 78 Hunnewell Ave Boston MA 02135

GARDNER, PETER JAGLOM, investment analyst, publisher; b. N.Y.C., June 3, 1958; s. Ralph David and Natalie (Jaglom) G.; m. Victoire Taittinger, June 22, 1984; children: Evan, Emma. BA, Middlebury (Vt.) Coll., 1980. Tech. analyst Dun & Bradstreet/Nat. CSS, N.Y.C., 1981; v.p. Servez-Vous (U.S.A.) Inc., N.Y.C., 1982-84; pres. Transatlantic Comml. Svcs., N.Y.C., N.Y., 1985-91; owner Northern Centinel, Kinderhook, N.Y., 1991—; dir. Gardner Internat., Inc., Quality Irish Foods, Ltd. Office: 115 E 82d St # 8B New York NY 10028-0831

GARDNER, ROBERT, writer, consultant; b. Redding, Conn., Feb. 21, 1929; s. Volney Paul and Mary Tyler G.; m. Natalie Candee Sanford, Sept. 10, 1949; children: John Thomas, Barbara Lee Conklin. BA cum laude, Wesleyan U., 1951; MA, Trinity Coll., 1957; Cert. Advanced Study, Wesleyan U., 1963. Adminstrv. asst. Am. Cyanamid, Idaho Falls, Idaho, 1951-52; tchr., coach Salisbury (Conn.) Sch., 1952-63, chair sci. dept., 1959-63, 68-69; developer Edn. Devel. Ctr., Newton, Mass., 1963-64, 66-68; pvt. practice cons. and author North Eastham, Mass., 1989—; cons. NSF-AID, Ajmer, India, 1967; tchr. physics workshop Colo. Sch. Mines, Golden, 1986, 88. Author: Experimenting with Sound and Music, 1991, Experimenting with Light, 1991, Famous Experiments You Can Do, 1990, Experimenting with Illusions, 1990, Experimenting with Inventions, 1990, More Ideas for Science Projects,1 989, Celebrating Earth Day, 1992, Crime Lab 101, 1992, (with Dennis Shortelle) The Future and Past, 1989, Projects in Space Science, 1988, and many others; contbr. articles to profl. jours. Recipient fellowships NSF, Wesleyan U., Bowdoin Coll., Rensselaer Poly. Inst., Providence Coll., 1985-63, 59, 73, 79, Klingenstein Found., Tchrs. Coll. Columbia U., 1983-84. Mem. Nat. Sci. Tchrs. Assn., Am. Assn. Physics Tchr., Sigma Xi. Home: 275 Seagull Ln North Eastham MA 02651-9999

GARDNER, SANDRA, writer; b. Everett, Mass., May 22, 1940; d. Morris Louis and Ruth (Davis) Shindell; m. Richard Platek, Nov. 6, 1959 (div. Sept. 1968); children: Barbara, Brenda; m. Lewis Gardner, Feb. 26, 1969; 1 child, Jonathan. AA in Liberal Arts, Boston U., 1959; BA magna cum laude, Hunter Coll., 1979. Freelance writer, editor Scholastic , Inc., N.Y.C., 1976-81; contbng. columnist, writer N.J. sect. N.Y. Times, N.Y.C., 1981-86; sr. staff writer U. Medicine & Dentistry of N.J., Newark, 1986-87; coord. external communications Overlook Hosp., Summit, N.J., 1987-91. Author: Six who Dared, 1981, Street Gangs, 1983, Teenage Suicide, 1986, rev. edit. 1990. Recipient 1st prize Social Issues Sigma Delta Chi, 1986, 3 Mercury Media awards, 1988-90, Spl. Media award Am. Heart Assn., N.J., 1990; named Commencement Speaker Stockton State Coll., Pomona, N.J., 1987, Woman of Achievement, N.J. Assn. Bus. and Profl. Women, 1986. Mem. N.J. Press Women (10 awards 1984-90), Nat. Fedn. Press Women (4 awrds 1988-91), Internat. Women Writers Guild. Jewish. Home: 779 Salem St Teaneck NJ 07666-5320

GARDNER, WALTER E., retail executive; b. N.Y.C., July 20, 1954; s. Walter E. and Joan (Quinlan) G. AD, Newbury Coll., Brookline, Mass., 1988; student, Eastern Nazarene Coll., Quincy, Mass., 1988—. Claims examiner Blue Cross/Blue Shield, Boston, 1973-76; calculation reviewer Prudential, Boston, 1976-79; cons. Wm. M. Mercer, Boston, 1979-80, Rand Assocs., Boston, 1980-82; asst. v.p., benefits dir. TJX Cos. Inc., Framingham, Mass., 1982—. Mem. New. Eng. Employee Benefits Coun. Home: 1340 Pleasant St Brockton MA 02401-2840

GAREY, JAMES ROBERT, aerospace engineer; b. Burbank, Calif., June 2, 1932; s. Robert Milton and Kathleen Margaret (Canning) G.; m. Kathleen, Jan. 7, 1956 (div. 1981); children: Michael, Daniel, Tamara, Scott, Pamela, Todd, Tracie; m. Joanne Carol Reposa, Jan. 30, 1982. BS in Aerospace Engring., Tex. A&M U., 1960; MS in Aerospace Engring., USAF Inst. Tech., 1972. Commd. 2d lt. USAFR, 1955; commd. capt. USAF, 1962, advanced through grades to lt. col., 1971, ret., 1979; sr. mem. tech. staff Anser Corp., Arlington, Va., 1979; sr. engr. Raytheon Corp., Bedford, Mass., 1979-85; sr. mem. profl. staff ISN Corp., Lexington, Mass., 1985-87; sr. cons. engr. Arthur D. Little, Inc., Cambridge, 1987—. Decorated Disting. Svc. medal, 1965, Air medal USAF, 1969-70, Meritorious Svc. medal, 1969, 79. Mem. AIAA (New Eng. sect. sec. 1989-90, vice chair 1990-91, chmn. 1991-92), Order of Daedalians (Minuteman chpt. treas. scholarship com. 1989-91). Republican. Roman Catholic. Home: 15 Putnam Rd Acton MA 01720 Office: Arthur D Little PSMC Acorn Park Cambridge MA 01720

GARFIELD, LESLIE JEROME, real estate executive; b. N.Y.C., Mar. 23, 1932; s. Jack and Anne (Weinert) G.; m. Johanna Rosengarten, Sept. 28, 1960; children: Clare Louisa, Jed Herbert, Cory Alexander. BA, U. Wis., Madison, 1953; MA, Harvard U., 1956; MBA, Columbia U., 1958. V.p. Pease & Elliman, Inc., N.Y.C., 1965-68, William A. White & Sons, Inc., N.Y.C., 1968-78; pres. Leslie J. Garfield & Co., Inc., N.Y.C., 1978—; bd. dirs. East N.Y. Savs. Bank. Chmn. bd. dirs. N.Y. Youth Symphony, 1986, pres. bd. dirs., 1975-86; bd. dirs. Carnegie Hill Neighbors, N.Y.C., 1985—; mem. Com. on Prints and Illustrated Books, Mus. Modern Art. Mem. Real Estate Bd. N.Y. (chmn. sales brokers com. 1985-86), The Drawing Soc. (bd. dirs.). Clubs: Century Assn., Nat. Arts, Harvard, Grolier. Office: 654 Madison Ave New York NY 10021-8404

GARGANO, MICHAEL LOUIS, computer science educator; b. N.Y.C., Oct. 14, 1947; s. Francis A. and Antionette G.; m. Phyllis A.; 1 child, Michael R. BA, MA, Bklyn. Coll., 1970; PhD, CUNY, 1975. Prof. Bklyn. Coll., N.Y.C., 1970-75; mktg. rsch. mgr. Equitable Life, N.Y.C., 1975-78; planning mgr. MetLife, N.Y.C., 1978-81; prof., chair PACE U., N.Y.C., 1978—; sr. rsch. scientist AIG, N.Y.C., 1988-90. Co-author: Design and Analysis of Expert Systems, 1989; contbr. articles to profl. jours. Mem. Internat. Neural Net Soc., IEEE, Am. Assn. of Artificial Intelligence, Assn. of Computing Machinery, Ops. Rsch. Soc. of Am., The Inst. of Mgmt. Scis., Nat. Coun. Tchrs. of Math, Math. Assn. of Am. Roman Catholic. Office: Pace U 1 Pace Plz New York NY 10038

GARGIONE, FRANK, electrical engineer; b. Perdifumo, Salerno, Italy, Oct. 18, 1938; came to U.S., 1955; s. Nicola and Carolina (Lembo) G.; m. Lucy Abarno, Aug. 5, 1967; children: Caroline, Angela, Nicole, Frank. BSEE in Communications, Drexel U., 1961; MSEE in Computer Option, U. Pa., 1965. Engr. missile and space div. GE, Phila., 1961-65; engr. vector div. United Aircraft, Trevose, Pa., 1965-67; engr., mgr. astroelectronics div. RCA, Princeton, N.J., 1967-88; mgr. astro-space div. GE, Princeton, 1988—. Contbr. articles in field to profl. jours. Fin. coun. mem. St. Joachim's Ch., Trenton, 1987—. Mem. AIAA, Am. Italian Hist. Assn. (treas. Cen. Jersey chpt. 1979—), Lions Club. Home: 239 Glenn Ave Trenton NJ 08648-3743 Office: GE Astrospace Div PO Box 800 Princeton NJ 08543-0800

GARGIUL, DONNA MARIE, economist; b. Auburn, N.Y., May 8, 1965; d. Donald E. and Jacqueline M. (Orlando) Scholz; m. Joseph A. Gargiul, Jr., July 11, 1987. BS in Applied Math. Econs., SUNY, Oswego, 1987; MA in Econs. and Fin., SUNY, Binghamton, 1989. Market rsch. specialist N.Y. State Electric and Gas, Binghamton, 1989; economist, planner Niagara Mohawk Power Corp., Syracuse, N.Y., 1989—. Mem. NAFE, SUNY Binghamton Alumni Assn., SUNY Oswego Alumni Assn., Omicron Delta Epsilon. Office: Niagara Mohawk Power Corp 507 Plum St Syracuse NY 13250-5001

GARGIULO, GERALD JOHN, psychoanalyst, writer; b. N.Y.C., Nov. 12, 1934; s. Fred Nunzio and Fanny Joy (Tarantino) G.; m. Julia Caldiero, Apr. 12, 1964; children: Paul Gerald, Connie Joy. BA in Philosophy, St. Bonaventure U., Orlean, N.Y., 1958; MA in Religious Studies, Wash. Theol. Union, Washington, 1962. Mem. faculty Manhattan Coll., N.Y.C., Riverdale, 1962-70; pvt. practice N.Y.C., Greenwich, Conn., 1970—; dir. The Inst. N.P.A.P., N.Y.C., 1988-92, pres. tng. inst., 1992—; assoc. editor The Psychoanalytic Review, N.Y.C., 1987—; pres. Coun. of Psychoanalytic Psychotherapists, N.Y.C., 1981-83; bd. dirs. N.Y. Ctr. for Psychoanalysis, 1973-75; mem. faculty Nat. Psychol. Assn. for Psychoanalysis, 1972—. Contbr. articles to profl. pubs. Bd. dirs. Psychoanalysts Against Nuclear Weapons, 1982-85; com. mem. Greenwich Nuclear Freeze Orgn., 1987-90. Fellow Inst. for Psychoanalytic Tng. & Rsch. (bd. dirs. 1976), Coun. of Psychoanalytic Psychotherapists; mem. Internat. Psychoanalytical Assn., Nat. Psychol. Assn. for Psychoanalysis, Conn. Poetry Soc. Home: 40-10 Ettl Ln Greenwich CT 06831 Office: 158 Greenwich Ave Greenwich CT 06830-6548

GARLAND, CARL WESLEY, chemist, educator; b. Bangor, Maine, Oct. 1, 1929; s. Cecil G. and Blandena Couillard (Wadell) G.; m. Joan A. Donaghy, July 30, 1955; children: Leslie J., Andrew E. B.S., U. Rochester, 1950; Ph.D., U. Calif.-Berkeley, 1953. Instr. chemistry U. Calif.-Berkeley, 1953; faculty MIT, 1953—, assoc. prof. chemistry, 1959-68, prof. chemistry, 1968—; vis. prof. U. Calif.-San Diego, 1972, U. Rome, 1974, Cath. U. Louvain (Belgium), 1977, Ben Gurion U., Israel, 1980, U. Paris, 1981, 82, U. Bordeaux, France, 1990; chmn. Gordon Research Conf. Orientational Disorder in Crystals, 1984. Author: (with D.P. Shoemaker, J.W. Nibler) Experiments in Physical Chemistry, 5th edit., 1989; editor: Optics and Spectroscopy, 1960-81, Liquid Crystals, 1991—; contbr. numerous articles to profl. jours. A.P. Sloan fellow, 1954-60; Guggenheim fellow, 1963. Fellow Am. Acad. Arts and Sci.; mem. Am. Phys. Soc. Home: 4 Edward St Belmont MA 02178-2343 Office: MIT Dept Chemistry Rm 6-237 Cambridge MA 02139

GARLAND, FLOYD RICHARD, minister; b. Ft. Wayne, Ind., Jan. 27, 1938; s. Floyd Elgie and Thlema Clara (Leasure) G.; m. Betsy Sanborn Aldrich, Sept. 7, 1963, (div. Oct. 1975); children: Craig William, Sarah Elizabeth; m. Katharine Adeline Wright, May 30, 1977 (div. Mar. 1991). BS in Hist., Purdue U., 1961; MDiv., Garrett Theol. Seminary, Evanston, Ill., 1964; MBA, Southeastern Mass. U., 1985. Ordained to ministry Meth. Ch., 1962. Student asst. Kelly Meth. Ch., Chgo., 1963-64; pastor Chester Heights Meth. Ch., Richmond, Ind., 1964-67, Hillsgrove United Meth. Ch., Warwick, R.I., 1967-75, St. Paul's United Meth. Ch., New Bedford, Mass., 1975-85, Portsmouth (R.I.) United Meth. Ch., 1985-91, Mathewson St. United Meth. Ch., Providence, 1991—; lectr., Salve Regina Coll., Newport, R.I., 1987-90; bd. dirs. Snem Fed. Credit Union, Northboro, Mass.; conf. statistician, So. New Eng. Conf. of United Meth. Ch., Boston, 1988—, pres. bd. trustees, 1979-85. Contbr. articles to profl. jours. Bd. dirs., v.p. Warwick Community Action, 1972-75; mem. Charter Rev. Commn., Warwick, 1972. Democrat. Home: 80 Grant Dr North Kingstown RI 02852-3619 Office: Mathewson St United Meth Ch 134 Mathewson St Providence RI 02903-1892

GARLAND, HOWARD, educator; b. Bklyn., June 22, 1946; s. Murray and Norma (Luft) G.; m. Eileen Mary Cohen, Aug. 21, 1968; children: Eric Lee, Adam Marc. BA, Bklyn. coll., 1968; MS, Cornell U., 1971, PhD, 1972. Asst. prof. Upsala Coll., East Orange, N.J., 1972-74; prof. U. Tex., Arlington, 1974-88; vis. prof. U. Ill., Champaign, 1985-86; prof., chair U. Del., Newark, 1988—. Contbr. over 30 articles to profl. jours. Mem. Internat. Assn. applied Psychology, Am. Psychol. Soc., Soc. I/O Psychology, Acad. Mgt. Home: 9 Falling Tree Ct Newark DE 19711-7462 Office: U Del Purnell Hall Newark DE 19716

GARLAND, JOAN BRUDER, social worker, psychologist; b. Cleve., Sept. 30, 1931; d. Henry Ignatius and Mary (Maher) Bruder; A.B., Mt. Holyoke Coll., 1952; postgrad. Wellesley Coll., 1952-53, U. Sao Paulo (Brazil), 1965-66; M.S., Sarah Lawrence Coll., 1974; M.S. in Social Work, Columbia U., 1977, PhD in Psychology, The Union Inst., 1986; Diplomate Clin. Social Work. m. Paul Griffith Garland, Aug. 28, 1954; children—Bonnie (dec.), Patrick, John, Cathryn. Grad. asst., chemistry dept. Wellesley (Mass.) Coll., 1952-53; chemist Polaroid Corp., Cambridge, Mass., 1953-54, 55-56; CAPES research fellow U. Sao Paulo, 1954-55; clin. instr. retardation N.Y. Med. Coll., Valhalla, 1978-80; social worker, psychiat. day treatment program Jewish Child Care Assn., Pleasantville (N.Y.) Cottage Sch., 1980; family research investigator Albert Einstein Coll. Medicine, Bronx, N.Y., 1982-86; pvt. practice, 1992—. Founder, v.p. Crime Victims Assistance Agy., Inc., 1981-83. Treas. council Girl Scouts, Sao Paulo, 1965-67; bd. dirs. PTA, 1972-73; bd. deacons Scarsdale (N.Y.) Congregational Ch., 1975; patient rep. White Plains (N.Y.) Med. Center, 1977. Cert. in family therapy, Center for Family Learning, Phila. Child Guidance Ctr.; cert. ind. social worker, N.Y. State, Conn. Fellow Soc. Clin. Social Work Psychotherapists; mem. APA, Nat. Assn. Social Workers, Acad. Cert. Social Workers, N.Y. Acad. Scis. Clubs: Mt. Holyoke, Wellesley (Palm Beach County). Home: 2156 Date Palm Rd Boca Raton FL 33432

GARLICK, THOMAS BRUCE, priest, chaplain, educator; b. N.Y.C., July 8, 1949; s. Bruce Robinson and Joan (Belliveau) G. AB, Boston Coll., Chestnut Hill, Mass., 1971; MEd, Fitchburg (Mass.) State Coll., 1974; MA, STB, U. Louvain, Belgium, 1984; MA, St. Bernard's Inst., Rochester, N.Y., 1985. Ordained priest Roman Cath. Ch., 1984. Assoc. pastor St. Anthony Ch., Dudley, Mass., 1984-88, Immaculate Conception Ch., Worcester, Mass., 1988-90; chaplain St. Vincent Hosp., Worcester, 1990—; adj. instr. Nichols Coll., Dudley. Home: 21 Heywood St Apt 6A Worcester MA 01604-5403 Office: St Vincent Hosp 25 Winthrop St Worcester MA 01604-4593

GARLOFF, SAMUEL JOHN, psychiatrist; b. Erie, Pa., Nov. 14, 1947. BS, Mansfield (Pa.) State Coll., 1969; MS, Johns Hopkins U., 1974; DO, Phila. Coll. Osteo. Medicine, 1978. Intern Walter Reed Army Med. Ctr., Washington, 1978-79; resident in psychiatry Dwight David Eisenhower Army Med. Ctr., Ft. Gordon, Ga., 1981-84; officer in charge USA Health Care Clinic, Rock Island, Ill., 1980-81; div. psychiatrist Ft. Hood, Tex., 1984-86; pvt. practice Pottsville, Pa., 1986—; med. dir. Drug and Alcohol Program Good Samaritan Regional Med. Ctr., Pottsville, 1986—, asst. med. dir., 1988-91, med. dir., 1991—; psychiat. cons. Operation Plus, Pottsville, 1987—, Hazelton (Pa.) Mental Health Ctr.; cons. Turning Point, Pottsville, 1986—, med. dir., 1988-91; clin. cons. III Corps Drug and Alcohol Program, Ft. Hood, Tex., 1984-85; instr. to physician asst. students, Rock Island, 1979-80, Ft. Hood, 1985; lectr., psychiat. nursing students, Ft. Gordon, Ga., 1982-84, family practice medicine residents, Ft. Hood, 1984-85. Chmn. spl. gifts com. St. Joseph Ctr. for Spl. Learning, 1989—; bd. dirs. Good Samaritan Found., 1989—, Schuylkill Unit Am. Cancer Soc., 1990—, St. Joseph's Ctr. Spl. Learning Devel. Bd., 1990—. Maj. U.S. Army Med. Corps, 1978-86. Fellow Am. Coll. Med. Quality (bd. cert.), Am. Acad. Pain Mgmt. (bd. cert.); mem. Am. Osteo. Assn., Am. Coll. Neuropsychiatrists, Assn. Mil. Osteo. Physicians and Surgeons, Pa. Osteo. Med. Assn., Schuylkill County Osteo. Med. Soc., Am. Osteopathic Acad. Addictionology. Home: 1759 Tall Oaks Rd Orwigsburg PA 17961-9543 Office: Good Samaritan Med Mall 700 Schuylkill Manor Rd Pottsville PA 17901-3849

GARMS, DAVID JOHN, federal official; b. Worthington, Minn., Oct. 19, 1942; s. Leonard John and Gladys Anna Hinkeldey; m. Dial Winifred Barnwell, June 9, 1971; children: Doria Jean, Diantha Barnwell. BA in Sociology, Gustavus Adolphus, St. Peter, Minn., 1964; MPA, U. Philippines, Manila, 1978. Rehab. officer U.S. AID, Saigon, Vietnam, 1967-71; program analyst devel. planning Africa Bur. U.S. AID, Washington, 1971-72; edn. officer U.S. AID, Dhaka, Bangladesh, 1972-76; asst. program officer U.S. AID, Manila, 1976-78; officer-in-charge India Affairs U.S. AID, Washington, 1978-81, officer-in-charge Sri Lanka/Nepal/Maldives Affairs, 1985-88; program officer U.S. AID, Lilongue, Malawi, 1981-85; chief office of program U.S. AID, Colombo, Sri Lanka, 1988—; sec. U.S.-India Joint Commn., Washington, 1978-80; mem. Peace Corps AID Task Force, Washington, 1986-88; chmn. Sr. Lanka Rehab. Task Force, Washington, 1987-88. Author: With The Dragon's Children, 1973. Mem. Am. Fgn. Svc. Assn., Sri Lanka Am. Soc. (pres. 1990-91), Fed. Exec. Inst. Assn. Lutheran. Office: Agy Internat Devel Colombo Dept of State Washington DC 20521

GARNER, CHARLES WILLIAM, educator; b. Pine Grove Mills, Pa., Apr. 18, 1939; s. Adam Krumrine and Blanche Ella (Gearhart) G.; m. Karyl J. Packer, Sept. 8, 1962; children: Ronald Adam, Juliet Paige. Student, U.S. Navy Electronics Airborne Sonar Sch., 1959; BS in Bus. Edn., Pa. State U., 1965, MEd in Higher Edn. Adminstrn., 1968, EdD in Vocat. Indsl. Edn., 1974. Adminstrv. asst. dept. psychology Pa. State U., 1965-75; asst. prof., site adminstr. March AFB, Calif. for So. Ill. U., 1975-77; asst. prof., coordinator Ft. Knox Ctr.- U. Louisville, 1977-78; assoc. prof., acting vice dean Rutgers U., Camden, N.J., 1978-79; assoc. prof. urban edn., chmn. dept. edn. Univ. Coll. Rutgers U., New Brunswick, N.J., 1978-81, assoc. prof. vocat. tech. edn. Grad. Sch. Edn., 1981-85, chmn. dept. vocat. tech. edn., 1982-85, assoc. prof. edn. adminstrn., 1985—; exec. dir. Vocat. Edn. Resource Ctr. Rutgers U., 1983-88, dir. continuing edn., 1987-89; mem. adv. com. 15th Air Force Noncommd. Officer Leadership Sch., Strategic Air Force Command, 1976-77; mem. N.J. state leadership team Leadership Tng. Inst.-Vocat. and Spl. Edn., 1980-81; mem. adv. council Vocat. Tng. Project, Eastern European Coalition Am., Perth Amboy, N.J., 1981-82; cons. IEEE. Author: Accounting and Budgeting in Public and Nonprofit Organizations: A Manager's Guide, 1991; contbr. articles to profl. jours.; co-editor: Occupational Edn. Forum, 1979-85; editorial reader: Jour. Indsl. Tchr. Edn., 1981; producer, host talk show pilot for public TV, 1979; producer, host: TV tape series Rutgers U.: Current Issues in Vocat. Edn., 1979. Served with USN, 1959-62. Grantee N.J. Dept. Edn. Div. Vocat. Edn., 1978-88; grantee HEW, 1979-80. Mem. AAUP, Am. Edn. Rsch. Assn., Am. Vocat. Assn. (editorial bd. Jours. Gen. and Related Instrn. 1982, trade and industry rsch. com. 1985-87), Acad. Mgmt., Am. Vocat. Edn. Rsch. Assn., Nat. Assn. Indsl. and Tech. Tchr. Educators, N.J. Assn. Vocat. Edn., Spl. Needs Pers. (exec. coun. 1980-81, pres. 1981-82), Vocat. Edn. Assn. N.J., Elks (exalted ruler 1972-73), Phi Delta Kappa, Omicron Tau Theta, Epsilon Pi Tau (trustee 1983-88). Home: 5673 Wismer Rd Pipersville PA 18947 Office: Dept Ednl Theory Policy Adminstrn New Brunswick NJ 08903

GARNER, CRAIG ANDREW, systems analyst, computer consultant; b. Newark, Mar. 28, 1950; s. Andrew David and Catherine (Culver) G.; m. Veleria Brown; children: Michelle Brown, Tammirah Brown. AS in Computer Sci., Essex County Coll., 1977; BS in Computer Sci., Kean Coll., 1980. Programmer AM Varitype, East Hanover, N.J., 1977-79, Monroe Systems for Bus., Morristown, N.J., 1979-80, Bell Labs. AT&T, Holmdel, N.J., 1981-83; programmer, analyst AT&T Communications, Piscataway, N.J., 1983—; adj. instr. Middlesex County Coll., Edison, N.J., 1982-84, Passaic County Coll., Paterson, N.J., 1982-84. Author: (poetry) Rhymes for Reasons, vols. I

and II, 1988; editor Newslink, 1987. Mem. Irvington (N.J.) Bd. Edn., 1987-89; pres. Park Place Block Assn., Irvington, 1988; dist. leader Dem. Orgn. Com., Irvington, 1991—. With USAF, 1967-71. Recipient Marcus Garvey award Soc. Black Engrs. Mem. NAACP. Home: 147 Park Pl # 1FL Irvington NJ 07111-2332 Office: AT&T Communications 290 Davidson Ave Rm W1G031 Somerset NJ 08875

GARNER, PETER WARD, marketing executive; b. Balt., Jan. 31, 1949; s. Wendell Richard and Barbara (Ward) G.; m. Barbara Ellen Sloves, Oct. 4, 1980; children: Joshua C., Samual A., Sarah E. BA in Psychology, Johns Hopkins U., 1971; MPH, Yale U., 1980. Behavioral counselor State of Conn., Middletown, 1971-74; mental health specialist Hamden (Conn.) Mental Health Svc., 1974-77; exec. dir. Regionald Mental Health Bd., Waterbury, Conn., 1979-82; mktg. cons. Aetna Life & Casualty, Hartford, Conn., 1982-84; mktg. adminstr. Aetna Life & Casualty, Hartford, 1984-88, mktg. officer, 1988-90, mktg. exec. health care cost mgmt. products and svcs., 1990—; cons. Mcpl. Police Acad., Meriden, Conn., 1973-78, Youth Svcs. Bur., East Hartford, Conn., 1976-82. Cubmaster Pack 73, Middletown, 1990. Mem. Am. Mktg. Assn. (exec.), Am. Mgmt. Assn., Sales and Mktg. Execs. Internat., Employee Benefits Inst. Home: 52 Harvard Ct Middletown CT 06457-4956 Office: Aetna Life & Casualty 151 Farmington Ave Hartford CT 06156-0001

GARNER, WILLIAM DARRELL, health services executive; b. High Point, N.C., Nov. 19, 1933; s. Talmadge Wade and Susie Jane (Vaughan) G.; m. Olga Marie Ramirez, Mar. 7, 1958; children: John Albert Rosales, William Dean Anthony, Leil Yvette. BSBA, U. N.C., 1955; MBA, U. Ga., 1967; PhD, George Washington U., 1991. Commd. 2nd lt. USAF, 1955, advanced through grades to col., 1975, ret., 1981; systems advisor Ryan Advisors and Cons., Washington, 1981-83; exec. dir. med. faculty assocs. George Washington U. Med Ctr., Washington, 1984—; advisor com. on faculty practice George Washington U., 1984—, mem./advisor com. on quality assurance, 1989—, advisor, health plan liaison com., 1989—, advisor, credentialling com., 1990—; mem. faculty Ctr. for Continuing Edn., Washington, 1988—; mem. George Washington U. Doctoral Assn., 1983—, treas., 1986-87, pres., 1987-89. Editor: Tactical Forces Employment in Southeast Asia, 1969, Tactical Forces Employment in the European Region, 1972, U.S. Air Forces in Europe Manual Aerial Combat Maneuvers and Tactics, 1973, NATO Air Defense Systems for the 1980s, 1978, Air Defense Systems in the Middle East, 1981, The Role of the Health Services Consultant, 1983. Decorated Def. Superior Svc. medal, Legion of Merit, D.F.C. with two bronze oak leaf clusters, Bronze Star with bronze oak leaf cluster, Air medal with three silver oak leaf clusters, Cross of Gallantry with palm (Republic of South Vietnam); recipient award for excellence in composition Am. Coll. Healthcare Execs., 1984. Mem. Am. Group Practice Assn., Med. Group Mgmt. Assn. (George Washington U. rep. to acad. practice assembly), University Club, Beta Gamma Sigma. Republican. Methodist. Home: 1104 Archery Dr Fort Washington MD 20744-6827 Office: George Washington U Med Ctr Med Faculty Assocs 2150 Pennsylvania Ave NW Washington DC 20037-2396

GARNETT, DIANNE KAY, educational fundraiser; b. Vincennes, Ind., Apr. 6, 1948; d. Wendell Allen and Doris Evelyn (Richter) Wampler; m. Robert Frederick Garnett Sr., June 24, 1976. BA, U. Evansville, 1969, MA, 1973. Systems analyst U. Evansville, Ind., 1969-74, dir. Project Computerized Vocat. Info. System, 1974-76, asst. dir. computer ctr., 1976-79, asst. prof. computing sci., 1979-81, dir. alumni rels., 1982-85, assoc. v.p. devel., 1985-89; systems analyst Whirlpool Corp., Evansville, 1981-82; v.p. devel. Colby-Sawyer Coll., New London, N.H., 1989—. Bd. dirs. Raintree Coun. Girl Scouts U.S., Evansville, 1989-90. Mem. Coun. for Advancement and Support of Edn., Rotary, Chi Omega. Home: 195 Newport Rd New London NH 03257-4237 Office: Colby-Sawyer Coll 100 Main St New London NH 03257-4648

GAROFALO, ROBERT CONRAD, retail executive; b. Woburn, Mass., Mar. 13, 1949; s. Carmine Anthony and Priscilla (Gifford) G.; m. Nancy Anne Boumenot, May 17, 1970 (div. Dec. 1984); 1 child, Derek Robert; m. Jerilyn Parla Rustici, Feb. 16, 1985; 1 child, Amanda Parla. Store mgr. Mammoth Mart, Salisbury, Mass., 1971-74; store mgr. Marshalls, West Roxbury, Mass., 1974-75, Canton, Mass., 1975-76; dist. mgr. Marshalls, Manchester, Conn., 1976-79; asst. regional mgr. Marshalls, Hamden, Conn., 1979-80; adminstrv. dir. Marshalls, Wakefield, Mass., 1981-85; regional dir. Marshalls, Bedford, N.H., 1985-87; regional dir. Marshalls, Exton, Pa., 1987-89, regional v.p., 1990—. Mem. 49ers, West Chester, Pa., 1988. Republican. Lutheran. Home: 1543 Mill Race Ln West Chester PA 19380

GAROFALO, ROBERT JOSEPH, music educator, conductor, author; b. Scranton, Pa., Jan. 25, 1939; s. Phillip Paul and Domenica (Casoria) G.; m. Ann Marie Bowling, Sept. 14, 1963; children: Michael, Roberta. BS in Music Edn., Mansfield (Pa.) U., 1960; MMus, Cath. U., 1963, PhD in Musicology, 1969. Music prof. Keene (N.H.) State Coll., 1966-67, Cath. U. Am., Washington, 1967—; co-founder, artistic dir. Eternal Winds Washington; conductor Heritage Americana, 1978-88; vis. prof. New England Conservatory, Syracuse U., U. Wis., U. Lethbridge, U. South Fla., U. Tenn., others. Author: Guide to Score Study for Wind Band Conductors, 1990, Blueprint for Band, 1983, Rehearsal Handbook for Band and Orchestra Students, 1983, Heritage Americana: Civil War Brass Band Music, 1983, Pictorial History of Civil War Era Musical Instruments and Military Bands, 1985; contbr. articles to profl. jours. Mem. Coll. Band Dirs. Nat. Assn. (past pres. Eastern div.), Nat. Cath. Bandmasters Assn., World Assn. Symphonic Bands and Ensembles. Home: 13249 Osterport Dr Silver Spring MD 20906-5912 Office: Cath U Am Sch Music Washington DC 20064

GAROIAN, CHARLES RICHARD, artist, educator; b. Fresno, Calif., Nov. 7, 1943; s. Kurken Makhtesi and Satenig Suzanne (Bezdigian) G.; m. Sherrie Elyce Alexanian, Jan. 27, 1968; children: Jason Aram, Stephanie Tamar. BA in Visual Art, Calif. State U., Fresno, 1968, MA in Visual Art, 1969; PhD in Edn., Stanford U., 1984. Art instr. and art curriculum coord. Los Altos (Calif.) High Sch., 1969-86; vis. lectr. U. Wash., Seattle, summer 1977; edn. dir. Pa. State U., Palmer Mus. of Art, University Park, 1986-90, asst. dir., 1990-91; assoc. prof. art edn. Sch. Visual Arts, Pa. State U., 1991—. Exhibits include San Francisco Mus. Modern Art, 1974, Charles Garoian, San Jose Mus. Art, 1975, Rites of Sculpture, Berkeley Mus. Art, 1976, New Adventures: Time and Space, Wash. State U., 1982; contbr. articles to profl. jours. Bd. dirs. Cen. Pa. Festival of Arts, State College, 1988-90; chmn. Com. for Pub Sculpture, 1988-91. Named Tchr. of the Yr. Mountain View/Los Altos High Sch. Dist., 1976; Pa. Coun. on Arts grantee, 1986, 87, 88, 90, 91; recipient Creative Programming award Nat. U. Continuing Edn. Assn., 1990, 91. Mem. Nat. Art Edn. Assn., Coll. Art Assn. Office: Pa State Univ Sch Visual Ar 102 Visual Arts Bldg University Park PA 16802

GARREAU, JOEL (ROLAND), writer; b. Pawtucket, R.I., Sept. 21, 1948; s. Roland Joseph and Gloria (Nadeau) G.; m. Adrienne Cook, May 21, 1976; children: Simone, Evangeline. Student, U. Notre Dame, 1969. Editor and art. dir. Style section Washington Post, 1970-74, domestic correspondent chief nat. desk, 1976-79, editor Outlook section, 1980-86, sr. writer, 1987—; asst. mng. editor The Trenton (N.J.) Times, 1974-76; cons. U.S. Nuclear Regulatory Commn., Washington, U.S. Dept. Transp., Washington, Am. Mktg. Assn., N.Y.C., Coldwell Banker, L.A., Urban Land Inst., Washington, Am. Inst. Architects, Washington, Brown U., Providence, NYU, N.Y.; speaker in field. Author: The Nine Nations of North America, 1981, Edge City: Life on the New Frontier, 1991. Office: Washington Post 1150 15th St NW Washington DC 20071-0002

GARRELICK, JOEL MARC, applied scientist in acoustics, consultant; b. N.Y.C., May 20, 1941; s. Samuel J. Garrelick and Phyllis Weidenbaum; m. Renee Brosell, Dec. 23, 1963; chilren: Kevin, Jenine, Daniel. BCE, CCNY, 1963, ME, 1965; PhD, CUNY, 1969. Lectr. CCNY, 1968-69; scientist Cambridge (Mass.) Acoustical Assocs., Inc., 1969-75, prin. scientist, 1976—, pres., 1990—. Contbr. articles to profl. jours. Fellow Acoustical Soc. Am.; mem. ASCE. Office: CAA Inc 80 Sherman St Cambridge MA 02140-3504

GARRETT, JAMES WILLIAM, computer company executive; b. Corpus Christi, Tex., Dec. 5, 1946; s. George Perce and Bulah Belle (Kerrel) G.; m. Barbara Merle Moore, July 1, 1972; 1 child, Eva Christine. BS, Ohio State U., 1969. Commd. 2d lt. USAF, 1969, advanced through grades to major, 1980, ret., 1988; dir. maintenance Techno-Scis. Inc., Greenbelt, Md., 1988—; sec./treas. Val Verde Airlines, Del Rio, Tex., 1989-91. Pres. Buena Vista PTO, 1990-91. Mem. Lions. Office: Techno Scis Inc 7833 Walker Dr # 620 Greenbelt MD 20770

GARRETT, JOYCE LYNN, education educator; b. Prineville, Oreg., Oct. 17, 1946; d. James Edward and Bettye Jeanne (Forbes) G. BA, U. Oreg., 1968, MS, 1973, MA, 1981, PhD, 1982; BS, Oreg. State U., 1970. Interim tchr. Colo. Sch. Deaf and Blind, Colorado Springs, 1969; 5th, 6th grade and behavior disorders tchr. Lincoln County Schs., Newport, Oreg., 1970-76; grad. teaching fellow U. Oreg., Eugene, 1977-82; supr. spl. edn. Creswell (Oreg.) Pub. Schs., 1978-80; asst. prof. edn. Weber State Coll., Ogden, Utah, 1982-84; assoc. prof. edn. Calif. State U., Chico, 1984-90, coordinator spl. edn. programs, 1986-87; assoc. prof. edn. Gallaudet U., Washington, 1990—; dir. resource specialist tchr. tng. project Calif. State U., Chico, 1985-87; program specialist cons. Modoc County Schs., Alturas, Calif., 1984; cons. classroom mgmt. vrious local sch. dists., 1980; v.p. programs State of Calif. Tchr. Educators, 1989-90. Mem. editorial bd. SE Regional Assn. Tchr. Educators Jour., 1991—; reviewer Jour. Action in Tchr. Edn., 1989—; contbr. articles to profl. jours. Vol. Spl. Olympics, Ogden, 1982-84, Nat. Zoo. Recipient Profl. Promise award Calif. State U., Chico, 1985. Mem. NEA, ASCD, Am. Edn. Rsch. Assn. (pres. spl. interest group invitational ednl. 1989-92), Assn. Tchr. Educators (mem. nat. meetings com. 1990—, chair publicity ocm. ann. meeting planning com., bd. dirs. 1993-96), Coun. Exceptional Children (v.p. Eugene chpt. 1979-80), Assn. Retarded Citizens (v.p. 1982-84). Office: Gallaudet U Dept Edn 800 Florida Ave NE Washington DC 20002-3660

GARRETT, MARGARET LUCRETIA, psychiatrist; b. Haddonfield, N.J., Sept. 11, 1931; d. Robert Young and Margaret (Davis) G. BS in Biology, Bucknell Coll., 1952; MD, U. Pa., 1956. Lic. psychiatrist, D.C. Intern Cooper Hosp., Camden, N.J., 1956-57; resident in psychiatry Yale-New Haven (Conn.) Hosp., 1959-62; mem. staff Met. Psychiat. Group, Washington, 1967-89; pvt. practice Washington, 1989—. Fellow Am. Psychiat. Assn.; mem. AMA. Office: 2501 Calvert St NW Apt 101 Washington DC 20008-2604

GARRIGLE, WILLIAM ALOYSIUS, lawyer; b. Camden, N.J., Aug. 6, 1941; s. John Michael and Catherine Agnes (Ebeling) G.; m. Jeannette R. Regan, Aug. 15, 1965 (div.); children: Maeve Regan, Emily Way; m. Rosalind Chadwick, Feb. 17, 1984; 1 child, Susan Chadwick. BS, LaSalle Coll., 1963; LLB, Boston Coll., 1966. Cert. civil trial specialist. Assoc. Taylor, Bischoff, Neutze & Williams, Camden, 1966-67, Moss & Powell, Camden, 1967-70; ptnr. Garrigle & Palm and predecessors, Cherry Hill, N.J., 1970—. With USAR, 1959-67. Mem. ABA, N.J. State Bar Assn., Burlington County Bar Assn., Camden County Bar Assn., Internat. Assn. Ins. Csl., Def. Rsch. Inst., Fedn. of Ins. & Corp. Counsel, Trial Attys. N.J., Camden County Inn of Ct. (sr.), Moorestown Field Club (N.J.), Atlantic City Country Club (Northfield, N.J.), Downtown Club (Phila.), Tavistock Country Club (Haddonfield, N.J.), Am. Bd. Trial Advs. (adv.), Inns of Ct. (chmn. Camden chpt.). Home: 223 E Main St Moorestown NJ 08057-2905 Office: Cherry Hill Plaza Ste 204 1945 State Hwy 70 Cherry Hill NJ 08034

GARRIGUES, GEORGE LOUIS, educator, journalist; b. L.A., Apr. 8, 1932; s. Charles Harris and Beulah Mae (Dickey) G.; children from previous marriage: Lisa Gale, Michael Charles, Rica Liane; m. Wanda Lau. BA in Govt., U. Calif., Riverside, 1957; MA in Journalism, UCLA, 1970. Reporter L.A. Times, 1957-66; info. officer International Labor Office, Geneva, 1967-69; prof. Western Wash. State Coll., Bellingham, 1970-72, Univ. So. Calif., L.A., 1972-74, Univ. of the Pacific, Stockton, Calif., 1975-77, Wayne State Univ., Detroit, 1977-81; mass communication dept. chair Univ. Bridgeport, Conn., 1982-90; prof. Univ. Bridgeport, 1982-91; chair communications dept. Lincoln U., Jefferson City, Mo., 1991-92. Mem. Soc. of Profl. Journalists. Democrat.

GARRISON, ELIZABETH JANE, artist; b. Elmira, N.Y., Feb. 11, 1952. BFA, Ringling Sch. Art and Design, 1973; postgrad., Mansfield U., 1976-78; MS, Fla. State U., 1980. Exhibits include Mus. Contemporary Art, The Netherlands, Mus. Fine Arts, St. Petersburg, Fla., Renwick Gallery, The Smithsonian Inst., Washington, and others; represented in permanent collections Yale U. Art Gallery, New Haven, Conn., Kunstgewerbe Mus., Berlin, Honolulu Acad. Arts. Nat. Endowment Arts fellows, 1981, 88. Home: PO Box 6670 Ithaca NY 14851-6670

GARRITY, EDWARD RICHARD, JR., materials engineer; b. Phila., Apr. 1, 1960; s. edward R. and Roseanne (Ferrara) G. BS in Matls. Engring., Drexel U., Phila., 1983, MS in Matls. Engring., 1985, PhD in Matls. Engring., 1989. Staff rsch. engr. Los Alamos (N.Mex.) Nat. Labs., 1986; cons. in matl. engring. Cherry Hill, N.J., 1983—; pres. 4-D Prototypes, Inc., Cherry Hill, 1990—; adj. asst. prof. Drexel U., 1989—, Rutgers U., Camden, N.J., 1990—; adj. prof. Temple U., Phila., 1991—. Contbr. articles to profl. jours. Sun Oil Corp. grantee, 1981, Los Alamos Nat. Lab. grad. student fellow, 1986. Mem. AIME, ASM, The Metals Soc. of AIME, Sml. Bus. Initiative Program of SBA, Pa. Gasoline Retailers Assn., Soc. for Advancement of Matls. and Process Engring., Matls. Rsch. Soc. Office: 4D Prototypes Inc PO Box 354 Voorhees NJ 08043-0354

GARRITY, WENDELL ARTHUR, JR., federal judge; b. Worcester, Mass., June 20, 1920; s. W. Arthur and Mary B. (Kennedy) G.; m. Barbara A. Mullins, May 24, 1952; children: W. Arthur III, Charles A., Anne M. Singleton, Jean M. Garrity Kennedy. A.B., Holy Cross Coll., 1941; LL.B., Harvard U., 1946. Bar: Mass. 1946, U.S. Dist. Ct. Mass. 1948, U.S. Supreme Ct. 1954. Law clk. to presiding justice U.S. Dist. Ct. Mass., 1946-47, asst. U.S. atty., 1948-50, U.S. atty., 1961-66, judge, 1966-85, sr. judge, 1985—; ptnr. Maguire, Roche & Leen, 1950-61; lectr. in field. Contbr. articles to profl. jours. Mem. Babson Recreation Ctr., Wellesley, Mass.; treas. Dem. Party, Wellesley, 1952-55; town coord. Kennedy Congl. Campaigns, 1952-60; coord. Wis. hdqrs. Kennedy Presdl. Campaign, 1960. Sgt. U.S. Army ETO. Recipient Rabb Human Rels. award Am. Jewish Community, 1979, Roger Baldwin award Mass. CLU Found., 1986, Meml. award 16th Ann. Martin Luther Breakfast, 1986. Mem. ABA. Mass. Bar Assn., Boston Bar Assn. (v.p. 1965-66), Clover Club, Harvard Club, Knights of Malta. Democrat. Roman Catholic.

GARROTT, IDAMAE T., state senator; b. Washington, Dec. 24, 1916; married; 2 children. AB, Western Md. Coll., 1936, LLD (hon.). Mem. Md. Ho. of Dels., 1979-87, mem. ways and means com., joint com. on energy; mem. Md. State Senate, 1987—, econ. and environ. affairs com., chmn. joint com. fed. rels., chmn. adv. com. on fed.-state local rels.; vice chair Montgomery County Senators. Author: Paying Our Way, Maryland State Taxes and You, 1958. Mem. Montgomery County Coun., 1966-74, chmn. planning com., 1970-74, pres., 1971; bd. dirs. Washington Met. Area Transit Authority, 1972-74; bd. dirs. Washington Suburban Transit Commn., 1971-74, chmn., 1972; bd. dirs. Met. Washington Coun. Govts., pres., 1974, chmn. land use com., 1969-74; bd. dirs. Solid Waste Mgmt. Agy. Met. Washington, 1969-74; pres. Montgomery County Humane Soc., 1976-77; bd. dirs. Wheaton Rescue Squad, 1982-84. Recipient John Dewey award, 1982, Humanitarian award Montgomery County Humane Soc., 1983, Cert. of Appreciation Montgomery County Edn. Assn., 1984, Horn Book award, 1985, Thomas B. Cook award, 1987, Md. Assn. of Deaf award, 1987. Office: Md State Senate State House Annapolis MD 21401

GARROW, DAVID JEFFRIES, author; b. New Bedford, Mass., May 11, 1953; s. Walter and Barbara Mae (Fassett) G.; m. Susan Foster Newcomer, Dec. 18, 1984. BA, Wesleyan U., Middletown, Conn., 1975; MA, Duke U., 1978, PhD, 1981. Instr. polit. sci. Duke U., Durham, N.C., 1978-79; vis. mem. Sch. Social Sci., Inst. Advanced Study, Princeton, N.J., 1979-80; asst. prof. polit. sci. U. N.C., Chapel Hill, 1980-84; assoc. prof. polit. sci. City Coll. N.Y., CUNY Grad. Ctr., 1984-87, prof., 1987—; vis. fellow Joint Ctr. Polit. Studies, Washington, 1984; sr. advisor Eyes on the Prize: Am.'s Civil Rights Years, PBS TV documentary broadcast, 1985-90; bd. mem. Martin Luther King, Jr. Papers Project, King Ctr., Atlanta, 1985—; fellow Twentieth Century Fund, 1991—. Author: Protest at Selma: Martin Luther King and the Voting Rights Act of 1965, 1978 (Chastain award 1979), The FBI and Martin Luther King, Jr.: From "Solo" to Memphis, 1981, Bearing the Cross: Martin Luther King, Jr. and the Southern Christian Leadership Conference, 1986 (Pulitzer Prize for Biography 1987, Robert F. Kennedy book award 1987); editor: The Montgomery Bus Boycott and the Women Who Started It: The Memoir of JoAnn Gibson Robinson, 1987; co-editor: The Eyes on the Prize Civil Rights Reader, 1987, 91; contbr. articles to publs. and profl. jours. Recipient NEH grant, 1984-85, Ford Found. grant, 1979-80, Lyndon B. Johnson Found. grant, 1979-80, Eisenhower World Affairs Inst. grant, 1985-86. Mem. Authors Guild, Am. Hist. Assn., Orgn. Am. Historians, Southern Hist. Assn., Phi Beta Kappa. Democrat. Home and Office: 200 Cabrini Blvd Apt PH9 New York NY 10033-1100

GARROW, WILLIAM CASSELMAN, health care consultant; b. Grand Rapids, Mich., Nov. 24, 1946; s. Kenneth Allan and Jean (McMullen) G. BA, Kalamazoo Coll., 1968; MA in Pub. Adminstrn., Syracuse U., 1970; MBA, U. Pa., 1975. CPA, Pa.; cert. fin. planner. Asst. dean Upstate Med. Ctr./SUNY, Syracuse, 1970-73; assoc. cons. Touche Ross & Co., Phila., 1975-78; asst. dir. Presbyn.-U. Pa. Hosp., &, 1978-82; mgr. Niessan Dunlap & Pritchard, CPA's, Colmar, Pa., 1982-84, Shotz, Miller & Glusman, P.C., Phila., 1984—. Contbr. articles to profl. jours. Mem. allocations rev. com. United Way, Phila., 1975-80; treas. Phoenix House Group Home for Girls, Phila., 1981-85, Phila. Citizens for Children and Youth, 1984-86; active Montgomery County Big Bros./Big Sisters, Norristown, Pa., 1986-91. Recipient award Wharton Sch. Health Care Adminstrn. Alumni Assn., 1984. Fellow Health Care Fin. Mgmt. Assn.; mem. AICPA, Pa. Inst. CPAs, Inst. Cert. Fin. Planners, Rotary (treas. new mems. class Phila. 1984, chmn. membership devel. com. 1987-88, bd. dirs. 1989-91). Home: PO Box 346 Bryn Mawr PA 19010-0346 Office: Shotz Miller & Glusman PC 1601 Market St Fl 2400 Philadelphia PA 19103-2391

GARRUTO, RALPH MICHAEL, research biologist, educator; b. Binghamton, N.Y., Nov. 20, 1943; s. Ralph Anthony and Josephine Janet (DiMartino) G.; m. Judith Dryden Sharp, Apr. 19, 1969; children: Jessica Anne, Jason Michael, John Ralph. BS, Pa. State U., 1966, MA, 1969, PhD, 1973. Cert. in epidemiology. Postdoctoral fellow NIH, Bethesda, Md., 1972-73, staff/sr. staff fellow, 1973-78, sr./supervisory rsch. biologist, 1978—; adj. prof. med. genetics U. South Ala. Coll. Medicine, Mobile, 1982—; adj. sr. scientist biol. anthropology Pa. State U., University Park, 1985—; founding mem. bd. trustees Nat. Mus. Health and Medicine Found., Washington, 1989-91; exec. sec. Commn. on Aging and the Aged, Zagreb, Yugoslavia, 1985-89; cons. Internat. ALS-MND Rsch. Found., Termine, Switzerland, 1991—. Co-editor: Biological Anthropology and Aging: An Emerging Synthesis, 1992, Dermatoglyphics: Science in Transition, 1991; contbr. articles to profl. jours.; patents pending for biol. agts. Recipient Merit award NIH, 1991, Spl. Achievement award, 1990, Commendation for Rsch., Guam Legislature, 1987; Wenner-Gren Found. leadership grantee, 1986; Alumni fellow Pa. State U., 1987. Fellow Am. Coll. Epidemiology, Am. Dermatoglyphics Assn. (sec.-treas. 1981-82, pres. 1987-89), Human Biology Coun. (exec. com. 1991—); mem. Soc. for Neurosci., World Fedn. Neurology (rsch. com. on neuroepidemiology). Office: NIH Bldg 36 Rm 5B-21 Bethesda MD 20892

GARTEL, LAURENCE MAURY, video computer photographer, artist; b. N.Y.C., June 5, 1956; s. Henry and Carol (Rosenblum) G. BFA, Sch. Visual Arts, 1977. Computer cover artist Computer Design mag., Littleton, Mass., 1981-82; instr. creative photography workshop Sch. Visual Arts, N.Y.C., 1978-83; computer cover illustrator Nikkei Computer mag., Tokyo, 1982, 83, 84, 85; computer illustrator Absolut Gartel for Absolut Vodka, Zoommag, 1986, School Arts mag., New Orleans, 1986; prof. computer graphics Sch. Visual Arts, N.Y.C., 1983—; judge Pan Pacific Computer Art Competition, Melbourne, Australia, 1985; speaker Computer Electronic Publ. Show, Chgo., 1990. Exhibits include Nikon House Gallery, N.Y.C., 1980, ACM Siggraph, Detroit, 1983, San Francisco, 1985, Dallas, 1986, computer art Mus. Art U. Okla., Norman, 1982, Long Beach Mus. Art (Calif.), 1983, Princeton U. Art Mus., 1983, Bronx Mus. Art, N.Y., 1987-88, Fine Arts Mus. of L.I., N.Y., 1988 and touring, Guild Hall Mus., East Hampton, N.Y., 1989, Joan Whitney Payson Gallery, Maine, 1989, U. So. Colo., 1990, N.Y. Telephone curated by Mus. of Modern Art, 1990, Gallery Internat., N.Y., 1990; art work in lending collection Mus. Modern Art, N.Y.C., 1981, Bibliotheque Nationale, Paris, 1985, Long Beach (Calif.) Mus., 1986, Norton Gallery Art, West Palm Beach, Fla., 1991, Ringling Sch. Art & Design, Sarasota, Fla., 1992; author: Laurence M. Gartel: A Cybernetic Romance, 1989; Musee Francais De la Photographie Bievres, France, 1992; contbr. articles to profl. jours. Recipient N.J. Art Dirs. Club award, 1985; Exptl. TV Ctr. grantee, 1979-90, Polaroid Corp. grantee, 1983-89, Intermedia Art Center grantee, 1984, Film and Video Arts residency Grantee, 1987, 89. Address: 270-16B Grand Central Pkwy Floral Park NY 11005

GARTENBERG, SEYMOUR LEE, retired recording company executive; b. N.Y.C., May 27, 1931; s. Morris and Anna (Banner) G.; m. Anna Stassi, Feb. 18, 1956; children: Leslie, Karen, Mark. BBA cum laude, CCNY, 1952. Asst. contr. Finlay Straus, Inc., N.Y.C., 1950-56; contr. Tappin's Inc., Newark, 1956; sr. v.p. Columbia House divsn. CBS, N.Y.C., 1956-65; exec. v.p. Columbia Records divsn. CBS, N.Y.C., 1967-73, v.p. fin., 1965-67; pres. CBS Toys Div., Cranbury, N.J., 1973-78; v.p. CBS/Columbia Group, N.Y.C., 1978—; sr. group v.p. CBS Records Group, 1979-87; exec. v.p. CBS Records Inc., 1987-91; ret., 1991. V.p., bd. dirs. City Coll. Fund; treas., bd. dirs. T.J. Martell Found. Leukemia, Cancer and AIDS Rsch. Mem. Inst. of Mgmt. Accts., Am. Mgmt. Assn., Mill Island Civic Assn., Am. Arbitration Assn. (panel mem.).

GARTH, JOHN CAMPBELL, physicist, researcher; b. N.Y.C., Sept. 26, 1934; s. Robert Campbell and Sarah Souther (Lingle) G.; m. Nancy Carolyn McCandless, Aug. 20, 1960; children: Lee McCandless, Lynn Virginia. BS in Engring., Princeton U., 1956; MS in Physics, U. Ill., 1958, PhD in Physics, 1965. Teaching asst. U. Ill., Urbana, 1956-59, NSF coop. fellow, 1959-60, rsch. asst., 1960-64; asst. prof. physics Worcester (Mass.) Poly. Inst., 1964-67; rsch. physicist Air Force Cambridge Rsch. Lab., Hanscom AFB, Mass., 1967-76; solid state physicist Rome Air Devel. Ctr. (named changed to Rome Lab. 1990), Hanscom AFB, 1976-91, Phillips Lab., Hanscom AFB, 1991—; presenter in field to profl. socs., symposia, confs., 1970—. Contbr. over 50 articles to sci. jours. Recipient Sci. Achievement award Rome Lab., 1976, Tech. Achievement award, 1981. Mem. IEEE (reviewer Conf. on Nuclear and Space Radiation Effects 1980-90), ASTM (E10.07 standards com. 1984—), Am. Phys. Soc., Am. Nuclear Soc. (session chmn. methods for neutral- and charged particles transport 1984, alt. session chmn. 1986). Evangelical. Home: 23 Morningside Ln Lincoln MA 01773-2703 Office: Phillips Lab PL/VTER Hanscom AFB MA 01731

GARTHOFF, RAYMOND LEONARD, diplomat, diplomatic historian and researcher; b. Cairo, Mar. 26, 1929; came to U.S., 1929; s. Arnold Alexander and Margaret Louise (Frank) G.; m. Vera Alexandrovna Vasilieva, Sept. 16, 1950; 1 child, Alexander Raymond. AB, Princeton U., 1948; MA, Yale U., 1949, PhD, 1951. Mem. rsch. staff RAND Corp., Washington, 1950-57; estimates officer CIA, Washington, 1957-61; with U.S. Dept. of State, Washington, 1961-79, ambassador, 1977-79; sr. fellow Brookings Instn., Washington, 1980—; mem. Am. Com. on U.S.-Soviet Rels., Coun. on Fgn. Rels. Author: Detente and Confrontation, 1985, Deterrence and Revolution in Soviet Military Doctrine, 1990, and 11 other books and monographs; editor, co-author, 55 books; contbr. articles to profl. jours. Recipient Arthur S. Flemming award Jaycees, 1965. Mem. Am. Assn. for the Advancement of Slavic Studies (coun. on fgn. rels.), Am. Assn. for the Promotion of Bulgarian Culture (hon chmn. 1989—), Soc. for Historians of Am. Fgn. Rels., Internat. Inst. for Strategic Studies, Acad. Polit. Sci., Assn. Diplomate Studies. Home: 2128 Bancroft Pl NW Washington DC 20008-4020 Office: Brookings Instn 1775 Massachusetts Ave NW Washington DC 20036-2188

GARVEY, MICHAEL STEVEN, veterinarian, educator; b. Chgo., Dec. 5, 1950; s. Charles Anthony and Jane O. G. BS in Vet. Medicine, U. Ill., 1972, DVM, 1974; cert. internship, The Animal Med. Ctr., N.Y.C., 1976, cert. med. residency, 1978; cert. advanced mgmt. program, Wharton Sch., U. Pa., 1992. Diplomate Am. Coll. Vet. Internal Medicine, Am. Coll Vet. Emergency and Critical Care. Staff veterinarian Bevlab Vet. Hosp., Blue Island, Ill., 1974-75; intern in medicine and surgery The Animal Med. Ctr., N.Y.C., 1975-76, resident in medicine, 1976-78; staff internist Bevlab Vet. Hosp., Blue Island, 1978-81; dir. medicine The Animal Med. Ctr., N.Y.C., 1981-83; chmn. dept. medicine The Animal Ctr., N.Y.C., 1983—; cons. Office of Animal Care, U. Chgo. Sch. Medicine, 1979—, Nat. Bd. Vet. Examiners, Schaumburg, Ill., 1981—, Mercy Coll. Animal Health Tech.,

Dobbs Ferry, N.Y., 1984—, Reader's Digest and Good Housekeeping mags., N.Y.C., 1984—; tech. cons. Sesame St., N.Y.C., 1990—; adv. bd. Profl. Examination Svc., N.Y.C., 1981—, vice-chmn., 1991—; vet. adv. panel Alpo Pet Foods, Inc., Allentown, Pa.,1981—; adj. prof. vet. medicine Tex. A&M U., 1986—; faculty assoc. U. Maine Animal Health Tech., Orono, 1976-78. Author: Animal Medical Center Hospital Formulary, 1990; author: (with others) Keeping Your Dog Healthy, 1985, Canine Emergencies, 1985, Symptoms of Illness in Dogs, 1985, Infectious and Contagious Diseases of Dogs, 1985, Feline Emergencies, 1985, Symptoms of Illness in Cats, 1985, Infectious and Contagious Diseases of Cats, 1985, Feeding the Sick Cat, 1989; editor: Canine Allergic Inhalant Dermatitis, 1982; cons. editor Small Animal Medicine, 1990; editorial review bd. Jour. of Am. Animal Hosp. Assn., 1985-90; contbr. articles to profl. jours. Dir. Blue Island Community Theatre, 1974-75, 78-80; treas. 440 E. 2d St. Owners' Corp., N.Y.C., 1985—. Mem. AVMA (del. 1990-91), Am. Animal Hosp. Assn., Am. Assn. Vet. Clinicians (pres. 1988-89, Pres. Gavel award 1989), Am. Coll. Vet. Emergency Critical Care, Am. Coll. Vet. Internal Medicine, Acad. Vet. Cardiology, N.Y. State Vet. Med. Soc., Soc. Comparative Endocrinology, Vet. Emergency Critical Care Soc., Vet. Med. Assn. N.Y.C. (Outstanding Svc. award 1984), Soc. Internat. Vet. Symposia (bd. dirs. 1990-92, pres. 1992—). Republican. Roman Catholic. Home: 440 E 62nd St Apt 2B New York NY 10021 Office: The Animal Med Ctr 510 E 62nd St New York NY 10021

GARVEY, RENEE J., director of admissions; b. Scranton, Pa., Jan. 30, 1964; d. Shirley Ann (Duffy) G. AS, Lackawanna Jr. Coll., Scranton, Pa., 1983; BS, Marywood Coll., Scranton, Pa., 1986; postgrad., U. Scranton, 1987—. Bus. instr. Northeast Inst., Scranton, Pa., 1986-88; community dir. March of Dimes, Dunmore, Pa., 1988-90; dir. of admissions Lackawanna Jr. Coll., Scranton, Pa., 1990—; textbook critic, Internat. Corr. Schs., Scranton, Pa., 1990—. Bd. dirs. Act 101 Program, NIE&LJC, 1986—; vol. Am. Heart Assn., Scranton, Pa., 1990, WVIA-TV, Pittston, Pa., 1990. Recipient full scholarship Lackawanna Jr. Coll., Scranton, Pa., 1981, Faculty of Yr. Northeast Inst., Scranton, Pa., 1988, Fundraising Records, March of Dimes, Dunmore, Pa., 1989; named The Natl. Dean's List, Marywood Coll., Scranton, Pa., 1985. Mem. Pa. Counselors Assn., Natl. Orgn. Admission Dirs. and Registrars, Phi Beta Lambda, Kappa Gamma Pi. Roman Catholic. Home: 1321 Brook St Scranton PA 18505-3907 Office: Lackawanna Jr College 901 Prospect Ave Scranton PA 18505-1870

GARVEY, RICHARD ANTHONY, lawyer; b. N.Y.C., Jan. 10, 1950; s. James Joseph Garvey and Janet Mary (Mooney) Rowse. AB, Boston Coll., 1972; JD, Harvard U., 1975. Bar: N.Y. 1976. Assoc. Simpson Thacher & Bartlett, N.Y.C., 1975-82, ptnr., 1982—. Mem. ABA, N.Y. State Bar Assn., Assn. Bar City N.Y., Phi Beta Kappa. Home: 35 Aviemore Dr New Rochelle NY 10804-4716 Office: Simpson Thacher & Bartlett 425 Lexington Ave New York NY 10017-3903

GARVIN, C(LARENCE) ALEXANDER, JR., economics educator; b. Clarksville, Tenn., Sept. 1, 1921; s. Clarence Alexander and Lena (Medcalf) G.; m. Alice Esther Hand, Sept. 4, 1970. BA in English, U. Tenn., 1942, PhD in Econs., 1973; MA in Internat. Rels., U. Chgo., 1948; MA in Math., U. Pitts., 1983. Adj. instr. mktg. Austin Peay State U., Clarksville, 1960-61; lab. instr. acctg. Vanderbilt U., Nashville, 1964-65; grad. teaching asst. in econs. U. Tenn., Knoxville, 1966-69; assoc. prof. econs. Indiana U. Pa., 1969-75, prof., 1975—; ptnr., gen. mgr. Garvin Furniture Co., Clarksville, 1948-62; mem. senate Indiana U. Pa., 1976-78, chmn. senate subcom. for faculty rsch., 1976-78; vis. fellow Sch. Econs. and Social Studies, U. East Anglia, Norwich, Eng., 1979-80; vis. prof. Am. U. in Cairo, 1984-86; presenter in field. Contbr. articles to profl. jours. Bd. dirs. Indiana U. Pa. Found., chmn. investment com., 1978-81; vestryman Trinity Episcopal Ch., Clarksville, 1961-62; vestryman Christ Episcopal Ch., Indiana, 1975-78, sr. warden, 1977-78, del. to dist. and diocesan conv., 1978-82; trustee Episcopal Diocese Pitts., 1978-81; vestryman St. Peter's Episcopal Ch., Blairsville, Pa., 1987-90, jr. warden, 1989-90, sr. warden, 1991—; Episcopal lay reader and minister, 1977—. Lt. USNR, 1942-46. Scholar Vanderbilt U., 1964-65. Mem. AAUP (pres. Indiana chpt. 1975-76), Am. Econ. Assn., Am. Math. Assn., Royal Econ. Soc., Western Econ. Assn., Ea. Econ. Assn. (area rep. 1974-78), Atlantic Econ. Soc. (exec. com. 1990—), Pa. Econ. Assn. (bd. dirs., sec.-treas. 1973-78), Omicron Delta Epsilon, Beta Gamma Sigma. Home: 293 N 7th St Indiana PA 15701-1809 Office: Indiana U Pa Dept Econs Indiana PA 15701

GARVIN, FLORENCE WARD, chemicals and petroleum company executive; b. Ft. Sam Houston, Tex., Oct. 6, 1928; d. Edward Joseph and Florence Emily (Bock) Ward; B.A., Our Lady of Lake U., San Antonio, 1949; postgrad. Trinity U., San Antonio, 1949-50; m. Sheldon R. Rappaport, Mar. 2, 1950 (div. July 1969); children—Bruce Ward, Lisa Lynn; m. 2d, Stefan J. Garvin, Oct. 3, 1981. Co-founder, asst. to pres. Pathway Sch., Norristown, Pa., 1961-68; adminstrv. dir. Neurosurg. Clinic for Children, Media, Pa., 1968-70; v.p. for devel. Vanguard Schs., Haverford, Pa., 1970-72; asst. to pres. Elwyn (Pa.) Inst., 1972-75; pvt. practice mgmt. cons., Media, 1976-78; cons. employee relations dept. E.I. DuPont de Nemours & Co., Inc., Wilmington, Del., 1978-85, sr. bus. assoc. internat. dept., 1985-89, mgr. bus. rels. devel., 1989-90, mgr. internat. human resources devel. human resources dept., 1990—. Pres. bd. dirs. Montgomery County Mental Health Clinics, 1965-68; bd. dirs. Phila. United Fund, 1969-72; bd. mgrs., sec. Garrett-Williamson Found., 1973-85; bd. dirs. Mary Campbell Center, Wilmington, 1978-81, trustee Wilmington Coll., 1981—; trustee Curtis Inst. Music, 1985-92. Home: 2 Yarmouth Ln Media PA 19063-4327 Office: DuPont Co. Bldg 708 Crp Wilmington DE 19898

GARWOOD, WILLIAM EVERETT, chemist researcher; b. Kirkwood, N.J., Oct. 25, 1919; s. Everett and Ethel Mary (Horner) G.; m. Betty Marie Spangberg, June 19, 1946; children: John Ernest, Christine Louise, Deborah Ann. BA in Chemistry, U. N.C., 1942; postgrad., Temple U., 1947-54. Rsch. scientist Mobil R & D Corp., Paulsboro, N.J., 1942-87; cons. Mobil R & D Corp., Paulsboro, 1987—; vis. scientist U. Ill., 1969; adj. prof. Glassboro (N.J.) State Coll., 1990—. Guest lectr.; author book; 112 patents in field; contbr. 27 articles to profl. jours. With USN, 1944-46. Mem. Am. Chem. Soc. (chmn. South Jersey sect. 1960), Phila. Catalysis Club, Rotary. Republican. Methodist. Office: Mobil R & D Corp Billingsport Rd Paulsboro NJ 08066-1003

GARY, NANCY ELIZABETH, nephrologist, academic administrator; b. N.Y.C., Mar. 4, 1937; d. Walter Joseph and Charlotte Elizabeth (Sayer) G. BS, Springfield (Mass.) Coll., 1958; MD, Med. Coll. Pa., 1962. Diplomate Am. Bd. Internal Medicine, Am. Bd. Nephrology. Resident Nassau County Med. Ctr., East Meadow, N.Y., 1962-64; resident St. Vincent's Hosp. and Med. Ctr., N.Y.C., 1964-65, chief renal sect., 1967-74; fellow in nephrology Georgetown U. Med. Ctr., Washington, 1965-67; instr. medicine NYU Sch. Medicine, N.Y.C., 1968-74; asst. prof. U. Medicine and Dentistry of N.J.-Rutgers Med. Sch., Piscataway, 1974-76, assoc. prof., 1976-81, prof., 1981-88, assoc. dean, 1981-87, exec. assoc. dean, 1987-88; dean Albany (N.Y.) Med. Coll., 1988-90; sr. med. adv. to adminstr. health care financing HHS, Washington, 1990-92; clin. prof. medicine George Washington U. Sch. Medicine, 1991—; prof. medicine, exec. v.p., dean Sch. Medicine Uniformed Svcs. U. Health Scis., Bethesda, Md., 1992—. Contbr. chpts. to books, articles to profl. jours. Robert Wood Johnson Health Policy fellow Nat. Acad. Sci. Inst. Medicine, 1987-88. Fellow ACP; mem. Assn. Am. Med. Colls. (coun. deans), AMA, Am. Soc. Nephrology, Alpha Omega Alpha. Office: Uniformed Svs U Health Scis Deans Office Sch Medicine 4301 Jone Bridge Rd Bethesda MD 20814-4799

GARZILLO, MARCELLO JOSEPH, construction and recording industry executive; b. Plainfield, N.J., Oct. 31, 1932; s. Anthony Frank and Rosemarie Louise (Guerino) G.; m. Alice Grace Fellows, Sept. 28, 1956; children: Mark, Steven, Paul, Cindy, Daniel, Laura, Matthew, Andrew, Keren, James. Student, Baylor U., 1955. Ptnr. M and A Builders, North Plainfield, N.J., 1956-76; owner, pres. Ambassador Constrn., Neshanic Station, N.J., 1976—, Marcello Records Internat., Neshanic Station, 1982—, MGG Music, Neshanic Station, 1982—, Stasia Music, Neshanic Station, 1982—. With U.S. Army, 1954-56. Mem. Grad. Club (sec. 1985-86). Home and Office: Ambassador Constrn/ Marcello Records Internat PO Box 550 Neshanic Station NJ 08853-0550

GASCHO, JOSEPH ALVIN, physician; b. Grand Island, Nebr., Feb. 20, 1947; s. Alvin and Cora Irene (Garber) G.; m. Barbara Sue Brunk, July 27, 1968; children: Joseph Alvin II, Susan Loring. BA in Natural Sci., Ea. Mennonite Coll., 1968; MD, U. Va., 1973. Diplomate Am. Internal Medicine, Am. Bd. Cardiovascular Disease. Intern U. Va., Charlottesville, 1973-74, resident in medicine, 1974-76, fellow in cardiology, 1976-77; fellow in cardiology U. Iowa, 1977-80; asst. prof. medicine U. Va. Sch. Medicine, Charlottesville, 1980-84, assoc. prof. medicine, 1984-86; assoc. prof. medicine Pa. State U. Coll. Medicine, Hershey, 1986—; dir. cardiology fellowship tng. program Pa. State U. Sch. Medicine, 1987—. Contbr. articles to profl. jours., books, monographs, publs. Chmn. local chpt. Am. Heart Assn., Charlottesville, 1984-85. Fellow Am. Coll. Cardiology, Am. Coll. Physicians; mem. Am. Heart Assn., Am. Fedn. Clin. Rsch., Am. Coll. Chest Physicians, Pi Mu Epsilon. Mennonite. Office: Hershey Med Ctr Hershey PA 17033

GASH, IRA ARNOLD, psychologist, educator; b. Newark, Nov. 19, 1930; s. Charles H. and Lillian (Shwam) G.; m. Sondra Regina Stetin, Mar. 30, 1958; children: Lauren Beth, Amy Leah. BA, NYU, 1952; MA, Columbia U., 1954, profl. diploma, 1958; PhD, Temple U., 1966. Rehab. counselor N.J. Rehab. Commn., Newark, 1956-59; project dir. Workman's Compensation Rehab., Trenton, N.J., 1959-60; psychologist Stevens Inst., Hoboken, N.J., 1965-69, Dept VA, Lyons, N.J., 1966-90; ind. cons. New Providence, N.J., 1968—; attending psychologist Essex County Guidance Ctr., East Orange, N.J., 1972-82; adj. faculty Seton Hall U., South Orange, 1990—; instr. Fairleigh Dickinson U., Rutherford, N.J., 1967-70; adj. lectr. Rutgers U., New Brunswick, N.J., 1968-70. Mem. Berkeley Heights (N.J.) Bd. Health; bd. dirs. Nova Psi, 1988-90. With U.S. Army, 1954-56. Mm. AACD, APA, Am. Bd. Profl. Disability Cons., Nat. Career Devel. Assn., Am. Rehab. Counselors Assn., N.J. Profl. Counselors Assn. Home: 82 Martins Ln Berkeley Heights NJ 07922-1713 Office: 29 South St New Providence NJ 07974-1996

GASINK, WARREN ALFRED, speech communication educator; b. Sioux City, Iowa, Sept. 1, 1927; s. George A. and Maud (Hatter) G.; children: Roxanne L. Cope, John A. Gasink. BA, Morningside Coll., 1953; MA, U. So. Calif., 1955; postgrad., UCLA, 1958-59. Educator Long Beach (Calif.) Community Coll., 1954-55, San Gabriel (Calif.) High Sch., 1956-58, Portland (Oreg.) State Coll., 1959-61, DuPont High Sch., Jacksonville, Fla., 1961-62, U. Maine, Orono, 1963-65; prof. speech communication East Stroudsburg (Pa.) U., 1965-91. With USN, 1945-48, USNR, 1950-51. Recipient Outstanding Leadership award Nat. Multiple Sclerosis Soc., 1990, also numerous forensic awards. Democrat. Methodist. Home: 61 Buttonwood Ct East Stroudsburg PA 18301

GASIOR, MICHAEL, financial executive; b. Middletown, Conn., July 8, 1960; s. Frederick and Barbara Jean (Zdankowski) G. BS, U. So. Calif., 1982; MBA, UCLA, 1984. Fin. cons. Shearson Lehman Bros., N.Y.C., 1984-86; v.p. Tucker Anthony and R.L. Day, Hartford, Conn., 1986-88; nat. mktg. dir. Barclays Bus. Credit, Hartford, 1989; pres. Am. Fin. Svcs., Middletown, Conn., 1989—. Author 7 textbooks on securities and markets, 1987-92. Tax commr. City of Middletown, 1987—. Mem. Nat. Assn. Security Dealers, Ins. Acctg. and Systems Assn., N.Y. Stock Exch. Republican. Roman Catholic. Office: Am Fin Svcs PO Box 959 Hartford CT 06143-0959

GASKIN, MARY, educational administrator; b. Mobile, Ala., June 16, 1925; d. Andrew and Hattie (Fornis) Burroughs; m. Leonard O. Gaskin, Dec. 10, 1951; children: Leonard Jr., Poppy. BA magna cum laude, Bklyn. Coll., 1971; MA, Columbia Ul, 1973; profl. diploma, St. John's U., Queens, N.Y., 1975. Tchr. blind N.Y.C. Pub. Schs., Bklyn., 1970-76, asst. dir., 1976-79, dir., 1979—; cons. New Orleans Pub. Schs., 1987, Anti-Defamation League B'nai B'rith, N.Y.C., 1989, Ctr. for Vocat. Edn., Akron, Ohio, 1980; adj. prof. NYU, 1984—. Editor curriculum documents: Occupational Education, 1991. Columbia U. scholar, 1988. Mem. Am. Vocat. Assn., Adminstrv. Women in Edn. Office: NYC Pub Schs 35-01 Union St Flushing NY 11354

GASQUE, WOODROW WARD, religious educator; b. Conway, S.C., Oct. 7, 1939; s. Claude Jackson and Catherine (Ward) G.; m. Laurel Sandfor, Aug. 25, 1961; 1 child, Catherine Michelle. BA, Wheaton (Ill.) Coll., 1960; BD, Fuller Theol. Sem., 1964, MTh, 1965; PhD, Manchester U., 1969. Asst. prof. Regent Coll., Vancouver, B.C., 1969-72; assoc. prof. Regent Coll., Vancouver, 1972-75, prof., 1975-90, v.p., prof., 1982-87; pres., prof. New Coll. Berkeley, Calif., 1979-82; provost, prof. Ea. Coll., Saint Davids, Pa., 1990—; adj. prof. Regent Coll., Vancouver, 1990—; vis. scholar Univ. de Lausanne, 1975-76, Princeton Theol. Sem., 1988-89; J. Omar Good Vis. Disting. prof. Juniata Coll., Huntingdon, Pa., 1987-88. Author: Sir William M. Ramsay, 1966, History of Interpretion Acts of Apostles, 1975, 90; co-editor: (20 vols.) New Internat. Greek Text Commentary Series, 1970; contbr. over 150 articles to profl. jours. Named Rsch. scholar Eahrhardt Found., Ann Arbor, 1988. Fellow Inst. Bibl. Rsch., Oxford Ctr. for Mission Studies; mem. Am. Coun. Higher Edn., Am. Acad. Religion, Soc. Bibl. Lit., Can. Soc. Bibl. Lit., Conf. on Faith and History, Tyndale Fellowship for Bibl. Rsch. Plymouth Brethren. Home: 1300 Eagle Rd Wayne PA 19087-3617 Office: Eastern Coll Saint Davids PA 19087

GASSER, JOHN RICHARD, food services executive; b. Buffalo, Sept. 22, 1941; s. Harold R. and Doris R. (Hopkins) G.; m. Beverley Blythe, June 21, 1965 (div. May 1977); children: John C., Bryce C., Elizabeth J.; m. Barbara D. Matteo, Nov. 4, 1977. EdB, SUNY, Buffalo, 1966. Various positions Buffalo and St. John, U.S. Virgin Islands, 1966-72; owner, chef The Sudbury Inn, Bethel, Maine, 1972-79; owner, broker Robert Crane Real Estate Assocs., Bethel, 1979-82; sales rep. John Sexton & Co., Orlando, Fla., 1982-83; mktg. assoc. Sysco of Cen. Fla., Ocoee, Fla., 1983-87; mgr. condo opers. Sunday River Ski Resort, Bethel; mktg. assoc. Maine Sysco, Newport, 1988-90; dir. N.E. Regional Tng. Sysco, Norton, Mass., 1990—. Mem. Bethel Rotary Club (charter), Elks Club. Republican. Home: 8 Pine St Norton MA 02766

GAST, DWIGHT V., writer, critic; b. Toledo, Apr. 23, 1951; s. Dwight and Natalie (Kowaleski) G. Student, U. Ill., 1968-71; BA, New Sch. for Social Research, N.Y.C., 1979, postgrad., 1979; postgrad., Villa Schifanoia, Florence, Italy, 1983. Playwright, dir., artist in residence Ill. Arts Council, Chgo., 1971-72; freelance writer Italy, 1978—; stringer AP and various mags., Florence, 1980-84. Author: Florence/Venice/Milan Access, 1991; editor Italy Haly mag., 1984, Diversion mag., 1985-87; contbr. to numerous books and travel guides; contbr. articles to popular and specialized mags. and newspapers; translator several books. Mem. Am. Soc. Journalists and Authors, Am. Soc. Mag. Photographers, Assn. Internat. Critiques Art, Nat. Book Critics Circle, Nat. Writers Union, N.Y. Travel Writers Assn., Soc. Am. Travel Writers. Home and Office: 265 Lafayette St New York NY 10012-4018

GASTER, DAVID ROBERT, management consultant, author; b. Oxford, Eng., Mar. 11, 1946; came to U.S., 1980; s. Benjamin Herman and Olga (Sinkko) G.; m. Leora S. Segal, July 27, 1979; children: Talia Elizabeth, Michael Andrew Shelley. Student, Poly. East London, 1990. Cert. airline transport pilot. Sales mgr. BG Plant Ltd., Oxford, 1967-69, sales dir., 1969-72; mng. dir. Aero Africa Svcs. Ltd., Nairobi, Kenya, 1972-77; sales dir. D & L Universal Ltd., Jersey, Eng., 1977-80; sr. trainer Grinder, De Lozier & Assocs., Santa Cruz, Calif., 1980-85; mng. dir. Pace Ltd., Henley-on-Thames, Eng., 1985-87, chmn., 1987-90; sr. cons. East West Cons., Lafayette, Calif., 1991—, Internat. Inst. for Learning, N.Y.C., 1991—; chmn. Pace Personal Devel., London, 1989—. Co-author: New Traditions in Business, 1991; also articles. Fellow Inst. Dirs.; mem. Inst. Mgmt. Cons., Brit. Assn. Aviation Cons., European Found. for Mgmt. devel., Brit.-Am. C. of C., Orgn. Devel. Network. Office: Internat Inst for Learning 110 E 59th St 6th Fl New York NY 10022

GASTON, DAVID MARK, investment advisor; b. Urbana, Ind., June 27, 1938; s. Russell Wilson and Lena Naomi (Herriman) G. BS, Johns Hopkins U., 1971; MBA, Drexel U., 1978. Chartered fin. analyst. Asst. trust officer Union Trust Co., Balt., 1963-67; asst. sec. Schroder Naess & Thomas, Balt., 1967-72; asst. treas. First Pa. Bank, Phila., 1972-76; asst. v.p. U.S. Trust Co., N.Y.C., 1976-81; v.p. Irving Trust Co., N.Y.C., 1981-86; pres. Gaston Capital Mgmt., Inc., N.Y.C., 1986—; trustee Clementine Lockwood Peterson Trust, 1992—. Dir. Bklyn. Philharm. Symphony Orch., 1981—. Office: Gaston Capital Mgmt Inc 82 Wall St Ste 1105 New York NY 10005-3682

GASTWIRTH, GLENN BARRY, association executive; b. N.Y.C., Sept. 18, 1946; s. Milton and Janette (Wasserman) G.; m. Joy Ann Binstock, Nov. 29, 1969; children: Sara Beth, Bradley Aaron. BA, Ohio State U., 1968; postgrad., NYU, 1968-69; Dr.Podiatric Medicine, N.Y. Coll. Podiatric Medicine, N.Y.C., 1974. Diplomate Am. Bd. Podiatric Surgery. Pvt.. practice podiatry Southgate, Mich., 1975-86, Tri-County Family Podiatrists, Pontiac, Mich., 1979-86; dir. sci. affairs Am. Podiatric Med. Assn., Bethesda, Md., 1986=92, dep. exec. dir., 1992—; editor-in-chief Jour. Am. Podiatric Med. Assn., 1989-91; exec. editor, 1991—. Pres. Cold Spring Sch. PTA, Potomac, Md., 1988-90. NIH fellow, 1968-69; N.Y.C. Dept. Pub. Health fellow, 1970. Fellow Am. Coll. Foot Surgeons, Am. Coll. Podiatric Med. Rev. (sec. 1990—); mem. Mich. Podiatric Med. Assn. (pres. 1981-82, Legion of Merit 1982), Am. Pub. Health Assn. (sect. council mem. 1972-74), Am. Diabetes Assn., Am. Podiatric Med. Assn. (ho. of dels. 1973-74, 80-86). Home: 12401 Willow Green Ct Rockville MD 20854-3044 Office: Am Podiatric Med Assn 9312 Old Georgetown Rd Bethesda MD 20814-1646

GATELY, MAURICE KENT, research immunologist; b. Omaha, Feb. 3, 1946; s. Harold Stephen and Alys Marie (Witt) G.; m. Celia Lin, July 8, 1972; children: Lynn Christine, Mark Stephen. BA, Johns Hopkins U., 1968, PhD in Microbiology, 1974, MD, 1975. Resident in pediatrics St. Louis Children's Hosp., 1975-76; rsch. fellow in pathology Harvard Med. Sch., Boston, 1976-79; sr. staff fellow NIH, Bethesda, Md., 1979-83; sr. scientist Hoffmann-La Roche, Inc., Nutley, N.J., 1983-85, rsch. investigator, 1985-88, rsch. leader, 1988—; ad hoc mem. contracts rev. com. Nat. Cancer Inst., Bethesda, 1982-83. Contbr. chpts. to books; contbr. articles to Sci., Jour. Immunology, Cell Immunology, Procs. Nat. Acad. Sci., others. Pres. Montville (N.J.) Soccer Assn., 1988-89. Helen Hay Whitney Found. fellow, 1976-79. Mem. AAAS, Am. Assn. Immunologists, N.Y. Acad. Scis. Office: Immunopharmacology Dept Hoffmann La Roche Inc 340 Kingsland St Nutley NJ 07110-1199

GATELY, ROBERT FRANCIS, civil engineer; b. Boston, Apr. 14, 1947; s. Francis Henry and Lillian Grace (Guida) G.; m. Dorothy Patricia Scahill, Oct. 10, 1975. BS, Northeastern U., Boston, 1975; MBA, Northeastern U., 1992. Registered profl. engr., Mass., Maine, R.I. Mem. Planning Bd., Hopedale, Mass., 1980—; clk. Cen. Mass. Regional Planning Commn., Worcester, 1984—; corp. mem. U.S.S. Mass. Meml. Commn., Fall River, 1986—. With USAF, 1966-69, Vietnam. Commendation medal USAF, 1969. Mem. Boston Soc. Civl Engrs., Mass. Soc. Profl. Engrs., Nat. Soc. Profl. Engrs., Am. Soc. Civil Engrs., Water Polution Control Fedn. (Alexandria, Va.), Boston Computer Soc. Republican. Roman Catholic. Home: 115 Dutcher St Hopedale MA 01747-1006 Office: Fay Spofford and Thorndike 191 Spring St PO Box 9117 Lexington MA 02173-9117

GATES, EARL DWIGHT, secondary education educator, consultant; b. Binghamton, N.Y., July 28, 1945; s. Dwight Mert and Cecile Viola (Fisk) G.; m. Shirley Mae Fonda, Jan. 28, 1968; children: Kimberly Anne, Timothy Earl, Susan Renee. AAS, SUNY, Canton, 1966; BS, SUNY, Oswego, 1977, MS, 1982. With USN, 1967-77, advanced through grades to E7, 1984; with USNR, 1978—; tchr. Madrid (N.Y.) Waddington High Sch., 1977-79, Greece Cen. Sch., Rochester, N.Y., 1979—, Hoover Drive Mid. Sch., Rochester; cons. Kevin Electronics, Plainview, N.Y., 1990—, Delmar Publishers, Albany, N.Y., 1986—; curriculum devel. N.Y. State Edn. Dept., Albany, 1984-87. Author: Introduction to Electronics, 1987, 91. Mem. Am. Vocat. Assn., Internat. Tech. Edn. Assn. (coun. supr., conf. chmn. 1989—), Internat. Graphic Arts Edn. Assn., N.Y. State Tech. Edn. Assn., Adminstrs. Vocat. Edn. Assn, Monroe County Tech. Edn. Assn. (sec. 1979-82), Rotary (vol. 1990—). Methodist.

GATES, RICHARD WADE, education educator; b. Buffalo, Dec. 21, 1934; s. Joseph David and Alice (Smith) G.; m. Marilyn Taylor, Aug. 11, 1967 (div. Dec. 1988); children: Julie, Matthew David. BS, State Coll., 1960, MS, 1962; MA, Syracuse U., 1968; PhD, U. Iowa, 1970. Tchr. Kenmore (N.Y.) Pub. Schs., 1960-66; prof. edn. St. Bonaventure U., 1970—. Bd. dirs. Olean (N.Y.) City Sch. Dist., 1983-91. With U.S. Army, 1953-55. Mem. Phi Delta Kappa. Republican. Home: 2085 Hillcrest Ave Olean NY 14760-9734 Office: St Bonaventure U Box AE Saint Bonaventure NY 14778

GATI, WILLIAM EUGENE, architect, designer and planner; b. Apr. 10, 1959; s. John and Edith Gati. Student, The Juilliard Sch. Of Music, 1965-77; BS in Architecture, CCNY, 1980, BArch cum laude, 1982; MS in Urban Planning, CUNY, 1985. Registered architect, N.Y. Freelance designer N.Y.C., 1978-83; designer Urban Living, Inc., N.Y.C., 1983-84, Robert L. Henry, Architect, N.Y.C., 1984-86, Glass & Assocs., N.Y.C., 1986-87; prin. architect William E. Gati, RA, AIA, N.Y.C., 1987—; prin. Architecture Studio, N.Y.C., 1991—; lectr. CCNY, 1985—; prof. Architecture N.Y. Inst. Tech., Old Westbury, 1985-89; instr. religious architecture, Cooper Union, N.Y.C., 1989; curator Fundamentals of Architecture, N.Y. Inst. Tech., 1987. Recent archtl. designs include: offices for Here's Life, N.Y.C., alterations to Calvary Bapt. Ch., N.Y.C., El Eden Ch., Bklyn., Living Word Christian Ctr., N.Y.C., All Saints Ch., Queens, N.Y.C., Dr. Aviles Med. Ctr., Queens, Tampellini Residence, Queens, expansion for Flushing Christian Sch., Queens, N.Y., El Eden Ch., Bklyn., Living Word Christian Ctr., N.Y.C., All Saints Ch., Queens, Dr. Aviles Med. Ctr., Queens, Tampellim Residence, Queens; author: Solar Energy Techniques, 1979 (AIA Recognition 1979), Frank L. Wright, 1981, Theory of Modern Architecture, 1981, Boston's Pub. Space, 1985, Vacant Lots, Architectural League N.Y.C., 1987; contbg. illustrator Jonathan Friedman Creations in Space, Fundamentals of Architecture. Chmn. religious architecture com., organized series: Places for Worship, N.Y.C. 1990; mem. planning bd. Kew Gardens. Mem. AIA, Mcpl. Art Soc. (assoc.), Archtl. League (assoc.), CCNY Alumni Assn. (v.p. 1983—), N.Y. Arts Group, Christian Architects Fellowship (pres.). Studio: 115-25 84th Ave Richmond Hill NY 11418

GATLIN, MICHAEL GERARD, lawyer, educator; b. Kittery, Maine, May 9, 1956; s. James Patrick and Florence (Lesperance) G.; m. Judith E. Ziman, Nov. 7, 1987; children: Vanessa Marie, Alexandra Elizabeth. BA, Framingham State Coll., 1978; JD, New Eng. Sch. Law, 1982. Bar: Mass. 1982, U.S. Dist. Ct. Mass. 1983, U.S. Ct. Appeals (1st cir.) 1983. Mem. adj. faculty dept. law Dean Jr. Coll., Franklin, Mass., 1986—; ptnr. McCarthy Gaynor & Gatlin, Framingham, Mass., 1988—. Bd. dirs., pres. Wayside Community Programs, Inc., Framingham, 1978—; bd. dirs. South Middlesex Consumer Assistance Office-Metrowest, Inc., Framingham, 1986—; mem. Framingham Planning Bd., 1992—. Recipient citation Mass. Ho. of Reps., 1984. Mem. Mass. Bar Assn., South Middlesex Bar Assn. (pres. 1991-92). Democrat. Home: 9 Hampden Rd Framingham MA 01701-2331 Office: McCarthy Gaynor & Gatlin 161 Worcester Rd Fl 2D Framingham MA 01701-5300

GATTA, JOHN JOSEPH, JR., English educator; b. Schenectady, N.Y., Feb. 15, 1946; s. John Joseph and Marie Loretta (Lajeunesse) G.; m. Julia Milan O'Brien, July 11, 1970. AB, U. Notre Dame, 1968; PhD, Cornell U., 1973. Prof. English U. Conn., Storrs, 1974—; vis. asst. prof. U. Mo., Columbia, 1973-74. Author: Gracious Laughter: The Meditative Wit of Edward Taylor, 1989 (Conf. of Christianity and Literature Book of the Yr. award 1989); contbr. articles to profl. jours. Fulbright lectureship, U. Dakar, Senegal, 1987-88; Woodrow Wilson fellow, 1968. Mem. MLA, Guild of Episcopal Scholars, Nathaniel Hawthorne Soc. Democrat. Episcopalian. Office: U Conn Dept English U-25 Storrs CT 06269

GAUM, CARL HENRY, civil engineer; b. N.Y.C., July 29, 1922; s. Conrad and Amanda (Schultz) G.; m. Ruth Ellen Banks, Feb. 26, 1955; children: Virginia Lee Collison, Carlann Ruth Fergusson. BCE, Rutgers U., 1949; postgrad., U. Okla. Registered profl. engr., N.J., Md., Pa. Hydraulic engr. U.S. Dept. Interior Geol. Survey, Trenton, Plainview, N.J., Tex., 1949-53; prin. Gaum Profl. Engrs., Trenton, 1953-59; supr. civil engrs. Bd. Engrs. for Rivers and Harbors, Washington, 1961-62; chif basin planning Ohio river div. Army Corps Engrs., Cin., 1962-68; chief interagy. & spl. studies Army Corps Engrs., Washington, 1968-73, chief cen. planning and mgmt., 1973-80; sr. water resources engr. Greenhorne & O'Mara, Greenbelt, Md., 1981-85; pres. Resources Engring. Inc., Arlington, Va., 1985-90; chief exec. officer Gaum & Assocs., Kensington, Md., 1985—; sr. advisor U.S. EPA, Wash-

ington, 1986-88. Author: Subsurface Facilities of Water Management, 1953. Chmn. citizens adv. com. City of Blue Ash, Ohio, 1963-65. Sgt. U.S. Army, 1942-45. Fellow ASCE (pres. nat. capitol sect. 1985-86, chmn. emergency assistance com. 1980-85, policy com. 1988-91, 1st chmn. water resources planning and mgmt. div. 1976), Am. Water Resources Assn.; mem. Internat. Assn. Navigation Congresses (chmn. 1969—, publ. com. 1991, Appreciation award 1977, 81), Wash. Soc. Engrs. (bd. dirs. 1990-91), Profl. Photographers Am. Inc., Internat. Freelance Photographers Orgn., Engrs. Coun. Md. (bd. dirs. 1988—). Democrat. Unitarian. Home and Office: 9609 Carriage Rd Kensington MD 20895-3619

GAUNA, MONICA COLLINS, family therapist; b. Takoma Park, Md., Oct. 31, 1963; d. Alexander Gillan and Jacqueline (Knott) C.; m. Guadalupe Gauna, June 13, 1987; 1 child, Alicia Janet. BS, Chaminade U., 1988; MA, Bowie State U., 1990. Salesman AMFAC Distbrs., Honolulu, 1987-88; counselor Washington Adventist Hosp., Takoma Park, Md., 1989-90; addictions counselor Prince George's County, Riverdale, Md., 1990-91; family therapist So. Area Youth Svcs., Temple Hills, Md., 1990-91, Kensington Wheaton (Md.) Youth Svcs., 1991—; cons. Prince George's County, Md., 1990—; owner Community Counseling Assocs., Upper Marlboro, Md., 1991—; mentor Project BEST, Temple Hills, 1991—. With U.S. Army, 1984-87. Mem. AACD, Juvenile Aid Vol. Alliance, People Against Child Abuse, Nat. Prevention Coalition, Nat. Assn. Multicultural Counseling. Republican. Roman Catholic. Office: So Area Youth Svcs 4305 St Barnabas Rd Ste 304 Temple Hills MD 20748-1849

GAUNTLETT, DONALD WAYNE, chemistry educator; b. Tremont, Pa., Mar. 10, 1940; s. William T. and Anna L. (Carl) G. BS in Edn., Kutztown U., 1962; MAT, Brown U., 1967; postgrad., La. State U., 1968-71, 73. Tchr. Tremont Borough Sch. Dist., 1963-65; prof. chemistry U. Pitts. at Johnstown, 1967-74, Wilkes Coll., Wilkes Barre, Pa., 1974-79, Millersville (Pa.) U., 1979-81, 84-87, Franklin and Marshall Coll., Lancaster, Pa., 1981, Bloomsburg (Pa.) U., 1982-83, Lehigh County Community Coll., Schneckville, Pa., 1987—. Mem. Am. Chemistry Soc., New Eng. Assn. Chemistry Tchrs., Sigma Xi. Republican. Office: Lehigh County Community Coll 2370 Main St Schnecksville PA 18078-9372

GAUTAM, KUL CHANDRA, international development executive; b. Amarpur-Isma, Gulmi, Nepal, Dec. 1, 1949; came to U.S., 1986; s. Om Prasad and Hima (Pandey) G.; m. Binata Dhital, June 24, 1973; children: Jyotsna, Biplav. Intermediate of Arts, Tri-Chandra Coll., Kathmandu, 1968; BA, Dartmouth Coll., 1971; MPA, Princeton (N.J.) U., 1973. Program officer UNICEF, UN, Phnom Penh, Cambodia, 1973-75, Jakarta, Indonesia, 1975-79; rep. UNICEF, UN, Vientiane, Laos, 1979-82, Port Au Prince, Haiti, 1982-86; chief program div. UNICEF, UN, N.Y.C., 1986-88, dir. planning, 1988—. Home: 186 Field Point Rd # 1B Greenwich CT 06830 Office: UNICEF 2 UN Plaza New York NY 10017

GAUTIERI, RONALD FRANCIS, pharmacology educator; b. Providence, Oct. 10, 1933; s. Emilio Guiseppe and Frances (Amalfitano) G.; m. Bernadette Howell, Jan. 20, 1962; 1 child, Anne Marie. BS, R.I. Coll. Pharmacy, 1955; MS, Temple U., 1957, PhD, 1960. Asst. prof. pharmacology Temple U., Phila., 1960-66, assoc. prof., 1966-70, prof., 1970—, chmn. dept., 1970—; med. legal cons., Phila., 1965—. Contbr. 55 articles on basic pharmacology to profl. jours. Invited participant Physiology Soc., 1971, 75. Mem. Am. Pharm. Assn., Am. Assn. Coll. Pharmacy, Am. Soc. Pharmacology & Exptl. Therapeutics, Am. Assn. Pharm. Scientists, Rotary Internat. Roman Catholic. Office: Temple U Sch of Pharmacy 3307 N Broad St Philadelphia PA 19140-5193

GAUTSCHY, GUDRUN DOROTHEA, learning disabilities educator; b. Hoya, Weser, Germany, July 22, 1944; arrived in U.S., 1952; d. Ferdinand and Mariechen (Bruns) Schwarz; m. Henry Philip Gautschy, June 8, 1968. BS, Montclair State U., 1980, MA, 1989. Dental asst. pvt. practice dental office, Chester, N.J., 1963-68; tchr. dental occupations Bergen County Vocat. Sch., Paramus, N.J., 1971-86, counselor, 1987-89; learning cons. Bergen County Vocat. Sch., Teterboro, N.J., 1989—. Mem. Bergen County Tech. Edn. Assn. (rec. sec. 1985—). Home: 35 Red Mine Rd Wanaque NJ 07465-2413

GAUVREAU, NORMAN PAUL, lawyer, state legislator; b. Burlington, Vt., Aug. 4, 1948; s. Norman O. and Dorothy (Daniels) G.; m. Evelyn A. Greenlaw, July 16, 1977; children—Jessica, Johanna. B.A., U. Maine, 1972; J.D., U. Maine Law Sch., 1975. Bar: Maine 1975. Assoc. Shiro & Jabar, Waterville, Maine, 1975-78; ptnr. Gauvreau & Thibeault, Lewiston, Maine, 1978-84, Andrews & Gauvreau, Lewiston, 1984-88, Whalen, Gauvreau & Blackburn, P.A., Lewiston, Maine, 1988-90, Gauvreau & Blackburn, P.A., 1990—. Bd. dirs. Abused Womens Shelter, Auburn, Maine, 1979-84; chmn. Lewiston Dem. City Com., 1984-86; mem. gov.'s council on Consumer Credit, 1976-78. Mem. ABA, Maine Trial Lawyers Assn., Androsroggin County Bar Assn. Lodge: Kiwanis (dir.). Office: Gauvreau & Blackburn PA PO Box 520 Lewiston ME 04243-0520 Other: Maine State Senate State House Sta 3 Augusta ME 04333

GAVALÁS, ALEXANDER BEARY, artist; b. Limerick, Ireland, Jan. 6, 1945; came to U.S., 1946; s. Emmanuel Zenon and Mary (Beary) G. Diploma, Sch. Art & Design, N.Y.C., 1963; student Manhattanville Coll., 1969-70, Guilmant Organ Sch., 1970, Kerpel Sch. Dental Tech., 1972. Cert. 20th Century Hudson River Artist. One man shows at Krasl Art Ctr., St. Joseph Mich., 1980, The Tweed Mus. Art, U. Minn., Duluth, 1980, Fine Arts Center of Clinton, Ill., 1980, Western Ill. U. Library Gallery, Macomb, 1981, Ft. Wayne Mus. Art, Ind., 1982, Mary Crest Coll., Eberdt Art Gallery, Davenport, Iowa, 1982, Arnot Art Mus., Elmira, N.Y., 1982, Queens Coll. Art Ctr., Flushing, N.Y., 1983; exhibited in group shows Taft Hotel, N.Y.C., 1964, J. Walter Thompson Art Gallery, N.Y.C., 1964, Hudson River Mus., Yonkers, N.Y., 1974-75, Far Gallery, N.Y.C., 1976-79, Eric Galleires, N.Y.C., 1981-82. Contbr. articles to profl. jours. Honorable mention Congl. record 88th congress for cultural contbr. to Life or Nation, 1964, award for work on spl. file Smithsonian Inst. from Harry Rand. Address: 65 Horton St Malverne NY 11565

GAVIN, JAMES MARTIN, consulting environmental engineer; b. Castlebar, Ireland, June 19, 1956; came to U.S., 1981; s. Seamus John and Eileen Lilian (Sheridan) G.; m. Margaret Gallagher, July 21, 1984; children: Sean McDermott, Aislinn Grace, Kara Sheridan. B of Engring., Univ. Coll. of Dublin, 1980. Registered profl. engr., N.Y., Conn.; chartered engr., Ireland. Project engr. Stearns & Wheler, Inc., Darien, Conn., 1982-84, office mgr., 1984-86; sr. project engr. Blasland, Bouck & Lee, White Plains, N.Y., 1986-88, mng. engr., 1988-89, assoc., 1989; v.p. Savin Engrs., P.C., Tarrytown, N.Y., 1989—. Mem. ASCE, Water Environ. Fedn., Instn. Engrs. Ireland. Roman Catholic. Home: 2 Old Lantern Dr Bethel CT 06801 Office: Savin Engrs PC 200 White Plains Rd Tarrytown NY 10591

GAW, JAMES RICHARD, corporate manager; b. Bklyn., Sept. 2, 1943; s. James A. and Catharine (Clough) G.; m. Lorraine Osenbruk, July 21, 1973; children: Sean James, Joshua Timothy, Desiree Ann. BA, L.I. U., 1965; MA, St. John's U., 1967. Cert. Health Cons. Underwriter Royal-Globe Ins. Co., N.Y.C., 1969-70; rep. Blue Cross/Greater N.Y., N.Y.C., 1970-75; mktg. specialist Community Health Plan, Albany, N.Y., 1975-78; dir., mktg. support Blue Cross/Northeastern N.Y., Albany, 1978-82, sr. advisor to pres., 1982-84; dir. program svcs. Empire Blue Cross/Shield, N.Y.C., 1984-89, dir. records mgmt., 1989-90; dir. adminstrn., 1990—; N.Y. state project dir. Blue Cross Assn., Chgo., 1979-83; preceptor Union U., Schenectady, N.Y., 1980-82. V.p. Cath. Charities, Albany, 1983-88; gov. Adirondack Mountain Club, Inc., Glen Falls, N.Y., 1980-83; mem. Nat. Com. on Alcohol & Drugs, Chgo., Washington, 1980-82; pres. Schoharie Family & Community Svcs., Cobleskill, N.Y., 1976-78; coord. Health Info. Sharing Project, Albany, 1979-81. With USMC, 1967-69, Vietnam. Recipient Svc. Award Recognition Schoharie Family and Community Svcs., 1988; grantee Nat. Inst. Drug Abuse, 1981-83. Mem. APHA, Internat. Facilities Mgmt. Assn., Assn. Records Mgmt. and Adminstrs., The Hastings Inst., N.Y. State Pub. Health Assn. Roman Catholic. Office: Empire Blue Cross/Shield PO Box 11800 Albany NY 12211-0800

GAWLAK, ALBERT A., wholesale products executive; b. Buffalo, N.Y., Oct. 19, 1962; s. Albert Anthony Gawlak and Patricia (Piskorowski) Gill. BA, Canisius Coll., 1987. Regional sales mgr. Park Electric Supply, Inc., Syracuse, N.Y., 1987—. Contbr. articles to profl. jours. Home: 14 Signal Hill Rd Fayetteville NY 13066-9674

GAWRON, VALERIE J., engineer; b. Kenmore, N.Y., Mar. 16, 1954; d. Stanley Carl and Jane Elizabeth (Garas) G. MA in Psychology, State U. Coll., 1977; MS in Indsl. Engring., SUNY, 1988, MBA, 1988; PhD in Engring. Psychology, U. Ill., 1980. Rsch. asst. State U. Coll., Geneseo, N.Y., 1976-77, U. Ill., Champaign, 1977-79; rsch. assoc. N.Mex. State U., Las Cruces, 1979-80; prin. engr. Calspan, Buffalo, N.Y., 1980—; mem. manpower & planning com. Nat. Security Indsl. Assn., Washington, 1988—. Contbr. to books and articles to profl. jours. Bd. dirs. Hemophilia Assn. We. N.Y., Buffalo, 1987-90; foster parent Foster Parent Plan Internat., 1988—. Mem. AIAA (com. standards life scis. & systems 1989—, human factors engring. wroking group 1990—), Aerospace Med. Assn., Aerospace Human Factors Assn. (charter 1990—), Assn. Aviation Psychologists (chmn. grants com. 1989—), Human Factors Soc., Mil. Ops. Soc., People for Ethical Treatment of Animals, Amnesty Internat. Democrat. Roman Catholic. Office: Calspan PO Box 400 Buffalo NY 14225-0400

GAWTHROP, ROBERT S., III, district judge; b. 1942. BA, Amherst Coll., 1964; JD, Dickinson Sch. Law, 1970. Law clk. to Ho. Lee F. Swope Harrisburg, Pa., 1969-70; mem. firm Gawthrop & Greenwood, West Chester, Pa., 1970-78; asst. dist. atty. Office Dist. Atty., West Chester, 1971-78, Wayne County, Pa., 1976-77; judge Ct. Common Pleas, Chester County, 1978-88; dist. judge U.S. Dist. Ct. (ea. dist.) Pa., 1987—; adj. prof. trial advocacy Dickinson Sch. Law, Carlisle, Pa., 1981-82. Contbr. articles to profl. jours. Bd. dirs. Am. Cancer Soc., The Phelps Sch.; mem. Pa. Horticultural Soc., Berks Grand Opera. 1st lt. Artillery OCS, 1965-67. Mem. ABA, Am. Judicature Soc., Federalist Soc. Law & Pub. Policy Studies, Nat. Dist. Attys. Assn., Pa. Bar Assn., Fed. Judges Assn., Fed. Bar Assn., The Savoy Co., The Ardensinges, Gilbert and Sullivan Players, Chester County Gilbert and Sullivan Soc., Orpheus club, Quarry Club, Italian Social Club, Appalachian Mountain Club, Delta Kappa Epsilon, Phi Mu Alpha. Office: US Dist Ct 7614 US Courthouse 601 Market St Philadelphia PA 19106-1510*

GAY, DAVID HOLDEN, project technician; b. Boston, Jan. 5, 1954; s. Ernest and Mary (Holden) G.; m. Ann Marie Grieve, June 19, 1982; 1 child, David C. Student, Northeastern U., Boston, 1972, 75, 80, 81, 83, 84, Lowell U., 1987-92, Lesley Coll., 1992—. Floor mgr. Harvard Coop. Soc., Cambridge, Mass., 1972-76; R&D tech. Polaroid Corp., Cambridge, 1976-85; project tech. Draper Lab., Cambridge, 1985—. Pres. R&D and Tech. Employee's Union, Belmont, Mass., 1990—; legis. agt. State of Mass., 1991—, legis agt. federal, 1991—. Roman Catholic. Home: 5 Decarolis Dr Tewksbury MA 01876 Office: Draper Lab 555 Technology Dr Cambridge MA 02139

GAY, NANCY BINGHAM, museum executive; b. Phila., May 22, 1923; d. James Julian and Anna Gertrude (Meng) B.; widowed, 1961, 76; children: Nancy, Susanne, Laurie, G. Bradford; stepchildren: Prudence, Stephanie. BS, U. Pa., 1944. Pres. Bergen Mus. Art and Sci., Paramus, N.J., 1970-76; exec. com. Pro Arte Chorale, Bergen County, N.J., 1977-82, 88—; pres. The Hermitage Historic House, Ho-Ho-Kus, N.J., 1978-86; v.p. devel. Old Barracks Mus., Trenton, N.J., 1986—; trustee Am. Labor Mus., Haledon, N.J., 1987—; legis. chair N.J. Historic Trust, Trenton, 1990—, trustee, sec. bd. dirs.; vice chmn. N.J. Com. for Humanities, New Brunswick, 1982-90; exec. dir. Mus. Coun. N.J., Trenton, 1985-90, Bergen County Cultural Commn., Hackensack, 1976-80; bd. dirs. Art Pride, Newark, 1986—. Bd. dirs. Ridgewood (N.J.) YWCA, 1978-89, Bergen County coun. Girl Scouts U.S., 1985-89. Recipient History Advocacy award N.J. Hist. Commn., 1988, Woman of Yr. award Soroptomists of No. Passaic Valley, 1991; named Woman of Influence in N.J., N.J. Monthly Mag., 1991. Mem. LWV, Am. Assn. Museums, Mid Atlantic Assn. Museums, Rep. Women for 90s, Nat. Trust Historic Preservation, Kappa Alpha Theta. Home: 337 Windsor Ter Ridgewood NJ 07450-2329 Office: Old Barracks Mus Barrack St Trenton NJ 08608-2006

GAYDOS, JOSEPH MATTHEW, congressman; b. Braddock, Pa., July 3, 1926; s. John and Elona (Magella) G.; m. Alice Ann Gray, Nov. 26, 1955; children: Joseph Matthew, Colleen, Kathleen, Kelly, Tammy. Student, Duquesne U.; LLB, U. Notre Dame, 1951. Bar: Pa. 1953. Mem. Pa. Senate for 45th Dist., 1967-68; dep. atty. gen. Pa., 1955; asst. solicitor Allegheny County, Pa.; gen. counsel dist. 5 United Mine Workers Am., then legal counsel dist. 50; mem. 90th-102nd Congresses from 20th Pa. dist., 1968—. Served with USNR, World War II, PTO. Mem. Allegheny County Bar Assn., Am. Legion, Cath. War Vets., VFW, Sons of Italy, McKeesport Am.-Slovak Club, Croatian Fraternal Union, Jednota, Polish Nat. Alliance, U. Notre Dame Alumni Soc. Democrat. Roman Catholic. Office: US Ho of Reps 2366 Rayburn House Office Bldg Washington DC 20515*

GAYDOS, MICHAEL EDWARD, IV, computer systems analyst, consultant; b. Trenton, N.J., Oct. 9, 1956; s. Michael Edward III and Gladys Rose (Fanny) G. BS, King's Coll., 1979; cert. in computer programming, Maxwell Inst., 1981. Programmer, cons. Wenz Systems, North Wales, Pa., 1982-83; programmer, analyst Internat. Computaprint Corp., Ft. Washington, Pa., 1984-89, analyst, 1990—; cons. trust system program Wenz Systems, North Wales, 1982-83. Sponsor G.O.P. Victory Fund, Washington, 1983—; benefactor The King's Coll. Ann. Fund, Wilkes-Barre, Pa., 1990—. Recipient Cert. of Recognition, Nat. Rep. Congl. Com. 1984, 86, Presdl. Achievement award 1987, Presdl. Cert. of Appreciation 1989, Cert. of Appreciation 1990—, Congl. Cert. of Appreciation 1991. Mem. Am. Mgmt. Assn., Men of Malvern Retreat League, Mikes of Am. Roman Catholic. Home: 501 Barrington Pl Lansdale PA 19446-5308 Office: Internat Computaprint Corp 475 Virginia Dr Fort Washington PA 19034-2792

GAYLE, JOSEPH CENTRAL, JR., computer information professional; b. N.Y.C., July 31, 1942; s. Joseph Sr. and Margaret Louemma (Smith) G.; m. Xenia Patricia Cockburn, June 22, 1968; children: Sean C., Melanie D. AS, CUNY, 1964; cert. with honors, Monroe Sch. Bus., 1963; cert., IBM Edn. Ctr., N.Y.C., 1974, Burroughs Edn. Ctr., Oakbrook, Ill., 1982, AT&T Edn. Ctr., Cin., 1983, AT&T Edn. Ctr., Atlanta, 1986. Treasury dept. clk. Tidewater Oil Co. subs. Getty Co., N.Y.C., 1962-64; computer operator analyst Chase Manhattan Bank, N.Y.C., 1966-68; sr. computer operator analyst Great Am. Ins. Co., N.Y.C., 1968-70; lead computer ops. analyst C.P.C. Internat. Co., Englewood Cliffs, N.J., 1970-71; asst. computer ops. supr. Irving Trust Bank, N.Y.C., 1971-77; computer ops. network supr. ABC, Hackensack, N.J., 1977-79, Warner Communications, N.Y.C., 1979-80; sr. system network supr. City Fed. Savs. and Loan, Somerset, N.J., 1980-82; sr. telecommunications cons. CIBA Geigy Corp., Ardsley, N.Y., 1982—; sr. computer specialist U.S. Army Data Processing Office Hdqrs., Hampton, Va., 1965-66; county supr. Bergen County Data Processing, Hackensack, 1975-80; computer sales cons. Computerland Micro Sales, Union, N.J., 1985-87; with AT&T Ednl. Ctr., Cin. and Fla., 1989. Contbr. articles to profl. jours. Town mem. Bd. Elections, Teaneck, N.J., 1978; sr. mem. Com. to Elect Bernie Brooks Mayor, Teaneck, 1980; county supr. Bergen County Civil and Criminal Justice System, Hackensack, 1980; state del. U.S. Congl. Adv. Bd., Washington, 1986. Served with U.S. Army, 1964-66. Recipient Nat. Peace award U.S. Army, 1966; Speaking of People honoree Ebony Mag. Publ., Chgo., 1981. Mem. Communications Mgrs. Assn., Sunguard Computer Disaster Group, Nat. Assn. Advancement Sci., N.Y. Acad. Scis., Nat. Space Soc., Am. Legion. Democrat. Club: Afro Civic League (Teaneck) (computer cons. 1983-86). Home: 628 George St Teaneck NJ 07666-5356 Office: CIBA-Geigy Corp 444 Saw Mill River Rd Ardsley NY 10502-2600

GAYLIN, NED L., psychology educator; b. Cleve., May 2, 1935; s. Harry C. and Fay I. G.; m. Rita Atran, June 30, 1957; children: Hilarie C., Ann E., Jed J., Daniel S. B.A., U. Chgo., 1956, M.A., 1961, Ph.D., 1965. Staff psychologist Inst. Juvenile Research, Chgo., 1965-68; counselor Bellefaire Children's Home, Cleve., 1953, Sonja Shankman Orthogenic Sch., Chgo., 1954-56; group worker, supr. Jewish Community Centers of Chgo., 1957-60; grad. research asst. Com. Human Devel., U. Chgo., 1959-60; intern Inst. Juvenile Research, Chgo., 1960-61, Counseling and Psychotherapy Research Center, U. Chgo., 1961-63; grad. teaching asst. dept. psychology U. Chgo., 1961-63; psychol. cons. State Ill., Rockford, 1961-64; psychotherapist, cons. Counseling and Psychotherapy Research Center, U. Chgo., 1963-65, psychol. cons., lectr., 1965; lectr. dept. social sci. S.E. Jr. Coll., Chgo., 1965-66; staff psychologist Inst. Juvenile Research, Chgo., 1965-68; psychol. cons. Peace Corps, No. Ill. U., DeKalb, 1966-68; chief psychologist S.W. Suburban Mental Health Assn., LaGrange, Ill., 1966-68; psychol. cons. Virginia Frank Child Devel. Center, Chgo., 1966-68; child clin. research psychologist NIMH, Bethesda, Md., 1968-70; lectr., cons. Washington Sch. Psychiatry, 1968-72; chmn. dept. family and community devel. Coll. Human Ecology, U. Md., College Park, 1970-77; prof., dir. family therapy tng. Coll. Human Ecology, U. Md., 1977—; mem. research com. Md. Community Coordinated Child Care, 1970-75. Contbr. articles in field to profl. jours. USPHS grantee, 1961-63; U. Chgo. fellow and scholar, 1954-56, 58-60; State Ill. edn. and tng. grantee, 1963-65. Mem. Nat. Council on Family Relations, Am. Psychol. Assn., Am. Assn. Marriage and Family Therapy, Groves Conf. on the Family, Assn. for Devel. of the Person Centered Approach, Sigma Xi. Home: 4617 Norwood Dr Bethesda MD 20815-5348 Office: U Md College Park MD 20742

GAYLIN, WILLARD, physician, educator; b. Cleve., Feb. 23, 1925; s. Harry C. and Fay (Baumgard) G.; m. Betty Schofer, June 15, 1947; children: Joan Deborah, Ellen Andrea. A.B., Harvard U., 1947; M.D., Western Res. U., 1951. Lic. psychiatrist, N.Y. Intern Cleve. City Hosp., 1951-52; resident psychiatry Bronx VA Hosp., 1952-54; faculty Columbia Psychoanalytic Sch., 1956—, clin. prof. psychiatry, 1972—; adj. prof. psychiatry Union Theol. Sem.; adj. prof. psychiatry and law Columbia Sch. Law, 1970; pres., founder The Hastings Ctr., Briarcliff Manor, N.Y., 1970—; vis. prof. Harvard U. Med. Sch., 1978. Author: The Meaning of Despair, 1968, In The Service of Their Country: War Resisters in Prison, 1970, Partial Justice: A Study of Bias in Sentencing, 1974, Caring, 1976, (with others) Doing Good: The Limits of Benevolence, 1978, Feelings: Our Vital Signs, 1979, The Killing of Bonnie Garland: A Question of Justice, 1982, The Rage Within: Anger in Modern Life, 1984, Rediscovering Love, 1986, Adam and Eve and Pinnocchio, 1990, The Male Ego, 1992; contbr. articles to profl. jours. Bd. dirs. Helsinki Watch., Nat. Bd. Planned Parenthood. Served with USNR, 1943-45. Recipient George E. Daniels medal of Merit for contbns. to psychoanalytic medicine, 1973; Elizabeth Cutter Morrow lectr. Smith Coll., 1970; Chubb fellow Yale U., 1972. Fellow Am. Psychiat. Assn.; mem. Inst. Medicine of NAS, Am. Psychoanalytic Assn., N.Y. Psychiat. Soc. Office: Hastings Center 255 Elm Rd Briarcliff Manor NY 10510-2207

GAYLOR, JAMES LEROY, biomedical research director; b. Waterloo, Iowa, Oct. 1, 1934; s. David P. and Lena (Livingston) G.; m. Marilyn Louise Gibson, Mar. 25, 1956; children—Douglas, Ann, Robert, Kenneth. B.S., Iowa State U., 1956; M.S., U. Wis., 1958, Ph.D., 1960. From asst. prof. to prof. biochemistry Cornell U., Ithaca, N.Y., 1960-77, chmn. biochemistry, molecular and cell biology sect., 1970-76; prof., chmn. dept. biochemistry U. Mo., Columbia, 1977-80; assoc. dir. life scis. rsch. E.I. duPont Cen. Rsch., Wilmington, Del., 1981-83, dir. health sci. rsch., 1984-85; dir. biol. rsch. E.I. duPont Pharms., Wilmington, Del., 1986-87; corp. dir. sci. and technology Johnson & Johnson, New Brunswick, N.J., 1987—; vis. prof. U. Ill., summers 1964-65; sabbatical leave U. Oreg. Sch. Medicine, 1966-67, U. Osaka, Japan, 1973-74; vis. lectr. La Molina, Peru, summer 1962; nutrition cons. Pew Found., Phila., 1986—; mem. bd. sci. counselors div. cancer prevention Nat. Cancer Inst., NIH, Bethesda, Md., 1987-91. Mem. various editorial bds.; contbr. over 150 rsch. articles to sci. jours. NIH fellow, 1958-60; spl. fellow, 1966-67; Guggenheim fellow, 1973-74. Mem. AAAS, Am. Chem. Soc., Am. Soc. Biochemistry and Molecular Biology, Am. Inst. Nutrition, Am. Heart Assn., Am. Assn. Pharm. Scientists. Office: Cosat Johnson & Johnson 410 George St New Brunswick NJ 08901-2021

GAYMAN, BENJAMIN FRANKLIN, lawyer; b. Carlisle, Pa., Jan. 18, 1947; s. Joseph Franklin and Mary E. (Fields) G.; m. Carol Ann Steinen, Nov. 26, 1971; children: Rebecca, Megan, Katie, Anna. BA, Dickinson Coll., 1968; JD, Georgetown U., 1974; LLM in Taxation, Boston U., 1979. Bar: N.H. 1975, U.S. Dist. Ct. N.H. 1975, U.S. Tax Ct. 1984. From assoc. to ptnr. Wiggin & Nourie, Manchester, N.H., 1975—; bd. dirs. Fleet Bank N.H., Nashua. Editor: Am. Criminal Law Rev., 1973-74. Trustee Manchester Girls and Boys Club, 1976—, Crotched Mountain Found., Greenfield, N.H., 1985—; dir., sec. Trust for N.H. Lands, 1987—, vice chmn. 1st lt. U.S. Army, 1968-71, Vietnam. Mem. ABA, N.H. Bar Assn. Home: 300 Steinmetz Dr Manchester NH 03104-1834 Office: Wiggin & Nourie PO Box 808 Manchester NH 03105-0808

GAYNOR, EDWARD BARRY, otolaryngologist; b. N.Y.C., Apr. 4, 1941; s. Norman N. and Mabel (Land) G.; m. Judith E. Greenberg, Apr. 15, 1968; children: Kenneth, Beth. AB, Adelphi U., 1962; MD cum laude, SUNY, Bklyn., 1966. Diplomate Am. Bd. Otolaryngology. Intern L.I. Jewish Hosp., New Hyde Park, N.Y., 1966-67, resident surgery, 1967-68; resident otolaryngology Temple U. Health Ctr., Phila., 1968-71; attending surgeon Temple U. Med. Ctr., St. Christopher's Hosp. Children, PHila., 1973-75; attending staff Park City Hosp., Bridgeport, Conn., 1985—, West Haven (Conn.) VA Hosp., 1980—; sr. attending surgeon Dept. Surgery, Sect. Otolaryngology, Norwalk, Conn., 1975—; mem. clin. faculty dept. otolaryngology Yale U. Sch. Medicine, New Haven, 1979—; asst. prof. otolaryngology Temple U., Phila., 1973-75. Contbr. articles to profl. jours. Bd. trustees, med. affairs com., laryngectomy group advisor Am. Cancer Soc., Fairfield County, 1979—. Maj. U.S. Army, 1971-73. Fellow ACS, Am. Acad. Otolaryngology, Triological Soc., Pan Am. Soc. Otolaryngology; mem. Conn. State Med. Soc., Fairfield County Med. Soc. Office: 40 Cross St Norwalk CT 06851

GBURZYNSKI, JOHN JOSEPH, federal agency administrator; b. Duluth, Minn., Mar. 2, 1943; s. Joseph Frank and Fern Josephine (Sharkey) G. BA, U. Minn., 1965, M in Indsl. Safety, 1980. Occupational safety and health specialist U.S. Postal Svc., Washington, 1968—. Sgt. USAF, 1965-68. Mem. Am. Soc. Safety Engrs. (cert. hazard control mgr., cert. hazardous materials mgr.), Duluth Kennel Club (bd. dirs. 1972-76), Am. Sealyham Terrier Club (bd. dirs. 1973-78), K.C., Pi Gamma Mu, Gamma Theta Upsilon. Roman Catholic. Office: US Postal Svc Hdqrs 475 LEnfant Pla SW Washington DC 20260-4231

GEBBIA, ROBERT JAMES, tax specialist; b. New Castle, Pa., Nov. 29, 1947; s. Joseph A. and Helen M. (Staransky) G.; m. Eileen A. Zuk, Oct. 2, 1971; children: Jamie, Christopher, Maria. BS, Youngstown State U., 1969; MBA, Canisius Coll., 1979. CPA. Tax law specialist IRS, Washington, 1972-74; IRS agt. IRS, Detroit and Buffalo, 1974-77; tax supr. Peat, Marwick, Mitchell, Buffalo, 1977-79, Coopers & Lybrand, Pitts., 1979-81; tax dir. UNC Resources, Falls Church, Va., 1981-85; sr. tax mgr. Occidental Petroleum, Tulsa, 1985-88; dir. taxes Carpenter Tech., Reading, Pa., 1988—; evening instr. Albright Coll., Reading, 1989—. With U.S. Army, 1970-71, Vietnam. Mem. Mfrs. Alliance for Productivity and Innovation, Pa. Chamber of Bus. and Industry, Tax. Execs. Inst. Home: 217 Logan Ave Reading PA 19610-2655 Office: Carpenter Tech PO Box 14662 101 W Bern St Reading PA 19612-4662

GECHTOFF, SONIA, artist; b. Phila., Sept. 25, 1926; d. Leonid and Etya (Freedman) G.; children—Susannah Kelly, Miles Kelly. BFA, Phila. Mus. Sch. Art, 1950. Instr. painting, drawing Calif. Sch. Fine Art, 1956-57; adj. asst. prof. art NYU, 1966-70; lectr. art Queens Coll., N.Y.C., 1970-74; assoc. prof. art U. N.Mex., 1974-75; artist-in-residence Skidmore Coll., summer, 1988, 89, 90, Adelphi U., N.Y., 1991; vis. artist Chgo. Art Inst., 1989. One-woman shows include DeYoung Mus., San Francisco, 1957, Ferus Gallery, Los Angeles, 1957, 59, Poindexter Gallery, N.Y.C., 1959, 60, Cortella Gallery, N.Y.C., 1976, 78, Gruenebaum Gallery, N.Y.C., 1979, 80, 82, 83, 87, Witkin Gallery, N.Y.C., 1984, 89, Gruenebaum Gallery, N.Y.C., 1985, Kraushaar Gallery, N.Y.C., 1990, Adelphi U., 1991, 871 Fine Arts Gallery, San Francisco, 1991, Adelphi U., 1991, Kraushaar Gallery, N.Y.C., 1992; group shows include, Guggenheim Mus., N.Y.C., 1954, San Francisco Mus. Art, 1953-58, Brussels World's Fair, 1958, 1st Paris Biennale, 1959, Whitney Mus., N.Y.C., 1959, 60, Sao Paulo (Brazil) Biennale, 1961, Nat. Gallery Am. Art Smithsonian Instn., 1976, Mus. Modern Art, N.Y.C., 1977, Aldrich Mus. Contemporary Art, Ridgefield, Conn., 1981, Bennington Coll., Vt., 1985, Weatherspoon Gallery, Greensboro, 1987, Gruneebaum Gallery, 1987; represented in permanent collections, San Francisco Mus. Modern Art, Guggenheim Mus., Mus. Modern Art, Met. Mus., N.Y.C., Balt. Mus. Art;

also pvt. and corp. collections. Ford Found. fellow Tamarind Inst., Los Angeles, 1963; recipient Purchase awards San Francisco Mus. Art, 1955-59; grantee Esther and Adolph Gottlieb Found. , 1987, Mid Atlantic NEA, 1988. Mem. Artists Equity N.Y. Address: 463 West St New York NY 10014

GECKLE, WILLIAM JUDE, physicist; b. Balt., May 26, 1955; s. Paul Thomas and Margaret Mary (Canning) G.; m. Suzanne Marie Rosch, Sept. 29, 1984; children: David, Theresa. BS magna cum laude, Loyola Coll., 1977; MS, Mich. State U., 1979. Physicist, sect. supr. applied physics lab. Johns Hopkins U., Laurel, Md., 1979—; mem. adv. bd. John K. Frost Ctr. for Imaging of Cells and Molecular Markers, John Hopkins U., 1990—; mem. McClurg Fellowship Com., Balt., 1990—. Contbr. numerous articles to profl. jours. NIH grantee, 1988. Mem. Computer Soc. of IEEE. Office: Johns Hopkins U Applied Physics Lab Laurel MD 20723

GEDEON, LUCINDA HEYEL, museum director; b. Port Chester, N.Y., Oct. 13, 1947; d. Philip H. and Isabel (Oldham) H.; m. Francis A. Sprout, Feb. 8, 1987. BA, Calif. State U., Long Beach, 1978; MA, UCLA, 1981, PhD, 1990. Asst. curator Grunwald Ctr. UCLA, 1978-81, asst. dir. Grunwald Ctr., 1981-83, acting dir. Grunwald Ctr., 1983-85; chief curator Ariz. State U. Art Museum, Tempe, 1985-91; dir. Neuberger Mus. SUNY, Purchase, 1991—. Author: (exhbn. catalogues) Tamarind: Los Angeles to Albuquerque, 1985, Fiber Concepts, 1989, (book) The Art of Leonard Lehrer, 1986; contbr. articles to profl. jours. Chairperson Tempe Mcpl. Arts Commn., Tempe, 1989-90; bd. dirs. Balboa Art Conservation Ctr., San Diego, 1986-91. CFA Rsch. grantee Ariz. State U. Coll. Fine Arts, 1990, Ariz. Commn. on the Arts Exhbn. grantee, 1987-88, 90-91, Inst. Museum Svcs. Conservation grantee, 1987-88, Ariz. Commn. on the Arts Symposium grantee, 1987-88, NEA Painting Conservation grantee, 1988-89; Edward A. Dickson History of Art fellow UCLA, 1984, Afro-Am. Studies fellow UCLA, 1984. Mem. Am. Assn. Museums, Coll. Art Assn., Am. Studies Assn., Museum Assn. Ariz. (bd. dirs. 1988-90). Office: Neuberger Mus SUNY Purchase NY 10577-1400

GEDER, LASZLO, neurologist, educator; b. Debrecen, Hungary, Aug. 11, 1932; came to U.S., 1974, naturalized, 1982; s. Joseph and Irene (Kardoss) G.; M.D., U. Debrecen, 1956, Ph.D., 1969; m. Julianna Toth, Sept. 22, 1956; children—Judith, Martha, Laszlo. Assoc. prof. dept. microbiology Med. Sch., U. Debrecen, Hungary, 1956-72; research assoc. Children's Hosp., Cin., 1964-65; Welcome research fellow dept. virology Med. Sch., U. Birmingham, Eng., 1970-71; acting head dept. microbiology, Ahmadu Bello U., Zaria, Nigeria, 1972-74; assoc. prof. dept. microbiology Coll. of Medicine, Pa. State U., Hershey, 1974-80; physician in neurology, dept. medicine Milton S. Hershey Med. Center, 1980-85, asst. prof. neurology dept. medicine, 1985—; dir. adult rehab. U. Hosp. Rehab. Ctr., 1988—; mem. Nat. Prostatic Cancer Project. Mem. Am. Soc. Microbiology, Am. Acad. Neurology, AAAS, N.Y. Acad. Scis., Sigma Xi. Presbyterian. Contbr. numerous articles on viral oncology to profl. jours. Home: 3360 Colebrook Rd Elizabethtown PA 17022-9075 Office: Pa State U Milton S Hershey Med Ctr Div Neurology Hershey PA 17033

GEESEMAN, ROBERT GEORGE, lawyer; b. Shreveport, La., Oct. 23, 1944; s. George Robert and Cora (Hamilton) Glasgow; m. Rosemary Monahan, Aug. 19, 1967; 1 child, Regan Glasgow. B.A., Yale U., 1966; J.D., U. Mich., 1969. Bar: Pa. 1969, U.S. Dist. Ct. (we. dist.) Pa. 1969, U.S. Supreme Ct., 1973, U.S. Tax Ct. 1979. Assoc. Blaxter, O'Neill, Houston & Nash, Pitts., 1969-75; ptnr. Lynch, Lynch, Carr & Kabala, Pitts., 1975-81, Lynch, Kabala & Geeseman, Pitts., 1981, Kabala & Geeseman, Pitts., 1981—; lectr. on tax law and employee benefits; legal adv. bd. Small Bus. Council Am. Mem. ABA (mem. profl. service corps. com. sect. on taxation, chmn. profl. corp. com. sect. econs.; bd. editors Withdrawal Retirement and Disputes, What You and Your Firm Should Know), Pa. Bar Assn., Allegheny County Bar Assn., Am. Soc. Law and Medicine, Am. Judicature Soc., Estate Planning Council, Pitts. Inst. Legal Medicine, Phi Delta Phi. Clubs: Rosslyn Farms Country, Rivers, Chartiers Country, Harvard-Yale-Princeton (Pitts.); Mory's (New Haven, Conn.); John's Island Country (Vero Beach, Fla.). Office: Kabala & Geeseman 200 1st Ave Pittsburgh PA 15222-1512

GEFFEN, ABRAHAM, physician, radiologist, educator; b. Atlanta, Sept. 22, 1916; s. Tobias and Heni (Rabinowitz) G.; m. Ethel Petegorsky, Mar. 28, 1948; children: David Barry, Robert Joseph, Sara Jane Geller. BA, Emory U., 1937; MD, Columbia U., 1941. Diplomate Am. Bd. Radiology. Intern Beth Israel Med. Ctr., N.Y.C., 1941-42; resident Mt. Sinai Med. Ctr., N.Y.C., 1946-47; asst. radiologist Mt. Sinai Hosp., N.Y.C., 1948-49; attending radiologist Beth Isreal Med. Ctr., N.Y.C., 1949-55, dir. radiology, 1955-75, sr. radiologist, 1976-87, cons., 1987—; prof. clin. radiology Mt. Sinai Sch. of Medicine, 1968—. Contbr. chpt. in book. Hon. v.p. Beth-El Synagogue, New Rochelle, N.Y., 1985. Maj. U.S. Army, 1942-45. Fellow Am. Coll. of Radiology; mem. AMA, N.Y. State Med. Assn., N.Y. Roentgen Soc., N.Y. State Radiol. Soc., Beth Israel Alumni Assn. (Alumnus of Yr. 1989), Mt. Sinai Alumni Assn., Phi Beta Kappa, Alpha Omega Alpha. Democrat. Jewish. Home: 28 Disbrow Ln New Rochelle NY 10804-3209

GEFFEN, FRANCES PEARL, educator, consultant; b. Bklyn., Aug. 22, 1919; d. Elias and Sadie (Katz) Avram; (widowed 1974); children: Joan Louise Friedman, Bonnie Ann Ashman. BA, Hunter Coll., 1939; MA, Hofstra U., 1960. Cert. elem. tchr., N.Y. Tchr. elem. Oceanside (N.Y.) Pub. Sch., 1959-82, Bridgehampton (N.Y.) Sch., 1988—; reading cons. Oceanside Schs., 1982-85. Lectr. Ctr. for Creative Retirement, L.I. U., Southampton, 1988—; active E. Hampton (N.Y.) and Sag Harbor Meals on Wheels, 1988-89; active bus tours and mus. shop Guild Hall, E. Hampton, 1988-89. Mem. LWV (edn. com. 1991-92), AAUW (rec. sec. East Hampton chpt. 1988-89), Hadassah (rec. sec. East Hampton chpt. 1988-89, Woman of the Yr. 1989, Love of a Lifetime award 1991-92). Republican. Home: 166 Gardiner Ave East Hampton NY 11937-1545

GEFFNER, DONNA SUE, speech pathologist, audiologist, educator; b. N.Y.C.; d. Louis and Sally (Weiner) G. BA magna cum laude, Bklyn. Coll., 1967; MA, N.Y. U., 1968, PhD (NDEA fellow), 1970, postgrad., Advanced Inst. Analytic Psychotherapy, 1973-75. Asst. prof. Lehman Coll., 1971-76; assoc. prof. dept. speech St. John's U., 1976-81, prof., 1982—, dir. Speech and Hearing Ctr., 1976—, chmn. dept. speech communication scis. and theater, 1983—, developer M.A. program in speech pathology and audiology; pvt. practice, 1980—; cons. to corp. execs.; TV producer and hostess NBC, 1977-78, CBS, 1978-79. Contbr. articles to profl. jours. and textbooks; issue editor Jour. Topics in Lang. Disorders, 1980; editor ASHA monograph, 1987. Emmy nominee for Outstanding Instrnl. Program, 1978; recipient award Pres.'s Com. on Employment of Handicapped, Pres's. medal for Outstanding Faculty Achievement St. Johns U., 1987; N.Y. State Edn. Dept. grantee, 1976-78, CUNY Rsch. Found. grantee, 1972. Fellow Am. Speech, Lang. and Hearing Assn. (legis. councillor 1978-87, 90—, Ednl. Standards Bd.); mem. N.Y. State Speech and Hearing Assn. (pres. 1978-80), Audiology Study Group N.Y. Office: St John's U Speech and Hearing Ctr Grand Central Pkwy Jamaica NY 11439

GEFFROY, MARC A., real estate, sales and finance associate; b. Boston, Nov. 14, 1961. BA in Econs., Haverford Coll., 1984; MBA in Fin., U. Pa., 1989. Assoc. J.P. Morgan & Co., N.Y.C., 1984-87; project mgr. Trammell Crow Co., Washington, 1989-91, L.A., 1991; sr. assoc. South Charles Realty, Balt., 1991—. Republican. Roman Catholic. Office: South Charles Realty 25 S Charles St Ste 1300 Baltimore MD 21201

GEFVERT, JILL MARIE HAGENBUCH, educator; b. Easton, Pa., Mar. 14, 1949; d. Llewellyn Maynard and Marie Eleanor (Hevener) Hagenbuch; 1 child, Sara E. BA, Westminster Coll., 1971; MA, Temple U., 1975, Cert. of Advanced Grad. Study, 1979. Tchr. Springfield (Pa.) Sch. Dist., 1971-72, William Penn Sch. Dist., Yeadon, Pa., 1972—. V.p. Meadows at Tinicum Community Assn., Phila., 1978-81. Mem. NEA, Pa. Edn. Assn., William Penn Edn. Assn. (v.p. 1989-91, pres. 1991—). Home and Office: William Penn Edn Assn PO Box 81 Darby PA 19023-0081

GEHL, ALICE ELVIRA, federal official; b. Washington, Feb. 11, 1936; d. Robert Benjamin Crump and Anita (Granai) Rinaldi; m. Edwin James Gehl, Jan. 12, 1958 (div. Jan. 1975); children: Elizabeth Jan, Rebecca Anne, Jeanne Marie, Donald Clifford. Student, Western Okla. State Coll., 1969-71, Air U., Gunter Air Force Sta., Ala., 1978-79. With Def. Lang. Inst., San Antonio, 1972-73, Wilford Hall USAF Med. Ctr., San Antonio, 1973-78; real estate assoc. Creative Realty, San Antonio, 1974-79; tng. clk. 3290th Tech. Tng. Group, San Antonio, 1978-79; clerical asst. U.S. Dept. Air Force, Washington, 1979-80, mgmt. asst., 1980-81; clerical asst. Office of Joint Chiefs of Staff, Washington, 1981-82; sec. health affairs Office of Sec. of Def., Washington, 1982-84; staff asst. Strategic Def. Initiative Orgn., Washington, 1984—. Cert. judge Miss Am. Pageant, Washington, 1989; tutor Operation Rescue, Washington, 1982-92; exec. sec. Mil. Aquabrats, San Antonio, 1976-77; chmn. ways and means com. Newburyport (Mass.) PTA, 1964-65. Recipient 1st pl. award Altus AFB Arts and Crafts Show, Ft. Clark Springs Photography Contest. Mem. NAFE, Federally Employed Women, Smithsonian. Republican. Lutheran. Home: 5611 Franconia Rd # 102 Alexandria VA 22310-2711

GEHRING, DAVID AUSTIN, physician, cardiologist; b. Bryn Mawr, Pa., Dec. 6, 1930; s. Harry Rittenhouse and Anne Gardiner (Bozarth) G.; m. Joan Helen Lotz, June 7, 1953 (div. Aug. 1982); children: David, Paul, Peter, Sue, Barbara, Eric; m. Victoria Marie Damiano, Sept. 2, 1982; children: Theresa, Judy Lynne, Michael Austin. BA magna cum laude, U. Pitts., 1952, MD, 1956. Diplomate Am. Bd. Internal Medicine. Commd. USN, 1956, advanced through grades to lt. comdr.; intern, then resident in internal medicine U.S. Naval Hosp. USN, Phila., 1956-60, mem. staff internal medicine U.S. Naval Hosp., 1960-61; chief internal medicine heart sta. U.S. Naval Hosp. USN, Annapolis, Md., 1961-63; resigned USN, 1963; cardiologist K.G.E. Med. Group, Woodbury, N.J., 1963-82; cardiologist, pres. Hobbs Cardiology, P.A., Hobbs, N.Mex., 1982-86; med. dir. Polk (Pa.) Ctr., 1986-91; physician, chief grade VA Med Ctr., Coatesville, Pa., 1991—; testing cardiologist Anthropometrics United Med. Group, Cherry Hill, N.J., 1974-82; clin. asst. prof. medicine Temple U. Hosp., Phila., 1975-82; adj. asst. prof. medicine Jefferson Meml. Coll., Phila., 1981-82; chief cardiac rehab. unit Lea Regional Hosp., Hobbs, 1982-86; chief med. svcs. 829th Sta. Hosp. USAR, Lubbock, Tex., 1984-86; cons. cardiology Oil City, Pa., 1986-91; staff Franklin (Pa.) Regional Med. Ctr., 1986-90, Oil City Area Health Ctr., 1986-91; teaching staff St. Joseph Hosp., Lancaster, Pa., 1991—. Author: EKG Workbook, 1972, EKG Workbook I, 1978; contbr. articles to profl. jours. Project dir. 23 Greater Del. Valley Reg. Med. Prog., Pa., 1971-75; mem. ACLS Inst. and affiliated faculty Pa. Heart Assn., 1986—, bd. dirs. N.W. chpt. 1988-91; bd. dirs. adv. com., chmn. personnel com. med. health, rehab., drugs and alcohol Venango County, Franklin, Pa., 1986-90, pres., 1988-89; mem. Health Care Adv. Com. to Congressman William F. Clinger, Jr., 23d Dist., Pa., 1989-91; lector St. Joseph Ch., Oil City, 1987-91, eucharistic min.. 1990-92; eucharistic min. St. Joseph Ch., Swedesboro, N.J., 1992—; mem. Pitts. Opera Soc. Lt. col. USAR, 1983-90. Recipient Outstanding Svc. award Am. Cancer Soc. N.J., 1967, Benjamin Berkowitz award N.J. Heart Assn., 1975, Nat. Def. Svc. medal 1975, USAR Components Achievement medal, 1988, Letter of Commendation, USAR, 1988, 90, Pres.'s medal of Merit, Rep. Task Force, 1984; Cert. of Apprecation, Sec. of State N.Mex., 1982, Venango County Commr.'s, 1987, 88, 89, 90, Polk Ctr. award of merit, 1991. Fellow Am. Coll. Cardiology, Am. Coll. Chest Physicians, Coll. Physicians of Phila., Am. Coll. Clin. Pharmacology, ACP (life, Recognition awards 1967-70); mem. AMA, Am. Geriatrics Soc., St. Jude Soc., Holy Name Soc., Assn. Miraculous Medal (promoter 1987—), Venango County Med. Soc. (pres. 1989-91), Franklin Club, Assn. Mil. Surgeons, Am. Coll. Physician Execs., Am. Legion. Democrat. Roman Catholic. Home: 138 Harvest Rd Swedesboro NJ 08085-1427 Office: VA Med Ctr 1400 Blackhorse Hill Rd Coatesville PA 19320-2097

GEHRINGER, RICHARD GEORGE, publishing executive; b. Newark, Oct. 31, 1949; s. George John and Constance Mary (Volz) G.; m. Phyllis Jean Salerno, Nov. 13, 1977; 1 child, Alexandra Rane. BS, U. S.C., 1972; MBA, St. John's U., Jamaica, N.Y., 1976. Mgmt. trainee Avdel Corp., Teterboro, N.J., 1972-74; purchasing analyst Resistoflex Corp., Roseland, N.J., 1974-76; staff acct. McGraw-Hill Pub. Co., Hightstown, N.J., 1976-78; bus. mgr., corp. real estate McGraw-Hill Inc., N.Y.C., 1979-80; asst. contr. McGraw-Hill Book Co., N.Y.C., 1980-81; contr. Oxford U. Press Inc., Fair Lawn, N.J., 1981-86; v.p., chief fin. officer Oxford U. Press Inc., N.Y.C., 1986—; fin. advisor Pi Kappa Alpha Fraternity, Columbia U., N.Y.C., 1988-89. Mem. Fin. Execs. Inst., Nat. Assn. Accts., Nat. Assn. Corp. Cash Mgmt. Republican. Roman Catholic. Home: 2920 Lake Boone Pl Raleigh NC 27608-1151 Office: Oxford U Press Inc 2001 Evans Rd Cary NC 27513-2009

GEIER, JOAN AUSTIN, writer, editor; b. Port Jervis, N.Y., Mar. 6, 1934; d. Charles Raymond and Gladys Elizabeth (Myers) Austin; m. Walter Henry Geier, Sept. 15, 1956; children: Charles Theodore, Robert Joseph, Elizabeth Madeleine. BA in Humanities, CUNY, 1966. Freelance writer N.Y.C., 1965—; asst. fashion editor Womens Wear Daily, N.Y.C., 1956-59; editor Crystal Highlights, Moundsville, W.Va., 1968-73; dir. spl. projects Folkworks, N.Y.C., 1987-90; critic Bklyn. Poetry Circle, 1980—. Author: Mother of Tribes, 1987, Garbage Can Cat, 1976; contbr. articles and poetry to pubIs. Devel., publicist vol. Nat Coalition for Relief of Liberia, Plainfield, N.J., 1990—; vol. foster care provider Spence Chapin, N.Y.C., 1990—; trustee Ecumenical Parish of Good Shepherd, Roosevelt Island, N.Y., 1982—; devel., publicist, teaching vol. Workshop in Bus. Opportunities, N.Y.C., 1965—. Recipient John Masefield award World Order of Narrative Poets, 1985, Basho award, 1990, Haiku award Shelley Soc., 1979, ORBIS/Rhyme Internat. award, England, 1991, Spl. award for Haiku Amelia Mag., 1985. Mem. Poetry Soc. of Am. (Gustav Davidson award 1982). Home: 556102H Main St New York NY 10044-0066

GEIER, PHILIP HENRY, JR., advertising executive; b. Pontiac, Mich., Feb. 22, 1935; s. Philip Henry and Jane (Gillen) G.; m. Faith Power, children—Hope, Johanna Geier. B.A., Colgate U., 1957; M.S., Columbia U., 1958. With McCann-Erickson, Inc., Cleve., 1958-60, N.Y.C., 1960-68; chmn. McCann-Erickson Internat. U.K. Co., London, 1969-73; exec. v.p. McCann-Erickson Europe, 1973-75; vice chmn. internat. ops. McCann Worldwide, London, 1973-75; vice chmn. internat. Interpublic Group of Cos., Inc., N.Y.C., 1975-77; pres., chief operating officer Interpublic Group of Cos., Inc., 1977-80, chmn., chief exec. officer, 1980—, pres., 1985—; dir. EAC Industries, Inc. Bd. dirs. Sch. Am. Ballet; trustee N.Y. Foundling Hosp., Boy's Club N.Y., MU of Delta Kappa Epsilon Found.; dean's adv. coun. Columbia Bus. Sch.; pres.' coun. Marymount Manhattan Coll. Mem. Am. Assn. Advt. Agys. (com. agy. mgmt.), Advt. Coun. (vice chmn. fin. com.), Coalition Svc. Industries. Clubs: Doubles (N.Y.C.); River (N.Y.C.); Sloane (London); Hurlingham (London). Office: Interpub Group Cos Inc 1271 Ave Of The Americas New York NY 10020-1300*

GEIGER, DAVID K., chemistry educator, researcher; s. Russell N. and Lucy (Aquino) G.; m. Hilda Cristina (Carrasco), Sept. 5, 1981; children: Matthew R., Mark S., Thomas M. BA, Franciscan U., Steubenville, Ohio, 1978; PhD, U. Notre Dame, Ind., 1983. Rsch. assoc. Radiation Lab. U. Notre Dame, Ind., 1983-85; asst. prof. SUNY, Geneseo, 1985-91, assoc. prof., 1991—. Contbr. articles to profl. jours. Edn. Found. grantee Exxon Found. of Rsch. Corp., 1988. Mem. Am. Chem. Soc. (grantee Petroleum Rsch. Fund 1990), Rochester Sect. of Am. Chem. Soc. Office: SUNY Dept of Chem Geneseo NY 14454

GEIGER, MARY ANN, historian; b. Detroit, Dec. 29, 1935; d. Clarence E. and Anne Grace (O'Neil) Knorpp; m. Thomas L. Geiger, Feb. 15, 1958; children: Garrett Thomas, Daniel C., Stephen Charles, Arthur Joseph. BS in Home Econs., U. Detroit, 1958; BS in Graphic Design, LaRoche Coll., Pitts., 1980. Self-employed fiber artist Knothings by Mary Ann, Valencia and Butler, Pa., 1975-91; exec. dir. Ctr. for History of Am. Needlework, Valencia, 1985—. Editor, writer C.H.A.N. Newsletter, 1985—; writer for Handspun Mag., 1983-86, Precious Fibers Mag., 1983-86; writer/compiler C.H.A.N. Pubs. on Counted Thread, 1991, 92. Mem. Spinners and Weavers Guild of Butler (founder, pres. 1980-85), Assoc. Artists of Butler (pres. 1970-80). Roman Catholic. Home: PO Box 377 RD 2 Valencia PA 16059 Office: Ctr for History Am Needlewk 6459 Old Rt 8 Butler PA 16001

GEIGER, PHILIP EARL, school system administrator; b. New Brunswick, N.J., June 12, 1947; s. Philip Murray and Ida May (Danley) G.; m. Mary Louise Rossi, Aug. 25, 1967 (div. 1974); children: Philip Jr., Robert; m. Roseann Meade, Mar. 21, 1975; children: Jennifer, Abigail. BA, Trenton State Coll., 1970; MA, Columbia U., 1972, MEd, 1973, EdD, 1980; MBA, U. Pa., 1987. Tchr. Corpus Christi Sch., South River, N.J., 1967-69; tech., asst. to prin. South Brunswick (N.J.) Pub. Schs., 1969-71; acting adminstrv. prin., asst. prin. Bordentown (N.J.) Twp. Pub. Schs., 1971-74; dir. adminstrv. svcs., asst. to supt. Scotch Plains (N.J.)-Fanwood Pub. Schs., 1974-77; supt. of schs. Galloway Twp. Pub. Schs., Absecon, N.J., 1977-84; pres. Am. Property Group, Atlantic City, 1984-88; supt. of schs. Lexington (Mass.) Pub. Schs., 1988-91, Piscataway (N.J.) Pub. Schs., 1991—; pres. Geiger & Assocs., Cons., Piscataway, 1972—. Contbr. articles to profl. jours. Pres. Atlantic Area Coun. Boy Scouts Am., Linwood, N.J., 1987-88; bd. dirs. Minuteman Coun. Boy Scouts Am., Stoneham, Mass., 1988-91; v.p. Atlantic Performing Arts Ctr., Atlantic City, 1984-88. Recipient Mgmt. Effectiveness award Am. Sch. and Univ. Mag., 1990, Disting. Svc. award N.J. Prins. and Suprs., 1983; Paul Harris fellow Lexington (Mass.) Rotary, 1991. Mem. ASCD, Am. Assn. Sch. Adminstrs., N.J. Assn. Sch. Adminstrs., The Wharton Exec. MBA Fund, The Wharton Club of Boston, Piscataway Rotary Club, Phi Delta Kappa (Disting. Svc. Key So. N.J. chpt. 1982). Home: 6 Oakwood Way Piscataway NJ 08854-3628 Office: Piscataway Pub Schs Willow Ave Piscataway NJ 08854-4425

GEIS, FLORENCE LINDAUER, psychology educator; b. Oakland, Calif., Apr. 3, 1933; d. Earl Sherman and Alma Frederica (Dahm) Lindauer; m. Jon Geis, 1954 (div. 1960). BA, U. Ariz., 1956; PhD, Columbia U., 1964. Rsch. assistantship Columbia U., N.Y.C., 1960-64, adj. asst. prof., summer 1964; asst. prof. psychology NYU, 1964-67; asst. prof. psychology U. Del., Newark, 1967-71, assoc. prof., 1971-82, prof. psychology, 1982—. Author: Studies in Machiavellianism, 1970, Personality Research Manual, 1978, Instructor's Guide for Personality Research Manual, 1978, Seeing and Evaluating People, 1982, Research on Seeing and Evaluating People, 1983, The Organizational Woman: Power and Paradox, 1992; contbr. articles to profl. jours., chpts. to books. Grantee Nat. Inst. Edn., 1979, U. Del., 1972; recipient Heritage Rsch. award Am. Psychol. Assn., 1991, E. Arthur Trabant award Women's Equity, 1989. Mem. AAUP, AAUW, APA, NOW, Am. Psychol. Soc., Ea. Psychol. Assn. Office: Univ of Del Dept Psychology Newark DE 19716

GEISENHEIMER, EMILE J., electronics industry executive, venture capitalist; b. New Orleans, June 27, 1947; s. Emile Adam and Arietta (Gore) G.; m. Susan Freier, Apr. 16, 1982; children: Geoffrey Graham, Timothy Adam. BS in Econs. and Fin., La. State U., 1973; MBA in Fin., U. Pa., 1975. Faculty fellow Wharton Sch., U. Pa., Phila., 1973-75; pres. Geisenheimer, Fletcher & Assocs., N.Y.C., 1973-75; sr. cons. Cresap, McCormick & Paget, Inc., N.Y.C., 1975-78; dir. planning/devel. Philips Med. Sys., Shelton, Conn., 1978-79; N.E. zone mgr. Philips Med. Sys., 1979-81, nat. sales mgr., 1981, v.p. sales and svc., 1981-84; pres. Philips Electronic Instruments, Mahwah, N.J., 1984-89; gen. ptnr. Nazem & Co., N.Y.C., 1989—; chmn. bd. dirs. Metrologix, Inc., 1989—, ServiScope Inc., 1990—, Tegal Inc., 1991—; bd. dirs. Spectranetics Corp., Spatial Tech. Inc., Tetrad Inc., UltraCision Inc. Mem. Rep. Nat. Com., 1983—. Mem. Sci. Apparatus Makers Assn. (bd. dirs. 1989—), Analytical Instruments Assn. (chmn. 1989—), Apple Ridge Country Club, Phi Kappa Phi, Beta Gamma Sigma. Republican. Congregationalist. Office: Nazem and Co 600 Madison Ave New York NY 10022-1615

GEISERT, GENE ALVIN, educator; b. Toledo, Ohio, July 22, 1927; s. George E. and Cora (Laconte) G.; children: Jean, Ann. BA in Ednl. Adminstrn., U. Toledo, 1951, MA in Ednl. Adminstrn., 1955; PhD in Ednl. Adminstrn., U. Mich., 1965. Tchr. Washington Twp. Schs., Toledo, 1951-56; prin. Sylvania (Ohio) Pub. Schs., 1956-60; supt. Alpena (Mich.) Pub. Schs., 1965-68, Wilmington (Del.) Pub. Schs., 1968-72, New Orleans Pub. Schs., 1972-80; assoc. prof. edn. adminstrn. St. John's U., N.Y.C., 1980—; pres. Think Network, N.Y.C., 1987—; cons. N.J. Pub. Employment Rels., 1980—; chief negotiator sch. dists. in N.J., Del., Mich., 1968-89; with U.S. Dept. Edn., 1988-89. Author: Corporation and Public Education in the Cities, 1982, Situation Approach to Leadership, 1982, Thinking Networks for Reading and Writing, 1987. With USN, 1945-47. Recipient Meritorious Svc. award Nat. Assessment of Edn., Brotherhood award Urban League of Greater New Orleans; selected as Ednl. Leader of the Century, Am. Assn. Sch. Adminstrs., 1976. Mem. AAUP, Assn. Supts. of Large City Schs. (chmn.), Nat. Assessment of Edn. Progress (chmn.), Am. Assn. Sch. Adminstrs. (chmn.), Phi Delta Kappa. Office: St Johns Univ Grand Central Pky Jamaica NY 11432-1043

GEISINGER, KURT FRANCIS, psychometrician, educator, dean; b. Danville, Pa., Jan. 11, 1951; s. Karl William and Florence Eva (Graber) G.; m. Janet Frances Carlson, Sept. 22, 1984. AB with honors, Davidson Coll., 1972; MS, U. Ga., 1974; PhD, Penn State U., 1977. Instr. Penn State U., University Park, 1975-76; dir., rsch. svcs. Bartell Assocs., State College, Pa., 1976-77; asst. prof. to prof. and chmn. dept. psychology Fordham U., Bronx, N.Y., 1977-92; dean of arts and scis. SUNY, Oswego, 1992—; vis. rsch. assoc. Ednl. Testing Svc., Princeton, N.J., 1976; cons. and expert witness, N.Y.C. Depts. of Law and Personnel, 1981—, Fox and Fox Counsellors at Law, N.Y.C., 1986—, Pub. Svc. Alliance of Can., Ottawa, 1987—; cons. Assessment Alternatives, Florham Park, N.J., 1987—. Contbr. articles to profl. jours. Mem. APA, Am. Psychol. Soc., Am. Ednl. Rsch. Assn., Nat. Coun. on Measurement in Edn., Northeastern Ednl. Rsch. Assn. (newsletter editor 1988-91, pres. 1986-89, bd. dirs. 1984-86), Phi Kappa Phi (Fordham U. chpt. pres. 1984-86), Psi Chi, Sigma Xi. Democrat. Lutheran. Home: 2134 Candlewood Dr Oswego NY 13126-2301 Office: SUNY-Oswego Sch Arts & Scis 601 Culkin Hall Oswego NY 13126

GEISLER, CAROL JOY, psychologist, clinician, researcher, educator; b. N.Y., Mar. 3, 1948; d. Arthur H. and Sylvia (Bittner) G. BS in Math., MIT, 1968; MS in Math., NYU, 1970, MA in Psychology, 1973, PhD in Psychology, 1982. Lic. psychologist, N.Y. Psychologist, clinician, supr. Bklyn. Community Counseling Ctr., 1977—; pvt. practice psychologist N.Y.C., 1982—; researcher, educator, supr. Sch. of Social Work NYU, N.Y.C., 1983—; cons. in field. Mem. APA (mem. at large rsch. sect. div. psychoanalysis), Am. Orthopsychiat. Assn., Soc. Psychotherapy Rsch., N.Y. State Psychol. Assn., Assn. for Psychoanalytic Self-Psychology. Democrat. Jewish. Office: NYU Sch Social Work 3 Washington Sq N New York NY 10003-6635 also: 150 W 13th St New York NY 10011

GEISMAR, ROBERT, banker, consultant; b. N.Y.C., Nov. 16, 1946; s. Leo William and Helen (Henninger) G.; m. Marie-Elaine Nancy Convertini, Mar. 24, 1973; children: Deanna Marie, Robert Matthew, Michelle Ann, Michael William. AA, St. Peter's Coll., 1982. Account rep. reconciliation dept. Depository Trust Co., N.Y.C., 1971-72; group leader syndicated loan dept. to broker loan dept. Morgan Guaranty Trust Co., N.Y.C., 1972-83; internat. banking officer capital/money markets loan svc. Westpac Banking Corp., N.Y.C., 1983-86; mgr. syndications, Corp. Fin. Group USA Can. Imperial Bank of Commerce, N.Y.C., 1986-89; banking cons., account rep. product svcs. McDonnell Douglas Corp. Info. Systems, Lyndhurst, N.J., 1989-91; banking and corp. cons., pres. Quantum Assocs., Palisades Park, N.J., 1991—. Pres. Palisades Park Little League, 1990, 91, coach, 1988, 89, team mgr., minor league rep., 1986, 87, 88; basketball coach St. Michael's CYO, Palisades Park, 1990. Sgt. USAF, 1967-71. Office: Quantum Assocs PO Box 408 Palisades Park NJ 07650-0408

GEISSLER, SUZANNE BURR, educator; b. Somerville, N.J., Nov. 12, 1950; d. Alfred Henry and Suzanne Judith (Golembeski) G. BA, Syracuse U., 1971, PhD, 1976; MA, Rutgers U., 1972; postgrad., Worcester Coll., Oxford U., 1973; MTS, Drew U., 1979. adj. prof. Upsala Coll., Sussex, N.J., 1979—; del. Episcopal Diocese of Newark Conv., 1989-91; mem. Diocese of Newark Com. on Constitution and Canons, Newark, 1991. Author: Jonathan Edwards to Aaron Burr, 1981, Lutheranism and Anglicanism in Colonial New Jersey, 1988. Mem. Bd. Edn., Florham Park, N.J., 1980-82. Mem. Am. Hist. Assn., Orgn. Am. Historians, U.S. Naval Inst., Navy League U.S., Aaron Burr Assn. (v.p.), Am. Soc. Ch. History, Hist. Soc. of Episcopal Ch., Chatham Club, Phi Beta Kappa. Republican. Home: 4 Midwood Dr Florham Park NJ 07932-1811 Office: Upsala Coll 44 Compton Rd Sussex NJ 07461-2647

GEJDENSON, SAM, congressman; b. Eschwege, Fed. Republic of Germany, May 20, 1948; s. Szloma and Julia G.; m. Karen Fleming; chil-

dren: Mia, Ari. AS, Mitchell Coll., 1968; BA, U. Conn., 1970. Mem. Conn. Ho. of Reps., 1974-78; coal broker, 1978-79; legis. liaison Conn. Office Policy and Mgmt., Hartford, 1979-80; mem. 97-102nd Congresses from 2d Conn. dist., 1981—. Office: US Ho of Reps 1410 Longworth House Office Bldg Washington DC 20515*

GEKAS, GEORGE WILLIAM, congressman; b. Harrisburg, Pa., Apr. 14, 1930; m. Evangeline Charas, 1971. B.A., Dickinson Coll., 1952, J.D., 1958. Bar: Pa. 1959. Asst. dist. atty. Dauphin County, Pa., 1960-66; mem. Pa. Ho. of Reps. from 103d dist., Harrisburg, 1966-74, Pa. Senate from 15th dist., Harrisburg, 1977-82, 98th-102d Congresses from 17th Pa. dist., Washington, 1983—; mem. House Jud. Com., House Select Com. on Intelligence. Chmn. March of Dimes, 1967; div. leader Cancer Crusade; v.p. United Ch. of Harrisburg; bd. dirs. Police Athletic League. Office: US Ho of Reps 1519 Longworth House Office Bldg Washington DC 20515*

GELATO, MARIE CATHERINE, physician; b. N.Y.C., July 7, 1947; d. Ignazio G. and Theresa (Lucera) G. BA, Hunter Coll., N.Y.C., 1969; MS, Mich. State U., 1972, PhD, 1975, MD, 1979. Diplomate Am. Bd. Internal Medicine, Am. Bd. Endocrinology. Postdoctoral fellow Max Planck Inst., West Germany, 1974-76; intern Dartmouth Med. Coll., Hanover, N.H., 1979-80; resident Dartmouth Med. Coll., Hanover, 1980-82; fellow endocrinology NIH, Bethesda, Md., 1982-85, sr. staff fellow, 1985-87; assoc. prof. dept. medicine SUNY, Stony Brook, 1987—; dir. clin. rsch. unit SUNY, Stony Brook, 1987—; cons. Hoffmann-LaRoche Inc., Nutley, N.J., 1987—. Contbr. articles on endocrinology to profl. jours. Mem. AMA, Am. Fedn. Clin. Rsch., Endocrine Soc., Sigma Xi. Office: SUNY Dept Medicine HSC T-15 060 Stony Brook NY 11794

GELB, JOSEPH DONALD, lawyer; b. Wilkes-Barre, Pa., Dec. 13, 1923; s. Edward and Esther (Fierman) G. m. Anne Mirman, July 3, 1955; children: Adam, Roger. Student, Pa. State Coll., 1943; BS, U. Scranton, 1950; LLB, George Washington U., 1952. Bar: D.C. 1954, Md. 1963, U.S. Supreme Ct. 1972. Adjudicator War Claims Commn., 1952-54; pvt. practice Washington and Md., 1954-69; ptnr. Gelb & Pitsenberger, Washington, 1969-74; prin. Joseph D. Gelb Chartered, Washington, 1974-80, Gelb, Abelson & Siegel, P.C., Washington, 1980-82; prin. Gelb & Siegel, P.C., Washington, 1982-85, prin. Joseph D. Gelb, Chartered, 1985—. Served with USAAF, 1943-46. Mem. ABA, Md. Bar Assn., D.C. Bar Assn., Assn. Trial Lawyers Am. Assn. Plaintiff's Trial Attys., Bethesda Country Club, B'nai B'rith, Masons. Home: 9620 Annlee Ter Bethesda MD 20817-1410 also: 525 N Ocean Blvd Pompano Beach FL 33062 Office: 1120 Connecticut Ave NW Washington DC 20036

GELB, JUDITH ANNE, lawyer; b. N.Y.C., Apr. 5, 1935; d. Joseph and Sarah (Stein) G.; m. Howard S. Vogel, June 30, 1962; 1 child, Michael S. B.A., Bklyn. Coll., 1955; J.D., Columbia U., 1958. Bar: N.Y. 1959, U.S. Dist. Ct. (so. dist. and ea. dist.) N.Y. 1960, U.S. Ct. Appeals (2d cir.) 1960, U.S. Ct. Mil. Appeals 1962. Asst. to editor N.Y. Law Jour., N.Y.C., 1958-59; confidential asst. to U.S. atty. ea. dist. N.Y., Bklyn., 1959-61; assoc. Whitman & Ransom, N.Y.C., 1961-70, ptnr., 1971—. Mem. ABA (individual rights sect., real property & trust law sect.), Fed. Bar Counsel, N.Y. State Bar Assn. (trusts and estates com.), N.Y. State Dist. Attys. Assn., Assn. of Bar of City of N.Y., Columbia Law Sch. Alumni Assn. (bd. dirs.), Girls, Inc. (resources com.), Princeton Club, Assn. Ex-mem. Squadron A Club. Home: 169 E 69th St New York NY 10021-5163 Office: Whitman & Ransom 200 Park Ave New York NY 10166-0005

GELB, RICHARD LEE, pharmaceutical corporation executive; b. N.Y.C., June 8, 1924; s. Lawrence M. and Joan F. (Bove) G.; m. Phyllis L. Nason, May 5, 1951; children: Lawrence N., Lucy G., Jane E., James M. Student, Phillips Acad., 1938-41; B.A., Yale, 1945; M.B.A. with Distinction, Harvard U., 1950. Joined Clairol, Inc., N.Y.C., 1950, pres., 1959-64; exec. v.p. Bristol-Myers Co., 1965-67, pres., 1967-76, chief exec. officer, 1972—, chmn. bd., 1976—; bd. dirs. N.Y. Times Co., N.Y. Life Ins. Co.; policy com. Bus. Roundtable; active Bus. Coun.; trustee Com. for Econ. Devel.; mem. Conf. Bd.; ptnr. N.Y.C. Partnerships, Inc. Charter trustee Phillips Acad., Andover; dir. Lincoln Ctr. for Performing Arts; mem., former dir. Coun. Fgn. Rels.; vice-chmn. bd. overseers, bd. mgrs. Meml. Sloan-Kettering Cancer Ctr.; chmn. bd. mgrs. Sloan Kettering Inst. Cancer Rsch.; vice-chmn., trustee N.Y.C. Police Found.; trustee N.Y. Racing Assn. Home: 1060 5th Ave New York NY 10128-0104 Office: Bristol-Myers Squibb Co 345 Park Ave New York NY 10154-0004

GELBEIN, JAY JOEL, accountant; b. Bklyn., Sept. 11, 1949; s. Leo and Sara (Eskolsky) G. B.S., Bklyn. Coll., 1972; M.S. with distinction, L.I. U., 1978; m. Marilyn Stern, Dec. 8, 1974; children—Moshe, Avi, Danielle. Cert. fin. planner. Appellate conferee IRS, N.Y.C., 1971-79; tech. mgr. Am. Inst. C.P.A.s, N.Y.C., 1979-81; pvt. practice acctg. and tax cons., Staten Island, N.Y., 1979—; prof. bus. Kingsborough Community Coll., Bklyn., 1981—; nat. tax lectr. C.P.A., N.Y. Mem. Am. Inst. C.P.A.s, N.Y. State Soc. C.P.A.s (mem. profl. service corp. com.), Inst. Cert. Fin. Planners. Author: Tax-wise Investing for High Income Taxpayers; contbr. to The Practical Accountant, 1991; co-author: Accounting Demonstration Problems Workbook. Home and Office: 13 President St Staten Island NY 10314-4119

GELERNT, IRWIN M., surgeon, educator; b. N.Y.C., Sept. 27, 1935; s. Lipman and Ray (Samuels) G.; married, June 11, 1960; children: Lee, Alicia, Michelle. BS, CCNY, 1957; MD, SUNY, N.Y.C., 1961. Diplomate Am. Bd. Surgery. Intern Bellevue Hosp. Cornel Med. Svc.; attending surgeon Mt. Sinai Hosp., N.Y.C., 1962-67, pres. attending staff, 1985-87; clin. prof. of surgery Mt. Sinai Sch. Medicine, N.Y.C., 1987—. Contbr. articles to profl. pubIs., chpts. to books. Trustee Manhattan Country Sch., N.Y.C., 1978-84. Named Physician of Yr., Nurses Assn. of Mt. Sinai Hosp., 1991. Fellow ACS, Am. Coll. Gastroenterology; mem. Found. Ileitis and Colitis (Man of Yr. 1983), Phi Beta Kappa, Alpha Omega Alpha. Office: 25 E 69th St New York NY 10021-4925

GELFAND, JEFFREY ALAN, physician, educator; b. N.Y.C., Sept. 13, 1946; s. Michael R. and Doris (Eichmann) G.; m. Janet Vullemier, Aug. 31, 1969; children: Jennifer, Lauren, Melissa. BS, U. Pa., 1967; MD, Tufts U., 1971. Bd. cert. internal medicine, 1976, infectious diseases, 1980, allergy and immunology, 1981. Intern Johns Hopkins Hosp., Balt., 1971-72, resident, 1972-73, chief resident, 1976-77; rsch. fellow NIH, Bethesda, Md., 1973-76; asst. prof. Tufts Univ. Sch. Medicine, Boston, 1977-82, assoc. prof., 1982-90, prof., 1991—; vice chmn. dept. medicine New Eng. Med. Ctr., Boston, 1991—. Contbr. articles to profl. jours. Lt. commdr. USPHS, 1973-76. Office: New England Med Ctr 750 Washington St #480 Boston MA 02111

GELFAND, STEVEN B., psychiatrist, neurologist; b. Bklyn., Oct. 6, 1948; s. Louis and Evelyn (Feldberg) G.; m. Susan Gelfand, Jan. 17, 1981; children: Danielle, Joshua. BS cum laude, N.Y. Inst. Tech., 1971; MS summa cum laude, Nova U., 1973; Profl. Diploma, L.I. Univ., 1975; MD, Universidad de Cetec, Santo Domingo, Dominican Republic, 1983. Lic. medicine, Pa., N.Y.; cert. sch. psychologist, N.Y.C. Various positions, 1973-79; clin. cons. psychology and hypnotherapy County Counseling, Rego Park, N.Y., 1978-79; chmn. bd. dirs. L.I. Coun. for Youth Devel., Melville, N.Y., 1978-79; sch. psychologist N.Y.C. Bd. Edn., Queens, 1980-81; resident psychiatry SUNY Downstate/King County Health Ctr., Bklyn., 1983-85; asst. clin. instr. dept. psychiatry SUNY Downstate/King County Health Ctr., 1983-85, resident neurology, 1985-88, asst. instr. neurology, 1985-88, resident psychiatry, 1988-89, dir. dept. neuropsychiatry, 1989—; floor psychologist, clin. supr. Boerum Hill Psychiat. Residence, Bklyn., 1974-76; instr. behavioral scis. N.Y. Inst. Tech., Old Westbury, 1974-80; instr. psychology adult edn. div. Adelphi U., Garden City, N.Y., 1979-80; exec. dir. P.R.I.C.E. Counseling Ctr., Farmingdale, N.Y., 1977-79. Contbr. articles to profl. jours. Grantee CETA program U.S. Govt., 1978-80. Mem. Assn. for Advanced Ethical Hyponosis, Am. Assn. Biofeedback Clinicians, Biofeedback Soc. Am., Joint Coalition Mental Health Workers, Am. Psychiat. Assn., Bklyn. Psychiat. Soc., Am. Acad. Neurology, Bklyn. Neurol. Soc., Assn. for Specialists in Group Work, Ethical Hypnosis Soc. Home: 105 Woodland Dr Oil City PA 16301-2040 Office: 9 Glenview Ave Ste 206 Oil City PA 16301-2174

GELIEBTER, ALLAN, psychologist, educator; b. Frankfurt, Germany, Jan. 22, 1947; came to U.S., 1950; s. Leo and Bella Geliebter. BS in Biology, CCNY, 1968; MA in Biology, Columbia U., 1970, M. Philosophy in Psychology, 1973, PhD in Psychology, 1976. From asst. prof. to assoc. prof. psychology Touro Coll., N.Y.C., 1976-1988, prof., 1988—, chmn. dept., 1981—; rsch. psychologist Obesity Rsch. Ctr. St. Luke's Roosevelt Hosp. Columbia U., N.Y.C., 1978—, dir. weight control and eating disorders, 1985—. Contbr. articles to profl. jours. Pres. Tenants Assn., N.Y.C., 1985—. NIH grantee, N.Y.C., 1981—. Mem. Am. Psychol. Assn., Ea. Psychol. Assn., Am. Soc. Clin. Nutrition, Internat. Assn. Study of Obesity. Jewish. Office: St Lukes Roosevelt Hosp 111 Amsterdam Ave New York NY 10023-7410

GELKE, KURT DAVID, furniture company executive; b. Ft. Campbell, Ky., Sept. 9, 1957; s. Donald Edward and Dolys Lee (Perry) G.; m. Eileen Margaret Fritz, May 23, 1987. BS, U.S. Mil. Acad., 1979; MBA, Harvard U., 1987. Registered engr.-in-tng., Pa. Commd. 2d lt. U.S. Army, 1979, advanced through grades to capt., 1983; resigned, 1984; mgr. N.Y. Telephone Co., Buffalo, 1984-85; mktg. specialist Moog Inc., East Aurora, N.Y., 1987-88; asst. to pres. Bush Industries, Jamestown, N.Y., 1988-90; v.p. mktg. and strategic planning Bush Industries, 1990—. Bd. dirs. Chautauqua County Pvt. Industry Coun., Jamestown, 1989—. Decorated Meritorious Svc. medal. Mem. Assn. Grads. U.S. Mil. Acad., Harvard U. Bus. Sch. Club Buffalo, Phi Kappa Phi. Republican. Roman Catholic. Home: Ll E Fairwood Dr Lakewood NY 14750 Office: Bush Industries 1 Mason Dr PO Box 460 Jamestown NY 14702-0460

GELLER, ANDREW MICHAEL, architect, designer; b. Bklyn., Apr. 17, 1924; s. Joseph Boris and Olga (Gernsten) G.; m. Shirley-Del Marie Morris, Oct. 22, 1944; children: Gregory Brook, Jamie Gail. V.p., design dir. Raymond Loewy/William Smith, N.Y.C., 1946-73; prin. archtl. firm, Northport, N.Y., 1973-83; v.p. Creative Design Internat., Riverdale, N.Y., 1983—; Mem. architects in schs. program, Nat. Commn. for Arts, Baldwin, N.Y., 1980—, AIA Hdqrs. Nat. Exhibit, Washington and N.Y., 1988. Designs include Lord and Taylor, Bloomingdale's, A&S, Stewarts, Higbees, Burdines, Richs, Gimbels, R.H. Macy's, Iveys, Sibleys, Filenes Market Basket stores; exhibited in Bklyn. Mus., Mus. of Modern Art N.Y., Guild Hall Princeton U., Soc. for Preservation of L.I. Antiquities, 1992. Chmn. Northport Archtl. Rev. Bd., 1976-79. Served with C.E. U.S. Army, 1941-45, ETO. Recipient House of Yr. award Interiors mag., 1960, Better Homes and Gardens, 1966, Cooper Union Alumnus'45. Mem. Am. Audubon Soc. (Humane medal 1938), Am. Forestry Assn. Home: 123 Highland Ave Northport NY 11768-1643

GELLER, HAROLD ARTHUR, earth and space sciences executive; b. Bklyn., June 14, 1954; s. Morris and Minnie (Kaplan) G. BS, SUNY, Albany, 1983; MA, George Mason Univ., 1992. Rsch. asst. SUNY at Downstate Med., Bklyn., 1972-74; rsch. asst. CUNY at Bklyn. Coll., 1974-75; engrng. aide FBI, Washington, 1977-78; lab. supr. ENSCO Inc., Springfield, Va., 1978-80; assoc. engr. Def. Systems Inc., McLean, Va., 1980-83; staff scientist/systems engr. Sci. Applications Internat. Corp., McLean, 1983-87; systems engr. Grumman Aerospace, Reston, Va., 1987-88, Sci. Applications Internat. Corp., McLean, 1988-90; rsch. asst. Naval Rsch. Lab., George Mason U., 1990-91; project mgr. Rsch. and Data Systems Corp., Greenbelt, Md., 1991-92; applications scientist Consortium Internat. Earth Sci. Info. Network, Washington, 1992—; computer cons., Burke, Va., 1986-87. Mem. AIAA (chmn. corp. liaison com. 1989-90, chmn. pub. affairs com. 1990-91). Democrat. Jewish. Office: Consortium Internat Earth Sci Info Network 1825 K St N W Washington DC 20006

GELLER, JANICE GRACE, nurse; b. Auburn, Ga., Feb. 25, 1938; d. Erby Ralph and Jewell Grace (Maughon) Clack; m. Joseph Jerome Geller, Dec. 23, 1973; 1 child, Elizabeth Joanne. Student, LaGrange Coll., 1955-57; BS in Nursing, Emory U., 1960; MS, Rutgers U., 1962. Psychiat. staff nurse dept. psychiatry Emory U., Atlanta, 1960; nurse educator Ill. State Psychiat. Inst., Chgo., 1961; clin. specialist in mental retardation nursing Northville, Mich., 1962; faculty Coll. Nursing Rutgers U., Newark, 1962-63, faculty Advanced Program in Psychiat. Nursing, 1964-66; faculty Coll. Nursing U. Mich., Ann Arbor, 1963-64; faculty, Teheran (Iran) Coll. for Women, 1967-69; clin. specialist psychiat. nursing Roosevelt Hosp., N.Y.C., 1969-70; faculty, guest lectr. Columbia U., N.Y.C., 1969-70; supr. Dept. Psychiat. Nursing Mt. Sinai Hosp., N.Y.C., 1970-72; pvt. practice psychotherapy N.Y.C., 1972-77, Ridgewood, N.J., 1977—; faculty, curriculum coord. in psychiat. nursing William Alanson White Inst. Psychiatry, Psychoanalysis and Psychology, N.Y.C., 1974-84; mem. U.S. del. of Community and Mental Health Nurses to People's Republic of China, 1983. Contbr. articles to profl. jours.; editorial bd. Perspectives in Psychiat. Care, 1971-74, 78-84; author: (with Anita Marie Werner) Instruments for Study of Nurse-Patient Interaction, 1964. Committeewoman Bergen County Rep. Com., 1989; mem. Rep. County Com., Bergen County, N.J. Recipient 10th Anniversary award Outstanding Clin. Specialist in psychiat.-mental health nursing in N.J., Soc. Cert. Clin. Specialists, 1982; Fed. Govt. grantee as career tchr. in psychiat. nursing, Rutgers U., 1962-63; cert. psychiat. nurse and clin. specialist, N.J., N.Y. Mem. AAAS, ANA (various certs.), N.J. Nurses Assn., Soc. Cert. Clin. Specialists in Psychiat. Nursing (chmn.), Coun. Specialists in Psychiat. Mental Health Nursing, Am. Group Psychotherapy Assn., Am. Assn. Mental Deficiency, World Fedn. Mental Health, Friends of Hermitage, Soc. Valley Hosp. of Ridgewood, AMA Aux., Bergen County Med. Soc. Aux., Coll. Club, Sigma Theta Tau. Address: 159 Fairmount Rd Ridgewood NJ 07450

GELLER, JEFFREY LAWRENCE, financier; b. N.Y.C., Sept. 23, 1953; s. Jerome Charles Geller and Harriet (Rogers) Blum; m. Karina Musheli, Nov. 22, 1990. BA, Columbia U., 1975, MBA, 1979. Sr. fin. analyst W.R. Grace & Co., N.Y.C., 1979-83, asst. to the pres., 1983; v.p. Bank of Am., N.Y.C., 1984-86; exec. v.p. Union Holdings, Inc., N.Y.C., 1986-91; pres., chief exec. officer Geller Ptnrs., Inc., N.Y.C., 1991—, also bd. dirs.; exec. v.p. Idle Wild Foods, Inc., Liberal, Kans., 1986-91, ZG Holding Corp., N.Y.C., 1986-91; v.p. Nat. Carriers, Inc., Liberal, 1986-91. Co-author: President's Private Sector Survey on Cost Control, 1983. Mem. com. Am. Cancer Soc., N.Y.C., 1982-86, Friends of Lenox Hosp., N.Y.C., 1985—, Children's Village, Dobbs Ferry, N.Y., 1985-87, Save Venice, Inc., N.Y.C., 1987—. Mem. Columbia Club, Rockefeller Club, Le Club.

GELLER, MATTHEW BRUCE, artist; b. N.Y.C.. BA, Conn. Coll., 1976; MFA, U. Del., 1978. Mem. faculty Sch. Visual Arts, N.Y.C.; co-chmn. TV and media panel N.Y. State Coun. on Arts; video curator Inst. for Art and Urban Resources; v.p. collaborative projects, cons. Nat. Endowment for Arts; vis. lectr. U. Calif., San Diego, 1987, Princeton U., 1988, Williams Coll., 1990; instr. sculpture U. Del., 1976-78, Del. Art Mus., 1978; instr. TV seminar Gt. Lakes Coll. Assn., 1983; artist-in residence Conn. Coll., 1983, 87, Rensselaer Poly. Inst., Art Inst. Chgo., St. Lawrence U., 1982-83, Cunningham Community for Arts, Mass. Exhibited in numerous group shows, including Barbara Gladstone Gallery, 1982, Young Hoffman Gallery, 1983, Jack Tilton Gallery, 3983, Cash/Newhouse Gallery, 1985, Queens Mus., 1986, New Mus., 1986, Art Gallery Hamilton, 1990, also numerous festivals; producer, writer, dir., editor videotapes including White Columns, 1981, Windfalls, 1982, Everglades City, 1985, Battery City Park, 1986, 8 arts and events programs World Fin. Ctr., 1987-90 Bees and Thoroughbreds, 1987, Split Britches, 1988. Recipient numerous awards, including silver medal Chgo. Film Festival, 1987, gold and silver medals Phila. Film Festival, 1987, silver award Houston Film Festival, 1988; fellow Am. Acad. Rome, 1991-92, Nat. Endowment for Arts, N.Y. State Visual Arts, Caps fellow Prix de Rome; numerous project fellowship and artist-in-residence grants Nat. Endowment for Arts, N.Y. State Coun. on Arts, also pub. and pvt. founds. Mem. Assn. Ind. Video and Film Producers.

GELLER, ROBERT, executive producer; b. Yonkers, N.Y., Nov. 12, 1931; s. Benjamin and Rose (Ptashek) G.; m. Marion Margolin, Nov. 25, 1958; children: Daniel Geller, Suzanne Geller. BA, NYU, 1953, postgrad., 1960-61, MA, 1987. Tchr. of English Yonkers (N.Y.) Sch., 1957-61; dept. chmn. Mamaroneck (N.Y.) Schs., 1961-68; dir. edn. Am. Film Inst., Washington, 1968-69; program coord. Community Film Workshops, 1969-70; project dir./assoc. dean Antioch/New Sch., N.Y.C., 1971-73; artistic dir. Sundance Inst., N.Y.C., Utah, 1980-82; exec. producer, pres. SeaCliff Prodns., Larchmont, N.Y., 1975—, Learning in Focus, Larchmont, 1975—; faculty Columbia U., 1987, 91-92; speaker 1992 Key West Lit. Seminar; cons. CBS, Polytel, Reeves Enter. Contbr. numerous articles to various publs. Recipient Peabody award U. Ga., 1981; John Hay fellowship William Coll., U. Chgo., 1960, 63; honored Mus. of Broadcasting. Democrat. Jewish. Office: Learning in Focus 4 Chatsworth Ave Larchmont NY 10538-2932

GELLER, ROBERT JAMES, advertising agency executive; b. N.Y.C., May 5, 1937; s. Jerome and Pearl (Klein) G.; m. Lois Dee Fromkin, June 9, 1968; children: Richard Evan, Stephen Laurence. BS CCNY, 1958. Account exec. Furman, Feiner & Co., N.Y.C., 1958-62; media supr. Interpublic Group of Cos., N.Y.C., 1962-64; asst. media dir. Foote, Cone & Belding, N.Y.C., 1964-69; pres. Adforce Inc., N.Y.C., 1970—. Contbr. numerous articles to profl. jours. Mem. Assn. Nat. Advertisers (mem. mgmt. policy com. 1980—, corp. membership com. 1990—), Am. Advt. Fedn. (bd. dirs. 1988—, mem. corp. membership com. 1989—, plans rev. com. 1990—, asst. sec. 1992—), Advt. Club N.Y.C. Republican. Home: 155 E 76th St New York NY 10021-2810 also: Ocean Rd Bridgehampton NY 11932 Office: Adforce Inc 235 E 42d St New York NY 10017

GELLERMAN, BRUCE EDWARD, reporter; b. Bklyn., Dec. 10, 1950; s. Seymour and Florence (Waxman) G. BA, Ohio State U., 1973; postgrad., Hebrew U., 1975-76. Sr. corr. Ctr. for Investigative Journalism, Washington, 1981-82; gen. assignment reporter Nat. Pub. Radio, Washington, 1982-83, sci. reporter, 1983-85, producer, 1986-87; bus. reporter Sta. WBUR-FM Radio, Boston, 1987-88; pub. affairs producer Sta. WORT-FM, Madison, Wis., 1980-82. Recipient awards Ohio State U., 1990, Corp. for Pub. Broadcasting, 1990, Investment Co. Inst., 1990, ABA, 1991, Pub. Radio News Dirs. 1991, Sci. Jounalism award AAAS, 1984, Pub. Svc. award Corp. Pub. Broadcasting, 1985, Investigative award UPI, 1982, award Milw. Press Club, 1983; Knight fellow U. Md., 1990, Travel fello Coun. for the Advancement of Sci. Writing. Mem. NATZ Assn. of Sci. Writers. Jewish. Home: 568 Green St Cambridge MA 02139-3120 Office: Sta WBUR-FM 630 Commonwealth Ave Boston MA 02215-2422

GELLERMANN, WILLIAM PRESCOTT, human systems development consultant; b. Seattle, June 2, 1929; s. John William and Mildred Emaline (Prescott) G.; m. Marjorie Phyfe, Sept. 14, 1968 (div. May 1980), m. Rita Ellen Hecht, Feb. 9, 1990. BA, U. Washington, 1950, MA in Bus. Adminstrn., 1953; PhD in Behavioral Sci. for Mgmt., UCLA, 1964. CPA, Wash. Sr. acct. Arthur Andersen & Co., N.Y.C., Detroit, 1953-58; asst. prof. SUNY, Buffalo, 1963-65, Cornell U., Ithaca, N.Y., 1965-68; adj. assoc. prof. City U. N.Y., Staten Island, 1972-78; pres. Dialogue Assocs., N.Y.C., 1972—; ethics task force chmn. Human Systems Devel. Consortium, 1982-88; co-dir. value and ethics in orgn. devel. study AAAS, 1984-86. Author: Values and Ethics in Organization and Human Systems Development, 1990; contbr. articles to profl. jours. and books. Mem. Am. Mgmt. Assn. (course leader 1980—), Internat. Orgn. Devel. Assn. (U.S. liaison 1989), N.Y. Orgn. Devel. Network, U.S. Orgn. Devel. Network, Orgn. Devel. Inst. (Outstanding Orgn. Devel. Cons. of Yr. 1984), Acad. Mgmt., Soc. for Bus. Ethics. Home: 372 Central Park W Apt 16C New York NY 10025-8211 Office: Principle-Ctred Assocs 372 Central Park W Apt 16C New York NY 10025-8211

GELLHORN, ALFRED, physician, educator; b. St. Louis, June 4, 1913; s. George and Edna (Fischel) G.; m. Olga Frederick, Aug. 4, 1939; children—Martha, Anne, Christina, Maria, Edna. Student, Amherst Coll., 1930-32, D.Sc. (hon.), 1969; M.D., Washington U., St. Louis, 1937; D.Sc. (hon.), CCNY, 1979, SUNY, 1984, Albany Med. Coll., 1986. Diplomate Am. Bd. Internal Medicine. Gen. surg. tng. Barnes Hosp., St. Louis, 1937-39; gynecology trainee Passavant Meml. Hosp., Chgo., 1939-40; fellow Carnegie Instn. of Washington, Balt., 1940-43; instr., later asst. prof. physiology Coll. Physicians and Surgeons, Columbia U., N.Y.C., 1943-45, asst., then assoc. prof. pharmacology, 1945-48, assoc. prof. clin. cancer research dept. medicine, 1948-52, assoc. prof. medicine, 1952-58, prof. medicine, 1958-68; prof. medicine and pharmacology, dean Sch. Medicine, also dir. Med. Ctr. U. Pa., Phila., 1968-73; dir. Ctr. Biomed. Edn., City Coll., v.p. for health affairs CUNY, 1974-79, emeritus, 1979—; dir. med. affairs N.Y. State Dept. Health, Albany, 1983—; sr. cons. Commonwealth Fund, N.Y., 1979-80, Aaron Diamond Found., 1987—; vis. prof. Harvard Sch. Pub. Health, 1980-83; physician Francis Delafield Hosp., N.Y.C., 1949-52, chief med. service, 1952-68; vis. prof. medicine Albert Einstein Med. Sch.; dir. Inst. Cancer Research, Columbia; bd. regents Nat. Library Medicine. Mem. ACP, Coll. Physicians Phila., Soc. for Clin. Investigation, Assn. Am. Physicians, N.Y. County Med. Soc., Am. Assn. Cancer Research (pres. 1962-63), Am. Soc. Pharm. and Exptl. Therapeutics, Inst. Medicine, Am. Soc. Biol. Chemistry. Office: State NY Dept Health Empire State Pla Albany NY 12237

GELMAN, BERNARD, journalist; b. Bronx, N.Y., June 16, 1933; s. Irving and Sonia (Berlinsky) G.; BBA cum laude, Coll. City N.Y., 1954; m. Anne Terese Westfield, Dec. 20, 1969. Asst. prodn. mgr. Master Matrix Service Co., N.Y.C., 1954; copywriter, traffic and prodn. mgr. S.T. Seidman & Co., Inc., advt. agy., N.Y.C., 1955; asst. advt. mgr. Olympic Radio & TV, Long Island City, N.Y., 1956-57; advt. and sales promotion mgr. Michael Lith, Inc., N.Y.C., 1958; copy chief Philip I. Ross Co., Inc., advt. agy., N.Y.C., 1959; free-lance writer by-line articles to Parade, Indpls. Star, Winnipeg Free Press, N.Y. Herald Tribune's Sunday mag., Success Unltd., Today, Irish Press, Manchester Evening News, 1959—; owner, editor Gelman Feature Syndicate, N.Y.C., 1962—. Mem. Nat. Writers Club (chpt. pres.), Soc. Am. Magicians, Internat. Brotherhood Magicians, Am. Soc. for Psychical Research, Internat. Guild Prestidigitators, Internat. Platform Assn., Eta Mu Pi. Home: 826 E 14th St Brooklyn NY 11230-2918 Office: POB 1370 Grand Central Sta New York NY 10163

GELMAN, DONALD, astronomy educator; b. Bklyn., Sept. 13, 1938; s. Samuel and Etta (Silverman) G.; m. Doraine Sills, Aug. 11, 1962; children: Sharon Beth, Deborah Lauren. BS, CUNY, 1964; MS, NYU, 1964, PhD, 1969. Rsch. physicist Kollsman Instrument Corp., Elmhurst, N.Y., 1961-64; sci. instr. CUNY, Bklyn., 1964; instr. physics L.I. U., C.W. Post Campus, Brookville, N.Y., 1964-69; asst. prof. physics L.I. U. C.W. POst Campus, Brookville, N.Y., 1969-73, assoc. prof., 1973-92; prof. L.I. U., C.W. Post Campus. Home: 11 Fielding Ave Huntington Station NY 11746-7139 Office: LI U CW POst Campus Brookville NY 11548

GELMAN, NORMAN IRA, public policy consultant; b. Pitts., Mar. 20, 1929; s. Jerome G. and Emma (Horovitz) G.; m. Esther Ann Paper, Aug. 29, 1951; children: Judith R., Sharon R. BA magna cum laude, U. Colo., 1951, MA, 1953. Editorial writer St. Petersburg (Fla.) Times, 1956-57; writer Congl. Quar., Inc., Washington, 1958-59; mem. profl. staff commerce com. U.S. Senate, Washington, 1959-61; mem. profl. staff Newmyer Assocs. Inc., Washington, 1961—, exec. v.p., 1985—. Pres. Am. Jewish Com., Washington, 1989-91, nat. exec. coun., 1989-92; bd. govs., 1992—, nat. adv. coun., 1992—; bd. dirs. Jewish Inst. for Nat. Security Affairs, Washington, 1977—, Jewish Community Coun., Washington, 1980-86; mem. Dem. Cen. Com., Montgomery County, Md., 1966-68. With U.S. Army, 1954-56. Phi Sigma Delta fellow U. Colo., 1951; congl. fellow Am. Polit. Sci. Assn., Washington, 1957-58. Mem. Pub. Affairs Coun., U. Colo. Grads. Coun., Phi Beta Kappa. Office: Newmyer Assocs Inc 1220 L St NW Ste 425 Washington DC 20005

GELOSO-BARONE, ROSALIA ANN, lawyer; b. Rye, N.Y., Apr. 21, 1962; d. Vincent M. and Patricia (Checca) G. BA in Journalism, Boston Coll., 1984; JD, Pace U., 1988. Bar: N.Y. 1988, Conn. 1988, U.S. Dist. Ct. (so. and ea. dists.) N.Y. 1988. Project asst. Fin. Acctg. Standards Bd., Stamford, Conn., 1984-85; legal asst. Merrill Lynch Realty, Inc., Stamford, 1985-86, U.S. Attorney's Office, N.Y.C., 1987-88; atty. Westchester County Attorney's Office, White Plains, N.Y., 1988—. Alumni admissions counselor Boston Coll., Fairfield County, Conn., 1984—. Recipient Merit Scholarship Pace Law Sch., 1986-88. Mem. ABA, N.Y. State Bar Assn., Conn. Bar Assn. Home: 208 Harris Rd Bedford NY 10507

GELSTON, STEPHANIE M., magazine executive; b. Freeport, N.Y., Feb. 7, 1960; d. Stephen and Majael (Baker) G. BS, Boston U., 1982. Editorial asst. Harvard U. Office of Devel., Cambridge, Mass., 1982-84, Harvard Mag., Cambridge, 1984-85; from copy editor to asst. mgn. editor Boston Bus. Jour., 1986-90, mgn. editor, 1990—. Mem. Soc. Profl. Journalists.

GELWICK, RICHARD LEE, theologian; b. Bristow, Okla., Mar. 9, 1931; s. Allen Garrett and Lenora Jean (Foster) G.; m. Beverly Prosser, May 14, 1955; children: Jennifer Gelwick Leucke, Allen Morrison Gelwick. BA, So. Meth. U., 1952; MDiv, Yale U., 1956; ThD, Pacific Sch. of Religion, Berkeley, Calif., 1965. Ordained to ministry United Ch. of Christ Maine Conf. Campus min., intern Temple U., Phila., 1954-55; asst. prof. religion Washington & Lee U., Lexington, Va., 1956-58; dir. religious activities Oberlin (Ohio) Coll., 1958-60; campus min. U. Calif., Berkeley, 1963-66; vis. lectr. Pacific Sch. Religion, 1965-66; asst. prof. religion Chapman Coll., Orange, Calif., 1966-67; adj. prof. Dayton (Ohio) U., 1970-71; chair religion and philosophy dept. Stephens Coll., Columbia, Mo., 1967-88; rsch. assoc. Bowdoin Coll., Brunswick, Maine, 1988-89; chair, assoc. prof. Coll. of Osteopathic Medicine U. New England, Biddeford, Maine, 1988—; chair Religion, Health and Med. Ethics Group, 1992-95; coord. Polanyi Soc., 1975—; cons. Soc. for Bioethics Consultation, 1990—. Author: The Way of Discovery, 1977, Credere Aude: Theory of Knowledge of Polanyi, 1965; editor: (jour.) Tradition and Discovery, 1983-91. Mem. education com. Maine Coun. Chs., 1992—, Cancer Adv. and Prevention Com. State of Maine, 1991—. Soc. for Values in Higher Edn. Dsciplinary Fellowship postdoctoral scholar, 1973-74; Rockefeller Found. doctoral fellow, 1962-63; Danforth Found. campus ministry fellow, 1960-62. Fellow Soc. for Values in Higher Edn.; mem. Soc. for Health and Human Values, Am. Acad. of Religion. Democrat. Home: RR5 2440 Cundy's Harbor Harpswell ME 04011 Office: U New England 11 Hillsbeach Rd Biddeford ME 04005

GEN, MARTIN, corporate executive; b. Feb. 14, 1926; s. Max and Gussie (Bluestone) G., m. Sara Tobin; children: Gilda Paul, Sam. Student, Syracuse U., 1946-50; BA, Pace U., 1950. Lic. pvt. detective. V.p., treas. Merlin, Inc., North Bergen, N.J., 1950-73; pres. Washmasters, Inc., North Bergen, 1950-73; v.p., treas. Expert Investigation and Protective Industries, Inc., Kenilworth, N.J., 1974—; pres. InterGlobal Trading, Kenilworth, N.J.; exec. dir. EIP, Inc., Kenilworth, N.J., 1973-74. Bd. dirs. Jewish Nat. Fund, Teaneck, N.J., 1986—, YMHA, Union, N.J., 1970, Fedn. Union County, N.J., 1970, Jewish Ednl. Ctr., Elizabeth, N.J., 1960. Served with USN, 1943-46, ETO, PTO. Named Man of Yr., YMHA. Mem. Am. Soc. Indsl. Security, Club 100. Home and Office: PO Box 195 Kenilworth NJ 07033-0195

GENABITH, RICHARD CARL, constable; b. Irvington, N.J., Sept. 21, 1946; s. Carl Henry and Elisabeth (Van Duin) G.; m. Debra Lynne Bentley, Oct. 26, 1986; children: Amanda Elisabeth, Erica Lynne. BA, Seton Hall U., 1969. Owner Mr. Softee Franchise (2), Irvington, 1965-72, AndRich Studios, Union, N.J., 1967—, RCG Cellular Enterprises, Inc., Union, 1987—; owner, ptnr. A&R Snowplowing, Union, 1970-78; constable Union Twp., 1974—; constable, ct. officer Spl. Civil Part Superior Ct. of N.J., Elizabeth, 1975—. Author computer software. Mem. Nat. Press Photographers, N.J. Press Photographers Assn., Irvington C. of C. (pres. 1989-91), Union C. of C., Ft. Myers Beach (Fla.) C. of C., Nat. Sheriffs Assn., Profl. Photographers Am., Profl. Photographers N.J., Optimists (past pres.), Elks (Newspaper Nat. 1st place award 1988, 90, 91, 92, state chmn., editor N.J. state chpt. 1987—, N.J. state assoc. 1987—), Mercedes Benz Club. Roman Catholic. Office: AndRich Studios PO Box 1249 Union NJ 07083-1249

GENATOSSIO, FRANCIS JOSEPH, financial planning company executive; b. Medford, Mass., Dec. 14, 1956; s. Samuel Lawrence and Mary (Roche) G.; m. Meredith Genatossio, 1990. BS, Bentley Coll., 1981. Bookkeeper Fidelity Fin. Corp., Quincy, Mass., 1978-79; acct. Capital Analysts of N.E., Quincy, 1979-81; office mgr. Capital Analysts of N.E., 1981-85, v.p. adminstrn., 1985-89, dir. ops., 1990—. Mem. South Shore C. of C. Office: Capital Analysts of NE 1266 Furnace Brook Pky Quincy MA 02169-4758

GENEROUS, ERIC YVES JACQUES, brokerage house executive; b. Nice, France, May 15, 1960; came to U.S. 1975; s. William Henry and Countess Denise (Calou de la Motte) Thiery G.; m. Rochanya Charlotte Hickman, July 23, 1983; children: Eric Nicholas Alexandre, William Joshua. Diploma, St. Mark's Sch., Southborough, Mass, 1978; BA in Economics, McGill Univ., 1983. Stockbroker Legg Mason Wood Walker, Balt., 1983-84; sr. v.p. Johnston, Lemon & Co., Washington, 1984-89; chief fin. officer & treas. Friedman, Billings, Ramsey & Co., Inc. (FBR & Co.), Washington, 1989—. Mem. St. John's Ch., Lafayette Sq., Washington. Mem. Univ. Club, Bellehaven Country Club. Home: 8806 Bel Air Pl Potomac MD 20854 Office: FBR & Company 1919 Pennsylvania Ave NW Washington DC 20006-3404

GENKIN, LARRY ALLEN, entrepreneur; b. Phila., Dec. 23, 1965; s. Stanley Harold and Susan (Gelb) G.; m. Lisa Ann Brett, Aug. 7, 1988. BS in Mktg., Advt. and Pub. Rels., Pa. State U., 1987. V.p. Food for Thought Caterers, Phila., 1987-90; pres. Sports Challenge U.S.A., Glenside, Pa., 1990—; dir. Nat. Inst. Personal Devel., Glenside, 1991—; seminar leader Performax, Mpls., 1990—. Mem. Toastmasters (Evaluator of Yr. award 1991).

GENNARI, F(RANK) JOHN, medical educator; b. Jersey City, May 18, 1937; s. Frank and Amelia (Sargia) G.; m. Emily Hewson Michie, Sept. 15, 1958; children: John Hewson, Jennifer Meade, Amelia Sargia. BS cum laude, Yale U., 1959, MD, 1963. Diplomate Am. Bd. Internal Medicine, Am. Bd. Nephrology. Intern U. Va. Hosp., Charlottesville, 1963-64, resident in medicine, 1964-66; fellow in nephrology Tufts-New Eng. Med., Boston, 1968-71; asst. prof. Sch. Medicine, Tufts U., Boston, 1971-75, assoc. prof., 1975-79; prof. medicine Coll. Medicine, U. Vt., Burlington, 1979—, dir. nephrology, 1979—, assoc. chair dept. medicine, 1987—. Co-author: Acid-Base, 1981, Acid-Base Disorders, 1987; contbr. articles to profl. publs., chpts. to books. Mem. exec. com. Vt. Heart Assn., 1982-85; mem. exec. com. Vt. Kidney Assn., 1980—, pres., 1984-86; mem. merit rev. bd. VA, Washington, 1989-92. Capt. Med. Corps, USAF, 1966-68. Grantee NIH, 1971—, Fogarty Internat., 1991. Mem. Am. Fedn. Clin. Rsch., Am. Soc. Clin. Investigation, Am. Soc. Nephrology, Am. PHysiol. Soc., Internat. Soc. Nephrology. Democrat. Office: U Vt Coll Medicine D305 Given Bldg Burlington VT 05405

GENOVESE, PHILIP WILLIAM, civil engineer; b. New Haven, Jan. 22, 1917; s. Anthony and Angelina (Ingianni) G.; m. Restituta Adelaide Buonocore, Jan. 25, 1947; children: A. Felicity Bruns, Philip A.V. BE, Yale U., 1938; MBA, U. New Haven, 1979. Registered profl. engr., Conn.; lic. land surveyor, Conn., N.Y. Field engr. Clarence M. Blair, Inc., New Haven, 1939-40, Bridgeport (Conn.) Hydraulic Co., 1940-41; design engr., ptnr. Argraves & Mort, New Haven, 1946-49; ptnr. Newman E. Argraves & Assocs., New Haven, 1949-54; pres. Philip W. Genovese & Assocs., Inc., Woodbridge, Conn., 1955—; bd. dirs. North Haven Nat. Bank, 1967-77, Conn. Nat. Bank, New Haven, 1967—; adv. bd. 1st Bank. Lt. comdr. CEC, USNR, 1941-46, PTO. Mem. ASCE (life), NSPE (bd. dirs. 1951-63), Conn. Soc. Profl. Engrs. (past pres., Outstanding Svc. award, Engr. of Yr. award), Conn. Engrs. in Pvt. Practice (pres. 1983-85), Bd. Supervision of Dams, Co. of C. (chmn. energy and environment com.), Farms Country Club (Wallingford, Conn.). Office: Philip W Genovese & Assocs Inc 88 Bradley Rd Woodbridge CT CT 06514-0330

GENOVESE, RICHARD, artist, photographer; b. N.Y.C., May 31, 1947; s. Henry Richard and Antoinette Josephine (Misiano) G. AAS, SUNY, Farmingdale, 1975; BA, C.W. Post Coll., 1978; L.I. U. Guest curator Bayville (N.Y.) Hist. Mus., 1991-92, Hempstead Harbor Artists Assn., Glen Cove, N.Y., 1986-89. Work exhibited French Embassy, N.Y.C., 1974; contbr. articles to art mags. Office: 76 Pine St Freeport NY 11520-3616

GENSHEIMER, CYNTHIA FRANCIS, economics educator; b. Bloomington, Ind., Feb. 16, 1953; d. Norman C. and Beverly (Cohen) Francis; m. Joseph M. Gensheimer, Dec. 27, 1975; children: Michael Francis, Lydia Jane. BA, U. Rochester, 1974; PhD, UCLA, 1979. Prin. analyst Congl. Budget Ofc., Washington, 1978-83; vis. asst. prof. Vassar Coll., Poughkekepsie, N.Y., 1989—. UCLA Found. fellow, 1974-77. Mem. Am. Econ. Assn., Nat. Tax Assn., Phi Beta Kappa. Office: Vassar Coll Poughkeepsie NY 12601

GENT, PAMELA JOYCE, special education educator; b. Youngstown, Ohio, Aug. 1, 1957; d. Paul Louis and Joyce Ann (Hunsinger) Pogany; m. Richard William Gent, Mar. 17, 1979; children: Stephanie R., Ethan R. BSEd, Youngstown State U., 1980; MEd, Kent State U., 1983, postgrad., 1984—. Cert. elem. tchr., spl. edn., neurodevel. therapy, Ohio. Tchr. Boardman (OHio) Local Schs., 1980-83; coordinating tchr. Children's Hosp. Akron (Ohio) Kent State U., 1983-84; grad. asst. Kent (Ohio) State U., 1985-88; coord. tchrs. Family Child Learning Ctr., Tallmadge, Ohio, 1984-85; asst. prof. spl. edn. Clarion U. Pa., 1988—; camp dir. Easter Seals Trumbull County, Warren, Ohio, summer, 1981, 83; instr. Walsh Coll., Canton, Ohio, summer 1988; cons. TRACES, Monmouth, Oreg., 1989-91; sr. assoc. Spec-Houser & Gent, Akron, 1989-91. Mem. North Cen. Evaluation Team, Youngstown, Ohio, 1991. Recipient Youngstown Ret. Tchrs. award Youngstown Ret. Tchrs. Assn., 1979; grantee Kent State U., 1988, Ohio Dept. Edn., 1988, Clarion U. Pa., 1990-91. Mem. Assn. Persons With Severe Handicaps, Coun. Exceptional Children, Am. Assn. Mental Retardation. Home: 208 E Ravenwood Ave Youngstown OH 44507-1921 Office: Clarion U Pa Spl Edn Ctr Clarion PA 16214

GENTILE, ANTOINETTE M., psychology educator, education educator; b. N.Y.C., Aug. 28, 1936; d. Michael and Ima-Mae G. BS, CUNY, Bklyn., 1958; MA, Ind. U., 1959, PED, 1967; PhD, SUNY, Stonybrook, 1972. Instr. R.I. Coll., Providence, 1959-62; prof. Tchrs. Coll. Columbia U., M.Y.C., 1964—. Co-author: Movement Sciences: Foundations for Rehabilitation, 1987; contbr. articles to profl. jours. Fellow AAHPERD, Am. Acad. Phys. Edn.; mem. AAAS, Am. Psychol. Assn., Soc. for Neurosci. Office: Columbia U Tchrs Coll 525 W 120th St New York NY 10027-6625

GENTILE, DOUG CHARLES, political activist, author, publisher; b. Youngstown, Ohio, Jan. 23, 1950; s. Willis Homer and Virginia Mae (Hunston) G.; m. Maria Cristina, Nov. 24, 1979; children: Paul, Peter. BA, Ohio State U., 1972; MPA, Kent (Ohio) State U., 1975. Investigator, demographics analyst U.S. Dept. of Labor, Phila., 1977-84; demographics analyst City of N.Y., 1984-88; record keeper, fin. analyst family owned bus. N.Y.C., 1988—; pres. Deleperso Corp., N.Y.C., 1989—; pro-bono lectr. in field; whistle blower activist City of N.Y. Contbr. numerous articles to profl. jours. Member Amnesty Internat. Urgent Action Network, N.Y.C., 1987—, Neighbors for Racial Harmony, Bay Ridge, N.Y. and Bklyn., 1990-91; mem., vol. Partnership for Homeless Shelter, Bay Ridge and Bklyn., 1987-88; mem. com. for democracy in Eastern Europe, 1988-89. Mem. Tertiary Soc. Forum (co-founder, populist). Methodist. Home and Office: 1754 73d St Brooklyn NY 11204

GENTILE, J. RONALD, educational psychology educator; b. Pottsville, Pa., Apr. 14, 1941; s. Joseph and Evelyn Marie (Warfield) G.; m. Patricia Koch, Sept. 7, 1963 (div. 1973); 1 child, Douglas Alan; m. Kay Burgher Johnson, Aug. 30, 1979. BS, Pa. State U., 1963, MS, 1964, PhD, 1967. Rsch. psychologist Walter Reed Army Inst. Rsch., Washington, 1967-69; prof. SUNY, Buffalo, 1969—, chair dept. ednl. psychology, 1971-72, 81, master Internat. Coll., 1977-79; dir. UNESCO and SUNY (Buffalo) program, Owerri, Nigeria, 1976-81. Author: (textbook) Educational Psychology, 1990, (children's book/cassette) Great Horse and Greater Horses, 1989, (cassette) Genteel Songs and Poems for Genteel People, 1991; pub., composer The Genteels, 1969—; contbr. over 50 articles to profl. jours. Capt. U.S. Army Med. Corps, 1967-69. Mem. Nat. Staff Devel. Coun., Am. Psychol. Soc., Am. Ednl. Rsch. Assn., Am. Fedn. Musicians. Office: SUNY at Buffalo 409 Baldy Hall Buffalo NY 14260

GENTILE, JOSEPH J., accountant; b. Bronx, N.Y., Feb. 5, 1958; s. Domenick George and Joan (Campus) G.;m. Susan Parisi, Nov. 28, 1981. BA in Pub. Acctg., Pace U., 1981. CPA, N.Y. Asst. mgr. Shopwell Inc., Rye, N.Y., 1975-81; mgr. Landry & Toole CPAs, White Plains, N.Y., 1981-90; prin. Joseph J. Gentile CPA, Mahopac, N.Y., 1991—; norm team chmn. Shopwell Inc., Rye, 1980-81. Recipient Community Svc. award Bronx (N.Y.) Hist. Soc., 1976. Mem. AICPA, N.Y. Soc. CPAs.

GENTILE, PAUL LOUIS, dean; b. Rochester, Pa., Nov. 26, 1940; s. Paul and Margaret A. (Ciclone) G.; m. Joyce A. Arnal, June 13, 1964; children: Paul L. III, Bradley E., Heather C. BS in Edn., California U. of Pa., 1962; MEd, Duquesne U., 1967; PhD, U. Pitts., 1981. Tchr. Aliquippa (Pa.) Jr. High Sch., 1962-67; guidance counselor Richland Sr. High Sch., Gibsonia, Pa., 1967-79; writer syndicated column Ednl. Mailbag, Pitts., 1971-72; dir. of guidance Pine-Richland Sch. Dist., Gibsonia, 1973-79; dir. of admissions and fin. aid Community Coll. of Allegheny County, Pitts., 1979-85, acting dean of students, 1985, dean of continuing edn., 1985—; mem. adj. faculty Community Coll. of Allegheny County, 1983-85, Duquesne U., 1989; mem. selection com. Senator Heinz, Naval Acad., Pitts., 1972-79; counselor edn., mem. adv. coun. Grad. Sch., Duquesne U., 1983-85. Member A.W. Beattie Bus. Edn. Study, Pitts., 1990-91; bd. dirs. North Hills Arts Festival, Pitts., 1985-87. With USCG, 1963-64. Mem. Nat. Assn. Continuing Edn. and Community Svcs., Pa. Assn. Adult and Continuing Edn., Pitts. Coun. on Higher Edn., Pennarama Edn. TV Group (rep. adv. bd. 1990), Rich Mars Rotary (exec. com. Mars chpt. 1981-90). Roman Catholic. Home: 1105 Woodhill Dr Gibsonia PA 15044-9231 Office: Community Coll Allegheny County 8701 Perry Hwy Pittsburgh PA 15237-5353

GENTNER, CLAUDIA ALENE, outplacement consultant; b. Hackensack, N.J., June 25, 1953; d. Raymond G. and Dorothy A. (Weber) Kreb; m. Kenneth L. Gentner, Oct. 4, 1975. BA, Ramapo Coll., 1977; MLS, Rutgers U., 1979. Mgr. client svcs. LPA Audits, Montvale, N.J., 1973-77; mgr. bus. info. ctr. Am. Cyanamid, Wayne, N.J., 1980-83; sr. v.p. Seagate Assocs. Inc., Paramus, N.J., 1983—; pres., chief exec. officer Outplacement Internat., Chgo., 1991-92, also bd. dirs. Contbr. articles to profl. jours. Mem. exec. bd. Bergen-Passaic Regional Libr. Coop., Hawthorne, N.J. Mem. Spl. Librs. Assn. Lutheran. Office: Seagate Assocs Country Club Pla W 115 Century Rd Paramus NJ 07652-1432

GENTRY, DONALD GUNN, railroad information systems executive; b. Mineola, N.Y., Aug. 11, 1940; s. James Norman and Clare (Gunn) G.; m. Jane Rash, Sept. 8, 1962; children: Donald G. Jr., Anne R. BS in Indsl. Engring., Ga. Inst. Tech., 1962; MS in Computer Sci., Navy Postgrad. Sch., 1969. Commd. ensign USN, 1962, advanced through ranks to capt., 1980; chief naval ops. fellow USN, Washington, 1972-73, Nat. War Coll., 1975-76, comdg. officer Patrol Squadron 24, 1977-78; head extended planning br. office of Chief Naval Ops. Navy Dept., Washington, 1979-81; fed. exec. fellow Coun. Fgn. Rels., Washington, 1981-82; exec. asst. and sr. aide to dep. chief naval ops. Navy Dept., Washington, 1982-83; comdg. officer U.S. Naval Air Sta., Bermuda, 1983-85; ret. USN, 1986; asst. v.p. info. systems Amtrak, Washington, 1986—. Decorated Legion of Merit. Republican. Office: Amtrak 400 N Capitol St NW Washington DC 20001-1511

GEOGHEGAN, JOSEPH EDWARD, electrical engineer; b. N.Y.C., Aug. 2, 1932; s. Roderick and Florence (Post) G.; m. Kathleen Bourké, Dec. 3, 1966. BEE, SUNY, Stony Brook, 1976; MBA, U. Phoenix, 1986. Engr. Otis Elevator Co., N.Y.C., 1956-66; sr. design engr. The Peelle Co., Bayshore, N.Y., 1966-78; sr. project engr. Westinghouse Electric Corp., Pitts., 1978-80; logistics mgr. Raytheon Co., Sudbury, Mass., 1980—; instr. Worcester (Mass.) Pub. Schs., 1991. Producer/host tv show Careers, 1983. Chmn. Northborough (Mass.) Coun. on Aging, 1988—; bd. dirs. The Audio Jour., Worcester, 1989—; com. mem. Reps., Northborough, 1989—; judge Mass. Academic Decathlon, 1986—. Sgt. U.S. Army, 1952-54. Mem. Toastmasters Internat. (area gov. 1988-89), Am. Legion.

GEOGHEGAN, MICHEL HENRY, United Nations official; b. Bradford, Yorks, Eng., Jan. 11, 1937; came to U.S., 1966; s. Thomas Anthony and Chantal Marie (de Nuchèze) G.; m. Anne Marie Geoghegan. BS in Econs., London Sch. Econs., 1960; MA, NYU, 1972. Third sec. British Fgn. Office and Svc., London, 1960-66, Brussels, 1962-64, Manila, Philippines, 1964-66, N.Y.C., 1966—; devel. economist UN Devel. Regional Svc., Middle East, 1972-78, Haiti and Rome, 1978-79, Sierra Leone, 1985-88, UN Hdqrs., 1989—; bd. dirs. Assn. World Edn., N.Y., Denmark, Earth Day Found., N.Y., Symphony for UN, N.Y.; chmn. Communication Coord. Com., N.Y., 1978—. Contbr. articles to profl. pubs.; author of poetry. With RAF, 1953-55. Mem. Club of Rome, Soc. for Internat. Devel. Roman Catholic. Home: 90-12 181st St Jamaica NY 11423 Office: UN Devel Program DC-1-1673 1 UN Pla New York NY 10017

GEORGE, ALBERT RICHARD, mechanical and aerospace engineer, educator; b. N.Y.C., Mar. 12, 1938; s. Albert Richard and Tekla (Kovtoun) G.; m. Carol Mae Frerichs, June 21, 1959; children—Albert Frederick, David Kovtoun, Amy Margaret. B.S.E., Princeton U., 1959, M.A., 1961, Ph.D., 1964. Vis. asst. prof. U. Wash., Seattle, 1964-65; asst. prof. Cornell U., 1965-69, asso. prof., 1969-77, prof., 1977—, asst. dir. mech. and aerospace engring. dept., 1972-77, dir., 1977-87, dir. mfg. engring. and productivity program, 1991—; head sect. BMW AG Automobile Mfrs., Fed. Republic of Germany, 1987-88; NRC sr. research assoc. NASA Ames Research Ctr., 1988; vis. sr. fellow U. Southampton, Eng., 1971-72; cons. in field. Contbr. articles to profl. jours. Mem. AIAA (assoc. fellow), ASME, Soc. Automotive Engrs., Am. Helicopter Soc., Sigma Xi. Congregationalist. Home: 119 Pine Tree Rd Ithaca NY 14850-6331 Office: Cornell U 208 Upson Hall Ithaca NY 14853-7501

GEORGE, HENRY HAMILTON, consulting company executive; b. Buffalo, Mar. 10, 1934; s. Henry H. and Alice (Williams) G.; m. Barbara Ann Balder, Sept. 6, 1960 (div. 1983); children: Elizabeth, Geoffrey. BSChemE, Lehigh U., 1956; PhD in ChemE, Rensselaer Polytech. Inst., 1960. Rsch. engr. E.I. DuPont, Richmond, Va., 1960-64, Celanese, Cumberland, Md., 1964-66; lab. supr. Celanese, 1967-69; mem. tech. staff Celanese, Summit, N.J., 1969-85; pres. Mercury Group Corp., Madison, N.J., 1985—. Contbr. to book chpts. and articles to profl. jours.; patentee (6) in field. Pres., Community Pool Corp., Berkeley Heights, N.J., 1980; mem. Madison Vol. Ambulance Corps, 1991—. Mem. AICE, Soc. Rheology, Soc. Plastic Engrs., Sigma Xi. Republican. Unitarian. Office: Mercury Group Corp 178 Greenwood Ave Madison NJ 07940-1304

GEORGE, JOEY RUSSELL, lawyer; b. Bklyn., Oct. 8, 1963; s. Jonas and Celeste Dorothy (Russell) G. BA, Howard U., 1985; JD, Harvard U., 1988. Bar: N.Y. 1989, Conn. 1989, U.S. Dist. Ct. (so. and ea. dists.) N.Y. 1989. Asst. prosecutor Queens County Dist. Atty., Kew Gardens, N.Y., 1988-90; asst. gen. counsel Exec. Office of the Pres., Office Mgmt. and Budget, Washington, 1990-91; assoc. dir. for policy The White House, Washington, 1991—. Trustee, Howard U., Washington, 1984-85; big bro., Big Bros. Am., Cambridge, Mass., 1986—. Mem. ABA, Ripon Soc. (pres. Harvard chpt. 1986-87, nat. v.p. 1987-88, bd. dirs. ednl. fund 1989—), Macon B. Allen Bar Assn., N.Y. State Bar Assn., Harvard Club, Phi Beta Kappa, Pi Sigma Alpha, Phi Alpha Theta. Republican. African Methodist Episcopalian. Home: 13129 225th St Jamaica NY 11413-1722 Office: The White House Washington DC 20500

GEORGE, PAMELA CARLSON, small business owner; b. Richmond, Va., Feb. 26, 1960; d. Morton Allen and Louise Irene (Garrett) Carlson; m. Steven Michael George, Apr. 19, 1986. BA, U. Del., 1982. With sales dept. Bloomingdale's, King of Prussia, Pa., 1982-84; advt. dir. Sachs Realty, Wilmington, Del., 1984-86; editor Town Talk, Wilmington, 1986-87; promotion asst. Sta. WDEL/WSTW, Wilmington, 1987-88, promotion dir., 1988-90; owner Creative Promotion, Wilmington, 1990—; cons. Caesar Rodney Half Marathon, Wilmington, 1991—, Family Times Family Festival, Wilmington, 1991, 92; coord. The County Fair, Wilmington, 1991. Columnist Out & About mag., 1988-89, Big Shot mag., 1990-91. Pub. rels. chair Del. Symphony Sizzler Fundraiser, Wilmington, 1990, chair, 1991; events chair mktg. com. United Way, Wilmington, 1991-92; program chair Taste of A Nation Homeless and Hungry Fundraiser, Wilmington, 1992—. Recipient Recognition award March of Dimes, 1989, Talleyville Jaycees, 1990, Achievement award Caesar Rodney Half Marathon, 1991. Mem. Pub. Rels. Soc. Am., Del. Media Soc., Wilmington Women in Bus. (chmn. pub. rels. 1991-92, bd. dirs. 1992-94), New Castle County C. of C. (account exec.), Wilmington Breakfast Club. Democrat. Episcopalian.

GEORGES, JOHN A., paper company executive; b. El Paso, Feb. 24, 1931; s. John A. and Opal (Biffle) G.; m. Zephera M. Givas, June 15, 1952; children: Mark, Andrew, Elizabeth. B.S., U. Ill., 1951; M.S. in Bus. Adminstrn, Drexel U., 1957. Exec. v.p. internat. and wood products and resources Internat. Paper Co., N.Y.C., 1979, vice chmn., 1980, pres., chief operating officer, 1981-85, chmn., chief exec. officer, 1985—, also dir.; bd. dirs. Warner Lambert Co., N.Y. Stock Exchange, Fed. Res. Bank N.Y. Dir. Bus. Council N.Y. State. Served with U.S. Army, 1953-55. Club: N.Y. Yacht. Office: Internat Paper 2 Manhattanville Rd Purchase NY 10577-2118

GEORGESCU, PETER ANDREW, advertising executive; b. Bucharest, Romania, Mar. 9, 1939; came to U.S., 1954, naturalized, 1954; s. V.C. Rica and Lygia (Bocu) G.; m. Barbara Anne Armstrong, Aug. 21, 1965; 1 son, Peter Andrew. A.B. cum laude, Princeton U., 1961; M.B.A., Stanford U., 1963. With Young & Rubicam, Inc., N.Y.C., 1963—; dir. mktg. Young & Rubicam, Inc., 1977-79; exec. v.p. Cen. Region Young & Rubicam, Inc., Chgo., dir., 1979-82; pres. Young & Rubicam Internat., N.Y.C., 1982-86, Young & Rubicam Advt., N.Y.C., 1986—, Young & Rubicam Inc., 1990—; bd. dirs. Briggs & Stratton, Inc. Member Council on Fgn. Relations, Am. Assn. Advt. Agencies (bd. dirs.), Internat. Advt. Assn., Inc. (bd. dirs.). Clubs: Princeton, Links, River (N.Y.C.); Racquet, Casino (Chgo.); Marks, Brooks (London). Home: 435 E 52d St New York NY 10022 Office: Young & Rubicam Inc 285 Madison Ave New York NY 10017-6401

GEORGOPOULOS, MARIA, architect; b. Moussata, Cefalonia, Greece, Apr. 2, 1949; came to U.S., 1973; d. Vassilios and Joulia Georgopoulos; m. Demetrios Georgopoulos (div. 1974). BArch, Nat. Poly. Sch. Greece, Athens, 1972; MS, Columbia U., 1976. Registered architect, N.Y., Greece. Project mgr. Architects Design Group, N.Y.C., 1976-79, Gruzen Samton Steinglass, N.Y.C., 1979-80; project dir. Lehman Bros., Kuhn Loeb Inc., N.Y.C., 1980-85; v.p. L.F. Rothschild Inc., N.Y.C., 1985-89, sr. project mgr., 1989-90; dir. of facilities mgmt. Dreyfus Corp., N.Y.C., 1990—. Mem. AIA, Am. Women Entrepreneurs, Greek Inst. Architects. Greek Orthodox. Club: Douglaston (N.Y.). Home: 14 Melrose Ln Flushing NY 11363-1221 Office: The Dreyfus Corp 200 Park Ave New York NY 10166-0005

GEPFERT, ALAN HARRY, management consultant, business educator, author; b. Cleve., Sept. 24, 1930; s. Joseph Harry and Freda Natalia (Schleicher) G.; m. Mary Caroline Austin, Aug. 26, 1959; 1 child: Grace Mary Cooper. BS in Engring. Adminstrn., Case Western Res. U., 1953, MS in Ops. Rsch., 1953, postgrad., 1953-56. Instr. Case Western Res. U., Cleve., 1953-58; mem. ops. rsch. cons. Case Western Res. U., 1953-58; dir. statis. rsch. Chgo. and North Western Rlwy., 1958-62; cons. McKinsey & Co., Inc., N.Y.C., 1962-70; exec. Mobil Oil, N.Y.C., 1970-86; prin. Strategic Systems Solutions, New London, N.H., 1986—; instr. Colby-Sawyer Coll., New London, 1992—. Author (with others) The Arts of Top Management, 1971, Turnaround Management, 1972, Strategic Planning For MIS, 1977; cons. editor Modern Railroads mag., 1959-70; contbr. articles to profl. jours. Trustee First Baptist Ch., White Plains, N.Y., 1969-70; dir. Pegasus Therapeutic Riding, Darien, Conn., 1985-88, Masonic Charity Found., Wallingford, Conn., 1989—, New London Hosp., 1990—. Mem. Inst. Mgmt. Scis. and Ops. Rsch. Soc. (mem. academic practitioner com. 1989—, chmn. joint edn. com. 1992—), Inst. Mgmt. Scis. (vice chmn. coll. on info. systems 1981-82, chmn. fin. com. 1964-65), Masons (32d degree), Shriners, Tau Beta Pi, Sigma Xi. Republican. Office: Strategic Systems Solutions 40 Little Sunapee Rd New London NH 03257

GEPHARDT, DONALD LOUIS, college dean; b. St. Louis, Mar. 27, 1937; s. Louis Andrew and Loreen Estelle (Cassell) G.; children: Lisa Diane, Francis Joseph. B of Music Edn., Drake U., 1959; BS, Juilliard Sch., N.Y.C., 1961; MS, Juilliard Sch., 1962; EdD, Washington U., St. Louis, 1978. Clarinet instr. Henry Street Settlement Music Sch., N.Y.C., 1961-64; music tchr. Wantagh (N.Y.) Elem. Schs., 1962-67; music tchr., band and orch. dir. W.C. Mepham High Sch., Bellmore, N.Y., 1967-70; assoc. prof. music, band and jazz ensemble conductor Nassau Community Coll., Garden City, N.Y., 1970-83, chmn. music dept., 1977-83, dean of instrn., 1984-90; dean sch. of fine and performing arts Glassboro (N.J.) State Coll., 1990—. Clarinetist Des Moines Symphony Orch., 1956-59, Aspen (Colo.) Festival Orchestra, 1959-60, Henry Schuman's Wind Ensemble Workshop, 1965-69, L.I. Symphony Orch., 1970-82; clarinetist Seuffert Band, 1962-90, Great Neck (N.Y.) Symphony, 1967-80; contbr. articles to profl. jours. Bd. dirs. L.I. Symphony, 1980-82; surrogate speaker Richard Gephardt for Pres., 1987-88. Mem. Music Educators Nat. Conf. (chpt. advisor 1970-83, 2-year coll. chmn. Eastern div. 1982-83), N.Y. State Sch. Music Assn. (chmn. rsch. 1982-84), N.J. Music Educators Assn., N.J. Alliance For Arts, Nassau

Music Educators Assn. (recording sec. 1968-69, 1st v.p. 1969-70, pres. 1970-71), Coll. Music Soc., Phi Mu Alpha Sinfonia. Democrat. Office: Glassboro State Coll Wilson 210 Glassboro NJ 08028

GEPHART, WILLIAM, professional society executive, singing educator; b. Spokane, Wash., July 5, 1913; s. Alva Roscoe and Pearl (Hartpence) G. AB, DePauw U., 1935; diploma, Juilliard Grad. Sch., 1940, Nat. Conservatory Music, Paris, 1950. Instr. singing Dalcroze Sch. Music, N.Y.C., 1949—, Union Theol. Sem., N.Y.C., 1961-73, Vassar Coll., Poughkeepsie, N.Y., 1968-69, 74-75, Hartford (Conn.) Conservatory, 1975-92; sec. Am. Acad. Tchrs. Singing, N.Y.C., 1972—. Home: 75 Bank St New York NY 10014-5900

GERACI, MICHAEL RALEIGH, communications company executive; b. Cleve., Mar. 4, 1937; s. Michael Christopher and Catherine Cecilia (Raleigh) G.; m. Mary-Therese Anne O'Connor, Aug. 1, 1964; children: Michael O'Connor, Christopher Raleigh, Gavin Hart. BS, John Carroll U., 1959. Mgr. pub. rels. Air Transport Assn., Washington, 1963-68; dir. advt. and pub. rels. Rolls-Royce N.Am., Inc., N.Y.C., 1968-73, Parsons & Whittemore, Inc., N.Y.C., 1973-76; mgmt. supr. Doremus & Co., N.Y.C., 1976-79; v.p. Ketchum Communications, Pitts., 1979-83; pres. Geraci Co., Inc., Pitts., 1983—. Contbr. numerous articles on advt., crisis communications mgmt. and bus. mktg. to profl. publs. Capt. U.S. Army, 1960-63. Mem. St. Clair Country Club. Republican. Home: 202 Orr Rd Pittsburgh PA 15241-2222

GERACI, PHILIP CHARLES, JR., book, pictorial publisher, computer consultant; b. Frederick, Md., Sept. 22, 1929; s. Philip Charles Geraci and Grace (Royston) Jones; m. Dorothy Schaffer, June 17, 1950; children: Philip James, Ronald Blair, Jeffrey Alan. BS, U. Md., 1953, MS, 196l. Instr. photography U. Md., College Park, 1953-57, prof. journalism, 1965-87; editor High Fidelity mag., Gt. Barrington, Mass., 1957-59, Airlift mag., Washington, 1959-65; pub. Free-Press, Burtonsville, Md., 1975-89. Author: Making Pictures for Publication, 1975, Photojournalism: New Images in Visual Communication, 1984, The Modern Mass Media Machine, 1987; also numerous articles to mags. and newspapers. With USAF, 1946-49.

GERARD, CLAUDE, advertising executive; b. Cumberland, Md., Oct. 17, 1918; s. Edgar Eston and Nettie June (Hardy) G.; m. Alice Marie Strickland, Oct., 1951 (div. 1961); children: Marie June, Helen Allen; m. Shirley Lee, July 17, 1970. BA, Johns Hopkins U., 1949, MA, 1951. Supr. Bur. Census, Washington, 1939-41; mgr., ptnr. Azrael Advt. Co., Balt., 1951-61; ptnr. Cahn Avis Gerard Roman, Balt., 1961-78; owner, ptnr. The Gerard Co., Hanover, Md., 1978—. Author: (self study courses) How to Take a Test, 1979, Marketing Recruitment, 1989. Lt. col. U.S. Army, 1946-51. Republican. Office: The Gerard Co 1334 Charwood Rd # G Hanover MD 21076-3113

GERBER, DONALD ALBERT, medical educator; b. N.Y.C., Apr. 10, 1932; s. J. August and Isabel (Globus) G.; m. Marica Lynn Getz, June 13, 1964; children: Susan E., Andrew J. AB, Columbia Coll., 1953; MD, Columbia U., 1957. Diplomate Am. Bd. Internal Medicine. Intern Osler Med. Svc. Johns Hopkins Hosp., Balt., 1957-58, asst. resident Osler Med. Svc., 1958-59; asst. resident in medicine Columbia Presbyn. Med. Ctr., N.Y.C., 1959-60; fellow in rheumatology Coll. Physicians and Surgeons Columbia U., N.Y.C., 1960-63; instr. SUNY Health Sci. Ctr., N.Y.C., 1963-64; asst. prof. SUNY Health Sci. Ctr. Bklyn., N.Y.C., 1964-69, assoc. prof., 1969—; clin. asst. dean SUNY Health Sci. Ctr., 1991—; chief arthritis clinic King's County Hosp., N.Y.C., 1972—; attending physician State U. Hosp., N.Y.C., 1966—; asst. to chmn. for ednl. affairs SUNY Health Sci. Ctr. at Bklyn. Med. Sch., N.Y.C., 1980—; spl. investigator Arthritis Found., 1963-66; prin. investigator rsch. grants NIH, 1966-78, 82-85. Contbr. articles to profl. jours. Fellow ACP, Am. Coll. Rheumatology; mem. Am. Fedn. for Clin. Rsch., N.Y. Rheumatism Assn. (v.p. 1976-77), N.Y. Arthritis Found. (med. and sci. com. 1971-74), Harvey Soc. Office: SUNY Health Sci Ctr Bklyn 450 Clarkson Ave # 42 Brooklyn NY 11203-2098

GERBER, GWENDOLYN LORETTA, psychologist, educator; b. Calgary, Alt., Can.; came to U.S., 1958; d. Ernest and Alma (Tesky) G. AB, UCLA, 1961, MA, 1964, PhD, 1967; cert. in psychoanalysis, NYU, 1970. Lic. psychologist, N.Y. Clin. psychologist Hillside Hosp., Glen Oaks, N.Y., 1970-73; asst. prof. psychology John Jay Coll. of Criminal Justice CUNY, N.Y.C., 1973-77, assoc. prof. psychology, 1977-90, prof., 1991—; pvt. practice in psychotherapy N.Y.C., 1970—. Contbr. chpts. to books and numerous articles to profl. jours. Fellow USPHS, 1962-63, 66-67, NIMH, 1967-69; grantee CUNY, 1989-92. Mem. APA (bd. dirs. div. 39 sect. III 1988-92, sec., mem. exec. coun. div. 39 sect. VI 1991-93, exec. com. div. 35 1991-93), N.Y. State Psychol. Assn. (pres. acad. div. 1989-90, coun. rep. 1991-93), N.Y. Acad. Sci. (vice chair psychology adv. com. 1990-92, chair psychology adv. com. 1992-93), Phi Beta Kappa, Chi Delta Pi. Office: John Jay Coll CUNY 445 W 59th St New York NY 10019-1104

GERDES, MICHELLE ANN, freelance designer; b. Trenton, N.J., Sept. 23, 1961; d. Paul and Kathryn (Sinchock) Kaniuka; m. Christopher John Gerdes, Apr. 5, 1986; 1 child, Andrew Paul. BA magna cum laude, Kean Coll. N.J., 1983. Asst. art dir. Medecommunications (div. Med. Econs. Co.), Oradell, N.J., 1983-84; sr. designer mag. Med. Econs. Co., Oradell, 1984-85, asst. art dir. mag., 1985-86; asst. art dir. Butterfly Originals, Mt. Laurel, N.J., 1986-87; design coord. J.B. Lippincott Co., Phila., 1987-88; asst. art dir. TV Guide, Radnor, Pa., 1988-91; freelance art dir. Sewell, N.J., 1991—. Recipient Cert. of Excellence award Art Dirs. Club of N.J., 1986, Merit award, 1987. Roman Catholic. Home and Office: 10 Hunter Ct Sewell NJ 08080-1674

GERDES, ROBERTO MAURICIO, sales and marketing professional; b. Mexico City, Apr. 25, 1948; came to U.S., 1976.; s. Mauricio Augusto and Carmel (Delagrave) G.; m. Linda Diane Swartz, Feb. 19, 1977; children: Michelle Angela, Marissa Erica. BA in Bus. Adminstrn., U. Ams., Cholula, Puebla, Mex., 1971. Account exec. McCann Erickson Stanton, Mexico City, 1971-74, Atlanta, 1974-76, N.Y.C., 1976-78; acct. supr. Doyle Dane Bernbach Inc., N.Y.C., 1978-79; v.p. accounts dir. Benton and Bowles Internat., Madrid, 1979-83, Benton and Bowles U.S.A., N.Y.C., 1983-86; exec. v.p. D'Arcy Masius Benton and Bowles Internat., Mexico City, 1986-87; dir. internat. sales UNIVISA Communications Group, N.Y.C., 1987-89; v.p. mktg. UNIVISA Inc., N.Y.C., 1989—; bd. mem. Servicios Tecnologicos Gageg, Agencias Canadienses y OccidenIales, MARCAR S.A., Noble and Assoc. Advt.; alt. dir. Internat. Coun. Nat. Acad. TV and Svcs., 1988-89. Contbr. article to profl. jour. Mem. Reforma Athletic Club (sec. 1971-75), Pueria de hierro (sec. 1979-82). Roman Catholic. Home: 129 E 82d St Apt 10-C New York NY 10028 Office: UNIVISA Communications Group 767 5th Ave Fl 12 New York NY 10153-1298

GERDTS, ABIGAIL BOOTH, art historian; b. New Milford, Conn., June 20, 1937; d. Frank Walter and Ruth Joan (Friedman) Booth; m. William H. Gerdts, July 23, 1976. BA, Radcliffe Coll., 1959; postgrad., Syracuse U., 1962-63. Membership sec. Corcoran Gallery of Art, Washington, 1959-61; rsch. asst. dept. painting Mus. of Fine Arts, Boston, 1961-62; registrar Lowe Art Ctr., Syracuse (N.Y.) U., 1962-63; curator Nat. Collection Fine Arts Smithsonian Instn., Washington, 1964-70, coord. bicentennial inventory of Am. paintings, 1970-77, coord. index of exhbns., 1977-78; pvt. practice cons. N.Y.C., 1978—; curator, archivist Nat. Acad. of Design, N.Y.C., 1980-89; dir., editor Winslow Homer Catalogue Grad. Ctr. CUNY, 1990—. Co-author: Winslow Homer in Monochrome, 1986; editor, contbg. author: Charles Sheeler, 1968, An American Collection...Nat. Acad. of Design, 1989; author, compiler: Directory to Bicentennial Inventory of American Paintings, 1976. Office: CUNY Grad Ctr 33 W 42d St New York NY 10036

GERHARD, HARRY E., JR., management and trade consultant; b. Phila., Aug. 7, 1925; s. Harry E. and Frances Jane (Edwards) G.; children: Susan Jillson, John, Barbara Thomas. Student, Muhlenberg Coll., 1943-44; AB, George Washington U., 1968, MA, 1969. Commd. ensign USN, 1943, advanced through grades to rear adm., 1971, exptl. test pilot, 1955-57; ret., 1976; exec. v.p., chief oper. officer Costa Line Cargo Svcs., Inc., N.Y.C., 1976-80; gen. mgr. Olayan Transp. Group, Dammam, Saudi Arabia, 1980-82; pres., owner Domestic & Overseas Countertrade & Cons. Svcs., Ltd., Washington, Pa., N.Y., 1983—; pres. Rsch. and Locating Assocs., Ltd., 1986—; arbitrator Adminstrv. Conf. of U.S. Nat. Assn. Securities Dealers, N.Y. Stock Exch., Soc. Maritime Arbitrators. Active Boy Scouts Am. Decorated Silver Star, D.F.C. (2), Meritorious Svc. medal (2), Air medals (16), Navy Commendation medal with combat v (2). Mem. Am. Arbitration Assn. (arbitrator), Assn. Naval Aviation, Air Force Assn., Am. Def. Preparedness Assn., Navy League U.S., Nat. Aero. Assn., Ret. Officers Assn., Order of Daedalians, Tailhook Assn., Cousteau Soc., Four C's, Fleet Res. Assn., Maritime and Environ. Cons., Mil. Order World Wars, Nat. War Coll. Alumni Assn., Soc. Maritime Arbitrators, Soc. Marine Cons., Soc. of Naval Architects and Marine Engrs., U.S. Def. Com., Am. Security Coun., Internat. Platform Assn., Greater Pitts. C. of C., Smaller Mfrs. Coun., Wings Club, N.Y. Yacht Club, Army Navy Club, Masons, Shriners. Republican. Lutheran. Address: Gateway Towers 20F Pittsburgh PA 15222-1133

GERING, RONALD CARL, human services administrator, psychotherapist; b. Trenton, N.J., June 19, 1945; s. Rudolph and Kathryn (Heidi) G.; children: Matthew Jason, Benjamin Michael. BA, Rutgers U., 1967; MA, Miami U., Oxford, Ohio, 1971. Rehab. counselor Mercer County Dept. Corrections, Trenton, 1971-72, dir. profl. svcs., 1972-75; program coord. family growth program Cath. Charities-Diocese of Trenton, 1975-82, clin. dir., 1982—; psychotherapist, Trenton and Princeton, N.J., 1989—; cons. Women's and Crisis Sevs., Flemington, N.J., 1988—; mem. med. team child care providers Harmony Sch., Prineton, 1991—. Mem. Ewing Twp (N.J.) Bd. Edn., 1984-88, chmn. edn. com., 1985-88; mem. Ewing Twp. Human Rels. Coun., 1984-86; bd. dirs. Ewing YMCA, 1977-80; mem. exec. com. Human Svcs. Adv. Coun. Mercer County, 1985—, vice chmn., 1987-89, chmn., 1989-90; mem. N.J. Gov.'s Task Force on Child Abuse, 1984—. Selected for Nat. Disting. Svc. Registry, 1990. Mem. AACD, Am. Assn. for Protection Children, Am. Assn. Mental Health Counselors, Am. Profl. Soc. on Abuse of Children, Nat. Victims Ctr. Home: 1 Wallace Ave Trenton NJ 08618-1955 Office: Cath Charities-Diocese of Trenton 39 N Clinton Ave Trenton NJ 08609-1096

GERJUOY, EDWARD, physicist, lawyer; b. Bklyn., May 19, 1918; s. Abraham and Clara (Hirsch) G.; m. Clark Jacqueline Reid, Aug. 26, 1940; children: Neil, David Leif. B.S. cum laude, CCNY, 1937; M.A., U. Calif., Berkeley, 1940, Ph.D., 1942; J.D. magna cum laude, U. Pitts., 1977. Bar: Calif. 1977, Pa. 1978. Asso. dir. sonar analysis group Div. War Research, Columbia, 1942-46; mem. faculty U. So. Calif., Los Angeles, 1946-51; vis. asso. prof. N.Y. U., 1951-52; mem. faculty U. Pitts., 1952-58, 64-82, prof. physics, 1964-82, prof. emeritus, 1982—; mem. Pa. Environ. Hearing Bd., 1982-86, cons. hearing examiner, 1987-89; of counsel Rose, Schmidt, Hasley & DiSalle, Pitts., 1987—; mem. research staff Gen. Atomic div. Gen. Dynamics Corp., San Diego, 1958-62; dir. plasma and space applied physics RCA Labs., Princeton, N.J., 1962-64; cons. Westinghouse Research Labs., 1952-58; mem. adv. com. health physics div. Oak Ridge Nat. Labs., 1967-71, chmn. com., 1971-74; asso. firm Tucker Arensberg Very & Ferguson, Pitts., 1978-80; vis. fellow Joint Inst. Lab. Physics, U. Colo., Boulder, 1970; cons. EPA, 1977-81; hearing examiner Pa. Environ. Hearing Bd., 1980-81; vis. scholar Stanford Math. Dept., 1987. Author: (with A. Yaspan) Reverberation, in series The Physics of Sound in the Sea, 1968; Editor: Physics Text Series, 1960-62, Jour. Comments on Atomic and Molecular Physics, 1971-74, Jurimetrics Jour. of Law Sci. and Tech, 1980-87; contbr. chpts. and numerous articles to tech. and legal lit. Bd. dirs. Pitts. ACLU, 1975-80, 92—. Fellow Am. Phys. Soc. (mem. panel on public affairs 1976-79, chmn. 1981), AAAS, AAUP, Inst. Physics, Phys. Soc. (Eng.); mem. ABA (chmn. phys. scis. com., sect. sci. and tech. 1976-77, mem. coun. sect. sci. and tech. 1977-80, 84, 87-91), Phi Beta Kappa, Sigma Xi, Order Coif. Home: 400 Richland Ln Pittsburgh PA 15208-2732 Office: Rose Schmidt Hasley & DiSalle 900 Oliver Pittsburgh PA 15222-2404

GERKE, PATRICIA ANN, advocacy educator; b. Camden, N.J., Feb. 23, 1961; d. Richard George and Dorothy Ann (Dougherty) G. BS in Human Ecology, Rutgers U., 1983; MA in Counseling, Rider Coll., 1992. Vol. coord. Assn. Retarded Citizens, Spokane, Wash., 1983-84, community edn. coord., 1984-85, employment support specialist, 1985-87; educator Bancroft, Inc., Haddonfield, N.J., 1987-88, self-advocacy coord., 1988-91; project coord. Speaking for Ourselves, Plymouth Meeting, Pa., 1991—; mem. rights and advocacy com. Internat. League Socs. for Persons with Mental Handicaps, Brussels, 1991; bd. advs. New Vision Mag.; lectr. in field. Mem. AACD, Assn. Retarded Citizens, South Jersey Outdoor Club, Phila. Folksong Soc. Home: 228 S Fellowship Rd Maple Shade NJ 08052-1819 Office: Speaking for Ourselves One Plymouth Meeting Plymouth Meeting PA 19462

GERLACH, JOHN THOMAS, university executive; b. McAdoo, Pa., Oct. 24, 1932; s. John Anthony and Mary Anne (Meshinsky) G.; m. Pamela Ann Wester (div. Oct. 1989); children: John Jr., Audrey, David. BS, Drexel U., 1955; MBA, U. Pa., 1961. Assoc. Booz, Allen & Hamilton, Chgo., 1961-67; corp. devel. v.p. General Mills, Mpls., 1967-78; pres. and founder Consumer Growth Capital, Mpls., 1978-82; pres. and chief oper. officer Horn & Hardart Co., N.Y.C., 1982-86; corp. fin. assoc. dir. Bear Stearns & Co., N.Y.C., 1986-88; v.p. Sacred Heart Univ., Fairfield, Conn., 1990—; adj. prof. Drexel Univ., Phila., 1988—; dir. Creighton Shirtmakers, Inc., Reidsville, N.C., 1980—; dir., audit com. mem. Uno Restaurant Corp., West Roxbury, Mass., 1987—, Am. Woodmark Corp., Winchester, Va., 1979—, Sec. Am. Fin. Enterprises, Mpls., 1977—. Author: (book) Successful Management of New Products, 1972, Corp. Restructuring of America, 1990. Dir. St. Mary's High Sch., Greenwich, Conn., 1988—; mem. bd. regents Investment Com., St. John's U., Collegeville, Minn., 1979—. Recipient Dean's medal, Coll. of Elec. Engring., Czech Tech. Univ., Prague, Czechoslovakia, 1991. Mem. Bridgeport Regional Bus. Coun., Fairfield C. of C. Home: 97 Oneida Dr Greenwich CT 06830-7127 Office: Sacred Heart Univ 5151 Park Ave Fairfield CT 06432-1000

GERLACH, WILLIAM C., sales executive; b. Wilkes Barre, Pa., Feb. 19, 1956; s. Roland Wendell and Elizabeth Ann (Roan) G. AAS, SUNY, Cobleskill, 1976; BS in Bus., Marist Coll., 1979. Salesman AB Dick, Poughkeepsie, N.Y., 1978, KD Hallmark, Hudson, N.Y., 1978-85; sales mgr. KD Office Works, Hudson, 1985—, sales mgr., ptnr., 1992—; cons. on many comml. projects. Coach, fundraiser CYO Basketball Program, Hudson, 1991-92; coach Columbia Youth Spl. Olympics, Hudson, 1985-86; bd. dirs. Hudson Jaycees, 1983. Named Agt.of Yr. Xerox Corp., 1988, 91, Agt. of 1st Quarter, 1989, Agt. of 3d Quarter, 1989, Agt. of 4th Quarter, 1990, Agt. of 1st adn 2d Quarters, 1991; named Mem. of Yr., Hudson Jaycees, 1983. Mem. Nat. Offices Products Assn., Columbia County Chamber (leadership class 1991-92), Cath. Youth Basketball, KC, Elks. Republican. Roman Catholic. Home: Box 157 Claverack NY 12513 Office: KD Office Works Healy Blvd Hudson NY 12534

GERLITZKI, GUENTHER JOHANNES, educator; b. Osterode, Germany, June 21, 1924; came to U.S., 1957, naturalized, 1963; s. Johann and Martha G.; m. Mary Lloyd, Aug. 28, 1956; children: Elizabeth Anne, Nicola Martha. Student Johann Wolfgang Goethe U., Frankfurt am Main, Germany, 1949-55; MA, NYU, 1959, PhD, 1966. Instr., NYU, 1959-64; assoc. prof. German, SUNY, Oswego, 1964-68, prof., 1968-90, prof. emeritus, 1990—, coordinator medieval studies, 1978-79. Bd. dirs. Cen. N.Y. Eye Bank and Rsch. Found., Syracuse, 1974-79; Oswego YMCA, 1979-82; bd. dirs. Oswego Meals on Wheels, 1976-90, v.p., 1982-90; pres. Am. Field Svc., Oswego, 1975. Recipient Disting. Teaching award NYU, 1963, Founders Day award, 1967; Danforth Found. tchr. fellow, 1963-64; SUNY fellow, 1967-68. Mem. MLA, Medieval Acad. Am., Am. Assn. Tchrs. German, Lit. Soc. N.Y., Delta Phi Alpha, Phi Sigma Iota, Alpha Phi Omega. Roman Catholic. Club: Lions (pres. 1976; mem. dist. cabinet 1974, 76-78, dir. 1982-84, 87—) (Oswego). Developer, script writer TV lang. films: Guten Tag, 1969, Mach mit, lern Deutsch, 1970; author: Guten Tag, Study Guide, 1969; Mach mit lern Deutsch, Textbook and Study Guide, 1970; Die Bedeutung der Minne in Moriz von Craûn, 1970. Home: 104 W 6th St Oswego NY 13126-2006

GERMAN, EDWARD CECIL, lawyer; b. Phila., Dec. 28, 1921; s. Samuel Edward and Reba (Trimble) G.; m. Jane Harlos, Sept. 2, 1950; 1 child, Jeffrey Neal. JD, Temple U., 1950. Bar: Pa. 1951. Ptnr. LaBrum & Doak, Phila., 1953-80, German, Gallagher & Murtagh, Phila., 1980—; cons., lectr. to law schools including Harvard U., U. Pa., Syracuse U., others; bd. dirs., mem. products liability, def. research coms. Def. Research Inst., Def. Research Regional Library Inst.; instr. Practicing Law Inst. Contbr. chpts. to books, articles to profl. jours. Dist. dir. United Fund Campaign, 1960; solicitor-counsel Civic Assns. Delaware County, 1955-60; sec. Haven Beach Assn., 1962-63, v.p., 1963-64; trustee Pop Warner's Little Scholars, 1968—; sec., treas. Henryville Conservation Club. Served with USAAF, 1942-46, with USAF, 1950-51. Mem. ABA (chmn. trial techniques com. 1969, mem. profl. and officers and dirs. liability law com. ins. sect. 1974—, pvt. antitrust litigation com. litigation sect. 1974—, subcom. miscellaneous malpractice re accts., bankers, etc. 1976—), Pa. Bar Assn. (com. unauthorized practice 1976—), Phila. Bar Assn. (mem. Pa. rules of civil procedure com. 1963-71, unauthorized practice law com. 1965—, common pleas ct. com. 1964-71, com. antitrust laws corp. sect., mem. Federal bench-bar conf.), Am. Law Firm Assn. (chmn. bd. 1985-86), Fedn. Ins. Counsel (bd. govs. 1960-62, v.p. 1962-63, sec.-treas. 1963-65, exec. v.p. 1965-66, pres. 1966-67, chmn. bd. 1967-68), Maritime Law Assn., U.S. Am. Legion, 40 and 8, Internat. Assn. Ins. Counsel (def. research com., profl. liability and malpractice com.), Internat. Assn. Humble Humbugs, Pa. C. of C., Phila. Def. Counsel Assn., Scribes, Phi Delta Phi. Lodges: Masons, Shriners. Clubs: Union League, Down Town, Maxwell Meml. Football, Union League (Phila.); Beach Haven (N.J.) Yacht; Little Egg Harbor Yacht; Urban (pres. 1987-88) (Phila.); Seaview Country (Absecon, N.J.); Little Mill Country; Belleplain Farms Shooting Preserve; India House; Founders Club. Home: 129 The Mews Haddonfield NJ 08033-1341 Office: German Gallagher & Murtagh 200 S Broad St Philadelphia PA 19102-3803

GERO, ANTHONY GEORGE, securities and commodities trader; b. London, May 31, 1936; came to U.S., 1947; s. Stephen Gero and Ilona (Braun) Von Rieger; m. Joan Selinger, Nov. 20, 1969 (div. 1980); m. Gale Gendason, Feb. 14, 1989; 1 child, Danielle Joy. BS, NYU, 1959; cert., Investment Bankers Inst. U. Pa., 1965. Reporter USIS Chilean Eartquake Relief/Am. Embassy, 1959-60; ptnr. Charles Plohn & Co., N.Y.C., 1960-67; v.p., dir. Internat. First Hanover Corp., N.Y.C., 1967-69; v.p. Drexel Burnham & Co., N.Y.C., 1971-80; 1st v.p. Prudential Securities, N.Y.C., 1981—; mem. U.S. Dept. Commerce, NDER, 1989—. Author: Precious Metals, 1985. Dir., treas. children's fund Commodities Exch. Ctr., N.Y.C., 1980—; chmn. NYMEX Charitable Trust, N.Y.C., 1990—. Recipient Cert., Holocaust Meml., 1991. Mem. N.Y. Produce Exch., N.Y. Merc. Exch. (bd. dirs., treas. N.Y.C. chpt. 1974—), Commodity Exch. Inc., N.Y. Coffe, Sugar and Cocoa Exch., N.Y. Cotton Exch., Commodity Fl. Brokers and Traders Assn. (chmn. 1990—), Investment Brokers Assn., Westchester County Police Revolver Age, Westchester County Sheriff's Assn., N.Y. Police Res. Assn. Republican. Home: 180 E End Ave New York NY 10128 Office: Prudential Securities 100 Gold St New York NY 10292

GERRA, MARTIN J(EROME), JR., economist, educator; b. N.Y.C., May 14, 1927; s. Martin Jerome and Margaret (Landi) G.; m. Anita Little, June 14, 1949; children: Ellen Gerra McCraney, Martin J. III. BS, Georgetown U., 1949; MA, Cath. U., 1954. Economist U.S. Bur. Labor Statis., Washington, 1949-51; mgr. demand analysis USDA, Washington, 1952-61; staff economist Lockheed Aircraft Corp., Marietta, Ga., 1962-64; mgr. internat. econs. IBM Corp., Armonk, N.Y., 1964-88; prof. econs. N.C. State U., Raleigh, 1989-91; adj. prof. Coll. of Notre Dame of Md., 1991—; bd. dirs. MedQ Corp., Washington. Bd. dirs., Westchester Svcs. for Hearing Impaired, N.Y.C., 1977-81. Social Sci. Rsch. Coun. fellow, 1956, Johnston fellow, Johns Hopkins U., 1958-59. Mem. Am. Econ. Assn. Home: 3505 Calvend Ln Kensington MD 20895-3110

GERRISH, CATHERINE RUGGLES, food company executive; b. Winona, Minn., July 10, 1911; d. Clyde O. and Frances (Holmes) Ruggles; m. Hollis G. Gerrish, Sept. 10, 1946. AB, Radcliffe Coll., 1932, AM, 1934; PhD, Harvard U., 1937. Rsch. asst. Harvard U., 1937-39; instr., asst. prof. econs. U. Ill., 1939-42, assoc. prof., 1946; economist Bur. Budget, Exec. Office President, 1943-45; asst. editor Quar. Jour. Econs., 1951-69; treas., v.p. Squirrel Brand Co., Cambridge, Mass., 1966—. Bd. dirs. The Cambridge Homes, pres., 1990-91. Mem. Am. Econ. Assn., Nat. Tax Assn., Coll. Club of Boston (pres. 1948-51), Radcliffe Alumnae Assn. (pres. 1953-55). Home: 207 Grove St Cambridge MA 02138-1096 Office: 17 Boardman St Cambridge MA 02139

GERRISH, EILEEN DEVINE, college administrator; b. Yonkers, N.Y., Dec. 17, 1950; d. Howard Francis and Laura Beatrice (Hotaling) Devine; m. John Peter Santoro (div.); children: Alyson Eileen, Jeffrey Michael; m. Timothy James Gerrish, Aug. 28, 1988; 1 child, Timothy Patrick. BA in Behavioral Sci., SUNY, Plattsburgh, 1973, MALS, 1991. Cons. promotions Chromalloy Photographics, St. Louis, 1975-76; asst. editor Adirondack Daily Enterprise, Saranac Lake, N.Y., 1976-83; dir. pub. rels. Paul Smith's (N.Y.) Coll., 1983-84; dir. community rels. North Country Community Coll., Saranac Lake, 1984—. Contbr. articles, photographs to profl. jours. Mem. Saranac Lake Cen. Sch. Bd., 1986-88, North Country Womyn, Saranac Lake, 1990; mem. bd. dirs. Saranac Lake Civic Ctr., 1990—. Recipient Citation for Excellence, Alumni Confedn. SUNY, Albany, 1985, One in a Million award SUNY Trustees, 1986, George Hodson award North County Community Coll., Saranac Lake, 1986; Ctr. for Women in Govt. fellow, Albany, 1989. Mem. Kiwanis (charter Saranac Lake chpt.), Saranac Lake Ski Club. Office: N County Community Coll 20 Winona Ave Saranac Lake NY 12983-2046

GERRISH, HOLLIS G., confectionery company executive; b. Berwick, Maine, June 23, 1907; s. Perley G. and Grace (Guptill) G.; A.B., Harvard U., 1930, postgrad. Bus. Sch., 1930-31; m. Catherine G. Ruggles, Sept. 10, 1946. With Squirrel Brand Co., mfg. confectioners, 1931—, pres., 1939-42, 46—. Bd. dirs. Middlesex-Cambridge (Mass.) Lung Assn., Cambridge YMCA, East End House, Cambridge Home for the Aged; trustee Lesley Coll., Cambridge; corp. mem. New Eng. Deaconess Hosp. Served as lt. comdr. USNR, 1942-46; capt. Res. Mem. Am. Soc. Candy Technologists, Cambridge Hist. Soc., Nat. Tax Assn., Mass. Audubon Soc. Episcopalian (trustee). Clubs: Harvard, Faculty, New England Confectioners, Norfolk Trout, Flycasters, Cambridge, Economy. Lodge: Rotary. Home: 207 Grove St Cambridge MA 02138-1096 Office: 10-12 Boardman St Cambridge MA 02139

GERRITY, DANIEL WALLACE, real estate developer; b. Albany, N.Y., Nov. 21, 1948; s. Joseph Warren and Phyllis Van Buren (Richard) G.; m. Maria Farley, May 30, 1970; children: Jeanne, Vera, Samuel. BA, U. Va., 1970; JD, Boston U., 1973; MS, Columbia U., 1977. Bar: Mass. 1973, N.Y. 1978. Atty. U.S. Dept. of HUD, Boston, 1973-75; real estate developer, pres. DWG Devel. Inc., N.Y.C., 1978-91, Boston, 1991—; sec.-treas. Salisbury Chevrolet, Inc., Scotia, N.Y., 1991—; pres. Marriner & Co., Boston, 1987—; dir. Saratoga Raceway, 1987—. Pres. Greenhope Housing, N.Y.C., 1986-91; bd. dirs. Community Svc. Soc., N.Y.C., 1990-91; trustee, treas. Preservation League of N.Y. State, Albany, 1980-88. Recipient Community Svc. award Pres. of the U.S., 1984, Young Lion award Sons of Italy, 1979; Equitable Life fellow, 1976-77. Office: 1 Dock Sq Boston MA 02109

GERRY, DALE FRANCIS, legislative assistant; b. Bangor, Maine, Apr. 18, 1950; s. Richard Woodman and Corrine (Paddock) G.; m. Dale Marie Ahearn, Dec. 22, 1976. BA, U. Maine, 1972. Dist. rep. Congressman William S. Cohen, Bangor, 1972-76, spl. asst., 1976-77; senate campaign coord. Congressman William S. Cohen, Portland, Maine, 1977-78; legis. asst. mil./communications./transp./maritime affairs Senator William S. Cohen, Washington, 1979—; cons. polit. candidates. Bd. dirs. Maine State Ballet, Bangor, 1976-79. Republican. Roman Catholic. Home: 4708 Tecumseh St College Park MD 20740 Office: Senator William S Cohen SH-322 Washington DC 20510

GERRY, JOHN FRANCIS, federal judge; b. Camden, N.J., Nov. 17, 1925; s. Francis P.; m. Jean June 21, 1952; children: Patricia, Kathleen, Ellen. A.B., Princeton U., 1950; LL.B., Harvard U., 1953. Solicitor Twp. of Mt. Laurel, N.J., 1971-72; judge Camden County Ct., 1972-73, N.J. Superior Ct., 1973-75; judge U.S. Dist. Ct. N.J., 1975-87, chief judge, 1987—. Mem. ABA, N.J. Bar Assn. Office: US Dist Ct 401 Market St # 588 Camden NJ 08102-1568*

GERRY, JOSEPH JOHN, priest, college chancellor, bishop; b. Millinocket, Maine, Sept. 12, 1928; s. Bernard Eugene and Blanche Agnes (McManemon) G. AB summa cum laude, St. Anselm's Coll., Manchester, N.H., 1950; postgrad., St. Anselm's Sem., 1954; MA, U. Toronto, 1955; PhD, Fordham U., 1959; LLD, Benedictine Coll., 1986, St. Anselm Coll., 1986; DD, St.

Joseph's Coll., Windham, Maine, 1990. Joined Order of St. Benedict, Roman Catholic Ch., 1948 ordained priest: Roman Catholic Ch., 1954. Asst. dean studies St. Anselm's Coll., 1958-59, dean studies, 1971-72; chancellor St. Anselm's Coll., N.H., 1972-86; consecrated bishop, 1986; auxiliary bishop Manchester, N.H., 1986-89; bishop Portland, Maine, 1989—. Home: 199 Western Promenade Portland ME 04102 Office: 510 Ocean Ave Portland ME 04103-4900

GERRY, ROGER GOODMAN, retired oral surgeon; b. Far Rockaway, N.Y., Feb. 26, 1916; s. Bernard Abraham and Edith Rose (Goodman) G.; A.B., U. N.C., 1936; D.M.D., U. Louisville, 1940; m. Peggy Newbauer, Nov. 6, 1944. Diplomate Am. Bd. Oral and Maxillofacial Surgery. Commd. lt. (j.g.) Dental Corps, USN, 1941, advanced through grades to capt., 1955; ret., 1965; dir. dental and oral surgery service Mt. Sinai Hosp. Services, City Hosp. Center, Elmhurst, N.Y., 1965-81; attending oral surgeon, head div. oral surgery Mt. Sinai Hosp., N.Y.C., prof. oral surgery Mt. Sinai Sch. Medicine, CUNY. Chmn. Planning Bd. Roslyn, N.Y. 1960-72; pres. Roslyn Landmark Soc., Roslyn Preservation Corp., 1964—. Spl. exhbn. in collection of Japanese Ceramics Met. Mus. Art, 1989-90; author: Catalogue of Japanese Ceramics, 1961; contbr. articles to profl. jours., Dictionaryof Art. Trustee Bryant Library, Village Roslyn, N.Y, Preservation League of N.Y. State. Recipient Howard C. Sherwood award Soc. for Preservation L.I. Antiquities, 1976, award Nat. Trust Historic Preservation, 1982, Ann. award Victorian Soc. in Am., 1985. Fellow Internat., Am. Coll. Dentists, Internat. Assn. Oral Surgeons, Met. Mus. Art (life), Brit. Assn. Oral and Maxillofacial Surgeons (hon.); mem. Am. Assn. Oral and Maxillofacial Surgeons, Am. Acad. Oral Pathology (emeritus), Am. Dental Assn. (hon.), Soc. Archtl. Historians, Japan Soc. Office: George Allen House 20 Main St Roslyn NY 11576-2131

GERSH, RICHARD LEON, insurance company executive; b. Boston, Jan. 29, 1952; s. Irving Stanley and Louise Bernice (Goldstein) G.; m. Claire Louise Menendez, Apr. 30, 1977; children: Jeremy Edward, Jacob Lee. BA, Boston U., 1975; MBA, U. Lowell, 1987. Claims supr., then comml. underwriter Sentry Ins., Concord, Mass., 1975-79; sr. mktg. rep. Alexander and Alexander, Boston, 1979-82; mgr. risk analysis Congoleum Corp., Portsmouth, N.H., 1982-84; dir. risk mgmt. New England Mut. Life Ins. Co., Boston, 1984-86, asst. v.p., 1986-89, 2d v.p., 1989—; bd. dirs. Newbury Ins. Co., Ltd., Hamilton, Bermuda. Mem. Soc. Property and Casualty Underwriters, Risk and Ins. Mgmt. Soc. Home: 3 Colonial Dr Westford MA 01886-4502 Office: New Eng Mut Life Ins Co 501 Boylston St Boston MA 02116-3706

GERSH, WAYNE DAVID, psychologist, cognitive behavior therapist; b. Bklyn., Sept. 7, 1949; s. Paul and Florence (Gelfand) G.; m. Barbara Marilyn Schwab, Apr. 20, 1981; children: Robert Schwartz, Jonathan Schwartz. BS, SUNY, Oneonta, 1971; MA, Calif. State U., Fresno, 1975; PhD, Adelphi U., 1977; postdoctoral clin. fellow, Inst. Behavior Therapy, 1981. Lic. psychologist, N.Y. Staff psychologist Suffolk Devel. Ctr., Melville, N.Y., 1978-81, Nassau Ctr. for Behavior Therapy, Massapequa, N.Y., 1980-81; clin. dir. Westchester Ctr. for Behavior Therapy, White Plains, N.Y., 1981—; psychol. cons. Am. Cancer Soc., White Plains, N.Y., 1987—, Almay Cosmetics Health Watch Coun., 1992—. Author: Psychological Treatment of Cancer Patients-A Cognitive Behavioral Approach, 1991; contbr. articles to profl. jours. Mem. APA, Westchester Psychol. Assn., Assn. for the Advancement of Behavior Therapy. Office: Westchester Ctr for Behavior Therapy 77 Tarrytown Rd White Plains NY 10607-1620

GERSHENFELD, MATTI KIBRICK, psychologist; b. Phila.; d. Hyman and Esther Kibrick; m. Marvin A. Gershenfeld, 1946 (dec. 1989); children: Robert, Howard, Richard, Kenneth. BA, U. Pa., 1947, MA in Govt. Adminstrn., 1951; EdD, Temple U., 1967. Lic. psychologist, Pa.; cert. marriage and family therapist. Pres. MKG Assocs., Elkins Park, Pa., 1975—, Couples Learning Ctr., Jenkintown, Pa., 1975—; adj. prof. Temple U., 1967—; grad. faculty mem. Pa. State U., Phila., dir. Inst. of Awareness; mem. organizing com., co-chair 1st Internat. Interdisciplinary Conf. on Women, Haifa, Israel, 1982. Author: Groups: Theory and Experience, 4th edit. 1989, Making Groups Work, 1983, How to Find Love, Sex and Intimacy after 50: A Woman's Guide, 1991; contbr. chpts. to Contemporary Marriage, 1986, Adult Development, 1984, Conservation of Marriage and the Family Studies, 1986. Active Phila. Planning Commn.; bd. dirs. Gratz Coll., Elkins Park, 1975—, Hillel Greater Phila.; mem. pres.' coun. Gwynedd (Pa.) Mercy Coll., 1981—; past pres. Am. Diabetes Assn., Phila., 1987-90, chair. Fellow Am. Psychol. Assn., Am. Assn. Marriage and Family Therapists; mem. Nat. Coun. on Family Rels., Pa. Coun. on Family Rels. (past pres.), Assn. State Couns. Nat. Coun. Family Rels. (past pres.), Eastern Coun. Psychologists (chair continuing edn.). Jewish. Home: 8302 Old York Rd Philadelphia PA 19117-1522 Office: Couples Learning Ctr Benson East A 13 Jenkintown PA 19046

GERSHENGORN, MARVIN CARL, physician, educator; b. N.Y.C.. M.D., NYU, 1971. Diplomate Am. Bd. Internal Medicine. Intern Strong Meml. Hosp., Rochester, N.Y., 1971-72, asst. resident in medicine, 1972-73; asst. prof. medicine NYU Sch. Med., 1976-80, assoc. prof., 1980-83; prof. medicine Cornell U. Med Coll., N.Y.C., 1983—; Abby Rockefeller Mauze disting. prof. Cornell U. Med Coll. Office: Cornell Univ Med Coll 1300 York Ave New York NY 10021-4896

GERSHMAN, ELIZABETH GIBSON, executive; b. Mansfield, Ohio, Oct. 16, 1927; d. Edward Douglas and Daisie Marie (Taylor) G.; m. Paul F. Cropper, Jr., Dec. 5, 1948 (div. Mar. 1953); m. James D. Gershman, June 29, 1957 (div. Mar. 1980); children: Katherine Anne, Taylor James. AA, Stephens Coll., Columbia, Mo., 1947; B Gen. Studies, U. Conn., Stamford, 1978. Freelance actress, N.Y.C., 1952-57; dir. Ft. Stamford Restoration, Stamford, 1972-77, Stamford Hist. Soc., 1977-82; pub. Knights Press, Inc., Stamford, 1983-92; v.p. spl. projects Triquest Devel. Corp., Stamford, 1992—; performing arts critic Stamford Trader, 1980-90, What To Do, arts newspaper, 1990—. Founder Ft. Stamford Corp., 1973-78; bd. dirs. Norwalk (Conn.) Symphony, 1972-79, Stamford Community Arts Coun., 1977-84, Stamford Mayor's Com. on Handicapped, 1981, Hist. Neighborhood Preservation, Stamford, 1985—; chmn. horizon com. Stamford Bicentennial Corp., 1973-77; mayoral appointee Fairfield County S.W. Regional Planning Area, 1977-80; program chmn. Conn. League Hist. Socs., 1978-80; publicity chmn. Stamford Bicentennial Purple Heart Com., 1982; pres. North Stamford Assn., 1986-88; elected mem. Bd. Reps. Stamford, 1981-83. Named One of 8 Outstanding Women in Conn., Fairfield County Adv., 1987; grantee NEH, 1978. Mem. Am. Booksellers Assn., Pub. Triangle, Conn. Critics Circle. Republican. Presbyterian. Office: Triquest Devel Corp 1 Landmark Sq Stamford CT 06901

GERST, ELIZABETH CARLSEN (MRS. PAUL H. GERST), university dean, researcher, educator; b. N.Y.C., June 10, 1929; d. Rolf and Gudrun (Wiborg) Carlsen; A.B. magna cum laude, Mt. Holyoke Coll., 1951; Ph.D., U. Pa., 1957; m. Paul H. Gerst, Aug. 3, 1957; children—Steven Richard, Jeffrey Carlton, Andrew Leigh. Instr. physiology Grad. Sch. Medicine, U. Pa., 1955-57, Cornell U. Med. Coll., N.Y.C., 1957-58; instr. Columbia Coll. Physicians and Surgeons, N.Y.C., 1959-61, asst. prof., 1961—, dir. Center Continuing Edn. in Health Scis., 1978-87, asst. dean continuing edn., 1984-87, dir. Office Med. Edn., N.Y. Acad. Med., 1987—; Authors: (with others) The Lung, Clinical Physiology and Pulmonary Function Tests, 1955, rev. edit., 1962. Pres. Citizen's Ednl. Council Tenafly, 1972-73; mem. Citizens Long-Range Planning Com., Tenafly Bd. Edn., 1973-77, chmn. supt. search, edn., tchr. hiring, personnel coms.; vice chmn. Tenafly Environ. Commn., 1972-77; trustee Tenafly Nature Center, 1972-80; bd. dirs., chmn. environ. quality Tenafly LWV, 1971-78; v.p. Bergen County LWV, 1973-75. Porter fellow Am. Physiol. Soc., 1956-57. Mem. Middle States Assn. Colls. and Schs. (team Commn. on higher edn., 1984—), Soc. Med. Coll. Dirs. of Continuing Med. Edn., Am. Physiol. Soc. (task force Women in Physiology 1973-75), N.Y. County Med. Soc. (com. on continuing med. edn. 1978—), Physiol. Soc. Phila., Harvey Soc., Biophys. Soc., Alliance Continuing Med. Edn., N.Y. Acad. Scis., AAAS, Phi Beta Kappa, Sigma Xi, Sigma Delta Epsilon. Unitarian. Home: 141 Tekening Dr Tenafly NJ 07670-1218 Office: Office Med Edn NY Acad Med 2 E 103d St New York NY 10029

GERST, PAUL HOWARD, physician; b. Sept. 24, 1927; s. David and Hilde (Werbel) G.; m. Elizabeth Carlsen, Aug. 3, 1957; children—Steven R., Jeffrey C., Andrew L. A.B., Columbia U., 1948, M.D., 1952. Diplomate: Am. Bd. Surgery, Am. Bd. Thoracic Surgery. Intern Columbia Presbyn. Med. Center, N.Y.C., 1952-53; resident Columbia Presbyn. Med. Center, 1956-62, mem. staff, 1962—; instr. physiology U. Pa., 1955-56; practice medicine specializing in surgery N.Y.C., 1962—; asst. clin. prof. surgery Columbia U., 1964-72; prof. surgery Albert Einstein Coll. Medicine, 1972—; dir. surgery Bronx-Lebanon Hosp. Center, N.Y.C., 1964—. Contbr. articles to profl. jours. Served to 1st lt. U.S. Army, 1953-55. USPHS postdoctoral fellow, 1955-56; Recipient Research Career Devel. award, 1964-65. Fellow A.C.S.; mem. Am. Physiol. Soc., N.Y. Soc. for Thoracic Surgery, N.Y. Surg. Soc., N.Y. Soc. for Cardiovascular Surgery, Am. Heart Assn. Home: 141 Tekening Dr Tenafly NJ 07670-1218 Office: Bronx Lebanon Hospital Center 1650 Grand Concourse Bronx NY 10457-7697

GERSTEIN, DORYNE SHARI (DORYNE SHARI DAVIS), advertising executive; b. Bklyn., Apr. 16, 1960; d. Israel Julius Morris and Maxine (Glassman) G. BA in English with honors, Rutgers Coll., 1982. Editorial asst. Mgmt. Acctg. mag. Nat. Assn. Accts., N.Y.C., 1982-83; advt. mgr. Mgmt. Acctg. mag. Nat. Assn. Accts., Montvale, N.J., 1983—; advt. and circulation mgr. Inst. Mgmt. Accts. (formerly Nat. Assn. Accts.), Montvale, 1987—. Mem. NAFE, Am. Mgmt. Assn., Small Mag. Pub. Group. Democrat. Jewish. Office: Inst Mgmt Accts 10 Paragon Dr Montvale NJ 07645-1718

GERSTEIN, ESTHER, sculptor; b. N.Y.C., May 20, 1924; d. Leon and Lillian (Peretz) Grizer; m. Leonard B. Gerstein, Mar. 31, 1946; children: Lee Steven, Laurie Susan. Student, Pratt Inst., 1941-42, NYU, 1942-43; pvt. study, various sculptors; student, Cooper Union, 1946-48. Asst. tchr. Art Students League, N.Y.C., 1944-46; painting tchr. pvt. sch. Great Neck, N.Y., 1961-63; founder, instr. sculpture and painting Studio 33, Westbury, N.Y., 1964-72; sculptor and painter pvt. studios, N.Y.C. and Boca Raton, Fla.; lectr. Norton Mus., Palm Beach, Fla., 1985. Exhibited in group shows at Hecksher Mus., Huntington, N.Y., Norton Mus., Palm Beach, Fla., Kellenberg Gallery, C.W. Post Coll., L.I., Firehouse Gallery, Nassau Community Coll., L.I., Lever House, N.Y.C., Grace Bldg., N.Y.C., Hofstra U., Lighthouse Gallery, Tequesta, Fla., Montoya Art Gallery, Palm Beach, Del-Aire Country Club, Boca Raton, Fla., Bocaire Country Club, Boca Raton, Polo Country Club, Boca Raton; one man show includes TV spl.; represented in numerous pvt. and corp. collections throughout U.S. Mem. Artists Guild Norton Mus., Contemporary Sculptors Guild, L.I. Craftsman's Guild.

GERSTENZANG, JAMES ROSE, journalist; b. N.Y.C., Oct. 8, 1947; s. Nathaniel M. and Miriam (Rosenbaum) G.; m. Eugenie C. Wetstein, July 27, 1974; children: Megan, Betsy. BA, Rutgers U., 1969. Reporter AP, San Francisco, 1970, Newark, 1970-73; editor, regional corr. AP, Washington, 1973-77, White House reporter, 1977-81, White House chief corr., 1981-84; Pentagon corr. Los Angeles Times, Washington, 1984-86, White House corr., 1986—. Mem. White House Corrs. Assn. (pres. 1983-84). Office: LA Times 1875 I St NW Washington DC 20006-5409

GERSTL, JOEL, sociology educator; b. Czechoslovakia, Aug. 20, 1932; came to U.S., 1938; s. Max and Claire (Ehrman) G.; m. Judith Jelinek, Dec. 18, 1966; children: Jonathan, Janis. BA, Columbia Coll., 1954, MA, 1958; PhD, U. Minn., 1959. Rsch. assoc. U. Mich., Ann Arbor, 1958-60; lectr. U. South Wales, Cardiff, Eng., 1960-62, Cambridge (Eng.) U., 1962-63; asst. prof. Purdue U., Lafayette U., 1963-65; assoc. prof. Temple U., Phila., 1965-68, prof., 1968—; vis. prof. King's Coll., London, 1987-88. Co-author: Profession without Community, 1969; co-editor: Professions for the People, 1976, Engineers and the Social System, 1969. Office: Dept Sociology Temple U Philadelphia PA 19122

GERSTNER, LOUIS VINCENT, JR., diversified company executive; b. N.Y.C., Mar. 1, 1942; s. Louis Vincent and Marjorie (Rutan) G.; m. Elizabeth Robins Link, Nov. 30, 1968; children—Louis, Elizabeth. B.A., Dartmouth Coll., 1963; M.B.A., Harvard U., 1965. Dir. McKinsey & Co., N.Y.C., 1965-78; exec. v.p. Am. Express Co., N.Y.C., 1978-81; vice chmn. bd. Am. Express Co., 1981-83, chmn. exec. com., 1983-85, pres., 1985-89, also bd. dirs.; chmn., chief exec. officer RJR Nabisco Inc., N.Y.C., 1989—; bd. dirs. Caterpillar Inc., The New York Times Co., AT&T, Bristol-Myers Squibb Co. Bd. dirs. Meml. Sloan Kettering Hosp., 1978-89, United Negro Coll. Fund, 1987-91, Lincoln Ctr. for Performing Arts, Am.-China Soc.; trustee Joint Coun. on Econ. Edn., 1975-87, chmn. 1983-85; mem. Bus. Roundtable; vice chmn., bd. dirs. New Am. Schs. Devel. Corp.; mem. adv. bd. Ctr. for Strategic and Internat. Studies; bd. dirs. Japan Soc., 1992—; trustee N.Y. Pub. Libr., 1991—; mem. The Bus. Coun., 1992. Mem. Coun. Fgn. Rels., Grocery Mfrs. Am., Next Century Schs. Found., N.Y. City Partnership. Office: RJR Nabisco Inc 1301 Ave Of The Americas New York NY 10019-6022

GERTZ, STEVEN MICHAEL, environmental engineer, consultant; b. Phila., Feb. 15, 1943; s. Sidney and Rose Gertrude (Smolen) G.; m. Thea Gail Sigismund, Aug. 20, 1967; children: Shira Jolene, Amira Rebecca. BSc, Phila. Coll. Phamacy & Sci., 1965; MSc, Drexel U., 1968, PhD, 1973. Environ. health specialist Phila. Health Dept., 1965-67, 68-69; sr. biophysicist Radiation Mgmt. Corp., Phila., 1972-74; ptnr. Porter-Gertz Cons., Ardmore, Pa., 1974-81; v.p. Roy F. Weston, Inc., West Chester, Pa., 1981-89; v.p., gen. mgr. Burns & Roe Environ. Svcs., Inc., King of Prussia, Pa., 1989—. Editor: Statistics in the Environmental Sciences, 1984; contbr. articles to profl. jours. Grad. fellow USPHS, 1967-68; recipient rsch. grants U.S. Army, 1969-70, NIH, 1971-72. Mem. ASTM (results advisor 1986—), Hazardous Materials Contrl Rsch. Inst., Bd. Hazard Control Mgmt. (cert. 1985—), Inst. Hazardous Materials Mgmt. (cert. 1985—, bd. examiners 1987—), Del. Valley Soc. for Radiation Safety (pres. 1977-78), Health Physics Soc. Home: 306 Bangor Rd Bala Cynwyd PA 19004-2804 Office: Burns & Roe Environ Svcs Inc 601 S Henderson Rd King Of Prussia PA 19406-3596

GERTZOG, IRWIN NORMAN, political scientist, educator; b. Bklyn., May 18, 1933; s. Benjamin and Sonia (Posnack) G.; m. Alice Solomon, Nov. 22, 1956; children: Joshua B., Rachel L. BA, Union Coll., Schenectady, 1954; PhD, U. N.C., 1965. Instr. polit. sci. Yale U., New Haven, 1964-65, asst. prof., 1965-71; Braun prof. polit. sci. Allegheny Coll., Meadville, Pa., 1971—; vis. prof. polit. sci. Princeton U., 1986-87, 91; cons. U.S. Congressman, Washington, 1965-80. Author: Congressional Women, 1984; editor: State and Local Government, 1970; mem. editorial bd. Women and Politics, 1989-90; contbr. articles to profl. jours. Vice chair Crawford County Bd. Welfare Assistance, Meadville, 1982-90; mem. exec. com. Crawford County Dem. Party, 1987—. With U.S. Army, 1956-58. Am. Polit. Sci. Assn. Congl. fellow, 1963-64; summer grantee NSF, 1968, NEH, 1986; Social Sci. Rsch. Coun. fellow, 1969-70. Mem. AAUP, Am. Polit. Sci. Assn., NOW. Jewish. Home: 468 Gilmore St Meadville PA 16335 Office: Allegheny Coll Dept Polit Sci Meadville PA 16335

GERVAIS, BARBARA ELIZABETH, educator; b. Waterbury, Conn., Mar. 1, 1951; d. John and Mary (Koban) Olear; m. Thomas Richard Gervais, July 19, 1975; 1 child, David Thomas. BS, U. Conn., 1973; MS, So. Conn. State U., 1976, postgrad., 1989. Tchr. Waterbury Pub. Schs., 1973—. Mem. NEA, Conn. Edn. Assn., Nat. Staff Devel. Coun., Elem. and Middle Sch. Prins. Assn. Conn., Phi Delta Kappa. Russian Orthodox. Home: 8 Newbridge Cir Cheshire CT 06410-4314

GERVAIS, PAUL NELSON, foundation administrator, psychologist, public relations executive; b. Augusta, Maine, June 28, 1947; s. Adrien and Phyllis (Sullivan) G. B in Bible and Doctrine/Ministerial Studies, Berean Coll., 1975; M, U. Maine, 1987; M in Marriage and Family Therapy, Coll. Clin. Family Sci., 1988; cert. in Constl. Law, U. Maine, 1969; Dr., N.Am. Biblical Sem., Buffalo, 1987; M. in Marriage and Family, San Antonio Theol. Sem., 1988; PhD in Psychology, San Antonio Theol. Sem., St. Paul, 1989; PhD in Marriage and Family Therapy, Minn. Grad. Sch., 1990. Cert. behavioral analyst, clin. supr.; registered clin. therapist; lic. marriage & family therapist, Tex. Reporter No. New Eng. div. News dept. NBC Radio div., N.Y.C., 1966-70; dir. pub. relations Kennebec Valley Med. Ctr., Augusta, 1970-73, Penobscot Bay Med. Ctr., Rockport, Maine, 1973-74; pres., chmn. bd. dirs. Ministry of Miracles Evangelistic Assn., Maine, 1975—; news dir. Maine Broadcasting System. Augusta, 1966-70; advisor, assoc. dir. pub. rels. state VA svcs., Maine, 1969-70; family counselor Gracelawn Meml. Pk., Auburn, Maine, assoc. dir., 1987; pres., chief exec. officer Motivational Resources, Critical Incident Response Unit, FBI, 1991. Pioneered one of first radio and TV health edn. programs from which proceeded other nat. and internat. programs in field. Active Rep. Nat. Com., Washington, 1987, Dole for Pres. Exploratory Com., 1987—, also adv. com., 1987, steering com. Campaign Am., 1987-88; mem. Presdl. Task Force, Washington, 1989, Rep. Senatorial Inner Circle, 1989—, U.S. Senatorial Club, Washington, 1989-90, Nat. Rep. Senatorial Com., Washington, 1990; chief exec. officer Gracelawn Meml. Park, Auburn, Maine, 1988—. Recipient vice-presdl. Citation Office of U.S. V.P. Hubert Humphrey, 1968, Malcolm T. MacEachern Citation Am. Health Congress, 1973; cert. in pub. rels. Chgo. chpt. Am. Hosp. Assn.; Presdl. Medal of Merit Pres. George Bush, 1989. Fellow Profl. Assn. Christian Counselors and Therapists; mem. AACD, Am. Acad. Family Therapists (exec. dir.), Publicity Club Boston (disting. bell ringer award 1974), Nat. Christian Counselors Assn. (mem. licensing bd., chmn. legal com.), Am. Mental Health Counselors Assn., Maine Network Associated Profl. Practitioners, Maine Assn. for Counseling and Devel. Baptist.

GESELL, GERHARD ALDEN, federal judge; b. Los Angeles, June 16, 1910; s. Arnold Lucius and Beatrice (Chandler) G.; m. Marion Holliday Pike, Sept. 19, 1936; children—Peter Gerhard, Patricia Pike. A.B., Yale, 1932, LL.B., 1935. Bar: Conn. 1935, D.C. 1941. With SEC, Washington, 1935-40; tech. adviser to chmn. SEC, 1940—; acted for Commn. as spl. counsel Temporary Nat. Econ. Com., study legal res. life ins. cos.; mem. Covington & Burling, Washington, 1941-67; judge U.S. Dist. Ct. D.C., 1968—; chief asst. counsel Joint Congl. Com. on Investigation Pearl Harbor Attack, 1945-46; Chmn. Pres.'s Com. on Equal Opportunity in the Armed Forces, 1962-64; chmn. com. on adminstrn. of justice D.C. Jud. Council, 1965-67; jud. mem. D.C. Commn. on Jud. Disabilities and Tenure, 1976-81. Co-author: Study of Legal Reserve Life Insurance Cos, 1940, Families and Their Life Insurance, 1940. Recipient Edward J. Devitt Disting. Svc. to Justice award, 1989. Mem. Am. Bar Assn., Am. Law Inst., Am. Coll. Trial Lawyers, Phi Delta Phi, Zeta Psi. Clubs: Lawyers (Washington), Met. (Washington); Casino (North Haven, Maine). Home: 3304 N St NW Washington DC 20007 Office: US Dist Ct US Courthouse 3d St & Constitution Ave NW Washington DC 20001

GESKIN, ERNEST S(AMUEL), science administrator, consultant; b. Dnepropetrovsk, Ukraine, USSR, June 4, 1935; came to U.S., 1977; s. Samuel A. and Rosa M. (Raskin) G.; m. Doris M. Osherenko, June 12, 1964; 1 child, Ellen. M in MetE, Inst. Mettalurgy, Dnepropetrovsk, 1957; PhD in ME, Inst. Steel and Alloys, Moscow, 1967. Engr. Inst. Automation, Dnepropetrovsk, 1957-67, mgr. lab., 1967-74; assoc. rsch. prof. George Washington U., Washington, 1977-78; assoc. prof. Clarkson Coll. Tech., Potsdam, N.Y., 1979-80; rsch. scientist, lab. mgr. Revere Rsch. Inc., Edison, N.J., 1981-83; dir. waterjet cutting lab. Revere Rsch. Inc., Edison, 1986—; spl. lectr. N.J. Inst. Tech., Newark, 1984-85, assoc. prof., 1986-90, prof. 1991—. Author/co-author over 80 papers and presentations; editor various symposia (Cert. Recognition, 1984, 89); 22 U.S. and USSR patents, 1969—. Mem. Iron & Steel Soc. AIME, Waterjet Tech. Assn., Sigma Xi. Office: NJ Inst Tech 323 King Blvd Newark NJ 07102

GESMER, HENRY, lawyer; b. Quincy, Mass., Apr. 1, 1912; s. Abraham Meyer and Esther Frances (Zide) G.; m. Bessie Nathanson, Nov. 24, 1940; children: Linda Schrank, Gabriel Myles, Ellen Frances Gesmer Hyde. BS, Harvard U., 1933, JD, 1936. Bar: Mass. 1936, U.S. Dist. Ct. Mass. 1937. Sr. ptnr. Brown, Rudnick, Freed & Gesmer, Boston, 1959—; dir. U.S. Trust Co., Boston. Hon. trustee Combined Jewish Philanthropies, Boston, 1965—; trustee Soc. Law Libr., Boston, 1988—; pres. assoc. Harvard U., Cambridge, Mass., 1987. Brandeis U. fellow, Waltham, Mass., 1988—. Mem. ABA, Mass. Bar Assn., Boston Bar Assn., Mass. Trial Lawyers Assn. Democrat. Jewish. Home: 111 Dane Hill Rd Newton MA 02161-2018 Office: Brown Rudnick Freed & Gesmer One Financial Ctr Boston MA 02111

GESS, NICHOLAS MICHAEL, prosecutor; b. N.Y.C., May 28, 1955; s. Karol Norbert and Mira (Mendelsohn) G. AB, Bowdoin Coll., 1977; JD, U. Maine, 1981. Bar: Maine, U.S. Ct. Appeals (1st cir.), U.S. Dist. Ct. Maine. Mgmt. trainee 1st Brunswick (Maine) Fed. Savings and Loan, 1977-78; asst. dist. atty. State of Maine, Portland, 1981-83; asst. atty. gen. State of Maine Dept. of Atty. Gen., Augusta, 1983-87; asst. U.S. atty. U.S. Atty.'s Office Dept. Justice, Portland, 1987-92, chief narcotics sect., 1992—. V.p. Cliff Island (Maine) Assn., 1990—. Office: US Dept Justice East Tower 6th fl Onn Hundred Mid St Plaza Portland ME 04101

GETCHELL, CHARLES WILLARD, JR., lawyer, publisher; b. Los Angeles, May 29, 1929; s. Charles Willard and Katharine (Fitch) G.; m. Angela Winthrop, Sept. 16, 1961; children—Katharine Chisholm, Emily Erskine, Sarah Fields. A.B., Stanford U., 1951, J.D., 1954. Bar: Calif. 1955, Mass. 1979, U.S. Dist. Ct. (no. dist.) Calif. 1960, Mass. 1984, U.S. Ct. Appeals, 9th cir. 1960. Atty., Air Materiel Force, Chateauroux, France, 1958-59; asst. U.S. atty. No. Dist. Calif., San Francisco, 1960-61; asst. mgr. Citibank, N.Y.C., Brussels, Belgium, 1961-68; v.p. Wood Struthers & Winthrop, N.Y.C., Brussels, 1969-77; ptnr. Gray, Wendell, Chalmers & Dahlen Boston, 1981—; pub. The Ipswich Press, Mass., 1980—. Transl.: European Monetary Unity: For Whose Benefit? (Pascal Salin), 1980. Contbr. occasional essays, verse in N.Y. Times, Boston Globe, Beverly Times. Mem. steering com. Bilderberg Meetings, The Hague, 1980-85; bd. dirs. Salzburg Seminar, 1985—. Served to lt. (j.g.), USNR, 1955-58. Mem. Belgian Am. Ednl. Found., Boston Bar Assn., Royal Soc. Polit. Economy. Republican. Clubs: Knickerbocker, Tavern, Myopia Hunt. Home: 828 Highland St Ipswich MA 01938-2737 Office: Ipswich Press PO Box 291 Ipswich MA 01938-0291

GETMAN, SHERYL MARIE, artist; b. Kalispell, Mont., Dec. 31, 1947; d. Dannie E. Loutherback and Shirley Jean (Barry) Michaelson; m. Daniel William Getman, Jan. 21, 1952; children: Guy Young, Crescent. Student, Ea. Mont. State Coll., 1968, 69, Calif State Coll., Fullerton, 1970, Mont. State U., 1974, 75, 76, Flathead Coll., Kalispell Mt., 1977, 78, Art Student's League, N.Y.C., 1988. Artist Jorgensen Pottery & Art Studio, Coram, Mont., 1978-83; owner, mgr. Spruce Park Truck Stop, Coram, 1980-83; pres., artist Sky Jordan Graphics, Kalispell, 1983-86; pres. Sky Jordan Restaurant Inc., Kalispell Mt., 1983-86; pres., artist Artistic Urges, Inc., Princeton, N.J., 1986—; v.p. Sky Deco Inc., 1989—; feature writer Penington (N.J.) Post, 1989, also freelance writer; pres. Sky East Inc., 1990—; instr. Reevaluation Counseling, Creativity Seminars, 1989—. Vol. Siddha Meditation Ctr. Mem. Nat. League Am. Pen Women, North Star Watercolor Soc. (bd. dirs. 1987-88). Unitarian. Home and Office: 342 Prospect Ave Princeton NJ 08540

GETTIER, EDMUND LEE, III, philosophy educator; b. Balt., Oct. 31, 1927; s. Edmund Lee Jr. and Clara Frances (Schuele) G.; m. Astrid Elizabeth Pfeiffer, Mar. 1957 (div. 1965); children: Evan E., Elizabeth L., Edmund L. IV, Sheila A., David B.; m. Lucia Milda Mingela, July 8, 1966; children: Daina N., Jonathan M. BA, Johns Hopkins U., 1949; PhD, Cornell U., 1961. Instr. to asst. prof. Wayne State U., Detroit, 1957-67; assoc. prof. to full prof. U. Mass., Amherst, 1967—. With U.S. Army, 1953-55. Mellon Post Doctoral Fellow, U. Pitts., 1964-65. Home: 16 Weatherwood Rd Amherst MA 01002-9802 Office: U Mass Dept Philosophy Amherst MA 01003

GETTIG, MARTIN WINTHROP, retired mechanical engineer; b. South Bend, Ind., Nov. 8, 1939; s. Joseph H. and Esther (Scheppele) G.; m. Nancy Caroline Buchannan, June 25, 1960 (dec. 1965). Student, Pa. State U., 1957-60, 89—. Process engr. Gettig Tech. Inc., Spring Mills, Pa., 1960-88. Inventor ultralight non-solid state miniature ignition systems for model aircraft employing small two cycle spark ignition engines. Staff sgt. Pa. N.G., 1961-67. Mem. NRA, Model Engine Collectors Assn., Soc. Antique Modelers and Model Airplanes, Acad. Model Awronautics, Univ. Club Pa. State U., Delta Phi. Republican. Lutheran. Home: PO Box 85 Boalsburg PA 16827-0085

GETTY, CHERYL, aerospace transportation executive; b. Teaneck, N.J., Nov. 18, 1951; d. Charles Robert and Katharine (Murray) G.; m. Robert B. Leventhal, Apr. 25, 1987; 1 child, Abigail Katharine. BA, St. Lawrence U., 1973; MPA, Am. U., 1976; EdS, George Washington U., 1986. Sr. cons. Tech. Assistance and Tng. Corp., Washington, 1976-79; dir. tng. Am. Ctr. for Quality of Work Life, Washington, 1979-81; mgr. personnel resources

Martin Marietta Corp., Bethesda, Md., 1981-86, dir. human resource devel., 1986—. Mem. ASTD, Human Resource Planning Soc. Home: 3831 Calvert St NW Washington DC 20007 Office: Martin Marietta 6810 Rockledge Dr Bethesda MD 20817

GETU, SEYOUM, mathematics educator; b. Deder, Harar, Ethiopia, July 21, 1941; came to U.S., 1974; s. Gonche and Ejigayehu (Tsadik) G.; m. Tsion Tesfaye, Sept. 14, 1974; children: Seble, Bruck, Amrote. BS, Haile Sellassie I U., Addis Ababa, Ethiopia, 1964; MS, U. Mich., 1967; PhD, U. MO., 1973; Profl. Deg. in Gen. Ops. Research, George Wash. U., 1982. Lectr. Haile Sellassie I U., 1967-70, asst. prof., 1973-74; asst. prof. Howard U., Washington, 1975-82, assoc. prof., 1982—. officer Ethiopian Community Ctr., Washington, 1981-82. Haile Sellassie fellow, 1965-67. Mem. Am. Math. Soc., Math. Assn. of Am., Washington Ops. Research and Mgmt. Sci., Nat. Assn. of Math. Home: 7724 Heritage Dr Annandale VA 22003-5309 Office: Howard U 2400 6th St NW Washington DC 20059-9997

GETZEL, JEFFREY ALAN, accountant; b. Bronx, N.Y., May 10, 1953; s. Carl J. and Rae (Grossman) G.; m. Micki Croce, Aug. 22, 1976; children: Melissa, Michael. BBA, Baruch Coll., 1971; MBA, Hofstra U., 1983. CPA, N.Y., N.J., Conn., Fla. Sr. acct. Druckman & Hill CPA, N.Y.C., 1971-76; mgr. Joseph D. Cooper & Co., Roslyn Heights, N.Y., 1976-79; ptnr. Gevirtz, Lesk & Getzel, Jericho, N.Y., 1979-83; pres., mng. ptnr. Jeffrey A. Getzel & Co., P.C., Woodbury, N.Y., 1983—. Treas. Am. Cancer Soc., Huntington Station, N.Y., 1989—, exec. bd. dirs., 1988—; trustee Temple Beth Torah, Melville, N.Y., 1990—, fin. com. chair, treas., 1991—. Mem. AICPA, N.Y. Soc. CPAs, Cold Spring Country Club (com. mem.). Jewish. Office: Jeffrey A Getzel & Co PC 130 Woodbury Rd Woodbury NY 11797-1409

GEVANTMAN, JUDITH, financial analyst, consultant; b. Pitts., May 25, 1949; d. Chaim and Charlotte Selma (Max) G. AB cum laude, Goucher Coll., Towson, Md., 1971; postgrad., NYU, 1971-74; MPA, Harvard U., 1977. Dep.dir. N.Y.C. Addiction Svcs. Agy., 1971-74; asst. v.p., supr. Moody's Investors Svc., N.Y.C., 1978-85; v.p., dir. mcpl. rsch. Wertheim, Schroder & Co., N.Y.C., 1986-87; v.p., mgr. fixed income rsch. Mabon, Nugent & Co., N.Y.C., 1988; ptnr. Rsch. Assocs., Bklyn., 1989—; chmn. bd. dirs. GemStone Investors Assurance Corp., 1990—; cons. Downstate Med. Sch., Bklyn.,1975, Harvard U. Med. Sch., Boston, 1976, Boston Mus. Sci., 1977. Bd. dirs. Bruekelen Owners Corp., Bklyn., 1982-83; alumni rep. Goucher Coll., 1985—; trustee Congregation Bnai Avraham, Brooklyn Heights, N.Y., 1988—. UN fellow U. Kans., 1970, Univ. fellow NYU, 1971-73; Senatorial scholar Md. Legislature, 1967-71; Urban Corp. grantee, 1970. Mem. Mcpl. Forum N.Y., Mcpl. Analyst Group N.Y., Harvard Club (N.Y.C.).

GHAI, RAJENDRA DURGAPRASAD, chemist; b. Lucknow, UP, India, Oct. 28, 1943; came to U.S., 1974; s. Durga Prasad and Satya Arora G.; m. Geetha Rajendra Subramanian, Jan. 18, 1968; children: Pranav, Nirupa. BS with honors, Gujarat U., Ahmedabad, India, 1964; MSc., M.S. U., Baroda, India, 1966, PhD, 1972. Rsch. scientist Sarabahai Squibb, Baroda, India, 1972-74; rsch. assoc. Dept. Biochemistry, Cell & Molecular Biology, Buffalo, N.Y., 1974-78; dir. Clin. Chem. Lab. Dept. OB/Gyn. Deaconess Hosp., Buffalo, 1977-78; rsch. assoc. Dept. Biochemistry Coll. Medicine U. South Ala., Mobile, 1978-80; instr. DO, Mobile, 1980-83; sr. staff scientist DO, Summit, N.J., 1989—; sr. rsch scientist Ciba-Giegy Corp., Summit, 1983-89. Contbr. numerous articles profl. jours. Recipient Fellowship World Health Orgn., 1967-71, Grant in Aid Nat. Inst. Health, Washington, 1980-85. Mem. AAAS, N.Y. Acad. Sci., Soc. of Biological Chemists, India (sec. 1973-74), Gerontological Soc. Am., Am. Soc. of Hypertension. Home: 250 Gallinson Dr New Providence NJ 07974-2725

GHALI, ANWAR YOUSSEF, psychiatrist, educator; b. Cairo, May 30, 1944; came to U.S., 1974, naturalized, 1980; s. Youssef and Insaf Wahba (Soliman) G.; m. Violette Fouad Saleh, May 23, 1968; 1 child, Susie. MD, Cairo U., 1966, DPM, 1970, DM, 1971. Diplomate Am. Bd. Psychiatry and Neurology; cert. adminstrv. psychiatry. Registrar in psychiatry Woodilee Hosp., Glasgow, Scotland, 1973-74; resident in psychiatry N.J. Med. Sch., Newark, 1974-77, instr., 1977-78, clin. asst. prof., 1978-79, asst. prof., 1979-83, clin. assoc. prof., 1983—; chief Outpatient Dept.-Community Mental Health Ctr., N.J. Med. Sch., Newark, 1978-86; dir. Emergency Psychiat. Svcs. Univ. Hosp., U. Medicine and Dentistry of N.J., Newark, 1986-87; med. dir. Profl. Counsel Ctr., Westfield, N.J., 1984-87; med. chief ambulatory psychiat. svcs. Elizabeth (N.J.) Gen. Hosp., 1987-89; dir. psychiat. tng. VA Med. Ctr., East Orange, N.J., 1989—, asst. chief psychiatry, 1990-91, assoc. chief psychiatry, 1991—. Contbr. articles to profl. jours. Recipient Exceptional Merit award Coll. Medicine & Dentistry, Newark, 1981. Mem. AMA, Christian Med. Soc., Am. Psychiat. Assn., N.J. Psychiat. Assn., N.Y. Acad. Scis. Republican. Presbyterian. Home: 22 Benvenue Ave West Orange NJ 07052-3202

GHATTAS, IGNATIUS, clergyman; b. Nazareth, Israel, Dec. 25, 1920. Educated, Holy Savior Sem., Saida, Lebanon. ordained priest, 1946; consecrated eparch Melkite Diocese of Newton, Mass., 1990. *

GHEZZO, MARIO, physicist, researcher; b. Trieste, Italy, Nov. 20, 1937; came to U.S., 1966; s. Francesco and Bruna (Sartori) G.; m. Marie I. Iagrossi, July 28, 1973. PhD, U. Trieste, 1962. Staff scientist Sprague Electric Co., North Adams, Mass., 1966-69; staff scientist R&D GE, Schenectady, N.Y., 1969—; mem. tech. adv. bd. Semiconductor Rsch. Corp., Research Triangle Park, N.C., 1986-90. Author: Advances in CMOS Processes, 1989; contbr. over 50 articles to profl. jours. Lt. Italian Forces Nuclear Def. Svc., 1963-64. Mem. IEEE, Electrochemical Soc., Soc. Mfg. Engrs. (sr.). Home: 404 Schauber Rd Ballston Lake NY 12019-2106 Office: GE KWB 1309 River Rd Schenectady NY 12309

GHIGLIERI, DOMINICK JAMES, consulting engineer; b. N.Y.C., Apr. 11, 1940; s. Dario Gaspare and Maria Teresa (Canepa) G. AAS, S.I. City Coll., 1960; BSEE, N.Y. Inst. Tech., 1962; LLB, LaSalle U., 1966; MA in Liberal Studies, NYU, 1979; DD, 1989. Ordained to ministry Universal Life Ch., 1974. Pvt. bus., cons. N.Y.C., 1967-77; cons. Dermot Reddy P.E., N.Y.C., 1977-88, Rhodes & Basso P.C., N.Y.C., 1988—. Author: Existential Zen Poetry, 1967. Radio warden, Civil Def., N.Y.C., 1964-70; vol. Peace Corps, U. N.Mex., 1963, Suicide Help Ctr., N.Y.C. Recipient Elec. Industry Participant award, Elec. Constrn. Panel, McGraw & Hill, 1982-87, Good Character award, City of N.Y., 1989. Fellow IEEE, Soc. Am. Magicians; mem. Instrument Soc., Psychology Club (past pres.), Manhattan Camera Club (pres. 1972). Home: 23 Bedford St New York NY 10014-4732 Office: Rhodes & Basso 38 E 30th St New York NY 10016-7316

GHIZ, JOSEPH A., Premier of Prince Edward Island; b. Charlottetown, P.E.I., Can., Jan. 27, 1945; s. Atallah Joseph and Marguerite (McKarris) G.; m. Rose Ellen McGowan; children—Robert, Joanne. B.Commerce, Dalhousie U., 1966, LL.B., 1969; LL.M., Harvard U., 1981; LLD (hon.) U. P.E.I., 1987. Bar: Can. Sr. ptnr. Scales, Ghiz, Jenkins & McQuaid, Charlottetown, 1969-81; leader Liberal opposition Party, Charlottetown, 1982-86; premier P.E.I., 1986—. Co-author: Towards A New Canada, 1978. Named to Queens Counsel, 1984. Mem. P.E.I. Law Soc. Anglican. Club: Charlottetown. Home: 122 N River Rd, Charlottetown, PE Canada C1A 3K8 Office: Office of Premier, PO Box 2000, Charlottetown, PE Canada C1A 7N8

GHOBASHY, OMAR ZAKI, lawyer; b. Cairo, Arab Republic of Egypt, Mar. 1, 1924; came to U.S., 1949; s. Ahmed and Bahia (Shawarbi) G. BA, Ain Shams U., Cairo, 1946; MA, NYU, 1953, PhD, 1955; MA, Columbia U., 1956; JD, Bklyn. Law Sch., 1960. Rep. of Yemen UN, N.Y.C., 1960-63; rep. of Arab States UN, 1977—; atty., bd. dirs. Moslem World League, N.Y.C., 1977—, Arab Rep. Egypt, United Arab Emirates and Arab govts., N.Y.C., 1964—; atty. for Indian tribes of N.Y. and Can., 1960—; atty., bd. dirs. Islamic Soc. N.Y., 1956-80; judge Philip Jessup Mooot Ct. on internat. law, 1992. Author books on internat. law, Am. Indians, Middle East; contbr. articles to profl. jours. Founder, sec. gen. Egyptian Club, 1963-70. Adopted as blood-brother by six nations of Iroquois confederancy. Mem. ABA (internat. law sect.), N.Y. State Lawyers Assn. (internat. law and immigration), N.Y. State Trial Lawyers Assn., N.Y. County Lawyers, Am. Immigration Lawyers, Westchester Bar Assn., Queens Bar Assn., Nat. Assn. Mfrs. (rep. UN),N.Y. Am. Soc. Intertnat. Law, Athletic Club (N.Y.C.), Westchester County Club (Rye, N.Y.). Home: 85 Wildwood Rd New Rochelle NY 10804-4712 Office: Ste 1117 122 E 42d St New York NY 10168

GHOSE, ARUP KUMAR, computational chemist, researcher; b. Malda, India, Feb. 26, 1951; came to U.S., 1981; s. Ajay Kumar and Uma Rani (Sinha) G.; m. Chandralekha Mittra, June 29, 1980; 1 child, Monalisa. PhD, Jadavpur U., Calcutta, 1978; postdoctoral, Tex. A&M U., 1981-84. Asst. rsch. scientist Tex. A&M U., College Station, 1984-85; rsch. investigator U. Mich., Ann Arbor, 1985-87; departmental head Nucleic Acid Rsch. Inst., Costa Mesa, Calif., 1987-89; sr. rsch. investigator Sterling Rsch. Group, Rensselaer, N.Y., 1990—; cons. Biodesign Inc., Pasadena, Calif., 1990. Contbr. articles to profl. jours. Mem. AAAS, Am. Chem. Soc., N.Y. Acad. Scis., IUPAC. Home: 66 Middlesex Dr Slingerlands NY 12159-9651 Office: 81 Columbia Tpke Rensselaer NY 12144-3411

GIACALONE, JOSEPH ANTHONY, economics educator, consultant; b. Bklyn., Sept. 10, 1938; s. Anthony Joseph and Mary (Sciuto) G.; m. Marianne Veronica Zimmermann, Dec. 29, 1962; children: Joseph A. Jr., Christine, Linda, Thomas. BA, Columbia U., 1960, PhD, 1971; MBA, St. John's U., N.Y.C., 1962. Instr. econs. St. John's U., Jamaica, N.Y., 1962-66, asst. prof., 1966-72, assoc. prof., 1972—, assoc. dean Coll. Bus. Adminstrn., 1972-85; Henry George chair in econs. St. John's U., N.Y.C., 1991—; dean St. John's U., Jamaica, N.Y., 1985-89; pres. Career Advancement Systems, Flushing, N.Y., 1985—; cons. to various univs. Contbr. articles to profl. jours., chpt. to book. Various offices St. Andrew Avellino Parish, Flushing, 1976—, Broadway-Flushing Homeowners Assn., 1978—. Recipient award for outstanding adminstrv. achievement St. John's U., 1986. Mem. Am. Econ. Assn., Nat. Assn. Bus. Economists, Econ. and Bus. History Assn., Beta Gamma Sigma, Omicron Delta Epsilon, Alpha Sigma Lambda, Alpha Chi Rho. Home: 33-54 167th St Flushing NY 11358 Office: St Johns U Dept Econs Jamaica NY 11439

GIACOBBE, PATRICK JAMES, data processing executive; b. Phila., Aug. 22, 1953; s. Matthew Anthony and Catherine (Owens) G.; m. Bernadette K. Roddy, June 21, 1978; children: Kevin, Brian. AS in Bus. Adminstn., Camden County Coll., 1986; BSBA, Thomas Edison U., 1989. Edn. specialist Itek Photcomposition, Nashua, N.H., 1971-71, Computer Automation, Dallas, 1977-80, Carterfone, Dallas, 1980-82; dist. svc. mgr. Syfa Data Systems, Moorestown, N.J., 1983-86; tng. mgr. Okidata, Mt. Laurel, N.J., 1986—; cons. Pubs. Ink, Blackwood, N.J., 1987—. Div. coord. Collingswood (N.J.) Youth Soccer League, 1989—, youth coach, 1989—. With USN, 1971-77. Mem. Soc. Tech. Communications, Nat. Assn. Desktop Pubs. Democrat. Roman Catholic. Home: 235 Cattel Ave Oaklyn NJ 08107-2310 Office: Okidata 532 Fellowship Rd Mount Laurel NJ 08054-3405

GIAEVER, IVAR, physicist; b. Bergen, Norway, Apr. 5, 1929; came to U.S., 1957, naturalized, 1963; s. John A. and Gudrun (Skaarud) G.; m. Inger Skramstad, Nov. 8, 1952; children: John, Anne Kari, Guri, Trine. Siv. Ing., Norwegian Inst. Tech., Trondheim, 1952; Ph.D., Rensselaer Poly. Inst., 1964. Patent examiner Norwegian Patent Office, Oslo, 1953-54; mech. engr. Can. Gen. Electric Co., Peterborough, Ont., 1954-56; applied mathematician Gen. Electric Co., Schenectady, 1956-58, physicist Research and Devel. Ctr., 1958-88; Inst. prof. Rensselaer Poly. Inst., Troy, N.Y., 1988—; also prof. U. Oslo, 1988—. Served with Norwegian Army, 1952-53. Recipient Nobel Prize for Physics, 1973; Guggenheim fellow, 1970. Fellow Am. Phys. Soc. (Oliver E. Buckley prize 1965); mem. IEEE, Norwegian Profl. Engrs., Nat. Acad. Sci., Nat. Acad. Engring. (V.K. Zworykin award 1974), Am. Acad. Arts and Scis., Norwegian Acad. Sci., Norwegian Acad. Tech. Office: Rensselaer Poly Ins Physics Dept Troy NY 12180-3590*

GIALANELLA, DONALD GEORGE, broadcast executive, artistic director, sculptor; b. Plainfield, N.J., June 9, 1956; s. Angelo George and Helena Joan (Kreminski) G.; m. Phyllis Clare Orlowski, June 25, 1988; children: Max Philip, Julian Andrew. Student, Montclair (N.J.) State U., 1974-77; BFA cum laude, Cooper Union, 1979. Art dir. South Coast Publs., San Diego, 1981-83; artist, animator ABC News/Sports, N.Y.C., 1983-84; assoc. network news graphics dir. ABC News, N.Y.C., 1984-85; broadcast graphics artistic dir. ABC Sports/Entertainment, N.Y.C., 1985—. Designer, producer (animation/graphics) Monday Night Football, 1990 (Emmy award 1990), (opening animation) Good Morning America, 1989. Recipient Elliot Lash Meml. prize Cooper Union, 1979, Page Design award Sigma Delta Chi, 1983, Gold Design award North County Press Club, 1984, Art Direction awards Art Direction mag., 1985; finalist Monitor Award Assn., 1986. Mem. Acad. TV, Arts and Scis. (Sports Emmy award 1990), Broadcast Designers Assn. Home: 9 Essex Ave Maplewood NJ 07040-1502 Office: ABC Sports 47 W 66th St Fl 8 New York NY 10023-6290

GIAMARTINO, GARY ATTILIO, management educator, consultant; b. Syracuse, N.Y., Feb. 19, 1952; s. Albert J. and Margaret M. (Palange) G.; m. Maryellen McDonald, July 23, 1988; children: Anna, Mary. AB, SUNY, Fredonia, 1974; MA, Western Ky. U., 1976; PhD, Vanderbilt U., 1979. Asst. prof. Coll. Charleston, S.C., 1979-84, The Citadel, Charleston, 1984-86; assoc. prof. mgmt. St. Joseph's U., Phila., 1986—, dir. Inst. Internat. Trade, 1990—; cons. various bus. and govt. orgns. Contbr. articles to profl. jours. Bd. dirs. Internat. Visitors Coun. Phila., 1991—; mem. adv. bd. Brazil U.S. Cen. Culture and Edn., Phila., 1986-90; mem. exec. com. East Pa. Ptnrs. Ams., Pittston, 1986—. Internat. Devel. fellow Kellogg Found., Ptnrs. Ams., 1988-90. Mem. Internat. Coun. Sml. Bus., U.S. Assn. Sml. Bus. and Entrepreneurs, Acad. Mgmt., Psi Chi. Home: 826 Kings Croft Cherry Hill NJ 08034-1110 Office: St Josephs U 5600 City Ave Philadelphia PA 19131-1395

GIAMBALVO, VINCENT, manufacturing company executive; b. Bklyn., Nov. 10, 1942; s. Frank and Anna (Pepey) G.; m. Rose Marie Esposito, Sept. 8, 1968; 1 child, Gina Marie. BA, Hunter Coll., 1966; MA, Northeastern U., 1970, PhD, 1973. Rsch. assoc. Northeastern U., Boston, 1972; asst. prof. behavioral sci. SUNY, N.Y.C., 1973-77; tng. specialist ADP Network Svcs., Ann Arbor, Mich., 1978-80; mgr. human resource devel. ADT Security Systems, Parsippany, N.J., 1981-88; dir. tng. and devel. Duro-Test Corp., Fairfield, N.J., 1989—; instr. Am. Soc. Tng. and Devel. cert. program Kean Coll., 1982-85; nat. and internat. sales and mktg. cons. Biofeedtrac Inc., Bklyn., 1984—. Contbr. articles on edn. and vision sci. to profl. jours. With USNR, 1964-71. NDEA Title IV fellow, 1968-71. Mem. ASTD (sec. Ann Arbor chpt. 1978-79, pres. 1980, leadership devel. coord. North N.J. chpt. 1989-90, pres.-elect 1991, pres. 1992), Am. Mgmt. Assn. Democrat. Roman Catholic. Home: 21 Eldor Ave New City NY 10956-1404 Office: Duro-Test Corp 9 Law Dr Fairfield NJ 07004-3200

GIANATASIO, DAVID JOHN, columnist, screenwriter; b. Bridgeport, Conn., Nov. 25, 1966; s. Dominick Andrew and Gloria (Takacs) G. BS, Boston U., 1988. Staff writer Ziff-Davis Publ., Boston, 1987-89; co-founder, editorial dir. Just Publ., Inc., Boston, 1990-92; staff writer Adweek Mag. Network, Boston, N.Y.C., 1989—. Author: (poetry) Bend Backward for Sharper Rezeption, 1992; co-author TV script, 1991; contbr. articles to profl. jours. Democrat. Office: Adweek Magazine Network 100 Boylston St Boston MA 02116

GIANGOLA, GARY, surgeon; b. N.Y.C., Feb. 2, 1955; s. John and Elena (Zollo) G.; m. Joan Evelyn Feierabend, Aug. 20, 1977; children: Gary, Vincent, Paul. BA, NYU, 1976, MD, 1980. Diplomate Am. Bd. Surgery. Surgical intern NYU Med. Ctr., N.Y.C., 1980-81, surgical resident, 1981-85, vascular surgical fellow, 1985-86, asst. prof. surgery, 1986—, attending surgeon, 1986—; attending surgeon Bellevue Hosp. Med. Ctr., N.Y.C., 1986—; svc. chief, vascular surgery Manhattan VA Med. Ctr., N.Y.C., 1990—; chief vascular surgery Manhattan VA Med. Ctr., N.Y.C., 1990—. Fellow Am. Coll. Surgeons; mem. Peripheral Vascular Surgery Soc., Internat. Soc. Cardio Vascular Surgery, Ea. Vascular Surgical Soc., N.Y. Cardiovascular Surgical Soc. Office: NYU Med Ctr 530 First Ave New York NY 10016

GIANNAROS, DEMETRIOS SPIROS, economist, educator; b. Karlovasi, Samos, Greece, Oct. 4, 1949; came to U.S., 1964; s. Spiridon Demetrios and Irene (Kiriakou) G.; m. Elizabeth Sampson, June 5, 1977; children: Edward, Spiros Jason. BA in Econs., U. Mass., 1972; MA in Econ. Devel., Boston U., 1976, MAPE in Polit. Econ., 1977, PhD in Econs., 1981. Mgr. Samos Imex Corp., Boston, 1974-77; asst. prof. econs. Suffolk U., Boston, 1977-79; prof. U. Hartford, West Hartford, Conn., 1980—; dir. exec. MPA program U. Hartford, West Hartford, 1986-88, assoc. to sr. v.p., dir. internat. studies, 1988-91; spl. asst. to pres. George Washington, U., Washington, 1988-89; cons. to pub. and pvt. orgns., 1977—; mem. bd. dirs. Coll. Southeastern Europe, 1992—. NSF grantee, 1983-84, U. Hartford Coffin grantee, 1983-8, Mellon Found. grantee, 1991-92; Am. Coun. on Edn. fellow, 1988-89. Fellow Am. Coun. on Edn. (mem. exec. bd. coun.); mem. Am. Econ. Assn., Internat. Econ. Assn., N.E. Bus. and Econs. Assn. (pres. 1990—), Helicon Soc. (pres., bd. dirs. 1975-78), Hellenic Assn., Paideia, World Affairs Coun. Greek Orthodox. Home: 56 Basswood Rd Farmington CT 06032-1142 Office: U Hartford Econs Dept 200 Bloomfield Ave West Hartford CT 06117-1500

GIANNONE, MICHAEL, podiatrist; b. Bklyn., Jan. 26, 1942; s. Louis Carmelo and Helen Dolores (Bassolino) G.; m. Ella Ann Valentine, Sept. 18, 1965; children: Louis Scott, Monica Susan, Michael Keith. BA, NYU, 1964; D of Podiatric Medicine, N.Y. Coll. Podiatric Medicine, 1970. Diplomate Am. Bd. Podiatric Surgery (credentials com. 1989—). Sec. Mt. Kisco (N.Y) Podiatry Group, P.C., 1972-78, v.p., 1978—; chief podiatry surg. staff No. Westchester Hosp., Mt. Kisco, N.Y. Fellow Am. Coll. Foot Surgeons. Republican. Roman Catholic. Home: 149 Broad Brook Rd Bedford Hills NY 10507-2235 Office: Mt Kisco Podiatry Group PC 91 Smith Ave Mount Kisco NY 10549-2810

GIANNOTTI, LOUIS JOHN, computer company executive, researcher; b. New Britain, Conn., Apr. 8, 1945; s. James Salvatore and Mary Teresa (Grossi) G.; m. Carleen Gladowski, Aug. 24, 1970; children: Louise Joy, Courtney Glad. BS in Naval Sci. and Math., U.S. Naval Acad., 1969; MS in Ops. Rsch. and Systems Analysis, U.S. Naval Postgrad. Sch., 1974. Cert. naval propulsion engr. Commd. ensign USN, 1969, advanced through grades to comdr., 1983; communications and ops. officer USS Hammberberg (DE 1015), Newport, R.I., 1969-72; engr. and exec. officer USS Glover (AGFF-1), Norfolk, Va., 1975-78; squadron engr., materials officer Destroyer Squadron Ten, Norfolk, 1978-79; from instr. to asst. prof. maths. U.S. Naval Acad., Annapolis, Md., 1979-82, chmn. computer sci. dept., 1984-86, dean of fin., 1986-87; exec. officer USS Farragut (DDG-37), Norfolk, 1982-84; comdg. officer USS Halyburton (FFG-40), Charleston, S.C., 1988-90; v.p. Decision System Techs. Inc., Greenbelt, Md., 1992—; rsch. analyst Adler Corp., Washington, 1980-82. Author, creator software integration automated combat decision system, data fusion system and tactical integration. Bd. dirs. Watergate Home Improvement Assn., Inc., Annapolis, 1986, pres., 1987, 92. Office: Decision System Techs Inc 6301 Ivy Ln Greenbelt MD 20770-1402

GIARDINA, ELSA GRACE V., cardiologist; b. Newark, Aug. 1, 1941; d. John and Elsa (Freda) G.; m. Alan L. Saroff, June 1, 1974; 1 child, John Saroff. AB, Bryn Mawr U., 1961; MD, NYU, 1965. Asst. prof. medicine Columbia U., N.Y.C., 1972-79, assoc. prof. medicne, 1980-87, prof. medicine, 1987—; mem. cardiorenal adv. com. Fed. Drug Adminstrn., Rockville, Md., 1984-88; mem. pharmacology study sect. NIH, Bethesda, Md., 1989—. Contbr. articles to profl. jours. Office: Columbia U 630 W 168th St New York NY 10032

GIARRUSSO, ALENA LOUISA, elementary and special education teacher; b. Pitts., Oct. 22, 1951; d. Nicholas Anthony and Antonina P. (Mazzotta) G. BE, Duquesne U., 1973; MEd, U. Pitts., 1974. Cert. elem. and spl. edn. tchr., Pa. Diagnostician Assn. for Children with Learning Disabilities, Pitts., 1975-77; tchr. of emotionally disturbed children Highland Sch., Bethel Park, Pa., 1974-77; resource tchr. Peters Twp. Mid. Sch., McMurray, Pa., 1977-91; trainer U. Pitts., 1980-82; elem. and spl. edn. tchr. Elm Grove Sch., McMurray, 1991—; adv. bd. Penn Star Computer System in Spl. Edn., Harrisburg, Pa., 1990-91; facilitator videotape Orientation to Peters Twp. Mid. Sch., 1990-91. Contbr. articles to profl. jours. Active Pitts. Ctr. Arts; dance study group South Side Presbyn. Ch., Pitts., 1991; usher Pitts. Pub. Theatre, 1981. Recipient Am. Legion Leadership award Immaculate Conception Sch., Pitts., 1965; fellow Dept. Def., 1973-74; Mainstreaming fellow U. Pitts., 1975. Mem. AACD, ASCD, Am. Liturgical Planning Holistic Approach, Am. Fedn. Tchrs., Am. Film Inst., Explorers CLub. Democrat. Roman Catholic. Office: Elm Grove Sch 225 Thompsonville Rd Canonsburg PA 15317

GIBBONS, ELIZABETH GILL, insurance company administrator; b. Newark, May 21, 1949; d. John Henry and Elizabeth Ann (Powers) G. BSBA, Montclair (N.J.) State Coll., 1983; MBA in Fin. Mgmt., Pace U., 1987. Nat. Assn. Ins. Commrs. coord. Prudential Capital Corp., Newark, 1983-84, MIS coord., 1984-86, assoc. investment mgr., 1986-88, investment mgr., 1988-90; dir. portfolio mgmt. group svcs. Prudential Ins. Co., Newark, 1990—. Foster parent Plan Internat. USA, N.Y.C., 1990—. Mem. NAFE, North Jersey Assn. for Female Execs. (bd. dirs. 1991—), Women's History Network. Office: Prudential Ins Co Two Gateway Ctr Newark NJ 07102

GIBBONS, JAMES MORTIMER, JR., orthopaedic surgeon, educator; b. Boston, Aug. 11, 1930; s. James M. and Rosemary (Mahon) G.; m. Louise Virginia Gibbons, Aug. 11, 1956; children: James, Brian, Christine, Louise, Timothy. AB, Boston U., 1953; MS, Tufts Coll., 1954; MD, N.Y. Med. Coll., 1958. Diplomate Am. Bd. Orthopedic Surgery; lic. physician, Mass. Intern Boston City Hosp., 1958-59; resident in orthopedics Lahey Clinic, Boston City Hosp., 1963-65; pvt. practice Mt. Auburn Hosp., Cambridge, Mass., Symms Hosp., Arlington, Mass.; clin. instr. orthopaedic surgery Harvard Med. Sch., Cambridge, Mass., Tufts Med. Sch., Boston. Lt. USN, 1960-62. Mem. Am. Acad. Orthopaedic Surgery, New Eng. Orthopaedic Soc. (pres. 1980). Roman Catholic. Home: 51 Winchester Rd Arlington MA 02174 Office: 300 Mt Auburn St Cambridge MA 02238

GIBBONS, JOHN SHERIDAN, financial analyst, consultant; b. Phila., Nov. 7, 1961; s. John Patrick and Patricia (Connor) G. BS, U. Houston, 1983, MBA, 1985. CPA, Tex., accredited tax advisor. Program analyst Singer-Link Fight Simulation, Houston, 1983-85; corp. acct. Rockwell Internat., Houston, 1986; cost analyst St. Luke Episcopal Hosp., Houston, 1987; fin. analyst Dun & Bradstreet, Plymouth Meeting, Pa., 1987—. Mem. AICPA, Soc. Pub. Accts. Republican. Office: IMS Am 660 W Germantown Pike Plymouth Meeting PA 19462-1048

GIBBONS, MARY PEYSER, civic volunteer; b. N.Y.C., Dec. 15, 1936; d. Frederick Maurice and Catherine Mary (McKelvey) Peyser; m. John Martin Gibbons, Dec. 26, 1955; children: Catherine Way, Mary Sloan, John, Fredericka Kerr, Myles. Ptnr. Gibbons & Bibow Assocs., Hartford, Conn., 1986-90; pres. Sefton & Sheil Ltd., Hartford, 1988—. Regent U. Hartford, 1988—, bd. trustees Hartford Art Sch., 1985—, v.p. 1991-92; pres. womens com. Wadsworth Atheneum, Hartford, 1978-80, bd. trustees, 1981-90, 91—; bd. dris. The Hartford Ballet, 1981—; vol. coms. Art Mus., U.S. and Can., 1982-91. Mem. Am. Assn. Mus. Vols. (pres. 1986-88, bd. dirs. 1982-90, contbr. articles to orgn. publs. 1986-88), U.S. Found., World Fedn. The Friends Mus., Hartford Club, Hartford Golf Club. Office: Sefton & Sheil Ltd 1130 Prospect Ave Hartford CT 06105-1124

GIBBS, CORA LEE, museum director; b. Prague, Czechoslovakia, June 22, 1924; d. Walter Wesley and Helen (King) Gethman; m. Julian Howard Gibbs, July 27, 1946 (wid. Feb. 1983); children: James, Judith, Jeffrey, Jonathan. BA, Smith Coll., Northampton, Mass., 1946; MA, Brown U., 1972. Researcher Index of Christian Art/Princeton (N.J.) U., 1947-50; lectr. Brown U., Providence, R.I., 1964-65; asst. curator of edn. Mus. of Art/R.I. Sch. Design, Providence, 1965-67, 70-71, curator of edn., 1971-80; lectr. Mead Art Mus., Amherst, Mass., 1981-84; exec. dir. Newport (R.I.) Art Mus., 1985—; bd. dirs. R.I. Arts Advocates, Providence; merit aid panelist State Coun. Arts and Humanities, Mass., 1981-84. Author various catalogues. Bd. dirs. Newport County YMCA, 1989—, Williamstown Regional Art Conservation, 1984-86. Recipient medal for Eminent Svc. Amherst coll., 1984. Mem. Rotary (treas. 1991), Northfield Mount Hermon Sch. (bd. dirs. 1982—), Japan-America Soc. (bd. dirs. 1987—). Democrat. Episcopalian. Office: Newport Art Mus 76 Bellevue Ave Newport RI 02840-7411

GIBBS, ELIZABETH VILLA, college program coordinator; b. Jamaica, N.Y., Aug. 27, 1935; d. Benjamin O. and Lucille D. (Wilcox) Villa; m. Wolcott Gibbs Jr., Jan. 4, 1958 (div. 1977); children: William Benjamin, Eric Wolcott; m. William A. Collins, June 21, 1980. BA, Wheaton Coll., Norton, Mass., 1957. Asst. editor Good Housekeeping, N.Y.C., 1958-63; free lance writer, 1970-77; city clk. City of Norwalk, Conn., 1977-81; grants coord. Norwalk Community Coll., 1985—. Author articles for various publs. Chmn. Norwalk Dem. Town Com., 1976-78; state cen. committeewoman, 1978-90; mem. Dem. Town Com., 1974—; exec. com. Maritime Ctr. at Norwalk, 1984—; treas. Norwalk Nagarote Sister City Com., 1985—. Mem. Nat. Coun. for Resource Devel., Devel. Assn. So. Conn. Office: Norwalk Community Coll 188 Richards Ave Norwalk CT 06854-1655

GIBBS, JUNE NESBITT, state senator; b. Newton, Mass., June 13, 1922; d. Samuel Frederick and Lulu (Glazier) Nesbitt; m. Donald T. Gibbs, Dec. 8, 1945; 1 child, Elizabeth. BA in Math., Wellesley Coll., 1943; MA in Math., Boston U., 1947; postgrad., U. R.I., 1981-84. Mem. Republican Nat. Com. from, R.I., 1969-80; sec. Republican Nat. Com., 1977-80; mem. R.I. State Senate, 1985—; mem. def. adv. com. Women in Services, 1970-72, vice chmn., 1972. Mem. Middletown Town Council, 1974-80, 82-84, pres., 1978-80. Served to lt. (J.G.) USNR, 1943-46. Home: 163 Riverview Ave Newport RI 02840-5324 Office: RI State Senate State Capitol Providence RI 02903

GIBBS, MICHAEL ERROL, city planner; b. Port of Spain, Trinidad and Tobago, Aug. 31, 1941; came to U.S., 1967; s. Neville and Carmen Amy (Steele) G.; m. Lynette Maud Greaves, Dec. 5, 1965 (div. 1987); children: Susan, Karen, Carolyn, Richard, Jeanette; m. Gloria Margaret Mitchell, May 27, 1990. Diploma, Ea. Caribbean Agrl. Inst., Trinidad, 1963; BA, U. Wisc., Oshkosh, 1971; MA, Ohio U., 1973. Agrl. asst. Govt. of Trinidad and Tobago, Arima, 1960-67; transportation planner Mid-Ohio Regional Planning Coun., Columbus, 1974-78, Jacksonville (Fla.) Area Planning Bd., 1978-79; prin. city planner Dept. of Planning Balt. City, 1979—. Founder, dir. West Indian Assn. of Md., Balt., 1981-83; dir. Festival of the West Indies, Balt., 1982, Trinidad and Tobago Cultural Festivals, Balt., 1989-91. Recipient Pres.'s citation City Coun. of Balt., 1983, Mayor's Citation award for svc. to community City of Balt., 1990. Mem. Managerial Profl. Soc. Balt., Md. Internat. Ethnic Ctr. (co-founder, pres. 1990-91), Trinidad and Tobago Assn. (co-founder, pres. 1988-90), Caribbean Sunset Social and Cultural Assn. (pres. 1983-87, treas. 1987-92). Roman Catholic. Home: 1610 Burnwood Rd Baltimore MD 21239 Office: Trinidad & Tobago Assn 2857 Greenmount Ave Baltimore MD 21218

GIBBS, MICHAEL JOHN, economics educator; b. Washington, July 16, 1962; s. Robert John and Wilhelmina (Fluhr) G.; m. Joetta Forsyth, Apr. 23, 1988; 1 child, Geoffrey. BA in Econs., U. Chgo., 1984, MA in Econs., 1984, PhD in Econs., 1989; postgrad., Harvard Bus. Sch., 1989. Cons., economist Ibbotson Assocs., Chgo., 1984-89; prof. econs. and organizational behavior Sch. Bus. Harvard U., Boston, 1989—. Earhart Found. fellow, 1984-85, 85-86, Bradley Found. fellow, 1986-87, 87-88, U. Chgo. fellow, 1986-87. Mem. Am. Econs. Assn., Acad. Mgmt. Home: 159 Hancock St Cambridge MA 02139-1726 Office: Harvard U Sch Bus Soldiers Field Boston MA 02163

GIBBS, RAYMOND WELDON, surgeon; b. Boston, Aug. 1, 1920; s. Raymond T. and Elizabeth (Weldon) G.; m. Dorothy Dawson; children: Virginia, Raymond W., Janet. SB, Boston U., 1943; MD, N.Y. Med. Coll., 1951. Instr. surgery Yale Med. Sch., 1953-54; sr. clin. instr. surgery Tufts Med. Sch., 1960-70; instr. Harvard Med. Sch., 1961-89; surgeon Harvard U. Dept. Athletics, 1957-90; surgical cons. Boston, 1957—. Fellow ACS, Am. Coll. Sports Medicine, Am. Burn Asn., Boston Surgical Soc., Mass. Med. Soc. Home: 67 Vermont St West Roxbury MA 02132 Office: State House Physician State House Boston MA 02133

GIBBS, WILLIAM PAUL, college administrator, cross-cultural educator; b. Sidney, Mont., May 10, 1952; s. Clyde L. and Edith Florence (Boyd) G.; m. Laurie Lee Furrer, Dec. 20, 1975; children: David, Adam, Kristen. Student, U. of the Pacific, 1970-72; BSc in Theology, Bethany Bible Coll., Santa Cruz, Calif., 1974; MA in Linguistics, U. Tex., Arlington, 1977; postgrad., Long Beach (Calif.) State U., 1980. Field linguist Summer Inst. Linguistics, Mex. and Guatemala, 1973-79; furlough coord., dir. pers. Wycliffe Bible Translators, Huntington Beach, Calif., 1979-81; area coord. Wycliffe Bible Translators, Portland, Oreg., 1981-85, assoc. N.W. regional dir., 1987-89; N.W. regional dir. Zondervan Corp., Vancouver, Wash., 1985-87; dir. pub. rels. Geneva Coll., Beaver Falls, Pa., 1989-90, dir. specialized enrollment, 1990—; instr. Geneva Coll., Clark Coll., Christian Heritage Coll., others, 1980—; advt. cons. Reform Presbyn Theol. Sem., Pitts., 1990-91. Author: The Ministry of Friendship, 1988; editor: Lay Representative Manual, 1985; designer, developer The Warmth Workshop, 1985; contbr. articles to profl. jours. Mem. adult Christian edn. bd. Chippewa Evang. Free Ch., Beaver Falls, 1990—, Sunday sch. tchr., 1989—. Gov.'s scholar State of Calif., 1970. Mem. Nat. Assn. Christian Coll. Admissions Pers., Christian Higher Edn. Profls. in Internat. Edn., Pa. Assn. Secondary Sch. and Coll. Admissions Counsellors. Republican. Home: RR 1 Box 52 New Galilee PA 16141-9601 Office: Geneva Coll College Ave Beaver Falls PA 15010

GIBER, DAVID J., industrial psychologist; b. Flushing, N.Y., June 23, 1954; s. Irwin J. and Harriette Lois (Freedman) G.; m. Brigitte Link, Sept. 8, 1985; 1 child, Samuel Leon. BA in Psychology, Stanford U., 1976; PhD in Psychology, Duke U., 1980. Lic. psychologist, Mass. Sr. human resource specialist Keane, Inc., Boston, 1982-85; dir. employee involvement N.Y. Airlines, N.Y.C., 1985-86; sr. pers. assoc. Goldman Sachs & Co., N.Y.C., 1986-87; bus. devel. mgr. Digital Equipment Corp., Maynard, Mass., 1988—; cons. Boston U., 1988—, Krent/Paffett Assocs., Boston, 1989—. Contbr. articles to profl. jours. Vol. Cath. Big Bros., N.Y.C., 1987. Mem. Am. Psychol. Assn. Home: 80 Waverley St Waltham MA 02154-7058 Office: Digital Equipment Corp Westminster MA 01473

GIBLIN, THOMAS PATRICK, labor union administrator; b. East Orange, N.J., Jan. 15, 1947; s. John Joseph and Theresa Elizabeth (Moran) G.; m. Mary Katherine Hughes, June 20, 1970; children: Thomas P. Jr., Noreen M., Edward M., Patrick F., Anne T. BA, Seton Hall U., 1969. Pres. Internat. Union of Oper. Engrs. Local 68, West Caldwell, N.J., 1975—; freeholder Essex County, Newark, 1977-78, 82-89, surrogate, 1990—. Candidate from 25th legis. dist. N.J. Assembly, 1973; treas. Essex County Dem. Com., Newark, N.J., 1979-82; alt. del. Dem. Nat. Conv., San Francisco, 1984, Atlanta, 1988; commr. N.J. Real Estate Commn., Trenton, 1979-82; lay adv. bd. St. Vincent Acad., 1984—; chmn. bd. trustees St. Barnabas Burn Found., 1989—, United Way Essex, 1976-82, 89—; bd. dirs. Essex unit Assn. Retarded Citizens, 1986—; trustee North Jersey Blood Ctr., 1991—. Named Man of Yr. United Cerebral Palsy, 1980; recipient Cert. of Merit, U.S. Dept. of Labor, 1979, Community Svc. award Frontiers Internat., 1985, Humanitarian award, N.J. Blood Ctr., 1988. Mem. N.J. Ins. Underwriting Assn. (bd. dirs. 1982-90). Democratic. Roman Catholic. Home: 40 Montague Pl Montclair NJ 07042-2820 Office: County of Essex Surrogate's Ct Hall of Records Newark NJ 07102

GIBOFSKY, ALLAN, physician, lawyer; b. N.Y.C., Sept. 7, 1949; s. Louis and Sally (Levy) G.; m. Karen Beth Sussman, June 5, 1982; children: Lewis Marshall, Esther Rachel, Laura Aimee. BS, Bklyn. Coll., 1969; MD, Cornell U., 1973; JD, Fordham U., 1985. Bar: N.Y. 1986, N.J. 1986, D.C. 1987; diplomate Am. Bd. Internal Medicine, Am. Bd. Legal Medicine; bd. cert. rheumatology 1980, legal med., 1987. Intern N.Y. Hosp., N.Y.C., 1973-74; resident in internal medicine N.Y. Hosp., 1974-77, fellow, 1977-79; asst. prof. medicine Cornell U. Med. Coll., N.Y.C., 1979-85; assoc. prof. medicine Cornell U. Med. Coll., 1985—, asst. prof. pub. health, 1985-90; assoc. prof. pub. health, 1990—; adj. assoc. prof. law Fordham Univ., N.Y.C., 1986—; v.p. med. and sci. affairs N.Y. Arthritis Found., 1984—, pres., 1989—; bd. govs. N.Y. Arthritis Found., Am. Bd. Legal Medicine, 1990—. Editor: Manual of Orthopedics and Rheumatology, 1981; contbr. articles to med. sci. and legal jours. Arthritis Found. rsch. grantee, 1975—; NIH rsch. grantee, 1977-82. Fellow ACP, Am. Coll. Legal Medicine (bd. govs. 1989—, treas. 1991—), Am. Coll. Rheumatology, N.Y. Acad. Medicine; mem. Nat. Health Lawyers Assn., N.Y. Rheumatism Assn (sec.-treas. 1985—), Soc. Salk Scholars CUNY (v.p. 1986—). Home: 425 E 79th St New York NY 10021-1037 Office: Hosp for Spl Surgery 535 E 70th St New York NY 10021-4872

GIBS, GABRIEL JOSEPH, investment company executive; b. Budapest, Hungary, Aug. 29, 1936; s. Laszlo and Ilona (Nadler) G.; m. Agnes Susan Hussar, Mar. 15, 1963; children: Jeffrey, Jodi. BS in Chemistry, CCNY, 1963; MBA in Fin., Pace U., Pleasantville, N.Y., 1974. Organic chemist Lederle Labs., Pearl River, N.Y., 1963-68; rsch. chemist St. Regis Paper Co., Lonza Inc., N.Y., 1968-75; mkt. devel. mgr. Lonza, Inc., Fair Lawn, N.J., 1975-86; pres. Volumetric Advisers, Pearl River, 1983—; chmn. bd. dirs. Volumetric Fund, Inc., 1978—. Patentee in field. Mem. Lions. Office: Volumetric Advisers 87 Violet Dr Pearl River NY 10965-1212

GIBSON, DAVID F., architect; b. Pine Bluff, Ark., July 28, 1944; s. Charlie W. Gibson and Margaret E. Frain. BS, U. Ark., 1970, BArch, 1971; MArch in Historical Preservation, Columbia U., 1975. Prin., founder David Gibson Assocs., N.Y., 1975-88; ptnr. Ryan Gibson Bauer Kornblath, P.A., N.Y.C. and Middletown, N.J., 1984-91; prin. Ehrenkrantz & Eckstut, Architects, N.Y.C., 1992—; resident architect Snug Harbor Cultural Ctr., S.I., 1979-84; asst. prof. Architecture N.J. Inst. Tech., 1976-80. Prin. works include restoration Rufus King Manor, Jamaica, N.Y., Snug Harbor Restoration, S.I., campus N.J. Inst. Tech., Microelectronics Ctr., Info. Tech. Ctr. Recipient Cert. of merit Mcpl. Arts Soc., 1979, Design award N.J. Soc. Architects, 1990; grantee Nat. Endowment Arts, 1979, N.Y. State Coun. on Arts, 1980. Mem. Art Deco Soc. N.Y. (pres. 1986-92). Office: Ehrenkrantz & Echstut 23 E 4th St New York NY 10003

GIBSON, DONALD BERNARD, literature educator; b. Kansas City, Mo., July 2, 1933; s. Oscar J. and Florine C. (Myers) G.; m. JoAnne Ivory, Dec. 14, 1963; children: David, Douglas. BA, U. Mo., Kansas City, 1955, MA, 1957; PhD, Brown U., 1962. Instr. Brown U., Providence, 1961-62; asst. prof. Wayne State U., Detroit, 1962-67; assoc. prof., then prof. U. Conn., Storrs, 1967-74; prof. lit. Rutgers U., New Brunswick, N.J., 1974—; cons. Ednl. Testing Svc., Princeton, N.J., 1980—. Author, editor 7 books lit. criticism; author: The Politics of Literary Expression, 1981, The Red Badge of Courage: Redefining the Hero, 1989. Recipient Fulbright award, 1962-64; grantee NEH, 1970-71, 92-93. Office: Rutgers U PO Box 5054 New Brunswick NJ 08903-5054

GIBSON, EDGAR THOMAS, surgeon, educator; b. Phila., Mar. 23, 1915; s. Albert and Mabel (Cave) G.; m. Helen Thombenson, Oct. 7, 1943; children: Ann, Barbara, Jeanne Rollins, Helen Tucker. BS, Villanova U., 1938; MD, Jefferson Med. Coll., 1942; postgrad., U. Pa., 1947-48. Resident surgery Cleve. Clinic, 1943-44, West Jersey Hosp., Camden, N.J., 1948-50; resident thoracic surgery Phila. Gen. Hosp., 1952-54; pres. staff Camden County Chest Hosp.; chmn. dept. surgery West Jersey Hosp. Group, 1975-78; staff mem. Our Lady of Lourdes Hosp., Camden, N.J.; instr. surgery Jefferson U., Phila. Pres. Camden County Heart Soc., 1960. Capt. U.S. Army, 1944-46, ETO. Fellow AMA, ACS, Am. Bd. Surgery, N.J. Soc. Surgeons; mem. Camden County Med. Soc. (pres.). Republican. Home: Box 36 Newage ME 04552

GIBSON, ERNEST WILLARD, III, state supreme court justice; b. Brattleboro, Vt., Sept. 23, 1927; s. Ernest William and Dorothy Pearl (Switzer) G.; m. Charlotte Elaine Hungerford, Sept. 10, 1960; children: Margaret, Mary, John. BA, Yale U., 1951; LLB, Harvard U., 1956. Bar: Vt. State's atty. Windham County, Vt., 1957-61; mem. Vt. Ho. of Reps., 1961-63, chmn. judiciary com., 1963; chmn. Vt. Pub. Svc. Bd., 1963-72; judge Vt. Superior Ct., 1972-83; justice Vt. Supreme Ct., 1983—. Chancellor Episcopal Diocese Vt., 1977—, trustee, 1973—, pres. bd. trustees, 1991—, dep. to gen. conv., 1976—. 1st lt., arty. U.S. Army, 1945-46, 51-53, Korea. Mem. Vt. Bar Assn. Home: 11 Baldwin St Montpelier VT 05602-2110 Office: Supreme Ct 111 State St Montpelier VT 05602-2700

GIBSON, JOSEPH WHITTON, JR., chemical company executive; b. Norristown, Pa., Feb. 24, 1922; s. Joseph Whitton and Nellie (Dear) G.; m. Norma Jean Stewart, Sept. 21, 1946; children: Joseph Whitton, Winn S. Gobeil, Philip B. BS, Worcester Poly. Inst., 1944; postgrad. in Electronics, Princeton U., 1944, M.I.T., 1945. With E. I. duPont de Nemours & Co., Wilmington, Del., 1946—; sr. research engr. E. I. duPont de Nemours & Co., 1961-79, sr. tech. specialist printing systems, imaging systems, 1979—. Contbr. articles to profl. jours. Treas. Mayfield Civic Assn.; v.p. Brandywine Babe Ruth; treas. Shellcrest Swim Club. Served to lt. USNR, 1944-46. Mem. Am. Assn. Textile Chemists and Colorists (Olney medal 1979), Am. Chem. Soc., Fiber Soc. (hon.), Internat. Platform Assn., Sigma Xi, Tau Beta Pi. Republican. Episcopalian. Home: 1215 Hillside Blvd Wilmington DE 19803-4211 Office: Photo Systems Lab 708 Chestnut Run Wilmington DE 19880

GIBSON, LAURINE CATALANO, counseling agency executive; b. Balt., Oct. 1, 1935; d. Vincent S. and Joanna F. (Jordanowski) Catalano; m. Robert E. Gibson, Aug. 26, 1961 (dec. 1988); children: Robert, Anita, Stephen. BS, Towson State U., 1958. Cert. consumer credit counselor; cert. fin. counseling exec. Tchr. Balt. County, 1958-59, Balt. City, 1959-61; pres. Consumer Credit Counseling Svcs. of S.E. Md., Inc., Bowie, 1980—. Author, producer (audio and video tape) Consumer Edn. for High Sch. Students, 1991. Mem. Internat. Credit Assn. of Greater Washington (bd. dirs. 1991—), Credit Profls. Internat. of the Nation's Capital (Credit Profl. of Yr. 1991). Office: Consumer Credit Counseling Svc SE Md Inc Ste 209 6911 Laurel Bowie Rd Bowie MD 20715

GIBSON, REGINALD WALKER, federal judge; b. Lynchburg, Va., July 31, 1927; s. McCoy and Julia Ann (Butler) G.; 1 child, Reginald S. B.S., Va. Union U., 1952; postgrad., Wharton Grad. Sch. Bus. Administrn., U. Pa., 1952-53; LL.B., Howard U., 1956. Bar: D.C. 1957, Ill. 1972. Agt. IRS, Washington, 1957-61; trial atty. tax div. U.S. Dept. Justice, Washington, 1961-71; sr. tax atty. Internat. Harvester Co., Chgo., 1971-76, gen. tax atty., 1976-82; judge U.S. Claims Ct., Washington, 1982—. Mem. bus. adbv. council Chgo. Urban League, 1974-82. Served with AUS, 1946-47. Recipient cert. award U.S. Dept. Justice Atty. Gen., 1969, recipient spl. commendation U.S. Dept. Justice Atty. Gen., 1970, Wall St. Jour. award, 1952, Am. Jurisprudence award, 1956; named Alumni of Yr. Howard U. Sch. Law, 1984. Mem. ABA, D.C. Bar Assn., Chgo. Bar Assn., Fed. Bar Assn., Nat. Bar Assn., Claims Ct. Bar Assn., J. Edgar Murdock Am. Inn of Ct. (taxation com.). Republican. Baptist. Club: Nat. Lawyers (Washington). Home: 6305 Chaucer Ln Alexandria VA 22304-3537 Office: US Claims Ct 717 Madison Pl NW Washington DC 20005-1011

GIBSON, SAM THOMPSON, internist, educator; b. Covington, Ga., Jan. 1, 1916; s. Count Dillon and Julia (Thompson) G.; m. Alice Chase, Oct. 31, 1942 (dec. Jan. 1971); children: Lena S., Stephen C., Judith Gibson Hammer, Lucy F.; m. Madge L. Crouch, Sept. 20, 1986. B.S. in Chemistry, Ga. Inst. Tech., 1936; M.D., Emory U., 1940. Diplomate: Am. Bd. Internal Medicine. Med. house officer Peter Bent Brigham Hosp., Boston, 1940-41, asst. resident medicine, 1946-47, asst. medicine, 1947-49; rsch. fellow medicine Harvard Med. Sch., 1941-42, spl. rsch. assoc., 1943, Milton fellow medicine, 1947-49; assoc. medicine George Washington U. Med. Sch., also George Washington U. Hosp., 1949-63, asst. clin. prof. medicine, 1963—, clin. asst. prof. medicine, Uniformed Svcs., Univ. Health Scis., 1980—; asst. med. dir. ARC Blood Program, 1949-51, assoc. med. dir., 1951-53, assoc. dir., 1953-56, dir., 1956-66; sr. med. officer ARC, 1957-67; asst. dir. div. biologics standards NIH, 1967-72; asst. dir. Bur. of Biologics, FDA, Bethesda, Md., 1972-74; asst. to dir. Bur. Biologics, FDA, Bethesda, Md., 1974-77, dir. div. biologics evaluation, 1977-83; dir. div. biol. product compliance Ctr. for Drugs and Biologics, 1983-85; assoc. dir. sci. and tech. Office of Compliance, Ctr. Drugs and Biologics, FDA, 1985-88; dir. sci. and tech. Office of Health Affairs FDA, Rockville, Md., 1988-89; cons. blood Naval Med. Sch., Nat. Naval Med. Center, Bethesda, 1950-63; mem. med. adv. bd. CARE-Medico, 1962-70, cons., 1970-89; chmn. U.S. com. for tranfusion equipment for med. use Am. Standards Assn., 1954-66, tech. adv. group transfusion equipment for med. use Nat. Commn. Clin. Lab. Standards/Am. Nat. Standards Inst., 1975-89; adviser orgn. blood transfusion services League Red Cross Socs., 1955-66. Contbg. editor: Vox Sanguinis Jour. Blood Transfusion, 1956-65; mem. adv. bd., 1965-76. Served from lt. (j.g.) to comdr., M.C. USNR, 1941-46; capt. Res. ret. Mem. AMA, AAAS, Internat., Am. socs. hematology, Nat. Health Coun. (dir. 1957-60, 61-64), Internat. Soc. Blood Transfusion (regional counselor 1962-66), Am. Fedn. Clin. Rsch., N.Y. Acad. Scis., Delta Tau Delta, Alpha Kappa Kappa, Alpha Chi Sigma, Tau Beta Pi, Phi Kappa Phi, Omicron Delta Kappa, Alpha Omega Alpha. Home: 5801 Rossmore Dr Bethesda MD 20814-2229

GIBSON, SCOTT CARTER, management company executive; b. Washington, Jan. 10, 1959; s. Paul Raymond and Janice Elizabeth (Carter) G. BS in Econs., U. Pa., 1980. Assoc. airline planning Pan Am. World Airways, N.Y.C., 1979-80, mgr. internat. schedules, 1980-81; dir. schedule planning N.Y. Air, N.Y.C., 1981-83, dir. planning, scheduling and systems, 1983-84; dir. airline planning Tex. Air Corp., Houston, 1984-86; dir. airline planning Continental Airlines, Houston, 1985-87, sr. dir. internat. mktg. and planning, 1987-88; staff mem. Dukakis for Pres., 1988; v.p., mng. dir. Interact-The Manchester Group, Washington, 1988-91; sr. v.p. Pacific Micronesia Corp., San Francisco, 1991—. Mem. Internat. Club, Wings Club. Democrat. Home: 1077 30th St NW Washington DC 20007-3829

GIBSON, STEPHEN LOWELL, investment executive; b. Salida, Colo., Nov. 12, 1963; s. C. P. and Carol A. (Mooney) G. AB, Princeton (N.J.) U., 1986. Rsch. asst. Bear, Stearns & Co., N.Y.C., 1986-87, assoc. economist, 1987-90; asst. v.p. Seligman Valuations, N.Y.C., 1990—. Nat. Merit schlar, 1982. Mem. Nat. Assn. Bus. Economists, Assn. for Investment Mgmt. & Rsch., N.Y. Soc. Security Analysts. Office: Seligman Valuations 130 Liberty St New York NY 10006-1198

GIDDINGS, CLIFFORD FREDERICK, corporate executive; b. East Dorset, Vt., May 28, 1936; s. Frederick Daniel and Natalie (Abbott) G. BA, U. Vt., 1958; MA, U. Wis., 1961; postgrad., Sorbonne U., Paris, 1958, U. Chgo., 1963-65. French master Lake Forest (Ill.) Acad., 1961-63; asst. head reference dept. The Newberry Library, Chgo., 1964-68, assoc. head reference dept., 1972-74; dir. library services Scott, Foresman and Co., Glenview, Ill., 1968-71; asst. mgr. Albert E. Barrett, Inc., Trenton, N.J., 1975-80, exec. v.p., 1980—. Fulbright scholar U.S. Dept. State, Grenoble, France, 1958-59. Mem. Associated Gen. Contractors of N.J., N.J. Asphalt Pavement Assn., Nat. Asphalt Pavement Assn., Utility and Transp. Contractors Assn. N.J. Episcopalian. Home: 66 Line Rd Trenton NJ 08690-1131 Office: Albert E Barrett Inc 2485 E State Street Ext Trenton NJ 08619-3389

GIDDINGS, WOOSTER PHILIP, surgeon, retired; b. Boston, Jan. 27, 1913; s. Harold Girard and Mildred Day (Potter) G.; m. Elizabeth Fisk, May 24, 1941; children: Robert F., Deborah, David G., James P. AB, Amherst Coll., 1934; MD, Harvard Coll., 1938. Diplomate Am. Bd. Surgery. Intern, asst. resident Mass. Gen. Hosp., Boston, 1938-42; resident, 1946; asst. in surgery %, Boston, 1947-50, Harvard Med. Sch., Boston, 1947-50; asst. prof. surgery Albany (N.Y.) Med. Coll., 1950-54; surgeon Putnam Meml. Hosp., Bennington, Vt., 1950-75; bd. dirs. emeritus First Vt. Bank, Brattleboro, Vt.; trustee Bennington Mus., 1960-88, trustee emeritus, 1988—. Assoc. editor: Surgery in World War II, 1955. Maj. M.C. AUS, 1942-46. Decorated Purple Heart, Bronze Star. Fellow Am. Coll. Surgeons; mem. New Eng. Surg. Soc., Excelsior Surg. Soc., Vt. State Med. Soc., Mass. Med. Soc. Home: RD 1 Pippin Knoll Bennington VT 05201

GIDLEY, THOMAS DUNNE, lawyer; b. Orange, N.J., Mar. 13, 1934; s. Edwin Louis and Dorothy Alice (Dunne) G.; m. Margaret Ann Devoe, Mar. 17, 1962 (div. Feb. 1988); children: Thomas Edwin, David Waterman; m. Betty Rohloff, Oct. 8, 1988. BA, Dartmouth Coll., 1956; LLB, Yale U., 1959. Bar: R.I. 1959, U.S. Dist. Ct. R.I. 1962, U.S. Supreme Ct. 1964, U.S. Ct. Appeals (1st cir.) 1968, Mass. 1985, U.S. Dist. Ct. Mass. 1985. Assoc. Hinckley, Allen, Tobin & Silverstein (predecessor firms Hinckley, Allen, Salisbury & Parsons and Hinckley & Allen), Providence, 1960-66, ptnr., 1966-85; ptnr. Gidley, Lovegreen & Sarli, Providence, 1985—. Contbr. articles to profl. jours. Mem. Bd. Fed. Examiners U.S. Dist. Ct., Providence, 1984—, legisl. study commn. med. malpractice Sate of R.I., Providence, 1985-86. Served to capt. R.I. N.G., 1959-70. Recipient Order of Commendation R.I. Supreme Ct., 1981. Fellow Am. Coll. Trial Lawyers; mem. ABA, R.I. Bar Assn., Nat. Health Lawyers' Assn., Am. Acad. Hosp. Attys., Internat. Assn. Def. Counsel, Hope Club, Barrington Yacht Club. Home: 4 White Birch Ln Barrington RI 02806-4932 Office: Gidley Lovegreen & Sarli 170 Westminster St Providence RI 02903-2101

GIEGERICH, PAUL RAYMOND, podiatrist; b. Queens, N.Y., Dec. 31, 1953; s. Edmund William and Mary J. (Cicione) G.; m. Nancy Jeanne Cooper, Aug. 20, 1977. BS in Biology, SUNY, Geneseo, 1976; D of Podiatric Medicine, Ill. Coll. Podiatric Medicine, 1980. Diplomate Am. Bd. Podiatric Surgery. Resident podiatric surgery Md. Podiatric Residency Program, Balt., 1980-82; podiatric physician self-employed Washington, 1982—; sec., treas. Parkwood Podiatric Residency Program, Clinton, Md., 1984-88; teaching staff Capitol Hill Hosp. Podiatric Residency Program, Washington, 1989—. Podiatric physician Dept. Health & Mental Hygiene, Md., D.C., 1980—, med. lectr., 1980—. Recipient Dedicated Svc. award Kappa Tau Epsilon, 1980. Fellow Am. Coll. Foot Surgeons; mem. Durlacher Nat. Podiatric Honor Soc., Am. Podiatric Med. Assn., D.C. Podiatric Med. Assn., Am. Coll. Foot Surgeons, Am. Diabetes Assn. Roman Catholic. Office: 3230 Pennsylvania Ave SE Washington DC 20020-3722

GIELEN, UWE PETER, psychology educator; b. Berlin, Aug. 15, 1940; s. Alfred and Ursula (Hackemesser) G. MA in Psychology, Wake Forest U., 1968; PhD in Social Psychology, Harvard U., 1976. Asst. prof. psychology York Coll./CUNY, N.Y.C., 1977-80; assoc. prof. psychology St. Francis Coll., Bklyn., 1980-87, chmn., dept. psychology, 1980-90, prof. psychology, 1987—; bd. dirs. Internat. Coun. Psychologists, Madison, Wis.; exec. bd. Soc. Cross-cultural Rsch. Co-author: The Kohlberg Legacy for the Helping Professions, 1991; sr. editor: Psychology in International Perspective, 1992; editorial bd. Moral Edn. Forum, 1988—; contbr. articles to profl. jours. Del. to UN Internat. Coun. Psychologists, N.Y., 1985—. Recipient rsch. grants H.F. Guggenheim Found., N.Y., 1986-88, Pacific Cultural Found., Taipei, Taiwan, 1986-87, Faculty Recognition award St. Francis Coll., Bklyn., 1984, 87. Mem. Bklyn. Psychol. Assn., Internat. Assn. Cross-cultural Psychology. Home: 472 Sackett St Brooklyn NY 11231-5019 Office: St Francis Coll 180 Remsen St Brooklyn NY 11201-4398

GIERER, VINCENT A., JR., tobacco and wine holding company executive; b. N.Y.C., Oct. 21, 1947; s. Vincent A. Sr. and Isabel (McEwen) G.; m. Josephine Lindenmayer; children: Gregory, Vincent, Beth. BBA, Iona Coll., 1969. CPA, N.Y. Audit supr. Ernst & Whinney, White Plains, N.Y., 1971-77; dir. fin. reporting U.S. Tobacco Inc., Greenwich, Conn., 1978-83, controller, 1983-86, sr. v.p., chief fin. officer, 1986-88, exec. v.p., chief fin. officer, 1988-90, pres., chief operating officer, 1990—, also bd. dirs.; pres., UST Inc. Mem. Wilton (Conn.) Newcomers; mgr. Little League, Wilton. Served with U.S. Army, 1969-71, Vietnam. Mem. Am. Inst. CPA's, Am. Mgmt. Assn., Fin. Execs. Inst. Roman Catholic. Office: UST Inc 100 W Putnam Ave Greenwich CT 06830-5342

GIESE, THEODORE LYNN, professional society administrator; b. Joplin, Mo., Feb. 11, 1945; s. Albert H. and Margaret E. (Key) G.; m. Patsy Ann Johnson, Aug. 11, 1968; children: Matthias John, Lydia Kay. BS in Physics, Mont. State U., 1968; MLS, U. Wis., Milw., 1972. Mfg. engr. Gen. Electric Med. Systems Vacuum Tube Ops., Milw., 1968-71; ref. libr. Minot (N.D.) State U., 1972-83; pub. info. specialist II Energy Rsch. Ctr., Grand Forks, N.D., 1983-85; bus. mgr. Abrasive Engring. Soc., Butler, Pa., 1989—; freelance photographer and writer Butler, Pa., 1985—; owner Meadowlark Tech. Svcs., Butler, Pa., 1988—. Viola player community/univ. orchs., Minot, S.D., Slippery Rock, Pa.; vocalist ch. choirs and community choral groups. Mem. Am. Soc. Assn. Execs. Lutheran. Home and Office: 108 Elliott Dr Butler PA 16001-1118

GIESE, WILLIAM HERBERT, tax accountant; b. Boston, Jan. 19, 1944; s. Robert Ewald and Harriet (Blaney) G.; m. Elaine Rabe, May 26, 1973; children: Amy Theiss, Katherine Clark, Lauren Stearns. BA, Amherst Coll., 1966; MBA, U. Pa., 1968. CPA. Staff acct. Price Waterhouse, Phila., 1968-70, sr. acct., 1970-73, mgr., 1973-79, ptnr., 1979—; speaker Wharton Tax Conf. Phila., 1988. Bd. dirs., fin. chmn. Dunwoody Home and Village, Newtown Square, Pa., 1990—; trustee Lankenau Hosp., Phila., 1990—; bd. dirs., past pres. North Ardmore Civic Assn.; past pres. Phila. Squash Racquets Assn., Bala Cynwyd; fin. chmn. 1989 U.S. Amateur Golf Tournament; treas. U.S. Squash Racquets Assn., Balt Cynywd, 1986-92. Mem. AICPA,

Pa. Inst. CPA's, Merion Golf Club (Ardmore, Pa.), Merion Cricket Club (Haverford, Pa.). Republican. Presbyterian. Home: 133 Edgewood Rd Ardmore PA 19003-2507 Office: Price Waterhouse 30 S 17th St Philadelphia PA 19103-4118

GIFFEL, TERRY CLYDE, media communications and technology educator; b. Terre Haute, Ind., Sept. 4, 1945; s. Harold H. and Ruth (Barnes) G.; m. Shari J. Austermiller, June 10, 1967; children: Barrett, Zachary. BS, Ind. State U., 1967, MS, 1970; PhD, U. Wis., 1976. Tchr. Brown County Pub. Schs., Nashville, 1967-68; asst. supr., audio-visual ctr. Ind. State U., Terre Haute, 1968-70; media specialist audio-visual svc. Miami U., Oxford, Ohio, 1970-74; specialist Bur. Audio-Visual Instrn. U. Wis. Extension, Madison, 1974-76; prof. media communication and tech. East Stroudsburg (Pa.) U., 1976—; coord. Inst. Communication Studies, East Stroudsburg, 1978-79; dir. Computers in Edn. Workshops, East Stroudsburg, 1981-86; cons. various sch. dists. and colls. scriptwriter slide set instructional Forces Creating the Kettle Moraine, 1975; contbr. articles and photographs to profl. jours. Mem. Pa. Assn. Ednl. Communications and Tech., Pocono Area Educators' Tech. Forum (co-founder), Alpha Phi Omega (hon.). Presbyterian. Office: East Stroudsburg U Dept Media Communication Tech East Stroudsburg PA 18301

GIFFEN, ROBERT HENRY, chemical engineer; b. Pottsville, Pa., Feb. 10, 1922; s. Florin McKee and Helen Marilla (Daggett) G.; m. Coral Bernice Hunter, Aug. 28, 1949; children: Susan Joan, Robert Henry Jr., Diana Maureen. BS, Newark Coll. Engring., 1943; MS, Iowa State U., 1947, PhD, 1951. Control chemist Gen. Chem. Co., Edgewater, N.J., 1943-44; chem. engr. U. Calif., Los Alamos, N.Mex., 1944-46; rsch. engr. Iowa State U., Ames, 1947-51; sr. engr. Westinghouse Electric, West Mifflin, Pa., 1951-57, supervising engr., 1957-69, mng. engr., 1969-72, adv. engr., 1972—. Sgt. U.S. Army, 1944-46. Mem. Am. Inst. Chem. Engrs. Home: 5188 Priscilla Dr Bethel Park PA 15102-2708 Office: Westinghouse Electric Corp PO Box 79 West Mifflin PA 15122-0079

GIGANTE, DINO VINCENT, small business owner; b. Boston, Apr. 17, 1934; s. Gabriel and Rita (D'Angelosante) G.; m. Doris I. Cosgrove, Feb. 24, 1957; children: Donna, Diane. BS in Pub. Mgmt., U. Mass., 1982; MBA, Anna Maria Coll., 1986. Cert. Safety Profl. Electronic technician Honeywell Corp., Brighton, Mass., 1957-58; marine electrician Bethlehem Steel Shipbuilding, Quincy, Mass., 1958-60, USN-Boston Naval Yard, 1960-66; elec. insp. supr. shipbldg. Quincy USN, 1966-72; compliance officer U.S. Dept. of Labor/OHSA, Boston, 1972-78, safety supr., 1978-84; area dir. U.S. Dept. Labor/OSHA, 1984-87, asst. regional adminstr., 1987-89; safety cons. Dino V. Gigante, Hingham, 1989—. Staff sgt. USAF, 1952-56, Korea. Mem. Am. Soc. Safety Engrs., Mass. Safety Coun., Soc. Fire Prevention Engrs. Home and Office: 45 Wanders Dr Hingham MA 02043-3456

GIGLIO, MARY ANN, executive secretary; b. Rochester, N.Y., Dec. 28, 1946; d. Samuel Paul and Ann Frances (Bianchi) G. NYS regents, Nazareth, Rochester, N.Y., 1960-64. Sec. Eastman Kodak Co., Rochester, N.Y., 1964-81, exec. sec. internat. div., 1981-83, exec. sec. photographic divsn., sr. exec. sec. to pres., 1983-90, sr. exec. sec. to chmn., pres. and chief exec. officer, 1990—. Docent Internat. Mus. Photography at George Eastman House. Roman Catholic. Office: Eastman Kodak Co 343 State St Rochester NY 14650-0229

GIGLIOTTI, JOANNE MARIE, arts administrator; b. Pitts., June 12, 1945; d. Joseph Francis and Anna Maria (Costantini) G.; children: Jennifer Lou Valli, Robert Joseph Valli. BFA, Carnegie-Mellon U., 1967; MEd, Pa. State U., 1978. Artist Philipsburg, Pa., 1967-78; dir. Hub Arts and Craft Centre, Pa. State U., 1978-80; art, framing cons. Eli's Art Gallery, State College, Pa., 1981-82; traveling exhbn. coord. Pa. Coun. on the Arts, 1981; founder, dir. The Fine Arts Connection, Inc., State College, Pa., 1980-82; founder, pres. The Fine Arts Connection, Inc., Washington, 1983-87; mgr. studio arts dept., resident assoc. program Smithsonian Instn., Washington, 1987—; lectr. Yale U., New Haven, 1990, Assn. of Coll. Unions Internat., 1967-78; tchr., instr. resident assoc. program Smithsonian Inst., 1984-87, Am. U., Washington, 1984-86; coord. Elizibehan Ednl. Festival, 1978; originator computer graphics symposium Infinite Illusions, 1990. Author: (with others) The Business of Art, 1989. Exec. sec. Smithsonian Inst. Womens Coun., 1990—, mem. Latino working com. 1991—; liason Women in Mus. Network, Am. Hist. Mus., 1990. Mem. Nat. Computer Graphics Assn., Am. Assn. of Mus., Phi Kappa Phi. Office: Smithsonian Instn Resident Assoc Program S Dillon Ripley Ctr 1100 Jefferson Dr SW Washington DC 20560

GIGLIOTTI, PETER MICHAEL, academic administrator, public information specialist; b. Bradford, Pa., Sept. 3, 1952; s. Francis Ralph Gigliotti and Alice Margaret (Bean) Plano; m. Ellen Jill Watson, Nov. 11, 1978; children: Nicholas Peter, Michael Richard. BA, St. Bonaventure U., 1974. Reporter, photographer, editor Pub. Opinion newspaper, Chambersburg, Pa., 1974-78, city editor, 1985-87, editor graphics/bus., 1987-88; dir. pub. infor. Pa. Dept. Community Affairs, Harrisburg, 1978-79; reporter Valley News-Dispatch, Tarentum, Pa., 1979; mng. editor Butler County News, Zelienople, Pa., 1979-81; asst. regional editor Herald Dispatch, Huntington, W.Va., 1981-85; W.Va. corr. USA Today, Huntington, 1982-85; dir. news svcs./advt. Shippensburg (Pa.) U., 1988—; mem. pres. cabinet Shippensburg U., 1988—, univ. community adv. coun., 1988—, black heritage com., 1988—, parents adv. bd., 1988—. Newsletter advisor Easter Seals of Franklin and Adams Counties Inc., 1989—; contbr. articles to mags. and newspapers. Founding advisor Operation Shipshape, Shippensburg, 1989; mem. pub. affairs com. Easter Seals of Franklin and Adams Counties Inc., Chambersburg, 1989, mem. crisis mgmt. com., 1990. Mem. Coll. and Univ. Pub. Rels. Assn. Pa., Coun. for the Advancement and Support of Edn. Office: Shippensburg U N Prince St Shippensburg PA 17257-1316

GIGLIOTTI, RICHARD JOSEPH, nuclear security executive; b. North Adams, Mass., June 15, 1945; s. Victor and Ida (Antenucci) G.; children: Gina Bianca, Victoria Marie, Richard Joseph Jr. BA, Norwich U., 1968; postgrad., Mass. State Coll., 1968-70. Police officer North Adams Police Dept., 1966-70, Wethersfield (Conn.) Police Dept., 1973-77; security supr. UNC Naval Products, Montville, Conn., 1977-78, corp. security dir., 1984—; mgr. security UNC Recovery Systems, Charlestown, R.I., 1978-80; dir. loss prevention Colt Firearms, Hartford, Conn., 1980-84; adj. faculty Ea. Conn. State U., Willimantic, 1989—, Mohegan Community Coll., Norwich, 1984—; guest lectr. various colls., univs., and corps., 1978—. Author: Security Design for Maximum Protection, 1984, Emergency Planning for Maximum Protection, 1991; contbr. articles to profl. jours. Active Gov.'s and Gen. Assembly's Task Force on Pvt. Security in Conn., 1983. 1st lt. U.S. Army, 1970-73. Recipient Chief Samuel Luciano award Mcpl. Police Tng. Coun., 1974. Mem. Internat. Assn. Chiefs Police, Am Soc. for Indsl. Security, Conn. Police Chiefs Assn., Hundred Club Conn. Roman Catholic. Office: PO Box 218 East Lyme CT 06333

GIL, JOAN, pathologist; b. Barcelona, Catalonia, Spain, June 26, 1940; came to U.S., 1976; s. Antonio and Petra (Camino) G.; m. Brigitte Sollereder, Aug. 12, 1970; children: Daniel J., Isadora B. Degree in medicine, U. Barcelona, 1964, D in Medicine, 1968; Habilitation in Anatomy, U. Berne, Switzerland, 1974. Mem. faculty dept. anatomy U. Berne, Switzerland, 1966-76; assoc. prof. dept. medicine and pathology U. Miami, Fla., 1976-77; assoc. prof. dept. medicine U. Pa., Phila., 1977-84; prof. dept. pathology Mt. Sinai Med. Sch., N.Y.C., 1984—; ad hoc cons. Health Effect Ins., NIH. Editor: Models of Lung Disease, 1990; mem. editorial bd. Exptl. Lung Rsch., 1979-88, Jour. Applied Physiology, 1983-89, Human Pathology, 1988—, Am. Jour. Physiology, Lung, Cell and Molecular Physiology, 1992—; also over 100 articles. Swiss Sci. Found. fellow, 1971-73; recipient Rsch. Career Devel. award Nat. Heart, Lung and Blood Inst., 1977-82. Mem. Am. Physiol. Soc., Am. Thoracic Soc., Internat. Stereology Soc., So. Soc. for Clin. Investigation. Roman Catholic. Office: Mt Sinai Med Ctr One Gustave L Levy Pl New York NY 10029-6504

GIL, REGINA KELLER, artist; b. Frankfurt, Fed. Republic of Germany, Dec. 17, 1948; came to U.S., 1950; d. Israel and Susan (Weisman) Keller; m. Joseph Gil, Dec. 26, 1970; children: Gideon Moses, Danielle Simone, Alexandra Caren. BA, CCNY, 1969; MA, Adelphi U., 1982. Staff artist Am. Inst. of Physics, N.Y.C., 1969; artist Murakami-Wolf Prodns., L.A., 1969-71; freelance illustrator, art dir. Y&R, D.D.B. & O., others, N.Y.C. and L.I., 1965—; instr. North Shore Community Arts Ctr., Great Neck, N.Y., 1981-84, North Shore YM-YWHA, Roslyn, N.Y., 1983-86, Great Neck Adult Edn., 1985—; pres./founder Artists Network of Great Neck, 1986-90; cons. Bd. of Coop. Ednl. Svcs.; invited speaker Holocaust Meml. Day, 1987, 91. Producer: (video programs) The Meat and Potatoes of Art, 1989, Vol. II, 1990; one-person show at Holocaust Mus., N.Y.; exhibited in group shows in N.Y.C., Parsons Sch. Design, CCNY, Soho Ctr., D & D Bldg., L.I. Adelphi U., Great Neck Libr., C.W. Post. U. Schwartz Gallery, North Shore Y, Bank of Great Neck, Guild Hall, Easthampton, others. Pres. PTA, Great Neck, 1978-84; trustee The Rehab. Inst., Mineola, N.Y., 1988-89; chmn. The Sr. Event, Great Neck, 1989; col. Childrens Living After-Sch. Prog., Great Neck, 1982-83. Grantee Office of Cultural Devel., 1989, 90, N.Y. State Coun. of the Arts, 1989; recipient Legis. Citation for Promotion of Arts, N.Y. State Assembly, 1990. Mem. Manhasset Artists Assn., Artists Network of Great Neck (bd. dirs.), Allied Artists of Am., Womanspace, Adelphi Art and Art History Assn., CCNY Art Alumni Assn. Jewish. Home and Office: 39 Shore Park Rd Great Neck NY 11023-2046

GILARDI, RICHARD D., lawyer; b. Pitts., June 12, 1936; s. Paul and Mary C. Gilardi; m. Carole Ann Herwood, July 30, 1960; children: Lynne T., Richard P. BA, Washington and Jefferson Coll., 1958; LLB, Duquesne U., 1962; postgrad. (fellow) U. Va. Sch. Law, 1962-63. Bar: Pa. 1964, U.S. Dist. Ct. (we. dist.) Pa. 1964, U.S. Ct. Appeals (3d cir.) 1967, U.S. Ct. Appeals (4th cir.) 1977. Assoc. Wilner, Wilner & Kuhn, Pitts., 1964-66, McArdle & McLaughlin, Pitts., 1967-69; sr. ptnr. Gilardi, Cooper & Gismondi, Pitts., 1969—; lectr. Duquesne U. Law Sch., 1964-66; instr. U. Va. Sch. Law, 1962-63. Pres. Allegheny County Alumni Assn., Washington and Jefferson Coll., 1967-68; mem. Washington and Jefferson Devel. Council, 1983—; mem. disciplinary bd. Supreme Ct. Pa. Mem. ABA, Pa. Bar Assn., Allegheny County Bar Assn., Acad. Trial Lawyers Allegheny County, Am. Mgmt. Assn., Am. Arbitration Assn., Am. Judicature Soc., Assn. Trial Lawyers Am., Western Pa. Trial Lawyers Assn., Pa. Trial Lawyers Assn. Clubs: St. Clair Country, Amen Corner, Fellows, Oyster Reef Golf, Rivers. Author: (with A. Pelaez) The Pennsylvania Comparative Negligence Act—An Alien Intruder in the House of Common Law; contbr. articles to profl. jours. Office: 808 Grant Pittsburgh PA 15219-1906

GILBANE, JEAN ANN (MRS. THOMAS F. GILBANE), construction company executive; b. Providence, Aug. 22, 1923; d. Vincent Thaddeus and Edna (Leary) Murphy; m. Thomas F. Gilbane, Sept. 12, 1946; children: Thomas, Robert, Richard, Jean, John, James. Student, Elmhurst Acad., 1941, Coll. New Rochelle, 1945. Sec. Gilbane Bldg. Co., Providence, 1950-81, treas., 1982—, also bd. dirs.; bd. dirs. Gilbane Properties, B.T. Equipment Co. Active Women's R.I. Hosp. Guild; mem. corp. Emma Bradley Hosp., Butler Hosp.; former trustee Coll. New Rochelle; bd. dirs. Women's Resource Ctr. South County; bd. dirs. So. County Hosp. Decorated lady Order Holy Sepulcher. Roman Catholic. Clubs: Dunes, Point Judith Country (bd. govs. 1985-88); Beach (Palm Beach); University, Wannamoisett. Home: 80 Don Ave Rumford RI 02916-2305 Office: Gilbane Bldg Co 7 Jackson Walkway Providence RI 02903-3623 also: Apt 402 N 400 S Ocean Blvd Palm Beach FL 33480

GILBERG, IRA MICHAEL, accountant, consultant; b. Balt., Apr. 30, 1967; s. Meyer and Pauline Marie (Petrone) G. BS in Acctg. and Fin., Towson State U., 1990. Cash flow supr. Gaff Games Inc., Ocean City, Md., 1986-87; fin. forecaster R.H. Macy, Owings Mills, Md., 1987-89; sr. acct., analyst M.S. Willett, Cockeysville, Md., 1989—; cons. Tool & Die Mfrs. Group, Balt., 1990—. Vol. ARC, Balt., 1991. Mem. Towson State U. Bus. Alumni. Republican.

GILBERG, KENNETH ROY, lawyer; b. Phila., Feb. 2, 1951; s. Leonard David and Roslyn (Tennis) G.; m. Nanci Jane Schwartz, Sept. 7, 1974. BA, Lebanon Valley Coll., 1973; JD, Widener U., 1976. Bar: Pa. 1976. Assoc. Pechner, Dorfman et. al., Phila., 1976-84, ptnr., 1984-87; ptnr. Myerson & Kuhn, Phila., 1988-89; prin. Kenneth R. Gilberg and Assocs., Bala Cynwyd, Pa., 1989-90, Mesirov, Gelman, Jaffe, Cramer & Jamieson, Phila., 1990—. Contbr. articles to profl. jours. Treas. Camp Exec. Bd. of Golden Slipper Club Charities. Recipient Meritorious Achievement award Pa. Sports Hall of Fame, 1974; named Most Valuable Player Mid-Atlantic Conf., 1973. Mem. Phi Alpha Delta (charter). Republican. Office: Mesirov Gelman Jaffe Cramer & Jamieson 1735 Market St Philadelphia PA 19103-7598

GILBERT, ALVIN EVERETT, agricultural economist, retired; b. Auburn, Maine, Nov. 27, 1925; s. Charles Everett and Lillian Ada (Hicks) G.; m. Janie Kathryn Thoresen, July 28, 1967; stepchildren: Anthony L. Bigbee, Brett Bigbee, Thomas P. Bigbee, Victoria L. Montes. BS in Gen. Agr., U. Maine, 1950, BS in Agrl. Econs., 1951. Warehouseman Miliken-Tomlinson Co., Lewiston, Maine, 1951-53; bookkeeper Nat. Biscuit Co., Portland, Maine, 1953-54; agrl. econ. U.S. Dept. Agriculture, Washington, 1954-82. Mem. Auburn City Coun., 1983-91. Mem. Grange (master 1983-88). Democrat. Unitarian. Home: HC 33 Box 240 Danville ME 04223-9705

GILBERT, CREIGHTON EDDY, art historian; b. Durham, N.C., June 6, 1924; s. Allan H. and Katharine (Everett) G. BA, NYU, 1942, PhD, 1955; DHL (hon.), Adelphi U., 1990. Jr. appts. Emory U., Louisville U., Ind. U., Ringling Mus., 1946-61; assoc. prof. Brandeis U., 1961-65, Sidney and Ellen Wien prof. history of art, 1965-69; prof. Queens Coll. City U. N.Y., 1969-77; Jacob Gould Schurman prof. history of art Cornell U., 1977-81; prof. Yale U., 1981—; Fulbright sr. lectr. U. Rome, 1951-52; Kress fellow Harvard Center for Italian Renaissance Studies, Florence, Italy, 1967-68; fellow Netherlands Inst. for Advanced Study, 1972-73; vis. prof. U. Leiden, 1974-75; Robert Sterling Clark vis. prof. Williams Coll., 1976; Zacks Found. vis. prof. Hebrew U. Jerusalem, 1985. Author: Michelangelo, 1967, Change in Piero della Francesca, 1968, History of Renaissance Art, 1972, The Works of Girolamo Savoldo, 1986, Poets Seeing Artists' Work: Instances from the Italian Renaissance, 1991; editor: Renaissance Art: Contemporary Essays, 1970, Italian Art 1400-1500, Sources and Documents, 1979, enlarged Italian edit., 1988; editor-in-chief: The Art Bulletin, 1980-85; translator: Complete Poems and Selected Letters of Michelangelo, 1963, 3d edit., 1979. Recipient Mather award Coll. Art Assn., 1964. Fellow Am. Acad. Arts and Scis., Ateneo Veneto (fgn.). Office: Yale U Dept History of Art 56 High St West Haven CT 06516-2019

GILBERT, DANIEL LEE, physiologist; b. Bklyn., July 2, 1925; s. Louis and Blanche (Lutz) G.; m. Claire Gilbert, July 26, 1964; 1 child, Raymond Louis. A.B., Drew U., 1948; M.S., State U. Iowa, 1950; Ph.D., U. Rochester, 1955. Instr. U. Rochester, 1955-56; instr. Albany Med. Coll., 1956-59, asst. prof. physiology, 1959-60; asst. prof. Jefferson Med. Coll., 1960-62, assoc. prof., 1962-63; research physiologist Nat. Inst. Neurol. Disorders and Stroke, NIH, Bethesda, Md., 1962—; head sect. cellular biophysics Nat. Inst. Neurol. and Communicative Diseases and Stroke, NIH, 1963-71; Bowditch lectr. Am. Physiol. Soc., 1964; organizer profl. symposia. Contbr. articles to profl. publs.; editor: Oxygen and Living Processes, 1981; co-editor: Squid as Experimental Animals, 1990. Served with U.S. Army, 1943-45. Decorated Purple Heart. Fellow AAAS; mem. Am. Chem. Soc., Am. Physiol. Soc., Am. Soc. Pharm. and Exptl. Therapeutics, Biophys. Soc., Corp. Marine Biol. Lab., Internat. Soc. Study Origin of Life, N.Y. Acad. Sci., Oxygen Club Greater Washington (pres. 1987-88), Oxygen Soc. (councilor 1987-89), Soc. Exptl. Biology and Medicine, Soc. Neurosci., Soc. Gen. Physiology, Undersea Med. Soc., Washington Soc. for History of Medicine (v.p. 1988-89, pres. 1989-90), Sigma Xi. Home: 10324 Dickens Ave Bethesda MD 20814-2137 Office: Nat Inst Neurol Disorders and Strokes Lab Biophysics NIH Bldg 9 Rm 1E124 Bethesda MD 20892

GILBERT, DENNIS CLARE, superintendent maintenance and tools; b. MEdina, N.Y., Dec. 15, 1952; s. Clare Claude and Rosemary Dora (Mallaber) G.; m. Denise Paulette Carney. Apr. 16, 1977; 1 child, Brendan James. BSME, GM Inst., 1978. Environ. engr. GM Corp., Harrison Div., Lockport, N.Y., 1978-82, maintenance supr., 1982-84, gen. supr. maintenance and tools, 1984-88, staff asst. personnel, 1988-90, personnel adminstr., 1990-91, supt. maintenance and tools, 1991—. Vol. Am. Cancer Soc., Niagara County, N.Y., 1990, Muscular Dystrophy, Buffalo, N.Y., 1989-91, Camp Good Days and Happy Times, Buffalo, 1990-91. With U.S. Army, 1972-74, Korea. Republican. Lutheran. Home: 5063 Saunders Settlement Rd Lockport NY 14094 Office: GM Corp Harrison Div 200 Upper Mountain Rd Lockport NY 14094

GILBERT, EDWARD WILLIAM, safety specialist; b. Rochester, N.Y., Jan. 29, 1938; s. Charles F. and Bertha (Faddis) G.; m. Ruth Hallows, Dec. 26, 1964; children: Cheryl A., Glena A. Student, Roberts Wesleyan Coll., 1957-59. Group leader Eastman Kodak Co., Rochester, 1959-74, safety technician, 1974-86, safety specialist, 1986—; mem. Environ. Speakers Team, Rochester, 1989—, Rochester Safety Coun., Nat. Safety Coun. Adv. bd. Project Outreach, Rochester; v.p. Brockport (N.Y.) Cen. Sch. Bd. Edn., 1988—; chmn. Monroe County Sch. Bd. Labor Rels. Com., 1991. Mem. Monroe County Sch. Bd. Assn., Environ. Info. Coun. Rochester. Office: Eastman Kodak Co Kodak Pk Rochester NY 14652-0001

GILBERT, JAMES EASTHAM, academic administrator; b. Bridgeport, Conn., July 1, 1929; s. Carl Ludwig and Anna Maude (Eastham) G.; m. Betty Lee Blankenship, Aug. 26, 1953; 1 child, Gregory Eastham. BS in Psychology, U. N.Mex., 1952, MA in Psychology, 1959; PhD in Psychology, Am. U., 1969. Interviewer Va. State Employment Service, Alexandria, 1952-53; tng. officer Nat. Security Agy., Washington, 1953-55; research psychologist Nat. Security Agy., Ft. Meade, Md., 1957-64, Hdqrs., Sec. to Air Staff, USAF, Washington, 1955-57; assoc. dean univ. adminstrn. Northeastern U., Boston, 1964-71; assoc. vice chancellor Ind. U.-Purdue U., Ft. Wayne, 1971-78; v.p. acad. affairs Pittsburg (Kans.) State U., 1978-86, interim pres., 1983; pres. East Stroudsburg (Pa.) U., 1986—; commr. Nat. Commn. for Study of Role and Future of State Colls. and Univs., Assn. State Colls. and Univs., Washington, 1985-86, vice chair pres.' commn. on tchr. edn. Contbr. to books on programmed learning, instrnl. aids, and higher edn. Mem. Am. Psychol. Soc., Am. Assn. Higher Edn., Soc. for Coll. and Univ. Planning, Rotary, Sigma Xi, Psi Chi, Phi Kappa Phi, Omicron Delta Kappa. Democrat. Home and Office: East Stroudsburg U 1 Clg Cir East Stroudsburg PA 18301

GILBERT, REAL PAUL, insurance company executive; b. Manchester, N.H., Feb. 10, 1938; s. Euclide Donat and Aurore (Gelinas) G.; m. Shirley A. Shackett, Apr. 24, 1965; children—David S., Nicole, Laurie-Ann. B.A., St. Anselm's Coll., 1969. Sales promotion Manchester Union Leader, Manchester, 1960-65, 1968-70; circulation dir. Loeb Newspapers, Lowell and Haverhill, Mass., 1965-69; sales and mktg. exec. Franklin Life Ins. Co., Springfield, Ill., 1970-75; pres. Gilbert Ins. Agy., 1969—, Words Translation Svcs., 1975—, QT Svcs. & Offices, Inc., Manchester, 1985—; dir. U.S. ops. Cooperants Mut. Life, Manchester, 1975-92. Ski editor The Liberator, Lowell, 1965-67; editor The Shield, The Compass. Contbr. articles to profl. jours. Officer Manchester Jaycees, 1965-69; pres. French Lang. Found., Manchester, 1984—, Action for Franco-Ams. of Northeast, Manchester, 1982—; state chmn. Nat. Battle of the Bands, project chmn. Manchester Winter Carnival, Inc. Mem. Manchester Assn. Life Underwriters (pres. 1977-78, bd. dirs. 1973-77, Nat. Pub. Service award 1979), N.H. Assn. Life Underwriters (pres. 1987—), Nat. Assn. Franco-Ams. (nat. v.p. 1985, bd. dirs. 1987). Republican. Roman Catholic. Clubs: Manchester Press, Jolliet (gov. 1984-88) (Manchester). Avocations: skiing; tennis; golf. Home: 308 Huse Rd PO Box 4185 Manchester NH 03108 Office: Gilbert Ins Agy PO Box 2000 83 Amherst St Manchester NH 03101

GILBERT, ROBERT PETTIBONE, retired physician, educator; b. Chgo., Sept. 29, 1917; s. Newell Clark and Charlotte Louise (Pettibone) G.; m. Anne Cribben Heneage, June 5, 1943 (div. 1964); children: Robert P., Diane H., Nancy C., Anne E., m. Brenda Drake, Oct. 2, 1964; children: Jane D., Newell C. BA, Haverford Coll., 1938; MD, Northwestern U., 1942. Diplomate Am. Bd. Internal Medicine. Cardiology fellow Stanford U. Med. Sch., San Francisco, 1947-48; instr. to assoc. prof. of Medicine Northwestern U. Med. Sch., Chgo., 1949-65; rsch. assoc. in Physiology U. Minn., Mpls., 1956-57; dir. edn. and rsch. Evanston (Ill.) Hosp., 1957-65; assoc. dean Jefferson Med. Coll., Phila., 1965-72, assoc. prof., 1965—; clin. prof. of Medicine and dir. student health Thomas Jefferson U., Phila., 1981-90. Contbr. articles to profl jours. Lt. USNR, 1943-46, PTO. Markle scholar Markle Found. and Northwestern U., 1952-57. Fellow Am. Coll. Physicians. Republican. Presbyterian. Home: 304 Keithwood Rd Wynnewood PA 19096-1224 Office: Thomas Jefferson U 1015 Walnut St Philadelphia PA 19107-5005

GILBERT, SHARON, artist; b. Bklyn., Feb. 15, 1944; d. Harry and Sylvia (Deitchman) G.; m. Vyt Bakaitis, Jan. 23, 1970; children: Elena, Ellery. Student, Skowhegan Sch., 1965; BFA, Cooper Union, 1966. Author: Three Mile Island Reproductions, 1979, Waste, 1980, '80 Faces, 1980, A Nuclear Atlas, 1982, Poison America, 1988, Green the Fragile, 1989, Urgent Life, 1990, Action Poses, 1991; solo exhbns.: Printed Matter, N.Y.C., 1980, Resnick Gallery, L.I. U., 1990, Rutgers U., New Brunswick, N.J., 1992; group shows: Albert-Ludwig U., Freiburg, Germany, 1980, Ctr. George Pompidou, Paris, 1985, Mus. Modern Art, N.Y.C., 1988-90, Vasarely Mus., Budapest, Hungary, 1990, others. Grantee Women's Studio Workshop, 1982, N.Y. Found. for Arts, 1989, Artists Space, 1990, Carl Schurz Hans German-Am. Inst., Freiburg, 1980. Mem. Artist Equity, Women's Caucus for Art (adv. bd. N.Y. chpt. 1979-83). Home and Studio: 323 Atlantic Ave Brooklyn NY 11201-5803

GILBERT, WALTER, molecular biologist; b. Boston, Mar. 21, 1932; s. Richard V. and Emma (Cohen) G.; m. Celia Stone, Dec. 29, 1953; children: John Richard, Kate. AB, Harvard U., 1953, AM, 1954; PhD, Cambridge U., 1957; DSc (hon.), U. Chgo., 1978, Columbia U., 1978, U. Rochester, 1979, Yeshiva U., 1981. NSF postdoctoral fellow Harvard U., Cambridge, Mass., 1957-58, lectr. physics, 1958-59, asst. prof. physics, 1959-64, assoc. prof. biophysics, 1964-68, prof. biochemistry, 1968-72, Am. Cancer Soc. prof. molecular biology, 1972-81, prof. biology, 1985-86, H.H. Timken prof. sci., 1986-87, Carl M. Loeb Univ. prof., chair dept. cellular and devel. biology, 1987—; chmn. sci. bd. Biogen N.V., Dutch Antilles, 1978-83, co-chmn., supervisory bd., 1979-81, chmn. supervisory bd., chief exec. officer, 1981-84; V.D. Mattia lectr. Roche Inst. Molecular Biology, 1976. Recipient U.S. Steel Found. NAS, 1968, Ledlie prize Harvard U., 1969, Warren triennal prize Mass. Gen. Hosp., 1977, Louis and Bert Freedman Found. N.Y. Acad. Scis., 1977, Prix Charles-Leopold Mayer Academie des Scis., Inst. de France, 1977, Nobel prize in chemistry, 1980, New Eng. Entrepreneur of Yr. award, 1991; co-winner Louisa Gross Horwitz prize Columbia U., 1979, Gairdner prize, 1979, Albert Lasker Basic Sci. award, 1979; Guggenheim fellow, 1968-69; hon. fellow Trinity Coll., Cambridge, U.K., 1991. Mem. Am. Phys. Soc., Nat. Acad. Scis., Am. Soc. Biol. Chemists, Am. Acad. Arts and Scis.; fgn. mem. Royal Soc. Office: The Biol Labs 16 Divinity Ave Cambridge MA 02138-2097

GILBOA, NISAN, physician; b. Balachna, Russia, Feb. 12, 1945; came to U.S. 1973; s. Schmuel and Mina (Lapp) G.; married, 1967; children: Amit, Noam, Keren. MD, Hebrew U., Jerusalem, 1973. Resident U. Oreg. Med. Sch., Portland, 1973-75; fellow U. Colo. Med. Sch., Denver, 1975-77; asst. prof. Union U. Med. Sch., Albany, N.Y., 1977, assoc. prof., to 1990; assoc. prof. medicine U. Pitts., 1990—; cons. Genentech Co., San Francisco, 1985; peer rev. com. Am. Heart Assn., 1985-89. Editor: Pediatric Nephrology, 1983; referee, reviewer med. and sci. jours.; contbr. articles to profl. jours. Am. Heart Assn./Am. Kidney Found. grantee, 1980-91. Office: Children's Hosp 3705 5th Ave Pittsburgh PA 15213

GILBORN, CRAIG ALFRED, museum director; b. Providence, R.I., Oct. 28, 1934; s. Iver S. and Lois (Woodhouse) G.; m. Alice Wolf, Aug. 30, 1958; children: Alexis Prince, Amanda Cee. BA, Mich. State U., 1957; MA, U. Del., 1961. Adminstr. programs div. Va. Mus. Fine Arts, Richmond, 1961-64; assoc. edn. div. Winterthur (Del.) Mus., 1964-69; exec. dir. Del. State Arts Coun., Wilmington, 1969-72; dir. Adirondack Mus., Blue Mountain Lake, N.Y., 1972—; trustee Shelburne (Vt.) Mus., 1987—; ex-officio bd. dirs. Adirondack Hist. Assn., Blue Mountain Lake. Author: Durant: The Fortunes and Woodland Camps of a Family in the Adirondacks, 1981, Adirondack Furniture and the Rustic Tradition, 1987 (Charles F. Montgomery award 1988), Blooms on Bedrock (photography), 1992. Commr. Gov.'s Commn. on The Adirondacks in the 21st Century, 1989-90. Disting. Svc. award SUNY, 1985. Mem. Am. Assn. Mus., Mid-Atlantic Assn. Mus. (pres. 1973-76), Am. Assn. for State and Local History, N.Y. State Assn. of Mus. Office: Adirondack Mus RR 28 Blue Mountain Lake NY 12812

GILCHREST, WAYNE THOMAS, congressman, former high school educator; b. Rahway, N.J., Apr. 15, 1946; s. Arthur and Elizabeth Gilchrest; m. Barbara Rawley; children: Kevin, Joel, Katie. AA in Liberal Arts, Wesley Coll., 1971; BA in History, Del. State Coll., 1973; postgrad., Loyola Coll., Balt., 1984—. Tchr. social studies Warren Hills Jr. High Sch., Washington, N.J., 1973-76; tchr. history St. Alban's City (Vt.) Elem. Sch., 1976-79, Kent County High Sch., Worton, Md., 1979-90; mem. 102 Congress from 1st Md. dist., 1991—. Vol. Nat. Forest Svc., Bitterroot Nat. Forest, Idaho, 1986-87. Sgt. USMC, 1964-68, Vietnam. Decorated Purple Heart, Bronze Star. Mem. Kent County Tchrs. Assn., VFW, Am. Legion, Mil. Order Purple Heart. Republican. Methodist. Office: US Ho of Reps 502 Cannon Hob Washington DC 20515-9995

GILDEA, BRIAN MICHAEL, lawyer; b. New Haven, Nov. 1, 1939; s. Thomas Michael and Lillian Frances (Reilly) G.; children: Larysa Albina, Stefan Bohdan. AS, New Haven U., 1964; BA, Providence Coll., 1967; JD, Suffolk U., 1970. Bar: Conn. 1970, U.S. Dist. Ct. Conn. 1971, U.S. Ct. Appeals (2d cir.) 1975, U.S. Ct. Appeals (3d cir.) 1979, U.S. Ct. Appeals (5th cir.) 1984, U.S. Supreme Ct. 1975. Legal adviser City of Boston, 1969-70; assoc. Celentano, Ivey & Gery, New Haven, 1970-73; ptnr. Celentano & Gildea, New Haven, 1973-74; pvt. practice, New Haven, 1974—. Bd. dirs. St. Mary's High Sch., New Haven, 1975-77; mem. Bethany (Conn.) Town Charter Commn., 1976; del. U.S./Japan Bilateral Session, 1988, U.S./China Joint Session on Trade and Econ. Law, 1987. With USAF, 1958-62. Recipient Svc. award Providence Coll., New Haven, 1979, Friar award St. Mary's Alumni Assn., 1980. Mem. ABA, Def. Rsch. Inst., Conn. Bar Assn., New Haven County Bar Assn., Am. Lawyers Assn. Democrat. Roman Catholic. Office: 512 Blake St New Haven CT 06515-1238

GILDEA, STEVEN JOSEPH, social services administrator; b. Bronx, N.Y., May 15, 1967; s. Arthur Thomas and Mary (Hanley) G. AA, Ocean County Coll., Toms River, N.J., 1987; BS in Health, Rutgers U., 1990. Sr. environ. therapist John L. Montgomery Med., Freehold, N.J., 1987-90; sr. house mgr. Devel. Disabilities Assn. N.J., Woodbridge, 1991—. Mem. Am. Assn. for Counseling and Devel. Roman Catholic. Home: 74 Rhode Island Dr Jackson NJ 08527-1454

GILES, JAMES T., federal judge; b. 1943. B.A., Amherst Coll., 1964; LL.B., Yale U., 1967. Mem. Nat. Labor Relations Bd., Phila., 1967-68; assoc. Pepper, Hamilton & Scheetz, 1968-79; judge U.S. Dist. Ct. (ea. dist.) Pa., Phila., 1979—. Mem. Fed. Bar Assn., Phila. Bar Assn. Office: US Dist Ct 8613 US Courthouse Independence Mall W Philadelphia PA 19106

GILES, THOMAS WILBUR, science educator; b. Millsboro, Pa., Aug. 29, 1939; s. Thomas Nelson and Frances (Muscavitch) G.; m. Kathleen Elaine Mensh, June 19, 1965; children: Elizabeth A., Thomas Ross. AB, Waynesburg Coll., 1961; MA in Phys. Sci., Mich. State U., 1968; EdD in Sci. Edn., Pa. State U., 1980. Cert. tchr., Pa. Tchr. chemistry Carroll County Schs., Westminster, Md., 1961-62; tchr. chemistry, physics West Greene Schs., Rogersville, Pa., 1962-63; tchr. sci., aht. Connellsville (Pa.) Schs., 1963-67; NSF grad. fellow AYI-Mich. State U., East Lansing, 1967-68; planetarium dir. Charleroi (Pa.) Schs., 1968-70; planetarium dir., sci. chmn. Hempfield Schs., Greensburg, Pa., 1970—; lectr., instr. dept. edn., dept. physics St. Vincent Coll., Latrobe, Pa., 1982—; instr. astronomy Westmoreland Community Coll., Youngwood, Pa., 1987—; presenter papers at profl. confs. Textbook reviewer Holt, Rinehart, Winston, 1986-90. Mem. NEA, Pa. Edn. Assn., Nat. Sci. Tchrs. Assn., Sch. Sci. and Math. Assn., Nat. Assn. Rsch. in Sci. Teaching, Waynesburg Coll. Alumni Assn. Mem. United Ch. of Christ. Office: St Vincent Coll 701 Fraser Purchase Rd Latrobe PA 15650-2667

GILFORD, LEON, business executive and consultant; b. Warsaw, Poland, Feb. 14, 1917; came to U.S., 1922, naturalized, 1928; m. Dorothy Jeanne Morrow, Mar. 31, 1950. BA, Bklyn. Coll., 1939; MA, George Washington U., 1949. Prin. scientist Ops. Rsch., Inc., Silver Spring, Md., 1960-71; chief statistician and dir. automatic data processing U.S. Tariff Commn., Washington, 1971-74; spl. asst. for reliability AEC, Germantown, Md., 1974-76; spl. asst. office of dir. U.S. Census Bur., Washington, 1977-81; v.p. R&D COBRO Corp., Wheaton, Md., 1982-90, also bd. dirs., 1982—; mem. panel quality control nat. welfare program Nat. Acad. Scis., 1986-87; mem. adv. com. Dept. Energy, Washington, 1981-84, mem. adv. coun. Nat. Ctr. for Edn. Stats., 1979; expert witness testimony to U.S. Congress and Fed. Cir. Ct. Contbr. articles to profl. jours. Capt. U.S. Army, 1942-46. Recipient Silver medal Dept. Commerce, 1956. Fellow AAAS, Am. Statis. Assn. (coun. 1968-70); mem. Washington Statis. Soc. (pres., v.p. 1963-65), Cosmos Club (Washington). Office: 1401 Rockville Pike # 380 Rockville MD 20852-1428

GILFRICH, JOHN VALENTINE, chemist; b. Springfield, Mass., Sept. 14, 1927; s. John Valentine and Irene Frances (Connery) G.; m. Nancy Jane Tucker, Jan. 23, 1954; children: John T., N. Lynn, Beth Ann, Robert H., Georgia Ann. BA, Am. Internat. Coll., 1949; postgrad., George Washington U., 1954-56. Analytical chemist Nat. Bur. Stds., Washington, 1948-51; phys. chemist Nat. Bur. Stds., 1951-52; analytical chemist Naval Ordnance Lab., Silver Spring, Md., 1952-60; phys. chemist Naval Ordnance Lab., 1960-66; research chemist x-ray optic br. Naval Research Lab., Washington, 1966-71; head spectrochem. analysis sect. Naval Research Lab., 1971-77, cons., 1977-81, assoc. head condensed matter physics br., 1981-82; ret.; part-time cons. Condensed Matter Physics Br., 1983-87; cons. research chemist Bethesda, Md., 1987—. Editor-in-chief X-Ray Spectrometry jour., 1986—; mem. editorial adv. bd. Spectroscopy and Spectral Analysis (Chinese) jour., 1990—; mem. editorial bd. Trace and Microprobe Techniques, 1982—; contbr. articles to profl. jours. With USAAF, 1946-47. Recipient Meritorious Civilian Service award Naval Ordnance Lab., USN, 1958. Fellow Am. Inst. Chemists (cert. profl. chemist), ACS (emeritus), Am. Crystalographic Assn., Microbeam Analysis Soc., Soc. for Applied Spectroscopy, Sigma Xi. Address: 8710 Lowell St Bethesda MD 20817-3218

GILINSON, PHILIP JULIUS, JR., retired laboratory administrator; b. Lowell, Mass., July 28, 1914; s. Philip Julius and Anna (Turnquist) G.; m. Hulda Einarsdottir, July 6, 1943; 1 child, Robert Alan. BS, MIT, 1936, MS, 1952. Registered profl. engr., Mass. Jr. engr. Heinze Electric Co., Lowell, 1936-38; engr. Pacific Mills Inc., Lawrence, Mass., 1938-40, Doelcam Corp., Newton, Mass., 1946-48; assoc. dir. C.S. Draper Labs., Cambridge, Mass., 1948-80; sr. cons. People's Republic China, Beijing, 1980-90; ret., 1990. Co-author: Magnetic and Electric Suspensions, 1974. Pres., bd. dirs. Scholarship Fund, Chelmsford, Mass., 1964. Lt. col. USAAF, 1940-46, ETO. Mem. Masons (master 1963-64), Sigma Xi. Luthran. Home: 8 Fuller Rd Chelmsford MA 01824-1818

GILJE, STEPHEN ARNE, academic administrator; b. Bklyn., June 16, 1949; s. Arne and Wladja (Trendowski) G.; m. June Anne Kelemecz, June 30, 1973; children: Kelly Anne, S. Scott. BS in Geology, SUNY, New Paltz, 1972; MA in Geology, SUNY, Binghamton, 1974. Rsch. phys. scientist U.S. Dept. Transp., Washington, 1974-77, rsch. hydrologist, 1977-82; sci. coord. U.S. Dept. Transp., McLean, Va., 1982-85; contract adminstr. Rsch. Found. SUNY, Albany, 1985-88; assoc. vice-provost SUNY, Binghamton, 1988—; spokesperson for animal rsch., Binghamton, 1988—; chair Instl. Rev. Bd., Binghamton, 1989—; mem. sponsored programs adv. com., Albany, 1991—. Contbr. articles on hydrologic rsch. to tech. publs. Mem. Nat. Coun. Rsch. Adminstrs., N.Y. State Acad. Scis., Soc. Rsch. Adminstrs., Assn. Univ. Tech. Adminstrs. Office: SUNY Binghamton Rsch/Sponsored Programs Binghamton NY 13901

GILKEY, CLINTON HOWARD, manufacturing company executive, civil engineer; b. Pitts., Sept. 23, 1938; s. Clarence and Bessie Mildred (Smith) G.; m. Madeleine Pelcher, Oct. 27, 1967 (div. July 1984); 1 child, Douglas; m. Samantha G. Gridley, Sept. 28, 1985. BSCE, Bucknell U., 1960; MSCE, Lehigh U., 1965. Engr. Dravo Corp., Pitts., 1962-63; teaching asst. Lehigh U., Bethlehem, Pa., 1963-65; engr., mgr. Combustion Engring., Windsor, Conn., 1965-76, dir., 1976-78; v.p. engring. Combustion Engring.-Bauer, Springfield, Ohio, 1978-82; engring. mgr. ABB Air Preheater, Inc., Wellsville, N.Y., 1982-88, mgr. purchasing, 1988-90, dir. heat recovery prodn., 1991—. 1st lt. U.S. Army, 1960-62, Korea. Mem. ASCE, ASME, Wellsville Country Club (bd. dirs., v.p. 1989—), Lions (sec. Wellsville 1989). Republican. Office: ABB Air Preheater Inc PO Box 372 Wellsville NY 14895-0372

GILL, CHARLES BURROUGHS, engineering educator; b. Sudbury, Ont., Can., Apr. 8, 1921; came to U.S., 1957; s. James Richard and Marion Pearl (Burroughs) G.; m. Mary Carolyn Somervill, Oct. 29, 1955; children: Catherine, Joseph. BSc, U. Toronto, Can., 1945; MSc, U. Mo., 1947, PhD, 1952. Smelter engr. Falcon Bridge (Ont., Can.) Nickel Mines Ltd., 1945-46; rsch. scientist U. Mo., Rolla, 1952-55; tech. supt. DeLoro (Ont., Can.) Smelting & Refining, 1955-57; prof. metall. engring. Lafayette Coll., Easton, Pa., 1957-89, prof. emeritus, 1989—. Author: Nonferrous Extractive Metallurgy, 1980, Material Beneficiation, 1991; co-inventor titanium plating. Mem. Assn. Profl. Engrs., Metals Soc. of AIME, Sigma Xi. Episcopalian. Home: 405 W Monroe St Easton PA 18042-1716

GILL, JOHN RAY, communications company executive; b. Milbank, S.D., Aug. 17, 1953; s. Ray Edwin and Margaret Irene (Steltz) G.; student Dakota Wesleyan U., 1971-73. Bookkeeper, Buford TV Inc., S.D., 1973-77, internal auditor, Tyler, Tex., 1977-80, asst. controller, 1980-81; controller Ind. Cablevision Corp., South Bend. 1981-83; controller CATV div. Buford TV Inc., 1983-86; ops. mgr. Broward Cablevision Inc., 1986-88, Jones Intercable Inc., Broward County, Fla., 1988-90, gen. mgr., Lancaster, N.Y., 1990—. Democrat. Methodist. Club: Mensa. Home: 1023 Northwood Dr Buffalo NY 14221-3855

GILL, THOMAS JAMES, III, physician, educator; b. Malden, Mass., July 2, 1932; s. Thomas James and Marguerite (Capobianco) G.; m. Faith Libbie Ettil, July 8, 1961; children: Elizabeth Ruth, Thomas James IV, Christopher Gregory. AB summa cum laude, Harvard U., 1953, MA in Chemistry, 1957, MD, 1957. Diplomate Am. Bd. Pathology. Asst. in pathology Peter Bent Brigham Hosp., Boston, 1957-58; intern N.Y. Hosp.-Cornell Med. Center, 1958-59; jr. fellow Soc. Fellows Harvard U., 1959-62; mem. faculty Harvard U. Med Sch., 1962-71, asso. prof. pathology, 1970-71; prof. pathology, chmn. dept. U. Pitts. Med. Sch., 1971-90; pathologist-in-chief Univ. Health Center Pitts., 1971-90, Maude L. Menten prof. exptl. pathology, 1988—, prof. human genetics, 1984—; cons. to govt. and industry; mem. sci. adv. bd. St. Jude Children's Research Hosp., Memphis, 1969-77, chmn., 1974-76; mem. allergy and immunology research com. Nat. Inst. Allergy and Infectious Diseases, 1973-76; mem. med. research service merit rev. bd. in immunology VA, 1976-79, chmn., 1977-79; mem. sci. adv. com. Damon Runyon-Walter Winchell Cancer Fund, 1978-81; mem. com. on animal models and genetic stocks NRC, 1978-86, chmn. com., 1983-86, mem. com. on rabbit genetic resources, 1979-80, mem. coun. Inst. Lab. Animal Resources, 1986—, mem. com. on preservation of lab. animal resources, 1985-90, com. on transgenic animals, 1991-92; mem. surgery, anesthesiology and trauma study sect. NIH, 1983-84; sci. adv. com. on immunology and immunotherapy Am. Cancer Soc., 1986-88; mem. Armed Forces Epidemiol. Bd., 1966-72; adj. prof. U. Milan, 1990—; nutrition found. Italy lectr., U. Milan, 1986—; trustee Am. Bd. Pathology, 1981-92, pres., 1992. Mem. editorial bd. several sci. and med. jours.; contbr. articles to profl. jours. Bd. dirs. Easter Seal Soc., Allegheny County, 1972-77, Univs. Asso. for Research and Edn. in Pathology, 1979-90. Recipient Lederle med. faculty award, 1962-65, research career devel. award NIH, 1965-71, cert. of appreciation for patriotic civilian svc. Dept. Army, 1973; Spl. Qualification in Pathology: Immunopathology, 1983; Disting. Scientist award in genetics S.W. Found. for Biomed. Research, 1986, Charter with medal U. Rijeka, 1990, medal U. Pitts., 1990; George H. Fetterman lectr. U. Pitts., 1981, George Hoyt Whipple lectr. U. Rochester, N.Y., 1984. Fellow Am. Soc. Clin. Pathologists, Assn. Pathology Chairmen (pres. 1978); mem. AMA, Am. Assn. Immunologists, Am. Assn. Pathologists, Am. Soc. for Molecular Biology and Biochemistry, Internat. Acad. Pathology, Am. Soc. Human Genetics, Transplantation Soc. (v.p. 1982-84), Am. Soc. for Immunology of Reprodn. (Disting. Investigator award 1991), Genetics Soc. Am., Internat. Soc. Immunology of Reprodn. (pres. 1992), Harvard Club N.Y.C., Harvard Club Boston, Harvard Club Western Pa., Fox Chapel Racquet Club, Pitts. Athletic Assn., Harvard Varsity Club, others. Home: 117 Crofton Dr Pittsburgh PA 15238-2503 Office: U Pitts Sch Medicine Pittsburgh PA 15261

GILL, WANDA EILEEN, academic administrator, consultant, playwright; b. Burlington, N.J., Feb. 7, 1945; d. Thomas Garfield Jr. and Marian Marie (Jeffries) W.; m. Bruce Leon Gill, Dec. 24, 1969; children: Candace Ellen, Kimberly Lea. BS, Va. State U., 1967; MA, U. Cin., 1969; MEd, Bowie (Md.) State U., 1982; EdD, George Washington U., 1987. Cert. tchr., D.C. Coord. med.-dental health careers Georgetown U. Sch. Medicine, Washington, 1977-79; coord. student svcs. Bowie State U., 1979-80, dir. student svcs., 1980—; cons. U.S. Dept. Edn., Washington, 1980-90; writer Metro Chronicle newspaper, Washington, 1987-88; proposal writer Coppin State Coll., Balt., 1989; mem. adv. bd. Planning A Needs Assessment Mgmt. System U. Ga., Athens, summer 1990. Author play The Cracker Box, 1990; also essays. V.p. Md. Women's Polit. Caucus, U. Md., 1988-90; pres. Community Crisis Coalition, Prince George's County, Md., 1989—, Md. Exec. Coun. for Econ. Oppotrunity, 1991-93. Danforth Found. fellow, 1967-69; named Outstanding Young Woman of Am., Outstanding Young Women of Am., 1979. Mem. U. Md. System Women's Forum (sec. 1989-91), Mideastern Assn. Ednl. Opportunity Program Pers. (Outstanding Svc. award 1990). Democrat. Baptist. Office: Bowie State U Jericho Park Rd Bowie MD 20715-3319

GILLAN, JOSEPH ANTHONY, chemicals executive; b. Amsterdam, N.Y., Feb. 19, 1940; s. Francis Joseph and Marie Katherine (Masten) G.; m. Mary Elizabeth Craig, 1965; children: Elizabeth Marie, Katherine Jane, Jennifer Ann. BA, Ithaca Coll., 1965. Reporter Rochester (N.Y.) Times-Union, 1960-62; pub. affairs advisor Champion Internat., N.Y.C., 1969-70; employee communications mgr. Babcock & Wilcox, N.Y.C., 1970-72; info. svcs. mgr. Johnson & Johnson, New Brunswick, N.J., 1972-74; sr. pub. affairs advisor Exxon Corp., N.Y.C., 1974-80; pub. affairs mgr. Exxon Chem. Europe, Brussels, 1980-83; asst. dir. pub. affairs Exxon Chem. Co., Darien, Conn., 1983—. Pres. Conn. Assn. for Children with Learning Disabilities, Norwalk, 1988—. With U.S. Army, 1961-64. Mem. Fairfield County MENSA, Thomas Wolfe Soc., N.Y. Road Runners Club.

GILLAN, MARIA MAZZIOTTI, poet, poetry center director; b. Paterson, N.J., Mar. 12, 1940; d. Arturo and Angelina (Schiavo) Mazziotti; m. Dennis P. Gillan, June 30, 1964; children: John Arthur, Jennifer Lisa. BA in Lit., Seton Hall U., 1961; MA in Lit., NYU, 1963; postgrad., Drew U., 1977-80. Poetry workshop leader Geraldine R. Dodge Found. Poetry Festival, Waterloo, 1986, 88, 90; with Geraldine R. Dodge Found. Com. of Poets, 1987—; Geraldine R. Dodge poetry tchr., 1986—; with poetry workshops connection between ethnicity and food Madison High Sch., 1988; poetry workshop leader Trenton State Writer's Conf., Trenton (N.J.) State Coll., 1988; panelist Pa. State Coun. on the Arts, 1988; poetry workshop leader Jamestown Community Coll., James Town, N.Y., 1989; dir. poetry ctr. Passaic County Community Coll., 1980—; presenter poetry Sta. WPFW, Nat. Pub. Radio, Washington, 1987, 88; presenter poetry to several orgns.; conductor poetry workshops Georgetown U., 1989, St. Norbert's Coll., Green Bay, Wis., 1990, So. Vt. Coll., Bennington, 1992. Author: Flowers From the Tree of Night, 1980, Winter Light, 1985, The Weather of Old Seasons, 1989, Luce D'Inverno, 1989, Cries of the Spirit, 1990, Taking Back My Name, 1991 (with others, anthologies) From the Margin: Readings in Italian-Americana, 1990, Lives in the Garden, 1989, Portraits of Poets, 1990, The Yearbook of American Poetry and Anthology of American Verse, 1986, The Dream Book, 1985 (Am. Book award 1986), The International Women Poets Anthology, 1990, Anthology of Italian-American Writers, 1989; editor Footwork: The Paterson Literary Rev., 1980—; mem. editorial bd. Voices in Italian Americana, 1992—; contb. articles and book revs. to profl. jours. Mem. bd. trustees Katharine Gibbs Sch., Dist. Alliance for Tourism, 1992; bd. dirs. Passaic County Cultural and Heritage Coun. Recipient Nat. Poetry Competiiton Commendation Chester H. Jones Found., 1989, Am. Literary Translators award, 1987, Editor's Choice award, 1985, Sri Chinmoy award, 1981, 82, 83, William Carlos Williams Contest award, 1972, 76; N.J. State Coun. on the Arts fellow in poetry, 1981, 85. Mem. Poets and Writers Inc., Poetry Soc. Am., Associated Writing Programs, Italian Am. Writers Assn., Modern Ethnic literature Soc. of the U.S., Assn. of Coll. & Univ. Arts Presenters. Home: 40 Post Ave Hawthorne NJ 07506-1809 Office: Passaic County Community Coll Poetry Ctr College Blvd Paterson NJ 07509

GILLELAND, LARUE WESLEY, journalism educator; b. St. Louis, Feb. 18, 1930; s. A. Wesley Gilleland and Agnes (Burd) Hutchison; m. Elizabeth Ross, June 22, 1962; children—Louise, Virginia, Michelle, Ross. Student, Central Mo. State, 1948-50; B.J., U. Mo., 1952, M.A., 1962. Reporter, Honolulu Advertiser, 1952-53; with advt.-dispatch dept. Los Angeles Times, 1953-54; newscaster sta. KVOO-TV, Tulsa, 1955; staff writer Comml. Appeal, Memphis, 1955-59; prof. U. Nevada-Reno, 1963-81, dept. chmn., 1976-81; prof. Northeastern U., Boston, 1981-82, dept. chmn., 1981-87, dir. Sch. Journalism, 1987-92, cons. 1992—; mem. accrediting Council Edn. in Journalism and Mass Communications, 1986-89. Author: GOSS Interviewing Technique, 1971; editor mag. Journalism Educator, 1969-76. Mem. central com. Washoe County Democratic Party, Reno, 1968-71; bd. dirs. Reno Philharmon. Symphony Orch., 1971-73. Mem. Soc. Profl. Journalists, Am. Soc. Journalism Sch. Adminstrs. (exec. dir. 1973-76, pres. 1979-80) service award 1980), Nev. State Press Assn., (service award 1981), New Eng. Press Assn. (bd. dirs 1982-92), Assn. for Edn. in Journalism (exec. com. 1979-80), Phi Kappa Phi, Kappa Tau Alpha. Home: 11 Three Ring Rd Scituate MA 02066-1441 Office: Northeastern U Sch Journalism Boston MA 02115

GILLER, ROBERT MAYNARD, physician; b. Chgo., Sept. 14, 1942; s. Edward M. and Lillian (Katz) G. Student, U. Ill., 1960-63, MD, 1967; postgrad., Columbia U., 1979—. Intern U. Ill., 1967-68; resident in internal medicine Cornell (N.Y.) Hosp., 1968-69; pvt. practice medicine specializing in preventive medicine Cornell (N.Y.) Hosp., N.Y.C., 1974—; faculty New Sch. Social Rsch., 1975—. Author: A Guide for Health, 1982, Medical Makeover, 1986, Maximum Metabolism, 1989. With M.C., U.S. Army, 1969-71. Fellow Am. Coll. Preventive Medicine, Internat. Acad. Preventive Medicine, Am. Acad. Family Physicians; mem. AMA (Physicians's Recognition award 1982). Office: 960 Park Ave New York NY 10028-0325

GILLESPIE, NICHOLAS JOHN, English scholar, educator; b. Bklyn., Aug. 7, 1963; s. John Thomas and Therese Agnes (Guida) G. BA in English, Psychology, Rutgers Coll., 1985; MA in English, Temple U., 1990; postgrad., SUNY, Buffalo, 1990—. Reporter Home News, New Brunswick, N.J., 1986; asst. editor Sterling Mags., N.Y.C., 1986-87; sr. assoc. editor Pilot Communications, N.Y.C., 1987-88; instr. Temple U., Phila., 1988-90, SUNY-Buffalo, 1990—. Contbr. short stories and articles to literary, popular mags.; editor Kiosk, 1990-91. Recipient Rutgers Alumni scholarship, 1985; Newton fellow Temple U., Phila., 1988, Presdl. fellow SUNY-Buffalo, 1990-93. Mem. MLA, Popular Culture Assn. Office: SUNY-Buffalo English Dept 305 Clemens Buffalo NY 14260

GILLESPIE, THOMAS FRANCIS, JR., collection industry executive; b. Phila., May 15, 1957; s. Thomas Francis and Marie H. (Scheer) G.; m. Debra Ann Townsend, May 6, 1978; children: Thomas III, Kevin, Tara. Assoc., Bucks County Community Coll., 1976. Buyer Gimbels, Phila., 1976-78; v.p. sales Fin. Collection Agys., Devon, Pa., 1978-86; pres., chief oper. officer Nat. Credit Mgmt. Corp., Cockeyville, Md., 1986—. Named finalist Entrepreneur of Yr. Inc. Mag., Merrill Lynch. Mem. Internat. Credit Assn., Ins. and Statis. Assn., Healthcare Fin. Mgmt., Balt. C. of C. Republican. Office: Nat Credit Mgmt Corp 10155 York Rd Ste 103 Cockeysville Hunt Valley MD 21030-3336

GILLESPIE, THOMAS WILLIAM, theological seminary administrator, religion educator; b. L.A., July 18, 1928; s. William A. and Estella (Beers) G.; m. Barbara A. Lugenbill, July 31, 1953; children: Robyn C., William T., Dayle E. B.A., George Pepperdine Coll., 1951; B.D., Princeton Theol. Seminary, 1954; Ph.D., Claremont Grad. Sch., 1971; DD (hon.), Grove City Coll., 1984; ThD (hon.), Theol. Acad. Debrecen, Hungary, 1988. Ordained to ministry Presbyterian Ch., 1954. Pastor 1st Presbyn. Ch., Garden Grove, Calif., 1954-66, Burlingame, Calif., 1966-83; pres., prof. N.T. Princeton (N.J.) Theol. Sem., 1983—. Served with USMC, 1946-47. Recipient A.A. Hodge prize in systematic theology Princeton Theol. Sem., 1953; Disting. Alumnus award Claremont Grad. Sch., 1984; Disting. Alumnus award Pepperdine U., 1986. Mem. Soc. Bibl. Lit. Republican. Lodge: Rotary Internat. (Burlingame). Home: Springdale 86 Mercer St Princeton NJ 08540-6819 Office: Princeton Theol Sem Office of Pres PO Box 552 Princeton NJ 08542-0552

GILLETTE, NORMAN JOHN, biology educator, retired; b. Cicero, N.Y., Mar. 17, 1911; s. Durward E. and Edna Mae (Wichie) G.; m. Elsie Himberg, Aug. 7, 1937; children: Elaine Susan, David Alan, Robert Kent. AB, Syracuse U., 1932, MA, 1933; PhD, U. Chgo., 1937. Assoc. prof. botany Univ. Idaho, Moscow, 1937-47, Syracuse (N.Y.) U., 1947-63; prof. biology SUNY, Oswego, 1963-76. Mem. Phi Beta Kappa, Sigma Xi, Gamma Alpha. Republican. Methodist. Home: PO Box 138 Rt # 3 Brown Dr Oswego NY 13126

GILLI, ANGELO CHRISTOPHER, SR., education consulting company executive; b. Windsor, Conn., Apr. 20, 1925; s. Saturno and Josephine (Magenta) G.; m. Lynne Marie Moore, Dec. 22, 1983. BS, Cen. Conn. State U., 1949; MA, U. Conn., 1952; EdD, SUNY, Buffalo, 1967. Instr. electronics, dept. chair New England Tech. Inst., 1953-55, Hartford Tech. Coll., 1955-63; prof., chair career program Niagara County Community Coll., 1963-65; assoc. prof. Rutgers U., New Brunswick, N.J., 1966-68; prof., co-chair vocat. edn. Pa. State U., University Park, 1968-76; prof. Tex. Southern U., Houston, 1976-79; prof. Coll. Technology SUNY, 1979-82; specialist Md. Dept. Edn., 1982-87; pres. IDEAS, Inc., Pasadena, Md., 1987—. Author 11 textbooks on electronics and edn., 1960—; book reviewer and newsletter editor: Edn. News, Mfg. Matters. With USNR, 1942-46. Mem. Am. Assn. Higher Edn. (life), Am. Vocat. Assn. (life). Home and Office: 8016 Tower Bridge Dr Pasadena MD 21122-6406

GILLI, LYNNE MARIE, academic administrator; b. Sidney, N.Y., May 4, 1954; d. Joseph Gerard and Marie Jane (Lese) Moore; m. Angelo Christopher Gilli, Sr., Dec. 22, 1983. BS, SUNY, Utica, 1978, MS, 1979; EdD, SUNY, Buffalo, 1983. Cert. ednl. adminstr. Tchr. Western Del. Bd. Coop. Ednl. Svcs., Sidney Center, N.Y., 1977-81; grad. asst. SUNY, Buffalo, 1981-82; specialist Div. Career and Tech. Edn. Md. State Dept. Edn., Balt., 1982-88, sect. chief, 1988-89, br. chief, 1989—. Contbr. articles to profl. jours. Mem. Am. Vocat. Assn. (life). Home: 8016 Tower Bridge Dr Pasadena MD 21122-6406 Office: Md State Dept Edn 200 W Baltimore St Baltimore MD 21201-2595

GILLILLAND, THOMAS, government official; b. Bladen, Nebr., Feb. 14, 1932; s. Whitney and Virginia (Wegmann) G.; m. Cora Lee Critchfield, Aug. 23, 1956; children: Shaun, Ruth, Virginia. Grad., Wentworth Mil. Acad., 1952; BA, Am. U., 1963, MA, 1967. Dep. dir. congl. liaison AID, Washington, 1969-75; congl. liaison officer USDA, Washington, 1975-76, dir. legis. affairs Animal and Plant Health Inspection Svc., 1976-83; dir. external affairs Fin. Mgmt. Svc. U.S. Dept. Treasury, Washington, 1983—. Contbr. mag. articles on barbershop music. Mem. Assn. Govt. Accts., Nat. Assn. Govt. Communicators (Blue Pencil award 1986), Soc. for Preservation and Encouragement Barbershop Quartet Singing in Am., Nat. Press Club. Republican. Presbyterian. Home: 300 E Broad St Falls Church VA 22046-3503 Office: US Dept Treasury Fin Mgmt Svc Washington DC 20227

GILLINGHAM, STEPHEN THOMAS, lawyer; b. St. Paul, May 30, 1944; s. Thomas Elmwood and Barbara Alice (Sickles) G.; m. Carolyn Jean Alvey, June 5, 1976; children: Kenneth, Brett. BA, Juniata Coll., 1966; JD, The George Washington Law Sch., 1969. Bar: Va. 1971. Tax specialist Price Waterhouse, Washington, 1969-71; tax law specialist IRS, Washington, 1971-77; sr. tax lawyer Internat. Paper Co., N.Y.C., 1977-83; dir. tax rsch. and planning The Singer Co., Stanford, Conn., 1983-88; tax counsel Am. Cyanamid Co., Wayne, N.J., 1988—; lectr. World Trade Inst., 1980—. Contbg. editor Tax Lawyer, 1984-88. With U.S. Army, 1970-75. Named one of Outstanding Young Men in Am., Jaycees, 1979. Mem. ABA, Va. Bar Assn., N.J. Tax Group (chmn. 1991—), Tax Execs. Inst. Home: 4 Northway Hartsdale NY 10530

GILLINSON, ANDREW STUART, communications executive; b. Stoke-on-Trent, Eng., Aug. 5, 1948; came to U.S., 1955; s. Roy Stuart and Joan Monica (Keatman) G.; m. Pamela Grant Hall, Dec. 11, 1971. AB, Brandeis U., 1969. From copywriter to sr. creative group supr. W.B. Doner & Co., Balt., 1970-78; v.p., creative Vansant Dugdale & Co., Balt., 1978-81; sr. exec. writer SmithKline Beckman, Phila., 1981-84; v.p. and creative dir. Foote

Cone & Belding, Phila., 1984-86; pres. Andrew Gillinson Communications, Wayne, Pa., 1986—. Active The English Speaking Union of the U.S., Phila., 1989, ARC, Phila., 1986. Mem. Am. Mktg. Assn.

GILLIS, DONALD PAUL, community theater director, producer; b. Providence, Apr. 12, 1941; s. Douglas Eugene and Anna Clementina (Broderick) G.; m. Diane Estelle Weldon, Oct. 10, 1964; children: Christopher Paul, Gregory Austin. BA, Providence Coll., 1972. Treas. Community Players Pawtucket, R.I., 1977-78, 88—, pres., 1984-85, choreographer, 1977—, producer, 1977—, dir., 1988, 90, also actor, dancer in prodns. MSgt. R.I. Air NG, 1963—. Mem. Am. Assn. Community Theatre. Democrat. Roman Catholic. Home: 115 Tremont St Pawtucket RI 02863-1421 Office: RI Air NG Quonset SAP North Kingstown RI 02852

GILLIS, RICHARD AUSTIN, university administrator; b. Brighton, Mass., May 9, 1953; s. Austin William and Louise (Scully) G.; m. Karen Jo Reiber, Aug. 7, 1988. B.Liberal Arts, Harvard U., 1985. Pub. info. asst. Mass. Housing Fin. Agy., Boston, 1979-82; coord. ednl. resources Harvard Med. Sch., Boston, 1983—, dir. ednl. resources, 1988—; cons. med. edn. tech., 1991—. Contbr. articles on edn. and orgns. to Boston Globe, 1985. Mem. Am. Mgmt. Assn. Democrat. Roman Catholic. Office: Harvard Med Sch 260 Longwood Ave Boston MA 02115-5720

GILLIS, WAYNE ANTHONY, dean; b. Niagara Falls, N.Y., Jan. 8, 1943; s. Donald V. and Margaret A. (Johnson) G.; m. Carol V. Lockwood; children: Kristine, David, Kathryn. AAS, SUNY, Morrisville, 1963; BS, Cornell U., 1965, PhD, 1971; MS, Okla. State U., 1968. Asst. prof. animal sci. dept. U. Guelph, Ont., Can., 1970-73; assoc. dir. animal prodn. div. Can. Dept. Agr., Ottawa, 1973-84; dean, prof. Platteville Coll. Agr. U. Wis., 1984-90; dean Sch. of Agr. and Natural Resources SUNY, 1990—; farmer, St. Isidore, Ont., Can., 1973-84; freelance animal judge, Eaton, N.Y., 1970—. Co-inventor meat tenderization method. Chairman Grant County Dems., Wis., 1989. Mem. N.Y. State Angus Assn. (bd. dirs. Earlville chpt. 1990—).

GILLISPIE, CHARLES COULSTON, history of science educator; b. Harrisburg, Pa., Aug. 6, 1918; s. Raymond Livingston and Virginia Lambert (Coulston) G.; m. Emily Ramsdell Clapp, Jan. 29, 1949. A.B., Wesleyan U., Middletown, Conn., 1940, M.A., 1942, D.Sc., 1971; student, MIT, 1940-41; Ph.D., Harvard U., 1949. Teaching fellow, tutor history Harvard U., 1946-47; faculty Princeton U., 1947-87, prof. history sci., 1959-67, Shelby Cullom Davis prof. European history, 1967-73, Dayton-Stockton prof. history, 1973-87, prof. emeritus, 1987—, chmn. dept. history, 1971-73, dir. program in history and philosophy of sci., 1960-66, 76-80; A.J. Balfour prof. history sci. Weizmann Inst., Israel, 1972; assoc. dir. studies Ecole des Hautes Etudes en Sciences Sociales, Paris, 1980-87. Author: Genesis and Geology, 1951, A Diderot Pictorial Encyclopedia of Trades and Industry, 2 vols, 1959, The Edge of Objectivity: An essay in the History of Scientific Ideas, 1960, Lazare Carnot, Savant, 1971, Science and Polity in France at the End of the Old Regime, 1980, The Montgolfier Brothers and the Invention of Aviation, 1783-1784, 1983, Monuments of Egypt, 1987; Editor-in-chief: Dictionary of Scientific Biography. Bd. mgrs. Bach Choir, Bethlehem, Pa., 1976-80. Served to capt. C.W.S. AUS, 1942- 45. Decorated officier Ordre des Palmes Académiques (France), 1989; fellow Am. Coun. Learned Socs., 1951-52, Guggenheim fellow, 1954-55, 70-71, NSF fellow, 1958-59, 62-63, fellow Ctr. for Advanced Study in Behavioral Scis., 1970-71; chaire d'histoire des Sciences, Fondation de France, 1980-82, 85-87. Fellow AAAS; mem. History Sci. Soc. (council 1952-55, 59-60, pres. 1964-66), Am. Acad. Arts and Scis., Académie Internationale d' Histoire des Sciences (v.p. 1965-68), N.Y. Acad. Scis. (hon. life mem.), Am. Philos. Soc., Phi Beta Kappa, Sigma Xi; corr. fellow Brit. Acad. Clubs: Princeton (N.Y.C.); Nassau (Princeton, N.J.), Franklin Inn (Phila.). Home: 3 Morgan Pl Princeton NJ 08540-2609

GILLMAN, RICHARD, company executive; b. Newark, June 5, 1931; s. Julius and Betty (Prager) G.; m. Shaldine Henoch, Apr. 3, 1960; children: Scott, Marc. B.B.A., U. Miami(Fla.), 1954; postgrad., Seton Hall U., 1950-51. Gen. ptnr. Edwards & Hanley, N.Y.C., 1966-74; v.p., dir. Bally Mfg. Corp., N.Y.C., 1974-79; now pres., COO Bally Mfg. Corp., Chgo.; chmn. bd. Bally's Park Place Inc., Atlantic City, N.J., 1979—; pres. Bally's casino hotels, Atlantic City, Las Vegas and Reno; dir. Waxman Industries, Cleve., 1975—. Bd. dirs. Atlantic City Casino Hotel Assn., 1983—; bd. dirs. Atlantic City Conv. Bur., 1983—, Miss. Am. Pageant, 1982. Mem. N.Y. Stock Exchange. Lodges: Binai B'rith; Masons. Home: Claridge 1 Vernon NJ 07044 Office: Bally's Park Pl Inc Park Pl and Boardwalk Atlantic City NJ 08401 also: Bally's 3645 Las Vegas Blvd S Las Vegas NV 89109-4307*

GILLY, PHILIP ALAIN, physician; b. Bklyn., Dec. 9, 1956; s. Jacques Michel and Elinore (Margolis) G.; m. Rondi Ellen Brower, Aug. 18, 1985. BA, Johns Hopkins U., 1978; MD, NYU, 1982. Diplomate Am. Bd. Family Practice. Intern, then resident in family practice St. Paul Hosp., Dallas, 1982-85; pvt. practice Dallas, 1985-86; civilian med. officer U.S. Army, Landstuhl, Fed. Republic Germany, 1986-90; family physician Community Health Plan, Hudson, N.Y., 1990—. Contbr. articles to med. jours. Mem. Am. Heart Assn. Recipient Physician's Recognition award AMA, 1985—. Fellow Am. Acad. Family Physicians; mem. N.Y. Acad. Scis. Democrat. Office: 713 Union St Hudson NY 12534-3001

GILMAN, BENJAMIN ARTHUR, congressman; b. Poughkeepsie, N.Y., Dec. 6, 1922; s. Harry and Esther (Gold) G.; m. Jane Prizant, Oct. 19, 1952 (div. 1978); children: Jonathan, Harrison, Susan, David (dec.), Ellen (dec.); m. Rita Gail Keller, Nov. 9, 1984; children: Alan Craig Kelhoffer, Eric Roy Kelhoffer. B.S., U. Pa., 1946; LL.B., N.Y. Law Sch., 1950. Bar: N.Y. 1952. Dep. asst. atty. gen. N.Y. Dept. Law, 1952-54, asst. atty. gen., 1954-55; partner firm Gilman & Gilman, Middletown, N.Y., 1955-72; counsel N.Y. Assembly's Com. on Local Finance, 1956-64; N.Y. Assemblyman 95th Dist., 1967-72; mem. 93d-97th Congresses from 26th N.Y. dist., 1972-82, 98th-102nd Congresses from 22d N.Y. dist., 1983—; mem. select com. on Hunger, Fgn. Affairs, Post Office and Civil Service coms., Select Com. on Narcotics; congl. rep. UN Law of Sea Conf., 1975-81, IMF Conf., 1975-78; del. U.S.-Mexican Interparliamentary Conf., 1976-87; mem. Ukrainian Famine Commn., 1986-91; co-chair U.S.-European Interparliamentary Conf.; mem. Presdl. Commn. on World Hunger, 1978-80, Ad-Hoc Com. on Irish Affairs, Republican Task Force on Handicapped and Task Force on Econ. Policy; mem. U.S.-Mex. Consultative Mechanism Subcom. on Narcotics Trafficking; U.S. rep. to 36th session UN Gen. Assembly; chmn. House Task Force on Missing in Action, 1983-85, vice chmn., 1985—; mem. World Hunger Yr. Bd.; mem. adv. com. N.Y. State Div. Youth's Start Ctr., 1962-67; mem. N.Y. State Southeastern Water Study Com., 1971-73, Lawyers' Com. for Civil Rights Under Law, 1963-75; mem. adv. com. Otisville Fed. Correctional Instn.; v.p., bd. dirs. Orange County Health Assn.; adv. council Lamont-Doherty Geol. Obs., Columbia U., 1979-82. Chmn. bd. dirs. Middletown Little League; bd. dirs. Goldenarea Hosp. Fund; bd. visitors U.S. Mil. Acad., 1973-83; lt. col. CAP. Served with USAAF, 1943-45; to col. USNG. Decorated D.F.C., Air medal. Mem. ABA, D.C. Bar Assn., N.Y. State Bar Assn., Assn. of Bar of City of N.Y., Middletown Bar Assn., Orange County Bar Assn., Assn. Trial Lawyers Am., VFW (past county comdr.), Am. Legion, Masonic War Vets. (lt. comdr.), Jewish War Vets., Forty and Eight, Air Force Assn., Internat. Narcotics Enforcement Officers, N.Y. Law Sch. Alumni (bd. dirs.), N.Y. Soc. in Washington (pres.), Grange, La Société des 40 Hommes et 8 Chevaux. Republican. Jewish. Lodges: Masons, Capitol Hill Shriners (pres.), Elks. Office: US Ho of Reps 2185 Rayburn House Office Bldg Washington DC 20515

GILMAN, JONATHAN CHARLES, financial planner; b. Norwich, Conn., July 30, 1953; s. Charles Murry and Mary Jane (Evans) G.; m. Beverly Ann Schilling, June 11, 1977; children: Nathan A., Nicholas, John. BA in Polit. Sci., Baldwin-Wallace Coll., 1977. V.p. Strategic Capital Corp, Gilman; sales rep. individual fin. svcs. div. Conn. Gen. Ins. Co. div. Cigna Corp., Bloomfield, Conn., 1977-84; pres., owner Gilman (Conn.) Fin. Svcs., 1985—, Gilman Planning Svcs., Inc., 1985—, Gilman Realty Co., 1987—; gen. agt. Chubb Life Am., Concord, N.H., 1985-86; ptnr. Gilman, Beckwith, Trantalis & Assocs., 1989-90; v.p. Strategic Capital Corp., Gilman, 1991—; registered rep. Robert Thomas Securities, Inc., N.Y.C., 1990—, Broad Reach Capital, Inc., Avon, Conn., 1985-90. Justice of peace Town of Bozrah, Conn., 1986; treas. Bozrah Rep. Town Com., 1987-90; chmn. Bozrah Econ. Devel. Commn., 1985, sec., 1986; chmn. Mohegan dist. Indian Trails coun. Boy Scouts Am., 1987-90, dist. vice-chmn. adminstrn., 1990—, mem. com. pack 77, 1990—, com. chmn. 1987-89; mem. Southeastern Conn. Econ. Devel. Coalition, 1991—; asst. scoutmaster Boy Scouts Am. Troop 77, Bozrah, 1992; chmn. large corp. gifts London Symphony Orch., 1991-92. Recipient Spark Plug award Boy Scouts Am., 1989, Oscar award Boy Scouts Am., 1990. Mem. Internat. Assn. Fin. Planners (mem. edn. com. Conn. chpt. 1986, Outstanding Com. Mem. award 1986, v.p. program com. 1987, at-large bd. dirs. 1987, chmn. spring conf.), Conn. Bus. and INdustry Assn., Eastern Conn. Area C. of C. (econ. devel. com. 1986—, govtl. affairs com. 1988—, pres. leadership program 1988-89), Rotary (chmn. internat. youth exch. program Norwich club 1988, co-chmn. Norwich Rose arts pancake breakfast 1989), Masons (worshipful master local lodge 1987). Home: 20 Gilman Rd Gilman CT 06336 Office: Gilman Fin Svcs 25 Gilman Rd Gilman CT 06336

GILMAN, NORMAN WASHBURN, organic chemist; b. Augusta, Maine, June 6, 1938; s. Frank A. Gilman and Helene D. (Washburn) Dorr; m. Diane P. Poulin, July 12, 1958; children: Craig S., Jennifer K. PhD, Princeton U., 1967. Rsch. investigator Hoffmann-LaRoche Inc., Nutley, N.J., 1968—. Cpl. USMC, 1956-59. Mem. AAAS, Am. Chem. Soc., Sigma Xi, Alpha Chi Sigma. Home: 5 Normandy Dr Wayne NJ 07470-2817 Office: Hoffmann-LaRoche Inc 340 Kingsland St Nutley NJ 07110-1199

GILMARTIN, JOHN A., medical products company executive; b. 1942. BS, Penn. State U., 1965; MBA, Havard U., 1967. With Pfizer Inc., 1966-79, v.p., group contr., 1967-79; with Millipore Corp., 1979—, contr., sr. v.p., pres., chief exec. officer, then also chmn. bd., chief oper. officer, 1986—. Office: Millipore Corp 80 Ashby Rd PO Box 255 Bedford MA 01730

GILMOND, JAMES EDWARD, headmaster, director of education; b. Worcester, Mass., May 8, 1949; s. Harry Frederick and Barbara Anne (Robinson) G. BA, Middlebury Coll., 197l; MEd, Assumption Coll., Worcester, 1975, MA, 1990. Cert. secondary English tchr., spl. edn. Head teller Guaranty Bank and Trust Co., Worcester, 197l-72; tchr. English Shrewsbury (Mass.) Jr. High Sch., 1972-75; asst. media coord. Polit. Cons., Inc., Westchester, N.Y., 1976; pub. rels. coord. Horizons for Youth, Sharon, Mass., 1977-79; program coord. Ashland (Mass.) Edn. Community Ctr., 1980; spl. edn. tchr. Devereux Sch., Rutland, Mass., 198l-82; team leader RZR, Inc., Concord, Mass., 1983-86; spl. edn. tchr. Burns Prep. Sch./YOU, Inc., Worcester, 1986-87, dir. edn., 1987-90; headmaster Burns Prep Sch./YOU Inc., Worcester, 1991—; cons., speaker John F. Kennedy Libr., Boston, 1988—; cons. Harmony (R.I.) Hill Sch., 1989—, Northboro/Southboro Schs. (Mass.), 1989—; cons. law related edn. program Dist. Ct. Dept., Boston, 1988—; state trainer Nat. Inst. for Citizen Edn. in Law, 1989—; mem. steering com. Juvenile Justice Initiative, Office Juvenile Justice and Delinquency Prevention, 1990—; nat. cons. in spl. edn. Juvenile Justice Initiative, 1990—. Co-editor: Language Arts Curriculum, K-12, 1975. Founder Worcester Area Law-Related Edn. Adv. Bd., 1989; co-founder Support and Encouragement Network for Spl. Educators, Worcester, 1989. Grantee John F. Kennedy Libr., 1987; law-related edn. fellow Mass. Supreme and Dist. Cts., 1988. Mem. Nat. Welfare League, Nat. Coun. for Social Studies, Nat. Assn. Secondary Sch. Prins., Assn. for Supervision and Curriculum Devel., Mass. Computer Using Educators, Mass. Assn. for Law-Related Edn. Office: Burns Prep Sch/YOU Inc 81 Plantation St Worcester MA 01604

GILMORE, BARBARA ELEANOR SALE, draftsman; b. Honolulu, Mar. 26, 1932; d. Charles Smith and Margaret Blake (Moss) Sale; m. Jerome N. Gilmore (div. 1960); children: Deborah Christine Gilmore Atchison, Daphne Victoria Gilmore McConnell. Student, Moore Inst. of Art, 1950-51, George Washington U., 1958-59, Smithsonian Inst., 1990. Draftsman Washington Suburban San. Commn., Hyattsville, Md., 1953-55, Michael Baker Jr. Inc., College Park, Md., 1957-59, Ewin Engring., Washington, 1959-62, Greenhorne & O'Mara, Riverdale, Md., 1962-66, Tallamy, Byrd, MacDonald & Lewis, Fairfax, Va., 1967-70, Daniel, Mann, Johnson & Mendenhall, Washington, 1973, Ben Dyer Assoc., Riverdale, Md., 1974, Hubbard & Hoffman, Riverdale, 1974, Assoc. Engrs., Silver Spring, Md., 1984—. Author: Portrait of A Modern City at the Turn of the Millenium, 1990 (Golden award, Hon. Mention). Vol. ARC, Washington, 1960-65. Republican. Episcopalian. Home: Apt 1227-A 8750 Georgia Ave Silver Spring MD 20910-3603 Office: Assoc Engrs Inc 8555 16th St Silver Spring MD 20910-2802

GILMORE, JOHN VAUGHN, JR., clinical psychologist; b. Boston, Aug. 6, 1948; s. John Vaughn and Eunice Chandler (Crocker) G. MDiv, Gordon-Conwell Sem., 1976; MTh, Princeton Theol. Sem., 1977; PhD, Mich. State U., 1984. Lic. psychologist, Calif. Clin. chaplain intern Princeton (N.J.) U. Med. Ctr., 1976-77; counseling intern Personality Dynamics, Southfield, Mich., 1978-79; psychologist Profl. Psychol. Cons., East Lansing, Mich., 1980-8l, Los Angeles County Dept. Mental Health, L.A., 1984-85; clin. psychology intern Psychol. Ctr., Pasadena, Calif., 198l-82; adminstrv. dir. I-Can Program, Pasadena, 1982-84; supervising psychologist Pacific Clinics, Pasadena, 1985-87; pres. John V. Gilmore Psychology Corp., Covina, Calif., 1988-89; forensic psychologist Taunton Secure Care Program, 1989—. Ednl. Testing Svc. rsch. grantee, 1976. Fellow Mass. Psychol. Assn.; mem. Am. Psychol. Assn., Am. Soc. for Psychology and Law. Office: Taunton State Hosp Howland Bldg Taunton MA 02780

GILMORE, ROBERT AMES, advertising executive; b. Brockton, Mass., Dec. 8, 1930; s. Wallace S. and Anna A. (Ames) G.; m. Janet L. Skinner, Dec. 24, 1951 (div. 1981); children: Amanda, Jon, Robert, Pamela, Holly, Julie, Peter, Keith. BS, Boston U., 1952, MS, 1953. Dir. WNET-TV, Providence, 1952-53; dir. of TV MIT, Cambridge, 1954-57; exec. prodn. dir. WHDH-TV, Boston, 1958-68; owner, pres. Robert Gilmore Assn., Inc., Dedham, Mass., 1969—; pres. The Gilmore Group.; producer Man, Ideas, Tech.-Nova, MIT, 1954. Dir. TV, Dateline Boston, 1964, City of N.Y. Traffic, 1966; dir. training videos including John Hancock, 1987, Dunkin Donuts, 1983, Data General, 1986; exec. producer Carrol Reed Ski, 1986, Head Skiis, 1987. Cons., producer Salvation Army, Boston, 1989—, Boston U. Ad Internat., 1987—. Recipient Telly award, 1988, 89. Mem. Advt. Club of Boston (producer, cons. 1978-79), MIT Faculty Club (life), Internat. TV Assn., New Eng. Producers Assn., Creative Club of Boston. Office: Gilmore Prodns 990 Washington Dedham MA 02026

GILMORE, RUSSELL STANLEY, curator, historian; b. Kansas City, Mo., Dec. 27, 1936; s. Howard Stanley and LaVange (Wescott) G. B.A. magna cum laude, Tex. Christian U., 1963; M.A. (Univ. fellow), U. Wis., Madison, 1965, Ph.D. (Vilas fellow), 1974. Supr. office field services State Hist. Soc. Wis., Madison, 1965-68; curator Wis. Vets. Mus., Madison, 1971-77; curator Army Mus. System, 1977—, curator-dir. Harbor Def. Mus. N.Y.C., Bklyn., 1980—; cons. Cambridge U. Press, 1983—. Author: Guarding America's Front Door: Harbor Forts in the Defense of New York City, 1983; also articles. Chmn. Museums Coun. N.Y.C., 1986-88. Served with U.S. Army, 1960-62. Recipient Smithsonian study award, 1976; Moncado prize Am. Mil. Inst., 1978; Army award for civilian service, 1985. Fellow Co. Mil. Historians; mem. Am. Assn. State and Local History (seminar fellow 1975), Com. Mil. Mus. Am., Council Am. Mil. Past, Am. Assn. Mus., Internat. Council Mus., Fortress Study Group (Gt. Britain), Orgn. Am. Historians, Soc. for History in Fed. Govt., Museums Council of N.Y.C. (chmn. 1986-88), Met. Hist. Structures Assn. (dir.), Ft. Hamilton Hist. Soc. (dir.), Armor and Arms Club N.Y.C. (hon.). Office: Harbor Def Mus Ft Hamilton Brooklyn NY 11252

GILMORE, THOMAS MEYER, trade association administrator, secretary; b. Millheim, Pa., Mar. 10, 1942; s. Harold Grant and Phyllis (Meyer) G.; m. Linda Steiglitz, June 23, 1972; children: Joshua Paul, Megan Elizabeth. BS, Lock Haven (Pa.) U., 1965; MS in Organic Chemistry, U. Del., 1970; PhD in Food Sci., Pa. State U., 1976. Instr. U. Del., Georgetown, 1967-72; prof. Del. Tech. & Community Coll., Georgetown, 1975-78; asst. prof. S.D. State U., Brookings, 1978-82; sr. food technologist Hershey (Pa.) Foods Corp., 1982-85; tech. dir. Dairy & Food Industry Supply Assn., Rockville, Md., 1985—; tech. rep. to ANSI/ISO TC-199 (safety and hygiene requirements for machinery). Contbr. articles to profl. jours. Vestry St. Pauls Episcopal Ch., Brookings, 1979-82; sr. warden, vestry, Grace Episcopal Ch., New Market, Md., 1987-90; pres. Brookings Lions, 1981. Mem. NEA (life), ASTM, Internat. Platform Soc., Am. Soc. Agrl. Engrs., Internat. Assn. Milk, Food, Environ. Sanitations, Am. Dairy Sci. Assn. (profl. sec. dairy food div. 1987-90), Inst. Food Tech. (counselor Washington chpt. 1987—, treas. Keystone chpt. 1985, exec. coun. dairy tech. div. 1987-88), N.E. Dairy Practice Coun., Internat. Dairy Fedn. (com. mem. experts on hygenic design dairy processing equip., chem. rep. to Fredrick Co. sludge task force). Democrat. Home: 4645 Lynn Burke Rd Monrovia MD 21770-9428 Office: Dairy & Food Industries 6245 Executive Blvd Rockville MD 20852-3938

GILMOUR, ROBERT ARTHUR, foundation executive, educator; b. L.A., Dec. 13, 1944; s. Leon and Helen (Lawrence) G.; m. Cathryn Anne Fontana, June 23, 1979; 1 child, Cathryn Elizabeth. AB magna cum laude, U. Calif., Davis, 1966; MA, Johns Hopkins U., 1969, PhD, 1972. Lectr. history U. Mich., Ann Arbor, 1970-72; asst. prof. U. Mich., 1972, Northwestern U., Evanston, Ill., 1972-75, Princeton (N.J.) U., 1975-81; rsch. fellow Am. Inst. for Econ. Rsch., Great Barrington, Mass., 1983; sr. assoc. Am. Inst. for Econ. Rsch., 1983-85; dir. rsch. Am. Inst. for Econ. Rsch., Great Barrington, Mass., 1985-91; chmn. faculty Am. Inst. for Econ. Rsch., Great Barrington, 1985-91, pres., chief exec. officer, 1991—. Author: The Other Emancipation, 1972, How to Cover the Gaps in Medicare, 1983, America's Unknown Enemy, 1984, How to Cover the Gaps in Medicare after Catastrophic Coverage, 1989; co-author: (with L. Pratt) Coping with College Costs, 1987; gen. editor monetary conf. series Progress Found., Carona, Switzerland, 1988—. Trustee Berkshire Community Coll. Found., Pittsfield, Mass., 1982-84; mem. AIER Corp., Great Barrington, 1985—, Fin. Com., Peru, Mass., 1987-90; counsel for charitable activities Progress Found., 1991—. Mem. AAAS, Am. Econ. Assn., Am. Fin. Assn., Phi Beta Kappa, Phi Kappa Phi. Office: AIER E C Harwood Libr Division St Great Barrington MA 01230-1115

GILPATRIC, LAWRENCE, education educator; b. Bridgeport, Conn., Aug. 3, 1948; s. Ralph Edwin and Doris Rose (McCormack) G.; m. Suzanne Bronstein, Aug. 10, 1975; children: Rebecca Lynn, Jeremy Todd, Brendan Scott. AS, Manchester Community Coll., 1978; BS, Charter Oak Coll., 1990; MS, Cen. Conn. State U., 1991. Cert. hotel administrator. Exec. chef Holiday Inns, New London, Conn., 1971-73; chef mgr. Szabo Food Svc., Hartford, Conn., 1973-74; chef instr. Assoc. Restaurants of Conn., Hartford, Conn., 1974-77; exec. chef Burning Tree Country Club, Greenwich, Conn., 1977-79; pres. Stowe's Pilot House Restaurant, West Haven, Conn., 1979-81; exec. chef Coveleigh Club, Rye, N.Y., 1981-84; gen. mgr. H. B. Brownson Country Club, Huntington, Conn., 1984-88; asst. prof. South Cen. Community Coll., New Haven, 1987—; interim gen. mgr. Winged Foot Golf Club, Mamaroneck, N.Y., 1991. Lector St. Vincent Ferrer Ch., Naugatuck, Conn., 1990—. With USMC, 1966-69. H. J. Heinz Grad. fellow The Edn. Found. of Nat. Restaurant Assn., 1991; recipient Silver Plate scholarship Nat. Inst. Foodservice Industry, 1977, Excellence in Edn. award, 1991. Home: 195 Evening Star Dr Naugatuck CT 06770-3507 Office: South Ctrl Community Coll 60 Sargent Dr New Haven CT 06511-5970

GILPATRICK, ELEANOR, educator; b. N.Y.C., Oct. 29, 1930; d. Murry and Essie (Hirsch) Gottesfocht. BA, CUNY, 1951; MA, New Sch. for Social Rsch., 1959; PhD, Cornell U., 1964. Instr. Cornell U., Ithaca, N.Y., 1963-64; rsch. asst. prof. U. Ill., Urbana, 1964-66; sr. rsch. assoc. Skill Advancement Inc., N.Y.C., 1966-67; dir. Health Svcs. Mobility Study, N.Y.C., 1968-78; assoc. prof. Hunter Coll. Sch. of Health Scis., N.Y.C., 1968-81, program dir. allied health svcs. adminstrn., 1982—; prof. Hunter Coll. Sch. of Health Scis., 1981—. Author: Grants for Non-profit Organizations, 1989, The Occupational Structure of N.Y.C. Municipal Hospitals, 1970, Structural Unemployment and Aggregate Demand, 1966; contbr. articles to profl. jours. Home: 302 W 12th St New York NY 10014-1945 Office: Hunter Coll 425 E 25th St New York NY 10010-2590

GILREATH, JERRY HOLLANDSWORTH, urban planner; b. Smithville, Tenn., Jan. 19, 1934; s. Homer Freeman and Wallee (Hollandsworth) G.; m. Ellen Johnston, June 15, 1974; 1 child, Kathryn Ann. BS, Mid. Tenn. State Coll., 1956; MS in Planning, U. Tenn., 1972. Editor UPI, Frankfurt, Fed. Republic of Germany, 1959-60; proofreader Jones Composition, Inc., Washington, 1961-62; publ. asst. Am. Geophysical Union, Washington, 1963-65; editorial asst. Library of Congress, Washington, 1965-67, mgmt. technician, 1968-69; community planner Nat. Capital Planning Commn., Washington, 1972—. Principal author numerous planning reports, 1976-85. With U.S. Army, 1956-59. Mem. Am. Planning Assn. Democrat. Club: Little Falls Swimming and Tennis (Bethesda, Md.). Home: 4806 Westway Dr Bethesda MD 20816-1726 Office: Nat Capital Planning Commn 801 Pennsylvania Ave NW # 301 Washington DC 20576-0001

GILREIN, SEAN MICHAEL, educational consultant; b. Worcester, Mass., June 29, 1960; s. James Anthony and Marie T. (Sheanan) G.; m. Sarah Jean Carpenter, Feb. 18, 1984; children: Christopher Jordan, Taryn Elizabeth. BS, Westfield State Coll., 1982; MEd, Worcester State Coll., 1988. Tchr. Project Coffee, Oxford, Mass., 1983-88, ednl. cons., 1986—, prin., 1988—; recruitment coord. High Performers Acad., 1984; curriculm supr. Project 50/50, 1984-88; adminstrv. liaison JTPA, 1988—; dir. Project Jobs, 1988-89. Mem. com. Project F.A.S.T., 1990—. Mem. Nat. Edn. Assn., Mass. Tchrs. Assn., Oxford Adminstr. Assn., Nat. Dropout Prevention Network, Mass. Assn. Pupil Transp., Nat. Diffusion Network (presenter). Democrat. Roman Catholic. Office: Project Coffee Main St Oxford MA 01540-2812

GILSDORF, MARY JO B., lawyer; b. Englewood, N.J., June 25, 1957; d. Robert Thomas and Nina Mae (Whitecap) G. BFA, U. Del., 1980; Paralegal Cert. with honors, Widener U., 1982; JD, Villanova U., 1989. Bar: Pa. 1989, U.S. Dist. Ct. (ea. dist.) Pa. 1989, N.J. 1989, U.S. Dist. Ct. N.J. 1989, C.C. 1990, U.S. Ct. Appeals (3d and D.C. cirs.) 1990, D.C. 1991. Paralegal Kassab, Cherry & Archibald, Media, Pa., 1982; paralegal Blank, Rome, Comisky & McCauley, Phila., 1982-86, law clk., 1987-89, assoc., 1989-91; assoc. Manko, Gold & Katcher, Bala Cynwyd, 1991—. Mem. ABA, Pa. Bar Assn., Phila. Bar Assn. (sec. environ. law com. 1989-92), N.J. Bar Assn., D.C. Bar Assn. Office: Manko Gold & Katcher 401 E City Ave Ste 500 Bala Cynwyd PA 19004-1167

GILSON, GILES PICKERING, fine arts, industrial arts, industrial design; b. Phila., July 19, 1942; s. Harry Rodgers and Francis Burrett (Iredell) G.; m. Betsy Cotton Gilson, Aug. 23, 1981; 1 child, Krys Cotton Gilson. Artist pvt. practice, Schenectady, N.Y., 1966—. Exhibits include Cooper, Hewitt Mus., N.Y.C., Met. Mus. Art, N.Y.C., Greenville (S.C.) County Mus. Art, Tampa (Fla.) Mus. Art, Kagan Gallery, Phila., Elements Gallery, N.Y.C., Seraph Gallery, Washington, DelMano Gallery, L.A., Contemporary Artisans Gallery, San Francisco, Ind. State U., Indpls., Carosell Bldg., St. Louis Mitchell Mus., Mt. Vernon, Ill., Arrowmont Show, Gatlinburg, Tenn. Art com. Empire State Aero Scis. Mus., Schenectady, N.Y., 1991. Recipient Spl. award Turned Object Show, Phila., 1981, Best Dimensional Display award, Growth Inc., N.Y.C., 1985, artist in residency award Mid Atlantic Found. for Arts, 1988. Mem. Am. Craft Coun., Sculpture Internat., Empire State Aero Scis. Mus. Home: 766 Albany St Schenectady NY 12307-1324

GIMARO, CHRISTOPHER ANDREW, real estate developer, consultant; b. Gwynedd, Pa., Aug. 21, 1964; s. Joseph F. and Gerry (Fields) G. BA in Acctg., Fin., Temple U., 1986. Prin. Gimaro Assocs. Ltd., Blue Bell, Pa., 1985—; gen. ptnr. The Montgomery Group Comfort Inn-Montgomcryville (Pa.) 1987—. Fundraiser asst. Temple Univ. Arts Music Festival, Ambler, Pa., 1991. Republican. Roman Catholic. Office: Gimaro Assocs Ltd 18 Sentry Pky Ste 1 Blue Bell PA 19422-2339

GIMBEL, MICHAEL MARC, alcohol/drug abuse services professional; b. Balt., Dec. 26, 1951; s. Milton and Frances (Buchman) G.; m. Stephanie Andrucci (div. Aug. 1981); m. Patricia Gaffney, Sept. 22, 1982 (separated Dec. 1991). Grad. high sch., Balt. Cert. addictions counselor, Md. Alcohol and drug counselor, dir. intake Synanon Found., Drug Treatment Program, Santa Monica, Calif., 1972-78; counselor drug program X-Cell, Inc., Balt., 1978-79; founder, counselor, dir. drug abuse program First Step, Inc., Randallstown, Md., 1979-80; dir. Balt. County Office Substance Abuse, Towson, Md., 1980—; edutor, speaker Sheppard Pratt Hosp. Edn. Ctr., Towson, 1984—; show host Comcast Cable TV, Towson, 1987—; host show on substance abuse Straight Talk, Fox 45; educator, lectr. Md. Assn. Pub. Schs., Annapolis, 1984—. Creator prevention programs Nat. Assn. Counties Achievement awards, 1985-91. Recipient Disting. Svc. awards Balt. County Med. Soc., Towson, 1984, MADD, Towson, Safety Coun. Md., Dir.'s Community Leadership award FBI, 1991. Mem. Internat. Narcotic Enforcement Officers Assn., Md. Assn. Supervision and Curriculum Devel.,

Employee Assistance Profls. Assn. Home: 9 Greenridge Rd Lutherville Timonium MD 21093-6121 Office: Balt County Office Substance Abuse 401 Washington Ave Rm 300 Baltimore MD 21204-4608

GIMINO, FREDERICK ANTHONY, psychologist, neuroscience researcher; b. N.Y.C., Feb. 2, 1948; s. Eloise (Pelachano) Gimino; m. Anne Marie Posey (div.); children: Marissa Anne, Frederick Anthony, Christina Marie; m. Barbara Mary Burt, June 1, 1979; children: Anthony, Christopher, Elizabeth, Katherine, Michael Patrick. BA, Manhattan Coll., 1970; MA, Hunter Coll., 1974; PhD, CUNY. Lic. psychologist, Pa. Lab technician Hunter Coll. CUNY, N.Y.C., 1972-74; instr. psychology Adelphi U., Garden City, N.Y., 1974-77; rsch. assoc. Inst. for Behavorial Rsch., Silver Spring, Md., 1979-80; instr. psychology Fordham U., N.Y.C., 1980-81; lectr. psychology Rosemont (Pa.) Coll., 1984-85; rsch. cons. Clin. Technologies, Mt. Kisco, N.Y., 1986; psychologist I Selinsgrove (Pa.) Ctr., 1986—; rsch. asst. N.Y. State Psychiat. Inst., N.Y.C., 1972-74; adj. lectr. psychology CCNY, N.Y.C., 1974-84; dir. rsch. Bridgeplaza Clinic, Queens, N.Y., 1981-83; bd. dirs. Behavior Rsch. Resources, N.Y.C., 1981-83; affiliated psychotherapist Cons., N.Y.C., 1981-86. Leader Boy Scouts Am., Northumberland, Pa., 1988—, Cub Scouts, Sunbury, Pa. Grad. fellow CUNY, 1977-81. Mem. Am. Psychol. Soc., Am. Psychol. Assn., Eastern Psychol. Assn., Psi Chi, Sigma Xi. Home: 654 Wallace St Northumberland PA 17857-1022

GIMMI, KENNETH JAMES, quality engineer; b. Phila., Feb. 9, 1948; s. Otto Gustav and Bertha Mary (McElhinney) G.; m. Patricia Eileen Edwards, Aug. 9, 1969; children: Andrew Michael, Stephen James, Krista Joy, Joel Mark. BA, Widener U., 1970; diploma in theology, Grace Theol. Sem., 1978. Cert. quality engr., quality auditor; ordained to ministry Bapt. Ch., 1991. Pastor Columbia (Pa.) Bible Ch., 1978-84; quality mgr. Machinery Products Inc., Lancaster, Pa., 1984-88; sr. quality assurance engr. Beretta USA Corp., Accokeek, Md., 1988—. Chmn. Sem. Extension Com., Potomac Bapt. Assn., Waldorf, Md., 1990-91. Mem. Am. Soc. Quality Control (sr., sect. edn. chmn. 1989-91, sec. 1990-91, gage and inspection instr. 1989, leadership quality improvement instr. 1990, stat. concepts instr. 1991). Republican. Home: 111BB Terry Dr Port Tobacco MD 20677 Office: QMT Quality Svcs Group PO Box 959 Bryans Road MD 20616-0959

GINDES, MARION E., clinical psychologist, consultant; b. Bklyn., July 14, 1939; d. Robert I. and Minna Alterwein; (div.); 1 child, Jessica Hornstein; m. David S. Palermo, June 29, 1980. Student, Smith Coll., 1957-59; BA, Barnard Coll., 1961; MS, PhD, Columbia U., 1965. Lic. psychologist, N.Y., Pa. Staff psychologist Bronx Mcpl. Hosp. Ctr., 1965-67; instr. Albert Einstein Coll. Medicine, 1965-67; dir. psychol. svcs. Coney Island Mental Health Ctr., Bklyn., 1967-69; asst. prof. Albert Einstein Coll. Medicine, 1970-72; asst. prof. psychology, 1972-80; dep. chairperson CUNY, Bklyn., 1973-76; vis. assoc. prof. Pa. State U., University Park, 1980-82; co-founder, bd. mem. Centre Valley Mgmt. Meadows Psychiat. Ctr., Centre Hall, Pa., 1981-85, cons. psychol. staff, 1985—; pres. Marion Gindes & Assocs., Cons., State College, Pa./N.Y.C., 1969—, 1991—; adj. assoc. prof. Pa. State U., 1982—; exec. com. Counseling Ministry of Christian Mission, State Coll., 1984-89; cons. Commonwealth Pa., 1989; conducted numerous psychol. workshops. Contbr. articles to profl. jours.; editor: Social Intervention, 1971; reviewer for maj. pub. cos. and profl. jours. Mem. Pa. Task Force on Women, N.Cen., 1986-87, Interdisciplinary Task Force on Alcoholism, State Coll., 1982-84; adv. bd. Parents Without Partners, State College, 1981-86; cons. Children & Youth Svcs., 1989. USPHS grantee, 1962-63, 64-65, NIMH grantee, 1969-70, Grant Found. grantee, 1970-75, CUNY grantee, 1977-79. Fellow Pa. Psychol. Assn., Cen. Pa. Psychol. Assn. (pres. 1989-90, exec. bd. 1986-91); mem. AAUW (bd. dirs. 1987-89), Am. Psychol. Assn., Eastern Psychol. Assn., Mental Health Profl. Pa. (v.p. 1982-83, pres. 1983-86), Am. Women Entrepreneurs, Sigma Xi, Kappa Delta Pi.

GINDI, ROGER ALAN, theatrical producer and manager; b. Bklyn., Jan. 19, 1952; s. Joseph M. and Elayne (Goldberg) G. BA, NYU, N.Y.C., 1973. Mgr. N.Y. Shakespeare Festival, N.Y.C., 1973-81; co. mgr. Gatchell & Neufeld, Ltd., N.Y.C., 1981-89; gen. mgr. Gindi Theatrical Mgmt., N.Y.C., 1989—; co. mgr. Hurlyburly, N.Y.C., 1984-85, Starlight Express, N.Y.C., 1986-89; gen. mgr. Nunsense, N.Y.C., 1985—, Our Country's Good, N.Y.C., 1991—. Producer: (play) Crazy He Calls Me, 1991. Mem. Assn. Theatrical Press Agts. and Mgrs. Democrat. Jewish. Office: Gindi Theatrical Mgmt 311 W 43d St Ste 605 New York NY 10036

GINDIN, IRINA, economist, consultant; b. Moscow, Sept. 11, 1938; came to U.S., 1976; d. Vasily and Anna (Khokhlovkin) Byalsky; m. Edward Gindin, Apr. 28, 1960; 1 child, Dmitry. MA equivalent, Inst. Nat. Economy, Moscow, 1961. Sr. economist Ministry of Coal Industry of USSR, Moscow, 1961-69; econ. affairs officer COMECON Secretariat, Moscow, 1969-75; econ. analyst Bankers Trust Co., N.Y.C., 1977, 82-86; pres. GBA Group, Internat. Bus. and Trade Cons., Syracuse, N.Y., 1991—; cons. Delphic Assocs., Inc., Washington, 1986-87, Tufts U. Fletcher Sch. Law and Diplomacy, Medford, Mass., 1987, Frost & Sullivan, Syracuse, 1986. Author monograph; contbr. articles to profl. jours. Mem. Am. Econ. Assn. Home: 3229 Isle of Pines Baldwinsville NY 13027 Office: GBA Group PO Box 364 Syracuse NY 13201

GINGL, MANFRED, manufacturing company executive; b. Weiz, Austria, July 2, 1948; arrived in Can., 1965; s. Friedrich and Margarete Gingl; married; 2 children. Toolmaker Speedex Mfg. div. Diematic Products, Concord, Ont., Can., 1965-77; mgr. Speedex Mfg. div. Magna Internat. Inc., Concord, 1977-78; mgr. Maple (Ont.) Stampings div. Magna Internat. Inc., 1978-80; gen. mgr. automotive ops. Magna Internat. Inc., Downsview, Ont., 1980-81; pres., chief oper. officer Magna Internat. Inc., Markham, Ont., 1981-88, pres., chief exec. officer, 1988—. Mem. Chrysler Supplier Roundtable, Ford Supplier Adv. Coun., GM Supplier Coun. Office: Magna Internat Inc, 36 Apple Creek Blvd, Markham, ON Canada L3R 4Y4

GINGOLD, DENNIS MARC, lawyer; b. Plainfield, N.J., June 23, 1949; s. Michael Richard and Sally (Weiss) G.; m. Anne Carol Pearson, Sept. 4, 1970; children: Stacy Michele, Samantha Anne. BA, Rollins Coll., 1971; JD, Seton Hall U., 1974; postgrad., Princeton U., NYU, 1974-75; LLM in Internat. Legal Studies, NYU, 1975; postgrad., SUNY, Buffalo, 1975-76. Bar: N.J. 1974, U.S. Dist. Ct. N.J. 1974, Colo. 1981, U.S. Dist. Ct. Colo. 1981, U.S. Ct. Appeals (10th cir.) 1984, U.S. Supreme Ct. 1985, D.C. 1989, U.S. Dist. Ct. D.C. 1989, U.S. Ct. Appeals (9th cir.) 1991. Atty.-advisor U.S. Compt. Currency, Washington, 1976-79; regional counsel 12th Nat. Bank Region U.S. Compt. Currency, Denver, 1979-80; ptnr. Gorsuch, Kirgis, Campbell, Walker & Grover, Denver, 1980-82, Kirkland & Ellis, Denver and Washington, 1982-85; lead banking ptnr. Squire, Sanders & Dempsey, Washington, 1985-88; ptnr. Foley, Hoag & Eliot, Washington, 1988-90, Ross and Hardies, Washington, 1990-91, Dickstein, Shapiro & Morin, Washington, 1991—; adj. prof. law U. Denver, 1981-82. Sr. mem. Seton Hall U. Law Jour., 1972-73. Named one of the Top 20 Banking Lawyers in U.S. Nat. Law Jour., 1983; Reginald Heber Smith fellow, 1975-76. Mem. D.C. Bar Assn., Colo. Bar Assn., N.J. Bar Assn., Denver Bar Assn., Banking Law Inst. (adv. coun. 1983-86), Denver Athletic Club, Bethesda Country Club. Home: 8712 Crider Brook Way Potomac MD 20854-4547 Office: Dickstein Shapiro & Morin 2101 L St NW 9th Fl Washington DC 20037

GINGRAS, DAVID ALAN, financial services company executive; b. Paterson, N.J., Mar. 18, 1946; s. Louis Dona and Carol Gilmore (Doyle) G.; m. Sarah Lynette Miller, Mar. 10, 1973; children: Thomas, Peter, Gail. BS, Phila. Coll. Textiles & Sci., 1969; MA, St. Joseph's U., 1973; MS in Acctg., U. Pa., 1975, MBA, 1976. Staff acct. Price, Waterhouse, Phila., 1969-72; nat. sales mgr. Burlington, Klopman, N.Y.C., 1973-79; acct. exec. Merrill Lynch, Newark, 1979-82; v.p. Merrill Lynch, N.Y.C., 1982-84, Shearson Lehman, Red Bank, N.J., 1984-86; pres., chief exec. officer Endowment Funding, Inc., Bala Cynwyd, Pa., 1987—. Mem. alumni bd. Phila. Coll. Textiles & Sci., 1971-76, 1988—; v.p., pres., Manhattan Coun. Boy Scouts Am., 1983-87; sponsor in perpetuity Ducks Unlimited. Recipient Silver Beaver award Manhattan coun. Boy Scouts Am., 1983, Whitney Young award, 1985, Silver Antelope, N.E. Region, 1988, God and Svc. award Nat. Protestant Com., 1986, Shofar award Nat. Jewish Com. on Scouting, 1990, George Meany award AFL-CIO, Nat. Sports Festival Steeplechase Champion, 1982, Eastern Masters 400 Meter Hurdles champion, 1983, and many other honors for athletics and civic svc. Mem. ASTD, Nat. Assn. Life Underwriters, Pa. Assn. Life Underwriters, Nat. Soc. Fund Raising Execs., Assn. of U.S. Army, SAR, Mil. Order of Fgn. Wars, New Eng. Soc., N.Y. St. George's Soc. N.Y., Vets. Corp. of Arty. (life, hereditary), N.Y. Guard (officer), Res. Officers Assn., Masons, Rotary Internat., Order of Lafayette. Republican. Presbyterian. Office: Endowment Funding Inc 208 Sycamore Ln Wallingford PA 19086

GINN, ROBERT JAY, JR., company president, episcopal priest; b. Council Bluffs, Iowa, Mar. 14, 1946; s. Col Robert Jay and Bette Jean (Bailey) G. BA, U. Nebr., Lincoln, 1968; MDiv, Harvard U., Cambridge, 1972. Allston-Burr Savior Tutor Quincy House Harvard Coll., Cambridge, Mass., 1973-75; dir. career svcs. Harvard U. Faculty of Arts & Scis., Cambridge, Mass., 1975-80, dir. personnel, 1981-85; pres. Vocations, Shrewsbury, Mass., 1985—; episcopal priest, Diocese of Western Mass., 1980—. Author: College Graduates Career Guide. 1981, Vocational Testing, 1979. Chmn. St. Thomas Fund, Boston, 1990—, Taylor Fellowship Program, 1990—. Mem. Am. Assn. Counseling & Devel.; chmn. Commn. on Campus Ministry, Radcliffe Coll. Career Svcs. Visiting Com. Republican. Episcopalian. Home: 45 Commons Dr Apt 33 Shrewsbury MA 01545-4956 Office: Vocations 9 Dartmoor Dr Shrewsbury MA 01545-1614

GINNARD, CHARLES RAYMOND, chemical company executive; b. Detroit, Oct. 2, 1947; s. Raymond John and Catherine (Wurscher) G.; m. Christine Fairfield, Nov. 15, 1969; children: Kelly, Janet, Matthew. BS in Chemistry, Wayne State U., Detroit, 1969. Analytical chemist DuPont Cen. Rsch., Wilmington, Del., 1969-83; rsch. adminstr. DuPont Cen. Rsch., Glenolden, Pa., 1984-86; personnel adminstr. DuPont Cen. Rsch., Wilmington, 1986—. Contbr. chpt. to book: Kolthoff's Treatise on Analytical Chemistry, 1982; contbr. articles to profl. jours. Bd. dirs. Yorklyn (Del.) Recreation Ctr., 1985-91; coach Sci. Olympiad, 1986-91. Mem. Am. Chem. Soc. (sec. local sect. 1978-79), Salem Aero Club (pres. 1977-79), Sci. Alliance, Sigma Xi.

GINSBERG, ALLEN, poet, photographer, musician; b. Newark, June 3, 1926; s. Louis and Naomi (Levy) G. A.B., Columbia U., 1948. With various cargo ships, 1945-56; co-dir. emeritus Kerouac Sch. Poetics; with Naropa Inst., Boulder, Colo.; disting. prof. Bklyn. Coll., 1986—. Assoc. with early Beat Generation prose-poets, 1945—; actor: motion picture Pull My Daisy, 1961, Don't Look Back, 1965, Guns of the Trees, 1962, Wholly Communion, 1965, Chappaqua, 1966, Renaldo and Clara, 1978; narrator: film Kaddish, NET, 1977; Author: Howl and Other Poems, 1955, Empty Mirror, 1960, Kaddish and Other Poems, 1960, Reality Sandwiches, 1963, Planet News, Poems, 1961-67, 1968, Indian Journals, 1970, The Fall of America: Poems of these States, 1973 (Nat. Book award 1974), The Gates of Wrath: Early Rhymed Poems 1948-51, 1973, Allen Verbatim, 1974, First Blues, 1975, Journals Early 50's Early 60's, 1977, Mind Breaths, Poems 1972-1977, 1978, As Ever: Correspondence A.G. and Neal Cassady 1948-68, 1978, Composed on the Tongue, Literary Conversations, 1967-77, 1980, Straight Hearts Delight: Love Poems and Selected Letters, 1980; author: Plutonian Ode, Poems 1977-1980, 1982, Collected Poems, 1947-80, 1984; White Shroud, poems, 1980-85, 1986, Annotated Howl, 1986; recs. include: Songs of Innocence and of Experience by William Blake Tuned by Allen Ginsberg, 1970, First Blues: Songs, 1982, Birdbrain, 1981, The Lion For Real, 1989; collaborated with Timothy Leary on works concerning anti-war new-consciousness movement. Gay activist. Guggenheim fellow in poetry, 1965-66. Mem. PEN (v.p. Am. chpt. 1987-88), Am. Inst. Arts and Letters. Buddhist. *

GINSBERG, BENJAMIN, political science educator; b. Poking, Fed. Republic of Germany, Apr. 1, 1947; came to U.S., 1949, naturalized 1955; s. Herman and Anna (Wolfstein) G.; m. Sandra Joy Brewer, Dec. 15, 1968; children: Cynthia, Alexander. BA, U. Chgo., 1968, MA, 1970, PhD, 1973. Asst. prof. govt. Cornell U., Ithaca, N.Y., 1972-78, assoc. prof., 1978-83, prof., 1983-91, dir. Survey Rsch. Facility, 1985-86, dir. Inst. Pub. Affairs, 1987-91, dir. Washington program, 1988-91; David Bernstein prof. polit. sci., dir. Ctr. Govt. Studies, Johns Hopkins U., Balt., 1992—; cons. N.Y. Times, N.Y.C., 1984-85. Author: Poliscide, 1976, The Consequences of Consent, 1982, Do Elections Matter?, 1985, The Captive Public, 1986, Freedom and Power in American Government, 1989, Politics by Other Means, 1990, American Government: Readings and Cases, 1992, The Fatal Embrace, 1992. Trustees' scholar U. Chgo., 1964-68; NIMH fellow U. Chgo., 1968-72; Jonathan Meigs grantee Cornell U., 1985, U.S. Dept. Justice grantee, 1984, Kellogg Found. grantee, 1987. Mem. Am. Polit. Sci. Assn. Jewish. Home: 212 Hanshaw Rd Ithaca NY 14850-2210 Office: Johns Hopkins U Mergenthaler Hall Baltimore MD 21218

GINSBERG, HAROLD SAMUEL, virologist, educator; b. Daytona Beach, Fla., May 27, 1917; s. Jacob and Anne (Kalb) G.; m. Marion Reibstein, Aug. 4, 1949; children: Benjamin Langer, Peter Robert, Ann Meredith, Jane Elizabeth. A.B., Duke U., 1937; M.D., Tulane U., 1941. Resident Mallory Inst. Pathology, Boston, 1941-42; intern, asst. resident Boston City Hosp., 4th Med. Service, 1942-43; resident physician, assoc. Rockefeller Inst., 1946-51; assoc. prof. preventive medicine Western Res. U. Sch. Medicine, 1951-60; prof. microbiology, chmn. dept. U. Pa. Sch. Medicine, 1960-73; prof. microbiology, chmn. dept. Coll. Phys. and Surg. Columbia, 1973-85, prof. microbiology and medicine, dir. section molecular pathogenesis of infection, 1986—; mem. commn. acute respiratory diseases Armed Forces Epidemiological Bd., 1959-73; cons. NIH, 1959-72, 75—, Army Chem. Corps, 1962-64, NASA, 1969-73, Am. Cancer Soc., 1969-73, mem. coun. on rsch. and pers., 1976-80; v.p. Internat. Com. on Nomenclature of Viruses, 1966-75; mem. space sci. bd., chmn. panel microbiology Nat. Acad. Sci., 1973-74; chmn. microbiology exam. com. Nat. Bd. Med. Examiners, 1974-79; mem. microbiology and infectious disease com. Nat. Inst. Allergy and Infectious Disease, NIH, 1976-81, chmn., 1979-81; co-chmn. Inst. Medicine, NAS Roundtable: AIDS: Modern Approaches Vaccines and Anti-Viral Drugs, 1989-92. Contbr. textbooks; co-author: Microbiology, 1967, 4th edit., 1990, Virology, 2d edit., 1988, Vaccines 88, Vaccines 89, Vaccines 90, Vaccines 91, Modern Approaches to New Vaccines, Including Prevention of AIDS; mem. editorial bd. Jour. Infectious Diseases, Jour. Immunology, Jour. Exptl. Medicine, Jour. Virology and Bacteriological Revs., Jour. Acquired Immune Deficiency Syndromes; editor: Jour. Virology, 1979-84, Cancer Research, 1978-82. Served to lt. col. M.C. AUS, 1943-46. Decorated Legion of Merit; recipient Disting. Svc. award Coll. Physicians and Surgeons, Columbia U., 1991. Fellow AAAS; mem. NAS, Inst. Medicine of NAS, Assn. Am. Physicians, Am. Acad. Microbiologists (chmn. bd. govs. 1971-72), Am. Soc. Clin. Investigation (councillor 1958-60), Am. Assn. Immunologists, Am. Soc. Microbiology (chmn. virology div. 1961-62, councillor div. 1977-81), Soc. Exptl. Biology and Medicine, Assn. Med. Sch. Microbiology Chairmen (pres. 1972-73), Harvey Soc. (pres. 1984coun. 1985-88), Cen. Soc. Clin. Research, Am. Soc. Biol. Chemists, Am. Soc. Virology (pres. 1983), Alpha Omega Alpha. Office: Columbia U Coll Physicians and Surgeons Dept Medicine 650 W 168th St New York NY 10032-3702

GINSBERG, MARK ALAN, psychologist; b. Bklyn., Sept. 23, 1944; s. Mac and Sophie (Rubin) G.; m. Pauline E. Speiglman, Nov. 24, 1974; children: Peter Kipp, Daivd Kipp, Matthew Kipp. BS, CCNY, 1966; MA, So. Ill. U., 1971, PhD, 1975. Lic. psychologist, N.Y. Counseling psychology intern Iowa State U., Ames, 1972-73; clin. pschology intern Health and Scis. Ctr. U. of Manitoba, Winnipeg, Can., 1973-74; program dir. CVS CYS Hutchings Psychiat. Ctr., Syracuse, N.Y., 1974-79; program dir. Adult Svcs. Hutchings Psychiat. Ctr., Syracuse, N.Y., 1979-81, dir. Psychology tng., 1981-90, chief psychologist, 1990—; pvt. practice psychologist, Syracuse, 1977—; adj. asst. prof. psychiatry Health Scis. Ctr. SUNY, 1975—; adj. asst. prof. Syracuse U., 1979—. Bd. dir. Alt. Route Inc., Syracuse, 1977-79; v.p. Madison County Community Svcs. Bd., Wampsville, N.Y., 1988—. Mem. Am. Psychol. Assn., N.Y. State Psychol. Assn., Cen. N.Y. Psychol. Assn. (sec. 1987-88), Eastern Evaluation Rsch. Soc. Democrat. Jewish. Home: PO Box 27 Canastota NY 13032-0027 Office: Hutchings Pschiat Ctr 620 Madison St Syracuse NY 13210-2338

GINSBERG, PHILLIP CARL, physician; b. Fairbanks, Alaska, June 1, 1954; s. Richard and Sondra (Soble) G.; m. Judith Carson, June 19, 1977; 1 child, Rachel Hope. BS in Biology, Villanova U., 1976; MS, Phila. Coll. Osteopath, 1985, DO, 1980. Diplomate Nat. Bd. Osteopathic Examiners; Am. Bd. Osteopathic Surgeons; cert. urological surgery. Intern Hosp. Phila. Coll. Osteopathic Medicine, Phila., 1980-81; resident Albert Einstein Med. Ctr., Phila., 1981-82; resident in urologic surgery Hosp. Phila. Coll. Osteopathic Medicine, Phila., 1981-85; pvt. practice Phila., 1985—; clin. assoc. prof. Phila. Coll. Osteopathic Medicine; med. dir. Urodiagnostics, Inc., Del. Valley Continence Ctr.; chmn. div. of urology, Phila. Geriatric Ctr., 1988, Albert Einstein Med. Ctr., 1989, Albert Einstein Med. Ctr.; cons. Nat. Cancer Inst. Contbr. numerous articles to profl. jours. Mem. AMA, Am. Osteo. Assn., Pa. Osteol. Assn., Pa. Med. Soc., Pa. Urology Assn., Am. Fertility Assn., Am. Urol. Assn., Mid Atlantic Urol. Assn., Phila. Urol. Soc., Lambda Omicron Gamma. Home: 724 Periwinkle Ln Wynnewood PA 19096-1650 Office: Albert Einstein Med Ctr 5401 Old York Rd Philadelphia PA 19141-3030

GINSBURG, DOUGLAS HOWARD, judge, educator; b. Chgo., May 25, 1946; s. Maurice and Katherine (Goodmont) G.; m. Claudia De Secundy, May 31, 1968 (div. Sept. 1980); 1 child, Jessica DeSecundy; m. 2d, Hallee Perkins Morgan, May 9, 1981; children: Hallee Katherine Morgan, Hannah Maurice Morgan. Diploma, Latin Sch. Chgo., 1963; BS, Cornell U., 1970; JD, U. Chgo., 1973. Bar: Ill. 1973, Mass. 1982, U.S. Supreme Ct. 1984, U.S. Ct. Appeals (9th cir.) 1986. Intern Covington & Burling, Washington, 1972; law clk. U.S. Ct. Appeals, Washington, 1973-74, U.S. Supreme Ct., Washington, 1974-75; prof. Harvard U., 1975-83; dep. asst. atty. gen. for regulatory affairs, Antitrust div. U.S. Dept. Justice, Washington, 1983-84, asst. atty. gen., Antitrust div., 1985-86; adminstr. for Info. and Regulatory Affairs Exec. Office Pres., Office Mgmt. and Budget, Washington, 1984-85; judge U.S. Ct. Appeals (D.C. cir.), 1986—; vis. prof. law Columbia U., N.Y.C., 1987-88; lectr. law Harvard U., Cambridge, Mass., 1987—; Found. prof. law George Mason U., Arlington, Va., 1988—; Charles J. Merriam vis. scholar, sr. lectr. U. Chgo., 1990. Author: Regulation of Broadcasting: Law and Policy Towards Radio, Television and Cable Communications, 1979, Antitrust, Uncertainty, and Technological Innovation, 1980; co-author: Regulation of the Electronic Mass Media, 1991; editor: (with W. Abernathy) Government, Technology and the Future of the Automobile, 1980; contbr. articles to profl. jours. Recipient Mecham prize scholarship U. Chgo. Law Sch., 1970-73; Casper Platt award U. Chgo. Law Sch., 1972. Mem. ABA (ex officio exec. coun. antitrust sect. 1985-86), Am. Econ. Assn., Am. Law and Econs. Assn., Ill. Bar Assn., Fed. Bar Assn. (exec. coun. banking com. 1983-87), Order of Coif, Phi Kappa Phi. Republican. Office: US Ct Appeals 3d St & Constitution Ave NW Washington DC 20001

GINSBURG, LEE ROBERT, organizational psychologist, management consultant; b. Phila., Aug. 21, 1942; s. Bernard and Betty (Friedman) G.; m. Margo Eisenberg, Aug. 21, 1965; children: Philip, Donald. BA, U. Pa., 1963; MA, Temple U., 1966, PhD, 1971. Staff asst. personnel rsch. Sun Oil Co., Phila., 1965-68; cons. MDC Psychol. Svcs., Phila., 1968-71; chief operating officer Mobix Corp., Cherry Hill, N.J., 1984-86; ptnr. Miller/Ginsburg, Phila., 1971-84, 86—; bd. dirs., First Exec. Bank, Phila. Co-author: Omega Management, 1979; contbr. articles to numerous publs. Pres., Penn Valley Jr. Sports Assn., Lower Merion, Pa., 1977-78; mem. Lower Merion Personnel Rev. Bd., 1984-89; trustee, Nat. Mus. Am. Jewish History, Phila., 1988. Mem. Soc. Indsl. and Orgnl. Psychology, Assn. Tng. and Devel., Acad. Mgmt., Boca Point Country Club. Republican. Jewish. Home: 6510 Via Rosa Boca Raton FL 33433-6435 Office: Miller Ginsburg 234 N Delaware Ave Philadelphia PA 19106-1401 also: 2499 Glades Rd # 209 Boca Raton FL 33431

GINSBURG, RUTH BADER, federal judge; b. Bklyn., Mar. 15, 1933; d. Nathan and Celia (Amster) Bader; m. Martin David Ginsburg, June 23, 1954; children: Jane Carol, James Steven. AB, Cornell U., 1954; postgrad., Harvard Law Sch., 1956-58; LLB Kent scholar, Columbia Law Sch., 1959; LLD (hon.), Lund (Sweden) U., 1969, Am. U., 1981, Vt. Law Sch., 1984, Georgetown U., 1985, DePaul U., 1985, Bklyn. Law Sch., 1987; DHL (hon.), Hebrew Union Coll., 1988, Amherst Coll., 1991; LLD (hon.), Rutgers U., 1991, Lewis & Clark U., 1992. Bar: N.Y. 1959, D.C. 1975, U.S. Supreme Ct. 1967. Law sec. to judge U.S. Dist. Ct. (so. dist.) N.Y., 1959-61; rsch. assoc. Columbia Law Sch., N.Y.C., 1961-62, assoc. dir. project internat. procedure, 1962-63; asst. prof. Rutgers U. Sch. Law, Newark, 1963-66, assoc. prof., 1966-69, prof., 1969-72; prof. Columbia U. Sch. Law, N.Y.C., 1972-80; U.S. Cir. judge U.S. Ct. Appeals, D.C. Cir., Washington, 1980—; Phi Beta Kappa vis. scholar, 1973-74; fellow Ctr. for Advanced Study in Behavioral Scis., Stanford, Calif., 1977-78; lectr. Aspen (Colo.) Inst., 1990, Salzburg Seminar, Austria, 1984; bd. dirs. Am. Bar Found., 1979-89, exec. com., 1981-89, sec., 1987-89; gen. counsel ACLU, 1973-80, bd. dirs., 1974-80. Author: (with Anders Bruzelius) Civil Procedure in Sweden, 1965; Swedish Code of Judicial Procedure, 1968; (with others) Sex-Based Discrimination, 1974, supplement, 1978; contbr. numerous articles to legal jours.; vol. editor: Business Regulation in the Common Market Nations, vol. 1, 1969. Mem. ABA, AAAS, Am. Law Inst. (council mem. 1978—), Coun. Fgn. Rels. Office: US Ct Appeals US Courthouse 3d St & Constitution Ave NW Washington DC 20001

GINSBURG, SIGMUND G., college and university administrator; b. N.Y.C., Oct. 12, 1937; s. Saul and Rose (Rich) G.; m. Judith Ann Jacobson, July 4, 1965; children: Beth Alison, David Grant. B.A. magna cum laude, Dartmouth Coll., 1959; postgrad., London Sch. Econs., 1959-60; M.P.A., Harvard U., 1961. Mgmt. intern Office of Sec. of Def., Washington, 1961-62; asst. to pres. Hudson Inst., 1964; asst. mgr. personnel adminstrv. services, mgmt. analyst Port Authority of N.Y. and N.J., 1964-66; sr. mgmt. cons. and spl. asst. to dep. mayor Office of the Mayor, City of N.Y., 1966-67; asst. city adminstr. Office of the Mayor, 1967-72; v.p. for adminstrn. and planning, treas. Adelphi U., Garden City, N.Y., 1972-78; v.p. for fin., treas. U. Cin., 1978-84, adj. prof. higher edn. adminstrn., bus. adminstrn., 1980-84; v.p. fin. and adminstrn. Barnard Coll., N.Y.C., 1984—; adj. assoc. prof. mgmt. Adelphi U., 1972-78; adj. asst. prof. CUNY, 1966-72; founder, dir. N.Y.C. Urban Fellowship Program, 1969-72; lectr. profl. meetings; mgmt. commentator Sta. WGUC, Cin., 1980; lectr. Fordham U., 1985—; instr. New Sch. Social Rsch., 1986, 91; mem. City Mgrs. Working Rev. Com. Cin. 2000 Plan, 1979-82; mem. citizen's adv. com. Wyo. Bd. Edn., 1980. Co-author: Managing the Higher Education Enterprise, 1980; author: Management: An Executive Perspective, 1982, Ropes for Management Success: Climb Higher, Faster, 1984; contbr. articles to profl. jours., chpts. to books. Served as lt. U.S. Army, 1962-64. Recipient Colby prize in govt. Dartmouth Coll., 1959, Merit award City of N.Y., 1969, Neil O. Hines publ. award NACUBO, 1992; Daniel Webster nat. scholar Dartmouth Coll., 1955-59; James B. Reynolds fellow Dartmouth Coll., 1959-60, Littauer fellow Harvard U., 1961. Mem. Phi Beta Kappa. Office: Barnard Coll 101 Milbank Hall 3009 Broadway New York NY 10027

GINSBURGH, BROOK, association administrator; b. Phila., Oct. 4, 1942; d. Harrison Stanford and Florence Virginia (Campbell) G. Diploma in nursing, Chestnut Hill Hosp., 1963. RN, Pa. Pediatric nurse Chestnut Hill Hosp., Phila., 1963-66; pediatric charge nurse Ea. Pa. Psychiatric Inst., Phila., 1967-69, Nazareth Hosp., Phila., 1970-76; adminstrv. asst. Subcontractors Assn. Del. Valley, Ardmore, Pa., 1977-79, exec. dir., editor monthly newsletter, pub. annual directory, 1980—. Treas. Condominium Bd. Dirs., 1991—. Mem. NAFE, Am. Soc. Assn. Execs., Pa. C. of C., Main Line C. of C. Office: Subcontractors Assn Del Valley 63 W Lancaster Ave PO Box 586 Ardmore PA 19003

GINTAUTAS, JONAS, physician, scientist, administrator; b. Justinava, Lithuania, Oct. 3, 1938; came to U.S., 1967; s. Jonas and Elena (Zaueckaite) Sinsinas; m. Kristina Zebrauskaite, June 13, 1970; children: Pasaka, Vadas. PhD, Northwestern U., 1976; MD, U. Juarez, Mex., 1984. Assoc. prof. Tex. Tech. U., Lubbock, 1975-77; assoc. prof. and dir. rsch. Tex. Tech. U. Health Scis. Ctr., Lubbock, 1979-82; dir. basic and clin. rsch., prof. neurology Brookdale Hosp. Med. Ctr., N.Y.C., 1985—; cons. Amtorg Corp., N.Y.C., 1987—, Raley Internat. Co., Boston, 1988—, Arrow Biomed Inc., Metuchen, N.J., 1988—. Editorial cons. Jour. Aphasia Agnosia Apraxia, 1979—; contbr. articles to profl. jours. Charter mem. Rep. Presdl. Task Force, Washington, 1982— (medal of honor 1982). Grantee more than $1 million for rsch. pvt. and govt. agys. Fellow Internat. Coll. Physicians and Surgeons (hon.); mem. Am. Biog. Inst. (dep. gov. 1987—), U.S. Senatorial Club (preferred). Roman Catholic. Home: 84-19 107 St Richmond Hill NY 11418 Office: Brookdale Hosp Med Ctr Linden and Rockaway Brooklyn NY 11212

GINTER, VALERIAN ALEXIUS, urban historian; b. Chgo., Nov. 4, 1939; s. Valerian Adalbert and Bernice (Podraza) G.; m. Linda Garner Tadlock,

Feb. 24, 1968 (div. 1973). BS in Speech, Northwestern U., 1962; postgrad., L.I.U., 1979-81. Investigator Acme Secret Service Ltd., Chgo., 1960-62; producer, dir. Sta. WAAY-TV, Huntsville, Ala., 1965-68; comml. coordinator CBS TV, N.Y.C., 1968-70; buyer SSC&B Lintas Worldwide, Furman-Roth Inc., SFM Media Corp., N.Y.C., 1970-79; prin. Ginter-Gotham Urban History, N.Y.C., 1981—. Author: Manhattan Trivia: The Ultimate Challenge, 1985; contbr. articles to profl. jours. Cons., tour designer, leader Mcpl. Art Soc., N.Y., 1975—, dir. video tng., St. Bart's Community House, N.Y.C., 1974-77. With U.S. Army, 1962-65. Mem. Theatre Hist. Soc., Victorian Soc. Am., Nat. Trust Historic Preservation, Soc. Archtl. Historians, Multi-lingual Guides' Assn. (Advisor to bd., sec. 1983-85). Roman Catholic. Home and Office: Ste 312 50 W 72d St New York NY 10023

GINTHER, LARUA JEANNE, psychologist, researcher; b. Highland, Ind., Oct. 29, 1958; d. Robert James and Leona (Bonneau) G.; m. George Carl Braun, July 28, 1990. BA, Purdue U., 1978; MA, U. Ala., 1981; D in Psychology, U. Hartford, Conn., 1990. Lic. psychologist, Conn. Sch. psychologist Simsbury (Conn.) Pub. Schs., 1984-88; intern Inst. of Living, Hartford, 1988-89; counselor John Dempsey Hosp., Farmington, Conn., 1989-90; rsch. assoc. U. Conn. Health Ctr., Farmington, 1990—; psychologist Charis Group, West Hartford, Conn., 1991—; cons. Community Food Pantry, Plainville, Conn., 1989—, Parkland Meml. Hosp., Dallas, 1991—. Contbr. articles to profl. jours. Mem. APA, Conn. Psychol. Assn., Conn. Assn. Sch. Psychologists, Phi Beta Kappa, Phi Kappa Phi, Psi Chi. Office: Charis Group 780 Farmington Ave West Hartford CT 06119-1619

GINZEL, ROLAND, artist; b. Lincoln, Ill., May 7, 1921; s. Mabel (Armstrong) G.; m. Ellen Lanyon, Sept. 4, 1948; children: Andrew, Lisa. BFA, Art Inst. of Chgo., 1948; MFA, U. Iowa, 1950; postgrad., Slade Sch., London, 1950-51, Cen. Sch. of Arts and Crafts, London, 1950-51. Faculty U. Chgo., 1954-58; prof. U. Ill., Chgo., 1958-88, prof. emeritus, 1988—; vis. prof. U. Wis., Madison, 1960, Columbia U., N.Y.C., 1985; instr. Parsons Sch. of Design, N.Y.C., 1985. One-man shows include Roy Boyd Gallery, Chgo., 1989, 91, Loyola U., Chgo., 1986, Gallery 400, 1986, U. Ill., Chgo., 1986, Dart Gallery, Chgo., 1978, 83, 86, Ill. State U., Normal, 1983, Boston U. Mus., 1979, Evanston (Ill.) Art Ctr., 1977, 55 Mercer Gallery, N.Y.C., 1975, Ill. State Mus., Springfield, 1975; exhibited in group shows at Am. Acad. Arts & Letters, N.Y.C., 1991, Columbia Coll. Art Gallery, 1988, Bernice Steinbaum Gallery, N.Y.C., 1986, State of Ill. Ctr. Gallery, Chgo., 1985, Art Inst. Chgo., 1979, 81, Smithsonian Instn. Chgo., Washington, 1979, others; represented in permanent collections including Art Inst. Chgo., Dallas Mus. Art, Mus. U. Mich., Ann Arbor, Mus. U. So. Calif., L.A., Purdue U., Lafayette, Ind., Sears Corp., Chgo., U. Ill., Urbana, others. Recipient Fulbright award, Academia de Belle Arti, Rome, 1962. Home and Office: PO Box 1045 Stockbridge MA 01262-1045

GIOBBI, CHAMBLISS MARTINO, composer; b. Mt. Kisco, N.Y., Feb. 14, 1963; s. Edward Gianchano and Elinor Ragland (Turner) G. BA in Music Composition, Boston U., 1986. Composer, librettist: The Nonetti, 1983, Knights Errant, 1985, Piano Concerto, 1986, (opera) The Holy Shroud, 1992; has works performed by Boston U. Symphony Orch., Boston Civic Symphony, Stanford Symphony Orch, Am. Opera Projects, Inc.; composer orchestral and operatic works. N.Y. Found. for the Arts fellow, 1991; ASCAP Found. grantee, 1991. Mem. Broadcast Music Inc. (awards 1985, 86), Am. Music Ctr. Home and Office: 114 Franklin St New York NY 10013

GIOELLO, DEBBIE ANN, fashion design educator; b. Yonkers, N.Y., Jan. 1, 1935; children: Debra Ann, Donna Maria. BS, Oswego (N.Y.) State U., 1970; MA, H. Lehman Coll., 1972. Lic. tchr. N.Y. Designer/stylist various fashion houses N.Y.C., 1952-80; pres. Gioello Ent., Yonkers, 1980—; prof. fashion design Fashion Inst. Tech., N.Y.C., 1968—, chmn. dept. fashion design, 1989—; lectr. various workshops, seminars. Writer, photographer "Real People at Work" series: Fashion Designer, 1976, Textile Designer, 1976, Custom Tailor, 1977, Advertising Copywriter, 1977; author: Production Term, 1978, Figure Types and Size Range, 1979, Profiling Fabrics, 1980, Designer/Stylist Handbook Vol. I and II, 1980, Designer/Stylist Croque Tracing Pad, 1980, Understanding Fabrics, 1982; author numerous video programs, other instructional books on fashion design; contbr. articles to profl. jours.; patentee in field. Recipient Proclamation award Mayor Angelo Martienlli, Yonkers, 1983; SUNY grantee, 1983; Dept. Energy Rsch. grantee, 1991. Mem. NAFE, Fashion Group, Artists Equity Assn., Nat. Assn. Women Artists. Home: 237 Van Cortlandt Park Ave Yonkers NY 10705-1520 Office: Fashion Inst Tech 27th St at 7th Ave New York NY 10001

GIOFFRE, JOSEPH D., savings and loan executive; b. Port Chester, N.Y., June 18, 1943; s. Joseph B. and Rose Gioffre; m. Kathryn R. Woodward, Oct. 10, 1964; children: Joseph, Kimberly. Supr. acctg. dept. Weshester Fed. Savs. and Loan, New Rochelle, N.Y., 1967=69; treas. Greenwich (Conn.) Fed. Savs. and Loan, 1969-74, v.p., contr., 1974-76, exec. v.p., 1976-80, chief adminstrv. officer, from 1980, now pres.; pres., chmn. Greenwich Fin Corp. Mem. fin. com. ARC, Greenwich., 1977—; bd. dirs. Jr. Achievement, 1977—. Mem. Fin. Mgrs. Soc. (pres. 1973-74), Kiwanis. Roman Catholic. Office: Greenwich Fin Corp 67 Mason St Greenwich CT 06830-5550*

GIOIELLA, RUSSELL MICHAEL, lawyer; b. Camden, N.J., Mar. 10, 1954; s. Michael S. and Mildred (Leonardo) G.; m. Nerissa M. Radell, June 28, 1980. BA summa cum laude, Cath. U., 1976; JD, NYU, 1979, MA, 1980. Bar: N.Y. 1980, U.S. Dist. Ct. (so. and ea. dists.) N.Y. 1980, U.S. Dist. Ct. (no. dist.) N.Y. 1982, U.S. Ct. Appeals (2d and 3d cirs.) 1980, U.S. Supreme Ct. 1984. Assoc. Litman, Kaufman and Asche, N.Y.C., 1979-84; ptnr. Litman, Kaufman, Asche and Lupkin, N.Y.C., 1985, Litman, Asche, Lupkin & Gioiella, N.Y.C., 1986—. Mem. steering com. N.Y. State Coalition to Abolish the Death Penalty. Mem. ABA, Assn. Bar City N.Y. (com. on product liability 1988-91, criminal cts. com. 1992—), N.Y. Criminal Bar Assn. (bd. dirs.), Nat. Assn. Criminal Def. Lawyers (ethics adv. com.), N.Y. State Assn. Criminal Def. Lawyers, Columbian Lawyers, Phi Beta Kappa. Democrat. Office: Litman Asche Lupkin & Gioiella 45 Broadway New York NY 10006-3007

GIONFRIDDO, PAUL, health care policy consultant; b. Middletown, Conn., May 25, 1953; s. Valentine Louis and Catherine (Pugliese) G.; m. Linda Hope Rammler, Aug. 7, 1982; children: Timothy, Larissa, Elizabeth, Benjamin. BA, Wesleyan U., 1975. Paralegal Conn. Legal Svcs., Meriden, 1977-78; mem. Conn. State Legislature, Hartford, 1979-89; mayor City of Middletown, 1989-91; cons. Agy. for Health Care Policy and Rsch., Washington, 1981—. Pres. People's Action for Clean Energy, Inc., Canton, Conn., 1976—; justice of peace City of Middletown, 1977—; mem. Conn. Environ. 2000 Com., Hartford, 1990—; corporator Middlesex Hosp. Recipient Outstanding Pub. Svc. award Assn. for Retarded Citizens, Conn., 1984, Ira Hiscock award Conn. Pub. Health Assn., 1985, Legislator of Yr. Caucus of Conn. Dems., 1987, Legis. Leadership award Conn. Assn. for Human Svcs., 1988, Conn. Coalition on Aging, 1990. Mem. APHA, Rockfall Found. Democrat. Roman Catholic. Home: 454 Ballfall Rd Middletown CT 06457-2331

GIOR, FINO (SERAFINO GIORDANO), electrology company executive; b. Hollywood, Calif., Sept. 8, 1936; s. Jack and Mary (Scorsone) G.; m. Carole Chalupa, Sept. 23, 1961; children: John, Maryann, James, Matthew. Student, St. John's U., Queens, N.Y., 1955-57; cert., Kree Inst. Electrology, Manhattan, N.Y., 1958. Pres. N.Y. State Electrologists, Inc., N.Y.C., 1978-79; founder, pres. Internat. Guild Profl. Electrologists Inc., High Point, N.C., 1979-84; pres. Advanced Electrology Clinics Am., Great Neck, N.Y., 1958—; advisor Internat. Guild Profl. Electrologists, Inc., 1980—; cons. and presenter various electrology-related orgns. Author: Modern Electrology, 1987, Official Standards For Electrology; contbr. articles to numerous nat. mags. and profl. publs. Sgt. U.S. Army N.G., 1954-59. Recipient Dr. Michele award, 1984. Mem. Internat. Guild of Electrologist Inc. (3d v.p.). Roman Catholic. Office: Advanced Electrology Mead Ln # 15 Roslyn NY 11576-2517

GIORDANO, ARTHUR ANTHONY, engineering executive; b. Boston, Sept. 28, 1941; s, Arthur and Anna (Latorella) G.; m. Diane Bunker, Aug. 22, 1964; children: Lisa, Amanda. BSEE, Northeastern U., 1964, MSEE, 1966; PhD in Elec. Engring., U. Pa., 1970. Engring. specialist GTE Sylvania, Needham, Mass., 1970-72; dept. mgr. GTE Sylvania, Needham, 1974-84; sr. tech. staff Stein Assocs., Waltham, Mass., 1972-74; v.p. systems CNR, Inc., Needham, 1985—; elec. engring. instr. Northeastern U., Boston, 1973-75, 78-79, 81-82, Tufts U., Medford Mass., 1980-81. Author: (with Fred Haber) Radio Science, 1972, (with Dr. F. Hsu) Least Square Estimation With Applications to Digital Signal Processing, 1985; co-inventor bi-polar area correlator; presenter in field; contbr. articles to IEEE Transactions on Communications Tech., IEEE Communications Mag., Radio Sci. Active Burlington (Mass.) Town meeting, 1985-88. Mem. IEEE (sr.), Internat. Union Radio Sci. (vice chmn. U.S. commision E 1978-81, chmn. 1981-84), Tau Beta Pi, Eta Kappa Nu. Roman Catholic. Office: CNR Inc 220 Reservoir St Needham MA 02194-3133

GIORDANO, PATRICIA SCHOPPE, interior decorator; b. Houston, Aug. 29, 1947; d. Conrad Joseph and Ellen Patricia (Condon) Schoppe; m. Natale Joseph, Apr. 17, 1971 (dec. Sept. 1989); children: Keith Joseph, Michael David, Ryan Peter, Todd Christopher. Student. U. Houston, 1965-67, NYU, 1969. Prin. Patricia S. Giordano Interiors, Ridgefield, Conn., 1975—; pub. speaker various floral design and horticulture workshops. Bd. dirs. Family and Children's Aid, Inc., Danbury, Conn., 1976-78, program rev. and nominating coms., 1978, head pub. rels. com., 1978-79, pres. aux., 1976-79; v.p. Twin Ridge Homeowner's Assn., Ridgefield, Conn., 1978-79, chmn., founder area beautification, 1978; pres. East Ridge Mid. Sch. PTO, 1988-89, PTA, 1991-92. Recipient award of Excellence Fed. Garden Clubs Conn., 1984, Tricolor award Nat. Council State Garden Clubs, 1984, Aboreal award Nat. Council State Garden Clubs, 1984, Hort. Excellence award Nat. Council State Garden Clubs, 1984. Mem. Allied Bd. Trade, Caudatowa Garden Club (v.p. 1987-89, 90, pres. 1991—). Republican. Roman Catholic. Club: Caudatowa Garden (v.p. 1987-89, 90-91).

GIORDANO, RICHARD VINCENT, chemical executive; b. N.Y.C., Mar. 24, 1934; s. Vincent and Cynthia (Cardetta) G.; m. Barbara Claire Beckett, June 16, 1956; children: Susan, Anita, Richard. B.A., Harvard U., 1956; LL.B., Columbia U., 1959; D.Comml. Sci., St. John's U., 1975. Bar: N.Y. 1961. Assoc. Shearman & Sterling, N.Y.C., 1960-63; asst. sec. Air Reduction Co. Inc., N.Y.C., 1963-64; v.p. distbr. products div. Air Reduction Co. Inc., 1964-65, exec. v.p., 1965-67; group v.p. Airco Inc. (now the BOC Group Inc.), 1967-71, pres., chief oper. officer, 1971-90, chief exec. officer, 1977-90, vice chmn., 1979—; mng. dir., chief exec. officer BOC Internat. Ltd., 1979-85; chmn., chief exec. officer, bd. dirs. BOC Group, Murray Hill, N.J., 1985-90; non-exec. dir. BOC Group, Murray Hill, 1991—; dep. chmn. Grand Met. PLC, London, 1991—; retired BOC Group, 1991; dir. Ga. Pacific Corp., Grand Met. Plc.; bd. dirs. Nat. Power Plc., Reuters Holdings Plc.; non-exec. dir. BOC Group, RTZ Corp. Plc. Decorated knight comdr. Order Brit. Empire. Mem. Assn. Bar City N.Y., Am. Iron and Steel Inst., Links Club (N.Y.C.). Address: BOC Group Inc 575 Mountain Ave New Providence NJ 07974

GIORDANO, SERAFINO See GIOR, FINO

GIPS, WALTER FULD, JR., manufacturing company executive; b. N.Y.C., May 24, 1920; s. Walter Fuld and Louise (Klee) G.; m. Ann Arenberg, June 19, 1948; children—Walter Fuld, Robert L., Donald H., Ellen C. B.A., Yale U., 1941; M.B.A., Harvard U., 1943. Asst. to v.p. U.S. Plywood, 1947-50; chmn. bd. Luminator Inc., 1950-69; chmn., pres., chief exec. officer, dir. Gulton Industries, Inc., Princeton, N.J., 1969-84; emeritus, dir. Gulton Industries, Inc., 1984—; dir. JPC Enterprises, Inc. Served to capt. U.S. Army, 1943-46. Mem. Harvard Bus. Sch. Club (Chgo.) (past pres. chpt.), Yale Club (N.Y.C.). Home: 92 Brookstone Dr Princeton NJ 08540-2435 Office: Independence Way Princeton NJ 08540

GIRARDI, LISA FLORIO, public relations specialist; b. Bayshore, N.Y., July 9, 1963; d. Joseph William and Jean Rosemary (Anzalone) Florio; m. Mark Girardi, June 20, 1987. BA, Daemen Coll., 1985; postgrad., SUNY, Albany, 1986—. Reporter, photographer Standard Press & Bennington Banner, Hoosick Falls, N.Y., 1985-86; spl. project asst. N.Y. State Easter Seal Soc., Albany, 1985-86, dir. spl. project assts., 1986-87; pub. rels. asst. Singer Advt. & Mktg., Buffalo, 1987-88, pub. rels. coord., 1988-89; tech. writer Calspan Corp., Buffalo, 1989-92; pub. rels. specialist Millard Fillmore Hosps., Buffalo, 1992—; mem. task force Allied Communications Talent for Literacy, Buffalo, 1990—. Contbr. articles to profl. jours. Mem. Profl. Communicators of Western N.Y., Pub. Rels. Soc. Am. (newsletter editor 1991—, bd. dirs.), Soc. Tech. Communications (pub. rels. chmn. 1991—), Lambda Iota Tau. Roman Catholic. Home: 1 Vincent Ave Buffalo NY 14218-1624 Office: Millard Fillmore Hosps 3 Gates Cir Buffalo NY 14209

GIRAUDIER, ANTONIO, artist, poet, writer, composer, pianist; b. Havana, Cuba, Sept. 28, 1926; naturalized U.S. citizen, 1969; s. Antonio Giraudier y Ginebra and Dulce Maria Milagros y Zorrilla; LittB, Belèn Jesuits, Havana, 1944, Vedado Inst., Havana, 1944; grad. U. Havana Law Sch., 1949; M in Painting (hon.), Accademia Italia, Parma, 1982; also pvt. student art. One-man exhbns. include Smolin Gallery, N.Y.C., 1965, New Masters Gallery, N.Y.C., 1967, Avanti Galleries, N.Y.C., 1968, 69, 71, 73, 75, Palm Beach (Fla.) Towers, 1969, U. Palm Beach, 1970, Marshall (Ill.) Pub. Library, 1975, Eastern Ill. U., 1975; two-man exhbns. include Welfleet Gallery, Cape Cod, Mass., 1967, Welfleet Gallery, Palm Beach, 1968, Avanti Galleries, 1972; numerous group exhbns., U.S. and Europe, 1964—, latest being Avanti Galleries, 1970-75, French Hosp. Art Show, 1970, Argosy Gallery, Miami, 1970, Am. Acad. Arts and Letters, N.Y.C., 1973, Portsmouth (Va.) Arts Coun., AAUW, N.Y. Poetry Forum, 1981, 82, Royal Trust Tower, Miami, 1989; represented in permanent collections Fordham U. at Lincoln Ctr., N.Y.C. and Bronx, N.Y., U. Palm Beach, Greenville (S.C.) Mus. Art, Maryhill (Wash.) Mus. Fine Arts, Ea. Ill. U., also numerous pvt. collections U.S. and Europe, including: Galeria de Arte Moderno, Santo Domingo, Dominican Republic, Museo Cubano de Arte y Cultura, Miami, Fla.; represented U.S.A. Piano Concert Expo, 1992, Pavilion, 1992; concert recital Palacio Viana, Cardob, 1992. Recipient Premier Prix de Printemps, Paris, 1959, hon. mention Praire Poet Collection, 1972, hon. mention Maj. Poets Contest, 1972; laureat Margerite d'Or, Paris, 1960, Danae Lit. designate, 1973; cert. of merit Am. Poets Fellowship Soc., 1973; numerous other awards. Hon. mem. L'Orientation litteraire, Paris; mem. Smithsonian Instn., Ill. State Poetry Soc. Author numerous published books poetry, U.S., Cuba, Spain, Argentina, Europe, Venezula, 1955—; contbr. poetry to compilations, anthologies; also songwriter, piano soloist, U.S. and abroad. Address: 215 E 68th St New York NY 10021

GIRLING, PETER MICHAEL, analyzer systems engineer, consultant; b. London, Jan. 28, 1937; came to U.S., 1981; s. Frederick Atto and Doris Winifred (Martin) G.; m. Sonia Mavis Hickson, 1962 (div.); 1 child, Philippa; m. Patricia Anne Wade, Apr. 28, 1972; children: Anna, Simon, Katherine, Siobhan. Spl. degree in chemistry, Imperial Coll., London, 1957; assoc., Royal Coll. Sci., London, 1968; higher nat. cert., Borough Poly., London, 1965. Chartered engr., U.K. Asst. master London County Coun., 1959-61; devel. chemist Burt, bolton & Haywood, Belvedere, Kent, Eng., 1961-63; applications chemist Cray Valley Products, St. Mary Cray, Kent, 1963-64; asst. chief engr. GEC-Elliott, London, 1964-70; engring. assoc. Esso Engring. (Europe) Ltd., New Malden, Surrey, Eng., 1970-81; sr. engring. assoc. Air Products & Chems. Inc., Allentown, Pa., 1981-90; sr. assoc. engr. Mobil R & d Corp., Princeton, N.J., 1990—; cons. Pskills, Allentown, 1975-91. Editor Process Control and Quality, 1990—; patentee in field. Sr. sci. officer CD Corps, London,, 1959-67; chmn. cub pack 8 Boy Scouts Am., Allentown, 1982-84. Fellow Inst. Measurement and Control (U.K.); mem. Instrument Soc. Am. (sr.). Office: Mobil R & D Corp PO Box 1026 Princeton NJ 08543

GIROLAMI, JAMES PAUL, podiatrist; b. Washington, Nov. 27, 1953; s. Andrew Joseph and Maria Regina (Caporaletti) G. BS, U. Md., 1975; D Podiatric Medicine, Ohio Coll. Podiatric Medicine, 1980. Diplomate Am. Bd. Podiatric Surgery. Resident in podiatric surgery Md. Podiatric Residency Program, Balt., 1980-82; pvt. practice, Washington, 1982—; dir. podiatric residency edn. program Parkwood Hosp., Clinton, Md., 1984-88; mem. teaching staff residency program Capitol Hill Hosp., Washington, 1989—; podiatrist, lectr. Dept. Health and Mental Hygiene, Balt., 1980-82. Clin. dir. City Mission Clinic, Cleve., 1978-79. Fellow Am. Coll. Foot Surgeons; mem. Am. Podiatric Med. Assn., D.C. Podiatric Med. Assn. (v.p. 1990—), Am. Diabetes Assn., Pi Delta, Phi Sigma. Office: 3230 Pennsylvania Ave SE Washington DC 20020-3722

GIRVIN, GERALD THOMAS, retired librarian, marine historian; b. Rochester, N.Y., Apr. 2, 1929; s. Stanley Frank and Marie Ann (Mulqueen) G.; student LeMoyne Coll., 1947-50; student St. Bernard's Sem., 1950-54; BA, St. John Fisher Coll., 1956; MS, State U. Coll. N.Y., 1960; postgrad. U. Rochester, 1960-62. Tchr. secondary English, Edison Tech. and Indsl. High Sch., Rochester, N.Y., 1956-57; libr. McQuaid Jesuit High Sch., Rochester, N.Y., 1957-68; media libr. Frederick Douglass Jr. High Sch., Rochester, 1968-69, Chestnut Ridge Sch., Churchville, N.Y., 1969-71; media specialist Churchville-Chili Jr. High Sch., Churchville, 1971-73, Churchville-Chili Sch. Dist., Churchville, 1973-78, Churchville-Chili Sr. High Sch., 1978-84, Chestnut Ridge Sch., 1984-91. Mem. NEA, N.Y. Edn. Assn., Marine Mus. Great Lakes at Kington, Circus World Mus., Rochester Maritime Inst., Internat. Lilac Soc., Great Lakes Hist. Soc., Great Lakes Maritime Inst., Steamship Hist. Soc. Am., Toronto Marine Hist. Soc., Detroit Marine Hist. Soc., Welland Canal Ship Soc. Roman Catholic. Contbr. articles to profl. jours. Home: 108 Delmar St Rochester NY 14606-2515

GISI, DAVID, sales manager; b. Sisseton, S.D., Sept. 13, 1950; s. Sebastian and Julia (Leboldus) G.; m. Lorraine R. Schodorf, Oct. 15, 1972; children: Jared, Jenna. AS, N.D. Sch. of Sci., 1971. Design engr. Morton (Ill.) Bldgs. Inc., 1972-79; sales mgr. Morton Bldgs. Inc., Phillipsburg, N.J., 1979—. Republican. Home: 4945 Wagner Dr Bethlehem PA 18017-8816 Office: Morton Bldgs Inc PO Box 126 Phillipsburg NJ 08865-0126

GISOLFI, ANTHONY MARIA, emeritus foreign language educator; b. San Felice a Cancello, Italy, Nov. 13, 1909; came to U.S., 1910, naturalized, 1924; s. Ernest E. and Vincenza (Prisco) G. m. Eleanor Hayes, June 29, 1935; children: Miriam Gisolfi D'Aponte, Diana Gisolfi Pechukas, Peter, Laura Gisolfi Gilbert. AB, CCNY, 1930; MA, Columbia, 1931, PhD in Italian Lit., 1959. Tchr. Spanish and Italian High Sch. of Music and Art, N.Y.C., 1937-64; assoc. prof. Spanish and Italian SUNY, Albany, 1964-76, emeritus, 1976—; lectr. Italian lang. and lit. Bronxville Adults Sch., 1980-90; regional specialist overseas br. Office of War Info., Eng. and Mediterranean, 1944-45; lectr. Italian, Sch. Gen. Studies, CCNY, 1947-63, Columbia, summers 1933, 58, 60-63. Author: On Classic Ground, 1962; The Essential Matilde Serao, 1968; Caudine Country: The Old World and an American Childhood, 1985; (with C. Coleman) Classical Italian Songs, 1955. contbr. to Columbia U. Dictionary of Modern European Lit., 1947, 2d edit., 1980; contbr. to A Concordance to Divine Comedy of Dante Alighieri, 1965; also contbr. articles, book revs., poetry translations to profl. jours. Mem. MLA, Am. Assn. Tchrs. Italian (v.p. 1959-60), Dante Soc. Am. Home: PO Box 225 Bronxville NY 10708-0225

GISOLFI (PECHUKAS), DIANA, academic administrator, art history educator; b. N.Y.C., Sept. 12, 1940; d. Anthony M. and Eleanor (Hayes) Gisolfi; m. Philip Pechukas, June 15, 1963 (div. Sept. 1991); children: Rolf, Maria, Sarah, Fiona (dec.), Amy. Student, Manhattanville Coll., 1958-60; BA magna cum laude, Radcliffe Coll., 1962; postgrad., Yale U., 1962-63; MA, U. Chgo., 1964, PhD, 1976. Instr. CUNY, 1967-68, Marymount Manhattan Coll., N.Y.C., 1977-79; asst. prof. Pratt Inst., Bklyn., 1979-84, assoc. prof., 1984-90, chair art history dept., 1980—, prof., 1990—; vis. asst. prof. Pratt Inst., 1976-79; dir. Pratt in Venice, Italy, 1984—; speaker Conv. on Veronese, Venice, 1988; invited participant, Veronese Reconsidered, CASVA, Washington, 1988. Illustrator (book) On Classic Ground, 1982; designer: (book) Caudine Country, 1987; contbr. articles on Veronese to Art Bull., Artibus et Historiae, Arte Veneta, others. Coord. Park Slope Freeze, Bklyn., 1984-86, Peace and Justice Com., St. Francis Xavier, 1984-86. Am. Philos. Soc. grantee, 1989. Mem. Coll. Art Assn., Caucus for Design History, Phi Beta Kappa. Democrat. Roman Catholic. Home: 843 President St Brooklyn NY 11215-1405 Office: Pratt Inst Dept Art History East 250 Brooklyn NY 11205

GISPANSKI, JOSEPH ANTHONY, JR., safety engineer trainer; b. Kittanning, Pa., Jan. 3, 1965; s. Joseph A. and Marie K. (Hromadik) G.; m. R. Jeanette Sidora, June 20, 1987. BS in Safety Sci., Indiana U. Pa., 1987. Cert. engr. trainer. Safety engr. trainer Hygiene Safety and Tng Inc, Kittanning, Pa. Mem. Am. Soc. Safety Engrs., Am. Indsl. Hygiene Assn., Nat. Environ. Tng. Assn. Office: Hygiene Safety and Tng Inc PO Box 837 Kittanning PA 16201-0837

GITLIN, MICHAEL, sculptor, educator; b. Capetown, South Africa, Apr. 23, 1943; came to U.S., 1970; s. Gershon and Miriam (Joffee) G.; divorced; children: Adam, Daniella. BA, Hebrew U., 1967; MFA, Pratt Inst., 1972. Drawing instr. Parsons Sch. Design, N.Y.C., 1976-77; sculpture instr. Bezalel Acad. Art., Jerusalem, 1977-78; sculpture and drawing instr. Parsons Sch. Design, N.Y.C., 1981-84; adj. prof. Bezalel Acad. Art, Jerusalem, 1985, Columbia U., N.Y.C., 1987; vis. prof. U. Calif., Davis, 1988. Numerous individual and group exhbns., permanent collections. Fellow Nat. Endowment for Arts 1985-86, Guggenheim 1987-88; recipient Israel Mus. Sandberg prize 1989. Home and Office: 290 Lafayette St # 1B New York NY 10012-3311

GITTELL, ROSS JACOBS, economics and public policy educator; b. N.Y.C., July 23, 1957; s. Irwin and Marilyn (Jacobs) G. AB, U. Chgo., 1979; MBA, U. Calif., Berkeley, 1981; PhD, Harvard U., 1989. Cons. Chase Econometrics, San Francisco, 1981-84; sr. cons. SRI Internat., Menlo Park, Calif., 1984-85; rsch. fellow Harvard U., Cambridge, Mass., 1985-87; dir. rsch. project Harvard U., Cambridge, 1987, lectr. econs., 1989—; asst. prof. and sr. rsch. assoc. New Sch. for Social Rsch., N.Y.C.; cons. Office Rsch., Calif. Assembly, Sacramento, 1980-81, Interface Inc., N.Y.C., 1980. Contbr. articles to profl. publs. Del. Ill. Dem. Conv., 1976, Dem. County Presdl. Conv., Ft. Worth, 1988. Mem. Am. Econ. Assn., Assn. for Pub. Policy Analysis and Mgmt., Nat. Assn. Bus. Economists, Phi Beta Kappa, Beta Gamma Sigma. Jewish. Office: New Sch Social Rsch Grad Sch Mgmt/Urban Policy 66 5th Ave New York NY 10011

GITTELMAN, MARTIN, clinical psychiatry educator; b. N.Y.C., Sept. 24, 1930; s. Philip and Frieda Gittelman; m. Lourdes Publico; children: Michelle, Maya Sofia. PhD in Clin. Psychology, Columbia U., 1966. Prof. clin. psychiatry N.Y. Med. Coll., Lincoln Health and Med. Ctr., Bronx, 1984—; cons. WHO, China, 1988, 90, 91, 92, Philippines, 1988, 90, West Africa, 1991, Vietnam, 1990. Mem. World Psychiat. Assn. (mem. edn. com.), World Assn. Psychosocial Rehab. (pres. 1991—). Office: NY Med Coll Dept Psychiatry 234 E 149th St Bronx NY 10451-5504

GITTERMAN, ALEX, social work educator; b. Kolomea, Poland; came to U.S., 1948; s. Paul and Fay (Hirsch) G.; m. Naomi Janet Pines, Sept. 1963; children: Daniel Paul, Sharon Lynn. B.A., Rutgers U., 1960; M.S.W., Hunter Coll., 1962; Ed.D., Columbia U., 1972. Div. dir. Bronx River Settlement, 1962-65; dir. East Side House Millbrook Ctr., Bronx, 1965-66; mem. faculty Columbia U., N.Y.C., 1966—, prof., 1972—; assoc. dean Columbia U., 1981-85; cons. Manhattan VA, N.Y.C., 1974-80, Family Service of Westchester (White Plains), N.Y., 1978-80, Bur. Child Welfare, 1977-80, Drug Abuse Prevention Program, Archdiocese of N.Y., 1985—. Contbr. articles to profl. jours.; author: (with L. Shulman) Mut. Aid Groups & The Life Cycle, 1985, (with C.B. Germain) The Life Model of Social Work Practice, 1980, Handbook of Social Work Practice with Vulnerable Populations, 1990. Recipient Hexter award Hunter Coll., 1981. Mem. Am. Orthopsychiat. Assn., Am. Pub. Health Assn., Soc. Hosp. Social Work Dirs., Com. on Social Work Edn., Nat. Assn. Social Workers. Democrat. Jewish. Office: Columbia U Sch Social Work 622 W 113th St # U New York NY 10025-7982

GITTLER, STEVEN, business law and education law educator, lawyer; b. May 21, 1926; m. Antonia Josephine, Aug. 7, 1954; 1 child, Jean Elizabeth. B.A., Lake Forest Coll., 1948; postgrad. U. Ill., 1950-51; M.A., Wash. State U., 1951; postgrad. U. Mich. Law Sch., 1954-55; Ed.D., SUNY-Buffalo, 1961. Bar: N.Y. 1981; U.S. Ct. Appeals (2d cir.) 1984, U.S. Supreme Ct. 1984. Instr., Mich. State U., East Lansing, 1953-54; from asst. prof. to prof. Buffalo State Coll., 1955—; assoc. Robert B. Moriarty, Esq., Buffalo, 1981-86; mediator/fact finder N.Y. State Pub. Employment Relations Bd., Albany, 1973—; arbitrator Am. Arbitration Assn., 1975—. Served to lt. col.

USAR, 1944-86. Mem. Nat. Orgn. Legal Problems of Edn. (dir. 1967-69), Erie County Bar Assn. Episcopalian. Home: 148 Autumnview Rd Buffalo NY 14221-1538 Office: Law Office 1260 Delaware Ave Buffalo NY 14209-2498

GITTLIN, ARTHUR SAM, industrialist, banker; b. Newark, Nov. 21, 1914; s. Benjamin and Ethel (Bernstein) G.; m. Fay Lerner, Sept. 18, 1938; children: Carol Franklin, Regina (Mrs. Peter Gross), Bruce David, Steven Robert. BCS, Rutgers U., 1938. Ptnr. Gittlin Bag Co. (name now changed to Gittlin Cos. Inc.), Livingston, N.J., No. Miami, Fla., N.Y.C., 1935-40; v.p., dir. Gittlin Bag Co., 1954—, chmn. bd., 1963—; v.p., dir. Abbey Record Mfg. Co., Newark, 1958-60; chmn., treas. Packaging Products & Design Co. (now PPD Corp.), Newark and Glendale, Calif., 1959-71, chmn. exec. com., treas., 1972—; chmn. Pines Shirt & Pajama Co., N.Y.C., 1960-85, Pottsville Shirt & Pajama Co. (Pa.), 1960—, Barrington Industries, N.Y.C., 1963-72, First Peninsula Calif. Corp., N.Y.C., 1964-68, Peninsula Savs. and Loan, San Francisco and San Mateo, Calif., 1964-68, Wall-co Imperial, Miami, Fla., 1965-87, Levin & Hecht, Inc., N.Y.C., 1966-72, Wallco of San Juan (P.R.), Brunswick Shirt Co., N.Y.C., 1966-72, Fleetline Industries, Garland, N.C., 1966-72, All State Auto Leasing & Rental Corp., Beverly Hills, Calif., 1968-72, Packaging Ltd., Newark, 1970-76, Kans. Plastics, Inc., Garden City, 1970-76, Bob Cushman Distbrs., Inc. (now Wallpapers Inc.), Phoenix, 1972-87, Wallpaper Supermarkets, Phoenix, 1976-80, Wallco Internat. Inc., Miami, 1976, Overwrap Equipment Corp., Fairfield, 1978-86, GCI Ala. Inc., Birmingham, 1981—; chmn. Wallpapers Inc., Oakland, Calif., 1982-86, Portland, Oreg., Honolulu, Denver, L.A. and Phoenix, 1982-86; pres. Covington Funding Co., N.Y.C., 1963—; vice chmn. bd. Peninsula Savs. and Loan Assn., San Mateo and San Francisco, 1964-67, chmn., 1967-68; chmn. bd., treas. Bob Cushman Painting & Decorating Co. (now Wallco West), Phoenix, 1972-86; treas., dir. Flex Pak Industries, Inc., Atlanta, 1973-76, Ploy Plax Films, Inc., Santa Ana, Calif., 1973-76; sec., chmn. exec. com. Zins Wallcoverings, Newark; ptnr. Benjamin Co., Livingston, N.J., Laurel Assocs. (Md.), Seaboard Realty Assocs., Miami, 1980—, GHG Realty Assocs., N.Y.C., 1980, Parkway Assocs., Miami, 1987—; ptnr., investors cons. Mission Pack, Inc., L.A.; vice chmn., dir., chmn. exec. com. Falmouth Supply, Ltd., Montreal, Que., Can., Ascher Trading Corp., Newark, Aptex, Inc., Newark; bd. dirs., fin. cons. Ramada Inns, Phoenix; bd. dirs., fin. cons. Aztar Inc., Phoenix; bd. dirs. Harris Paint & Wall Covering Super Marts, Miami, Morgan Hill Mfg. Co., Reading, Pa., Douglas Gardens Home for the Aged, Miami. Chmn. N.C. com. B'nai B'rith, 1940; treas. N.C. Fedn. B'nai B'rith Lodges, 1941-43, v.p., 1943-44, pres., 1944-47; mem. com. to rev. dept. banking and ins. N.J. Commn. on Efficiency and Economy in State Govt., 1967-69; trustee Benjamin Gittlin Charity Found., Newark, BAMA Master Retirement Program, Hillel Found. at Rutgers U., Temple Emanuel, Miami, hon. v.p., bd. dir.; founders bd. Miami Gardens Home Aged. Jewish (pres., trustee B'nai Abraham, Livingston N.J., trustee Temple Emanuel, Miami, 1987—). Clubs: Greenbrook Country (Caldwell, N.J.), Turnberry Yacht and Golf (Turnberry Isle, Fla.), Westview Country (Miami, Fla.). Lodge: B'nai B'rith. Home: 59 Glenview Rd South Orange NJ 07079-1060 also: 9801 Collins Ave Bal Harbour FL 33154 Office: 2875 NE 191st St Miami FL 33180-2803 also: 21 Penn Plz New York NY 10001 also: 70 S Orange Ave Livingston NJ 07079

GIULIANI, PETER, consultant; b. Tuscany, Italy, Jan. 4, 1907; s. John and Caterino (Tolomei) G.; m. Paulne Marie Provost, May 8, 1943; children: John Paul, Peter Arthur. LLD (hon.), Worwich U., 1980. Bar: Vt. 1928. Assoc. counsel Nat. Life Ins. Co., Montpelier, Vt., 1935-71; trust. U. Vermont, Burlington; fellow Norwich U., Northfield, Vt., 1981-90. Chmn. Ways and Means Com. Vt. Gen. Assembly, Montpelier, 1966-84. S.Sgt. USMC, 1942-45., U.S. Republican. Roman Catholic. Home: 15 College St Montpelier VT 05602-3634 Office: McKee Giuliani & Cleveland 94 Main St # 1st Montpelier VT 05602-2905

GIULIANI, RUDOLPH W., lawyer, former government official; b. N.Y.C., May 28, 1944. A.B., Manhattan Coll.; J.D., NYU. Law clk. U.S. Dist. Ct. Judge, N.Y.C., 1968-70; asst. U.S. atty. So. Dist. N.Y.; exec. asst. U.S. atty., chief narcotics sect., and chief spl. prosecutions sect. Dept. Justice, assoc. dep. atty. gen., 1975-77; assoc. atty. gen., 1981-83; U.S. atty. U.S. Dist. Ct. (so. dist.), N.Y., 1983-89; mem. firm Patterson, Belknap, Webb and Tyler, N.Y.C., 1977-81, White & Case, N.Y.C., 1989-90, Anderson Kill Olick & Oshinsky PC, N.Y.C., 1990—. Rep. candidate for mayor N.Y.C., 1989. Office: Anderson Kill Olick & Oschinsky 666 3d Ave New York NY 10017

GIUNTA-MANGE, ANITA DIANE, psychologist; b. Long Branch, N.J., Mar. 10, 1960. Student, NYU, 1977-79; BA in Psychology Cum Laude with Distinction, Boston U., 1981; MA in Clin. Psychology, Calif. Sch. of Profl. Psychology, Fresno, 1983, PhD in Clin. Psychology, 1985. Lic. psychologist, N.Y., Fla.; lic. sch. psychologist, N.Y. Rsch. asst. sociology dept. Boston U., 1979-80, rsch. asst. psychology dept., 1980-81; staff asst. Newton-Wellesley-Weston-Needham Community Mental Health and Retardation Ctr., Newtown Centre, Mass., 1980-81, Apt. Living Program, Allston, Mass., 1981; therapist and test examiner Fresno Unified Sch. Dist., 1982-83, Fresno City Coll. Assessment Ctr., 1982-83; tchr. Fresno City Coll., 1984; psychology intern Pilgrim Psychiatric Ctr., West Brentwood, N.Y., 1984-85; psychologist Inpatient Unit Creedmoor Psychiat. Ctr., Queens Village, N.Y., 1985-86; assoc. psychologist Queens Village Community Svcs., 1986-88, field supr. for psychology intern, 1987-88; adj. asst. prof. St. John's U., Queens, 1986; psychol. test examiner Patchogue (N.Y.) Sch. Dist., 1987-88; psychologist Sunrise Psychiat. Clinic, Amityville, N.Y., 1988-90; pvt. practice West Babylon and Patchogue, 1987—. Contbr. article to local newspaper. Mem. APA, Psi Chi. Roman Catholic. Office: 393 Sunrise Hwy West Babylon NY 11704-5909

GIVENS, JANET EATON, writer; b. N.Y.C., July 5, 1932; d. Irving Daniel and Matilda (Schmelzle) E.; m. Richard Ayres Givens, Aug. 24, 1957; children—Susan Ruth, Jane Lucile. B.A., Queens Coll., 1953; M.A., Columbia U., 1955. Lic. tchr., N.Y. Tchr. pub. elem. schs., Silver Spring, Md., 1953-55, Mamaroneck, N.Y., 1955-59; supr. prospective tchrs., part-time lectr. Queens Coll., N.Y.C., 1959-68. Author: The Migrating Birds, 1964; Something Wonderful Happened, 1982; Just Two Wings, 1984; contbg. author: Tensions Our Children Live With, 1959. V.p. PTA, Pub. Sch. 219, Queens, N.Y., 1972-73, del. to United Parents Assn., 1971-72, editor PS 219 News, 1971-73. Home: 14711 68th Rd Flushing NY 11367-1332

GIWA, LATEEF OLAKUNLE, thoracic surgeon, educator; b. Offa, Kwara, Nigeria, Apr. 1, 1943; came to U.S., 1969; s. Alhaji Sani and Rabiat (Abegbe) G.; m. Adikat Kofo Disu, Dec. 27, 1968 (div.); 1 child, Abdul Lateef; m. Amudat Adunni Musa, Feb. 7, 1981; children: Femi Hafiz, Tayo Muizz. GCE, Fed. Sch. Sci., Lagos, Nigeria, 1963; MB, BS., U. Ibadan, Nigeria, 1968. Diplomate Am. Bd. Surgery, Am. Bd. Thoracic Surgery. Intern Lagos (Nigeria) Gen. Hosp., 1968-69, Manchester (Conn.) Meml. Hosp., 1969-70; surg. resident L.I. Jewish Hosp., New Hyde Park, N.Y., 1970-74; cardiothoracic resident Montefiore Hosp. & Med. Ctr., Bronx, N.Y., 1974-76; asst. prof. surgery SUNY, Stony Brook, 1976-80; sr. lectr. in surgery U. Ilorin, Nigeria, 1980-84; pvt. practice L.I., 1984—; attending surgeon L.I. Jewish Hosp., New Hyde Park, 1985—, Deepdale Gen. Hosp., Little Neck, N.Y., 1984—. Contbr. articles to profl. jours. Fellow Am. Coll. Surgeons, Am. Coll. Angiology, Am. Coll. Cardiology, Am. Coll. Chest Physicians. Islamic. Office: Lateef O Giwa MD 99 Tulip Ave Ste 109 Floral Park NY 11001

GIZIS, EVANGELOS JOHN, biochemist; b. Tinos, Greece, Apr. 1, 1934; came to U.S. 1960; s. John Constantine and Anna (Sigalas) G.; m. Frances C. Murray, Oct. 21, 1967; children: John, Alexander, Paul-Robert. BS in Chemistry, Athens U., 1957; MS in Food Sci., Oreg. State U., 1962, PhD in Food Sci., Biochemistry, 1963. Postdoctoral fellow Mich. State U., E. Lansing, 1964-65; fellow Carnegie-Mellon U., Pitts., 1965-66; biochemist L.I. Jewish Hosp., N.Y.C., 1966-70; rsch. collaborator Brookhaven (N.Y.) Nat. Lab., 1967-69; acting pres., dean CUNY, Hostos CC, Bronx, 1970-77; chemist VA Hosp., Bklyn., 1970-73; adj. prof. Nutrition Dept. NYU, N.Y.C., 1978—; v.p. Queens Coll., CUNY, Flushing, 1986—; acting pres., v.p. CUNY, Borough of Manhattan Community Coll., 1977-86; title III evaluator Community Coll. of Balt., 1980—. Contbr. articles to profl. jours. Mem. Am. Inst. Nutrition, Inst. Food Technologists, Am. Chem. Soc., Soc. for Exptl. Biology and Medicine. Greek Orthodox. Home: 427 Ryder Rd Manhasset NY 11030-2761 Office: Queens Coll 65-30 Kissena Blvd Flushing NY 11367

GLADKIN, PETER, computer company executive; b. Watenstadt, Germany, July 19, 1947; came to U.S., 1951; s. Nikolai and Antonina (Duchina) G.; m. Victoria Ann Ervin, Sept. 21, 1975; children: Peter Giles, Michael Alexander. BS in Chemistry, U. Ill., Chgo., 1969; MBA, Northwestern U., 1976; M in Bus., Harvard U., 1989. Forensic chemist Ill. Racing Bd., Chgo., 1969-70; tech. rep. Crown Cork & Seal, Chgo., 1970-71; analytical sales rep. Hewlett Packard, Chgo., 1971-75; gen. mgr. USSR Hewlett Packard, Moscow, 1975-78; product line mgr. Hewlett Packard, Boeblingen, Germany, 1978-80; nat. accounts mktg. mgr. Hewlett Packard, Boston, 1980-86, gen. mgr. info. systems, 1986—; bd. dirs. Ctr. for Health-care Info. Mgmt., Chgo. Contbr. articles to profl. jours. Founding mem. Orthodox Children's Camp, Rockford, Ill., 1964—. Mem. Am. Chem. Soc., Am. Mensa Ltd., Am. Assn. Individual Investors, Internat. Assn. Fin. Planners, Nat. Account Mktg. Assn. (bd. dirs. 1984—, pres. 1986), Concord Country Club, Beta Gamma Sigma. Republican. Russian Orthodox. Office: Hewlett Packard 3000 Minuteman Rd Andover MA 01810-1099

GLAESSMANN, DORIS ANN, county official; b. Northampton, Pa., Feb. 18, 1940; d. Frank G. and Theresa (Fischl) Zwikl; m. Edward Glaessmann, Sept. 1, 1962; children: Edward Jr., Robert F. Grad. high sch., Northampton, 1958. Sec., bookkeeper John F. Moore Agy., Inc., Allentown, Pa., 1958-64; ct. clk. Criminal div. Clk. of Cts. Office, Allentown, 1968-69, asst. dep. clk., 1969-76, chief dep. clk., 1976-82; clk. of cts. Lehigh County Criminal and Civil divs., Allentown, 1982—. Den mother, sec. Cub Scout Pack 140, Allentown, Pa., 1973-78; mem., past bd. dirs. Quota Club Allentown, 1983—; mem. coun. St. Peter's Evang. Luth. Ch., Allentown, 1984-89. Mem. Nat. Assn. County Recorders and Clks., Internat. Assn. Clks., Recorders, Election Ofcls. and Treas., Pa. Prothonotaries and Clks. Assn. (past pres.), Pa. Elected Women's Assn. (past sec.-treas., past pres. Lehigh Valley chpt.). Democrat. Home: 945 E Lynnwood St Allentown PA 18103-5250 Office: Lehigh County 455 Hamilton St PO Box 1548 Allentown PA 18105-1548

GLANZ, RUTH, audiovisual communications professional; b. N.Y.C., Nov. 28, 1928; d. Joseph and Miriam (Greenfield) Ginsberg; m. Lawrence Goldstein, Feb. 22, 1951 (div. 1978); children: Beth Erica Goldstein McKee, Donna Lee, Tina Cindy; m. Spencer Glanz, June 11, 1989. BA, CUNY, 1949, MS, 1975. Asst. dir. audiovideo Equitable Life Assurance Soc., N.Y.C., 1975-77; dir. audiovisual comms. Associated Merchandising Corp., N.Y.C., 1977-92; videographer, editor, adj. prof. Hunter Coll. CUNY, N.Y.C., 1969-75. Producer over 1000 multi-image and video programs. Pres. PTA, 1963-64; coord. Women Strike for Peace, Manhattan, 1967-69. Mem. Internat. TV Assn., Assn. for Multi-Image Internat., Fashion Group, Internat. Home Fashion and Design Assn.

GLASBERG, H(ERBERT) MARK, psychiatrist; b. N.Y.C., Oct. 11, 1939; s. Joseph and Elsa (Haber) G.; m. Paula Drillman, June 19, 1960; children: Scot Bradley, Hilary Jennifer. BA, Yeshiva U., 1953; MS, Columbia U., 1954; MD, SUNY, 1958. Diplomate Nat. Bd. Med. Examiners, Am. Bd. Psychiatry and Neurology. Intern Maimonides Hosp. N.Y.C., 1958-59; resident in psychiatry Kings County Hosp., N.Y.C., 1959-60; resident in internal medicine Kingsbridge VA Hosp. of Columbia U. Coll. Med. Program, N.Y.C., 1960-61; resident Payne Whitney Psychiat. Clin., N.Y. Hosp., 1963-65, fellow, 1965-66; spl. rsch. fellow Nat. Inst. Mental Health, 1966-68, Cornell U. Med. Sch., N.Y. Hosp.; pvt. practice medicine specializing in psychiatry, N.Y.C., 1968—; attending physician dept. of psychiatry Columbia U. Coll. of Physicians & Surgeons; instr. Cornell U. Med. Sch., 1966-68; assoc. prof. psychiatry Mt. Sinai Sch. Medicine, 1968—; dir. psychiat. outpatient svcs. Beth Israel Hosp., N.Y.C., 1968-74, assoc. attending psychiatrist, 1968-74; attending psychiatrist St. Vincent's Hosp., N.Y.C., 1974—, chief psychiat. emergency and cons. svcs., 1974-75; examiner Am. Bd. Psychiatry & Neurology, 1988—. Cons. mem. panel of ind. psychiatrists N.Y.C. Mental Health Info. Svc., 1968—. Mem. Manhattan physicians com. United Jewish Appeal, 1970—; mem. com. admission selection Cornell U. Med. Coll., Ctr. Alumni Assn. N.Y. Hosp. Lt. col., M.C., AUS, 1961-63. Fellow ACP, Am. Psychiat. Assn. (internat. platform com. 1980—), N.Y. Acad. Scis., N.Y. Acad. Medicine; mem. APA, AAAS, Am. Psychosomatic Soc., Soc. for Adolescent Psychiatry, Internat. Platform Assn. Home and Office: 14 E 73d St New York NY 10021

GLASBERG, MEYER SAMUEL, lawyer, accountant; b. Phila., Dec. 16, 1916; s. Harry and Mary (Cooper) G.; m. Jean Carlin, Dec. 13, 1942 (dec. Apr. 1991); 1 child, Mark R. Student, Temple U., 1939, BSC, 1979; JD, Temple U., Phila., 1939. Bar: Pa. 1979, U.S. Dist. Ct. Pa. 1979; CPA, Pa. CPA pvt. practice, Phila., 1944-67, Brown and Co., Phila., 1967-73, J.K. Lasser and Co., Phila., 1973-77, Touche Ross and Co,, Phila., 1977-79; lawyer pvt. practice, Phila., 1979-91. Mem. Pa. Bar Assn., Phila. Bar Assn. Office: 5 St James Ct Philadelphia PA 19106

GLASER, ALVIN, manufacturing company executive; b. New Bedford, Mass., Jan. 8, 1932; s. Morris and Jennie (Brody) G.; m. Rosalyn S.F. Clasky, Jan. 20, 1963; children: Iris, Linda, Marjorie, Jeffrey. Student pub. schs., New Bedford. Mgr. Morris Glaser Glass Co., New Bedford, 1949—; treas. Glaser Inc., 1964—, pres. Glaser Glass Corp., 1985—; corporator Compass Bank. Mem. Dartmouth (Mass.) Youth Commn. Mem. Nat. Glass Assn., New Bedford C. of C., Masons, Order Eastern Star, Shriners, B'nai B'rith, Moose. Home: 2 Ann Ave North Dartmouth MA 02747-3253 Office: 1265 Purchase St New Bedford MA 02740-6695

GLASER, JUDITH ENTINE, communications company executive; b. Phila., June 23, 1946; d. Martin and Rose (Cole) Entine; m. Richard David Glaser, Jan. 18, 1970; children: Rebecca Amy, Joshua Ari. BA, Temple U., 1967; MS, Drexel U., 1969; postgrad., Harvard U., 1968, 78, Fairfield (Conn.) U., 1979-81. Learning cons. Hahnemann Hosp., Phila., 1969-70, Bess Stone Ctr., Lawrence, Kans., 1970-73, Judy Glaser & Assocs., Fairfield, 1973-84; communications cons., pres., 1984—; nat. speaker ASTD, ISA, Benchmaking and Best Practices, Wharton Exec. Edn., Nat. Soc. Pharm. Sales Trainers, Nat. Acctg. Soc. Sr. editor: Random House Business Dictionary, 1989; contbr. articles to profl. jours. Dir. pub. rels. Brandeis U. Nat. Women's Com., Fairfield, 1973-77, Holistic Health Conf., Westport, Conn., 1981; mem. coun. Cablevision, 1979—. Recipient Entrepreneurial Excellence award hon. mention Women's Entrepreneurial Network, Quality cons. award Union Carbide Co., Linde Mgmt. Devel., 1991. Mem. ASTD, Am. Mgmt. Assn., Instructional Systems Assn. (v.p. pub. rels. 1991-92, mem. employability task force 1989-92). Office: Benchmark Comm Inc 106 Picketts Ridge Rd West Redding CT 06896

GLASER, MICHAEL SCHMIDT, literature and writing educator; b. Chgo., Mar. 20, 1943; s. Milton A. and Rona (Schmidt) G.; m. Patricia Carlson, June 18, 1966 (div. July 1974); children: Brian, Joshua, Daniel; m. Kathleen Nancy Webbert, May 8, 1975; children: Amira, Eva. BA, Denison U., 1965; MA, Kent State U., 1967, PhD, 1971; postdoctoral student, U. Calif., San Diego, 1974-75. Teaching fellow Kent (Ohio) State U., 1966-70; asst. prof. St. Mary's Coll., St. Mary's City, Md., 1970-74, assoc. prof., 1974-82, chmn. dept. Arts and Letters, 1979-81, prof. English, 1982—; dir. Oxford Program and Festival of Poets and Poetry, St. Mary's City, Festival of Poets and Poetry, St. Mary's City, 1980—; active Poet-in-the-Schs. project, Md. State Arts Coun., Balt., 1985—; bd. dirs. Poetry Com. of Washington. Author: A Lover's Eye, 1989, 2d edit., 1991; editor: The Cooke Book, 1987. Bd. dirs. St. Mary's County Arts Coun., St. Mary's County Women's Ctr.; chmn. St. Mary's County Housing Authority, 1985-89. Mem. MLA, The Writer's Ctr. Home: PO Box 1 Saint Marys City MD 20686-0001 Office: St Mary's Coll Montgomery Hall Saint Mary's City MD 20686

GLASER, PAUL RUSSEL, podiatric surgeon; b. Bklyn., June 23, 1945; s. Paul R. and Mary Margaret (Hopkins) G.; m. Carolyn Winnifred Kane, Aug. 10, 1968; children: Paul R. II, Alana Lee. BS, L.I. U., 1968; D Podiatric Medicine, Ill. Coll. Podiatric Medicine, 1972. Diplomate Am. Bd. Podiatric Surgery, Am. Bd. Podiatric Orthopedics, Am. nat. Bd. Podiatry Examiners. Resident in surgery Ohio Coll. Podiatric Medicine, Cleve., 1972-73, N.Y. Coll. Podiatric Medicine, N.Y.C., 1973-74; pvt. practice Huntington, N.Y., 1974—; cons. Diabetes Assn. L.I., Melville, N.Y., 1985—, N.Y. Athletic Club, N.Y.C., 1983—, N.Y. State Supreme Ct. Arbitration, Riverhead, 1983—; co-dir. dept. surgery L.I. SurgiCtr., 1988—; ofcl. Meadowlands Vitalis Invitational Track, 1985-91. Fellow Am. Coll. Foot Surgeons, Suffolk Acad. Medicine; mem. Am. Coll. Podopediatrics, Suffolk County Podiatric Med. Soc. (pres. 1985-87). Republican. Roman Catholic. Office: 76 E Main St Ste 3 Huntington NY 11743-2837

GLASER, ROBERT EDWARD, electrical engineer; b. Balt., Mar. 12, 1954; s. Stanley and Helen (Sherbow) G. BES, Johns Hopkins U., 1975, MSE, 1977, PhD, 1981. Lic. FCC radiotelephone operator. Dir. R&D Telesaver, Inc., Owings Mills, Md., 1981-85; pres. IC Engring., Inc., Owings Mills, 1986—; cons. in field; part-time lectr. Johns Hopkins U., 1986—. Inventor distributed processing telephone switching system; contbr. Handbook of Software Engineering, 1984; contbr. articles to profl. jours. Pres. Randallstown Amateur Radio Club, Md., 1980—. Mem. IEEE, IEEE Computer Soc. Office: IC Engring Inc PO Box 321 Owings Mills MD 21117-0321

GLASER, ROBERT LEONARD JR., investor; b. Highland Park, Ill., Mar. 29, 1960; s. Robert Leonard and Nancy Lehman (Field) G. BS, Roger Williams Coll., 1982. Rsch. analyst John Blair & Co., N.Y.C., 1982-84; pres., owner Lehmann Bldg. Co., Peoria, Ill., 1984-89, Nu-Media, Inc., Westport, Conn., 1986—, Glaser Holding Ltd., Westport, 1986—. Dir., treas. Nat. Alliance of Drug Free Athletes, Portland, Maine, 1990—. Office: Glaser Holding Ltd 1771 Post Rd E Ste 300 Westport CT 06880-5658

GLASER, ROBERT VINCENT, investment company executive; b. Rochester, N.Y., June 16, 1951; s. Robert E. Glaser and Mary L. (Bates) Greenman. BA in Polit. Sci., U. Buffalo, 1973; MBA, NYU, 1978. Trainee The Chase Manhattan Bank, N.A., N.Y.C., 1973-76, asst. v.p., 1976-79; v.p. credit, mktg. officer The Chase Manhattan Bank, N.A., Manama, Bahrain, 1979-81, v.p., regional instnl. mgr., 1981-83; mem. mgmt. com. Investcorp Group, Manama, N.Y.C., 1983—; also bd. dirs.; bd. dirs. Color Tile Inc., Burnham Svcs. Corp., Catherines Stores Corp., Dellwood Foods Inc., Fox Photo Inc., Gucci Am., Inc., Guccio Gucci S.p.A., N.Y. Dept. Stores of P.R. Mem. University Club, Doubles Club, Rockefeller Ctr. Club, Grand Champions Club, Mosimann's Club. Office: Investcorp Internat Inc 37W Fl 280 Park Ave New York NY 10017-1288

GLASGOLD, ALVIN I., physician; b. N.Y., Apr. 28, 1936; s. Jeanne (Brown) Ovis; m. Joyce Padrusch; children: Mark, Ellen, Robert. MD, N.Y. Med. Coll., 1961. Diplomate Am. Bd. Facial Plasitc and Reconstructive Surgery, Am. Bd. cosmetic Surgery, Am. Bd. Otolaryngology-Head and Neck Surgery. Intern Beth Israel Hosp., N.Y.C., 1961-62; resident Bronx Vet.'s Hosp. and Columbia U. Coll. Physicians and Surgeons, 1962-66; chmn. Dept. Otolaryngology-Head and Neck Surgery St. Peter's Med. Ctr., New Brunswick, N.J., Robert Wood Johnson Univ. Hosp., New Brunswick; attending physician Manhattan Eye, Ear and Throat Hosp., N.Y.C.; assoc. clin. prof. surgery UMDNJ-Robert Wood Johnson Med. Sch., New Brunwicks; chmn. Facial Plastic sect. N.J. Acad. Ophthalmology and Otolaryngology, 1980-88; chmn. ann. facial plastic symposium N.J. Acad. Ophthalmology and Otolaryngology, 1983-88; co-chmn. external rhinoplasty course Manhattan Eye, Ear and Throat Hosp., AAFPRS, 1989, 90; instr. rhinoplasty Mt. Sinai Hosp., 1986-88; mem. bd. govs. Am. Acad. Ophthalmomogy and Otolaryngology, 1981-84. Author: (book) Application of Biomaterials in Facial Plastic Surgery, 1991. Fellow Am. Acad. Facial Plastic and Reconstructive Surgery, Am. Acad. Cosmetic Surgery (pres., bd. dirs. Facial Plastic Surgery Info. Svc., Inc., credentials com.), Am. Coll. Surgeons, Am. Acad. Otolaryngology-Head and Neck Surgery (instr. revision rhinoplasty-external approach 1990, bd. govs. 1981-84), Am. Soc. Head and Neck Surgery, Am. Soc. Liposuction Surgery. Home: 31 River Rd Highland Park NJ 08904

GLASHOW, SHELDON LEE, physicist, educator; b. N.Y.C., Dec. 5, 1932; s. Lewis and Bella (Rubin) G.; m. Joan Glashow; children: Jason David, Jordan, Brian Lewis, Rebecca Lee. AB, Cornell U., 1954; AM, Harvard U., 1955, PhD, 1958; DSc (hon.), Yeshiva U., 1978, U. Marseille, 1982, Adelphi U., 1989, Bar Ilan U., 1989, Gustave Adolphus Coll., 1989. NSF fellow U. Copenhagen, Denmark, 1958-60; rsch. fellow Calif. Inst. Tech., 1960-61; asst. prof. Stanford U., 1961-62; asst. prof., assoc. prof. U. Calif. at Berkeley, 1962-66; mem. faculty Harvard U., 1966—, prof. physics, 1967—, Higgins prof. physics, 1979—, Mellon prof. scis., 1988—; disting. vis. scientist Boston U., 1984—; cons. Brookhaven Nat. Lab., 1966-73, 75—; mem. sci. policy com. CERN, 1979-84; vis. prof. U. Marseille, 1971, MIT, 1974-80, Boston U., 1983; affiliated sr. scientist U. Houston, 1983—; univ. scholar Tex. A&M U., 1983-86. Author: (with Ben Bova) Interactions, 1988; contbr. articles to profl. jours. and popular mags.; editor-in-chief for physics Quantum mag., 1989—. Pres. Andrei Sakharov Inst., 1980-85, Nat. Com. for Excellence in Edn., 1985-88. Recipient J.R. Oppenheimer Meml. prize, 1977, George Ledlie prize, 1978, Nobel prize in physics, 1979, Castiglione di Sicilia prize, 1983; NSF fellow, 1955-60, Sloan fellow, 1962-66, CERN vis. fellow, 1968. Fellow Am. Phys. Soc., AAAS; mem. Am. Acad. Arts and Scis., Nat. Acad. Scis., Sigma Xi. *

GLASNER, DANIEL MAYER, consultant; b. Uniontown, Pa., Mar. 20, 1940; s. Samuel and Jenny (Solomon) G.; m. Elaine Neysa Goldstein, June l, 1958; children: Robert Carl, Michael Lee. BA, John Hopkins U., 1960; MS in Indsl. Psychology, Purdue U., 1962, PhD in Indsl. Psychology, 1963. Cert. mgmt. cons. Indsl. psychologist Eli Lilly & Co., Indpls., 1963-66; cons. The Hay Group, Phila., 1967-77, 78-86, 92—, Effective Orgn., West Chester, Pa., 1977-78; exec. BankEast Corp., Manchester, N.H., 1986-91; adj. prof. Drexel U., Phila., 1977-78. Com. chair BIA of N.H., Concord, 1989—; bd. dirs. United Way of Greater Manchester, 1989—; incorporator Fidelity Health Assocs., Manchester, 1989—; bd. overseers N.E. Regional Lab., Andover, Mass., 1991—. Mem. APA, Am. Arbitration Assn. (panelist), Am. Compensation Assn., Inst. Mgmt. Cons., Sigma Xi. Republican. Home: 178 Liberty Hill Rd Bedford NH 03110-5630 Office: Independence Pl 15 Constitution Dr Ste 100 Bedford NH 03110-6006

GLASOW, E. THOMAS, French language educator; b. Rochester, N.Y., Dec. 5, 1947; s. Edward Richard and Ethel Marie (Preece) G. MA in English, State U. Coll., 1972; MA in French, U. Buffalo, 1982, PhD in French, 1985. Cert. secondary tchr., N.Y. Teaching asst. Govt. of France, Amiens, 1972-73; tchr. high sch. Ripley (N.Y.) Cen. Sch., 1975-80; teaching asst. English U. de Paris VII, 1982-83; lectr. French SUNY, Buffalo, 1986—; freelance translator Amadeus Press, Portland, Oreg., 1989—. Translator: Marc-Antoine Charpentier, 1991, 19th Century Italian Opera, 1991, Olivier Messiaen, Music and Color, 1992; opera critic Opera News, N.Y.C., 1973—; contbg. reviewer, writer Opera Quar., Durham, N.C., 1990—. Recipient Deems Taylor award ASCAP, 1992. Mem. MLA, Met. Opera Guild. Office: SUNY 910 Clemens Hall Buffalo NY 14260

GLASS, BURTON JOEL, physician, general surgeon; b. N.Y.C., Aug. 26, 1945; s. Charles and Lucille (Krisberg) G. BA, NYU, 1967; MD, U. Md., Balt., 1971. Diplomate Nat. Bd. Med. Examiners. Intern pediatrics Nassau County Med. Ctr., 1971-72, resident in pediatrics, 1972-73, resident in gen. surgery, 1973-77; physician, gen. surgeon Burton J. Glass MD, P.C., Rockville Centre, N.Y., 1979—; cons. Island Peer Review Orgn., Lake Success, N.Y., 1990—. Fellow ACS; mem. Nassau County Med. Soc. (bd. censors 1991—), Nassau Acad. Medicine, N.Y. State Med. Soc., Nassau Surg. Soc. Office: Burton J Glass MD PC 24 Maple Ave Rockville Centre NY 11570

GLASS, JOHN SHELDON, manufacturing executive; b. Glens Falls, N.Y., Mar. 10, 1936; s. John Wilbur and Josephine Emily (Sheldon) G.; m. Sharon Brackett, June 20, 1987; children by previous marriage: John S., Sarah S. AB, Union Coll., Schenectady, 1958; MS, MIT, 1960. Asst. sec. No. Nigeria Ministry of Econ. Planning, Kaduna, 1960-62; mgr. product devel. Polaroid Corp., Cambridge, Mass., 1962-68; mktg. mgr. Millipore Corp., Bedford, Mass., 1968-76; dir. investor relations Millipore Corp., Bedford, 1976-85; v.p. Millicorp, Bedford, 1985—; bd. dirs., exec. com. Protein Databases, Inc.; founder, dir. Glyko, Inc. Pres., regional gov. Sloan Club MIT, Cambridge, 1980-86; mem. Carroll Wilson award com., 1985-86. Recipient Frank Bailey prize, Union Coll., 1958; Eliphalet Nott scholar, 1958; MIT fellow in Africa, 1960-62. Mem. Nat. Investor Rels. Inst. (bd. dirs. 1978-83), Kaduna Club, Race Club, Phi Beta Kappa, Kappa Psi. Home: 48 Main St Boxford MA 01921-2502 also: Kattskill Bay NY 12801 Office: Millipore Corp 80 Ashby Rd Bedford MA 01730-2271

GLASS, PHILIP, composer, musician; b. Balt., Jan. 31, 1937; s. Benjamin C. and Ida (Gouline) G.; divorced; children: Juliet, Zachary. AB, U. Chgo., 1956; MS in Composition, Julliard Sch. Music, 1964; composition student with, Nadia Boulanger, Paris, 1964-66. Composer in residence Pitts. Pub. Schs., 1962-64; founder, performer Philip Glass Ensemble, 1968—; former taxi cab driver. Various European concert tours, 1968—, U.S. tours, 1972—; founder: (record co.) Chatham Sq. Prodns., N.Y.C., 1972; recs. include Music in 12 Parts, 1971-74, North Star, 1977, Glassworks, 1982, Facades, The Photographer, Solo Piano, Songs from the Trilogy, others; composer: (operas) (with Robert Wilson) Einstein on the Beach (European tour), 1976, Akhnaten, 1984, Mishima, 1985, Satyagraha, 1985, (with Robert Morau) Juniper Tree, 1985, Songs from Liquid Days, 1986, The Making of the Representative for Planet 8, The Fall of the House of Usher, The Palace of the Arabian Nights, Hydrogen Jukebox, 1991, The Mysteries and What's So Funny, 1991, (film music) Koyaanisqatsi, 1982, The Thin Blue Line, 1989, (theatre music) The CIVIL WarS, 1984, ceremonial music for 1984 Olympics, (symphonic works) The Light, The Canyon, Itaipu; played at Met. Opera, Nov. 1976; has collaborated with Paul Simon, Allen Ginsberg. Recipient Broadcast Music Industry award, 1960, Lado prize, 1961, Benjamin award, 1961-62, Young Composer's award Ford Found., 1964-66; named Musician of Yr., Musical Am. mag., 1985; composition grantee Fulbright, 1966-67, Found. for Contemporary Performance Arts, 1970-71, Changes, Inc., 1971-72, Nat. Endowment for the Arts, 1974-75, Menil Found., 1974. Mem. ASCAP, SACEM (France). Office: care Internat Prodn Assoc 853 Broadway Rm 2120 New York NY 10003-4703*

GLASS, WERNER BOTHO, former chemical engineering researcher; b. Berlin, Fed. Republic of Germany, May 27, 1927; came to U.S., 1947; s. George and Anna (Wolff) G.; m. Lois Dorothy Satz, Aug. 24, 1952; children: Alan, Donald, Kenneth. Cert., U. l'Aurore, Shanghai, China, 1947; BChemE, Syracuse U., 1950; SM, MIT, 1951, ScD, 1956. Rsch. leader Esso Rsch. and Engring. Co., Linden, N.J., 1956-63; assoc. dir. rsch. Ionics, Inc., Watertown, Mass., 1963-67; staff advisor Exxon Rsch. and Engring. Co., Linden, 1967-70; sr. staff advisor Exxon Rsch. and Engring. Co., Florham Park, N.J., 1970-86; ret., 1986—. Recipient chpt. award Am. Inst. Chem. Engrs., 1949, Lingquist medal Swedish Acad. Sci., 1980. Democrat. Jewish. Home: 913 The Blvd Westfield NJ 07090

GLASSER, ISRAEL LEO, federal judge; b. N.Y.C., Apr. 6, 1924; s. David and Sadie (Krupp) G.; m. Grace Gribetz, Aug. 24, 1952; children—Dorothy, David, James, Marjorie. LL.B., Bklyn. Law Sch., 1948; B.A., CUNY, 1976. Bar: N.Y. 1948. Fellow Bklyn. Law Sch., 1948-49, instr., 1950-52, asst. prof. law, 1952-53, asso. prof., 1953-55, prof., 1955-74, adj. prof., 1974, dean, 1977-82; judge U.S. Dist. Ct. N.Y., 1982—; judge N.Y. State Family Ct., N.Y.C., 1969-77. Mem. ABA, Assn. of Bar of City of N.Y. Office: US Dist Ct 225 Cadman Plz E Brooklyn NY 11201

GLASSER, MARC SETH, data processing executive; b. Bklyn., May 22, 1952; s. Israel and Julia (Birstein) G.; m. Donna Lynn Camp; 1 child, Ethan. BS in Math., Rensselaer Polytech. Inst., 1973; MS in Computer Sci., NYU, 1977. Programmer trainee Mfrs. Hanover Trust Co., N.Y.C., 1973-74, programmer, 1974-76, sr. programmer, 1976-79, programmer, analyst, 1979-82, sr. programmer, analyst, 1982-85, tech. officer, 1985-90, info. systems officer, 1990—. Mem. Amateur Press Assn. of N.Y. Unltd., Empiricon (vice-chmn. 1978). Home: PO Box 1252 Bowling Green Station New York NY 10274 Office: Chemical Bank 55 Water St New York NY 10041

GLASSER, STEPHEN ANDREW, publishing executive, lawyer; b. Memphis, July 27, 1943; s. Melvin A. and Esther (Kron) G.; m. Lynn Schreiber, Dec. 30, 1965; children: Susan, Laura, Jeffrey, Jennifer. BA cum laude, Colgate U., 1965; JD, U. Mich., 1968. Bar: D.C., 1968. Asst. dir. Practising Law Inst., N.Y.C., 1968-71; exec. v.p., exec. editor N.Y. Law Pub. Co., N.Y.C., 1971-77; pres. Law & Bus. Inc. div. Harcourt Brace Jovanovich, N.Y.C., 1977-86, Prentice Hall Law & Bus. div. Simon & Schuster Profl Info Group, Englewood Cliffs, N.J., 1986—. Co-founder, editor, publisher Legal Times of Washington, 1978-86. Mem. ABA, D.C. Bar Assn., Assn. Bar City N.Y., Phi Beta Kappa. Home: 86 Highland Ave Montclair NJ 07042-1910 Office: Prentice Hall Law & Bus 270 Sylvan Ave Englewd Clfs NJ 07632-2513

GLASSMAN, LAWRENCE S., plastic surgeon; b. June 20, 1953. BA, Johns Hopkins U., 1975, MD, 1978. Diplomate Am. Bd. Surgery, Am. Bd. Plastic Surgery. Surgeon Columbia Presbyn. Med. Ctr., N.Y.C., 1978-83; plastic surgeon Montefiore Med. Ctr. and Albert Einstein Coll. of Medicine, Bronx, N.Y., 1983-85; clin. instr. surgery Albert Einstein Coll. of Medicine, 1985—; plastic surgeon, owner Ctr. for Ambulatory Plastic Surgery, N.Y.C., 1985—; plastic surgeon Good Samaritan Hosp., Suffern, N.Y., 1985—, Nyack (N.Y.) Hosp., 1988—, St. Anthony Community Hosp., Warwick, N.Y., 1985—, Chilton Meml. Hosp., Pompton Plains, N.J., 1985-89. Contbr. articles to profl. jours. Fellow ACS; mem. AMA, Am. Soc. Plastic and Reconstructive Surgery, Am. Assn. Surgery of the Hand, Med. Soc. Rockland County, Phi Beta Kappa, Alpha Omega Alpha. Office: 125 S Main St New City NY 10956

GLASSMOYER, THOMAS PARVIN, lawyer; b. Reading, Pa., Sept. 4, 1915; s. James Arthur and Margaretha (Parvin) G.; m. Frances Helen Thierolf, May 9, 1942; children—Deborah Jane Beck, Nancy Parvin Brittingham, Wendy Jean Barber. A.B., Ursinus Coll., 1936, LL.D. (hon.), 1972; LL.B., U. Pa., 1939. Bar: Pa. 1940. Law clk. Common Pleas Ct. 6, Phila., 1939-40; assoc. Murdoch, Paxson, Kalish & Green, Phila., 1940-42; atty. Dept. Justice and Office Price Adminstrn., 1942-43; assoc. Schnader, Harrison, Segal & Lewis, Phila., 1946-50, ptnr., 1950-87, counsel, 1988—, chmn. pension com., 1969-84, chmn. tax dept., 1972-84, chmn. investment com., 1984-86, chmn. bd. trustees of Retirement Trust, 1986-89; lectr. NYU Inst. Fed. Taxation; adv. bd. U. Pa. Tax Conf. Author: (with Sherwin T. McDowell) Legal Problems in Tax Returns, 1949; editor-in-chief U. Pa. Law Rev., 1938-39. Past pres. Upper Dublin Twp. PTA Council; mem. Zoning Bd. Adjustment Upper Dublin Twp., Montgomery County, Pa., 1957-59, bd. commrs., 1959-71, pres., 1968-69; mem. Upper Dublin Environ. Control Bd., 1972-82; bd. dirs. Ursinus Coll., Collegeville, Pa., 1956—, 1st v.p., 1978-81, pres., 1981-90, chmn. exec. com., 1981—; bd. dirs. Wissahickon Valley Watershed Assn., 1974-76; trustee Bernard G. Segal Found., Phila., 1969—, Charlotte W. Newcombe Found., Princeton, N.J., 1982—. Served to 1st lt. JAG Dept., AUS, 1943-46. Recipient Eagle Scout award, Boy Scouts Am. Life Fellow Pa. Bar Found.; mem. ABA, Pa. Bar Assn. (ho. of dels. 1982-88, coun. sect. taxation), Phila. Bar Assn. (sect. taxation), Fed. Bar Assn., Judge Advs. Assn., Pa. Folklife Soc. (bd. dirs., sec.), Nat. Assn. Coll. and Univ. Attys., Assn. Governing Bds. Univs. and Colls., Nat. Audubon Soc., Bucks County Hist. Assn., Quakertown Hist. Soc., U.S. Golf Assn., Lawyers Club of Phila., Manorlu Club, Mfrs. Golf and Country Club, Oak Terrace Country Club, Union League, Order of Coif. Republican. Lutheran. Home: 1648 N Hills Ave Willow Grove PA 19090-4231 Office: Schnader Harrison Segal & Lewis 1600 Market St Ste 3600 Philadelphia PA 19103-4247

GLATIS, GEORGE W., international engineering company executive; b. Lynn, Mass., Sept. 1, 1933; m. Anastasia Glatis; children: Gina, Christopher. BS in Mgmt., Boston U.; MBA, George Washington U. With corp. mktg. dept ITT, Washington; chmn. bd. Wheeler Industries, Inc., Washington, 1969-82; pres., chief exec. officer Gladon Internat., Inc., Landover, Md., 1982—. With USN. Office: Gladon Internat Inc 8201 Corporate Dr Ste 800 Landover MD 20785

GLATT, MITCHELL STEVEN, corporate executive; b. N.Y.C., Sept. 2, 1957; s. Herbert and Gloria (Comita) G.; m. Randy Ginsburg, Oct., 1987. BA, NYU, 1978, MBA, 1980. Agt. trainee Internat. Creative Mgmt., N.Y.C., 1980-81; exec. asst. to chmn. bd. Bozell, Jacobs, Kenyon & Eckhardt, Inc., N.Y.C., 1981-87; mktg. exec. Magla Products Inc., Chatham, 1987—. Cons. Statue of Liberty Ellis-Island Found., N.Y.C., 1983-87, Juvenile Diabetes Found., N.Y.C., 1987; adv. bd. NYU Sch. of the Arts, 1990. Recipient Commendation Advt. Women of N.Y., N.Y.C., 1986. Mem. Am. Mgnt. Assn. Clubs: Manhattan Yacht (N.Y.C.); Greenbrook Country (West Caldwell, N.J.). Office: Magla Products Inc 700 Shunpike Rd Chatham NJ 07928-2199

GLAUBINGER, LAWRENCE DAVID, manufacturing company executive, consultant; b. Newark, Nov. 26, 1925; s. Samuel I. and Pauline (Sandler) G.; m. Lucienne Lefebvre, Nov. 11, 1967. BS with honors, Ind. U., 1949; MBA, Columbia U., 1977. Adminstrv. asst. to pres. Ronson Inc., Newark, 1949-51; mdse. mgr. United Mchts., N.Y.C., 1951-65; v.p. Marietta Silk Mills (Pa.), 1965-66; pres., chief exec. officer Channel Textile Co. Inc., Bradford, Vt., 1966-75; chmn. bd., chief exec. officer Stern & Stern Industries, Inc., N.Y.C., 1977—, also bd. dirs.; pres. Lawrence Econ. Cons. Inc., Hallandale, Fla., 1977—; bd. dirs. Leucadia Nat. Corp., Marisa Christina, Inc., House of Ronnie, Inc., Transp. Capital Corp., Gordon's Deep Discount. Bd. overseers Columbia U. Sch. Bus., chmn. ann. funds campaigns, 1980-82; bd. dirs. Ind. U. Found.; bd. overseers Ind. U. Ctr. Entrepreneurship and Innovation. Served with USCGR, 1943-46. Mem. Hoosier Hundred, Ind. U. Dean's Assos., Columbia U. Bus. Assocs., Campaign for Columbia (co-chmn. bus. sch.), Am. Arbitration Assn., Princeton Club (N.Y.), Green Brook Country, Beta Gamma Sigma. Republican. Jewish. Home: 437 Golden Isles Dr Hallandale FL 33009-7556 Office: Stern & Stern Industries Inc 708 3d Ave New York NY 10017

GLAZER, CHARLES THOMAS, public relations executive; b. McKeesport, Pa., May 6, 1951; s. Frank John and Mary (Panko) G.; m. Jacquelyn Youhon, June 30, 1973; 1 child, Brian Thomas. BA in Journalism, Pa. State U., 1973; postgrad, U. N.C., 1982-83. Various positions in broadcasting, radio and TV Pitts., 1969-74; sect. exec. Boy Scouts Am., Pitts., 1974-78; mgr. meetings Instrument Soc. Am., Research Triangle Park, N.C., 1978-84; v.p. convs. and edn. Bldg. Owners and Mgrs. Assn., Internat., Washington, 1984-89; sr. account exec. Ketchum Pub. Rels., Pitts., 1989—. Mem. Pa. State Sch. Communications Alumni Soc. (bd. dirs.), Assn. Corp. Growth, Pub. Rels. Soc. Am. Republican. Roman Catholic. Home: 711 Adele Dr Irwin PA 15642-2668 Office: Ketchum Pub Rels 6 Ppg Pl Pittsburgh PA 15222-5406

GLAZER, DAVID ANDREW, lawyer, entrepreneur, marketing executive; b. Boston, Mar. 2, 1953; s. Nelson Sumner and Esther (Greenberg) G.; m. Sharon Ann Henderson, July 18, 1981; children: Michael H., Russell H. BA in Polit. Sci., SUNY, Oneonta, 1975; JD, Am. U., 1978; MS in Fin. Services, Am. Coll., Bryn Mawr, Pa., 1984; MBA, George Washington U., 1985. Bar: Va. 1978, U.S. Supreme Ct. 1983. CLU; chartered fin. cons.; cert. fin. planner, Research atty. Research Group, Inc., Charlottesville, Va., 1978-80; editor Lawyer's Coop. Pub. Co., Washington, 1980-82; dir., mktg. counsel Acacia Group, Washington, 1982-86; chief exec. officer No. Va. Fin. Group, Inc., Alexandria, Va., 1986-87; adj. faculty Georgetown U., Washington, 1982-87, George Washington U., 1986-87; dir. advanced mktg. CHUBB Life Am., Concord, N.H., 1986-90; v.p. mktg. svcs. Home Life Ins. Co. N.Y., 1990-91; pres. Md. Fin. Group, Balt. and Commonwealth Fin. Group, Washington, 1991—. Author, editor: Federal Regulation of Employment Service, 1982; author: Wage Continuation Plans as an Executive Fringe Benefit, 1990. Mem. Am. Soc. CLU's, Inst. Cert. Fin. Planners (cert.), Internat. Assn. Fin. Planners. Bd. dirs. Acacia Employees Fed. Credit Union, 1985-86; coach community flag football teams. Jewish. Office: 3 Bethesda Metro Ctr Bethesda MD 20814-5330

GLAZER, PENINA MIGDAL, college dean, history educator; b. Roosevelt, N.J., Jan. 27, 1939; d. Benjamin and Rebecca (Marshak) Migdal; m. Myron Peretz Glazer; children: Joshua, Jessica. BA, Douglass Coll., 1960; MA, Rutgers U., 1961, PhD, 1970. From asst. to assoc. prof. history Hampshire Coll., Amherst, Mass., 1970-81, acting pres., 1982, 84, dean of faculty, 1976-84, prof. history, 1981—, dean faculty, 1989—, v.p., 1989—; bd. dirs. Nat. Yiddish Book Ctr., Amherst, 1984—; mem. grad. faculty U. Mass., Amherst, 1981—, adv. bd. Everywoman's Ctr., 1989—. Co-author: Sociology: Inquiring Into Society, 1977, Understanding Society, 1978, Unequal Colleagues, 1987, The Whistleblowers, 1989. Russell Sage Found. grantee, 1979-80, Rockefeller Found. grantee, 1972, MacArthur Found. grantee, 1992; Gilman fellow Carnegie Found., 1973. Mem. Mass. Found. for Humanities and Pub. Policy (bd. dirs. 1989—). Office: Hampshire Coll West St Amherst MA 01002-2954

GLAZIER, RAYMOND EARL, JR., social research executive, health policy analyst; b. Coshocton, Ohio, Nov. 14, 1941; s. Raymond Earl Sr. and Dorothy Opal (Baker) G.; m. Martha Lane MacLeish, Sept. 15, 1963 (div. 1973); 1 child, Andrew Baker; m. Debra Lee Medeiros, May 1, 1983; 1 child, Daniel Ray. BA in Social Rels. magna cum laude, Harvard U., 1964, postgrad., 1964-65; All But Dissertation in PhD, Heller Sch. of Brandeis U., 1990. Anthropology field asst. Aro Hosp., Abeokuta, Nigeria, 1961-62; co-dir., stats. dept. Age Ctr. of N.Eng., Boston, 1964; ednl. games designer Abt Assocs., Inc., Cambridge, Mass., 1965-66; curriculum designer Abt Assocs., Cambridge, Mass., 1966-69, dep. area mgr., human devel. area, 1972-75, founder and editor-in-chief, Games Cen., 1969-78, mktg. mgr., Abt Books Div., 1978-80, dir. corp. communications, 1980-84, mgr., corp. mktg. svcs. and sr. health policy analyst, 1985-91, mgr. disability and rehab. related rsch., 1991—; tech. assistance coord., 1991—; AIDS rsch. presentor, Westboro (Mass.) State Hosp., 1987; ednl. game cons. dept. nutrition, U. Lavale, Quebec City, Can., 1976; reader Simulation and Games, Beverly Hills, Calif., 1969-79, Simulation/Gaming, Moscow, Idaho, 1971-78. Author: How to Design Educational Games, 6 edits. 1969-76, Life of the Egba Yoruba, 1973, Life of the Kwakiutl Indians, 1972, Mobility-Impaired Americans' Needs for Adaptive Housing Features, 1988; pub. numerous class room games; contbr. articles on AIDS and public policy to jours. and mags., disability and access issues to mags. and newspapers. Pres. Info. Ctr. for Individuals with Disabilities, Boston, 1984-90, v.p., 1991—, trustee, 1977—; mem. housing com. Boston Ctr. for Ind. Living, Boston, 1985-87. Woodrow Wilson Nat. fellow, 1964, NSF fellow, 1964-65; ind. student rsch. grantee NSF, 1962-64. Mem. Am. Anthropol. Assn., Nat. Spinal Cord Injury Assn., Mass. Assn. of Paraplegics, Nat. Head Injury Found., Mass. Head Injury Assn. Home: 59 Underwood St Belmont MA 02178-4021 Office: Abt Assocs Inc 55 Wheeler St Cambridge MA 02138-1168

GLEIM, ROBERT ALAN, aerospace engineer; b. Harrisburg, Pa., July 29, 1968; s. James Earl and Eldora Effie (Fansler) G.; m. Faith Darlene Daugherty, June 29, 1991. BS in Aerospace Engring., Pa. State U., 1990. Design engr. Pa. State U., University Park, 1988-89, GE, Valley Forge, Pa., 1990—; pvt. cons., Valley Forge, 1990—. Designer 2 seat sport aircraft (Bird of Prey). Mem. AIAA, Pa. Soc. Profl. Engrs., Sigma Gamma Tau (treas. 1989-90), Tau Beta Pi. Republican. Home: 3000 W Valley Forge Cir King Of Prussia PA 19406-1149

GLENCER, SUZANNE THOMSON, science educator; b. Monongahela, Pa., Feb. 7, 1942; d. John Cuddy and Sue Elizabeth (DeForrest) Thomson; m. May 9, 1970 (div.). BS in Zoology, Pa. State U., 1964; MEd in Biology, Calif. (Pa.) State U., 1968; postgrad., U. Pitts., 1970-84. Biology, health instr. Allegheny Community Coll., Pitts., 1969-85; instr. Pa. State U., New Kensington, 1978-84; sci. tchr. Northgate Sch. Dist., Bellevue, Pa., 1967—, also drug/alcohol coord., 1978—; cons. area sch. dists., Pitts., 1990—; speaker numerous local orgns., Pitts., 1985—. Author: Adventures of Atom, 1985, Concepts in Kindness, 1987; contbr. articles to local newspaper, 1980—; writer and presenter numerous grants. Bd. dirs. Animal Friends, Pitts., 1974-84, Am. Cancer Soc., Pitts., 1979-83, Teen Recreation Fedn., Bellevue, 1989—; mem. adv. bd. Citizens Against Substance Abuse, Bellevue, 1990—. Named Outstanding Young Educator, North Hill's Jaycees, 1979, Pa. Outstanding Young Educator, State of Pa. Jaycees, 1979, Pa. State Tchr. of Yr., Dept. Edn., 1982, Citizen of Yr., Pitts. City & Suburban Life, 1982, Citizen of Yr., Pa. Police, 1989; recipient Nat. Drug Free Sch. award Pres. Bush, 1989. Mem. NEA, Pa. State Edn. Assn. Republican. Roman Catholic. Home: The Ter Box 617 RR # 1 Fombell PA 16123 Office: Northgate Sch Dist 589 Union Ave Pittsburgh PA 15202-2999

GLENDENING, PARRIS NELSON, county executive, educator; b. Bronx, N.Y., June 11, 1942; m. Frances Anne Hughes, Nov. 21, 1976; 1 child, Raymond Hughes. AA, Broward County Jr. Coll., 1962; BA, Fla. State U., Ft. Lauderdale, 1964; MA, Fla. State U., Tallahassee, 1965; PhD, Fla. State U., Ft. Lauderdale, 1967. Asst. prof. Univ. of Md., College Park, 1967-72; assoc. prof. Univ. of Md., 1972—; coun. mem. Hyattsville City Coun., Md., 1973-74, Prince George's County Coun., Upper Marlboro, Md., 1974-82; coun. chmn. Prince George's County Coun., 1980, 81, county exec., 1982—; commr. State of Md.'s Chesapeake Bay Critical Area Commn., 1984—; bd. dirs. World Trade Ctr., 1990—; mem. Bd. of Visitors U. Md.'s Sch. of Pub. Affairs, 1990—; bd. trustees Ptnrs. for Livable Places, 1990—. Author:(with Mavis Mann Reeves) Controversies of State and Local Political Systems, 1972, Pragmatic Federalism, 1977, 2nd edit., 1984; contbr. numerous articlesto profl. pubs. Del. to Dem. nat. Conv., San Francisco, 1984, Atlanta, 1988, N.Y.C., 1992; bd. govs., steering com. Am.'s Clean Water Found. Recipient numerous awards, including City and State mag., Prince George's County, Prince George's High Sch. Prins. assn., State Assn. Retarded Citizens, Nat. Bus. League So. Md., Spanish Speaking Communities Md., Inc., Rotary Internat., Md. Assn. Psychol. Svcs., Elizabeth and David Scull award for disting. leadership to Washington met. region Coun. Govts., 1991. Mem. AAUP, AAAS (profl. ethics group 1988—), Am. Polit. Sci. Assn., ASPA (profl. ethics com. mem. 1989—, chmn. 1991-92, SIAM mem. 1991—), Nat. Coun. Elected County Execs. (1st v.p. 1989-90, pres. 1991-92), Md. Assn. Counties (pres. 1987-88), Nat. Assn. Counties (bd. dirs. 1992—, vice chmn. intergovtl. rels. policy steering com. 1987-90, chair 1990—, taxation and fin. steering com. 1984-87). Home: 6824 Pineway Hyattsville MD 20782-1157 Ofice: Prince George's County 14741 Gov Oden Bowie Dr Upper Marlboro MD 20772

GLENN, JOHN WILLIAM, JR., vocational educator; b. Buffalo, Feb. 23, 1944; s. John William and Frances Elizabeth (Sparling) G.; m. Diane Mary Johnson, Aug. 9, 1969 (div. 1989); 1 child, Rosemary Frances. AAS, Paul Smith's Coll., 1965; BEd, SUNY, Buffalo, 1969, MS in Edn., 1971; DEd, Pa. State U., 1973. FSA supr. SUNY, Buffalo, 1965-69; instr. Erie Community Coll., Buffalo, 1969-71; div. head gen.-vocat. techs. State Tech. Inst. of Memphis, 1971-73; dir. dept. vocat.-tech. edn. SUNY Coll. of Tech., Utica, 1976-82, SUNY, Oswego, 1982—; cons. N.Y. State Dept. Edn., Albany, 1980—; program rev. cons. N.Y., R.I., Pa. Contbr. articles to profl. jours.; editorial bd. Am. Tech. Edn. Assn., 1984—. Vice pres. Onondaga chpt. Father's Rights Assn. N.Y.State, Syracuse, 1989—; bd. dirs., treas. Pvt. Industry Coun. of Oneida County, Utica, 1979-82. Mem. Am. Vocat. Assn. (dir. 1987-90, Outstanding Svc. award Tech. Edn. div. 1990, Disting. Leadership award 1990, Svc. award 1990), N.Y. State Occupational Edn. Assn. (Disting. Svc. award 1989, pres. 1984-86), Nat. Coun. for Occupational Edn. (pres. 1978-79), Am. Tech. Assn. (v.p. 1983-84, Coll. of Cons.), Joint Coord. Coun. for Occupational Edn. (chmn. 1982-84). Republican. Roman Catholic. Office: SUNY Coll at Oswego 208 Rich Hall Oswego NY 13090

GLESER, LEON JAY, statistics educator; b. St. Louis, Dec. 17, 1939; s. Sol M. and Goldine T. (Cohnberg) G.; m. Marilyn B. Zolotor, June 8, 1969; 1 child, Kimberly A. BA, U. Chgo., 1960; MS, Stanford U., 1962, PhD, 1963. Asst. prof. math, stats. Columbia U., N.Y.C., 1963-65; asst. prof. stats. The Johns Hopkins U., Balt., 1965-69, assoc. prof. stats., 1969-72; assoc. prof. stats. Purdue U., West Lafayette, Ind., 1972-77, prof. stats., 1977-89; prof. maths., stats. U. Pitts., 1989—; vis. rsch. fellow Ednl. Testing Svc., Princeton, N.J., 1971-72; vis. prof. dept. biostats., Harvard U. Sch. Pub. Health, Boston, 1979-80; vis. math. statistician, Nat. Inst. Standards and Tech., Gaithersburg, Md., 1987—. Assoc. editor jours., including Psychometrika, 1972-79, Matrix Analysis and Applications, 1989—, Statis. Sci., 1991—; author: (with C. Derman and I. Olkin) A Guide to Probability Models and Applications, 1973, Probability Models and Applications, 1980; co-editor: Contributions to Probability and Statistics, Essays in honor of Ingram Olkin, 1989; contbr. articles to profl. jours. Grantee NSF, 1979-88, 89—. Fellow Am. Statis. Assn. (editor jour. 1971-74, 86-91), Inst. Math. Stats., Royal Statis. Soc.; mem. Psychometric Soc., Internat. Statis. Inst., Internat. Chemometrics Soc. (N.Am. chpt.), Sigma Xi. Office: U Pitts Dept Math and Stats Pittsburgh PA 15260

GLEZEROV, VALERY, pathologist; b. Leningrad, Russia, June 28, 1939; came to U.S., 1980; s. Zusja Mendel and Asna Boruch (Lotzov) G.; m. Yelena Usrael Dvorkin, Aug. 3, 1940; 1 child, Marina. MD, Pediatric Med. Sch., Leningrad, Russia, 1963; PhD, Inst. Exptl. Medicine, Leningrad, Russia, 1970. Physician Mil. Svc., USSR, 1963-65, Pediatric Med. Sch., Leningrad, USSR, 1965-79; dir. lab. Hosp. #2, Leningrad, USSR, 1969-79; lab. technologist Mount Sinai Hosp., N.Y.C., 1981-82; resident physician Lenox Hill Hosp., N.Y.C., 1982-85, chief resident, 1985-86; fellow Mount Sinai Sch. at Elmhurst, Queens, N.Y., 1986-87; attending physician Mount Sinai Sch. at Elmhurst, Queens, 1987-89, chief cell immunology, 1989-90, dir. clin. pathology, 1990—. Contbr. articles to profl. jours. Lt. Med. Corps, 1963-65, USSR. Fellow Am. Soc. Clin. Pathology; mem. N.Y. Acad. Scis., N.Y. Pathol. Soc. Republican. Jewish. Office: Mt Sinai at Elmhurst 79-01 Broadway Elmhurst NY 11373

GLIATTA, REV. RONALD, school administrator; b. Bronx, N.Y., Feb. 7, 1950; s. Albert and Connie (Santo) G. BA, Immaculate Conception Sem., 1972; MA, St. John Sem., 1977; cert. edn. and guidance, Boston State Coll., 1983. Ordained priest Roman Cath Ch., 1977. Assoc. pastor St. Francis Parish, Toronto, Can., 1977-79; assoc. prin. Columbus High Sch., Boston, 1979-81; dir. sem. edn. Scotus Friary, Boston, 1981-85; appointed Official of Congregation for Doctrine of the Faith Vatican City, Rome, 1985-86; prin. Serra Cath. High Sch., McKeesport, Pa., 1986-89; sec. formation and edn. St. Bonaventure Friary, Brighton, Mass., 1989—; counselor Interfaith Rehab. Ctr., Boston, 1975; adv. bd. U.S. Am. Family Found., Boston, 1980-83; mem. rsch. bd. advisors Am. Biog. Inst., 1989 (inscribed in Internat. Book of Honor 1989). counselor advisor Malden Mass. Juvenile Dist. Ct., 1982-83. Mem. Am. Assn. Guidance Counselors, Mon-Yough C. of C. Home and Office: 466 Lincoln St Marlborough MA 01752-2090

GLICK, ALAN HARVEY, psychology educator, hypnotherapist; b. Balt., May 15, 1934; s. Louis S. and Flora (Laderberg) G. BA, U. Md., 1956, MA, 1961, EdD, 1968. Lic. profl. counselor. Speech pathologist Baltimore County Pub. Schs., Md., 1960-68; assoc. prof. psychology New Community Coll. of Balt., 1968—; dir. Md. Ctr. Hypnosis, Luthville Timon, 1986—. Mem. Am. Assn. Counseling and Devel., Am. Assn. Counselors and Therapists, Am. Assn. Clinically Cert. Mental Health Counselors, Nat. Guild for Hypnosis. Office: New Community Coll Balt 2901 Liberty Heights Ave Baltimore MD 21215

GLICK, IRVIN DAVID, education educator; b. Hanover, Pa., Mar. 23, 1935; s. Abe Frank and Lena Rebecca (Blumenthal) G.; m. Helen Davis, June 11, 1959; children: Robert Michael, Leanne Sue. BA with honors, U. Md., 1960, MEd, 1965, PhD, 1969. Cert. tchr., Md., Ohio. Mem. mgmt. staff Robert Hall, Inc., Boston, 1960-62; tchr. Annapolis (Md.) Jr. High Sch., 1962-63; NDEA fellow U. Md., College Park, 1963-66; prof. U. Toledo, 1966-75; assoc. dean profl. studies SUNY, Oswego, 1975-77, acting dean profl. studies, 1977-78, v.p., dean of students, 1978-83, prof. edn. and communication studies, 1983—, asst. provost for spl. projects, 1983—; cons. State of Ohio, Columbus, 1969-72, various sch. dists. in Ohio, 1969-74; convener, moderator Nat. Issues Forums, Oswego, 1987—. Author: Communication Studies, 1989; co-author: A Qualitative Study of Excellence in Teaching, 1982, 3 other books; contbr. articles to profl. publs. Founder Oswego Hosp. Century Club, 1979; program chair Oswego Rotary Club, 1983-86. With USAF, 1953-57, Korea, Japan. Mem. Phi Delta Kappa (historian Oswego chpt. 1991—), Phi Alpha Theta, Phi Kappa Phi. Democrat. Jewish. Home: RR 3 Box 196 Oswego NY 13126-9535 Office: SUNY Oswego Oswego NY 13126

GLICK, JOSEPH, psychologist, educator; b. N.Y.C., Nov. 27, 1935; s. Percy Elias and Rose Alma (Goldman) G.; m. Jacqueline Orsat; 1 child, Jonathan. BA, Brandeis U., 1956; MA, Clark U., 1958, PhD, 1964. Asst. prof. Yale U., New Haven, 1964-68; assoc. prof. U. Minn., Mpls., 1968-70; assoc. prof. Grad. Ctr. CUNY, N.Y.C., 1970-72; prof. psychology Grad. Ctr. CUNY, 1972—; pres. Glick Assocs., N.Y.C., 1988—; cons., researcher various polit. campaigns. Author: The Cultural Context of Learning and Thinking, 1971; editor: Social Cognition, 1978; contbr. numerous articles to various publs. Democrat.

GLICK, KENNETH JOEL, real estate executive; b. Bklyn., Nov. 10, 1951; s. Daniel and Selma (Levine) G.; m. Mary Ann D'Antonio, Nov. 29, 1975; children: Melissa, Scott, Jennifer, Lori. Student, St. John's U., 1969-71, Hebrew U., Jerusalem, Israel, 1971, CUNY, 1971-73. Lic. real estate broker, N.Y. Asst. constrn. supt. Glick Constrn. Corp., Lake Success, N.Y., 1975-80, constrn. supt., 1980-83; dir. property mgmt. Mereda Realty Corp. div. Glick Orgn., Lake Success, 1983-84, v.p. mgmt. and devel., 1984-90; ptnr. Mereda Realty Corp., Lake Success, 1987—, chief oper. officer, 1987—, sr. v.p., 1990—. Vol. police officer Villages of Rockville Centre and Floral Park, N.Y., 1970-74, Forest Hills Ambulance Corps., 1975-81; advisor B'nai

B'rith Youth Orgn., 1969-71. Mem. Nat. Assn. Home Builders, Registered Apt. Mgr. Jewish. Office: Mereda Realty Corp 1983 Marcus Ave Lake Success NY 11042-1080

GLICK, MARK ALAN, lawyer, educator; b. Chgo., Mar. 26, 1955; s. Alan and Marilyn Glick; m. Alba Cruz, June 30, 1985; 1 child, Amanda. BA summa cum laude, UCLA, 1978, MA, 1980; MA, New Sch. Social Rsch., 1982, PhD in Econs., 1985. Bar: N.Y., 1991. Assoc. prof. econs. U. Utah, Salt Lake City, 1985—; rsch. economist Jerome Levy Econ. Inst., N.Y.C., summer 1988; atty. antitrust dept. Skadden, Arps, Slate, Meagher & Flom, N.Y., 1990—; adj. prof. econs. John Jay Coll. CUNY, 1982-84. Contbr. articles to profl. jours. Rsch. com. grantee U. Utah, 1986. Mem. N.Y. Bar, Am. Econs. Club. Home: 868 1st Ave Salt Lake City UT 84103-3828 Office: Skadden Arps Slate Meaghan & Flom 919 3d Ave New York NY 10022

GLICK, MYRNA JOAN, psychologist; b. Newark, Aug. 7, 1936; d. Harry and Ida (Alter) Bergman; m. Carl Salamensky, Aug. 21, 1955 (dec. 1971; m. Joseph M. Glick, Oct. 14, 1972; children: Shelley, David. BA, William Patterson Coll., 1966; MA, Columbia U., 1967, PhD, 1975. Lic. psychologist, N.J. Chmn. child study team Franklin Lakes (N.J.) Schs., 1969-85; psychotherapist Pascack Mental Health Clinic, Park Ridge, N.J., 1975-76; pvt. practice Pompton Plains, N.J., 1977—. Mem. NEA, Am. Psychol. Assn., N.J. Psychol. Assn., Morris County Psychol. Assn. Jewish. Office: 933 State Rt 23 Pompton Plains NJ 07444-1039

GLICKMAN, EDWARD ALAN, real estate company executive; b. Bklyn., Apr. 30, 1957; s. Paul Joseph and Constance (Scheman) G.; m. Diana Pauline Keat, July 8, 1984; children: Eric, Alexander. B. Applied Sci., U. Pa., 1978, BS in Econs., 1978; MBA, Harvard U., 1981. V.p. Shearson Lehman, N.Y.C., 1981-85, Smith Barney, N.Y.C., 1985-89; exec. v.p. and chief fin. officer Presdl. Realty Corp., White Plains, N.Y., 1989—. Bd. dirs. Neighbors Together Corp., Bklyn., 1985—, pres. 1989-91. Mem. Harvard Club. Office: Presdl Realty Corp 180 S Broadway White Plains NY 10605

GLICKMAN, JAMES A., English language educator, writer; b. Davenport, Iowa, Dec. 29, 1948; s. Eugene David and Elaine Jeanne (Ginsberg) G.; m. Elissa Deborah Gelfand, Oct. 14, 1982; 1 child, Daniel Gelfand. BA in English Lit., Yale U., 1970; MFA in Fiction Writing, Iowa Writers Workshop, 1972. Instr. U. Ariz. Law Sch., Tucson, 1972, Radcliffe Seminars, Cambridge, Mass., 1985-88; prof. Community Coll. R.I., Lincoln, 1973—. Author short stories. Home: 51 Mcgilpin Rd Sturbridge MA 01566-1230

GLICKMAN, MARLENE, social organization administrator; b. Evansville, Ind., May 13, 1936; d. Morris Jack and Sarah (Krawll) Foreman; m. Marshall Levi Glickman, Jan. 9, 1956; children: Cynthia Anne, Joseph Leonard. Student, Ohio State U., 1954-56. Area dir. The Am. Jewish Com., Buffalo, 1982—. Pres. Human Rights Adv. Coun., Western N.Y., 1988—; bd. dirs. YWCA, Buffalo and Erie County, 1990—, Western N.Y. Commn. for Martin Luther King Jr., 1991—; mem. United Way Agy. Allocations Com.; chairwoman Towns and Villages div. United Way, 1981; pres. N.E. Lakes Coun. Union Am. Hebrew Congregations, 1982-86, Meals on Wheels of Buffalo and Erie County, 1981-83, Coun. Congl. Pres.-Erie County, 1979-81, Temple Beth Am., 1978-80, Sisterhood Temple Beth Am., 1969-71, 76-77; vice chair gen. campaign United Jewish Appeal, 1980, chair woman's div., 1979. Recipient Abraham Pugash Community Rels. award for establishing Kosher Meals on Wheels, Jewish Family Svc., Buffalo and Erie County, N.Y., 1975. Mem. Union Am. Hebrew Congregations (bd. dirs.), Commn. on Synagogue Music, Nat. Cantorial Placement Commn., Hadassah (life), Assn. Reform Zionists Am. (del. to Israel 1987), Brandeis Women's Com., Nat. Coun. Jewish Women (life, Hannah G. Solomon award 1985), Assn. Jewish Community Rels. Workers, Jewish Communal Svc. Assn. Office: The Am Jewish Com 3407 Delaware Ave Buffalo NY 14217-1421

GLICKMAN, NORMAN J., ecomomist, urban policy analyst; b. Bklyn., July 27, 1942; s. Harry and Beatrice (Frankel) G.; m. Elyse M. Pivnick, May 8, 1983; children: Katy Rose, Madeline Claire. BA, U. Pa., 1963, MA, 1967, PhD, 1969. Prof. urban and regional planning U. Pa., Phila., 1980-82; Hogg prof. urban policy U. Tex., Austin, 1983-89; prof. urban planning Rutgers U., New Brunswick, N.J., 1989, dir. Ctr. for Urban Policy Rsch. State of N.J., 1989—; vis. scholar U.S. Dept. HUD, Washington, 1978-79; fellow Netherland Inst. for Advanced Studies, Wassenaar, The Netherlands, 1981-82; sr. rsch. scholar Internat. Inst. for Applied Systems Analysis, Laxenburg, Austria, 1977. Co-author: The New Competitors, 1989 (Top 10 Bus. Week 1989). Chmn. Econ. Devel. Commn., Austin, 1985-89. Recipient Lindback award U. Pa., 1976, named Disting. Fulbright Prof., Monterrey (Mex.) Inst. of Tech., 1985; fellow Japan Found., 1976. Mem. EEFMS (charter), Regional Sci. Assn. (v.p. 1988-89), Am. Econ. Assn. Office: Rutgers U Ctr for Urban Policy Rsch PO Box Piscataway NJ 08855-0489

GLICKMAN, PAULA RIVLIN, public relations and marketing executive; b. N.Y.C.; d. Harry Nathaniel and Eugenie (Graciany) Rivlin; m. Ivan Melvin Glickman, Oct. . 21, 1962; children: Allison, Michael, Ellen. BS, Cornell U., 1958; postgrad., Harvard U., 1955. Editor The MacMillan Co., N.Y.C., 1961-66; dir. communications, mktg. and sales Arista Imports, N.Y.C., 1968-72; editor Kraus-Thompson Orgn., Ltd., Millwood, N.Y., 1982-84; mgr. Companion of N.Y. a Mutual of Omaha Co., Rye, N.Y., 1984-88; dir. external affairs St. Vincent's Hosp. and Med. Ctr. of N.Y, Harrison, 1988-91; dir. info. svcs. Dept. Health, Westchester County, N.Y., 1991—. Chmn. Cornell Tradition, Westchester, N.Y., 1986-88; area chairperson Cornell Alumni Admissions Ambassadors Network, Rye, Port Chester, N.Y., 1970—; bd. dirs. Am. Cancer Soc, Westchester, 1986-88. Mem. Pub. Rels. Soc. Am., Healthcare Pub. Rels. and Mktg. Soc., Women in Communications, Cornell Club (bd. govs. 1983—). Home: 85 Allendale Dr Rye NY 10580-2403 Office: Dept Health 112 E Post Rd White Plains NY 10601

GLICKMAN, ROSALIND HELEN, interior designer; b. Apr. 29, 1937; d. Benjamin and Dorothy (Altman) Estner; m. Ronald Harvey Glickman, FEb. 22, 1960; children: David Seth, Deborah Lynn. BS in Edn., Boston U., 1958; Cert. in Interior Design, R.I. Sch. Design, 1978. Cert. tchr., Mass. Tchr. 1st grade Dedham (Mass.) Pub. Schs., 1958-61; Sunday sch. tchr. Temple Emeth, Chestnut Hill, Mass., 1962-63; tchr. 1st grade Tenacre Country Day Sch., Wellesley, Mass., 1962-63; kindergarten tchr. Solomon Schechter Day Sch., Newton, Mass., 1973-74; interior designer Drapery Elegance Corp., Auburndale, Mass., 1975—. Pres. Sisterhood, Temple Emeth, 1974-75. Recipient recognition award Boston U. Gen. Alumni Assn., 1989. Mem. Am. Soc. Interior Designers, Boston Curtain and Drapery Club, Boston U. Sch. Edn. Alumni Assn. (pres. 1984-86), Boston U. Women Grads. Club (v.p. 1988-91, pres. 1991—), Women's League (v.p. 1977-79). Home: 121 Bonad Rd Chestnut Hill MA 02167-3601 Office: Drapery Elegance Corp 339 Auburn St Newton MA 02166-1907

GLICKSMAN, MICHAEL LEWIS, psychologist; b. N.Y.C., Mar. 15, 1941; s. William and Julia (Wachs) G.; m. Marcia Spence, Feb. 4, 1979; 1 child, Noah Stafford. BA, Hofstra U., 1962; MA, U. Toledo, 1964; postgrad., NYU, 1968. Psychologist Narcotic Addiction Control Commn., N.Y.C., 1967-71; clin. asst. prof. psychiatry SUNY Downstate Med. Ctr., Bklyn., 1971-74; psychologist Office Mental Retardation and Devel. Disabilities, Bklyn., 1977-80, Rockland Children's Psychiat. Ctr., Goshen, N.Y., 1980-82, Middletown (N.Y.) Psychiat. Ctr., 1982—; cons. Crystal Run Village, Inc., Middletown, N.Y., 1991—. Contbr. articles to profl. jours. and hobby-related periodicals. NIMH fellow, 1963-64. Mem. Internat. Steamboat Soc., Aquatic Gardeners Assn., Hudson Valley Antique Radio and Phonograph Soc. (bd. dirs.), Orange County Antique Auto Club, Messerschmitt Owners Club. Democrat. Jewish. Home: 147 Highland Ave Middletown NY 10940-4729 Office: Middletown Psychiat Ctr Monhagen Ave Middletown NY 10940-6212

GLICKSTEIN, ARTHUR F., psychologist; b. Bklyn., Nov. 18, 1927; s. Samuel and Esther (Beckman) G.; m. Beverly Florence Teitelbaum, Sept. 13, 1953; children: Susan, Lisa and Karen (twins). BA, Bklyn. Coll., 1948; MA, U. Ky., 1951, PhD, 1959. Lic. Psychologist, Conn. Clin. psychology trainee VA Hosp., Lexington, Ky., 1951-52; clin. psychology officer U.S. Army Mental Hygiene Clinics, Ft. Polk, Ft. Riley, La., Kans., 1952-56; staff psychologist Norwich (Conn.) State Hosp., 1957-61; dir. psychol. dept. Newington (Conn.) Childrens Hosp., 1961-68; pvt. practice Newington, 1957—; cons. South Windsor (Conn.) Pub. Sch., 1968—, Newington Police Dept., 1979—, Southfield Project, Newington, 1980—. Pres. Temple Sinai, Newington. 1st lt. Med. Svc. Corps, 1952-56. Mem. APA, Am. Assn. Marriage and Family Therapists, Nat. Register Health Svc. Providers in Psychology, Conn. Psychol. Assn. (former pres.), Conn. Assn. Marriage and Family Therapists (former bd. dirs.). Democrat. Jewish. Home: 70 Dover Rd Newington CT 06111-1014 Office: 1268 Main St Ste 107 Newington CT 06111-3088

GLIJANSKY, ALEX, psychiatrist; b. Caracas, Venezuela, Oct. 6, 1948; came to U.S., 1975; s. Natalio and Ghenea (Rechtman) G.; m. Belinda Matyas, Aug. 12, 1973; children: Ghena, Avi. MD, Universidad Cen. de Venezuela, 1971, MS, 1974. Resident in psychiatry Hahnemann U., Phila., 1978; med. dir. Fishtown/Lower Kensington Mental Health Ctr., Phila., 1978-82; assoc. psychiatrist Mental Health Ctr. Abington (Pa.) Meml. Hosp., 1982—; asst. prof. dept. Mental Health Scis., Hahnemann U., Phila., 1978—. Mem. edn. com., bd. dirs. Schechter Hebrew Day Sch., Phila., 1985—. Mem. Am. Psychiat. Assn., Pa. Psychiat. Soc., Phila. Psychiat. Soc., Phila. Assn. for Psychoanalysis, Philmont Country Club. Office: 8302 York Rd Ste #9 Elkins Park PA 19117

GLIKLICH, JERRY, physician, educator; b. Jelenia Góva, Poland, May 6, 1948; came to U.S., 1958; s. Henry and Henia (Gotajner) G.; m. Jane Salmon, Sept. 12, 1976; children: David, Benjamin. AB, Columbia U., 1969, MD, 1975. Intern N.Y. Hosp., N.Y.C., 1975-76, resident, 1977-78; fellow in cardiology Presbyn. Hosp., N.Y.C., 1978-81, attending physician, 1981—, assoc. clin. prof., 1991—; asst. prof. medicine Columbia U., N.Y.C., 1981-91; cons. in field. Contbr. articles to profl. jours. Mem. ACP, Am. Coll. Cardiology, Phi Beta Kappa. Office: Presbyn Hosp 161 Ft Washington Ave New York NY 10032

GLIMCHER, ARNOLD B., art executive; b. Duluth, Minn., Mar. 12, 1938; s. Paul and Eva (Fishman) G.; m. Mildred Louise Cooper, Dec. 20, 1959; children: Paul William, Marc Cooper. B.A., Mass. Coll. Art., 1969; postgrad., NYU Sch. Psychology, Boston U. Founder, owner Pace Gallery, Boston, 1961-63; founder, pres. Pace Gallery, N.Y.C., 1963—; founder Pace Editions, 1968—. Author: Louise Nevelson, 1972, paperback edit., 1976; (with Paul Vitz) Modern Art and Modern Science: The Parallel Analysis of Vision, 1983; motion picture producer: Gorillas in the Mist, The Good Mother; producer, director: The Mambo Kings.; contbr. articles to art jours. Fellow Israel Mus. (chmn. devel. com. 1976-77); mem. Am. Acad. Arts and Letters, Art Dealers Officier des Arts et Lettres Assn. Am. (bd. dirs.). Office: Pace Gallery 32 E 57th St New York NY 10022-2513

GLINES, JOHN, playwright, producer; b. Santa Maria, Calif., Oct. 11, 1933; s. Denzil Cassius and Ellen Antoinette (Lanza) G. BA, Yale U., 1955. Writer Captain Kangaroo, N.Y.C., 1965-71, Sesame St., N.Y.C., 1979-81; project dir. Stamp Out AIDS, N.Y.C., 1986—; artistic dir. The Glines, Inc., N.Y.C., 1976—; cons. for developing children's TV series, 1972-78. Author: (plays) On Tina Tuna Walk, 1988, In Her Own Words, 1989, Men of Manhattan, 1990, Chicken Delight, 1991, Body and Soul, 1991; producer (plays) Torch Song Trilogy, 1981-85, As Is, 1985. Recipient numerous awards as producer of Torch Song Trilogy. Mem. Broadway Cares (founding trustee), Producers Group (steering com. 1990-91). Democrat. Office: 240 W 44th St New York NY 10036

GLISAN, EILEEN WYDO, Spanish educator; b. Uniontown, Pa., Dec. 27, 1956; d. Andy Sr. and Sophie (Sabo) Wydo; m. Roy Allen Glisan, May 17, 1980; 1 child, Nina Andreya. BS in Secondary Edn., Calif. (Pa.) U., 1979; MA in Hispanic Linguistics, U. Pitts., 1982, PhD in Hispanic Linguistics, 1983. Cert. tchr. Spanish and French, Pa.; cert. oral proficiency tester and trainer for Spanish. Spanish/French tchr. Jefferson (Pa.)-Morgan Jr./Sr. High, 1979-80; teaching asst.-fellow U. Pitts., 1980-84; instr. Spanish U. Pitts., 1984-85; assoc. prof. Spanish Ind. U. of Pa., 1985—; cons. to sch. dists., 198—. Author: (in Spanish) Enlaces, 1991, (with others) Adapting a FLES Approach...1991; contbr. articles to profl. jours. Mem. North Allegheny Fgn. Lang. Adv. Coun., Wexford, Pa., 1987—. Grantee U.S. Dept. Edn., Ind. U. of Pa., 1986. Mem. N.E. Conf. on Teaching of Langs. (bd. dirs. 1991-94), Pa. State Modern Lang. Assn. (v.p. 1990—), Appalachian Educator's Soc. (exec. coun. 1987—), Am. Coun. on Tchrs. of Langs., Am. Assn. of Tchrs. of Spanish and Portugese, Allegheny Fgn. Lang. Assn., Alpha Mu Gamma (Excellence in Spanish/French 1979). Orthodox Catholic. Home: 2537 Glenwood Dr Wexford PA 15090-7939 Office: Indiana U of Pa 472 Sutton Hall Indiana PA 15701

GLITMAN, ERIK WAYNE, management consultant; b. Nassau, The Bahamas, July 23, 1959; s. Maynard Wayne and Gunda Christine (Amundsen) G.; m. Diane Lynn Kirson, Aug. 14, 1983. BA in Environ. Studies, Johnson (Vt.) State Coll., 1981; BA in Econs., U. Vt., 1985; MA in Internat. Affairs, Am. U., 1987. With The Lane Press, Burlington, Vt., 1981-85; intern Stein Assocs., Rockville, Md., 1986, assoc., 1987; cons. Booz Allen & Hamilton, Bethesda, Md., 1987-88; sr. cons. Kaiser Assocs., Vienna, Va., 1988-89; pres., prin. Fletcher Mountain Group, Burlington, Vt., 1989—; pres. Vt. Cons. Network, Burlington, 1991—. Mem. Smuggler's Notch Vol. Ski Patrol and Ski Sch., Jeffersonville, Vt., 1979—; exec. dir. Vt. Gov.'s Com. on Economy and Efficiency in State Govt., 1990. Mem. Am. Mgmt. Assn. (assoc.), Soc. Competitive Analyst Profls. Office: Fletcher Mountain Group 383 College St Burlington VT 05401-8344

GLITZ, DONALD ROBERT, insurance underwriting executive; b. Uniontown, Pa., Sept. 30, 1944; s. Joseph William and Helen (Keblis) G.; m. Frances Antonia Sante, Aug. 24, 1968; children: Kristin, Allison, Derek. BA in Econ., Pa. State U., 1969; MA in Liberal Studies, SUNY, Stonybrook, 1976. CPCU. Underwriter comml. ins. CIGNA, Pitts., 1969-73; sr. underwriter comml. ins. CIGNA, Garden City, N.J., 1973-77, mgr. comml. ins., 1977-79; dir. underwriting N.E. region CIGNA, Radnor, Pa., 1979-81, dir. product mgmt. N.E. region, 1981-82; dir. packages product mgmt. CIGNA, Phila., 1982-87, dir. underwriting western area, 1987-89, dir. underwriting western and cen. area, 1989-90, dir. casualty underwriting world-wide, 1990—; vice chmn. Eastern Regional Office underwriting com. Indsl. Risk Insurers, Hartford, Conn., 1986-89; ins. instr. Villanova U., 1983-85. V.p. Student Govt. Assn. Pa. State U., Fayette, 1966; basketball ofcl. Lionville (Pa.) Youth Assn., 1990. With U.S. Army, 1962-65. Fellow CPCU Soc.; mem. Nittany Lions Club. Home: 118 Taylors Mill Rd Downingtown PA 19335-1637

GLOCK, MARVIN DAVID, retired psychology educator; b. San Jose, Ill., Nov. 19, 1912; s. David William and Lydia (Gruensfelder) G.; m. Elva Ruth Snell, Apr. 13, 1941; children—Carol Sue, Sandra Kay. Student, Blackburn Coll., 1930-32; A.B., U. Nebr., 1934; M.S., U. Ill., 1935-38; Ph.D., State U. Iowa, 1947. Tchr. Edison (Neb.) High Sch., 1934-36; prin. Mason City (Ill.) Community High Sch., 1936-41; asst. prof. edn. Mich. State U., 1947-49; prof. ednl. psychology Cornell U., Ithaca, N.Y., 1949-83, prof. emeritus, 1983—; cons. in communication skills; cons. in communications skills. Author: (with J.S. Ahmann and Helen Wardeberg) Evaluating Elementary School Pupils, 1960, (with J.S. Ahmann) Evaluating Pupil Growth: Principles of Tests and Measurements, 6th edit, 1980, Readings in Educational Psychology, 1971, Measuring and Evaluating Educational Achievement, 2d edit, 1975, PROBE: An Audiotutorial College Reading Program, 3d edit, 1984, PROBE II: An Audio tutorial Reading Program, 1978; author numerous sci. papers. Lt. USN, 1942-45. Fulbright fellow Sri Lanka, 1962-63; recipient numerous research grants. Fellow Am. Psychol. Assn.; mem. Sigma Xi, Phi Kappa Phi. Presbyterian. Home: 101 Homestead Ter Ithaca NY 14850-6217

GLOSBAND, DANIEL MARTIN, lawyer; b. Salem, Mass., July 3, 1944; s. Leon Glosband and Ruth Pauline (Wentworth) Glosband School; m. Merrily Cotton, Dec. 23, 1967; children: Alexander, Gabriel, Oliver. BA, U. Mass., 1966; JD, Cornell U., 1969. Bar: Mass. 1969, U.S. Dist. Ct. Mass. 1970, U.S. Ct. Appeals (1st cir.) 1971, U.S. Dist. Ct. Conn. 1971, U.S. Dist. Ct. Vt. 1974, U.S. Supreme Ct. 1982. Assoc., then ptnr., firm Widett & Widett, Boston, 1969-75; ptnr. Goldstein & Manello, Boston, 1976-87, Goodwin, Procter and Hoar, Boston, 1988—. Contbr. numerous articles on bankruptcy to profl. jours. Fellow Am. Coll. Bankruptcy, Am. Bar Found., Mass. Bar Found.; mem. Mass. Bar Assn. (chmn. bankruptcy com. 1980-83), Boston Bar Assn. (chmn. bankruptcy com. 1977-80), ABA (sect. on corps., chmn. internat. bankruptcy com. 1990—). Democrat. Jewish. Home: 34 Atlantic Ave Swampscott MA 01907-2404 Office: Goodwin Procter & Hoar Exchange Pl Boston MA 02109-2808

GLOSSER, JEFFREY MARK, lawyer; b. 1936; married; 1 child. BS in Econs. with distinction, U. Pa., 1958; JD, Harvard U., 1961. Bar: D.C. 1962. Law clk. U.S. Ct. Claims, 1963-64; assoc. Emery & Wood, Washington, 1965-69; ptnr. Jeffrey M. Glosser, P.C., Washington, 1969-86, Whiteford, Taylor & Preston, Washington, 1987—; instr. continuing legal edn. courses sponsored by D.C. Bar, 1976—. Mem. ABA (adminstrv. law sect., mem. various coms.), D.C. Bar Assn. (mem., numerous coms.), Fed. Bar Assn. (U.S. Claims Ct. com.), Fed. Cir. Bar Assn. (rules com. 1985—). Office: Whiteford Taylor & Preston 888 17th St NW Washington DC 20006-3939

GLOSSER, WILLIAM LOUIS, lawyer; b. Johnstown, Pa., Aug. 30, 1929; s. Saul I. and Eva (Hurwitz) G.; m. Patricia Freeman, Feb. 5, 1932; children: Alix Paul, Jill P., Jonathan. BS Temple U., 1951; LLB, U. Pa., 1954. Bar: Pa. 1954, Fla. 1956, U.S. Dist. Ct. (we. dist.) Pa. 1956, U.S. Dist. Ct. (so. dist.) Fla. 1957. Assoc. Broad and Cassel, Miami Beach, Fla., 1956-57; sole practice, Coral Gables, Fla., 1957-61, Johnstown, Pa., 1962—; magistrate judge U.S. Dist. Ct. (we. dist.) Pa., 1973—; corp. sec., dir. Glosser Bros., Inc., Johnstown, 1969-85; of counsel Smorto, Persio, Zadzilko, Sibert & Webb, Johnstown, 1988—. Bd. dirs. Lee Hosp., Johnstown; mem. Johnstown adv. council Pa. Human Relations Commn.; pres. United Jewish Fedn. Johnstown, 1970-75; chmn. fund drive United Way, 1985, pres., 1987-88; bd. dirs. Mt. Aloysius Coll., 1980-84. Served with U.S. Army, 1954-56. Mem. Pa. Bar Assn., Fla. Bar Assn., Cambria County Bar Assn., Pa. Bar Assn., Greater Johnstown C. of C. (pres. 1985), Rotary; B'nai B'rith (pres. lodge 1965-67, 83-84). Jewish. Home: 521 Luzerne St Johnstown PA 15905-2324 Office: Smorto Persio Zadzilko & Webb 4th Fl 410 Main St Johnstown PA 15901

GLOVER, LAURICE WHITE, psychoanalyst, musician; b. Los Angeles, Oct. 15, 1930; d. Lawrence Francis and Alice Violet (King) White; B.A., Occidental Coll., 1951; M.S. in Social Work, Columbia U., 1956; cert. in psychoanalysis and psychotherapy Postgrad. Ctr. Mental Health, N.Y.C., 1971, cert. in supervision of psychoanalysis, 1975; student pipe organ Norman Wright, Robert Owen, Virgil Fox; m. Norman James Glover, Aug. 18, 1956 (div. 1963), remarried, 1983; stepchildren—Valerie Scott, Norman James, Susan Charlotte, John Thomas. Pvt. practice psychoanalysis, N.Y.C., 1968—; faculty and sr. supr. psychoanalysis Postgrad. Ctr. Mental Health, N.Y.C., 1976—, asst. dean of tng., 1982—, tng. analyst, 1985—; asst. clin. prof. psychiatry Albert Einstein Coll. Medicine, Yeshiva, U., N.Y.C., 1975—; adj. asst. prof. psychology Bronx Community Coll., 1974; tng. analyst Nat. Psychol. Assn. for Psychoanalysis, 1974-76; psychoanalysis faculty Nat. Inst. Psychotherapies, 1978—; faculty, sr. supr. psychoanalysis, tng. analyst Tng. Inst. Mental Health Practitioners, 1979-84. Organist, choir dir. Throggs' Neck Lutheran Ch., Bronx, N.Y., 1964-67; jazz organist Hotel Barbizon for Women, 1965-66; organist, choir dir. 4th Ave. Meth. Ch., Bklyn., 1967—74. Mem. Soc. Clin. Social Workers, Nat. Assn. Social Workers, Am. Group Psychotherapy Assn., Am. Guild Organists, Am. Theatre Organists Soc., Am. Fedn. Musicians. Contbr. articles to profl. publs. Office: 271 Central Park W New York NY 10024-3020

GLOVER, NORMAN JAMES, engineering executive; b. Bklyn., Feb. 6, 1929; s. Norman James and Livia Delfine (Bongiorni) G.; B.S. in Engring. (Killough scholar), Columbia U., 1950; postgrad. 1953-56; postgrad. U. Alaska, 1950, Harvard U., 1968-69, Naval War Coll., 1970; m. Laurice White, 1956 (div. 1963), remarried, 1983; m. Ellen Janet Wilson, 1964 (div. 1980); children: Valerie, Norman James, Susan, John. Engr., Alaska Rd. Commn., 1950-51; engr., supt., v.p. Heydt Constrn. Co., N.Y.C., 1955-60; v.p., mgr. fgn. ops., dir. constrn. Thompson-Starrett Co., N.Y.C., 1960-66; pvt. engring. practice, N.Y.C., 1961-64; v.p., engr. Viking Devel., Boston, 1966-70; Sheraton Corp., Boston, 1970-76, exec. v.p. design and devel., 1971-75; v.p., dir. ops. ITT Community Devel. Corp., Palm Coast, Fla., 1976-77; v.p. ITT Land Corp., 1975-77; v.p. Palm Coast Utilities Corp., 1975-77; pres. Ramada Devel. Corp., Phoenix, 1977-79; v.p. Ramada Inns, Inc.; v.p., mng. dir. Beaver Creek Devel., Vail (Colo.) Assocs. Inc., 1979-83; pres., mgr. dir. Internat. Cons. and Engrs., P.C., N.Y., 1980—; mem. steering com. performance concept in building Building Research Inst.-Nat. Acad. Scis. Mem. adv. council Columbia U. Faculty Engring. and Applied Sci.; bd dirs. Beaver Creek Metro Dist., 1980-82; chmn. selection bd. A/E/CM Svcs., N.Y. State Facilities Devel. Corp., 1986-87. Lt. comdr. USCGR, 1951-54. Registered profl. engr., N.Y., N.J., Ariz., Maine, Va., Ga., Fla., Ind., Tex., Colo., Mont., Alaska, Mass., Oreg., Md., Ala., Mo., Minn., Ky., Wis., Mich. Chartered engr., U.K. Fellow Inst. Structural Engrs. (U.K.), Soc. Am. Mil. Engrs., ASCE (task com. structural applications of plastics, pub. works com. urban plan and devel. div., com. constrn. standards); mem. Boston Soc. Civil Engrs., Mass. Soc. Profl. Engrs., Arctic Inst. N.Am., Am. Soc. Quality Control, ASTM, Constrn. Specifications Inst., Am. Mgmt. Assn., U.S. Naval Inst. Clubs: Vail Athletic; Univ. (Boston); Columbia (N.Y.C.); Cavalry (Bahrain); Ariz. Athletic (Phoenix). Author papers, tech. reports. Office: 271 Central Park W New York NY 10024-3020

GLOVER, RON K., business information services company executive; b. Newark, Ohio, May 11, 1940; s. Edward M. and Lucy Arzela (Luther) G.; m. Karolyn S. Zimerman, 1958 (div.); children: Kara, Ronna; m. Rosemarie Ann Montagna, Dec. 20, 1986; children: Ronald, Jr. BS, Rio Grande Univ., 1961; cert. advanced mgmt. program, Harvard U., 1983, D. Bus. Mgmt. (hon.), 1989. With Am. Express Co., 1970-90; dist. sales mgr. Card div. Service Establishment Sales, Atlanta, 1970-71; regional dir. Card div. Corp. Card and Gold Card Sales, Chgo., 1971-72; dir. Card div. Mktg. and Sales, Mexico City, Mex., 1972-73; v.p., gen. mgr. Card div. Mexico City, Mex., 1973-76; regional v.p. Card div. Asia, Pacific, Australia, Singapore, 1976-78; sr. v.p. Card div. Card Mktg. U.S.A., N.Y.C., 1978-79, Europe, Middle East, Africa, London, 1979-82; exec. v.p. Consumer Fin. Services div. Worldwide Mktg. and Strategic Planning, N.Y.C., 1982-83; pres. Travel Related Services, Japan, Tokyo, 1983-85; chmn., chief exec. officer Health Carecard Inc., Austin, Tex., 1985-86; pres. Travelers Cheque Group, N.Y.C., 1986-90, Dun & Bradstreet Bus. Credit Svcs., 1990—. Bd. dirs. Rio Grande (Ohio) U., Lake Erie Coll., Painesville, Ohio. Republican. Presbyterian. Office: Dun & Bradstreet Info Svcs One Diamond Hill Rd Murray Hill NJ 07974

GLUBO, LES JAY, podiatrist; b. Bklyn., Mar. 16, 1951; s. Aaron and Blanche (Rosenthal) G.; m. Lauren Gail Wolfe, May 13, 1979; children: Heather, Jessica. BA, Adelphi U., 1973; D Podiatric Medicine, N.Y. Coll. Podiatric Medicine, 1981. Diplomate Am. Bd. Podiatric Surgery. Tchr. Nassau Ctr. Emotionally Disturbed Children, Woodbury, N.Y., 1973-77; resident in podiatric surgery Luth. Hosp. Balt., 1982; podiatrist Giardina and Glubo, P.C., Balt., 1983-85; pvt. practice N.Y.C., 1985—. Fellow Am. Coll. Foot Surgeons; mem. Am. Podiatric Med. Assn., N.Y. State Podiatric Med. Assn. (N.Y. div. exec. bd. 1986—, treas. 1988-90, v.p. 1990-92, pres. 1992—), Am. Podiatric Sports Medicine Assn., Am. Assn. Hosp. Podiatrists. Home: 533 Churchill Rd Teaneck NJ 07666 Office: Grand Ctrl Footcare Ste 1201 122 E 42d St New York NY 10168

GLUCK, CAROL, history educator; b. Newark, Nov. 12, 1941; d. David E. and Doris S. Newman; m. Peter L. Gluck, May 1, 1966; children: Thomas Edward, William Francis. Student, U. Munich, 1960-61, U. Tokyo, 1972-74; BA, Wellesley Coll., 1962; MA, Columbia U., 1970, PhD, 1977. Asst. prof. Columbia U., N.Y.C., 1975-83, assoc. prof., 1983-86, prof., 1986-88, George Sansom prof. history, 1988—; vis. rsch. assoc. faculty law Tokyo U., 1978-79, 85-86, 92; vis. prof. Harvard U., Cambridge, Mass., 1991; publs. bd. Columbia U. Press, N.Y.C., 1991—; co-dir. NEH project Asia in the Core Curriculum, N.Y.C., 1987—; chair instnl. grants subcom. Japan Found., 1986—; disting. lectr. N.E. Area Coun., 1988, Japan Soc. for Promotion Sci., 1989. Author: Japan's Modern Myths, 1985 (Fairbank prize 1986, Trilling award 1987); co-editor: Showa: The Japan of Hirohito, 1992; adv. bd. Jour. Japanese Studies, 1989—; contbr. numerous articles to profl. publs. Mem. com. rsch. librs. N.Y. Pub. Librs., 1987—; mem. Coun. on Fgn. Rels. Woodrow Wilson Found. fellow; Fulbright grantee, 1985-86; Japan Found. grantee; Fgn. Area fellow. Fellow Am. Acad. Arts and Scis.; mem. Am. Hist. Assn. (coun. 1987-90), Assn. Asian Studies (coun. 1981-84, nominating com. 1985-86), Japan Soc. (bd. dirs. 1990—), Asia Soc. (trustee 1992—), Phi Beta Kappa. Office: Columbia U East Asian Inst 420 W 118th St New York NY 10027-7213

GLUCK, NANCY DEPROSPO, special event planner; b. Paterson, N.J., Apr. 2, 1959; d. Carl William and Rita Marie (McGillick) DeProspo; m. Barry Martin Gluck, Sept. 12, 1987. AAS in Bus. Adminstrn., Ocean County Coll., Toms River, N.J., 1981. Sales rep. Broadcast Alternatives, Inc., Toms River, 1979-84; interviewer Nat. Talent Assocs., Fairfield, N.J., 1984-85; sales rep. R&H Assocs., Tinton Falls, N.J., 1985-87; bus. mgr. Coast Imported Car Corp., Toms River, 1987-88; exec. Nu Skin Internat., Inc., Provo, Utah, 1990—; owner Affairs of the Heart, Inc., Lanoka Harbor, N.J., 1987—; N.J. state coord. Assn. of Bridal Cons., New Milford, Conn., 1990—; instr. Affairs of the Heart, Inc., Lanoka Harbor, 1990—. Mem. Optimist Club of Toms River (pres.-elect 1991-92). Roman Catholic. Home: 407 Elizabeth Ct Lanoka Harbor NJ 08734-9269 Office: Affairs of the Heart Inc 407 Elizabeth Ct Lanoka Harbor NJ 08734-9269

GLUCKSBERG, SAM, psychology educator; b. Montreal, Que., Can., Feb. 6, 1933; came to U.S., 1945; s. Murray and Sonia (Afrin) G.; children: Matthew, Kenneth, Nadia Glucksberg. BS, CCNY, 1956; PhD, NYU, 1960. Instr. NYU, N.Y.C., 1958-60; chair psychology dept. Princeton (N.J.) U., 1974-80, from instr. to prof., 1963—; cons., Princeton, 1980—. Author: Psychology, 5th edit., 1991; editor Jour. Exptl. Psychology: Gen., 1984-89; author 80 sci. articles and book chpts. Capt. U.S. Army, 1958-63. Fellow APA (pres. div. exptl. psychology 1988-89), AAAS, Soc. Exptl. Psychologists (sec.-treas. 1987-90). Home: 29 Bainbridge St Princeton NJ 08540-3901 Office: Princeton U Dept Psychology Princeton NJ 08544-1010

GLUCKSTAL, LEONARD, construction company executive; b. Bklyn., Nov. 29, 1947; s. Alfred Eugene Miriam (Cohen) G.; m. Michelle L. Weiss, May 25, 1950 (div. 1977); children: Kevin David, Corey Benjamen; m. Anita Elizabeth Cimochowski, Feb. 13, 1982. BSCE, U. Miami, 1970. Project mgr. Laurence J. Rice, Inc., Hempstead, N.Y., 1970-75; pres. Lenelle Constrn. Corp., Huntington, N.Y., 1975-78; project mgr. E.W. Howell, 1978-79, Waywest Devel., N.Y.C., 1979-82; v.p. Pickwick Devel., N.Y.C., 1982-85, Silver Edge Constrn., N.Y.C., 1985-90, The Columns, Inc., N.Y.C., 1988-90; pres. Golden Rule Constrn., N.Y.C., 1990—. Office: Golden Rule Constrn 270 Lafayette St # 1310 New York NY 10012

GLUSKER, DONALD LEONARD, chemicals manager; b. Chgo., Oct. 6, 1930; s. Albert Joseph and Anne (Goldsmith) G.; m. Jenny Pickworth, Dec. 18, 1955; children: Ann, Mark, Katharine. BS, U. Calif., Berkeley, 1951; PhD, Oxford (Eng.) U., 1954. Postdoctoral fellow Calif. Inst. Tech., Pasadena, 1954-56; sr. scientist Rohm and Haas Co., Phila., 1956-61, lab. head, 1961-68, rsch. supr., 1968-72; rsch. dir. Rohm and Haas Co., Spring House, Pa., 1972-76, rsch. mgr. various depts., 1976-90, mgr. polymer and resins synthesis rsch. dept., 1990—. Patentee in field. Mem. Pa. selection com. Rhodes Trust, Phila., 1963-68, 90—. NSF fellow, 1954; Rhodes Trust scholar, 1951. Mem. Am. Chem. Soc. (petroleum rsch. fund adv. bd. Washington chpt. 1977-80, polymer award selection com. 1983-86), Am. Assn. Rhodes Scholars. Democrat. Home: 1011 Anna Rd Huntingdon Valley PA 19006 Office: Rohm and Haas Co 727 Norristown Rd Spring House PA 19477

GLYNN, TIMOTHY KEVIN, record and video producer; b. Terryville, N.Y., Nov. 29, 1964; s. Raymond Edward and Margaret (Collette) G. AAS in Electronics, Suffolk U., 1986; student, SUNY, Stony Brook, 1990—. Foreman Superior Stone, Port Jefferson Station, N.Y., 1986-89; freelance producer Terryville, 1989—; mgr. Deja-VU, Port Jefferson Station, 1985-91; jr. audio engr. Sanctum Stuios, Lake Rok, N.Y., 1987-90. Author, engr. (mus. rec.) Deja-VU, 1989, vol. II, 1991. Mem. Young Reps., Port Jefferson Station, 1991. Mem. Nat. Acad. Rec. Arts and Scis. (edn. com. 1991—). Roman Catholic. Home: 8 Newport Dr Port Jefferson Station NY 11776-3319

GLYNN, WILLIAM THOMAS, JR., entrepreneur, lawyer; b. Newark, Feb. 6, 1921; s. William T. Marie (Grant) G.; m. Jean Patricia Bagger, June 20, 1953; children: William T. III, Diane P., Thomas M., Denis C., Michael C., Timothy G., Sharon A., Kathleen T. BBA, St. Bonaventure (N.Y.) Coll., 1943; JD, Fordham U., 1950. Bar: N.J. 1949, N.Y. 1952, Fed. Dist. Ct. 1949. Acct. various orgns., 1946-52; v.p., treas. Wah Chang Corp. (now Teledyne, Inc.), N.Y.C., 1952-69; exec. v.p. Benilite Corp., N.Y.C., 1969-79; pres. Multi Resources Internat., N.Y.C., 1969-81; chmn. Hitox Corp., Corpus Christi, Tex., 1974-83; chmn., pres. Applied Microwave Devices Corp., Belmar, N.J., 1983-90; pres. GMK Resources, Inc., Wall, N.J., 1990—, DMN, Inc., Wall. Mayor, commr. Allenhurst, N.J., 1970-80, 84-88; pres. bd. edn., Allenhurst, 1966-70; mem. planning bd., bd. adjustment, Allenhurst, 1980-84. With U.S. Army, 1943-46, ETP, with USAR, 1951-66. Home: 121 Racquet Rd Wall NJ 07719

GOBLE, ALFRED THEODORE, physicist, educator; b. River Falls, Wis., Jan. 24, 1909; s. Lloyd and Carolyn Nelle (Green) G.; m. Ethel Theo Frank, July 31, 1935; children: Robert Lloyd, Louis Frank, Jonathan Charles. BA, U. Wis., 1929, PhD, 1933. Instr., asst. prof. U. Tulsa, 1934-37; from asst. prof. to assoc. prof. Alfred (N.Y.) U., 1937-44; rsch. assoc. radio rsch. lab. Harvard U., Cambridge, Mass., 1944-45; from assoc. prof. to prof. Union Coll., Schenectady, N.Y., 1945-74, chmn., 1966-71, emeritus prof., rsch. prof., 1974—; vis. asst. prof. Princeton (N.J.) U., 1942-43; vis. rsch. assoc. Clarendon Lab. Oxford (England) U., 1964, 71; cons. Revere Copper and Brass, Ramo-Wooldridge, STL Aerospace Corp. Co-author: (with D.K. Baker) Modern Physics, 1962, 2d edition, 1971. Mem. Am. Phys. Soc., Optical Soc. Am., Am. Assn. Physics Tchrs., Sigma Xi. Home: 1366 Mcclellan St Schenectady NY 12309 Office: Union Coll Dept Physics Schenectady NY 12308

GOCEK, MATILDA ARKENBOUT (MRS. JOHN A. GOCEK), librarian; b. Hoboken, N.J., Feb. 18, 1923; d. Jacob Richard and Mathilda (Meyer) Arkenbout; m. Harry Francis Decker, May 15, 1939 (div. Nov. 1955) children: Ruth Ann Decker Robinson, Dianne Karen Decker McKinstrie; m. John A. Gocek, Nov. 18, 1956; 1 son, John Jacob. AA, Orange County Community Coll., 1961; BA, SUNY, New Paltz, 1964; MLS, SUNY, Albany, 1967. Libr. dir., Monroe (N.Y.) Free Libr., 1958-61, Tuxedo Park (N.Y.) Libr., 1963-76; historian Town of Tuxedo, 1973-76; dir. Suffern Free Libr., 1977-90; pres.; chief exec. officer Libr. Rsch. Assocs. Inc., 1990—; libr. cons. Tuxedo Union Free Sch., 1967-69. Editor: Libr. Rsch. Assocs., 1968. Vice chmn. Montgomery Expdn. Meml. Observance, 1973. Bd. dirs. Tuxedo Park Sch.; trustee, pres. Mus. Village of Orange County (N.Y.), 1980-83. Mem. Orange-Sullivan Pub. (pres. 1967-70), N.Y. Library Assn., Southeastern N.Y. Libr. Reference Resource Coun., Libr. Assn. Rockland County (N.Y.) (goals com. 1977, exec. bd. 1980-83), Ramapo Catskill Libr. System Assn. (exec. bd. 1986-88). Home: RD 5 Box 41 Dunderberg Rd Monroe NY 10950 Office: Dunderberg Rd Monroe NY 10950

GOCHMAN, EVA RUTH, psychologist; b. Vienna, Austria; came to U.S., 1938; d. David and Josefine (Heiss) Grubler; m. Stanley I. Gochman, Jan. 15, 1956; children: David, Julie. BA, Hunter Coll., 1951; MA, Columbia U., 1952; PhD, Adelphi U., 1957. Diplomate Am. Bd. Psychology. Rsch. cons., staff mem. Topeka (Kans.) State Hosp., 1956-57; psychologist Lyons (N.J.) VA Hosp., 1958-59; chief psychologist Somerset County Guidance Ctr., Somerville, N.J., 1959-64; dir. youth and parent svcs. Bergen Ctr. Psychol. Svcs., Englewood, N.J., 1964-67; field assessment officer Peace Corps Tng. Ctr., P.R., 1968-69; assoc. prof. U. P.R., Cayey, 1969-74; ednl. specialist in rsch. St. Elizabeth's Hosp., Washington, 1974-80, acting dir. mother and infant program, 1981-87; dir. parent and infant program Commn. Mental Health Svcs., Washington, 1987—; lectr. various orgns. Contbr. numerous articles to profl. jours. Mem. APA (chair Com. Infant Mental Health, div. psychoanalysis), World Mental Health Assn., World Assn. Infant Psychiatry and Allied Disciplines. Office: Parent & Infant Devel Progr 51 N St NE Ste 700C Washington DC 20002-3323

GODA, JOHN MICHAEL, insurance broker; b. Pitts., Aug. 18, 1964; s. John Jr. and Rose Ellen (Rufft) G. BA, Grove City Coll., 1986. Account exec. Conover & Assocs., Inc., Pitts., 1986-88, sales mgr., 1988-90; v.p. sales Harte, Hawke & Zupsic, Inc., Pitts., 1990—; pres. Young Agts. Pitts., Pa., 1989-91; dir. Ind. Agts. Pitts., Pa., 1989-91. Editor: Young Agents Outlook, 1989-91. Youth counselor Coalition for Christian Outreach. Mem. Ins. Club Pitts., Profl. Ins. Agts., Young Agts. Pitts., Ind. Agts. Pitts. Office: Harte Hawke & Zupsic 336 First St Pittsburgh PA 15215

GODDARD, ROBERT CLYDE, clinical psychologist, supervisor, educator; b. N.Y.C., July 9, 1951; s. Philip H. and Yvette Elaine (Schwartz) G. BA in Psychology, Kenyon Coll., 1974; MA in Psychology, U. So. Miss., 1978, PhD in Clin. Psychology, 1980. Lic. psychologist, Mass.; cert. psychology, N.H. Practicum student U. So. Miss., Hattiesburg, 1977-79; therapist, intern Shoreline Mental Health Clinic, Essex, Conn., 1979-80; intern in clin. psychology Conn. Valley Hosp., Middletown, 1979-80; sch. psychologist Concord (N.H.) Pub. Sch. Dist., 1982, Portsmouth (N.H.) Pub. Sch. Dist., 1982-83; youth and family therapist Strafford Guidance Ctr., Dover, N.H., 1983-85; pvt. practice Manchester and Dover, N.H., 1981-85; tng. dir. Family Therapy Inst. So. N.H., Bedford and Dover, N.H., 1987—, exec. dir., 1985—; cons. Notre Dame Coll., Manchester, N.H., 1983-87; asst. prof. St. Anselm Coll., Manchester, 1980-82, Merrimack Valley Coll., U. N.H., Manchester, 1982; adj. faculty mem. Ea. Conn. State Coll., Willimantic, 1980, U. So. Miss., McComb, 1978-79; instr. U. So. Miss., Hattiesburg, 1977-79; lectr. child abuse and neglect issues. Editor: N.H. Jour. Counseling and Devel., 1983—; contbr. numerous articles to profl. jours. Chmn. Strafford Regional Child Abuse Assn. Assessment Team, 1984-85. Mem. APA, Am. Assn. Marriage and Family Therapy (approved supr., clin. mem.), AACD, N.H. Assn. Counseling and Devel. (exec. bd. 1983—), No. New Eng. Assn. Counselor Edn. and Supervision (exec. bd., treas. 1983-84), Assn. Humanistic Edn. and Devel., N.H. Mental Health Counselors Assn. (pres. 1985-86), N.H. Marriage and Family Counselors Assn. (pres. 1987-88). Home: 65 Derryfield Ct Manchester NH 03104-4548 Office: Family Therapy Inst 360-10A Rt 101W Bedford NH 03104

GODDARD, THOMAS GLEN, lawyer, public affairs professional; b. Wichita Falls, Tex., Aug. 8, 1955; s. Glen and Florence Ellen (Cowgill) G.; m. Alice Ann Milton, May 31, 1981 (div. 1986); m. Barra Kahn, June 14, 1987. BA in Polit. Sci., U. Ariz., 1976, JD, 1979. Bar: Ariz. 1979, U.S. Dist. Ct. Ariz. 1979, U.S. Ct. Appeals (9th cir.) 1979. Assoc., Law Offices of Walter B. Nash, III, P.C., Tucson, 1979-81; pvt. practice, Tucson, 1981; spl. asst. to Ariz. Gov. Bruce Babbitt, Tucson, 1981-83; state legis. counsel Assn. of Trial Lawyers of Am., Washington, 1983-85; dir. Alliance for Consumer Rights, N.Y.C., 1985-86; pres. Goddard Pub. Affairs Corp., Tucson, 1986-90; exec. dir. Tucson Adminstrs., Inc., 1989; counsel, govt. and media rels. Nat. Assn. Ins. Commrs., Washington, 1990—. Contbr. articles and columns to legal publs. Recipient William Spaid Meml. award U. Ariz. Coll. Law. Mem. Blue Key, Phi Kappa Phi. Office: Nat Assn Ins Commrs Ste 309 444 E Capitol St NW Washington DC 20001-1512

GODDESS, LYNN BARBARA, real estate broker; b. N.Y.C., Mar. 3, 1942; d. Eugene Daniel and Hazel Cecile (Kinzler) G.; divorced. BS, Columbia U., 1963, postgrad., 1964-66. Coord. John M. Burns Assembly Campaign, N.Y.C., 1963; dir. spl. events, projects Kenneth B. Keating Senatorial Campaign, N.Y.C., 1964; dist. dir. fund raising Muscular Dystrophy Assn. Am. Inc., N.Y.C., 1965-66; exec. acct. fund raising, pub. relations Victor Weingarten Co., N.Y.C., 1966-67, Oram Group (formerly Harold L. Oram Inc.), N.Y.C., 1967-70; dir. devel. City Ctr. Music Drama Inc., N.Y.C., 1970; sales person Whitbread-Nolan, N.Y.C., 1971-73; from asst. v.p. to sr. v.p. Cross and Brown Co., N.Y.C., 1973-1985; sr. dir. Cushman & Wakefield, Inc., N.Y.C., 1985—. Trustee Young Adult Inst. Mem. Nat. Soc. Fund Raisers, Assn. Fund Dirs., Real Estate Bd. N.Y. (named Most Ingenious Broker Yr. 1975), Women's Forum. Office: Cushman & Wakefield Inc 1166 Ave of the Americas New York NY 10036-2708

GODFREY, GEORGE CHEESEMAN, II, surgeon; b. Atlantic City, Oct. 15, 1926; s. William M. and Elizabeth (Uzzell) G.; m. Evelyn Fry, Sept. 20, 1952; children: Cheryl Lynn, George Cheeseman III. Student St. Bonaventure Coll., 1944, U. Ky., 1945; AB, Colgate U., 1948; MD, Jefferson Med. Coll., 1952. Intern, Atlantic City Hosp., 1952-53; resident in gen. surgery U.S. VA Hosp., Ft. Howard, Balt., 1953-57; practice medicine specializing in surgery, Somers Point, N.J., 1957—; chief gen. and trauma surgery, dir. dept. surgery Shore Meml. Hosp., Somers Point, 1973-76, dir. surgery, 1982-87; instr. surgery Jefferson Med. Coll., Phila., 1958-84; cons. in orthopedics and neurology N.J. Div. Disability Determinations, N.J. Rehab. Program, 1960—; physician FAA Tech. Center, part-time, 1977—, med. mgr., 1982-85; pres. Shore Surg. P.A., Atlantic Indsl. Med. Assocs. Contbr. article to profl. jours. Pres. Linwood (N.J.) Bd. Edn., 1972-73; mem. Atlantic County United Way, Atlantic County YMCA, Atlantic Performing Arts. Served with U.S. Army, 1944-46. Recipient Disting. Service award N.J. Jr. C. of C., 1960, Maroon Citation, Colgate U. Diplomate Am. Bd. Surgery, Nat. Bd. Med. Examiners. Fellow ACS; mem. AMA, Am. Trauma Soc., Am. Soc. Abdominal Surgeons, Aerospace Med. Assn., Am. Occupational Med. Soc., N.J., Atlantic County Med. Socs., Atlantic Indsl. Med. Physicians (pres.), Chainede Rotesseurs, Atlantic City Country Club, Marriott Seaview Country Club, Resorts Internat. Racquet Club, Kiwanis, Masons, Shriners, KT, Phi Kappa Tau, Phi Beta Pi. Methodist. Home: 112 Glenside Ave Linwood NJ 08221-2424 also: 5550 N Ocean Dr Singer Island FL also: 674 Shore Rd Somers Point NJ 08244 also: 1616 Pacific Ave Atlantic City NJ also: 705 White Horse Pike Absecon NJ 08201

GODFREY, HENRY PHILIP, immunologist, experimental pathologist; b. Poughkeepsie, N.Y., Aug. 7, 1941; s. Joseph and Mildred (Hoffman) G.; m. Ginger Schnaper, May 6, 1977; children: Thomas Owen, David Stuart. BA cum laude, Harvard U., 1961, MD cum laude, 1965; PhD, U. Birmingham, Eng., 1980. Diplomate Am. Bd. Med. Examiners. Intern Barnes Hosp., St. Louis, 1965-66; USPHS surgeon NIH, Bethesda, Md., 1966-70; Moseley travel fellow Harvard U., Cambridge, Mass., 1970-72; hon. rsch. fellow U. Birmingham, 1970-78; lectr. U. Copenhagen, 1972-75; asst. prof. SUNY, Stony Brook, 1975-82; assoc. prof. pathology N.Y. Med. Coll., Valhalla, 1982-88, prof. pathology, 1988—. Abstract editorial bd. Transplantation Procs., Stony Brook, 1981—; editorial bd. Lymphokines, N.Y.C., 1982-87; contbr. articles to sci. jours. Grantee Anna Fuller Fund, 1970-72, Kroc Foun., 1976-79, Nat. Cancer Inst., 1979—, Burroughs Wellcome, 1988. Mem. Am. Assn. Immunologists, Brit. Soc. Immunology, Am. Soc. Microbiology, N.Y. Acad. Scis., Harvey Soc. Office: Dept Pathology NY Med Coll Valhalla NY 10595

GODINO, RINO LODOVICO, petroleum and chemical company executive; b. N.Y.C., Mar. 21, 1925; s. Enrico and Emily (Forneron) G.; m. Dolores Estelle Pagano; children: Diane C., Marc L. B Chem. Engring., NYU, 1950, M Chem. Engring., 1952, cert. exec. mgmt., 1967. Registered profl. engr., N.J., Pa., Ill. Instr. NYU, 1950-51; process design engr. Foster Wheeler USA Corp., N.Y.C., 1951-62; chief process engr. Foster Wheeler USA Corp., Livingston, N.J., 1962-72; mgr. process design Foster Wheeler Energy Corp., Livingston, N.J., 1972-73, dir. design and devel., 1973-81, v.p., 1981—; v.p., gen. mgr. Petrochemical Cons. Can., Ltd. subs. Foster Wheeler Energy Corp., 1979—; bd. dirs., KBC, Inc., New Orleans, Fractionation Rsch., Inc. Patentee in field; contbr. articles to tech. publs. Elder, First Waldensian Ch. N.Y., N.Y.C., 1950; rep., Protestant Coun. Chs., N.Y.C., 1954. Decorated Bronze Star medal, 3 Battle Star medals, Combat Infantry Man's badge. Mem. Am. Inst. Chem. Engrs., Nat. Soc. Profl. Engrs., Internat. Brotherhood Magicians, Soc. Am. Magicians, Tau Beta Pi, Phi Lambda Upsilon. Office: Foster Wheeler USA Corp Perryville Corp Pk Clinton NJ 08809

GODLESKI, JOHN JOSEPH, pathologist; b. Nanticoke, Pa., July 24, 1943; s. John and Sophie (Pretko) G.; m. Mary Lou Moss, June 14, 1969; children: Teresa Louise, Daniel Peter. BS, King's Coll., Wilkes-Barre, Pa., 1965; MD, U. Pitts., 1969. Intern, resident Mass. Gen. Hosp., Boston, 1969-71; rsch. fellow Harvard Sch. Pub. Health, Boston, 1971; USPHS officer EPA, Research Triangle Park, N.C., 1971-73; asst. prof. Med. Coll. of Pa., Phila., 1973-78; asst. prof. Brigham & Women's Hosp., Boston, 1978-85, assoc. prof., 1985—. Contbr. 50 articles to profl. jours. Rsch. grantee NIH, 1979—. Roman Catholic. Home: 421 Conant Rd Weston MA 02193-1830 Office: Brigham & Womens Hosp 75 Francis St Boston MA 02115-6195

GODLEWSKI, JAMES BERNARD, educator, consultant; b. Wilkes-Barre, Pa., Nov. 22, 1952; s. Stanley William and Alberta Theresa (Baloga) G.; m. Theresa Anne Boblick, July 9, 1983; children: Michael James, Matthew Joel, Kristofer John. BA in History, Elem. Edn., Wilkes U., 1974, MS in Elem Edn., 1977; EdD in Elem Edn., Temple U., 1987. Cert. elem. tchr., elem. prin., computer specialist, Pa. Educator Wallenpaupack Area Sch. Dist., Hawley, Pa., 1975—; sports writer The News Eagle, Hawley, 1975-90; prin. Godlewski Assocs., Wilkes-Barre, 1991—; adj. faculty Pa. Dept. Edn., Harrisburg; adj. prof. Pa. State U., 1990; pres. MAKS Computer Solutions, Inc. Co-author: (workbook) Reading to Think, 1989; contbr. articles to profl. jours. Mem. Econ. Devel. Coun. Northeastern Pa., 1987. Mem. NEA, PTA, Internat. Coun. Computers for Educators, Nat. Coun. Social Studies, Assn. for Devel. Computer Based Instructional Systems, Assn. Supervision, Curriculum and Devel., Assn. Tchrs. Computers, Math, and Sci., Nat. Mid. Schs. Assn., Pa. Coun. Tchrs. Math., Northeastern Pa. Assn. Math Tchrs., Pa. State Ednl. Assn., Pa. Assn. Supervision, Curriculum and Devel., Northeastern Pa. Amateur Computer Club, Wallenpaupack Area Ednl. Assn., Twins Found., KC, Temple Owl Club, Phi Delta Kappa. Republican. Roman Catholic. Home: 212 Bowman St Wilkes Barre PA 18702-5405 Office: Wallenpaupack Area Sch Dist PO Box 17 Hawley PA 18428-0017

GODWIN, JOSEPH LAWRENCE, porcelain designer, artist, writer; b. Ithaca, N.Y., Dec. 29, 1947; s. Charles John and Margaret-Jane (Copeland) G.; m. Ursula Petermann, July 31, 1987. BFA, U. Mass., 1970. Potter Copeland Pottery, Pepperell, Mass., 1971-75, Internat. Cultural Found., Tarrytown, N.Y., 1975-78; apprentice potter ShinSangHo Pottery, Piok Che, Korea, 1978; vis. potter Tsukamoto Pottery, Mashiko, Japan, 1979, Garrison (N.Y.) Art Ctr., 1980; potter Millwood, N.Y., 1981; porcelain designer, prodn. Joseph Godwin Porcelains, Pepperell, 1982—; clay instr. Geneseo Art Ctr., Ayer, Mass., 1983-84, Groton (Mass.) Ctr. for Arts, 1983, Decordova Mus., Lincoln, Mass., 1985, Brookfield (Conn.) Art Ctr., 1986. Copyrighted polychrome slip-carved porcelain, 1984; works in museum collections including Mus. of Fine Arts, Boston, 1985, Currier Gallery, Manchester, N.H., 1990. Mem. League of N.H. Craftsmen, Soc. Arts and Crafts. Home and Office: Studio House Gallery 54 Jewett St Pepperell MA 01463

GODWIN, R. WAYNE, chemicals company executive; b. 1941. BS, Rensselaer Poly. Inst.; PhD, Duke U. With Celanese Corp., 1966-86; With BASF Corp., 1986—, pres. structural materials, 1986-87, pres. fibers div., corp. exec. v.p., 1987. Office: BASF Corp Fibers Div PO Drawer D Williamsburg VA 23187

GODWIN, RALPH LEE, JR., real estate executive; b. Raleigh, N.C., July 20, 1954; s. Ralph Lee Sr. and Hilda Faye (Sellars) G. BS in Commerce, U. Va., 1976; MBA, Dartmouth Coll., 1982. Fgn. exchange trader N.C. Nat. Bank, Charlotte, 1976-78; mgr. N.Y. office 1st Nat. Bank Atlanta, N.Y.C., 1979-80; assoc. corp. fin. Goldman Sachs & Co., N.Y.C., 1982-84; assoc. Eastdil Realty, Inc., N.Y.C., 1984-88; dir. Jones Lang Wootton, U.S.A., N.Y.C., 1988—; pres. Centurion Devel. Corp., Wilmington, N.C., 1976—; officer Eastdil Equities, Inc., N.Y.C., 1984-86. Recipient Devel. cert. DARE Inc., Wilmington, 1984, 88. Mem. Real Estate Bd. N.Y., N.C. Soc. N.Y., U. Va. Alumni Assn., Dartmouth Coll. Alumni Assn. Wykagyl Country Club, N.Y. Athletic Club, Downtown Athletic Club, Regency Whist Club, Omicron Delta Kappa. Republican. Episcopalian. Office: Jones Lang Wootton USA Apt 5-F 101 E 52d St 20th Fl New York NY 10022

GOE, ERIC A., physician; b. N.Y.C., Jan. 21, 1948; s. George and Frieda H. (Zisca) G.; m. Carole A. Ryan, June 7, 1969; children: Deirdre, James, Siobhan. BS, Rensselaer Polytech. Inst., 1969; MD, Albany Med. Coll., 1973. Diplomate Am. Bd. Family Practice; cert. added qualifications in geriatrics. Pvt. practice Orlando, Fla., 1976-87; clin. instr. Fla. Hosp. Family Practice Residing, Orlando, 1976-91; asst. clin. prof. U. S.Fla., Tampa, 1976-91; clin. dir. Park Care Community Health Ctr., Orlando, 1987-90; med. dir. Community Health Plan, Glens Falls, N.Y., 1990—; dir. Fla. Acad. of Family Physicians, 1987-90. Editorial rev. bd.: Family Practice Rsch. Jour., 1987—. Named Preceptor of Yr., Fla. Hosp., Orlando, 1987-88. Fellow Am. Acad. Family Physicians (grant reviewer); mem. Warren County Med. Soc., Med. Soc. State of N.Y., N.Y. State Acad. of Family Physicians. Office: Community Health Plan 694 Upper Glen St Glens Falls NY 12801

GOELET, ROBERT G., business executive; b. Sandricourt, France, Sept. 28, 1923; s. Robert Walton and Anne Marie (Guestier) G.; m. Alexandra Gardiner Creel, Sept. 9, 1976. A.B., Harvard U., 1945. Chmn. R.I. Corp.; pres. Goelet Realty Co.; v.p. Goelet Corp.; dir. Chem. Bank, Chem. Banking Corp. Trustee Am. Mus. Natural History, 1958—, pres., 1975-88, chmn., 1988-89, Boscobel Restoration Inc., 1976—; trustee French Inst.-Alliance Française N.Y., 1951—, pres., 1967—; trustee N.Y. Zool. Soc., 1951—, pres., 1971-75; trustee Phipps Houses, 1959—, Carnegie Instn., Washington, 1980—, St. Catherine's Island Found., 1981—, Edward John Noble Found., 1981—, Mus. Comparative Zoology, 1980—. Office: 22 E 67th St New York NY 10021-5829

GOELLER, CHRISTINE JANE, systems consultant; b. Newark, N.J., Nov. 21, 1951; d. John Henry and Laura (Cusimano) G.; m. Kelvin John Granberg, July 30, 1977. BA cum laude, Rutgers U., 1973; MA, Montclair State Coll., 1977. Programmer Diecomp, Inc., South Plainfield, N.J., 1973-74, Automated Data Assocs., Rahway, N.J., 1974-75; grad. asst. Montclair State Coll., Upper Montclair, N.J., 1976-77; programmer analyst Burns and Roe, Inc., Paramus, N.J., 1977-78; system analyst Airco, Inc., Murray Hill, N.J., 1978-82; sr. system cons. CIBA-GEIGY Corp., Summit, N.J., 1982—. Contbr. articles to profl. jours. Mem. Assn. Computing Machines, N.Y. Acad. Sci. Roman Catholic. Home: 78 Westover Ave West Caldwell NJ 07006-7723 Office: CIBA-GEIGY Corp 556 Morris Ave Summit NJ 07901-1398

GOELLER, LEO F., telecommunication consultant; b. Rockbridge County, Va., Aug. 14, 1925; s. Leo F. and Mildred (Searson) G.; m. Nan Rubright; children: Lawrence N., James D. BEE, U. Va., 1953, MEE, 1954; postgrad., Stevens Coll., 1959, Rutgers U., 1966-67. Radio writer, announcer, technician various stations, various cities, 1943-49; engr. Bell Telephone Labs., Whippany, Holmdel, N.J., 1954-66, RCA, Camden, N.J., 1967-74; prin. Communication Resources, Haddonfield, N.J., 1974—. Patentee in field; author books/articles on telephone switching. Pfc. USAF, 1949-50. Mem. IEEE. Home: PO Box 2018 326 E Cottage Ave Haddonfield NJ 08033 Office: Communication Resources PO Box 2018 Haddonfield NJ 08033

GOELZER, DANIEL LEE, lawyer; b. Milw., Feb. 14, 1947; s. Gerald Howard and Roberta (Hart) G.; m. Angela C. Carcone, Jan. 9, 1988; children: Christina H., Mary E.; 1 child by previous marriage, Michael W. BBA, U. Wis., 1969, JD, 1973; LLM, George Washington U., 1979. Bar: Wis. 1973, U.S. Dist. Ct. (we. dist.) Wis. 1973, U.S. Ct. Appeals (7th cir.) 1974, U.S. Ct. Appeals (2d, 9th and D.C. cirs.) 1975, U.S. Supreme Ct. 1976, D.C. 1979. Auditor, Touche, Ross & Co., Milw., 1969-70; law clk. judge U.S. Ct. Appeals, Chgo., 1973-74; atty. SEC, Washington, 1974-78, exec. asst. to chmn., 1978-83, gen. counsel, 1983-90; ptnr. Baker and McKenzie, Washington, 1990—; adj. prof. law Georgetown U. Law Ctr., 1986—. Contbr. articles to law jours. Served with USAR, 1969-75. Mem. ABA, Fed. Bar Assn., AICPA. Republican. Congregationalist. Avocation: amateur radio. Home: 5941 Searl Ter Bethesda MD 20816-2022 Office: Baker & Mckenzie 815 Connecticut Ave NW Washington DC 20006-4004

GOEPFERT, ROBERT HAROLD, music educator; b. N.Y.C., Oct. 30, 1935; s. Harold Frederick and Agnes Annie (Mischke) G. BEE, The Cooper Union, 1957; MMus, New Eng. Conservatory, Boston, 1967; MusAD, Boston U., 1981. Piano tchr. Brookline (Mass.) Music Sch., 1959; performing pianist, 1959—; piano tchr. Boston U., 1972-74, Tufts U., Medford, Mass., 1968-86; prof. music Anna Maria Coll., Paxton, Mass., 1968—. Editor/founder Spectrum, 1985—. F.H. Beebe travel grantee Beebe Found., 1967. Mem. Kappa Gamma Lambda. Office: Anna Maria Coll Sunset Ln Worcester MA 01612-1198

GOETCHEUS, JOHN STEWART, orthopaedic surgeon; b. Cin., May 14, 1938; s. Lester Frederick and Elizabeth (Gibson) G.; m. Janice Berg, July 13, 1963; children: Amy, Gregory. BA, DePauw U., 1960; MD, Case Western Res. U., 1964. Cert. Nat. Bd. Examiners, Am. Bd. Orthopaedic Surgery. Surgeon USAF, Edwards, Calif., 1966-68; resident orthopaedic surgery Yale New Haven Hosp., Yale Sch. Medicine, 1968-71; pvt. practice orthopaedic surgery Essex, Conn., 1971—; cons. orthopaedic surgery West Haven (Conn.) Vets. Hosp., 1970—; clin. instr. orthopaedic surgery Yale Med. Sch., New Haven, 1970—. Elected mem. regional Dist. 4 Bd. Edn., Essex, Deep River, Chester, 1983-89; mem. bd. visitors DePauw U., Greencastle, Ind., 1990-93. Fellow Ea. Orthopaedic Assn. (bd. dirs. 1991); mem. Am. Acad.

Orthopaedic Surgeons. Republican. Home: 14 Partridge Ln Essex CT 06426 Office: Middlesex Tpke PO Box 697 Essex CT 06426

GOFF, ROBERT EDWARD, health plan executive; b. Worcester, Mass., Nov. 19, 1952; s. Julius Lewis and Doris (Katz) G.; m. Jill P. Galber, Aug. 19. 1978 (dec. Aug. 1982); m. Jinny Sue Yaver, June 30, 1985; 1 child, Blake Adam. BBA with honors, Northeastern U., Boston, 1976; MBA with honors, Babson Coll., 1978; cert., Cornell U., 1981. Adminstrv. dir. Adirondack PSRO Inc., Glens Falls, N.Y., 1977-80; v.p. No. Met. Hosp. Assn., Newburgh, N.Y., 1980-83, Good Samaritian Hosp., Suffern, N.Y., 1983-85; exec. dir., chief exec. dir. WellCare N.Y., Inc., Newburgh, 1985-90; pres. Wellcare Leasing Corp., Newburgh, N.Y., 1990—, Well Care Med. Mgmt. Inc., 1992—; bd. dirs. Wellcare Mgmt. Group Inc.; pres. Wellcare Med. Mgmt.; cons. in field. Bd. dirs. Hospice Care, Inc. Recipient Vigil Honor award Order Arrow, 1969, Eagle Scout award Boy Scouts Am., 1970. Mem. Hudson Valley Hosp. Exec. Assn. (pres., bd. dirs. 1982-85), Healthcare Fin. Mgmt. Assn., Am. Coll. Hosp. Adminstrs., Beta Gamma Soc. Home: RR 1 Wappingers Falls NY 12590-9801 Office: WellCare NY 130 Meadow Ave Newburgh NY 12550-3030

GOFFINET, EDWARD PETER, JR., chemical engineer; b. Louisville, Nov. 15, 1930; s. Edward Peter and Evelyn Marie (Barnes) G.; m. Patricia Rae Baumann, Feb. 23, 1953 (dec. July, 1989); children: Pamela Kay, Terri Ann. BS in Chem. Engring, Notre Dame U., 1952. Registered profl. engr., Del. Chem. engr. E.I. Du Pont de Nemours, Louisville, Ky., 1952-60, Wilmington, Del., 1960-63; div. head E.I. Du Pont de Nemours, Wilmington, 1963-72, sr. cons., 1972-83, sr. rsch. assoc., 1983-86, rsch. fellow, 1986-91, sr. tech. fellow, 1991—; vis. prof. U. Del., Newark, 1981-84. Patentee process for making monovinylacetylene,, process for making acetylene, separation of polymers from solutions, separation of ethylene-propylene copolymer, process for polymerization of monomers. With CIC, U.S. Army, 1952-54. Recipient achievement medal Am. Inst. Chemists, 1952; named Ky. Col., State of Ky., 1968; scholar Am. Inst. Chem. Engrs., 1950. Home: 2403 Annwood Dr Wilmington DE 19810-2715 Office: EI Du Pont de Nemour & Co Exptl Sta Box 80269 Wilmington DE 19880

GOFFMAN, MARTIN, small business owner, consultant; b. Phila., June 22, 1940; s. Benjamin and Evelyn D. (Pollack) G.; m. Renee Cooperstein, Nov. 28, 1965; children: Robert, Vivian, Deborah. BA, Temple U., 1961, MS, 1963, PhD, 1965. Rsch. chemist ASARCO Inc., South Plainfield, N.J., 1965-78, sr. rsch. chemist, 1978-82, sect. head, 1982-85; prin. Martin Goffman Assocs., Edison, N.J., 1985—; pres., CEO Dellview U.S.A. Med., Inc., Piscataway, N.J., 1990—, also bd. dirs. Inventee in field. AEC fellow, 1963. Mem. Assn. Cons. Chemists (v.p. N.Y.C. chpt. 1989-90), Electrochem. Soc. (past pres. Met. N.Y. chpt.), Am. Chem. Soc., Assn. Ind. Info. Profls. Office: 3 Dellview Dr Edison NJ 08820-2545

GOGAN, JAMES WILSON, corporate executive; b. Springhill, N.S., Can., May 19, 1938; m. Mary Maureen Richards, Oct. 26, 1963; children: James Richard, Mary Monique, John Paul, Suzanne Maureen. B in Commerce, Dalhousie U., Halifax, N.S., 1959. With H.R. Doane, Amherst, New Glasgow and Antigonish, N.S., Can., 1959-62; chief fin. officer Empire Group, Stellarton, N.S., Can., 1962-74; exec. v.p. Empire Group, Stellarton, N.S., 1975-85, pres., 1985—; chmn., bd. dirs. Sobey Leased Properties Ltd., Island Realty Ltd.; pres., bd. dirs. Armdale Mall Ltd., Bridge Str. Motors Ltd., Empjan Holdings Ltd., Empro Ltd., Internat. Properties Ltd.; vice chmn., bd. dirs. Halifax Devels. Ltd.; pres., bd. dirs. Empire Co. Ltd., Armdale Mall Ltd., Bridge St. Motors Ltd., Empjan Holdings Ltd., Empro Ltd., Internat. Properties Ltd.; sec., bd. dirs. Kepec Holdings Ltd., Sobey Found., Atlantic Motors Ltd., Empire Theatres Ltd.; v.p., bd. dirs. A.S.C. Investments Ltd., Lunenburg Investments Ltd., E.C.L. Investments Ltd., Granville Devels. Ltd.; bd. dirs. Sobeys Inc., Barclays Bank Can., Hannaford Bros. Co., Consumers Distbg. Co. Ltd., Crombie Ins. (U.K.) Ltd., Lawton's Drug Stores Ltd., The Sobey Art Found., Atlantic West London Ltd. Sec., treas. United Appeal, New Glasgow; charter mem. YMCA/YWCA Pictou County; chair fin. and adminstrn. parish coun. St. John The Bapt. Roman Cath. Ch.; mem. bd. govs., exec. com., investment com. St. Francis Xavier U. Mem. Lloyd's of London (underwriting), Fin. Execs. Inst. Can., Gyro Club (past pres.), Abercrombie Golf and Country Club. Roman Catholic. Office: Empire Co Ltd, 115 King St, Stellarton, NS Canada B0K 1S0

GOGLIETTINO, JOHN CARMINE, insurance company executive; b. Danbury, Conn., Sept. 5, 1952; s. Nicholas and Josephine (Staffieri) G.; m. Deborah Ann Russo, Sept. 25, 1976. BA in History, Western Conn. State Coll., 1975. Sales rep. Met. Life Ins. Co., Danbury, 1978-81; account exec. Thomas A. Settle, Inc., Danbury, 1981-88, Hodge Ins. Agy., Danbury, 1988—. Editor: (newspaper) Yankee Doodler, 1983-84. Rec. sec. State of Conn. Bd. Vet. Medicine, Hartford, 1984—; candidate Danbury Dem. Town Com., 1986, mem., 1988—, fin. chmn. 1990-92, treas., 1992—; active Italian Heritage Soc.; trustee, v.p. Scott-Fanton Mus., 1985-91. Recipient Statesman award Conn. Jaycees 1983, Disting. Svc. award 1990, City of Danbury 1990; named one of Outstanding Young Men of Am. Jaycees, 1982, 90, Conn. Outstanding Young Citizens award Channel 30 and Conn. Jaycees. Mem. Life Underwriters Assn. (cert. 1982), Health Underwriters Assn., Danbury Ins. Men Orgn., Western Conn. State Coll. Alumni Assn. (activator memberships 1985-87), No. Fairfield County Bus. People Assn., Danbury Jaycees, Kiwanis (v.pl, pres. Danbury Club 1984-86), Elks, Americo Vespucci Club (trustee). Roman Catholic. Home: PO Box 2598 Danbury CT 06813-2598 Office: Hodge Ins Agy 283 Main St Danbury CT 06810-6607

GOH, DAVID SHUH-JEN, psychology educator; b. Nanjing, Kiangsu, China, July 9, 1941; came to U.S., 1967; s. Yinghwa and Pei-sue (Cho) G.; m. Jane C.; children: Alice, Nancy, Tiffany. BA, Nat. Taiwan C.K. U., 1963; MS, Ill. State U., 1969; PhD, U. Wis., 1973. Psychologist Lincoln (Ill.) Devel. Ctr., 1969-70; asst. prof. U. Wis., La Crosse, 1973-75; assoc. prof. Cen. Mich. U., Mt. Pleasant, 1975-80; prof., chmn. So. Ill. I., Carbondale, 1980-88; prof. CUNY, Queens Coll., Flushing, 1988—. Author: Psychological Testing Vol. 1, 2, 1988; contbr. articles to profl. jours. Fellow APA; mem. Asian Am. Psychol. Assn. (pres. 1989-91), and numerous others. Home: 34 Angler Ln Port Washington NY 11050-1702 OFfice: CUNY Queens Coll Flushing NY 11367-0904

GOKAY, MICHAEL ALAN, assistant director; b. Burlington, Vt., Nov. 10, 1951; s. Clarence Orbis and Dorothy (Francis) Trainor; children: Elizabeth Guy, Emily Michael. BS in Indsl. Edn., Temple U., 1981; MEd in Supervision, U. Pitts., 1982. Electrician Port Jervis (N.Y.) Electric Co., 1973-75; elec. foreman Barrier Industries, Port Jervis, 1976-77; indsl. electrician J.O. Ryder Rendering, Inc., Matamoras, Pa., 1977-78; tchr. Del. Valley High Sch., Milford, Pa., 1978-80, Parkway West Area Vocat.-Tech. Sch., Oakdale, Pa., 1980-84; supr. Cumberland-Perry Area Vocat.-Tech. Sch., Mechanicsburg, Pa., 1984-85; asst. dir. Upper Bucks County Area Vocat.-Tech. Sch., Perkasie, Pa., 1985—; instr. indsl. machines I and II, Allegheny County Community Coll., Oakdale; instr. elec. constrn. Del. Valley High Sch., Milford; owner A&Z Electric Co., Matamoras. Home: 15 Mattis St Hellertown PA 18055-2812 Office: AVTS 3115 Ridge Rd Perkasie PA 18944-3830

GOLAR, MARTHA L., lawyer; b. Suffern, N.Y., Sept. 12, 1953. BA, Cornell U., 1974; JD, NYU, 1978. Assoc. atty. Marshall, Bratter, Greene, Allison & Tucker, N.Y.C., 1978-80, Lipkowitz & Plaut, N.Y.C., 1980-82; sr. staff atty. Joseph E. Seagram & Sons Inc., N.Y.C., 1982—. Pres. Condominium Assn., N.Y.C., 1986—. Mem. N.Y. Women's Bar Assn. (pres. 1991-92, treas. 1990-91, sec. 1989-91, bd. dirs. 1985-91), Assn. of Bar of City of N.Y. (lawyers in transition com., mil. affairs and justice com.). Office: Joseph E Seagram & Sons 800 3d Ave New York NY 10022-7604

GOLASZEWSKI, RICHARD STANLEY, economic consulting firm executive; b. Torrington, Conn., Aug. 28, 1947; s. Edward and Josephine (Cappetta) G.; m. Debra Susan Brendlinger, May 19, 1979; children: Richard Paul, Jesse Robert. BS in Acctg. magna cum laude, La Salle Coll., 1975; MPA, U. Pa., 1977. Sr. economist Acumenic Rsch. and Tech., Bethesda, Md., 1980-83; economist Gellman Rsch. Assocs., Jenkintown, Pa., 1977-80, exec. v.p., 1983—; cons. FAA, Washington, 1979—, NASA, Washington. Author: (monographs) Single ATC System Western Europe, 1989, Economic and Financial Analysis of Airbus Industry, 1990. Dir. Help Inc., Phila., 1980-83. Capt. U.S. Army, 1966-72, Vietnam. Morgantuau fellow Wharton Sch., 1975-77. Mem. NAS (com. mem. tranps. rsch. bd. 1990-91), AIAA, Transp. Rsch. Forum, Am. Helicopter Soc., Vietnam Helicopter Pilots Assn. Office: Gellman Rsch Assocs 115 West Ave Ste 201 Jenkintown PA 19046-2031

GOLD, ALLEN MORTON, biochemist, educator; b. Chgo., May 25, 1930; s. Joseph and Sadie (Zerulnik) G.; m Joyce B. Zeitlin, June 15, 1952. BA, U. Chgo., 1951; PhD, Harvard U., 1955. Scientist Worcester Found. Exptl. Biology, Shrewsbury, Mass., 1956-57; fellow Columbia U., N.Y.C., 1957-62, faculty, 1962--. Contbr. articles to scholarly and profl. jours. Mem. Am. Soc. for Biochemistry and Molecular Biology, Am. Chemical Soc., Harvey Soc. Office: Columbia U Dept Biochemistry/Molecular Biophysics 630 W 168th St New York NY 10032-3702

GOLD, DENNIS CHARLES, psychologist; b. Bklyn., Jan. 1, 1952; s. Jack Martin and Sarah (Rives) G.; m. Elyse Mindy Wax, June 1, 1975; children: Narayan, Kienan. BA, SUNY, Binghamton, 1973; PhD, U. Mo., 1977. Lic. psychologist, Pa. Asst. prof. psychology Kings Coll., Wilkes-Barre, Pa., 1977-84; sr. psychologist N.E. Pa. Counseling Ctr., Kingston, Pa., 1984—; cons. psychologist Red Rock Job Corps, Lopez, Pa., 1979-88; rsch. psychologist Luzerne County Mental Health and Mental Retardation, Wilkes-Barre, 1988-90; presenter profl. workshop Transformations, Switzerland, 1983. Author: (with others) Psychology and Performing Arts, 1991. Bd. dirs. Child-Adolescent Spl. Svc. Program, Wilkes-Barre, 1988—. Mem. APA, Pa. Psychol. Assn., Internat. Assn. Play Therapists, Nat. Register Health Svc. Providers in Psychology. Office: NE Pa Counseling Ctr 676 Wyoming Ave Kingston PA 18704-3857

GOLD, FAY HELFANO, artist; b. N.Y.C., Oct. 15, 1907; d. Solomon and Esther (Aston) Helfano; 1 child, David Gold. Painter Richard Hayley Lever Studio, N.Y.C., 1919—; actress, 1979—, poet, 1941—, playright. One-woman shows include Norlyst Gallery, N.Y.C., 1946, Roko Gallery, N.Y.C., 1949, 51, Partita Gallery, Southampton, N.Y., 1956 (first prize drawing competition), Village Art Ctr., N.Y.C., 1964, John Myers Gallery, 1964; exhibited in group shows at Pa. Acad. Fine Arts, 12961, Silvermine Guild, 1961-62, Jersey City Mus., 1961, Audubon Artists, 1962, 66, 67, 69, Eastern States Exhibition Mass., 1963, Soc. of Four Arts, Fla., 1963, Okla. Printmakers Soc., 1964, 69, Nat. Acad. Design, 1966. Yaddo grantee, Saratoga Springs, N.Y., 1949; recipient Popular prize Mcpl. Art Ctr., 1939, John J. Karpnick prize, Audubon Artists, 1964. Mem. Art Students League, Artists Equity Assn., Am. Watercolor Soc. Address: Box 256 Times Sq Sta New York NY 10108

GOLD, HILARY ALEXANDER, college administrator; b. London, July 10, 1931; came to U.S., 1949; s. Frank David and Anne (Joseph) G.; m. Arlene Jeanne Herman, Apr. 10, 1954; children: Jonathan, Laurence (dec.). BA, Bklyn. Coll., 1955, MS, 1956; EdD, Columbia U., 1960. From asst. prof. to prof. Bklyn Coll., 1964-71, prof., chmn. student affairs, 1971—; assoc. dean Sch. of Gen. Studies Bklyn. Coll., 1968-69, dean, 1969-71; dean of students Bklyn. Coll., 1971-73; v.p. Student Affairs and Svcs., Bklyn. Coll., Campus Affairs Bklyn. Coll., 1979-89; grand marshal Bklyn. Coll., 1982—; v.p. Student Life Bklyn. Coll., 1989—; v.p. Bklyn. Coll. Student Ctr. Corp., 1971—. Co-author: (with others) Influence of Ressentiment, 1965, Society's Children, 1967; contbr. numerous articles to profl. jours. Mem. Borough Pres. Task Force Racial Relations, Bklyn., 1988—, Lt. Gov.'s Adv. Panel, N.Y., 1991—. Recipient award for Exemplary Svc., N.Y. City Coun., 1983; multiple other awards from student and civic groups; grantee: Fed. Title III, NSF, Xerox, Newcomb Found. and many others. Fellow Bklyn. Coll.; Mem. Coun. for Advancement and Support of Edn. (spl. achievement award 1984), Bklyn. Coll. Alumni Assn. (exec. bd. and bd. dirs. 1973—, Alumnus of Yr. 1976) Kappa Delta Pi, Phi Delta Kappa, Alpha Sigma Lambda. Home: 2321 E 65th St Brooklyn NY 11234-6319 Office: Bklyn Coll Bedford Ave # H Brooklyn NY 11222-3102

GOLD, PHRADIE KLING See KLING, PHRADIE

GOLD, R. ILISE, human development counselor and trainer; b. N.Y.C., Dec. 23, 1954; d. Allen and Ellen (Borenstein) Wisser; m. Robert James Gold, Apr. 5, 1981; children: Alanna Elizabeth, Davin Michael. MEd in Counseling, Northeastern U., Boston, 1982; BA in Edn./Psychology, U. Bridgeport, Conn., 1976; acting, Lee Strasberg Theatre Inst., N.Y.C., 1977. Career counselor U. Mass., Boston, 1978-79; staff rels. asst. and internal recruiting Citibank, N.A., N.Y.C., 1978-81; rsch. cons. Bit-Tel Investment Co., Portland, Oreg., 1981-82; career cons. Career & Life Strategies, Inc., Westport, Conn., 1982-84; career and life planning specialist Ilise Gold Assocs., Westport, Conn., 1984—; pres. Ilise Gold Prodns., 1991—. Contbr. articles to mags. Mem. Am. Assn. Counseling and Devel., Nat. Career Devel. Assn., Career Planning and Adult Devel. Network, World Future Soc., Acad. Profl. Consultants and Advisors, Entrepreneurial Women's Network. Office: Ilise Gold Assocs 164 Kings Hwy N Westport CT 06880

GOLD, WILLIAM ELLIOTT, health care management consultant; b. Bklyn., Oct. 21, 1948; s. Theodore David and Debra (Fridovich) G.; m. Nili Rachel Scharf, June 1, 1972; children: Avitai, Doria Michelle. BA, SUNY, Stony Brook, 1970; MSS, Hebrew U. of Jerusalem, Israel, 1972; PhD, U. Minn., 1982. Rsch. asst. Hebrew U. of Jerusalem, 1971-72; cons. Dept. Health, Mpls., 1973-74; researcher Mt. Sinai Hosp., Mpls., 1973-74; hosp. adminstrn. instr. U. Minn., Mpls., 1974-75; coord., dir. Blue Cross/Blue Shield Greater N.Y. HMO, N.Y.C., 1975-85; pres. ANCHOR, Chgo., 1985-88; v.p. Rush-Presbyn. St. Luke's Med. Ctr., Chgo., 1985-88; pres. Gold Health Strategies, Inc., N.Y.C., 1988—; vice chmn. The HMO Group, 1987-88; steering com. U. Mo.-KC Nat. Ctr. for Managed Care Adminstrn., Kansas City, 1986—; chmn. N.Y. Bus. Group on Health Managed Care Task Force, N.Y.C., 1989—; asst. adj. prof. Columbia U., N.Y.C., 1989—. Co-editor in chief Managing Employee Health Benefits, 1992. Fellowship Caldwell B. Esselstyn Found., 1991-92. Home: 225 W 71st St Apt 32 New York NY 10023 Office: Gold Health Strategies Inc 250 Park Ave Ste 1300 New York NY 10177

GOLDBERG, ALAN JEFFREY, healthcare management consultant; b. Brookline, Mass., Sept. 7, 1949; s. Bernard and Shirley Thelma (Kooris) G.; m. Beverly Ronda Swartz, Aug. 13, 1972; children: James, Marissa. BS in Indsl. Engring. and Ops. Rsch., U. Mass., 1971; M Engring., Rensselaer Poly. Inst., 1972. Mgmt. systems engr. HARICOMP, Providence, 1972-74, asst. dir., 1974-76; dir. devel. Applied Mgmt. Systems, Inc., Burlington, Mass., 1976-80, dir. bus. svcs., 1980-84, v.p., 1984-85, pres., 1985—; bd. dirs. edn. subs. Mass. Med. Soc., Boston, 1980-81. Editor, contbg. author: Hospital Departmental Profiles, 1980, co-editor, contbr., 2d edit., 1985 (Book of Yr. award 1986), 3d edit., 1990; contbg. author: Productivity and Performance Management, 1989. Recipient lifetime achievement award Am. Hosp. Assn., 1990. Fellow Health Care Info. and Mgmt. Systems Soc. of Am. Hosp. Assn. (pres. 1979, bd. dirs. 1977-79, chmn. 1979, tech. publ. award 1985); mem. Health Care Mgmt. Assn. (bd. dirs., program chmn. 1990, membership chmn. 1991), Am. Coll. Health Care Execs. Democrat. Jewish. Office: Applied Mgmt Systems Inc 5 New England Executive Park Burlington MA 01803-5009

GOLDBERG, ALAN MARVIN, toxicologist, educator; b. Bklyn., Nov. 20, 1939; s. William and Celia Ida (Rudman) G.; m. Helene Schoenbach, Aug. 14, 1960; children—Michael David, Naomi Jill. BS, Bklyn. Coll. Pharmacy, 1961; PhD in Pharmacology, U. Minn., 1966. Research asst. U. Wis., 1961-62; research asst. U. Minn., 1962-66; research assoc. Inst. Psychiat. Research Ind. U., 1966-67, asst. prof. dept. pharmacology, 1967-69; asst. prof. environ medicine Johns Hopkins U., Balt., 1969-71, assoc. prof., 1971-78, prof. dept. environ. health scis., 1978—, assoc. chmn. dept., 1978-80, acting dir. div. toxicology, 1979-80, dir. div. toxicology, 1980-82, dir. Ctr. Alternatives to Animal Testing, 1981—, assoc. dean research, Sch. Pub. Health, 1984—; prin. rsch. scientist Chesapeake Bay Inst., 1979-84; mem. health hazard evaluation team of chem. waste dumps State of Tenn., 1980; mem. EPA Rev. Panel, 1980-82. Mem. editorial bd. Jour. Am. Coll. Toxicology, In Vitro Toxicology. Contbr. articles to profl. jours. Recipient award Ind. Neurol. Soc., 1967, Russel and Burch award Human Soc. of U.S., 1991; named Disting. Alumnus, L.I. Univ., 1992. Mem. AAAS, Am. Soc. Pharmacology and Exptl. Therapeutics, Soc. Neurosci. (pres. Balt. chpt. 1971-73), Am. Soc. Neurochemistry, Am. Epilepsy Soc., Internat. Soc. Neurochemistry, Soc. Toxicology, Internat. Study Group on Memory Disorders, Internat. Union Pharmacology, Office of Tech. Assessment Panel on Alternatives to Animal Use in Rsch. Testing and Edn. and Frontiers in Neuroscience, Nat. Acad. Sci., Inst. for Lab. Animal Resources. Home: 2231 Crest Rd Baltimore MD 21209-4227 Office: 615 N Wolfe St Baltimore MD 21205-2103

GOLDBERG, ALLAN SETH, podiatrist; b. Astoria, N.Y., Mar. 18, 1955; s. Samuel and Rita Lee (Stein) G.; m. Cindy Ilene Levy, Oct. 19, 1985; children: Samuel, Jaclyn. BS in Biology, Applied Math. and Stats., SUNY, Stony Brook, 1976; DPM cum laude, N.Y. Coll. Podiatric Medicine, 1981. Assoc. prof. postdoctoral edn., coord. residency edn. N.Y. Coll. Podiatric Medicine, N.Y.C., 1991—. Mem. Am. Mensa, Am. Coll. Foot Surgeons (assoc.), Am. Coll. Med. Quality (affiliate). Home: 10 Mitchell Ave Flushing NY 11803-3019

GOLDBERG, BERNARD ARTHUR, management consultant; b. Bronx, N.Y., Aug. 4, 1944; s. Harold and Sarah (Schwartz) G.; m. Sandra Lee Allison, Nov. 5, 1966; children: Caren C., Dawn A., Wendy R. BA in Biology, L.I. U., 1966. Mem. sales and sales mgmt. staff gen. systems div. IBM, Phila., 1970-80; pres. Mktg. Resources Internat., Bensalem, Pa., 1980-82; exec. v.p. Internat. Computerized Telemarketing, Langhorne, Pa., 1982-86; pres. B.A. Goldberg Cons. and Direct Mktg. Pubs., Yardley, Pa., 1986—. Author: Business-to-Business Direct Marketing, 1987, How To Manage and Execute Telephone Selling, 1989, The Lead Generation Handbook, 1991; author, editor newsletter The Bus. Mktg. Notepad, 1990. Capt. inf. U.S. Army, 1966-70. Mem. Dir. Mktg. Assn. (vice chmn. bus. coun. 1985-86). Office: Direct Mktg Publishers 1304 University Dr Morrisville PA 19067-2829

GOLDBERG, BEVERLY RAPPAPORT, hospital fundraising professional; b. Jersey City, N.J., Dec. 20, 1931; d. Max and Minnie (Resnick) Rappaport; m. Nolan Metz Goldberg, Feb. 14, 1954; children: Jan Ellen Goldberg Spiro, Steven Charles, Chris Andrew. BS, Beaver Coll., 1953. Cert. Assn. Health Care Philanthropy, Fund Raising Exec. Editorial asst. Springfield (N.J.) Sun, 1953-54, Times Chronicle Newspaper, Jenkintown, Pa., 1962-63; pub. rels. writer, then pub. rels. asst. Abington (Pa.) Meml. Hosp., 1963-74, asst. dir. pub. rels. and devel., 1974-87, dir. devel., 1987—; bd. dirs. 1st Am. Savs., Jenkintown. Trustee Beaver Coll., chair inst. advancement com. 1988-91. Recipient Publs. Excellence award Hosp. Assn. Pa., 1975, 77, 79, 81, 84, Golden Disc award Alumnae Assn. Beaver Coll., 1976. Mem. Assn. Healthcare Philanthropy (region bd. dirs. 1991—), Nat. Soc. Fund Raising Execs. Office: Abington Meml Hosp 1200 Old York Rd Abington PA 19001-3788

GOLDBERG, CARL, psychotherapist; b. N.Y.C., Jan. 21, 1938; s. Samuel and Mollie (Hecht) G. BA, Am. Internat. Coll., 1960; MA, U. Wyo., 1961; PhD, U. Okla., 1966; cert. in analytic psychotherapy, Washington Sch. Psychiatry, 1970. Assoc. clin. prof. dept. Psychiatry George Washington U. Med. Sch., Washington, 1974-81; dir. group Psychotherapy program Mt. Sinai Hosp. Svcs., Elmhurst, N.Y., 1981-85; assoc. clinical prof. dept. Psychiatry Albert Einstein Coll. Medicine, N.Y.C., 1981—; psychotherapist pvt. practice, N.Y.C., 1980—; coord. group Psychotherapy Tng. Program St. John's U., N.Y.C., 1988-91; adj. assoc. prof. psychology St. John's U., 1988-91, NYU, 1988—; clin. assoc. CUNY, Psychol. Ctr., 1982; rsch. assoc. Psychohistory Forum, 1986—; bd. advisors, vis. faculty Change Inst. Human Growth, Montreal, 1978—, N.Y. City for Psychodrama Tng., 1976—. Author and co-editor of 10 books; contbr. over 90 articles to profl. jours. Home and Office: Lobby C 305 E 24th St New York NY 10010

GOLDBERG, CONRAD STEWART, data processing executive; b. N.Y.C., June 10, 1943; s. Hyman and Ruth (Horowitz) G.; m. Regine Gluck, June 18, 1967; children: Meredith Aileen, Brian Craig. BS in Physics, CCNY, MA in Physics, 1967, PhD in Physics, 1974. Programming mgr. Control Data Corp., N.Y.C., 1969-73; data processing coord. Harcourt Brace Jovanovich, N.Y.C., 1973-74, systems devel. mgr., 1976-82; mgr. Grumman Data Systems, Bethpage, N.Y., 1974-76; dir. bus. systems Tambrands, White Plains, N.Y., 1982—. Home: 6 Baylor Cir White Plains NY 10605 Office: Tambrands Inc 777 Westchester Ave White Plains NY 10604

GOLDBERG, DAVID ELLIOTT, chemistry educator; b. Scranton, Pa., July 26, 1932; s. Maurice Max and Adele Helen (Jacobson) G.; m. Illeana B. Rosner, July 5, 1959; children: Jeffrey Miles, Amy Lynn. BS, George Washington U., 1954; PhD, Pa. State U., 1959. Mem. faculty Pa. State U., University Park, 1958-59; mem. faculty chemistry Bklyn. Coll., 1959—. Author: Chemistry, Reactions, Structure, Properties, 1972, 3000 Solved Problems in Chemistry, 1987, Assembly Language Programming, 1987, Chemistry Foundations, 1990, others. Mem. Am. Chem. Soc., Royal Soc. Chemistry, Phi Beta Kappa, Sigma Xi, Phi Lambda Upsilon, Phi Epsilon Pi. Office: Bklyn Coll Bedford Ave H Brooklyn NY 11222-3102

GOLDBERG, EDWARD, glass and aluminum company executive; b. Phila., May 22, 1929; s. Benjamin Nathan and Katie (Rabinowitz) G.; m. Sherry Block, Feb. 3, 1951; children: Denise Mindy, Neal Bruce, Susan. BSBA, St. Joseph's Coll., Phila., 1951. Sales H. Perilstein Glass Co., Phila., 1951-53; asst. gen. mgr. Standard Glass Co., Detroit, 1953-60; gen. mgr. Susquehanna Glass Co., Oneonta, N.Y., 1960-66; contract mgr. Utica Glass Co., Utica, N.Y., 1966-70; gen. mgr. Utica Glass Co., Utica, 1970-77; v.p. Chromalloy-Am. Corp., King of Prussia, Pa., 1977-82; pres., chief executive officer No. Glass Systems, Inc., Utica, 1982—. Mem. Flat Glass Mktg. Assn. (dir. 1982—), Am. Subcontractors Assn. (dir. 1985—), Sealed Insulate Glass Mfrs. Assn. (dir. 1978-80), Construction Specifications Inst., Mohawk Valley Builders Exchange (Annual Appreciation award 1976, pres. 1974-76, dir. 1982-89), Fort Schuyler Club, Peale Club, Shriners, Knights of Pythias. Republican. Jewish. Home: 1201 Bismark Way PO Box 11 King of Prussia PA 19406 Office: Northern Glass Systems Inc 725 Varick St PO Box 528 Utica NY 13503-0528

GOLDBERG, ERWIN B., advertising executive, marketing executive; b. Bklyn., Apr. 20, 1945; s. David and Adele (Littenberg) G.; m. Diane Burko, Sept. 4, 1966; 1 chld, Jessica Burko-Goldberg. Dir. advt. Life Assurance Corp. Pa., Phila., 1976-77; sales promotion mgr. Nat. Liberty Corp., Valley Forge, Pa., 1977-80; v.p. McAdams & Ong Advt., Phila., 1980-81; pres. Arau & Goldberg Advt., Phila., 1982-85; v.p., gen. mgr. Lefton Direct, Phila., 1985—. Bd. dirs. Phila. Child Guidance Clinic, 1987-90, Phila. Young Plawrights Festival, 1988—. Mem. Direct Mktg. Assn., Phila. Direct Mktg. Assn. Democrat. Jewish. Home: 510 S 46th St Philadelphia PA 19143-2102 Office: Lefton Direct Rohm & Haas Bldg Independence Mall W Philadelphia PA 19106

GOLDBERG, GERALDINE ELIZABETH, biokinesiologist; b. Neptune, N.J., Mar. 22, 1939; d. Albert Voorhees and Katherine Irene (Mulholland) McCormick; m. Arthur Goldberg, July 1, 1961. BS cum laude, East Stroudsburg U., 1967; MA in Psychology, Fairleigh Dickinson U., 1971. Staff clin. psychologist Youth Devel. Clinic, Newark, 1971-75; psychotherapist in clin. psychology Mental Health Cons. Ctr., N.Y.C., 1975-85; human resources specialist AGE Corp., Livingston, N.J., 1979—; sec. bd. dirs. AGE Corp., Livingston, 1977—, v.p., 1980—. Mem. N.J. Assn. Profl. Psychologists (past pres.), Am. Psychol. Assn. (assoc.), N.J. Psychol. Assn. (assoc.).

GOLDBERG, HAROLD HOWARD, psychologist, educator; b. N.Y.C., Apr. 30, 1924; s. Julius and Fannie (Somers) G.; m. Roslyn Jacobowitz, June 26, 1948; children: Barbara Balsam, Susan Pitcher, Lisa. BA, NYU, 1948, MA, 1949; PhD, AMW U., Tulsa, 1970. Cert. psychologist, sch. psychologist, sch. adminstr. Psychotherapist in pvt. practice N.Y.C., 1949—; chief psychologist Queens-Island Reading Ctrs., N.Y.C., 1959-62; sch. adminstr. League Sch./Rsch. Ctr. for Seriously Emotionally Disturbed, Bklyn., 1967-78; acting dir. Community Guidance Svc., N.Y.C., 1977-78; acting dir. Am. Inst. for Psychotherapy and Psychoanalysis, N.Y.C., 1977-78, mem. faculty, 1974-78; mem. faculty Greenwich Inst. for Psychotherapy and Psychoanalysis, N.Y.C., 1978—. Founder, editor Jour. Clin. Issues in Psychology, 1969-78, Profl. Digest of N.Y. Soc. Clin. Psychology, 1965-69, News and Notes, 1963-65; editor Newsletter for the N.Y. Soc. Clin. Psychologists, 1965-69. With USAF, 1942-45. Mem. Am. Psychol. Assn., N.Y. Soc. Clin. Psychologists (pres. 1972-73), N.Y. Psychol. Assn., Am. Assn. Marriage and Family Therapy, Psi Chi, Phi Delta Kappa, Kappa Delta Pi. Office: 105 E 63d St 3-A New York NY 10021

GOLDBERG, HAROLD SEYMOUR, electrical engineer, academic administrator; b. Bklyn., Jan. 22, 1925; s. David and Rose (Maslow) G.; m. Florence Meyerson, May 29, 1949; children: Lawrence, Irene. B.E.E. (Schweinberg scholar), Cooper Union, 1944; M.E.E., Poly. Inst. Bklyn., 1949; student, Columbia U. Engring. draftsman Cole Electric Products Co., 1944-45; radio engr. Press Wireless, Inc., 1945-47; asst. project engr. Radio Receptor Co., 1947-48; project engr. No. Radio Co., 1948-50; mgr. prodn. test, test equipment design sects. Allen B. DuMont Labs., Inc., 1950-56; mgr. engring. fabrication dept. Emerson Radio & Phonograph Corp., 1956-57; chief devel. engr. Consol. Avionics Corp., Westbury, N.Y., 1957-59; engring. mgr. data systems EPSCO, Inc., Cambridge, Mass., 1959-62; v.p. research Lexington Instruments Corp., Waltham, Mass., 1962- 66; prin. research engr. AVCO-Research div., Everett, Mass., 1966-68; ops. mgr. Orion Research Inc., 1968-70; v.p. applications Analogic Corp., Wakefield, Mass., 1970-71; ops. mgr. Data Precision Corp., Danvers, Mass., 1971-72; pres. Data Precision Corp., 1972-82; v.p. Analogic Corp., 1979-85; pres. Acrosystems Corp., Beverly, Mass., 1985-88; assoc. dean Gordon Inst., Wakefield, Mass., 1988—; cons. Wakefield, 1988—. Served with AUS, 1945-47. Recipient award of distinction Poly. Inst. N.Y., 1980, John Fluke Sr. Pioneer award, 1989; N.Y. State Vets scholar, 1957. Fellow IEEE (chmn. Boston group on medicine and biology 1965-66, mem. exec. com. Boston sect. 1967-69, vice chmn. Boston 1969-70, chmn. Boston 1970-71, internat. bd. dirs. 1971-75, 89-90, v.p. 1975, dir. Electro 1975-89, treas. tech. activities bd. 1991, citation of honor U.S. Activities Bd. 1978); mem. Instrumentation and Measurement Soc. of IEEE (sec.-treas. 1983, pres. 1985-87), Tau Beta Pi. Home: 10 Alcott Rd Lexington MA 02173-1950 Office: Audubon Rd Wakefield MA 01880-1203

GOLDBERG, IRA, concrete company executive; b. Bklyn., Oct. 8, 1948; s. Herbert and Evelynne (Stahl) G.; m. Ellen Bien, Dec. 27, 1970; children: Brian, Robin. BA, Bklyn. Coll., 1970. Pres. Alberg Custom Contracting Inc., Manalapan, N.J., 1970—; chief exec. officer Bomanite of N.J. Inc., Manalapan, 1984—. Office: Bomanite of NJ Inc 699 Tennent Rd Manalapan NJ 07726

GOLDBERG, JOSEPH (JIM), mortgage banker; b. Phila., May 6, 1953; s. Leonard and Joyce (Goldstein) G.; m. Cynthia Anne Hullihen, Mar. 29, 1979; children: Joshua R., Michael I., Emily C. BS, U.S. Mil. Acad., 1975; MBA, Monmouth Coll., 1983. Loan officer Guild Mortgage Corp., Rockville, Md., 1986-87, Douglas Michaels Mortgage Svc., Silver Spring, Md., 1987-88, CenTrust Mortgage Corp., Rockville, 1988-89; mortgage banker Mortgage Mgmt. Assocs., Inc., Severna Park, 1989-90, James Madison Mortgage Co., 1990-91; Margaretten Co., Inc., Rockville, 1991—. Contbr. articles to profl. jours. Bd. dirs. Hallowell Homeowners Assn., Olney, Md., 1987-90, pres. 1989. Maj. USAR. Mem. Res. Officers Assn. (pres. chpt. 19 Washington dist.), Assn. U.S. Army, Young Bankers Com., Masons, B'Nai Shalom of Olney Men's Club (v.p. 1992—). Republican. Jewish. Home: 17136 Old Baltimore Rd Olney MD 20832-2502 Office: Margaretten Co Inc 30 W Gude Dr Ste 130 Rockville MD 20850-1161

GOLDBERG, JOSEPH PHILIP, government official; b. Bklyn., May 1, 1918; s. Max and Fanny (Steltzer) G.; B.S.S., CCNY, 1937; M.A., Columbia U., 1938, Ph.D., 1950; m. Selma Takiff, Aug. 22, 1943; children: Seth M., Lise A. Instr. econ. history CCNY, 1937-39; high sch. tchr., N.Y.C., 1938-42; economist Bur. Labor Stats., Washington, 1942; econ. adviser Nat. War Labor Bd. and Wage Stblzn. Bd., Washington, 1943-46; labor adviser Office of Housing Expediter, 1946-48; staff dir. joint congl. com., 1948; div. chief Bur. Labor Stats., Labor Dept., Washington, 1949-51, spl. asst. to commr. of labor stats., 1954-86; with Wage Stblzn. Bd., 1951-53; instr. Am. U., 1948-49; research asso. Harvard U., 1957, U. Mich., 1964-69, ILO Inst. Indsl. Relations Studies, 1973—; U.S. del. 22 ILO maritime and internat. labor confs., 1956-85; cons. on maritime industry U.S. Dept. Labor, 1986—. Pres., J.F. Kennedy High Sch. PTA, 1968-69, New Hampshire Estates, 1956-57, trustee schs. Montgomery County, 1957-62, 86—; arbitrator, consumer protection Md. State Atty. Gen.; mediator Washington Mediation Svc., Docent-Smithsonian Inst.. Recipient research grants Yale Fund, Harvard, U. Mich., Ford Found.; Meritorious Service award Labor Dept., 1963, 85, Commr.'s Eminent Service award, 1973. Mem. Indsl. Relations Research Assn. (pres. D.C. chpt. 1963-64, mem. nat. exec. bd. 1973-76), Am. Econ. Assn., AAAS, Phi Beta Kappa. Author: The Maritime Story, 1958; (with others) Collective Bargaining and Technological Change in American Transportation, Monograph on Modernization in the Maritime Industry, 1971; Productivity Bargaining in the Private Sector, 1975; The Law and Practice of Collective Bargaining, 1976; Frances Perkins, Isadore Lubin and the Bureau of Labor Statistics, 1980; The AFL and a National Bureau of Labor Statistics, 1983; The First One Hundred Years of the Bureau of Labor Statistics, 1985; contbr. articles to profl. jours. Home: 707 Stonington Rd Silver Spring MD 20902-1549 Office: Bicentennial Bldg Washington DC 20212

GOLDBERG, KENNETH PHILIP, mathematics educator, consultant; b. Bklyn., Dec. 9, 1945; s. Edward and Dolores Goldberg; m. Jeanne D. Smith; children: Timothy, Rebecca, Andrew. BA, NYU, 1967, MS, 1969; PhD, Mich. State U., 1973. Cert. secondary math. tchr., N.Y. From asst. to assoc. prof. NYU, N.Y.C., 1973-82, prof. use of tech. in teaching of math., 1982—. Author: Push Button Mathematics, 1984, Commodore 64 Logo, 1986, (with others) Basic Statistics, 1979, revised edit., 1990, Micros for Parents, 1984. Mem. Assn. Math. Tchrs. N.Y. State (pres. 1991-92), Nat. Coun. Tchrs. Math. Office: NYU Dept Math Edn 239 Greene St Bldg 200 New York NY 10003-6601

GOLDBERG, MALCOLM, physics educator; b. Reading, Pa., Oct. 8, 1936; s. Nathan Thomas Goldberg and Mary G. (Horowitz) Kaiserman; m. Margaret L. Sapphire, Mar. 16, 1959 (div. 1977); children: Loren Natalie, Jill Leslie Goldberg-Laplante; m. Ruth Nuba, Nov. 2, 1986; stepchildren: Robyn Lee Stukalin, Daniel G. Stukalin. BS, Queens Coll., 1958; MS, U. Conn., 1960; MA, SUNY, Stony Brook, 1965, PhD, 1971. Physics assoc. Brookhaven Nat. Lab., Upton, N.Y., 1960-71; prof. physics Westchester Community Coll., Valhalla, N.Y., 1971—; program assoc. NSF, Washington, 1976-77, chmn. physical scis. dept., 1978—; cons. in sci. edn. Author monographs; contbr. 10 sci. articles on radiation effects in solids to profl. publs. Mem. AAAS, Am. Assn. Physics Tchrs., Nat. Sci. Tchrs. Assn., Sigma Xi. Office: Westchester Community Coll 75 Grasslands Rd Valhalla NY 10595-1636

GOLDBERG, MARC EVAN, biotechnology executive; b. Boston, Mar. 14, 1957; s. Ray Allan and Thelma (Englander) G.; m. Pamela Francine Winer, June 11, 1983; children: Frederick Warren, Alyssa Rachel, Meredith Hayley. AB, Harvard U., 1979, MBA, JD, 1983. Bar: Mass, 1985. Mgr. bus. devel. Genetics Inst., Inc., Cambridge, Mass., 1983-87; v.p. fin. and corp. devel., chief fin. officer, treas. Safer, Inc., Newton, Mass., 1987-91; pres., chief exec. officer Mass. Biotech. Rsch. Inst., Worcester, Mass., 1991—; founder Mass. Biotech. Coun., bd. dirs., 1985—, pres., 1985-87, 90-92; bd. dirs. Neo Phyte Inc., Can., TSI Corp., Worcester. Mem., prin. author Gov.'s Task Force on Biotechnology, 1991—; mem. pres.'s circle Beth Israel Hosp., 1985-88; trustee Worchester State Coll., 1991—, Harvard Yearbook Pubs., 1981—; mem. exec. adv. bd. Harvard Varsity Club, 1982—, Town of Wellesley adv. com., 1992—; bd. dirs. Newton Centre (Mass.) Neighborhood Assn., 1987-89. Mem. Mass. Bar Assn. Office: Mass Biotech Rsch Inst One Innovation Drive Worcester MA 01605

GOLDBERG, MARTIN, physician, educator; b. Phila., Sept. 15, 1930; s. Samuel and Esther (Schreibman) G.; m. Lynn Taksey, June 17, 1951 (dec. Aug. 31, 1976); children: Meryl I., Karen L., Dara S.; m. Marion Lindblad, May 26, 1978; 1 son, David S. BA, Temple U., 1951, MD, 1955; MA (hon.), U. Pa., 1971. Diplomate: Am. Bd. Internal Medicine (chmn. nephrology com. 1976-79, bd. govs. 1976-79), Nat. Bd. Med. Examiners. Intern Phila. Gen. Hosp., 1955-56, resident, 1957-59, sr. attending physician, 1970-76; resident Cleve. Clinic, 1956-57; fellow nephrology Hosp. U. Pa., Phila., 1959-61; sr. attending physician Hosp. U. Pa., 1962-79; mem. faculty U. Pa. Sch. Medicine, 1960-79, prof. medicine, 1970-79, chief renal electrolyte sect., 1966-79, acting chmn. dept. medicine, 1975-76; sr. attending physician Phila. VA Hosp., 1968-79; Gordon and Helen Hughes Taylor prof. medicine U. Cin., 1979-86; chmn. internal medicine U. Cin. Coll. Med. and Hosp., 1979-86; prof. medicine Temple U. Sch. Medicine, Phila., 1986—, dean, vice pres., 1986-89; mem. sci. adv. bd. Nat. Kidney Found., 1970-76; chmn. kidney council Am. Heart Assn., 1973-74; study cons. NIH, 1968-72, 82-85; bd. mgrs. St. Christopher's Hosp. Children, 1986-89. Mem. editorial com.: Jour. Clin. Investigation, 1969-70, Kidney Internat, 1972-74, Jour. Mineral and Electrolyte Metabolism, 1977—; mem. editorial bd. dirs. Am. Journal of Hypertension, 1990—; physician-editor Nephrology MKSAP Am. Coll. Physicians, 1991—. Recipient Alumni prize Temple U. Sch. Medicine, 1955, Lindback award for distinguished teaching U. Pa., 1972; Disting. Med. Scientist of Yr. award Med. Alumni Temple U. Sch. Medicine, 1985; Research Career Devel. award NIH, 1963-70; research grantee NIH, 1962-89; research grantee John Hartford Found., 1970-73. Fellow A.C.P. (nat. sci. program com. 1976-81), Am. Coll. Clin. Pharmacology; mem. Assn. Am. Med. Colls. (council of deans), Assn. Am. Physicians, Am. Soc. Clin. Investigation, Am. Physiol. Soc., Am. Fedn. Clin. Research (chmn. eastern sect. 1967), Am. Soc. Nephrology (sec.-treas. 1975-78), Interurban Clin. Club, Internat. Soc. Nephrology (council 1975-84), Am. Clin. and Climatological Assn., Coll. Physicians Phila., Alpha Omega Alpha. Office: Temple U Health Scis Ctr Nephrology Parkinson Pavilion Philadelphia PA 19140

GOLDBERG, MELVIN A., non-profit organization executive. BS, CCNY; MA, Columbia U. Dir. sales, planning and rsch. DuMont TV Network; dep. dir. evaluation USIA; dir. rsch. Westinghouse Broadcasting Co.; v.p., dir. rsch. Nat. Assn. Broadcasters; v.p. rsch. and new bus. devel. John Blair & Co.; prin. Melvin A. Goldberg, Inc.; v.p. primary and social rsch. ABC TV; v.p. news, social and tech. rsch. ABC Mktg. and Rsch. Svcs., ABC, Inc., v.p. market planning, tech. and social rsch.; exec. dir. Electronic Media Rating Coun., N.Y.C., 1985—; lay mem. ABA Commn. on Pub. Understanding About the Law and the Pub. Participation Resource Group,. U.S. Congress Office Tech. Assessment. Editorial bd. TV Quar. Mem. NATAS, Am. Assn. Pub. Opinon Rsch., Radio-TV Rsch. Coun. (past pres.), Market Rsch. Coun., Internat. Radio and TV Soc. Office: Electronic Media Rating Coun 509 Madison Ave New York NY 10022-5501

GOLDBERG, MICHAEL H., magazine publisher; b. Bklyn., June 7, 1949; s. Isidore Sol and Harriet (Taub) G.; m. Iris Andrea Feigeles; children: Jenna, Sarie. BA in English, L.I. U., 1970; MS in TV Prodn., Bklyn. Coll., 1973. Free-lance video producer, 1970-79; account exec. Nat. Telephone Directory Co., Union City, N.J., 1979-84; nat. accounts dir. ABC, N.Y.C., 1984-86; regional mgr. Gorman Pub. Co., N.Y.C., 1986-87; pub. Media Horizons Inc., N.Y.C., 1987-89, Dear Doctor Mag., 1989—; v.p., group pub. Howmark Publs., Elizabeth, N.J., 1990—. Mem. Nat. Assn. Broadcasters. Home: 22 Burnet Hill Rd Livingston NJ 07039-3607

GOLDBERG, MORTON HAROLD, oral and maxillofacial surgeon, educator; b. Springfield, Mass., Mar. 24, 1933; s. Joseph Frank and Lena (Bendett) G.; m. Phyllis Zeller, June 19, 1955; children: James, Julie, David. BS, U. Mass., 1954; DMD, Harvard U., 1958; MD, Albany Med. Coll., 1961. Intern Albany (N.Y.) Hosp., 1961-62; resident in oral and maxillofacial surgery Bellevue Hosp., 1962-64; pvt. practice, Hartford, Conn., 1964—; clin. prof. oral and maxillofacial surgery U. Conn., Farmington, 1978—. Author: Oral and Maxillofacial Infections, 1981, 2d edit., 1987. 2d Lt. U.S. Army. Recipient oral surgery award Bellevue Hosp., 1982. Mem. Am. Assn. Oral and Maxillofacial Surgery (Geis award 1991), Hartford Dental Soc. (pres. 1975-76), Alpha Omega Alpha. Office: Gillett Oral Surgeons 85 Seymour St Hartford CT 06106-5501

GOLDBERG, MYRON ALLEN, physician, psychiatrist; b. Bronx, June 4, 1942; s. Marcus and Rose (Spiegel) G. AB, Hunter Coll., 1965; MD, Universidad del Noreste, Tampico, Mexico, 1979. Staff psychiatrist, forensic unit Bronx-Lebanon Hosp., Bronx, N.Y., 1985-86, team leader inpatient unit, 1986-88, chief physician geriatric svcs., dept. psychiatry, 1986—; clin. instr. Albert Einstein Coll. of Medicine, Bronx, 1986—, team leader inpatient unit, 1991-92, unit chief inpatient svc., 1992—. Inventor fluid pressure relief valve, 1973. Judicial del. Dem. Coop City Club, Bronx, 1986; exec. com. Dem. Club, Bronx, 1987-88 and other offices. Recipient recognition Crotona Park Community Mental Health Ctr., 1986. Mem. Am. Psychiatric Assn., AMA. Democrat. Hebrew. Home: 12024B Aldrich St Bronx NY 10475-4502

GOLDBERG, ROSELEE, art historian; b. Durban, Republic of South Africa; came to U.S., 1975; d. Allan and Pauline Annie (Hackner) G.; m. Dakota Jackson, Nov. 8, 1979; children: Zoe, Pierce. BA, U. Witwatersrand, Johannesburg, Republic of South Africa, 1967; MA, Courtauld Inst., London U., 1970. Dir. Royal Coll. of Art Gallery, London, 1972-75; curator The Kitchen Ctr. for Video, Music and Dance, N.Y.C., 1978-80; cons., freelance curator, 1980—; lectr. NYU, N.Y.C., 1988—. Author: Performance Art, 1979, 88. Critics grantee, NEA, 1978. Mem. Internat. Assn. Art Critics, Coll. Art Assn. Home: 327 E 18th St New York NY 10003

GOLDBERG, SHELDON AARON, retired air force officer; b. Detroit, Aug. 29, 1938; s. Jacob and Bessie Rebecca (Halperin) G.; m. Waltraud Lina Reinhard, Sept. 3, 1959; children: Kerstin Waltraud, Richard Allan, Steven Lawrence. BA, U. Puget Sound, 1967; MA, U. Wis., 1968, U. Md., 1985; postgrad., U. Md., 1985—. Enlisted USAF, 1956, advanced through grades to lt. col., 1977, retired, 1985, various operation assignments, 1956-75; USAF liaison officer Fed. Rep. Germany Gen. Staff Coll., Hamburg, 1975-78; air policy staff officer Hdqtrs. Allied Forces Cen. Europe, Brunssum, The Netherlands, 1978-81; chief nat. security studies div. Air Command and Staff Coll., Maxwell AFB, Ala., 1981-83; chief dept. curriculum devel. Air War Coll. Sch. of Assn. Programs, Maxwell AFB, 1983-85; staff cons. Inst. Def. Analyses, Alexandria, Va., 1985-86. Editor: Strategic Appraisal of Western Europe for the 17th, 18th and 19th Edits., 1984-86, Military Leadership for 18th and 19th Edits., 1985-86. Sec. Jaycees, Lakewood, Wash., 1965-67; mem. Jaycees of U.K., Oxford, 1971-72. Recipient non-resident scholarship Univ. Wis. Grad. Sch., Madison, 1967-68; decorated two Disting. Flying Crosses, USAF, 1969-70, 17 Air Medals, USAF, 1969-70, three Meritorious Svc. Medals, USAF, 1978, 83, 85, Def. Meritorious Svc. Medal, USAF, 1981. Mem. Air Force Assn. (life mem.), Ret. Officers Assn. (life mem.), Internat. Studies Assn., European Community Studies Assn., Pi Gamma Mu (life mem.), Pi Sigma Alpha, Phi Kappa Phi. Jewish. Home: 2967 Gracefield Rd Silver Spring MD 20904-1668

GOLDBERG, STEPHEN Z., chemistry educator; b. Bklyn., May 26, 1947; s. Irving and Fay (Segal) Goldberg. AB with distinction, Cornell U., 1968; PhD, U. Calif., Berkeley, 1973. Asst. prof. Adelphi U., Garden City, N.Y., 1975-80, assoc. prof., 1980-86, prof. chemistry, 1986—. Mem. AAAS, Am. Chem. Soc., Am. Crystallographic Assn., N.Y. Acad. Sci.

GOLDBERG, STEVEN SELIG, education law educator; b. Bklyn., Jan. 8, 1950; s. Harry Louis and Ruth (Bartnofsky) G. BA, SUNY, Binghamton, 1970; JD, Bklyn. Law Sch., 1973; MA, Columbia U., 1976; PhD, U. Pa., 1985. Bar: Pa. 1974, U.S. Dist. Ct. (ea. dist.) Pa. 1976, U.S. Ct. Appeals (3d cir.) 1976, Nebr. 1980. Legal editor Prentice-Hall, Inc., Englewood Cliffs, N.J., 1974-75, CCH, N.Y.C., 1975; atty. Camden (N.J.) Regional Legal Svcs., 1976, Edn. Law Ctr., Phila., 1976-80; fellow psychology grad. tng. program U. Nebr., Lincoln, 1980-81; pvt. practice Phila., 1982-85; asst. prof. edn. law U. N.D., Grand Forks, 1986-88; assoc. prof. Beaver Coll., Glenside, Pa., 1988—; lectr. U. Pa., Phila., 1990—; mem. profl. adv. bd. Montgomery County (Pa.) Assn. for Children with Learning Disabilities, Pa. Assn. Children with Learning Disabilities; cons. right to edn. asistance group Pa. Dept. Edn. Author: Special Education Law, 1982; editor: Readings on Equal Education, 1990l co-host, producer show Sta. KFJM Pub. Radio U. N.D., 1987; producer videotapes; contbr. articles to profl. jours. Mem. ABA, Am. Ednl. Rsch. Assn. (chair edn. law 1989-90), Nat. Orgn. Legal Problems in Edn. Jewish. Office: Beaver Coll Church and Easton Rds Glenside PA 19038

GOLDBERG, VICTOR PAUL, law educator; b. 1941. BA, Oberlin (Ohio) Coll., 1963, MA, 1964; PhD, Yale U., 1970. From asst. to full prof. U. Calif., Davis, 1967-83; prof. Northwestern U., Evanston, Ill., 1983-88; prof., co-dir. Ctr. Law and Econ. Studies Columbia U., N.Y.C., 1988—; assoc. prof. U. Calif., Berkeley, 1977; prof. U. Va., Charlottesville, 1981; mem. Inst. for Advanced Study, Princeton, N.J., 1978-79. Fellow Ctr. for Study of Pub. Choice, Blacksburg, Va., 1975-76. Office: Columbia U Sch Law 435 W 116th St New York NY 10027-7201

GOLDBERGER, GEORGE STEFAN, finance executive; b. Oradea, Romania, July 3, 1947; came to U.S., 1962; s. Ladislau and Margareta (Schwartz) G.; 1 child, David Michael. BS in Systems Engring., Bklyn. Polytechnic U., 1969; MBA in Fin., U. Pa., 1975. Systems analyst Grumman Corp., Bethpage, N.Y., 1969-73; ops. analyst Internat. Paper Co., N.Y.C., 1973-74; mgmt. cons. Booz, Allen & Hamilton, N.Y.C., 1975-77; asst. to chmn. W.R. Grace & Co., N.Y.C., 1977-85; pres. Citizens Against Govt. Waste, Washington, 1986-89; chief oper. officer Pres.'s Pvt. Sector Survey on Cost Control (Grace Commn.), Washington, 1986-89; dir. mergers and acquisitions Figgie Internat., Inc., Willoughby, Ohio, 1989-90; pres. Goldberger & Assocs., Inc., N.Y.C., 1991—. Contbr. articles to publs. Republican. Jewish.

GOLDBERGER, NEAL MICHAEL, anesthesiologist; b. Schenectady, N.Y., Jan. 7, 1957; s. Alfred Lewis and Helen Sylvia (Cohen) G.; m. Lee Ann Soowal, Sept. 20, 1987. BA, U. Pa., 1978; MD, Tufts U., 1982. Diplomate Am. Bd. Anesthesiology. Resident in anesthesia Letterman Army Med. Ctr., San Francisco, 1982-86; chief of anesthesia Blanchfield Army Hosp., Ft. Campbell, Ky., 1986-90; anesthesiologist Hartford (Conn.) Anesthesiology Assocs., 1990—; anesthesiologist, pain specialist Hartford Hosp., 1990—; med. dir. Pain Therapy Cons., Farmington, Conn., 1992—; clin. fellow pain U. Cin., 1985; clin. fellow pain Vanderbilt U., Nashville, 1988-89, asst. clin. prof. anesthesia, 1989-90. Contbg. author: Contemporary Issues in Chronic Pain Management, 1991. Maj. USAR, 1978—. Mem. Am. Soc. Anesthesiologists. Office: Hartford Anesthesiology Assocs Ste 306 85 Seymour St Hartford CT 06106-5501

GOLDBLATT, BARRY LANCE, manufacturing executive; b. Palo Alto, Calif., July 29, 1945; s. Samuel and Joan Charlotte (Morton) G. BS, U. So. Calif., 1967, MBA, 1968. Supr. market rsch. for brands Procter & Gamble Co., Cin., 1968-71; mgr. market rsch. Personal Products Co. subs. Johnson & Johnson, 1971-74; assoc. dir. consumer rsch. Johnson & Johnson Baby Products Co., Skillman, N.J., 1974-87; dir. market rsch. Johnson and Johnson Dental Care Co., New Brunswick, N.J., 1987-89, Johnson and Johnson Consumer Products, Inc., Skillman, 1989—. Bd. dirs. New Brunswick Hot Line, 1973; vol. Urban Cons. Group, 1977—. Recipient Cert. of Recognition Nat. Symposium Hispanic Bus. and Economy, Chgo., 1981, Cert. of Appreciation U. So. Calif., L.A., 1981. Mem. U. So. Calif. MBA's, U. So. Calif. Commerce Assocs., Advt. Rsch. Found., Am. Mktg. Assn., Assn. MBA Execs., Am. Philatel. Soc., U. So. Calif. Assocs., U. So. Calif. Alumni Club, Skull and Dagger, Zeta Beta Tau. Republican. Club: U. So. Calif. Alumni of N.J. (pres.). Home: 20 Andrews Ln Princeton NJ 08540-7633 Office: Johnson & Johnson 199 Grandview Rd Skillman NJ 08558-1311

GOLDBLATT, IRWIN LEONARD, chemical research; b. N.Y.C., Jan. 22, 1940; s. Samuel and Ruth (Schreiber) G.; m. Mildred Rita; children: Naomi, Mark, Sarah. B of Chem. Engring., CCNY, 1962; MS, Brandeis U., 1967; PhD in Chemistry, Brandies U., 1973. Chemist Polaroid Corp., Cambridge, Mass., 1962-64, Mithras Inc., Cambridge, Mass., 1964-68; rsch. assoc. chemistry Exxon Rsch. and Devel., Linden, N.J., 1968-86; mgr. prodn. devel. Castrol Inc., Piscataway, N.J., 1987—. Patentee in field; contbr. articles to profl. jours. Mem. AAAS, Am. Soc. Health Engring., Am. Soc. Testing and Materials, Soc. Tribology and Lubrication Engring. (sec.). Office: Castrol Inc 240 Centennial Ave Piscataway NJ 08854

GOLDEMBERG, ROBERT LEWIS, chemist; b. Passaic, N.J., Sept. 18, 1925; s. Maurice and Elizabeth (Grimberg) G.; children: Sharanne Ruth, Kathleen, David R. BSChemE, Princeton U., 1948. Sr. chemist Coty, Inc., N.Y.C., 1950-58; rsch. dir. Shulton, Inc., Clifton, N.J., 1958-64, Lanvin-Charles of the Ritz, Norwalk, Conn., 1964-67; dir. tech. svcs. Van Dyk & Co., Belleville, N.J., 1967-73; pres. Rakuma Labs., Inc., S. Hackensack, N.J., 1973—; dir. Continuing Edn. Ctr., Inc., S. Hackensack, 1975-84; prs. Trion Chem. Corp., Clifton, 1981-85; v.p. rsch. Oral Rsch. Labs. Inc., N.Y.C., 1985-88. Sgt. inf. U.S. Army, 1944-46, ETO, PTO. Fellow Soc. Cosmetic Chemists; mem. Am. Chem. Soc., N.Y. Acad. Scis. Home: PO Box 2083 South Hackensack NJ 07606

GOLDEN, BALFOUR HENRY, private investor; b. Bangor, Maine, Aug. 23, 1922; s. Samuel Henry and Helen (Rybier) G. m. Emma Jane Krakauer, June 22, 1956; children: Peter Balfour, Betsy Jane, Robert Henry. AB cum laude, Bowdoin Coll., 1944; postgrad., Columbia U., 1945-47. Pres. Golden Food Svcs. Corp., N.Y., 1951-70, N.J., 1951-70, Iowa, 1951-70; Pres. Golden Co. of Maine, 1952-70, Golden Base Svcs. Corp., S.C., 1952-70, Plaza Eats, Inc., N.Y., 1958-70, Dubonnet Restaurant Corp., N.Y., 1960-70; cons. food svc., 1970-74; pres. Guardian Food Svc. Corp., N.Y.C., 1974-85, Ropes Tremblay, Inc., N.Y.C., 1986—. Mem. exec. bd. Ridgewood (N.J.)-Glen Rock coun. Boy Scouts Am. With AUS, 1943-45. Mem. New Eng. Soc. in N.Y.C., N.Y. Restaurant Assn. (dir.), Williams Club, Phi Beta Kappa. Home: 325 Beechwood Rd Ridgewood NJ 07450-2306

GOLDEN, CHARLES JOSH, neuropsychologist, consultant; b. L.A., Nov. 8, 1949; s. Joseph Arnold and Jennie (Elnai) G.; m. Heather Phillips, Oct. 26, 1986; children: Zarabeth, Leila, Chloe. BA, Pomona Coll., 1971; PhD, U. Hawaii, 1975. Diplomate Clin. Psychology and Neuropsychology. Asst. prof. U. S.D., Vermillion, 1975-78; assoc. prof. Med. Ctr. U. Nebr., Omaha, 1979-83, prof. Med. Ctr., 1983-87; prof. Drexel U., Phila., 1987-90; dir. neuropsychology, dir. program ops. Schien Assocs., Milford, Pa., 1990—. Author: Diagnosis and Rehabilitation in Clinical Neuropsychology, 1979, 2d edit., 1981, Clinical Interpretation of Object Tests, 1981, 2d edit., 1989, Luria-Nebraska Neuropsychology, 1981, 2d edit., 1985; editor Internat. Jour. Clin. Neuropsychology, 1981—. Fellow APA (div. bd. dirs. 1978-81), Nat. Acad. Neuropsychologists (pres. 1980-82). Home: PO Box 1565 Milford PA 18337-2565 Office: 221 Broad St Milford PA 18337-1099

GOLDEN, FRED STEPHAN, financial executive; b. Phila., Oct. 5, 1945; s. Gilbert and Constance Carolyn (Berman) G.; m. Nan Eve Melnicoff, May 24, 1967; children: Michael, Gil, Heath. BS, Lehigh U., 1967; MBA, Temple U., 1969. CPA, Pa. Sr. staff acct. Laventhol Horwath, Phila., 1967-70; mgr. S.P. Halbert & Co., Ambler, Pa., 1970-73; prin. F.S. Golden, CPA, Mgmt. Cons., Plymouth Meeting, Pa., 1973-80; fin. v.p. Pennbrook/Abbotts, Phila., 1980-82, Confab Corp., Wayne, Pa., 1982-88; exec. v.p., chief fin. officer Pilot Air Freight Corp., Lima, Pa., 1988—. Contbr. articles to profl. publs. Troop leader Springhouse (Pa.) Boy Scouts Am., 1979-89. Mem. AICPA, Pa. Inst. CPAs, CPAs in Bus., Edn. and Govt., Friends of Franklin Inst., Phila. Zool. Soc. Office: Pilot Air Freight Corp PO Box 97 Lima PA 19037-0097

GOLDEN, JACQUELYN D., business/computer educator; b. Clarksdale, Miss.. AA in Gen. Edn., Coahoma Jr. Coll., 1984; BS in Computer Sci., Miss. Valley State U., 1986; MS in Vocat.-Tech. Edn., SUNY, Oswego, 1990. Cert. bus. education, vocational/tech. edn., elem. edn. N.Y. Tutor spl. programs Miss. Valley State U., 1985-86; substitute tchr. Clarksdale Pub. Sch. System, 1986; typist II Syracuse (N.Y.) City Sch. Dist., 1986-87, tchr. asst., 1987-88, tchr., tchr. asst., 1988-90, tchr., tchr. perceiver specialist, 1990-91; technology instr. gifted program Syracuse City Schools, 1990—. Songwriter, arranger. Mem. Ch. of God in Christ.

GOLDEN, JOHN JOSEPH, JR., manufacturing company executive; b. New Milford, Conn., Jan. 13, 1943; s. John Joseph and Anne Munroe (Hope) G.; m. Carolyn Joan Pachesa, May 29, 1965 (div. July 1984); children: Elizabeth Susan, Jennifer Leigh, John Joseph III, Matthew Benjamin; m. Ethel M. O'Neill Pierry, June 8, 1991; 1 stepchild, Michael Joseph. BS, MIT, 1966. V.p. systems devel. Quantum Computing Corp., Newton, Mass., 1968-70; mgr. computer ops. Polaroid Corp., Cambridge, Mass., 1970-75; dir. info. processing Schering-Plough Corp., Kenilworth, N.J., 1975-78; dir. info. systems Compugraphic Corp., Wilmington, Mass., 1978-80; dir. info. systems electro-optics div. Honeywell, Lexington, Mass., 1981-83; dir. adminstrn. electro-optics div. Honeywell, Wilmington, Mass., 1983-87; dir. materials electo-optics div. Honeywell, Marlboro, Mass., 1987-90; gen. mgr. Micracor, Concord, Mass., 1990—. With USAR, 1964-70. Mem. Assn. for Computing Machinery, IEEE, MIT Alumni Orgn., Mass. Iota Tau Assn. (treas. 1970—), Optical Soc. Am. Roman Catholic. Home: PO Box 761 North Andover MA 01845-0761 Office: Micracor Concord MA 01742

GOLDEN, REYNOLD STEPHEN, family practice physician, educator; b. Herkimer, N.Y., Jan. 11, 1937; s. Harold Theodore and Ethel Anne (Myers) G.; m. Gale Holtz, Nov. 26, 1959 (div. May 1978); children: Nathan Myers, Jennifer Lynn (dec.), Laura Beth (Lieba); m. Ellen Jean Moore, Sept. 9, 1978; children: Melissa Nan, Benjamin Harold. AB cum laude, Harvard Coll., 1958; MD, SUNY, Syracuse, 1962. Diplomate Am. Bd. Family Practice, Am. Bd. Internal Medicine. Intern Lankenau Hosp., Phila., 1962-63; resident in internal medicine SUNY, Syracuse, 1963-66; pvt. practice Utica, N.Y., 1966-78; dir. family practice residency St. Elizabeth Hosp., Utica, 1978-92, St. Francis Hosp., Poughkeepsie, N.Y., 1992—; clin. assoc. prof. dept. family medicine SUNY, Syracuse, 1991—; cons. residency assistance program, Kansas City, Mo., 1988—; charter mem. N.Y. State Coun. on Grad. Med. Edn., N.Y.C., 1988-90. Editor N.Y. Family Physician, 1987-92. Mem. N.Y. State Acad. Family Physicians (chmn. bd. dirs. 1988-89, pres. 1992-93, Presdl. Citation 1985, 86, 88), Cen. N.Y. Acad. Medicine (pres. 1977-79, Golden Torch award 1989). Jewish. Office: Family Health Ctr 2209 Genesee St 4 Jefferson Plaza Poughkeepsie NY 12601

GOLDEN, ROBERT CHARLES, brokerage executive; b. Bklyn., July 12, 1946; s. Charles Joseph and Audrey (Griffin) G. BS in Acctg., Fordham U., 1968, MBA in Fin., 1978. V.p. internal audit Walston & Co., Inc., N.Y.C., 1969-73; v.p.-fin. Acan X-Ray Co., Inc., Detroit, 1973-76; exec. v.p. Prudential Securities Inc., N.Y.C., 1976—. Bd. dirs. Cath. Guardian Soc., Bklyn. and Queens, N.Y., 1985—; trustee Xaviarian High Sch., Bklyn. Recipient citation Coun. of City of N.Y., Fanciscan Heritage award Franciscan Sisters of the Poor at Pla. Hotel, 1987, Apple award Prudential Pacesetters, 1989, St. Francis Xavier Soc. award, Xaverian Bros., 1990, Thomas J. Cuite award, Irish Am. Heritage Wk. Com. of N.Y.C. Hall, 1991, Crystal Shield award Salvation Army, 1992; named Educator of Yr. Assn. of Tchrs. of N.Y., 1986, Cath. Guardian Soc. Humanitarian of Yr., 1985, Chief Brehon of the Great Irish Fair, 1992; named to Diocesan Ct. of Honor, Diocese of Bklyn. Mem. Securities Industry Assn., Mcpl. Club Bklyn., St. Patrick Soc. of Bklyn., Emerald Assn. L.I. (pres.), Fort Hamilton Hist. Soc., Acad. Magical Arts, The Friendly Sons St. Patrick City N.Y., Cathedral Club of Bklyn. (past pres.), Bay Ridge Mens Club, Fordham U. Pres. Club, Ancient Order of Hibernians (div. 22), KC, Bayfort Benevolent Assocs. (past pres.), Bklyn. Club. Roman Catholic. Home: 33 Columbia Ave Staten Island NY 10305-3739 Office: Prudential Securities Inc 100 Gold St New York NY 10292-0002

GOLDEN, ROBERT EDWARD, college dean, writer, consultant; b. St. Louis, Mar. 2, 1945; s. Robert Edward and Marion (O'Brien) G.; m. Barbara Masana, Oct. 6, 1967 (div. 1986); 1 child, Matthew. AB, U. Mich., 1967; MA, U. Rochester, 1970, PhD, 1972. Asst. assoc. prof. Rochester (N.Y.) Inst. Tech., 1971-89, assoc. dean, 1980-84, chair Lang., Lit. and Communications div., 1984-89; dean Coll. of Arts and Scis. Shippensburg (Pa.) U., 1989—; cons. corp., audit and operational analysis Xerox Corp., Rochester, 1978-80. Co-author: (with Mary Sullivan) Flannery O'Connor and Caroline Gardon; A Reference Guide, 1976; (with Katherine Mayberry) For Argument's Sake, 1990; contbr. articles on Am. lit. and ednl. use of computers to profl. jours. Chair, bd. dirs. Writers and Books, Rochester, 1988-89. Mem. Am. Assn. of Higher Edn., Coun. of Coll. Arts and Scis., Am. Conf. of Acad. Deans, Modern Lang. Assn., Phi Beta Kappa. Home: 125 W Pomfret St Carlisle PA 17013-3219 Office: Shippensburg U Shippensburg PA 17257

GOLDEN, RONALD AARON, physician, nephrologist; b. Kew Gardens, N.Y., Apr. 5, 1943; s. Max and Sally (Hoffman) G.; m. Ruthe Susan Feigenbaum, Mar. 11, 1967; children: Meredith Lynn, Lauren Hillary, Jessica Amy. BS, Hobart Coll., 1963; MD, NYU, 1967. Diplomate Am. Bd. Internal Medicine, Am. Bd. Nephrology. Attending nephrologist Booth Meml. Hosp., Queens, N.Y., 1974—, Montefiore Med. Ctr., Bronx, N.Y., 1974—; cons. Union Hosp., Bronx, Pelham Bos Gen. Hosp., St. Barnabas Hosp., Astoria Gen. Hosp., La Guardia Hosp., 1975—. Lt. comdr. USN, 1972-73. Mem. Am. Soc. Nephrology, Internat. Soc. Nephrology, Renal Physicians Assn. Jewish. Office: Nephrology Assoc PC 1874 Pelham Pky S Bronx NY 10461

GOLDEN, STEPHEN EDWARD, II, hospital chief financial officer; b. Carthage, N.Y., Oct. 9, 1949; s. Stephen E. and Theresa M. (Mandronico) G.; m. Rosemary A. Stowell, Apr. 20, 1968; (div. 1981); children: Ellen M., Stephen E. III. BS in Acctg., U. Rochester, N.Y., 1971. CPA, N.Y. Audit mgr. Deloitte, Haskins & Sells, Rochester, 1971-79; sr. audit mgr. Peat Marwick, Syracuse, N.Y., 1979-86; chief fin. officer Auburn (N.Y.) Meml. Hosp., 1986—. Com. chmn. United Way, Syracuse, 1980—; pres. Star Lake (N.Y.) Protective Assn., 1988-90. Mem. Healthcare Fin. Mgmt. Assn. (pres. cen. N.Y. chpt. 1986—), Inst. Internal Auditors (bd. dirs. local chpts. 1975-86), N.Y. State Soc. CPA's (bd. dirs. 1977-79).

GOLDENBERG, DAVID MILTON, experimental pathologist, oncologist; b. N.Y.C., Aug. 2, 1938; s. Leo and Lillie (Spivak) G.; m. Hildegard Gruenbaum, Apr. 28, 1961; children: Eva, Deborah, Denis, Neil, Lee. Student, Shimer Coll., 1954-56; BS, U. Chgo., 1958; ScD, U. Erlangen-Nuremberg, Fed. Republic of Germany, 1965; MD, U. Heidelberg, Fed. Republic of Germany, 1966. Assoc. rsch. prof. pathology U. Pitts. Med. Sch., 1968-70; assoc. prof. pathology Temple U. Med. Sch., Phila., 1970-72, U. Ky. Med. Ctr., Lexington, 1972-73; prof., dir. div. exptl. pathology U. Ky., Lexington, 1973-83; pres. Ctr. for Molecular Medicine and Immunology, Newark, 1983—; adj. prof. medicine and surgery N.J. Med. Sch., U. of Medicine and Dentristry of N.J., Newark, 1983—; mem. VA Merit Rev. Bd. for Oncology, Washington, 1974-77; exec. dir. Ephraim McDowell Community Cancer Network, Lexington, 1975-80; pres. Ephraim McDowell Cancer Rsch. Found., 1978-80; sec./treas. Ky. Cancer Commn., Frankfort, 1978-80; mem. sci. adv. bd. German Fund for Cancer Rsch., Bonn, 1980—; chmn. bd. Immunomedics, Inc., Morris Plains, N.J., 1983—; mem. exptl. immunology study sect. NIH, Bethesda, Md., 1980-83; adj. prof. N.J. Med. Sch., Newark, 1983—. Author more than 600 articles, book chpts., abstracts, 1962—; assoc. editor Cancer Rsch. mag.; mem. editorial bd. Tumor Biology, Antibody, Immunoconjugates and Radiopharms., Jour. Nuclear Medicine and Allied Scis. Recipient Rsch. Found. award U. Ky., 1978, Outstanding Investigator grant Nat. Cancer Inst., 1985—, N.J. Pride award in sci. and tech. N.J. Monthly, 1986, Excellence in Cancer Rsch. award N.J. Senate and Assembly, 1985-86, Otto Herz Meml. lectureship Tel Aviv U., 1991, 3M/Mayneord Meml. lectureship Brit. Inst. Radiology, 1991. Hon. mem. Argentine Cancer Assn. Jewish. Office: Ctr Molecular Medicine & Immunology 1 Bruce St Newark NJ 07103-2709

GOLDENBERG, MARVIN MANUS, pharmacologist, pharmaceutical developer; b. N.Y.C., July 7, 1935; s. Jacob and Sarah Goldenberg; m. Esther K. Gelman, Sept. 8, 1957; children: Sol Jeffrey, Lisa Shari. BS, Bklyn. Coll. Pharmacy, 1957; MS, Temple U., 1959; PhD, Med. Coll. Pa., 1965. Lic. pharmacist, N.Y., Pa. Group leader Norwich-Eaton Pharms., Norwich, N.Y., 1965-80; dir. immunopharmacology rsch. Merck Sharp & Dohme, Rahway, N.J., 1980-85, asst. dir. clin. rsch., 1985-88; dir. ophthalmic R&D Am. Cyanamid, Pearl River, N.Y., 1988-89, dir. ophthalmic rsch., 1989-91; pres., v.p. pharm. product devel. and mfg. Reedand Carnrick div Reed and Carnick div. Block Drug Co., Jersey City, N.J., 1991—; grant reviewer NIH, Bethesda, Md., 1978-89, fellowship reviewer, 1984-89. Author: The Role of Arachidonic Acid Oxygenation Products, 1984, Gastric Cytoprotection with Prostaglandins, 1985; contbr. numerous articles to profl. jours.; inventor on numerous pats. Pres. Temple, Norwich, N.Y., 1972. Fellow Am. Soc. for Pharmacology, Am. Gastroent. Assn., Inflammation Rsch. Assn., Soc. of Clin. Pharmacology; mem. Am. Assn. Pharm. Scientists, Masons (pres. Norwich, N.Y. 1975). Office: Block Drug Co 257 Cornelison Ave Jersey City NJ 07302-3113 also: 721 Shackamaxon Dr Westfield NJ 07090

GOLDENBERG, MYRNA GALLANT, English language and literature educator; b. Bklyn., Mar. 8, 1937; d. Harry and Fay (Solomon) Gallant; m. Neal Goldenberg, Jan. 27, 1957; children: Elizabeth, David Brian, Eve Lisa. BS cum laude, CCNY, 1957; MA, U. Ark., 1961; PhD, U. Md., 1987. Faculty, dept. English Montgomery Coll., Rockville, Md., 1971—, chmn. dept., 1979-81, coord. gen. edn., 1981-90, coord. women's studies program, 1990—; lectr. humanities Johns Hopkins U.; co-dir. FIPSE project: Integrating Scholarship of Women in Curricula of Selected Md. Community Colls., 1988-90; chmn. Montgomery County Commn. on Humanities, 1984-91; chmn. Title IX adv. com. Montgomery County Pub. Schs., 1985-89; lectr. in field. Contbg. author/author: Common and Uncommon Concerns: The Complex Role of Community College Department Chairpersons/Enhancing Department Leadership, 1990, Different Horrors/Same Hell: Women Remembering the Holocaust, Thinking Unthinkable: Human Meanings of the Holocaust, 1990; contbg. editor: Belles Lettres, 1989—; editor: Community Coll. Humanities Rev.; contbr. articles to profl. jours. Recipient Disting. Humanities Educator award Community Coll. Humanities Assn., 1989, Outstanding Faculty Mem. award Montgomery Coll., 1990, Teaching award Md. Assn. for Higher Edn., 1991; acad. adminstrn. fellow Am. Coun. on Edn., 1981-92, Lowenstein-Wiener fellow U. Md., 1983. Mem. MLA, Assn. Jewish Studies, Nat. Coun. Tchrs. English, History Edn. Soc., Phi Kappa Phi. Home: 9328 Garden Ct Rockville MD 20854-3962

GOLDENBERG, SHERRI ROBERTA, advertising account executive; b. Hartford, Conn., Nov. 11, 1964; d. Benjamin Lewis and Minnie Mary (Novack) G. Student, Bradley U., 1982-84, U. Hartford, 1984-86. Account exec. media and prodn. coord. Jonathan & Williams Advt., West Hartford, 1986-89; account exec. Arnold Fortuna Lane Advt., Hartford, 1990—; account exec. JW-Adlink Recruitment Advt.; media coord. recruiting advt. plans. Active in Big Brothers/Big Sisters Am. Mem. Internat. Gem Minerals and Fossil Soc., Ad Club of Hartford, Conn. Art Dirs. Club. Home: 26 Oakwood Ave West Hartford CT 06119-2175

GOLDENSOHN, BARRY NATHAN, poet, English educator; b. N.Y.C., Apr. 26, 1937; s. Joseph Benjamin and Shirley (Friedburg) G.; m. Lorrie Myer, Aug. 5, 1956; children: Matthew, Rachel. BA, Oberlin (Ohio) Coll., 1957; MA, U. Wis., 1959. Instr. IIT, Chgo., 1959-61, Kent (Ohio) State U., 1961-62; co-founder, tchr., dir. Pacific High Sch., Portola Valley, Calif., 1962-65; tchr. Goddard Coll., Plainfield, Vt., 1965-70; vis. prof. Writers Workshop, U. Iowa, Iowa City, 1970-72; tchr. Goddard Coll., 1972-77; dean humanities and arts Hampshire Coll., Amherst, Mass., 1977-82; prof. English Skidmore Coll., Saratoga Springs, N.Y., 1982—. Author: (books of poetry) St. Venus Eve, 1972, Uncarving the Block, 1978, The Marrano, 1988, Dance Music, 1992; editor: Swift's Gullivers Travels, 1961; contbr. articles to profl. jours., poetry in periodicals and anthologies. NEH grantee, 1977-78; Vt. Coun. of Arts grantee; N.Y. Found. for the Arts grantee. Home: 11 Seward St Saratoga Springs NY 12866-1001 Office: Skidmore Coll English Dept Saratoga Springs NY 12866

GOLDFARB, MURIEL GORDON, psychotherapist, consultant; b. N.Y.C., Oct. 1, 1934; d. Martin and Sally (Gordon) Nathan; m. Robert W. Goldfarb, June 7, 1953; children: Kevin, Leda, Shanna, Kim. AA, Nassau Community Coll., 1966; BA, Hofstra U., 1972; counseling diploma, Postgrad. Ctr. Mental Health, N.Y.C., 1974. Psychiatric nurse Phoenix House, N.Y.C., 1969-71; psychotherapist No Shore Cornell Hosp., Manhasset, N.Y., 1974-76; pvt. practice psychotherapist N.Y.C., 1976—; founder, pres. Woman's Counseling Svc., N.Y.C., 1976-80, Counseling By Mail, N.Y.C., 1983—; cons. on psychol. issues various nat. mags., tv., radio, 1976—; workshop presenter. Mem. Southampton (N.Y.) Lake Preservation Assn., 1985—. Mem. AACD. Office: 2109 Broadway New York NY 10023-2130

GOLDFARB, RICHARD MARC, advertising and communications executive; b. Bklyn., Oct. 19, 1953; s. Oscar and Betty (Fagenbaum) G. BA, Bklyn. Coll., 1976. Sta. rels. supr. SESAC, N.Y.C., 1975-77; v.p. mktg. svcs. Ed Libov Assocs., N.Y.C., 1978-84, v.p., gen. mgr. ELA Entertainment, 1978-84; dir. advertiser sales Viacom Enterprises, N.Y.C., 1984-85; sr. v.p., gen. mgr. Bocass Communications, N.Y.C., 1985-86; v.p. Turner Broadcasting Sales, N.Y.C., 1986-90, sr. v.p., 1990—. Co-producer Com. Restoration of Ellis Island and Statue of Liberty, Liberty Island, N.Y., 1983. Mem. NATAS, Internat. Radio and TV Soc., Advertiser Syndicated TV Assn. (rep. 1985—, bd. dirs.), Advt. Club N.Y., Am. Film Inst., Cousteau Soc., Nat. Geog. Soc. Home: 300 E 93d St New York NY 10128 Office: Turner Broadcasting 420 5th Ave New York NY 10018-2702

GOLDFARB, STANLEY, internist, educator; b. N.Y.C., Dec. 18, 1943; s. Robert Melvin and Mary Ann (Siegel) G.; m. Rayna Lynne Block, Aug. 30, 1970; children: Rachael, Michael. AB, Princeton U., 1965; MD, U. Rochester, 1969; MS, U. Pa., 1986. Asst. prof. U. Pa., Phila., 1974-84, assoc. prof., 1984-88, prof. medicine, 1988—; mem. nephrology bd. Am. Bd. Internal Medicine, Phila., 1988—. Editor: Hormones, Autocods and Kidney, 1991. Bd. dirs. Nat. Kidney Found. Pa., Phila., 1988-90. Capt. USNG, 1970-76. NIH grantee, Washington, 1984-88; recipient Vol. award Nat. Kidney Found., N.Y.C., 1990. Mem. Am. Soc. Clin. Investigation. Home: 801 Muirfield Rd Bryn Mawr PA 19010 Office: U Pa 3400 Spruce St Philadelphia PA 19104

GOLDFELD, DORIAN, mathematics educator; b. Marburg, Germany, Jan. 21, 1947; came to U.S., 1950; s. Saul and Helen Goldfeld; m. Iris Anshel; children: Dahlia Anne, Ada Pearl. BS in Engring., Columbia U., 1967, PhD, 1969. Miller fellow U. Calif., Berkeley, 1969-71; postdoctoral fellow Hebrew U., Jerusalem, 1971-72; lectr. Tel Aviv U., 1972-73; mem. Inst. Advanced Study, Princeton, N.J., 1973-74; vis. prof. Scuola Normale Superiore, Pisa, Italy, 1974-76, Harvard U., Cambridge, Mass., 1982-83; asst. assoc. prof. MIT, Cambridge, 1976-82; assoc. prof. U. Tex., Austin, 1983-85; prof. Columbia U., N.Y.C., 1985—. Editor: Higher Mathematics From An Elementary Point of View, 1982, Automorphic Functions and Selbergs Trace Formula, 1988. Sloan Found. fellow, 1977-79; recipient prize Vaughn Found., Houston, 1985. Mem. Am. Math. Soc. (Cole prize in number theory 1987), Math. Assn. Am. Office: Columbia U Dept Math New York NY 10027

GOLDFISCHER, SIDNEY LEO, dean, pathologist, researcher, educator; b. N.Y.C., Dec. 28, 1926; s. Samuel and Ida (Lerner) G.; m. Lillian Birenbaum, Feb. 27, 1955 (dec. June 1974); children: Carl, Susan, Michael, Madeline; m. Cleo Mullas Dana, Oct. 12, 1990. BS, Columbia U., 1958; MD, NYU, 1961. Asst. prof. Albert Einstein Coll. of Medicine Yeshiva U., N.Y.C., 1967-70, assoc. prof. Albert Einstein Coll. of Medicine, 1970-74, prof. Albert Einstein Coll. of Medicine, 1974—, dir., indsl. liaison Albert Einstein Coll. Medicine, 1983—, acting chair pathology dept. Albert Einstein Coll. Medicine, 1984—, assoc. dean sci. ops. Albert Einstein Coll. Medicine, 1989—. Contbr. articles to profl. jours. Pres. HistoChem. Soc., 1982-83, N.Y. State Electron Microscopy Soc., 1986. Jewish. Office: Yeshiva U Albert Einstein Coll Medicine 1300 Morris Park Ave Bronx NY 10461-1924

GOLDFRANK, MRS. HERBERT J. See KAY, HELEN

GOLDFRANK, LEWIS ROBERT, physician; b. N.Y.C., Sept. 8, 1941; s. Herbert John and Helen (Colodny) G.; m. Susan M. Harrington, Aug. 29, 1964; children: Michelle, Andrew, Jennifer, Rebecca. BA, Clark U., 1963; MD, U. Brussels, Belgium, 1970. Resident Montefiore Hosp., Bronx, N.Y., 1971-73; dir. emergency medicine Morrisania Hosp., Bronx, 1973-76, North Cen. Bronx Hosp., 1976-79, Montefiore Hosp., 1976-79, Bellevue Hosp., Manhattan, N.Y., 1979—, NYU Med. Ctr., Manhattan, 1979—; dir. N.Y. City Poison Ctr., Manhattan, 1979—; bd. dirs. Soc. Acad. Emergency Medicine, 1990—. Author, editor: Goldfrank's Toxicologic Emergencies, 4th edit., 1990, Emergency Doctor, 1987, Diagnostic Testing in the Emergency Department, 1984. Recipient Am. Med. Writer's Assn. Hon. Mention, 1988, Hal Jayne Acad. Excellence award Soc. Acad. Emergency Medicine, 1990. Fellow Am. Coll. Emergency Physician, Am. Acad. Clin. Toxicology, Am. Coll. Physicians; mem. Am. Bd. Med. Toxicology (dir., chmn. 1985—). Home: 55 Grace Ln Ossining NY 10562-2129 Office: Bellevue Hosp Ctr First Ave & 27th St New York NY 10016

GOLDIN, DANIEL, government agency administrator; b. N.Y.C., July 23, 1940; m. Judith Linda Kramer; children: Aerial, Laura. BS in Mech. Engring., City Coll. N.Y., 1962. Rsch. scientist Lewis Rsch. Ctr., NASA, Cleve., 1962-67; with TRW, from 1967, mem. tech. staff, 1967; then v.p., gen. mgr. space and tech. group TRW, Redondo, Calif.; adminstr. NASA, Washington, 1992—. Office: NASA Office of Adminstr Washington DC 20546*

GOLDIN, HARRISON JACOB, financial consultant; b. N.Y.C., Feb. 23, 1936; s. Dr. Harry and Anna E. (Eskolsky) G.; m. Diana Stern, Nov. 20, 1966; children—Daniel, Matthew, Jonathan. A.B., summa cum laude, Princeton U., 1957; LL.B., Yale Law Sch., 1961. Bar: N.Y. 1961, U.S. Dist. Ct. (so. dist.) N.Y. 1964, U.S. Ct. Appeals (2nd cir.) N.Y. 1965. Atty. U.S. Dept. Justice, Washington, 1961-63, Davis Polk & Wardwell, N.Y.C., 1963-69; N.Y. State senator, Albany, 1966-73; comptroller City of N.Y., 1974-89; now pvt. practice cons. Goldin Assocs., N.Y.C.; lectr. Columbia Law Sch., N.Y.C., 1974-89; adj. prof. law N.Y. Law Sch., N.Y.C., 1983-89, Cardoza Law Sch., 1983-89; adj. prof. acctg. NYU, 1982-89. Woodrow Wilson fellow Harvard U., 1957-58. Mem. Council on Fgn. Relations, Order of Coif, Phi Beta Kappa. Democrat. Jewish. Home: 150 E 73d St New York NY 10021 Office: Goldin Assocs 767 Fifth Ave 28th Fl New York NY 10153

GOLDIN, JUDAH, Hebrew literature educator; b. N.Y.C., Sept. 14, 1914; s. Gerson David and Rachel (Robkin) G.; m. Grace Avis Aaronson, June 21, 1938; children: Robin Elinor (dec.), David Lionel. BSS, CCNY, 1934; diploma, Sem. Coll., 1934; MA, Columbia, 1938; MHL, Jewish Theol. Sem., 1938, DHL, 1943, HLD, 1968; MA, Yale, 1958; DD, Colgate U., 1973; HLD, Jewish Inst. Religion, Hebrew Union Coll., 1986. Ordained rabbi, 1938. Lectr., vis. assoc. prof. Jewish lit. and history Duke, 1943-45; assoc. prof. religion U. Iowa, 1946-52; dean, assoc. prof. Agada Sem. Coll., Jewish Theol. Sem., 1952-58; adj. prof. religion Columbia, 1955-58; prof. Jewish studies Yale, 1958-62, prof. classical Judaica, 1962-73; prof. postbibl. Hebrew lit. U. Pa., Phila., 1973-85, prof. emeritus, 1985—. Author: The Two Versions of Abot de Rabbi Nathan, 1945, Hillel the Elder, 1946, The Period of the Talmud, 1949, The Fathers, 1955, The Living Talmud, 1957, The Three Pillars of Simeon the Righteous, 1958, A Philosophical Session in a Tannaite Academy, 1965, The End of Ecclesiastes, 1966, The Song at the Sea, 1971, Profile of Aqiba ben Joseph, 1976, The First Pair, 1980, Freedom and Restraint of Haggadah, 1986; editor: The Jewish Expression, 1970, The Munich Mekilta, 1980. Am. Philos. Soc. grantee, 1957, 71; Guggenheim fellow, 1958; Fulbright fellow, 1958, 64-65; Am. Council Learned Socs., 1978. Fellow Am. Acad. Jewish Research, Am. Acad. Arts and Scis.; mem. Am. Schs. Oriental Research, Conn. Acad. Arts and Scis., Oriental Club Pa., Phi Beta Kappa. Home: 405 Thayer Rd Swarthmore PA 19081-1230 Office: U Pa Oriental Studies Dept Philadelphia PA 19104

GOLDIN, LEON, artist, educator; b. Chgo., Jan. 16, 1923; s. Joseph P. and Bertha (Metz) G.; m. Meta Solotaroff, July 30, 1949; children—Joshua, Daniel. B.F.A., Art Inst. Chgo., 1948; M.F.A., U. Iowa, 1950. From Instr. to assoc. prof. Columbia U., 1964-82, prof., 1982—, chmn. dept. painting and sculpture, 1973-75, 77-80; former tchr. Calif. Coll. Arts and Crafts, Phila. Coll. Art, Queen's Coll., Cooper Union; vis. prof. painting Stanford, summer 1973. Exhibited one man shows, Oakland Art Mus., 1955, Felix Landau Gallery, Los Angeles, 1956, 57, 59, Galleria L'Attico, Rome, 1958, Kraushaar Galleries, N.Y.C., 1960, 64, 68, 72, 84, 88, 90, U. Houston, 1981; rep. permanent collections, Bklyn. Mus., City Mus. St. Louis, Worcester Mus., Addison Gallery Am. Art, Pa. Acad. Fine Arts, Los Angeles County Mus., Santa Barbara Mus., Oakland Art Mus., Munson Proctor Inst., Va. Mus. Fine Arts, Portland (Maine) Mus., Everson Mus., Syracuse, N.Y., U. Ark., Okla. Art Center. Served with AUS, 1943-46, ETO. Recipient Prix de Rome Am. Acad. Rome, 91955-58, Jennie Sesnan gold medal Pa. Acad. Fine Arts, 1966; Tiffany grantee, 1951; Fulbright scholar to France, 1952; Guggenheim fellow, 1959; Nat. Endowment for Arts grantee, 1967, 80; Nat. Inst. Arts and Letters grantee, 1968; N.Y. Caps grantee, 1981. Mem. Nat. Acad. Design (elected 1991). Home: 438 W 116th St New York NY 10027-7203

GOLDMACHER, JEFFERY A., human resources professional; b. Bronx. N.Y., Jan. 25, 1956; s. Donald William and Sandra Agnes (Rosenberg) G.; m. Ava Lee Gaster, Aug. 14, 1976 (div. June 1988); 1 child, Michael; m. Betsy Ann Morris, Sept. 25, 1988. BA, Hofstra U., 1978; MPA, C.W. Post Coll., 1980. Spl. projects mgr. Fiberglass Resources Corp., Farmingdale, N.Y., 1974-76; asst. buyer M. Fortunoff of Westbury, N.Y., 1976-80; registered rep. Equitable Life/Buxton Agy., 1981-83; personnel mgr., office mgr. Law Offices of Mark Schwarz, N.Y.C., 1983-86; personnel mgr. Winfred M. Berg, Inc., East Rockaway, N.Y., 1986-88; dir. human resources Crest Uniform Co., Inc., N.Y.C., 1988—; cons. in field, 1983—. Mem. Am. Mgmt. Assn., Soc. of Human Resources Mgrs., Soc. Human Resource Planners. Home: 160 E 84th St New York NY 10028-2008

GOLDMAN, ALFRED EMMANUEL, marketing research consultant; b. Bklyn., Dec. 19, 1925; s. Samuel and Julia (Schwartz) G.; m. Adele Lieb, Mar. 30, 1952; children: Julia Madelaine, Marshall Scott. BS, CCNY, 1949, MA, cert. in clin. sch. psychology, 1950; PhD in Clin. Psychology, Clark U., 1955. Research clin. psychologist Boston State Hosp., 1953-54; asst. prof. Northeastern U., Boston, 1954-55; research assoc. Sch. Public Health, Harvard U., 1955-56; asst. dir. psychol. services Norristown (Pa.) State Hosp., 1956-60; dir. rsch. devel. Nat. Analysts Inc., 1960-64, exec. v.p., dir. rsch., 1964-70; pres. Nat. Analysts div. Booz Allen and Hamilton Inc., 1970-82, sr. v.p., 1982-91; pvt. practice mktg. rsch. cons Bryn Mawr, Pa., 1991—; founding chmn. Coun. Am. Survey Rsch. Organs, 1975-77. Author: The Group Depth Interview: Principles and Practice, 1986; contbr. articles in field to various publs. Served with USAAF, 1944-46. Fellow Am. Psychol. Assn.; mem. Phi Beta Kappa.

GOLDMAN, ANDREW, architect; b. N.Y.C., June 21, 1947; s. Harry and Ida (Gurman) G. BA, Amherst (Mass.) Coll., 1968; postgrad., Columbia U., 1968-69; MArch, Harvard U., 1971. Designer Perkins & Will, Architects, N.Y.C., 1972; sr. assoc. Maitland/Strauss Architects, P.C., Greenwich, Conn., 1973-80; assoc. Ulrich Franzen Architects, N.Y.C., 1981-82; sr. assoc. Prentice & Chan, Ohlhausen, N.Y.C., 1983-87; founding prin. N.Y.C., 1987-88; ptnr. Kevin Hom + Andrew Goldman Architects P.C., N.Y.C., 1989—. Playwright Dabones of Babylon, 1983, A Second Brilliance, 1987, Fast, 1991; contbr. articles to profl. jours. Recipient O'Neill Theatre award O'Neill Theatre Ctr., 1974. Mem. AIA.

GOLDMAN, ARNOLD, proto-type electronics specialist; b. Chgo., July 8, 1931; s. Samual and Nettie (Cohen) G.; m. Merald Greta Flecker, Mar. 7, 1953; children: Richard Seth, Steven Adam. Student, N.Y. Inst. Tech., 1956-57. With RCA Inst., N.Y.C., 1952-53, AT&T Bell Labs., Holmdel, N.J., 1953—. Com. chmn. Boy Scouts Am., Howell, 1972-74. With USN, 1953-54, Korea. Jewish. Home: 54 Sunset Dr Howell NJ 07731 Office: AT&T Everetts Corner Rd Holmdel NJ 07733

GOLDMAN, ARNOLD DAVID, psychiatrist, educator; b. Phila., Sept. 29, 1933; s. Abraham and Kate (Kossel) G.; m. Marilyn Esther Venitsky, June 23, 1957; children: Audrey, Shari, Rachel, Daniel. BA, U. Pa., 1954; MD, Hahnemann U., 1958. Diplomate Am. Bd. Psychiatry and Neurology, qualified in geriatric psychiatry. Intern Lower Bucks County Hosp., Bristol, Pa.; resident Eastern Pa. Psychiat. Inst., 1961-63, Hahnemann Hosp., Phila., 1963-64; dir. psychiatry Hahnemann div. Phila. Gen. Hosp., 1970-74; dir. inpatient psychiatry Albert Einstein Med. Ctr. So. Div., Phila., 1975-80; head consultation-psychiat. svcs. Cooper U. Hosp., Camden, N.J., 1980-85; chief psychiatry West Jersey Health Systems, Voorhees, N.J., 1988—; pvt. practice, Voorhees, 1964—; clin. prof. psychiatry Robert Wood Johnson Med. Sch., U. Medicine and Dentistry N.J., Piscataway, 1989—. Sr. asst. surgeon USPHS, 1959-61. Fellow Am. Psychiat. Assn.; mem. AMA, Am. Psychoanalytic Assn., N.J. Psychiat. Assn. (councilor 1986-90, membership chmn. 1988—), Coun. Phila. Psychiatric Soc. (liaison 1987—), Alpha Omega Alpha. Home: 514 Old Gulph Rd Narberth PA 19072-1621 Office: 100 Carnie Blvd Ste 1B Voorhees NJ 08043-4512

GOLDMAN, ERNEST HAROLD, computer engineer; b. Lynn, Mass., Oct. 4, 1922; s. Samuel Abraham and Julia (Portnoy) G.; m. Muriel Lyons, Dec. 19, 1948; children: Robyn S., Wayne A. BS, USCG Acad., 1943; postgrad., Princeton U., MIT, 1943; MS, Harvard U., 1949, DSc, 1952. Instr. in elec. engring. Harvard U., Cambridge, Mass., 1950-51; sr. engr. IBM, Poughkeepsie, N.Y., 1951-57; rsch. dir. IBM, Yorktown Hgts., N.Y., 1958-64; lab. mgr. IBM, Fishkill, N.Y., 1965-74; program mgr. IBM Corp. Hdqrs., Armonk, N.Y., 1975-81; adj. full prof. Pace U., Pleasantville, N.Y., 1974-82; vis. prof. Rutgers U., New Brunswick, N.J., 1990; Bannow-Wahlstrom prof. computer engring. U. Bridgeport, Conn., 1982—; cons. in field. Contbr. articles to profl. jours. Lt. USCG, 1943-47. Recipient Bowdoin prize Harvard U., 1950. Mem. IEEE, Computer Soc., Assn. for Computer Machinery, Spl. Interest Group Computer Communications, Harvard Club of Fairfield County, Rsch. Soc. Am., Sigma Xi. Home: 4 Regulation Rd West Redding CT 06896-1225 Office: U Bridgeport Bridgeport CT 06604

GOLDMAN, IRA STEVEN, gastroenterologist; b. Bronx, N.Y., May 19, 1951; s. George David and Belle (Hans) G.; m. Niki Ellen Kantrowitz, Jan.

20, 1980; children: Zachary, Joshua. BA, U. Rochester, 1973; student, Oxford U., 1972; MD, Columbia U., 1977. Diplomate Am. Bd. Internal Medicine, Subspecialty Gastroenterology. Internal medicine intern Columbia Presbyn. Med. Ctr., N.Y.C., 1977-78, resident in internal medicine, 1978-80; fellow in gastroenterology and liver diseases Sch. Medicine U. Calif., San Francisco, 1980-83; instr. in anatomy Columbia U., N.Y.C., 1978; asst. prof. medicine U. Calif., San Francisco, 1983-85, Med. Coll. Cornell U., N.Y.C., 1985-91; attending physician North Shore Univ. Hosp., Manhasset, N.Y., 1985—; mem. physicians adv. bd. Am. Liver Found., L.I., 1985—; mem. sci. adv. commn. L.I. chpt. Nat. Found. for Ileitis and Colitis, 1985-91. Reviewer jours. Gastroenterology; contbr. articles, book chapts., case reports, and abstracts to profl. jours., sci. meetings. Recipient Am. Liver Found. Rsch. fellowship award, 1982, Nat. Insts. Health, Clin. Investigator award, 1983. Fellow ACP, Am. Coll. Gastroenterology; mem. Am. Fedn. for Clin. Rsch., Am. Assn. for Study of Liver Diseases, Med. Soc. of the State of N.Y., Nassau County Med. Soc., Nassau County Acad. Medicine, Alpha Omega Alpha. Office: North Shore Univ Hosp 300 Community Dr Manhasset NY 11030-3800

GOLDMAN, JANICE GOLDIN, psychologist, educator; b. Phila., Feb. 15, 1938; d. Samuel and Dorothea (Berenson) Goldin; m. Arthur S. Goldman, Aug. 31, 1958; children: Jill Ann Goldman-Callahan, Joshua N., Jennifer S. BA, U. Pa., 1960, MA, 1962; MS, Hahnemann Med. Coll., 1972, D in Psychology, 1975. Lic. psychologist, Pa. Chief psychologist Charles Peberdy Child Psychiatry Ctr. Hahnemann U., Phila., 1975-87, from clin. asst. to assoc. prof., 1985-87; pvt. practice Jenkintown, Pa., 1977—; cons. Haverford (Pa.) State Hosp., 1982, Assn. for Mental Health Affiliates with Israel, 1984, 86; mem. profl. adv. bd. Pub. Radio Sta WHYY, Phila., 1984-86; workshop leader Women's Ctr. of Montgomery County, Jenkintown, 1982—. Contbr. articles to profl. jours. Board dirs. Assn. for Mental Health Affiliate with Israel, nationwide, 1984-88, Or Hadash Synogogue, Wyncote, Pa., 1989. Mem. Am. Psychol. Assn., Am. Family Therapy Assn., Nat. Register Health Svc. Providers, Phila. Soc. Clin. Psychology (sec. 1977-79), Pa. Psychol. Assn., Internat. Soc. for Study of Multiple Personality and Dissociative Disorders, Phila. Soc. Clin. Hypnosis, Amnesty Internat., Phi Beta Kappa. Democrat. Office: Foxcroft Sq Apts 1250 Greenwood Ave Jenkintown PA 19046

GOLDMAN, JERRY STEPHEN, lawyer; b. Bklyn., Sept. 7, 1951; s. Bernard I. and Charlotte (Emerling) G.; m. Lisa Steinberg, Mar. 28, 1981; children: Rachel Dawn, Samantha. BA with honors, NYU 1973; JD, Boston U., 1976; LLM in Taxation, Temple U., 1983. Bar: Mass. 1977, N.Y. 1977, U.S. Dist. Ct. (ea. and so. dists.) N.Y. 1980, U.S. Supreme Ct. 1981, Pa. 1982, U.S. Tax Ct. 1983, U.S. Ct. Appeals (3d cir.) 1983, U.S. Dist. Ct. (ea. dist.) Pa. 1983, U.S. Ct. Appeals (2d cir.) 1992. Sr. asst. dist. atty. Kings County Dist. Atty.'s Office, Bklyn., 1976-82; pvt. practice, N.Y.C. and Phila., 1982—; dir., pres. Huntingdon Brook Community Assn., Bucks Co, Pa., 1985-89. Bd. dirs., counsel Citizen's Crime Commn., Phila., 1983—; atty. Phila. Vol. Lawyers for the Arts, 1983—; chmn. Upper Southampton Planning Commn., 1984-90. Mem. ABA, N.Y. State Bar Assn., Mass. Bar Assn., Pa. Bar Assn., Phila. Bar Assn. Jewish. Avocations: cross-country skiing, music. Office: 1520 Locust St Philadelphia PA 19102-3193 also: 17th Fl 277 Broadway New York NY 10007 also: Ste 409 1 Fairway Plz Huntingdon Valley PA 19006

GOLDMAN, JOEL J., lawyer, oil and gas drilling company executive; b. N.Y.C., Sept. 7, 1940; s. Myron and Pearl (Jacobs) G.; m. Jane I. Stalker, July 23, 1973; children: Elizabeth Ann, Rebecca Lynn. BS, U. Va., 1962, JD, Syracuse U., 1965. Bar: N.Y. 1966, U.S. Dist. Ct. (we. dist.) N.Y. 1966. Law clk. Myron Goldman, N.Y.C., 1965; staff atty., chief trial counsel Legal Aid Soc. Rochester, N.Y., 1966-73; ptnr. Kaman, Berlove, Marafioti, Jacobstein & Goldman, Rochester, 1973—; lectr. family law; spl. investigator N.Y. State Spl. Commn. on Attica, 1972; mem. panel arbitrators Am. Arbitration Assn.; mem. faculty Nat. Bus. Inst., 1985—. Referee, Ea. Assn. Inter-Collegiate Football Ofcls., 1974—, v.p. Empire chpt., 1988, pres. 1989. Fellow Am. Acad. Matrimonial Lawyers; mem. ABA, N.Y. State Bar Assn. (exec. com. family law sect. 1982, mem. exec. com. 1981—), Monroe County Bar Assn. (chmn. family law sect. 1982, exec. com. 1981-86), Assn. Trial Lawyers Am. Jewish. Author continuing edn. materials. Contbg. editor Bender's Forms for Civil Practice, 1986, Medina's Bostwick, 1986. Home: 67 Mountain Rd Rochester NY 14625-1816 Office: Kaman Berlove Marafioti Jacobstein & Goldman 13 S Fitzhugh St Ste 400 Rochester NY 14614-1485

GOLDMAN, JUDITH, writer, editor; b. Chgo.; d. Emmanuel M. and Irene (Mirotsnic) G. BA, Bard Coll., 1964; postgrad., Ill. Inst. Tech., 1965. Editor Print Collector's Newsletter, N.Y.C., 1970-73; mng. editor Artnews, N.Y.C., 1973-75, contbg. editor, 1975—; curator Whitney Mus. of Am. Art, N.Y.C., 1978-91. Author: Windows at Tiffany: The Art of Gene Mone, 1980, American Prints: Porcess & Proofs, 1981, Jasper Johns Prints: 1977-1981, 1981, Jasper Johns: 17 Monotypes, 1982, Frank Stella, Fourteen Prints with Drawings, Collages, and Working Proofs, 1983, James Roseinquist, 1985. McDowell Colony fellow, 1976; NEA grantee, 1978. Home: 525 W End Ave New York NY 10024-3207

GOLDMAN, LAWRENCE, biophysicist; b. Boston, May 6, 1936; s. Theodore Taft and Sophye (Altshuler) G.; m. Faith Kordis, July 11, 1968 (div. 1978); 1 child, Ann. BS summa cum laude, Tufts U., 1958; PhD, UCLA, 1964. Postdoctoral trainee Columbia U., 1964-65; asst. prof. U. Md., College Park, 1965-67, Balt., 1967-70; vis. scientist Lab. Biophysics, NIH, Bethesda, Md., 1967-70; assoc. prof. Sch. Medicine U. Md., 1970-77, prof. physiology, 1977—, prof. biophysics, 1977—; Fulbright sr. prof. Universtat des Saarlandes, 1987-88. Contbr. numerous sci. articles on biophysics of electrically excitable membranes to profl. jours. Recipient Carmichael prize in physiology Tufts U., 1958; NSF fellow, 1958-59, NIH fellow, 1960-64, 64-65, NIH spl. rsch. fellow, 1972-73, NATO sr. fellow U. London, 1970. Fellow AAAS; mem. Biophys. Soc., Am. Inst. Biol. Sci., Am. Physiol. Soc., Soc. Gen. Physiologists, Soc. Neurosci., Phi Beta Kappa. Office: U Md Sch Medicine Dept Physiology Baltimore MD 21201

GOLDMAN, LAWRENCE PAUL, financial services professional; b. Chgo., June 12, 1942; s. Dan E. and Louise (Paul) G.; m. Darlene J. Lewis, July 6, 1963; children: Dawn Marie, Gregory Allen. Diploma, South Bend Coll. Commerce, 1963. CLU, Fellow Life Mgmt. Inst. Trainee office supr. John Hancock Fin. Svcs., No. Ind., 1963-65; office supr. John Hancock Fin. Svcs., Kenosha, Wis., 1965-67, Chgo., 1967-70; supr., field adminstr. John Hancock Fin. Svcs., Boston, 1970-91; sr. coord. fin., 1991—. Mem. Water Safety Inst. ARC, Michigan City, Ind., 1960-67. Recipient Highest award for Bravery Am. Vets., Gary, Ind., 1962. Mem. FLMI Soc. Atlanta. Jewish. Home: 37 Oak Dr Upton MA 01568

GOLDMAN, LAWRENCE SAUL, lawyer; b. Phila., Mar. 25, 1942; s. Ephraim Lederer and Belle Joan (Finkelstein) G.; m. Kathi Sue Schleifer, June 20, 1965; children: Carolyn, Jonathan. BA, Brandeis U., 1963; JD, Harvard U., 1966. Bar: N.Y. 1966. Asst. dist. atty. New York County, N.Y.C., 1966-71; asst. gen. counsel N.Y. State Commn. To Investigate N.Y.C., 1971-72; ptnr. Goldman & Hafetz, N.Y.C., 1972—; cons. N.Y.C. Commn. on Police Corruption, 1972. Contbg. author: Criminal Trial Advocacy, 1980—. Trustee Congregation Rodeph Sholom, N.Y.C., 1983—; bd. dirs. William F. Ryan Community Health Ctr., N.Y.C., 1986-88; mem. N.Y. State Commn. on Judicial Conduct, 1990—, mem. adv. com. on the criminal procedure law. Recipient Man of Yr. award Hogan Assocs., 1984. Mem. N.Y. Assn. Criminal Def. Lawyers (dir., pres. 1987-89), N.Y. Criminal Bar Assn. (pres. 1982-85), Nat. Assn. Criminal Def. Lawyers (bd. dirs., chair ethics adv. com.), Harvard Club. Democrat. Office: 60 E 42d St New York NY 10165

GOLDMAN, MARILYN BARBARA, career and outplacement counselor; b. Bklyn., Feb. 9, 1943; d. Philip and Eleanor (Silverberg) Gavrin; m. Stuart Douglas Goldman, Aug. 9, 1964; children: Seth Jay, Jennifer Beth. BA, Bklyn. Coll., 1964; MA, Pa. State U., 1975. Cert. counselor, career counselor. Exec. dir. Job Options Inc., Harrisburg, Pa., 1976-78; pres. Horizons Unltd. Inc., Washington and Rockville, Md., 1978—. Author: The Work You Do: What It Says About You; staff writer Career Counselor column, 1990—. Women's Ednl. Equity Act grantee U.S. Dept. Edn., Washington, 1976-78. Mem. AACD, Met. Area Career and Life Planning Network, Employee Assistance Program Practioners Inc., Md. Assn. Career Devel. Office: Horizons Unltd Inc 1133 15th St NW Ste 1200 Washington DC 20005-2710

GOLDMAN, PHYLLIS E., psychology educator. BA, Rutgers U., 1966; MA, Seton Hall U., 1969; MS, Stevens Inst. Tech., 1978; EdD, Seton Hall U., 1983. Rsch. asst. Rutgers Univ., Newark, 1965-66; counselor N.J. Dept. of Labor and Industry, Newark, 1967-69; prof., psychology County Coll. of Morris, Randolph, N.J., 1969—; pvt. practice cons., 1978—. Editor: (book) Dimensions of Work and Human Behavior, 1980, 85, (jour.) Morris Manager, 1988, 89, 90; contbr. articles to profl. jours. Mem. speakers bur. County Coll. of Morris, Randolph, 1976—; bd. advisors Cath. Community Svcs., Newark, 1978-80. Mem. Am. Mgmt. Assn., Psi Chi, Kappa Delta Pi, Phi Delta Kappa. Office: County Coll of Morris Rt 10 & Center Grove Rd Randolph NJ 07869

GOLDMAN, RICHARD PAUL, educator; b. N.Y.C., Mar. 31, 1935; s. Edward and Dorothy (Myer) Goldman; m. Claire Elaine Taylor, Aug. 16, 1975; stepchildren: Lisa Backe, Nina Backe. BA magna cum laude, Yale U., 1956; MA, Middlebury Coll., 1965. Tchr., adminstr. Wilbraham (Mass.) Acad., 1959-72; assoc. headmaster Germantown Friends Sch., Phila., 1972—; cons. The Franklin Group, 1985—. Editor: (book) Sportswriters' Choice, 1959, (mag.) Studies in Education, 1972—; author: Profession at Risk, 1988; contbr. articles to profl. jours. Trustee Friends Coun. on Edn., Phila., Wilbraham & Monson Acad., 1988. Mem. Council for Advancement and Support of Edn., Phi Beta Kappa. Democrat. Jewish. Club: Yale. Home: 107 W Allens Ln Philadelphia PA 19119-4101

GOLDMAN, RONALD FRANK, consulting mechanical engineer; b. Brookline, Mass., July 11, 1947; s. William Wolf and Molly (Levias) G. BSME, Columbia U., 1969. Registered profl. engr., Mass., N.H. Engr. DuPont, Wilmington, Del., 1969-71; self-employed musician N.Y.C., 1972-77; engr. R.G. Vanderweil Engrs., Boston, 1978-79, BR&A Consulting Engrs., Boston, 1979-80; musician, pub. Circle of Sound Music, Boston, 1990—; founder, exec. dir. Circumcision Resource Ctr., Boston, 1991—; owner, prin. Goldman Engring., Boston, 1981—; seminar leader Belmont (Mass.) Ctr. for Psychol. Growth, 1991; lectr. Inteface, Cambridge, Mass., 1992; counselor Circumcision Resource Ctr., Boston, 1992; mem. Adv. Coun. to Internat. Symposia on Circumcision, San Anselmo, Calif., 1992. Singer, musician, songwriter, producer, pub. (mus. album) Bridge to the Unknown, 1990; contbr. articles to profl. jours. Dir., big bro. Jewish Big Bro. Assn., Newton, Mass., 1984-85; mem. Brookline Town Meeting, 1986-92; cons. Adv. Coun. on Pub. Health, Brookline 1990-92; tutor Jewish Vocat. Svc., Brookline, 1989-90. Mem. ASHRAE, Broadcast Music Inc. (writer, pub.), Sierra Club, Amnesty Internat., Appalachian Mountain Club. Office: Circumcision Resource Ctr PO Box 232 Boston MA 02133

GOLDMAN, SAMUEL, family counselor; b. N.Y.C., Mar. 6, 1931; s. Jacob and Rose (Greenberg) G.; m. Isalene Silensky, Mar. 29, 1961; 1 child, Melanie Hope. BA in Edn., L.I. U., 1955; MS in Edn., Hunter Coll., N.Y.C., 1960; MA in Counseling, Manhattan Coll., 1983. Cert. guidance counselor, N.Y. Tchr. Elem. Sch. PS 81, Bronx, Riverdale, N.Y., 1955-81; family counselor Isalene Family Counseling Svc., Riverdale, 1981—, network coord., 1981—, newsletter editor, 1981—, video therapist, 1981—; chpt. leader United Fedn. Tchr., Bronx, 1955-70. Treas. Benjamin Franklin Reform Dem. Club, Riverdale, 1967-68. Mem. AACD, N.Y. State Assn. Counseling and Devel. (seminar sponsor, facilitator, Cert. of Appreciation 1988). Office: Isalene Family Counseling Svc Riverdale Sta PO Box 62 Bronx NY 10471-0062

GOLDMAN, STEPHEN SHEPARD, health science administrator; b. Brockton, Mass., Nov. 24, 1941; s. Maurice and Ethel Goldman; m. Karen Mary Tack, May 27, 1977; 1 child, Matthew. BA, Northeastern U., 1964; MS, U. Ill., 1966, PhD, 1970. Asst. prof. NYU Med. Ctr., N.Y.C., 1978-90; postdoctoral fellow NIH, Bethesda, Md., 1970-72, staff fellow, 1972-78, adminstr. cardiac function br., 1990—. Mem. Am. Physiology Soc., Am. Heart Assn., Am. Soc. for Neurochemistry. Office: NIH Nat Heart Lung & Blood Inst Cardiac Function Br 7550 Wisconsin Ave Bethesda MD 20892-0001

GOLDRING, ELIZABETH, environmental media artist, poet; b. Forest City, Iowa, Feb. 13, 1945; d. James C. and Vera (Farrington) Olson; 1 child, Jessica Tova Farrington Goldring. BA cum laude, Smith Coll., 1967; MEd, Harvard U., 1978. Art tchr. St. Louis Pub. Schs.; exhibits developer The Children's Mus., Boston, 1973-76; fellow Ctr. for Advanced Visual Studies MIT, Cambridge, Mass., 1977—, exhibits and projects dir. Ctr. for Advanced Visual Studies, 1977—, lectr. Dept. of Architecture, 1989; co-dir. Sky Art Conf., CAVS, MIT, 1981-86, project dir. Desert Sun/Desert Moon, 1986. Prin. works include ICA, Boston, 1976, Documenta 6, Kassel, 1977, Smithsonian Institution, Washington, 1978, Secession, Vienna, 1979, Musee de l'art Moderne del la Ville de Paris, 1985, Desert Sun/Desert Moon, Lone Pine, Calif., 1986, (eye/sight interactive installations) Lights/Orot, Yeshiva U. Mus., N.Y.C., 1988, Kunstverein Karlsruhe, Fed. Republic Germany, 1988, Celebration of Light, Savonlinna, Finland, 1989, Washington Project for the Arts, 1989, A Visual Language for the Blind, 1991; contbr. articles to publs; artist/producer (tapes) The Inner Eye-From the Inside Out (audiotapes) International Alarm, 1982, Der Hahnenschrei, 1983, Coyote, 1986, Kikeriki, 1989. NEA InterArts grantee, 1985, Diabetes Rsch. and Edn. grantee, 1986; recipient award for article New Eng. Jour. Optometry, 1990. Office: MIT Ctr Adv Visual Studies MIT W-11 40 Massachusetts Ave Cambridge MA 02139-4132

GOLDSCHMID, MARY TAIT SEIBERT, economist, consultant; b. Oxford, Ohio, July 15, 1947; d. Joseph Charles and Elizabeth Colville (Tait) Seibert; m. Harvey Jerome Goldschmid, Dec. 21, 1973; children: Charles Maxwell, Paul MacNeil, Joseph Tait. Student, London Sch. Econs., 1968; BA, Smith Coll., 1969; MBA, Columbia U., 1973, PhD, 1975. Security analyst Argus Research, N.Y.C., 1969-70; economist Chase Manhattan Bank, N.Y.C., 1970-71, Exxon Corp., N.Y.C., 1974-86, Goldschmid P.C., N.Y.C., 1986—; asst. prof. Coll. of Mt. St. Vincent, N.Y.C., 1988—; econ researcher Personal Capciation, N.Y.C., 1986—. Contbr. articles to profl. jours. Trustee Riverdale Sr. Svcs., 1990—, Riverdale Country Sch., Bronx, 1986-90, pres. Parents Assn., 1986-87. Mem. Am. Econs. Assn., Women's Fin. Assn., Nat. Assn. Bus. Economists. Clubs: Cosmopolitan, Riverdale Yacht. Home: 691 W 247th St Bronx NY 10471-3224

GOLDSCHMIDT, PETER GRAHAM, business development consultant, physician; b. Cardiff, Wales, Feb. 18, 1945; came to U.S., 1970; s. Heinz Joachim Siefried and Marjorie (Sweet) G. DMS, Poly. Cen. London, 1968; MB, BS, U. London, 1970; MPH, Johns Hopkins U., 1971, DPH, 1980. Rsch. assoc. Johns Hopkins U. Sch. Hygiene and Pub. Health, Balt., 1972-75; v.p., dir. Policy Rsch. Inc., Balt., 1974-81, Quality Standards in Medicine, Inc., Bethesda, Md., 1986-90; dir. health svcs. rsch. and devel. svc. VA, Washington, 1981-86; pres. World Devel. Group, Inc., Bethesda, 1986—; bd. dirs. Policy Rsch. Inst., Balt., 1978-87, Quality Standards in Medicine, Inc., Boston; pres. Health Improvement Inst., Bethesda, 1991—. Contbr. numerous articles to profl. jours. Recipient various grants. Mem. AMA, APHA, Ops. Rsch. Soc. Am., Balt.-Washington Venture Group. Office: World Devel Group 5101 River Rd Apt 1913 Bethesda MD 20816-1574

GOLDSMITH, CATHY ELLEN, special education teacher; b. N.Y.C., Feb. 18, 1947; d. Eli D. and Gertrude A. G. BS, NYU, 1968, MA in Elem. Edn., 1971, MA in Ednl. Psychology, 1974. Cert. physs. handicapped, K-6 elem. edn. tchr., N.Y. Formerly tchr. learning disabled, emotionally disturbed adolescents N.Y.C. Bd. Edn., now tchr. trainable retarded children. Represented in permanent collections Bobst Libr. NYU. Bd. dirs. United Jewish Appeal, Fedn. Jewish Philanthropies, B'nai B'rith Hillel Jewish Assn. Coll. Youth. Recipient Charles Oscar Maas Essay award in Am. History, 1968, Disting. Alumni Svc. award NYU, 1987. Mem. Nat. Profl. Assn. in Edn., Coun. for Exceptional Children, Coun. for Learning Disabilities, Found. for Exceptional Children, Orton Dyslexia Soc., N.Y. State-N.Y.C. Assn. Tchrs. Handicapped, NYU Alumni Leadership Coun. (rec. sec.), Pi Lambda Theta (past pres.). Home: 3 Washington Square Village Apt 12J New York NY 10012-1807

GOLDSMITH, JOHN GRAHAM, architect; b. Englewood, N.J., Nov. 26, 1947; s. Samuel Lunt and Sybil (Graham) G.; m. Katherine Goldsmith, Dec. 20, 1975; children: Laura, Stephany, Sage, Courtney, Graham. BA, Syracuse (N.Y.) U., 1970, BArch, 1971; MArch, U. Pa., 1972. Registered architect, Vt., N.H., Maine, Conn., Mass., Fla., N.Y. Architect Vollmer Assocs., N.Y.C., 1972-74, J. Graham Goldsmith, Assocs., Stowe, Vt., 1974-79, Wiemann Lamphere, Architects, Burlington, Vt., 1978-83, J. Graham Goldsmith, Architects, Burlington, 1983—. Co-chmn. architects and engrs. United Way, Burlington, 1990—. Mem. AIA, NCARB, Vt. chpt. AIA. Office: J Graham Goldsmith 7 Kilburn St Burlington VT 05401-4750

GOLDSMITH, LOWELL ALAN, medical educator; b. Bklyn., Mar. 29, 1938; s. Isidore Alexander and Ida (Kaplan) G.; m. Carol Amreich, June 11, 1960; children: Meredith, Eileen. AB, Columbia Coll., 1959; MD, SUNY, Bklyn., 1963. Diplomate Am. Bd. Dermatology. Intern, then resident in medicine UCLA Med. Ctr., 1963-65; resident in dermatology Harvard Med. Sch., Boston, 1967-69; asst. prof. dermatology Harvard U. Med. Sch., Boston, 1970-73; asst. in dermatology Mass. Gen. Hosp., Boston, 1970-71, asst. dermatologist, 1971-73; assoc. prof. medicine Duke U. Med. Ctr., Durham, N.C., 1973-78, prof., 1978-81; James H. Sterner prof. dermatology Sch. Medicine and Dentistry, U. Rochester, N.Y., 1981—, chief dermatology unit, 1981-87, acting chmn. dept. medicine, 1985-87, chmn. dept. dermatology, 1987—; mem. dermatology adv. com. FDA, 1983-87; chmn. Gordon Rsch. Conf. on Epithelial Differentiation and Keratinization, 1987; mem. gen. medicine A study sect. USPHS, NIH, 1988-92, chmn. 1990-92; chmn. med. adv. bd. Nat. Ichthyosis Found., 1981-85, Nat. Alopecia Areata Found., 1981-87, 90—; bd. dirs. Monroe Community Hosp., Rochester, Ctr. Alternatives Animal Testing, Balt.; chmn. NIH Consensus Conf. on Diagnosis and Treatment of Early Melanoma, Bethesda, 1992. Author, editor: Biochemistry and Physiology of the Skin, 1983, 2d edit., 1991; mem. editorial bd. Archives Dermatology, 1982-92, Clinics in Dermatology, 1982, Jour. Investigative Dermatology, 1987-92, Seminars in Dermatology, 1991—; also numerous articles. With USPHS, 1965-67. Recipient Rsch. Career Devel. award USPHS, 1975-80; Macy Found. fellow, 1978-79. Mem. Assn. Am. Physicians, Am. Soc. Clin. Investigation, Soc. Investigative Dermatology (bd. dirs.), N.Y. State Soc. Dermatology (pres. 1985-89), Buffalo-Rochester Dermatology Soc. (pres. 1987), Assn. Profs. Dermatology (bd. dirs. 1984-87, pres.-elect 1990-92), Am. Bd. Dermatology (bd. dirs. 1993—), Nat. Ichthyosis Found. (chmn. mem. adv. bd. 1981-85), Rochester Dermatology Soc., Rochester Acad. Medicine, Polish Dermatol. Assn. (hon.), Alpha Omega Alpha. Office: U Rochester Dept Dermatology 601 Elmwood Ave # 697 Rochester NY 14642-9999

GOLDSMITH, MAXINE IRIS, library administrator; b. Tarrytown, N.Y., Apr. 25, 1947; d. Abraham Herman and Florence (Levinsky) Kaplan; m. Brian P. Goldsmith, Apr. 3, 1971; children: Scott, Leslie. BS, Russell Sage Coll., 1969; MLS, Rugers U., 1970. Reference librarian McGraw-Hill, Inc., N.Y.C., 1970-71; periodicals librarian N.J. State Libr., Trenton, 1971-76; librarian N.J. Div. Criminal Justice, Trenton, 1976-77; libr. adminstr. N.J. Dept. Higher Edn., Trenton, 1978—; bd. dirs. adv. com. Sch. Communications, Info. & Libr. Svc., Rutgers U., New Brunswick, N.J. Editor: (index) Popular Periodicals Index, 1975-91; author: (bibliography) Going to College in New Jersey, 1978, 80, 91. Bd. dirs. after sch. program Hopewell Valley YMCA, Pennington, N.J., 1988—. Mem. Spl. Librs. Assn. (pres. Princeton-Trenton chpt. 1985-86, sec.-treas. edn. div. 1989-91, chair edn. div. 1992-93), Hadassah (fin. sec. Lawrence chpt. 1987—). Jewish. Home: 16 Brandon Rd Trenton NJ 08638-1126 Office: NJ Dept of Higher Edn 20 W State St CN542 Trenton NJ 08625

GOLDSMITH, MERWIN, actor, theater director; b. Detroit, Aug. 7, 1937; s. Max Harold and Alice Flora (Singer) G.; m. Susan Leigh Benson, Mar. 1966 (div. 1969). BA in Theater, UCLA, 1960; student, Bristol Old Vic Theatre Sch., Bristol. Appeared in (stage prodns.) Auntie Mame, 1958, License to Murder, 1964, The Tempest, Trap for a Lonely Man, Phaedra, Gentlemen Prefer Blondes, 1965, Billy Budd, 1967, Fiddler on the Roof, 1968-69, Minnie's Boys, 1970, Much Ado About Nothing, Pal Joey, 1973, Last of the Red Hot Lovers, 1974, Hedda Gabler, 1975, Oklahoma!, 1978, Death of a Salesman, The Importance of Being Ernest, 1982, Hello, Dolly!, 1983, La Boheme, 1984, The Taming of the Shrew, 1985, Hamlet, 1986, Grand Hotel, The Musical, 1991, Merry Widow, 1991, Learned Ladies, 1991; (films) Shamus, 1972, Boardwalk, 1979, So Fine, 1981, Blue Heaven, 1984, Making Mr. Right, 1986, (TV) All My Children, Ryan's Hope, The Guiding Light, Search for Tomorrow, As the World Turns, Another World, Wide World of Mystery, The Connection; dir. stage Dirty Linen, 1977, Vanities, 1980, Me & My Girl, 1988-89, Grand Hotel, 1991. Served with USAFR. Nominated Best Actor in a Mus. award Variety Critics Poll, 1972, Best Supporting Actor in a Mus. award, 1973; nominee Best Actor Mus., Joseph Jefferson Awards, 1972. Mem. AFTRA, SAG, NARAS (Grammy awards voter), Actors Equity Assn., The Players Club. Office: Silver Kass & Massetti 145 W 45th St New York NY 10036-4008

GOLDSMITH, MORTIMER MICHAEL, transportation and purchasing executive; b. Binghamton, N.Y., June 22, 1950; s. Mortimer M. Goldsmith and Agnes E. (Igoe) Munson; m. Mary Ellen Mahoney, July 1, 1970 (div. Mar 1973); m. Susan G. Bartholomew, Apr. 24, 1976; children: Monique Yvonne, Matthew Mortimer. Student profl. related classes, various. Cert. police officer, S.C.; cert. import/export documention. Regional mgr. Nat. Freight Inc., Vineland, N.J., 1978-81; regional v.p. Thurston Motor Lines, Charlotte, N.C., 1981-87; v.p. sales Friedmans Express, Wilkes Barrer, Pa., 1987-89; transp. and purchasing dir. Harper Collins Pubs., Scranton, Pa., 1989—. Vol. Big Bros. Am., Greenville, S.C., 1977; lay leader Faith United Meth. Ch., Fairmont Twp., Pa., 1987—; with exec. series LEadership Wilkes Barre, 1988; sch. dir. Northwest Area Sch. Dist., Shickshinny, Pa., 1991—, pres. bd. dirs. 1991-92. With USMC, 1968-70, Vietnam. Recipient citation Work with Missing/Exploited Children U.S. Senate, 1975, proclamation Gov. Joe Frank Harris, 1975. Mem. Nat. Film Carriers Northeastern Pa., Traffic Club (bd. dirs. 1990), Coun. of Logistics Mgmt. (cert.). Republican. Home: RR 2 Box 2179 Shickshinny PA 18655-9680

GOLDSMITH, VICTOR, marine geologist, environmental educator; b. N.Y.C., Sept. 22, 1940; s. Herman and Rosa (Friedman) G.; 1 child, Jason. BS, Bklyn. Coll. CUNY, 1962; MS, Fla. State U., 1966; PhD, U. Mass., 1972. Researcher Lamont-Doherty Geol. Obs., Nyack, N.Y., 1961-64; petroleum geologist Amoco, New Orleans, 1966-67; prof. marine geology Coll. William and Mary, Williamsburg, Va., 1972-80, Israel Nat. Oceanographic Inst., Haifa, 1980-87; prof. geology and geography Hunter Coll., CUNY, 1988—, exec. officer PhD program earth, environ. scis., 1992; mem. N.Y. State Coastal Task Force, Albany, 1990-92, N.Y. and N.J. Oil Spill Adv. Com., N.Y.C., 1990—. Contbr. over 88 articles to sci. jours. Recipient over 30 rsch. grants. Fellow Explorers Club; mem. N.Y. Acad. Scis. (chmn. geoscis. sect. 1990-91). Jewish. Office: Hunter Coll Geology and Geography Dept 695 Park Ave New York NY 10021-5085

GOLDSTEIN, BERNARD DAVID, physician, educator; b. Bronx, N.Y., Feb. 28, 1939; s. Leon Louis and Emily (Bergen) G.; m. Joyce Lee Cohen, June 2, 1963; children—Lara, Ross. B.S., U. Wis., 1958; M.D., NYU, 1962. Diplomate Am. Bd. Toxicology, Am. Bd. Internal Medicine, Am. Bd. Hematology. Intern, asst. resident, resident 3d and 4th (NYU) med. divs. Bellevue Hosp., N.Y.C., 1962-65; NIH postdoctoral research fellow dept. medicine NYU Med. Ctr., N.Y.C., 1965-66; instr. in medicine Sch. Medicine, NYU, 1968-70, asst. prof. depts. environ. medicine and medicine, 1970-75, assoc. prof., 1975-80; attending physician Bellevue and Univ. Hosps., N.Y.C., 1968-80; prof., chmn. dept. environ. and community medicine U. Medicine and Dentistry, N.J.-Robert Wood Johnson Med. Sch., Piscataway, 1980—; dir. grad. program in pub. health U. Medicine and Dentistry, N.J.-Robert Wood Johnson Med. Sch., 1982-89, dir. environmental and occupational health scis. inst., 1985—; asst. adminstr. for research and devel. EPA, Washington, 1983-85; dir. Nat. Inst. Environ. Health Scis. Ctr. of Excellence, 1988—; chmn. clean air sci. adv. com. EPA, 1982-83; mem. toxicology study sect. NIH, 1980-84, chmn. 1982-84; mem. bd. sci. dirs. Risk Sci. Inst., 1986—; chmn. com. molecular markers NAS, 1986-89, on risk assessment methodology NAS, 1990—, on role of physician in occupational and environ. medicine Inst. Medicine, NAS, 1986—, on enhancing role of primary care practitioners in environ. and occupational health Inst. Medicine, NAS, 1989; chmn. ad hoc com. on dioxin, EPA, 1988-89; vice chmn. sci. group on methodology for sci. evaluation chems., 1989—; chmn. mem. working group

on Air Quality Guidelines for Major Urban Air Pollutants, 1985; mem. health rev. com. Health Effects Inst., 1987—; mem. nat. adv. environ. health effects coun. NIH, 1987-91; bd. dirs. Lovelace Inst., Weston Inc., Internat. Life Sci. Inst. Contbr. articles to profl. jours., chpts. to books. Fellow Am. Coll. Preventive Medicine, ACP.; mem. NAS Inst. Medicine, WHO Commn. on Health and Environment, Am. Soc. Clin. Investigation. Home: 417 Prospect St Westfield NJ 07090-4007 Office: U Medicine Dentistry NJ Robert Wood Johnson Med Sch Dept Environ Community Medicine Piscataway NJ 08854

GOLDSTEIN, DONALD MAURICE, historian, educator; b. N.Y.C., Dec. 15, 1932; s. Max A. and Jean M. Goldstein; B.A., U. Md., 1954, M.A., 1962; M.S., Georgetown U., 1963; M.P.A., George Washington U., 1965; Ph.D., U. Denver, 1970; grad. War Coll., 1973, Air Command and Staff Coll., 1965; m. Mariann Norma Zinck, Aug. 5, 1961; children—Tammie, Timmie, Tommie, Teri. Commd. 2d lt. U.S. Air Force, 1955, advanced through grades to lt. col., 1972; comdr. missile site, Taiwan, 1958-59; staff officer U.S. Strike Command, 1961-64; research assoc. Airstaff Pentagon; assoc. prof. history USAF Acad., 1965-71, asst. track coach, 1965-71; ret., 1977; assoc. prof. history Troy (Ala.) State U., 1971-74; prof. aerospace studies U. Pitts., 1975-77, assoc. prof. public and internat. affairs, 1975—, dir. placement and alumni, 1977-85, assoc. dean, 1985—. Decorated Soldiers medal, Meritorious Service medal with 2 oak leaf clusters, Joint Service Commendation medal, Air Force Commendation medal with oak leaf cluster. Mem. Am. Hist. Assn., Internat. Studies Assn., Am. Soc. Public Adminstrs., Am. Polit. Sci. Assn., Air Force Assn., Omicron Delta Kappa, Phi Kappa Phi, Phi Alpha Theta, Sigma Nu. Roman Catholic. Club: Toastmasters. Author: Ennis C. Whitehead Aerospace Commander, 1970; Adolph Hitler in the Perspective of the American Press, 1961; Adolph Hitler Adminstrator of a Society, 1965; (with others) Miracle at Midway, 1982, Target Tokyo: The Story of the Surge Spy Ring in Japan, 1984; collaborator: At Dawn We Slept: The Untold Story of Pearl Harbor, 1981; Pearl Harbor: The Verdict of History, 1985, December 7, 1941: the Day the Japanese Attacked Pearl Harbor, 1988, God's Samurai Lead Pilot at Pearl Harbor, 1990, Fading Victory: The Diary of Matome Ugaki, 1991, The Way it Was: A Pictorial History of Pearl Harbor, 1991, The Williwar War: The Arkansas National Guard in World War II, 1992. Asst. editor papers on fgn. policy for House Com. on Internat. Affairs, 1947-54. Contbr. articles on def. policy and nat. security affairs to profl. jours. Home: 2146 Meadowmont Dr Upper St Clair Pittsburgh PA 15241 Office: U Pitts Grad Sch Pub Int Affairs Dean's Office Forbes Complex 3G-35 Pittsburgh PA 15260

GOLDSTEIN, DORIS MUELLER, librarian, researcher; b. Somerville, N.J., Mar. 11, 1942; d. Henry Frederick and Sophie (Lages) Mueller; m. Steven Morris Goldstein, July 4, 1971. BA, U. Nebr., 1964, MA, 1966; cert., Goethe U., Frankfurt, Fed. Republic Germany, 1966; MLS, U. Md., 1973. Vol., instr. Peace Corps, Addis Abeba, Ethiopia, 1966-68; cataloger Libr. of Congress, Washington, 1968-69; instr. Bowie (Md.) State Coll., 1969-72; libr. Kennedy Inst. of Ethics Georgetown U., Washington, 1973-81, dir. libr. and info. svcs., 1981—, dir. Nat. Reference Ctr. for Bioethics Lit., 1984—; cons. dept. nursing George Mason U., Fairfax, Va., 1984-89; adj. faculty mem. in libr. sci. U. Md., 1990. Author: Bioethics: A Guide to Information Sources, 1982; editor Scope Note Series, 1985—; contbr. articles to profl. jours. Ford Found. grantee, 1964. Mem. Spl. Librs. Assn., Med. Libr. Assn., D.C. Libr. Assn., Phi Beta Kappa, Alpha Lambda Delta, Delta Phi Alpha, Beta Phi Mu (pres. Iota chpt. 1985-86). Office: Georgetown U Kennedy Inst Ethics Washington DC 20057

GOLDSTEIN, ELEANOR, artist, social worker; b. N.Y.C., May 2, 1935; d. Benjamin and Gertrude (Bober) Kronish; m. Alvin Goldstein, Dec. 27, 1959; children: Eric, Michael, Eileen. BA, Bennington (Vt.) Coll., 1957; MSW, Columbia U., 1981. Cert. social worker, N.Y. Asst. dir. Westchester Student Adv. Coalition, White Plains, N.Y., 1981-82, exec. dir., 1982-85; free lance artist Hastings-on-the-Hudson, N.Y., 1985—. Bd. dirs. Hastings-on-the-Hudson Recreation Commn., 1976-78; v.p. Hastings Learning Disabilities Com., 1974-76; organizer Hastings Com. for Youth, Inc., 1976-79. Mem. Hudson River Contemporary Artists, Nat. Assn. Women Artists, Hastings League Women Voters (bd. dirs. 1973-75). Home and Office: 1 Chester Ter Hastings Hdsn NY 10706-3907

GOLDSTEIN, FRED, accountant; b. N.Y.C., Aug. 24, 1924; s. Max and Mary (Frisch) G.; m. Roslyn Weissman, Dec. 24, 1953; children: Lori Beth, Barry Mark. BBA cum laude, CCNY, 1950; MBA, NYU, 1952. CPA. Ptnr. Wertheim & Co., N.Y.C., 1959—; lectr. Found. Acctg. Edn., N.Y.C., 1986. Pres. South Park Civic Assn., Roslyn, 1962-63, Temple Sinai Brotherhood, Roslyn, 1979-80, of Temple Sinai, 1987-89; mem. exec. bd. N.Y. Fed. Union, N.Y. State chpt. Union of Am. Hebrew Congregations. Decorated Bronze Star, Purple Heart. Mem. AICPA, N.Y. State Soc. CPAs, Jewish Chautauqua Soc. (life). Jewish. Home: 34 Peachtree Ln Roslyn Heights NY 11577-2416 Office: Wertheim & Co 225 W 34th St New York NY 10122-0008

GOLDSTEIN, GARRY ARNOLD, internist, occupational medicine physician; b. Norfolk, Va., Jan. 4, 1931; s. Sam Ralph and Sarah (Kaminsky) G.; m. Carol Michael Hayes, June 26, 1958; children: Beth Allison Goldstein Oliphant, Brad L., Steven R. BA, Duke U., 1952; MD, U. Va., 1959. Med. intern U. Ala., 1959-60, asst. resident in medicine, 1960-61; rsch. fellow in medicine Beth Israel Hosp., Harvard Med. Sch., Boston, 1961-62, chief resident in medicine, 1963-64; postdoctoral fellow in biochemistry MIT, Cambridge, 1962-63; pvt. practice, 1964-89; med. dir. Holmes Transp. Co. of New Eng., 1980-85; regional med. examiner UPS, 1980-85; med. dir. GM C.P.C., Framingham, Mass., 1985-89, GM B.O.C., Wilmington, Del., 1989—. Contbr. articles to profl. jours. Past dir. Algonquin Coun. Boy Scouts of Am., Framingham Country Club; corporator Framingham Union Hosp. With U.S. Army, 1952-54; sr. asst. surgeon USPHS, 1959—. Recipient Cert. of Merit, ARC, 1954. Mem. AMA, Am. Coll. Occupational Medicine, Del. Coll. Occupational Medicine, Am. Diabetes Assn., Am. Heart Assn., Mass. Med. Soc., Del. Med. Soc., New Castle County Med. Soc., Del. Acad. Medicine, Radley Run Country Club, Beta Beta Beta. Jewish. Office: GM BOC/LAD Boxwood & Centerville Rds Wilmington DE 19806

GOLDSTEIN, HENRY, fund raising, management and public relations consultant; b. N.Y.C., Nov. 6, 1933; s. Morris and Frances (Sholdar) G.; children: Janet, Jonathan. BS in Journalism, NYU, 1954, postgrad., 1958-61. Campaign dir. United Community Chest, Paterson, N.J., 1956-58, Greater N.Y. Fund, N.Y.C., 1958-64; with The Oram Group, Inc., N.Y.C., 1964—, pres., chief exec. officer, 1978—; adj. prof. Grad. Sch. Mgmt. and Urban Professions New Sch. Social Rsch., N.Y.C. Co-author: Dear Friend: Mastering the Art of Direct Mail Fund Raising; columnist Non-profit Times. Bd. dirs., mem. adv. com. Nat. Assn. Drug Abuse Problems; mem. scholarship awards com. Jackie Robinson Found.; bd. dirs. Soho Repertory Theater Co., Inc.; Berkshire Theatre Festival. With U.S. Army, 1954-56. Mem. Nat. Soc. Fund Raising Execs., Pub. Rels. Soc. Am., 60 East Club, N.Y. Road Runners Club. Office: 275 Madison Ave New York NY 10016-1101

GOLDSTEIN, HOWARD BERNARD, investment banker, advertising and marketing executive; b. Bronx, N.Y., Dec. 4, 1943; s. Maurice and Matilda Goldstein; B.F.A., Pratt Inst., 1970; m. Susan Nadine Goldberg, June 25, 1967; children—Jill Alecya, Brett Adam. Art dir. Fairfax Advt. div. Ogilvy & Mather, Inc., N.Y.C., 1968-72; creative dir. Hoffman Advt., N.Y.C., 1972-80, Miller, Addison, Steele, Inc., N.Y.C., 1980-82; pres. Gould Advt., Cliffside Park, N.J., 1969—; registered securities broker,1969, br. officer tax shelter coordinator E.F. Hutton & Co., Inc., 1983-85; registered security broker, sr. v.p., mem chmn.'s coun., dir.'s coun. Lehman Bros. Shearson Lehman Bros., Inc., 1985—, guided portfolio mgmt. Lehman Bros. Shearson Lehman Bros., Inc., 1985—. Winston Tower 200, Condominium Assn.; mem. Internat. Assn. Fin. Planning, Inst. Cert. Fin. Planners, Coll. Cert. Fin. Planners, Denver Grad. Police & Fire Acad. of Bergen County, N.J., June 12, 1986. Fin. officer N.J. State Police Office of Emergency Mgmt., Cliffside Park, 1986; spl. police officer Cliffside Park Police Dept., N.J. State Police Benevolent Assn., 1986—; mem. steering com. Coalation Bus., Labor and Community Orgns. of N.Y., 1992; mem. Rep. Senatorial Inner Circle , 1992.; mem. Graphic Artists Guild, 1976-80, Bronx County Hist. Soc., 1968-71, Cliffside Park Baseball Assn., 1979—, coach, 1981, 83; sponsor Project High Frontier, U.S. Govt., 1986, sustaining mem. Rep. Nat. Com., 1981—; preferred mem. U.S. Senatorial Club, 1984—; Sachs art scholar, 1955; Exhibited Bronx Hist. Soc. photo show, N.Y.C., 1970; paintings at Soc. of Illustrators show, 1971-72; numerous other shows. Recipient medal for art service Youth Friends Assn., 1961, Ga. Pacific award, 1978. Mem. Tenafly Rifle and Pistol Club Inc., Nat. Rifle Assn. Jewish. Clubs: Fort Lee Racquetball. Lodge: Bnai Brith. Address: 200 Winston Dr Cliffside Park NJ 07010

GOLDSTEIN, IRVING ROBERT, mechanical and industrial engineer, educator, consultant; b. Jersey City, N.J., Apr. 28, 1916; s. David and Anna (Krug) G.; m. Natalie E. Glattstein, Jan. 30, 1949; children: Barbara Joy, David Lee. BSME, Newark Coll. Engring.; MSME, Stevens Inst. Tech., 1947. Registered profl. engr., N.J., Calif. Field worker, N.J. Dept. Edn., 1938-39, indsl. engr., Maidenform Co., 1939-40, cost analyst, William Bal Corp., 1940-41, resident insp. N.Y. Ordinance Dist., 1941-43, sales rep., Eagle Hosiery Co., 1946-47, instr. dept. indsl. and mgmt. engring. N.J. Inst. Tech., 1947-50, asst. prof., 1950-55, assoc. prof., 1955-70, prof., 1970-81, prof. emeritus, 1981—, prof. dept. info. sci. and systems, Fairleigh Dickinson U., 1992—; cons. engr. Irving R. Goldstein, P.E., Springfield, N.J., 1967—; lectr. in field; examiner profl. engring. exam State of N.J., 1967-82; rep. Am. Nat. Standards Inst., 1970-83, Engr. Joint Coun. Com. for Am. Bicentennial, 1975-78; vice-chmn. N.J. Engrs. Com. for Student Guidance, 1981-83, state meetings coord., 1974-81, treas., 1983-86. Contbr. articles to profl. jours. Served with U.S. Army, 1943-46, ETO. Fellow Inst. Indsl. Engrs. (life, dir. work measurement and method engring div. 1970-73, conf. chmn. 1973-81, publs. chmn. 1966-70, Phil Carroll Achievement award 1975, pres. Met. N.J. chpt. 1977-78, v.p. rsch. and edn. 1968-73, 75-76, 79-81, chmn. bd. gov.'s Metro N.J. chpt. 1966-68, 81-82, faculty advisor N.J. Inst. Tech. U. chpt. 1962-77, Disting. Svc. award Met. N.J. chpt. 1970, 76, 85, Walter Salabun award 1989, historian Metro N.J. chpt. 1980—, dir. student affairs Dist. 2, 1989-90); mem. ASME (life), Ops. Rsch. Soc. Am., Inst. Mgmt. Scis., Nat. Soc. Profl. Engrs., Prodn. Ops. Mgmt. Soc., N.Y. Acad. Scis., Order of Engr., Alpha Pi Mu, Pi Tau Sigma. Address: 21 Janet Ln Springfield NJ 07081

GOLDSTEIN, JEFFREY HASKELL, psychology educator; b. Norwalk, Conn., Aug. 11, 1942; s. Robert and Sylvia (Schwartz) G. BA, U. Conn., 1964; MS, Boston U., 1966; PhD, Ohio State U., 1969. Prof. psychology Temple U., Phila., 1973—; vis. prof. Inst. of Edn. U. London, 1987-89, U. Utrecht (The Netherlands), 1990—; cons. British Toy and Hobby Assn., London, 1987—, Toy Mfrs. Europe, 1990—. Author: Aggression and Crimes of Violence, 1986; co-author: Psychology: An Introduction, 1990; editor: Sports, Games and Play, 1989; editor jour. Current Psychology, 1988-89. Fellow Am. Psychol. Assn. Am. Psychol. Soc., Internat. Soc. for Rsch. on Aggression (Idiodynamics award); mem. Nat. Toy Coun. (Eng.). Office: Temple U Dept Psychology Philadelphia PA 19122

GOLDSTEIN, JEFFREY MARC, pharmacologist; b. Bronx, N.Y., May 9, 1947; s. Joseph and Shirley (Scher) G.; B.S. in Biology, Colo. State U., 1970; M.S. in Biology, Seton Hall U., 1973; Ph.D. in Neurosci., U. Del., 1980; m. Robin Small, Aug. 22, 1971; children—Kevin Alan, Neal David. Asso. scientist Schering Corp., Bloomfield, N.J., 1970-76; prin. pharmacologist ICI Pharms. Group, Wilmington, Del., 1976—. Mem. AAAS, N.Y. Acad. Scis., Am. Soc. Pharmacology and Exptl. Therapeutics, Soc. Neurosci., Sigma Xi. Research and publs. in field. Home: 4 Curry Ct Wilmington DE 19810-3312 Office: ICI Pharms Group Wilmington DE 19897

GOLDSTEIN, JOEL SAMUEL, information systems company executive, consultant; b. Bayonne, N.J., Sept. 28, 1942; s. Philip and Beatrice Leah (Cohan) G.; m. Vicki Rose Goldstein, Nov. 26, 1968 (div.); 1 child, David Eric; m. Rebecca Goldstein, Jan. 5, 1980. BS in Mgmt., Rutgers U., Newark, 1970. Sr. programmer Prudential Ins. Co., Newark, 1963-71; sr. cons. ITT Data Svcs., Paramus, N.J., 1969-71; project mgr. Consol. Edison, N.Y.C., 1971-73; mgr. tech. support N.Y. Telephone, N.Y.C., 1973-75, Mut. Benefit Life Ins. Co., Newark, 1977-80; v.p. system devel. Communications Internat., N.Y.C., 1975-76; sr. cons. Coopers & Lybrand, N.Y.C., 1976-77; v.p. info. systems RCA, N.Y.C., 1980; pres., chief exec. officer Responsive Systems Co., Morganville, N.J., 1981—; bd. dirs. TRIDEX; lectr. nat. and internat. seminars, 1989—. Contbr. articles to profl. jours. and mags. With U.S. Army, 1964-66. Mem. Computer Measurement Group (nat. program com. 1989—, bd. dirs. N.E. region 1991—), Assn. for Computing Machinery (chmn. program com. 1982-83), Am. Mgmt. Assn. (div. pres.), Soc. Info. Mgmt., Knauer DB2 User Group (chmn. spl. interest group 1990-91), Delaware Valley DB2 User Group (program com. 1991—). Office: Responsive Systems Co 281 Hwy 79 N Morganville NJ 07751-1157

GOLDSTEIN, JOEL WILLIAM, federal agency administrator; b. Chgo., June 5, 1939; s. Harold and Adeline (Laskin) G.; m. Marcia Ruth Gray, June 4, 1963; children: Lauren, Daniel. BA, Grinnell Coll., 1961; MA, U. Kans., 1963, PhD, 1966. Asst. prof. Carnegie-Mellon U., Pitts., 1966-74; health scientist adminstr. NIMH, Rockville, Md., 1974-85; dep. assoc. adminstr. Alcohol, Drug Abuse and Mental Health Adminstrn., Rockville, 1985—. Contbr. articles to profl. jours. USPHS fellow, 1963-66; Falk Med. Fund grantee, 1969, 70. Mem. Soc. Experimental Social Psychology, Am. Psychol. Assn. Home: 11610 Gowrie Ct Rockville MD 20854-3623 Office: ADAMHA 5600 Fishers Ln Rm 13103 Rockville MD 20857-0001

GOLDSTEIN, JOSHUA, playwright; b. Washington, July 4, 1953; s. Joseph and Sonja (Lambek) G.; m. Marilene Simone Phipps, July 3, 1988. Student, Antioch Coll., 1972-73; BA, Yale U., 1976. Reporter contbr. New Republic Mag., Washington, 1978; playwright Transatlantic, New Haven, 1982, Presumed World, New Haven, 1984-86; staff writer Embassy TV, L.A., 1985; playwright Martin Night, New Haven, 1985-86, Hate, Boston, 1988-89; scriptwriter In the Red, New Haven, 1990; playwright The End, New Haven, 1991, Our Baby's First Seven Years, New Haven, 1991; scriptwriter: Moonlight Rides, New Haven, 1992.

GOLDSTEIN, KENNETH K., journalism educator, editor, writer; b. N.Y.C., Apr. 4, 1926; s. Morris B. and Rebecca (Bagdan) G.; m. Irene Frances, May 4, 1956; children: Marianne Elaine, Gordon Mitchell. BA, Kent State U., 1948; MA, U. Mich., 1951; cert. in sci. writing, Columbia U., 1966. Cub reporter N.Y. Daily News, N.Y.C., 1942-43; reporter Washtenaw Post-Tribune, Ann Arbor, Mich., 1950-51; copy chief New World Pub. Rels., N.Y.C., 1948-50; resident playwright Erie (Pa.) Playhouse, 1951-53; reporter, columnist Erie Dispatch-Herald, 1953-56; sci. editor, corr. UPI-Movietone, N.Y.C., 1956-63; editor, producer, sci. writer CBS-TV, N.Y.C., 1963-68; prof., assoc. dean Grad. Sch. Journalism Columbia U., N.Y.C., 1968—; cons. editor Sci. Digest, N.Y.C., 1979-82, GEO Mag., N.Y.C., 1979-82; writer Family Weekly USA Weekend, N.Y.C., 1982-83. Author: The World of Tomorrow, 1967, New Frontiers of Medicine, 1974; editor: California Science: A Reporter's View, 1969; contbr. articles to numerous jours. Bd. dirs. Armstrong Meml. Found., 1969—; mem. environ. health com. N.Y. Acad. Medicine, 1988; mem. media com. Am. Inst. Physics. 1st lt. USAF. Decorated D.F.C., Air medal; Sloan-Rockefeller Found. fellow Columbia U., 1965-66; recipient Mayor's Commendation award City of N.Y., 1964, Hopwood awrd in drama, 1951. Fellow N.Y. Acad. Sci.; mem. Nat. Assn. Sci. Writers. Jewish. Office: Columbia U Grad Sch Journalism New York NY 10027

GOLDSTEIN, LARRY SAMUEL, marketing educator; b. N.Y.C., May 21, 1943; s. Harry and Ida (Cohen) G.; m. Margaret Frenkel, June 12, 1966; children: Avram, Akiva. BBA, CUNY, 1965; MA, Columbia U., 1967; MBA, CUNY, 1978, PhD, 1980. Asst. prin. Beth Jacob Schs., Bklyn., 1967-69; sales mgr. Olivetti Corp., N.Y.C., 1969-71; mktg. mgr. C. Itoh & Co., Inc., N.Y.C., 1971-73; instr. Montclair State Coll., Upper Montclair, N.J., 1973-78; assoc. prof. Iona Coll., New Rochelle, N.Y., 1978—; cons. SBA, N.J., 1974-78, New Rochelle Planning Com., 1979, Tri-Star Component Products, Bronx, N.Y., 1985-87, Chase Manhattan Bank, White Plains, N.Y., 1989; chmn. dept. mktg. Iona Coll., 1983-90. Contbr. articles to profl. jours. Mem. Community Planning Bd. # 3, Manhattan, 1967-71. Mem. Am. Mktg. Assn., Point-of-Purchase Advt. Inst., Educom, Direct Mktg. Assn., Beta Gamma Sigma. Home: 74-10 175th St Flushing NY 11366 Office: Iona Coll Dept of Mktg 715 North Ave New Rochelle NY 10801-1890

GOLDSTEIN, LEONARD BARRY, dentist, educator; b. Seaford, N.Y., Feb. 6, 1944; s. Jacob Martin and Adele (Pelzner) G.; m. Phyllis Lynn Kerwin, June 25, 1967; children: Marcie Ilene, Sherri Elysse. Student, Ind. U., 1961-63; DDS, Case Western Reserve U., 1967; Cert. in Orthodontics, Dewey Sch. Orthodontics, N.Y.C., 1969; PhD in Electro-Medicine, City U., Los Angeles, 1988. Diplomate Am. Acad. of Pain Mgmt. Gen. practice dentistry Smithtown, N.Y., 1969—; attending orthodontist Abe Stark Philanthropies Dental Clinic, Bklyn., 1970-77; guest prof. Dept. Phys. Edn. Queens Coll., N.Y., 1979—; guest lectr. Dept. Phys. Edn. Queensboro (N.Y.) Community Coll., 1980—; dir. dental services Good Samaritan Profl. Services, St. James, N.Y., 1979—, v.p. med. bd., 1979—; attending dental staff St. John's Episc. Hosp., 1980—, Community Hosp. Western Suffolk, 1980—; bd. dirs. L.I. Ctr. for Cranio-Facial Pain, Smithtown. Contbr. articles to profl. jours. Served to capt. Dental Corps, U.S. Army, 1967-69. Recipient fellowship in removeable prosthetics U.S. Army Dental Corps, 1967. Fellow Acad. Stress and Chronic Disease, Acad. Gen. Dentistry, Am. Endodontic Soc.; mem. Am. Equilibration Soc., Am. Coll. Sports Medicine, Internat. Acad. Preventive Medicine, Cranial Acad. of Am. Osteopathic Soc., Am. Orthodontic Soc., Internat. Soc. Orthodontists, Am. Dental Soc., Cronio-Mandibular Study Club of N.Y., L.I. Gnathological Study Club, Northeastern Gnathological Soc. Home: 178 Alexander Ave PO Box 217 Nesconset NY 11767 Office: 50 Route 111 Smithtown NY 11787-3700

GOLDSTEIN, MARJORIE TUNICK, special education educator; b. Port Chester, N.Y., Oct. 20, 1940; d. Abraham and Gertrude (Gluckman) Tunick; m. Herbert Goldstein, May 27, 1973. BA, Syracuse U., 1961; MA, George Washington U., 1968; PhD, Yeshiva U., N.Y.C., 1979. Spl. edn. tchr. Lancaster (Pa.) City Pub. Schs., 1962-63, Hempfield Union Schs., Landisville, Pa., 1963-64, Montgomery County (Md.) Pub. Schs., 1964-65; edn. specialist U.S. Office Edn., Washington, 1965-69; coord. field ops. Curriculum R&D Ctr., Yeshiva U., N.Y.C., 1969-78; supr. spl. edn. E. Ramapo Cen. Sch. Dist., Spring Valley, N.Y., 1978-79; adj. asst. prof. Herbert Lehman Coll., Bronx, 1980-83; spl. edn. coord. Ednl. Improvement Ctr./NE, W. Orange, N.J., 1981-83; assoc. prof. William Paterson Coll. of N.J., Wayne, N.J., 1983—; spl. needs book reviewer Instr. mag., N.Y.C., 1984-90; co-developer entry level cert. tests Pa. Ednl. Testing Svc., Princeton, 1985-88. Cons. editor Career Devel. for Exceptional Individuals, 1988—. Contbr. articles to profl. jours. Office Spl. Edn. and Rehab. Svc./Dept. Edn. grantee, 1987-90; named Educator of Yr., Morris County ARC, 1991, N.J. Assn. Retarded Citizens, 1991. Mem. ASCD, Coun. Exceptional Children (N.J. div. on career devel. sec. 1988), Am. Assn. Mental Deficiency, Am. Ednl. Rsch. Assn., N.J. Assn. Supervision and Curriculum Devel. (assoc. exec. dir. 1984-85, 86-87, 89-91). Office: William Paterson Coll NJ 300 Pompton Rd Wayne NJ 07470-5172

GOLDSTEIN, MARTIN BARNET, osteopathic physician, psychiatrist; b. N.Y.C., Jan. 9, 1933; s. Samuel Eli and Bessie Leah (Kurman) G.; m. Nov. 23, 1963. BS in Pharmacy, L.I. U., 1955; DO, Chgo. Coll. Osteo. Medicine, 1959. Diplomate Am. Osteo. Bd. Neuropsychiatry, Am. Bd. Sexology. Intern Met. Hosp., Phila., 1959-60; pvt. practice Phila., 1960—; pres., chief exec. officer Neuro-Rsch. Inc., Phila., 1978-84, Lafayette Psychiat. Assocs., Whitemarsh, Pa., 1981-84; chmn. bd. dirs. Equibank Del., Wilmington, 1987-89; bd. dirs. Equimark, Pitts., 1985-89. Editor Jour. Med. Aspects Human Sexuality, 1986-90; contbr. over 100 articles to med. jours. Mem. Penn Valley (Pa.) Civic Assn., 1966—. Fellow Am. Coll. Neuropsychiatrists, Am. Acad. Clin. Sexologists; mem. Am. Osteo. Assn. (editorial referee Jour. 1966—), Am. Psychiat. Assn., Pa. Osteo. Med. Asssn., Phila. Osteo. Med. Assn., Philadelphia County Osteo. Soc. Republican. Jewish. Office: 2400 Chestnut St Apt 2506 Philadelphia PA 19103-4323

GOLDSTEIN, MARVIN NORMAN, physician; b. Balt., Aug. 10, 1940; s. Manuel Quezon and Sylvia (Wagenheim) G.; m. Athene Schuffmann, July 1, 1962; children: Joshua, Claire. AB summa cum laude, Western Md. Coll., 1960; MD, U. Md., 1964. Diplomate Am. Bd. Psychiatry and Neurology. Intern in internal medicine U. Chgo. Hosp., 1964-65; resident in neurology Strong Meml. Hosp., U. Rochester, N.Y., 1965-68; chief resident in neurology Strong Meml. Hosp., U. Rochester, 1967-68; asst. attending neurologist, instr. U. Md. Hosp., Balt., 1968-69, Johns Hopkins Hosp., Balt., 1969-70; asst. prof. neurology and anatomy U. Rochester Sch. Medicine and Dentistry, 1970-74, clin. asst. prof. neurology and anatomy, 1974-78, clin. assoc. prof. neurology and anatomy, 1978—; sr. attending neurology The Genesee Hosp., Rochester, 1978—; instr. in neurology and anatomy U. Rochester Sch. Medicine and Dentistry, 1965-68, Sch. Medicine, Georgetown U., Washington, 1968-70; staff neurologist U.S. Naval Hosp., Bethesda, 1968-70; med. staff exec. com. The Genesee Hosp., Rochester, 1989-90. Contbr. articles to profl. jours. Bd. dirs. Rochester Area Multiple Sclerosis, Rochester, 1972-78: adult edn. com. Temple Beth El, Rochester, 1985-90. Lt. comdr. USNR, 1968-70. Grantee NIH, 1972-74. Fellow Am. Acad. Neurology, Royal Soc. Medicine; mem. Am. Epilepsy Soc., Am. Acad. Clin. Neurophysiology, Sigma Xi. Home: 20 Varinna Dr Rochester NY 14618-1508 Office: 220 Alexander St Rochester NY 14607-4004

GOLDSTEIN, MILTON, art educator; b. Holyoke, Mass., Nov. 14, 1914; s. Jacob Bernard and Sarah (Peskin) G.; m. Mollie Brick. Student, Northeastern U., 1934-35, Art Students League, 1939-41, 46-49. Part-time instr. Art. Students League, N.Y.C., 1948-65; instr. graphics arts dept. Adelphi U., Garden City, N.Y., 1953-56, asst. prof., 1956-59, assoc. prof., 1959-65, prof., 1965-85, prof. emeritus, 1985. Represented in permanent collections Mus. Modern Art, Pila. Mus. Art, Met. Mus., Bklyn. Mus., Smithsonian Nat. Mus., Libr. Congress, and other pub. and pvt. collections in Am. and Europe; several one-man shows (nat. prizes and purchase awards); inventor color printing method for making color etchings. With U.S. Army, 1942-45. Guggenheim fellow, 1950. Fellow Royal Soc. Arts; mem. Soc. Am. Graphic Artists, Art Student League (life). Home: 56 16 219th St Bayside NY 11364 Office: Adelphi U Dept Art and Art History Blodgett Hall Rm 302 Garden City NY 11530

GOLDSTEIN, MILTON HOUSEMAN, rehabilitation facility administrator; b. Bklyn., Jan. 10, 1937; s. Benjamin and Gertrude (Houseman) G.; m. Ella Stickle Goldstein, Sept. 18, 1961; children: Cindy Goldstein Getty, Alan Goldstein. BS, NYU, 1959. Vocat. trainer United Cerebral Palsy Assn., Roosevelt, L.I., N.Y., 1959-61; workshop supr. Internat. Ctr. for Disabled, N.Y.C., 1961-63; exec. dir. Gateway Industries Inc., Kingston, N.Y., 1963-65, The Workshop Inc., Menands, N.Y., 1965-82; pres. MGA Assocs., Albany, N.Y., 1982-85; exec. dir. Challenge Industries Inc., Ithaca, N.Y., 1985—; mem. adv. bd. N.Y. State Sch. Indsl. and Labor Rels., Cornell U., Ithaca, 1987—; v.p. Finger Lakes Indsl. Ctr., Ithaca, 1988-90; bd. dirs. N.Y. State Assn. Rehab. Facilities, Albany, 1986-89. With U.S. Army N.G., 1957-63. Mem. Tompkins County Mental Health Assn. (pres. 1990-91), Tompkins County C. of C. (bd. dirs. 1988—, v.p. 1990-91, chmn. bd. 1992), Rotary. Home: 29 Hunter Ln Ithaca NY 14850-9662 Office: Challenge Industries Inc 402 E State St Ithaca NY 14850-4498

GOLDSTEIN, MINDY SUE, biologist; b. N.Y.C., July 20, 1952; d. Seymour and Ida (Silver) Zibitt; m. Jerome Sydney Goldstein, Aug. 5, 1972; children: Ila Beth, Cori Anne. BS cum laude, NYU, 1974, MS, 1978, PhD, 1983; postgrad., SUNY, Stony Brook, 1983-85. Staff scientist Applied Genetics, Freeport, N.Y., 1985-87; mgr. lab. svcs. Collaborative Labs., East Setauket, N.Y., 1987—. Patentee absorbable bandage. Mem. Am. Soc. for Cell Biology, AAAS, N.Y. Acad. Sci. Jewish. Office: Collaborative Labs 3 Technology Dr East Setauket NY 11733

GOLDSTEIN, NAOMI, psychiatrist; b. N.Y.C., Apr. 24, 1932; d. Eli and Caroline (Kleppner) G.; m. Franklin Feldman, June 3, 1956; children: Sarah, Eve, Jacob. AB, Vassar Coll., 1952; MD, N.Y. Med. Coll., 1956. Diplomate Am. Bd. Psychiatry and Neurology. Pvt. practice N.Y.C., 1960—; psychiat. adminstr. N.Y.C. Probation Methadone Clinic, Bernstein Inst., 1970-72; dir. Supreme and Criminal Ct. Psychiat. Clinics, 1968-72; staff psychiatrist Liaison Svc. Bellevue Hosp., 1972-74; chief psychiatry Met. Correction Ctr. Fed. Bur. Prisons, N.Y.C., 1974-78; attending psychiatrist Bellevue Hosp., 1978-90; clin. prof. psychiatry Med. Sch. NYU, N.Y.C., 1990—; clin. prof. psychiatry NYU Med. Sch., N.Y.C., 1990—; pres. Am. Bd. Forensic Psychiatry, Balt., 1988-89; mem. N.Y. State Bd. profl. Med. Conduct, Albany, 1978—, chmn., 1982-84; lectr. Columbia Law Sch., Columbia U., N.Y.C., 1988; mem. bd. advisors Fed. Correctional Instn., Otisville, N.Y., 1980-85. Contbr. articles to profl. jours. Fellow Am. Psychiat. Assn. (trustee-at-large 1982-85, pres. N.Y. County dist. br. 1985-86), N.Y. Acad. Medicine, Am. Acad. Psychiatry and The Law, Assn.

Women Psychiatrists, Am. Med. Women's Assn.; mem. AMA, Acad. Hon. Soc. N.Y. Med. Coll., Phi Beta Kappa. Jewish. Office: 16 E 79th St New York NY 10021-0150

GOLDSTEIN, NEIL WARREN, filmmaker; b. Washington, June 3, 1950; s. Alfred Frank and Tillie (Garber) G.; m. Janice Posatery Burke, Mar. 28, 1981; 1 child, Evan Benjamin. BA, Washington U., St. Louis, 1972, MA, 1974. Dir. instl. tech. Childrens Hosp., L.A., 1975-82; chief exec. officer Corp. Disabilities and Telecommunication, L.A., 1982-88; chmn. East Coast chpt. Corp. Disabilities and Telecommunication, Phila., 1988—; pres. Central Coast Community TV, L.A., 1982, Concept Works, Inc., L.A. 1980-82; co-founder Lyme Project, Phila., 1988—; vice chmn. Pub. Health Planning Group, Phila., 1988. Dir., producer film festival Superfest, 1976-88 (CC Robinson award 1987); exec. producer TV spl. Superfest, 1982-89 (Emmy 1986, Gov. award 1989); dir., producer TV spl. Breaking Ground, 1987 (Gov. award 1988, Presdl. Commendation 1988, Emmy nominee), Amnesty, KTLA-TV, 1988, Lyme Disease: In Our Own Backyard, N.J. Network, 1991. Vol. Westside YMCA, West Los Angeles, Calif., 1982-84; bd. dirs. Ranch Owners Assn., Tehachapi, Calif., 1984-88; adv. com. Sch. Bd. Upper Moreland Twp., 1990-91; co-chair health issues adv. com. Montgomery County, 1992. Grantee Corp. Pub. Broadcasting, L.A., 1987, Am. Film Inst., L.A., 1988. Mem. Soc Motion Picture & TV Engrs., Dirs. Guild, Acad. TV. Home: 1930 Cathedral Rd Huntingdon Valley PA 19006-5006 Office: Lyme Project CDT East PO Box 618 Bryn Athyn PA 19009-0618

GOLDSTEIN, NORMAN ROBERT, safety engineer; b. Boston, June 5, 1928; s. Myer and Janet Katherine (Bornstein) G.; B.Sc., Northeastern U., 1951; M.Sc., Franklin and Marshall Coll., 1956; m. Charlotte Lipson, Sept. 15, 1948; children—Sue Ellen, David, Julie. Registered prof. engr. N.J., Pa., Mass.; cert. safety specialist; cert. safety exec. World Safety Orgn. Various engrng. positions RCA, Lancaster, Pa., 1951-67, mem. tech. staff David Sarnoff Research Center, 1967-70; co-founder, v.p. Engineered Inspection System, Inc., Robbinsville, N.J., 1970-89; founder, prin. N.R. Goldstein & Assocs., Robbinsville, 1989—; lectr. various local colls.; instr. Realtor's Inst.; mem. standards panel Commn. on Consumer Product Safety. Pres., Men's Club, Temple Beth El, Lancaster, 1958, Eden Civic Assn., 1960; bd. dirs. Jewish Community Center, Lancaster, Princeton Jewish Center, Temple Beth Chaim, West Windsor, N.J.; conciliator N.J. HOW Program; dist. commr. Boy Scouts Am., 1973-76. Served with C.E., U.S. Army, 1945-47. Recipient award of merit Stony Brook dist. George Washington coun. Boy Scouts Am., 1976. Fellow Nat. Acad. Forensic Engrs.; mem. ASTM, NSPE, N.J. Soc. Profl. Engrs., Am. Soc. Safety Engrs. (profl. grade), World Safety Orgn. (cert. safety specialist, cert. safety exec.), Bldg. Ofcls. and Code Adminstrs., Sigma Pi Sigma. Republican. Clubs: Engineers (Trenton). Lodges: Lions (past pres. West Windsor, past gov. internat. dist. 16B, editor jour.), K.P., B'nai Brith. Contbr. numerous articles to profl. jours.; patentee in U.S. and fgn. countries. Office: N R Goldstein & Assoc 1200 Rt 130 Robbinsville NJ 08592

GOLDSTEIN, RICHARD A., manufacturing company executive; b. 1942; married. BBA, U. Mass.; LLB, Boston U.; LLM, Harvard U. Atty. Choate Hall & Stewart, 1968-70; spl. asst. to cabinet mem. U.S. Govt., Washington, 1970-73; assoc. Arnold & Porter, Washington, 1973-75; staff atty., gen. couns. Lever Bros. Co., 1975-80, v.p. adminstrv. asst. to chmn., 1980-84; chmn., CEO Unilever Can. Ltd., 1984-89; pres., CEO Unilever U.S. Inc., N.Y.C., 1989—. Office: Unilever US Inc 390 Park Ave New York NY 10022-4613*

GOLDSTEIN, RUBIN, consulting scientist; b. N.Y.C., Mar. 29, 1933; s. Sam and Ray (Faier) G.; m. Sylvia Fay Galitzer, June 3, 1956; children: Lori Jean, Susan May, Pamela Joy. AB in Physics, Princeton U., 1955; AM in Physics, Harvard U., 1956, PhD in Physics, 1960. Rsch. assoc. in applied physics and instr. applied math. Harvard U., Cambridge, Mass., 1960; asst. prof. nuclear engrng. U. Calif. Berkeley, Berkeley, 1960-65; physicist Brookhaven Nat. Lab., Upton, N.Y., 1965-71; cons. staff physicist Combustion Engrng., Windsor, Conn., 1971-73, sr. cons. physicist and area mgr., 1973-79, prin. cons. scientist and mgr., 1980-82, sr. prin. cons. scientist, 1983-86; cons. scientist Goldstein Cons., West Hartford, Conn., 1987—; cons. in field. Contbr. over 55 articles to tech. jours., books. Princeton U. scholar, 1951-55, Harvard U. fellow, 1955-57, NSF fellow, 1958-60. Mem. Am. Nuclear Soc. (exec. com. of math. and computation div., honors and awards com.), Am. Phys. Soc., Phi Beta Kappa, Simga Xi. Home: 8 E Normandy Dr West Hartford CT 06107-1405 Office: Goldstein Cons 8 E Normandy Dr West Hartford CT 06107-1405

GOLDSTEIN, SIDNEY, sociology educator, demographer; b. New London, Conn., Aug. 4, 1927; s. Max and Bella (Hoffman) G.; m. Alice Dreifuss, June 21, 1953; children: Beth Leah, David Louis, Brenda Ruth. BA, U. Conn., 1949, MA, 1951; PhD, U. Pa., 1953. Instr. sociology U. Pa., 1953-55; mem. faculty Brown U., Providence, 1955—, prof. sociology, 1960—, George Hazard Crooker univ. prof., 1977—, chmn. dept. sociology and anthropology, 1963-70, dir. Population Studies and Tng. Ctr., 1965-89; demographic advisor Chulalongkorn U., Bangkok, 1968-69; research fellow Inst. Contemporary Jewry, Hebrew U. Jerusalem, 1969—; sr. fellow East-West Population Inst., Honolulu, 1976, 82, 90; scholar-in-residence Rockefeller Study Ctr., Bellagio, 1990; sr. vis. scholar Hebrew U., 1990; vis. fellow Australian Nat. U., Canberra, 1977; cons. UN Econ. and Social Commn. for Asia and Pacific, 1971-72, 77-82, Nat. Ctr. Health Stats., 1970-77, Internat. Program Population Analysis, Smithsonian Instn., 1971-76; mem. U.S. Bur. Census Adv. Com., 1965-71, Rand Corp., 1975-83; mem. nat. com. research on 1980 census Social Sci. Research Council, 1981-88; mem. governing bur. Com. Internat. Cooperation in Nat. Research in Demography, 1981—; mem. com. on population Nat. Research Council of Nat. Acad. of Scis., 1983-87; chmn. nat. tech. adv. com. on Jewish population studies Council Jewish Fedns., 1984—; co-chmn. internat. sci. com. on 1990 census surveys of world Jewry, Jerusalem, 1988—. Author: Patterns of Mobility, 1910-1950, 1958; Consumption Patterns of the Aged, 1960; The Norristown Study: An Experiment in Interdisciplinary Research Training, 1961; (with K.B. Mayer) The First Two Years: Problems of Small Business Growth and Survival, 1961; Migration and Economic Development in Rhode Island, 1958; (with Calvin Goldscheider) Jewish Americans, 1968; Urbanization in Thailand, 1947-1960, 1970; The Demography of Bangkok, 1972; (with V. Prachuabmoh and A. Goldstein) Urban-Rural Migration Differentials in Thailand, 1974; (with A. Speare and W. Frey) Residential Mobility, Migration and Metropolitan Change, 1975; Circulation in the Context of Total Mobility in Southeast Asia, 1978. Editor: (with D.F. Sly) Basic Data Needed for the Study of Urbanization, 1975; The Measurement of Urbanization and the Projection of Urban Population, 1975; Patterns of Urbanization: Comparative Country Studies, 1977; (with wife) A Test of the Potential Use of Multiplicity in Research on Population Movement, 1979; Population Mobility in the People's Republic of China, 1985; Surveys of Migration in Developing Countries: A Methodological Review, 1981; Migration and Fertility in Peninsular Malaysia, 1983; Urbanization in China, 1985; (with wife) Migration in Thailand: A Twenty-Five Year Review, 1986; (with C. Goldscheider) The Jewish Community of Rhode Island: A Social and Demographic Survey, 1988; Comparative Migration Patterns to Shanghai and Bangkok, 1989, Urbanization in China, 1982-1987, The Role of Migration and Reclassification, 1990, (with wife) Permanent and Temporary Migration Differentials in China, 1991, Demographic Issues and Data Needs for Mega-City Research, 1991. Bd. dirs. Jewish Fedn. R.I., 1964-68, 78-82, 85— . Bur. Jewish Edn., Providence, 1959-82; bd. dirs. Council of Jewish Fedns., 1987—, Guggenheim fellow, 1961-62; Harrison fellow, 1953; Social Sci. Research Council fellow, 1961-62; Fulbright scholar, Denmark, 1961-62; recipient Disting. Svc. medal Chulalongkorn U., 1969, Disting. Svc. medal Mahidol U., 1991, CJF Recognition award, 1992; sr. research awardee NAS, 1983. Mem. Am. Sociol. Assn., Population Assn. Am. (pres. 1975-76), Assn. Jewish Demography and Stats. (dir.), Am. Statis. Assn., Internat. Union Sci. Study of Population (chair com. urbanization and population distbn. 1971-76), Assn. Sociol. Study of Jewry, Phi Beta Kappa. Home: 95 Kiwanee Rd Warwick RI 02888-4040 Office: Brown U Providence RI 02912

GOLDSTEIN, SIMEON HAI FISCHEL, real estate broker; b. N.Y.C., Dec. 26, 1915; s. Herbert S. and Rebecca V. (Fischel) G.; m. Naomi R. Ginsburg, Aug. 27, 1942; children: Deborah J. Goldstein Stepelman, Seth M., Jonathan D. BA, Columbia Coll., 1936; MS, Columbia U., 1938. From bldg. mgr. to exec. dir. Harry & Jane Fischel Found. & affiliates, N.Y.C., 1936-86; broker assoc. J. Clarence Davies Realty Co., Inc., N.Y.C., 1986-89; real estate broker Simeon H.F. Goldstein, N.Y.C., 1989—. Contbr. articles to profl. jours. Rep. nominee N.Y. State Legis., Bronx, 1946, 48, 50, 52, 54, 55; v.p. Citizens Housing & Planning Coun. of N.Y., 1989—; mem. community planning bd. Bronx, 1963-83, 1990—, chmn. Bd. #4 in past, currently chmn. econ. devel. com. of Bd. #11; pres. Pelham Pkwy. Rep. Club, Bronx, 1976—; bd. dirs. Jewish Community Coun. of Pelham Pkwy., 1981—, Congregation Kehal Adas Yeshurun, Bronx, 1980—; del. Assn. Bronx Jewish Community Couns., 1989-91; exec. coun. Commn. on Synagogue Rels., UJA- Fedn. Jewish Philanthropies. Mem. Bronx County Hist. Soc. (charter). Home: 2222 Holland Ave Bronx NY 10467-9402 Office: 250 W 57th St Ste 2318 New York NY 10107-0258

GOLDSTEIN, THEODORE PHILIP, chemist; b. Balt., Feb. 23, 1928; s. Isadore A. and Leah (Rankin) G.; m. Nadine Edelstein, Sept. 11, 1968. BA, Johns Hopkins U., 1951, MA, 1958, PhD, 1961. Chemist U.S. Army Chem. Corps, Edgewood, Md., 1952-55, Sinai Hosp., Balt., 1955-56; rsch. chemist Mobil Oil, Paulsboro, N.J., 1961-63; sr. rsch. chemist Mobil Oil, Princeton, N.J., 1963-75; assoc. Mobile R&D Corp., Princeton, 1975—. Assoc. editor Organic Geochemistry, 1977-82. Fellow Am. Assn. Chemists; mem. AAAS, Am. Chem. Soc., Catalysis Soc. Am., Monterey Study Group, Sigma Xi. Office: Mobile R&D Corp PO Box 1026 Princeton NJ 08543-1026

GOLDSTONE, BETTE PERILSTEIN, education educator; b. Phila., Dec. 29, 1947; d. Paul K. and Norma (Marrus) Perilstein; m. Peter Jay Goldstone, Aug. 31, 1975; children: Avra Sharon, Rebecca Hannah. BA, U. Pa., 1969; MEd, Boston U., 1971; EdD, Temple U., 1982. Cert. elem. and early childhood tchr., Pa. Tchr. Get Set Ctrs., Phila., 1969-70, Solomon Schechter Sch., Phila., 1971-74; teaching asst. Temple, Phila., 1974-76, instr., 1977; instr. Beaver Coll, Glenside, Pa., 1979-87, asst. prof. edn., 1988—; exhbn. dir. book illustration Beaver Coll., Glenside, Pa., 1986-90; cons. to suburban and city sch. dists., 1989—; coord. children's lit. speaker series, 1986—; presenter at nat. and state confs. Author: Lessons to be Learned, 1984; contbr. articles to profl. publs. Mem. Nat. Coun. Tchrs. English, Internat. Reading Assn., Children's Lit. Assn., Children's Lit. Assembly, Phila. Coun. of Reading Round Table (steering com. 1989-91). Democrat. Jewish. Office: Beaver Coll Edn Dept Church Rd Glenside PA 19038

GOLDWYN, JUDITH S., civic worker; b. N.Y.C., Apr. 1, 1940; d. Raymond B. and Rosetta (Van Gelder) Schlessel; BA, NYU, 1962; MA, L.I. U., 1973; m. Ronald M. Goldwyn, Aug. 20, 1961; children: Ira D., Laura-Jill. Tchr., Gt. Neck, N.Y., 1972-77; owner The Word Factory, Gt. Neck, 1977-86; exec. dir. Ronald McDonald House L.I., 1986—; cons. Temple Beth-El of Great Neck Outreach program, 1989—. V.p. pub. rels. Gt. Neck United Community Fund, 1983-86, dir., 1983-89; producer United Community Players, 1986-88; bd. dirs. Russell Gardens Assn., 1988—. Mem. Nat. Soc. Fundraising Execs., Gt. Neck Village Bus. Assn. (pres.), L.I. Coalition for Fair Broadcasting, Gt. Neck C. of C. (dir.). Office: Ronald McDonald House LI 26707 76th Ave New Hyde Park NY 11040-1433

GOLDZUNG, HAROLD JOHN, clergyman; b. Mineola, N.Y., Dec. 20, 1933; s. George Joseph and Anna Elizabeth (Hartman) G.; m. Mary Ellen Hesselink, Aug. 18, 1956; children: Kathleen Goldzung Vanden Oever, Constance Jean Goldzung Eckart, Harold John. AB, Hope Coll., 1955; MDiv, N.B. Theol. Sem., 1958. Ordained to ministry Reformed Ch., 1958. Pastor Old Saratoga and Bacon Hill Reformed Chs., Schuylerville, N.Y., 1958-66, Second Reformed Ch., Schenectady, 1966-74, Grove Reformed Ch., North Bergen, N.J., 1974—; pres. Synod of Albany, Schenectady, 1968; sec. Classis of Schenectady, 1970-74; pres. Classis of Palisades, 1975. Chairperson Counseling Svcs., Palisade Gen. Med. Ctr., North Bergen, N.J., 1987, first vice chmn. bd. govs., 1991; chmn. bd. govs. Palisade Gen. Med. Ctr., 1992; mem. adv. bd. Salvation Army, 1875—. Recipient Men's Svc. award Grove Ch. Consistory, North Hudson County, N.J., 1990. Mem. Hudson County Ministerial Assn. (past chmn., pres. 1987-90, sec. 1990—). Home: 1136 46th St North Bergen NJ 07047-2906

GOLEY, MARY ANNE, fine arts program director; b. Washington, July 1, 1945; d. Alfred Victor and Beatrice (Tabinski) G. BA, U. Md., 1967; MA, Case Western Res., 1973, postgrad., 1975. Asst. registrar Nat. Mus. Am. Art, Washington, 1968-70; dir., fine arts program Fed. Res. Bd., Washington, 1975—; fine arts cons. Fed. Res. Bank, Miami, Fla., 1979, Jacksonville, 1988, Dallas, 1992; pres. bd. dirs. Arlington (Va.) Arts Ctr., 1987-90, guest curator, 1986; mem. Presdl. Task Force on Arts and Humanities, 1981; guest dir. Nat. Mus. Am. Art, 1976-77, John White Alexander; archivist Inventory Am. Paintings, Nat. Mus. Am. Art, 1971; pub. Def. Inst. Bull., 1989; lectr. in field. Contbr. to exhibition catalogues Fed. Res. Bd. Recipient Fgn. Decoration, Queen Beatrix, The Netherlands, 1982, Grand Duke of Luxembourg, 1988. Mem. Am. Assns. Mus., Archives Am. Art, Artable, Assn. Profl. Mus. Art Advisors, Charles Rennie Mackintosh Soc. Office: Fed Res Bd Fine Arts Program 20th and Constitution Ave Washington DC 20551

GOLIA, PETER R., insurance executive; b. N.Y.C., Aug. 14, 1926; s. Nicola and Josephine (DeTata) G.; m. Elizabeth Mastrantone, Sept. 26, 1953; children: Regina, Peter R., Annette, Jean Marie. BS, Manhattan Coll., 1949. Marine claims adjuster W.J. Roberts, Inc., N.Y.C., 1951-53, Fire Assn. Phila., N.Y.C., 1953-54; asst. v.p. Adams & Porter Inc., N.Y.C., 1954-70; sr. v.p. Adams & Porter Inc., 1981—; v.p. Whitehall Brokerage, Inc., Ter Bush & Purnell, Bache Ins. Svcs., Inc./Prudential, N.Y.C., 1970-81. With U.S. Army, 1946-47. Mem. Assn. Average Adjusters of U.S. (full mem., chmn. 1990-91, ann. subscriber London), Maritime Law Assn. of U.S. Republican. Roman Catholic. Home: 51 Summit St White Plains NY 10607-1208 Office: Adams & Porter Inc 1 World Trade Ctr Ste 8433 New York NY 10048-0070

GOLL, GILLIEN, actress; b. Newark, May 31; s. Aaron and Florence (Deutch) G. AB, Barnard Coll.; MA, Hunter Coll. writer, dir. Theatre for the Forgotten, L.I., N.Y., 1978-80; story editor Stigwood/Yellen Prodns., N.Y.C., 1981-83; acting educator Total Theatre Lab, N.Y.C., 1989-90, Fordham U., N.Y.C., 1990—. Author, dir.: (plays) Fascination Rhythm, The Want Ads: A Dramatic Reading for Four Voices; author: (plays) Bizarre Search ... For Murder, 'Cause They'll Be Dying on Bandstand; actor appearing in Unfinished Business, The War of the Worlds, But Most of Us Cry in Movies, A Christmas Carol, Seize the Day, Saturday Night Live, Metaphysical Vaudeville, Looking Up, Wildflowers, others; dir. I'm Dreaming or Am I?, All the Way Home; actor, co-dir., producer Apartment Stories, 1991; artistic dir. The Centaur Stage, 1990—. Mem. SAG, AFTRA, Actors' Equity Assn., N.Y. Women in Film. Office: The Centaur Stage PO Box 1693 New York NY 10025

GOLLAND, JEFFREY H., psychologist, psychoanalyst, educator; b. Bklyn., Apr. 28, 1941; s. Gerald Edward and Rose Alice (Finkelstein) G.; m. Patricia Elaine Yeager, July 14, 1969 (div. July 1991); children: David Hamilton, Richard Morris. A.B. cum laude, Brandeis U., 1961; A.M., NYU, 1962, Ph.D., 1966; cert. in psychoanalysis, N.Y. Freudian Soc., Inc., 1973. Lic. psychologist, N.Y. From psychologist to chief psychology Brooke Gen. Hosp., San Antonio, 1966-68; psychologist-in-charge out patient clinic Bellevue Psychiat. Hosp., N.Y.C., 1968-70; instr. psychiatry NYU Med. Ctr., 1968-70; asst. prof. edn. Baruch Coll. CUNY, 1970-75, chmn. dept., 1974-79, assoc. prof., 1975—; solo practice psychoanalysis and psychology, N.Y.C., 1968—; field supr. psychotherapy Rutgers Grad. Sch. Psychology, Piscataway, N.J., 1975-85; with faculty Am. Inst. for Psychoanalysis and Psychotherapy, N.Y.C., 1976-84, N.Y. Freudian Soc., 1984—. Author book chpts. and revs. Contbr. articles to profl. jours. Trustee Brandeis U., Waltham, Mass., 1985-89, The Village Temple, N.Y.C., 1984—; pres. emeritus 145 Fourth Ave. Tenants Assn., N.Y.C., 1977—. Served to capt. U.S. Army Res., 1966-68. Recipient Founders Day award NYU, 1967. Mem. Am. Psychol. Assn., N.Y. Freudian Soc. (treas. 1984-90), Brandeis U. Alumni Assn. (bd. dirs. 1976-91, pres. 1985-89), Phi Delta Kappa. Democrat. Jewish. Avocations: tennis, running, skiing. Home: 145 4th Ave New York NY 10003-4906 Office: CUNY Baruch Coll Box 505 17 Lexington Ave New York NY 10010

GOLOB, DAVID RICHARD, II, investor, consultant; b. La Jolla, Calif., Jan. 1, 1968; s. David Richard and Mary Katherine (Moynihan) G. AB in Chemistry, Harvard U., 1989. Bus. analyst McKinsey & Co., N.Y.C., 1989-91; assoc. Gen. Atlantic Ptnrs., N.Y.C., 1991—. Mem. Harvard Club N.Y.C., Japan Soc. N.Y., Phi Beta Kappa.

GOLOMB, CLAIRE, psychology educator; b. Frankfurt am Main, Germany, Jan. 30, 1928; came to U.S., 1958; d. Chaskel and Fanny (Monderer) Schimmel; m. Dan S. Golomb, Feb. 24, 1954; children: Mayana, Anath. BA, Hebrew U., Jerusalem, 1954; MA, New Sch. for Social Rsch., 1959; PhD, Brandeis U., 1969. Instr. psychology Wellesley (Mass.) Coll., 1969-70; asst. prof. Brandeis U., Waltham, Mass., 1971-74; assoc. prof. psychology U. Mass., Boston, 1974-77, prof., 1977—. Author: Young Children's Sculpture and Drawing, 1974, The Child's Creation of a Pictorial World, 1992. Mem. Am. Psychol. Assn., Jean Piaget Soc. Office: U Mass Harbor Campus Boston MA 02125

GOLOMB, RICHARD MOSS, lawyer; b. Phila., Oct. 24, 1958; m. Marci Cohen. BS in Polit. Sci., Am. U., 1980; JD, Nova U., 1983. Bar: Pa. 1984, N.J. 1984, U.S. Dist. N.J. 1984. Law clk. to presiding justice Camden, N.J., 1983-84; assoc. Romisher & Phillips, Phila., 1984-85, Kreithen Baron & Miller, Phila., 1985-89; ptnr. Kreithen, Baron, Villari & Golomb, Phila., 1989—. Mem. Phila. Dem. Exec. Com.; vice chmn. young lawyers div. Fedn. Allied Jewish Appeal, 1989, chmn. Chai div., 1990, mem. Nat. Young Men's Cabinet, 1992—; bd. dirs. Young Leadership Coun., 1990—. Fellow Acad. Advocacy; mem. ABA, Pa. Bar Assn., Phila. Bar Assn., Pa. Trial Lawyers Assn. (bd. govs.), Assn. Trial Lawyers Am., Phila. Trial Lawyers Assn. (bd. govs. 1990—). Jewish. Home: 205 Wiltshire Rd Wynnewood PA 19096-3332 Office: Kreithen Baron Villari & Golomb 1201 Chestnut St 10th Fl Philadelphia PA 19107

GOLOVSKOY, VAL SEMION, linguist, educator; b. Moscow, Feb. 25, 1938; came to the U.S., 1981; m. Julia I. Bosky, Oct. 17, 1986. MA, Inst. Cinematography, Moscow, 1966, U. Mich., 1983. Editor, writer art pub. house, Moscow, 1965-74, Cinema Art, Moscow, 1974-78, Soviet Screen Mag., Moscow, 1978-80; asst. editor New Russian Word, N.Y.C., 1983-84; vis. prof. U. Ariz., Tucson, 1985; writer, broadcaster Voice of Am., Washington, 1986-88; lang. and cultural instr. Fgn. Svc. Inst., Washington, 1989—; vis. prof. Queens Coll., N.Y.C., 1983-85. Author: Behind the Soviet Screen, 1986; contbr. articles to profl. jours. Bd. dirs. Litfund, Washington, 1986—. Grantee Queens Coll., 1983-84, Kennan Inst., Washington, 1985. Mem. Am. Assn. Tchrs. Slavic and East European Langs., Am. Assn. for Advanced Soviet Studies. Republican. Home: 4141 N Henderson Rd # 605 Arlington VA 22203

GOLUB, SAMUEL JOSEPH, textile sciences consultant; b. Middleboro, Mass., July 25, 1915; s. Solomon Harry and Bessie (Caplan) G.; m. Faye Goldstein, Sept. 21, 1940; children: Shepard Carl, Joan Nancy Golub Cohen. BS, U. Mass., Amherst, 1938, MS, 1940; PhD, Harvard U., 1945. Assoc. prof. biology U. Mass., Ft. Devens, 1945-46; biology editor Webster's Dictionary, Springfield, Mass., 1946-48; asst. prof. Brandeis U., Waltham, Mass., 1949-56; sr. rsch. assoc. Fabric Rsch. Labs., Dedham, Mass., 1956-59; assoc. dir. ACH Fiber Svc., Boston, 1959-63; asst. dir. Albany Internat. Rsch. Co., Dedham, 1963-85; cons. on textile scis., Newton, Mass., 1985—. Contbr. articles to profl. jours.; patentee in textile field. Chmn. Am. Cancer Soc., Newton, 1970. Recipient Civilian Meritorious Svc. award USN, 1945; grantee Rogoff Found., 1974. Fellow Am. Inst. Chemists; mem. ASTM (hon. 1980, chmn. com. on dists. 1971-72, com. D13, 1972-78, com. on standards 1973-76, task groups 1960-85), Fiber Soc., Am. Assn. Textile Chemists and Colorists, Internat. Wool Textile Assn. (tech. rep. for U.S. 1972-78), Phi Kappa Phi. Home and Office: 38 Myerson Ln Newton MA 02159-3509

GOMERY, DOUGLAS, communications educator, writer; b. N.Y.C., Apr. 5, 1945; s. John Edgar and Julia (Halsted) G.; m. Marilyn L. Moon, Jan. 13, 1973. BS, Lehigh U., 1967; MA, U. Wis., 1970, PhD, 1975. Asst. prof. mass communication U. Wis., Milw., 1974-79, assoc. prof., 1980; assoc. prof. U. Md., College Park, 1981-87, prof., 1987—; sr. researcher media studies project Woodrow Wilson Ctr. for Internat. Scholarship, Washington, 1988—; vis. prof. Northwestern U., Evanston, Ill., 1980, U. Iowa, Iowa City, 1982, U. Utrecht, The Netherlands, 1990, 92; cons. Am. Film Inst., Washington, 1982—. Author: High Sierra, 1979, (with Annette Michelson) The Art of Moving Shadows, 1989, (with Robert C. Allen) Film History: Theory and Practice, 1985, The Hollywood Studio System, 1986, (with Phil Cook and L.W. Lichty) American Media, 1988; editor: The Will Hays Papers, 1987, Movie History: A Survey, 1991, Shared Pleasures, 1992, The Future of News, 1992; mem. editorial bd. Cinema Jour., 1983—, Jour. Media Econs., 1989—, Jour. Film and Video, 1983—; contbg. editor Screen, London, 1984-89, Iris, Paris, 1983-89; editor Marquee, 1991; also over 300 articles. Cons. Joint Com. on Landmarks Washington, 1983, 85, 86, 90, NEH, 1980—, Nat. Endowment Arts, 1980—, Md. State Hist. Preservation Office, 1988, Voice of Am., Nat. Gallery Art., Wis. Dept. Revenue, 1978; trustee Am. Film Inst., 1986-89. Mem. Theatre Hist. Soc. (chmn. Weiss award com. 1984-87, Weiss prize 1988, bd. dirs. 1987-89), Soc. Cinema Studies, Univ. Film and Video Assn. (editorial bd. jours. 1983—), Broadcast Edn. Assn. Home: 4817 Drummond Ave Bethesda MD 20815-5428 Office: U Md Dept Communication Arts and Theatre College Park MD 20742

GÔMEZ-ROSA, ALEXIS, poet, writer, and foreign language educator; b. Santo Domingo, Dominican Republic, Sept. 2, 1950; came to U.S., 1983; s. Juan Francisco Gómez Rivera and Altagracia de la Rosa de Gómez; m. Bárbara García, Feb. 12, 1976 (div.); children: Berenice, Yelidã. BA, NYU, 1989, postgrad., 1990—. Community liaison Northern Manhattan Coalition for the Immigrants Rights, N.Y.C., 1987-89; tchr. Spanish Caribbean Ednl. Ctr., N.Y.C., 1988—; dir. poetry workshop Casa de Teatro, Santo Domingo, 1976-78; instr. in poetry Boston/Dorchester (Mass.) Pub. Sch., 1984-85; editor of the collected poetry Luna Cabeza Caliente. Author: Oficio de Post-Muerte, 1973, High Quality, Ltd., 1985, Contra la pluma la espuma, 1990, Tiza & Tinta, 1990. Mem. Latin-Am. Written Inst., N.Y.C., Asociacion Dominicana de Escritores. Home: 514 W 176th St # 4B New York NY 10033-8446

GOMOLL, ALLEN WARREN, cardiovascular pharmacologist; b. Chgo., July 10, 1933; s. Herbert Fredrick and Sara Evelyn (Cowan) G.; m. Elaine L. Kirkpatrick, Sept. 17, 1955; children: Gary A., Lisa E. BS in Pharmacy, U. Ill., Chgo., 1955, MS, 1958, PhD, 1961. Instr. U. Ill. Coll. Medicine, Chgo., 1960-61, asst. prof., 1961-66; group leader Mead Johnson, Evansville, Ind., 1966-70, sect. leader, mgr., 1970-81; prin. rsch. scientist Bristol-Myers, Evansville, 1981-84; rsch. fellow Bristol-Myers, Wallingford, Conn., 1984-90; sr. rsch. fellow Bristol-Myers Squibb, Princeton, N.J., 1990—. Reviewer Life Scis., 1973—, Jour. Med. Chemistry, 1975—, Circulation, 1989—; contbr. sci. articles to profl. jours. Fellow Am. Coll. Cardiology, Am. Heart Assn. Coun. Circulation and Basic Sci. Coun.; mem. Am. Soc. Pharmacology & Exptl. Therapy, Internat. Soc. Heart Rsch., Sigma Xi. Office: Bristol-Myers Squibb PRI PO Box 4000 Princeton NJ 08543-4000

GOMORY, RALPH EDWARD, mathematician, manufacturing company executive, foundation executive; b. Brooklyn Heights, N.Y., May 7, 1929; s. Andrew L. and Marian (Schellenberg) G.; m. Laura Dumper, 1954 (div. 1968); children: Andrew C., Susan S., Stephen H. BA, Williams Coll., 1950, ScD (hon.), 1973; postgrad., Kings Coll., 1950-51, Cambridge U., Eng., 1950-51; PhD, Princeton U., 1954; LHD (hon.), Pace U., 1986; DSc (hon.), Poly. U., 1987, Syracuse U., 1989, Worcester Poly. U., 1989, Carnegie-Mellon U., 1989. Rsch. assoc. Princeton U., 1951-54, asst. prof. math., Higgins lectr., 1957-59; with IBM, Yorktown Heights, N.Y., 1959-86; dir. math. scis., rsch. div. IBM, Armonk, 1968-70, dir. rsch., 1970-86, v.p., 1973-84, sr. v.p., 1985-89, sr. v.p. for sci. and tech., 1986-89, also mem. corp. mgmt. bd., 1983-89, dir. Asia Pacific Group, 1982-88; pres. Alfred P. Sloan Found., N.Y.C., 1989—; Andrew D. White prof.-at-large Cornell U., 1970-76; bd. dir. Bank of N.Y., Lexmark Internat., Inc., Washington Post Co., Ashland Oil, Inc.; mem. adv. coun. dept. math. Princeton, 1982-85, chmn., 1984-85; mem. adv. coun. Sch. Engrng. Stanford U., 1978-85; chmn. vis. com. div. applied scis. Harvard U., 1987-91; mem. White House sci. coun., 1986-89, Coun. on Fgn. Rels.; chmn. adv. com. to Pres. on High Temperature Superconductivity, 1987-88; mem. coun. on grad. sch. Yale U., 1988—; mem. vis. com. elec. engrng. and computer sci. MIT, 1988-90; mem. Pres.' Coun. Advisors on Sci. and Tech., 1990—; researcher in integer and linear programming, non-linear differential equations. Trustee Hampshire Coll., 1977-86, Princeton U., 1985-89, Alfred P. Sloan Found., 1988-89; mem.

governing bd. Nat. Rsch. Coun., 1980-83; mem. com. on mandatory retirement in higher edn. Nat. Rsch. Coun., 1989-90, chmn., 1990. With USN, 1954-57. Recipient Lanchester prize Ops. Rsch. Soc. Am., 1964, Harry Goode Meml. award Am. Fedn. Info. Processing Socs., 1984, John Von Neumann Theory prize Ops. Rsch. Soc. Am. and Inst. Mgmt. Scis., 1984, IRI medal Indsl. Rsch. Inst., 1985, Engring. Leadership Recognition award IEEE, 1988, Nat. Medal of Sci., 1988; IBM fellow, 1964. Fellow Econometric Soc., Am. Acad. Arts and Scis.; mem. Nat. Acad. Scis. (coun. 1977-78, 80-83, com. sci., engring. and pub. policy 1985—), Nat. Acad. Engring. (coun. 1986-92), Am. Philos. Soc. (coun. 1986-92). Home: 260 Douglas Rd Chappaqua NY 10514-3100 Office: Alfred P Sloan Found 630 5th Ave New York NY 10111-0242

GOMPERZ, PAUL ANDREAS, insurance company executive; b. Vienna, Austria, July 26, 1937; came to U.S., 1941; s. Theodore and Marguerite (Berstl) G.; m. Janet Massey Santelman, Apr. 4, 1964; 1 child, M. Elizabeth. BA, Columbia U., 1958; postgrad., U. So. Calif., L.A., 1962-68. CLU; chartered fin. cons. Mgmt. trainee Union Bank, L.A., 1962-64, credit mgr., fin. analyst, 1964-65; sales agt. Lincoln Nat. Life, L.A., 1965-67; v.p. Planned Equity Corp., L.A., 1968-71; regional v.p. Planned Equity Corp., East Orange, N.J., 1971-76; exec. v.p. Planned Equity Corp., East Orange, 1976-78, pres., 1978-83; pres. Voluntary Benefit Systems Corp. Am., Millburn, N.J., 1983—. Dir. YMCA of the Oranges, Maplewood, West Essex and Sussex County, Inc., 1977—, vice chmn., 1981-85, chmn., 1985-89 (named Layman of Yr. 1986); dir. Columbia Univ. Club of No. N.J., 1980—, pres., 1980-82, sec., 1982-89, pres. 1989—; mem. ins. com. Columbia Alumni Fedn., 1982—. Lt. USAF, 1958-61, USAFR, 1961-65. Recipient Alumni medal Alumni Fedn. Columbia Univ., N.Y., 1985. Mem. Nat. Assn. Life Underwriters, Million Dollar Round Table. Democrat. Congregational. Home: 272 Hartshorn Dr Short Hills NJ 07078-1915 Office: Voluntary Benefit Systems Corp of Am Ste 304 343 Millburn Ave Millburn NJ 07041

GONG, NANCY YEE, glass artist, small business owner; b. Rochester, N.Y., June 8, 1957; d. Don S. and Sue H. (Tang) G.; m. Peter W. Fisk, July 10, 1983. Student Sch. for Am. Craftsmen, Rochester Inst. Tech., 1973-78; student, Champlain Coll., 1975-76, Empire State Coll., 1976-77, Naples Mills Sch. Arts & Craft, 1976. Proprietor, artist Gong Glass Works, Rochester, N.Y., 1979—; presenter glass art tech. workshos and confs. Rochester Mus. & Sci Ctr., 1979-83; spl. projects coord. Pyramid Art Gallery, Allofus Art Workshop, Inc., Rochester, 1979-86; instr. stained glass techniques Rochester Mus. & Sci. Ctr., 1979-86; participant Narcissus Quagliata's Design Workshop, San Francisco, 1978, ALLOFUS Art Workshop, Inc., Rochester, 1976-80, PORTCON '82 Art Glass Conf., San Diego, 1982, Environ. Art Glass Conf., Oklahoma City, 1989, Profl. Art Glass Sem., San Antonio, 1990, Pub. Art Politics and Processes Symposium, Arts for Greater Rochester, 1990, Glass Art Soc. Conf., Monterey, Calif., Corning, N.Y., Huntington, W.Va., Toronto, Ont., Can., 1978—; cons., bd. dirs. Arts for Greater Rochester Speakers Bur., 1990. Exhibited at Lincoln First Plaza Gallery, Rochester, Meml. Art Gallery U. Rochester (Excellence award 1981), Glassmasters Guild Finalist N.Y.C., 1981, Oakland County Cultural Offices, Southfield, Mich., 1987, Glass Growers Gallery, Erie, Pa., Kunst Art & Form Internat., Vienna, Austria, Galerie, N.Y., Greater Rochester International. Airport (finalist 1990); select projects include Meml. Art Gallery Rochester, Women's Coun. Room, Cornell U. Ithaca Faculty Club, Paychex, Inc., GM, Genesee Region Home Care Assn. Hospice Unit, Eastman Kodak Co., Lodge at Woodcliff, Monroe C.C., Duke U. Fuqua Sch. Bus. Conf. Ctr., Malarkey's on the Lake. Bd. dirs. Arts for Greater Rochester, 1991. Mem. AIA, Am. Soc. Interior Designers, Interior Design Soc., Glass Art Soc., Arts for Greater Rochester, Meml. Art Gallery Univ. Rochester, Am. Crafts Coun. Home and Studio: Gong Glass Works PO Box 10344 Rochester NY 14610

GONNELLA, ELEANOR ANN, internist, emergency medicine physician; b. Newark, June 22, 1954; d. Angelo Michael and Eleanor (Fabbo) Gonnella; m. Robert P. Sheridan, June 27, 1982; children: Diana, Victoria. BS, Upsala Coll., 1976; MD, U. Cen. Del Este, Dominican Republic, 1982. Cert. ACLS, ATLS. Resident Perth Amboy (N.J.) Gen. Hosp., 1982-85, asst. chief resident in medicine, 1985; emergency rm. dr. Raritan Bay Med. Ctr., Perth Amboy, 1985-91, Gen. Hosp. Ctr. at Passaic, N.J., 1991—; instr. Advanced Cardiac Life Support, N.J., 1991—. Mem. Am. Coll. Emergency Physicians (publicity com. 1991); Med. Soc. N.J. (coun. on pub. health 1984-85), Essex County Med. Soc. Roman Catholic.

GONSALVES, GREGORY JAY, art director; b. Warwick, R.I., Sept. 12, 1968; s. Joseph and Madeline (Sanquist) G. Student, R.I. Sch. Design, 1986—. With Blazing Graphics, Inc., Cranston, R.I., 1986-87, graphic designer, 1987-88, art dir., 1988—; freelance creative dir., Warwick, 1988—. Active Amnesty Internat., N.Y.C., 1987—. Named Best of Nation Internat. Youth Skill Olympics, 1988; recipient Silver medal in Design Internat. Youth Skill Olympics, 1988, Nat. Skill Olympics, 1986, Gold medal in Design Vocat. Indsl. Clubs Am., 1986. Mem. Am. Inst. Graphic Arts. Mem. Christian Ch. Home: 1099 Main Ave Warwick RI 02886-1940

GONYO, MARILYN E., education educator; b. Perth Amboy, N.J., Oct. 29, 1943; d. John M. and Catherine (Kozak) G. BA, Glassboro (N.J.) State Coll., 1965; MA, Kean Coll., Union, N.J., 1968; EdD, Rutgers U., 1976. Cert. elem. tchr., reading tchr., cons., learning disabilities tchr., tchr. of handicapped, supr., prin., sch. adminstr., N.J. Asst. prof., coord. learning disabilities programs Montclair (N.J.) State Coll., 1974-81; cons. Child Diagnostic Ctr., Woodbridge, N.J.; ednl. specialist N.J. Dept. Edn., Trenton, 1981-85; prof. edn., dir. Learning Ctr., Georgian Court Coll., Lakewood, N.J., 1985—. Mem. N.J. Gov.'s Conf. Com. for Libr. and Info. Svc.; mem. juvenile conf. com. Twp. of Woodbridge; judge oratorical contest. Recipient Disting. Svc. award Rutgers U., 1986. Mem. N.J. Assn. Learning Cons. (past pres., Anita McKean Svc. award 1985), N.J. Coun. for Learning Disabilities (pres.), Internat. Reading Assn. (past pres. Middlesex coun.), N.J. Reading Tchrs. Assn., N.J. Schoolwomen's Club (past pres.), Phi Delta Kappa, Delta Kappa Gamma, Kappa Delta Pi, Alpha Delta Kappa. Home: 10 E William St Fords NJ 08863-2208 Office: Georgian Ct Coll Lakewood NJ 08701

GONZALEZ, RAUL, healthcare company executive; b. Chgo., Oct. 2, 1948; s. Paul A. and Emily (Herrera) G. BSBA, Lakeland Coll., Sheboygan, Wis., 1973; MBA, Pepperdine U., 1985. Salesman Reynolds and Reynolds Co., Elk Grove, Ill., 1973-74; with credit dept. Mobil Oil Corp., Schaumburg, Ill., 1974-76; supr. ops. J & J-Personal Products Co., Wilmington, Ill., 1976-79; ops. mgr. east region Baxter Health Cre, Edison, N.J., 1979—. With USN, 1966-69, Vietnam. Mem. Am. Mgmt. Assn. Republican. Roman Catholic. Office: Baxter Health Care Renal Div 49 Distribution Blvd Edison NJ 08817

GONZALEZ, ZOE MIRELLA, elementary education educator; b. Habana, Cuba, July 5, 1958; came to U.S., 1967; d. Pablo Andres and Aristel G. BA in English magna cum laude, St. Peter's Coll., 1980; EdM summa cum laude, Rutgers U., 1984. Cert. tchr. Asst. mgr. Grand Hyatt-New York, N.Y.C., 1980-82; tchr. Bayonne (N.J.) Bd. Edn., 1985—. Co-author: (children's book) A Story from Widg, 1991. Mem. NEA, People for the Ethical Treatment of Animals, Am. Mus. Natural History, World Wildlife Fund, The Humane Soc. of the U.S. Home: 425 61st St West New York NJ 07093-2247 Office: 18 W 26th St Bayonne NJ 07002-3897

GONZALEZ-ACUNA, JOSE, physician, researcher; b. Havana, Cuba, Dec. 12, 1952; came to U.S., 1961; s. J. Cepero and Rosa (Pina) G.-A.; m. Ellen Feathers; 1 child, Evan Alexander. MD, Temple U., 1985. Med. resident JFK Med. Ctr., Edison, N.J., 1985-88; med. dir. Immediate Care Group, Lawrenceville, N.J., 1988-90, Hill Refrigeration Co., Trenton, N.J., 1990—; exec. dir. Health Sense, Inc., Plainsboro, N.J., 1989-90; exec. dir. Project Faith, Inc., Trenton, 1990—, founder MED-COMM health system for the poor, 1991. Bd. dirs. N.J. Citizens Alliance Fire Safety, Trenton, 1990-91, Mercer County Hispanic Assn., Trenton, 1989-91. Mem. AMA, Am. Acad. Family Physicians, Undersea Med. Soc. Republican. Roman Catholic. Office: 1213 Hamilton Ave Trenton NJ 08629

GONZÁLEZ-CRUZ, LUIS FRANCISCO, hispanic literature educator; b. Cárdenas, Matanzas, Cuba, Dec. 11, 1943; came to U.S., 1965; s. Francisco and Alicia Maria (De La Cruz) González Estenoz. BS, I. Jose Smith Coll., Cardenas, 1960; Pub. Health Lab. Technician, U. Havana, Cuba, 1963; MA, U. Pitts., 1968, PhD, 1970. Lab. technician Mass. Gen. Hosp., Boston, 1968; Spanish instr. Point Park Coll., Pitts., 1968-69; Hispanic lit. instr. Pa. State U., New Kensington, 1969-71, asst. prof., 1971-74, assoc. prof., 1974-79, prof., 1979—; nat. dep. Circulo de Cultura Panamericano, Verona, N.J., 1988-90; lit. cons. Teatro Avante, Miami, 1990—. Chief editor Lit. Jour. CONSENSO, Pa. State, 1977-81; mem. editorial bd. six lit. jours. in U.S. and abroad; author: (poetry) Shooting Gallery, 1975, (poetry) Disgregaciones, 1986, (lit. criticism) D'Ors. Fervor del método, 1988; five other books devoted to Pablo Neruda, César Vallejo, Federico Garcia Lorca, Virgilio Pinera and Cuban Theater in the U.S. Recipient Short-Story prize Revista Chicano-Riqueña, 1980, Poetry prize Revista Mairena, 1981, Critcism award Am. Coun. of Learned Socs., 1984; named Finalist (lit. criticism) Golden Letters awards, 1987. Mem. MLA, NRC (review panelist), NEH (reviewer grant proposals 1982—), Am. Assn., Tchrs. Spanish Portuguese, Fla. Endowment Humanities (official evaluator internat. hispanic theater festival). Home: 220 N Dithridge St Apt 1203 Pittsburgh PA 15213-1428 Office: Pa State U 3550 7th Street Rd New Kensington PA 15068-1798

GOOD, ALLEN HOVEY, acquisitions broker, real estate broker; b. Boston, July 5, 1930; s. Herbert Shelley Good and Elizabeth (Hovey) Jack; m. Catherine Forrester Campbell, June 25, 1959 (div. June 1975); children: Alison Good Ross, Forrester Hovey; m. Joan Duffey Meyers, June 12, 1976; stepchildren: Robert Whitney Meyers Jr., Mary Meyers Miller. AB in English, Bus. Adminstrn., U. Mass., 1955. Ea. region sales mgr. Sandpaper, Inc., Rockland, Mass., 1956-67; pres. A.H. Good Corp., Summit, N.J., 1967-75, Chemdyne, Inc., Summit, 1975-84; v.p. Mid-Atlantic Bus. Brokers, Florham Park, N.J., 1984-86; pres. Atlantic Nat. Acquisitions & Mergers, Inc., Mountainside, N.J., 1987—; cons. Pfizer, Inc., N.Y.C., 1983; subst. instr. Fairleigh-Dickensen Grad. Sch., Madison, N.J., 1986; mem. Lic. Exec. Soc., Norwalk, Conn., 1988-89. Editor Newsletter Summit Tennis Club, 1977; patentee: skin lotion, 1982, skin cleanser, 1985. Mem. Rep. Club, Short Hills, N.J., 1957-59, N.J. Symphony Jr. Com., 1959-60, Mantoloking Yacht Club, 1959-75. Mem. Summit Tennis Club. Home: 149 Kent Place Blvd Summit NJ 07901-4709 Office: Atlantic Nat Acquisitions and Mergers, Inc 1450 Rt 22 Mountainside NJ 07092-2603

GOOD, DANIEL JAMES, manufacturing executive; b. Chgo., Apr. 4, 1940; s. Archibald and Lillian (Senft) G.; m. Marlene Emma Breithaupt, Oct. 14, 1961; children: Julie, Laura. B.S., DePaul U., 1961; postgrad., U. Chgo., 1963. Assoc. Warburg Paribas Becker, Chgo., 1964-71, v.p., 1968-71, mgr. corp. fin., 1971-78, mng. dir., 1976-78, gen. mgr. investment banking, 1978-80, sr. vice chmn., 1980-82, co-chmn. mgmt. com., 1983-84; pres., chief operating officer A.G. Becker Paribas Inc., N.Y.C., 1983-84; exec. v.p., head mergers and acquisitions, dir. E.F. Hutton & Co., Inc., N.Y.C., 1984-86; pres., chief exec. officer E.F. Hutton LBO, Inc., N.Y.C., 1986; mng. dir., dir. merchant banking group Shearson Lehman Bros. Inc., N.Y.C., 1986-89; chmn. Good Capital Co., Inc. (mcht. bank), N.Y.C., 1989; vice chmn. Golden Cat Corp.; bd. dirs. Molex Inc., Gilbert Engring. Co., S.G. Warburg & Co. Ltd., London, Paribas, S.A., Paris; chmn. bd. dirs. Associated Stationers, Inc., Golden Cat. Corp., Bridgeport Machines, Inc. Bd. dirs. Lincoln Park Zool. Soc.; mem. gov. bd. Chgo. Orchestral Assn. Mem. Council on Fgn. Relations. Clubs: Chicago, Casino, Mid-Am, Econ. (Chgo.); Winter (Lake Forest, Ill.); Exmoor Country (Highland Park, Ill.); Econ., Bond (N.Y.C.).

GOOD, JOHN LEON, III, health care executive; b. Melrose, Mass., May 12, 1943; s. John Leon Jr. and Pearl McLean (Phelps) G.; m. Susan Ruth Butterfield, Apr. 9, 1967; children: Travis James, Bonnie Elizabeth. Student, Bentley Coll., 1960-62; BS, Gordon Coll., 1966; MRE, Gordon Conwell Theol. Sem., 1970; MBA, New Hampshire Coll., 1980. Dir. pub. relations Gordon Coll., Wenham, Mass., 1964-67; dir. coll. and alumni relations, asst. to v.p. Gordon Coll., Wenham, 1970-78; dir. devel. Lexington (Mass.) Christian Acad., 1967-70; dir. community relations and devel. Beverly (Mass.) Hosp., 1978-84, v.p., 1984—; pres. North Shore Emergency Med. Svc., Inc., Lynn, Mass., 1986-89; trustee Beverly Nat. Bank, 1987—. Contbr. articles to profl. jours. and publs. Chmn. exec. commn. Am. Heart Assn., 1987; sec., clk., North Shore Community Arts Found., Beverly, 1982—, bd. dirs. 1982—; vol. Essex Fire Dept., 1970—, lt. 1986-87; mem. Essex Rep. Town Com., 1972-82, 84-85, chmn. 1974-80; mem. Beverly Community Coun., 1979—, Beverly Cable TV Program Commn., 1981-85; bd. dirs. Beverly Sch. for the Deaf, 1980—, Am. Cancer Soc., 1979-80, v.p., 1980; bd. dirs. Greater Beverly Red Cross, 1981—. Fellow Nat. Assn. for Hosp. Devel.; mem. New Eng. Assn. for Hosp. Devel. (pres. 1988-90, spl. presdl. citation 1986), Mass. Soc. for Fund Raising Execs., Nat. Soc. for Fund Raising Execs., Am. Coll. of Healthcare Execs., Am. Coll. Healthcare Mktg., Acad. for Health Svc. Mktg., Rotary (pres. 1986-87), North Shore Press Club, B'nai B'rith (Man of Yr. 1982). Republican. Baptist. Home: 85 Martin St Essex MA 01929-1218 Office: Beverly Hosp 85 Herrick St Beverly MA 01915-1776

GOOD, REBECCA MAE WERTMAN, learning and behavior disorder counselor, nurse; b. Barberton, Ohio, May 13, 1943; d. Frederick Daniel Wertman and Freda Beam Wertman Lombardi; m. William Robert Good Jr., Aug. 15, 1964; children: William Robert III, John Joseph, Matthew Stephan. RN, Akron Gen. Med. Ctr., Ohio, 1964; BS in Psychology, Ramapo Coll., Mahwah, N.J., 1986; MA in Counseling, NYU, 1990. RN, N.Y. Relief supr., pm psychiat. nurse F.D.R. VA Hosp., Montrose, N.Y., 1971-72; geriatric charge nurse Westledge Extended Care Facility, Peekskill, N.Y., 1972-77; infirmary and ICF nurse St. Dominics Home, Orangeburg, N.Y., 1981-83; allergy and immunology nurse Dr. Andre Codispoti, Suffern, N.Y., 1979-89; rsch. asst. counselor NYU, Manhattan, N.Y., 1989-90; Rockland advocate Student Advocacy Inc., White Plains, N.Y., 1989-90; exec. dir. Rockland County Assn. for Learning Disabled, Orangeburg, 1990-91; life skills counselor Bd. Coop. Edn., West Nyack, N.Y., 1991—; counselor of learning and behavior disorders Suffern, 1991—; hospice nurse United Hospice Rockland, 1991—. Co-chmn. Rockland County Coord. Coun. for Developmentally Disabled Offenders, New City, N.Y., 1990—; mem. bd. visitors Rockland Children's Psychiat. Ctr., orangeburg, 1991—; mem. U.S. Congressman Benjamin Gilman's Handicapped Adv. Com., Rockland County, 1985—; pres. Spl. Edn. PTA of Ramapo Cen. Sch. Dist., 1982-86. Ramapo Coll. of N.J. Pres.'s scholar, 1986. Mem. AACD, Rockland County Assn. for Children with Learning Disabilities (pres. 1986-88), N.Y. Assn. for the Learning Disabled (sec. 1988-89), Westchester Putnam Rockland Assn. for Counseling and Devel., N.Y. State Assn. for Counseling and Devel., Assn. Bds. Visitors N.Y. State Facilities for the Mentally Disabled Inc., Hospice Nurses Assn., Rockland County Psychol. Soc. Inc., Dist. 17 N.Y. State Nurses Assn. Episcopalian. Home: 18 Mary Beth Dr Suffern NY 10901-6432

GOOD, SHARON, publisher; b. Bklyn., June 23, 1950; d. Sam and Selma (Karp) G. BA, Hofstra U., 1972. Ptnr., pub. Excalibur Pub., N.Y.C., 1990—; freelance photographer, 1977—. Author, illustrator Alpha, Beta and Gamma, 1991, (with others) By Actors, For Actors, 1991; contbr. short stories to mags.; contbr. photography to mags. and anns.; co. mgr., performer Gingerbread Players and Jack, 1977-87; actress various roles, 1966-88. Mem. NAFE, COSMEP (Internat. Assn. Ind. Pubs.), New Age Pub. and Retailing Alliance, Pub. Mktg. Assn. Office: Excalibur Pub 434 Ave of the Americas # 790 New York NY 10011-8411

GOOD, VIRGINIA JOHNSON, real estate executive; b. Onancock, Va., Mar. 1, 1919; d. Obed Wilbur and Sallie Mildred (Deyerle) Johnson; m. William Dennis Good, Jan. 14, 1941 (dec. Apr. 1970). Bus. cert., Elon College, N.C., 1937; real estate cert., U. Miami, 1973; student, Montgomery County Jr. Coll., 1974. Acct. Carolina Biol. Supply Co., Elon College, N.C., 1935-39, Sears Roebuck, Richmond, Va., 1939-40, Ritchie Electric, Charlottesville, Va., 1940-41; mgmt. investor Dr. & Mrs. William D. Good Real Estate, Washington and Gaithersburg, Md., 1941-70, Good Properties, Washington and Miami Beach, Fla., 1970—, Dennis Apts., Miami Beach, Fla., 1972—; Mem. D.C. Apt. Owners/Mgmt. Assn., Washington, 1970-84, Miami Beach Apt. Owners Assn., 1970-86, North Shore Apt. Owners Assn., Miami Beach, 1986-88. Exec. com. Anti Rock Quarry, Dawsonville, Md., 1959, Save Our Coast, Miami Beach, 1982-86; mem. Montgomery County Hist. and Geneal. Soc., Rockville, Md., 1977—, Nat. Geneal. Soc., 1980—, Greater Miami Geneal. Soc., Miami, 1982—, Va. Hist./Geneal. Soc., Richmond, 1988—, Bradley Blvd. Civic Assn., Bethesda, Md., 1989. Mem. La Gorce Country Club, Miami Beach, Columbia Country Club (Chevy Chase, Md.), DAR, Nat. Soc. So. Dames, United Daus. of Confederacy, Nat. Soc. Colonial Dames of XVII Century, Nat. Huguenot Soc. Mem. United Church of Christ. Home: 5310 La Gorce Dr Miami FL 33140-2134 Office: 5723 Bradley Blvd Bethesda MD 20814-1033

GOODALE, JENNIFER PAINE, public relations specialist; b. Buenos Aires, May 30, 1962; came to U.S., 1962; d. Thomas Trefethen Goodale and Nancy Ellen Hall. BA, Barnard Coll., 1984. Customer svc. rep. Van Mosman Merchandising, N.Y.C., 1984-87; coord. cultural affairs Philip Morris Cos. Inc., N.Y.C., 1986-90, cultural affairs specialist, 1990—. Fund raiser, class agt. Taft Sch., Watertown, Conn., 1980—; assoc. Next Wave Assn., Bklyn. Acad. Music, 1990-92; bd. dirs. Voice Theater, 1991-92; mem. jr. com. Am. Ballet Theatre. Office: Philip Morris Cos Inc 120 Park Ave New York NY 10017-5523

GOODE, CARON BANTA, therapist, educational consultant, writer; b. Lawton, Okla., Oct. 12, 1951; s. Julius Henry and Georgia (Gorman) Banta; m. Philip C. Chinn (div.); 1 child, Kristin; m. Thomas O. Goode, Dec. 21, 1986. BS, Okla. Coll. Liberal Arts, 1971; MEd, Our Lady of the Lakes U., 1973; EdD, George Washington U., 1983. Tchr., speech therapist Alamo Heights Sch. Dist., San Antonio, 1972-74, edn. diagnostician, 1974-76; spl. edn. cons. Region XI Svc. Ctr., Ft. Worth, 1976-78; rsch. assoc. Spl. Olympics, Inc., Washington, 1978-81; dir. counseling and edn. Seton Ctrs., Inc., Falls Church, Va., 1982; pvt. edn. and psychol. trainer, cons., 1982-86; pvt. therapist, researcher Center Harbor, N.H., 1986—; bd. dirs. New Found. for Children, Center Harbor; writer Zephyr Press, Tucson, 1991—; rschr., writer and cons. UFO Orgns., 1989—. Author: Mind Fitness for Esteem/Excellence, 1991; contbr. articles to profl. jours. Mem. ASCD, Assn. Past Life Therapy, Assn. Humanistic Psychology, The Global Assn. for Transforming Edn., Nat. Assn. for Edn. of Early Childhood. Home and Office: PO Box 1496 Center Harbor NH 03226

GOODE, CYNTHIA BAIRD, corporate executive; b. Bayshore, N.Y., Nov. 6, 1957; d. Robert Breckenridge and Esther Madelyn (Steere) Baird; divorced; children: Emily Amanda, Miles Cary. BA, Purdue U., 1980. Sous chef Greensleeves Restaurant, Indpls., 1981-82, LaRotisserie Restaurant, Milw., 1982-84; treas., v.p., sec. Robert B. Baird Div., Southampton, N.Y., 1987—; also bd. dirs. Robert B. Baird & Co., Inc., Southampton; v.p., treas. Polyesther Corp., Southampton, 1987—. Contbr. to cook book: You Can't Be Too Rich or Too Thin: Hamptons Cooking, 1988. Mem. Parrish Art Mus., Smithsonian Instn., Shinnecock Yacht Club, Southampton Ballet Co., Southampton Peconic Beach Club. Home: 84 Camberly Rd East Hampton NY 11937-1406 Office: Polyester Corp Robert B Baird Div PO Box 5076 Southampton NY 11969-5076

GOODE, W. WILSON, mayor; b. Seaboard, N.C., Aug. 19, 1938; m. Velma Williams; children: Muriel, Wilson, Natasha. Student, Morgan State Coll., Balt.; MPA, U. Pa. Probation officer, bldg. maintenance supr., ins. claims adjuster; exec. dir. Phila. Council Community Advancement; head Pa. Pub. Utility Commn., 1978; mng. dir. City of Phila., 1980-83, mayor, 1984—. With U.S. Army. Democrat. Office: City Hall #215 Philadelphia PA 19107

GOODE-ELMAN, ALICE NEUFELD, English educator; b. Bronx, N.Y., June 6, 1949; d. Lewis and Hilda (Rifkin) Neufeld; m. Richard Elman, Apr. 9, 1978; 1 child, Lila Neufeld Elman; 1 stepchild, Margaret. BA, SUNY, Stonybrook, 1970, MA, 1971, PhD, 1979. Prof. humanities Suffolk Community Coll., Selden, N.Y., 1975—, head dept. humanities, 1990—. Contbr. articles to profl. jours., book reviews. NEH grantee, 1983; SUNY-Albany/Ford Found. and UUP/NYS Labor Mgmt. Com. grantee, 1991. Mem. MLA, NOW, Nat. Women's Studies Assn., SUNY Women's Exec. Coun. Home: PO Box 216 Stony Brook NY 11790-0216

GOODELMAN, RUTH N., sculptor; b. Johnstown, Pa., Sept. 28, 1914; d. Samuel and Annie (Kaplan) Nisenson; m. Leon Goodelman, Jan. 13, 1945 (dec. Dec. 1957); children: Peggy Martin, Suzy. Cert., Traphagen Sch. of Design, 1933; student, Columbia U., 1934; studied with, Bella Artes, 1975, Kyle Smith Studio, 1985. Dancer, choreographer Eternal Rd., N.Y.C., 1936-38; fashion designer N.Y.C., 1932-68; pub. Med. Rsch. Press, N.Y.C., 1958-75; tchr. fashion art Fashion Inst. Tech. Parson's Sch. Design, N.Y.C., 1971-74; freelance sculptor N.Y.C., 1975—. Mem. Nat. Assn. Women Artists, N.Y. Artist Equity Assn., Stone Sculpture Soc. of N.Y., Sculptors League, Orgn. of Ind. Artists. Home: 24E E 11th St New York NY 10003-4436

GOODEN, DWIGHT EUGENE, professional baseball player; b. Tampa, Fla., Nov. 16, 1964; s. Dan and Ella Mae G.; m. Monica Colleen Harris, Nov. 21, 1987. Pitcher minor league teams, Kingsport, Little Falls and Lynchburg, 1982-83, N.Y. Mets, Nat. League, 1984—; mem. Nat. League All-Star Team, 1984-86, 88. Named Pitcher of Yr., Carolina League, 1983, Rookie of Yr., Nat. League, 1984, Rookie Pitcher of Yr., Nat. League, 1984; winner Cy Young award Nat. League, 1985; first major league pitcher to record 200 strikeouts in each of first 3 seasons. Office: care NY Mets William A Shea Stadium Roosevelt Avenue St Flushing NY 11368-2132*

GOODENOUGH, DAVID JOHN, radiology educator; b. Reading, Berks, Eng., Oct. 3, 1944; came to U.S., 1959; s. Douglas Frank and Irene Hilda (Booth) G.; m. Marjorie Evelyn Reed, Sept. 7, 1963; children: Jennifer, Meredith. BS, U. Chgo., 1967, PhD, 1972. Instr. radiology U. Chgo., 1972-73; vis. assoc. FDA Bur. Radiol. Health, Rockville, Md., 1973-74; asst. prof. radiology Johns Hopkins U., Balt., 1974-75; assoc. prof., dir. div. radiology physics George Washington U., Washington, 1975-84, prof. radiology, 1985—, co-dir. Inst. Med. Imaging, 1990—; cons. NIH, Bethesda, Md., 1975—, VA, Washington, 1975—, Inst. Radiol. Imaging Scis., Myersville, Md., 1984—; expert Internat. Atomic Energy Agy., Vienna, Austria, 1990—. Editor: Diagnostic Images in Medicine, 1983; contbr. articles to profl. jours.; patentee in field. Recipient Svc. Citation, Soc. Photooptical Engrs., San Diego, 1974, Sci. Citation, Radiol. Soc. N.Am., Chgo., 1977, Medal Presentation, Internat. Congress Radiology, Paris, 1989, Certs. of Commendation, Philippines Nuclear Regulatory Agy., Manila, 1991, Philippines Dept. Radiation Health, Manila, 1991. Mem. AAUP, Assn. Univ. Radiologists, Soc. Magnetic Resonance Medicine, Soc. Photo Optical Instrumentation, Soc. Nuclear Medicine. Republican. Methodist. Home: 3917 Crow Rock Rd Myersville MD 21773 Office: George Washington U Dept Radiology 901 23d St NW Washington DC 20037

GOODES, MELVIN RUSSELL, manufacturing company executive; b. Hamilton, Ont., Can., Apr. 11, 1935; s. Cedric Percy and Mary Melba (Lewis) G.; m. Arlene Marie Bourne, Feb. 23, 1963; children: Melanie, Michelle, David. B in Commerce, Queen's U., Kingston, Ont., Can., 1957; MBA, U. Chgo., 1960. Rsch. assoc. Can. Econ. Rsch. Assocs., Toronto, Ont., 1957-58; market planning coord. Ford Motor Co. Can., Oakville, Ont., 1960-64; asst. to v.p. O'Keefe Breweries, Toronto, 1964-65; mgr. new product devel. Adams Brands div. Warner-Lambert Can., Scarborough, Ont., 1965-68; area mgr. Warner-Lambert Internat., Toronto, 1968-69; regional dir. confectionary ops. Warner-Lambert Europe, Brussels, 1969-70; pres. Warner-Lambert Mex., 1970-76; pres. Pan-Am. zone Warner-Lambert Internat., Morris Plains, N.J., 1976-77, pres. Pan-Am. and Asian zone, 1977-79; pres. consumer products div. Warner-Lambert Co., Morris Plains, N.J., 1979-81, sr. v.p., pres. consumer products group, 1981-83, exec. v.p., pres. U.S. ops., 1984-85, pres., chief operating officer, 1985-91, chmn., chief exec. officer, 1991—, also bd. dirs., chmn. bd., chief exec. officer, 1991—; bd. dirs. Chem. Banking Corp., Chem. Bank, Unisys; mem. exec. adv. council Nat. Ctr. Ind. Retail Pharmacy, 1984-85. Bd. dirs. Coun. on Family Health, N.Y.C., 1981-86, Advt. Edn. Found., N.Y.C., 1989-91; mem. fin. com. Joint Coun. on Econ. Edn., 1984—, mem. exec. com., 1986—; mem. Internat. Exec. Svc. Corps., 1989—; mem. adv. coun. Sch. of Bus. Queen's U., Kingston, Ont., Can., 1980-84; trustee Drew U., Madison, N.J., 1985-88, Queen's U., 1988—. Fellow Ford Found., 1958, Sears, Roebuck Found., 1959. Mem. nat. Wholesale Druggists Assn. (assoc. adv. com.), Nat. Assn. Retail Druggists (exec. adv. coun. 1983-85), Pharm. Mfrs. Assn. (bd. dirs. 1989-91), Proprietary Assn. (v.p. 1983-88, bd. dirs., mem. exec. com. 1981-88), Nat. Alliance Bus. (bd. dirs. 1984-86), Plainfield Country Club (N.J.), Econ. (N.Y.C.). Unitarian. Office: Warner-Lambert Co 201 Tabor Rd Morris Plains NJ 07950-2693

GOODHARTZ, GERALD, law librarian; b. N.Y.C., Oct. 23, 1938; s. Jack and Anna (Sperling) G.; m. Carol Scialli, Aug. 18, 1969; children: Joanna, Allison. BSCE, CCNY, 1961; MLS, U. So. Calif., 1970. Night reference asst. Assn. Bar of City of N.Y., 1956-61; library asst. Cravath, Swaine & Moore, N.Y.C., 1961-65; head librarian Rosenman, Colin, Freund, Lewis & Cohen, N.Y.C., 1965-69, Keatinge & Sterling, L.A., 1969-70, Kaye, Scholer, Fierman, Hays & Handler, N.Y.C., 1970—; library planning cons. Olympic Towers, N.Y.C., 1975; lectr. in field. Mem. ABA, Am. Assn. Law Libraries (cert.), Law Library Assn. Greater N.Y., Assn. Law Librarians of Upstate N.Y., Spl. Libraries Assn., ALA, Am. Soc. Info. Scientists, Am. Mgmt. Assn., Assn. Info. Mgrs., Nat. Micrographics Assn. Office: Kaye Scholer Fierman Hays & Handler 425 Park Ave New York NY 10022-3506

GOODHUE, MARY BRIER, lawyer, state senator; b. London, 1921; naturalized, 1942; d. Ernest and Marion H. (Hawks) Brier; m. Francis A. Goodhue, Jr., May 15, 1948 (dec. Sept. 1990); 1 child, Francis A. III. BA, Vassar Coll., 1942; LLB, U. Mich., 1944. Bar: N.Y. 1945. Assoc. Root, Clark, Buckner & Ballantine, N.Y.C., 1945-48; asst. counsel N.Y. State Crime Commn., N.Y.C., 1951-53, Moreland Commn., N.Y.C., 1953-54; mem. firm Goodhue, Arons & Neary and predecessors, Mt. Kisco, 1955—; mem. N.Y. State Assembly from 93d Dist., 1975-78, N.Y. State Senate, 1979—. Trustee, Presbyn. Hosp., N.Y.C., Westchester Mental Health Assn.; N.Y. del. Nat. Women's Conf., Houston, 1977. Mem. ABA, West Bar Assn., No. Westchester Bar Assn. Office: 126 Barker St Mount Kisco NY 10549-1500 Also: McLain St Mount Kisco NY 10549 Also: NY State Senate Albany NY 12224

GOODLAND, KATHARINE, English educator, military career officer; b. Estherville, Iowa, Jan. 10, 1958; d. Fayette Paul and Sarah Josephine (Stevenson) G. BS, U.S. Mil. Acad., 1980; MA, Purdue U., 1990. Commd. 2d lt. U.S. Army, 1980, advanced through grades to capt., 1984; platoon comdr. 9th Div. Arty., Ft. Lewis, Wash., 1980-81, legal officer, 1981-83; protocol officer Ft. Sill Okla., Lawton, 1984-85; pers. officer 1-32d Field Arty., Hanau, Fed. Republic of Germany, 1985-86, battery comdr., 1986-88, ops. officer, 1988; instr. U.S. Mil. Acad., West Point, N.Y., 1990—. Mem. Modern Lang. Assn., Nat. Coun. Tchrs., Shakespeare Assn. Am., Phi Kappa Phi. Home: US Mil Acad West Point NY 10996

GOODLING, WILLIAM F., congressman; b. Loganville, Pa., Dec. 5, 1927; m. Hilda Wright; children: Todd, Jennifer. B.S., U. Md.; M.S., Western Md. Coll.; doctoral studies, Pa. State U. Various teaching positions including prin. West York Area High Sch.; supt. Spring Grove Area Schs.; supr. student tchrs. Pa. State U.; mem. 94th-102nd congresses from 19th Pa. Dist., 1975—; mem. edn. and labor coms., com. on budget Congress from 19th Pa. Dist. Served with Armed Forces, 1946-48. Republican. Methodist. Club: Lions. Office: 2263 Rayburn House Office Bldg Washington DC 20515

GOODMAN, ABBIE REBECCA, executive; b. Pitts., Jan. 17, 1961; d. Stephen Richard and Marjorie (Connors) Goodman; m. Laurence D. Shind, Sept. 8, 1990. BA, Chatham Coll., 1982. Pub. outreach coord. Mayor's Office Cable Communications, Boston, 1982-84; project mgr. Mass. Corp. Ednl. Telecommunications, Boston, 1984-86, mktg. dir., 1986-88; cons. Mass. Office Internat. Trade and Investment, Boston, 1988-91, exec. dir., 1991—; cons. Bishoff-Solomon Communications, Boston. Pres. Mass. Women's Polit. Caucus, Boston, 1989-90; bd. dirs. Jackson Mann Community Sch., Boston, 1984-88; life mem. Hadassah, Boston, 1983—. Jewish. Office: Mass Office Internat Trade 100 Cambridge St Ste 902 Boston MA 02202

GOODMAN, ALFRED NELSON, lawyer; b. N.Y.C., Jan. 21, 1945; s. Bernard R. and Mildred (Schlanger) G. BS in Mech. and Aerospace Scis., U. Rochester, 1966; JD, Georgetown U., 1969. Bar: N.Y. 1970, D.C. 1971, U.S. Supreme Ct. 1974. Patent examiner U.S. Patent Office, Washington, 1969-71; assoc. Roylance, Abrams, Berdo & Goodman, Washington, 1971-74, ptnr., 1975—. Mem. Am. Patent Law Assn., ABA, Bar Assn. of D.C. (chmn. patent, trademark and copyright law sect. 1984-85, bd. dirs. 1985-86). Home: 4948 Sentinel Dr Bethesda MD 20816-3510 Office: Roylance Abrams Berdo & Goodman 1225 Connecticut Ave NW Ste 315 Washington DC 20036-2680

GOODMAN, BRIAN WILLIAM, financial services company executive; b. Liverpool, Eng.; came to U.S., 1955; s. Thomas William and Kathleen Mary (Carter) G.; m. Marilyn Byrnes, Aug. 6, 1960 (div. 1986); children: Alistair Raphael, Nicholas Seth. MA, Cambridge U., Eng., 1955; fellow, Yale U., 1955-57; Anglo-Am. Mktg. Program, Harvard Bus. Sch., 1968. Info. officer British Govt., N.Y.C., 1958-60, comml. officer, 1960-70; asst. v.p. Barclays Bank PLC, N.Y.C., 1970-74, v.p., 1974-85, cons., 1985-87; cons. Group of Thirty, N.Y.C., 1985-87; pres. N. Am. Eurofi, PLC, Ossining, N.Y., 1988—. Sec. Ea. U.S. Rugby Union, N.Y., 1958-72; trustee Royal Coll. Surgeon's Found., N.Y., 1982—. Mem. Am. Mgmt. Assn. (internat. coun. 1976—, Service award 1991), Appalachian Mtn. Club, N.Y.-N.J. Trail Conf. Office: Eurofi PLC 762 Kitchawan Rd Ossining NY 10562-1127

GOODMAN, DAVID BARRY POLIAKOFF, physician, educator; b. Lynn, Mass., June 1, 1942; s. Nathan and Eva (Poliakoff) G.; children—Derek, Alex. A.B., Harvard Coll., 1964; M.D., U. Pa., 1968, Ph.D., 1972. Intern dept. pathology U. Pa. Hosp., Phila., 1971-72; assoc. pediatrics and biochemistry U. Pa. Sch. Medicine, Phila., 1972-73, research asst. prof., 1973-76, assoc. prof., 1980-82, prof. pathology and lab. medicine, 1982—, dir. div. lab. medicine, 1980-83; asst. prof. internal medicine Yale U. Med. Sch., New Haven, 1976-79, assoc. prof., 1979-80; cons. NSF, VA, Ctr. Oral Health Research, U. Pa. Contbr. numerous articles to profl. jours.; mng. editor: Metabolic Bone Disease and Related Rsch., 1981-90; editor Hormonal Regulation Epithelial Transport Ions and Water, 1981, Technology Impact: Potential Directions for Laboratory Medicine, 1984. Recipient Achievement award Upjohn Co., 1968; Roland Jackson scholar, 1964-68; Pa. Plan scholar, 1968-72. Fellow N.Y. Acad. Scis. (Lamport award 1981); mem. Acad. Clin. Lab. Physicians and Scientists, AAAS, Am. Assn. Pathologists, Am. Fedn. Clin. Research, Am. Heart Assn., Am. Physiol. Soc., Am. Soc. Bone and Mineral Research, Soc. Devel. Biology, Soc. Neurosci. Home: 1201 Grenox Rd Wynnewood PA 19096-2218 Office: U Pa Hosp Dept Pathology and Lab Med Founders 7.102 3400 Spruce St Philadelphia PA 19104-4220

GOODMAN, ELAINE IRIS, public relations executive; b. Phila., Sept. 28, 1963; d. Martin Sylvan and Barbara (Sack) G. BA, Temple U., 1985. Pub. rels. account exec. JRA Mktg. Communications, Phila., 1985-87; pub. rels. counselor FCB/Lewis, Gilman & Kynett, Inc., Phila., 1988-92; sr. account exec. Leu Lane Advt. & Pub. Rels., Bala Cynwyd, Pa., 1992—. Active polit. affairs com. Young Leadership Coun., FAJA, Phila., 1987; core com. mem. Young Jewish Leadership Concepts, Phila., 1990—; fundraiser U.S. Holocaust Meml. Mus., Phila. Scholar Soc. Profl. Journalists, Phila. 1981; recipient Gold Circle Merit award Am. Soc. Assn. Execs., 1988, 89. Mem. LWV Phila.Pub. Rels. Soc. Am. (chair Pepperpot com. 1992, editor chpt. newsletter 1988-90, award program judge 1991, Pepperpot Merit award 1988, 89, Pepperpot award 1991, Drumbeater award 1990-91), World Affairs Coun. Phila. Office: Levlane Advtg and Pub Relsc 1 Belmont Ave Bala Cynwyd PA 19004

GOODMAN, JACOB ELI, mathematician; b. Lynn, Mass., Nov. 15, 1933; s. Saul Lederman and Sarah (Glassman) G.; m. Josephine Leona Fox, Aug. 24, 1973; children: Rachel Elizabeth, Naomi Susan. BA, NYU, 1953; MA, Columbia U., 1955, PhD, 1967. Asst. prof. math. CUNY, N.Y.C., 1967-72, assoc. prof. math., 1973-80, prof. math., 1981—. Editor: (book) Discrete Geometry and Convexity, 1985, Discrete and Computational Geometry: Papers From the DIMACS Special Year, 1991; co-editor-in-chief Discrete & Computational Geometry, 1985—; mem. editorial bd. Computational Geometry: Theory and Applications, 1990—; contbr. numerous articles to math. jours. Recipient Lester R. Ford award Math. Assn. Am., 1990, Fulbright rsch. award, 1991. Mem. Am. Math. Soc. Jewish. Office: CUNY City Coll Dept of Math New York NY 10031

GOODMAN, JORDAN ELLIOT, journalist; b. N.Y.C., Sept. 13, 1954; s. Elliot Raymond and Norma (Bromberg) G.; m. Suzanne Kay Koblentz, June 20, 1981; 1 child, Jason Koblentz. Student, London Sch. Econ., 1974-75; BA, Amherst Coll., 1976. Editor in chief Info Mag., N.Y.C., 1977-79; sr. reporter Money Mag., N.Y.C., 1979—; commentator Fin. News Network, N.Y.C., 1985-91, Cable News Network, N.Y.C., 1989-90, Mutual Broadcasting System, Washington, 1990—, NBC News, 1991—; regional dir. Soc. Profl. Journalists, Chgo., 1989-90. Author: Dictionary of Finance and Investment Terms, 1986, rev., 1990, Barron's Finance and Investment Handbook, 1987, rev., 1991. Mem. Common Cause, N.Y.C., 1985—. Mem. Mid-Atlantic Club, N.Y.C. Fin. Writers Assn., N.Y. Deadline Club (pres. 1986-87). Democrat. Jewish. Home: 438 3d St Brooklyn NY 11215-2952 Office: Money Mag 1271 Ave of the Americas New York NY 10020-1300

GOODMAN, MICHAEL B(ARRY), communications educator; b. Dallas, July 10, 1949; s. Harold A. and Dora (Einhorn) G.; m. Karen E. Kailenta, June 4, 1977; children: 1 stepchild, Craig Cook, 1 child, John David. BA, U. Tex., 1971; MA, SUNY, Stony Brook, 1972, PhD, 1979. Adj. instr. SUNY, Old Westbury, 1976-79; adj. asst. prof. N.Y. Inst. Tech., N.Y.C., 1976-82, N.Y.U., 1979-81; asst. prof. SUNY, Stony Brook, 1979-81, Northeastern U., Boston, 1982-86; assoc. prof., dir. M.A. in corporate communication Fairleigh Dickinson U., Madison, N.J., 1986—; cons. in communications to numerous orgns. in U.S.; conducts seminars and workshops on written communication, 1979—; conf. chmn. Internat. Profl. Communication Conf., Phila., 1993. Author: William S. Burroughs: An Annotated Bibliography, 1975, Contemporary Literary Censorship: The Case History of Burroughs Naked Lunch, 1981, Write to the Point: Effective Communication in the Workplace, 1984, William S. Burroughs: A Research Guide, 1990; contbr. articles and revs. to profl. jours. and lit. mags.; assoc. editor Issues in Corp. Communication, IEEE Transactions on Profl. Communications, 1990, 91; cons. reader for College English. Vice-pres. Friends Sem. PTA, N.Y.C., 1990-91. Named to Resident Faculty Nat. Faculty Excellence in Teaching English Program, Vassar Coll., 1984. Mem. IEEE Profl. Communication Soc. (adminstrv. com.), Nat. Coun. Tchrs. English, Soc. for Tech. Communication (sr. mem.), Modern Lang. Assn., Am. Mgmt. Assn., Assn. for Bus. Communication, Authors Guild, Authors League. Home: 470 2d Ave New York NY 10016-9112 Office: Fairleigh Dickinson U 285 Madison Ave Madison NJ 07940-1099

GOODMAN, NEAL ROBERT, international educator, consultant; b. Jersey City, May 13, 1947; s. Leo and Beatrice (Gering) G.; m. Varda Armoni, June 20, 1971; children: Jennifer, Laurie. BA, St. Peter's Coll., 1969; MA, CCNY, 1970; PhD, NYU, 1977. Faculty St. Peter's Coll., Jersey City, 1971—; prof. St. Peter's Coll., 1986—; pres. Global Dynamics, Inc., Randolph, N.J., 1984—. Author: Intercultural Training, 1987, Doing Business With Japan, 1991, Doing Business With Germany, 1991, Internationalizing the Curriculum, 1991. Mem. ASTD, Soc. Intercultural Edn. Tng. and Rsch. (treas. 1988-92, exec. bd. 1988-92), Nat. Soc. for Performance Instrn., Am. Sociol. Assn., Nat. Assn. Foreign Student Affairs, Inst. for Internat. Edn. Home: 19 Wilkinson Rd Randolph NJ 07869-3418 Office: St Peters Coll 2641 Kennedy Blvd Jersey City NJ 07306

GOODMAN, PAMELA BETH, assistant stockbroker; b. Phila., Dec. 28, 1964; d. Donald A. and Reeta (Stern) G. BA, Morley Coll. Art, London, 1985, European Sch. Bus., London, 1985, City U. of London, 1985, Muhlenberg Coll., 1986. Account mgr. MCI Telecommunications, Bala Cynwyd, Pa., 1986-87; asst. broker and mgrs. asst. Merrill Lynch Consumer Markets, Phila., 1986—; asst. to mgr. Merrill Lynch, Phila., 1988-89. Inventor boardgames. Mem. World Affairs Coun., Phila., 1984, Better Bus. Bur., Phila., 1986. Scholarship Detra Assn., 1982. Mem. Muhlenberg Bus. Club (v.p. 1982-83), Federated Allied Jewish Appeal, Nat. Assn. of Securities Dealers, N.Y. Stock Exch. (registered rep.), Am. Stock Exch. (registered rep.), Chgo. Bd. of Options Exch. Home: # 1 Mary Watersford Rd Bala Cynwyd PA 19004

GOODMAN, RICHARD, executive; b. Hanover, N.H., Jan. 9, 1931; s. Benjamin Samuel and Anna (Tapper) G.; widower; children: Jane, Susan, David. BA, Dartmouth U., 1953; MA, Wesleyan Coll., 1955; EdD, Harvard U., 1961. Tchr. Middletown (Conn.), 1955; teaching prin. Meriden (N.H.), 1957-59; supt. Miford (N.H.), 1961-65; exec. dir. New England Sch. Div. Coun., Cambridge, Mass., 1965-69; supt. Wellesley, Mass., 1969-76; exec. dir. N.H. Sch. Bds., N.H. Sch. Adminstrs., U. N.H. Edn. Svc. Ctr., Durham, 1976—. Sgt. U.S. Army, 1955-57. Mem. AASA. AEFA, ASCD.

GOODMAN, RICHARD SHALEM, lawyer, orthopedic surgeon. BA, Alfred (N.Y.) U., 1955; MD, N.Y. U., 1960; JD, Touro Coll., 1987. lic. N.Y. 1961—, Calif. 1961—. Intern Ind. U. Med. Ctr., Indianapolis, 1960-61; resident in gen. surgery Bronx Mcpl. Hosp. Ctr., 1961-62; resident in orthopedics N.Y.C. Med. Ctr. and various others, 1964-67; attending physician St. John's Hosp., Smithtown, N.Y., 1967—; asst. prof. SUNY, Stony Brook, 1971-88; pres. staff Community Hosp. of We. Suffolk, 1967—; cons. to numerous bus., govt. agys., and ins. cos.; presenter, speaker, and panelist in fields. Author: Proof of Facts; contbg. author: Handling Soft Tissue Injury Cases: Medical Aspects, 1988, Medical and Hospital Negligence; contbr. articles to med. and legal jours.; bd. editorial cons. Medical Malpractice Prevention. Trustee Alfred U., 1978-84. Fellow Am. Acad. Orthoped. Surgeons, Am. Coll. Legal Med. (mem. policy and planning com., program chmn. annual meeting 1988—); mem. Am. Bd. Othorped. Surgery (cert. 1969), Ea. Orthoped. Assn., Am. Soc. Law and Med., Am. Coll. Sports Med., Am. Rheumatism Assn., Suffolk County Med. Soc., N.Y. State Med. Soc., Internat. Coll. Surgeons, PanAm. Med. Assn., Arthritis Found., N.Y. State. Soc. Orthoped. Surgeons, N.Y. U. Bellevue Orthoped. Alumni Assn., Am. Acad. Legal and Industrial Med. (bd. govs.), Bach Aria Group (bd. dirs. 1970-88), University Club. Office: 285 E Main St Smithtown NY 11787-2912

GOODMAN, ROBERT PHILIP, jewelry company executive, real estate broker; b. Brookline, Mass., Apr. 3, 1950; s. Warren Philip and Laura Bernice (Freeman) G.; children: Laura Michele, Michael Lee. BS summa cum laude, U. Md., 1990. Cert. paralegal. Mgr. Kay Jewelers, Inc., Alexandria, Va., 1973-80; pres. Fallston (Md.) Jewelers, 1980-81, Robert's Jewelers, Inc., Balt., 1981—; broker Am. Bus. Brokers, Inc., Towson, Md., 1991—. Mem. Jewelers of Am., Md., DC and Va. Tri-State Jewelers Assn., Alpha Sigma Lambda. Republican. Jewish. Office: Am Bus Brokers Inc 905 York Rd Baltimore MD 21204-2514

GOODMAN, ROY MATZ, state senator, business executive; b. N.Y.C., Mar. 5, 1930; s. Bernard A. and Alice (Matz) G.; m. Barbara Christine Furrer, June 28, 1955; children: Claire Goodman Pellegrini, Leslie Alice, Randolph Bernard. BA cum laude, Harvard U., 1951, MBA with distinction, 1953; LHD (hon.), Pratt Inst., 1991. Assoc. buying and new bus. dept. Kuhn, Loeb & Co. Investment Bankers, 1955-60; pres. Ex-Lax Distbg. Co., Inc., 1962-71, chmn. bd., 1971-75, also bd. dirs., 1975-80; mem. N.Y. State Senate, 1968—; sr. asst. majority leader, chmn. investigations, taxation and govt. ops. com.; past chmn. legis. com. on pub.-pvt. coop.; chmn. Senate spl. com. on arts and cultural affairs ; mem. Senate task force on def. spending and N.Y. Ins. Exchange; mem. fin., rules, cities, edn., crime and correction and transp. coms., subcom. on libs.; pres. Goodman Family Found.; pres. Roycemore Inc., 1968-70, also bd. dirs.; pres. Drug Devel. Corp., 1968-70, bd. dirs.; bd. dirs. 1st Empire State Corp.; mem. Bklyn. adv. bd. Chem. Bank N.Y. Trust Co., 1963-65; commr. fin., fin. adminstr. City of N.Y., 1966-68; mem. mayor's cabinet and supercabinet, 1966-68; chmn. Housing and Urban Devel. Com., 1968-76, State Charter Revision Commn. for N.Y.C., 1972-76; adj. prof. pub. adminstrn. Baruch Coll. CUNY, 1975. Mem. N.Y.C. Banking Commn., 1966-67; past trustee N.Y.C. Police Pension Fund, N.Y.C. Fire Dept. Pension Fund; chmn. Parents Com., Dalton Schs. Devel. Program; past trustee, mem. Brotherhood-In-Action; trustee Heart Research Found.; exec. asst. to chmn. N.Y. State Assembly Jud. Com., 1963-64; asst. to atty. gen. State N.Y., 1960; pres. 9th A.D. Rep. Club, 1963-64; del. N.Y. State Rep. Convs., 1966-86, Rep. Nat. Conv., 1968, 72, 76, 80, 84, 88, 92. Presdl. Elector, 1984; chmn. N.Y. County Rep. Com., 1981—, treas., 1965; mem. N.Y. Rep. State Com., exec. com.; N.Y. State co-chmn. Bush-for-Pres. campaigns, 1988, 92, Bush-Quayle Nat. Fin. Com., 1988, 92; candidate for Mayor of N.Y.C., 1977; past trustee Barnard Coll.; trustee Carnegie Hall Soc., Inc., Carnegie Hall Corp., Columbia Coll. Pharm. Scis., L.I. Coll. Hosp., N.Y. Com. Young Audiences, United Jewish Appeal, Tel Aviv U.; presdl. appointee to Nat. Commn. Fine Arts, 1985-89, Nat. Coun. Arts, 1989; fellow Met. Mus. Art; patron Met. Opera; sponsor N.Y. Philharm. Soc.; trustee Temple Emanu-El; bd. dirs. N.Y. Legis. Svc., Inc., 1990; past bd. dirs. Freedom House, Dalton Sch.; mem. council advisors N.Y. Com. for Young Audiences, Harvard Com. on Univ. Resources, John F. Kennedy Sch. Govt. adv. bd; mem. com. Harvard U. Overseers to Visit John F. Kennedy Sch. Govt. Lt. USNR, 1953-56. Recipient Disting. Service award (Young Man of Yr.) Jaycees, 1966, Mt. Scopus citation Hebrew U., Jerusalem, 1968, Scroll of Honor United Jewish Appeal, 1970, Kennedy Ctr. award for Disting. Leadership in Arts-in Edn., Nat. Arts Club Citation of Merit, Medal of Merit City U., 1972, Man of Yr. award Brotherhood-in-Action, 1972, Humanitarian award Soc. for Prevention Cruelty to Children, 1976, citation for community service Odyssey House, 1976, Our Town newspaper award for leadership in City Charter revision, 1976, Fiorello H. LaGuardia Meml. award, 1979-80, citation for outstanding service N.Y. Young Rep. Club, 1982, Disting. Alumni award Hunter Coll. Elem. Sch. Parents Assn., 1985, Service awards N.Y. Police Found. and N.Y. Fire Safety Found., 1986, Patriotic Service award U.S. Treasury Dept.; named to honor scroll Columbia Assn. of N.Y.C. Police Dept., 1979, N.Y. State Rep. of Yr. Ripon Soc., 1972; named Statesman Father of Yr. award, 1984, named to Econ. Hon. Soc. St. John's U. Mem. Anti-Defamation League (bd. govs. N.Y.), Am. Young Pres.'s Orgn., Fin. Analysts Fedn., N.Y. Soc. Security Analysts, Council Fgn. Relations, Assn. Harvard Alumni (past dir.), Omicron Delta Epsilon (hon.). Clubs: City, Century Assn., Harvard Bus. Sch. (N.Y.C.); Senate of N.Y. State; Harvard (gov.); Century Country (Purchase, N.Y.); Fort Orange (Albany, N.Y.)Dutch Treat. Home: 1035 5th Ave New York NY 10028-0135 Office: 270 Broadway Rm 2400 New York NY 10007-2375 also: NY State Senate Legislative Office Bldg Albany NY 12247

GOODMAN, WALLACE RICHARD, principal; b. Buffalo, Aug. 7, 1941; m. Christine S. Goodman, June 29, 1968; children: Aaron D., Matthew P., Timothy M. BS, SUNY, Fredonia, 1964; MS, Ithaca Coll., 1968. Cert. ednl. adminstr. Music educator Lancaster (N.Y.) Cen., 1964-65, Edward Town Jr. High, Sanborn, N.Y., 1965-68, Williamsville (N.Y.) Cen., 1968-69, Niagara-Wheatfield Cen., Sanborn, N.Y., 1969-80; prin. jr. high Wilson (N.Y.) Cen. Sch., 1980—; v.p. Sch. Adminstrs. Region 12, Buffalo, 1985-87, pres., 1987-89; bd. dirs. Am. youth Symphony and Chorus. Conductor Sanborn (N.Y.) Fire Co. Band, 1966—. Recipient Medal of Honor, Mid-West Nat. Band Assn., 1971, Citation of Excellence, Nat. Band Assn., 1976; named Outstanding Educator, Wheatfield Jaycees. Mem. Wilson Hist. Soc. (bd. dirs.), PTA (life), Masons (past master, jr. warder). Republican. Episcopalian. Home: 2722 Maple Rd Wilson NY 14172

GOODMAN, WILLIAM RICHARD, insurance adjusting company executive; b. Staunton, Va., Sept. 19, 1930; s. Harry and Ruth (Meyer) G.; m. Alice Helene Katzenstein, June 13, 1954; children: Harvey, Laurie, Barry. BS, U. Md., 1952; JD, U. Balt., 1955. Pub. ins. adjuster, lawyer Goodman-Gable-Gould Co., Balt., 1952-73, v.p., 1973-85, pres., 1985—, chmn. bd., 1989—. Chmn. Balt. County Indsl. Devel. Commn., 1967-69; mem. Met. Transit Authority, Balt., 1969-71, bd. rev. Dept. Transp., Md., 1971-76, Md. Racing Commn., 1984. Mem. Nat. Assn. Pub. Ins. Adjusters (dir., v.p., pres., chmn. bd. dirs., Disting. Service award 1987). Democrat. Jewish. Home: 7811 Park Heights Ave Baltimore MD 21208-4322 Office: Goodman Gable Gould Co 6 Reservoir Cir Baltimore MD 21208-1309

GOODMAN-MILLER, DOROTHY VICTORY, music company executive; b. Kingstree, S.C., May 7, 1945; d. Willie Israel and Ila Mai (Mitchum) Goodman; m. Saul Jacob Weitz, May 3, 1965 (div. 1970); m. Elijah Miller, Jan. 13, 1972; children: Michael E., Titus M., Abraham Gabriel, Andrew Israel, Uttara. PsyD, Internat. U., Los Altos, Calif., 1990. Producer, writer, recording artist William David's Swami Records, Bklyn., 1963; with Bklyn. Eagle News, 1963-64; writer, recording artist Amy Records/Screen Gems, N.Y.C., 1963-65; editor Negro Book Club/Afro Am. Woman, N.Y.C., 1965—; adolescent social worker Greer Sch., Hope Farm, N.Y., 1966; sec., adminstrv. asst. Vassar Coll., Poughkeepsie, N.Y., 1968; corres. Harlem Valley Times, Lake Amenia, N.Y., 1968; sec., cons. Inst. for Human Factors in Space, Arlington, Va., 1989—; pres. Goodman Prodns., Arlington, Va., 1985—; cons., writer Orleans Records, New Orleans, 1983—; concert sponsor, cons. Great Day Chorale, Bklyn., 1991; cons. Black Heritage Book Club, 1990-91; dir., founder Elye Goodman Archives for Rsch. on African-Asian Ams., 1989—. Author book of poetry: Blue Springs and Other Seasons, 1987; contbg. author book: Venceremos Brigade, 1970; songwriter numerous songs include: I Wrote You a Letter, 1963; contbr. articles in field of psychopathology of racial predjudice, ethnic rsch. Sponsor Children's Internat., South India, 1990-91; founder, dir. Multi-Ethnic, Multicultural Community Children's Play Group. Named Miss Beaux Arts finalist Ophelia De Vore Alumni, 1964; recipient Silver Poet award World of Poetry, 1988. Mem. Nat. Assn. for Rsch. in Schizioprenia and Depression, S.I. Alliance for the Mentally Ill, Am. Mental Health Fund, S.I. Children Mental Health Soc., S.I. Inst. for the Arts and Scis., Brit. Assn. of Cemeteries in South Asia, Manic Depressive-Depression Assn. Home: 3 Lockman Pl Staten Island NY 10303-2024 Office: Goodman Prodns 1101 N Highland St # 503 Arlington VA 22201-2854

GOODRICH, CHAUNCEY GLENN, professional society administrator; b. Silver Creek, N.Y., Aug. 26, 1928; s. Chauncey E. and Gladys D. (Stolts) G.; m. Alene Lois Braun, Jan. 12, 1952; children: Linda, Sharon, Dale, Lisa. BA, SUNY, Fredonia, 1950; MEd, SUNY, Buffalo, 1956. Tchr. Kenmore (N.Y.) Pub. Schs., 1955-65, sch. prin., 1965-86; chief exec. officer Med. Socs. N.Y., Niagara Falls, 1989—. Sgt. USAF, 1950-53. Office: Med Socs NY PO Box 488 Niagara Falls NY 14302-0488

GOODRICH, ISAAC, neurosurgeon, educator; b. Milledgeville, Ga., Sept. 19, 1939; s. Ellis and Frieda (Bergman) G.; AA, Ga. Mil. Coll., 1959; BS, U. Ga., 1961; MD, Med. Coll. Ga., 1964; m. Dianne L. Brittain, Aug. 28, 1965; children: Mindy Anne, Scott David, Jennifer Gale. Intern, Columbia-Presbyn. Med. Center, N.Y.C., 1964-65, resident in neurosurgery, Yale-New Haven Med. Center, 1967-71; practice medicine specializing in neurosurgery, New Haven, 1971—; instr. neurosurgery, Yale U. Med. Sch., 1970-71, asst. clin. prof., 1978-86; assoc. clin. prof., 1986—; attending neurosurgeon Yale-New Haven Hosp., 1973—, Hosp. St. Raphael, 1971—; mem. courtesy staff Milford Hosp., 1986—; cons. staff Vets. Meml. Med. Ctr., VA Hosp., 1986—, West Haven, 1990—. Served as capt., U.S. Army, 1965-67. Decorated Bronze Star, Air Medal. Cert., Am. Bd. Neurol. Surgery; recipient AMA Physicians Recognition Award for Continuing Med. Edn., 1969, 72, 75, 78, 81, 85, 88; Disting. Alumni award Ga. Mil. Coll., 1980. Fellow ACS, Internat. Coll. Surgeons, Royal Soc. Medicine; mem. Congress of Neurol. Surgeons, New Eng. Neurosurg. Soc., Pan Pacific Surg. Assn., Am. Assn. Neurol. Surgeons, AMA, Conn. State Med. Soc., New Haven City, New Haven County med. assns., AAAS, N.Y. Acad. Scis. Jewish. Designated hon. citizen, Boys Town, Nebr., 1971; contbr. articles, papers to med. publs., meetings. Home: 264 Rimmon Rd Woodbridge CT 06525-1847 Office: 60 Temple St New Haven CT 06510

GOODRICH, JAMES TAIT, neuroscientist, pediatric neurosurgeon; b. Portland, Ore., Apr. 16, 1946; s. Richard and Gail (Josselyn) G.; m. Judy Loudin, Dec. 27, 1970. Student, Golden West Coll., 1971-72; A.A., Orange Coast Coll., 1972; B.S. cum laude, U. Calif.-Irvine, 1974; M.Phil., Columbia U., 1979, Ph.D., 1970 M.D., 1980; Diplomate Am. Bd. Neurological Surgery. Neuroscientist, pediatric neurosurgeon N.Y. Neurol. Inst., N.Y.C., 1981-86; dir. div. pediatric neurosurgery Albert Einstein Coll. Medicine, N.Y.C., 1986—. Contbr. articles to profl. jours. Recipient Roche Labs. award in neuroscis., 1978, Mead-Johnson award, 1978, Bronze medal Alumni Assn. Coll. Physicians and Surgeons, 1980, Sandoz award for outstanding research, 1980; Willamette Industries scholar; NIH grantee. Fellow Royal Soc. Medicine (London); mem. Internat. Soc. Pediatric Neuro-Surgeons, Worshipful Soc. Apothecaries (London), N.Y. Acad. Medicine (Melicow award 1980), Am. Assn. History of Medicine (Sir William Osler medal 1977-78), AMA, Brit. Brain Research Assn., European Brain Research Assn., Friends of Columbia U. Libraries, Friends of Osler Library of McGill U., N.Y. Acad. Scis., Am. Assn. Neurol. Surgeons, Am. Assn. Neurological Surgery (chmn. sect. on history of neurological surgery), Congress Neurol. Surgeons, Med. History Soc. N.J., ISIS History of Sci. Soc., Soc. for Bibliography of Natural History (London), Columbia Presbyn. Med. Soc., U. Calif. Alumni Assn., Soc. Ancient Medicine, AAAS, Am. Osler Soc., Les Amis du Vin, South Coast Wine Explorers Club (past chmn.), Friends of Bacchus Wine Club (past chmn.), Dionysius Council of Presbyn. Hosp. of N.Y.C., Sigma Xi, Alpha Gamma Sigma. Research on neuronal regeneration, brain reconstruction and craniofacial reconstruction. Home: 214 Everett Pl Englewood NJ 07631-1650 Office: Albert Einstein Coll Medicine Montefiore Med Ctr Div Pediatric Neurosurgery Bronx NY 10467

GOODRIDGE, NOEL HERBERT ALAN, chief justice; b. St. John's, Nfld., Can., Dec. 18, 1930; s. William Prout and Freda Dorothy (Hayward) G.; m. Isabelle Patricia Galway, Jan. 22, 1956; children: Alan Edward, William Herbert, Douglas Noel, Maria. BA, Dalhousie U., Halifax, Nova Scotia, 1951, LLB, 1953. Admitted to bar 1953. Assoc., ptnr. Stirling, Ryan and Goodridge and predecessors, St. John's, 1953-75; puisne judge trial div. Supreme Ct. Nfld., 1975-86; judge Ct. Martial Appeal Ct., 1981—; chief justice Ct. of Appeal of Supreme Ct. Nfld., 1986—. Mem. Can. Bar Assn. (pres. Nfld. br. 1972-74, exec. mem. 1975), Can. Judges Conf. (exec. mem. 1978-80), Can. Jud. Coun., Kinsmen Club (pres., life mem., gov. Atlantic Provinces), Rotary (hon.). Mem. Anglican Ch. Can. Home: 71 Rennies Mill Rd, Saint John's, NF Canada A1C 3P9 Office: Supreme Ct, Ct of Appeals PO Box 937, Saint John's, NF Canada A1C 5M3

GOODSELL, JAMES NELSON, journalist; b. Evanston, Ill., June 7, 1929; s. Nelson Jesse and Jean (Wilson) G.; m. Alice Louise Forn, Aug. 26, 1953 (div.); children: Paul Nelson, Amy Jean, Victoria Louise; m. Rhoda Merle Ford, July 24, 1982. BA, Principia Coll., 1951; MA, Mex. City Coll., 1953; PhD, Harvard U., 1966. Reporter The Chgo. Sun, 1947, The Cin. Post, 1955-56; reporter The Christian Sci. Monitor, Boston, 1957-62, Latin Am. editor, 1962-85; editorial advisor Sta. WGBH-PBS, Boston, 1984; anchor, editor Monitor Radio The Christian Sci. Monitor, Boston, 1985-87, Latin Am. corrd., World Monitor, 1987-89, anchor, editor El Monitor de Hoy (TV), 1989—. Editor: Castro's Personal Revolution, 1973. Cpl. U.S. Army, 1953-55. Recipient Maria Moors Cabot award Columbia U., 1968, Peabody award, 1985, Emmy nomination, 1988. Mem. Am. Hist. Assn., Lat. Am. Studies Assn., Conf. on Latin Am. History, Coun. of the Ams., Royal Soc. of Arts, Coun. on Fgn. Rels., Inter-Am. Press Assn. (Fgn. Corr. award 1969, 72, 82), Overseas Press Club (Fgn. Corr. award 1967, 70), Sigma Delta Chi (Fgn. Corr. award 1966). Office: The Christian Sci Monitor El Monitor de Hoy One Norway St Boston MA 02115

GOODSON, MARK, television producer; b. Sacramento, Jan. 24, 1915; s. Abraham Ellis and Fannie (Gross) G.; children by previous marriages: Jill, Jonathan, Marjorie. BA, U. Calif., 1937. Announcer, newscaster, dir. Sta. KFRC, San Francisco, 1938-41; radio announcer, dir. N.Y.C., 1941-43; radio dir. U.S. Treasury War Bond Dr., 1944-45; chmn. bd. Goodson Newspaper Group. Formed Goodson-Todman Prodns., 1946; originated radio shows Winner Take All, 1946, Stop the Music, 1947, Hit the Jackpot, 1947-49; creator of TV game programs What's My Line, It's News to Me, The Name's the Same, I've Got a Secret, Two for the Money, The Price is Right, Password, Match Game, To Tell the Truth, Family Feud, Child's Play, others; producer TV film series The Web, The Rebel, Richard Boone Theater, Branded. Trustee Mus. Broadcasting, 1985—; bd. dirs. Am. Film Inst., 1975—. Recipient Nat. TV award Gt. Brit., 1951, Emmy award Acad. TV Arts and Scis., 1951, 52, Sylvania award, Daytime Emmy Lifetime Achievement award., 1989-90. Mem. Acad. TV Arts and Sci. (pres. N.Y.C. 1957-58), Phi Beta Kappa. Office: 375 Park Ave New York NY 10152-0002 also: 5750 Wilshire Blvd Los Angeles CA 90036

GOODSON, RICHARD CARLE, JR., chemist, hazardous waste management consultant; b. Toledo, June 22, 1945; s. Richard Carle Goodson Sr. and Norma (Buehler) Robinson; m. Deborah Ann Hart, Mar. 29, 1969 (div. Feb. 1978); 1 child, Geoffrey Carle; m. Thelma Agnes Matthews, Nov. 22, 1978. BS in Chemistry, Union Coll., 1967; MS in Inorganic Chemistry, U. Conn., 1970. Dist. engr. Drew Chem. Corp., Boonton, N.J., 1972-74; product supr. Drew Chem. Corp., Boonton, 1974-75, regional tech. supr., 1975-76; chief chemist, tech. dir. Environ. Waste Removal, Waterbury, Conn., 1976-79; gen. mgr., dir. tech. lab. Conn. Treatment Corp., Bristol, Conn., 1979-82; pres., owner Goodson Assocs., Avon, Conn., 1982—; dir. ops., corp. dir. waste mgmt. and regulatory compliance Hampden Mathieu Chem. Co., Springfield, Mass., 1990—. Mem. Am. Chem. Soc. Republican. Home and Office: 51 Anvil Dr Avon CT 06001-3218

GOODSPEED, SCOTT WINANS, hospital administration executive; b. Boston, Jan. 6, 1954; s. Robert Fall and Joanne (Way) G.; m. Mary Ellen McDonough, Sept. 25, 1976; children: Kathleen, Brendan. BS, Ithaca Coll., 1976; postgrad., Harvard U., 1977; MHA, U. Minn., 1980. Rsch. asst. adminstrn. health svcs. dept. Ithaca (N.Y.) Coll., 1974-75; statistician, br. mgr. Bur. Vital Records and Health Stats., Concord, N.H., 1976-78; adminstrv. resident R.I. Hosp., Providence, 1979-80; planning assoc. Elliot Hosp., Manchester, N.H., 1980-82; dir. planning, systems and cost containment Elliot Hosp., Manchester, 1982-83, v.p. adminstrv. svcs., 1983-86, sr. v.p., chief oper. officer, 1986-90, acting chief exec. officer, 1989-90, pres., chief exec. officer, 1990—; bd. dirs. N.H. Imaging Svcs., Inc, 1989—, N.H. Lithotripter Ctr., Inc., 1989—; instr. Rivier Coll., Nashua, N.H., 1982—; clin. faculty assoc. U. N.H., Durham, 1982—, U. N.C., Chapel Hill, 1982—; bd. dirs. NH Imaging Svcs., Inc., NH Lithotripter Ctr., Inc.; presenter in field. Contbr. articles on strategic and bus. planning and quality assurance to profl. jours. Mem. Task Force on Planning, N.H. Hosp. Assn.,1 980-84; mem. N.H. Gov.'s Com. on Long-Term Care, 1981; bd. dirs. Mancester Assn. Retarded Citizens, Inc. 1982-84, N.H. div. Am. Cancer Soc., 1990—, N.H. div. Am. Cancer Soc., 1990—, United Way Greater Manchester, 1984-90, chmn. venture grant com., 1986-87, chmn. nominating com., 1988; bd. dirs. Cypress Med. Park Condominium Assn., 1985—, Stat Care, 1985-88, chmn. bd., 1987-88;/ Gov.'s appointee N.H. Job Tng. Coun., 1988—. Recipient James A. Hamilton award U. Minn., 1980, Vernon E. Weckwerth award, 1982, Emerging Leaders in Healthcare award The Healthcare Forum-Korn/Ferry Internat., 1992; named one of Outstanding Young Men of Am., U.S. Jaycees, 1980. Fellow Am. Coll. Health Care Execs. (regent's adv. coun. 1988—); mem. Am. Assn. Hosp. Planning and Mktg., Am. Hosp. Assn., Soc. Hosp. Planning Am., Freestanding Ambulatory Surgery Assn., Am. Mgmt. Assn., Greater Manchester C. of C. (Leadership Manchester program 1988, chmn. health and edn. div. membership div. 1989—, bd. dirs. 1990—), U. Minn. Alumni Assn., Rotary. Home: 41 Wellesley Dr Bedford NH 03110-4532 Office: Elliot Hosp 955 Auburn St Manchester NH 03103-3599

GOODWILL, DONALD JOSEPH, systems analyst, consultant; b. North Tonawanda, N.Y., Apr. 30, 1944; s. Oland Stuart and Myrle Elizibeth (Walker) G.; m. Maureen E. Johnson. PhD in Physics, SUNY, Buffalo, 1969. Researcher U.S. Dept. of State, Washington, 1976-85; systems analyst Quant-m Corp., Buffalo, 1984—; MIS dir. Trek, Inc., Medina, N.Y., 1990—. Inventor inertia drive. Home: 4671 Griswold St Middleport NY 14105-9635 Office: Trek Inc 3932 Salt Works Rd Medina NY 14103-9598

GOODWIN, ELIZABETH TANNER, dentist, researcher; b. Biddeford, Maine, May 15, 1957; d. Charles Victor and Shirley (Mewer) Tanner; m. Kurt Joseph Goodwin, July 5, 1980; children: Sarah Joy, Megan Elizabeth, Michael Patrick. BA in Zoology and BS in Chem. Engring., U. Maine, 1979; DMD, Tufts U., 1982. Researcher USPHS/Tufts U., Boston, 1979-82; gen. practice dentistry USPHS, Uinalhaven, Maine, 1982-85; researcher USPHS, Boston, 1985—; dentist Dr. Norman Rogers, Methven, Mass., 1986—; research task team Pub. Health Service, Boston, 1986—; educator dentistry Mass. Edn. Dept., Georgetown, Mass., 1986—. Organizer Hotline: Rape, Suicide, Drugs, Alcohol, Orono, 1977-79, Adopt-a-Grandparent, Groveland, Mass., 1985—; pres. Health Council, Vinalhaven, 1983, 84-85; mem., sec. Mothers Against Drunk Driving, Georgetown, 1985—; mem. Mothers Against Nuclear War, Boston, 1986—. Mem. ADA, Am. Acad. Gen. Dentists, Acad. of Women Dentists (Woman Dentist of Yr. 1983-85), Mass. Dental Soc. of Merrimac Valley, Phi Beta Kappa, Phi Kappa Phi. Presbyterian. Club: Young Profls. with Children (Georgetown) (sec. 1985-86, pres. 1986—). Lodge: Order of Eastern Star (Worthy Assoc. Matron 1983-85). Home: PO Box 193 Groveland MA 01834-0193

GOODWIN, JAMES ALTON, JR., athletic association executive; b. Hartford, Conn., Dec. 8, 1949; s. James Alton and Jane Morgan (Bacon) G.; m. Emily Janeway Apthorp, Dec. 17, 1983; children: Morgan Janeway, Robert Alton, Liza Williams. BA in History, Williams Coll., 1971; MA in History, Plattsburg (N.Y.) State Coll., 1980. Tchr. White Mountain Sch., Littleton, N.H., 1974-76; venue mgr. Lake Placid (N.Y.) Olympic Organizing Com., 1979-80; cross country mgr. Olympic Regional Devel. Authority, Lake Placid, 1981-85; exec. dir. Adirondack Trail Improvement Soc., Keene Valley, N.Y., 1986—, Adirondack Ski Touring Coun., Lake Placid, N.Y., 1986—. Author guidebook: Northern Adirondack Ski Tours, 1982; editor guidebook: Guide to ADK Trails, 1985; contbr. articles to profl. jours. Trustee Keene Valley Neighborhood House, 1992. With U.S. Army, 1971-73. Mem. U.S. Ski Assn., Adirondack Mtn. Club (bd. govs. 1978-80, 3d v.p. 1981-82). Republican. Home: HCR #1 Box 63A Alstead Hill Rd Keene NY 12942-9706 Office: Adirondack Ski Touring Coun PO Box 843 Lake Placid NY 12946-0843

GOODWIN, MAURICE ROY, otolaryngologist; b. Bklyn., Nov. 28, 1911; s. Harris and Mary Goodwin; married, Sept. 21, 1933; children: Sheilah Helen, Lynne Ellen. BSc, NYU, 1928; MD, DDS, Vienna and Graz (Austria) U., 1931; postgrad., NYU, 1956-57. Diplomate Am. Bd. Otolaryngology. Assoc. mem. staff of otolaryn. surgery Bronx (N.Y.) Meml. Hosp., 1960—; mem. staff of otolaryn. surgery Our Lady of Mercy/Pelham Hosps., Bronx, 1961—; cons. in otolaryn. surgery Albert Einstein Hosp., Westchester Surgery Med. Ctr., Bronx, 1961—. Contbr. articles to profl. jours. Fellow ACS, AAAS, Am. Coll. of Chest Physicians, Am. Acad. of Facial and Reconstructive surgery, Am. Acad. of Otolaryn. & Head & Neck Surgery, Internat. Coll. Surgeons. Republican.

GOODWIN, MILDRED, education educator; b. N.Y.C., Dec. 3, 1926; d. Meyer and Rae (Garfield) Lieberman; m. Louis Goodwin, June 20, 1948; children: Robert, Barbara Peled. BA in English Edn., Jersey City State Coll., 1962, MA in Reading Edn., 1967, cert. libr. media specialist, 1980; postgrad., Fordham U., 1970-80. English tchr. Snyder High Sch., Jersey City, 1962-67; asst. prof. lang. arts and edn. Jersey City (N.J.) State Coll., 1967-91, assoc. prof., 1991—, chmn. div. adminstrv. curriculum and instrn., 1983-89; film critic local community newspaper, Concordia, 1991—; dir., pronouncer Hudson County Spelling Bee, Jersey City, 1968-88; presenter in field. Vol. Am. Red Cross, Jersey City, 1960's. Mem. Brandeis Univ. Women's Club (study group dir.). Home: 10 Andrew Johnson Dr # C Cranbury NJ 08512-4808 Office: Jersey City State Coll 2039 Kennedy Blvd Jersey City NJ 07305-1527

GOODWIN, PHILLIP KNOWLES, bank executive; b. N.Y.C., July 13, 1934; s. Fred Howard and Phyllis (Knowles) G.; m. Diana Mitchell Tilt, Dec. 10, 1960; children: Chris K., Scott M. BA in Polit. Sci., Yale U., 1956. Credit trainee N.Y. Trust Co., N.Y.C., 1956-59; personnel adminstr., various other official positions Chem. Bank New York Trust Co., N.Y.C., 1959—; regional pres. Chem. Bank, Albany, N.Y., 1986—. Pres. Northeastern Assn. of Blind, Albany, 1988—, Palace Performing Arts Corp., Albany, 1989—. With U.S. Army, 1959-63. Mem. Ft. Orange Club, Schuyler Meadows Club. Republican. Presbyterian. Home: 34 Folmsbee Dr Albany NY 12204 Office: Chem Bank 41 State St Albany NY 12204

GOODWIN, ROLF ERVINE, lawyer; b. Bethlehem, Pa., May 2, 1956; s. Francis Black and Grethe Julie (Andresen) G.; m. Nancy Elspeth Sarstedt, Feb. 2, 1991. AB, Harvard Coll., 1978; JD, NYU, 1982. Bar: N.H. 1982. Assoc. Hamblett & Kerrigan P.A., Nashua, N.H., 1982-87; ptnr. Deasy & Dwyer P.A., Nashua, N.H., 1988—. Pres., trustee Community Music Sch., Nashua, 1984—; trustee Nashua Symphony Assn., 1983—; bd. dirs. Harvard Pierian Found., Inc., Cambridge, Mass., 1990—; admissions chmn. Harvard-Radcliffe Club N.H., 1983—. Mem. Nashua Bar Assn., N.H. Bar Assn. (ethics com., com. on revision of rules of profl. conduct). Home: 3 Belfast St Nashua NH 03063 Office: Deasy & Dwyer PA 400 Amherst St Nashua NH 03063

GOODWIN, SUSAN ANN, academic administrator; b. Boston, June 9, 1944; d. Herbert Franklin and Elizabeth (Dunlap) G.; m. Michael L. Finson, June 20, 1968 (div. 1972); m. 2d Samuel Brackston Hinchey, Jan. 20, 1973. BA, Wellesley Coll., 1966; MA, Boston U., 1967; PhD, Tufts U., 1975. Assoc. prof. U. Lowell (now U. Mass. Lowell), 1977-78, spl. asst. to pres., 1977-78, dir. info. systems, 1978-80, acting dean rsch., dir. rsch. found., 1980-81, v.p. for adminstrn., 1981-84, v.p. adminstrn. and fin., 1984-91, vice chancellor adminstrn. and fin., 1991—; bd. dir. Pvt. Industry Coun., Lowell, 1983—. Bd. dirs. Merrimack Valley United Fund, Lawrence, Mass., 1980-86. Office: U Mass Lowell MA 01854

GOODYEAR, EDWARD STEPHEN, JR., marketing communications executive; b. Waterbury, Conn., Nov. 30, 1954; s. Edward Stephen Sr. and Dorothy Ann (Bassford) G.; m. Barbara Diane Greene, Oct. 1,1988; 1 child, Marc Patrick Couture Jr. BS in Communications, Emerson Coll., 1977; MS in Communications, Fairfield U., 1984. Dir. O'Neal and Prelle, Hartford, Conn., 1983-85, Keiler Pub. Rels., Farmington, Conn., 1985-88; v.p. Chaffee-Bedard, Providence, 1988-89; prin. Greene Communications, Londonderry, N.H., 1989—; mgr. mktg. communications Agfa Corp., Wilmington, Mass., 1990—. Contbr. articles to profl. jours. Press sec. Hanlon for Congress campaign, Conn., 1982. Mem. Pub. Rels. Soc. Am. (pres. Conn. chpt. 1987-88), Internat. Pub. Rels. Assn., Counselors Acad. Republican. Home: 15 Raintree Dr Londonderry NH 03053-2513 Office: Agfa Corp 200 Ballardvale St Wilmington MA 01887-1069

GOODYEAR, FRANK H(ENRY), JR., art association administrator; b. N.Y.C., Jan. 5, 1944; s. Frank Henry and Alison (Harrison) G.; m. Elizabeth Wanton Balis, July 6, 1944; children: Frank Henry III, Alison H., Grace Wanton. B.A., Yale, 1966; M.A., Winterthur Program, Early Am. Culture, U. Del., 1969. Curator R.I. Hist. Soc., Providence, 1969-72; curator Pa. Acad. Fine Arts, Phila., 1972-82, acting exec. dir., 1982-83; pres. Pa. Acad. Fine Arts, 1983—; chmn. com. on Yale U. Art Gallery and Brit. Art Ctr. Yale U. Coun.; mem. governing bd. Yale U. Art Gallery; dir. Conservation Ctr. for Art and Hist. Artifacts. Mem. editorial bd. Cambridge Monographs on Am. Artists; contbr. articles profl. jours. Lectr., bd. dirs. Fairmount Park Art Assn. Mem. Am. Assn. Museums (legis. com.). Office: Pa Acad Fine Arts Broad & Cherry Sts 118 N Broad St Philadelphia PA 19102-1598

GOODYEAR, JOHN LAKE, artist, educator; b. Los Angeles, Oct. 22, 1930; s. Ronald Ralph and Lillian Katherine (Lake) G.; m. Anne Marie Dixon, July 14, 1953; children: Sarah, Amy. B.Design, U. Mich., 1952, M.Design, 1954. Mem. faculty dept. art U. Mich., Grand Rapids, 1956-62, U. Mass., 1962-64; mem. faculty visual arts dept. M.G.S.A., Rutgers U., New Brunswick, N.J., 1964—; prof. art Douglass Coll., Rutgers U., 1976—. Exhbns. include III Bienal de Arte, Medellin, Colombia, 1972, The Jewish Mus., N.Y.C., 1970, Mus. Modern Art, N.Y.C., 1965, Martha Jackson Gallery, N.Y.C., 1960, Neuberger Mus., Purchase, N.Y., 1980, 89, Princeton Gallery Fine Arts, 1987, Jersey City Mus., 1991, Snyder Fine Art, N.Y.C., 1992; represented in permanent collections, Mus. Modern Art, N.Y.C., Met. Mus., N.Y.C., N.J. State Mus., Whitney Mus. Am. Art, N.Y.C., Guggenheim Mus., N.Y.C., Milw. Art Ctr., Nat. Mus. Am. Art, Washington. Served with U.S. Army, 1954-56. Graham Found. for Advanced Studies in Fine Arts fellow, 1962, 70; Center for Advanced Visual Studies, M.I.T. fellow, 1970-71; Pub. Commn. fellow, Trenton, N.J., 1991. Office: MGSA Rutgers U Visual Art Dept New Brunswick NJ 08903

GOODYEAR, JOHN LEE, insurance broker; b. Snowshoe, Pa., Sept. 15, 1936; s. Willis Lee and Anne Rose (Rackovan) G.; m. Rose Marie Toner, Oct. 24, 1959; children: Jeanne (dec.), John II, James, Judith, Jeffrey. BA, Villanova U., 1958; postgrad., U. Miami Sch. of Law, 1962-64. CLU. Regional group mgr. Provident Mut. Life Ins. Co., Phila., 1961-75; pres. Alexander & Alexander Benefits Svcs., Inc., N.Y.C., 1975—; dir. health strategies group Alexander Cons. Group, Greenwich, Conn., 1983-85; sect. chmn. CLU Edn., N.Y.C., 1976-77. Dir. Christian confrat. doctrine St. Theresa Parish, Briarcliff, N.Y., 1974-76. Capt. USMC, 1958-61. Mem. Sleepy Hollow Country Club (pres. 1988-89), N.Y. Athletic Club, Shinnecock Hills Golf Club. Republican. Roman Catholic. Home: 2 Highview Rd Ossining NY 10562-2201 Office: Alexander & Alexander Svcs 1185 Ave of the Americas New York NY 10036-2601

GOON, DICKSON BING, component engineer; b. Boston, Feb. 16, 1954; s. Bing Soon and Chun Mi (Wong) G.; m. Tip Nar Woo, June 16, 1985; children: Matthew Y.,Wayne Y. BSEE Northeastern U., 1977; MS in Mgmt. Worcester Poly. Inst., 1986. Jr. asst. civil engr. City of Boston, 1972; trademark research tech. Thomson & Thomson, Boston, 1973; electronic tech. C.S. Draper Lab., Cambridge, 1974-77; component engr. Honeywell Inc., Billerica, Mass., 1977-80; component engr. GenRad Inc., Concord, 1980-86; sr. component engr. Modicon Inc., North Andover, Mass., 1986—. Mem. IEEE (student sec. 1977), Chinese-Am. Civic Assn. Democrat. Home: 7 Mill St Burlington MA 01803-2601 Office: Modicon Inc 1 High St North Andover MA 01845-2699

GOOT, JOANNE GUNVOR, nursing educator, researcher; b. Bklyn., Feb. 20, 1953; d. Erik Gunnar and Anita Johanna (Söderlund) Karlman; m. Robert Andrew Goot, Apr. 21, 1990; 1 child, Andrew Gunnar. BSN, CUNY, 1974; MSN, pediatric nurse practitioner, SUNY, Stony Brook, 1992. RN, N.Y. Sr. staff nurse recovery room Bellevue Hosp., N.Y.C., 1974-77, head nurse, 1977-80; sr. staff nurse post anesthesia care unit St. Vincent's Hosp., N.Y.C., 1980-81; instr., rsch. nurse II, Univ. Hosp. at Stony Brook, 1981-92. Mem. Am. Soc. for Post Anesthesia Nursing, Sigma Theta Tau (Kappa Gamma chpt.). Lutheran. Home: 5316 N 105th Plz Apt 8 Omaha NE 68134

GOOTMAN, NORMAN, pediatrics educator; b. Phila., Feb. 6, 1933; m. Phyllis Myrna Adler; children: Sharon, Craig. BS, U. Vt., 1954, MD, 1958. Diplomate Am Bd. Pediatrics, Am. Bd. Pediatric Cardiology. Intern in pediatrics Bronx (N.Y.) Mcpl. Hosp. Ctr., 1958-59, resident in pediatrics, 1959-60; rsch. fellow in pediatric cardiology Albert Einstein Coll Medicine, Bronx, 1960-61, 64-65; clin. assoc. prof. pediatrics Downstate Med. Ctr., 1965-72; assoc. prof. pediatrics Sch. Medicine, Health Scis. Ctr. SUNY, Stony Brook, 1972-75, prof. pediatrics Sch. Medicine, Health Scis. Ctr., 1975-89; prof. pediatrics Albert Einstein Coll. Medicine, 1989—; vis. prof. physiology Health Sci. Ctr., SUNY, Bklyn., 1991—; chief div. pediatric cardiology Schneider Children's Hosp., L.I. Jewish Med. Ctr., Queens Hosp. Ctr. Affiliation, 1965-90; cons. Queens Hosp. Ctr., 1965—, dept. pediatrics South Shore div. St. John's Episcopal, 1977—, dept. pediatrics Peninsula Hosp. Ctr., 1977—, Jamaica Hosp., 1978—, Huntington Hosp., 1978—, Cen. Gen. Hosp., 1981—, Winthrop Univ. Hosp., 1983—, L.I. Jewish Med. Ctr., 1991—; presenter numerous nat. and internat. confs. Author numerous chapts. in books; contbr. over 100 articles to profl. jours. Trustee L.I. Heart Coun., 1988; co-chmn. Nassau chpt. Am. Heart Assn., 1983-85, rsch. com., 1974—, coun. on basic sci., 1985—, coun. on cardiovascular disease in the young, 1985—, bd. dirs., 1985—. Capt. U.S. Army, 1962-64. Grantee Am. Heart Assn., 1970-89, L.I. Med. Ctr., 1988-90. Fellow Am. Coll. Cardiology, Am. Soc. Pediatrics; mem. N.Y. Acad. Sci., N.Y. Med. Soc., N.Y. Heart Assn., Soc. for Pediatric Rsch., Am. Physiol. Soc. (chmn. continuing edn. com.), Nassau Pediatric Soc. (pres. 1986-87), Am. Physiologic Soc., Am. Pediatric Soc.. Home: 2 Country Village Ln Manhasset Hills New Hyde Park NY 11040 Office: SUNY Health Sci Ctr Dept Physiololgy Box 31 450 Clarkson Ave Brooklyn NY 11203

GOOTMAN, PHYLLIS MYRNA ADLER, physiologist, educator; b. N.Y.C.; d. Albert S. and Ida (Krieger) Adler; m. Norman Gootman, June 1, 1958; children: Sharon Hillary, Craig Seth. BA in Zoology cum laude, Barnard Coll. Columbia U., 1959; PhD, Yeshiva U., 1967. Rsch. assoc. dept. physiology and biophysics U. Wash., Seattle, 1963; instr. dept. physiology Albert Einstein Coll. Medicine, Bronx, N.Y., 1968-70, asst. prof., 1970-73; asst. prof. Downstate Med. Ctr. SUNY, Bklyn., 1973-75, assoc. prof., 1975-81, prof. sch. grad. studies, dept. physiology, 1981—; vis. prof. dept. physiology and biophysics Albert Einstein Coll. Medicine, 1989—; vis. asst. prof., 1973-76; cons. in pediatrics Schneider Children's Hosp. L.I. Jewish-Hillside Med. Ctr., New Hyde Park, 1976—. Co-editor: Perinatal Cardiovascular Function, 1983; editor: Developmental Neurobiology of the Autonomic Nervous System, 1986; contbr. articles and revs. to profl. jours. John Miles Davidson fello in physiology Albert Einstein Coll. Medicine, 1973. Mem. AAAS, Soc. for Neuroscis., Biophys. Soc., Am. Physiol. Soc. (animal care and experimentation com. 1989—), Am. Heart Assn., Am. Inst. Biol. Scis., Microcirculatory Soc., Soc. for Experimental Biology and Medicine, Am. Assn. for Lab. Animal Sci., Internat. Soc. for Devel. Neuroscis., Royal Soc. Medicine, Sigma Xi. Office: SUNY Health Sci Ctr Bklyn Dept Physiology Box 31 450 Clarkson Ave Brooklyn NY 11203-2098

GOPPELT, JOHN WALTER, physician; b. Saginaw, Mich., Jan. 20, 1924; s. Paul Gustave and Marion LeRoy (Payne) G.; m. Martha Keller Rowland, Mar. 31, 1956; 1 child, Edmund H. B.S., MIT, 1949; M.D., U. Pa., 1955. Diplomate Am. Bd. Psychiatry and Neurology. Rotating intern Bryn Mawr Hosp., Pa., 1955-56; resident in psychatry Inst. of Pa. Hosp., Phila., 1956-59; practice medicine, specializing in psychiatry, Haverford, Pa., 1959—; from instr. to assoc. dept. psychiatry Sch. Medicine, U. Pa., Phila., 1960-74. Contbr. articles to profl. jours. Chmn. Drug and Alcohol Council of Delaware County, Media, Pa., 1979-83; committeeman Republican Party, Haverford Twp., Pa., 1980. Served with U.S. Army, 1943-46. Recipient Legion of Honor award Chapel of Four Chaplains. Mem. AMA, Am. Psychiat. Assn., N.Y. Acad. Scis., Math. Assn. Am., Sigma Xi. Avocation: mathematics. Address: Exeter Rd Haverford PA 19041

GORALSKI, DONALD JOHN, public relations executive, counselor; b. Buffalo, Apr. 21, 1957; s. John Bernard and Irene (Kazmierczak) G.; m. Debra Marie Buser, Aug. 11, 1984. BA, Canisius Coll., 1980. Community svc. rep. western N.Y. chpt. March of Dimes Birth Defects Found., Buffalo, 1981-82, pub. relations dir., 1982-83; pub. relations dir. no. Jersey chpt. March of Dimes Birth Defects Found, Fairfield, N.J., 1983-84; pub. relations dir. Ellis Singer, Greve, St. Paul, Minn., 1984-87, Ellis Singer Group, Buffalo, 1984-87; sr. pub. relations officer Nat. Ctr. for Earthquake Engring. Rsch., Buffalo, 1987—; guest lectr. U. Buffalo, Buffalo State Coll., Medaille Coll., 1984-88, Canisius Coll., 1990. Mem. spl. events com. Am. Cancer Soc., Western N.Y. chpt., 1985-86; mem. mktg. subcom. St. Mary's Sch. for Deaf, 1987; mentor Pub. Rels. Student Soc. of Am., Buffalo, 1989-91; mem. Allied Communications Talent for Literacy, Buffalo, 1990-91; mem. meeting and event planners coun. Univ. at Buffalo, 1992. Mem. Pub. Rels. Soc. Am. (bd. dirs. Buffalo-Niagara chpt. 1987-91, pres.-elect 1992), Pub. Rels. Assn. Western N.Y. (treas. 1986-87, v.p. 1987-88, pres. 1989, pub. rels. and comm. exec. steering com. 1987-90, 92). Home: 12 Morton Dr Buffalo NY 14226-3338 Office: Nat Ctr Quake Engring Rsch U Buffalo Red Jacket Quad Buffalo NY 14261

GORCZYCA, FRYDERYK EMIL, mechanical engineering educator; b. New Bedford, Mass., Oct. 11; s. Frank and Marja (Skrzyniasz) G.; m. Stasia Koss, July 4, 1955; children: Diane Gorczyca Patrick, Ann Marie Gorczyca Vogel. BSME, Southeastern Mass. U., 1958; MS, Northeastern U., 1962. Registered profl. engr., Mass. Prof. mech. engring. Southeastern Mass. U., North Dartmouth, 1958—. Author: Application of Metal Cutting Theory, 1987. With U.S. Army, 1952-54, Korea. Recipient Tchr. of Yr. award Southeastern Mass. U. Faculty Fedn., 1988, citation for outstanding performance Commonwealth of Mass., 1990. Mem. ASME (treas. Providence sect. 1974-76), Soc. Mfg. Engrs. (cert., pres. SE Mass. chpt. 1974-75), Am. Soc. Engring. Edn., Polish and Am. World War Vets. Assn. (treas. New Bedford post 1982-92). Home: 103 County Rd East Freetown MA 02717-1629 Office: Southeastern Mass U Mech Engring Dept North Dartmouth MA 02747

GORDESKY, MORTON, lawyer; b. Egg Harbor, N.J., Apr. 11, 1929; s. Benjamin and Rose (Suskin) G.; m. Marcelline D. Fallick, June 8, 1952 (div. 1982); children: Benjamin Todd, Nancy Hope Hafuta. BS, Temple U., 1950; JD, Rutgers U., 1954. Bar: Pa. 1955, U.S. Dist. Ct. (ea. dist.) Pa. 1958, U.S. Dist. Ct. Md. 1991, U.S. Ct. Appeals (3rd cir.) 1983, U.S. Ct. Appeals (4th cir.) 1990, U.S. Supreme Ct. 1983. Sole practice, Phila., 1954—. Mem. Phila. Dem. Com., 1956-68, mem. lawyer's com., fundraiser. Served with U.S. Army, 1954-56. Mem. Phila. Bar Assn., Amvets (judge adv. 1961-64), Greater Phila. C. of C., Am. Legion. Jewish. Lodges: KP, B'nai Brith. Office: 3131 Fl 1700 Market St Philadelphia PA 19103-3931

GORDON, ARLENE CAHN, clinical psychologist; b. Hartford, Conn., June 12, 1958; d. Herbert and Theresa (Lighton) C.; m. Michael Gordon, Oct. 16, 1988; children: Jeremy Gordon, Carmel Gordon. BA in Communications, U. Pa., 1980, MS in Secondary Edn., 1980; MA in Sch. Psychology, Adelphi U., 1986, PhD in Clin. Psychology, 1988. Tchr. English, drama dir. Penn Charter Sch., Phila., 1980-83; psychology intern Elizabeth (N.J.) Gen. Med. Ctr., 1987-88; psychol. counselor Fairleigh Dickinson U., Madison, N.J., 1988-91; psychotherapist West Orange, N.J., 1989—. Contbr. chpt. in book. Mem. Am. Psychol. Assn., N.J. Psychol. Assn. Home: 15 Dogwood Dr West Orange NJ 07052-1016

GORDON, BARRY, cognitive neurologist and neuroscientist; b. Phila., Mar. 16, 1951. BA, Pa. State U., 1971; MD, Thomas Jefferson U., 1973;

MA, Johs Hopkins U., 1980, PhD, 1981. Intern N.Y. Hosp., 1973-74; resident Johns Hopkins Hosp., Balt., 1974-77; assoc. prof. neurology Johns Hopkins U., Balt., with Mind/Brain Inst. Office: Johns Hopkins Univ Meyer 222 600 N Wolfe St Baltimore MD 21205

GORDON, CAMERON ELLIOTT, economist; b. N.Y.C., Dec. 27, 1962; s. Elliott and Barbara Ann (Steplar) G.; m. Kathryn Lee Marsland, Sept. 19, 1987. BA, Wesleyan U., Middletown, Conn., 1984; MPhil in Econs., CUNY, 1992. Rsch. asst. Coun. Econ. Priorities, N.Y.C., 1985-87; cost-benefit analyst Dept. Environ. Protection Bur. Water Supply, 1987-89; economist joint com. on taxation U.S. Congress, Washington, 1989-92; economist U.S. Adv. Commn. on Intergovtl. Rels., Washington, 1992—. Home: 2032 Belmont Rd NW Apt 107 Washington DC 20009-5413

GORDON, DAVID JEREMY, medical scientist; b. Chgo., Aug. 11, 1946; s. Irving Arthur and Arline Shirley (Leavitt) G.; m. Susan Ellen Weisbach, Aug. 12, 1984. BS, U. Chgo., 1967, PhD in Chemistry, 1971, MD, 1973; MPH in Epidemiology, U. N.C., 1981. Med. intern U. Calif., San Diego, 1973-74; staff assoc. Nat. Heart, Lung & Blood Inst., Bethesda, Md., 1974-77; med. officer Nat. Heart, Lund & Blood Inst., Bethesda, Md., 1977—. Contbr. articles to profl. jours. With USPHS, 1973—. Fellow Am. Heart Assn. (coun. epidemiology); mem. USPHS Commd. Officers Assn., Phi Beta Kappa. Office: NIH Nat Heart Lung & Blood Inst DHVD 7550 Wisconsin Ave Bethesda MD 20892

GORDON, DORIS (YETTA), association administrator; b. N.Y.C., June 8, 1928; d. Sam and Edith (Schneiderman) Cohen; m. Nathan Noah Gordon, Dec. 25, 1959 (dec. June 1987); children: Monte Galt, Julie Ayn. BBA, CCNY, 1948; postgrad., Hunter Coll., 1950. Jr. exec. W. T. Grant Co., N.Y.C., 1948-49; bookkeeper various cos. N.Y.C., 1949-53; tchr. L.A. schs., 1951, N.Y.C. schs., 1953-60, Md. schs., 1960; nat. coord. Libertarians for Life, Montgomery County, Md., 1976—. Publisher newsletter LFL Reports, 1981—; contbr. articles to profl. jours. Active Right to Life movement. Mem. Internat. Soc. for Individual Liberty. Libertarian. Home and Office: Libertarians for Life 13424 Hathaway Dr Silver Spring MD 20906-3221

GORDON, FLORENCE SHANFIELD, mathematics educator; b. Montreal, Que., Can., Mar. 11, 1942; came to U.S., 1968; d. Morris and Jean (Rubacha) Shanfield; m. Sheldon P. Gordon, June 27, 1965; children: Craig, Kenneth. BSc with honours in Math., McGill U., Montreal, 1963, MSc in Math. Stats., 1964, PhD in Math. Stats., 1968. Asst. prof. C.W. Post Coll., L.I. U., Greenvale, N.Y., 1968-71, Adelphi U., Garden City, N.Y., 1982-83; assoc. prof. math. N.Y. Inst. Tech., Old Westbury, 1983—; mem. precalculus reform project NSF, 1991—. Author: (book and software) Statistics through the Eye of the Computer, 1993; editor: (monograph) Statistics for the 21st Century, 1992; contbr. articles on stats. to profl. jours. Mem. Math. Assn. Am., Am. Statis. Assn., Am. Math. Soc. Home: 61 Cedar Rd East Northport NY 11731-4128 Office: NY Inst Tech Old Westbury NY 11568

GORDON, GERD STRAY, historian, educator, writer; b. Stavanger, Norway, Nov. 15, 1912; came to U.S., 1948; d. Johannes and Ella (Stray) Johansen; m. Johan Vogt (div.); children: Mette Wernøe, Gerd Ada Vogt, Christina Isaksen; m. Raymond Gordon; 1 child, Karen Allyn. Student, Oslo U., 1937-41; BA, Fla. State U., 1960; MA, U. Pitts., PhD, 1978. Cert. tchr., Fla., Pa. Accredited corr. Aftenposten-Norsk Dameblad, Oslo, 1948-55; tchr. Panama C.Z. Schs., Panama Episc. Sch., 1960-61, Am. Coop. Sch., Tunis, Tunisia, 1962-64; tchr. Am. Internat. Sch., Bangkok, 1965-68, Djakarta, Indonesia, 1968-69; tchr. Am. Sch., New Delhi, India, 1969-70, Pitts. Pub. Sch. System, 1970-83; freelance lectr., 1983—; lectr., Slippery Rock (Pa.) Coll., U. Kans., Lawrence, Vanderbilt U., Nashville; presenter, Symposium of Scandinavian Historians. Author: Kvinnen Idag (Woman Today), 1952; contbr. articles to numerous publs including Dictionary of Scandinavian History, 1986. Dem. ofcl., Denver, 1952-57, election judge, 1954-58; bd. dirs., rep., Planned Parenthood, Denver and Pitts., 1952-89; participant Citizen Day Com. signed S.P. Kinney II Denver Woman's Press Club, 1965, Senate of Pa., 1985. Resistance worker during German occupation of Norway, World War II. Recipient Outstanding Citizen award Norwegian Resistance; Ella Lyman Cabot Trust grantee U. Pitts. Mem. Denver Women's Press Club (bd. dirs. 1952—), Pitts. U. Historian Alumnae Orgn., Fla. State U. Alumnae Assn., AAUW (bd. dirs. Pitts. chpt. 1984—), LWV (past bd. dirs. Denver and Pitts. chpts.), Countryside Garden Club (bd. dirs. 1970—). Home: 224 Rockingham Rd Pittsburgh PA 15238-3014

GORDON, HARRY WILLIAM, pharmacologist, consultant; b. N.Y.C., Mar. 3, 1924; s. Abraham and Elsie (Cheskin) G.; m. Rosalind Weinberg, Jan. 21, 1950; 1 child, Bebe Gail. BS, L.I. U., 1948; PhD, Georgetown U., 1952. Pharmacologist, toxicologist NYU-Bellevue Med. Ctr., N.Y.C., 1952-55; rsch. assoc. Colgate-Palmolive Co., Jersey City, 1955-57; asst. dir. R & D, Block Drug Co., Jersey City, 1957-59; dir. R & D, St. Barnabas Med. Ctr., Newark, 1959-62, mem. clin. rsch. com., 1962-65; v.p., dir. R & D, Schmid Labs., Inc., N.Y.C., 1962-76; v.p., sci. dir. Del Labs, Inc., Farmingdale, N.Y., 1976-91; cons. to drug and cosmetic industry, 1991—; cons. Interboro Gen. Hosp., N.Y.C., 1965-70. Contbr. numerous articles to sci. jours., including NAS. Fellow AAAS; mem. Am. Pharm. Assn., Am. Chem. Soc., N.Y. Acad. Scis. Home: 1832 Cornelius Ave Wantagh NY 11793-3207

GORDON, IRWIN GLENN (YASHAD), archivist; b. Bklyn., Dec. 7, 1965; s. David Grodenchik and Roslyn Muriel (Cutler) G. BA in Judaic Studies summa cum laude, Bklyn. Coll., 1989; postgrad. in Libr. and Info. Sci., Pratt Inst., Bklyn., 1991—. Libr. asst., govt. documents Gideonse Library, Bklyn. Coll., 1987; substitute tchr. Bklyn., 1989-90; asst. librarian Advt. Rsch. Found., N.Y.C., 1990-91; contbg. staff mem. Hatikvah newspaper B'nai B'rith Abe Stark Hillel House, Bklyn., 1986-87, asst. editor, 1987, editor-in-chief, 1988-89, editor emeritus, 1989. Jewish. Home: 2790 W 5th St Apt 1E Brooklyn NY 11224-4167

GORDON, JAQUELYN RUTH (ANMA), poet, artist, designer; b. Boston, Dec. 29, 1943; d. John Edward and Ruth Lillian (Bucknell) Chism; m. Lansing A. Gordon, May 22, 1964 (div. 1968); 1 child, Trilby Spring. BFA, Mass. Coll. Art, 1984. Jewelry designer Swank Inc., Attleboro, Mass., 1967-72, 78-80; doll designer Hasbro-Bradley, Pawtucket, R.I., 1972-74, 75-76, Mattel, Hawthorne, Calif., 1974-75; jewelry designer Clementine Co., Warwick, R.I., 1984-85, Donley Co., North Attleboro, Mass., 1987-89; home health aide to the elderly Walpole Vis. Nurse Assn., 1989—. Author, illustrator: Dream of a Middle Aged Girl, 1986. Grantee Attleboro Arts Lottery Coun., 1987, 91.

GORDON, JEFFREY MARK, dental educator and researcher; b. N.Y.C., Aug. 10, 1952; s. Benjamin and Selma (Gold) G.; m. Gloria Goldberg; 1 child, Melissa. BA/Math. summa cum laude, Queens Coll., 1973; DMD, Harvard U., 1977, M Med. Sci., 1980. Cert. periodontics. Staff mem. Forsyth Dental Ctr., Boston, 1980-81; asst. prof. Fairleigh Dickinson U., Hackensack, N.J., 1981-86; assoc. prof. Fairleigh Dickinson U., Hackensack, 1987-90; dir. dental rsch. TKL Rsch., Inc., Paramus, N.J., 1990—; cons. periodontal rsch. ctr. Gainesville, 1984-90. Contbr. articles to profl. jours. Recipient rsch. grants in field, 1981—. Mem. Am. Dental Assn., Am. Acad. Periodontolgy, Internat. Assn. Dental Rsch., Am. Soc. Microbiology, Phi Beta Kappa. Home: 56 Huff Ter Montvale NJ 07645-1037 Office: 130 Kinderkamack Rd River Edge NJ 07661-1931

GORDON, JEFFREY NEIL, law educator; b. Richmond, Va., June 18, 1949; s. Irving Leonard and Viola Anne (Clayman) G. BA, Yale U., 1971; JD, Harvard U., 1975. Bar: N.Y. 1977, U.S. Dist. Ct. (so. and ea. dists.) N.Y. 1978, U.S. Ct. Appeals (2nd cir.) 1979, D.C. 1981. Reporter Rocky Mount News, Denver, 1971-72; law clk. to judge U.S. Ct. Appeals (10th cir.), Denver, 1975-76; assoc. Cleary, Gottlieb, Steen & Hamilton, N.Y.C., 1976-78; spl. asst. to gen. counsel, atty. advisor U.S. Treasury, Washington, 1978-81; prof. law NYU, N.Y.C., 1982-88, Columbia U., N.Y.C., 1988—; co-dir. Ctr. Law and Econ. Studies, Columbia U. Contbr. articles to profl. jours. Bd. dirs. employees fed. credit union NYU, 1983-86. Recipient Exceptional Svc. award U.S. Dept. Energy, 1982. Mem. ABA, Am. Law Inst., Assn. of Bar of City of N.Y., Harvard Club, Mory's Club (New Haven), Phi Beta Kappa. Democrat. Jewish. Home: 410 Riverside Dr Apt 81 New York NY 10025-7923 Office: Columbia Law Sch 435 W 116th St New York NY 10027-7201

GORDON, KURTISS JAY, computer programmer; b. N.Y.C., July 20, 1940; s. Kurt Jacoby and Jeannette (Goldstein) G.; m. Rebecca Courtney Parks, Aug. 15, 1964; children: Geoffrey, Sara, Cynthia. BS in Physics, Antioch Coll., 1964; AM in Astronomy, U. Mich., 1966, PhD in Astronomy, 1969; MS in Elec. and Computer Engring., U. Mass., 1985. Rsch. assoc. Nat. Radio Astronomy Obs., Charlottesville, Va., 1969-70; asst. prof. astronomy Hampshire Coll., Amherst, Mass., 1970-76, assoc. prof., 1976-85; sr. postdoctoral rsch. assoc. computer and info. sci. dept. U. Mass., Amherst, 1985-87, sci. applications coord. Univ. Computing Svcs., 1987—. Contbr. articles to profl. publs.; author, co-author computer programs. Mem. IEEE, Am. Astron. Soc., Assn. Computing Machinery, Sigma Xi (sec. U. Mass. chpt. 1986—),. Office: Univ Computing Svcs U Mass Amherst MA 01003

GORDON, LOIS GOLDFEIN, English language educator; b. Englewood, N.J., Nov. 13, 1938; d. Irving David and Betty (Davis) Goldfein; m. Alan Lee Gordon, Nov. 13, 1961; 1 son, Robert Michael. B.A. (Nat. Merit supplementary scholar, Barbour scholar), U. Mich., 1960; postgrad., Columbia U., 1960-61; M.A., U. Wis., 1962, Ph.D. (Dissertation Completion fellow), 1966. Teaching asst. U. Wis., 1962-64; lectr. CCNY, 1964-66; asst. prof. U. Mo., Kansas City, 1966-68; asst. prof. English Fairleigh Dickinson U., Teaneck, N.J., 1968-71; assoc. prof. Fairleigh Dickinson U., 1971-75, prof., 1975—, chmn. dept. English and comparative lit., 1982-90; cons. U. Mo. Press, 1968-69, Doubleday Inc., 1974, Fairleigh Dickinson U. Press, 1975—, Prentice Hall, 1977—, Duke U. Press, 1986—, Cambridge U. Press. Author: Stratagems to Uncover Nakedness: The Dramas of Harold Pinter, 1969, Donald Barthelme, 1981, Robert Coover: The Universal Fiction-Making Process, 1983, American Chronicle: Six Decades in Am. Life, 1920-79, 1987, Seven Decades in American Life, 1920-89, 1990, Harold Pinter: A Casebook, 1990; asst. editor: Lit. and Psychology, 1968-71; contbr. book revs. to profl. jours. and newspapers. Research grantee U. Mo., 1968, Fairleigh Dickinson U., 1985, 89. Mem. Internat. Bach Soc., MLA, PEN, Internat. League Human Rights, Acad. Am. Poets. Jewish. Home: 300 Central Park W New York NY 10024-1513 Office: Fairleigh Dickinson U Dept English Teaneck NY 07666

GORDON, MARK, actor, theater director, theater educator; b. N.Y.C., May 19, 1926; s. Jacob and Sarah (Benin) G.; m. Barbara Glenn, Oct. 13, 1955; 1 child, Keith. Student, Theater Sch. Dramatic Arts, N.Y.C., 1946-47, Actors Lab., Los Angeles, 1947-50, Am. Theater Wing, N.Y.C., 1950-54, Drama Lab., N.Y.C., 1954-55. Workshop dir., actor Compass Players, Chgo., 1955-56; ind. theatrical and film actor, 1955—, ind. theatrical dir., 1969—; guest prof. theater Carnegie-Mellon Univ., Pitts., 1969-70, Columbia Univ., N.Y.C., 1970-71, High Sch. Performing Arts, N.Y.C., 1970-72, Finch Coll., N.Y.C.; head M.B.K. Prodns., N.Y.C., 1982—. Playwright: (with others) Glorious Age, 1975; actor numerous Broadway prodns. including Desire Under the Elms, Of Mice and Men, Mr. Roberts, The Devils, off-Broadway prodns. include The Iceman Cometh, The Man Who Never Died...Joe Hill, TV appearances include Mary Tyler Moore, Hawaii 5-O, Kojack, Dick Van Dyke, film appearances include Take the Money and Run, A New Leaf, Don't Drink the Water, Ninth Configuration; dir. Broadway prodn.: Before You Go (named Best Comedy Dir. on Broadway 1969), off-Broadway prodns. for Los Angeles Actors Theater, Carnegie Recital Hall, Playwrites Horizon, participating dir. Actors Studio; dir. numerous TV commls. Recipient numerous Andy awards, Clio nominations, Contribution to Comedy in Chgo. medal Univ. Chgo.; Rockefeller grantee Ctr. Opera of Mpls., 1963-64; scholar Am. Theater Wing. Mem. AAUP, AFTRA, Dirs. Guild Am., Screen Actors Guild, Actors Equity Assn., Nat. Acad. TV Arts and Scis., Soc. Stage Dirs. and Choreographers. Office: MBK Prodns 323 W 83d St New York NY 10024

GORDON, MARTIN ELI, physician, educator; b. Kiev, Russia, Aug. 15, 1921; came to U.S., 1922; s. Isadore and Belle Gordon; m. Evelyn E. Gordon, Mar. 17, 1946; children: Jeffrey I., Judy I. Dienstag. BS, Kent State U., 1943; MD, Yale U., 1946. Diplomate Am. Bd. Internal Medicine, Nat. Med. Bds. Intern U. Chgo. Clinics, 1946-47; jr. to chief med. resident VA Hosp., Newington, Conn., 1949-51; acting chief to chief gastroenterology sect. VA Hosp., West Haven, Conn., 1953-54; cons. gastroenterologist dept. univ. health Yale Univ., New Haven, 1954-72; clin. instr. to clin. prof. medicine Yale Sch. Medicine, New Haven, 1951—; pvt. cons. gastroenterologist various hosps., Conn., 1955—; cons. practice in gastroenterology and travel medicine New Haven, 1955—; pres. Med. Films, Inc., New Haven, 1956—; assoc. fellow Pierson Coll., Yale U., 1979—; sem. chmn., exhibitor 1st and 2nd Internat. Conf. Travel Medicine, Zurich, Atlanta, 1988, 91; trustee Yale Med. Libr., 1989—; internat. jury judge various film festivals. author, producer, dir. various med. ednl. films, 1971—; contbr. articles to profl. jours. Med. advisor Am. Cancer Soc., Conn., 1967, 90, Experimental Five Yr. BA Internat. Program, Yale U., 1966-67. Sr. asst. surgeon USPHS, 1947-49. Recipient Svc. award Am. Cancer Soc., Conn., 1967, 71. Fellow Am. Coll. Physicians (Laureate award 1991 Conn. chpt., audiovisual and sci. coms.), Am. Coll. Gastroenterology (archives com. 1991—); mem. AMA (div. ednl. devel.), Am. Soc. Gastrointestinal Endoscopy (past chmn. archieves and sci. coms.), Am. Soc. Tropical Medicine and Hygiene (ad hoc com. on tng. aids), Yale Alumni Assn. (del. to nat. 1989—), Sigma Xi. Office: Med Films Inc PO Box 8548 New Haven CT 06531-8548

GORDON, MICHAEL, lawyer; b. Newark, Oct. 12, 1953; s. Carl and Rose (Katz) G.; m. Arlene Cahn, Oct. 16, 1988; children: Jeremy, Carmel. BA, Columbia U., 1975; JD, Rutgers U., 1979. Bar: N.J. 1980, U.S. Dist. Ct. N.J. 1980, U.S. Ct. Appeals (3d cir.) 1984. Adj. prof. Montclair State Coll., Upper Montclair, N.J., 1978-79; atty. N.J. Dept. of Environ. Protection, Trenton, 1979-80; sole practice Montclair, 1980-83; ptnr. Gordon, Gordon P.C., West Orange, N.J., 1983—; spl. environ. counsel cities of Newark, Ridgefield, Montclair and Lafayette, N.J.; vis.lectr. Rutgers U., Newark, 1985. Vol. atty. Legal Services of Essex, Newark, 1984—, Essex County Dem. Com., 1987; dem. candidate U.S. House of Reps. 11th dist. of N.J., 1990; mem. Govs. Emergency Solid Waste Task Force, 1990. Recipient Cert. of Achievement, Ironbound Com. Against Toxic Waste, Newark, 1985, Outstanding Vol. award Essex Newark Legal Services, 1985. Mem. Assn. Trial Lawyers Am., N.J. State Bar Assn., N.J. Assn. Trial Lawyers (chmn. environ. law com. 1986-88). Club: Columbia (North Jersey). Office: 80 Main St West Orange NJ 07052-5414

GORDON, MORRIS AARON, medical mycologist, microbiologist; b. Waterbury, Conn., Apr. 3, 1920; s. Samuel and Anna (Rubinstein) G.; m. Ruth Kathryn McKee, May 22, 1945 (div. 1970); children: Barbara Jean, David Spencer, Sarah Elizabeth. BS, City Coll. N.Y., N.Y.C., 1940; MS, U. Chgo., 1942; PhD, Duke U., 1949. Diplomate Am. Bd. Microbiology; cert. lab. dir., N.Y. Lab. officer Regional Hosp., U.S. Army, Camp Blanding, Fla., 1945-46; mycologist Communicable Disease Ctr., Atlanta, 1949-54; biol. warfare specialist Chem. Corps Training Command, Fort McClellan, Ala., 1954-55; assoc. prof. microbiology Med. Coll. S.C., Charleston, 1955-59; sr. to prin. rsch. scientist, dir. mycology labs. N.Y. State Dept. Health, Albany, 1959—, dir. clin. microbiology & mycology labs., 1983-87, dir. emeritus clin. microbiology labs., 1987—; study sect. NIH, Washington, 1971-75; adv. com. Brown-Hazen Awards, N.Y.C., 1974-78; cons. VA Hosp., Albany, 1959—; rsch. prof. Albany Med. Coll., 1975—. Author: Laboratory Identification of Pathogenic Fungi, 1970; founder/editor Bull. Med. Mycol. Soc. Ams., 1976—; contbr. articles to profl. jours. Lt. comdr. USPHS, 1949-54. Recipient various rsch. grants NIH, teaching fellowship Duke U., 1947-49; Fulbright professor, 1978, Inter-Am. fellow La. State U., 1959. Mem. Med. Mycol. Soc. Ams. (pres. 1978-79, Benham award 1988), Internat. Soc. Human and Animal Mycology (v.p. 1982-85, Georg award 1991), Am. Soc. Microbiology (pres. mycology sect.), Sigma Xi (pres. Albany chpt. 1972). Home: 9 Leaf Rd Delmar NY 12054-2607 Office: NY State Dept Health Wadsworth Labs PO Box 509 Albany NY 12201-0509

GORDON, MYRON, psychologist; b. Bklyn., Apr. 12, 1920; s. Samuel E. and Bella (Horowitz) Goldfarb; B.S.S., CCNY, 1941, M.S., cert. in clin. psychology, 1942; fellow Rochester (N.Y.) Guidance Center, 1942-43; Ph.D., N.Y.U., 1952; m. Jetta Hendel, Nov. 10, 1949; children—Tamar, Eve. Staff psychologist Kings County Hosp., Bklyn., 1947-48; staff psychologist Queens Coll. Ednl. Clinic, 1949-53, psychologist Queens Speech and Hearing Center, 1953-54; cons. psychologist Children's Day and Night Shelter, N.Y.C., 1953-59; asso. prof. student personnel Queens Coll., 1961-83; practice in individual and group psychotherapy, 1952—; co-chmn. Queens County Mental Health Soc., 1969-76. Served with USAAF, 1943-45, AUS, 1945-46. Mem. Am. Psychol. Assn., Am. Group Psychotherapy Assn., Am. Profs. Peace in Middle East, N.Y. Soc. Clin. Psychologists (exec. bd. 1957-60), Queens Psychologists in Psychotherapeutic Practice (pres. 1957-58). Author: Theme-Centered Interaction: An Original Focus on Counseling and Education, 1971; Making Meetings More Productive, 1981. Editor Teaching-Learning Jour., 1974-76. Home: 41 Slocum Cres Flushing NY 11375-5236 Office: 114-06 Queens Blvd Forest Hills NY 11375

GORDON, PAUL DAVID, investment company executive; b. Everett, Mass., May 31, 1941; m. Arthur B. and Caterine D. (Cronin) G.; m. Dorothy L. Trepaney, July 4, 1970; children: Paul Jr., Michelle, Jeffrey, Christopher. AA in Extension Studies, Harvard U., 1985. Cert. registered options prin. series 4, series 63, gen. securities prin. Nat. Assn. Securities Dealers, series 12, series 7 N.Y. Stock Exch., commodity assoc. person Chgo. Bd. Trade, real estate broker, Mass., notary pub., Mass. Margin clk. PaineWebber Inc., Boston, 1959-63, regional margin mgr., 1964-69, ops. mgr., 1970-85, asst. br. mgr., v.p. adminstrn., 1986—; arbitrator N.Y. Stock Exch., N.Y.C., 1987—. Mem. exec. com. Boston Securities Cashiers Assn., 1976; assoc. mem. Jobs for Mass. Inc. Office: PaineWebber Inc 265 Franklin St Boston MA 02110-3113

GORDON, PAULA ROSSBACHER, musician, educator, producer, arts consultant; b. Fort Riley, Kans., Aug. 3, 1953; d. John Robert and Nancy (Fray) Rossbacher; m. Douglas Seth Gordon, June 19, 1976. BMus, Mansfield (Pa.) U., 1975, MS, 1980; postgrad., Pa. State U., Westminster Choir Coll. Cert. Yamaha music tchr. Grad. asst. Mansfield U., 1975-76; pers. and pub. rels. dir. McCarthy Ent., Williamsport, Pa., 1981; gen. mgr. Williamsport Symphony Orch., 1982-87; producer, exec. dir. Theatre by the Sea, Cape May, N.J., 1986-89; arts cons. N.Y., Pa., N.J., 1985—; owner, designer Gordon Graphics, Williamsport, 1988—; freelance performer/pianist, 1975—; arts cons., 1985—. Co-author: A History of Trinity Church, 1989. Bd. dirs. Coll./Community Arts Coun., Mansfield, 1974, Williamsport Players, 1980; activ ministry devel. com. Trinity Episc. Ch., 1991—, dir. pastoral ministry, 1992—. Republican. Episcopalian. Home and Office: 1024 Packer St Williamsport PA 17701-3427

GORDON, RICHARD H., professional hockey team executive. Mng. gen. ptnr., gov. Hartford Whalers. Office: Hartford Whalers 242 Trumbull St 8th Fl Hartford CT 06103*

GORDON, RICHARD LEWIS, mineral economics educator; b. Portland, Maine, June 19, 1934; s. Benjamin M. and Sara I. Gordon; m. Nancy Ellen Helfand, June 8, 1958; children: David William, Benjamin Mark. A.B., Dartmouth Coll., 1956; Ph.D., MIT, 1960. Econ. analyst Union Carbide Corp., 1960-64; asst. economist First Nat. City Bank, N.Y.C., 1964; mem. faculty Pa. State U., State College, 1964—, prof. mineral econs., 1970—; Shell lectr. on energy econs. Surrey (Eng.) U., 1981; bd. dirs. Ctr. for Energy and Mineral Policy, 1987—; Micasu U. endowed fellow in mineral econs., 1990. Author: The Evolution of Energy Policy in Western Europe, 1970, U.S. Coal and the Electric Power Industry, 1975, Coal in the U.S. Energy Market, 1978, An Economic Analysis of World Energy Problems, 1981, Reforming the Regulation of Electric Utilities, 1982, World Coal Economics, Policies and Prospects, 1987. Recipient Scholars medal The Pa. State U., 1989; decorated officer with honors 1st class Decoration of Andres Bello, Venezuela, 1989. Mem. AIME (chmn. council econs. 1973 Mineral Econs. award), Internat. Assn. Energy Economists, Am. Econ. Assn., Econometric Soc., Royal Econ. Soc., AAAS. Jewish. Home: 429 Kemmerer Rd State College PA 16801-6408 Office: Pa State U 204 Walker Dr State College PA 16801-7082

GORDON, ROBERT DANA, transplant surgeon; b. N.Y.C., Jan. 25, 1945; s. Gerson George and Muriel Ruth (Danish) G.; m. Linda Susan Gordon, July 9, 1970; children: David Charles, Daniel Lawrence. BA, Amherst Coll., 1966; MD, Cornell U., 1971. Diplomate Am. Bd. Surgery. Intern in surgery Mass. Gen. Hosp., Boston, 1971-72, resident in surgery, 1972-74, 77-78; vis. scientist transplantation biology unit Clin. Rsch. Ctr., Harrow, U.K., 1974-76; rsch. fellow Mass. Gen. Hosp./Harvard Med. Sch., Boston, 1974-76; clin. fellow Harvard Med. Sch., Boston, 1977-78; asst. prof. surgery U. Colo., Denver, 1979-83; asst. prof. surgery U. Pitts., 1983-88, assoc. prof. surgery, 1988-92; prof. surgery, chief liver transplant svc. Emory Univ., Sch. Medicine, Atlanta, 1992—; attending surgeon Presbyn. U. Hosp., Children's Hosp. Pitts; cons. surgeon Pitts. VA Med. Ctr.; chmn. fgn. rels. com. United Network Organ Sharing, Richmond, Va., 1987-90. Bd. dirs. Pitts. chpt. ARC. Fellow ACS; mem. Internat. Soc. Cardiovascular Surgery, Cen. Surg. Assn., Soc. Univ. Surgeons, Am. Soc. Transplant Surgeons (chmn. med. data rev. com.), Transplantation Soc., Pan Am. Med. Assn. (pres. sect. organ transplantation), Pa. Soc. Biomed. Rsch. (bd. dirs. 1991—). Office: U Pitts Transplantation Div/Surgery 3501 5th Ave Pittsburgh PA 15213-3301

GORDON, SCOTT (HARRY SCOTT BUEHLMEIER), entertainer; b. Dumont, N.J., Oct. 12, 1949; s. Harry Gordon and Florence Victoria (Bielawski) B.; m. Dian Mary Kenlon, Nov. 10, 1973. Grad. high sch., Mahwah, N.J. Pres. Scott Gordon Enterprises, Inc., Paramus, N.J., 1974—; performer, writer The Uncle Floyd Show, West Orange, N.J., 1976—; audio cons. Playhouse on the Mall, Paramus, N.J., 1974, make-up cons. Ken's Costumes, Fair Lawn, N.J., 1976—. Author: Editor (profl. mag.) Psychicos, 1978-80; author (column) Vibrations, 1987; maker radio commls.: San Antonio Rose with Willie Nelson, B-52s, Labour of Lust, First Exposure; engr. (radio programs) The Italian American Serenade, The Colavita Music Hall, Italian Melodies, Sunday Funnies; air personality Remember When, 1987—; entertainer Nickelodeon Turkey TV. Mem. AFTRA, Psychic Entertainers Assn. (bd. dirs. 1978-80, founder), Soc. Broadcast Engrs., Audio Engring. Soc., Circle Tri Corbies, The Radio Repertory Co. of Am. Office: Scott Gordon Enterprises Inc PO Box 791 Paramus NJ 07653-0791

GORDON, TIMOTHY WILLIAM, communications executive; b. Wilmington, Del., Jan. 18, 1965; s. Richard Wallace Gordon and Barbara (Bateson) Woolley; m. Serena Charlotte Morrissey, Dec. 31, 1990. BA in English, Lake Forest Coll., 1986. Dir. membership Soc. Tech. Communication, Arlington, Va., 1987-88; dir. communications Nat. Assn. Pediatric Nurse Assocs. and Practitioners, Cherry Hill, N.J., 1988—. Editor, writer The Pediatric Nurse Practitioner, 1989—. Mem. Soc. Tech. Communication (membership mgr. Del. Valley chpt. 1990—), Am. Soc. Assn. Execs., Phila. Mus. Art, Brandywine Conservancy. Republican. Home: 1011 Baltimore Pike Chadds Ford PA 19317 Office: Nat Assn Pediatric Nurse Assocs and Practitioners 1101 Kings Hwy N Ste 206 Cherry Hill NJ 08034-1912

GORDON, TINA, sculptor, art therapist; b. N.Y.C.; d. Abraham and Rose (Scoff) Schapiro; m. Norman B. Gordon (div.); children: Jane, Judith, Marc. BA in Fine Arts, Goddard Coll., 1972; postgrad., NYU, 1978-80; student, Nat. Acad. Art, N.Y.C., 1981-83, Parsons Sch. Design, N.Y.C., 1983-88. Art tchr. East River Montessori Sch., N.Y.C., 1969-72; instr. Nassau Community Coll., 1973-76; art therapist Manhattan Psychiat. Ctr., N.Y.C., 1977-87. Exhibited in shows at Nat. Acad. Art, 1977, 78, 80, Nat. Art Club, N.Y.C., 1978, 79, 80, 83, 88, Thompson Gallery, N.Y.C., Salamagundi Art Club, N.Y.C., 1979-90, Pen and Brush, N.Y.C., 1984-89, L.I. Artists Guild, 1970, 71, 72, numerous others; commns. for Manhattan Psy. Ctr. Mem. Salmagundi Art Soc. (Elliot Liskin award in sculpture 1984, 86), Nat. Assn. Women Artists, Pen and Brush (Merit award 1985, 87, 88, 89), Am. Soc. Contemporary Artists, Burr Artists, Allied Artists, Knickerbocker Artists (Roman Bronze award 1981, 83), Nat. Sculpture Soc. (assoc.). Home: 24 5th Ave New York NY 10011-8858

GORDON, WALTER KELLY, provost, English language educator; b. Bklyn., Jan. 25, 1930; s. William Benjamin and Grace Adele (Kelly) G.; m. Lydia Caroline Fruchtman, Aug. 29, 1959; 1 child, Karyn Gay. A.B., Clark U., 1950; M.A., U. Pa., 1956, Ph.D., 1961. Instr. Cedar Crest Coll., 1959-61; faculty Rutgers U., Camden, 1961—; prof., dean coll. Rutgers U., 1974-81, acad. dean, provost Camden campus, 1981—; cons. Campbells Soup Co., 1976—. Author: (with J.L. Sanderson) Exposition and the English Language, 1963, 2d edit., 1968, Literature in Critical Perspectives, 1969. Bd. dirs. Walt Whitman Internat. Poetry Center, 1974-77. Served to lt. USNR, 1951-56. Recipient Lindback award for disting. teaching, 1970. Home: 2803 Salem Dr Riverton NJ 08077-4027 Office: Rutgers U Camden Coll Arts & Scis 379 Armitage Hall Camden NJ 08102

GORE, JAYAVANT PRABHAKAR, mechanical engineering educator, researcher; b. Pune, Maharashtra, India, Apr. 4, 1956; came to U.S., 1980; s. Prabhakar G. and Nalini P. (Kelkar) G.; m. Medha J. Kirtane; children: Athurva, Ohm. BE, Pune U., 1978; MS, Pa. State U., 1982, PhD, 1986. Asst. engr. Tata Engring., Pune, 1978-80; grad. asst. Pa. State U., University Park, 1980-83, 84-85; systems engr. Singer Corp., Silver Spring, Md., 1983-84; rsch. fellow U. Mich., Ann Arbor, 1985-87; asst. prof. U. Md., College Park, 1987—; cons. Fusion Systems Inc., Rockville, Md., 1988-91, Shell Rsch. Corp., Houston, 1991—. Contbr. articles to profl. jours. Presdl. Young Investigator rsch. grantee, 1991. Mem. ASME (Best Paper award, 1987), AIAA, Internat. Combustion Inst., Internat. Assn. Fire Safety Sci. Home: 2440 Kestral Blvd Apt E West Lafayette IN 47906-6536 Office: U Md Dept Mech Engring College Park MD 20742

GOREN, ALEXANDER MIRCEA, investment company executive; b. Bucharest, Romania, Feb. 19, 1940; came to U.S., 1984; s. Avram and Stella (Cukier) G.; m. Rina Attar, Nov. 20, 1966 (div. 1983); children: Andrea Y., Elisabeth J.; m. Brooke Weinstein, June 24, 1984; 1 stepchild, Brett Kroeger. BA, Harvard U., 196l, postgrad., 1979; MBA, Columbia U., 1963. Asst. v.p. fin. Brinco, Montreal, Que., Can., 1963-64; investment officer Royal Trust Co., Montreal, 1964-65; head rsch. Caboto S.p.a., Milan, 1965-66; gen. mgr. Sosicom Srl, Milan, 1966-70; mgr. Eurodollar loans Keyser Ullman, Ltd., London, 1970-73; gen. mgr., chief exec. officer Mediterranean Car Agy., Ltd., Tel Aviv, 1973-84; gen. ptnr. Goren Bros., N.Y.C., 1985—; bd. dirs., vice chmn. N.Y. and Fgn. Securities, N.Y.C., 1987-90; bd. dirs., chmn. exec. com. Marcade Inc., N.Y.C., 1986—. Bd. govs. Ben Gurion U. of Negev, 1980—; bd. dirs. N.Y.C. Outward Bound Ctr., 1990—, The Tilton Sch., 1990—. Mem. Harvard Club N.Y.C. Jewish. Office: 805 3d Ave 26th Fl New York NY 10022

GORENSTEIN, SHIRLEY SLOTKIN, anthropologist, educator; b. N.Y.C., Mar. 4, 1928; d. Harry and Mary (Pfeffer) Slotkin; m. Samuel Gorenstein, July 3, 1948; children: Ethan Ezra, Gabriel William. B.A., Queen's Coll., 1949; M.A., Columbia U., 1953, Ph.D., 1963. Lectr. anthropology Columbia U., N.Y.C., 1963-71; asst. prof. Columbia U., 1971-74, assoc. prof., 1974-75; prof. anthropology Rensselaer Poly. Inst., Troy, N.Y., 1975—; chmn. dept. sci. tech. studies Rensselaer Poly. Inst., assoc. dean Sch. Humanities and Social Scis., 1975-90. Author works in field. Mem. N.Y. State Bd. for Hist. Preservation, 1976-85. Mem. Am. Anthropol. Assn. (exec. bd. 1976-79), Soc. Am. Archaeology., Soc. Profl. Archaeologists (bd. standards 1983-86). Office: Rensselaer Poly Inst 5506 Sage Lab Troy NY 12180-3590

GOREWITZ, RUBIN LEON, accountant, financial consultant; b. Bklyn., June 7, 1924; s. Isadore Asa and Esther (Tickotzki) G.; children: Shalom, Heshi, Marian Esther. BBA, CCNY, 1951. CPA, N.Y. Acct. J. Sherago & Co., CPAs, N.Y.C., 1942-48; sr. acct. Leonard A. Shair, CPA, N.Y.C., 1948-56; contr. Herold Radio & Electronics Co., Mt. Vernon, N.Y., 1956-59; pvt. practice acctg. and fin. cons., N.Y., 1959—; staff acct., cons. N.Y. State Coun. Arts; founder, former treas., dir. Mudsummer, Inc., Expts. in Art & Tech., Inc., The Real U. of Sts., The Real Gt. Soc.; treas. 21c Corp.; bd. dirs. Robert Rauschenberg, Inc., Untitled Press, Inc., Cloud Mgmt. Internat., Inc., Change, Inc.; cons. new bus. ventures; controller, advisor to Peter Max and his corp. entities. Founder, past treas., dir. Abstract Ballet Comtempo, Inc.; founder, past dir. Storytime Dance Theatre, Inc.; founder, treas., dir. Jazz Composers Orch., Found. for Devel. and Preservation of Cultural Arts, Opera Today, Inc., Inst. for Chamber Music, Inc., Traditional Jazz Band Co., Inc., Found. for Vital Arts, Creative Dance Found., Modern Dance Artists, Inc., Seamus Murphy Dance Found., Yuriko Dance Found., Daniel Nagrin Dance Found., Intermedia Found.; founder, dir. Cunningham Dance Found.; treas. Lightyears, Inc.; founder, fin. advisor Martha Graham Ctr., Chimera Dance Found., New World Workshop, Dance Theatre Found., Search, Inc.; Ctrs. for Change; chmn. bd. Dance Notation Bur.; bd. dirs. Dance Theatre Workshop, Change Inc. Concert Artists Guild; founder, pres. Artists' Rights Today, Inc.; fin. advisor Performance Group, Living Theatre, Open Theatre, Found. Contemporary Performing Arts, Music Drama Theatre, Cantor's Assembly Am.; adv. dir. Modern Dance Found., Hackensack; lectr., writer and lobbyist on rights of artists. With AUS, 1943-45, ETO. Mem. AICPA, N.Y. State Soc. CPAs, Nat. Assn. Cost Accts. (past dir. N.Y.C. chpt.). Home and Office: 186 Lawrence Rd PO Box 256 Accord NY 12404 also: 35 W 65th St New York NY 10023

GORHAM, JOHN PATRICK, accounting educator; b. N.Y.C., Mar. 6, 1942; s. Peter Mark and Kathleen Mary (O'Brien) G.; m. Maureen A. O'Sullivan, Apr. 24, 1965; children: Maureen, John, Bernadette, Patrick, Monica. BBA, Manhattan Coll., 1963; MA, CCNY, 1970; MBA, NYU, 1973, PhD, 1980. Tchr. St. Helena High Sch., Bronx, N.Y., 1966-68, Ardsley (N.Y.) High Sch., 1968-69; computer programmer Bklyn. (N.Y.) Union Gas Co., 1969-70; prof. acctg. Bronx (N.Y.) Community Coll., 1970—. Author: Bookkeeping-Simplified and Self Taught, 1983. Mem. Phi Delta Kappa. Roman Catholic. Home: 110 Brown Rd Scarsdale NY 10583-5660 Office: Bronx Community Coll 181 Street and Univ Ave Bronx NY 10453

GORIN, ROBERT MURRAY, JR., educator; b. Mineola, N.Y., Oct. 29, 1948; s. Robert Murray and Vivian Margaret (Schleider) G. AB, Xavier U., 1970, MA, 1970; MS in Edn., Hofstra U., 1974; MA, Fordham U., 1978; PhD, St. Louis U., 1980; postgrad. Yale U., Harvard U., Johns Hopkins U., Civil War Inst., Gettburg Coll. Tchr. social studies Bellmore-Merrick (N.Y.) Central High Sch. Dist., 1974-77, 78-83, Rockville Centre (N.Y.) Union Free Sch. Dist., 1977-78, Manhasset (N.Y.) Pub. Sch., 1983—; fellow Robert A. Taft Inst. Govt., 1976, Soc. for Values in Higher Edn.; adj. asst. prof. history Hofstra U., 1986—. Cert. N.Y. State Edn. Dept. With USAR, 1968-69. Mem. Am. Hist. Assn., So. Hist. Assn., Orgn. Am. Historians, Orgn. History Tchrs., Center for Study Presidency, Am. Heritage Soc., Moral Edn. Assn., Soc. for History Edn., Nat. Coun. for Social Studies (ethics adv. com. 1982-91), N.Y. State, L.I. Couns. for Social Studies, Inst. Society, Ethics and Life Scis., Am. Assn. State and Local History, N.Y. Hist. Soc., Soc. of Civil War Historians, Assn. for Supervision and Curriculum Devel., The Civil War Soc., Nat. Coun. History Edn. Assn. for Preservation of Civil War Sites, Moral Edn. Assn., Taft Assocs., Met. Opera Guild, Civil War Round Table N.Y., Phi Alpha Theta. Republican. Roman Catholic. Home: 51 Somerset Ave Garden City NY 11530-1145

GORLIN, RENA ANN, writer; b. Bklyn., Dec. 27, 1957; d. Philip and Sylvia (Levy) G.; m. Raymond R. Plante, 1991. BA magna cum laude, Brandeis U., 1979; JD, Am. U., 1982. Legal editor and reporter BNA's Patent, Trademark and Copyright Jour. Bur. Nat. Affairs, Inc., Washington, 1983; legal editor and reporter U.S. Law Week, Washington, 1983-86; sr. copywriter Bur. Nat. Affairs, Washington, 1986—; freelance editor and copywriter, Washington area, 1986—. Author: Codes of Professional Responsibility, 1986, 2d edit., 1990. Mem. law com. Anti-Defamation League B'nai Brith, Washington, 1980; vol. Big Sisters, Waltham, Mass., 1976-78; moot ct. judge Cath. U. Law Sch. competitions, Washington, 1985—. Mem. Washington Ind. Writers, Soc. for Health and Human Values. Office: BNA Sales and Mktg Div 1231 25th St NW Washington DC 20037-1157

GORMAN, IDA NIEBAUER, magnetic resonance technologist; b. Fairview, Pa., Dec. 7, 1949; d. Ferdinand Oscar and Julia Catherine (Bausch) Niebauer; m. Philip Thomas Gorman, June 14, 1975; children: Jennifer Lynn, Chad Michael. BA in Biology, Mercyhurst Coll., 1971; postgrad., Pa. State U., Hershey. Jr. rsch. technician dept. surgery M.S. Hershey (Pa.) Med. Ctr., 1971-73, rsch. technician, 1973-78, sr. rsch. pacemaker technician, 1978-83, rsch. technician dept. radiology, 1984, sr. rsch. technician, 1984-86, rsch. support asst. dept. radiology, 1986-89; magnetic resonance technologist, spectroscopist York (Pa.) Imaging Ctr., 1989—. Author: (manual) Basic Index and Troubelshooting Guide to Cardiac Pacing, 1983, (manuscript) T2 Weighted Image Manipulation to Accent Pathology, 1991; contbr. articles to profl. jours. Sec. St. Theresa Home/Sch. Assn., New Cumberland, Pa., 1987-89; lector St. Theresa Ch., New Cumberland, 1989-91. Scholar Mercyhurst Coll., 1967-71. Mem. AAAS, N.Y. Acad. Sci. Roman Catholic. Home: 5004 Balmoral Ct Mechanicsburg PA 17055 Office: York Imaging Ctr 1640 S Queen St York PA 17403

GORMAN, JAMES LOU, baseball team executive; b. Providence; s. Mary Lou Gorman. AB, Stonehill Coll.; MA, Bridgewater (Mass.) State Coll. From dir. player devel. to v.p., asst. gen. mgr. Kansas City Royals, 1968-76; v.p., dir. baseball ops. Seattle Mariners, 1976-78, gen. mgr., 1978-80; v.p., dir. baseball ops. N.Y. Mets, 1980-84, former sr. v.p., gen. mgr., from 1984; now sr. v.p., gen. mgr. Boston Red Sox. Bd. dirs. Stonehill Coll.; bd. visitors Mass. Maritime Acad.; alumni coun. Bridgewater State Coll. Capt. USNR. Named to Stonehill Coll. Hall of Fame, R.I. Gridiron Hall of Fame. Office: Boston Red Sox 4 Yawkey Way Boston MA 02215-3496

GORMAN, MARGARET MARY, psychology consultant and educator; d. Vincent A. and Margaret (Thomser) G. BA in English, Trinity Coll., 1939; MA in Philosophy, Fordham U., 1952; PhD in Ednl. Psychology, Cath. U., 1958. Tchr. Acads. of the Sacred Heart, 1942-56; prin. parochial sch. St. Katherine's Sch., Torresdale, Pa., 1957-59; chmn. dept. psychology, prof. psychology Newton Coll. of the Sacred Heart, 1959-75; psychol. cons. U.S. Army, Ft. Monmouth, N.J., 1962—, USAF, Montgomery, Ala., 1967—; adj. prof. psychology, theology Boston Coll., 1981—. Bd. dirs. Newton Community Svc. Ctr., 1969-77, pres., 1974-76; commr. Newton Human Rights Commn., 1970-74, chair, 1972-74; trustee Mass. Sch. Profl. Psychology, 1976—, chair bd. trustees, 1978—. Fellow Mass. Psychol. Assn. (sec. 1968-71, bd. dirs. 1973-75); mem. APA (div. 36 religious issues), Soc. for the Psychol. Study of Social Issues, Soc. for the Sci. Study of Religion, Assn. for Moral Edn., Boston Coordinating Coun. on Drug Abuse. Home: 55 Lee Rd Chestnut Hill MA 02167-3932 Office: Boston Coll Chestnut Hill MA 02167

GORMAN, MARILYN GRACE, marketing and communications professional; b. Springfield, Mass., Sept. 8, 1966; d. Philip W. Jr. and Marion N. Gorman. BSBA in Mktg., Western New Eng. Coll., 1988. Pub. rels. asst. Western New Eng. Coll., Springfield, 1986-88; selling specialist J.C. Penney, Inc., Springfield and Warwicke, 1984—; pub. affairs asst. Metro. Life Ins. Co., Warwick, R.I., 1988-91; mktg. analyst Metro. Property & Casualty Ins. Co., Warwick, R.I., 1991—. Mem. Am. Mktg. Assn., Pub. Rels. Soc. Am. (membership chmn. 1991—). Office: Metro Property & Casualty 700 Quaker Ln # 350 Warwick RI 02886-6669

GORMAN, RAYMOND JAMES, health facility administrator, consultant; b. Waterbury, Conn., June 11, 1953; s. Raymond J. Sr. and Josephine (Stokna) G.; m. Sylvia Joan McFall, May 25, 1991. AA, Mattatuck Community Coll., Waterbury, 1980; M in human svcs. adminstrn., Antioch New Eng. Grad. Sch., Keene, N.H., 1990. Program assoc. Am. Cancer Soc., Watterbury, 1973-75; exec. dir. Am. Cancer Soc., New Britain, Conn., 1975-77; program specialist Conn. Dept. Mental Health, Hartford, 1977-80; dir. adminstrv. svcs. Community Mental Health Affiliates, New Britain, 1980-86; asst. regional adminstr. Conn. Dept. Mental Health, Newington, 1986-91; exec. dir. Conn. Assn. Child Caring Agencies, Hamden, 1991—; cons. South Pub. Health Svcs., Southington, Conn., 1989—. Bd. dirs. Human Resources Assn., New Britain, 1986-88, Help Us Grow, Southington, 1987-89; mem. Robinson House Adv. Bd., 1991—. Mem. NRA. Office: Conn Assn Child Caring Agencies 1400 Whitney Ave Hamden CT 06517-2499

GORMAN, ROBERT SAUL, architect; b. N.Y.C., June 28, 1933; s. Philip and Lillian (Weiss) G.; B.Arch., M.Arch., Yale U., 1966; m. Judith Alice Albaum, July 2, 1965; children—Melissa, Sasha William Shannon. Apprentice to Frank Lloyd Wright, 1953-56; designer Eero Saarinen, Hamden, Conn., 1961-67; architect, planner Victor Gruen Assos., N.Y.C., 1967-69, Juster/Pope, Architects, Shelburne Falls, Mass., 1977-78; architect Robert Gorman Assos., Architects, Planners, Solar Energy Cons., Richmond, N.H., 1969-80; founder, prin. Rawson Place Architects, 1980-89; founder, prin. Green River Architects, 1989—; cons. Bklyn. Coll., 1967-69. Served with AUS, 1956-58. Frank Lloyd Wright Found. fellow, 1953-56. Mem. AIA (Design award 1972). Pioneer in solar energy archtl. applications; architect, planner many projects. Home: Richmond Rd Richmond NH 03470 Office: Green River Architects Box 817 RR4 Brattleboro VT 05301

GORMLEY, GERARD MAJELLA, data processing executive; b. Phila., Sept. 17, 1957; s. Francis John and Maryann Dolores (Mancini) G. BA in Chemistry, LaSalle U., Phla., 1979; MA in Computer Sci., Villanova U., 1991. Chemist William H. Rorer, Ft. Washington, Pa., 1979-81, Lemmon Pharm., Sellersville, Pa., 1981; chemist Smith, Kline, Beecham, Phila., 1981-83, system mgr., 1983-90; pres. Aardvark Automation, Phila., 1990—; computer cons. Smith, Kline, Beecham, 1990—, McNeil Labs., Ft. Washington, Pa., 1991—. Ben Franklin Tech. Ctr. grantee, 1990-91. Office: Aardvark Automation 250 Ross Rd King Of Prussia PA 19406

GORMLEY, JAMES JOHN, editor; b. Montreal, Que., Can.; s. Edward Patrick and Audrey Mary (Keller) G. BA, CUNY, 1989. Editor, writer SUNY Health Sci. Ctr., Bklyn., 1988-89; med. prodn. editor Simon & Schuster, Appleton & Lange Div., Norwalk, Conn., 1990-91; prodn. editor Plenum Pub. Corp., N.Y.C., 1992—. Author: (poems, with others) Poetic Voices of America, 1990; editor-writer newsletter Clin. Practice Mgmt. Plan News, 1988-89. Mem. Conn. Press Club, Golden Key Nat. Honor Soc. Home: care Juliana Gonzalez Gormley 811 New York Ave Apt 1103 Brooklyn NY 11203

GORRIARAN, AL JUAQUIN, army officer; b. Havana, Cuba, Oct. 29, 1955; arrived in U.S., 1960; s. Adolf and Mary Ellen (Pedraza) G.; m. Nancy Wynne Mattison, Oct. 16, 1976 (div. Oct. 1980); 1 child, Calvin; m. Eden Joy Hart, Oct. 29, 1955. BA in Pub. Adminstrn., Calif. State U., Chico, 1982; MBA, Webster U., 1986; MPA, Troy (Ala.) State U., 1990. Commd. 2d lt. U.S. Army, 1982, advanced through grades to capt., 1986; adminstrv. officer 4th Brigade, Ft. Jackson, S.C., 1983; comdr. C. Co. Reception Sta., Ft. Jackson, 1984-86; human resources officer 8th Infantry Div., Bad Krueznach, Fed. Republic Germany, 1986-87; comdr. 226th Postal Co., Munich, Fed. Republic Germany, 1988-90, U.S. Army Recruiting Co., Saratoga, N.Y., 1990-91; ops. officer U.S. Army Recruiting Battalion, Albany, N.Y., 1991—; instr. City Colls. Chgo., Bad Krueznach, 1986-87, Munich, 1988-90. Contbr. articles to profl. jours. Mem. Adjutant Gen. Corps. Assn. Home: 98B Elsmere Ave Delmar NY 12054-4316 Office: US Army Recruiting Batt 21 Aviation Rd Albany NY 12205-1131

GORRIN, EUGENE, lawyer; b. Irvington, N.J., Apr. 22, 1956; s. Harry and Ruth (Goldberg) G. BA, Rutgers U., 1978; JD, George Washington U., 1981; LLM in Taxation, NYU, 1982. Bar: N.J. 1981, U.S. Dist. Ct. N.J. 1981, U.S. Tax Ct. 1982, U.S. Supreme Ct. 1985. Assoc. Ozzard, Rizzolo, Klein, Mauro & Savo, Somerville, N.J., 1982-83; Assoc. Levine, Furman & Davis, East Brunswick, N.J., 1984-88; ptnr. Cole, Schotz, Bernstein, Meisel and Forman, P.A., Hackensack, N.J., 1988—. Mem. ABA (taxation sect.), N.J. Bar Assn. (taxation sect.), U.S. Supreme Ct. Hist. Soc., Phi Alpha Delta. Home: 2607 Frederick Ter Union NJ 07083-5603 Office: Cole Schotz Bernstein Meisel and Forman PA Court Pla N 25 Main St Hackensack NJ 07601-7037

GORSKI, ROBERT ALEXANDER, chemist, consultant; b. Passaic, N.J., Nov. 24, 1922; s. Stephen T. and Wanda P. (Amlicke) G.; m. Helen Marie Thompson, Aug. 19, 1944; children: Robert J., Mary Ann B., Mark G., Stephen J., Paul F. BA in Sci., La Salle U., 1947; MS in Chemistry, U. Pa., 1948, PhD in Phys. Chemistry, 1951. Chemist DuPont, Wilmington, Del., 1951-53; rsch. chemist DuPont Freon Products Lab., Wilmington, Del., 1953-60, sr. rsch. chemist, 1960-70, rsch. assoc., 1970-78, tech. assoc., 1978-85; cons. DuPont Fluorochemicals Lab., Wilmington, Del., 1985-91; ret., 1991—. Author book chpt.; contbr. articles to profl. jours.; patentee solvents. With U.S. Army, 1943-46, ETO. Mem. Am. Chem. Soc., ASTM, Nat. Geog. Soc., KC, Sigma Xi. Republican. Roman Catholic. Home: 735 Harvard Ln Newark DE 19711-3134

GORT, MICHAEL, economics educator; b. Minsk, USSR, Sept. 30, 1923; came from China to U.S., 1937; m. Elizabeth Ann Mitchell, June 15, 1957; children: William Henry, Adam Michael. AB, Bklyn. Coll., CUNY, 1943; AM, Columbia U., 1951, PhD, 1954. Lectr. in econs. U. Calif., Berkeley, 1951-54; mem. research staff Nat. Bur. Econ. Research, N.Y.C., 1954-57; assoc. prof. fin. U. Chgo., 1957-62; cons. Dept. Commerce, Washington, 1962-63; prof. econs. SUNY, Buffalo, 1963—; vis. prof. econs. Northwestern U., Evanston, Ill., 1967-68; sr. research staff mem. and dir. research program in indsl. orgn. Nat. Bur. Econ. Research, N.Y.C., 1971-75; pres. Michael Gort Assocs., Buffalo, 1977—. Author: Diversification and Integration in American Industry, 1962, Changes in the Size Standard of Business Firms, 1964; contbr. articles to profl. jours. Fellow Social Sci. Research Council, 1950-51. Mem. Am. Econ. Assn., Royal Econ. Soc., European Assn. for Research in Indsl. Econs. Home: 71 Smallwood Dr Buffalo NY 14226-4028 Office: SUNY Dept of Econs North Campus Buffalo NY 14260

GORTLER, LEON BERNARD, chemist; b. Des Moines, Jan. 30, 1935; s. Louis and Ruth (Dvorsky) G.; m. Selma Ruth Bass, June 12, 1960; children: Jan Maret, Andrew Ian, Jocelyn Patrice. AB, U. Chgo., 1957, BS, 1957, MS, 1957; PhD, Harvard U., 1962. Postdoctoral fellow U. Calif., Berkeley, 1961-62; instr. Bklyn. Coll., Bklyn., N.Y., 1962-65, asst. prof., 1965-69, assoc. prof., 1969-73, prof., 1973—; chmn. Dept. Chemistry, Bklyn. Coll., 1984-87. Author: Techniques and Experiments in Organic Chemistry, 1977. Mem. Am. Chem. Soc. (Div. of History chmn. 1982-83), History of Sci. Soc., Sigma Xi. Office: Brooklyn Coll Dept Chemistry Brooklyn NY 11210

GORUP, GREGORY JAMES, marketing executive; b. Kansas City, Kans., Mar. 27, 1948; s. Mike and Helen F. Gorup; m. Kathleen Susan Grogan, Apr. 12, 1986; children: Michael Thomas, Ryan Nicholas. BA in Econs., St. Benedict Coll., 1970; MBA, U. Pa., 1972. Market analyst product planning and devel. dept. Citibank, N.Y.C., 1972-73, market planning officer corp. product mgmt. div., 1973-74, product mgr. securities services, 1974-75; v.p., dir. product devel. Irving Trust Co. N.Y.C., 1975-80, mgr. product mgmt. dept., 1980-81; v.p. mktg. Credit Suisse, U.S. area, 1981-84; sr. cons. Wesley, Brown and Bartle, N.Y.C., 1985-86; bank mktg. mgr. Digital Equipment Corp., N.Y.C., 1986-87; money mktg. mgr. Reuters N.Am., 1987-88; pres. Gorup Assocs., 1989-91; dist. v.p. Nat. Computer Systems, N.Y., 1991—. Mem. Am. Mgmt. Assn., Ducks Unltd., Wharton Bus. Sch. Club, Princeton Club N.Y., Orienta Beach Club. Republican. Roman Catholic. Home: 47 Kingsbury Rd New Rochelle NY 10804-4718 Office: 29 Tulip Tree Ln Mamaroneck NY 10543

GORZYNSKI, EUGENE ARTHUR, microbiologist, educator; b. Buffalo, N.Y., Oct. 8, 1919; s. Charles Stanley and Helen Mary (Prolejko) G.; m. Ruth Repp, Jan. 10, 1946; children: David, Timothy, Kathleen. BA in Biology, U. Buffalo, 1949, MA in Bacteriology, 1953; PhD in Microbiology, SUNY, Buffalo, 1968. Registered specialist microbiologist. Rsch. microbiologist Children's Hosp., Buffalo, 1947-65; sr. cancer rsch. scientist Roswell Park Meml. Inst., Buffalo, 1969-73; asst. dir. Erie County Pub. Health Lab., Buffalo, 1968-75; prof. microbiology and pathology SUNY Sch. Medicine and Biol. Scis., Buffalo, 1969—; dir. microbiology VA Med. Ctr., Buffalo, 1975—. Author: (with others) Methods in Immunodiagnosis, 1973, Medical Microbiology, 1982, Oral Microbiology and Immunology, 1988; contbr. articles to profl. jours. With U.S. Army, 1941-46, ETO, col. ret. Res. Fellow AAAS, Am. Acad. Microbiology, Infectious Diseases Soc. Am. Democrat. Roman Catholic. Office: VA Med Ctr 3495 Bailey Ave Buffalo NY 14215-1129

GOSDIS, SHERRY, credit manager; b. Joseph, Utah, Apr. 22, 1947; d. Duane Barney and Stella (Wilcock) Kirkwood; children: Loni, Krisy, T. Shane. Grad. magna cum laude, N.Y. Inst. Credit, 1982; postgrad., Fordham U., 1983. Collector, investigator Crocker United Bank, N.Y.C., 1978-81; credit analyst Rosenthal & Rosenthal Inc., N.Y.C., 1981-84; asst. treas., sr. analyst Comml. Credit Corp., N.Y.C., 1984-86; asst. v.p., sr. analyst Congress Talcott, N.Y.C., 1986-89; asst. mgr. credit Liz Claiborne Inc., N.Y.C., 1989—. Mem. Progressive Credit Club, Futures Credit Club, Designers Credit Group, Meadowlands Credit Group. Home: 16 Chatham Rd Hewitt NJ 07421-1604 Office: Liz Claiborne Inc One Claiborne Ave North Bergen NJ 07047

GOSKOWSKI, FRANCIS MICHAEL, English educator; b. Carbondale, Pa., Feb. 12, 1950; s. Frank Michael and Helen Katherine (Antonyak) G. BA, U. Scranton, 1972, MA, 1976. Lectr. in English U. Scranton, Pa., 1974-75; instr. to assoc. prof. English Lackawanna Jr. Coll., Scranton, 1975—, chmn. dept. humanities, 1980-89, 91—; off-premise instr. Internat. Corr. Schs., Scranton, 1989—; tutor gifted student program Scranton Sch. Dist., 1987, 89. Reviewer Best Sellers, 1975-80. Lector Sacred Heart Ch., Forest City, Pa., 1968—. Mem. Nat. Assn. Tchrs. English, Northeastern Pa. Writing Coun., Alpha Sigma Nu. Democrat. Roman Catholic. Home: 301 Hudson St Forest City PA 18421-1411 Office: Lackawanna Jr Coll 901 Prospect Ave Scranton PA 18505

GOSS, JOEL FRANCIS, writer; b. Pawnee, Okla., Nov. 15, 1955; s. William Richard and Mary Ann (Webb) G. BA, U. Tenn., 1985. Staff writer Sta. WDXB, Chattanooga, 1970-73, Sta. WGOW, Knoxville, Tenn., 1973-75; writer, dir. V.T. Films, Knoxville, 1974-76; writer Hi-Test Films, Knoxville, 1976; freelance writer N.Y.C., 1976-80; writer, mgr. Improvisation, Inc., N.Y.C., 1980-84; writer, producer CB Prodns., N.Y.C., 1984; mng. dir. Albuquerque '49, N.Y.C., 1983—; v.p. Buster Keaton Archive, N.Y.C., 1985—; cons. Rohauer Films, London, 1985-88, Am. Theatre Wing, N.Y.C., 1987; film instr. Brown Sch., Knoxville, 1976; chmn. Film com., Knoxville, 1974-76. Author: Albuquerque '49, 1973, (with Michael Kaluta) The Shadow, 1992; screenplays: The Prairie Traveler, 1986, Manhattan Underground, 1987, Bard of Broadway, 1988, Sandhogs, 1991, Battling Butler, 1991; translator tng. manuals: Construzione Aerounaticle, 1973; co-screenwriter (with Raymond Rohauer), researcher Buster Keaton-A Hard Act to Follow, 1987; writer Spectacular Days of Radio, 1990, (with Martin Connor) Madame Sherry, 1989, Cat Guthrie in Concert, 1992, The Rich Conaty Radio Show, 1992; restored dialog to film (with Bruce Goldstein) The Donovan Affair (1929), 1992; co-producer Am. Hepatitis Assn. Benefit, 1989; promotions writer CNN Headline News, Sandy Hook Found. Vol. Nat. Music Theatre Network, N.Y.C., Washington, 1985, 87, Nat. Theatre Wing, N.Y.C., 1987, Muscular Dystrophy Assn., N.Y.C., 1987. Grantee U. Tenn., 1975, CB Prodns., 1984. Mem. Buster Keaton Soc. Office: 310 Riverside Dr Ste 323 New York NY 10025

GOSS, JOHN REED, III, education educator; b. Lewistown, Pa., Mar. 21, 1955; s. John Reed and Dorothy (Williams) G.; m. Janet L. Smalley, Aug. 16, 1986. BS in Econs. and Sociology, Pa. State U., 1977; MA, Indiana U. Pa., 1982; MS in Edn., Elmira Coll., 1988; PhD, The Am. U., 1991. Exec. dir. Odyssey, Inc., Lewistown, Pa., 1977-81; exec. v.p. CHRIE, University Park, Pa., 1983-86, Arts Coun. Tompkins County, Ithaca, N.Y., 1986-88; rsch. fellow Am. U., Washington, 1988—; adj. faculty Averett Coll., Danville, Va., 1990—, The Am. U., Washington, 1991—, Nat.-Louis U., 1991—; cons. in field. Mem. bd. edn. Mifflin County Sch. Dist., Lewistown, Pa., 1977-86; mem. County Dem. Com., Mifflin County, 1979-85; candidate Pa. Ho. of Reps., 82d Dist., 1982. Recipient Mellon Travel award Am. U., Washington, 1991. Mem. Philosophy of Edn. Soc., Am. Ednl. Rsch. Assn., Washington Assn. Profl. Anthropoligists. Episcopalian. Home: 4010 Spruell Dr Kensington MD 20895-1345

GOSSAGE, THOMAS LAYTON, chemical company executive; b. Nashville, May 7, 1934; s. Walker E. and Mildred (Davis) G.; m. Virginia Eastman, July 27, 1957; children: Laura Eastman, Virginia Lowry. BS, Ga. Inst. Tech., 1956, MS, 1957. Process engr. Humble Oil Co., 1957; asst. dir. govt. rels. Monsanto Rsch. Corp., Dayton, Ohio, 1961-66; dir. rsch. and devel. mktg. Monsanto Rsch. Corp., Dayton, 1966-68; group mktg. dir. Monsanto Co. New Enterprises div., St. Louis, 1968-70; pres., chief exec. officer Aqualon Group, a unit of Hercules Inc., 1989-91; asst. gen. mgr. plasticizers div. Monsanto Indsl. Chems. Co., 1977, gen. mgr. plasticizers div., 1977-79, gen. mgr. detergents and phosphates, 1979-80, asst. mng. dir., 1980-81, v.p., mng. dir., 1981-83; group v.p., mng. dir. Monsanto Internat., St. Louis, 1983-86; group v.p., sr. v.p. Monsanto Chem. Co. div. Monsanto Co., St. Louis, 1986-88; pres. Hercules Splty. Chems. Co., a unit of Hercules, Inc., 1988-89; chmn., chief exec. officer Hercules Inc., 1991—; pres., chief exec. officer The Aqualon Group, a unit of Hercules, 1989—; chmn., chief exec. officer Hercules Inc., 1989—; also bd. dirs. Hercules, Inc.; mem. adv. coun. Law Engring. Co., Atlanta. 1st lt. USAF, 1957-60. Mem. Chem. Mfrs. Assn. (bd. dirs.), Conf. Bd., Bus. Roundtable, Ga. Tech. Adv. Bd. Home: 8 Wood Rd Wilmington DE 19806-2022 Office: Hercules Inc Hercules Plz Wilmington DE 19894-0001

GOSSAGE, WAYNE, library administrator, management consultant, recruiter; b. Bellingham, Wash., June 13, 1926; s. Coy Dell and Sadie Fay (Campbell) G.; m. Grace Villella, July 3, 1950; children: Leslie Anne, Gordon. BS, U. Wash., 1947; MS, Columbia U., 1951, MA, 1969. Asst. head adult svcs. East Orange (N.J.) Pub. Libr., 1951-54; head adult svcs.

Levittown (N.Y.) Pub. Libr., 1954-55; dir. Warner Libr., Tarrytown, N.Y., 1956-63; asst. libr. Tchrs. Coll., Columbia U., N.Y.C., 1964-67; dir. Bank St. Coll. Edn. Libr., N.Y.C., 1967-80; pres. Gossage Regan Assocs., Inc., N.Y.C., 1980—; libr. cons. Gossage Regan Assocs., Inc., N.Y.C., 1980—; cons. to corp. librs., univs., assns., founds., chs., pubs., govt. agys. Contbr. articles to profl. jours. Vice pres. Hist. Soc. Tarrytown, 1960-61; trustee Harvard Libr., N.Y., 1978—; mem. alumni trustee nominating com. Columbia U., 1974-76; bd. advisors Pratt Inst. Sch. Info. and Libr. Sci., 1988—. With USNR, 1944-46. Coun. on Libr. Resources fellow, 1978-79; recipient Disting. Community Svc. award Tarrytown, 1962. Mem. ALA (notable books coun. 1961-62, chmn. edn. and behavioral scis. sect. 1975-76, Ralph Shaw arward for libr. lit. jury 1975-76, chmn. Wilson indexes com. 1978-81, Mudge citation com. 1985-87), N.Y. Libr. Assn. (v.p. resources and tech. svcs. sect. 1974-75, legis. com. 1974-75, pres. coll. and univ. librs. sect. 1978-79), N.Y. Libr. Club (pres. 1990-91), Spl. Libr. Assn. (chmn. div. social sci. 1975-76), Columbia U. Sch. Libr. Svcs. Alumni Assn. (sec.-treas. 1974-76, pres. 1977-78), Archons of Colophon (convenor 1989-90). Home: 382 W Clinton Ave Irvington NY 10533-2132 Office: Gossage Regan Assocs Inc 25 W 43d St Ste 812 New York NY 10036-7406

GOSSARD, WILLIAM H(ERBERT), JR., federal agency program administrator; b. Hickory, N.C., Dec. 2, 1945; s. William Herbert and Zelma Charlotte (Parnell) G.; m. Cara Stirling, Feb. 14, 1976; children: Jace Stirling, Michelle Reneé, Kathryn Jean-Marie. BA, Ottawa U., 1967; MPA, Ball State U., 1971. Mgmt. analyst U.S. Dept. Transp./Fed. R.R. Administrn., Washington, 1971-77; program mgr. U.S. Nat. Transp. Safety Bd., Washington, 1977—; pres. Med. Mktg. and Mgmt. Svcs., Centreville, Md., 1991—; cons. AIHS, 1991—. Contbr. to nat. and internat. publs. Sr. exec. fellow Harvard U., 1985. Mem. Lions. Republican. Presbyterian. Home and Office: Med Mktg and Mgmt Svcs RD 4 Box 656 Centreville MD 21617

GOSSELIN, KENNETH JAMES, healthcare executive; b. Woburn, Mass., Mar. 12, 1960; s. Edward J. Collins and Florence (Bursey) Gosselin; m. Stephanie Jeanne Moalli, Aug. 10, 1985; children: Christopher James Collins, Emily Jeanne Marie. AB, Boston Coll., 1982; M in Healthcare Adminstrn., Xavier U., 1985. Adminstrv. resident Elliot Hosp., Manchester, N.H., 1985-86; program dir. Nat. Med. Enterprises, L.A., 1986-88; asst. exec. dir. Synernet, Inc., Portland, Maine, 1988—; treas. Compass, Inc., Portland, Maine, 1989—. Mem. Am. Coll. Healthcare Execs., Maine Hosp. Assn., Rotary (Portland), Portland C. of C. Republican. Roman Catholic. Home: 39 Shady Run Ln Cumberland ME 04021

GOSSELIN, PETER GORDON, reporter; b. Rochester, N.Y., May 22, 1951; s. Robert E. and Ruth (Smith) G.; m. Katherine W. Hazard, 1989. BA in Philosophy, Brown U., 1976; MBA in Econs., Columbia U., 1984. Reporter Catskill (N.Y.) Daily Mail, 1975, The Transcript, North Adams, Mass., 1976-79; labor reporter Providence Jour.-Bull., 1979-83; investigative reporter Boston Globe, 1985-89, Washington Bur. Boston Globe, 1989—. Recipient George Polk award L.I.U., 1986, 87. Office: Boston Globe 2000 Pennsylvania Ave NW Washington DC 20006-1812

GOSSELIN, ROBERT EDMOND, pharmacologist, educator; b. Springfield, Mass., Sept. 2, 1919; s. A. Edmond and Grace (Pettengill) G.; m. Ruth L. Smith, June 26, 1948 (dec. Dec. 1977); children—Peter Gordon, Andrea Lee; m. Patricia S. Whitaker, July 25, 1981. A.B., Brown U., 1941; Ph.D., U. Rochester, 1945, M.D., 1947. Med. intern Yale service Grace-New Haven Hosp., 1947-48; instr. pharmacology U. Rochester, 1948-52, asst. prof. pharmacology, scientist atomic energy project, 1954-56; prof. dept. pharmacology and toxicology Dartmouth Med. Sch., 1956-89, prof. emeritus, 1989—, chmn. dept., 1956-75; dir. poison info. center Hitchcock Hosp., 1957-82; cons. USPHS, 1959-63, U.S. Army Chem. Corps, 1954-59; mem. toxicology study sect. USPHS, 1964-68; mem. toxicology adv. bd. U.S. Consumer Product Safety Comm., 1978-85. Contbr. articles to profl. jours. Pres. Norwich Devel. Assn., 1965. Served with AUS, 1944-46; to capt., M.C. AUS, 1952-54. Mem. Am. Physiol. Soc., Am. Soc. Exptl. Pharmacology and Therapeutics, AAAS, Toxicology Soc., Phi Beta Kappa, Sigma Xi. Home: The Holm Hanover NH 03755 Office: Dartmouth Med Sch Hanover NH 03756

GOSSELS, CLAUS PETER ROLF, lawyer; b. Berlin, Aug. 11, 1930; came to U.S., 1941; s. Max and Charlotte (Lewy) G.; m. Nancy Lee Tuber, June 29, 1958; children: Lisa Rae, Amy Devra, Daniel Joshua. AB, Harvard U., 1951, LLB, 1954. Bar: Mass. 1955, U.S. Dist. Ct. Mass. 1957, U.S. Ct. Appeals (1st cir.) 1957, U.S. Supreme Ct. 1965. Assoc. Sullivan & Worcester, Boston, 1956-65; mem. Zelman, Gossels & Alexander, Boston, 1965-72, Weston, Patrick, Willard & Redding, Boston, 1972—; master Superior Ct., Mass., 1984—. Co-author, editor: Vetaher Libenu, 1980. Moderator Town of Wayland, Mass., 1982—. With U.S. Army, 1954-56. Mem. Mass. Bar Assn., Boston Bar Assn., Mass. Moderators Assn. (bd. dirs. 1990—), Mass. Acad. Trial Lawyers. Jewish. Home: 32 Hampshire Rd Wayland MA 01778-1021 Office: Weston Patrick Willard & Redding 84 State St Boston MA 02109-2202

GOSSETT, OSCAR MILTON, advertising executive; b. N.Y.C., May 27, 1925; s. Oscar Percival and Helen (Deutsch) G.; m. Anna C. Scheid, May 29, 1949; children—Susanne, Michael, Thomas, Lorraine, James M. Student, Stevens Inst. Tech., 1943-44, 46-47, Columbia U., 1947-48, Northwestern U. With Compton Advt., Inc., 1949—, pres., from 1968—, chmn. bd. and chief exec. officer, 1971-83; chmn. bd., chief exec. officer Compton Communications Holding Co., from 1982, Saatchi & Saatchi Compton Worldwide, from 1982; co-chmn., formerly co-chief exec. officer Saatchi & Saatchi Advt. Worldwide, now exec. dir., dir. N.Am. ops. Nat. chmn. Religion in Am. Life; bd. dirs. Eye Bank for Sight Restoration, Nat. Ctr. for Health Edn.; communications cons. to dean Harvard Sch. Pub. Health. Served as officer USNR, 1943-46. Mem. Am. Advt. Fedn. (bd. govs.), Advt. Women of N.Y. (1st hon. male mem.). Methodist. Inventor mobile of solar system. Office: Saatchi & Saatchi Advt Worldwide 375 Hudson St New York NY 10014-3658*

GOSSETT, ROBERT FRANCIS, JR., merchant banker; b. San Antonio, Tex., Nov. 19, 1943; s. Robert Francis and Anne Elizabeth (Donnell) G.; m. Pauline Washington Gillespie, June 27, 1964; children: Robert Francis III, Frank Morgan Gillespie. BA, U. Tex., 1964; JD, Georgetown U., 1967; MBA, U. Pa., 1969. Assoc., investment bank div. Merrill Lynche, Pierce, Fenner & Smith, N.Y.C., 1969-74; v.p. Oppenheimer Properties, Inc., N.Y.C., 1974-78; exec. v.p., dir. Loeb Rhoades Hornblower Capital Corp., N.Y.C., 1978-81; chmn. bd., pres. Vance Capital Corp., N.Y.C., 1981—; gen. ptnr. First San Bernardio Assoc., Ltd., Long Beach, Calif., 1979—, First Riverside (Calif.) Assoc., 1980—, First Portland assoc., Beaverton, Oreg., 1980—, Vance Pioneer Assoc., St. Paul, 1982—, Corp. Realty Income Fund I, Ltd., N.Y.C., 1986—; chmn. bd. dirs. Colton Leasing Corp., Houston, 1983—, Minn. Street Assoc., Inc., St. Paul, 1988—. Mem. CampFire Club. Office: Vance Capital Corp 406 E 85th St New York NY 10028-6302

GOSSMANN, HANS-JOACHIM L., physicist, researcher; b. Schwandorf, Germany, Sept. 15, 1955; m. Yae-Lea Yueh, Oct. 3, 1987; 1 child, Mona. MS, SUNY, Albany, 1979, PhD, 1984; diploma, U. Wuerzburg, Germany, 1981. Postdoctoral mem. tech. staff AT&T Bell Labs., Murray Hill, N.J., 1984-85, mem. tech. staff, 1985—. Contbr. chpts. to books, more than 60 articles to profl. jours. Fellow Bohmische Phys. Soc.; mem. Am. Vacuum Soc. (award 1984), Materials Rsch. Soc., Am. Phys. Soc. Office: AT&T Bell Labs 600 Mountain Ave New Providence NJ 07974-2010

GOTAY, CAROLYN COOK, information specialist; b. New Brunswick, N.J., Feb. 12, 1951; d. Richard Cairns and Winifred Louise (Imhof) Cook; m. Mark Joseph Gotay, May 14, 1973; children: Alexander Joseph, Maria Elisa. BA cum laude, Duke U., 1973; MA, U. Md., 1975, PhD, 1977. Asst. prof. Gettysburg (Pa.) Coll., 1977-79, U. Calgary, Alta., Can., 1979-84; health scientist adminstr. Nat. Cancer Inst., Bethesda, Md., 1984-88; rsch. assoc. Western Consortium for Pub. Health, Berkeley, Calif., 1988-89; sr. info. specialist The Emmes Corp., Potomac, Md., 1990-92; assoc. prof. U. Hawaii Cancer Rsch. Ctr., Honolulu, 1992—; vis. scholar U. Calif., San Francisco, 1988-89; reviewer Social Sci. & Medicine Jour., 1984—; mem. panel, chair Nat. Cancer Inst., Toronto, Ont., Can., 1986—. Author: The Grant Seekers Handbook, 1990, The Quality of Life Handbook, 1990, rev., 1992; contbr. articles to profl. jours. Alta. Heritage Found. scholar, 1985-88, grantee, 1985-88, NIH grantee, 1991—. Mem. APA, APHA. Home: 1329 Maleko St Kailua HI 96734 Office: Cancer Rsch Ctr Hawaii 1236 Lauhala St Honolulu HI 96813

GOTH, ROBERT WILLIAM, plant pathologist; b. Phillips, Wis., May 10, 1927; s. William Edward and Rose (Dolezalek) G.; m. Joyce Marie Nelson, Dec. 29, 1954; children: Valerie, Robert W. Jr., Stephen. BS, U. Wis., Superior, 1954; MS, U. Minn., 1958, PhD, 1961; postgrad., U. Calif., Davis, 1965-66. Rsch. plant pathologist USDA, Beltsville, Md., 1961—. Author: (with others) Fungal Wilts of Plants, 1981. Sgt. U.S. Army, 1945-52. Grad. scholar Tozer Found., 1959. Mem. Am. Phytopath. Soc. (sec. treas. Potomac div. 1981-84, v.p. 1984-85, pres. 1985-86), Potato Assn. Am. (pres. pathology sect. 1983), Sigma Xi, Gamma Alpha. Office: Potato Assn Am HH13 Bldg 011 Barc-W Beltsville MD 20705

GOTLIEB, ALLAN E., former ambassador; b. Winnipeg, Man., Can., Feb. 28, 1928; s. David Phillip and Sarah (Schiller) G.; m. Sondra Kaufman, Dec. 20, 1955; children: Rebecca, Marcus, Rachel. B.A., U. Calif., 1949; LL.B., Harvard U., 1954; M.A., B.C.L. (Vinerian Law scholar), Oxford U., 1956; LLD (hon.), various schs. Bar: Eng. 1956. Fellow Wadham Coll. and univ. lectr. in law Oxford U., 1954-56; joined Can. Dept. External Affairs, 1957; 2d sec. Can. mission to UN, Geneva, 1960-62; 1st sec. Can. del. 18 Nation Disarmament Conf., 1962-64; head legal div. Dept. External Affairs, 1965-66; asst. under sec. for external affairs and legal adviser, 1967-68, dep. minister communications, 1968-73, dep. minister manpower and immigration, 1973-76; chmn. Can. Employment and Immigration Commn., 1976-77; under sec. Dept. External Affairs, 1977-81; Can. ambassador to U.S., Washington, 1981-89; vis. prof. polit. sci. Carleton U., 1966-71; adj. prof. internat. relations, 1975-78; vis. fellow All Souls Coll., Oxford, 1975-76, William Lyon Mackenzie King vis. prof. Harvard U., 1989, Claude Bissell vis. prof. U. Toronto, 1989; former Gov. Internat. Devel. Rsch. Ctr., Nat. Film. Bd., ; chmn. Can. Coun., Burson-Marsteller, Exec. Cons. Ltd., Ottawa; bd. dirs. Alcan, Hollinger Corp., Champion Internat. Corp., Macmillan Inc.; mem. adv. bd. Bank of Montreal, The Investment Co. Am., Nestle Enterprises Ltd, Hollinger Inc.; cons. Stikeman, Elliott, Toronto; adviser Pepper, Hamilton & Scheetz, Washington. Author: Disarmament and International Law, 1965, Canadian Treaty-Making, 1968, Human Rights, Federalism and Minorities, 1979, Impact of Technology on the Development of International Law, 1982; editor: Human Rights, Federalism and Minorities, 1979; contbr. articles to profl. jours.; editor: Harvard Law Rev., 1950-51; chmn. exec. com. Sat. Night Mag. Decorated officer Order of Can., companion Order of Can.; recipient Outstanding Achievement award Govt. Can., 1983, Haas Internat. award U. Calif. Regents, 1985,. Address: Commerce Ct W Ste 5300, PO Box 85, Toronto, ON Canada M5L 1B9

GOTOWKO, JOHN FRANCIS, pharmacist; b. North Tonawanda, N.Y., Sept. 20, 1950; s. Frank Richard and Helen Rose (Mis) G.; m. Carolyn Elizabeth Cardone, Dec. 28, 1973; children; Joseph Francis, Andrew Francis. BS in Chemistry, Niagara U., 1968-72; MS in Med. Tech., SUNY, Buffalo, 1973-75, BS in Pharmacy, 1981, MBA, 1983. Registered pharmacist, N.Y. Clin. chemist Milland Fillmore Hosp., Buffalo, 1975-82; staff pharmacist Roswell Park Cancer Ctr., Buffalo, 1982-85; dir. pharmacy West Seneca (N.Y.) Devel. Ctr., 1985—; community pharmacist Kare Drugs, Buffalo, 1985-86, Pete N' Larry's Pharmacy, Williamsville, N.Y., 1986—; instr. chemistry Erie C.C., Buffalo, 1986; instr. bus., Amherst, N.Y., 1987—, Bryant & Stratton Bus. Coll., Buffalo, 1983-86; owner, pres. RPD Cons., North Tonawanda, N.Y., 1985—; appointed assoc. faculty sch. pharmacy SUNY, Buffalo, 1988—. Chmn. bd. Concerned Taxpayers of North Tonawanda, 1990—; asst. coach Little League Baseball, North Tonawanda, 1990. Cadet 1st lt. U.S. Army Res., 1969-81. Faculty scholar SUNY, 1968-72, Niagara U., 1968-72; Army ROTC Program scholar, 1969-71. Mem. Am. Pharm. Assn., Am. Soc. Cons. Pharmacist, Am. Soc. Clin. Chemistry, Nat. Assn. Retail Druggist, Western N.Y. Hosp. Assn., Concerned Taxpayers of North Tonawanda (founder, dir. 1990-91), Beta Gamma Sigma. Democrat. Roman Catholic. Home: 72 Dale Dr North Tonawanda NY 14120 Office: West Seneca Devel Ctr 1200 East & West Rd West Seneca NY 14224

GOTSCH, JOHN WARREN, fund raising executive; b. New Rochelle, N.Y., Feb. 17, 1937; s. Charles Stephen and Alta Margaret (Moore) G.; m. Gail S. Brock (div.); 1 child, Sybil Gabriella. BA in Sociology and Anthropology, Hobart Coll., 1963. Cert. fund raising exec. Dir. rsch. and devel. N.J. P.R. Congress, Trenton, 1972-82; dir. devel. Am. Hungarian Found., New Brunswick, N.J., 1982-84; asst. prin. devel. and alumni rels. Xaverian High Sch., Bklyn., 1984-87; sr. cons. Ketchum Inc., Pitts., 1987-90, Robert F. Semple Assocs., Nutley, N.J., 1990-91; v.p., corp. officer Aging In Am. Inc., Bronx, 1992—; fund raising coun. Archdiocese of Anchorage, 1991—; capitol campaign dir. Planned Parenthood/Essex County, Newark, N.J., 1990-91, Kingston (N.Y.) Boys Club, 1989; mgmt. cons. Calif. Health Dept., Sacramento, 1988. Contbr. articles to profl. jours. Trustee Princeton (N.J.) Pro Musica, 1991—; mem. N.J. State Health Planning Coun., Trenton; v.p. Del. Valley Regional Tourism Coun., Trenton, 1984, Roebling (N.J.) Summit Conf. Com., 1984. With U.S. Army, 1958-60. Named to Athletic Hall Fame Gill/St. Bernard's Sch., Gladstone, N.J., 1986. Mem. Nat. Soc. Fund Raising Execs., Assn. Healthcare Philanthropy, Coun. Advancement and Support Edn. Republican. Byzantine Catholic. Home: 214 6th Ave Roebling NJ 08554 Office: Aging in Am 1500 Pelham Pky Bronx NY 10461

GOTSCH-THOMSON, SUSAN DOROTHEA, college dean; b. Oak Park, Ill., Aug. 9, 1942; d. Richard Emil and Mildred H. (Peckat) Gotsch; m. Ronald Bruce Thomson, June 10, 1973; 1 child, Jessica Jin Hwa. BA, Valparaiso U., 1964; MA, Bryn Mawr Coll., 1974, PhD, 1977. Asst. prof. Tuskegee (Ala.) U., 1977-80; from asst. prof. to assoc. prof. Glassboro (N.J.) State Coll., 1980-89; assoc. dean of the coll. Beaver Coll., Glenside, Pa., 1989—, dean continuing edn., 1991—. Mem. sch. bd. Gateway Regional High Sch., Woodbury Hts., N.J., 1988—. Office: Beaver Coll Glenside PA 19038

GOTTA, ALEXANDER WALTER, anesthesiologist, educator; b. Bklyn., Apr. 10, 1935; s. A. Walter and Helen C. (Bruskewic) G.; m. Colleen A. Sullivan, July 17, 1965; 1 child, Nancy C. B.S. summa cum laude, St. John's U., 1956; M.D., NYU, 1960. Diplomate Am. Bd. Anesthesiology, Am. Bd. Med. Examiners. Intern, U. Chgo., 1960-61; resident Boston City Hosp., 1961-62, N.Y. Hosp.-Cornell U., N.Y.C., 1962-64; instr. anesthesiology Cornell U., 1964-66, asst. prof., 1978-79; dir. anesthesia St. Mary's Hosp., Bklyn., 1968-78; asst. prof. SUNY-Bklyn., 1968-78, assoc. prof., 1978-85, prof., 1985—; dir. anesthesia L.I. Coll. Hosp., Bklyn., 1983-90; dir. anesthesia Kings County Hosp. Ctr., 1990—; speaker in field. Contbr. articles to profl. jours. Served to capt. U.S. Army, 1966-68, Vietnam. Fellow N.Y. Acad. Medicine (chmn. anesthesia sect. 1990), Am. Coll. Anesthesiologists, Am. Soc. Anesthesiologists (ho. of del. 1986—); mem. N.Y. Soc. Anesthesiologists (bd. dirs. 1983—, chmn. sci. program com.), N.Y. Soc. Critical Care Medicine (pres. 1985), Assn. Univ. Anesthesiologists. Republican. Roman Catholic. Club: Brooklyn. Avocation: History. Home: 29 Ascot Ridge Rd Great Neck NY 11021-2912 Office: Kings County Hosp Ctr 451 Clarkson Ave Brooklyn NY 11203-2097

GOTTFELD, GUNTHER MAX, urban mass transit official, consultant; b. Berlin, June 13, 1934; came to U.S., 1941; s. William James and Charlotte Jeanette (Less) G.; m. Linda Stratton Keene, Oct. 26, 1969 (div. Jan. 1976); children: Deborah Charlotte, David William; m. Ann Richmond, July 13, 1985. BS, Shephard Coll., 1958; MA, Am. U., 1960. Transp. planner Nat. Capital Trnasp. Agy., Washington, 1961-63; cons. Stockholm Transit Authority, 1963-64; fed. liaison officer Mass. Bay Transp. Authority, Boston, 1965-70; sr. transp. planner Md. Mass Transit Adminstrn., Balt., 1970-74, intergovtl. coordinator, 1974—. Mem. Am. Pub. Transit Assn. (mem. legis. com. 1981—), Md. Mass Transit Adminstrn., Am. Rd. and Transp. Builders Assn. (mem. pub. transit council 1986—, mem. legis. watch com. 1986—), Internat. Union Pub. Transport. Democrat. Jewish. Home: 5301 Hesperus Dr Columbia MD 21044-1808 Office: Md Mass Transit Adminstrn 300 W Lexington St Baltimore MD 21201-3418

GOTTFRIED, BENJAMIN FRANK, manufacturing executive; b. Phila., Apr. 13, 1939; s. Harry Nathan and Sylvia (Chernow) G.; divorced; 1 child, Hal. Student, U. Md., 1973-74, 79-80, Cen. Tex. Coll., 1974-75. Enlisted U.S. Army, 1959; served as chief warrant officer U.S. Army Engrs., 1959-79, ret., 1979; regional maintenance mgr. Avis Truck Leasing, Balt., 1979-82; svc. mgr. Hale Truck and Trailer Equipment, Marlton, N.J., 1982-85; sr. dir. svc. Iveco Trucks N.Am., Bensalem, Pa., 1985—. Author: (with others) Fleet Equipment, 1986, Transport Topics, 1987. Decorated Purple Heart, Bronze Star, Commendation Medal, Meritorious Svc. Medal. Mem. DAV (life), Hon. Order Ky. Cols, Fraternal Order Police. Jewish. Home: 303 N Elmwood Rd Marlton NJ 08053

GOTTLIEB, ARNOLD, dentist; b. N.Y.C., Jan. 8, 1926; s. Samuel J. and Matilda (Gross) G.; m. Joan F. Rigler, June 27, 1947; children: Susan, Jeffrey, Jane. Student, CCNY, 1943-45; DDS cum laude, U. Pitts., 1949. Pvt. practice reconstructive dentistry N.Y.C., 1949—; vis. dentist Heart House hosp.,1 948-49; attending dental surgeon Harlem Eye and Ear Hosp., 1955-65, chief dental cons., 1966-68; lectr. Fedn. Dentair, Austria, AIMS, China, Russia; presenter at profl. confs.; bd. dirs. Haptentech. Contbr. articles to profl. jours. Past v.p. community synagogue, Rye, N.Y.; founder, pres. Homeowners Assn., Pine Ridge, Rye, 1989-90. Capt. U.S. Army, 1951-53. Mem. ADA, Fedn. Dentaire Internat., Myodentronic Soc. N.Y. (past sec., treas.)Fedn. Dentair, Am. Internat. Med. Soc., Sea Pines Country Club (Hilton Head Island, S.C.), Pound Ridge Tennis Club, B'nai Brith (past pres. Henry Hudson Lodge), Omicron Kappa Upsilon. Jewish. Home: 211 Ferris Hill Rd New Canaan CT 06840

GOTTLIEB, H. DAVID, podiatrist; b. Washington, Mar. 2, 1956; s. Julius J. and Charlotte (Papernik) G.; m. Wendy Ilene Weisbard, June 17, 1979; children: Jason, Cheryl. BA, Cornell U., 1978; DPM, Pa. Coll. Podiatric Medicine, 1982. Diplomate Nat. Bd. Podiatry Examiners, Am. Acad. Pain Mgmt., Am. Coun. Cert. Podiatric Physicians and Surgeons. Podiatrist Dr. Julius J. Gottlieb, P.C., Washington, 1982-91; prin. H. David Gottlieb, DPM, P.C., Washington, 1991—. Author (book chpt.) Laser Surgery of the Foot, 1988. Mem. Chevy Chase (D.C.) Citizens Assn., 1982—; den master Cub Scouts Am., Gaithersburg, Md., 1991-92; pres. Young Couples Club Gaithersburg Hebrew Congregation, Gaithersburg, 1984-85. Felow Acad. Ambulatory Foot Surgery; mem. APHA, Am. Podiatric Med. Assn., Am. Assn. Podiatric Physicians and Surgeons, Am. Running and Fitness Assn., Internat. Soc. Podiatric Laser Surgery (assoc.). Office: 3900 Mckinley St NW Washington DC 20015-2993

GOTTLIEB, JULIUS JUDAH, podiatrist; b. Jersey City, May 27, 1919; s. Joseph Uziel and Gussie (Farber) G.; m. Charlotte Papernik, Oct. 18, 1942; children: Sheldon, Cynthia, Lorinda, David, Jonathan. Student, NYU, 1938-39, Ill. Coll. Podiatric Medicine, 1940-42; DPM, Ohio Coll. Podiatric Medicine, 1943. Diplomate Am. Podiatric Med. Specialties Bd. Pvt. practice podiatric medicine Washington, 1943—; past cons. Army Footwear Clinic. Co-inventor fiberglass foot prosthetics and plastic shoe lasts. Chmn. com. Nat. Capital area council Boy Scouts Am., 1969-73; pres. Franklin Knolls Citizens Assn., 1963. Recipient Shofar award Boy Scouts Am. Fellow Acad. Ambulatory Foot Surgeons (region 8 sci. chmn. 1987-88), Nat. Coll. Foot Surgeons (founding); mem. Am. Podiatric Med. Assn., Am. Pub. Health Assn., Am. Coll. Podopediatrics, Am. Podiatric Circulatory Soc., Am. Bd. Foot Surgeons (founding diplomate), D.C. Podiatric Med. Soc. (past pres.), Am. Assn. Foot Specialists (past pres., Foot Specialist of the Yr. 1973), Am. Assn. Individual Investors, Internat. Platform Assn., Am. Physicians Fellowship Inc. for Medicine in Israel, Columbia Heights Bus. Men's Assn. (past pres.), Chevy Chase Citizens Assn., B'nai B'rith. Republican. Jewish. Home: 15812 Ancient Oak Dr Gaithersburg MD 20878-2110 Office: 3900 Mckinley St NW Washington DC 20015-2993

GOTTLIEB, KRISTA, lawyer; b. Prague, Czechoslovakia, June 26, 1955; came to U.S., 1965; d. Paul and Krista (Podzimkova) G.; m. F. Joseph Coveney, Oct. 11, 1980; 1 child, David O. BA in Polit. Sci. cum laude, Barnard Coll., 1976; JD, Albany Law Sch., 1979. Bar: N.Y. 1980, U.S. Dist. Ct. (so., ea. and we. dists.) N.Y. 1980. Assoc. Fisher & Fisher, Bklyn., 1979-82, Reich, Rosen, Barrison & Felzen, N.Y.C., 1982-83, Moritt, Wolfeld & Resnick, Garden City, N.Y., 1983-85; ptnr. Mattar & D'Agostino, Buffalo, 1986—. Mem. NAFE, Women's Bar Assn., N.Y. State Bar Assn., Ask Women, Erie County Bar Assn. Office: Mattar & D'Agostino 17 Court St Ste 600 Buffalo NY 14202

GOTTLIEB, LEONARD SOLOMON, pathology educator; b. Boston, May 26, 1927; s. Julius and Jeanette (Miller) G.; m. Dorothy Helen Apt, Mar. 23, 1952; children: Julie Ann, William Apt, Andrew Richard. A.B., Bowdoin Coll., 1946; M.D., Tufts U., 1950; M.P.H., Harvard U., 1969. Diplomate: Am. Bd. Anatomic Pathology. Intern and resident in pathology Boston City Hosp., 1950-55; asst. chief pathology U.S. Naval Hosp., Chelsea, Mass., 1955-57; assoc. pathologist Mallory Inst. Pathology, Boston, 1957-66, assoc. dir., 1966-72, dir., 1972—; prof. pathology Boston U. Sch. Medicine, 1970—, chmn. dept., 1980—; dir. Mallory Inst. Pathology Found., 1980—; lectr. Harvard U., 1963—; dir. student faculty exch. program Boston U. and Hebrew U., Hadassah Med. Sch., 1988—. Gen. editor Biopsy Pathology Series, Chapman and Hall; mem. editorial bd. Am. Jour. Surgical Pathology; contbr. over 125 articles on exptl. and human gastrointestinal and liver diseases. Mem. bd. govs. Hebrew U. of Jerusalem, 1991—; sci. adv. bd. Boston chpt. Israel Cancer Rsch. Fund, 1991—. Served to lt. M.C., USNR, 1955-57; to lt. comdr. 1960-63. Named Hon. Mem. Faculty Medicine The Hebrew U., 1987; James Bowdoin scholar, 1945. Mem. Am. Assn. Pathologists, Am. Assn. Study of Liver Disease, U.S.-Can. Acad. Pathology, Am. Soc. for Cell Biology, Am. Gastroent. Assn., New Eng. Soc. Pathologists (pres. 1968-69), Am. Soc. Clin. Pathology, Mass. Soc. Pathology, Coll. Am. Pathologists, Am. Physicians Fellowship, Inc. for Medicine in Israel (pres. 1990—), Am. Friends of Hebrew U. of Jerusalem (pres. New Eng. region 1989—). Office: Mallory Inst Pathology 784 Massachusetts Ave Roxbury MA 02118-2383

GOTTLIEB, LESTER M., real estate and securities company executive; b. N.Y.C., May 3, 1932; s. Samuel and Eva (Schoenfeld) G.; m. Sarah Dean Tompkins, Dec. 4, 1967; children: Cynthia Anne, Curtis Tompkins; children by previous marriage: Mark Albert, Alyssa Beth, Adine Julia. BA, CCNY, 1954; postgrad. NYU, 1956. With IBM, 1956-69, mgr. bus. planning for systems devel. div., 1967-69; pres. Data Dimensions, Inc. 1969-84, vice chmn., 1984-90; pres. CAMAC Equities, Ltd. and CAMAC Securities, Ltd., 1981-91, Old Greenwich, Conn., 1981—; adj. asst. prof. econs. U. Bridgeport; nat. lectr. Assn. Computing Machinery. Pres. Woodlands-Worthington Taxpayers Assn., 1962-68; bd. dirs. North Greenwich Assn. 1973-74, Ctr. for Internat. Mgmt. Studies. Nat. Bd. YMCA's 1972—, Greater N.Y. YMCA; bd. dirs. City Coll. Fund, 1990—. With AUS, 1954-56. Recipient Leo Klauber award, Mark Asa Abbott award. Fellow Am. Sociol. Soc.; mem. Acad. Polit. Sci., Am. Arbitration Assn. (comml. arbitrator 1981—), CCNY Alumni Assn. (bd. dirs. 1983—, pres. alumni varsity assn. 1987-88, Alumni Svc. award). Republican. Club: Landmark (charter mem.), Masons. Mem. editorial bd. Jour. Computer Ops., 1965-69, Mgmt. Tech. mag., 1983-84. Home: Weavers Hill Greenwich CT 06831 Office: 1455 E Putnam Ave Old Greenwich CT 06870-1307

GOTTLIEB, MARTIN MORRIS, logistics engineer; b. Eastchester, N.Y., Nov. 8, 1959; s. Walter and Rose Toby (Weitman) G.; m. Jeri Beth Slavin, Oct. 9, 1988. BA in Studio Art, SUNY, Binghamton, 1982; BSEE, Northeastern U., Boston, 1985; SM in Mgmt., MIT, 1990. Mfg. engr. Atex subs. Kodak Co., Bedford, Mass., 1985-86; mfg. engr. Laser Metric Systems, Cambridge, Mass., 1986-87; tech. svcs. mgr. The 660 Corp., Boston, 1987-88; mfg. cons. Kontron Instruments, Everett, Mass., 1990; process supr. Hewlett Packard Co., Andover, Mass., 1990-92, logistics engr., 1992—; bd. dirs. Art Savvy, Boston. Tustee Temple Sinai, Brookline, Mass., 1989—. Recipient Presl. Sports award Pres. Coun. Phys. Fitness, 1991; Bronze medal U.S. Tae Kwon Do Union, 1992. Mem. Nat. Assn. Watch and Clock Collectors, Wodehouse So., MIT/Sloan Club Boston. Office: Hewlett Packard Co 3000 Minuteman Rd Andover MA 01810

GOTTLIEB, ROBERT ADAMS, publisher; b. N.Y.C., Apr. 29, 1931; s. Charles and Martha (Keen) G.; m. Maria Tucci, Apr. 26, 1969; children—Roger, Elizabeth, Nicholas. B.A., Columbia, 1952; postgrad., Cambridge (Eng.) U., 1952-54. Editor-in-chief, v.p. Simon & Schuster, 1955-68; editor-in-chief Alfred A Knopf, Inc., N.Y.C., 1968-87, exec. v.p., 1968-73, pres., 1973-87; editor New Yorker mag., 1987-92. Mem. Phi Beta Kappa. Office: care New Yorker Mag Inc 20 W 43d St New York NY 10036

GOTTSCHALK, BERNARD, physicist; b. Frankfurt, Main, Germany, Jan. 6, 1935; came to U.S., 1938; s. Ernst and Rose (Hamburger) G.; m. Jane Climenko, June 27, 1962; children: Adam, Arthur, Alexander. BS in Physics, Rensselaer Polytechnic Inst., 1955; MS, PhD, Harvard U., 1962. Postdoctoral fellow Harvard U., Cambridge, Mass., 1962-65; from asst. prof. to prof. Northeastern U., Boston, 1965-80; sr. rsch. fellow Cyclotron Lab. Harvard U., 1981—, mem. proton therapy coop. group, 1984—; vis. scientist Stanford Linear Accelerator Ctr., Palo Alto, Calif., 1971-72, 79-81, Max Planck Inst. CERN, Geneva, Switzerland, 1974-75. Contbr. articles to Phys. Letters, Nuclear Physics, Phys. Rev. Grantee NSF, 1965-80. Mem. Am. Phys. Soc. Democrat. Jewish. Office: Harvard Cyclotron Lab 44 Oxford St Cambridge MA 02138-1998

GOTTSCHALK, WALTER HELBIG, mathematician, educator; b. Lynchburg, Va., Nov. 3, 1918; s. Carl and Lula (Helbig) G.; m. Margaret Hemsworth, Aug. 27, 1952; children: Heather, Steven. B.S., U. Va., 1939, M.A., 1942, Ph.D. in Math, 1944; M.A. (hon.), Wesleyan U., Middletown, Conn., 1964. From instr. to prof. math. U. Pa., 1944-63, chmn. dept., 1955-58; prof. math. Wesleyan U., 1963-82, prof. emeritus, 1982—, chmn. dept., 1964-69, 70-71; Mem. Inst. Advanced Study, Princeton, 1947-48; research assoc. Yale U., 1960-61. Author: (with G.A. Hedlund) Topological Dynamics, 1955; Mem. editorial bd.: Math. Systems Theory, 1967-75; Contbr. articles to profl. jours. Mem. Am. Math. Soc. (asso. editor proc. 1954-56, asso. sec. for East 1971-76), Math. Assn. Am., Soc. Indsl. and Applied Math., AAUP, Phi Beta Kappa, Sigma Xi. Democrat. Unitarian. Home: 500 Angell St Apt 414 Providence RI 02906-4455

GOTTSMAN, EARL EUGENE, academic administrator; b. Carrollton, Ohio, July 6, 1946; s. Herman Louis and Dora Samatha (Lotz) G.; m. Janice Marie Howard, Oct. 12, 1974; children: Kevin Lee, Kendra Louise, Kelly Lynn. BS, Ohio State U., 1968; MS, Iowa State U., 1972. Instr., rsch. asst. Iowa State U., 1968-71; prof. Capitol Coll., Laurel, Md., 1972-77, acad. dean, 1977-85, v.p. for acad. affairs, 1985—; adj. prof. No. Va. Community Coll., Annandale, 1975-77; bd. mem. Engring. Manpower Commn., Washington, 1985—; chmn. Fred J. Berger Award Com., Washington, 1990-91. Recipient James H. McGraw award Glencoe Divsn. Macmillan/McGraw-Hill Publ. Co., 1991. Mem. Am. Soc. Engring. Edn. (immediate past chair engring. tech. div.). Methodist. Office: Capitol Coll 11301 Springfield Rd Laurel MD 20708-9759

GOUGER, DALE BARTLETT, psychiatrist; b. Schenectady, N.Y., Oct. 17, 1942; s. Thomas Arthur and Gladys (Bartlett) G.; m. Carol Ann Burian, July 15, 1967; 1 child, Robert Dale. BS, Lebanon Valley Coll., 1965; MD, Jefferson Med. Ctr., 1969. Intern Reading Hosp. and Med. Ctr., West Reading, Pa., 1969-70; resident in psychiatry Sheppard & Pratt Hosp., Towson, Md., 1973; pvt. practice Reading Psychiat. Ctr., West Reading, Pa., 1973—; med. dir., Family Guidance Ctr., Reading, Pa., 1986—; psychiat. cons., Threshold Day Care Ctr., Reading, 1988—. Fellow Phila. Coll. Physicians; mem. Am. Psychiat. Assn., Lancaster Kennel Club, Am. Shetland Sheepdog Assn. Democrat. Lutheran. Home: RR 2 Box 2347 Mohnton PA 19540-9525 Office: Reading Psychiat Ctr 301 S 7th Ave Reading PA 19611-1410

GOUGH, JOHN FRANCIS, lawyer; b. Phila., Nov. 28, 1934; s. John Joseph and Honora Veronica (Garrity) G.; m. Natalie Smith, Mar. 8, 1984; children: David, Robert, J. Joseph II, Richard, Jonathan, Kristin. AB cum laude, St. Joseph's U., 1957; JD, Yale U., 1960. Bar: Pa. 1961, U.S. Dist. Ct. (ea. dist.) Pa. 1961, U.S. Ct. Appeals (3d cir.) 1961, U.S. Supreme Ct. 1967. Assoc. Erskine, Barbieri & Sheer, Phila., 1960-65, White and Williams, Phila., 1965-68; ptnr. White and Williams, 1968-80, Toll, Ebby & Gough, Phila., 1980-87; ptnr., chmn. corp. dept. Abrahams & Loewenstein, Phila., 1987-88; ptnr. Hoyle, Morris & Kerr, Phila., 1988-92, Montgomery, Mccracken, Walker & Rhoads, Phila., 1992—; mem. exec. com. Ea. Dist. Bankruptcy Conf., 1989—; faculty co-chmn. and lectr. Temple Grad. Sch. Law, Phila., 1989—; lectr. U. Pa., Wharton Grad. Sch., 1987—. Contbr. to Temple Law Quar.; author course materials for profl. and ednl. orgns. Pres., Highfield Sch. PTA, Plymouth, Pa., 1966-68, Greene Twp. Montessori Sch., Phila., 1979-80. Mem. ABA, Pa. Bar Assn., Phila. Bar Assn. (pres. Jr. Bar Assn. 1964-65), Am. Assn. Hosp. Attys., Pa. Assn. Hosp. Attys., Hosp. Attys., S.E. Pa. (pres. 1977-79), Nat. Health Lawyers Assn., Union League of Phila., Yale Club of Phila. Office: Montgomery MCracken Walker & Rhoads Three Parkway 20th Fl Philadelphia PA 19102

GOUGHER, RONALD LEE, foreign language educator; b. Allentown, Pa., July 27, 1939; s. Samuel Franklin and Beatrice Dorothy (Shanaberger) G.; 1 child, Robert. BA, Muhlenberg Coll., 1961; MA, Lehigh U., 1964; postgrad. Stanford U., 1963, Harvard U., 1964, U. Pa., 1964-75; advanced cert. Goethe Inst., Munich, 1969. Chmn. fgn. lang. dept. Parkland High Sch., Allentown, Pa., 1961-65; instr. German, Lehigh U., 1965-69; assoc. prof. German, West Chester U., Pa., 1969—, dir. internat. edn., 1974-83, chmn. dept. fgn. langs., 1977—; campus dir. Expt. in Internat. Living 1972—; treas. Pa. Consortium Internat. Edn., 1978-83, pres., 1983-86; coord.-chairperson Assn. Depts. Fgn. Langs., State System Higher Edn., Pa., 1984-88, citizen amb. Linquistis Del. to China, 1991, 92; lectr. in field. Bd. dirs. Peters Valley Crafts Ctr.; active Congress-Bundestag Youth Exchange Program, 1988-92, Citizen Ambassador Program, China, 1991, 92. Fulbright travel grantee, 1963, 69, travel grantee Soros Found., 1990, 91, 92; recipient numerous grants for fgn. langs. and internat. studies, programs NEH, Rockefeller Found.; recipient Chapel of Four Chaplins award, 1981. Mem. Am. Assn. Tchrs. German, Am. Coun. Teaching Fgn. Langs., NE Conf. Teaching Fgn. Lang., Internat. Platform Assn., Smithsonian Instn. Republican. Lutheran. Author numerous publs. in German lang. and lit., individualizing instrn. in fgn. langs.; co-editor, Individualization Fgn. Lang. Learning in Am., 1970-75. Home: 3309 Windsor Dr Thorndale PA 19372-1038 Office: West Chester U Dept Fgn Langs West Chester PA 19380

GOUGHLER, DONALD H., social services association executive; b. New Castle, Pa., June 27, 1945; s. E.H. and Nellie G. (Campbell) G.; m. Susan M. McGeary, Aug. 24, 1968; 1 child, Jordan C. BA in Speech, Westminster Coll., 1968; MSW, U. Pitts., 1976. Lic. social worker, Pa. Dir. therapeutic recreation Woodville State Hosp., Carnegie, Pa., 1971-76; aide to congressman U.S. Ho. of Reps., Pitts., 1975-76; exec. dir. Mon Valley United Health Svcs., Inc., Monessen, Pa., 1984-85; dep. dir.. Southwestern Pa. Area Agy. on Aging, Inc., Monessen, 1977-83; exec. dir. Southwestern Pa. Area Agy. on Aging, Inc., 1985-86, chief operating officer, 1986-88; exec. v.p., chief exec. officer Southwestern Pa. Human Svcs., Inc., 1988—; cons. Transplant Recipients Internat. Orgn., Pitts., 1985-88; mem. profl. adv. coun. Alzheimer's Disease Alliance, Pitts., 1988—; pres. Monessen House, Inc., Elderly Housing, 1988—; mem. adv. coun. Sch. Social Work, U. Pitts., 1988—; adj. faculty W.Va. U. Grad. Sch. Social Work, 1991—. Contbr. articles to profl. jours. Mem. inclusions com., Mon Valley United Way, 1986-89, division chmn., 1989; fundraiser, Mon Valley chpt. Am. Heart Assn., 1988. 1st lt. U.S. Army, 1968-71. Mem. Rotary Internat. Democrat. Office: Southwestern Pa Human Svcs Eastgate 8 Monessen PA 15062

GOULBOURNE, DONALD SAMUEL, JR., healthcare administrator, social worker; b. New Rochelle, N.Y., Apr. 5, 1950; s. Donald Samuel Sr. and Girthel (Grayson) G.; 1 child, Antoine Donald. BA, Columbia Union Coll., 1973; MS, Columbia U., 1977; cert., Yeshiva U., 1984. Lic. social worker, N.Y. Tchr.'s asst. New Rochelle Bd. Edn., 1974-75; clin. social worker Family & Children Svcs., Stamford, Conn., 1977-79; social work coord. Einstein Coll. Medicine Nat. Health Svc. Corps., N.Y.C., 1979-84; dir. dept. social svc. Einstein Coll. of Medicine, N.Y.C., 1984-89; dir., chief adminstr. Lincoln Ave Clinic/Guidance Ctr., New Rochelle, 1989—; vol. group leader Minority Task Force on AIDS, N.Y.C., 1987—; counselor to adult patients Community of New Rochelle, 1989—. Vice pres. bd of mgrs. Westchester Townhouse Condominium Assn., Yonkers, N.Y., 1986—. Lt. comdr. USPHS, 1980—. Mem. Nat. Assn. Social Workers, Soc. Clin. Work Psychotherapist, Inc. Democrat. Baptist. Home: 21 Clinton Ave New Rochelle NY 10801-3305 Office: Guidance Ctr 95 Lincoln Ave New Rochelle NY 10801-3912

GOULD, CHARLES HOWARD, construction management educator, consultant; b. Youngstown, Ohio, Aug. 12, 1935; s. Howard Ball and Florilla (Tibbits) G.; m. Lady Claire Allen, Aug. 17, 1959 (div. Feb. 1965); 1 child, Stephen; m. Susanna Derby Black, June 17, 1967; children: Charles H. Jr. (dec.), Katherine. BCE, Rensselear Poly. Inst., 1957; MCE, U. Mich., 1979. Registered profl. engr., N.Y., D.C. Field engr. Raymond Internat., Plattsburgh, N.Y., Liberia, 1961-64; project mgr. Raymond Internat., N.Y.C., Liberia, 1964-70; v.p. Mergentine Corp., Washington, Edmonton, Alta., Can., 1970-77; sr. v.p. Mergentine Corp., Flemington, N.J., 1980-85; lectr. U. Mich., Ann Arbor, 1977-80; assoc. prof. N.J. Inst. Tech., Newark, 1985-88; assoc. prof. constrn. mgmt. U. Maine, Orono, 1988—; cons. Bechtel Corp., Ann Arbor, 1978-80. Author: Fundamentals of Construction Cost Estimating, 1988, Computer Applications in Construction Management, 1992. Lt. USN, 1957-61. Decorated knight comdr. Order of African Redemption (Liberia). Mem. ASCE, Am. Soc. Engring. Edn., Assoc. Gen. Contractors (assoc.), Moles. Methodist. Home: 100 Ridgeview Dr Bangor ME 04401-7051 Office: U Maine 220 E Anx Orono ME 04473

GOULD, DONALD EVERETT, chemicals company executive; b. Concord, N.H., May 19, 1932; s. Everett Luther and Gladys (Wilcox) G.; B.S. in Chem. Engring., U. N.H. 1954; postgrad. math. Rutgers U., 1955-59; m. Marilyn Bachelder, June 13, 1953; children—Barbara, Allen, Douglas. Devel. chem. engr. plastics div. Union Carbide Co., Bound Brook, N.J., 1954-59, tech. service engr., Bound Brook and Wayne, N.J. 1959-64, mgr. tech. service indsl. bag dept., Wayne, 1964-66, mgr. tech. services indsl. fabricated products dept. 1966-67, mktg., mgr. indsl. bags, 1967-69, sr. packaging engr., 1969-72, mgr. packaging, 1972-74, mgr. distbn. safety and regulations, 1974-79, staff engr. for packaging, 1980-85, sr. staff engr. packaging, labeling, 1985-91, prin. engr. packaging, labeling, and regulations, 1991—. Mem. Packaging Inst. (vice chmn. films, foils and laminations com. 1962-64, chmn. 1964-66, sect. leader bottle containers, chmn. bag com. 1975-78, 85-88, exec. com. chem. packaging 1985—), Am. Soc. Quality Control, Chem. Mfrs. Assn. (chmn. distbn. work group), Am. Council for Chem. Labeling, Inst. Packaging Profls. (vice chmn. films), Alpha Chi Sigma. Club: Packanack Lake Country. Contbr. articles profl. jours., also to Ency. Engring. Materials and Processes. Home: 98 Lake Dr E Wayne NJ 07470-4253 Office: River Rd PO Box 670 Bound Brook NJ 08805-0670

GOULD, HARRY EDWARD, JR., industrialist; b. N.Y.C., Sept. 24, 1938; s. Harry E. and Lucille (Quartucy) G.; m. Barbara Clement, Apr. 26, 1975; children: Harry Edward, III, Katharine Elizabeth. Student, Oxford U., 1958; B.A. cum laude, Colgate U., 1960; postgrad., Harvard Bus. Sch., 1960-61; M.B.A., Columbia U., 1964. Assoc. in corp. fin. dept. Goldman, Sachs & Co., N.Y.C., 1961-62; exec. asst. to sr. v.p. ops. Universal Am., N.Y.C., 1964-65; sec., treas. Young Spring & Wire Corp., Detroit, 1965-67, exec. v.p., chief operating officer, 1967-69, also dir.; v.p. adminstrn. and fin. Universal Am. Corp., 1968-69; mem. exec. com., v.p., sec.-treas. Daybrook-Ottawa Corp., Bowling Green, Ohio, 1967-69; dir., mem. exec. com. Am. Med. Ins. Co., N.Y.C., 1966-74; pres., chmn., chief exec. officer, dir. Gould Paper Corp., N.Y.C., 1969—; chmn. bd., dir. Samuel Porritt & Co., East Peoria, Ill., 1969—, Computer Copies Corp., N.Y.C., 1970-73, Ingalls Mfg., Inc., Ceres, Calif., 1971—, McNair Mfg., Inc., Chico, Calif., 1972—, Hawthorne Paper Co., Kalamazoo, 1974—, Weiss Mfg., Inc., Chico, 1974—, Vrisimo Mfg., Inc., Ceres, 1974—; chmn. bd. Lewis & Gould Paper Co., Inc., Northfield, Ill., 1975-78; chmn., pres., chief exec. officer Signature Communications Ltd., Los Angeles and N.Y.C., 1986—; chmn. exec. com., dir. Richard Lewis Paper Corp., Northfield, 1992—; bd. dirs. Reinhold-Gould GmbH, Hamburg, Germany, 1969—; ltd. ptnr. Hardy & Co. (mem. N.Y. Stock Exch.), N.Y.C., 1973-78; bd. dirs., chmn. exec. com. Richard Lewis Paper Corp., Northfield, Ill., 1992—. Co-chmn. Pacesetter's com. Boy Scouts Am., 1966-69; participant as U.S. Pres.'s rep. UN E-W Trade Devel. Commn., 1967; mem. N.Y. Gov.'s Task Force on N.Y. State Cultural Life and Arts, 1975—; pres. Harry E. Gould Found., N.Y.C., 1971—; mem. nat. council Colgate U., 1973-76, trustee, mem. budget, devel., fin. and student affairs coms., 1976—; mem. adv. bd. Columbia U. Grad. Sch. Bus., 1980—; bd. dirs. United Cerebral Palsy Rsch. and Ednl. Found., 1976—, Nat. Multiple Sclerosis Soc., 1977—, N.Y.C. Housing Devel. Corp., 1977—; USO of Met. N.Y., 1981; bd. dirs. Housing N.Y. Corp., 1986—, vice chmn., 1987—; bd. dirs., chmn. exec. com. Cinema Group, Inc., L.A., 1979-86, chmn., pres., 1982-86; mem. Dem. Nat. Fin. Coun., 1974-78, also vice chmn. exec. com., chmn. budget and audit coms.; treas. N.Y. State Dem. Com., 1976-77; mem. mayor's citizens com. Dem. Nat. Conv., 1976; mem. U.S. Pres.'s Export Coun. (exec. com., chmn. export expansion subcom., mem. export promotion subcom.), 1979-82; mem. exec. br. Acad. Motion Picture Arts and Scis., 1985—; nat. trustee, mem. exec. com. Nat. Symphony Orch., Washington, 1978—; trustee Riverdale Country Sch., 1990—. Mem. Nat. Paper Trade Assn. (dir., mem. printing paper com. 1973—), Paper Mchts. Assn. N.Y. (dir. 1972—), Paper Distbn. Coun., Young Pres. Orgn., Paper Club N.Y., Fin. Execs. Inst., Columbia U. Grad. Sch. Bus. Alumni Assn. (dir. 1980—), Phi Kappa Tau. Clubs: Pres.'s N.Y. (co-chmn. assocs. div. 1964-68), City Athletic, Harvard, Harvard Business, Friars, Marco Polo (N.Y.C.); Les Ambassadeurs (London); Rockrimmon Country (Stamford, Conn.). Home: 25 Sutton Pl S New York NY 10022 also: Cherry Hill Farm 429 Taconic Rd Greenwich CT 06831 Office: Gould Paper Corp 315 Park Ave S New York NY 10010-3607

GOULD, HARVEY ALLEN, physics educator; b. Oakland, Calif., Sept. 4, 1938; s. Mauri and May (Kleiner) G.; m. Patti Orbuch, Sept. 29, 1974; children—Joshua, Emily, Evan. B.A., U. Calif.-Berkeley, 1960, Ph.D., 1966. Postdoctoral research Nat. Bur. Standards, Washington, 1966-67; asst. prof. physics U. Mich., Ann Arbor, 1967-71; assoc. prof. physics Clark U., Worcester, Mass., 1971-81, prof., 1981—. Contbr. articles to profl. jours. Mem. Am. Phys. Soc., Am. Assn. Physics Tchrs. Office: Clark U Physics Dept 950 Main St Worcester MA 01610-1477

GOULD, JACK RICHARD, oil industry technical executive, consultant; b. Bklyn., Feb. 28, 1922; s. Morris and Sylvia (Mitchell) Gold; m. Ruth Lynn Schnitzer, Oct. 21, 1945; children: Kenneth Alan, Michelle Ann. BA, Bklyn. Coll., 1943; MS, Pa. State U., 1947, PhD, 1949. Chemist Montrose Chem. Co., Newark, 1943-45; rsch. chemist Houdry Process Corp., Marcus Hook, Pa., 1949-51; group leader Reaction Motors, Inc., Rockaway, N.J., 1951-56; sect. head Stauffer Chem. Co., Chauncey, N.Y., 1956-63; dir. of rsch. Metalsalts, Inc., Hawthorne, N.J., 1963-64; staff v.p. of rsch. and engring. M.W. Kellogg Co., Piscataway, N.J., 1964-69; sr. environ. scientist Am. Petroleum Inst., Washington, 1969-91, cons., 1991—; cons. Marine Spill Response Corp., Washington, 1991—. Inventor of chems., chem. processes, high energy rocket propellants, pesticides; editor: Oil Spill Studies, 1985; contbr. articles to profl. jours. Pres. Greater Washington chpt., RP Found. Fighting Blindness, Rockville, Md., 1972-84, trustee, 1984—; organizer Internat. Oil Spill Confs., 1969—. Recipient Hon. Cert. for Outstanding Svcs., Internat. Oil Spill Confs., 1991. Mem. Am. Chem. Soc. (editor petroleum chem. div. Preprints, 1973-76), N.Y. Acad. Scis., AAAS, Marine Tech. Assn., Sigma Xi. Home: 6021 Neilwood Dr Rockville MD 20852-3703

GOULD, JAMES WARREN, international relations educator; b. Boulder, Colo., May 14, 1924; s. Douglas W. and Elsa (Dohne) G.; m. Anne Garrison, Jan. 5, 1951; children: Robert D., Steven C., Christopher W., C. Linn, Elizabeth A. Cert. des etudes, U. Paris, 1946; AB, U. Pa., 1946; MA, Fletcher Sch. Law and Diplomacy, 1947, PhD, 1955. Fgn. svc. officer U.S. Fgn. Svc., Sumatra, Hong Kong and Java, 1947-52; internat. oil legislator Mobil Oil Co., N.Y.C., 1955; asst. prof. internat. relations Claremont (Calif.) Men's Coll., 1955-60; assoc. prof. Scripps Coll., Claremont, 1960-64, prof., 1967-90, prof. emeritus, 1990; Fulbright prof. U. Munich, 1960-61. Author: The U.S. and Malaysia, 1969, Americans in Sumatra, 1960, American Interests in Sumatra, 1955, Report 350th Anniversary Celebrations Barnstable, 1991. Chair Hist. Commn. Town of Barnstable, 1992; exec. dir. UN Assn.-U.S.A. Cape Cod and Islands, 1990; historian Cotuit Hist. Soc., 1989; founder Cape Cod Citizens for a Peaceful Solution in the Middle East, 1990; mem. interfaith coun. Cape Cod Coun. Chs., 1991; sec. study com. Cohut Hist. Dist., 1991. Sgt. U.S. Army, 1941-45, ETO. Fellow Asia Found., 1953; Fulbright Found., 1959, Danforth Found., 1963. Mem. Consortium on Peace Rsch. and Edn., Conf. Peace Rsch. in History, Internat. Peace Rsch. Assn., UN Assn. (So. Calif. v.p. 1965—). Mem. Soc. of Friends.

GOULD, LAWRENCE ALREN, cardiologist; b. Bklyn., N.Y., Dec. 15, 1930; s. Raymond and Lola G.; m. Roberta Barkley, Mar. 31, 1957; children: Julie, Bruce. BA, Bklyn. Coll., 1952; MD, NYU Sch. Medicine, 1956. Diplomaet Am. Bd. Internal Medicine, Am. Bd. Cardiology. Intern Kings County Hosp., Bklyn., 1956-57; resident Bronx (N.Y.) VA Hosp., 1959-62, asst. chief cardiology, 1965-67, chief cardiology, 1967-69; chief rsch. lab. Misericordia Hosp., 1969-74; chief cardiology Methodist Hosp., Bklyn., 1974-91, acting dir. medicine, 1991—. Contbr. over 300 articles on cardiology to profl. jours. Capt. U.S. Army Med. Corps, 1957-59. Mem. N.Y. Cardiol. Soc. (pres. 1980-81). Home: 4 Effron Pl Great Neck NY 11020-1412 Office: Methodist Hosp 506 6th St Brooklyn NY 11215-3502

GOULD, PHILIP, art history educator; b. N.Y.C., Oct. 17, 1922; s. Moses and Hattie (Furst) G.; m. Feb. 4, 1950; children: Gregory, Nicholas, Genia, Elka. BA, NYU, 1949; Doctorate de l'Univ., Sorbonne, Paris, 1953. Instr. art history Columbia U., N.Y.C., 1954-63; prof. art history Sarah Lawrence Coll., Bronxville, N.Y., 1959-92; vis. prof. Pratt Inst., Bklyn., 1973, Fordham U., Bronx, 1968, Parsons Sch. Design, 1988, Taiwan Nat. U., 1976, U. Calif., Berkeley; lectr. USIS, various locations; sr. tech. advisor UN Devel. Programme, Beijing, China, 1989; assoc. mem. Columbia U. Seminar on Traditional China, 1992-95. Author essays. With USMC, 1943-45; PTO. Fulbright fellow, 1958-59, Summer Seminar, 1966, Travel grantee, 1975-76. Mem. Soc. Archtl. Historians, Am. Assn. Mus. Home: 15 Claremont Ave New York NY 10027-6814 Office: Sarah Lawrence Coll Bronxville NY 10708

GOULD, ROBERT BRYAN, computer consultant; b. San Jose, Calif., Apr. 12, 1956; s. Stanley George and Patricia Jane (Lee) G. Grad. high sch., Santa Clara, Calif. Archtl. draftsman Cor-Lon Co., San Jose, Calif., 1977-79; owner, operator RBG Drafting Svc., San Jose, 1979-84; gen. contractor Datum Constrn. Corp., San Jose, 1980-84; theatrical electrician The King & I, N.Y.C., 1984-85; theatrical stage mgr. Dreamgirls, N.Y.C., 1985-87, Legs Diamond, N.Y.C., 1988-89; editor The League of Am. Theatres, N.Y.C., 1989-90; prodn. mgr. Phantom of the Opera/Les Miserables, N.Y.C., 1990-91; owner, computer cons. Datum Computer Svc., N.Y.C., 1991—; computer cons. CBS, N.Y.C., 1990—. Author, editor: (compendium of U.S. and Can. theatres) Stage Specs: A Guide to Legit Theatres, 1990. Mem. Internat. Alliance Theatrical Stage Employees (theatrical stagehand 1978—, sec., treas. 1982-83), Actors' Equity Assn. (theatrical stage mgr. 1987—).

GOULD, WAYNE CURTIS, podiatrist; b. Framingham, Mass., May 20, 1960; s. Victor Arthur Gould and Beryl P. (Kilton) Samia; m. Shirley Anne Ulmer, July 9, 1983; children: Carolyn Marie, Ryan Curtis. Student, Stetson U., 1981; BS, Dr. William Scholl Coll., D of Podiatric Medicine, 1985. Resident in surgery Bapt. Meml. Specialty Hosp., Memphis, 1985-86; podiatrist pvt. practice Dover, N.H., 1986—; coun. mem. Am. Diabetes Assn., Alexandria, Va., 1986—; surg. staff mem. Seacoast Outpatient Surgery Ctr., Somersworth, N.H., 1987—, Wentworth Douglas Hosp., Dover, 1990—. Named Biology Student of the Yr., Stetson U., 1980. Assoc. Am. Coll. Foot Surgeons; mem. Am. Podiatric Assn., Am. Diabetes Assn., Appalachian Mountain Club. Office: Wayne C Gould DPM 750 Central Ave Dover NH 03820-3412

GOULD, WILLIAM ALLEN, computer science educator; b. Clearfield, Pa., Dec. 3, 1941; s. William Lewis and Edna Elizabeth (Passmore) G.; m. Priscilla Annette McVay, June 12, 1965; children: Robert, Kenneth, Sharon, James, Jason. BS, Elizabethtown Coll., 1963; MA, Pa. State U., 1965, EdD, 1971. From instr. to assoc. prof. Shippensburg (Pa.) U., 1966-71, prof., 1971—, asst. dir. Computer Ctr., 1970-83, dir. Computer Ctr., 1983—. Office: Shippensburg U Computer Ctr Shippensburg PA 17257-2299

GOULD, WILLIAM HENRY MERCUR, environmental systems sales/marketing professional; b. Pitts., Dec. 23, 1951; s. Curtis E.L. Gould and Linda (McKoy) Stewart; m. Marguerite DeVilliers, June 12, 1983; children: Emma Lesley, Benjamin Cooper DeWet. BA, U. Denver, 1976. Sales rep. W.H. Potter Co., Wayne, Pa., 1975-77, v.p., 1977-81; regional sales mgr. Environ. Products div. Dresser Industries, Houston, 1981-85; supt. Turner Constrn. Co., Phila., 1985-88; dir. mktg. Nat. Constrn. Svcs., Inc., Frazer, Pa., 1988-89, sales and mktg. profl. indsl. machinery and equipment, 1989-90; sales and mktg. mgr. Global Environmental Corp., Plumsteadville, Pa., 1990-92; v.p. sales and mktg. TexCon Environ. Inc., Greenville, S.C., 1992—; turnkey indsl. air pollution control and energy recovery systems, biofiltration indsl. odor control systems. Pres. Landmark Homeowners Assn., Malvern, Pa., 1983-85; bd. dirs. Hug the Earth environ. edn. orgn., 1989—. Democrat. Unitarian. Office: TexCon Environ Inc 817 Spruce Ave West Chester PA 19382

GOULDER, CAROLJEAN HEMPSTEAD, psychologist; b. Houston, Minn., Apr. 9, 1933; d. Orson George and Jean Helen (Lischer) Hempstead; m. L. Lynton Goulder, Jr., May 26, 1956 (div. 1978); children: Jean Virginia, David Thomas, Ann Rachel; m. John T. Blake, Apr. 12, 1986. BS, Hamline U., 1956; CAGS, R.I. Coll., 1975, MA in Sch. Psychology, 1972; postgrad., Nova U., 1977-78. Cert sch. psychologist, R.I. Dept. head, instr. Highsmith Hosp., Fayetteville, N.C., 1956-57; instr. nursing New Eng. Deaconess Hosp., Boston, 1957-58; dir. psychol. svcs. Burrillville Sch. Dept., Harrisville, R.I., 1972-79, sch. psychologist, 1972—; coord. presch. handicapped, 1985-86; lectr. pediatric problems Sturdy Meml. Hosp., Attleboro, Mass., 1970-72; cons. Wheeler Sch., Providence, 1970-73. Chmn. 2d Congl. Ch. Sch., Attleboro, Mass., 1962-65, mem. religious edn. com., kindergarten com. and choir, 1965; active 1st Unitarian Ch., Providence, 1982—. Mem. R.I. Sch. Psychologists Assn., Nat. Assn. Sch. Psychology, Am. Psychol. Assn. (assoc.), Mass. Psychol. Assn. (assoc.), Coun. for Exceptional Children, Delta Kappa Gamma. Office: AT Levy Sch Spl Svcs Office Harrisville RI 02830

GOUNARD, BEVERLEY ELAINE, psychologist; b. Hamilton, Ont., Can., Nov. 24, 1942; came to U.S., 1971; d. Cyril and Lily Gladys (Rickard) Roberts; m. Jean-Francois Gounard, Aug. 19, 1967 (div. 1989); children: Anne-Marie Christine, Emilie Sarah Marie. BA, McMaster U., 1964; MA, Queens U., Can., 1968; PhD, U. Waterloo, 1971. Lic. psychologist, N.Y. 1974. Asst. prof. psychology SUNY, Buffalo, 1971-78, rsch. cons., 1978-81, affirmative action compliance coord., 1981-82; pvt. practice psychologist Buffalo, 1982—. Contbr. articles to profl. jours. Ont. Mental Health Found. Rsch. fellow, 1970-71, SUNY fellow, 1977-78. Mem. APA, AAUW, Can. Psychol. Assn., N.Y. State Psychol. Assn., Psychol. Assn. Western N.Y., Gerontol. Soc. Am., Sigma Xi. Office: 67 Mead St North Tonawanda NY 14120-4496

GOUNARIS, ANNE DEMETRA, biochemistry educator, researcher; b. Boston, Oct. 27, 1924; d. Demetrios Themistocles and Kaliope (Gouvalaris) G. R.N. Mass. Gen. Hosp., 1946; A.B., Boston U., 1955; Ph.D., Harvard U., 1960. Research assoc. Brookhaven Nat. Lab., Upton, N.Y., 1960-62, Carlsberg Lab., Copenhagen, 1962-64, Rockefeller U., N.Y.C., 1964-66; prof. Vassar Coll., Poughkeepsie, N.Y., 1966-90, prof. emeritus, 1990—; vis. fellow Mass. Gen. Hosp., Boston, 1978-83; vis. scientist Strangeways Research Lab., Cambridge, Eng., 1980-81. Contbr. articles to profl. jours. NIH grantee, 1968-71, 1972-76; Ann Horton Fellow, 1980-81; named Collegium Disting. Alumnae, Boston U., 1974. Mem. AAAS, AAUP, Am. Chem. Soc., Am. Soc. Biol. Chemists, Protein Soc., Phi Beta Kappa, Sigma Xi.

GOUNE, STEVEN ETIENNE, financial executive; b. French Cameroon, Nov. 4, 1956; s. Martin and Marie Guilefeng (Goune) Donkeng; m. Cathy Lorraine Mounts, Dec. 23, 1982; 1 child, Jennyfer Celine. BS, Normandy Bus. Sch., LeHavre, France, 1980; MBA, Pa. State U., 1983. Cert. acct., France. Contr. Louis Dreyfus Corp., Paris, 1979-82; sr. cons. Deloitte Haskins & Sells, Washington, 1983-84; fin. systems mgr. Satellite Bus. Systems, McLean, Va., 1984-85; asst. staff mgr. Bell Atlantic-C&P Telephone, Washington, 1985-87; bus. fin. mgr. John Short and Assocs., Columbia, Md., 1987-89; chief fin. officer Govt. Investment Mgmt. Corp., Washington, 1989—; bd. dirs. Inst. on African Affairs, Washington, 1990—. Contbr. articles to profl. jours. Speaker D.C. Pub. Schs., 1990-92. Mem. Am. Mgmt. Assn., Inst. Mgmt. Accts., Treasury Mgmt. Assn. Roman Catholic. Home: 5911 Norham Dr Alexandria VA 22310 Office: Govt Investment Mgmt Corp 1730 Rhode Island Ave NW Washington DC 20036

GOURDJI, JOSEPH, writer; b. Baghdad, Iraq, Aug. 16, 1926; s. Menashi Gourdji and Naima (Jacob) Nahom; m. Anna Roitberg, Nov. 15, 1964; children: Naomi (dec.), Pamela, Benjamin. Ice skater Hollywood Ice Revels, Hollywood Films, Sonja Henie, N.Y.C., L.A., 1944-47; programmer, systems analyst, EDP dept. mgr. Western Union, others, N.Y.C., 1960-72; artist Jacque Seligman, N.Y.C., 1947-57; antique dealer Antique Ctr. Am., N.Y.C.,

1972-79; freelance jewelry designer own line, Trifari, Monet, Dauplaise, others, N.Y.C., 1979-89; writer poetry, prose N.Y.C., 1947—; pub. Buy the Poem monthly, Forest Hills, N.Y., 1990—. Author poems. Office: Buy the Poem Parkside Station PO Box 4078 Forest Hills NY 11375

GOURLEY, THEODORE JOSEPH, JR., educational organization administrator; b. Paterson, N.J., Aug. 17, 1944; s. Theodore Joseph and Josephine Veronica (Radigan) G.; m. Mona Lee Tonaaino, June 25, 1966 (dec. Oct. 1979); 1 child, Katrina Coleen; m. Marlene Ann Fisher, July 7, 1979; children: Theodore J. III, Jonathan Samuel. BA, Wilkes U., 1966; MA, Trenton State Coll., 1970; EdD, Temple U., 1976. Cert. elem. and secondary tchr., sch. supt., prin., spl. edn. Spl. edn. tchr. New Egypt (N.J.) Sch., 1966-68, Mount Laurel (N.J.) Schs., 1968-71; coord. spl. edn. Burlington County Co-Tech. High Sch., Mt. Holly, N.J., 1971-72; spl. edn. supr. Ednl. Improvement Ctr., Pitman, N.J., 1972-77; pres., co-founder Olympics of the Mind, Creative Competitions Inc., Glassboro, N.J., 1979-83; dir. gifted edn. N.J. State Dept. Edn., Trenton, 1977-83; assoc. exec. dir. Ednl. Info. & Resource Ctr., Sewell, N.J., 1983—; mem. roundtable Project XL, U.S. Patent/Trademark Dept. Commerce, Washington, 1988—; mem. governance bd. Nat. Engring. Design Challenge, Alexandria, Va., 1989—. Author: Cognetics, 1984, Problems, Problems, Problems, 1982, Marsville: The Cosmic Village, 1991; contbr. articles to profl. publs. Ednl. Policy fellow George Washington U., 1979. Mem. Nat. Assn. Gifted Children, Coun. for Exceptional Children, Creative and Inventive Thinking Assn.(mem. adv. bd. 1988—), Jr. Engring. Tech. Soc. (dir., bd. dirs. 1986—). Roman Catholic. Office: Ednl Info & Resource Ctr 606 Delsea Dr Sewell NJ 08080-9399

GOURLIE, JONATHAN WILLIAM, insurance company executive; b. Springfield, Mass., June 22, 1942; s. Robert Donald and Marion E. (Jones) G.; m. Nancy Christine Gray, June 13, 1964; children: Heather Lynn Walton, Christine Marion. BS in Math., Union Coll., Schenectady, N.Y., 1964; MBA, Babson Coll., 1980. From tech. staff to dir. John Hancock Life, Boston, 1964-77; asst. to pres. Colonial Penn Life, Phila., 1977-79; dir. planning Am. Inst. P and L Underwriters, Malvern, Pa., 1980-89; sr. bus. analyst US Healthcare, Blue Bell, Pa., 1989—. Town coord. Rep. Congl. Campaign, Framingham, Mass., 1970, 72. Republican. Presbyterian. Office: US Healthcare 980 Jolly Rd Blue Bell PA 19422

GOVERN, FRANK STANLEY, health care executive, educator; b. Plainfield, N.J., May 18, 1951; s. Fred John and Jane Louise (Schweitzer) G.; m. Patricia Loretta Hermanns, Aug. 19, 1972; children: Jason, Heather. AAS, Middlesex County Coll., 1973; BA, Salem State Coll., 1979; MAS, Johns Hopkins U., 1981. Asst. adminstrn. Circle Terrace Hosp., Alexandria, Va., 1981-84; chief exec. officer Tyrone (Pa.) Hosp., 1984-85; pres., chief exec. officer Charles River Hosp., Wellesley, Mass., 1985-86; dir. fin. and adminstrn Joint Ctr. Radiation Therapy, Boston, 1986—; instr. Northeastern U., Boston, 1986—; lectr. Harvard Med. Sch., Boston, 1986—. Contbr. articles to profl. jours. Founder, pres. Citizens for Excellence in Edn., Beverly, Mass., 1991. Capt. USAF, 1974-76. Mem. Am. Coll. Health Care Execs., Am. Med. Group Mgmt. Assn., Soc. Radiation Oncology Adminstrn., Am. Hosp. Assn. Home: 145 Hale St Beverly MA 01915 Office: Joint Ctr Radiation Therapy 50 Binney St Boston MA 02115

GOWAN, DONALD ELMER, religion educator; b. Cleghorn, Iowa, Jan. 31, 1929; s. Elmer G. and Lucile O. (Woodcock) G.; m. Darlene G. Rogers, Dec. 28, 1958; children: Douglas, Pamela. BA, U. S.D., 1951; BD, U. Dubuque, 1957; PhD, U. Chgo., 1964. Computer programmer Gen. Electric Co., Richland, Wash., 1951-54; pastor Presbyn. Ch., Princeton, Iowa, 1955-59; head Bible dept. North Tex. State U., Denton, 1962-65; mem. faculty Pitts. Theol. Sem., 1965—, Robert Cleveland Holland prof. O.T., 1985—. Author: When Man Becomes God, 1975, The Triumph of Faith in Habakkuk, 1976, Bridge Between the Testaments, 1976, Reclaiming the Old Testament for the Christian Pulpit, 1980, Shalom, 1984, Ezekiel, 1985, Eschatology in the Old Testament, 1986, From Eden to Babel: Genesis 1-11, 1988. Mem. AAUP, Soc. Bibl. Lit., Phi Beta Kappa. Presbyterian. Office: Pitts Theol Sem 616 N Highland Ave Pittsburgh PA 15206-2596

GOWANS, ALAN, historian, writer; b. Toronto, Ontario, Can., Nov. 30, 1923; came to U.S., 1948; BA, U. Toronto, 1946; MFA, Princeton U., 1948, PhD, 1950; PhD, Princeton U., 1950. Art history dept. chmn., Winterthur Program assoc. Univ. Del., 1956-66; history dept. in art chmn. Univ. Victoria, Can., 1967-88; vis. prof. Harvard Univ., Edinburgh, Univ. Cin., Tufts Univ. and several other universities, 1964-89. Author numerous books including: The Comfortable House: Suburban Architecture in North America 1890-1930, 1986, Styles and Types of North American Architecture: Social Function and Cultured Expression, 1992; contbr. articles to profl. jours. Mem. Soc. of Archtl. Historians (pres. 1970-74, dir. 1974-80). Home & Office: Nat Images of NAm Living 5242020 F St NW Washington DC 20006-4234

GRABEL, LAWRENCE, actuarial company executive; b. Mt. Vernon, N.Y., May 24, 1947; s. Hyman and Mildred (Fisher) G.; m. Donna Marie Sclafani, Sept., 1965 (div. Jan. 1978); children: Ian, Adam. BS in Math., CCNY, 1970. Enrolled actuary. Asst. actuary Pension Planning Co., N.Y.C., 1970-76; pension actuary Warner Communications, Inc., N.Y.C., 1976-77; pres. Ibex Pension Actuaries, Ic., N.Y.C., 1978—. Contbr. articles to profl. jours. Dir. Com. Retirement Income Security Protection, N.Y.C., 1985-87. Mem. Am. Soc. Pension Actuaries (govt. affairs com. 1986—, chmn. ann. conf. 1989, gen. conf. chmn. 1990-91, bd. dirs. 1991), Am. Acad. Actuaries. Office: Ibex Pension Actuaries Inc 11th Fl 33 Irving Pl New York NY 10003-2332

GRABILL, GLORIA ELIZABETH, social worker, county agency administrator; b. Passaic, N.J., Sept. 17, 1938; d. Vanel and Alice Gertrude (Asgill) Perry; m. James Ray Grabill, Sept. 17, 1967; children—Jill-Allyson, Jefferson Perry. B.A., Rutgers U., 1965, M.S.W., 1973. Community worker Task Force, Passaic, N.J., 1965-66; caseworker Passaic County Bd. Social Services, Paterson, N.J., 1965-67, casework supr., 1967-75, supr. staff devel. and tng., chmn. edn. leave com., 1975—, affirmative action officer, 1974—, corrective action, and tng. com. chmn., 1982—; trustee, tchr. Rutherford Unitarian Soc. (N.J.), 1966-67; chmn. social service com. Head Start, Paterson, 1973-74. Mem. adv. com. Spl. Aid for Girls Expecting, Paterson; inspirational choir Union Bapt. Ch. of Passaic. Recipient Commendation Passaic County Bd. Social Services, 1983. 89. 90; Cert. of Appreciation, 1986. Mem. Nat. Assn. Social Workers, Am. Pub. Welfare Assn., Nat. Staff Devel. and Tng. Assn., Acad. Cert. Social Workers, Am. Assn. for Affirmative Action (com. on inquiry). Democrat. Home: 8 Tara Ln Montville NJ 07045-9650 Office: Passaic County Bd Social Svcs 80 Hamilton St Paterson NJ 07505-2017

GRABOWSKI, EDWARD JOSEPH JOHN, chemist; b. Jamaica, N.Y., Apr. 23, 1940; s. Edward John and Mary Frances (Sulczynski) G.; m. Lenore Edith Rampino, June 24, 1961; 1 child, David Christopher. BS, MIT, 1961; PhD, U. Rochester, 1965. Sr. chemist Merck & Co., Inc., Rahway, N.J., 1965-72, rsch. fellow, 1972-75; sr. rsch. fellow Merck & Co., Inc., Rahway, 1975-79, sr. investigator, 1979-85, dir., 1985-87, sr. dir., 1987—. Contbr. 60 articles to profl. jours.; 30 patents in field. Pres. FCPS, N.Y.C., 1981-85. Mem. Am. Chem. Soc., European Photochem. Assn., Royal Soc. Chemistry, Internat. Congress of Heterocyclic Chemistry. Home: 741 Marcellus Dr Westfield NJ 07090-2012 Office: MSDRL Merck & Co Inc PO Box 2000 Rahway NJ 07065-0900

GRABOWSKI, JOSEPH JAMES, chemistry educator; b. Elkridge, Md., Nov. 4, 1956; s. Raymond Peter and Mae Ethel (Miller) G.; m. Paula Jane Noeth, July 16, 1977. BA in Chemistry, U. Md., Baltimore County, 1978; PhD in Organic Chemistry, U. Colo., 1983. Rsch. technician Lab. for Chem. Dynamics, U. Md., Balt., 1978; teaching asst. chemistry dept. U. Colo., Boulder, 1978-79, rsch. asst., 1979-83; postdoctoral fellow Harvard U., Cambridge, Mass., 1983-84, asst. prof., 1984-88, assoc. prof., 1988-91, founder, chmn. deptl. teaching fellow program, 1988-91; assoc. prof. dept. chemistry U. Pitts., 1991—; cons. Crystal Diagnostics Systems, Woburn, Mass., 1986, Alcon Labs., Ft. Worth, 1989. Contbr. articles to profl. jours. Deacon, sec. exec. com. 1st Congl. Ch., Sharon, Mass., 1990—. Recipient Presdl. Young Investigator award NSF, 1986. Fellow AAAS; mem. Am. Chem. Soc., Am. Soc. for Mass. Spectrometry (VG instruments rsch. award 1986). Home: 1027 E End Ave Pittsburgh PA 15221 Office: Dept Chemistry U Pitts Pittsburgh PA 15260

GRACE, CHARLES BROWN, JR., investment executive; b. Evanston, Ill., Apr. 11, 1934; s. Charles Brown and Nancy Brewster (Dougherty) G.; children: Ingrid Wiese, Charles Brown III, Melissa Dewitt, Gerd Morris. BA, Princeton U., 1956; MBA, U. Pa., 1962. Assoc. Drexel and Co., Phila., 1958-60; instr. U. Pa., Phila., 1961-63; cons. Booz Allen and Hamilton, N.Y.C., 1963-64; mng. dir. Smith Barney and Co., N.Y., Paris, 1965-76; pres. Ashbridge Corp., Phila., 1976—; bd. dirs. Neutronics, Exton, Pa., Ashbridge Corp., Phila., Heintz Investment Co., Wilmington, Del. Bd. dirs. French Am. Found., N.Y.C.; overseer Univ. Mus., Phila. 1st lt. USMC, 1956-58. Mem. Knickerbocker Club (bd. govs.), Phila. Club, Racquet Club, Gulph Mills Golf Club. Home: 1272 St Mathews Rd Chester Springs PA 19425-2702 Office: Ashbridge Corp 1515 Market St Ste 1420 Philadelphia PA 19102-2331

GRACE, JOHN KENNETH, business executive; b. Washington, Nov. 12, 1945; s. Walter Kenneth and Muriel (Hess) G.; m. Patricia McCabe, Nov. 23, 1974; children: Christopher, Jennifer. BA, Tufts U., 1968; MBA, NYU, 1972. Account exec. Young & Rubicam, Inc., N.Y.C., 1969-71; v.p., group mgmt. supr. Grey Advt., Inc., N.Y.C., 1972-87; v.p. mktg. and food Nutri/System Inc., Willow Grove, Pa., 1987-88; exec. v.p. Lippincott & Margulies, Inc., N.Y.C., 1988-91, also bd. dirs.; pres., chief exec. officer JKG Assocs., Inc., Darien, Conn., 1992—. Bd. overseers Tufts U., 1991—.

GRACE, L(INDA) A(NN), artist, designer; b. N.Y.C., Feb. 23, 1952; d. William John and Jeannette Mary (Caldrone) Haberland; m. John Joseph Drummond, May 12, 1989; 1 child by previous marriage, Richard Damien. Student, Cornell U./Les Ataliers, Paris, 1985, Iona Coll., 1986; BFA, Coll. New Rochelle, 1986. Pres. Interscenes, Inc., New Rochelle, 1979—; graphic designer Grace Designs, New Rochelle, 1987—; owner Panel Art, Ltd., New Rochelle, 1987—; pvt. tutor Artist's Studio, New Rochelle, 1988—; instr. arts and crafts workshop Thorton Donovan Sch., 1987; lectr. Coll. New Rochelle, 1986, 90. Group shows include Les Ataliers, Paris, 1985, Coll. New Rochelle, 1985, 86, 90, 91 (1st prize award juried alumnae exhibit 1990), Lawrence Gallery, 1987, 88, 90, 92; represented in permanent collections Talon Corp., Paris, Viols Estate, Paris, Godfrin Estate, Belgium, Ferioli Estate, Italy, Grace Industries, Benevento Estate, Durante Estate, others. Lutheran. Studio: Studio D 303 Centre Ave New Rochelle NY 10805

GRACE, THOMAS LEE, healthcare administrator, nurse; b. Huntingdon, Pa., Mar. 29, 1955; s. Robert Leroy and Mary Elizabeth (Isenberg) G.; m. Renee Lee Ramsey, Oct. 20, 1979; 1 child, Elliott Lee. ASN, Robert Morris Coll., 1978; diploma in nursing, Sewickley (Pa.) Valley Hosp., 1979; BSN, LaRoche Coll., 1984; M in Pub. Mgmt., Carnegie Mellon U., 1985. RN, Pa. Staff nurse ortho dept. McKeesport (Pa.) Hosp., 1979-80; staff nurse emergency rm. Allegheny Gen. Hosp., Pitts., 1980-81; flight nurse Life-Flight-Allegheny Gen. Hosp., Pitts., 1981-85; chief flight nurse Aries-Fairfax Hosp., Falls Church, Va., 1985-86; coord. emergency svcs. Fairfax Hosp., Falls Church, 1986-87; flight program dir. Pennstar U. Pa. Med. Ctr., Phila., 1987-91; asst. adminstr. Hosp. of U. Pa., Phila., 1991—. Inventor crico ventilation device; contbr. articles to profl. jours. Mem. Huntingdon Vol. Fire Dept., 1972—, Valley Ambulance Authority, Coraopolis, Pa., 1977-79; del. Cen. Dist. Fireman's Assn., Tyrone, Pa., 1983—; scoutmaster Sewickley Meth. Ch. Troop Boy Scouts Am., 1978-79. With U.S. Army, 1973-76. Mem. Nat. Flight Nurses Assn. (pres.), Emergency Nurses Assn., Am. Mgmt. Assn., Am. Legion. Democrat. Home: 594 Forest Rd Wayne PA 19087-2322

GRADY, GREGORY, lawyer, banker; b. Takoma Park, Md., Oct. 10, 1945; s. Francis Joseph Grady and Deane (McGehee) Black; m. Carol Love Harrison, Feb. 25, 1978; children: Olivia Love, Blake McGregor, Harrison Edwards. BA in Econs., U. Va., 1969; JD, Tulane U., 1972. Bar: D.C. 1973, U.S. Ct. Appeals (D.C. cir.) 1973, U.S. Ct. Appeals (4th cir.) 1975, U.S. Supreme Ct. 1976, U.S. Ct. Appeals (5th cir.) 1977, U.S. Ct. Appeals (10th cir.) 1979, U.S. Ct. Appeals (11th cir.) 1981, U.S. Ct. Appeals (6th cir.) 1982, U.S. Dist. Ct. 1988. Staff atty., supervisory atty. FPC, Washington, 1972-74; assoc. Littman, Richter, Wright & Talisman, P.C., Washington, 1974-79; mem. Wright & Talisman, P.C., Washington, 1979—, v.p., 1983—; bd. dirs. Bank of Franklin (Miss.). Mem. ABA, Fed. Energy Bar Assn., D.C. Bar Assn. Republican. Episcopalian. Home: 666 Live Oak Dr Mc Lean VA 22101-1569 Office: Wright & Talisman PC 1200 G St NW Ste 600 Washington DC 20005-3802

GRAEFF, DAVID WAYNE, maintenance executive, consultant; b. West Reading, Pa., Oct. 24, 1946; s. Wayne Samuel and Sara (Spohn) G.; m. Linda Ruth Lohrke, Aug. 17, 1968; children—Hether, Rebecca, Matthew. B.S.M.E., Ind. Inst. Tech., 1969. Lic. in sewage treatment plant and waterworks, Pa. Maintenance engr. Central Soya, Decatur, Ind., 1969-71; mfg. engr. Nat. Seal div. Fed. Mogul, Van Wert, Ohio, 1971-73; facilities engr. Kawecki Berylco div. Cabot, Van Wert, Ohio, 1973-76; plant engr. Willson Products div. E.S.B., Reading, 1976-78; maintenance supt. Brush-Wellman Inc., Reading, 1978—; maintenance cons. Maintenance Inc., Fleetwood, Pa., 1976—. Vice comr. USCG Aux., Reading, 1983-84, cert. marine examiner, 1982—, info. system officer, 1984. Mem. AICE, Soc. Mfg. Engrs., Am. Water Works Assn., Am. Inst. Plant Engrs., Am. Assn. Energy Engrs., Am. Chem. Soc., Environ Engrs. & Mgrs. Inst., Pa. Soc. Profl. Engrs., Ducks Unltd., Moose, Theta Xi. Republican. Lutheran. Home: 815 N Forest St Fleetwood PA 19522-1021 Office: Brush-Wellman Inc Shoemakersville Rd Shoemakersville PA 19555-1414 also: PO Box 973 Reading PA 19603

GRAF, JEFFREY HOWARD, cardiologist; b. N.Y.C., Apr. 6, 1955; s. Rudolf F. and Bettina L. (Knisbacher) G.; m. Roberta Ruth Rubin, June 26, 1982; children: Allison, Daniel, Russell. BA magna cum laude, NYU, 1976, MD, 1980. Diplomate Am. Bd. Cardiology, Am. Bd. Internal Medicine. Cardiology fellow Mt. Sinai Med. Ctr., N.Y.C., 1983-86; cardiologist educator Mt. Sinai Sch. Medicine, N.Y.C., 1986—; cons., 1986—. Fellow Am. Coll. Cardiology; mem. Phi Beta Kappa, Alpha Omega Alpha. Office: 1111 Park Ave New York NY 10128

GRAF, KERMIT WILMER, education administrator; b. Sheboygan, Wis., Sept. 25, 1952; s. Wilmer and Florence (Brill) G. BS, U. Wis., Milw., 1974; MS, U. Wis., La Crosse, 1978; postgrad., U. Ariz., 1984, 88. 4-H youth agt. and assoc. prof. youth devel. U. Wis. Extension, Elkhorn, 1974-84; exec. dir. Cornell Coop. Extension-Rockland, Thiells, N.Y., 1984-89, Cornell Coop. Extension-Suffolk, Riverhead, N.Y., 1990—; met. adv. com. Cornell Coop. Extension, Ithaca, N.Y., 1990—, mktg. commn., 1987—; mem. Nassau/Suffolk Health Systems, 1991—; chair L.I. Harvest Festival, Riverhead, 1991—. Co-author: Creative Marketing, 1989; creator/producer (slide/tape) Producing the One Act Play, 1982, Mime the Silent Art, 1982; writer (video) Orientation to Cornell, 1991. Mem. L.I. Assn. for AIDS Care, Huntington, N.Y., 1991—, L.I. Assn., Commack, N.Y., 1990—, Partnership for a New L.I., Commack, 1992. Recipient Disting. Svc. award N.Y. State Assembly, 1989, Rockland County Legislature, 1989, Managerial Leadership award Epsilon Sigma Phi, 1988, Outstanding Young Man of Am. award, 1985, Adminstrv. Studies scholarship Farm Found., 1981. Mem. Nat. Assn. Extension 4-H Agts., Epsilon Sigma Phi. Home: 46 Tariff St Sayville NY 11782 Office: Cornell Coop Ext 246 Griffing Ave Riverhead NY 11901

GRAF, PETER GUSTAV, accountant, lawyer; b. Vienna, Austria, June 19, 1936; came to U.S. 1940, naturalized, 1945; m. Rosalie Greenbaum, Apr. 6, 1963; 1 child, Paul Evan. B.S. in Econs., U. Pa., 1957; Ll.B., NYU, 1960, Ll.M., 1962. Bar: N.Y. 1960; C.P.A., N.Y. Tax acct. J.K. Lasser & Co., N.Y.C., 1961-62; with Joseph Graf & Co., N.Y.C., 1962—, ptnr., 1966—; v.p., founder, dir. AGS Computers Inc., N.J., 1967—; ptnr., founder, treas., dir. Nardin Gallery, Inc., Cross River, N.Y.; founder Cable Systems USA Assocs., W.Va., Pa. and Ohio; founder USA Mobile Communications, Inc., Cellular USA Inc., USA Ventures Ltd. Mem. Am. Inst. C.P.A.s, N.Y. State Soc. C.P.A.s, N.Y. State Bar Assn. Home: 87 Holly Pl Briarcliff Manor NY 10510-2107 Office: Joseph Graf & Co 6 E 43d St New York NY 10017-4609

GRAFF, DAVID AUSTIN, chiropractor; b. Mpls., Sept. 24, 1949; s. Austin Joseph and Aleen Marie (O'Donnell) G.; m. Barbara Ruth Paterson, Jan 15, 1983. Student, U. Wis., Stevens Point, 1967-70; D Chiropractic Medicine, Palmer Coll., 1974; postgrad., Nat. Coll. of Chiropractic, Lombard, Ill., 1988-91. Diplomate Nat. Bd. Chiropractic Examiners. Extern Caputo Chiropractic Clinic, Plainview, N.Y., 1975; chiropractor Bahan & Bahan Chiropractic Health Ctr., Derry, N.H., 1976—; instr. N.Y. Chiropractic Coll., Old Brookville, 1975; nutritional cons. Bahan & Bahan Profl. Assn., Derry, N.H., 1976—, treas., 1984—. Editor: Textbook on spinal X-Rays, 1975. Mem. N.H. Chiropractic Assn., Whole Health Inst. Office: Bahan & Bahan Chiropractic Health Ctr Box 186 33 Crystal Ave Derry NH 03038

GRAFF, HETTIE WESTBROOK MURPHY, university administrator; b. Wallace, N.C., Feb. 16, 1928; d. William Faison and Josephine Hodges (Martin) Murphy; m. William Hastings Graff, July 12, 1948; children: William Hastings, Richard Westbrook, Cynthia Todd McKay. BA in Elem. Edn., Antioch Coll., 1975; MEd in Ednl. Media, Temple U., 1979. Cert. media specialist; cert. elem. tchr. CCTV operator Conwell Mid. Magnet Sch., Sch. Dist. Phila., 1965-75; tchr. reading Simon Gratz High Sch., Phila., 1975-80; trainer Provident Nat. Bank, Phila., 1980-81; instructional developer, cons. Phila., 1981-85; mgr. learning resources Coll. Health, Phys. Edn., Recreation and Dance, Temple U., Phila., 1986-88; dir. learning resources Temple U., Phila., 1988—; cons. Nat. Steel, Parsipanny, N.J., 1982-83, Pitney Bowes, Cherry Hill, N.J., 1981-84, Motorola Electronics, Phoenix, 1984-85. Producer multi-image show Conwell School Documentary, 1971, School District Documentary, 1974; author: Documents in Banking, 1984; coord. teaching asst. orientation program, 1989. Vol. Internat. Visitors' Ctr., Phila., 1982—. Mem. Assn. for Ednl. Communication and Tech., Nat. Soc. Performance and Instrn., Profl. and Orgn. Devel. Network, Am. Assn. Higher Edn. Democrat. Episcopalian. Home: 517 Smithfield Ave Philadelphia PA 19116-1035 Office: Temple U Coll Health Phys Edn Recreation Dance 220 Pearson Hall Philadelphia PA 19122

GRAFF, RANDY, actress; b. Bklyn., May 23, 1955. Grad., Wagner Coll. Profl. theater debut in Gypsy, Village Dinner Theater, Raleigh, N.C.; appeared in Godspell, Raleigh; other appearances include Pins and Needles, Roundabout Theatre, N.Y.C., 1978, Something, Wonderful Westchester Regional Theatre, Harrison, N.Y., 1979, Sarava, Mark Hellinger Theatre, N.Y.C., 1979, Coming Attractions, Playwrights Horizons, Mainstage Theatre, N.Y.C., 1980, Keystone, McCarter Theatre, Princeton, N.J., 1981, A... My Name is Alice, Village Gate Theatre, N.Y.C., 1984, Amateurs, Playhouse in the Park, Cin., 1985, Fiorello!, Goodspeed Opera House, East Haddam, Conn., 1985, Absurd Person Singular, Phila. Drama Guild, Phila., 1986, Les Miserables, Broadway Theatre, N.Y.C., 1987, City of Angels, Va. Theatre, N.Y.C., 1989; also appeared in TV series episodes, programs. Recipient Drama Desk award, 1990, Antoinette Perry award for best featured actress in musical, 1990. Office: care Chris Boneau 165 W 46th St Ste 600 New York NY 10036-2501*

GRAFTON, ROBERT BRUCE, program director science; b. Rochester, N.Y., May 15, 1935; s. Corydon Melvin and Beatrice (Hawes) G.; m. Carolyn Kolb Grafton, July 8, 1967 (div. Dec. 1990); children: Geoffrey Backus, Benjamin Robert. ScB, Brown U., Providence, R.I., 1958, PhD, 1967. Prof. U. Mo., 1967-71; visiting lectr. Leicester (England) U., 1970-71; prof. Trinity Coll., Hartford, Conn., 1971-75; program mgr. Office Naval Rsch., N.Y.C., 1975-78, Arlington, Va., 1978-86; program dir. NSF, Washington, 1986—; program com. COMPSAC Conf., Chgo., 1983-86. Facilitator New Beginnings, Washington, 1990—; Lt. USN, 1958-62. Recipient Svc. award IEEE Computer Soc., 1985. Office: Nat Sci Found 1800 G St NW Washington DC 20550-0002

GRAHAM, AARON RICHARD, educational educator; b. St. Petersburg, Fla., Apr. 4, 1944; s. Willie and Willie Mae (George) G.; m. Janet Lorraine Wilkins, June 21, 1969; children: Andrea Yvonne, Aaron Richard II. AA, St. Petersburg Jr. Coll., 1965; BS, N.C. Cen. U., 1967; MS in Edn., Akron U., 1969; EdD, Fordham U., 1990. Cert. prin., sch. adminstr., N.J. Sci. tchr. Nat. Tchr. Corps, Akron, Ohio, 1967-69, Akron Pub. Schs., 1969-71; biology tchr. Palisades Park (N.J.) Pub. Schs., 1973-77; program coord. N.J. Dept. Edn., Bergen County, 1977-83, ednl. planner, 1983-89; asst. dir. curriculum and instrn. Bergen County Tech. Schs., Hackensack, 1989-91; asst. prof. adminstrn., curriculum and instrn. Jersey City State Coll., 1991—; cons. Bergen County Tech. Schs., 1991—; mem. adv. com. Acad. Advancement of Teaching and Mgmt., Edison, N.J., 1991—; presenter U. Coun. for Ednl. Adminstrn., Scottsdale, Ariz., 1989. Trustee Teaneck (N.J.) Libr. Bd., 1983—; mem. Bergen County Human Rels. Coalition, 1987—, v.p., 1991—. Mem. ASCD, N.J. Staff Devel. Coun., Nat. Staff Devel. Coun., Urban League (Svc. award 1987, bd. dirs. 1982—), Phi Delta Kappa. Home: 86 Church St Teaneck NJ 07666-4932

GRAHAM, ALBERT DARLINGTON, JR., educational administrator; b. Camden, N.J., July 28, 1948; s. Albert Darlington and Betty Jane (Belancin) G. BS cum laude, Union Coll., Barbourville, Ky., 1970, MA, 1973; EdM, Johns Hopkins U., 1977; EdD, Calif. Western U., 1980; MA, Glassboro State Coll., 1991; PhD, LaSalle U., 1992. Cert. supt., prin., supr., sch. bus. adminstr., secondary social studies tchr., in student personnel svcs., N.J. Tchr. social studies Penns Grove (N.J.) Mid. Sch., 1970-82, coord. career edn., 1974-75, chmn. social studies dept., 1978-82; athletic dir. Penns Grove High Sch., Carneys Point, N.J., 1983-85, coord. gifted and talented program, 1986-87, dir. guidance, vice prin. in charge curriculum, fin.-instrn., 1982—. Mem. Carneys Point Twp., 1979-84, 81—; mayor Carneys Point Twp., 1992; mem. Salem County (N.J.) Bd. Chosen Freeholders, 1985-87, N.J. Gov.'s Coun. on Phys. Fitness and Sports, 1986—; chmn. Carneys Point Sewerage Authority, 1981-85, 91—, Salem County Selective Svc. Bd., 1982—; pres. Salem County Assn. Local Govt., 1983-84, Village Arms Sr. Citizens Complex, Carneys Point, 1984—; pres. Carneys Point Rep. Club, 1981-84; trustee Salem Community Coll., 1987-91, Union Coll., 1992—. Recipient Govt. James D. Black Sr. award for Acad. Cxcellence, Blackwell Meml. award in polit. sci., Medallion award for Excellence in Ednl. Adminstrn.; named to Outstanding Young Men of Am., 1978. Mem. ASCD, N.J. Pins. and Suprs. Assn. (svc. and leadership award 1984), N.J. League Municipalities (svc. and leadership award 1984), South Jersey Assn. Freeholders (svc. and leadership award 1985), Penns Grove High Sch. Alumni Assn. (treas. 1975—), Exch. Club (pres. Penns Grove 1984-85), Masons (32d degree), Elks (leading knight Penns Grove 1986-87), Mensa, Phi Delta Kappa, Iota Sigma Nu, Gamma Beta Phi, Phi Delta Gamma. Methodist. Home: Wiley Rd Harding Hwy Carneys Point NJ 08069 Office: Penns Grove High Sch Harding Hwy Penns Grove NJ 08069-2279

GRAHAM, BARBARA F., writer, editor; b. Ann Arbor, Mich., Mar. 24, 1950; d. Myron and Lolita June (Stein) Fink; m. Peter Collier Graham, Dec. 14, 1975 (div. Dec. 1990); children: Trevor Collier, Dana Courtney. BA in Asian History, Northwestern U., 1971; MA in East Asian Studies, U. Mich., 1973. Asst. to dir. The Conf. Book, N.Y.C., 1974; asst. to project planning mgr. C. Itoh & Co. Inc., N.Y.C., 1974-75; asst. to pres. Marshalsea Assoc. Inc., N.Y.C., 1975-76; writer, researcher free lance, Ann Arbor, Boston, 1976—; mgr. editorial programs Polygen Corp., Waltham, Mass., 1985—; editor Polygen Corp. now Molecular Simulations, Inc., Waltham, 1985—. Editor Chem. Design Automation News, 1985—. Mem. AAAS, N.Y. Acad. Scis. Unitarian. Home: 1 Aberdeen Rd Weston MA 02193-1732 Office: Molecular Simulations Inc 200 5th Ave Waltham MA 02154-8704

GRAHAM, BERNARD ALLEN, human resources executive, clergyman, consultant; b. Montrose, Pa., Aug. 20, 1933; s. Otis M. and Florence I. (Tinklepaugh) G.; m. Glendora L. Bunnell, June 26, 1954; children: David N., Doreen R., Wendy L. BTh, Bapt. Bible Sem., Clarks Summit, Pa., 1956; BA in Edn., Wheaton (Ill.) Coll., 1954; postgrad., SUNY, Binghamton, 1958-60. Ordained to ministry, Bapt. Ch., 1958. Info. system analyst IBM Corp., Endicott, N.Y., 1957-64, resource planner, 1964-80, in mgmt. and employee devel., 1980—; pastor Elk Lake Community Ch., Springville, Pa., 1954-71, East Bridgewater Community Ch., Montrose, 1973-86; cons. to industry and govt., 1983—; adj. faculty SUNY, Binghamton, 1982—. Author various management programs. Chair faculty Broome County Devel. Yr. 2000, SUNY, Binghamton, 1990. Mem. Am. Soc. for Tng. and Devel. (dir. planning 1988-89, bd. dirs. 1986—, pres. 1990). Republican. Home: RR 5 Box 146 Montrose PA 18801-9351

GRAHAM, CHARLES, JR., physiology educator; b. Balt., June 17, 1940; s. Charles Raymond and Matilda Pat (Layman) G.; m. Patricia Ellen Cole, Jan. 20, 1962; children: Charles R., Kelly Patricia, Michael E., Kerri M. BS, Loyola Coll., Balt., 1962; PhD, U. Del., 1967. Instr. Loyola Coll., Balt., 1966-67, asst. prof., 1967-71, assoc. prof., 1971-77, prof., 1977—; lab. dir. Med. Eye Bank, Balt., 1974-85. Contbr. articles to Corneal Physiology. Fellow Wilmer Inst.; mem. Am. Soc. Zoologists, Nat. Assn. Advisors for Health Professions. Democrat. Roman Catholic. Office: Loyola Coll 4501 N Charles St Baltimore MD 21210-2601

GRAHAM, DAVID, physician; b. Sunderland, England, Dec. 24, 1947; came to U.S., 1973; s. Terence and Eveline (Partridge) G.; children: Amanda, Lisa, David. MB, ChB, Edinburgh U., 1972. Bd. cert. Ob-gyn. and Radiology. Intern ob-gyn. Johns Hopkins Hosp., Balt., 1973-74, resident radiology, 1974-77, fellow radiology, 1977-78, asst. prof. ob-gyn./radiology, 1980-83; resident ob-gyn. McMaster Univ., Hamilton, Ont., 1978-80; assoc. prof. ob-gyn. Univ. Rochester, N.Y., 1983-88; dir. prenatal ultrasound Union Meml. Hosp., Balt., 1989—; med. dir. Med. Ultrasound Imaging Svcs., Stratford, N.J., 1982—. Contbr. chpts. to books and articles to profl. jours. Pres. Medigrafix, Inc., Ellicott City, Md., 1990—; v.p. Acutel, Inc., Columbia, Md., 1991. Fellow Am. Coll. Obstetricians and Gynecologists, Royal Coll. Surgeons; mem. Am. Inst. Ultrasound in Medicine (sr.). Office: Med Ultrasound Imaging Svcs 1406B Crain Hwy S # 304 Glen Burnie MD 21061-4027

GRAHAM, DONALD EDWARD, publisher; b. Balt., Apr. 22, 1945; s. Philip L. and Katharine (Meyer) G.; m. Mary L. Wissler, Jan. 7, 1967; children: Liza, Laura, William, Molly. B.A., Harvard U., 1966. Formerly with Newsweek mag.; with The Washington Post, 1971—, asst. mng. editor sports, 1974-75, asst. gen. mgr., 1975-76, exec. v.p., gen. mgr., 1976-79, pub., 1979—; pres., chief exec. officer The Washington Post Co., 1991—; dir. Washington Post Co., Bowaters Mersey Paper Co. Ltd. Trustee Fed. City Council, 1976. Served with U.S. Army, 1966-68. Mem. Am. Antiquarian Soc. Office: Washington Post Co 1150 15th St NW Washington DC 20071-0002*

GRAHAM, FRANCES KEESLER (MRS. DAVID TREDWAY GRAHAM), psychologist, educator; b. Canastota, N.Y., Aug. 1, 1918; d. Clyde C. and Norma (Van Surdam) Keesler; m. David Tredway Graham, June 14, 1941; children: Norma, Andrew, Mary. B.A., Pa. State U., 1938; Ph.D., Yale U., 1942. Acting dir. St. Louis Psychiat. Clinic, 1942-44; instr. Barnard Coll., 1948-51; research assoc. Sch. Medicine, Washington U., St. Louis, 1942-48, 53-57, U. Wis., Madison, 1957-64; asso. prof. pediatrics and psychology U. Wis., 1964-68, prof., 1968-86, Hilldale research prof., 1980-86; prof. U. Del., Newark, 1986—; Cons. Nat. Inst. Neurol. Diseases and Blindness perinatal research br.; mem. exptl. psychology research review com. NIMH, 1970-74, NRC, 1971-74; mem. bd. sci. counselors NIMH, 1977-81, chmn., 1979-81; mem. Pres.'s Commn. for Study of Ethical Problems in Medicine and Biomed. and Behavioral Research, 1980-82. Mem. editorial bd. Jour. Exptl. Child Psychology, 1964-67, Child Devel., 1966-68, Jour. Exptl. Psychology, 1968-73, Psychophysiology, 1968-73; contbr. articles to profl. jours. Recipient Rsch. Scientist award NIMH, 1964-89, Disting. Alumna award Pa. State U., 1983, Wilbur L. Cross medal Yale U., 1992. Mem. AAAS (chmn. sect. psychology 1979), APA (coun. 1975-77, pres. div. physiol. and comparative psychology 1978-79, G. Stanley Hall award 1982, Disting. Scientist award 1990), NAS, Am. Psychol. Soc. (William James fellow 1990), Soc. Rsch. Child Devel. (council 1965-71, pres. 1975-77, Disting. Sci. Contbns. award 1991), Soc. Psychophysiol. Rsch. (dir. 1968-71, 72-75, pres. 1973-74, Disting. Contbns. award 1981), Soc. Exptl. Psychologists, Soc. Neurosci., Psychonomic Soc., Acoustical Soc. Am., Internat. Soc. Devel. Psychobiology, Sigma Xi. Home: 311 Dove Dr Newark DE 19713-1211

GRAHAM, JOHN FRANCIS, insurance company executive; b. Phila., July 28, 1948; s. Joseph Aloyuious and Mary Veronica (Forsythe) G.; m. Janet Lynn Jacobs, Sept. 16, 1972; children: Ryan David, Michael Joseph, Lindsay Joan. BS, La Salle Coll., 1970; MEd, Temple U., 1972. Tchr. Sch. Dist. Phila., 1970-72; salesman ins. Internat. Services Plan Inc. and Millburn Mgmt. Corp., Verona, N.J., 1972-78; pres., chief exec. officer Internat. Services Plan Inc. and Millburn Mgmt. Corp., Verona, 1978-87; chmn. bd. dirs. Fairview Ins. Assocs. Inc. (formerly Millburn Mgmt. Co.), Verona, 1987—. Trustee N.Y. Coll. Podiatric Medicine, N.Y.C., 1975—, Karen Anne Quinlan Ctr. Hope, Mt. Arlington, 1982—, Livingston Symphony Orch., N.J., 1984—, Internat. Sch. Commerce, Nutley, N.J., shareholder, 1983—; chmn. Comml. Lines Deregulation Act 1982, 1982. Co-recipient Karen Anne Quinlan Ctr. Hope Meml. award, 1984. Mem. Profl. Ins. Agts. Assn. N.J. (sec.-treas. 1979-81), Ind. Ins. Agts. Assn. N.J. Democrat. Roman Catholic. Office: Fairview Ins Assocs Inc 25 Fairview Ave Verona NJ 07044-1341

GRAHAM, JOHN WEBB, lawyer; b. Toronto, Ont., Can., Sept. 10, 1912; s. George Wilbur and Rosaline (Webb) G.; m. Velma Melissa Taylor, June 19, 1941 (dec. Nov. 5, 1971); children: Edward Samuel Rogers (stepson), Ann Taylor; m. Natalia Nikolaevna Popowa, July 15, 1976. Student, Upper Can. Coll., 1920-30; B.A., Trinity Coll., U. Toronto, 1933, D.S. Litt., 1981; Barrister-at-law, Osgoode Hall Law Sch., Can., 1936; LLB, York U., 1991. Bar: Queen's counsel 1956. Corp. trust officer Toronto Gen. Trusts Corp., 1936-39; solicitor Daly, Thistle, Judson & McTaggart, Toronto, 1946-48; gen. counsel Imperial Life Assurance Co. Can., Toronto, 1949-58; ptnr. Payton, Biggs & Graham, Toronto, 1958-77, Cassels Brock, 1977-84; ptnr. Cassels, Brock & Blackwell, 1984-88, of counsel, 1988—; chmn. bd. Rogers Telecom. Ltd., Rogers Comm. Inc., Rogers Cable TV Ltd., Rogers Broadcasting Ltd.; vice chmn. Cantel Inc.; bd. dirs. numerous cos. including Scorfin Inc. Mem. exec. com. Trinity Coll., Toronto, 1960-71, also chmn., 1966-69; Pres. St. Paul's Progressive Conservative Assn., 1957-61. Served with Royal Canadian Armoured Corps, 1939-46, ETO. Decorated Efficiency Decoration, 1944; hon. lt. col. Gov. Gen's Horse Guards, 1970-75. Mem. Canadian Bar Assn., County of York Law Assn., Lawyers Club Toronto, Assn. Life Ins. Counsel, Canadian Tax Found., Estate Planning Coun. Toronto, Progressive Conservative Bus. Men's Club Met. Toronto (v.p. 1968-70), Sigma Chi (internat. pres. 1971-73). Mem. Conservative party. Mem. Anglican Ch. Can. Clubs: Albany, Toronto Hunt, York, Royal Canadian Mil. Inst. (Toronto hon. pres.); Empire of Can. Office: Ste 2100, 40 King St W, Toronto, ON Canada M5H 3C2

GRAHAM, KATHARINE, newspaper executive; b. N.Y.C., June 16, 1917; d. Eugene and Agnes (Ernst) Meyer; m. Philip L. Graham, June 5, 1940 (dec. 1963); children: Elizabeth Morris Graham Weymouth, Donald Edward, William Welsh, Stephen Meyer. Student, Vassar Coll., 1934-36; AB, U. Chgo., 1938. Reporter San Francisco News, 1938-39; mem. editorial staff Washington Post, 1939-45, mem. Sunday circulation and editorial depts., pub., 1969-79; pres. Washington Post Co., 1963-73, 77, chmn. bd., 1973—, chief exec. officer, 1973-91; co-chmn. Internat. Herald Tribune; bd. dirs. Reuters Founders Share Co. Ltd., Urban Inst., Fed. City Coun. Life trustee U. Chgo.; hon. trustee George Washington U. Fellow Am. Acad. Arts and Scis.; mem. Am. Soc. Newspaper Editors, Nat. Press Club, Coun. Fgn. Rels., Overseas Devel. Coun., Met. Club, Cosmopolitan Club, 1925 F Street Club. Home: 2920 R St NW Washington DC 20007-2920 Office: Washington Post Co 1150 15th St NW Washington DC 20071-0002

GRAHAM, KENNETH ROBERT, psychologist, educator; b. Phila., June 5, 1943; s. Edgar and Margit (Leafgreen) Graham; m. Michele Carolyn Monroe, Aug. 10, 1968; children: Mark Andrew, Richard Alan. BA, U. Pa., 1964; PhD, Stanford U., 1969. Lic. psychologist, Pa. Asst. prof. Muhlenberg Coll., Allentown, 1970-77, assoc. prof., 1977-84, prof., 1984—, psychology dept. head, 1984—; rsch. psychologist Unit for Exptl. Psychiatry Inst. of Pa. Hosp., Phila., 1969-70; adjunct asst. prof. U. Pa., Phila., 1969-70; cons. smoking cessation various hosps., 1985—. Author: (text) Psychological Research, 1977; contbr. over 30 articles to profl. and sci. jours. Bd. dirs., pres. Lehigh Valley Child Care, Allentown, 1979-85; advisor Pathways (Conf. of Chs.), Allentown, 1989—, N.E. Pa. Synod Luth. Ch. in Am., Wescosville, Pa., 1989—. Mem. Am. Psychol. Assn. (pres. div. psychol. hypnosis 1980-81), Am. Soc. Clin. Hypnosis (asst. editor Jour. Clin. Hypnosis 1974—), Soc. for Clin. and Exptl. Hypnosis, Kiwanis Club (pres. Allentown, 1991-92). Democrat. Office: Muhlenberg Coll Psychol Dept Allentown PA 18104

GRAHAM, SHELDON MARCELLUS, deputy comptroller; b. N.Y.C., July 22, 1954; s. Leonard and Rosie (Chapman) G. BS in Bus. Adminstrn., Drexel U., 1977; MBA Corp. Fin., Pace U., 1985. CPA, N.Y. Acct. Laventhal & Horwath, N.Y.C., 1977-79; auditor treasury div. Chem. Bank, N.Y.C., 1979-82; dep. comptr. State N.Y. Mortgage Agy., N.Y.C., 1982—. Mem. AICPA, N.Y. State Soc. CPAs. Roman Catholic. Home: 1293 Crescent Ave Roselle NJ 07203 Office: State NY Mortgage Agy 260 Madison Ave New York NY 10016

GRAINGER, NESSA, artist; b. Atlantic City, N.J., Sept. 15; d. Barnet and Pauline (Gittelman) Posner; m. Murray Grainger; children: Richard Greenbaum, Margie Friedman. BFA, Phila. Mus. Sch., 1950; postgrad., Tyler Sch. Art, Phila., 1954-55, Pa. Acad. Art, Phila., 1962-64. One-woman shows include The Interchurch Ctr., N.Y.C., 1992; exhibited in group shows at Douglas Coll. Women's Ctr., N.J., 1990. Recipient Grumbacher Gold medal Catherine Lorillard Wolfe Art Assn., 1985, Best Landscape 1986, First prize Essex Watercolor Soc., Award of merit Perkins Art Ctr., 1987, First prize for abstract watercolor Miniature Art Soc. of N.J., 1988. Mem. Nat. Assn. of Women Artists (pres. 1989-91, medal of honor 1973, Molly M. Canaday award, Kopet award), N.J. Watercolor Soc. (pres. 1982-84, 1986-88, silver medal of honor 1985, Forbes award 1985, ODS award 1987, Mitzuki Kovacs award 1988), Phila. Watercolor Club, Knickerbocker Artists, Allied Artists of Am., Audubon Artists (v.p. watermedia 1988, Koffler award 1987, silver medal 1989), Catherine Lorillard Wolf Art Soc., Am. Soc. of Contemporary Artists (Doris Kreindler award), Soc. Exptl. Artists. Home: 212 Old Turnpike Rd Califon NJ 07830

GRALISH, TOM, photographer; b. Mount Clemens, Mich. Formerly journalistic photographer Las Vegas Valley Times, then with UP; picture editor and staff photographer Phila. Inquirer, 1983—. Recipient Pulitzer Prize for Feature Photography, 1986. Office: Phila Inquirer 400 N Broad St Philadelphia PA 19130-4099*

GRALLO, RICHARD MARTIN, research psychologist; b. Winthrop, Mass., Feb. 15, 1947; s. Frederick Michael and Jennie A. (Ferrario) G.; A.B., Boston Coll., 1969; M.S. (John A. Lyons fellow), M.I.T., 1972; M.A., N.Y.U., 1976, PhD, 1988. Instr. philosophy Goddard Coll., Plainfield, Vt., 1974; teaching asst. stats. N.Y.U., 1978, research asst. Teaching Performance Center, 1977-79, evaluation specialist Inst. for Developmental Studies, 1979-80, instr. tests and measurement dept. ednl. psychology, 1979-87, research assoc. Inst. for Developmental Studies, 1980—; mem. faculty philosophy of sci. New Sch. for Social Research, N.Y.C., 1978; mem. faculty dept. edn. Coll. Human Services, N.Y.C., 1983—, dir. advanced standing program; cons. N.Y.C. Bd. Edn.; rsch. psychologist N.J. Med. Sch. Knighted Order of St. John of Jerusalem, 1986. Mem. Am. Psychol. Assn. (asso.), N.Y. Acad. Scis. (mem. psychology sect. adv. com.), Phi Delta Kappa. Contbr. articles on ednl. research to profl. jours. Home: 1257 E 7th St Plainfield NJ 07062-1907

GRAM, ANITA MARIE, psychologist; b. Temple, Tex., July 7, 1950; d. Bernard Joseph and Marjorie L. (Gray) G. B. Music Edn., U. Kans., 1973, MS in Edn., 1980; PhD, U. Tex., 1986. Lic. psychologist, Mass. Music therapist U. Iowa Psychiat. Hosp., Iowa City, 1973-78; psychology intern McLean Hosp., Belmont, Mass., 1985-86; psychologist Lindemann Ctr., Boston, 1987-88, Charles River Hosp., Wellesley, Mass., 1986—. Mem. APA, Internat. Soc. Multiple Personality & Dissociation, New Eng. Soc. Multiple Personality & Dissociation, Kappa Delta Pi, Phi Kappa Lambda. Democrat. Office: Charles River Hosp 203 Grove St Wellesley MA 02181-7498

GRAMMENOPOULOS, ANTHONY FILIOS, architect; b. Nairobi, Kenya, Sept. 8, 1948; came to U.S., 1973; s. Filios and Helen (Wideson) G. BA with honors, U. Newcastle, England, 1972; MArch, Yale U., 1977. Registered architect, N.Y. Archtl. asst. Yutaka Murata Architects, Tokyo, Japan, 1972-73; Skidmore Owings & Merrill, Washington, 1973-74, Justin Henshell Architects, N.Y.C., 1978-79; prin. architect McClintock, Grammenopoulos, Soloway Architects, N.Y.C., 1980—; visiting critic Yale U., New Haven, 1980—. Contbr. articles to profl. jours. Office: MGS Architects 611 Broadway # 528 New York NY 10012-2608

GRAMS, ARMIN EDWIN, psychologist, educator, retired; b. Chgo., Oct. 20, 1924; s. Adolf and Anna Caroline (Mueller) G.; m. Norma Mueller, Aug. 23, 1947; children: Paul, Elisabeth Louise Haxby, James Carlton, John Frederick. BS, Concordia Coll., 1945; MA, DePaul U., 1947; PhD, Northwestern U., 1952. Lic. psychologist, Vt. Tchr., prin. various elem. schs., Chgo., 1945-49; instr. dept. edn. and psychology DePaul Univ., Chgo., 1949-52, asst. prof. dept. edn. and psychology, 1952-55; assoc. prof. dept. psychology LaCrosse (Wis.) State Coll., 1955-57; assoc. prof., Inst. Child Devel. Univ. Minn., Mpls., 1957-62; prof. The Merrill Palmer Inst. of Human Devel. and Family Life, Detroit, 1962-71; prof. dept. human devel. Univ. Vt., Burlington, 1971-90, prof. emeritus, 1990—; psychologist Dyslexia Meml. Inst., Chgo., 1950-55; mem. bd. dirs. Search Inst., Mpls., 1958-86, chair, 1972-79; guest prof. Eberhard-Karls-Univ., Tubingen, Germany, 1968-69; human devel. cons. Gen. Learning Corp., Chgo., 1984—;. Author: Children and Their Parents, 1963, Facilitating Learning and Individual Development, 1966, Changes in Family Life, 1968, Sex Education: A Guide for Teachers and Parents, 2d edit., 1970; contbr. over 50 articles to profl. jours. Mem. Govs. adv. coun. Vt. Office on Aging, Waterbury, 1977-80; Vt. del. Nat. Rural Aging Strategy Conf., DesMoines, 1979; Vt. state coord. White House Conf. on Families, Washington, 1979-81. Mem. APA, Nat. Coun. in the Aging (bd. dirs. 1988-90), Assn. for Gerontology in Higher Edn. (exec. com. 1987—, pres. elect 1991—). Home: 134 Spear St S Burlington VT 05403-6146 Office: U Vt Living/Learning Ctr C-150 Burlington VT 05405-0384

GRANAI, EDWIN, state senator; b. Barre, Vt., Aug. 16, 1931; m. Joanne Dawson; 3 children. BA in Econs., Antioch Coll.; MDiv., Yale U. Ordained to ministry Presbyn. Ch.; cert. shopping ctr. mgr. Pastor Stepney (Conn.) Meth. Ch., 1956-57; office mgr. Procter & Gamble, N.Y.C. and Cin., 1957-69; owner Little Prof. Book Ctrs., Vt., 1969-76; mem. Vt. Ho. of Reps., 1974-78; gen. mgr. Univ. Mall, Finard, Vt., 1979-90; mem. Vt. State Senate, 1991—; majority whip, asst. Dem. leader Vt. Ho. of Reps., 1976-78; mem. fin. com., govt. ops. com. Vt. State Senate, 1991—; cons. v.p. Fianrd & Co., 1991—; bus. cons., 1976-79. Dem. candidate Gov., Vt., 1978; chmn. Vt. Dem. Orgn., 1981-85; trustee Antioch Coll.; active United Way, Ronald McDonald House; minister nursing homes; hospice, bereavement counselor. Mem. Am. Booksellers Assn., Rotary (past pres.), C. of C. Home: 106 Killarney Dr Burlington VT 05401 Office: VT State House Montpelier VT 05602

GRANATH, HERBERT A., television industry executive; b. N.Y.C., 1928. Grad., Fordham U., 1954. Pres. Capital Cities/ABC Video Enterprises, Inc., N.Y.C.; chmn. ESPN Cable Network; co-chmn. Arts & Entertainment Cable Network, Lifetime Cable Network. Office: Capital Cities/ABC Video Enterprises Inc 77 W 66th St New York NY 10023-6201*

GRANATIR, WILLIAM LOUIS, psychiatrist; b. Phila., Apr. 1, 1916; s. Jacon and Anna (Stein) G.; m. Mildred Silver, July 4, 1941; children: John Robert, Joseph Paul, Thomas Alan, Charles Elliot. BA, U. Pa., 1936; MD, Hahnemann Med. Coll., Phila., 1941. Diplomate Am. Bd. Psychiatry and Neurology. Intern Mt. Sinai Hosp., Phila., 1941-42; resident St. Elizabeths Hosp., Washington, 1946-48; psychiatrist St. Elizabeth's Hosp., Washington, 1946-48; dir. Washington Inst. Mental Hygiene, 1948-50; pvt. practice Washington, 1950—; supervising tng. analyst Washington Psychoanalytic Inst., 1965-78, supervising analyst, 1982—; clin. prof. George Washington U. Med. Sch., 1979—. Flight surgeon U.S. Army Air Corps, 1942-46. Fellow Am. Psychiat. Assn.; mem. Am. Psychoanalytic Assn. (life mem.), Washington Psychoanalytic Soc. (pres. 1973-75). Office: 4545 Connecticut Ave NW Washington DC 20008-6042

GRAND, RICHARD JOSEPH, pediatrics educator; b. N.Y.C., Feb. 1, 1937; s. Milton Joseph Harold and Pearl Grand; m. Myra M. Grand, Mar. 21, 1965; children: Peter, Julia, Joseph. AB magna cum laude, Harvard U., 1958, AM, 1976; MD, NYU, 1962. Diplomate Am. Bd. Pediatrics, Am. Bd. Pediatric Gastroenterology. Intern in pediatrics Bellevue Hosp., N.Y.C., 1962-63; mem. pediatrics staff Children's Hosp., Boston, 1963-64, 66-67; clin. assoc. NIH, Bethesda, Md., 1964-66; rsch. fellow Children's Hosp., Mass. Gen. Hosp., MIT, 1967-70; from asst. to assoc. prof. pediatrics Harvard U. Med. Sch., Boston, 1970-83; chief gastroenterology Children's Hosp., Boston, 1976-83; prof. pediatrics Tufts U., Boston, 1983—, assoc. dir. Digestive Disease Ctr., 1984—; chief pediatric gastroenterology and nutrition New Eng. Med. Ctr. and Tufts U., Boston, 1983—; mem. sci. adv. bd., rsch. devel. com. Crohn's and Colitis Fedn. Am., N.Y.C., 1985—. Editor: Pediatric Nutrition: Theory and Practice, 1987. Mem. com. on nutrition Mass. Med. Soc., Waltham, 1984—. Sr. asst. surgeon USPHS, 1964-66. Mem. Am. Gastroent. Assn., Am. Assn. for the Study of Liver Disease, N.Am. Soc. for Pediatric Gastroenterology (pres. 1988-90), Am. Pediatric Soc., Am. Soc. for Clin. Nutrition, Am. Inst. Nutrition, Am. Liver Found. (bd. dirs. 1980-90). Office: New Eng Med Ctr Box 213 750 Washington St Boston MA 02111-1854

GRANDE, JOSEPH ANTHONY, college administrator, educator; b. Malden, Mass., Sept. 4, 1932; s. Genuino J. and Ida (Tricca) G.; m. Marguerite Rose Edwards, July 12, 1985. BS summa cum laude, Buffalo State Tchrs. Coll., 1953; MA, U. Buffalo, 1955; PhD, U. Notre Dame, 1971. Tchr. D'Youville Coll., Buffalo, 1958-75, 81-86, div. chair, 1975-81, asst. v.p. acad. affairs, 1986-90, v.p. acad. affairs, 1990—. Co-author: Second Looks: Pictorial History of Buffalo and Erie County, 1987; author booklet and articles. Chmn. Erie County Preservation Bd., 1989—; historian Village of Kenmore, N.Y., 1981-85. Recipient Outstanding Achievement award in edn. Nat. Columbus Com., Buffalo, 1985. Mem. Buffalo and Erie County Hist. Soc. (chmn. adv. bd. 1980—, Owen Augsburger award 1980), Buffalo Coun. on World Affairs (dir., pres. 1969-71), Tonawanda-Kenmore Hist. Soc. (pres. 1975-78), Amherst Colony Mus., Western N.Y. Higher Edn. Consortium of Vice Presidents, Buffalo Yacht Club. Office: D'Youville Coll 320 Porter Ave Buffalo NY 14201-1084

GRANDGENT, CHARLES MALCOLM, software engineer; b. Amityville, N.Y., Feb. 23, 1953; s. Roland and Dorothy (MacKersie) G.; m. Carol Marie Haynes, June 28, 1985; children: Thomas, Suzanne. AS in Elec. Engring., NW Conn. Community Coll., 1976; cert. computer systems specialist, Air U., 1976. Programmer Patterson Oil Co., Winsted, Conn., 1974-77; contract programmer Data Power, Inc., Terryville, Conn., 1977-78; systems programmer Talley Industries, Thomaston, Conn., Norcross, Ga., 1978-79; sr. systems programmer Honeywell, Waltham, Mass., 1979-81; mgr. applications software NEC Info. Systems, Acton, Mass., 1981-85; sr. mem. tech. staff Gould-Modicon, North Andover, Mass., 1985-89; mgr. system software PictureTel Corp., Peabody, Mass., 1989—. Contbr. article to profl. jours. Mem. Am. Radio Relay League, Rosicrucian Order, Traditional Martinist Order. Democrat. Home: 50 Westvale Dr Concord MA 01742-2935 Office: PictureTel Corp One Corporation Way Peabody MA 01960

GRANDON, RAYMOND CHARLES, physician; b. Carlisle, Pa., Nov. 27, 1919; s. Frank Leonard and Teresa (Libonat) G.; m. Doris May New, June 8, 1945; children: Raymond, S. Suzanne, David. BS, Dickinson Coll., 1942; MD, Jefferson Med. Coll., 1945. Intern St. Lukes Hosp., Bethlehem, Pa., 1945-46; resident internal medicine Harrisburg (Pa.) Hosp., 1948-50; dir. Hahneman Affiliate Faculty, Harrisburg, 1958-64; assoc. prof. div. medicine Hahneman affiliate faculty Harrisburg Hosp., 1958-64; preceptor Physician Asst. program Hahneman Med. Coll. Physician's, 1975-76; clin. asst., prof. medicine Pa. State U. Milton S. Hershey Med. Ctr., 1979-80, clin. assoc. prof. medicine, 1980-89; mem. Corp. Pa. Blue Shield, 1975-92, Bd. Health Rsch. Inst. Pa., 1971-83, Bd. Health Corp. Pa. Skilled Nursing Home, 1970. Contbr. articles to Jour. AMA. Mem. Govnrs. Commn. Alcoholism, Pa., 1954-56; clinician Alcohol Counseling Ctr., Pa. Dept. Health, 1954-59. Recipient Founders award, Pa. Med. Soc. Auxiliary, 1984, Seilbert Meml. award, Harrisburg Acad. Medicine, 1957. Mem. ACP (life), AMA (del. 1972—), Am. Soc. Internal Medicine (trustee 1983-86, mem., pres. socio-econ. rsch. edn. found. 1985-86), Pa. Med. Soc. (pres. 1981-82), Pa. Soc. Internal Medicine (pres. 1974-76), Dauphin County Med. Soc., Med. Bur. Harrisburg (pres. 1971-76), Jefferson Med. Coll. Alumni Assn. (exec. com. 1960-85), Am. Heart Assn. (coun. clin. cardiology 1945—), Am. Diabetes Assn., N.Y. Acad. Scis., World Med. Assn., Assn. Life Ins. Med. Dirs. Am., Forum for Med. Affairs (pres. 1991), Pa. State Bd. Med. Edn. and Licensure, Phi Kappa Sigma, Phi Chi. Office: 131 State St Harrisburg PA 17101-1087

GRANET, IRVING, mechanical engineering educator, consultant; b. Bklyn., July 2, 1924; s. Samuel and Ida Granet; m. Arlene Janet Wertheim, June 23, 1951; children: Ellen Jill, Kenneth Mark, David Bruce. B Mech. Engring., Cooper Union, 1944; MME, Poly. U., N.Y.C., 1948; grad., Oak Ridge Sch. Reactor Tech., 1956. Registered profl. engr., N.Y. Engr. Lloyd Rogers & Co., N.Y.C., 1944-45; engr., dir. nuclear engring. Foster Wheeler Corp., N.Y.C., 1947-59; project engr. Republic Aviation Corp., Farmingdale, N.Y., 1959-73; v.p., chief engr. EMS Devel. Corp., Farmingdale, 1973-76; assoc. prof. N.Y. Inst. Tech., Old Westbury, 1976-77; prof. mech. engring. Queensborough Community Coll., CUNY, Bayside, 1977—; cons. Fairchild Republic Corp., Farmingdale, 1980-88. Author: Elementary Applied Thermodynamics, 1965, Fluid Mechanics for Engineering Technology, 1971, Strength of Materials for Engineering Technology, 1973, Thermodynamics and Heat Power, 1974, Modern Materials Science, 1980, Statics and Strength of Materials, 1982, Technical Mechanics, 1983, Termodinamica (Spanish edit.), 1988; also over 60 articles. With USAAF, 1945-47. Mem. ASME (life). Office: Queensborough Community Coll 56th Ave & Springfield Blvd Bayside NY 11364

GRANGER, ROBERT ALAN, mechanical and aerospace engineering educator, consultant; b. Evanston, Ill., Aug. 7, 1928; s. Robert Alan and Kathleen (Buehr) G.; m. Ruth Nickerson, Oct. 17, 1951; children—Eric Carl, Erin Allyson. B.A., Pomona Coll., 1955; M.S. Drexel Inst. Tech., 1959; Ph.D., U. Md., 1970. Sr. research scientist Martin Co., Balt., 1955-60; prin. engr. Boeing Co., Renton, Wash., 1975; prof. mechanical and aerospace engring. U.S. Naval Academy, Annapolis, Md., 1960—, discipline dir., 1972-75; cons. NASA, Boeing Co.; vis. prof. U. Petroleum and Minerals, Saudi Arabia, 1977-79, U. Zurich, Switzerland, 1978, Yale U., 1989; dir. Vortex Dynamics Symposium von Karman Inst., Brussels, Belgium; dir., prin. lectr. Introduction to Wing Flutter Symposium, 1991. Author: Fluid Mechanics, 1985, Unified Method of Aeroelasticity, 1986, Experiments in Fluid Mechanics, 1986, Design of Spacecraft, 1988, Introduction to the Flutter of Winged Aircraft, 1992. Contbr. over 400 articles to profl. jours. Served with U.S. Army, 1950-52, Korea. Ford Found. fellow, 1965. Hon. mem. Inst. Modern Physics (Athens, Greece); mem. AIAA, Kappa Mu Epsilon, Alpha Gamma Sigma. Republican. Avocations: Composing; mountain climbing; writing; tennis; swimming. Home: 950 Mastline Dr Annapolis MD 21401-6860 Office: US Naval Acad Mech Engring Dept Annapolis MD 21402

GRANICK, LOIS WAYNE, association administrator; b. Weatherford, Okla., Mar. 5, 1932; d. Johnny Wayne and Lois Bernice (Wells) Cox; m. Robert Eugene Granick, June 6, 1951; children—Bruce, Leslie Granick Knipling, Jeffrey, Andrea. Student, U. N.Mex., 1949-51. Programmer, systems analyst Documentation, Inc., Bethesda, Md., 1961-66; cons. Mexican Govt., Mexico City, 1966-69; info. specialist Autocomp, Inc., Bethesda, 1970-72; dir. Autocode div. of Autocomp, Inc., Bethesda, 1972-73; exec. editor Psychol. Abstracts APA, Washington, 1974-90; dir., PsycINFO APA, 1977-90, spl. advisor, 1990-92. Mem. Am. Soc. Info. Sci., Nat. Fedn. Abstracting and Info. Svcs. (bd. dirs. 1977-82, pres. 1980-81), Nat. Info. Standards Orgn. (bd. dirs. 1991-92), Info. Sci. Abstracts (bd. dirs. 1978-79), Info. Industry Assn. (bd. dirs. 1982-89, chmn. 1988), Assn. Info. and Dissemination Ctrs., Internat. Coun. Sci. and Tech. Info. (gen. sec. 1986-89). Home: 5414 Center St Bethesda MD 20815-7101 Office: APA 100 N Carolina Ave SE Washington DC 20003-1841

GRANIERI, GEORGE JOHN, marketing executive; b. Newark, Sept. 7, 1939; s. Sam and Mary (Marone) G.; m. Elizabeth M. Czyzewski, July 20, 1963; children: Mark, Lynn. BSEE, N.J. Inst. Tech., 1961. Engr. GE, Valley Forge, Pa., 1961-62, I.T.T. Fed. Labs., Nutley, N.J., 1962-63, Lockheed Electronics, Plainfield, N.J., 1963-65, Am. Standard, Piscataway, N.J., 1965-68, 70-71; engr. MICT RCA Solid State, Somerville, N.J., 1968-75, 77-80; with mktg. Harris Semiconductor, Melbourne, Fla., 1980-81; v.p. mktg. Siemens Components, Iselin, N.J., 1981-88; v.p. mktg. integrated cir. systems dept. Std. Micro Systems, Long Island, 1989-91, AT&T Microelectronics, Reading, Pa., 1989-91; with Integrated Circuit Systems, Inc., Valley

Forge, 1991—. Contbr. numerous articles to profl. jours.; patentee. Home: 14 Howell Ave Piscataway NJ 08854

GRANOFF, GARY CHARLES, lawyer, investment company executive; b. N.Y.C., Feb. 2, 1948; s. N. Henry and Jeannette (Trum) G.; m. Leslie Barbara Resnick, Dec. 21, 1969; children: Stephen, Robert, Joshua. BBA in Acctg., George Washington U., 1970, JD with honors, 1973. Bar: N.Y., 1974, Fla., 1974, U.S. Dist. Ct. (so. dist.) N.Y., 1976. Assoc. Dreyer & Traub, N.Y.C., 1973-75; ptnr. Ezon, Langberg & Granoff, N.Y.C., 1975-78, Granoff & Walker, N.Y.C., 1982—; pvt. practice N.Y.C., 1978-81; pres., also bd. dirs. Elk Assocs. Funding Corp., N.Y.C., 1979—, GCG Assocs., Inc., N.Y.C., 1982—; atty. del. to U.S.-China Joint Session on Trade, Investment and Econ. Law, Beijing, 1987. Campaign vol. Mondale for Pres., N.Y.C., 1984; fundraiser Robert Garcia for Congress, N.Y.C., Dem. Senatorial Campaign Com., N.Y.C., 1987-88; active N.Y. Lawyers for Dukakis com., 1988; chmn. N.Y.C. chpt. George Washington U. Nat. Law Ctr. Leadership Gifts Com. With USAR, 1969-75. Mem. N.Y. State Bar Assn., Fla. Bar Assn., Assn. Bar City N.Y., People-to-People Internat., George Washington U. Alumni Assn. (chmn. N.Y.C. chpt.), North Shore Country Club. Club: North Shore Country. Office: Granoff & Walker 600 3d Ave Ste 3810 New York NY 10016

GRANOVETTER, MARK, sociology educator; b. Jersey City, Oct. 20, 1943; s. Sidney and Violet (Greenblatt) G.; m. Ellen Susan Greenebaum, June 14, 1970; 1 child, Sara. AB, Princeton (N.J.) U., 1965; MA, Harvard U., 1967, PhD, 1970. Asst. prof. Johns Hopkins U., Balt., 1970-73; from asst. to assoc. prof. Harvard U., Cambridge, Mass., 1973-77; from assoc. prof. to prof. SUNY, Stony Brook, 1977—. Author: Getting A Job, 1974; series editor Cambridge U. Press, 1986—; contbr. articles to profl. jours. Ctr. for Advanced Study fellow, 1977, J.S. Guggenheim Found. fellow, 1981. Office: SUNY Dept of Sociology Stony Brook NY 11794-4356

GRANSTON, DAVID WILFRED, publishing company executive; b. Schenectady, N.Y., Dec. 5, 1939; s. Arnold Andrew and Edna (Nickerson) G.; BA, Colgate U., 1958; MBA, Syracuse U., 1960; m. Priscilla Day, June 10, 1961; 1 child, David Wilfred. Supr. E.I. DuPont De Nemours & Co., Inc., Parlin, N.J., 1961-62; sr. fin. analyst Bendix Corp., N.Y.C., 1963-69; controller Allied Chem. Corp., N.Y.C., 1969-71; v.p. finance Thomas Borthwick Sons, Ltd., N.Y.C., 1972-78; v.p., chief fin. officer N.Y. Times Syndication Sales Corp., N.Y.C., 1978-82; chief fin. officer, assoc. dir. Consumers Union, Mt. Vernon, N.Y., 1983—. Served with USCGR, 1960. Colgate U. War Meml. scholar, 1954-58. Mem. Colgate U. Alumni Club (L.I.) (pres. 1975-76), L.I. Wydanch Club, Creek Club (Locust Valley, N.Y.) (bd. govs. treas., house com.), Northport (Maine) Yacht Club (vice commodore), Windham (N.Y.) Mountain Club, L.I. Club, Creek Club (bd. govs., treas., house com.). Home: PO Box 368 Piping Rock Rd Locust Valley NY 11560 Office: Consumers Union Corp 101 Truman Ave Yonkers NY 10703-1057

GRANT, CAROL SAWYER, nonprofit trust executive; b. Worcester, Mass., Mar. 22, 1962; d. Joseph Francis and Barbara Ann (Hosey) Sawyer; m. Alexander Galt Grant, June 23, 1990. BA, Trinity Coll., Hartford, Conn., 1984; EdM, Harvard U., 1990. Asst. dir. John F. Kennedy Sch. Govt., Harvard U., Cambridge, Mass., 1987-89; dir. communications Trust for Pub. Land, Boston, 1991—. Mem. Women in Devel. Greater Boston, Harvard Club N.Y. Democrat. Home: 36 Pleasant St Dover MA 02030-2049

GRANT, CONRAD JOSEPH, physicist; b. Corpus Christi, Tex., Apr. 2, 1956; s. Conrad Joseph and Deirdre Patricia (Tierney) G.; m. Monica Lane Vekeman, June 17, 1978; children: Michael, Stephen, Brendan, Matthew. BS in Physics, U. Md., 1978; MS in Applied Physics, Johns Hopkins U., 1982, MS in Computer Sci., 1984. Physicist Applied Physics Lab., Johns Hopkins U., Laurel, Md., 1978—, sect. supr., 1984-87; asst. group supr. Applied Physics Lab., Johns Hopkins U., Laurel, 1987—. Contbr. articles to profl. jours. Pres. Mt. Airy Area Jaycees, 1987; CPR instr. Am. Heart Assn., Frederick, Md., 1981-89; coun. mem. St. Michael's Church, Poplar Springs, Md., 1990—. Mem. Assn. Naval Engrs., U.S. Naval Inst., Navy League of the U.S. Republican. Roman Catholic. Home: 6854 Runkles Rd Mount Airy MD 21771-7320 Office: Johns Hopkins U Applied Physics Lab Laurel MD 20723-6099

GRANT, EDWARD, employment services executive; b. Bklyn., Apr. 10, 1936; s. David and Deborah (Jablow) G.; m. Helene Clarke, Mar. 12, 1961; children: Robin, Fran, Andrew. BBA in Mktg., Hofstra U., 1958. Pres., founder Career Employment Svcs., Inc., Westbury, N.Y., 1960-91; exec. v.p. Career Horizons, Inc., Stamford, Conn., 1991—; 1060—. Contbr. articles to bus. jours. Bd. trustees Temple Emanu-el, East Meadow, 1980—; mem. L.I. Com. for Soviet Jewry, Carle Place, N.Y., 1983—; chmn. Nassau Community Coll. Adv. Coun., Garden City, N.Y., 1983—, bd. dirs. Nassau Community Coll. Found., 1988—; program chmn. Dist. Citizen award dinner Nassau County coun. Boy Scouts Am., 1985; bd. dirs. L.I. March of Dimes, 1989—; mem. corp. devel. com. Hofstra U., 1989—. With USAFR, 1958-64. Recipient Svc. award, L.I. Employment Agy. Coun., 1977, Ohio Assn. of Pers. Cons., 1980, Outstanding Contbn. award, N.J. Assn. of Pers. Cons., 1982. Mem. Nat. Assn. Pers. Cons. (mem. Speakers Bur. 1977—, bd. dirs. 1968—), Assn. of Pers. Cons. (N.Y. bd. dirs. 1968—, Svc. award 1983), Nat. Assn. of Temporary Svcs., Cert. Pers. Cons. Soc., Hofstra U. Alumni Assn., L.I. Assn., East Meadow C. of C., Am. Diabetes Assn. L.I. Home: Crescent So 260 Fox Hunt Oyster Bay Cove NY 11791 Office: Career Employment Svcs Inc 1600 Stewart Ave Westbury NY 11590-6611

GRANT, FREDERICK ANTHONY, investment banker; b. Jacksonville, Ill., Sept. 4, 1949; s. Irwin Herbert and Emma Eleanor (Voelker) G.; m. Patricia Johns (div. Dec. 1982); 1 child, Frederick Peter. BA, Ariz. State U., 1972; MBA, U. Chgo., 1975. Assoc. Bacon, Whipple & Co., Chgo., 1976-80; v.p. Security Pacific Capital Markets, N.Y.C., 1980-84, Shearson Lehman Bros., N.Y.C., 1984-86; sr. v.p. C.J. Lawrence, Morgan Grenfell, N.Y.C., 1986-89; pres., chief exec. officer KSG Internat., N.Y.C., 1989-92; pres. CEO TLC Capital Ptnrs., Inc., N.Y.C., 1992—; guest lectr. Columbia U., N.Y.C., 1985-86. Bd. dirs. alumni bd. U. Chgo., 1987—. Mem. UN Assn. (econ. policy coun. 1989), Korean Econ. Inst. Am. (adv. coun. 1990—), Chgo. Club, Racquet and Tennis Club (N.Y.C.).

GRANT, GERALD, sociology and education educator; b. Syracuse, N.Y., Feb. 3, 1938; s. G. Edward and Ruth Almira (Smith) G.; m. Judith Hawley Dunn, July 22, 1961; children: Katharine Grant Rooney, Sarah Ruth, Robert Ashton. B Social Studies, John Carroll U., 1959; MS, Columbia U., 1960; EdD, Harvard U., 1972. Edn. editor Washington Post, 1961-67; teaching fellow Harvard U., Cambridge, Mass., 1968-72; prof. sociology and edn. Syracuse (N.Y.) U., 1972—; mem. com. on edn. issues Nat. Assn. Ind. Schs., Boston, 1981-87. Co-author: The Perpetual Dream, 1978, On Competence, 1979; author: The World We Created at Hamilton High, 1988; editor Rev. Rsch. in Edn., 1991-92. Co-founder Wescott East Neighborhood Assn., Syracuse; vol. cook Unity Kitchens, Syracuse; co-chmn. Onondaga Citizens League for Study Edn.; co-pres. Levy Mid. Sch. Parent-Tchr.-Student Orgn. With USMC, 1960-61. Nieman fellow Harvard U., 1967-68, Spencer fellow Nat. Acad. Edn., 1974-79; fellow Ctr. for Advanced Study in Behavioral Scis., Stanford, Calif., 1988-89. Mem. Am. Sociol. Assn., Am. Ednl. Rsch. Assn. Roman Catholic. Office: Syracuse U 257 Huntington Hall Syracuse NY 13244-2340

GRANT, IAN STANLEY, engineering company executive; b. Auckland, New Zealand, Apr. 1, 1940; came to U.S., 1969; s. Edmund William and Tui (Hadfield) G.; m. Josephine Anne McHardy, Apr. 23, 1962 (div. June 1972); children: Megan Anne, Philippa Jane; m. Joan McCabe, Apr. 28, 1973. BEng, U. New Zealand, 1962; MEng, U. New South Wales, Sydney, Australia, 1968. Engr. Electricity Commn. New South Wales, Sydney, 1962-69, GE, Pittsfield, Mass., 1969-72; with Power Techs. Inc., Schenectady, N.Y., 1972—, dept. mgr., 1986—, v.p., 1989—. Contbr. articles to profl. jours. Fellow IEEE; mem. Conf. Internat. des Grandes Reseaux Electriques (convenor 1986—), Mohawk Golf Club. Republican. Episcopalian. Home: 1163 Avon Rd Schenectady NY 12308-2405 Office: Power Techs Inc 1482 Erie Blvd Schenectady NY 12305-1000

GRANT, MICHAEL KEVIN, medical diagnostic computer firm executive; b. Passaic, N.J., Feb. 16, 1961; s. Richard Thomas and Judith Lenore (Blanda) G.; m. Virginia Mary Holman, Sept. 1, 1984; 1 child, Jennifer Lynne. BA in Psychology, Marquette U., 1983; MBA in Mktg. and Sales Mgmt., Nova U., 1986. Mgr. bus. and trade shows IBM Corp., Boca Raton, Fla., 1983-85, bus. planner PC-based systems, 1985-86; systems engr. IBM Corp., West Orange, N.J., 1987-89; product mktg. mgr. The Ultimate Corp., East Hanover, N.J., 1989-90, dir. N.Am. sales support, 1990-91, dir. mktg. and bus. devel., 1991; v.p. mktg. Computer Support of N.Am., Basking Ridge, N.J., 1991—; founder, pres. Clin. Diagnostyx Corp., West Milford, N.J., 1991—. Campaign coord. IBM Corp./United Way, 1983-89. Mem. Am. Mgmt. Assn. Republican. Roman Catholic. Office: Clin Diagnostyx Corp PO Box 8 Mountain Lakes NJ 07046

GRANT, ROBERT BRUCE, history educator; b. N.Y.C., Oct. 3, 1933; s. Albert L. and Rose Dorothy (Livingston) G.; m. Frances Dancygier, Sept. 6, 1953; children: Ruth, Paul. BA, NYU, 1955; MA, Columbia U., 1957, EdD, 1970. Tchr. New Rochelle (N.Y.) High Sch., 1957-60, Roslyn (N.Y.) High sch., 1960-67; asst. prof. Tchrs. Coll., Columbia U., N.Y.C., 1969-71; MAT dir. Trinity Coll., Washington, 1971-72; assoc. prof. to prof. Framingham (Mass.) State Coll., 1972-79, assoc. dean, 1979-80, v.p. acad. affairs, 1980-84, prof. history and edn., 1984—. Author: The Black Man Comes to the City, 1972, Surveying the Land, 1991. Trustee Danforth Mus. Art, Framingham, Mass., 1982-87; mem. adv. bd. Performing Arts Ctr. of Greater Framingham, 1983-84. Coe fellow, 1966, NDEA fellow, 1967-69. Mem. Mass. Tchrs. Assn., Orgn. Am. Historians, Nat. Coun. for Social Studies. Office: Edn Dept 100 State St Framingham MA 01701-2471

GRANT, ROBERT JAMES, animal nutritional research manager; b. Ogallala, Nebr., Nov. 24, 1937; s. Joseph Michael and Florence Maude (Caudy) G.; m. Patricia Louise Davidson, Dec. 29, 1962; 1 child, Shawna Lee. BS in Animal Prodn., Colo. State U., 1960; MS in Animal Sci., Cornell U., 1970, PhD in Animal Nutrition, 1973. Rancher and farmer pvt. practice, Crook, Colo., 1960-68; group mgr. nutritional rsch. Hoechst-Roussel Agri-Vet Co., Somerville, N.J., 1973—. Contbr. articles to profl. jours. Mem. Nat. Spinal Cord Soc., Fergus Falls, Mont., 1983—. Recipient Ford Found. Grad. Student Exchange award U. Philippines, Coll. Agr., Los Baños, Philippines, 1970-72; 1st and 2nd pl. trophies, Nat. Livestock Judging Contest, 1960. Mem. Am. Soc. Animal Sci., N.Y. Acad. Scis., Poultry Sci. Assn., Am. Registry Profl. Animal Scientists, Animal Health Orgn. (com. mem. 1974—), U.S. English, Statue of Liberty-Ellis Island Found. Office: Hoechst-Roussel Agri-Vet Co Rt 202-206 Somerville NJ 08876

GRANT, STEPHEN ALLEN, lawyer; b. N.Y.C., Nov. 4, 1938; s. Benton H. and Irene A. Grant; m. Anne. K. Bagley, Feb. 11, 1961 (div. Nov. 1975); children: Stephen, Katharine, Michael; m. Anne-Marie Laignel, Dec. 8, 1975; children: Natalie, Elizabeth, Alexandra. AB, Yale U., 1960; LLB, Columbia U., 1965. Bar: N.Y. 1965, U.S. Supreme Ct. 1969. Law clk. to judge U.S. Ct. Appeals (2d cir.), N.Y.C., 1965-66; assoc. Sullivan & Cromwell, N.Y.C., 1966-73, ptnr., 1973—. Mem. Japan-U.S. Friendship Commn., U.S.-Japan Conf. on Cultural and Ednl. Interchange. Lt. (j.g.) USNR, 1960-62. Mem. ABA, N.Y. State Bar Assn., Assn. of Bar of City of N.Y., Coun. Fgn. Rels. Clubs: Down Town, Links. Home: 1021 Park Ave New York NY 10028-0959 Office: Sullivan & Cromwell 125 Broad St New York NY 10004-2400

GRANT, SUSAN IRENE, lawyer; b. N.Y.C., Apr. 27, 1953; d. Walter Arnold and Beatrice L. (Thalheimer) G.; m. Brian A. King, June 24, 1990. BA, NYU, 1974; JD, Columbia U., 1977. Bar: N.Y. 1978, U.S. Dist. Ct. (ea. dist.) N.Y. 1978. Assoc. Law Offices of Rita Eredics, Esq., Flushing, N.Y., 1977-78; staff atty. The Dreyfus Corp., N.Y.C., 1978-85; asst. gen. counsel Prudential-Bache Securities Inc., N.Y.C., 1985-89, asst. v.p., 1986-89; asst. gen. counsel, assoc. v.p. Prudential Mut. Fund Mgmt., Inc., N.Y.C., 1987-89; asst. counsel First Investors Corp., N.Y.C., 1989—. Mem. ABA, N.Y. State Bar Assn., Am. Corp. Counsel Assn. Home: 301 E 78th St New York NY 10021-1322 Office: First Investors Corp 95 Wall St New York NY 10005-4201

GRANT, WILLIAM PACKER, JR., banker; b. Orange, N.J., July 18, 1942; s. William Packer and Ruth Katherine (Dwyer) G.; m. Maureen Ann Mele; May 20, 1972; children: William Packer III, Michael Charles. Student, U. Pa., 1960-63. Adminstrv. asst. fiscal svcs. Fed. Res. Bank N.Y., N.Y.C., 1972-76, spl. asst. fiscal services, 1976-85, chief safekeeping div., 1985-86, chief automated payments div., 1986-87, spl. asst. electronic payments, 1987—; pres. WPG Enterprises, 1990—. Editor newsletter Update, 1987-90. Mem. Comdr.'s Club DAV, Washington, 1983—, Am. Space Frontier Com., Washington, 1984-88, Ams. for the High Frontier, 1988—, Rep. Nat. Com., Washington, 1981—; commr. Little Falls Youth Wrestling, 1988-90; co-founder, dir. Hornets Wrestling Club, 1990. With U.S. Army, 1964-66. Recipient Spl. Commendation in connection with internat. direct deposit program Social Security Adminstrn. Mem. Am. Security Coun., Internat. Platform Assn., Little Falls Athletic Club, Deer Lake Club, Phi Sigma Kappa. Republican. Roman Catholic. Home: 159G Main St Little Falls NJ 07424-1440 Office: Fed Res Bank NY 33 Liberty St New York NY 10005-1011

GRANVILLE, CHARLES STRECKER, data processing executive; b. Cin., Aug. 9, 1951; s. Arthur and Joan (Strecker) G.; m. Regina Catherine Carroll, Aug. 3, 1974; children: Melanie Carroll, Colin Joseph. BSBA, Babson Coll., Wellesley, Mass., 1973; MBA, Babson Coll., 1976. Cert. data processing profl., system profl. Mktg. product mgr. Burroughs, Lexington, Mass., 1976-77; software mgr. Tech. Mgmt., Inc., Lexington, 1977-80; MIS dir. Orgn. for Indsl. Research, Waltham, 1980-85; dir. sales/mktg. Orgn. for Indsl. Research, 1985; pres. Reach Intelligence Sys., Amesbury, Mass., 1985; co-founder, chief exec. officer, pres. CimTelligence Corp., Lexington, Mass., 1985—; lectr. in field. Contbr. articles to profl. jours. Mem. Soc. Mfg. Engrs. (sr. mem.), Bos-Ten CEO Network, Beta Gamma. Home: 13 Bartkus Farm Concord MA 01742-5218 Office: CimTelligence Corp One Forbes Rd Lexington MA 02173

GRAPIN, JACQUELINE G., newspaper writer; b. Paris, Dec. 15, 1942; came to U.S., 1985; d. Jean and Raymonde (Ledru) G.; m. Michel Le Goc, June 4, 1971; children: Claire, Julien. Degree, Institut d'Etudes Politiques, Paris, 1966; Degree in Law, U. Paris, 1967; Auditeur, Inst. des Hautes Etudes de Def. Nat., Paris, 1980. Staff writer LeMonde, Paris, 1967-81; dir.-gen. Interevia Pub. Group, Geneva, 1982-86; pres. The European Inst., Washington, 1986—; econ. cor. Le Figaro, Washington, 1987; prof. Inst. d'Etudes Politiques, Paris, 1974-77. Author: La Guerre Civile Mondiale, 1977, Radioscopie des Etats-Unis, 1980, Fortress America, 1984, Pacific America, 1987; assoc. editor World Paper, Boston, 1980—; contbr. articles to profl. jours. Trustee Aspen Inst. for Humanistic Studies, N.Y.C., 1981—. Recipient Prix Vauban Inst. des Hautes-Etudes, Paris, 1977. Mem. Internat. Inst. Strategic Studies London. Club: Nat. Press, Kenwood Golf (Washington); Polo (Paris). Home: 85 Rt de Villette, 1231 Geneva Switzerland Office: The European Inst 4745 Massachusetts Ave NW Washington DC 20016-2345

GRASS, ALEXANDER, retail company executive; b. Scranton, Pa., Aug. 3, 1927; s. Louis and Rose (Breman) G.; m. Lois Lehrman, July 30, 1950; children: Linda Jane, Martin L., Roger L., Elizabeth Ann; m. Louise B. Gurkoff, Apr. 26, 1974. LLB, U. Fla., 1949. Bar: Fla. 1949, Pa. 1953. Pvt. practice Miami Beach, Fla., 1949-51; v.p. Rite Aid Corp., Shiremanstown, Pa., 1952-66; pres. Rite Aid Corp., 1966-69, 77-89, chmn., chief exec. officer, 1969—; chmn. Super Rite Foods, Inc., 1983—; bd. dirs. Hasbro Industries. Mem. nat. exec. com. United Jewish Appeal, 1968-79, nat. vice chmn., 1970-79, gen. chmn., 1984-86, chmn. bd. trustees, 1986-88; pres. Harrisburg (Pa.) Jewish Fedn., 1970-72; chmn. Israel Edn. Fund, 1975-78; bd. dirs. Pa. Right to Work Found., 1972-74, Harrisburg Hosp., 1977-81; vice chmn. Harrisburg Hosp., 1988—; mem. Pa. Coun. Arts, 1982; bd. dirs. Keystone State Games, 1982—, Israel Ctr. Social and Econ. Studies, 1983; trustee Jerusalem Inst. Mgmt., 1983; mem. exec. com. Jewish Agy. for Israel, 1984-88, bd. govs. 1984-90; treas. United Israel Appeal, 1986-90; exec. com. Am. Jewish joint dist. com., 1986—. With USNR, 1945-46. Recipient Disting. Alumnus award U. Fla., 1992. Mem. Nat. Am. Wholesale Grocers Assn. (bd. dirs. 1971-73), Nat. Assn. Chain Drug Stores (bd. dirs. 1972—, chmn. 1985-86). Jewish (dir. temple). Home: 4025 Crooked Hill Rd Harrisburg PA 17110-9458 Office: Rite Aid Corp PO Box 3165 Harrisburg PA 17105-3165

GRASS, MARTIN LEHRMAN, business executive; b. Harrisburg, Pa., Feb. 17, 1954; s. Alex and Lois (Lehrman) G.; m. Jody Harrison, Mar. 24, 1959; children: Leila Rose, Sharla Harrison. BA, U. Pa., 1976; MBA, Cornell U., 1978. V.p. real estate Rite Aid Corp., Shiremanstown, Pa., 1978-81, v.p. corp. planning and devel., 1981-84, sr. v.p. corp. planning and devel., 1984-87, exec. v.p., 1987-89, pres., chief oper. officer, 1989—, also bd. dirs.; vice chmn. super Rite Foods Inc. Office: Rite Aid Corp PO Box 3165 Harrisburg PA 17105*

GRASSI, JOSEPH F., lawyer; b. N.Y.C., Dec. 6, 1949. BA, Queens Coll., 1970; JD, NYU, 1974. Bar: N.Y. 1974. Assoc. Milbank, Tweed, Hadley & McCloy, N.Y.C., 1976-79; asst. corp. counsel Corp. Counsel of N.Y.C., 1979-83; pvt. practice N.Y.C., 1983-89; ptnr. McDonough Marcus Cohn & Tretter, P.C., N.Y.C., 1989—. Mem. ABA, N.Y. County Lawyers' Assn. Home: 7002 Boulevard E Guttenberg NJ 07093-4929 Office: McDonough Marcus Cohn & Tretter PC 600 3d Ave New York NY 10016-1901

GRASSI, LOUIS C., accountant; b. Bklyn., Sept. 25, 1955; s. Salvatore R. and Lena (Cestone) G.; m. Kathy Siciliano, July 3, 1982; 1 child, Alessandra. BBA, Queens Coll., 1977. C.P.A., N.Y. Staff acct. Pustorino, Puglisi & Co., N.Y.C., 1977-79; sr. acct. Peat Marwick Mitchell & Co., N.Y.C., 1979-81; mng. ptnr. Castellano, Grassi & Co., Westbury, N.Y., 1981-87; pres., chief exec. officer Biscotti, Grassi & Co., Valley Stream, N.Y., 1987—; vice chmn. bd. EAC, Inc., Mineola, N.Y., 1987—. Editor Jour. of Constn. Acctg. and Taxation. Mem. N.Y. State Soc. CPAs (exec. bd., dir. blood dr. 1989), Constn. Fin. Mgmt. Assn. (bd. dirs. 1989—), Profl. Liability Commn. (chmn. 1990—), Associated Acctg. Firms Internat. (exec. bd. 1988—), North Hills County Club, Strathmore Vandervilt Country Club (pres.). Republican. Roman Catholic. Office: Biscotti Grassi & Co 76 S Central Ave Valley Stream NY 11580-5405

GRASSO, RICHARD A., stock exchange executive. BS in Acctg., Pace U.; postgrad. cert. advanced mgmt., Harvard U., 1985. Mem. staff N.Y. Stock Exch., 1968-73, dir. listing and mktg., 1973-77, v.p. corp. svcs., 1977-81, sr. v.p. corp. svcs., 1981-83, exec. v.p. mktg. group, 1983-86, exec. v.p. capital markets, 1986-88; pres., chief operating officer N.Y. Stock Exchange, 1988—; overseer ops. N.Y. Future Exchange; coord. Depository Trust Co., Nat. Securities Clearing Corp.; bd. dirs. Securities Industry Automation Corp. Office: NY Stock Exch 11 Wall St New York NY 10005-1916*

GRÄTON, MILTON STANLEY, covered bridge builder and restorer; b. Turnerville, Conn., Dec. 16, 1908; s. Austin S. and Catherine A. (Fay) G.; m. Doris Isabel Howe, Nov. 8, 1935; children: June Ellen Gräton Meitz, Arnold Milton, Isabel Doris Gräton Dittrich, Austin Sumner IV, Stanley Edward. Grad. high sch., Winchedon, Mass. Carpenter, heavy equipment operator Gräton Assocs., Ashland, N.H., 1926-88, owner, 1950-90, cons., 1990—. Author: The Last of the Covered Bridge Builders, 1978, The Building of Zehnder's Holz-Brücke, 1980; prin. works include Turkey Jim, Campton, N.J., 1958, Stoughton, Weathersfield, Vt., 1959, Bagley, Warner, N.H., 1965, Durgin, Sandwich, N.H., 1967, Union St., Woodstock, Vt., 1968-69, Flint, Tunbridge, Vt., 1969, New England Coll., Henniker, N.H., 1972, Waitsfield Village, Waitsfield, Vt., 1973, Bedell, Haverhill, N.H., 1974-79, Blair, Campton, 1975, Downers, Weathersfield, 1976, Pine Brook, Waistfield, 1977, Holz-Brucke, Frankemuth, Mich., 1980, Blow-Me-Down, Cornish, N.H., 1981, New Hall or Graton, Rockingham, Vt., 1982, Dingleton Hill, Cornish, 1983, Van Trans Flat, Rockland, N.Y., 1984-85, Gilbertville, Ware and Hardwick, Mass., 1986-87, Knights Ferry, Calif., 1988-89, Gräton Squam River, Ashland, 1989-90, Packard-Hill, Lebanon, N.H., 1990-91, wooden covered bridges, many others. Chmn. Sch. Bd. Ashland, 1961. Honoree Ofcl. Day of Recognition N.H. Gov. Walter Petersen, 1970, Royal & Ancient Order Bridge Stretchers, 1973, Notable Ams. Bicentennial Era, 1976. Mem. Nat. Soc. Preservation Covered Bridges (hon. life), Vt. Soc. Engrs. Republican. Home and Office: Gräton Assocs RFD US Rte 3 Ashland NH 03217

GRAU, JOHN MICHAEL, trade association executive; b. St. Joseph, Mich., May 22, 1952; s. Otto R. and Esther P. (Spitzer) G.; m. Gayle Luedeman, May 7, 1983. BBA, U. Mich., 1974. Realty specialist HUD, Washington, 1974-75; field rep. Nat. Elec. Contractors Assn., San Mateo, Calif., 1975-76, chpt. mgr., Milw. chpt., 1976-85, asst. exec. v.p., Bethesda, Md., 1985-86, exec. v.p., CEO, 1986—; chmn., trustee Nat. Elec. Benefit Fund, Washington, 1986—; co-chmn. Coun. Indsl. Rels., Washington, 1986—; bd. mem. Plan for Settlement Jurisdictional Disputes in Constrn. Industry, Washington, 1986—. V.p. Elec. Contracting Found., Bethesda, 1989—. Fellow Acad. Elec. Contracting (bd. mem. 1986—); mem. Am. Soc. Assn. Execs., U.S. C. of C. (Com. of 100 1990—). Lutheran. Home: 7514 Heatherton Ln Potomac MD 20854-3222 Office: Nat Elec Contractors Assn 3 Bethesda Metro ctr Bethesda MD 20814-3202

GRAU, MARCY BEINISH, former banking consultant; b. Bklyn., Aug. 7, 1950; d. Joseph Beinish and Gloria (Rosenbaum) Bennett; m. Bennett Grau, Nov. 19, 1978; 2 children. AB with high honors, U. Mich., 1971; postgrad., Columbia U., 1972, N.Y. Inst. Fin., 1973. Asst. to chmn. Bancroft Convertible Fund, N.Y.C., 1973-75; precious metals trader J. Aron & Co., N.Y.C., 1975-81, mgr. metals mktg., 1981-83; v.p. Goldman, Sachs & Co/J. Aron, N.Y.C., 1983-88; investment banking cons., N.Y.C., 1988-90. Editor Precious Metals Rev. and Outlook, 1980—; contbr. article to profl. jours. Vol. worker pediatrics dept. Lenox Hill Hosp., N.Y.C., 1978-79; asst. The Holiday Project, The Hunger Project, N.Y.C., 1978-83; vol. Yorkville Common Pantry, N.Y.C., 1984,; tutor Yorkville Neighborhood Assn., N.Y.C., 1984; assoc. Child Devel. Ctr., N.Y.C.; trustee Congregation B'Nai Jeshurun, 1989—, pres., 1991—. Mem. Phi Beta Kappa. Democrat. Jewish. Home and Office: 300 W End Ave New York NY 10023-8156

GRAUER, WILLIAM KALE, III, aeronautical engineer; b. Abington, Pa., May 27, 1958; s. William Kale II and Margret Joy (Conard) G.; m. Karen Patricia Gesler, Apr. 7, 1990; 1 child, William Kale IV. BS in Aero. Engring., Embry-Riddle Aero. U., 1980; MBA, Drexel U., 1985. Registered profl. engr., Pa. Aero. engr. Boeing Helicopters, Phila., 1979—. Inventor, patentee walking device for handicapped. Pres., chief exec. officer Working, Inc. (innovative engring. for the disabled), Media, Pa., 1991; scoutmaster troop 503 (handicapped) Boy Scouts Am., Wilmington, Del., 1987-90. Recipient Outstanding Svc. award Kiwanis Club Del., 1989, Young Engr. of Yr. award Phil. Engrs. Club, 1991. Mem. AIAA (sr., pres. 1989-90, Hilliard Paige Lectureship award 1989), Am. Helicopter Soc. (Lichten Competition finalist 1981). Republican. Lutheran. Home: 2 W Rampart St Media PA 19063-5219

GRAVA, DONALD WALTER, JR., investment banker; b. New Haven, Apr. 8, 1955; s. Donald W. Sr. and Audrey (Florio) G.; m. Susan M. Palazzi, July 15, 1977. BA in Econs., Yale U., 1977; MBA, NYU, 1981. Staff acct. Coopers & Lybrand, N.Y.C., 1977-79; sr. fin. analyst GK Techs., Inc., Greenwich, Conn., 1979-80; sr. planning analyst Kennecott Corp., Stamford, Conn., 1980-82; asst. v.p. A.G. Becker Paribas, N.Y.C., 1982-84; 1st v.p. ELM Securities, Inc., N.Y.C., 1984-87; pres., founder The Versailles Group, Ltd., Westport, Conn., 1987—, also bd. dirs. Mem. Westport Rowing Club (founding mem. 1987), Assn. Yale Alumni, Power Ten N.Y. Club, Yale Club (Eastern Fairfield County). Office: The Versailles Group Ltd PO Box 552 Westport CT 06881

GRAVATT, CHRIS-TINA MILLEN, maker heirloom miniature quilts; b. Trenton, N.J., Jan. 22, 1947; d. Edward George and Frances Claire (Ferber) Millen; divorced; children: Lisa Adele Gravatt McBryde, Carrie Anne Gravatt. Grad. high sch., Trenton, N.J., 1965. Seamstress Morrisville, Pa., 1968-75; quilt artist Morrisville, Phila., 1979-84; antique quilt restorer, conservationist Phila., 1980-90, maker heirloom miniature quilts, 1985—. Author: Heirloom Miniatures, 1990; exhibited in group shows at Mus. of Am. Folk Art, N.Y.C., 1991, Dollywood, Pigeon Forge, Tenn., 1991, Am. Quilt Soc. Mus., Puducah, Ky., 1991, Decatur Ho., Washington, 1991, Mus. of Am. Quilts and Textiles, San Jose, Calif., 1990-91, Hanwerken Zonder Gretzen Needlework Fair, The Netherlands, 1990, The Golden Lion, Antwerp, Belgium, 1988, Houston Quilt Festival, Houston, 1987, Paisley (Scotland) Mus. and Art Galleries, 1986. Pres. Wild Geese Quilters, Phila., 1983-86, founder, 1981; co-pres. Head Ho. Craftsmen's Assn., Phila., 1984-86. Recipient over 50 awards, ribbons and prizes various quilt shows and contests, N.Y., Conn., Pa., Md., N.C., 1976—. Mem. Nat. Quilter's Assn.,

Am. Quilter's Soc., Am. Quilt Study Group, British Quilter's Guild, Heartstring Quilters. Home: 1308 E Columbia Ave Philadelphia PA 19125-3213

GRAVE, FLOYD KERSEY, music educator; b. Yonkers, N.Y., Jan. 20, 1945; s. Thomas Brooks and Elizabeth (France) G.; m. Margaret Helen Grupp, Aug. 29, 1973. MusB, Eastman Sch. Music, 1966; MA, NYU, 1968, PhD in Musicology, 1973. Asst. prof. music U. Va., Charlottesville, 1974-81; assoc. prof. music Rutgers U., New Brunswick, N.J., 1981—, asst. chmn. grad. studies in performance dept., 1987—, dir. grad. studies, 1990—, mem. senate, 1989—, faculty rep. to bd. trustees, 1990—; vis. prof. NYU, N.Y.C., 1983, Princeton (N.J.) U., 1984. Author, editor: Vogler, Keyboard Music, A-R edits., 1986; co-author: In Praise of Harmony, 1988, Joseph Haydn: A Guide to Research, 1990; contbr. numerous articles and revs. to Am. and European music rsch. jours. Recipient James C. Healey medal NYU Alumni Assn., 1973; Ford fellow, 1967-69, fellow Rutgers Coll., Rutgers U., 1981—; grantee German Acad. Exch. Svc. Munich, 1973-74, Darmstadt, 1979, Am. Philos. Soc., Vienna, Stockholm, 1979. Mem. Am. Musicological Soc. (pres. Greater N.Y. chpt. 1984-86), Coll. Music Soc., Soc. for Music Theory, Internat. Soc. for Study of Time. Home: 78A Cedar Ln Highland Park NJ 08904-2040 Office: Rutgers U Grad Program in Music Douglass Campus Chapel Dr New Brunswick NJ 08903

GRAVER, SUZANNE LEVY, English educator; b. N.Y.C., Aug. 17, 1936. BA summa cum laude, CUNY, 1957; MA, U. Calif., Berkeley, 1960; PhD, U. Mass., 1976. Tchr. English Berkeley High Sch., 1960-61, Culver City High Sch., 1961-62; asst. prof. Berkshire Community Coll., 1966-72; vis. asst. prof. Tufts U., 1976-78; assoc. ind. study Empire State Coll., SUNY, 1978; lectr. Williams Coll., Williamstown, Mass., 1976, 78-82, coord. writing workshop, 1981-85, asst. prof., 1983-87, chair dept. women's studies, 1988-89, assoc. prof. English, 1988-91, assoc. dean faculty, 1990-91, prof., dean of the faculty, 1991—; univ. fellow U. Mass., Amherst, 1974-76, Am. Coun. Learned Socs. fellow, 1985-86, 89-90, Nat. Humanities Ctr. fellow, 1989-90; manuscript reader Ind. U. Press, Victorian Studies; fellowship and grants application reader NEH, Nat. Humanities Ctr., The Grad. Ctr., CUNY. Author: George Eliot and Community : A Study in Social Theory and Fictional Form, 1984, and numerous essays and revs. in Victorian lit. and culture. NEH fellow, 1985. Mem. AAUP, ACLU, NOW, Modern Lang. Assn. (rep. to del. assembly 1988-91), Amnesty Internat., Wilderness Soc., Northeast Modern Lang. Assn. (chair English novel sect. 1980). Office: Williams Coll PO Box 141 Williamstown MA 01267-0141

GRAVES, DENISE BROWNE, psychologist, educator; b. Phila., May 5, 1948; d. John Andrew Jr. and Hattie Louise (Walton) Browne; m. Michael Alexander Graves, Aug. 29, 1970; children: Daren Alexander, Camar Andrew. BA, Swarthmore (Pa.) Coll., 1969; PhD, Harvard U., 1975. Asst. prof. clin. psychology program NYU, 1975-79; asst. prof. Univ. Rafael Urdaneta, Maracaibo, Venezuela, 1980-85; dept. chair Univ. Rafael Urdoneta, Maracaibo, Venezuela, 1983-85; asst. prof. dept. ednl. founds. Hunter Coll. CUNY, 1986-90, assoc. prof., 1990—, dept. chair, 1991—; cons. Children's TV Workshop, N.Y.C., 1987—, Women's Action Alliance, N.Y.C., 1989, 90—. Contbr. articles to profl. jours. and chpts. to books. Active Coalition 100 Black Women, Lower Fairfield County, Conn., 1987—, Jack and Jill of Stamford-Norwalk. Mem. Am. Psychol. Assn., Soc. for Rsch. Child Devel., Internat. Communication Assn., Am. Ednl. Rsch. Assn. Office: CUNY Hunter Coll Dept Ednl Founds 695 Park Ave New York NY 10021-5085

GRAVES, HOWARD DWAYNE, army officer, academic administrator, educator; b. Roaring Springs, Tex., Aug. 15, 1939; s. Tommy J. and Velma Lee (Clifton) G.; m. Gracie Pauline Newman, June 29, 1963; children: Gigi Reneé Graves Kail, Gregory Howard. BS in Mil. Sci., U.S. Mil. Acad., West Point, N.Y., 1961; BA, Oxford (Eng.) U., 1963, MA, 1968, M of Letters, 1971. Registered profl. engr., Wis. Commd. 2d lt. U.S. Army, 1961, advanced through grades to lt. gen., 1989; instr., then asst. prof. and assoc. prof. dept. social scis. U.S. Mil. Acad., West Point, 1970-73; mil. asst. to sec. def. Washington, 1973-76; comdr. 54th Engr. Bn., V Corps, U.S. Army Europe, 1976-78; student U.S. Army War Coll., Carlisle Barracks, Pa., 1978-79, spl. asst. to dep. comdt., 1979; comdr. 20th Engr. Brigade, XVIII Airborne Corps, Ft. Bragg, N.C., 1980-82; asst. div. comdr. 1st Inf. Div., Ft. Riley, Kans., 1982-83; dep. chief of staff, engr. U.S. Army Forces Command, Ft. McPherson, Ga., 1983-84; dep. dir. strategy plans and policy directorate Office Dep. Chief of Staff for Ops. and Plans; asst. army ops. dep. Orgn. Joint Chiefs of Staff, Washington, 1984-86, vice dir. joint staff, 1986-87; comdt. U.S. Army War Coll., Carlisle Barracks, 1987-89; asst. to chmn. Joint Chiefs of Staff, Washington, 1989-91; supt. U.S. Mil. Acad., West Point, 1991—. Decorated D.S.M., Def. D.S.M., Legion of Merit with oak leaf cluster, Bronze Star with 2 oak leaf clusters, Air medal (5), Meritorious Svc. medal with oak leaf cluster. Home: Quarters 100 West Point NY 10996 Office: US Mil Acad Office of the Supt West Point NY 10996-5000

GRAVES, MICHAEL, architect; b. Indpls., July 9, 1934; s. Thomas Browning and Erma Sanderson (Lowe) G.; children by previous marriage: Sarah Browning, Adam Daimhin. BS in Architecture, U. Cin., 1958, hon. doctorate, 1982; MArch, Harvard U., 1959; postgrad. (Acad. fellow), Am. Acad. in Rome, 1960-62; LHD (hon.), Boston U., 1984; HHD (hon.), Savannah Coll. Art and Design, 1986; DFA (hon.), RISD, 1990, N.J. Inst. Tech., 1991. Lectr. architecture Princeton (N.J.) U., 1962-67, assoc. prof., 1967-72, Schirmer prof. architecture, 1972—; pres. Michael Graves, Architect, Princeton, 1964—; architect in residence Am. Acad. in Rome, 1979. Exhibited in group shows Mus. Modern Art, N.Y.C., 1967, 68, 75, 78, 79, 80, 81, 84, Cooper-Hewitt Mus., N.Y.C., 1976, 78, 79, 80, 82, 85, 87, Triennale, Milan, Italy, 1973, 85, Roma Interrotta, Rome, 1978, Venice Biennale, Italy, 1980, Met. Mus. of Art, 1985, 86, 87, Emory U. Mus. Art and Archeology, Atlanta, 1985; one-man shows include U. So. Calif., 1981, No. Ill. U., 1982, Inst. for Architecture and Urban Studies, N.Y.C., 1982, Colby Coll., Maine, 1983, Moore Coll. Art, Phila., 1983, Fla. Internat. U., Miami, 1983, Pa. State U., University Park, 1984, Royal Inst. Brit. Architects, Heinz Gallery, London, 1984, Wadsworth Athaneum, Hartford, Conn., 1984, Carleton Coll., Northfield, Minn., 1986, W.Va. U., 1986, Hamilton Coll., Clinton, N.Y., 1987, Archivolto Gallery, Milan, Italy, 1987, U. Va.-Charlottesville, 1987, U. Md.-College Park, 1988, Duke U. Mus. Art, Durham, N.C., 1988, Butler Inst. Art, Youngstown, Ohio, 1989, Deutsches Architekturmuseum, Frankfurt, Dem. German Republic, 1989, Washington Design Ctr., 1989, Syracuse U. Sch. Architecture, 1990, Kunstnernes Hus, Oslo, 1990; designer archtl. projects: Newark Mus., 1968, Rockefeller House, 1969 (Progressive Architecture Design award 1970), Hanselmann House, 1967 (AIA Nat. Honor award 1975), Gunwyn Ventures Office, 1971 (AIA Nat. Honor award 1979), Snyderman House, 1972 (Progressive Architecture Design award 1976), Crooks House, 1976 (Progressive Architecture Design award 1977), Schulman House, 1976 (AIA Nat. Honor award 1982), Fargo (N.D.)-Moorhead (Minn.) Cultural Ctr., 1977-79 (Progressive Architecture Design award 1979), Chem-Fleur Inc., 1977 (Progressive Architecture Design award 1978), Warehouse Renovation (Graves House), 1977, 85 (Progressive Architecture Design award 1978), Plocek House, 1978 (Progressive Architecture Design award 1979), pvt. residence in Green Brook, N.J., 1978 (Progressive Architecture Design award 1980), Sunar Showrooms, N.Y.C., 1979, Chgo., 1979, Houston, 1980, L.A., 1980, N.Y.C., 1981 (Interiors award 1981), London, 1985, Loveladies Beach House, 1979 (Progressive Architecture Design award 1980), Environ. Edn. Ctr., 1980 (Progressive Architecture award 1983), Portland (Oreg.) Bldg., 1980 (AIA Nat. Honor award 1983), Pub. Library, San Juan Capistrano, Calif., 1980 (AIA Nat. Honor award 1985), Newark Mus. Master Plan and Renovation, 1982, Humana Bldg., Louisville, 1982 (Interiors award 1985, AIA Nat. Honor award 1987), Emory U. Mus. Art and Archaeology, 1982 (Interiors award 1985, AIA Nat. Honor award 1987), Riverbend Music Ctr., 1983, Whitney Mus. Am. Art, N.Y.C., 1984, Diane Von Furstenberg Boutique, 1984, Erickson Alumni Ctr., W.Va. U., 1984, Clos Pegase Winery, Calif., 1984 (AIA Nat. Honor award 1990), San Francisco Conservatory Music, 1984, Sotheby's Tower, N.Y.C., 1985, Aventine Devel., La Jolla, Calif., 1985, Shiseido Health Club, Tokyo, 1985, Disney Co. Corp. Office Bldg., Burbank, Calif., 1985, Crown Am. Hdqrs., Johnston, Pa., 1985, Walt Disney World Dolphin and Walt Disney World Swan Hotels, Fla., 1986 (Progressive Architecture award 1989), Youngstown (Ohio) Hist. Ctr. Industry and Labor, 1986 (Progressive Architecture Design award 1987), Brisbane (Calif.) Civic Ctr., 1986, 10 Peachtree Place, Atlanta, 1987, Henry House, Rhinebeck, N.Y., 1987 (Progressive Architecture award 1989), U. Va. Arts and Sci. Bldg., Charlottesville, 17, Sporting Club at The Bellevue, Phila., 1987, St. Mark's Ch., Cin., 1987, Portside Dist. Condominium Tower, Yokohama, Japan, 1987, Momochi Dist. Apt. Bldg., Fukuoka, Japan, 1987, Sporting Club at the Bellevue, Phila., 1987, St. Marks's Ch., Cin., 1987, Portside Dist. Condominium Tower, Yokohama, Japan, 1987, Momochi Dist. Apt. Bldg., Fukuoka, Japan, 1987, Metropolis Master Plan, L.A., 1988, Metropolis Phase I Office Bldg., L.A., 1988, Stores and Galleries for Lenox, Tysons Corner, 1988, Palm Beach, 1988, N.Y., 1988, Mpls., 1988, Costa Mesa, 1989, Frandfurt, 1989, Phila., 1989, Nashville, 1989, Kansas City, 1990, Midousuji Minami Office Bldg., Osaka, 1988, Healdsburg Pla. Hotel, Calif., 1988, 89, Fed. Triangle Devel. Site Competition, Washington, 1988, Tajima Office Bldg., Toyko, 1988, Hotel N.Y., Euro Disneyland, France, 1988, Inst. for Theoretical Physics U. Calif. at Santa Barbara, 1989, Venice, Calif. Pub. Libr., 1989, Detroit Inst. of Arts Master Plan, 1989, Apt. Bldgs., Brussels, 1989, 500 Forest Golf Club, Japan, 1989, Indpls. Art League, 1989, Emory U. Mus. of Art and Archeology Addition, Atlanta, 1989, Obihiro Mixed-Use Complex, Japan, 1990, Kasumi Group R & D Ctr., Japan, 1990, Fukoka (Japan) Internat. Office Project, 1990, Kasumi Group Rsch. and Tng. Ctr., Tsukuba City, Japan, 1990, Isetan Dept. Store, Yokohama, Japan, 1990, Clark County Libr., Las Vegas, 1990, Denver Cen. Libr., 1991, others; designer furniture, textiles and artifacts: Sunar, 1980-83, V'Soske, 1979-80, Alessi, 1981—, Baldinger Archtl. Lighting, 1983—, Swid Powell, 1985—, Steuben, 1986—, Tiffany, 1986, Munari, 1986—, WMF, 1987—, Atelier Internat., 1987—, Vorwerk, 1987—, Tajima, 1987, Dunbar Furniture, 1989, Arkitektura, 1989—; monographs include Michael Graves, Academy Editions, 1979, Michael Graves: Buildings and Projects, 1966-1981, 1981, Michael Graves: Buildings and Projects 1982-89, 90; illustrator: The Great Gatsby, Arion Press, 1984. Trustee Am. Acad. Rome. Recipient Rome prize Am. Acad. in Rome, 1960-62, Arnold W. Brunner Meml. prize in architecture, 1981, Silver Spoon award Boston U., 1984, Euster award, 1984, Ind. Arts award, 1984, Henry Hering Meml. medal Am. Sculpture Soc., 1986, N.J. Gov.'s Pride award, 1991, Walt Whitman Creative Arts award, 1991, also 38 N.J. Soc. Architects AIA awards, 15 Progressive Architecture Design awards; named. Interiors Designer of Yr., 1981. Fellow AIA (8 awards), Soc. Fellows Am. Acad. in Rome (trustee); mem. Am. Acad. Inst. Arts and Letters. Office: 341 Nassau St Princeton NJ 08540-4692

GRAVES, RUTH PARKER, educator; b. Port Arthur, Tex., Oct. 19, 1934; d. Thomas B. and Eunice (Chardin) Parker; m. Glenn R. Graves, Aug. 8, 1956; 1 child, Christopher. BA, Baylor U., 1956; MA, U. Tex., 1961; postgrad., George Washington U., 1963-64. Migrant labor advisor Tex. State AFL-CIO, Austin, 1959-61; pub. info. officer Pres.'s Com. on EEO, Washington, 1961-63; teaching fellow George Washington U., Washington, 1963-64; labor desk coord. Dem. Nat. Conv., Washington, 1965-67; program analyst U.S. OEO, Washington, 1965-67, dir. migrant div., 1967-72; ind. cons. and lectr., 1972-75; pres. Reading is Fundamental, Inc., Washington, 1975—; nat. adv. coun. Ctr. for the Book, Libr. of Congress, 1977—; adv. bd. Kidwave Radio Network, Phila., 1990—; lectr. in field. Editorial adv. bd. Child Mag., N.Y.C., 1989—; editor: The RIF Guide to Encouraging Young Readers, 1987; contbr. articles to profl. jours. Recipient William A. Jump award, U.S. Govt., 1971, Jeremiah Ludington Literacy Leadership award Ednl. Paperback Assn., 1982, Manhattan Literacy Coun. award, 1986, Internat. Reading Assn. Literacy award, 1987, As They Grow award Parents Mag., 1991; named Bookwoman of the Yr. Woman's Nat. Book Assn., 1987. Office: Reading is Fundamental 600 Maryland Ave NW #500 Washington DC 20024

GRAVES, THOMAS ASHLEY, JR., ; b. Buffalo, July 3, 1924; s. Thomas Ashley and Esther (Brittain) G.; m. Zoe Ann Wasson, June 12, 1962; children: Thomas, Stephen, Mary, Andrew, Elizabeth. BA, Yale U., 1945; MBA, Harvard U., 1949, DBA, 1958; LLD, U. Pa., 1975; LittD(hon.), Coll. of Charleston, 1976; LLD, Christopher Newport Coll., 1986, Wesley Coll., 1990. Asst. dean, assoc. dir. doctoral program Harvard. Grad. Sch. Bus. Adminstrn., 1950-60; dir. IMEDE, Internat. Mgmt. Devel. Inst., Lausanne, Switzerland, 1960-64; assoc. dean, dir. Internat. Center for Advancement of Mgmt. Edn., Stanford Grad. Sch. Bus., 1964-67; assoc. dean Harvard Grad. Sch., 1967-71; pres. Coll. William and Mary, Williamsburg, Va., 1971-85; dir., chief exec. officer, trustee Henry Francis du Pont Winterthur Mus., Del., 1985-92; bd. dirs. Reynolds Metals Co., Del. Trust Co. Served with USNR, 1943-46. Mem. Harvard Club (N.Y.C.), Wilmington Club, Wilmington Country Club, Phi Beta Kappa (hon.), Phi Sigma (hon.), Beta Gamma Sigma (hon.). Home: 2305 W 11th St Wilmington DE 19805

GRAVES, WILLARD LEE, electrical engineer; b. Springfield, Mo., Nov. 19, 1940; s. Willard Lee and Winifred Elizabeth (Yadon) G.; m. Carol Gevecker, June 23, 1962; children: Karen Richardson, Paul Willard. AB, BS, Drury Coll., Springfield, 1962; BSEE, Johns Hopkins U., 1965, MS, 1967, PhD, 1972. Registered profl. engr., Md. Engr. City of Springfield, 1958-62; chmn. dept. computer sci. Towson (Md.) State U., 1971-77; study mgr. U. Md., Balt., 1977-80; dir. cardiology div. systems computing Johns Hopkins Hosp., Balt., 1980—; rsch. assoc. Johns Hopkins U., 1962-65, assoc. rsch. scientist, 1965-71, assoc. prof. engring., 1973—, asst. prof. medicine, 1980—, asst. prof. biostats., 1982—; owner, mgr. Computation Cons., Balt., 1963—; v.p. Envirometrics, Pitts., 1967—; exec. v.p. Rhntek Inc., Balt., 1991—. Author books, also articles. Communicator Md. Med. Eye Bank, Balt., 1967—. Grantee NIH, 1990. Mem. Balt. Engring. Soc. (bd. dirs. 1987). Home: 220 Chancery Rd Baltimore MD 21218-2501 Office: Johns Hopkins U Charles and 34th Sts Baltimore MD 21218

GRAVES, WILLIAM P. E., editor; b. Washington, Dec. 27, 1926; s. Ralph A. and Elizabeth (Evans) G.; m. Joyce Witmyer. BA in English Lit., Harvard U., 1950. Joined Fgn. Svc., Dept. State, 1950; svc. in Fed. Republic Germany and Japan, resigned as consul, 1954; from legend writer to sr. asst. editor Nat. Geographic mag., Washington, 1956-90, editor, 1990—. With USN, World War II. Office: Nat Geographic 17th and M Sts NW Washington DC 20036

GRAY, ARNOLD LEE, accountant; b. Cobleskill, N.Y., Sept. 1, 1945; s. Ford and Margaret Robbins (Kling) G.; m. Anne Marie Traino, Nov. 18, 1972; children: Jane M., Beth E., Ethan F., Claire A. AAS, SUNY, Cobleskill, 1966; BS, SUNY, Albany, 1968, MS, 1970. CPA, N.Y. Tax mgr. Deloitte & Touche, Rochester, N.Y., 1971-78, Richmond, Va., 1978-79, Washington, 1979-80; sr. mgr. Coopers & Lybrand, Rochester, 1980-85; tax mgr. Davie, Kaplan & Braverman, P.C., Rochester, 1985-87; pres. Postgate, Perry & Gray, P.C., Rochester, 1987-91; pvt. practice Rochester, 1991—. Author: Matthew Bender's NY Tax Service, 1985; contbr. articles to profl. jours. Pres. Am. Heart Assn., Genesee Valley chpt., 1984-86, bd. dirs. N.Y. State Affiliate, 1984-86; arbitrator N.Y. Stock Exch., Western N.Y.; vice chmn. Rochester Jaycees, 1977-78. With USMC, 1968-70. Recipient Disting. Svc. award Rochester Jaycees, 1978, Dir. of Yr., 1978; named Outstanding Young Men of Am. U.S. Jaycees, 1978, 80-81. Office: Gray CPA 144 Exchange Blvd Ste # 600 Rochester NY 14614

GRAY, BRIAN ANTON, personnel consulting company executive; b. Phila., Apr. 13, 1939; s. Cecil James and Bertha LaVerne (Renfrow) G.; m. Linda Ann Cooper, June 3, 1967; children: Brian Anton Jr., Christina Dion. BA, Cheyney U. Pa., 1964; MA, Howard U., 1972. Pers. officer Howard U. and Hosp., Washington, 1967-76, dir. pers. svcs., 1982-91; coord. corp. coll. rels. Miller Brewing Co., Milw., 1976-79; chief exec. officer BG and Assocs., Bethesda, Md., 1991—. Mem. nominating com., chmn. bd. dirs. Montgomery Coll., Rockville, Md., 1988-91; 2d v.p. bd. dirs. Bur. Rehab., Lanham, Md., 1988—. Mem. Am. Compensation Assn., Soc. for Human Resource Mgmt. (cert. sr. profl. in human resources), Nat. Assn. Pers. Cons., Nat. Assn. Health Svcs. Execs., Montgomery County C. of C., Chevy Chase C. of C. Democrat. Home: 10112 Langhorne Ct Bethesda MD 20817 Office: BG and Assocs PO Box 34162 Bethesda MD 20827-0162

GRAY, CHARLES AUGUSTUS, banker; b. Syracuse, N.Y., Sept. 16, 1928; s. Charles William and Elizabeth Marie (Koch) G. Cert., Am. Inst. Banking, 1958, Sch. Bank Adminstrn., 1961. Cert. internal auditor. With Mchts. Nat. Bank & Trust Co. of Syracuse, 1946-77, auditor, 1959-77, v.p., 1970-77; N.Y. State dir. Bank Adminstrn. Inst., 1970-72; regional auditor cen. N.Y. region Irving Bank Corp., 1977-82, v.p. cen. N.Y. region, 1982-89. Treas. Upper N.Y. Synod, Luth. Ch. in Am., 1966-87, Upstate N.Y. Synod, Evang. Luth. Ch. in Am., 1988—; treas. Luth. Found. Upstate N.Y., 1977-78, bd. dirs., 1980—; pres. Interfrat. Alumni Coun., Syracuse U., 1980-83. Mem. Bank Adminstrn. Inst. (pres. central N.Y. chpt. 1970-72), Inst. Internal Auditors (treas. cen. N.Y. chpt. 1974-76, pres. 1985-86), Lions (pres. local club 1973-75), Masons, Shriners. Republican. Home and Office: 1321 Westmoreland Ave Syracuse NY 13210-3436

GRAY, CLAYTON HOWARD, minister, seminary official; b. Auburn, Maine, June 19, 1912; s. Fred Howard and Edna (Whitney) G.; m. Virginia Marsden, Dec. 2, 1935; children: David Thomas, Stephen Marsden, Virginia Susan. Student, Gordon Coll., 1929-30, Bapt. Bible Sem., Clarks Summit, Pa., 1962-70; BTh, Burton Theol. Sem., 1964; postgrad., 1989—. Ordained to Bapt. ministry, Sept. 26, 1933, Dundas Prince Edward Island, Can. Pastor 3 home mission s in New Brunswick, Prince Edward Island, Can., 1930-34, Fundamentalist Bapt. Ch., Lynn, Mass., 1935-41, Park Ave Bapt. Ch., Binghamton, N.Y., 1941-44, First Bapt. Ch., Butler, Pa., 1950-62; dir. alumni and ch. relations Bapt. Bible Sem., Clarks Summit, 1962-70; exec. dir. Soc. for Propagation of Bapt. Principles, Fleetville, Pa., 1970—; from dean to pres. Empire State Bapt. Sem., Liverpool, N.Y., 1973-86; pastor Fleetville (Pa.) Bapt. Ch., 1986-88, pastor emeritus, 1988—; pres. emeritus Empire State Bapt. Sem., 1986—. Mem. Grace Bapt. Fellowship N.Am. (founder), Gen. Assn. Regular Bapt. Chs. (v.p. 1936), Pa. Assn. Regular Bapt. Chs. (coun. of 10 1950-62), Empire State Fellowship Regular Bapt. Chs. (coun. of 10 1942-49). Republican. Home: PO Box 84 Fleetville PA 18420-0084

GRAY, DAVID MARTIN, power plant service company executive; b. Sycamore, Ill., Oct. 21, 1933; s. Ambrose John and Roseanne (Towle) G.; m. Ann Bloor, Feb. 5, 1955; children: Judith, Sarah, Andrew. BS in Physics, U. Ill., 1960. Product mgr. Combustion Engring., Inc., Windsor, Conn., 1974-76, mgr. adminstrn., 1976, dir. ops. control, 1976-79, dir. comml. svcs., 1979-82, dir. product support, 1982-84; v.p. ops. OX CE Fuel Co., Windsor, 1984-86; v.p. bus. devel. ABB CE Svcs., Inc., Windsor, 1986-90, v.p. fossil svcs., 1990-91, pres., 1991—. Comdr. USNR, 1952-81. Mem. Am. Soc. Naval Engrs. Roman Catholic. Office: ABB CE Svcs Inc PO Box 568 Windsor CT 06095

GRAY, DAVID WILLIAM, human resource executive; b. Sacramento, Calif., June 25, 1948; s. William and Ruth Evelyn (Davis) G.; m. Kathleen Marie Mead, Jan. 30, 1970; children: Jennifer, Rebecca, Peter. BA, Calif. State U., Chico, 1973, MA, 1978. Coord. coop. edn. and internship Calif. State U., 1973-80; dir. pers. Coopers & Lybrand, Sacramento, 1980-84; dir. adminstrn. Coopers & Lybrand, Washington, 1984-89, ptnr., prin., 1989—; cons. U.S. Civil Svc. Commn., 1975-80. Pres. Calif. Coop. Edn. Assn., 1979; mem. exec. bd. D.C. Spl. Olympics, 1985—. 1st lt. USMCR, 1970-73. Office: Coopes & Lybrand 1800 M St NW Washington DC 20036

GRAY, DON, artist; b. San Francisco, June 16, 1935; s. Leslie George and Mildred Marie (Koester) G.; m. Jessie Benton Evans, Oct. 13, 1960. BA in Art, Ariz. State U., 1957; MA in Art, U. Iowa, 1962. Prof. artist and poet Florida, N.Y., 1962—; assoc. prof. art Pace U., Briarcliff, N.Y., 1981-85; asst. prof. art Ladycliff Coll., Highland Falls, N.Y., 1971-81; producer/moderator Artist and Critic, Manhattan Cable TV, 1975—; participant TV programs comparing Rembrandt/Van Gogh self-portraits, evaluations of 19th and 20th century art. Art critic: Art World mag., 1982—; exhibited in many galleries and univs., N.Y., Ariz., N.Mex.; author of poems. Grantee Inst. for Urban Resources, N.Y., 1981. Mem. Coll. Art Assn. Home and Office: 8711 E Pinnacle Peak Rd # 223 Scottsdale AZ 85255-3555

GRAY, EDWARD BARTON, JR., surgeon, educator; b. Newton, Mass., May 22, 1924; Edward Barton and Mary Josephine (White) G. ; m. Mary Frances Dawson, May 24, 1952; children: Stephen Francis, Catherine Rose, Carol Ann. Student, Harvard, 1946, MD, 1948. Diplomate Am. Bd. Surgery. Intern Peter Bent Brigham Hosp., Boston, 1949-50, asst. resident surgery, 1950-51, 53-56, chief resident surgeon, 1956-57, sr. assoc. in surgery, 1957—; practice medicine specializing in gen. surgery Peter Bent Brigham Hosp., Stoughton, Mass., 1959—; instr. surgery Harvard Med. Sch., Boston, 1957—; chief of surgery Cardinal Cushing Hosp., Brockton, Mass., 1967-74; mem. staff Goddard Meml. Hosp., Stoughton; pres. Park Surg. Assocs., 1969—; asst. clin. prof. surgery Tufts Med. Sch., Boston, 1971—; mem. exec. com. Region VII, Comprehensive Health Planning Agy., Middleboro, Mass., 1972-74; chmn. profl. adv. com. Brockton Regional Cancer Registry, 1982—; chmn. cancer com. Cardinal Cushing Gen. Hosp., 1980—; mem. exec. com. Brockton Multi-Svc. Ctr.; exec. com., chmn. approvals com. Nat. Cancer Commn., 1986-89, ea. states chmn., 1984-89, Mass. state chmn., 1983-86; trustee Packard Manse. Contbr. articles to profl. jours. Capt., M.C., USAF, 1951-53. Fellow ACS (state liaison chmn.); mem. AMA, Boston Surg. Soc. (exec. com. 1989-95), Mass. Med. Soc. (councilor Plymouth dist.), Plymouth County Med. Soc. (v.p., pres. 1973-74), Soc. Surg. Oncology, New Eng. Surg. Soc. (exec. com. 1986—), New Eng. Cancer Soc. (exec. com. 1985-87), Am. Soc. Clin. Oncology, Kiwanis. Roman Catholic. Home: 2 Button Cove Rd Hingham MA 02043-1933 Office: 966 Park St Stoughton MA 02072

GRAY, ERNEST P(AUL), physicist, educator; b. Vienna, Austria, Mar. 12, 1926; came to U.S., 1940; s. Cornel and Alice (May) G.; m. Miriam Neuberger, June 27, 1954; children: Peter L., Robert L. BA, Cornell U., 1947, PhD, 1952. Teaching asst. Cornell U., Ithaca, N.Y., 1944, rsch. asst., 1946-48, 50-51; rsch. asst. Los Alamos (N.M.) Sci. Lab., 1946; mathematician Nat. Bur. Standards, Washington, 1946; physicist Applied Physics Lab. Johns Hopkins U., Silver Spring, Md., 1948, 51—; adj. prof. Johns Hopkins U., Balt., 1964—; William S. Parsons vis. prof. Johns Hopkins U., Balt., 1968-69, 84-85. Contbr. articles to profl. jours. Chmn. edn. com. Allied Civic Group, Silver Spring, 1965-79, v.p., 1976-78; pres. Huntington Civic Assn., Silver Spring, 1966-67. With AUS, 1944-46. Recipient William Cawton award Allied Civic Group, 1978; fellow AEC, 1948-50, William S. Parsons fellow, 1957-58. Mem. AAAS, Am. Phys. Soc., Am. Contract Bridge League. Home: 412 Kimblewick Dr Silver Spring MD 20904-6320 Office: Applied Physics Lab Johns Hopkins Rd Laurel MD 20723-1140

GRAY, GEORGE FRANCIS, bank professional; b. Balt., Nov. 18, 1956; s. Barrett A. and Erma-Louise A. (Blount) G. BS in Bus. Adminstrn., Morgan State U., 1978. Cert. fin. counselor. Supr. Equitable Life Assurance Soc. of the U.S., Hunt Valley, Md., 1979-84, Buck Cons., Silver Spring, Md., 1984-88; benefits counselor Fed. Res. Bank, Balt., 1988-90, supr. payroll and personnel records, 1990—; mentor Lake Clifton High Sch., Balt., 1991—. Home: 3722 Pinelea Rd Pikesville MD 21208 Office: Fed Res Bank 502 S Sharp St Baltimore MD 21201

GRAY, JOHN ROBERT, data processing executive; b. Sale, Cheshire, Eng., May 11, 1952; came to U.S., 1988; s. Percy Norman and Eunice (Moffat) G.; m. Denise Janet Haynes, Sept. 5; children: Rebecca Louise, Oliver John. Grad. high sch., Sale. Internat. mktg. mgr. Redifussion Computers, Crawley, Eng., 1975-82; gen. mgr. Philips Bus. Systems, Colchester, Eng., 1982-86, Philips T.D. Systems, Apeldoorn, The Netherlands, 1986-88; pres. Philips Info. Systems Inc., Dallas, 1988-90, Capitol Disc Interactive, Washington, 1990—; dir. Capitol Multi Media, Washington, 1991—; chmn. Paperless Prose Inc., Gaithersberg Md., 1991—. Author Lives & Times, 1991. Coach Nat. Youth Sports Coaches Assn., Md., 1991. Recipient Maestro award Softlab Assn., Munich, 1988. Mem. CDI Assn. Am. (dir. 1991), Interactive Multi Media Assn., O. Salians Rugby Union Club (2d team capt. 1980-82), Jaguar Enthusiasts Club. Home: 12521 Triple Crown Rd North Potomac MD 20878 Office: Capitol Disc Interactive 2121 Wisconsin Ave Washington DC 20007

GRAY, JOHN WILLARD, management consultant; b. Kittanning, Pa., Sept. 17, 1935; s. Turney Willard and Nettie Jane (Cornman) G.; m. Patricia Joan George, Aug. 11, 1956; children: John Willard Jr., Robin Elizabeth. BA in Bus., Marietta Coll., 1957. Claims rep. Liberty Mutual Ins. Co., Buffalo, 1957-61; claims supr. Liberty Mutual Ins. Co., 1962-65; claims examiner Liberty Mutual Ins. Co., Boston, 1966-68, tng. dir., 1969-71; chief exec. officer Gray's Enterprises, Kittanning, 1971—, Friendship Inn-Motel, Kittanning, 1971—, Friendship Estates Real Estate, Kittanning, 1971—, Leadership Mgmt., Inc., Kittanning, 1971—. Bd. dirs. Armstrong County (Pa.) Tourist Bur., 1985—; mem. adv. bd. Pa. 4-H Club, Armstrong County, 1985-90; mem. exec. bd. Pa. State U., 1985-90; bd. dirs. Crooked Creek Horse Park, Ford City, 1982—. With U.S. Army, 1957-58, 61-62. Mem. Am. Endurance Riding Conf. (10th Nat. award 1990), Eastern Competitive Trail Riding Assn (4000 Miles award 1990), Internat. Arabian Horse Assn. (Legion of Honor 1989, 90), Ea. Competitive Trail Riding Assn.

(bd. dirs.), Pa. Arabian Horse Assn. (Champion Endurance Trail Horse award 1989, 91), Ft. Armstrong Horsemen's Assn. (bd. dirs. 1980—). Republican. Lutheran. Office: Gray's Enterprises Friendship Plz RD 6 Box 279G Kittanning PA 16201

GRAY, LAWRENCE NEAL, plastic surgeon; b. Chgo., May 28, 1953; s. Samuel Howard and Gloria (Crohn) G.; m. Ruth Soper, Aug. 31, 1980; children: Evan, Whitney, Andrew. BA, Washington U., St. Louis, 1975; MD, Ind. U., Indpls., 1979. Diplomate Am. Bd. Plastic Surgery. Resident in gen. surgery Boston U., 1979-82; resident in plastic surgery Loyola U., Maywood, Ill., 1982-85; plastic surgeon Atlantic Plastic Surgery Assocs., Portsmouth, N.H., 1985—. Mem. AMA, Am. Soc. Plastic and Reconstructive Surgeons, Am. Assn. Hand Surgeons, New Eng. Soc. Plastic and Reconstructive Surgeons, Portsmouth Med. Soc. (pres. 1989-92), N.H. Med. Soc., Rockingham County Med. Soc. Jewish. Office: Atlantic Plastic Surgery Assocs 330 Borthwick Portsmouth NH 03801

GRAY, OSCAR SHALOM, lawyer; b. N.Y.C., Oct. 18, 1926. BA, Yale U., 1948, JD, 1951. Bar: Md. 1951, D.C. 1952, U.S. Supreme Ct. 1952. Atty.-adviser legal adviser's office U.S. Dept. State, Washington, 1951-57; sec. Nuclear Materials and Equipment Corp., Apollo, Pa., 1957-64, treas., 1957-67, v.p., 1964-71, dir., 1964-67; spl. counsel Presdl. Task Force on Communications Policy, Washington, 1967-68; cons. U.S. Dept. Transp., Washington, 1967-68, acting dir. office environ. impact, 1968-70; sole practice Washington, 1970—, Balt., 1971—; adj. prof., professorial lectr. Law Ctr. Georgetown U., Washington, 1970-71; lectr. Cath. U. Am., Washington, 1970-71; assoc. prof. U. Md., Balt., 1971-74, prof., 1974—; vis. prof. U. Tenn., 1977. Author: Cases and Materials on Environmental Law, 1970, 2d edit., 1973, supplements, 1974, 75, 77; (with F. Harper and F. James Jr.) The Law of Torts, 2d. edit., 1986, semi-ann. supplements, 1987-92; (with H. Shulman and F. James Jr.) Cases and Materials on the Law of Torts, 3d edit., 1976; contbr. articles to legal jours. Mem. ABA, Am. Law Inst. (adviser restatement third of torts-products liability), D.C. Bar Assn., D.C. Fedn. of Civic Assns. (parliamentarian 1991-92), Selden Soc. (state correspondent Md.), Order Coif, Phi Beta Kappa. Office: 500 W Baltimore St Baltimore MD 21201

GRAY, PAUL EDWARD, academic official; b. Newark, Feb. 7, 1932; s. Kenneth Frank and Florence (Gilleo) G.; m. Priscilla Wilson King, June 18, 1955; children: Virginia Wilson, Amy Brewer, Andrew King, Louise Meyer. SB, MIT, 1954, SM, 1955; Sc.D., Mass. Inst. Tech., 1960. Mem. faculty MIT, 1960-71, 90—, Class of 1922 prof. elec. engring., 1968-71, dean Sch. Engring., 1970-71, chancellor, 1971-80, pres., 1980-90; mem. MIT Corp., 1971—, chmn., 1990—; dir. Shawmut Nat. Corp., Boston, The New Eng., Boston, A.D. Little Inc., Cambridge, Boeing Co., Seattle, Eastman Kodak Co., Rochester. Trustee Wheaton Coll., Mass., 1971, chmn. bd. trustees, 1976-87; trustee Kennedy Meml. Trust; mem. corp. Mus. of Sci., Boston; bd. dirs. Nat. Action Coun. for Minorities in Engring.; corporator Woods Hole Oceanographic Inst. 1st lt. AUS, 1955-57. Fellow Am. Acad. Arts and Scis., IEEE (publs. bd. 1969-70); mem. NAE, AAAS, Mex. Nat. Acad. Engring. (corr.), Sigma Xi, Eta Kappa Nu, Tau Beta Pi, Phi Sigma Kappa. Mem. United Ch. Christ. Office: MIT Office Chmn of Corp 77 Massachusetts Ave Cambridge MA 02139-4307

GRAY, PAULETTE STYLES, biologist; b. Chattanooga, Feb. 21, 1943; d. Paul Styles and Louise (Hill) Dennis; m. Walter Leonard, May 10, 1964; children: Walter Leonard Jr., Daniel Allen. BS, Tuskegee Inst., 1966; MS, Atlanta U., 1976, PhD, 1978. Asst. prof., dir., electron microscopy lab. Atlanta U., 1978-79; research assoc. U. Kaiserslautern, Fed. Rep. Germany, 1979-81; instr. U. Maryland, Kaiserslautern, 1980-82; supr. clin. microbiology sect. Landstuhl Army Regional Med. Ctr., Fed. Rep. Germany, 1981-82; exec. sec. Nat. Cancer Inst. div. of Extramural Activities, Bethesda, Md., 1983-84, spl. review officer, 1984—, chief, rev. logistics br., 1988—; mem. Nat. Cancer Inst. Div. Extramural Activities awards com., Bethesda, 1983—, exec. sec. working group of subcom. on agenda adv. bd., 1989—, adv. com. Comprehensive Minority Program, Bethesda, 1983—; chmn. orgn. subcom. NIH Women's Adv. com., Bethesda, 1986-88; assignee profl. devel. health sci. adminstr. program NIH, Bethesda, 1986-88. Contbr. articles to profl. jours. Tchr. Sun. Sch. Alfred St. Bapt. Ch., Alexandria, Va., 1982-89, supt., 1988-89; judge sci. and engring. fair Fairfax County pub. schs., 1984-89; speaker Med. Coll. Ga., Augusta, 1985. Recipient Lederle Labs. award, 1977, H.E. Finley Meml. award Atlanta U., 1978, Outstanding Performance award Nat. Cancer Inst., 1983—; Josiah Macy Jr. fellow, 1979, Hon. Fulbright Hays fellow, 1979-81. Mem. Am. Soc. Zoology, Nat. Inst. Sci., Atlanta U. Ctr. Honor Soc. (biology), Am. Assn. Cancer Research, Inc., Beta Kappa Chi, Alpha Kappa Alpha. Office: Nat Cancer Inst 5333 Westbard Ave Bethesda MD 20892-0001

GRAY, ROBERT CURTIS, political science educator, writer; b. East Chicago, Ind., June 13, 1946; s. Robert Alton and Mildred (Savage) G.; m. Sandra Gail Edwards, Dec. 21, 1968 (div. Feb. 1988). BA in Govt., U. Tex., 1968, PhD in Govt., 1975. Instr. Franklin and Marshall Coll., Lancaster, Pa., 1972-75, asst. prof., 1975-80, assoc. prof., 1980-90, chmn. dept. govt., 1982-86, 88-91, prof., 1990—; asst. for nuclear planning Office of Sec. of Def., Washington, 1979-80; cons. Congl. Rsch. Svc., Washington, 1983-88; rsch. assoc. Internat. Inst. for Strategic Studies, London, 1987. Co-author: Nuclear Strategy & Arms Control, 1982; co-editor: American Foreign Policy Since Detente, 1984; N.Am. editor Def. Analysis, 1990—; contbr. articles to profl. jours. and chpts. in books. Bd. dirs. Jr. Achievement Lancaster-Lebanon, Pa., 1990—, Econ. Devel. Co., Lancaster, 1991—, Leadership Lancaster, 1992—. H.B. Earhart Found. fellow, 1970-71, NSF fellow, 1971-72, Internat. Affairs fellow Coun. Fgn. Rels., 1979-80. Mem. Internat. Studies Assn. (governing bd. security studies sect. 1989-92), Brit. Politics Group. Home: 27 Tanglewood Dr Reading PA 19607-3365 Office: Franklin and Marshall Coll Dept of Govt PO Box 3003 Lancaster PA 17604-3003

GRAY, ROBERT KEITH, communications company executive; b. Hastings, Nebr., Sept. 2, 1923; s. Garold C.J. and Marie (Burchess) G. BA, Carleton Coll., 1943; MBA, Harvard U., 1949; D.Bus.(hon.), Marymount Coll., 1981; LLD (hon.), Hastings Coll., 1982; HHD (hon.), Creighton U., 1989. Assoc. prof. fin. Hastings Coll., Nebr., 1950-51; prof. U. So. Calif., Los Angeles, 1952; spl. asst. sec. navy, 1954; spl. asst. to Pres. Eisenhower White House, Washington, 1955-57, appointments sec., 1958; sec. Eisenhower Cabinet, Washington, 1959-60; v.p. Hill & Knowlton, Inc., Washington, 1961-64, sr. v.p., 1965-70, exec. v.p., 1971-76, vice chmn., 1977-81; chmn. Hill & Knowlton, Inc., 1991—; founder, chmn. Gray and Co. Pub. Communications Internat. (merger Hill and Knowlton, Inc.), Washington, 1981-86; chmn., chief exec. officer Hill and Knowlton Pub. Affairs Worldwide, Washington, 1986—, Hill and Knowlton USA, Washington, 1986—; chmn., pres. Gray and Co. II, Washington, 1988—; chmn. Gray Investment Properties, Inc., Washington, 1988—; chief exec. officer, pres. Member Services Co., Washington, 1988—; chmn, chief exec. officer Powerhouse Leasing Corp., Washington, 1988—; bd. dirs. 1st Am. Bank, Mid-South Broadcasting Co. Author: Casebook on Organization and Operation of a Small Business Enterprise, 1950, Eighteen Acres Under Glass, 1962; also articles; subject of cover story U.S. News and World Report, 1985. mem. pub. info. adv. coun. World Wildlife Fund; bd. dirs. Freedoms Found., Valley Forge, Pa.; trustee Fed. City Coun., Washington; mem. nat. adv. bd. Am. U.; dir. emeritus Wolf Trap Found.; bd. dirs. Eisenhower World Affairs Inst.; mem. internat. adv. bd. Internat. Inst. for Peace through Tourism; bd. councilors Sch. Bus. Adminstrn., U. So. Calif.; mem. pvt. sector pub. rels. com. and internat. coun., USIA, 1981—; dir. communications Reagan-Bush Campaign, Washington, 1980; co-chmn. Presdl. Inaugural, Washington, 1981; hon. chmn. for 1989 Bush-Quayle Inaugural, 1985; adv. bd. Ctr. Strategic and Internat. Studies, Commn. on Bicentennial of U.S. Constn., 1988; mem. bd. Alliance to Save Energy; adv. com. Presdl. Debates, 1988, Pub. Edn. Task Force of Pub./Pvt. Careers Project at the Kennedy Sch. Govt. Harvard U.; mem. steering com. Nat. Air and Space Mus. joint project with the Ctr. for Democracy; mem. Com. for Single Six-Yr. Presdl. Term; prin. benefactor Gray Ctr. Communications Arts, Hastings Coll., Neb. Comdr. USN, 1944-46, now Res. Decorated knight comdr. Order of Merit (Italy); Medaille de Vermeil, Mayor of Paris, 1982; recipient Disting. Nebraskalander award, 1985; named Marketer of Yr., Adweek Mag. Republican. Episcopalian. Clubs: 1925 F St., George Town (chmn.) (Washington). Lodge: Masons. Home: 4953 Rock Spring Rd Arlington VA 22207-2705 Office: Hill & Knowlton Inc Washington Harbour 1730 Rhode Island Ave NW # 612 Washington DC 20036-3101

GRAY, SHEILA HAFTER, psychiatrist, psychoanalyst; b. N.Y.C., Oct. 19, 1930; m. Oscar Shalom Gray, Apr. 8, 1967. MD, Harvard U., 1958. cert. Washington Psychoanalytic Inst., 1969. Intern St. Elizabeths Hosp., Washington, 1958-59; resident McLean Hosp., Belmont, Mass., 1959-61; clin. and rsch. fellow Mass. Gen. Hosp., Boston, Mass., 1961-62; staff psychiatrist Chestnut Lodge, Inc., Rockville, Md., 1962-64; practice medicine, specializing in psychiatry and psychoanalysis Washington, 1964—; clin. asst. prof. psychiatry U. Md. Sch. Medicine, Balt., 1968-75, clin. assoc. prof., 1975-83, clin. prof., 1983—; instr. Washington Psychoanalytic Inst., 1971-75, teaching analyst, 1975—; mem. staff U. Md. Hosp., Balt.; physician mem. Commn. on Mental Health, Superior Ct. of D.C., 1972—; bd. govts. Nat. Capital Reciprocal Ins. Co., 1981—; cons. Walter Reed Army Med. Ctr., Washington, 1983—. Mem. Mayor's Adv. Com. on Mental Health Svcs. Reorgn., Washington, 1984; mem. adv. panel for Mayor's Environ. Design Awards Program, 1988-89; mem. exec. com. D.C. Fedn. Civic Assns., 1984—, asst. rec. sec., 1985, rec. sec., 1986-88, 2nd v.p., 1989-90, pres., 1991—; v.p. programs Women's Equity Action League Met. D.C., 1986; commr. D.C. Adv. Neighborhood Commn., 1986-88. Fellow Am. Psychiat Assn.; mem. Am. Psychoanalytic Assn. (diplomate Bd. of Profl. Standards), Washington Psychiat. Soc. (councillor 1981-83), Med. Soc. D.C. (exec. bd. 1982, House of Delegates, 1992—), Washington Psychoanalytic Soc. (chmn. bd. dirs. psychoanalytic clinic and councillor ex officio 1987-90), Palisades Citizens Assn. (bd. dirs 1980—), treas. 1983-84, pres. 1984-86). Office: PO Box 40612 Palisades Sta Washington DC 20016

GRAY, THADDEUS IVES, investment analyst; b. N.Y.C., Nov. 30, 1959; s. Cleve and Francine (du Plessix) G. BA, U. Pa., 1981; MBA, NYU, 1989. Chartered fin. analyst. Investment analyst Abbott Capital Mgmt. L.P., N.Y.C., 1989—. Mem. N.Y. Soc. Security Analysts. Roman Catholic. Home: 106 E 85th St New York NY 10028

GRAY, WILLIAM H., III, association executive, former congressman; b. Baton Rouge, Aug. 20, 1941; m. Andrea Dash, Apr. 17, 1971; children—William H. IV, Justin Yates, Andrew Dash. B.A., Franklin and Marshall Coll., 1963; M.Div., Drew Theol. Sem., Madison, N.J., 1966; Th.M., Princeton Theol. Sem., 1970; postgrad., U. Pa., 1965, Temple U., 1966, Oxford U., 1967. Ordained to ministry Baptist Ch.; asst. minister Bright Hope Baptist Ch., Phila., 1963-64; dir. 1st Baptist Ch., Montclair, N.J., 1964-65; co-pastor, sr. minister Union Baptist Ch., Montclair, 1966-72; asst. prof., dir. St. Peter's Coll., Jersey City, 1970-74; sr. minister Bright Hope Baptist Ch., 1972—; lectr. Jersey City State Coll., 1968, Rutgers U., 1971, Montclair State Coll., 1970-72; mem. 96th-101st Congresses from 2d Dist. Pa.; House Majority Whip; pres. United Negro Coll. Fund, N.Y.C., 1991—; chmn. house budget com., 1985—; mem. house appropriations com. Congl. Black Caucus, Nat. Economic Commn.; vice chmn. Dem. Leadership Coun. Trexler Found. scholar, 1962; Rockefeller Protestant fellow, 1965. Mem. Phila. Pastor's Conf., Phila. Baptist Assn., Progressive Nat. Baptist Assn., Am. Baptist Conv., Alpha Phi Alpha. Democrat. Club: Frontier Internat. Lodges: Masons, Elks. Office: United Negro Coll Fund 500 E 62d St New York NY 10021-8309*

GRAY-ALDRICH, GRETCHEN ELISE, health administrator and nurse; b. Corinth, N.Y., Oct. 18, 1934; d. Bertrand Leroy and Ethel Isabel (Gilbert) Gray; m. Leland D. Aldrich, Feb. 10, 1956; children: Ginger Lee, Leland Duane, Cheryl Jean, Melody Joy. Diploma in Nursing, Union U., Albany, N.Y., 1955; B Profl. Studies, Empire State Coll., Saratoga, N.Y., 1985; MS in Health Adminstrn., Russell Sage Coll., 1990. RN, N.Y. Med. and surg. staff nurse Saratoga Hosp., 1955-60; office nurse Leo F. Giordano, M.D., Hadley, N.Y., 1960-62; med., surg. and operating room nurse Adirondack Regional Hosp., Corinth, N.Y., 1969-75, dir. insvc., 1975-77, asst. dir. nursing, 1977-79, dir. nursing, 1979-81; coord. rsch. project N.Y. Rsch. Found. for Mental Hygiene, Albany, 1984; cons. on health and adminstrv. nursing Hatcher Rsch. Assocs., Voorheesville, N.Y., 1984-85; cons. health adminstrn. and med. nursing N.Y. State Office Mental Health, Albany, 1985—, chmn. office mental health state wide infection control nurses com., 1986—; mem. adv. bd. needlestick prevention pilot program N.Y. State Dept. Health, Albany, 1990—. Elder Rockwell Falls Presbyn. Ch., Lake Luzerne, N.Y., 1969; commr. Gen. Assembly, Albany Presbytery, Presbyn. Ch. U.S.A., Rochester, 1971; bd. dirs. Adirondack Regional Hosp., Corinth, 1981-89; founder, bd. dirs. Upper Hudson Primary Care Consortium, Warrensburg, 1987—, Adirondack Regional Primary Care Ctr., Corinth, 1987—. Mem. N.Y. State Pub. Health Assn., Health Care Mgrs. Assn. Northeastern N.Y., Phi Kappa Phi. Republican. Home: 5114 Park Ave Hadley NY 12835 Office: NY State Office Mental Health Bur of Health Svcs 44 Holland Ave Albany NY 12205-5035

GRAYSON, DARRYL STEPHEN, marketing professional, vice-president; b. Miami Beach, Fla., Nov. 3, 1961; s. Charles Phillip and Edith (Hirshfeild) Greenberg. BA, SUNY, Binghamton, 1983; MBA, Fordham U., 1990. Mktg. analyst Pan Am. Trade Corp., N.Y.C., 1983-85; product mgr. Citibank, N.Y.C., 1985-87; v.p. dir. mktg, sales. Deak Internat., N.Y.C., 1988—; cons., 1991—; speaker, panelist at investment seminars and conventions. Mem. Direct Mktg. Assn., Internat. Assn. Fin. Planners. Home: 1354 1st Ave Apt 4D New York NY 10021-4465

GRAZE, ROBERT L., association executive; b. Bridgeport, Conn., June 8, 1936; s. Eugene E. and Marion E. (Barnish) G.; m. Sharon M. Morgan, May 30, 1968. BS, U. Bridgeport, 1958, MS, 6th Yr. diploma, 1960; postgrad., NYU, 1962-65. Asst. to chancellor U. Bridgeport, 1960-66; v.p. Ind. Coll. Funds Am., N.Y.C., 1966-88; exec. dir. Assn. Corp. Travel Execs., Parsippany, N.J., 1988—. Recipient Outstanding Vol. award Am. Heart Assn., Conn., 1989, All Heart award, 1991. Mem. Am. Soc. Assn. Exec. (cert.), N.Y. Soc. Assn. Execs., Am. Soc. Travel Agts. Republican. Roman Catholic. Home: 36 Wintergreen Dr Easton CT 06612-2127 Office: Assn Corp Travel Execs PO Box 5394 Parsippany NJ 07054-6394

GRAZIANO, JOSEPH HAROLD, scientist, educator; b. Roslyn, N.Y., Mar. 8, 1947; s. Nicholas Joseph and Eleanor (Wright) G.; m. Florence Cicack, June 24, 1967 (div.); children: Joseph, Michelle; m. Mary J. Murphy; 1 child, Caitlin. BS in Biology, L.I. U., 1967; PhD in Physiology, Rutgers U., 1971; postdoctoral, Rockefeller Univ., 1971-73. Asst. prof., lab. med. biochemistry Rockefeller Univ., 1973-74; vis. asst. prof. The Rockefeller Univ., N.Y.C., 1974-78; asst. prof. pharmacology and pediatrics Cornell Univ., N.Y., 1974-78; assoc. prof. pharmacology and pediatrics Cornell Univ., 1978-79; assoc. prof. pharmacology Columbia Univ. Coll. of P & S, N.Y.C., 1979-90, prof. pharmacology, 1990-91; prof. pharmacology and pub. health, head div. environ. sci. Columbia Univ., N.Y.C., 1991—; bd. mem. Instnl. Rev. Bd., Columbia Univ., N.Y.C., 1990—; toxicology cons. WHO, Europe, 1988; com. mem. Nat. Inst. of Environ. Health Sci. Rev. Com., 1989—. Contbr. articles to profl. jours. Mem. AAAS, APHA, Am. Soc. Hematology, N.Y. Acad. Scis., Soc. Occupational and Environ. Health, Soc. Pediatric Rsch., Soc. Toxicology. Office: Columbia U 630 W 168th St New York NY 10032-3702

GREBOW, PETER ERIC, chemist; b. N.Y.C., Nov. 25, 1946; s. Karl and Shirley Grebow; m. Marjorie Ruth Siegel, Aug. 16, 1969; children: Stephen, Daniel. AB, Cornell U., 1967; MS in Chemistry, Rutgers U., 1969; PhD in Chemistry, U. Calif., Santa Barbara, 1973. Postdoctoral fellow Coll. of Physicians & Surgeons Columbia U., N.Y.C., 1973-75; various rsch. positions Revlon Health Care, Tuckahoe, N.Y., 1975-82, dir. drug disposition, 1982-86; dir. drug disposition Rorer Pharm. Corp., Ft. Washington, Pa., 1986-88, v.p. drug devel., 1988-90; dir. drug devel. Cephalon, Inc., West Chester, Pa., 1991-92; v.p. drug devel. Cephalon, Inc., 1992—. Mem. AAAS, Am. Chem. Soc.

GREBOWSKY, JOSEPH MARK, physicist; b. Hazelton, Pa., Aug. 20, 1941; s. Joseph Anthony and Mary (Dagilus) G.; m. Margaret Louise Alpert, June 21, 1963; children: Bret, Amorette. BS in Physics, Manhattan Coll., 1963; MS in Physics, Pa. State U., 1965, PhD in Physics, 1968. Physicist Naval Ordinance Lab., White Oak, Md., 1963; rsch. asst. Pa. State U., University Park, 1963-65; astrophysicist Goddard Space Flight Ctr., NASA, Greenbelt, Md., 1968—. Contbr. articles to profl. jours. Mem. Am. Geophysical Union. Buddhist. Home: 10902 Devin Pl Kensington MD 20895-2302

GRECCO, PATRICK RONALD, psychologist; b. Bronx, Jan. 14, 1949; s. Nicholas Peter and Rose (DiLorenzo) G.; m. Barbara Charlton, Aug. 15, 1981; children: Elizabeth, Nicholas. BA, NYU, 1970; MA, Columbia U., 1976, MEd, 1977; PhD, Calif. Sch. Profl. Psychology, 1980. Lic. psychologist, N.Y., Pa. Vol. U.S. Peace Corps, Niger, West Africa, 1970-71; caseworker Mission of the Immaculate Virgin, S.I., N.Y., 1971-74; with N.Y. State Dept. Social Svcs., N.Y.C., 1974-75; mental health technician St. Vincents Med. Ctr. of S.I., 1976-77; vocat. rehab. counselor N.Y.State Dept. Edn., S.I., 1977-80; lectr., counselor Chestnut Hill Coll., Phila., 1985-86; clin. cons. U. Pa., Ctr. for Cognitive Therapy, Phila., 1985-88; psychologist Charles Drew Community Mental Health Ctr., Phila., 1986-87, N.Y. Foundling Hosp., S.I., 1987—; counselor Fresno City Coll., 1983-84; doctoral intern Merced County Community Mental Health Ctr., 1982-83, The Bridge, Merced, 1981-82; postdoctoral fellow med. sch. U. Pa., 1984-85. Fellow Am. Psychol. Assn. Office: NY Foundling Hosp 119 Tompkins Ave Staten Island NY 10304-2601 also: 52 W Ferry St New Hope PA 18938

GRECO, ALBERT NICHOLAS, communications educator; b. Trenton, N.J., June 15, 1945; s. Albert Charles and Nellie Marie G.; m. Elaine Anne Rovegno, Aug. 10, 1968; children: Albert, Timothy, John, Robert. BA, Duquesne U., 1967, MA, 1969; EdD, NYU, 1982. Teaching grad. asst. Duquesne U., 1967-68; tchr. Dwight-Englewood (N.J.) Sch., 1968-79, chmn. dept., 1970-73, dir. testing, 1973-75, prin. summer sch., 1970-78, prin. high sch., 1975-78, dir. devel., 1978-79; exec. dir. Met. Lithographers Assn., N.Y.C., 1979-83; adj. instr. Bergen Community Coll., 1970-78; adj. prof. NYU, 1980-83, dir. Ctr. for Graphic Communications Mgmt. and Tech., 1983-85, assoc. prof., assoc. dean Gallatin div., 1985—; exec. dir. Lithographic Industry Scholarship, Edn. and Devel. Fund., 1982-83. Author: Business Journalism: Management Notes and Cases, 1988, Advertising Management and The Business Publishing Industry, 1991; editor NYU Press Bus. mag. pub. series; co-editor: Editorial Excellence; contbr. articles to profl. jours. Bd. dirs. Book Industry Study Group. Recipient Cert. of Recognition Edn. Coun. of Graphic Arts Industry, 1985. Mem. Internat. Communications Assn., Soc. for Scholarly Pub., Assn. Edn. in Journalism and Mass Communication, Phi Alpha Theta. Roman Catholic. Home: 183 S Queen St Bergenfield NJ 07621-2636 Office: NYU Gallatin div 715 Broadway 6th Fl New York NY 10003-6806

GRECO, CHARLES, clinical social worker; b. Bklyn., Feb. 13, 1949; s. Erasamus C. and Nelda W. (Hartley) G.; m. Frances Belli, Aug. 24, 1974; 1 child, Jonathan Charles. BA, L.I. U., 1975, MA, 1977; MSW, Fordham U., 1979. Cert. clin. social worker, N.Y.; bd. cert. diplomate clin. social work. Clin.. social worker Cath. Charities, Laurel, N.Y., 1979-84; dir. YMCA, Centerach, N.Y., 1974; pvt. practice, psychotherpaist Rocky Point, N.Y., 1984—; social work cons. Suffolk Co. (N.Y.) Librs., 1984—, clin. social worker St. John's Cath. Sch., Center Moriche, N.Y., 1989—. With U.S. Army, Vietnam, 1968-71. Mem. NASW (mem. inquiry com. 1989—). Office: 7 Westchester Dr Rocky Point NY 11778-8809

GREELEY, RICHARD STILES, environmental consultant; b. Framingham, Mass., Dec. 25, 1927; s. Sidney Foote and Annette (Stiles) G.; m. Loretta Betke, June 16, 1951; children: Richard S. Jr., Benjamin Betke. BS, Harvard U., 1949; MS, Northwestern U., 1951; PhD, U. Tenn., 1959. Group leader Oak Ridge (Tenn.) Nat. Lab., 1954-60; dir. rsch. The Mitre Corp., McLean, Va., 1960-80; v.p. R. F. Weston, Inc., West Chester, Pa., 1980-82; pres. The Greeley Tech. Group, West Chester, Pa., 1982-89; gen. mgr. R. E. Wright Assocs., Inc., King of Prussia, Pa., 1989—. Author: Computer Techniques, 1975, Solar Heating & Cooling, 1981. Ltjg. USN, 1951-54. Mem. Am. Chem. Soc. Home: 418 Round Hill Rd Wayne PA 19087-4728

GREELEY, SEAN MCGOVERN, trust company executive; b. New Brunswick, N.J., Nov. 8, 1961; s. Horace James Jr. and Patricia Louise (McGovern) G.; m. Kristin Elisabeth Lindefjeld, June 20, 1987; children: Elisabeth Lindefjeld, Anna Barlinn. BSBA, Monmouth Coll., 1983. With Dean Witter Reynolds, N.Y.C., 1983-85; acct. exec. U.S. Trust Co., N.Y.C., 1985-87, fin. officer, 1987-90, asst. v.p., 1990—. Mem. Tau Kappa Epsilon (pres., bd. dirs. 1984-90, cons. bd. fin. 1986-90). Republican. Home: 14 North St Rumson NJ 07760-1610 Office: US Trust Co NY 770 Broadway New York NY 10003

GREEN, ADOLPH, playwright, lyricist; b. N.Y.C., Dec. 2, 1915; s. Daniel and Helen (Weiss) G.; m. Phyllis Newman, Jan. 31, 1960; children: Adam, Amanda. Student pub. schs., N.Y.C. Writer, author: (Broadway musicals with Betty Comden) On the Town, 1944-45, Billion Dollar Baby, Two on the Aisle, Wonderful Town, Take Me Out to the Ball Game, Good News, Barkleys of Broadway, Band Wagon, Singing in the Rain, Bells are Ringing, 1960, Do Re Mi, 1960, Subways are for Sleeping, 1962, Fade Out-Fade In, 1964, (with Betty Comden and Jules Styne) Say Darling, 1959, The Cockeyed Tiger, 1977, On the Twentieth Century, 1978, The Will Rogers Follies, 1991 (Tony award, 1991; (screenplays with Betty Comden) What a Way to Go, Auntie Mame; co-author: (with Betty Comden) Applause; writer-dir.: (with Betty Comden) By Bernstein, 1975, Lorelei; TV prodns. include Peter Pan, Wonderful Town; appeared as actor in: (with Betty Comden) film Simon, 1979 (Co-recipient Donaldson award for Wonderful Town 1953, Tony award for co-writer music and lyrics for Hallelujah, Baby, 1968, Tony award for co-writer book Applause, 1970, Tony awards for best book of musical (with Comden) and for best score (with Comden and Coleman) for On the Twentieth Century 1978; named to Songwriters Hall of Fame 1980). Home: 211 Central Park W New York NY 10024-6020

GREEN, ALAN IVAN, psychiatrist; b. Norwalk, Conn., Nov. 7, 1943; s. H. Howard and Irene G.; m. Frances S. Cohen, Oct. 9, 1983. AB, Columbia Coll., 1965; MD, Johns Hopkins U., 1969. Intern Beth Israel Hosp., Boston, 1969-70; staff assoc. Nat. Inst. Mental Health, Washington, 1970-72; dir. biomed. rsch. Spl. Action Office for Drug Abuse Prevention Exec. Office of Pres., Washington, 1972-73, cons., 1973-75; resident in psychiatry Mass. Mental Health Ctr., Boston, 1973-75, 81-82, assoc. dir. psychopharmacology, 1982—; adminstrv. dir. Commonwealth Rsch. Ctr., Boston, 1986—; asst. prof. psychiatry Harvard U., Boston, 1984—. Contbr. sci. articles to profl. jours. Recipient Milton Fund award Harvard Med. Sch., 1988. Mem. Am. Psychiat. Assn., Mass. Psychiat. Soc. Office: Mass Mental Health Ctr 74 Fenwood Rd Boston MA 02115-6106

GREEN, ALLAN, cinematographer; b. Bklyn., Aug. 12, 1928; s. Edward and Doris (Steinberg) G.; married May 19, 1956 (div.); children: Michael, Lisa, Mark. BA, L.I. U., 1948. Freelance dir. photography Pearl River, N.Y., 1958—. With U.S. Army, 1951-53. Mem. Rockland Astronomy Club. Home: 110 Pascack Rd Pearl River NY 10965

GREEN, BENNETT DONALD, quality assurance specialist; b. N.Y.C., Nov. 24, 1950; s. John Jerome and Leona Pearl (Gillman) G.; m. Deborah Lynn Stephen, Dec. 23, 1972; children: Rebecca Lynn, John Stephen, Sara Elizabeth. BS, Rensselear Poly. Inst., 1972, MS, 1974; Exec. MBA, Claremont Grad. Sch., 1988. Cert. quality engr. Am. Soc. Quality Control. Sr. mfg. analyst internat. div. Bristol Myers, Syracuse, N.Y., 1974-77; sect. mgr. sterilization Baxter-Travenol Labs., Deerfield, Ill., 1977-78, quality control supr., 1978-82, quality assurance plant mgr. Hyland Therapeutics div., 1982-85; dir. quality assurance NeoRx Corp., Seattle, 1985-87; dir. Genzyme Corp., Cambridge, Mass., 1987-91, v.p. quality assurance and control, 1991—. Referee U.S. Soccer Fedn., Mass., 1992—. Mem. Am. Soc. for Quality Control, Parenteral Drug Assn., Regulatory Affairs Profl. Soc.

GREEN, BERT FRANKLIN, JR., psychologist; b. Honesdale, Pa., Nov. 5, 1927; s. Bert Franklin and Emily May (Brown) G.; m. Hasseltine Beck Robinson, Apr. 29, 1961 (div. 1974); children—Malcolm Edward. A.B., Yale, 1949; M.A., Princeton, 1950, Ph.D., 1951. Mem. psychology group Lincoln Lab., Mass. Inst. Tech., 1951-62, leader, 1958-62; cons. RAND Corp., 1961; prof. psychology Carnegie Inst. Tech., Pitts., 1962-69; head psychology dept. Carnegie Inst. Tech., 1962-67; prof. psychology Johns Hopkins, Balt., 1969—. Author: Digital Computers in Research, 1963.

Mem. Am. Psychol. Assn., Am. Statis. Assn., Psychometric Soc., Psychonomic Soc., AAAS. Home: 311 Eastway Ct Baltimore MD 21212-4710

GREEN, BILL, congressman; b. N.Y.C., Oct. 16, 1929; m. Patricia Freiberg; children: Catherine, Louis. A.B. magna cum laude, Harvard U., 1950, J.D. magna cum laude, 1953. Bar: D.C. 1953, N.Y. 1954. Law sec. to judge U.S. Ct. Appeals (D.C. cir.), 1955-56; practice law N.Y.C., 1956-70; counsel N.Y. State Joint Legis. Com. on Housing and Urban Devel., 1961-64; mem. N.Y. State Assembly, 1965-68; regional adminstr. HUD, 1970-77; mem. 95th-102d Congresses from 15th N.Y. dist., 1979—. Founding trustee Jewish Assn. for Svcs. to Aged; trustee Montefiore Med. Ctr., New Sch. for Social Rsch.; sec. F.D. Roosevelt Meml. Commn.; co-chair Nat. Commn. on Severely Distressed Pub. Housing Projects; mem. U.S. Holocaust Meml. Coun.; mem. domestic cabinet UJA/Fedn. of Jewish Philanthrophies, N.Y. Lt. JAGC, U.S. Army, 1953-55. Office: US Ho of Reps 2301 Rayburn House Office Bldg Washington DC 20515 also: 60 E 42d St Rm 2306 New York NY 10165-0015*

GREEN, DAVID EDWARD, librarian, priest, translator; b. Adrian, Mich., June 22, 1937; s. Edward Robert Alexander and Fannie Amelia (Nadler) G.; m. Sharon Weiner, June 1, 1961; children: Alexis Ann, Philip DeWitt. BA, Harvard U., 1960; BD, Div. Sch. of Pacific, Berkeley, Calif., 1963; MLS, U. Calif., Berkeley, 1970. Ordained priest Episc. Ch., 1964. Assoc. librarian Grad. Theol. Union, Berkeley, 1970-82; libr. dir. Gen. Theol. Sem., N.Y.C., 1982—. Translator many German theol. works. Mem. Am. Theol. Libr. Assn., N.Y. Area Theol. Libr. Assn., Beta Phi Mu. Home and Office: 175 9th Ave New York NY 10011-4924

GREEN, EDWARD CROCKER, health consulting firm executive; b. Washington, Nov. 29, 1944; s. Marshall and Lispenard Seabury (Crocker) G.; m. K. Shannon McCaffray, Sept. 22, 1967 (div. 1977); 1 child, Timothy A. BA, George Washington U., 1967; MA, Northwestern U., 1968; PhD, Cath. U. Am., 1974; postdoctoral, Vanderbilt U., 1978-79. Asst. prof. W.Va. U., Morgantown, 1976-78; devel. cons. various orgns., Washington, 1979-86; mgr. internat. programs John Short & Assocs., Columbia, Md., 1986-88; mgr. and researcher The Futures Group, Washington, 1988—; social scientist Acad. for Ednl. Devel., Swaziland, 1981-84; personal services contractor U.S. AID, Swaziland, 1984-85. Author: Planning Psychiatric Services for Southern Africa, 1979; editor: Practicing Development Anthropology, 1986; contbr. 55 articles to profl. jours. Mem. adv. council Health Communications for Child Survival Acad. for Ednl. Devel., Washington, 1985—. Recipient Praxis award Washington Assn. Profl. Anthropologists, 1982, 83; NIMH postdoctoral fellow, 1978-79; research grantee Sigma Xi, 1971. Fellow Am. Anthrop. Assn.; mem. N.Y. Acad. Scis., Soc. Med. Anthropology, Soc. Applied Anthropology, Nat. Council for Internat. Health, Sigma Xi Soc. Club: Swaziland Theatre (Mbabane) (social dir. 1982-83). Home and Office: 2807 38th St NW Washington DC 20007

GREEN, FRED WALLACE, insurance company executive; b. Boston, Nov. 24, 1945; s. John Davidson and Helga Matilda (Ober) G.; m. Carol Jayne Budlong, Nov. 17, 1968; children: Joshua Davidson, Jessica Jayne. BS in Marine and Elec. Engring., Mass. Maritime Acad., 1966; MBA, Northeastern U., 1971. CPCU. Marine engr. Marine Engrs. Benefits Assn., Boston, 1966-72; auditor Coopers and Lybrand, Boston, 1972; acct., asst. treas., v.p. Abington (Mass.) Mutual Ins. Co., 1972-80, sec., sr. v.p., 1980-82, exec. v.p., sec., 1982-84; pres., chief exec. officer Abington Mutual Ins. Co., Brockton, Mass., 1984—; chmn., chief exec. officer, pres. Abington Casualty Ins. Co., East Greenwich, R.I., 1984—, Patrons Fire Ins. Co. of R.I., East Greenwich, R.I., 1989—; lectr. Stonehill Coll., Mass. Maritime Acad., 1989—. Mem., past pres. North Attleboro (Mass.) Jaycees, 1970-81 (Jaycee of Yr. 1972); trustee, past chmn. Mass. Jaycees Charitable Trust, Marlboro, 1974-81, Brockton Area Pvt. Ind. Coun./Regional Employment Bd., 1983—, Met. South C. of C., Brockton, 1984—; dir. Old Colony YMCA, Brockton, 1985-91, Southeastern Mass. Supts. Ctr., 1989-92, People's Savs. Bank, Brockton, 1990—; mem. Mass. Dept. Edn., Sch. Bus. Ptnr. Program, Quincy, 1990—. Mem. New Eng. Assn. Mutual IKns. Accts. (pres. 1977-78), Soc. Chartered Property and Casualty Underwriters, Jaycees Internat. Senate (Outstanding Young Leader 1976). Republican. Episcopalian. Home: 236 East St Foxboro MA 02035 Office: Abington Mutual Ins Co 120 Liberty St Brockton MA 02401

GREEN, GERARD LEO, priest, educator; b. Batavia, N.Y., July 27, 1928; s. George Leo and Marian (Powers) G.; BS, Mt. St. Mary's Coll., 1952; MA, St. Bonaventure U., 1958; postgrad. (NSF fellow) U. Notre Dame, summers 1961, 62, U. Buffalo, 1965-66; Ed.M., SUNY, 1968. Lab. technician Eastman Kodak Co., 1947-48; chemist Xerox Co., 1952; ordained priest Roman Catholic Ch., 1956; parish asst Diocese Buffalo, 1956-59; instr. chemistry Bishop Turner High Sch., Buffalo, 1959-74, dir. sci., 1959-70, 72-74; adminstr. Our Lady of the Rosary Parish, Wilson, N.Y., 1968; adminstr. St. Barnabas Parish and Sch., Depew, N.Y., 1973-75, pastor, 1976-90, prelate of honor, 1984, mem., supr., leader tng. team, 1979-90; pastor Sts. Peter and Paul Parish, Hamburg, N.Y., 1990—. Mem. sci. curriculum com. Dept. Edn. Diocese Buffalo, 1960-70, chmn. diocesan chemistry textbook evaluation com., 1961-70, mem. diocesan pastoral council for handicapped, 1976-82, sec., 1978-79, diocesan regional coord., 1979-80, mem. diocesan fin. com., 1984—, diocesan priests coun., 1990—; mem. Diocesan Cons. Parish Computers, 1983—, Diocesan Bd. Priests Retirement, 1985-91; mem. Sch. Bd. St. Francis High Sch., 1992—; diocesan bd. dirs. for TV prodn., 1986—; chaplain Hyview Fire Co., 1976-81, Cheektowaga Police PBA, 1976-90, West End Fire Co., 1977-90, Depew Village Fire Co., 1980-88; mem. Western N.Y. Sci. Congress Com., 1960-74, sec., 1968, co-chmn., 1969, chmn., 1972-73, state chmn., 1970; mem. gen. chemistry exam. com. N.Y. State Edn. Dept., 1970-73; mem. Maryvale Schs. Planning Bd., 1977-79; cons. sci. facilities in secondary schs.; mem. local IUE-AFL-CIO Scholarship Fund Com., 1968-71. Mem. dist. com. Boy Scouts Am., Buffalo, 1957-74; bd. dirs. Tifft (Conservation) Farm, 1978-82. Served with AUS, 1946-47. Recipient Disting. Service award in sci. edn., 1975. Mem. Sci. Tchrs. Assn. N.Y. (dir. 1971-73), Nat. Cath. Edn. Assn. Clubs: Order of Arrow, KC. Author articles. Address: 66 E Main St Hamburg NY 14075

GREEN, HARVEY, history educator; b. Buffalo, Sept. 15, 1946; s. Herman and Bessie Green; m. Susan Reynolds Williams, June 21, 1980. BA, U. Rochester, 1968; MA, Rutgers U., 1970, PhD, 1976. Historian Strong Mus., Rochester, N.Y., 1976-83; v.p. interpretation Strong Mus., Rochester, 1983-89; assoc. prof. history Northeastern U., Boston, 1989—. Author: Light of the Home, 1983, Fit for America, 1986, The Uncertainty of Everyday Life 1915-1945, 1992; mem. editorial bd. Northeastern U. Press, 1990—; contbr. articles to profl. jours. Trustee Landmark Soc. Western N.Y., Rochester, 1985-89; bd. overseers Strawberry Banke Mus., 1991—. Univ. fellow Rutgers U., 1973; NEH grantee, Washington, 1982, 83, 85. Mem. Orgn. Am. Historians, Am. Studies Assn. (coun. mem. New Eng.), Am. Hist. Assn., Am. Assn. State and Local History (coun. mem., cons. various museums 1987—). Office: Northeastern U 249 Meserve Hall Boston MA 02115

GREEN, HOPE STUART, public television executive; b. Boston, July 26, 1944; d. Edwin T. and Jean C. (Porter) G.; m. Robert G. Arns, May 4, 1985. AB, Bryn Mawr Coll., 1966. Various devel. and personnel positions Sta. WGBH-TV, Boston, 1966-72; dir. devel. Mass. Eye and Ear Infirmary, Boston, 1972-74, Sta. KCTS-TV, Seattle, 1974-80; pres. Vt. ETV, Colchester, 1980—; cons. several TV stas., 1972—, Pacifica Found., L.A., 1984. Mem. Ea. Ednl. TV Network (trustee 1980—), Nat. Assn. Public TV Stas. (bd. dirs. 1989—). Office: WETK Ethan Allen Ave Colchester VT 05446-3105

GREEN, JOHN HAMPSON, educational administrator; b. Cambridge, Mass., Mar. 19, 1932; s. Lawrence Waldo and Rose Emily (Pollard) G.; m. Betty Harrison, Sept. 3, 1956; children: Douglas, Susan, Mark. BS, Bridgewater State Coll., 1954; MEd, Northeastern U., 1960; Cert. Advanced Study, U. Conn., 1964. Cert. ednl. adminstr., Conn., Mass. Prin. Suffield (Conn.) Pub. Schs., 1960-66, supt. schs., 1966-69; dir. edn. Greater Hartford (Conn.) Process, Inc., 1970-74; sr. rsch. assoc. Nat. Inst. Edn., Washington, 1974-75; pres., exec. dir. Edn. Collaborative for Greater Boston, Brookline, Mass., 1975—; cons. Inst. Ednl. Leadership, Washington, 1977-89; edn. tech. assoc. Harvard Grad. Sch. Edn., Cambridge, Mass., 1987-88. Chmn., Conn. Instructional TV coun., Hartford, 1964-65; gubernatorial appointee Mass. Spl. Legisl. Commn. on Unequal Ednl. Opportunity, Boston, 1978-80; mem. edn. adv. com. Dukakis Gubernatorial Campaign, Boston, 1982. Sgt. AUS, 1956-58. Nat. Edn. Policy fellow, 1969-70. Mem. Mass. Orgn. Ednl. Collaboratives (pres. 1986-88), Conn. Assn. Sch. Supts. (chmn. legisl. com. 1968-69), Am. Assn. Sch. Adminstrs. (leadership adv. com.), Mass. Assn. Sch. Supts. Home: 10 Windemere Rd Wellesley MA 02181-4821 Office: Edn Collaborative Greater Boston 20 Kent St Brookline MA 02146-7353

GREEN, JOYCE HENS, federal judge; b. N.Y.C., Nov. 13, 1928; d. James S. and Hedy (Bucher) Hens; m. Samuel Green, Sept. 25, 1965 (dec.); children: Michael Timothy, June Heather, James Harry. B.A., U. Md., 1949; J.D., George Washington U., 1951. Bar: D.C. 1951, Va. 1956, U.S. Supreme Ct. 1956. Practice law Washington, 1951-68, Arlington, Va., 1956-68; ptnr. Green & Green, 1966-68; judge Superior Ct., D.C., 1968-79, U.S. Dist. Ct. for D.C., 1979—. Co-author: Dissolution of Marriage, 1986, supplements, 1987-89; contbr. supplements Marriage and Family Law Agreements, 1985-89. Trustee D.C. div. Am. Cancer Soc., 1963-76. Named Woman Lawyer of Yr., 1979. Fellow Am. Bar Found., Am. Acad. Matrimonial Lawyers; mem. Fed. Judges Assn. (bd. dirs.), ABA, Va. Bar Assn., Bar Assn. D.C., D.C. Bar, D.C. Women's Bar Assn. (pres. 1960-62), Exec. Women in Govt. (chmn. 1977), Kappa Beta Pi, Phi Delta Phi (hon.). Club: Nat. Lawyers (Washington). Office: US Dist Ct US Courthouse 3d St & Constitution Ave NW Washington DC 20001

GREEN, JUDITH, writer; b. N.Y.C.; d. Arthur and Rose (Fields) Heiman; m. William J. Green (dec.); children: Christina Fields, Nicholas Wiliam. BA, Vassar Coll., 1958. Copywriter BBDO, N.Y.C., 1958-63. Author: The Young Marrieds, 1962, Winners, 1981, Sometimes Paradise, 1987, Unsuitable Company, 1991. Mem. Author's Guild. Home: 555 Park Ave New York NY 10021-8166

GREEN, JULIA LYNNE, financial services professional; b. Mpls., Nov. 17, 1959; d. Kenneth and Roberta (Pinsky) G. BA, Mt. Holyoke Coll., 1980; postgrad., Harvard U., Boston U. Staff asst. Harvard Coll., Cambridge, Mass., 1980-81; promotion asst. MIT Press, Cambridge, 1981-82; freelance proofreader O'Reilly Assocs., Newton, Mass., 1987; sr. sec. dept. computer sci. Boston U., 1986-87; sr. sec. mut. series fund State St. Bank, Boston, 1987-89; trans. processor mut. series fund Boston Fin. Data Svcs., Quincy, Mass., 1990-92; account specialist Zweig, Boston Fin. Data Svcs., Quincy, 1990—. Organizer Mass Pirg, Amherst, 1977-78. Mem. WGBH, Mt. Holyoke Club Boston, Quill and Scroll. Home: 107 Spring St Apt 3A Watertown MA 02172-3471

GREEN, JULIUS CURTIS, business manager; b. Balt., Dec. 23, 1957; s. Julius and Barbara Ann (Harrison) G.; m. Sheila Lynn Wray, July 2, 1988. BS in Acctg., U. Balt., 1983, MBA in Fin., 1989; postgrad., George Washington U. Law Ctr., 1991—. CPA, Md. Receptionist U. Md., Balt., 1981-83; legis. auditor State of Md., Annapolis, 1983-86; dir. aux. svcs. Morgan State U., Balt., 1986-88, George Washington U., Washington, 1988—; bd. dirs. Eastern Assn. Coll. Aux. Svcs., Staunton, Va., 1989-90; cons. in field. Treas. Com. for Curt Anderson, Balt., 1983-89; mem. 43/44 Legis. Com., Balt., 1985—. With USAF, 1976-80. Recipient Air Force commendation, 1979; named Outstanding Vet., U. Balt., 1981. Democrat. Baptist. Office: The George Washington U 2121 I St NW Washington DC 20052

GREEN, JUNE LAZENBY, federal judge; b. Arnold, Md., Jan. 23, 1914; d. Eugene H. and Jessie T. (Briggs) Lazenby; m. John Cawley Green, Sept. 5, 1936. JD, Am. U., 1941. Bar: Md. 1943, D.C. 1945. Claims adjuster Lumbermans Mut. Casualty Co., Washington, 1942-43, claims atty., 1943-47; pvt. practice Washington, 1947-68, Annapolis, Md., 1950-68; judge U.S. Dist. Ct. D.C., 1968—; mem. spl. ct. Regional Reorganization Railroad Act, 1987—; examiner bar, Washington, 1963-68. Named Woman Lawyer of Yr., 1965; recipient Lifetime Achievement award Alumni Assn. of Am. U., 1986. Mem. ABA, Md. Bar Assn., Bar Assn. D.C. (bd. dirs. 1966-68, award 1984), Women's Bar Assn. D.C. (pres. 1955-57), Kappa Beta Pi. Home: 464 W Joyce Ln Arnold MD 21012-2207 also: 550 N St NW Washington DC 20024 Office: US Courthouse 3D Constitution Ave NE Washington DC 20002-5618

GREEN, LEON MORTON, psychiatrist; b. Berkeley, Calif., July 3, 1949; s. Morton and Elizabeth Ann (Griffith) G.; m. Gwendolyn Gail Ditmars, June 5, 1971 (div. Sept. 1975); m. Mary Ann Donahue, May 3, 1980; stepchildren: Jill Robin Swartz, Meghan Marie Swartz. BA, U. Kans., Lawrence, 1971; cert., Leningrad State U., USSR, 1972; BSM, U. S.D., 1974; MD, George Washington U., 1976. Diplomate Am. Bd. Med. Examiners. Intern C.S. Wilson Meml. Hosp., Johnson City, N.Y., 1976-77; resident Shephard Eno Pratt Hosp., Towson, Md., 1977-79, fellow, 1979-80; psychiatrist Associated Psychiatric Svcs., Newark, Del., 1980-81; pvt. practice Wilmington, Del., 1981—. Adv. bd. Mental Health Assn. in Del., Wilmington, 1988-90; hon. bd. mem., 1983-88. Mem. AMA, AAAS, Am. Psychiat. Assn., Psychiat. Soc. Del. (sec. 1983-85, pres. 1986-87), Com. for Sci. Investigation Claims of Paranormal. Democrat. Office: 1601 Milltown Rd Wilmington DE 19808-4047

GREEN, LISA MICHELE, copy editor; b. Freeport, N.Y., June 4, 1957; d. Richard and Annette Theresa (DeGrace) G.; divorced. BA in Psychology, Adelphi U., 1980. Pers. recruiter, adminstrv. asst. Lloyd Personnel Cons., Great Neck, N.Y., 1979-82; sec./advt. coord. Biomed. Information Systems, Inc., N.Y.C., 1982-83; editorial asst. Scholastic, Inc., N.Y.C., 1983-85; editorial prodn. asst. McGraw-Hill, Inc., N.Y.C., 1985-87; jr. copywriter, proofreader Siebel/Mohr, Inc., N.Y.C., 1987-88; proofreader/copyeditor AC&R Advt., Inc., N.Y.C., 1988-90; copy editor Doubleday Book & Music Clubs, Garden City, N.Y., 1990-91; copy editor, jr. copywriter Lintas: Mktg. Communications, Inc., N.Y.C., 1991—. Copyeditor: Bruce Springsteen: The Boss, 1985. Democrat. Jewish. Office: Lintas Mktg Comm One Dag Hammarskjold Plz New York NY 10017

GREEN, MAURICE RICHARD, neuropsychiatrist; b. Chgo., Oct. 28, 1922; divorced; children: Melissa, Suzanne, Constance. BS, Northwestern U., 1942; BM, Northwestern U. Med. Sch., 1945, MD, 1946; cert. in Psychoanalytic Tng., William Alanson White Inst., N.Y.C., 1954. Diplomate Am. Bd. Psychiatry and Neurology. Intern Passavant Hosp., Chgo., 1945-46; resident in psychiatry Bronx (N.Y.) VA Hosp., 1948-51; cons. psychiatrist Brookwood Hall, East Islip, L.I., N.Y., 1955-58; staff psychiatrist Psychiatric Clinic Ct. Spl. Sessions, 1956-60; cons. psychiatrist Bleuler Psychotherapy Ctr., Queens, N.Y., 1956-68; research psychiatrist, mem. psychiat. epidemiology sect. William Alanson White Inst., N.Y.C., 1968-72; attending geriatric psychiatrist Albert Einstein Med. Sch., 1974-76; attending child and adolescent psychiatry Harlem Hosp. of Columbia Presbyn. Med. Ctr., N.Y.C., 1974-75; med. dir. geriatric and family psychiatry Lincoln Hosp., 1974-76; chief psychiatrist Family Ct. Services div. South Beach Psychiat. Ctr., S.I., N.Y., 1976-80; sr. attending psychiatrist Columbia-Presbyn. at St. Luke's-Roosevelt Hosp., N.Y.C., 1978—; cons. psychiatrist Liaison-Consultation Service NYU Med. Ctr., N.Y.C., 1985-86; psychiatrist spl. evaluation and treatment unit Rockland Psychiat. Ctr., 1985-87; mem. faculty William Alanson White Inst., N.Y.C., 1957—; cons. Goddard Coll., 1961-68; assoc. attending psychiatrist Bellevue Hosp., 1962-85, presently attending physician; supervisory and tng. analyst William Alanson White Inst., 1962—; clin. prof. child and adolescent psychiatry NYU Med. Sch., 1964—; mem. med. bd. Roosevelt Hosp., 1965-76; prin. investigator Diamox-Thiamine Research Unit Nathan S. Kline Research Inst., 1987; med. dir. Neurologic Systems, Inc., 1987; presidium Inst. for Brain Function Research, Inc., 1987; mem. Treatment Innovations Task Force-Soc. for Traumatic Stress Studies, 1987. Author: Interpersonal Psychoanalysis: Selected Papers of Clara Thompson, 1971, Psicoanalisi interpersonale, 1972, L'Esperiencze Prelogica, 1972, Violence and the Family, 1980; (with Edward S. Tauber) Prelogical Experience, 1959; assoc. editor Contemporary Psychoanalysis jour., 1968—; contbr. articles to profl. jours. Project dir. Nathan Kline Rsch. Inst., 1988—. Fellow Am. Psychiat. Assn. (com. on aging N.Y. Dist. br.), Am. Acad. Psychoanalysis, Am. Orthopsychiat. Assn. (publs. com. Anniversary Vol. 1968-71), Am. Acad. of Child and Adolescent Psychiatry (com. on hospitalization of children, nat. legis. network 1982-86), N.Y. Acad. Medicine; mem. AMA, N.Y. Coun. on Child Psychiatry, N.Y. Soc. Clin. Psychiatry, William Alanson White Psychoanalytic Soc., Physicians for Social Responsibility, Nat. Assn. Patients Rights and Advocacy, Inst. Brain Function Rsch., Soc. Biol. Psychiatry. Home and Office: 275 Central Park W 15-D New York NY 10024

GREEN, MICHAEL ENOCH, chemistry educator, academic administrator; b. N.Y.C., Nov. 5, 1938; s. George A. and Esther (Gladstone) G.; m. Nihal Kustimur, Oct. 12, 1974; 1 child, Omar. BA, Cornell U., 1959; MS, Yale U., 1961, PhD, 1964. Rsch. assoc. Calif. Inst. Tech., Pasadena, 1963-64; vis. lectr. Mid. East Tech. U., Ankara, Turkey, 1964-66; mem. chemistry faculty CUNY, N.Y.C., 1966, asst. prof., 1966-70, assoc. prof., 1973-83, prof., 1984—, dept. chair, 1990—. Co-author: Safety in Working with Chemicals, 1978, Use of Estimates in Solving Chemistry Problems, 1990; contbr. articles to profl. jours. Mem. Am. Chem. Soc., Am. Phys. Soc., N.Y. Acad. Scis. (chair biophysics sect. 1987-88), Biophys. Soc. Office: CUNY 138th St & Convent Ave New York NY 10031

GREEN, MICHAEL KENT, educator; b. Monette, Mo., May 23, 1951; s. Kenneth L. Green and Evelyn m. (Hagebusch) Smith; m. Margaret M. Weast; 1 child, Megan E. BA, U. Kans., 1973; MA, U. Chgo., 1975, PhD, 1979. Asst. prof. Marquette U., Milw., 1979-81; asst. prof. SUNY, Oneonta, 1981-88, assoc. prof., 1988—; dir. Internat. Studies SUNY, Oneonta, 1988—. Contbr. articles to profl. jours. Rsch. grant SUNY Rsch. Found., 1985, W.B. Ford grant, 1987, 90, Profl. Devel. grant United Univ. Professions, 1988-89. Mem. Am. Philos. Assn., N.Am. Kant Soc., Coun. for Employee Rights and Responsibilities, N.Am. Soc. for the Study of J.J. Roussear, Popular Cultural Assn, Dante Soc., Am. Soc. for Eighteenth Century Studies. Office: SUNY Philosophy Dept Oneonta NY 13800

GREEN, NORMAN MARSTON, JR., minister; b. Oakland, Calif., June 27, 1932; s. Norman Marston and Gladys Marian (Meads) G.; m. Dolores Antoinette Taylor, June 27, 1953; children: Russell Norman, Cynthia Louise, Sharon Marie, Deona Lynn. BA, U. Calif., Berkeley, 1954; BD, Berkeley Bapt. Div. Sch., 1957; postgrad., U. Chgo., 1957-59; DMin, Ea. Bapt. Theol. Sem., Phila., 1982. Ordained to ministry Am. Baptist Ch., 1957. Pastor Grace Bapt. Ch., Downers Grove, Ill., 1959-62; field rep. Am. Bapt. Home Mission Soc., Valley Forge, Pa., 1962-66, field dir., 1966-76; dir. office planning resources Am. Bapt. Nat. Ministries, Valley Forge, Pa., 1977—; recording clk. Cen. Bapt. Ch., Wayne, pa., 1986-90, treas., 1990—; sec.-treas. Assn. of Statisticians of Am. Religious Bodies, 1987—; championship statistician Masters Long Distance Running com. The Athletic Congress/USA, 1988—. Joint author: Local Church Planning Manual, 1977, Key Steps in Local Church Planning, 1980, Churches and Church Membership in the United States 1990, 1992. Inspector of elections Tredyffrin Twp., Berwyn, Pa., 1976-81; grand prix coord. Mid-Atlantic Athletics Congress, Phila., 1991—; U.S. del. World Assn. Vet. Athletes, 1988—. Recipient Otto T. Essig award The Athletics Congress/USA, 1990, Male Athlete of the Yr. age 50-54, 1982-87, age 55-59, 1987-91. Mem. Am. Bapt. Ministers Coun., Phila. Masters Track and Field Assn. (life), Religious Rsch. Assn., Mid-Atlantic Athletics Congress (v.p. 1988—), Am. Running and Fitness Assn. (pres. 1991—). Democrat. Home: 405 Curtis Ct Wayne PA 19087 Office: National Ministries PO Box 851 Valley Forge PA 19482-0851

GREEN, RAYMOND FERGUSON ST. JOHN, marketing and advertising executive; b. Phila., Aug. 15, 1950; Raymond Silvernail and Rose Dorathea (Basile) G.; BA in Psychology, Lafayette Coll., 1972; postgrad. Temple U., 1972-75; m. Lisa Rose Wardzinski, June 24, 1972; children: Katharine Amanda, Ian Ferguson Paul. Prodn. asst. Franklin Broadcasting Co., Phila., 1972-73, asst. sec., 1973-75, v.p. corp. affairs, 1975-78, exec. v.p., 1978-84; pres., gen. mgr., COO Franklin Broadcasting Co., 1983-88, pres. Magnetik Prodns., Inc., 1982-88; pres. Greenrose Corp., 1988—, also bd. dirs.; sec./treas. Liebert & Co.; bd. dirs. Young Audiences Eastern Pa., co-chmn., 1989-90. Associated Bio-Med. Svcs.; dir. Northwestern Corp., 1988—; v.p. Amica Co., 1985—; treas. NW Ctr. MH/MR, 1986—. Mem. adv. bd. Phila. Boys Choir & Chorale, 1986—, Musical Fund Soc. of Phila. Mem. Northwest Center; mem. Musical Fund Soc. Phila., Phila. Art Alliance. Mem. Ea. Montgomery County Assn. Realtors, TV Radio Advt. Club, Internat. Soc. Bacchus (trustee, chmn. Phila. chpt. 1988-91), Center Internat. Gastronomic Studies (trustee), N.G. Assns. of U.S. and Pa., Phila. Art Alliance, Colonial Phila. Hist. Soc., Union League Club, Commonwealth Club, Rotary. Roman Catholic. Office: 644 Germantown Pike Lafayette Hill PA 19444-1642

GREEN, RAYMOND ROBERT, hospital administrator; b. Appleton, Wis., Aug. 26, 1946; s. Robert Louis and Leone Frances (Van Eperen) G.; m. Angelina Gladys Kiratzopoulos, May 26, 1969 (div. 1986); 1 child, Christopher James; m. Eileen Harrison, Apr. 18, 1992. BBA, U. Wis., 1972. Employment mgr. Jersey City med. Ctr., 1973-75; dir. personnel Riverside Gen. Hosp., Secaucus, N.J., 1975-81; v.p. adminstrn. Meadowlands Hosp. Med. Ctr., Secaucus, 1981-89; v.p. human resources Lawrence Hosp., Bronxville, N.Y., 1990—. With USN, 1965-69. Mem. Asst. Hosp. Dirs. Assn. N.J., N.J. Assn. Hosp. Pers. Adminstrs., Nat. Assn. Hosp. Recruiters (founder, charter mem., treas. 1975-76), N.J. Assn. Profl. Recruiters (founder, pres. 1973-75), Am. Hosp. Assn., Assn. Hosp. Human Resource Adminstrs., Am. Soc. Healthcare Human Resource Adminstrs. (pres. 1992). Roman Catholic. Office: Lawrence Hosp 55 Palmer Ave Bronxville NY 10708-3491

GREEN, RAYMOND S(ILVERNAIL), retired radio station executive; b. Torrington, Conn., Jan. 1, 1915; s. Percy Alexander and Amy (Silvernail) G.; m. Rose Basile, June 20, 1942; children: Carol Rae Green Hoffman, Raymond Ferguson. Student, Julius Hartt Sch. Music, 1934-37; studied violin with, Sarah Newton, 1925-33; voice with, Royal Dadmun, 1934-38, Giuseppe Boghetti, 1938-41, Alfredo Martino, 1942-50; coached with, Frederick Kitzsinger, 1946, Stuart Ross, 1947, Dr. Ernst Knoch, 1947-50; D.H.L. (hon.), Cabrini Coll., 1982; D.Mus. (hon.), Combs Coll., 1984; D.F.A. (hon.), New Sch. Music, 1984. Producer, dir. musical programs NBC, N.Y.C., 1941-47; prodn. mgr. NBC, 1948; gen. mgr. Sta. WFLN, Phila., 1949-66; pres. Franklin Broadcasting Co., Phila., 1966-82, chmn. bd., 1982-88; owner, operator conservation tree farm, Washington, Vt. Pres. Phila. Art Alliance, 1966-73, chmn. bd., 1973-77, hon. pres., 1977; exec. v.p. Schuylkill Valley Nature Ctr., 1970-90; bd. dirs. Presser Found., 1985—, Mus. Fund. Soc., Union League Phila.; v.p., chmn. Eugene Ormandy Archive, U. Pa., assoc. trustee, 1989—; trustee Valley Forge Mil. Acad. Found., 1989-92. Maj. USAAF, 1942-46. Decorated commendatore Order of merit Italian Republic; recipient William Penn Human Rights award, 1982, George Washington Medal Freedoms Found. at Valley Forge. Fellow Royal Soc. Arts (London); mem. Broadcast Pioneers (pres. 1965-66, life dir.), Musical Fund Soc. Phila. (pres. 1983-86, bd. dirs.), Am. Forestry Assn., Pa. Soc. Clubs: Franklin Inn, Philobiblon, Union League (bd. dirs. 1984-88), Phila. Cricket (Phila.). Home: 308 Manor Rd Lafayette Hill PA 19444-1741 Office: Greenrose Corp 3138 Butler Pike Plymouth Meeting PA 19462

GREEN, RICHARD MICHAEL, surgeon; b. Rochester, N.Y., Feb. 26, 1944; s. Leonard and Edith (Grossman) G.; m. Barbara Sue Lipson, June 26, 1967; 1 child, Debra. BA, Colgate U., 1966; MD, U. Rochester, 1970. Diplomate Am. Bd. Surgery, Am. Bd. Vascular Surgery. Resident in surgery U. Rochester, 1970-76, vascular surgeon, 1976-89, chief, vascular surgery, 1989—. Contbr. articles to profl. jours. Capt. U.S. Army Res. Mem. Soc. for Vascular Surgery, Internat. Soc. for Cardiovascular Surgerg (mem. chmn. 1989), Am. Coll. Surgeons, Centra Surgical, Ea. Vascular Soc. (sec. 1989—), Alpha Omega Alpha. Home: 58 Whitestone Ln Rochester NY 14618 Office: 125 Lattimore Rd Rochester NY 14620

GREEN, ROBERT EDWARD, neurosurgeon, writer; b. N.Y.C., Mar. 30, 1921; s. Bud and Anna Marie (vonHinken) Green; m. Beverly Jane Horn, Oct., 1945; children: James Kimball, Gwynneth Marie, Thomas Carter, Cathlin Louise. BA, Columbia U., 1941; MD, Cornell U., 1944. Diplomate Am. Bd. Neurol. Surgery. Intern U. Chgo. Clinics, 1944-45, resident, 1945-46; resident in neurosurgery Johns Hopkins Hosp., Balt., 1948-51, instr. neurosurgery, 1950-51; attending neurosurgeon St. Barnabas Med. Ctr., Newark, 1951-64, Hosp. Ctr. at Orange, N.J., 1951—; chief div. neurosurgery Med. Ctr. at Livingston, Newark, N.J., 1964—, trustee, 1981-90, dir. neurosurgical edn. and resident tng., 1989—; chief div. neurosurgery Hosp. Ctr. at Orange, N.J., 1959—; cons. neurosurgeon St. Mary's Hosp., Orange, 1966—, Montclair Community Hosp. (N.J.), 1964—. Author, mem. editorial bd: A History of Neurological Surgery, 1951; writer, narrator tape recording Forever Green -50 Years of Songs by Buddy Green, 1983; contbr.

med. articles to publs. Capt. M.C., U.S. Army, 1946-47, ETO. Fellow ACS, Internat. Coll. Surgeons; mem. Am. Assn. Neurol. Surgeons, Congress Neurol. Surgeons, N.J. Neurol. Soc. (pres. 1961-62, peer rev. com. 1983—), Chaine des Rotisseurs (Regional Bailli, N.E. 1979-81), Chaine des Rotisseurs (Chambellan 1982-86, hon. 1986—, asst. regional Bailli, N.E., 1988-90, regional Bailli, N.E, 1990—, bd. dirs., Ordre Mondial de Gourmets Degostateurs Consul Regional N.E. 1991—). Republican. Congregationalist. Office: 22 Old Short Hills Rd Livingston NJ 07039-5605

GREEN, ROSE BASILE (MRS. RAYMOND S. GREEN), poet, author, educator; b. New Rochelle, N.Y., Dec. 19, 1914; d. Salvatore and Caroline (Galgano) Basile; m. Raymond S. Green, June 20, 1942; children: Carol-Rae Green Sadano, Raymond Ferguson St. John. BA, Coll. New Rochelle, 1935; MA, Columbia U., 1941; PhD, U. Pa., 1962; LHD (hon.), Gwynedd-Mercy Coll., 1979, Cabrini Coll., 1982. Tchr., Torrington High Sch., Conn., 1936-42; writer, researcher Fed. Writers Project, 1935-36; freelance script writer Cavalcade of Am., NBC, 1940-42; assoc. prof. English, univ. registrar Tampa U., Tampa, 1942-43; spl. instr. English, Temple U., Phila., 1953-57; prof. dept. English, Cabrini Coll., Radnor, Pa., 1957-70, chmn. dept., 1957-70. Author: Cabrinian Philosophy of Education, 1967, (criticism) The Italian-American Novel, 1972, (poetry books) To Reason Why, 1971, Primo Vino, 1972, 76 for Philadelphia, 1975, Woman, The Second Coming, 1977, Lauding the American Dream, 1980, Century Four, 1981, Songs of Ourselves, 1982, (transl.) The Life of Mother Frances Cabrini, 1984, The Pennsylvania People, 1984, Challenger Countdown, 1988, Five Hundred Years of America, 1492-1992, 1992; editor faculty jour. A-Zimuth, 1963-70. Exec. dir. Am. Inst. Italian Studies; dir. lit. com. Phila. Art Alliance; bd. dirs., trustee Free Libr. of Phila.; v.p., dir. Nat. Italian-Am. Found.; chair Nat. Adv. Coun. Ethnic Heritage Studies; adv. bd. Women for Greater Phila.; dir. Balch Inst. Phila. Decorated cavalier Republic of Italy; named Woman of Yr. Pa. Sons of Italy, 1975, Disting. Dau. of Pa., 1978; recipient Nat. Amita award for lit., 1976, Nat. Bicentennial award for poetry DAR, 1976, other awards for contbns. to lit. and edn. Fellow Royal Soc. Arts (London); mem. AAUW (dir.-at-large), Am. Acad. Polit. and Social Sci., Acad. Am. Poets, Acad. Polit. Sci., Am. Studies Assn., Ethnic Studies Assn., Nat. Council Tchrs. English, Am.-Italy Soc. (dir. 1952—), Eastern Pa. Coll. New Rochelle Alumnae (pres. 1951-54), Cosmopolitan Club, Kappa Gamma Phi. Home: 308 Manor Rd Lafayette Hill PA 19444-1741

GREEN, RUTH R., retired health agency administrator; b. N.Y.C.; d. William and Ethel (Trachtenberg) Relkin; m. Darwin Green, Sept. 2, 1950; children: Robert L., Sandor A. BS, CCNY, 1950; MA, Columbia U., 1952. Intake counselor Vocat. Rehab. div N.Y. State, N.Y.C., 1950-51; asst. adminstr., dir. counseling N.Y. League for the Hard of Hearing, N.Y.C., 1951-79, exec. dir., 1979-92; ret., 1992; advisor Vocat. Rehab. Commn. on Deafness, 1986—. Advisor N.Y.C. Bd. Edn. Adv. Com. Occupational Edn., 1976—. Fellow World Rehab. Fund., 1979. Mem. APA, ACA, Nat. Rehab. Assn., Nat. Rehab. Counseling Assn., Am. Speech, Hearing and Lang. Assn. (clin. cert. bd. 1987-89), Am. Deafness and Rehab. Assn., IACS (site visitor, bd. dirs. 1991-92). Home: 1669 Hendrickson Ave Merrick NY 11566-2828

GREEN, STEPHEN JOEL, columnist; b. Boston, Oct. 13, 1940; s. Hyman and Anne Rose (Marcus) G.; m. Barbara Kaufman, Aug. 6, 1965 (div. 1989); children: Jennifer Lara, Alison Rebecca; m. Virginia Nash Durrin, Oct. 28, 1990. BA, Northeastern U., Boston, 1963. Editor Danvers (Mass.) Herald, 1963-65; reporter Providence Jour., 1965-66, Washington Star, 1966-71, Washington Post, 1971-77; city desk editor Miami News, 1977-79; politics editor San Diego Union, 1979-83, editorial writer, 1983-84; mng. editor, columnist Copley News Service, Washington, 1984—. With USNG, 1963-68. Mem. Soc. Profl. Journalists, White House Corrs. Assn., Nat. Press Club. Home: 4926 Sedgewick St NW Washington DC 20016-2326 Office: Copley News Svc 1100 National Press Bldg Washington DC 20045

GREEN, WARREN ARTHUR, health facility administrator; married. B, U. Pitts., 1966, M, 1968. Adminstrv. asst. Eye and Ear Hosp. Pitts., 1966, asst. exec. dir., 1971-72, assoc. exec. dir., 1972-77; adminstrv. resident Homestead (Pa.) Hosp., 1967-68; chief ops. svc. Naval Hosp., Portsmouth, Va., 1968-71; v.p., gen. dir. Albert Einstein Med. Ctr., Phila., 1977-81; sr. v.p., gen. dir. Daroff div. Mt. Sinai Hosp., Mpls., 1981-83; pres. Mt. Sinai Hosp.; now, pres. Sinai Hosp. Balt. Mem. APHA, Am. Hosp. Assn., Hosp. Assn. Pa. Office: Sinai Hosp Balt 2401 W Belvedere Ave Baltimore MD 21215*

GREEN, WILLIAM ANTHONY, builder and developer; b. Balt., Aug. 3, 1951; s. Irvin Green and Lillian Leola (Sparrow) Keene; m. Cynthia Diane (div.); m. Bonnie Lou Fisher. Student, Howard Community Coll., Columbia, Md., 1978, 86, Coll. Notre Dame, Balt., 1989—. Owner, operator Green & Co. Antiques & Art, Balt., 1967-73; asst. mgr. Rosa Bonheur Meml. Park, Balt., 1967-69, owner, 1979—; owner Westport Cemetery Corp., Balt., 1983-87, Belair Meat & Poultry Co., Balt., 1985-87; gen. ptnr. Featherbed Partnership, Balt., 1987-89; pres., owner Acquest Homes, Inc., Balt., 1984—; prin. William A. Green Real Estate Devel., Balt., 1987—. Bd. dirs. Linwood Children's Ctr., Ellicott City, Md.; mem. 1980, Foster Care Review Bd., Ellicott City, 1989-93. Decorated Royal duke of Trabzon by Prince Eugenios of the Lascaris-Comnena Dynasty, Trabzon, Turkey, 1987. Mem. Homebuilders Assn. of Md., Howard County C. of C., Rotary Club (Ellicott City pres. 1989-90). Office: Acquest Homes Inc 3100 Timanus Ln Ste 101 Baltimore MD 21207-2871

GREEN, WILLIAM EDWARD, medical administrator; b. Rockville Ctr., N.Y., June 14, 1943; s. Edmund Francis and Mary Margaret (Strupel) G.; m. Martha Ann Sweeney, Sept. 21, 1968; children: William Edward Jr., John Patrick. AAS in Bus. Adminstrn., Nassau Community Coll., 1965; BS in Econs. and Bus., Hofstra U., 1967; M Profl. Studies in Health Care Adminstr, L.I. U., 1979. Adminstrv. asst. VA Med. Ctr., Northport, N.Y., 1974-76; asst. med. adminstr. VA Extended Care Ctr., St. Albans, N.Y., 1976-77, VA Med. Ctr., Bklyn., 1977-80; pub. health advisor USPHS, N.Y.C., 1980-81; chief med. adminstrn. office VA Outpatient Clinic, Bklyn., 1981-83; asst. med. adminstr. VA Med. Ctr., Bronx, 1983-86, program mgmt. officer, 1986; patient adminstr. Hqrs NYARNG, Latham, N.Y., 1987-91; exec. officer 244th Med. Group NYARNG, 1991—. Lt. col. Med. Svc. Corps., U.S. Army. Fellow Am. Acad. of Med. Adminstrs. (diplomate); mem. Alliance of ARNG Health Care Profls., Am. Acad. Med. Adminstrs. (state dir. 1984-89, regional dir. 1989-91), Assn. Mil. Surgeons U.S. (pres. N.Y. chpt. 1987, v.p. 1986), DAV (life), Res. OFficers Assn., Assn. U.S. Army, Gold Key, Upsilon Gamma Alpha. Republican. Roman Catholic. Home: 365 Smith St Freeport NY 11520-3228 Office: Hdqrs 244th NY-ARNG 355 Marcy Ave Brooklyn NY 11206-4811

GREENAWALT, DONALD RALPH, vocational school educator; b. Lancaster, Pa., July 7, 1931; s. Ralph Theodore and Mina (Kroll) G.; m. Isabelle Diane Bradley, Aug. 15, 1953; children: Renee, Donna. BS in Vocat. Edn., Elizabethtown Coll., 1973; MS in Edn., Temple U., 1976. Cert. tchr. machine shop, Pa. Machinist Armstrong World Industry, Lancaster, 1949-70, apprentice instr., coord., 1976—; tchr. Lancaster County Vo-Tech, Willow Street, Pa., 1970-76. Cpl. U.S. Army, 1952-54. Mem. Pa. Vocat. Assn., Am. Vocat. Assn., Tall Cedars of Lebanon, Masons, Lancaster Lodge of Perfection, Reading Consistory, Shriners. Republican. Presbyterian. Home: 316 Homecrest Dr Willow Street PA 17584-9449

GREENAWALT, PEGGY FREED TOMARKIN, advertising executive; b. Cleve., Apr. 27, 1942; d. Bernard H. and Gyta Elinor (Arsham) Freed; m. Gary Tomarkin, Aug. 7, 1966 (div. 1981); children: Craig William, Eric Lawrence; m. William Sloan Greenawalt, Oct. 31, 1987. BS, Simmons Coll., 1964. Asst. account exec. Howard Marks/Norman, Craig & Kummel, Inc., N.Y.C., 1964-66; account exec. Shaw Bros. Advt. Co., N.Y.C., 1966-67; copywriter Claire Advt. Co., N.Y.C., 1967; ptnr. Copywriters Coop., Hartsdale, N.Y., 1970-73; copy chief Howard Marks Advt., N.Y.C., 1973-80; sr. copywriter Wunderman, Ricotta & Kline, N.Y.C., 1980-82; v.p., assoc. creative dir. Ayer-Direct (N.W. Ayer), N.Y.C., 1982-84; sr. v.p., creative dir. D'Arcy Direct (D'Arcy, MacManus & Masius), N.Y.C., 1984-86; creative and mktg. cons., 1986-87; pres. Tomarkin/Greenawalt, Inc.; judge Clio Awards. Author: Kiss, The Real Story, 1980. Dem. dist. Leader. Mem. Direct Mktg. Creative Guild, Direct Mktg. Assn., Women in Communications, Direct Mktg. Club N.Y., Westchester Assn. Women Bus. Owners (pres.). Office: 45 E 30th St New York NY 10016-7323

GREENAWALT, WILLIAM SLOAN, lawyer; b. Bklyn., Mar. 4, 1934; s. Kenneth William and Martha Frances (Sloan) G.; m. Jane DeLano Plunkett, Aug. 17, 1957 (div. May 1986); m. Peggy Ellen Freed Tomarkin, Oct. 31, 1987; children: John DeLano, David Sloan, Katherine Downs. A.B., Cornell U., 1956; LL.B., Yale U., 1961. Bar: N.Y. 1962, U.S. Dist. Ct. (so. and ea. dists.) N.Y. 1962, U.S. Ct. Apls. (2d cir.) 1962, U.S. Supreme Ct. 1966. Assoc. Sullivan & Cromwell, N.Y.C., 1961-65; N.E. regional legal svcs. dir. U.S. Office Econ. Opportunity, N.Y.C., 1965-68; assoc. Rogers & Wells, N.Y.C., 1968-69, ptnr., 1969-77, sr. ptnr., 1977-81; sr. ptnr. Halperin, Shivitz, Eisenberg, Schneider & Greenawalt, N.Y.C., 1981-86, Eisenberg Honig Fogler Greenawalt & Davis, N.Y.C., 1986-91, Bangser Klein Rocca & Blum, N.Y.C., 1991—; lectr. in field. Bd. editors: Yale Law Jour., 1959-61; contbr. articles in field to profl. jours. Chmn., Applied Resources Inc., N.Y.C., 1968-70; chmn. Community Aid Employment Ex-Offenders, Westchester, N.Y., 1971; pres. Westchester Legal Svcs., 1971-74; bd. dirs, 1975-91; mem. N.Y. State Gov.'s Task Force Elem. and Secondary Edn., 1974-75; mem. Pres. Carter's Task Force Criminal Justice, 1976; panel comml. arbitrators Am. Arbitration Assn., 1977—, adv. coun. N.Y. State Senate Dems., 1978—; asst. treas. N.Y. State Dem. Party, 1990—; mem. Greenburgh Recreational Commn., 1976-83, Statewide Spl. Commn. on Polit. Ethics (Dem. Party), 1986-87; mem. Statewide Spl. Commn. on Election Law and Campaign Spending Reform, 1989—; pres. Westchester Crime Victims Assistance Agy., 1981-82; commr. Taconic State Parks, Recreation and Historic Preservation Commn., 1984—, chmn., 1989—; vice-chmn. N.Y. State Coun. on Parks, Recreation and Hist. Preservation, 1989—; moderator Scarsdale Congl. Ch., 1988-90. Lt. comdr. U.S. Navy, 1956-58, Res., 1961-68. Fellow N.Y. Bar Found.; mem. ABA, N.Y. State Bar Assn. (chmn. com. on availability of legal svcs. 1968-70, chmn. action unit #3 1979-81, chmn. spl. commn. on alternatives to jud. resolution of disputes 1981-85), Assn. Bar City N.Y., Nat. Legal Aid and Defenders Assn., Sphinx Head, Aleph Samach, Phi Alpha Delta, Chi Psi, County Tennis of Westchester Club (pres. 1979-80) (Scarsdale, N.Y.), Yale Club. Democrat. Congregationalist. Office: 230 Park Ave New York NY 10169-0005

GREENAWAY, FREDERICK THOMAS, adult education educator; b. Rakaia, New Zealand; came to U.S., 1973; s. Norman and Thelma Beryl (Pluck) G. BS with honors, U. Canterbury, Christchurch, New Zealand, 1969, PhD, 1973. Rsch. assoc. Mich. State U., Lansing, Mich., 1973-74, Syracuse U., Syracuse, N.Y., 1974-80; asst. prof. Clark U., Worcester, Mass., 1980-86, assoc. prof., 1986—, chair, dept. chem., 1990—. Author: numerous rsch. papers. Office: Clark U 950 Main St Worcester MA 01610-1473

GREENBAUM, BRUCE, podiatrist; b. Bklyn., Oct. 24, 1964; s. Robert H. and Doris (Orenstein) G. BA, SUNY, Binghamton, 1985; DPM, Pa. Coll. Podiatric Medicine, 1989. Resident Met. Hosp., Springfield, Pa., 1989-90. Active Am. Diabetes Assn., 1990—. Mem. Am. Podiatric Med. Assn., N.Y. Podiatric Med. Assn., Am. Coll. Foot Surgeons (assoc.), Am. Bd. Podiatric Surgery (assoc.). Jewish. Office: 525 Neptune Ave Brooklyn NY 11224-4063

GREENBAUM, DAVID, real estate development and management executive; b. Bayreuth, Fed. Republic of Germany, Nov. 16, 1946; came to U.S., 1952; s. Herman and Dora (Goldfinger) G.; m. Linda Ruth Malament, Nov. 28, 1969; 1 child, Rebecca Hope. BS in Chemistry, CUNY, 1967; MS in Edn. Adminstrn., Pace U., 1974. Asst. prin., tchr. N.Y.C. Bd. of Edn., Bklyn., 1968-84; pres. Prospect Ct. Realty Corp., Bklyn., 1983—; exec. dir. Midwood Devel. Corp., Bklyn., 1985-88. Mem. com. memberships Community Bd. # 6, Bklyn., 1985, 87; bd. chair Bklyn. Bd. NYANA, 1985-87. Home: 377 Clinton St Brooklyn NY 11231-3602 Office: Propect Ct Realty Corp 485 Court St Brooklyn NY 11231-4016

GREENBERG, AARON ROSMORIN, public relations executive; b. Bklyn., July 5, 1932; s. J. George and Etta (Rosmarin) G.; m. Felice Barmash, June 29, 1958; children: Beth Susan, Marc David. BA in Journalism, Emory U., 1954; MS in Journalism, Columbia U., 1955; postgrad., NYU, 1964-65. Editor Fairchild Pubs., N.Y.C., 1955-56; account exec. Ruder & Finn, Inc., N.Y.C., 1958-61, dir. research, 1963-72; dir. pub. Yeshiva U., N.Y.C., 1961-62; dir. research Am. Stock Exchange, N.Y.C., 1972; v.p. William G. Hetherington & Co., Newark, 1973-78; pres. Livingston (N.J.) Pub. Relations, Inc., 1978—; contbg. editor Book of Knowledge, Encyclopaedia Britannica; instr. Fairleigh-Dickinson U., Madison, N.J., 1980-81; sports corr. West Essex Tribune, Livingston, N.J., 1981—. Mem. adv. commn. on Cable TV, Livingston, 1978-81, adv. commn. on energy, Livingston, 1981-83, adv. commn. transp., Livingston, 1983-85; chmn. adv. council parks & recreation, Livingston, 1985—. Served to sgt. U.S. Army, 1956-58. Mem. Livingston C. of C. (dir.). Jewish. Office: Livingston Pub Rels Inc PO Box 82 Livingston NJ 07039-0082

GREENBERG, ALLAN CARL, college administrator, historian; b. Bklyn., Aug. 24, 1940; s. Leon Abraham and Stella (Goldsmith) G.; m. Marie-Christine Brigitte Jacoberger, Aug. 9, 1979 (dec. May 1989); 1 child, Sean. BA, Cornell U., 1962, MA, 1964; PhD, U. Ill., 1967. Asst. prof. So. Meth. U., Dallas, 1967-68; vis. asst. prof. Ind. U., Bloomington, 1968-69, Rutgers U., New Brunswick, N.J., 1969-70; from asst. prof. to prof. history, polit. sci. Curry Coll., Milton, Mass., 1970—, dir. continuing edn., 1971-74, registrar, 1975—; cons. Dada Archive and Rsch. Ctr., U. Iowa, Iowa City, 1981—; bd. govs. Free U. Ireland, Dublin, 1991—. Author: Artists and Revolution, Dada and the Bauhaus, 1917-1925, 1979; contbr. chpts. to books. Treas., asst. chair, chair Milton Arts Lottery Commn., 1983-87, 89—, chair ACCLAIM, Milton, 1983-85; coll. rep. Milton Community Schs. Adv. Bd., 1981-90. Mem. Am. Hist. Assn., Conf. for Cen. European History, Am. Assn. Coll. Registrars and Admissions OFficers, New. Eng. Assn. Coll. Registrars and Admissions Officers. Home: 122 Old Oaken Bucket Rd Scituate MA 02066 Office: Curry Coll 1030 Blue Hill Ave Milton MA 02186-2330

GREENBERG, ALLAN JEFFREY, accountant; b. Wilkes-Barre, Pa., Jan. 31, 1960; s. Martin and Sondra (Garber) G.; m. Susan Greenberg, Apr. 4, 1987; children: Zachary, Jayne. BS, Ind. U. of Pa., 1982; postgrad., Loyola U., Balt., 1992—. CPA, Md. Sr. supr. Laventhol & Horwath, Washington, 1983-90; mng. dir. Friedman & Fuller, Balt., 1990—. Mem. audit rev. com. United Way, Balt., 1989-91; chm. acctg. div. Associated Jewish Charities, Balt., 1991-92; bd. dirs. Santa Claus Anonymous, Balt., 1990—. Mem. AICPAs, Md. Inst. CPAs. Republican. Office: Friedman & Fuller 22 E Fayette St Baltimore MD 21202

GREENBERG, DAVID GORDON, family and parenting services executive; b. Port Chester, N.Y., Mar. 25, 1947; s. Milton L. and Alice R. (Gordon) G.; m. Susan Stein, June 13, 1976; children: Sarah, Jacob. BA, Antioch Coll., Yellow Springs, Ohio, 1970; PhD, Union Inst., Cin., 1978. Substance abuse specialist Sch. Dist. Phila., 1976-85; dir. parenting dept. Frankin Maternity Hosp., Phila., 1985-88; dir. dept. family & parenting Hosp. Phila. Coll. Osteo. Medicine, 1988—; dir. Planned Parenthood S.E., Phila, 1987—. Photographer Mt. Airy Express & Learning Tree, Phila., 1984—. Recipient Speical Recognition award March of Dimes, Phila., 1991. Home: 7128 Crittenden St Philadelphia PA 19119-1214 Office: Osteopathic Med Ctr 4150 City Ave Philadelphia PA 19131-1610

GREENBERG, FRANK EDGAR, sports administrator, attorney; b. Phila., Mar. 28, 1933; s. Allen Lewis and Sonya (Dessen) G.; m. Anne Schwab, Mar. 31, 1966 (div. 1986); children: Jeff I., Scott H. BS in Econs., U. Pa., 1955, LLB, 1960. Assoc. Katz, Slifkin & Bernstein, Phila., 1960-61; ptnr. Katz, Slifkin & Greenberg, Phila., 1961-82; sole practitioner Frank E. Greenberg & Assocs., Phila., 1982-84; ptnr. Bernstein, Fox, Greenberg & Semanoff, Phila., 1984-88; of counsel Semanoff & Hendler, Phila., 1988-90, Jenkintown, Pa., 1990—; exec. v.p. The Athletics Congress, Indpls., 1984-88, pres. 1988-92. Bd. dirs. U.S. Olympic Com., 1988, Pacific Conf. Games, 1988, Pan Am. Games. 1st lt. U.S. Army, 1955-57/. Robert Geigengach award The Athletic Congress, 1984. Mem. Phila. Sports Congress (exec. com.), Phila. Masters Assn. (sec., bd. dirs.), Friends of Penn Relays, Track and Field Hall of Fame (pres. 1988—). Home: 111 S California Ave Apt 302 Atlantic City NJ 08401-6452 Office: Semanoff & Hendler 610 Old York Rd Ste 200 Jenkintown PA 19046-2837

GREENBERG, GEOFFREY ANDREW, hair colorist, beauty consultant; b. Bklyn., Mar. 25, 1948; s. Jack Jay and Eleanor (Toubin) G. Student, Rider Coll., 1965-67, Arts Students League of N.Y., 1968-73, Sch. of Visual Arts, N.Y., 1973-74, H.B. Studio, N.Y., 1976-78. Art restoration apprentice Marjak Studios, N.Y.C., 1968-69; owner, tchr. Chelsea Artist Workshop, N.Y.C., 1974-76; hair colorist Saks Fifth Ave, N.Y.C., 1981-86, 86-90, Yves Claude Hair, N.Y.C., 1983-86, Suga Salon, N.Y.C., 1990—, Clives Summers Salon, N.Y.C., 1990—, Salon Ishi, N.Y.C., 1992—. Art Students League of N.Y. scholar, 1968. Home: 55 Perry St # 4M New York NY 10014

GREENBERG, HARVEY ROY, psychiatrist; b. Phila., June 27, 1935; s. Murry Harry and Dora (Cohen) G.; m. Sharon Messitte; children: Matthew, Paul, Nicholas. AB, Columbia Coll., N.Y.C., 1955; MD, Cornell U., 1959; psychoanalysis degree, N.Y. Med. Coll., 1970. Diplomate Am. Bd. Psychiatry and Neurology. Internship N.Y. Hosp. Cornell U. Med. Ctr., N.Y.C., 1959-60; resident in psychiatry NYU/Bellevue Med. Ctr., 1960-63; Pvt. practice psychiatry and psychoanalysis N.Y.C., 1965—; supervising psychiatrist, lectr. adolescent psychiatry Bronx Children's Psychiat. Ctr., Bronx, N.Y., 1975—; clin. prof. psychiatry Albert Einstein Med. Coll., Bronx, 1981—; faculty L.I. Inst. Psychoanalysis, L.I., N.Y., 1986—; residency Bellevue Psychiat. Hosp., NYU Med. Ctr., N.Y.C., 1963-65. Author: Emotional Illness in the Family, 1989; contbr. articles to profl. jours. Capt. U.S. Army, 1963-65. Fellow Am. Psychiat. Assn. (film com. 1977—), Am. Acad. Psychoanalysis; mem. Am. Soc. Adolescent Psychiatry, N.Y. Med. Soc. Home and Office: 320 W 86th St New York NY 10024-3139

GREENBERG, HENRY MORTON, physician, educator; b. N.Y.C., Oct. 5, 1940; s. David and Flora (Budnick) G.; m. Barbara Helene Brown, June 20, 1965; children: Lisa, Jeffrey Oliver. BA, U. Pa., 1961; MD, Tufts U., 1965. Intern St. Elizabeth Hosp., Boston, 1965-66; resident St. Lukes Hosp., N.Y.C., 1968-70; fellow in cardiology Roosevelt Hosp., N.Y.C., 1970-72, co-dir. CCU, 1972-79; dir. coronary care unit Roosevelt site St. Lukes Roosevelt Hosp., N.Y.C., 1979—; from instr. to assoc. clin. prof. of medicine Columbia U. Coll. Physicians & Surgeons, N.Y.C., 1972-87, assoc. prof. clin. medicine, 1987—. Editor: Sudden Coronary Death, 1982, Clinical Aspects of Life Threatening Arrhymias, 1984; contbr. articles to profl. jours. With USPHS, 1966-68, Peace Corps physician, Cameroon, West Africa. Fellow ACP, Am. Coll. Cardiology, Am. Heart Assn. (coun. clin. cardiology), N.Y. Acad. Scis. (conf. com. co-chmn. 1990-92). Office: St Lukes Roosevelt Hosp 428 W 59th St New York NY 10019

GREENBERG, JAY RICHARD, molecular biologist; b. Davenport, Iowa, Aug. 23, 1943; s. Abraham and Ruth Kramer (Mason) G.; divorced; children: Jay, Rachel. BS, U. Chgo., 1964, PhD, 1968. Postdoctoral fellow Inst. Cancer Rsch., Phila., 1968-73; staff scientist Worcester Found. for Exptl. Biology, Shrewsbury, Mass., 1973-83, sr. scientist, 1983-86; assoc. rsch. scientist Yale U., New Haven, 1986-90; sr. rsch. assoc. U. Rochester, N.Y., 1990—; cons. NIH, Bethesda, Md., 1982, 83; grant reviewer NSF, Washington, 1973, reviewer for numerous jours. Contbr. articles to profl. publs. NIH fellow, 1968; grantee NIH, NSF, 1974—; recipient Cancer Rsch. award Mass. div. Am. Cancer Soc., 1974. Mem. Am. Soc. Cell Biology, Am. Soc. Biochemistry and Molecular Biology. Office: U Rochester Hutchinson Hall Rochester NY 14627

GREENBERG, LEON, mathematician; b. N.Y.C., Sept. 8, 1931; s. Herman and Bertha (Sorin) G.; m. Jeanette Berman, Dec. 26, 1955; children: Wendy, Lise, David, Beth. BS, CCNY, 1953; MA, Yale U., 1955, PhD, 1958; MA (hon.), Brown U., 1964. Instr. Brown U., Providence, R.I., 1958-60, asst. prof., 1960-63, assoc. prof., 1963-64; assoc. prof. U. Md., College Park, 1964-66, prof., 1966—; mathematician Nat. Bur. Standards, Washington, 1964-67; vis. mem. Courant Inst./NYU, 1963; Lady Davis Vis. Prof., Hebrew U., Jerusalem, 1978. Contbr. articles to profl. jours. Recipient NATO fellowship NSF, Copenhagen, 1960, grants ONR, Providence, 1960-64, NSF, College Park, 1966-80. Mem. Siam. Office: U of Md Math Dept College Park MD 20742

GREENBERG, LINDA, librarian; b. Phila.; d. George and Sarah (Elkins) G. BA, Temple U., 1965; MS, Drexel U., 1968. Cert. profl. libr., N.J. Reference libr. AT&T Bell Labs., Whippany, N.J., 1968-72; info. specialist Bell Labs. Bus. Info. Systems, Piscataway, N.J., 1972-74; cataloger Newark Pub. Libr., 1974-75; editor, tech. liaison N.Y. Times Info. Svc., Parsippany, N.J., 1975-83; rsch. info. specialist Merrill Lynch & Co., N.Y.C., 1983-87; sr. info. specialist Merrill Lynch and Co., N.Y.C., 1987-90, mgr. tech. svcs., 1990—. Mem. ALA, Am. Soc. Info. Sci., Spl. Librs. Assn. Office: Merrill Lynch Libr 24th Fl World Fin Ctr 250 Vesey St New York NY 10281-1012

GREENBERG, MARK LAWRENCE, humanities educator; b. N.Y.C., July 2, 1948; s. Arnold J. and Ruth (Krotman) G.; m. Vivian Naphtali, June 25, 1972; children: Erica Hilary, Alison Laura. BA cum laude, CUNY, 1971; AM in English, U. Mich., 1972, PhD in English, 1978. Asst. prof. Saginaw (Mich.) Valley U., 1977-79; asst. prof. Drexel U., Phila., 1979-84, assoc. prof., 1984-91, prof. humanities, 1991—; vis. assoc. prof. Swarthmore (Pa.) Coll., 1987; cons. Unisys Corp., Blue Bell, Pa., 1988-89; NEH cons. Phila. Coll. Pharmacy and Sci., 1991—; mem. editorial adv. bd., rev. editor Modern Lang. Studies, Brown U., 1982—. Author, editor: Literature and Technology, 1992; editor: Approaches to Blake's Songs, 1989; guest editor: New Models for Literature and Sci., 1990; contbr. articles to profl. jours. Recipient Meritorious Ind. Study Coun. award Nat. U. Continuing Edn. Assn., 1988; NEH fellow Princeton U., 1981. Mem. Soc. Lit. Scis. (pres. 1989-91), Modern Lang. Assn. (chair exec. com. lit. and sci. 1989), Coun. Editors Learned Jours., Am. Soc. 18th Century Studies. Home: 2255 Deerpath Rd Huntingdon Valley PA 19006-5905 Office: Drexel U Dept Humanities Philadelphia PA 19104

GREENBERG, MELANIE HOPE, illustrator; b. N.Y.C., Dec. 28, 1954; d. Lawrence Leopold and Ruth (Gerber) G. Student, Hunter Coll., 1971-72, 75-76. Adminstrv. asst. Framing Gallery The Picture Show, N.Y.C., 1976-77; framing design cons. Gaines Am., N.Y.C., 1977-78; freelance paste-up mech. artist audio-visual, mags., newspapers, book design, 1980-90; product designer greeting cards, stationary, giftware, kitchenware, games, 1990—. Author, illustrator: At the Beach, 1989, My Father's Luncheonette, 1991 (AIGA Book Show 1990), Celebrations: Our Jewish Holidays, 1991; illustrator: It's My Earth Too!, 1992. Mem. Soc. Children's Book Writers, The Children's Book Illustrators Group (steering com., publicity dir., bull. bd. dir.).

GREENBERG, MICHAEL RICHARD, urban studies and community health educator; b. N.Y.C., Aug. 22, 1943; s. Sydney Saul and Mildred (Saletra) G.; m. Gwendolyn Barker, Jan. 19, 1978; children: Seana Suggs, Heather Suggs, Joshua Suggs, Alexandra Greenberg. BA, CUNY, 1965; MA, Columbia U., 1966, PhD, 1969. Asst. prof. Columbia U., N.Y.C., 1969-71; assoc. prof. Rutgers U., New Brunswick, N.J., 1971-73, prof., 1973-78, disting. prof., 1978-82, prof. urban studies and community health, 1982—; dir. pub. policy Hazardous Substure Mgmt. and Rsch. Ctr., Newark, 1984—; co-dir. pub. health N.J. Grad. Progam in Pub. Health, New Brunswick, 1983—; dir. policy Environ. Occupational Health Sci. Inst., New Brunswick, 1985—. Author: Urbanization and Cancer Mortality, 1983, Public Health and the Environment, 1988, Environmental Risk and the Press, 1989 (award 1988), Environmental Reporter's Handbook (award 1989). Recipient Spl. Merit award EPA, 1977. Mem. APHA, Soc. for Epidemiol. Rsch., Assn. of Am. Geographers, Soc. for Risk Analysis. Home: 228 Lawrence Ave Highland Park NJ 08904-1838 Office: Rutgers U Dept Urban Studies Livingston Campus New Brunswick NJ 08903

GREENBERG, MILTON, political scientist, educator; b. Bklyn., Feb. 20, 1927; s. Samuel and Fannie (Schnell) G.; m. Sonia B. Brown, June 20, 1948; children: Anne Greenberg Bookin, Nancy R. B.A., Bklyn. Coll., 1949; M.A., U. Wis., 1950, Ph.D. (univ. scholar), 1955. Instr. polit. sci. U. Tenn., Knoxville, 1952-55; asst. prof. Western Mich. U., Kalamazoo, 1955-59; assoc. prof. Western Mich. U., 1959-64, prof., 1964, chmn. polit. sci. dept., 1965-69; dean Coll. Arts and Scis., Ill. State U., Normal, 1969-72; v.p. acad. affairs, dean faculties Roosevelt U., Chgo., 1972-80; provost, v.p. acad. affairs Am. U., Washington, 1980—, interim president and provost, 1990-91; pres. assoc. Cleve. Met. Svcs. Commn., 1957; cons. Citizens for Mich. (constl. reform movement), 1960. Author: (with J.C. Plano) The American Political Dictionary, 1962, 8th edit., 1989, (with others) The Political Science

Dictionary, 1973; contbr. to Colliers Yearbook, 1959—; mem. editorial adv. bd. Ednl. Record, 1985—; cons. editor ASHE-ERIC Higher Edn. Reports, 1986—; contbr. articles to profl. jours. Mem. Mich. Gov.'s Commn. on Legis. Apportionment, 1962, Kalamazoo Community Rels. Bd., 1964-65; mem. bd. dirs. Combined Health Appeal of Nat. Capital Area, 1982—, v.p., 1983-85, pres., 1986-88. Social Sci. Rsch. Coun. grantee, 1959, 61. Mem. Am. Polit. Sci. Assn., Midwest Polit. Sci. Assn. (exec. coun. 1972-75), Middle States Assn. Colls. and Schs. (cons.-evaluator 1983—), Law and Soc. Assn., AAUP, Am. Assn. Higher Edn., North Cen. Assn. Colls. and Schs. (commn. on instns. higher edn. 1975-80, exec. bd. 1979-80, cons.-evaluator 1975-80), Nat. Coun. Chief Acad. Officers, Am. Coun. on Edn. (exec. com. 1983-85, chmn. 1985). Office: Am U 4400 Massachusetts Ave NW Washington DC 20016-8001

GREENBERG, MORTON IRA, federal judge; b. Phila., Mar. 20, 1933; s. Harry Arnold and Pauline (Hofkin) G.; m. Barbara-Ann Kissel, May 29, 1987; children from first marriage: Elizabeth, Suzanne, Lawrence. AB, U. Pa., 1954; LLB, Yale U., 1957. Bar: N.J. 1958, U.S. Dist. Ct. N.J. 1958, U.S. Ct. Appeals (3d cir.) 1972, U.S. Supreme Ct. 1973. Law clk.office of atty. gen. State of N.J., Trenton, 1957-58, dep. atty. gen., 1958-60, asst. atty. gen., 1971-73; pvt. practice, Cape May, N.J., 1960-71; judge law div. Superior Ct. N.J., New Brunswick, 1973-76; judge chancery and gen. equity divs. Superior Ct. N.J., Trenton, 1976-80, judge appellate div., 1980-87; judge U.S. Ct. Appeals (3d cir.), Trenton and Phila., 1987—. Office: US Ct Appeals US Courthouse 402 E State St Trenton NJ 08608-1507

GREENBERG, RICHARD ALAN, psychiatrist, educator; b. Phila., Mar. 28, 1946; s. Benjamin and Natalie (Kaplan) G.; m. Laudelina Lahom, June 23, 1979; children: Eric Michael, Jason Paul. AB, Albright Coll., 1968; MD, Thomas Jefferson U., 1973. Diplomate Am. Bd. Psychiatry and Neurology. Resident in psychiatry Jefferson-Del. State Hosp., 1973-76; pvt. practice Bethesda, Md., 1979-86, Washington, 1986—; staff psychiatrist Psychiat. Inst. D.C., Washington, 1976—, pres. med. staff, 1985—; lectr. psychiatry George Washington U., Washington, 1979—, assoc. clin. prof., 1981—; chmn. Ann. Greenbrier Psychopharmacologic Conf., White Sulphur Springs, W.Va.; chief physician, dir. evaluation svcs. Clin. Neurosci. Program, Washington, 1987—. Fellow Am. Pschiat. Assn.; mem. AMA (med. staff sect.), Washington Psychiat. Soc., Med. Soc. D.C. (health svcs. facilities com. 1984—). Democrat. Roman Catholic. Home: 10544 Hunters Way Laurel MD 20723-5724 Office: 2112 F St NW Ste 406 Washington DC 20037-2715

GREENBERG, SAUL NORMAN, orthodontist, educator; b. Bklyn., June 20, 1923; s. Paul and Rebecca (Kaplan) G.; m. Joan Ratner (dec.); children: Stephen, Andrew, David; m. Sheila Pollack, Apr. 8, 1984. BA, Bklyn. Coll., 1943; DDS, NYU, 1947; Cert. in Orthodontics, Columbia U., 1955. Diplomate Am. Bd. Orthodontists. Chmn. orthodontics Inst. for Grad. Dentists, N.Y.C., 1975-80; chief orthodontics dept. Flushing (N.Y.) Hosp., 1980—; prof. orthodontist NYU Coll. Dentistry, 1987—. Author: So You Want To Be A Dentist, 1964; contbr. articles to profl. jours. 1st lt. U.S. Army, 1951-53. Fellow Am. Coll. Dentists; mem. Am. Assn. Orthodontists, ADA, Omicron Kappa Upsilon. Home: 50 Hillpark Ave Great Neck NY 11021 Office: 143-33 Sanford Ave Flushing NY 11355-2049

GREENBERG, SHELDON BURT, plastic and reconstructive surgeon; b. Bklyn., July 8, 1948; s. Morris and Lillian (Liss) G.; m. Andrea R. Levy, Feb. 10, 1991. BS, Muhlenberg Coll., 1970; MD, Chgo. Med. Sch., 1974. Diplomate Am. Bd. Otolaryngology, Plastic Surgery. Resident in surgery Lenox Hill Hosp., N.Y.C., 1974-75; resident in otolaryngology Met. Hosp., Manhattan Eye and Ear Hosp., N.Y.C., 1978; resident in plastic surgery Akron (Ohio) City Hosp., 1978-80, fellow in hand surgery, 1980; pvt. practice, Norwalk, Conn., 1981—. Fellow Am. Coll. Surgeons, Am. Soc. Plastic and Reconstructive Surgeons; mem. Conn. Med. Soc., Fairfield County Med. Soc., Fairfield Men's Club. Republican. Jewish. Office: 40 Cross St Norwalk CT 06851-4647

GREENBERG, STEVEN MOREY, lawyer; b. Jersey City, Apr. 9, 1949; s. Joseph and Rhoda (Weisenfeld) G. AB cum laude, Syracuse U., 1971; JD, U. Pa., 1974. Bar: N.J. 1974, U.S. Dist. Ct. N.J. 1974, N.Y. 1980, U.S. Dist. Ct. (so. dist.) N.Y. 1986, U.S. Dist. Ct. (ea. dist.) N.Y. 1986, U.S. Ct. Appeals (3d cir.) 1987, U.S. Ct. Claims 1989. Assoc. Carpenter, Bennett & Morrissey, Newark, 1974-77; assoc. firm Cole, Berman & Belsky, Rochelle Park, N.J., 1977-79; pvt. practice Hackensack, N.J., 1979—; atty. Bergenfield (N.J.) Rent Leveling Bd., 1985-89, 92—. Trustee, past chmn. youth activities com. Jewish Ctr. of Teaneck, N.J., 1978—; dir., v.p. JH & RC Sr. Housing, Inc., Jersey City, 1992—; trustee, past pres., past v.p., past sec. Sam Gorovoy Group Care Home for Sr. Adults, Bergenfield, N.J., 1983—; mem. adv. bd. dirs. Jewish Home and Rehab. Ctr., Jersey City and River Vale, N.J., 1982-90, chmn. pers. com., 1986—, governing body, 1986—, exec. com., 1987—, v.p., 1992—; trustee Jewish Family Svc., Inc. of Bergen County, 1986—, treas., 1990-92, v.p., 1992—; trustee The Solomon Schechter Day Sch. of Bergen County, 1986-87, Bergenfield Mus. Soc., 1989—, Teaneck Jewish Meml. Assn., 1990-92, v.p., 1990-92, pres., 1992—; mem. Jewish Community Rels. Coun. No. N.J., 1986—; mem. N.J. regional adv. bd. Anti-Defamation League of B'nai B'rith, 1989—, exec. com., 1989—; mem. Teaneck Jewish Community Coun., 1989—; mem. community advocacy program UJC Resource Coun., 1991—. Recipient Second Century award Jewish Theol. Sem. Am., 1988. Mem. ABA, N.J. Bar Assn., Bergen County Bar Assn., Assn. Transp. Practitioners, Phi Kappa Phi, Pi Sigma Alpha. Home: 96 Westminster Ave Bergenfield NJ 07621-3916 Office: 2 University Plaza Dr Hackensack NJ 07601-6202

GREENBERG, WILLIAM MICHAEL, psychiatrist; b. Bklyn., Oct. 19, 1946; s. Benjamin Greenberg and Marilyn (Berger) Hamberg; m. Wendy Faith Megerman, June 14, 1992. BA, Queens Coll., 1968; postgrad., U. Medicine & Dentistry N.J., 1974-76; MD, Albert Einstein Coll. Medicine, 1978. Diplomate Am. Bd. Psychiatry and Neurology. Computer programmer Western Electric Co., N.Y.C., 1970-73; rsch. asst. Bklyn. Jewish Hosp., 1973-74; resident in psychiatry Bronx (N.Y.) Mcpl. Hosp. Ctr., 1978-83, house staff pres., 1981-82; acting med. dir. Met. Ctr. for Mental Health, N.Y.C., 1983; staff psychiatrist Bronx Psychiat. Ctr., 1983-84; dir. psychiatry clinic North Cen. Bronx Hosp., 1984-88; psychiatrist, cons. Montefiore Mental Health Svcs. at Rikers Island, East Elmhurst, N.Y., 1985-86; pvt. practice Bronx, 1985-88; chief psychiatrist, attending staff mem. Bergen Pines County Hosp., Paramus, N.J., 1988—; asst. clin. prof. Albert Einstein Coll. Medicine, Bronx, 1988-90; vis. asst. prof. Med. Coll. Pa., 1990—. Asst. editor Community Psychiatrist, 1985-89; mem. editorial bd. Einstein Quar. Jour. Biology and Medicine, 1987—; contbr. articles to profl. jours.; reviewer for profl. jours. Union rep. Com. Interns and Residents, N.Y.C., 1979-81; speaker's bur. Physicians for Social Responsibility, N.Y.C., 1982-84, Bergen Pines County Hosp., 1988—. Rock Sleyster Meml. scholar AMA, 1977; recipient Bergen Pines Psychiatry Residency Teaching award, 1991. Mem. AAAS, APHA, Am. Psychiat. Assn., Am. Assn. Community Psychiatrists, Assn. for Advancement of Philosophy and Psychiatry. Office: Bergen Pines County Hosp Div Psychiatry Paramus NJ 07652

GREENBERGER, DANIEL MORDECAI, physics educator; b. N.Y.C., Sept. 29, 1933; s. Eugene and Frances (Goldfein) G.; m. Suzanne Marie Dohm, July 18, 1987. BS, MIT, 1954; MS, U. Ill., 1956, PhD, 1958. Asst. prof. Ohio State U., Columbus, 1960-61, U. Calif., Berkeley, 1961-63; from asst. prof. to assoc. prof. CCNY, N.Y.C., 1963—, prof.; Chief organizer, chmn. Internat. Conf. Fundamental Problems in Quantum Theory, N.Y. Acad. Scis., 1986. Editor: New Techniques in Quantum Measurement Theory, 1987; contbr. articles to profl. jours. 1st lt. U.S. Army, 1958-60. Recipient Fulbright Prof. award, 1986, Humboldt Sr. Scientist award Humboldt Found., 1988; NSF postdoctoral fellow, 1961-62. Mem. Am. Assn. Physics Tchrs., Am. Phys. Soc., Sigma Xi. Democrat. Jewish. Office: CUNY Dept Physics 137th St & Convent Ave New York NY 10031

GREENBERGER, JOSH, computer consultant, writer; b. Czechoslovakia, Sept. 25, 1948; came to U.S., 1951; s. Solomon and Pearl (Stern) G. Grad., Comml. Programming Unltd., N.Y.C., 1968. Computer cons. various corporations, N.Y., N.J., 1985—; cons. Goddard Inst. Space Studies, N.Y.C., 1973-74. Author: Human Intelligence Gone Ape, 1990; author, editor, pub. Theories and Fantasies, 1986, A Thin Line Between Theory and Fantasy, 1983; author various screenplays, 1986—; contbr. articles to profl. jours. Jewish.

GREENBIE, BARRIE BARSTOW, landscape architect, author, educator; b. N.Y.C., Mar. 29, 1920; s. Sydney and Marjorie (Barstow) G.; m. Vlasta Koran, July 20, 1965; children: Ingrid, Marnie, Andrea. BS in Drama, U. Miami, 1953; MS in Urban and Regional Planning, U. Wis., 1968, PhD, 1972. Asst. prof. drama Skidmore Coll., Saratoga Springs, N.Y., 1953-58; designer J. Gordon Carr Assocs., N.Y.C., 1959-63; pres., designer Portapavilion Structures, Ltd., N.Y.C., 1960-68; planner Max Anderson Assocs., Madison, Wis., 1968-69; prof. landscape architecture and regional planning U. Mass., Amherst, 1970-89, prof. emeritus, 1989—. Author: Design for Diversity, 1974, Spaces: Dimensions of the Human Landscape, 1981, Space and Spirit in Modern Japan, 1988. With U.S. Army, 1943-46, PTO. Home: 15 Cortland Dr Amherst MA 01002-3401

GREENBLATT, ARTHUR EDWIN, college president; b. Balt., Jan. 16, 1942; s. Rena (Zvares) G.; m. Lynda M. Chernack, Nov. 3, 1962 (div.); children: Clifford, Brian, Joshua; m. Sandra Leet Hetzel, May l, 1987; 1 child, Rosannah. BFA, Md. Inst., 1963; MEd, Towson State U., 1970. Tchr. art Howard County Pub. Schs., Ellicott City, Md., 1963-70; dir. field experiences Md. Inst. Coll. Art, Balt., 1970-73, 75-77; asst. dir. curricular coordination Alliance Ind. Colls. Art, Kansas City, Mo., 1974-75; acad. dean Ctr. for Creative Studies Coll. Art and Design, Detroit, 1978-89; pres. Montserrat Coll. of Art, Beverly, Mass., 1989—; panel moderator art workshops, 1988—. Bd. dirs. Balt. Assn. for Retarded Children, 1971-74; bd. dirs., pres. Young Audiences Mich., Detroit, 1985-87; bd. dirs., treas. Detroit Focus Gallery, 1986—. Mem. Nat. Art Edn. Assn., Am. Assn. for Higher Edn., Nat. Coun. Art Adminstrs. (chmn. 1984-86), Mich. Art Edn. Assn. Jewish. Office: Montserrat Coll Art PO Box 26 Beverly MA 01915-0026

GREENBLATT, RENA MATISON, psychologist, psychoanalyst; b. N.Y.C., Sept. 2, 1955; d. Sumner Eliot and Shirley (Volin) Matison; m. Edward Robert Greenblatt, May 22, 1983; children: Daniel Matison, David George. BA, Columbia U., 1978; PhD, CUNY, 1985. Rsch. fellow Columbia U., N.Y.C., 1980-81, rsch. worker, 1980-84; fellow of psychology in psychiatry N.Y. Hosp., Cornell Med. Ctr., White Plains, N.Y., 1984-86; sr. psychologist, cons. The Jewish Bd. of Family and Children's Svcs., N.Y.C., 1986-88; adj. asst. prof. CUNY, N.Y.C., 1990—; adj. lectr. CUNY, N.Y.C., 1981-84; cons. Family Health Assocs., N.Y.C., 1988—; adj. asst. prof. NYU, N.Y.C., 1991—. Mem. Inst. for Psychoanalytic Tng. and Rsch. Candidate Orgn. (profl. liaison 1990—), Am. Psychol. Assn. (div. psychoanalysis), Orton Soc. for Dyslexia. Office: 420 E 64th St # 1D New York NY 10021-7853

GREENBLATT, ROBERT IRA, physician; b. Bklyn., Mar. 10, 1953; s. BEnjamin and Esther Molly (Weissband) G.; m. Rhonda Ann Okin, Aug. 7, 1975; children: Michael, Scott, Carolyn. BS, L.I. U., 1975; MD, U. So. Calif., 1978. Pvt. practice Union, N.J. Office: Ideal Profl Pk 2333 Morris Ave Ste B6 Union NJ 07083

GREENBLATT, WALTER CHARLES, food service executive, entrepreneur; b. Milw., June 18, 1956; s. Ray Harris and Betty (Goldsmith) G.; m. Esther Helen Schor, July 4, 1981; children: Daniel, Jordan. BA summa cum laude, Yale U., 1978; MA with first class honors, Oxford U., 1980; MBA with distinction, Harvard U., 1982. Cons. Bain & Co., Boston, 1981-85; chief exec., founder, chmn. bd. dirs. La Cart Inc., N.Y.C., 1985—; mentor/speaker NYU Stern Bus. Sch. Entrepreneurs' Exch., 1992. Recipient McLaughlin prize Yale U., 1977, Chauncey Brewster Tinker prize, 1978, Wrexham prize, 1978, Exceptional Distinction award. Phi Beta Kappa. Home: 112 Lake Ave Metuchen NJ 08840 Office: La Cart Inc 600 W 28th St New York NY 10001

GREENDLINGER, MICHAEL LEONARD, accountant; b. N.Y.C., Jan. 5, 1938; s. Samuel and Frances (Rubin) G.; m. Arlene Norma Ebner (div. 1983); children: Risa Jill, Stacy Lynn. BBA, Adelphi U., 1960. CPA, N.Y. Ptnr. Clarence Raines & Co., N.Y.C., 1970-77, Hertz Herson & Co., N.Y.C., 1977-87, Bachman Schwartz & Abramsen, N.Y.C., 1987-90; chief exec. officer Kaleidoscope Internat., Ltd., N.Y.C., 1990—. Instr. Adopt-A-Class, Queens, 1987-90. Mem. AICPAs, N.Y. State Soc. CPA (chmn. comml. credit com. 1982-85, chmn. apparel and textile com. 1987-90), Exchequer Credit Club (pres.). Office: Kaleidoscope Internat Ltd 261 5th Ave New York NY 10016-7602

GREENE, ALLEN STEVEN, financial consultant; b. Bronx, N.Y., Dec. 20, 1946; s. Seymour Ira and Ruth Eileen (Sands) G.; m. Sandra Joyce Kruse, Mar. 7, 1970 (div.); m. Veronique C. Maas, Sept. 8, 1985; children: Peter, Sari, Jérémie. BBA, CCNY, 1968; MBA, CUNY, 1971. Asst. treas. Bankers Trust Co., N.Y.C., 1968-71; asst. v.p. Am. Bank & Trust Co., N.Y.C., 1971-73, v.p., sr. credit officer, 1973-76; v.p. Bank Leumi Trust Co. of N.Y., N.Y.C., 1976-77; pres. Allen S. Greene & Co., Inc., N.Y.C., 1977-90; bd. dirs. Elmwood Fed. Savs. Bank, VSB Bancorp, Inc., chmn. bd.; chief exec. officer VSB Bancorp, Inc., Valley Savs. Bank. Office: Valley Savs Bank 15 Vervalen St Closter NJ 07624-2688

GREENE, BARNETT ALAN, anesthesiologist; b. N.Y.C., July 30, 1907; s. Harris and Sarah (Frischman) G.; m. Lee Adelman, Dec. 24, 1932; children: Stuart A., William H. BSc cum laude, CCNY, 1929; MD cum laude, NYU, 1934. Diplomate Am. Bd. Anesthesiology. Intern, house officer Lincoln City Hosp., Bronx, N.Y., 1934-36, resident in anesthesiology, 1936-39; anesthesiologist Bklyn. Cancer Inst., Dept. Hosps. of N.Y.C., 1939-47; dir. dept. anesthesiology Prospect Heights Hosp., Bklyn., 1939-46, Unity Hosp., Bklyn., 1940-75, Bklyn. Hebrew Home and Hosp. for Aged, 1939-75, Adelphi Hosp., Bklyn., 1939-74, Bklyn. Women's Hosp., 1946-75, Cumberland Hosp. of Dept. of Hosps. City of N.Y., 1955-70; physician Luth. Hosp., Bklyn., 1963-78; pres. Greene, Berkowitz and Goffen, Physicians, P.C., 1971-81, Barnett A. Greene, M.D. P.C., 1978—; clin. assoc. prof. anesthesiology SUNY Downstate Med. Ctr., 1958-75; clin. practice examiner Am. Bd. Anesthesiology, 1946-52; vis. anesthesiologist Kings County Hosp., 1951-55, acting dir. dept. anesthesiology, 1951-55; attending anesthesiologist Bklyn.-Cumberland Hosp. Med. Ctr., 1970-75, emeritus, 1975—; chmn. bd. trustees Bklyn. Women's Hosp. Clinic, 1975-78; mem. malpractice mediation panel Kings County Supreme Ct., 1978-90. Contbr. articles to profl. publs. Maj. Med. Corps, U.S. Army, 1943-46. Decorated Bronze Star. Fellow Am. Anesthesiologists, N.Y. Acad. Medicine; mem. AMA, N.Y. State Med. Soc. (mem. com. on peer rev. 1981, com. on operating rm. safety 1981-83), Kings County Med. Soc. (McAteer prize 1940, mem. continuing edn. com. 1977-80), Phi Beta Kappa, Alpha Omega Alpha. Jewish.

GREENE, BEVERLY ANN, clinical psychologist; b. Orange, N.J., Aug. 14, 1950; d. Samuel and Thelma G. BA, NYU, 1973; postgrad. Marquette U., 1973-74; MA, Adelphi U., 1977, PhD, 1983. Lic. psychologist, N.Y., N.J. Fellow in psychology Mental Retardation Inst., N.Y. Med. Coll., Valhalla, N.Y., 1974-76; psychol. cons. Williamsburg Child Devel. Ctr., Bklyn., 1976-78; psychology intern East Orange VA Med. Ctr., 1978-79; rsch. asst. dept. neurosci. N.J. Coll. Medicine and Dentistry, Vet.'s Hosp., 1979-80; psychology trainee, Children's Partial Hospitalization Unit, Brookdale Hosp. and Med. Ctr., 1980; cert. sch. psychologist N.Y.C. Bd. Edn., 1980-82, staff psychologist, 1982-84; sr. psychologist, dir. inpatient child and adolescent psychol. svcs. King's County Psychiat. Hosp., 1984-89; supervising psychologist Community Mental Health Ctr., U. Medicine and Dentistry N.J., Newark, 1989-91; clin. instr. in psychiatry Downstate Med. Sch., 1982-85, clin. asst. prof., 1985-89, acting dir. Children's Inpatient Unit, 1985-86; clin.asst. prof. dept. psychiatry U. Medicine and Dentistry of N.J., Newark, 1989-91; assoc. clin. prof. dept. psychology St. Johns U., N.Y., 1991—. Contbr. articles to profl. jours.; co-author books. Martin Luther King scholar, 1968-72, NIMH fellow, 1976-77. Fellow APA (co-chari continuing edn. Women's div. 1991—, diversity in clin. psychology task force, fellow div. clin. psychology, co-editor dev. 44 ann. pub.), Am. Psychol. Assn.; mem. Internat. Neuropsychol. Soc., Nat. Assn. Black Psychologists, N.Y. Assn. Black Psychologists, Nat. Assn. Women in Psychology (Women of Color Psychologies Publ. award, 1991), Am. Orthopsychiat. Assn., N.Y. Assn. Women in Psychology, N.Y. Coalition of Hosp. and Instnl. Psychologists. Office: 26 St Johns Pl Brooklyn NY 11217-3240

GREENE, EDWARD ALLEN, retired public affairs executive; b. Waco, Tex., May 25, 1926; s. James Floyd and Marie Louise (Dupres) G.; m. Elizabeth Ann Love, Oct. ll, 1952; children: Edward Allen Jr., Deborah Ann Greene Lord, Judith Love Greene Murray, Philip James. BA, George Washington U., 1950. Reporter Washington Evening Star, 1950-52; asst. pub. rels. Assn. Gen. Contractors Am., Washington, 1952-58; pub. affairs asst. Am. Waterways Operators, Washington, 1958-60; pub. info. specialist USPHS, Washington, 1960-61; pub. affairs office interim dep. U.S. Army C.E., Washington, 1961-91. Author: D-Day: The Greatest Invasion, 1969. V.p. Park View Citizens Assn., 1968, pres. 1969-70, 85-86. Mem. Nat. Press Club, Constrn. Writers Assn. (pres. 1977-78, Silver Hard Hat award 1989). Republican. Roman Catholic. Home: 3226 Park View Rd Chevy Chase MD 20815-5644

GREENE, HERMAN PAUL, JR., retired engineer; b. Albany, N.Y., June 5, 1936; s. Herman Pellitier and Catherine C. (Hayes) G. BS in Bldg. Constrn., Rensselaer Poly. Inst., 1958. Jr. engr. N.Y.S. Dept. Pub. Works, Albany, 1958-59, asst. sanitary engr., 1959-63, sr. sanitary engr., 1963-68; sr. sanitary engr. N.Y. State Office of Gen. Svcs., Albany, 1968-73; assoc. mech. constrn. engr. N.Y.S. O.G.S., Albany, 1973-91; supr. constrn. and start-up N.Y. State Waste to Energy Burn Plant, Albany Answers Project. Mem. Nat. Soc. Prof. Engrs. Roman Catholic. Home: 50 Peck Rd Lot 27 Wynantskill NY 12198-8727

GREENE, HOWARD ROGER, educational consultant; b. New Haven, Conn., July 26, 1937; s. Charles and Freda (Miller) G.; m. Donna Gurian (div.); m. Laurie Ann Sheldon, Apr. 16, 1975; children: Adam Scott, Matthew West, Katharine Amanda, Andrew Charles. BA, Dartmouth Coll., 1959; MA, NYU, 1961; MEd, Harvard U., 1964. Tchr. Hopkins Grammar Sch., New Haven, 1961-63; teaching fellow Harvard U., Cambridge, Mass., 1963-64; admissions dean Princeton (N.J.) U., 1964-69; ednl. cons., 1969—; exec. dir. AIFS Scholarship Found., Greenwich, Conn., 1990—, also trustee, 1989—. Author: Scaling the Ivy Wall, 1987, Beyond the Ivy Wall, 1990. Active 1st Presbyn. Ch. New Canaan, Conn., 1988—, elder, 1992—; trustee New Canaan Country Sch., 1989—; class officer Dartmouth Coll., 1990—. Mem. Am. Acad. Dramatic Arts (trustee 1984—), Harvard Club N.Y. Home: Wildwood Dr Wilton CT 06897-1620

GREENE, JESSE J., JR., treasurer; b. N.Y.C., Mar. 7, 1945; s. Jesse Johnson and Ann (Cox) G.; m. Christine Sofijczuk, Aug. 6, 1972; children: Bryan Michael, Colin Jesse. BSME, NYU, 1969, MSME, 1971; JD and MBA in Bus., Columbia U., 1975. Engr. Grumman Aerospace, Bethpage, N.Y., 1969, IBM Corp., Yorktown Heights, N.Y., 1971-72; tax atty. IBM Corp., Armonk, N.Y., 1975-83, asst. treas., 1991—; tax atty. IBM Credit Corp., Stamford, Conn., 1983-91, v.p., 1989-91. NDEA fellow NYU, 1970; N.Y. State Regents scholar, 1963. Mem. ABA, ASME, N.Y. State Bar Assn.

GREENE, JOHN ROBERT, history and communication educator, author; b. Syracuse, N.Y., Apr. 13, 1955; s. John Charles and Margaret Ann (Tozer) G.; m. Patty Nan Messer, June 9, 1979; children: Thomas John, Christopher Edward. BA, St. Bonaventure (N.Y.) U., 1976, MA, 1978; PhD, Syracuse (N.Y.) U., 1983. Assoc. prof. Cazenovia (N.Y.) Coll., 1979—, co-chair Ctr. for Life Studies, 1991-92; adj. instr. Univ. Coll., Syracuse U., 1981-92. Author: The Crusade: The Presidential Election of 1952, 1985, The Limits of Power: The Nixon and Ford Administrations, 1992; editor: The Quest: A Guide to the Job Interview, 1991; chpts. in books; contbr. articles to profl. jours. Lay reader St. James Ch., Syracuse, 1971—. Harry S Truman Libr. grantee, 1980, 86, Rockefeller U. grantee, 1988, Gerald R. Ford Found. grantee, 1992. Mem. AAUP, Am. Hist. Assn., Speech Communication Assn., Ctr. for Study of Presidency, Alpha Sigma Lambda. Roman Catholic. Office: Cazenovia Coll Box F Cazenovia NY 13035

GREENE, JOSEPH NATHANIEL, JR., former foundation executive, former diplomat; b. N.Y.C., Apr. 9, 1920; s. Joseph N. and Nanine (Pond) G.; m. Edith Cowles, Mar. 21, 1942 (div. Aug 1960); children: Alice W., Nancy W., Edith E.; m. Christine O'Hara, Apr. 22, 1961; children—Joanna, John, stepdau. Susan O'Hara. Grad., Hotchkiss Sch., 1937; B.A., Yale U., 1941. Asst. instr. Phillips Acad., 1941; U.S. fgn. service officer, 1942-73; assigned to Montreal, Ottawa, Rome, Trieste; desk officer for Italy, Dept. State Washington; assigned to Singapore, Bonn; dep. dir. exec. secretariat Dept. State, Washington, 1956; spl. asst. to Sec. State, 1957-59; assigned Imperial Def. Coll., London, 1960; counselor embassy, dep. chief mission Lagos, Nigeria, 1961-63; minister-counselor, dep. chief mission Am. embassy, New Delhi, 1963-68; dep. adminstr. Bur. Security and Consular Affairs, 1968-69, dep. asst. sec. state internat. orgn. affairs, 1969-70; minister-counselor, dep. chief mission Am. embassy, London, 1970-71; diplomat-in-residence Brandeis U., Waltham, Mass., 1971-72; minister-counselor in charge U.S. interests, Cairo, 1972-73; pres. Seven Springs Center, Mt. Kisco, N.Y., 1973-82; mem. internat. adv. com. Am. Security Bank, 1978-82. Mem. Bryam com. Nature Conservancy, 1973-81; mem. program coun. Ctr. for Internat. Studies and Liberal Arts, Conn. Coll., 1991—; bd. dirs. High Hopes Therapeutic Riding, Inc., 19991—; bd. corporators, mem. devel. com. Lawrence and Meml. Hisp., New London, Conn., 1983-92. With USNR, 1944-46. Mem. Council Fgn. Relations. Clubs: Met. (Washington); Yale (N.Y.C.). Home: 138 Joshuatown Rd Lyme CT 06371-3120

GREENE, KAREN SANDRA, singer, actress, educator; b. N.Y.C., Jan. 7, 1942; d. Nathan and Natalie (Barashick) Stein; m. Richard Greene, July 1, 1962 (div. 1980); children: Barry Randall, Lauren Jennifer. BA, U. Conn., 1988. Singer, dancer, Broadway actress N.Y.C., 1960-62; pres., educator Karen Greene Studios, A Class Act, Tigre Video Prodns., Norwalk, Conn., 1962—; pres., dir. voice On Stage Acad., Ltd., Westport, Conn., 1982-84; dir., educator theater arts Westport YMCA, 1981-85; producer, dir. A Class Act, Tigre Prodns., 1962—; educator Temple Shalom, Norwalk, 1975-87; dir. theater arts Bridgeport (Conn.) Jewish Ctr., 1985; dir. Norwalk Jewish Ctr., 1985, Wilton (Conn.) Children's Theater, 1988-90; educator music and drama St. Luke's Sch., New Canaan, Conn., 1989-90; educator voice, acting, adult edn. Norwalk and Westport (Conn.) Bds. Edn., 1990—. Voiceover artist nat. performing tours; dir., vocalist soc. band Shades of Greene. Coord. Southwestern Conn. Women's Issues Conf., 1988; active women's equal rights, pro-choice, NOW, Women's Empowerment, Fairfield County, Conn.; active animal rights advocate; Conn. rep. Friends of Animals, others. Mem. NOW, AFTRA, SAG, Actor's Equity Assn., Internat. Platform Assn., Internat. TV Assn., Women's Empowerment, N.E. Anti-Vivisect. Soc., People for the Ethical Treatment of Animals, Greenpeace. Home and Office: 4 Suburban Dr Norwalk CT 06851-1612

GREENE, LYNNE JEANNETTE, fashion designer; b. Albany, N.Y., Aug. 27, 1938; d. Zebulon Stevens and Helen Matilde (Maier) Robbins; m. Stanley E. Greene, Jan. 31, 1962 (dec. June 27, 1987); 1 child, Stuart Nathaniel; m. Michael Alan Karlan, Sept. 29, 1991. Student, Goucher Coll., 1956-57; BA, Parsons Sch. Design, 1960. Asst. designer Haymaker Sportswear (David Crystal), N.Y.C., 1959-61; designer Craig Craely Sportswear and Dresses, N.Y.C., 1961-63, Flair Lingerie, N.Y.C., 1964-66; designer, owner Kaleidoscope Lingerie, N.Y.C., 1966-67; head designer Contessa/Monique/Fisher Lingerie, N.Y.C., 1967-71; creative dir. Eye of the Peacock Sportswear; head designer, owner Lynne Greene Designs Retail, Montclair, N.J., 1972-74; designer, pres. Little Greene Apples Inc., Montville, N.J., 1971—; designer, dir. mktg. Lady Lynne Lingerie, Guy Laroche Lingerie, N.Y.C., 1973—; lingerie critic Pratt Inst., 1984—. Patentee in field; illustrator books, pamphlets in fashion and packaging fields; commn. artist and illustrator. Active participant Montville Soccer Assn, 1972-88, fund drives for Am. Heart Assn., Cancer Inc. Mem. The Fashion Group. Republican. Unitarian Universalist.

GREENE, MARGARET MCCAFFREY, actress, writer, director; b. Paisley, Scotland; came to U.S., 1938.; m. Stanley (Mark) W. Greene (dec.). Student, Temple U., 1948. Writer, actress Kovacs on Corner/Sta. WPTZ-TV, Phila., 1950; with Charade Parade with Ed McMann, Phila., 1951; producer Plays and Players, Phila., 1952; writer, actress Marge and Jeff/Dumont Network, N.Y.C., 1954-55; actress Candid Camera, N.Y.C., 1960-67. Producer world premiere stage prodn. Stalag 17, Phila, 1952; writer, dir., producer mus. Lady Lily at Ford's Theater starring Tessie O'Shea, 1978; guest appearances include Jack Paar Show, Merv Griffin Show, Johnny Carson Show; appeared in TV soap operas Another World, All My Children, As the World Turns; panelist shows Twenty Questions, One Minute Please; appeared in over 100 TV commls. Mem. Screen Actors Guild, AFTRA, Writers Guild Am., Dirs. Guild, Dramatists Guild. Home and Office: 915 Wynnewood Rd # 2C Witherbee Ct Pelham Manor NY 10803

GREENE, MICHAEL EDWARD, insurance and investment products consultant; b. Bklyn., Jan. 26, 1935; s. Bertram H. and Marion B. (Longo) G.; m. Anastasia D. Moshovos, Aug. 31, 1957; children: Michele, Victoria, Michael, Christine, Stacy, Roxanne. Assoc. in Mktg., U. Hartford, 1960. CLU, chartered fin. cons. With group sales and underwriting Hartford (Conn.) Life, 1958-65, dir. sales, 1965-77; asst. v.p., dir. sales Hartford (Conn.) Life VA, 1977-80, v.p., dir. sales, 1980-84; v.p., broker, dir. sales Hartford Life, Simsbury, Conn., 1985-87; sr. v.p., ins. ops. Thomson McKinnon, N.Y.C., 1984-85; v.p. Skandia Life Am. Corp., Westport, Conn., 1987-89; pvt. practice ins. and investment products cons. MEG Co., 1989—; chmn. investment products mktg. Life Ins. Mktg. Research Co., 1984—, com. mem. 1980—; chmn. Annuity Mgrs. Roundtable, 1985. Mem. Housing Authority, Thompsonville, Conn., 1961, mem. Bd., Edn., Cherry Hill, N.J., 1969-70. Served with U.S. Army, 1953-55. Republican. Roman Catholic. Club: N.Y. Athletic. Home: 139 Apple Hl Wethersfield CT 06109-3505 Office: Am Skandia Life Assurance Corp Tower One Corp Dr Shelton CT 06484

GREENE, PHILIP JAMES, lawyer; b. Washington, Nov. 12, 1961; s. Edward Allen and Elizabeth Ann (Love) G.; m. Elise Marie Greene. BA, Mt. St. Mary's Coll., 1983; JD, Loyola U., New Orleans, 1986. Bar: Md., Pa., D.C. Assoc. McNamee, Hosea & Scott, P.A., Greenbelt, Md., 1986-88; assoc. gen. counsel U.S. Dept. Commerce/Office of Chief Counsel/Tech, Washington, 1988—; bur. counsel Nat. Tech. Info. Svc., Springfield, Va., 1988—. Writer, editor: (mag.) Headliners, 1988-89. Named to Outstanding Young Men of Am., 1990. Mem. Md. State Bar Assn., D.C. Bar Assn., Pa. Bar Assn., La. Soc., Loyola U. Alumni Assn. (bd. dirs. 1989—), Chestnut Lodge Golf Soc. (bd. dirs. 1987—). Republican. Roman Catholic. Home: 18050 Ohara Cir Olney MD 20832-1455 Office: US Dept Commerce RM 4610 14th St and Constitution Ave NW Washington DC 20230

GREENE, RICHARD H., journalist; b. Milford, Conn., Aug. 12, 1955; s. Eugene Harold and Bebe (Bender) G.; m. Katherine Barrett, Feb. 21, 1981; children: Benjamin, Sandra. BS in Journalism, Northwestern U., 1977. Researcher Forbes mag., N.Y.C., 1977-79, reporter, 1979-81, staff writer, 1981-82, assoc. editor, 1982-84, contbg. editor, 1984-89; freelance writer, N.Y.C., 1984—. Co-author: The Man Behind the Magic, 1991; contbg. editor Fin. World; columnist Glamour; contbr. articles to Fin. World, Glamour, Ladie's Home Jour., Reader's Digest, Redbook, also others. Recipient Amos Tuck medal Dartmouth Coll., 1978, award for excellence in fin. journalism N.Y. Soc. CPAs, 1984, 91, cert. of merit, 1987. Mem. Am. Correctional Assn. Home and Office: 25 Waterside Plz Apt Gg New York NY 10010-2621

GREENE, RICHARD MYRON, physician; b. Rochester, Minn., Oct. 11, 1953; s. Laurence Francis and Rosalyn (Ravits) G.; m. Kathryn Soult, Apr. 27, 1985; children: Alexandra, Ashley. BA, Colgate U., 1976; MD, Chgo. Med. Sch., 1984. Intern Columbus Hosp, Chgo., 1984-85; resident in dermatology Mayo Clinic, Rochester, Minn., 1986-89; clin. instr. dermatology U. Rochester, 1989—; attending physician Strong Meml. Hosp., Rochester Gen. Hosp. Contbr. articles to med. jours. Mem. AMA, Monroe County Med. Soc., N.Y. State Med. Assn., Minn. Med. Assn. (pres. resident physician sect. 1988-89), Zumbro Valley Med. Assn. Home: 8 Split Rock Rd Pittsford NY 14534-1814 Office: 1655 Elmwood Ave # 120 Rochester NY 14620

GREENE, ROBERT JAY, surgeon, oncologist; b. Phila., Jan. 17, 1930; s. Samuel Robert and Kathryn (Purisch) G.; m. Edith Morse, Dec. 27, 1952 (div. 1961); children: Steven, Linda, Karen; m. Barbara Lee Bassin, May 21, 1962; 1 child, David. AB, U. Pa., 1950; MD, Harvard U., 1954. Diplomate Am. Bd. Surgeons. Sr. surgeon St. Luke's Hosp., New Bedford, Mass., 1962—. Capt. U.S. Army, 1956-58. Fellow ACS; mem. Am. Soc. Clin. Oncology, Mass. Med. Soc. Democrat. Jewish. Home and Office: New Bedford Surg Assocs Inc 49 Hawthorne St New Bedford MA 02740

GREENE, ROBERT WARREN, education educator, real estate broker; b. Boston, Apr. 17, 1928; s. Benjamin Martin and Mary (Wilson) G.; m. Elizabeth Ann Army, Sept. 11, 1956; 1 child, Mary Elizabeth. BS, Worcester State Coll., 1954; MEd, Northea. U., 1956; PhD, U. Conn., 1965. Notary public, Mass. Tchr. math. Shrewsbury (Mass.) High Sch., 1954-60; supr. sci. edn. Campus Sch., Fitchburg (Mass.) State Coll., 1960-65, asst. to acad. dean, 1965-67, dir. placement, registrar, 1967-74, chmn. grad. program in sch. adminstrn., 1968-76, prof. edn. and sch. adminstrn., 1976—; pres. Greene & Greene Properties, Worcester and Hyannis, Mass., 1978—; bd. dirs., incorporator United Educators Life Ins. Corp., Framingham, Mass., 1974-86. Chmn. bd. trustees Shrewsbury Pub. Libr., 1968-76; pres. Shrewsbury Fed. Credit Union, 1968-74, also past pres., incorporator; mem. personnel bd. edn. Roman Cath. Diocese of Worester, 1978-84; chmn. bd. dirs. Worcester Area Mental Retardation Bd., 1987—. With USN, 1951-53. Mem. Assn. for Supervision and Curriculum Devel., Mass. State Coll. Placement Dirs. (chmn. 1974-75), Mass. Tchrs. Assn. (bd. dirs. 1964-76), Fitchburg State Coll. Faculty Assn. (pres. 1971-75), Holy Cross Coll. Cath. Alumni Assn., Econ. Club (Worcester), Kappa Delta Pi (faculty advisor 1979—). Democrat. Home: 16 Laurel Ave Shrewsbury MA 01545 Office: Fitchburg State Coll Pearl St Fitchburg MA 01420-3338

GREENEBAUM, LEONARD CHARLES, lawyer; b. Langgoens, Fed. Republic Germany, Feb. 6, 1934; came to U.S. 1937, naturalized, 1952; s. Norbert and Henny Lisa (Greenbaum) G.; m. Barbara Rosendorf, Feb. 10, 1957; children: Beth Lynn, Cathy Sue, Steven I. BS cum laude in Commerce, Washington and Lee U., 1956, JD cum laude, 1959. Bar: D.C. 1959, Va. 1959., Md. 1965. Atty. Sachs, Greenebaum & Tayler and predecessor firms, Washington, 1959-64, ptnr., 1964-75, mng. ptnr., 1975-90; ptnr., D.C. coord. litigation Baker & Hostetler, Washington, 1990—; arbitrator Am. Arbitration Assn., Washington, 1975—; mem. Washington and Lee U. Law Coun. Chmn. bd. Davis Meml. Goodwill Industries, Washington, 1979-82; bd. dirs. Coun. for Ct. Excellence. Capt. U.S. Army, 1957. Recipient Svc. to Handicapped People award Davis Meml. Goodwill Industries, 1982. Fellow Am. Bar Found.; mem. D.C. Bar Assn., Md. Bar Assn., Assn. Trial Lawyers Am., Internat. Platform Assn., Jud. Conf. D.C. Cir., Univ. Club (Washington), Bethesda Country Club (Md.), Wild Dunes Club (Charleston, S.C.), George Town Club (Washington), Order of Coif, Phi Delta Phi. Jewish. Home: 6121 Shady Oak Ln Bethesda MD 20817-6027 Office: Baker & Hostetler 1050 Connecticut Ave NW Washington DC 20036-5303

GREENFEST, ROBERT, investment banking executive; b. Bklyn., Dec. 6, 1960; s. Melvin and Elaine G.; m. Jaye B. Brager, Jan. 15, 1983. BBA in Fin., George Washington U., 1982, MBA in Fin. and Investments, 1984. Loan officer C.B.T. Factors Corp., N.Y.C., 1982-83; futures trader Fin. Futures Day Traders, Washington, 1984-86; asst. v.p. Washington Bank, Falls Church, Va., 1986-88, Mellon Bank, Rockville, Md., 1988-89; v.p. Nat. Capital Cos., Washington, 1989—, Potomac Securities, Inc., Washington, 1989—; mem. adv. bd. U.S. Small Bus. Adminstrn., Washington, 1989—; guest speaker 48th Annual Conv., Nat. Assn. Homebuilders, 1992. Mem. Nat. Assn. Securities Dealers (lic.). Jewish. Office: Nat Capital Cos 1850 M St NW #1040 Washington DC 20036

GREENFIELD, CHERYL S., auditor; b. Bethpage, N.Y., Apr. 29, 1959; d. Sidney S. and Elaine (Schwab) G. BS, SUNY, Buffalo, 1981, MBA, 1983. CPA, N.Y., Maine. Audit sr. Coopers and Lybrand, Albany, N.Y., 1982-87; acctg. mgr., audit mgr. Schenectady (N.Y.) Trust Co., 1987-88; audit mgr. Schatz, Fletcher & Assocs., Augusta, Maine, 1988—. Treas. Big Bros./Big Sisters, Waterville, Maine, 1989-90. Mem. AICPA, Nat. Assn. Accts. (regional treas. 1989-91, regional v.p. 1991-92, chpt. officer, pres., v.p., sec. Albany chpt. 1982-88, dir. Bangor Waterville chpt. 1988—), Maine Bankers Assn., Savs. Bank Assn. Maine. Office: Schatz Fletcher & Assocs One Weston Ct Augusta ME 04330

GREENFIELD, DANIEL PAUL, psychiatrist; b. Newark, July 29, 1945; s. Leonard Sidney and Dorothy (Katzin) G.; m. Marguerite Rodgers, Oct. 31, 1946; children: Jeremy Samuel, Sarah Elizabeth, Katherine Rebecca. BA, Oberlin Coll., 1967; MD, U. N.C., 1971; MPH, Harvard U., 1975, MS, 1977. Intern, gen. med. officer USPHS Hosp., S.I., N.Y., 1971-74; resident in preventive medicine Harvard Sch. of Pub. Health, Boston, 1974-77; resident in psychiatry N.Y. Hosp.-Cornell Med. Ctr., White Plains, 1977-80; asst. prof. Rutgers Med. Sch., Piscataway, N.J., 1980-86; med. dir. Future Health Systems, Inc., Summit, N.J., 1986-90; mng. ptnr. Brown & Greenfield, Physician Cons., Florham Park, N.J., 1990—; pvt. practice Millburn, N.J., 1980—; cons. Prudential Ins. Co. Am., Parsippany, N.J., 1990-92, N.J. Dept. Health, Trenton, 1980—; clin. assoc. prof. Albert Einstein Coll. Medicine/Montefiore Med. Ctr., Bronx, 1986—; mem. drug and alcohol coun. N.J. Gov.'s Office, Trenton, 1985—; mem. bd. trustees Community Health Law Project, East Orange, N.J., 1990—. Contbr. articles to profl. jours. Mem. Com. on Drug Awareness, Millburn, 1987-90. Fellow N.J. Acad. Medicine; mem. AMA, Am. Psychiat. Assn., Am. Acad. Psychiatry and Law, Am. Soc. Addiction Medicine, Med. Soc. N.J. (com. chmn. 1982-88), Am. Occupational Medicine Assn. Democrat. Jewish. Office: Brown & Greenfield Physician Cons 256 Columbia Tpke Ste 210 Florham Park NJ 07932

GREENFIELD, HELEN MEYERS, real estate executive, publishing company executive, inspection and test service executive; b. Albany, N.Y., 1908; d. Stephen Ferencevich Meyers and Catherine (Bronkov) Ferencevich Meyers; m. Frank L. Greenfield, Apr. 1, 1929; children: Stuart Franklin, Val Shea. Grad., Baker's Bus. Sch., 1924. Accounts supr. George G. McCaskey Co., N.Y.C., 1924-29; spl. assignments purchasing dept. McCall's Pub. Co., N.Y.C., 1929, Fgn. Affairs Publs., Inc., N.Y.C., 1929-31; with purchasing dept. Glidden-Buick Corp., N.Y.C., 1931-32; interviewer U.S. Govt. Civil Works Adminstrn., N.Y.C., 1931-32; supr. filing and payroll systems Houston St. Project Ctr., N.Y.C., 1933-36; with dept. accounting Reuben H. Donnelley Co., N.Y.C., 1936-37; supr. layouts, makeup prins. of semi-monthly publs. Tide Publs., Inc., N.Y.C., 1939-41; asst. to purchasing agt., supr. maintenance perpetual inventory Hopeman Bros., N.Y.C., 1941-43; with money order div., corr. dept. U.S. Govt., P.O. Dept., N.Y.C., 1943-44, 1941-43; v.p. Frank L. Greenfield Co., Inc., N.Y.C., 1945-59, All Purpose Chair Corp., N.Y.C., 1950-55; pres. VAL Equipment, Inc., N.Y.C., 1950-62; v.p. Am. Testing Labs., Inc., N.Y.C., 1950-63; supr. personnel, purchases Irving Lampert Co., N.Y.C., 1951-52; account assignment coordinator, advt. contracts dept. Newsweek, N.Y.C., 1960-78; owner, operator Princess Helen Antiques; pres. Helen M. Greenfield Realty Corp., 1968-79; bus. cons., 1979—. Active New York Heart Assn.; founder, coord., show producer, dir. and hostess ann. banquet honor of Dr. Manuel Cabral, composer-dir. Mt. Laurel Ctr. Performing Arts, 1960-84; assoc. mem. Nat. Trust for Hist. Preservation; mem. Staten Island Hist. Soc., Staten Island Inst. of Arts and Scis.; mem. Statue of Liberty-Ellis Island Found. Inc. Named Hon. Princess Helene Evening Star by chief Rising Sun, Chief and High Priest of all N. and S. Am. Indian Tribes and Couns., 1947. Mem. Internat. Platform Assn. Club: Order Eastern Star (past matron).

GREENFIELD, MEG, journalist; b. Seattle, Dec. 27, 1930; d. Lewis James and Lorraine (Nathan) G. BA summa cum laude, Smith Coll., 1952; Fulbright scholar, Newnham Coll., Cambridge (Eng.) U., 1952-53; DHL (hon.), Smith Coll., 1978, Georgetown U., 1979, Wesleyan U., 1982, Williams Coll., 1987, Princeton U., 1990. With Reporter mag., 1957-68, Washington editor, 1965-68; editorial writer Washington Post, 1968-70, dep. editorial page editor, 1970-79, editorial page editor, 1979—; columnist Newsweek, 1974—. Recipient Pulitzer prize for editorial writing 1978. Mem. Am. Soc. Newspaper Editors, Phi Beta Kappa. Home: 3318 R St NW Washington DC 20007-2309 Office: Washington Post Co 1150 15th St NW Washington DC 20005-2780

GREENFIELD, ROBERT THOMAS, JR., physician; b. Washington, July 8, 1933; s. Robert Thomas and Auis Aileen (Gadson) G.; m. Wilma Sue Robertson, Sept. 25, 1953; children: Kimberly, Karyn, Robert III, Richard, Brian, Ashley. BS, Howard U., 1954, MD, 1958. Diplomate Am. Bd. Ob/Gyn. Intern Madigan Gen. Hosp., Tacoma, 1958-59; resident Freedmen's Hosp., Washington, 1963-67, pres. ob-gyn., 1963-67; pvt. practice Washington, 1968—; instr. ob/gyn. Howard U., Washington, 1967—, Georgetown U., Washington, 1980—; mem. State Health Coord. Com., Washington, 1976-80; pres. med. staff Columbia Hosp. for Women, Washington, 1984-86. Capt. M.C., U.S. Army, 1958-63. Fellow Am. Coll. Ob/Gyn. (chmn. D.C. sect. 1978-80), Am. Coll. Surgeons; mem. NCCAP (life), Washington Med. Soc., Internat. Coll. Surgeons, Urban League, Alpha Omega Alpha. Democrat. Roman Catholic. Office: Drs Clark & Greenfield Chartered 665 E St SW Washington DC 20024

GREENFIELD, STEVEN E., executive; b. Chgo., Mar. 6, 1947; s. Sidney I. and Rose (Walner) G.; m. Mary McComb, Dec. 13, 1969; children: Tamara, Sara. BA in Polit. Sci., Cornell Coll., 1989; MA in Social Planning, Goddard Coll., 1974. Assoc. dir. Human Svcs. Planning Coun., Schenectady, N.Y., 1972-79; exec. dir. Schenectady Girls Club, 1979-88, Assn. Community Living Agys. in Mental Health, Albany, N.Y., 1988—; peer regional network Nat. Ctr. Disabilities Advocates, Newark, N.J., 1991. Pres. Agy. Exec. Assn., Schenectady, 1986, Congregation Agndat Achim, Schenectady, 1991—; bd. dirs. Alcoholism Coun. Schenectady County, 1986-88, Northeast Parent-Child Soc., Schenectady, 1985-88. Recipient Youth Svc. award, B'nai Brith, Schenectady, 1987. Mem. Mental Health Assn. N.Y. State (bd. dirs. 1988—), Internat. Assn. Psycholsocial Rehab. Svcs. Democrat. Jewish. Home: 1440 Clifton Park Rd Niskayuna NY 12309-4314 Office: ACLAIMH 260 Washington Ave Albany NY 12210-1312

GREENFIELD, VAL SHEA, ophthalmologist; b. N.Y.C., Apr. 20, 1932; s. Frank Lynne and Helen (Meyers) G. Student, Brown U., 1948-49, 50-51, St. John's U., 1949; BA cum laude, Bklyn. Coll., 1952; MD, Yale U., 1956. Diplomate Am. Bd. Ophthalmology; lic. to practice med. Pa., N.Y., and N.J., 1959—. Intern Walter Reed Army Hosp., Washington, 1956-57; asst. chief U.S. Army Dispensary, Phila., 1957-59, chief, 1959-60; postgrad. preceptorship in ophthal. under co-chief ophthal. Presbyn.-U. Pa. Med. Ctr., Phila., 1963-66; practice medicine specializing in obstetrics Phila., Riveride, N.J., 1960-63; practice medicine specializing in ophthalmology Phila., 1966—; assoc. dir., lectr. in neuro-ophthalmology Hahneman U., Phila., 1978—, assoc. clin. prof. Robert Wood Johnson Med. Sch. of N.J. U. of Medicine and Dentistry, 1988—; attending surgeon in ophthalmology Frankford and Rolling Hills Hosps., Phila, 1970—; asst. to assoc. prof. Ophthalmology Hahneman U. Sc. Medicine, 1977-88; lectr. Biblical topics U.S., Israel, Europe, New Zealand, USSR.; guest speaker TV stas., clubs. Contbr. articles to profl. jours., chpts. to textbooks. Bd. deacons Community Ch., Mt. Laurel Chapel, 1974—. Served to capt., M.C., U.S. Army, 1955-60. Inducted into Chapel of 4 Chaplains, Temple U., 1981; inducted Hon. Brave Cherokee Indians by Chief Rising Sun, Chief and High Priest of all N. and S. Am. Indian Tribe and Couns., 1947; recipient AMA Physicians Recognition award in Continuing Med. Edn., 1974-92 (award tri-annually). Fellow ACS, Phila. Coll. Physicians; mem. AMA, Pa. Med. Soc., Phila. County Med. Soc., Am. Assn. Ophthalmology, Pa. Acad. Ophthalmology, Pan-Am. Soc. Ophthalmology, Soc. Contemporary Ophthalmology, Christian Med. Soc., Am. Soc. Cataract and Refracture Surgery, Internat. Platform Soc., Am. Judeo-Christian Fellowship, Alpha Kappa Kappa. Democrat. Office: 4500 Arthur Kill Rd Staten Island NY 10309-1318

GREENHALL, ARTHUR MERWIN, retired zoologist; b. N.Y.C., Aug. 6, 1911; s. Harry Arthur and Florine (Aufhauser) G.; m. Elizabeth Rusk Jones, Feb. 28, 1942; children: Paul Rusk, Alice Rusk Greenhall Feavyear. BA, U. Mich., 1934, MS, 1935; postgrad., Columbia U., 1939-41, NYU, 1941. Cert. tchr., N.Y. Dir. Portland (Oreg.) Zool. Park, 1942-47; gen. curator Detroit Zool. Park, 1947-53; curator Nat. Mus., Port of Spain, Trinidad, 1953-63; zoologist Ministry of Agriculture, Trinidad, Tobago, 1954-63; zoologist fish and wildlife lab. Nat. Mus. Natural History, Washington, 1963-68; animal health officer UN, Mexico City, 1963-77; zoologist U.S. Fish and Wildlife Svc., Washington, 1963-88, Office Scientific Authority, Washington, 1977-88; ret. U.S. Fish and Wildlife Svc., Washington, 1988; rsch. assoc. Am. Mus. Natural History, N.Y.C., 1967—; cons. Pan Am. Health Orgn., Washington, 1988—, Internat. Union Conservation Nature, 1976—; mem., consul UN Task Force Mission, 1966. Co-author: Review of Bats Trinidad and Tobago, 1961, Bats of Argentina, 1983, Natural History of Vampire Bats, 1988, Field Guide to South American Mammals,, 1992, House Bat Management, 1982. Layman mem. Curriculum Coun. Pub. Schs. Portland, 1942-47; chief animal control Civilian Def. City of Portland, 1942-47. Fellow Linnean Soc. London; mem. Trinidad Tobago Field Naturalists Club (life), Am. Assn. Icthyologists and Herptologists (life) Am. Soc. Mammalogists (life), Bat Conservation Internat., Phi Sigma, Chi Gamma Phi, Beta Beta Beta. Office: Am Mus Natural History Central Park St W New York NY 10026-4355

GREENHOUGH, JOHN HARDMAN, business forms executive; b. London, Aug. 6, 1939; arrived to Can., 1949; s. Thomas Chaplin and Rena (Pilling) G.; married, 1962; children: Peter, Jennifer. BA in English and Econs., Wilfrid Laurier U., Waterloo, Ont., Can., 1962. With Maclean Hunter Ltd., Toronto, Ont., 1962-72, 81-82, various sales and mktg. positions, bus. publs. div., 1962-68, group pub., 1969-72; founding pub. Can. Data Systems Mag. Toronto, Ont., 1969; v.p. printing Maclean Hunter Ltd., Toronto, Ont., 1981-82; group pres. printing Maclean Hunter Ltd., 1990—; v.p., gen. mgr. Data Bus. Forms Ltd., Brampton, Ont., 1972-80, chmn., CEO, 1992—; chmn. Davis & Henderson Ltd., Toronto; bd. dirs. Gen. Bus. Forms Ltd., Edmonton, Alta., Can., Transkrit Corp., Brewster, N.Y. Mem. Can. Bus. Forms Assn. (past v.p., bd. dirs. 1982-88). Office: Data Bus Forms Ltd, 2 Shaftsbury Ln, Brampton, ON Canada L6T 3X7

GREENKY, SETH RICHARD, personal manager, composer, screenwriter; b. Manhattan, N.Y., Feb. 25, 1948; s. Alfred M. and Adele Grace (Novikoff) G.; children: Nicole M. Williams Greenky. BA in Psychology, Monmouth Coll., 1970; DD, Universal Life Ch., Modesto, Calif., 1977. V.p. Talent Recon/Solid Sounds Mgmt., N.Y.C., 1971-73; touring musician, 1972; sales mgr. Bell Sounds Studios, N.Y.C., 1973-75; pres. The Harlem Angels, N.Y.C., 1990—, Green Key Music/Mgmt., N.Y.C., 1975—; cons. RCA, Sound Ideas, Sound Mixers, ODO, Media Sound, Dimensional Sound, Electric Lady Studios, Sire Records, A & M, Arista, Bell Records, Polygram, Elektra/Asylum, Motown Records. Author: Letters to the Predaotr, 1991; (screenplays) If I Spent the Night with Your, 1983-84, The Shape of Thyngs, 1984; dir. 31st and 3rd, TV pilot, 1987-88; composer numerous songs, 1963—; inventor Shampoo Discs, 1982, Humane Canteen for Dogs, 1987, Ear Snaps, 1990, Exfoliation Tape, 1990, Drawer Chair, 1991. Mem. ASCAP (Songwriter's award 1975), Nat. Conf. Personal Mgrs., Broadcast Music Inc.

GREENLEES, THOMAS WILLIAM, surgeon; b. N.Y.C., Aug. 2, 1926; s. William and Theresa (Kensler) G.; m. Taeko Atsumi, June 21, 1960; children: Christine, Lisa. BA, Cornell U., 1945; MD, N.Y. Med. Coll., 1949; MPH, Harvard U., 1983. Diplomate Am. Bd. Surgery. Intern Flower Fifth Ave Hosp., N.Y.C., 1949-50; resident Met. Hosp., N.Y.C., 1950-51, 53-56; pres. Schonarie County Surg. Assocs., Cobleskill, N.Y., 1960-85; med. dir. Textron Corp., Wilmington, Mass., 1985—; attending physician occupational medicine U. Hosp., Boston, 1985—. Bd. dir. Mohawk Valley Econ. Devel. Dist., N.Y. State, 1970—, SUNY Found., Cobleskill, N.Y., 1986—. Lt. comdr. USNR, 1956-59, Japan. Fellow ACS, Am. Coll. Occupational Medicine; mem. AMA, New Eng. Occupational Med. Assn. (pres. 1990). Methodist. Home: PO Box 910 Cobleskill NY 12043-0910

GREENLY, COLIN, artist; b. London, Jan. 21, 1928; came to U.S., 1939, naturalized, 1948; s. Arthur John and Caroline Matilda (Fantini) G.; m. Laurie Ann Zadek, May 8, 1976; 1 child, Katharine Lydia Caro Herman. A.B., Harvard U., 1948; postgrad., Columbia U. Sch. Painting and Sculpture, 1951-53, Am. U. Grad. Sch. Fine Arts, 1956. dir. art Madeira Sch., Greenway, Va., 1955-68; Dana prof. fine arts Colgate U., 1972-73; vis. artist numerous colls., univs. One-man shows, Corcoran Gallery Art, Washington, 1968, Royal Marks Gallery, N.Y.C., 1968, 70, Everson Mus., Syracuse, N.Y., 1971, Andrew Dickson White Mus., Cornell U., 1972, Picker Gallery, Colgate U., 1973, Finch Coll. Mus., N.Y.C., 1974, group shows include, Mus. Modern Art, N.Y.C., 1953, 73, De Cordova Mus., Lincoln, Mass., 1965, Des Moines Art Center, 1967, Nat. Collection Fine Arts, Washington, 1968, Krannert Art Mus., Champaign, Ill., 1969, 74, Emmerich Gallery Downtown, N.Y.C., 1972, John Weber Gallery, N.Y.C., 1975, Whitney Mus. Am. Art, N.Y.C., 1978, N.Y. State Mus., Albany, 1981; represented in permanent collections, Albright Knox Art Gallery, Buffalo, Corcoran Gallery Art, Des Moines Art Center, Everson Mus., High Mus. Art, Atlanta, Mus. Modern Art, N.Y.C., Phila. Mus. Art, Nat. Gallery Art, Washington, Nat. Collection Fine Arts, Washington, Herbert F. Johnson Mus., Ithaca, N.Y.; restoration and contemporary adaptation of: Hulse Barn, Campbell Hall, N.Y. Nat. Endowment Arts grantee, 1967; Com. for Visual Arts grantee, 1974; Creative Artists Public Service program fellow N.Y.C., 1972, 78. Mem. Nat. Audubon Soc., Nature Conservancy, Wilderness Soc., Nat. Trust for Hist. Preservation. Address: RD 1 Box 545 Campbell Hall NY 10916

GREENO, J(OHN) LADD, management consultant; b. Syracuse, N.Y., June 6, 1949; s. John Stuart and Mary Jane (Pfohl) G.; m. Grace-Marie Misiano, Feb. 7, 1981; children: Meredith, Jane. BBA, U. Okla., 1971; postgrad., U. Hawaii, 1975; MBA, Harvard U., 1978. Ensign USN, 1971, advance through grades to lt., 1975, surface warfare officer, 1971-76; human resource mgmt. specialist Human Resource Mgmt. Sch. USN, Memphis, 1975; human resource mgmt. specialist Human Resource Mgmt. Ctr. USN, Honolulu, 1976, resigned, 1976; cons. Arthur D. Little, Inc., Cambridge, Mass., 1977—, dir., 1985—, v.p., 1986—; mng. dir. Arthur D. Little, Inc., 1989—; bd. dirs. TM Cons. S.A., Madrid, Arthur D. Little Can. Ltd. Author: Environmental Auditing: Fundamentals and Techniques, 1985, Environmental, Health and Safety Auditors Handbook, 1988, Guide to Effective Environmental Auditing, 1991; contbr. author Environmental Auditing Handbook, 1984. With U.S. Navy, 1971-76. Mem. Environ. Auditing Roundtable (founding mem., chmn. steering com. 1984-85, Extraordinary Svc. award 1991). Home: 32 Stone Root Ln Sudbury MA 01776-1370 Office: Arthur D Little Inc 15 Acorn Park Cambridge MA 02140-2301

GREENSPAN, ALAN, economist; b. N.Y.C., Mar. 6, 1926; s. Herman Herbert and Rose (Goldsmith) G. BS summa cum laude, NYU, 1948, MA, 1950, PhD, 1977. Pres., chief exec. officer Townsend-Greenspan and Co., Inc., N.Y.C., 1954-74, 77-87; mem. cons. Council Econ. Advisers, 1970-74, chmn., 1974-77; cons. Congressional Budget Office, 1977-87; mem. Pres.'s Econ. Policy Adv. Bd., 1981-87; chmn. Nat. Commn. on Social Security Reform, 1981-83; mem. Task Force on Econ. Growth, 1969, Pres.'s Fgn. Intelligence Adv. Bd., 1983-85; Commn. on an All-Vol. Armed Force, 1969-70; Commn. on Fin. Structure and Regulation, 1970-71; cons. U.S. Treasury, 1971-74, Fed. Res. Bd., 1971-74; mem. econ. adv. bd. Sec. of Commerce, 1971-72; mem. central market system com. SEC, 1972; mem. GNP rev. com. Office Mgmt. and Budget; sr. adviser panel on econ. activity Brookings Instn., 1970-74, 77-87; chmn. bd. govs. Fed. Res. System, 1987—; mem. bd. economists Time mag., 1971-74, 77-87; adj. prof. Grad. Sch. Bus. Adminstrn., NYU, 1977-87. Mem. Nixon for Pres. Com., 1968-69, dir. domestic policy research; personal rep. of Pres.-elect to Bur. Budget for transition period, chmn. task force on fgn. trade policy.; Bd. overseers Hoover Instn. on War, Revolution and Peace, 1973-74, 77-87. Recipient John P. Madden medal, 1975; joint recipient Pub. Service Achievement award, 1976, William Butler Meml. award, 1977. Fellow Nat. Assn. Bus. Economists (past pres.). Clubs: Hillcrest Country (L.A.); Metropolitan (Washington); Century Country, Harmonie. Office: FRS 20th Constitution Ave NE Washington DC 20551-0001

GREENSPAN, ALAN GEORGE, systems analyst; b. N.Y.C., Aug. 26, 1943; s. Philip and Gertrude (Pinn) G.; m. Sara Theodora Schlessinger, Feb. 12, 1972; children: Eve, Michael. BS, NYU, 1965. Sr. systems analyst Phila. (Pa.) Dept. of Health, 1982—. Buddhist. Home: 2527 Naudain St Philadelphia PA 19146-1031 Office: City of Phila OMHMR 1101 Market St Philadelphia PA 19107-2934

GREENSPAN, JOEL DANIEL, neuroscience researcher and educator; b. Chgo., Nov. 30, 1952; s. Dan and Helen (Ross) G.; m. Deborah Ann Barringer, Apr. 17, 1982. BS, Rollins Coll., 1974; MS, Fla. State U., 1976, PhD, 1980. NIH postdoctoral fellow U. N.C., Chapel Hill, 1980-83, asst. prof., 1984-87; asst. prof. neurosci., neurosurgery, physiology SUNY Health Sci. Ctr., Syracuse, 1987—. Contbr. articles to Somatosensory Rsch., Jour. of Neurosci., Jour. Comparative Neurology, Spinal Afferent Processing, Issues in Pain Mgmt. Grantee NIH, 1984-87, NSF, 1988—. Mem. Soc. for Neurosci., Internat. Assn. for Study of Pain, Am. Pain Soc., N.Y. Acad. Sci. Office: SUNY Health Sci Ctr 3118 Weiskotten Hall Syracuse NY 13210

GREENSPAN, LEON JOSEPH, lawyer; b. Phila., Feb. 10, 1932; s. Joseph and Minerva (Podolsky) G.; m. Irene Gordon, Nov. 2, 1958; children: Marjorie, David, Michael, Lisa. AB, Temple U., 1955, JD, 1958. Bar: N.Y. 1959, U.S. Supreme Ct., 1969, N.J. 1985, Fla. 1985, Pa. 1986, Conn., 1991. Pvt. practice law, White Plains, N.Y., 1959-64; ptnr. Greenspan & Aurnou, White Plains, 1964-77; ptnr. Greenspan & Jaffe, White Plains, 1978-87; ptnr.

Greenspan, Jaffe & Rosenblatt, Whiteplains, 1987-91; ptnr. Greenspan & Rosenblatt, 1992—; counsel Brown, Boston; lectr. Fla. Bar CLER Program, 1991, 92; atty. Tarrytown (N.Y.) Housing Authority. Pres. Hebrew Inst., White Plains; vice chmn. ann. dinner NCCJ. Recipient Pres.'s award Union Orthodox Synagogues, 1982; honoree Hebrew Inst., White Plains, 1983. Mem. ABA, Westchester County Bar Assn., White Plains Bar Assn., N.Y. State Trial Lawyers Assn., Criminal Cts. Bar Assn. Westchester County. Home: 14 Pinebrook Dr White Plains NY 10605-4713 Office: 180 E Post Rd White Plains NY 10601-4910

GREENSPAN, SARA THEODORA, administrative assistant; b. Balt., June 21, 1940; d. Clifford Moses and Reba Eve (Schulman) Schlesinger; m. Alan George Greenspan, Feb. 12, 1972; children: Eve Rebecca, Michael Philip. BA, Temple U., 1966, MEd, 1971; postgrad., Family Inst., Phila., 1987-89. Psychology supr. Phila. State Hosp., 1971-74; with crisis intervention Phila. Com. for Homeless, 1985-86; adminstrv. asst. Hosp. of the U. of Pa., Phila., 1989—. Mem. Soka-Gakkai Internat.-USA. Buddhist. Home: 2527 Naudain St Philadelphia PA 19146 Office: Hosp of the U of Pa 3400 Spruce St Philadelphia PA 19104

GREENSPAN, STANLEY IRA, psychiatrist; b. N.Y.C., June 1, 1941; m. Nancy Thorndike; children: Elizabeth, Jake, Sarah. BA cum laude, Harvard U., 1962; MD, Yale U., 1966. Intern SUNY Upstate Med. Ctr., Syracuse, 1966; resident in psychiatry Psychiat. Inst., Columbia Presbyn. Med. Ctr., N.Y.C., 1967; fellowship in adolescent and child psychiatry Hillcrest Children's Ctr., Children's Hosp. Nat. Med. Ctr., 1969; cons. to student health George Washington U., 1969; clin. practice child/adult psychiatry and psychoanalysis, 1970—; clin. prof. psychiatry, behavioral sci. and pediatrics George Washington U. Med. Sch., 1982—; rsch. psychiatrist Lab. Psychology, NIMH, 1970, Mental Health Study Ctr., NIMH, 1972-74, asst. chief, 1974, acting chief, 1974-75, chief, 1975-82; dir. Clin. INfant Devel. Program, NIMH, 1975-82; chief Clin. Infant Devel. Rsch. Unit, Lab. Psychology and Psychopathology, IRP, NIMH, 1982-84; chief Clin. Infant/Child Devel. Rsch. Ctr., DMCH, HRSA and NIMH, 1984-86; founder Nat. Ctr. for Clin. Infant Programs, pres. 1975-84, chmn. diagnostic classification com.; others. Editorial bd.: Jour. Am. Psychoanalytic Assn., Jour. Preventive Psychiatry, Jour. Psychoanalytic Inquiry, Infant Mental Health Jour., Jour. Psychotherapy Practice and Rsch.; author, editor of monographs and books; contbr. chpts. to books and articles to profl. jours. Past mem. Surgeon Gen.' Task Force on Infant Mortality; past regional v.p. World Assn. for Infant Psychiatry and Allied Disciplines. Recipient Edward A. Strecker award for outstanding contbrs. to Am. psychiatry, Pub. Health Svc. Spl. Recognition award, Heintz Hartman prize for contbrs. to psychoanalysis. Fellow Am. Psychiat. Assn. (Ittleson prize for outstanding contbrns. to child psychiatry rsch.); mem. Am. Psychoanalytic Assn. (chmn. com. on program liaison, cert. in adult, child and adolscent psychoanalysis 1979), Am. Coll. Psychiatry, Am. Coll. Psychoanalysis. Office: 7201 Glenbrook Rd Bethesda MD 20814

GREENSPON, JEFFREY MARK, psychology and neuroscience educator, researcher; b. Hartford, Conn., Apr. 2, 1952; s. Gilbert Eli and Florence (Sprinczeles) G.; m. Anne Marie Gomez, July 1, 1984; children: Alex, Emma. BS, Coll. of William and Mary, 1975; MS, Clark U., 1977, PhD in Psychology, 1982. Instr. Hobart and William Smith Colls., Geneva, N.Y., 1979-82, asst. prof., 1982-84, assoc. prof., 1984-91, prof., 1991—; chair psychology dept. Hobart and William Smith Colls., Geneva, 1987-91; reviewer Prentice Hall Pubs., 1982-85, 86—. Contbr. numerous articles to profl. jours. Bd. dirs. Geneva Home Improvement Corp., 1981-89. Andrew W. Mellon Found. grantee Hobart and William Smith Coll. 1986. Mem. N.Y. Acad. Sci. Home: 6 Sunset Dr Geneva NY 14456-1424 Office: Hobart and William Smith Coll Geneva NY 14456

GREENSTEIN, ABRAHAM JACOB, mortgage company executive, accountant; b. Munich, Fed. Republic of Germany, May 5, 1949; came to U.S., 1950; s. Morris and Bella (Yeger) G.; m. Ruth Sanik, June 5, 1974; children: Pinchus, Yisroel, Shlomo. BS in Acctg., Bklyn. Coll., 1972. Sr. auditor State Comptrollers Office, N.Y.C., 1972-75; asst. dir. Office of Spl. Dep. Comptroller, N.Y.C., 1978-82; sr. v.p. fin. N.Y.C. Housing Devel. Corp., 1983-88, appointed exec. v.p., 1988—; treas. Housing Assistance Corp., N.Y.C., 1985—, Housing for N.Y. Corp., N.Y.C., 1986—. Trustee Congregation Chasdi Gur, Bklyn., 1982-87. Mem. Am. Mgmt. Assn., Govt. Fin. Officers Assn., Council of State Housing Agys., Mortgage Bankers Assn. Jewish. Office: NYC Housing Devel Corp 75 Maiden Ln New York NY 10038-4810

GREENSTEIN, EDWARD THEODORE, veterinarian; b. N.Y.C., Mar. 1, 1923; s. William and Rose (Spitzer) G.; m. Betty Lesser, May 30, 1946; children: Lynn, Donald, Reva. AA in Agr., SUNY, Farmingdale, 1943; student, L.I. U., 1945-48; DVM, Cornell U., 1952. Pvt. practice, Victor, N.Y., 1952-59; lab. animal veterinarian U. Rochester, N.Y., 1959-64; lab. animal veterinarian, toxicologist Woodard Rsch. Corp., Herndon, Va., 1964-67; sr. rsch. scientist Bristol Labs., Syracuse, N.Y., 1967-75; expert cons. Nat. Cancer Inst., Bethesda, Md., 1975-77; univ. veterinarian Rutgers U., Piscataway, N.J., 1977-87; dir. lab. animal svcs. Bio/dynamics Inc., East Millstone, N.J., 1987—; cons. on lab. animal medicine Eastman Dental Dispensary, Rochester, 1960-62, Beecham Lab., Parsippany, N.J., 1977-87, Gen. Foods Corp., Cranbury, N.J., 1981-87, Exxon Biomed. Sci. Lab., East Millstone, 1983-87; speaker in field. Contbr. articles to sci. jours. Cons. Seeing Eye Found., Morristown, N.J., 1978; mem. subcom. N.J. Gov.'s Commn. on Sci. and Tech., Trenton, 1983-84; expert witness N.J. Bd. Vet. Examiners, Newark, 1984—. Tech. sgt. AUS, 1943-45; MTO. Named Man of Yr. YMCA, Syracuse, N.Y., 1975. Mem. AVMA, Am. Coll. Lab. Animal Medicine (diplomate), Am. Soc. Lab. Animal Practice (chmn. pub. info. com. 1982-83, Continuing Edn. award 1988-89), Am. Assn. for Lab. Animal Sci. (founder, v.p. Upstate N.Y. br. 1964, founder, pres. N.J. br. 1987, lectr. tech. tng. course 1991), Assn. Primate Veterinarians, N.Y. Acad. Scis. Jewish.

GREENSTEIN, JOEL ROBERT, educational administrator, photographer; b. Bklyn., Aug. 11, 1937; s. Jack and Esther (Deutsch) G. BA, Queens Coll., 1960; cert. comml. photography, N.Y. Inst. Photography, 1967. Lic. tchr., N.Y. Grad. rsch. asst. U. Buffalo, 1960-61; tchr. N.Y.C. Bd. Edn., Bklyn., 1965-68, Bur. for Edn. of Physically Handicapped, Bklyn., 1974-75; sr. vocat. evaluator Internat. Ctr. for Disabled, N.Y.C., 1968-74, North Shore Univ. Hosp., Manhasset, N.Y., 1976; work supr. Post Grad. Ctr., N.Y.C., 1977-82; tng. coordinator N.Y.C. Dept. EPA, 1983-84; rehab. counselor Jewish Guild for Blind, N.Y.C., 1984-86; coordinator vocat. svcs. Vocat. Instruction Project, Bronx, N.Y., 1986—. Photography exhibited in one man shows and group shows (prize 1961, 64, 72, 73). Recipient 1st prize for photography N.Y. Pub. Library, 1965; Bkln. Mus. grantee, 1977, 79. Mem. Assn. Vocat. Rehab. Advs., Park West Photographic Soc. (v.p. 1971, 1st place award 9 times), Psi Chi. Home: 44 W 72d St New York NY 10023

GREENWALD, DOROTHY I., art educator; b. Harrison, Ark., Sept. 22, 1920; d. George W. and Caroline (Brown) Neal; student Sch. of Cosmetology, Miami, Okla., 1938-39, Craft Students League, N.Y.C., 1958-62; m. Harry Greenwald, Apr. 17, 1949. Owner, operator beauty salon and ladies ready to wear stores, 1940-58; instr. ceramic dept. Craft Student League, N.Y.C., 1962-80, Queens Museum Sch. of Art, Flushing, N.Y., 1980—; past chmn. Craft Students League of YWCA of N.Y.; chmn. crafts dept. Rockland Ctr. for Arts, West Nyack, N.Y.; pres., treas. Greenwald Electro-Mech. Cons., Inc., Whitestone, N.Y. Recipient awards Rockland Center for Art, 1972, L.I. Guild of Craftsmen, 1972, Artist-Craftsmen N.Y., 1975. Mem. World Craft Council, Am. Craft Council, Artist-Craftsmen N.Y. (pres. 1972-75), L.I. Guild of Craftsmen. Republican. Home: 16625 Powells Cove Blvd Whitestone NY 11357-1528

GREENWALD, HERBERT, advertising consultant; b. N.Y.C., Mar. 30, 1910; s. Nathan and Minnie (Lieb) G.; m. Carrie Weisberg, June 15, 1935; children: John, Mark. Student, Art Students League, N.Y.C., 1927-30. Art dir. Bloomingdales, N.Y.C., 1931-33, Montgomery Ward, N.Y.C., 1933-35; fashion art dir. Macy's Dept. Store, N.Y.C., 1936-39; creative advt. mgr. Macy's Dept. Store, 1942-45; exec. art dir. Gimbels Dept. store, N.Y.C., 1940-42; v.p. Amos Parrish & Co., Inc., N.Y.C., 1945-59; pres. Herbert Greenwald Assocs., N.Y.C., 1959—; mem. adv. com., N.Y. High Sch. of Art and Design, N.Y.C., 1942—; mem. faculty Sch. of Retailing, NYU, 1952-57; lectr. Sch. Bus., CCNY, 1954-55. Author: (textbooks) Fashion Illustration, 1961, Independent Retailing, 1976, (with others) Fashion Advertising and Promotion, 1992. Capt. aux. police, N.Y.C. Police Dept., 1950-60. Cited for distinctive contbns. to retail advt. Nat. Retail Mchts. Assn., N.Y.C., 1958. Mem. Soc. Illustrators (spl. award for contbg. to edn. 1965). Home: 2914 Jerome Ave Bronx NY 10468-1645 Office: Greenwald Assocs 521 5th Ave New York NY 10175-0003

GREENWALD, MICHAEL JAY, certified public accountant, tax consultant; b. N.Y.C., June 12, 1953; s. Allyn and Helen (Feiler) G.; m. Jo Ann Landesberg, Apr. 1, 1979; children: Lisa Ann, David Harmon, Max Aaron. BA, Yale U., 1975, M.Pub. and Pvt. Mgmt., 1981. CPA, Conn., N.Y. Tax specialist Coopers & Lybrand, Stamford, Conn., 1981-84; dir. taxes Daseke & Co., Inc., Westport, Conn., 1984-85; sr. tax mgr. Kenneth Leventhal & Co., N.Y.C., 1985-88; v.p. Starrett Housing Corp., N.Y.C., 1988-91; ptnr. Schneider & Greenwald, N.Y.C., 1991—. Contbr. articles to profl. jours. Mem. fin. com. Juvenile Diabetes Found. Internat., N.Y.C., 1983-85; nat. bd. mem. Christmas in April USA, Washington, 1991—. 2d lt. U.S. Army, 1977-79. Mem. AICPA, Conn. Soc. CPA's, N.Y. State Soc. CPA's, Assn. of Yale Alumni (del. 1990—). Jewish. Home: 32 Pebble Ln Roslyn Heights NY 11577 Office: Schneider & Greenwald 461 Fifth Ave New York NY 10017

GREENWALD, THOMAS EDWARD, investment company executive; b. Akron, Ohio, Jan. 25, 1960; s. Louis Joseph and Jeanne Marie (Campeau) G.; m. Mary Perna, June 22, 1985; children: Marissa Nancy, Joseph Francis. BS in Mktg. and BA in Communications, Canisius Coll., 1982. Sales rep. Office Automation, Williamsville, N.Y., 1982-83; assoc. v.p. Dean Witter Reynolds, Buffalo, 1983—. Dir. alumni bd. Canisius Coll., 1984-90. Mem. Bond Club of Buffalo (pres. 1990). Roman Catholic. Home: 204 Rambling Rd East Amherst NY 14051 Office: Dean Witter Reynolds 610 Norstar Bldg Buffalo NY 14202

GREENWALT, WILLIAM EARL, JR., insurance agent; b. Harrisburg, Pa., Aug. 14, 1962; s. William Earl and Roberta Marie (Masseau) G.; m. Mary Frances Bakos, Mar. 2, 1985; children: William E. III, Michael Paul, Nicole Marie. BS in Acctg., Pa. State U., 1986. Account rep. Interactive Fin. Svcs., Phila., 1986-89, Wausau Ins. Co., Harrisburg, 1989—. Bd. dirs. Building Wishes-Make a Wish Found., Lancaster, Pa., 1990—; baseball coach, York, Pa., 1980-82. Republican. Roman Catholic. Office: Wausau Ins Co 2201 Forest Hills Dr Ste 6A Harrisburg PA 17112-1089

GREENWAY, ROBERT CHARLES STUART, counselor, educator; b. Westmoreland County, Pa., Apr. 13, 1928; s. William Harold and Elisabeth Edith (Stuart) G.; m. M. Elinor Watts, Dec. 19, 1957; children: Pamela Stuart, Robert Stuart. BS, U. Va., 1960; MS, Boston U., 1964; postgrad., Harvard U., 1966-69, 90; MA, Columbia U., 1974. Cert. sch. psychologist. Interpreter Dept. of the Army, Paris, France, 1955-58; tchr. Long Branch (N.J.) Pub. Schs., 1960-61, Westport (Conn.) Pub. Schs., 1961-63; counselor New Canaan (Conn.) Pub. Schs., 1963-65; counselor Bedford (Mass.) Pub. Schs., 1965-72, dir. counseling, 1972-75, counselor, advanced placement dir., 1975—. With U.S. Army, 1945-47. Kellogg fellow Columbia U., 1972. Mem. New England Historic Geneal. Soc., Heraldry Soc., Stewart Soc., St. Andrews Soc., Greenway Family Assn., Phi Delta Kappa. Home: 10 Munroe Rd Lexington MA 02173

GREENWAY, ROBERT STUART, computer engineer; b. Long Branch, N.J., Dec. 26, 1960; s. Robert Charles Stuart and Mary Elinor (Watts) G. BS, Cornell U., 1983; MS, U. Wis., 1984; MBA, Worcester Poly. Inst., 1991. Prin. engr. Data Gen. Corp., Westboro, Mass., 1985—. Office: Data Gen 4400 Computer Dr Westborough MA 01580-0001

GREENWAY, WILLIAM CHARLES, electronics executive, design engineer; b. Worcester, Mass., Feb. 28, 1958; s. Christopher W. and Beatrice C. (Masitis) G.; m. Joy Ann Montgomery, May 5, 1984; children: Ariel, Ann, Christopher. BSEE, U. Mass., 1982; MS in Mech. Engring., Syracuse (N.Y.) U., 1987, MBA, 1990. Registered profl. engr., N.Y. Mem. mfg. mgmt. program GE, Somersworth, N.H., 1982-84; supr. assembly start GE, Syracuse, 1984-85, systems analyst, 1985-86, sr. systems engr., 1986-87; mfg. mgr. Leybold Inficon, East Syracuse, N.Y., 1987-88; v.p. ops. S&S Inficon, Liverpool, N.Y., 1988-90, exec. v.p., 1990-92, pres., 1992—. Patentee therapy imaging system, DSH exposure control. Mem. IEEE, Am. Soc. Quality Control, Am. Prodn. and Inventory Control Soc., Soc. Photo-Optical Instrumentation Engr. Home: 1000 Tulip St Liverpool NY 13088-5051 Office: S&S Inficon Inc 121 Metropolitan Dr Liverpool NY 13088-5335

GREENWELL, KEVIN JAMES, accountant; b. Havre de Grace, Md., Mar. 31, 1958; s. James Cyriacus and Mildred Joanne (Heller) G.; m. Mollie Kay Frances Banz, May 15, 1982. AA in Bus. Adminstrn., Harford Community Coll., Bel Air, Md., 1979; BS in Acctg., U. Balt., 1981. CPA, Md. Acct. Deloitte Haskins & Sells, Balt., 1981-83; comm. fin. auditor Union Trust Co. of Md., Balt., 1983-84; acct. Stegman & Co., Pub. Accts., Balt., 1984-85, McGrow, Pridgeon & Co., Pub. Accts., Towson, Md., 1985-86; asst. contr. McCall Handling Co., Balt., 1986-87; acct., cons. Bradley Assocs., Pub. Accts., Lutherville, Md., 1987-89; acct. Clark and Anderson, Pub. Accts., Glen Burnie, Md., 1989—. Contbr. (with others) article to mag. Active Laurel Valley Homeowners' Assn., Abingdon, Md., 1985—, Glenangus Homeowners' Assn., Bel Air, 1991—. Recipient Wall St. Jour. Student Achievement award Harford Community Coll., 1979; U. Balt. Found. fellow U. Balt. Edn. Found., 1979. Mem. AICPA, KC, Md. Assn. CPAs (acctg. and auditing conf. com. 1991—, pub. rels. com. 1989-91, membership com. 1992—). Republican. Roman Catholic. Home: 2705 Long Meadow Dr Abingdon MD 21009-1156

GREENWOOD, AUDREY GATES, librarian; b. Buffalo, Mar. 27, 1917; d. Marc Herbert and Genevieve Cecelia (Naab) Gates; B.A., D'Youville Coll., 1939; B.S. in Library Sci., Cath. U. Am., 1940, M.A., 1944; m. Clayton Edward Greenwood, Sept. 2, 1944; children—Mary Ellen, Nancy Jane, Susan Jean. Head librarian Gonzaga High Sch., Washington, 1940-45, Southeastern U. Evening Sch., 1941-45; reference librarian Cath. U. Am., evenings 1942-43; librarian St. Joseph's Collegiate Inst., Buffalo, 1945-46; head librarian Canisius High Sch., Buffalo, 1949-50; head librarian Eden (N.Y.) Central Schs., 1950-83, coordinator state and fed. funds, 1969-83, dir. adult edn., 1973-83. Mem. Eden Tchrs. Assn. (past pres.), Erie County Ednl. Assn. (past v.p.), NEA, N.Y. State Tchrs. Assn., N.Y. State United Tchrs. (state del. 1992—, legis. chmn. Western zone, chmn. retirees of western N.Y. 1984-88, pres. retirees of western N.Y. 1989—), mem. ROC com. 1985-88, mem. editorial bd. The Active N.Y. State United Tchrs. Retiree, mem. Commn. 100, retiree del. 1992—), N.Y. State Retired Tchrs. Assn. (pres. Southtowns chpt. 1987—, legis. commn. 1987—, historian western zone 1988—, del. 1991—), Am. Fedn. Tchrs. (nat. del.), Sch. Librarians Assn. Western N.Y. (past pres.), N.Y. Educators Assn., Delta Kappa Gamma. (state legis. chmn., state fin. com. 1991—), Beta Zeta (v.p. 1986-89, pres. 1989—). Democrat. Roman Catholic. Home: 3688 Briarwood Ct Hamburg NY 14075-2247

GREENWOOD, FRED HENRY, aerospace management consultant, engineer; b. Vienna, Austria, May 14, 1927; came to U.S., 1940; s. Walter George and Illona Greenwood; m. Eva Pollenz, Sept. 8, 1951; children: Susan, Jeffrey, John. B Mech. Engring., CCNY, 1951; MSME, U. Conn., 1958; program mgmt. diploma, Rensselaer Poly. Inst., 1975. Analytical engr. Westinghouse Electric Corp., Lester, Pa., 1951-54; program mgr. Hamilton Standard div. United Techs. Corp., Windsor Locks, Conn., 1954-87; aerospace cons., West Hartford, Conn., 1987—; cons. Grumman Aerospace Corp., Bethpage, N.Y., 1987-88, Dornier GmbH, Friedrichshafen, Germany, 1987—, Carleton Tech. Inc., Orchard Park, N.Y., 1987—, CJB Devels. Ltd., Portsmouth, Eng., 1988-89, European Space Agy., Noordwijk, The Netherlands, 1988-89, ILC Dover Inc., Frederica, Del., 1989, United Techs. Corp., Hartford, Conn., 1990—, Umpqua Rsch. Co., Myrtle Creek, Oreg., 1990—; chmn. 6th Internat. Conf. on Environ. Systems, San Diego, 1976. Author, editor: The Program Management System Guide, 1982; author: Water Quality Standards, 1989; also articles. Mem. West Hartford Bd. Tax Rev., 1990—. Recipient Pub. Svc. medal NASA, 1981, Snoopy award NASA Astronauts, 1982, Internat. Conf. on Environ. Systems award Soc. Automotive Engrs., 1990. Assoc. fellow AIAA (life sci. and systems tech. com.); mem. ASME (crew systems tech. com.), Hartford Ski Club (pres. 1974-75), Tau Beta Pi, Pi Tau Sigma.

GREENWOOD, JOHN EDWARD DOUGLAS, investment banker, lawyer; b. Blundell Sands, Lancashire, Eng., Mar. 4, 1923; came to U.S., 1948; s. Arthur and Mabel (Hunt) G.; m. Charlotte Elizabeth Sabey, May 25, 1946; children: Marcia Barbara, Douglas Charles William. B in Commerce with honors, McGill U., 1948; JD, Yale U., 1951. Bar: N.Y. 1952. Jr. legal assoc. Milbank, Tweed, Hope & Hadley, N.Y.C., 1951-52, Chadbourne, Hunt, Jaeckel & Brown, N.Y.C., 1952-54; with legal dept. Creole Petroleum Corp., N.Y.C., 1954-55; assoc. corp. fin. Bacon Stevenson & Co., N.Y.C., 1955-59; v.p. E.F. Hutton & Co., N.Y.C., 1959-60; pres., founder Can. Alpha Lessors Ltd., Mont., Can., 1960-63; ptnr., sr. v.p. Eastman Dillon Union Securities, N.Y.C., 1963-72; prin. Blyth Eastman Dillon & Co., N.Y., 1972-78; pvt. investor, 1978—; bd. dirs. Electromotive, Inc., Chantilly, Va.; chmn. investment adv. com. Am. Capital Fin., L.P., 1992; U.S. rep. fin. IAEA, World Confs., Copenhagen, Paris, 1975, Stockholm, 1976, Salzberg, 1977. Mem. Rep. Boosters Club, N.Y., 1965—; patron Winslow Therapeutic Riding, Inc., Warwick, 1982—, Warwick Hist. Soc., 1984—; sec., dir. Friends of McGill, Inc., N.Y., 1952-60; treas., trustee Tuxedo Park (N.Y.) Sch., 1961-63; U.S. rep. Internat. Atomic Energy Assn. Confs., Copenhagen and Paris, 1974, Srockholm, 1975, Salzberg, 1997. With Royal Can. Navy, 1941-45. Mem. Am. Nuclear Energy Coun. (bd. dirs. Washington 1976-78), Atomic Indsl. Forum, Links Club of N.Y., Univ. Club of Montreal, Racquet and Tennis Club of N.Y., Leash Club of N.Y., Tuxedo Club of Tuxedo Park, N.Y., Capitol Hill Club of Washington, Bond Club of N.Y. Episcopalian. Home and Office: 19 Park Ave Warwick NY 10990-1702

GREENWOOD, SCOTT ALSON, insurance agency executive; b. Fitchburg, Mass., Apr. 4, 1949; s. Robert B. and Lois (Stevenson) G.; m. Elaine Mary Tuttle, June 20, 1970; children: Jessica, Jocelyn, Benjamin. BA in Econs., Marietta (Ohio) Coll., 1971. Treas. S.A. Greenwood & Son, Inc., Winchendon, Mass., 1971-82, pres., 1982-83; v.p. Heritage Ins. Agy., Gardner, Mass., 1983-90, pres., 1990—. Co-inventor electronic vision trainer. Trustee Murdock Fund, Winchendon, 1980—; dir. W.P. Clark Meml., Winchendon, 1979-80. Home: 9 Weathers Ln Bolton MA 01470 Office: Heritage Ins Agy 90 Parker St Gardner MA 01440-0219

GREENWOOD, SUSAN FOWLE, sociology educator; b. Newburyport, Mass., Apr. 21, 1941; d. Harry Winfield and Elsie Edith (Dudley) Fowle; m. Michael Sargent Greenwood, June 10, 1961; children: Willard P. II, Davis F. Cert. in liberal arts, Katharine Gibbs Sch., 1961; BA, U. Maine, 1986, MA, 1989. Lic. social worker, Maine. Sec. physics dept. Brown U., Providence, 1961-63; sec. physics dept. Yale U., New Haven, 1963-66, adminstrv. asst. physics dept., 1966-67; vol. coord., caseworker Ouachita Children's Ctr., Hot Springs, Ark., 1977-84; part-time instr. U. Maine, Orono, 1987—; cons. Myers-Briggs Type Indicator, Orono, 1987—. President LWV, Middlebury, Vt., 1972-74, Hot Springs, 1976-78, Ctr. for Noetic Studies, Orono, 1989-90, sec., 1991; bd. govs. Ouachita Meml. Hosp., 1977-82; chair social concerns com. Orono Meth. Ch., 1990-91. Mem. Am. Sociol. Assn., Soc. for Sci. Study of Religion, Assn. for Psychol. Type. Democrat. Home: 129 Bennoch Rd Orono ME 04473-1121 Office: U Maine Dept of Sociology Orono ME 04469-0124

GREER, BILLY LOUIS, laboratory manager; b. Trinidad and Tobago, Aug. 26, 1959; came to U.S., 1960; s. Billy Louis Greer and Aura Magdalena (Rodriguez) Harter; m. Nancy Ellen Willard, May 22, 1982; children: Lane Elizabeth, Glen Ryan. BS in Biology, Hampden-Sydney Coll., 1981. Lab. supr. Comml. Testing & Engring. Co., Norfolk, Va., 1981-82; br. mgr. Comml. Testing & Engring. Co., Balt., 1982-85, mgr. Balt. ops., 1985—; relief housecounselor Bello Machre, Inc., Glen Burnie, Md., 1986—; mem. subcom. on coal transp. Chem. Transp. Adv. Com., Washington, 1989. Mem. Md. Coal Assn. (sec./treas., v.p., pres.). Office: Comml Testing & Engring Co 7609 Energy Pky Ste 1002 Baltimore MD 21226-1737

GREER, EDWARD GABRIEL, theatre director, drama educator; b. Cambridge, mass., Apr. 10, 1920; s. Louis Chaim and Mollie (Eisenman) Greenberg. BA, Harvard U., 1941; postgrad., Yale U., 1941-42. Asst. curator theatre dept. Mus. Modern Art, N.Y.C., 1944; stage mgr. Chautauqua (N.Y.) Opera Co., 1944; instr. New Sch. Social Rsch., N.Y.C., 1954-56; assoc. prof. drama dept. Syracuse (N.Y.) U., 1974—; instr. Am. Theatre Wing, U. Wash.; lectr. Vassar Coll., Hammond, Mus., North Salem, N.Y.; advisor N.Y. State Coun. on Arts. Dir. (plays) Music at Night, Murder in the Cathedral, The Little Clay Cart, Dr. Faustus, Elektra, The Tempest, The Importance of Being Earnest, Wasters of the Moon, All That Fall, Edward II, Gallows Humour, American Blues, The Beaux Stratagem, She Stoops to Conquer, A Flea in Her Ear; English narrator Obraztsov Russian Puppet Theatre, Moscow Art Theatre, Comedie Francaise, N.Y.C. Ctr.; recorded Lang. for Daily Use, 1965. With U.S. Army, WW II. Fulbright fellow, 1950-51. Mem. Actors Equity Assn., Soc. Stage Dirs. and Choreographers, Actors Studio (dirs. unit 1960-65).

GREER, GORDON BRUCE, lawyer; b. Butler, Pa., Feb. 17, 1932; s. Samuel Walker and Winifred (Fletcher) G.; m. Nancy Linda Hannaford, June 14, 1959; children: Gordon Bruce, Alison Clark. BA, Harvard U., 1953, JD cum laude, 1959. Bar: Wis. 1959, Mass. 1961. Assoc. Foley, Sammond & Lardner, Milw., 1959-61; assoc. Bingham, Dana & Gould, Boston, 1961-67, ptnr., 1967—. Bd. dirs. The Colonial Group, Inc. Served to maj. USAFR. Mem. ABA, Mass. Bar Assn., Boston Bar Assn. Republican. Clubs: Brae Burn Country; Federal, Harvard (Boston). Editor Harvard Law Rev., vols. 71, 72. Home: 45 Fieldmont Rd Belmont MA 02178-2606 Office: Bingham Dana & Gould 150 Federal St Boston MA 02110-1745

GREGAN, JOHN PATRICK, finance executive, small business owner; b. Sigourney, Iowa, Nov. 24, 1947; s. Raymond Stephen and Ellen Mary (O'Brien) G.; m. Rhonda Mason Weissberg, Nov. 19, 1977; children: Brien Geoffrey, Audrey Jane. BA in Acctg., St. Ambrose Coll., Davenport, Iowa, 1970. Internal revenue agt. IRS, Davenport, Iowa, 1970-71; computer audit specialist OIO (office of internal ops.), Washington, 1971-79; tax acct. SMATAX Corp., Waldorf, Md., 1979—; Md. del. to Internat. Soc. Pub. Accts. Conv., 1987, 92. Diplomate, Rome, 1973. Mem. Nat. Soc. Pub. Accts., Md. Soc. Pub. Accts., Nat. Assn. Enrolled Agts., Va. Soc. Enrolled Agts., D.C. Soc. Enrolled Agents, Md. Soc. Enrolled Agts. Democrat. Catholic. Home: 1014 Forest View Dr Waldorf MD 20601-2001 Office: SMATAX Corp 1014 Forest View Dr Waldorf MD 20601-2001

GREGG, J. ROBBY, JR., human resources executive, consultant; b. Bethesda, Md., July 29, 1961; s. James R. and Edith (Jackson) G. BA in Communications, Wake Forest U., 1983. Mktg. sales intern Wrangler, Greensboro, N.C., 1985; brand mktg. asst. Hanes, Winston-Salem, N.C., 1985-87; acct. mgr. Intersec Pers., Washington, 1987-89; recruiting mgr. The Choice for Temporaries, Washington, 1989-91; branch mgr. ADIA, Rosslyn, Va., 1992—; pres. Progressive Personnel Human Resource Cons., Washington, 1990—. contbr. articles to profl. jours. Vol. D.C. Commission for Women, 1990—, Am. Diabetes Assn., 1991—, Mentor Programfor Youth, 1992. Recipient Good Guy award D.C. Commn. for Women, 1991. Mem. Metro. Washington Temporary Svcs. Assn., Washington Area Wake Forest Alumni Assn. Democrat. Home: 2349 Ashmeade Pl NW Washington DC 20009

GREGG, JUDD, governor of New Hampshire, former congressman; b. Nashua, N.H., Feb. 14, 1947; m. Kathleen MacLellan, 1973; children—Molly, Sarah, Joshua. A.B., Columbia U., 1969; J.D., Boston U., 1972, LL.M., 1975. Bar: N.H. 1972. Practice law Nashua, N.H.; mem. 97th-100th Congresses from 2d N.H. dist., Washington, 1981-89; governor of N.H., Concord, 1989—; mem. N.H. Gov.'s Exec. Council, 1978-80. Pres. Crotched Mountain Rehab. Found. Office: Office of Gov 208-214 Statehouse Concord NH 03301

GREGORIAN, VARTAN, academic administrator; b. Tabriz, Iran, Apr. 8, 1934; came to U.S., 1956; s. Samuel B. and Shushanik G. (Mirzaian) G.; m. Clare Russell, Mar. 25, 1960; children: Vahe, Raffi, Dareh. Grad., Coll. Armenien, 1955; BA, Stanford U., 1958, PhD, 1964; hon. degree, Boston U., 1983, Brown U., 1984, Johns Hopkins U., 1987, NYU, 1987, U. Pa., 1988, U. Dartmouth, 1989. From instr. to asst. prof. to assoc. prof. history San Francisco State Coll., 1962-68; assoc. prof. UCLA, 1968; from assoc. prof. to prof. U. Tex., 1968-72, dir. spl. programs, 1970-72; Tarzian prof. Armenian and Caucasian history U. Pa., Phila., 1972-80; dean U. Pa. (Faculty Arts and Scis.), 1974-79, provost, 1978-80; pres. N.Y. Pub. Library, 1981-88; prof.

New Sch. for Social Research, N.Y.C., 1984—; prof. History and Near Eastern studies NYU, 1984—; pres. Brown U., Providence, R.I., 1989—; mem. Nat. Humanities Faculty, 1970—; bd. dirs. Inst. for Advanced Study, Boston U., 1975—, Trinity Sch., 1982—, J. Paul Getty Trust. Author: The Emergence of Modern Afghanistan, 1880-1946, 1969. Internat. League of Human Rights, 1984—, Vassar Coll., 1987; chmn. bd. visitors Grad. Sch. and Univ. Ctr., CUNY, 1984—, N.Y. Pub. Libr. Recipient Danforth E.H. Harbison Teaching award 1969, Cactus Teaching award 1971, award of distinction Phi Lambda Theta and Phi Delta Kappa, 1980, Silver Cultural medal Italian Ministry Fgn. Affairs, 1977, Gold medal of honor City and Province of Vienna (Austria), 1976, 1st Disting. Humanist award Pa. Humanities Council, 1983, Gold medal Nat. Inst. Social Scis., 1985; Am. Philos Soc. grantee, 1965, 66; fellow Social Sci. Research Council, 1960, Ford Found. Fgn. Area Tng., 1960-62, Am. Council Learned Socs.-Social Sci. Research Council, 1965, John Simon Guggenheim Found., 1971-72, Social Sci. Research Council, 1971-72, Am. Council Edn., 1973, Nat. Fellowship award Fellowship Commn., Phila., 1984; decorated Officier de l'Ordre des Arts et Lettres, France, 1986. Mem. ALA, Am. Hist. Assn. (program chmn. 1972), Am. Philos. Soc., Internat. Fedn. Library Assn. (co-chmn. program com. 1985), Assn. Advancement Slavic Studies (program chmn. Western Slavic Conf. 1967), Mid-East Studies Assn., Council on Fgn. Relations, Acad. of Medicine. Clubs: Grolier, Round Table. Office: Brown U Office of President Providence RI 02912*

GREGORIO, ROBERT DOMENIC, accountant; b. N.J., Oct. 6, 1966; s. Domenic Joseph and Maryann Virginia (Peccini) G. BSBA in Acctg. magna cum laude, Glassboro State Coll., 1989, postgrad., 1991—. Acct. Computer Scis. Corp., Mt. Laurel, N.J., 1989—. Mem. C. of C. of So. N.J., Bally's Holiday Health and Fitness Club, Gamma Tau Sigma. Home: 56 Jobs Ln Williamstown NJ 08094-1314

GREGORY, HAROLD ANTHONY, editor; b. Beachmont, Mass., Apr. 2, 1919; s. George and Akaby (Pashigian) Krikorian. BA, Mexico City Coll., 1948; MA, Boston U., 1950. Adminstrv. pub. info. officer, pvt. to 1st lt. U.S. Army, 1941-46; translator, producer Radio Edn. Unesco 2d Gen. Conf., Mexico City, 1947-48; pub. info. specialist Worcester (Mass.) Chpt. ARC, 1953-58; lectr. art history and Spanish Anna Maria Coll., Paxton, Mass., 1960-63; tchr. Worcester Pub. Schs., 1962-79; journalist Armenian Mirror Spectator, Watertown, Mass., 1952-76; freelance writer Worcester Telegram & Gazette; asst. prof. Spanish Quinsigamond Community Coll., Worcester, 1983-84; editor, photographer The Messenger, Worcester, 1984—; columnist Camp Edward News, 1941-42. Author (epic poem) Concord Revisited; one-man shows include Wordscape; playwright Freedom's Ptnr.-Freedom's Choice; spl. collection of lit. and artistic publs. Worcester Pub. Libr. Founder, researcher The Concordian Party of Am. Survey, Worcester, 1973. Recipient St. Vartan award Diocese of Armenian Ch. of Am., N.Y.C., 1990. Mem. ASCAP, Res. Officers Assn. U.S., Disable Am. VETS, NEA, AAAS, N.Y. Acad. Scis., Newspaper Inst. Am., Knights of Vartan, Arshavir Lodge No. 2, Worcester Br. Armenian Students Assn. Republican. Armenian. Home: PO Box 1221 Worcester MA 01601-1221

GREGORY, JULIA PAIGE, financial advisor; b. Louisville, Sept. 7, 1952; d. Frank J. and Mary Elizabeth (Haws) Gerdnic; m. Warren Thomas, Oct. 1, 1977; children: Katharine Elizabeth, Scott Elliott. BA in Internat. Affairs, George Washington U., 1974; MBA, U. Pa., 1980. Asst. mgr. Chem. Bank, N.Y., 1976-78; sr. v.p. Dillon, Read & Co. Inc., N.Y.C., 1980-90; prin. J.P. Gregory & Co., Inc., N.Y.C., 1991-92; mng. dir., corp. fin. Prime Charter Ltd., N.Y.C., 1992—. Mem. benefit com. Unitarian Ch. All Souls, N.Y.C., 1991, 92, audit com., 1992—. Mem. Wharton Exec. Leadership Gift Com., Wharton Club. Home: 105 Fifth Ave New York NY 10003 Office: Prime Charter Ltd 1120 Ave of the Americas One Exchange Plz New York NY 10006

GREGORY, MYRA MAY, educator, religious organization administrator; b. N.Y.C., Sept. 21, 1912; d. Thomas and Anna (Collins) G. Diploma, Maxwell Tchrs. Tng. Sch., Bklyn., 1933; BS in Edn., Bklyn. Coll., 1940, MA in History, 1952. Cert. music tchr. Tchr. N.Y.C. Bd. Edn., Bklyn., 1943-75; social worker Berean Bapt. Ch., Bklyn., 1932-48, supr., 1932—, fin. sec. Sunday sch., 1935—; bd. dir. Berean-Vacation Bible Sch., Bklyn.;tchr. Protestant Coun., N.Y.C., 1940-81; bd. dir. Recreation Bedford-Stuyvesant Area Project, Bklyn. Author poems (Golden Poet award 1988). Bd. mgrs. Bklyn. Sunday Sch. Union, 1974—, Seminar for Christian Teaching, Bklyn., 1974-86; pres. Coun. of Chs. of the City of N.Y., Bklyn., 1984-86; bd. dirs. Bklyn. Div. Coun. of Chs., 1984—. Named Tchr. of Yr. Community Sch. Bd. Dist. 14, Bklyn., 1973, Outstanding Tchr. Stuyvesant Div. of the Bklyn. Sunday Sch. Union, 1977, Educator/leader, Berean Bapt. Ch., 1977; recipient Ecumenism citation, Borough Pres.'s Office, Bklyn., 1985. Mem. Am. String Tchrs. Assn., Am. Viola Soc., Assn. Childhood Edn. Internat., Assn. for Supervision and Curriculum Devel. Democrat. Home: 1139 Lincoln Pl Brooklyn NY 11213-3527

GREGORY, R(ICHARD) THOMAS, artist, photographer; b. Balt., July 27, 1948; s. Richard Henry and Betty Mae (Bley) G. Student, Grossmont Coll., 1971-73; BFA in Art Edn., Md. Inst., 1974, MFA in Art Edn., 1976. Photographer Photo Balt. '77, 1977-78; photographer Photographic Survey Md., Balt., 1979-80; assoc. prof. Essex Community Coll., Balt., 1980—; pres. SoBo Publs., Balt., 1981—; photographer Mayor's Offic eof Folk Life, Balt., 1987-88; instr. photography Smithsonian Institution, Washington, 1976-79. Artist photographic mural Balt. subway, 1983. Recipient Best in Show award Md. Annual Photo Exhbn. Md. Gen. Assembly, 1986, Disting. Artist award Life of Md. Gallery, Balt., 1985. Mem. Am. Soc. Mag. Photographers, Soc. for Photographic Edn. Republican. Home and Office: 911 Light St Baltimore MD 21230-4015

GREGUS, LINDA ANNA, government official; b. Hartford, Conn., Mar. 24, 1956; d. Steven and Sylvia Christine (Ramunno) G. AB, Bowdoin Coll., 1978; MA in Law and Diplomacy, Tufts U., 1985. Vol. VISTA, Phoenix, 1978-79; research asst. Econ. Research Assocs., Boston, 1979; ops adminstr. CRT Inc., Hartford, Conn., 1980-82; program officer U.S. Dept. of State, Washington, 1986-90; analyst CIA, Washington, 1990—. Recipient Milo Peck Scholarship Town of Windsor, Conn., 1984. Republican. Home: 1904 Wilson Ln Mc Lean VA 22102-1958

GREGWARE, JAMES MURRAY, financial planner; b. Plattsburgh, N.Y., Dec. 17, 1956; s. John William and Patricia Ann (Murray) G.; m. Kathleen Mary Stanley, June 23, 1979; children: Ryan James, Kailee Michelle. BA in Bus. and Psychology, SUNY, Potsdam, 1979. Cert. investment advisor, stockbroker, fin. planner. Commodities trader The Exch., Plattsburgh, 1979-82; stockbroker, collections supr., loan officer Champlain Valley Fed. Savs., Plattsburgh, 1982-84; fin. planner, securities instr. New Life Fin. Services, Waterville, Maine, 1984-87; stockbroker Investacorp, Inc., Waterville and Pittsfield, Mass., 1985-89; pres. Fin. Designs & Mgmt., Inc., Manchester, N.H., 1985—; pres. Eastern Fin. Group, Waterville, 1984-87, Pittsfield, 1987—; stockbroker, fin. planner Investment Ctr. Inc., 1989—; investment mgr. Comfed Savs. Bank, Pittsfield, Mass., 1990-91; pres. Comtrust, Pittsfield, Mass., 1991—. Mem. Nat. Assn. Security Dealers, Coll. Fin. Planning. Republican. Roman Catholic. Home: 11 Riverwind Dr Rexford NY 12148-1223 Office: Comtrust 1450 East St Pittsfield MA 01201-5319

GREIF, TONI ANNE, mortgage banker; b. N.Y.C., June 2, 1954; d. Murray W. and Adele (Buchsbaum) G. BA in Psychology, Fairfield U., 1976; MBA, U. Conn., 1981. Various positions to asst. auditor Conn. Bank and Trust Co., N.A., Norwalk, 1972-76; various positions including br. mgr. Old Greenwich br. People's Bank, Bridgeport, Conn., 1976, asst. v.p., until 1983; exec. v.p. Williamsburg Mortgage Corp., Greenwich; sr. v.p. Bank of Darien, Conn., until 1987; founder, owner, pres., chief operating officer Sound Beach Fin. Corp., Riverside, Conn.; ad hoc prof. real estate fin. Norwalk (Conn.) Community Coll., also mem. friends bd. Bd. dirs. United Way Greenwich; bd. rep. United Way Tri-State; past pres. Lifeline Southwestern Conn.; mem. adv. bd. Youth Shelter; mem. Norwalk Community Coll. Found., Inc.; former mem. bd. dirs. S.W. Fairfield County chpt. Am. Cancer soc.; former mem. aadv. coun. Fairfield County Coop. Found. Recipient Disting. Svc. award Greenwich Jaycees, 1981, Outstanding Personal Achievement Alumni merit award Fairfield U., 1985, Bravo award YMCA/Town of Greenwich, 1988. Mem. Women in Mgmt. (bd. dirs., past pres.), Am. Mgmt. Assn., Nat. Assn Bank Women, Greenwich Bd. Realtors, Stamford Bd. Realtors, Kiwanis (bd. dirs., chmn. community devel. com.). Office: Sound Beach Fin Corp 1171 E Putnam Ave Riverside CT 06878

GREIFER, AARON P., chemistry educator; b. Passaic, N.J., Sept. 29, 1919; s. Morris and Mamie (Margolis) G.; m. Rita Weiss, Mar. 14, 1943; children: Roberta, Margaret. BA, Ohio State U., 1942; MA, Columbia U., 1948. Chemist Elwood Ordnance Plant, Joliet, Ill., 1942-43; rsch. assoc. Ohio State U., Columbus, 1944; chemist Kellex Corp., N.Y.C., Jersey City, 1948-49; supervising chemist Fed. Telephone & Radio Corp., Clifton, N.J., 1951; scientist GE Co., Syracuse, N.Y., 1951-56; sr. mem. tech. staff RCA, Needham, Mass., 1956-60; project leader Clevite Corp., Cleve., 1961-64; staff scientist Sperry Rand Corp., Blue Bell, Pa., 1964-81; instr. Del. County Community Coll., Media, Pa., 1983-84; lectr. Villanova (Pa.) U., 1984—. Co-author (with others): Magnetism and Magnetic Materials, 1967; contbr. to Landolt-Bornstein III/46, 1970. Sgt. U.S. Army, 1945-46. Recipient Cert. of Appreciation, U.S. Sec. War, 1945. Fellow Am. Inst. Chemists; mem. Am. Chem. Soc., Am. Phys. Soc., Toastmasters Internat. (Club Pres. of Yr. dist. 38 1980). Home: 51 Golfview Rd Ardmore PA 19003-1625

GREIG, RUSSELL G., biochemist; b. Oban, Scotland, June 11, 1952; came to U.S. Oct. 1976; s. Thomas Greig and Olive (MacLennan) Sharp; m. Linda Griglione, Nov. 6, 1982; children: Russell, Andrew. BS in Biochemistry, Univ. Manchester, England, 1973, PhD in Biochemistry, 1977. Research/teaching assoc. Univ. Oreg., Eugene, 1977; research fellow Univ. British Columbia, Vancouver, 1978-80; assoc. sr. investigator Smith Kline & French Labs., Upper Merion, Pa., 1980-82, advanced to group dir., 1989-91; v.p. project mgmt. Smith Kline Beecham, King of Prussia, Pa., 1991—; adj. prof. Dept. of Pathology, Univ. Pa., 1986—. Author: numerous articles in profl. pubs. and mags. Fulbright Hayes Scholar, 1977. Mem. Am. Assn. for Cancer Research. Home: 117 Sugartown Rd Devon PA 19333-1609 Office: Smith Kline & French Labs Four Falls Corp Ctr PO Box 1510 King Of Prussia PA 19406

GREINER, WILLIAM ROBERT, university administrator, educator, lawyer; b. Meriden, Conn., June 9, 1934; s. William Robert and Dolores (Quinn) G.; m. Carol A. Morrissey, Aug. 24, 1957; children—Kevin Thomas, Terrence Alan, Daniel Robert, Susan Lynn. B.A., Wesleyan U., Conn., 1956; M.A. in Econs., Yale U., 1959, J.D., 1960, LL.M., 1966. Bar: Conn. 1961, N.Y. 1973. Asst. prof. Sch. Bus., U. Wash., 1960-64; assoc. prof. Sch. Mgmt., U. Wash., 1964-67; assoc. prof. Sch. of Law, SUNY, Buffalo, 1967-69, prof., 1969—, assoc. provost, 1970-74, assoc. dean, 1975-80; assoc. v.p. acad. affairs SUNY, Buffalo, 1980-83, interim v.p. acad. affairs, 1983-84, provost, 1984—, pres., 1991—; cons. in field. Author: (with Harold J. Berman) Nature and Functions of Law, 1966, 72, 80; contbr. articles to profl. jours. Home: 359 Troy Del Way Buffalo NY 14221-3335 Office: SUNY Buffalo NY 14260

GRELL, LEWIS ADAM, association executive; b. New Castle, Pa., June 15, 1932; s. Adam Lewis and Mildred Mae (Barris) G.; m. Pamela L., June 9, 1961; children: Lewis Jr., Holly, Lynn, Jon. BS in Elem. Edn., Slippery Rock Coll., 1953; MEd, U. Pitts., 1957, EdD, 1963. Tchr. New Castle (Pa.) Sch. Dist., 1953, 55-59, prin., 1959-63; prin., dir. summer sch. Oak Park (Ill.) Elem. Sch. Dist., 1963-66; asst. supt. Am. Sch. Internat. Sch. of Hague (The Netherlands), 1966-68; supt. Eden (N.Y.) Cen. Schs., 1968-72, Am. Sch. of Hague, 1972-81, Hamburg (N.Y.) Cen. Sch. Dist., 1981-89; exec. dir. Assn. Advancement Internat. Edn., New Wilmington, Pa., 1989—; chmn. Mid. States Accrediting Com., Frankfurt, Germany, 1987, European Coun. Internat. Schs., London, 1978-80; cons. Am. Sch. Brasilia, 1987; speaker in field. Contbr. articles to profl. jours. Chmn. We. N.Y. Fin. & Legis. Com., Lancaster, 1984-87, Subcom. Sch. Aid, Albany, N.Y., 1983-85. With USN, 1953-55. Office: AAIE THompson House Westminster Coll New Wilmington PA 16172

GREMELSBACKER, JOHN ANDREWS, real estate developer; b. Glen Cove, N.J., Oct. 20, 1942; s. Eugene and Margaret (Mizveski) G.; m. Linda Montfort, May 30, 1969; children: Laura Jane, Lynsey, Courtney. BA in History, L.I.U., 1974; MS in Orgn. and Mgmt., Cen. Conn. State U., 1989; postgrad., Yale U., 1991—. Mem. Youth Svcs. Commn., Cheshire, Conn., 1980-82, Cheshire Vol. Fire Dept., 1976—, Mass. Environ. Edn. Soc., Boston, 1988—; chmn. Environ. Commn., Cheshire, 1986-91; treas. G.O.P. # 5, Waterbury, Conn., 1991—; pres. John Gremelsbacker Inc., Cheshire, 1978—; bd. dirs. Conn. Realty, Cheshire. Author: How to Build Your Own Home, 1989; author music; inventor environ. recycler, 1990. Mem. Rep. Town Com., Cheshire, 1985, Rep. Nat. Com., Washington, 1988; coach Park n Recreation Girls Softball, Cheshire, 1980; bd. dirs. Cheshire Theatre Ensemble, 1989; officer C.W. Post Jud. Bd., 1968. Cpl. USMC, 1960-64. Named Coach of Yr., Cheshire Park n Recreation Dept., 1991. Mem. DAV, Am. Legion, Tau Kappa Epsilon (treas. 1968-69). Republican. Roman Catholic. Home: 595 Broad Swamp Rd Cheshire CT 06410

GRENA, BARBARA WASZAK, artist, educator; b. N.Y.C., Jan. 24, 1942; d. Felix and Wanda Barbara (Skowron) W.; m. William Milon, Apr. 8, 1961; children: Geraldine, Veronica, Mary Ann. Fine Arts Cert., Washington Sch. Art, Chgo., 1974. Instr. Monmouth County Pk. System, N.J., 1992; demonstrator Monmouth County Festival Arts, 1986-92, Manasquan River Art Groups, 1992, various art groups; juror for various artist orgns. Exhbns. include Georgian Ct. Coll., N.J., Pastel Soc. Am., N.Y., Salmagundi Club, N.Y., AT&T Bell Labs Hdqs., Holmdel, N.J., Prudential Hdqs., N.J., Monmouth Arts Festival, Tinton Falls, N.J., Guild Creative Art, Shrewsbury, N.J., Monmouth Mus., Lincroft, N.J., Thompson Pk. Visitors Ctr., Lincroft, Town Hall, Little Silver, N.J., Ocean County Open Exhbn., Island Heights, N.J.; represented in collections The Evergreen Gallery, Spring Lake, N.J., The Right Angle Gallery, Freehold, N.J., Spectrum Gallery, Port Pleasant Beach, N.J., Serendipity Gallery and Seagirt (N.J.) Gallery, Matawan, N.J., Soundview Gallery, Port Jefferson, N.J., in numerous corp. and pvt. collections. Mem. NOW, Pastel Soc. Am., Women in Arts, Guild Creative Art, Ocean County Artist Guild, Monmouth Art Found. Home and Studio: 3 Ramsey Rd Middletown NJ 07748

GRENACHE, CLAUDE LAURENT, priest; b. Leominster, Mass., Oct. 27, 1937; s. Lucien Ernest and Gladys Muriel (Ayotte) G. BA, Assumption Coll., Worcester, Mass., 1959; STB, U. Catholique de Lyon, Lyons, France, 1962; STL, Idem, Lyons, 1964. Mem. Augustinians of the Assumption, Roman Cath. Ch., ordained priest, 1966; lic. tchr. for secondary edn., Sherbrooke, Que., Can. Tchr. high sch. College D' Alzon, Bury, Que., 1964-67; highschool tchr. Coll. du Mont-Ste-Anne, Sherbrooke, 1967-72; dir./pastor Sanctuaire du Sacré-Coeur, Beauvoir, Que., 1972-78; pres. Fedn. of Shrine Directors, Montreal, 1975-78; cons. Episcopal Conf. of Que., Montreal, 1967-78; pastor Ch. of Our Lady of Guadalupe, N.Y.C., 1984-88; coord. multicultural edn. Assumption Coll., Worcester, 1989-92, dir. campus ministry, v.p. for religious affairs, 1992—; vicar provincial Augustinians of the Assumption, Brighton, Mass., 1984—; mem. Priests' Coun., Sherbrooke, 1972-78; trustee Assumption Coll., 1984-89, Ecumenical Dialogue with Bapt. Ch. (No. Conf.), N.Y.C., 1984-89. Home: 50 Old English Rd Worcester MA 01609-1300 Office: Assumption College 500 Salisbury St Worcester MA 01609-1232

GRENNELL, ROBERT LOVELL, psychology educator; b. Irving, N.Y., July 28, 1910; s. John Chapman and Emma (Brehn) G.; student SUNY, 1930; BS, Pa. State U., 1934; MA, Cornell U., 1937; EdD, NYU, 1950; m. Elinor Thorsen, Aug. 16, 1941; children: Donna L., Susanne T., John C. Tchr., Morrisville Pub. Schs., Pa., 1928-32, Silver Creek High Sch., N.Y., 1934-35; tchr., psychologist, research dir. Rockville Centre Pub. Schs., L.I., N.Y., 1935-42; vocat. adviser, psychologist-counselor U.S. VA, Buffalo, 1946-47; prof. edn. and psychology State Univ. Coll., Fredonia, N.Y., 1947-74, prof. emeritus, 1974—. Mem. Bd. Edn., Lake Shore Central Sch. system, Angola, N.Y., 1957-60; mem., chmn. Town of Brant Planning Bd., 1964-89. Capt. AUS, 1942-46; lt. col. USAF Res., ret. Mem. Am. Psychol. Assn., N.Y. State, Psychol. Assn., Western N.Y. Psychol. Assn., Ret. Officers Assn., Air Force Assn., Phi Delta Kappa. Home: 995 Milestrip Rd Irving NY 14081-9522 Office: State U Coll Thompson Hall Fredonia NY 14063

GRENQUIST, PETER CARL, publishing executive; b. East Orange, N.J., Feb. 15, 1931; s. Ernst Alexander and Carmela (Anastasia) G.; m. Barbara Ross Krone, Dec. 20, 1967; children: Carl Robert, Louisa Beatrice. B.A., Dartmouth Coll., 1953; M.A., Columbia U., 1957, Ph.D., 1963. Vice pres. Am. Assembly, Columbia U., 1957-62; dir. Spectrum Books, Prentice-Hall, Inc., 1962-70; v.p. coll. divsn. Prentice-Hall, Inc., 1970-72, corp. v.p., 1972—, pres. Trade Book divsn., 1972-80; CEO Arco Pub., Inc. (subs.), 1981-85; gen. mgr. gen. books divsn. McGraw-Hill Book Co., 1986-89; exec. dir. Assn. Am. Univ. Presses, Inc., N.Y.C., 1990—. Served to lt. (j.g.) USNR, 1953-56. Woodrow Wilson fellow, 1956-57. Mem. Devon Yacht Club, Phi Beta Kappa. Office: Assn Am Univ Presses Inc 584 Broadway New York NY 10012-3229

GRESHAM, STEPHEN DEANE, investment company executive; b. Balt., Nov. 20, 1960; s. Glen Edward and Phyllis Elaine (Kilmer) G. BA in Orgnl. Behavior with distinction, Brown U., 1983. Security analyst Cen. Group Can. and One Jefferson Street, Inc., Ellicottville, N.Y., 1980-82; v.p. One Jefferson Street, Inc., Ellicottville, N.Y., 1982-83; sr. account exec. Advest, Inc., Ellicottville, 1983-85; portfolio mgr. Advest, Inc., Hartford, Conn., 1985-87, v.p. investment mgmt., 1987-90, mng. dir., 1990-91; mng. dir. Systematic Fin. Mgmt., Inc., Ft. Lee, NJ, 1991—; dir. mktg. Boston Security Counsellors, 1987-89; bd. dirs. Preferred Mgrs. from Advest, Hartford, Advest Managed Portfolio Svc., Hartford, Master Portfolio from Advest, Decision Maker from Advest. Bd. dirs. AIDS Project Hartford, 1989-90. Mem. Assn. Investment Mgmt. Sales Execs., Ellicottville Area C. of C. (pres., bd. dirs. 1985-87). Office: Systematic Fin Mgmt Inc 2 Executive Dr Fort Lee NJ 07024

GRESS, ROSE MARIE, food products executive; b. Scranton, Pa., Sept. 19, 1930; d. Harry Stephan and Oricia Elizabeth (Simco) Ezak; m. Edward James Gress, Feb. 28, 1950; children: James Michael, Gary Edward, Glenn Jay, Jeffrey Paul, Keith Stephan. Grad. tech. high sch. and comtometer sch., Scranton, Pa. With Am. News, Scranton, 1949-50; comptometer operator W.L. Maxon Co., Old Forge, Pa., 1950-54; pres. J & R Inc., Clarks Summit, Pa., 1970—, Gress Poultry, Inc., Scranton, 1976—, Gress Frozen Foods, Scranton, 1980—, West Ridge Enterprises, Scranton, 1988—. V.p. St. Joseph's Ctr., Scranton, 1958; vol. Merch Hosp., Scranton, 1960; mem. pres.'s circle U. Scranton, 1980—; officer bd. dirs. St. Francis of Assisi, Scranton, 1980—. Club: Scranton Country (Clarks Summit). Avocations: golf, swimming, gourmet cooking, travel, reading. Home: 231 N 3rd St Apt 206 Philadelphia PA 19106-1221 Office: Gress Poultry Inc 141 S Dewey Ave Scranton PA 18504-1998

GRESSER, MARK GEOFFREY, podiatrist; b. Flushing, N.Y., Feb. 28, 1958; s. Herbert David and Adele (Davidson) G.; m. Monika Jean MacLean, Sept. 9, 1990. BS, BA, SUNY, Stony Brook, 1980; D of Podiatric Medicine, N.Y. Coll. Podiatric Medicine, 1984. Diplomate Am. Bd. Podiatric Orthopedics, Nat. Bd. Podiatry Examiners. Resident in podiatry Foot Clinics N.Y., N.Y.C., 1985; podiatrist North Country Podiatry, Miller Place, N.Y., 1986—, Ctr. Moriches, N.Y., 1988—; Assoc. Am. Coll. Foot Surgeons, 1987—. Mem. Suffolk County Handicapped Adv. Bd., Hauppauge, N.Y., 1991. Mem. Am. Podiatric Med. Assn., N.Y. State Podiatric Med. Assn. (dir.), Miller Pl.-Mt. Sinai C. of C. Democrat. Jewish. Office: N Country Podiatry 765-3 Route 25A Miller Place NY 11764-2738

GRESSER, SEYMOUR GERALD, sculptor, publications consultant; b. Balt., May 9, 1926; s. Simon Solomon and Sara (Williams) G.; m. Evângeline Ruth Wilson, July 4, 1950 (div. June 1976); children: Moshe, Terence, Rachel, Daniel. BS in Zool. Scis., Md. U., 1949, MA in English Lit. and Creative Writing, 1972. Publs. cons. Systems Documentation, Silver Spring, Md., 1975—; artist in residence Wesley Theol. Sem., 1992—; tech. publs. cons. System Devel. Corp./Unisys, McLean, Va., 1984-86; artist in residence Wesley Theol. Sem., Washington, 1992. One and two man shows include Daedal Fine Arts Gallery, Fallston, Md., 1983, Sweetbriar (Va.) Coll., 1985, Duke U. & Bryant Ctr. Gallery, Durham, 1986, Montpellier Cultural Art Ctr., Laurel, Md., 1988, Howard Community Coll. Gallery, Columbia, Md., 1989; group exhbns. include Athena Gallery, New Haven, 1965-73, City Art Outdoor Exhibit, Washington, 1979, Art Barn Gallery, Washington, 1990, Open Studio Gallery, N.Y.C., 1984, Slavin Gallery, Washington, 1986, Strathmore Hall Exhbn., 1988, Wesley Theol. Sem., Washington, 1992, others; represented in permanent collections including Antioch Coll., St. John the Divine Cathedral Gallery, Eliot House Harvard U., Pierson Coll. Yale U., Henry D. Blair Jr. Collection, George Mladinich Coll., Fairfield Coll., Olga Knoepke Collection. Sculpture resident S.D. Coun. for Arts, NEA, 1981, Colgate U., 1989, Thomas Johnson Sch., 1990. Home and Studio: 1015 Ruatan St Silver Spring MD 20903

GRETES, FRANCES CONSTANCE, information specialist; b. Norfolk, Va., Dec. 5, 1948; d. Ernest Peter and Demetra S. (Semon) G.; B.A. in Fine Arts, Coll. William and Mary, 1970; M.Librarianship, Emory U., 1973. Archtl. librarian John Portman & Assoc., Atlanta, 1973-76; adminstrv. librarian U.S. Army Libraries, Grafenwoehr, W. Ger., 1976-79; army librarian Pentagon, Washington, 1980; mktg. coordinator, info. dir. Skidmore, Owings & Merrill, N.Y.C., 1980-86; info. broker, 1983—, dir. profl. communications, 1986-87; dir. info. svcs., 1987—. Recipient cert. of achievement U.S. Dept. Army, 1979. Mem. Spl. Libraries Assn., Art Libraries Soc. N.Am., Assn. Real Estate Women, Hellenic Am. C. of C. Greek Orthodox. Author: Directory of International Periodicals and Newsletters on the Built Environment. Contbr. articles to profl. jours.

GRETHEN-GOLD, KIM L., producer; b. Schenectady, N.Y., Feb. 24, 1963; d. Donald DeVere and Marie Elizabeth (Freeman) G.; m. Mark R. Gold, June 11, 1988. BFA in Theatre, Hofstra U., 1985; M of Applied Psychology, NYU, 1991. Free-lance theatre electrician various off-Broadway, film and TV productions, N.Y.C., 1985-91; head gaffer Lifetime Channel's Regis Philbin Show and Attitudes, N.Y.C., 1987; freelance assoc. producer video, 1991—. Mem. Am. Assn. Counseling and Devel. Democrat.

GRETZ, STEPHEN RANDOLPH, finance company executive; b. Phila., May 26, 1948; s. William Edward and Janis (Dobson) G.; m. Connie Vigneri, June 24, 1972. BS, Trinity Coll., 1970; MBA, U. Pa., 1972. Asst. treas. trust dept. Chase Manhattan Bank, N.Y.C., 1972-75; 2d v.p. sales mgr. Bache, Halsey, Stuart, N.Y.C., 1975-76; 2d v.p., sr. mktg. research mgr. Bache, Halsey, Stuart, Shields, N.Y.C., 1976-78; dir. mktg. communications Personal Capital Planning Group subs. Merrill Lynch, N.Y.C., 1978-80; mcpl. product mgr. Merrill Lynch, N.Y.C., 1981-83, dir. mktg. research, 1984-85, dir. emerging investor services, 1986-88; group v.p. taxable debt. Merrill Lynch, Pierce, Fenner & Smith, N.Y.C., 1988—. County committeeman S.I. Reps., 1974-79; bd. dirs. S.I. Bot. Gardens, 1987—, pres., 1991—; bd. dirs. Vis. Nurses Assn. S.I., 1983-84, pres., 1985-86, chmn., 1986—. Mem. Devon Yacht Club, Richmond County Country Club, Maidstone Club. Roman Catholic. Office: Merrill Lynch Pierce Fenner & Smith 250 Vesey St New York NY 10281-1012

GREUEL, DAVID PAUL, publisher, owner; b. Bemidji, Minn., Dec. 4, 1945; s. Gregory and Jeanette Marie (Cyr) G.; m. Judith Courtney, June 30, 1975 (div. Aug. 30, 1988); m. Mary Alice Sykora, May 28, 1989. BA, Harvard Coll., 1967. Mktg. dir. Ind. Sch. Press, Wellesley, Mass., 1971-87; owner Wayside Pub., Concord, Mass., 1987—. Editor: Anthology AP French, 1988. 1st lt. U.S. Army, 1968-71. Mem. Harvard Club-Concord, Thoreau Club-Concord. Republican. Roman Catholic. Home: 208 Boxborough Rd Stow MA 01775 Office: Wayside Pub 129 Commonwealth Ave Concord MA 01742-2010

GREULICH, ROBERT CHARLES, insurance company marketing executive; b. Milw., July 1, 1958; s. Richard Paul and Shirley Ann (Knapp) G.; m. Kathleen Ann Olsen, Sept. 19, 1980; children: Stephanie Rae, Christopher Ryan. Asst. mgr. Toy Fair, Des Moines, 1973-77; mgr., buyer Gen. Novelty, Des Moines, 1977-80; agt. The Equitable, Des Moines, 1980-81, asst. dist. mgr., 1981-83, dist. mgr., 1983-84, registered rep., 1984—; regional mktg. dir. The Equitable, Chgo., 1988-90; nat. mktg. mgr. The Equitable, N.Y.C., 1990—; pres. Diversified Retirement Svcs., Des Moines, 1990-91; asst. agy. mgr. The Equitable, Northbrook, Ill., 1991—; cons. Flexsoft 401(k) Inc., N.Y.C., 1990—. Mem. Nat. Assn. Life Underwriters, Nat. Assn. CLUs. Republican. Roman Catholic. Home: 16 W 630 Mockingbird Ln Townhouse 20-G Hinsdale IL 60521

GREW, EDWARD STURGIS, geologist, educator; b. Boston, May 29, 1944; s. James Hooper and Alma (Clayburgh) G.; m. Priscilla Croswell Perkins, June 14, 1975. BA, Dartmouth Coll., 1965; PhD, Harvard U., 1971. Rsch. assoc. U.S. Geol. Survey, Washington, 1971-72; project assoc. U. Wis., Madison, 1972-75; asst. rsch. geologist UCLA, 1975-83; Humboldt fellow Ruhr U., Bochum, Germany, 1983-84, 85; from asst. to assoc. rsch. prof. U. Maine, Orono, 1984—; participant 7 Antarctic rsch. expeditions, 1972-88; invited scientist Nat. Inst. Polar Rsch., Tokyo, 1988-89; interacademy exch. scientist Inst. Geology Ore Deposits, Moscow, 1987, 90. Contbr. numerous articles to profl. jours. Fulbright scholar U. Melbourne, Australia, 1978; Indo-Am. Program fellow Nat. Geophysical Rsch. Inst., Hyderabad, India, 1980-81; recipient Antarctic Svc. medal NSF. Fellow Geol. Soc. Am., Mineralogical Soc. Am., Explorers Club; mem. Am. Geophys. Union, Mineralogical Soc. Great Britain, Mineralogical Assn. Canada. Home: 2A N Main St Orono ME 04473-1731 Office: U Maine 110 Boardman Hall Orono ME 04473

GREW, ROBERT RALPH, lawyer; b. Metamora, Ohio, Mar. 25, 1931; s. Edward Francis and Coletta Marie G.; m. Anne Gano Bailey, Aug. 2, 1958; 1 child, Christopher Adam. AB, U. Mich., 1953, JD, 1955. Bar: Mich. 1955, N.Y. 1958. Assoc., Carter, Ledyard & Milburn, N.Y.C., 1957-68, ptnr., 1968—; lectr. legal problems in banking and in venture capital investments Practising Law Inst. Mem. Pilgrims of U.S., English Speaking Union (nat. v.p. 1989—), ABA, N.Y. State Bar Assn. (chmn. health law com. 1986-89), Assn. of Bar of City of N.Y. Republican. Clubs: Union, Down Town Assn., Lansdowne (London). Office: Carter Ledyard & Milburn 2 Wall St New York NY 10005-2001

GREWE, JOHN MITCHELL, orthodontist, educator; b. Eau Claire, Wis., Feb. 6, 1938. BS, U. Minn., 1960, DDS, 1962, MSD in Oral Pathology, 1964, PhD in Anatomy, 1966, Cert. in Orthodontics, 1967. Pvt. practice dentistry Eau Claire, then Mpls., 1962-66; mem. dental staff U. Minn., 1967, VA Hosp. and Univ. Hosp., Iowa City, Iowa, 1968-69; practice orthodontics Univ. Md., 1969-77; pvt. practice orthodontics Towson, Md., 1977—; asst. prof., chmn. pediatric dental div. U. Minn., 1966-67, U. Iowa, Iowa City, 1967-69; assoc. prof. Coll. Dental Surgery, U. Md., Balt., 1969-75, prof., chmn. dept. orthodontics, 1969-78, part-time clin. prof., 1978-85; consulting orthodontist Johns Hopkins Hosp., Children's Hosp., Mercy Hosp.; cons. NIH, 1974, 76—, WHO, 1974-77, others. Contbr. articles to profl. jours.; assoc. editor Md. State Dental Jour. Fellow Internat. Col. Dentists, Am. Coll. Dentists; mem. AAAS, ADA, Internat. Assn. Dental Rsch., Am. Assn. Orthodontics, Internat. Soc. Cranio-Facial Biology, Am. Soc. Dentistry for Children, Md. Soc. Dentistry (past pres.), Md. Soc. Orthodontics (past pres.), Fedn. Dentaire Internat., Sigma Xi.

GREY, FRANCIS JOSEPH, accountant, accounting company executive, educator; b. Yeadon, Pa., Nov. 30, 1931; s. William and Delia (Mullin) G.; m. Marlene M. Ward, June 24, 1961; children: Francis Joseph Jr., Melissa Ann. BS in Econs., Villanova U., 1958. CPA. Tax profl. Coopers & Lybrand, Phila., 1958-64, tax ptnr. in charge, 1964-72, mng. ptnr. tax, 1972—; mem. devel. com. Villanova (Pa.) U., 1972—; bd. dirs. Del. County Hosp., Upper Darby, Pa.; adj. prof. Villanova Law Sch. Author: Tax Planning for Real Estate, 1978, 88, Pa. Taxation of Corporations, 1980; contbr. articles to profl. jours. Adv. com. Wharton Sch. Tax Conf., Phila., 1970-88, Internat. Bus. Forum, Phila., 1980-88. Sgt. U.S. Army, 1952-53, Korea. Mem. AICPAs, Pa. Inst. CPAs (v.p. 1988), Internat. Fiscal Assn. (treas. 1975), Phila. C. of C. (bd. dirs. 1975—), Phila. Country Club (bd. dirs. 1980-84), Union League of Phila., Locust Club, Beta Gamma Sigma. Republican. Roman Catholic. Office: Coopers & Lybrand 2400 11th Ctr Philadelphia PA 19133

GREYTAK, DAVID EDWARD, economist, educator; b. Butte, Mont., Jan. 13, 1941; s. Martin A. and Alda S. Greytak; B.A., St. Edwards U., 1963, cum laude; M.A., Washington U., St. Louis, 1965, Ph.D., 1968; m. Linda Friedlander, Apr. 3, 1971; children—Eric, Emily. Asst. prof., 1969-73, assoc. prof., 1973-78, prof. econs., 1979—; dir. Met. Studies program, Syracuse (N.Y.) U., 1987—, sr. lectr. Universidad Complutense de Espana, Madrid, Spain, 1975-76; vis. prof. urban econs. Inst. de Estudios de Administracion Local, Madrid, 1975-76; vis. lectr. pub. economy and mcpl. devel. Inter Univ. Ctr. Econs. Studies, Gadjah Mada U., Yogyakarta, Indonesia, 1991; prin. rsch. scientist and vis. assoc. prof. polit. economy Johns Hopkins U., Balt., 1977-78, rsch. dir. subcom. on state econ. devel. Center for Met. Planning and Rsch., 1977-78; cons. to U.S. and fgn. govt. on local govt. fin., regional devel., 1972—; mem. N.Y. State Adv. Coun. Econ. Info. and Rsch., 1988—. Fulbright Hayes fellow, 1975-76. Mem. Am. Econ. Assn. Regional Sci. Assn. (counsellor 1979-81), N.E. Regional Sci. Assn. (pres. 1977-78), Nat. Tax Assn. Author: The Environment for Small Business and Entrepreneurship in SBA Region II With Emphasis on New York and New Jersey, 1981; contbr. chpts. to books on econs.; contbr. articles to profl. jours. Office: Syracuse U 400 Maxwell Hall Syracuse NY 13244-1090

GRIBBEN, CAROLYN ECKHAUS, college counselor; b. Easton, Pa., Jan. 22, 1957; d. Howard and Jean (Stander) Eckhaus; m. Les Ira Gribben, Aug. 13, 1988. BS in Psychology summa cum laude, CUNY, 1977; MA, Columbia U., 1978; PhD, Fordham U., 1991. Counselor Bklyn. Coll., CUNY, 1980-87; counselor Kingsborough Community Coll., CUNY, Bklyn., 1978-80, instr./counselor in student devel., 1987—; mem. adv. bd. SUNY/CUNY, 1991—. Mem. AACD, Nat. Career Devel. Assn., Am. Coll. Pers. Assn.

GRIDLEY, MARY THERESA, realtor; b. Albany, N.Y., July 27, 1935; d. John J. and Helen Marie (Smith) Zeller; m. Ronald James Gridley, Apr. 30, 1960; children: Laurel Alison Tcherkezian, David Laurence. Student, Sorbonne U., Paris, 1955-56; BA, Marymount Coll., 1957; BS, SUNY, Albany, 1961; postgrad., Russell Sage Coll., 1974-76. Cert. real esates sales agent, tchr., N.Y. With sales reservations Am. Airlines, Albany, 1957-58; speech tchr. John Robert Powers Sch., Albany, 1957-58; tchr. French lang. Hackett Jr. High Sch., Albany, 1958-60, Van Corlaer Jr. High Sch., Schenectady, N.Y., 1960-64, Mont Pleasant High Sch., Schenectady, 1976-80; realtor Veronica W. Lynch, Inc., Schenectady, 1984—. Fundraiser Am. Heart Assn., Albany, 1978-92, ARC, Cancer Soc., Schenectady Mus.; pres. Women's League Symphony Execs., 1973-92, v.p., treas.; bd. dirs. Dominion House Family YWCA and Child Svc. Agy., Schenectady, 1972-80, Our Ladies Charity, Symphony Orch.; active Sunnyview Hosp. Aux., 1982—, St. Clare's Hosp. Aux., 1980—, Rep. Com., 1982—. Named Hon. Vol. of Yr., Jr. League, 1974-75, Hon. Heart Ball Chmn., Am. Heart Assn., 1991; recipient Kaye Rosendaal award Civic Vol. Yr., 1977. Mem. AAUW (v.p.), Jr. League Schenectady (exec. com. 1972-76), Gardener's Workshop (treas. 1977-92, pres., exec. com.), N.Y. State Assn. Realtors, Nat. Assn. Realtors, Schenectady Bd. Realtors, Capitol Region Multiple Listing Svc., Nat. Trust Historic Preservation (real estate affiliate), Mohawk Golf Club, Schenectady Racquet Club. Roman Catholic. Home: 708 Marks Ln Schenectady NY 12309 Office: Veronica W Lynch Inc 5 S Church St Schenectady NY 12305

GRIEFEN, JOHN ADAMS, artist, educator; b. Worcester, Mass., Nov. 24, 1942; s. Robert John and Faith (Adams) G.; m. Paulette Joy Hunsicker, Sept. 27, 1970; 1 child, Katherine Abigail Jacqueline. Student, Chgo. Art Inst., 1964-65, Bennington Coll., 1965-66; B.A., Williams Coll., 1966; post-grad., Hunter Coll., 1966-68. Instr. Bennington Coll., 1968-69, Great Neck Adult Edn., N.Y., 1971-76. One-man shows Kornblee Gallery, 1969, 70, 73, Deitcher O'Reilly Gallery, N.Y.C., shows, William Edward O'Reilly Inc., N.Y.C., Martha Jackson Gallery, N.Y.C., Frank Watters Gallery, Sydney, Australia, 1979, Salander O'Reilly Galleries, N.Y.C., 1981, 82, 84, 85, 91, Harcus-Hrakow Gallery, Boston, Phyllis Kind Gallery, Chgo., B.R. Kornblatt Gallery, Balt., Diane Brown Gallery, Washington, 1978, Sunne Savage Gallery, Boston, 1979, Williams Coll. Mus. Art, Williamstown, Mass., 1980, Martin Gerard Gallery, Edmonton, Alta., Can., 1981, Gallery Moos Ltd., Toronto and Calgary, 1981, Edmonton Art Gallery, 1984, Hirondelle Gallery, N.Y.C., 1986, Salander O'Reilly Galleries, L.A., 1991; exhibited group shows Indpls. Mus. Art, Phoenix Mus., Sydney Mus., Whitney Mus. Purdue U., N.Y. Mus. Modern Art, Santa Barbara Mus., Boston Mus. Fine Arts; represented in pub. collections Larry Aldrich Mus. Contemporary Art, Allen Art Mus., Arthur A. Anderson Co., Bank of Ill., Calgary (Can.), Boston Mus. Fine Arts, Bklyn. Mus., Carnegie Inst. Mus. Art, Chase Manhattan Bank, Continental Resources Inc., Hines Indsl., Boston, N.Y.C., Washington, Dallas, Hirshhorn Mus. and Sculpture Garden, Washington, Met. Mus. Art, Michner Collections-U. Tex., Musnson-William-Proctor Art Inst., Mus. Modern Art, Newark Mus. Fine Arts, Reader's Digest Assn. Inc., Rose Art Mus., Brandeis U., Rothmans Art Gallery, St. Lawrence U., Sydney Mus., Australia, Whitney Mus., Williams Coll. Art Mus., Worcester Mus. Art, Mass., Met. Mus. Art, N.Y.C., Vassar Coll. Mus. Art, Poughkeepsie, N.Y. Home: 57 Laight Rd New York NY 10013 Office: care Salander O'Reilly Galleries 20 E 79th St New York NY 10021-0187

GRIEGER, RONALD DEAN, superhard materials company executive; b. Francesville, Ind., Feb. 2, 1945; s. Orval C. and Evelyn M. (Nickels) G.; children: Scott, Khara. BS, Ind. State U., 1967; PhD, Purdue U., 1973. Sr. project engr. Specialty Materials GE, Worthington, Ohio, 1973-76, mgr. diamond engr. Speciality Materials, 1976-80; mgr. advance process engr. Lighting GE, Cleve., 1980-82; mgr. x-ray engr. Medical Systems GE, Milw., 1982-85; mgr. ops. GTE Valdiamant, Ann Arbor, Mich., 1985-87; v.p. Phoenix Crystal Corp., Ann Arbor, Mich., 1987-89, Tempo Tech. Corp., Somerset, N.J., 1990—; adj. faculty Columbus (Ohio) Tech., 1975-76; cons., Ann Arbor, 1987-89. Vol. goods to needy, Social Svcs., Ann Arbor, 1989-90. Mem. Am. Chem. Soc. Office: Tempo Tech Corp 500 Apgar Dr Somerset NJ 08873-1155

GRIESA, THOMAS POOLE, federal judge; b. Kansas City, Mo., Oct. 11, 1930; s. Charles Henry and Stella Lusk (Bedell) G.; m. Christine Pollard Meyer, Jan. 5, 1963. A.B. cum laude, Harvard U., 1952; LL.B., Stanford U., 1958. Bar: Wash. 1958, N.Y. 1961. Atty. Justice Dept., 1958-60; with firm Symmers, Fish & Warner, N.Y.C., 1960-61, Davis Polk & Wardwell, N.Y.C., 1961-72; partner Davis Polk & Wardwell, 1970-72; judge U.S. Dist. Ct. So. Dist. N.Y., 1972—. Mem.: Stanford Law Rev., 1956-58. Bd. visitors Stanford Law Sch., 1982-84. Served to lt. (j.g.) USCGR, 1952-54. Mem. Bar Assn. City N.Y., Union Club N.Y.C. Christian Scientist. Office: US Dist Ct US Courthouse Foley Sq New York NY 10007-1501

GRIESAR, WILLIAM HOWARD, lawyer; b. N.Y.C., Dec. 2, 1932; s. Otto Jonas and Ruby (Ozer) G.; m. Agnes Joan Mastrangelo, June 8, 1962; children: William, Katherine, Peter. BA, U. Va., 1955, LLD, 1958. Assoc. Rogers, Hoge & Hills, N.Y.C., 1959-65, ptnr., 1965-83; v.p., gen. counsel The Rockefeller Univ., N.Y.C., 1983—. Home: 60 Southlawn Ave Dobbs Ferry NY 10522-3520 Office: The Rockefeller Univ 1230 York Ave New York NY 10021-6341

GRIESEDIECK, ELLEN, artist, photographer, designer; b. St. Louis, Jan. 26, 1948; d. Joseph Edmund and Judith (Powers) G.; m. Samuel Felton Posey, Sept. 11, 1979; children: John Jameson, Judith Campbell. BFA, U. Colo., 1970. Designer Newman's Own Labels, Westport, Conn., 1983—; contbg. photographer Sports Illustrated, People mag., Road and Track mag., others. Solo exhbns. include Galerie de Poche, Paris, 1990, Gallery Henoch, N.Y.C., 1985, 89; group shows include Seagram's Co. Exhbn., N.Y.C., 1980, Soc. Illustrators Ann. Show, 1977, 78, 79, Royal Orleans Hotel, New Orleans, 1978, Spectrum Fine Art, N.Y.C., 1979; photographer, illustrator: Golf: The Passion and the Challenge, 1977, King of the Road, 1978; paintings featured in book Summer, 1990. Chorus mem. Berkshire Choral Inst., 1991—.

GRIESINGER, DAVID HADLEY, physicist; b. Cleve., Mar. 27, 1944; s. Frank Kern and Barbara (Ginn) G.; m. Harriet Ely, Dec. 27, 1969; 1 child, Benjamin Day. BA, Harvard U., 1966, PhD in Physics, 1976. Prin. design cons. Lexicon Inc., Waltham, Mass., 1976—. Inventee in field; contbr. numerous articles to profl. jours. Mem. Audio Engring. Soc., Acoustical Soc. Home: 23 Bellevue Ave Cambridge MA 02140-3634 Office: Lexicon Inc 100 Beaver St Waltham MA 02154-8440

GRIFFIN, BOB FRANKLIN, lawyer, state legislator; b. Braymer, Mo., Aug. 15, 1935; s. Benjamin Franklin and Mildred Elizabeth (Cowan) G.; m. Linda Charlotte Kemper, Aug. 18, 1957; children: Julie Lynn, Jeffrey Scott. BS, U. Mo., 1957, JD, 1959. Bar: Mo. 1959. Pros. atty. Clinton County, Plattsburg, Mo., 1963-70; mem. Mo. Ho. of Reps., 1970—; speaker pro tem, 1977-80, speaker, 1981—; pvt. practice law Cameron, Mo., 1983—; of counsel Polsinelli, White, Vardeman & Shalton, Kansas City, Mo., 1990—. Mem. exec. com. Nat. Conf. State Legislators, 1981—; mem. exec. com. Council of State Govts., past chmn. midwestern legis. conf.; mem. Dem. Legis. Leaders Caucus, 1981—; bd. dirs. State Legis. Leaders Found. Served to capt. JAGC, USAF, 1959-62. Mem. Mo. Bar Assn., Clinton County Bar Assn., Order of Coif, Phi Alpha Delta. Methodist. Office: 223 E 3D St Cameron MO 64429

GRIFFIN, JAMES DONALD, mayor; b. Buffalo, June 29, 1929; s. Thomas J. and Helen M. (O'Brien) G.; m. Margaret Ellen McMahon., May 4, 1968; children—Maureen, Megan, Thomas. Grad., Erie County Tech. Inst., 1958. With feed mills and grain elevators Buffalo; now engr. Buffalo Creek R.R.; mem. Ellicott Dist. Council, 1961-65, N.Y. State Senate, 1967-77; mayor City of Buffalo, 1977—. Served to lt. U.S. Army, 1951-53, Korea. Mem. Buffalo C. of C. Democrat. Roman Catholic. Club: K.C. Office: 65 Niagara Sq Buffalo NY 14202-3330*

GRIFFIN, JO ANN THOMAS, financial planner, fiduciary tax specialist; b. Dallas, July 20, 1933; d. John Baxton and Joan Marion (Ament) Thomas; m. John Barrett Brown, June 29, 1963 (div. 1972); children: John Barrett Jr., Daniel Thomas; m. Thomas Reese Griffin, Jan. 25, 1976; stepchildren: Gregory Crawford, Kevin Bradley. BA, U. Miss., 1955; BS magna cum laude, Lamar U., 1964; MEd, U. Del., 1972. Cert. fin. planner. Site mgr. Motivational Ctr., Inc., Wilmington, Del., 1976-78; asst. dir. Indochinese social svcs. Associated Cath. Charities, New Orleans, 1978-79; dir. continuing edn. St. Mary's Dominican Coll., New Orleans, 1979-80; with fin. mgmt. U.S. Dept. Agr., New Orleans, 1981; tax auditor IRS, New Orleans, Phila., Del., 1981-86; revenue agt. IRS, Wilmington, Del., 1987—; tax specialist Horty & Horty, CPA's, Wilmington, 1986-87. Docent Winterthur, New Orleans Mus. Art, Wilmington and New Orleans, 1966-85; sustaining mem., advisor Jr. League of Wilmington, 1989—; lay reader, mem. outreach com. Epsic. Ch. Diocese of Del., Wilmington, 1971—; regent Vieux Carre chpt. DAR, New Orleans, 1984; bd. dirs. Neighborhood Watch, New Orleans, 1983-85. Recipient Grad. Scholarship award AAUW, 1971, Sustained Superior Performance award IRS, New Orleans, 1984, Spl. Achievement award IRS, Wilmington, 1988, 89, Customer Svc. awards, 1989, 90. Mem. Am. Soc. Women Accts. (sec. 1986-89), Del. Valley Soc. Cert. Fin. Planners, Wilmington Tax Group, Estate Planning Coun. Del., Wilmington Women in Bus., Rotary, Blue and Gold Club. Democrat. Episcopalian. Home: 900 N Broom St Apt 16 Wilmington DE 19806-4546 Office: IRS 409 Silverside Rd Wilmington DE 19809

GRIFFIN, KATHERINE HOEH, librarian; b. Cleve., Oct. 22, 1959; d. Richard Charles and Dolores Marie (Bencina) Hoeh; m. Kenneth John Griffin, Aug. 31, 1985; 1 child, Owen Arthur. BA, Hiram Coll., 1981; MA, Northeastern U., 1984. Asst. libr. Mass. Hist. Soc., Boston, 1985—. Mem. NOW, Soc. Archtl. Historians, New England Archivists (print coord. 1990, membership com. 1991), Boston Archivists Group, Phi Beta Kappa. Home: 11 Boylston St Jamaica Plain MA 02130-2115 Office: Mass Hist Soc 1154 Boylston St Boston MA 02215-3695

GRIFFIN, KATHLEEN CHRISTINA, assistant dean; b. N.Y.C., Oct. 5, 1948; d. James Joseph and Anna Mary (Cusack) G. BA, Pace U., 1983; MA, So. Ill. U., 1984. Various civil svcs. positions N.Y.C., 1970-83; teaching fellow Boston U., 1985-86; acad. counselor Pace U., N.Y.C., 1986-89, asst. dean, 1989—, instr. English, 1988—; instr. English Fordham U., Bronx, N.Y., 1988. Mem. Nat. Assn. Acad. Affairs Adminstrs., Modern Lang. Assn., Pi Lambda Theta, Phi Kappa Phi, Sigma Tau Delta (chpt. pres. 1982-83). Democrat. Roman Catholic. Home: 2515 University Ave Bronx NY 10468-4003 Office: Sch Edn Pace U 1 Place Pla New York NY 10038

GRIFFIN, MARGARET ELIZABETH, early childhood and art educator; b. Lansing, Mich., Dec. 3, 1952; d. Sumner Albert and Barbara Jane (Hammill) G. BA, U. Tenn., 1975, MS, 1978; PhD, Mich. State U., 1982. Asst. prof. Iowa State U., Ames, 1982-84, Beaver Coll., Glenside, Pa., 1984-91; project dir. Kaleidoscope-Settlement Music Sch., Phila., 1990—; cons. HeadStart, Phila., 1988—, Pew Charitable Trusts, Phila., 1990, Fedn. Day Care Svcs, 1986—. bd. trustees Kimberton Waldorf Sch., Pa., 1990—. Mem. Mid-Atlantic Assn. for Edn. of Young Children (governing bd.), Dela. Valley Assn. for the Edn. of Young Children (pres.), Nat. Assn. Early Childhood Tchr. Educators, Soc. for Rsch. in Child Devel., Am. Ednl. Rsch. Assn. Office: Kaleidoscope-Settlement Music Sch 416 Queen St Philadelphia PA 19147-3094

GRIFFIN, PRISCILLA LORING (MRS. JOHN J. GRIFFIN), wax manufacturing company executive; b. Winchester, Mass., Apr. 1, 1930; d. John Alden and Madeleine (Libby) Loring; m. John J. Griffin, Jan. 27, 1951; children: Patricia, Michael, Peter. Student, Pembroke Coll., Brown U., 1947-49, Katherine Gibbs Coll., 1949-50. Adminstrv. asst., asst. treas. Roger A. Reed, Inc., Reading, Mass., 1971-72, pres., treas., 1972-87, chmn. bd., treas., 1987—; trustee Roger A. Reed, Inc. Profit Sharing and Trust, 1968. Chair Camp Fire Girls of Reading, 1964-66, mem. state bd., 1966-68; mem. Reading Town Meeting, 1957-68, Small Bus. Task Force; sec. Friends of Libby Mus. Mem. New Eng. Women Bus. Owners Assn. Industries Mass., Small Bus. Assn. New Eng., LWV (chmn. Ipswich club 1969-70). Unitarian. Club: Ipswich Bay Yacht. Home: Mountain Shadows PO Box 406 Melvin Village NH 03850-0406 Office: 167 Pleasant St Reading MA 01867

GRIFFIN, WILLIAM DALLAS, chemistry educator; b. Plainfield, N.J., Jan. 1, 1925; s. Ralph Eastman and Jessie Young (Dallas) G.; m. Margaret Ann Rutledge, Oct. 31, 1947; children: William Jr., Richard, Lawrence, Robert, Jeffrey, John. BSc, Rutgers U., 1948. Scientist Allied Chem. Corp., Morristown, N.J., 1948-71; sr. chemist Pavelle Corp., West Caldwell, N.J., 1972-73; sci. lab. supr. County Coll. of Morris, Randolph, N.J., 1973-90, lectr. chemistry, 1975-90, part-time adj. prof. chemistry, 1990—. Patentee in field. 1st lt. USAAF, 1943-45. Fellow Photographic Soc. Am. Home: 35 Terry Dr Morristown NJ 07960-4713

GRIFFITH, C. WAYNE, business executive, consultant; b. Wilkes-Barre, Pa., Nov. 11, 1935; s. Cromwell and Mildred (Albeck) G.; m. Jacqueline M. Jones, Feb. 18, 1956; children: W. Douglas, Laurel J., Beverly C., Dwight M. BA in Econs., Wilkes U., 1959; MBA in Mktg., Northwestern U., 1964. Dir. sales and mktg. AMP, Inc., Harrisburg, Pa., 1960-72; group v.p. internat. Burndy Corp., Norwalk, Conn., 1972-76; group v.p. and exec. v.p. Leeds and Northrup, North Wales, Pa., 1976-78; chmn., pres. and founder Xylogies, Inc., Burlington, Mass., 1978-83; chmn., chief exec. officer and founder Acorn Mgmt. Assoc., Inc., Weston, Mass., 1984—, Coll. Counsel, Inc., Natick, Mass., 1986—; bd. dirs. Precision Connector Designs, Peabody, Mass., DataCon, Inc., Burlington. Author: Marketing for Success, 1971, International Discoveries, 1975. Precinct cpt. Republican Party, Cook County, Ill., 1962-65. Sgt. U.S. Army, 1953-55. Mem. Am. Electronics Assn. (vice chmn. 1980-82, chmn. 1982-84)., Mass. High Tech. Coun., New England Small Bus. Assn. Republican. Home: 63 Black Oak Rd Weston MA 02193-1127 Office: Coll Counsel 220 N Main St Natick MA 01760-1100

GRIFFITH, DANIEL ALVA, geography educator; b. Pitts., Nov. 15, 1948; s. Donald Sanford and Mary Jane (McClain) G.; m. Diane Elaine Swartz, Jan. 3, 1970; children: Darren Lee, Michele Renee. BS, Indiana U. of Pa., 1970, MA, 1972; MS, Pa. State U., 1985; PhD, U. Toronto, Ont., Can., 1978. Instr. Ryerson Polytech. Inst., Toronto, 1975-78; from asst. prof. to full prof. SUNY, Buffalo, 1978-88; prof. geography Syracuse (N.Y.) U., 1988—, dir. stats. program, 1991-92; vis. EPA/EMAP rsch. affiliate stats. dept. Oreg. State U., Corvallis, 1990, 91, 92; dep. dir. N.Y. State program in geographic info. and analysis Syracuse U., 1989-90; ASI dir. NATO Sci. Affairs, Brussels, 1979-80, 81-82, 85. Author: Spatial Autocorrelation, 1987, Advanced Spatial Statistics, 1988, Statistical Analysis for Geographers, 1991; editor books; contbr. numerous articles to rofl. jours. NSF grantee, 1981, 83-84, 85, 88-90, 92-93; Fulbright fellow, 1992—. Mem. Am. Statis. Assn., Regional Sci. Assn., Assn. Am. Geography (chair 1987-88, Nystrom Dissertation award 1980). Democrat. Methodist. Home: 5270 Wethersfield Rd Jamesville NY 13078 Office: Syracuse U Geography Dept Syracuse NY 13244-1160

GRIFFITH, EMLYN IRVING, lawyer; b. Utica, N.Y., May 13, 1923; s. William A. and Maud A. (Charles) G.; m. Mary L. Kilpatrick, Aug. 13, 1946; children: William L., James R. AB, Colgate U., 1942; JD, Cornell U., 1950; also hon. degrees. Bar: N.Y. 1950, U.S. Supreme Ct. 1954. Pvt. practice law Lockport, N.Y., 1950-52, Rome, N.Y., 1952—; bd. dirs. various corps. and founds.; treas. N.Y. State Photonics Devel. Corp., 1989—. Contbr. articles to profl. jours. in U.S. and U.K. Mem. N.Y. State Bd. Regents, 1973—, Gov.'s Com. on Librs., 1976-78; co-chmn. State Conf. Professions, 1974-77, 85-90; mem. Forum Edn. Orgn. Leaders, 1978-80, Intergovtl. Adv. Coun. on Edn., 1982-86; del. to China-U.S. Joint Session on Trade and Law, Beijing, 1987, Soviet-Am. Conf. on Comparative Edn., Moscow, 1988, N.Y. State-USSR Lawyers Conf., Moscow, 1990; pres. Nat. Assn. State Bds. Edn., 1979-80; pres. Nat. Welsh-Am. Found., 1981-83; v.p. Hon. Soc. Cymmrodorion, London, 1988—; trustee, bd. pensions United Presbyn. Ch., 1966-72, Aerospace Edn. Found., 1979—. Maj. USAAC, 1942-46. Recipient Alumni Disting. Service award Colgate U., 1975, Exceptional Service citation Air Force Assn., 1980; Doolittle fellow Aerospace Edn. Found., 1988. Fellow Am. Bar Found., N.Y. Bar Found. (recipient Root-Stimson award for pub. svc.. 1986—, bd. dirs. 1989—); mem. ABA (com. pub. edn. 1974—), N.Y. State Bar Assn. (ho. dels. 1974-76, com. lawyer competency 1986-89, co-chmn.. com. atty. professionalism, 1989-, mem. bd. editors Bar Jour. 1986-), Oneida County Bar Assn. (pres. 1974-75), State Conf. County Bar Officers (chmn. 1974-76), Osgoode Soc. Can., Selden Soc. Eng., Rome Club, Fort Orange Club of Albany, Colgate Club N.Y.C., Cornell Club of N.Y., Phi Gamma Delta Internat. (pres. bd. trustees 1982-86, dir., v.p. edn. found. 1986—,). Office: 225 N Washington St Rome NY 13440-5724

GRIFFITH, F. LEE, III, lawyer; b. Buffalo, Sept. 3, 1947; s. Forrest Lee Jr. and Helen Elizabeth (Lines) G.; m. Jayne Walker, Apr. 30, 1989; children: Amanda, Abigail. BA, Williams Coll., 1969; JD cum laude, Boston U., 1972. Bar: Conn. 1972. Assoc. Day, Berry & Howard, Hartford, Conn., 1972-78; ptnr. Day, Berry & Howard, Stamford, Conn., 1979—, exec. com., 1989—. Mem. numerous bar and profl. assns. Office: Day Berry & Howard 1 Canterbury Stamford CT 06901

GRIFFITH, JAMES JOSEPH, physician; b. Mt. Vernon, N.Y., Aug. 16, 1927; s. John Joseph and Mathilda (Kelly) G.; m. Sylvia Ann Hurzeler, Oct. 3, 1953 (div. 1976); children: Gregory, Paul, Kate. AB, Columbia Coll., 1948; MD, SUNY, 1952. Diplomate Am. Bd. Internal Medicine. Intern Hartford (Conn.) Hosp., 1952-54; resident in internal medicine Norwalk (Conn.) Hosp., 1954-55; practice medicine specializing in internal medicine Norwalk, Conn., 1955—; mem. staff, dir. Norwalk Med. Group, P.C., Norwalk, 1964-88; bd. dirs. Alcoholism and Drug Dependency Council Mid-Fairfield County, Westport, Conn. Served with USNR, 1945-46. Mem. ACP, Fairfield County Med. Assn. Democrat. Roman Catholic. Office: Norwalk Med Group PC 40 Cross St Norwalk CT 06851-4647

GRIFFITH, MADLYNNE VEIL, controller; b. Johnstown, Pa., Jan. 2, 1951; d. J. Donald and Mary Jane (Veil) G.; 1 child, Philip Bryce. BA, St. Mary's Coll., 1973; MBA, U. Notre Dame, 1975; doctoral candidate, Pa. State U., 1985—. Cost and budget analyst U. Mich., Ann Arbor, 1980-81; acct. U. N.C., Wilmington, 1981, Johnstown Med. Devel. Corp., 1982-83; controller Mt. Aloysius Coll., Cresson, Pa., 1983—. Republican. Roman Catholic. Office: Mt Aloysius Coll Cresson PA 16630

GRIFFITH, MARY LOUISE KILPATRICK (MRS. EMLYN I. GRIFFITH), civic leader; b. Gadsden, Ala., Mar. 22, 1926; d. Lewis A. and Willie (Reid) Kilpatrick; m. Emlyn I. Griffith, Aug. 13, 1946; children: William L., James R. AB, Huntingdon Coll., 1947. Pres. Evergreen Twig, Rome, N.Y., 1966-67, Rome Home, 1973-75; Rome Coll. Found., 1990—; mem. Bd. Edn. Rome City Sch. Dist., 1967-77; pres. Rome Coll. Found., 1990—; del. U.S. China Joint Session on Trade and Law, Beijing, 1987, Soviet-Am. Conf. on Comparative Edn., Moscow, 1988; mem. Gov.'s Conf. on Librs., 1990. Bd. dirs. Utica Coll. Found., 1974-80, George Jr. Republic, 1974-88, Pub. Broadcasting Coun. Cen. N.Y., 1977-83, Rome Art and Community Ctr., 1978-84, 1st Presbyn. Ch., Rome, 1979-85, Cen. N.Y. Assn. for the Blind and Visually Impaired, 1988—, Kirkland Coll. Coun., 1967-75, Rome chpt. Am. Field Svc., 1969-77, Utica Symphony Orch., 1989—. Recipient Rose for Living award Rotary Club, 1973, Civic award for conspicuous pub.

service Colgate U., 1978. Mem. AAUW, PEO (pres. 1965-66), Nat. Soc. Lit. and Arts., Wednesday Morning Club (pres. Rome, N.Y. 1968-70). Home: Golf Course Rd Rome NY 13440-7554

GRIFFITH, OWEN WENDELL, biochemistry educator; b. Oakland, Calif., June 19, 1946; s. Charles H. and Gladys C. (Farrar) G. BA, U. Calif., Berkeley, 1968; PhD, Rockefeller U., 1975. Asst. prof. Cornell U. Med. Coll., N.Y.C., 1978-81, assoc. prof., 1981-87, prof., 1987-92; prof., chmn. biochemistry Med. Coll. of Wis., Milw., 1992—; mem., chmn. med. biochemistry study sect. NIH, Bethesda, Md., 1988—. Contbr. over 100 articles to profl. jours. Grantee NIH. Mem. Am. Chem. Soc., Am. Soc. Biochemistry and Molecular Biology, Am. Soc. Pharmacology and Exptl. Therapeutics. Office: Dept Biochemistry Med Coll Wis 8701 Watertown Plank Rd Milwaukee WI 53226

GRIFFITH, REESE ANN, corporate communications executive; b. Cambridge, Md., Apr. 8, 1959; d. William Martin Andrews and Eva Rosalie (Henry) Fowler; m. Schieffelin Stephen Schuyler, July 28, 1978 (div. 1980); m. Michael Robert Griffith, Nov. 5, 1983 (div. 1985). BA in Mass Communications, Towson State U., 1982; postgrad., Johns Hopkins U., 1988-92. Reporter, sch. editor The Star Democrat Newspaper, 1976-77; pub. affairs sr. rep. Blue Cross and Blue Shield of Md., Balt., 1980-85, mgr. community rels., 1985-87; pub. affairs exec. First Nat. Bank of Md., Balt., 1987-89, human resources exec., 1989—; assoc. faculty Johns Hopkins U. Editor: Lifelines, 1991. Bd. dirs., publicity chair Marylanders Against Youth Suicide, Balt., 1985—; mem. pub. rels. subcom. Greater Balt. Com., 1989-90. Recipient Excellence award external video Md. chpt. Internat. Assn. Bus. Communicators. Mem. Pub. Rels. Soc. Am. (APR, Best in Md. United Way program 1985, 87), Internat. TV Assn. (bd. dirs., publicity). Democrat. Baptist. Home: 1321 Kenton Rd Baltimore MD 21234-6012

GRIFFITH, STEVEN MORGAN, playwright, actor; b. Greenville, S.C., Mar. 31, 1961; s. Robert Warren Griffith and Shirley Ann (Hall) Anderson. BA in Speech and Theatre, Lander Coll., 1983. Actor Nettle Creek Players, Hagerstown, Ind., 1982, Ft. Harrod Drama Prodns., Harrodsburg, Ky., 1983-86, Savannah (Ga.) Theatre Co., 1984-85, Ark. Repertory, Little Rock, 1986, Ky. Contemporary Theatre, Louisville, 1987, Lincoln Boyhood Drama Assn., Lincoln City, Ind., 1987, Blue Apple Players, Louisville, 1987, Playhouse in the Park, Cin., 1987-88, Westbank Cafe, N.Y.C., 1989. Playwright: The Water Tower, 1990 (Playwrighting award Drama League N.Y. 1991).

GRIFFITH, WILLIAM HARRY, carpet distributor executive; b. Collingdale, Pa., July 3, 1931; s. William Harry and Edna-Mae (Stickley) G.; m. Helen Marie Hill, Mar. 2, 1957; children: William Harry, Robert Francis. AS, U. Pa., 1960. Salesman Glanz Behm and Herring, Phila., 1950-72; Salesman Magee Glanz Carpet, Bloomsberg, Pa., 1972-90, v.p. sales, 1990—. Pres. Coun. Civic Assn., Colwick, N.J., 1962, Hunt Tract Civic Assn., Cherry Hill, N.J., 1970. With USN, 1951-55. Mem. Excelsior Consistory, Shriners, Royal ORder of Scotland. Republican. Baptist. Home and office: 410 Holly Glen Dr Cherry Hill NJ 08034

GRIFFITHS, ANTHONY F., telecommunications industry executive; b. Rangoon, Burma, July 19, 1930; s. David Thomas and Margaret (Tompkins) G.; children: Jennifer, Stephanie, David, Michael. BA, McGill U., Can., 1954; MBA, Harvard U., 1956. With Can. Resins & Chems., Ltd., Montreal, Que., Can., from 1956, Can. Curtiss Wright, 1958-59, P.S. Ross & Ptnrs., 1959-60; mktg. mgr. Consumers Glass Co., Ltd., 1960-65, v.p., 1965-68, exec. v.p., 1968-71; pres., chief exec. officer Jonlab Investments, Ltd., Toronto, 1971-73; chmn., chief exec. officer Can. Cablesystems, Ltd., 1973-79; fin. and mgmt. cons. Connor, Clark & Co. Ltd., Toronto, 1979; vice-chmn. to chmn. exec. com. Harding Carpets Ltd., Toronto, 1979-85; pres., chief exec. officer Mitel Corp., Kanata, Ont., Can., 1985-87, 1991—, also chmn. bd. dirs.; chmn. bd. Mitel Corp., 1987-91, pres., chmn., chief exec. officer, 1991—. Mem. Soc. Fin. Analysts. Anglican. Office: Mitel Corp, 350 Legget Dr, Kanata, ON Canada K2K 1X3

GRIFFITHS, PETER BOYD, construction company executive; b. Binghamton, N.Y., Dec. 31, 1956; s. Charles Northup and Elizabeth Hope (Wiltsie) G.; m. Sandra Jayne Smith, Feb. 4, 1984. AB in Econs., Lafayette Coll., 1980. Asst. mgr. Household Fin. Corp., Binghamton, 1980-82; asst. v.p. Binghamton Slag Roofing, 1982-84; pres. Weathermaster Roofing Co., Binghamton, 1984—; bd. dirs. Assoc. Bldg. Contrs. of the Triple Cities, 1988-91, v.p., 1991, pres., 1992; bd. dirs. SEPP, Inc., 1991—. Trustee Local 203 Tng. Fund, Binghamton; bd. dirs. Binghamton Symphony Orch., 1986—, chmn. nominating com., 1988-89, 90—, exec. com., 1989-90; active Broome Community Coll. Found., Binghamton, 1985-91; active Harpur forum SUNY Binghamton Found., 1988—. Mem. Nat. Roofing Contrs., N.Y. State Bus. Coun., Broome County C. of C., N.Y. State Roofing Contrs. Assn. (sec. 1989—), Rotary (sgt.-at-arms 1987, treas. local club 1988-91, v.p. 1991—). Republican. Presbyterian. Home: 1566 Stevens Rd Binghamton NY 13903-6208 Office: Weathermaster Roofing Co PO Box 2131 Binghamton NY 13902-2131

GRIFFITHS, ROBERT BUDINGTON, physics educator; b. Etah, India, Feb. 25, 1937; s. Walter Denison and Margaret (Hamilton) H. A.B., Princeton U., 1957; M.S., Stanford U., 1958, Ph.D., 1962. Postdoctoral fellow U. Calif. at San Diego, 1962-64; asst. prof. Carnegie-Mellon U., Pitts., 1964-67; assoc. prof. Carnegie-Mellon U., 1967-69, prof. physics, 1969—, Otto Stern prof., 1979—. NSF postdoctoral fellow, 1962-64; Alfred P. Sloan research fellow, 1966-68; J.S. Guggenheim fellow, 1973; recipient Sr. Scientist award Humboldt Found., 1973, A. Cressy Morrison award Acad. Scis., N.Y., 1981, Dannie Heineman prize for math. physics, 1984. Mem. Am. Phys. Soc., Am. Sci. Affiliation, U.S. Nat. Acad. Scis., Phi Beta Kappa, Sigma Xi. Presbyterian. Office: Carnegie-Mellon U Physics Dept Pittsburgh PA 15213

GRIFFITHS, ROLAND REDMOND, biology educator; b. Glen Cove, N.Y., July 19, 1946; s. William and Sylvie (Redmond) G.; children: Sylvie, Jeannie, Morgan. BS, Occidental Coll., 1968; PhD, U. Minn., 1972. Asst. prof. Johns Hopkins U., Balt., 1972-78; assoc. prof. Johns Hopkins U., 1978-86, prof. behavioral biology and neuroscience, 1987—; cons. WHO, Geneva, 1981—, pharm. cos., 1982—. Contbr. articles to profl. jours., book chpts. to books in field. Recipient numerous grants Nat. Inst. on Drug Abuse, Rockville, Md. Office: Johns Hopkins Univ Sch of Medicine 5510 Nathan Shock Dr Baltimore MD 21224

GRIGALONIS, MARY LOU, educator; b. Pottsville, Pa., Aug. 14, 1962; d. John Joseph and Mary Louise (Scholtes) Lisowski; m. Gregory F. Grigalonis, Dec. 10, 1961. BS, Bloomsburg U., 1984; postgrad., Kutztown U., 1987—. Cert. spl. edn. tchr., Pa. Tchr. spl. edn. Gallows Hill Ednl. Ctr., Easton, Pa., 1984, Wiley House, Bethlehem, Pa., 1985, Berks County Intermediate Unit, Reading, Pa., 1986-90, Kutztown (Pa.) Area Sch. Dist., 1990-91, East Penn Sch. Dist., 1991—. Vol. ARC, 1985, Am. Cancer Soc., 1986—. Fellow NEA, Pa. State Edn. Assn., Berks County Intermediate Unit Edn. Assn., Kutztown Area Tchrs. Assn., East Penn Area Tchrs. Assn. Republican. Roman Catholic. Home: 332 Welby Dr Schnecksville PA 18078-9500 Office: East Pa Sch Dist 640 Macungie Ave Emmaus PA 18049-2130

GRIGELY, JOSEPH CONSTANTINE, JR., English language educator; b. Springfield, Mass., Dec. 16, 1956; s. Joseph Constantine and Anne Mary (Arlotta) G. AB, St. Anselm's Coll., 1978; DPhil, Oxford U., 1984. Assoc. prof. English Gallaudet U., Washington, 1983—; Mellon postdoctoral fellow in English Stanford (Calif.) U., 1985-87. Author: The Reconfigured Self, 1967. Mem. MLA. Office: Gallaudet U Dept of English 800 Florida Ave NE Washington DC 20002-3660

GRIGGS, SHIRLEY ANN, educator, consultant; b. Detroit, Sept. 15, 1931; d. Cecil W. and Ann (Wynand) G. AB, U. Mich., 1953; MA, Northwestern U., 1956; EdD, Columbia U., 1967. Tchr. South Lake Jr. High Sch., St. Clair Shores, Mich., 1953-55; counselor, asst. prin. Pershing and Eastern High Schs., Detroit, 1956-69; prof. St. John's U., N.Y.C., 1969—; study dir. Human Affairs Rsch. Ctr., N.Y.C., 1970-75; cons. Urban Affairs Ctr., N.Y.C., 1975-78; cons.-evaluator N.Y.C. Pub. Schs., 1975—. Author: Counseling and Learning Style, 1985; editor: (jour.) Counseling and Devel., 1985-88. Regional chair United Way Found., Detroit, 1968; conv. coord. AACD, Detroit, 1968; bd. mgrs. Chappaqua, N.Y. condominium, 1984—. Recipient Faculty Merit award St. John's U., 1989, 90. Mem. AAUP, AACD, Am. Psychol. Assn. Roman Catholic. Office: St Johns U Utopia Pkwy & Union Tpke Jamaica NY 11439

GRIGGS, STEPHEN LAYNG, management consultant; b. Morristown, N.J., Nov. 30, 1947; s. Paul Newton and Frances Hulbert (Layng) G.; m. Margaret Anne Hastings, Nov. 27, 1970; children: Jocelyn Hastings, Diana Hastings. BSME, Villanova (Pa.) U., 1969; MS, MIT, 1971; MBA, Harvard U., 1974. Mem. tech. staff Bell Telephone Labs., Holmdel, N.J., 1969-72; div. mgr. Norlin Industries, Carlisle, Pa., 1974-77, contr., chief fin. officer, 1977-79; sr. assoc. Booz Allen & Hamilton, N.Y.C., 1979-82; v.p. ops., chief fin. officer Phys. Acoustics Corp., Princeton, N.J., 1982-83; sr. ptnr. KSM Group Inc., Short Hills, N.J., 1983-88; pres. The Tewksbury Group Inc., Oldwick, N.J., 1988—. Mem. IEEE, Am. Assn. Clin. Chemists, Soc. of Competitive Intelligence Profls., Am. Soc. for Materials, Soc. for the Advancement of Materials and Process Engring., Hunterdon County Hist. Soc., Sigma Xi, Tau Beta Pi, Pi Tau Sigma. Republican. Episcopalian. Office: Tewksbury Group Inc PO Box 48 Oldwick NJ 08858-0048

GRIGLAK, MARTIN SAMUEL, union executive; b. Pitts., Jan. 13, 1927; s. Martin A. and Fannie (Nieberg) G.; m. Rita J. Pernatozzi, Nov. 24, 1949; children: Nancy Ann, Martin J., James R., Janet Lee. Student, Pa. State U., 1946-47, Waynesburg Coll., 1947-48. With Bell of Pa., Connellsville, Pa., 1950-60, Fedn. of Telephone Workers, Connellsville, Pa., 1952-62; exec. sec. Fedn. of Telephone Workers, Phila., 1962-66, exec. bd., 1960-84; pres. Western div. Fedn. of Telephone Workers, Connellsville, 1960-84; internat. staff rep., arbitrator, negotiator Communications Workers of Am., Dist. 13, Connellsville, 1984—; lectr. various univs.; cons. to Republic of China-Taiwan, 1986, 88 for Asian Am. Free Labor Inst. Contbr. articles to profl. jours. Bd. trustees Forbes Health Systems, Pitts.; chmn. bd. dirs. Highlands Hosp. and Health Ctr., Connellsville, 1990—; pres., bd. trustees Connellsville State Hosp., 1975, 78, 81, bd. trustees, 1971-85; active in past various major presdl., gubernatorial and senatorial campaigns. Recipient commendation Republic of China. Min. Interior, 1986. Mem. K.C., Elks. Democrat. Roman Catholic. Home: 206 S 9th St Connellsville PA 15425-2908 Office: Communications Workers Am 516 W Crawford Ave Connellsville PA 15425-2533

GRIGNON, ALBINA YVONNE, college administrator; b. Cohoes, N.Y., Dec. 22, 1949; d. Joseph Paul and Aline Bernadette (Senecal) Bourgeois; m. Wilfred Henry Grignon III, Aug. 26, 1972; children: Scott, Eric, Brian. BA, SUNY, Albany, 1971, MS, 1972. Asst. to dean grad. studies SUNY, Albany, 1972-80, asst. dean pub. affairs, 1980-83, asst. provost Rockefeller Coll., 1983-87, asst. dean sch. of bus., 1987—; advisor Cohoes Sch. Dist., 1988-90; lectr. Pub. Svc. Tng. program, Albany, Bklyn., Wilton, 1987-90. Chair Women's Concern Com., Albany, 1990-92; exec. coun. mem. Parnts Adv. Com., Cohoes 1989-91, Cohes Sch. Bd. 1992-95; chair Save for Am., Cohoes, 1992; mem. PTA Cohoes, 1989-92, Faculty Parent Com.; commr. Cohoes Youth League. Recipient Bread & Roses award Coun. of Women's Groups, 1991. Mem. N.Y. State Assn. Women in Higher Edn. (exec coun. 1990-92), Evergreen Golf League, SUNY Alumni Assn. (co-chair com.). Home: 50 James St Cohoes NY 12047 Office: SUNY-Albany Sch of Bus 1400 Washington Ave Albany NY 12222

GRIGORIADIS, MARY, artist; b. Jersey City, June 23, 1942; d. George and Anna (Peliotis) Livitsanos; m. Michael D. Grigoriadis, July 25, 1965; 1 child, Vanessa Maia. B.A., Barnard Coll., 1963; M.A., Columbia U., 1965. One person shows A.I.R. Gallery, N.Y.C., 1972, 75, 76, 78, 80, 82, 84, 86, 89, Helen Shlien Gallery, Boston, 1978, 81, 83, Douglas Coll., 1979, O.K. Harris Gallery, N.Y.C., 1976, Gallery K, Washington, 1978; exhibited in group shows Aldrich Mus. Ridgefield, Conn., 1981, Alternative Mus., N.Y.C., 1980, Bklyn. Mus., 1977; Albright Knox Gallery, 1977, Am. Acad. Arts and Scis., 1974, Whitney Mus. Am. Art, 1973, The Guild Hall Mus., East Hampton, 1987, The Muse Found. Phila., 1988, Va. Mus. Fine Arts, 1990, Franklin Furnace, 1991. Founding mem. A.I.R. Gallery, N.Y.C., 1972-90, exec. com., 1983-85. Represented in permanent collections: 1st Nat. Bank of Chgo., Chase Manhattan Bank, Athens, Prudential Ins. Co., Hoffman LaRoche Corp., Best Products, Richmond, Va., Allen Meml. Art Mus. Vorres Mus., Athens, Cabot Corp., Boston, Va. Mus. of Fine Arts, Richmond, 1989. N.Y. Found. for the Arts, fellow. Home: 382 Central Park W Apt 20P New York NY 10025-6039

GRILLO, JOANN DANIELLE, mezzo-soprano; b. Bklyn., May 14, 1939; d. John Daniel and Lucille Ann (De Pierre) G.; m. Richard Kniess, July 23, 1967; 1 child, John Richard. BS in Music, Hunter Coll., 1976; studied voice with Marinka Gurewich, Daniel Ferro, Lorenzo Anselmi, Joan Dornemann, Loretta Corelli, Franco Iglesias.; also courses, Met. Opera. Founder, mng. dir. Ambassadors of Opera and Concert World Wide, 1981—. Appeared in Aida, Madame Butterfly, N.Y. City Opera, 1962, with Paris Opera, Teatro San Carlo, Naples, Italy, Zurich (Switzerland) Stadttheatre, Opera of Marseille, France, 1964, Frankfort (Fed. Republic of Germany) Opera as Carmen, Amneris and Jocasta, 1967-68, Amneris in Aida at Teatro Municipal, Rio di Janeiro, 1989; European debut in Werther at Gran Teatro Liceo, Barcelona, Spain, 1963, 78; debut with Met. Opera, N.Y.C., 1963, resident artist, 1963—; debut with Vienna Staatsoper as Carmen, 1978, English debut in Verdi Requiem at Buxton Festival, 1991; performed Carmen with Paris Opera, 1981; appearances include Met. Opera, Vienna Staatsoper, Paris Opera, Paris Opera Comique, Amsterdam Opera, Hamburg Staatsoper, Deutsche Oper am Rhein, Opera of Madrid, Internat. Festival Split, Bellas Artes Mexico City, Israel nat. Opera, Dallas Civic Opera, Washington Opera Soc., N.Y.C. Opera, Opera Nice, Washington Opera Soc., Phila. Opera, Cin. Opera, others; roles include in Don Carlos, Il Trovatore, Carmen, Samson et Dalila, Damnation de Faust, Die Walkure, Das Rheingold, Gotterdammerung, Tannhauser, others; toured U.S. for Civic Concert Orgn., 1959, 1961; presented concerts in Europe, Latin Am. and Far East. Kathryn Long scholar Met. Opera. Roman Catholic. Office: Ambs of Opera 240 Central Park S Ste 16M New York NY 10019-1413

GRIM, WAYNE MARTIN, pharmaceutical company executive, consultant; b. York, Pa., Apr. 12, 1930; s. Oreb Elmore and Elizabeth (Clarkson) G.; m. Norma Bricker Grim, Aug. 30, 1942; children: Sharon, Michael. BS in Pharmacy, Phila. Coll., 1952, MS in Pharmacy, 1954; PhD in Pharm. Chemistry, U. Mich., 1959. Pharmacy lic., Pa. Sr. scientist Merck Sharp and Dohme Rsch. Laboratories, Rahway, N.J., 1954-56; sr. scientist Merck Sharp and Dohme Rsch. Laboratories, West Point, Pa., 1959-64, mgr., Pharm. Devel., 1964-67; mgr. devel. labs. Merck Sharp and Dohme Rsch. Laboratories, Hoddesdon, Eng., 1967-68; dir. pharm. devel. MSDRL, West Point, Pa., 1968-75, sr. dir. pharm. rsch., 1975-78; rsch. dir. to v.p. Wm. H. Rorer Inc., Ft. Washington, Pa., 1978-88; pres. Wayne M. Grim Assn., Doylestown, Pa., 1988—; cons. Wayne M. Grim Assocs., Doylestown, Pa., 1988—; adjunct prof. Phila. Coll. Pharmacy, 1990—. Patentee in field; contbr. articles to profl. jours. Fellow Am. Found. Pharm. Edn., U. Mich., 1956-59. Mem. Am. Pharm. Assn., Am. Assn. Pharm. Scientists, Am. Soc. Hosp. Pharmacists, N.Y. Acad. Sci., AAAS, Rho Chi, Sigma Xi. Democrat. Mem. United Meth. Ch. Home and Office: 2990 Yorkshire Rd Doylestown PA 18901-1667

GRIMES, DARRELL JAY, microbiologist; b. Keota, Iowa, Sept. 26, 1944; s. Darrell Mac and Martha Virginia (Burton) G.; m. Beverly I. Stutzman, July 25, 1964 (div. 1980); children: Bret, Terence, Christopher; m. Brenda Lee Baldwin Youngren, Sept. 20, 1981 (div. 1992); children: Brianna Youngren, Darin J. Grimes, Lauren J. Grimes. BA in Biology, Drake U., 1966, MA in Biology, 1968; PhD in Microbiology, Colo. State U., 1971. Asst. to assoc. prof. U. Wis., LaCrosse, 1971-80; vis. assoc. prof. U. Md., College Park, 1980-83, rsch. assoc. prof., 1983-87; prof. microbiology U. N.H., Durham, 1987-90, sea grant coll. dir., 1987-90, marine inst. dir., 1987-90, Jackson estuarine lab. dir., 1989-90; microbiologist U.S. Dept. Energy, Washington, 1990—; exec. sec. biotechnology rsch. subcom., FCCSET Fed. Coordinating Coun. for Sci., Engring. and Tech., Washington, 1991—; cons. in field. Editorial bd. Applied and Environ. Microbiology, 1988—; assoc. editor Estuaries, 1989—; contbr. articles to profl. jours. Fellow Am. Acad. Microbiology; mem. Am. Soc. for Microbiology, Am. Elasmobranch Soc. (charter, treas. 1985-89), Estuarine Rsch. Fedn., Am. Geophys. Union, Nat. Assn. of State Univ. and Land Grant Colls. (bd. dirs. marine div. 1987-90), Sigma Xi, Beta Beta Beta. Republican. Methodist. Office: Dept Energy Environ Sci Div ER-74 Washington DC 20585

GRIMES, GARY WAYNE, biology educator; b. Henderson, Ky., Oct. 28, 1946; s. Jack and Dorothy Lee G.; m. Suzanne; children: Ross, David. PhD, Ind. U., 1972. Asst. prof. Hofstra U., Hempstead, N.Y., 1973-78; assoc. prof. Hofstra U., Hempstead, 1978-83, prof., 1983—. Author: Cellular Aspects of Pattern Formation, 1991; contbr. numerous articles to sci. jours. Office: Hofstra U Dept of Biology Hempstead NY 11550

GRIMES, HOWARD WARREN, publisher; b. Denver, Feb. 18, 1922; s. Oscar E. and Myrtle (Griffin) G.; m. Frances Brauff, Oct. 31, 1953; 1 child, Laura Elizabeth. BS in Chem. Engring., Columbia U., 1950. Pres., pub. Vandergrift (Pa.) News Pub. Co., Inc., 1955—. With USN, 1942-46. Home: 14 Morgan Dr Leechburg PA 15656-1038

GRIMM, JAY VAUGHN, stockbroker; b. Sabetha, Kans., Jan. 28, 1926; s. Ben W. and Emma (Hunzeker) G.; m. Teresa McGarry, July 29, 1956; children: Katherine, Cordelia, Jay Jr. BA, U. Kans., 1949; LLB, Yale U., 1952. Bar: N.Y. 1953. Pres. Grimm & Davis, Inc., N.Y.C., 1962—, Royal/Grimm & Davis, N.Y.C., 1982-90. With USN. Decorated Purple Heart. Mem. N.Y. Soc. Security Analysts. Democrat. Home: 950 Park Ave New York NY 10028-0320 Office: Grimm & Davis Inc 17 Battery Pl New York NY 10004-1101

GRINDON, ARTHUR ST. LEGER, film studies educator; b. St. Louis, June 2, 1949; s. Arthur St. Leger and Claire (Elmore) G.; m. Elizabeth Fuller, June 21, 1969 (div. 1973); m. Sharon Lloyd, July 25, 1986; 1 child, Blake Zoe. BA in History, U. Calif., Berkeley, 1971; MA, NYU, 1978, PhD, 1986. Film libr. Audio Brandon Films, Oakland, Calif., 1972-75; audio visual coord. cinema studies dept. NYU, N.Y.C., 1977-80, adminstrv. asst. to chair cinema studies dept., 1980-87; asst. prof. film studies, dept. theater, dance, film-video Middlebury (Vt.) Coll., 1987—; presenter in field. Contbr. articles to profl. jours. Mem. Am. Studies Assn., Assn. Ind. Film & Video, Soc. Cinema Studies (sec.-treas. 1990—). Democrat. Home: 33 Chipman Park Middlebury VT 05753-1321 Office: Middlebury Coll Dept Theater Dance Film Middlebury VT 05753

GRINER, NORMAN, film director, graphic designer; b. N.Y.C, July 11, 1932; s. Samson and Rosa (Hien) G.; m. Barbara Helen Bankoff (div. 1964); m. Jane Conway Dillard, 1966; children: Julia Louise Griner, Joanna Laura Griner. BFA, Cooper Union, 1952. Art dir., designer The Macmillan Co., N.Y.C., 1952-53, 55-56, Esquire Mag., N.Y.C., 1956-57, The N.Y. Times, N.Y.C., 1957; art dir. CBS-TV, N.Y.C., 1957-59; designer, photographer, owner, dir. Horn/Griner, Inc., N.Y.C., 1957-74; dir., owner Griner/Cuesta & Schrom, N.Y.C., 1974—. Dir., producer Oye Willie, 1981. Bd. dirs. York Theatre Co., N.Y.C., 1985—; mem. Cen. Park Conservancy, N.Y.C., 1981—, Civitas, N.Y.C., 1983—, Carnegie Hill Neighbors, N.Y.C., 1985—. Cpl., U.S. Army, 1953-55. Recipient numerous awards Art Dirs. Club, Cannes Film Festival, Clio awards, etc., 1959—. Mem. Dirs. Guild Am., Cooper Union Advancement Soc., Nat. Arts Club, Cooper Union Alumni Assn. (bd. dirs. 1967-71). Office: Griner/Cuesta & Schrom 49 E 21st St New York NY 10010-6213

GRINSTEIN, BENJAMIN, physicist, educator; b. Mexico City, Aug. 23, 1958; came to the U.S., 1980; s. Marcos and Rosa G.; m. Rebeca Marcus, Apr. 26, 1980; children: Jonathan D., Gabriel A. MS, Cinvestav-IPN, Mexico City, 1980; PhD, Harvard U., 1984. Postdoctoral rsch. assoc. Calif. Inst. Tech., Pasadena, 1984-87, Lawrence Berkeley (Calif.) Lab., 1987-88; asst. scientist Fermi Nat. Accelerator Lab., Batavia, Ill., 1988-89; assoc. prof. Harvard U., Cambridge, Mass., 1989-92; sr. scientist Superconducting Super Collider Lab, Dallas, 1992—. Alfred P. Sloan Found. grantee, 1990. Mem. Am. Phys. Soc. Jewish. Office: Superconducting Super Collider Lab 25550 Beckleymeade Ave MS-2001 Dallas TX 75237

GRIPPE, PETER JOSEPH, sculptor, artist, printmaker; b. Buffalo, Aug. 8, 1912; s. Leonard and Josephine G.; m. Florence Berg, Apr. 21, 1940; 1 stepchild, Ronald Roseman. Student, Albright Art Sch., 1923-25, Art Inst. of Buffalo, 1929-35, Atelier 17, 1944-47. Student tchr. Art Inst. of Buffalo, 1934-35; sculptor, painter Fed. Art Projects, N.Y.C., 1939-42; sculptor Black Mtn. (N.C.) Coll., 1948; designer Pratt Inst., Bklyn., 1949-50; sculptor Smith Coll., Northampton, Mass., 1951-52; dir., isntr. Atelier 17, N.Y.C., 1951-54; sculptor, printmaker Brandeis U., Waltham, Mass., 1953-77; ret., 1977—; Represented in permanent collections at Mus. Modern Art, Whitney Mus. of Am. Art, Libr. of Congress, Bklyn. Mus., Albright Art Gallery, Toledo Mus. of Art, Phila. Mus., Walker Art Ctr., Print Coun., U.S. Info. Ctr., Brandeis U., Nat. Gallery of Art, Univ. of Mich., R.I. Sch. of Design, Chapman Meml. Ctr., Addison Gallery of Art; one man exhibitions include Orrefors Galleries, N.Y.C., 1942, Willard Gallery, N.Y.C., 1944-46, Peridot Gallery, N.Y.C., 1957, 59, Nordness Gallery, N.Y.C., 1960, Cantor Art Gallery, Worcester, Mass., 1986, Sid Deutsch Gallery, N.Y.C., 1991. Commissions include design of Brandeis Creative Arts Award Medallion, 1954, mural for P.R. Info. Ctr., N.Y.C., 1958, 7 ft. bronze sculpture for Theodore Shapiro Forum, 1963, for Simons Coll. Sci. Bldg., Boston, 1973; conceived the project: 21 Etchings and Poems, 1960. Recipient Purchase prize Bklyn. Mus., 1947, First prize for Print, Met. Mus. of Art, 1952, Sculpture award Nat. Coun. for U.S. Art, 1955, Sculpture award R.I. Arts Festival, 1961, Guggenheim fellowship in Sculpture, 1964. Studio: 28100 Main Rd Orient NY 11957-1111

GRISANTI, EUGENE PHILIP, flavors and fragrances company executive; b. Buffalo, Oct. 24, 1929; s. Nicholas D. and Victoria (Pantera) G.; m. Anne Couming, June 29, 1953; children: Marylee, Christopher, Eugene Paul. A.B. magna cum laude, Holy Cross Coll., 1951; LL.B., Boston U., 1953; LL.M., Harvard U., 1954. Bar: Mass. 1953, N.Y. 1954. Mem. firm Fulton, Walter & Halley, N.Y.C., 1954-60; gen. atty. Internat. Flavors & Fragrances Inc., N.Y.C., 1960-64, sec., gen. atty., 1964-70, v.p., sec., gen. atty., 1970-74; pres. Internat. Flavors & Fragrances, N.Y.C., 1974-79; sr. v.p., dir. Internat. Flavors & Fragrances Inc., N.Y.C., 1979-85, chmn., pres., chief exec. officer, 1985—. Mem. Fragrance Found. (bd. dirs.), Cosmetic Toiletry and Fragrance Assn. (bd. dirs.). Clubs: Larchmont Yacht, Winged Foot Golf; University (N.Y.C.). Office: Internat Flavor & Fragrances Inc 521 W 57th St New York NY 10019-2905*

GRISCOM, DAVID LAWRENCE, research physicist; b. Pitts., Nov. 1, 1938; s. Samuel B. and Margaret (Deuser) G.; m. Catherine Anne-Marie Godeux, Sept. 12, 1970; children: Laurent Samuel, Celine Ann. BS in Physics, Carnegie Mellon U., Pitts., 1960; PhD in Physics, Brown U., Providence, 1966. Rsch. assoc. Physics Dept Brown U., 1966-67; from postdoctoral assoc. to rsch. physicist Naval Rsch. Lab., Washington, 1967—; program mgr. Def. Advanced Rsch. Projects Agy., Arlington, Va., 1981-83; editorial adv. bd. Jour. Non-Crystalline Solids, 1981—; mem. NASA Microgravity Discipline Working Group, 1988—. Contbr. numerous articles to profl. jours.; Co-editor Defects in Glasses, 1986. Recipient Sci. achievement award Washington Acad. Scis., 1974 (physical scis. award 1974), publication award Naval Rsch. Lab., Washington, 1979,86. Fellow Am. Ceramic Soc. (chmn. glass and optical materials div. 1991-92); mem. AAAS, Am. Physical Soc. Democrat. Roman Catholic. Office: Naval Research Lab Code 6505 Washington DC 20375

GRISHAM, LARRY RICHARD, physicist, consultant; b. Henderson, Tex., Feb. 2, 1949; s. James Marion and Eva Fay (Powell) G.; m. Jacqueline Lea Criswell, June 24, 1972; children: Austin Nathanial, Rachel Nicole, Hilary Jane. BS in Physics, U. Tex., 1971; PhD in Physics, Oxford (Eng.) U., 1974. Postdoctoral fellow Princeton (N.J.) U., Plasma Physics Lab., 1974-75, staff rsch. physicist, 1975-82, rsch. physicist, 1982-89, prin. rsch. physicist, 1989—, head beam physics, 1988—; cons. Northrop Corp., L.A., 1985, Phys. Dynamics, La Jolla, Calif., 1986-88, Teledyne Brown Engring., Huntsville, Ala., 1989—. Contbr. numerous articles to profl. jours. Mem. N.J. Rhodes Scholar Selection Com., Morristown, 1986—. Recipient Tex. Exec. Centennial Honored Alumnus award U. Tex., Austin, 1985; winner Westinghouse Sci. Talent Search, Washington, 1967; Rhodes scholar, 1971; Woodrow Wilson found. fellow, 1971. Mem. AAAS, Am. Phys. Soc., Phi Beta Kappa.

Methodist. Home: 2 Dennick Ct Princeton NJ 08540-2202 Office: Princeton Univ Plasma Physics Lab PO Box 451 Princeton NJ 08543-0451

GRISSOM, GAIL COFFIN, psychotherapist; b. Bryn Mawr, Pa., July 4, 1942; d. Roy Riddell and Catharine (Pfingst) Coffin; m. Grant R. Grissom, July 7, 1969; children: Erik, Merry. BA, U. Wis., 1964; MA, Bryn Mawr Coll., 1975; MPS, N.Y. Theol. Sem., 1980. Pvt. practice psychotherapy Wallingford, Pa., 1980-89, Media, Pa., 1989—. Fellow Am. Orthopsychiat. Assn.; mem. C.G. Jung Found., Am. Assn. Marriage and Family Therapists. Home and Office: 275 Ridley Creek Rd Media PA 19063

GRISWOLD, BENJAMIN HOWELL, IV, investment banker; b. Balt., Sept. 4, 1940; s. Benjamin Howell and Leith (Symington) G.; m. Page Lee Hufty, May 19, 1979 (div.); children: Belinda J., Anna B., Benjamin H., Alexander P.; m. Wendy Goodyear, Apr. 25, 1987. AB, Princeton U., 1962; MBA, Harvard U., 1967. Security analyst Alexander Brown & Sons, Balt., 1967-70, dir. research, 1971-74, dir. trading, 1975-80, head div. equity, 1981-83, vice chmn., 1984-86, chmn., 1987—; mem. adv. com. regional firms N.Y. Stock Exchange, 1987. Trustee Johns Hopkins U., Balt., 1988, Walters Art Gallery, Balt., 1988, Concord (Mass.) Acad., 1987, Peabody Conservatory, Balt., 1986. 1st lt. U.S. Army, 1963-75. Mem. Links Club N.Y.C., Md. Club. Republican. Episcopalian. Office: Alex Brown & Sons Inc 135 E Baltimore St Baltimore MD 21202-1646*

GRISWOLD, DENNY (MRS. J. LANGDON SULLIVAN), editor, publishing executive; b. N.Y.C.; m. J. Langdon Sullivan, September 24, 1951. BA, Hunter Coll.; MA, Radcliffe Coll. Mem. editorial staff Bus. Week mag., N.Y.C.; mng. editor Forbes mag., N.Y.C.; founder, editor-at-large Pub. Rels. News, N.Y.C., 1944—. Author: The PR Handbook, 1948. Bd. dirs. USO, Internat. Ctr. N.Y. Fellow Pub. Rels. Soc. Am.; mem. Women Execs. in Pub. Rels. (founder), Women's Forum (130 awards). Office: Pub Rels News 127 E 80th St New York NY 10021-0333

GRISWOLD, GARY NORRIS, engineering company executive; b. Fairbanks, Feb. 12, 1947; s. Norris Rockwell and Margaret Moore (Kennedy) G.; m. Lois Ruth Brinkman, June 17, 1967; children: Mark David, Melissa Robin. BS, U. Wash., 1970; MS, Union Coll., 1980. Cert. in data processing. Computer programmer Knolls Atomic Power Lab., Schenectady, N.Y., 1972-75; sr. systems analyst State of N.Y., Albany, 1975-79; mgr. mgmt. info. systems devel. Phoenix Data Systems, Inc., Albany, 1979-85; pres. InfoLogic Software, Inc., Troy, N.Y., 1985—; adj. asst. prof. Union Coll., 1980-83; cons. on mgmt. info. systems. Mem. IEEE, Assn. Computing Machinery. Office: 1223 Peoples Ave Ste 5405 Troy NY 12180-3511

GROARK, EUNICE, state official; b. Sharon, Conn., Feb. 1, 1938; m. Thomas Groark; children: Eunice, Marie, Virginia. BA, Bryn Mawr Coll., 1960; grad., Univ. Conn. Law Sch., 1965. Lt. gov. Conn., 1991—. Mem. Conn. Bar Assn. Office: Lt Governor's Office State Capitol Rm 304 Hartford CT 06106*

GRODBERG, MARCUS GORDON, drug research consultant; b. Worcester, Mass., Jan. 27, 1923; s. Isaac and Rosalie (Hirsch) G.; m. Shirley Florence Merkle, Apr. 15, 1951; children: Joel David, Kim Gordon, Jeremy Daniel. AB, Clark U., Worcester, 1944; MS, U. Ill., 1948. Jr. research chemist Schenley Labs Inc., Lawrenceburg, Ind., 1944-47; research and devel. chemist Marine Products Co., Boston, 1948-50, Brewer and Co. Inc., Worcester, 1950-55; tech. dir. Gray Pharm. Co. Inc., Newton, Mass., 1955-58; dir. research and devel. Colgate Hoyt Labs., Canton, Mass., 1958-89; cons. Newton, 1989—. Author: Fluorides; patentee in field. Asst. leader Cub Scouts, Newton, 1960-62, fund raiser United Fund, Newton, 1960-62. Mem.Internat. Assn. Dental Research, Am. Chem. Soc., Acad. Pharm. Scis., Am. Pharm. Assn.,N.Y. Acad. Scis., others. Jewish. Home: 111 Hyde St Newton MA 02161-1243 Office: Colgate Hoyt Labs One Colgate Way Canton MA 02021

GRODEN, GERALD, psychologist; b. Cambridge, Mass., Apr. 11, 1931; s. Eugene and Ruth (Patten) G.; A.B., U. Vt., 1957, M.A., 1960; Ph.D., Purdue U., 1963; m. June Handwerger, Mar. 28, 1975; 1 son, John. Instr., then asst. prof. dept. neurology Ind. U. Med. Sch., Indpls., 1963-66, asso. faculty mem. dept. psychology, 1964-66, U. R.I. extension, Providence, 1966—, clin. assoc. prof., Kingston, 1969—; dir. psychology dept. R.I. Hosp. Child Devel. Center, Providence, 1966-78; dir. Groden Ctr., Providence, 1976—; dir. Behavioral Assocs., Providence, 1980—; cons. in field; bd. dirs. Sophia Little Home, R.I. Protective and Advocacy System, Providence, 1975—; mem. R.I. Gov.'s Adv. Commn. on Mental Retardation, R.I. Gov.'s Adv. Commn. on Children and Youth, R.I. Senate Adv. Commn. on Early Intervention. Served with USNR, 1952-54. State of R.I. grantee, 1972. Mem. AAAS, Am., Eastern, New Eng., R.I. (dir.) psychol. assns., Sigma Xi. Contbr. articles in field to profl. jours. Home: 99 Fosdyke St Providence RI 02906-3537 Office: 80 Mt Hope Ave Providence RI 02906

GRODY, GARY LANCE, psychologist, consultant; b. N.Y.C., May 29, 1949; s. Phil and Gladys (Lustig) G.; m. Eileen Natalie Bloom, Jan. 27, 1980; children: Ian, Lindsay. BA in Liberal Arts, Hofstra U., 1971; MA in Psychology, New Sch. for Social Rsch., 1974; PhD in Clin. Psychology, U.S. Internat. U., 1977. Pvt. practice Lawrence, N.Y., 1977—; chief psychol. svcs. Oncology Dept. Bklyn.-Caledonian Hosp.; founder Med. Weight Control Ctr. Lawrence; dir. Health Through Edn. Stress Mgmt. Co., Lawrence; co-dir. Med. Cons. Nat. Inst. Weight Control, Massepequa, N.Y.; mem. adj. faculty psychology L.I. U., Bklyn., Greenville, N.Y., 1977-87; TV corr. Sta. Cable 12 News, L.I., 1988—. Featured writer-columnist Nassau-Herald newspaper, 1987-89. Mem. profl. adv. bd. Nat. Epileptic Found., Hampstead, N.Y., 1980—. Named Most Popular U. Prof. in N.Y.C. Village Voice newspaper, 1985; recipient Nat. award winner in facial memory. Mem. APA, N.J. Psychol. Assn. Office: 290 Central Ave Lawrence NY 11559

GROFF, HAROLD ALLEN, electrical engineering educator; b. Wilkes-Barre, Pa., Apr. 23, 1931; s. Edmund L. and Adeline H. (Kapp) G.; m. Evelyn M. Williams, Dec. 23, 1965; children: Alex, Jeff. BSEE, Bucknell U., 1957; postgrad., Temple U., 1961. Engr., mgr. RCA, Camden, N.J., 1957-63, Western Union Co., N.Y.C., 1964-70; mgr. GTE Internat., Milan, 1970-76; dir. Infranav Ltd., Rio de Janeiro, 1976-78; project mgr. R.M. Parsons, Pasadena, Calif., 1978-80; prof. elec. engring. chmn. dept. telecommunications Pa. State U., Lehman, 1980—. Mem. NE Pa. Regional Econ. Devel. Coun.; mem. edn. bd. Nat. Cable TV Ctr. and Mus. With USN, 1948-52, Korea. Bell of Pa. faculty fellow, 1988—. Mem. IEEE, Soc. Cable TV Engrs., Nat. Assn. Radio and Telecommunications Engrs. (bd. dirs. 1990—), Am. Soc. Engring. Edn. Office: Pa State U Box PSU Lehman PA 18627

GROFF, JAMES B., association executive; b. Buffalo, June 17, 1932; m. Anne Marie Mekosh, Dec. 6, 1958; children: Kathleen, David, Daniel, Nancy. BS in Civil Engring., Union Coll., Schenectady, 1954; MS in San. Engring., U. Mich., 1963. Commd. ensign USN, 1955, advanced through grades to capt., 1975; comdg. officer Constrn. Bn. 301 USN, Quang Tri, Run, 1969-70; officer Shore Pollution Abatement Program Naval Facilities Engring. Command, Alexandria, Va., 1972-74; officer environ. protection program USN, Washington, 1974-77; dep. exec. dir. Am. Water Works Assn., Washington, 1979-85; exec. dir. Nat. Assn. Water Cos., Washington, 1985—. Decorated Bronze Star. Mem. Am. Water Works Assn. Office: Nat Assn Water Cos 1725 K St NW Ste 1212 Washington DC 20006-1401

GROFF, JOHN MARSHALL, museum director; b. Bryn Mawr, Pa., Aug. 12, 1951; s. Marshall Irwin and Jacqueline (Hires) G.; m. Diane M. Flewelling, Nov. 18, 1973. BA, Bates Coll., 1973; MA, U. Del., 1981, cert. mus. studies program, 1981. Registrar/asst. curator Phila. (Pa.) Maritime Mus., 1977-84; dir. Osterville (Mass.) Hist. Soc., 1984-89; rsch. cons. Phila., 1989-90; exec. dir. colonial hist. house WYCK, Phila., 1990—; mem. Hist. Commn., Barnstable, Mass., 1987-89, chmn., 1989; bd. mem. Mus. Coun. of Phila., 1991—, chmn. membership com., 1979-84. Co-author: George R. Bonfield, 1978, The Titantic & Her Era, 1982; writer (newspaper) Cape Code Arts and Antiques, 1985. Trustee Osterville (Mass.) Free Libr., 1987-89. Recipient H.F. duPont Winterthur fellowship Winterthur (Del.) Mus., 1975-76. Mem. Soc. for the War of 1812 (dir. 1980, 84, 90), Am. Assn. for State and Local History, Pa. Soc. Sons of the Revolution, The Garden Conservancy, Phi Beta Kappa. Episcopalian. Office: WYCK 6026 Germantown Ave Philadelphia PA 19144-2191

GROH, LEANNA WHEATON, retired education educator; b. Owego, N.Y., July 5, 1916; d. Frank Ransome and Ina Loretta (Parker) W.; m. Robert Lawless Groh, May 13, 1939; children: Robert M., Ellin L., David T., Charles S., James F. BS, Cornell U., 1937. Cert. tchr., N.Y. Tchr. Geneva (N.Y.) High Sch., 1955-64, B.O.C.E.S., Stanley, N.Y., 1965-72; cons. Head Start, Geneva, 1965—, PennYan (N.Y.) Day Care Ctr., 1968-70. Author: (desk-top publs.) Lent-Hill Folks, Only a Little Way, From Boy to Man, World War II Letters, More Later--War II Letters, When You and I Were Young. Vol. Geneva Hist. Soc., 1978; bd. dirs. Ontario Day Care Ctr., Geneva, 1973, others. Mem. N.Y. State Retired Tchrs. Assn., N.Y. State Home Econs. Tchrs. Assn. Am. Vocat. Assn., Cornell U. Alumni Assn., Yates Coun. Geneal. and Hist. Soc., Finger Lakes Geneal. Soc., others. Home: 1275 Arrowhead Beach Rd Dresden NY 14441-9701

GROLLMAN, SIGMUND SIDNEY, physiology educator; b. Stevensville, Md., Feb. 12, 1923; s. Ellis Phillip and Rachel Naomi (Krystal) G. BS, U. Md., 1947, MS, 1949, PhD, 1952. Cert. biochem. physiology. Teaching asst. U. Md. Zoology Dept., College Park, 1947-49, instr., 1949-51, asst. prof., 1952-55, assoc. prof., 1955-58, prof., 1958-84, chair div. physiology, 1966-73, dir. grad. studies, 1973-83, prof. emeritus, 1984; pres. Sigmund Grollman Ltd., Balt., 1970—. Author: (textbook) The Human Body--Its Structure and Function, 1964, 4th rev. edit., 1984, (manual) Anatomy and Physiology, 1960-84, Experimental Mammilian Physiology, 1971-83; contbr. articles to profl. jours. Active Am. Jewish Congress, N.Y.C., Am. Israeli Pub. Affairs Com., Washington. Sgt. U.S. Army, 1940-43, ETO. Fellow Am. Coll. Sports Medicine; mem. Soc. Exptl. Biology and Medicine, N.Y. Acad. Sci., Sigma Xi. Home: 4001 N Charles St Baltimore MD 21218-1749 Office: Sigmund Grollman Ltd 9727 Mt Pisgah Rd Apt 1511 Silver Spring MD 20903-2013

GROM, BOGDAN, sculptor, painter, illustrator; b. Devincina, Trieste, Italy, Aug. 26, 1918; came to U.S., 1957; s. Miro and Frida (Dolenc) G. Diploma, Fine Arts Acad., Venice, Italy, 1944. Prof. State Gymnasium, Ptuj, Yugoslavia, 1945-47, Gymnasium and Tchrs. Prep. Sch., Trieste, 1947-53; free-lance artist Trieste, 1953-57; designer Printex Corp., Ossining, N.Y., 1957, Masta Displays Inc., New York, 1957-59; free-lance artist North Salem, N.Y. and Englewood, N.J., 1959—; vis. prof. Prat Inst., N.Y.C., 1960, Bklyn. Community Coll., 1962; dir. art North Salem Gallery Ltd.; lectr. art revs. Rai, Trieste; pres. No. Jersey Sculptors Assn., Tenafly, N.J., 1976-78. Author: (book) Slovene Ornaments, 1949, (art portfolio) Trieste and Its Karst, 1957; illustrator (books) Tom Sawyer, 1947, Huckleberry Finn, 1948. Bd. dirs. North Jersey Art Ctr., Tenafly, N.J., 1976-78. Recipient art teaching award European Recovery program, 1954, design award Westchester chpt. AIA, 1985. Mem. Am. Coll. Assn., Am. Medallic Sculptors Assn., Fedn. Internat. de la Medaille. Home and Studio: 416 Cumberland St Englewood NJ 07631

GRO MAMBO ANGELA NOVANYON IDIZOL See LEWIS, JOCELYA

GROMILLER, JAMES WILLIAM, retired management consultant; b. Altoona, Pa., June 27, 1931; s. James Francis and Avelline (Filtz) G.; m. Trudy Fox, Feb. 23, 1957; children: James P., Nancy G. Newhams, Andrew B., Matthew J. BA in Journalism, Pa. State U., 1953, MA in Commerce, 1954. Supervising auditor corp. auditing GE, Schenectady, N.Y., 1959-65; cons. corp. bus. analysis GE, N.Y.C., 1965-68; mgr. fin. and planning GE, Danville, Ill., 1968-74; mgr. fin. transit vehicle products GE, Erie, Pa., 1974-79; cons. bus. productivity improvement GE, Fairfield, Conn., 1979-84. Home: 145 Bayberry Ln Easton CT 06612

GROMOSIAK, PAUL, mathematics educator; b. Niagara Falls, N.Y., Aug. 21, 1942; s. John and Anna (Rimanosky) G. BS in Chemistry, Niagara U., 1964. Chemist Eastman Kodak, Rochester, N.Y., 1965, Durez Plastics div. Occidental, North Tonawanda, N.Y., 1966-68; tchr. Niagara Falls Bd. Edn., 1969-89; author Western N.Y. Wares, Inc., Buffalo, 1990—; guest lectr. Ctr. of Renewal, Stella Niagara, N.Y., 1991—. Author: Soaring Guls and Bowing Trees, 1990, Answers to the 100 Most Common Questions About Niagara Falls, 1990, Zany Niagara, 1992. Vol. historian Schoellkopf Geol. Mus., Niagara Falls, 1984—. Mem. Old Fort Niagara Assn. (life), Niagara County Hist. Soc., Buffalo Friends of Olmsted Parks. Home: 5819 Grauer Rd Niagara Falls NY 14305-1455

GRONBACH, ROBERT CHARLES, hospital system executive; b. Bklyn., May 18, 1928; s. Charles Herman and Martha (Lenzing) G.; m. Cynthia Kathleen Grant; 1 child, Garth Grant. BS, CCNY, 1951, MA, 1952. Personnel asst. IBM, N.Y.C., 1951-52; personnel rep. TWA, Queens, N.Y., 1955-58; personnel dir. Hartford (Conn.) Hosp., 1958-68, asst. hosp. dir. and dir. employee relations, 1969-81, v.p., employee relations, 1982-86; v.p. human resources Conn. Health Sys. and Hartford Hosp., 1987—; adj. prof. and assoc. curriculum chmn. Hartford Grad. Ctr., 1976—; adj. lectr. U. Conn. Sch. Bus., Hartford, 1973-76. Contbr. articles to profl. jours. Bd. dirs., chmn. personnel com. Hartford YMCA, Immediate Med. Care Ctr., Inc., H.H. Real Estate Corp., H.H. Mgmt. Svcs. Corp. Mem. Conn. Hosp. Assn. (bd. dirs.), Am. Hosp. Assn., Am. Soc. Healthcare Human Resource Execs. (bd. dirs. 1965-67, pres. 1967), Med. Ctr. Employee Relations Assn. (pres. 1968-71). Home: 48 Stonepost Rd Glastonbury CT 06033-4139 Office: Conn Health System 55 Farmington Ave Hartford CT 06105-3711

GRONCKI, PAUL J(OHN), economist, bank executive; b. Schenectady, N.Y., Jan. 27, 1949; s. Paul Albert and Lillian (Urban) G.; m. Michelle Marianne Tokarczyk, Aug. 25, 1979. BS in Econs., SUNY, Albany, 1971; MA, SUNY, Stony Brook, 1974, PhD in Econs., 1981. Economist N.Y. Dept. Labor, N.Y.C., 1972-74; assoc. scientist Brookhaven Nat. Lab., Upton, N.Y., 1976-82; economist econs. dept. Citibank, N.Y.C., 1982-83, asst. v.p., product mgr., 1983-86, asst. v.p. product devel. Focus, 1986-87, asst. v.p. credit design Focus, 1987, v.p. strategic mktg. programs pvt. banking group, 1987-89; v.p. info. planning Citicorp Fin. Inc. (Md.), Balt., 1989; v.p., dir. analysis and planning mktg. group The Pvt. Bank subs. Bankers Trust Co., 1990-91; v.p. mgmt. cons. PSI, 1992—; cons. fund raising Women's Quarterly Rev., N.Y.C., 1984-86. Vice chair Hudson Group-N.Y. regional office Dem. Nat. Com., N.Y.C., 1982-88; chair campaign Village Inds. Dems., N.Y.C., 1984; cons. Bus. Vols. for the Arts/Arts and Bus. Coun., N.Y.C., 1986-89; pres. Chelsea Reform Dem. Club, 1988-89, 91; chair N.Y. State New Dem. Coalition, 1990-91, pres. coop. bd., 1989, 91—; leader 64th Assembly Dist., Part A, Dem. Party. Mem. Am. Econs. Assn., Am. Mktg. Assn., N.Y. Assn. Bus. Economists (sec. 1986-88, v.p. and pres. elect. 1988-89), Bank Mktg. Assn., Pub. Works Forum, Chelsea Waterside Pk. Assn., 504 Dem. Club, Ams. for Dem. Action, NOW. Roman Catholic. Home: 601 N Eutaw St Apt 716 Baltimore MD 21201-4530

GRONENBORN, ANGELA MARIA, research scientist, chemist; b. Cologne, Germany, May 11, 1950; came to U.S., 1988; d. Jakob and Maria (Simons) G.; m. G. Marius Clore, Dec. 12, 1981; 1 child, Katharina Rachel Rebecca. Diploma, U. Cologne, Germany, 1975, PhD, 1978. Rsch. scientist Med. Rsch. Coun., London, 1978-84; group leader Max Planck Inst., Munich, Germany, 1984-88; sect. chief NIH, Bethesda, Md., 1988—. Contbr. over 200 articles to sci. jours. Recipient Award in Biol. Scis., Wash. Acad. Scis., 1989. Office: Bldg 2 Rm 123 NIH Bethesda MD 20892

GRONICH, DAN NEAL JONATHAN, real estate broker, consultant, investor; b. Buffalo, Nov. 30, 1942; s. Harry E. and Claire (Kamen) G.; m. Judith Krolick, Dec. 20, 1964 (div. 1976); 1 child, Amanda; m. Beverly Moyer Gronich, July 29, 1977. BS, Columbia U., 1964; MBA, NYU, 1968. CPA, N.Y. Tax specialist Deloitte & Touche (formerly Touche Ross & Co., N.Y.C., 1967-72; real estate broker Rudnick Brett Wyckoff, N.Y.C., 1972-76, dir. comml. leasing, 1976; chmn. Gronich & Co., Inc., N.Y.C., 1976—, Gronich World Trade Corp., 1990—. Bd. dirs. N.Y.C. Pub. Devel. Corp., 1984-89, exec. com. mem., 1989, fin. com. mem., 1986-89, devel. com. mem., 1987-89. Winner of the Most Ingenious Deal of the Yr. award Real Estate Bd. of N.Y., 1991. Mem. AICPA, Soc. Indsl. and Office Realtors (v.p. N.Y.C. chpt. 1987-90, pres. 1990—), Real Estate Bd. N.Y. Inc. (bd. govs. 1985—, exec. com. 1988—, treas. 1989—). Office: Gronich & Co Inc 575 5th Ave Fl 21 New York NY 10017-2491

GRONKA, M(ARTIN) STEVEN, educational association executive, film producer; b. Westchester, Pa., Apr. 30, 1952; s. Martin Joseph and Dorothy Elizabeth (Snyder) G. BA in Arts and Scis., U. Del., 1974, MBA, 1982, postgrad. in econs., 1982; postgrad. in div., Westminster Theol. Sem., 1976. Prodr., dir. Synthetic Imagery, Princeton, N.J., 1987-90, Masterworks Prodns., Newark, Del., 1989—; vice chmn., CEO Found. Against Smoking & Tobacco, Newark, 1988—; chmn., pres. Advance Am. Found., Cape May Court House, N.J., 1989—; cons. pub. rels. Cape May (N.J.) Harbor Marine & Resort, 1990—. Prodr., art dir. 3-D computer-animated opening Am.'s Cup Opening, 1988; co-prodr. music video, film Please Save Us the World, UN Global Youth Forum, 1992. Bd. dirs. Cape May Ctr. Pub. Policy, 1989—; com. 100 to Honor Law EnforcementOfficers, Cape May, 1991. Mem. U. Del. Bus. and Econ. Alumni Assn. (founding 1000), Stone Harbor Hobie Cat Sailors Assn. (commodore), Les Ami Du Vin Internation Wine Club (life). Presbyterian. Home: 6 S Dillwyn Rd Newark DE 19711 Office: Advance Am Found PO Box 843 Cape May Court House NJ 08210

GROOM, DONALD JOSEPH, human resources executive; b. Barberton, Ohio, Aug. 7, 1947; s. Leo and Mildred (Pantzar) G.; m. Carla A. Forman, Jan. 31, 1976; children: Kevin A., Melissa R. BS in Indsl. Mgmt., U. Akron, 1970; MBA, Ohio State U., 1975. Sr. fiscal analyst, liaison Ohio Legis. Budget Office, Columbus, 1976-77; dir., employment Ohio State U., Columbus, 1977-78, dir., compensation, 1978-80; personnel mgr., corp. office and dist. ctr. Gold Circle Stores, Columbus, 1980-81; regional personnel mgr. Gold Circle Stores, Cin., 1981-85; dir. human resources Atlanta Specialty Retailing, Atlanta, 1985-87; v.p. human resources Retail Ventures, Inc., Pitts., 1987—. 1st lt. U.S. Army, 1970-72, Vietnam, maj. res. Mem. Am. Soc. Personnel Adminstrn., Pitts. Personnel Assn. Home: 2544 Clubhouse Dr Wexford PA 15090-7955

GROOMS, ROBERT P., advertising executive; b. Bryn Mawr, Pa.; s. Chester Middleton and Eleanor (Kearney) G.; m. Patricia Van Akerley, Oct. 2, 1947; children: Carol A., Paul A. Dipl. in Advt. Design, Phila. Coll. Art, 1948; BA, U. of the Arts, Phila., 1983; B.Sociology, Beaver Coll., Glenside, Pa., 1988. Editorial asst. The Sat. Evening Post-Curtis Publs., Phila., 1951-53; asst. art dir. Farm Jour.-Farm Jour. Inc., Phila., 1953-56; art dir. Lewis & Gilman Inc., Phila., 1956-59, The Hary P. Bridge Co., Phila., 1959-72; owner, designer Bob Grooms Design, Jenkintown, Pa., 1972—. With U.S. Army, 1943-45; PTO. Mem. Phila. Sketch Club, VFW (chaplain 1991), Am. Legion (comdr. 1968). Home and Office: 307 West Ave Jenkintown PA 19046-2027

GROSCH, LUCIA LEOKADIA, nurse, retired; b. Essen, Fed. Republic of Germany, Aug. 31, 1911; came to U.S., 1913; d. John Hugo and Bertha (Burrush) Hirsch; m. William Ernest Albers, May 29, 1936 (dec. Mar. 1958); children: Diana, John; m. Jason Grosch, Nov. 22, 1964. Grad., Bklyn. Girls' Sch., 1928; diploma, N.Y.C. Sch. Nurses, 1963. Ordained deaconess Holy Orth. Ch. Am., 1962; consecrated to priesthood and episcopate, 1980; declared archbishop matriarch, 1985. Charge nurse Byrd S. Coler Hosp., Welfare Island, N.Y., 1964-65; pvt. duty nurse Gotham Agy., N.Y.C., 1965-68; charge nurse Cross County Hosp., Westchester County, N.Y., 1968-71; sec. Gutenburg Press, Preston Hollow, N.Y., 1948-58. Editor Mercury newsletter, 1973—; author sermons and lectures for Metro. Coll. of Soc. Rosicrucians Inc. Am.. Mem. Holy Orth. Ch. Am., 1955—. Mem. Soc. Rosicrucians Inc. Am. (declared Hierophantia of Metro. Coll. 1973, declared Supreme Magus 1985). Home: Box 192B Preston Hollow NY 12469 Office: Soc Rosicrucians Inc Am 10 E Chestnut St Kingston NY 12401

GROSMAN, ALAN M., lawyer; b. Newark, Mar. 13, 1935; s. Charles M. and Grace (Fishman) G.; m. Bette Bloomenthal, Dec. 27, 1967; children: Ellen, Carol. B.A., Wesleyan U., 1956; M.A., Yale U., 1957; J.D., N.Y. Law Sch., 1965. Bar: N.J. 1965, U.S. Dist. Ct. N.J. 1965, U.S. Sup. Ct. 1969. Ptnr., Grosman & Grosman and predecessors, Short Hills, N.J., 1965—; asst. prosecutor Essex County, N.J., 1968-69; mem. family part practice com. N.J. Supreme Ct., 1984-88, mem. dispute resolution task force, 1987-88, com. on women in the cts., 1991—; chmn. N.J. World Trade Coun., 1975-77; lectr. in field. Mem. ABA (chmn. alimony, maintenance and support com. family law sect. 1983-87), N.J. State Bar Assn. (exec. editor N.J. Family Lawyer, 1980-91, mem. exec. com. family law sect. 1980—, chmn. sect. 1987-88), Am. Acad. Matrimonial Lawyers (pres. N.J. chpt. 1983-85, nat. bd. govs. 1984-88, editor Jour. AAML 1980-90), Essex County Bar Assn. (chmn. family law com. 1970-72), Rep. Club, Inc. (counsel 1988—), N.Y. Law Sch., Millburn-Short Hills Rep. Club, Inc., Phi Beta Kappa. Reporter New Haven Jour., 1959-60, Newark Evening News, 1961-62; contbr. articles to profl. jours. Address: 75 Main St Ste # 304 Millburn NJ 07041

GROSOF, MIRIAM SCHAPIRO, mathematics educator; b. N.Y.C., Dec. 2, 1932; d. Meyer and Lillian (Milgram) Schapiro; m. Gerard M. Grosof, June 6, 1952 (div. 1971); children: Benjamin N., David H. AB summa cum laude, Barnard Coll., 1952; MA in Math., Columbia U., 1953; PhD, Yeshiva U., 1966. Lectr. math. Columbia U., N.Y.C., 1953-58; rsch. assoc. math. edn. Yeshiva U., N.Y.C., 1966-68, asst. prof., 1968-71, assoc. prof., 1971-83, prof. edn. and math., 1983—; adj. assoc. prof. math. Pace U., N.Y.C., 1974-80, adj. prof. 1980—; cons. in field, 1982—; dir. curriculum devel. project NSF, Yeshiva U., 1971-72, adminstr. insvc. program, 1967-73. Author: (with H. Sardy) A Research Primer for the Social and Behavioral Sciences, 1985; contbr. articles to profl. jours. Fellow NSF, 1952-53, 64, 65, 66; Grad. fellow AAUW, 1958-59. Mem. Am. Stats. Assn., Math. Assn. of Am., Assn. for Women in Math., Nat. Coun. of Tchrs. of Math., Phi Beta Kappa. Office: Yeshiva U 245 Lexington Ave New York NY 10016

GROSS, BEATRICE SCHAAP, education educator, consultant, writer; b. N.Y.C., Jan. 23, 1935; married; 2 children. BA in Am. Studies, Syracuse U., 1956; MS in Edn., Bank Street Coll. Edn., N.Y.C., 1958. Cert. pre-sch. and elem. tchr. Adj. faculty NYU, N.Y.C., 1968-81, New Sch. Social Research, N.Y.C., 1983-87; vis. prof. Vassar Coll., 1985; assoc. prof. humanities SUNY, Old Westbury, 1972-76; cons. to govt., industry and founds., 1976—; participant univ. seminars Columbia U. Author: Radical School Reform, 1970, Will it Grow in a Classroom?, 1974, The Children's Rights Movement, 1977, The New Old, 1978, Teaching Under Pressure, 1979, Towards Improved Compensatory Education, 1982, Independent Scholarship: Promise, Problems and Prospects, 1983, The Great School Debate: Which Way for American Education, 1985; syndicated columnist: The Family Viewpoint, 1979-82; co-editor: Ind. Scholarship newsletter; contbr. articles to profl. jours.; author teaching materials McGraw Hill, Sci. Research Assocs. Program adv. Beacon Coll., 1978-82; assoc. dir. Writers in the Pub. Interest, 1981—; assoc. project dir. Ind. Scholars Project, 1982—; adj. assoc. prof. La Quardia Community Coll., 1992—; exec. com. Womanspace, Great Neck, N.J. Recipient Disting. Achievement award Ednl. Press Assn. Am., 1974; Faculty Exchange scholar SUNY, 1975. Mem. Am. Soc. Journalists and Authors. Home: 17 Myrtle Dr Great Neck NY 11021-1807

GROSS, DAVID JOHN, biophysicist, educator; b. Chester, Ill., June 14, 1953; s. Kenneth John and M. Aileen (Barnard) G.; m. Julie Kay Cox, July 28, 1979. BS in Physics, U. Ill., 1975, MS in Physics, 1977, PhD in Physics, 1982. Postdoctoral assoc. dept. applied and engring. physics Cornell U., Ithaca, N.Y., 1982-86; asst. prof. dept. biochemistry and molecular biology U. Mass., Amherst, 1986-92, assoc. prof., 1992—. Contbr. articles to Modern Cell Biology, Biophys. Jour., Cell Regulation, Procs. NAS. Mem. AAAS, Am. Phys. Soc., Am. Soc. Cell Biology, Biophys. Soc. Office: Dept Biochemistry & Molecular Biology U Mass Amherst MA 01003

GROSS, DONALD, principal; b. Pottsville, Pa., Aug. 6, 1947; s. Jerome J. and Vevee (Strauss) G.; m. Ann Elizabeth Wallace, Apr. 14, 1973. BS in Edn., Ohio U., 1969; MA, Ohio State U., 1971; EdD, Lehigh U., 1988. Tchr. Champaign (Ill.) Pub. Schs., 1974-76; prin. Urbana (Ill.) Sch. Dist., 1976-78, Bloomsburg (Pa.) Area Sch. Dist., 1978-88, Cinnaminson (N.J.) Twp. Schs., 1988-91, Valley Cen. Sch. Dist., Montgomery, N.Y., 1991—; pvt. practice cons.; adj. prof. Lehigh U., Bethlehem, Pa., 1988. Capt. U.S. Army, 1969-78. Mem. Assn. Supervision and Curriculum Devel., Nat. Assn. Secondary Schs., N.J. Prin. and Suprs. Assn., N.J. Assn. Supervision and Curriculum Devel., Elks. Jewish. Office: Valley Cen Sch Dist 1189 Rt 17K Montgomery NY 12549

GROSS, FELIKS, sociologist, educator, author; b. Cracow, Poland, June 17, 1906; came to U.S., 1941; s. Adolf and Augusta (Alexander) G.; m. Priva

Baidaff, July 25, 1937; 1 child, Eva Helena Gross Friedman. LLM, Jagiellonian U., 1930; LLD, Jagiellanian U., 1931. Bar: Poland 1937. Sec., gen. Cen. Ea. European Planning Bd., 1941-45; editor New Europe and World Reconstrn. jour., N.Y.C., 1942-45; prof. sociology grad. ctr. Bklyn. Coll., N.Y.C., 1946-77, prof. emeritus, 1977—, resident prof. CUNY grad. ctr., 1988—; vis. prof. NYU, 1945-68; vis. prof., dir. Inst. Internat. Affairs, U. Wyo., Laramie, summers 1945-52; vis. prof. Woodrow Wilson Sch. Fgn. Affairs, U. Va., Charlottesville, 1951, 54-56, U. Vt., Burlington, 1957; sr. Fulbright prof. U. Rome, 1957-58, 64-65, 74; lectr. other European, Am. univs.; mem. rsch. coun. Fgn. Policy Rsch. Inst., Phila., 1966—; vis. prof. Columbia U., N.Y.C., 1973; lectr. U. Florence, 1977, Italian Fgn. Office, Rome; cons. Nat. Com. on Causes and Prevention of Violence, 1968. Pres., Taraknath Das Found., N.Y., 1965; hon. pres. CUNY Acad. Humanities and Scis., 1985, Internat. Labor Office of the League of Nations, Geneva, 1930; co-founder, bd. dirs. Non-Profit Coordinating Com. N.Y., 1984-86. Author: Nomadism, 1936; Polish Worker, 1945; Foreign Policy Analysis, 1954; Seizure of Political Power, 1957; Valori Sociali e Struttura, 1967; World Politics and Tension Areas, 1967; Violence in Politics, 1973; Il Paese, Values and Social Change in an Italian Village, 1974; The Revolutionary Party, 1974; Ethnics in the Borderland, 1979; Ideologies, Goals and Values, 1986; Working Class and Culture (in Polish), 1986, others; contbr. numerous articles to profl. jours. Carnegie scholar, Paris, 1931; Pub. Affairs Found. NYU, 1962-63; grantee Sloane Found., 1963, Fulbright, 1956-57, 64-65, 74, City U. Rsch. Found., 1971-74, NSF, 1972, Rockefeller Found., 1974; recipient Golden Cross of Phoenix, King of Greece, 1963, Ethnic New Yorker award N.Y.C., 1987, Polonia Restituta, Pres. of Poland, 1991, Alfred Jurzykowski Prize award for scholarship contbn. Mem. Polish Inst. Arts and Sci. (pres. 1988), Internat. League Rights of Man (dir. 1960), Am. Sociol. Assn., Acad. Polit. Sci., N.Y. Acad. Sci., Polish Acad. Ssis. (fgn. mem.), Authors League, Sigma Xi. Home: 310 W 85th St New York NY 10024-3819 Office: Polish Inst Arts and Scis of Am 208 E 30th St New York NY 10016-8202

GROSS, FREDYE WRIGHT, fundraising executive; b. Dallas, Jan. 7, 1949; d. William Larry and Fredonia (Robinson) Wright; m. John R. Murphy, Feb. 15, 1981 (div. Feb. 1992); m. Adam Anthony Gross, July 11, 1992. BA, U. Tex., 1971. Pub. info. dir. Aurora Higher Edn. Ctr., Denver, 1973-77; pub. rels. dir. Colo. Hist. Soc., Denver, 1977-78; promotion dir. San Francisco Examiner, 1978-81; exec. dir. Friends of the Balt. Symphony, 1982-84; sales and mktg. assoc. Coldwell Banker Comml. Real Estate, Balt., 1985-89; dir. resource devel. The Enterprise Found., Columbia, Md., 1989—; pres. bd. dirs. Md. Art Place, Balt., 1984—; nat. mem. visual arts adv. bd. Coll. Santa Fe, N.Mex., 1992—. Contbr. photogrphy to newspaper and mags. Trustee Balt. Mus. Art, 1989—, Md. Inst. Coll. Art, Balt., 1984—; mem. capital campaign com. Salvation Army, Balt., 1988; co-chair benefit Assoc. Black Charities, Balt., 1991; mem. comml. real estate com. Greater Balt. Bd. Realtors, 1986-89. Recipient pub. svc. awards; Spl. Events award Assn. Newspaper Promoters, 1980; Photography award Denver Art Mus., 1975, others. Mem. Parks and People Found., Balt. Country Club. Democrat. Episcopalian. Office: The Enterprise Found 500 American City Bldg Columbia MD 21044

GROSS, GEORGE, lawyer, publishing executive; b. Vari, Hungary, May 1, 1934; s. David and Julia (Klien) G.; m. Marcy A. Lynn, May 6, 1966 (div. 1980); children: Julian A., Alexandra L. BA, U. Conn., 1959; LLB, Boston U., 1962. Bar: Conn. 1962, D.C. 1963. Counsel housing, urban devel. subcom. Ho. of Reps., Washington, 1969-74, exec. dir. budget com., 1974-78; dir. fed. rels. Nat. League of Cities, Washington, 1978-84; adminstr. N.Y.C. Human Resources Adminstrn., 1984-86; exec. dir. N.Y. State Fin. Control Bd., N.Y.C., 1986-88; v.p. govt. affairs Mag. Pubs. Am., Washington, 1989—. With U.S. Army, 1959-61. Mem. River Bend Golf and Country Club (Great Falls, Va.). Democrat. Home: 4620 N Park Ave Bethesda MD 20815-4549 Office: Mag Pubs Am 1211 Connecticut Ave NW Washington DC 20036-2701

GROSS, GEORGE, JR., entrepeneur; b. Pitts., Aug. 4, 1941; s. George Sigfred and Mildred (Wildermuth) G.; m. Margaret Ann Chatham, Mar. 31, 1973; 1 child, Michael George Gross; stepson, Edward Klause. Student, St. Leo's, Pitts., 1955, N. Catholic, Pitts., 1959. Terminal mgr. Eazor Express Inc., Pitts., 1969-70, Interstate Truck Svc., Martins Ferry, Ohio, 1970-71; mgr. spl. svd. div. Eastern Express, Terre Haute, Ind., 1971-72; terminal mgr. Eazor Express Inc., Pitts., 1972-74, dir. spl. com. div., 1974-77, v.p. spl. commodity div., 1977-79; v.p. sales mktg. W.F.W. Co., Youngstown, Ohio, 1979-83; ptnr. Gribble Trucking, Somerset, Pa., 1983-86; owner Gemm Enterprises Inc., Pitts., 1986—; asst. perm. mgr., mgmt. trainee, truck driver, Eazor Express, Inc., Pitts.; mechanic, Lennon's Svc., Pitts. Democrat. Roman Catholic. Office: Gemm Enterprises Inc McKnight East Plz # 1 Ste 2006 Kinvara Dr Pittsburgh PA 15237

GROSS, HARRIET SHARON, psychiatrist; b. Phila., Oct. 25, 1958; d. Norman Robert and Joan Sheila (Paull) G.; m. Richard Lynn Bowman; children: Amanda Meredith Bowman, Jessica Paige Bowman. BA, Wellesley (Mass.) Coll., 1979; MD, Med. Coll. Pa., Phila., 1983. Diplomate Nat. Bd. Med. Examiners; lic. psychiatrist Pa., bd. cert. psychiatry, 1991. Resident in adult psychiatry SUNY/Health Scis. Ctr., Syracuse, 1983-84; resident in child and adolescent psychiatry dept. mental health scis. Hahnemann U., Phila., 1985-87; resident in adult psychiatry dept. mental health scis. Hahnemann U., 1987-90; staff child, adolescent and adult psychiatrist C.A.T.C.H., Inc., Community Mental Health Ctr., Phila., 1990—. Recipient Winifred B. Stewart Meml. prize, Med. Coll. Pa., 1983. Mem. Am. Psychiatric Assn. Office: CATCH Inc 1409 11 Lombard St Philadelphia PA 19146

GROSS, HENRY, management consultant; b. Havana, Cuba, Jan. 13, 1949; came to U.S. 1960.; s. Enrique Sibrower and Emma (Revilla) G. AB, Dartmouth U., 1971; MBA, Amos Tuck U., Hanover, N.H., 1972. Sr. product mgr. Colgate-Palmolive, N.Y.C., 1972-76; mktg. mgr. Frito-Lay, Inc., Dallas, 1976-78; dir. mktg. C & C Cola, Inc., Elmwood, N.J., 1978-79; sr. dir. mktg. Revlon, Inc., N.Y.C., 1979-83; gen. mgr. Rainbow Programming, Woodbury, N.Y., 1984-86; pres. Gross & Assocs., N.Y.C., 1987—; bd. dirs. Rent-A-Wreck, Inc., Los Angeles, Harvard Tech., Inc., N.Y.C., 320-57 Corp., treas., N.Y.C. Contbr. articles to profl. jours. Mem. Internat. Radio and TV Soc., Nat. Cable TV Assn., Cable TV Adminstrn. and Mktg. Soc. Republican. Clubs: Yale (N.Y.C.), Vertical (N.Y.C.). Office: Gross Assocs 320 E 57th St New York NY 10022-2948

GROSS, IAN, academic pediatrician, neonatologist; b. Pretoria, Republic of South Africa, Oct. 15, 1943; came to U.S., 1971; s. Kenneth and Gladys Bakst (Cooper) G.; m. Melanie Belman, Dec. 3, 1967; children: David Anthony, Adam Charles. BS, U. Witwatersrand, Johannesburg, Republic of South Africa, 1963, MBBCh, 1967; MA (hon.), Yale U., 1985. Diplomate Am. Bd. Pediatrics, Am. Bd. Neonatal-Perinatal Medicine. Rotating intern Johannesburg Gen. Hosp., 1968; pediatric resident U. Witwatersrand Hosps., Johannesburg, 1970-71, Children's Hosp. Harvard Med. Sch., Boston, 1971-73; postdoctoral fellow in pediatrics Yale U., New Haven, Conn., 1973-74; asst. prof. Yale U. Sch. Medicine, New Haven, 1974-78, assoc. prof., 1978-85, prof., 1985—; dir. Newborn Spl. Care Unit, Yale New Haven Hosp., 1982—; mem. study sect. NIH, Bethesda, Md., 1981-85, adv. bd. Mead Johnson Symposia, Evansville, Ind., 1985—, Hood Found., Boston, 1988—. Contbr. over 60 jour. articles and book chpts. Named Most Disting. Med. Grad. U. Witwatersrand, Johannesburg, 1967; James Hudson Brown fellow, Yale U., 1973; rsch. grantee NIH and Am. Heart Assn. Fellow Am. Acad. Pediatrics; mem. Soc. Pediatric Rsch., Am. Physiol. Soc., Am. Thoracic Soc., Perinatal Rsch. Soc. Office: Yale Sch Medicine 333 Cedar St New Haven CT 06510-3289

GROSS, IRWIN LEE, lawyer, corporate executive; b. Phila., Nov. 23, 1943; s. Nathan Gross and Helen (Hecht) Rappoport; m. Linda Cohen, June 29, 1969; children: Elizabeth Shana, Gabriella Lynne. BS, Temple U., 1965; JD, Villanova U., 1968. Bar: Pa. 1968, U.S. Dist. Ct. (ea. dist.) Pa. 1969. Asst. dist. atty. Office Dist. Atty., Phila., 1970-71; ptnr. Nissenbaum, Gross & Rudolph, Phila., 1971-74, LaCheen, Doner, LaCheen & Gross, Phila., 1974-76, Irwin L. Gross P.C., Phila., 1976-81; exec. v.p., bd. dirs. Internat. Mobile Machine Corp., Phila., 1981-84; pres., chief exec. officer, chmn. bd. dirs. Internat. Cogeneration Corp., Phila., 1984—; bd. dirs. Power Spectrum Inc. Bd. dirs. Boys Town of Jerusalem, Phila., 1985—, Soc. Hill Synogogue. Capt. USAR, 1968-75. Mem. ABA, Phila. Bar Assn., Middle States Ind. Power Producers Assn. (v.p.). Republican. Jewish. Club: Golden Slipper (Phila.) (bd. dirs.). Office: ICC Technologies 441 N 5th St Philadelphia PA 19123-4008

GROSS, JULIE, public relations professional; b. N.Y.C., Aug. 11, 1959; d. Herbert N. Gross and Beverly (Silbert) Ross; m. Darryl Gelfand, Sept. 3, 1987. BA in English, Barnard Coll., 1981. Pub. relations rep. Commodity Exchange, Inc., N.Y.C., 1981-85; acct. exec. Hill & Knowlton, N.Y.C., 1985-87; pub. rels. dir. Childreach, Long Beach, N.Y., 1987—. Office: Childreach 162 W Park Ave # 2 Long Beach NY 11561

GROSS, MARY ANNE, author, educator; b. Cornwall, N.Y., Aug. 10, 1943; d. Anthony Louis and Anne Malvina (Buckneberg) Gross; m. Angelo Carl Ferraro, Jan. 31, 1974; children: Antonia Anne, Daniel James. BA, BS, SUNY, New Paltz, 1965. Cert. tchr., N.Y. Tchr. pub. and pvt. schs., N.Y., 1965-75. Author: Baking Bread the Way Mom Taught Me, 1979; editor: Mother, These Are My Friends, 1969, Ah, Man, You Found Me Again, 1972. Founder Save Our Streams, Woodbury Falls, N.Y., 1986. Recipient Ray Bergman Trout Unlimited Conservation award, 1989. Mem. Kappa Delta Pi. Home: Box 597 Yesterdays Village Highland Mills NY 10930

GROSS, MICHAEL RAYMOND, public relations professional; b. Lewiston, Maine, Jan. 6, 1952; s. Raymond Emerton and Esther Louise (Proctor) G.; m. Stephanie Jean Lufkin, Sept. 25, 1976; children: James Michael, David Thomas. Student, U. So. Maine, 1970-72; BA in Journalism, U. Maine, Orono, 1974; cert. in media law, U. Maine, Portland, 1976. Pub. rels. assoc. Penobscot Bay Med. Ctr., Rockport, Maine, 1974-76; program dir., news dir. Sta. WRKD-AM-FM, Rockland, Maine, 1976-81; reporter, news anchor, state house news reporter Sta. WABK-AM-FM, Gardiner, Maine, 1981-83; communications cons., family tchr. Hinckley (Maine) Home Sch. Farm, 1983-86; communications specialist Maine Agrl. Experiment Sta., Orono, 1986—; instr. Univ. Coll., Bangor, Maine, 1987-90; cons. Sci. and Engring. Ctr., Orono, others. Contbg. author: The Shore Village Story, 1976; contbr. articles to profl. publs.; writer, designer ann. reports. Bd. dirs. Maine Sea Foods Festival, Rockland, 1977-79. Mem. Agrl. Communicators in Edn. (state rep. 1987—, nat. program com. 1989-90), Maine Pub. Rels. Coun., Maine Assn. Broadcasters (news and feature awards 1977-81), Maine Press Assn., Rockland Area Jaycees, Camden Civic Theater. Republican. Episcopalian. Home: 54 Oak Grove St Bangor ME 04401-7053 Office: Maine Agrl Experiment Sta Rm 1 WInslow Hall Orono ME 04469-0163

GROSS, NATHAN, oral and maxillofacial surgeon; b. Phila., May 17, 1933; s. Samuel and Anna (Badner) G.; m. Bernice Gross; children: James H., Jeffrey H. DMD, Temple U., 1957; postgrad., U. Pa., 1959-60. Diplomate Am. Bd. Oral and Maxillofacial Surgery. Assoc. pathology U. Pa. Sch. Dental Medicine, Phila., 1961-66; instr. oral surgery U. Pa. Sch. Dental Medicine, 1961-62, instr. oral pathology, 1964-67, instr. oral surgery, 1964-67; lectr. oral surgery/oral pathology Camden County Coll., Blackwood, N.J., 1980-83, Camden County Voc. Sch., Blackwood, 1981-83; instr. oral surgery Temple U., Albert Einstein Med. Ctr., Phila., 1969—; assoc. prof. dept. surgery Sch. Medicine and Dentistry of N.J., Stratford, N.J.; surg. and pathology cons. William Kessler Meml. Hosp., Hammonton, N.J., 1979—; chief oral/maxillofacial surgery Kennedy Meml. Hosp. Am. Cancer Soc. research fellow, 1960-63. Fellow Am. Assn. Oral and Maxillofacial Surgeons, Am. Coll. Oral and Maxillofacial Surgeons, N.J. Soc. Oral and Maxillofacial Surgeons, Del. Valley Soc. Oral and Maxillofacial Surgeons, Internat. Assn. for Maxillofacial Surgery, Rotary. Office: 3 N White Horse Pike Somerdale NJ 08083-1798

GROSS, PETER ALAN, epidemiologist, researcher; b. Newark, Nov. 18, 1938; s. Meyer P. and Nathalie (Bass) Denburg) G.; m. Regina Teri Gittlin, May 30, 1964; children: Deborah Karen, Michael Philip, Daniel Brian. BA cum laude, Amherst Coll., 1960; MD, Yale U., 1964. Diplomate Am. Bd. Internal Medicine. Intern Yale-New Haven Hosp., 1964-65, jr. resident, 1965-66; sr. resident Peter Bent Brigham Hosp., Boston, 1968-69; research and edn. assoc. Va Hosp., West Haven, Conn., 1971-73, acting chief infectious disease sect., 1972-73; chief infectious disease sect. VA Hosp., West Haven, Conn., 1973-74; chief infectious disease sect. Hackensack (N.J.) Med. Ctr., 1974—, chmn. dept. medicine, 1980—, chmn. med. bd., 1986; prof. medicine N.J. Med. Sch., Newark, 1981—, vice chmn. dept. medicine, 1989-90; assoc. clin. prof. medicine Columbia U. Coll. Physicians and Surgeons, N.Y.C., 1971-81, asst. clin. prof., 1974-77; asst. prof. medicine Yale U. Shc. Medicine, New Haven, 1971-74; ad hoc reviewer rsch. grants NIH, Nat. Inst. Allergy and Infectious Diseases; investigator Ctr. for Biologic Evaluation and Rsch. FDA, 1974—; mem. clin. indicators task force Joint Commn. on Accreditation of Healthcare Orgns., 1987-89. Authro: Gram Strain Recognition, 1975, 2d edit., 1980; mem. editorial bd. Jour. Clin. Microbiology, 1980—, Infection Control, 1980-90; assoc. editor Clin. Performance and Quality Health Care, 1992—. Served to lt. comdr. USPHS, CDC, 1966-68. NIH fellow Yale U., 1969-71. Mem. AAAS, ACP (task force on adult immunization), Infectious Disease Soc. Am. (fellow, clin. affairs com.), Am. Acad. Microbiology, Am. Soc. Virology, Am. Soc. Microbiology, Soc. Hosp. Epidemiologists Am. (councillor 1986-88, v.p. 1992). Republican. Jewish. Office: Hackensack Med Ctr Hackensack NJ 07601

GROSS, PRIVA BAIDAFF, art historian, retired educator; b. Wieliczka, Poland, June 19, 1911; came to U.S., 1941, naturalized, 1955; d. Israel and Leopolda (Friedman) Baidaff; Ph.M., Jagellonian U., Cracow, Poland, 1937; postgrad. (N.Y. U. scholar 1945-47), N.Y. U. Inst. Fine Arts, 1945-48; m. Feliks Gross, July 25, 1937; 1 dau., Eva Helena Gross Friedman. Mem. faculty Queensborough Community Coll., CUNY, 1961-81, assoc. prof. art history, 1971-81, ret., 1981, co-chmn. art and music dept., 1966-68, chmn. art dept., 1968-74, dir. coll. gallery, 1968-77. SUNY grantee, 1967. Mem. AAUW (dir. 1972-76, 1980-82), Coll. Art Assn. Am., Soc. Archtl. Historians, Gallery Assn. N.Y. State (dir. 1972-73), N.Y. State Assn. Jr. Colls., AAUP, Polish Inst. Arts and Scis. Am., Council Gallery and Exhbn. Dirs. (dir. 1970-72). Contbr. articles, revs. to profl. publs. Home: 310 W 85th St New York NY 10024-3819

GROSS, ROBERT EMANUEL, collateral loan broker; b. N.Y.C., May 13, 1920; s. Solomon Sidney and Estelle (Prager) G.; m. Gloria Polansky, Dec. 30, 1942 (dec. Feb. 1986); children: Gary, Kenneth. BA, Franklin and Marshall Coll., 1942. Sec. Sol S. Gross Co. Inc., N.Y.C., 1943-71; pres. S&G Gross Co. Inc., N.Y.C., 1971—. Mem. Collateral Loan Brokers Assn. (sec.-treas. 1982—). Office: S&G Gross Co Inc 486 8th Ave New York NY 10001

GROSS, SONJA KELLER, research scientist, chemist; b. Trutnov, Czechoslovakia, Feb. 2, 1926; came to U.S., 1947; d. Otto and Olga (Wolfner) Keller; m. Dec. 19, 1949 (dec. Jan. 22, 1991); 1 child, Mark, Donald. BS, MIT, 1950; MA, Harvard U., 1951, PhD, 1954. Asst. prof. Simmons Coll., Boston, 1957-62; lectr. Boston U., 1962-63; scholar Radcliffe Inst., Cambridge, Mass., 1966-68; rsch. assoc. MIT, Cambridge, 1968-71; scientist E.K. Shriver Ctr., Waltham, Mass., 1971—. Contbr. articles to profl. jours. Named Scholar, Radcliffe Inst., 1966-68; grantee NIH, 1959-63. Mem. Am. Chem. Soc., N.Y. Acad. Scis., Sierra Club, Mass. Audubon Soc. Office: E K Shriver Ctr 200 Trapelo Rd Waltham MA 02154-6332

GROSS, STANLEY JAY, psychologist, consultant; b. Bklyn., Sept. 25, 1927; s. Albert S. and Selma G. (Krebs) G.; m. Carol Jacobs, Dec. 29, 1955 (div. Jan. 1975); children: Elizabeth, David, Jennifer; m. Julia L. McVay, Aug. 29, 1978. BBA, Baruch Coll., 1950; MA, Columbia U., 1953, EdD, 1959. Postdoctoral fellow U. Ill., Chgo., 1972-73; cen. treas. Baruch Coll., N.Y.C., 1953-55; social sci. instr. Orange County Community Ctr., Middletown, N.Y., 1956-58; assoc. dean students SUNY, Buffalo, 1958-61; dean students Rockford (Ill.) Coll., 1961-66; prof. counseling psychology Ind. State U., Terre Haute, 1966-88; clin. fellow Harvard Med. Sch., Boston, 1987; pvt. practice, Quincy, Mass., 1988—; instr. Tchrs. Coll. Columbia U., N.Y.C., 1955-56; cons. Addictions, Family and Recovery, Plymouth, Mass., 1987—; lectr Tufts U., Medford, Mass., 1991. Author: Of Foxes and Henhouses, Licensing and the Health Professions, 1984. With USN, 1945-46, U.S. Army, 1950-52. Mem. APA, Mass. Psychol. Assn., Avanta Network. Office: 110 W Squantum St Ste 17 Quincy MA 02171-2131

GROSS, STEVEN, medical marketing communications and device company executive; b. Jersey City, Aug. 12, 1946; s. Milton and Mildred G.; children: Meredith Paige, Sharlee Beth. CEO, founder pharm. advt./communications DevCom, Inc.; CEO, founder MDDM, Inc.; v.p. Women's Internat. Ctr. Office: DevCom Inc 1700 Russell Rd Paoli PA 19301-1260

GROSSBARD, ARTHUR JEROME, automotive supplies executive; b. N.Y.C., Mar. 30, 1938; s. Louis and Sara (Jacobs) G.; m. Sondra H. Marin, Mar. 20, 1966. BS, NYU, 1962, MBA, 1965. V.p., gen. mgr. A.T.I., Inc., Milford, Conn., 1972-77; prin. owner Economy Svc. Ctrs. Am., Miami, Fla., 1977-87; v.p., gen. mgr. Accurate Equipment Co., N.Y.C., 1987—; mktg. dir. Clearway Automotive Group, N.Y.C., 1987—; v.p., regional dir. Midas, Inc., Chgo., 1966-72. Office: Clearway Auto Group 21110 Hillside Ave Jamaica NY 11427-1719

GROSSBART, TED ALAN, clinical psychologist; b. Detroit, June 3, 1946; s. Samuel Alexander and Mary (Spilkin) G.; m. Rosely Traube, Feb. 9, 1974; children: Zachary, Matthew. AB, U. Mich., 1967; MA, Boston U., 1972, PhD, 1972. Diplomate Am. Bd. Med. Psychotherapists; lic. psychologist, Mass. Pvt. practice Boston, 1970—; instr. Harvard Med. Sch., Boston, 1973—; sr. assoc. clin. supr. Beth Israel Hosp., Boston, 1973—. Author: Skin Deep: A Mind/Body Program for Healthy Skin, 1986. Bd. advisors Boston HELP. Mem. APA, Am. Bd. Med Psychotherapists (bd. advisors), Soc. for Clin. and Exptl. Hypnosis. Home: Goodwin's Landing Marblehead MA 01945 Office: 466 Commonwealth Ave Apt 201 Boston MA 02215-2710

GROSSBERG, DAVID BURTON, cardiologist; b. Bronx, N.Y., Oct. 28, 1956; s. Jules Harold and Florence (Greenbaum) G.; m. Karen Leslie Sonin, Apr. 17, 1988; 1 child, Samuel Benjamin. BA, SUNY, Binghamton, 1977; MD, SUNY, Syracuse, 1981. Diplomate Am. Bd. Internal Medicine, Am. Bd. Cardiology. Resident in internal medicine Overlook Hosp.Columbia U. Coll. Physicians and Surgeons, Summit, N.J., 1981-84; asst. clin. prof. medicine George Washington U., Washington; adj. asst. prof. medicine Baylor U. Sch. Medicine; staff physician St. Mary's Hosp., East Orange, N.J., 1982; internist Sumter County Pub. Health, Wildwood, Fla., 1984-86; cardiology fellow Albany (N.Y.) Med. Ctr. Hosp., 1986-88; cardiologist Md. Cardiology Assoc., Silver Spring, 1988-91; pvt. pracitce Silver Spring, Rockville, Md., 1991—; mem. dir. Ctrl. Fla. Ambulance Svcs., Sumterville, 1984-85; assoc. attending staff Washington Adventist Hosp., Shady Grove Adventist Hosp., Holy Cross Hosp., Suburban Hosp., Laurel Hosp.; co-investigator Gusto Trial-Thrombo Cytic Therapy Post. Recipient Elsbeth Kroeber Meml. award N.Y. Biology Tchrs. Assn., 1973, Regents scholar, 1973. Fellow Am. Coll. Cardiology, Am. Coll. Chest Physicians; mem. ACP, Physicians for Social Responsibility, Md. Med. Soc. (alternate del. 1991), Sierra Club (vol. physician Wilderness Project 1982), Audubon Soc., Md. Soc. Cardiology, Montgomery County Med. Soc. Office: 2415 Musgrove Rd Ste 307 Silver Spring MD 20904

GROSSE-MIDDELDORF VIOLA, BIRGIT ELISABETH, language educator; b. Essen, Germany, May 22, 1958; came to U.S., 1982; d. Herman and Elisabeth (Rautenberg) G.-M.; m. Robert Viola, Oct. 25, 1982; children: Liv, Lars. Diploma, Freie U., Berlin; ArtsD, SUNY, Stonybrook, 1990. Adj. prof. German SUNY, Stonybrook, 1990—; adj. prof. comparative lit. Hofstra U., Helmstead, N.Y., 1991—. Home: 237 Springville Rd Hampton Bays NY 11946 Office: Comparative Lit Dept Hofstra U Hempstead NY 11550

GROSSI, RALPH EDWARD, agricultural organization executive, farmer, rancher; b. San Rafael, Calif., Feb. 16, 1949; s. James Joseph and Rose Marie (Halter) G.; m. Judy Arlene Lamb, Sept. 9, 1972; children: Amy, Erin, Kathryn. BS, Calif. Poly. State U.-San Luis Obispo, 1971. Mng. ptnr. Marindale Dairy, Novato, Calif., 1971-87, Marindale Ranch, Novato, 1987—; pres. Am. Farmland Trust, Washington, 1985—, also bd. dirs.; founder, bd. dirs. Marin Agrl. Land Trust, Marin County, Calif., 1980-90, chmn., 1980-82; pres. Marin County Farm Bur., 1979-81; mem. water adv. com. Calif. Agr., Sacramento, 1979-81, U.S. Implementation Bd. of N.Am. Waterfowl Mgmt. Plan, Washington, 1988—. Mem. adv. com. Sch. Agr., Calif. Poly. State U., 1988; bd. dirs. Wildlife Habitat Enhancement, Washington, 1989—; v.p. Alpha Gamma Rho Found., Kansas City, Mo., 1991—. Recipient Feinstone Environ. award Sol Feinstone Awards Com., 1985. Mem. Soil and Water Conservation Soc., Calif. Farm Bur. Fedn. (Outstanding Young Farmer and Rancher award 1976), Inst. for Alternative Agr. (pres.' coun. 1990—). Republican. Presbyterian. Office: Am Farmland Trust 1920 N St NW # 400 Washington DC 20036-1601

GROSSMAN, ALLEN NEIL, publishing executive; b. Bklyn., May 14, 1946; s. William Lester and Shirley Miriam (Jacobson) G.; m. Pamela Jean Pearson, June 8, 1969; children: Steven Mueller, Elizabeth Jane. AB, Princeton U., 1968; JD, Harvard U., 1971. Bar: Pa. 1971, N.J. 1973. Assoc. Dechert Price & Rhoads, Phila., 1971-73, Smith Stratton Wise & Heher, Princeton, N.J., 1973-75; ptnr. Smith Stratton Wise & Heher, 1975-81; dir. bus. devel. Dow Jones Info. Svcs. Group, Princeton, 1981-91, exec. dir. bus. ops. and devel., 1991-92; exec. dir. mktg. and devel. Dow Jones Bus. Info. Svcs. Group, Princeton, 1992—; dir. Integrated Communications Systems, Inc., Roswell, Ga., 1982-92, DataTimes Corp., Oklahoma City, 1989—. Dir. Princeton Area United Way, 1978-79; mem. Princeton Regional Bd. Edn., 1980-84, 86-91, Coun. of Princeton U. Community, 1990-92; coach Princeton Youth Soccer Assn., 1984-91. Mem. ABA, Alumni Cou. Princeton U., Princeton Club N.Y. Democrat. Jewish. Home: 39 Tyson Ln Princeton NJ 08540-4141 Office: Dow Jones Bus Info Svcs Group PO Box 300 Princeton NJ 08543-0300

GROSSMAN, ANNE CHOTZINOFF, archivist, translator; b. N.Y.C., Feb. 21, 1930; d. Samuel and Pauline (Heifetz) Chotzinoff; m. Herbert Grossman, Mar. 5, 1951; 1 child, Elizabeth Ellen. Grad., Katharine Gibbs Sch., N.Y.C., 1948. Assoc. producer NBC-TV Opera, N.Y.C., 1949-52, 54-57; translater NBC-TV, N.Y.C., 1964; editor S.N. Behrman's People in a Diary, N.Y.C., 1972; lit. asst. to Irene Mayer Selznick, N.Y.C., 1975-87; co-editor Kitty (by Kitty Carlisle Hart), N.Y.C., 1984-89; archivist for Vladimir and Wanda Toscanini Horowitz, N.Y.C., 1989—. Translator operas Tosca, Madame Butterfly, Merry Wives of Windsor, Falstaff, Lucia di Lammermoor, La Serva Padrona, also others; numerous lieder of Schubert, Schumann, Beethoven, Mozart, also others. Jewish. Home: 20 Ocean Walk West Gilgo Beach New York NY 11702

GROSSMAN, FRED, financial company executive; b. N.Y.C., Sept. 25, 1921; s. Andrew and Lena Grossman; m. Shirley Glickman, June 19, 1949; children: Lynn, Steven. BS, NYU, 1949. CPA, N.Y. Acct. S.D. Leidesdorf & Co., N.Y.C., 1951-60; exec. v.p. Starwood Corp., N.Y.C., 1961-84; pres. F.G. Asset Mgmt. Inc., N.Y.C., 1984—. 1st lt. USAF, 1942-46, PTO. Mem. AICPA, N.Y. Soc. CPAs. Office: FG Asset Mgmt Inc 635 Madison Ave # 16 New York NY 10022-1009

GROSSMAN, JERROLD B., pharmaceuticals executive; b. N.Y.C., Oct. 23, 1947. BA, Fairleigh Dickinson U., 1969, MBA, 1973; D of Profl. Studies in Bus. Mgmt., Pace U., 1989. Gen. mgr. Nomis Svc. Stores, Bklyn., 1969-72; fin. analyst Irving Trust Co., N.Y.C., 1972-74; sr. adminstr. Greater N.Y. blood program ARC, N.Y.C., 1974-79; dir. mktg., sales and biologics resources N.Y. Blood Ctr., 1979-85; v.p., dir. mktg. N.Am. Immuno-U.S., Inc., N.Y.C., 1985-90; pres. Genesis Bio-Pharm., Inc., Tenafly, N.J., 1990—. Author: Overview of Plasma Derivative, 1984, (ency. sect.) Impact of Technology on the Plasma Derivative Industry, 1989, Blood and Plasma Industry, 1992. Bd. dirs. Temple Sinai Bergen County. Sgt. N.Y. Nat. Guard, 1969-75. Mem. Am. Assn. Blood Banks.

GROSSMAN, MICHAEL ROSS, surgeon, podiatrist; b. Phila., June 16, 1962; s. Robert and Joy Carol (Marton) G. BA in Biol Basis of Behavior, U. Pa., 1985; BS, DPM, William Scholl Coll., Chgo., 1990. Pvt. practice Phila.; adj. faculty Pa. Coll. Podiatric Medicine, Phila., 1991—. Contbr. articles to profl. jours. Mem. Pa. Podiatric Med. Assn., Am. Podiatric Med. Assn., Am. Podiatric Med. Postgrad. Assn., Fedn. Allied Jewish Appeal, Alzheimer's Assn. Greater Phila. Home: 200 Tower Ln Narberth PA 19072-1128

GROSSMAN, RICHARD LESLIE, bank consultant; b. N.Y.C., Oct. 8, 1948; s. Louis and Sylvia (Wallach) G.; m. Helene Blass, June 7, 1970;

children: Stephen Gregory, Jessica Eileen. BA, Hunter Coll., 1970; MBA, NYU, 1976. Cert. cash mgr. Sr. analyst N.Y. Blue Cross, N.Y.C., 1970-74; asst. v.p. Nat. Bank N. Am., N.Y.C., 1974-81, European Am. Bank, N.Y.C., 1981-85, Fidelity Bank, Phila., 1985-88; cons. Earnings Performance Group Inc., Short Hills, N.J., 1988—. Asst. den leader Boy Scouts Am., Holland, Pa., 1988-89. Recipient appreciation certs. Boy Scouts Am., 1989. Mem. Nat. Treasury Mgmt. Assn. Republican. Jewish. Home: 31 Forrest Dr Southampton PA 18966-2155 Office: Earnings Performance Group 830 Morris Tpke Short Hills NJ 07078-2675

GROSSMAN, STEPHEN LEWIN, administrative law judge; b. Newark, Dec. 2, 1935; s. Harold and Eve Rae (Levine) G.; m. Ann Elisabeth Marks, July 28, 1960; children: Michael W., Kenneth L., Helane M. BA, Vanderbilt U., 1957; JD, Columbia U., 1962. Bar: D.C. 1963. Atty. ICC, Washington, 1962-65; pvt. practice law, 1965-66; supervisory atty. ICC, Washington, 1966-70, mem. rev. bd., 1970-72; asst. gen. counsel U.S. Dept. Transp., Washington, 1972-75; adminstrv. law judge FERC, Washington, 1975—; faculty advisor Nat. Jud. Coll., Reno, Nev., 1984; vis. lectr. Govt. Law Ctr., Albany Law Sch., 1991. Mem. bd. editors Judge's Jour., 1989-92. Mem. adv. com. Montgomery County Master Plan, 1989, 90; chmn. Wheaton (Md.) Revitalization Strategy Com., 1983—. Capt. USNR, 1957-59, 85, mem. Res. ret. Mem. ABA, Fed. Adminstrv. Law Judges Conf. (pres. 1990-92). Home: 1617 Arbor View Rd Silver Spring MD 20902-1408 Office: FERC 825 N Capitol St NE Washington DC 20002-4277

GROSSMANN, ELIHU DAVID, chemical engineering educator; b. Phila., Nov. 29, 1927; s. Julius and Sophie R. (Stern) G.; m. Doris Martin, Dec. 19, 1954; children: Lois D., Mark M., Michele. BSChemE, Drexel U., 1951, MSChemE, 1956; PhD, U. Pa., 1965. Chem. engring. instr. Drexel U., Phila., 1952-56, from asst. to assoc. prof. chem. engring., 1956-81, prof. chem. engring., 1981—; cons. U.S. Army, 1961-83, numerous indsl. cos., 1952—; expert witness for law and ins. firms, 1961—. Co-author: Farm & Field Wastes, 1974; contbr. articles to profl. jours. Patentee in field. Bd. dirs. Jewish Campus Activities Bd., Phila., 1974—; bd. overseers Gratz Coll., 1992; speaker Lower Merion (Pa.) Sch. Dist. Resource Group, 1970-76. With U.S. Army, 1946-47. Mem. AAUP, Am. Soc. Engr. Edn. (Young Engr. Tchrs. Paper Contest award 1957), Am. Chem. Soc., Am. Inst. Chem. Engrs., B'nai Brith, Tau Beta Pi, Sigma Xi, Phi Lambda Upsilon.

GROSSO, GINO, psychiatrist; b. Turin, Italy, Aug. 29, 1948; came to U.S., 1956; s. Nicholas Andrea and Mary (D'Amico) G.; m. Eileen Wood, Feb. 3, 1979; children: Amanda, Susannah. BA cum laude, Syracuse U., 1971; MD, SUNY Health Scis. Ctr., Bklyn., 1975. Cert. adult psychiatry, forensic psychiatry, geriatric psychiatry, sleep disorders medicine; accredited clin. polysomnographer (physician sleep specialist). Resident in psychiatry Hosp. of U. Pa., Phila., 1976-79; fellow in forensic psychiatry Hosp. of U. Pa., 1978; pvt. practice Phila.; med. assoc. Forensic Neuropsychiat. Office of Cecil Harris, DO, DSc, Ltd, Phila., 1985-91; pvt. practice Exton, Pa., 1991—; attending psychiatrist Einstein Med. Ctr., Phila., 1979-85, dir. med. student teaching program, 1979-82; cons. Phila. Ct. Common Pleas, 1979-88; med. dir. Phila. Mental Health Clinic, 1979-87; fellow sleep medicine Med. Coll. Pa., Phila., 1985-87; med. dir. emergency psychiatry screening program Helene Fuld Med. Ctr., Trenton, 1988-92; dir. psychiat. peer rev. dept. TAO, Inc. (subs. Blue Cross-Blue Shield), 1992—. Bd. dirs., sec. New Horizons Montessori Sch., ft. Washington, Pa., 1988-91. Mem. Am. Psychiat. Assn., Am. Sleep Disorders Assn., Am. Acad. Psychiatry and Law, Acad. Psychosomatic Medicine, Am. Geriatrics Soc., Am. Assn. for Geriatric Psychiatry.

GROSSVOGEL, DAVID I., writer, educator; b. San Francisco, June 19, 1925; s. Rene Gur and Ada (Bloom) Grossvogel; m. Anita Vidussoni (div.); children: Steven, Deborah; m. Jill Elyse Jaross. BA, U. Calif., Berkeley, 1949; cert. d'univ., U. Grenoble, France, 1950; MA, Columbia U., 1951, PhD, 1954. Instr. Columbia U., N.Y.C., 1954-56; asst. prof. Harvard U., Cambridge, Mass., 1956-60; assoc. prof. Cornell U., Ithaca, N.Y., 1960-64, prof., 1964-70, Goldwin Smith prof. comparative lit. and romance studies, 1970—. Author: The Self-Conscious Stage, 1958, Four Playwrights & a Postscript, 1962, Limits of the Novel, 1968, Divided We Stand, 1970, Mystery and Its Fictions, 1979, Dear Ann Landers, 1987; co-author: Changing Channels: America in TV Guide, 1992; editor: Diacritics, 1971-76. With USAF, 1943-45. Fulbright fellow, 1949-50, Fulbright Postdoctoral fellow, 1959-60, Guggenheim fellow, 1964-65. Mem. Phi Beta Kappa. Office: Cornell U 288 Goldwin Smith Ithaca NY 14853

GROSSVOGEL, JILL ELYSE, graphic designer, French art researcher; b. N.Y.C., Feb. 23, 1945; d. Jesse Jacobs and Blossom Hope (Rubenstein) Spitz; m. Richard Jaross, 1966 (div. 1971); m. David I. Grossvogel, June 22, 1974. Diplome, Faculté d'Aix-Marseilles, 1965; BA, Hunter Coll., 1966, MA, 1970; PhD, Cornell U., 1974. Graphic designer Harper & Row Pubs., N.Y.C., 1966-69; curator SUNY-Binghamton Art Mus., 1977-80; graphic designer Martin & Grossvogel, Ithaca, 1984—; freelance cons. art museums, 1979-91; teaching assoc. div. modern lang. Cornell U., Ithaca, 1990—; instr. Ithaca Coll., 1974-75; instr. dept. communication Cornell U., 1984-85; cons. Musée de Pont-Aven, France, 1981-91. Author: Claude Emile Schuffenecker: Margin and Image, 1979, Form and Fragmentation in French Art from Neo-Classicism to Neo-Impressionism, 1991. Recipient Gold award Strathmore Paper Co., 1988, 89; SUNY-Binghamton Found. travel grantee, Brittany and Paris, 1979; N.Y. State Coun. on Arts fellow Met. Mus., 1978-80. Democrat. Jewish. Home: 247 Valley Rd Ithaca NY 14850-6152

GROSVENOR, GILBERT MELVILLE, journalist, educator, business executive; b. Washington, May 5, 1931; s. Melville Bell and Helen (Rowland) G.; m. Donna C. Kerkam, June 16, 1961 (div.); children: Gilbert Hovey II, Alexandra Rowland; m. Wiley Jarman, June 1, 1979; 1 child, Graham Dabney. BA, Yale U., 1954; D Pub. Service (hon.), George Washington U., 1983; LHD (hon.), U. Colo., 1983, Curry Coll., 1984; LLD (hon.), Coll. Wooster (Ohio), 1983; LHD (hon.), William and Mary Coll., 1987, Miami U., Oxford, Ohio, 1988, Syracuse U., 1989, R.I. Coll., 1991. With Nat. Geog. Soc., 1954—, trustee, 1966—, v.p., 1966-80, assoc. editor, 1967-70, editor, 1970-80, pres., 1980—, chmn. bd., 1987—; bd. dirs. White House Hist. Assn., Conservation Fund, Chevy Chase Bank, FSB, Chesapeake & Potomac Telephone Co., Charles Allmon Trsut, Inc., Marriott Corp., Ethyl Corp.; former fellow Yale Corp. Trustee Nat. Wildflower Rsch. Ctr., Fed. City Coun., B.F. Saul Real Estate Trust, N.Y. Zool. Soc.; past vice chmn. Pres.'s Commn. Ams. Outdoors.; chmn., found. bd. Alexander Graham Bell Assn. for Deaf; bd. dirs. Am. Farmland Trust; bd. visitors Coll. William and Mary; ann. corp. mem. Children's Hosp.; mem. Pres.'s Commn. Environ. Quality, Washington Cathedral chpt. Recipient Editor of Year award Nat. Press Photographers Assn., 1975; Disting. Achievement award U. So. Calif. Sch. Journalism and Alumni Assn., 1977. Mem. Assn. Am. Geographers, Explorers Club, Newcomen Soc., Alfalfa Club, Alibi Club, Cosmos Club, Chevy Chase Club (Md.). Office: Nat Geographic Soc 17th & M Sts NW Washington DC 20036

GROTH, RICHARD HENRY, chemistry educator, consultant; b. New Britain, Conn., Oct. 14, 1929; s. Henry and Nellie Emma (Otterbein) G.; m. Joyce Lorraine Weaver, June 6, 1959; children: Eileen Lesley, Kathleen Joyce. BS, Cen. Conn. State U., 1951; PhD, Ohio State U., 1956. Postdoctoral assoc. Duke U., Durham, N.C., 1956-57; from asst. prof. to assoc. prof. U. Hartford, Conn., 1957-70; from assoc. prof. to prof. Cen. Conn. State U., New Britain, 1970—, dept. chmn., 1975-84; cons. Pratt & Whitney Aircraft, East Hartford, Conn., 1961—, Conn. State Police Forensic Sci. Lab., Meriden, Conn., 1983—. Author: Chemistry and Environment, 1974, Fundamentals of Chemistry, 1978; contbr. numerous articles to profl. jours.; patentee gels and their creation. Chmn. Cons. Com. for Adult Edn., Meriden, 1977—, Bruce Mahan Scholarship Com., New Britain, 1983—. Summer Insts. on Sci. Edn. grantee Conn. State Dept. Higher Edn., 1985-89, Instrumentation grantee Conn. State Dept. Edn., 1990. Fellow AAAS; mem. AAUP, Am. Chem. Soc. (sect. chair 1970-71, mem. exec. bd. 1960-82). Home: 75 Coe Ave Meriden CT 06450-3854 Office: Cen Conn State U Copernicus Hall New Britain CT 06050

GROTTA, SANDRA BROWN, interior designer; b. Detroit, June 7, 1934; m. Louis William Grotta, Sept. 8, 1955. Student U. Mich., 1952-55, N.Y. Sch. Interior Design, 1964. Pres. S.G. Interiors, New Vernon, N.J., 1964—. Mem. Am. Soc. Interior Designers.

GROVE, MICHAEL JAMES, management and marketing consultant; b. Chgo., June 21, 1958; s. James Frederick and Judith Elaine (Prater) G. BS cum laude, Boston U., 1989, MBA, 1991. Founder, cons., dir. ops. The Consulting Collaborative, Inc., Boston, 1980-89; founder Global TradeNet, Inc., Boston, 1992—; bd. dirs. Ctr. for Art Therapies. Dir. telemarketing and fund raising L. DiCara for Mayor campaign, Boston, 1983; bd. dirs. Ctr. for Creative Art Therapies, Inc., Boston, 1986-89. Recipient Alumni award Boston U., 1989, MBA scholar, 1989. Mem. New Eng. Nonprofit Mgmt. Assn. (mktg. and membership coord. 1986-88), Phi Beta Delta. Address: PO Box 270 B/U Sta Boston MA 02215

GROVER, JAMES ROBB, chemist, editor; b. Klamath Falls, Oreg., Sept. 16, 1928; s. James Richard and Marjorie Alida (Van Groos) G.; m. Barbara Jean Ton, Apr. 14, 1957; children: Jonathan Robb, Patricia Jean. BS summa cum laude, U. Wash., Seattle, 1952; PhD, U. Calif., Berkeley, 1958. Rsch. assoc. Brookhaven Nat. Lab., Upton, N.Y., 1957-59, assoc. chemist, 1959-63, chemist, 1963-67, chemist with tenure, 1967-77, sr. chemist, 1978—; cons. Lawrence Livermore (Calif.) Nat. Lab., 1962; assoc. editor Ann. Revs., Inc., Palo Alto, Calif., 1967-77; vis. prof. Inst. for Molecular Sci., Okazaki, Japan, 1986-87; vis. scientist Max-Planck Inst. für Strömungsforschung, Göttingen, Fed. Republic Germany, 1975-76. Contbr. numerous articles to profl. jours. With USN, 1946-48. Mem. Am. Chem. Soc. (chmn. nuclear chemistry and tech. 1989), Am. Phys. Soc., Triple Nine Soc., Sigma Xi, Phi Beta Kappa, Phi Lambda Upsilon, Zeta Mu Tau, Pi Mu Epsilon. Libertarian. Presbyterian. Home: 20 Brewster Hill Rd East Setauket NY 11733-1426 Office: Brookhaven Nat Lab Dept Chemistry Upton NY 11973-5000

GROVER, MARK DONALD, computer scientist; b. Augusta, Maine, July 12, 1955; s. Donald William and Aletha D. (Wells) G. BA, U. Fla., 1976; MS, Northwestern U., 1978, PhD, 1982. Instr. Northwestern U., Evanston, Ill., 1978-81; mem. tech. staff TRW Def. Systms, Redondo Beach, Calif., Fairfax, Va., 1981-85; sr. computer scientist Advanced Decision Systems, Arlington, Va., 1985-89; prin. software engr. Oberon Software Inc., Cambridge, Mass., 1990—; program chmn. Nat. Symbolics User Group Conf., Washington, 1986; presenter to confs. in field. Contbr. articles to sci. jours. Vol. cert. emergency med. technician. Mem. IEEE, Assn. for Computing Machinery, Am. Assn. for Artificial Intelligence, NRA (life), Phi Beta Kappa, Tau Beta Pi. Office: Oberon Software Inc One Memorial Dr Cambridge MA 02142

GROVER, ROBINSON ALLEN, philosophy educator; b. N.Y.C., Feb. 15, 1936; s. Allen and Beatrice (Beard) G.; m. Nancy Dow, Jan. 1980. BA, Yale Coll., 1958; MA, Brown U., 1961, PhD, 1969; M of Legal Studies, Yale U., 1976. Asst. prof. U. Conn., Torrington, 1969-76, assoc. prof., 1976—, dir. Torrington campus, 1982-88. Mem. AAUP, Am. Philos. Assn., Internat. Hobbes Assn. Home: PO Box 633 Simsbury CT 06070-0633 Office: U Conn Torrington Campus University Dr Torrington CT 06790-2619

GROVER, WILLIAM JOSEPH, insurance consulting executive, safety engineer; b. Springfield, Mass., Sept. 5, 1948; s. William Joseph and Alma Marie (Rioux) G.; m. Nancy Faye Buchanan, Oct 23, 1976; children: Jennifer L. Collins, Jill E. Collins. BS in Indsl. Mgmt., U. Lowell, 1970. Sr. loss control rep. Aetna Life & Casualty, Albany, N.Y., 1970-74; loss control supr. Reliance Ins. Co., Canandaigua, N.Y., 1974-76; dir. casualty loss control Reliance Ins. Co., Phila., 1977-81, asst. sec. loss control, 1981-84, sec. loss control, 1984-86; v.p. Controlled Risk Svcs., Thorofare, N.J., 1986-89, Creative Risk Svcs., Berlin, N.J., 1989—; constrn. safety com. Am. Ins. Svcs. Group, N.Y.C., 1977-86; security com., 1979-86. Mem. Am. Soc. Safety Engrs. Office: Creative Risk Svcs Inc 272 S Whitehorse Pike PO Box 40 Berlin NJ 08009-0040

GROVES, HURST KOHLER, lawyer, oil company executive; b. Indpls., Mar. 30, 1941; s. John Hurst and Mary Ellen (Sisco) G.; m. Marilyn Anne Woislaw, Nov. 17, 1967; children: Jennifer, Catherine. AB, Princeton U., 1963; JD, U. Mich., 1967. Bar: Ind. 1967, N.Y. 1968. Assoc. Cravath, Swaine & Moore, N.Y.C. and Paris, 1967-77; with Mobil Oil Corp. and subs. cos., 1977—; sr. counsel Mobil Oil Corp., N.Y.C., 1977-80; gen. counsel Mobil Sekiyu K.K., Tokyo, 1980-84; sr. counsel Mobil South Inc., N.Y.C., 1984-88; v.p. Mobil Sales & Supply Corp., N.Y.C., 1988-90, Fairfax, Va., 1990-91; asst. gen. counsel internat. sales and supply Mobil Oil Corp., N.Y.C., 1988-90, Fairfax, Va., 1990-91; asst. gen. counsel exploration and producing div., 1991—. Vice chmn., treas. U.S.-Japan Trade Study Group, Tokyo, 1983-84; bd. dirs. Prospect Park West Assn., Bklyn. Fellow Am. Bar Found.; mem. ABA (chmn. energy law com. of internat. law and practice sect. 1988—), Assn. of Bar of City of N.Y., Internat. Bar Assn., Internat. Law Assn., Am. C. of C. in Japan (chmn. investments com. 1982, bd. govs. 1984), Tokyo Am. Club, Heights Casino, Lawrence Beach Club, Columbia Club, Princeton Club. Episcopalian. Office: Mobil Oil Corp 3225 Gallows Rd Fairfax VA 22037-0002

GROW, ROBERT THEODORE, economist, association executive; b. Newton, Mass., Aug. 14, 1948; s. William and Lempi (Kangas) G.; m. Anita L. Capps, Nov. 20, 1982; 1 child, Margaret Celia. BS magan cum laude, U. Mass., 1970, MS, 1973. Regional econs. Southeastern Va. Planning Dist. Commn., Norfolk, 1973-80; dir. met. coord. Met. Washington (D.C.) Coun. Govts., 1980-85; exec. dir. Washington/Balt. Regional Assn., Washington, 1985—; chmn. met. com. Capital Area chpt. Am. Planning Assn., Washington, 1988-89. Mem. Md. Indsl. Developers Assn., Va. Econs. Devel. Assn., Balt. Econ. Soc. (mem. steering com. 1992), Phi Kappa Phi. Office: Washington/Balt Reg Assn 1129 20th St NW Ste 200 Washington DC 20036

GRUBB, FARLEY WARD, economic history educator; b. Kennewick, Wash., Sept. 14, 1954; s. Forrest Ward Grubb and Bernice Edna (Schmale) Sadler. BA, U. Wash., 1977; AM in Econs., U. Chgo., 1981, PhD in Econs., 1984. Foreman Olympic Prefabricators, Seattle, 1976-78; lectr. Roosevelt U., Chgo., 1982-83, U. Chgo., 1983; asst. prof. econ. history U. Del., Newark, 1983-88, assoc. prof., 1988—. Contbr. articles to profl. jours. Mem. Am. Econ. Assn., Econ. History Assn., Cliometrics Soc. Republican. Office: U Del Dept Econs Newark DE 19715

GRUBER, ARNOLD, meteorologist; b. N.Y.C., Feb. 28, 1940; s. Leon and Esther (Lieber) G.; m. Phyllis E. Rubin, Aug. 11, 1962; children: Suzanne L., Martin H. BS, CUNY, 1962; MS, Fla. State U., 1964, PhD, 1968. Rsch. scientist Boeing Co., Seattle, 1969-70; rsch. meteorologist NOAA, U.S. Dept. Commerce, Washington, 1970-76, supr. meteorologist, 1976—; vis. prof. U.S. Naval Acad., Annapolis, Md., 1990-91; mem. various profl. coms. Author: From Weather Vanes to Satellites: An Introduction to Meteorology, 1983; also articles. Fellow Am. Meterol. Soc. (chair com. on hurricanes and tropical meteorology 1979-81), Am. Geophys. Union, Sigma Xi. Office: NOAA/NESDIS World Weather Bldg Washington DC 20233

GRUBER, BARBARA MIKLOS, accountant; b. Bridgeport, Conn., July 10, 1946; d. Louis and Helen (Karcsinski) Miklos; m. Jon Olsen Gruber, Nov. 16, 1974; children: Jeffrey Charles, Kevin Jon. BS, U. Bridgeport, 1971. CPA, Pa. Staff acct. Cooper's and Lybrand, New Haven, 1971-74; acctg. mgr. Montgomery Bar Assn., Norristown, Pa., 1984-87; law office adminstr. McTighe, Weiss, Norristown, 1987-88; cons. Collegeville, Pa., 1989—. Home: 5013 Coldsprings Dr Collegeville PA 19426-3410

GRUBER, DOUGLAS LLOYD, small business owner; b. Bklyn., Apr. 2, 1920; s. Henry Jr. and Adeline Helen (Long) G.; m. Ruth Mary Manecke, Sept. 23, 1953 (div. Sept. 1979); children: Mary Elizabeth, Cathryn; m. Priscilla Jane Hubbert, Sept. 29, 1984. BA, Columbia U.-Columbia Coll., 1941, MS, 1942. Assoc. editor The N.Y. Sales Exec. Mag., N.Y.C., 1946-49; mng. editor McGraw-Hill Corp., N.Y.C., 1950-55; pres., owner All-Tame Animals, Inc., 1956-88, G. Lloyd Douglas, Inc., 1988—. Lt. comdr. USN, 1942-46, ETO, PTO. Republican. Episcopalian. Home: 2219 Westminster Manor Ln Sun City Center FL 33573

GRUBER, ROSALIND H., counseling psychologist; b. Bronx, N.Y., Feb. 10, 1943; d. Lazarus L. and Beatrice (England) G.; B.A. cum laude, SUNY, New Paltz, 1974; M.A., Suffolk U., 1978. Nat. Cert. Counselor; lic. clin. social worker. Sch. registrar Assn. Help Retarded Children, N.Y.C., 1968-70; counselor Neighborhood Youth Corps, Poughkeepsie, N.Y., 1971-73; liaison Govt. Subsidized Housing, Cambridge, Mass., 1975-77; dir., counselor Aradia Counseling, Boston, 1978-91; ptnr.-owner real estate investment co., 1982—; producer C3 TV, South Yarmouth, Mass., 1990—; dir., owner Clearview Counseling, Brookline, Mass., 1991—; student supr. Suffolk U., Lesley Coll., Boston U. Mem. Nat. Assn. Social Workers, Am. Personnel and Guidance Assn., Assn. Humanistic Edn. and Devel., Mass. Mental Health Counselors Assn., Assn. Women in Psychology, U.S. Power Squaron. Home: PO Box 1056 Barnstable MA 02630 Office: 308A Harvard St Brookline MA 02146 also: 420 Marstons Ln Cummaquid MA 02637 also: 41 Babbling Brook Rd Centerville MA 02632

GRUENBERG, ELLIOT LEWIS, electronics company executive; b. N.Y.C., Mar. 16, 1918; s. Lewis and Sadie (Schoenbrun) G.; m. Ruth Frankel, Apr. 19, 1947. BEE, CCNY, 1938. Engr., inspector U.S. Signal Corps Line Inspection, Newark, N.J., 1939-43; quality control mgr. Tech. Devices, Roseland, N.J., 1943-48; sr. engr. J.H. Bunnell, Bklyn., 1948-51, Freed Radio, N.Y.C., 1951; sr. engr., mgr. W.L. Maxson, N.Y.C., 1951-58; sr. engring. mgr. Fed. Systems div. IBM, Bethesda, Md., 1958-73; cons. West New York, N.J., 1974-79; chmn. BroadCom, Inc., Secaucus, N.J., 1979-88, also bd. dirs.; chmn., pres. CompFax Corp., West N.Y., N.J., 1988—. Editor: Handbook of Telemetry and Remote Control, 1967; inventor SYNAPZ Microwave Communications, radar, electronic telecommunications, telemetry, BGET Secure Communications, OTIC Digital Transmission Bandwidth Compression; patentee in field; contbr. articles to profl. jours. Fellow Am. Inst. Aeronautics and Astronautics (assoc.); mem. IEEE (sr. life mem. 1940—). Democrat. Mem. Ethical Culture. Home: 6040 Blvd 30G E West New York NJ 07093-3860

GRUENBERG, MARK JONATHAN, correspondent; b. Chgo., Jan. 17, 1953; s. Robert and Ruth (Schwartz) G. BA, U. Chgo., 1975. Writer profiles The Congress Project, Washington, 1972; editor in chief Chgo. Maroon, 1973-74; corr. Chgo. Daily News, 1973-75; researcher Congl. Quarterly, Washington, 1975-79; Washington columnist Ill. Issues Mag., 1977-79; reporter Middletown (N.Y.) Times Herald Record, 1979-81, Port Jervis Bur. chief, 1980-81, dep. editor editorial, 1981; Washington corr. Ottaway News Svc., 1981—. Bd. trustees Temple Micah, 1984-86. Recipient award of excellence N.Y. State Pubs. Assn., 1981, 83. Mem. Westchester Bridge Assn., Regional Reporters Assn. (bd. dirs. 1990—), Chgo. Daily News Alumni Assn. Jewish. Home: 4000 Cathedral Ave NW Washington DC 20016-5249 Office: Ottaway News Svc 1025 Connecticut Ave NW Washington DC 20036-5405

GRUFFERMAN, SEYMOUR, medical educator, researcher; b. N.Y.C., Nov. 29, 1937; s. Leo and Claire (Eisdorfer) G.; m. Sue Young Sook Kimm, Dec. 23, 1967. BS, CUNY, 1960; MD, SUNY, Syracuse, 1964; MPH, Harvard U., 1968, MS, 1974, DrPH, 1979. Diplomate Nat. Bd. Med. Examiners, Am. Bd. Pediatrics. Intern U. Ill. Research and Ednl. Hosps., Chgo., 1964-65; resident in pediatrics N.Y. Hosp.-Cornell Med. Ctr., N.Y.C., 1965-67; asst. prof., head Dept. Pub. Health, Gondar (Ethiopia) Pub. Health Coll. Haile Selassie I U., 1971-73; epidemiologist Mgmt. Scis. for Health, Cambridge, Mass., 1973-74; teaching fellow, Dept. Epidemiology Harvard Sch. Pub. Health, Boston, 1975-76; asst. prof. pediatrics Duke U. Med. Ctr., Durham, N.C., 1976-81, assoc. prof., 1981-87, asst. prof. Dept. Medicine, chief Clin. Epidemiol. Div. Dept. Pediatrics, 1984-87; dir. Epidemiology and Biostats. Unit Comprehensive Cancer Ctr. Duke U., 1976-87, dir. Cancer Prevention and Control Program, also exec. com., 1981-87; attending pediatrician Duke U. Hosp., 1976-87; dir. epidemiology study program Sch. Medicine Duke U., 1978-87; prof. dept. epidemiology grad. sch. pub. health U. Pitts., 1987-88; prof. and chmn. dept. clin. epidemiology and preventive med. U. Pitts. Sch. Medicine, 1988—; adj. assoc. prof. dept. epidemiology Sch. Pub. Health, mem. grad. faculty U. N.C., Chapel Hill, 1982-87; mem. admissions com. Harvard Sch. Pub. Health, 1974-76, search com. for dir. internat. health program, 1975; mem. 3d yr. curriculum com. Sch. Medicine, Duke U., 1976-78; med. records com. Duke U. Med. Ctr., 1977-87, clin. cancer edn. program com., 1978-87; mem. intergroup Rhabdomoysarcoma study com., 1978—; mem. commn. on cancer N.C. Sec. Human Resources, 1979-81; pub. edn. com. N.C. div. Am. Cancer Soc., 1984-87; mem. sci. com. Nat. Coun. on Radiation Protection & Measurements, 1985-89; ad hoc mem. Epidemiology and Disease Control Study Sect. NIH, 1978, chmn. epidemiology and tech. transfer subcom. of AIDS rsch. rev. com., 1987-91; mem. numerous spl. rev. and ad hoc coms., participant workshops, confs. Nat. Cancer Inst., NIH, Nat. Inst. Allergy and Infectious Diseases; cons. Research Triangle Inst., N.C., 1977-78, Burroughts Wellcome Co., 1979-87, Internat. Agy. for Rsch. on Cancer, worldwide, 1981-90, tropical disease rsch. program WHO, 1981, Rockefeller Found., 1982, Plough, Inc., Memphis, 1985—; invited lectr. Assn. Tchrs. Preventive Medicine, 1982, M.D. Anderson Hosp. and Tumor Inst., Houston, 1982, Leukemia, Soc. Am., 1984. Reviewer Jour. Clin. Epidemiology, Jour. Nat. Cancer Inst., Am. Jour. Epidemiology, New Eng. Jour. Medicine, others; contbr. articles to profl. jours. Served to maj. USAF, 1968-71. Grantee NIH, 1974-75, 77-79, 77-80, 80-83, 80-85, 83-85, 86-88, 87-88, 87-92, Dept. HHS, 1989—, Am. Family Corp., 1980-85, A.W. Mellon Found., 1981-84, 85-87; Individual Rsch. fellow NIH; recipient Preventive Oncology Acad. award Nat. Cancer Inst., 1980-85. Fellow Am. Coll. Epidemiology; mem. Am. Assn. Cancer Edn., Am. Assn. Cancer Rsch., Am. Soc. Preventive Oncology, Children's Cancer Study Group, Pediatric Oncology Group, Soc. Epidemiol. Rsch. (student prize paper award 1979), Dandie Dinmont Terrier of Am. Home: 432 Morewood Ave Pittsburgh PA 15213-1814 Office: U Pitts Sch Medicine M-200 Scaife Hall Pittsburgh PA 15261

GRUHL, ANDREA MORRIS, librarian; b. Ponca City, Okla., Dec. 9, 1939; d. Luther Oscar and Hazel Evangeline (Anderson) Morris; m. Werner Mann Gruhl, July 10, 1965; children: Sonja Krista, Diana Krista. B.A., Wesleyan Coll., 1961; M.L.S., U. Md., 1968; postgrad., Johns Hopkins U., 1970-71, U. Md., 1968, 71-73. Tchr. Broward County, Fla., Dept. Def. Montgomery County (Md.), 1961-66; libr. Prince Georges County (Md.) Pub. Libr., 1966-68, 81-83, U. Md., College Park, 1970-72; art history researcher Joseph Alsop, Washington, 1972-74; libr. Howard County Pub. Libr., Columbia, Md., 1969-70, 74-79; European exch. staff Libr. of Congress, Washington, 1982-86; cataloger fed. documents GPO, Washington, 1986—; mem. women's program adv. com., processing dept. rep. Libr. of Congress, 1983-86, mem. ofcl. del. to Internat. Fedn. Libr. Assns. ann. conf., Munich, 1983, Chgo., 1985; state del. White House Conf. on Librs., 1978, 90. Indexer, editor: Learning Vacations, 3d edit., 1980; LCPA Index to Libr. of Congress Info. Bull., 1984. Trustee Howard County Community Coll., 1989—, Howard County Pub. Libr., Columbia, Md., 1979-87; publ. chmn. LWV of Howard County, Md., 1974; citizen's rep. for Howard County and exec. bd. Balt. Regional Planning Council Libr. Com., 1976-79; Friends of the Libr., Howard County, Md., pres., 1976; vol. Nat. Gallery of Art Libr., Washington, 1978-80. Mem. ALA (mem. trustee assn. 1982-87, catologing sect. 1988—, govt. documents roundtable 1988—, fed. librs. roundtable, internat. rels. roundtable), Assn. Libr. Collections and Tech. Svcs. of ALA, Art Librs. Soc. N. Am. (coord. mems. publ. exhbn. 1980-82), Libr. Congress Profl. Assn. (coord. ann. staff art show 1982, 83, chmn. libr. sci. group 1985-87), Libr. Congress Am. Fedn. State County and Mcpl. Employees Union 1477 (program chmn. 1984-86), Md. Libr. Assn. (pres. trustee div. 1982-83), Assn. Community Coll. Trustees, Md. Assn. Community Coll. Trustees (sec. 1991-92). Democrat. Lutheran. Home: 5990 Jacobs Ladder Columbia MD 21045-3817 Office: Govt Printing Office Washington DC 20401

GRUMER, EUGENE LAWRENCE, oil company executive; b. N.Y.C., May 25, 1940; s. Joseph and Ruth (Vermus) G.; m. Susan Kay Moldavi, June 13, 1964 (div. 1982); children: Sondra, Elliott, Warren; m. Diana Karsenty, June 24, 1984. BS in Fuel Tech., Pa. State U., 1961, BSChemE, 1962; MSChemE, MIT, 1964, postgrad., 1965. Registered profl. engr., Tex. Rsch. engr. Celanese Chem. Co., Corpus Christi, Tex., 1965-67; sr. process analysis engr. Celanese Chem. Co., Corpus Christi, 1969-70; econs. engr. Celanese Rsch. Co., Summit, N.J., 1967-69; mgr. ops., planning and econs. Hess Oil Virgin Islands Corp., St. Croix, V.I., 1971-83; adminstrv. asst., process engr. Amerada Hess Corp., Woodbridge, N.J., 1983-86, coord. planning and ref. econs., 1990—; mgr. econs. and planning Amerada Hess Corp., Port Reading, N.J., 1986-90. Scholarship Eastern Gas and Fuel Assn., 1957; fellowship MIT, 1962. Mem. Am. Assn. of Cost Engrs. (local dir., cert.), Am. Chem. Soc., Am. Inst. Chem. Engrs., Phi Kappa Phi, Omicron Delta Kappa, Tau Beta Pi, Sigma Xi. Home: Maddaket 7 Scotch Plains NJ 07076 Office: Amerada Hess Corp 1 Hess Plz Woodbridge NJ 07095-1229

GRUNBERG, ROBERT LEON WILLY, nephrologist; b. Bucharest, Romania, July 23, 1940; came to U.S., 1972, naturalized, 1977; s. William A. and Isabelle L. (Rosen) G.; m. Donna M. Fishman, Oct. 19, 1975; children: Wendie I., Andrea B. MD, U. Orleans-Tours, France, 1969. Diplomate Am. Bd. Internal Medicine, Am. Bd. Nephrology. Intern, then resident in cardiology Vichy (France) Hosp., 1968-72; resident in internal medicine Albert Einstein Med. Ctr., Phila., 1972-74; fellow in nephrology-hypertension Hahnemann Univ. Hosp., Phila., 1974-76, sr. clin. instr. then asst. clin. prof. div. nephrology, 1976; pvt. practice medicine specializing in nephrology Allentown, Pa., 1976—; assoc. attending physician Allentown Hosp. (now Lehigh Valley Hosp.), St. Luke's Hosp., Bethlehem, Pa., Lehigh Valley Hosp. Ctr. (now Lehigh Valley Hosp.), Allentown; attending charge div. nephrology Easton (Pa.) Hosp.; courtesy staff Hahnemann Med. Coll. and Hosp.; dir. Renal Dialysis Ctr. at Easton (Pa.) Hosp., 1989. Fellow Am. Coll. of Physicians; mem. AMA (Physician's Recognition award 1976, 79, 82, 85, 88, 89-92), ACP, Pa. Med. Soc., Am. Soc. Nephrology, Am. Soc. Artificial Internal Organs, Internat. Soc. Hypertension, Internat. Soc. Nephrology, Assn. for Advancement Med. Instrumentation, Internat. Soc. for Peritoneal Dialysis, Nat. Kidney Found., N.Y. Acad. Scis. Office: 50 S 18th St Easton PA 18042-3912 also: 401 N 17th St Allentown PA 18104

GRUNBERGER, DEZIDER, biochemist, researcher; b. Kosice, Czechoslovakia, May 29, 1922; came to U.S., 1968; s. Louis and Janka (Gluck) G.; m. Marta Herman, Dec. 23, 1948; children—George, Ivan. M.Sc., U. Prague, 1950; Ph.D., Acad. Sci., Prague, 1956, D.Sc., 1968. Head dept. Acad. Sci., Prague, Czechoslovakia, 1956-64, head dept., 1965-68; asst. prof. George Washington U., Washington, 1964-65; prof. biochemistry and biophysics Columbia U., N.Y.C., 1968—; E. and J. Michaels prof. Weizmann Inst., Rehovot, Israel, 1983. Author: Molecular Biology of Mutagens and Carcinogens, 1983; editor: Mechanisms of Cellular Transformations by Carcinogenic Agents, 1987; assoc. editor: Pharmacology and Therapeutics Cancer Communications; contbr. 172 articles to profl. jours; U.S. patent for preparation and use of caffeic acid phenethyl ester. Leukemia Soc. U.S.A. scholar, 1972-77, Rockefeller Found. scholar, 1981; grantee NIH, EPA, Am. Cancer Soc. Mem. Am. Soc. Biol. Chemists, Am. Assn. Cancer Research, Am. Chem. Soc., Harvey Soc., N.Y. Acad. Sci., AAAS. Office: Columbia U 701 W 168th St New York NY 10032-2704

GRUNBLATT, HILDA RUTH, translator, editor; b. Bklyn., Mar. 20, 1922; d. Samuel and Anna (Robson) Waterman; m. Jacques Grunblatt, Nov. 27, 1947 (dec. Jan. 1989); children: Ellen Miriam, Jesse Elliott, Mark Henry. BA, Bklyn. Coll., 1943. Tchr. N.Y.C. Bd. of Edn., Bklyn., 1946-49; med. asst., bookkeeper Offices of Dr. Jacques Grunblatt, North Creek, N.Y., 1949-75; freelance co-translator and editor North Creek, 1981—. Editor, co-translator: Seven Hills, 1981, The Shattered Dream, 1989, Hells, 1991. Organizer, vol. Town of Johnsburg Headstart, Johnsburg, N.Y., 1962-73; vol. Lit. Vols. Am., Glens Falls, 1990—; bd. dirs. Warren County Planned Parenthood, Glens Falls, 1966-75, Adirondack Ctr. for the Arts, Blue Mountain Lake, N.Y., 1966-75, Warren County Homemaker Svc., Glens Falls, 1967-75. Recipient Golden Poet award World of Poetry, 1985, 87. Mem. AAUW, Temple Beth-El. Jewish. Home: PO Box 25 North Creek NY 12853

GRUNES, ROBERT LEWIS, engineering consulting firm executive; b. Bklyn., Aug. 15, 1941; s. Abe and Doris (Dicker) G.; m. Eleonora Grasselli, Oct. 14, 1972; children: Natalie, Daniel, Ian. BS in Engring., Poly. Inst. Bklyn., 1963, MS in Engring., 1965, PhD in Phys. Metallurgy, 1970. Registered profl. engr., N.Y., N.J., Pa. Engr. Pratt & Whitney div. United Aircraft Corp., East Hartford, Conn., 1963; rsch. fellow Poly. Inst. Bklyn., 1963-64, rsch. assoc., 1966-70; rsch. engr. Lewis Rsch. Ctr. NASA, Cleve., 1965; pres. R. L. Grunes & Assocs., Inc., N.Y.C., 1970—; mem. adj. faculty N.J. Inst. Tech., Newark, 1974-78. Author: Pollution Control Market and Industries, 1971; contbr. articles to profl. jours. 1st lt. CE U.S. Army, 1964-66. Mem. ASME, ASCE, ASTM, Metall. Soc. Office: R L Grunes & Assocs Inc 521 5th St New York NY 10017

GRUPPE, CHARLES CAMILLE, artist; b. N.Y.C., July 1, 1928; s. Paulo Mezdag and Camille Louise (Plasschaert) G.; divorced. BFA, Columbia U., 1954, MFA, 1955. Free-lance artist, U.S.A., Europe, 1960—. Numerous one-man shows, group shows in Boothbay Harbor, Maine, Stamford, Conn., Key West, Fla., Palm Beach, Fla., and Barcelona, Spain; represented in over 5,000 pvt. collections; workshops include Jupiter, Fla., Marathon, Fla., Greenwich, Conn., Oyster Bay, L.I., Hilton Head, S.C., 1991. With USAAF, 1946-47, PTO. Fulbright Found. fellow, 1957; Columbia U. fellow, 1958; Huntington Hartford Found. fellow, 1959. Mem. Nantucket Art Assn., North Shore Art Assn., Salmagundi Art Assn., Hudson Valley Art Assn., Silvermine Guild. Avocations: stamp collecting, travel. Home and Office: 3 Beaverbrook Rd PO Box 841 Lyme CT 06371

GRUSHOW, IRA, English educator; b. N.Y.C., Apr. 11, 1933; s. Asher and Sadie (Greenstein) G.; m. Jane Ducat, Aug. 1965; children: Alexander, Sophia. BA, CCNY, 1954; MA, Yale U., 1956, PHD, 1963. Instr. English Carnegie Inst. Tech., Pitts., 1960-62; instr. English Franklin & Marshall Coll., Lancaster, 1962-63, asst. prof., 1963-68, assoc. prof., 1968-85, prof., 1985-91, Alumni prof. English Belles Lettres and Lit., 1991—. Author: Imaginary Reminiscences of Sir Max Beerbohm, 1984; contbr. articles and revs. to profl. jours. Mem. AAUP, Am. Soc. 18th Century Studies, Modern Lang. Assn., Hist. Soc. Cocalico Valley (pres. 1984-86). Democrat. Jewish. Office: Franklin and Marshall Coll Lancaster PA 17604

GRUSON, HIROKO TSUBOTA, multinational search company executive, management consultant; b. Tokyo, Japan, Jan. 10, 1940; came to U.S., 1961; d. Midori and Matsu (Hayashi) Tsubota; m. Michael Gruson, July 11, 1964; children: Rudolf, Andreas, Sebastian, Matthias, Florian, Konrad. Student, Tsuda Coll., Tokyo, 1958-61; BA, Benedictine Coll., 1962; MSW, Columbia U., 1964; postgrad., F.U., Berlin, 1965-66; EdD, Columbia U., 1971. Borough dir. N.Y. Svc. for Orthopedically Handicapped, 1964-65; asst. prof. sociology CUNY, 1971-74; dep. chief personnel UN, N.Y.C., 1974-86; sr. v.p., mng. dir. Japan practice Boyden Internat., N.Y.C., 1986-89; mng. dir. multinat. exec. search A.T. Kearney Inc., N.Y.C., 1989-91; pres. Tsubota Gruson Multinational Exec. Search, N.Y.C., 1991—. Bd. dirs. 850 Park Ave Corp., N.Y.C., 1985-87. Recipient Mobilization for Youth award, 1963-64, YWCA The Class of 1988 Acad. of Women Achievers. Mem. Japan Soc., Asia Soc., Japanese C. of C., Nippon Club. Roman Catholic. Home and Office: 850 Park Ave New York NY 10021-1845

GRUSZKA, JAMES RICHARD, educational director; b. Buffalo, N.Y., Sept. 12, 1948; s. Richard Bernard and Jane Rita (Baginski) G.; m. Donna Lee Bartolone, MAr. 19, 1988; children: Kimberly Ann, Andrew Joseph. AS, Kemper Coll., 1968; BS, SUNY, Buffalo, 1987. Cert. dir. facilities mgmt. Advt. liaison Buffalo Courier Express, 1970-76; pipefitter, welder United Assn. Plumbers and Pipefitters, Niagara Falls, N.Y., 1976-85; tchr. Buffalo Pub. Schs., 1987-89; quality assurance engr. Cooper Industries, Turbo-Compressor Div., Buffalo, 1989-90; dir. facilities Amherst (N.Y.) Cen. Sch. Dist., 1990—. Maj. USAF, 1969—. Am. NRA (life), Inst. Plant Engrs., N.Y. State Assn. Supts. of Schs. Bldg. and Grounds, N.Y. State Militia Assn., Air Force Assn. (life), Experimental Aircraft Assn., Aircraft Owners and Pilots Assn. Home: 126 Brookdale Dr Williamsville NY 14221 Office: Amherst Cen Sch System 55 Kings Hwy Amherst NY 14226

GRUZLESKI, THOMAS FLOYD, engineering manager; b. Johnson City, N.Y., Oct. 3, 1945; s. Floyd Thomas and Lottie (Svarney) G.; m. Nancy Gail Wychules, Sept. 2, 1967; children: Jason Thomas, Audra Kristen, Laura Gail. BS in Aerospace Engring., Rensselaer Poly. Inst., 1967. Registered profl. engr., N.Y. With Link Flight Simulation Corp., Binghamton, N.Y., 1966-73; sr. engr. Link Flight Simulation Corp., Binghamton, 1973-80; gen. dept. mgr. Link Flight Simulation div. CAE Corp., Binghamton, 1988—; engring. cons. Mitsubishi Precision Co., Kamakura, Japan, 1969-70. League dir. So. Tier Hockey Assn., Endicott, N.Y., 1973-75; quartermaster Troop 236 parents com. Boy Scouts Am., Endwell, N.Y., 1986—. Mem. AIAA (sr., treas. 1986-88). Democrat. Episcopalian. Home: 453 Chrysler Rd Endicott NY 13760-1001 Office: Link Flight Simulation Div PO Box 1237 Binghamton NY 13902-1237

GRYCE, DAVID CONRAD, lawyer; b. Danbury, Conn., Jan. 16, 1955; s. Walter I. and Barbara Ann (Bacon) G.; m. Patricia Ann Brown, Aug. 13, 1983, 1 child, Julie Ann. BA, Brown U., 1977; JD, U. Denver, 1983. Bar: Colo. 1983, D.C. 1988, U.S. Dist. Ct. (Colo.) 1983, U.S. Ct. Appeals (10th cir.) 1983, U.S. Dist. Ct. D.C. 1989, U.S. Ct. Appeals (fed. and 5th cirs.) 1989. Assoc. Koransky, McCullough and Friedman, P.C., Denver, 1983-85; sole practice Evergreen and Lakewood, Colo., 1985-87; assoc. Mason, Fenwick & Lawrence, Washington, 1988-90, ptnr., 1991—. Mng. editor Intellectual Property Law Jour., 1990—. Named to Order of St. Ives, 1983. Mem. ABA, Assn. Univ. Tech. Mgrs., Colo. Bar Assn., Denver Bar Assn., Assn. Trial Lawyers Am., Bar Assn. D.C., U.S. Trademark Assn., Am. Intellectual Property Law Assn. Republican. Office: Mason Fenwick & Lawrence 1225 I St NW # 1000 Washington DC 20005-3944

GRYNBAUM, BRUCE B., physician, medical facility administrator; b. Anapa, Russia, May 25, 1920; came to U.S., 1939; s. Maurycy and Gertrude (Wytrzyc) G.; m. Alice Anigstein, Sept. 3, 1943 (widowed 1977); children: Steven, Gail Ann; m. Joan Brandon Reid, Dec. 5, 1981. MD, Columbia U., 1943. Med. Diplomate. Dir. rehab. medicine N.Y.C. Dept. Hosp., 1950-70; dir. rehab. medicine svc. Beekman Downtown Hosp., N.Y.C., 1950-83; assoc. dir. rehab. medicine svc. Bellevue Hosp., N.Y.C., 1950-58, dir. rehab. medicine svc., 1958-87; prof. clin. rehab. medicine N.Y.U. Sch. Medicine, N.Y.C., 1968—; vice chmn. Dept. Rehab. Medicine, clin. dir. Rusk Inst. N.Y.U. Med. Ctr., 1983—; exec. com. Cen. Labor Rehab. Coun., N.Y.C., 1969—; bd. mem. N.Y. State Labor Community Svcs. Agy., 1986—; v.p. med. affairs World Rehab. Fund, 1989—. With U.S. Army, 1944-46. Recipient Silver Bicentennial medal Columbia U. Coll. Physicians and Surgeons, 1967, Disting. Clin. award Am. Acad. Phys. Medicine and Rehab., 1987, Howard A. Rusk award Aux. to Rusk Inst., 1990. Mem. Am. Acad. Phys. Medicine and Rehab., N.Y. Acad. Medicine, APHA, AMA, N.Y. Soc. Phys. Medicine and Rehab., Union League Club. Office: Rusk Inst Rehabilitation 400 E 34th St New York NY 10016

GSCHWINDT DE GYOR, PETER GEORGE, economist; b. Budapest, Hungary, Jan. 1, 1945; came to U.S., 1975; s. George and Marie Henrietta (Haggenmacher) G.; m. Michele Herman, Oct. 14, 1972; children: Henrik, Marie. MA in Econs., Brussels U., Belgium, 1967. Grad. trainee Samuel Montagu and Co., London, 1967-69; dep. mgr. Europe Chase Manhattan Bank, London, 1970; credit officer Banque de Commerce (Chase), Antwerp and Brussels, 1971-75; ops. officer IMF, Washington, 1975-80, economist, 1980—. Dir. Hosp. Relief Fund for Caribbean, Chevy Chase, Md., 1982—. Decorated knight Magistalis Grace Sovreign Mil. Order Malta, Rome, 1975. Mem. Am. Conf. on Religious Movements, European Conf. on Religious Movements (dir. Brussels 1991—). Roman Catholic. Home: 10108 Fleming Ave Bethesda MD 20814

GUALTIERI, DEVLIN MICHAEL, physicist, researcher; b. Utica, N.Y., Dec. 11, 1947; s. Gregory Thomas and Stephanie M. (Gondek) G.; m. Anne V. Perretta, May 29, 1971; children: Michael, Marianne. BS, Syracuse U., 1970, PhD, 1974. Weizmann fellow U. Pitts., 1976-77; staff physicist Materials Rsch. Ctr. Allied-Signal, Inc., Morristown, N.J., 1977-81; sr. rsch. physicist Elec. Materials & Devel. Lab. Elec. Materials and Devices Lab., Morristown, N.J., 1983-88; sr. rsch. physicist Applied Physics Lab. Allied-Signal, Inc., Morristown, N.J., 1988—. Patentee in field. Mem. AAAS, IEEE (sr.), Am. Phys. Soc., Am. Assn. for Crystal Growth (treas. Mid-Atlantic sect. 1982-83), Sigma Xi, Phi Kappa Phi. Roman Catholic. Home: 12 Moore St Ledgewood NJ 07852 Office: Allied Signal Inc PO Box 1021 Morristown NJ 07962

GUALTIERI, JOSEPH PETER, museum director; b. Royalton, Ill., Dec. 25, 1916; s. Simone and Teresa (Toracca) G.; m. Marie E. MacDonald, Nov. 21, 1939; children: Ricardo Simone, Renee Marie; m. Angeline Lanzetta, Sept. 19, 1987. Diploma, Art Inst. Chgo., 1939; postgrad. study in, Italy, 1969-70. Tchr. art Hull House, Chgo., 1942, Lyman Allyn Mus., New London, Conn., 1945-46, Eastern Conn. State U., Willimantic, Conn., summers 1950-52, Hillyer Coll., Hartford, Conn., 1957-58, Norwich (Conn.) Art Sch., 1943-79; tchr. Norwich Free Acad.; dir. Slater Meml. Mus., Norwich, 1962—. One-man exhbns. include, Chgo. Art Inst., 1941, Contemporary Art Gallery, N.Y.C., 1951, Nexus Gallery, Boston, 1965, Parnassus Gallery, Chgo., 1941-42, Cummings Art Center, New London, Conn., 1979. Bd. dirs. Otis Library, Norwich, 1975-81; mem. Norwich Charter Revision Com. Recipient 1st prize Chgo. Art Inst., 1941, Logan medal, 1941; purchase prize Pa. Acad. Fine Arts, 1948, 51; prize Eastern States Exposition Conn. Artists, 1951. Mem. Conn. Acad. Fine Arts, United Italian Soc. (chmn.). Democrat. Roman Catholic. Home: 167 Liberty St Pawcatuck CT 06379-1335 Office: Slater Meml Mus 108 Crescent St Norwich CT 06360-3556

GUARE, JOHN, playwright; b. N.Y.C., Feb. 5, 1938; s. John Edward and Helen Clare (Grady) G.; m. Adele Chatfield-Taylor. AB, Georgetown U., 1961; MFA, Yale U., 1963; PhD (Hon.), Georgetown U., 1991. Seminar in writing fellow Saybrook Coll., Yale U., New Haven, 1977-78, adj. prof., 1978-81; lectr. NYU, CCNY; vis. artist Harvard U., 1990-91. Seminar in writing fellow, Saybrook Coll., Yale U., New Haven, 1977-78; adj. prof., 1978-81; lectr. NYU, CCNY. Author: (plays) Muzeeka, 1968 (Obie award 1968), Cop-out, 1969, House of Blue Leaves, 1971, Marco Polo Sings a Solo, 1973, Landscape of the Body, 1977, Rich and Famous, 1977, Bosoms and Neglect, 1979, Lydie Breeze, 1982, Gardenia, 1982, Women and Water, 1985, Moon Over Miami, 1988, Six Degrees of Separation, 1990, Four Baboons Adoring the Sun, 1992; co-adapter, lyricist: (plays) Two Gentlemen of Verona, 1971; author: (with others) (screenplay) Taking Off, 1970, (screenplay) Atlantic City, 1981; playwright-in-residence N.Y. Shakespeare Festival, 1976-77; co-editor Lincoln Ctr. Rev. Recipient Variety Poll award for most promising playwright N.Y. Drama Critics, 1968-69, N.Y. Drama Critics award for best Am. play, 1971, Obie award for best play, 1971, Outer Critics Circle prize for playwriting, 1971, N.Y. Drama Critics award for best musical, 1972, Tony awards for best musical and best libretto, 1972, Jefferson award, 1977, Best Screenplay award N.Y. Film Critics, 1981, Best Screenplay award Los Angeles Film Critics, 1981, Best Screenplay award Nat. Film Critics, 1981, award of merit Am. Acad. Arts and Letters, 1981, Venice Film Festival Grand prize, 1981, N.Y. Drama Critic's Circle award, 1991; nominated Acad. award, 1981. Fellow N.Y. Inst. Humanities; mem. Dramatist Guild Council, Am. Acad. Inst. Arts and Letters. Address: care R Andrew Boose 1 Dag Hammarskjold Pla New York NY 10017

GUARINI, FRANK J., congressman; b. Jersey City, Aug. 20, 1924; s. Frank J. and Caroline (Critelli) G. Grad., Columbia U. Midshipmen's Sch., 1944; B.A., Dartmouth Coll., 1947; J.D., NYU, 1950, LL.M., 1955; postgrad. advanced law program, Acad. Internat. Law, The Hague, Netherlands. Bar: N.J., U.S. Supreme Ct., Ct. Internat. Trade, U.S. Ct. Appeals, U.S. Tax Ct. Mem. 96th-102nd Congresses from 14th N.J. Dist., 1979—, mem. ways and means com., subcom. on trade, budget com., chmn task force on urgent fiscal issues, and select com. on narcotics abuse and control; Majority Whip-at-Large 96th-101st Congresses from 14th N.J. Dist., mem. adv. bd. U.S. Internat. Ct. of Trade; mem. N.J. Senate, 1966-72; chmn. air and water pollution com., pub. health com., appropriations com., com. on law revision; mem. transp. com., com. on instns. and agys. N.J. Senate. Co-author: New Jersey Rules of Evidence; contbr. numerous articles to profl. publs. Chmn. bd. regents St. Peter's Coll., Jersey City; mem. coun. on govt. Fairleigh Dickinson U.; mem. exec. com. Christ Hosp., Jersey City; fund chmn. Urban League Hudson County; bd. dirs. Hudson County Mental Health Assn., Hudson County Health and Tb League; mem. nat. bd. govs. ARC, also pres. Jersey City chpt.; trustee Hudson County Bar Found. Served to lt. (s.g.) USNR, World War II, PTO. Fellow ABA; mem. Fed. Bar Assn., Inter-Am. Bar Assn., Hudson County Bar Assn. (trustee), N.J. State Bar Assn. (gen. coun.), Hudson County C. of C. and Industry (exec. com.), Hague Acad. Internat. Law (trustee), Assn. Am. Trial Lawyers (nat bd. govs.), N.J. Assn. Trial Lawyers (chmn. exec. com.), Dante Alighieri Soc., UNICO, Rotary (dir.), Columbus Citizens Club, Bergen Carteret Club, Univ. Club of Jersey City, Hudson County Club of Jersey City (bd. govs.), Phi Delta Phi (pres.), Alpha Delta Phi. Democrat. Office: US Ho of Reps Rm 2458 Rayburn House Office Bldg Washington DC 20515

GUARINO, MARSULA GAIL, humanities educator; b. Jamestown, N.Y., Jan. 9, 1942; d. Carl Harold and Valerae Elsie (Sundell) Munson; m. Michael James Guarino, July 5, 1965; children: Michael Alexander, Amy Beth. BA in English, U. Rochester, 1964; MA in English, SUNY, Fredonia, 1967. Tchr. English, Jamestown High Sch., 1964-65, Southwestern Cen. Sch., Lakewood, N.Y., 1966-69; career counselor CETA, Chautauqua County and YWCA, Jamestown, 1974-76; substitute tchr. Jamestown Pub. Schs., 1976-81; instr. humanities Jamestown Community Coll., 1981—, actress, reader Reader's Theater, 1986-90. Mem. Chautauqua County Airport Commn., 1983-86; campaign worker Ted Smith for County Exec. Com., 1987; vol. Amicae-Hotline for Rape and Battering, Jamestown, 1990. Recipient Faculty award of excellence Jamestown Community Coll., 1986. Mem. Community Coll. Humanities Assn. Democrat. Episcopalian. Home: 127 Wilton Ave Jamestown NY 14701-7845 Office: Jamestown Community Coll Falconer St Jamestown NY 14701-3614

GUARINO, MICHAEL J., medical educator; b. Phila., Dec. 30, 1953; s. Angelo A. and Clorinda (Fioravanti) G.; m. Patricia A. Tedesco, July 3, 1976; children: Andrew, Robert, Jeffrey, Suzanne. BS in Chemistry, St. Joseph's U., 1975; MD, Thomas Jefferson U., 1979. Diplomate Am. Bd. Internal Medicine, Am. Bd. Med. Oncology. Fellow, instr. in medicine Strong Meml. Hosp. U. Rochester (N.J.), 1982-84; assoc. mem. staff dept. medicine Med. Ctr. Del., Wilmington, 1984—; instr. medicine Thomas Jefferson U., Phila., 1984—; chmn. cancer com. Meml. Hosp. Salem (N.J.) County, 1985—; med. dir. Hospice Salem County, Salem, 1986—; dir. protocol office cancer ctr. Med. Ctr. Del., Wilmington, 1988—, mem. bone marrow transplant team, 1989—. Mem. AMA, Am. Soc. Internal Medicine, Am. Assn. Clin. Oncology. Democrat. Roman Catholic. Office: Med Oncology Assn 1941 Limestone Rd Wilmington DE 19808

GUARNESCHELLI, PHILIP GEORGE, human resources executive, lawyer; b. Bklyn., May 17, 1932; s. Nicola and Amelia (Addeo) G.; m. Frances Ann Jacobs, Nov. 14, 1957; children: N. Timothy, Philip W., Peter N., Ann J. BA, Gettysburg Coll., 1954; JD, Dickinson Sch. Law, 1959. Bar: D.C. 1960. Attorney AMP Inc., Harrisburg, Pa., 1959-72, mgr. indsl. rels., 1972-80, v.p. indsl. rels., 1980-89, corp. v.p. human resources, 1989—. Bd. dirs. Capital Blue Cross, Harrisburg, 1985—, Harrisburg Med. Mgmt. Inc., 1988—; bd. overseers Widener U. Sch. Law, Harrisburg, 1990—. Mem. Mfr.'s Assn. for Productivitiy and Innovation-Human Resources Coun. II (vice chmn. 1991), D.C. Bar Assn., Country Club of Harrisburg (bd. govs. 1982-84). Republican. Roman Catholic. Home: 4724 Laurel Dr Harrisburg PA 17110-3244 Office: AMP Inc 441 Friendship Rd Harrisburg PA 17111-1204

GUBERMAN, RONALD MARK, podiatrist; b. Queens, N.Y., Dec. 13, 1960; s. Jack Solomon Guberman and Edith Lee (Stall) Grey; m. Denise Michele Reich, Aug. 16, 1986; 1 child, Ashley Nicole. BA, SUNY, Binghamton, 1983; D of Podiatric Medicine, N.Y. Coll. Podiatric Medicine, 1987. Resident Wyckoff Hts. Hosp., Bklyn., 1987-89, co-chief resident, 1988-89, assoc. dir. podiatric med. edn., 1989—, attending podiatric physician, 1989—; attending podiatric physician New Rochelle (N.Y.) Hosp., 1991—; pvt. practice Mamaroneck, Ridgewood, N.Y., 1989—. Author: (with others) Clinics in Podiatric Medicine, 1987, 89. Mem. Am. Coll. Foot Surgeons (assoc.), Am. Bd. Podiatric Surgery, N.Y. Acad. Scis., Am. Acad. Podiatric Sports Medicine. Office: 143 Mamaroneck Ave Mamaroneck NY 10543-3712 Office: 1670 Putnam Ave Ridgewood NY 11385

GUBERNATIS, THOMAS FRANK, SR., electrical buyer; b. Balt., Sept. 16, 1947; s. Elmer Charles and Agnes Elizabeth (Haupt) G.; m. Susan Marie Furst, Apr. 4, 1970; children: Thomas F. Jr., Marie E., Elaine K. BS, U. Balt., 1971. Project mgr. H.A. Harris Co., Towson, Md., 1971-79; estimator, purchasing Blumenthal-Kahn Elec. Co., Owings Mills, Md., 1979-88; prof. buyer Brown & Heim Inc., Lansdowne, Md., 1988—. Coord. South Carroll Alcohol and Drug Awareness Team, Sykesville, Md., 1980—, Concerned Citizens/Carroll County, 1981-83; treas. Carroll County Crime Solvers, 1983-91; 3d v.p. No. MADD, Balt., 1986-87. With USNR, 1966-72. Recipient Good Citizen award Md. State Police, 1982, Bro. Kenneth award Mt. St. Joseph, Balt., 1965. Mem. KC. Democrat. Roman Catholic. Home: 5915 Forest Ct Sykesville MD 21784

GUBSER, DONALD URBAN, materials scientist, educator; b. Alton, Ill., Dec. 21, 1940; s. Urban Alvin and Myrtle Helen (Grabbe) G.; m. Virginia Lee McCarthy, Aug. 12, 1967; children: Michael Donald, Andrea Denise. BS, U. Ill., 1963, MS, 1964, PhD, 1969. Rsch. physicist Naval Rsch. Lab., Washington, 1969-72, head sect. superconductivity, 1972-81, head br. metal physics, 1981-87, supr. div. materials sci. and tech., 1987—; prof. George Washington U., Washington, 1978—; head sect. condensed matter sci. NSF, Washington, 1985-86; Mem. adv. bd. N.Y. State Superconductivity Inst., Buffalo, 1990—, Ill. Ctr. for Superconductivity, Urbana, 1990—, Nat. Magnet Lab., Tallahassee, 1991—. Editor Jour. Superconductivity, 1988—. Recipient Meritorious Civilian Svc. award USN, 1983. Fellow Am. Phys. Soc.; mem. Metall. Soc., Materials Rsch. Soc., Sigma Xi. Home: 4923 Gainsborough Dr Fairfax VA 22032-2317 Office: Naval Rsch Lab Code 6300 4555 Overlook Ave SW Washington DC 20375-0002

GUBSER, LYN M., electronic publishing company executive; b. McMinnville, Oreg., July 9, 1939; s. Ivan M. and Orva A. (McFetridge) G.; m. Shirley Curtis, Dec. 23, 1967 (div. 1973); children: Elizabeth Joy, William C.; m. Diane K. Riese, Apr. 14, 1974; children: Kimberly K., John R. BS, Oreg. State U., 1961; MS, U. Oreg., 1963, PhD, 1968. Assoc. dean Coll. Edn., U. Ariz., Tucson, 1971-75; dean Coll. Edn., Western Ill. U., Macomb, 1975-78; exec. dir. Nat. Coun. Accreditation Tchr. Edn., Washington, 1978-83, Assn. Ednl. Communications and Tech., Washington, 1983-86; pres. Pembrooke Mortgage Corp., Alexandria, Va., 1987-89, Am. Insights, Inc., Alexandria, Md., 1991—; U.S. rep. Internat. Coun. on Ednl. Media, Paris, 1983-86; instrnl. tech. liaison person State Edn. Commn. China, Beijing, 1984-86; mem. adv. bd. Walt Disney EPCOT Ctr, Orlando, Fla., 1983-86; cons. to over 25 internat. corps. Founding editor TechTrends mag., 1984; columnist on edn. and tech. Alexandria Gazette Packet, 1987-90; contbr. numerous articles on tech., mgmt. and higher edn. to profl. jours. Bd. dirs. young astronauts program White House Initiative, Washington, 1984-87. Recipient Disting. Achievement award Am. Assn. Colls. for Tchr. Edn., 1978, Assn. for Humanistic Edn., 1979; Excellence in Communications award Greater Washington Soc. Assn. Execs., 1985. Mem. Rotary, Phi Delta Kappa. Home and Office: 603 Beverly Dr Alexandria VA 22305-1302

GUBSER, PETER ANTON, political scientist, writer, educator; b. Tulsa, May 9, 1941; s. Eugene Herbert and Mary (Douglass) G.; m. Annie Yeni-Komshian, Aug. 15, 1969; children: Sasha Mary-Helen, Christi Valerie. BA, Yale U., 1964; MA, Am. U. Beirut, 1966; PhD, Oxford (Eng.) U., 1970. Rsch. fellow U. Manchester, Eng., 1970-72; assoc. rsch. scientist Am. Insts. for Rsch., Washington, 1972-74; asst. rep. Ford Found., Beirut, 1974-77; pres. Am. Near East Refugee Aid, Washington, 1977—; lectr. various govt. and non-govt. instns., 1977—; bd. dirs. Internat. Svc. Agys, Washington, 1982—, Am. Coun. for Voluntary Internat. Action, 1984—; adj. prof. Georgetown U., Washington, 1990—. Author: Politics and Change at Karak, Jordan, 1973, Jordan: Crossroads of Middle East Events, 1983, Historical Dictionary of Hashemite Kingdom of Jordan, 1991. Bd. dirs. Internat. Coll., Beirut, 1982—, Nat. Coun. on U.S.-Arab Rels., Washington, 1985—. Mem. Am. Polit. Sci. Assn., Middle East Inst., Middle East Studies Assn. Democrat. Mem. Christian Ch. Office: Am Near East Refugee Aid 1522 K St NW # 202 Washington DC 20005-1270

GUCCIONE, SAMUEL ANTHONY, engineering educator; b. Granite City, Ill., May 31, 1941; m. Linda Tooley; children: Diane M., Christine M. BSEE, U. Ill. at Urbana, Champaign, 1964; MSEE, UIUC, Urbana, Ill., 1970; postgrad., Temple U., 1988—. Assoc. engr. Douglas Aircraft Co., Huntington Beach, Calif., 1964-65; aerospace engr. McDonnell-Douglas Corp., St. Louis, 1965-67; engr. Magnavox Co., Urbana, 1967-70; rsch. engr. Electromagnetic Compatibity Analysis Ctr., Annapolis, Md., 1970-74; instr., dir. engring. tech. Del. Tech. and Community Coll., Dover, 1974—; adj. faculty Parkland Jr. Coll., Champaign, 1970; ednl. cons. Tech. Coll., Lima, Peru, 1980-81, Altoona (Pa.) Area Vocat. Sch., 1983; accreditation cons. Bunker Hill Community Coll., Boston, 1982. Contbr. articles to profl. jours. Mem. Soc. Mfg. Engr. (sr.), Phi Delta Kappa. Office: Del Tech & Community Coll 1832 N DuPont Hwy Dover DE 19901

GUDEON, ARTHUR, podiatrist; b. N.Y.C., Feb. 27, 1935; s. Samuel and Mina (Kaminsky) G.; m. Loretta Bachrach, June 16, 1957 (div. 1976); children: Karla, Marilyn, Adam; m. Susan Steinmetz, Apr. 8, 1979; 1 child, Andrea. BA, NYU, 1956; D Podiatric Medicine, N.Y. Coll. Podiatric Medicine, 1960. Diplomate Am. Bd. Podiatric Surgery. Pvt. practice podi-

atry Family Podiatry of Rego Park, N.Y., 1960—; sr. faculty, mem. residency selection com. St. Joseph's Hosp. Catholic Med. Ctr., N.Y.C., 1980—; dep. examiner N.Y. State Bd. Podiatry, 1981; podiatry chmn., mem. adv. coun. for occupational edn. N.Y.C. Bd. Edn., 1980—. Vol. local health fairs, sch. programs, sports events, N.Y., 1965—. Fellow Am. Coll. Foot Surgeons (pres. N.Y. div. 1990—), Am. Assn. Hosp. Podiatrists; mem. APHA, N.Y. State Podiatric Med. Assn. (chmn. sci. affairs com. Queens div. 1984—, chmn. N.Y. state sci. affairs com. 1986-90, Podiatrist of Yr. 1969, 74), Am. Soc. Podiatric Med. Assts. (hon., bd. dirs. 1983—, Podiatrist of Yr. 1989), Am. Podiatric Med. Assn., Am. Podiatric Sports Medicine Acad. Democrat. Jewish. Office: Family Podiatry Rego Park 91-35 63d Dr Rego Park NY 11374

GUEFT, BORIS, health facility administrator, educator; b. Cannes, France, Nov. 10, 1916; came to U.S., 1917; s. Amshel and Nina (Oussoltseff) G.; m. Eula Mae Respess, June 25, 1943; children: Nina, Esther, Michael. AB, Columbia U., 1938; MD, NYU, 1941. Intern Sinai Hosp., Balt., 1941-42; resident New Britain Gen. Hosp., 1942-43, fellow, 1946-47; resident, fellow Mt. Sinai Hosp., N.Y.C., 1947-50; lab. dir. Fairfield State Hosp., Newtown, Conn., 1950-55; dir. pathology VA Hosp., Cin., 1955-58; prof. pathology Albert Einstein Coll. Medicine, Bronx, N.Y., 1958-71; lab. dir. Union Hosp., Bronx, 1970-90, Hebrew Hosp. for Chronic Sick, Bronx, 1980—; cons. pathology and electron microscopy Bronx-Lebanon Hosp., Bronx, 1975-90; adj. prof. N.Y. Med. Coll., Valhalla, 1975—. Contbr. numerous articles to profl. jours. Capt. M.C., U.S. Army, 1943-46, ETO. Decorated Bronze Star. Fellow ACP, Am. Assn. Pathologists, Sigma Xi. Home: 25 Vanderbilt Rd Scarsdale NY 10583-7218 Office: Hebrew Hosp Chronic Sick Bronx NY 10475

GUENTHER, KENNETH ALLEN, business association executive, economist; b. Rochester, N.Y.; s. Walter K. and Erna (Ahrenz) G.; m. Lilly Hoesli, Jan. 11, 1964; 1 child, Christine R. B.A. cum laude, U. Rochester, 1957; postgrad., Johns Hopkins U. Sch. Advanced Internat. Studies, 1957-58, Rangoon Hopkins Ctr., Burma, 1958-59, Yale U., 1959-60. Internat. economist Dept. Commerce, Washington, 1960-65; fgn. service officer Dept. State, Washington, 1965, 68-69, Santiago, Chile, 1966-68; spl. asst. to Senator Jacob Javits U.S. Senate, Washington, 1969-73; exec. dir. Inter-Am. Devel. Bank, Washington, 1973-74; asst. spl. trade rep. White House, Washington, 1974-75; asst. to bd. govs. Fed. Res System, 1975-79; assoc. dir. Ind. Bankers Assn. of Am., Washington, 1980-82, exec. dir., 1982-85; exec. v.p., 1985—; vice chmn. Ind. Bankers Assn., Am. Bancard Inc., Arlington, Va., 1990; bd. dirs. Ind. Bankers Assn., Community Banking Network Inc., Ind. Bankers Securities Corp. Inc. Contbr. articles on banking to profl. jours. Served with U.S. Army, 1961-66. Recipient spl. achievement award Fed. Res. System, 1977, presdl. pen for work on Monetary Control Act, 1980. Mem. Bretton Woods Com. (exec. com. 1989-91), Exchequer Club (recorder), St. Albans Tennis Club. Office: Ind Bankers Assn Am 1 Thomas Cir NW Ste 950 Washington DC 20005

GUERRERO, MARIO, JR., architect, consultant; b. Bklyn., July 21, 1962; s. Mario and Migdalia (Roman) G.; m. Isabel Bachiller, July 9, 1988; children: Erica Nazario, Mario III. B of Archtl. Tech., N.Y. Inst. of Tech., 1985. Community assoc. div. alternative mgmt. program N.Y.C. Housing Preservation and Devel., 1985-87, asst. project devel. coord. rent housing maintenance, 1987-89, city planner SRO devel., 1989-91, asst. architect div. homeless housing devel., 1991—; archtl. cons Top Gun Constrn. Inc., N.Y.C., 1991—. Editor Throne newsletter, 1986-89. Treas. 1867-69 7th Ave Tenants Assn., N.Y.C., 1990-92; founder, pres. Latin Inter-Cultural Collegiate Orgn., N.Y. Inst. Tech., 1980-83. Named Parent of the Yr., PTA, 1991. Roman Catholic. Home: 1867-69 7th Ave New York NY 10026 Office: NYC Dept Housing and Preservation and Devel 75 Maiden Ln New York NY 10038

GUERRETTE, RICHARD HECTOR, priest, management consultant; b. Bristol, Conn., June 26, 1930; s. Hector and Leona (Marcel) G. BA, St. Mary's Sem. and U., 1955; MA, U. Notre Dame, 1971; STM, Yale U., 1971; PhD, U. Conn., 1981. Ordained priest Roman Cath. Ch., 1959. Lectr., researcher Ecumenical Continuing Edn. Ctr., Yale U., New Haven, 1972-73; adj. prof. Goddard Coll., Plainfield, Vt., 1980-81, Vt. Coll. Norwich U., Montpelier, Vt., 1981-83, 90—; lectr., rsch. fellow Yale U. Div. Sch., New Haven, 1971, 84-87; lectr., researcher U. Conn., West Hartford, 1984-89; dir., cons. EquiPax Ctr. Human and Ethical Resources, Newport, Vt., 1988—; dir., curator EquiPax Art Gallery, Newport, 1989—; dir., psychotherapist EquiPax Counseling Svcs., Newport, 1988—; resource cons. Vt. Dept. Edn., Montpelier, 1988—; invited lectr. at internat. confs. Author: A New Identity for the Priest: Toward An Ecumenical Ministry, 1971, The Emmanuel Servant Community: Study of Social Movement Organization, 1981; contbr. articles on corp. and mgmt. ethics to profl. publs., articles on theology and liturgy to religious publs.; book reviewer Jour. Bus. Ethics, 1988. Named for Disting. Svc. in Counseling and Devel., The Nat. Disting. Svc. Registry, 1989-90. Mem. AACD, Soc. Advancement Socio-Econs. Office: EquiPax Ctr Human/Ethical Resources 30 Coventry St Newport VT 05855-2128

GUERRIERI, KEVIN SCOTT, telecommunications executive, consultant; b. New Carrollton, Md., Aug. 16, 1962; s. Harry Joseph and Mildred Louise (Sexton) G. BS, U. Md., 1987. Account exec. Automation Electronics Corp., Greenbelt, Md., 1988-89; br. mgr. Automation Electronics Corp., Capital Heights, Md., 1989-90; regional mgr. Innovative Tech. Inc., Silver Spring, Md., 1990-91, U.S. Fiberline Communications, Calverton, Md., 1991-92. Mem. Suburban Lions Club (jr.). Home: 403 Burnt Mills Ave Silver Spring MD 20901-4404

GUETZKOW, DANIEL STEERE, computer company executive; b. Ann Arbor, Mich., May 19, 1949; s. Harold S. and Lauris (Steere) G.; m. Diana Gulbinowicz, April, 1979. Student, Columbia U., 1967-70; BSBA in Accountancy, Thomas Edison State Coll., 1989; MS in Bus. and Mgmt., Acctg. Systems, U. Md., 1991. CPA, D.C.; cert. mgmt. acct. Prodn. mgr. Rehrig-Pacific, Inc., L.A., 1975-78; maintenance mgr. Setco, Inc., Culver City, Calif., 1978-79; plant mgr. Veneer Tech., Inc., L.A., 1979; co-founder, chief fin. officer, chief ops. officer, exec. v.p. Netword, Inc., Riverdale, Md., 1981—; also dir. Netword, Inc., Riverdale. Author: (book) Indemnification of Officers and Directors, 1988, (software) Telemarketing Database Mgr., 1984-86, Systems Accounting Control, 1985, Electronic Mail Switcher, 1982, 84, Compute Marginal IRS Tax Rate Using Linear Programming Sensitivity Analysis, 1989, Working Capital Liquidity Mgmt. Simulation, 1990, Use of Information Theory to Determine When to Post Audit Capital Budgeting Decisions, 1991, Leading/Lagging Paradigm for Classifying Performance Indicators for Total Quality Management, 1991; contbr. articles to profl. jours. Mem. AICPA, D.C. Inst. CPAs (chief fin. officers and mgmt. cons. svcs. coms.), Ops. Rsch. Soc. Am., Inst. Mgmt. Accts., Md. Assn. CPAs, Nat. Assn. Corp. Dirs. Office: Netword Inc PO Box 840 Riverdale MD 20738-0840

GUGEL, CRAIG THOMAS, advertising executive; b. Detroit, Jan. 18, 1954; s. Paul Walter and Patricia Angela (Sullivan) G. BA, U. Windsor, Ont., Can., 1976. Asst. br. mgr. Mich. Nat. Bank, Livonia, 1975-77; analyst media research Kenyon & Eckhardt, Inc., Birmingham, Mich. and N.Y.C., 1977-81; supr. media rsch. Kenyon & Eckhardt, Inc., N.Y.C., 1981-82; v.p., asst. dir. media rsch. McCann-Erickson, Inc., N.Y.C., 1982-84; v.p., dir. media rsch. Foote, Cone & Belding, Inc., N.Y.C., 1984-86; sr. v.p., corp. dir. media resources Bozell, Jacobs, Kenyon & Eckhardt, Inc., N.Y.C., 1986-88; sr. v.p., dir. media research Backer Spielvogel Bates, Inc., N.Y.C., 1988-91, sr. v.p., exec. dir. media rsch. and tech., 1991—. Mem. Am. Assn. Advt. Agts. (media rsch. com.), Media Rsch. Dirs. Assn., Advt. Rsch. Found. (various coms.), Agy. Media Rsch. Coun., Advt. Club of N.Y., Radio and TV Rsch. Coun., Am. Mgmt. Assn., Advt. Info. Svcs. (bd. dirs. 1987-90, 91—). Office: Backer Spielvogel Bates Inc 405 Lexington Ave New York NY 10174-0002

GUGGENHEIMER, JAMES, dentist, educator; b. Belgrade, Yugoslavia, Mar. 4, 1936; came to U.S., 1938; s. Siegfried and Eta (Rubowitz) G.; m. Constance Fitzgerald, Mar. 27, 1969; children: Paul, Peter, Gregor. BS, CCNY, 1958; DDS, Columbia U., 1962. Diplomate Am. Bd. Oral Medicine. Intern VA Hosp., Albany, N.Y., 1962-63; resident oral surgery Strong Meml. Hosp., Rochester, N.Y., 1963-64; fellow oral medicine Phila. (Pa.) Gen. Hosp., 1964-66; asst. prof. Univ. Pitts. (Pa.) Sch. Dental Medicine, 1966-70, assoc. prof., 1970-76, prof., 1976—; mem. active staff Presbyn. Univ. Hosp., Pitts., 1968—, Montefiore Univ. Hosp., Pitts., 1968—; dir. Div. Oral Medicine, Pitts., 1977—; affiliate mem. Pitts. Cancer Inst., 1986—. Mem. profl. edn. com. Am. Cancer Soc., Pitts., 1986; bd. dirs. Am. Chronic Pain Assn., Pitts., 1989. Mem. APHA, Am. Assn. Dental Rsch., Omicron Kappa Upsilon. Home: 971 Wellesley Rd Pittsburgh PA 15206-1728 Office: Univ Pitts Sch Dental Med 3501 Terrace St Pittsburgh PA 15261-0001

GUI, JAMES EDMUND, architect; b. Wooster, Ohio, Aug. 13, 1928; s. Harry Ludwig and Mabel Josephine (Olson) G.; B.Arch., Ohio State U., 1954; m. Anne Louise Outram, Oct. 15, 1955; children—Linda Anne, Jeffrey Allen. Asso. firm Charles F. McKirahan & Assocs., Architects, Ft. Lauderdale, Fla., 1958-63; chief specifications Architects Collaborative, Cambridge, Mass., 1963-67; propr. James E. Gui, Archtl. and Specifications Cons., Belmont, Mass., 1967—; cons. Architects Collaborative, Benjamin Thompson & Assocs., Cambridge Seven Assocs., Archtl. Resources Cambridge, Inc., Harvard, MIT, others. Mem. AIA, Constrn. Specifications Inst., Boston Soc. Architects, Mass. Assn. Architects. Cons. Juilliard Sch. Music, Lincoln Center, N.Y.C.; U.S. Pavillion Expo 67, Montreal; New Eng. Aquarium; Children's Hosp. Med. Center; Harvard U. Law Sch. Complex (2d award Constrn. Specifications Inst.); Harvard Gutman Library, Harvard Obs.; Kirkland Coll.; Berkshire Community Coll.; Tufts U. Dental Health Center; Independence Nat. Hist. Park Visitors Center; Wilmington Jewish Community Center (1st award Constrn. Specifications Inst.); Faneuil Hall Marketplace, Boston; Harborplace, Balt.; Seaport Market, N.Y.C.; Harvard Kennedy Sch. Govt., Cambridge; Ordway Music Theater, Mpls. Address: 965 Concord Ave Belmont MA 02178

GUIBORD, LINDA BERGENDAHL, fundraiser, entrepreneur; b. Glen Cove, N.Y., June 1, 1946; d. Eigil and Lillian Gertrude (Bettine) Bergendahl; m. Robert Farnum, Oct. 16, 1971 (div. 1988); children: Heidi, Garth. BA, L.I. U., 1969; MA, SUNY, Stony Brook, 1984. Asst. curator Nat. Pk. Svc., Mastic, N.Y., 1980-84; office mgr. Coogan, Swanson and Lange, Burlington, Vt., 1985-87; rsch. officer U. Vt., Burlington, Vt., 1987—; pres. Impact Info., Burlington, 1991—. Founder Brookhaven Hist. Dists., Patchoque, N.Y., 1978, Community Connection Program, Burlington, 1988, Holiday Basket Program, Burlington, 1988; mem. Colchester (Vt.) Sch. Task Force, 1991. Mem. New Eng. Rsch. Devel. Assn. Home: Oak Circle Dr Colchester VT 05446

GUIDETTE, CHRISTOPHER LINO, public relations executive; b. Springfield, Mass., Dec. 19, 1946; m. Mary Regina McAvoy, Jan. 2, 1971; children: Regina, Molly, Kevin. BA, Am. U., 1968; MA, Rutgers U., 1981. Accredited Pub. Rels., 1990. Writer AP, Charleston, W.Va., 1971-72; writer, editor The Home News, New Brunswick, N.J., 1973-80; city editor The Home News, New Brunswick, 1980-83; dir. communications N.J. Gen. Assembly, Trenton, 1983-86; dir. pub. rels. Prudential Ins. Co., Newark, 1986-88; dir. corp. communications Ins. Svcs. Office, Inc., N.Y.C., 1988—. Author: Mass Media Crisis and Political Change, 1980; editor: Lotteries, 1989. Mem. Highland Park (N.J.) Borough Coun., 1984-87; mem. Highland Park Planning Bd., Highland Park Zoning Bd. Adjustment, 1984-87; dir. Opera Theater of N.J., 1985-87. With U.S. Army, 1969-71, Vietnam. Mass Communications fellow NEH Tufts U., Harvard U., 1978; recipient Interpretive Writing 1st place award N.J. Press Assn., 1974. Mem. Pub. Rels. Soc. Am., Soc. Profl. Journalists.

GUIDOS-MARUSKIN, MARIE, real estate broker, appraiser; b. Eldersville, Pa., Oct. 18, 1937; d. Silvester Joseph and Katherine (Orenchuk) Kanzius; m. Paul Joseph Guidos, Nov. 14, 1959 (div. May 1985); children: Anne Kay, Paul Joseph Jr., Lori Beth, Robert John; m. Albert Frank Maruskin, May 27, 1989; stepchildren: Lynn Marie, Elizabeth Jane. Degree in secretarial sci., Pa. Comml. Coll., Washington, Pa., 1956. Lic. real estate sales, broker; cert. gen. appraiser, Pa. Sec. several employers, Washington, Pa., 1956-72; sales assoc. Bennett Real Estate, Washington, 1972, J.C. McCleery Agency, Washington, 1972-73, Loren W. Carl Agency, Washington, 1973-79; broker/owner Guidos Real Estate, Washington, 1980—; mem. Job Retention Job Force, Wash. Pa., 1990—, Wash. County Coun. on Econ. Devel., 1988—. Adv. bd. Pitts. Nat. Bank, Wash., Pa., 1982—; bd. dirs. United Way of Wash. County, 1983-89, United Way of Southwestern Pa., Pitts., 1987-89, Wash.-Greene Assn.for Blind, 1983-86; officer, charter mem. Zonta, Wash., 1985-86. Mem. Nat. Assn. of Realtors, Pa. Assn. of Realtors, Greater Wash. Bd. of Realtors (treas. 1980, 81, sec. 1982, v.p. 1983, pres. 1984, realtor of yr. 1984), Pitts. Ind. Fee Appraisers, Kiwanis. Republican. Mem. Orthodox Ch. America. Office: Guidos Real Estate 98 E Maiden St Washington PA 15301-4912

GUILD, RICHARD SAMUEL, trade associations management company executive; b. Boston, Nov. 5, 1925; s. Walter Rayford and Anna (Hollander) G.; BS, Boston U., 1949; m. Susan Jane Coughlin, July 3, 1965; children: Laura Ann, Linda Jean. With Guild Assocs., Inc., Boston, 1949—, mng. dir., 1960-65, pres., 1965—; owner Copypro, 1975—; treas. Resource Matching System, Inc., 1982-83; exec. sec. New Eng. Marine Trade Assn., 1963, Liquified Petroleum Gas Assn. New Eng., 1972-1985; mng. dir. Shoe Pattern Mfrs. Assn., 1951—, Mass. Automatic Merchandising Coun., 1964—, Tel. Answering Assn. New Eng., 1983; exec. v.p. Am. Boat Builders and Repairers Assn., 1979-90; treas. Wet Ground MICA Assn., 1983-87. With USNR, 1944-45. Cert. assn. exec. Mem. Multiple Assn. Mgmt. Inst. (past pres.), Am. Soc. Assn. Execs. (past bd. dirs.), N.Am. Paddlesports Assn. (exec. v.p. 1987-90), Boston Soc. Assn. Execs. (past pres.), Def. Orientation Conf. Assn., Soc. Mgmt. of Profl. Computing (exec. sec. 1985—), New Eng. Honda Automobile Dealers Assn. (exec. sec. 1985), Acura Dealers of N.E. (exec. sec. 1989). Home: 5 Glengarry St Winchester MA 01890-2511 Office: 100 Boylston St Boston MA 02116-4610

GUILLARD, ROBERT RUSSELL LOUIS, biological oceanographer, consultant; b. N.Y.C., Feb. 5, 1921; s. Robert Lilliard Russell and Suzanne (DeMoura) Guillard; m. Elizabeth Davenport, May 1954 (div. 1962); m. Ruth Fredericks Stimson, Dec. 6, 1962. BS, CCNY, 1941; MS, Yale U., 1951, PhD, 1954. Elec. engr. Navy Yard, N.Y.C., 1941-46; instr. physics NYU, 1946, CCNY, 1946-49; grad. asst. dept. plant sci. Yale U., New Haven, 1950-53; rsch. assoc. U. Hawaii, Honolulu, 1954-55; aquatic microbiologist U.S. Fish and Wildlife Svc., Milford, Conn., 1955-58; from assoc. to sr. scientist Woods Hole (Mass.) Oceanographic Inst., 1958-81; sr. scientist Bigelow Lab. Ocean Scis., West Boothbay Harbor, Maine, 1981—; dir. Provasoli-Guillard Ctr. for Culture of Marine Phytoplankton, West Boothbay Harbor, Maine, 1985-89; cons. Pigeon Point Rsch. Ctr., Pescadera, Calif., 1974-76; instr. marine botany Marine Biol. Lab., Woods Hole, 1967-70, 78, 79. Corr. (jour.) Marine Ecology, 1981—; contbr. articles to profl. jours. Hooker-Eaton fellow Yale U., 1954, summer fellow, Woods Hole Oceanographic Inst., 1954; recipient Darbaker award, Bot. Soc. Am., 1968. Fellow AAAS; mem. Phycol. Soc. Am. (editorial bd. 1974-77, 81-85), Internat. Phycol. Soc. (exec. coun. 1974-77), Am. Soc. Limnology and Oceanography (editorial bd. 1983-86). Home: River Rd Box 523 RR1 Boothbay ME 04537 Office: Bigelow Lab for Ocean Scis McKown Pt West Boothbay Harbor ME 04575

GUILLÉN, JORGE EDUARDO, classical guitarist, educator; b. Caracas, Venezuela, Oct. 2, 1957; came to U.S., 1984; s. Evangelio and Dominga (Huizi) G.;m. Kim Ann Sechrest, Oct. 19, 1991. Diploma 16th Century Music, Centro Superior Estudios Musicales, Caracas, 1976; diploma guitar performance, U. Centro Occidental, Barquisimeno, Venezuela, 1977, Escuela de Musica J.A. Lamas, Caracas, 1984. Dir. Proyecto Alfa, Caracas, 1979-84; radio producer Emisora Cultural de Caracas, 1979-84; TV producer C.A. Venezolana de TV, Caracas, 1979-84; tchr. music V.M.I. Music, Washington, 1985-87; guitar instr. Guitar Gallery, Washington, 1987-90; assoc. prof. music U. D.C., Washington, 1988—; mus. dir. Hispanic Inst. for Arts, Washington, 1987-88; endorser GHS Strings Corp., Battle Creek, Mich., 1987—. Performer long play Reminicencias Latinas, 1980; performer, producer audio tape Audio Terapia, 1981; composer: Two Venezuelan Waltzes, 1990. Recipient Gran Sol de Oriente, Caracas, 1982. Home: 3133 Connecticut Ave NW # 408 Washington DC 20008 Office: U DC 4200 Connecticut Ave Bldg 36 Washington DC 20008

GUILLEN, MAURO FEDERICO, sociology and management educator; b. Leon, Spain, Sept. 30, 1964; came to U.S., 1987; s. Julian and Maria Flor (Rodriguez) G. BA in Polit. Economy, U. Oviedo (Spain), 1987, D Polit. Economy cum laude, 1991; MA, Yale U., 1989, M in Philosophy, 1990; PhD in Sociology, 1992. Instr. Yale U., New Haven, 1989-91, grad. affiliate Calhoun Coll.., 1990-92; asst. prof. internat. mgmt. and sociology MIT Sloan Sch. Mgmt., Cambridge, 1992—; rsch. affiliate Ctr. for European Studies, Harvard U., 1992—. Author: The AIDS Disaster, 1990 (Gustavus Myers award outstanding book on human rights 1991), La Profesion de Economista, 1989. Organizer Grad. Employees and Studen Orgn. at Yale, New Haven, 1991-92. Fulbright fellow Inst. of Internat. Edn., 1989-92, John D. Rockefeller 3d fellow Program on Nonprofit Orgns., Yale U., 1989. Mem. Am. Sociol. Assn., Internat. Sociol. Assn., Health and Human Rights Group (Europe). Roman Catholic. Home: 950 Massachusetts Ave # 602 Cambridge MA 02139 Office: Sloan Sch Mgmt E52-MIT 50 Memorial Dr Cambridge MA 02139

GUILLEN, MICHAEL ARTHUR, mathematical physicist, educator, writer, television journalist; b. L.A.; s. Marin Arthur and Betty Guillen; m. Laurel Lucas, Sept. 7, 1991. BS in Physics with distinction, UCLA; MS in Physics, Math. and Astronomy, Cornell U., PhD in Physics, Math. and Astronomy, 1982. Tchr. physics and math. Core Curriculum Program Harvard U., Cambridge, Mass., 1985—; sci. editor Sta. WCVB-TV, Boston, 1985—, ABC-TV program Good Morning Am., N.Y.C., 1988—; sci. correspondent ABC News, N.Y.C., 1990—; tech. advisor Metro Goldwyn Mayer; participant numerous ednl. improvement programs; sci. cons. MGM/VA; mem. adv. bd. AIP. Author: Bridges to Infinity: The Human Side of Mathematics, 1984; contbr. articles to numerous newspapers and mags. including N.Y. Times, Washington Post, Sci. Digest, Sci. News, Psychology Today, Esquire; chief cons. NOVA TV show A Mathematical Mystery Tour; host/writer (TV spls.) Time, Tides and Tuning Forks (Emmy award, Ohio State award), To Be or Not to Be: Endangered Species of New England (Ohio State award), Heads or Tails: Predicting the Unpredictable, 1987, Greenland Polar Ice Cap, 1991 (Ohio State award), War in the Gulf: Answering Children's Questions, 1991 (ACT award, Nat. TV Critics award, Dupont-Columbia U. award); formerly sci., tech. contbr. CBS Morning News; TV spls. include Laetrile: The Last Chance. Recipient Danforth award for disting. teaching Harvard U., 1989, 90, Broadcast Media award for overall excellence AIAA, 1987. Mem. AAAS (chmn. sci. and math. edn. symposium), NAS (chmn. scis. and humanities conf., com. rsch. in math., sci. and tech. edn.), Leonardo Da Vinci Soc. (founder), Phi Eta Sigma, Sigma Pi Sigma, Pi Mu Epsilon. Office: ABC-TV 47 W 66th St New York NY 10023

GUILMETTE, LARRY GENE, real estate executive; b. Randolph, Vt., May 23, 1948; s. Eugene Albert and Lorretta (Sherman) G.; m. Janet Reed, June 10, 1972; 1 child, Taylor Reed. AS, Northwestern Conn., 1972; BFA magna cum laude, Syracuse U., 1975. R.P.A., Bldg. Owners and Mgrs. Inst. Internat. Dir. custodial svcs. Am. Sch. for the Deaf, West Hartford, Conn., 1976-81; bldg. mgr. One Am. Plaza, The Farley Co., Hartford, Conn., 1981-83, City Place, Bronson & Hutensky, Hartford, 1983-86; v.p. ops. Bronson & Hutensky, Hartford, 1986-87; v.p. property mgmt. svcs. The Farley Co., Hartford, 1987-91; v.p., ptnr. Excelsior Group, Hartford, 1991—. Mem. BOMA Greater Hartford (sec.-treas. 1986-88, v.p. 1988-90, pres. 1990—), Mid-Atlantic Conf. BOMA (bd. dirs. 1985—), Environ. Mgmt. Assn. Internat. (pres. 1980, Mem. of Yr. 1982). Office: The Excelsior Group 40F Weston St Hartford CT 06120-1538

GUIMOND, ROBERT WILFRID, medical physiology educator, lawyer; b. Fall River, Mass., Sept. 4, 1938; s. Romeo A. and Jeannette (Boissoneault) G.; m. Elaine Brodie, July 13, 1963; children: Jefferson, Jameson. BA in History, U. R.I., 1961, PhD in Physiology, 1970; JD, New Eng. Sch. Law, 1978. Bar: Mass. 1978, U.S. Dist. Ct. Mass. 1980, U.S. Ct. Appeals (1st cir.) 1980, U.S. Supreme Ct. 1983. Asst. prof. zoology U. R.I., Kingston, 1970-71; prof. biology Boston State Coll., 1971-82; prof. biology U. Mass., Boston, 1982—; sole practice law, Boston and Fall River, 1978—. Mem. Conservation Law Found. Mem. Am. Physiol. Soc., ABA, Am. Soc. Law and Medicine, Am. Forestry Assn., Nature Conservancy. Democrat. Roman Catholic. Home: 307 Montgomery St Fall River MA 02720-4221 Office: U Mass Harbor Campus Biology Dept Boston MA 02125

GUISELEY, KENNETH BALM, chemist; b. Auburn, N.Y., July 20, 1933; s. Percival and Louie (Balm) G.; m. Elizabeth Ann Schnackenberg, Sept. 1, 1956; children: Cynthia Anne, Pamela Jeanne, David Lawrence. BA in Chemistry, Hartwick Coll., 1955; PhD in Organic Chemistry, Syracuse U., 1960. Postdoctoral fellow Syracuse (N.Y) U., 1960-61; sr. chemist Marine Colloids, Inc., Rockland, Maine, 1961-74; dir. polymer rsch. Marine Colloids div. of FMC, Rockland, 1974-82; sr. rsch. assoc. FMC BioProducts, Rockland, 1982-90, rsch. fellow, 1990—. Contbr. articles to profl. jours. Chmn. Hope (Maine) Planning Bd., 1973; active Nativity Luth. Ch., Rockport, Maine, 1964-72. Fellow Am. Inst. Chemists; mem. Am. Chem. Soc. (carbohydrate div.). Republican. Office: FMC BioProducts 191 Thomaston St Rockland ME 04841-2129

GULATI, DHIRAJ, telecommunications executive; b. Kashgar, China, Oct. 14, 1949; came to U.S., 1964; s. Prem. N. and Sudarshan (Ahuja) G.; m. Nilu Walia, Apr. 30, 1979; children: Vikant, Neyha. BEE, CUNY, 1978; MBA in Fin., Pace U., 1982. Subscriptions mgr. UN, N.Y.C., 1971-82; mktg. dir. Rochester (N.Y.) Telephone Corp., 1982—. Mem. Rochester Bus. Opportunity Coun., Rotary. Office: Rochester Telephone Corp 180 S Clinton Ave Rochester NY 14646-0001

GULATI, JAGDISH, medical educator; b. India, Apr. 1, 1942; came to U.S., 1963; m. Maggie Smith, Dec. 1967 (div. 1976); 1 child, Sunita. MS, U. Pa., 1965, PhD, 1970. Postdoctoral fellow NIH, Bethesda, Md., 1972-78; asst. prof. Albert Einstein Coll. Medicine, Bronx, N.Y., 1978-84, assoc. prof., 1984-91, prof., 1991—; dir. Molecular Physiology Lab., Bronx, 1978-91. Contbr. over 35 articles to profl. publs. Mem. Biophys. Soc., Am. Physiol. Soc., Soc. Gen. Physiologists, Physiol. Soc. U.K. Office: Albert Einstein Coll of Medicine 1300 Morris Park Ave Bronx NY 10461-1924

GULIA, JOSEPH PAUL, business advisor; b. N.Y.C., Apr. 11, 1934; s. Joseph Giacinto and Lena Marie (Fassi) G.; m. Anneliese Mueller, May 10, 1958 (div. 1984); children: Peter Joseph, Gregory Paul, Carol Anne, Audrey Louise. BA, Cornell U., 1955; MBA, NYU, 1962. CPA, N.Y. Adminstrv. acct. IBM Corp., N.Y.C., 1958-59; pub. acct. CPA Firms, N.Y.C., 1959-64; auditor Westchester County, White Plains, N.Y., 1964-68, dep. com. fin., 1968-71, 1st dep. com. fin., 1971-75; comptroller City of Yonkers, N.Y., 1975-76; fin. adminstr. Mt. Vernon Pub. (N.Y.) Pub. Schs., 1976-84; commr. fin. Westchester County, White Plains, 1984-91; prin. Joseph P. Gulia, CPA, Scarsdale, N.Y., 1992—. Treas. Eastchester (N.Y.) Rep. Town Com., 1978-83; mem. Zoning Bd. of Appeals, Eastchester, 1980-87. Mem. AICPA, N.Y. Soc. CPAs (Disting. Pub. Svc. award 1976, named Outstanding CPA in N.Y. Govt. 1990), N.Y. Govt. Fin. Officers Assn., Govt. Fin. Officers Assn., Nat. Italian Am. Found., Cornell Club Westchester. Republican. Roman Catholic. Home and Office: 114 White Rd Scarsdale NY 10583-6212

GULKA, JOHN MATTHEW, computer consulting company executive; b. Schuylkill Twp., Pa., Dec. 8, 1953; s. John and Mary Ann (Litto) G.; m. Nina Maria Mandzy, Feb. 16, 1980. B.S., George Mason U., 1976. Jr. systems analyst COV VEC, Richmond, Va., 1978-79; sr. systems analyst Commonwealth of Va., Richmond, 1979-80; cons. CGA Computer Inc., Washington, 1980-82, account mgr., cons., 1982-84, tech. dir., Falls Church, Va., 1984-86; tech. dir. CAP Gemini Am., Vienna, Va., 1986; founder, pres. EXXCEL, Inc., Alexandria, 1987-88; sr. assoc. Booz, Allen & Hamilton, Inc., Bethesda, Md., 1988-90; mgr. ops. and engring. info. systems, INTELSAT, Washington, 1990—; ptnr. NVP Gems, Alexandria, Va., 1975—, Nova Gems, Alexandria, 1986—. Mem. Data Processing Mgmt. Assn., Am. Soc. Pub. Adminstrn. (pres. Interuniv. Student Assn. 1974-76, pres. local chpt. 1975-76). Republican. Roman Catholic. Avocations: conchology; gemology; music; photography; enophile and collector. Home: 4607 Kling Dr Alexandria VA 22312-1511 Office: 3400 International Dr NW Washington DC 20008-3006

GULL, THEODORE RAYMOND, astrophysicist, science facility manager; b. Hot Springs, S.D., Aug. 17, 1944; s. Albert Henry and Virginia Irene (Sieger) G.; m. Hazel Joy Constantine, July 1, 1967; children: Michael Stephen, Matthew Christopher. BS in Physics, MIT, 1966; PhD in Astronomy, Cornell U., 1970; MBA, Loyola U., 1985. Rsch. assoc. Yerkes Obs.

U. Chgo., Williams Bay, Wis., 1970-72; asst. astronomer Kitt Peak Nat. Obs., Tucson, 1972-75; prin. engr. Lockheed Electronics Corp., Houston, 1975-77; astrophysicist Goddard Space Flight Ctr., NASA, Greenbelt, Md., 1977—, ASTRO-1 mission scientist, 1982-91, assoc. chief Lab. for Astronomy & Solar Physics, 1985—, dep. prin. investigator space telescope imaging spectrograph, 1986—, acting 2d gen. instrument project scientist, 1988-90; cons. Nat. Geographic, Washington, 1975—, D.C. Heath & Co., Lexington, Mass., 1991—. Contbr. over 150 articles to profl. jours. Chairperson guidance rev. com. Howard County Sch. System, Columbia, Md., 1988. Recipient Goddard Space Flight Ctr award of merit, 1991. Mem. Am. Astron. Soc., Internat. Astron. Union, Astrophys. Soc. of Pacific, Sigma Xi, Alpha Sigma Nu. Democrat. Methodist. Home: 9275 Brush Run Columbia MD 21045-5302 Office: Code 680 Goddard Space Flight Ctr Greenbelt MD 20771

GULLA, ROBERT JOSEPH, investment executive; b. Cambridge, Mass., Dec. 9, 1935; s. Patrick Joseph and Adeline Mary (Ventura) G.; m. Sylvia Mary Morrone, Aug. 15, 1959; children: Robert, Gregory, Steven, Andrea. BS in Bus., Providence Coll., 1957. Sales exec., registered rep. Merrill Lynch Pierce Fenner & Smith, Boston, 1959-75; sr. acct. exec., asst. v.p. Merrill Lynch Pierce Fenner & Smith, Providence, 1971-73, sales mgr., 1971-75; resident officer, asst. v.p. Kidder Peabody & Co., Inc., Providence, 1975-78, v.p., 1978-88, sr. v.p., 1988-91; mng. dir. Kidder Peabody & Co., Inc., N.Y.C., 1991—. Trustee Westerly (R.I.) Libr., 1985 (Disting. Svc. award 1985), Westerly Hosp., 1990—; pres. Dante Soc., Westerly, 1986; advisor Westerly Ctr. for Arts, 1989; exec. bd. mem. Cath. Charity Fund, Providence, 1991. Recipient Bishops award Cath. Found., 1990; named Patron of Youth, YMCA, 1990. Mem. R.I. Assn. Investment Firms (pres. 1979). Roman Catholic. Office: Kidder Peabody & Co Inc 1200 Fleet Ctr Providence RI 02903

GULLETTE, ETHEL MAE BISHOP (ETHEL MAE BISHOP), pianist; b. St. Paul, Mar. 29, 1908; d. Clarence Eugene and Alma (Beckman) Bishop; m. William Brandon Gullette, Sept. 5, 1936; children: Ethel Mae, Charlene Ann. MusB, MacPhail Sch. Music, Mpls., 1928; BA, U. Minn., 1931; diploma, Juilliard Sch. Music, 1936; pvt. study piano with Donald N. Ferguson, James Friskin. Pianist and accompanist in concerts and radio appearances, Midwest U.S., 1925-33; voice accompanist Juilliard Sch. Music, also pvt. piano tchr., N.Y.C., 1933-47; duo-pianist, accompanist Fairfield County, Conn., 1951—, also Hartford, Conn., N.J. and N.Y.C., 1967—; concert pianist, Ea. U.S., 1953—; 30 concerts Fairfield Hills Hosp., Newtown, Conn., 1957-71; concerts, Savannah, Ga., Hilton Head Island and Beaufort, S.C., 1972; accompanist Darien Troupers, 1968, 69, New Canaan High Sch. Summer Theater, 1972-73; concert appearances include Dallas, 1983, Scottsdale, Ariz., 1985, Lebanon, Bridgeport, Greenwich, New Canaan, Norwalk and Darien, Conn., 1980—; mem. New Canaan Piano Quartet, 1960-68, New Canaan Town Players, 1952-88, accompanist, 1958-63, 73; mem., accompanist Nutmeg Music Theatre, 1957-61, Demi-Opera Co., Brookfield Summer Theatre, Conn., 1961, many others. Bd. govs., rehearsal pianist Norwalk Symphony Orch., 1955-62; mem. New Canaan Community Concerts Assn., 1954-88, membership chmn., 1967-69, bd. dirs. 1961-69, 84-88; active fund drives charitable orgns.; co-pres. New Canaan High Sch. Parent's Coun., 1964-65. Recipient Hon. Golden Eaglet award Southwestern Coun. coun. Girl Scouts U.S.A., 1985; also citations for work in Am. Cancer Soc. and ARC drives. Mem. N.Y. Singing Tchrs. Assn., New Canaan Hist. Soc. (photographer gown exhibits 1968-86), Darien Community Assn. (bd. dirs. 1982-84, chmn. duo piano group 1962-64, 82-84, sec. duo piano group 1984-86), New Canaan Libr., New Canaan Audubon Soc., Norwalk Symphony Orch. Women's Assn. (mem. bd. 1976-82), Am. Shakespeare Guild, AAUW (charter 1970—, named Outstanding Mem. Conn. chpt. 1980), Friends N.Y. Philharm. Orch. (New Canaan chmn. 1968-71), Fairfield County Panhellenic Coun., Juilliard Alumni Assn., U. Minn. Alumni Assn. (past dir. N.Y.), New Canaan Community Concerts Assn. (hon. life, Membership and Svc. award 1974, citation for 25 yrs. outstanding achievements 1979), Mu Phi Epsilon (recognition as 50 yr. mem. 1977), Delta Zeta (alumni charter; pres. local alumnae chpt. 1961-63, treas. 1982-84; named Outstanding New Eng. Alumna 1980, Nat. Woman of Yr. 1982; recipient Golden Rose 50 yr. mem. award 1981, New Eng. Cert. Achievement, 1989, Very Spl. Delta Zeta Alumna award, 1990; ann. alumna svc. award established in her name by Fairfield County chpt. 1983). Congregationalist. Clubs: Schubert (St. Paul); Atlantic Beach (L.I., N.Y.); Schubert of Fairfield County (duo piano group sec. 1980-82). Home: 225 Essex Meadows Essex CT 06426

GULLO, JOHNNI LEE, pharmacologist; b. Marlton, N.J., May 24, 1962; d. John Joseph and Josephine Mary (Anastasi) G.; m. David James Brown, May 14, 1988; 1 child, Ashley Nicole. BA in Biology, Rutgers U., 1984. Lab. technician II U. Pa. Sch. Medicine, Phila., 1984-87; teaching rsch. specialit III U. Medicine and Dentistry of N.J., New Brunswick, 1987-88; pharmacologist Wyeth-Ayerst Rsch., Princeton, N.J., 1988-90, sr. pharmacologist, 1990-92; assoc. rsch. scientist Bristol-Myers Squibb Rsch. Inst., 1992—. Author, co-author papers and abstracts in field. Mem. Sigma Delta Tau (sgt.-at-arms New Brunswick chpt.). Republican. Roman Catholic. Home: 1211 Stoneridge Cir Helmetta NJ 08828-1138

GULLOTTA, THOMAS P., human services executive, writer; b. Hartford, Conn., Dec. 23, 1948; s. Pasquale Thomas and Rita (Cague) G.; m. Geraldine Gullotta, Apr. 7, 1971 (div. 1975); m. Christianne Frankenfeld, Dec. 4, 1976; 1 child, Bernard. BA, U. Conn., 1971; MSW, Trinity Coll., 1975, MA, 1974. Clin. dir. Town of Glastonbury, Conn., 1975-81; C & E dir. USMHS, Danielson, Conn., 1981-84; chief exec. officer Child & Family Agy., New London, Conn., 1984—; mem. adv. coun. child welfare program St. Joseph's, Westfield, Conn., 1983-90; mem. study human svcs. commn. State of Conn., 1985-87. Author: Adolescent Life Experience, 3d edit., 1983—, Today's Marriages & Families, 1986; editor Jour. Primary Prevention, 1980—. Mem. Conn. Bd. of Edn., Glastonbury, 1981-86, Town Coun., Glastonbury, 1986-91. Recipient Disting. Svc. award Friends of Glastonbury Youth, 1981. Mem. Assn. Prevention Profls. (Disting. Svc. award 1981), NASW (chair pub. rels. com. Conn. chpt. 1980-83), Rotary. Republican. Home: 221 Keeney St Glastonbury CT 06033-1409 Office: Child & Family Agy 255 Hempstead St New London CT 06320-6290

GULOTTA, GERALD DAVID, industrial designer; b. Rockford, Ill., Apr. 17, 1921; s. Peter Rouselle and Lillian Elizabeth (Ingrassia) G.; m. Laura Anahid Babayan, Feb. 3, 1961; 1 child, Lisa Francesca. B in Indsl. Design, Pratt Inst., 1975. Designer Towle Silver Smiths, New Buryport, Mass., 1950-52, Eva Zeisel Studio, N.Y.C., 1952-53, George Nelson Design, N.Y.C., 1954-55; freelance designer N.Y.C., 1955-61; designer Raymond Lowey/William Smith, N.Y.C., 1961-62; freelance designer and cons. N.Y.C., 1962—; adj. instr. in indsl. design Pratt Inst., Bklyn., 1954-65, adj. prof., 1965-85; design edn. cons. Ministry of Econs., Lisbon, Portugal, 1974; tchr. design edn. workshop U. Guadajara, Mex., 1976-77; lectr. in field. Cpl. inf. U.S. Army, 1941-45, ETO. Democrat. Home: 22 W 26th St New York NY 10010-2023

GULOTTA, VICTOR, marketing executive; b. Bklyn., Mar. 14, 1954; s. Jerry and Joan (Holzhausen) G.; m. Donna Sheinberg, Aug. 21, 1987. BA in English, SUNY, Buffalo, 1978. Advt., promotion mgr. Prometheus Books, Inc., Buffalo, 1977-80, asst. editor, 1978-80, dir. advt., promotion, 1981-87, v.p. advt., promotion, 1983-87; advt. copywriter H.E. Harris & Co. (subs. Gen. Mills Co.), Boston, 1980-81; v.p. mktg. Bob Adams, Inc. Pub., Boston, 1987-89, v.p. promotion and publicity, 1989-91; proprietor Blithedale Antiquarian Books, Newton, Mass., 1988-92; sales dir. Bromer Booksellers, Inc., Boston, 1991—. Author: (with Brandon Toropov) Banned: Classical Erotica, 1992; editor Prometheus News and Revs. newsletter, 1984-86; book rev. editor Free Inquiry mag., 1982-87. Mem. Manuscript Soc., Mass. and R.I. Antiquarian Booksellers, Boston Mus. Fine Arts. Democrat. Home: 254 Auburndale Ave Newton MA 02166-1619

GULYAS, BELA JANOS, science administrator, physiology researcher; b. Szekesfehervar, Hungary, Apr. 14, 1938; came to U.S., 1957; s. Kelemen and Majsa (Margit) G.; m. Mary B. Tretheway, Aug. 30, 1962; children: Anne M., Lisa G., Catherine E. BS, Moravian Coll., 1962; MS, W.Va. U., 1965; PhD, U. Colo., 1968; postgrad., U. Wash., 1970. Instr. Georgetown U. Sch. Medicine and Dentistry, Washington, 1970-71; sr. staff fellow Nat. Inst. Child Health and Human Devel., NIH, Bethesda, Md., 1971-74, sr. investigator, 1974-82, sect. chief, 1982-84; health sci. adminstr. Div. Rsch. Grants, NIH, Bethesda, 1984-88; health sci. adminstr., sci. rev. adminstr. Nat. Ctr. for Rsch. Resources, NIH, Bethesda, 1988—. Editor: Autocrine and Paracrine Mechanisms in Reproductive Endocrinology, 1989; contbr. articles to profl. jours. Mem. AAAS, Am. Fertility Soc., Am. Assn. Anatomists, Soc. for the Study Reproduction, Develop. Biology. Home: 14401 Kings Grant St Gaithersburg MD 20878-2572

GUMAN, WILLIAM JOHN, aerospace technology executive; b. Greenwich, Conn., June 23, 1929; s. William and Elsa (Hammermann) G.; m. Elsie Ruth Kramer, June 19, 1954; children—William F., Gloria G. B. Aero. Engring., Rensselaer Poly. Inst., 1952, M. Aero. Engring., 1954, Ph.D., 1965. Asst. prof. aero. engring. Rensselaer Poly. Inst. Troy, N.Y., 1956-59; prin. research engr. Republic Aviation, Farmingdale, N.Y., 1959-65; mgr. electric space propulsion Fairchild Rep. Co., Farmingdale, 1965-78, mgr. rsch. and devel. planning, 1978-82, dir. rsch. and devel. tech., ops., 1982-85, dir. adv. products devel., 1985-87; dir. constract rsch. and devel. corp. tech. Grumman Corp., Bethpage, N.Y., 1987-90, corp. strategic and market planning, 1990—; adj. asst. prof. physics and engring. C.W. Post Coll., Greenvale, N.Y., 1960-62. Contbr. articles to profl. jours. Inventor pulsed plasma propulsion system. Recipient Cert. of Recognition NASA, 1976; Regional award Inst. Aero. Scis.; winner Ricketts Research prize Rensselaer, Poly. Inst., Troy, N.Y., 1952. Fellow AIAA (assoc., tech. com. electric space propulsion 1966-68, 78-80, Tech. Excellence award 1977); mem. Nat. Security Indsl. Assn. (bd. dirs. N.Y. chpt. 1985-87, panel mem. research engring. com., Washington, 1983-87), Sigma Xi. Avocations: photography, high fidelity, competitive ballroom dancing. Home: 26 Gaymore Ln Commack NY 11725-1306

GUMBEL, BRYANT CHARLES, broadcaster; b. New Orleans, Sept. 29, 1948; s. Richard Dunbar and Rhea Alice (LeCesne) G.; m. June Carlyn Baranco, Dec. 1, 1973; children: Bradley Christopher, Jillian Beth. BA, Bates Coll., 1970. Writer Black Sports mag., N.Y.C., 1971; editor Black Sports mag, N.Y.C., 1972; sportscaster KNBC-TV, Burbank, Calif., 1972-76, sports dir., 1976-81; sports host NBC Sports, N.Y.C., 1975-82; co-host Today Show NBC, N.Y.C., 1982—. Recipient Emmy award, 1976, 77, Golden Mike award, Los Angeles Press Club, 1978, 79, Edward R. Murrow award Overseas Press Club, 1988. Mem. AFTRA. Office: NBC Today Show 30 Rockefeller Pla New York NY 10112*

GUMBER, PAUL MICHAEL JAMES, security consultant, commercial pilot; b. Steubenville, Ohio, Oct. 28, 1962; s. Chester Stephen Sr. and Carole Rita (Egan) G. Cert. pilot. Office clk. U.S. Dept. Commerce, Bur. Census, Erie, Pa., 1990; owner, pres. Control Lab, Erie, Pa., 1987—. Rep. del. Model Legislature/YMCA, Harrisburg, Pa., 1979. Recipient Best Bill (sponsor), Model Legislature/YMCA, 1979. Democrat. Roman Catholic. Home: 233 E Sixth St Upper East Apt Erie PA 16507 Office: Control Lab PO Box 1865 Erie PA 16507

GUMBINNER, PAUL S., advertising and executive recruitment agency executive; b. N.Y.C., Aug. 30, 1942; s. Paul G. Gumbinner and Ruth (Gumpert) Coben; m. Nancy Levin (div. 1978); children: Elizabeth Susan, Jeffrey Michael; m. Amye Hope Price, Sept. 12, 1982. BS, Temple U., 1964. Asst. account exec. Richard K. Manoff, N.Y.C., 1964-66; account exec. DKG, Inc., N.Y.C., 1966-68; v.p. Kenyon & Eckhardt, N.Y.C., 1969-73; sr. v.p. McCaffrey & McCall, N.Y.C., 1974-77; pres. Anesh, Viseltear, Gumbinner, N.Y.C., 1977-82, The Gumbinner Co., N.Y.C., 1982—. Contbr. articles to Ad Week, Advt. Age. Pres. Friends Emelin Theatre, Mamaroneck, N.Y., 1976-78; v.p. Larchmont (N.Y.) Pub. Library, 1975-77. Recipient Effie award Am. Mktg. Assn., 1985. Mem. Ad Club N.Y. (guest lectr.). Democrat. Office: The Gumbinner Co 254 E 49th St New York NY 10017-1579

GUMERMAN, STEVE HOWARD, rehabilitation psychologist; b. Phila., Mar. 7, 1957; s. Alvin and Dolores (Bralow) G.; m. Debra Gumerman; children: Frank, Lee. BA in Psychology, Temple U., 1980, MEd in Counseling Psychology, 1984. Lic. psychologist; nat. cert. counselor; cert. vocat. evaluator. Psychologist Giuffre Med. Ctr., Phila., 1983-84; sr. cons. U.S. Social Security Adminstrn., Div. Vocat. Rehab., 1986—; sr. rehab. counselor Continental Rebab. Resources, Phila., 1984—. Author: Encyclopedia of Special Education, 1987; contbr. articles to profl. jours. Mem. AACD, Am. Psychol. Assn. Home: 402 Audubon Ter Philadelphia PA 19116-2730

GUMPRIGHT, HERBERT LAWRENCE, JR., dentist; b. Newport, R.I., Apr. 23, 1946; s. Herbert Lawrence and Helen Marie (Broderick) G.; m. Cynthia Randolph Williams, June 16, 1972 (div. Apr. 1987); children: Broderick J., Tyler H. BS, U. R.I., 1968; DDS, NYU, 1972. Lic. dentist, Mass. Intern Waterbury (Conn.) Hosp. Affiliate Yale U. Sch. Medicine, 1972-73; assoc. Ronald J. Dowgiallo, DMD, Harwichport, Mass., 1973-78; pvt. practice Brewster, Mass., 1978—; producer, host Your Dental Health, Community Access TV, 1978-91. Fellow Acad. Gen. Dentistry; mem. Am. Dental Soc., Mass. Dental Soc., Cape Cod Dist. Dental Soc. (treas. 1988-90, v.p. 1989, pub. rels. com. chmn. 1988-91). Office: 2452 Main St Box 1108 Brewster MA 02631

GUND, AGNES, art museum administrator. Pres. Mus. of Modern Art, N.Y.C., 1991—. Office: care Museum Modern Art 11 W 53d St New York NY 10019-5498

GUNDERSHEIMER, WERNER LEONARD, library director; b. Frankfurt, Hesse, Fed. Republic of Germany, Apr. 7, 1937; s. Herman Samuel and Frieda (Siegel) G.; m. Karen Rosenwald, Oct. 16, 1939; children: Joshua, Benjamin. BA, Amherst Coll., 1959, DHL (hon.), 1984; MA, Harvard U., 1960, PhD, 1963; MA (hon.), U. Pa., 1971; DHL (hon.), Williams Coll., 1989, Muhlenberg Coll., 1991. Asst. prof. history U. Wis., Madison, 1963-64; jr. fellow in history Harvard U., Cambridge, Mass., 1962-66; asst. prof. U. Pa., Phila., 1966-68, assoc. prof., 1968-72, prof., 1972-85, chmn. history dept., 1976-78; vis. prof. Tel Aviv (Israel) U., 1982; adj. prof. of History Amherst (Mass.) Coll., 1986—; dir. Folger Shakespeare Library, Washington, D.C., 1984—; trustee Rosenbach Mus. and Library, Phila., 1969-89, The Medici Found., Princeton, N.J., 1984—, Brit. Inst. of the U.S., Washington, 1985-90. Author: Life and Works of Louis LeRoy, 1966, Ferrara: The Style of a Renaissance Despotism, 1973, Art and Life of the Court of Ercole I d'Este, 1972; editor: The Italian Renaissance, 1965; contbr. articles to profl. jours. Trustee Shakespeare Theatre at the Folger, Washington, 1985-92, PEN/Faulkner Found., 1990—; cons. NEH, 1982—. Fellow Inst. for Advanced Study, 1970-71, Guggenheim fellow, 1974-75, I Tatti fellow Harvard Ctr. for Renaissance Study, 1974-75. Mem. Am. Hist. Assn., Ind. Rsch. Libr. Assn. (pres. 1991—), Renaissance Soc. Am., Med. Acad. Am. Democrat. Jewish. Clubs: Harvard, Grolier. Home: 2903 32nd St NW Washington DC 20008-3526 Office: Folger Shakespeare Libr 201 E Capitol St SE Washington DC 20003-1004

GUNERMAN, PENNY ANN, pension administrator; b. Mahopac, N.Y., May 14, 1953; d. Walter Paul and Ruth Christine (Dellairo) Bleda; m. Thomas Richard Gunerman, July 7, 1973; children: John Robert, Thomas Joseph. Student, SUNY, Delhi, 1972, Syracuse U., 1979. Mktg. rep. RLC Electronics, Inc., Mt. Kisco, N.Y., 1972-75; program coord. Syracuse (N.Y.) U. Coll. of Visual and Performing Arts, 1975-79; pension mktg. mgr. Braun Assocs., Actuarial Co., Syracuse, 1979-81; life ins. agt. MONY, Syracuse Assocs., 1981—; pres. pension cons. Gunerman Assocs., Inc., Cazenovia, N.Y. Mem. N.Y. Employee Benefits Coun. Mem. Am. Soc. Pension Actuaries, Syracuse Assn. Life Underwriters, Willow Bank Yacht Club, Thunderbird Ski Club. Office: Gunerman Assocs Inc Carriage Ln Cazenovia NY 13035-1329

GUNKEL, CARROLL REESE, clergyman; b. Balt., Mar. 3, 1937; s. John George Jr. and Gertrude Agnes (Huhn) G.; m. Barbara Gail Hall, Oct. 14, 1961; children: Susan, Stephanie, Christopher. BS, Loyola Coll., Balt., 1958; MDiv, Wesley Theol. Sem., Washington, 1961; PhD, St. Mary's U. and Sem., Balt., 1980. Ordained to ministry Meth. Ch., 1961. Pastor Idlewylde United Meth. Ch., Towson, Md., 1958-61; assoc. pastor Northwood-Appold United Meth. Ch., Balt., 1961-63; pastor Trinity United Meth. Ch., Catonsville, Md., 1963-75, University United Meth. Ch., College Park, Md., 1975-83, Bethesda (Md.) United Meth. Ch., 1983-89; dir. devel. Asbury Meth. Village, Gaithersburg, Md., 1989-91; asst. to pres. and chief exec. officer Asbury Village, Gaithersburg, 1992—; adj prof. philosophy Catonsville Community Coll., 1969-89. Author: Into the House of the Lord, 1973, The Unlikely Bride, 1976, They Met the Master, 1980; contbr. articles to religious mags. Mem. Md. Gov.'s Spl. Task Force on Life Preservation, Balt., 1972-73; chaplain Balt. County Police and Fire Depts., Towson, 1968-75; pres. bd. trustees Bd Child Care, Balt., 1980-83; chair Balt. Conf. Bd. Higher Edn., Washington, 1985-89; exec. bd. Ecumenical Inst. of St. Mary's U. and Sem. Named Clergyman of Yr., Bethesda C. of C., 1989. Mem. Nat. Planned Giving Assn., Masons (chaplain 1966-75). Office: Asbury Meth Village 201 Russell Ave Gaithersburg MD 20877-2801

GUNN, G. GREG, insurance executive; b. Washington, Sept. 10, 1958; s. W. Guy and Emily (Hamby) G. BS, Pa. State U., 1980. Cert. ins. counselor. Account exec. Byerly Ins. Agts. & Brokers, Inc., Lemoyne, Pa., 1980-83, v.p., 1983-88; pres. Penn Property & Casualty, Inc., Lemoyne, 1988—; pres. Am. Subcontractors Assn. Central Pa., 1988-89, exec. com. 1985-89; chmn. Central Pa. Ins. Com., Harrisburg, 1988. Contbr. articles to profl. jours. Mem. Profl. Ins. Agts. Assn., Capital Area Agts. Assn., Assoc. Pa. Constructors (bd. dirs.), Shriners. Republican. Methodist. Home: 22 Paddock Ln Camp Hill PA 17011-1268 Office: Penn Property & Casualty PO Box 620 Lemoyne PA 17043-0620

GUNN, WILLIAM JOHN, graphic designer; b. Brookline, Mass., Nov. 27, 1920; s. Francis and Katherine (McGrory) G.; m. Mary Eileen Kelly, Aug. 16, 1944; children: Eileen, John, Kathleen, Nora. Diploma, Mass. Coll. Art, 1942; spl. student, Calif. Sch. Fine Arts, 1944-45. Pres. Gunn Assocs., Inc., Boston, 1946-86; bd. dirs. Mass. Coll. Art Found., Boston; lectr. in field. Chmn. Norwell (Mass.) Cub Scout pack Boy Scouts Am., 1957, Boy Scout troop, Norwell, 1958-61. Cpl. USMCR, 1942-45. Decorated Silver Star, Purple Heart with 2 gold stars; recipient Golden T-square award Boston Art Dirs. Club, 1968, William J. Gunn award Creative Club of Boston, 1985. Mem. Creative Club of Boston (chmn. various coms. 1954-91, William J. Gunn award established 1985), Mass. Coll. Art Alumni Assn. (bd. dirs. Boston chpt. 1987-91, treas., Disting. Alumnus 1988). Roman Catholic.

GUNNISON, HUGH, counseling educator; b. Mt. Kisco, N.Y., Nov. 26, 1929; s. Hugh and Constance Hopkins (Frost) G.; m. Patricia Bushner, June 22, 1988; children: Jonathan, Stanley H. BA in English, St. Lawrence U., 1952, MEd in Counseling, 1959; EdD, Syracuse U., 1964. Diplomate Internat. Acad. Profl. Counselors and Psychotherapists. Asst. prof. psychology Onondoga Community Coll., Syracuse, 1962-64; lectr. Syracuse (N.Y.) U., 1964-65; prof. counseling St. Lawrence U., Canton, N.Y., 1965-78, 79—, dir. London programme, 1991-92; prof. counseling George Peabody Coll.-Overseas Div. Vanderbilt U., Cambridge, Eng., 1978-79. Contbr. articles to profl. jours. With USCG, 1952-56. Mem. APA, AACD, Nat. Bd. Cert. Counselors (cert.), Cert. Clin. Mental Health Counelors (cert.).

GUNTER, JOHN DAVID, chemist; b. Durham, N.C., Nov. 18, 1947; s. June Uriah and Elizabeth (Kerr) G.; m. Patricia Jean Hadden, July 10, 1971; children: Davis, Christopher, Andrew. AB in Chemistry, U. N.C., 1969; MS in Organic Chemistry, N.C. State U., 1973, PhD in Inorganic chemistry, 1976. Vis. asst. prof. N.C. State U., Raleigh, 1976-77; chemist Tenn. Eastman Co., Kingsport, 1977-79, sr. chemist, 1979-87, devel. assoc., 1988; tech. assoc. Eastman Kodak Co., Rochester, N.Y., 1989-91, dept. mgr., 1991—. Mem. Am. Chem. Soc. Presbyterian. Home: 145 Caversham Woods Pittsford NY 14534 Office: Eastman Kodak Co B-30 Fl 8 Kodak Pk Rochester NY 14652-3403

GUNTHER, GEORGE LACKMAN, state senator, natureopathic physician; b. Bridgeport, Conn., Nov. 22, 1919; s. George and Gwendolyn (Cliff) G. ; m. Priscilla A. Staples, June 5, 1941; children: Pattie K., Karla Gwen (Mrs. R. Mazzey), Lance Inder. Grad., Nat. Coll. Drugless Physicians, Chgo., 1942. Intern Chgo. Gen. Health Svc., 1940-41; pvt. practice natureopathic medicine Chgo. Gen. Health Svc., Bridgeport, 1943-44, Stratford, Conn., 1944—; mem. Conn. Senate, Stratford, Conn., 1944—, 1967—, dep. minority leader, 1971-72, 75-76, 78-80, 87—, dep. majority leader, 1973-74, asst. minority leader, 1977-80, minority leader, 1981-82, dep. minority leader, 1987-92; Chmn., Stratford Conservation Commn., 1960-71; mem. Stratford Citizens Council on Edn., 1961—; mem. Stratford Bd. Edn., 1957-61; mem. Stratford Town Council, 1960-65; mem. Conn. Bd. Natureopathic Examiners, 1946-49; mem. Stratford Drug Adv. Com., 1971—; mem. Capitol Restoration Commn.; mem. L.I. Sound Study Com. of New Eng. River Basins Commn.; vice chmn. natural resources com. Nat. Conf. State Legislatures, 1976-77; mem. Environ. Regional com. The Council of State Govts.; vice chmn. Atlantic State Marine Fisheries Commn. legislator div., BiState L.I. Sound Marine Resources com.; mem., state chmn., bd. dirs. Am. Legis. Exchange Coun. Bd. dirs. Stratford P.A.L., Sterling Community Center, Stratford Red Cross; bd. assocs. U. Bridgeport. Recipient Am. Motors Conservation award Am. Motors Corp., 1966; named Water Conservationist of Year for Conn., Conn. State League of Sportsmen and Conservation Clubs, Nat. Wildlife Fedn. and Sears and Roebuck Found., 1966; Nat. Water Conservationist of Year, Nat. Wildlife Fedn. and Sears and Roebuck Found., 1966; Outstanding Service award Seymour Fish and Game Club, 1966; Outstanding Civic Leader of Am., 1967; Legis. Conservationist of Year for Conn., Conn. State League Sportsmen, Nat. Wildlife Fedn. and Sears and Roebuck Found., 1969; Citizen of Year award Stratford Civitan Club, 1970; Arthur Rickerby Meml. award Ecology League Conn., 1972; Legion of Honor award Internat. Order DeMolay, 1972; Raymond J. O'Connor Meml. Community Service award Stratford Jaycees, 1974; Conservation award SHAME, Inc., 1974; AFL-CIO Citation Conn., Am. Fedns. tchrs., 1974, Young Rep. Conn. Legislator of Yr. award, 1977, Heritage Group Councils award, 1979, award Conn. Optometric Soc., 1979, legis. award Fairfield County League of Sportsmen, 1980, Legislator of Yr. Conn. Police Chiefs Assn., 1982, Legislator of Yr. award Nat. Rifle Assn., Environ. Conservations award L.I. Sound Am., 1986, Commdr's Cross of the Order of Merit Fed. Republic Germany, 1987, numerous others. Mem. Stratford Antique Gun Collectors Assn. (organizer, 1st pres.), Conn. Campers Assn., Stratford YMCA, P.T.A., Center Sch. Father's Club, Milford C. of C. (hon.), Bridgeport Boat Owners Assn. (hon.), Conn. Campers Assn., So. Conn. Sportsmen's Assn., Protect Your Environment, Theta Sigma (hon.), Sigma Phi Kappa. Masons, Shriners, Lions (life, past pres., past officer, Outstanding Service Achievement award, Master Key award), Pootatuck Yacht Club (hon.). Office: Conn State Senate State Capitol Bldg Hartford CT 06106

GUNTHER, MICHAEL JOHN, police officer; b. Lakewood, N.J., July 4, 1949; s. John and Fran (Windeler) G.; m. Maryann Margaret Costello, Mar. 6, 1971; children: Michael John II, Chris Edward. AA, Ocean County Coll., 1973; BA, Stockton State Coll., 1977. Master well driller Windeler and Gunther Corp., Howell, N.J., 1971-75; police officer Howell Police Dept., 1975—; co-owner Manalapan Bowling Mgmt. Co.; mem. of SWAT, Howell Police, 1990—, mem. pistol league, 1991—. Exempt vol. fireman Southard Fire Dept., Howell, 1968-75; bd. dirs. Pop Warner Football, Howell, 1990—. With USNR, 1968-75. Recipient Police Excellent award Howell Twp., 1990, Police Life Saving award Howell Twp. chief of police, 1991, Mayor award, 1991, Hon. Police award Howell Twp., 1991, Ann. Merit award 200 Club, 1991, Merit award Am. Police Hall of Fame, 1991. Mem. NRA, Candlewood Swim Club. Republican. Methodist. Office: Howell Twp Police Dept PO Box 580 Howell NJ 07731

GUNTON, JAMES DOUGLAS, college dean; b. Medford, Oreg., Mar. 28, 1937; s. Harold N. Gunton and Hazel M. Gold Scanlan; m. Margaret R. Taylor, June 24, 1962; children: Deborah, James, Michael. BA in Chemistry, Linfield Coll., McMinnville, Oreg., 1958; BA in Physics, Oxford U., Eng., 1961; PhD in Physics, Stanford U., 1966. Asst. prof. physics Temple U., Phila., 1968-73, assoc. prof. physics, 1973-76, prof. physics, 1976-88, dir. Ctr. for Advanced Computational Sci., 1985-88; dean Coll. Arts and Scis. Lehigh U., Bethlehem, Pa., 1988—. Author: Dynamics of Metastable and Unstable States, 1983; contbr. articles to profl. jours. Rhodes scholar 1958, Danforth fellow 1962, Woodrow Wilson fellow 1958. Fellow Am. Phys. Soc. Office: Lehigh Univ Maginnes Hall Bethlehem PA 18015

GUPTA, ANIL KUMAR, educator; b. New Delhi, India, Sept. 24, 1949; came to U.S., 1975; s. Charan Dass and Chandra (Prabha) G.; m. Rekha

Yeshwant Talcherkar, July 6, 1975; 1 child, Rahul. B in Tech., Indian Inst. Tech., Kanpur, India, 1970; diploma Bus. Adminstrn., Indian Inst. Mgmt., Ahmedabad, India, 1972; D in Bus. Adminstrn., Harvard U., 1980. Area sales mgr. Hindustan Lever Ltd., Bombay, India, 1972-73, product mgr., 1973-75; asst. prof. sch. mgmt. Boston U., 1980-86; assoc. prof. strategic mgmt. U. Md., College Park, 1986-92, prof. strategic mgmt., 1992—; cons. numerous U.S. and European corps. Contbr. articles to profl. jours.; editorial bd.: Jour. High Tech. Mgmt. Rsch., Acad. Mgmt. Rev. Recipient Broderick prize for Excellence in Rsch., Boston U., 1984, Allen J. Krowe prize for Excellence in Teaching, U. Md., College Park, 1989. Mem. Am. Acad. Mgmt. (Glueck Best Paper award in bus. policy and planning 1991), Inst. Mgmt. Scis., Strategic Mgmt. Soc. Home: 12603 Pentenville Rd Silver Spring MD 20904-3526 Office: U Md Coll Bus and Mgmt College Park MD 20742

GUPTA, GIRISH CHANDRA, electrical engineer, consultant; b. Dhuri, Punjab, India, May 13, 1941; came to U.S., 1972; s. Hans Raj and Parsini Devi (Agarwal) G.; m. Adarsh Bala Agarwal Gupta, Aug. 24, 1968; children: Sona, Serena. Faculty in sci., Govt. Coll., Malerkotla, India, 1959-61; BSEE, M.L. Nehru Engring. Coll., Allahabad, India, 1965. Registered profl. engr., Pa. Lectr. Thapar Polytechnic, Patiala, Punjab, 1965-67; elec. engr., sub divisional officer Punjab State Electricity Bd., Patiala, 1967-72; engr. design and constrn. for nuclear power plants Stone & Webster Engring. Corp., N.Y.C., Pa., 1980—; sr. power designer EBASCO Services Inc., N.Y.C., 1978-80; elec. engring., cons. Stone & Webster Engring. Corp., N.Y.C., 1980—. Mem. Ctrl. Jersey India Assn. Hindu. Office: Stone & Webster Engring Corp 1-Penn Plaza 250 W 34th St New York NY 10116

GUPTA, RAM SWAROOP, engineering educator; b. Uttar Pradesh, India, Mar. 22, 1940; came to U.S., 1979; s. Narain Das and Sona (Bai) G.; m. Saroj Bala, June 13, 1964; children: Apurv, Sukirti, Sudipti. B of Engring. with hons., Jabalpur Univ., India, 1961; M of Engring., Roorkee Univ., India, 1964; PhD, Polytechnic Univ., N.Y.C., 1983. Registered profl. engr., R.I., Mass. Asst. exec. engr. Nat. Projects Constrn. Corp., New Delhi, 1962-64; sr. rsch. officer Planning Commn. Govt. of India, New Delhi, 1964-72; Colombo Plan fellow Queensland Irrigation and Water Supply Commn., Brisbane, Australia, 1972; hydrology expert Govt. of Liberia, Monrovia, West Africa, 1974-79; pres. Delta Engrs., Inc., Bristol, R.I., 1986—; prof. Roger Williams Coll., Bristol, 1981—. Author: Hydrology and Hydraulic Systems, 1989; contbr. articles to profl. publs. Mem. R.I. Bd. Cert. of Operators of Waste Water Treatment, R.I., 1983-86. Mem. ASCE, Providence Engring. Soc., Water Pollution Control Fedn. Home: 423 Sowams Rd Barrington RI 02806-2745 Office: Roger Williams College Bristol RI 02809

GUPTA, RAMESH KUMAR, electrical engineering executive; b. Dhuri, Punjab, India, Nov. 13, 1953; came to U.S., 1980; s. Hans R. and Parsini Gupta; m. Nitu Gupta, Jan. 10, 1982; 1 child, Raman. BSc with honors, Punjab U., Chandigarh, India, 1974; MScEE, U. Alta., Edmonton, Can., 1976, PhDEE, 1980; MBA, U. Pa., 1989. Mem. tech. staff Comsat Labs., Clarksburg, Md., 1980-85, staff scientist, 1985-87, assoc. mgr., 1987-89, sr. scientist, 1989-90, mgr. microwave components, 1990—. Mem. editorial bd. Comsat Tech. Rev., 1989—; contbr. tech. articles and papers to profl. publs.; inventor, patentee in field. Merit scholar Punjab U., 1970-74; Centennial fellow Alta. Govt. Telephones, 1976-79, Dissertation fellow U. Alta., 1979-80. Mem. IEEE (sr.), IEEE Microwave Theory and Techniques Soc. (chmn. Washington chpt. 1988-89), AIAA. Office: Comsat Labs 22300 Comsat Dr Clarksburg MD 20871

GUPTA, RAVI CHANDRA, venture capitalist, international marketing and business strategy specialist; b. Mombasa, Kenya, Nov. 11, 1956; s. Satish Chandra and Krishna (Balkishen) G. BA with honors, Delhi U., India, 1978; cert. in tech. mgmt., Loughborough U. Tech., U.K., 1978; student internat. mgmt., Manchester Bus. Sch., U.K., 1979; MBA, U. Pa., 1987. Mgmt. trainee, then internat. mktg. cons., then regional mgr. mktg. Turner & Newall Group, Manchester, 1978-83; mktg. mgr. Coralie Electronics Gould Corp. USA, New Delhi, India, 1983-85; v.p. investment banking First Asian Securities/First Growth Group, N.Y.C. and Bridgewater, N.J., 1987-90; bus. mgr. Trespa N.Am., Advanced Tech. Group, Hoechst Celanese Corp., Bridgewater, 1990—; mem. innovative constrn. technologies program Sch. of Architecture, MIT, Cambridge,1 990-91. Invitee Duke of Edinburg's Award Scheme, 1985; featured in articles in Forbes Mag., 1986, USIA mag., 1987. Mem. Constrn. Specifications Inst., Assn. of Indians in Am. (exec. com. N.Y. chpt. 1989). Office: Trespa N Am Advanced TechGroup Rte 202-206 Bridgewater NJ 08876

GUPTA, SUBHASH CHANDRA, metallurgical engineer; b. Doggadda, Utter Prad, India, Aug. 12, 1941; came to U.S., 1967; s. Shiv Dayal and Munni Devi Gupta; m. Madhu, Apr. 28, 1967; children: Sharad, Paresh. BS, U. Rajasthan, Jaipur, India, 1962; BE in Metallurgy, Indian Inst. Sci., Bangalore, 1964, ME, 1966; MBA, Renssalaer Poly. Inst., Troy, N.Y., 1985. Lectr. dept. of metallurgy Indian Inst. Sci., Bangladore, 1966-67; metall. engr. The Bendix Corp., Utica, N.Y., 1968-70; sr. metall. engr. The Bendix Corp., Utica, 1973-74, mgr. metallurgy, 1974-76, mgr. metallurgy, reliability, 1976-82; plant metallurgist Kelsey Hayes Co., Utica, N.Y., 1970-73; mgr. engring. Allied Corp., Utica, N.Y., 1982-85; mgr. metallurgy Allied Signal, Utica, 1985-88, Lucas Aerospace Power Transmission Corp., Utica N.Y., 1988—. Mem. ASM Internat. (named Outstanding Young Mem., 1975), Am. Soc. for Quality Control, Rotary Internat. Republican. Hindu. Home: 50 Imperial Dr New Hartford NY 13413-3210 Office: Lucas Aerospace Power 211 Seward Ave Utica NY 13502-5799

GUPTA, VENU GOPAL, psychology educator; b. Hoshiar Pur, Punjab, India, Apr. 3, 1934; came to U.S., 1966; s. Ram Dass and Ram Piari Aggarwal; m. Sunita Gupta, Nov. 29, 1961; children: Sunil, Sanjiv. BA with 1st class honors, Punjab U., 1953, MA 1st class 1st, 1955, MEd 1st class 1st, 1959; BEd, Delhi U., 1958; PhD, Ga. State U., 1974. Cert. counselor, Pa. Lectr. Colls. Punjab and Kurukshetra U. India, 1955-63; teaching and rsch. fellow U. Alta., Edmonton, Can., 1963-66; asst. prof. psychology U. Wis., Stevens Point, 1966-68; asst. prof. psychology and counseling Ea. Ky. U., 1968-72; teaching and rsch. fellow Ga. State U., 1972-74; prof. psychology Kutztown U. Pa., 1974—. Subject of interviews on radio and TV. Recipient Cert. of merit Dictionary Internat. Biography, 1970. Mem. AAAS, AACD, AAUP, Internat. Coun. Psychologists, Internat. Assn. Applied Psychology, Internat. Assn. for Cross-cultural Psychology, Internat. Coun. on Edn. for Teaching, Am. Psychol. Assn., Am. Ednl. Rsch. Assn., Am. Assn. for Counselor Edn. and Supervision, Am. Mental Health Counselors Assn., Phi Delta Kappa. Home: 744 Highland Ave Kutztown PA 19530-1306 Office: Kutztown U of Pa Dept Psychology Kutztown PA 19530

GURFEIN, STUART JAMES, jewelry manufacturing company executive; b. N.Y.C., Mar. 24, 1947; s. Louis J. and Ruthe (Jacobs) G.; divorced; children: Scott Eric, Heather Gill; m. Kathryn Merine, Apr. 4, 1981; children: Kody Allana. BS, Cornell U., 1968; MBA, Columbia U., 1970. Account exec. Cunningham & Walsh Advt., N.Y.C., 1970-71; v.p. Gurfein Bros. Inc., N.Y.C., 1971-82, M. Fabrikant & Sons, N.Y.C., 1983-86; chmn. A.B.L. Jewelers Inc., N.Y.C., 1986—, Jeffrey Stevens, Inc., N.Y.C., 1988—; bd. dirs. Flyabl, Inc. Bd. dirs. Nat. Found. for Advancement in Arts, 1985—. Mem. Friars Club, Plumb Club. Office: ABL Jewelers Inc 562 5th Ave # 4 New York NY 10036-4801

GURFEL, BENOR, comptroller; b. Beltz, Bessarabia, Romania, Aug. 7, 1932; came to U.S., 1986; s. Leizer and Rebecca (Reznik) G.; m. Dorit Fish, Oct. 12, 1957; 1 child, Eli. PhD in Econs., Ural Polytech. Inst., Sverdlovsk, Russia, 1967. Registered profl. engr., Russia. Assoc. prof. Ural Polytech. Inst., 1968-72; MIS mgr. Ministry of Industry, Tallinn, Estonia, 1972-77; assoc. prof. Ben-Gurion U., Israel, 1977-82; project leader Ctr. Econs. Devel., Israel, 1983-86; mgr. of info. La-Salle Internat., Chgo., 1986-88; comptroller Balt. Hebrew U., 1988—; cons. Ministry of Energy, Israel, 1983-86. Contbr. articles to profl. jours. Mem. Royal Soc. Eng., Econometric Soc., Computer Entrepreneurs Assn. Am. Office: Balt Hebrew U 5800 Park Heights Ave Baltimore MD 21215

GURIAN, MAL, telecommunications executive; b. N.Y.C., Nov. 17, 1926; s. George Joseph and Rose (Graff) G.; m. Gloria Dickler; children: Randy Harlan, Nancy Ellen Newman. Ptnr. Mal Gurian Assocs., N.Y.C., 1946-77; v.p. Radio Telephone Corp., N.Y.C., 1960-83; sr. v.p. Aerotron, Inc., Raleigh, N.C., 1965-81; v.p. Oki Advanced Communications, Hackensack, N.J., 1981-84; pres. Oki Telecom, Fairlawn, N.J., 1984-88, Cartell, Inc., Romulus, Mich., 1988, Cellcom Cellular Corp., Fairfield, N.J., 1989-91; CEO Universal Cellular, Inc., Anaheim, Calif., 1992—; bd. dirs. Oki Telecom, Cartell, Inc., Universal Cellular, Inc. Life mem. Old Tappan (N.J.) First Aid Corps, 1966—. Cpl. USMC, 1943-46. Decorated Air medal. Fellow Radio Club of Am. (v.p. 1976—, Spl. Svcs. award 1986, Sarnoff citation 1988, Fred Link award 1989); mem. Assoc. Pub. Safety Communications Officers, Nat. Assn. of Bus. and Ednl. Radio (bd. dirs. 1977-84, Chmn.'s award 1986). Home: 14 Old Farmstead Rd Chester NJ 07930-9663

GURLAND, DORIS FANETTE, psychologist; b. Worcester, Mass., Sept. 29, 1924; d. Frank and Sema (Sorin) Hurwitch; m. Joseph Gurland, Dec. 23, 1948; children: Lisa, Johanna. BS, Wheelock Coll., Boston, 1950; MEd, R.I. Coll., 1964. Cert. clin. and sch. psychologist, R.I. Dir. Nursery Sch., Jewish Community Ctr., Providence, 1957-60; clin. psychologist R.I. Dept. Mental Health, Cranston, 1969-79; sch. psychologist Pleasant View Sch., Providence, 1979—; bd. dirs. Improvise!, Providence. A founder, bd. dirs. Looking Glass Theater, Providence, 1960-72; founding mem. 1st cancer support group in R.I., 1975; bd. dirs. ACLU, Providence, 1986-88. With USNR, 1944-46. Grantee R.I. Dept. Edn., 1964-66. Mem. R.I. Sch. Psychologists Assn. (com. for internat. conf. 1990), R.I. Audubon Soc., Mass. Audubon Soc., Maine Audubon Soc., R.I. Ornithol. Assn., Brookline Bird Club. Home: 43 Blackstone Blvd Providence RI 02906-5413

GURMAN, INA RUTH, educator; b. Passaic, N.J., Jan. 9, 1944; d. Benjamin and Frieda (Bell) Greenhause; m. Laurence Allan Gurman, June 15, 1969; children: Andrew Lowell, Jessica Leigh. BA, Douglass Coll., 1965; MA, Rutgers U., 1972; postgrad., Georgian Court Coll., 1988-89. Spanish and English lang. tchr. Edison Jr. High Sch., West Orange, N.J., 1965-67; teaching asst. Rutgers Univ., New Brunswick, N.J., 1967-69; spanish tchr. Monmouth Regional High Sch., Tinton Falls, N.J., 1969—; tchr. English Am. Inst. for Foreign Study, Howell, N.J., summer 1988, Interstudy, Howell, summers 1986, 87. Pres. Congregation Ahavat Achim Sisterhood, Howell, N.J., 1987-90. Recipient Tchr. Recognition award Gov. of N.J., 1991-92. Mem. NEA, Fgn. Lang. Educators of N.J., N.J. Edn. Assn., Monmouth Region Edn. Assn., Am. Assn. Tchrs. of Spanish and Portuguese.

GURNEY, ALBERT RAMSDELL, playwright, novelist, educator; b. Buffalo, Nov. 1, 1930; s. Albert Ramsdell and Marion (Spaulding) G.; m. Mary Forman Goodyear, June 8, 1957; children: George, Amy, Evelyn, Benjamin. BA, Williams Coll., 1952, DDL (hon.), 1984; MFA, Yale U., 1958; LLD, Buffalo State U., 1992. Mem. faculty MIT, 1960—, prof. lit., 1970—. Contbr. works to Best Short Plays, 1955-56, 57-58, 69, 70, 92; author: (plays) The Golden Fleece, 1969, Public Affairs, 1970, Scenes From American Life, 1971, Children, 1974, Richard Cory, 1976, The Middle Ages, 1977, The Wayside Motor Inn, 1977, The Golden Age, 1980, The Dining Room, 1981, What I Did Last Summer, 1982, The Perfect Party, 1985, Another Antigone, 1985, Sweet Sue, 1986, The Cocktail Hour, 1988, Love Letters, 1988, The Old Boy, 1991, The Fourth Wall, 1992, (teleplays) O Youth and Beauty, 1979, The Hit List, 1988, (musical play) The Snow Ball, 1991; (novel) The Gospel According to Joe, 1974, (novel) Entertaining Strangers, 1977, (novel) The Snow Ball, 1984, The Perfect Party, 1985, Another Antigone, 1985, Sweet Sue, 1986, The Cocktail Hour, 1988, Love Letters, 1988, (teleplay) The Hit List, 1988, (musical play) The Snow Ball, 1991, The Old Boy, 1992, The Fourth Wall, 1992. Served with USNR, 1952-55. Recipient N.Y. Drama Desk award, 1971, Rockefeller Playwrights award, 1977, Playwriting award Nat. Endowment Arts, 1981-82, Award of Merit Am. Acad. and Inst. Arts and Letters, 1987. Mem. Authors League Am., Writers Guild. Home: Wellers Bridge Rd Roxbury CT 06783-1616 Office: 120 W 70th St Apt 3C New York NY 10023-4417

GURNEY, JOHN STEVEN, illustrator; b. Lancaster, Pa., Jan. 11, 1962; s. Allan Bruce and Caroline Edith (Whitside) G.; m. Kathleen Ann Gatto, Sept. 20, 1987. BFA, Pratt Inst., 1984. Freelance illustrator Bklyn., 1984—. Illustrator (children's book) The Temptation of Wilfred Malachy, 1985, The Night Before Christmas, 1988, On Our Way to Market, 1991, Hansel & Gretel, 1991, Over the River and Through the Woods, 1992. Democrat. Roman Catholic. Home and Office: 261 Marlborough Rd Brooklyn NY 11226-4511

GURSKY, MARY PATRICIA (TRICIA GURSKY), educational administrator; b. Uniontown, Pa., Sept. 27, 1960; d. Edward Joseph and Margaret Ann (Gaddis) G. BS in Edn., California U. Pa., 1986, MS in Counselor Edn., 1988. Instructional I teaching cert. in secondary English, Pa. Sec., receptionist Household Fin. Corp., Uniontown, Pa., 1980; clk. typist West Penn Power Corp., Connellsville, Pa., 1980-82; exec. sec. Nemacolin, Inc., Farmington, Pa., 1982-83; salesperson Hess's Dept. Store, Uniontown, Pa., 1984; grad. asst. California U. Pa., 1987-88; mental health therapist Albert Gallatin Psychol. Svcs., Uniontown, Pa., 1988—; dir. W.Va. Career Inst., Lemont Furnace, Pa., 1987—; in-svc. presenter Albert Gallatin Svcs., Uniontown, Pa., 1988—. Mem. Mental Health Assn., Uniontown Bus. and Profl. Women (corr. sec. 1991-92, young careerist), Uniontown C. of C. (co-chair Ambassadors 1990—, mem. edn. coun. 1988—), Uniontown Rotary. Democrat. Roman Catholic. Home: PO Box 117 Brier Hill PA 15415-0117 Office: W Va Career Inst 200 College Dr Lemont Furnace PA 15456-9608

GURVITCH, HELEN W., county official; b. N.Y.C., Apr. 3, 1924; d. Nathan and Sophie (Benenson) Weiner; widowed; children: Donna McLaughlin, Howard. BA, CUNY, 1946. Dir. purchasing Town of Clarkstown, New City, N.Y., 1968-70; purchasing supr. East Ramapo Sch. Dist., Spring Valley, N.Y., 1970-74; commr. purchasing County of Rockland, New City, 1974—. Bd. dirs., treas. Am. Lung Assn. of Hudson Valley, White Plains, N.Y. Mem. N.Y. Assn. Purchasing Ofcls. (pres.), N.Y. State Assn. of Counties (bd. dirs.). Home: 101 Gedney St Nyack NY 10960-2209 Office: County of Rockland 18 New Hempstead Rd New City NY 10956-3637

GUSHARD, KEITH LEE, reporter; b. Meadville, Pa., May 1, 1958; s. Ernest John and Elizabeth Alice (Lobins) G. BA in Communications, Pa. State U., 1980. Disk jockey Sta. WMGW-AM, WZPR-FM, Meadville, 1980-82, reporter, 1982-85; affiliate news corr. ABC Radio News, 1982-85; reporter, fill-in city editor Meadville Tribune, 1985—. Mem. Rotary (sec. Vernon Twp. chpt. 1989). Republican. Presbyterian. Office: Meadville Tribune 947 Federal Ct Meadville PA 16335-3286

GUSOFF, PATRICIA KEARNEY, elementary school educator; b. Phila., Jan. 25, 1951; d. William Anthony and Helen Frances (Budnik) Kearney; m. Ronald Gusoff, June 22, 1975; children: Wayne Kenneth, Howard Brandon. BS in Edn., Temple U., 1973, MEd, 1977, EdD, 1988. Cert. elem. tchr., supr., adminstr., Pa., N.J. Elem. sch. tchr. Sch. Dist. Phila., 1973-89, elem. sci. tchr., 1989-90, basic skills tchr., 1990—, tchr. remedial work primary grades, 1990—; asst. facilitator, tutor William McKinley Elem. Sch., Phila., 1992—. Coord. sch. recycling Phila. Pride, 1990—. Mem. ASCD (assoc.), Pa. ASCD, Phila. Fedn. Tchrs. Home: 1119 Hedgerow Ln Philadelphia PA 19115

GUSSOW, JOHN ANDREW, lawyer; b. Bklyn., May 11, 1946; s. Emanuel M. and Jean M. (Gumpert) G.; children—Jerome A., Charles E. A.B., Dickinson Coll., 1967; J.D., Syracuse U., 1970. Bar: N.Y. 1971. Trial atty. civil div. Dept. Justice, N.Y.C., 1970-75; assoc. Melvin D. Kraft P.C., N.Y.C., 1975-76; asst. gen. counsel, asst. sec. M. Lowenstein Corp., N.Y.C., 1976-82, assoc. gen. counsel, asst. sec., 1982—; small claims arbitrator Civil Ct. Richmond County; mem. N.Y. State Cable TV Commn., 1984-86, ptnr. Hart and Gussow, 1986-87; ptnr., Gussow and Emma, 1987-91; Law chmn., mem. exec. com. Richmond County (N.Y.) Republican Com.; Rep. candidate for dist. atty. Richmond County, 1983; commr. N.Y. State Cable TV Commn., 1984-91; bd. dirs. Staten Island Acad., Camelot Found., Staten Island Community TV, S.I. Symphony; mem. community bd., law chmn. Richmond County Rep. Com. Mem. ABA, Assn. Bar City N.Y., Textile Lawyers Assn., Customs Bar Assn., N.Y. State Bar Assn., Richmond County Bar Assn., Am. Arbitration Assn. (nat. panel). Jewish, Congregates B'nai Israel. Lodge: Richmond County Kiwanis. Home: 50 Yacht Club Cv Staten Island NY 10308-3531 Office: Gussow & Emma 32 Narrows Rd S Staten Island NY 10305-2832

GUSTAFSON, GAYLE LEE, software writer; b. Burlington, Iowa, Nov. 10, 1959; d. Louis Frederick and Fern (Nelson) Gustafson; m. Gary Robert Ferreira, May 16, 1992. BS in Computer Sci. and Bus., Boston U., 1986. Documentation specialist Raytheon Co., Sudbury, Mass., 1982-87; software tech. writer Concurrent Computer, Tinton Falls, N.J., 1987-88; cons. AT&T, Lincroft, N.J., 1988-89, Holmdel, N.J., 1990—; cons. IBM Nordiska Lab., Stockholm, 1989-90; software writer EJV Ptnrs., L.P., N.Y.C., 1991—. Mem. ACM, IEEE, Assn. of Women in Computing, Soc. Tech. Communicators (chpt. leader, newsletter mgr. 1990-91, judge 1990). Lutheran. Home: 822 Stafford Ave Staten Island NY 10309-2336

GUSTAVSON, HENRY BRADFORD, architectural executive; b. Bronxville, N.Y., Dec. 16, 1954; s. Henry Berthil and Shirley (Losee) G.; m. Ruby Schwartz, Nov. 13, 1982; children: Henry Eric, Richard Solomon. BArch, BFA, Syracuse U., 1977; MBA, Fordham U., 1981. Draftsman Henry Loheac & Assocs., Scarsdale, N.Y., 1977-79, Gibbons, Heidtmann & Salvador, White Plains, N.Y., 1979; project mgr. David Paul Helpern, P.C., N.Y.C., 1979-85; owner Gustavson/Dundes, N.Y.C., 1985—; chmn. Design Review Bd., White Plains, 1985—.

GUSTIN, WILLIAM ARNETT, earth science and geography educator; b. Tuscola, Ill., Sept. 9, 1960; s. Veit Ivan and Nola Claire (Swinford) G.; m. Leisa Kay Gauer, Dec. 31, 1988; 1 child, Christopher Shaun. BS in Geography and History, Ind. State U., 1983, MA in Geography, 1988. Assoc. coord. Climatology Lab. Climatology Lab. Ind. State U., Terre Haute, 1983-88; prof. earth sci. and geography California U. Pa., 1988—; dir. Earth Scis. Computer Applications Lab., Southwestern Pa. Inst. Regional and Econ. Devel., California U. Pa., 1990—. Mem. Am. Meteorol. Soc., Assn. Am. Geographers, Assn. Am. Weather Observers, Ind. Acad. Sci., Pa. Geog. Soc., Nat. Weather Assn. Baptist. Home: RR 1 Box 126 Fredericktown PA 15333-8904 Office: Dept Earth Scis California U Pa California PA 15419

GUSTINA, CHARLES FRANCIS, interior designer, photographer; b. Manchester, Conn., Aug. 25, 1957; s. Francis Joseph Jr. and Patricia Winifred (Wilson) G. BA in Fine Arts, Georgetown U., 1979; postgrad., Pratt Inst., 1979-82. Designer Kohn Pedersen Fox Conway Assn., N.Y.C., 1981-85; sr. designer Miller Orgn., Inc., N.Y.C., 1985-86, Owen & Mandolfo, Inc., N.Y.C., 1987-88, Perkins & Will, N.Y.C., 1988-90; owner, designer Charles F. Gustina Design, N.Y.C., 1985—; owner, photographer Carlo Foto, N.Y.C., 1990—; design cons. Hellmuth, Obata, & Kassabaum, P.C., N.Y.C., 1991-92, Clark, Tribble, Harris & Li, N.Y.C., 1986, Noel Jeffrey, Inc., N.Y.C., 1985. Photographer Opus I, 1990, Opus II, 1991. Office: 200 Waverly Pl # 2 New York NY 10014

GUSTON, SHEILA E., association executive; b. Paterson, N.J., Mar. 21, 1936; d. Jack and Jean (Fuchs) Eckhaus; m. Herbert M. Guston, June 9, 1957; children: Debra E., Judith M., David H. BS, Fairleigh Dickinson U., 1957; MA, William Paterson Coll., 1974. Cert. assn. exec. Dir. N.J. region B'nai B'rith Women, Clifton, 1976-87; exec. dir. Alpha Omega Internat. Dental Fraternity, N.Y.C., 1987—. Mem. N.Y. Soc. Assn. Execs. (bd. dirs.), Am. Soc. Assn. Execs. (devel. com), NAFE, B'nai B'rith Women (coun. pres. 1972-73). Home: 7 Wichita Path Oakland NJ 07436-3818 Office: Alpha Omega 347 5th Ave # 703 New York NY 10016-5010

GUTHRIE, JAMES RUSSELL, magazine publishing executive, marketing executive; b. East Orange, N.J., Oct. 18, 1940; s. David Russell and Janet MacFarlane (Walker) G.; m. Ann Louise Trattner, Sept. 21, 1968; children: Elizabeth Trattner, MacLean Ann. BS in Econ., U. Pa., 1962, MA in Am. Civilization, 1988. Acct. exec. Ted Bates, N.Y.C., 1963-66; sr. acct. exec. Sullivan, Stouffer, Colwell & Bayles, N.Y.C., 1966-69; acct. supr. Foote Cone and Belding, N.Y.C., 1969-70, v.p. acct. supervision, 1970-72, v.p. mgmt. supervision, 1972-78, sr. v.p. group mgmt. supervision, 1978-81; pres., chief oper. officer John Emmerling, Inc., N.Y.C., 1981-87; exec. v.p. mktg. Magazine Pubs. Am., N.Y.C., 1987—; exec. dir. Pubs. Info. Bur., N.Y.C., 1990—. Author poetry and speeches; contbr. numerous articles to profl. jours. Bd. dirs. Congl. Ch., New Canaan, Conn., 1977-80, chmn. bd. trustees, 1981, chmn. stewardship, 1980. With U.S. Army, 1963-68. Mem. U. Pa. Alumni Assn., U. Pa. Friars Honor Soc., Union League Club N.Y., Ad Club N.Y. (advt. coun. campaigns rev. com.), Lake Club New Canaan, Coral Beach Club Bermuda, St. Andrews Soc. N.Y. Republican. Home: 33 Canoe Hill Rd New Canaan CT 06840-3702 Office: Mag Pubs Am 575 Lexington Ave New York NY 10022-6102

GUTHRIE, JOHN FRANCIS, electronics executive; b. Balt., Sept. 22, 1957; s. James Vincent and Claire Bernadette (Ray) G.; m. Patricia Ann Bathon, June 16, 1984; children: Caroline Frances, Kathleen Lauren, Rebecca Marie. BA, Loyola Coll., Balt., 1979, MBA, 1984. CPA, Md. Underwriter Fidelity and Deposit, Balt., 1979-81; sr. cons. Deloitte Haskins and Fells (now Deloitte and Touche), Balt., 1982-86; v.p. fin., chief fin. officer Communication System Tech., Inc., Columbia, Md., 1986—; also bd. dirs. Communicaiton System Tech., Inc., Columbia, Md. Bd. dirs. subcom. United Way, Balt., 1990—. Mem. Balt.-Washington Venture Capital Group, Assn. for Corp. Growth, Md. Assn. CPAs, Am. Assn. CPAs. Republican. Roman Catholic. Office: CSTI 9740 Patuxent Woods Dr Columbia MD 21046-1533

GUTHRIE, WILLIAM DAVID, dean, consultant; b. Trenton, N.J., Nov. 26, 1935; s. John Munro and Helen (Young) G.; m. Evelyn Rue, Aug. 16, 1958; children: Kathryn, Kristin. BS, Trenton State Coll., 1957, MA, 1960; PhD, NYU, 1975. Educator sci. Trenton Pub. Schs., 1957-58; educator physics and math. Hopewell Valley Cen. High Sch., Pennington, N.J., 1958-59; supr. sci. and math. N.J. State Dept. Edn., Trenton, 1959-65; assoc. dean Rider Coll., Lawrenceville, N.J., 1965—; cons. sci. and math. Designer: Amman Jordan Sci. Edn. Ctr. Natural History Hall, N.J. State Mus.; contbr. articles and chpts. to profl. jours. Moderator, Presbytery New Brunswick, N.J. Fellow N.J. Sci. Tchrs. Assn.; mem. N.J. Assn. Colls. for Tchr. Edn. (pres. 1982-84), N.J. Acad. Sci. (exec. com. 1984—), N.J. Coun. Edn. (exec. com. 1988-90), Am. Ednl. Rsch. Assn., Phi Delta Kappa (faculty advisor). Home: 8 Poor Farm Rd Pennington NJ 08534-3801 Office: Rider Coll Lawrenceville Rd Trenton NJ 08648-4308

GUTIERREZ, ADOLFO OSVALDO, electrical engineer; b. Santiago, Chile, Nov. 21, 1959; came to U.S., 1986; s. Adolfo R. and Gladys (Gajardo) G.; m. Jimena Vargas, Jan. 3, 1987; 1 child, Adolfo E. BSc in Elec. Engring., Physics, U. Chile, Santiago, 1985, MSc in Elec. Engring., 1986; PhD in Engring. Physics, Rensselaer Polytech. Inst., 1991. Staff scientist Intersci., Inc., Troy, N.Y., 1989—. Mem. IEEE, Optical Soc. Am., Am. Phys. Soc., Sigma Xi (assoc.). Office: 105 Jordan Rd Troy NY 12180

GUTIERREZ, PETER LUIS, biophysicist, educator, researcher; b. Monteria, Colombia, June 9, 1939; s. Pedro Antonio and Fanny Edith (Hogg) G.; m. Sarah Ann Hanchett, Sept. 2, 1966; children: Fanny Elizabeth, Ann Carolynn. BS, Wheaton Coll., 1962; MS, Calif. State U., L.A., 1970; PhD, So. Ill. U., 1973. Engring. asst. Automatic Electric, North Lake, Ill., 1962-64; engr.-writer Hycon Mfg. Co., Monrovia, Calif., 1965-67; spl. doctoral asst. So. Ill. U., Carbondale, 1972; staff biophysicist Nat. Biomed. Electron Spin Resonance Spectroscopy Ctr., Milw., 1974-78; assoc. prof. oncological pharmacology Cancer Ctr., U. Md., Balt., 1978—. Editorial bd. Free Radical Medicine and Biology, 1992—; sci. reviewer Molecular Pharmacology Jour., 1985—, Brit. Jour. Cancer, 1986—, Chemico-Biol. Interactions, 1988—; contbr. articles to sci. publs. Mem. Am. Chem. Soc., Am. Assn. Cancer Rsch., Internat. Soc. for Free Radical Rsch., Biophys. Soc. Republican. Baptist. Office: Univ Md Cancer Ctr 655 W Baltimore St Baltimore MD 21201-1509

GUTMAN, I. CYRUS, transportation consultant, business executive; b. Perth Amboy, N.J., Mar. 28, 1912; s. Leon and Jennie (Levine) G.; m. Mildred B. Largman, July 21, 1940; children: Harry L., Peggy Sheren, Richard J.S. BS in Econs., Johns Hopkins U., 1932. Dist. mgr. Motor Freight Express, Inc., Phila., 1933-40; v.p., treas., gen. mgr. Modern Transfer Co., Inc., Allentown, Pa., 1940-67, dir. nat. sales, 1967-70; v.p. Atlantic div. Nat. Resource Recovery Corp., 1982—; mem. labor panel Am. Arbitration Assn., 1980—; bd. dirs. Eastern Industries, Inc., Wescosville, Pa., 1967-76. Pres. Lehigh County Indsl. Devel. Corp., 1959-85, Lehigh's Econ. Advancement Project, Inc., 1960-85; chmn. Lehigh County Indsl. Devel.

Authority, 1966-82; mem. adv. com. Central Pa. Teamsters Pension and Health and Welfare Funds, 1969-76; mem. nat. resources com., nat. alumni schs. com. Johns Hopkins; mem. Lehigh-Northampton Counties Joint Planning Commn., 1962-82; chmn. Allentown Sch. Dist. Authority, 1966-86; mem. Lehigh and Northampton Transp. Authority, 1972-74; chmn. Allentown Non-Partisan Com. for Local Govt.; mem. Eastern Conf. Joint Area Com.; assoc. mem. Nat. Jewish Welfare Bd.; hon. bd. mem. Allentown Jewish Community Ctr., 1986—; exec. com. Citizens for Lehigh County Progress, 1965—; chmn. central campaign planning com. Lehigh Valley Hosps., 1966-67; adv. com. Good Shepherd Workshop; adv. bd. Allentown citadel Salvation Army, treas., 1971-80; pres. bd. assocs. Muhlenberg Coll., v.p., 1971-73, pres. 1974-76; bd. assocs. Cedar Crest Coll., 1972—; gen. adv. com. Lehigh County Vocat.-Tech. Sch., Lehigh County Community Coll., 1977; mem. Lehigh County Rep. Exec. Com.; trustee Allentown Hosp., 1970-82, hon. trustee, 1982-87, hon. mem., 1987; hon. Lehigh Valley Hosp. Ctr., 1987—; trustee, Swain Sch., 1977-80; bd. dirs. Lehigh Valley Jr. Achievement, United Fund, Allentown, Jewish Fedn. Allentown, 1953-60, Wiley House, 1969-80; bd. dirs. Lehigh Valley Public TV, Sta. WLVT, 1980—, vice chmn., 1984-88, chmn. 1989—; past trustee Rabbi Louis M. Youngerman Found., Internat. Assn. Machinists Local 1099 Dist. Pension Plan, Phi Sigma Delta Found.; hon. adv. bd. Lehigh Valley Assn. for Retarded Children, 1969-70; mem. adv. bd. Lehigh Valley Ctr. for Performing Arts, 1975-77. Recipient St. Patrick's Day award Lehigh Valley, 1961, Civic Svc. commendation Whitehall C. of C.; Golden Deeds award Allentown Exchange Club, 1972, Disting. Citizens Sales award Sales and Mktg. Execs., Allentown and Bethlehem, 1976, Outstanding Svc. award Lehigh Valley Traffic Club, 1978, citation Pa. Ho. of Reps., 1982, City of Allentown, 1982, Americanism award Anti-Defamation League and B'nai Brith, 1985, citation Assn. for Blind and Visually Impaired, 1985, citation Lehigh County Vocat. Tech. Sch., 1986; Jack Houlihan Community Vol. award Lehigh County United Way, 1985, Presdl. proclamation through Gov. Thornburgh, Pa., 1986; Cyrus Gutman Scholarship established by Lehigh County Bus. and Indsl. Community Johns Hopkins U., 1983; I. Cyrus Gutman Day proclaimed in honor Allentown, Bethlehem, Easton, Pa. Mem. Allentown C. of C. (Disting. Svc. award 1967, past bd. dirs.), Traffic and Transp. Assn. Pitts., Met. Traffic Assn. N.Y., Cen. Pa. Motor Carriers Assn. (v.p., exec. com.), Pa. Soc., Am. Trucking Assn. (gov. Regular Common Carrier Conf. 1968), Eastern Labor Adv. Assn. (v.p.), Am. Arbitration Assn. (labor panel 1980—), Hon. First Defenders, Johns Hopkins Alumni Assn. (past sec., past pres. Phila. area), Lehigh County Hist. Soc. (exec. com. 1968-71), Nat. Fedn. Temple Brotherhoods, Berkleigh Country Club (hon. mem., past pres.), Lehigh Valley Club, Locust Midcity Club, Traffic and Transp. Club, Traffic Club Phila., Traffic Club Balt., N.Y. Traffic Club, Livingston Club, Masons, B'nai Brith, Omicron Delta Kappa, Pi Delta Epsilon, Zeta Beta Tau. Home and Office: 800 Hausman Rd Allentown PA 18104-9393

GUTSCH, WILLIAM ANTHONY, JR., astronomer; b. Newark, Jan. 14, 1946; s. William Anthony and Mary (Ellenback) G. B.S., St. Peter's Coll., 1967; M.S., U. Va., 1973, Ph.D., 1978. Staff astronomer Rochester Museum and Sci. Ctr., N.Y., 1973-82; chmn. Am. Mus.-Hayden Planetarium, N.Y.C., 1982—; cons. in field, lectr. in field; news columnist Rochester Times-Union, 1980-84; sci. reporter Sta.-WOKR-TV, Rochester, N.Y., 1976-82; sci. corr. Sta.-WABC-TV, N.Y.C., 1982-84, sci. editor, 1984-86; on-air meteorologist ABC Network, 1986—; sci. columnist Gannett, 1980-90; cons. U. Santiago, Chile, 1982. Author: The Search for Extraterrestrial Life, 1991, other books; also newspaper articles, TV news and planetarium scripts. Recipient award of svc. U. Santiago, 1982, City of Buenos Aires, 1983, City of San Juan, 1991, City of Jaharta, Indonesia, 1991; Emmy nominee, 1987. Mem. Am. Astron. Soc., Am. Meteorol. Soc., Am. Assn. Physics Tchrs., Internat. Planetarium Soc. (pres.-elect 1992).

GUTTMAN, CHARLES MARTIN, chemist; b. Cin., Apr. 11, 1939; s. Ervan Edward and Eva (Bloom) G.; m. Judith Atwood, Sept. 15, 1960 (div. Mar. 1970); children: Hannah, Harry; m. Evelyne Lee Barry, Feb. 15, 1975; 1 child, Damiana. BA, Earlham Coll., Richmond, Ind., 1961; PhD, Brandeis U., Waltham, Mass., 1967. Rsch. assoc. Bell Labs., Summit, N.J., 1967-68; rsch. chemist N.I.S.T. Polymer Div., Gaithersburg, Md., 1968—. Mem. ASTM (task chmn. 1970—. Jewish. Office: NIST Polymer Div Gaithersburg MD 20879

GUTTMAN, GILDA RAE, writer, humanities and theatre arts educator; b. N.Y.C., Jan. 5, 1951; d. Morris Hiram and Louise (Wasserman) Dobrin; m. Bruce Guttman, July 5, 1971. BSEd, NYU, 1971, PhD, 1982; MSEd, Long Island U., 1973; postgrad., Shakespeare Inst., Stratford-on-Avon, 1975. High sch. tchr. drama N.Y.C. Bd. Edn., 1972-80; free lance dir., designer of lighting and sets, 1980-85; arts and entertainment editor Derry (N.H.) News, 1985-90; adj. prof. humanities N.H. Coll., Salem, 1986—; adj. prof. puppetry and ednl. theatre Hesser coll., Manchester, N.H., 1990—; adj. prof. theatre Plymouth State Coll., 1992—; adj. women's history and puppetry Mt. Ida Coll., Newton, Mass., 1990—; lighting designer Bklyn. Arts and Cultural Assn., 1982; historian Am. Community Theatre Assn., 1984-86; community TV coord. CTV-20, Londonderry, N.H., 1986-88, producer, 1984-87; guest speaker opera Music Masters, Londonderry, 1989-90; creative cons. for multi media presentations. Writer, photographer Manchester mag.; photographer Harcourt, Brace & Jovanovich, 1988, N.H. Gateways, Nashua C. of C., 1990—; founder, mem. NYU Creative Arts Team, 1975-80; dir., artistic dir. Mus. and Drama Co., 1985-88; feature writer, editor N.H. Assn. Realtors Newsletter, 1989, Highnotes, Nashua Symphony Assn. Newsletter, 1991—, Higgins Herald, N.H. Coll. Newsletter; contbr. hundreds revs., articles to popular mags., newspapers. Pres. N.H. Community Theater Assn., Concord, 1986-88; mem. Animal Rescue League N.H., 1990—; bd. dirs. N.H. Friendship Chorus, 1988—, trustee, 1988—; trustee Nashua Symphony Assn., 1990—. Recipient Bicentennial Medal U.S. Bicentennial Com., 1988. Mem. N.H. Press Assn. (bd. dirs., chair better newspaper contest, editor NHPA Handbook), Federated Arts (communications com., newsletter and calendar editor 1990—), New Eng. Press Assn. (conv. com.), New Eng. Collegiate Press Assn. (founder, exec. dir. 1992—), Women in Communication, Inc. (v.p. fin. 1987-88), U.S. Inst. Theatre Tech., Alpha Psi Omega. Jewish. Home: 12 Dan Hill Rd Londonderry NH 03053-3130

GUTTMAN, HELENE NATHAN, research executive; b. N.Y.C., July 21, 1930; d. Arthur and Mollie (Bergovoy) Nathan. BA, Bklyn. Coll., 1951; AM, Harvard U., 1956; MA, Columbia U., 1958; PhD, Rutgers U., 1960. Chartered chemist Royal Soc. Chemistry; registered profl. animal scientist. Rsch. technician Pub. Health Rsch. Inst., N.Y.C., 1951-52; control bacteriologist Burroughs-Wellcome, Inc., Tuckahoe, N.Y., 1952-53; vol. researcher Haskins Labs., N.Y.C., 1952-53; rsch. asst. Haskins Labs., 1953-56, rsch. assoc., 1956-60, staff microbiologist, 1960-64; lectr. dept. biology Queens Coll., N.Y.C., 1956-57; rsch. collaborator Brookhaven Nat. Labs., Upton, L.I., N.Y., 1958; guest investigator Botanisches Institut der Technisches Hochschule, Darmstadt, Germany, 1960; rsch. assoc. dept. biol. scis. Goucher Coll., Towson, Md., 1960-62; vis. asst. rsch. prof. dept. medicine Med. Coll. Va. Richmond, 1960-62; asst. prof., then assoc. prof. dept. biology NYU, 1962-67; from assoc. prof. to prof. dept. biol. scis. U. Ill.-Chgo., 1967-75, prof., 1969-75; prof. dept. microbiology U. Ill. Med. Sch., 1969-75; assoc. dir. for rsch. Urban Systems Lab. U. Ill., 1975; expert Office of Dir. Nat. Heart, Lung and Blood Inst., NIH, Bethesda, Md., 1975-77; coordinator rsch. resources Office Program Planning and Evaluation Nat. Heart, Lung and Blood Inst., NIH, 1977-79; dep. dir. Sci. Adv. Bd., Office of Adminstr., EPA, 1979-80; program coordinator, post-harvest tech., food safety and human nutrition, sci. and edn. adminstrn. USDA, 1980-83, assoc. dir. Beltsville Human Nutrition Rsch. Ctr., Agrl. Rsch. Svc., 1983-89; pres. HNG Assocs., 1983—; animal care coord. Nat. Program Staff, Agr. Rsch. Svc./USDA, Beltsville, Md., 1989—. Sr. author: Experiments in Cellular Biodynamics, 1972; co-editor (proceedings) First Joint USA-USSR Joint Symposium on Blood Transfusion, Moscow, USSR (Oct. 18-20, 1976), DHEW Publ. No. (NIH) 78-1246, 1978; editorial bd. Jour. Protozoology, 1972-75, Jour. Am. Med. Women's Assn., 1978-81; sr. editor: Science & Animals: Addressing Contemporary Issues, 1989; editor: Guidelines for Well-being of Rodents in Research, 1990; contbr. articles to profl. jours. and books. Mem. edn. com. Ill. Commn. on Status Women, 1974-75; cons. EPA, sci. adv. bd., 1974-79; bd. dirs. Du Page County Comprehensive Health Care Agy., 1974-75. Andelot fellow Harvard U., 1956, Rutgers scholar Rutgers U., 1960; recipient Thomas Jefferson Murray prize Theobald Smith Soc., 1959; spl. award for work in Germany Deutscher Forschungs Gemeinschaft, 1960; Fellow Dazian Found., 1956; research grantee. Fellow AAAS, Am. Inst. Chemists (com. chmn.), Am. Acad. Microbiology, N.Y. Acad. Scis.; mem. Soc. Am. Bacteriologists (pres.'s fellow 1957), Tissue Culture Assn. (com. chmn. Nat. Capital Area br. 1988-90), Am. Soc. Neurochemistry, Am. Soc. Biol. Chemistry, Neurosci. Soc., Am. Soc. Microbiologists, Am. Soc. Cell Biology (past com. chmn.), Am. Soc. Clin. Nutrition, Soc. Protozoology (past mem. exec. com., past jour. editorial bd.), Soc. Exptl. Biology and Medicine, Assn. Women in Sci. (past mem. exec. bd., past com. chmn.), Fed. Orgn. Profl. Women (past task force chmn., past pres.), Univ. and Coll. Women Ill. (past v.p.), Am. Running and Fitness Assn. (bd. dirs., mem. editorial bd.), Sigma Xi, Sigma Delta Epsilon (past coord. regional ctrs.). Home: 5607 Mclean Dr Bethesda MD 20814-1021 Office: Nat Program Staff Agrl Rsch Svc USDA BARC W Bldg 002 Rm 105 Beltsville MD 20705

GUTZEIT, FRED ERNST, artist, educator; b. Cleve., Oct. 30, 1940; s. Fritz Carl and Emmy (Rosner) G. Cert. grad., Cleve. Inst. Art., 1962; MA in Painting, Hunter Coll., CUNY, 1979. Prof. Lacoste Sch. Art, France, 1984, 85, L.I. U., Bklyn, 1985-88; mem. 55 Mercer St. Artists, Inc., N.Y.C., 1982-85; vis. assoc. prof. Pratt Inst., 1985—. One-man shows include Herbert F. Johnson Mus., Ithaca, N.Y., 1977, Cleve. Inst. Art, 1977; exhibited in group shows at Alrich Mus., Ridgefield, Conn., 1975-82, Allan Stone Gallery, N.Y.C., 1984, Nat. Arts Club, N.Y.C., 1986, L.I. U., Bklyn., 1986, Washington County Mus. Fine Arts, Hagerstown, Md., 1986, Cleve. Inst. Art, 1988, Bklyn. Bot. Gardens Gallery, Bklyn., 1988, Pratt Manhattan Gallery, N.Y.C., 1989, Nat. Bldg. Mus., Washington, 1990, Mona Bismarck Found., Paris, 1991, others. Cleve. Art Mary C. Paige travelling scholar, Mexico, 1962-63. Home and Studio: 264 Bowery New York NY 10012

GUY, BRUCE MICHAEL, financial executive; b. Salem, Mass., Nov. 27, 1949; s. Roland Joseph and Simone M. (Parent) G.; m. Patricia Dorothy Greene, Oct. 6, 1974; children: Brian T., Shawn M. BS, Salem State Coll., 1973; MBA, Suffolk U., 1978; Cert., Brown U., 1979. CMA. Fin. ops. officer Salem (Mass.) Savs. Bank, 1971-79; comptroller New Eng. Bd. Higher Edn., Wenham, Mass., 1979-80; exec. v.p., treas. Progressive Consumers Fed., Saugus, Mass., 1980-90; cons., pres., prin. Fin. Mgmt. Assocs., Wenham, Mass., 1990—; asst. prof. acctg. and finance, Salem State Coll., 1991—. Office: Fin Mgmt Assocs PO Box 2692 South Hamilton MA 01915

GUYETT, ROBERT LOSEE, specialty chemicals and metals executive; b. Dobbs Ferry, N.Y., Jan. 10, 1937; s. Howard Lynn Guyett; m. Susan Weisser, Jan. 31, 1959; children: Gregory L., Keith L. BA, Williams Coll., 1958; MBA, Rutgers U., 1959. With Pogson Peloubet (merged with Price Waterhouse, 1963), 1959-63; sr. tax mgr. Price Waterhouse, 1963-76; sr. auditor Stamford, Conn., 1963-65; tax mgr. Europe Brussels, 1968-71; sr. tax mgr. Phila., 1972-76; v.p., treas. LTV Corp., Dallas, 1976-86; dir. taxes, 1976-79, asst. treas., fin. and tax, 1979-83, v.p., controller, 1983-86, v.p., treas., 1986; sr. v.p. fin., chief fin. officer Fluor Corp., Irvine, Calif., 1987-91; sr. v.p. fin., chief fin. officer Engelhard Corp., Iselin, N.J., 1991—, also bd. dirs.; founder, bd. dirs. Concorde Bank N.A., Dallas; bd. dirs. Newport Corp. Mem. Am. Inst. CPA's, Nat. Assn. Accts., Fin. Execs. Inst., Tax Exec. Inst., Internat. Fiscal Assn., Beta Theta Pi. Clubs: Williams (N.Y.C.); Huntington Valley Country (Phila.) (treas., bd. govs. 1974-76), Santa Ana Country Club. Office: Engelhard Corp 101 Wood Ave Iselin NJ 08830

GUZMAN, RODOLFO MANUEL, energy consultant; b. Caracas, Venezuela, Jan. 7, 1966; came to U.S., 1989; s. Manuel A. and Marina M. (Maeer) G.; m. Julianna Szabo, June 15, 1991. Degree in Mech. Engring. summa cum laude, U. Simon Bolivar, Caracas, 1988; MBA with distinction, Wharton Sch. U. Pa., 1991. Ops. analyst Petroquimica de Venezuela S.A., Caracas, 1988-89; energy cons. Arthur D. Little Inc., Cambridge, Mass., 1991—. Palmer scholar. Roman Catholic. Home: 200 Ledgewood Dr Apt 208 Stoneham MA 02180

GUZZARDI, WALTER PETER, book publishing company executive; b. Washington, June 18, 1950; s. Walter Peter and Anne Bannister (Woods) G.; m. Isabel Ruth Geffner, Oct. 10, 1984; children: Samuel Geffner, William Spector. BA, SUNY, Stony Brook, 1972. Advt. mgr. St. Martin's Press, N.Y.C., 1974-76; advt. and promotion assoc. Bantam Books, N.Y.C., 1976-78, sr. editor, 1982-87; editor Penguin Books, N.Y.C., 1978-80, Dell Pub. Co., N.Y.C., 1980-82; v.p., editorial dir. Harmony Books/Crown Pubs., N.Y.C., 1987—. Office: Harmony Books 201 E 50th St New York NY 10022-7703

GWINN, GERALDINE B., interior designer; b. Columbia, Pa., Mar. 3, 1952; d. William W. and Darlene Mae (Brubaker) Martin; m. David Loren Gwinn, June 13, 1970; children: Angela Marie, Jeremy Todd. Interior Design Diploma, LaSalle U., 1974. Owner, prin. A Touch of Class, Lititz, Pa., 1980-87; interior designer Bareville Furniture, Leola, Pa., 1981-87, Design Detail Interiors, Lancaster, Pa., 1987—. Mem. Am. Soc. Interior Designers (professional). Republican. Office: Design Detail Interiors 1368 Harrisburg Pike Lancaster PA 17601-2613

GYLLENHAMMAR, PEHR GUSTAF, business executive; b. Gothenburg, Sweden, Apr. 28, 1935; s. Pehr and Aina (Kaplan) G.; M.Law, U. Lund, 1959; MD honoris causa, U. Gothenburg, 1981; Tech D honoris causa, Brunel U., 1987, ED honoris causa, Tech. U. Nova Scotia, 1988; D Soc. Sci. honoris causa, U. Helsinki, 1990; m. Christina Engellau; children: Cecilia, Charlotte, Oscar, Sophie. With Ins. Co. Amphion, 1961-64; asst. adminstrv. mgr. Ins. Co. AB. Skandia, 1965-66, v.p., 1966, dep. mng. dir., 1968-70, mng. dir., chief exec., 1970; mng. dir., chief exec. officer AB Volvo, Gothenburg, 1971-83, chmn., chief exec. officer, 1983-90, exec. chmn., 1990—, also bd. dirs.; vice chmn. bd. Skandinaviska Enskilda Banken; dir. United Techs. Corp., Kissinger Assocs. Inc., Pearson plc, Reuters Holdings PLC, Régie Nat. des Usines Renault SA, Procorida AB; chmn. bd. Swedish Ships Mortgage Bank; mem. Internat. advisory com. Chase Manhattan Bank. Mem. Fedn. Swedish Industries (dir.). Author 5 books. Office: AB Volvo, S-40508 Gothenburg Sweden

HAACKE, HARRY HENRY, insurance company executive; b. N.Y.C., Mar. 5, 1928; s. Harry H. and Ruth P. (Ford) H.; married, Sept. 1, 1951; 1 child, Robert D. BA, St. Lawrence U., Canton, N.Y., 1952. Underwriter Ins. Co. N.Am., N.Y.C., 1954-62, Royal Globe Ins. Group, N.Y.C., 1962-68; sr. v.p., broker Marsh & McLennan, N.Y.C., 1968-81; pres., broker Rollins Wrightson Co., N.Y.C., 1981-88; sr. v.p., broker Johnson & Higgins, N.Y.C., 1988—. Republican. Home: 8 Candlewood Springs New Milford CT 06776 Office: Johnson & Higgins 125 Broad St New York NY 10004

HAAG, DAVID EARL, banker; b. Lebanon, Pa., May 21, 1946; s. Thomas B. and Helen (Fortna) M.; m. Joan Mary Brubaker, July 5, 1969; children: Jeffrey, Jessica. BS in Fin., Pa. State U., 1968; postgrad., U. Del., 1986-88. With Bank of Pa., Reading, 1971—, regional mktg. mgr., 1990—. Speaker United Way, Reading, 1992; fund raiser St. Joseph Hosp., Reading, 1992, Pa. State U., 1992; dir.,pres. Berks Gymnastics Team. Capt. U.S. Army, 1968-71, Vietnam. Decorated Purple Heart, V. Silver Star, Bronze Star for Valor. Mem. Reading Mktg. Assn., Internat. Airborne Soc., Am. Legion, VFW, DAV. Office: Bank of Pa 50 N 5th St Reading PA 19601

HAAG, EUGENE PAUL, accountant; b. N.Y.C., Apr. 27, 1937; s. Eugene Christian and Johanna (Kloz) H.; m. Judith Ann Thornton, Sept. 10, 1960; children: Julia (dec.), Eugene Jr., Jonathan, Jason, Jessica. BA in Acctg., Duke U., 1960. CPA, N.Y.; cert. tax profl. Am. Inst. Tax Studies. Tax. mgr. Arthur Andersen & Co., N.Y.C., 1962-69; owner Eugene Paul Haag, CPA, Yonkers, N.Y., 1969—; seminar leader Found. for Acctg. Edn., N.Y.C., 1987—. V.p., dir. Community Aid for Retarded Children, Buchanan, N.Y., 1969-79; cons. Assn. for Performing Arts, Yorktown Heights, N.Y., 1978-80. With U.S. Army, 1960-62. Mem. AICPA, N.Y. State Soc. CPAs (seminar leader 1987—, com. on individual income taxes 1987—), Nat. Soc. Tax Profls., Nat. Tax Assn., Tax. Inst. Am., Alpha Kappa Psi. Republican. Roman Catholic. Home: 178 Somerston Rd Yorktown Heights NY 10598-2218 Office: Eugene Paul Haag CPA 540 Palmer Rd Yonkers NY 10701-5207

HAAG, FRED GEORGE, mechanical engineer; b. Weehawken, N.J., May 11, 1931; s. Frederick Christian and Charlotte (Kupker) H.; m. Dorothy Belle Dodson, Dec. 14, 1957; children: Ellen, Catherine. ME, Stevens Inst. Tech., Hoboken, N.J., 1953; MS, Rensselaer Poly. Inst., 1958, D Engring. Sci., 1964. Registered profl. engr., N.Y. Engr. Oak Ridge (Tenn.) Sch. Reactor Tech., 1953-54; supervising engr. Knolls Atomic Power Lab., Schenectady, 1955-67; assoc. prof. Union Coll., Schenectady, 1967-72; dir. Bur. Air Resource Tech. Svcs. N.Y. State Environ. Conservation, Albany, 1972-79; power generation planner N.Y. State Pub. Svc. Commn., Albany, 1979—; adj. prof. Union Coll. Schenectady, 1977—. Office: NY State Pub Svc Commn 3 Empire State Plz Albany NY 12223-0001

HAAG, JAMES JOSEPH, state government executive, researcher; b. Detroit, Aug. 5, 1941; s. Joseph Floyd and Margaret Elizabeth (Wassman) H.; m. Marie Thresa Heimerdinger Haag, Dec. 30, 1966; children: William James, Christina Marie, James Michael. AB, U. Detroit, 1963; MPA, Wayne State U., 1966. Cert. Internal Auditor. Rsch. assoc. Citizens Rsch. Coun. of Mich., Detroit, 1965-68; rsch. supr., asst. dir. Bur. Pub. Adminstrn. U. Maine, Orono, 1968-73; prin. assoc., doord. publs. N.Y. Legis. Commn. on Expenditure Review, Albany, 1973-87, dir., 1987—; instr., tchr. Legis. Commn. on Expenditure Review Inservice Training Program lectures, panel presentations, 1985—; mem. peer review team Tenn. State Comptrollers Office, Nashville, 1986. Author: Maine Municipal Charter Series Guides, 1971. Mem. North Colonie Schs. Ad Hoc Com. to Study Pupil Population Needs, Newtonville, N.Y., 1989; leader Our Lady of Assumption Ch. music group, Latham, N.Y., 1974-80. Recipient Achievement in Audit Methods award Legis. Commn. on Expenditure Review staff awards com., Albany, N.Y., 1990. Mem. Am. Soc. Pub. Adminstrn., Inst. Internal Auditors, Govtl. Rsch. Assn., Nat. Legis. Program, Evaluation Soc., Am. Evaluation Soc. Office: NYS Legislative Commn on Expenditure Review 111 Washington Ave Albany NY 12210

HAAGA, DAVID ANDREW FOGEL, psychologist; b. Washington, July 25, 1961; s. Paul Galarneaux and Virginia Mary (Coughlan) H.; m. Candice Ann Fogel, June 7, 1987; 1 child, Kevin Fogel. BA, Harvard U., 1983; MA, U. So. Calif., 1985, PhD, 1988. Lic. psychologist, Md., D.C. Rsch. asst. prof. psychology in psychiatry U. Pa., Phila., 1988-89; asst. prof. dept. psychology The Am. U., Washington, 1989—. Contbr. articles to profl. jours. U. So. Calif. fellow, 1985-86; rsch. grantee NIH, 1985-86, 86-87, The Am. U., 1990. Mem. AAUP, ACLU, Assn. for Advancement Behavior Therapy, Am. Psychol. Assn., Soc. for the Exploration Psychotherapy Integration. Democrat. Home: 2022 Rockland Ave Rockville MD 20851-2440 Office: The American Univ Dept Psychology 4400 Massachusetts Ave NW Washington DC 20016-8062

HAAHR, JORN CHRISTIAN, electrical engineer, consultant; b. Skive, Denmark, Nov. 3, 1935; came to U.S., 1963; s. Peder Christian and Inger Marie (Jensen) H.; m. Joan Gluckauf, June 29, 1963; children: Paul, Berit, Marit. MSEE in Power Systems, Tech. U. Denmark, Copenhagen, 1963. Assoc. engr. New England Electric System, Boston, 1963-66; engr. Am. Electric Power Svc. Corp., N.Y.C., 1966-73, sect. head, 1973-84; program mgr. Systems Control Inc., N.Y.C., 1984-90; cons. engr. Ebasco Svcs. Inc., N.Y.C., 1990—. Mem. IEEE (contbr. articles). Office: Ebasco Svcs Inc 2 World Trade Ctr New York NY 10048

HAAN, RICK ALLAN, computer company executive; b. Grand Rapids, Mich., Sept. 21, 1953; s. Jerry Dale and Jeanine E. (Barthiaume) Hodges; m. Linda Rae Zane, Aug. 8, 1976; children: Justin, Aaron, Michelle. BA, Harvard U., 1975; MBA, U. Mich., 1977. V.p. R. Shriver Assocs., Parsippany, N.J., 1977-82; sr. v.p., gen. mgr. DSI Datatrak Systems Inc., Parsippany, 1982—. Mem. Morris Twp. (N.J.) Bd. Adjustment, 1988—. Mem. Harvard Club N.J. (exec. com. 1988—). Office: DSI Datatrak Systems Inc 10 Sylvan Way Parsippany NJ 07054

HAARMEYER, DAVID ALAN, computer programmer/analyst, educator; b. Buffalo, Oct. 30, 1958; s. Robert Charles and Irene (Gorniak) H.; m. Valerie Jean Frank, May 14, 1983; children: Melinda Jane, Carolyn Nicole. BS in Mgmt., SUNY, Buffalo, 1980, MBA, 1986. Cert. data processor. Software cons. DVH Software Devel., Kenmore, N.Y., 1986—; programmer/analyst Ecology and Environment, Lancaster, N.Y., 1988—; computer instr. Kenmore-Tonawanda (N.Y.) Sch. Dist., 1990—. Treas. Alliance Men's Fellowship, Kenmore Alliance Ch., 1990—. Mem. Data Processing Mgmt. Assn. (publicity dir. 1989-91), sec. 1991—). Republican. Home: 352 W Hazeltine Ave Buffalo NY 14217-2542 Office: Ecology and Environment 368 Pleasant View Dr Lancaster NY 14086-1397

HAAS, ELEANOR A. (MRS. PETER RALPH HAAS), marketing and business development consultant; b. Jersey City; d. Nicholas Mark and Eleanor (Cochran) Alter de Csanytelek; m. Peter Ralph Haas, Oct. 22, 1966. BA, Smith Coll., 1953. Account exec. Ruder & Finn, Inc., N.Y.C., 1966-68; founder, pres. The Haas Group, Inc., N.Y.C., 1968-86, HTL Ventures, Inc., N.Y.C., 1986—; v.p., dir. HMG Planning The Howard Marlboro Group, N.Y.C., 1988-91; v.p., dir. planning and devel. The S Group, Inc., 1992—; adj. assoc. prof. dept. journalism NYU, 1980-83, lectr. Sch. Continuing Edn., 1981-83, adv. bd. Sail Adventures in Learning, Inc. (SAIL). Mem. NATAS, Am. Mktg. Assn., Advt. Women N.Y., Advt. Club N.Y. Office: HTL Ventures Inc 120 E 56th St Ste 630 New York NY 10022-3607

HAAS, JACQUELINE CRAWFORD, lawyer; b. St. Louis, Nov. 9, 1935; d. Ernest Augustus and Nora (Fullard) Crawford; m. Karl Alan Haas, Jan. 27, 1962 (dec. Mar. 1986); children: James Andrew, Susan Jennifer, David Reid, Peter Crawford. AB, Cornell U., 1957; LLB, Harvard U., 1961. Bar: N.Y. 1962, U.S. Dist. Ct. (so. dist.) N.Y. 1963, U.S. Ct. Appeals (2d cir.) 1968, Mass. 1972. Assoc. Lord, Day & Lord, N.Y.C., 1961-63; atty. family ct. div. Legal Aid Soc., Bklyn., 1964-66; exam. atty. N.Y.C. Dept. of Investigation, 1966-68, exec. asst. to commr., 1969-71; pvt. practice Weston, Mass., 1971—; mem. Greater Boston com. Harvard U. Law Sch. Fund, Cambridge, Mass., 1976—. Del. Mass. Dem. Issues Conv., 1983, 85, 87, 89, Mass. Dem. Nominating Conv., 1984, 86; vice chmn., mem. Dem. Town Com., Weston, 1984-86; chmn. bd. Roxbury-Weston Programs, Inc., 1982-84, mem. family com., 1973-75; active community coordinating coun., 1982-85; METCo. Weston, Weston Housing Needs com. 1991—. Mem. ABA (civil practice and procedure of the antitrust sect.), Mass. Bar Assn., Assn. of Bar of N.Y.C., Harvard Law Sch. Assn. Mass. (v.p. 1991—). Democrat. Episcopalian. Office: 42 Partridge Hill Rd Weston MA 02193-1750

HAAS, JERE DOUGLAS, nutritional sciences educator, researcher; b. Lancaster, Pa., Sept. 15, 1945; s. Jacob Charles and Dorothy Louise (Graeter) H.; m. Sharon Faye Pitt, June 22, 1968; children: Jeremy Michael, Jonathan Andrew. AB, Franklin and Marshall Coll., 1967; MA, Pa. State U., 1970, PhD, 1973. Trainee in human biology USPHS, Peru, 1971-73; asst. prof. anthropology U. Mass., Amherst, 1973-75; asst. prof. nutrition Cornell U., Ithaca, N.Y., 1975-80, assoc. prof., 1980-87, prof., 1987—, also dir. human biology program; hon. rsch. fellow anatomy dept. U. Aberdeen, Scotland, 1982; vis. prof. Food Rsch. Inst., Stanford (Calif.) U., 1988-89; mem. com. on nutrition during pregnancy and lactation Inst. Medicine, NAS, 1988-90. Editor: Human Population Biology, 1989; mem. editorial bd. Human Biology, 1984-88, Annals Human Biology, 1985—, Am. Jour. Human Biology, 1990—; contbr. over 100 articles to profl. jours., chpts. to books. Rsch. grantee NSF, Bolivia, Peru, 1975-88, NIH, N.Y., Kans., Guatemala, 1978-91. Fellow Human Biology Coun. (exec. com. 1981-85); mem. Am. Assn. Phys. Anthropologists (v.p. 1992-94), Am. Inst. Nutrition, Am. Soc. Clin. Nutrition. Office: Cornell U Savage Hall 211 Ithaca NY 14853-6301

HAAS, KENNETH FRED, physician, administrator; b. Bronx, N.Y., 1946. MD, Albany, 1972. Diplomate Am. Bd. Internal Medicine, Am. Bd. Gastroenterology. Intern medicine Montefiore Hosp. and Med. Ctr., Bronx, 1972-73, resident in medicine, 1973-75, fellow in Ge, 1975-77; attending physician Freehold Area Hosp, N.J., 1977—, Monmouth Med. Ctr., Long Branch, N.J., 1977—, Jersey Shore Med. Ctr., Neptune, N.J., 1977—; asst. chief medicine Centrastate Med. Ctr. (formerly Freehold Area Hosp.). Office: 77755 Schanck Rd Apt B1 Freehold NJ 07728 also: 1400 Rte 35 Ocean NJ 07712

HAAS, KENNETH GREGG, orchestra executive; b. Washington, July 8, 1943; s. Philip and Eunice (Dillon) H.; children: Elizabeth, Amanda; m. Signe L. Johnson, Mar. 23, 1990; 1 child, John Kenneth. A.B., Columbia U., 1964. Asst. to mng. dir. N.Y. Philharm., 1966-70; asst. gen. mgr. Cleve. Orch., 1970-75, gen. mgr., 1976-87; gen. mgr. Cin. Symphony Orch., 1975-

76; mng. dir. Boston Symphony Orch., 1987—; mem. music panel Ohio Arts Council, 1975-79, chmn. challenge grant panel, 1985-86; co-chmn. orch. panel Nat. Endowment Arts, 1982-85, co-chmn. music overview panel, 1982-85, chmn. music challenge grant panel, 1984-85; trustee Cleve. Ballet, 1974-77. Trustee Laurel Sch., 1985-87; mem. nat. adv. com. Mandel Ctr. for Non-Profit Instns., Case Western Res. U., 1985—; adv. trustee Cleve. Inst. Music, 1985-87; overseer New England Conservatory, 1990—. Mem. Am. Symphony Orch. League (dir. 1980-82, 92—, exec. com. 1981-82), Mgrs. Maj. Orchs. U.S. and Can. (chmn. 1980-82). Office: Boston Symphony Orch Symphony Hall 301 Massachusetts Ave Boston MA 02115-4511

HAAS, RAE MARIE, accountant; b. Butte, Mont., July 27, 1929; d. Samuel Siliman and Bessie Helen (Pielaet) Carruthers; m. John Everett Haas, June 5, 1948 (div. July 1982); children: John David, Susan Rae, Doris Ann, Caroline Marie. CPA, Va. Dir. adminstrv. services Supt. Pub. Instrn., Helena, Mont., 1971-75; dir. internal services with Mont. Commr. of Labor, Helena, 1976-77; prin. Haas and Assocs., Helena, 1978-82; fin. adminstr. Dunaway, McCarthy & Dye, Washington, 1983; acct. Roberts, Halt & Co., Alexandria, Va., 1984-85, DeBoe & Stone, CPA's, Arlington, Va., 1986-89; contr. S.L. Hinson Assoc., Alexandria, Va., 1989; gen. mgr. Rock Creek Cemetery, Washington, 1990—. Treas. Episcopal Diocese Mont., Helena, 1982-83; mem. coun. Helena Model Cities, 1970; mem. Mont. Milk Control Bd., 1980-82; pres., bd. dirs. Hunting Creek Club Condominium, 1987-90. Mem. AICPA, Am. Soc. Women Accts., Am. Women's Soc. CPA's (local pres., bd. dirs. 1984-87, nat. bd. dirs. 1991—). Home: 45 Hawthorne Ct NE Washington DC 20017 Office: Rock Creek Cemetery Rock Creek Church Rd Washington DC 20011

HAAS, RICHARD JOHN, artist; b. Spring Green, Wis., Aug. 29, 1936; s. Joseph Francis and Marie (Nachreiner) H.; m. Cynthia Dickman (div. 1970); m. Katherine Sokolnikoff, 1980; 1 child, Gregory Alexander. BS, U. Wis., Milw., 1959, PhD (hon.), 1991; MFA, U. Minn., 1964. Instr. art U. Minn., Mpls., 1963-64; asst. prof. Mich. State U., 1964-69; instr. printmaking Bennington (Vt.) Coll., 1968-79; mem. fine arts faculty Sch. Visual Arts, N.Y.C., 1977-81; instr. fresco painting Skowhegan (Maine) Sch. Painting and Sculpture, 1982, 84. Numerous murals commd., 1975—, including Times Tower, N.Y.C., 1979, NYU Ctr. for Continuing Edn., 1979, Wentworth Hotel, Melbourne, Australia, 1980, Centre Theatre, Milw., 1981, Town & Country Mall, Houston, 1982, N.Y. Pub. Libr., 1982, Citycorp Ctr., N.Y.C., 1984, Harry Cain Tower, Miami Fla., 1985, Quadrangle Mus. complex Smithsonian Instn., 1986, Williams Coll. Mus. Art, 1988, Home Savs. Am., Forest Hills, N.Y., 1989, Bradenton, Aventura, Vero Beach, Fla., 1990, Pasadena, Calif., 1990, 91. Bd. dirs. Pub. Art Fund; bd. govs. Skowhegan Sch. Painting and Sculpture; trustee Hudson River Mus., Yonkers, N.Y., N.Y. State Preservation League; mem. adv. bd. Billboard Mus. Am. Recipient award Mcpl. Art Soc., 1977, medal of honor AIA, 1977, Doris C. Freedman award City of N.Y., 1989; fellow Nat. Endowment for Arts, 1978, Guggenheim fellow, 1983. Office: 361 W 36th St New York NY 10018-6408

HAAS-WILSON, DEBORAH ANN, economist; b. N.Y.C., Dec. 23, 1955; d. Walter M. and Carol Ann (Steinberg) H.; m. Lawrence A. Wilson, July 26, 1981; children: Carrie, Matthew. BA in Econs., U. Mich., 1979; MA in Econs., U. Calif., Berkeley, 1981, PhD in Econs., 1983. Rsch. asst. Congl. Budget Office, Washington, 1977-78, Dept. Health and Human Svcs., Washington, 1979; teaching assoc. U. Calif., Berkeley, 1980-82, rsch. asst., 1981, 82-84; cons. Dept. Energy, Washington, 1980; instr. econs. Sacramento City Coll., 1982; postdoctoral fellow Brandeis U., Waltham, Mass., 1987-88; asst. prof. Smith Coll., Northampton, Mass., 1984-91, assoc. prof., 1991—; mem. Agy. for Health Care Policy and Rsch. Grant Rev. Com., Dept. Health and Human Svcs.; referee for The Am. Econ. Rev., The Rev. Econs. and Statistics, The Jour. Bus. and Econ. Statistics, The Jour. Health Econs., The Jour. Indsl. Econs. Contbr. articles to profl. jours. Home: 77 Pleasantview Ave Longmeadow MA 01106-1019 Office: Dept of Econs Smith Coll Northampton MA 01063

HABECK, FREDERIC HARVEY, sales executive; b. Milw., Mar. 20, 1933; s. Edgar Alfred and Edna (Koehn) H.; m. Sharon Lee Fuchs, Aug. 6, 1966 (div. 1978); 1 child, Deborah Ann. BA, Knox Coll., Galesburg, Ill., 1956. Sales rep. Parke Davis Pharm., Detroit, 1958-68; sales mgr., mktg. mgr. Marine Colloids, Inc., Rockland, Maine, 1968-78; regional mgr. Fidco, Inc., White Plains, N.Y., 1978—; mem. sales mktg. D.A. Ent., Huntington Beach, Calif., 1978—. Mem. Inst. Food Tech., Food and Drug Law Inst. Home: 21342 Green Spray Ln Huntington Beach CA 92646-7560

HABENICHT, WENDA, sculptor, artist; b. Elkhart, Ind., June 7, 1956; d. Robert H. Habenicht and Susanna Frink. BA in Studio Arts cum laude, Beloit Coll., 1978, MA Teaching, 1979; MFA, Columbia U., 1981. Resident Va. Ctr. for Creative Arts, Sweet Briar, 1988. One-man shows include Va. Ctr. for Creative Arts, 1988, Toronto (Ont., Can.) Sculpture Garden, 1989; exhibited in numerous group shows, including Phila. Art Alliance, 1982, Bklyn. Mus., 1983, Bruce Mus., Greenwich, Conn., 1985, Inst. for Art and Urban Resources, N.Y.C., 1986, Snug Harbor Cultural Ctr., S.I., N.Y., 1987, Hillwood Art Gallery, L.I. U., Brookville, 1988, Sculpture Tour U. Tenn., Knoxville, 1990, Socarates Sculpture Park, L.I. City, N.Y., 1987; work cited in numerous publs. Grantee Ill. Art Coun., 1982, Artists' Space, 1985, 86, 87, Artist Fellowship, Inc., 1986. Mem. Internat. Sculpture Ctr., Coll. Art Assn., Orgn. for Ind. Artists, Phi Beta Kappa. Home and Studio: RD 1 Box 203 Worcester NY 12197

HABENSTREIT, ABRAHAM ISAAC, educational administrator; b. N.Y.C., July 12, 1937; s. Sidney and Alice (Kaplan) H.; m. Barbara Ziegler, Aug. 24, 1958; children: David, Shelly. BA, CCNY, 1959. Newspaper reporter Bergen Record, Hackensack, N.J., 1959-61; advt. copywriter Fred Wittner Co., N.Y.C., 1961-63; dir. pub. rels. Long Island U., Bklyn., 1963-66; staff assoc. Bedford-Stuyvesant Restoration, Bklyn., 1966-68; assoc. dean, adminstr. CUNY, N.Y.C., 1968-78; dir. pub. rels. New Sch. for Social Rsch., N.Y.C., 1978-85; dir. pub. affairs Albert Einstein Coll. Medicine, N.Y.C., 1985—. Home: 101 Clark St Brooklyn NY 11201-2746 Office: Albert Einstein Coll Med 1300 Morris Park Ave Bronx NY 10461-1924

HABER, BRUCE MICHAEL, sales representative; b. N.Y.C., Jan. 29, 1957; s. Emanuel and Millicent (Lobel) H.; m. Susan Ann Eilertson, Oct. 17, 1982; children: Sarah Elizabeth, Amy Lynne. BS, U. Conn., 1979. From acct. rep. and supr. to group sales mgr. Savin Corp., Boston, 1979-87; dist. sales mgr. Alco Office Products Co., Providence, 1987-89, Boston, 1989—; lectr. Profl. Sec. and Office Mgrs. Forum, Boston, 1990. Mem. Boston C. of C. (lectr. Expo 1989). Home: 2 Forest Ln Norfolk MA 02056 Office: A-Copy Alco Office Products World Trade Ctr Ste 626 Boston MA 02210

HABER, EMANUEL MILTON, podiatrist, small business owner; b. Newark, July 20, 1958; s. Abe and Julyette (Felder) H.; m. Shari Faith Yagoda, May 31, 1987. BA in Biology, Case Western Res. U., 1980; DPM, Ohio Coll. Podiatric Medicine, 1984. Diplomate Am. Bd. Podiatric Surgery. Resident in podiatry St. Michael's Med. Ctr., Newark, 1984-85; assoc. Waldwick (N.J.) Podiatry Ctr., P.A., 1985-86, v.p., 1986-88, pres., 1988—; mem. staff Valley Hosp., Ridgewood, N.J., 1986—, Barnert Meml. Hosp., Paterson, N.J., 1989—; mem. adj. faculty Ohio Coll. Podiatric Medicine, Cleve., 1988—, U. Osteo. Medicine, Des Moines, Iowa, 1988—. Contbr. articles to profl. jours. Board trustees Temple Israel Ridgewood, 1990—. Fellow Am. Soc. Podiatric Medicine, Am. Coll. Ft. Surgeons; mem. Am. Podiatric Med. Assn., N.J. Podiatric Med. Assn., Am. Coll. Podopediatrics, Am. Assn. Hosp. Podiatrists, Internat. Coll. Podiatric Laser Surgery (assoc.), N.J. Pub. Health Assn., APHA, Lions (chmn. multiple sclerosis com. Waldwick chpt. 1990-91, chmn. program com. 1990-91). Office: Waldwick Podiatry Ctr 168 Franklin Tpke Waldwick NJ 07463-1802

HABER, PIERRE CLAUDE, psychologist; b. Landau, Germany, June 8, 1931; s. Kurt S. and Hedwig (Kuhn) H.; came to U.S., 1943, naturalized, 1949; B.A., Bklyn. Coll., 1952; M.A., Duke U., 1953; Ph.D., U. Paris, 1956; Counselor, dir. adult edn. Central Sch. Dist. 2, Yorktown Heights, N.Y., 1956-59; psychologist Manpower Devel. Program, Bklyn., 1959-65; asst. prof. Queens Coll., 1965-70; exec. sec., exec. dir. Psychology Soc., N.Y.C., 1970—; cons. forensic psychologist N.Y. State, 1978—; assoc. prof. Jersey City State Coll., 1967-80. Mem. APA, Am., N.Y. State personnel and guidance assns., Psychology Soc., N.Y. Assn. Public Sch. Adult Educators (v.p. 1957-59), Pi Delta Phi. Republican. Jewish. Contbr. to Compton's Ency., also articles to profl. jours. Home and Office: 100 Beekman St New York NY 10038-1810

HABERMEHL, LAWRENCE LEROY, philosophy educator; b. Joplin, Mo., June 13, 1937; s. Roland William and Ruth Esther (Kelly) H.; m. Kathryn J. Barnes, June 8, 1958 (div. 1974); children: Elizabeth Anne, R. William, Edward Hale; m. Sue Ellen Lovejoy, Sept. 16, 1989. AB, Phillips U., 1959; BD, Union Theol. Sem., 1961; PhD, Boston U., 1967. House mgr. Boston Seaman's Friend Soc., 1963-65; teaching fellow Boston U., 1965-66; asst. prof. philosophy Am. Internat. Coll., Springfield, Mass., 1966-73, assoc. prof., 1973—. Author/editor: Morality in the Modern World, 1976. Mem. AAUP, Am. Philos. Assn., Metaphys. Soc. Am., Common Cause, Amnesty Internat. Unitarian-Universalist. Home: 15 S Park Ave East Longmeadow MA 01106-1129 Office: Am Internat Coll Dept Philosophy Springfield MA 01109

HABIB, EDMUND J., aerospace engineer; b. Dover, N.H., May 24, 1927; s. Joseph and Nadine (Elias) H.; m. Mary Lou Spang, July 31, 1954; children: David, Judy, Bonnie, Lisa, Sharon. BSEE, Cath. U. of Am., 1949, MS, 1952, postgrad., 1966. Br. head Goddard Space Flight Ctr., NASA, Washington, 1958-62, assoc. div. head, 1962-72; dir. adv. com. res. NASA Hdqrs., Washington, 1973-74; dir. adv. sat. engr. Comsat Corp., Washington, 1974-77; asst. v.p. engring. Am. Sat. Co., Rockville, 1977-82; v.p. engring. Sat. System Engr., Rockville, 1982-85; pres. Fairchild Com. Syst., Frederick, Md., 1985-88; sr. dir. engring. Fairchild Space Co., Germantown, Md., 1988—. Inventor tone ranging system. Mem. IEEE, AIAA (medal 1972), Am. Rocket Soc., Planetary Soc., Sigma Xi (hon.). Home: 7201 Deer Lake Ln Rockville MD 20855-1987

HACHIDA, HOWARD MITSUGI, military officer; b. Honolulu, Sept. 15, 1953; s. Stanley Takashi and Charlotte Ritsuko (Imada) H.; m. Sandra Busto, July 18, 1981; children: Daniel, Peter. MS, Air Force Inst. & Tech., Dayton, Ohio, 1982. Commd. 2d. lt. USAF, 1977, advanced through grades to major, 1988; ops. research analyst Air Force Operational Test and Evaluation Ctr., Albuquerque, 1982-86, USAF Hdqr. Studies and Analyses, Washington, 1986-90; mem. Joint Staff, The Pentagon, Washington, 1990—. Mem. Ops. Research Soc. of Am. Home: 8720 Whitson Ct Springfield VA 22153-1268

HACKER, JON CHRISTOPHER, designer, glass manufacturing company executive; b. Dayton, Ohio, Oct. 9, 1950; s. Homer Owen and Lydia Sarah (McLean) H. BS in Indsl. Design, U. Cin., 1973. Designer Henry Dreyfuss Assocs., N.Y.C., 1973-74, J.C. Penney Co., Inc., N.Y.C., 1974-76; sr. product mgr. Dansk Internat. Designs, Mt. Kisco, N.Y., 1976-79, v.p., dir. design, 1985-87; mgr. design GAF Corp., N.Y.C., 1979-80; prin. Christopher Hacker Design, N.Y.C., 1980-81; exec. design dir. Estee Lauder Co., N.Y.C., 1981-85; v.p., design dir. Steuben Glass div. Corning (N.Y.) Inc., N.Y.C., 1987—. Mem. Indsl. Designers Soc., Am. Inst. Graphic Artists. Office: Corning Inc Steuben Glass 717 Fifth Ave New York NY 10022

HACKETT, HARRY LEONARD, financial consultant; b. Southampton, N.Y., May 20, 1942; 020; s. Harry Leonard and Sarah Helen (Culver) H.; m. Barbara McCall Hare, Jan. 20, 1965; children: Sarah Louise, Harry Leonard. B of Econ., U. Pa., 1964. Cert. fin. planner. With Morgan Guaranty, N.Y.C., 1966-68; fin. cons., v.p. Merrill Lynch, Smithtown, N.Y., 1968—. Treas., bd. dirs. Boy Scouts Am. Troop 3, Smithtown, 1983-85; trustee, deacon, First Presbyn. Ch., Huntington, N.Y., 1979-83, pres. deacons, 1981. 1st lt. U.S. Army, 1964-66. Mem. Wharton Club of L.I. (bd. dirs. 1988-91). Republican. Home: 11 Thatch Pond Rd Smithtown NY 11787-1844 Office: Merrill Lynch 50 Rte III Smithtown NY 11787

HACKETT, JEAN MARIE, actress; b. York, Pa., Aug. 28, 1956; d. Burtis M. and Linda (Leanza) H. BFA, NYU, 1979; Cert., Royal Acad. Dramatic Art, London, 1978. Film and TV roles include L.A. Law, Ingeborg in Anna, Amy in Finally Mine and Jane in Vieux Carre; plays include A Streetcar Named Desire, Cyrano de Bergerac, Richard III, Arms and the Man, The Taming of the Shrew, Hamlet, The Winter's Tale, The Legend of Oedipus, Arturo Ui, Room Service, George and Frederick, The Matchmaker, Hopscotch, The Front Page, Who Killed by Bald Sister Sophie, Dying to Love, Home Fires, A Collage of Tennessee Williams, House Music, others. Mem. SAG, Actor's Equity Assn. Democrat. Episcopalian. Home: 3452 Oak Glen Dr Los Angeles CA 90068-1314

HACKEY, DORIS PLUMMER, educator, consultant; b. Washington, Feb. 25, 1928; d. Garnett Augustus and Hannah (Hoes) Plummer; m. George Edward Hackey, Nov. 24, 1946; children: Craig, George Jr. BA, Antioch U., 1978; MA, Hood Coll., 1986. Substitute tchr. Montgomery County Pub. Schs., Rockville, Md., 1946-56, tchr. specialist, 1972—; tchr., dir. Clinton Day Nursery, Rockville, Md., 1956-70; tchr. Rockville Daycare Assn., 1970-72. Editor The Lifesaver, 1980— (award 1984-89). Sec. Edward Taylor School, Boyds, Md., 1953; exec. sec. Gaithersburg (Md.) High Sch., 1966; worker Dem. party, 1985-87; presenter John Wesley United Meth. Ch., Clarksburg, Md., 1989. Mem. NEA (del., presenter young children conf. 1989), Md. State Tchrs. Assn., Montgomery County Alliance Black Sch. Educators, Nat. Black Child Devel. Inst., Merrymakers. Republican. Roman Catholic. Home: 23714 Clarksburg Rd Clarksburg MD 20871-9243 Office: Montgomery County Pub Schs 4910 Macon Rd Rockville MD 20852-2228

HACKMAN, ELMER ELLSWORTH, III, engineering company executive; b. Phila., Mar. 22, 1928; s. Elmer Ellsworth and Leone (Hershberger) H.; m. Edna Lucile Oaks, Apr. 4, 1953; children: Matthew Ellsworth, Christian Lee. BS in Chemistry, Juniata Coll., Huntington, Pa., 1949; MS in Chem. Engring., U. Pa., 1957; PhD in Chemistry, U. Del., Newark, 1967. Registered profl. engr., Pa., Del. Engr. Sinclair Refining Co., Chem. Corps., Am. Viscose Corp., 1949-54; asst. mgr. splty. chems. Chem. Div. of Atlantic Refining Co., Phila., 1954-55; from mgr. rsch. projects to mgr. environ. tech. Thiokol Chem. Corp., Elkton, Md., 1958-73; pres. NST/Engrs., Inc., Wilmington, Del., 1973—; seminar leader McGraw Hill, N.Y.C., 1979-82; cons. in field. Author: Toxic Organic Chemicals Destruction and Waste Treatment, 1979; patentee in field; contbr. articles to profl. jours. Air Force Office Sci. Rsch. grantee, 1965-67. Mem. Am. Inst. Chem. Engrs., Am. Chem. Soc., Sigma Xi. Lutheran. Office: NST/Engrs Inc PO Box 2857 Wilmington DE 19805-0857

HACKMAN, MARTIN ROBERT, chemist; b. N.Y.C., Mar. 20, 1942. BS in Chemistry, Bklyn. Coll., 1965; MA in Chemistry, CUNY, 1973. Rsch. chemist Technicon, Inc., Ardsley, N.Y., 1966-68; applications chemist Princeton Applied Rsch., Inc., Princeton, N.J., 1969; scientist Hoffmann La Roche Inc., Nutley, N.J., 1969-85; tech. adminstr. Whithall Labs., Hammonton, N.J., 1985-86; rsch. scientist Anaquest, Inc., Murray Hill, N.J., 1986—; mem. governing bd. Eastern Analytical Symposium, Montchanin, Del., 1978—. Contbr. articles to profl. publs. With USAR, 1965-71. Mem. ASTM, Am. Chem. Soc. Office: Anaquest Inc 100 Mountain Ave New Providence NJ 07974-2005

HACKNEY, SHELDON, university president. Pres. Univ. of Penn., Phila. Address: Univ of Penn Office of Pres 34th and Spruce Sts Philadelphia PA 19104*

HADDAD, ERNEST MUDARRI, lawyer; b. Boston, Oct. 30, 1938; s. Abraham and Elaine (Mudarri) H.;m. Kathleen L. Tracy; 1 child, Barton Edward; children from previous marriage: Scott Cochrane, Mark Mudarri. BA, Trinity Coll., Hartford, Conn., 1960; LLB, Boston U., 1964. Bar: Mass. 1964, U.S. Dist. Ct. Mass. 1966, U.S. Supreme Ct., 1981. Assoc. Springer, Goldberg, Hyman & Levenson, Boston, 1964-66; asst. dean and mem. faculty sch. law Boston U., 1966-71; asst. sec., gen. counsel Exec. Office Human Svcs., Boston, 1971-75; gen. counsel Blue Cross and Blue Shield Mass. Inc., Boston, 1976-80; sec., gen. counsel The Mass. Gen. Hosp., Boston, 1981—; gen. counsel Gen. Hosp. Corp., McLean Hosp. Corp., Spaulding Rehab. Hosp. Corp., MGH Profl. Svcs. Corp., MGH Health Svcs. Corp., MGH Inst. Health Professions, Inc., McLean Health Svcs., Inc.; bd. dirs. Codman Co., Inc., 1966-88. Adminstrv. editor Boston U. Law Rev., 1963, Spl. Tribute from editors, 1971. Program chmn., mem. exec. com. Boston Study Group, 1979—, mem. Nat. Def. Exec. Res. Unit Fed. Emergency Mgmt. Agy., 1971-91, Dept. Labor, 1970-81; trustee Social Polcy Rsch. Corp., 1981—, chmn. pub. policy com. 1981-84, bd. dirs. 1980-84; chmn. social svcs. rev. com., mem. support policies com. United Way Massachusetts Bay, 1978-81; mem. exec. com., bd. dirs. Friendly Aid-Chest and Coun. Wellesley, 1968-76, bd. dirs. and host parent ABC Program Inc., 1975-81; mem. gov.'s task force on Reorgan. State Govt., 1981-82; bd. mgrs. New Eng. Home for Little Wanderers, 1978-79. Recipient Spl. Appreciation award Boston U. Student Bar Assn., 1971, 150th Anniversary award Trinity Coll., 1973, Trinity Coll. Alumni medal for Excellence, 1990. Mem. ABA (forum com. health law, antitrust law and legal edn.-bar admissions sects.), Am. Acad. Hosp. Attys., Am. Corp. Counsel Assn., Am. Soc. Law and Medicine, Nat. Assn. Coll. and Univ. Attys., Nat. Health Lawyers Assn., Mass. Bar Assn., Boston Bar Assn., Trinity Club Boston (pres. 1989-91), Union Boat Club. Home: 144 Mt Vernon St Boston MA 02108-1128 Office: Mass Gen Hosp Trustees' House Boston MA 02114

HADDAD, JAMES HENRY, chemical engineering consultant; b. Willimantic, Conn., Jan. 30, 1923; s. William Addy and Nellie (Birbarie) H.; m. Isabel Serrano, Feb. 3, 1962; children: Frederick William, Francis Xavier. BS in Engring., Yale U., 1944. Chem. engr. Conn. Hard Rubber Co., New Haven, 1943-44; engr. rsch. dept. Mobil Rsch. Devel. Corp., Paulsboro, N.J., 1944-52; engr. engring. dept. Mobil Rsch. Devel. Corp., N.Y.C., 1952-70; engring. cons. Mobil Rsch. Devel. Corp., Princeton, N.J., 1971-89; ind. cons. worldwide chem. processing/solids systems Chem. Processing/Solids Systems, Princeton Junction, N.J., 1989—. Contbr. articles to profl. publs.; patentee in field. Mem. budget com., trustee Princeton Area Communities United Way, 1977-90. Mem. Am. Chem. Soc., Am. Inst. Chem. Engrs., Alpha Chi Sigma. Republican. Roman Catholic. Home and Office: 45 Van Wyck Dr Princeton Junction NJ 08550

HADDAD, THURAYYA HANNA, language educator; b. Salt, Jordan, May 21, 1939; came to U.S., 1973; d. Hanna Salameh and Karma Eisa H. BA, Beirut Arab U., Lebanon, 1971; MS, Georgetown U., 1976; MA, George Washington U., 1978. Prin. Ministry of Edn. Amman, Jordan, 1966-72; tchr. Arabic Fgn. Svc. Inst., Washington, 1974-82; lectr. Arabic George Mason U., 1986-87, Georgetown U., 1978-84; prof. Arabic Johns Hopkins U., Washington, 1978—; cons. Fgn. Mission Bd., Richmond, Va., 1984--; cert. examiner Fgn. Svc. Inst., 1978-82. Author: Spoken Arabic, 1984; contbr. articles to profl. jours. Mem. Middle East Studies Assn., Middle East Inst., Am. Assn. Tchrs. Arabic (exec. bd. 1986). Democrat. Roman Catholic. Home: 1 Broomall Ct Silver Spring MD 20906 Office: Johns Hopkins U 1619 Massachusetts Ave NW Washington DC 20036-2213

HADDEN, MARTHA J., interior designer; b. Salem, Mass., Jan. 12, 1951; d. Franklin J. and Emily M. (Tolisano) H.; m. John P. Treadwell, Nov. 25, 1977. AS in Interior Design, Garland Jr. Coll., Boston, 1971; student, Boston Archtl. Ctr., 1972-75; grad. Interior Environ. Design, New England Sch. Art & Design, Boston, 1979. Draftsman Payette Assoc., Boston, 1971-73,78, Dellea Engring., Inc., Boston, 1974-77; interior designer Antranig Der Marderosian, Inc., Boston, 1979-80, Hadden Assocs., Marblehead, Mass., 1980—. Recipient Excellence in Architecture award New Eng. regional coun. AIA, 1983. Mem. Am. Soc. Interior Designers (profl. mem., Interior Design Project award New Eng. chpt. 1992), Inst. Bus. Designers (profl. mem., v.p. pub. rels. New Eng. chpt. 1990-92, pres.-elect 1992-93, cert. of appreciation 1992), Nat. Coun. Interior Design Qualification (juror 1988-90, master juror 1990—). Office: Hadden Associates 22 School St Marblehead MA 01945-3327

HADDOCK, JORGE, industrial engineering educator, consultant; b. Caguas, P.R., Aug. 15, 1955; s. Jorge and Francisca (Acevedo) H.; m. Maria A. Valentin, June 7, 1980; children: M. Angelique, D. Alexander. BSCE, U. P.R., 1978; MS in Mgmt. Engring., Rensselaer Poly. Inst., 1979; PhD in Indsl. Engring., Purdue U., 1981. Instr. engring. U. P.R., Mayaguez, 1978-81; asst. prof. U. P.R., Rio Piedras, 1981-83, Clemson (S.C.) U., 1984-86; asst. prof. indsl. engring. and ops. rsch. Rensselaer Poly. Inst., Troy, N.Y., 1986-90, assoc. prof., 1990—; cons. Sistema, Inc., San Juan, P.R., 1980, Mgmt. and Janitorial Svcs., San Juan, 1982-83, Computer Data Svcs., San Juan, 1982, Baxter-Travenol Labs., Maricao, P.R., 1982, Citibank, N.A., San Juan, 1982, Michelin Tires, Greenville, S.C., 1986, Globe Internat., Buffalo, 1988, Jiffy Lube, Albany, N.Y., 1990, Bendix, Green Island, N.Y., 1990, also others; participant numerous workshops, confs. and meetings. Author: User-Oriented Operations Research Methodologies, 1987, (with S. Bohl) Instructor's Manual for Engineering Economy, 1989; mem. editorial bd. Internat. Jour. Computer Simulation; contbr. articles to profl. jours., chpts. to books. Bd. dirs. Hispanic Outreach Svcs., Albany, 1990-92. Recipient numerous grants. Mem. Inst. Indsl. Engrs. (sr., pres. Capital-Berkshire chpt. 1989-90, bd. dirs. 1990—, Outstanding Young Indsl. Engr. award 1990), Ops. Rsch. Soc. Am., Inst. Mgmt. Scis. (assoc.), Soc. Computer Simulation, Nat. Acad. Engring. Mex. (corr.), KC (3 degree, chancellor Clemson 1985-86), Tau Beta Pi (charter sec.-treas. Piedmont chpt. 1985-86). Home: 102 Old Coach Rd Clifton Park NY 12065-7617 Office: Dept Decision Scis-Engring Syst Rensselaer Poly Inst Troy NY 12180-3590

HADDOCK, ROBERT LYNN, information services company executive, marketing professional, writer; b. Vallejo, Calif., May 12, 1945; s. Orville Walter and Lee Ellen (Alexander) H. BA, Union Coll., 1967; postgrad., NYU, 1977-81. Editor So. Pub. Assn., Nashville, 1969-74, controller, 1974-75; mktg. analyst Bus. Publs. div. Prentice-Hall, Englewood Cliffs, N.J., 1975-78, bus. mgr., 1978-81; bus. mgr. Ziff-Davis Pub. Co., N.Y.C., 1981-82, dir. bus. devel., 1982-83; pres. Personal Access, Inc., N.Y.C., 1983-84; v.p., dir. product devel. Citicorp Global Report, N.Y.C., 1984-86, v.p., dir. mktg., 1986-88; v.p., dir. product devel. Citibank, N.A., N.Y.C., 1989-90; v.p., dir. product devel. and mktg. Enhanced Telephone Svcs., Inc., N.Y.C., 1990-91; pres. M-Power Corp., N.Y.C., 1991—. Author: The Broken Web, 1973, How to Stop Smoking, 1974; inventor database accessing system, 1983, enhanced telephone, 1989. Mem. Am. Assn. Artificial Intelligence, Information Industry Assn., Mensa. Home: 105 W 13th St Apt 15F New York NY 10011-7848

HADDY, FRANCIS JOHN, physician, educator; b. Walters, Minn., Sept. 6, 1922; s. Thomas J. and Frances (Shaheen) H.; m. Theresa Eileen Brey, Sept. 21, 1946; children: Richard, Carol, Alice. Student, Luther Coll., Decorah, Iowa, 1940-42; B.S., U. Minn., 1943, B.M., 1946, M.D., 1947, M.S. in Physiology, 1949, Ph.D. in Physiology (Am. Heart Assn. fellow), 1953. Diplomate: Am. Bd. Internal Medicine. Intern Mpls. Gen. Hosp., 1946-47; fellow internal medicine Mayo Found., 1949-51; asst. prof. physiology and medicine Northwestern U. Med. Sch., 1953-61; clin. investigator VA Research Hosp., Chgo., 1957-59; prof. physiology, chmn. dept., asso. prof. medicine U. Okla. Med. Center, 1961-66; prof. physiology, chmn. dept. Mich. State U., East Lansing, 1966-76; prof. physiology Uniformed Services U., Bethesda, Md., 1976—; chmn. dept. physiology Uniformed Services U., 1976-87; mem. cardiovascular study sect. NIH, 1963-69; tng. com. Nat. Heart and Lung Inst., NIH, 1970-73; mem. atherosclerosis and hypertension adv. com. Nat. Heart, Lung and Blood Inst., NIH, 1983-86; rsch. com. Am. Heart Assn., 1974-80; mem. life scis. adv. com. NASA, 1986—, chmn., 1988—, sr. scientist NASA/Johnson Space Ctr. S.C. med. scis. div., Houston, 1989-90. Mem. editorial bd.: Am. Jour. Physiology, 1963-69, 80-86, Jour. Applied Physiology, 1963-69, Procs. Soc. Exptl. Biology and Medicine, 1969-72, Circulation Research, 1975-81, Microvascular Research, 1978-81, Hypertension, 1978-81. Recipient Med. Sci. Achievement award Am. Heart Assn., 1987. Fellow Am. Coll. Nutrition (ann. award 1986); mem. Am. Physiol. Soc. (steering com. circulation group 1972-75, chmn. com. on coms. 1974-77, mem. coun. 1976-79, pres. 1981, fin. com. 1983-89, chmn. fin. com., 1985-89, select com. on animal care 1988-91, Carl J. Wiggers award 1966, chmn. long range planning com. 1990—), Am. Soc. Clin Investigation, Fedn. Am. Socs. Exptl. Biology (bd. dirs. 1980-83, treas. 1990—), Internat. Union Physiol. Scis. (U.S. nat. com. 1976-79, 81-84), Nat. Hypertension Assn. (trustee 1979—), Nat. Acad. Scis. (basic biomed. scis. panel, com. on nat. needs for biomed. and behavioral rsch. personnel, inst. medicine 1983-86), Assn. Chmn. Depts. Physiology (chmn. animal welfare com. 1986-87). Home: 10804 Whiterim Dr Potomac MD 20854-1784

HADERER, HARRY W., II, automotive dealer importer; b. Boston, July 17, 1962; s. Edward G. and Margaret M. (Mancini) H. and Patrick and Costantinos Pryles; m. Drew Lendt; children: Xenia Mercedes, Aristotle Costantinos. BA in Communications, Stanford U., 1984; BSBA, Menlo

Coll., 1986. Tech. svc. dir. Park Porsche Audi Inc., Lawrence, Mass., 1980-86; consumer svc. adminstr. Audi of Am. Inc., Troy, Mich., 1986, sr. warranty adminstr., 1986-88; owner The Motorcar Galleries, Inc., Topsfield, Mass., 1988-91; v.p./treas. Greenfield (Mass.) Volkswagen, 1991—; bd. dirs. MCG Imaging, Boston. Editor (newsletter) The Progressive, 1986-90. Republican. Greek Orthodox. Office: The Motorcar Galleries Inc 94 Central PO Box # 97 Topsfield MA 01983

HADERMANN, ALBERT FELIX, physical chemist; b. N.Y.C., Mar. 20, 1938; s. Felix Theodore and Hilda Elsie (Krumrein) H.; m. Dianne Cecil Lawson, Apr. 20, 1963; children: Sylvia, Theodore, Krista, Cynthia. BS, CCNY, 1959; PhD, Am. U., 1970. Sr. chemist Melpar Inc., Falls Church, Va., 1963-67; asst. prof. Am. U., Washington, 1971-74; sr. scientist Dynamac, Rockville, Md., 1974-77; prin. scientist Sci. Applications Inc., McLean, Va., 1977-84; v.p. rsch. Gen. Tech. Applications, Inc., Manassas, Va., 1984-90; pres. Hadermann Cons., Inc., Ijamsville, Md., 1990—; bd. dirs. Gen. Tech. Applications, Inc., Manassas, Va., 1983-90. Contbr. articles to profl. jours. With U.S. Army, 1961-63. Mem. AAAS, Am. Chem. Soc. Office: Hadermann Cons Inc 11609 Browningsville Rd Ijamsville MD 21754-9126

HADLEY, ELIZABETH HARRISON, lawyer, health policy analyst; b. Lawrence, MA, May 20, 1955. BA, Yale U., 1977, MPH, 1989; JD, U. Calif., Berkeley, 1981. Asst. atty. gen. State of Conn. Office of the Atty Gen., Hartford, 1984-87; program analyst U.S. Dept. Health & Human Svcs., Washington, 1989—. Bd. dirs. Guilford (Conn.) Land Conservation Trust, 1984-88, Washington Com. for the Frontier Nursing Svcs., 1990—. Mem. Phi Beta Kappa. Office: US Dept Health & Human Svcs 200 Independence Ave SW Washington DC 20201

HADLEY, JANE BYINGTON, psychotherapist; b. N.Y.C., Apr. 24, 1929; d. David and Ruth (Johnson) Millar; m. Arthur Twining Hadley, Feb. 24, 1979; children: Elisabeth Danish, Caroline Thies. BA, U. Va., 1951; MA, Columbia U., 1967; analytic tng., Met. Ctr. for Mental Health, 1970-73. Intern Queens Coll., 1969; pvt. practice psychotherapy N.Y.C., 1971—. Bd. dirs. Planned Parenthood of N.Y. Mem. Am. Psychol. Assn., Cosmopolitan Club, Doubles Club, Edgarton Yacht Club. Democrat. Episcopalian.

HADLOCK, CHARLES ROBERT, mathematics educator; b. Bklyn., Apr. 19, 1947; s. Charles Henry and Anna Marie (Osmers) H.; m. Joanne Theresa Miscione, Aug. 26, 1967; children: Charles James, Theresa Anne. BS, Providence Coll., 1967; MA, U. Ill., 1968, PhD, 1970. Asst. prof. math. Amherst (Mass.) Coll., 1970-76, Bowdoin Coll., Brunswick, Maine, 1976-77; sr. cons. Arthur D. Little, Inc., Cambridge, Mass., 1977-79, mgr. safety and environ. risk, 1979-90; prof. and chmn. math. scis. Bentley Coll., Waltham, Mass., 1990—; cons. in risk analysis and environ. mgmt. Author: Field Theory and Its Classical Problems, 1979 (MAA Book award 1985), Ecuaciones Diferenciales Ordinarias, 1977; contbr. articles to profl. jours. Scoutmaster Lincoln Boy Scouts Am., Mass., 1980-84; trustee Providence Coll., 1971-75; chmn. risk analysis rev. panel NSF, 1984-85. Fulbright-Hays Commn. lectureship, 1976. Mem. ASME, Math. Assn. Am., Soc. for Indsl. and Applied Math. Home: Sandy Pond Rd Lincoln MA 01773-2005 Office: Bentley Coll Dept Math Scis Waltham MA 02154

HADZOR, THOMAS BAYLOR, university administrator; b. Pitts., July 29, 1954; s. Paul Willey and Maxine Gertrude (Gobelman) H.; m. Debra Ann Price, July 14, 1979; children: Sarah, Rebecca, Robert, Thomas. BA, Muhlenberg Coll., Allentown, Pa., 1976; MA, Mich. State U., 1979. Dir. annual giving, coord. spl. programs Mercersburg (Pa.) Acad., 1979-81; dir. devel., dir. capital campaign Scranton (Pa.) Prep. Sch., 1981-86; dir. capital campaign Wilkes U., Wilkes-Barre, Pa., 1986-87, exed. dir. devel., 1987-88, v.p. for devel., 1988—; mem. alumni coun. Mercersburg Acad., 1990—. Bd. dirs. Leadership Wilkes-Barre, 1990—; com. co-chair Dallas (Pa.) Playground Project, 1988; deacon, pub. rels. chair, asst. chmn. bd., chmn. bd. Huntsville (Pa.) Christian Ch., 1981—. Mem. Coun. for Advancement and Support of Edn. (instl. coord.), N.E. Pa. Ednl. Devel. Coun. Democrat. Mem. Disciples of Christ Ch. Home: Box 518 RD 1 Upper Demunds Rd Dallas PA 18612 Office: Wilkes U 170 S Franklin St Wilkes Barre PA 18766-0001

HAEDO, JORGE ALBERTO, service company executive; b. Buenos Aires, Dec. 3, 1945; came to U.S., 1969; s. Rodolfo and Aida Leonor (Muro) H.; m. Cristina Monica Mann, Feb. 7, 1973; 1 child, Karina Michelle. Grad. high sch., Buenos Aires. Regional ops. mgr. United Health Svc. (formerly Crothall Hosp. Svcs.), Newark, Del., 1971-79; assoc. dir. support svcs. Mt. Sinai Hosp., N.Y.C., 1979-80; chmn., chief exec. officer Shifa Svcs., Inc., Hackensack, N.J., 1980—. Home: 85 Margetts Rd Spring Valley NY 10977-6119 Office: Shifa Svcs Inc 540 Hudson St Hackensack NJ 07601-6637

HAFEN, ELIZABETH SUSAN SCOTT, physicist; b. Springfield, Mo., July 25, 1946; d. George William and Wealtha Belle (Chaplin) Scott; m. Clifford Henry Hafen, Jr., Nov. 27, 1970. B.S., Iowa State U., 1968, Ph.D., 1973. Instr. physics MIT, Cambridge, 1973-78, asst. prof., 1978-82, assoc. prof., 1982-83, prin. research scientist physics dept./lab. Nuclear Sci., 1983—. Contbr. articles to profl. jours. Mem. Am. Phys. Soc., New Eng. Hist. Geneol. Soc. Democrat. Methodist.

HAFETS, RICHARD JAY, lawyer; b. N.Y.C., Apr. 23, 1951; s. Meyer Hafets and Marilyn (Glanzrock) Bell; m. Claire Margolis, June 18, 1972; children: Brooke, Amy. BS in Bus. summa cum laude, Am. U., Washington, 1973, JD magna cum laude, 1976. Bar: Md. 1976, U. S. Dist. Ct. Md. 1976, U.S. Ct. Appeals (4th cir.) 1976, U.S. Supreme Ct. 1981. Assoc. Piper & Marbury, Balt., 1976-84, ptnr., 1984—, head labor practice, 1990—, chmn. hiring and assoc. coms., 1988—. Labor atty. Balt. Symphony Orch., 1986—; bd. mem., gen. counsel Am. Cancer Soc., Balt., 1983-89; bd. mem. Md. Ballet, Balt., 1978-80. Mem. ABA, Md. Bar Assn., Balt. City Bar Assn., Order of Coif. Home: 7346 Narrow Wind Way Columbia MD 21046-1262 Office: Piper & Marbury 36 S Charles St Baltimore MD 21201-3020

HAFFNER, DEBRA WYNNE, public health service administrator; b. Morristown, N.J., Aug. 1, 1954; d. Saul and Harriet (Kupferstein) H.; m. Ralph Tartaglione, Mar. 13, 1982; 1 child, Alyssa. BA, Wesleyan U., 1975; MPH, Yale U., 1979. Resource dir. Population Inst., Washington, 1975-77; spl. asst. USPHS, Rockville, Md., 1978-80; dir. community svcs. Planned Parenthood, Washington, 1981-84; dir. info. and edn. Ctr. for Population Options, Washington, 1985-88; exec. dir. Sex Info. and Edn. Coun. of the U.S., N.Y.C., 1988—. Author: Sex Education 2000, 1990, Winning the Battle, 1991; (booklet) How To Talk To Your Children About AIDS, 1989; (monograph) AIDS and Adolescents, 1987. Dir. Title IX Com., Rockville, 1983-84, Nat. Family Planning Assn., 1988-90 (Disting. Svc. award 1990), Nat. Leadership Coalition on AIDS, 1990—, Westport (Conn.) Unitarian Ch.; commr. Commn. on Women, Rockville, 1980-83. Recipient Pioneer award Coalition for Sexuality and Disability, 1990. Mem. APHA (coun. 1987—, chair population and family planning sect.), Am. Assn. Sex Educators, Counselors and Therapists, Soc. for Sci. Study of Sex. Office: Sex Info & Edn Coun of U S 130 W 42d St Ste 2500 New York NY 10036

HAFKENSCHIEL, JOSEPH HENRY, JR., cardiologist, educator; b. Youngstown, Ohio, Apr. 2, 1916; s. Joseph Henry and Anna Marie (Conroy) H.; m. Lucinda Buchanan Thomas, July 18, 1942 (dec. 1983); children—Joseph Henry III, Benjamin A. Thomas, Mark Conroy, John Proctor; m. Carol MacDonald Smith Rush, Jan. 25, 1985. A.B., Swarthmore Coll., 1937; M.D., Johns Hopkins U., 1941. Diplomate Am. Bd. Internal Medicine. Intern, U. Pa. Hosp., Phila., 1941-42, resident, 1948-49, fellow in cardiology, 1949; instr. pharmacology U. Pa. Sch. Medicine, Phila., 1946-47, instr. medicine, 1949-51, assoc. medicine, 1951-66; cardiovascular disease physician in pvt. practice, Phila., 1949-65, Palo Alto, Calif., 1969-78; med. dir. West Coast Office Sandoz Pharm., San Francisco, 1965-67; staff physician Cowell Student Health Service Stanford U., Calif., 1967-69, clin. instr. medicine, 1966-69, asst. to assoc. prof., 1969-84, emeritus clin. assoc. prof. medicine, 1984—; staff physician Extended Care Service VA Med. Ctr., Palo Alto, 1978-84. Contbr. articles to profl. jours. Pres. Peninsula Meml. and Funeral Soc., Palo Alto, 1984. Served to maj. M.C., USAAF, 1942-46. Fellow Coll. Physicians Phila., ACP, Am. Heart Assn., Royal Soc. Medicine; mem. Air Force Assn., Mus. Soc., Am. Irish Hist. Soc., Am. Legion (post comdr. 1960-62), Sigma Xi. Republican. Roman Catholic. Clubs: Stanford Faculty; San Francisco Golf; Merion Golf; Gulph Mills Golf, Ballybunion Golf (Ireland). Avocations: world travel, golf, gardening, art history. Home: 870 Lesley Rd Villanova PA 19085-1118

HAFNER, MICHAEL JOHN, financial analyst; b. La Crosse, Wis., Apr. 22, 1963; s. Eugene John and Barbara JoAnn (Smikla) H. BSCE (magna cum laude), Marquette U., 1985; MSCE, U. Minn., 1986; MBA, U. Chgo., 1991. Structural engr. Skidmore, Owings & Merrill, Chgo., 1986-89; fin. analyst IBM, Essex Jct, Vt., 1991—. Mem. ASCE. Roman Catholic. Home: 5 S Meadow Dr Burlington VT 05401-5375 Office: IBM Dept 842/Bldg 615-2 Essex Junction VT 05452

HAFT, MARILYN GEISLER, lawyer; b. N.Y.C, Aug. 1, 1943; d. Frank and Sarah (Engelsohn) Geisler; m. Kenneth W. Bowser; 1 child, Samantha Danielle. BA, Bklyn. Coll., 1965; JD, NYU, 1968. Bar: N.Y. 1969, U.S. Supreme Ct. 1973, D.C. 1978. Staff counsel ACLU Nat. Office, N.Y.C., 1970-76; dep. counsel govt. ops. com. U.S. Congress, Washington, 1976-77; assoc. dir. office of pub. liaison The White House, Washington, 1977-78, dep. counsel to v.p. Walter Mondale, 1978-79; N.Y. Primary campaign dir. Re-election for Carter/Mondale, N.Y.C., 1979-80; U.S. rep. Mission to the U.N., N.Y.C., 1980-81; sole practice entertainment law N.Y.C., 1981-89; of counsel Summit, Rovins & Feldesman, N.Y.C., 1989-90; ptnr. Fischbein, Badillo & Wagner, N.Y.C., 1990—; film producer Barking Dog Prodns., N.Y.C., 1987—. Author: Time Without Work, 1984; author, editor: Prisoner's Rights Sourcebook, 1972, Rights of Gay People, 1973; producer (film) In a Shallow Grave, 1988, Preston Sturges: The Rise and Fall of an American Dreamer, 1990. Democrat. Jewish. Home: 111 E 10th St New York NY 10003-7514 Office: Fischbein Badillo & Wagner 909 3rd Ave New York NY 10022-4731

HAFTEL, JAN, jewelry designer; b. Phila., Oct. 16, 1954; d. Leonard Cohen and Eva (Wolk) DeCinque; m. Lawrence E. Haftel, July 22, 1973. AA, Community Coll., Phila., 1973. Prin. Jan's Gems, Phila., 1987—. Mem. Soc. of Craft Designers (2nd place award 1991). Jewish.

HAGAN, FRANK EDWARD, sociology educator; b. Pitts., June 19, 1945; s. Frank E. and Dolores (Thiel) H.; m. Mary Ann Szymanowski, Aug. 27, 1966; 1 child, Shannon Kate. BA in Sociology, Gannon U., Erie, Pa., 1966; MA in Sociology, U. Md., 1968; PhD in Sociology, Case Western Res. U., Cleve., 1975. Instr. Slippery Rock (Pa.) U., 1968-71; sr. rsch. assoc. Case Western Res. U., Cleve., 1973-75; instr. to prof. criminal justice dept. Mercyhurst Coll., Erie, 1975—, dir. criminal justice dept., 1978-79, dir., prof. grad. program in adminstrn. of justice, 1980—. Author: Research Methods in Criminal Justice, 1989, Criminology, 1986, 2nd edit. 1990; co-editor (with Marvin Sussman) Deviance and the Family, 1988. Mem. Mayor's Police Task Force, Erie, Pa., 1990. Mem. Am. Soc. Criminology, Acad. Criminal Justice Scis. (nat. chmn. rsch. com. 1984), Am. Sociol. Soc., Northeastern Acad. Criminal Justice, Pa. Acad. Criminal Justice. Democrat. Roman Catholic. Office: Grad Program Adminstrn Just Mercyhurst Coll Erie PA 16546

HAGAN, KENNETH JAMES, historian, museum director; b. Oakland, Calif., Feb. 20, 1936; married; 3 children. AB, U. Calif., Berkeley, 1958; MA %, U. Calif., 1964; PhD in History, Claremont Grad. Sch., 1970. Instr. Claremont Men's Coll., 1968-69; asst. prof. Kans. State U., 1969-73; asst. prof. U.S. Naval Acad., 1973-77, assoc. prof., from 1977, now prof., archivist; dir. U.S. Naval Acad. Mus. Author: American Gunboat Diplomacy and the Old Navy, 1877-1889, 1973, This People's Navy: The Making of American Sea Power, 1990; co-author: Americal Foreign Policy, 1977; editor: In Peace and War, Interpretations of Am. Naval History, 1975-78; contbr. Ency. of Am. Fgn. Policy, 1978; contbg. author to other publs. on Am. diplomatic and naval history. Office: US Naval Acad Mus Annapolis MD 21402*

HAGAN, WILLIAM JOHN, JR., chemistry educator, historian; b. Port Washington, N.Y., May 17, 1956; s. William John Sr. and Kathleen Marie (Grysk) H. BA in Chemistry, Bowdoin Coll., 1978; MS in Chemistry, Rensselaer Inst. Tech., 1983, PhD in Chemistry, 1985, MS in History, 1986. Postdoctoral fellow U. Rochester, N.Y., 1985-87; asst. prof. St. Anselm Coll., Manchester, N.H., 1987—; vis. prof. Rennselaer Poly. Inst., Troy, 1988. Contbr. articles to profl. jours. Texaco Corp. fellow Rensselaer Poly. Inst., 1982; St. Anselm Coll. grantee, 1988. Mem. AAAS, Am. Chem. Soc., History of Sci. Soc., Am. Soc. Photobiology, Internat. Soc. Study of the Origin of Life, Sigma Xi. Roman Catholic. Office: St Anselm Coll 87 St Anselm Rd Manchester NH 03102

HAGEDORN, ALFRED ARTHUR, III, organic chemist; b. Colorado Springs, Colo., Dec. 17, 1948; s. Alfred Arthur and Beatrice Dorothy (Mead) H.; m. Myrna Lee Sult, Aug. 13, 1972. AB in Chemistry cum laude, Cornell U., 1969; PhD in Chemistry, Mich. State U., 1974. Rsch. assoc. dept. chemistry Columbia U., N.Y.C., 1974-76; lectr. dept. chemistry Rutgers U., New Brunswick, N.J., 1976-80, asst. prof. dept. chemistry, 1980-82; sr. rsch. chemist Berlex Labs., Inc., Cedar Knolls, N.J., 1982-86, scientist, 1987-88, sect. head chem. devel., 1988—; bd. dirs. Mid-Colo. Investment Co., Inc., Colorado Springs. Contbr. articles to profl. jours.; patentee in field. Predoctoral fellow NSF, 1970-73, postdoctoral fellow NIH, 1974-75; grantee Petroleum Rsch. Fund, 1978-82. Mem. AAAS, Am. Chem. Soc., N.Y. Acad. Sci., Sigma Xi, Alpha Chi Sigma. Republican. Home: 57 Eardley Rd Edison NJ 08817-3054 Office: Berlex Labs Inc 110 E Hanover Ave Cedar Knolls NJ 07927

HAGEMAN, RICHARD PHILIP, JR., educational administrator; b. Derby, Conn., Dec. 21, 1941; s. Richard Philip and Jane Elizabeth (Serafinowicz) H.; children: Margaret Anne, Sheila Marie. BS, Cen. Conn. State U., 1964; MS, U. Bridgeport, 1968, profl. diploma, 1972. Cert. counselor Nat. Bd. Cert. Counselors; cert. tchr., Conn. Tchr. Stony Brook Sch., Stratford (Conn.) Bd. Edn., 1964-69, elem. sch. guidance counselor, 1969-81, secondary sch. guidance counselor, 1981-83; asst. prin. Stratford (Conn.) Acad., 1983-90; prin. Whitney Sch., 1990—; lectr. edn. Fairfield U. Grad. Sch. Edn., 1971—; head counselor Stratford Continuing Edn. Program, 1983-91, chief examiner Gen. Ednl. Devel., 1986-91; assessor, trainer Beginning Educator Support and Tng. program Conn. State Dept. of Edn.; mem. adv. bd. counselor edn. Fairfield (Conn.) U., 1970-74; co-chmn. Stratford Juvenile Deliquency Prevention Team, 1979-81. Mem. Youth Adv. Bd. Stratford, 1981-85, chairperson, 1984-85; radio announcer Sta. WMNR, Monroe, Conn., 1982—. Mem. AACD, ASCD, NEA (life), Stratford Edn. Assn. (pres. 1978-79), Am. Sch. Counselor Assn., New Eng. Assn. Specialists Group Work (pres. 1982-83), Nat. Assn. Elem. Sch. Prins., Phi Delta Kappa. Roman Catholic. Democrat. Office: Whitney Sch 1130 Huntington Rd Stratford CT 06497-2796

HAGEMAN, WILLIAM EUGENE, pharmacologist; b. Glendale, Ohio, Sept. 2, 1939; s. William Henry and Dorothy Mae (Van Camp) H.; m. Rita Jean Berssenbruegge, Aug. 15, 1964; children: Leticia Lynn, Holly Lynn, Daniel William, Christa Jeanette. Student, De Pauw U., 1958-60; BS in Pharmacy, U. Cin., 1963; MS, U. Pitts., 1966, PhD, 1968. Sr. scientist McNeil Labs., Ft. Washington, Pa., 1968-73, group leader, 1974-80; prin. scientist McNeil Pharm., Spring House, Pa., 1980-86, Janssen Rsch. Found., Spring House, 1987-90, R. W. Johnson Pharm. Rsch. Inst., Raritan, N.J., 1990—; chmn. steering com. Cardiovascular Pharmacol. Discussion Group, 1977-85. Mem. Physiol. Soc. Phila., Am. Soc. Pharmacol. and Exptl. Therapeutics, Inflamation Rsch. Assn. (co-chmn. poster com. 1986, 88, 80, chmn. continuing edn. com. 1990-92), Pulmonary Rsch. Group. Mem. Pentacostal Ch. Office: RW Johnson Pharm Rsch Inst Rte 202 Raritan NJ 08869-0602

HAGEN, DANIEL RUSSELL, physiologist; b. Springfield, Ill., Sept. 29, 1952; s. Robert William and Russella Mae (Lane) H.; m. Rosemary Ellen Simonetta, Mar. 25, 1978; children: Matthew, Mark, Lane, Elise. BS, U. Ill., 1974, PhD, 1978. Rsch. assoc. Cornell U., Ithaca, N.Y., 1978; asst. prof. Pa. State U., University Park, 1978-84, assoc. prof., 1984—; vis. assoc. prof. U. Wis., Madison, 1988-89. Mem. editorial bd. Jour. of Animal Sci., 1983-86; contbr. over 27 articles to profl. jours. Mem. AAAS, Am. Soc. for Animal Sci., Soc. for Study of Reprodn., Soc. for Study of Fertility. Office: Pa State U 324 Henning Bldg University Park PA 16802

HAGEN, JAMES ALFRED, marketing executive; b. Forest City, Iowa, Mar. 27, 1932; s. Archie M. and Catherine E. (McGuire) H.; m. Mary King, Aug. 16, 1958; children: Joseph Patrick, Margaret Mary. B.A., St. Ambrose Coll., 1956; M.A., Iowa State U., 1958. Asst. gen. freight agt. Mo. Pacific R.R., St. Louis, 1958-62; dir. mktg. research, v.p. corp. devel. So. Rwy., Washington, 1963-71, 76-77; assoc. adminstr. econs. Fed. R.R. Adminstrn., Washington, 1971-74; pres. U.S. Rwy. Assn., Washington, 1974-76; sr. v.p. mktg. and sales Consol. Rail Corp., Phila., 1977-85, chmn. bd., pres., chief exec. officer, 1989—; exec. v.p. sales and mktg. distbn. services group CSX Transp., 1985-88; pres. distbn. services group CSX Transp., Balt., 1988-89; mem. bus. adv. com. Northwestern U. Transp. Ctr. Mem. Nat. Freight Transp. Assn., Am. Soc. Transp. and Logistics. Roman Catholic. Home: 1315 Wrenfield Way Villanova PA 19085-2061 Office: Consol Rail Corp 6 Penn Plz Philadelphia PA 19103*

HAGENBRUCH, HARRIET ANN, education librarian; b. N.Y.C.; d. Abraham and Augusta (Kiel) Cohen); m. Arthur Hagenbruch; children: Arthur, Michael, Lee-Ann, Eric, Carl. BA, Hunter Coll.; MLS, L.I. Univ. Cert. sch. media specialist; cert. pub. libr. Paraprofl. libr. East Meadow (N.Y.) Sch. Dist., 1982-86, sch. media specialist, 1986-88; edn. libr. Curriculum Materials Ctr. Hofstra U., Hempstead, N.Y., 1988—. Mem. ALA, Nassau County Libr. Assn. (v.p. acad. and pres.-elect 1991—), Assn. Coll. Rsch. Librs. (exec. bd. 1990—, chmn. Edn./Curriculum Materials Ctr. Librarians 1990—), Assn. Coll. Rsch. Librs. N.Y. Home: 545 Pontiac Rd East Meadow NY 11554-5418 Office: Hofstra Univ 1000 Fulton Ave Hempstead NY 11550-1009

HAGENSTEIN, PERRY REGINALD, economist; b. St. Paul, Sept. 25, 1931; s. Edwin Bernhardt and Harriet J. (Raschke) H.; m. Ann Hill, Oct. 20, 1956; children: Jonathan, Randall, Edwin, Elizabeth. BS, U. Minn., St. Paul, 1952; MF, Yale U., 1953; PhD, U. Mich., 1963. Forester Fordyce (Ark.) Lumber Co., 1956-58; rsch. economist U.S. Forest Svc., Upper Darby, Pa., 1960-66; sr. policy analyst U.S. Pub. Land Law Review Commn., Washington, 1966-70; rsch. fellow Harvard U., 1970-71; exec. dir. New England Natural Resources Ctr., Boston, 1971-77; pres. Resources Issues, Inc., Wayland, Mass., 1977—; trustee New Eng. Natural Resources Ctr. Author numerous articles in profl. jours. With U.S. Army 1953-56 (Fed. Republic Germany). Mem. Soc. Am. Foresters, Am. Economics Assn., Am. Forestry Assn. (bd. dirs. 1976—, pres. 1984-86), Forest Hist. Soc. (bd. dirs. 1983-89), Cosmos Club. Home: 15 Bennett Rd Wayland MA 01778-2703 Office: PO Box 44 Wayland MA 01778-0044

HAGER, EDWARD PAUL, developer; b. Pottsville, Pa., Jan. 15, 1948; s. Edward Louis and Pauline Ann (Macalush) H. BA magna cum laude, St. Charles Borromeo, Phila., 1970. Dist. exec. Hawk Mountain coun. Boy Scouts Am., Reading, Pa., 1971-78, sr. dist. exec. Hawk Mountain coun., 1978-80, devel. dir. Hawk Mountain coun., 1980-83; fin. dir. Nassau county coun. Boy Scouts Am., Roslyn, N.Y., 1983-85; dir. devel. Luth. Home, Topton, Pa., 1985—. Campaign worker United Way So. Schuykill, Pottsville, Pa., 1977-79, United Way Berks County, Reading, 1982, 85-91; com. chmn. Hawk Mountain coun. Boy Scouts Am., 1986-89. Named one of Outstanding Young Men Am., 1977; recipient St. George award Nat. Cath. Com. on Scouting, 1978. Mem. Nat. Soc. Fundraising Execs. (bd. dirs. northeastern Pa. chpt. 1986—, v.p. 1988, pres. 1989-90, nat. bd. dirs. 1991, nat. assembly 1992), Rotary (bd. dirs. West Reading chpt. 1980-83, Reading chpt. 1990—, dist. Rotary Found. group study exch. 1991—), Luth. Brotherhood (br. v.p. 1991—). Roman Catholic. Home: 404 Race St Macungie PA 18062-1029 Office: Luth Home at Topton Topton PA 19562

HAGER, MARY HASTINGS, nutritionist, educator, consultant; b. Upland, Calif., Mar. 27, 1948; d. Howard Benjamin and Miriam Agnes (Sahlmann) Hastings; m. Douglas Francis Hager, Jan. 4, 1982; children: Marghet Janet, Bettina Miriam. BS in Foods and Nutrition, U. Del., 1971; MS in Nutrition and Dietetics, U. Calif., Davis, 1973, PhD in Nutrition, 1978. Registered, lic. dietitian. Nutritionist U. Calif. Sch. Medicine, Davis, 1973-74; staff scientist Procter and Gamble Co., Cin., 1978-83, devel. staff, 1986-87; asst. prof. Coll. of Mount St. Joseph, Cin., 1983-85, Tex. Christian U., Ft. Worth, 1987-89; vis. lectr. Rutgers U., New Brunswick, N.J., 1989-90; assoc. prof. Coll. of St. Elizabeth, Morristown, N.J., 1991—; cons. IGA Grocers, Cin., 1984-85, Hoffman-LaRoche Corp., Nutley, N.J., 1989-90, Procter and Gamble Co., Cin., 1990—. Contbr. articles and abstracts to profl. publs. Chmn. bd. dirs. Greater Cin. Nutrition Coun., 1985-86; mem. edn. task force Am. Heart Assn., Ft. Worth, 1988-89, pub. edn. com. Am. Cancer Soc., Ft. Worth, 1988-89. Grad. fellow Procter and Gamble Co., 1975-78; Amy Rextrew scholar U. Del., 1970; grantee Tex. Christian U. Rsch. Fund, 1988. Mem. AAAS, Am. Inst. Nutrition (rsch. award 1978), Am. Dietetic Assn., Am. Physiol. Soc., Soc. for Nutrition Edn., N.J. Nutrition Coun., Sigma Xi. Democrat. Episcopalian. Home: 9 Jay Dr Randolph NJ 07869-4102 Office: Dept of Home Econs Coll of St Elizabeth Morristown NJ 07960

HAGER, WAYNE RICHARD, chemical engineering educator; b. Balt., Sept. 6, 1941; s. Richard Anton and Evelyn Veronica (Kofron) H.; m. Deanna Doris Driskill, Oct. 21, 1962 (div. 1988); m. Mary Ann Rees, Jan. 14, 1989; children: Suzanne, Sharon, Brooke, Matthew, Jeffrey, Sara. BS in Chem. Engring., U. Utah, 1963; MS in Chem. Engring., U. Idaho, 1971, PhD in Chem. Engring., 1972. Engr. E.I. DuPont de Nemours & Co., Wilmington, Del., 1963-64, 66-69; from asst. prof. to prof. U. Idaho, Moscow, 1972-88; prof., head gen. engring. dept. Pa. State U., University Park, 1988-91, head Sch. Engring. Tech. and Commonwealth Campus Engring., 1991—; cons. in field. Contbr. articles to profl. jours. 1st lt. U.S. Army, 1964-66. Fellow NDEA, 1969-72; Fulbright scholar U. Mauritius, Indian Ocean, 1985-87. Mem. Am. Soc. Engring. Edn., Fulbright Assn., Am. Inst. Chem. Engrs., Pa. Acad. Sci., Am. Assn. Community and Jr. Colls. Roman Catholic. Home: 752 W Aaron Dr State College PA 16803-3117 Office: Pa State Univ 245 Hammond Bldg University Park PA 16802

HAGERTY, GEORGE JAMES III, university administrator, educator, consultant; b. Quincy, Mass., Dec. 15, 1952; s. George James Jr. and Madeleine Louise (Hogan) H.; m. Laura Theresa D'Ambrosio, July 1, 1978; children: Matthew G., Emily C., Andrew J. AB, Stonehill Coll., 1975; MA, Harvard U., 1976, EdD, 1978. Program dir. Boston Sch. Dist., 1976-78; post-doctoral fellow U. Md., College Park, 1978-79; program officer D.H.E.W. Bur. of Edn. for the Handicapped, Washington, 1980-81; br. chief U.S.D.E. Office of Spl. Edn. Programs, Washington, 1981-83, U.S.D.E., Compliance and Enforcement, Washington, 1983-85; dir. acad. devel. Stonehill Coll., North Easton, Mass., 1985-89, assoc. prof. polit. sci. and edn., 1985—; ptnr. Taylor, Hagerty & Assoc., Inc., Washington, 1986—; dir. corp. found. and govt. rels. Stonehill Coll., North Easton, Mass., 1989—; bd. dirs. Brockton Vis. Nurse Assn.; bd. trustees Notre Dame Acad., Hingham, Mass., 1987—, Old Colony Hospice Assn., Stoughton, Mass., 1985—; program expert U.S. Dept. Edn., Washington, 1990—; instr. Harvard U., Cambridge, Mass., 1992—. Contbr. articles to profl. jours. and book chpts. Apptd. Mass. Coun. on Disabilities, 1990—. Recipient Nat. Leadership award Nat. Coun. on Disabilties, 1989; Nat. fellowship U. Coun. for Edn. Adminstrn., 1978. Mem. Coun. for Exceptional Children, Phi Delta Kappa. Roman Catholic. Home: 11 Wagon Wheel Rd Taunton MA 02780-4369

HAGEY, WALTER REX, banker; b. Hatfield, Pa., July 24, 1909; s. Justus T. and Martha Mabel Hagey; m. Dorothy E. Rosenberger, Oct. 17, 1931; 1 child, Donald C. Student, U. Pa., 1931-36; LLB, La Salle Extension U., 1938; STB, Temple U., 1943; grad., Stonier Grad. Sch. Banking Rutgers U., 1951; LLD, Muhlenberg Coll., 1963. With Fidelity Bank (formerly Fidelity-Phila. Trust Co.), 1929—, asst. sec., 1948—, asst. v.p., 1957-66, v.p., 1966-74. Supply pastor Eastern Pa. Synod Lutheran Ch. Am., 1950-80, treas., 1950-80, now Luth. Synod S.E. Pa.; treas. Luth. Synod Northeastern Pa., 1969-70; pres., dir. Phila. Luth. Social Union; treas. Luth. Laymens Movement for Stewardship of United Luth. Ch., 1959-63; mem. bd., exec. com. Luth. Council in U.S., 1962-74; mem. bds., treas. home missions, inner missions, Christian edn. Eastern Pa. Synod, Luth. Ch. Am., 1950-69; vice chmn. adminstrn. and fin. Luth. Ch. in Am., 1972-78, mem. bd. pensions, 1978-84 , v.p. Bd. Am. Missions, 1972-78; bd. dirs., adv. bd. Muhlenberg Med. Center; bd. dirs., chmn. Prosser Found., 1968-89; bd. dirs., treas. Luth. Retirement Homes, 1978-82; mem. com. for investments Luth. Ch. in Am., 1978-82; bd. dirs., sec. Silver Spring-Martin Luther Sch., 1976-89; treas. Bethesda House, 1950-69; treas., registrar Luth. Lay Acad., 1981—; treas. The Auxiliary-Luth. Theol. Sem. at Phila., 1986-89, The Religious Tercente-

nary Com., 1982-89. m. Am. Inst. Banking, Phila. Estate Planning Council, Pa. Council Chs. (dir. 1954-70), Pa. Soc., Luth. Hist. Soc. Eastern Pa., Men of Mt. Airy Sem. (pres. 1976-86), Pa. Bible Soc. (treas., sec., now pres., dir. 1971—), Rotary, Elm (sec. 1951-63), Midday Club, Anglers (Phila.). Home: 510 E Lawn Ave Lansdale PA 19446-1523

HAGGERTY, JAMES JOSEPH, aerospace and science writer; b. Orange, N.J., Feb. 1, 1920; s. James Joseph and Anna (Morahan) H.; student pub. schs.; m. Marian Smith Mitten, Nov. 20, 1962 (dec. Jan. 1989); children: Karin, James Joseph, Brian. Reporter Orange (N.J.) Daily Courier, 1938-40; mil. editor Am. Aviation Publs., 1948-53; aviation editor Collier's, 1953-56; free-lance writer on sci. and aerospace subjects, 1956—; editor Aerospace Year Book, 1957-70; aerospace editorial cons. Aerospace Industries Assn., 1974—, NASA, 1975—, Pres. Commn. on Space Shuttle Challenger Accident, 1986. Served with USAAF, 1942-48. Decorated D.F.C., Air medal with clusters. Mem. Aviation Space Writers Assn. (past pres.), AAAS, Air Force Assn. Clubs: Bethesda Country; Touchdown (Washington). Author: First of the Spacemen, 1960; Spacecraft, 1961; Flight, 1964; The U.S. Air Force: A Pictorial History in Art, 1965; Man's Conquest of Space, 1965; Food and Nutrition, 1966; Apollo Lunar Landing, 1969; Hail To The Redskins, 1973; Aviation's Mr. Sam, 1973. Address: 502 H St SW Washington DC 20024

HAGGERTY, WARREN H., JR., mayor; m. Liza Pettinato; children: Matthew, Elizabeth, Patrick. BS in Pub. Adminstrn., Kutztown U. Legis. asst. Pa. Ho. of Reps., 1978-82; asst. to mayor of Reading Pa., 1982-86; councilman, 1986, apptd. mayor of Reading, 1987, elected mayor, 1987, 91. Mem. adv. bd. Hawk Mountain Coun., Boy Scouts Am. Mem. Nat. League of Cities, Pa. League of Cities, Govt. Fin. Officers Assn. Office: 815 Washington St Reading PA 19601-3637*

HAGNER, SAMUEL BENEDICT, psychiatrist; b. Phila., Nov. 1, 1925; s. George Wills Sr. and Evelyn (Benedict) H.; m. Elizabeth Jean Cunningham, July 22, 1950; children: Martha H. Leathe, David G., Thomas C. AB, Oberlin Coll., 1949; MD, Temple U., 1954; grad., Phila. Psychoanalytic Soc., 1969. Diplomate Am. Bd. Psychiatry and Neurology. Intern Germantown Hosp., Phila., 1954-55; resident in psychiatry Temple U., Phila., 1955-58, rsch. asst. Sch. Medicine, 1958-65, instr. Sch. Medicine, 1958-69; pvt. practice, Phila. and Dover, N.H., 1958—; chief dept. psychiatry Wentworth-Douglass Hosp., Dover, 1982-83, cons., 1969-91; cons. Family Svc. Phila., 1961-69; examiner Social Seucrity Disability Unit, Concord, N.H., 1978—. Contbr. articles to profl. jours. Staff sgt. U.S. Army, 1944-46. Fellow Am. Psychiat. Assn. (life); mem. N.H. Psychiat. Soc. (continuing edn. com. 1972-76, peer rev. com. 1975-76, exec. coun. 1977-79), N.H. Med. Soc. Office: 113 Locust St Dover NH 03820-3793

HAGOOD, LOUIS R., publisher; b. Tampa, Mar. 6, 1944; s. Louis R. and Mary (Carter) H.; m. Patricia Carr, June 29, 1965; 1 child, Caroline Newport. BA, Duke U., 1965; MBA, CUNY, 1967. Mgr. info. Engring., Aerospace and Banking, N.Y.C. and, Calif., 1965-69; mgmt. scientist Singer Co., N.Y.C., 1970-73; ops. mgr. Citibank, N.Y.C., 1974-80; freelance mgmt. cons. N.Y.C., 1981-84; pub. Oxbridge Communications, N.Y.C., 1985—. Mem. Nat. Arts Club, Newsletter Assn., Direct Mktg. Assn., Director Pubs. Forum. Home: 34 Gramercy Park E New York NY 10003-1731 Office: Oxbridge Communications 150 5th Ave New York NY 10011-4311

HAGUE, ALBERT FREDERICK, data processing company executive; b. Newburgh, N.Y., Jan. 28, 1947; s. Albert Victor and Mary Wood (Salmon) H.; m. Carol Patricia Beretta, July 26, 1966; 1 child, Paula Marie. AAS, Orange County Community Coll., Middletown, N.Y., 1975. Fin. clk. IBM, Hopewell Junction, N.Y., 1970-72; prodn. analyzer IBM, 1972-79, with dept. tech. support, 1979-81, plans & controls auditor, 1981-83, staff asst., 1983-85, prodn. control mgr., 1985-88, staff planner, 1988—. Sgt. USAF, 1966-70, Vietnam. Decorated Commendation medal. Mem. Am. Assn. Individual Investors, Moose. Republican. Roman Catholic. Home: 411 Lattintown Rd Marlboro NY 12542

HAGUE, PAUL RICHARD, geologist, consultant; b. Worcester, Mass., Sept. 26, 1940; s. Gustaf Frederick and Ruth Jordan (McDonald) H.; m. Christine Carr, July 19, 1968; 1 child, Emily. BS in Geology, U. Mass., 1973. Field engr. Pratt & Whitney, Inc., Hartford, Conn., 1966-67; engr. asst. Worcester Poly. Inst., Alden Rsch. Labs., Holden, Mass., 1967-69; sedimentologist, dir. Normandeau Assoc., Bedford, N.H., 1974-79; geologist Geophysical Survey Systems, Inc., Salem, N.H., 1980-82; founder, prin. Geoscan, Weare, N.H., 1983—; also bd. dirs. Geoscan; Dir.: (music video) Suzanne's Lament, 1972; photographer: (book) Reader's Digest Book on Canada, 1978. Mem. Weare Conservation Commn., 1987, 91—, Weare Recycling and Transfer Sta. Commn., 1990. Petty officer USN, 1960-66, Vietnam. Mem. Geol. Soc. Am., Soc. Exploration Geophysicists, N.H. Geol. Soc. (charter mem.). Zen Buddhist. Home and Office: Geoscan 35 Abijah Bridge Rd Weare NH 03281-4805

HAGUE, WILLIAM, priest; b. Honolulu, Jan. 19, 1952; s. James Duncan and Henriette Catherine (Reitsma) H.; m. Jane Milliken, May 31, 1981; children: James Duncan, Christopher Hathaway. BA, U. Va., 1974; MDiv, Va. Theol. Sem., 1980; DMin, Hartford (Conn.) Sem., 1987. Ordained to ministry Episcopal Ch., 198l. Rector Christ Episcopal Ch., Kensington, Md., 1989—. Mem. City Tavern. Home and Office: 3902 Everett St Kensington MD 20895-3818

HAHN, CELIA ALLISON, writer, editor; b. Cleve., Jan. 3, 1931; d. Latham Lee and Celia (Fisher) A.; m. Robert H. Hahn, June 24, 1961; children: David L., Allison L. BA summa cum laude, Smith Coll., 1953; postgrad., Union Theol. Sem., 1953-55, Yale Div. Sch., 1957-58; DD (hon.), Gen. Theol. Sem., 1990. Dir. religious edn. St. Andrew's Ch., Meriden, Conn., 1957-58, Grace Ch., Silver Spring, Md., 1958-63; editorial cons. Project Test Pattern, Washington, 1972-74; editor in chief Alban Inst., Washington, 1974—. Author: Lay Voices in an Open Church, 1985, Sexual Paradox, 1991; co-author: The Male-Female Church Staff, 1990, numerous others. Mem. Phi Beta Kappa. Democrat. Home: 11453 Washington Pla W Reston VA 22090 Office: The Alban Inst 4125 Nebraska Ave NW Washington DC 20016-2700

HAHN, CELIA FERNER, broadcaster; b. Sioux City, Iowa, Mar. 21, 1942; d. Arnold Erland and Celia Evelyn (Wright) F.; m. Curtis Henry Hahn, Feb. 6, 1966; children: Cathy Celia, Christopher Curtis. BA, State U. Iowa, 1964. asst. to pres. Cranbrook Ednl. Community, Bloomfield Hills, Mich., 1972-78; owner WLDM Radio, 1978— and WNNZ Radio, 1987—, Westfield, Mass. Mem. Greater Westfield Area C. of C. (pres. 1985), corporator Westfield Atheneum, Westfield Boys & Girls Club, Woronoco Savings Bank, (charter) Zonta of Greater Westfield. Episcopalian. Clubs: Westfield Woman's (program chmn. 1980-82); Williston Parents Assn. (v.p. 1983-84), Western Mass Bus. Womans Alliance. Avocations: swimming, solar energy, travel, reading. Home: Pineridge Dr Westfield MA 01085-4524 Office: Celia Communications Inc 249 Union St # 1248 Westfield MA 01085-2492

HAHN, DAVIS MILFORD, medical oncologist; b. Balt., Mar. 24, 1946; s. Theodore John and Odessa (Milford) H.; m. Anne Peter, Sept. 11, 1976; children: William Milford, John Hammond. BA, Johns Hopkins U., 1967; MD, U. Va., 1971. Intern Vanderbilt U. Hosp., Nashville, 1971-72, resident, 1972-74; chief med. oncology Good Samaritan Hosp., Balt., 1977—; asst. prof. medicine U. Md. Hosp., Balt., 1978—. Elder Second Presbyn. Ch., Balt., 1986—. Lt. comdr. USPHS, 1974-77. Recipient Med. Oncology fellowship Nat. Cancer Inst., 1977. Mem. Am. Coll. Physicians, Am. Soc. Clin. Oncology, Am. Soc. Internal Medicine. Office: Good Samaritan Hosp Ste 107 5601 Loch Raven Blvd Baltimore MD 21239

HAHN, FRED, emeritus political science and history educator; b. Stankov, Czechoslovakia, May 28, 1906; s. Emil and Helen (Wilhelm) H.; came to U.S., 1939, naturalized, 1947; D.Law and Polit. Sci., U. Prague, 1929; M.A., Columbia U., 1951; m. Edith H. Friedman, Dec. 25, 1949; children: Susan Ann, Jeanette Emily. Atty., Prague, Czechoslovakia, 1929-39; self-employed, N.Y.C., 1941-62; lectr. Fairleigh Dickinson U., Rutherford, Madison, N.J., 1962-64; assoc. prof. Trenton (N.J.) State Coll., 1964-69, prof., 1969-77, emeritus, 1977—; guest prof. U. Frankfurt, Germany, 1968-69, summer 1971, 73, 75; assoc. Inst. on East Central Europe, Columbia U., 1980—. Fulbright grantee, 1968-69, summer 1973. Mem. Am. Hist. Assn., Am. Assn. for Advancement Slavic Studies, Czechoslovakia Acad. Arts and Scis., Soc. for History Czechoslovak Jews (dir.), Internat PEN. Author: Marxist and Utopian Socialists, 1965, History of Russia, 1968, Stürmer, 1978; co-author several books; contbr. articles to profl. jours. Home: 780 W End Ave New York NY 10025-5549

HAHN, JOHN CHARLES, insurance cliams representative; b. Middletown, N.Y., July 6, 1943; s. John William and Eva Kay (Terwilliger) H.; m. Margaret Ward, Dec. 12, 1969 (div. Apr. 1977); m. Pamela Kay Legenos, Apr. 18, 1987. Student, Orange County Community Coll., 1961-63, Rider Coll., 1963-66. Benefits adminstr. Phelps Dodge Corp., Suffern, N.Y., 1966-70; cliams rep. Nationwide Ins. Co., Syracuse, N.Y., 1970—. Mem. planning bd. Town of Mamakating, Wurtsboro, N.Y., 1991—; bd. dirs. Basha Kill Area Assoc., Cuddebackville, N.Y., 1985—; v.p. Sullivan County Environ., Liberty, N.Y., 1990—; vol. Bis Bros./Big Sisters Orange County, Newburgh, N.Y., 1983—. Home: PO Box 212 Summitville NY 12781 Office: Nationwide Ins Co 2 Summit Ct Fishkill NY 12524-1333

HAHN, JOHN WILLIAM, insurance company executive; b. N.Y.C., July 12, 1940; s. Ferdinand J. and Evelyn H. H. (Hauser) H.; m. L. Dale Mazza; children: Nancy, John. BA, CUNY, 1962; postgrad., Harvard U., 1973. With Atlantic Mut. Cos., N.Y.C., 1963—, v.p., adminstrv. svcs., 1974-78; sr. v.p., adminstrv. svcs. Atlantic Mut. Cos., Roanoke, Va., 1978-85; exec. v.p., adminstrn. Atlantic Mut. Cos., Madison, N.J., 1985—; exec. com., bd. dirs. Ins. Value Added Network Svcs., Conn., 1985-92; mem. stds. com. Agy. Co. Orgn. for R&D; bd. dirs. Crestar Bank, Roanoke, Va. Mem. Am. Mgmt. Assn., Ins. Acctg. Statis. Assn., Marines Meml. Assn., Harvard Club (N.Y.C.), Roanoke (Va.) Country Club, Hidden Valley Country Club (Va.). Office: Atlantic Mut Cos 3 Giralda Farms Madison NJ 07940-1004

HAHN, LORNA, political organization executive, author; b. Phila., June 16; d. Charles William and Belle Herman; m. Walter F. Hahn; 1 child, Randolph P. BA, Temple U.; MA, U. Pa., PhD in Internat. Rels., 1962. Instr. Temple U., Phila.; researcher Spl. Ops. & Rsch. Office, Washington; rsch. coord. Hist. Evaluation & Rsch. Orgn., Washington; dir. Masters program Am. U., Washington; exec. dir. Assn. Third World Affairs, Washington, 1968—; v.p. Internat. Fedn. for Protection of Religious, Linguistic & Ethnic Minorities, Washington, 1987—; pub. Third World Forum, 1976—; advisor Save Cambodia, Inc.,Washington, 1980—; lectr. Cath. U., Washington, 1965-66, Howard U., Washington, 1971-73, 82-83. Author: North Africa: Nationalism to Nationhood, 1960, Undergrounds in Insurgency, Revolutionary and Resistance Warfare, 1964, Morocco: Old Land, New Nation, 1966, An Historical Dictionary of Libya, 1981; author numerous monographs, articles and reviews; frequent guest on talk shows. Advisor Dem. candidates. Recipient Scholarship medal Phi Gamma Mu. Mem. Dems. 2000. Mem. Unitarian Ch. Office: Assn Third World Affairs 1629 K St NW Washington DC 20006

HAHN, NORMAN JACOB, engineer; b. Indpls., Mar. 20, 1965; s. Jerome Byron and Sara Francis (Troutman) H. BS in Aerospace Engring., Pa. State U., 1988. Experimental engr. Hamilton Standard div. United Techs. Corp., Windsor Locks, Conn., 1988—; sr. exptl. engr. Mem. AIAA, Pa. State U. Alumni Assn. Republican.

HAHN, ROGER CARL, chemistry educator; b. Cleve., Feb. 20, 1932; s. Walter Carl and Winona (Cornell) H.; m. Bessie King, June 9, 1962 (div. 1982); children: Angela, Michael, Belinda; m. Estelle Guilbault, Aug. 10, 1985. BA, Oberlin Coll., 1953; PhD, Ohio State U., 1960. Asst. prof. U. S.D., Vermillion, 1960-63; asst. prof. Syracuse (N.Y.) U., 1965-71, assoc. prof. chemistry, 1971—; researcher in field. Contbr. articles to profl. publs.; patentee synthesis of highly pure stereoisomers of glycidol derivatives. With U.S. Army, 1953-55. NIH postdoctoral fellow, 1963-65. Mem. Am. Chem. Soc. Office: Syracuse U Chemistry Dept 1-014 CST Syracuse NY 13244-4100

HAHN, STEPHEN WALTER, English educator; b. Lawrence, Mass., Apr. 23, 1950; s. Alfred Elden and Theresa Lily (O'Connell) H.; m. Meredith L. Handren, Oct. 5, 1968 (div. July 1970); 1 child, Emil (dec.); m. Lori Van Decker, Aug. 16, 1985. BA in English and Philosophy, Amherst Coll., 1975; MA in English, Rutgers U., 1975, PhD in English, 1983. Assoc. dir. writing program English dept. Rutgers U., New Brunswick, N.J., 1983-84; asst. prof. William Paterson Coll., Wayne, N.J., 1984-90, assoc. prof., 1990—; dir. freshman writing William Paterson Coll., Wayne, 1988-91, dir. gen. edn., 1992—. Editor The Friend: Comment on Romanticism Jour., 1991—; contbr. articles to profl. jours. N.J. State Coll. faculty fellow Princeton U., 1991-92. Mem. N.J. Coll. English Assn. (2nd v.p. 1989-90, 1st v.p. 1990-91, pres. 1991—), Wordsworth Trust Am. (v.p. 1991—), Phi Beta Kappa. Office: William Paterson Coll English Dept Wayne NJ 07470

HAHNER, MORITZ JULIUS, utility company executive; b. Jersey City, May 6, 1931; s. Moritz J. and Lillian M. (Hoth) H.; m. Joan E. Gundlach, July 15, 1955; children: Scott, Gail, Douglas. AA, Jersey City Jr. Coll., 1955; BA, Rutgers U., 1966. Mgr. med. dept. Pub. Svc. Gas and Electric, Newark, 1966-74, asst. mgr. employee benefits, 1974-76, mgr. employee benefits, 1976-92, dir. corp. benefits, 1992—. Mem. Health Svcs. Orgnl. Study Commn., State of N.J., 1988-89; chmn. bd. dirs. Hosp. and Health Planning Coun. Met. N.J.; chmn. info. and referral svc. United Way of Essex and West Hudson; v.p. N.J. Health Careers; v.p. bd. trustees, chmn. exec. com., chmn. fin. com. Boys' Club of Union; sect. leader Greater Newark Hosp. Devel. Fund.; chmn. employee stock ownership plan devel. com. Tax Reduction Act; chmn. bd., chief exec. officer Hospice, Inc. Mem. Am. Gas Assn. (chmn. compensation and benefits com. 1988-89, mem. human resource mgmt. com. 1988-89, mem. task force 1988-89), Coun. Social Agencies of Newark (v.p., mem. exec. com., chmn. nominating com.). Republican. Lutheran. Home: 373 Iroquois Dr Bricktown NJ 08724 Office: Pub Svc Elec & Gas Co 80 Park Plz Newark NJ 07102-4106

HAIG, ROBERT LEIGHTON, lawyer; b. Plainfield, N.J., July 30, 1947; s. Richard Randall and Edith (Remington) H. AB, Yale U., 1967; JD, Harvard U., 1970. Bar: N.Y. 1971, U.S. Dist. Ct. (so. and ea. dists.) N.Y., U.S. Ct. Appeals (2d cir.). Assoc. Kelley Drye & Warren, N.Y.C., 1970-79, ptnr., 1980—. Co-author: Preparing for and Trying the Civil Lawsuit, 1987, Federal Civil Practice, 1989, Federal Litigation Guide, 1992 (chpt. in book); mem. bd. editors Fed. Litigation Guide Reporter, 1989—. Mem. legis. com. Com. for Modern Cts., N.Y.C., 1986—; mem. exec. coun. N.Y. State Conf. Bar Leaders, 1988-90. Recipient award for excellence in continuing legal edn. Assn. Continuing Legal Edn. Adminstrs., 1991. Fellow Am. Bar Found., N.Y. Bar Found.; mem. ABA (del. 1991—), Assn. Bar City N.Y. (chmn. com. judiciary 1989-92, com. on jud. adminstrn. 1989-92), N.Y. County Lawyers Assn. (exec. com. 1986—, v.p. 1986-92, pres. 1992—, dir. 1985—, chmn. com. on supreme ct. 1984-86, chmn. fin. com. 1988-90, lectr. 1984—), N.Y. State Bar Assn. (chmn. com. on fed. cts. 1986-88, del. 1988—, chmn. comml. and fed. litigation sect. 1988-90, lectr. 1985—, exec. com. 1991—). Office: Kelley Drye & Warren 101 Park Ave New York NY 10178-0002

HAIGHT, DONALD ALEXANDER, counselor, educator; b. Neptune, N.J., Sept. 29, 1946; s. Donald Everett and Doris Florence (Crelin) H.; m. Diane Kaye Bott, June 6, 1970; children: David Andrew, Alison Sara. BA, Lebanon Valley Coll., Annville, Pa., 1968; MEd, Springfield (Mass.) Coll., 1969, Cert. of Adv. Study, 1970; EdD, U. Fla., 1972. Nat. cert. counselor. Prof. counselor edn. SUNY, Plattsburgh, 1972—. Contbr. articles to profl. jours., chpts. to books. Mem. N.Y. State Assn. for Counseling and Devel. (pres. 1991—). Presbyterian. Office: SUNY Plattsburgh 104 Ward Hall Plattsburgh NY 12901

HAILEY, ANTHONY EUGENE, production administrator; b. Harrisburg, Pa., July 30, 1959; s. Richard Mathew and Medeline Elizabeth (Pearson) H.; m. Cynthia Stephens, June 10, 1989. BS in Chem. Engring., U. Tenn., 1982. Rsch. engr. E.I. DuPont, Aiken, S.C., 1982-84; process engr. E.I. DuPont, Richmond, Va., 1984-86; rsch. engr. E.I. DuPont, Parkersburg, W.Va., 1986-88; tech. rep. E.I. DuPont, Wilmington, Del., 1988-89, mktg. specialist, 1989-91, area supt. prodn., 1992—. Mem. Nat. Soc. Black Engrs., Soc. Automotive Engrs., Brandywine Profl. Assn. (chair membership com. Wilmington chpt. 1991—).

HAILEY, JACOB JOSEPH, bank executive; b. Phila., Feb. 2, 1949; s. Eugene Peter and Mary Frances (Smith) H. BA in Econs., St. Joseph's U., 1971, BA in History, Polit. Sci., 1971. Adminstr. Cath. Social Svcs., Phila., 1971-72; adminstrv. asst. Pa. House Reps., Harrisburg, 1972-74; chief budget analyst Pa. State House Appropriations Com., Harrisburg, 1974-76; banking officer Beneficial Savings Bank, Phila., 1976-84, asst. v.p., 1984—. Author: Reflections on the Nature of Man, 1971. Candidate Phila. City Coun., 1975, Phila. Dem. City Com., 1976. Mem. Greater Broad and Olney Bus. Assn. (dir. 1980—), Nat. Jesuit Honors Soc., St. Joseph; U. Alumni Assn. (bd. govs. 1980-86), Roman Catholic. High Sch. Alumni Assn. Roman Catholic. Home: 1912 Pine St Philadelphia PA 19103 Office: Beneficial Bank 5700 N Broad St Philadelphia PA 19141

HAILPERN, BRENT TZION, computer scientist; b. Denver, Jan. 11, 1955; s. Jacob and Maxine S. (Rothchild) H.; m. Susan M. Gunn, June 19, 1977; 1 child, Joshua M. BS summa cum laude, U. Denver, 1976; MS, Stanford U., 1978, PhD, 1980. Rsch. staff mem. IBM T-J Watson Rsch. Ctr., Yorktown Heights, N.Y., 1980-84, mgr., 1984-85, sr. mgr., 1985-90; sr. tech. cons. IBM T-J Watson Rsch. Ctr., Yorktown Heights, 1991—; programming cons. IBM Corp. Hdqrs., Armonk, N.Y., 1990-91; adv. bd. Columbia U. Ctr. Adv. Tech. Sci., N.Y., 1991—. Author book; contbr. chpts. to books and articles to profl. jours.; patentee in field. Treas. Katonah (N.Y.) Village Improvement Soc., 1989-91. Gates Found. scholar, 1974-76; fellow NSF, 1976-79, Fannie and John Hertz Found., 1979-80. Mem. IEEE (sr., program chmn. 26th ann. Lake Arrowhead workshop 1987, computer editorial bd. 1989—), Assn. for Computing Machinery (spl. interest group onprogramming lang., sec.-treas. 1989-91, vice chmn. for confs.1991—, local arrangements chmn. 1990, conf. chmn. 1991, program com. 1992), Internat. Fedn. Info. Processing (working group 2.2). Office: IBM T-J Watson Rsch Ctr PO Box 704 Yorktown Heights NY 10598

HAINES, ELIZABETH JOAN, programmer/analyst; b. Boston, Jan. 7, 1958; d. Daniel Lawrence and Catharine Caroline (Weaver) McCue; m. John Edward Haines, May 12, 1979; children: Patricia, Michael, Jeffrey. BA in Romance Lang. magna cum laude, Boston Coll., 1979; postgrad., Babson Coll., 1984, Oxford U., Eng., 1976. Sr. programmer, analyst Prime Computer, Framingham, Mass., 1987—. Author (with Carolyn (McGue) Gordon): children's workbook: ABC Sticker Designs, 1991. Home: 53 James St Bellingham MA 02019 Office: Prime Computer MS 10-80 500 Old Connecticut Path Framingham MA 01701

HAINES, MICHAEL ROBERT, economist, educator; b. Chgo., Nov. 19, 1944; s. James Joshua and Anne Marie (Welch) H.; m. Patricia Caroline Foster, Aug. 19, 1967 (div. Dec. 1986); children: James, Margaret. BA, Amherst Coll., 1967; MA, U. Pa., 1968, PhD, 1971. Asst. prof. econs. Cornell U., Ithaca, N.Y., 1972-79; vis. lectr. econs. U. Pa., Phila., 1979, rsch. assoc. prof. Sch. Pub. and Urban Policy, 1979-80; assoc. prof. econs. Wayne State U., Detroit, 1980-86, prof., 1986-90; Banfi Vintners Disting. prof. econs. Colgate U., Hamilton, N.Y., 1990—; cons. NIH, Bethesda, Md., 1980-84, 90, 91, The World Bank, Washington, 1983; rsch. affiliate Population Studies Ctr. U. Mich., 1990—; rsch. assoc. Nat. Bur. of Econ. Rsch., 1987—. Author: Economic-Demographic Interrels. in Developing Agrl. Regions, 1977, Fertility and Occupation, 1979, Fatal Years, 1991; contbr. articles to profl. jours. NIH grantee, 1974-77, 78-82, 89—. Mem. Internat. Union for Sci. Study Population, Econ. History Assn. (bd. editors 1987-91), Social Sci. History Assn. (bd. dirs. 1983-85, treas. 1985—), Am. Econ. Assn., The Cliometrics Soc. (bd. editor 1988—), Population Assn. Am., Am. Statis. Assn. Episcopalian. Avocations: numismatics, wine, book collecting. Office: Colgate U Dept Econs 13 Oak Dr Hamilton NY 13346-1338

HAINLINE, LOUISE, vision scientist, psychology educator; b. New London, Conn., Apr. 22, 1947; d. Wilmer Roger and Ina Lucien (Kart) H. BA, Brown U., 1969; MA, Harvard U., 1971, PhD, 1973. Asst. prof. psychology Bklyn. Coll., CUNY, 1972-80, assoc. prof., 1981-84, prof., 1985-91, Broeklundian prof. psychology, 1991—; asst. prof. Grad. Ctr., CUNY, 1978-80, assoc. prof., 1981-84, prof., 1985—; dir. Infant Study Ctr., Bklyn. Coll., CUNY, 1972—, dir. early evaluation program, 1986—, dir. Applied Vision Inst., 1991—. Author chpts. in books; contbr. articles to profl. jours. NIH grantee, 1974—, NSF grantee, 1974-75, 90—, March of Dimes grantee, 1979-81, CUNY grantee, 1977—. Mem. AAAS, APA, Assn. for Women in Sci., Am. Psychol. Soc., N.Y. Acad. Scis., Phi Beta Kappa (chpt. pres. 1991—), Sigma Xi. Office: CUNY Bklyn Coll Bedford Ave # 4 Brooklyn NY 11210-1120

HAINLINE, WALLACE F., art director, graphic designer, photographer; b. Paola, Kans., Nov. 25, 1906; s. Wallace M. and Mary Ellen (Powers) H.; children: John M., Ann E., M. Ellen. Student, Art Inst., 1927-28. Designer Carson, Pirie, Scott & Co., Chgo., 1927-29; art dir. Better Homes & Gardens Successful Farming Mag. Meredith Pub. Co., Des Moines, 1930-50, House Beautiful Mag., N.Y.C., 1950-57; owner Corp. Advt. Packaging, Photography, N.Y.C., 1957-89. Mem. Am. Inst. Graphic Arts (bd. dirs.), Art Dirs. Club, N.Y. (bd. dirs.), Art Dirs. Club Chgo., Socl Illustrators, Mt. Kisco Country Club. Office: Wallace F Hainline Assocs 27 North Way Chappaqua NY 10514-2212

HAIPT, MILDRED MARY, education educator; b. Newark, Oct. 15, 1928; d. Carl and Theresa (Messner) H. BS magna cum laude, Fordham U., 1950, MA, 1957; PhD, U. Md., 1972. Cert. social studies tchr. grades 7-12, N.Y., cert. in sch. adminstrn. and supervision, N.Y. Tchr. of homebound Newark (N.J.) Bd. Edn., 1950-51; tchr. social studies Ursuline Acad., Bethesda, Md., 1956-59, Wilmington, Del., 1959-61; asst. prin. The Ursuline Sch., New Rochelle, N.Y., 1962-64; supr. student tchrs. Univ. Md., Baltimore County, 1971-72; prof. edn. Coll. New Rochelle, N.Y., 1961—; chairperson, bd. mem., trustee Acad. Mt. St. Ursula, Bronx, N.Y., 1988—. Recipient Edn. Professions Devel. Act fellow Fed. Govt., 1969-71. Mem. N.Y. Assn. Tchr. Educators (treas. 1986—), Tchr. Inst. Mamaroneck (policy bd. mem. 1983—, higher edn. rep.), Assn. Tchr. Educators Commn. on Edn. Tchr. Educators, World Edn. Fellowship (pres. U.S. sect. 1989—), N.Y. State Tchr. Edn., Cert. and Practices Bd. Democrat. Roman Catholic. Home: 39 Willow Dr New Rochelle NY 10805-2319 Office: Coll of New Rochelle 29 Castle Pl New Rochelle NY 10805-2308

HAIRSTON, ROBERT CONWAY, microbiology educator, clinical microbiologist; b. N.Y.C., Aug. 26, 1951; s. Herman Robert and Dorothea Helen (Eberhart) H. AD, Harrisburg Area Community Coll, Pa., 1971; BS in Biology, Pa. State U., 1973; MS in Biology, Shippensburg U., 1978. Cert. in environ. protection and foodborne disease control Ctr. for Disease Control. Tchr. Carson Long Inst., New Bloomfield, Pa., 1973-77; prof. microbiology Harrisburg Area Community Coll., 1981—; clin. microbiologist Hershey (Pa.) Med. Ctr., 1985—; cons. Pa. Dept. Environ. Protection, Harrisburg, 1984-90. Treas. Pa. Two Yr. Coll. Biologists, Harrisburg, 1987-88; v.p. Cen. Pa. Microbiology Assn., Harrisburg, 1985-86. Mem. East Pa. Am. Soc. Microbiology. Home: 1401 Montfort Dr Harrisburg PA 17110-3016 Office: Harrisburg Area Community Coll 3300 N Cameron Street Rd Harrisburg PA 17110-2999

HAJDINYAK, JOHN STEVEN, financial executive; b. Bethlehem, Pa., Jan. 6, 1953; s. John Joseph and Anna (Haas) H.; m. Karen Ann Bobin, Sept. 18, 1982. BS in Acctg., Lehigh U., Bethlehem, Pa., 1974; MBA in Fin., Fairleigh Dickinson U., 1978. Cost acct. Colgate-Palmolive Co., Jersey City, 1974-76; fin. analyst Warner Lambert Co., Morris Plains, N.J., 1976-78, sr. cost acctg. analyst internat., 1978-80, cost acctg. mgr. internat. div., 1980-85, mgr. internat. pricing, 1985-89, dir. internat. pricing and sourcing, 1989—. Republican. Methodist.

HAJEK, BRADLEY CARR, country club administrator; b. Hagerstown, Md., Sept. 1, 1963; s. Richard Joseph and Glenna Ruth (Smith) H.; m. Angela Marie Plotner, Apr. 2, 1984 (div. Jan. 1988). AA in Mgmt., Hagerstown Jr. Coll., 1983; BS in Hospitality Mgmt., Fla. Internat. U., 1984. Line cook Sheraton Inn, Hagerstown, 1980-83; rest supr. Miami Marriott-Airport, Miami, Fla., 1983-84; asst. mgr. Taco Bell div. Pepsi Co., Greensboro, N.C., 1985, Magic Pan, Bethesda, Md., 1986-87, Chestnut Ridge Country Club,

Lutherville, Md., 1987-88, Suburban Club of Balt., 1989—. Writer, performer (albums) Standing on the Edge, 1989, Higher Ground, 1990, Living in America, 1991. Mem. Club Mgrs. Assn. Am. Home: 101 Fitz Ct Unit 202 Reisterstown MD 21136 Office: Suburban Club Balt County 7600 Park Heights Ave Baltimore MD 21208-4399

HAJJAR, JEAN-JACQUES JOSEPH, engineer; b. Beirut, Lebanon, Sept. 27, 1961; came to U.S., 1979; s. Joseph Yacoub and Nora Joseph (Haladjian) H. BS, MIT, 1983, MS, 1985, PhD, 1989. Sr. devel. engr. Analog Devices, Wilmington, Mass., 1989–; cons. Polaroid Corp., Waltham, Mass., 1985-87; instr. MIT, Cambridge, 1983-88. Contbr. articles to profl. jours. Recipient Guillemin Prize MIT, Cambridge, 1983; Grass Instrument fellow, Quincy, Mass., 1985, MIT Dept. of EE fellow, 1985. Mem. IEEE, The Electrochemical Soc., Eta Kappa Nu, Tau Beta Pi, Sigma Xi. Home: 4 Canal Park Apt 802 Cambridge MA 02141-2208 Office: Analog Devices 804 Woburn St Wilmington MA 01887-3462

HAKALA, THOMAS JOHN, financial planner, accountant; b. Bayonne, N.J., July 6, 1948; s. John R. and Anna J. (Vida) H.; m. Marilynn Freund, Aug. 15, 1976; children: Lauren V., John C. AB in History, Georgetown U., 1970; JD, St. John's U., 1975; postgrad., NYU, 1975-80. Bar: N.J. 1975, N.Y. 1976. Supr. Weeden & Co., N.Y.C., 1970-73; mgr. Coopers & Lybrand, N.Y.C., 1975-87; sr. mgr. KPMG Peat Marwick, N.Y.C., 1987-89, ptnr., 1989—; bd. advisers Jour. Taxation of Estates and Trusts, N.Y.C., 1990—. Contbr. articles to profl. jours. Mem. Edison (N.J.) Republican Club, 1991—. Mem. AICPA, Ocean Beach and Yacht Club, Phi Delta Phi. Republican. Roman Catholic. Home: 8 Whitewood Rd Edison NJ 08820-3202 Office: KPMG Peat Marwick 599 Lexington Ave New York NY 10022-6030

HAKIM-ELAHI, ENAYAT, obstetrician, gynecologist; b. Teheran, Iran, Nov. 23, 1934; came to U.S., 1959, naturalized, 1973; s. Mohamed-Ali and Masoomeh Rahimi; M.D., Med. Sch., Teheran, 1959; lic. physician, Maine, Conn., Vt., N.Y., N.H., Calif.; diplomate Am. Bd. Ob-Gyn. m. Renate Emsters, Nov. 15, 1967; 1 child, Cristina. Intern, Queens Hosp. Ctr., N.Y.C., 1960, resident in internal medicine, 1961, resident in ob-gyn, 1961-64, resident in radiotherapy of gynecologic cancer, Am. Cancer Soc. fellow Queens div., 1965; resident in gynecology Cancer Rsch. Inst., Columbia-Presbyn. Med. Ctr., N.Y.C., 1964-65; practice medicine specializing in ob-gyn, N.Y.C., 1968—; mem. staff Booth Meml. Med. Ctr., Flushing, N.Y., N.Y. Hosp., N.Y.C., Jamaica (N.Y.) Hosp., Univ. Hosp., Stonybrook ; med. dir. Margaret Sanger Ctr., N.Y.C., 1973—, Planned Parenthood of N.Y.C., 1977—; asst. prof. ob-gyn Cornell U. Med. Coll., N.Y.C., 1973—; dir. Dept. of Ob-Gyn LaGuardia Hosp., 1990—. Served with U.S. Army, 1965-67. Fellow ACS, Am. Coll. Obstetricians and Gynecologists, Internat. Coll. Surgeons, Am. Fertility Soc.; mem. Am. Soc. Gynecol. Laparoscopists, Am. Soc. Colposcopy and Cervical Neoplasia, Am. Pub. Health Assn., Am. Coll. Physician Execs., Assn. of Reproductive Health Profls., Royal Soc. Medicine (London), World Med. Assn., N.Y. State Med. Soc., Queens Gynecol. Soc. Contbr. articles to profl. jours.

HALBERSTADT, ROBERT BILHEIMER, optometrist; b. Stockertown, Pa., Feb. 11, 1918; s. Joseph Victor and Lillian (Bilheimer) H.; O.D., No. Ill. Coll. Optometry, 1939; m. Mary Margaret Gassner, Nov. 9, 1940; children: Mary Diane Seip, Victoria Milou Mackenzie. Optometrist, Nazareth, Pa., 1940—; cons. Optometry Whitehall-Coplay Sch. Dist., 1966-78, Pathway Sch., Norristown, Pa. 1966-67, Miller Clinic, Stroudsburg, Pa., 1971-74, Learning Center, Scranton (Pa.) Pub. Schs., 1971-72; staff optometrist, cons. Allentown State Hosp., 1967-68; extern Gesell Inst., New Haven, 1967-68. Active Lehigh Valley Assn. for Brain Damaged Child, 1965-68; 2d Assn. for Brain Damaged Children, 1966-68; program chmn. Lehigh Valley Assn. for Children with Learning Disabilities, 1969-74, bd. dirs., 1971-74, 1st v.p., 1973-74; mem. Council Exceptional Children; with Friendship House, Scranton, 1973-75; mem. pres.'s club Ill. Coll. Optometry, 1973—, Century Club, 1976—; mem. nat. pilot project team on formation fo spl. edn. model Intermediate Sch. Unit 20 of Pa., 1980-81; mem. Nazareth Area Residents for Clean Air, 1991. With USNR, 1944-46. Mem. Optometric Extension Program (state dir. 1950-58, regional dir. 1958-84, life mem. Pioneer Fund 1987—), Pa. Optometric Assn. (treas. 1948-57). Address: 116 S Broad St Nazareth PA 18064

HALBRECHT, KENNETH ASHLEY, marketing professional; b. Teaneck, N.J., Oct. 19, 1960; s. Irving Daniel and Dorothy Anne (Welter) H. BS in Econs., U. Pa., 1983; MBA, Fordham U., 1988. Programmer IBM, White Plains, N.Y., 1983-85, project mgr., 1985, fin. analyst, 1985-87; mktg. rep. IBM, N.Y.C., 1987—, mgr. internat. opportunities, 1989-92; pres., treas. 210 E. 21st St. tenant's corp. coop., N.Y.C., 1987—. Capt. Sigma Chi Derby Days, Ronald McDonald House, Phila., 1982; coord. Network for Humanities, N.Y., N.J., 1987-89; mentor N.Y. Partnership, N.Y.C., 1991-92. Grantee IBM, 1985-88. Mem. Beta Gamma Sigma, Sigma Chi (exec. com. 1981-83). Republican. Episcopalian. Office: IBM 33 Maiden Ln New York NY 10038

HALDAR, DIPAK, biochemist, cell biologist; b. Bankura, India, Dec. 8, 1937; came to U.S., 1969; s. Bhola Nath and Renuka (Mitra) H.; m. Jaya Sarkar, July 3, 1963; children: Joydeep, Deeya. PhD, U.Calcutta, 1963, U. London, 1966. Postdoctoral fellow McMaster U., Hamilton, Ont., Can., 1966-69; vis. scientist McMaster U., Hamilton, Ont., 1973-74; asst. mem. St. Jude Children's Rsch. Hosp., Memphis, 1969-71; lectr. biochemistry Calcutta (India) U., 1971-73; vis. investigator Pub. Health Rsch. Inst. City of N.Y., 1974-75; asst. prof. biol. sci. St. John's U., Jamaica, N.Y., 1975-79, assoc. prof., 1979-83, prof., 1983—. Contbr. articles to sci. jours. Grantee NSF, 1982, 84, 88-92, NIH, 1986-88. Mem. AAAS, Am. Soc. Cell Biology, Am. Soc. Biochemistry and Molecular Biology. Office: St Johns U Jamaica NY 11439

HALDEMAN, CHARLES WALDO, III, senior staff engineer; b. Phila., June 9, 1936; s. Charles Waldo Jr. and Anna Freemont (Douglass) H.; m. Louise Stephenson, June 27, 1959; children: Charles Waldo, George Stephenson. BS, MIT, 1959, MS, 1959, ScD, 1964. Rsch. asst. MIT Naval Supersonic Lab., Cambridge, Mass., 1959-64; staff engr. MIT Aerophysics Lab., Cambridge, Mass., 1964-79, assoc. dir., 1979-82; staff engr. MIT Lincoln Lab., Lexington, Mass., 1982-87, sr. staff engr., 1987—; v.p. engring., cons. Megatech Corp., Billerica, Mass., 1971-82. Contbr. numerous articles and rsch. papers to scientific jours.; patentee in field including Wavy Tube Heat Pumping, Vacuum Cleaning. Mem. Am. Inst. Aero. and Astronautics. Office: MIT Lincoln Lab 244 Wood St Lexington MA 02173

HALE, JUDSON DRAKE, SR., editor; b. Boston, Mar. 16, 1933; s. Roger Drake and Marian (Sagendorph) H.; m. Sara Huberlie, Sept. 6, 1958; children: Judson Drake, Daniel, Christopher. B.A., Dartmouth Coll., 1958; D Journalism (hon.), New Eng. Coll., 1984; LittD (hon.), Franklin Pierce Coll., 1987; LHD (hon.), Keene State Coll., 1989. Asst. editor Yankee, Inc., Dublin, N.H., 1958-61; asst. editor Yankee, Inc., 1961-63, mng. editor, 1963-69, mng. editor, v.p., 1970—, also dir.; editor-in-chief, 1970—; editor, v.p. Old Farmers Almanac; dir. Solar Environ. Scis., Inc. Author: Inside New England, 1982, The Education of a Yankee, 1987; editor: That New England, 1968; editor The Best of Yankee mag., 1985, The Best of The Old Farmer's Almanac, 1991; mem. editorial bd. Dartmouth Alumni Mag. Trustee MacDowell Colony; bd. dirs. Task Force for Hist. Preservation in N.H. Served with AUS, 1955-57. Mem. Cheshire County Dartmouth Alumni Club, Dublin Lake Club, Phi Kappa Psi. Republican. Episcopalian. Home: Valley Rd Dublin NH 03444 Office: Yankee Pub Inc Main St Dublin NH 03444-9999

HALE, RICHARD THOMAS, JR., investment banking company executive; b. Abington, Pa., July 17, 1945; s. Richard Thomas Sr. and Elizabeth (Parrish) H.; m. Eleanor Armsted Gibson, July 27, 1969; children: Delia, Thomas, Gibson. BA, Yale U., 1968; MBA, U. Pa., 1972. Securities analyst Girard Bank, Phila., 1972-74, Robert Garrett & Sons, Balt., 1974, Alex Brown & Sons, Balt., 1974—; v.p. Alex Brown & Sons, 1980-82, prin., 1983-85, mng. dir., 1986—, asset mgmt. div. head, 1988—; pres. Guilford Assn., Balt., 1986-89. Trustee Burn Mawr Sch., 1983—, v.p., 1990—. Lt. USN, 1968-70. Mem. Balt. Security Analysts. Soc. (pres. 1982-83), Maryland Club, Elkridge Club, Brook Club (N.Y.C.), Casino Club (Nantucket). Democrat. Episcopalian. Home: 224 Northway Baltimore MD 21218-1140 Office: Alex Brown & Sons Inc 135 E Baltimore St Baltimore MD 21202-1646

HALE, ROBERT GRAHAM, consulting company executive; b. Waterbury, Conn., Apr. 20, 1934; s. Randal Lewis and Doris Vivian (Dimock) H.; m. Pauline Marie Schweizer, June 12, 1954; children: Robert G. Jr., Kathleen Marie, David Stephen. BS, Tchrs. Coll., New Britain, Conn., 1956; MS, Cen. Conn. State U., 1964; cert. advanced studies, Syracuse U., 1967. Tchr. Manchester (Conn.) Pub. Schs., 1956-58; tchr. Branford (Conn.) Pub. Schs., 1958-67, dir. instrnl. svcs., 1967-80; edn. cons. Conn. Dept. Edn., Hartford, 1980-90, asst. div. dir., 1990-92; pres. R.G. Hale Cons., Madison, Conn., 1992—; chmn. bd. dirs. So. Ednl. Communications Assn. Ctr. for Instrnl. Tech., Columbia, S.C., 1988-89. Editor: Educational Media and Special, 1979. Mem. Madison (Conn.) Bd. Edn., 1988. Recipient pub. svc. award Madison Jaycees, 1983, award Conn. Ednl. Media Assn., 1985. Mem. ALA, Assn. for Ednl. Communications and Tech. (pres. 1978-80), Lions. Home and Office: R G Hale Consulting 76 Fairview Dr Madison CT 06443-2347

HALEGUA, ALFREDO, sculptor; b. Montevideo, Uruguay, May 4, 1930; arrived in U.S., 1959; s. Jaime and Raquel (Albagli) H.; m. Raquel Serebrier, Sept. 8, 1957. BFA in Painting, Sculpture, Prints, Sch. Plastic Arts, Montevideo, 1950, MFA with honors, 1952. Art critic Semanario Arts Newspaper, Montevideo, 1956-58; art critic weekly arts supplement El Bien Publico, Montevideo, 1958-59; traveling fellow Nat. Commn. Fine Arts, Montevideo, 1959-60; prof. sculpture Am. U., Washington, 1964-65; Mem. adv. panel Md. Arts Coun., 1971-72. 16 major one-man shows in U.S. and fgn. countries including Balt. Mus. Art, 1962-63, 68; exhibited in over 150 group shows including Corcoran Gallery Art, Washington, 1965, Mus. Contemporary Art, 1981; prin. works include 5 sculpture fountains, City of Charlotte, N.C., 1987; represented in permanent collections 22 major mus. and pub. places, including Nat. Gallery Art, Washington, Kennedy Ctr., Washington; author: The Magic Line, 1988. Recipient 16 awards and honors, including first prizes and gold medal. Mem. Internat. Sculpture Soc. Home and Studio: 2601 30th St NW Washington DC 20008

HALES, CHARLES ALBERT, physician; b. Greeley, Colo., Apr. 27, 1941; s. Charles A. and Dorothy G. (Henkle) H.; m. Mary Ann Little, June 12, 1965; children: Samuel, Christopher, John. BA, Emory U., 1962, MD, 1966. Diplomate Am. Bd. Internal Medicine, Am. Bd. Pulmonary Disease. Intern Boston City Hosp., resident I; resident II U. Calif., San Francisco; Harvard pulmonary fellow Mass. Gen. Hosp., Boston; assoc. prof. medicine Harvard Med. Sch., Boston, 1979—; physician Mass. Gen. Hosp., 1990—. Lt. comdr. USNR, 1968-70. Mem. Am. Thoracic Soc., Am. Physiology Soc., Am. Soc. Clin. Investigation, Am. Heart Assn. (chmn. cardiopulmonary coun. 1991—).

HALEY, MICHAEL JOHN, training company executive; b. Detroit, Apr. 12, 1948; s. Edgar John and Acelia Olive (Young) H.; m. Terry Ann Morley, Feb. 20, 1970 (div. 1985); children: Patrick, Shannon. Student, Lawrence Inst. Tech., Southfield, Mich., 1970-71, U. Wis., 1987. Journeyman lineman Am. Line Bldrs. App. Tng., Detroit, 1966-70; line design technician Henkels & McCoy Elec. Contrs., Ortonville, Mich., 1971-72; gen. foreman Harlan Elec. Co., Southfield, Mich., 1972-74, 79-80; tng. crew foreman L.A. Dept. Water/Power, 192-83; project mgr. NUS Tng. Corp., Gaithersburg, Md., 1983-88, tng. and devel. mktg. mgr., 1988-89; tech. tng. cons. TRA-Tech Cons. Svc., Frederick, Md., 1989-90, pres., 1990—; cons. in tng. City of Burbank, Calif., 1986-88, N.Y. State. Elec. & Gas, 1988-90; tech. tng. specialist N.Y. Power Authority, White Plains, N.Y., 1990-91. Author: (video/text) Safety in Overhead Lines, 1984, Overhead Line Maintenance, 1985, High Voltage Maintenance/Safety, 1988. CPR instr. ARC, Detroit, 1979. Mem. Internat. Brotherhood of Elec. Workers, Am. Soc. Safety Engrs., Inter-Utility Tng. Assn. Democrat. Roman Catholic. Home: 7083 Jasper Dr # C Middletown MD 21769-7540 Office: Tra-Tech Cons Svcs Inc 5300 Westview Dr Ste 305 Frederick MD 21701-8374

HALFEN, ABRAHAM, physician, obstetrician/gynecologist; b. Caracas, Venezuela, June 18, 1947; came to U.S., 1981; s. Jacob and Sarah (Hoires) H.; m. Josie Roque, Aug. 12, 1985; children: Audrey, David. BS, Herzl-Bialik, Caracas, 1964; MD, Cen. U. Venezuela, Caracas, 1971. Resident in ob-gyn. Concepcion Palacios Maternity Hosp., Caracas, 1971-75; fellow in reproductive endocrinology and infertility Columbia U. Coll. Physicians and Surgeons, N.Y.C., 1981-83; attending obstetrician/gynecologist SUNY, Stony Brook, 1983-85, asst. attending, 1985—; pvt. practice ob-gyn, infertility reproductive endocrinology East Setauket, N.Y., 1985—. Mem. Am. Fertility Soc., Pacific Coast Fertility Soc., Suffolk Acad. Medicine, Am. Coll. Internat. Physicians, Internat. Am. Coll. Physicians and Surgeons, N.Y. Acad. Scis.

HALL, ALDEN BARKER, retired surgeon; b. Burlington, Vt., July 2, 1927; s. Charles Erwin and Adeline Lane (Tower) H.; m. Audrey Helen Schramm, June 14, 1955; children: Alden, Benjamin, A. Jean. BA, Princeton U., 1949; MA, Amherst (N.Y.) Coll., 1951; MD, U. Rochester, 1955. Diplomate Am. Bd. Surgery. Intern and resident surgeon Bellevue Hosp., N.Y.C., 1955-61; attending surgeon Newton (N.J.) Meml. Hosp., 1961—, chief dept. surgery, 1970-72, chief staff, 1972-74, med. dir., 1986—; vice chmn. Atlantic Health Systems, Chatham, N.J., 1992—; bd. dirs. North Jersey Physicians Rev., Parsippany; v.p. med. affairs Newton Meml. Hosp., 1985—. With U.S. Army, 1945-47. Fellow ACS; mem. Am. Coll. Physician Execs., Rotary (bd. dirs. 1983-89), Soc. Surgeons of N.J. Republican. Home: 498 Ridge Rd Newton NJ 07860-9651 Office: Schmidt-Fletcher Med 175 High St Newton NJ 07860

HALL, CHRISTOPHER GEORGE LONGDEN, marketing executive; b. Coventry, Eng., June 7, 1956; came to U.S., 1980; s. Alfred Frederick and Margaret Anne (Robinson) H.; m. Avril Jacqueline Wardell, July 3l, 1982. MA, Oxford U., 1977, DPhil, 1980; MS in Bus., Columbia U., 1983. Asst. to chmn. Gold Fields Am. Corp., N.Y.C., 1980-83; pres. Hall Mgmt. Assocs., San Francisco, 1983-87, Congden and Carpenter Co., Seekonk, Mass., 1987-88; mng. dir. Petralex Stainless Ltd., Malvern, Pa., 1985-86; v.p. planning Levinson Steel Co., Pitts., 1988-89; v.p. mktg. Thypin Steel Co., N.Y.C., 1989—; internat. commercial arbitrator Am. Arbitration Assn., 1991—. Author: Britain, America and Arms Control, 192l-1937, 1987. Councilman City of Oxford (Eng.), 1979-8l. Mem. United Oxford and Cambridge Univs. Club (London). Episcopalian. Office: Thypin Steel Co 49-49 30th St Long Island City NY 11101

HALL, DAVID, newspaper editor; b. Lebanon, Tenn., Mar. 7, 1943; s. Hal Turner Hall and Mildred (Durham) Hall Carson; m. Suzanne Lovell, Sept. 5, 1964; children: Carson, Matthew, Amanda. BJ, U. Tenn., 1965, MA in Econs., 1966. Fin. news reporter, asst. fin. editor, Middle East corr., editorial writer, asst. mng. editor Chgo. Daily News, 1966-78; asst. mng. editor Chgo. Sun-Times, 1978; mng. editor St. Paul Pioneer Press, 1978-82; exec. editor St. Paul Pioneer and Dispatch, 1982-84; editor, v.p. The Denver Post, 1984-86, editor, sr. v.p., 1986-88; editor, v.p. The Record, Hackensack, N.J., 1988-92; editor The Plain Dealer, Cleve., 1992—. With U.S. Army, 1967-69, Vietnam. Recipient Disting. Alumni award Castle Heights Mil. Acad., Lebanon, 1984. Mem. Am. Soc. Newspaper Editors, Soc. Profl. Journalists. Presbyterian. Office: 145 Senlac Hills Dr Chagrin Falls OH 44022-3254

HALL, DAVID BENJAMIN, statistician; b. Ithaca, N.Y., Jan. 17, 1951; s. Charles Edwin and Shirley Elizabeth (Auringer) H.; m. Barbara Jean Protts, June 22, 1985; children: Brittany, Daniel, Matthew. AB, Colgate U., 1973; MS, Cornell U., 1976, PhD, 1983. Math. statistician FDA, Rockville, Md., 1978-81; chief biostatistics arctic investigations lab. Ctrs. for Disease Control, Anchorage, 1981-87; chief biometrics div. viral diseases Ctrs. for Disease Control, Atlanta, 1987-91; sr. statistician Boehringer Ingelheim Pharms., Ridgefield, Conn., 1991—; adj. asst. clin. prof. U. Hawaii Sch. Pub. Health, Manos, 1985-87; alternate mem. Ctrs. for Disease Control Institutional Rev. Bd., Atlanta, 1988-91; adv. com. anti-inflammatory drugs, FDA, Rockville, 1989-91. Author: (with others) Statistics, 1991; contbr. articles to profl. jours. Mem. Am. Statis. Assn. (pres. Alaska chpt. 1985-86, Outstanding mem. 1989), Biometrics Soc. Home: 10 Farview Rd Brookfield CT 06804

HALL, DEBORAH JANE, investment executive; b. New Haven, Conn., Apr. 24, 1952; d. Almon Blakeslee and Harriet Ellis (Penniman) H.; m. James Cameron Woods, Jan. 20, 1990. AB cum laude, Mount Holyoke Coll., 1974; MBA, U. Va., 1976. 2d v.p. Chase Manhattan Bank, N.Y.C., 1976-82; mng. dir. Prudential Investment Corp., Newark, N.J., 1982—. Office: Prudential Investment Corp 100 Mulberry St Newark NJ 07102-4004

HALL, DENNIS GENE, optics educator; b. Belleville, Ill., Mar. 7, 1948; s. Eugene and Mildred (Klein) H.; m. Rita Mae Winkelmann, June 12, 1970; children: Katherine, Christine, Gregory. BS in Physics, U. Ill., 1970; MS in Physics, So. Ill. U., 1972; PhD in Physics, U. Tenn., 1976. Asst. prof. physics So. Ill. U., Edwardsville, 1976-78; sr. engr. McDonnell Douglas Corp., St. Louis, 1978-80; asst. prof. Inst. Optics U. Rochester, N.Y., 1980-82, assoc. prof., 1982-87, prof., 1987—; grad. fellow Oak Ridge (Tenn.) Associated Univs., 1975. Contbr. articles to profl. publs., chpts. to books; patentee in field. Capt. USAFR, 1973-89. Fellow Internat. Soc. Optical Engring., Optical Soc. Am. (bd. dirs. 1991—); mem. Am. Phys. Soc., Materials Rsch. Soc. Office: U Rochester Inst Optics Rochester NY 14627

HALL, FREDERICK KEITH, chemist; b. Leeds, Eng., Jan. 3, 1930; naturalized, 1976; s. Frederick Stanley and Mary Elizabeth (Stocks) H.; m. Patricia Ellison, Aug. 25, 1956; children: Simon Keith, Stephanie Jane, Andrew Nicholas. B.S. with 1st class honors, U. Manchester, 1951; Ph.D., U. Leeds, 1954; grad., Advanced Mgmt. Program, Harvard U., 1979. Research chemist Courtaulds (Can.) Ltd., 1956-58, asst. tech. mgr., 1958-60, tech. mgr., 1960-63, plant mgr., 1963-66; dir. tech. service Internat. Paper Co., 1966-70, asst. dir. research center, 1970-72, dir. primary process, 1972-75, corp. dir. research, 1975-77; dir. S & T labs., 1977-79, chief scientist, 1979—. Served with Brit. Army, 1953-55. Fellow TAPPI (pres. 1991—), Royal Soc. Chemistry, Textile Inst., Am. Inst. Chemists; mem. Chem. Inst. Can., Can. Pulp and Paper Assn., Tuxedo Club. Office: Internat Paper Co Corp Research Ctr Longmeadow Rd Tuxedo Park NY 10987

HALL, GRACE ROSALIE, physicist, educator, literary scholar; b. Meriden, Conn., July 15, 1921; d. George John and Grace Cleora (Gleason) White; m. Eldon Conrad Hall, July 2, 1948; children: Brent Channing, Pamela Rosalie, Craig Gleason, Gordon Timothy. BS in Chemistry, Eastern Nazarene Coll., 1946; MA in Physics, Boston U., 1946, doctoral studies in physics, 1946-53; MA in English, Simmons Coll., 1975. Bookkeeper Cherry & Webb Co., Providence, 1939-42; sec. to registrar Eastern Nazarene Coll., Quincy, Mass., 1942-44, instr. physics, chemistry, 1945-46; teaching fellow physics Boston U., 1946-49; instr. physics lab. Northeastern U., Boston, 1956-57; asst. prof. physics Eastern Nazarene Coll., Quincy, 1957-61, asst. prof. chemistry, 1969, asst. prof. phys. sci., 1974; instr. Shakespeare Barrington (R.I.) Coll., 1984; tchr. Westwood (Mass.) Seminar, 1975; ch. sch. dir. First Parish, Westwood, 1977-81; chair seminar U. Louisville, 1988. Author: (chpt. in book) Webs & Wardrobes, 1987; contbr. articles to profl. jours. Dir. Norfolk Assn. for Retarded Citizens, 1978-79; judge High Sch. Sci. Fairs, North Quincy, Mass., 1960-64, 69-76, REgional Sci. Fairs, Bridgewater, mass., 1960-62. Recipient Faculty scholarship Eastern Nazarene Coll., 1943-45, Libr. Family of Yr. award City of Quincy, 1960. Mem. MLA (session participant 1978, 84), Shakespeare Assn. of Am. (seminar participant 1988-92), Christianity and Lit. Assn., Children's Lit. Assn. (scholarly rsch. and writing 1978—), MIT Women's League (editor activities guide and newsletter, 1989-92), New Eng. Hist. Geneal. Soc., Mus. Fine Arts.

HALL, HOWARD KINGSLEY, sport psychology educator, researcher; b. Middlesbrough, Yorkshire, Eng., Apr. 5, 1967; came to U.S., 1981; s. Joe and Mabel (Ball) H. BA with honors, North Staffordshire Polytech., Stafford, Eng., 1979; postgrad., Leeds (Eng.) Carnegie, 1981; MS in Phys. Edn., North Tex. State U., 1984; PhD in Kinesiology, U. Ill., 1990. Asst. prof. U. Colo., Boulder, 1988-89, Syracuse (N.Y.) U., 1989—. Contbr. articles to profl. jours. Mem. AAHPERD, Assn. for Advancement of Applied Sport Psychology, N.Am. Soc. for Psychology of Sport and Phys. Activities. Home: 24A Ball Rd Syracuse NY 13215-1602 Office: Syracuse U Dept Health Phys Edn 840 Comstock Ave Syracuse NY 13210-2810

HALL, JANE ANNA, writer, model; b. New London, Conn., Apr. 4, 1959; d. John Leslie Jr. and Jane Dezzie (Green) H. Grad. model, Barbizon Sch., 1976. Model Barbizon Agy., New Haven, 1977; employed by dir. of career planning Wesleyan U., Middletown, Conn., 1985-86; free lance writer, poet, 1986—; poetry contest judge Saybrook 25th Anniversary Celebration, Acton Pub. Libr., 1992. Author: Cedar and Lace, 1986, Satin and Pinstripe, 1987, Fireworks and Diamonds, 1988, Stars and Daffodils, 1989, Sunrises and Stone Walls, 1990, Mountains and Meadows, 1991; founder, editor: Poetry in Your Mailbox newsletter, 1989—; one-woman shows include Westbrook (Conn.) Pub. Libr., 1989, 90, 91. Sunday sch. tchr. 1st Congl. Ch., Westbrook, 1977-90, asst. supt., dir. Christian edn., 1979-84; poetry reader Congl. Ch., Broad Brook, Conn., 1988; group poetry reader and displayer Westbrook Pub. Libr., 1989, 91, reader Night of Thousand Stars readathon, 1990; group poetry displayer Acton Pub. Libr., Old Saybrook, Conn.,1990, judge poetry contest 25th anniversary celebration, 1992. Recipient 2d prize Conn. Poetry Soc., 1983, Cert. Merit for Disting. Svc. to the Community, 1989, Cert. World Leadership, 1989. Mem. Internat. Platform Assn., Romance Writers Am. (Conn. chpt.), Conn. Poetry Soc. (pres. Old Saybrook chpt. 1989-91, world poetry chmn. 1989). Home and Office: PO Box 629 Westbrook CT 06498

HALL, JOSEPH LINDLEY, electrical engineer; b. Boston, Jan. 22, 1936; s. William Mott and Sarah (Redfern) H.; m. Nancy C. King, June 18, 1961; children: David M., Michael K., William L., Thomas S. BA in Physics, Williams Coll., 1959; SB, SM in Elec. Engring, MIT, 1959, PhD in Elec. Engring., 1963. Asst. prof. MIT, Cambridge, 1963-64, Johns Hopkins U., Balt., 1964-66; mem. tech. staff AT&T Bell Labs., Murray Hill, N.J., 1966—. Assoc. editor Jour. Acoustical Soc. Am., 1981-83; editor: Peripheral Auditory Mechanisms; contbg. author: Hearing Research and Theory, 1981. Bd. dirs. Summit (N.J.) Speech Sch., 1976-81. Fellow Acoustical Soc. Am. Office: AT&T Bell Labs Rm 2D 546 600 Mountain Ave New Providence NJ 07974-0636

HALL, KENNETH OCTAVIUS, university official and dean, educator; b. Jamaica, W.I., Apr. 24, 1941. BA in History with honors, U. W.I., Kingston, 1966; postgrad. dipl. in internat. rels., U. W.I., Trinidad, 1967; MA in History, Queen's U., Kingston, Ont., 1969, PhD in History, 1971. Tchr. Rusea High Sch., Lucea, Jamaica, W.I., 1961-63; teaching asst. div. social sci. U. W.I., Trinidad, 1966-67; instr history Queen's U., Kingston, Ont., 1969-71; asst. prof. history SUNY, Oswego, 1971-73, assoc. prof. history, 1973-84, prof. history, 1984-86, asst. provost, 1982-84; from asst. provost to asst. provost for acad. programs SUNY Cen. Adminstrn., 1982-90; v.p. acad. affairs (acting) SUNY, Old Westbury, 1989-90, v.p. acad. affairs, dean faculty and prof. Am. studies, 1990—; adminstrv. officer Ministry of Agr., Jamaica, 1966; chief rsch. and conf. sect. Caribbean Community Secretariat, Georgetown, Guyana, 1975-76, dir. adminstrn. and gen. svcs. div., 1976-77; vis. prof. U. W.I., Mona, 1972-73; adj. prof. history Hobart & William Smith Colls., Geneva, N.Y., 1974; prof. Caribbean studies SUNY-Albany, 1986-89; advisor to vice chancellor U. W.I., 1986—; advisor Office Internat. Programs SUNY-Albany, 1984—; cons. ALCAN, Jamaica Ltd., 1988—; cons. in field. Author: Imperial Proconsul: Sir Hercules Robinson and South Africa, 1881 to 1889, 1980, The Group of 77: Strengthening Its Negotiating Capacity, 1979; editor: Makers of the Twentieth Century, 1982; contbr. articles to profl. jours., chpts. to books. Jamaican Tchrs. scholar; Can. Internat. Devel. Agy. grad. fellow; Rsch. Found. of SUNY summer fellows; IFDA rsch. fellow. Mem. African Studies Assn., Am. Hist. Assn., Caribbean Historians Assn., Royal African Soc., N.Y. African Studies Assn., N.Y. Latin Am. Studies Assn., African Studies Assn. of W.I., African Heritage Assn. Office: SUNY Coll at Old Westbury 223 Store Hill Rd Old Westbury NY 11568-1706

HALL, MARCIA JOY, non-profit organization administrator; b. Long Beach, Calif., June 24, 1947; d. Royal Waltz and Norine (Parker) Stanton; m. Stephen Christopher Hall, March 29, 1969; children: Geoffrey Michael, Christopher Stanton. AA, Foothill Coll., 1967; student, U. Oreg., 1967-68; BA, U. Washington, Seattle, 1969. Instr. aide Glen Yermo Sch., Mission Viejo, Calif., 1979-80; market rsch. interviewer Rsch. Data, Framingham, Mass., 1982-83; adult edn. instr. Community Sch. Use Program, Milford, Mass., 1982-83; career info. ctr. coord. Milford High Sch., 1983-86; corp.

rels. dir. Sch. Vols. for Milford, Inc., 1985-86; NE area coord. YWCA of Annapolis and Anne Arundel County, Severna Park, Md, 1987-89; exec. dir. West Anne Arundel County C. of C., Odenton, Md., 1989—. Pres. PTO, Mission Viejo, 1979-80, Milford, 1981-84; consumer assistance vol., Calif. Pub. Interest Rsch. Group, 1977-78. Mem. NAFE, Internat. Platform Assn., Toastmasters (treas. 1988—, pres. 1989—). Home: 507 Devonshire Ln Severna Park MD 21146-1017

HALL, MICHAEL LEE, federal government agency grants administrator; b. San Antonio, Jan. 2, 1946; s. John Edward and Lorraine Louise (Horn) Hall; m. Joy Lynn Schmidt, Aug. 28, 1966. BA, U. Tex., 1968, MA, 1972; MA, Johns Hopkins U., 1974, PhD, 1977. Asst. prof. Centenary Coll. La., Shreveport, 1976-80; assoc. prof. Centenary Coll. La., 1980-87, chmn. dept. English, 1980-83; program officer Nat. Endowment for the Humanities, Washington, 1987-88; asst. dir. for seminars div. fellowships and seminars Nat. Endowment for the Humanities, 1988—; humanities adminstr. Nat. Endowment for the Humanities, Washington, 1985-87; instr. (part-time) Georgetown U., Washington, 1989; dir. summer seminar for secondary sch. tchrs. Nat. Endowment for the Humanities, Centenary Coll. La., Shreveport, 1984. Co-editor: LIT: Literature and Interpretive Techniques, 1986; poetry editor Poet Lit. Mag., Oklahoma City, 1985—; contbr. articles and revs. on Brit. lit. to profl. jours. Nat. Endowment for the Humanities fellow in residence U. Chgo, 1978-79. Mem. MLA, Nat. Coun. Tchrs. English, John Donne Soc. Democrat. Presbyterian. Office: Nat Endowment for the Humanities 1100 Pennsylvania Ave NW Washington DC 20506-0005

HALL, N. JOHN, English educator; b. Orange, N.J., Jan. 1, 1933; s. Norman C. and Lucille (Hertlein) H.; m. Marianne Gsell Hall, Oct. 13, 1968; 1 child, Jonathan G. AB, Seton Hall U., 1955; PhD, NYU, 1970. Prof. English Bronx Community Coll. and Grad. Sch., CUNY, N.Y.C., 1970—, disting. prof., 1983—. Author: Salamundi: Byron, Allegra, and the Trollope Family, 1975, Trollope and His Illustrators, 1980; editor: Rossetti and His Circle, 1987, Zuleika Dodbsok 1985, The Letters of Anthony Trollope (2 vols.), 1983, Trollope: A Biography, 1991, others. NEH fellow, 1974, Guggenheim Found. fellow, 1977, 84, Am. Coun. Learned Soc. fellow, 1982. Mem. Modern Lang. Assn. Home: 44 W 10th St New York NY 10011-8762

HALL, PAMELA ELIZABETH, psychologist; b. Jacksonville, Fla., Sept. 10, 1957; d. Gary Curtiss and Ollie (Banko) H. BA, Rutgers U., 1979; MS in Edn., Pace U., 1981, PhD in Psychology, 1984. Lic. psychologist, N.Y., N.J., Calif. Profl. asst. Dr. Donald Wiedis, N.Y.C., 1980-81; psychology extern St. Vincent's Med. Ctr., N.Y.C., 1981-82; intern in clin. psychology Elizabeth (N.J.) Gen. Med. Ctr., 1982-83, staff psychologist, 1983-85; staff psychologist J.F.K. Med. Ctr., Edison, N.J., 1985-87; pvt. practice Summit and Perth Amboy, N.J., 1985—; sr. supervising psychologist Muhlenberg Med. Ctr., Summit, N.J., 1987-90; founder, pres. N.J. Chpt. for Study of Multiple Personality & Dissociation, Perth Amboy, 1988—. Mem. Mayor's Com. on Substance Abuse, Perth Amboy, 1987. Named Henry Rutgers scholar, 1979. Mem. APA, Am. Soc. Clin. Hypnosis, Internat. Soc. for Study of Multiple Personality Dissociation (pres. N.J. chpt. 1988—), Pace U. Alumni Assn., Rutgers U. Alumni Assn., Psi Chi. Home: 192 State St PO Box 1820 Perth Amboy NJ 08862-1820

HALL, PETER ANDREW, university educator, writer; b. Montreal, Quebec, Can., Aug. 11, 1950; came to U.S., 1975; s. Paul Frank Thomas and Cosette (Henderson) H. BA, U. Toronto, 1972; MPhil, Balliol Coll. Oxford, Eng., 1974; AM, Harvard U., 1978, PhD, 1982. Legis. aide Canadian Parliment, Ottawa, Ontario, Can., 1974-75; rsch. assoc. Harvard Bus. Sch., Boston, 1979-80; asst. prof. govt. dept. Harvard U., 1982-87; Paul Sack assoc. prof. Harvard Bus. Sch., 1987-89, govt. prof., 1989—; sr. rsch. assoc. Center for European Studies, Cambridge, 1982—; cons. Royal Commn. on Econ. Prospects of Can., Ottawa, 1984-85, Office of Tech. Assessment (U.S. Congrss), Washington, 1990-91. Author: Governing the Economy, 1986 (Woodrow Wilson award 1987); editor: The Political Power of Economic Ideas, 1989; co-editor; Developments in French Politics, 1990. Chair Joint Com. on Western Europe of the Soc. Sci. Rsch. Coun., N.Y.C., 1989—; mem. Steering Com. Coun. for European Studies, N.Y.C., 1988—. Recipient Book award, Policy Studies Assn., 1987; German Marshall Fund fellowship, German Marshall Fund, Washington, 1986; Samuel H. Beer award, British Politics Group, 1983; Tozzer prize, Harvard U., 1982. Mem. Am. Polit. Sci. Assn. (mem. program com. 1987, 90), World Politics (editorial bd. 1991—), Comparative Polit. Studies (editorial bd. 1991—). Episcopalian. Office: Ctr for European Studies 27 Kirkland St Cambridge MA 02138

HALL, RICHARD CLAYTON, psychologist, consultant, researcher; b. Pitts., Apr. 29, 1931; s. Clayton LeClaire and Genevieve (Gorman) H.; m. Doris Margaret Bjorkland, Aug. 26, 1963; children: Karen, Janice, Dorothy. BS in Psychology with honors, Trinity Coll., 1952; MS, U. Pitts., 1959, PhD, 1963. Lic. psychologist, Pa. Rsch. psychologist Polk (Pa.) Ctr., 1963-68, dir. behavior modification programs, 1968-75, chmn. subcom. human rights for behavior mgmt. procedures, 1987-89, staff psychologist, 1989-91; ind. researcher Key West, Fla., 1975-84, Polk, Pa., 1985—. Contbr. articles to profl. jours. With U.S. Army, 1953-55. NSF Coop. Grad. fellow, 1959. Mem. Am. Psychol. Assn., Sigma Xi, Pi Gamma Mu. Democrat. Episcopalian. Home: 101 Elm St Polk PA 16342

HALL, ROBERT J., newspaper executive; b. Phila.. BS in accounting, Drexel U. CPA in 1968. With Inquirer & Daily News, Phila., Pa., 1973-85; exec. v.p. & gen. mgr. Detroit Free Press, Detroit, Mich., 1985, pub., chmn.; pub., chmn. Phila. Inquirer and Daily News, Phila., Pa., 1990—. Bd. of Trustees at Drexel U., vice chmn. of the Greater Phila. First Corp., chmn. of the Phila. Comm. for the 1994 World Cup Bid and chmn. of the Fairmount Pk. Historic Houses Project. mem. of the Bd. of the Police Athletic League, Greater Phila. C. of C., Phila. Convention and Visitors Bur., Phila. Sports Congress, Met. Sunday Newspapers and Newspapers First Corp. Office: The Phila Inquirer 400 N Broad St Philadelphia PA 19103*

HALL, SAMUEL M., JR., career educator, career development consultant; b. Saginaw, Mich., Dec. 23, 1937; s. Samuel M. and Marie Hall; m. Mary Josephine Fisher, Aug. 13, 1973; 1 child, John Anthony. AA, Ferris Inst., Big Rapids, Mich., 1962; AB, Western Mich. U., Kalamazoo, 1963; MA, Mich. State U., 1965. Coord. sch. dropout program Lansing (Mich.) Sch. System, 1964-65; dir. career devel., asst. prof. edn. Langston (Okla.) U., 1965-66; edn. advisor U.S. Office of Edn., Washington, 1966-67; dir. career planning and placement, acad. counselor Del. State Coll., Dover, 1967-70; dir. career svcs. Howard U., Washington, 1970—; editorial advisor Career-Vision Mag., N.Y.C., 1988-90; feature author Black Collegian, New Orleans, 1985; mem. adv. bd. Kinexus. Author: Planning and Implementing the Careers Conference, 1975; contbr. articles to mags.; interviewed on radio and TV. Co-pres. Ind. Living for the Handicapped, Washington, 1990-91; v.p. Belmont Living for the Handicapped, Washington, 1990-91; mem. Mayor's Youth Adv. Task Force, Washington, 1983-86; dep. dir. Summer Jobs Program, Washington, 1980; chair recognition com. Howard U., 1986-87, chair career counseling panel, 1989—. Recipient Outstanding Svc. award 1987, Middle Atlantic Placement Assn., 1985, Ed Parrish award, 1989. Mem. Alpha Phi Alpha (house mgr. 1964-65, corr. sec. 1964-65), Alpha Phi Omega Svcs. Orgn. (chpt. advisor 1968-70). Home: 217 Rittenhouse St NW Washington DC 20011-1468 Office: Howard U Student Resource Ctr 6th and Bryant Sts NW Washington DC 20059

HALL, STANLEY ECKLER, international financial consultant; b. Cooperstown, N.Y., Jan. 10, 1934; s. Wesley Claude and Cynthia Helen (Eckler) H.; m. Jewel Irene Breiner, Aug. 10, 1957; children: Brian Vernon, Sandra Jewel, Nancy Jane Cynthia. BS, St. Lawrence U., 1955, MEd, 1967; BSEE, Purdue U., 1959; MS, Clarkson U., 1970. Sales engr. GE, Schenectady, N.Y., 1959-62, supr. sales tng., 1962-64; dir. Operation Enterprise Am. Mgmt. Assn., Hamilton, N.Y., 1964-65; dir. devel. St. Lawrence U., Canton, N.Y., 1965-70; v.p. devel. Hiram (Ohio) Coll., 1970-72; v.p. univ. devel. Purdue U., West Lafayette, Ind., 1972-74; v.p. planning and devel. Hartwick Coll., Oneonta, N.Y., 1974-78; v.p. pub. affairs Colgate U., Hamilton, N.Y., 1978-88; sr. v.p. Brakeley, John Price Jones, Stamford, Conn., 1988-91; pres. Brakeley Recruiting, Stamford, 1989-91, Leatherstocking Cons., Cooperstown, N.Y., 1991—. State chmn. N.Y. Crusade Am. Cancer Soc., Syracuse, 1970; trustee Purdue Found., 1972-74, Catskill Mt. Edn. Ctr., Stamford, N.Y., 1974-78; v.p., bd. dirs. Purdue Rsch. Found., West Lafayette, 1972-74; bd. dirs. Bassett Hosp. Found., 1985—, Hyde Hall Restoration, Cooperstown, 1988—. 1st lt. U.S. Army, 1955-57. Recipient Disting. Alumni citation St. Lawrence U., Canton, 1990. Mem. St. Lawrence Alumni Assn. (exec. coun. 1991—), Native Sons of Cooperstown, Adirondack Mountain Club, Sigma Chi (life). Republican. Presbyterian. Home: 1 Elm St Cooperstown NY 13326-1213 Office: Box 721 Cooperstown NY 13326

HALL, STEVEN EDWARD, medicinal chemist; b. Detroit, Aug. 24, 1954; s. Herbert William and Marcia Jean (Bowles) H.; m. Jane Elizabeth Tennant, Oct. 29, 1976; children: Michelle, Rachel. BS, Cen. Mich. U., 1976; PhD, MIT, 1982. Rsch. chemist Quaker Oats Chems. Div., Barrington, Ill., 1976-78; rsch. asst. MIT Dept. Chemistry, Cambridge, Mass., 1978-82; rsch. investigator Squibb Inst. Med. Rsch., Princeton, N.J., 1982-87, sr. rsch. investigator, 1987-88, rsch. group leader, 1988-91; assoc. dir. Bristol-Myers Squibb Pharm. Rsch. Inst., Princeton, N.J., 1991—; reviewer in field. Inventor/patentee in field; contbr. articles to profl. jours. Deacon Abiding Presence Luth. Ch., Ewing, N.J., 1987—. Mem. Am. Chem. Soc. (sec.-treas. fall symposium Princeton sect. 1983, 84-85), N.Y. Acad. Sci. Office: BMS Pharm Rsch Inst PO Box 4000 Princeton NJ 08540

HALL, WANDA JEAN, mental health professional, consultant; b. Miami, Okla., July 3, 1943; d. Max Calvin Kinnaman and Dorothy D. (Peck) Fadler; m. James Marvin Hall, Apr. 10, 1964 (div. Feb. 1965); m. George Edward Hall, Mar. 21, 1973; children: Heather Renata, Sam. AA, Stephens Coll., Columbia, Mo., 1963; BS, Kans. U., Pittsburg, 1965; MS, New Sch. for Social Rsch., N.Y.C., 1991. Asst. psychologist Parsons (Kans.) State Hosp., 1966-67; hosp. care investigator N.Y. Dept. Social Work, N.Y.C., 1968-70; social worker Drug Abuse Program, Amsterdam, The Netherlands, 1970-74; dir. Washington Park Co-op Presch., N.Y.C., 1974-75; project dir. Manhattan Devel. Ctr., N.Y.C., 1975-77; pvt. practice as human devel. specialist, N.Y.C., 1978-81; community rels. coord. Orange County Dept. Mental Health, Goshen, N.Y., 1981—; parenting cons. Teens Exploring Parenting, Inc., Middletown, N.Y., 1990-91; instr. Orange County Community Coll., Middletown, 1990-91. Producer, host radio show Conversation on Epilepsy, Radio Sta. WGNY, 1981; dir., narrator mental health skits Forum Players, 1980; producer, host 5 TV series Love from the 26,000 Club, 1983. Bd. dirs. Orange County Coalition for Choice, Warwick, N.Y., 1991, Orange County Task Force on Child Abuse/Neglect, 1984-89, Ct. Apptd. Spl. Assts., 1987—; bd. dirs. Bandwagon Community Ctr., chair pers., 1990-91; mem Planned Parenthood, Orange County, N.Y., 1989—, Safe Homes, Orange County, 1987—; co-founder Orange County Parenting Coalition, 1990-91; mem. Middletown Coun. Community Agys., 1980—; mem. Interagy. Coun. Child Sexual Abuse. Recipient DWI Alcohol Safety award N.Y. State Alchol Bur., Albany, 1986, Community Svc. award Youth Bur., Goshen, 1987, ZONTA scholarship award, 1989, Community Svc. award Otisville (N.Y.) State Correction, 1989. Mem. NAACP. Methodist. Office: Orange County Dept Mental Health Drawer 471 Harriman Dr Goshen NY 10924

HALL, WILLIAM SMITH, JR., land surveyor; b. Milford, Conn., Nov. 10, 1941; s. William Smith and Elizabeth (Brodeur) H.; m. Joy Collette Herrick, Sep. 13, 1969; children: William Smith 3d, Amber-Dawn. Student, U. Conn., 1959-60; AS in Civil Engring., Hartford State Tech. Coll., 1972. Lic. land surveyor, Conn.; cert. sr. civil engring. technician, Conn. Rodmantransitman Mcpl. Engring. Dept., Milford, 1960-67; road insp., survey party chief Mcpl. Engring. Dept., Trumbull, Conn., 1967-70; transitman, party chief Leonard Surveyors, Norwalk, Conn., 1970; transitman Donald Disbrow, P.E. & RLS, Hamden, Conn., 1970-72; land surveyor Kasper Assocs., PE & LS, Bridgeport, Conn., 1972-77; owner, mgr., land surveyor Hall Surveyors, Plymouth, Conn., 1973—; mem. adv. com. civil dept. Hartford (Conn.) State Tech. Coll., 1984—, surveying instr., 1991—; com. mem. film on land surveying A Matter of Degrees, 1983-86. Capt. Woodmont Vol. Fire Co. 5, Milford, 1969; chmn. bd. trustees Terryville Congl. Ch., Plymouth, 1986; mem. Plymouth Zoning Bd. Appeals, 1980—, vice chmn., 1985—, acting chmn., 1988. Mem. Conn. Assn. Land Surveyors (sec. 1979-82, pres. 1982-84, county bd. dirs. 1984—, Appreciation awards 1984), Surveyor's Proprietor's Coun. (sec.-treas. 1989, v.p. 1990, pres. 1991). Democrat. Office: 350 Lk Plymouth Blvd Plymouth CT 06782

HALLARD, WAYNE BRUCE, economist; b. Plainfield, N.J., Dec. 28, 1951; s. Donald Jay and Patricia (Adelmann) H.; m. Grace Elizabeth Farrell, Apr. 29, 1972 (div. 1979); 1 child, Travis; m. Deborah Jane Russo, Aug. 16, 1987. Student, Brown U., 1970-71; AA in Bus., Union Coll., 1977; BS in Econs., Fairleigh Dickinson U., 1980, MBA in Econs., 1984; postgrad., N.Y.U., 1984-87. Store mgr. Wine Art of N.J., Watchung, 1972; staff mgr. Bell Atlantic, Newark, 1972—; cons. N.J. Coun. of Savs. Instns., West Orange, 1987—, F.A. Russo Assocs., Scotch Plains, N.J., 1989—. Trustee, treas. Lehmen Found., Newark, 1979-84; bd. dirs., treas. Vol. Ctr. of Greater Essex County, 1990—; mem. Mental Health Assn., East Orange, 1979-80, Newark Mus., 1987—; trustee, past sec., treas. Newark Jaycees Internat. Senators Scholarship Found., 1986—; umpire Scotch Plains-Fanwood Youth Baseball Assn., 1982—; trustee, past pres. Brotherhood Temple Sharey Tefilo Israel, South Orange, N.J., 1980—. With USAFR, 1971-80. Recipient Cert. of Appreciation Cts. and Corrections Assn. N.J. 1982; named One of Outstanding Young Men of Am., 1981, 83, 85, 86, 88. Mem. Am. Econ. Assn., Greater Newark C. of C. (bd. dirs. 1980-82), Telephone Pioneers Am., Am. Sealyham Terrier Club, Garden State All Terrier Club (treas.), Mastiff Club Am., B'nai B'rith, Delta Mu Delta. Republican. Jewish. Home: 518 Jerusalem Rd Scotch Plains NJ 07076-2011 Office: Bell Atlantic 540 Broad St Newark NJ 07102-3178

HALLBERG, BUDD JAYE, management consulting firm executive; b. Ottumwa, Iowa, Oct. 2, 1942; s. Melvin Kenneth and Janet Berina (Dowden) H.; m. Diana May Pierce, Dec. 30, 1962; children: Cynthia Ann Hallberg-Walker, Amy Christine. BA, Parsons Coll., 1965; MA, Goddard Coll., 1980; diploma, Command & Gen. Staff Coll., 1981; cert., Wharton Sch., 1984. Account exec. Francis I. duPont & Co., Moline, Ill., 1966-69; sales mgr. Francis I. duPont & Co., N.Y.C., 1969-70; br. mgr. Francis I. duPont & Co., Toledo, 1970-71; v.p. Dominick & Dominick, Inc., N.Y.C., 1971-72, Hornblower & Weeks, Inc., N.Y.C., 1972-74; mem. N.Y. Mercantile Exchange, N.Y.C., 1974-76; dir. U.S. Commodity Future Trading Commn., Washington, 1976-83; v.p. Heinold Commodities, Inc., N.Y.C., 1983-85; pres. SCAN Mgmt. Inc., Gettysburg, Pa., 1985—. Contbr. articles to profl. jours. Fund raiser Rep. Party, Old Greenwich, Conn., 1974, St. Saviours Episcopal Ch., Old Greenwich, 1975. Maj. USAR. Mem. Futures Industry Assn., Nat. Futures Assn. (assoc.), Army & Navy Club Wash., N.Y. Athletic Club, Rotary. Home: 320 Spangler School Rd Gettysburg PA 17325-8639 Office: SCAN Mgmt Inc Drawer 4835 Gettysburg PA 17325-4835

HALLEE, NEAL DAVID, agricultural engineer; b. Waterville, Maine, Oct. 21, 1943; s. Florian Francis and Constance Yvette (Tardiff) H.; m. Margaret Anne Chasse, Aug. 26, 1967; children: Richard Francis, Margaret Elizabeth. BS, U. Maine, Orono, 1966, MS, 1968; PhD, Pa. State U., 1981. Registered profl. engr., Maine. Instr. and rsch. assoc. dept. agrl. engring. U. Maine, Orono, 1966-68; rsch. assoc. dept. agrl. engring. Pa. State U., University Park, 1973-74; extension agrl. engr. U. Maine Coop. Extension, Orono, 1968—. Co-author: Potato Storage Design and Management, 1984. Mem. Am. Soc. Agrl. Engrs. (Blue Ribbon award, 1987), Potato Assn. Am., KC. Roman Catholic. Home: 27 Cromwell Dr Orono ME 04473-1127 Office: U Maine Extension 116 Libby Hall Orono ME 04473

HALLER, LEE HIGDON, psychiatrist; b. Pitts., Aug. 19, 1947. BA in Psychology, U. Mich., 1968, MD, 1972. Diplomate Am. Bd. Psychiatry and Neurology. Rotating intern Wayne County Gen. Hosp., Eloise, Mich., 1972-74; resident in gen. psychiatry Duke U. Med. Ctr., Durham, N.C., 1973-74; fellow child psychiatry Children's Psychiat. Hosp./U. Mich., Ann Arbor, 1975-77; pvt. practice Rockville, Md., 1979—; clin. asst. prof. psychiatry dept. psychiatry Georgetown U. Med. Ctr., Washington, 1979—, George Washington U. Med. Ctr., Washington, 1979—. Contbr. numerous articles to profl. jours. With U.S. Army, 1977-79. Mem. Am. Psychiat. Assn., Am. Acad. Psychiatry and the Law, Am. Soc. for Adolescent Psychiatry, Am. Acad. Child Psychiatry, Montgomery County Med. Soc., Phi Rho Sigma Med. Fraternity. Home and Office: 15225 Shady Grove Rd # 305 Rockville MD 20850-3234

HALLER, ROBERT TERRENCE, marketing, advertising and public relations consultant; b. N.Y.C., May 20, 1930; s. Harry and Fay Haller; m. Charlotte Haller, Dec. 17, 1957; children: John D., William B. BS, NYU, 1955; diploma, U.S. Army War Coll., 1980; MA, Cen. Mich. U., 1981. Account exec. BBDO, 1955-62; account supr. Interpub. Group: Pritchard Wood, 1962-65; advt. mgr. Savarin Coffee, 1965-66; account supr. McCaffrey & McCall, Inc., 1966-67; advt. mgr. Simplicity Pattern Co., 1967-69; pres. Fashion Scene, Inc., 1969-79; v.p., mgmt. supr. Ogilvy & Mather, Inc., N.Y.C., 1970-82; pres., creative dir. CFI Advt. & Pub. Rels., N.Y.C. and Hamlin, Pa., 1982—; asst. prof., program dir. advt. and pub. rels. Marywood Coll., Scranton, Pa., 1988—. Author: Creative Firepower, 1987; contbr. author Broadcasting mag., Media Rev., Am. Mktg. Assn., North County News; account exec. DuPont, Air France, Eagle Pencil, 1955-62; account supr. Smith Bros., Beck Beer, Caryl Richards, Faberge, 1962-65, Quaker Oats and Quaker Life cereal, 1966-67; mgmt. supr. Sears, Roebuck & Co., Panasonic, Matsushita Electric, Am. Express, Longines, Owens Corning Fiberglas, 1970-82. With U.S. Army, col. inf. USAR, ret. Decorated Legion of Merit. Mem. Am. Advt. Fedn., Pub. Rels. Soc. Am., Am. Legion, Res. Officers Assn., Civil Affairs Assn., 77th Army Res. Command Assn., NYU Vets. Alumni Assn. (pres. 1957-59), NYU Club (bd. govs.), Alpha Delta Sigma (Nat. Advt. honor). Republican. Home: RR 5 Box 5154F Lake Ariel PA 18436 Office: CFI Advt & Pub Rels 38 Maple Ln # 489 Hamlin PA 18427

HALLIDAY, LAURA ALICE MCCARTY, vocational education administrator; b. Lehighton, Pa., Aug. 11, 1928; d. Eugene James and Edna Elizabeth (Goldsworthy) McCarty; m. James G. Halliday (wid.); 1 child, Bonnie Lynn Filo. BS, Mansfield U., 1950; MEd, Lehigh U., 1962; DEd, Pa. State Univ., 1971. Cert. dir. vocat. edn., supr., tchr., Pa. Tchr. East Penn Sch. Dist., Emmaus, Pa., 1950-59; vocat. cons. Bur. of Vocat. Edn./Pa. Dept. Edn., Harrisburg, 1959-90; dir. vocat. edn. Bristol (Pa.) Twp. Sch. Dist., 1990—; adj. instr. Pa. State U., University Park, 1971-72, Lehigh U., Bethlehem, 1974; mem. profl. adv. com. Pa. Dept. Edn., Harrisburg, 1990—. Contbg. author curriculum guides in field, 1971—. Recipient edn. grant Pa. Dept. Edn., 1968-69. Mem. Am. Vocat. Assn. (life), Pa. Vocat. Assn. (life, com. mem. 1976-89, 90—), Am. Home Econs. Assn. (life), Pa. Home Econs. Assn. (life), Nat. Assn. Home Econs. State Suprs., Order of Eastern Star (life, past matron 1958), Omicron Nu. Home: 3623 Ironstone Rd Bethlehem PA 18017-1209 Office: Bristol Twp Sch Dist 800 Coates Ave Bristol PA 19007-5899

HALLIWELL, WILLIAM HENRY, veterinary pathologist; b. Pitts., Oct. 15, 1939; s. Henry John and Agnes Patricia (McCarthy) H.; divorced; children: Andrea C., Michael M. DVM, Auburn U., 1964; PhD, U. Mo., 1971. Lic. veterinarian, N.C., Ala., Fla., Mo. Pvt. practice vet. medicine Garner, N.C., 1964-65; from asst. prof. to prof. U. Mo., Columbia, 1968-76; pathologist Lovelace Found., Albuquerque, 1976-78, WestPath Labs., Ft. Collins, Colo., 1978-84; dir. pathology Hoffmann La Roche, Nutley, N.J., 1984-89, Schering-Plough, Inc., Kenilworth, N.J., 1989—. Contbr. over 50 articles to profl. jours., chpts. to books. Capt. USAF, 1965-68. Mem. Am. Coll. Vet. Pathology (cert.). Republican. Lutheran.

HALLMAN, RICHARD DOUGLAS, biology educator; b. Kitchener, Ont., Can., Aug. 11, 1951; came to U.S., 1977; s. Kenneth Franklin and Lillian Mary (Perschbacher) H.; m. Diane Brower, Jan. 8, 1978. BA in Psychology, U. Waterloo (Can.), 1974; MA in Biol. Sci., Hunter Coll., 1987. Lab. technician Ont. Water Resources Commn., Toronto, Can., 1970, 71; tech. asst. U. Göttingen (Fed. Republic of Germany), 1971-72; child care worker Whitby (Can.) Psychiat. Hosp., 1975-77; survey technician Lovell-Belcher Surveyors, N.Y.C., 1977-81; math. and sci. tchr. Jr. High Sch. 123, Bronx, N.Y., 1981-83; biology tchr. Forest Hills High Sch., Queens, N.Y., 1983—; curriculum developer Forest Hills High Sch., Queens, 1984-88. Recipient City of Waterloo scholarship, 1968, Govt. Ont. scholarship, 1969; N.Y. State Regents fellow, 1985, Am. Soc. Biochemistry and Molecular Biology fellow, 1991. Mem. N.Y. Biology Tchrs. Assn., Alumni Assn. Hunter Coll. Office: Forest Hills High Sch 67-01 110th St Forest Hills NY 11375

HALLOCK, GILBERT VINTON, physician; b. Worcester, Mass., Oct. 23, 1925; s. Robert Palmer and Mildred Estelle (Amidon) H.; m. Eleanor Marion Sjogren, Aug. 2, 1953 (div. Dec. 1982); children: Peter Benjamin (dec.), Candyce H. Cummings, Jason Palmer. Student, Clark U., 1946-48; AB, Harvard U., 1950; MD, Tufts U., 1954; postgrad., Med. Coll. pa., 1978. Intern Worcester City Hosp., 1954-55; med. dir., assoc. med. dir., dir. profl. svcs. and info. Astra Pharm. Products, Inc., Worcester, 1956-73; assoc. med. staff Good Samaritan Hosp., Suffern, N.Y., 1975-77, Worcester City Hosp., 1969-83; asst. physician dept. mental health Commonwealth of Mass., Worcester State Hosp., 1980-83; with security svc. Calif. Plant Protection, Inc., Worcester, 1984-85; assoc. dir. profl. svcs. Lederle Labs. div. Am. Cyanamid Co., Pearl River, N.Y., 1976-78, assoc. dir. med. adv. dept., 1974-76; med. dir., cons. Bioevaluation, Inc., N.Y.C., 1974; dir. med. svcs. Dome Labs. Div., Miles Labs., West Haven, Conn., 1974; incorporator, dir., pres. Student Internat. Svc. Found., Inc., Boston, 1969-72; cons. pharmacology The Meml. Hosp., Worcester, 1965-83, Worcester City Hosp., 1977-83; mem. rsch. com., bd. dirs. Med. Rsch. Inst. Worcester, Inc., 1969-83. Bd. dirs. Armed Forces Com. of Worcester County, Inc., v.p., 1984-85, pres., 1985-86; sr. vice comdr. Worcester Vets. Coun., 1985, comdr., 1986; mem. Auburn Community Health Coun.; past treas., v.p., pres. Julia Bancroft Sch., Auburn PTA; mem. ex-officio bd. trustees Am. Police Hall of Fame and Mus.; mem. Rep. Nat. Com., Nat. Rep. Congl. Com.; mem. adv. bd. First Bapt. Ch. Worcester; mem. Bd. Health, Auburn, 1972-75; mem. Conservation Commn., 1972-73. With USAAF, 1943-45, col. Res., 1950-85. Fellow Assn. Anesthetists of Gt. Britain and Ireland; mem. ADA, APHA, AMA (Physician's Recognition award 1969, 72, 75, 78, 81), Royal Soc. Health, Drug Info. Assn., Am. Soc. Anesthesiologists, Am. Soc. Regional Anesthesia, Internat. Anesthesia Rsch. Soc., Am. Dental Soc. Anesthesiology, Indsl. Med. Assn., Am. Profl. Practice Assn., Am. Med. Writers' Assn., Assn. Med. Dirs., Am. Soc. Law and Medicine, Am. Coll. Gen. Practice, World Med. Assn., Orthomolecular Med. Soc., Am. Holistic Med. Assn. Republican. Baptist. Home: 16 Duncannon Ave Apt 2 Worcester MA 01604-5128

HALLOCK, SUZY, counselor; b. Moline, Ill., Mar. 26, 1942; d. Warren Arthur Hallock and Norma Anita (Ames) Nytes; m. Timothy Butterworth, June 26, 1966 (div. May 1976); children: Elizabeth Brook, Benjamin Clark. AB, Mount Holyoke Coll., 1964; MEd, Lesley Coll., 1978; Cert. Advanced Grad. Studies, U. Vt., 1988. Lic. counselor, Vt.; cert. reality therapist. English tchr. MacDuffie Sch., Springfield, Mass., 1964-66; 2d grade tchr. Horton Pub. Sch., Pittsboro, N.C., 1966-67, Elm Hill Sch., Springfield, Vt., 1967-68; tchr. adult basic edn. Bellows Falls (Vt.) High Sch., 1969-75; admissions counselor Hartford (Conn.) Coll. for Women, 1973-76; writer, reporter Keene (N.H.) Sentinel, Brattleboro (Vt.) Reformer, 1975; counselor Woodstock (Vt.) Union High Sch., 1976—; pvt. practice counselor Norwich & South Pomfret, Vt., 1978—; dir. Dept. Counseling and Health, Woodstock, Student Peer Counselor Program, Woodstock; sr. faculty assoc. Inst. Reality Therapy, L.A., 1985—, practicum supr., faculty assoc., 1978—; instr. Inst. Reality Therapy in Ireland, Dublin, Cork, Waterford. Case author: What Are You Doing?, 1980, Control Theory in the Practice of Reality Therapy, 1989; contbr. articles to profl. jours. Mem. Woodstock Child Protection Team, 1990-91; negotiator Woodstock Union Tchrs. Assn., 1986-91. Named Educator of Yr., Woodstock Community and Sch. Assn., 1983. Mem. NEA, Am. Assn. Sch. Counselors, Vt. Assn. Sch. Counselors, Vt. Assn. Counseling and Developments (Guzetta award 1991), Vt. Edn. Assn., New Eng. Assn. Coll. Admissions Counselors (Outstanding Counselor 1986). Democrat. Home: Donegal On The Stage Rd South Pomfret VT 05067 Office: Woodstock High Sch Woodstock VT 05091

HALLORAN, LEO AUGUSTINE, retired financial executive; b. Schenectady, N.Y., Apr. 2, 1931; s. Leo Augustine Halloran and Helen (O'Hare) Pagel; m. Marilyn Elizabeth Gobeli, Dec. 29, 1956; children: Patricia Garvey, Michael, Kevin. AB in Econs., Union Coll., Schenectady, N.Y., 1953. With fin. mgmt. program Gen. Electric Co., Schenectady, 1956-60, mem. corp. audit staff, 1961-64, mgr. fin., 1965-70; mgr. fin. Consumer Products Group, Fairfield, Conn., 1971-75; sr. v.p., chief fin. officer Gen. Electric Capital Corp., Stamford, Conn., 1976-89, ret., 1990; bd. dirs. Kidder Peabody, N.Y.C. Sgt. U.S. Army, 1953-55. Mem. Fin. Execs. Inst., Woodway Country Club, Landmark Club. Address: 524 E 72nd St New York NY 10021

HALLOUN, ELYSSA NADIA, guidance counselor, psychologist, educator; b. Cambridge, Mass.. BA, BS cum laude, U. Mass., 1975; MS, MEd, Suffolk U., 1977; cert. advanced grad. study, Boston State Coll., 1980. Cert. guidance counselor, guidance dir., spl. subject tchr., K-12 music tchr., secondary tchr., vocat. guidance counselor, social studies tchr., Mass.; cert. guidance counselor, guidance dir., N.H.; cert. occupational edn., social studies, biligual tchr., coord. adult practical arts programs, Calif. Lectr. U. Mass., Harvard U., Cambridge, 1973-74; asst. to dir. admissions A Better Chance, Boston, 1975; advisor, tchr., curriculum developer Arlington (Mass.) Pub. Schs., 1975-78; acad. and student affairs counselor Graham Jr. Coll., Boston, 1976-77; guidance counselor Malden (Mass.) Pub. Schs., 1978-79; vocat. guidance counselor Old Colony Regional Vocat. Tech. High Sch., Rochester, Mass., 1978-79; student svcs. U. Calif. San Diego, La Jolla, 1981-86; guidance counselor San Diego City Schs., 1986; instructional material developer San Diego State U. Found., 1986; guidance counselor, dept. head Seabrook (N.H.) Sch. Dist. SAU 21, 1986—; guest lectr. Boston State Coll., 1974-80; participant in preparation vocat. material for govtl. and ednl. orgns. HEW, 1979; mem. Gov.'s Task Force on Vocat. Counseling and Comprehensive Guidance Curriculum, Mass., N.H. Mem. AACD (N.H. del. nat. convs. 1988-91), Am. Sch. Counselors Assn., N.H. Sch. Counselors Assn. (v.p. mid. sch. counseling 1987-88, v.p. elem. sch. counseling 1988-89, pres.-elect 1989-90, pres. 1990-91), Nat. Assn. for Armenian Studies and Rsch. (exec. bd. membership and publicity coms.), N.H. Seacoast Sch. Counselors Assn., N.H. Assn. Counseling and Devel., N.H. Assn. for Career Devel., N.H. Marriage and Family Counseling Assn. Home: PO Box 964 Hampton NH 03842-0009 Office: Seabrook Elem Sch Walton Rd Seabrook NH 03874-4517

HALPERIN, DONALD MARC, state senator, lawyer; b. Bklyn., July 25, 1945; s. Charles and Gladys (Solomon) H.; m. Brenda Stibel, June 22, 1969; children: Jeremy Nehemiah, Rebecca Ruth. BA in Sociology, Rutgers U., 1967; JD, Bklyn. Law Sch., 1970, Tel Aviv U., 1978. Bar: N.Y. 1972, Fla. 1975. Counsel Fuchsberg & Fuchsberg N.Y.C., 1974-80, Gaffin & Mayo, 1981-83, Seiden, Stempel & Bennett, 1983—; mem. N.Y. State Senate, N.Y.C., 1971—; Mem. Legis. Commn. on Expenditure Rev., Pub. Auth. Control Bd. Recipient Masada award State of Israel Bonds, 1974, Pub. Service award N.Y. State Jewish Wars Vet., 1975, Cert. of Achievement, Nat. Dist. Atty. Assn., 1976. Mem. Nat. Fedn. Italian Am. Orgns. (hon.), Nat. Conf. Ins. Legislators (past pres.). Democrat. Jewish. Office: Community Office 1600 Sheepshead Bay Rd Brooklyn NY 11235-3824 Other: NY State Senate Legislative Office Bldg Albany NY 12247

HALPERIN, GEORGE BENNETT, educator, retired naval officer; b. N.Y.C., Aug. 7, 1926; s. George and Muryal (Lesser) H.; m. Ellen Elizabeth Barber, Dec. 18, 1957 (div. 1988); children: Gail Susan, Thomas Allyn. BS, U.S. Naval Acad., 1950; MBA, Stanford U., 1958; postgrad., Naval War Coll., Newport, R.I., 1965-66; MA in History, U. Vt., 1976; MEd, Harvard U., 1979; postgrad., Oxford U., 1987-88, St. Catherine's Coll., 1987-88. Commd. ensign U.S. Navy, 1950, advanced through grades to comdr., 1965; dir. systems and standards div. Naval Supply Ctr., Oakland, Calif., 1963-65; freight terminal officer Naval Support Activity, Danang, Vietnam, 1966-67; supply officer Naval Air Sta., Barbers Point, Hawaii, 1967-70; ret., 1970; tchr. History Stowe (Vt.) High Sch., 1972-80, asst. prin., 1975-76; tchr. John F. Kennedy Sch., Berlin, 1980-86; Chmn. Lamoille South Dist. Profl. Growth Com., 1977-78. Decorated Navy Commendation medal. Mem. Navy League U.S., U.S. Naval Acad. Alumni, Army-Navy Country Club, Oxford Soc., Harvard Club, Hanover Country Club.

HALPERIN, JEROME ARTHUR, pharmaceutical convention executive; b. Paterson, N.J., Feb. 21, 1937; s. Harry Nathan and Frieda (Niestat) H.; m. Barbara Anne Hott, Sept. 1, 1963; children: Alicia Jennifer Odom, Rachel Elizabeth. BS, Rutgers U., 1958; MPH, Johns Hopkins U., 1962; MS, MIT, 1974. Commd. officer USPHS, 1958, advanced through grades to asst. surgeon gen. (rear adm.), 1983; staff pharmacist USPHS Hosps., Dept. HEW, Albuquerque and N.Y.C., 1958-61; radiol. health specialist Calif. Health Dept., Berkeley, 1962-65; dir. states agreement Bur. Radiol. Health, Rockville, Md., 1965-66; dir. indsl. radiation and air hygiene Kans. Dept. Health, Topeka, 1966-68; regional rep. Bur. Radiol. Health, Chgo., 1968-71; dir. Northeastern Radiol. Health Lab., FDA, HEW, Winchester, Mass., 1971-73; dep. assoc. dir. new drug evaluation Bur. Drugs, FDA, HEW, Rockville, Md., 1974-77, dep. dir., 1977-82; acting dir. Office of Drugs Nat. Ctr. for Drugs and Biologics FDA, Rockville, 1982-83; v.p. tech. CIBA Consumer Pharms., Edison, N.J., 1983-89; exec. dir. U.S. Pharmacopeial Conv., Inc., Rockville, Md., 1989—; nat. bd. advisors U. Ariz. Coll. Pharmacy, Tucson, 1986—; adv. bd. U. Calif. Drug Studies Unit, San Francisio, 1983—; chmn. Conf. on Pharmacy 21st Century Va., 1984; cons. WHO, 1979—. Contbr. articles to profl. jours. Mem. Bd. Health, Hoffman Estates, Ill., 1971; bd. dirs. Perspective Woods Citizen Assn., Olney, Md., 1977-80. Named Alumnus of Yr. Rutgers U., 1981; recipient Outstanding Service award Federally Employed Women's Assn., 1983. Fellow Am. Pub. Health Assn., AAAS; mem. Am. Assn. Pharm. Scientists (charter, treas.), Drug Info. Assn., Am. Pharm. Assn. Jewish. Office: US Pharmacopeial Conv Inc 12601 Twinbrook Pky Rockville MD 20852-1790

HALPERN, ALFRED IRVING, trade association executive; b. Boston, July 25, 1925; s. Philip and Ida (Saleson) H.; m. Elaine Frank, Dec. 9, 1951 (dec. 1987); children: Wendy Halpern Morrison, Deborah Lee, John David. AB, Harvard U., 1948. Mem. adminstrn. and sales staff Bristol Rubber Co., Boston, 1948-54; New Eng. sales mgr. Am. Biltrite Rubber Co., Inc., Trenton, N.J., 1955-71; sales mgr., then v.p. contract sales Joseph Silverman and Co., Inc., Boston, 1972-87; exec. dir. Northeast Flooring Contractors Assn., Inc., Newton Highlands, Mass., 1988—. Co-chmn. Vocat. Adjustment Ctr., Boston, 1973-80; pres. Greater Boston Assn. Retarded Citizens, 1983-85. Cpl. USAAF, 1943-46, Brazil. Recipient Pres.'s award Greater Boston Assn. Retarded Citizens, 1979, 82. Mem. New Eng. Soc. Assn. Execs., Am. Mensa. Jewish. Home: 250 Hammond Pond Pky Apt 108N Chestnut Hill MA 02167-1533

HALPERN, FREDERICK MICHAEL, real estate developer; b. Bayreuth, Germany, Feb. 26, 1948; s. Sam and Gladys (Landau) H.; m. Cheryl Miriam Feldman, June 12, 1977; 3 children. BS, U. Pa., 1971. Ptnr. The Halpern Orgn., Woodbridge, N.J., 1971—; dir. State Bank of S. Orange, N.J.; council mem. N.J. Investment Council. Founder Citizens for Am., Washington; trustee Washington Inst. for Near East Policy, Stern Coll. for Women of Yeshiva U.; reg. bd. dirs. Anti-Defamation League of B'nai B'rith. Mem. Am. Israel Pub. Affairs Com. (exec. com.), Nat. Assn. Indsl. and Office Park Developers, Beaver Creek Club. Republican. Jewish. Office: The Halpern Orgn 90 Woodbridge Center Dr Woodbridge NJ 07095-1142

HALPERN, JOSHUA BARUCH, chemistry educator; b. Bklyn., Jan. 21, 1946; s. Nathan W. and Bertha (Hotkins) H.; m. Judith Ann Cassidy, July 2, 1974. BA, Johns Hopkins U., 1966; PhD, Brown U., 1972. Postdoctoral assoc. Notre Dame Radiation Lab., South Bend, Ind., 1971-73; sci. asst. U. Bielefeld, Fed. Republic Germany, 1973-77; asst. rsch. prof. Howard U., Washington, 1977-79, asst. prof., 1979-84, assoc. prof., 1984-90, prof., 1990—; dir. D.C. Space Grant Consortium, Washington, 1991—. Mem. Am. Chem. Soc., Am. Phys. Soc., Optical Soc. Am. Office: Howard U Dept Chemistry Washington DC 20059

HALPERN, MIMI, neuroscientist; b. Antwerp, Belgium, June 19, 1938; came to U.S., 1941; d. Marcel and Clara (Strulovici) H.; m. Ariel Halpern, June 11, 1961 (dec. Dec. 1985); children: Joann, Jeffrey. AB, Oberlin Coll., 1960; PhD, Adelphi U., 1964. Teaching asst. psychology dept. Oberlin Coll., 1959-60; teaching and rsch. asst. psychology dept. Adelphi U., 1960-61, rsch. asst., 1961-63, instr., 1963-64; assoc. rsch. scientist SUNY Downstate Med. Ctr., 1964-67, instr. anatomy & cell biology dept., 1967-69, asst. prof. anatomy & cell biology dept. and grad. program in biol. psychology, 1969-74, assoc. prof., 1974-79; prof. SUNY Health Sci. Ctr. (formerly Downstate Med. Ctr.), Bklyn., 1979—, asst. dean Sch. Grad. Studies, 1975-83; assoc. dean Sch. Grad. Studies SUNY Health Sci. Ctr. (formerly Downstate Med. Ctr.), 1983-90; dir. grad. program in biol. psychology SUNY Health Sci. Ctr. (formerly Downstate Med. Ctr.), Bklyn., 1976-85, co-dir. grad. program neural and behavioral sci. Sch. Grad. Studies, 1985-90. Contbr. articles to profl. jours.

HALPERN, SIDNEY, history educator; b. Phila., Jan. 18, 1927; s. Bernard M. and Sophie (Swidler) H.; AB, U. Pa., 1947, MA, 1950, PhD, 1964; MA, Harvard U., 1949; DCL (hon.), U. Vascondurias; m. Phyllis C. Schachter, Dec. 21, 1951; children: Baruch, Nikki. Vice pres. Loyalty Life Ins. Agy., Inc., 1954-67, sec., dir., 1965-67; exec. v.p. Plymouth Mut. Life Ins. Co., 1954-57, pres., dir. 1957-67; pres. editor, pub. Mercury Books, Inc., 1961-67; asst. v.p. George Washington Life Ins. Co., 1965-67; asst. prof. history Temple U., Ambler, Pa., 1967-76, assoc. prof., 1976-83, prof., 1983—, dir. Ambler Campus, 1971-75, dean campus, 1975-82, prof., 1982—; pres. Provident Pub. Co., 1969—. Mem. Adath Zion, Zionist Orgn. Am., Jewish Def. League, Phi Beta Kappa, Sigma Rho, Order Conrad III. Author: Caesar and the Aurelii Cottae, the Passions of Caesar and Christ, Salvation is from the Jews, On His Father's Business, Cyrus ha'Maschiah, The Hinge of History: Genocidal Anti-Semitism From Ararat To Arafat; contbr. articles to psychoanalytic jours. Home: 1025 Friendship St Philadelphia PA 19111-4113 Office: Temple U Ambler PA 19002

HALPERN, STANTON DAVID, maintenance supplies company executive; b. Bklyn., July 23, 1949; s. Samuel and Cecelia (Strum) H.; m. Lauri Beth Newman, July 22, 1973; children—Lauren Rachel, Joshua Seth. B.A., Hofstra U., 1971. Notary Pub., N.Y.; lic. pesticide applicator, N.Y. Sales rep. Halbro Control Industries, Farmingdale, N.Y., 1971-79, dir. mktg., 1980-82, chief exec. officer, exec. v.p., 1982—. Contbr. articles to profl. jours. Republican committeeman 145th ea. dist., Huntington, N.Y. Recipient Nat. Honor Soc. award H. Frank Carey High Sch., 1965-67; J.F.K. Meml. Citizenship award Sachs Furniture, 1967; Outstanding Salesmanship award Dale Carnegie Inst., 1973. Mem. Internat. Platform Assn., Internat. Sanitary Supply Assn., Am. Mgmt. Assn., L.I. Assn. environ. com.), 110 L.I. Action Group. Lodge: Masons. Home: 4 Wilmington Dr Melville NY 11747-4014 Office: Halbro Control Industries 2090 Route 110 Farmingdale NY 11735-1714

HALPERSON, MICHAEL ALLEN, office products company executive; b. Boston, Sept. 11, 1946; s. Bertram David and Rose (Doolan) H. AB, Union Coll., 1968; MA in Teaching, U. Mass., 1970. Asst. to group v.p. Plymouth Rubber Co., Inc., Canton, Mass., 1972-73; corp. dir. pers. and indsl. rels. Plymouth Rubber Co., Inc., Canton, 1973-79, mgr. mktg., cons. products, 1979-81, dir. sales and mktg., 1981-85, v.p., 1985-92; v.p., gen. mgr. Plymouth Office Products a Hon Industries Co., Pawtucket, R.I., 1992—; bd. dirs., v.p. Cape Cod Sea Camps, Inc., Capt. Del. Assocs., Inc., Brewster, Mass.; bd. dirs., treas. Camp Wono, Inc., Brewster. Bd. dirs. Canton Assn. Industries, Inc., 1977-92, Neponset Valley Nursing Assn., Inc., 1979—, Neponset Valley Health Systems, Inc., Norwood, Mass., 1982—, chmn., 1990—; bd. dirs. Southwood Community Hosp., Inc., Norfolk, Mass., 1985—, Norfolk-Bristol Homemakers Svc., Inc., 1980—; bd. dirs. Norwood Hosp., Inc., 1983—, chmn., 1988-90. Mem. Nat. Office Products Assn., Office Products Mfrs. Assn. (bd. dirs. 1985—, pres. 1989, chmn. 1990). Home: PO Box 390 Sharon MA 02067-0390 Office: 255 Main St Ste 510 Pawtucket RI 02860

HALPIN, JAMES RICE, librarian; b. N.Y.C., May 24, 1935; s. James H. and Frances Seward (Round) H.; m. Roberta Anne Ibach, Aug. 28, 1971; children: Keith James, Robin Carrie. Student, Washington Coll., Md., 1954-57; BA, Parsons Coll., 1959; MLS, L.I. U., 1965. Trainee, libr. Farmingdale (N.Y.) Pub. Libr., 1962-65; bus. social sci. libr. Rochester (N.Y.) Pub. Libr., 1965-69; reference libr. North Babylon (N.Y.) Pub. Libr., 1969; br. libr. Sunnyside Libr., Linden, N.J., 1969-70; head reference svcs. Newburgh (N.Y.) Free Libr., 1970—; reference cons. Ramapo Catskill Libr. System, 1980-90. With U.S. Army, 1959-62. Mem. ALA, Southeastern N.Y. Libr. Resources Coun. (trustee 1986—), Orange Libr. Assn. (pres. 1983-85, award 1985). Office: Newburgh Free Libr 124 Grand St Newburgh NY 12550-4615

HALPIN, PETER, information systems specialist, programmer; b. Orange, N.J., Jan. 28, 1938; s. Thomas A. and Ethel Rita (Matthews) H.; m. Joan Elizabeth Wu, Nov. 21, 1964; children: Eric Glenn, Gary Kevin. BSME, N.J. Inst. Tech., 1959. Engr. State of N.Y., Babylon, 1959-60, U.S. Army Engring. Rsch. and Devel. Lab., Ft. Belvoir, Va., 1961-62; vol. Peace Corps, Arecibo, P.R., Brattleboro, Vt., 1963; sci. bibliographer Libr. of Congress, Washington, 1964; phys. scientist U.S. Def. Tech. Info. Ctr., Alexandria, Va., 1965-66; tech. info. specialist U.S. EPA, Washington, 1966-69, Rsch. Triangle Park, N.C., 1969-78; tech. info. specialist U.S. Dept. Health and Human Svcs., Washington, 1978-84, program analyst, 1984—; freelance programmer Washington, 1990—. Author: (with others) Air Pollution, 3d edit., 1977, (thesaurus) Standard Air Pollution Classification Network, 1978; contbr. articles to profl. jours. Tutor Homeless Children's Tutorial Project, Washington, 1990—. With U.S. Army, 1960-62. Mem. Am. Soc. for Info. Sci. (chmn. Carolinas chpt. 1973-74), Mensa. Home: 921 Welham Green Rd Great Falls VA 22066-1517

HALSEY, MARTHA TALIAFERRO, Spanish language educator; b. Richmond, Va., May 5, 1932; d. James Dillard and Martha (Taliaferro) H. A.B., Goucher Coll., 1954; M.A., U. Iowa, 1956; Ph.D., Ohio State U., 1964. Asst. prof. Pa. State U., University Park, 1964-70, assoc. prof., 1970-79, prof. Spanish, 1979—; vis. Olive B. O'Connor prof. lit. Colgate U., Hamilton, N.Y., 1983. Author: Antonio Buero Vallejo, 1973; editor: Madrugada, 1969, Hoy es fiesta, 1978, Los inocentes de la Moncloa, 1980, El enganao, Caballos desbocaos, 1981, (with Phyllis Zatlin) The Contemporary Spanish Theater: A Collection of Critical Essays, 1988; editor: Estreno, 1992—; gen. editor (Spanish play series) Estreno Contemporary, 1992—; mem. editorial bd. Modern Internat. Drama, 1968-75, Ky. Romance Quar., 1970-76; contbr. articles to profl. jours. Am. Philos. Soc. grantee, 1970, 78; Inst. for Arts and Humanistic Studies grantee, 1977. Mem. MLA, South Atlantic MLA, Am. Assn. Tchrs. Spanish and Portuguese, N.E. Modern Lang. Assn., Phi Beta Kappa, Phi Sigma Iota, Sigma Delta Pi. Democrat. Episcopalian. Clubs: Fellowship of Reconciliation, Episcopal Peace Fellowship, Nuclear Freeze Group. Home: 151 W Prospect Ave State College PA 16801-5248 Office: Dept Spanish Pa State U State College PA 16802

HALTERMANN, WILLIAM HENRY, JR., financial advisor; b. Englewood, N.J., Nov. 6, 1948; s. William Henry and Mary Bryan (Mellon) H.; m. Deirdre Sheridan, Apr. 8, 1989; children: William Henry III, Victoria J. BA, Hamilton Coll., 1970; MBA, Columbia U., 1979. 2d v.p. Chase Manhattan Bank, N.Y.C., 1973-78; assoc. Paine Webber, N.Y.C., 1979-81; mng. dir. Dean Witter Reynolds, N.Y.C., 1981-89; pres. HRBA, Inc., Windham, N.Y., 1990—; adj. asst. prof. Rensselaer Poly. Inst., Troy, N.Y., 1991—. Founder Ski Windham Disabled Ski Program, 1982—; mem. Albany (N.Y.) Coun. for Bus. Devel., 1991—. Mem. Albany-Colonie Regional C. of C. Office: HRBA Inc PO Box 494 Windham NY 12496

HAM, INYONG, industrial engineering educator; b. Hwangzu, Korea, Dec. 22, 1925; came to U.S., 1954, naturalized, 1975; s. Dukjung and Kwangdo (Kim) H.; m. Hyunduk Kim, Nov. 14, 1949; children: Taewoo, Taewuk. B.Engring., Seoul Nat. U., Korea, 1948; M.Sc., U. Nebr., 1956; Ph.D., U. Wis., 1958, hon. doctorate, Nanjing Aero. Inst., People's Republic China, 1988. Prof. indsl. engring. Pa. State U., University Park, 1958—, FANUC prof., 1989—, Disting. prof., 1991—; dir. Mfg. Rsch. Ctr., 1990—; dir. industry and asst. min. of industry Republic of Korea, Seoul, 1960-62; cons. Asian Productivity Orgn., Tokyo, UN Indsl. Devel. Orgn., World Bank, others; Fulbright prof. USSR, 1981; cons. prof. Xian Jiatong U., People's Republic China, 1981, Beijing Inst. Tech., People's Republic China, 1985; chair, vis. prof. U. Tokyo, 1989, Russel Severance Springer vis. prof. U. Calif., Berkeley, 1991. Author: Design of Cutting Tools, 1968; Group Technology, 1985. Recipient CAM-I award Computer Aided Mfg. Internat., 1978, Disting. Svc. citation, U. Wis., 1985. Fellow ASME, Inst. Indsl. Engring. (mfg. systems div. award 1981); mem. N.Am. Mfg. Rsch. Inst. (pres. 1985-86), Internat. Inst. Prodn. Engring. Rsch. (coun. 1983-85), Soc. of Mfg. Engrs. (Internat. Edn. award 1985, Albert M. Sargent Progress award 1990), Korea Scientist and Engrs. in Am. (pres. 1973-74). Home: 980 Mccormick Ave State College PA 16801-6529 Office: Pa State U Dept Indsl Engring University Park PA 16802

HAMA, MARY YOSHIKO, economist; b. Karuizawa, Japan, Jan. 3, 1945; came to U.S., 1952; d. Francis Ryosuke and Clara Harue (Morita) H.; m. Thomas Patrick McLoughlin, June 4, 1977; 1 child, Christopher F. BS, U. Calif., Berkeley, 1967; MS, U. Minn., 1969; postgrad., U. Md., 1985—. Economist Bur. Labor Stats. U.S. Dept. Labor, Washington, 1969-74; economist Human Nutrition Info. Svc. USDA, Hyattsville, Md., 1974—. Contbr. articles to profl. publs. Mem. Am. Coun. Consumer Interests, Am. Agrl. Econs. Assn., So. Agrl. Econs. Assn., Am. Statis. Assn. Office: USDA HNIS 6505 Belcrest Rd Hyattsville MD 20782-2011

HAMAKER, JOEL BRIGHAM, business executive; b. Washington, Mar. 19, 1946; s. Kenton Darrell and Mary Josephine (Cline) H. BS, Mich. State U., 1969; MA, Va. Poly. Inst. and State U., 1974; postgrad., Columbia Pacific U., 1991—. Planner, designer Stottler, Staff & Assocs., Lanham, Md., 1969-72; assoc. planner Md. Dept. of Planning, Frederick, 1974-78; agt. Hyde & Co., Bethesda, Md., 1980-84; prin. Delphi Solutions Group, Bethesda, 1984—; cons. Town of Thurmont, Md., 1974-76. Author: Money Management Mastery, 1983, Learning Unconditional Acceptance, 1989; co-creator board game Off The Wall, 1991. Member Frederick City Beautification Program, 1976, Bethesda Ever Green, 1991; bd. dirs. Internat. Meditation Soc., Frederick, 1974-77. Va. Poly. Inst. & State U. scholar, 1972; recipient Performance Cert., Integrated Awareness Group, 1990. Mem. ASTD, Assn. for Transpersonal Psychology, Assn. for Humanistic Psychology, Nat. Soc. for Performance and Instruction. Office: Delphi Solutions Group PO Box 154 Glen Echo MD 20812-0154

HAMBEL, HENRY PETER, security consultant; b. Bklyn., Apr. 11, 1951; s. Henry Thomas and Doris Ada (Mawhinney) H.; m. Carole Ann. AAS in Criminal Justice, Suffolk County Community Coll., 1977; BS in Criminal Justice, Pacific Western U., 1988, PhD in Criminal Justice with emphasis in Forensic Psychology, 1992; postgrad., Newport U. Sch. of Law, 1992—. Park ranger Suffolk County Park's Dept., Sayville, N.Y., 1973; deputy sheriff Suffolk County Sheriff's Dept., Riverhead, N.Y., 1973-80; police officer, undercover narcotics detective Suffolk County Police Dept., Yaphank, N.Y., 1980-88; pres., owner The Housewatch Agy., Eastport, N.Y., 1982-88; security cons. pvt. practice, Eastport, N.Y., 1988—; ind. security cons. Author: Last Call: The Party's Over: The Reality of Alcohol and Other Drug Use, 1992. Mem. APA, Nat. Law Enforcement Acad./Am. Police Acad. (Honors fellow 1991), Am. Soc. Indsl. Security (cert. protection profl.), Nat. Assn. Chiefs of Police, Internat. Police Assn. (life), Am. Psychology and Law Soc., Ret. Detectives Assn. Suffolk County, Ret. Police Assn. N.Y., Fraternal Order of Police. Summer Home: Box 925 Eastport NY 11941-0925 Winter Home: 700 SE 22d St Homestead FL 33033

HAMBLETON, GEORGE BLOW ELLIOTT, management consultant; b. Balt., Dec. 20, 1929; s. John Adams Hambleton and Margaret (Elliott) Carey; m. Janet Findlay MacLaren, Mar. 17, 1962 (dec. 1991); children: Anne Carey, Charles MacLaren, James Elliott. AB, Princeton U., 1952; program for mgmt. devel., Harvard U., 1964. Various positions with Latin American div. Pan Am, 1955-62; asst. div. service mgr. Pan Am, Miami, Fla., 1963-64; dir. USSR Pan Am, Moscow, 1966-70; dir. internat. affairs Pan Am, Washington, 1971-76; dir. comml. sales Pan Am, N.Y.C., 1977-80; v.p. mktg. N.Y. Airways, N.Y.C., 1976-77; exec. dir., vice chmn. Project Orbis, Inc., N.Y.C., 1980-83; pres. Andrews MacLaren Inc., N.Y.C., 1983-86; dep. asst. sec., dep. dir. gen. U.S. and fgn. comml. svc. Dept. Commerce, Washington, 1986-88; sr. v.p. Mgmt. Internat. Inc., Westport, Conn., 1988—; bd. dirs. Flight Found., Inc., Washington, Andrews MacLaren Ltd., Northants, Eng., Envirogas Vehicle Systems Inc., N.Y. Dir. Fgn. Policy Discussion Group, Washington, 1975—; mem. N.J. Conservation Found., 1987; mem. adv. com. East-West Trade, U.S. Dept. Commerce, 1973-79; mem. dist. export coun. U.S. Dept. Commerce, Conn., 1989—. 1st lt. U.S. Army, 1952-55, Korea. Mem. Fgn. Policy Assn., River Blindness Found. (Houston), Aircraft Owners and Pilots Assn., Upper Raritan Watershed Assn., Brook Club (N.Y.), Met. Club (Washington), Naval and Mil. Club (London), Md. Club (Balt.), Princeton Club (N.Y. and Washington), Essex Hunt Club (Far Hills, N.J.), Greenspring Valley Hunt Club (Balt.), Harvard Bus. Sch. Club (Washington, v.p. 1973-76), Wings Club (N.Y.), Aero Club (Washington). Republican. Episcopalian. Home: Stone Valley Farm 163 Burrell Rd Lebanon NJ 08833 Office: Mgmt Internat Inc 21 Stony Brook Rd Westport CT 06880

HAMBLETT, STEPHEN, newspaper publishing executive; b. 1934. BA, Harvard U., 1957. With Providence Jour. Co., 1957—, various sales and mgmt. positions, 1957-69, asst. v.p., 1974-79, from v.p. mktg. corp. devel. to exec. v.p., 1979-85, pres., asst. pub., 1985-87, chmn., pub., chief exec. officer, 1987—. Office: Providence Jour Co 75 Fountain St Providence RI 02902-0050

HAMBURGER, MARY ANN, medical management consultant; b. Newark, Aug. 25, 1939; d. Herman and Sylvia (Strauss) Marcus; div. June 1966; children: Bruce David, Marc Laurence. AA, U. Bridgeport (Conn.), 1960. Office mgr. Millburn, N.J., 1970-84; propr., mgr. Mary Ann Hamburger, Assocs., med. mgmt. cons. co., Maplewood, N.J., 1984-; tchr. adult edn. South Orange Maplewood Bd. Edn., 1975-83; cons. Wellcare of N.Y.; profl. physician recruiter, N.Y., N.J. Mem. NAFE. Democrat. Jewish. Home and Office: 74 Hudson Ave Maplewood NJ 07040-1403

HAMBURGER, ROBERT JAY, internist, educator; b. Phila., May 30, 1941; s. Jacob Robert and Freda (Lindenheim) H.; m. Marilyn Gardner; children: Keith Robert, Eric Gardner Norman. BS, Mich. State U., 1963; MD, Tulane U., 1967. Diplomate Am. Bd. Internal Medicine. Intern U. Pa. Hosp., Phila., 1967-68; med. resident Hosp. U. Pa., Phila., 1968-69, renal fellow, 1969-71; staff physician Boston VA Med. Ctr., 1976-81, chief renal sect., 1981—; assoc. prof. medicine Tufts U. Sch. Medicine, 1976—. Editor nephrology texts, 1987. Lt. col. U.S. Army, 1971-76. Mem. Am. Soc. Nephrology, Internat. Soc. Nephrology, Alpha Omega Alpha. Home: 28 Old Colony Rd Wellesley MA 02181 Office: Boston VA Med Ctr 150 S Huntington Ave Boston MA 02130

HAMDAN, LAWRENCE ANISE, investment banker, lawyer; b. South Orange, N.J., Aug. 31, 1961; s. Ali A. and Dorothea E. (Nevola) H. AB magna cum laude, Princeton U., 1983; MBA with high distinction, Harvard U., 1989, JD magna cum laude, 1989. Bar: N.Y. 1990. Rsch. analyst Brown Bros. Harriman & Co., N.Y.C., 1983-84; pres. FLYERS Svcs. Inc., Cambridge, Mass., 1985-89; assoc. First Boston Corp., N.Y.C., 1989—. Author: F.L.Y.E.R.S., 1985, Youth Trends, 1987. Baker scholar Harvard Bus. Sch., 1989. Mem. Phi Beta Kappa. Roman Catholic. Office: First Boston Corp Park Avenue Pla New York NY 10055

HAMEL, BRUCE ROGER, business executive; b. Laconia, N.H., July 31, 1951; s. Roger Robert and Roxanna (Harmon) H.; m. Marcia Doris Matthews, Oct. 8, 1977; 1 child, Marc Matthew. BS in Bus. Adminstrn., U. N.H., 1977; U. William & Mary, 1983. Plant mgr. Agway Petroleum Corp., Norwich, Vt., 1977-81; dist. mgr. Energy North Inc., Manchester, N.H., 1983-86; pres. The Home Beautivul, Inc., Laconia, N.H., 1986—. Mem. Exchange Club Lakes Region (bd. dirs. 1991-93), Beta Gamma Sigma. Republican. Office: The Home Beautiful Inc RR 1 Box 350 Laconia NH 03246-9126

HAMEL, JAMES VICTOR, engineering consultant; b. Rochester, N.Y., Apr. 21, 1944; s. Victor Joseph and Georgiana (Northrop) H.; m. Elizabeth Ann Mecke, Apr. 7, 1967; 1 child, Omar Quinn. BSCE, U. Pitts., 1965, PhD in Civil Engring., 1970; SMCE, MIT, 1966. Registered profl. engr., Pa., W.Va., Ohio, N.Y., N.J., Minn., S.D., N.D., Mont., Wyo., Ky., geologist, N.C. Rsch. engr. U. Pitts., 1967-69; asst. prof. S.D. Sch. Mines and Tech., Rapid City, 1969-72; cons. U.S. Army Corps Engrs., Omaha, 1970-73; project engr. Gen. Analytics, Inc., Monroeville, Pa., 1972-73; cons. engr. Hamel Geotech. Cons., Monroeville, 1973—. Contbr. articles to profl. jours. Union Carbide scholar, 1961-65; NSF grad. trainee, MIT, 1965-66. Fellow ASCE (bd. dirs. Pitts. sect. 1983-86, Pitts. Civil Engr. of Yr. 1990); mem. Soc. Mining Engrs., Assn. Engring. Geologists, Internat. Assn. Engring. Geology, Internat. Soc. Rock Mechanics, Internat. Soc. Soil Mechanics and Found. Engring., U.S. Comm. on Large Dams. Home and Office: Hamel Geotech Cons 1992 Butler Dr Monroeville PA 15146-3918

HAMER, WALTER JAY, chemical consultant, science writer; b. Altoona, Pa., Nov. 5, 1907; s. Jessie James and Naomi Gertrude (Roland) H.; m. Alma Robinson, Mar. 19, 1941; 1 child, Margaret. BS, Juniata Coll., Huntingdon, Pa., 1929, DSc (hon.), 1966; PhD, Yale U., 1932. Asst. instr. Juniata Coll., 1926-29; postdoctoral fellow Yale U., New Haven, 1932-34;

rsch. assoc. MIT, Cambridge, 1934-35; rsch. chemist Nat. Bur. Standards, Washington, 1935-50, chief electrochemistry, 1950-70, dir. Electrolyte Ctr., 1968-72; chem. cons., Washington, 1972—; adj. prof. Georgetown U., Cath. U., Georgetown U., Cath. U., govt. agys. commerce and agriculture, 1940-50; rsch. chemist Manhattan Project, Washington, 1943-45; adj. examiner Civil Svc. Commn., 1948-50; cons. U.S. Dept. Def., 1951-53; vis. panel mem. Electrochemistry Lab., U. Pa., Phila., 1962-63; lectr. univs. and govt. agys. Author: (monographs) Standard Cells, 1965, Theoretical Activity Coefficients, 1968; co-author: (monograph) Halogen Acids Electrolytic Conductances, 1970; editor: Electrochemical Constants, 1953, The Structure of Electrolytic Solutions, 1959. Recipient cert. of merit Manhattan Project, 1945, OSRD, 1945; Superior Accomplishment award U.S. Dept. Commerce, 1954, 62, 65, Disting. Svc. gold medal, 1966; 1st prize for paper IEEE, 1955. Mem. The Electrochem. Soc., Inc. (hon., v.p. 1960-63, pres. 1963-64, Robert T. Foley award Nat. Capital sect. 1991), Yale Chemists Assn. (pres. 1958-61), Am. Camellia Soc. (accredited judge), Cosmos Club. Republican. Episcopalian. Home and Office: 407 Russell Ave Apt 305 Gaithersburg MD 20877-2829

HAMERMAN, DAVID JAY, gerontologist, educator; b. N.Y.C., Apr. 20, 1925; s. Joseph and Bertha (Broder) H. MD, NYU, 1948. Diplomate Am. Bd. Internal Medicine. Intern Mt. Sinai Hosp., N.Y.C., 1948-49; resident in medicine Mt. Sinai Hosp., Montefiore, N.Y., 1949-51; chief resident in medicine Mt. Sinai Hosp., N.Y.C., 1951-52; dir. arthritis program Albert Einstein Coll. Medicine, N.Y.C., 1956-68, prof. medicine, 1968—; chmn. dept. medicine Montefiore Hosp. Albert Einstein Coll. Medicine, N.Y.C., 1968-79, head div. geriatrics, 1983-89, dir. Resnick Gerontology Ctr., 1990—. Author: Primer on Connective Tissue, 1968; contbr. articles to profl. jours. Capt. U.S. Army, 1953-55. Markle Found. scholar, 1957-62; Sinsheimer Found. fellow, 1963-68, Fogarty Inst. Internat. fellow, 1980-81; recipient Geriatric Leadership Acad. award Nat. Inst. on Aging, 1986—. Fellow ACP; mem. Am. Soc. for Clin. Investigation, Assn. Am. Physicians. Office: Montefiore Med Ctr 111 E 210th St Bronx NY 10467-2490

HAMID, ANSLEY, anthropologist, educator; b. San Fernando, Trinidad, W.I., July 25, 1944; came to U.S., 1973; s. Abdul and Isabella H.; m. Vera Mehta, Oct. 27, 1969 (div. 1980); children: Rahul, Jyotin; m. Vanessa Lee, June 16, 1987; 1 child, Deshana. BA with honors, London Sch. Econs., 1968; MA, MPhil, Columbia U., 1976, MEd, 1977, PhD, 1980. Tchr. Naparima Coll., Trinidad, 1963-65; rsch. asst. Inst. Social Rsch., Bombay, India, 1968-69; edn. officer Ministry Edn., North Ea. State, Nigeria, 1971-73; rsch. asst., rsch. assoc. Columbia U., N.Y.C., 1975-79; rsch. assoc. UN Study Caribbean Migration, N.Y.C., 1982; fellow Rsch. Inst. Study of Man, N.Y.C., 1983—; rsch. scientist N.Y. State Office Mental Health/Psychiat. Inst., N.Y.C., 1985; adj. asst. prof. John Jay Coll. Criminal Justice/CUNY, N.Y.C., 1985-87, prof. anthropology, 1987—; social worker Telegraph Hill Neighbourhood Coun., London, 1970-71, Hale House for Infants, N.Y.C., 1984, Colonial Park Community Svc., Inc., N.Y.C., 1985-87; vis. asst. prof. anthropology NYU, 1981; adj. prof. anthropoogy Borough Manhattan Community Coll., 1985; internal rev. bd. Addiction Rsch. and Treatment Ctr., Bklyn.; presenter at profl. confs. Contbr. to profl. publs. Grantee Ford Found. 1977, NIH 1978, U.S. Dept. Commerce Bur. of Census 1990, 91, Guggenheim Found. 1990, 91. Office: John Jay Coll 445 W 59th St New York NY 10019-1104

HAMILL, ELIZABETH ALLISON (LIZ HAMILL), songwriter; b. Belleville, Ill., Mar. 16, 1959; d. Janet Francis (Becherer) Filardo. BA, Dickinson Coll., 1982; MusM, New Eng. Conservatory Music, 1986. Account exec. WPC, Boston, 1986-88; music tchr. Hamill Music Studio, Cambridge, Mass., 1989—; songwriter Hamillet Music Prodn., Cambridge, Mass., 1988—. Editor: The Advancing Guitarist, 1987; songwriter, co-producer (recording, CD, cassette) Liz Hamill, 1992. Office: Hamillet Music Prodns PO Box 689 Cambridge MA 02238

HAMILTON, ANTHONY ROBERT, public relations executive; b. Brentwood, Essex, Eng., July 1, 1936; came to U.S., 1952; s. Archibald Robert and Pamela Alice (Dawson) H.; m. Judith Redfern, Sept. 5, 1969 (div. 1990); 1 child, Austin. BA in Broadcasting, U. Fla., 1961. Reporter, photographer Sta. WFLA-TV, Tampa, Fla., 1961-69, news mgmt., 1969-79; pub. info. mgr. GTE Fla., Tampa, Fla., 1980-88; dir. media rels. GTE Corp., Stamford, Conn., 1989—. Mem. founding bd. Planned Parenthood Hillsborough County, Tampa, 1985-87; bd. dirs. Mus. Sci. Industry, 1986-88; chmn. Mayor's Franklin St. Mall Adv. Com., Tampa, 1987-88; mem. Mayor's Coun. Youth Drug Abuse, Stamford, 1989-90. Recipient Golden Image award Fla. Pub. Rels. Assn., 1983. Mem. Fairfield County Pub. Rels. Soc. (v.p. 1991-92, pres. 1992—), Soc. Profl. Journalists (chpt. pres. 1965), Radio TV News Dirs. Assn. Republican. Episcopalian. Home: 9 Ralph St Stamford CT 06902-7805 Office: GTE Corp 1 Stamford Forum Stamford CT 06904

HAMILTON, BROOKS WITHAM, retired journalism educator; b. Boston, Dec. 31, 1918; s. Harold Cyrle and Elvyra (Witham) H.; m. Marion Jean Treglown, Mar. 27, 1948; children: Stephen Brooks, Faith Hamilton Griffith, Harold Cyrle II, Pennell W. AB in Polit. Sci., Bates Coll., 1941. Reporter, city editor Daily Kennebec Jour., Augusta, Maine, 1941-47, 52; asst. prof. U. Maine, Orono, 1952-58, assoc. prof., 1958-68, prof., 1968-85, prof. emeritus, 1985—, chmn. faculty senate, 1963-65; exec. editor Maine Pub. Broadcast Network, Orono, 1968-74; cons. on maritime affairs. Author: Mad Hooligan Story, 1989; contbr. articles to profl. jours. With USCG, 1942-46. Fellow New Eng. Acad. Journalists; mem. Soc. Profl. Journalists, Assn. for Edn. in Journalism, Sigma Delta Chi (Yankee Quill award 1982). Home: PO Box 320 Stillwater ME 04489-0320 Office: U Maine 106B Lord Hall Orono ME 04473

HAMILTON, CHRISTOPHER JOHN, health industry executive; b. Bexley, Kent, Eng., Feb. 21, 1947; s. John Philip and Hilda Ivy (Cutts) H.; m. Marian Joyce Clark, Oct. 5, 1968; children: Matthew John, Eleanor Jane. With export sales dept. Marley Tile Co., Sevenoaks, Kent, 1968-70, Amalgamated Dental Co., London, 1970-73; mktg. mgr. Dentsply Internat., London, 1974-76, sales and mktg. dir., 1976-82; internat. sales dir. Dentsply Internat., Weybridge, Eng., 1982-83; gen. mgr. Dentsply Internat., York, Pa., 1986-88; internat. sales and mktg. dir. Ceramco Inc., N.J., 1989—. Mem. Chartered Inst. Mktg., Inst. of Export, British Dental Trade Assn. (exhbn. com. 1982-86). Home: RR 3 Box 205 Dallastown PA 17313-9605 Office: Dentsply Internat 1200 S Pleasant Ave Dallastown PA 17404

HAMILTON, DAVID JOHN, business planning manager; b. Bryn Mawr, Pa., Apr. 28, 1956; s. John A. and Eleanor N. Hamilton; m. Janet Ellen Gardner, Aug. 3, 1986; 1 child, Sara Ashley. BME, U. Del., 1978; MBA, Widener U., Chester, Pa., 1981. Registered profl. engr., Del.; cert. in prodn. and inventory mgmt., cert. computer systems integrator. Prodn. engr. Stuart Pharms., Wilmington, Del., 1978-79, planning asst., 1979; planner, scheduler Stuart Pharms., Newark, 1979-80, supr. inventory and materials control, 1980-83, plant systems coord., 1983-84; prodn. systems adminstr. ICI Pharms., Wilmington, 1984-85; materials mgr. ICI Pharms., Pasadena, Calif., 1985-88; mgr. bus. planning ICI Films, Wilmington, 1988—; instr. Widener U., Chester, 1983-85, 88—; MRP II project leader Stuart Pharms., Wilmington, 1983-85. Author: Cycle Counting: An Approach to Inventory Record Accuracy, 1981; contbr. articles to profl. jours. Mem. Rep. Nat. Com., 1977-81; v.p. Woodside Pines, Arcadia, Calif., 1985-88. Mem. Am. Prodn. and Inventory Control Soc. (v.p. bd. dirs. 1984-85, 89—, instr., 1988, 89), Nat. Soc. Profl. Engrs., Inst. Indsl. Engrs., Am. Soc. Quality Control, Am. Assn. Artificial Intelligence, Del. Assn. Profl. Engrs., Coun. Logistics Mgmt. Republican. Lutheran. Home: 112 Haddington Way Hockessin DE 19707-1810 Office: ICI Americas Inc Concord Pike & New Murphy Wilmington DE 19897

HAMILTON, GEORGE ERNEST III, lawyer, trustee; b. Washington, Oct. 19, 1926; s. George Ernest Jr. and Marian (Hamilton) H.; m. Doreen Wessel Booth, June 26, 1954; children: Winifred, George Ernest IV, Christopher, Merrick. BS, Georgetown U., 1949, JD, 1952. Bar: D.C., Md. Law clk. U.S. Ct. Appeals (D.C. cir.), Washington, 1952-53; asst. U.S. atty. Washington, 1953-55; assoc. Hamilton & Hamilton, Washington, 1955-60, ptnr., 1960-80; pres. Hamilton, P.A., Washington, 1980—; trustee Alexander & Margaret Stewart Trusts, Washington, 1988—. Bd. dirs. Children's Hosp. Nat. Med. Ctr., 1960-83, chmn., pres., 1970-74; bd. dirs., gen. counsel Am. Cancer Soc., Washington, 1959—; bd. dirs. Potomac Sch., 1972-76, Louise Lisner Home, 1987—. With USAF, 1945. Recipient Frank H. Weitzel award Am. Cancer Soc., 1989. Mem. ABA, D.C. Bar Assn., Md. Bar Assn., Montgomery County Bar Assn., Barristers Club, Lawyers Club, Met. Club, Chevy Chase Club (pres. 1987-88), Alfalfa Club, Chesapeake Bay Yacht Club, Talbot Country Club. Home: 3500 Hamlet Pl Chevy Chase MD 20815-4816 Office: 20 Chevy Chase Cir NW Washington DC 20015-2979

HAMILTON, HOWARD BRITTON, engineer, educator; b. Augusta, Kans., Oct. 28, 1923; s. Silas Howard and Ora (Barker) H.; m. Geraldine E. Karr, Jan. 27, 1943; children—Stephen P., Jana L., John V., Christopher H. B.S., U. Okla., 1949; M.S., U. Minn., 1955; Ph.D., Okla. State U., 1962; postgrad., U.S. Army Command and Gen. Staff Coll., 1969, Indsl. Coll. Armed Forces, 1971. Registered profl. engr., Pa., Ohio. Engr. Gen. Electric Co., Schenectady, 1949-53; prof., head elec. engring. dept. U. Wichita, 1955-64; unit chief mfg. research Boeing Co., Wichita, 1958-60; chief of party U. Pitts.-U.S. AID at U. Santa Maria, Valparaiso, Chile, 1964-66; prof., head elec. engring. dept. U. Pitts., 1966-73, prof. engring., 1973-84, chmn., 1984-86, prof. emeritus, 1986—; cons., 1986—; lectr. in power system interconnection, Bogota, Colombia, 1969; Ford Found. cons. U. Santa Maria, 1968; OAS lectr. computer analysis Santa Maria U., Chile, 1972. Author: Power Processing (Electric Machinery Analysis), 1970, Economic Control and Operation, Power Systems, 1971, Experiments and Principles of Systems Engineering, 1971. Served to capt. AUS, World War II; col. Res. ret. Decorated Air medal, Purple Heart; recipient Prisoner of War medal. Fellow IEEE (counselor student br., sec., treas., vice chmn., chmn. Wichita sect., dir., chmn. Pitts. sect. 1972-73, dir. region II, 1977-78, mem.-at-large U.S. activity bd., conduct com. 1979-89, chmn. history com. 1985-88, 92—); mem. Phi Eta Sigma, Eta Kappa Nu, Sigma Tau, Tau Beta Pi. Home: 1422 Oak St Oakmont PA 15139-1014 Office: U Pitts 348 Benedum Hall Pittsburgh PA 15261-2234

HAMILTON, HOWARD HENRY, educational administrator; b. Glen Cove, N.Y., May 27, 1935; s. Howard Henry and Josephine (Coddington) H.; m. Rosemarie Margaret Adinolfi, June 16, 1972; children: Sharon, Francis, Lyn, Marie. BS in Bus. Mgmt., Providence Coll., 1957; MS in Counseling, St. John's U., 1966. Asst. to plant mgr. Circle Wire & Cable Co., Syosset, N.Y., 1958-59; fin. adminstr. Sperry Rand, New Hyde Park, N.Y., 1959-61; asst. admissions, records, fin. aid St. John's U., Jamaica, N.Y., 1961-66; dep. dir. univ. admissions Fairleigh Dickinson U., Rutherford, N.J., 1966-91; pres. Ednl. Svcs. Internat., 1991—; chmn. Becton Dickinson & Co., Internat. Scholarship Com. Chmn. bd. dirs. Psychotherapy Assocs., Bayonne, N.J., 1983—; advisor Circle of K. Kiwanis; pres. Kiwanis Club of Rutherford, 1980-81. Recipient Achievement award Fairleigh Dickinson U., Svc. award Korean Student Assn., 1984. Mem. Nat. Assn. Fgn. Student Advisors, Nat. Assn. Coll. Admission Counselors (Svc. award 1970-75), N.J. Assn. Coll. Admission Counselors (pres. 1981-82, Svc. award 1970-85), Middle States Assn. Collegiate Registrars and Officers of Admission (treas. 1986-87), Hotel and Restaurant Soc. (hon. life), Sigma Pi. Home: 306 N Mountain Ave Montclair NJ 07043-1019

HAMILTON, HUGHBERT CLAYTON, psychologist, educator; b. Cedar Rapids, Iowa, Mar. 6, 1903; s. Leslie S. and H. Belle (Clayton) H.; m. Mildred Eckhardt, May 31, 1940. B.A., Cornell Coll., 1925; M.A., Columbia, 1926, Ph.D., 1929. Mem. faculty Temple U., 1928—, prof. psychology, 1946-70, chmn. dept., 1962-70, dir. psychology lab., 1930-70, editor univ. publs., 1945-69, prof. emeritus, 1970—. Contbr. articles to profl. jours. Fellow Am., Pa. psychol. assns., A.A.A.S.; mem. Eastern Psychol. Assn., Psychonomic Soc., AAUP, Midwestern Psychol. Assn., Sigma Xi. Home: 5720 Wissahickon Ave Philadelphia PA 19144-5606

HAMILTON, J. SCOTT, economic consultant; b. Indpls., Aug. 4, 1961; s. Harry Wayne Hamilton and Bonnie (Jean) Davis; m. Susan Rodgers, Aug. 5, 1990. BA in Econs., Ind. U., 1984. Editorial asst. The Am. Spectator, Washington, 1985-87; sr. policy analyst Assn. Am. R.R., Washington, 1987-90; sr. assoc. DRI/McGraw Hill, Boston, 1990—. Libertarian. Home: 40 Commonwealth Rd Watertown MA 02172-1319 Office: DRI/McGraw Hill 24 Hartwell Ave Lexington MA 02173-3144

HAMILTON, JAMES ARTHUR, biomedical researcher, biophysics educator; b. Lewistown, Pa., Oct. 21, 1947; s. Joseph Arthur and Margaret (Gray) H.; m. Malinda Sue McLendon, May 28, 1983; 1 child, Lianna Renee. BS in Chemistry cum laude, Juniata Coll., 1969; PhD in Chemistry, Ind. U., 1974. Rsch. chemist Eastman Kodak, Rochester, N.Y., 1969; assoc. instr. Ind. U., Bloomington, 1969-74, rsch. asst., 1971-74, asst. prof. continuing edn. chemistry, 1975, postdoctoral fellow, 1976-78; asst. rsch. prof. medicine and biochemistry Boston U. Sch. Medicine, 1978-85, assoc. rsch. prof. medicine and biochemistry, 1986-91, prof. biophysics, 1991—. Assoc. editor Lipids, 1990—; contbr. over 50 articles to profl. jours. Recipient Nat. Rsch. Svc. award NIH, 1976, Shared Instrument grantee, 1990, prin. investigator grantee, 1991-96. Mem. Biophys. Soc., Am. Chem. Soc. Democrat. Presbyterian. Office: Boston U Sch Medicine Biophysics 80 E Concord St Roxbury MA 02118-2394

HAMILTON, JAMES THEODORE, educational management educator; b. Springfield, Ohio, Sept. 16, 1931; s. Thomas Fleming and Emilie (Gebauer) H.; m. Gretchen Worley, June 8, 1957; children: Heidi, Eric, Heather. BA, Miami U., 1953; BS, Ohio State U., 1955, MA, 1956; PhD, Case Western Reserve U., 1963. Prof. ednl. mgmt. Univ. Bridgeport, Conn., 1966—; dir. doctoral program Univ. Bridgeport, 1990—, chmn., dept. ednl. mgmt., 1990—; councillor Atlantic Coun. of U.S., Washington, 1988—; dir. controlled testing ctr. for Miller analogies test and grad. records exam, Univ. Bridgeport, 1970—. Contbr. articles to profl. jours. Chater commn. Town of Fairfield, Conn., 1986. Recipinet six fed. and state grants. Mem. AACD, Am. Ednl. Rsch. Assn., Delta Sigma Phi, Phi Delta Kappa, Pi Gamma Mu, Phi Mu Alpha. Home: 66 Adams Rd Fairfield CT 06430-3018 Office: Dept Ednl Mgmt Univ Bridgeport 380 University Ave Bridgeport CT 06604-5692

HAMILTON, JOHN BRUCE, aerospace company executive; b. Summit, N.J., Sept. 5, 1943; s. John Burns Hamilton and Dorothy (Bucher) Conover; m. Lillian Roberta Gladding, Oct. 10, 1966 (div. June 1983); m. Patricia Ann Smith, Jan. 6, 1986. AB, Dartmouth Coll., 1966. Mgr. Bonwit Teller, N.Y.C., 1966-67, Allied Stores, N.Y.C., 1967-71; dir. Singer Co., N.Y.C. and Wayne, N.J., 1971-75; v.p. Citicorp, N.Y.C., Huntington, N.Y., and New Orleans, 1975-81; v.p. Lillian Vernon Co., Mt. Vernon, N.Y., 1982-85; chief exec. officer C.E. Conover & Co., Fairfield, N.J., 1986—. Office: CE Conover & Co Inc 333 Passaic Ave West Caldwell NJ 07006-8035

HAMILTON, JOSHUA PEARRE, chemical company executive; b. Nashville, July 24, 1938; s. John P. and Susan (Gordon) H.; m. Judith H. Jones, May 27, 1960; children: Sarah Springer, Susan Peck, Virginia. BE, Vanderbilt U., 1960. With prodn. dept. Union Carbide, Texas City, Tex., 1960-71; with distbn. dept. Union Carbide, various locations, 1971-85; dir. of quality splty. chems. div. Union Carbide, Danbury, Conn., 1985—. 1st It. USAR, 1960-68. Conservative. Methodist. Home: 181 Mimosa Cir Ridgefield CT 06877

HAMILTON, LISA, advertising manager; b. Bridgeport, Conn., Jan. 8, 1961; d. James J. and Margaret M. (Bachmann) Otzel; 1 child, Gary James. AA, Lasell Coll., 1981. Advt. artist Post Pub. Co., Bridgeport, 1981-84; advt. sales account exec. Bridgeport Post Newspaper, 1984-89, life mgr., 1989-90, retail advt. mgr., 1990—. Mem. christian edn. com. Lordship Community Ch., Stratford, Conn., 1989—. Mem. New Eng. Newspaper Assn. Home: 235 Reed St Stratford CT 06497-3524 Office: Post Pub Co 410 State St Bridgeport CT 06604-4560

HAMILTON, PATRICIA ANN, magazine editor, writer; b. Chgo., Sept. 15, 1930; d. Charles Anson and Anna (Critchfield) Wardley; m. Lloyd Alexander Hamilton Jr., Aug. 23, 1952; children: Diana Hope, Lloyd Alexander III, Andrea Margeurite. AB, Conn. Coll., 1962; MA, Columbia U., 1972. Copywriter Houghton Mifflin Co., Boston, 1952-54, Kenyon & Eckhardt, San Francisco, 1954-55, William Morrow Co., N.Y.C., 1955-57; editor, writer Editors Unltd., Greenwich, Conn., 1970-79; editor D&B Reports mag. Dun & Bradstreet Corp., N.Y.C., 1979—. Contbr. articles to New York Times. Mem. bd. of visitors Walnut Hill Sch., Natick, Mass., 1991. Mem. Am. Soc. Mag. Editors, Pequot Yacht Club. Home: 180 River Rd Nyack NY 10960-4904 Office: Dun & Bradstreet Corp 299 Park Ave New York NY 10171-0002

HAMILTON, RICHARD FREEMAN, tourism association executive; b. North Conway, N.H., Feb. 13, 1936; s. Carroll Eastman and Esther (Brackett) H.; m. Sandra Elaine Hakanson, Aug. 25, 1962; children: Lisa Ann, Trevor Alan, Scott Andrew. Grad. high sch., Conway, N.H. Sales mgr. Ea. Slope Inn, North Conway, 1960-63; asst. mgr. Indianhead Ski Resort, Bessemer, Mich., 1963-66; exec. dir. Ski 93 Assn., Lincoln, N.H., 1966-70; pres. White Mountains Attractions Assn., North Woodstock, N.H., 1970—; v.p. Attractions Svcs. Corp., North Woodstock, 1971—; mgr. White Mountains News Bur., North Woodstock, 1972—; pres. Ski The White Mountains Assn., North Woodstock, 1976—. Photo editor: Saving Great Stone Face, 1984; author, photographer: N.H. Scenes and Seasons, 1989. Recipient Appreciation/Recognition award Woodstock (N.H.) Vitalization Assn., 1985; named N.E. Travel Person of Yr., Yankee Mag., Dublin, N.H., 1986. Mem. Nat. Press Photographers Assn., Nat. Stereoscopic Assn., Ea. Ski Writers Assn., Soc. Am. Travel Writers, Assn. Travel Mktg. Execs. (cert.), N.H. Travel Coun. (founder, bd. dirs., pres. 1973-81, N.H. Travel Person of Yr. 1982), New England U.S.A. Found. (bd. dirs., pres. 1985-87), Coun. Regional Execs., N.H. Hist. Soc., Lincoln-Woodstock Rotary. Republican. Episcopalian. Home: 11 Woodside Ave Littleton NH 03561-2811 Office: White Mountains Attractions Rt 112 North Woodstock NH 03262

HAMILTON, ROBERT WILLIAM, physiologist; b. Stanton, Tex., June 5, 1930; s. Robert William and Lois Rogers H.; m. Beverly Luth Cooper, Jan. 23, 1954 (dec. 1970); children: Kitty, Lucy Hamilton Kantor, Sally; m. Kathryn Ann Faulkner, 1972. BA, U. Tex., 1951; MS, Tex. A&M, 1958; PhD, U. Minn., 1964. Lab. mgr., investigator Union Carbide Corp., Tarrytown, N.Y., 1964-75; v.p. R&D Tarrytown Labs., Ltd., 1975-76; cons., pres. Hamilton Rsch., Ltd., Tarrytown, 1976—; cons., researcher NOAA, USN, USAF, NAASA, OSHA, 1964—; cons. Japanese Maritime S-D Force, Yokosuka, 1989—, Swedish Navy, Horsfjerden, 1978—, German GKSS Lab., Geesthacht, 1980-91. Editor (symposium proc.) Decompression from Deep Dives, 1976; author: (with others) Encyclopedia Britannica, 1970; co-author: DCAP Decompression Computation Program and Manual, 1980—; co-inventor, patentee neon as a diving gas. Scoutleader Explorers, Anchorage, 1951-55; vestry warden Christ Episcopal Ch., Tarrytown, 1977-80, 90—; exec. com., sec. Undersea/Hyperbaric Med. Soc., Bethesda, Md., 1981-86, 90; committeeman Nat. Fire Protection Assn., Boston, 1988—. Maj. USAF, 1951-55, 68-69, Vietnam. Decorated DFC; recipient Stover-Link award Undersea Med. Soc., 1977, Award for Profl. Excellence, Aerospace Indsl. Life Scis. Assn., 1972, Oceaneering award Undersea/Hyperbaric Med. Soc., 1988./. Mem. Undersea Med. Soc. (charter, awards 1977, 88), Aerospace Med. Assn. (committeeman), N.Y. Acad. Scis. (sect. chair 1975-75), Am. Physiology Soc. European Undersea Biomed. Soc., South Pacific Underwater Med. Soc., Inst. of Diving. Democrat. Episcopalian. Home and Office: 80 Grove St Tarrytown NY 10591-4138

HAMILTON, THOMAS MICHAEL, marketing executive; b. Bronxville, N.Y., Jan. 8, 1947; s. Harold Thomas and Mary Theresa (Byrne) H.; m. Kathryn Borys, May 24, 1984. BS, SUNY, Buffalo. Sales mgr. Herk, Inc., N.Y.C., 1971-73; account exec. William Esty Co., Inc., N.Y.C., 1973-77, account supr., 1977-80, v.p., assoc. dir. sales promotion, 1980-83, sr. v.p., dir. sales promotion, 1983-88; pres. Hamilton Promotions, Inc., Katonah, N.Y., 1988-89; v.p. mktg. Harrington, Righter & Parsons Inc., N.Y.C., 1989—. Fundraiser United Way of Greater N.Y., 1976-84; council mem. HIP Consumer Council, N.Y.C., 1985; mem. North East Katonah (N.Y.) Community League, 1987—. Served to 1st lt. USAF, 1968-71. Mem. Mktg. Communications Execs. Internat. (bd. dirs. 1983-86), Promotion Mktg. Assn. Am. (bd. dirs. 1986—, exec. com. 1987—, vice-chmn. 1989-90, chmn.-elect 1990-91, chmn. bd. 1991—). Office: Harrington Righter Parsons 110 E 59th St New York NY 10022-1304

HAMILTON, WILLIAM ERNEST,
Dec. 11, 1951; s. Zeb Thomas and Irene (Hinners) H.; m. Deborah Yvett Sillman, Dec. 18, 1982; children: Marian Irene, Joseph Zebulon. BS, Tex. Tech. U., 1974; MS, Ohio State U., 1979; PhD, SUNY, Syracuse, 1983. Rsch. assoc. SUNY, Syracuse, 1979-82; instr. Onondoga Community Coll., Syracuse, 1982-83; asst. prof. biology Pa. State U., New Kensington, Pa., 1983—. Contbr. articles to profl. jours. Mem. U.S. Soil Ecology Soc. Office: Pa State Univ 3550 7th Street Rd New Kensington PA 15068-1798

HAMLEN, ROBERT PAUL, physical chemist; b. Newark, Oct. 1, 1929; s. Paul F. and Frances M. (Mears) H.; m. Jean L. Gleisner, Dec. 27, 1952; children: Kathleen, Richard, William, Michele. BS in Chemistry, Lafayette Coll., 1951; PhD in Phys. Chemistry, John Hopkins U., 1956; postgrad., Harvard U., 1978. Rsch. scientist Linde div. Union Carbide, Tonawanda, N.Y., 1956-60; staff mem., then mgr. electrochemistry GE R & D Ctr., Schenectady, N.Y., 1960-73; lab. dir., then gen. battery div. Exxon Enterprises, Linden, N.J., 1973-82; founder, pres. Alupower, Inc. div. Alcan Aluminum Ltd., Bernardsville, N.J., 1983-90, sr. cons., 1990-92; dir. Power Sources div. U.S. Army Electronics Tech. & Devices Lab, Ft. Monmouth, N.J., 1992—; speaker in field. Contbr. articles to profl. publs.; patentee in field. Mem. Am. Chem. Soc., Electrochem. Soc. Home: 15 Harvey Dr Bernardsville NJ 07924-1803 Office: US Army ET&D Lab SLCET-P Fort Monmouth NJ 07703-5601

HAMLETT, JAMES GORDON, electronics engineer, management consultant and educator; b. Utica, N.Y.. BSEE, Syracuse U., 1947-49; BSBA, SUNY, Syracuse, 1985; MBA, City U., Seattle, 1991. Cert. vocat. edn. tchr., N.Y. Engr.-writer Warner, N.Y., Inc., Syracuse, 1952-54; vocation edn. tchr. evenings adult edn. Syracuse Cen. Tech. High Sch., 1956-62; project leader GE, Syracuse, 1955-90; mgmt. cons. Syracuse, 1990—; vol. job interview cons. to laid off employees GE, 1991—; lectr. Syracuse U., 1980-81, Queens U., Kingston, Ont., Can., 1976; presenter in field. Author: Your Television Set, 1953, Engineering-Related Abbreviations, 1980-84 (VIP award 1980); editor Syracuse SCANNER, IEEE, 1959-68. Prin. Flood Contorl Com., Town of Onondaga, N.Y., 1962; tennis coach U.S. Jaycees, North Syracuse, N.Y., 1968; mem. steering com., sec., exec. com. L.C. Smith Coll. Engring. and Computer Sci, Syracuse U. With U.S. Army, 1942-45, ETO. Fellow Soc. for Tech. Communications (internat. stem mgr. 1980, exec. com.); mem. IEEE (life sr., exec. com., Cert. 1981), Entrepreneurs of Am., N.Y. Acad. Scis. (cert. 1985), Am. Mgmt. Assn., Syracuse GE Engrs. Assn., Syracuse U. Alumni Assn., Empire State Coll. Alumni Assn. (pes. Syracuse area alumni/student assn.),City U. Alumni (life), Vets. Battle of the Bulge (life, historian, treas.). Home: 330 Everingham Rd Syracuse NY 13205-3258

HAMLIN, CARY LEE, psychiatry educator, psychopharmacologist; b. Port Allegany, Pa., Oct. 15, 1949; s. Leon Cary and Dorothy Jane (Doll) H.; m. Elizabeth Carr, July 3, 1977; children: Karin, Jane Kiley, Adam. BS in Chemistry, U. Pitts., 1971, MD, 1975; diploma in Psychiatry, Dartmouth U., 1978. Diplomate Am. Bd. Psychiatry and Neurology. Resident in internal medicine Robert Wood Johnson Med. Sch., Piscataway, N.J., 1979-80; asst. clin. prof. Psychiatry U. N.J., Piscataway, 1980-86; pvt. practice Chester, N.J., 1986—; mem. Psychiatry staff Morristown (N.J.) Meml. Hosp., 1983—; asst. clin. prof. Columbia U., N.Y.C., 1986—; dir. anxiety clinic Fair Oaks Hosp., Summit, N.J., 1982-86, assoc. dir. outpatient rsch., 1983-86. Sr. author (book chpt.) Anxiolytics—Response Predictions, 1984; contbr. articles to profl. jours. Mem. AAAS, Am. Psychiat. Assn. Office: 500 Rte 24 Chester NJ 07930

HAMMACK, FLOYD MORGAN, sociology educator; b. Vancouver, Wash., Dec. 2, 1944; s. Charles Wesley and Dorothy (Morgan) H.; m. Nancy Marie Walker, Apr. 9, 1977; children: Andrew, Philip. BA, U. Oreg., 1966, MA, 1969; PhD, Fla. State U., 1973. Instr. NYU, N.Y.C., 1971-72, asst. prof., 1972-79, assoc. prof. ednl. sociology, 1979—; co-chair seminar on higher edn. Columbia U., N.Y.C., 1988—. Co-editor: Education and Society, 1990; contbr. articles to profl. publs. Office: NYU 300 East Bldg New York NY 10003

HAMMEL, EILEEN NOEL, business owner; b. Phila., Nov. 28, 1964; d. John William and Joan Barbara (Kennedy) H. Grad. high sch., Phila. Asst. mgr. Enterprise Six Corp., Upper Darby, Pa., 1983-84, mgr., 1984-85, fashion cons., coord., 1985-87; beauty and fashion image cons. Tim

Mahoney, N.Y.C., 1987-89; founder, pres. Perfect Style, Phila., 1985—; fashion image curriculum adviser U. Ohio, 1990. Author: (manual) The Perfect Image, 1985, Perfect Make-up Magic, 1990; contbr. articles to profl. publs. Fundraiser Patti Cassidy Forsyth Fund, Swarthmore, Pa., 1990; campaigner Dem. Orgn., Phila., 1983-85. Mem. Assn. Fashion and Image Cons., Internat. Platform Soc. Roman Catholic. Office: Perfect Style 7616 City Line Ave Ste 220 Philadelphia PA 19151-2007

HAMMEL, FRANK ELLIOTT, writer; b. Auburn, N.Y., Sept. 15, 1959; s. John Elliott and Mary Beatty (Sutter) H.; m. Munn Harris, Nov. 29, 1980; 1 child, Martha Ann. BA, U. S. Fla., 1982; MSJ, Columbia U., 1984. Mng. editor Ski Bus., Ski New Eng., Darien, Conn., 1987-89; assoc. editor Supermarket Bus., N.Y.C., 1985-87. contbr. articles to Snow Country, Ski Bus., Supermarket Bus.; freelance writer N.Y. Times, The Advocate, The Fairfield County Advocate. Recipient Jesse H. Neal award, Assn. Bus. Pubrs., 1991, Cert. of Merit, 1989, 90. Mem. N. Am. Ski Journalists Assn., Ea. Ski Writers Assn. Home: 46 W 71st St # 3A New York NY 10023-4225

HAMMELL, THOMAS JAMES, engineering psychologist, educator; b. New Brunswick, N.J., May 8, 1944; s. Arthur Francis and Margaret Regina (O'Reilly) H.; m. Ruth Karoline Haberkern, June 29, 1968; children: Thomas James, Darren Richard. B in Engring., Stevens Inst. Tech., Hoboken, N.J., 1966, M of Mgmt. Sci., 1968; PhD in Psychology, U. Conn., 1974. Sr. rsch. psychologist electric boat div. Gen. Dynamics, Groton, Conn., 1968-73; v.p. R & D, gen. mgr. elec. assocs. div. Ship Analytics, Inc., North Stonington, Conn., 1973-88; pres., chief scientist Paradigm Assocs., East Lyme, Conn., 1988—; mem. adj. faculty dept. psychology U. Conn., Groton, 1981—; sr. staff cons. Nat. Maritime Rsch. Ctr., Kings Point, N.Y., 1974-87; mem. panel, industry chmn. NRC, NAS, Washington, 1984; chmn. various profl. worldwide conf. sessions, 1980-90; expert witness on human factors for various legal firms, 1991; cons. Port of Rotterdam, The Netherlands, 1990—. Contbr. numerous articles to profl. publs. Mem. Am. Psychol. Assn., Human Factors Soc. Office: Paradigm Assocs 35 Heritage Rd East Lyme CT 06333-1109

HAMMEN, CARL SCHLEE, zoology educator; b. Newark, Aug. 26, 1923; s. Roy Merrill and Bertha Ida (Schlee) H.; m. Edna Ruth Graham, 1949 (div. 1961); children: Charles Scott, Carol Graham; m. Susan Chandler Lum, Oct. 13, 1962; children: Ralph (dec.), John, Elizabeth. BA, St. John's Coll., Annapolis, Md., 1947; MA, Columbia U., 1949; MS in Biol. Scis., U. Chgo., 1952; PhD in Zoology and Biochemistry, Duke U., 1958. Instr. biology and chemistry Mitchell Coll., Statesville, N.C., 1949-51; prof. biology and math. Cedarville (Ohio) Coll., 1952-53; biologist VA Hosp., Martinsburg, W.Va., 1953-54, Army Chem. Ctr., Edgewood, Md., 1954-56; assoc. prof. biology Newark State Coll., Union, N.J., 1958-60, Adelphi Coll., Garden City, N.Y., 1960-63; assoc. prof. zoology U. R.I., Kingston, 1963-71, prof. zoology, 1971—. Author: (book) Elementary Quantitative Biology, 1972, German translation, 1975, Japanese translation, 1976, Marine Invertebrates: Comparative Physiology, 1980; contbr. 49 tech. papers and rev. articles to profl. publs. Lt. (j.g.) USN, 1943-46, PTO. Rsch. grantee (3 instns.) NSF, 1959-66, U. R.I. rsch. com., 1972, 79; Noyes Found. fellow U. Chgo., 1952; NSF postdoctoral fellow Duke U. Marine Lab., 1959, 63; Fulbright scholar, Morocco, 1984. Mem. Am. Physiol. Soc., Am. Soc. Zoologists, Sigma Xi. Office: U RI Dept Zoology Kingston RI 02881

HAMMER, THOMAS ALLEN, trade association executive; b. Houston, Aug. 15, 1947; s. Lloyd Allen Jr. and Charlotte (Hinds) H.; m. Jennifer Florer, Dec. 27, 1969; children: Adam Thomas, Samantha Jeneane. BA in History, Marietta (Ohio) Coll., 1969; MBA in Fin., George Washington U., 1974. Asst. cashier, br. mgr. First Va. Bank, Falls Church, 1970-74; economist Mitsubishi Internat. Corp., Washington, 1974-75; asst. dir. nat. affairs Am. Farm Bur. Fedn., Washington, 1975-78; govt. rels. advisor Nelson & Harding, Washington, 1978-80, Pope, Ballard & Loos, Washington, 1980; exec. asst. for transition U.S. Dept. Agr., Washington, 1980-81, dep. asst. sec. for internat. affairs and commodity programs, 1981-82; govt. rels. advisor Heron, Burchette, Ruckert & Rothwell, Washington, 1982-87; pres. Sweetener Users Assn., Washington, 1987—. Contbr. articles to profl. jours. Pres. bd. trustees The Barker Found., Washington, 1991—. Lt. (j.g.) USN, 1969-70. Mem. Commodity Club Washington, Sugar Club, Food Group. Republican. Episcopalian. Home: 3231 Valley Ln Falls Church VA 22044 Office: Sweetener Users Assn 2100 Pennsylvania Ave NW Washington DC 20037

HAMMERMAN, DAVID LEWIS, biology educator; b. Bklyn., Dec. 19, 1935; s. Sam and Gertrude (Sussman) H.; m. Gail Stern, Dec. 22, 1963; children: Craig, Robin, Evan. BS, CCNY, 1957; MS, NYU, 1959, PhD, 1962. Rsch. asst. dept. medicine NYU, N.Y.C., 1958-59, fellow dept. biology, 1959-62, instr. dept. biology, 1962; asst. prof. dept. biology L.I. U., Bklyn., 1962-66, assoc. prof. dept. biology, 1966-71, prof. dept. biology, 1971—; cons. div. natural history Bklyn. Inst. Arts and Sci., 1963, Ednl. Testing Svc., Princeton, N.J., 1977-85, W. B. Saunders, Phila., 1990; mem. adv. com. on higher edn. 13th Congl. Dist., Bklyn., 1968-70. Author: Laboratory Exercises in Physiology, Laboratory Exercises in Advanced Vertebrate Physiology, Case Studies in Pathology, Laboratory Exercises in Pathophysiology; contbr. articles to profl. jours. Grantee NSF, 1969, 72, U.S. Office Edn., 1971-72. Mem. AAAS, Am. Soc. Zoologists, Niagara Soc., Sigma Xi. Office: Long Island Univ Dept Biology Brooklyn NY 11201

HAMMETT, JAMES LINCOLN, JR., business and computer consultant; b. Willimantic, Conn., Aug. 2, 1943; s. James Lincoln and Kathryn Wesley (Campbell) H. BSME, Worchester (Mass.) Poly., 1965; MSME, Cornell U., 1966; MBA, Babson Coll., 1977. Systems engr. Exxon Rsch. and Engring., Florham Park, N.J., 1966-73; sr. sales application engr. The Foxboro (Mass) Co., 1973-77; mktg. mgr. Tesdata Inmet, Indian Harbour Beach, Fla., 1977-78; dir. corp. planning EMC Controls, Hunt Valley, Md., 1978-82; pres. Entre Computer Ctr., Timonium, Md., 1982-89, Systems Internat., Timonium, 1990—. Vice pres. Oreg. Ridge Nature Ctr., Hunt Valley, Md., 1990—. Office: Systems Internat 221 Deer Fox Ln Lutherville Timonium MD 21093-4342

HAMMOND, DUANE ALLEN, graphic designer, consultant; b. Nashua, N.H., Nov. 3, 1940; s. Robert Lee and Lilla (Watson) H.; m. Sandra Rines; children: Donna May, Lorrie Lee, Brian David. AS, Mus. Sch. Fine Arts, 1964. Art dir. Daniel Eneguess Assocs., Peterboro, N.H., 1964-65, Drum Advt., Jaffrey, N.H., 1965-66; asst. art dir. Graf & Co., Boston, 1966-68; pres., chief exec. officer Hammond Design Assoc., Milford, N.H., 1968—. Mem. Zoning Bd. Adjustment, Milford, N.H., 1989-91; chmn. Souhegan Valley Assn. for the Handicapped, Amherst, N.H., 1988-92. With U.S. Army, 1959-67. Recipient of more than 50 1st pl. awards in graphic excellence from advt. and graphic assns., 1984-91. Mem. Rotary, Advt. Club of N.H. (Best of Show Design award 1982, 86), Creative Club of N.H., Boston Art Dirs. Club. Democrat. Unitarian Universalist. Home: 1 Chestnut St Milford NH 03055-3806 Office: Hammond Design Assoc 79 Amherst St Milford NH 03055-4031

HAMMOND, ELEANOR AGNES MERRIAM, historical society curator; b. Long Beach, Calif., July 25, 1924; d. Walter Scott Merriam and Grace Lavinia (Carpenter) Merriam Atwood; m. John Stephen Hammond, July 27, 1952 (div. 1965); children: Beth Ellen, Laura Jean Hammond Kulmala. AB, Wheaton Coll., 1946; AM, Mt. Holyoke Coll., 1947; postgrad., Bridgewater State Coll., 1967-75. Tchr. Northfield (Mass.) High Sch., 1947-54, Greenfield (Mass.) High Sch., 1963-64, Middleborough (Mass.) High Sch., 1964-69; libr. Meml. Jr. High Sch., Middleborough, 1969-86; curator Aptucxet Trading Post Mus./Bourne (Mass.) Hist. Soc., 1989—; speaker in field. Mem. Monument Beach (Mass.) Civic Assn., 1985—, Friends of Coun. on Aging, Bourne, 1991—. Mem. Wareham Bus. and Profl. Woman's Orgn. (pres. 1980-83, Bus. Woman of Yr. 1989), Mass. Fedn. Bus. and Profl. Women Found. (state chair 1985-86), Mass. Fedn. Bus. and Profl. Women (state chair coun. on future of women in workplace 1987-91, dist. nominating com. chmn. 1991-92), Mass. Archaeol. Soc. (state edn. chmn. 1991—), Aptucxet Garden Club (awards chair 1991—). Office: Aptucxet Trading Post Mus Aptucxet Rd Buzzards Bay MA 02532-5434

HAMMOND, JANE LAURA, law librarian, lawyer; b. nr. Nashua, Iowa; d. Frank D. and Pauline (Flint) H. B.A., U. Dubuque, 1950; M.S., Columbia U., 1952; J.D., Villanova U., 1965. Bar: Pa. 1965. Cataloguer Harvard Law Library, 1952-54; asst. librarian Sch. Law, Villanova (Pa.) U., 1954-62, librarian, 1962-76, prof. law, 1965-76; law librarian, prof. law Cornell U., Ithaca, N.Y., 1976—; adj. prof. Drexel U., 1971-74; mem. depository library council to pub. printer U.S. Govt. Printing Office, 1975-78; con. Nat. Law Library, Monrovia, Liberia, 1989. Fellow Am. Libr.Assn.; mem. Am. Assn. Law Librs.(sec. 1965-70, pres. 1975-76), Coun. Nat. Libr. Assn. (sec.-treas. 1971-72, chmn. 1979-80), ALA, ABA (com. on accreditation 1982-87, coun. sect. legal edn. 1984-90), PEO. Episcopalian. Office: Cornell Law Libr Myron Taylor Hall Ithaca NY 14853

HAMMOND, RED, artist; b. Niagara Falls, N.Y., Sept. 26, 1947; s. Norman Louis and Virginia (Finley) H.; m. Meryl Rebecca Dunn, July 1, 1970 (div. Sept. 1984); m. Anne Marlin Baxter, Oct. 17, 1987. BFA, SUNY, Buffalo, 1970. Affiliate Salander-O'Reilly Galleries, Inc., N.Y.C., 1970—; vis. artist San Francisco Art Inst., 1982, U. Wis., Madison, 1984, U. Buffalo, 1986, U. Maine, Portland, 1990-91. With U.S. Army, 1967-69. Grantee NEA, 1981-82, 87-88, Gottlief Found., 1990. Mem. Franklin Broadway Loft Residence Assn. (pres. N.Y.C. chpt. 1991—), Downtown Washington Market Assn. (bd. dirs. N.Y.C. chpt. 1991—). Home: 54 Franklin St New York NY 10013-4009

HAMOSH, MARGIT, biology educator; b. Dresden, Germany, Aug. 13, 1933; came to U.S., 1965; d. Jacob Katz and Clara (Heitner) Segenreich; m. Paul Hamosh, Oct. 21, 1954; children: Ada, Leora Y., Tamar D. MS in Microbiology, Hebrew U., Jerusalem, 1956, PhD in Biochemistry, 1959. Instr. biochemistry Hadassah med. Sch., Hebrew U., 1961-64, asst. prof. biochemistry, 1964-65; vis. scientist NIMH, 1965-67, NIH, NIAMD, Bethesda, Md., 1967-74; asst. prof. anatomy Med. Ctr., Georgetown U., Washington, 1974-76, rsch. assoc. in physiology and biophysics, 1976-79, assoc. prof. pediatrics, 1979-84, prof. pediatrics, 1984—, chief div. devel. biol. nutrition, 1988; mem. pulmonary disease adv. com. NHLBI-NIH, Bethesda, 1980-84; mem. maternal child rsch. com. NICHD-NIH, Bethesda, 1986-90; chmn. nutrition during lactation com. Nat. Acad. Scis., Washington, 1988-90, mem. nutrition during pregnancy and lactation com., 1989-92; mem. editorial bd. Nutrition, Jour. Pediatric Gastro Nutrition, Biol. Neonate; vis. prof. Heritage Found., Can., 1985. Author: Lingual and Gastric Lipases, 1990; editor: Human Lactation, Vol. 2, 1986; contbr. articles to profl. jours., chpts. to books. Advisor Project Hope, Child Hosp., Crackow, Poland, 1985. Named Hon. Citizen, City of Oaxaca, Mex., 1986. Mem. Am. Thoracic Soc. (mem. nat. rsch. rev. ctr. 1984-90), Am. Coll. Nutrition (editorial bd., mem. pediatrics coun. 1982-84), Am. Fedn. Clin. Rsch., Am. Inst. Nutrition, Am. Physiol. Soc., Am. Soc. Clin. Nutrition, Endocrine Soc., Perinatal Rsch. Soc. (mem. coun. 1983-85), Internat. Soc. Rsch. Human Milk Lactation (pres. 1987-89). Democrat. Jewish. Office: Georgetown U Pediatric Dept 3800 Reservoir Rd NW Washington DC 20007

HAMPAR, BERGE, molecular scientist; b. N.Y.C., Aug. 20, 1932; s. Yervant and Dikranouhi (Antreasian) H.; m. Nancy C. Tucker, July 11, 1977 (div. 1987). BA, Columbia U., 1954, DDS, 1960; JD, U. Balt., 1984. Bar: Md. 1985, D.C. 1988. Postdoctoral Columbia U., N.Y.C., 1960-62; scientist Nat. Inst. Dental Rsch., NIH, Bethesda, Md., 1962-67; dir. grade Nat. Cancer Inst. NIH, Bethesda, Md., 1967-86; pres. Bio-Molecular Tech., Inc., Frederick, Md., 1986—. Contbr. over 70 articles to publs. Lt. (j.g.) USN, 1954-56. Mem. Am. Assn. Immunology, Am. Soc. Virology. Office: Bio-Molecular Tech Inc 5340 Spectrum Dr Frederick MD 21701-7337

HAMPSON, MARY JOAN, microbiologist; b. Buffalo, Apr. 18, 1947; d. Allan James and Marian Anita (Tripodi) Williams; m. Augustua D., June 21, 1967 (div. 1975); children: Augustus, Rebecca. BS, Quinnipiac Coll., Hamden, Conn., 1972. With Miles, Inc., West Haven, Conn., 1976—; mgr. quality assurance standards Miles, Inc., 1984—; cons. in field. Bd. dirs. Friends of Orch. New England, New Haven, 1985-86, treas., 1986-90. Mem. Am. Soc. Microbiology, Soc. Indsl. Microbiology, Perenteral Drug Assn., Artspace (bd. dirs., v.p. fin. 1988—), Jr. League, Yale Figure Skating Club (pres., treas., bd. dirs. 1984—), New Haven Symphony Orch. (bd. dirs. 1991—). Republican. Roman Catholic. Office: Miles Inc Pharm Div 400 Morgan Ln West Haven CT 06516-4175

HAMPSON, THOMAS LEE, church organization executive; b. Oakdale, Calif., Nov. 17, 1948; s. Lee G. and Margaret (Crumpacker) H.; m. Anita Morano; 1 child, Thomas D. BA, U. Notre dame, 1971, MA, 1973; MA in Edn., Washington U., St. Louis, 1982. Tchr. St. Joseph's High Sch., South Bend, Ind., 1975-81; assoc. dir. Office on Global Edn., Ch. World Svc., Balt., 1982—. Co-author: Make a World of Difference, 1989, Tales of the Heart, 1990; contbr. articles to various periodicals. Mem. devel. edn. com. Interaction, 1984-89; chmn. nat. adv. com. World Food Day, Washington, 1988-89; chmn. social action com. Corpus Christi Ch., Balt., 1983-88. Recipient Tchr. of Yr. award St. Joseph High Sch., 1980, Social Justice award Midwest chpt. Order of St. Joseph, 1980, Wilber award for Make A World of Difference Religious Pub. Rels. Coun., 1990. Mem. Nat. Assn. Ecumenical Staffs, Nat. Assn. for Social Studies Edn., Nat. Assn. for Curriculum Devel. Democrat. Roman Catholic. Office: Ch World Svc 2115 N Charles St Baltimore MD 21218

HAMPTON, MARK, interior designer; b. Indpls., June 1, 1940; s. Mark and Alice (Burkert) H.; m. Duane Flegel, July 11, 1964; children: Catharine, Alexa. Student, London Sch. Econs., 1961; BA, DePauw U., 1962; MFA, N.Y. Inst. Fine Arts, 1967; DFA, DePauw U., 1986. Cert. A.S.I.D. With David Hicks, London, 1961, Mrs. Henry Parish II, N.Y.C., 1962-63, McMillen, Inc., N.Y.C., 1969-75; pres. Mark Hampton Inc., N.Y.C., 1976—; restorer-decorator White House, Washington, Blair House, Washington, Gov.'s Mansion, Albany, N.Y., Gracie Mansion, N.Y.C., Nat. Gallery of Art, Washington, Nat. Acad. Design, N.Y.C., Am. Acad., Rome, Camp David, v.p.'s home, Washington, various pvt. houses, apts., hotels, offices, trains, boats, planes. Author, illustrator: Mark Hampton on Decorating, 1989 (Book-of-the-Month Club selection 1989); illustrator: Apple's Europe. Trustee Am. Acad. in Rome. Mem. Am. Soc. Interior Designers, Com. for the Preservation of the White House. Mem. Soc. of Friends. Home: 1001 Park Ave New York NY 10028-0935 Office: Mark Hampton Inc 654 Madison Ave New York NY 10021-8404

HANACHÉ, MARIE ADELE, physician; b. N.Y.C., Aug. 9, 1932; d. Jean élie and Marjorie (Yabroudi) H.; divorced; children: Marjorie DeVries, Suzanne Sullivan, William DeVries, Patricia DeVries, Jennifer DeVries. BA, Coll. New Rochelle, 1953; MD, George Washington U., 1957. Intern Nassau County Med. Ctr. (formerly Meadowbrook Hosp.), 1957-58; physician VA Hosp., Amarillo, Tex., 1958-60; pvt. practice Jericho, N.Y., 1961-69, Rockville Ctr., N.Y., 1983-89; med. dir. Carle Pl. (N.Y.) Schs., Union Free Sch. Dist. #11, 1961—, Hofstra U., Hempstead, N.Y., 1986—; cons. physician A. Holly Patterson Geriatric Ctr., Uniondale, N.Y., 1970-91. Mem. AMA, Am. Acad. Family Practice, Am. Coll. Health Assn., Med. Soc. N.Y. State, Nassau County Med. Soc. Roman Catholic. Office: Hofstra Univ 1000 Fulton Ave Hempstead NY 11550

HANBURY, RAYMOND FRANCIS, JR., psychologist, consultant; b. Jersey City, Mar. 28, 1945; s. Raymond Francis and Rose Ann (Doorley) H.; m. Patricia Ann Delaney, Mar. 9, 1974; children: Amy, Kim. BS, St. Peter's Coll., 1967; MA, Seton Hall U., 1969; PhD, NYU, 1980. Lic. psychologist, N.J.; diplomate, fellow Am. Bd. Med. Psychotherapists; diplomate Am. Bd. Vocat. Experts; cert. addictions specialist, rehab. counselor. Adj. asst. prof. dept. psychiatry Mt. Sinai Sch. Medicine, N.Y.C., 1980—; pvt. practice Manasquan, N.J., 1989; dir. clin. svcs. Mt. Sinai Med. Ctr., N.Y.C., 1970-90; dir. rehab. psychology dept. JFK Johnson Rehab. Inst., Edison, N.J., 1990—; adj. asst. prof. psychology Pace U., White Plains, N.Y., 1980-82; cons. Spring Lake Heights (N.J.) Police Dept., 1989—, VA Med. Ctr., Bronx, N.Y., 1978-79; crisis intervention specialist Mid-Bergen Community Mental Health Ctr., Paramus, N.Y., 1980-89; clin. dir. critical incident stress debriefing team Monmouth-Ocean County, N.J., 1990—. Cons. editor Psychology Addictive Behaviors, 1987—; mem. editorial bd. Advances in Alcohol and Substance Abuse, 1990—; contbr. articles to profl. jours. Fellow Rehab. Svcs. Adminstrn., 1967-69. Mem. APA, N.J. Psychol. Assn., N.J. Acad. Psychology, Soc. Psychologists in Addictive Behaviors (pres. 1989-91, newsletter editor 1989—), Am. Acad. Health Care Providers in Addictive Disorders (nat. adv. bd. 1990—). Roman Catholic. Office: JFK Johnson Rehab Inst 65 James St Edison NJ 08820-3903

HANCKE, KAREN LEE, consultant; b. Endicott, N.Y., May 28, 1967; d. Peter John and Sonja Ruth (Eliassen) H. BS in Commerce, U. Va., 1989. Cons. Anderson Cons., Washington, 1989—. Tutor Temple Sinai-Gen. Scott Homeless Families Tutoring Program, Washington, 1989-90. Mem. Nat. Soc. for Performance & Instrn., U. Va. Club of Washington, U. Va. Alumni Assn., Arlington Women's Soccer League, delta Gamma Alumnae Assn. of No. Va. Democrat. Presbyterian. Home: 6835C N Washington Blvd Arlington VA 22213-1122 Office: Andersen Cons 1666 K St NW Washington DC 20006-2803

HANCOCK, CHARLES CAVANAUGH, JR., scientific association administrator; b. Riverside, Calif., Oct. 19, 1935; s. Charles Cavanaugh and Mary Elizabeth (Riordan) H.; m. Barbara Jean Nelson, Jan 31, 1987: children from previous marriage: Christopher Alan, Stephen Edward. B.S. in Chem. Engring, Stanford U., 1958; M.S. in Indsl. Engring, Tex. Tech U., 1967. Commd. 2d lt. U.S. Air Force, 1958, advanced through grades to lt. col., 1974; worldwide locations in research and devel. and logistics, to, 1979, ret., 1979; exec. officer Am. Soc. Biochem. and Molecular Biology, Bethesda, Md., 1979—; also mgr. Jour. Biol. Chemistry. Decorated Meritorious Service medal with 3 oak leaf clusters. Mem. AAAS, Inst. Indsl. Engrs. (sr.), Coun. Engring. and Sci. Soc. Execs., Conv. Liaison Coun. (chmn. 1991-92), Profl. Conv. Mgmt. Assn., Coun. Biology Editors, Sigma Xi, Alpha Pi Mu. Office: Am Soc Biochem & Molecular Biology 9650 Rockville Pike Bethesda MD 20814-3998

HANCOX, DAVID ROBERT, audit administrator, educator; b. Albany, N.Y., Aug. 1, 1951; s. Robert F. and Elaine C. (Morgart) H.; m. Judith A. Gaylord, Jan. 17, 1975; children: Robert, Bradford, Ryan D. AS, Hudson Valley Community Coll., 1973; BBA, Siena Coll., 1975. Cert. internal auditor. State auditor N.Y. State Comptr., Albany, 1974—; lectr. Albany Bus. Coll., 1982-83, Schenectady (N.Y.) Community Coll., 1988, Siena Coll., Loudonville, N.Y., 1991—, Russell Sage Coll., Albany, 1992—; dir. state audits N.Y. State Comptr., 1989—. Mem. Assn. Govt. Accts. (pres. N.Y. Capital chpt. 1986-87, bd. dirs., 1987-89, Arlington, Va. regional v.p. 1990—, Gold award 1991), Inst. Internal Auditors (Albany chpt. bd. govs. 1988-90). Roman Catholic. Home: 21 Magnolia Ter Albany NY 12209-1714 Office: N Y State Comptr AE Smith Bldg Albany NY 12236

HANCOX, ROBERT ERNEST, financial services company executive; b. Newark, Apr. 6, 1943; s. Ernest E. and Laverne (Bruguiere) H. m. Judith Hale, Aug. 6, 1966; children: Jennifer Susan, Elizabeth Jane. B.A., Lycoming Coll., 1965; M.B.A., Fairleigh Dickinson U., 1970; Ph.D., Pace U., 1981. Coord. mgmt. devel. State Farm Ins. Cos., Wayne, N.J., 1965-66, asst. personnel mgr., 1968-70, pers. supt., 1970-72, regional pers. mgr., 1972-76, regional pers. dir., 1976-81; v.p. CIGNA Corp., 1981-83, Penn Mut. Life Ins. Co., 1983-87; exec. v.p., chief operating officer ICMA Retirement Corp., Washington, 1987-88, pres., chief exec. officer, 1988—; bd. dirs. The Daro Group Inc., CPAs, Inc., Pub. Adminstrn. Holding Corp., ICMA RC Svcs., Inc., 777 North Capitol Corp., ICMA Retirement Trust, ICMA Retirement Corp.; assoc. prof. Seton Hall U., 1970-74, Fordham U., 1974-81. Trustee Lycoming Coll.; bd. dirs. Ctr. for Pub. Adminstrn. and Svc. Inc. Mem. Acad. Mgmt., Indsl. Gerontology Rsch. Inst. (bd. dirs.). Republican. Methodist. Office: ICMA Retirement Corp 777 N Capitol St NE Washington DC 20002-4239

HAND, BRIAN EDWARD, science association administrator; b. DuBois, Pa., Mar. 16, 1963; s. Homer Edward and Patricia Ann (Delaco) H. BA, Pa. State U., 1985; MA, Cath. U., 1989. Asst. to city mgr. City of DuBois, 1983; coord. Coun. Commonwealth Student Govts., University Park, Pa., 1984-85; exec. dir. United Way, DuBois, 1985-87; teaching asst. Cath. U. of Am., 1987-89; asst. dir. Nat. Blood Found., 1989-91; treas. LTG Assocs., Washington, 1985—; exec. dir. Del. County, Pa. unit Am. Cancer Soc., 1992—. Bd. dirs. DuBois Campus Alumni Soc., 1985-87, sec., 1986-87; active in DuBois Area Hist. Soc., 1983-87; pres. Student Govt. Assn. Pa. State U.-DuBois, 1982-83; mem. Profl. Assn. United Way of Pa., 1986-87, campaign coord., 1989; pres. DuBois Commmunity Theatre, 1986; commr. Adv. Neighborhood, Washington, 1991. Recipient Eric A. and Josephine Walker award Pa. State U. 1983, Outstanding Young Alumni award Pa. State U.-DuBois, 1987. Mem. Assn. Founds. Group, Rotary (chmn. scholarship com. Dubois club 1986). Home: 1300 S Farmview Dr Apt G-33 Dover DE 19901-7764 Office: 280 N Providence Rd Media PA 19063-3585

HAND, PAUL EDGAR, agricultural cooperative executive; b. Carmel, Maine, Jan. 14, 1931; s. Edgar Austin and Irene Marie (Cyr) H.; m. Georgette Cyr, Feb. 15, 1931; children: Karen Matejik, Deborah Fisher, Charlene Wright, Cheryl Gordon, Paul, David. BS, U. Maine, 1952, Ms, 1955; PhD, Penn State U., 1960. Instr. Penn State U., Univ. Park, Pa., 1955-57; economist Interstate Milk Producers, Phila., 1957-68; asst. gen. mgr. Interstate Milk Producers, Southampton, Pa., 1968-82; gen mgr. Interstate Milk Producers, Southampton, 1982-87; gen. mgr. Atlantic Dairy Coop., Southampton, 1987—; cons. Agrl Coun. Calif., Sacramento, 1968-71. 1st lt. U.S. Army, Inf., 1952-54, Korea. Decorated Legion of Merit. Mem. Am. Agrl. Econs. Assn., Reserve Officers Assn. (life), Phila. Soc. for Promoting Agr. (treas. 1963). Republican. Roman Catholic. Office: Atlantic Dairy Coop 1225 Industrial Hwy Southampton PA 18966-4022

HAND, PETER JAMES, neurobiologist, educator; b. Oak Park, Ill., Jan. 5, 1937; s. James Harold and Edna Mae (Watson) H.; m. Mary Minnis, Sept. 16, 1958; children—Katherine Patricia, Carol Jane, Margaret Anne, Robin Lynn, Stephen Douglas, Peter James; m. Carol Louise Corson, Oct. 23, 1976; m. Christine L. Arnold, Sept. 19, 1986. V.M.D., U. Pa., 1961, Ph.D., 1964. Mem. faculty U. Pa., Phila., 1964—, prof. anatomy, 1979—, head dept. anatomy, 1980-87, 91—; mem. NIH rev. com. Regional Primate Ctrs., 1985-89. Contbr. articles on neurobiology to profl. publs. Pres. USO Council, Cape May, N.J., 1972-73, nat. del.; trustee Mid-Atlantic Ctr. for Arts, Cape May, 1973-74; bd. dirs. Cape May Taxpayers Assn., 1972-74, Univ. City Hist. Soc., Phila., 1978-80. NIH grantee, 1970-82, 86—. Mem. Am. Assn. Anatomists, Am. Assn. Vet. Anatomists, Soc. Neurosci. (pres. Phila. chpt. 1984-85), Internat. Brain Rsch. Orgn., World Assn. Vet. Anatomists, Internat. Assn. for Study of Pain, Am. Assn. Acupuncture, Internat. Coll. Acupuncture and Electro-Therapeutics, Sigma Xi, Alpha Psi (trustee 1965-87). Democrat. Home: PO Box 144 Wycombe PA 18980-0144 Office: U Pa Sch Vet Medicine Philadelphia PA 19104

HAND, ROBERT STEPHENS, retired chemical engineer; b. Shubuta, Miss., Nov. 18, 1915; s. Albert Powe and Rhoda Catherine (Stephens) H.; m. Jeanne Catherine Nealon, Apr. 22, 1946; children: Rita Catherine, Robert Stephens Jr. BS, Millsaps Coll., 1936; MS, MIT, 1938. Devel. engr. West India Chems., Ltd., Matthewtown, Inagua, 1938-40; hydrosulfite plant supt. Va. Smelting Co., West Norfolk, 1940-42; plant site engr. Miss. Agrl. and Indsl. Bd., Jackson, 1946-51; project engr. E.I. DuPont de Nemours & Co., Jackson, Miss., 1951-80; author, pub. R.S. Hand Co., Chadds Ford, Pa., 1990-92. Author of 10 books. V.p. Kennett Twp. Civic Assn., Chester County, Pa., 1959. Lt. USN, 1942-46. Mem. Am. Inst. Chem. Engrs. Republican. Methodist. Home and Office: 6 Nine Gates Rd Chadds Ford PA 19317-9258

HANDEL, BERNARD, accountant, actuarial and insurance consultant, lawyer; b. N.Y.C., Sept. 25, 1926; s. Louis and Sarah (Brody) H.; m. Shirley M. Krom. BBA, CUNY; J.D., Pace U. With Eisner & Lubin, C.P.A.s, N.Y.C., 1946-52; v.p. Davis Assocs., N.Y.C., 1952-56; pres. Handel Group div. H.D.L. Assocs., Inc., Poughkeepsie, N.Y., 1956—, Hudson Valley Planning, Poughkeepsie, 1961—; dir. Bankers Assurance Co., 1984—. Bd. dirs. Dutchess County chpt. ARC; bd. dirs. Hudson Valley Health Systems Agy., pres., 1982-84; bd. dirs. Dutchess County Health Planning Council, 1976—; treas. Dutchess County Assn. Sr. Citizens, 1976; past insp. N.Y. State Athletic Commn.; mem. N.Y. State Hosp. Rev. and Planning Council, 1978—; bd. dir. Am. Health Planning Assocs., 1982-85; trustee Vassar Bros. Hosp., 1986—, vice-chmn., 1991-92; bd. dirs. Bardavon Opera House, 1985—. Served with U.S. Army, 1945-46. Mem. Internat. Found. Employee Benefit Plans (chmn. cons. com., chmn. health care svc. com. 1980-83, 88-90, chmn. health care data base com., 1986-87, dir. 1981-83, 85-87, 90-91), ISCEBS (fellow, gov. council 1982-84), N.Y. State Soc. CPAs, Nat. Assn.

Securities Dealers, Am. Pension Conf., Soc. Benefit Plan Adminstrs., ABA, N.Y. State Bar Assn. Clubs: Rotary, Amrita. Author books and articles in field. Office: PO Box 709 53 Academy St Poughkeepsie NY 12602

HANDEL, GERALD SEIDMAN, sociology educator; b. Cleve., Aug. 8, 1924; s. Louis and Pearl (Seidman) H.; m. Ruth Alice Doman, Feb. 5, 1956; children: Jonathan, Michael J. AB, U. Chgo., 1947, AM, 1951, PhD, 1962. Rsch. assoc. U. Chgo., 1952-56; asst. dir., then v.p. Social Rsch. Inc., Chgo., 1956-66; sr. staff assoc. Ctr. for Urban Edn., N.Y.C., 1966-67; assoc. prof. CUNY, 1967-73, prof., 1973—. Author: Social Welfare in Western Society, 1982; co-author: Family Worlds, 1959, Workingman's Wife, 1959, The Child and Society, 5th edit., 1989; editor: The Psychosocial Interior of the Family, 1967, 3d edit., 1985, Childhood Socialization, 1988; co-editor: The Apple Sliced: Sociological Studies of New York City, 1984, Qualitative Methods in Family Research, 1992. Mem. Am. Sociol. Assn., Eastern Sociol. Soc., Soc. Study of Symbolic Interaction, Am. Psychol. Assn. Office: CUNY Convent Ave New York NY 10031

HANDLER, DOUGLAS PERRY, economist; b. Phila., Oct. 17, 1957; s. Robert and Claire (Fischer) H.; m. Allison Joy Rubin, Mar. 31, 1984; children: Phillip, Daniel. AB, Dickinson Coll., 1978; MA, Georgetown U., 1981. Economist Bd. Govs., Fed. Res. Bd., Washington, 1982-85; dir. short-term forecasting WEFA Group (formerly Wharton Econometrics), Phila., 1985-87; mgr. econometric analysis Dun & Bradstreet Corp., N.Y.C., 1987—; asst. adj. prof. Sacred Heart U., Fairfield, Conn., 1988—; econ. adv. bd. mem. Coun. on Credit Risk, N.Y.C., 1989—; mem. N.Y. State Adv. Coun. on Econ. Info. and Rsch., Albany, 1988—. Contbr. articles Bus. Econs., 1988, 90, Confederation Svc. Industries, 1988, 91, Comml. Lending Rev., 1992. Mem. Nat. Assn. Bus. Economists (fin. roundtable (sec./treas. 1988—), N.Y. Assn. Bus. Economists, Econ. Club Conn. (program chmn. 1987-88, membership chmn. 1988—), Nat. Bus. Econ. Issues Coun. Office: Dun & Bradstreet Corp 299 Park Ave New York NY 10171-0002

HANDLER, MARK S., retail executive; b. 1933; married. Student, U. Ill.; B.S., Roosevelt U., 1957; M.S., N.Y.U., 1958. With R.H. Macy & Co. Inc., N.Y.C., 1958—; mdse. adminstr. Bamberger's (subs. R. H. Macy & Co. Inc.), Newark, 1962-65, v.p., mdse. adminstr., 1965-67, sr. v.p. merchandising, 1967-71, pres., 1979, chmn., chief exec. officer, 1979-80, also bd. dirs.; pres., dir. R. H. Macy & Co. Inc., N.Y.C., 1980-92; co-chmn. R.H. Macy & Co. Inc., N.Y.C., 1992—. Served with U.S. Army, 1953-55. Office: R H Macy & Co Inc 151 W 34th St New York NY 10001-2124

HANDLEY, RAY, professional football coach; b. Artesia, N.Mex., Oct. 8, 1944; m. JoAnne Handley; children: Donnie, Cami. BA in History, Stanford U., M degree. Asst. coach Stanford U., 1967, linebackers coach, 1970-74; dir. jr. varsity football U.S. Mil. Acad., 1968-69; offensive coord. Air Force Acad., 1975-78; running backs coach N.Y. Giants, 1983-91, also former offensive coord., head coach, 1991—. Office: New York Giants Giants Stadium East Rutherford NJ 07073*

HANDSCHUMACHER, ROBERT EDMUND, biochemistry educator; b. Abington, Pa., Oct. 16, 1927; m. Joan A. Goddard; children: Kurt, Mark. BSChemE, Drexel Inst., 1949; MS in Biochemistry, U. Wis., 1951, PhD in Biochemistry, 1953. Postdoctoral fellow Lister Inst., 1953-54; postdoctoral fellow pharm. Yale U. Sch. Medicine, New Haven, 1955-56, asst. prof. pharm., 1956-60, assoc. prof. pharm., 1960-64, dir. div. biol. scis., 1969-72, chmn. dept. pharm., 1974-77, prof. pharm., 1964—; chmn. Eleanor Roosevelt Internat. Fellowship Com., 1966-73, Am. Cancer Soc. Coun. Rsch. Grants, 1977-78, sci. rev. com. Ludwig Cancer Unit, Brussels, 1980-84, health and med. care com. Commn. Acad. Sci., 1984—; sec., treas. Am. Assn. Cancer Rsch., Phila., 1982-88; rsch. prof. Am. Cancer Soc., 1977—; Philips Meml. lectr. Meml. Sloan-Kettering, N.Y.C., 1985; chmn. exp. therap. adv. bd. B-W Fund, 1990—; coun. mem. Nat. Inst. Environ. Health Scis., 1987—. Author 250 articles, book chpts., etc. Sci. dir. Anna Fuller Fund, Yale U. Sch. Medicine, 1973-88; chmn. Samuel Roberts Noble Found. Adv. Bd., Okla., 1982-90; mem. bd. govs. Yale U. Press, New Haven, 1989—. Fellow AAAS; mem. Conn. Acad. Sci. & Engring. (charter). Democrat. Lutheran. Home: 97 Great Harbor Rd Guilford CT 06437-3036 Office: Yale U Sch Medicine 333 Cedar St New Haven CT 06510-3289

HANDSHAW, GORDON FRANK, financial analyst; b. Smithtown, N.Y., June 12, 1950; s. George A. and Genevieve (Gumbus) H.; m. Rosemarie Margiotta, June 28, 1981; children: Darran, Daniel. Student, SUNY, Stony Brook, 1968-71. Underwriter N.Y. Life Ins. Co., Hicksville, 1971; mgr. Bank of Suffolk County, St. James, N.Y., 1971-73, Bank of Babylon, West Islip, N.Y., 1974-77; asst. v.p. Citibank, Melville, N.Y., 1978-89; v.p. Apple Acceptance Corp., Bethpage, N.Y., 1990—. Commr. Miller Place (N.Y.) Fire Dist. (chief 1988), 1989—. Mem. N.Y. Marine Trades Assn. Republican. Office: Apple Acceptance Corp 185 Central Ave Bethpage NY 11714-3931

HANDSPICKER, BRIAN DEWITT, software engineer, architectural designer; b. McAllen, Tex., July 19, 1957; s. Brian Purdy and Jacqueline Ann (Colclough) H.; m. Janet Elizabeth Morehouse. Student, Bates Coll., Lewiston, Maine, 1975-79. Software engr. Computer Systems Engring., Burlington, Mass., 1979-80, Prime Computer, Framingham, Mass., 1980-84; mem. tech. staff Banyan Systems, Westboro, Mass., 1984-86; prin., software engr. Digital Equipment Corp., Littleton, Mass., 1986-91, tech. program mgr., 1991-92, advanced devel. tech. leader, 1992—; acctg. group leader Am. Nat. Standards Inst. X3T54, 1988-90; framework group chair Open Software Found. Mgmt. Spl. Interest Group, 1989-91, chair, 1991—; dep. chair. X/Open System Mgmt. Group, 1990—. Office: Digital Equipment Corp 550 King St Littleton MA 01460-1289

HANDWERGER, SANDRA, physician, educator; b. Boston, Mar. 17, 1955; d. Abraham and Betty (Tigar) H. BA, Vassar Coll., 1976; MD, Columbia U., 1980. Intern, resident Beth Israel Med. Ctr., N.Y.C., 1980-83, fellow in infectious diseases, 1985-86, attending physician, 1986—, asst. chief div. infectious diseases, 1990—; asst. prof. medicine Mount Sinai Sch. Medicine, N.Y.C., 1986—; postdoctoral fellow in microbiology Rockefeller U., N.Y.C., 1983-85. Contbr. articles to profl. jours. Recipient Rsch. Merit award Pfizer Pharm., 1986. Mem. Am. Soc. for Microbiology. Office: Beth Israel Med Ctr 16th St & First Ave New York NY 10003

HANDY, ELLEN JOAN, art historian; b. Schenectady, N.Y., Mar. 11, 1961; d. Rollo LeRoy and Toni Esther (Scheiner) H. AB, Barnard Coll., 1980; MFA, Princeton (N.J.) U., 1983, postgrad. Asst. master Rockefeller Coll., Princeton U., 1982-84; lectr. Tyler Sch. Art, Temple U., Phila., 1986, Phila. Coll. Art, 1985-87; reviewer Arts Mag., N.Y.C., 1982-92; rsch. asst. and cataloger Canadian Ctr. for Architecture, Montreal, 1985-87; sr. rsch. asst. Dept. Prints and Photographs, Met. Mus. Art, N.Y.C., 1987-89; lectr. Sch. Visual Arts, N.Y.C., 1991; faculty mem. Sotheby's Am. Arts Course, N.Y.C., 1989-91; chmn., dept. art Bard Coll., Annandale On Hudson, N.Y., 1991—; lectr. dept. edn. Met. Mus. Art, N.Y.C., 1987-92; cons. curator for photography exhbn., The Chrysler Mus., Norfolk, Va., 1993; cons., rev. panel for photog. terminology Art and Architecture Thesaurus, Williamstown, Mass., 1989. Contbr. numerous articles to profl. mags.; author (photography entries) The Reader's Catalog, 1989-90. Grantee Australian Consulate, 1989, Princeton U., London, 1983. Mem. ACLU, Coll. Art Assn. Home: 163 E 87th St # 1E New York NY 10128 Office: Bard Coll Dept Art Annandale On Hudson NY 12504

HANDY, MARY CATHERINE LIPHAM, infosystems specialist; b. Bowdon, Ga., Sept. 16, 1947; d. James Cliff and Mildred Elizabeth (Garrett) Lipham; m. H. Brooks Handy, Oct. 28, 1990. BA, W. Ga. Coll., 1969; MA, U. Ga., 1971. Archivist Md. Hall of Records, Annapolis, 1972-79; residential assessor Md. State Dept. of Assessments and Taxation, Annapolis, 1978-84; mem. task force Md. State Dept. of Assessments and Taxation, 1983-84; comml. indsl. trainee Md. State Dept. of Assessments and Taxation, Upper Marlboro, 1984-86; instr. telecommunications procedures Md. State Dept. of Assessments and Taxation, 1986-87; comml. indsl. assessor Md. State Dept. of Assessments and Taxation, Annapolis, 1986. Mem. Condominium Covenants Com., 1980-82, bd. dirs. 1982-83. Ford Found. fellow, 1969-70. Mem. Internat. Platform Assn., Nat. Trust for Hist. Preservation, Md. Assn. Assessing Officers (parliamentarian), Davidsonville Ballroom Dance Club. Home: 1552 Crofton Pky Crofton MD 21114-1533 Office: Md Dept Assessments and Taxation 301 W Preston St Baltimore MD 21201-2305

HANDY, ROLLO LEROY, economics educator, research executive; b. Kenyon, Minn., Feb. 20, 1927; s. John R. and Alice (Kispert) H.; m. Toni Scheiner, Sept. 17, 1950; children—Jonathan, Ellen, Benjamin. B.A., Carleton Coll., Northfield, Minn., 1950; M.A., Sarah Lawrence Coll., 1951; postgrad., U. Minn., 1951-52; Ph.D., U. Buffalo, 1954. Mem. faculty U. S.D., 1954-60, prof. philosophy, head dept., 1959-60; assoc. prof. Union Coll., Schenectady, 1960-61; mem. faculty SUNY-Buffalo, 1961-76, prof. philosophy, 1964-76, chmn. dept., 1961-67, chmn. div. philosophy and social scis., 1965-67, provost faculty ednl. studies, 1967-76; pres. Behavioral Rsch. Council, 1976-84, Am. Inst. Econ. Rsch., 1977-91; pres. emeritus Am. Inst. Econ. Rsch., Great Barrington, Mass., 1991—. Author: Methodology of the Behavioral Sciences, 1964, Value Theory and the Behavioral Sciences, 1969, The Measurement of Values, 1970, (with Paul Kurtz) A Current Appraisal of the Behavioral Sciences, 1964; (with E.C. Harwood) rev. edit., 1973, Useful Procedures of Inquiry, 1973; Co-editor: (with E.C. Harwood) Philosophical Perspectives on Punishment, 1968, The Behavioral Sciences, 1968, The Idea of God, 1968. Served with USNR, 1945-46. Mem. AAUP (chpt. pres. 1964-65), Am. Anthrop. Assn., Am. Philos. Assn., Mind Assn., Philosophy Sci. Assn. Office: Am Inst Econ Rsch Great Barrington MA 01230

HANES, DONALD KEITH, cooperative executive; b. Oregon, Ill., Apr. 4, 1933; s. Harold Samuel and Ruth Lucille (Burke) H.; m. Patricia Elsberg, July 30, 1960; children: Deborah Ann, Dawn Michele, Katherine Elizabeth. BS in Journalism and Communications, U. Ill., 1955. Publs. advt. mgr. Watt Pub. Co., Mt. Morris, Ill., 1957-61; agrl. promotion specialist Portland Cement Assn., Chgo., 1961-65; asst. dir. advt. and pub. relations Am. Breeders Service, DeForest, Wis., 1965-68; dir. info. and edn. Farm Electrification Council, Oakbrook, Ill., 1968-71; dir. pub. relations Nat. Council Farmer Coops., Washington, 1971-74, v.p. pub. relations, 1974-82, v.p. communications, 1982-90; v.p., mem. instnl. rels. Nat. Coun. Farmer Coops., Washington, 1990—; bd. dirs. Coop. Devel. Found., Washington, 1986—, United Coop. Svcs., Washington, 1980-81, 89, vice chmn. bd., 1981-83, 84-85, 90—, del.-at-large, 1983-84, 88, chmn. bd., 1985-87; chmn. Md. Coop. Law Coalition, 1983-88. Producer (film) From This Land, 1979 (Cine Golden Eagle award 1979, Gold Camera U.S. Indsl. Film Festival 1980), (video) Cooperative Benefits, 1992. Served to capt. USAR, 1955-65. Recipient Coop Month Communications award Nat. Planning com. for Coop Month, 1984. Mem. Coop Communicators Assn. (pres. 1975-76, H.E. Klnefelter award 1979), Agrl. Rels. Coun. (Founders award 1977, pres. 1982-83), Advt. Coun. Coops. (pres. 1982-84, Leadership award 1984), Am. Agrl. Editors Assn. (assoc.), Nat. Agrimktg. Assn. (co-founder Chesapeake chpt. 1982, bd. dirs. 1982-84). Republican. Methodist. Club: Nat. Press (Washington). Lodge: Masons. Home: 1100 Cedrus Way Rockville MD 20854-5534 Office: Nat Coun Farmer Coops 50 F St NW Ste 900 Washington DC 20001-1530

HANES, LEE DUNCAN, mental health facility administrator; b. Kansas City, Mo., June 2, 1927; d. Elmer Lee and Edna Beryl (Ingram) Duncan; widowed; 1 child: William Duncan. BS in Pharmacy, U. Kansas City, Mo., 1949; BS in Medicine, U. Mo., 1952; MD, U. Kans., 1954. Diplomate Am. Bd. Psychiatry and Neurology; lic. psychiatrist, Kan., Mo., N.Y. Intern St. Luke's Hosp., Kansas City, 1954-55; pvt. practice Kansas City, 1955-56; resident in psychiatry Greater Kansas City Mental Health Found., 1956-59; asst. clin. dir. Psychiat. Receiving Ctr., Kansas City, 1959-62; supervisory positions various mental health ctrs. Mo., 1962-69; asst. commr. of mental health N.Y. State Dept. of Mental Hygiene, 1969-70; dir. St. Lawrence Psychiat. Ctr., Ogdensburg, N.Y., 1970—; mem. adv. bd. St. Lawrence County Mental Health Bd., 1970-75; mem. adv. com. Comprehensive Community Mental Health Ctr., Watertown, N.Y., 1970-90, acting dep. ops. commr. Office of Mental Health, 1983; clin. instr. pathology, 1950-52, psychiatry U. Mo., Columbia, 1959-62; asst. clin. prof. psychiatry U. Mo., Columbia, 1962-69. Author: (with R. Epps) Day Care of Psychiatric Patients, 1964; contbr. articles to profl. jours. Bd. dirs. Ogdensburg Boys Club, 1973—, Ogdensburg Bicentennial com., 1973-76, St. Lawrence County Economic Devel. Coun., 1977-81; active Augsbury Inst. Inc. for Youth and Families, 1990—; vice chmn. Ogdensburg Arts Festival, 1975; mem. community adv. bd. of Ogdensburg Correctional Facility, 1982—, regional planning adv. coun. 1989—; mem. St. John's Episcopal Ch. Vestry, 1985-88. Recipient Ogdensburg VFW Citation, 1974, St. Lawrence U. North Country Citation, 1976; named Hon. Parade Marshall Seaway Festival, 1979, Ogdensburg C. of C. Citizen of Yr., 1985. Fellow Am. Psychiat. Assn. (life), Am. Orthopsychiat. Assn. (life); mem. AMA (Physicians Recognition award 1991), Am. Group Psychotherapy Assn., Assn. of Mental Health Adminstrs., Am. Assn. Of Psychiatric Adminstrs., N.Y. State Assn. of Facility Dirs. (Exceptional Achievement award 1986), Assn. of Mental Health Adminstrs. (cert.), Zonta (hon.). Home and Office: St Lawrence Psychiat Ctr Station A Box 146 Ogdensburg NY 13669

HANESIAN, DERAN, chemical engineer, chemistry and environmental science educator, consultant; b. Niagara Falls, N.Y., Sept. 26, 1927; s. Vahan and Anna (Kabasakalian) H.; m. Eva Hanesian. B.Ch.E., Cornell U., 1952, Ph.D., 1961. Registered profl. engr., N.Y., N.J. Prodn. engr. E.I. duPont de Nemours, Niagara Falls, 1952-57; research engr. E.I. duPont de Nemours, Deepwater, N.J., 1960-63; prof. dept. chem. engring., chemistry and environ. sci. N.J. Inst. Tech., 1963—, chmn. dept. chem. engring., chemistry and environ. sci., 1975-88; research engr. E.I. duPont, 1964-66, Exxon, Florham Park, N.J., 1967-70; tchr. Celanese, 1977, 80, Algerian Petroleum Inst., 1978; vis. prof. U. Edinburgh, 1981, Erevan Poly. Inst., Armenia, USSR, 1983; acting dep. dir., vis. prof. Ctr. for Plastics Recycling Rsch. Rutgers U., Piscataway, N.J., 1989—. Served with U.S. Army, 1945-46. Recipient Robert Van Houten award N.J. Inst. Tech., 1977; Fulbright grantee Erevan Poly. Inst., Armenia, USSR, 1982, Deutscher Akademischer Austauschdienst grantee, 1981-82, NSF grantee, 1967, 72, 91. Fellow Am. Inst. Chem. Engring.; mem. Am. Chem. Soc., Am. Soc. Engring. Edn. (Middle Atlantic AT&T Found. award 1986), Order of the Engr., Sigma Xi, Omega Chi Epsilon, Alpha Chi Sigma, Tau Beta Pi, Omicron Delta Kappa. Armenian Apostolic. Home: 51 Shepard Pl Nutley NJ 07110-2730 Office: NJ Inst Tech 323 Dr Martin Luther King Jr Blvd Newark NJ 07102

HANEY, JOHN BENJAMIN, speech communications educator; b. Milw., May 2, 1931; s. F. Earl McKinley and Edith (Heizer) H.; m. Diane Hope Dutton, July 18, 1959; children—Steven Arthur, John Frederic. B.S., Miami U., Oxford, Ohio, 1952; M.A., U. Mich., 1954, Ph.D., 1960. Commd. 2d lt. USAF, 1954, advanced through grades to capt., 1960; asst. prof. English, chief TV div. U.S. Air Force Acad., Colorado Springs, 1961-64; resigned, 1964; assoc. prof. speech U. Ill., Chgo., 1964-68, prof., 1968-71, dir. Office Instructional Resources, 1964-71; prof. communication arts and scis., 1971—, also dir. instructional devel. Queens Coll., CUNY, 1971-84. Author: (with Eldon Ullmer) Educational Communications and Technology, 3d edit., 1980; director Queens Pub. TV. Democratic Party leader, Manhasset, N.Y. Mem. Internat. Communication Assn. (past pres.), Soc. Programed and Automated Learning (past pres.), Assn. Ednl. Communications and Tech. (book rev. editor AV Communication Rev. 1973-78), Phi Mu Alpha Sinfonia, Omicron Delta Kappa, Kappa Phi Kappa, Alpha Epsilon Rho, Phi Eta Sigma. Episcopalian. Home: 39 Hawthorne Pl Manhasset NY 11030-2019 Office: CUNY Queens Coll Flushing NY 11367

HANEY, JUDITH LOUISE, printing and marketing company executive; b. Allentown, Pa., Aug. 26, 1946; d. Willard Lester and Madeline Adele (Ranck) Brobst; m. Robert Hoffman Benfer, Jr., Feb. 9, 1968 (div. 1974); 1 child, Michele Lee; m. Todd Henry Haney, Feb. 5, 1977. BS in Elem. Edn., Kutztown (Pa.) U., 1974. Tchr. Allentown Sch. Dist., 1974-79; mem. support staff Mchts. Bank N.A. div. 1st Fidelity N.J., Allentown, 1979-90; retail loan officer, mgr. customer svcs. CC Direct Mktg. Svcs., A Christmas Club Co., Easton, Pa., 1990—. Mem. support staff Walkathon, Allentown, 1986-90, Allentown Literacy Coun., 1987-90. Republican. Lutheran. Home: 16 S Muhlenberg St Allentown PA 18104-6217 Office: CC Direct Mktg Svcs A Christmas Club Co 100 Kuebler Rd Easton PA 18042-9288

HANF, CHARLES DAVID, surgeon; b. N.Y.C., Oct. 20, 1950; s. Nathan and Florence (Rothstein) H.; m. Arline Helen Reinking, Apr. 9, 1988; 1 child, Jennifer. SB, MIT, 1972; MD, Creighton U., 1977. Diplomate Am. Bd. Surgery. Resident surgery Creighton U., Omaha, 1977-82; pvt. practice surgery Omaha, 1982-85; fellow trauma and critical care Md. Inst. EMS Systems, Balt., 1985-86; pvt. practice surgery Long Beach, Calif., 1986-87; dir. surg. critical care Montefiore Med. Ctr., Bronx, N.Y., 1987—. Fellow ACS; mem. Soc. Critical Care Medicine. Office: Montefiore Med Ctr 111 E 210 St Bronx NY 10467

HANFORD, CRAIG BRADLEY, army officer; b. Washington, Sept. 4, 1953; s. Lexie Bernard and Doris Alma (Davis) H.; m. Cassandra Hurse, Jan. 30, 1988. BS in Gen. Engring., U.S. Mil. Acad., 1975; MS in Systems Mgmt., U. So. Calif., 1982; MS in Info. and Computer Sci., Ga. Inst. Tech., 1985; grad., Def. Systems Mgmt. Coll., Ft. Belvoir, 1987, Armed Forces Staff Coll., Norfolk, Va., 1990. Cert. engr.-in-tng.; lic. gen. securities rep. Nat. Assn. Securities Dealers, ins. rep., Ga. Commd. 2d lt. U.S. Army, 1975, advanced through grades to lt. col., 1992; chief Tech. Transfer Office, U.S. Army Inf. Systems Engring. Command, Ft. Belvoir, Va., 1985-86; exec. officer, software engr. Office Program Exec. Officer, Standard Army Mgmt. Info. Systems, 1987-88; comdr. A Co., 4th Bn., 58th Aviation Regt., 1988; chief contract monitoring sect. Joint Ops. Planning and Execution System program DCA, Washington, 1990-91; exec. officer Def. Systems Support Orgn. Def. Info. Systems Agy., Washington, 1991—. Decorated Meritorious Svc. medal with three bronze oak leaf clusters. Mem. Army Aviation Assn. Am., Armor Assn., Assn. for Computing Machinery, IEEE Computer Soc., Nat. Black MBA Assn., Rocks (life), Kappa Alpha Psi (life). Office: DISA DSSO/JAX 701 S Courthouse Rd Arlington VA 22204

HANGER, WALLACE CARLTON, JR., government official; b. Danville, Va., Mar. 31, 1955; s. Wallace Carlton and Maude Florence (Yates) H. BS, Radford U., 1977; MS, Fla. Inst. Tech., 1987. Tchr. bus. Roanoke County Pub. Schs., Roanoke, Va., 1977-78; quality assurance specialist U.S. Army Def. Ammunition Ctr. and Sch., Savannah, Ill., 1979-83; chief quality assurance sect. U.S. Army Europe, Bremerhaven, Fed. Republic Germany, 1986-88; ops. rsch. analyst U.S. Army Materiel Systems Analysis Activity, Aberdeen Proving Ground, Md., 1983-86, lead ops. rsch. analyst, 1988-91, sci./tech. assessor, 1991—; cons. on tech. edn. Harford County Schs., Aberdeen, Md., 1983-86; cons., advisor U.S. Army Chem. Rsch. and Devel. Ctr., Edgewood, Md., 1983-88. Recipient Exceptional Performance award U.S. Army Depot Systems Command, 1982, U.S. Army Europe, 1987; Sustained Superior Performance award U.S. Army Materiel Command, 1983. Mem. Ops. Rsch. Soc. Am., Am. Def. Preparedness Assn., Soc. Logistics Engrs., Am. Soc. for Quality Control, U.S. Naval Inst., CAP (sr.), Chantilly Manor Club (Cecil County, Md.), Masons. Republican. Baptist. Home: 66 Sunnyside Dr Port Deposit MD 21904-1675 Office: Army Material Systems AMXSY-R Aberdeen MD 21005-5071

HANGLEY, WILLIAM THOMAS, lawyer; b. Long Beach, N.Y., Mar. 11, 1941; s. Charles Augustus and Faustine Charmillot H.; m. Mary Dupree Hangley, July 24, 1965; children: Michele Dupree, William Thomas, Katherine Charmillot. BS in Music, SUNY-Coll. at Fredonia, 1963; LLB cum laude, U. Pa., 1966. Bar: Pa. 1966, U.S. Ct. Appeals (3d cir.) 1966, U.S. Dist. Ct. (ea. dist.) Pa. 1966. Assoc. Schnader, Harrison, Segal & Lewis, Phila., 1966-69; mem. Hangley Connolly Epstein Chicco Foxman & Ewing, Phila, 1969—; judge protem Phila. Ct. of Common Pleas, 1991—; mem. adv. bd. Pub. Interest Law Ctr. Phila. Contbr. articles to profl. publs. Bd. dirs. Ams. for Dem. Action, 1972-81. Fellow Am. Coll. Trial Lawyers; mem. ABA (co-chmn. litigation sect. com. on fed. procedure 1990—), Pa. Bar Assn. (corp. and litigation coms., securities and antitrust subcoms., ho. dels. 1989—), ACLU, Phila. Bar Assn., Racquet Club (Phila.), Order of Coif. Roman Catholic. Office: Hangley Connolly Epstein Chicco Foxman & Ewing 1515 Market St Philadelphia PA 19102-1509

HANHAUSEN, EDWARD HENRY, ophthalmologist; b. Jersey City, Aug. 18, 1926; s. Edward and Louise (Bechtle) H.; m. Ethel Doris Ashworth, June 17, 1950; children: Sheryl Ann, Jeffrey Edward. BS, Ursinus Coll., 1946; MD, U. Pa., 1950. Intern Temple U. Hosp., Phila., 1950-51, resident, 1951-54, instr. ophthalmology, 1954-55, instr. to assoc. prof., 1958-80; sr. attending ophthalmologist Bryn Mawr (Pa.) Hosp. Capt., U.S. Army, 1956-58, ETO. Office: 418 E Lancaster Ave Wayne PA 19087

HANIG, CARL JESSE, ophthalmologist; b. Bronx, N.Y., July 14, 1955; s. Albert and Louise (Assael) H. BA summa cum laude, Columbia U., 1976; MD, SUNY, Bklyn., 1980. Diplomate Am. Bd. Ophthalmology. Resident internal medicine Nassau Hosp., Mineola, N.Y., 1980-81; resident ophthalmology SUNY Health Sci. Ctr., Syracuse, N.Y., 1981-84, clin. asst. prof. ophthalmology, 1985—; fellow ophthalmology-plastic surgery Manhattan Eye, Ear and Throat Hosp., N.Y.C., 1984-85. Asst. editor Ophthalmic Plastic and Reconstructive Surgery, 1986. Fellow Am. Acad. Ophthalmology, Phi Beta Kappa. Jewish. Office: 742 James St Syracuse NY 13203

HANKIN, WILLIAM HENRY, psychiatrist; b. Phila., Apr. 12, 1946; s. William Henry and Martha Willets (Parry) H.; m. Joanne Clara D'Orsaneo; children: Evan Andrew, Christina A. Student, Swarthmore Coll., 1964-65, 66-67, City Coll. San Francisco, 1972-73; BA, Temple U., 1979, MD, 1983. Diplomate Am. Bd. Psychiatry and Neurology, Nat. Bd. Med. Examiners. Intern in medicine and psychiatry Balt. City Hosp., 1983-84; resident in psychiatry Johns Hopkins U. and Hosp., Balt., 1984-87; staff psychiatrist Cape Counseling Svcs., Cape May Court House, N.J., 1987-90, dir. psychiatry, 1989-90; mem. med. staff Burdette Tomlin Meml. Hosp., Cape May Court House, 1987—; cons. Francis Scott Key Med. Ctr., Balt., 1986-87; presenter in field. With U.S. Army, 1969-71, Vietnam. Decorated Bronze Star; Temple U. President's scholar, 1979. Mem. Am. Psychiat. Assn., Am. Assn. Community Psychiatrists, N.J. Psychiat. Assn., Far South Jersey Psychiat. Soc., U.S. Croquet Assn., Phi Beta Kappa. Office: 307 Stone Harbor Blvd Ste 6 Cape May Court House NJ 08210-0954

HANKINSON, JAMES FLOYD, business executive; b. Weymouth, N.S., Can., Sept. 21, 1943; s. J. Scott and Edith Ann (Journeay) H.; m. Grace Mary Buck, July 16, 1966; children—Mary Grace, John Scott. B. Commerce, Mount Allison U., Sackville, N.B., 1964; C.A., Ontario Inst. Chartered Accountants, 1969; M.B.A., McMaster U., Hamilton, Ont., 1970. Asst. to dir. acctg. CP Rail, Montreal, Que., 1973-74, asst. dir., 1974-75; dir. acctg. CP Rail, Montreal, 1975-79; comptroller Can. Pacific Ltd., Montreal, 1979-81; v.p. fin. and acctg. Can. Pacific Enterprises Ltd., 1981-85; chmn., chief exec. officer Can. Pacific Securities Ltd., 1981-85; group v.p. Can. Pacific Ltd., 1985-88; exec. v.p. Can. Pacific Ltd., Toronto, Ont., 1988-90; pres., chief oper. officer Can. Pacific Ltd., Toronto, 1990—; bd. dirs. Can. Pacific Enterprises Ltd., Can. Pacific Forest Products Ltd., Can. Pacific Ltd., Can. Pacific Securities Ltd., Can. Pacific Securities (Ont.) Ltd., Can. Pacific Express & Transport, Fording Coal Ltd., Laidlaw Inc., Marathon Realty Co. Ltd., PanCan. Petroleum Ltd., United Dominion Industries, Inc., United Dominion Industries Ltd. Office: Can Pacific Ltd, 123 Front St W Ste 800, Toronto, ON Canada M5J 2M8

HANKS, DAVID ALLEN, art consulting company executive; b. St. Louis, Dec. 13, 1940; s. Stanley and Elizabeth (Dixon) H. BA, Washington U., 1962, MA, 1965. Assoc. curator Am. Decorative Arts/Art Inst. Chgo., Ill., 1969-74; curator dept. Am. art Phila. (Pa.) Mus. of Art, 1974-77; guest curator Smithsonian Instn., Washington, 1977-80; pres. David A. Hanks and Assocs., N.Y.C., 1980—; bd. mem. Fabric Workshop, Phila. Author: The Decorative Designs of Frank Lloyd Wright, 1979, Innovative Furniture in America, 1981, Frank Lloyd Wright: Preserving and Architectural Heritage, 1989, Donald Deskey: Toward a Modern Design, 1989. Recipient Travel grant Graham Found. for Advanced Study in Fine Arts, 1974, rsch. fellowship Nat. Endowment for the Arts, 1976. Mem. Century Club. Home: 800 5th Ave New York NY 10021-8970 Office: David A Hanks and Assocs 200 Park Ave S New York NY 10003-1503

HANKS, ROBERT J., investment executive; b. Utica, N.Y., Mar. 3, 1943; s. Marius Darrow and Pauline (Rogers) H.; m. Katharine Schroeder, May 11, 1991; children: Andrew, Elizabeth, Jonathan. BS, Syracuse U., 1967, MBA, 1969. V.p. GTE Corp., Stamford, Conn., 1969-82, Conrac Corp., Stamford, 1982-84; chief exec. officer Tech. Svc. Group, Melbourne, Fla., 1985-87; pres. RJH Assocs., Inc., Westport, Conn., 1988—, also bd. dirs.; prin. BCP Investment Co., Boston, 1991—, also bd. dirs.; bd. dirs. VPD, Inc., Sacramento, Ecologica Ineternat., Inc., Bedford, N.H., 1991—; pres., dir. BCP Ventures, Inc., Bedford, 1992—; gen. ptnr. New Eng. Growth Fund I, L.P.,

Indonesia Growth Fund I, L.P. Mem. Dalton Club (bd. dirs. 1991-92). Office: BCP Investment Co 313 Congress St Boston MA 02210

HANLEN, JOHN GARRETT, artist; b. Winfield, Kans., Jan. 1, 1922; s. Homer Hartford and Etta Belle (Garrett) H. Student, Pa. Acad. Fine Arts, 1939-43, 46-50; student (3 traveling fellowships), Barnes Found., Merion, Pa., 1942, 43, 47. gen. critic painting Pa. Acad. Fine Arts, 1953-86; prof. drawing, painting Moore Coll. Art, Phila., 1954-83. Exhibited in group shows including, Pa. Acad. Fine Arts anns., 1948—, Detroit Art Inst., 1959, Moore Coll. Art, Phila., 1968, Penn Mus., Harrisburg, Pa., 1971, Rosenfeld Gallery, Phila., 1979, one-man shows include, Peale House, Phila., 1966; Woodmere Art Mus., Chestnut Hill, Pa., 1973; represented in permanent collections, Library of Congress, Pa. Acad. Fine Arts, War Dept. of Combat Art, Moore Coll. Art, Woodmere Art Mus. Served with Signal Corps, AUS, 1943-46, CBI. Decorated Chinese Bronze Star; Tiffany Found. fellow, 1950; Edwin Austin Abbey fellow, 1951; Moore Coll. Art grantee, 1980; Percy M. Owens Meml. for Disting. Pa. Artist, 1986. Mem. Fellowship Pa. Acad. Fine Arts, Woodmere Art Mus. (fine arts com. 1975-85). Home: E Logan St Apt 2004 Philadelphia PA 19144-3017

HANLEY, RAYMOND JOSEPH, health services researcher; b. Seattle, May 9, 1955; s. Raymond Joseph and Opal Evelyn (Ramsland) H.; m. Kimberly Jordan Votava, May 15, 1987; children: Lindsey, Michael. BA, U. Wash., 1977, MPA, 1983. Rsch. tech. dept. Psychiatry and Behavioral Scis., U. Wash., Seattle, 1978-83; policy rsch. assoc. Asst. Sec. Planning and Evaluation, Dept. Health/Human Svcs., Washington, 1983-85; sr. rsch. analyst The Brookings Institution, Washington, 1985—; cons. The Urban Inst., Washington, 1989-90, Lewin/ICF, Washington, 1990, Commonwealth Fund Commn. on Elderly People Living Alone, Balt., 1989; v.p. Grad. Sch. of Pub. Affairs, U. Wash., Seattle, 1982-83. Co-author: Caring for the Disabled Elderly: Who Will Pay?, 1988; author: (with others) Long-Term Care and Social Insurance, 1991, Financing Long-Term Care: Problems and Progress, 1990; contbr. articles to profl. jours. Bd. dirs. Fremont Community Clinic, Seattle, 1981. Scholarship Lucky Stores, 1973; fellowship Dept. Health and Human Svcs., 1983. Mem. APHA, Gerontol. Soc. Am., Am. Soc. Aging, Am. Soc. for Pub. Adminstrn. Democrat. Roman Catholic. Home: 9302 Flower Ave Silver Spring MD 20901-3440 Office: The Brookings Instn 1775 Massachusetts Ave NW Washington DC 20036-2188

HANLEY, THOMAS AQUINAS, JR., executive recruiter; b. Bklyn., June 23, 1954; s. Thomas Aquinas and Anne Renee (Churchill) H.; m. Laura Patricia Boyd, Aug. 4, 1979; children: Thomas Aquinas III, Theresa Anne, William Joseph. BS in Biology, Rensselaer Poly. Inst., 1975, postgrad., 1976-77; JD, N.Y. Law Sch., 1983. Engr. Am. Electric Power Svc. Corp., Canton, Ohio, 1977-78; recruiter Halbrecht & Co., N.Y.C., 1978-80; pres., founder Resource Control Systems Corp., N.Y.C., 1982-89, Smith Hanley Assocs., Inc., N.Y.C., 1980—. Author: (software) Placement Power, 1983. Fundraiser Rensselaer Poly. Inst., Troy, N.Y., 1988—. Mem. Westchester Hills Golf Club. Roman Catholic. Office: Smith Hanley Assocs 99 Park Ave New York NY 10016

HANLON, DAVID PATRICK, hotel and casino executive; b. Cin., Nov. 23, 1944; children: Lara Suzanne, David Jeffrey. BS in Hotel Adminstrn., Cornell U., 1966; MBA in Fin., MS in Acctg., U. Pa. Wharton Sch., 1971; cert. advanced mgmt. program, Harvard Bus. Sch., 1986. Salesman Smith, Barney, Harris, N.Y.C. and Los Angeles, 1972-75; dir. project fin., dir. corp. fin. Fluor Corp., 1975-78; treas., chief fin. officer, v.p. ops. and adminstrn., exec. v.p. Caesars World, Inc., Los Angeles, 1978-84; pres. Harrah's East Hotel/Casino, Atlantic City, 1984-88; pres., chief exec. officer Resorts Internat. Casino Hotel (now Merv Griffin's Resorts), Atlantic City, 1988—. Mem. N.J. Olympic Com., Ptnrship. N.J., Govs. Council Physical Fitness, N.J. Alcoholic Beverage Study Commn. Mem. Casino Assoc. N.J. (chmn.), Casino Reinvestment Devel. Authority. Office: Resorts Internat Hotel Inc N Carolina Ave & Boardwalk Atlantic City NJ 08404 also: Equestrian Ctr Moss Mill Rd Smithville NJ 08201*

HANN, KIMBERLY MARIE, oil company performance and compliance manager; b. Chambersburg, Pa., Apr. 29, 1959; d. Paul Ira and Peggy Ann (Cormany) H. BSBA in Mktg., Shippensburg U., 1981; AA in Acctg., Harrisburg (Pa.) Area Community Coll., 1987; MBA, Kutztown U., 1990. Word processing technician St. Joseph's Hosp., Lancaster, Pa., 1981-82; sr. acct. Am. Water Works Svc. Co., Hershey, Pa., 1982-86; acct. Atlantic Pipeline Co., Sinking Spring, Pa., 1986-87, sr. acct., adminstrv. analyst, 1987-88; cost analyst Atlantic Refining & Mktg. Co., King of Prussia, Pa., 1988-89; mktg. analyst Sun Refining & Mktg. Co., Phila., 1989-91; mgr. performance and compliance Sun Co. Inc. (R&M), Phila., 1991—. Mem. Nat. Assn. Accts. (mem. retention 1987-89), Am. Bus. Women's Assn. (treas. 1985-87). Republican. Roman Catholic. Office: Sun Co Inc (R&M) 10/11 Penn Ctr 1801 Market St Philadelphia PA 19103

HANNA, CHARLOTTE, management science educator; b. Burlington, Vt., July 26, 1951; d. John T. and Dorothea (Smith) H.; m. W. Scott Bassage, Sept. 18, 1982; 1 child, John Oliver. BA, Bennington Coll., 1974; MA, PhD, Stanford U., 1985. Asst. acad. planning Vt. State Colls., Burlington, 1975-76; fin. aid adminstr. Antioch Coll. West, San Francisco, 1977-78; teaching fellow Stanford (Calif.) U., 1979-84; assoc. prof. Trinity Coll. Vt., Burlington, 1986—; cons. Digital Equipment Corp., South Burlington, Vt., 1988-89; chmn. faculty affairs coun. Trinity Coll., Burlington, 1988—. Contbr. articles to profl. jours. Bd. dirs. Baird Ctr. for Children and Families, Burlington, 1988—; tutor literacy program Barre Learning Ctr., Washington County, Vt. Mem. Bus. and Profl. Womens Club, Ea. Acad. Mgmt. Home: RR 1 Box 5C East Calais VT 05650-9702 Office: Trinity Coll Vt 208 Colchester Ave Burlington VT 05401-1422

HANNA, EDGAR E., microbiologist, immunologist; b. Anniston, Ala., Sept. 2, 1933; s. Edgar E. Sr. and Nellie (Wheeler) H.; m. Norma J. Rushin, 1960; children: Natalie, Monica, Charles. BS, Tuskegee U., 1959; MS, U. Minn., 1964, PhD, 1967. NIH predoctoral fellow in microbiology and immunology U. Minn., Mpls., 1964-67; postdoctoral fellow NIH, Bethesda, Md., 1967-69; asst. prof. Med. Coll. of Va. Commonwealth Univ., Richmond, 1969-70; sr. staff fellow in molecular genetics lab. Nat. Inst. Child Health and Human Devel.-NIH, Bethesda, 1970-75, sr. investigator, 1975-83, chief of sect. devel. and molecular immunity lab., 1983-90, sr. microbiologist, sci. rev. adminstr. div. sci. rev., 1990—; mem. adv. coun. Group Health Assn., Inc., Washington, 1971—; Burroughs-Wellcome vis. prof. Morehouse Coll., 1976, King Chavez Parks vis. prof. State of Mich./Wayne State U., 1990-91. Mem. editorial bd. Infection and Immunity, 1982-86. With U.S. Army, 1953-56. Fellow Am. Acad. Microbiology (bd. govs. 1985-88); mem. AAAS, Am. Assn. Immunologists (membership com. 1982-85), Am. Soc. Microbiology (chmn. immunology div. 1980-82), Internat. Endotoxin Soc. (charter), Sigma Xi. Office: NIH 9000 Rockville Pike Bethesda MD 20892-0001

HANNA, EDUARDO ZACARIAS, pharmaceutical company executive; b. Formosa, Argentina, Apr. 9, 1941; came to U.S., 1981; s. Jose and Dorotea (Cabili) H.; m. Clara Isabel Altman, Mar. 23, 1970; children: Claudio M., Perla Y., Andrea C. Pharmacist degree, Pharmacy & Chemistry Sch., La Plata, Argentina, 1964; Biochemist degree, Exacts Sciences Sch., La Plata, Argentina, 1969; Indsl. Adminstrn. degree, Econ. Sciences Sch., Sao Paulo, Brazil, 1980. Quality assurance inspector Eli Lilly & Co., Buenos Aires, 1968; prodn. mgr. Merck Sharp & Dohme & Co., Buenos Aires, 1970; tech. dir. Norwich Eaton Pharmaceuticals, Inc., Buenos Aires, 1973; indsl. dir. Norwich Eaton Pharmaceuticals, Inc., Sao Paulo, 1976; dir. internat. tech. svcs. Norwich Eaton Pharmaceuticals, Inc., Norwich, N.Y., 1981; prof. Institute D'Elia, Buenos Aires, 1971. Named prof. Sec. Edn. Argentina, 1971. Mem. Pharm. Assn. Sao Paulo (prof. 1978), Chem. and Pharm. Soc., Sao Paulo (prof. 1980), Pharm. Mfg. Assn. U.S.A., Pharm. and Biochem. Assn. Argentina. Home: 55 Hillview Dr Norwich NY 13815-1013

HANNA, LOUIS JAMES, securities trader; b. Camden, N.J., Sept. 27, 1967; s. James William and Angela (Notarfrancesco) H. BA in Econs., Rutgers U., 1990. Lic. securities trader. Specialist clk. Wallace/Park Ave Securities, Phila., 1987; adminstrv. asst. Albert Nipon, Phila., 1988-89; registered rep. 1st Investors Corp., Stratford, N.J., 1989; rsch. asst. Mergers & Acquistitions Database, Phila., 1990; trading asst. John Louis Securities Group, Phila., 1990-91; loan technician trading and corp. banking support J.P. Morgan Del., Newark, 1991—. Internat. Ladies Garment Worker's scholar, 1985. Mem. Fin. Mgmt. Assn., Catholic Philopatrian Soc. Republican. Roman Catholic. Home: 400 Dearborne Ave Blackwood NJ 08012-4532

HANNA, SAMIR A., pharmaceutical company executive; b. Cairo, Egypt, May 1, 1934; m. Aida Kamel, May 1, 1966; children: Gihan A., Mark. BA in Pharmacy and Pharm. Chemistry, Cairo U., 1956, Diploma in Phytochemistry, 1963, Diploma in Mfg. and Indsl. Pharmacy, 1966; PhD in Pharm. Scis., Assiut U., Cairo, 1970. Sect. head Drug Rsch. and Control Ctr., Cairo, 1963-70; lectr. N.D. State U., Fargo, summer 1972; dir. quality control Natcon Chems., N.Y.C., 1971-74; dir. analytical R&D Endo Labs Inc., E.I. DuPont, N.Y.C., 1974-79, Bristol Labs., Syracuse, N.Y., 1979-83; dir. analytical R&D Bristol-Myers Co., Syracuse, 1983-86, v.p. quality assurance, 1986-90; v.p. worldwide quality control Bristol-Myers Squibb Co., N.Y., N.J., 1990—; lectr. Ctr. for Profl. Advancement, N.J., 1977—; mem. antibiotic/vet. subcom. USP Com. of Revision. Contbr. chpts. to books, articles to profl. jours. Mem. Acad. Pharm. Scis., Am. Chem. Soc., Am. Pharm. Assn., Assn. Ofcl. Analytical Chemists, Parenteral Drug Assn., Egyptian Pharm. Assn. Home: 6 Elm Ct Trenton NJ 08648-5128 Office: Bristol-Myers Squibb Co PO Box 4755 Syracuse NY 13221-4755

HANNAH, DUNCAN RATHBUN, artist; b. Mpls., Aug. 21, 1952; s. James Blain and Rosemary (Rathbun) H. Student, Bard Coll., 1971-73; BFA, Parsons Sch. Design, 1975. instr. Sch. Visual Arts, N.Y.C., 1989-91. Works represented in permanent collections, including Met. Mus. Art, N.Y., Chase Manhattan Bank, N.Y., Chem. Bank, N.Y., Grand Rapids (Mich.) Art Mus., McDonalds Corp., Ill., Merrill Lynch, N.Y., Nynex, N.Y., Readers Digest, N.Y., Mpls. Inst. Art, Bristol Meyers, J.C. Penney, Champion Paper; shows include Semaphore Gallery, N.Y., 1983-86, Phyllis Kind Galleries, N.Y. and Chgo., 1988-89, Charles Cowles Gallery, N.Y., 1989, 91, Tatistcheff Galleries, N.Y. and L.A., 1991. Home: 160 W 71st St New York NY 10023-3901

HANNAH-ROSS, DIANNE LORRAINE, educational administrator; b. Somers Point, N.J., July 16, 1954; d. Lewis Pernell and Essie (Boose) Hannah; m. Herman Hannah Ross, July 20, 1987 (dec. Nov. 1990). BS, Northeastern U., Boston, 1977; MA, Howard U., 1979. Residene hall counselor Howard Univ., Washington, 1979-82; asst. libr., receptionist Am. Bankers Assn., Washington, 1982-84; ednl. adminstrn. Stockton State Coll., Pomona, N.J., 1984—. mem. youth adv. bd., Sunday sch. tchr. New Mount Calvary Bapt. Ch., 1984—; mem. adv. bd. Coll. Outreach, 1984—; mem. Weynouth Twp. Graduation Com., 1988—; mem. Martin Luther King Jr. Day Celebration com. Twp. of Galloway, 1988—. Recipient Outstanding Achievement in Commuter Student and Adult Learner Svcs. award Commn. XVII, 1991. Mem. AACD, Am. Coll. Pers. Assn., Assn. for Multicultural Counseling and Devel., Assn. Coll. Unions Internat., Nat. Clearinghouse for Commuter Programs, NAACP, Nat. Coun. Negro Women, Alpha Kappa Alpha. Office: Stockton State Coll Jimmie Leeds Rd Pomona NJ 08240-9999

HANNALLAH, RAAFAT SAMY, anesthesiologist; b. Egypt, Sept. 17, 1944; m. Isis Hannallah; children: David, Michael. MB, B Ch, Cairo U., 1966. Residency McGill U., Montreal, Can., 1968-73; prof. anesthesiology and pediatrics Sch. Medicine George Washington U.; vice chmn. anesthesiology Children's Nat. Med. Ctr., Washington; Diplomate Am. Bd. Anesthesiology. Fellow Royal Coll. Physicians and Surgeons of Can. Office: Children's Nat Med Ctr 3800 Reservoir Rd NW Bldg 2phc Washington DC 20007-2196

HANNAN, JOSEPH FRANCIS, financial executive; b. Paterson, N.J., Aug. 30, 1945; s. Joseph Francis and Margret (Condon) H.; m. Grace Mary Costantin, July 1, 1972. AA, Edward Williams Coll., 1975; BS, Fairleigh Dickinson U., 1977. CPA, N.J. Acct., mem. staff Jersey Cen. Power & Light, Morristown, N.J., 1976-77; acct., mem. staff to mgr. Touche, Ross & Co., CPAs, Newark, 1977-84; audit mgr. Weiner & Co., CPAs, Morristown, N.J., 1984-87; v.p. fin., treas., chief fin. officer Weeks Marine, Inc., Cranford, N.J., 1987—, Healy Tibbitts Builders Inc., San Francisco, 1987—. Vice-chmn. Historic Preservation Com., Pompton Lakes, N.J., 1990—. Mem. AICPA, N.J. Soc. CPAs, Constrn. Fin. Mgmt. Assn. (dir. 1982-87). Office: Weeks Marine Inc 216 North Ave E Cranford NJ 07016-2441

HANNAN, MICHAEL JOSEPH, economic and statistics educator; b. Pitts., Jan. 24, 1963; s. John Francis and Marie Laura (Garcia) H.; m. Laura Victoria Misencik, Aug. 10, 1985. BA in Econs., U. Pitts., 1984; PhD in Mineral Resource Econs., W.Va. U., 1988. Sr. rsch. asst. Regional Rsch. Inst., Morgantown, W.Va., 1984-88; asst. prof. econs. U. Pa., Edinboro, 1988—; conf. presenter Pa. Econ. Assn., Johnstown, 1990, Am. Assn. Geographers, Toronto, Can., 1990, Applied Econometric Assn., Washington, 1988, Pitts. Modeling and Simulation, Pitts., 1988. Author: (with others) Industry Structure and Capacity, 1989; contbr. articles to profl. jours. Presenter North Coast Bus. Week, Erie, 1989-90. Rsch. grant Edinboro U., 1991, Pa. State System of Higher Edn., 1991. Mem. Am. Econ. Assn., Pa. Econ. Assn., Phi Kappa Phi, Lambda Chi Alpha. Democrat. Roman Catholic. Office: Dept Bus & Econs U Pa Edinboro PA 16444

HANNENBERG, VERA LOSEV, educational administrator; b. N.Y.C., Dec. 9, 1923; d. Saul and Gussie (Gerstein) Losev; m. Sidney Hyman Hannenberg, Oct. 7, 1945 (dec.); children: Alexander A., Leo R.W. BA cum laude, Bklyn. Coll., 1944, MS in Edn., 1972; Cert., NYU, 1976. Lic. sch. adminstr. N.Y. Coord. occupational planning N.Y.C. Bd. Edn., 1972-76, dir. planning, evaluation and rsch./occupational edn., 1977-80, dir. Office Occupational Edn., 1980—; supr. remedial reading Manpower Devel. Tng. Program, N.Y.C. Bd. Edn., 1966-71; mem. N.Y. State Coun. on Vocat. Edn., 1987—. Contbr. articles to profl. jours. Named Disting. Vocat. Educator of the Yr. N.Y. State Edn. Dept., 1989; recipient Disting. Svc. Plaque, U.S. Job Corps, Washington, 1985, 90. Mem. Am. Vocat. Assn., Nat. Assn. Local Adminstrs. in Vocat. Edn., N.Y. State Occupational Edn./Adminstrn. Assn. Home: 1224 E 8th St Brooklyn NY 11230-5106 Office: NYC Bd Edn 110 Livingston St Brooklyn NY 11201-5065

HANNEVIG, VERONICA ANN, rehabilitation counselor; b. Bronx, N.Y., July 28, 1942; d. Hans Rayfield Hannivig and Sophie Magdalene (Bela-Drob) Burgio; m. David Lawrence Seroka, June 23, 1962 (div. 1986); children: Stephanie, Kathryn, Veronica, Josephine, David, Geraldine, Derek. Student, U. Nev., 1980, Tarrant County Jr. Coll., 1983-87; BS, U. Tex. Health Sci. Ctr., 1987; MS, U. Scranton, 1990. Cert. rehab. counselor. Instructional aide Adolescent CareUnit, Grand Prairie, Tex., 1985-86; substance abuse counselor DARCO Drug Svcs., Inc., Dallas, 1987-88; adolescent therapist N.E. TriCounty Mental Health/Mental Retardation, Carbondale, Pa., 1989, mental health rehab. counselor, 1990; rehab. specialist Comprehensive Rehab. Assocs., Mechanicsburg, Pa., Marietta, Ga., 1990—; cons. Bread of Life Ministry, Harrisburg, Pa., 1991-92; advisor U. Scranton (Pa.) Rehab. Program, 1988-89; grant writer N.E. TriCounty Mental Health/Mental Retardation, 1990, Domestic Abuse Women's Network, Kent, Wash., 1982. Den mother Boy Scouts Am., Arlington, Tex., 1985. Mem. AACD, Nat. Ctr. for Homeopathy.

HANNIGAN, EUGENE JOSEPH, civil engineer; b. Camden, N.J., May 8, 1939; s. John William and Florence Bernadette (Connor) H.; m. Marie N. Valenzo, Jan. 21, 1967; children: Lori Ann, Patricia Ann, Amy Elizabeth. BS in Civil Engring., Drexel U., 1962; MS in Civil Engring., Purdue U., 1964. Registered profl. engr., Pa., N.J., Ohio, W.Va. Project engr. D'Appolonia Cons. Engrs., Inc., Pitts., 1964-67; project engr., v.p. Engring. Mechanics, Inc., Pitts., 1967-73; owner, prin. engr. Eugene Hannigan Cons. Engrs., Monroeville, Pa., 1973-86; pres. Hannigan Engring. Assocs., Inc., Monroeville, 1986—; adj. asst. prof. dept. civil engring. U. Pitts.; mem. Parents Coun. St. Francis Coll., Loretto, Pa.; former evening lectr. Allegheny County Community Coll. Mem. edn. com., parish coun. St. Bernadette's Roman Cath. Parish, 1978-83, pres., 1982-83; pres. Parent-Tchrs. Guild, St. Bernadette's Roman Cath. Sch., 1978—. Mem. ASCE (Pitts. young engr. of yr. award 1970, past pres. Pitts. sect., past sec.-treas. dist. 4 coun., past chmn. nat. com. student svcs., past mem. nat. com. fellowships, scholarships, grants and bequests, past mem. exec. com. Edn. Div.), ASTM, Nat. Soc. Profl. Engrs., Am. Arbitration Assn. Home: 4434 Marywood Dr Monroeville PA 15146-1326 Office: 502 Laurel Dr Monroeville PA 15146-1136

HANNIGAN, JOHN DAVID, paper industry consultant; b. Portland, Maine, Aug. 3, 1947; s. George Edward and Esther June (Gray) H.; m. Claudia Elizabeth Balcerzak, Apr. 28, 1979; children: John David Jr., Nicole Marie, Julie Elizabeth. Supr. ops. control Internat. Paper Co., Hanover, Md., 1971-84; customer svc. mgr. Union Camp Corp., Trenton, N.J., 1984-86; sales rep. Met. Co., Dayton, N.J., 1986-87, St. Joseph Paper Co., Balt., 1987-88; packaging broker Gray Co., Mitchellville, Md., 1988—. Patentee in field. With U.S. Army, 1965-69, Vietnam. Mem. Mensa. Roman Catholic.

HANNON, JOHN ROBERT, investment company executive; b. Atlanta, Aug. 9, 1945; s. George Franklin and Elizabeth (Broadfield) H.; m. Jackie Lyn Wagner, Apr. 28, 1984; children: Kimberly, Melissa. BA, Duke U., 1967. CFA, CLU, CPCU. Group sales rep. The Prudential Ins. Co. of Am., Charlotte, N.C., 1967-69, group ins. mgr., 1969-72; assoc. dir. group ins. The Prudential Ins. Co. of Am., Newark, 1972-74; regional group mgr. The Prudential Ins. Co. of Am., Jacksonville, Fla., 1974-79, dir. group mktg., 1979-81; v.p. group credit mktg. The Prudential Ins. Co. of Am., Newark, 1981-83; v.p. group ins. mktg. The Prudential Ins. Co. of Am., Roseland, N.J., 1983-85, v.p. group credit ins. ops., 1985-87, v.p. corp. group mktg. communications, 1987-88; sr. v.p. Prudential Capital Corp., Newark, 1988-91, Prudential Investment Corp., Newark, 1991; pres. Prudential Affiliated Investors, Newark, 1991-92, chmn., chief exec. officer, 1992—; mem. bd. dirs. CSI Asset Mgmt., Inc., Enhanced Inestment Technologies, Inc., Hallmark Capital Mgmt., Inc., Mercator Asset Mgmt., Inc., PruTimber Investments, Inc., PCM Internat., Prudential Asia Investments, Ltd., Jennison Assos. Capital Corp.; visiting faculty bus. sch. U. North Fla., Jacksonville, 1979-80. Elder Lakewood Presbyn. Ch., Jacksonville, 1977-81; deacon First Presbyn. Ch., Caldwell, N.J., 1987-90, elder, 1990—; vol. campaign U.S. Senate Challenger, State of Fla., 1980; mem. Nat. Eagle Scout Assn. Served with USN, 1963-67. Mem. Fin. Analysts Fedn., Assn. Investment Mgmt. and Rsch., N.Y. Soc. Security Analysts, Mensa, Rudder Club (commodore 1979-80), University. Republican. Clubs: Rudder (commodore 1979-80), University. Home: 100 Garfield Ave Madison NJ 07940 Office: Prudential Affiliated Investors 20th Fl 751 Broad St Newark NJ 07102-3777

HANNUM, DAVID LAWRENCE, training and development professional; b. Detroit, May 6, 1945; s. John Andrew and Ruth (Life) H.; m. Mary Ellen Oltesvig, Apr. 19, 1968; children: James K., Charles M. BS, Regis Coll., Denver, 1982; MBA, Fairleigh Dickinson U., 1984; M cert. in project mgmt., George Washington U., 1991. Instr. Mich. Bell., Detroit, 1971-78, mgr. tng., 1978-80; with course devel. dept. AT&T, Denver, 1980-82; systems test mgr. AT&T, Parsippany, N.J., 1982-84; project mgr. AT&T, Morris Plains, N.J., 1984-89; mgr. tng. AT&T, South Plainfield, N.J., 1989-91; NCR Network Edn. Ctr., West Columbia, S.C., 1991—; co-owner Pocono Craft Loft, Tannersville, Pa., 1986—; trainer Engring. Soc. Detroit, 1979; assoc. prof. County Coll. of Morris, Dover, N.J., 1984-85. Author various computer tng. courses. Leader, trainer, commr. Boy Scouts Am., Mich., Colo., N.J., Pa., 1975-90. With USNR, 1962-63. Mem. IEEE, IEEE Computer Soc. (assoc. editor, columnist Micro mag. 1982-86), ASTD, Profl. Picture Framers Assn., Hobby Industries Assn., Assn. for Craft and Creative Industries. Office: NCR Network Edn Ctr 3245 Platt Springs Rd West Columbia SC 29170-2517

HANRAHAN, JOHN JOSEPH, scientist; b. New London, Conn., Mar. 19, 1932; s. John James and Celia (Cunningham) H.; m. Mary Ellen Ruddy, Aug. 24, 1957; children: Margaret, Maureen, Brian, Mary Kathryn. BA in Math. with honors, U. Conn., 1954, MS in Physics, 1962; diploma with distinction, Naval War Coll., 1987. Computer analyst Electric Boad div. Gen. Dynamics Corp., Groton, Conn., 1960-62; supr. ops. rsch. and analysis Naval Underwater Systems Ctr., New London, Conn., 1962-87; sr. scientist Bolt Beranek & Newman, Inc., New London, 1987—. Author: Predicting Convergence Zone Formation in the Deep Ocean. Proceedings of Internat. Congress on Underwater Acoustics, 1987; co-author Bottom-Interacting Ocean Acoustics, 1980. Capt. USAF, 1955-57. Fellow Acoustical Soc. Am.; mem. Assn. Hibernians, Sigma Pi Sigma. Roman Catholic. Office: BBN Systems and Tech Union Station New London CT 06320

HANRAHAN, JOYCE YANCEY, educational administrator; b. Fyffe, Ala., Sept. 29, 1933; d. Wallace Odell and Nellie Lee (Raughton) Yancey; m. Edward John Hanrahan, Nov. 12, 1960. BA, U. Ala., University, 1955; MEd, U. N.H., 1964, 68; postgrad., Boston U., U. Calif., Boston U., Harvard. Cert. tchr., prin., N.H., N.J., Maine, Wis. Tchr. pub. schs., Madison, Wis., Durham, N.H., 1960-68; prin. Little Harbour Sch., Portsmouth, N.H., 1969-72, York (Maine) Elem. Sch., 1978-84; ednl. field agt. New Eng. Program in Tchr. Edn., Durham, 1972-75; exec. dir. Community Day Care Ctr., Portsmouth, 1975-76; cons. N.H. Child and Family Svcs., Concord, N.H., 1976-78; headmistress lower sch. Internat. Sch., Brussels, 1984-87; head lower sch. Shady Side Acad., Pitts., 1987-89; asst. head, prin. Short Hills (N.J.) Campus, The Pingry Sch., 1989—; mem. accrediting com. European Coun. Internat. Schs., 1984-87; cons. on early childhood edn. and child care related issues, New Eng., 1970-84; participant numerous TV panels on edn. related issues, 1970-84; ptnr. J & J Hanrahan, rare books. Writer, dir. TV program on child care as polit. issue,. Mem. Portsmouth City Coun., 1972-76, C. of C., N.H. Gov.'s Task Force on Mental Health of Children, 1976-80, N.H. Early Childhood Task Force, Concord, 1972-80; bd. dirs. N.H. Charitable Trust, Concord, 1974-84, United Fund, Children's Mus., SPNEA, AAA-NH, numerous others. Fellow U.S. Govt., U. N.H., 1968-69, NEH, Ga. Inst. Tech., 1980, Prin.'s Ctr., Harvard U. Sch. Edn., 1984, Aspen Inst., 1990. Mem. ASCD, Nat. Assn. Ind. Schs., Harvard Prin.'s Ctr., Antiquarian Booksellers Assn. AM., Nat. Assn. Edn. Young Children. Home: 320 White Oak Ridge Rd Short Hills NJ 07078-1158

HANSEL, JOHN PARKER, manufacturing executive; b. Cranford, N.J., Sept. 11, 1924; s. Charles Francis and Kathryn (Denman) H.; m. Frances Morris Soule, July 20, 1945; children: Carla, Parker, Peter, Turner, David. BA, Princeton U., 1946. Sales engr. Filtrine Mfg. Co., Bklyn., 1947-54; pres. Filtrine Mfg. Co., Waldwick, N.J. and Harrisville, N.H., 1954—; founder, chief exec. officer Nat. Bus. News, Harrisville, N.H., 1964—, Elm Rsch. Inst., Harrisville, 1967—. Editor: (2 films) Dutch Elm Disease, 1975 (Golden Eagle award); inventor accident proof drinking fountain. Chmn. No-East-West Hwy., Dublin, N.H., 1972—; bd. dirs., v.p. Bus. and Indsl. Assn., Concord, N.H., 1980—; bd. dirs. Monadnock Mental Health, Keene, N.J., 1980-90. Served to 1st lt. USMC, 1943-45. Republican. Episcopalian.

HANSEN, BARBARA CALEEN, scientist, physiology educator; b. Boston, Nov. 24, 1941; d. Reynold L. and Dorothy (Richardson) Caleen; m. Kenneth Dale Hansen, Oct. 8, 1976; 1 son, David Scott. B.S., UCLA, 1964, M.S., 1965; Ph.D., U. Wash., 1971. Asst. prof. then assoc. prof. U. Wash., Seattle, 1971-76; prof., assoc. dean U. Mich., Ann Arbor, 1977-82; assoc. v.p. acad. affairs and research, dean grad. sch. So. Ill. U., Carbondale, 1982-85; v.p. for grad. studies and research U. Md., Balt. and Baltimore County, 1985-90; prof. physiology, dir. obesity, diabetes and aging rsch. ctr. U. Md., 1990—; mem. adv. com. to dir. NIH, Washington, 1979-83; mem. joint health policy com. Assn. Am. Univs., Nat. Assn. State Univs. and Land-Grant Colls., Am. Council on Edn., Washington, 1982-86; mem. nutrition study sect. NIH, 1979-83; mem. program com. Inst. Medicine-Nat. Acad. Scis., Washington, 1982-84; mem. Armed Forces Epidemiology Bd. Contbr. articles to profl. jours.; editor: Controversies in Obesity, 1983; chpts. on physiology. Mem. adv. com. Am. Bur. Med. Advancement China, N.Y.C., 1982-85, Robert Wood Johnson Found., Princeton, N.J., 1982-91. U. Pa. Inst. Neuroscis. fellow, 1966-68; Arthur Patch McKinley scholar of Phi Beta Kappa, 1964. Mem. Am. Physiol. Soc., Inst. Medicine of Nat. Acad. Scis., Am. Inst. Nutrition, Am. Soc. for Clin. Nutrition, Internat. Assn. for Study Obesity (pres. 1986-90), N.Am. Assn. for Study Obesity (pres. 1984-85, 1986-90), Nat. Assn. State Univs. and Land Grant Colls. (chairperson coun. on rsch. policy and grad. edn. 1986-87), Phi Beta Kappa. Republican. Presbyterian. Office: U Md Sch Medicine MSTF6-00 10 S Pine St Baltimore MD 21201-1192

HANSEN, JEANNE BODINE, counselor; b. Reading, Pa., Nov. 26, 1930; d. George Smith and Emily Irene (Miller) Bodine; m. Richard Forrest Bean, May 27, 1951 (div. 1963); children: Mary, Christopher, David; m. Benjamin

John Hansen, May 21, 1965; 1 child, Clara. AB, U. Chgo., 1950; MEd, Towson State U., 1972. Nat. cert. counselor. Tchr. First Luth. Sch., Towson, Md., 1961-62, Balt. County Bd. Edn., Towson, Md., 1962-71; adminstrv. asst. John F. Kennedy Inst., Balt., 1972-73; employment counselor, manpower specialist State of Md., Balt., 1973-87, health benefits counselor, 1987-90; instr. Palmer Sch., Balt., 1990-91. Bd. dirs. Balt. Luth. High Sch., Towson, 1977-80, ACTS Ministry, Inc., Towson, 1988—; block capt. Towson Manor Village, 1991—. U. Chgo. scholar. Mem. Am. Assn. for Counseling and Devel., Assn. for Adult Devel. and Aging, Md. Assn. for Counseling & Devel., Women of First Luth. (rep.), Luth. Women's Missionary League (co-chmn. 1991—). Home: 216 Maryland Ave Baltimore MD 21286-5214

HANSEN, PER KRISTIAN, management consultant; b. Oslo, Feb. 17, 1932; s. Kristian and Gudrun Marie (Nordal) H.; m. Charlotte Berta Kretzschmar, July 18, 1964; children: Karin, Christian, Elisabeth. BSCE, Stanford U., 1955, MSCE, 1956. Engr., estimator Bechtel Corp., San Francisco, 1957-67, supt., 1967-72; constrn. mgr. Bechtel Power Corp., San Francisco, 1972-78; mgr. of constrn. Bechtel Power Corp., Ann Arbor, Mich., 1978-84; v.p. Bechtel Constrn., Inc., Gaithersburg, Md., 1984-86; pres. CPH Assocs., Inc., Gaithersburg, 1987—; mem. industry adv. com. to sch. of constrn. engring. and mgmt. Purdue U., Lafayette, Ind., 1982-84. Served as lt. C.E., 1950-53. Mem. ASCE, Norwegian Am. C. of C., Constrn. Mgmt. Assn. Am., San Francisco Engrs., Montgomery County C. of C. Lutheran. Home: 11604 Flints Grove Ln Gaithersburg MD 20878-2409 Office: CPH Assocs Inc 444 N Frederick Ave Ste 303 Gaithersburg MD 20877-2432

HANSEN, PETER HENRY, marketing executive; b. Bronx, N.Y., July 17, 1954; s. Henry Ernst and Geraldine Mae (Wells) H.; m. Lauren Dustin, May 10, 1985 (div. Mar. 1989); m. Katherine Southall, Aug. 31, 1991. BA in Polit. Sci., Trinity Coll., Hartford, Conn., 1976. Account exec. Supreme Artists, N.Y.C., 1976-78, Multi-Dimensional Arts, Albany, N.Y., 1978-80; dir. spl. projects U.S. Com. for UNICEF, N.Y.C., 1980-89; dir. devel. and mktg. Dance Theatre of Harlem, N.Y.C., 1989—; lectr. NYU Sch. Continuing Edn. Trustee The Vertex Found., San Diego, 1991—. Home: 427 Jersey Ave Jersey City NJ 07302-4346 Office: Dance Theatre of Harlem 247 W 30th St New York NY 10001-2801

HANSEN, PETER T., marketing professional director; b. Boston, Apr. 9, 1943; s. Walter O. Hansen and Dorothy A. (Bryant) Coleman; m. Patricia M. Lowden, Aug.12, 1967; children: Ryan N., Karyn J. BS, Rivier Coll., 1978, MBA, 1981. Product devel. engr. to v.p. mktg. Bemis Co., Inc., Nashua, N.H., 1967—; chmn. bd. dirs. N.H. Shippers Coop., Manchester, N.H., 1978-82. With USN, 1961-65. Home: 82 Amherst St Amherst NH 03031 Office: Bemis Co Inc Haines St Extension Nashua NH 03060

HANSEN, THOMAS DUANE, mental health executive; b. York, Pa., Sept. 19, 1944; s. Frederick Arthur and Blanche (Rohrbaugh) H.; m. Kay Ellen Koontz, Dec. 29, 1973; 1 child, Jared Thomas. BS, U. Md., 1970; MSW, U. Conn., 1973; PhD, U. of Maine, 1989. Lic. clin. social worker. Case worker Children's Svcs., York, Pa., 1972-73; chief program officer Community Action Program, Annapolis, Md., 1975-76, case work supr., 1976-79; sole practice mental health cons. Stonington, Maine, 1981-89; asst. prof. U. of Maine, Orono, 1989-91; exec. dir. Rural Health Ptnrs., Blue Hill, Maine, 1991—. Author: Life is a Moody Rainbow, 1970, Shades and Shadows, 1972; contbr. articles to profl. journals. With U.S. Army, 1961-64. Recipient Rural Health Outreach award Office of Rural Health Policy, 1991. Mem. Nat. Council-Family Relations (pres. 1984-88), Nat. Assn. of Social Workers, Am. Orthopsychiat. Assn. Democrat. Mem. Unitarian Universalist Ch. Home: RR 3 Box 32-H Ellsworth ME 04605 Office: Rural Health Ptnrs PO Box 309 Blue Hill ME 04614

HANSON, DAVID BIGELOW, construction company executive, engineer; b. Cambridge, Mass., Feb. 24, 1946; s. David B. Jr. and Kathleen M. (Roscoe) H.; m. Colleen Marie Barrett, Oct. 31, 1969; children: Matthew Joseph, Joshua David. BS in Civil Engring., U. Mass., 1968; postgrad., Templeton Coll., 1989. Supt. Bechtel Corp., San Francisco, 1968-71; project engr. Dwight Bldg. Co., Hamden, Conn., 1971-74; cost engring. mgr. HBE Corp., St. Louis, 1974-79, dir. project devel., 1979-81, v.p., 1982-84; v.p. Bassett Constrn. Co., Pueblo, Colo., 1981-82; dir. procurement and estimating Turner Internat. Industries, Inc., N.Y.C., 1984-85, v.p. procurement and estimating, 1986, v.p., gen. mgr., 1986-89; v.p., gen. mgr. Healthcare div. Turner Constrn. Co., N.Y.C., 1989-91; v.p., gen. mgr. Turner Constrn. Co., Detroit, 1991—; bd. dirs. Turner Info. Systems, N.Y.C. Mem. adv. bd. Regional Alliance for Minority and Women Businesses, N.Y.C., 1989-91. Mem. ASCE, Nat. Soc. Profl. Engrs., Associated Gen. Contractors (internat. constrn. com. 1987-89), Detroit Golf Club, Economic Club of Detroit. Republican.

HANSON, DAVID JUSTIN, sociology educator, college administrator; b. Orlando, Fla., Aug. 10, 1941; s. George Dewey and Clair (Cameron) H.; m. Carol Ann Wenger, Aug. 1,1 964; 1 child, Cynthia Denice. BA cum laude, Fla. State U., 1963; MA, Syracuse U., 1967, PhD, 1972. Asst. prof. sociology SUNY Coll Arts & Sci., Potsdam, 1968-76, assoc. prof., 1976-82, chair dept. sociology, 1977-85, prof., 1982—, dir. MA program in human svc., 1983-88, dir. of assessment, 1989—; alcohol and alcohol abuse cons. for 3d edit. Books for Coll. Librs., ALA, Chgo., 1985-86. Contbr. numerous articles to profl. jours. V.p. Alcohol and Substance Abuse Coun. of St. Lawrence County, Inc., Canton, N.Y., 1987—. Recipient Award for Excellence, N.Y. State Sociol. Assn., 1987; grantee Rsch. Found. of SUNY, Albany, 1984. Mem. Phi Kappa Phi (pres. Potsdam chpt. 1991—), Alpha Kappa Delta, Phi Eta Sigma. Home: 10 Drumlin Dr Potsdam NY 13676-1636 Office: SUNY Coll Arts and Sci Pierrepont Ave Potsdam NY 13676-2027

HANSON, DAVID PARKER, business education educator; b. Rheinbeck, N.Y., Nov. 9, 1939; s. Earl Parker and Charlotte (Leeper) H.; m. Barbara Rullan, Sept. 10, 1962; children: James, Carol; m. Laurel Ann McGough, May 10, 1986; children: Stephen, Daniel. BA, Haverford (Pa.) Coll., 1961; MA, U. Fla., 1966, PhD, 1970; JD cum laude, U. Mich., 1976. Asst. prof. polit. sci. Western Mich. U., Kalamazoo, 1969-74; assoc. Burlingham, Underwood & Lord, N.Y.C., 1976-78; atty., advisor U.S. Maritime Adminstrn., Washington, 1978-82; assoc. prof. internat. bus. Duquesne U., Pitts., 1982—. Lt. (j.g.) USNR, 1961-64. NDEA fellow U. Fla., 1965-68. Office: Duquesne U Sch Bus Adminstrn Pittsburgh PA 15282

HANSON, KATHARINE HEARD, association executive; b. Santa Monica, Calif., Jan. 30, 1947; d. Townsend and Rose (Loring) Heard. BA, Stanford U., 1969; MBA, Boston U., 1971. Asst. dir. div. of Instl. rsch., Office of the Pres. Boston U., 1971-73; v.p., dir. budget U. Mass. System, Boston, 1973-78; exec. dir. Consortium on Financing Higher Edn., Cambridge, Mass., 1978—; bd. dirs. Boston Five Cents Savs. Bank, New Eng. Edn. Loan Mktg. Corp., Braintree, Mass., Audion, Inc., Washington. Contbr. articles to profl. jours., chpts. to books; editor: Higher Education in a Changing Economy, 1990. Trustee Stanford U., 1984-89. Recipient Svc. award Stanford Assocs., 1987. Mem. Stanford Centennial Group of D.C., N.H. Audubon Soc., Appalachian Mtn. Club, Stanford Club of Boston, Nat. Commn. on Testing, Stanford Assocs. (bd. govs. 1989—). Office: Consortium on Fin Higher Ed 238 Main St #307 Cambridge MA 02142

HANSON, KENNETH RALPH, biochemist, retired; b. Birmingham, Eng., Sept. 7, 1930; s. William George and Nora Elizabeth (Laity) H.; m. Betty Ruth Crump, June 13, 1958; children: Patrick S.C., Gaelen E. BSc in Organic Chemistry, U. Liverpool, Eng., 1951, PhD in Organic Chemistry, 1954. Fellow in enzymology NRC, Ottawa, Ont., Can., 1956-58; fellow in bichemistry Jane Coffin Childs Sch. Medicine/NYU, N.Y.C., 1958-60; asst., asso. and full biochemist Dept. Biochemistry and Genetics, Conn. Agrl. Expt. Sta., New Haven, Conn., 1960-69, sr. biochemist, 1974-91; ret. Dept Biochemistry and Genetics, Conn. Agrl. Expt. Sta., New Haven, Conn., 1991. Contbr. numerous articles to profl. jours. Japan Soc. Promotion Sci. fellow. Mem. Phytochem. Soc. N.Am. (pres. 1972-73), Am. Soc. Plant Physiologists, Am. Soc. Biol. Chemistry and Molecular Biology. Home: 595 Saddle Ridge Rd Orange CT 06477-2024

HANSON, PEG, graphic designer, writer, illustrator, psychic; b. Detroit, Sept. 14, 1946; d. Heber C. and Kathryn (Shields) Hizar; children: William Andrew, Peter Christopher. Student, Cranbrook Art Inst., 1958-60, Universidad de Mex., 1963, Mich. State U., 1964-67. Writer, illustrator, designer Leisure mag., Bauston Spa, N.Y., 1974-75; designer Van de Car DePoor & Johnson Advt., Albany, N.Y., 1975; prodn. mgr. Children's Design Ctr., Saratoga Springs, N.Y., 1975; creative dir. Kellert Advt., Albany, 1975-77; ad mgr. Higerson Bury & Sons, Bennington, Vt., 1977-86; owner Peg Hanson & Assoc., Albany, 1986—; mktg. dir. United Way Northeastern N.Y., 1987-90; graphic arts mgr. Elliot Publs., Inc., 1990-91; owner Peg Hanson Visual Comm., 1991—. Mem. Rensselaerville (N.Y.) Hist. Soc., 1989—; pub. rels. com. Ronald McDonald House; bd. dirs. Rensselaerville Libr. Howard and Bush grantee; recipient Strathmore Paper Graphics award. Mem. Internat. Assn. Bus. Communications, Internat. House of Printing Craftsmen, Nat. Assn. Desktop Pub. Home: RR 1 Box 10 Rensselaerville NY 12147-9502 Studio: 2173 Methodist Hill Rd RR 1 Box 10 Rensselaerville NY 12147-9502

HANSON, ROBERT DELOLLE, lawyer; b. Harrisburg, Pa., Dec. 13, 1916; s. Henry W. A. and Elizabeth (Painter) H.; B.A., Gettysburg Coll., 1939; LL.B., Dickinson Law Sch., 1942; m. Barbara Esmer, Apr. 22, 1949. Admitted to Pa. bar, 1942; practiced in Harrisburg, 1946—; solicitor, Dauphin County, 1958-76, Dauphin County Redevel. Authority, 1959—. Pres. Family and Children's Service of Harrisburg, 1956-57; mem. Harrisburg Sch. Bd., 1952-57, Dauphin County Housing Authority, 1960; gen. chmn. Tri-County United Fund, 1969, pres., 1971-72; trustee Gettysburg Coll., 1974—, sec., 1980, vice chmn., 1983-86; pres. Keystone area council Boy Scouts Am., 1980-82 (Silver Beaver award 1980, Eagle award 1990). Served from 2d lt. to maj. inf. AUS, 1942-46; ETO. Recipient Alexis de Tocqueville award United Way Am., 1991Others award Salvation Army, 1992; decorated Bronze Star, Purple Heart. Mem. Am., Pa. (sec., treas. taxation sect. 1948-59), Dauphin County (dir. 1958-59) bar assns., Gettysburg Coll. Alumni Assn. (treas. 1958, 59, v.p. 1968-71, pres. 1971-72), Phi Beta Kappa. Lutheran (pres. council of congregation 1953, 54, 55, 57, 58, 59). Clubs: Masons (33 deg., past master, pres. bd. trustees 1982-85), Execs. (pres. 1953), Tuesday, Harrisburg Rotary (pres. 1979). Home: 2500 N 2d St Harrisburg PA 17110 Office: 100 Chestnut St Ste 307 Harrisburg PA 17101-2542

HANSON, RONALD LEE, biochemist; b. Lincoln, Nebr., Feb. 2, 1944; s. Lester Eugene and Gladys (Diessner) H. BA, U. Minn., 1965; PhD, U. Wis., 1970. Postdoctoral fellow Med. Sch. Harvard U., Boston, 1970-72; asst. prof. Columbia U., N.Y.C., 1972-79; sr. scientist Sandoz, Inc., East Hanover, N.J., 1979-81; mem. sr. sci. staff Sandoz Rsch. Inst., East Hanover, 1981-87; sr. rsch. investigator Bristol-Myers Squibb, New Brunswick, N.J., 1987—; sr. investigator N.Y. Heart Assn., 1973-77. Contbr. articles to profl. jours.; inventee in field. NSF fellow, 1965-69, NIH fellow, 1970-72; grantee NSF, 1974-76, NIH, 1976-79. Mem. AAAS, Am. Soc. Biochemistry and Molecular Biology, Phi Beta Kappa. Office: Bristol Myers Squibb 1 Squibb Dr New Brunswick NJ 08903

HANSON, SIMON PETER, chemical engineering educator; b. Torquay, Eng., June 13, 1953; came to U.S., 1969; s. Jack Aubrey and Eliza Ellen (Hall) H.; m. Nancy Ann Dean, Dec. 7, 1980. SB, MIT, 1974, ScD, 1982. Asst. prof. chem. engring. U. Ariz., Tucson, 1983-89; mng. dir. A. Best Co., Tucson, 1989-90; dir. rsch. and devel. Ikonotek, Scottsdale, 1990-91; rsch. engr. Consolidation Coal Co., Pitts., 1991—. Halcon Internat. fellow, 1976. Mem. AIAA (sr.), Am. Inst. Chemists, Am. Inst. Chem. Engrs., Combustion Inst., Sigma Xi. Home: 1750 Village Green Dr Clairton PA 15025-3052 Office: R&D Consol Coal Co Library PA 15129

HANSON, THOMAS EARL, biology educator; b. Lincoln, Nebr., Jan. 25, 1941; s. Earl Thomas and Martha Elinor (Howells) H.; m. Marlene Ann Schicker, Jan. 30, 1964; children: Kimberly Ann, Christopher Earl. BA, So. Ill. U., 1964; PhD, Mich. State U., 1969. Rsch. asst. biology dept. Calif. Inst. Tech., Pasadena, 1969-73; asst. prof. Temple U., Phila., 1974—. Author: (chpt.) Development of Drosophila, 1992; contbr. articles to profl. jours. NIH fellow, 1970, grantee, 1975; recipient Johnson & Johnson Co. award, 1964. Democrat. Home: 102 Walnut St Jenkintown PA 19046-3126 Office: Temple U Biology Dept 12th & Norris St Philadelphia PA 19122

HANSSON, RICHARD JOHN, lawyer; b. Jersey City, Apr. 20, 1952; s. Robert Wesley and Roberta Loretta (O'Brien) H.; m. Jacqueline Jean Brookes, Sept. 27 1990; children: Heather Brookes, Timothy Richard. BS in Acctg., St. Peter's Coll., 1975; JD, Seton Hall U., 1987. Bar: N.J. 1988. Acct., mgr. The Quaker Oats Co., Elizabeth, N.J., 1975-81; paramedic University Emergency Med. Svcs., Newark, N.J., 1983—; sole practice law Roselle, N.J., 1987—; chief exec. officer EMS Theory and Practice, Roselle, 1989—; expert witness emergency med. svc. theory and practice, Roselle, 1990—. Co-founder, pres. Union Twp. Vols., 1979; treas., v.p. Roselle Vol. Ambulance, 1972-79. Mem. Nat. Assn. EMTs, N.J. Bar Assn., N.J. Trauma Awareness Found. (bd. dirs. 1989—). Home and Office: 242 W 5th Ave Roselle NJ 07203-1140

HANTHO, CHARLES HAROLD, textile executive; b. Lethbridge, Alta., Can., 1931; m. Phyllis Mae Weir, 1957; children: Karl Alan, Mark Albert, Jon Andrew, Heather Gale. BSChemE, U. Alta., Can., 1953. With C-I-L Inc., Can., 1953—; tech. asst. C-I-L Inc., Edmonton, Alta., 1953; with plastics sales dept. C-I-L Inc., Toronto, 1954-61, salesman, 1961-64; with plastics sales dept. C-I-L Inc., Brampton, Ont., 1964-67; with plastics sales dept. C-I-L Inc., Montreal, Que., 1964-67, gen. mgr. plastics, 1968-71, v.p., dir., 1973-81; dep. chmn. C-I-L Imperial Chem. Industries P.L.C. C-I-L Inc., London, 1976-78; pres. C-I-L Inc., Montreal, Que., 1981-82, chief exec. officer, 1982—, chmn., 1985-88; ret., 1988; pres., chief oper. officer Dominion Textile Inc., Montreal, 1989—, chief exec. officer, 1989, chmn., pres., 1990—, also bd. dirs.; bd. dirs. Dofasco Inc., Inco Ltd., TransAlta Utilities Corp. Bd. dirs. Montreal YMCA Found. Fellow Can. Acad. Engring.; mem. Soc. Chem. Industry (past chmn.), Can. Mfrs. Assn. (past chmn.), Can. Chem. Producers' Assn. (past chmn.), Mt. Royal Club, Toronto Club, St. George's Golf and Country Club, Mt. Bruno Golf Club, Can. Club Montreal (bd. dirs.). Office: 1950 Sherbrooke St W, Montreal, PQ Canada H3H 1E7

HANTON, E(MILE) MICHAEL, public and personnel relations consultant; b. Gary, Ind.; s. Zachary and Maria (Suciu) H. AB, Ind. U., 1951, MA, 1955; grad. sr. USAF profl. mil. edn. course, USAF Air War Coll., 1968. Various prodn. positions U.S. Steel Corp., Gary, 1940, 41, 50; prodn. contr. Douglas Aircraft Corp., Santa Monica, Calif., 1946-47; classified advt. mgr Weaver Pub. Co., Santa Monica, 1947-48; reporter Muncie (Ind.) Evening Press, 1952, Gary Post-Tribune, 1952-53; head cashier Office Lake County Treas., Gary, 1955-60; pub. and pers. rels. cons. Gary, 1960—, Plattsburgh, N.Y., 1968—; asst. prof. State U. Coll. Arts & Scis., Plattsburgh, 1966-67; cons. community rels. and fund raising. Author: The New Nurse, 1973. With USAAF, 1941-45, USAF active res. 1945-69, ret. Decorated Air medal, Purple Heart. Mem. Am. Med. Writers Assn., Assn. Edn. in Journalism and Mass Communications, Health Scis. Communications Assn., Am. Acad. Advt., Gary C. of C., Plattsburgh C. of C., Air Force Assn., Res. Officers Assn., Nat. Arts Club, Steel Club, Caterpillar Club, Flying Boot Club. Office: PO Box 803 Plattsburgh NY 12901-0803

HANTULA, RICHARD MICHAEL, editor; b. Mt. Clemens, Mich., Nov. 13, 1945; s. Wilho Nick and Lyyli Ingrid (Luoma) H.; m. Irina Leonidovna Belodedova, July 26, 1974; 1 child, Elias. BA, U. Mich., 1967; AM, Harvard U., 1969, PhD, 1976. Translator Cambridge, Mass., 1976-77; sr. editorial asst. Macmillan Ednl. Co., N.Y.C., 1977-78, assoc. editor, 1978-80, translation editor, 1980, sr. editor, 1980-91; sr. editor P.F. Collier, Inc., N.Y.C., 1991-92; mng. editor, 1992—; Editor, translator: The Rule of Empress Anna, 1982; contbr. articles to profl. jours. Mem. AAASS, N.Y. Acad. Scis., Am. Mus. Natural History, Phi Beta Kappa. Office: P F Collier Inc Editorial Div 866 3d Ave New York NY 10022-6221

HAO, OLIVER JING, civil engineer; b. Kunming, Yunan, China, May 11, 1946; came to U.S., 1969; s. S.L. and Y. (Zen) H.; m. Cathy C. Tang. Mar. 24, 1979; children: Melissa B., Christina A. BS, Cheng Kung U., 1968; MS, Colo. State U., 1971; PhD, U. Calif., Berkeley, 1982. Registered profl. engr., Ohio, Ind. Instr. Non Commissioned Army Sch., Taipei, Taiwan, 1968-69; rsch. asst. Colo. State U., Ft. Collins, 1969-71, Iowa State U., Ames, 1971-73; dir. rsch. SIEW, Inc., Columbus, Ind., 1973-78; rsch. asst. U. Calif., Berkeley, 1978-81; asst. prof. U. Md., College Park, 1982-87, assoc. prof., 1987—; cons. Environ, Inc., Washington, 1984, Aepco, Inc., Bethesda, Md., 1982-85, Aneptek Co., Natick, Mass., 1989. Contbr. articles to profl. jours. Initiation grantee NSF, Washington, 1983. Mem. ASCE (assoc. editor Jour. Environ. Engring. 1990—), Am. Water Works Assn., Internat. Water Pollution Assn., Water Pollution Control Fedn. Assn., Environ. Engring. Profls. Avocation: reading. Home: 14431 Pebblestone Dr Silver Spring MD 20905-5978 Office: U Md Dept Civil Engring College Park MD 20742

HAPEMAN, JOHN WILLIAM, psychologist; b. Scranton, Pa., Oct. 22, 1942; s. John Wetherby and Ruth Lillian (Jones) H.; m. Judith Anne Bonnert, Sept. 29, 1961; children: John F., Wayne D., Mark D., Jeffrey R., Brian T. AA in Mech. Design, Johnson Tech. Inst., 1961; BA in Psychology, Alvernia Coll., 1988; MA in Counseling Psychology, U. Pa., Kutztown, 1991. Exptl. technician Sprague & Henwood Corp., Scranton, Pa., 1961-62; electronic & mech. technician NCR Corp., Avola, Pa., 1962-73; owner, operator J.W. Hapeman Cash Register Sales & Svc., Mill City, Pa., 1973-77; svc. mgr. Reading (Pa.) Bus. Equipment, 1977-78; svc. mgr., sales rep. Capital Cash Register Co., Reading, 1978-83; researcher, riflemaker J.W. Hapeman Gunsmithing, Kutztown, Pa., 1983-91; counselor Kutztown U. of Pa., 1990—; counselor pvt. practice Fleetwood, Pa., 1991—; dir. One Another Ministries, Fleetwood, Pa., 1991—; cons. counselor Family Life Svcs., Topton, Pa., 1991—; cons. Christian Counseling Assocs., Ephrata, Pa. Mem. Am. Assn. Counseling & Devel., Christian Counseling Assn. Home and Office: 134 Spook Ln Fleetwood PA 19522

HAPKE, BRUCE WILLIAM, planetary scientist, educator; b. Racine, Wis., Feb. 17, 1931; s. William E. and Blanche V. (Pulda) H.; m. Joyce Zellinger, June 18, 1954; children: Kevin, Jeffrey, Cheryl. BS, U. Wis., 1953; PhD, Cornell U., 1962. Sr. rsch. assoc. ctr. radiophysics and space rsch. Cornell U., Ithaca, N.Y., 1960-62; prof. dept. geology and planetary sci. U. Pitts., 1962—; rsch. assoc. Carnegie Mus. Natural History, Pitts.; prin. investigator Appolo Lunar Samples; mem. TV sci. team NASA Mariner 10 Mission; guest scientist TV sci. team NASA Viking Lander Mission; cons. NASA. Contbr. articles to profl. jours. Lt. USNR, 1953-55. Asteroid #3549 Hapke named in his honor, 1988. Mem. AAAS, Am. Geophys. Union, Am. Astron. Soc. (chmn. div. planetary scis. 1988-89), Internat. Astron. Union. Office: U Pitts 321 Old Engineering Hall Pittsburgh PA 15260-3332

HAPPEL, JOHN, chemical engineer, researcher; b. Bklyn., Apr. 1, 1908; s. John and Emilie (Weinkauf) H.; m. Dorothy Merriam, 1951; children: Jill, George, Ruth. BS, MIT, 1929, MS, 1930; DChemE, Poly. Inst. Bklyn., 1948. Registered profl. engr., N.Y. With Socony Vacuum Oil Co., 1930-48; prof. chem. engring., chmn. dept. chem. engring. NYU, N.Y.C., 1949-73, prof. emeritus, 1973—; adj. prof. Columbia U., N.Y.C., 1973—, spl. rsch. assoc., 1976—; pres. Catalysis Rsch. Corp.; mem. bd. mgrs. Mohonk Consultations, Inc.; mem. petroleum industry war coun., 1942-45; mem. tech. com. in charge on constrn. and operation of world's largest butadiene plant for synthetic rubber, 1942-47; cons. petroleum chems. various cos. Author: Chemical Process Economics, 1958, 2d edit. (with Donald Jordan), 1974, (with Howard Brenner) Low Reynolds Number Hydrodynamics, 1965, 2d edit., 1973, paperback edit., 1983; translator: (with M.F. Delleo, Jr., G. Dembinski, A.H. Weiss) Catalysis by Non-Metals (from Russian by O.V. Krylov), 1970, (with Miguel Hnatow and Laimonis Bajars) Base Metal Oxide Catalysts, 1977, Isotopic Assessment of Heterogeneous Catalysis, 1986; assoc. editor: Chem. Engring. Jour.; mem. editorial adv. bd. Ency. Chem. Processing and Design, Oxidation Communications, Chem. Engring. Jour.; contbr. articles to profl. jours., chpts. to tech. books; patentee in field. Recipient Certificate of Distinction Poly. Inst. Bklyn.; Tyler award N.Y. sect. Am. Inst. Chem. Engrs.; Vols. 82, 83 Chem. Engring. Communications honored 80th birthday. Fellow N.Y. Acad. Scis. (v.p. 1977), Am. Inst. Chem. Engrs. (Founders award 1987); mem. Am. Chem. Soc. (Honor Scroll), Nat. Acad. Engring., Chemists Club, Sigma Xi, Alpha Chi Sigma, Phi Lambda Upsilon, Tau Beta Pi. Episcopalian. Home: 69 Tompkins Ave Hastings On Hudson NY 10706-3944 Office: Columbia U New York NY 10027

HARAMATI, AVIAD, physiology and biophysics educator, researcher; b. Jerusalem, Jan. 25, 1954; came to U.S., 1956; s. Amnon and Dinah (Eliezri) H.; m. Claire Zeller, May 30, 1982; children: Talia, Ariel, Natan. BS, Bklyn. Coll., 1975; PhD, U. Cin., 1979. Postdoctoral fellow Mayo Clinic, Rochester, Minn., 1979-82, instr., 1981-82, asst. prof., 1982-85; asst. prof. Sch. of Medicine Georgegown U., Washington, 1985-87, assoc. prof. Sch. of Medicine, 1987-92; prof. Sch. of Medicine Georgetown U., Washington, 1992—; mem. rsch. com. Nat. Kidney Found., Washington, 1990—. Contbr. numerous articles to profl. jours. Recipient Day Meml. Rsch. award Nat. Kidney Found., 1989, 90. Mem. Kemp Mill Synagogue (v.p. 1991—). Office: Georgetown U Sch Medicine 3900 Reservoir Rd NW Washington DC 20007-2187

HARARI, CARMI, clinical psychologist, psychoanalyst; b. N.Y.C., Dec. 4, 1920; s. Ezra and Dina (Katz) H.; m. Clara Soshen, June 19, 1942 (div.); children: Karen Tarnofsky, Michelle Chino; m. Sarah Zaraleya Kurzweil, Dec. 31, 1979. BSS in Psychology, CCNY, 1946; MA in Clin. Psychology, NYU, 1947; EdD in Psychology of Family Life, Columbia U., 1968; cert. in psychoanalysis, 1978. Lic. psychologist, N.Y. Sch. psychologist N.Y.C., 1946-47; clin. psychologist VA Hosps. and Clinics, N.Y.C., 1947-50; lectr., asst. prof. NYU, Columbia U., CUNY, Met. Inst. Psychoanalytic Studies, N.Y.C., 1948-82; pvt. practice N.Y.C., 1950—; staff psychologist N.Y.C. Children's Ct., 1950-52, chief psychologist, 1953-57; dir. Community Consultation Svcs., N.Y.C., 1957-75; staff psychologist, 1957-70; exec. dir. Humanistic Psychology Ctr. of N.Y., N.Y.C., 1973—; dir. Interactions: Psychol. Svcs., New City, N.Y., 1990—; cons. various schs., N.Y.C., 1956-75, Ministry Social Welfare, Israel, 1961, Office Disability Determinations, N.Y. State Dept. Social Svcs., 1970—, others; adj. prof. various N.Y. colls., 1975-82; dir. internat. devel., mem. exec. bd. Assn. Humanistic Psychology, 1969-80; exec. sec. N.Y. Soc. Clin. Psychologists, 1967-69, pres. 1970-72; NGO rep. Internat. Coun. Psychologists, UNESCO, 1980—, bd. dirs. internat. liaison, 1988—; treas. Psychologists for Social Responsibility, Washington, 1982-88. Author book chpts.; contbr. articles to profl. jours. and newsletters. Organizer, leader Group Psychotherapy Found., N.Y.C. Around the World Study Tour, 1966; chair adv. bd. Women's Ctrs. for Occupational Devel., N.Y.C., 1969-71; trustee Psychol. Svc. Ctr. N.Y., Soc. Clin. Psychologists, N.Y.C., 1969-72; organizer, leader internat. confs. humanistic psychology, Denmark, Eng., France, Iceland, Ger., India, Israel, Japan, Mex., Netherlands, Norway, Sweden, USSR, 1969-76; bd. dirs. Assn. for Humanistic Psychologists, Humanistic Psychology Inst., San Francisco, 1970-76; adv. bd. Identity House, N.Y.C., 1972-73. With USAF, 1942-45. Recipient War Svc. scholarship, N.Y. State, 1952. Fellow APA (div. pres. Humanistic Psychology Found. 1971-73, coun. rep. 1974-77, 78-81, 85-88, 91—, pres. proposed div. transpersonal psychology 1982-83, chmn. subcom. on psychology of peacemaking 1988-90, mem. com. on internat. rels. in psychology), Am. Orthopsychiat. Assn., Interam. Psychology Soc., Internat. Assn. for Cross Cultural Psychology, World Fedn. Mental Health, Internat. Assn. Applied Psychology (sec.-treas. div. polit. psychology 1990); mem. Phi Delta Kappa, Kappa Delta Pi. Home: 10 Wyndam Ln New City NY 10956-4527 Office: Wnydham Inst 19 E 34th St New York NY 10001

HARBACH, RALPH EDWARD, entomologist, researcher; b. Streator, Ill., Mar. 23, 1948; s. Edward Ralph and Lorraine (Marrow) H.; m. Roberta Louise Crampton, Mar. 14, 1970; children: Paul Edward, Andrea Lynn. BS, Western Ill. U., 1971, MS, 1972; PhD, U. Ill., 1976. Bd. cert. entomologist. Rsch. assoc. N.C. State U., Raleigh, 1976-79; entomologist Walter Reed Army Inst. Rsch., Washington, 1980-84, Armed Forces Rsch. Inst. Med. Sci., Bangkok, 1985-88; mgr. biosystematics unit Walter Reed Army Inst. Rsch., Washington, 1988—; rsch. assoc. Smithsonian Instn., Washington, 1983-86, 89—. Author: Taxonomists' Glossary of Mosquito Anatomy, 1980, The Mosquitoes of the Subgenus Culex in Southwestern Asia (Diptera: Culicidae), 1988; asst. editor Mosquito Systematics. Grantee Dept. Def. In-House Lab. Ind. Rsch., 1986, 91, 92. Mem. AAAS, Entomol. Soc. Am., Am. Mosquito Control Assn., Entomol. Soc. Washington (membership sec. 1983), Am. Mosquito Control Assn., Sigma Xi. Office: Walter Reed Army Inst Rsch Biosystematics Unit MSC Smithsonian Instn Washington DC 20560

HARBISON, JAMES PRESCOTT, research physicist; b. Phila., Apr. 5, 1951; s. Robert James III and Elizabeth (Thompson) H.; m. Susan Foster, June 17, 1973; children: Thomas Foster, Daniel Robert, Elizabeth Thompson Harbison. AB in Physics, Harvard Coll., 1973, SM in Applied Physics, 1974, PhD in Applied Physics/Materials Sci., 1977. IBM postdoctoral fellow Harvard U., Cambridge, Mass., 1977-78; mem. tech. staff Bell Labs., Murray Hill, N.J., 1978-84, Bellcore, Red Bank, N.J., 1984—. Contbr. articles to profl. jours.; patentee in field. Mem. Am. Phys. Soc., Am. Vacuum soc., Minerals, Metals and Materials Soc., Materials Rsch. Soc. Unitarian. Home: 53 Tyson Dr Fair Haven NJ 07704-3036 Office: Bellcore NVC 3X-211 331 Newman Springs Rd Red Bank NJ 07701-7040

HARBIT, DOUGLAS ALAN, historic preservationist; b. Hampton, Iowa, Dec. 14, 1949; s. William Glen and Edythe Marie (Harvey) H.; life ptnr. Terry Hanlen, Aug. 10, 1985. BA, COE Coll., Cedar Rapids, Iowa, 1972; MPA, George Washington U., 1975. Dir. bus. svcs. Oakland (Calif.) Dept. Devel., 1975-76; asst. dir. Dept. Devel., Newport News, Va., 1976-84; v.p. Carley Capital Group, Washington, 1984-87; dir. fin. svcs. Nat. Trust for Historic Preservation, Washington, 1987—; guest lectr. Columbia U., N.Y.C., 1988—. Active County Task Force on Village Zoning, Prince George's County, Md., 1991; treas. South of Sligo Citizens Assn., Takoma Park, Md., 1991. Mem. Urban Land Inst., Coun. Urban Econ. Devel. Democrat. Home: 708 Auburn Ave Silver Spring MD 20912-5853 Office: Nat Trust Hist Preservation 1785 Massachusetts Ave NW Washington DC 20036-2117

HARDEE, LEWIS JEFFERSON, JR., educator; b. Wilmington, N.C., Jan. 17, 1937; s. Lewis Jefferson and Dorothy (Dosher) H. BA, U. N.C., 1959, MA, 1971. Instr. Am. Acad. Dramatic Arts, N.Y.C., 1970-84; assoc. prof. Wagner Coll., S.I., N.Y., 1984—; music dir., composer in residence Penny Bridge Players, Bklyn., 1981-84, music dir. Wagner Coll. Theatre, S.I., 1984—. Composer Revolution!; composer, lyricist The Prince and the Pauper, 1978, Treasure Island, 1979, Christopher Columbus, 1981, 82, published as Christopher Columbus His Story, 1991, Hansel and Gretel, 1981, Nothing to Hide, 1982, Robin Hood, Build Me A Bridge, 1983, Goldilocks, 1983, Sweet Land of Liberty, 1986, The Little Prince, 1987. Bd. dirs. The Lambs, N.Y.C., 1987—, Inter-Cities Performing Arts, Inc., Union City, N.J., 1988-89, Brunswick Performing Arts Ctr., Inc. Southport, N.C., 1989—. With U.S. Army, 1960-62. Grantee Meet the Composer, Inc., 1982, N.C. Coun. for Arts, 1976; recipient Award of Merit Eleanor Gay Lee Gallery Found., 1983. Mem. ASCAP, Nat. Assn. Tchrs. Singing, Dramatists Guild, Assoc. Artists Southport (hon. life). Home: 320 E 57th St New York NY 10022-2948 Office: Wagner Coll Grymes Hill Staten Island NY 10301

HARDIMAN, JOSEPH RAYMOND, investment banker; b. Salisbury, Md., May 27, 1937; s. Leonard Roy and Virginia Mildred (Darden) H.; m. Katherine McCampbell, Mar. 23, 1963; children: Katherine Hughes, Elizabeth Gore. BA, U. Md., 1959, LLB, 1962. Bar: Md. 1962. Law clk. to Hon. Hall Hammond Md. Ct. of Appeals, 1962-63; assoc. Miles & Stockbridge, Balt., 1963-68; exec. v.p., sec., dir. Robert Garrett & Sons, Inc., Balt., 1968-75; gen. partner Alex. Brown & Sons, 1975-87, mng. dir., 1984-87; pres., chief exec. officer Nat. Assn. of Securities Dealers, Inc., 1987—; bd. dirs. NASDAQ, Inc., NASD Market Svcs. Inc. Bd. dirs. Arthritis Found., Md., 1975-79, pres., 1976-78; bd. dirs. Balt. Urban Coalition, 1975-78, U. Md. Med. System, 1980-86; bd. dirs. Fund for Ednl. Excellence, 1984-91; mem. steering com. Baltimore County Charter Rev. Commn., 1977-78; trustee St. Paul's Sch. for Girls, 1978-86, Securities Industry Found. Econ. Edn., 1988—; mem. adv. bd. Vanderbilt U. Fin. Markets Rsch. Ctr., 1988—, U. Calif. Securities Regulation Inst., 1988—; bd. visitors U. Md. Sch. Law, 1990—. Mem. Md. Club, Elkridge Club, Met. Club, Links Club (N.Y.C.), Order of Coif, Phi Delta Theta, Omicron Delta Kappa. Home: 8 Bowen Mill Rd Baltimore MD 21212-1053 Office: Nat Assn Securities Dealers 1735 K St NW Washington DC 20006-1516

HARDIMAN, THERESE ANNE, lawyer; b. Chestnut Hill, Pa., Mar. 2, 1956; d. Edward Joseph and Grace Joan (Shaw) Hardiman; m. David J.P. Malecki, Feb. 3, 1990; 1 child, Christine Mary; BA in History, BA in Psychology, Mt. St. Mary's Coll., 1978; JD, Thomas M. Cooley Law Sch., 1983. Bar: Pa. 1983, U.S. Dist. Ct. (ea. dist.) Pa. 1983, U.S. Ct. Appeals (3d cir.) 1984, U.S. Dist. Ct. (mid. dist.) Pa. 1989. Staff rsch. asst. Internat. Brotherhood of Teamsters, Washington, 1978-79; law clk. Richard R. Rashid, Atty. at Law, Lansing, Mich., 1981-82; law clk. Pearlstine, Salkin, Hardiman & Robinson, Landsdale, Pa., 1981; staff asst. Employment Rels. Bd., Mich. Dept. Civil Svc., Lansing, 1982; mem. Pearlstine, Salkin, Hardiman & Robinson, Landsdale, 1983-86; v.p. Edward J. Hardiman & Assocs. P.C., 1986—. Editor-in-chief Pridwin, 1978, layout editor, 1977. Recipient Golden Key award, Delta Theta Phi, 1981; Outstanding Student award Student Bar Assn., Thomas M. Cooley Law Sch., 1982. Mem. ABA, Assn. Trial Lawyers Am., Pa. Assn. Trial Lawyers, Pa. Bar Assn., Monroe County Bar Assn., Montgomery County Bar Assn., Delta Theta Phi. Republican. Roman Catholic. Office: RR 40 Box 850 Pocono Pines PA 18350

HARDING, DARLENE CAROL, mathematics and foreign language educator; b. Springfield, Minn., May 9, 1945; d. Lyle Lynn and Ruth Elizabeth (Hensch) Stark; m. Richard M. Harding, July 3, 1975; children: Richard Walker, Daniel Aaron. BS, St. Cloud U., 1967, MA, Ball State U., 1975; postgrad., SUNY, Buffalo, 1987—. Cert. tchr., N.Y. Tchr. Spring Lake Park (Minn.) High Sch., 1967-69, Dept. Def. Overseas Schs. various countries, 1969-75, Woodbridge (Va.) High Sch., 1983-85; asst. prof. math. and fgn. lang. Medaille Coll., Buffalo, 1985—; v.p. bd. dirs. Walker Estates, Batavia, N.Y., 1988—. Mem., officer German-Am. Assn., Bamberg, Fed. Republic Germany, 1977-78, Osterholz-Scharmbeck, Fed. Republic Germany, 1978-79; pres. bd. dirs. Garmisch Am. Montessori Sch., 1982. Recipient Pushkin award Def. Lang. Inst., 1980. Mem. ASCD, Nat. Coun. Tchrs. Math., Math. Assn. Am., Am. Ednl. Rsch. Assn., Clarence Bus. and Profl. Women's Orgn., Clarence (N.Y.) Swim Club, Episcopal Ch. Women Club. Republican. Episcopalian. Home: 4630 Pine Mnr Clarence NY 14031-2225 Office: Medaille Coll 18 Agassiz Cir Buffalo NY 14214-2695

HARDING, ENOCH, JR., clothing executive; b. Greenville, S.C., Apr. 7, 1931; s. Enoch and Nell (Evans) H.; m. Sarah Tomlinson, Dec. 26, 1953 (div. 1978); children: Enoch III, Earle T., David H., Elizabeth W.; m. Virginia Black, Sept., 1978. BS, Presbyn. Coll., Clinton, S.C., 1953. Div. mgr. Stone Mfg. Co., Columbia, S.C., 1955-62, Oxford Industries, Columbia, 1962-71; div. pres. Kellwood Co., N.Y.C., 1971-77, 83—; pres. Vanity Fair Mills, Reading, Pa., 1977-83. Vice chmn. Midlands Tech. Coll., Columbia, 1961-71. 1st lt. U.S. Army, 1953-55. Mem. Union League Club N.Y.C. Home: 118 Sylvan St Chapin SC 29036-8790

HARDMAN, JOHN HERBERT, school counselor; b. Pitts., May 6, 1929; s. Carl Deffabaugh and Elsie Mary (Schilling) H.; m. Jeannine Beatrice Mower, Jan. 31, 1952; children: Janice, Jay, Jeffrey. BS, U. Pitts., 1952, MEd, 1954. Cert. sch. counselor. Asst. dean of students U. Pitts., 1952-59; counselor Mt. Lebanon Pub. Schs., Pitts., 1959-65; instr. (part-time) Pa. State U., Pitts., 1959-65; counselor North Hills Sch. Dist., Pitts., 1965—; developer, dir., owner Falcon Youth Camp, Carrollton, Ohio, 1959-84; developer Shared Acres, Carrollton, 1988—; presentor state and nat. levels counseling and camping, 1960-75. Contbr. articles to profl. jours. Mem. Common Cause, Washington, 1972; parent rep. Pitts. City Schs., 1972-78; mem. com. mgmt. Pitts. YMCA, Deer Valley Family Camp, 1958-64; at-large bd. dirs. U. Pitts., 1987—; elder Presbyn. Ch. With U.S. Army, 1946-48. Mem. AACD, NEA, Pa. State Edn. Assn. Republican. Presbyterian. Home: 2019 Arnold Acres Dr Pittsburgh PA 15205-4105 Office: North Hill Sch Dist 55 Rochester Rd Pittsburgh PA 15229-1188

HARDMAN, KATHLEEN GOLDIE BROWN, nurse; b. Newark, June 17, 1915; d. Henry Jay and Kathleen Goldie (Burner) Brown; m. Ike Quebec, June 17, 1936 (div. 1950). BS, Howard U., 1984; MA, U. of D.C., 1989. RN, N.Y., D.C. Staff nurse Harlem Hosp., Manhattan, N.Y., 1937-42, Morrisania Hosp., Bronx, N.Y., 1942-45; pvt. duty nurse N.Y. area, 1945-50; staff nurse D.C. Gen., 1950-51; pub. health nurse D.C. Pub. Health Nursing Svc., 1951-63; RN, bus. coord. Robert F. Blythe, M.D., P.C., Washington, 1964—, Silver Spring, Md., 1991—; cons., educator various health programs; speaker Nat. Ctr. for the Black Aged Estate, Washington. Represented in pub. and pvt. collections Dept. Agrl. Grad. Sch., Washington, 1968-80; developed and produced needlework, products for crochet and knitting exhbns. Active voter registration activities, Washington, 1950—, recruitment for health svc. occupations, 1950—, neighborhood watch and safety programs, 1950—, tenants and community based polit. coun. programs, 1950—; mem., pres. Christian basic Bible study class, mem. scholarship com., mem. ch.'s renovation com. Takoma Park Bapt. Ch. Mem. Nat. Assn. Parliamentarians (treas. Sartwell unit), LWV, Internat. Toastmistress Club (held all offices 1940-50), Lambda Kappa Mu (1st anti basileus 1947-50, program dir. 1947-50, youth dir. 1943-47). Republican. Home: 120 Jefferson St NW Washington DC 20011-6628

HARDMAN, WILLIAM VICTOR, JR., marketing professional; b. Oklahoma City, Okla., Oct. 20, 1945; s. William Victor and Naomi Doll (Chell) H.; m. Linda Carl, Nov. 16, 1967 (div. Aug. 1969); 1 child, Amy Lynn; m. Christine Shannon, June 2, 1973; children; Vanessa, William Maxwell. A in Electronics, Comml. Radio Inst., 1966. Electronic tech. Bendix Radio Corp., Balt., 1965-66; salesman Coulter Electronics, Pitts., 1970-72; br. mgr. Semiconductor Specialists, Pitts., 1972-74; regional mgr. KW Electronics Sales, Pitts., 1974-87, mktg. mgr., 1987—; pres. Circuit Breakers, Inc., Pitts. Bd. dirs. Hampton Community Libr., Allison Park, Pa., 1990, sec., 1991. With U.S. Army, 1966-69. Republican. Episcopalian. Home: 2500 Tall Timber Dr Allison Park PA 15101-3033 Office: Circuit Breakers Inc/KW Electronics 4068 Mount Royal Blvd Allison Park PA 15101

HARDY, DAVID WALTER, journalist; b. Plainfield, N.J., June 7, 1942; s. John Walter and Abigail Penelope (Jones) H.; m. Lyn Yolanda Nicolls, Dec. 16, 1967; children: Dalyn Gail, David Walter Jr. BA, Fairleigh Dickinson U., 1964. Sports reporter Courier-News, Plainfield, 1964-67; reporter N.Y. Daily News, N.Y.C., 1967-69; reporter Washington Post, 1969-71, asst. dir. employee rels., 1971-72; investigative and polit. reporter N.Y. News, N.Y.C., 1973—. Recipient N.Y. State Investigative Reporting award UPI, 1985. Mem. Nat. Assn. Black Journalists, Newspaper Guild N.Y. (chmn. human rights com. local 3, 1985, exec. bd. 1989—), N.J. State House Corrs. Assn., Sigma Delta Chi (feature writing award N.J. chpt. 1986). Episcopalian.

HARDY, DONNA DEE, music educator; b. McKeesport, Pa., Aug. 5, 1941; d. Daniel Hale and Maryland Virginia (Brant) H. MusB, U. Mich., 1964, MusM, 1971, postgrad.; MA, U. Pitts., 1989. Tchr. music Wayne (Mich.) Area Sch. Dist., 1964-66; music cons. Livonia (Mich.) Area Sch. Dist., 1966-68; choral dir. L'Anse (Mich.) Area Sch. Dist., 1968-71; Orff supr. Copper County Intermediate Sch. Dist., Hancock, Mich., 1971-74; music instr. Union Coll., Lincoln, Nebr., 1979-80; mem. adj. faculty Pa. State U., McKeesport, 1980-84; instr. music Shippensburg (Pa.) U., 1984-92, asst. prof. music, 1992—; vis. prof. Colegio Adventista de Etudie Superiores, Alajuela, Costa Rica, 1980; cons. music edn. various orgns. in Pa., Mich.; dir. Cumbelaires Shippensburg U. at White House, Washington, also in Taiwan, London, Seville, Spain, U.S. Pavilion, 1992. Author: Music Mixtures, 1977; contbr. papers to profl. publs. Mem. Pa. Music Educators Assn., Music Educators Nat. Coun. Republican. Seventh-day Adventist. Home: 2510 Grandview Ave Mc Keesport PA 15132-7828 Office: Dept Music Shippensburg Univ Shippensburg PA 15132

HARDY, JUNE DORFLINGER, painter, photographer, interior designer; b. N.Y.C., Feb. 2, 1929; d. William Francis Dorflinger, Jr. and Katheryn (Hait) Dorflinger Manchee; m. John Alexander Hardy, Jr., May 26, 1956. Grad., Briarcliff Jr. Coll., 1949; student, Parsons Sch. Design, 1949-50, N.Y. Sch. Interior Design, 1953-54, 87-89, Nat. Acad. Art-Art Students League, 1966-85, Columbia U., 1963. Asst. tchr. Peck Sch., Morristown, N.J., 1950-51; with pers. dept. McGraw Hill, Inc., 1951-52; editorial asst., then asst. editor Better Homes and Gardens mag., 1951-52, 1952-57; editorial asst., then asst. editor Successful Farming mag., 1952-57; freelance portrait painter and photographer, 1969-89; tchr. drawing and pastel painting Onteora Club, N.Y., 1977; mem. Twilight Park Exhbn. Com., 1983-87. Nat. Home Fashions League scholar, 1953; recipient 1st prize portrait in oil Twilight Park Art Show, 1976, 79, first prize figurative painting-pastel portrait, 1989, 1st prize portrait photography, 1977, 2d prize pastel landscape, 1979, 2d prize for flower photography, 1982, 3d prize oil portrait, 1987; 1st prize for flower photography Onteora Garden Club Show, 1982, 1st and 2d prizes for photography Twilight Park Art Show, 1985, 1st prize a pastel portrait, 1989. Mem. Art Students League (life), Colony Club (chmn. entertainment 1979-84), Onteora Club, Naples Art Assn. Republican. Episcopalian. Address: 14 Sutton Pl S New York NY 10022 also: Lions Gate 2919 Gulf Shore Blvd N Naples FL 33940

HARDY, MAURICE G., medical and industrial equipment manufacturing company executive; b. 1931. Dir. European ops. Pall Corp., 1962-72, v.p. European ops., 1972-75; exec. v.p. Pall Corp., Glen Cove, N.Y., 1975-85, pres., COO, 1985-89, pres., CEO, 1989—, also bd. dirs. Office: Pall Corp 30 Sea Cliff Ave Glen Cove NY 11542-3634*

HARDY, RALPH W. F., biochemist, biotechnology executive; b. Lindsay, Ont., Can., July 27, 1934; s. Wilbur and Elsie H.; m. Jacqueline M. Thayer, Dec. 26, 1954; children: Steven, Chris, Barbara, Ralph (dec.), Jon. B.S.A., U. Toronto, 1956; M.S., U. Wis.-Madison, 1958, Ph.D., 1959. Asst. prof. U. Guelph, Ont., Can., 1960-63; research biochemist DuPont deNemours & Co., Wilmington, Del., 1963-67, research supr., 1967-74, assoc. dir., 1974-79, dir. life scis., 1979-84; pres. Bio Technica Internat., Inc., Kansas City, Kans., 1984-86; pres., chief exec. officer Boyce Thompson Inc., Ithaca, N.Y., 1986—; dep. chmn. Bio Technica Internat., Inc., 1986-90, cons., bd. dirs., 1990—; mem. exec. com. bd. agr. NRC, 1982-88, mem. commn. life scis., 1984-90, bd. biology, 1984-90, com. on biotech., 1988—, bd. sci. technol. internat. devel., 1990—, chmn. com. on biol. control, 1992—, chmn. com. on biol. nitrogen fixation, 1992—; mem. com. genetic experimentation Internat. Coun. Sci. Union, 1981—; mem. sci.adv. com. U. S. Dept. Energy, 1991—; mem. alternative agr. res. commercialization bd. USDA, 1992—. Author: Nitrogen Fixation, 1975, A Treatise on Dinitrogen Fixation, 3 vols, 1977-79; mem. editorial bd. sci. jours.; contbr. over 150 articles to sci. jours. Mem. biotech. exec. bd. Cornell U., 1986—, adv. coun. Vet. Coll., 1989—, mem. governing bd. Cornell Ctr. for Environment, 1991—; chmn. Nat. Agr. Biotech. Coun., 1988—. Recipient Gov. Gen.'s Silver medal, 1956, Sterling Henricks award 1986; WARF fellow, 1956-58; DuPont fellow, 1958-59. Mem. Indsl. Biotech Assn. (bd. dirs. 1986-89), Agr. Rsch. Inst. (bd. govs. 1988-91), Am. Chem. Soc. (exec. com. biol. chemistry div., Del. award 1969), Am. Soc. Biol. Chemists and Molecular Biologists, Am. Soc. Plant Physiology (exec. com. 1974-77), Am. Soc. Agronomy, Am. Soc. Microbiology. Episcopalian. Home: 330 The Pky Ithaca NY 14850-2249 Office: Boyce Thompson Inst Tower Rd Ithaca NY 14853-1801

HARDY, THOMAS GEORGE, chemical agricultural products and fertilizer company executive; b. Nyiregyhaza, Hungary, July 13, 1945; s. Andrew Hardy and Magda (Gordon) Heller; m. Jeanne Sloan, Nov. 17, 1980. BA with honors, U. Sydney, Australia, 1966; MBA, U. Pa., 1969. Ptnr. McKinsey and Co. Inc., N.Y.C., Paris, Tokyo, 1969-84; exec. v.p. Trans-Resources Inc., N.Y.C., 1985—; bd. dirs. Laser Industries Ltd., Haifa Chems. Ltd., Cedar Chems. Bd. dirs. March of Dimes, N.Y.C., 1982—. Mem. Univ. Club. Jewish. Office: Trans-Resources Inc 9 W 57th St New York NY 10019-2600

HARDY-BEIERL, BARBARA, English educator; b. N.Y.C.; m. Christopher Beierl, July 12, 1986. BA, CCNY, 1964; MA, San Francisco State U., 1967; PhD, Wayne State U., 1972. Cert. secondary sch. tchr., N.H. Editorial asst. Farrar, Strauss, Giroux, N.Y.C., 1962-64, U. Calif. Press, N.Y.C., 1964-65; grad. asst. San Francisco State U., 1966-68; asst. prof. Wayne State U., Detroit, 1968-72, SUNY, Oswego, 1972-79; fellow Harvard U., Cambridge, Mass., 1979-81, lectr., 1981-84, writer, editor, cons. Grad. Sch. Edn., 1986-90; editor Alliance for Ind. Scholars, Cambridge, 1990—; faculty U. N.H., St. Anselm Coll., 1987-89, Adult Learning Ctr., Nashua, 1992—. Author: Dramatic Quicklyisms, 1980; co-author: Connecting Civic Education and Language Education, 1991. Mem. N.Y. Coll. English Assn. (pres.), Coll. English Assn. (bd. dirs.). Home: 5 Shetland Rd Nashua NH 03062-3017

HARGADON, BRO KEVIN, psychologist, educator; b. N.Y.C., Mar. 29, 1930; s. Michael James and Mary Theresa (Houlihan) H. BA, Cath. U. Am., 1952, MS, 1961, PhD, 1969. Lic. clin. psychologist. Tchr. La Salle Acad., Providence, 1952-57, Hillside Hall, Troy, N.Y., 1957-59, De La Salle Coll., Washington, 1960-70; staff psychologist No. Va. Mental Health Inst., Falls Church, Va., 1970-77; pvt. practice Washington, 1977-80; exec. dir. Lincoln Hall, Somers, N.Y., 1980-81; prof. Manhattan Coll., Bronx, N.Y., 1981—; bd. mem. Archdiocesan Cons. Svc., Washington, 1973-74; cons. Bklyn. (N.Y.) Archdiocese, 1987—. Contbr. articles to profl. jours. Recipient Disting. Svc. award D.C. Psychol. Assn., Washington, 1973. Mem. APA, Assn. Psychology Type, Psychology Religious Interests, Phi Beta Kappa, Sigma Xi. Home: 4415 Post Rd Bronx NY 10471-3499 Office: Manhattan College Bronx NY 10471

HARGENS, CHARLES WILLIAM, III, electrical engineer, consultant; b. Phila., Oct. 21, 1918; s. Charles William Jr. and Marjorie (Garman) H.; m. Mary K. Johnson, June 14, 1941; children: William Garman, Mary Van Deusen, Roger Snow. SB, MIT, 1941. Registered profl. engr., Pa. Design engr. Lockheed Aircraft, Burbank, Calif., 1941-42; group engr. Gilfillan Bros., L.A., 1942-43; vis. staff mem. MIT Radiation Labs., Cambridge, 1942-44; group engr. RCA, Camden, N.J., 1945-47; sr. engr., tech. dir., inst. fellow Franklin Inst. Labs., Phila., 1947-88; assoc. prof. Temple U., Phila., 1976-77, Drexel U., Phila., 1978-87; noise control cons. air mgmt. div. City of Phila., 1978—; rsch. assoc. Wills Eye Hosp., 1970; cons., prof. acoustics; invited lectr. U. Wis., 1962, 63, 64. Co-author: Studies in Medicine, Physics and Voice, 1968, (chpts.) Bioengineering and the Skin, 1981; contbr. articles to Jour. Ophthalmic Surgery, Jour. Acoustical Soc. Am., Investigative Dermatology, Indsl. Rsch., Electronics, Jour. Instrument Soc. Am., Jour. Franklin Inst., IEEE Transactions. Mem. adv. com. Spring Garden Coll., Phila., 1972-76; rsch. assoc. Bd. of City Trusts, 1970. Recipient Diploma, War Manpower Commn., 1944, Citation Mayor City of Phila., 1974. Fellow IEEE (Phila. Sect. Appreciation award 1972); mem. ASTM (Citation 1982), Franklin Inst. (com. sci. and arts 1981), MIT Alumni Assn. (life, Bronze Beaver award 1976), Numerical Control Soc. (founder), Sigma Xi. Episcopalian. Home and Office: 1006 Preston Rd Philadelphia PA 19118-1333

HARGREAVES, DAVID WILLIAM, communications company executive; b. Akron, Ohio, May 4, 1943; s. William B. and Helen Grace (Slusser) H.; m. Sandra Jean Tessier, Sept. 4, 1965; children: Kristen Elizabeth, Cinda Anne, Gregory David. BSEE, U. Maine, Orono, 1965; MBA, U. Rochester, 1967. Sales engr. Mobile Communications div. Gen. Electric, Lynchburg, Va., 1970-74, mgr. systems projects, 1974-75, mgr. systems bids/proposals, 1975-78; mgr. internat. mktg. Gen. Electric Powerline Carrier Bus., Lynchburg, 1978-80; gen. mgr. Gen. Electric Microwave Link Operation, Owensboro, Ky., 1980-84; mng. dir. Alpha Telecom div. Alpha Industries, Methuen, Mass., 1984-86; pres. Dynatech Tactical Communications, Inc. (formerly Controlonics Corp.), Hudson, N.H., 1986—; conductor seminars in field. Contbr. articles to profl. jours. Chmn. bd. Gen. Electric United Way Pacesetter campaign, Lynchburg, 1978; advisor Jr. Achievement project bus., Owensboro, 1982, 83. Served to capt. U.S. Army, 1968-70, Vietnam. Decorated Bronze Star, D.S.C., 1970. Mem. Am. Mktg. Pres.'s Assn., Massibesic Yacht Club, Eta Kappa Nu, Tau Beta Pi. Republican. Home: 191 Buttrick Rd Hampstead NH 03841-2183 Office: Dynatech Tactical 16 Hampshire Dr Hudson NH 03051

HARGROVE, JOHN R., federal judge. BA, Howard U., 1947; LLB, U. Md., 1950. Sole practice, Balt., 1950-55; asst. U.S. atty. Dist. Ct. Md., Balt., 1955-57, dep. U.S. atty., 1957-62; assoc. judge People's Ct, Balt., 1962-63; ptnr. Howard & Hargrove, Balt., 1963-68; assoc. judge Municipal Ct., Balt., 1968-71; adminstrv. judge Dist. Ct., Balt., 1971-74; assoc. judge Balt. Circuit Ct., Balt., 1974-84; judge, U.S. Dist. Ct. Md., Balt., 1984—. Served with AUS, 1943-46. Office: US Dist Ct 101 W Lombard St Baltimore MD 21201-2626*

HARGROVE, MICHAEL B., transportation executive; b. Georgetown, Ky., Apr. 15, 1941; s. B. Walton and Zellaca Mae (Isbell) H.; m. F. Marion Hanson, June 25, 1966. BS in Chemistry, U. Ky., 1963, MS in Econs., 1966, PhD in Econs., 1971. Chemist Ky. Hwy. Dept., Frankfort, 1963-64; rsch. asst. Ky. Hwy. Labs., Lexington, 1964-65; teaching asst. U. Ky., Lexington, 1965-66, rsch. assoc., 1966-68; lectr. U. Md., College Park, 1968-71, asst. prof., 1971-77; prin. Tempus Assocs., University Park, Md., 1974-79; mgr., engring. economist Assn. Am. R.R.s, Washington, 1979-84, dir., engring. economist, 1984—. Contbr. articles to profl. jours. U. Md. rsch. fellow, 1977. Mem. Am. Econs. Assn., Am. Statis. Assn., Am. R.R. Engring. Assn., Transp. Rsch. Forum, Decision Sci. Inst. Democrat. Methodist. Home: 61 St Andrews Rd Severna Park MD 21146-1433 Office: Assn Am RRs 50 F St NW Washington DC 20001-1530

HARING-SMITH, TORI, English and theatre educator; b. Chgo., Jan. 1, 1953; d. Philip Smyth and Jacqueline (Kolle) Haring; m. Robert Henry Smith, June 1, 1974; 1 child, Whitney Patrick Haring-Smith. BA, Swarthmore Coll., 1974; MA, U. Ill., 1977, PhD, 1980. Teaching asst. U. Ill., Urbana, 1975-80; asst. prof. Brown U., Providence, 1980-86, assoc. prof. English, 1986—, assoc. prof. theatre, 1987—, dir. writing fellows program, 1982-91; freelance ednl. cons., Providence, 1981—, theatre dir., Providence, 1986—. Author: A.A. Milne, 1982, A Guide to Writing Programs, 1984, From Farce to Melodrama, 1985; also numerous articles on pedagogy, lit. and theatre. Recipient sr. class citation Brown U., 1984, 85, 86; fellow Watson Found., 1974, Lilly Found., 1981, Wriston fellow Brown U., 1984. Mem. Coun. on Coll. Composition and Communication (exec. com. 1987-89), Nat. Coun. Writing Program Adminstrs. (exec. com. 1985-88, dir. cons. evaluator program 1986-88), Assn. for Theatre in Higher Edn. Office: Brown U Dept Theatre PO Box 1897 Providence RI 02912-0001

HARITON, MORRIS BERNARD, accountant; b. Washington, May 2, 1911; s. Barney Meilah and Anna (Taishoff) H.; m. Edith G. Hariton, Dec. 2, 1964 (dec.); children: Nancy H. Gewitz, Richard B. Hariton; m. Irma G. Levy, Sept. 26, 1965. MCS, Southeastern U., 1934. CPA, D.C. Acct., ptnr. Verkouteren, Hariton & Ricketts, Washington, 1935-50; acct., ptnr. M.B. Hariton & Co., Washington, 1950-85, Hariton, Mancuso & Jones, Washington, 1990—; pres. D.C. Inst. CPAs, 1966-67, Estate Planning Coun., Washington, 1964-65; chmn. Bd. of Accountancy, Washington, 1965-66. Office: Hariton Mancuso & Jones 1101 17th St NW Washington DC 20036

HARITOS, DOLORES JEAN, nursing educator; m. Peter T. Haritos. RN, New Eng. Meml. Hosp., 1950; BSN, MSN, Boston U., 1968, EdM, 1958; EdD, Boston Coll., 1980. Cert. nursing adminstr. Commd. USAF, 1951, advanced through grades to col., 1977; assoc. dir. sch. nursing Peter Bent Brigham Hosp., Boston, 1958-61; dir. sch. nursing Whidden Meml. Hosp., Everett, Mass., 1964-67; coord. Headstart Community Action Coun., Chelsea, Mass., 1967-68; dir. No. Essex Community Coll. Ctr. Nursing Edn., Haverhill, Mass., 1968—; cons. Bunker Hill Community Coll., Quincy Jr. Coll., Bristol Community Coll., North Shore Community Coll., Quinsigamond Community Coll., Mass. Bay Community Coll. Author: (oral histories) Historical Biographies, First Chief Nurses of Corps, Air Force; editor (newsletter) Mass./R.I. League Nursing News MARILN News, 1989—; mem. editorial bd. Jour. Nursing History, Boston U., 1986-89. Mem. adv. com. to nursing prog., Mass. Bay Community Coll., Boston, 1989—. Col. USAF, 1951-88. Recipient Citation for Outstanding Leadership, Mass./R.I. League Nursing, 1984, Citation for Outstanding Performance, Commonwealth Mass., 1984, Meritorious Svc. medal for Outstanding Leadership and Svc. to USAF Nurse Corps, 1982. Mem. ANA, Am. Assn. History Nursing Employers, Nat. League Nursing (accreditation vis. 1984—, mem. nat. bd. rev. 1982-85), Assn. Mil. Surgeons, USAF War Coll. Alumni Assn., Res. Officer Assn., Army/Navy Club D.C., Am. Legion. Office: No Essex Community Coll Elliott Way Haverhill MA 01830

HARKE, DOUGLAS JAMES, college administrator, physicist; b. Edmonton, Alta., Can., Apr. 18, 1942; s. Alvin Herbert and Donna (Henkelman) H.; m. Diana Katherine Archer, Aug. 21, 1964; children: Douglas Jr., Russell, Andrew. BSc, U. Alta., 1963; MA in Edn., Washington U., 1964; MS, PhD, Purdue U., 1969. Tchr. Washington High Sch., South Bend, Ind., 1965-67; asst. prof. SUNY, Geneseo, 1969-74, dean grad. studies, 1974-88, dir. rsch., 1988—; bd. dirs. Sci. Trial Project, Rochester, N.Y., 1972-76. Author: Tests in Physics, 1973; contbr. articles to profl. jours. Office: SUNY Erwin # 205 Geneseo NY 14454

HARKINS, HERBERT PERRIN, otolaryngologist; b. Scranton, Pa., Aug. 13, 1912; s. Percy Stoner and Myra (Perrin) H.; B.S., Lafayette Coll., 1934;

M.D., Hahnemann Med. Coll., 1937; M.Sc., U. Pa., 1942; m. Anna Catherine Shepler, July 16, 1938; children—Herbert P., Sally Anne, Nancy Shepler. Lectr. otolaryngology Hahnemann Med. Coll., 1939-44, asso. prof., 1944-51, prof. head dept. otolaryngology, 1951; asst. prof. otolaryngology Grad. Sch. Medicine, U. Pa., 1951—; sr. staff otolaryngology Lankenau Hosp. Bd. Studies in Higher Edn. Trustee, Lafayette Coll. Served as comdr. U.S. Navy, 1945-48; Res. Diplomate Am. Bd. Otolaryngology. Fellow A.C.S., Am. Otorhinol. Soc. Plastic Surgery; mem. Am. Soc. Ophthalmic and Otolaryngologic Allergy (pres.), Am., Pa. acads. ophthalmology and otolaryngology, Coll. Physicians Phila., Phila. Laryngol. Soc., Phila County Med. Soc., AMA, Am. Laryngol., Rhinol. and Otol. Soc. Clubs: Union League, Phila. Country, Bachelors Barge. Contbr. numerous articles on ear, nose and throat to med. jours. Home: 701 Woodleave Rd Bryn Mawr PA 19010-1708 Office: Lankenau Med Bldg Wynnewood PA 19096

HARKINS, IGNATIUS JOHN, III, real estate developer, business owner; b. Wilmington, Del., Nov. 13, 1936; s. Ignatius John II and Irma Jane (Masten) H.; m. Lois Ann Morano, 1954 (div. 1965); children: John, Lois Ann, Patricia; m. Charlotte Stradley Jackson, 1967 (div. 1981); m. Roseann Hildebrandt, Nov. 2, 1981. Grad. high sch., Wilmington. Constrn. mgr. Todd Constrn., Newark, Del., 1965-75; sales agt. Quigley Real Estate, Wilmington, 1961-65; owner Chestnut Hill Builders, Inc., Newark, 1972—, I.J. Harkins Realty, Inc., Newark, 1965—; chmn. Del. Real Estate Commn., Dover, 1969-73. Mem. Home Builders Assn. of Del. (pres. 1985-86), Nat. Home Builders Assn., New Castle County Bd. Realtors, Nat. Assn. Realtors, Cecil County Md. Bd. Realtors, Del. Saengerband. Office: 248 E Chestnut Hill Rd Newark DE 19718-0001

HARKINS, MICHAEL E., state official; b. Wilmington, Del., Apr. 23, 1941; m. Helen White, 1964; children: Christine, Kelly, Amy. BA, Holy Cross Coll., 1963. Sec. State Del. Dover, 1985—. Office: Del Dept State Townsend Bldg Dover DE 19901

HARKNESS, KENNETH KOHLSAAT, computer executive; b. Evanston, Ill., Jan. 2, 1934; s. Edward Malcolm and Cynthia Gates (Kohlsaat) H.; m. Antoinette Murphey, Apr. 12, 1958; children: Amy, Sara, Jennifer. BA in Econs., Williams Coll., 1956; MBA, Harvard U., 1962. Group product mgr. Maxwell House Div. Gen. Foods, White Plains, N.Y., 1962-69; pres. Wilson Tennis Div. PepsiCo., Inc., Chgo., 1970-80; chief exec. officer Revell, Inc., L.A., 1980-83; pres. Game div. Atari, Inc., Sunnyvale, Calif., 1983-85; exec. v.p. Softsel Computer Products, L.A., 1985-88; pres., chief exec. officer Guidance Techs., Inc., Pitts., 1989—, also bd. dirs. Lt. USN, 1956-60, CBI. Mem. Software Pubs. Assn., Sporting Goods Mfg. Assn. (bd. dirs. 1975-80). Republican. Home: 805 Heather Ln Winnetka IL 60093-1316 Office: Guidance Techs Inc 800 Vinial St Pittsburgh PA 15212-5100

HARKNESS, SAMUEL DACKE, III, materials scientist; b. Oct. 28, 1940; s. Samuel Dacke Jr. and Jane Margaret (Morin) H.; m. Christine Lee Hotchkiss, Dec. 28, 1963; children: Samuel, Laura, Matthew. B in Metall. Engring., Cornell U., 1963; PhD in Materials Sci., U. Fla., 1967; MBA, U. Pitts., 1983. Rsch. engr. dept. space power Atomics Internat., Canoga Park, Calif., 1963-64; mgr. radiation effects Argonne (Ill.) Nat. Lab., 1967-73, assoc. dir. fusion, 1976-79; mgr. materials tech. sect. Combustion Engring., East Windsor, Conn., 1973-76; mgr. materials tech. div. Bettis Atomic Power Lab., West Mifflin, Pa., 1979-90; gen. mgr. systems, processes and techs. div. Westinghouse Sci. & Tech. Ctr., Pitts., 1990—. Editor: Radiation Effects, 1975; contbr. 75 articles to profl. jours. Coach Youth Soccer, Peters Twp., Pa., 1982-85; mem. Sch. Bd., Peters Twp., 1983-86. Alfred P. Sloan scholar Cornell U., 1958-63; Engring. fellow U. Fla., 1964-67. Fellow Am. Soc. Metals; mem. AIME (Metall. Soc. awards com. 1970-73, Robert Lansing Hardy Gold Medal award 1969), Am. Nuclear Soc. (materials sci. adv. bd. 1974-77). Home: 160 Maple Ln Canonsburg PA 15317-2648 Office: Westinghouse Electric Corp 1310 Beulah Rd Pittsburgh PA 15235-5098

HARLAN, LEONARD MORTON, merchant banker; b. Newark, June 1, 1936; s. Harold Robinson and Doris Harriet (Siegler) H.; m. Elizabeth Nan Kramon, Aug. 27, 1969; children: Joshua, Noah. BME, Cornell U., 1959; MBA with distinction, Harvard U., 1961, DBA, 1965. Lic. real estate broker, N.Y., N.J. Security analyst Donaldson, Lufkin & Jenrette, Inc., 1965-69, v.p., 1968-69; founder, chmn. bd. The Harlan Co., Inc. (formerly Harlan, Betke & Myers, Inc.), N.Y.C., 1969—; dir. Ryland Group, Inc., 1984—; pres. Castle Harlan, Inc., 1987—; gen. ptr. Legend Capital Group, 1988—; bd. dirs. Del. Group of Mutual Funds, 1988—, Del. Mgmt. Holdings, Inc., 1988—; chmn. Long John Silver's Holdings, Inc., 1989-92, bd. dirs., 1989—; guest lectr. Harvard U. and Columbia U. grad. schs. bus. adminstrn., 1968—, others; adj. prof. banking and real estate N.Y. U. Real Estate Inst., 1968—, Grad. Sch. Bus. Adminstrn., 1976-80; adj. prof. bus. adminstrn. Columbia U. Grad. Sch. Bus. Adminstrn., 1980—; trustee North Country Sch./CTT, 1989—. Editorial bd. Real Estate Rev. Jour., 1971-84; contbr. articles to profl. jours. Mem. Pres.'s Com. on Indsl. Innovation, 1978; mem. Urban Devel. Action Grant Task Force, HUD, 1984; mem. exec. com. N.Y. chpt. Am. Jewish Com., 1975-80, Central N.J. chpt., 1980—, treas., 1988—, nat. budget commn., 1987; mem. Cerberus Soc. (N.Y.C. Citizens Budget Commn.), 1983-88; trustee N.Y.C. Citizens Budget Commn., 1988—. Recipient Charles B. Shatuck Meml. award Am. Inst. Real Estate Appraisers, 1967, 72; Disting. Tchr. award NYU, 1979; Ford Found. fellow, 1964-65; Zurn fellow, 1962-63. Mem. Harvard Bus. Sch. Alumni Coun., Harvard Bus. Sch. Alumni Assn. (v.p. 1991-93, bd. dirs. 1989—), Harvard Club N.Y. (admissions com. 1973-75), Harvard Bus. Sch. Club Greater N.Y. (v.p. N.Y.C. chpt. 1977-79, bd. dirs. 1989—), Harvard Club of Princeton, Cornell Club of Princeton. Office: Castle Harlan Inc 150 E 58th St New York NY 10155

HARLAN, MARK EVAN, musician; b. Santa Monica, Calif., Oct. 8, 1953; s. Mahlon Moore Harlan and Eunice Dale (Johnson) Taylor; m. Renée Ann Caso, May 17, 1984. BA in Music, U. Calif., Santa Barbara, 1978; MusM, New Eng. Conservatory Music, 1981. Staff musician dance dept. Loyola Marymount U., L.A., 1976-77; accompanist various dance studios and U., Boston, 1979-84; pianist, accordionist Klezmer Conservatory Band, Boston, 1984-90; piano tchr. Dana Hall Sch., Wellesley, Mass., 1988—; faculty artist, tchr. Bates Dance Festival, Lewiston, Maine, 1989—; music dir. New Opera Theater Ensemble, Boston, 1990-91; musician, composer pvt. practice, Boston, 1985—; faculty artist Cultural Edn. Collaborative, Boston, 1989-90. Composer numerous works. Freedom writer Amnesty Internat., N.Y., 1989—; com. mem. Cambridge (Mass.) Recycling Com., 1989-91, Cambridge Food Coop., 1983-85. Mem. Am. Fedn. Musicians, Boston Musicians Assn. Home: 38 Thingvalla Ave Cambridge MA 02138

HARLEY, NAOMI HALLDEN, radiation specialist, environmental medicine educator; b. N.Y.C., Aug. 4, 1932; d. Carl Edward and Ida Wilson (Palmer) Hallden; m. John Henry Harley, Sept. 11, 1964. B.S., Cooper Union, N.Y.C., 1959; M.S., NYU, 1967, Ph.D., 1971, A.P.C., 1983. Phys. scientist U.S. Atomic Energy Commn., N.Y.C., 1951-65; research prof. environ. medicine NYU, 1965—; council mem., sci. com. chmn. Nat. Council on Radiation Protection and Measurement, Washington, 1982—. Contbr. articles to profl. jours. USPHS fellow, 1965. Mem. AAAS, Health Physics Soc., N.Y. Acad. Scis., NYU Alumni Club. Democrat. Office: NYU Sch of Medicine Dept Environ Medicine 550 1st Ave New York NY 10016-6402

HARLLEE, JOHN, author, former naval officer; b. Washington, Jan. 2, 1914; s. William Curry and Ella Florence (Fulmore) H.; m. Jo-Beth Carden, Sept. 10, 1937 (dec. April 1985); 1 son, John; m. Helen Tewksbury King, Oct. 19, 1986. B.S., U.S. Naval Acad., 1934; grad., Naval War Coll., 1950. Commd. ensign U.S. Navy, 1934, advanced through grades to rear adm.; comdr. motor torpedo squadron 12, 1943-44; mem. (Naval Congl. Liaison Unit), 1948-49; comdr. destroyer U.S.S. Dyess, 1949-50, comdr. destroyer div. 152, 1955-56, comdr. U.S.S. Rankin, 1958, ret., 1959; v.p. Edward I. Farley & Co., Inc., N.Y.C., 1960-61; mem. Fed. Maritime Commn. (and predecessor), 1961-69, chmn., 1963-69; exec. dir. San Francisco Twin Bicentennial, 1974-75; mgmt. cons. shipping Orgn. Ams. for Energy Independence, 1975-77. Author: Marine and Manatee, 1983, Terror and Triumph, 1990; contbr. articles to profl. jours. Chmn. Citizens for Kennedy and Johnson, No. Calif., 1960. Decorated Silver Star, Legion of Merit with combat V, Commendation ribbon with combat V, Presdl. Unit citation with bronze star; recipient Spl. Commendation Fed. Bar Assn., 1969. Mem. SAR, Sons Republic Tex., Tex. State Soc. Washington, Nat. Press Club (Washington), Tex. Breakfast Club (charter), Chevy Chase Club (Md.), Army Navy Club (Washington). Presbyterian. Home: 8101 Connecticut Ave # 408 Bethesda MD 20815-2810

HARMAN, SIDNEY, audio and video company executive; b. 1918. Sec. of commerce, 1977-80; with Harman Internat. Industries, Inc. (formerly Harman-Kardon, Inc.), now chmn. bd., CEO. Office: Harman Internat Industries 1101 Pennsylvania Ave NW Washington DC 20004*

HARMAN, THEODORE CARTER, physicist, researcher; b. Warsaw, Ind., July 22, 1929; s. Seward W. and Bernice E. (Irvine) H.; m. Marilyn Irene Axline, Aug. 3, 1957; children: Elizabeth, Janet, Kathryn, Thomas. AB, Manchester Coll., 1951; MS, Purdue U., 1953. Project leader Battelle Meml. Inst., Columbus, Ohio, 1953-58; asst. group leader Lincoln Lab. MIT, Lexington, 1959-65, 66-78, sr. staff mem. Lincoln Lab., 1978-87, staff mem. Lincoln Lab., 1987—; program mgr. Def. Project Rsch. Agy. U.S. Dept. Def., Washington, 1965-66. Author: (with J.M. Honig) Thermoelectric and Thermomagnetic Effects, 1967; (with I. Melngailis) Narrow Gap Semiconductors, 1974; (with others) Physics and Chemistry of II-VI Compounds, 1967; editor: Jour. Electronic Materials, 1972—; contbr. articles to High Purity Indium Antimonide, Liquidus and Solidus Lines in Semiconductors. Fellow Am. Phys. Soc., Am. Inst. Physics; mem. IEEE (publs. com. 1991—), The Minerals, Metals and Materials Soc. (publs. com. 1984—, electronic materials com. 1965—), Sigma Xi. Office: MIT Lincoln Lab 244 Wood St Lexington MA 02173-9108

HARMATZ, MORTON GERALD, psychology educator; b. N.Y.C., Mar. 25, 1939; s. Harry J. and Louise (Hershenfeld) H.; m. Lynne Deckered, Dec. 20, 1969 (div. 1982); 1 child, Mark D.; m. Robin Lynes, June 21, 1992. BA, Ohio State U., 1960; MS, U. Wash., 1962, PhD, 1963. Lic. Clin. psychologist, Mass. Asst. prof. U. Mass., Amherst, 1964-71; assoc. prof. U. Mass., 1971-77, full prof., 1977—; cons. Westfield (Mass.) Community Support Svcs., 1975—, Sprinfield (Mass.) Mental Health Assn., 1986—. Author: Abnormal Psychology, 1978, Human Sexuality, 1983; contbr. articles to publs. Fellow Am. Psychopathological Assn.; mem. Am. Psychol. Assn. Office: U Mass Psychology Dept Tobin Hall Amherst MA 01003

HARMELIN, STEPHEN JOSEPH, lawyer; b. Phila., May 7, 1939; s. Louis M. and Ethel (Katz) H.; m. Gisela H. Kiesel, Jan. 20, 1971; children: Alison Kate, Melina Alexis. BA cum laude, U. Pa., 1960; LLB, Harvard U., 1963. Bar: Pa. 1964, U.S. Supreme Ct. 1968. Atty. broadcast bur. FCC, Washington, 1964; aide White House, Washington, 1964-65; assoc. Dilworth, Paxson, Kalish & Dilks (name now Dilworth, Paxson, Kalish & Kauffman), Phila., 1965-70, ptnr., 1970-86, co-chmn. corp. dept., 1986-91, mng. ptnr., 1991—; bd. dirs. Analytics Inc., Willow Grove, Pa.; chmn. Publicker Industries, Greenwich, Conn., 1980-84; lectr. Phila. Coll. Art, 1970-72. Spl. asst. dist. atty. City of Phila., 1970; commr. Pa. Conv. Ctr. Authority, Phila., 1989; gen. counsel Pa. Legis. Reapportionment Commn.; trustee Thomas Skelton Harrison Found., Phila., 1982, Found. of the Phila. Heart Inst., 1988; bd. dirs. Phila. div. Am. Cancer Soc., 1986, crusade chmn., 1987-88. With USCGR, 1963-69. Mem. ABA, Phila. Bar Assn., Union League Club. Republican. Jewish. Office: Dilworth Paxson Kalish & Kauffman Mellon Bank Ctr Ste 3200 1735 Market St Philadelphia PA 19103

HARMON, CAROLINE HOFF, business executive; b. Elizabeth, N.J., Apr. 4, 1927; d. Carl Herman and Marie (Bergmann) Hoff; m. Paul C. Harmon, Sept. 12, 1959. BS in Mgmt. magna cum laude, NYU, 1961, postgrad. Sch. of Law, 1961-62, MA in Edn., 1964, postgrad. in Arts and Sci., 1964-68. Corp. sec., office mgr. Nat. Coll. Club Program, N.Y.C., 1957-59; asst. to v.p. sales Fawcett-Dearing Printing Co., N.Y.C., 1959-60; asst. to corp. sec. U.S. Industries, Inc., N.Y.C., 1960-66; adminstr. Nigerian project NYU, 1966-68; asst. to v.p. and corp. sec. Celanese Corp., N.Y.C., 1968-72; mgr. corp. EEO program Internat. Paper Co., N.Y.C., 1973-75; dir. EEO program ABC, N.Y.C., 1975-77; pres. Brantwood Corp., Short Hills, N.J., 1978—; chief acct. Trevcon, Inc., Liberty Corner, N.J., 1987—; cons. IBM, GE Credit, Joseph Seagram and others, 1977-87; author, leader nation-wide seminars Am. Mgmt. Assn. and NYU Sch. Continuing Edn., 1975-81. Contbr. chpt. to book and articles to profl. jours. Bd. dirs. Women's Equity Action League, N.J., 1972-78; com. chairperson Am. Assembly of Collegiate Schs. Bus., St. Louis, 1973-76; researcher Pres. Kennedy Commn. on the Status of Women, 1963. Recipient NYU Pres.'s Cert. of Achievement, 1961. Mem. Am. Mgmt. Assn., Am. Arbitration Assn. (arbitration panel mem. 1974-78), N.Y.C. C. of C. and Industry (chmn. subcom. on minorities and women in mgmt. 1974-75), N.J. Bus. and Industry Assn., Phi Chi Theta (v.p. 1966-70, pres. 1970-74, dir. profl. programs 1974-78, bd. dirs. 1989—, Hall of Fame 1989). Office: 2 Brantwood Ter Short Hills NJ 07078-1814

HARMON, JAMES ALLEN, investment banker; b. N.Y.C., Oct. 12, 1935; s. Bert and Belle (Kirschner) H.; m. Jane Elizabeth Theaman, Aug. 11, 1957; children—Deborah Lynn, Douglas Lee, Jennifer Ann. B.A., Brown U., 1957; M.B.A., Wharton Grad. Sch., U. Pa., 1959. With N.Y. Hanseatic Corp., N.Y.C., 1959-74, sr. v.p., 1969-74; gen. partner Wertheim & Co., Inc., N.Y.C., 1975—, vice chmn., 1980-86, chmn., 1987—, chief exec. officer, 1988—; bd. dirs. Schroders plc, London, Securities Industry Assn.; bd. dirs., chmn. nominating com. Questar Corp., Salt Lake City; mem. adv. com. on internat. capital markets N.Y. Stock Exch. Bd. dirs. Internat. Tennis Hall of fame; trustee Brown U. Home: 43 Kettle Creek Rd Weston CT 06883-2208 Office: Wertheim Schroder & Co Inc 787 7th Ave New York NY 10019-6018

HARMON, RICHARD L., theatrical designer, educator; b. N.Y.C., Nov. 3, 1950; s. Jerome W. and Rhya (Saper) H.; m. Jan M. Huebner, May 17, 1986; 1 child, Julia. Student, Temple U., 1968-69, L.I. U., 1969-70; BFA, NYU, 1973, MFA, 1974. Instr., designer, tech. dir. U. Ark., Fayetteville, 1976-78; vis. asst. prof., designer Cornell U., Ithaca, N.Y., 1978-79; mem. faculty Parsons Sch. Design, N.Y.C., 1980-81; vis. lectr., designer U. Calif., Santa Barbara, 1981-82; vis. specialist in lighting design William Paterson Coll., Wayne, N.J., 1983-84; resident designer New Federal Theatre, N.Y.C., 1984—, prodn. mgr., 1984-85; designer, tech. dir. SUNY, Old Westbury, 1985-87; vis. asst. prof., designer Bucknell U., Lewisburg, Pa., 1987-88; asst. prof., designer Hofstra U., Hempstead, N.Y., 1989—; freelance designer numerous univs., colls., regional theatres. Designer sets, lights and/or costumes over 100 theatrical prodns., various univs. and Off-Broadway. Recipient AUDELCO award for excellence in Black Theatre, 1991. Mem. United Scenic Artists. Studio: 167 W 72nd St New York NY 10023-3221 Office: Hofstra U Dept Drama & Dance Hempstead NY 11550

HARMON, RICHARD WINGATE, management consultant; b. Exeter, N.H., July 16, 1958; s. William Wingate and Elaine (Waters) H.; m. Kathleen Hayward Harmon, Aug. 8, 1987; 1 child, David Wingate. BS in Adminstrn., U. N.H., 1981; MBA in Adminstrn., N.H. Coll., 1986. Lic. security dealer. Pilot, operator New Eng. Aviation, Sanford, Maine, 1981-82; founder, owner Harmon Aviation, Exeter, N.H., 1988—; owner, pres. Harmon Realty Investments, Exeter, 1985—; founder, owner Exeter Storage Depot, Inc., 1989—; owner, pres. Harmon-Waters, Exeter, 1982—; venture capital cons., constrn. mgmt. cons., bus. turnaround cons., bus. start-up cons. Mem. Aircraft Owners and Pilots Assn., Exptl. Aircraft Assn., Seaplane Pilots Assn., Exeter Area C. of C., N.H. Coll. Alumni Assn., U. N.H. Alumni Assn., Sigma Alpha Epsilon. Office: Harmon-Waters 23 Garfield St Exeter NH 03833

HARMON, W. DAVID, academic administrator; b. Akron, Ohio, Feb. 21, 1943; s. W.D. Sr. and Joy Marie (Johnson) H.; m. Patricia Ann Stewart, Nov. 12, 1963; children: David Christopher, Mark Aric. BS, SUNY, Buffalo, 1964; MS, Hofstra U., 1970; PhD, St. John's U., Jamaica, N.Y., 1980. Tchr. East Meadow (N.Y.) Sch. Dist., East Meadow, 1964-70; assoc. dir., counseling ctr. St. John's U., Jamaica, N.Y., 1970—; instr. SUNY, Old Westbury, 1984—; cons. Rudolph Clark Assocs., Westbury, 1985—, N.Y.C. Police Dept., 1986, Am. Assn. Retired Persons, Queens, N.Y. 1987; adj. assoc. prof. psychology, St. John's U., Jamaica, N.Y. Commissioner Nassau County Human Rights Commn., Mineola, N.Y., 1986—; asst. leader Ethical Humanist Soc. L.I., 1989—; bd. dirs. St. Mary's Children and Family Svcs., Syosset, N.Y. Mem. Am. Coll. Personnel Assn., Assn. Non-White Concerns in Counseling, Com. on Multi-Cultural Affairs, Am. Psychol. Assn., Nat. Assn. Neuro-Linguistic Programmers. Republican. Club: 100 Black Men of Nassau/Suffolk, Inc. (Westbury) (2d v.p.). Home: 199 W Seaman Ave Freeport NY 11520-1540 Office: St John's U Counseling Ctr Grand Central and Utopia Pkwys Jamaica NY 11439

HARMOND, RICHARD PETER, educator; b. N.Y.C., Mar. 19, 1929. BA, Fordham U., 1951; MA, Columbia U., 1954, PhD, 1966. Assoc. prof. St. John's U., N.Y.C., 1957—. Co-author: Long Island as America, 1977; co-editor: Technology in the 20th Century, 1983, editor: (newsletter) L.I. Archives Conf., 1982—, assoc. editor: L.I. Hist. jour., 1988—; contbr. articles to profl. jours. With U.S. Army, 1951-53. Mem. Orgn. Am. Historians, Soc. History of Tech. Office: St John's U Jamaica NY 11439

HARNER, JAMES PHILIP, agricultural educator; b. Quakertown, Pa., May 1, 1943; s. George B. and Elsie (Smith) H.; m. Lois Carol Miller, May 29, 1965; children: Duane, Sheri. BS, Del. Valley Coll. Agr. & Sci., 1965; MS, U. Md., 1967; PhD, U. Ill., 1972. Herd supr. U. Md., Ellicott City, 1967-68; dairy supt. Cornell U., Dryden, N.Y., 1971-77; farm mgr. Meridale (N.Y.) Farms, 1977-78; dairy supt., asst. prof. Delaware Valley Coll., Doylestown, Pa., 1978-86; rsch. farm mgr., asst. dir. animal care dept. Rutgers U., New Brunswick, N.J., 1986—. Treas. Trinity Luth. Ch., Ithaca, N.Y., 1975-77. Recipient Hon. Garden State degree N.J. State Future Farmers Am., 1988. Mem. Am. Dairy Sci. Assn., N.E. Soc. Agrl. Rsch. Mgrs., Gamma Sigma Delta, Delta Tau. Alpha. Home: 20 Stacey Dr Doylestown PA 18901-3340 Office: Rutgers U NJAES/Cook Coll Animal Care Program PO Box 231 New Brunswick NJ 08903-0231

HARNETT, CRAIG CURTISS, executive; b. Tenafly, N.J., June 2, 1952; s. William Watkins and Betty Van-Reese (Curtiss) H.; m. Barbara Ruth Hunzinger, Aug. 10, 1974; children: Kelly Ericson, William Curtiss. BA, Rutgers U., 1974; MBA, NYU, 1976. CPA N.Y. Corp. trust adminstr. Chem. Bank, N.Y.C., 1974-75; staff acct. Price Waterhouse, N.Y.C., 1976-78, sr. acct., 1979-81, mgr., svc. mgr., 1981-86; chief fin. officer Wolper Ross & Co. Ltd., N.Y.C., 1986-87; corp. controller, north Am. Reuters, N.Y.C., 1988; supr., chief operating officer, chief fin. officer Revelation Techs., N.Y.C., 1989; sr. v.p., chief fin. officer Hearst/ABC-Viacom Entertainment Svcs., N.Y.C., 1989-90, group v.p. fin. and tech., chief fin. officer, 1990—. Coach Cranford (N.J.) Basketball League, 1987-90, Cranford Little League Baseball, 1986-91; mem. audit com. Presbyn. Ch., Cranford, 1987-88, chmn. audit com., 1989. Mem. Internat. Radio and Television Soc., AICPA, AM. Mgmt. Assn., N.Y. State CPA's Assn., Broadcast Fin. Mgrs. Assn., Rutgers Alumni Assn. Democrat. Home: 1 Hampton St Cranford NJ 07016

HAROLD, PAUL DENNIS, state senator; b. Boston, Sept. 5, 1948; s. Joseph Robert and Marguerite (Burke) H. BA, U. Mass., 1970; JD, Suffolk U., 1973; M of Pub. Adminstrn., Harvard U., 1981. Councillor City of Quincy, Mass., 1976-79; senator State of Mass., Boston, 1979—; bd. dirs. Nat. Council Internat. Visitors, Washington, 1987—. Bd. dirs. Boy Scouts Am., Boston, 1982—. Recipient German-Marshall Fund award, 1986; named Outstanding Leader, Boston Jaycees, 1984. Mem. Quincy Bar Assn. Democrat. Roman Catholic. Clubs: Union, Univ. (Boston). Home: 66 Furnace Brook Pky Quincy MA 02169-2303 Office: Mass State Senate 507 State House Boston MA 02133

HARPER, DELPHINE BERNICE, health care executive; b. Boston, Sept. 6, 1947; d. James Albert and Bernice (Bell) Garnett; m. John Henry Redd III, Dec. 31, 1966 (div. May 1972); 1 child, John; m. Morris Harper, Aug. 18, 1975; children: Michele, Kimberly. Cert. acctg., Boston Sch. Bus., 1966; BS, Northeastern U., 1973; postgrad., L.I. U., 1975-76. Lic. real estate agt., D.C., Md. Asst. Admissions Office Northeastern U., Boston, 1968-71; adminstrv. asst. to dir. Assn. for Better Housing, Boston, 1971; community organizer Roxbury Multi Svc. Ctr., Boston, 1971-72; unit mgr. Peter Bent Brigham Hosp., Boston, 1972-74; mgmt. analyst State of Mass., Boston, 1974-75; proprietor Kimele's Wine & Cheese, Cambridge, Mass., 1978-79; real estate agt. Bd. Realtors, D.C., Md., 1983-86; program officer, asst. dir. resident svcs. Dept. Housing, 1986-88; v.p. ops., mgmt. officer Health Care Systems Corp., Silver Spring, Md., 1988—. Bd. dirs. Dem. Nat. Com., Washington, 1988; mem. Kennedy Ctr., 1989—. John F. Kennedy scholar Northeastern U., Boston, 1971-73, Martin Luther King scholar, 1970-71. Mem. Am. Mgmt. Assn., Greater WAshington Edn. Telecommunication Assn., Women in Arts, Smithsonian Assocs., Nat. Trust for Hist. Preservation, Nat. Geog. Soc., Nat. Assn. Investors Corp., N.Y. Met. Opera Guild, Archaeol. Inst. Am., N.Y. Mus. Natural History, Phi Beta Kappa.

HARPER, EDWIN LELAND, manufacturing executive; b. Belleville, Ill., Nov. 13, 1941; s. Horace Edwin and Evelyn Ruth (Wright) H.; m. Lucy Davis, Aug. 21, 1965; children: Elizabeth Allen, Peter Edwin. BA with honors, Principia Coll., 1963; PhD, U. Va., 1968. Guest scholar Brookings Instn., Washington, 1965-66; lectr. Rutgers U., 1966-68; staff Bur. of Budget, Washington, 1968-69; sr. cons. Arthur D. Little, Inc., Washington, 1969; spl. asst. to pres. of U.S., 1969-72; asst. dir. Domestic Coun., Washington, 1970-72; v.p. INA Corp. (now CIGNA), Phila., 1973-74; pres., chief exec. officer Air Balance, Inc., Chgo., 1975; sr. v.p. strategic planning, chief adminstrv. officer Certain Teed Corp., 1976-78; v.p. Emerson Electric Co., St. Louis, 1978-81; dep. dir. Office of Mgmt. and Budget; asst. to pres. of U.S. Washington, 1981-82, 82-83; chmn. Pres.'s Coun. on Integrity and Efficiency in Govt., 1982-83, Fed. Property Rev. Bd., 1982-83; dir., exec. v.p. Dallas Corp. (formerly Overhead Door Corp.), 1983-86; sr. v.p., chief fin. officer Campbell Soup Co., Camden, N.J., 1986-89, exec. v.p., 1989-91; dep. exec. dir. platform com. Rep. Conv., 1976; mem. Pres.'s Commn. on Pers. Interchange, Washington, 1976-79, 81-83, Pres.'s Commn. on Indsl. Competitiveness, 1983-86, Pres.' Commn. Exec., Legis. and Judicial Salaries, 1987; chmn. White Hose Fellows Selection Com., Phila., 1990, 91; bd. dirs. Phila. Suburban Corp. Contbr. articles to profl. jours. Bd. dirs. Principia Coll., Valley Forge Mil. Acad., Penjerdel, Salvation Army, Phila., Eisenhower World Affairs Inst. Recipient Louis Brownlow award, 1969, Exec. Govt. award Opportunities Industrialization Corp. Am., 1982, Person of Yr. award Washington chpt. Inst. Internal Auditors, 1982, Spl. Commendation Assn. Fed. Investigators, 1983; Ford Found. grantee, 1965. Mem. Nat. Acad. Pub. Adminstrn., Fin. Execs. Inst., U.S. C. of C. (econ. policy com.), Union League, Raven Soc., Omicron Delta Kappa. Republican. Office: 3 Benjamin Franklin Pky Philadelphia PA 19102-1322

HARPER, JAMES WELDON, III, financial consultant; b. Frederick, Md., Mar. 3, 1937; s. James Weldon, Jr. and Mildred Mary (Conaway) H.; student Duke U. Coll. rep. Time, Inc., 1955-59; jr. exec. trainee Merrill Lynch Pierce Fenner and Smith, N.Y.C., 1959-60; v.p. fin. planning Haight and Co. Inc., Washington, 1961-72; pres. fin. cons. Weldon Enterprises Ltd., Washington, 1972—; pres. U.S. Energy Conservation Service, Inc.; cons. Aries Corp.; nat. coord. Nat. Planned Giving Assocs., Inc., 1983—; bd. dirs. 6 cos., 1962-91; involved in 113 corps., 98 partnerships. Conservator Nat. Real Estate Trust for Health Care, Inc. Served with U.S. Army, 1959. Methodist. Author three manuals on consulting instrumental in the formation of. Office: Weldon Enterprises Ltd PO Box 1061 Main Station Washington DC 20013

HARPSTER, NORMAN RAY, financial executive; b. Balt., July 29, 1951; s. Norman Ray and Phyllis (Weaver) H.; m. Diane Noon, Oct. 18, 1975; children: Amy. Lauren. BA in Econs., Lafayette Coll., 1973; MBA, U. Va., 1975. With Air Products and Chems Inc., Allentown, Pa., 1975—, mgr. fin. analysis Process Gas div., 1980-81, contr. Process Gas div., 1981-87, contr. Environ/Energy Systems, 1987-91, chief fin. officer, 1991—. Bd. dirs. Pa. Stage Co., Allentown, 1984—. Republican. Presbyterian. Home: 1680 Sunderland Dr Bethlehem PA 18015-9371 Office: Air Products and Chems Inc 7201 Hamilton Blvd Allentown PA 18195-9642

HARRELL, JERRY A., counselor; b. Warsaw, Ind., Aug. 27, 1961; s. Homer L. and Dorothy L. Harrell; m. Gay Lynn Williams. BS, Ball State U., 1985; MS, West Chester U., 1992. Assoc. min. Del. Valley Christian Ch., Media, Pa., 1986-90; transporter Riddle Meml. Hosp., Media, 1990—; intern counselor Del. County Community Coll., Media, 1991; mem., bd. dirs. Indian Lake Camp, Darlington, Md., 1986-90, dir. sr. high, 1989-90. Chmn. edn. West Chester (Pa.) Christian Ch., 1991—. Mem. AACD (student), Nat. Career Devel. Assn. (student), Assn. for Specialists in Group Work (student). Home: 274 Glen Riddle Rd D-204 Media PA 19063

HARRICE, NICHOLAS CY (NICHOLAS PSIHARIS), commercial radio and television announcer; b. Chgo., Mar. 1, 1915; s. Peter and Vasiliki (Anargyros) Psiharis; student Sch. Commerce, Northwestern U., 1934-38; child by previous marriage, Lincoln Peter; m. 2d, Helena Seroy, Dec. 12, 1959; 1 child, Melanie Samantha. Concession barker Chgo. World's Fair, 1934; with Samuel Insull ABC Network, 1935; announcer, copywriter, newsman, programmer Sta. WLS, Chgo., 1936-42; news broadcaster Sta. WGN, Chgo., 1942-45; freelance comml. announcer, N.Y.C., 1945—; contract comml. announcer "and, they are mild!" segment Pall Mall cigarette advt. campaign for radio and TV, 1946-70; product spokesman for GM, Proctor & Gamble, DuPont Co., Miller Brewing Co., Alka-Seltzer, Kaiser-Fraser; announcer radio programs for Walter Winchell, Grand Cen. Sta., Cavalcade of Am., The Big Story, H.V. Kaltenborn, Wednesday Night Fights, William L. Shirer, RCA Victor Show, The Thin Man, Quick as a Flash; producer What's the Good Word; pres. Stair Mountain Prodns. Recipient Sargent Oratorical award, 1935; Clio award, 1962; 1st place Gold medal sabres Ill. Fencers League, 1936, Amateur Fencers League Am., 1936; mem. champion sabre team Amateur Fencers League Am., 1935. Mem. SAG (bd. dirs. 1966-69), AFTRA (bd. dirs. 1956-60). Clubs: Lambs, Deru, Lynx, Friars, Advt. (N.Y.C.). Home: Teton Valley Highlands Box 400 Moose WY 83012

HARRIGAN, GAIL LABRUZZA, corporate controller, consultant; b. Hartford, Conn., Oct. 24, 1951; d. Stinnard Harry and Irene Theresa (Page) H.; m. Robert Andrew Castonguay, Aug. 21, 1971 (div. May 1980); 1 child, Eric Thomas Castonguay; m. Gary Douglas LaBruzza, Jan. 13, 1984. Student, U. Conn., 1969-71, Post Coll., 1981-83. Customer svc. rep. Conn. Bank and Trust, Bristol, Conn., 1971-72; claims analyst Conn. Gen. Life Ins., Bristol, Conn., 1972-74; office mgr. CMCW, Inc., Canton, Conn., 1977-81; corp. controller Mirror Polishing & Plating, Waterbury, Conn., 1981—; owner, ptnr. Gateway Svcs., Harwinton, Conn., 1989—, G&G remodeling, 1987—. Mem. Garden Writers Am. Home: 166 Wildcat Hill Rd Harwinton CT 06791-2114 Office: Mirror Polishing & Plating 346 Huntingdon Ave Waterbury CT 06708-1419

HARRINGTON, BOB (ROBERT WILLIAM), critic, social worker; b. Richmond Hill, N.Y., Oct. 2, 1950; s. Jean Alexander and Josephine (Borruso) H. BA, SUNY, Oneonta, 1972. Sr. caseworker Nassau County Dept. Soc. Services, Mineola, N.Y., 1977-85; probation officer Nassau County Dept. Probation, Mineola, 1985—; theater and cabaret critic, theater editor L.I. and N.Y. Nightlife mags., Deer Park, N.Y., 1981-91; cabaret and music critic Back Stage, N.Y.C., 1984—; cabaret and theater critic New York Post, N.Y.C., 1986—. Columnist Agt. & Mgr. Mag., N.Y.C., 1991—. Recipient Am. Legion Citizenship award Am. Legion, Oneonta, 1972. Mem. Manhattan Assn. of Cabaret (v.p. 1985—, Spl. Outstanding Contbns. award, 1986), Outer Critics Circle (bd. dirs. 1984—), Soc. of Singers (bd. dirs. 1987-91), Drama Desk, Am. Theater Wing Tony Voter, Hearts and Voices (adv. bd. 1992—). Roman Catholic. Home: 1710 Kroll Rd East Meadow NY 11554-1608 Office: 210 South St New York NY 10002-7807

HARRINGTON, DONALD P., radiologist; b. St. Louis, Jan. 20, 1941; s. Paul and Louise (Anderson) H.; m. Mary Reilly, Nov. 21, 1966; children: Anne, Katie. BS, U. of Ariz., 1962; MD, Marquette U. Sch. of Medicine, 1966. Diplomate Am. Bd. Radiology, Am. Bd. Nuclear Medicine. Intern Milw. County Gen. Hosp., 1966-67; resident in radiology Mpls. VA Hosp., 1967-70; fellow in cardiovascular radiology U. Minn., Mpls., 1970-71; staff radiologist and chief cardiovascular radiologist Mpls. VA Hosp., 1971-72; staff radiologist Johns Hopkins Hosp., Boston, 1972-79; cardiovascular and interventional radiologist Brigham and Women's Hosp., Boston, 1979-87, dir. cardiovascular and interventional radiology sect., 1987-91; cardiovascular and interventional radiologist U. of Calif. San Francisco Hosps. and Clinics, 1985-86, Ft. Miley VA Hosp., San Francisco, 1985-86; radiologist-in-chief U. Hosp. SUNY at Stony Brook, 1991—; instr. U. of Minn. Sch. Medicine, 1971-72; asst. prof. Johns Hopkins U. Sch. Medicine, 1972-79, assoc. prof., 1979; assoc. prof. Harvard Med. Sch., 1979-91; vis. assoc. prof. U. of Calif., San Francisco Sch. Medicine, 1985-86; prof. and chmn. Sch. of Medicine SUNY, Stony Brook, 1991—; lectr. various assn. meetings. Author: (with others) Pediatric Nuclear Medicine, 1974, Cardiac Diagnostic Procedures for the Clinician, 1982, Vascular and Interventional Radiology, 1983, Shackelford's Textbook on Surgery of the Alimentary Tract, 1983, The Guide to Cardiology, 1984, Non-Invasive Imaging Techniques in Cardiovascular Disease, 1985; contbg. editor Am. Jour. Roentgenology, 1978—, Cardiovascular Intervention Radiology, 1980—; contbr. articles to profl. jours. Fellow Coun. Cardiovascular Radiology Am. Heart Assn. (chmn. Nominating Com. 1986-88); mem. Soc. Nuclear Medicine, Johns Hopkins Med. Soc., Soc. Cardiovascular and Interventional Radiology (chmn. Rules Com. 1982-84), Inter-Am. Coll. Radiology, New Eng. Angiographic Soc. (pres. 1981-82), Rsch. Counc. Am. Heart Assn., A ssn. U. Radiologists, Soc. Thoracic Radiology, Long Island Radiological Soc., Suffolk County Med. Soc., Soc. of Chmn. of Acad. Radiology Depts. Office: SUNY Dept Radiology Sch Medicine Health Scis Ctr 4 092 Stony Brook NY 11794-8460

HARRINGTON, EDWARD F., judge; b. 1933. AB, Holy Cross Coll., Worcester, Mass., 1955; JD, Boston Coll., 1960. Law clk. to Hon. Paul C. Reardon Mass. Superior Ct., 1960-61; spl. trial atty. criminal div. U.S. Dept. Justice, 1961-65, atty.-in-charge Strike Force Against Organized Crime, 1970-73; asst. U.S. atty. Mass., 1965-69; assoc. Offices of Paul T. Smith, Boston, 1961, Offices of Melvin Louison, Taunton, Mass., 1969; mem. firm Peloquin, McKeon & Reilly, Boston, 1973-75, Gargan, Harrington & Markham, Boston, 1975-77; U.S. atty. Mass., 1977-81; mem. firm Sheridan, Garrahan & Lander, Framingham, Mass., 1981-88; dist. judge Mass., 1988—. Contbr. articles to profl. jours. Chmn. Alcoholic Beverages Control Commn., 1975-77; nominee Dem. Party for Atty. Gen., Mass., 1974, Rep. Party for Atty. Gen., Mass., 1986; campaign chmn. Shriver for Pres. Campaign Com., 1976; advisor Nat. Commn. on Violence, 1968-69; cons. Nat. Commn. on Rev. of Nat. Policy Toward Gambling, 1974-76; bd. dirs. Mass. Com. Against Child Abuse, 1979-81, Charitable Irish Soc., 1985-86; mem. St. Joseph's Parish Coun., 1975-77. Lt. (j.g.) USN, 1955-57; with USNR, 1957-72. Recipient Letter of Commendation FBI Dir. Edgar Hoover, 1968. Mem. ABA, Mass. Bar Assn., South Middlesex Bar Assn. Office: US Courthouse Rm 1134 Boston MA 02109*

HARRINGTON, GARY MICHAEL, English educator; b. Butte, Mont., Sept. 18, 1953; s. Daniel Raymond and Marie E. (Twomey) H. BA, U. Mont., 1976, MA, 1979; PhD, U. Toronto, Ont., Can., 1984. Grad. fellow U. Toronto, 1980-83; asst. prof. English, Mont. Coll. Mineral Scis. and Tech., Butte, 1984-88, Salisbury (Md.) State U., 1988—; lectr. Delmarva Libr. Series, 1988—. Author: Faulkner's Fables of Creativity, 1991; contbr. articles, essays and revs. to profl. jours. Tutor Project Read, Salisbury, 1991. Summer fellow NEH, 1989, 91. Mem. N.E. Modern Lang. Assn., South Atlantic Modern Lang. Assn., Faulkner Soc., Am. Lit. Assn., Soc. for Study So. Culture, Am. Conf. for Irish Studies. Office: Salisbury State U English Dept 1101 Camden Ave Salisbury MD 21801-6800

HARRINGTON, GERARD, III, public relations executive, business consultant; b. N.Y.C., Nov. 13, 1956; s. Gerard Jr. and Sue Leah (Sayer) Harrington Salomon; m. Elizabeth Baker Taylor, Sept. 24, 1983; 1 child, David Gerard. BS, Northwestern U., 1978. News writer Ind. TV News Assn., N.Y.C., 1978-79, mng. editor, 1979-80; news writer, producer Cable News Network, Atlanta, 1980-83, exec. producer, 1983-84; news dir. Sta. WTZA-TV, Kingston, N.Y., 1984-86; contbg. editor Crain's N.Y. Bus., N.Y.C., 1986-88; bus. reporter Poughkeepsie (N.Y.) Jour., 1987-88; pres., chief exec. Harrington Assocs. Inc. affiliate Ruder Finn Inc., Kingston, 1988—; mem. adv. coun. Krissler Bus. Inst., 1990—; adj. prof. communications Marist Coll., 1991—; mng. editor The Trends Jour., 1992—. Co-editor: Problems in Law of Mass Communications, 1978; writer TV documentary A Finite World, 1982 (Best TV program award Populaton Action Coun. 1982); producer TV documentary Parricide: The Saddest Murder, 1983; developer Hudson ValleyOpoly bd. game, 1991; contbr. articles to profl. jours. Bd. dirs. Ulster Performing Arts Ctr., Kingston, 1988—. Recipient award for outstanding prodn. of major breaking news event Cable New Network, 1983, Outstanding News Programming award N.Y. State Broadcasters Assn., 1986, Gold Eclat award for pub. rels. excellence Hudson Valley Area Mktg. Assn., 1991. Fellow Socio-Econ. Rsch. Inst. Am.; mem. Soc. Profl. Journalists, Pub. Rels. Soc. Am., Assn. for Creative Devel. Officers, Profl. Communicators Hudson Valley, C. of C. Ulster County, Nat. Trust for Historic Preservation, Regional Plan Assn., Hudson Valley Internat. Trade Assn., Hudson Valley Direct Mktg. Assn., Hudson Valley Area Mktg. Assn. (bd. dirs. 1988—). Office: 57 Fairmont Ave Kingston NY 12401-5221

HARRINGTON, GERI SPOLANE, advertising agency executive; b. New Haven, Conn.; d. Frederick A. and Evelyn Cynthia (Ritchie) Spolane; m. Don Harrington (dec. 1979); children: Peter Tynus, John Jeffrey. B.A., Smith Coll. Mkt. rsch. analyst Good Housekeeping Mag., N.Y.C., 1959-60; writer, analyst Bur. Applied Social Rsch. Columbia U., 1961-64, Dept. Commerce, Washington, 1964-67, Ted Bates, Inc., N.Y.C., 1967-69; copywriter Grey Advt., 1970-72; sr. writer Doherty, Clifford, Shenfield & Steers, 1972-74; pres. Don Harrington Assocs., Wilton, Conn., 1975—. Author: The College Cookbook, 1975, revised edit., 1982, updated edit., 1988, Summer Garden, Winter Kitchen, 1976, The Salad Book, 1977, The Woodburning Stove Book, 1977, revised edit., 1979, Grow Your Own Chinese Vegetables, 1978, revised edit., 1984, Fireplace Stoves, Hearth and Inserts, 1980, Total Warmth, 1981, Never Too Old, 1981, The Medicare Answer Book, 1982, Cash Crops for Thrifty Gardners, 1984, The Health Insurance Answer Book, 1985, Real Food, Fake Food and Everything In Between, 1987, The Asthma Self Care Book, 1991.Trustee, Wilton Library Assn.; ombudsman Medicare-Conn., 1982-83; v.p. Wilton Playshop; past v.p. Wilton PTA. Mem. Nat. Press Club, Authors Guild, Inst. Food Technologists. Huxley Inst. Mem. Congl. Ch. Avocations: gardening, rock hunting, travel, swimming. Office: Don Harrington Assocs 29 Merwin Ln Wilton CT 06897-2599

HARRINGTON, KENNETH ALAN, data processing executive; b. Bennington, Vt., Nov. 24, 1948; s. Gerald Fred and Gertrude (Scott) H.; m. Lea Michelle Luchetti, Sept. 26, 1981; children: Mattison, Gabriel, Lucas. BSBA, U. Vt., 1970; MBA in Mktg. and Fin., U. Pa., 1978. Sales and mktg. staff N.Y. Tele. and AT&T, N.Y.C., 1970-76; assoc., cons. Booz Allen & Hamilton, N.Y.C., 1978-81; dir. strategy Plessey, N.Y.C., 1981-83; v.p. internat. Plessey Peripheral Systems, Irvine, Calif., 1983-86; pres. Spitz Inc., Chaddsford, Pa., 1986-89; v.p. market strategy UNISYS, Blue Bell, Pa., 1989-92; v.p. mktg. and strategy JWP Info. Svcs., Canton, Mass., 1992—. Bd. dirs. Walden Sch., Swarthmore, Pa., 1991-92. Office: WP Information Svcs 70 Shawmut Rd Canton PA 02021

HARRINGTON, MATTHEW JEROME, public relations company executive; b. Boston, May 25, 1962; s. John Michael and Ellen Patricia (White) H.; m. Elizabeth Ann Abell, Aug. 16, 1986; children: Elizabeth Phelps, Lauren Shippen. BA, Denison U., 1984. Account exec. Daniel J. Edelman Inc., N.Y.C., 1984-85; sr. account exec. R.C. Auletta Inc., N.Y.C., 1985-87; v.p. Dewe Rogerson Inc., N.Y.C., 1987-91; v.p., dir. investor rels. Edelman Pub. Rels. Worldwide, N.Y.C., 1991—. Fellow Nat. Investor Rels. Inst.; mem. Brit.-Am. C. of C., Pub. Rels. Soc. Am., Univ. Glee Club N.Y.C. Democrat. Roman Catholic. Office: Edelman Pub Rels Worldwide 1500 Broadway New York NY 10036-4015

HARRINGTON, MICHAELE MARY, watermedia artist, graphic designer, consultant; b. Boston, June 27, 1946; d. William Gerard and Jadwiga (Jerasonek) H.; m. Jeffrey Fancher Nicoll, Sept. 12, 1970; children: Heather Anne, James Craig William. BFA cum laude, Mass. Coll. Art, 1968. Prodn. mgr. R.H. Stearns Co., Boston, 1968-69; layout artist Grossman's, Braintree, 1971-72, Bradlee's, Braintree, 1973; asst. art dir. Canton (Mass.) Advt. Agy., 1973-78; watermedia artist, graphic designer, illustrator Hyattsville and Darnestown, Md., 1978—; mem. faculty Rockville Arts Place, 1990—; demonstrator, studio and workshop tchr., 1988—; design cons. KBL Group, Silver Spring, Md., 1986—; book illustrator Denlinger Pubs., Ltd., Fairfax, Va., 1986. Exhibited in group shows So. Watercolor Soc., Pensacola, Fla., 1982, Am. Watercolor Soc., N.Y.C., 1983, 90, Catherine Lorillard Wolfe Arts Club, N.Y.C., 1983, 84, Midwest Watercolor Soc., Davenport, Iowa, 1983, Mid-Atlantic Regional, Balt., 1983, 84, 86, 87, 89, 91, New Orleans Art Assn., 1984, Dundalk Coll., Md., 1985, San Diego Watercolor Soc., 1990, North Coast Collage Soc., Pitts., Watercolor Soc., Rocky Mountain Nat., 1991; one-person shows Montpelier Cultural Arts Ctr., Laurel, Md., 1982, Friendship Gallery, Chevy Chase, Md., 1990, Artshowcase Gallery, Balt., 1991, 92, Rockville Civic Ctr. Mansion Galleries, 1992; represented in permanent collections including Washington Health Ctr., Coast Guard Art Collection of Smithsonian Instn., Washington. Juror art in pub. places program Md.-Nat. Capital Parks and Planning Commn., Hyattsville, Md., 1980-81. Recipient Juror's choice award Md. Fedn. Art, 1982, 2d place award New Orleans Art Assn., gold medal Catherine Lorrilard Wolfe Arts Club, 1984, Abstract award Md. Nat. Found., 1989, Zeber Exptl. award North Coast Collage Soc., 1991. Mem. The Art League (Grumbacher Gold Medal 1991), Balt. Watercolor Soc. (award 1989), Potomac Valley Watercolorists (juried), Coast Guard Artists Program.

HARRINGTON, PHILLIP JOHN, JR., insurance company executive; b. Marshall, Mich., Apr. 20, 1957; s. Phillip John and Myra Lee (Ekdahl) H.; m. Kathie Marie Jackovitz, Aug. 20, 1983; children: Katherine Elizabeth, Anna Christine. BS summa cum laude, Western Mich. Univ., 1979; MS, Cornell U., 1983. Fellow N.Y. State Senate, Albany, 1981-82, legis. asst., 1982-86, spl. asst. to dep. majority leader, 1986-88; dir., mut. fund rsch. Prudential Ins. Co. of Am., Newark, N.J., 1988-89, dir., enterprise planning, 1989-90, v.p., govt. rels., 1990—; bd. dirs. N.Y. State HMO Conf., Latham, N.Y. Life Ins. Co. Guaranty Corp., N.Y.C.; exec. com. Industry Adv. Com., Nat. Conf. of Ins. Legislators, Brookfield, Wis., 1990—. Co-author: A Handbook of Educational Variables, 1985. Coun. mem. Faith Luth. Ch., New Providence, N.J., 1990—. Community Ambassador City of Kalamazoo, Mich., 1978-79. Mem. Minisink Club. Lutheran. Home: 75 Orchard Rd Chatham NJ 07928-2031 Office: Prudential Ins Co Am 751 Broad St Newark NJ 07102-3777

HARRINGTON, ROBERT DUDLEY, JR., printing company executive; b. Worcester, Mass., Dec. 19, 1932; s. Robert Dudley and Anne Victoria Harrington; m. Melissa Banks Hubner, Mar. 25, 1978. AB, Brown U., 1955; MBA, Columbia U., 1957. With Morgan Guaranty Trust Co., N.Y.C., 1957-59; v.p. Faulkner, Dawkins & Sullivan, N.Y.C., 1959-69; pres. Printers Express Co., Inc., Darien, Conn., 1976—. Mem. N.Y. Yacht Club, Edgartown Yacht Club, Round Hill Club, Edgartown Reading Rm., Holland Lodge, Athelstan Lodge, The Pilgrims. Office: Printers Express Co Inc 110 Post Rd Darien CT 06820-2911

HARRINGTON, ROBERT SUTTON, astronomer, researcher; b. Newport News, Va., Oct. 21, 1942; s. Jean Carl and Virginia Hall (Sutton) H.; m. Betty Jean Maycock, July 25, 1976; children: Amy Lucile, Ann Charon. BA, Swarthmore Coll., 1964; PhD, U. Tex., 1968. Astronomer U.S. Naval Observatory, Washington, 1968-85, supr. astronomer, 1985—. Mem. Internat. Astron. Union, Am. Astron. Soc. Office: US Naval Obs Washington DC 20392-5100

HARRIS, ALFRED PETER, art director, painter; b. Toronto, Ont., Can., Apr. 4, 1932; s. Louis Derwood and Phyllis Ometa (Weir) H. Diploma in Drawing and Painting, Ont. Coll. Art, Toronto, 1955; LLD (honoris causa), Brock U., St. Catharines, Ont., 1985. Display designer T. Eaton Co., Toronto, 1955-57; dir. Rodman Hall Arts Ctr., St. Catharines, 1960—; pres. Ont. Assn. Art Galleries, Toronto, 1971-72; mem. com. monuments Sec. of State, Ottawa, Ont., Can., 1968-69. Exhibited at Windsor Art Gallery, 1977, Gallery Stratford, 1985; one-man shows at Roberts Gallery, 1969-70, 73, 75, 77-79, 81-85, 87, 91. Mem. Can. Art Mus. Dirs. Organ.,Ont. Assn. Art Galleries (Fenn award 1987), St. Catharines Club. Office: Rodman Hall Arts Centre, 109 St Paul Crescent, Saint Catharines, ON Canada L2S 1M3

HARRIS, ALLEN, lawyer, educator; b. Bklyn., Feb. 3, 1929; s. Edward and Minnie (Herzog) H.; m. Susanne T. Berger, Sept. 1, 1957. B.A., N.Y.U., 1949; J.D., Columbia U., 1954. Bar: N.Y. 1954, Mo. 1968, U.S. Sup. Ct. 1966, U.S. Ct. Mil. Appeals 1956, U.S. Tax Ct. 1954, U.S. Ct. Appeals (2d cir.) 1955, U.S. Dist. Ct. (so. dist.) N.Y. 1955, (ea. dist.) N.Y. 1957. Assoc. Newman and Newman, N.Y.C., 1954-55, Garey and Garey, N.Y.C., 1955-56; asst. dist. atty. New York County, 1956-59; 1st asst. counsel, trial counsel, coordinating com. on discipline First Jud. Dept., N.Y. State Sup. Ct., 1959-62; law sec. to justice N.Y. State Sup. Ct., 1962-63; gen. counsel, labor negotiator United Board and Carton Corp., N.Y.C., 1963; asst. counsel N.Y. State Commn. on Investigation, 1963-65; assoc. dir. Inst. Jud. Adminstrn., N.Y.U., 1965-67; prof. law, dir. community legal edn., dir. legal research, dir. legal assistance to inmates clinic, dir. public service project in law enforcement U. Mo., Kansas City, 1967-69; prof. law Bklyn. Law Sch., 1969-72; counsel N.Y. State Study Commn. for N.Y.C., 1972; spl. asst. atty. gen. N.Y. State, 1972-76; sole practice, N.Y.C., 1976-79; sr. law asst., appellate div. First Jud. Dept., N.Y. State Sup. Ct., N.Y.C., 1979—; cons. for legal matters N.Y. State Select Com. on Correctional Instns., 1971-72; dir. spl. projects N.Y.C. Patrolmen's Benevolent Assn., 1978; cons. to police in Kansas City, 1968-69; mem. faculty appellate judges seminars N.Y. U., 1965-67; involved in numerous hearings. Served as 1st lt., inf. U.S. Army, 1951-53; col. JAGC. Decorated Combat Infantryman's badge; recipient N.Y. State Conspicuous Service cross. Mem. ABA, N.Y. State Bar Assn., Nat. Dist. Attys. Assn., N.Y. State Dist. Attys. Assn., Assn. Bar City N.Y., N.Y. County Lawyers Assn., Fed. Bar Council, Richmond County Bar Assn., Kansas City Bar Assn., Mil. Order World Wars, Res. Officers Assn. U.S., AAUP, Internat. Assn. Chiefs Police. Jewish. Club: City. Contbr. articles to encys. and legal jours. Home: 700 Victory Blvd Apt 18D Staten Island NY 10301-3533 Office: Appelate Div Ct House 25th St and Madison Ave New York NY 10010

HARRIS, BENJAMIN LOUIS, chemical engineer, consultant; b. Savannah, Ga., Aug. 1, 1917; s. Raymond Branson and Edith (Kontner) H.; m. Janet Diekmann, Oct. 4, 1942; children: Benjamin S., Stefanie Harris Hunt, Deborah Harris Kommalan, Penelope Harris Clifton, Rebecca Harris Gutin. BE, Johns Hopkins U., 1938, PhD, 1941; diploma, Indsl. Coll. Armed Forces, Washington, 1965. Registered profl. engr., Md. Asst. prof. Johns Hopkins U., Balt., 1946-53; commd. 2d lt. U.S. Army, advanced through grades to col., 1968; with R&D Command U.S. Army, Edgewood Arsenal, Md., 1952-66; dep. asst. dir. defense R&D U.S. Army Office Sec. Def., Alexandria, Va., 1966-70; tech. dir. U.S. Army Office Sec. Def., Aberdeen, Md., 1970-81; advanced through grades to col. USAR; pres. Engring. Rsch. Co. of Glenarm, Md., 1981-83; cons. in field, 1981—; pres. Profl. Engrs. Bd., Md., 1987-88, v.p., 1988—. Editor St. George Philatelec Soc. Newsletter; patentee in field, contbr. articles to profl. jours. Mem. Gov.'s Exec. Adv. Coun., Md., 1988—; exec. bd. Balt. Area coun. Boy Scouts Am., 1964—; mem. adv. com. USCG, NRC, Washington, 1967-77; com. ethics and professionalism Nat. Coun. Examiners Engring. and Surveying. Recipient Silver Beaver award Boy Scouts Am., 1952, Silver Antelope award, 1987, Disting. Eagle award, 1976, Lamb award Luth. Ch., 1964, St. George award Cath. Ch., 1983. Fellow AAAS, Am. Inst. Chem. Engrs.; mem. SAR, Order Founders and Patriots Am., Sons and Daus. of Pilgrims, Soc. Boonesborough, St. George Soc. Balt., St. Andrews Soc. Balt., Mil. Order World Wars (past comdr. Balt. chpt.), Ret. Officers Assn., Res. Officers Assn., Chem. Corps Regtl. Assn. Democrat. Lutheran. Home and Office: 11323 Glen Arm Rd Glen Arm MD 21057-9434

HARRIS, BERNICE EISEN, investment executive, educator; b. N.Y.C., June 24, 1927; d. Harry and Clara (Eisen) H. BS in Engring., N.J. Inst. Tech., 1948; MBA in Econs., NYU, 1954, postgrad., 1954-69. Rsch. asst. Shell Chem. Corp., N.Y.C., 1949-53; statis. dir. rsch. dept. Young & Rubicam, N.Y.C., 1957-60; quality control supr. McGraw Hill div. F.W. Dodge, N.Y.C., 1965-66; reorgn. adminstr. Shearson Lehman, N.Y.C., 1984-90; fin. asst. Spectrum Source Corp., N.Y.C., 1990—; adj. asst. prof. Lubin Grad. Sch., Pace U., N.Y.C., 1978-87; with H&R Block, N.Y.C., tax seasons, 1990, 91. Mem. Lenox Hill Dem. Club, N.Y.C., 1983—. Episcopalian.

HARRIS, BRIAN CRAIG, lawyer; b. Newark, Sept. 8, 1941; s. Louis W. and Lillian (Frankel) H.; m. Ellen M. Davis, Aug. 20, 1978; children: Andrea, Keith. BS, Boston U., 1963; JD, Rutgers U., 1966. Bar: N.J., 1968, D.C. 1968, U.S. Ct. Appeals (3d cir.) 1968, N.Y. 1984, U.S. Ct. Appeals (2d cir.) 1985. Asst. corp. counsel Newark, 1968-70; assoc. Braff, Litvak & Ertag, East Orange, N.J., 1970-72; ptnr. Braff, Litvak, Ertag, Wortmann & Harris, East Orange, 1972-85, Braff, Ertag, Wortmann, Harris & Sukoneck, Livingston, N.J., 1985-91, Braff, Harris & Sukoneck, 1991—; adj. lectr. law and medicine Seton Hall U., South Orange, N.J., 1982-83, trial preparation Rutgers U., Newark, 1983, strategy of def. United Tech. Corp., Chgo., 1986. Chmn. Essex County Heart Assn., East Orange, 1972-73; mem. adv. com. Llewellyn Park, West Orange, N.J.; sustaining mem. Product Liability Adv. Coun., Inc.; contbg. mem. Nat. Ileitis Found., N.Y.C., 1983—. Mem. ABA, N.Y. State Bar Assn., N.J. Bar Assn., Essex County Bar Assn., N.Y. Trial Lawyers Assn., Essex County Trial Lawyers Assn., Middlesex County Trial Lawyers Assn., Assn. Trial Lawyers Am., Def. Rsch. Inst., N.J. Trial Lawyers Assn., N.J. Def. Assn. Named Master of the Inns of Ct., Arthur J. Vanderbilt Sect., 1988. Jewish. Club: Green Hollow Tennis (East Hampton, N.Y.), Orange Lawn Tennis (South Orange, N.J.). Avocations: running, basketball, theater, tennis, study of mil. strategy of land forces in World War II. Home: Llewellyn Pk West Orange NJ 07052-5402 Office: Braff Harris & Sukoneck 570 W Mt Pleasant Ave Livingston NJ 07039-1619 also: 233 Broadway Ste 970 New York NY 10279

HARRIS, BURTON HENRY, surgeon; b. N.Y.C., Jan. 30, 1941; s. Mark and Nettie (Bilsky) H.; m. Marian Lichtiger, 1962 (div. 1973); children: David, Robert, Eileen; m. Kathleen Mary Donnelly, Nov. 28, 1973; 1 child, Mark. BA, Hobart Coll., 1961; MD, SUNY, N.Y.C., 1965. Intern, resident, and chief resident in surgery SUNY, 1965-71; chief resident in pediatric surgery Children's Hosp., Columbus, Ohio, 1971-73; prin. Drs. Wilkinson, Webb & Harris P.A., Jacksonville, Fla., 1973-81; dir. Kiwanis Pediatric Trauma Inst. New Eng. Med. Ctr., Boston, 1981—; chief div. pediatric surgery New Eng. Med. Ctr., Boston, 1985—; Orvar Swenson prof. pediatric surgery Tufts U. Sch. Medicine, Boston, 1981—. Editor: Progress in Pediatric Trauma, 1985, 87, 89; contbr. articles to profl. jours. Med. advisor Profl. Golf Assn. Tour, Ponte Vedra, Fla., 1977—. Brig. gen. USAR, 1966—. Decorated Legion of Merit, D.S.M.; NIH fellow, 1961-64, Am. Cancer Soc. clin. fellow, 1971-73. Fellow Am. Coll. Surgeons (chpt. pres. 1980-81, State com. chmn. 1989—), Am. Coll. Emergency Physicians, Am. Cancer Soc., Am. Pediatric Surg Assn., Am. Acad. Pediatrics, Soc. Pediatric Trauma (pres. elect. 1989—); mem. Ea. Assn. for the Surgery Trauma (pres. 1989-90), Am. Trauma Soc. (dir. 1986—), Internat. Soc. Aeromed. Svcs. (pres. 1988—), Wellesley (Mass.) Country Club. Republican. Office: New Eng Med Ctr Box 344 750 Washington St Boston MA 02111-1526

HARRIS, CYRIL MANTON, physicist, engineering and architecture educator, consulting acoustical engineer; b. Detroit; s. Bernard O. and Ida (Moss) H.; m. Ann Schakne, July 12, 1949; children: Nicholas Bennett, Katherine Anne. B.A., UCLA, 1938, M.A., 1940; Ph.D., MIT, 1945; Sc.D. (hon.), N.J. Inst. Tech., 1981, Northwestern U., 1989. Rsch. asst. Carnegie Instn. Washington, 1941; mem. staff Bell Telephone Labs., 1945-51; cons. Office Naval Research, London, Eng., 1951; Fulbright lectr. Tech. U., Delft, Holland, 1951-52; Charles Batchelor prof. elec. engring., prof. architecture and past chmn. div. archtl. tech. Columbia U.; now prof. emeritus; vis. Fulbright prof. U. Tokyo, 1960; acoustical cons. Met. Opera House, N.Y.C., John F. Kennedy Ctr. Performing Arts, Washington, Krannert Ctr. Performing Arts, U. Ill., Powell Symphony Hall, St. Louis, Nat. Acad. Scis. Auditorium, Washington, Minn. Orch. Hall, Mpls., Nat. Ctr. Performing Arts, Bombay, Avery Fisher Hall, N.Y. State Theater reconstructions, Lincoln Ctr., N.Y.C., Symphony Hall, Salt Lake City; past dir. Inst. Theatre Tech.; mem. noise control group, mem. com. on undersea warfare NRC, 1955-57, mem. bldg. adv. bd., 1977-79; mem. coun. hearing and bio-acoustics Armed Forces-NRC, 1953-55; mem. adv. panel 213 to Nat. Bur. Standards, 1966-69, chmn., 1969-71. Author: (with V.O. Knudsen) Acoustical Designing in Architecture, 1950, rev., 1980, Handbook of Noise Control, 1957, 2d edit., 1979, 3d edit retitled Handbook of Acoustical Measurements and Noise Controls, 1991; Shock and Vibration Handbook, 3d edit., 1987, Dictionary of Architecture and Construction, 1975; Historic Architecture Sourcebook, 1977, Illustrated Dictionary of Historic Architecture, 1983; Handbook of Utilities and Services for Buildings, 1990; contbr. articles to profl. jours.; editorial adv. bd.: Physics Today, 1955-66. Bd. dirs. Armstrong Meml. Research Found., 1976—; hon. v.p., trustee St. Louis Symphony Soc., 1977—; mem. nat. adv. bd. Utah Symphony Orch., 1976-85. Recipient Franklin medal, 1977; Emile Berliner award, 1977; Hon. award U.S. ITT, 1977; Wallace Clement Sabine medal, 1979; AIA medal, 1980; Gold Medal Audio Engring. Soc., 1984; award of honor for sci. and tech. City of N.Y., 1985; Alumni award UCLA, 1989. Fellow Acoustical Soc. Am. (pres. 1964-65, assoc. editor jour. 1959-70, Gold medal 1987), IEEE, Audio Engring. Soc. (hon.); mem. NAS, NAE, Am. Inst. Physics (mem. governing bd. 1965-66), N.Y. Acad. Scis. (v.p. 1988-91, pres. 1991—, chmn. bd. 1992—), Am.

Philos. Soc., Sigma Xi, Tau Beta Pi. Office: Columbia U Mudd Bldg New York NY 10027

HARRIS, DWAYNE MATTHEW, real estate manager; b. Neptune, N.J., Jan. 12, 1967; s. Phyllis (Eppes) H. BSBA, Seton Hall U., 1990. Adminstr. First Fidelity Bancorp., Newark, N.J., 1988-89; regional v.p. Primerica, Totowa, N.J., 1989-90; first level mgr. Rappaport Bros. Inc., Freehold, N.J., 1990—; pres. Harris Enterprises, Atlantic Highlands, N.J., 1990—. Editor newsletter Out-West, 1986. Organizer Young Dems., Seton Hall U., 1988. Named Outstanding Young Man in Am., Outstanding Ams., 1989. Mem. Internat. Traders, Premier Club, Sigma Pi (pres. 1987-88). Methodist. Home: 73 Ave A Atlantic Highlands NJ 07716-1061

HARRIS, ELIZABETH CLAUDIA, guidance director, psychology educator; b. Cleve., Nov. 16, 1942; d. Ernest Charles and Claudia Frances (Tebbs) H.; m. Charles Matthew Rice, Jan 6, 1962 (div. 1965); children: Christopher Michael Rice, Adam Peter Rice. BS, Brigham Young U., 1983; MA in Edn., U. Colo., 1987. Cert. ednl. specialist. Sch. counselor Tooele (Utah) Sch. Dist., 1986-88; dir. guidance Islesboro (Maine) Sch. Dept., 1989—; counselor in field, Islesboro, 1989—; adult edn. tchr. Islesboro Sch. Dept., 1990-91. Ambulance driver Islesboro Ambulance Assn., 1989—; accompanist Islesboro Community Chorus, 1989—. Mem. Am. Assn. Counseling & Devel., Am. Sch. Counselor Assn., Assn. Mormon Counselors & Psychotherapists, Assn. Measurement & Evaluation in Edn. Mem. LDS Ch.

HARRIS, FRANCESCA TREPPEDA, art director; b. White Plains, N.Y., Dec. 29, 1958; d. Frank J. and Gemma M. (Russo) T.; m. Daniel O. Harris, Aug. 10, 1985. AAS, Fashion Inst. of Tech., 1980; student, NYU, 1986. Designer, art dir. Ziff Davis Publ. Inc., N.Y., 1981-85; art dir. Grey Direct Mktg. Inc., N.Y., 1985-86; assoc. creative dir. Ed Sobel & Assocs. Inc., N.Y., 1986-88; sr. art dir. Gross, Townsend, Frank, Hoffman, N.Y., 1988-90, S.J. Weinstein Assocs. Inc., N.Y.C., 1990—; creative cons. Advt. Women of N.Y., 1987, sr. art dir., 1988; sr. art dir. E.R. Squibb & Sons Inc., DuoDerm, 1988, SmithKline Beecham, Massengill, 1989, Merck Sharp & Dohme Noroxin, 1990, Genzume Biotherapeutics, Ceredase, 1992, Armour Pharms. Monoclatep Regeneron, 1992. Art dir. American Movie Classics Mag., Creative/AD: Berlitz Intern., 1986, DigitalNews Mag., 1986, Stray Cats, 1984. Recipient Award of Excellence Grey Direct Mktg., N.Y., 1985, RX Club award, 1990. Mem. Trout Unltd., Theodore Gordon Fly Fishing, Salty Flyrodders, Caanan Pine Grove Assn., Am. Inst. of Graphic Arts, Fashion Inst. Tech. Alumni Assn. Democrat.

HARRIS, FREDERICK JOHN, educator; b. N.Y.C., July 29, 1943; s. Frederick and Anna (Guttmann) H. BA, Fordham U., 1965; MA, Columbia U., 1966, PhD, 1969. Asst. prof. Fordham U., N.Y.C., 1970-79, assoc. prof., 1979-84, prof. French and comparative lit., 1984—, chmn. div. humanities, 1979-85; bd. dirs. Fordham U. Press, N.Y.C.; mem. adv. com. Krieg und Literatur/War and Literature. Author: André Gide-Romain Rolland: Two Men Divided, 1973, Encounters with Darkness: French and German Writers on World War II, 1983; contbr. articles to profl. jours. Mem. MLA, Am. Assn. Tchrs. French, Internat. Comparative Lit. Assn., Am. Comparative Lit. Assn., Soc. Des Amis d'André Gide, Stewart Hall (v.p. 1989-90, bd. dirs.). Roman Catholic. Office: Fordham U Lincoln Center Campus New York NY 10023

HARRIS, JAMES FULBRIGHT, retired pharmacist; b. Atlantic City, Sept. 16, 1929; s. James Handy Jr. and Annie Paige (Fulbright) H.; m. Gisele Turnier, Aug. 18, 1956; children: Bertrand, Emmanuel. BS in Pharmacy, Howard U., 1956. Registered Pharmacist, Washington. Community pharmacist Colbert Pharmacy, Washington, 1956-57, Standard Pharmacy, Washington, 1958-61; staff pharmacist D.C. Gen. Hosp., Washington, 1961-68; cons. pharmacist D.C. Medicaid Drug Program, Washington, 1968-91; retired, 1991; chmn. D.C. Dept. Human Svcs. Bd. Pharmacy, Washington, 1981-84, D.C. Dept. Human Svcs. Pharmacy and Therapeutics Com., 1981-91; cons. D.C. Drug Substitution Com., Washington, 1982-91. treas. SEEDS Haiti Inc., Washington, 1989—. Sgt. U.S. Army, 1952-54, Korea. Mem. Am. Pharm. Assn., Am. Soc. Hosp. Pharmacies, Washington Pharm. Assn. (A.H. Robins Bowl of Hygea award 1984, mem. exec. com. 1985—, exec. dir.), D.C. Soc. Hosp. Pharmacies, Assn. Black Hosp. Pharmacists, Nat. Pharm. Assn., Chi Delta Mu. Democrat. Home: 1405 Kalmia Rd NW Washington DC 20012

HARRIS, JEFFREY EARL, economist, physician; b. Phila., May 12, 1948; s. Samuel and Anita (Charney) H.; m. Johanna M. Lieb, Aug. 8, 1971; children: Zoe K., Luke J. AB, Harvard U., 1969; MD, U. Pa., 1974, PhD, 1975. Resident, fellow Mass. Gen. Hosp., Boston, 1974-77, clin. assoc., 1977—; asst. prof. MIT, Cambridge, 1976-80; assoc. prof. MIT, 1980—; vis. prof. Harvard Sch. Pub. Health, Boston, 1988-89; cons., editor U.S. Surgeon Gen., Office on Smoking and Health, 1978-88; cons. Atty. Gen. Can., Ottawa, 1988-90; mem. Nat. Rsch. Coun., Diesel Impacts Study Com., 1980-81, Inst. Medicine, Com. on Nat. Strategy Toward AIDS, 1986. Editor U.S. Surgeon Gen.'s Reports on Smoking and Health, 1979-83; contbr. articles to profl. jours., chpts. in books. Mem. Town Meeting, Brookline, Mass., 1986—, fin. adv. com. mem., 1986-90; invited faculty U.S. Ho. of Reps. Com. on Ways and Means,, Issues Seminar, 1989; physician mem. Mass. Bd. Registration in Medicine, Boston, 1978-80. Grantee, Robert Wood Johnson Found., 1988-89, Am. Cancer Soc., 1985-87, Nat. Cancer Inst., 1985-86; USPHS Rsch. Creer Devel. award, 1980-85. Mem. N.Y. Acad. Scis., Am. Statis. Assn., Am. Econ. Assn., Am. Pub. Health Assn., Skating Club of Boston, Bay State Speed Skating Club. Home: 52 Hedge Rd Brookline MA 02146-7551 Office: MIT E52-252G Cambridge MA 02139

HARRIS, JOHN KENNETH, lawyer; b. N.Y.C., Nov. 13, 1948; s. John Joseph and Maryan Harley (Smith) H.; m. Susan Joan Krieger, Apr. 2, 1983; children: Keighley Simons, Tracey Allison. BA, U. Va., 1970; JD, Villanova U., 1975; LLM in Taxation, NYU, 1979. Bar: Pa. 1975, U.S. Tax Ct. 1979, U.S. Dist. Ct. (ea. dist.) Pa. 1980, N.J. 1985, U.S. Dist. Ct. N.J. 1985. Assoc. MacElree, Harvey, Gallagher & Featherman, West Chester, Pa., 1979-83, Fellheimer, Eichen & Goodman, Phila., 1983-84, Archer & Greener, P.C., Haddonfield (N.J.) and Phila., 1984-88, Fox, Rothschild, O'Brien & Frankel, Phila. and Princeton (N.J.), 1988-90; of counsel White and Williams, Phila. and Westmont, N.J., 1990—; counsel Benjamin Franklin Bridge Lighting Corp., Phila., Camden, N.J., 1987. Bd. dirs. Jr. Achievement of Cen. Jersey, 1990; v.p. Cen. Chester County YMCA, West Chester, Pa., 1983; mem. Camden County Tax Com., vice chmn., 1992-93. Lt. USN, 1970-79, comdr. USNR, 1985—. Mem. N.J. State Bar Assn. (taxation sect.), Greater Phila. C. of C. (small bus. coun.), C. of C. of So. N.J. (small bus. action com.), Racquet Club. Home: 49 Warwick Rd Haddonfield NJ 08033-3704 Office: White and Williams 222 Haddon Ave Ste 300 Collingswood NJ 08108-2828

HARRIS, JOHN PATRICK, engineering consultant; b. Phila., Apr. 20, 1942; s. John Patrick and Helen Marie (O'Neill) H.; m. Patricia Mary Jordan, Nov. 18, 1972; children: Sean Patrick, Kathleen Martha, Erin Jordan. Cert. in Russian studies, Syracuse U., 1964; BA, Northeastern U., 1977, MA, 1978. Prodn. mgr. Am. Opinion mag., Belmont, Mass., 1969-75; editor Jour. Saranac Lake Placid (N.Y.), 1970-71; govt. contracts adminstr. Linguistic Systems Inc., Cambridge, Mass., 1975-76; print coord. Brown, Daltas & Assocs., Cambridge, 1976-83; cons. in info. mgmt., pub. affairs, emergency preparedness Stone & Webster Engring. Corp., Boston, 1983-89; nuclear tng. coord., emergency preparedness coord. L.I. (N.Y.) Power Authority, 1991—; mem. bus. adv. coun. Rivier Coll., Nashua, N.H., 1988—; bus. advisor Jr. Achievement Inc., Boston, 1989. Newspaper columnist, 1982—. Treas. Winchester Hist. Soc., 1979-80; nuclear cons. Mass. Republican Com., 1988—; loaned exec. assoc. United Way Massachusetts Bay, 1988; merit badge counselor Boy Scouts Am., Lawrence, Mass., 1989—; elected mem. Mass. Gov.'s Coun., 1990—; v.p. Essex County Rep. Com., 1989—; elected mem. Andover Rep. Com., 1988—; del. Rep. Nat. Conv., 1992. Mem. Am. Nuclear Soc., Essex Club (Beverly, Mass., pres. 1985-88), Middlesex Club (bd. dirs. 1992—). Roman Catholic. Home and Office: 31 Lincoln Cir Andover MA 01810

HARRIS, LOUISE, writer; b. Warwick, R.I., 1903; d. Samuel P. and Faustine M. (Borden) H. AB, Brown U., 1926; pvt. study organ with T. Tertius Noble, N.Y.C., 1938-42. Sec. Samuel P. Harris, Inc., 1928-42; tchr. piano and organ, ch. organist, recitalist Providence, 1928-50; founder, curator C.A. Stephens Collection; researcher Youth's Companion. Author: A Comprehensive Bibliography of C.A. Stephens, 1965, None But the Best, 1966, A Chuckle and A Laugh, 1967, The Star of the Youth's Companion, 1969, The Flag Over the Schoolhouse, 1971, Our Great American Story-Teller, 1978, Old Glory-Long May She Wave, 1981, Time for the Truth, 1987; compiler: Under the Sea in the Salvador (C.A. Stephens), 1969, C.A. Stephens Looks at Norway, 1970, Charles Adams Tales (C.A. Stephens), 1973, Little Big Heart (C.A. Stephens), 1974. Mem. R.I. Hosp. Corp.; 1st founder Brown U. Med. Sch. Recipient Statue of World Culture, Italy, 1984. Mem. Nat. Archives Assocs., Am. Guild Organists, Hymn Soc. Am., Audubon Soc., Brown Alumnae Assn., Nat. Trust Historic Preservation, Am. Bicentennial Rsch. Inst., Am. Heritage Soc., Am. Mus. Natural History, Smithsonian Instn. Assocs., Nat., Western R.I. Home: 395 Angell St Apt 111 Providence RI 02906-4064 Office: Brown U PO Box 1926 Providence RI 02912-0001

HARRIS, MARTIN SEYMOUR, electrical engineer; b. Bklyn., Mar. 15, 1935; s. Harry and Eva (Greenspan) Heimowitz; m. Vivian M. Shifrin, June 29, 1957; children: Kathy Lynn Harris Galante, Vicki Sue. BEE, Cooper Union, 1957. Sr. engr. Sperry Gyro Corp., Lake Success, N.Y., 1957-68; dir. programs Telephonics Corp., Huntington, N.Y., 1968-80, Electronic Assocs., Inc., West Long Branch, N.J., 1980-83; program mgr. Norden Systems, Melville, N.Y., 1983-85; dir. programs Loral Control Systems, Archbald, Pa., 1985—. Mem. Assn. Old Crows, Am. Def. Preparedness Assn., Assn. of U.S. Army, Navy League of U.S., Project Mgmt. Inst. Republican. Jewish. Home: PO Box 625 Dalton PA 18414-0625 Office: Loral Control Systems John F Kennedy Blvd Archbald PA 18403

HARRIS, MELVA J., management consultant; b. Montgomery, Ala., Dec. 25, 1944; d. Clisby Harris and Flore (Smith) Poole. BBA, Baruch Coll., 1980; MA, N.Y. Inst. Tech., N.Y.C., 1991. Supr. ops. AT&T, N.Y.C., 1967-83; pres. Harris Devel. Cons., East Windsor, N.J., 1984—; cons. Mercer County Coll. Small Bus. Devel. Ctr., Trenton, N.J., 1988—. Bd. chmn. Mercer County Pvt. Industry Coun., Trenton, 1990-92; pres., chief exec. officer Trenton Granville Acad.; bd. trustee Mill Hill Child and Family Devel. Ctr., Trenton. With U.S. Air Force, 1963-67. Recipient Officer Outstanding Svc. award Mercer County Pvt. Industry Coun., 1991; named Outstanding Bus. and Profl. Woman, N.Y. Dist. Bus. and Profl. Women's Orgn., 1986. Mem. N.Y. Met. Am. Soc. Tgn. and Devel. (pres. elect 1991—), Nat. Speakers Assn., Princeton Area C. of C. (bd. dirs.), N.Y. Speakers Assn. Home and Office: Harris Devel Cons 834 Jamestown Rd Hightstown NJ 08520-5604

HARRIS, MICALYN SHAFER, lawyer; b. Chgo., Oct. 31, 1941; d. Erwin and Dorothy (Sampson) Shafer. AB, Wellesley Coll., 1963; JD, U. Chgo., 1966. Bar: Ill. 1966, Mo. 1967, U.S. Dist. Ct. (ea. dist.) 1967, U.S. Supreme Ct. 1972, U.S. Ct. Appeals (8th cir.) 1974, N.Y. 1981, N.J. 1988. Law clk. U.S. Dist. Ct., St. Louis, 1967-68; atty. The May Dept. Stores, St. Louis, 1968-70, Ralston-Purina Co., St. Louis, 1970-72; atty., asst. sec. Chromalloy Am. Corp., St. Louis, 1972-76; pvt. practice, St. Louis, 1976-78; gen. counsel S.B. Thomas, Inc.; div. counsel CPC N.Am., 1978-84; corp. counsel and asst. sec. CPC Internat., Englewood Cliffs, N.J., 1984-88; assoc. counsel Weil, Gotshal & Manges, N.Y.C., 1988-90; pvt. practice, 1991; v.p., sec., gen. counsel Xian Corp., 1991—. Mem. ABA (chair corp. counsel com. past, chmn. corporate counsel com., past securities law com., tender offers and proxy statements subcom.), Ill. Bar Assn., N.Y. State Bar Assn. (securities regulation com. and computer law com.), Bar Assn. Met. St. Louis (past chmn. TV com.), Mo. Bar Assn. (past chmn. internat. law com.), Am. Corp. Counsel Assn. N.J. (past bd. dirs. and chmn. bus. law com.), Am. Corp. Counsel Assn. N.Y. (mergers and acquisitions com., corp. law com.). Address: 625 N Monroe Ridgewood NJ 07450

HARRIS, MILES FITZGERALD, meteorologist; b. Brunswick, Ga., Feb. 2, 1913; s. James Madison and Louise (Fitzgerald) H.; m. Marguerite Bertice Leonard, May 13, 1938; children: Ann Louise, Theresa Geraldine, Emily Leland. BSc in Meteorology, NYU, 1944, MSc in Meteorology, 1957. Weather observer U.S. Weather Bur., Macon, Ga., 1932-35, Savannah, Chattanooga,, Macon,, Washington, 1937-42; cadet/clk. South Atlantic Steamship Line, Savannah, 1935-37; meteorologist U.S. Weather Bur., Washington, 1944-45; hurricane forecaster U.S. Weather Bur., San Juan, P.R., 1945-48; spl. projects meteorologist U.S. Weather Bur., Washington, 1948-51, rsch. meteorologist, 1951-61, head editing and pub. br., 1961-66; phys. scientist, chief Sci. Info. Br. Environ. Sci. Svcs. Adminstrn., Washington, 1966-70; editor Mon. Weather Review, 1968-70; editor Am. Meterol. Soc., Boston, 1970-83, ret., 1983; Editor, writer, cons. Earth Sci. Curriculum Project, Boulder, Colo., 1964-67. Author: Man Against Storm, 1962, Getting to Know the World Meterological Organization, 1966, Opportunities in Meteorology, 1972, Investigating the Earth, 1967-84; contbg. author Ency. of Earth Scis., 1976; contbg. author and editor John Hale, A Man Beset by Witches, 1992. Mem. Am. Meteorol. Soc. Democrat. Congregationalist. Home: 40 Lothrop St Beverly MA 01915-5150

HARRIS, PAUL SMITH, human resources professional; b. Santa Monica, Calif., Nov. 29, 1935; s. Wallace Albert and Henrietta (Smith) H.; m. Jill B. Hall, Sept. 15, 1956 (div. June 1974); children: Gregory A., Geoffrey A.; m. Nancy Lynn Cherry, Sept. 9, 1975; 1 child, Doug B. BA in Psychology, U. Utah, 1958; postgrad., UCLA, 1961-63. Mgr. employment Western Airlines Inc., L.A., 1956-64; mgr. selection Am. Airlines Inc., N.Y.C., 1964-66; mgr. adminstrn. IBM, Princeton, N.J., 1966-72; dir. orgn. planning and devel. CNA Fin. Corp., Chgo., 1972-76; v.p. human rsch. developer W.E. Walker Stores Inc., Jackson, Miss., 1976-80; pres. Harris Cons., Inc., Salt Lake City, 1980-83; dir. pers. Americas div. Intercontinental Hotels, Washington, 1983-88; v.p. orgn./devel. and human svcs. Showboat Casino/Hotel, Atlantic City, N.J., 1988—. Bd. dirs. C. of C., Middlesex County, N.J., 1970-71, Chgo. Alliance of Businessman, 1974-75. Mem. Masons (master mason Mt. Moriah # 2 Utah, 32 degree). Republican. Christian Scientist. Office: Showboat Hotel Casino 801 Boardwalk Atlantic City NJ 08401-7599

HARRIS, PENNY SMITH, developer, fund raising executive; b. Old Town, Maine, Apr. 6, 1941; d. Owen Halbert and Louise Marion (Whitten) Smith; m. Parker Fred Harris, June 22, 1963 (div. 1991); children: Susan Leslie, Nancy Lynne. BS in Sociology, U. Maine, 1963; MS in Bus. Mgmt., Husson Coll., 1984. Social worker Elizabeth Lund Home, Burlington, Vt., 1964-65; pub. sch. tchr. Essex Junction, Vt.; asst. dir. devel., corp. support mgr. Maine Pub. Broadcasting Network, Bangor, 1985-89; dir. devel. Eastern Maine Med. Ctr., Bangor, 1989—. Mem. task force on campaign fin. Sen. George Mitchell, Augusta, Maine, 1983; mem. All Am. City selection award jury Nat. Civil League, N.Y.C., 1987; bd. dirs. Greater Bangor United Way, 1990—; trustee U. Maine System, 1991—. Mem. LWV (pres. Bangor-Brewer chpt. 1979-81, state pres. 1982-85, nat. bd. dirs. 1986-88, sec. nat. bd. dirs. 1988-90, project dir. TV polit. debates Bangor 1988—, project dir. Nat. Security and You Conf., Portland, Maine 1983), U. Maine Alumni Assn. (v.p. bd. dirs. 1991—). Democrat. Methodist. Lodge: Rotary. Home: 325 Garland St Bangor ME 04401-5538 Office: Ea Maine Healthcare 489 State St Bangor ME 04401-6616

HARRIS, PHILIP EDWIN, brokerage house executive, consultant; b. New Rochelle, N.Y., Sept. 9, 1947; s. Charles Marvin and Claire (Meier) H.; m. Ruth Beall, Sept. 12, 1970; children: Philip, Robert, Mark, Lauren. Student, Am. Sch., Lugano, Switzerland, 1966; BS in Psychology, Bus. Adminstrn., Baldwin-Wallace, 1970; MBA, Adelphi U., 1985. Real estate broker Poly-Little Realtors, Denver, 1973-75; salesman div. coffee Nestle, L.A., 1975-78; sales mgr., mgr. Bronx area M&H Food Broker, White Plains, N.Y., 1978-82; stockbroker Laidlaw Adams & Peck, N.Y.C., 1982-84; v.p., br. mgr. Laidlaw Adams Peck & Fahnstock, Manasquan, N.J., 1984-88; v.p., br. mgr. Baird Patrick & Co., Spring Lake, N.J., 1988-89, N.Y.C., 1989-91; v.p. equities, co. mgr. Mid-State Securities, Red Bank, N.J., 1991—; food broker cons., Tarrytown, N.Y., 1980-91. Leader youth group Sherman Oaks (Calif.) Luth. Ch., 1976-78; treas. Hillcrest Civic Assn., Tarrytown, 1983-85; mem. coun. St. Marks Luth. Ch., Elmsford, N.Y., 1983-85; umpire South Wall (N.J.) Little League, 1989-91. Mem. Am. Contract Bridge League, Nat. Assn. Securities Dealers. Republican. Home: 1236 Oak Rd Manasquan NJ 08736-2010 Office: Mid State Securities 137 Broad St Red Bank NJ 07701-1923

HARRIS, RANDY HAYES, telecommunications consultant; b. High Point, N.C., Oct. 13, 1956; s. Hayes Rush and Bernice Elverse Harris; 1 child, Randy Hayes Jr. BS in Polit. Sci., Rutgers U., 1982. Instr. writing Rutgers U., New Brunswick, N.J., 1982-84; computer operator AT&T Communications, Piscataway, N.J., 1984-85; communications cons. Mktg. and System Devel. Corp., Lyndhurst, N.J., 1985-88; sr. communications analyst Chem. Bank of N.Y.C., N.Y.C., 1988—; cons. Joyce Dudley Assocs. Mem. NAACP. Baptist. Home: 128 Wayne St Jersey City NJ 07302-3478

HARRIS, RAYMOND JESSE, retired government official; b. Van Buren, N.Y., Dec. 28, 1916; s. Francis Elbert and Anna Marie (Selinsky) H.; A.B., Harvard U., 1940, postgrad., 1940-42; postgrad. U. Pa., 1952-54, 59-60; m. Rosalba Emilia Prestianni, Jan. 7, 1950 (dec. 1989). Cert. drafter U.S. State Dept., Washington, 1947, vice consul Am. consulate, Palermo, Italy, 1947-50, Munich, Germany, 1950-51; personnel technician, information officer City of Phila., 1952-59, adminstrv. asst. to water commr., 1959-79; ret., 1979; Republican committeeman 59th ward, City of Phila., 1986—. Served with USAAF, 1942-45; ETO. Named Water Dept. Supr. of Year, 1971, 72, 73, 76; recipient Ted Moses award Pa. Water Pollution Control Assn., 1978. Mem. Am. Water Works Assn., Archeol. Inst. Am., Am. Acad. Polit. and Social Sci., Nat. Trust Historic Preservation, Pa. Hist. Soc., Acad. Polit. Sci., Am. Anti-Vivisection Soc., Planetary Soc., Harvard of Phila. Club, Germantown Rep. Club. Home: 275 W Tulpehocken St Philadelphia PA 19144-3209

HARRIS, ROBERT CHARLES, lawyer; b. N.Y.C., Feb. 24, 1952; s. Bert and Mildred (Adelson) H.; m. Melody S. Rich, Sept. 1, 1974; children: Betsy Abigail, Mitchell Neal, Emily Nina. BA, SUNY, Stony Brook, 1974; JD, NYU, 1978. Bar: N.Y. 1979. Assoc. Linden and Deutsch, N.Y.C., 1978-87; ptnr. Leavy, Rosensweig & Hyman, N.Y.C., 1987—. Trustee Young Israel of West Hempstead, N.Y., 1985—, officer, 1987—. Recipient Yitzchak Altus prize SUNY, Stony Brook, 1974. Mem. ABA, N.Y. State Bar Assn., Assn. of the Bar of the City of N.Y., Order of the Coif, Phi Beta Kappa. Jewish. Office: Leavy Rosensweig & Hyman 11 E 44th St New York NY 10017-3608

HARRIS, ROBIN ROSE, treasury analyst; b. Southbridge, Mass., May 4, 1963; d. George Wilfred and Florence Rachel (Corriveau) Mailloux; m. Clifford Lloyd Harris, Sept. 1, 1985; 1 child, Jonathan James. BS in Bus. Mgmt., N.H. Coll., 1985. Credit analyst Ekco Group, Inc., Nashua, N.H., 1986; treasury analyst Ekco Group, Inc., Nashua, 1987—. Mem. Nat. Investor Rels. Inst. (Boston chpt.). Democrat. Office: Ekco Group Inc 98 Spit Brook Rd Ste 102 Nashua NH 03062-5738

HARRIS, ROGER CLARK, psychiatrist, consultant; b. Washington, Aug. 27, 1938; s. Lester Wilbur and Margaret Elizabeth (Gilligan) H.; m. Ann Marie Dorman, Sept. 22, 1962; children: Laura Colleen, Gregory Scott Henry. BS, U. Md., 1961; postgrad., U. Md., College Park, 1961-62; MD, U. Md. Sch. Medicine, Balt., 1964-68. Diplomate Am. Bd. Med. Examiners, Am. Bd. Psychiatry and Neurology. Intern Washington Hosp. Ctr., 1968-69; resident in psychiatry Med. Sch. U. Md., 1969-72; staff psychiatrist Portsmouth (Va.) Psychiat. Ctr., 1972-73, Larry H. Dizmang and Assoc., Annapolis, Md., 1973-74; pvt. practice Annapolis, 1974-75; prin. Roger C. Harris Group Practice of Psychiatry and Assocs., Annapolis, 1975—; pres. Chesapeake Comprehensive Counseling Ctrs., Inc., Washington and Balt., 1988—; co-founder Psychiatry Consultation Svc. of Baltimore City Police Dept., 1970-72; chief psychiatry svc. Anne Arundel Gen. Hosp., Annapolis, 1978-81; asst. clin. prof. psychiatry U. Md. Sch. Medicine, 1973—; acting dir. of outpatient clinic U. Md. Emergency Psychiat. Svcs., 1971-72, chief resident, 1971-72; primary founder Hosp. Inpatient Svcs., Anne Arundel Gen. Hosp. Mem. Disability Rev. Bd. for Anne Arundel County, 1985-87, Orgn. of Physicians for Social Responsiblity, 1985—. Recipient Cert. Appreciation Arundel Lodge, Inc., Annapolis, 1988, Mitchell Scholarship, Alpha Tau Omega Social Fraternity, College Park, Md., 1960. Mem. Chesapeake Bay Psychiat. Soc., Am. Psychiat. Assn., Md. Psychiat. Soc., Anne Arundel County Med. Soc., Am. Group Psychotherapy Assn., Orthopsychiat. Assn., Epping Forest Boat Club, Young Foresters Orgn., Alpha Tau Omega (sec. 1958-60). Democrat. Presbyterian. Home: 338 Severn Rd Annapolis MD 21401-6650 Office: Chesapeake Comprehensive Counseling Ctr 8 Willow St Annapolis MD 21401-3147

HARRIS, RUTH ELLEN BEALL, nursing researcher, educator; b. Hamilton, Ohio, Jan. 6, 1947; d. F. Wayne and Edythe Edna (Gerlach) Beall; m. Philip Edwin Harris, Sept. 12, 1970; children: Philip Michael, Robert Scott, Mark Edward, Lauren Elizabeth. Diploma, Fairview Park Hosp. Sch. Nsg., 1968; BA, BS, Baldwin-Wallace Coll., 1970; BSN, MS in Nursing, U. Colo., Denver, 1973, 75; PhD, NYU, 1985. RN, N.Y., N.J. Critical care nurse various hosps., N.Y. and N.J.; asst. clin. prof. nursing UCLA, 1976-78; asst. prof. nursing Adelphi U., 1978-85; assoc. prof. Seton Hall U. Coll. Nursing, South Orange, N.J., 1986—; vis. prof. Sch. Nursing Boston U., 1986; staff nurse various nursing registries; rsch. asst. VA Hosp., L.A., 1980-81; mem. coun. on dialysis and transplantation Nat. Kidney Found., 1979—; cons., presenter, researcher, speaker in field. Co-editor Scholarly Inquiry for Nursing Practice: An Internat. Jour.; contbr. articles to profl. publs. Probation counselor Jefferson County Ct., Denver, 1974-76; vol. inoculation program ARC, L.A., 1976; group counselor Sherman Oaks Luth. Ch., 1976-78; tchr. CPR classes Am. Heart Assn., 1976-82. Grantee HEW, 1974-75, Adelphi U., 1980, 81, Am. Heart Assn., 1983, F.A. Davis/Nat. League Nursing, 1983; rsch. fellow Jersey Shore Heart Inst., 1990—. Mem. ANA (coun. nurse researchers 1979), N.J. State Nurses Assn., AACN (bd. dirs. N.Y.C. chpt. 1979-85, mem. various coms.), Am. Heart Assn. (mem. sci. coun. on nursing 1988, coun. on nursing practice N.Y.C. chpt. 1979-81, merit award 1983), Sigma Theta Tau, Alpha Tau Delta (Gamma Tau faculty advisor 1978-79). Home: 1236 Oak Rd Manasquan NJ 08736-2010

HARRIS, SANDRA ANN, fundraiser; b. Lisbon, Portugal, Mar. 20, 1944; came to U.S., 1963; d. Colin G. and Adelajda J. (Zamoyska) H. BA in Media Studies summa cum laude, Fordham U., 1983. Mgr. London Arts Gallery, 1970-73; capital campaign dir. Sta. WNET-TV, N.Y.C., 1974-78; found., corp. relations dir. Cornell Med. Ctr. The N.Y. Hosp., N.Y.C., 1978-81; devel., mktg. mgr. Sta. WNYC-TV, N.Y.C., 1981-82; individual gifts dir. N.Y.C. Opera, 1983-84; devel. dir. Am. Woman's Econ. Devel. Corp., N.Y.C., 1984-86; pvt. practice fundraising N.Y.C., 1986-88, 91—; dir. devel. Inst. for the Advancement of Health, N.Y.C., 1988-90. Mem. Nat. Soc. Fundraising Execs. (cert.), Alpha Sigma Lambda. Home and Office: 333 W 57th St New York NY 10019-3159

HARRIS, SANDRA LEE, psychology educator; b. Seattle, Apr. 15, 1942; d. William Wolf and Felice (Deitchman) H. BA, U. Md., 1964; PhD, SUNY, Buffalo, 1969. Asst. prof. psychology Douglass Coll., New Brunswick, N.J., 1969-73; assoc. prof. Douglass Coll., Rutgers U., New Brunswick, N.J., 1973-79, dir. Douglas Devel. Ctr., 1972-88, exec. dir., 1988—; assoc. prof. dept. clin. psychology GSAPP, Rutgers U., Piscataway, N.J., 1974-79, prof., 1979-86, prof. II, 1986—, chmn. dept. clin. psychology, 1987—. Co-author: Psychopathology and Society, 1975, Educating the Developmentally Disabled, 1986; author: Families of the Developmentally Disabled, 1983. Fellow Am. Psychol. Assn.; mem. Am. Assn. Mental Deficiency, Soc. for Pediatric Psychology, Assn. for Advancement of Behavior Therapy. Office: GSAPP PO Box 819 Rutgers Univ Piscataway NJ 08855-0819

HARRIS, SUSANNA, immunologist, retired; b. Bklyn., May 11, 1919; d. Barnet and Rebecca (Goodman) Shapiro; m. T.N. Harris, Dec. 26, 1940; children: Joseph D., Elizabeth. BA, Bklyn. Coll., 1940; BS, Drexel U., 1942; PhD, U. Pa., 1948. Instr. bacteriology U. Pa. Sch. Medicine, Phila., 1948-51, asst. prof. pediatrics rsch., 1951-54, assoc. prof. immunology in pediatrics, 1954-82. Contbr. articles in profl. jours. Mem. Am. Acad. Microbiology, AM. Assn. Immunology, Sigma Xi. Home: 5112 Woodbine Ave Philadelphia PA 19131-2405 Office: Children's Hosp Rm 5002 Wood Bldg 34th Civic Ctr Blvd Philadelphia PA 19104

HARRIS, WALTE DAVIS, surgeon; b. Lexington, Ky., June 29, 1936; s. Bascom Thomas and Kathryn (Freed) H.; m. Betty Mae Kinsey, May 11, 1963; children: John B., Summer P. BS, U. Ky., 1958; MD, Vanderbilt U., 1962; MS in Otorhinolaryngology, U. Mich., 1968; MBA, U. Ky., 1988. Diplomate Am. Bd. Otorhinolaryngology. Pvt. practice physician, surgeon Lexington, 1970-89; asst. med. dir. Provident Life and Casualty, Chattanooga, 1989-90; med. dir. Aetna Health Plans, Hartford, Conn., 1990—.

Major Med. Corps, U.S. Army, 1968-70, Vietnam. Fellow Am. Coll. Surgeons, Am. Soc. Head and Neck Surgeons. Republican. Home: 438 Main St Old Saybrook CT 06475

HARRIS, WENDELL V., English educator; b. Oklahoma City, Jan. 8, 1932; s. Mark Thomas and Rubie (Voelker) H.; m. Harriett Rutledge, Aug. 24, 1954. BA in Philosophy, U. Okla., 1954, MA in English, 1957; PhD in English, U. Wis., 1961. Instr. to prof. of English Univ. Colo., Boulder, 1961-70; assoc. provost No. Ill. Univ., DeKalb, Ill., 1970-78; acting provost No. Ill. Univ., DeKalb, 1978-79; dept. head English Pa. State Univ., University Park, 1979-85, prof. English, 1985—. Author: British Short Fiction/19th Century, 1979, Omnipresent Debate, 1981, Interpretive Acts, 1988, Dictionary of Concepts in Literary Criticism and Theory, 1992; contbr. articles to profl. jours. 1st lt. U.S. Army, 1955-57. Recipient fellowship Nat. Endowment Humanities, 1976, Guggenheim, 1985-86. Fellow Royal Soc. Arts, Inst. for the Arts and Humanities Studies. Office: Dept English Pa State Univ State College PA 16802

HARRIS, WILEY LEE, financial services executive; b. Lynchburg, Va., Jan. 15, 1949; s. Willie M. Harris; m. Thelma E. Thomas, June 28, 1991. BS in Indsl. Sociology, Yale U., 1971. Human resources trainee GE, Lynchburg, 1972-74; equal employment opportunity mgr. GE, 1974-77; human resources mgr. GE Info. Svcs. Co., Chgo., 1977-79, Rockville, Md., 1979-87; compensation mgr. GE Fin. Svcs. Co., Stamford, Conn., 1987—. Mem. NAACP, Lynchburg, 1980—. Recipient Civic Achievement award NAACP, Lynchburg, 1986, Employment Achievement, State of Va., Richmond, Va., 1980. Mem. Internat. Assn. for Employee Benefits, Am. Compensation Assn., Am. Soc. for Personnel Adminstrn. Republican. Office: GE Fin Svcs 260 Long Ridge Rd Stamford CT 06927-0001

HARRIS, WILLIAM NORMAN, music educator; b. Washington, Sept. 8, 1952; s. Clarence Norman and Helen Lucy (Holsey) H. BMEd, Millikin U., 1974; MA, various, 1987. Elem. gen. music tchr. Montgomery County Pub. Schs., Rockville, Md., 1974—; producer, dir. spring musical theatre, Poolesville (Md.) Jr./Sr. High Sch., 1986-91. Former mem. Montgomery County Masterworks Chorus, U. Md. Chorus; actor, singer Montgomery Coll., Summer Dinner Thetre, Rockville, 1988, 89, 90; artistic dir., choral master Damascus (Md.) Theatre Co.; singer U.S. Postal Svcs. (Black Hist. Month's Observances) Hdqrs., Washington, 1986-88; dir. children's chorus for PYE Panda Earth Day Expo '90. Fellow NEA, Music Educators Nat. Conf.; mem. Phi Mu Alpha Sinfonia, Beta Theta chpt. (treas. 1972-74). Democrat. Methodist. Home: 19256 Misty Meadow Ter Germantown MD 20874-5367

HARRIS, WILLIAM NORTH, consulting company executive; b. Augusta, Maine, Oct. 7, 1938; s. Charles Miller and June Annette (Freeman) H.; m. Lorrayne Thomas (div.); 1 child, Timothy Edward Harris; m. Susan K. Behnke, 1985. Student, Cornell U., 1956-57; BSBA, Boston U., 1961; MBA, Northwestern U., Evanston, Ill., 1966. Mgr. MIS Sears Roebuck & Co., Chgo., 1966-70; sr. mgr. Price Waterhouse & Co., Chgo., 1970-75; dir. info. svcs. Hammermill Paper Co., Erie, Pa., 1975-81; dir. MIS Kendall Co., Boston, 1981-84; dir. info. svcs. Coca-Cola USA, Atlanta, 1984-86; v.p. Citibank N.A., N.Y.C., 1986-87; chmn. Behnke, Harris & Assoc., Inc., Atlanta, N.Y.C., 1987—. Contbr. articles to profl. jours. Mem. County Rep. Com., Erie, 1975-80. Mem. Am. Mgmt. Assn. (info. systems coun.), N.Y.C. Computer Exec. Roundtable, Deane Hill Country Club (Knoxville, Tenn.), Ashford Club (Atlanta), Cornell Club (N.Y.C.), World Trade Club (Atlanta), 191 Club (Atlanta). Republican. Episcopal. Office: Behnke Harris & Assocs Inc 5696 Peachtree Pky Norcross GA 30092 also: 575 Madison Ave Ste 1006 New York NY 10022

HARRISES, ANTONIO EFTHEMIOS, biology educator; b. Manchester, N.H., Sept. 12, 1926; s. Efthemios John and Gramato (Kerageorge) H.; m. Mary Catherine Dennig, Aug., 1957; children: Anthony, Gregory, Stephen, Susan and Sally (twins). BA, St. Anselms' Coll., 1950; MS, U. N.H., 1952; PhD, U. Notre Dame, Ind., 1957. Prof. U. So. Miss., Hattiesburg, 1957-69, Salem (Mass.) State Coll., 1969—; dir. nuclear medicine tech. program Salem State Coll., 1981-91. Author: Monogenetic Trematoda. Cpl. USAAF, 1944-46, ETO. Am. Soc. Parasitologists, Helminthological Soc. Washington, Sigma Xi. Office: Salem State Coll Biology Dept Salem MA 01970

HARRISON, CHARLES ROBERT, JR., technical writer, consultant; b. Balt., Jan. 19, 1957; s. Charles Robert Sr. and Shirley Ann (Hobbs) H. BA, U. Md., Catonsville, 1980, MA, 1984; postgrad., Johns Hopkins U., 1990—. Mgmt. analyst Housing Authority of Balt. City, 1985-87, tech. writer, 1987—; tchr. Catonsville C.C., 1991—, Essex C.C., 1991—; records mgmt. cons. Inst. for Internat. Programs, Johns Hopkins U., Balt., 1987, Dept. Housing and Community Devel., Balt., 1984-87; graphics cons. Balt. Heritage, Inc., 1980-81. Researcher book The Uncertain Triumph, 1984. Pres. Kensington Improvement Assn., Catonsville, 1991-92; mem. S.W. Coalition, Arbutus, Md., 1991-92; mem. Ridgeway Dem. Club, Catonsville, Md., 1991. Recipient Gov.'s citation State of Md., 1977, Gov.'s citation State of Ala., 1977; Dean's scholar U. Md., 1982. Mem. Assn. Records Mgrs. and Adminstrs. (bd. dirs. 1987-89, Plaque 1989), Soc. Tech. Communicators. Democrat. Home: 817 Warwick Rd Catonsville MD 21229

HARRISON, COLIN YOUNG, magazine editor, novelist; b. N.Y.C., Nov. 27, 1960; s. Earl Grant Jr. and Jean Spencer (Young) H.; m. Kathryn Elizabeth Lang, Oct. 28, 1988; children: Sarah Esme, Walker Earl. BA in English, Haverford (Pa.) Coll., 1982; MFA in English, U. Iowa, 1986, postgrad., 1987. Grad. teaching asst. U. Iowa, Iowa City, 1984-87; writer Columbia U., N.Y.C., 1987-88; assoc. editor Harper's Mag., N.Y.C., 1988—. Author: Break and Enter, 1990; editor: What's Going on Here?, 1991. Mem. Corp. of Haverford Coll., 1990—. Exxon fellow, 1986, Michener fellow, 1987; book named to Notable Books of 1990 N.Y. Times Book Rev. Mem. Author's Guild. Mem. Soc. of Friends. Office: Harper's Magazine 666 Broadway New York NY 10012

HARRISON, DONALD, newspaper editor; b. Phila., May 14, 1928; s. Martin and Diana (Feinstein) H.; m. Grace Wagner, Sept. 7, 1952; children—Eric Ethan, Lori Ann, Ellen Wendy. BA, U. Pa., 1949. City editor Phila. Jewish Times, 1949-51; mng. editor News of Delaware County, 1954-63; asst. city editor Phila. Bull., 1963-69, city editor, 1969-72, editorial writer, 1972-73, editor arts and culture, 1973-79, regional editor, 1979-81, asst. mng. editor, 1981-82; assoc. editor editorial pages Phila. Daily News, 1982-87, dep. editor editorial pages, 1987—; lectr. journalism U. Pa., 1960. Editor: From the Letters of Robert S. Gerdy (1942-45), 1969. Served with AUS, 1951-53. Recipient Lowell Mellett award for critical evaluation of journalism, 1985. Mem. Pa. Soc. Newspaper Editors, Nat. Conf. Editorial Writers, Franklin Inn Club, Soc. Profl. Journalists (past pres. Greater Phila. profl. chpt.). Home: 1434 Westwood Ln Wynnewood PA 19096-3839

HARRISON, EARL DAVID, lawyer, real estate executive; b. Bryn Mawr, Pa., Aug. 25, 1932; divorced; 1 child, H. Jason. BA, Harvard U., 1954; JD, U. Pa., 1960. Bar: D.C. 1960. Pvt. practice Washington; exec. v.p. Washington Real Estate Corp., 1986—. Capt. U.S. Army, 1954-57. Decorated Order of Rio Branco (Brazil); Order of Merit (Italy). Mem. ABA, D.C. Bar Assn., Washington Assn. Realtors, Montgomery County Md. Assn. Realtors, Nat. Assn. Realtors, Harvard Club of D.C., U. Pa. Club of D.C. Home: 3249C Sutton Pl NW Washington DC 20016-3507 Office: 777 14th St NW Ste 305 Washington DC 20005-3282

HARRISON, EDWARD THOMAS, JR., chemist; b. Norfolk, Va., Mar. 4, 1929; s. Edward Thomas and Mabel (Weaver) H.; B.S., Va. State U., 1951, M.S., 1958; Ph.D., George Washington U., 1981; m. Bertha Mae Neal, Dec. 30, 1962; children—April, Edward. With NIH, 1959—, biologist Nat. Inst. Dental Research, 1962-64, chemist, 1964—. Served with AUS, 1951-53. USPHS fellow, 1960-61. Mem. AAAS, Am. Inst. Biol. Scis., Tissue Culture Assn., Va. Acad. Scis., N.Y. Acad. Scis., Fedn. Am. Scientists, Internat. Platform Assn., Brazilian-Am. Cultural Inst., Alpha Phi Alpha. Democrat. Episcopalian. Author articles in field. Home: 438 Quackenbos St NW Washington DC 20011-1308 Office: Lab Cellular Devel and Oncology Nat Inst Dental Research NIH Bethesda MD 20205

HARRISON, FRANCIS PATRICK, procurement officer; b. Phila., June 12, 1950; s. Francis Patrick and Margaret Ann (Gutbrod) H.; m. Christine Mary Fedorko, Aug. 27, 1977; children: Sara Christine, Joel Francis P. Student, Allentown Coll., 1968-71; BA in Labor Studies, Rutgers U., 1978; MS in Bus., Va. Commonwealth U., 1983. Cert. purchasing mgr. Asst. mgr. Home Unity Savs. and Loan, Phila., 1971-73; salesman Reynolds Metals Co., Phila., 1973-78, Gary's Stereo, Richmond, Va., 1978-80; purchaser Va. Electric and Power Co., Richmond, 1980-83; mgr. procurement Am. Satellite Co., Rockville, Md., 1983-85; cons. Harrison Assocs., Silver Spring, Md., 1985-86; purchasing officer IMF, Washington, 1986—; cons. MCL, Inc., La Grange, Ill., 1985-86. Mem. Nat. Assn. Purchasing Mgmt., Am. Mgmt. Assn. Roman Catholic. Home: 10715 Glenwild Rd Silver Spring MD 20901-1604 Office: IMF 700 19th St NW Washington DC 20431-0002

HARRISON, GREGORY ARNOLD, safety and fire protection engineer; b. Balt., July 16, 1944; s. Harry Melvin and Marie (Conway) H.; m. Constance Ann Godfrey, Sept. 17, 1977 (div. 1983). BS in Fire Protection, U. Md., 1966, MS in Civil Engring., 1970; MS in Engring. Adminstrn., George Washington U., 1979; clarinet studies with Sidney Forrest, Peabody Conservatory. Registered profl. engr., Md., Calif. Fire protection/safety engr. Goddard Space Flight Ctr., NASA, Greenbelt, Md., 1967-69; gen. engr. Naval Ship Engring. Ctr., DOD, Hyattsville, Md., 1969-71; fire/safety engr. Nat. Bur. Standards, Gaithersburg, Md., 1972-75; safety/fire prevention engr. Arabian Am. Oil Co., Dhahran, Saudi Arabia, 1975-77; fire protection engr. U.S. Nuclear Regulatory Commn., Bethesda, Md., 1977-82, licensing project mgr. for Clinton Nuclear Power Sta., 1982-83; project engr. Tenera L.P., Bethesda, 1983-84; pres., owner Gregory A. Harrison, P.E. & Assocs., Gaithersburg, 1984—; assoc. Forensic Tech., Inc., Annapolis, Md., 1982-90, Tech. Analysis Corp., McLean, Va., 1987—, Tech. Adv. Svc. 4 Atty., Ft. Washington, Pa., 1980-90. Author: (archtl. ency.) Stair and Ramp Safety, 1989; contbr. articles to profl. jours. Vol. fireman Rockville (Md.) Vol. Fire Dept., 1989, Ellicot City (Md.) Vol. Fire Dept.; pres. Diamond Farms Homeowners Assn., Gaithersburg, 1978-83; mem. Rep. Nominating Com., Washington, 1983—; clarinetist Greg Harrison Jazz Band. Recipient Cost Reduction award, NASA, 1968. Mem. Bldg. Ofcls. and Code Adminstrs., Am. Soc. Safety Engrs., Soc. Fire Protection Engrs., Nat. Fire Protection Assn. (adv. coun. 1973). Republican. Methodist. Home: 16209 Kimberly Grove Rd Gaithersburg MD 20878-2279

HARRISON, HAROLD, electrical engineer; b. Bklyn., May 15, 1948; s. Fredrick Philip and Esther Gussie (Siegel) H.; m. Nancy Gene Goldstein, Oct. 15, 1972 (div. 1979); 1 child, Jamie Scott. BSEE, Northwestern U., Chgo., 1974. Elec. engr. N.Y.C. Transit, Bklyn., 1973-80, project cons., 1975-80; owner Harrison Contracting Corp., N.Y.C., 1980—. Alderman Dem. Party, Bklyn., 1978-79. Decorated Silver Star, Bronze Star, Purple Heart. Mem. Aircraft Owners and Pilots Assn. (treas. 1980), KP (pres. 1984-85). Jewish. Home: 1665 Brooklyn Ave Brooklyn NY 11210 Office: Harrison Contr Corp 1817 Madison Pl Brooklyn NY 11229

HARRISON, LOIS SMITH, hospital executive, educator; b. Frederick, Md., May 13, 1924; d. Richard Paul and Henrietta Foust (Menges) S.; m. Richard Lee Harrison, June 23, 1951; children: Elizabeth Lee Boyce, Margaret Louise Wade, Richard Paul. BA, Hood Coll., 1945; MA, Columbia U., 1946. Counselor CCNY, 1945-46; founding adminstr., counselor, instr. psychology and sociology Hagerstown (Md.) Jr. Coll., 1946-51, registrar, 1946-51, 53-54, instr. psychology and orienta, 1954-56; registrar, instr. psychology, Balt. Jr. Coll., 1951-54; bus. mgr., acct. for pvt. med. practice Hagerstown, 1953—; trustee Washington County Hosp., Hagerstown, 1975—; chmn. bd. Washington County Hosp., 1986—; bd. dirs. Home Fed. Savs. Bank, Hagerstown, 1983—; speaker ednl. panels, convs. hosp. panels and seminars. Author: The Church Woman, 1960-65. Trustee Hood Coll., Frederick, 1972—, chmn. bd., 1979—; mem. Md. Gov.'s Commn. to Study Structure and Ednl. Devel. Commn., 1971-75; pres. Washington County Coun. Ch. Women, 1970-72; appointee Econ. Devel. Commn., County Impact Study Commn. Bd.; bd. dirs. Md. Hosp. Assn. Quality Coun. Bd., Md. Chs. United, 1975—; chmn. bd. dirs. Md. Hosp. Edn. Inst., 1988—; pres. Ch. Consistory. Recipient Alumnae Achievement award Hood Coll., 1975, Washington County Woman of Yr. award, AAUW, 1984, Md. Woman of Yr. award, 1984, Md. Woman of Yr. award Francis Scott Key Commn. for Md.'s 350th Anniversary, 1984; named one of top 10 women Tri-State area, Herald-Mail Tri-State newspaper, 1990. Mem. Hagerstown C. of C. Democrat. Mem. United Ch. Christ. Home: 12835 Fountain Head Rd Hagerstown MD 21742-2748 Office: Washington County Hosp Hagerstown MD 21740

HARRISON, MATTHEW CLARENCE, JR., manufacturing executive, author; b. West Point, N.Y., Aug. 19, 1944; s. Matthew Clarence and Roberta A. (Grigg) H.; m. Judith A. Cole, Dec. 31, 1971; children: Cecily E., Page C. BS, U.S. Mi. Acad., 1966; MA, Am. U., 1972; cert. spl. studies in mgmt. and bus. adminstrn., Harvard U., 1985. Commd. 2nd lt. U.S. Army, 1966, advance through grades to lt. col.; chief oper. officer Wedtech Corp., Debtor-in-Possession, N.Y.C., 1986-89; mng. dir. Buccino & Assocs., Inc., N.Y.C., 1989-90; pres. CEPA Cons., Ltd., Rye Brook, N.Y., 1990-91; COO Berger Aindustries, Inc., Maspeth, N.Y., 1992—. Author: (book) Feeding Frenzy, 1989. Decorated Silver Star, five Bronze Stars, two Purple Hearts. Mem. West Point Soc. of N.Y. (bd. govs. 1991—), Alpha Phi Theta (historian's hon. soc.). Episcopalian. Office: CEPA Cons Ltd 24 Hawthorne Ave Rye Brook NY 10573-2927

HARRISON, MICHAEL ALLEN, marketing executive, consultant; b. West Islip, N.Y., Mar. 9, 1960; s. Hugh Allen and Theresa Ann (Filippelli) H.; m. Gabriella Sue Goldberg, 1991. BBA, Hofstra U., 1982, MBA, 1992. Acct. McCall Pub. Co., N.Y.C., 1982-84; dir. ops. Hofstra Health Dome, Hempstead, N.Y., 1984-88; dir. mktg. Hofstra Health Dome, Hempstead, 1988-92; pres. Turnstyles, U.S.A., L.I.; nat. panelist Mktg. Health Promotion Series, 1991. Editor: Enlightened Eating for Better Health, 1988; pub. Health Promotion as Corporate Strategy, 1992. Cons. L.I. Heart Coun., Lifeline: L.I. Mem. L.I. Assn.

HARRISON, ROBERT WILLIAM, zoologist, educator; b. Napoleon, Ohio, Nov. 3, 1915; s. Charles Foster and Goldie Dell (Fahrer) H.; m. Marion Murlless Billings, May 30, 1943 (div. 1973); children: Suzanne Harrison Marchetti, Elizabeth A. Harrison Greene, Barbara A. Harrison DiOrio; m. Ruth Lightner Hastings, July 31, 1974 (div. Nov. 19, 1980). AB, Oberlin Coll., 1938; postgrad., Springfield (Mass.) Coll., 1938-39; MA, Wesleyan U., Middletown, Conn., 1941; MS, Yale U., 1942, PhD (Nat. Cancer Inst. rsch. fellow), 1949. Asst. in biology Springfield Coll., 1938-39; asst. Wesleyan U., 1939-41, vis. assoc. prof., 1957; asst. in zoology Yale U., New Haven, 1941-42, 46-48, rsch. asst. pathology Med. Sch., 1942; instr. zoology U. R.I., Kingston, 1949-50, asst. prof., 1950-56, assoc. prof., 1956-65, prof., 1965-77, prof. emeritus, 1977—, assoc. dean div. univ. extension, 1968-69, acting dean, 1969-70, acting chmn. dept. zoology, 1974-75; cons. Crime Lab.; vis. spl. instr. Brown U., 1958. Bd. dirs. Animal Rescue League So. R.I.; mem. Rep. Town Com. of South Kingstown, R.I., 1962-66, chmn. bipartisan com. on town adminstrn. Town Coun., 1966; pres. Friends of U. R.I. Libr. Capt. USNR, 1942-46. AEC grantee, 1962; Physiol. Soc. rsch. fellow U. Ill., 1959. Mem. AAUP, AAAS, Am. Inst. Biol. Scis., R.I. Assn. Health, Phys. Edn. and Recreation (hon. life), N.Y. Acad. Scis., Am. Soc. Zoologists, Am. Coll. Sports Medicine, Ret. Officers Assn., Nat. Ret. Tchrs. Assn., Am. Assn. Ret. Persons, Commodore Point Judith Yacht Club, South County Chamber Singers Club, U.S. Yacht Racing Union, Sigma Xi, Phi Kappa Phi. Congregationalist. Home: 40 Dockray St Wakefield RI 02879-3915 Office: U RI Dept Zoology Kingston RI 02881

HARRISON, WILLIAM SHAW, retired social sciences educator, education facility director; b. Milton, Mass., Mar. 30, 1922; s. Walter Thatcher and Alice Julian (Shaw) T.; children: William Shaw, Robert Caarter, John Richard, James Edward. AB in Govt., Harvard U., 1948. Enlisted man U.S. Army, 1942, advanced through grades to capt., 1950; resigned, 1951; mgr. Jordan Marsh Dept. Store, 1952-54; tchr., varsity coach Milton Acad., 1953-56; prof. social scis., varsity coach Lowell (Mass.) Technol. Inst., 1957-63; prof. nat. security policy and future studies U. Lowell, 1963-87; ret., 1987; owner Golden Golf War Coll., Dracut, Mass., 1987—, The Golden Ideas War Coll., Dracut, 987—; cons. on creativity, 1991—. Decorated Silver Star medal, Legion of Merit. Mem. Assn. Former Intelligence Officers, World Future Soc., Am. Security Coun. (nat. adv. bd.), 17th Airborne Div. Assn., Am. Legion, NRA, Harvard Varsity Club. Congregationalist. Home and Office: 120 Skyline Dr Ste 16 Dracut MA 01826

HARRIS-WARRICK, RONALD MORGAN, neurobiology and behavior educator; b. Berkeley, Calif., July 28, 1949; s. Morgan and Marjorie Ruth (Mason) H.; m. Rebecca Lamar, Apr. 5, 1975; children—Sheridan, Thomas. B.A. in Biol. Scis., Stanford U., 1970, Ph.D. in Genetics, 1976. Postdoctoral fellow NIH, Stanford U., Calif., 1976-78; Muscular Dystrophy Assn. postdoctoral fellow Harvard U., Boston, 1978-80; asst. prof. neurobiology Cornell U., Ithaca, N.Y., 1980-86; assoc. prof., 1986—. Recipient Guggenheim fellow, 1986-87. Contbr. articles to profl. jours. Mem. AAAS, Soc. for Neurosci., Internat. Soc. Neuroethology, Sierra Club, Audubon Soc., Phi Beta Kappa. Avocations: camping; skiing; mountaineering; music. Office: Sect Neurobiology and Behavior Cornell U Seeley Mudd Hall Ithaca NY 14853

HARROD, B(ILLY) J(OE), professional association executive; b. Olney, Tex., Jan. 30, 1933; s. Palmer Francis and Euna Pearl (Dunagan) H. MusB, North Tex. State Coll., 1954; MusM, Ind. U., 1959, Dr. Mus. Edn., 1961. Cert. tchr., Tex. Mgr. trade and edn. div. Alexander Broude Inc., N.Y.C., 1971-79; dir. ednl. div., assoc. editor Summy Birchard Pubs., Princeton, N.J., 1978-80; asst. to exec. dir. ASCE, N.Y.C., 1980-82; mgr. spl. projects Am. Assn. Engring. Socs., N.Y.C., 1982-83, acting exec. dir., 1984; mng. dir. Soc. Women Engrs., N.Y.C., 1984—, acting exec. dir., 1985—. Bd. dirs. Engring. Socs. Libr., N.Y.C., 1986-92. With U.S. Army, 1954-56. Named Knight Ofcl., Pres. Republic of Liberia, 1966, one of the Men of Achievement, 1989. Mem. Am. Soc. Assn. Execs., Am. Assn. Engring. Socs. (bd. dirs.), N.Y. Soc. Assn. Execs., Council Engring. and Sci. Soc. Execs., Soc. Women Engrs. (affiliate), Sigma Phi Epsilon, Alpha Chi, Phi Theta Kappa. Democrat. Presbyterian. Office: Soc of Women Engrs 345 E 47th St Rm 305 New York NY 10017-2330

HARSHBARGER, SCOTT, state attorney general; b. New Haven, Dec. 1, 1941; s. Luther Henry and Marian (Masemore) H.; m. Elizabeth Elliott, June 15, 1963; children—Michael, Benjamin. B.A., Harvard U., 1964, LL.B., 1968. Bar: Mass. 1968. Assoc. Goodwin, Procter & Hoar, Boston, 1968-70; dir. Lawyers' Com., Boston, 1970-72; dep. chief counsel Mass. Defenders, Boston, 1972-75; chief pub. protection bur. Office Mass. Atty. Gen., Boston, 1975-78; chief counsel State Ethics Commn., Boston, 1978-80; assoc. Posternak, Blankstein & Lund, Boston, 1980-82; former dist. atty. Middlesex County, Mass., Cambridge, from 1983; now atty. gen. Commonwealth of Mass.; pres. bd. dirs. Justice Resources Inst., Boston, 1979-84; former lectr. Boston U. Law Sch., from 1980. Mem. Boston Bar Assn. (chmn. urban affairs sect. 1980-82), Nat. Dist. Attys. Assn. (chmn. policy com. 1983—). Democrat. Mem. Ch. of Brethren. Office: Office of Atty General 1 Ashburton Pl Rm 2010 Boston MA 02108-1518*

HART, ALAN ROBERT, small business owner; b. Albany, N.Y., Dec. 14, 1947; s. Courtland and Perpetua (Cools-Lartigue) H.; m. Dianne Lynn Van Ness, Sept. 4, 1976; children: Heather, Patrick. AS in Math. Sci., Hudson Valley Community Coll., Troy, N.Y., 1972; BS in Chemistry, Rennselaer Poly. Inst., 1974. Chemist N.Y. State Food Lab., Albany, 1974-75; quality assurance mgr. Sterling Drug, Inc., East Greenbush, N.Y., 1975-91; owner Plastic Extruded Parts, Nassau, N.Y., 1992—. Inventor continuous strip marker. Den leader Cub Scout Pack 166, Nassau, 1988—; chmn. Nassau Village Planning Bd., 1982—. With U.S. Army, 1967-70. Mem. Am. Soc. Quality Control (cert. quality engr., sr. mem., past sec. Albany chpt., past treas.). Roman Catholic. Home: 3 Kosey St PO Box 124 Nassau NY 12123 Office: Plastic Extruded Parts Inc PO Box 124 Nassau NY 12123-0124

HART, AMY S., performing artist, actress; b. Racine, Wis., Feb. 14, 1962; d. John P. Hartl and Sylvia Frances Hormann Alper; 1 child, Jason Alexander Hart Cotroneo. BA in Drama, Music, Bennington (Vt.) Coll., 1984. Mime Animal Crackers Theatre Co., Racine, Wis., 1978-80, Friends Mime Co., Milw., 1978; set designer Comic Light Opera, Milw., 1983; actress Pecos Road Cafe, Santa Fe, N.Mex., 1984-85; dancer Aria Edry Dance Co., Amherst, Mass., 1986; sch. programmer New Eng. Puppetry Series, Amherst, Mass., 1986-87; actress/playwright Enchanted Circle Theatre, Northampton, Mass., 1987—; solo performing artist Amy Hart Co., Haydenville, Mass., 1991—. Playwright: Voices from Birth to Burial, 1990, Queen of Hearts, 1991, Dance of the Earth, 1987; author poetry book: I Want to Say Something, 1979 (Wis. Acad. Sci. Arts and Letters 1st place.). Home and Office: PO Box 16 Haydenville MA 01039

HART, C(HARLES) W(ILLARD), JR., zoologist, curator; b. Farmville, Va., Jan. 30, 1928; s. Charles Willard and Etta Catharine (Sawyer) H.; m. Margaret Waddell Gordon, Sept. 17, 1957 (div. Jan. 1958); m. Nancy Dabney Gardner, June 9, 1962. BA, Hampden-Sydney (Va.) Coll., 1949, BS, 1950; postgrad., Fla. State U., 1950-52, 53-54; MA, U. Va., 1951. Instr. biology Washington Coll., Chestertown, Md., 1954-55, Randolph Macon Woman's Coll., Lynchburg, Va., 1955-56; med. editor Smith, Kline & French Labs., Phila., 1956-58; editor sci. publs. Acad. Natural Scis., Phila., 1958-70, dir. water pollution studies, 1968-74; asst. to dir. Natural History Mus., Smithsonian Instn., Washington, 1974-79, curator dept. invertebrate zoology, 1979—, dep. chmn., 1985-88, chmn. dept., 1988-91. Co-author: (with Janice Clark) An Interdisciplinary Bibliography of Freshwater Crayfishes from Aristotle Through 1987, 1989; co-editor: (with P. Holt and R. Hoffmann) The Distributional History of the Biota of the Southern Appalachians, Part I: Invertebrates, 1969; (with S. L. H. Fuller) Pollution Ecology of Freshwater Invertebrates, 1974, Pollution Ecology of Estuarine Invertebrates, 1979; contbr. numerous articles to profl. jours. Mem. Phila. Rep. Com., 1966. Fellow AAAS; mem. Am. Soc. Zoologists (com. on rsch. in systematic biology 1974-78), Crustacean Soc. (treas. 1981-85), Biol. Soc. Washington (editor 1978-80, sec. 1986-88), Assn. Southeastern Biologists (editor 1961-72, pres. 1970-71), Coun. Biology Editors (treas. 1968-71), Cosmos Club, Phi Beta Kappa, Sigma Xi. Episcopalian. Home: 6449 Walters Woods Dr Falls Church VA 22044

HART, DEAN EVAN, research optometrist; b. Westbury, N.Y., Nov. 4, 1957; s. Ronald Warren and Beatrice (Rosenblitt) H. AAS in Ophthalmic Dispensing, Erie Community Coll., 1980; BS in Gen. Studies, N.Y. Inst. Tech., 1981; MA in Biology, Hofstra U., 1983; postgrad. researcher, U. Calif., Berkeley, 1985; OD, SUNY Coll. Optometry, N.Y.C., 1987. Lic. in ophthalmic dispensing and contract lens fitting, N.Y.; lic. optician, Fla.; cert. Am. Bd. Opticianry. Dir. Low Vision Clinic, instr. refraction and optics Columbia U. at Harlem Hosp. Med. Ctr., N.Y.C., 1988—; assoc. rsch. scientist Harkness Eye Inst., Columbia U. Coll. Physicians and Surgeons, 1989—; dir., asst. med. advisor Tristate Consumer Ins. Co.; numerous presentations in field. Contbr. articles and abstracts to sci. jours., chpts. to books. Grantee Optometric Ctr. N.Y., 1984, Sola-Barnes-Hind, 1984, 85; travel fellow Nat. Eye Inst., 1985. Fellow Am. Acad. Optometry; mem. Am. Optometric Assn., Contact Lens Assn. Ophthalmologists, Internat. Soc. for Contact Lens Rsch., Assn. for Rsch. in Vision and Ophthalmology, N.Y. Acad. Scis., Contact Lens Soc. N.Y. State. Home: 9925 NW 65th Ct Tamarac FL 33321-3341 Office: Woodbury Optical Group 185 Woodbury Rd Hicksville NY 11801-3029

HART, GURNEE FELLOWS, investment counselor; b. Chgo., Apr. 26, 1929; s. Percival Gray and Marguerite May (Fellows) H.; B.A. cum laude, Pomona Coll., 1951; M.B.A., Stanford U., 1955; m. Marjorie Walker Leigh, Apr. 23, 1966. With Willis & Christy, Los Angeles, 1955-65; investment counsel Scudder, Stevens & Clark, Inc., L.A., 1965-67; with Scudder, Stevens & Clark, N.Y.C., 1967—, ptnr., 1972-85, mng. dir., 1985—. Vice chmn. bd. dirs., mem. exec. com., trustee N.Y. Philharm.; bd. dirs. Lincoln Center for the Performing Arts, Inc., 1981-86; chmn. Friends of N.Y. Philharm., 1975-82; bd. dirs., v.p. Berkshire Farm Center and Svcs. for Youth, 1972-83; trustee Pomona Coll., 1982—. Served to 1st lt., inf. U.S. Army, 1951-53; Korea. Decorated Bronze Star. Mem. N.Y. Soc. Security Analysts, St. Andrew's Soc. State of N.Y., Soc. Mayflower Desc., Century Assn., Univ. Club, Phi Beta Kappa. Republican. Episcopalian. Home: 133 E 64th St New York NY 10021-7045

HART, HERBERT MICHAEL, military officer; b. St. Louis, Oct. 19, 1928; s. Herbert Malcolm and Helen Genevive (Quigley) H.; m. Teresa Keating, Oct. 13, 1958; children: Bridget, Erin, Bret, Tracy, Megan, Michael, Patrick. BS in Journalism, Northwestern U., 1951. Commd. 2d lt. USMC, 1951, advanced through grades to col., 1972; infantry platoon, co. and bn. comdg. officer USMC, Republic of Korea, 1952, 53, Vietnam, 1969-70; head profl. edn. Dept. Navy, Washington, 1977-78; head hist. br. Marine Corps.

Hqrs., Washington, 1973-77, dep. dir. pub. affairs, 1978-80, dir. pub. affairs, 1980-81, ret., 1981; dir. pub. affairs Res. Officers Assn. of U.S., Washington, 1982—; cons. Office of History U.S. Army Corps Engrs., 1981—; mem. adv. bd. ad hoc com. Nat. Park Svc., 1985—, com. on Cemeteries and Memls. VA, 1987-92. Author 9 mil. history books; editor ROA Nat. Security Report, 1983—; mem. editorial bd. Mil. History mag., 1983—. Decorated 2 Purple Heart medals, 2 Legion of Merit medals; recipient Award of Merit Am. Assn. State and Local History, 1976, Cultural Achievement award Sec. of Interior, 1979, Conservation Svc. award Sec. Interior, 1986. Fellow Co. Mil. Historians; mem. Potomac Westerners (pres. 1974-75, 84-85), Res. Officers Assn. U.S. (life), Marine Corps Res. Officers Assn. (life), Marine Corps Combat Corres. Assn. (life), Marine Corps Hist. Found. (charter, bd. dirs. 1983-87), Assn. U.S. Army, Nat. Pk. Svc. Employee and Alumni Assn. (life), VFW (life), Am. Legion (life), Ret. Officers Assn. (life), 1st Marine Div. Assn. (life), 3rd Marine Div. Assn. (life), Coun. Am. Mil. Past. (co-founder 1966, exec. dir. 1971—), Western History Assn. (charter), Apollo Soc. (bd. dirs. 1983-87), Am. Civil Def. Assn. (bd. advisors 1991—), Am. Mil. Inst. (trustee 1978-83), K.C., Nat. Press Club, Soc. Profl. Journalists, Theta Xi (life). Republican. Roman Catholic. Home: 3218 Hallran Rd Falls Church VA 22041-2411 Office: Res Officers Assn US 1 Constitution Ave NE Washington DC 20002-5655

HART, KENNETH EINAR, psychology educator, researcher; b. Sudbury, Ont., Can.; s. Leo and Kaija Elizabeth (Hohter) H. BA, Laurentian U., Sudbury, Ont., 1978; MA, Lakehead U., Thunder Bay, Can., 1981; PhD, U. Houston, 1987. Teaching fellow U. Houston, 1982-86; rsch. asst. U. Tex. Med. Sch., Houston, 1985; postdoctoral fellow Uniformed Svcs. U., Bethesda, Md., 1986; dir. rsch. Hofstra U. Health Dome, Hempstead, N.Y., 1987; asst. prof. psychology Hofstra U., 1987—. Cons. editor Jour. Applied Social Psychology, 1987, Psychol. Reports, 1988, Am. Jour. Community Psychology, 1990, Health Psychology, 1991; contbr. articles to profl. jours. Hofstra U. grantee, 1987, Lakehead U. scholar, 1980. Mem. APA, Assn. for Advancement of Behavior Therapy, So. Soc. Philosophy and Psychology, Western Psychol. Assn., Soc. for Behavioral Medicine, Soc. for Advancement of Social Psychology. Office: Hofstra U Hempstead NY 11550

HART, PAUL, dean of students, educator, poet; b. Elizabeth, N.J., Dec. 28, 1955; s. James Joseph and Alice Eugenia (McLaughlin) H. BA, Kans. State U., 1976, MA, 1979; ArtsD, Drake U., 1983; M in Spiritual Therapy, The New Sem., 1985. Tchr. Bd. Edn., Linden, N.J., 1976-77; grad. instr. Kans. State U., Manhattan, 1977-79; residence dir. U. Nebr., Lincoln, 1979-80; exec. dir. Communication Help Ctr., Union, N.J., 1980-81; teaching fellow Drake U., Des Moines, 1981-83; instr. Des Moines Area Community Coll., 1981-83, Union County Coll., Cranford, N.J., 1983-84; dir. grad. housing U. N.H., Durham, 1984-87; dean, prof. Rutgers U., Newark, 1987—; cons., trainer Gay Counseling Svc., Manhattan, Kans., 1974-76, FONE crisis intervention ctr., Manhattan, 1973-79; cons. Municipal Drug Coun., Manhattan, 1975-76, AIDS Action and Edn. Com., New Brunswick, N.J., 1988-90, Fund for the Improvement of Post Secondary Edn. Alcohol Grant, New Brunswick, 1990—; dir. Drug Edn. and Counseling Ctr., Manhattan, 1975-76. Author: A Crossing, 1983; Anthology of Magazine Verse and Yearbook of American Poetry, 1984; contbr. articles and poetry to newspapers and jours. Vol. AIDS Walk, N.Y.C., 1987—, Gay and Lesbian Community Ctr., N.Y.C., 1989—. Recipient Best Undergrad. Publ. award Coord. Coun. Literary Mags. in Nation, 1975. Mem. Ocean County Poets Coop., Acad. Am. Poets, Am. Coll. Pers. Assn. (mem. steering com.), Assn. Religious and Values Issues in Counseling. Home: 434 West 19th St Apt 4D New York NY 10011 Office: Rutgers Univ 91 Bleeker St Newark NJ 07102-1912

HART, RICHARD OLIVER, software engineer; b. Boston, June 27, 1949; s. Oliver Marion and Virginia Gaylord (Swift) H.; 1 child, Abigail Madeline. BS, U. Conn., 1972, MS, 1975, PhD, 1987. Instr. U. N.H., Durham, 1975, U. Conn., Storrs, 1976-80; prin. engr. Digital Equipment Corp., Nashua, N.H., 1980—. Mem. steering com. N.H. River campaign, Concord, 1985-90; mem. Amherst (N.H.) Conservation Commn., 1988—; exec. dir. Nelson Village Dancers, 1988-91. Mem. IEEE, IEEE Posix (printing standards working group), Assn. for Computing Machinery, Am. Canoe Assn., Nat. Speleological Assn., Appalachian Mountain Club. Republican. Congregationalist. Home: 51 Christian Hill Rd Amherst NH 03031-3313

HART, SEAN TIMOTHY, psychologist, social worker, consultant, psychotherapist; b. Poughkeepsie, N.Y., Feb. 23, 1953; s. Joseph Charles and Theresa Evelyn (Chester) H.; m. Diane Romagnani, June 23, 1979. BS, U. Scranton, Pa., 1975; MSW, Fordham U., 1977; D in Clin. Psychology, Chgo. Sch. of Profl. Psychology, 1989. Lic. social worker, Conn. Clin. social worker Dutchess County Mental Hygiene, Poughkeepsie, 1977-81; clin. social worker Med. Sch. Northwestern U., Chgo., 1983; resident in psychology Conn. Valley Hosp., Middletown, 1986-87; staff psychologist Brook Hollow Health Care Ctr., Wallingford, Conn., 1987-89; program dir. Hosp. of St. Raphael, New Haven, 1989-91; clin. dir. Guenster Rehab. Ctr., 1991—; prin. psychotherapist Chelsea Counseling Ctr., Wappings Falls, N.Y., 1978-81, Scranton Psychotherapy Group, New Haven, 1990—. Mem. APA, Am. Acad. Health Care Providers in Addictive Disorders, Soc. Personality Assessment. Home: 16 Quail Hollow Ln Bristol CT 06010-4888

HARTE, ANDREW DENNIS, transportation company executive, travel agent; b. Bronx, N.Y., Jan. 23, 1946; s. Bernard and Gertrude (Romm) H. BA, Hunter Coll., 1968; MS in Spanish, SUNY, New Paltz, 1975; MS in English, SUNY-New Paltz, 1979; MA in French, NYU, 1975; MS in Reading, L.I. U., 1979. Cert. tchr., 48 states. Tchr. Hendrick Hudson Sch., Montrose, N.Y., 1968-69, Mahopac Schs., N.Y., 1969-70, Croton-Harmon Schs., N.Y., 1970-83; owner Dominion Limousine Corp., Thornwood, N.Y., 1989—; mem. local com. N.E. Conf. on Teaching Fgn. Langs., N.Y.C., 1979-83. Mem. Am. Assn. Tchrs. French (life), Am. Assn. Tchrs. Spanish and Portuguese (life), N.Y. State Assn. Fgn. Lang. Tchrs. (life, bd. dirs. 1983-86), Mensa (life), Phi Delta Kappa (life, editor, historian). Office: Dominion Limousine Corp PO Box 328 Peekskill NY 10566-0328

HARTELL, JOHN, artist, retired art educator; b. Bklyn., Jan. 30, 1902; s. John and Madeline (Engskjen) H.; m. Sylvia Muller, Sept. 10, 1928; children: Mari Hartell Quint, Karin Hartell Cattarulla. BArch, Cornell U., 1925; pograd., Royal Acad. Fine Arts, Stockholm, 1926-27. Instr. architectur Clemson (S.C.) U., 1927-28; assoc. prof. U. Ill., Urbana, 1928-30; prof. architecture Cornell U., Ithaca, N.Y., 1930-68; prof. art Cornell U., Ithaca, 1939-68, chmn. art dept., 1939-59, prof. emeritus, 1968—; mem. McDowell Colony, Peterborough, N.H., summers 1929-30. One-man shows Kraushaar Galleries, 1943—, Cornell U., Dallas Mus. Fine Arts, Hofstra U., Lehigh U., Meml. Art Gallery, Rochester, N.Y., Munson-Williams-Proctor Inst., Syracuse Mus. Fine Arts, also others; exhibted in group shows Albright Knox Gallery, Birmingham Mus., Butler Inst. Am. Art, Carnegie Inst., Art Inst. Chgo., Cin. Mus., St. Louis Art Mus., Indpls. Mus. Art, Walker Art Ctr., Whitney Mus. Am. Art, numerous others; represented in permanent collections in univs., cos., pvt. collections. Recipient award Ill. Wesleyan U., 1950, N.Y. State Fair, 1951, Munson-Williams-PRoctor Inst., 1952, Cortland County Fair, 1952, Meml. Art Gallery, 1953. Democrat.

HARTER, DONALD HARRY, research administrator and medical educator; b. Breslau, Germany, May 16, 1933; came to U.S., 1940; naturalized, 1945; s. Harry Morton and Leonor Evelyn (Goldmann) H.; m. Lee Grossman, Dec. 18, 1960 (div. 1976); children: Kathryne, Jennifer, Amy, David; m. Rikki Horne, May 18, 1985 (div. 1986); m. Marjorie Brandt Dahlin, Oct. 12, 1990. A.B., U. Pa., 1953; M.D., Columbia U., 1957. Diplomate: Am. Bd. Psychiatry and Neurology. Intern in medicine Yale-New Haven Med. Center, 1957-58; asst. resident, then resident neurology N.Y. Neurol. Inst., 1958-61; guest investigator Rockefeller U., 1963-66; mem. faculty Columbia Coll. Physicians and Surgeons, 1960-75, prof. neurology and microbiology, 1973-75; vis. fellow Clare Hall, Cambridge, Eng., 1973-74; attending neurologist N.Y. Neurol. Inst., Presbyn. Hosp., 1973-75; Charles L. Mix prof. Northwestern U., 1975-85, Benjamin and Virginia T. Boshes prof. neurology, 1985-88, chmn. dept. neurology, 1975-87; chmn. dept. neurology Northwestern Meml. Hosp., Chgo., 1975-87; dir. rsch. scholars program Howard Hughes Med. Inst./NIH, Bethesda, 1989—; vis. sci. officer Howard Hughes Med. Inst., 1986-87, sr. sci. officer, 1987—; clin. prof. neurology George Washington U. Sch. Medicine and Health Scis., 1987—; mem. adv. com. on fellowships Nat. Multiple Sclerosis Soc., 1976-79, chmn., 1977-79, rsch. programs adv. com., 1989—; mem. Nat. Commn. on Venereal Disease, HEW, 1970-72; mem. med. adv. bd. Am. Parkinson Disease Assn., 1976-90, Myasthenia Gravis Found., 1980-87; mem. sci. adv. coun. Nat. Amyotrphic Lateral Sclerosis Found., 1978-85; mem. sci. rev. com. Amyotrophic Lateral Sclerosis Assn., 1987-91, chmn. 1989-91; mem. bd. sci. counselors Nat. Inst. Dental Rsch. NIH, 1990—; sr. sci. advisor Amyotrophic Lateral Sclerosis Assn., 1992—. Mem. editorial bd. Neurology, 1976-82, Anns. of Neurology, 1983-89; mem. adv. bd. Archives of Virology, 1975-81. Recipient Joseph Mather Smith prize Columbia U., 1970, Lucy G. Moses award, 1970, 72; Am. Cancer Soc. scholar, 1973-74; USPHS spl. fellow, 1963-66, Guggenheim fellow, 1973. Mem. Am. Soc. Clin. Investigation, Am. Neurol. Assn., Soc. Exptl. Biology and Medicine, Assn. Univ. Profs. Neurology, Infectious Disease Soc. Am., Soc. Neurosci., Am. Acad. Neurology, Am. Assn. Immunologists, Am. Soc. Microbiology, Am. Assn. for History Medicine, Am. Soc. Virology, Royal Soc. Medicine (U.K.)., Cosmos Club, Yale Club N.Y.C., Univ. Club Chgo., Univ. Club Washington, Phi Beta Kappa, Sigma Xi. Home: 2475 Virginia Ave NW Apt 503 Washington DC 20037-2639 Office: Howard Hughes Med Inst 6701 Rockledge Dr Bethesda MD 20817-1813 also: Howard Hughes Med Inst 1 Cloister Ct Bethesda MD 20814

HARTFORD, BRIAN ARNOLD, insurance executive; b. Haverhill, Mass., Apr. 7, 1943; s. Arnold Alfred and Janice Mary (Haley) H.; m. Jeanne Gerber, Feb. 14, 1987 (dec. 1990); 1 child, Laura Ann Klein. Student, Boston U., 1961-64; A in History, Adelphi U., 1966. LUTCF; lic. in life, health, property, casualty ins. Md., Pa., Va., D.C. Buyer trainee B. Altman & Co., N.Y.C., 1965-66, jr. buyer, 1969-71; sales mgr. Wm. Intner Co., Queens, N.Y., 1971-72; store mgr. trainee Lerner Shops, N.Y.C., 1972-73; store mgr. Lerner Shops, Springfield, Va., 1973-76, Wheaton, Md., 1976-78; store mgr./area mgr. Lane Bryant, Landover, Md., 1978-83; sales mgr. ins. Durham Life Ins. Co., Springfield, Va., 1983-87; ins. agt./broker Morgan Fin., Inc., Columbia, Lutherville, Md., 1987—; lectr. in field. Contbr. articles to profl. jours. Vol. counselor Washington Hosp. Ctr., 1990—; transplant team vol. Johns Hopkins Hosp., 1991—. Recipient Cert. of Excellence Sandimmune Photo Essay Contest, 1991. Mem. Nat. Assn. Life Underwriters, Life Underwriters Polit. Action Com., No. Va. Assn. Life Underwriters (bd. dirs. 1986-90), Balt. Assn. Life Underwriters, Order of Demolay (life), Masons, Am. Legion. Republican. Home: 5914-602 Watch Chain Way Columbia MD 21064 Office: Morgan Fin 1300 York Rd #200 Lutherville MD 21093

HARTFORD, ROBERT LIONEL, industrial/organizational psychologist; b. Cambridge, Mass.; s. Lionel C. and Alberta M. Hartford. BA in Psychology with honors, U. Calif., Santa Cruz, 1978; MA in Indsl./Organizational Psychology, U. So. Fla., 1982, PhD in Indsl./Organizational Psychology, 1987. Teaching asst. U. So. Fla., Tampa, 1979-81, course instr., 1981-83; human resources cons. GTE Data Svcs., Tampa, 1983-86, Pers. Designs, Inc., Grosse Pointe, Mich., 1987-90; staff dir. human resources NINEX Corp., White Plains, N.Y., 1990—. Mem. APA, Soc. Indsl./Organizational Psychology, Metro N.Y. Assn. Applied Psychology, Assn. for Participation and Quality. Office: NYNEX Corp 1113 Westchester Ave Rm 275 White Plains NY 10604-3510

HARTL, WILLIAM PARKER, oil company executive; b. Boston, May 9, 1935; s. Emil Martin and Elizabeth (Parker) H.; m. Judith Ford, Feb. 9, 1985. BA, Boston U., 1964. Exec., Ashland Oil Europe, Inc., Geneva, 1968-72, dir. fin. communications Ashland Oil, Inc., N.Y.C., 1972—; dir. Communications Strategy Group Inc., Boston. Mem. Manhattan adv. bd. Salvation Army. Served to maj. USA, 1956-63, ETO. Recipient Disting. Svc. award Investment Edn. Inst., 1981, Nat. Assn. Investment Clubs, 1979. Mem. Am. Mgmt. Assn., Nat. Investor Rels. Inst. (chmn. bd. 1977-78), Fin. Communications Soc. (pres. 1983), Investor Rels. Assn. (pres. 1991-92), Petroleum Investor Rels. Assn. (sec.-treas. 1992—), N.Y. Soc. Security Analysts, Assn. Investment Mgmt. Rsch., Pub. Rels. Soc. Am., Internat. Assn. Bus. Communicators, Am. Petroleum Inst., Nat. Alumni Coun. Boston U., University Club, Met. Club N.Y.C., Columbian Lodge. Republican. Presbyterian. Office: Ashland Oil Inc 535 Madison Ave New York NY 10022-4212

HARTLEY, BARON MANNING, food products executive, consultant; b. Salem, Mass., Aug. 4, 1924; s. Cyril and Gertrude Marion (Long) H.; m. Pat Kraly, June 20, 1953 (dec. Jan. 1975); children: Baron Manning Jr., Sarah Ann; m. Bess Kraly MacNeille, Nov. 3, 1979. BS, Boston U., 1947, MBA, 1949; cert. advanced mgmt., Worcester PolyTech, 1962. Mgmt. trainee Am. Optical, Southborough, Mass., 1949, supt., 1950-54, asst. gen. mgr., 1955-57, ops. asst. exec. v.p., 1958-62; v.p. Crown Box Co., Willmington, N.C., 1962-63; mgr., dir. United Fruit, Boston, 1963-77; v.p. Chiquita Brands, Boston, 1978-89; ret., 1989; mem. Diebold Rsch. Group., N.Y.C., 1967-88, adv. bd., 1970-75. Contbr. articles to profl. publs. Asst. chmn. hosp. dirve, Southbridge, 1958; active United Way, Div. CHMM, Southbridge and Boston, 1959—; mem. Peabody Mus., Essex Inst. Boston Mus. Sci., Boston Mus. Fine Arts, New England Aquarium, Southborough Land Found. Recipient teaching fellowship, Boston U., 1947-49. Mem. Soc. for Info. Mgmt., Jaycees (dir. 1957-58, pres. Southbridge chpt. 1955-56), Manley Bus. Assocs. (pres. Boston 1987—). Home: 3 Granuaile Rd Southborough MA 01772-1421 Office: 250 E 5th St # 1200 Cincinnati OH 45202-5190

HARTLEY, DUNCAN, fund raising executive; b. Sept. 27, 1941; s. Harold Shephard and Catherine Carmichael (Hursley) H.; m. Adrienne Ashley, Aug. 19, 1971. BA, U. Mich., 1964; MA, Wayne State U., Detroit, 1966, PhD. Instr. English dept. Wayne State U., 1969-71; asst. prof. William Paterson Coll., 1971-74; adminstr. ednl. resources, chpt. liaison Young Pres.'s Orgn., N.Y.C., 1974-78; dir. planned giving Carroll Coll., Waukesha, Wis., 1978-80; dir. capital gifts Greater N.Y. Coun. Boy Scouts Am., N.Y.C., 1980-84; dir. individual giving, exec. dir. pres.'s coun. Meml. Sloan-Kettering Cancer Ctr., N.Y.C., 1984—. Co-editor, author: The Sociology of the Arts, 1974. Mem. Princeton Club of N.Y., Audiophile Soc. Presbyterian. Home: 26 Misty Mountain Rd Randolph NJ 07869-4729 Office: Meml Sloan Kettering Ctr 1275 York Ave New York NY 10021-6094

HARTMAN, CHARLES HENRY, association executive, educator; b. Red Lion, Pa., Feb. 1, 1933; s. Earl Eugene and Jeannette (Kline) H.; m. Patricia A. Cooper, Aug. 3, 1956 (div. May 1974); children: Elizabeth Jean, Amy Joan; m. 2d Catherine M. Wheeler, June 7, 1975; children: Eric Michael, Jennifer Leigh, David Wheeler, Scott Andrew. BS, Millersville U., 1954; MA, Mich. State U., 1958, EdD, 1962. Tchr. Hollidaysburg Pub. Schs., Pa., 1956-57; assoc. prof. Ill. State U., Normal, 1959-62; vis. lectr. edn. U. Wis., Madison, 1962-63, Milw., 1963-64; dir. edn. Automobile Safety Found./Hwy. Users Fedn., Washington, 1964-70; dep. adminstr. Nat. Hwy. Traffic Safety Adminstrn., U.S. Dept. Transp., Washington, 1970-73; pres. Motorcycle Safety Found., Irvine, Calif., 1973-84; also pres. Touchstone Mgmt. Svcs., Delta, Pa., 1984-88; pres. Strategic Mgmt. and Communications Group, Delta, 1991—; exec. v.p. AAAHPERD, Reston, Va., 1988-90; exec. dir. Am. Coll. Health Assn., Balt., 1990—; lectr. bus. adminstrn. Capital Campus, Pa. State U., Middletown, 1987-88; dir. Nat. Safety Coun., Chgo., 1976-79, vice chmn. traffic conf., 1976-78; presdl. appointee Nat. Hwy. Safety Adv. Commn., Washington, 1977-80; gov.'s appointee Pa. Task Force on Alcohol and Hwy. Safety, 1981-82; vice chmn. Alliance for Traffic Safety, 1981-83, chmn. 1983-85; mem. policy commn. Hwy. Users Fedn.; cons. Nat. Assn. Women Hwy. Safety Leaders, Md. State Edn. Dept., 1969-70; bd. dirs. Lincoln Intermediate Unit #12, 1987-89, 91—; speaker pub. meetings U.S. and abroad. trustee Nat. Motorcycle Fund; pres. Howard County C. of C., Columbia, Md., 1985-87; sch. dir. Red Lion (Pa.) Area Schs., 1986—, also pres. sch. bd., 1988, v.p. 1989—. With AUS, 1954-56, ETO. Recipient Traffic Safety Educator of Yr. award Wis. Traffic Edn. Assn., 1972, Sec.'s award U.S. Dept. Transp., 1973. Fellow Am. Acad. Safety Edn. (pres. 1975-76); mem. NEA, Am. Soc. Assn. Execs. (vice-chmn. evaluation com. 1984-85, chmn. 1985-86), Soc. Automotive Engrs., Pres. Assn./Am. Mgmt. Assn., Am. Driver and Traffic Safety Edn. Assn., York 2000 Commn., Assn. for Advancement of Automotive Medicine, Pa. Sch. Bds. Assn., Phi Delta Kappa. Republican. Home: RR 2 Box 133 Delta PA 17314-9614 Office: Am Coll Health Assn PO Box 28937 Baltimore MD 21240-8937

HARTMAN, ELLIOTT MORGAN, JR., educator, museum director; b. North Hornell, N.Y., Aug. 11, 1938; s. Elliott M. and Katherine (Rowley) H.; m. Pamela Kay Gowan, Feb. 10, 1962; children: Lynne Fitzpatrick, Elliott M. III. BA, Colgate U., 1960; MA, Columbia U., 1971, postgrad. Sci. high sch. tchr. No. Tonawanda bd. edn., N.Y., 1963-65; prof. Westchester Community Coll., Valhalla, N.Y., 1965—; adj. prof. SUNY, Purchase, 1981, Columbia U., 1989, 91—; dir. Westchester Mus. Natural History, Valhalla, 1984—; adminstr. NSF Grant; cons. NSF, 1980-81. Co-Editor: GNATHOS, N.E. Region of Soc. for Coll. Sci. Tchrs., 1987—; contbr. editor Columbia Encyclopedia, N.Y.C., 1973-74; author: (monograph) Beach Forms & Coastal Processes, 1975, (book) Laboratory Studies in Astronomy, 1985; contbr. numerous articles to profl. jours. and publs. Speaker, cons. Westchester County Boy Scouts Am. Yonkers; program speaker on Fossils to various Westchester County Elem. Schs., 1989-91; mgr./coach Earl Schiff Little League, Spring Valley, N.Y., 1974-79. Recipient Innovative Edn. award SUNY Faculty Senate, 1972, Sci. Inst. award NSF, 1965; NSF Local Course Improvement grantee, 1981. Mem. Soc. for Coll. Sci. Tchrs. (state mem. co-chair, N.E. regional steering com.-mem. 1986—, councilor-at-large 1992—), Nat. Sci. Tchrs. Assn., Royal Astron. soc. of Can., Astron. Soc. of the Pacific, Nat. Assn. of Geology Tchrs. Home: 5 Deerwood Rd Spring Valley NY 10977-1002 Office: Westchester Community Coll 75 Grasslands Rd Valhalla NY 10595-1636

HARTMAN, GEORGE EITEL, architect; b. Ft. Hancock, N.J., May 7, 1936; s. George Eitel and Evelyn (Ritchie) H.; m. Ann Burdick, May 22, 1965; children—Sarah, Joshua. B.A., Princeton, 1957, M.F.A., 1960. Registered architect, Md., Washington, Va. Pvt. practice architecture, 1964-65; ptnr. Hartman-Cox Architects, Washington, 1965—; Design critic Cath. U. Am., 1964-69, U. Md.; Kea Disting. prof. architecture N.C. State U., 1973-74, prof. architecture, 1977; chmn. adv. coun. Princeton U. Sch. Architecture, 1985-87; mem. architecture rev. panel Fgn. Bldg. Office, Dept. State, 1991—. Works include EURAM office bldg, Washington, Waterfront Center, Washington; Brewer residence, Chevy Chase, Md., Conant residence, Potomac, Md., Nat. Humanities Center, Raleigh, N.C., Nat. Permanent Bldg., Washington, 1001 Pennsylvania Ave, Washington; Folger Shakespeare Library, Washington, Immanuel Presbyn. Ch., McLean, Va., Sumner Sch., Washington, H.E.B. hdqrs., San Antonio, Market Square, Washington, Franklin Sq., Washington, Pa. Plaza, Washington, U.S. Embassy, Kuala Lumpur, Malaysia, Chrysler Mus., Norfolk, Va. Served to 2d Lt., F.A. AUS, 1957. Recipient Louis Sullivan award for architecture, 1972, 75 Nat., State and Local Design awards, 1967—; fellow Am. Acad. in Rome, 1977-78. Fellow AIA (pres. Washington chpt. 1975, chmn. nat. capitol com. 1976, chmn. nat. com. on design 1977, AIA Nat. Honor award 1970-71, 81, 83, 89, AIA Firm award 1988); mem. U.S. Commn. Fine Arts, Cosmos Club (pres. 1985). Home: 47 W Lenox St Bethesda MD 20815-4208 Office: Hartman Cox Architects 1025 Thomas Jefferson St NW Washington DC 20007-5201

HARTMAN, HEDY ANN, museum chief executive officer; b. Sept. 24, 1954; d. Alan Stuart Hartman and Joan Marcia (Lederman) Hartman Goldsmith; m. Jon Abbott Mersereau, Nov. 27, 1976 (div. June 1981); m. William Bainbridge Everett, June 2, 1984 (div. Jan. 1990). B.A. with distinction, U. Pa., 1975; M.A., U. Wash., 1982, Ph.C., 1983. Researcher Am. Mus. Natural History, N.Y.C., 1974; curatorial asst. Univ. Mus., U. Pa., Phila., 1974-75; instr. Children's Mus., Indpls., 1976; curatorial asst. Indpls. Mus. Art, 1975-76; program adminstr. statewide services S.C. State Mus., Columbia, 1977-80; pres. Hartman Planning & Devel. Group Ltd., Bellevue, Wash., 1980-88; exec. dir. Nat. Bicycle Ctr., Redmond, Wash., 1989-90; pres., chief exec. officer Staten Island Inst. Arts and Scis., N.Y., 1990—. S.C. state rep. Southeastern Mus. Conf., 1979-80; bd. dirs. Staten Island C. of C., 1992—, Staten Island Jewish commentary ctr., 1991—. Author: Funding Sources and Technical Assistance for Museums and Historical Organizations, 1979; Fund Raising for Museums, 1985. Editor: Official Museum Guide to Products and Services, 1980. Mem. Am. Assn. Museums, Am. Assn. State and Local History (bd. dirs. 1983-86), Western Museums Conf. (bd. dirs. 1980-83), Wash. Mus. Assn. (bd. dirs. 1985-90, sec. 1986-90), Mid-Island Rotary Club of Staten Island (treas. 1991—). Office: SI Inst of Arts & Scis 75 Stuyvesant Pl Staten Island NY 10301-1998

HARTMAN, HENRY BOB, psychologist; b. Bronx, Nov. 9, 1951; s. Seymour Maurice and Esther (Seifer) H.; m. Susan Lynn Solomon, July 3, 1985; children: Jenna, Elana. BA, NYU, 1973; MA, St. John's U., 1974; PhD, Hofstra U., 1979. Lic. psychologist, N.Y. Dep. dir., psychologist, asst. Psychiatry Svcs. Ctr., Inc., White Plains, N.Y., 1974-84; prin. Dr. Henry B. Hartman, White Plains, 1979—; psychologist St. Cabrini Nursing Home, Dobbs Ferry, N.Y., 1989—. Office: 12 Old Mamaroneck Rd White Plains NY 10605-2010

HARTMAN, HOPE JANINE, educational psychologist, researcher, consultant; b. Cin., Sept. 30, 1947; d. Philbert H. and Lillian J. (Roth) H.; m. Dennis Charles Haas, Aug. 24, 1969 (div. 1985); m. Michael Jeffrey Holub, Oct. 13, 1985; 1 child, Alicia Dawn. BA, Ohio State U., 1969; PhD, Rutgers U., 1980. Rsch. dir., IAPC Montclair State Coll., Upper Montclair, N.J., 1974-76, asst. prof., asst. dir. Project Thistle, 1984-85; rsch. coord. Rockland Community Coll., Suffern, N.Y., 1977-81; rsch. specialist Newark Bd. Edn., 1981-84; assoc. prof., dir. Peer Tutoring & Coop. Learning Program City Coll. of CUNY, N.Y.C., 1986—; cons. State Dept. Edn., Hartford, Conn., 1985-86. Editor, author: (newsletter) Cogitare, 1984-88; contbr. articles to profl. jours. Co-founder Youth Ctr., Hopatcong, N.J., 1977. Recipient Disting. Paper award N.E. Ednl. Rsch. Assn., 1983; Aaron Diamond Found. grantee, 1988, 91, Leon Lowenstein Found. grantee, 1988, Exxon Found. grantee, 1990. Mem. APA, Am. Ednl. Rsch. Assn., ASCD. Office: CCNY 138th St & Convent Ave New York NY 10031

HARTMAN, JENNIFER WEAVER, community college administrator; b. Decatur, Ga., Mar. 10, 1947; d. John R. and Bette (Farmer) Weaver; m. Gary E. Hartman, June 15, 1968; children: Bradley Harris, Brooke Morgan. BS, Pa. State U., 1969. Mgmt. trainee Woodward & Lothrop, Washington, 1969-70, asst. buyer, 1971-72; exec. dir. YWCA, Gettysburg, Pa., 1975-77, program dir., 1978-84, exec. dir., 1984-89; dir. Gettysburg Ctr.-HACC, 1989—; sec. Adams County Coun. Community Svcs., Gettysburg, 1986-87; v.p., founder Survivors, Inc., Gettysburgh, 1981—; mem. steering com. YWCA Capital Campaign, 1978-81; adv. bd. dirs. Admas County Nat. Bank, 1992. Area coordinator Adams County United Way, 1973; v.p. Friends of the Library, 1974-76; mem. Martin Luther King Celebration Com., 1981-87. Recipient Outstanding Alumni award Pa. State, 1989. Mem. AAUW (recipient women making a difference award 1984), Gettysburg Personnel Assn. Democrat. Lutheran. Home: 70 Park Ave Gettysburg PA 17325-8473 Office: Gettysburg Ctr 902 Biglerville Rd Gettysburg PA 17325-7244

HARTMAN, KENNETH SHANE, software management consultant; b. Houston, Apr. 3, 1955; s. Kenneth Swift and Virginia Lee (Shane) H. Student, MIT, 1981-85. Assoc. dir. tech. Palladian Software, Cambridge, Mass., 1985-86; dir. tech. Palladian Software, Cambridge, 1986-87, v.p. R&D, 1987-88; dir. tech. SPR, Inc., Burlington, Mass., 1988—. Republican. Office: SPR Inc 77 S Bedford St Burlington MA 01803-5154

HARTMAN, KEVIN JOHN, metallurgical engineer; b. Alpena, Mich., Oct. 9, 1960; s. Gary John and Mary Ellen (Henry) H. BS in Engring. Materials and Metallurgy, U. Mich., 1982, MSE in Metallurgy, 1984. Process engr. Howmet Corp., Plymouth, Mich., 1984-85, Hampton, Va., 1985-86, Dover, N.J., 1986-88; metall. engr. "A" Hamilton Standard, Windsor Locks, Conn., 1988—; adj. prof. County Coll. Morris, Randolph, N.J., 1986-88. Mem. United Comml. Travellers, Alpena, 1978—. Mem. Metall. Soc. of AIME (nominating com. N.J. chpt. 1988-89), Am. Soc. for Metals (chmn. student affairs Hartford chpt. 1988—, nat. mem. found. 1990—, course instr. 1990—), Am. Welding Soc. Republican. Episcopalian. Office: Hamilton Standard Space and Sea Systems 1 Hamilton Rd Windsor Locks CT 06096-1000

HARTMAN, LEE ANN WALRAFF, educator; b. Milw., Apr. 21, 1945; d. Emil Adolph and Mabelle Carolyn (Goetter) Walraff; m. Patrick James Hartman, Oct. 5, 1968; children: Elizabeth Marie, Suzanne Carolyn. BS, U. Wis., 1967; postgrad., U. R.I., 1972-73, Johns Hopkins U., 1990. Cert. tchr., Wis., Md. Educator Port Wash. Bd. Edn., Wis., 1967-68; instr. ballet YWCA, Wilmington, Del., 1977-78; tutor Md. Study Skills Inst., Columbia, 1984-86; tchr. Howard County Bd. Edn., Columbia, 1985—. Contbr. ar-

ticles to profl. jours. Bd. dirs. Columbia United Christian Ch., 1980-83; mem. Gifted and Talented Com., Columbia, 1980-90, Lang. Arts Com., 1985—, USCG Officers Wives Club, 1970-72, Hosp. Aux., 1980-91, Columbia, Md., 1985—, Bay St. Louis, Miss., 1970-72; troop leader Girl Scouts U.S., Columbia, 1980-91. Mem. AAUW (exec. bd. 1985—), Home Hosp. Tchrs. Assn. Md. Home: 5070 Durham Rd W Columbia MD 21044-1445 Office: Howard County Bd Edn Rt # 108 Columbia MD 21044

HARTMAN, MARY LOUISE, information services librarian; b. Toledo, Ohio, Mar. 18, 1942; d. Carl Leo and Marie Louise (Weis) Campbell; m. Charles Martin, June 27, 1964; children: Christine, Katherine, Jeffrey, John. BA in History, Rosary Coll., River Forest, Ill., 1964; MLS, Rutgers U., 1980. Info. svcs. librarian Princeton (N.J.) Pub. Libr., 1983—; on-line rsch. svcs. cons. East Windsor, 1987—. Co-founder Pax Christi N.J., Middletown, 1981; pres. Assn. for Rights of Catholics in the Ch., Delran, N.J., 1989—, editor newsletter, 1988. Mem. Women's Ordination Conf., Call to Action, Nat. Assn. Lay Ministry, Nat. Assn. Lay Leaders, Corpus. Roman Catholic. Office: Assn for Rights of Cath PO Box 912 Delran NJ 08075

HARTMAN, ROBERT WILLIAM, government official; b. N.Y.C., Jan. 7, 1938; s. Eugene and Ella (Schweitzer) H.; m. Rhona Cohen, Jan. 31, 1960; children: Peter Adam, Michael Gordon. BA, Queens Coll. N.Y., 1958; AM, Harvard U., 1961, PhD, 1964. Tchr. Upward Bound program Brandeis U., Waltham, Mass., 1966, asst. prof. econs., 1963-68; Brookings econ. policy fellow HEW, Washington, 1968-69; rsch. assoc., sr. fellow Brookings Instn., Washington, 1969-82; sr. analyst for budget process Congl. Budget Office, Washington, 1982-91, acting dep. dir., 1987-91, asst. dir. spl. studies div., 1991—; vis. lectr. Grad. Sch. Pub. Policy, U. Calif., Berkeley, 1975-76; mem. budget group Carter-Mondale Transition Staff, Washington, 1976-77. Author: Credit for College, 1971, Reforming School Finance, 1973, Setting National Priorities, 1974, 75, Pay and Pensions for Federal Workers, 1983. Recipient Excellence in Teaching award Brandeis U.; Univ. fellow Harvard U., Earhart Found. fellow. Mem. Assn. for Pub. Policy Analysis and Mgmt. (policy coun. 1986-90, chmn. nominating com. 1990). Home: 4803 Langdrum Ln Bethesda MD 20815-5412 Office: Congl Budget Office Washington DC 20515

HARTMAN, THOMAS JEFFERY, data processing executive; b. Phoenixville, Pa., Mar. 17, 1966; s. John Edwin and Mary Lou (Rehberg) H. AAS in Data Processing, Montgomery County Comm. Coll., Blue Bell, Pa., 1986. Computer operator Montgomery County Community Coll., Blue Bell, Pa., 1986-87; data processing/technologies mgr. Waterloo Gardens, Inc., Exton, Pa., 1988—; notary public in field. Mem. Internat. Mgmt. Coun. (notary pub.), Phi Theta Kappa. Republican. Methodist. Home: 402 Village Walk Exton PA 19341-1242 Office: Waterloo Gardens Inc 200 N Whitford Rd Exton PA 19341-2099

HARTMANN, ROBERT SANKEY, hospital administrator, health care communications executive; b. Long Beach, Calif., June 9, 1948; s. Robert Trowbridge and Roberta (Sankey) H.; m. Ruth Eva Satterthwaite, Dec. 9, 1978; children: Daniel Satterthwaite, David Trowbridge. BA cum laude in Speech/Drama, Occidental Coll., 1969; MA in Speech/Drama, 1971; student in acting, Guildhall Sch. Music and Drama, London, 1970; mgmt. devel. course Harvard Bus. Sch., 1974. Spl. asst. to chmn. Nat. Endowment for Arts, Washington, 1973-78; lobbyist for Daniel J. Edelman, Washington, 1978; creative dir., lobbyist Hill and Knowlton, Washington, 1978-81; sr. v.p. Ruder Finn & Rotman, Washington, 1981-84; dir. pub. rels. World Wildlife Fund, Washington, 1984-86; sr. v.p. and dir. public rels. Abramson Assocs., Inc., 1986-90; dir. communications,devel., govt. rels. and vol. svcs. Nat. Rehab. Hosp., Washington, 1990—. Recipient award of achievement Soc. for Tech. Communications, N.C., 1982; Paul Zucker award for excellence in communications, 1983, 84; named Outstanding Young Man Am., 1983. Mem. Pub. Relations Soc. Am. (Thoth award 1984), Internat. Assn. Bus. Communicators (Gold Quill award 1984), Nat. Press Club, Capitol Hill Club. Home: 5023 Worthington Dr Bethesda MD 20816-2748 Office: Nat Rehab Hosp 102 Irving St NW Washington DC 20010-2949

HARTNETT, JOHN F., manufacturing corporation owner; b. Cleve., July 2, 1937; s. John F. Hartnett and Jean Katherine (Nieman) Mackert; divorced; children: Christine, Heather, Cynthia, John IV. Student, John Carroll U., 1955-63. Salesman Kurt J. Lesker Co., Pitts., 1963-70, gen. mgr., 1970-77; chief exec. officer M-TEK, Pitts., 1977—, Vacuum Research Corp., Pitts., 1987—, UDG, Inc., 1989—; bd. dirs. Kurt J. Lesker Co., Fuji Seiki (Japan). Mem. Instrument Soc. Am., Sci. Apparatus Mfrs. Assn. (mem. exec. com. 1987—), Am. Vacuum Soc., Measurement, Control and Automation Assn. (chmn. 1990—). Office: M-TEK 2419 Smallman St Pittsburgh PA 15222-4609

HARTT, STANLEY HERBERT, lawyer, sales executive; b. Montreal, Que., Can., Nov. 11, 1937; s. Maurice and Rose Gertrude (Gallay) H.; m. Linda Joan Bloomfield, Sept. 5, 1961; children: Heather Ann, Michael John, James David, Douglas Andrew. BA, McGill U., 1958, MA, 1961, B of Civil Law, 1963. Bar: Que. 1965. Mem. firm Stikemar, Elliott, Tamaki, Mercier & Robb, Montreal, Que., Can., 1965-71, ptnr., 1971-85; dep. min. fin. Govt. of Can., 1985-88, chief of staff to Prime Min. Mulroney, 1985-88, 1989; chmn., pres., CEO Campeau Corp., Toronto, Can., 1990—; lectr. Sir George Williams U., 1962-65; lectr. labor law and policy McGill Indsl. Rels. Ctr., 1965-67; lectr. labor law Faculty of Law McGill U., from 1972; prof. history Labour Coll. Can., 1963, 65-66. Recipient MacDonald Travelling Scholarship U. Paris, 1963, Bar of Paris prize, 1965. Office: Campeau Corp, 5800 40 King St W, Toronto, ON Canada M5H 3Y8 also: 320 Bay St 5th Fl, Toronto, ON Canada M5H 2P2*

HARTWELL, DAVID GEDDES, publishing consultant, educator, writer, anthologist; b. Salem, Mass., July 10, 1941; s. Henry Geddes and Constance Elizabeth (Nash) H.; m Patricia Lee Wolcott, Aug. 30, 1969 (div. 1992); children: Alison Wolcott, Geoffrey Solan. BA, Williams Coll., 1963; MA with distinction, Colgate U., 1965; PhD in Comparative Medieval Lit., Columbia U., 1973. Ptnr. Dragon Press, 1973-78, proprietor, 1978—; sci. fiction editor New Am. Libr., 1971-73, Berkley Pub./G.P. Putnam & Sons, 1973-78, G.K. Hall & Co., 1975-86, Tor Books, 1984—; instr. Stevens Inst. Tech., 1973-76, Clarion Sci. Fiction Writing Workshop, Seattle, 1984, 86, 90; vis. prof. Harvard U., 1987, 88, 89, 91; dir. sci. fiction Pocket Books/Simon & Schuster, 1978-83, Arbor House, 1984-88, William Morrow, 1988-91; co-publisher Entwhistle Books, 1967-82; cons. Waldenbooks Otherworlds Club, 1983-84; cons. sci. fiction Book-of-the-Month Club, 1989; judge Readeroon Small Press Awards, 1989; adminstrv. cons. Turner Tomorrow Awards, 1990-91. Co-editor: (with L.W. Currey) The Battle of the Monsters, 1977, (with Kathryn Cramer) Christmas Ghosts, 1988, (with Kathryn Cramer) The Spirits of Christmas, 1989; editor: The Dark Descent, 1987 (World Fantasy award 1988), Foundations of Fear, 1992, (with Kathryn Cramer) Masterpieces of Fantasy & Enchantment, 1988, The World Treasury of Science Fiction, 1988, (with assistance of Kathryn Cramer) Masterpieces of Fantasy & Wonder, 1989, Foundations of Fear, 1992. Recipient Hugo award nominee for Best Sci. Fiction Editor, 1982, 83, 84, 87, 88, 89, 90, World Fantasy award nominee, Spl. award, 1977, 87, 88, World Fantasy award for Best Anthology, 1988, Sci. Fiction Chronicle Poll winner for Best Editor Books, 1987, 88, 89. Mem. Internat. Assn. for the Fantastic in the Arts, Modern Lang. Assn., PEN Am. Ctr., Sci. Fiction Rsch. Assn. Congregationalist. Home and Office: David G Hartwell Inc 153 Deerfield Ln N Pleasantville NY 10570-1430

HARTWELL, FREDERIC PECK, magazine editor, consultant; b. Evanston, Ill., Feb. 21, 1947; s. William Frederic and Catherine Alice (Arvidson) H.; m. Marie Hartwell-Walker, Aug. 17, 1968; children: Jennifer Rebecca, Adam Frederic, Toby David, Emily Susan. BS, U. Mass., 1974. Lic. master electrician, Mass. Owner, operator Hartwell Electric, Chgo., 1976-79, Amherst, Mass., 1979-82; electrician Hampshire Coll., Amherst, 1982-86, head electrician, 1989-90; elec. inspector Town of Amherst, 1982-89, Town of Pelham (Mass.), 1986—; editor Electrical Constrn. and Maint. Mag., Overland Park, Kans., 1990—; sec., mem., Mass. Elec. Code Adv. Com., Boston, 1987—. Author: Understanding NEC Rules on Swimming Pools, Spas, and Hot Tubs, 1991, 1993 NEC Changes, 1992; contbr. articles in field. Active town meeting Town of Amherst, 1983-91. Mem. Nat. Fire Prevention Assn. (elec. sect., prin. mem., sec. Nat. Elec. Code Comm. Code Making Panel 9, 1990—), Internat. Assn. Elec. Inspectors (Paul Revere chpt., exec. com. 1991—). Republican. Congregationalist. Home: 60 N Whitney St Amherst MA 01002 Office: EC&M Mag/Intertec 9800 Metcalf Ave 707 Westchester Ave Overland Park KS 66212

HARTWIG, THOMAS LEO, civil engineer; b. Pitts., June 16, 1952; s. Leo William and Bertha Barbara (Lukas) H.; m. Cynthia L. Grupp, 1987; children: Adam T. and Megan K. (twins). BSCE, U. Notre Dame, 1974. Registered profl. engr., Pa. Mgr. infiltration, inflow Duncan, Lagnese & Assoc., Pitts., 1974-76, ops. engr., 1976-80, mgr. ops. div., 1980-81, mgr. ops., assoc., 1981, v.p., 1981-83, v.p., mgr. mcpl. environ. engring., 1983-86, sr. v.p., mgr. mcpl. environ. engring., 1986—, also bd. dirs. Mem. ASCE, Water Pollution Control Fedn., Nat. Soc. Profl. Engrs., Water Pollution Control Assn. Pa. (program co-chmn. 1983), Profl. Engrs. in Pvt. Practice, Western Pa. Pollution Control Assn. (1st v.p.), Chi Epsilon. Democrat. Roman Catholic. Home: 9131 Ridgefell Ave Pittsburgh PA 15237-4853 Office: Killam Assocs DLA div 100 Allegheny Dr Warrendale PA 15086-7565

HARTY, EMMETT JOSEPH, investment company executive; b. Bklyn., Aug. 15, 1946; s. John Patrick and Harriet Mary (Gallagher) H.; m. Kathleen Anne Romanski, Sept. 20, 1975; children: Emmett Joseph Jr., Faith Anne. BSc, U. Windsor, Ont., Can., 1968. Mgr. preferred stock div. Weeden & Co., N.Y.C., 1974-78, First Boston, N.Y.C., 1978-79, Dean Witter Reynolds, N.Y.C., 1979-81; salesperson Drexel Burnham, N.Y.C., 1981-83, Becker Paribas, N.Y.C., 1983-84; prin., mgr. Alex Brown & Sons, Inc., N.Y.C., 1984-89; pres. Parallax Group, Westport, Conn., 1989, Parallax Group, Inc., Westport, Conn., 1991—; mng. dir. Smith Barney Harris Upham, N.Y.C., 1989-90; cons. U.S. Treasury, Washington, 1990-92; mem. Option Coop., N.Y.C., 1991—. Author: (booklet) Preferred Stocks, 1978, Americus Trust-Primes & Scores, 1987, Prime/Scores-Percs/Leaps, 1991. Sponsor, initiator Jason Found. Maritime Ctr. at Norwalk, Conn., 1990-91; chmn. ann. giving Greens Farms Acad., Westport, 1990-92. With USMC, 1969-72. Home: 325 Bayberry Ln Westport CT 06880 Office: Parallax Group Inc 315 Post Rd W Westport CT 06880

HARTZELL, GEORGE TURNER, construction company executive; b. Washington, Pa., Feb. 11, 1920; s. Milton Brindle and Maude (Turner) H.; m. Anna Pearl Reamer, Dec. 30, 1941; children: Elaine Ann Hartzell Nagle, Susan Kay Hartzell Perry, Anita Dawn Hartzell MacNeill. BSc, Dickinson Coll., 1942; MSc, Shippensburg U., 1982. Chemist Wyeth Inc., Phila., 1942-44, biochemist, 1946-50; supr. Pa. Dept. Labor, Chambersburg, 1950-60; pres. Hartzell Constrn. Co. Inc., Fayetteville, Pa., 1960—; pres. Pa. Home Owners Warranty Coun., 1977-78, Greene-Guilford Environ. Assn., Fayetteville, 1987-92; instr. Pa. State U., Mont Alto Campus, 1986. Pres. Franklin County chpt. ARC, 1974, Franklin County Legal Aid Soc., 1987, 88, 89, 90, 91, 92; mem. Chambersburg (Pa.) Sch. Bd., 1976-82, 90-94. Sgt. U.S. Army, 1944-46. Mem. Am. Chem. Soc., Realtors Assn., Franklin County Builders Assn. (sec. 1986-87, pres. 1988-89), Nat. Assn. Home Builders, U.S. Power Squadron (comdr. Susquahannoc, 1978), Lions (pres. Scotland, Pa. club 1960), Elks. Republican. Lodges: Lions (pres. Scotland, Pa. club 1960), Elks. Office: Hartzell Constrn Co Inc 5125 Lincoln Way E Fayetteville PA 17222-1098

HARVATIN, ANTHONY CHRISTOPHER, construction executive; b. Carbondale, Pa., Mar. 6, 1951; s. Anthony and Julia (Gerchman) H.; m. Candace Anne Coile; 1 stepchild, Amber Baker. BS, Pa. State U., 1972. Estimator AC&S, Inc., King of Prussia, Pa., 1974-78; sales engr. AC&S, Inc., Wilmington, Del., 1978-85, br. mgr., 1985—; trustee Local Union #42 Pension Fund, Wilmington, 1985—, Welfare Fund, 1985—, Apprentice Fund, 1985—; screening com. Del. Investment Found., Wilmington, 1989—. Mem. ASHRAE. Republican. Roman Catholic. Home: 1010 Summit View Dr Newark DE 19713-1124 Office: AC&S Inc 3315 Old Capitol Trl Wilmington DE 19808-6295

HARVEY, ALEXANDER, II, federal judge; b. Balt., May 3, 1923; s. Fred B. and Rose (Hopkins) H.; m. Mary E. Williams, Feb. 24, 1951; children: Elizabeth H., Alexander IV. BA, Yale U., 1947; LLB, Columbia U., 1950. Bar: Md. 1950. Assoc. Ober, William, Grimes & Stinson, Balt., 1950-66, ptnr., 1953-66; asst. atty. gen. Md., 1957-58; judge U.S. Dist. Ct. Md., 1966-86, chief judge, 1986-91; Mem. Gov. Md. Com. to Study Blue Sky Law of Md., 1961; mem. character com. Ct. Appeals Md. 8th Jud. Cir. Bd. dirs. Balt. Symphony Assn., 1966-68; pres., dir. Balt. Opera Guild, 1960; bd. dirs. Balt. Coun. Social Agys., 1957-63; trustee Ch. Home and Hosp., Balt., 1952-71. 1st lt. AUS, World War II, ETO. Mem. Am., Md., Balt. bar assns., Phi Beta Kappa. Episcopalian (vestry 1967-70). Home: 7300 Brightside Rd Baltimore MD 21212-1011 Office: US Dist Ct 101 W Lombard St Baltimore MD 21201-2626

HARVEY, CALVIN REA, lawyer; b. Saxonburg, Pa., Sept. 25, 1943; s. Howard F. and Evelyn (Rea) H.; m. Patricia McCabe, May 31, 1987; children: Jesse F., Matthew N. AB, Washington and Jefferson Coll., 1965; JD, George Washington U., 1968. Bar: Pa. 1968. Ptnr. Buchanan Ingersoll Profl. Corp., Pitts., 1968—. Mem. ABA, Pa. Bar Assn., Allegheny County Bar Assn., Am. Coll. Real Estate Lawyers, Duquesne Club. Presbyterian. Home: 27 Buckingham Pl Pittsburgh PA 15215-1504 Office: Buchanan Ingersoll 5800 USX Tower Pittsburgh PA 15219

HARVEY, CHARLES ERNEST, accountant, consultant; b. Lewiston, Maine, Apr. 26, 1963; s. Arthur Wallace and Patricia Helen (Wilgus) H.; m. Lisa Anne Dietz, Feb. 20, 1988. BABA, Gordon Coll., 1986; MBA, Pepperdine U., 1987. CPA, Mass. Staff cons. Deloitte & Touche, Boston, 1987-90; sr. auditor Gillette Co., 1990—; tax, bus. cons., 1987—. Mem. choir 1st Bapt. Ch. Manchester (Mass.)-by-Sea, 1988—, ch. auditor. Recipient Elijah Watt Sells High Distinction award, 1989; music scholar Gordon Coll., 1981-82, leadership grantee, 1981-86, Bares scholar Pepperdine U., 1986-87. Mem. AICPA, Mass. Socv. CPAs (gold medal 1989), Am. Mensa, Inst. Internal Auditors, Nat. Soc. Tax Profls. Baptist. Home: 254 E Lothrop St Beverly MA 01915-3742 Office: Gillette Co Prudential Tower Bldg Boston MA 02199

HARVEY, LESLIE LEO (LES HARVEY), composer; b. Worcester, Mass., Apr. 3, 1926; s. Herbert Erwin and Mary Agnes (Nagle) H.; m. Gladys Teresa Smith, Aug. 3, 1946 (div. 1972); children: Kathleen, Edith, Karen, Thomas, Debra, Mary. Assoc., Worcester Jr. Coll., 1951. Singer Major Bowes Original Amateur Hour, N.Y.C., 1939-42; recording artist Mel-O-Dee Records, N.Y.C., 1947-55; radio-TV personality W.T.A.G. W.N.E.B. Worchester, Worcester, Boston, N.Y.C., 1955-70; freelance writer Worcester Telegram & Gazette, 1970-80; pres. Boston Theatrical Agy., 1972-82, Boston Town Prodns., 1982—; mem. Broadcast Music, Inc., N.Y.C., 1980—; pub. writer Peer So. Music, N.Y.C., 1980—. Author: (album) To Rose with Love,1990; composer: Sons of Rosie Kennedy, 1980, In Boston, She's a Lady, 1985, To Rose with Love, 1985, You Gotta Be More Irish Than Harvard, 1988, In Boston Town, 1990, I'm a Man You Don't Meet Everyday, 1990, Rosie, 1990, The Mistletoe Society, 1991; contbr. articles to newspapers. Candidate Gov.'s Coun. Mass., 1980. With USN, 1943-46, PTO. Decorated World War II Victory medal with 8 Battle Stars. Mem. DAV, U.S. Hist. Soc., The Mistletoe Soc., Irish Charitable Soc., Mus. Fine Arts. Democrat. Roman Catholic. Home: 5991 NW 16th Pl # 8 Fort Lauderdale FL 33313 Office: Boston Town Prodns PO Box 372 Boston MA 02101

HARVEY, MARY BIRD, university official; b. Atlanta, May 8, 1929; d. Frank Elmer and Mary Bird (Hyde) Horner; m. Henry Bell Harvey, Jr., Dec. 20, 1950; children: Janice Devan, Henry Bell III, Kenneth Harry. AB, Wesleyan Coll., Macon, Ga., 1951; MA, Pa. State U., 1974. Libr. microforms aide Pa. State U., University Park, 1979-84, rsch. coord. Devel. Office, 1984-86, rsch. mgr., 1986—. Mem. Am. Prospect Rsch. Assn., New Eng. Prospect Rsch. Assn., Cen. Pa. Geneal. Soc. (sec. 1977-79, pres. 1983-84), Md. Hist. Soc., Soc. Ark and Dove, Centre County Hist. Soc. Democrat. Methodist. Office: Pa State U Devel Rsch 5 Old Main University Park PA 16802-1502

HARVEY, NEIL See PERLISH, HARVEY NEIL

HARVEY, RAYMOND NORMAN, economics educator; b. Lockport, N.Y., Apr. 18, 1832; s. Albert Adam and Carrie (Buehring) H.; m. Mary Lou Kovach, Apr. 5, 1958; children: James R., Emily E. BSBA, Ashland (Ohio) U., 1961; MEd, SUNY, Buffalo, 1963. Tchr. Buffalo Pub. Schs., 1963-64; prof. econs., coord. dept. econs. Niagara County Community Coll., Sanborn, N.Y., 1964—. Sunday sch. tchr., supt., bd. dirs. Lockport Alliance Ch., 1980-90. Cpl. U.S. Army, 1952-54. Mem. N.Y. State Econs. Assn., Nat. Econs. Assn. Home: 6367 Badger Dr Lockport NY 14094-5947 Office: Niagara County Community 3111 Saunders Settlement Rd Sanborn NY 14132-9460

HARVEY, ROSE MARIE, stock broker; b. Bellefonte, Pa., July 23, 1924; d. Charles Joseph and Frances (Bruno) Nelo; m. Norman Richard Harvey, Mar. 31, 1948; children: Michael David, Patricia Arlana Harvey Johnson, Stephen Wayne, Joseph Walter II, Daniel Thomas. Student, Pa. State U., 1943-45, N.Y. Inst. Fin. Registerld rep. all U.S. exchanges, SEC Corrometal Products, Bellefont; lic. life ins. rep., Pa. Sec. Cerro Metal Products, Bellefonte, 1942-60, Green Ellis and Anderson, State College, Pa., 1960-64, Clark Dodge & Co., State College, 1964; registered rep. Josephthal & Co., State College, 1965-82, Prudential Bache, State College, 1982-84, Shearson Lehman, State College, 1984-90, Investment Mgmt. and Rsch., Inc., State College, 1990—; treas., bd. dirs. GHM & Assocs., Inc., State College, 1990—; bd. dirs., v.p. sales Art Alliance Cen. Pa., Lemont, 1992. Precinct chmn. Centre County Rep. Com., Bellefonte, 1960—; mem. Shade Tree Commn., Bellefonte Borough, 1980-91, Med. Commn., 1980—. Roman Catholic. Home: 207 W Linn St Bellefonte PA 16823 Office: Investment Mgmt & Rsch Inc 220 Regent Ct Ste D1 State College PA 16801

HARVEY, W(ILLIAM) ANDRÉ, sculptor; b. Hollywood, Fla., Oct. 9, 1941; s. Edmund H. and Jeanne B. (Bright) H.; m. Roberta Rush, Jan. 12, 1964. BA, U. Va., 1963. Bronze sculptures include Rain Before Morning, 1985, Flying Frog, 1985, The Sunbathers, 1986, Helen, 1987, A Gathering of Emporers, 1988, Carolyn with Cattle Egrets, 1989; exhibited in group shows including Nat. Sculpture Soc., N.Y.C., 1983, 85, 88, 89, 91, Del. Art Mus., Wilmington, 1989, Brandywine River Mus., Chadds Ford, Pa., 1991; represented in permanent collections including Sara Lee Corp., Memphis, Hunter Mus., Chattanooga, De Bartolo Corp., Youngstown, Ohio, Meijer Corp., Grand Rapids. Mem. Nat. Sculpture Soc. (Joel Meissner award 1980, Tallix Foundry award 1989), Artists Equity, Internat. Sculpture Ctr., Internat. Ctr. for Wildlife Art and Nature in Art. Studio: PO Box 8 Rockland Rd Rockland DE 19732

HARVEY, WILLIAM MORRIS, media consultant; b. Bklyn., Mar. 4, 1942; s. Ned and Sandy (Margolis) H.; m. Lynn Haas, 1961 (div. 1965); 1 child, Nicole; m. June Lillian Skinner, May 5, 1986. BA in Philosophy, Bklyn. Coll., 1963; postgrad., NYU, 1963-64. Media rsch. analyst Grey Advt., Inc., N.Y.C., 1963; asst. mgr. media rsch. Kenyon & Eckhardt, Inc., N.Y.C., 1964; mgr. media rsch. Interpub., Inc., N.Y.C., 1964-65; mgr. planning Arbitron, Inc., N.Y.C., 1965-67; v.p. broadcast devel. C.E. Hooper, Inc., N.Y.C., 1967-69; exec. v.p. Brand Rating Index, Inc., N.Y.C., 1969-71; pres. New Electronic Media Sci., Inc., Woodstock, N.Y., 1972—, Unltd. Prodns. Inc., Woodstock, 1979—; bd. dirs. Human Effectiveness Inst., Woodstock, 1976—; cons. Bristol-Myers, Inc., N.Y.C., 1978-83, ABC-TV, Inc., N.Y.C., 1978-85, U.S. Army Delta Force, Carlisle, Pa., 1980-83, chmn. Computerized Telemarketing, Inc., N.Y.C., 1983-8, Unltd. Positive Communications, Inc., 1988—; cons. IBM, L.A., 1989—, CBS-TV, N.Y.C., 1989—, AT&T, N.Y., 1990—. Author: Mind Magic, 1976, The Theory of the Conscious Universe, Plan for Motion Picture Electronic Marketing; newsletter editor The Mktg. Pulse, 1979—; inventor in field; co-producer TV programs The Pope at Castel Gondolfo, The New Television, Cable Convention News. Chmn. Plans for Am. Com., Woodstock, 1975, First World State Com., Woodstock, 1983—; bd. dirs. cultural affairs Sino-Am. Cultural Consortium, L.A., 1982—; cons. The Papal Project to End War, N.Y.C., 1983-86; chmn. Internat. Ratings Svc./Global Tracking Svc., 1990—. Office: Unltd Positive Communications Inc 11 N Chestnut St New Paltz NY 12561-1706

HARWOOD, BERNICE BAUMEL, artist, community volunteer; b. Bklyn., Mar. 6, 1923; d. Max and Mildred (Weinberger) Baumel; m. Daniel J. Harwood, Aug. 23, 1947; children: René Gordon, Felice Spodick. BS in Art Edn., Hofstra U., 1973, MA in Spl. Edn., 1975; student, Ruth Leaf Studio, Douglaston, N.Y., 1980-87, Studio Camitzer, Valdottavo, Italy, 1983. Artist in residence Syossett (N.Y.) Sch. Dist., 1986. Exhibited in one-woman shows at Calkins Gallery, Hofstra U., 1985, Graphic Eye Gallery, Port Washington, N.Y., 1989; exhibited in group shows at Hutchins Gallery, C.W. Post U., Greenvale, N.Y., 1982, Albrecht Mus., St. Joseph, Mo., 1986, Monmouth (N.J.) Mus. Art, 1986, Foxhall Gallery, Washington, 1987, Elaine Benson Gallery, Bridghampton, N.Y., 1989, Daruma Gallery, Cedar Hurst, N.Y., 1991; others; works included in pvt. collections including IBM, Bethlehem, Pa., Am. Stock Exchange, N.Y.C., Chase Manhattan (N.Y.) Bank; illustrator: Five Towns, 1962. Chairperson LWV, Woodmere, N.Y., 1957-61; v.p. Nat. Coun. Jewish Women, Lawrence, N.Y., 1976-81; committeewoman Dem. Party, Woodmere, 1962-84; mem. bd. advisors Nassau County Mus. Fine Art, 1981-88. With WAVES, 1944-46. Recipient art awards, including 2d prize Emily Lowe Gallery, Hofstra U., 1984, award of excellence Long Beach (N.Y.) Art League, 1987. Mem. Nat. Assn. Women Artists (juror 1988-90, Leila Sawyer award 1983), N.Y. Artists Equity, Long Beach Art League, Prints Plus Etc. N.Y. Democrat. Jewish. Home: 835 Fiske St Woodmere NY 11598-2429 also: 41 Windsor Ln Boynton Beach FL 33436

HARWOOD, COLIN FREDERICK, business executive; b. Manchester, Lancashire, Eng., July 17, 1937; s. Frederick George and Nancy Irene (Livick) H.; m. Heather Norah Littlewood, Aug. 2, 1958. BSc, Chelsea Coll., 1963, PhD, 1969. Sci. tchr. St. Johns Coll., Nassau, The Bahamas, 1963-66; sci. adviser IIT Rsch. Inst., Chgo., 1969-77; asst. v.p. R&D Pall Corp., L.I., N.Y., 1977—. Patentee in field; contbr. articles to profl. jours. Recipient Honors Chem. Processing Vaaler award, 1986. Home: 17 Southland Dr Glen Cove NY 11542-1026 Office: Pall Corp 30 Sea Cliff Ave Glen Cove NY 11542-3634

HARWOOD, WILLIAM BRADFORD, public relations executive; b. Balt., Feb. 23, 1925; s. Richard Roberts and Willyhyde (Hart) H.; m. Ruth Anne Lawless; children: Ellen Marvin Uzenoff, Janet Howard Peditto. BA, Marshall U., Huntington, W.Va., 1950. Editor/writer AP, Balt., 1946-58; with The Martin Co., Cape Canaveral, Fla., 1958-62; asst. dir. pub. relations Martin Marietta Corp., Balt., 1962-67; dir. pub. relations Martin Marietta Corp., N.Y.C., 1967-74, Bethesda, Md., 1974-83; exec. dir. pub. relations Martin Marietta Corp., 1983-84, v.p. pub. rels., 1984-90; cons., 1990—; pres. HARCO, Inc., pub. rels. counselors, Bethsda, 1990—; bd. dirs. Samaritan Inns Devel. Found.; mem. pub. rels. com. pvt. sector USIA, 1987—. Bd. dirs. Washington Ballet, 1988—, Cathedral Choral Soc., Washington, 1987-91, Media Inst., 1989—. 2d lt. USAAC, 1943-45. Recipient Christopher award, AP, 1956. Mem. Air Force Assn., AIAA, Arthur Page Soc., Pub. Rels. Seminar, Nat. Press Club. Home and Office: 6311 Swords Way Bethesda MD 20817-3350

HASBROUCK, KENNETH EDWARD, professional society administrator; b. Gardiner, N.Y., June 30, 1916; s. Josiah LeFevre and Agnes (Riley) H.; m. Alice Jackson, July 10, 1948; children: Kenneth Edward Jr., Charles Jackson. B in Edn., SUNY, New Paltz, 1946; MA, NYU, 1946. Social studies tchr. various schs., 1941-42, 46-72; pres. Huguenot Hist. Soc., New Paltz, 1960—, also bd. dirs.; pres. Young-Morse Historic Site, Poughkeepsie, N.Y., 1979—; historian Ulster County, N.Y., 1960—. Author: Street of the Huguenots, 1952, History of Gardiner, N.Y., 1955, The Hasbrouck Family in America, Vols. I & II, 1961, Vol. III, 1974, Vol. IV, 1984, Vol. V., 1987, The Bevier Family in America, 1970, Three Hundred Years of the VerNooy Family in America, 1971, The Crispell Family in America, 1976, Vol. II, 1984, Vol. III, 1989, The Giraud-Gerow Family in America: First Four Generations in America, 1981, Vol. II, 1982, Vol. III, 1986; contbr. articles to mags. and newspapers. Named Alumnus of Yr. Coll. New Paltz, 1984. Mem. Huguenot Soc. Am., New England Geneal. Soc., N.Y. Geneal. and Biographical Soc., Holland Soc. N.Y., St. Nicholas Soc., Sons Am. Revolution, Huguenot Hist. Soc., Hasbrouck Family Assn. (pres. 1957-71). Office: Huguenot St PO Box 339 New Paltz NY 12561-0339

HASE, RICHARD ARTHUR, pastor, consultant; b. Little Rock, June 24, 1945; s. Helmut Gustva and Maxine Olivia (Schnipper) H.; m. Elizabeth Jean Wheeler, May 30, 1986; 1 child, Jason R.; 1 stepchild, Timothy Bacon. AA, St. Paul's Coll., Concordia, Mo., 1965; BA, Concordia Coll., River Forest, Ill., 1968; MDiv, Concordia Theol. Sem., Springfield, Ill., 1975. Ordained to ministry of Gospel Luth. Ch., Mo. Synod, 1975. Dir. christian edn. Zion Luth. Ch., Brainard, Minn., 1967-68; tchr., dir. athletics Our Shepherd Luth. Ch., Birmingham, Mich., 1968-71; pastor Mt. Olive Luth. Ch., Balt., 1975-86, Berea Luth. Ch., Balt., 1981-86; staff organizer Baltimorian United Leadership Devel., Balt., 1986-88; pastor Nazareth Luth. Ch., Balt., 1986-87; dir. of ministry Balt. Urban Ministry Coalition Luth. Ch., Mo. Synod, 1988-91; sr. pastor St. Paul's Luth. Ch., Glen Burnie, Md., 1991—; mem. pastoral staff Johns Hopkins Hosp., Balt., 1975-87; cons. urban ministry Southeastern Dist. Luth. Ch., Balt., 1980—; bd. dirs. Luth. Mission Soc. Md., Balt., 1976-78. Author: Vision for Urban Ministry, 1989; editor: Study of Urban Ministry, 1982. Organizer, team mem. Balt. Commonwealth Agts., 1985-88; chairperson cycling program Am. Lung Assn. Md., Balt., 1988-91, chairperson spl. events, 1989-91; bd. dirs. 4x4 Community Assn., Balt., 1982-86, Balt. United in Leadership Devel., 1985-91. Named Fundraiser of the Yr., Am. Lung Assn., 1991, Spl. Event Chairperson of the Yr., Am. Lung Assn., 1990; recipient Recognition award Senate of Md., 1986, Balt. City Coun., 1988. Mem. Interdenominational Ministerial Alliance (treas. Balt. chpt. 1987-89), Balt. Urban Ministry Coalition (pres. 1982-84, 85-86), Forum for Clergy in Black Ministry, Glen Burnie Ministerial Alliance. Home: 271 Hemingway Ln Severna Park MD 21146 Office: St Pauls Luth Ch 308 Oak Manor Dr Glen Burnie MD 21061

HASEGAWA, TOMOHIRO, electrical engineer; b. San Francisco, Nov. 26, 1962; s. Akira and Miyoko (Okada) H.; m. Shirley Shiaoning Young, Sept. 28, 1986; 1 child, Audrey Kei Hueymiin. BSEE, MSEE, MIT, 1985. Data clk. Bell Labs., Murray Hill, N.J., 1979-80; computer programmer Ctr. for Space Rsch., MIT, Cambridge, Mass., 1981-82; coop. engrng. intern Hewlett Packard Co., Andover, Mass., 1982-85, rsch. and design engr., 1985—; coll. recruiter Hewlett Packard Co., Andover, 1987—. Inventee (with others) pulsed doppler flow mapping apparatus; contbr. articles to profl. jours. Recipient Raymond Freany Meml. award Town of New Providence (N.J.), 1980; MIT scholar, 1984-85. Mem. Straight Down Volleyball Club, Eta Kappa Nu, Tau Beta Pi. Home: 22 Avery Ln Andover MA 01810-6401 Office: Hewlett Packard Co 3000 Minuteman Rd Andover MA 01810-1099

HASEK, JOHN ALLAN, police lieutenant; b. Pitts., Apr. 5, 1936; s. John Joseph and Gertrude Ruth (Heinen) H.; m. Paula Kathleen SMith, May 29, 1970; 1 child, Keith Allan. A of Adminstrv. Criminal Justice, Alleg. Community Coll., 1982. Patrolman West View Police Dept., Pitts., 1967-73; sgt. Allegheny Regional Narcotic Task Force, Pitts., 1973-74; drug agt. DEA/Joint Narcotic Task Force, Pitts., 1974-75; police sgt. West View Borough Police Dept., Pitts., 1978-89; police lt. West View Borough Police Dept., 1989—; police coord. West View Vol. Fire Dept., Pitts., 1984-91; steering com. Chem. People, North Hills, Pitts., 1984-87. Democrat. Methodist. Home: 1 Lipp Ave Pittsburgh PA 15229-2001 Office: West View Police Dept 441 Perry Hwy Pittsburgh PA 15229-1889

HASHEMI, REZA ATTAR, systems and computer science educator; b. Mashhad, Khorassan, Iran, Feb. 27, 1947; came to U.S., 1972; s. Mohammad-Mehdi and Malakeh (Parvaneh) Hashemi-Attar; m. Zarrin Nasrin Negahban Zafaranlou, Feb. 1, 1973; children: Omead, Navead. BS in Physics, U. Mashhad, 1969; MS in Physics, U. N.Mex., 1973, MSEE and Computer Sci., PhD in Physics, 1977. Lectr. U. Mashhad, 1970-71; rsch. assoc. U. N.Mex., Albuquerque, 1977-79; mem. tech. staff AT&T Bell Labs., Allentown, Pa., 1979-89; assoc. prof. systems and computer sci. Howard U., Washington, 1989—; vis. prof. N.C. A&T State U., Greensboro, 1988-89. Contbr. articles to profl. jours. V.p. MSA, Albuquerque, 1975-76; co-founder Iranian Cultural Soc., Lehigh Valley, Pa., 1983-88. Mem. Am. Soc. Engrng. Educators, Sigma Xi. Home: 8932 Edgewood Dr Gaithersburg MD 20877-1544 Office: Howard U LKD-2113 2300 6th St NW Washington DC 20059-0001

HASHÍMOTO-SINCLAIR, YOKO, theater arts educator, makeup and costume designer; b. Kamakura, Japan, Aug. 20, 1939; came to U.S., 1966; d. Naoaki Hashimoto and Kimie Hamada; m. Thomas Alexander Sinclair, Aug. 20, 1978; 1 child, Karen Hashimoto. BA in English Lit., Aoyama Gakuin U., Tokyo, 1964, MA in English Lit., 1966; MA in Theater Arts, U. Mich., 1967, PhD in Theater Arts, 1972. cert. 19-20th Century Drama, Oxford U., England, 1974, Contemporary Drama, London U., 1975. Teaching fellow speech and theater arts U. Mich., Ann Arbor, 1967, 70; asst. prof. speech communication and theater West Chester (Pa.) U., 1969-70, assoc. prof., 1970—; artistic dir./designer Beaver Coll. Theater Palyshop, Glenside, Pa., 1970-79; artist-in-edn. Del. State Arts Coun., Wilmington; lectr., condr. workshops on theatrical costume design and makeup; costume & makeup designer for drama, musical, opera and dance. Recipient Travelling Grant to U.S. award Am. Coll. Woman's Assn., 1966; Barbour scholarship U. Mich., 1966-69; recipient Meritorious Costume Design award Am. Coll. Theater Festival, 1987, 91, 92. Mem. Costume Soc. of Am., Chesapeake Region U.S. Inst. Theater Tech., East Cen. Theater Conf. Home: 1065 Kerwood Rd West Chester PA 19382-7438 Office: West Chester U Dept Theater West Chester PA 19383

HASIUK, CYNTHIA LEE, nurse practitioner, psychotherapist; b. Hartford, Conn., Oct. 8, 1950; d. Leslie Eugene and Joan Lee (Carrington) Stevens; m. Walter Hasiuk, Aug. 13, 1976. LPN, Mesa (Ariz.) Community Coll., 1972; ADN, Mohegan Community Coll., Norwich, Conn., 1977; BSN, U. Hartford, 1984; MA in Counseling, St. Joseph Coll., 1987. Cert. adult nurse practitioner, advanced practice RN. Adult nurse practitioner Dr. Edward Sawicki, Internist, Willimantic, Conn., 1983-88, U. Conn., Storrs, 1988-91; advanced practice RN Hartford Hosp., 1991—; pvt. practice in psychotherapy Amston, Conn., 1987—; Cert. adult nurse practitioner, advanced practice RN. Mem. AACD, Am. Mental Health Counselor Assn., Conn. Nurse Practitioner Group, Iota Upsilon (v.p. 1989-90), Sigma Theta Tau. Home: 54 Crouch Rd Amston CT 06231

HASKELL, BARBARA, curator; b. San Diego, Nov. 13, 1946; d. John N. and Barbara (Freeman) H.; m. Leon Botstein; 1 child, Clara Haskell Botstein. BA, UCLA, 1969. Dir. UCLA Exptl. Arts Festival, 1966; asst. registrar Pasadena (Calif.) Art Mus., 1969, curatorial asst., 1970, asst. curator, 1970, assoc. curator, 1970-72, curator painting and sculpture, 1972-74, dir. exhbns. and collections, 1974; curator painting and sculpture Whitney Mus. Am. Art, N.Y.C., 1975—. Author: Arthur Dove, 1974, Marsden Hartley, 1980, Milton Avery, 1982, Blam! The Explosion of Pop, Minimalism and Performance 1958-64, 1984, Georgia O'Keefe: Works on Paper, 1985, Ralston Crawford, 1985, Charles Demuth, 1987, Donald Judd, 1988, Burgoyne Diller,1990, also collection catalogs. Named Woman of Yr., Mademoiselle mag., 1973. Office: Whitney Mus Am Art 945 Madison Ave New York NY 10021-2705

HASKIN, DAYTON WILLIAM, English educator, researcher; b. Ann Arbor, Mich., Sept. 14, 1946; s. Dayton William and June Kathryn Haskin; m. Margaret Ann Thomas, 1990; 1 child, Thomas Henry. BA, U. Detroit, 1968; MA, Northwestern U., 1970; BD with honors, U. London, 1975; PhD, Yale U., 1978. Instr. in English John Carroll U., University Heights, Ohio, 1970-72; assoc. prof. Boston Coll., Chestnut Hill, Mass., 1978—; seminar mem. Ctr. on Culture & the Economy, Chestnut Hill, 1988—. Contbr. numerous articles to profl. jours. Mem. Modern Lang. Assn., John Donne Soc. (exec. bd. 1990—), Milton Soc. Am. Office: Boston Coll Carney Hall 442 Chestnut Hill MA 02167

HASLEM, JOHN ARTHUR, finance educator; b. St. Louis, Aug. 16, 1934; s. John R. and B. (Morris) H.; m. Jane Nehf, Aug. 5, 1955; children: John A. Jr., James R., Jeffrey A. AB, Duke U., 1956; postgrad., Harvard U., 1956-57; MBA, U. N.C., 1961, PhD, 1967. Fellow, instr., rsch. asst. U. N.C., Chapel Hill, 1960-65; asst. prof. U. Wis., Madison, 1965-69; assoc. prof. U. Md., College Park, 1969-76, chmn. fin. coll. bus. and mgmt., 1972-73, 78-84, asst. dean for acad. affairs coll. bus. and mgmt., 1973-78, prof. fin., 1976—; cons. Dir. Supersonic Transport Devel., Washington, NASA, Greenbelt, Md., and various pvt. sector orgns.; cons., expert witness U.S. Dept. Justice, Washington. Author: Bank Funds Management, 1984, Commercial Bank Management, 1985, The Investor's Guide to Mutual Funds, 1988; co-editor: Financial Markets: Instruments and Concepts, 2d edit., 1986; contbr. articles to profl. jours. Fellow Found. for Econ. Edn.; mem. Am. Fin. Assn., Fin. Mgmt. Assn. (pres. student chpts. 1983-84), Cosmos Club, Alpha Tau Omega, Beta Gamma Sigma, Alpha Kappa Psi, Delta Sigma Pi. Home: 2025 Hillyer Pl NW Washington DC 20009-1005 Office: U Md Coll Bus and Mgmt College Park MD 20742

HASMAN, GARY FRANCIS, computer science educator; b. Rochester, N.Y., Oct. 22, 1946; s. Edward Donald and Ruth Freda (Lochner) H.; m. Joanne Patsynski, June 21, 1969 (div. 1973); 1 child, John Edward; m. Isabel Nebot-Alemany, May 26, 1979. BS in Indsl. Engrng., Okla. State U., 1972, M. Indsl. Engrng., 1974; MS in Computer Sci., Rochester Inst. Tech., 1990. Asst. prof. computer sci. Alfred (N.Y.) U., 1988-92; pres. Garisa Consulting, Alfred Station, N.Y., 1992—; cons. Gallanter Rsch. Svcs., Mamaroneck, N.Y., 1989—. Author: Thoughts, 1984. Capt. USAF, 1966-86. Alfred U. grantee, 1990. Mem. ACM, Am. Assn. for Artificial Intelligence, Computer Soc. of IEEE, Consortium for Computing in Sml. Colls., Alpha Pi Mu. Republican. Roman Catholic. Home: 5910 State Route 21 Alfred Station NY 14803-9709 Office: Alfred Univ 5921 Rt 21 Alfred Station NY 14803-9709

HASPEL, MARTIN VICTOR, scientist; b. N.Y.C., Aug. 24, 1945; s. Leo A. and Estelle S. (Freeman) H.; m. Linda Strachman, June 12, 1967; 1 child, Moshe. BA, Yeshiva U., 1967; PhD, Pa. State U., 1974. Dir. hybridoma rsch. Biotech. Rsch. Inst., Rockville, Md., 1982—; adj. prof., microbiology U. Md., College Park, 1989—. Patentee in field. Virology fellow Pa. State U. Coll. Medicine, 1974-75, immunopathology fellow and asst. mem. Scripps Clin. Rsch. Inst., La Jolla, Calif., 1975-80, sr. staff fellow NIH, Bethesda, Md., 1980-82. Mem. Am. Soc. Microbiology, Am. Assn. Immunologists, Am. Assn. Pathologists, Am. Assn. Neuropathologists, Am. Assn. Cancer Rsch., Soc. Gen. Microbiology, Irish Setter Club Am., Sierra Club (life), Capital Dog Tng. Club, Potomac Irish Setter Club. Office: Biotech Rsch Inst 1330A Piccard Dr Rockville MD 20850-4330

HASSAN, AFTAB SYED, scientific research director; b. Lahore, Punjab, Pakistan, Apr. 20, 1952; came to U.S., 1976; s. Maqsud Syed and Saliha Aktar Hassan. BSCE with distinction, U. Engring. and Tech., Lahore, 1973; postgrad. in aerodyns., Colo. State U., 1976; MS, George Washington U., 1977; PhD, Columbia Pacific U., 1985. Scientist in ocean, coastal and environ. engrng. George Washington U., 1977-84; tech. asst. George Washington U., Washington, 1979-84, asst. prof., 1980-85; chmn. math. and sci. Emerson Prep. Inst., Washington, 1979-89; acad. coord. Ctr. for Minority Student Affairs, Georgetown U. Med. Sch., Washington, 1983-87; v.p. Met. Acctg. Assocs., Washington, 1987-88; acctg. mgr. Washington Info. Group, 1988-91; owner Met. Acctg. and Rsch., Washington, 1988-91; sr. tech. editor and author Betz Pub. Co., Rockville, Md., 1991—, designer new products, dir. sci. rsch., 1991—; bd. dirs. French Pastries, Inc., Washington, McPherson News and Gift, Washington; rsch. assoc. Chesapeake Bay Tidewater Adminstrn. in Fish Physiology, part-time 1979-88; prof. reasoning and problem solving Sch. for Summer and Continuing Edn., Georgetown U., 1983—; acad. specialist Drew/UCLA Med. Sch. Program, 1985-87; acad. cons. for Grad. Record Exam/Med. Coll. Admission Test, Morgan State U., 1989—. Author: Preparation for the MCAT, 6th edit., 1992, author, editor Betz Pub. Co., Bethesda, Md., 1984—. Mem. ASCE, NSPE, Am. Soc. Engrng. Edn., Am. Inst. Profl. Bookkeepers, Soc. Am. Mil. Engrs., Nat. Soc. Tax Profls., Amnesty International, Habitat for Humanity Internat., Hosp. for Sick Children, Cancervive, The Salvation Army, People for the Ethical Treatment of Animals. Recipient Merit award Nat. Assn. Chiefs of Police, Leaders in Community Svc. award Am. Biog. Inst., 1990. Mem. ASCE, NSPE, Am. Soc. Engrng. Edn., Am. Inst. Profl. Bookkeepers, Soc. Am. Mil. Engrs., Nat. Soc. Tax Profls., Nat. Law Enforcement Acad. (hon. mem.). Home: Ste 291 4401-A Connecticut Ave NW Washington DC 20008

HASSEL, JAMES CRAIG, counselor; b. Wilkes-Barre, Pa., Nov. 15, 1960; s. Robert Ward and Eleanor I. (Krommes) H. BS, King's Coll., Wilkes-Barre, Pa., 1987; MS, U. Scranton, 1990. Cert. rehab. counselor. Peer counselor N.E. Pa. C.I.L., Scranton, 1988-90; rehab. counselor United Rehab. Svcs., Wilkes-Barre, 1990; drug and alcohol counselor Cath. Soc. Svc., Wilkes-Barre, 1990—. Mem. Nat. Rehab. Assn., Nat. Assn. Ind. Living, Nat. Rehab. Counseling Assn., Pa. Rehab. Counseling Assn. (bd. dirs.). Home: 50 Waller St Wilkes Barre PA 18702-3429

HASSETT, CAROL ALICE, psychologist; b. Bklyn., Apr. 19, 1947; d. Joseph and Anna (Portanova) Lusardi; m. John J. Hassett, June 29, 1968; 1 child, John J. BS, St. John's U., 1968; MEd, Hofstra U., 1974, PhD in Psychology, 1981. Cert. advanced emergency med. technician, pre-hosp. critical care technician; permanently cert. tchr., N.Y. Tchr. Day Elem. Sch., Bklyn., 1968-69; psychologist Nassau County Dept. Drug and Alcohol also Mental Health Assn. Nassau County, East Meadow, N.Y., 1981-84; chief supervising psychologist Queens Outreach Project, 1985—; pvt. practice clin. psychology, 1984—; from adj. asst. prof. to adj. assoc. prof. Hofstra U., 1980—. Contbr. articles to profl. jours. Trustee, pres. Malverne (N.Y.) Pub. Libr., 1986—; vice chair, bd. dirs. Malverne Vol. Ambulance Corps, 1976—; bd. govs. Kings County Cadet Corps, 1966-72. Mem. APA, Nassau County Psychol. Assn. (mem. bd. dirs. 1986—). Republican. Roman Catholic. Home: 105 Franklin Ave Malverne NY 11565-1926 Office: 230 Hilton Ave Hempstead NY 11550

HASSETT, JAMES MANNING, small business owner, psychology educator; b. N.Y.C., June 22, 1947; s. John and Jean (Manning) H.; m. Patricia Ann Dugan, Nov. 26, 1977; 1 child, Eileen. BS in Psychology, Fordham U., 1969; MA in Psychology, Harvard U., 1971, PhD in Psychology, 1975. Asst. prof. Wellesley (Mass.) Coll., 1974-75, Boston U., 1974-84; assoc. editor Psychology Today, N.Y.C., 1977-80; cons. editor Addison-Wesley Pub., Reading, Mass., 1984; rsch. psychologist Sci. Systems, Inc., Cambridge, Mass., 1984-85; pres. Brattle Systems, Inc., Arlington, Mass., 1985—; adj. assoc. prof. Boston U., 1985—. Author: A Primer of Psychophysiology, 1978, Psychology in Perspective, 1984, (with others), 2d edit., 1989; contbr. articles to profl. jours. NSF fellow, 1969; recipient Sci. Writers award ADA, 1978. Office: Brattle Systems Inc 927 Massachusetts Ave Arlington MA 02174-4622

HATCH, FREDERICK TASKER, chemicals consultant; b. Boston, Aug. 27, 1924; s. Frederick Southard and Beatrice (Tasker) H.; m. Virginia Weeks, Mar. 3, 1946; children: Daniel F., Daphne A., Deborah J., Douglas E. BA, Dartmouth Coll., 1944; MD, Harvard U., 1948; PhD, MIT, 1960. Diplomate Nat. Bd. Med. Examiners. Intern Roosevelt Hosp., N.Y.C., 1948-49; rsch. fellow Columbia U., N.Y.C., 1949-52; established investigator Am. Heart Assn./Mass. Gen. Hosp., Boston, 1960-65; sr. scientist, sect. leader Lawrence Livermore (Calif.) Nat. Lab., 1965-80, asst. assoc. dir., 1980-87, cons., 1987—; mem. lipid metabolism adv. com. Nat. Heart, Lund and Blood Inst., Bethesda, Md., 1968-73. Assoc. editor Lipids Jour., 1964-73; author chpts. in books; contbr. numerous articles to profl. jours. Secretary Land Conservation Task Force, Meredith, N.H., 1989-90. Capt. USAR, 1952-55. Fellow Am. Inst. Chemists; mem. Am. Chem. Soc., Am. Soc. Biochemistry and Molecular Biology, Environ. Mutagen Soc., Arteriosclerosis Coun. of Am. Heart Assn. (exec. com. 1971-73). Home and Office: 27 Pease Rd Meredith NH 03253-5509

HATCH, MARY WENDELL VANDER POEL, interior decorator, non-profit organization executive; b. N.Y.C., Feb. 6, 1919; d. William Halsted and Blanche Pauline (Billings) Vander Poel; m. George Montagu Miller, Apr. 5, 1940 (div. 1974); children: Wendell Miller Steavenson, Gretchen Miller Elkus; m. Sinclair Hatch, May 14, 1977 (dec. July 1989). Pres. Miller Richard, Inc., Interior Decorators, Glen Head, N.Y., 1972—; bd. dirs. Eye Bank Sight Restoration, N.Y.C., 1975—, pres., 1980-88, hon. chair, 1988—; bd. dirs. Manhattan Eye Ear and Throat Hosp., N.Y.C., 1966—, v.p., 1978-90; sec. Cold Spring Harbor Lab., N.Y., 1985-89, 92—, bd. dirs., 1985-90; chair DNA Learning Ctr., 1991—; bd. dirs. Cold Spring Harbor Lab, 1991—, sec., 1992—. V.p. North Country Garden Club, Nassau County, N.Y., 1979-81, 1983-85; dir. Planned Parenthood Nassau County, Mineola, N.Y., 1982-84, Hutton House C.W. Post Coll., Greenvale, N.Y., 1982—; chair Hutton House, 1992—. Recipient Disting. Trustee award United Hosp. Fund, 1992. Mem. Colony Club (N.Y.C.), Church Club (N.Y.C.), Piping Rock Club (Long Island), Order St. John Jerusalem (N.Y.C.). Republican. Episcopalian. Home: Mill River Rd # 330 Oyster Bay NY 11771-2712

HATCH, PATRICIA ANN, banker; b. Keene, N.H., Dec. 15, 1950; d. David and Gladys Marie (Guertin) Peaks; m. William W. Hatch, Feb. 21, 1981; children: Kathleen Marie, John Thomas. Assoc., Becker Jr. Coll., 1970; grad., Maine/N.H./Vt. Sch. Banking, 1981. Sec. Vt. Nat. Bank Brattleboro, 1970-72, Baybutt Constrn. Corp., Keene, N.H., 1972-73; exec. sec. Cheshire County Savs. Bank, Keene, 1973-81, dir. retirement accounts, 1981-84, retirement accounts officer, 1984-91; asst. v.p. retirement accts., 1991—. Recipient Elden J. Murray Meml. award Maine-N.H. Sch. Savs. Banking, 1981. Mem. VFW Aux., Fin. Women Internat. Congregationalist. Office: Cheshire County Savs Bank 194 W St PO Box # 746 Keene NH 03431

HATFIELD, THOMAS BARLOW, manufacturing company executive; b. Indpls., Oct. 28, 1933; s. Thomas F. and Kathleen D. (Ziegler) H.; m. Edith A. Arnold, Jan. 24, 1959; children: Sharon M., Kenneth S., Michael A. BSME, Purdue U., 1956; Cert. Indsl. Mgmt., Worcester Poly., 1977-81. Proposal engr. Cincinnati Milacron-Heald, Worcester, Mass., 1956-64; regional sales mgr. Cincinnati Milacron-Heald, Brussels, Belgium, 1964-69; mktg. mgr. Cincinnati Milacron-Heald, Biggleswade, Eng., 1969-74, Worcester, 1974-88; v.p. mktg. Moore Spl. Tool Co., Inc., Bridgeport, Conn., 1988-91; v.p. sales and mktg. Fellows Corp., Springfield, Vt., 1991—; tech. advisor automated mfg. equip. tactical adv. com. U.S. Dept. Commerce, Washington, 1989—. With U.S. Army, 1956-58. Republican. Roman Catholic. Home: 32 Pinewood Village West Lebanon NH 03784 Office: Fellows Corp Precision Dr PO Box 851 Springfield VT 05156

HATHAWAY, CARMRID GLASTON, horseman, real estate investor; b. Tarboro, N.C., Feb. 8, 1922; s. Carmrid Glaston and Estelle (Pittman) H.; m. Margaret Tryphena Deese, June 20, 1944; children: Joyce Elaine, Carmrid Glaston III. Student, George Washington U., 1941-42, Naval Air Tng. Ctr., 1944; BS in Mil. Sci. and Bus. Adminstrn., U. Md., 1971. Lic. pilot, real estate, Md. Enlisted USN, 1942, advanced through grades to capt., 1965, ret., 1975; comdg. officer naval air sta. USN, Grosse Ile, Mich., 1967-69; comdg. officer naval tng. ctr. USN, Washington, 1972-75; pres. Harness Racing Inc., Suitland, Md., 1975—; chmn. bd. dirs. Activities Investments, Inc., Washington; adv. com. Md. Standardbred Race Fund; mem. Md. Racing Commn., 1984-85. Adv. com. Md. Racing Commn., 1984-85; mem. Md. Standard Bred Race Fund, 1984-85. Mem. Ret. Officers Assn., U.S. Trotting Assn., Standard Bread Breeders Md. (bd. dirs. 1980-), Standardbred Race Fund (adv. com), Md. Harness Horseman's Assn. (bd. dirs. 1979-), Cloverleaf Standard Bred Owners Assn., U. Md. Alumni Assn. Internat. Baptist. Club: Commd. Officers (Andrews AFB, Md. and Washington D.C.). Home: 4406 Ridgecrest Dr Suitland MD 20746-3750 Office: Activities Investments Inc 3352 Upland Ter NW Washington DC 20015-2445

HATHEWAY, ROBERT JAMES, association executive, human resources consultant; b. Springfield, Mass., June 2, 1946; s. Ralph MacClean and Jeanne Ann (Provost) H.; m. Margaret Mary Coffey, July 19, 1969; children: David, Kate. BS, Boston U., 1968, MS, 1971. Exec. asst. Mass. Dept. Pub. Welfare, Boston, 1976-77; asst. dir. Office for Children, Boston, 1977-80; exec. dir. Assn. Tng. and Employment Profls., Inc., Windsor Locks, Conn., 1980—, New England Community Action Assn., Windsor Locks, 1980—, Low Income Planning Agy., Hartford, Conn., 1981-86; pres. RJH Assocs., Windsor Locks, 1986—; engring. analyst Pratt & Whitney Aircraft, East Hartford, Conn., 1968-69; mem. housing fin. agy. Commonwealth of Mass., Boston, 1974-79; mem. adv. coun. on vocat. edn. State of Conn., Hartford, 1985-86. Author: Changes in Zoning, 1975, Contemporary Direction in Human Resource Management, 1990; editor Thrust, 1981-88; polit. editor Holyoke Transcript-Telegram, 1969-73. Dir. govtl. and pub. rels. Mass. Mcpl. Assn., Boston, 1973-76; dir. United Labor Orgn., Hartford, 1986—; active United Cerebral Palsey South Cen. Conn., Wallingford, 1991. With U.S. Army, 1968-74. Named Outstanding Contbr., Mass. Mayor Assn., 1976. Democrat. Home: 50 Bretton Rd West Springfield MA 01089 Office: Assn Tng and Employment Profls Inc 56 Main St PO Box 636 Windsor Locks CT 06096

HATKOFF, CRAIG MITCHELL, real estate executive, educator; b. Albany, N.Y., Mar. 19, 1954; s. Leon and Doris (Wildove) H. BA magna cum laude, Colgate U., 1976; MBA, Columbia U., 1978. Mng. dir. Chem. Bank, N.Y.C., 1978-89; mng. ptnr. Victor Capital Group, N.Y.C., 1989—; adj. prof. bus. Columbia U., N.Y.C., 1990—. Mem. Albany Academy (nat. adv. bd.), Columbia Bus. Sch. Alumni Assn. (bd. dirs.), Phi Beta Kappa. Office: Victor Capital Group 885 3rd Ave New York NY 10022-4834

HATSOPOULOS, GEORGE NICHOLAS, mechanical engineer, thermodynamicist, educator; b. Athens, Greece, Jan. 7, 1927; came to U.S., 1948, naturalized, 1954; s. Nicholas and Maria (Platsis) Hatzopoulos; m. Daphne Phylactopoulos, June 14, 1959; children: Nicholas, Marina. Student, Nat. Tech. U., Athens, 1945-47; BS, MS, MIT, 1950, ME, 1954, ScD, 1956; ScD (hon.), N.J. Inst. Tech., 1982; LHD (hon.), U. Lowell, 1991. Instr. MIT, 1954-56, asst. prof. mech. engrng., 1956-58, assoc. prof., 1959-63, sr. lectr. in mech. engrng., 1963-90; founder, pres. CEO, chmn. bd. dirs. Thermo Electron Corp.; developer, mgr. and marketer products based on thermodynamic technologies of heat transfer and energy conversion, Waltham, Mass., 1956; mem. governing coun. Nat. Acad. Engring, Nat. Assn. for Engrs.; mem. adv. bd. program tech. and econ policy Kennedy Sch. Govt., Harvard U.; exec. com. Nat. Bur. Econ. Rsch., mem. govs. adv. coun. on econ. growth and tech.; adv. coun. The Internat. Ctr. in N.Y., Inc.. Author: Principles of General Thermodynamics, 1965, Thermionic Energy Conversion, vol. 1, 1973, vol. 2, 1979; contbr. numerous articles to profl. jours. Bd. dirs. Bolt Beranek & Newman, Maliotis Found., Ctr. for Policy Rsch., Am. Coun. for Capital Found., Congl. Econ. Leadership Inst.; dir. NRC Bd. on Sci., Tech., Econ. Policy, 1990-92; vice chmn. Am. Bus. Conf.; trustee Boston Mus. Sci.; chmn. Fed. Res. Bank Boston, 1988-89; chmn. Coll. Yr. in Athens, Inc.; corp. mem., 1987-92; tech. witness numerous Senate and Congl. Hearings. Recipient Am. Achievement Golden Plate award, 1961, Corp. Leadership award MIT, 1980, Master Entrepreneur Inc. award, 1989, Businessperson of the Yr., New Eng. Bus. Mag., 1989, Inventor of the Yr., Boston Mus. Sci., 1990, Entrepreneurship award Internat. Ctr. in N.Y.C., 1991, Medallion for entrepreneurship Beta Gamma Sigma, U. Lowell, 1992. Fellow IEEE, AIAA, ASME (chmn. exec. com. div. energetics 1968-69), Nat. Acad. Engring., Am. Acad. Ars and Scis.; mem. Sigma Xi, Pi Tau Sigam (Gold medal award 1960), Sigma Chi, Beta Gamma Sigma (Medallion for Entrepreneurship). Greek Orthodox. Home: Tower Rd Lincoln MA 01773-3210 Office: Thermo Electron Corp 81 Wyman St Waltham MA 02254-9046

HATTEN, MARK WILLIAM, computer hardware-software company executive; b. Newark, Oct. 17, 1957; s. William and Gertrude (Hayes) H.; m. Marion Clarke, May 31, 1987. BS Elec. Engring. Tech., Thomas Edison State U., 1992. Cust engr. IBM, Lyndhurst, N.J., 1979-80; tooting engr. IBM Semiconductor, Essex June, Vt., 1980-81; with instrumentation ITT DCD, Clifton, N.J., 1981-89, ATE engr., 1989; systems engr. ATT, 1989-90, prodn. mgr., 1991—. Home: 145 Lincoln St Montclair NJ 07042-4429

HATTIS, PHILIP DAVID, aerospace engineer; b. Chgo., July 18, 1952; s. Bernard Sidney and Janis (Wolfson) H.; m. Beverly Kardon, June 27, 1981; 1 child, Valerie. BSME, Northwestern U., Evanston, Ill., 1973; MS in Aeronautics, Calif. Tech. Inst., Pasadena, 1974; PhD in Aeronautics/Astronautics, MIT, 1980. Draper Fellow C.S. Draper Lab., Inc., Cambridge, Mass., 1974-80, tech. staff, 1980-81, prog. mgr., 1981-85, sect. chief, 1985-88, div. staff, 1988—. Co-editor: (newsletter) Aerospace New Eng., 1988-91; contbr. articles to profl. jours. Fellow AIAA (assoc., chmn. New Eng. sect. 1989-90, treas. 1987-88, coun. dir. 1984-87, space systems tech. com. 1990—), AAAS, ASME, Soc. Aerospace Engrs. (com. 1987—); mem. Sigma Xi, Tau Beta Pi. Office: CS Draper Lab Inc 555 Technology Sq # 4E Cambridge MA 02139-3563

HATTON, DONALD H., product service executive; b. Chgo., Jan. 11, 1938; s. Coy Z. and Christine (Fabry) H.; m. Arlene Rose Evangelos, Oct. 22, 1961; children: Mark, Phillip, Denise. Diploma in electronic tech., DeVry Tech., 1959; assoc. in acctg., Wright Coll., 1961. Design engr. U.S. Berkel, La Porte, Ind., 1959-61; computer engr. Allstate Ins. Co., Niles, Ill., 1961-66; mgr. publ. and tng. Warwick Electronics, Niles, 1966-76; dir. svcs. Sanyo

Mfg., Forrest City, Ark., 1977-83; staff v.p. Electronic Industries Assn., Washington, 1983—. With U.S. Army, 1961-63. Mem. Internat. Vocat. Orgn. (U.S. tech. del. 1985—), Vocat. Indsl. Clubs of Am. (exec. steering com. 1990—, amb. 1986—). Office: Electronic Industries Assn 2001 Pennsylvania Ave NW Washington DC 20006-1813

HATZES, ROBERT LOUIS, JR., decorative table linens company executive; b. Washington, June 23, 1953; s. R. Louis and Maylou (Renaud) H.; m. Korry Kay Ovian, Mar. 6, 1982; children: Robert K., Nicholas G., Nina M. BSBA, Butler U., 1974. Freelance photographer Washington, 1976-80; catering mgr. Sue Fisher Caterers, Rockville, Md., 1980-81; entrepeneur Party Cloths Inc., Bethesda, Md., 1982—. Republican. Office: Party Cloths Inc 2426 Linden Ln # 204 Silver Spring MD 20910

HAUBER, PATRICIA ANNE, educator; b. Phila., Feb. 16, 1953; d. Frederick Joseph and Dorothy Marie (Delaney) Hauber. AA, Montgomery County Community, Blue Bell, Pa., 1973; BS, Bloomsburg U., 1975; MEd, Lehigh U., 1985, elem. prin. cert., secondary prin. cert., 1990. Tchr. North Penn Sch. Dist., Lansdale, Pa., 1975-85; sci. coord., tchr. St. Jude Sch., Chalfont, Pa., 1985—. Instr., trainer ARC, CPR programs, Lansdale, Pa., 1979—. Mem. AAAS, ASCD, Pa. Sci. Tchrs. Assn., Pa. Assn. for Supervision and Curriculum Devel., Phi Delta Kappa. Democrat. Roman Catholic. Home: 391 Huckleberry Ln Harleysville PA 19438-2334 Office: St Jude Sch 323 W Butler Ave Chalfont PA 18914-2329

HAUCK, NEIL TOD, architect; b. Babylon, N.Y., Apr. 9, 1954; s. William John and Ingrid Martha (Hellmers) H.; m. Ann Frances Banks, June 18, 1978; children: Megan Ann, Peter Tod. BSE in Civil Engring., Princeton U., 1976; M Architecture, U. Va., 1979. Registered architect, N.Y., Conn.; nat. cert. archtl. registration bds. Draftsman Donald A. Swofford, Architect, Charlottesville, Va., 1979-80; designer Kevin Roche John Dinkeloo and Assocs., Hamden, Conn., 1980-83; assoc. David Bruce Falconer and Assocs., Darien, Conn., 1983-84; ptnr. Falconer Scofield and Hauck Architects, Darien, 1984-88; pres. and founder Neil Hauck Architects, P.C., Darien, 1988—; commr. Conn. Soc. of Architects Edn. Commn., New Haven, Conn., 1992-94. Dir. Darien C. of C. Bd. Dirs., 1990—; chmn. 1st Ch. Congregational Bd. of Music, Fairfield, Conn., 1991-92; mem. Princeton U. Alumni Schs. Com. Recipient 10/10 and Under Exhbn. award, Design award Conn. Soc. Architects/AIA, 1990. Mem. AIA, Nat. Trust for Hist. Preservation, Conn. Soc. of Architects, Rotary Internat. of Darien. Home: 86 Lalley Blvd Fairfield CT 06430-6604 Office: Neil Hauck Architects PC 859 Post Rd Darien CT 06820-4603

HAUCK, RICHARD HENRY, science educator; b. Harrisburg, Pa., Apr. 19, 1930; s. George Washington and Kathryn Irene (Daniels) H.; m. Gilda Tan, Jan. 19, 1977; children: Richard Daniels, Richelle Kathryn, Richenda Elaine. BS, Shippensburg State Coll., 1957; MSc, U. Bridgeport, 1963; EdD in Secondary Edn., Wade Hampton Coll., 1989. Tchr. pub. schs., L.A., 1957-59, Harrisburg, Pa., 1959-61, Conn., 1961-74, Morgan City, La., 1979-82, Dillsburg, Pa., 1984-85; with S.E. Asia sci. edn. survey South Korea, The Philippines, Hong Kong, Malaysia, Borneo, 1974-77; instr. Prin. Tech. DCTS, Harrisburg, 1986-87; substitute tchr. Cumberland County Schs., 1987-90; sci. tchr. York Springs Sch. System, Pa., 1990-91; chemist rsch. and devel. staff Gen. Dynamics Corp., 1964-65; fgn. edn. mgr. Clinton (Conn.) Nat. Bank, 1964-66; cons. fed. edn. projects LEARN and MONIES; audio-visual and ednl. closed circuit TV dir. Montville-Groton Pub. Sch. (Conn.), 1965-69; pres. Ednl. Research Assocs., Old Saybrook, Conn., 1969-79, Morgan City, La., 1979-82, Mechanicsburg, Pa., 1982-85; instr. chemistry and physics U.S. Nat. Def. Cadet Corps, New Bloomfield, Pa., 1982-84; v.p. Hauck Bros. Ltd., Mechanicsburg, Pa., 1979-86. Editor: Raintree Illustrated Sci. Ency., 1978-80 . Liaison Middlesex Sch. and Cumberland Valley Bd. Edn., 1990-91; bd. dirs. World Monies Mus. With Pa.NG, 1947-56, USAF, 1952-53, U.S. Army, 1982-84. Recipient Recognition cert. Pa. State Sci. Fair., 1960. Mem. AAAS, NEA, Nat. Sci. Tchrs. Assn., Pa. State Ednl. Assn., Gt. Ea. Numis. Assn., New Eng. Numis. Assn. (bd. dirs.), N.Y. Acad. Scis., Conn. Ednl. Media Assn. (founding mem.), Am. Legion (life), Mensa (exec. com., ednl. proctor, deputy LOCSEC 1991—), SAR, Lions (charter Tiger Island club), Masons. Republican. Episcopalian. Office: PO Box 1366 Mechanicsburg PA 17055-1366

HAUCK, WILLIAM EDWARD, education educator, psychologist; b. Pa., July 5, 1932; s. Lewis William and Margaret Alice (Freas) H. BS in Math. and Physics, U. Pitts., 1954, MEd in Edn. Psychology, 1962; PhD in Counseling & Edn. Psychology, U. Wis., Madison, 1969. Cert. tchr. in English, math., phys. scis., social studies; cert. sch. psychology, counseling, Pa.; lic. psychologist, Pa. Dir., overseas adult edn. Armed Svcs., Kassel, Fed. Republic Germany, 1954-57; tchr., math. and English Churchill Area Schs., Pitts., 1957-61; rsch. assoc. Bucknell U., Lewisburg, Pa., 1961-63; rsch. assoc., teaching asst. U. Wis., Madison, 1963-67; assoc. coord., Project SESAME-Title III Bucknell U., Lewisburg, Pa., 1967-69, prof. edn., 1969—; psychologist Five-County Psychol. Svcs., Lewisburg, Pa., 1985—. Author: Fractions, 1966, Decimals and Percents, 1966, Review of Trigonometry, 1968; co-author: (manual) Brief Algebra Review Manual, 1967, Algebra Review Manual, 1967; reviewer Harper Collins Publishers, 1990—; contbr. numerous rsch. articles to refereed jours. With U.S. Army, 1954-56. Recipient Lindback award, Bucknell U. Mem. Am. Ednl. Rsch. Assn. (div. rsch. and instrn., div. counseling), APA (div. sch. psychology, div. counseling), Nat. Assn. Sch. Psychologists. Home: RD 1 Box 138-C Danville PA 17821 Office: Bucknell U Lewisburg PA 17837

HAUFT, AMY GILBERT, artist; b. Cin., Apr. 9, 1957; d. Neil Edward and Eleanor (Snyder) H. BFA, U. Calif., Santa Cruz, 1980; postgrad., Skowhegan Sch. Painting, Maine, 1981; MFA, Art Inst. Chgo., 1983. asst. prof. Tyler Sch. Art, Phila., 1989—; vis. lectr. Princeton (N.J.) U., 1989; vis. artist Calif. Inst. Arts, Valencia, 1988. Exhibited in group shows including Mus. Contemporary Art, Chgo., 1987, ArtPark, Lewiston, N.Y., 1988, Bklyn. Mus., 1990, and in one-woman shows including P.S.I. Mus., Long Island, 1987, New Mus., N.Y.C., 1989, Contemporary Arts Forum, Santa Barbara, Calif., 1990, Ctr. for Arts Wesleyan U., Middletown, Conn., 1990, Berland/Hall Gallery, N.Y.C., 1991. Grantee Flintridge Found., 1989, Artmatters, Inc., 1989, 88, ArtPark, 1988, N.Y. State Coun. Arts, 1987. Studio: 1155 Manhattan Ave Brooklyn NY 11222

HAUGE, RICHARD ANDREW, attorney, state senator; b. Wilmington, Del., Feb. 9, 1956; s. Erling B. and Louise Mills (Faircloth) H.; m. Rhonda Ann Denny, Jan. 2, 1981; children: Andrew Jr., Ryan Alexander. BS in Acctg., U. Del., 1977; JD, Duke U., 1981. Bar: Del. 1981, U.S. Dist. Ct. Del. 1983, U.S. Ct. Appeals (3d cir.) 1988. Assoc. Funk, Franta & Hauge, Newark, Del., 1981-85; first asst. county atty. New Castle County, Wilmington, 1985-86, county atty., 1986-89; assoc. The Linpro Co., Wilmington, 1989-90, Green, Ward & Krapf, Wilmington, 1990—; mem. Del. Senate, 1988—. Republican. Office: Del State Senate Legislative Hall Dover DE 19901 also: Green Ward & Krapf 3801 Kennett Pike Ste D-200 PO Box 3700 Wilmington DE 19807

HAUGE, SHARON KAYE, mathematician, educator; b. Gt. Bend, Kans., July 7, 1943; d. Marguerite (Salmans) Horyna. BA, Ft. Hays State U., 1964; MS in Math., Okla. State U., 1966; PhD in Math., Am. U., 1976, MSTM in Ops. Rsch., 1982. Mathematician U.S. Naval Rsch. Lab., Washington, 1969-72; prof. math. U. D.C., Washington, 1977—; adj. prof. math. Am. U., Washington, 1977—; systems cons. Author: Mathematics in the Marketplace, 1988, (textbook series) Solving World Problems in Mathematics, 1982; contbr. articles to profl. jours. resource person D.C. Pub. Schs., 1986—; vol. to homeless lst Bapt. Ch., Silver Spring, Md. Mem. Math. Assn. Am., Am. Math. Soc., Assn. for Women Mathematicians. Office: U DC Dept Math 4200 Connecticut Ave NW Washington DC 20008-1174

HAUGHTON, DOMINIQUE MARIE ANNICK, statistician, educator; b. Neuilly, Hauts de Seine, France, May 4, 1955; came to U.S., 1978; d. Paul Denis Raoul and Monique (Tixier) Boudier; m. Jonathan Henry Haughton, Sept. 18, 1979. Math. Maitrise, Paris VII U., 1976, Math. DEA, 1977; PhD in Math., MIT, 1984. Mem. Ecole Normale Supérieure, Paris, 1975-78, 79-80; teaching asst. MIT, Cambridge, Mass., 1979-83; asst. prof. Swarthmore (Pa.) Coll., 1983-84, Temple U., Phila., 1987-91; assoc. prof. math. Bentley Coll., Waltham, Mass., 1991—. Translator, Springer Verlag, Heidelberg, Fed. Republic Germany, Siam, Phila., Plenum, N.Y.C., Birkhauser, Cambridge, 1982—. Sachs Found. scholar Harvard U., 1978-79. Mem. Am. Statis. Assn., Am. Math. Soc., Inst. Math. Stats., Math. Assn. Am. Office: Bentley Coll Dept Math Scis Waltham MA 02154

HAUKE, PAUL RICHARD, management consultant; b. Orange, N.J., Apr. 24, 1951; s. Rudolph Benedict and Helen Clementine (Pecci) H.; m. Sophie Ann Harcar, Nov. 12, 1977; children: Matthew Blake, Pamela Lynn, Eric Jordan. BA, Monmouth Coll., 1973, MBA, 1976. Registered pub. acct., N.J. Pres. Pacryn Enterprises, Oakhurst, N.J., 1971-73, Sense Appeal Dimensions Internat., N.Y.C., 1973-75; auction-appraisal assoc. O. Rundell Gilbert Garrison, Hudson, N.Y., 1975-77, B.G. Coates Assoc., Rumson, N.J., 1975-77; mktg. and sales cons. Di Feo/Hagen Dealer Group, N.J., 1977-81; pres. Arapex Chem. Co., Asbury Park, N.J., 1981-86; gen. mgr. Interstate Mgmt. Assocs., Toms River, N.J., 1986-89; pres. Am. Bus. Concepts, Point Pleasant, N.J., 1989—; cons. U.S. Auto Fleet Sales/Rental Car Buy Back Programs, Margolis/Chase/Neuer, Verona, N.J., Dunn, Pashman, et al, Hackensack, N.J., 1991—; bd. dirs. Royce Real Estate Partnerships, Freehold, N.J. Author: Hotel/Motel Sales Hotel Motel Banquets Sales Manual, 1984, Telecommunication Marketing Phone Technology Today, 1989, Consumer Satisfaction Indexes CSI Improvement Guide, 1991. Organizer voter registration drive, Monmouth County, N.J., 1974—, local work incentive programs, Monmouth County, 1977—; participant Landlord/Tenant Rev., Monmouth and Ocean Counties, N.J., 1980—. Recipient Hon. Mention, W.F. Cody and Co., 1985; named Bus. Planner of the Yr., A&M Mgmt., 1986. Mem. Am. Mgmt. Assn. N.Y., Assn. MBA Execs. N.Y., Nat. Auto Dealers Assn. (assoc.), Nat. Auctioneers Assn. Nebr. Office: Am Bus Concepts Inc 145 South St (Rt 79) Freehold NJ 07728

HAUPTMAN, HERBERT AARON, mathematician, educator, researcher; b. N.Y.C., Feb. 14, 1917; s. Israel and Leah (Rosenfeld) H.; m. Edith Citrynell, Nov. 10, 1940; children: Barbara, Carol Hauptman Fullerton. BS in Math., CCNY, 1937; MA, Columbia U., 1939; PhD, U. Md., 1955, PhD (hon.), 1985; PhD (hon.), CCNY, 1986, U. Parma, Italy, 1989, D'Youville Coll., 1989, Bar-Ilan U., Israel, 1990, Columbia U., 1990. Statistician U.S. Census Bur., Washington, 1940-42; civilian instr. electronics and radar U.S. Army Air Force, Boca Raton, Fla., 1942-43, 46-47; physicist, mathematician Naval Rsch. Lab., Washington, 1947-70; head math. biophysics lab. Med. Found., 1970-72, exec. v.p., rsch. dir., 1972-85; pres., res. dir. Med. Fedn. Buffalo, 1985-87, pres., 1988—; also bd. dirs., 1972—; prof. biophys. sci. SUNY, Buffalo, 1970—, chmn. bd. dirs.; with N.Y. State Inst. on Superconductivity, 1988—; mem. sci. adv. bd. BioCryst, 1989—; math. instr. U. Md., 1958-70; chmn. Inter Congress Symposium Direct Methods in Crystallography, Buffalo, 1976; pres. Assn. Ind. Rsch. Insts., 1979, 80, mem. nominating com., 1982; mem. U.S.A. Nat. Com. for Crystallography, 1979-81, 82-85, 88, 89; mem. nat. adv. com. Comprehensive Regional Ctr. for Minorities CCNY, 1989—; mem. adv. bd. for disting. scientist. Author: (with J. Karle) Solution of the Phase Problem., 1953, Crystal Structure Determination: The Role of the Cosine Seminvariants, 1972, Dir. Methods in Crystallography, Proceeding of the 1976 Intercongress Symposium, 1978; contbr. chpts. to books, articles to profl. jours. Trustee Buffalo Gen. Hosp., 1990—; chmn. communications com. Philos. Soc. Washington, 1966-67, corr. sec., 1967-69, pres., 1969-70. Served to lt. (jg.) USNR, 1943-46. Sr. fellow for Travel, Lectures and Rsch. in Italy NATO, 1973; grantee NSF, 1972-92; recipient Belden prize (gold medal) in Math., 1935, RESA award in Pure Scis., 1959, Citizen of Yr. award Buffalo Evening News, 1986, Schoelkopf award Am. Chem. Soc., 1986, Gold Plate award Am.Acad. Achievement, 1986, Nat. Libr. Medicine medal, 1986, Law Sch. award Maimomides Chabad House, 1986, others, (with J. Karle) Patterson award, 1984, Nobel Prize in Chemistry, 1985; honoree Western New York Man of Yr. Buffalo C. of C., 1986, YMCA Dinner, 1986, 90th Nobel Ann. Dinner, 1991; inductee Nobel Hall Sci. Mus. Sci. and Industry, 1986, Townsend Harris Hall Fame, 1989; guest of honor Roswell Park Meml. Inst., 1985, YMCA Luncheon, 1986, others; invited guest Am. Nobel Convocation, 1987, 88, Weizmann Nat. Dinner, 1988, others. Fellow Washington Acad. Scis., Jewish Acad. Arts and Scis. (medal 1986); mem. AAAS, Am. Math. Soc., Am. Phys. Soc., Am. Crystallographic Assn. (mem. Fankuchen award com. 1988), Math. Assn. Am., U.S. Nat. Acad. Scis., Cosmos Club, Saturn Club (guest of honor 1985), Sigma Xi (sec. Buffalo chpt. 1971-72), Phi Beta Kappa. Office: Med Found Buffalo 73 High St Buffalo NY 14203-1196

HAUPTMAN, LAURENCE MARC, history educator; b. N.Y.C., May 18, 1945; s. David and Frieda (Landesman) H.; m. Ruth Jacobs, May 23, 1970; children: Beth, Eric. BA, NYU, 1966, MA, 1968, PhD, 1971. Instr. SUNY, New Paltz, 1971-73, asst. prof., 1973-77, assoc. prof., 1977-82, prof., 1982—; hist. cons. for Am. Indian nations including Pequot Tribe of Conn., 1987, Oneida Nation of Wis., 1986, Seneca Nation of Indians, N.Y., 1985; expert witness Senate select com. on Indian Affairs, U.S. Congress, 1990, House subcom. on interior and insular affairs, 1990. Author: The Iroquois & the New Deal, 1981, The Iroquois Struggle for Survival, 1986, Formulating American Indian Policy in New York State, 1988; editor: Neighbors & Intruders, 1978, The Oneida Indian Experience: Two Perspectives, 1988, The Pequots in Southern New England, 1990, The Iroquois Indians and the Civil War: From Battlefield to Reservation, 1992. Recipient Peter Doctor Meml. award Peter Doctor Fellowship Found. of Iroquois Indians, 1987, NYS-UUP Award for Excellence in Teaching, 1991. Mem. Am. Hist. Assn., Orgn. Am. Historians, Western History Assn., Am. Soc. for Ethnohistory, N.Y. State Hist. Assn., Am. Soc. for State & Local History, Pa. Hist. Assn. Home: 2 Sarafian Rd New Paltz NY 12561-3816

HAUPTMAN, THEODORE, lawyer; b. Detroit, July 11, 1952; s. Isadore and Eva (Stanaslowski) H.; m. Maureen Mary Choder, June 15, 1974; children: Jonathan Evan, Adam Craig, Allyson Ivy. BS, Phila. Coll. Textiles and Scis., 1974; JD, U. Detroit, 1978. Bar: Pa., 1978, U.S. Dist. Ct. (ea. dist.) Pa. 1978. Asst. mgr. Robert Bruce Inc., Phila., 1974-75; assoc. Allen Rothenberg Law Offices, Phila., 1978-79, Sacks & Basch Assocs., Phila., 1979-80, Ronald Abrams Law Offices, Phila., 1980-81, Kreithen, Baron & Miller, Phila., 1981-87; ptnr. Miller, Hauptman & Melvin, Phila., 1987—. Articles editor U. Detroit Law Rev., 1976-78. Mem. Phila. Bar. Assn. (mem. lawyer reference com. 1985-87, arbitration com. 1985-87), Del. County Bar Assn., Phila. Trial Lawyers Assn. Republican. Jewish. Lodges: B'nai B'rith. Home: 29 Penn Cir Southampton PA 18966-2339 Office: Miller Hauptman & Melvin 1234 Market St Philadelphia PA 19107-3727

HAUSER, CARL, architect; b. Williamsport, Pa., Apr. 27, 1949; s. Carl William and Clara Jane (Vollman) H.; m. Corinne Calesso, Sept. 18, 1983. BArch., U. Ariz., 1972; MArch., U. Ill., 1974. Registered profl. architect N.Y., Calif. Asst. prof. U.N.C., Charlotte, 1974-77; assoc. The Arroyo Group, Pasadena, Calif., 1977-78; project architect Robinson, Mills & Williams, San Francisco, 1978-81; project mgr. Perkins & Will, N.Y.C., 1981-84; project dir. Swanke, Hayden, Connell Architects, N.Y.C., 1985-90; prin. CRSS Architects, Inc., L.A., 1991; constrn. mgmt. cons. Mayor's Office Dir. of Constrn., N.Y.C., 1992—; adj. assoc. prof. N.Y. Inst. Tech.; adj. faculty N.Y. Sch. Interior Design, N.Y.C. Mem. AIA, Met. Ctr., Nat. Inst. for Archtl. Edn., Assn. Collegiate Schs. of Architecture. Democrat. Home: 1192 1st Ave Apt 6-E New York NY 10021

HAUSER, CHRISTOPHER GEORGE, lawyer; b. Syracuse, N.Y., May 5, 1954; s. W. Dieter and Nancy (Keating) H. BA, Washington & Jefferson Coll., 1976; JD, Dickinson Sch. Law, 1979. Bar: Pa. 1979, U.S. Dist. Ct. (we. dist.) Pa. 1981, N.Y. 1987, U.S. Supreme Ct. 1992. Legal asst. Pa. Dept. of Justice, Harrisburg, 1978-79; assoc. McDowell, McDowell, Wick & Daly, Bradford, 1979-83, ptnr., 1983—; broker, owner Re/Max Alpine Sales, Ellicottville, N.Y., 1991—; pres. Alpine Sales and Rental Mgmt., Inc., Ellicottville, N.Y., 1987—; chmn. adv. bd. Office Econ. Community Devel., Bradford, 1988—. Chmn. campaign Bradford Area United Way, 1984, v.p. 1987-89, pres., 1990-92; chmn. Downtown Bradford Revitalization Corp., 1986—, Bradford Parking Authority, 1986—; pres. Alleghany Highlands coun. Boy Scouts Am., Falconer, N.Y., 1986-88, Bradford Area Jaycees, 1983-85; dir. Bradford Econ. Devel. Corp., 1987—, Exchange Club, 1989—. Recipient Outstanding Svc. award Bradford Area United Way, 1985, Silver Beaver award Allehany Highlands coun. Boy Scouts Am., 1990, Founder's award Order Arrow Boy Scouts Am., 1991; named Bus. Person of Yr. Bradford C. of C., 1986, One of Outstanding Young Men of Am. U.S. Jaycees, 1983. Mem. N.Y. Bar Assn., Pa. Bar Assn., McKean County Bar Assn. (treas. 1984-86), Pennhills Club (sec. 1985-90, pres. 1990-92), Bradford Club. Republican. Episcopalian. Home: 104 Congress St Bradford PA 16701-2228 Office: McDowell Wick Daly Gallup Hauser & Hartle 50 Boylston St PO Box 361 Bradford PA 16701

HAUSER, STEWART BARRY, customs broker; b. N.Y.C., Mar. 1, 1942; s. David and Mary (Rapapport) H.; m. Zoe L. Hauser, Mar. 25, 1978 (div. Dec. 1990); children: David, Rebecca. AB, Brown U., 1963; MBA, NYU, 1968. Pres. D. Hauser Inc., N.Y.C., 1964—. Mem. Nat. Brokers Assn. (chairperson 1990, pres.), N.Y. Brokers Assn. (v.p. 1990). Jewish. Office: D Hauser Inc Ste 1951 One World Trade Ctr New York NY 10048

HAUSER, WILLARD ALLEN, neurology and epidemiology educator; b. Cleve., Mar. 6, 1937; s. Willard E. and Annabelle (Garnett) H.; m. Leeana Belle Gregory, June 13, 1963 (div. 1986); children: Bernard, Rachel, Michael. AB, Western Res. U., 1958; MD, St. Louis U., 1962; postgrad., Northwestern U., 1962-66, Mayo Grad. Sch., 1968-70. Rsch. asst. Mayo Clinic, Rochester, Minn., 1968-69, rsch. assoc., 1969-70; asst. prof. U. Minn., Mpls., 1970-74, assoc. prof., 1974-79; assoc. prof. Columbia U., N.Y.C., 1979-84, prof. neurology/epidemiology, 1984—; cons. NIH, Washington, 1972—; mem. com. Internat. League Against Epilepsy, Brussels, 1988—; sr. vis. scientist Mayo Grad. Sch., 1980—. Author books in field; editor rsch. articles. Mem. profl. adv. bd. Epilepsy Found. Am., Washington, 1987—, N.Y. Epilepsy Assn., N.Y.C., 1982-86. Capt. U.S. Army, 1966-68. Grantee NIH, 1969—, Epilepsy Found. Am., 1979—; NATO/Italian CNR fellow, 1990-92. Fellow Am. Acad. Neurology, Am. Neurol. Assn., Am. Epilepcy Soc., Am. Epidemiology Soc. Office: Columbia U 630 W 168th St New York NY 10032-3702

HAUSMAN, HOWARD, electronics executive; b. N.Y.C., July 4, 1945; s. Edward A. and Bella (Bloom) H.; divorced; children: Lawrence Stuart, Bradley Russel. BSEE, Poly. Inst. N.Y., 1967, MSEE, 1971. Computer programmer Harry Kahn Assocs., Great Neck, N.Y., 1965-67; engr. Airborne Instruments Lab., Deer Park, N.Y., 1967-72; dept. head Miteq Inc., Hauppauge, N.Y., 1972-81; pres. Labred Electronics Corp., Bohemia, N.Y., 1981—; mem. tech. cons. com., local adv. counsel 2d supervisory dist. Bd. Coop. Ednl. Services, Suffolk County, N.Y., 1986—; cons. Arista Devices, Inc., Ronkonkoma, N.Y., 1974-81; instr. Hofstra U., Hempstead, N.Y., 1971-78; lectr. Poly. U., Farmingdale, N.Y., 1978—. Contbr. articles to profl. jours. Mem. IEEE (sr.), AIAA (sr.), AAAS, Nat. Contracts Mgmt. Assn., N.Y. Acad. Scis., Am. Inst. Aeronautics and Astronautics (sr.). Home: 14 Ray Ln Smithtown NY 11787 Office: Labred Electronics Corp 55 Cabot Ct Hauppauge NY 11788-3788

HAUSMAN, SUZANNE IRIS, graphic designer; b. Rochester, N.Y., Mar. 26, 1938; d. Jack Louis and Julia (Goldblatt) Sokol; m. George Hausman, June 7, 1959 (div. 1977); children: Jeffrie Laurence, Jody Lee. BFA, Rochester Inst. Tech., 1959; student, Sch. Am. Craftsmen, 1959-61, Sch. Visual Arts, 1965-70. Printer, retoucher Eastman Kodak Co., Rochester, N.Y., 1956-59; graphic designer, illustrator Lefevre Studio, Rochester, 1959-61; instr. Bklyn. Mus. Sch., 1972-76; art dir., sr. designer Gibbs and Hill, Inc., N.Y.C., 1975-83; graphic designer N.Y.C. Pub. Devel. Corp., 1984-87; dir. graphics, photographic svcs. N.Y.C. Dept. Transp., 1987-89; graphics and display coord. Rockefeller Ctr. Mgmt. Corp., N.Y.C., 1989—; freelance designer, N.Y.C., 1983-84; designer FDC, Bklyn., 1984—, YWCA, Bklyn., 1987-88, Hayden/Wegman, N.Y.C., 1990—. Designer, illustrator: Yes, Virginia, 1970; designer, craftsman of jewelry; works included in exhibits including: Kirkland Art Ctr., Clinton, N.Y., 1970, Munson-Williams-Proctor Inst., Utica, N.Y., 1961, Rochester Meml. Art Gallery, 1969. Mem. Am. Crafts Coun. Home: 1669 Glenwood Rd Brooklyn NY 11230-1713 Office: Rockefeller Ctr Mgmt Corp 1230 Ave Of The Americas New York NY 10020-1513

HAUSSLEIN, ROBERT WILLIAM, chemical engineer; b. N.Y.C., Sept. 17, 1937; s. Robert Frederick and Edith Wilhelmina (Arndt) H.; m. Evelyn Bryan Bullitt, June 18, 1960; children: Robert, Thomas, Evelyn. SB, MIT, 1958, PhD, 1965. Asst. dir. rsch. Amicon Corp., Lexington, Mass., 1964-71; sr. mgr. rsch. Polaroid Corp., Cambridge, Mass., 1971-88; v.p. Hyperion Catalysis, Cambridge, 1989—. Mem. Am. Chem. Soc. Home: 20 Slocum Rd Lexington MA 02173-5622 Office: 38 Smith Pl Cambridge MA 02138

HAUTH, WILLARD ELLSWORTH, III, manufacturing executive; b. Boston, May 20, 1948; s. Willard Ellsworth Jr. and Jeanne Margaret (Ginther) H.; m. Pamela Sue Matheny, Feb. 26, 1983; children: Grant Marcus, Stefanie Lynn. BS in Ceramic Engring., Alfred (N.Y.) U., 1970, MS in Ceramic Sci., 1974. Rsch. and devel. engr. Babcock and Wilcox, Augusta, Ga., 1971-74, Corning Glass Works, Buckhannon, W.Va., 1974-75; ceramics scientist Los Alamos (N.Mex.) Nat. Lab., 1975-80; rsch. and devel. projects mgr. Battelle Columbus (Ohio) Labs., 1980-83; rsch. and devel. mgr. Dow Corning Corp., Midland, Mich., 1983-89; sr. v.p. rsch. devel. and engring. Advanced Refractory Techs., Inc., Buffalo, 1990—; pres. Materials Tech. Assocs., Los Alamos, 1973-76. Capt. U.S. Army, 1971-79. Fellow Am. Ceramic Soc. (trustee 1987—, Schwartzwalder P.A.C.E. award 1983); mem. Nat. Inst. Ceramic Engrs. (pres. 1983-84, trustee 1987—), ASTM, Am. Soc. Materials, Model A Ford Restorers Club. Home: 482 Fillmore Ave East Aurora NY 14052-1722 Office: Advanced Refractory Techs Inc 699 Hertel Ave Buffalo NY 14207-2341

HAUVER, LARRY KING, art educator; b. Big Spring, Tex., May 16, 1945; s. Robert Russell and Grace Margaret (Plunkard) H.; m. Donna May Davidson, Aug. 25, 1973; children: Janice May, Emily Anne. BS, Frostburg State U., 1967. Advanced profl. cert. in art, elem. and secondary sch. Art educator Frederick County Bd. Edn., Frederick, Md., 1967—. Campaign chmn. Com. to Elect Galen R. Calgett, Frederick, 1982-89; bd. dirs. Frederick Educators Found., Inc., 1989-91. Named Outstanding Art Educator, Md. Art Edn. Assn., 1986. Mem. NEA, Md. State Tchrs. Assn. (pres.'s adv. coun. 1989-91), Frederick County Tchrs. Assn. (pres. 1989-91, chmn. polit. action com. 1986, Outstanding Tchr. 1985). Democrat. Home: 7905 Edgewood Farm Rd Frederick MD 21702 Office: Yellow Springs Elem Sch 5740 Industry Ln Frederick MD 21702

HAVENS, TIMOTHY MARKLE, investment advisory firm executive; b. New Haven, Oct. 20, 1945; s. Walter Paul and Ida Markle (Hessenbruch) H.; children: Paul Markle, David Stockdale. BA, U. Pitts., 1969. V.p. Drexel Burnham Lambert, Phila., 1970-79; pres. Newbold's Asset Mgmt., Phila., 1979—; bd. dirs. Federal Union, Washington, 1982—, Game Conservation Internat., San Antonio, United Asset Mgmt. Corp.; mem. adv. bd., Phila. Coll. Physicians. Trustee Independence Hall Assn., Phila. Served with USAR, 1968-74. Mem. Racquet Club (Phila.), Merion Cricket Club, (Haverford, Pa.). Republican. Episcopalian. Avocation: hunting. Home: 418 Fishers Rd Bryn Mawr PA 19010-3606 Office: Newbold's Asset Mgmt Inc 937 Haverford Rd Bryn Mawr PA 19010-3819

HAVERLY, DOUGLAS LINDSAY, librarian, historian; b. Stamford, N.Y., Apr. 16, 1925; s. De Forest Ward and Amy Elizabeth (Lindsay) H. Student, Albany Bus. Coll., 1948, Alfred U., 1948-49, Russell Sage Coll., 1950-52. Libr. N.Y. State Libr., Albany, 1949-77; with Bur. Testing N.Y. State Dept. Edn., Albany, 1978-82; ret., 1982; pres., curator Donald C. Ringwald Marine Navigation Ltd., Albany, 1987—. With USN, 1943-54. Mem. Steamship Hist. Soc. (budget dir. 1973-76, bd. dirs. 1977-80, organizer Hudson Valley chpt. 1974, chmn. 1975-78, libr. 1990—), Hudson River Mareitime Ctr., Sons and Daus. of Pioneer Rivermen, Palatines to Am. (historian N.Y. chpt. 1991—), Herkimer (N.Y.) Hist. Soc., Schoharie County Hist. Soc. (life), Clan Lindsay Soc. (life), N.Y. Hist. Soc., Ulster County Geneal. Soc., Van Aken/Auken Newsletter. Home and Office: Steamship Hist Soc of Am 23 Wedgewood Dr Loudonville NY 12211

HAVILLAND, BEN, lawyer, policy specialist; b. Charleston, W.Va., Mar. 11, 1924; s. Benjamin Charles and Elizabeth (Battreall) Grosscup; A.B., Wittenberg U., 1948; J.D., U. Wash., 1953; m. Michele Drapeau, Sept. 16, 1950; children—Stephen John, Lance. Admitted to Wash. State bar, 1954, D.C. bar, 1973, U.S. Supreme Ct. bar; practice law, 1954—; prof. bus. law Palomar Coll., San Diego County, Calif., 1956-59; adj. prof. internat. Sch. Law, Washington, 1975; specialist policy and procedures, program mgr. fgn. mil. sales U.S. Air Force, Washington, 1967—. Active, Boy Scouts Am. Served with USNR, 1942-45, USMCR, 1945-59, maj. ret. Decorated Peruvian Cross Aero. Merit; recipient Outstanding Service to Conservation

award Hartford Ins. Co., 1973, Silver Beaver award Boy Scouts Am., Silver Wresth awards; hon. pilot, Guatemala. Mem. Alpha Phi Omega, Phi Sigma Alpha, Beta Theta Pi. Episcopalian. Author: Earthquakes and Cities, 1950. Home: 4214 River Rd NW Washington DC 20016-4535 Office: Hdqrs USAF (PRI) Washington DC 20330

HAVIR, BRYAN THOMAS, urban planner; b. Allentown, Pa., Feb. 9, 1963; s. Donald John and Ruth Mary (Schmoyer) H. BA in Polit. Sci., History, Pa. State U., 1985, M of Pub. Adminstrn., 1990; postgrad., Delaware Valley Coll., 1990—. Planning intern City of Allentown, 1984-85; legal researcher Pa. State U., University Park, 1985; enforcement officer zoning and code South Whitehall Twp., Allentown, 1985-86; asst. site planner Montgomery County Planning commn., Norristown, Pa., 1986-87; asst. planner Mercer County Planning Bd., Trenton, N.J., 1987-88; planning dir., zoning code enforcement officer Warwick Twp., Jamison, Pa., 1988-90; coord. community devel. Evesham Twp., Marlton, N.J., 1991—. Asst. scoutmaster Boy Scouts Am., Allentown, 1980—; mem. Lehigh County Hist. Soc.; bd. dir. Bucks County Agrl. Land Preservation Bd., 1990. Mem. Am. Planning Assn., Am. Soc. Pub. Adminstrn., Urban Land Inst., Ams. for Dem. Action, Pa. State U. Alumni Assn., Keystone Soc., Nat. Eagle Scout Assn., Acad. Polit. Sci. Democrat. Congregationalist. Home: 41 Southwark Ct Southampton PA 18966-2549 Office: Evesham Twp Adminstrn Bldg 125 E Main St Marlton NJ 08053-2104

HAVLICEK, FRANKLIN J., communications executive; b. N.Y.C., July 18, 1947; s. Raymond Joseph and Rosalia Maria (Zona) H.; m. Louise Sferrazza, July 15, 1950. BA, Columbia U., 1968, JD, 1973, MA, 1977, MPhil, 1980; cert., Internat. Inst. Human Rights, Strasbourg, France, 1972. Bar: N.Y. 1974, U.S. Dist. Ct. (so. and ea. dists.) N.Y. 1974, U.S. Ct. Appeals (2d cir.) 1975, U.S. Supreme Ct. 1979, D.C. 1990. Atty. Battle & Fowler, N.Y.C., 1973-78; spl. advisor to Mayor of N.Y.C., 1978-82; ptnr. Seham, Klein, Zelman, N.Y.C., 1982-84; dir. labor rels. NBC, N.Y.C., 1984-88; v.p. indsl. rels. and pers. Washington Post, 1988—; adj. prof. Sch. Internat. & Pub. Affairs Columbia U., N.Y.C., 1978—; chmn. Sunnyside Found., 1981-91. Editor: Collective Bargaining, 1979, Presidential Selection, 1982, Election Communications, 1984; contbr. numerous articles on law, govt., communications to mags., newspapers. Mem. chmn.'s task force on NLRB, Washington, 1976-77; exec. com. N.Y. Gov.'s Task Force on Schs. and Bus., 1986-88; counsel Vietnam Veterans Meml. Commn., 1982-85, State Commn. on Dioxin, 1983-85; candidate for U.S. Senate in N.Y., 1986; bd. dirs. World Affairs Coun. of Washington; mem. U.S.-U.S.S.R. Emerging Leaders Summit, 1988, 90; bd. dirs. World Affairs Coun., 1991—, Internat. Peace Acad., 1989-90, World Media Colloquium UNESCO, 1989; U.S. Tech. expert ILO, 1990. With U.S. Army, 1968-70. Ford Found. fellow, 1977. Mem. ABA, Assn. of Bar of City of N.Y., Am. Polit. Sci. Assn., Am. Acad. Polit. Sci., Czechoslovakian Soc. Arts and Scis., N.Y. Acad. Scis. Roman Catholic. Club: City N.Y. (trustee 1985-87). Home: 3364 Tennyson St NW Washington DC 20015-2443 Office: Washington Post Co 1150 15th St NW Washington DC 20071-0002

HAVRILKO, JO-ANN P., nurse, songwriter; b. Hazleton, Pa., Aug. 14, 1942; d. Joseph Andrew and Anna R. (Keeler) Miller; m. Vincent M. Havrilko, Oct. 19, 1961; 1 child, Vincent R. Diploma, Pottsville Hosp. Sch. Nursing, 1963; student, St. Joseph's Coll., Maine. RN, Pa. Staff nurse Hazleton Gen. Hosp., 1963-80, head nurse, 1980—; dir. New Wine Ministries gospel trio, Herald interdenominational Christian theater group. Songwriter, music performed by numerous artists; performer, songwriter My Life is in Your Hands, Lord, 1990. Active in prison ministry with gospel trio. Mem. ANA (cert. med.-surg. nurse), Pa. Nurses Assn., BMI. Republican. Home: PO Box 59 Kelayres PA 18231 Office: Hazleton Gen Hosp E Broad St Hazleton PA 18201

HAWES, JOHN KENNEDY, college administrator; b. N.Y.C., Mar. 18, 1930; John Kennedy and Helen Rita (Thor) H.; m. Suzanne Law, Dec. 26, 1968; children: Mary Jane, John Brenden. MA, Manhattan Coll., 1960; MS, Iona Coll., 1962; PhD, St. John's U., 1972. Assoc. prof. CUNY, N.Y.C., 1968-76; dean of instruction Passiac Community Coll., Paterson, N.J., 1976-81; v.p. acad. affairs. acad. dean. Office: St Francis Coll 180 Remsen St Brooklyn NY 11201-4398

HAWES, WILLIAM FRANCIS, music educator, consultant; b. Phila., Aug. 7, 1940; s. Charles Erwin and Margaret (Cassel) H.; m. Kay Ramsey, May 20, 1961; children: Kenneth, Kerry Beth. BS in Edn., West Chester (Pa.) U., 1962; MA, Columbia U., 1967. Cert. music tchr., N.Y. Tchr. Lakeland Cen. Schs., Shrub Oak, N.Y., 1962-70, Carmel (N.Y.) Cen. Schs., 1970—; dir. music, organist Drew United Meth. Ch., Carmel; cons. in music Phila. Coll. Bd., 1987—. Cert. lay speaker United Meth. Ch. Mem. Am. Choral Dirs. Assn., Internat. Assn. Jazz Educators, Am. Guild English Handbell Ringers, Music Educators Nat. Conf., N.Y. State Sch. Music Assn., N.Y. chpt. Am. Choral Dirs. Assn. Home: Tiger Trail E RD #10 Carmel NY 10512 Office: Carmel High Sch 30 Fair St Carmel NY 10512-1398

HAWKES, CAROL ANN, academic administrator; b. N.Y.C.; d. Howard N. and Lavinia M. (Lally) H. B.A., Barnard Coll., 1943; M.A., Columbia U., 1944, Ph.D., 1949. Dir. acad. English liberal arts div. Katharine Gibbs Sch., N.Y.C., 1950-57; prof. English, chmn. dept. English and comparative lit. Finch Coll., N.Y.C., 1957-75; v.p. for ednl. affairs, dean of coll. Hartwick Coll., Oneonta, N.Y., 1975-80; pres. Endicott Coll., Beverly, Mass., 1980-87; dean Sch. Arts and Scis., Western Conn. State U., Danbury, 1987—; Trustee Norwich U., Hartwick Coll.; adv. bd. Harvard Sch. Dental Medicine. Author: Master's Degree Programs and the Liberal Arts College, 1968. Mem. MLA, LWV, Modern Humanities Research Assn., Am. Assn. Higher Edn., Phi Beta Kappa. Clubs: Princeton (N.Y.C.); Columbia U. of New Eng. Office: Western Conn State U Sch Arts and Scis Danbury CT 06810

HAWKES, ELIZABETH H., curator; b. Wilmington, Del., Aug. 12, 1943; d. Sidney Whittington and Betty Armstrong (Boyce) Handy; m. Robert W. Hawkes, Feb. 12, 1971. BA, Mary Washington Coll., 1965; MA, U. Del., 1969. Asst. curator Del. Art Mus., Wilmington, 1968-80, assoc. curator, 1980-90, curator John Sloan collection, 1977-90; ind. curator, West Chester, Pa., 1991—. Author: American Painting and Sculpture: Delaware Art Museum, 1975. Co-editor: A Small School of Art: The Students of Howard Pyle. Mem. Assn. Am. Mus., Mid-Atlantic Mus. Assn. Office: 715 N Creek Rd West Chester PA 19380-1908

HAWKESWOOD, WILLIAM GORDON, anthropology educator; b. Auckland, New Zealand, Nov. 1, 1951; s. Kenneth G. and Lois D. (Kirkman) H.; m. Phyllis S. Herda, June 10, 1988. BA, U. Auckland, 1979, MA with honors, 1984; M. Philosophy, Columbia U., 1988, PhD, 1991. Adj. prof. John Jay Coll., N.Y.C., 1990; adj. asst. prof. York Coll., N.Y.C., 1991—, Columbia U., N.Y.C., 1991, SUNY, Purchase, 1991—. Author: One of the Children, 1992; contbr. articles to profl. jours. Presidents fellow Columbia U., 1984-89. Fellow Royal Anthrop. Inst.; mem. Am. Anthrop. Assn., Am. Ethnol. Soc., Soc. for Med. Anthropology, Soc. for Urban Anthropology, New Zealand Assn. Social Anthropologists, Royal Polynesian Soc.

HAWKINS, BRIAN LEE, academic administrator, educator; b. Lafayette, Ind., Aug. 5, 1948; s. Robert H. and Majorie Joan (Bradley) H.; m. Lisa Ellen Herrick, Dec. 30, 1970; children: Timothy, Steven. BA, Mich. State U., 1970, MA, 1972; PhD, Purdue U., 1975. Asst. prof. U. Tex., San Antonio, 1975-76, asst. dean of bus., 1976-81; assoc. v.p. acad. affairs Drexel U., Phila., 1981-86, assoc. v.p. computing and telecommunications, 1984-86; v.p. Brown U., Providence, 1986—, spl. asst. to pres., assoc. provost acad. planning, 1990—; trustee EDUCOM, Washington, 1986-90, chmn. bd., 1989-90. Author: Managerial Communication, 1981; editor: Managing & Organizing Info Resources on Campus, 1990. Office: Brown U PO Box 1885 Providence RI 02912-0001

HAWKINS, (WILLIAM) BRUCE, physics educator; b. Rochester, N.Y., Sept. 8, 1930; s. William Bruce and Doris (Dickinson) H.; m. Ruth Ann Elsaesser, June 3, 1957; children: Judith Lisbie, Patricia Joan. BA, Amherst Coll., 1951; PhD, Princeton U., 1954. NSF fellow ETH, Zürich, Switzerland, 1954-55; instr. Yale U., New Haven, 1955-57; asst. prof. Oberlin (Ohio) Coll., 1957-61; asst. prof. Smith Coll., Northampton, Mass., 1961-68, assoc. prof., 1968-87, prof., 1987-92, emeritus prof., 1992—. Clk. of devel. Friends Gen. Conf., Phila., 1985-91. Mem. Am. Phys. Soc., Am. Assn. Physics Tchrs., Cat Acoustical Soc., Assn. for Computing Machinery, Sigma Xi. Democrat. Mem. Soc. of Friends. Office: Smith Coll Physics Dept Clark Science Ctr Northampton MA 01063

HAWKINS, CHARLES EARL, III, association executive; b. Jefferson City, Mo., Feb. 20, 1943; s. Charles E. and Colette (Ellis) H.; m. Martha Jean Youkey, June 11, 1966; children: Charles E. IV, Jennifer Lee. BS, Fla. So. Coll., 1965. Dir. mem. svcs. Nat. Crushed Stone Assn., Washington, 1968-71; v.p. govt. rels. Nat. Sand and Gravel Assn., Silver Spring, Md., 1972-83; v.p. govt. affairs Associated Builders and Contractors, Washington, 1984-90, sr. v.p., 1991—. Com. chair Mt. Zion United Meth. Ch., Highland, Md., 1982-88; dir. Congl. Charity Tennis Tournament, 1988—, Congl. Charity Golf Tournament, 1989—; com. mem. St. Mathews United Meth. Ch., Bowie, Md., 1991-92; treas. St. Catherines' Pub. Watershed Assn., Md., 1990—. 1st lt. U.S. Army, 1966-68, Vietnam. Mem. Am. Soc. Assn. Execs. (bd. dirs. 1991-92), Woodmont Rod and Gun Club, Nat. Assns. Exec. Club, Chester Rive Yacht and Country Club, Tully's Fancy Hunting Club, Jefferson Islands Club (exec. v.p. 1987—). Office: Associated Builders and Contractors 729 15th St NW Washington DC 20005

HAWKS, IRENE KAMINSKY, psychologist; b. N.Y.C., Jan. 19, 1945; d. Anatole and Lydia (Judey) K.; m. Robert E. Hawks, Sept. 3, 1966. BA, Syracuse U., 1966; MA, NYU, 1973, PhD, 1984. Diplomate Am. Bd. Cert. Counselors; lic. psychologist, N.Y. Interviewer N.Y. State Employment Svc., N.Y.C., 1966-74; counselor N.Y. Assn. for New Ams., N.Y.C., 1974-78; psychology intern Cabrini Med. Ctr., N.Y.C., 1979-80; coord. counseling svcs. Bramson Orgn. for Rehab. thru Tng., N.Y.C., 1977-82; psychology extern Karen Horney Clinic, N.Y.C., 1986-87; supr. learning disability CUNY, N.Y.C., 1984-90; psychologist N.Y.C., 1981—, Inst. for Psychotherapeutic Advancement, N.Y.C., 1987—, Jewish Bd. Family and Children's Svcs., N.Y.C., 1990—; presenter Am. Coun. for Learning Disabilities Internat. Conf., 1986. Mem. APA (presenter 1978, 80), N.Y. State Psychol. Assn. (presenter 1987), Am. Assn. Mental Health Counselors, N.Y. Soc. Clin. Psychologists.

HAWLEY, FRANK JORDAN, JR., venture capital executive; b. Roanoke Rapids, N.C., Oct. 3, 1927; s. Frank Jordan and Mary (Miller) H.; m. Alethea Wood, Sept. 12, 1959; children: Frank J. III, Mark R., Andrew D., Stuart W., Alethea S. BS in Physics, U. N.C., 1949; MBA, Harvard U., 1955. Rsch. analyst Eaton & Howard, Inc., Boston, 1955-59; banking assoc. Lazard Freres, N.Y.C., 1959-64; portfolio mgr. Stein, Roe & Farnham, N.Y.C., 1964-69; exec. v.p. Laidlaw Coggeshall, Inc., N.Y.C., 1969-74; gen. ptnr. Foster Mgmt. Co., N.Y.C., 1974-82; mng. ptnr. Saugatuck Capital Co., Stamford, Conn., 1982—; chmn. bd. Morgan Products Ltd., Oshkosh, Wis., Med. Rehab. Inc., Tallahassee, Fla.; mem. mgmt. com. Atlantic Cellular LP. Vice pres., treas. New Canaan (Conn.) YMCA, 1981-85; trustee Chocorua Chapel Assn., Squam Lake, N.H.; bd. visitors U. N.C., Chapel Hill, trustee Kenan Inst. Pvt. Enterprise of U. N.C. Lt. (j.g.) USN, 1950-53, Korea. Mem. Conn. Venture Capital Assn. (exec. com. 1983—), Links Club, Harvard Club (N.Y.C.), New Canaan Country Club, New Canaan Field Club, Mill Reef Club (Antigua), Phi Beta Kappa. Republican. Episcopalian. Home: 613 Silvermine Rd New Canaan CT 06840-4325 Office: Saugatuck Capital Co 1 Canterbury Grn Stamford CT 06901-2032 also: Morgan Products Ltd 25 Tri-State Internat Ste 325 Lincolnshire IL 60069

HAWLEY, JEAN GANNETT, publisher; b. Augusta, Maine, Jan. 16, 1924; d. Guy Patterson and Anne (Macomber) G.; m. Roger Chilton Williams, Oct. 11, 1945 (div. 1952); children: Roger Chilton Jr. (dec.), Guy G., Timothy A.; m. Sumner A. Hawley, Dec. 21, 1970. Student, Bradford Jr. Coll., 1942-43; DBA (hon.), Portland U., 1958; LHD (hon.), Colby Coll., 1959, Nasson Coll., 1959; LLD (hon.), Bates Coll., 1980. Exec. v.p., mgr. nat. advtg. Guy Gannett Pub. Co., Portland, Maine, 1953, pres., 1954-78, pub., 1959—, also chmn. bd. dirs. Recipient Deborah Morton award Westbrook Coll., 1965. Office: Guy Gannett Pub Co 1 City Ctr PO Box 15277 Portland ME 04101

HAWRYLKO, EUGENIA ANNA, allergist, immunologist, researcher; b. N.Y.C., Feb. 7, 1942; d. Nicholas and Ludmila (Pavlov) H.; m. Raymond James Aab, Aug. 17, 1974; children: Allison Eugenia, Elizabeth Adele. AB, Vassar Coll., 1962; MD, NYU, 1966. Diplomate Am. Bd. Allergy and Immunology. Intern, resident Bellevue Hosp., N.Y.C., 1966-68; rsch. fellow Harvard Med. Sch., Boston, 1968-69; rsch. fellow Trudeau Inst., Saranac Lake, N.Y., 1969-73, asst. mem., 1973-74; rsch. assoc., assoc. Sloan-Kettering Inst., N.Y.C., 1974-81; clin. fellow in allergy and immunology N.Y. Hosp. Cornell Med. Ctr., N.Y.C., 1978-80; instr. clin. medicine NYU Med. Ctr., N.Y.C., 1981—; clin. asst. attending Bellevue (N.Y.) Hosp., 1981—; chief allergy and immunology labs. L.I. Coll. Hosp., Bklyn., 1982-88; pvt. practice N.Y.C.; mem. adv. com. on clin. investigation immunology and immunotherapy Am. Cancer Soc., 1978-82. Contbr. articles to profl. jours. Recipient Faculty Rsch. award Am. Cancer Soc., 1976-81. Fellow Am. Acad. Allergy and Immunology, Am. Coll. Allergists and Immunologists; mem. Am. Assn. Immunologists, N.Y. Allergy Soc., Vassar Club. Office: 160 E 32d St New York NY 10016

HAY, GEORGE AUSTIN, actor, producer, director, musician, artist; b. Johnstown, Pa., Dec. 25, 1915; s. George and Mary Louise (Austin) H. B.S., U. Pitts., 1938; postgrad., U. Rochester, 1939; M.Litt., U. Pitts., 1948; M.A., Columbia U., 1948. dir. Jr. League hosp. shows, N.Y.C., 1948-53. Producer, dir. off-Broadway prodns., 1953-55; motion picture casting dir. for Dept. Def. films, Astoria Studios, N.Y., 1955-70, motion picture producer-dir., U.S. Dept. Transp., Washington, 1973—; group exhbns. of paintings and sculpture include, Lincoln Ctr., N.Y.C., 1965, Parrish Art Mus., Southampton, N.Y., 1969, Carnegie Inst., 1972, Duncan Galleries, N.Y.C., 1973, Bicentennial Exhbn. Am. Painters, Paris, 1976, Chevy Chase Gallery, 1979, Watergate Gallery, 1981, Le Salon des Nations a Paris, 1983; rep. permanent collections, Met. Mus. Art, N.Y.C., Library Congress, also, pvt. collections; bibliog. reference to works pub. in History of Internat. Art, 1982; author, illustrator: Seven Hops to Australia, 1945, The Moving Image, A Career in Pictures, 1990; Dir.: Bicentennial documentary Highways of History, 1976; dir.: film World Painting in Museum of Modern Art, 1972; Composer: Rhapsody in E Flat for piano and strings, 1950; writer: TV program Nat. Council Chs., 1965; Broadway appearances include: What Every Woman Knows, 1954; original Broadway run of Inherit the Wind, 1955-57; created role of Prof. Fiveash in premiere of The Acrobats, White Barn Theater, Westport, Conn., 1961; feature films include: Murder, Inc., 1960, Pretty Boy Floyd, 1960, The Landlord, 1970, Child's Play, 1971, Chekhov's The Bet, 1978, Being There, 1980, No Way Out, 1986, Her Alibi, 1988; TV appearances include Am. Heritage, 1961, Americans-A Portrait in Verses, 1962, Naked City, 1962, U.S. Steel Hour, 1963, Another World, 1965, Edge of Night, 1968, As the World Turns, 1969, Love Is a Many-Splendored Thing, 1972, The Adams Chronicles, 1976, A Woman Named Jackie, 1991; piano soloist in concerts and recitals, 1937; performer Cruise Ship, Europe, 1938; author, illustrator: The Arts Scene; entrepreneur in mgmt. of property, portfolio of stocks and bonds; contbr. articles to periodicals. Apptd. time adv. panel, pres.'s coun. Coll. William and Mary; mem. World Affairs Coun., Am. Archtl. Found.; bd. govs., trustee Hist. Home of Pres. James Monroe; mus. donor Am. doctor's office turn-of-century period preservation; bd. dirs. Washington Film Coun. With AUS, 1942-46, PTO. Recipient Loyal Svc. award Jr. League, 1953, St. Bartholomew's Silver Leadership award, 1966, Gold medal Accademia Italia, 1980, Smithsonian Instn. Pictorial award, 1982; Fed. Govt. Honor award in recognition 35 yrs. dedicated svc., 1990; subject of biog. work: Austin Hay, Adventures of a Christmas Child, 1970. Mem. NATAS, AFTRA, SAG, Am. Artists Profl. League, Allied Artists Am., Internat . Bach Soc., Beethoven Soc., Nat. Soc. Arts and Letters, Music Libr. Assn., Actors Equity Assn., Nat. Assn. Investors, Nat. Trust Hist. Preservation, SAR, Nat. Parks and Conservation Assn., Shakespeare Oxford Soc., St. Andrew's Soc., Victorian Soc. (bd. dirs.), Cambria County Hist. Soc., Am. Philatelic Soc., Am. Mus. Moving Image, English Speaking Union, Nat. Arts Club (N.Y.C.), Players Club (N.Y.C.), Nat. Travel Club, Columbia U. Club, Nat. Press Club, Arts Club, Classic Car Club Am., Nat. Naval Med. Command, Sigma Chi, Phi Mu Alpha. Home: 2022 Columbia Rd NW Washington DC 20009-1352 Office: US Dept Transp 400 7th St SW Washington DC 20590-0002 also: Hay Ave Johnstown PA 15902

HAYASHIDA, MOTOI, psychiatrist, educator; b. Tokyo, Feb. 6, 1932; came to U.S., 1959; s. Toyoji and Takako Hayashida; m. Hiroko Nakagawa, July 16, 1960; chldren: Tetsu, Naoto. MD, Keio U., Tokyo, 1958, ScD, 1967. Diplomate Am. Bd. Psychiatry and Neurology. Rotating intern Hahnemann U. Hosp., Phila., 1959-60; resident in psychiatry Middletown (N.Y.) State Hosp., 1960-62, Phila. Gen. Hosp., 1962-64; chief alcoholism treatment unit VA Med. Ctr., Phila., 1982-86; clin. assoc. prof. dept. psychiatry U. Pa., Phila., 1988—; cons., speaker on alcoholism. Contbr. articles on alcoholism to med. jours. Recipient Meritorious Svc. award VA, 1987; Fulbright scholar, Tokyo, 1959-62. Mem. Am. Psychiat. Assn., Am. Soc. Addiction Medicine (cert.), N.Y. Acad. Scis., Japanese Med. Soc. Am. (bd. dirs.), Japan-U.S. Garioa/Fulbright Alumni Assn. (adv. coun.). Office: VA Med Ctr University Ave Philadelphia PA 19104

HAYASI, NISIKI, physicist; b. Niigata City, Japan, Mar. 12, 1929; came to U.S., 1963; s. Matsuki and Fuku (Fukushima) H.; m. Chikako Nomura, Nov. 21, 1952; children: Fujio, Kay Keiko Makishi. AB, First Coll., Tokyo, 1949; SB, SM, U. Tokyo, 1952, PhD, 1962. Tech. ofcl. Japanese Ministry Transp., Tokyo, 1952-61; tech. ofcl. Japanese Premier's Office, Tokyo, 1961-62, br. mgr., 1962-64; postdoctoral assoc. NASA Ames Rsch. Ctr., Moffett Field, Calif., 1964-65; program mgr., staff scientist Lockheed Corp., Marietta, Ga., 1965-70; mgr. advanced tech. Langston div. Harris Corp., Cherry Hill, N.J., 1971-74; sr. mng. dir. Fgn. Ops. div. SPS Techs., Inc., Jenkintown, Pa., 1975; exec. dir. Tech. Transfer Cons., Cherry Hill, N.J., 1975—; pres. Culti Corp., Cherry Hill, 1977—; vis. asst. prof. U. Cin., 1963-64; exec. cons. Tomoku Co., Ltd., Tokyo, 1974-78; NAS-NRC postdoctoral rsch. assoc. 1964, 65. Contbr. numerous articles to profl. jours.; patentee in U.S., France, Netherlands, Fed. Republic Germany, Japan. Pres. Japanese Sch. Greater Phila. PTA, 1973-74; dir. Japanese Assn. of Greater Phila., 1990-91. Japanese Govt. overseas fellow, 1963; U. Pa. scholar, 1971-73. Fellow AIAA (assoc.); mem. Ambs. Club, Sigma Gamma Tau. Home and Office: Culti Corp 16 Locust Grove Rd Cherry Hill NJ 08003

HAYDEN, BRUCE P., real estate counselor; b. Saginaw, Mich., Sept. 9, 1915; s. Bruce Lynn and Glenna (Pancoast) H.; m. Margaret McBeth, June 28, 1940; children: Lynn Hayden Wadhams, Ann Hayden Hamilton, Robert McBeth. BS, U.S. Naval Acad., Annapolis, Md., 1938. Trainee to v.p. Conn. Gen. Life Ins. Co., Hartford, 1938-72; chmn. Hayden, Tolzmann & Assocs., Bloomfield, Conn., 1972—; trustee Corp. Property Investors, N.Y.C., 1972-91, Nooney Real Estate Trust, St. Louis, 1982-91. Mem. Am. Soc. Real Estate Counselors (pres. 1987). Office: Hayden Tolzmann & Assocs Inc PO Box 708 Bloomfield CT 06002-0708

HAYDEN, GEORGE ALLEN, retired science administrator; b. Kansas City, Mo., Feb. 25, 1928; s. Roscoe C. Hayden and Minnie M. (Jones) Mims; m. Ida L. White, June 29, 1957; 1 child, Julie. BA, U. Kans., 1950; MS, Howard U., 1960, PhDd, 1966. Postdoctoral fellow Sloan-Kettering Cancer Inst., Rye, N.Y., 1966-68; rsch. scientist ARC, Bethesda, Md., 1968-71; administrator Nat. Heart, Lung and Blood Inst., NIH, Bethesda, 1971-89, annuitant Minority Access to Rsch. Careers program, 1989—, sr. staff advisor, 1992. Recipient Dirs.'s award NIH, 1985, EEO award NIH, 1986. Mem. AAAS, Am. Chem. Soc., Internat. Soc. Hypertension in Blacks, Sigma Xi. Home: 1312 Juniper St NW Washington DC 20012-1441

HAYDEN, JOSEPH A., JR., lawyer; b. Newark, Apr. 2, 1944; s. Joseph A. and Mary (Giblin) H.; m. Donna Heinrich, Aug. 26, 1967; children: Kathryn Elizabeth, Patrick Jsoeph; m. Katharine Jackson Sweeney, July 19, 1987. Student, Boston Coll., 1966; JD magna cum laude, Rutgers U., 1969. Bar: N.J. 1969, U.S. Dist. Ct. N.J. 1969, N.Y. 1981. Law sec. to chief justice N.J. Supreme Ct., Trenton, 1969-70; dep. atty. gen. organized crime and spl. prosecution sect. Div. Criminal Justice, Atty. Gen.'s Office, Trenton, 1970-73; pvt. practice Newark, Hoboken and Weehawken, N.J., 1973—. Counsel to Essex County Dem. Party, 1976-80. Fellow Am. Coll. Trial Lawyers, Am. Bar Found.; mem. N.J. State Bar Assn., Assn. Criminal Def. Lawyers N.J. (trustee 1985—, founder, 1st pres.). Democrat. Home: 811 Hudson St Hoboken NJ 07030-4202 Office: Hayden Perle & Silber 1500 Harbor Blvd Weehawken NJ 07087

HAYDEN, MICHAEL JOSEPH, retail chain official; b. Somers Point, N.J., Apr. 4, 1964; s. John Francis and Carmen (Moreno) H. BS, SUNY, Oswego, 1987; AS, Mohawk Valley Community Coll., Utica, N.Y., 1984. Cert. secondary tchr., N.Y. Guard Ft. Ontario Hist. Park, Oswego, 1988-90, N.Y. State Parks, Oswego, 1988-90, Recreation and Hist. Preservation, Oswego, 1988-90; tchr. global studies Notre Dame High Sch., Utica, N.Y., 1989-90; sales leader Sears Roebuck and Co., New Hartford, N.Y., 1991—. Named an Outstanding Coll. Student of Am., KC, 1989. Mem. Wilson Ctr., Am. Assn. State and Local History, Oswego's Men Honor Soc. Roman Catholic. Home: 502 W Dominick St Apt 7 Rome NY 13440-4819

HAYDEN, NEIL STEVEN, communications company executive; b. Bronx, N.Y., May 23, 1937; s. Aaron Alexander and Selma (Turtletaub) H.; m. Elaine Charlotte Lawson, July 3, 1960 (div. 1975); children: Stephanie, Jennifer, Aaron II; m. Carolyn Sue Carper, May 8, 1975 (div. 1985); m. Ellen Maxine Sulcov, Feb. 4, 1990. Student, U. Fla., 1955-58; student, U. Miami, Fla., 1958. With copy staff Miami Herald, 1958; reporter Albany Herald, 1959, Hickory Daily Record, Hickory, N.C., 1959-60; editor The Jackson Herald, Jefferson, Ga., 1960-62; editor, publ. The Hartwell Sun, Hartwell, Ga., 1962-67; publ. Athens Banner-Herald & The Daily News, Athens, Ga., 1967-72; pres., publ. Huntington Herald-Dispatch & Huntington Advertiser, Huntington, W.Va., 1972-76, Statesman and Capital Jour., Salem, Oreg., 1976-79, Courier-Post, Camden, N.J., 1979-80, The Bulletin, Phila., 1980-82; pres., chief operating officer Herald Examiner, Hearst Community Newspapers, L.A., 1982-84; pres. AD/SAT, Inc., N.Y.C., 1984-92; with Capital Devel. Assocs., Inc., Fair Lawn, N.J., 1992—. Bd. dirs. World Affairs Council Phila.; bd. dirs. Police Athletic League; mem. Phila. Orchestra Council; bd. dirs. Phila. Conv. & Visitors Bur.; mem. Greater Phila. Partnership;adv. bd. Haddonfield (N.J.) Symphony Soc. Mem. Am. Newspaper Publs. Assn., Am. Soc. Newspaper Editors; Nat. Newspaper Assn., Advt. Counc. Newspaper Com., Am. Coun. on Edn. for Journalism and Mass Communications; Women in Communications, Inc., Calif. Newspaper Publs. Assn., Greater Phila. C. of C. (bd. dirs.), Newsletter Pub. Assn. Home: 749 Rivenwood Rd Franklin Lakes NJ 07417-1443 Office: Capital Devel Assocs Inc 2-14 Fair Lawn Ave Fair Lawn NJ 07410-1300

HAYDEN, ROBERT RUSSELL, educational administrator, education educator; b. Aug. 14, 1934; s. John Joseph and Eleanore (Wade) H.; m. Kathryn Ann Murphy, June 14, 1958; children: John, Frances, Keelin, Robert. BA, Siena Coll., Loudonville, N.Y., 1955; MA, SUNY, Albany, 1959, EdS, 1968, PhD, 1972. Adj. prof. Schenectady (N.Y.) County Community Coll., 1970-72, Hudson Valley Community Coll., Troy, N.Y., 1974-79; dir., prof. semester Siena Coll., 1973-77, asst. prof. edn., 1973-79, assoc. prof., 1980-85, head dept., 1977-91, asst. v.p. acad. affairs, 1979—, prof., 1985—; cons. in field. Contbr. articles to ednl. publs. chmn. Town of Hoosick Community Ctr., Hoosick Falls, N.Y., 1961-68; vice-chmn. Rensselaer Mental Health Bd., Troy, 1978-80; active Rensselaer Community Svcs Bd., 1989—. With U.S. Army, 1955-57, Japan. ESEA fellow, 1966-69. Mem. Am. Assn. Tchr. Educators, Northeastern Ednl. Rsch. Assn., Coun. Basic Edn., Ea. Ednl. Rsch. Assn. Roman Catholic. Office: Siena Coll Rte 9 Loudonville NY 12211

HAYDOCK, MICHAEL DAMEAN, commissioner; b. Schenectady, N.Y., Sept. 3, 1940; s. Louis and Olive Ann (Keenan) H.; divorced. AA, U. of State of N.Y., Albany, 1974; BA, SUNY, Albany, 1975. Various pos. in bldg. dept. City of Schenectady, 1965-70, bldg. insp., 1970-71; zoning adminstr. Town of Niskayuna, N.Y., 1971-80; bldg. insp. City of Poughkeepsie, N.Y., 1980-86; bldg. commr. City of Albany, 1986—; instr. in code enforcement State of N.Y., various locations, 1986—. Contbr. articles to Nat. Bldg. Ofcls. and Code Adminstrn. mag., 1983—, Dutchess County Hist. Soc. Yearbook, 1986. With U.S. Army, 1959-62. Mem. N.Y. State Firefighting and Code Enforcement Pers. Standards and Edn. Commn., N.Y. State Bldg. Ofcls. Conf. (pres. Capital Dist. area 1988-89, 2d state v.p. 1991—), Am. Legion. Democrat. Office: City Albany Bldg Dept City Hall Eagle St Albany NY 12207

HAYEK, WILLIAM EDWARD, investment counsel, financial consultant; b. Bronx, N.Y., Aug. 24, 1947; s. William Andrew and Mary Rita (Smith)

H.; m. Ellen Marie Becker, Sept. 12, 1970; children: Bradford Andrew, Timothy Wescott. BS, Seton Hall U., 1969; MS in Econs., Fairleigh Dickenson U., 1972; MS in Fin., Bucknell U., 1974; postgrad. fiduciary law, Northwestern U., 1975. Registered investment advisor; cert. fin. planner. Sr. trust officer Midlantic Nat. Bank, Englewood and Newark, 1969-75; v.p., sr. trust officer First Nat. Bank of N.J., Totowa, 1975-80; pres., sr. v.p. trust div. mgr. Commonwealth Nat. Bank, 1980-82; pres., chmn. WEHCO Fin. Svcs. Group Ltd., 1985—; exec. v.p., dir. Centurion Capital Mgmt. Co., Inc., 1989-91; pres., chmn. Main St. Mgmt. Co., Dover, Pa., 1991—. Bd. dirs. Pa. Coalition of AIDS Orgns.; chmn., bd. dirs. York AIDS Project; bd. dirs. ABC Advocates. Mem. Inst. Cert. Fin. Planners, Lions Club, Kiwanis (pres. 1973-75). Home: 118 Maplewood Dr Dover PA 17315-1332 Office: Main St Mgmt Co 8 N Main St Dover PA 17315-1210

HAYES, ANDREW PATRICK, marketing professional; b. Newark, June 29, 1958; s. Charles Hartkoff Jr. and Marjorie Kathryn (Meyerstein) H. BA, Denison U., 1981. Sales engr. Iverson Bros-Hardinge, Des Plaines, Ill., 1982-83; mktg. mgr. Kern Importers, Elk Grove, Ill., 1983-84; sales engr. Warner & Swasey Co., Westmont, Ill., 1981-82, 84-86; account exec. AT&T, Chgo., 1986-88; sales mgr. AT&T, Brookfield, Wis., 1988-90; regional mgr. agts. AT&T, Parsippany, N.J., 1990—. Mem. Young Irish Fellowship, Chgo., 1983-87, Young Reps. Orgn., Chgo., 1983-87; pres. Chgo. Lacrosse Club, 1985-88, Midwest Club Lacrosse Assn., 1986-87.

HAYES, CAROL J., biology educator; b. N.Y.C., Dec. 13, 1940; d. Arnold C. and Regina (Tighe) H. BS in Biology, St. Joseph's Coll., Bklyn., 1961; PhD in Physiology, NYU, 1975. Research asst. Booth Meml. Hosp., Flushing, N.Y., 1961-63; research assoc. Cornell U. Med. Sch., N.Y.C., 1963-65; instr. biology St. Joseph's Coll., 1965-68, asst. prof., 1968-75, assoc. prof., 1975-80, prof., 1980—, chmn. dept. biology, 1976—. NSF research fellow Ill. Inst. Tech., 1968-69. Mem. AAAS, Internat. Assn. Chronobiology, N.Y. Acad. Scis., N.Y. Zool. Soc., Sigma Xi. Office: St Joseph's Coll 245 Clinton Ave Brooklyn NY 11205-3688 also: St Joseph's Coll 155 Roe Blvd Patchogue NY 11772

HAYES, DIAHANN FOWLER, artist, hotel service professional; b. Detroit, May 20, 1959; d. Charles Robert and Margaret Ann (Sullivan) Fowler; m. William Clifton Hayes II, Feb. 13, 1981; children: William Clifton III, Laurance Charles. Student, Corcoran Sch., Washington, 1980. Graphic designer Sta. WHUR, Washington, summer 1974; merchandising display coord. Jos. A. Bank Clothiers, Washington, 1982-83; guest svc. rep. Capital Hilton, Washington, 1983-84, Washington Hilton, 1986—; mem. adv. com. Spl. Edn. Dept., Washington, 1991. Exhibited in group shows at Galex 25, Chgo., 1991, Monsernat Gallery, N.Y.C., 1991, Wetherholt Gallery, Washington, 1991. Mem. Washington Projects for the Arts, Internat. Assn. Visual Arts, Surface Design Assn., Art on Video. Democrat. Roman Catholic. Home and Office: Universal Arts 1727 Swann St NW Washington DC 20009-5536

HAYES, E(VERETT) RUSSELL, anatomy educator; b. Pomeroy, Ohio, Feb. 5, 1917; s. Everett R. and Mildred (Russell) H.; m. Nancy Padan, Mar. 4, 1946; children: Anne, Alan, Kevin. AB, Ohio U., 1938; PhD, Ohio State U., 1947. Instr. U. Buffalo, 1945-48; asst. prof. Ohio State U., Columbus, 1948-54, assoc. prof., 1954-57; assoc. prof. SUNY, Buffalo, 1957-62, prof. anatomy, 1962-85, prof. emeritus, 1985—. Contbr. articles to profl. publs. Mem. Am. Assn. Anatomists, Am. Soc. Zoologists (assoc. editor Jour. Morphology), Histochem. Soc., Biol. Stain Commn., Am. Soc. Cell Biology. Home and Office: 6599 Bear Ridge Lockport NY 14094

HAYES, GEORGE STEPHEN, non-profit organization executive; b. Sullivan, Ind., May 27, 1947; s. George Edward and Olive Maxine (Stafford) H.; m. Paula Malsack, June 6, 1978 (div. Apr. 1985). BA, Ind. U., 1969; MAgr, Tex. A&M U., 1972. World Alliance youth dir. YMCA, Geneva, Switzerland, 1969-71; devel. edn. dir. internat. div. USA YMCA, N.Y.C., 1975-81; community organizer Greater Lafayette Community Ctr., Ind., 1971; reporter Keene (N.H.) Evening Sentinel, 1972; rsch. asst. Tex. A&M U., College Station, 1971-72; publ. dir. Kansas City (Mo.) Mus. History and Sci., 1973-74; cons. devel. program UN, 1977-82; internat. program dir. Am. Field Svc., 1982-85; pres., founder Am. Ctr. Internat. Leadership, Balt., 1985—. Founder Infant Formula Campaign/Nestles Boycott, Mpls., 1976; field dir. McCloskey Presdl. Campaign, Concord, N.H., 1972; bd. dirs. Ch. World Svc., 1979-81, N.Y.C., Interlink News Svc., N.Y.C., 1980-86. Community fellow Kettering Inst., 1980; recipient AFS Pesce D'Oro award, 1984, Aspen Inst. fellowship, 1991. Office: Am Ctr Internat Leadership 401 E Pratt St Ste 2432 Baltimore MD 21202-3039

HAYES, JAMES B., magazine executive. Student, Georgetown U., 1959. Promotional writer Sports Illustrated, 1959-60, N.Y. sales rep., 1960-63, Phila. sales rep., 1963-67, Detroit assoc. mgr., sales rep., 1967-72, Detroit mgr., 1872-77, N.Y. mgr., 1977-79, advt. sales mgr., 1979-82; advt. sales mgr. Money, 1982-84; pub. Discover, from 1984; now pub. Fortune, N.Y.C. Office: Fortune Time & Life Bldg Rockefeller Ctr New York NY 10020*

HAYES, JOHN BRUTON, JR., brokerage house executive; b. N.Y.C., Feb. 12, 1942; s. John Bruton and Muriel Mary (Spink) H.; m. Susan Joan Steele, Sept. 11, 1982; children: John B. III, Andrew Steele, Caitlin Corbett. BS, Manhattan Coll., 1964. Retail sales Edwards & Hanly, N.Y.C., 1968-70; retail, dealer sales Merrill Lynch, N.Y.C., 1970-74; nat. dealer sales mgr. Bache Halsey Stuart, N.Y.C., 1974-76; mgr., founder unit trust dept. Weeden & Co., N.Y.C., 1976-79; asst. to pres. Carroll, McEntee, McGinley, N.Y.C., 1978-79; v.p. Am. Liquid Trust, N.Y.C., 1978-79; founder, mgr. syndicate, sales unit trusts Bear Stearns & Co., N.Y.C., 1979-82; v.p., mgr. syndicate, sales unit trusts Thomson-McKinnon Securities, N.Y.C., 1982-89; v.p. sales and mktg. Prudential-Bache Securities, 1989-90; registered investment advisor JBH, Inc., 1990—; mng. dir. Parallax Group Inc., 1991—. Contbr. to and interviewed for articles in profl. jours. Mem. Mcpl. Bond Club of N.Y., Unit Trust Assn. (bd. dirs. 1980). Republican. Roman Catholic. Clubs: Metropolitan (N.Y.C.); Rockaway Hunting (Cedarhurst, N.Y.); Nat. Golf Links (Southampton, N.Y.); Brooklawn Country (Fairfield, Conn.). Home: 230 Longmeadow Rd Fairfield CT 06430-1763 Office: 315 Post Rd W Westport CT 06880

HAYES, JOHN EDWARD, broadcasting executive; b. Niagara Falls, N.Y., Sept. 14, 1941; s. John H. and Margaret (Wilson) H.; m. Jean Wheeler, Jan. 1, 1964; children: John Jr., Janice. BS in Broadcasting, U. Fla., 1963. State capital bur. chief Sta. WTVJ-TV, Miami, 1963-67; exec. asst. Fla. Dept. Consumer Svcs., 1967-71; state capitol bur. chief Sta. WTVT-TV, Tallahassee, 1971-77; asst. news dir. Sta. WTVT-TV, Tampa, Fla., 1977-79; news dir. Sta. WBRC-TV, Birmingham, Ala., 1979-82, Sta. KNTV-TV, San Jose, Calif., 1982-83; v.p., gen. mgr. Sta. KLAS-TV, Las Vegas, Nev., 1983-87; gen. mgr. Sta. WIVB-TV, Buffalo, 1987-89; pres. Jour. Broadcasting of Charlotte (N.C.) Co., 1989-93; v.p. TV Providence Jour. Co., 1993—. Recipient Nat. Headliners award Headliners Club, 1973, Emmy award TV Acad. Arts and Sci., 1982. Presbyterian. Office: Providence Jour Co 75 Fountain St Providence RI 02902

HAYES, NICHOLAS, congressional aide; b. N.Y.C., Sept. 4, 1947; s. John Anthony Jr. and Josephine (Hurley) H. BA, Trinity Coll., 1969. V.p. Hurley-Johnson Corp., N.Y.C., 1970-78, Longwood Assocs., Syosset, N.Y., 1978-80; exec. dir. campaign financing Sen. Jacob K. Javits, N.Y.C., 1980-81; sr. asst. for congl. relations and legis. U.S. Dept. Housing, Washington, 1981-82; adminstrv. asst. to Congressman Hamilton Fish Jr., Washington, 1982—. Mem. Nat. Horse Show Assn. Am. (bd. dirs. 1973—). Republican. Roman Catholic. Office: US Ho of Reps Rayburn Bldg 2269 Washington DC 20515

HAYES, NORMAN ROBERT, JR., lawyer; b. Schenectady, N.Y., Apr. 12, 1948; s. Norman Robert Sr. and Ethel May (Blair) H.; m. Alice S. Margitan, Oct. 14, 1972; children: Robert, Charles. BS, Clarkson U., 1970; JD, Union U., 1973. Bar: N.Y. 1974, U.S. Dist. Ct. (no. dist.) N.Y. 1974, U.S. Supreme Ct. 1978. Ptnr. Wemple, Daly, Casey, Hayes, Watkins & Harter, Schenectady, 1973-86, Hayes & Casey, Clifton Park, 1986—; pres. S.P.B. Industries, Clifton Park, N.Y., 1979—; chmn. Active Industries Inc.; bd. dirs. Saratoga Econ. Devel. Corp., Saratoga Springs, N.Y., Home Funding Finders Inc., Clifton Park, N.Y. Pres. County Knolls South Civic Assn., Clifton Park, 1975-76. Served to capt. U.S. Army, 1973-74. Mem. ABA, N.Y. State Bar Assn., Schenectady County Bar Assn. Republican. Home: 20 Timberwick Dr Clifton Park NY 12065-6225 Office: Hayes & Casey 258 Ushers Rd Clifton Park NY 12065-1400

HAYES, WILBUR FRANK, biology educator; b. Rhinelander, Wis., Nov. 10, 1936; s. Wilbur Mead and Evelyn (Stritesky) H.; m. Dawn Olivia Waldorf, July 21, 1979 (div. Feb. 1991); stepchildren: Lynn, Robert, Dana, Richard, Gary, Kevin. BA, Colby Coll., 1959; MS, Lehigh U., 1961, PhD, 1965. Postdoctoral fellow Yale U., New Haven, 1965-67; asst. prof. biology Wilkes Coll., Wilkes-Barre, Pa., 1967-71, assoc. prof., 1971—; vis. prof. Northeastern U., Boston, 1987-88. Contbr. articles to profl. jours. Chmn. bd. dirs. Northeastern Pa. chpt. A. Heart Assn., Wilkes-Barre, 1986-87. Mem. Am. Soc. Zoologists, Pa. Acad. Sci., Electron Microscope Soc. Am., Sigma Xi (pres. Wilkes Coll. club chpt. 1976-77, sec., treas. 1984-87, 88-91). Republican. Congregationalist. Home: 47 Stanley St Wilkes Barre PA 18702-2308 Office: Wilkes U Dept Biology Wilkes-Barre PA 18766

HAYMANN, MARY DUNN, foreign language educator; b. New London, Conn., Feb. 22, 1945; d. Joseph Sinon and Mary (Casserly) Dunn; m. Francois Bernard Haymann, Feb. 17, 1968; children: Bettina, Laura. BA, Simmons Coll., 1966; MA, Rutgers U., 1984, PhD, 1990. French tchr. Newton (Mass.) South High Sch., 1966-68; ESL tchr., asst. to cultural attache U.S. Embassy, Cen. Africa Republic, 1968-69; editor, legal translator Law Office Frank Boas, Brussels, 1970-72; freelance tech. translator France, U.S., 1972-80; teaching asst., French dept. Rutgers Univ., New Brunswick, N.J., 1981-82; instr., French dept. Caldwell (N.J.) Coll., 1979-86; v.p. fin. F.H. Techs., Inc., Verona, N.J., 1984—; instr. French dept. Rutgers Univ., New Brunswick, 1990-91; asst. prof. French dept. Caldwell (N.J.) Coll., 1991—. Contbr. articles to profl. jours. Mem. AAUW, Am. Assn. Tchrs. of French, Modern Lang. Assn., Soc. des Amis de Colette, Soc. des Profs. France (bd. dirs. 1990—).

HAYNES, GARRY LOCKLYN, consulting actuary; b. Atlanta, Apr. 6, 1953; s. Thomas Vandiver and Peggy Louise (Cobb) H.; m. Deborah Elaine Hatcher, Mar. 22, 1975; children: Carolyn Elaine, Brian Patrick, Kevin Scott. BBA, Ga. State U., Atlanta, 1975. Cons. actuary Buck Cons., N.Y.C., summers 1981-87, Washington, 1987—; actuary Meidinger, Charlotte, N.C., 1980-81, Louisville, 1975-80. Pres. Waverly Crossing Community Assn., Chantilly, Va., 1989-91. Mem. Soc. Actuaries, Am. Acad. Actuaries, Conf. of Actuaries in Pub. Practice. Home: 4313 Galesbury Ln Chantilly VA 22021-3636 Office: Buck Cons 1850 K St NW # 205L Washington DC 20006-2213

HAYNES, JOHN EARL, historian; b. Plant City, Fla., Nov. 22, 1944; s. John Milner and Elizabeth (Farmer) H.; m. Janette Marie Murray; children: Joshua, Amanda, John. BA, Fla. State U., 1966; MA, U. Minn., 1968, PhD, 1978. Tax policy advisor Gov. of Minn., St. Paul, 1971-77; legis. aide U.S. Senator Wendell Anderson, Washington, 1977-78, U.S. Rep. Martin Sabo, Washington, 1979-83; dir. tax analysis fin. dept. State of Minn., St. Paul, 1983-85, asst. commr. for tax policy revenue dept., 1985-87; historian Libr. of Congress, Washington, 1987—. Author: Communism and Anti-Communism, 1987, Dubious Alliance, 1984. Del. to state conv. Minn. Dem.-Farmer-Labor Party, 1976. Maj. USAR, 1966-90. Leadership fellow Bush Found., 1974, Woodrow Wilson fellow Woodrow Wilson Found., 1967. Mem. Am. Hist. Assn., Orgn. Am. Historians, Historians of Am. Communism, Phi Beta Kappa. Anglican. Home: 3100 King Tree St Silver Spring MD 20902-2402

HAYNES, NORRIS MICHAEL, psychology educator; b. Port of Spain, Trinidad, May 11, 1950; came to U.S., 1970; s. Melville and Audrey (Corke) H.; m. Monica H.; children: Nadine, Felixcia, Norrissa. BA, SUNY, Plattsburgh, 1972, MA, 1975; PhD, Howard U., 1978, MBA, 1981. Lic. psychologist Conn., Washington. Tchr., counselor Montreal (Can.) High Sch., 1973-75; sr. psychologist Sound Systems Intervention Inc., Washington, 1977-81; asst. prof. Howard U., Washington, 1981-85; dir. of rsch., sch. devel. program, Child Study Ctr. Yale U., New Haven, Conn., 1985—, asst. prof., 1989—; adj. prof. So. Conn. State U., New Haven, 1988—. Contbr. articles to profl. jours. Fulbright scholar, 1971. Mem. APA, Am. Ednl. Rsch. Assn., Beta Gamma Sigma, Phi Delta Kappa. Home: 105 Westwood Rd New Haven CT 06515-2244 Office: Yale Child Study Ctr 230 S Frontage Rd New Haven CT 06515

HAYNES, SEAN AARON RUSSEL, electrical engineer; b. East Meadow, N.Y., Sept. 15, 1968; s. Thomas Frances Haynes and Eileen Robin Shadoff Jagoe. BSEE, Northeastern U., Boston, 1991. Co-op engr. GE Aerospace ASD, Burlington, Mass., 1988-91; engr. Gen. Dynamics Electric Boat, Newport, R.I., 1991—. Author software: Tandy Sound Digitizer, 1991, Checkbook Organizer, 1992. Mem. IEEE. Democrat. Office: Gen Dynamics Elec Boat 2 Corporate Pl D702 Middletown RI 02840

HAYNES, THOMAS BERANEK, filmmaker, lawyer; b. Boston, Apr. 30, 1956; s. Leo Leroy and Phyllis May (Knight) Beranek; m. Jean Reed, Aug. 7, 1982. BA, Dartmouth Coll., 1978; JD, U. Chgo., 1981. Bar: Ill. 1983. Law clk. U.S. Ct. Appeals (2d cir.), Bridgeport, Conn., 1981-82, U.S. Ct. Appeals (7th cir.), Chgo., 1982-83; atty. Schiff Hardin & Waite, Chgo., 1983-88; pres. Enzo Provolone Prodns., Inc., 1989—. Mng. editor U Chgo. Law Rev., 1980-81; writer, producer, dir. An Insect, 1977, What Dread Hand?, 1991. Mem. fgn. affairs com. Chgo. Coun. on Fgn. Rels., 1985-90; bd. govs. Chgo. Symphony Orch., 1986-90. Mem. ABA, Chgo. Bar Assn., Am. Judicature Soc. (bd. dirs. 1984-88), Harvard Club of Boston, Internat. Club of Chgo. Democrat. Episcopalian. Office: PO Box 7596 FDR Sta New York NY 10150-1913

HAYNES, THOMAS MORRIS, philosophy educator; b. Waukesha, Wis., Oct. 24, 1918; s. George Albert and Lois (Morris) H.; m. Jane Louise Riggs, Sept. 12, 1942; children: Christopher Thomas, Jonathan Marshall, Carolyn Martha. AB, Butler U., 1941; PhD, U. Ill., 1949. Indsl. engr. RCA, Indpls., 1942-44; research and devel. engr. P.R. Mallory, Indpls., 1944-46; postdoctoral fellow Faculty Law U. Paris, 1949-50; instr. philosophy U. Ill., 1950-51; research asst. U. Ill. (Coll. of Law), 1950-51; instr. philosophy Lehigh U., 1952-54, asst. prof., 1954-61, asso. prof., 1961-69, prof., 1969-83, prof. emeritus, adj. prof., 1983-91. Mem. Am. Philos. Assn., AAUP, N.Y. Acad. Scis., Environ. Def. Fund, World Wildlife Fund, Nat. Resources Def. Coun., The Wilderness Soc., Nat. Wildlife Fedn. (assoc.), Union Concerned Scientists (sponsor), Phi Beta Kappa, Phi Kappa Phi. Home: 640 High St Bethlehem PA 18018-4047 Office: Lehigh U Dept Philosophy Phil Bldg #15 Bethlehem PA 18015

HAYS, DAN ANDREW, physicist; b. Dallas Center, Iowa, July 12, 1939; s. Leonard Andrew and Florence (Orton) H.; m. Judith Ann Delp, Aug. 23, 1964; children: Andrew, David. BS, Iowa State U., 1961; MS, Rutgers U., 1963, PhD, 1966. Postdoctoral fellow U. Pitts., 1966-68; mem. rsch. staff Xerox Corp., Rochester, N.Y., 1968-80, prin. scientist, 1980—. Contbr. articles to profl. jours. Recipient Ednl. Svc. award Plastics Inst. Am., 1975, Xerox Pres. award, 1981, Chester F. Carlson award, 1991; RCA fellow, 1964-66, Andrew Mellon fellow, 1966-68. Mem. Am. Phys. Soc., Electrostatic Soc. Am., Imaging Sci. and Tech. Methodist. Office: Xerox Corp 0114-22D 800 Phillips Rd Webster NY 14580-9791

HAYS, DIANA JOYCE WATKINS, consumer products company executive; b. Riverside, Calif., Aug. 29, 1945; d. Donald Richard and Evelyn Christine (Kolvoord) Watkins; m. Gerald N. Hays, Jan 30, 1964 (div. Jan. 1970), 1 child, Tad Damon. BA, U. Minn., 1975, MBA, 1982. Dir. environ./phys. sci. Sci. Mus. Minn., St. Paul, 1972-76; dir. mktg. rsch. No. Natural Gas Co., Omaha, 1977-78; mktg. asst., asst. product mgr. Gen. Mills, Inc., Mpls., 1978-81; product mgr. ortho pharms. Consumer Products div. Johnson & Johnson, Raritan, N.J., 1981-82, product dir. home diagnostics, 1982-86; mktg. dir. new market devel. Consumer Products div. Becton Dickinson & Co., Franklin Lakes, N.J., 1986-90; dir. home diagnostics worldwide program Becton Dickinson Advanced Diagnostics Div. Becton Dickinson & Co., Balt., 1990—; founder, pres. Exec. Computing Solutions, Inc., Balt., 1991—; chmn. energy exhibit com. Assn. Sci.-Tech. Ctrs., Washington, 1974-75. Producer Ecologenie, 1975. Recipient Tribute to Women and Industry award YWCA, 1989. Mem. Am. Mktg. Assn., NAFE, Twin Mgmt. Forum, Am. Assn. of Health Svcs. Mktg., Capital PC User Group, Beta Gamma Sigma (life). Republican. Roman Catholic. Office: Becton Dickinson & Co Advanced Diagnostic Div 10 Loveton Cir Sparks MD 21152

HAYS, JAMES FRED, geologist, educator; b. Little Rock, July 10, 1933; s. Orren Lee and Virginia (Russell) H.; m. Diane Lee Huntoon, Dec. 22, 1956; 1 dau., Lee Anne. A.B., Columbia U., 1954; M.S. (NSF fellow), Calif. Inst. Tech., 1961; Ph.D., Harvard U., 1966. Geologist U.S. Geol. Survey, 1961; guest investigator Geophys. Lab., Carnegie Instn. of Washington, 1965; Soc. Fellows jr. fellow Harvard U., 1963-66, asst. prof. geology, 1966-69, assoc. prof., 1969-72, prof., 1972-84, chmn. dept. geol. scis., 1981-82; dir. div. earth scis. NSF, 1982-87, sr. sci. advisor, 1987-91, dir. earth scis. div., 1991—; cons. NASA Astronaut Tng. Program, 1969-73; mem. NASA Lunar Sample Analysis Planning Team, 1973-76; chmn. Lunar and Planetary Rev. Panel, 1978-81; prin. investigator Apollo Lunar Sample Program; vis. prof. chemistry and geology Ariz. State U., 1978-79; mem. Harvard Ctr. for Earth and Planetary Physics., 1970-84; adminstrs. bd. Harvard and Radcliffe Colls., 1976-78; mem. sci. adv. bd. Mt. St. Helens Nat. Volcanic Monument, 1983-87; mem. adv. com. on mining and minerals research Dept. Interior, 1983-85; mem. Working Group for U.S.-Peoples' Republic of China Agreement for Cooperation in Earth Scis., 1982-87; exec. sec. Pres.'s Com. on Nat. Medal Sci., 1987-91. Assoc. editor: Nature of the Solid Earth, 1970, Jour. Geophys. Research, 1978-80, 83-85. Served to capt. USNR, 1954-59. NSF grantee, 1974-82; NASA grantee, 1971-82. Fellow Geol. Soc. Am. (councilor 1988-91), Mineral. Soc. Am.; mem. AAAS (councilor 1989-92), Am. Geophys. Union, Am. Assn. Petroleum Geologists, Geol. Soc. Washington, Geochem. Soc., Potomac Geophys. Soc., Meteoritical Soc., Am. Ornithologists Union, Naval Res. Assn., Phi Beta Kappa, Sigma Xi. Clubs: Harvard (N.Y.C., D.C.), Cosmos. Home: Rt 4 Box 94E Warrenton VA 22186 Office: Div Earth Scis NSF Washington DC 20550

HAYS, ROBERT ALEXANDER, lawyer; b. Westerly, R.I., June 20, 1944; s. William Henry and Margaret Elizabeth (Tefft) H.; m. Norma Marie Camerlin, Aug. 23, 1969; children—Stephanie Rebecca, Gregory Alexander. AS, Mitchell Coll., 1967; BS, NYU, 1969, MS, 1970; JD, Widener U., 1976. Bar: N.J. 1976, U.S. Dist. Ct. N.J. 1976, U.S. Patent Office 1974, U.S. Ct. Appeals (fed. cir.) 1982, Calif. 1989. Mem. tech. staff RCA, Moorestown, N.J., 1970-73, patent atty., Princeton, N.J., 1973-78, resident patent counsel, Cherry Hill, N.J., 1978-80; group patent counsel Perkin-Elmer, Norwalk, Conn., 1980-84; patent counsel ITT, Shelton, Conn., 1984-86, patent atty. Pitney Bowes, Stamford, Conn., 1986-88; sr. patent atty. Hughes Aircraft Co., L.A., 1988—. Mem. L.A. Patent Law Assn., Tau Beta Pi, Eta Kappa Nu. Office: Hughes Danbury Optical Systems Inc 100 Wooster Hts Danbury CT 06810-7588

HAYS, THOMAS CHANDLER, holding company executive; b. Chgo., Apr. 21, 1935; s. Marion C. and Carolyn (Reid) H.; m. Mary Ann Jergens, June 8, 1958; children—Thomas, Michael, Paul, Jennifer. B.S., Calif. Inst. Tech., 1957, M.S., 1958; M.B.A. with high distinction (Baker scholar), Harvard U., 1963. Ops. research analyst Lockheed Corp., Los Angeles, 1963-64; product mgr. Andrew Jergens Co. (formerly subs. Am. Brands), Cin., 1964-70; v.p. mktg. Andrew Jergens Co. (formerly subs. Am. Brands), 1970-78, exec. v.p., 1978, pres., chief exec. officer, 1979-80; v.p. mktg. Am. Tobacco Co. (subs. Am. Brands), 1980-81, exec. v.p., 1981-85, pres., 1985-87, pres., chief operating officer, 1985-86, chief exec. officer, 1986-87, chmn., 1987-88; pres., chief operating officer Am. Brands, Inc., 1988—, also bd. dirs.; bd. dirs. Am. Tobacco, Acushnet Co., Gallaher Ltd., Golden Belt Mfg. Co., MasterBrand Industries, Inc., MCM Products, Inc., ACCO World Corp., Am. Brands Internat. Corp., Am. Tob. Internat. Corp., Am. Franklin Co., Jim Beam Brands Co., Franklin Life Ins. Co. Trustee, treas. Cin. Country Day Sch., 1978-80; trustee The Andrew Jergens Found., trustee Five-Town Found.; bd. dirs., treas. Meml. Community Ctr., 1965-75. 1st lt. USAF, 1958-61. Republican. Presbyterian. Clubs: Cin. Country, Darien Country, Bel Air Bay, Tokeneke.

HAYS, THOMAS R., electronics executive; b. MacFarlan, W.Va., July 14, 1915; s. William R. and Myra (Wilson) H.; m. Jeane Ligney, May 11, 1945; children: Thomas R. Jr., Sharon Hays Stricchiola, Jeane Anne Hays Nerlino, Bonnie Hays Erlichman. BSEE, Ohio U., 1937; cert., Nothwestern U. Inst. Mgmt., 1959. Registered profl. electrical engr. Student engr. RCA Corp., Camden, N.J., 1937-38, radar and sonar engr., 1938-45; dist. sales mgr. Tube div. RCA Corp., Harrison, N.J., 1946-56; sales mgr. Picture Tube div., Receiving Tube div., Solid State div., Memory Products div. RCA Corp., Somerville, N.J., 1956-60, mktg. mgr. Solid State div., 1960-75; mgr. major accts. RCA Corp., Somerville, 1975-80; pres. Tom Hays, Inc., Madison, N.J., 1980—; realtor Coldwell Banker, 1986—; pres. Tom Hays, Inc., 1980—. Bd. dirs. Madison YMCA, 1982—; bd. dirs., v.p. Madison Meth. Ch., 1985—, pres. bd. trustees, 1988; mem. long range planning com. Morris County Bd. Realtors, 1988—, YMCA, 1989. Republican. Lodge: Rotary (v.p., bd. dirs., 1985—, pres.-elect, 1988, pres., 1989-90). Home: 20 Beverly Rd Madison NJ 07940-2817 Office: Coldwell Banker 20 Beverly Rd Madison NJ 07940-2817

HAYS, WILLIAM PAUL, music educator; b. Westville, Okla., Feb. 11, 1929; s. Paul and Olive Freda (Kern) H.; m. Dorothea Richter, Aug. 23, 1958; 1 child, Marie Elizabeth. MusB, U. Ark., 1950; MusM, Ind. U., 1952; pvt. study organ with, A. Marchal, Paris, 1957-58, 63-64; D Sacred Music, Union Theol. Sem., N.Y.C., 1970. Asst. prof. Hendrix Coll., Conway, Ark., 1952-53; organist-choirmaster Pulaski Heights Meth. Ch., Little Rock, 1952-53; assoc. prof. Union Coll., Barbourville, Ky., 1954-66; organist-choirmaster United Presbyn. Ch., Garden City, N.Y., 1966-68; lectr. Union Theol. Sem., N.Y.C., 1970-72; prof. organ music Westminster Choir Coll., Princeton, N.J., 1972—; vis. prof. Trenton (N.J.) State Coll., 1987; free lance lectr. and recitalist. Editor: 20th-Century Views of Music History, 1972; contbr. articles and revs. to profl. jours. and encys. Mem. AAUP, Am. Bach Soc., Am. Musciol. Soc., Organ Hist. Soc., Music Tchrs. Nat. Assn. (pres. ea. div. 1979-82, nat. organ chair 1986-91, nat. exec. bd. 1979—). Home: 443 W 50th St New York NY 10019-6507 Office: Westminster Choir Coll Princeton NJ 08540

HAYTHE, WINSTON MCDONALD, lawyer, educator, consultant, real estate investor; b. Reidsville, N.C., Oct. 10, 1940; s. McDonald Swann and Henrietta Elizabeth (East) H.; m. Glenann Leigh Rogers, Aug. 17, 1963 (div. 1977); children: Sheila Elaine, Kevin McDonald, Rhonda Leigh. BS, S.W. Mo. State U., 1963; JD, Coll. William and Mary, 1967; postgrad., U. Va. Grad. Sch. Law, 1968-69. Bar: Va. 1967, D.C. 1969. Assoc. Rhyne & Rhyne, Washington, 1969-72; sr. trial atty. AEC, Washington, 1972-73; asst. gen counsel, sr. atty. Consumer Produce Safety Commn., Washington, 1973-82; staff dir. legal office EPA, Washington, 1982-83, 050, 1985-91; sr. atty. Nat. Enforcement Tng. Inst., 1991—; legis. fellow U.S. Senate, Washington, 1983-85; adj. prof. law U. Md., College Park, 1978— mem. law faculty U.S. Army Judge Adv. Gen.'s Sch., Charlottesville, Va., 1969—; cons. Barrister Enterprises, Washington, 1978—. With JAGC, U.S. Army, col. Res. Recipient Excellence in Teaching award U. Md., 1992. Mem. Va. State Bar Assn., D.C. Bar Assn., Fed. Bar Assn. (chmn. nat. com. 1981—), Coll. William and Mary Law Sch. Assn. (bd. dirs. 1988—), Kappa Mu Epsilon. Republican. Presbyterian. Home: 2141 P St NW Apt 402 Washington DC 20037-1031 Office: US EPA 401 M St SW Washington DC 20460

HAYWARD, CHARLES WILLIAM, heavy equipment dealer executive; b. St. John's, Can., June 2, 1937; s. Frank R. and Anna C. (Kapelley) H.; m. Mary Bridget Sullivan, Nov. 24, 1962; children: Anne Louise, Maureen Leslie, Mark William. B in Commerce, Dalhousie U., Halifax, N.S., 1958; MBA with honors, Harvard U., 1966. Audit clk. Doane Raymond, New Glasgow, N.S., Can., 1958-61; mgr., staff chartered acct. Doane Raymond, Grand Falls, Nfld., 1961-64; cons. Doane Raymond, Halifax, 1966-68, ptnr., 1968-86; exec. v.p. N.S. Tractors & Equipment Ltd., Halifax, 1986—; bd. dirs. J&D Equipment Ltd., Tractors & Equipment, Ltd., Halifax Water Commn. Contbr. articles to profl. jours.; co-author: Computer Aided Design, 1966. Bd. dirs. N.S. Art Gallery 1984-88, Sacred Heart Sch., 1984-87. Fellow Inst. Chartered Accts. N.S. (pres. 1973-74, Berman Meml. prize 1960), bd. chmn. Can. Inst. Chartered Accts. (standard setting bds. 1983-87); mem. Inst. Chartered Bus. Valuators Can., Inst. Mgmt. Cons. Atlantic Can., Asburn Golf (bd. dirs. 1985-89) Club, Halifax (pres. 1984-85) Club,

Cathedral Laymen's Assn. (pres. 1984-86). Liberal. Anglican. Office: NS Tractors & Equipment Ltd, 3575 Kempt Rd, Halifax, NS Canada B3K 5J2

HAYWARD, GEORGE J., lawyer; b. Kingston, Pa., Dec. 30, 1944; s. Ralph R. and Martha P. (Tamkus) H.; m. Nancy E. Goldsmith, 1967 (div. 1974); children: Benjamin G., Jennifer R., Christopher D.; m. Jennifer M. Jordan, Feb. 23, 1985; children: George J.J., John G.J. BA, King's Coll., 1966; JD, Harvard U., 1969. Bar: Pa. 1970, N.Y. 1980, N.J. 1988. Assoc. Montgomery, McCracken, Walker & Rhoads, Phila., 1969-71, Wolf, Block, Schorr & Solis-Cohn, Phila., 1971-73; gen. counsel AAMCO Industries, Inc., Bridgeport, Pa., 1973-78; asst. counsel, sec., dir. DeLorean Motor Co., N.Y.C., 1979-83; gen. counsel Internat. Distbn. Ctrs. Inc., North Bergen, N.J., 1983-86, Carrier Industries Inc., Elizabeth, N.J., 1986—. Mem. ABA, Pa. Bar Assn., N.Y. State Bar Assn., N.J. Bar Assn. Club: Harvard (N.Y.C.). Home: 55 Stonewall Cir White Plains NY 10607-1834 Office: Carrier Industries Inc 1-71 North Ave E Elizabeth NJ 07201

HAYWARD, HAROLD, civil engineer, consultant; b. N.Y.C., Jan. 11, 1920; s. Israel and Sadie Lillian (Blum) Horwitz; B.C.E. cum laude, Coll. City N.Y., 1941; M.C.E., N.Y.U., 1949; m. Dorothy Rose Anderson, Aug. 18, 1946; children—H. Garrett, Susan Hayward Wrobel, Rael Joanne Hayward Cantline, Margaret Elizabeth, Carol Anne. Engr.-in-charge Elwyn E. Seely & Co., N.Y.C., 1941-44, Elson T. Killam, N.Y.C., 1946-49; city engr. City of Beacon, N.Y., 1951-54; partner Wiesenfeld Hayward & Leon, N.Y.C., 1954-61, Hayward & Pakan Assos., Poughkeepsie, N.Y., 1961—. Vice chmn. Poughkeepsie Parking Authority, 1965-72, chmn., 1972-76; chmn. bd. dirs. Dutchess County chpt. Am. Heart Assn., 1978—. Bd. dirs. Rehab. Programs Inc., 1965-70, hon. dir., 1970—. Served to lt. (j.g.) USNR, 1943-46. Registered profl. engr., N.Y. Mem. Cons. Engrs. Council, Nat. Soc. Profl. Engrs., Dutchess County Art Assn. (treas. 1967). Clubs: Masons, Rotary (pres.-elect Poughkeepsie 1979), Kevin Barry Irish (Poughkeepsie, treas. 1978, pres. 1980). Works include structural engring. on St. John's Ch., Collegeville, Minn., Arlington Sewage Treatment Plant, Poughkeepsie, Town of Poughkeepsie Water System. Home: 35 Adriance Ave Poughkeepsie NY 12601-4923 Office: Hayward & Pakan Assocs 321 Main Mall Poughkeepsie NY 12601-3125

HAYWARD, JANE, museum curator; b. Orange, Conn., Aug. 13, 1918; d. Lawrence Herbert Hayward and Julia Ellen (Woodruff) Elliot. BFA, U. Pa., 1952, MA, 1954; PhD, Yale U., 1958; ArtsD (hon.), Stonehill Coll., 1980. Tech. illustrator Am. Viscose Corp., Phila., 1945-54; rsch. asst. Yale U. Art Gallery, New Haven, 1958-61; instr. Conn. Coll., New London, 1961-64, asst. prof., 1964-67; curator Lyman Allyn Mus., New London, 1961-65; Clawson Mills fellow Met. Mus. Art, N.Y.C., 1967-69, assoc. curator, 1969-74, curator, 1974—; adj. prof. Columbia U., N.Y.C., 1971—. Co-author articles in Ency. Britannica, World Book Ency., monographs. Trustee Stonehill Coll., North Easton, Mass., 1972-79. Recipient Monticello prize Yale U., 1956; Am. Coun. Learned Socs. fellow, 1966-67; Cresson scholar Pa. Acad. Fine Arts, 1940, 42. Fellow Internat. Ctr. Medieval Art (life, bd. dirs. 1977-86); mem. Census Stained Glass Windows in Am. (bd. dirs. 1979—), Coll. Art Assn., Internat. Corpus Vitrearum (Am. rep. 1956—, pres. Am. bd. 1982—). Republican. Episcopalian. Office: Met Mus Art Cloisters Fort Tryon Pk New York NY 10040

HAYWARD, RICHARD WILLIAM, insurance agent; b. Waterbury, Conn., Jan. 9, 1932; s. George Arthur and Mary (Dennison) H.; m. Mildred Ann Makl, Feb. 1, 1957 (div. 1978); children: Mark Andrew, Polly Pepper Hayward Miller, Kirsten Hayward Stone, Elizabeth Hayward Mute, Ian Andrew. Student, U. Conn., U. Hartford, Quinne Coll. pres. Waterbury Life Underwriters, 1963; v.p. Conn. State Life Underwriters, Hartford, 1968-69. Chmn. Woodbury Bd. Fire Commrs., 1984-91, capt. Woodbury Fire Dept., 1967-70; house chmn. Glebe House Mus., Woodbury, 1978-85; concert mgr. Conn. Choral Soc., Woodbury, 1990-91; mem. St. Paul's Choir, Woodbury, 1963-91. Democrat. Episcopalian. Home and Office: 11 Scratchville Rd Woodbury CT 06798-2925

HAYWARD, TERESA CALCAGNO, educator; b. N.Y.C., Jan. 28, 1907; d. Vito and Rosalie (Amato) Calcagno; m. Peter Hayward, Feb. 6, 1932; children: Nancy, Peter. BA, Hunter Coll., 1929; MA, Columbia U., 1931. Tchr. romance langs. Jr. High Sch. 164, N.Y.C., 1936-57, Jr. High Sch. 141, Riverdale, N.Y., 1957-71; tchr. English to Japanese women Nichibei Fujinkai, Riverdale, 1972—, chmn. Riverdale chpt., 1976-92, Manhattan, 1992—. Bd. dirs. Riverdale chpt. UN Assn., 1973—; mem. Hunger and Social Outreach com. Christ Ch., Riverdale. Democrat. Episcopalian. Avocations: concerts, piano, art lectures, travel.

HAYWOOD, ANNE MOWBRAY, pediatrics, virology, and biochemistry educator; b. Balt., Feb. 5, 1935; d. Richard Mansfield and Margaret (Mowbray) H. BA in Chemistry, Bryn Mawr Coll., 1955; MD, Harvard U., 1959. Cert. Am. Bd. Pediatrics. Intern pediatrics U. Calif. Med. Ctr., San Francisco, 1959-60; postdoctoral fellow biochemistry dept. Columbia U., N.Y.C., 1961-62; postdoctoral fellow div. biology Calif. Inst. Tech., Pasadena, 1960-61, 62-64; asst. prof. microbiology, microbiology dept. Northwestern U. Med. Sch., Chgo., 1964-66, Yale U. Med. Sch., New Haven, 1966-73; resident pediatrics U. Wash., Seattle, 1974-75, pediatric infectious disease fellow, 1975-76; pediatric infectious disease fellow Vanderbilt U., Nashville, 1976-77; assoc. prof. pediatrics and microbiology U. Rochester (N.Y.), 1977-85, assoc. prof. pediatrics, microbiology, medicine, 1985—; vis. asst. prof. Rockefeller U., N.Y.C., 1971-72; vis. scientist biophysics unit Agrl. Rsch. Coun., Cambridge, Eng., 1972-74, Inst. for Immunology and Virology, U. Zürich (Switzerland), 1987; vis. assoc. prof. dept. zoology U. Calif., Davis, 1986. Co-author: Practice of Pediatrics, 1977, Infections in Children, 1982, Liposome Letters, 1983, Practice of Pediatrics, 1987, Molecular Mechanisms of Membrane Fusion, 1988, Membrane Fusion, 1991, Encyclopedia of Human Biology, 1991, Cell and Model Membrane Interactions, 1991. Fogarty Internat. Ctr. Sr. fellow NIH, 1987, European Molecular Biology Orgn. fellow, 1973-74, NIH Spl. fellow, 1971-73, Am. Cancer Soc. Postdoctoral fellow, 1960-62; Harvard Med. Sch. scholar, 1955-59, Harriet Judd Sartain scholar, 1955-59, N.Y. Alumnae scholar Bryn Mawr Coll., 1951-55. Mem. Biophys. Soc., Am. Soc. for Biochem. and Molecular Biology, Infectious Diseases Soc. Am. Democrat. Office: U Rochester Med Ctr PO Box 777 Rochester NY 14642

HAYWORTH, CURTIS BENJAMIN, chemical engineer; b. Vienna, Austria, Dec. 1, 1920; came to U.S., 1938; s. Siegmund and Rose Hayworth; children: Steven, Karen. B in Chem. Engring., CCNY, 1944; M in Chem. Engring., NYU, 1947, ScD, 1949. Registered profl. engr., N.Y. Analyst Allied Chem. Corp., Wilmington, Del., 1944-45; tech. supr. lab. Allied Chem. Corp., Edgewater, N.J., 1945-48; rsch. chem. engr. Allied Chem. Corp., N.Y.C., 1948-53; asst. mgr. devel. rsch. Allied Chem. Corp., Marcus Hook, Pa., 1953-55; asst. dir., dir. Allied Chem. Corp., Morristown, N.J., 1955-61, asst. tech. dir., 1961-63, asst. dir. Cen. Rsch. Lab., 1963-70; v.p. World Patent Devel. Corp., N.Y.C., 1970-71, pres., 1971-75; valuation engr. U.S. Treasury, Mountainside, N.J., 1975—. Contbr. articles to profl. jours.; patentee in field. Mem. Am. Inst. Chem. Engrs., Am. Chem. Soc., Sigma Xi. Home: PO Box 1447 Morristown NJ 07962-1447

HAYWORTH, SCOTT DAVID, physician; b. N.Y.C., Apr. 4, 1956; s. Henry Charles and Anne (Sinnreich) H.; m. Nan Alison Sutter, June 21, 1981; 1 child, William. AB, Princeton U., 1978; MD, Cornell U., 1984. Diplomate Am. Bd. Ob/Gyn., Nat. Bd. Med. Examiners. Intern Mt. Sinai Hosp., N.Y.C., 1984-85, resident physician, 1985-87, chief resident, 1987-88; physician Mt. Kisco (N.Y.) Med. Group, 1988—; co-chmn. laser com. No. Westchester Hosp., 1991—, mem. pharmacy and therapeutics com., 1990—. Contbr. chpt. to book and articles to profl. jours. Fellow NIH, 1981, David Barr, 1981. Fellow Am. Coll Ob-Gyn.; mem. Westchester Ostetrical Soc., Internat. Soc. Gynecologic Endoscopy, Gynecologic Laser Soc. Office: Mt Kisco Med Group 34 S Bedford Rd Mount Kisco NY 10549

HAZARD, GEOFFREY CORNELL, JR., law educator; b. Cleve., Sept. 18, 1929; s. Geoffrey Cornell and Virginia (Perry) H.; m. Elizabeth O'Hara; children: James G., Katherine W., Robin P., Geoffrey Cornell III. BA, Swarthmore Coll., 1953, LLD (hon.), 1988; LLB, Columbia U., 1954; LLD (hon.), Gonzaga U., 1985, U. San Diego, 1985, Ill. Inst. Tech., 1990. Bar: Oreg. 1954, Calif. 1960, Conn. 1982. Assoc. Hart, Spencer, McCulloch, Rockwood & Davies, Portland, Oreg., 1954-57; exec. sec. Oreg. Legis. Interim Com. Jud. Adminstrn., 1957-58; assoc. prof. law, then prof. U. Calif., Berkeley, 1958-64; prof. law U. Chgo., 1964-71; prof. law Yale U., 1971—, prof. mgmt., 1979-83, acting dean Sch. Orgn. and Mgmt., 1980-81, Sterling prof. law, 1986—; mem. Adminstrv. Conf. U.S., 1971-78. Author: (with David W. Louisell and Colin Tait) Pleading and Procedure, 1962, 6th edit., 1989, Research in Civil Procedure, 1963, (with Fleming James) Civil Procedure, 4th edit., 1992, Ethics in the Practice of Law, 1978, (with W. William Hodes) Law of Lawyering, 2d edit. 1990, (with Susan Koniak) Law and Ethics of Lawyering, 1990, also articles.; editor: Law in a Changing America, 1968, (with Deborah Rhode) Legal Profession: Responsibility and Regulation, 1985. Served with USAF, 1948-49. Fellow Am. Bar Found. (exec. dir. 1964-70, Rsch. award 1986), Am. Acad. Arts and Scis.; mem. ABA (cons. code jud. conduct 1970-72, reporter standards jud. adminstrn. 1971-77, reporter model rules of profl. conduct 1978-83), Am. Law Inst. (reporter restatement of judges 1973-81, dir. 1984—), Nat. Legal Aid and Defender Assn., Inst. Jud. Adminstrn., Am. Judicature Soc., Selden Soc., Calif. State Bar, Conn. Bar Assn., Assn. Bar City N.Y., Phi Beta Kappa. Episcopalian. Home: 452 Humphrey St New Haven CT 06511-3711

HAZARD, NANCY, executive; b. Washington, Dec. 26, 1944; d. John Newbold and Susan (Lawrence) H. BA in Art History, Carleton Coll., 1967; postgrad., Noboru Kubo Studio, Kyoto, Japan, 1969, Alfred U., 1970. Sole proprietor Nancy's Studio (a pottery bus.), Leverett, Mass., 1969-74; instr. Elms Coll., Chicopee, Mass., 1973-74; extension solar tech. Energy Edn. Ctr., Coop. Ext. Svc., Amherst, Mass., 1979-81; sole proprietor Hazard & Sun (design build co.), Greenfield, Mass., 1981-89; instr. Cornerstones, Brunswick, Maine, 1984-88; dir. Cornerstones, Springvale, Maine, 1988, Northeast Sustainable Energy Assn., Greenfield, 1989—; bd. dirs. NE Solar Energy Assn., Brattleboro, Vt., 1985-89. Contbr. articles to profl. jours. Bd. dirs. Wllowman Hill, Deerfield, Mass., 1978-89; com. mem. Appalachian Mountain Club, Hadley, Mass., 1984-89. Office: Northeast Sustainable Energy Assn 23 Ames St Greenfield MA 01301-2429

HAZELL, PETER BRIAN REGINALD, agricultural economist, researcher; b. Halstead, Essex, England, June 21, 1944; s. Reginald George and Phyllis Rose (Smith) H.; m. Jill Nancy Matthews, June 29, 1969 (div. Mar. 1978); m. Joan Ann Straker, Feb. 1, 1981. BS, Seale-Hayne Coll., England, 1965; MS, Cornell U., 1968, PhD, 1970. Sr. rsch. assoc. U. Newcastle-Upon-Tyne, U.K., 1970-72; economist World Bank, 1972-79; rsch. fellow Intenat. Food Policy Rsch. Inst., Washington, 1979-84, program dir., 1984-86; sr. economist World Bank, Washington, 1986-88, prin. economist, 1988—. Author: (with others) Project Evaluation in Regional Perspective: A Study of an Irrigation Project in Northwest Malaysia, 1982, Risky Agricultural Markets: Price Forecasting and the Need for Intervention Policies, 1984, Crop Insurance for Agricultural Development: Issues and Experience, 1986, Mathematical Programming for Economic Analysis in Agriculture, 1986, Variability in Grain Yields: Implications for Agricultural Research and Policy in Developing Countries, 1989, The Green Revolution Reconsidered: The Impact of High-Yielding Rice Varieties in South India, 1991; contbr. over 50 articles to profl. jours. Mem. Phi Kappa Phi. Office: World Bank 1818 H St NW Washington DC 20433-0002

HAZELTON, JOHN RICHARD, clinical engineer; b. Carbondale, Pa., Sept. 8, 1946; s. S. Richard Hazelton and Anna (Haag) London; children: Julie, Andy. Assoc., Pa. State U., Scrantonwn, 1966; postgrad., Pa. State U., State College, 1966-67, Pa. State U., Middletown, 1967-68. Engring. technician Weston Instruments, Archbald, Pa., 1969-71; supr. biomed. engring. Community Med. Ctr., Scranton, 1971-82, asst. dir. plant svcs., 1982-87, dir. clin. engring., 1987—. Chmn. bd. Hemlock Grove United Meth., Greentown, Pa., 1987-91, chmn. trustees, 1978-87. Mem. Clin. Engring. Soc. of Pa. (pres. 1991), Biomed. Soc. Ea. Pa. (pres. 1985-91). Home: PO Box 234 Greentown PA 18426-0234

HAZLETT, DAVID CHARLES, financial consultant; b. Washington, Sept. 30, 1962; s. Arthur William and Nanette (Zimmerman) H.; m. Jacqueline Cheryl Dalton, June 18, 1988; 1 child, Diane Amber. BA in Bus. Mgmt., Marietta Coll., 1987. Fin. cons. Artnan Enterprises, Vienna, Va., 1987-88; pres. David C. Hazlett Cons., Vienna, 1988-90; controller The Burning Tree Club, Bethesda, Md., 1990—. Mgr. Vienna Men's Softball League, 1990—. Mem. Tau Kappa Epsilon. Republican. Office: The Burning Tree Club 8600 Burdette Rd Bethesda MD 20817

HAZY, JAMES KENT, telecommunications company executive; b. Butler, Pa., Apr. 19, 1955; s. Emil J.C. and Loretta (Klemm) H.; m. Ellen Rose Neary. BS, Haverford (Pa.) Coll., 1978; MBA in Fin. with distinction, U. Pa., 1988. Data ctr. supr. South Cen. Bell, New Orleans, 1978-80; project mgr. Bus. Info. Systems, New Orleans, 1980-83; with AT&T, Parsippany, N.J., 1984-85; project mgr. AT&T, Somerset, N.J., 1986-88; bus. devel. dist. mgr. AT&T, Morristown, N.J., 1989-92; sr. investment mgr. AT&T Ventures Corp., Short Hills, N.J., 1992—. Active ARC (treas. bd. dirs. Raritan Valley chpt.)./. DAV scholar, 1978, K.C. scholar, 1978. Mem. AAAS, IEEE, Assn. Computing Machinery, N.Y. Acad. Scis., Sci. Inst., People to People Internat., Wharton Club. Office: AT&T Ventures Corp Bldg 1 Rm 16402 101 JFK Pkwy Short Hills NJ 07078

HEAD, GEORGE LEWIS, vocational educator; b. Seattle, Mar. 25, 1941; s. Edward Deering and Virginia Elita (MacLafferty) H. BA, U. Wash., 1959; MA, U. Pa., 1967, PhD, 1968. CPCU, CSP, CLU, ARM. With Ins. Inst. Am., Malvern, Pa., 1967-83, v.p., 1984—. Author: Insurance to Value, 1970 (C.A. Kulp award 1970), Essentials of Risk Control, 1988 (C.A. Kulp award 1988), Essentials of Risk Management, 1991, Essentials of Risk Financing, 1992. Mem. Risk and Ins. Mgmt. Soc. (Goodell award 1987), Pub. Risk Mgmt. Assn., Am. Risk and Ins. Assn., Soc. CPCUs, Soc. CLUs, Am. Soc. Safety Engrs., Am. Soc. Healthcare Risk Mgmt., Human Factors Soc., Risk Mgmt. Inst. Baptist. Office: Ins Inst of Am 720 Providence Rd Malvern PA 19355-0770

HEADRICK, THOMAS EDWARD, lawyer, educator; b. East Orange, N.J., June 28, 1933; s. Lewis Barnard and Marian Elizabeth (Rogers) H.; m. Mary Margaret Shontz, June 27, 1957; children—Trevor, Todd. B.A., Franklin and Marshall Coll., 1955; B.Litt., Oxford (Eng.) U., 1958; LL.B., Yale U., 1960; Ph.D., Stanford U., 1975. Bar: Conn. 1960, Calif. 1962. Asst. dir. Ansonia (Conn.) Redevel. Agy., 1959-60; law clk. to justice Wash. State Supreme Ct., Olympia, 1960-61; assoc. firm Pillsbury, Madison & Sutro, San Francisco, 1961-64; mgmt. cons. Emerson Cons., London, 1964-66, Baxter, McDonald & Co., Berkeley, Calif., 1966-67; asst. dean Stanford U. Law Sch., 1967-70; v.p. acad. affairs Lawrence U., 1970-76; dean law sch. U. at Buffalo, 1976-85; prof. law SUNY, Buffalo, 1976—, interim dean arts and letters faculty, 1990; cons. Nat. Endowment for Humanities, NSF; legal commentator Sta. WKBW-TV, 1978-80. Author: The Town Clerk in English Local Government, 1962; co-editor Law and Policy. Mem. Law and Soc. Assn., Policy Studies Orgn., Phi Beta Kappa. Office: SUNY Buffalo Law Sch 411 O'Brian Hall Buffalo NY 14260

HEAL, GEOFFREY MARTIN, economics educator; b. Bangor, Wales, Apr. 9, 1944; s. Thomas John and Gwen Margaret (Owen) H.; m. Felicity Margaret Heal, Sept. 16, 1967 (div. 1979); 1 child, Bridget Margaret; m. Graciela Chichilnisky; 1 child, Natasha Sable. BA, Cambridge U., 1966, PhD, 1969. Dir. studies Christs Coll., Cambridge U., 1967-73; prof. econs. Sussex U., Brighton, Eng., 1973-81, head dept. econs., 1976-81; mng. editor Rev. Econ. Studies, London, 1973-78; prof. Essex U., Colchester, Eng., 1981-83; exec. dir. Fin. Telecommunications, London, 1984-89; prof. grad. sch. bus. Columbia U., N.Y.C., 1983—; vice dean for acad. affairs grad. sch. bus. Columbia U., 1991—; pres. Sci. Internat., N.Y.C., 1990—; cons. U.K. Dept. Energy, London, 1973-76, U.S. Dept. Energy, Washington, 1976-78, OPEC Sec. Gen., Vienna, Austria, 1979-81. Author: The Theory of Economic Planning, 1973, Public Policy and the Tax System, 1979, Economics Theory and Exhaustible Resources, 1979, Linear Algebra and Linear Economics, 1980, The Evolving International Economy, 1987, Oil In The International Economy, 1991. Fellow Econometric Soc., 1973, Royal Soc. Arts, 1984; NSF grantee. Home: 335 Riverside Dr New York NY 10025-3421 Office: Columbia U Bus Sch Uris Hall New York NY 10027

HEALD, BRUCE DAY, educator; b. Boston, June 5, 1935; s. Henry M. and Muriel D. (Day) H. m. Helen Peaslee, May 21, 1960; children: William Forristall III, Craig, Eric Bentley, Allyson Kaye. A.A., Boston U., 1956; B.S. in Music Edn., Lowell State U., 1959; M.A., Columbia Pacific U., 1984, Ph.D., 1985. Supr. music Ashland-Meredith Union 2, Meredith, N.H., 1959-64; dir. music, lectr. fine arts Belknap Coll., Center Harbor, N.H., 1963-65; dir. bands Plattsburgh (N.Y.) City Schs., 1969-70; supr. music Inter-Lakes Sch. Dist., Meredith, 1965-69, dir. music edn., 1970-77; dir. instrumental music Kennebunk (Maine) High Sch., 1977-79; prodn. mgr. Annalee Mobilitee Dolls, Meredith, 1979-81; lectr. English and journalism Moultonborough Acad., 1981-86; dir. music Congl. Ch., Laconia, N.H., 1985—; chair English dept. Holy Trinity Sch., Laconia, 1987—; mentor Columbia Pacific U., 1986—; instr. music N.H. Coll., Manchester, 1988—. Author: Follow the Mount, 1968, 1970, Postmaster of the Lake, 1971, Mail Service on the Lake, 1980, Steamboats in Motion, 1984, New Hampshire Learnin' Days, 1987, Boats 'n Ports I & II, 1989, Landmarks and Legacy, 1990, The Boston See Party, 1991; composer Kennebunk Concert March, The Hills of Old N.H., Moultonboro Concert March, Cascades, Trilogy. Commr. Parks and Playgrounds, Meredith, 1966-69; selectman Town of Meredith, 1971-76. Served with USMC, 1954-62. Mem. NEA, N.H. Tchrs. Assn., Nat. Catholic Edn. Assn., Masons, Order Eastern Star. Republican. Home: PO Box 1052 Meredith NH 03253-1052 Office: Holy Trinity Sch Laconia NH 03254

HEALD, DARREL VERNER, Canadian federal judge; b. Regina, Sask., Can., Aug. 27, 1919; s. Herbert Verner and Lottie (Knudson) H.; m. Doris Rose Hessey, June 30, 1951; children: Lynn, Brian. B.A., U. Sask., 1938, LL.B., 1940. Bar: Called to Sask. bar 1941. Partner firm Noonan, Embury, Heald, Molisky and Gritzfeld, Regina, until 1964; atty. gen. and provincial sec. Province Sask., 1964-71; MLA for Lumsden dist. Sask. Legislative Assembly, Regina, 1964-71; judge trial div. Fed. Ct. Can., Ottawa, Ont., 1971-75; judge Fed. Ct. Appeal, Ottawa, 1975—. Served with RCAF, 1941-45. Home: 44 Aleutian Rd, Ottawa, ON Canada K2H 7C8 Office: Fed Ct Appeal, Supreme Ct Bldg/Ste 71, Ottawa, ON Canada K1A 0H9

HEALEY, JOHN ANDREW, physics educator; b. Waterbury, Conn., July 20, 1939; s. John Joseph and Bernice Ruth (Mahoney) H.; m. Marjorie Ann Taylor, Sept. 3, 1966 (div. 1973); children: Laura Jean, Elizabeth Ann. BS in Physics, Fairfield U., 1961; MS in Physics, St. John's U., 1964. Grad. asst. St. John's U., Jamaica, N.Y., 1961-63, rsch. asst., 1962; physics instr. U. Conn., Waterbury, 1964-74, asst. prof. physics, 1974—; chmn. faculty Staff Assn. of U. Conn. at Waterbury, 1991—. Bd. dirs. New Opportunities for Waterbury, 1969-71; mem. task force Conn. Commn. for Higher Edn., Hartford, Conn., 1972-73; sec. Waterbury Higher Edn. Com., 1978-86; mem. adv. com. Higher Edn. Ctrs., Waterbury, 1979-89. Mem. AAUP (pres. local chpt. 1968-69, state sec.-treas. 1969-70, state pres. 1970-72), Sigma Pi Sigma. Home: 44 Flood Bridge Rd Southbury CT 06488-2249 Office: U Conn 32 Hillside Ave Waterbury CT 06710-2288

HEALEY, TIMOTHY CRAIG, coast guard officer; b. Chgo., May 22, 1950; s. Gerald and Phyllis M. Healey; m. Paula Dzenis; children: Jonathan, Kristin. BS, U.S. Coast Guard Acad., 1972; MBA in Transp., Golden Gate U., 1978. Commd. vice 2d lt. U.S. Coast Guard, 1968, advanced through grades to lt. comdr., 1982; sr. insp., material USCG Marine Safety Office, Balt., 1986; resident insp. USCG at Bethlehem Shipyard Corp., Sparrows Point, Md., 1986-88; chief mcht. marine vets. br. Mcht. Vessel Personnel div. USCG, Washington, 1989-90; chief safety, oversight sec. Ship Design br. USCG, Washington, 1990-91; sr. project mgr. Oil Pollution Act Spl. Staff, USCG, Washington, 1991-92. Contbr. articles to profl. jours. Bd. govs. Grace Episcopal Day Sch., Silver Spring, Md., 1985-88, chair bd. govs., 1988-91. Mem. Soc. Naval Architects and Marine Engrs., Marine Tech. Soc., USCG Acad. Alumni Assn., Golden Gate U. Alumni Assn. Home: 1447 Crestridge Dr Silver Spring MD 20910

HEALY, DAVID GEORGE, college administrator; b. Mpls., June 3, 1949; s. George Robert and Dorothy Ann (Kohli) H.; m. Marjorie Jo Norgaard, Aug. 4, 1973 (div. 1980); 1 child, Andrew; m. Denise Trucdiep Pham, Nov. 12, 1983; children: Travis, Mai Ann. BA, Lawrence U., 1972; MBA, Coll. William and Mary, 1976. Asst. budget dir. Coll. Williamand Mary, Williamsburg, Va., 1973-75, dir. svcs., 1975-80; asst. v.p. adminstrn. U. Md., College Park, 1980-83; system mgr. Continental Cable, Richmond, Va., 1980; v.p. fin. Goucher Coll., Towson, Md., 1983-90; v.p. for adminstrn. and treas. Williams Coll., Williamstown, Mass., 1990—; dir. First Agrl. Bank, Pittsfield, Mass., S.C.U.U.L. Ins., Hamilton, Bermuda, Berkshire Housing Devel. Corp., Pittsfield, Mass. Mem. Econ. Devel. Commn., Williamstown, Mass., 1990—. Mem. Nat. Assn. Coll. and Univ. Bus. Officers, Ea. Assn. Coll. and Univ. Bus. Officers (bd. dirs. 1989—). Office: Williams Coll Main St # 458 Williamstown MA 01267-2602

HEALY, GERALD BURKE, otolaryngologist; b. Boston, Mar. 31, 1942; s. Gerald E. and Margaret C. (Burke) H.; m. Anne Herron, June 3, 1991; children: Elisabeth, Laurie. AB cum laude, Boston Coll., 1963; MD, Boston U., 1967; MBA (hon.), Harvard U., 1990. Diplomate Am. Bd. Otolaryngology, Am. Bd. Laser Surgery, Nat. Bd. Med. Examiners; lic. physician, Mass., Pa. Surg. intern Univ. Hosp., Boston, 1967-68, resident in surgery, 1968-69, resident in otolaryngology, 1969-72; instr. otolaryngology Boston U. Sch. Medicine, 1974-75, asst. prof., 1975-77, assoc. prof., 1977-83, prof., 1983—; assoc. dir. otolaryngology Boston VA Hosp., 1975-76; assoc. otolaryngologist-in-chief The Children's Hosp., Boston, 1976-79, otolaryngologist-in-chief, 1979—; instr. otolaryngology Tufts U. Sch. Medicine, 1975-88; assoc. prof. otolaryngology Harvard Med. Sch., 1988—, prof. otology and laryngology, 1988—; assoc. staff Mass. Eye and Ear Infirmary, Boston, 1984-881 chief otolaryngology Valley Forge Army Med. Ctr., Phoenixville, Pa., 1972-73, William Beaumont Army Med. Ctr., El Paso, 1973-74; assoc. dir. otolaryngology Boston City Hosp., 1975-76; bd. dirs. Am. Bd. Otolaryngology, 1986—; mem. com. on certification Am. Bd. Med. Specialists, 1988—. Reviewer Jour. Pediatrics, 1976—, Pediatrics, 1977—, New Eng. Jour. Medicine, 1979—, Annals of Otology, Rhinology and Laryngology, 1982-88, The Laryngoscope, 1986-88; mem. editorial bd. Internat. Jour. Pediatric Otolaryngology, 1979—, The Laryngoscope, 1988—, Annals of Otology, Rhinology and Laryngology, 1988—. Maj. U.S. Army, 1972-74. Fellow ACS, Am. Coll. Chest Physicians, Am. Acad. Pediatrics; mem. Am. Bd. Emergency Medicine (bd. dirs. 1988—), Am. Soc. Pediatric Otolaryn. (pres. 1987), Am. Laryngol. Assn. (exec. coun. 1985—), Am. Broncho-Esophagological Assn. (exec. coun. 1983—, pres. 1990-91), Am. Acad. Otolaryngology-Head and Neck Surgery (chmn. outcomes com. 1991), Am. Acad. Facial Plastic and Reconstructive Surgery, Soc. Univ. Otolaryngologists, Mass. Med. Soc., New Eng. Otolaryn. Soc., Pediatric Otolaryn. Study Group. Office: Childrens Hosp 300 Longwood Ave Boston MA 02115-5737

HEALY, JAMES B., hospitality consultant; b. N.Y.C., July 2, 1930; BS in Bus. Adminstrn., SUNY-Albany, 1977; MA, William Paterson Coll., Wayne, N.J., 1978; m. Phyllis Cordasco, Feb. 27, 1967; 1 son, Brendan J. Cert. hotel adminstr. Chief purser Am. Export Lines, N.Y.C., 1951-60; hotel and restaurant exec., N.Y. and N.J., 1960-79; assoc. prof., assoc. dean, dir. Sch. Hotel, Restaurant and Tourism Mgmt., Coll. Bus. Adminstrn., Fairleigh Dickinson U., Rutherford, N.J., 1979-90; with Hospitality Cons., Wayne, N.J., 1990—; cons. airlines, Caldwell (N.J.) Coll., others. Served to lt. USNR, 1952-69. Recipient UN Commendation medal, 1952, FDU Alumni Great Tchr. award, 1987; commendation Kings Park Youth, L.I., 1973, Instituto Professionale Alberghe iro di Stato, Formia, Italy, 1986. Mem. Am. Acad. Polit. Scientists, Am. Polit. Sci. Assn., AAUP, Res. Officers Assn., Chaine des Rotisseurs, Assn. Hospitality Fin. Mgmt. Educators, Council Hotel, Restaurant and Instl. Edn., U.S. Naval Acad. Found., Naval Res. Assn., Airline Passengers Assn., Alumni Assn. William Paterson Coll., Internat. Geneva Assn., Delta Mu Delta, Eta Sigma Delta. Roman Catholic. Author: The Challenge of Change in Higher Education, 1979; The HRI Degree, 1982; The Northern Ireland Dilemma: An American Irish Imperative, 1989; International Marketing for U.S. Hotels in a Changing Environment; Hotel Restaurant Education in Transition; others. Home: 519 Bloomfield Ave Caldwell NJ 07006-5550

HEALY, JAMES CASEY, lawyer; b. Washington, Feb. 19, 1956; s. Joseph Francis Jr. and Patricia Ann (Casey) H. BS, Spring Hill Coll., 1978; JD, Emory U., 1982. Bar: Ga. 1983, Conn. 1983, U.S. Dist. Ct. Conn. 1984, U.S. Tax Ct. 1984, U.S. Supreme Ct. 1987. Assoc. Gregory & Adams, Wilton, Conn., 1982-87, ptnr., 1988-89, mng. ptnr., 1990—; spl. counsel Wilton Police Commn., 1986-89; mem. Parks and Recreation Commn. Bd.

dirs. Mark Lavin Meml. Offshore Med. and Safety Found., Empire, Mich., 1987—, Village Market Inc., 1988-90; chmn. leadership giving program United Way, 1991—; active various charity and athletic orgns. Mem. ABA, State Bar of Ga., State Bar of Conn. (young lawyer's real property/land use sect. com.), Stamford/Norwalk Regional Bar Assn., Silver Spring Country Club. Republican. Roman Catholic. Office: Gregory & Adams 190 Old Ridgefield Rd PO Box 190 Wilton CT 06897

HEALY, JULIA SCHMITT, artist; b. Elmhurst, Ill., Mar. 28, 1947; d. Albert Leo and Louise Anne (Tilly) Schmitt; m. Richard Healy, Apr. 6, 1973 (div. Aug. 1990); children: Patrick, Katharine. BFA, Sch. of the Art Inst. Chgo., 1970, MFA, 1972; student various including, U. Chgo., Yale U., Dalhousie, Univ., NYU. Dir. Eye Level Gallery, Halifax, N.C., 1974-76; artist, tchr. Studio in a Sch., N.Y.C., 1989—; adj. prof. Sch. of the Art Inst. of Chgo., 1970-72, Ocean County Coll., Toms River, N.J., 1979-81, Pratt Inst., Bklyn., 1991—; art adv. bd. Chancerllor's Bd., N.Y.C. Pub. Schs.; mem. edn. com. Snug Harbor Cultural Ctr., Staten Island, N.Y., 1991—; dir. The Art Lab, Staten Island, 1990—, Alice Austen House, Staten Island, 1990—. Columnist: (syndicated) Artmakers, 1990—; exhbns. include Staten Island Mus., 1989, Newhouse Ctr. for Contemporary Art, 1987; over 50 group exhbns., three maj. pub. commns. Mem. Community Bd. Waterfront Com., Staten Island, 199—; vol. Project Hospitality, Staten Island, 1989—. Recipient artist's grant Staten Island Coun. on the Arts, 1987, 91, Can. Coun., Ottawa, 1976-78, fellowship Yale Summer Sch. of Music and Art, 1969, Weissglass award Staten Island Mus. Mem. Artists Space, The New Mus., The Tibetan Mus., The Mudlane Soc. Home: 294 Edgewater St Staten Island NY 10305-4934

HEALY, MARTIN JOHN, academic administrator; b. N.Y.C., Apr. 5, 1939; s. John and Kathleen Ann (Hanley) H.; m. Ann Marie Brennan, Aug. 15, 1964; children: Lisa Ann, John Paul. BA, St. John's U., Jamaica, N.Y., 1964, MS, 1969. Writer Sta. WNEW, N.Y.C., 1958-60; writer, producer Sta. WCBS, N.Y.C., 1960-67; v.p. communications and pub. affairs St. John's U., 1968—. Mem. Internat. Radio and TV Soc. Roman Catholic. Home: 15 Cross Rd Manhasset NY 11030-1449 Office: St Johns U Grand Central & Utopia Pkwy Jamaica NY 11439

HEALY, ROBERT DANFORTH, manufacturing executive; b. Northhampton, Mass., Apr. 17, 1939; s. Frederick Clark and Myrtle Frances (Clark) H.; m. Mary Jane Guilcher, Apr. 22, 1978. Machinist Pratt and Whitney Aircraft, E. Hartford, Conn., 1963-67; plant mgr. Ridge Tool Co., Cromwell, Conn., 1967-71; owner CVS Industries, Chesterfield, Mass., 1971-73; v.p., ptnr. Quabbin Industries Inc., Chicopee, Mass., 1972-92; pres. Seth Alden Healy's Sons, Inc., Williamsburg, Mass., 1992—; ptnr. Industrial Airpark Assn., Chicopee, 1981—, Am. Gravure Engraving, Holyoke, Mass., 1985-91, Pro-Mac Engring. Inc., Chicopee, 1987-92, Quabbin Internat. Inc., Richmond, Calif., 1987-92. Mem. ASME. Republican. Home: 16 North St Williamsburg MA 01096-9304

HEANEY, MICHAEL FRANCIS, JR., correction officer; b. N.Y.C., Oct. 3, 1938; s. Michael Francis and Margaret (Lyons) H.; m. Doris E. Kivlehan, Nov. 22, 1960 (div. Oct. 1976); children: Michael P., Todd C., Daniel J., Michele M. Ryan F. Student, Bklyn. Coll., 1960-61, John Jay Coll., 1985-86, Empire State Coll., 1986-87; BS in Criminal Justice, Southwest U., 1991. Diesel mechanic MaBSTOA-Transic Authority, N.Y.C., 1961-83; correction officer N.Y. State Dept. Corrections, N.Y.C., 1983—; mem. exec. bd. Transport Workers Union, N.Y.C., 1965-83. With U.S. Merchant Marines, 1954-60. Mem. Am. Fedn. Police (nat. v.p. jails and corrections 1991—), Am. Jail Assn. (field rep. 1991—), Am. Correctional Assn., Am. Assn. Correctional Tng. Personnel, Am. Soc. Law Enforcement Tng., Am. Merchant Marine Vets. Assn., Nat. Assn. Investigative Specialists, Internat. Assn. Correction Officers, Internat. Criminal Investigators Assn., Fraternal Order of Police, NRA, KC. Republican. Roman Catholic. Home: 273 Lincoln Ave Staten Island NY 10306-3358 Office: Arthur Kill Correction Ctr 2911 ARthur Kill Rd Staten Island NY 10309-1197

HEANUE, ANNE ALLEN, librarian; b. Ft. Oglethorpe, Ga., Feb. 7, 1940; d. James Edward and Mary (Dennean) Allen; m. Kevin E. Heanue, July 20, 1963; children: Mary, Brian, Patricia. BA cum laude, Dunbarton Coll., 1962; MA, Georgetown U., 1966; MS in Libr. Sci., Cath. U. Am., 1976. Libr. Deloitte Haskins and Sells, Washington, 1977-79; asst. to dir. Am. Libr. Assn., Washington, 1979-81, asst. dir., 1981-84, assoc. dir., 1984—. Bd. dirs. Alexandria (Va.) LWV, 1967-78; chmn. Alexandria Spl. Edn. adv. com., 1978-79; mem. Alexandria Gypsy Moth Control Commn., 1991—. Mem. ALA, Am. Soc. Access Profls., Am. Soc. Assn. Execs. D.C. Libr. Assn., Beta Phi Mu, Pi Gamma Mu. Roman Catholic. Home: 610 Pullman Pl Alexandria VA 22305-1226 Office: ALA 110 Maryland Ave NE Washington DC 20002-5626

HEARN, CHRISTINE AGNES, theology educator; b. Phila., Mar. 6, 1950; d. Raymond Robert and Agnes Farley (McCole) H. BS in Elem. Edn., Gwynedd-Mercy Coll., 1975; MA in Religious Studies, St. Charles Sem., 1984; Advanced Cert. in Spiritual Direction, Neumann Coll., Aston, Pa., 1992. Nurses' aide St. Christopher Hosp., Phila., 1974-75; tchr. jr. high sch. St. Philip Neri Sch., Lafayette Hill, Pa., 1975, Our Lady of Calvary Sch., Phila., 1975-78, St. Christopher Sch., Phila., 1978-85; theology tchr. Paul VI High Sch., Haddonfield, N.J., 1983-85; retreat coord. CYE-Phila. Archdiocese, 1985-90; adj. prof. Cabrini Coll., Radnor, Pa., 1990—; religion prof. Holy Cross High Sch., Delran, N.J., 1992—; workshop presenter, religion cons. in field. Mem. Thomas Merton Soc., Spiritual Dirs. Internat., Am. Assn. Counseling and Devel., St. Mary Parish, Women's Ordination Conf. Roman Catholic. Home: Stoney Run 11-F Maple Shade NJ 08052 Office: Holy Cross High Sch 5035 South Rte 130 Delran NJ 08075

HEARN, ROSAMOND ERNST, music service executive; b. Boston, Sept. 17, 1924; d. Harry Benjamin and Mary (Downey) E.; divorced; children: Robert D., Diane G., Mary R., Kathleen Anne. Student, Boston U., 1940-42, Longy Sch. Music, 1947-49, Am. Conservatory Music, 1966-71, 74-77; music fellow, U. Colo., 1974-75. Lab. technician Consol. Rendering Co., Boston, 1942-52; organist, choir dir. Mass., Conn. and Ill., 1948-72; asst. condr., accompanist Am. Conservatory of Music, Chgo., 1970-73; organist, choir dir. Sacred Heart Ch., Lombard, Ill., 1973-78; mgr. music store Manhattan Sch. Music, 1978-79; organist Colesville Presbyn. Ch., Silver Spring, Md., 1979—; gen. ptnr., mgr. Allegro Music Service, Silver Spring, 1985—; mgr. choral music dept. Lyon Healy Co., Chgo., 1975-78; mgr. choral, vocal, organ depts. Harris Music Co., Rockville, Md., 1979-85. Columnist Mitzi's Merit Series, 1984—. Mem. Am. Guild Organists (bd. dirs. 1967-70), Am. Choral Dirs. Assn. (workshop coordinator), Music Educators Nat. Conf., Choristers Guild, Music Industry Council, Silver Spring C. of C., Delta Omicron (Outstanding Service to Music Profession 1968). Office: Allegro Music Svc 1398 Lamberton Dr Silver Spring MD 20902-3421

HEARTH, BLAIR ANTHONY, fundraiser, clergyman; b. Fall River, Mass., Apr. 23, 1950; s. Theodore Frederick and Jacqueline (Blair) H.; m. Amy Hill. BA, Stetson U., DeLand, Fla., 1972; MDiv, Garrett Theol. Sem., Evanston, Ill., 1976. Ordained elder United Meth. Ch. Assoc. pastor St. Paul's United Meth. Ch., Tallahassee, Fla., 1976-78, First United Meth. Ch., Ormond Beach, Fla., 1978-81; exec. dir. Halifax Urban Ministries, Daytona Beach, Fla., 1981-85; regional dir. N.Y.C. Easter Seal Soc., 1985-87; dir. devel./planned giving Mt. Sinai Med. Ctr., N.Y.C., 1987-90; nat. dir. planned giving Nat. March of Dimes Found., White Plains, N.Y., 1990—; adj. prof. philosophy and religion Bethune Cookman Coll., Daytona Beach, 1981-85; v.p. N.Y. Conf. United Meth. Found., White Plains, 1988-91; treas. Planned Giving Group of Greater N.Y., N.Y.C., 1987-91; cons. Religious News Svc., N.Y.C., 1987-91. Founder, pres. Nova House, Daytona Beach, 1983-85; mem. adv. bd. Bethel Homes, Ossining, N.Y., 1988-91. Mem. AAAS, N.Y. Acad. Scis., Nat. Soc. Fund Raising Execs., Meth. Fedn. for Social Action, Forth Interest Group. Democrat. Home: 45 Van Cortlandt Ave Ossining NY 10562 Office: March of Dimes Birth Defects Found 1275 Mamaroneck Ave White Plains NY 10605

HEARTT, CHARLOTTE BEEBE, university official; b. N.Y.C., Nov. 12, 1933; d. Stacey Kile and Charlotte Beebe; BA, Wellesley Coll., 1954; m. William Hollis Peirce, 1954; children: Daniel Converse, William Kile; m. Stephen Heartt, 1962; children: Thomas Beebe, Sarah Lincoln. Intern Office of V.p. Richard Nixon, Washington, 1953; asst. in Computing Numerical Analysis Lab. U. Wis., Madison, 1954-56; dir. fund raising Boston Arts festival, 1961; sec. to dean coll. rels. Radcliffe Coll., Cambridge, Mass., 1961-62; sec. to chmn. dept. city planning Harvard U., Cambridge, 1962; Fulbright program adviser, study abroad adviser Brandeis U., 1966-71, dir. office internat. programs, 1971-75, dir. found. and corp. rels., 1976-79; dir. corp. rels., asst. dir. devel. Smith Coll., Northampton, Mass., 1979-81, dir. devel., 1981—. Mem. Commonwealth Task Force on the Open Univ., 1973; bd. dirs. Council on Internat. Ednl. Exchange, 1973-77, mem. exec. com., 1975-77; Boston Area Seminar for Internat. Students, 1973-76; mem. adv. com. New England Colls. Fund, 1981—; bd. trustees Berkshire Sch., 1989—. Mem. Sect. on U.S. Study Abroad (nat. sec., regional rep. 1972-74), Nat. Assn. Fgn. Student Affairs (nat. commr. liaison), Nat. Assn. Women Deans, Adminstrs. and Counselors (internat. students and programs com. 1974-76), Nat. Soc. Fund Raisers, Council for Advancement and Support Edn. Home: 51 Belmont Ave Northampton MA 01060-3705 also: 133 E 65th St New York NY 10021 Office: Smith Coll Devel Office Clark Hall 50 Elm St Northampton MA 01063-0001

HEATH, HARRIET ELIZABETH, developmental psychologist, parent educator; b. Ithac, Mich., Feb. 22, 1928; d. Glenn McKinley and Margaret (Woodruff) Frye; m. Douglas H. Heath, June 15, 1952; children: Russell, Wendilee O'Brien, Annemarie Sanchez. BA, Cornell (Iowa) Coll., 1949; PhD, Bryn Mawr Coll., 1976. Lectr. U. Del., Newark, 1978-79; dir. Parent Early Edn. Ctr., Wilmington, Del., 1979-81; psychologist William Penn Sch. Dist., Yeadon, Pa., 1977-83, Moorestown (N.J.) Friends Sch., 1983-86; dir. curriculum and tng. Edn. for Parenting, Phila., 1981-89; cons., researcher, writer Haverford, Pa., 1983—; dir. The Parent Ctr., dept. human devel. Bryn Mawr (Pa.) Coll., 1981—; cons. Delaware County Nursing Mothers, Ardmore, Pa., 1983—; counselor family rels. Phila. Yearly Meeting, 1985—. Author: Learning About Parenting, Learning to Care, 1983, Parents Planning, 1983, Fulfilling Lives, 1991. Fellow Am. Orthopsychiat. Assn., Am. Psychol. Assn. Mem. Soc. of Friends. Home: 223 Buck Ln Haverford PA 19041-1106 Office: The Parent Ctr Dept Human Devel Bryn Mawr Coll Bryn Mawr PA 19010

HEATH, ROBERT EVERETT, retail executive; b. Franklin, N.H., June 5, 1941; s. Everett Morrill and Madeline Shirley (White) H.; m. Sarah Strudivant, June 23, 1963 (div. July 1982); 1 child, Holly Michelle. BS, U. N.H., 1963. Lic. real estate broker N.H. Clerk E.M. Heath Inc., Centre Harbor, N.H., 1955-64; mgr. E.M. Heath Inc., 1964-74, pres., gen. mgr., 1975—; ptnr. BREV, Centre Harbor, 1986—; bd. dirs. BankEast, Manchester, N.H., 1980-89, Associated Grocers of New England, Manchester, 1977-90, chmn. of bd. 1990—. Capt. Centre Harbor Fire Dept., 1962—; trustee Centre Harbor Congl. Ch., 1964-78; treas. Centre Harbor N.H., 1964—, Bay Dist., Centre Harbor, 1968-78. Office: E M Heath Inc RR 25 Center Harbor NH 03226-9805

HEATH, ROGER CHARLES, state senator, writer; b. Franklin, N.H., Jan. 21, 1943; s. Everett M. and Madeline (White) H.; m. Sharon Lunn, Aug. 6, 1967. BS, No. Ariz. U., 1966. Tchr. pub. schs., N.H., Ariz., N.Y., 1966-69; mgr. E.M. Heath Stores, Inc., N.H., Ariz., N.Y., 1969-73, now dir., treas., 1969-73; mem. N.H. Ho. of Reps., 1979-84; mem. N.H. Senate, 1984—, chmn. ways and means com., 1985-87, asst. majority whip, 1988—. Author: The Policital Spectrum, The Language of Politics, 1978; contbr. articles to nat. mags. Chmn. natural resources com. N.H. Rep. Platform Com., 1983; vice chmn. N.H. Pub. Radio Adv. Bd., Concord, 1981-84; commr. Ednl. Commn. of States, 1985-87; del Coun. of State Govts., Eastern Regional Conf., 1985, Coun. of State Govts. Environ. Task Force; commr. Atlantic States Marine Fisheries Commn.; chmn. Christa McAuliffe Planetarium Commn., 1989-92. Mem. Nat. Coun. State Legislatures, Am. Legis. Exch. Coun. (membership coord., chmn. nat. task force on edn. 1985—), Nat. Conf. State Legislatures (internat. trade com.), Gun Owners N.H. (bd. dirs., v.p. 1980-84), Mead Wilderness Base HIgh Adventure Program (adv. com.), Winnipesaukee Sportsmen's Club (bd. dirs. 1983-87), Masons. Home: Grove St Center Sandwich NH 03227 Office: NH State Senate State Capitol Concord NH 03301

HEATHERTON, TODD FREDERICK, psychology educator; b. Lethbridge, Alta., Can., Feb. 9, 1961; came to U.S., 1990; s. Frederick G. L. and Marlene E. Sandercock; m. Patricia Ryrie Dickson, June 24, 1989. BSc, U. Calgary, 1984; MA, U. Toronto, 1986, PhD, 1989. Rsch. assoc. Social Sci. and Humanities Rsch. Coun. fellow Case Western Res. U., Cleve., 1989-90; asst. prof. dept. psychology Harvard U., Cambridge, Mass., 1990—. Contbr. numerous articles to profl. jours. Nat. Sci. and Engring. Rsch. Coun. scholar, 1985-87, 87-89, Ont. Grad. scholar, 1987-88. Mem. Am. Psychol. Soc., Am. Psychol. Assn., Soc. for Personality and Social Psychology. Office: Harvard U Dept Psychology 33 Kirkland St Cambridge MA 02138-2044

HEATLEY, CONNIE FRANCES, association executive; b. Bronx, N.Y., Oct. 10, 1942; d. Salvatore Charles and Mary Moscatiello LaMotta; m. Michael H. Heatley; children: Ray, Peter, David. BA, SUNY, Albany, 1969; postgrad., Fordham U., 1974. Activities coord. San Diego Assn. for the Retarded, 1970-72; edn. program dir. Edn. Ctrs. of Newark Archdiocese, 1973-79; dir. communications tng. Riverside Eating Disorder Clinic, Secaucus, N.J., 1979-84; communications coord. Sun Chem. Corp., N.Y.C., 1984-86; pub. relations dir. Nat. Coffee Assn., N.Y.C., 1986-87; v.p. pub. rels. Direct Mktg. Assn., N.Y.C., 1987-92, sr. v.p. pub. rels., 1988—. Recipient Silver-Mercury award Nat. Media Conf., 1988, finalist Mercury award, 1989, cert. of Merit, Internat. Assn. of Bus. Communicators, cert. of Excellence, Gold award Internat. Astrid awards, 1991, Apex award for publ. excellence, 1991. Mem. Pub. Rels. Soc. Am., Women in Communications, Am. Soc. Assn. Execs. (assoc.). Episcopalian. Office: Direct Mktg Assn 11 W 42d St New York NY 10036-8096

HEATON, DEBORAH MCGANN, graphic designer, small business owner; b. Phila., Nov. 8, 1957; d. Thomas H. and Evelyn (Garnett) McG.; m. Clayton E. Heaton, Apr. 8, 1989. BS, U. N.C., Greeensboro, 1979; MFA, Tyler Sch. of Art, 1983. Mech. artist, designer Kingswood Group, Ardmore, Pa., 1979-81; instr. Tyler Sch. of Art, Phila., 1981-83; owner McGann Design Co., Wayne, Pa., 1981-87, 88—; art dir. Boyd Tamney Cross, Wayne, 1983-87, Lyons, Inc., Wilmington, Del., 1987-88; adj. asst. prof. Drexel U., Phila., 1989-91; tng. cons. Quark, Inc., Bear, Del., 1991—. Mellon Found. grantee, 1983; recipient Pica award Printing Industries the Carolinas, 1979, Gold award Inst. of Am. Bus. Comm., 1990, 91. Mem. Am. Inst. Graphic Arts, Advt. Club Del. (Merit award 1987, 90, 91), Sierra Club (chair com. Del. chpt. 1990-92, vice-chair 1992—, del. appalchian regional conservation com. 1991—).

HEATON, DONALD SLADE, financial executive; b. Framingham, Mass., Aug. 2, 1946; s. Richard Harry and Bernice E. (Marble) H.; m. Renate Regina Sanden, June 16, 1968; 1 child, Jennifer Stacey. BBA, Boston U., 1968, MBA, 1970. CPA, Mass. Sr. mgr. KPMG Peat Marwick, Boston, 1970-79; corp. contr., chief acctg. officer Cabot Corp., Boston, 1979-90; v.p., group chief fin. officer Fidelity Capital, Boston, 1990—. Sgt. USAR, 1970-76. Named to Hall of Fame, Boston U., 1968. Mem. AICPA, Fin. Exec. Inst., Mass. Soc. CPAs, Boston U. Alumni Assn. (dir. 1970-91, pres. 1990-92), Boston U. Nat. Alumni Coun. Home: 5 Tara Rd Southborough MA 01772-1444 Office: Fidelity Investments 82 Devonshire St # 25 D Boston MA 02109-3614

HEATON, LARRY CADWALDER, II, sales executive; b. Benton, Ill., Oct. 26, 1956; s. Larry Cadwalder and Dorothy Jean (Brooks) H.; m. Veronica Louise Edens, May 30, 1987; children: Larry Cadwalder III, Davin Bryce, Jonathan Wade. BSBA, U. Ill., 1979. Mgr. food, beverage Poison Apple Rock Theater, Champaign, Ill., 1979-80; gen. mgr. Cochrane's Restaurant, Urbana, Ill., 1980; sales rep. Profl. Retirement Programs, Inc., Jacksonville, Fla., 1981, dir. sales, 1981-82; product specialist U.S. Surg. Corp., Norwalk, Conn., 1982, sales rep., 1983, regional sales dir., 1984-89, divisional sales dir., 1989—. Lt. USMCR, 1975-80. Mem. NRA, Am. Mgmt. Assn., Internat. Platform Assn., Am. Legion, Blues Alley Music Soc., Centurion Club, Porsche Club, Mensa, Delta Chi. Republican. Methodist. Home: 9200 Broken Timber Way Columbia MD 21045-2310 Office: US Surg Corp 150 Glover Ave Norwalk CT 06850-1346

HEAVNER, ANN DENISE, banker; b. Cumberland, Md., Sept. 19, 1956; d. William Harmon and Ramona Fern (Mauzy) H.; m. David Straup Slick, July 25, 1981; children: Jessica Heavner Slick, Katherine Victoria Slick, Elizabeth Ann Slick. BA, Loyola Coll., Balt., 1978; cert., Md. Banking Sch., Balt., 1984. Cert. corp. cash mgr., Md. Asst. ops. officer First Nat. Bank Md., Balt., 1979-81; corp. banking officer Union Trust Bank, Balt., 1981-83, asst. v.p., 1983-85; v.p. Signet Bank Md., Balt., 1985—. Sec. Shepherd of the Glen Luth. Ch. Council, Glenwood, Md., 1986, Md. 4H All-Stars. Mem. Nat. Assn. Bank Women, Exec. Women's Network. Republican.

HEAVNER, MARTIN LUTHER, environmental professional, educator, journalist; b. Cumberland, Md., Dec. 3, 1955; s. Robert Perrin and Willetta May (Stine) H.; m. Gale Lynn Wright, June 17, 1978. AA, Potomac State Coll., 1975; BS in Journalism, W.Va. U., 1977; MBA, Frostburg State U., 1992. Editor Pasquino Newspaper, Keyser, W.Va., 1974-75; feature writer W.Va. Univ. News Svc., Morgantown, W.Va., 1976-77; copy editor intern Richmond (Va.) Times-Dispatch, summer 1976; graphic artist Suburban Newspapers, Inc., Silver Spring, Md., 1977; info. coord. Govt. Insts., Inc., Rockville, Md., 1977-79, mgr. communications, 1979-85, v.p., 1985—; writer, photographer Ijamsville, Md., 1986—. Co-editor: Energy Reference Handbook, 1978; exec. editor Waste Minimization Report newsletter, 1986—; contbr. articles to profl. jours.; photographer various mags. Vol. Montgomery County Recycling Hotline, Rockville, 1992. Recipient Photography Grand prize Antietam Photo Salon, 1988, Nat. Pk. Svc., 1987, Photography Star award N.I.H. Camera Club, 1987. Mem. Frederick Camera Clique, Latent Image Workshop (Photography Best of Show award 1983), C & O Canal Assn., Internat. Assn. Bus. Comms., Nat. Environ. Tng. Assn., Met. Washington Soc. Environ. Profls. Democrat. Methodist. Office: Govt Insts Inc 4 Research Pl Ste 200 Rockville MD 20850

HEBALD, CAROL, poet, writer; b. N.Y.C., July 6, 1934; d. Henry Hebald and Ethel (Miller) Lifland. BA magna cum laude, high honors English, CUNY, 1969; MFA, U. Iowa, 1971. Actress Broadway, off-Broadway, TV, N.Y.C., 1952-64; English instr. U. Northern Iowa, Cedar Falls, 1971-72; asst. prof. Utica Coll. of Syracuse (N.Y.) U., 1972-75; creative writing instr. NYU, 1975-76; vis. lectr. U. Wis., Madison, 1976-77; asst. prof. U. Kan., Lawrence, 1977-79; assoc. prof. U. Kan, 1980-84; vis. prof. Warsaw U., Poland, 1981-82; writer-in-residence MacDowell Colony, Peterborough, N.H., summers 1976-78, Millay Colony, summers 1977, 84, Va. Ctr. for Creative Arts, Sweet Briar, summers 1981, 83-85, Edward Albee Found., Monlauk, N.Y., summer 1984. Author: Three Blind Mice/Two Short Novels, 1989; (plays) Martha, 1990, The Fat Lady, 1989; contbr. poems to Antioch Rev., N.Am. Rev., Mass. Rev. Recipient William Bradley Otis fellowship Disting. Contbns. to Am. Lit., 1969, The Elias Lieberman Poetry award, 1969, The Ralph Weinburg Poetry award, 1968, The Theodore Goodman Short Story award, 1968; recipient Pen Am. Fund N.Y. State Coun. on the Arts, 1985, recipient Kans. Quar. Seaton award Kans. Quar, 1986, McGraw Hill Nomination Editor's Book award Pushcart Prize, 1986-88; creative writing grantee Utica Coll., 1974-75, The Wis. Arts Bd., 1976, U. Kans. Rsch. Fund, 1978. Mem. PEN, Authors Guild of Am., Poets and Writers, Inc., Phi Beta Kappa. Home and Office: 1375 E 18th St Brooklyn NY 11230-7543

HEBER, RUTH R., psychologist, consultant; b. Lodz, Poland, June 27, 1935; came to U.S., 1957; d. Moses Zwi and Ryna (Glucklich) Borenstein; m. Jacob Heber, 1955 (div. 1982); children: Ron, Sheldon, Lorraine; m. Lawrence Walter Kullman, 1987. BA in Psychology, CUNY, 1972; MS in Ednl. Psychology and Guidance, Yeshiva U., 1974, PhD in Devel. Psychology, 1979. Lic. psychologist, N.Y. Adj. instr. Jersey City State Coll., N.Y., 1976-77; instr. psychology Pace U., N.Y., 1980-81; rsch. assoc. New Careers Tng. Labs. Grad. Sch. and Univ. Ctr. N.Y., 1978-80; staff psychotherapist North Suffolk Mental Health Ctr., N.Y., 1980-82; supervising psychologist, clinic and program coord. Creedmoor Psychiat. Ctr., N.Y., 1982-88; dir. East Side Consultation Ctr., N.Y.C., 1988—; adj. asst. prof. psychology Queens Coll., CUNY, 1981-83, adj. asst. prof. dept. edn. and community svcs., 1987; cons., lectr. Humanistic Psychology Ctr., N.Y., 1983—; East Coast conf. coord. Assn. for Transpersonal Psychology, 1983-86; lectr. psychiatry Mt. Sinai Sch. Medicine, CUNY, 1990—; supr. psychiat. residents Mt. Sinai Med. Ctr., N.Y.C., 1989—; adj. prof. The Union Inst. Grad. Sch. Cin., 1991—; pvt. practice; presenter, guest speaker, workshop leader. Mem. APA (pres. proposed div. transpersonal psychology 1987-88, program chmn. humanistic psychology div. 1988-89, treas. 1989—, Am. Acad. Psychotherapists, Internat. Coun. Psychologists, Internat. Assn. Applied Psychology, Internat. Assn. Cross-Cultural Psychology, Am. Group Psychotherapy Assn., Am. Soc. Psychosomatic Ob-Gyn, Ea. Group Psychotherapy Assn., Assoc. Alumni Mt. Sinai Med. Ctr., Phi Beta Kappa, Psi Chi, Kappa Delta Pi, Delta Phi Alpha. Office: 200 E 33rd St Apt 4I New York NY 10016

HEBERT, CHARLES ALEXANDRE, information broker; b. Terre Haute, Ind., Feb. 11, 1906; s. Joseph Alexandre and Mabel (Chewning) H. BA, U. N.C., 1934; MA, NYU, 1950, postgrad., 1951—. Engr. Bell Telephone Labs., N.Y.C., 1929-49; officer, lt. comdr. USN, 1941-46; asst. v.p. Engring. Rsch. Assoc., Arlington, Va., 1947-48; owner Rsch. Svc., N.Y.C., 1950—. Author: Carrier Telefon System, 1938, Annotated Bibliography of Audio-Visual Aids for Management Development Programs, 1958; patentee in field. Mem. Soc. Historique Acadienne. Office: Rsch Svc PO Box 20322 Columbus Cir Sta New York NY 10023-1484

HEBERT, DONNA MARIE, food product executive; b. Worcester, Mass., June 20, 1951; d. Charles George and Lena Marie (Diliddo) Olson; m. Raymond Louis Hebert, June 17, 1972; children: Wendy Ann, Daniel Raymond. Student, Quinsigamond Community Coll., Worcester, 1969-70, Assumption Coll., Worcester, 1970-72. Sales person F.W. Woolworth, Worcester, 1967-69; researcher State Mutaul Life Ins., Worcester, 1969-70; bus. office pers. Assumption Coll., Worcester, 1970-73; pres. Stage Stop Candy, Ltd., Dennis Port, Mass., 1982—. Treas. troop 82 Boy Scouts Am., South Dennis, Mass., 1988—; Eucharistic Min. Recipient Bronze Pelican, Diocesan Scout Office, Fall River, 1990. Mem. Dennis C. of C., Cape Cod Pers. Assn., D-Y Band Parents (exec. bd.). Roman Catholic. Office: Stage Stop Candy Ltd 411 Main St Dennis Port MA 02639

HEBERT, WILLIAM HARVEY, financial consultant; b. Newark, N.J., Aug. 14, 1929; s. William Hector and Margaret (Kehoe) H.; m. Margaret M. Jasper, Aug. 21, 1954 (div. 1976); children: William Harvey, Jr., Christine Elizabeth; m. Barbara A. Osmond, Dec. 27, 1986. BS in Edn., Worcester State Coll., 1952, MEd, 1956; PhD, U. Conn., 1968; LLD (hon.), Ricker Coll., 1977, Worcester State Coll., 1979. Tchr. Joslin Elem. Sch., Oxford, Mass., 1954-55, Sr. High Sch., Shrewsbury, Mass., 1955-59; asst. exec. dir. Mass. Tchrs. Assn., Boston, 1959-64, exec. dir., 1964-83; chmn. bd. United Educators, Inc., Framingham, Mass., 1983-85; account exec. Mgmt. Recruiters, Braintree, Md., 1988; dir. edn. Greater Boston C. of C., 1988-90; spl. cons. Phila. Fin. Advisors, Canton, Mass., 1991—. Trustee Worcester (Mass.) State Coll. Capt. USMC, 1948-54, Korea. Democrat. Roman Catholic. Home: 61 Shrine Rd Norwell MA 02061-2235

HECHINGER, FRED MICHAEL, newspaper editor, columnist, foundation executive; b. Nuremberg, Germany, July 7, 1920; came to U.S., 1937, naturalized, 1943; s. Julius and Lilly (Niedermaier) H.; m. Grace Bernstein; children: Paul David, John Edward. Student, NYU, 1937-38; AB, CCNY, 1943; postgrad., U. London, 1945; LLD, Kenyon Coll., 1955; LLD (hon.), Bates Coll., 1963, U. Notre Dame, 1963, Knox Coll., 1966; LHD (hon.), Bard Coll., 1956, Wash. Coll., 1965, Wilkes Coll., 1968, St. Joseph's Coll., 1970, Rider Coll., 1972, Paine Coll., 1972, Trinity Coll., 1973, CCNY, 1977, SUNY, 1986, Marymount Manhattan Coll., 1987, Mercy Coll., 1988, Franklin Pierce Coll., 1990, Conn. Coll., 1991. Corr. London Times Ednl. Supplement, 1946-47; ednl. columnist Washington Post, 1947-50; edn. editor, fgn. corr., cons. to pub. Sunday Herald, Bridgeport, Conn., 1947-50; fgn. corr. Overseas News Agy., 1948-50; spl. writer This Week mag., 1946-59; edn. editor N.Y. Herald Tribune, 1950-56; assoc. pub. The Sunday Herald, Bridgeport, Conn., 1956-59; edn. editor The N.Y. Times, N.Y.C., 1959-69; mem. editorial bd. The N.Y. Times, 1969-77, asst. editorial page editor, 1976, edn. columnist, 1978-90; sr. advisor Carnegie Corp., N.Y.C., 1991—; pres. N.Y. Times Co. Found., 1977-90; also bd. dirs.; contbg. editor Saturday Rev., 1977-78; adj. prof. CUNY, 1974-78; cons. edn. and cultural relations div. U.S. Mil. Govt., summers 1948, 49; Served with Office Mil.

Attache Am. Embassy, London; also with Brit. War Office, 1944-46. Author: New Approaches, 1955, An Adventure in Education, 1956, Worrying About College, 1958, The Big Red Schoolhouse, 1959, A Better Start, 1986, Fateful Choices, 1992; (with Grace Hechinger) Teen-age Tyranny, 1963, Pre-School Education Today, 1966, The New York Times Guide to N.Y.C. Private Schools, 1968, Growing Up in America, 1975; edn. editor Parents mag., 1957-59; contbr. to Change mag. Pres. N.Y. Times Neediest Cases Fund, 1977-90; bd. dirs. Acad. Ednl. Devel.; mem. Pres.'s Commn. on Fgn. Langs. and Internat. Studies, 1978-79; vice chmn., bd. dirs. Carnegie Corp.; bd. dirs. N.Y., Fgn. Policy Assn.; mem. adv. bd. Yale-New Haven Tchrs. program, Stanford U., Stanford and the Schs. program. Recipient Brit. Empire medal, George Polk Meml. award, 1950, 51, 90, Fairbanks award, 1952, Townsend Harris medal, 1968, Soc. Silurians editorial writing award, 1971, 76, Disting. Alumni medal, 1973, Disting. Service award Council Chief State Sch. Officers, Disting. Svc. medal Tchrs. Coll. Columbia U., 1990; Carnegie Found. Advancement of Teaching fellow, 1980-82; recipient Horace Mann Guardian award, 1983, James Bryant Conant award, 1989. Mem. Edn. Writers Assn. (pres. 1956, awards 1948, 49, 52, 64, 68, 73, 74, 76), Century Assn. Club, Phi Beta Kappa. Office: 437 Madison Ave New York NY 10022-7001

HECHINGER, JOHN W., JR., home improvement company executive; b. 1950; married. BBA, Boston U., 1972. With Hechinger Co., Landover, Md., 1972—, v.p. real estate devel., from 1982, pres., COO, until 1990, pres., CEO, 1990—, also bd. dirs. Office: Hechinger Co 1616 McCormick Dr Landover MD 20785*

HECHT, EUGENE, physics educator; b. Bklyn., Dec. 2, 1938; s. Irving and Mollie (Balinsky) H.; m. Carolyn Eisen, June 18, 1960; children: Amy Allison, Jennifer Michal, Jamey Adam. BS, NYU, 1960; MS, Rutgers U., 1963; PhD, Adelphi U., 1967. Engr. RCA Astroelectronics, N.J., 1960-63; prof. physics Adelphi U., Garden City, N.Y., 1967—. Author: Optics, 1974, Schuams Outline in Optics, 1975, Physics in Perspective, 1980, The Mad Potter of Biloxi: G.E. Ohr, 1989. Recipient Art Book of Yr. award Art Librs. Am., 1990. Office: Dept Physics Adelphi U Garden City NY 11530

HECHT, JAMES LEE, writer, researcher, consultant; b. N.Y.C., Dec. 21, 1926; s. Leo and Edith (Hoffheimer) H.; m. Amy Blatchford, Oct. 10, 1953; children: Charles B., Margaret W. BChemE, Cornell U., 1949; MS, Ga. Inst. Tech., 1951; PhD, Yale U., 1955. Rsch. engr., rsch. supr., rsch. assoc., sr. rsch. assoc. E.I. du Pont de Nemours & Co., Wilmington, Del., 1953-85; adj. prof., dir. Project for the Study of Am. Future U. Del., Newark, 1986—. Author: Because It is Right: Integration in Housing, 1970, Rubles and Dollars: Strategies for Doing Business in the Soviet Union, 1991. Recipient Pub. Svc. award U.S. Dept. Interior, 1979. Mem. Am. Chem. Soc. (chmn. Western N.Y. sect. 1965-66), Del. Coun. for U.S.-USSR Rels. (chmn. 1987-90). Democrat. Episcopalian. Home: 111 S Spring Valley Rd Wilmington DE 19807-2448

HECHT, PATRICIA LAYTON, elementary school educator, author, consultant; b. Toms River, N.J., Apr. 19, 1935; d. Harry J. and Elsie Graham (Pile) Layton; m. Kenneth Parker Keller, Apr. 14, 1956 (div. 1969); children: Alexandra Niles Keller Calabrese, Corinne Graham, Jennifer Layton. BS, Douglass Coll., 1956; MA in History, Rutgers U., 1960; postgrad., Monmouth Coll., 1981. Cert. elem. tchr., N.J. 1st grade tchr. Ladd On-Base Schs., Fairbanks, Ala., 1956-57; English, history tchr. Elizabeth (N.J.) Schs., 1957; 1st grade tchr. Middletown (N.J.) Twp. Schs., 1958, 1st, 2d grade tchr., 1958-60, 8th grade history tchr., 1960-61; pvt. tutor Middletown, 1961-64; editor The Monmouth Unitarian, Lincroft, N.J., 1969-70; 2d grade tchr. Elberon Sch., Long Branch, N.J., 1972-87, 1st grade tchr., 1987-91, 1st grade tchr. computer sci. tech., 1991—; critic reader Scott Foresman Co., Glenview, Ill., 1990-91; curriculum writing Long Branch Schs., 1972-92. Author: Math Made Easy For Grade One, 1991, The Little Vowel Books, 1991, Nicholas Niles Was Born Today, 1991, Mainly Lame-Brain Listening Games, 1991; author (play) Lincoln, 1990; researcher, author McHugh Genealogy, 1966, My Mother's Family: A Niles-Pile Genealogy, 1970. Recipient Golden Apple Tchr. award Cable TV Network, 1989, N.J. Tchr. of Month award, 1989. Mem. NEA, NOW, Long Branch Schs. Edn. Assn. (Elberon rep. 1990-91), N.J. Edn. Assn., Nat. Trust for Hist. Preservation. Home: 390 Ocean Ave # 2A Long Branch NJ 07740 Office: Elberon Sch Park Ave Long Branch NJ 07740

HECHT, ROBERT WILLIAM, insurance executive; b. Jackson, Miss., Feb. 26, 1945; s. William Frederick and Rose M. (Cardell) H.; m. Maryann Cavalieri, Oct. 29, 1969 (div. 1982); children: Matthew Laurence, Graham T.; m. Roberta M. Waterson, Aug. 6, 1983; 1 child, Michele L. Anderson. AA with honors, Fairleigh Dickinson U., 1978; postgrad., Thomas A. Edison State U., 1989—. From claims adjuster to claims supr. N.J. Mfgs. Ins. Co., West Trenton, 1970-91, sr. tech. trainer, 1991—. With U.S. Army, 1966-70, Vietnam. Mem. Soc. Ins. Trainers and Educators, Am. Soc. of Trainers and Developers. Methodist. Home: 29 Greenbrier Rd Levittown PA 19057-3305 Office: NJ Mfrs Ins Co Sullivan Way Trenton NJ 08628-3401

HECK, ALBERT, JR., broadcasting executive; b. Wilkes-Barre, Pa., Jan. 25, 1927; s. Albert and Ethel (Wilcox) Gould; m. Jane M. Heck, Dec. 1975; children: Bruce Craig, Scott. Grad. high sch., Asbury Park, N.J. Mgr. Walter Reade Theatres, Asbury Park; promotion mgr. Asbury Park Press; sales mgr. House Beautiful Mag., N.Y.C.; N.Y. sales mgr. Look Mag., N.Y.C.; dist. sales NBC Radio Network, N.Y.C.; v.p. mktg. sales Radio Advt. Bur., N.Y.C.; pres. Radio Network Assn., N.Y.C. Office: Radio Network Assn 1700 Broadway New York NY 10019-5905

HECK, RONALD MARSHALL, chemical engineer; b. Balt., Sept. 23, 1943; s. Joshua H. and Rita Mercedes (Young) H.; m. Barbara Thompson, June 16, 1990; children: Ron, Kimberly, Teresa. BS in Chem. Engring. cum laude, U. Md., 1965, PhD in Chem. Engring., 1969. Rsch. chem. engr. Celanese Chem. Co., Corpus Christi, Tex., 1969-72; sr. rsch. chem. engr. Englehard Industries, Menlo Park, N.J., 1972-77; sect. head Engelhard Industries, Menlo Park, N.J., 1977-84; engring. mgr. Engelhard Industries, Union, N.J., 1984-87; group leader Englehard Industries, Menlo Park, 1987—. Contbr. articles to profl. jours.; patentee in field. Mem. Kingwood Twp. Sch. Bd., N.J., 1975, pres., 1978. Mem. Am. Inst. Chem. Engrs., Air and Waste Mgmt. Assn., Soc. Automotive Engrs. Home: 269 Kingwood Station Rd Frenchtown NJ 08825-1035 Office: Englehard Corp 2655 Route 22 W Union NJ 07083-8598

HECKERT, PAUL CHARLES, sociologist, educator; b. Lewistown, Pa., May 30, 1929; s. Paul Kester and Clara Belle (Plessinger) H.; A.B., Catawba Coll., 1951; B.D., Lancaster Theol. Sem., 1954; M.S., Cornell, 1959, Ph.D., 1964; m. Sara Mae Raezer, Sept. 6, 1952; children—Paul Andrew, Druann Maria, Daniel Alex, Nathanael Alan, Diane Manette. Ordained minister United Ch. of Christ, 1954; missionary United Ch. of Christ, Honduras, 1954-60; clergyman various Methodist chs., N.Y., 1960-64; asso. prof. sociology, also chmn. dept. Catawaba (N.C.) Coll., 1964-68, prof., 1968-72, also chmn. joint dept. sociology with Livingstone Coll., Salisbury, N.C.; prof., chmn. dept. sociology Frostburg (Md.) State Univ., 1972-87; prof., 1987—; del. Rowan Coop. Christian Ministry, 1968-72; mem. leadership devel. com. Pa. West Conf., United Ch. of Christ, 1973-78. Bd. dirs. Salisbury Rowan Community Service Council, 1971-72. Served with AUS, 1948-50. Ford fellow, summer 1968, NASA/ASEE summer faculty fellow, 1969, 77, AEC summer faculty fellow, 1973; NEH grantee, 1975, 79, 83, 86. Mem. Am. Sociol. Assn., Rural Sociol. Soc., AAAS, Phi Kappa Phi, Alpha Kappa Delta, Sigma Delta Pi, Delta Tau Kappa. Contbr. book revs. to profl. jours. Home: 13 N Woodlawn Ave Cumberland MD 21502-7254 Office: Frostburg State U Frostburg MD 21532

HECKLER, JOHN MAGUIRE, stockbroker; b. Meriden, Conn., Nov. 11, 1927; s. George Ernest and Mary Catherine (Maguire) H.; m. Sheryl Jean Bills, Nov. 30, 1985; children: Belinda West, Alison Anne, John Maguire. AB, Fairfield U., 1951; postgrad. Fordham U., 1951-53, Harvard U., 1953-54. Exec. Maguire Homes, M. W. Maguire, 1954-62; instl. salesman Harris Upham & Co., Boston, 1962-68; resident mgr. Middendorf, Colgate & Co., Boston, 1968-70; chmn., chief exec. officer Boston Instl. Services, Inc., 1971—; dir. Europension Boston Assocs.; chmn. Spur Publs., Inc., 1989—; mem. N.Y. Stock Exch., 1970—. Campaign asst. Congressman Bradford Morse, 1960. Served with USCG, 1945-47. Republican. Episcopalian. Clubs: Harvard (Boston); Middleburg and Piedmont (Va.) Hunt; Capitol Hill (Washington). Office: Sears Crescent Sq Brookline MA 02146-7410

HECKMAN, JOANN, small business owner; b. Newton, N.J., Feb. 23, 1950; d. James Richard and Frances Margaret (Bertram) H. AS in Communications, Centenary Coll., 1982, BA in Communications and Journalism cum laude, 1984. Cert. clin. hypnotherapist. Co-owner, pres. The Crystal Works, Hackettstown, N.J., 1987-91; internat. assn. counselor, therapist Hypnotherapy & Hollistic Awareness, Hackettstown, 1991—. Mem. NAFE, AAUW, Internat. Assn. Counselors & Therapists, Am. Assn. Counseling and Devel., Nat. Guild Hypnotists, Phi Theta Kappa (Merit cert. 1982), Alpha Chi. Republican. Mem. Unitarian Universalist Ch. Home: 313 Shore Rd PO Box 114 Budd Lake NJ 07828 Office: Hypnotherapy & Holistic Awareness 110 Grand Ave Ste 7 Hackettstown NJ 07840-7101

HEDAYA, ROBERT JOSEPH, psychiatrist; b. Bklyn., Mar. 13, 1952; s. Joseph Hedaya and Carol Sarah (Harary) Maleh; m. Mindy Bess Seligman, Sept. 25, 1971; children: Adam Joshua, Caroline. BA cum laude, SUNY, Buffalo, 1974, MD, 1979. Diplomate Am. Bd. Psychiatry and Neurology. Resident tng. Georgetown U. Hosp., Washington, 1979-83; asst. clin. prof. psychiatry Georgetown U. Hosp., Washington, Md., 1983—; resident tng. NIMH, Bethesda, Md., 1982-83, cons., 1988-89; pvt. practice Chevy Chase, Md., 1983—; mem. attending staff dept. psychiatry Holy Cross Hosp., Silver Spring, Md., 1983-90; guest speaker Holy Cross Hosp., Silver Spring, 1983—; cons. NIMH, Bethesda, 1988-89. Coach Children's Soccer League, Rockville, 1984-85; mem. Com. for Accurate Middle East Reporting in Am., Washington, 1985—. Arthur, Inc. grantee, 1984. Mem. AMA, Am. Psychiat. Assn., Am. Group Psychotherapy Assn. Jewish. Office: 4701 Willard Ave Ste 222 Bethesda MD 20815-4637

HEDBERG, FRANKLIN AUGUSTIN, academic administrator, journalist; b. Caracas, Venezuela, Apr. 30, 1946; s. Hollis Dow and Frances (Murray) H.; children: James Augustin, Helen Mary. BA, Columbia U., 1973, MA, 1975, M.S. Journalism, 1976, PhM in English Lit., 1977. Copyboy Kansas City (Mo.) Star, 1964-65, market reporter, 1965-66; editor-in-chief Reports Mag., World Edn., N.Y.C., 1974-77; writer, editor Time-Life Books, Alexandria, Va., 1977-81; staff writer Money Mag., Time Inc., N.Y.C., 1981-84; sr. editor Money Mag., Time-Warner, N.Y.C., 1984-89; dir. publs. The Lawrenceville (N.J.) Sch., 1991—; adj. prof. English NYU, 1985-89; adj. prof. Columbia U. Grad. Sch. Journalism, N.Y.C., 1987-88; instr. No. Va. Community Coll., Alexandria, 1977-81; seminar instr. Radcliffe Publishing Program, Harvard U., Cambridge, Mass., 1985. Author: Faith Under Fire and the Revolutions in Eastern Europe, 1992. Trustee 1st Presbyn. Ch., Morrisville, Pa., 1987-90. Recipient Nat. Press Club award for best consumer journalism, 1982, Bagehot fellowship in bus. and fin. journalism, Columbia U., 1985. Home: 725 Crown St Morrisville PA 19067 Office: The Lawrenceville Sch Lawrenceville NJ 08648

HEDERMAN, REA S., publisher. Pub. N.Y. Rev. of Books. Office: NY Rev Books 250 W 57th St New York NY 10107-0001*

HEDGE, JEANNE COLLEEN, health physicist; b. Scottsburg, Ind., May 30, 1960; d. Paul Russell and Barbara Jean (Belshaw) H. BS in Environ. Health, Purdue U., 1983. Chemistry and health physics technician Marble Hill Nuclear Generating Sta., Pub. Svc. Ind., Madison, 1983-84; radiation protection asst. Pub. Svc. Electric and Gas Co., Hancock's Bridge, N.J., 1984-85, radiation protection technician, 1985-89, engr., 1989-90, lead engr., 1990-91, sr. staff engr., 1991—; mem. People to People Internat. Citizen Ambassador Exch., People's Republic China, 1988. Recipient 5th Kup green belt Am. Tae Kwan Do Moo Duk Kwan, 1991. Mem. AAAS, APHA, NOW, Am. Nuclear Soc., Health Physics Soc., Tau Beta Sigma.

HEDGEPETH, CHESTER MELVIN, JR., university dean; b. Richmond, Va., Oct. 28, 1937; s. Chester M. Sr. and Ethel (Carter) H.; m. Thelma Washington, Aug. 16, 1969; 1 child, Chester III. BA, Blackburn Coll., 1960; MA, Wesleyan U., 1966; EdD, Harvard U., 1977. Tchr. English Maggie L. Walker High Sch., Richmond, 1960-65; instr. English Va. Union U., Richmond, 1965-68, Coll. St. Thomas, St. Paul, 1969-70, Macalester Coll., Mpls., 1970-71; asst. prof. English Va. Union U., Richmond, 1972-75, Va. Commonwealth U., Richmond, 1978-83; dean arts and sci. U. Md. Ea. Shore, Princess Anne, Md., 1983—. Author: Theories of Social Action in Black Literature, 1968, 20th Century Afro-American Writers and Artists, 1991; sr. editor Md. Rev., 1986—. Trustee bd. Wicomico Presbyn. Ch., 1986-89. Grantee NEH, 1971, Va. Found. Humanities, 1978, Md. Humanities Coun., 1988. Mem. Phi Delta Kappa, Sigma Pi Phi. Office: U Md Ea Shore Princess Anne MD 21853

HEDLUND, ROBERT L., state senator, automobile executive; s. Robert and Joanne (Sarni) H. Student, Quincy Jr. Coll., Wentworth Inst. Tech. Pres. Hedlund Motors Sales, Inc., Braintree, Mass., 1979—; senator Norfolk-Plymouth Dist.; mem. commerce & labor com., pub. safety com., taxation com., couties com. Mass. State Senate, 1991—. Vol. Avi Nelson for U.S. Senate campaign, 1978; Norfolk County coord. Phil Crane for Pres. campaign, 1980; Hingham coord. Ray Shamie for U.S. Senate campaign, 1984; state chmn. Mass. Fedn. Young Reps., 1987-90; co-chmn. Debra Tucker for U.S. Congress campaign, 1988; del. Rep. Nat. Conv., Atlanta, 1988; mem. exec. bd. Mass. Rep. State Com., 1988-90; treas. Hull Rep. Town Com., 1988-90; mem. Weymouth Rep. Town Com., 1990—; mem. adv. coun. South Shore Elder Svcs., 1991—; mem. govt. adv. bd. Beacon Hill Inst., 1991—; appointee Local Govt. Adv. Coun., 1991—, Commn. Future of State Colls. and Community Colls., 1991—. Mem. Nat. Fedn. Ind. Bus., South Shore C. of C. (govt. affairs com. 1987-90), Sierra Club, Boston Area Bicycle Coalition. Address: 1662 Commercial St East Weymouth MA 02189

HEDLUND, RONALD DAVID, vice provost, researcher, educator; b. Joliet, Ill., June 16, 1941; s. Henry Gustav and Betty Marie (Nelson) H.; m. Ellen Louise Parrish, Aug. 22, 1964; children: Karen Marie, David Peter. BA, Augustana Coll., 1963; MA, U. Iowa, 1964, PhD, 1967. Asst. prof. U. Wis., Milw., 1967-73, assoc. prof., 1973-77, dir. social sci. rsch. facility, 1978-80, prof., 1977-89, assoc. dean of rsch. Grad. Sch., 1980-89; vice provost of rsch., prof. U. R.I., Kingston, 1989—; co-chair rsch. network R.I. Partnership Sci. & Tech., Providence, 1990—; bd. dirs. Econ. Innovation Ctr., Newport, R.I. Contbr. numerous articles to profl. jours. Mem. Kingston Fire Dist. Study Com., 1990. NSF grantee, 1967, 77, 84, Ford Found. grantee, 1985. Mem. Am. Polit. Sci. Assn., Nat. Coun. Univ. Rsch. Adminstrs., Midwest Polit. Sci. Assn. (exec. coun. 1987-90), Soc. of Rsch. Adminstrs., Southern Polit. Sci. Assn., Western Polit. Sci. Assn. Lutheran. Office: U RI Rsch Office 70 Lower College Rd Kingston RI 02881-1316

HEDMAN, FREDERICK ALVIN, accountant, lawyer; b. Evansville, Ind., July 29, 1937; s. Fritz Algot and Marjorie Eugenia (Copenhaver) H.; m. Juanita Nazareno Martinez, June 5, 1989. BS in Acctg., U. Balt., 1963, JD, 1969. Bar: Md. 1974, U.S. Supreme Ct. 1980. Operating acct. HUD, Washington, 1964—; sole practice, Bel Air, Md., 1974—. Recipient Silver award Boy Scout Am., N.Y.C., 1955. Mem. Assn. Govt. Accts. (bd. dirs. Montgomery-Prince Georges chpt. 1983—, Certs. of Merit 1977-91, Unsung Hero award 1979), Md. State Bar Assn., Harford County Bar Assn. Republican. Methodist. Home: 218 Fulford Ave Bel Air MD 21014-3814 Office: HUD 451 7th St SW Washington DC 20410

HEDSTROM, ERIC LEONARD, JR., management consultant; b. Buffalo, June 2, 1922; s. Eric L. and Mary (Warren) H.; m. Eloise Gilbert Herrick, Jan. 7, 1950; children: Mitchell W., Gilbert S., Roger W. BE, Yale U., 1947. Pres. Cooper Paper Box Corp., Buffalo, 1947-59; internat. v.p. Graphic Controls Corp., Buffalo, 1959-83; internat. mgmt. cons. Buffalo, 1983—. Chmn. strategic planning adv. coun. Erie Community Coll., 1984-90; pres., bd. dirs. Boys and Girls Clubs of Erie County, Episcopal Community Svcs.; v.p., bd. dirs. Western N.Y. Grantmakers Assn., former vich-chmn., bd. dirs. United Way Buffalo and Erie County. Capt. USAAF, 1943-46, PTO. Recipient awards Boys Clubs Am., community svc. award NCCJ. Mem. Crag Burn Golf Club, Plantation Golf Club, Phi Gamma Delta. Home and Office: 465 Girdle Rd East Aurora NY 14052-1226 also: 715 Harrington Lake Dr Venice FL 34293

HEDSTROM, MITCHELL WARREN, banker; b. Buffalo, Apr. 14, 1951; s. Eric Leonard and Eloise (Herrick) H.; m. Zoe C. Dyson, Apr. 28, 1990. BS, Northeastern U., Boston, 1975; MS, MIT, 1977. Account officer Citibank, N.A., N.Y.C., 1978-80; sr. account officer Citibank, N.A., 1980-82, asst. v.p., 1982-84, v.p., 1984—. Mem. Coun. on Fgn. Rels., Coral Beach and Tennis Club. Republican. Episcopalian. Home: 515 E 72d St New York NY 10021-4032 Office: Citibank NA 399 Park Ave New York NY 10043-0001

HEEKS, ROBERT EUGENE, chemical engineer; b. Rochester, N.Y., Jan. 19, 1928; s. John A. and Marie Laura (Lomb) H.; m. Shirley Cathrine Stam, July 16, 1955; children: Leslie G., Robert E. Jr., Mark A., Kathleen M., Elizabeth M. AB in Chemistry, U. Rochester, 1952, MScheme, 1954, PhDChemE, 1957. From engr. to mgr. photo engr. Xerox Corp., Rochester and Webster, N.Y., 1956-86, ret. contract mgr., 1987—; bd. dirs., cons. Brightline Photo Products, Tampa, Fla., 1973-85. Patentee in field. Mem. AICE, Am. Chem. Soc., Soc. Photog. Scientists and Engrs., Canandaigua Yacht Club (chmn. 1981-92), Sigma Xi. Republican. Roman Catholic. Home: 87 Hillcrest Dr Penfield NY 14526-2451

HEER, EDWIN LEROY, insurance executive; b. American Falls, Idaho, Aug. 19, 1938; s. Edwin Frederick and Kathryn Irene (Franks) H; m. Jacqulin S. Jefford, May 23, 1960 (div. Mar. 1978); 1 child, Kevin Jack; m. Judith Lee Overton-Jones, Jan. 2, 1980. BS, U. Alaska, 1963; MBA, St. Mary's U. Tex., San Antonio, 1976. Asst. actuary Aetna Life & Casualty Co., Hartford, Conn., 1963-68; assoc. actuary Ins. Co. of N.Am., Phila., 1968-72; asst. v.p. USAA, San Antonio, 1972-78; v.p., corp. actuary W.R. Berkley Corp., Greenwich, Conn., 1978-91; sr. v.p., chief corp. actuary W.R. Berkley Corp., Conn., 1991—; bd. dirs. Union Standard Ins. Co., Dallas, Signet Reins. Co., Morristown, N.J. Fellow Casualty Actuarial soc.; mem. Am. Acad. Actuaries, Soc. Chartered Property Casualty Underwriters (cert.). Republican. Lutheran. Home: 44 Strawberry Hill Ave Stamford CT 06902-2632 Office: W R Berkley Corp 165 Mason St Greenwich CT 06830-6608

HEERWAGEN, HERBERT ALFRED, lawyer; b. Newark, Nov. 20, 1910; s. Arthur and Margaret (Juban) H.; m. Doris Louise Richardson, May 26, 1939 (div. 1965); children: Peter D., David R., Nancy L., John R.; m. Margaret Knoll Anderson, Dec. 17, 1977. Student, Dickinson Coll., 1928-30; AB, Cornell U., 1932, JD, 1934. Bar: N.Y. 1934. Assoc. firm Davies, Hardy, Ives & Lawther, and predecessors, 1934-44, 46-57, ptnr., 1958-77, Windels, Marx, Davies & Ives, 1978-82, of counsel, 1983-84; sec. Birmingham Corp., 1982-83. Assoc. editor Cornell Law Quar., 1932-33, editor-in-chief, 1933-34. Mem. New Castle Recreation Commn., Chappaqua, N.Y., 1957-69, chmn., 1965-67; past sec., chmn. Manhattan coun., past trustee, trustee emeritus Big Bros. Inc., Big Bros./Big Sisters of N.Y.C., Inc.; trustee, sec. Ox Hollow Found., Inc., 1964-84; trustee Bar Harbor Festival Corp., 1975—; vol. Overlook Hosp., Summit, N.J., 1986—. Served with AUS, 1944-46. Recipient Boardman prize Cornell U. Law Sch., 1933, McKinney prize, 1934. Mem. ABA, ACLU, Acad. Polit. Sci., Cornell U. Law Assn., Nat. Audubon Soc., Bedford Audubon Soc., Amnesty Internat. U.S., Sierra Club, Order of Coif, Phi Beta Kappa, Phi Kappa Phi. Home: 133 Parker Ave Maplewood NJ 07040-1811 Office: 156 W 56th St Ste 220 New York NY 10019-3800

HEERWAGEN, PETER H., financial and investment management company executive, lawyer; b. Summit, N.J., Aug. 16, 1945; s. Elwood J. and Grace S. (Stager) H.; m. Phyllis R. Burnham, June 21, 1969; children: Matthew B., Elizabeth A. BA, Boston U., 1968; JD, Syracuse U., 1972. Bar: N.Y. 1973. Exec. v.p., chief investment officer The Ayco Corp., Albany, N.Y., 1972—. Bd. dirs. Albany Med. Ctr., 1985—, Albany Inst. History and Art, 1989—. Mem. N.Y. State Bar Assn., Schuyler Meadows Club. Office: Ayco Corp 1 Wall St Albany NY 12205-3894

HEFFERNAN, CAROL FALVO, English educator; b. Bklyn., Nov. 7, 1944; d. Leo Joseph and Mary (Cappiello) Falvo; m. Thomas Farel Heffernan, Mar. 21, 1970; 1 child, Geoffrey Farel. AB, Barnard Coll., 1965; MA, U. Wis., 1968; PhD, NYU, 1973. Instr. Monmouth Coll., West Long Branch, N.J., 1968-69, Adelphi U., Garden City, N.Y., 1969-72, Nassau Community Coll., Garden City, 1972-73; asst. prof. U.S. Merchant Marine Acad., King Point, N.Y., 1973-76; asst. prof. Rutgers U., Newark, 1976-82, assoc. prof., 1982—; vis. prof. Trinity Coll., Dublin, Ireland, 1981. Author: The Phoenix at the Fountain, 1988; editor: Le Bone Florence of Rome, 1976; contbr. articles to profl. jours. Rsch. grantee Rutgers U., 1978, 79, 85, N.J. Dept. Higher Edn., 1984-86. Mem. AAUP, Modern Lang. Assn., Medieval Acad. Am., New Chaucer Soc., Renaissance Soc. Am., Internat. Courtly Lit. Soc. Office: Rutgers U Dept English Newark NJ 07102

HEFFERNAN, ROBERT VINCENT, legislative staff member; b. Burlington, Vt., Dec. 30, 1955; s. Vincent William and Roberta Ida (Masse) H. BA in Communication-print Journalism, The Am. U., 1977. Profl. staff mem. U.S. Senate Com. Govtl. Affairs, Washington, 1974-81; exec. v.p., sec./treas. Conn. Florists Assn., Monroe, 1989—; staff dir. Conn. Ctr. for Farming, Plants & Flowers, Botsford, 1990—. Author: CABINETMAKERS: Story of The Three-Year Battle to Establish the U.S. Department of Education, 1983. Bd. dirs. Monroe C. of C., 1985—. Mem. Am. Soc. Assn. execs., Soc. Am. Florists, Conn. Soc. Profl. Journalists. Democrat. Roman Catholic. Home: 480 Litchfield Rd New Milford CT 06776-2009 Office: Conn Florists Assn 590 Main St Monroe CT 06468-2882

HEFFNER, RALPH H., agricultural products company executive; b. 1938. Farmer Jersey Acres Farm Inc., Pine Grove, Pa.; formerly vice chmn. Agway Inc., now chmn.; bd. dirs. Curtice-Burns Foods Inc. Office: Agway Inc PO Box 4933 Syracuse NY 13221-4933*

HEFLER, PETER RICHARD, transportation executive; b. Boston, May 22, 1940; s. William Abbott and Geradine Martha (Doyle) H.; m. Janet Kay Hefler, Apr. 28, 1979; 1 child, Brien Peter. BA, U. Mass., 1963; MBA, Adelphi U., 1975. Exec. dir., mgr. Transit Express, Inc., Springfield, Mo., 1989—; nat. advt. dir. Transit Performance mag., 1989—. Maj. USAF, 1963-86. Mem. Wason North Bus. Assn. (pres. 1989-91, bd. dirs. 1986-88, 91-92), New Eng. Passenger Transp. Assn. (bd. dirs. 1986-90, 2d v.p. 1990-91, 1st v.p. 1992-93), Air Force Assn., N.Y. Athletic Club, Wings Aviation Club (N.Y.C.). Home: 152 Abbott St Springfield MA 01118 Office: Transit Express Inc 2840 Main St Springfield MA 01107

HEGEMAN, JAMES ALAN, corporate executive; b. Indpls., Jan. 8, 1943; s. Frank Anderson and Helene Anna (Sudbrock) H.; BS in Acctg. cum laude, U. Tenn., 1973; MBA, Harvard U., 1975. CPA, Tenn.; m. Catherine Louise Mallers, May 1, 1966 (div. 1973); 1 child, Christopher Scott; m. Janet Lee Scherf Nystrom, May 24, 1986. Pres., chmn. Nat. Rent-A-Cycle, Inc., Indpls., 1964-68, Fairfield Electronics Corp., Indpls., 1965-68; gen. mgr. H & R Block, Inc., Knoxville, Tenn., 1967-73; asst. contr. Rohm & Haas, Inc., Knoxville, 1973-75; v.p. Gerson Co., Middleboro, Mass., 1975-76; contr. Acton Corp. (Mass.), 1976-79; chief exec. officer Acton Films, Inc., N.Y.C., Telaction Phone Corp., Palisades Park, N.J., 1976—; corp. contr. Golden Eye Seafoods, Inc., New Bedford, Mass., 1977-78; chief fin. officer Simon Konover & Assocs., K&P Mgmt., Inc., Anthony Assocs. (all West Hartford, Conn.), 1978-79; v.p. fin. Audio Specialists, Inc. and Sound Playground, Newington, Conn., 1979—; fin./mgmt. cons. Standex Internat. Corp., Salem, N.H., 1979-84; chief cons. APC Skills Co., Palm Beach, Fla., Alexander Proudfoot Co., Chgo., 1984; chief fin. officer State St. Technologies, Hartford, Conn., 1984—; pres. LWC Industries, Inc., Miami, Fla., also dir.; treas., dir. Kenmore Rd. Assn., 1987—; bd. dirs. Window Corp. Am. Mem. Ind. Rep. Cen. Com., 1967-68; bd. govs. U. Tenn., 1975-79; named to Tenn. gov.'s staff Tenn. Col. Continental Grain Co. Fellow, 1973; Cabot fellow, 1974. Mem. Am. Film Inst., Am. Inst. CPA's, Tenn. Soc. CPA's, U. Tenn. Alumni Assn. (pres.), Wally Byam Caravan Club Internat. (pres. region 1, internat. bd. trustees), Beta Alpha Psi. Lutheran. Club: Harvard (Boston). Home and Office: 58 Kenmore Rd Bloomfield CT 06002-2111

HEGER, FRANK JOSEPH, structural design engineer; b. Bklyn., Aug. 13, 1927; s. Frank Joseph and Philomena (Schmitz) H.; m. Anne Amelia Mulholland, July 4, 1950; children: John, Robert, Elizabeth, Thomas. SB, MIT, 1948, SM, 1949, ScD, 1962. Registered profl. engr., Ala., Calif., Fla., Ga., Ill., Ind., Iowa, Maine, Md., Mass., Mich., Minn., N.H., N.J., N.Y.,

N.C., Ohio, Pa., S.C., Va. Structural design engr. Ford Bacon & Davis Inc., N.Y.C., 1949-55; asst. prof. structural design MIT, Cambridge, 1955-63; sr. prin. Simpson Gumpertz & Heger Inc., Arlington, Mass., 1963—; lectr. in field. Contbr. articles to profl. jours. Recipient Spl. Award for Excellence Am. Inst. Steel Constrn., 1968, Cert. of Appreciation, U. Lowell (Mass.), 1979, James F. Lincoln Arc Welding Found. award, 1981, Reese Structural Rsch. award ACI, 1984, many others. Fellow ASCE (mem. std. practice for std. installation direct design of soil/precast concrete pipe interaction systems com.), ACI (mem. com. 344 - design of circular prestressed concrete structures, past New Eng. chpt. pres.), ASTM (mem. com. C13 on concrete pipe, Award of Merit); mem. Boston Soc. of Civil Engrs. Sect. of ASCE (past dir., chmn. loads adv. com.), Boston Assn. Structural Engrs. (past pres.), Transp. Rsch. Bd., Am. Water Wks. Assn., Am. Concrete Pipe Assn., Wire Reinforcement Inst. Office: Simpson Gumpertz & Heger 297 Broadway Arlington MA 02174-5394

HEGERLE, HENRY ALOYSIUS, engineering administrator; b. Pitts., Nov. 18, 1937; s. Harry A. and Helen (Thieret) H. Student, Carnegie Inst. Tech., 1956-59; BSEE, Carnegie Mellon U., 1971, M. Pub. Mgmt., 1987. Registered profl. engr., Pa. Owner Hegerle Inc., Pitts., 1967-80; plan examiner City of Pitts. Dept. Pub. Safety, 1980-82, plan examiner, tng. officer, 1982-90, asst. chief engring., 1990—; voting mem. Coun. Am. Bldg. Officials Certification Com., Falls Church, Va., 1985—. A founder, incorporator Hilltop/Allentown Civic Assn., Pitts., 1973; active Knoxville Community Orgn., Pitts., 1981; dist. commr. Boy Scouts Am., 1978—. Mem. BOCA Internat. (coms.), Pa. Bldg. Officials Conf. (pres. 1985-86), Commonwealth Bldg. Officials (pres. 1985-86), Internat. Assn. Elec. Inspectors (bd. dirs. western Pa. chpt.). Roman Catholic. Home: 211 Charles St Pittsburgh PA 15210-1603 Office: City of Pitts Dept Pub Safety 1600 W Carson St Pittsburgh PA 15219-1031

HEGGESTAD, HOWARD EDWIN, plant pathologist; b. Stoughton, Wis., July 24, 1915; s. Erick A. and Gunda (Veium) H.; m. Dolores Andersen, June 10, 1939; children: Arnold, Margot, David. PhB, U. Wis., 1940, PhD, 1944. Instr. horticulture U. Wis., Madison, 1944-46; agronomist USDA, Greeneville, Tenn., 1946-55; agronomist, rsch. leader USDA, Beltsville, 1955-66, chief air pollution lab., 1966-75, plant pathologist rsch., 1975-84, biol. sci. collaborator, 1990—; cons. Electric Power Rsch. Inst., Palo Alto, Calif., 1979-81. Assoc. editor: Jour. Environ. Quality, Plant Disease Reporter, Phytopathology; contbr. articles to profl. jours. and books. Lutheran. Home: 3112 Castleleigh Rd Silver Spring MD 20904-1713

HEGHINIAN, ELIZABETH ALBAN TRUMBOWER, artist, educator; b. N.Y.C., Jan. 11, 1917; d. Eli Cadwallader and Maria Lucas (Coyle) Trumbower; m. Aram Lincoln Heghinian, Aug. 24, 1957; children: Elizabeth Alban, Marie Hunazant. Student, Pratt Inst., 1938; BS magna cum laude, NYU, 1950, MA, 1952, PhD, 1957; postgrad. Bklyn. Inst. Arts and Scis., 1963-66, Bklyn. Mus. Art Sch., L.I. U., 1963-66, Fairleigh Dickinson U., 1970; studied under Richard Mayhew, Geogiana Brown Harbeson, Edith Fetterolf, Katheryn I. Young, Howard W. Arnold, I.-Ching Ku. Indsl. designer Belle Kogan Assos., 1938-40; art dir. Norscross Pubs., 1940-42; buyer for battle damaged U.S. naval vessels and equipment Arma Corp., 1942-45; dir. arts and crafts YWCA Camp Program, 1946; designer Cosmopolitan Crafts, Camp Fire Outfitting Co., 1946-47; faculty N.Y. U., 1947-61, asst. prof. edn., 1957-61; v.p. Hudson Machinery Co., Inc., Internat. Graphic Arts Equipment Dealers, 1975—; v.p. Hudson Machinery Co. Inc., 1975—; specialist consultation svcs. nat. arts and crafts com. Boys' Clubs Am., 1949-65; rsch. and practicum in remedial reading techniques N.Y.C. Pub. Sch., Bklyn., 1966-68; exhibited in group shows Pratt Inst., 1936-38, N.Y. U., 1948-52; represented in permanent collection Bklyn. Mus. Art Sch., pvt. collections. Mem. nat. adv. com. on recreation programs and activities arts and crafts sect. Nat. Recreation Assn., 1958-62; pres. Camp Jefferson, Inc., N.Y.C.; dir. Camp Jefferson, Palisades Interstate Park, N.Y., 1945-86 ; active town wide camping and sch. year program Girl Scouts U.S.A., 1969-73; mem. N.Y. Assn. for Brain Injured Children, 1963-86 . Recipient Founders Day certificate, N.Y. U., 1950. Mem. Am. Watercolor Soc. (asso.), AAUW, Nat. Congress Parents and Tchrs., Tenafly Nature Center Assn., Palisades Interstate Park Camp Dirs.' Assn., Pi Lambda Theta, Kappa Delta Pi, Epsilon Pi Tau. Author: The Contribution of Craft Activities to the Philosophy and Objectives of Boys Clubs of America, 1957; (monograph) Crafts in Boys' Clubs, 1958. Address: 52 Howard Park Dr Tenafly NJ 07670

HEIBEL, PATRICIA MARIE, marketing coordinator, photographer; b. Northfield, Minn., July 29, 1956; d. Richard Henry and Irene (Graff) L. BS in Indsl. Tech., U. S. Maine, 1991. Cert. chromatographer, spectroscopist, microscopist. Bookeeper First Nat. Bank, Northfield, Minn., 1974-78; R&D engring. technician Sheldahl Inc., Northfield, 1978-83; sr. technician 3 M Co., St. Paul, Minn., 1983-85; analytical chem. technician 3 M Co., St. Paul, 1985-88; photographer, technician Woodard & Curran, Inc., Portland, Maine, 1988-90; mktg. coord. T.Y. Lin Internat., Falmouth, Maine, 1991—; cons. Prodn. Tech. Ctr., USM, Gorham, Maine, 1990—; owner, mgr. Art Seen, Scarborough, Maine, 1990—. Photographer: (books) The Best of Photography, 1989 (finalist), The Best of Photography, 1990 (finalist). Recipient Best of Show award, Photographic Soc. Am., 1986; named Photographer of Yr. 3M Camera Club, St. Paul, 1987, Nat. Winner, Fuji Film Corp., 1987, winner Internat. Art Competition, N.Y.C., 1990. Mem. Am. Soc. Safety Engrs., Epsilon Pi Tau. Office: T Y Lin 5 Fundy Rd Falmouth ME 04105

HEIBERGER, MICHAEL H., academic administrator, optometrist; b. Bklyn., Oct. 14, 1940; s. Samuel and Kitty (Silverberg) H.; m. Surelle H. Coleman, June 23, 1968; children: Alexander, Elizabeth. BS, Bklyn. Coll., 1961, Pa. Coll. of Optometry, 1966; OD, Pa. Coll. of Optometry, 1967; MA, NYU, 1971. Asst. dir. Optometric Ctr. of N.Y., N.Y.C., 1967-71, assoc. dir., 1971-78; v.p. student affairs Coll. of Optometry SUNY, N.Y.C., 1971-84, v.p. planning Coll. of Optometry, 1984—. Home: 7 Burbank Ct Greenlawn NY 11740-2141 Office: SUNY Coll of Optometry 100 E 24th St New York NY 10010-3610

HEIFETZ, LOUIS JAMES, education and psychology educator, researcher; b. Cambridge, Mass., June 8, 1947; s. Edward and Hannah (Leavitt) H.; m. Benita Ann Blachman, June 24, 1973. BA in Psychology, Yale U., 1969; PhD in Clin. Psychology, Harvard U., 1974. Rsch. psychologist Behavioral Edn. Projects, Inc., Cambridge, Mass., 1971-73; lectr., asst. prof. psychology dept. Yale U., New Haven, 1973-77; assoc. prof. Sch. Edn. Syracuse (N.Y.) U., 1978-89, prof., 1989—; data-analysis cons. U.S. Dist. Ct. Conn., Hartford, 1975-78; measurement cons. Am. Guidance Svc., Circle Pines, Minn., 1980; pres. bd. dirs. Disability Awareness: An Empowering Ministry, Elmira, N.Y., 1987—. Author: Steps to Independence, 5 vols., 1976-77; author articles, monographs and chpts. to books. Grantee N.Y. Office Mental Retardation and Devel. Disabilities, 1979-80; Fulbright fellow, 1985. Mem. APA, Am. Assn. on Mental Retardation. Office: Syracuse U Sch Edn 805 S Crouse Ave Syracuse NY 13244-2280

HEILBERG, ROBERT, wholesale hardware distribution executive; b. N.Y.C.; s. Adolf and Clara (Winter) H.; m. Muriel Seiler; children: Wendy Beth, Neil Howard. BBA, NYU. Pres., founder Diamond Hardware Co., Woodhaven, N.Y., 1955—. Inventor artificial limb for above knee amputation. V.p. Peninsula Counseling Ctr., 1988—. Named Coach of Yr. Lawrence High Sch., 1978; recipient Tower of David Govt. of Israel, 1967, Hosp. Service award VA, 1968, Diamond Club award Yeshiva Dov Revel, 1972-76, Presdl. Council Stanley Tools Mfg. Co., 1986-87. Mem. United Jewish Y's of L.I. (bd. dirs., pres. 1986, 87, 88), Williamsburg YM-YWHA (treas. 1976—), Camp Hatikvah (treas. 1980—), Harvey Gardens Coop. (pres. 1958-59), United Jewish Assn. Fedn. (trustee 1982—, Leadership Achievement award N.Y. 1991), Fedn. Jewish Philanthropies (Life award 1970). Lodge: B'nai B'rith (pres. 1967-69, Man of Yr. 1980). Lodge: B'nai B'rith (pres. 1967-69, Man of Yr. 1980).

HEILMAN, CARL EDWIN, lawyer; b. Elizabethville, Pa., Feb. 3, 1911; s. Edgar James and Mary Alice (Bechtold) H.; m. Grace Emily Greene, Nov. 29, 1934 (div. 1952); children: John Greene, Elizabeth Greene; m. Claire Virginia Phelps, Oct. 10, 1952 (dec. June 1990); m. Marie Wilmot Russ, Nov. 23, 1990. BA, Lafayette Coll., Easton, Pa., 1932, MA, 1933; JD magna cum laude, U. Pa., 1939. Bar: N.Y. 1940, Pa. 1940, Mass. 1973, U.S. Supreme Ct. 1960. Tchr. English, Easton High Sch., 1934-36; assoc. Dwight, Harris, Koegel & Caskey, N.Y.C., 1939-42; atty. OPA, Washington, 1942-43; atty. N.Y. Gov.'s Commn. to Investigate Workmen's Compensation Law, N.Y.C., 1943-44; assoc. Dewey, Ballantine, Bushby, Palmer & Wood, N.Y.C., 1944-59, ptnr., 1959-73; counsel to firm Csaplar & Bok, Boston and San Francisco, 1973-90. Trustee Upsala Coll., East Orange, N.J., 1970-73. Fellow Am. Bar Found.; mem. ABA, Nat. Trust for Hist. Preservation, Order of Coif. Republican. Episcopalian. Home: 750 Washington Rd Apt 1402 Pittsburgh PA 15228-2054

HEILMANN, CHRISTIAN FLEMMING, corporate executive; b. Penang, Malaysia, Apr. 26, 1936; came to U.S., 1977; s. Poul Bent and Hedvig Buchwald (Moller) H.; m. Marilyn Mildred Harter, July 9, 1959 (div. 1973); children: Christian Philip, Nicholas John, Claire Marie; m. 2d, Judith Lucy Tucker, Sept. 15, 1973; children: Per Flemming, Niels Henrik. M.A., Cambridge (Eng.) U., 1957. Mng. dir., chief exec. officer Metal Box South Africa Ltd., Johannesburg, 1970-77; v.p. Continental Can Co., Stamford, Conn., 1977-78; pres. Continental Group Europe, Brussels, Belgium, 1978-80, Continental Diversified Industries, Stamford, Conn., 1980-81; exec. v.p., chief adminstrv. officer Continental Group, Inc., Stamford, 1982-84; dir., pres., chief exec. officer Am. Can Can. Inc. (named changed to Onex Packaging Inc. 1986), Rexdale, Ont., 1984-89; chmn., chief exec. officer Brockway Standard, Inc., Atlanta, 1989—; mem. adv. coun. U. Toronto Bus. Sch., 1985-92; bd. dirs. Porter Chadburn Inc.; chmn. New Highwall Metal Spinning & Stamping Co., Inc., 1991. Mem. Danish-Am. Soc. (bd. dir.), Greenwich Country Club.

HEILOMS, MAY (MRS. SAMUEL HEILOMS), painter; naturalized U.S. citizen, 1932; d. Mark A. and Eugenie (Mogilensky) Levinson; m. Samuel Heiloms, June 12, 1938. Student, Hunter Coll., 1929, Art Students League. Adviser Ford Found. Program in Humanities, 1958, 59; invited juror exhbn. Am. Acad. Arts and Letters. Exhibited paintings, Pa. Acad., Bklyn. Mus., Cleve. Mus., Denver Mus., Silvermine Guild, Butler Inst. Am. Art, Nat. Acad., Nat. Arts Gallery, Mexico Mus. Fine Arts, Okla. City Mus., others, one-man shows, Monmouth Guild, 1960, Bennett Coll., 1961, Silvermine Guild Conn., Jeanette Nessler Gallery, N.Y.C., East Central State Mus., Okla., Cortland Art Center, N.Y., Paducah Art Guild, Ky., Warder Pub. Library, Springfield, Ohio, Five Corners Library, Hudson Gallery, N.Y.C., Muhlemberg Library, N.Y., Mus. Fine Arts, Mexico City, Nat. Mus. Sports, N.Y.C., Loeb Center, N.Y. U., 1979, 80, Custom House Twin Towers Gallery, N.Y.C., 1980, 81, others, also univs. and colls., traveling shows, Cleve. Mus. Art, Allbright Art Gallery, Buffalo, Dallas Mus. Art, Corcoran Gallery, Rochester Meml. Art Gallery, Columbia Mus. Art, also Lisbon, Portugal, Naples, Italy, Athens, Greece, Brussels, Belgium, also, Museo De Bellas Artes, Buenos Aires, Argentina, paintings permanent collections, Phila. Mus. Art, Samuel S. Fleisher Meml. Art Found., Ludwig Bowman Collection, Collectors of Am. Art, Norfolk Mus. Art, Safed State Mus., Israel, Bat Yam Museum, Israel, Okla. City Mus., Denny Collection, Kenny Internat. Found., also pvt. collections. Recipient prize for oil Jersey City Mus., 1950, 51, 59, 63, 1st prize, medal, 1956; prize Painters and Sculptors N.J., 1952, 55, 75; Bocour prize, 1958; prize for oil, 1960, 62; prize Bklyn. Soc. Artists, 1957; Atwood Klinger prize for abstract oil Nat. Assn. Women Artists, 1954; Patricia Murphy prize, 1958; E. Morse Genius prize for watercolor, 1960; M. Grumbacher prize oil, 1961; Sarah E. Good prize oil, 1962; Bainbridge prize watercolor, 1963; prize watercolor Bklyn. Soc. Artists, 1958; Nat. Soc. Painters in Casein, prize casein, 1962; prize, 1967, 70, 73; prize for oil Painters and Sculptors N.J., 1964; prize for watercolor Nat. Assn. Women Artists, 1966; M.H. Steiglitz prize Nat. Soc. Painters in Casein, 1966; prize (oil) Am. Soc. Contemporary Artists, 1967, 68, 71, 80; Windsor Newton prize, 1980; prize for acrylic Nat. Soc. Painters in Casein and Acrylic, 1974; memorabilia on microfilm Archives Am. Art; memorabilia on microfilm Smithsonian Instn.; prize for oil Painters and Sculptors N.J., 1975; prize for oil Nat. Arts, 1975, 76; Bocour prize for oil Bergen County Mus., 1982; prize for oil Allied Artists, 1983; Emily Lowe award for oil Audubon Artists, 1988, Silver medal of honor for oil, 1990. Fellow Royal Acad. Arts (Eng.); mem. Am. Painters and Sculptors (dir.), Painters and Sculptors N.J. (hon. life pres.), Audubon Artists (v.p., Stephen Hirsch Meml. award Prize for Oil, 1987), Painters in Casein (dir.), Artists Equity, Nat. Assn. Women Artists, Bklyn. Soc. Artists, Casein Soc., Allied Artists (officer exec. bd.), Watercolor Soc. Ala., Am. Soc. Contemporary Artists (1st v.p.), Knickerbocker Artists, Silvermine Guild, N.Y. Soc. Women Artists (chmn. membership com.), Art Students League, Manhattan Gallery Group, Am. Soc. Contemporary Artists (Simmons award 1984, 1st prize for oil 1985). Studio: 340 W 28th St New York NY 10001

HEIM, BRUCE KENNEDY, business owner, real estate developer; b. Glen Cove, N.Y., Nov. 7, 1941; s. Benjamin Hooke and Janet (Scott) H.; m. Susan Boal Shepard; children: Frances Heim Patterson, John William VIII, Benjamin Louis, Janet Patricia. BS, U.S. Mil. Acad., 1963; MBA, Pa. State U., 1970. Co-owner Killinger, Leonard & Heim, State College, Pa., 1971-77, Heim, Henderson & Bruce, State College, 1977-81; owner Keystone Real Estate Corp., State College, 1981—; bd. dirs. regional bd. Mellon Bank, State College, UniMart, State College, Unico, State College. Bd. dirs., sec. Second Mile, State College, 1977—; bd. dirs. Pa. Centre Stage, State College, 1988—. Capt. inf. U.S. Army, 1963-69, Vietnam. Republican. Episcopalian. Office: Keystone Real Estate Group 444 E College Ave Ste 560 State College PA 16801-5571

HEIMAN, MICHAEL KENNETH, environment, planning and geography educator; b. N.Y.C., July 29, 1949; s. Martin Udo and Ruth Kitt (Heimann) H.; m. Paula Deborah Bourla, June 24, 1979; children: Jonathan Eli, Eric Samuel. BS, SUNY, Stony Brook, 1971; MS, Cornell U., 1975; MA, U. Calif., Berkeley, 1978, PhD, 1983. Outdoor recreation planner U.S. Army Corps Engrs., N.Y.C., 1972; teaching assoc., lectr. U. Calif., Berkeley, 1979-82; vis. assoc. prof. Cornell U., Ithaca, N.Y., 1980—; asst. prof. Syracuse (N.Y.) U., 1983-89; assoc. prof. environ. studies and geography Dickinson Coll., Carlisle, Pa., 1989—; sr. rsch. fellow Rockefeller Inst. Govt., Albany, N.Y., 1987-88; cons., contbr. World Book Ency., Chgo., 1987—, Ency. Americana, Hawleyville, Conn., 1990—. Author: The Quiet Evolution: Power, Planning, and Profits in N.Y. State, 1988, Coastal Recreation in California, 1986; contbr. articles to profl. jours., chpts. to books. Cons. grassroots citizen environ. group N.Y., La., Pa., 1986—. Recipient Environ. Justice award Pa. Environ. Network, 1990. Mem. Am. Planning Assn., Assn. Am. Geographers (pres. socialist geography spl. group 1991—), Assn. Collegiate Sch. of Planning, Sigma Xi. Jewish. Office: Dickinson Coll Environ Studies James Center Carlisle PA 17013

HEIMANN, JOSHUA GAINES, commercial banker; b. N.Y.C., Mar. 1, 1959; s. John Gaines and Margaret Edith (Fechheimer) H.; m. Karen Olin, July 26, 1987; 1 child, Alexandra Rand. BA, Hampshire Coll., 1982; MBA, NYU, 1988. Mgmt. assoc. Rep. Nat. Bank of N.Y., N.Y.C., 1982-85, asst. treas., 1985-86, asst. v.p., 1986-88; v.p. Rep. Nat. Bank of N.Y., 1988-92; v.p. and regional ops. officer Republic Nat. Bank of N.Y., Buenos Aires, 1992—; v.p., regional ops. officer Rep. Nat. Bank N.Y. Trustee Citizens Budget Commn. Mem. Young Mortgage Bankers Assn. Democrat.

HEIMBAUGH, JAMES ROSS, hotel executive; b. Monett, Mo., Jan. 27, 1918; s. James Ross and Sarah Jeanette (Hayes) H.; m. Ruby Virginia Murphy, Aug. 17, 1946; children: Judy Rae, David Ross. Grad., U. Ill., 1941; summer hotel course, Cornell U., 1952. With Hilton Hotels, 1948-56; sales mgr. Palmer House, Chgo., 1955-60; officer, exec. v.p. charge sales, mktg. and advt. Tisch Hotels Co., 1961-72; pres., dir. Americana Hotels, N.Y.C., 1972-79; owner, pres. James R. Heimbaugh's Assocs. Inc., 1979—. Served with USNR, 1941-46. Decorated Bronze Star. Mem. Am. Hotel and Motel Assn. (chmn. conv. liaison com. 1977—), Hotel Sales Mgmt. Internat., Am. Soc. Assn. Execs. (disting. service award 1986), Sales Execs. Club N.Y.C. (dir., Man of Year award 1975). Presbyterian. Clubs: Skeeters (N.Y.C.); Masons. Home: 1600 Parker Ave Fort Lee NJ 07024-7050 Office: J R Heimbaugh and Assocs Inc PO Box 1910 596 Andersen Ave Ste 204 Cliffside Park NJ 07010

HEIN, AUGUST HENRY, transportation company executive; b. Buffalo, May 21, 1931; s. August and Rose (Versch) H.; m. Barbara Bruce Jackson, Nov. 27, 1958; 1 child, August Howard. BS in Edn., SUNY, Buffalo, 1958; grad., U.S. Army Command-Staff Coll., Ft. Leavenworth, Kans., 1969, Nat. Def. U., Washington, 1976; MS in Social Sci., Coll. of Pacific, 1977. Cert. tchr., N.Y. Tchr. Maryvale High Sch., Cheektowaga, N.Y., 1958-60; asst. mgmt. rep. Bethlehem Steel Co., Lackawanna, N.Y., 1960-76; v.p. labor rels. Nitec Paper Corp., Niagara Falls, N.Y., 1976-80, N.F.T. Metro Systems, Buffalo, 1980—; pres. Eagle-Cambridge Mgmt. Cons., Depew, N.Y., 1987—; baseball scout Pitts. Pirates; bd. dirs. Buffalo Devel. Corp.; v.p. Eagle Sports, Inc. Bd. dirs. Lancaster (N.Y.) Sch., 1979-85, Buffalo Devel. Corp., 1980—; regional coord. U.S. Mil. Acad., West Point, N.Y., 1980—; chmn. loaned execs. United Fund, Buffalo, 1987. Col. U.S. Army. Mem. Am. Legion (athletic dir. Depew), Lions (v.p. Buffalo), K.C. Republican. Roman Catholic. Home: 39 Michele Dr Depew NY 14043-1408 Office: NFT Metro Systems 181 Ellicott St Buffalo NY 14043

HEINDL, DENNIS DUANE, manufacturing company executive; b. St. Mary's, Pa., June 30, 1942; s. Harold H. and Marion M. Heindl; student public schs., Ridgway area; m. Rose E. DeGroat, Oct. 13, 1962; 1 dau., Paula. Press operator Keystone Carbon Co., St. Mary's, 1959-61; sales mgr. Nat. Molded Products, St. Mary's, 1963-70; founder, owner, pres. Compacted Powdered Metals, Ridgway, Pa., 1970—, Atlas Pressed Metals, Du Bois, Pa., 1975—, Laurel Mfg. Inc., Du Bois, 1980—; owner radio Sta. WLMI, 1988—; dir. Keystone Nat. Bank; pres. Laurel Media Inc. Served with USN, 1960-62. Roman Catholic. Club: Elks (past exalted ruler). Home: 602 Hyde Ave PO Box 146 Ridgway PA 15853 Office: PO Box J Du Bois PA 15801

HEINE, HAROLD WARREN, chemistry educator; b. Highland Park, N.J., Sept. 14, 1922; s. Charles William and Elizabeth (Gabriel) H.; m. Marjorie Anne Boote, Aug. 1, 1953; children: Katharine, Elizabeth, Eric. BSc, Rutgers U., 1944, PhD, 1948. Prof. chemistry Bucknell U., Lewisburg, Pa., 1948—, chair dept., 1970-86; cons. NIH, 1965-69; guest prof. U. Heidelberg (Fed. Republic Germany), 1969-70; vis. prof. Union Carbide, Tarrytown, N.Y., 1973, U. Auckland (New Zealand), 1987. Contbr. numerous articles to profl. jours. Asst. scoutmaster Boy Scouts Am., Highland Park, 1940-44, scoutmaster, Lewisburg, 1957. Recipient E. Harris Harbison award for gifted teaching and rsch. Danforth Found., 1970, Mfg. Chemist Catalyst award Mfg. Chemists Assn., 1980; named Sr. Faculty fellow NSF, U. Koln, Germany, 1960-61. Mem. Am. Chem. Soc. rsch. award 1987), Council on Undergrad. Rsch. (pres. chem. div. 1988-90). Home: 944 Curtin Ave Lewisburg PA 17837-1717 Office: Dept Chemistry Bucknell U Lewisburg PA 17837

HEINE, LEONARD M., JR., investment executive; b. N.Y.C., Nov. 14, 1924; s. Leonard Max and Elise (Frey) H.; BS in Econs., U. Pa., 1948; m. Sandra Fleming, Oct. 14, 1966; children: Michael Kenneth, Nancy Ellen, Thomas Charles, Christopher Altman. Salesman, Lehman Bros., N.Y.C., 1952-58; sales mgr. L.F. Rothschild, N.Y.C., 1958-62; gen. ptnr. R.J. Buck & Co., N.Y.C., 1962-70; pres., founder, chmn. Mgmt. Asset Corp., Westport, Conn., 1970-90; investment mgr. chmn., pres. LMH Fund Ltd., 1983—; pres. Heine Mgmt. Group Inc., 1983—; chmn., pub. Weston (Conn.) Voice. Treas., Weston Pub. Libr., 1980-81; trustee St. Mary's Hosp., West Palm Beach, Fla., Norwalk Hosp.; bd. dirs. Fairfield Home Elderly; nat. commr. Anti-Defamation League; bd. dirs. St. Mary's Hosp., West Palm Peach, Fla., Ballet Fla.; trustee Albert Einstein Coll. Medicine's Soc. Founders. With U.S. Army, 1943-46. Decorated Purple Heart, Combat Inf. badge. Mem. Am. Soc. Profl. Cons., Birchwood Country Club (Westport), U. Pa. Club (N.Y.C.), Palm Beach Country Club (Fla.). Republican. Office: Heine Mgmt Group 1175 Post Rd E Westport CT 06881

HEINEMANN, PETER, painter, educator; b. Denver, Apr. 22, 1931; s. Arthur Mason Heinemann and Stella Irene Diana (Peckham) Cohen; m. Gisella Gross (div. Aug. 1970); children: Mark Elliot, Johanna Ellen; m. Marie Savettieier. Student, Black Mt. Coll., 1948-49. Tchr. Sch. Visual Arts, N.Y.C., 1960—. One-person shows include roko Gallery, 1954, 56, 59, Hacker Gallery, 1963, Gallery 120, 1983, Gallery Schlesinger, 1985, 87, 89, 92. Recipient Creative Artists Program grant, 1972, 74, 77, NEA grantee, 1983, N.Y. Found. for Arts grantee, 1986; recipient Nat. Inst. Arts and Letters Childhassam Purchase award, 1972. Office: Sch Visual Arts 209 E 23rd St New York NY 10010-3901

HEINER, DENNIS GRANT, manufacturing company executive; b. Ogden, Utah, Aug. 18, 1943; s. Grant and Mary (Stoker) H.; m. Margo Proctor, Dec. 17, 1970; children: Shalayna, Bryce James, Jillian, Brittany. BA, Weber State Coll., 1969; MBA, Brigham Young U., 1971; M in Mktg., Northwestern U., 1983; cert. strategic mktg. mgmt., Harvard U., 1985. V.p. mktg., gen. mgr. Sportplay, Inc., Salt Lake City, 1971-72; dir. mktg. adminstrn. and fin. Sno-Jet, Inc., Burlington, Vt., 1972-74; v.p. fin. Glastron Boat Co., Austin, Tex., 1974-78, v.p. fin. and adminstrn., 1978-79; v.p. fin. Delmar Window Coverings, Westminster, Calif., 1979-81, pres., 1981-84; pres. window coverings div. Beatrice Cos., Inc., Westminster, Calif., 1984-85; group v.p. U.S. Household Prducts div. Black & Decker, Shelton, Conn., 1985-86, exec. v.p., pres., 1986-92; exec. v.p., pres. security hardware group Black & Decker, Anaheim, Calif., 1992—; bd. dirs. Raytech Corp., Trumbull, Conn. Bd. dirs. Jr. Achievement, Austin, 1978-79. Mem. Young Pres.' Orgn. (So. Calif. and Fairchester chpts.). Republican. Mormon. Office: Black & Decker Corp 516 E Santa Ana St Anaheim CA 92803

HEINLE, ROBERT ALAN, physician; b. Tarentum, Pa., Oct. 26, 1933; s. Edward William and Mary Alice (Purvis) H.; B.S., U. Pitts., 1955, M.D., 1959; m. Barbara Klimeck, Aug. 23, 1958; children—Richard, Jeffrey, Ronald, Robert, Thomas, Timothy. Intern, U. Pitts. Health Center, 1959-60, resident, 1962-65; research fellow in medicine Peter Bent Brigham Hosp., 1965-67; research asso. in medicine Harvard Med. Sch., 1967-68; asst. prof. medicine U. Rochester (N.Y.) Med. Sch., 1968-71, asso. prof., 1971-75, clin. asso. prof., 1975—; dir. cardiovascular lab. Genesee Hosp., Rochester, 1975—; sr. asso. physician Strong Meml. Hosp., Rochester, 1975—; cons. Am. Heart Jour., 1973—; NIH research fellow, 1965-68. Bd. dirs. Blue Cross in Rochester, Blue Shield in Rochester. Served with U.S. Army, 1960-62. Fellow ACP, Am. Coll. Cardiology; mem. Am. Heart Assn., AMA, Am. Fedn. Clin. Research, Rochester Individual Practice Assn. (dir.), Phi Beta Kappa, Omicron Delta Kappa, Alpha Omega Alpha. Republican. Roman Catholic. Home: 415 Warren Ave Rochester NY 14618-4319 Office: 224 Alexander St Rochester NY 14607

HEINS, MAURICE HASKELL, mathematics educator; b. Boston, Nov. 19, 1915; s. Samuel and Rose (Golbert) H.; m. Hadassah Wagman, Aug. 25, 1940; children: Sulamith Hannah, Samuel David. A.B. summa cum laude, Harvard U., 1937, Henry Russell Shaw travelling fellow, 1937-38, M.A., 1939, Ph.D., 1940. Asst. Inst. for Advanced Study, 1940-42; asst. prof. Ill. Inst. Tech., 1942- 44; mathematician Office Chief of Ordnance War Dept., 1944-45; asso. prof. Brown U., 1946-47, prof., 1947-58; prof. math. U. Ill., Urbana, 1958-74; also distinguished prof., chair complex analysis U. Md., College Park, 1974-86, prof. emeritus, 1987—; vis. prof. U. Calif., Berkeley, 1963-64; exchange prof. Paris IV, 1979; President's fellow, 1952-53; Fulbright Research scholar attached to the Faculté des Sciences, U. Paris, 1952-53; mem. Inst. for Advanced Study, 1956-57. Author: Selected Topics in the Classical Theory of Functions of a Complex Variable, 1962, Complex Function Theory, 1968, Hardy Classes on Riemann Surfaces, 1969; contbr. articles to profl. jours. Recipient Bowdoin prize, 1940. Fellow Am. Acad. Arts and Scis.; mem. Am. Math. Soc. (coun. mem., editor Proc. 1962-68), London Math. Soc., Phi Beta Kappa, Sigma Xi. Home: 3304 Winnett Rd Bethesda MD 20815-3202

HEINS, ROBERT WILLIAM, health facility administrator; b. N.Y.C., Jan. 20, 1933; s. Fred August and Clara G. (Johnson) H.; m. Anna Sabatello, Jan. 14, 1956 (div. Nov. 1982); children: Kurt, Tom, Margie, Bill; m. Deanna McCandless, Dec. 1982; stepchildren: Myla, Sara. Patient accounts mgr. Childrens Hosp. of L.A., 1963-67, UCLA Hosp. & Clinics, Westwood, Calif., 1967-69; dir. fin. U. Calif. Hosps. & Clinics, San Francisco, 1969-72; cons. Herman Smith Assocs., Hinsdale, Ill., 1972-73; dir. fin. N.C. Meml. Hosp., Chapel Hill, 1973-74; dir. med. svc. plan U. Mich. Sch. of Medicine, Ann Arbor, 1974-76; exec. dir. med. svc. plan U. N.C. Sch. of Medicine, Chapel Hill, 1976-78; dir. med. svc. plan U. Tex. Health Svcs. Ctr., Dallas, 1978-85; med. sch. cons. Shared Med. Systems, Malvern, Pa., 1985-86; assoc. dean fiscal affairs Tex. Tech. U. Sch. of Medicine Health Svcs. Ctr., Lubbock, 1986-89; adminstr. Laconia (N.H.) Clinic, 1989-90; asst. v.p. bus. affairs Childrens Nat. Med. Ctr., Washington, 1990-91; adminstr. Laconia Clinic, 1991—; bd. dirs. Lakes Region Mental Health, Inc. Sgt. USMC,

1950-54, Korea. Mem. Med. Group Mgmt. Assn. (chmn. govt. rels. com. 1984-89), Healthcare Fin. Mgmt. Assn., Am. Hosp. Assn., Rotary. Lutheran. Office: Laconia Clinic 724 Main St Laconia NH 03246-2767

HEINSOHN, ROBERT JENNINGS, mechanical engineering educator; b. Bklyn., Aug. 28, 1932; s. Rudolf H.B. and Grance (Jennings) H.; m. Anne L. Heinsohn, July 30, 1955; children: Janet Glass, Elizabeth Cohen. BSME, RPI, 1954; MSME, MIT, 1955; PhD, Mich. State U., 1963. With Pratt & Whitney, East Hartford, Conn., 1955-56, Johns Hopkins U., Balt., 1956-58, Mich. State U., East Lansing, 1958-63; prof. Pa. State U., University Park, 1963—; cons. in field. Author: Industrial Ventilation: Engineering Principles, 1991. Capt. USAF, 1954-58. Mem. ASME, ASHRAE, Am. Acad. Environ. Engrs. (diplomate). Home: 4104 W Whitehall Rd Pennsylvania Furnace PA 16865-9721

HEINTZELMAN, CAROL ANN, social work educator; b. Allentown, Pa., Sept. 24, 1942; d. Allen George and Emma Amanda (Strauss) H. BA, Muhlenberg Coll., 1965; MSW, Howard U., 1970; D of Social Work, Cath. U., 1980. Lic. social worker, Pa. Group worker Luth. Social Svcs., Bklyn., 1966-68; supr. Dept. of Pub. Welfare, Winchester, Va., 1970-71; instr. social welfare and sociology Shepherd Coll., Shepherdstown, Pa., 1971-75; asst. prof. of social work Elizabethtown (Pa.) Coll., 1976; prof. social work Millersville (Pa.) U., 1978—. Bd. dirs. East region Luth. Social Svcs., Lititz, Pa., 1979-85, 86—. Mem. AAUW, NASW, Coun. on Social Work Edn., Pa. Assn. of Undergrad. Social Work Educators, Pa. Soc. of Teaching Scholars, Delta Kappa Gamma. Democrat. Lutheran. Home: 11 Townsend Ct Lancaster PA 17603 Office: Millersville U Millersville PA 17551

HEINZEN, BERNARD GEORGE, lawyer; b. Hendricks, Minn., Sept. 8, 1930; s. Bernard Martin and Thelma Harrington (Bowers) H.; m. Maryann Mullen, Aug. 25, 1978; children from previous marraige: John Masters, Robert Kenneth (dec.), James Warren, William Martin. BA, Carleton Coll., 1953; LLB, NYU, 1956. Bar: Minn. 1956, U.S. Supreme Ct. 1969, Pa. 1978. Atty., legal adviser U.S. Dept. State, Washington, 1956-58; assoc. Dorsey & Whitney, Mpls., 1960-65, ptnr., 1966-76; spl. asst. atty. gen. State of Minn., St. Paul, 1967-70; gen. counsel Consol. Rail Corp., Phila., 1976-77; counsel Harvey, Pennington, Herting & Renneisen, Ltd., Phila., 1977-83; pres. Bernard G. Heinzen, Ltd., Phila., 1978—; ptnr. Stassen, Kostos & Mason, Phila., 1983-85; adviser U.S. del. to Geneva Conf. on Law of the Sea, 1958. Contbr. Stanford Law Rev., 1959; assoc. editor NYU Law Rev., 1955-56. Mem. Citizens Com. on Pub. Edn., Mpls., 1964-76; exec. com. state cen. com. Minn. Rep. Party, 1967-71. 1st lt. U.S. Army, 1957-60. Mem. ABA, Phila. Bar Assn., Minn. State Bar Assn. (chmn. com. on ins. 1970-73), Am. Judicature Soc., World Affairs Coun. Phila., Citizens League (Mpls.), Racquet Club Phila., Union League Phila., Mpls. Club, Phi Beta Kappa. Republican. Episcopalian. Home: 1901 Walnut St Philadelphia PA 19103-4664 Office: 1 Liberty Pl Ste 2500 1650 Market St Philadelphia PA 19102

HEIR, KAL M., financial executive; b. Jersey City, Sept. 30, 1919; s. Michael and Bessie H.; m. Rosamond; children: Jeffrey, Marilyn, Brian. BS, N.J. State Tchrs. Coll., 1940. Mgr. Chun King Inc., Duluth, Minn., 1953-56; eastern sales mgr. Mead Johnson Co., Evansville, Ind., 1956-59; v.p. mktg. Technical Tape Inc., New Rochelle, N.Y., 1959-62; pres. Golden Fleece Sales, N.Y.C., 1962-70, Evergreen Merchandising Inc., N.Y.C., 1962-88; cons. to U.S. food and drug cos. N.Y.C., 1988—; dir. Evergreen Sales Internat., N.Y.C., 1988-89; philanthropist State of Israel-Hewbrew Scholarship Endowment N.J. State Tchrs. Coll. Author: Creative Selling, 1960. With U.S. Army, 1942-44. Recipient Presdl. medal N.J. State Tchrs. Coll., 1990. Mem. Jewish War Vet., Bnai Brith, Sales Exec. club. Republican. Jewish. Home: 2903 N Palm Aire Dr Pompano Beach FL 33069-3406

HEISEL, RALPH ARTHUR, architect; b. St. Louis, Sept. 17, 1935; s. Ralph Alonzo and Marie Lucille (Hadfield) H.; m. Janet Clevenger Scott, Aug. 4, 1962; children: Jean Marie, Arthur Scott. BS, Ga. Inst. Tech., 1957, BArch, 1958; MArch, U. Pa., 1961. Registered architect, N.Y., Fla., Ga., Conn., N.J. Designer Bodin and Lamberson, Architects, Atlanta, 1961, Fry Drew & Ptnrs., Architects, London, 1962-64; sr. assoc. I.M. Pei and Ptnrs., Architects, N.Y.C., 1964-86; pres. Heisel Assocs., Architects P.C., N.Y.C., 1986—; vis. critic various univs. Prin. works (for I.M. Pei & Ptnrs.) include Paul Mellon Ctr. for the Arts, The Choate Sch., Wallingford, Conn., Johnson & Johnson Baby Products Co. Hdqrs., N.J., Sunning Plaza Office and Apt. Complex, Hong Kong, Raffles City Hotel, Office and Shopping Complex, Singapore, The Morton H. Meyerson Symphony Ctr., Dallas, (for Heisel Assocs.) Barell Residence, Kingspoint, N.Y., St. David's Episc. Ch., N.Y., Wildwood Pla., Atlanta, Winsland House, Singapore. Mem. bd. dirs. Palmer House Group Home for the Handicapped, Larchmont, N.Y., 1980—, bd. of archtl. rev., Larchmont. Served to 1st lt. USAF, 1958-60. Recipient Design award, N.J. Bus. and Industry Assn., 1982. Mem. AIA (design awards com., Nat. Designs award 1974, 91), N.Y. State Assn. Architects, Nat. Trust for Hist. Preservation, Nat. Coun. Archtl. Regis. Bds., Univ. Club (Larchmont). Home: 2 Acorn Ln Larchmont NY 10538-1901 Office: Heisel Assocs Architects PC 611 Broadway New York NY 10012-2608

HEISER, WAYNE, engineering executive; b. Phila., Oct. 14, 1952; s. Martin Francis and Carol Rosalie (Kulp) H.; m. Donna Andredi, May 5,l 1979 (div. Jan. 1985); m. MaryAlice Emma Schaeffer, Dec. 28, 1985; 1 child, Danielle. AA, Montgomery County Coll., 1972; BSME, Spring Garden Coll., 1974. Engr. Bethlehem (Pa.) Steel Corp., 1974-85; maintenance specialist Logan Aluminum Inc., Russellville, Ky., 1985-90; mgr. plant engring. and maintenance T.B. Woods Sons Co., Chambersburg, Pa., 1990-92; mgr. maintenance Anchor Hocking Packaging Co., Glassboro, N.J., 1992—. Pres., chief exec. officer Hope Luth. Ch., Russellville, 1989. Named to Honorable Order of Ky. Colonels. Mem. Am. Foundrymen's Soc. Republican. Home: 379 Ragged Edge Rd Chambersburg PA 17201 Office: Anchor Hocking Packaging Co 70 Sewell St Glassboro NJ 08028

HEISER, WILLIAM ELLWOOD, financial executive, consultant; b. Hanover, Pa., Sept. 25, 1950; s. Ellwood Duvall and Helen Regina (Slagle) H.; m. Pamela Ann Klunk, Aug. 19, 1972; children: Andrew, Jonathan, Maria. BS, Mt. St. Mary's Coll., Emmitsburg, Md., 1972. CPA, Pa. Sr. acct. Price Waterhouse & Co., Balt., 1971-75; contr. United Consol. Industries, Hanover, Md., 1975-78; mgr. Harry Ness & Co., York, Pa., 1978-82; v.p. J.H. Schuler Co., Hanover, Pa., 1982-89; v.p. fin. R.H. Sheppard Co., Hanover, 1989—, also bd. dirs.; bd. dirs. St. Onge Ruff & Assocs., York. Bd. dirs. Strand Capitol Ctr. for Performing Arts, York, 1982; bd. dirs. Hanover Adams Rehab. and Tng. ctr., New Oxford, Pa., 1987—, pres. 1990—; pres. coun. Sacred Heart Cath. Ch., Spring Grove, Pa., 1988-91. Mem. AICPA, Pa. Inst. CPA's, PaHaGaCo Lake Assn., Bon Air Country Club, KC. Democrat. Home: RD 3 Box 3673 Spring Grove PA 17362

HEISERER, ALBERT, JR., automotive educator, small business owner; b. Bklyn., Nov. 27, 1937; s. Albert Charles and Alice (Bonin) H.; m. Rosemarie E. Pollinger, May, 17, 1958; children: Albert A., Alicia R., Lawrence H. AAS Auto & Diesel Tech., SUNY, Farmingdale, 1957; BA in Biology & Math., Dowling Coll., 1975; postgrad., CUNY, 1976-77. Cert. tchr., N.Y. Tech. researcher Fairchild Engine Div., Deer Park, N.Y., 1957-59; owner, operator A&A Shell, Williston Park, N.Y., 1959-65; tractor trailer driver United Parcel Svc., Maspeth, N.Y., 1965-72; teaching asst. Dowling Coll. Marine Sci. Program, Oakdale, N.Y., 1973; student tchr. Wilson Tech.-B.O.C.E.S., Lindenhurst, N.Y., 1977; automotive & diesel tchr. Middle Country Sch. Dist., Centereach, N.Y., 1977-88; owner, pres. Personal Mechanic, Ronkonkoma, N.Y., 1983-87; freelance religious writer Ronkonkoma, N.Y., 1987—; adj. prof. Suffolk Community Coll., Selden, N.Y., 1988—. Contbr. articles to mags. Chmn., organizer Meals on Wheels, 1982-87; pres., organizer Fish of Ronkonkoma, 1975—, Aid Assn. for Luth., 1986—; v.p. C. of C.; mem. Shepherds Inn Soup Kitchen, 1986—, all Lake Ronkonkoma. With USCGR, 1954-62, USCGA, 1977-82. Recipient Eleanor Roosevelt Community Svc. award, Gov. Cuomo N.Y. 1985, Mid. Country Cen. Sch. Dist. award 1986, 87. Mem. Nassau-Suffolk Counselors Assn., Suffolk Co. Vocational Educators Assn., N.Y. State United Tchrs. Assn., NRA, Am. Legion. Republican. Lutheran. Home and Office: 17 Peter Rd Ronkonkoma NY 11779-4316

HEISHMAN, STEPHEN JAY, psychology researcher and educator; b. Louisville, Apr. 22, 1953; s. J.W. and Ruth (Seewer) H.; m. Pamela D. Alexander, Oct. 24, 1987; children: Allison Brady, Alexander Tate, Nathaniel Jay. BA, Vanderbilt U., 1975; PhD, U. Louisville, 1985. Asst. prof. psychology St. Anselm Coll., Manchester, N.H., 1982-86; postdoctoral fellow dept. psychiatry sch. medicine Johns Hopkins U., Balt., 1986-88, instr. dept. psychiatry sch. medicine, 1988—; staff scientist Nat. Inst. on Drug Abuse Addiction Rsch. Ctr., Balt., 1988-91, rsch. psychologist, 1991—; cons. FAA, 1989—, Nat. Coffee Assn., N.Y.C., 1990-91; lectr. Md. State Dept. Edn., 1990. Contbr. numerous articles to profl. jours. Mem. AAAS, Am. Psychol. Assn., Ea. Psychol. Assn., Behavioral Pharmacology Soc. Democrat. Presbyterian. Office: NIDA Addiction Rsch Ctr PO Box 5180 Baltimore MD 21224-0180

HEISLER, ELWOOD DOUGLAS, hotel executive; b. Wilmington, Del., June 29, 1935; s. Elwood Dean and Laura Matilda (Hutchison) H.; B.A., Mich. State U., 1957; postgrad. Johns Hopkins U., 1979—. Asst. mgr. Kents Restaurants, Atlantic City, 1957; mgr. Korean Mil. Adv. Group Officers' Club and Housing Office, Tague, 1958-59; innkeeper Treadway Inns Corp., N.Y., Mass., Colo., Ohio, Va., Del., 1960-68, Holiday Inns, Inc., Lansing and Troy, Mich., 1969-77; gen. mgr. Quality Inns, Inc., Towson, Md., 1977-89; gen. mgr. Quality Stes. Hotel, Mt. Laurel, N.J., 1989—. Mem. SAR, St. George's Soc. of Baltimore, Soc. of Sons of St. George of Phila., German Soc. of Md., German Soc. of Pa., L'Amicale-Soc. Francaise de Baltimore, Supreme Court Hist. Soc., Hist. Soc. of Delaware, Md. Hist. Soc., Nantucket Hist. Assn., Burlington County N.J. Hist. Soc., Md. Retired Officers Assn., sec. Md. state adv. council Future Bus. Leaders of Am./Phi Beta Lambda; bd. dirs. Gunpowder Youth Camps, Inc.; mem. Balt. Council on Fgn. Affairs, Ea. Shor Soc. of Balt. (v.p.), Nat. Cathedral Assn., Md. Press Club. Served to 1st U.S. Army, 1957-59. Named Top Ten Innkeeper Holiday Inns Internat., 1975; Md. Bus. Person of the Year, Future Bus. Leaders of Am., 1981, Bus. Person of Year nat. chpt., 1981, award of Merit Baltimore County C. of C., 1982, Paul Harris fellow Rotary Found., 1983, Outstanding Service award Md. Future Bus. Leaders of Am., 1984, Baltimore Mayor's Citation, 1984. Mem. Am. Hotel and Motel Assn., N.J. Hotel and Motel Assn., Hotel Sales Mgmt. Assn., Balt. County C. of C. (v.p.). Republican. Congregationalist. Clubs: Univ., Towson Rotary (pres.), Advt. of Balt. (bd. govs.). Clubs: Baltimore Yacht. Author manual for resort ops., 1965; author: The Rising Sun of the Japanese Hotel Industry, 1980. Home: 316 Spring Hill Ave Wilmington DE 19809-1658 Office: 515 Fellowship Rd Mount Laurel NJ 08054-3404

HEISLER, STANLEY DEAN, lawyer; b. The Dalles, Oreg., Jan. 11, 1946; s. Donald Eugene and Roberta (Van Valkenburgh) H. BA, Willamette U., 1968, JD, 1972. Bar: Oreg. 1972, U.S. Ct. Claims 1972, U.S. Tax Ct. 1972, U.S. Ct. Appeals (9th cir.) 1972, D.C. 1973, U.S. Ct. Appeals (fed. cir.) 1973, U.S. Ct. Mil. Appeals 1973, N.Y. 1985, U.S. Supreme Ct. 1985. Assoc. Heisler & Van Valkenburgh, The Dalles, 1973-74; ptnr. Heisler, Van Valkenburgh & Coats, The Dalles, 1975-81, Heisler & Heisler, The Dalles, 1982-84, Cohen & Shalleck, N.Y.C., 1985-88, Phillips, Nizer, Benjamin, Krim & Ballon, N.Y.C., 1988-91, Squadron, Ellenoff, Plesent & Lehrer, N.Y.C., 1991—. Speechwriter Sec. of State Tom McCall, Salem, 1965, Gov. Tom McCall, Salem, 1966-68; speechwriter, legis. asst. U.S. Senator Bob Packwood, Washington, 1969-73; vice chmn. Pres.'s Air Quality Adv. Bd., Washington, 1973-76. Mem. ABA, N.Y. State Bar Assn., Assn. of Bar of City of N.Y., Arlington Club, Univ. Club (N.Y.C. and Portland, Oreg.). Republican. Home: 201 E 69th St Apt 12K New York NY 10021-5469 Office: Squadron Ellenoff Plesent & Lehrer 551 5th Ave New York NY 10176-0001

HEISTAND, COLEEN RENEE, educator; b. Harrisburg, Pa., Apr. 21, 1948; d. Joseph Edward and Millie Melicent (Miller) Kelly; m. Donald Fry Heistand, June 11, 1977. BS in English Edn., Shippensburg U., 1969, MEd in Reading, 1978, MEd in Adminstrn., 1988. Cert. tchr., adminstr., Pa. Tchr. Lower Dauphin Sch. Dist., Hummelstown, Pa., 1969—; from coord. secondary gifted program to elem. prin. Lower Dauphin Sch. Dist. Mem. ASCD, Internat. Reading Assn., Capital Reading Assn., Keystone Reading Assn., NEA, Pa. State Edn. Assn., Lower Dauphin Edn. Assn. Office: Lower Dauphin Sch Dist 291 E Main St Hummelstown PA 17036-1799

HEISTER, ROBERT JOHN, JR., lawyer, military reserve officer; b. Pitts., June 29, 1953; s. Robert John Sr. and Margaret Elaine (Walton) H. BA, U. Pitts., 1976; JD, Duquesne U., 1984. Bar: Pa. 1984, U.S. Dist. Ct. (we. dist.) Pa. 1984, U.S. Ct. Appeals (3d cir.) 1988, U.S. Supreme Ct. 1988. Sr. law clk. to presiding judge Commonwealth Ct. Pa., Pitts., 1984-86; asst. dist. atty. Allegheny County, Pitts., 1986—. Lt. comdr. USNR, 1977—. Named Law Student of Yr. western chpt. Pa. Trial Lawyers Assn., 1983. Mem. ABA, Allegheny County Bar Assn., Pa. Bar Assn., Pa. Dist. Atty.'s Assn., U.S. Naval Inst., Res. Officer Assn. (judge adv. gen. 1985-86), Nat. Dist. Attys. Assn., Univ. Club, Masons, Shriners, Phi Delta Theta (province pres. 1985—). Democrat. Presbyterian. Office: Office Dist Atty Narcotics Unit 401 Courthouse Pittsburgh PA 15219

HEITNER, JOHN A., English educator, writer; b. Bklyn., May 7, 1931; s. Samuel and Constance (Stannage) H.; m. Susanne James, 1956 (div. 1985); children: Randall, Steven, Wendi. BA cum laude, Hofstra U., 1959; MA, Cornell U., 1960; PhD, U. Rochester, 1968. Instr. SUNY, Albany, 1962-65; assoc. prof. Cen. Conn. State U., New Britain, 1965—; lectr. Am. lit. N.W. U., Lanzhou, People's Republic of China, summer 1990, Chingdao (People's Republic of China) U., summer 1990. Author: The Search for the Real Self, 1978, At the Edge of Consciousness, 1987; contbr. articles and poems to profl. jours. Chmn. Caucus of Local Party Presdl. Nominations, New Britain, 1976; del. Dem. Congl. Caucus, New Britain, 1976, Dem. State Caucus, Southington, Conn., 1972. 1st lt. USMC, 1951-54. N.Y. State Coll. Teaching fellow N.Y. State Regents, 1959-61. Mem. AAUP, Melville Soc., Hawthorne Soc., Mark Twain Circle, Kappa Delta Pi. Mem. Eckankar Ch. Office: Cen Conn State U Stanley St New Britain CT 06050

HELBERG, SHIRLEY ADELAIDE HOLDEN, artist; b. Solvay, N.Y., Mar. 9; d. Isaac Edgar and Gladys Evelyn (Tucker) Holden; student Syracuse U.; m. Burton Edvard Helberg; children: Keir Holm, Kristin Vaughan, Kecia Tucker, Kandace Holden, Kraig Brownlee. BE, Johns Hopkins U., 1969; MFA, Md. Inst. Art, 1975. Tchr. various schs. in N.J. and Pa.; tchr. Manchester (Pa.) Pub. Schs., 1965-84, Balt. City Schs., 1988—. One-woman art show U. Va., Charlottesville, 1974, Cayuga Mus. Art and History, Auburn, N.Y., 1974, Hist. Soc. York Mus., Pa., 1977, York Coll., 1984, Country Club of York. Bd. dirs. York (Pa.) Arts Coun., 1964-66. Mem. NEA, Nat. League Am. Pen Women (Pa. State art chmn. 1972-74, pres. Pa. orgn. 1974-76, nat. scholarship chair 1976—, registrar 1986-88, 5th v.p. 1988-90, chmn. nat. sch. com. 1990-92, Disting. Svc. award 1978, 80, 82, 84, 86, 88, 90, Disting. Achievement award 1988), NEA, Pa. State Edn. Assn., Internat. Platform Assn., Harrisburg, York Art Assns., Pa. Watercolor Soc., Johns Hopkins Faculty Club. Republican. Methodist. Home: RR 4 Spring Grove PA 17362-9804 also: 727 S Ann St Baltimore MD 21231

HELD, JAMES ROBERT, policy analyst; b. Apr. 16, 1961; m. Pamela M. Held. BS, Siena Coll., 1983; MS, Rensselaer Poly. Inst., 1986, PhD, 1988. Mem. Am. Econ. Assn., Nat. Tax Assn., Tax Inst. of Am. Home: 45 Euclid Ave Delmar NY 12054-1226 Office: NY State Dept Econ Devel 1 Commerce Ave Albany NY 12245-0001

HELDENBRAND, KEITH, administrator; b. Columbus, Ohio, Dec. 7, 1950; s. Ladd Lee and Anne (Maier) H.; m. Christina Beckstead, Sept. 19, 1987. BA in Polit. Sci., Am. U., 1973; M in Internat. Adminstrn., Sch. for Internat. Tng., 1980. Aadminstr. tuberculosis control U.S. Peace Corps, Kabol, Afghanistan, 1973-74; surviellance officer small pox eradication U.S. Peace Corps, Gondar, Ethiopia, 1974-75; ops. officer WHO, Jakarta, Indonesia, 1978-79; tech. officer WHO Regional Office for the Western Pacific, Manila, Philippines, 1979-82; recycling coord. Land Reclamation, Inc., Westbrook, Maine, 1983-85; systems analyst Def. Logistics Agy., Columbus, 1985-87; treas. Land Reclamation, Inc., Westbrook, 1988—; bd. dirs. Intown Portland Exch. Mem. Greater Portland C. of C. (govtl. affairs com. 1990-92), Nat. Solid Waste Mgmt. Assn., N.H. Resource Recovery Assn., Maine Resource Recovery Assn., Assn. of Vt. Recycles. Republican. Home: 63 North Rd Cumberland Center ME 04021 Office: Land Reclamation Inc 84 Warren Ave Westbrook ME 04092

HELFAND, ARTHUR E., podiatrist; b. Phila., Jan. 12, 1935; s. Nathan H. and Esther (Farbman) H.; m. Myra Werner, May 23, 1976; children—Jennifer Bess, Lewis Aaron. D.Podiatric Medicine, Temple U., 1957. Diplomate Am. Bd. Podiatric Orthopedics, Am. Bd. Podiatric Pub. Health (exec. dir.). Pvt. practice Phila., 1957—; active staff James B. Giuffre Med. Ctr., Phila., 1958-89, coord. dept. podiatry, 1959-68, co-chief, 1968-78, chief, 1978-89, dir. podiatric edn., 1968-89; dir. clin. rsch. Pa. Coll. Podiatric Medicine, Phila., 1963-64, prof. podiatry, coord. clinics, 1964-70, prof. podiatry, chmn. dept. community health and aging, 1970—; mem. staff Thomas Jefferson U. Hosp., Phila., 1973—; cons. podiatry dept. surgery Phila. VA Hosp., 1973-82, 89—; adj. prof. medicine Jefferson Med. Coll., Phila., 1976—, adj. prof. orthopedic surgery, podiatry, vis. assoc. prof. community health and preventive medicine, 1977-79; cons. in field. Mem. editorial bd. Rehab. Today, 1990—; contbr. 236 articles to profl. jours. Recipient Lifetime Achievement award Podiatry Mgmt., 1991. Fellow ACP, Am. Pub. Health Assn., Pa. Pub. Health Assn., Royal Soc. Health; mem. Am. Geriatrics Soc., Am. Coll. Foot Orthopedists, Am. Soc. Podiatric Medicine, Am. Podiatry Assn. (pres. 1982-83), Pa. Podiatry Assn., Phila. County Podiatry Soc., Am. Soc. Podiatric Dermatology, Del. Valley Diabetes Assn., Am. Assn. Hosp. Podiatrists, Gerontol. Soc., Am. Med. Writers Assn., Am. Hosp. Assn., AMA, Temple U. Alumni Assn., Internat. Acad. Preventive Medicine, Am. Assn. Diabetes Educators, AAUP, Am. Assn. Colls. Podiatric Medicine. Home: 9 Hansen Ct Narberth PA 19072-1712 Office: Pa Coll Podiatric Medicine Race at 8th St Philadelphia PA 19107

HELFAND, ROBERT YISRAEL, therapist; b. Bronxville, N.Y., Jan. 1, 1955; s. Arnold and Dorothy (Barkin) H.; m. Colleen Klose, June 24, 1978 (div. 1983); m. Cathleen Helfand, Oct. 19, 1985; children: David Jon, Amanda Eytana. BA in Social Sci., SUNY, New Paltz, 1977; MS in Counseling and Human Resources, U. Bridgeport, 1980; PhD in Edn. and Behavioral Sci., Columbia Pacific U., 1984. Cert. marriage and family therapist, Conn. Guidance counselor intern New Fairfield High Sch., New Fairfield, Conn., 1979-80; co-therapist Leela Panoor, MD, 1983-85; psychotherapist Brookfield Ctr. for Wholistic Health, Brookfield, Conn., 1980-86; employee assistance program counselor Control Data Corp., Mpls., 1987--; IBM health instr. Johnson & Johnson Health Management, Mt. Vernon, N.Y., 1987--; founder, exec. dir. Danbury Personal Counseling, Danbury, Conn., 1984--; pres. Men's Counseling Ctrs., Washington and Danbury, Conn.; cons. Personal Devel. Inst., Danbury, 1980-81. Com. chmn. Candlewood Hills Tax Dist., New Fairfield, Conn., 1980-84; mental health chmn. Danbury United Way, 1988. Mem. AACD, Employee Assistance Profls. Assn., Employee Assistance Soc. N.Am., Acad Family Mediators (sr. mem.), Am. Assn. Marriage and Family Therapists (clin. mem.), Assn. Religious Communities, Am. Mental Health Counselors Assn., Am. Soc. Group Psychotherapy (psychodramatist in tng.). Jewish. Office: Danbury Personal Counseling 35 Padanaram Rd Danbury CT 06811-3701

HELFERICH, GERARD MARION, book editor; b. Troy, N.Y., May 22, 1954; s. William Henry Helferich and Marion (Flint) Rehn; m. Teresa Avila Nicholas, Aug. 28, 1977. BA, Swarthmore Coll., Pa., 1976. Assoc. editor Doubleday & Co., N.Y.C., 1981-82; acquisition editor Hearst Books, N.Y.C., 1982-83; editor Facts on File, N.Y.C., 1983-86, exec. editor, 1986-88, v.p., assoc. pub., 1988-91; v.p., editor-in-chief of gen. reference Prentice Hall, N.Y.C., 1991—. Office: Prentice Hall Reference 15 Columbus Cir New York NY 10023-7706

HELINGER, MICHAEL GREEN, mathematics educator; b. Syracuse, N.Y., Feb. 5, 1947; s. Harley George and Marion Irene (Green) H.; m. Susan Jessie McRae, Apr. 13, 1974 (div. Feb. 1987). BS with distinction, Clarkson U., Potsdam, N.Y., 1968, MS, Rensselaer Poly. Inst., Troy, N.Y., 1969. Instr. Clinton Community Coll., Plattsburgh, N.Y., 1969-73, asst. prof., 1974-86, assoc. prof. math., 1987—; life ins. agt. William LaCount Assocs., Franklin United Life, Plattsburgh, 1980-84; owner, mgr. Sue's Beauty Salon, Plattsburgh, 1984; pres., treas. Helinger Rentals, Inc., Plattsburgh, 1976—; owner B&M Firewood Co., 1990—; mem. acad. affairs com. Clinton Community Coll., 1970-72, 75—, chmn. 1971-72, 86-90, gen. edn. com., 1990—, chmn., 1990—. Vol. Clinton Correctional Facility, Dannemora, N.Y., 1971-75, 88—; apptd. ministerial servant Jehovah's Witnesses, 1991—. Recipient Cert. of Appreciation, Clinton Correctional Facility, Dannemora, 1989, 92. Mem. Math. Assn. Am., N.Y. State Math. Assn. Two-Yr. Colls., Math. League (team founder, coach 1984—, mem. state com. for Math. League Exam 1992—), Ski Club (advisor 1985—), Pi Mu Epsilon. Home: RR 2 Box 197 Peru NY 12972-9419 Office: Clinton C C Plattsburgh NY 12901

HELLAND, GEORGE ARCHIBALD, JR., government official, former equipment manufacturing company executive, management consultant; b. San Antonio, Nov. 28, 1937; s. George Archibald and Ruth (Gorman) H.; m. Josephine Howell, June 9, 1962 (div. 1989); children: Jane Elizabeth, Thomas Gorman; m. Antonia Scott Day, Nov. 24, 1990. BS in Mech. Engring., U. Tex., 1959; MBA with distinction, Harvard U., 1961. Registered profl. engr., Tex. With Cameron Iron Works, Inc., Houston, 1961-77, asst. sales mgr., 1963, dist. sales mgr., 1964, dist. sales mgr., U.K., Africa, 1965, product mgr., 1966, plant mgr., Leeds, Eng., 1967, mgr. oil tool products, 1968, v.p., 1969-75, exec. v.p., 1975-77; with Weatherford International, Inc., Houston, 1977-79; v.p. Weatherford Internat., Inc., 1977, pres., chief exec. officer, dir., 1978-79; pres. McEvoy Oilfield Equipment Co. (name changed to Sii McEvoy div. Smith Internat., Inc. 1980), Houston, 1979-85; pres. McCall Industries, Inc., Houston, 1986-87, bd. dirs.; gen. mgmt. cons., 1987-90; dep. asst. sec. of energy for export assistance U.S. Dept. Energy, Washington, 1990—; pres. Lockwood Corp., Gering, Nebr., 1986-87; chmn. bd. dirs. SIE Internat., Inc., Ft. Worth; prin. Innova Ptnrs., 1988-90; bd. dirs. Reiton Corp. Bd. dirs. Briarwood Sch., Houston; trustee S.W. Rsch. Inst.; mem. exec. com. Jr. Achievement of S.E. Tex. Recipient Five Outstanding Young Texans award Tex. Jr. C. of C., 1972; named Outstanding Young Houstonian Houston Jr. C. of C., 1972; Disting. Grad. Sch. Engring. U. Tex., 1977. Mem. ASME, Am. Inst. Mining, Metall. and Petroleum Engrs., Am. Petroleum Inst. (bd. dir.), Inst. Gas Engrs. (U.K.), Tex. Soc. Profl. Engrs., Am. Wellhead Equipment Assn. (pres. 1967), Petroleum Equipment Suppliers Assn. (pres. 1976-77), Houston C. of C., Brit. Am. Bus. Assn. (bd. dir.), Tau Beta Pi, Phi Eta Sigma, Pi Tau Sigma, Sigma Nu, Friars Soc. Presbyterian. Home: 2622 W Lane Dr Houston TX 77027-4914 Office: US Dept Energy Rm 7A029 1000 Independence Ave SE Washington DC 20585-0001

HELLER, DAVID R., osteopath; b. Feb. 7, 1953; s. Samuel E. and Beatrice (Bucks) H.; m. Colleen Ford, Apr. 8, 1989; children: Benjamin, Rachel. BA, U. N.H., 1975; BS, Rutgers U., 1979; DO, Southeastern Coll. Osteo., 1985. Intern Humana Hosp. Palm Beaches, West Palm Beach, Fla., 1985-86; resident La. State U. Med. Ctr.-Charity Hosp., New Orleans, 1985-88; emergency physician, med. dir. Emergency Med. Svc. Exeter (N.H.) Hosp., 1988—. Author emergency med. paper. Recipient Upjohn Achievement award Upjohn Co., 1985. Fellow Am. Osteo. Assn., Am. Coll. Emergency Physicians (v.p. N.H. chpt. 1989-91); mem. N.H. E-911 Task Force (chmn. 1991-92), Sigma Sigma Phi. Office: Exeter Hosp 10 Buzell Ave Exeter NH 03833

HELLER, GERALD MARK, accountant; b. New Britain, Conn., Mar. 28, 1964; s. Gerald Thomas and Sophia (Kita) H. AS in Mgmt., Bentley Coll., 1986, BS in Acctg., 1986. CPA, Mass. Auditor Kennedy and Lehan, Boston, 1986-88, Deloitte and Touche, Boston, 1989—. Mem. AICPA, Mass. Soc. CPAs. Roman Catholic. Office: Deloitte and Touche 125 Summer St Boston MA 02110-1616

HELLER, MICHAEL D(AVID), poet, critic, educator; b. N.Y.C., May 11, 1937; s. Peter Frank and Martha Rose (Rosenthal) H.; m. Doris Whytal, June 6, 1962 (div. 1976); m. Jane Augustine, Mar. 5, 1979. BS, Rensselaer Poly. Inst., 1959; MA in English, NYU, 1986. Mem. faculty, acad. coord. Am. Lang. Inst./NYU, N.Y.C., 1967—; poet Poets in Pub. Svcs., 1971-86; cons. Poetry in Pub. Places, N.Y.C., 1971-80, Ucross (Wyo.) Found., 1990-91. Author: Knowledge, 1980, COnviction's Net of Branches, 1985, In the Builded Place, 1990; contbr. poetry, criticisms to various publs. N.Y. Coun. on Arts fellow, 1976; NEH Poet/Scholar, 1980, summer seminar, 1986; N.Y. Found. on Arts fellow, 1989. Mem. PEN, MLA, Poetry Soc. Am. (DiCastagnola award 1980), Am. Acad. Poets, Poets and Writers. Home: PO Box 1289 New York NY 10009-0981 Office: Am Lang Inst NYU 1 Washington Sq N New York NY 10003-6635

HELLER, PAMELA, artist; b. Cleve., Apr. 28, 1954; d. Milton Stanford and Rita Heller: m. Peter Sebok, Oct. 11, 1981; 1 child, Anna. BFA, Cleve. Inst. Art, 1979. model cons. Carnegie Hall, N.Y.C., 1985, Thomas Jefferson Meml. Found., Charlotteville, Va. One-woman shows at Broadway Windows, N.Y.C., 1986, Installation for Cleve. Ctr. for Contemporary Art, 1988, Installation for Lawrence Oliver Gallery, Phila., 1988, Installation for Sculpture Space, Utica, N.Y., 1991, internat. selected group exhbns., 1983—; photo editor various publs. Artists Space Project grantee, N.Y.C., 1986, Individual Artists Fellowship grantee Nat. Endowment for Arts, Washington, 1987, Sculpture Space Project grantee, Utica, 1991. Home: 112 6th Ave Brooklyn NY 11217-3571

HELLER, PETER, educator, author; b. Vienna, Austria, Jan. 11, 1920; came to U.S., 1944; s. John and Margarete (Steiner) H.; m. Katrina Burlingham, 1944 (div. 1951); 1 child, Anne; m. Christiane Menzel, Aug. 20, 1951; children: Joan, Didi, Stephen, Eve. Licentiate of Music, McGill Conservatory, Montreal, Canada, 1944; BA, McGill U., 1944; MA, Columbia U., 1945, PhD, 1951. Instr. Columbia U., N.Y.C., 1947-48, Harvard U., Cambridge, Mass., 1948-51; from assoc. prof. to Commonwealth prof. U. Mass., Amherst, 1954-68, prof. German and comparative lit., chair German & Slavic, 1968-71; prof. German and Comparative Lit. SUNY, Buffalo, 1968-91, prof. emeritus, 1991—. Author: Dialectics and Nihilism, 1968, Studies on Nietzsche, 1980, A Child Analysis with Anna Freud, 1990; editor: (series) Modern German Studies, Literature and the Sciences of Man. Home: 280 Brompton Rd Buffalo NY 14221-5943

HELLER, STEPHEN RICHARD, chemist, scientific database specialist; b. N.Y.C., Jan. 5, 1943; s. Sanford and Ethel (Sinowitz) H.; m. Rachelle, June 14, 1964; children: Joshua, Adam, Matthew. BS, SUNY, Stony Brook, 1963; PhD, Georgetown U., 1967. Chemist NIH, Bethesda, Md., 1967-72, EPA, Washington, 1972-84, USDA, Beltsville, Md., 1984-89, 90—; database mgr. Maxwell-Macmillan Co., Moscow, Russia, 1989-90. Author: 8 Chemistry Books; contbr. 124 sci. papers to profl. jours. Recipient Gold medal EPA, 1976. Mem. Am. Chem. Soc. (div. coun. 1986—), Internat. Union of Pure and Applied Chemistry (chmn. database com. 1990—). Jewish. Home: 2413 Lillian Dr Silver Spring MD 20902-4955 Office: USDA ARS Bldg 005 10300 Baltimore Ave Beltsville MD 20705-2325

HELLER, STEVE, computer programmer; b. Phila., Apr. 17, 1949; s. Leonard Heller and Sali (Green) Neff; m. Judith Iris Schwartz, June 3, 1984. BA in Natural Scis., Shimer Coll., 1970. Asst. dir. R&D Gen. Instrument Corp., Towson, Md., 1974-76; sr. programmer, analyst Quotron Systems, Inc., N.Y.C., 1976-77; dir. software devel. Micro Corp., Phila., 1978-82, New Lang. Assocs., N.Y.C., 1982-84; cons. Citibank CBT&EG, Melville, N.Y., 1984, Sperry Corp., Great Neck, N.Y., 1984-87, Spencer Orgn., Inc., Westwood, N.J., 1986-88; product mgr. ICM Svcs., Inc., Great Neck, 1987-89; dir. R&D Liberty Computer Systems, Westbury, N.Y., 1989-91; sr. cons. Systems Strategies, Inc., N.Y.C., 1991—. Author: Large Problems, Small Machines, 1992; contbr. articles to profl. jours. Mem. Assn. for Computing Machinery.

HELLERMAN, MARVIN LAWRENCE, toy manufacturing executive; b. N.Y.C., Sept. 14, 1927; s. Julius and Pauline (Kaffko) H.; m. Claire Ellen Travis, June 3, 1962; children: Jeffrey, Lee. BBA, Pace U., 1950. Pub. acct. N.Y.C., 1951-53; dir. ops. Master Artists Materials, Bklyn., 1953-57; pres. Lawrence Art Craft, N.Y.C., 1957-59; controller, sales mgr. Pyro Plastics Corp., Union, N.J., 1959-63; pres. Marvin L. Hellerman Co., N.Y.C., 1963-65; v.p. Ideal Toy Corp., N.Y.C., 1965-77; pres. Tara Toy Corp., Hauppauge, N.Y., 1977-88, Marv Hellerman Inc., N.Y.C., 1977-90, Marvlee Inc., North Lindenhurst, N.Y., 1989—. Bd. dirs. Grace Harbor Assn., Kings Point, N.Y., 1986-88; trustee Temple Emanuel, Kings Point, 1983-88; mem. president's coun. Brandeis U., Waltham, Mass., 1977—, coord. Toy Industry Dinner, N.Y.C., 1975-85; mem. president's coun. NYU, N.Y.C., 1988—. With U.S. Army, 1945-46. Mem. L.I. Assn.

HELLIKER, STEVEN A., theatrical lighting company executive; b. Teaneck, N.J., Apr. 9, 1948; s. Albert Francis and Stella (Maciejewski) H.; m. Diane Mosolino, Oct. 23, 1982; 1 child, Alaina. BA, William Paterson Coll., 1970. Stage mgr. Lily Turner Prodns., N.Y.C., 1970-79; sales mgr. Bash Theatrical Lighting Supply, North Bergen, N.J., 1980-84, v.p., 1985—; pres. Bash/Prodn. Assocs., Orlando, Fla.; nat. sec. Theatre and TV Bd., N.Y.C., 1985-87. Mem. Illuminating Engring. Soc. (nat. sec.). Avocations: music, theatre history. Office: Bash/Prodn Assocs 6469 Conroy Rd Orlando FL 32835-3503

HELLING, CHARLES SIVER, soil scientist, researcher; b. Madelia, Minn., Jan. 9, 1940; s. Siver Hage and Lila Evelyn (Wiborg) H.; m. Sharon Ann Thormodson, Aug. 1, 1964; 1 child, Michael Charles. BA in Chemistry, St. Olaf Coll., Northfield, Minn., 1961; MS in Soil Sci., U. Wis., 1963, PhD in Soil Sci., 1966. Rsch. assoc. agronomy dept. Cornell U., Ithaca, N.Y., 1965-67; soil scientist Agrl. Rsch. Svc., USDA, Beltsville, Md., 1967—. Contbr. numerous articles to sci. jours. Treas., pres. Beltsville Citizens Assn., zoning chmn.; treas Beltsville Swimming Club, Inc.; mem. citizens' adv. com. Md. Nat. Capital Park and Planning Commn., Prince George's County. Recipient Superior Svc. award USDA, 1974, Fed. Lab. Consortium award for excellence in tech. transfer Office Nat. Drug Control Policy, 1991. Mem. Am. Soc. Agronomy, Soil Sci. Soc. Am., Weed Sci. Soc. Am., Coun. for Agrl. Sci. and Tech. Lutheran. Home: 11307 Emack Rd Beltsville MD 20705-2623

HELLINX, WILLY BERNARD, management executive; b. Rumst, Antwerp, Belgium, Dec. 8, 1945; came to U.S., 1986; s. Albert and Maria (Claes) H.; m. Nechama Ben-Meshiah, Dec. 30, 1985; children: Monique, Dorian. BSChemE, Bijzondere Sch. Tech. Engrs., Antwerp, 1966; postgrad., U. Leuven, 1975. Prodn. mgr. Papeteries de Belgique S.A., Duffel, Belgium, 1968-79; dir. mfg. Lithorex N.V., Erembodegem, Belgium, 1979-86; project mgr. Webcraft Techs. Inc., N. Brunswick, N.J., 1986-89; dir. internat. bus. Blava Inline Inc., Tappan, N.Y., 1989; v.p. internat. bus. Webcraft Games Inc., N. Brunswick, 1989—. Comdr. Belgian Army, 1967-68. Named Knight in the Order of the Crown, Ministry of Def., Belgium, 1978, Knight in the Order of Leopold II, 1986. Home: 54 Ingramstreet Forest Hills Gardens NY 11375 Office: Webcraft Games Inc Rte 1 and Adams Station North Brunswick NJ 08902

HELMETAG, CARL, ski manufacturing company executive; b. Phila., Feb. 6, 1948; s. Carl and Marjorie (Dearnley) H.; m. Patricia L. Kay, Aug. 8, 1970; children: Krista, Molly. BA, U. Wis., 1970; MBA, U. Pa., 1974. Asst. to pres. Singer Co., N.Y.C., 1974-76, Rossignol Ski Co., Williston, Vt., 1976-78; v.p. fin. Skis Dynastar, Colchester, Vt., 1978-84, exec. v.p., 1984—; pres. tri-state distbrs., 1987—. Lt. (j.g.) USN, 1970-72. Mem. Ski Industries Am. (bd. dirs. 1989—), Lake Champlain C. of C. (bd. dirs. 1985). Office: Skis Dynastar Hercules Dr Colchester VT 05446-1548

HELMS, JANET ELTESER, psychology educator, consultant, researcher; b. Kansas City, Mo., May 19, 1947; d. Brown Jerry and Elteser (Barnes) H. BA, U. Mo., 1968, MA, 1971; PhD, Iowa State U., 1975. Lic. psychologist, Md., D.C. Asst. prof., counseling psychologist Counseling Ctr. Wash. State U., Pullman, 1975-77; from asst. to assoc. prof. So. Ill. U., Carbondale, 1977-81; assoc. prof. U. Md., College Park, 1981-83, prof., 1983—. Author: Practioners Guide, 1982, (manual) Training Manual for Diagnosing Racial Identity, 1991, A Practitioner's Guide to the Edwards Personal Preference Schedule, Black and White Racial Identity: Theory, Research, and Practice, A Training Manual for Diagnosing Racial Identity in Social Interactions, A Race is a Nice Thing to Have: A Guide to Being a White Person or Understanding the White Persons in Your Life, 1992; editor: Black and White racial Identity, 1990; mem. editorial bd. Jour. Counseling Psychology, 1981—. Recipient Janet E. Helms award Columbia U., 1991. Fellow APA (sec. div. 17 1987-90,); mem. Assn. Black Psychologists, African Am. Writers' Guild of D.C. Office: Dept Psychology U Md College Park MD 20742

HELWIG, GEORGE JAMES, securities trader/dealer; b. N.Y.C., July 19, 1935; s. George Bernard and Florence Mary (Murphy) H.; m. Betty Jane McLaughlin, Sept. 21, 1963; children: George Hunter, Andrew Hunter, Kathryn. BS, Columbia U., 1962. Comml. artist Nat. Broadcasting Co., N.Y.C., 1955-60; sr. systems analyst Chase Manhattan Bank, N.Y.C., 1962-63, E. F. Hutton & Co., N.Y.C., 1963-64, Eastman Dillon Union Securities, N.Y.C., 1964-66; mgr. Peat, Marwick, Mitchell, N.Y.C., 1966-71; v.p. Swiss Am. Corp., N.Y.C., 1971-73, pres., chief exec. officer, 1984—, also bd. dirs.; pres., chief exec. officer Swiss Am. Securities Inc., N.Y.C., 1973—, also bd. dirs.; bd. dirs. Credit Suisse Asset Mgmt., N.Y.C. Pres. N.Y. Lung Assn., 1990—, pres. elect, 1988-90, v.p., 1985-88, Fanwood Sch. for Deaf Children, Westchester, N.Y., 1986—. Mem. Metro Pres. Orgn., Union League Club, Sleepy Hollow Country Club. Office: Swiss Am Securities 100 Wall St Fl 4 New York NY 10005-3701

HELWIG, RALPH DANIEL, management consultant; b. Pitts., Mar. 25, 1946; s. Ralph William and Mary Catherine (Hall) H.; m. Frances Patricia Maul, Aug. 8, 1970. Student, Sophia U., 1967; BS in Chemistry, U. Pitts., 1968, MBA in Mktg., 1969. Ptnr. Bagnell, Batcher & Assocs., Pitts., 1968; rsch. analyst DuPont Co., Wilmington, Del., 1969-72; sr. rsch. assoc. Predicasts, Inc., Cleve., 1972-74; compt. Disco, Washington, 1974-76; dir. mktg. svcs. Pfizer Med. Systems, Columbia, Md., 1976-78; dir. ops. Psych Systems, Inc., Balt., 1979-81; exec. v.p. Computer Terminal Svcs., Canton, Ohio, 1982-84; pres., owner Econ. Strategies, Ltd., Ellicott City, Md., 1978—; affiliate ptnr. Bus. Cons. Group, Balt., 1988-90. Pres. Cleveland Heights (Ohio) Neighborhood Assn., 1973. Mem. Am. Cons. League, Svc. Corps of Ret. Execs./Active Corp. Execs. (v.p. 1987-89), Howard County C. of C., Rotary (pres. Woodlawn Westview chpt. 1989). Republican. Roman Catholic. Office: Econ Strategies Ltd PO Box 1358 Ellicott City MD 21041-1358

HEMAN, ROBERT JEROME, JR., printing company executive, association executive; b. Lowell, Mass., Nov. 15, 1926; s. Robert Jerome and Ethyl Bein (Pentz) H.; m. Constance Anne Bodwell, Sept. 18, 1954; children: Roberta, Dawn, Kevin. Student, Suffolk U., 1947-48, Suffolk Law Sch., 1948-50, Worcester Poly. Inst., 1957. Supr., quality control and quality assurance David Clark Co., Worcester, 1956-60; mgr., quality control and quality assurance Harrington & Richardson, Inc., Worcester, 1960-64; dir., quality control and quality assurance Gardner and Am. Optical Corp., Southbridge, Mass., 1964-75; gen. mgr. Acme Blue Print Co., Inc., Worcester, 1975-85, pres. and owner, 1985—. Dir. bd. trustees Pub. Libr., Worcester, 1987—; corporator Worcester Art Mus.; mem. City Beautification Com., Worcester, 1991—, Target Worcester, 1991—. With USN, 1943-46, PTO. Mem. DAV (life), VFW, Elks (life, Elk of Yr. 1985-86, chpt. pres., state pres., editor Mass. Elks News, 1982-86, Grand Loge (rep.). Roman Catholic. Home: 143 Lovell St Worcester MA 01603-2554 Office: Acme Blue Print Co 102 1/2 Grove St Worcester MA 01605

HEMATI, NEYRAM, engineering educator; b. Tehran, Iran, Aug. 18, 1960; came to U.S., 1978; s. Iraj and Katayoon (Zaryab) H.; m. Shirin Zartoshty, Aug. 7, 1981; children: Maziar Sam, Kaveh Kevin. BS, Iowa State U., 1982; MEngring., Cornell U., 1984, PhD, 1988. Teaching asst. Cornell U., Ithaca, N.Y., 1983-86, rsch. asst., 1984-88; asst. prof. engring. Drexel U., Phila., 1988—; ind. cons., Bryn Mawr, Pa., 1990—. Reviewer for several pub. cos.; contbr. articles to profl. jours. Drexel U. rsch. scholar, 1991. Mem. ASME, IEEE, Soc. Automotive Engrs., Cornell Soc. Engrs., Sigma Xi, Pi Tau Sigma.

HEMBERGER, GLEN JAMES, university band director; b. Boulder, Colo., Jan. 18, 1962; s. James Frank and Jacqueline Ann (Kent) H.; m. Linda Dawn Thomas, June 3, 1989. BME, U. Colo., 1985, MMus, 1989. Cert. music tchr., Colo. Dir. bands Thornton (Colo.) Sr. High Sch., 1985-87; grad. asst. U. Colo. Bands, Boulder, 1987-89; assoc. dir. bands U. R.I., Kingston, 1989—; clinician Rocky Mountain Drum Major Camp, Denver, 1982-90, R.I. Music Educators' State Conv., 1992; adjudicator Colo. Bandmasters Judging Assn., Denver, 1984-89, N.E. Scholastic Band Assn., Boston, 1989—; guest condr. high schs., honor bands, clinics, 1984—; guest condr. U.S. Coast Guard Band, Charter Oak High Sch. Honor Band, R.I. Jr. High All-State Band, Community Bands, 1991—; founder So. New Eng. High Sch. Honor Band, 1991. Contbr. articles to profl. jours. Mem. Olympic All-Am. Marching Band, L.A., 1984. Mem. Coll. Band Dirs. Nat. Assn., Music Educators Nat. Conf., R.I. Music Educators Assn., New Eng. Coll. Band Assn. (R.I. state chmn.), Nat. Band Assn., World Assn. for Symphonic Bands and Ensembles, Kappa Kappa Psi, Tau Beta Sigma. Home: 940 Quaker Ln Apt 803 East Greenwich RI 02818-5023 Office: U RI Band Fine Arts/Music Dept Kingston RI 02881-0801

HEMELESKI, JOHN PETER, academic administrator; b. Orange, N.J., Nov. 5, 1927; s. William Joseph and Susan (Mulherin) H.; m. Barbara Ann Eash, May 5, 1962; children: Amy, Patricia, Barbara, Karen, John, William, Thomas. BA in Communications and Journalism, U. Denver, 1950. Editor weekly newspapers Colo. and, N.Mex., 1950-52; fin. investigator Dun & Bradstreet, Inc., East Orange, N.J., 1953-59; supr. pub. rels. The Newark Mus., 1959-63; assoc. dir. pub. rels. Newark Coll. of Engring., 1963-75; acad. adminstr. N.J. Inst. Tech., Newark, 1963—; cons. in field, N.J., 1965-75. Court appointed mem. Juvenile Rels. Coun., Essex County, N.J., 1975-80; implementator Gov.'s N.J. Pride Mobile Mus. and Jersey Jubilee, 1984-88; fundraiser United Way, and others, N.J., 1985-88. With U.S. Army, 1945-47, ETO. Recipient Cert. of Appreciation, N.J. Assn. Tchrs. of English, 1969. Mem. Pub. Rels. Soc. Am. (chmn. juried competitions, exec. com., ednl. instns. sect., nominating chmn., accreditation chmn. N.J. chpt., dir., governing bd., sec., treas. 1972-83), Nat. Assn. Accts., Am. Coll. Pub. Rels. Assn., Internat. Am. Bus. Communicators. Home: 126 Parkview Dr Bloomfield NJ 07003-2936

HEMELRIKE, CORNEILLE YVON, management and international trade consultant; b. N.Y.C., Dec. 12, 1944; s. Charles and Yvonne (Auxila) H.; m. Francoise Wyseur, Jan. 13, 1968 (div. Mar. 1970); 1 child, Emmanuelle Beatrice. B Polytech. Studies, Jury Cen. d'Homologation, Belgium, 1965; MS, U.L.B., Belgium, 1968; MS in Computer Sci. Equiv, I-B-M, Belgium, 1970; LLB, LaSalle Extension U., Chgo., 1972. Tech. cons. Law & Bus. Offices, Brussels, 1967-74; mgmt. and bus. cons. Law & Bus. Offices, Newcastle, Australia, 1975-77; inside mgmt. cons. W&J Sloane, Inc., Washington, 1977; mgmt. cons. Washington, 1978-79; asst. to pres., adminstr. Am. Chartering & Trade Corp., Washington, 1979-80; cons. adminstr., mgmt./internat. bus. cons. Lykes Bros. Steamship Co., Washington, 1980-85; internat. bus. and mgmt. cons., sr. ptnr., v.p. Law & Bus. Offices, Washington, 1985—. Republican. Roman Catholic. Home: 4323 Mahan Rd Silver Spring MD 20906-4772

HEMENWAY, DAVID, public health educator; b. N.Y.C., Mar. 14, 1945; s. Henry Harold and Marjorie Sophie (Wilson) H.; m. Nancy Lou Williams, Sept. 12, 1969; 1 child, Brett Turner. BA, Harvard Coll., 1966; MA, U. Mich., 1967; PhD, Harvard U., 1974. Mgmt. intern Office of Sec. Defense, Arlington, Va., 1967-68; Washington correspondent Consumers Union, Washington, 1969; asst. prof. Boston U., 1973-75; sr. lectr. Harvard Sch. Pub. Health, Boston, 1975—; dep. dir. Harvard Injury Control Ctr., Boston, 1987—; chair, injury prevention coun. Nat. Assn. for Pub. Health Policy, S. Burlington, Va., 1988—. Author: Industrywide Voluntary Product Standards, 1975, Monitoring and Compliance, 1985, Prices and Choices, 1988. Injury Rsch. fellow Pew Found., 1986. Mem. APHA, Am. Econ. Assn., Am. Coun. Consumer Interests, Assn. for Pub. Policy Analysis and Mgmt., Am. Soc. for Health Svcs. Rsch. Home: 28 Adams St Brookline MA 02146-3168 Office: Harvard Sch Pub Health 677 Huntington Ave Boston MA 02115-6023

HEMILY, PHILIP WRIGHT, science administrator; b. Newaygo, Mich., June 2, 1922; s. Philip Bernard and Gertrude Bernice (Wright) H.; m. Marion L. McLatchy, June 19, 1949 (div. Aug. 1979); children: Brendon, Laurenne, Valerie. BS in Engring., U. Mich., 1947; DSc, U. Paris, 1953. Instr. in math. Auburn (Ala.) U., 1947-49; rsch. assoc. Nat. Ctr. Sci. Rsch., Paris, 1953-57; program officer, dep. dir. Office Internat. Affairs, NSF, Washington, 1957-65; sci. counselor U.S. Mission to OECD, Paris, 1965-73; sci. officer Bur. Oceans & Internat. Environ. & Sci. Affairs, Dept. of State, Washington, 1974-76, 83; dep. asst. sec. gen. sci. affairs div. NATO, Brussels, 1976-83; interim dir. com. on internat. orgns. & programs Office Internat. Affairs, NAS, Washington, 1991—; cons. Bur. Oceans & Internat. Environ. & Sci. Affairs, Dept. of State, 1984-87, Office Internat. Affairs, NAS, 1984-90, Carnegie Commn., N.Y.C., 1990-91. Editor: Science and Future Choice, 1979, UNESCO Science Programs, 1984; author publs. in field. 1st lt. U.S. Army, 1983-86. Recipient Einstein medal UNESCO, 1991. Fellow AAAS; mem. Am. Crystallographic Assn. Office: Office Internat Affairs NAS 2101 Constitution Ave NW Washington DC 20418-0001

HEMINGWAY, ALFRED HENRY, JR., lawyer; b. Leominster, Mass., Aug. 4, 1942; s. Alfred Henry and Therese Constance (Barriere) H.; m. Julie Ellen Murphy, June 10, 1967 (dec. May 1986); children: Kathryn Therese, Jessica Lee, Sara Clifford, Kevin Krober; m. Karen Ann Pate, July 9, 1989. BS, Worcester Poly. Inst., 1964; MS, U. Mass., 1970; JD, Stanford U., 1971. Bar: Calif. 1972, N.Y. 1973, U.S. Dist. Ct. (so. dist.) N.Y. 1974, U.S. Dist. Ct. (ea. dist.) N.Y. 1974, U.S. Dist. Ct. (ea. dist.) Mich. 1982, U.S. Ct. Appeals (2d cir.) 1975, U.S. Ct. Appeals (fed. cir.) 1973, U.S. Patent Office 1973, U.S. Supreme Ct. 1985, U.S. Dist. Ct. (ea. dist.) Wis. 1984. Assoc. Davis, Hoxie, Faithfull & Hapgood, N.Y.C., 1971-74, Morgan, Finnegan, Pine, Foley & Lee, N.Y.C., 1974-76, Bryan & Bollo, Stamford, Conn., 1976-79, Arthur, Dry & Kalish, N.Y.C., 1979-81, Offner & Kuhn, N.Y.C., 1981-82; mem. Felfe & Lynch, N.Y.C., 1982—, Stanford Law Rev., 1969-70. Contbg. author: Practicing Law in New York City, 1975. Served to capt. U.S. Army, 1966-68. Mem. Calif. Bar Assn. Home: PO Box 7262 Wilton CT 06897-7262 Office: Felfe & Lynch 805 3d Ave New York NY 10022

HEMMERDINGER, H. DALE, real estate executive; b. Washington, Oct. 31, 1944; s. Monroe Elliott Hemmerdinger and Carol Phyllis (Weil) Haussamen; m. Elizabeth Gould, June 25, 1969; children: Damon John, Katherine Molly. BA, NYU, 1967, postgrad., 1967-68. Cert. real estate broker, N.Y. Pres., chief exec. officer The Hemmerdinger Corp., N.Y.C., 1968—, Atco Properties & Mgmt., Inc., N.Y.C., 1968—; bd. dirs. Realty Found. of N.Y., N.Y.C., Mchts. Bank of N.Y.; speaker in field. Contbr. articles on real estate to Crain's N.Y. Bus., other profl. jours. Commr. conciliation and appeals bd. City of N.Y., 1978-84; mem. Dem. County Com., N.Y.C., 1978—, N.Y. State Senate Adv. Com., 1980—, N.Y. State Fin. Control Bd., 1990; mem. N.Y. State Senate Adv. Coun. on State Productivity, 1990; gov. Citizens Housing and Planning Coun., N.Y.C., 1982—; mem. exec. com. Assn. for Better N.Y., N.Y.C., 1984—; trustee, mem. exec. com. Nightingale Bamford Sch., N.Y.C., 1985—; trustee, mem. exec. com. Police Found., 1986—, also treas. Mem. Real Estate Bd. N.Y., Manhattan C. of C., Queens C. of C., Harmonie Club (pres. 1985-86), Sky Club, Univ. Club, Commanderie de Bordeaux, Town Tennis Club, N.Y. Yacht Club. Office: Atco Properties & Mgmt Inc 555 5th Ave New York NY 10017-2416

HEMMINGS, JEFFREY PORTER, investment company executive; b. Schenectady, N.Y., June 12, 1941; s. Harry Richard and Dorothy Van Dyck (Dickie) H.; m. Maria Monette Wiglesworth, May 18, 1974; children: Emery Van Dyck, Anne Kavanaugh. BS, St. Lawrence U., 1963. Salesperson E.F. Hutton & Co. Inc., N.Y.C., 1969-88; account v.p. Paine Webber Inc., White Plains, N.Y., 1988—. Pres. Silvermine Community Assn., Norwalk, Conn., 1992—. Lt. (j.g.) USN, 1963-67, Vietnam. Mem. Country Club of New Canaan, New Canaan Winter Club. Republican. Congregationalist. Home: Echo Hill Rd New Canaan CT 06840 Office: Paine Webber Inc 11 Martine Ave White Plains NY 10606

HEMMINGS, MADELEINE BLANCHET, association administrator; b. Bryn Mawr, Pa., Aug. 14, 1942; d. Wilfred Loyola and Feroline (Sissenere) Blanchet; m. Richard Bagot Hemmings, Mar. 14, 1970; 1 child, Laurie Cornwall Hemmings. Cert. lang. and linguistics, U. Fribourg, Switzerland, 1961; BS, Cornell U., 1976. Owner Hallmark of Pa., Harrisberg, Pa., 1964-70; assoc. dir. human resources Cornell U., Ithaca, N.Y., 1972-77; policy dir. employee benefits NAM, Washington, 1977-79; policy dir. edn. C. of C. of the U.S., Washington, 1979-83; v.p. policy Nat. Alliance of Bus., Washington, 1983-85; pres. West Va. Roundtable, Charleston, W.Va., 1985-87; exec. dir. Nat. Assn. of State Dirs. of Vocat. Edn., Washington, 1987—; cons. Edn. Policy, Washington, 1979—; bd. dirs. Aslan Farms, Brookeville, Md. Author: The New Job Training Partnership Act, 1982. Campaign mgr. Connie Cook for Congress, Ithaca, N.Y., 1984; sponsor U.S. Pony Club, Olney, Md., 1987-92. Mem. U. S. C. of C. (edn. com.), Cornell Pres.' Club, Greater Washington Soc. Assn. Execs. (Am. chief exec. coun. 1989—). Republican. Roman Catholic. Home: 3600 Sundown Rd Brookeville MD 20833-1200 Office: 1616 P St NW Ste 340 Washington DC 20036

HEMSING, JOSEPHINE CLAUDIA, performing arts administrator; b. Paris, France, June 5, 1953; d. Albert E. and Esther (Davidson) H.; m. Daniel F. Cameron, Sept. 22, 1990. Student, Sorbonne U. de Paris, 1972-73; BA, Sarah Lawrence Coll., 1974; postgrad., CUNY, 1982—. Dep. dir. distbn. ASCAP, N.Y.C., 1975-81; assoc. dramaturg and festival coordinator Städtische Bühnen Freiburg, Fed. Republic Germany, 1981-82; publicity asst. Audrey Michaels Pub. Relations, N.Y.C., 1983; publicity assoc. N.Y. Philharmonic, N.Y.C., 1984-85; publicist The Carson Office, N.Y.C., 1985-89; publicist, personal rep. for performing artists Hemsing Assocs., N.Y.C., 1989—. Mem. prodn. staff for New Russian Chamber Orch., N.Y.C., 1976-79, Encompass Music Theatre, N.Y.C., 1978-79, Wallgraben Theater on Tour, U.S.,A., 1980, Rodger Hess Prodns., N.Y.C., 1982, John Hart Assoc., N.Y.C., 1982, Peter Witt Players Prodns., N.Y.C., 1982-83, numerous Broadway and off-Broadway shows including How I Got That Story, 1982, Twice Around the Park, 1983, Diary of a Madman, 1989; NBC-TV documentary Missiles Go Home, 1981; numerous published translations. Democrat. Home: 440 E 79th St Apt 9L New York NY 10021-1401 Office: 401 E 80th St Apt 29K New York NY 10021-0654

HENAHAN, DONAL, music critic; b. Cleve., Feb. 28, 1921; s. William Anthony and Mildred (Doyle) H. Student, Kent U., 1939-40, Ohio U., 1940-42; B.A., Northwestern U., 1948; postgrad., U. Chgo., 1949, Chgo. Sch. Music, 1950-57; MusD (hon.), Providence Coll., 1990. With Chgo. Daily News, 1947-67, music critic, 1957-67; with N.Y. Times, 1967-91, chief music critic, 1980-91, ret., 1991; mem. vis. com. U. Chgo., 1978-80. Served to 1st lt. USAF, 1942-45. Decorated Air Medal with 3 oak leaf clusters; recipient Pulitzer Prize for Criticism, 1986. Poynter fellow Yale U., 1983.

HENBEST, ROBERT LEROY, retired bank and insurance company executive; b. Elmira, N.Y., Aug. 25, 1923; s. Edmund James and Helen Mae (Yost) H.; m. Grace Edith Rowley; children: Judith H. Bayer, Jacqueline Lee, William H., R. Theodore E. Student, Lycoming Coll., 1943, Elmira Coll., 1950, 52, U. Conn., 1951, U. Hartford, 1953; diploma, Wharton Bus. Sch., 1955. Ins. mgr. Henbest Ins. Service, Elmira, 1941-42, 45-47; pres. Henbest & Morrisey, Inc., Elmira, 1945-89; bank dir. Elmira Savs. Bank, 1987-89; now ret. Chmn. Chemung County Safety Orgn.; worked for United Fund; mem. Clemens Ctr. Performing Arts, Arnot Art Gallery, North Presbyn. Ch.; vol. Retired Sr. Vol. Program, MEdicare/Medicaid Assistance Program, claims counselor Courier Arnot-Agden Med. Ctr.6. Decorated DFC, Air medal with four oak leaf clusters, Presdl. citation with oak leaf cluster. Mem. Chemung County Ins. Agts. Assn. (pres. 1958), Am. Legion, Curtis Wright Air Force Assn. (chpt. v.p.), Profl. Ins. Agts. Assn., Ind. Agts. Assn., Chemung C. of C., 15th Air Force Assn., 451st Bomb Group Assn., Masons. Republican. Home: 92 Roricks Glen Pky Elmira NY 14905-1921 Office: Henbest & Morrisey 305 E Water St Elmira NY 14901-3473

HENDERSON, COLE, financial consultant; b. Syracuse, N.Y., Apr. 12, 1960; s. Gerald Scott and Nancy Jean (Webster) H.; m. Renae Ann Battelene, Oct. 18, 1986; 1 child, Erika Nicole. BS in Pub. Acctg., Syracuse U., 1982. Jr. acct. The Conran Stores, Inc., New Rochelle, N.Y., 1982; fin. planner MML Investors, Inc., Syracuse, 1983-85; sales rep. Cen. N.Y. Bldg. Products, Syracuse, 1986; fin. cons. Shearson Lehman Bros., Syracuse, 1987—; mem. fin. planning coun. Shearson Lehman Bros., 1989-92. Com. person Rep. Party, Syracuse, 1989-92; coord. youth edn. program Salvation Army, Syracuse, 1991-92. Mem. Syracuse U. Young Alumni Assn., Syracuse U. Sch. Mgmt. Alumni Assn. (co-founder), Syracuse U. Alumni Assn. (bd. dirs. 1989—). Republican. Office: Shearson Lehman Bros Mchts Bank Bldg 220 S Warren St Syracuse NY 13202

HENDERSON, DANIEL GARDNER, electrical engineer; b. Norfolk, Va., Oct. 25, 1941; s. Mac Daniel and Edith (Bosemberg) H.; m. Lois Barr, June 24, 1966; children: Sondra Kaye, Janine Michelle. AA in Sci., Chipola Jr. Coll., Marianna,Fla., 1963; BSEE, U. Tenn., 1965. With assoc. staff Applied Physics Lab. Johns Hopkins U., Laurel, Md., 1965-71; with sr. staff Applied Physics Lab. Johns Hopkins U., Laurel, 1971-81, prin. staff Applied Physics Lab., 1981—. Mem. Assn. Old Crows (Gold Cert. of Merit 1983, Cert. of Appreciation 1986), U.S. Naval Inst., Tailhook Assn., Tau Beta Pi. Repub-

lican. Baptist. Home: 7921 Anfred Dr Laurel MD 20723-1136 Office: Johns Hopkins U Applied Physics Lab Johns Hopkins Rd Laurel MD 20723

HENDERSON, DOUGLAS BOYD, lawyer; b. Pitts., Sept. 21, 1935; s. Arthur G. and Mildred E. (Rickenbach) H.; m. Olivia Lauer, July 6, 1957; children: Scotland Weaver, Keith Arthur, Heather Alice Atkinson. B.S. in Indsl. Engring., Pa. State U., 1957; J.D. with honors, George Washington U., 1963. Bar: Va. 1962, D.C. 1963. Mfs. agt. firm Arthur G. Henderson & Assos., Pitts., 1957-59; patent agt. Swift & Co., Washington, 1959-62; law clk. to Hon. Donald E. Lane U.S. Ct. Claims, Washington, 1962-63; asso. firm Irons, Birch, Swindler & McKie, Washington, 1963-65; founding partner firm Finnegan, Henderson, Farabow, Garrett & Dunner (and predecessors), Washington, 1965—; mem. adv. coun. U.S. Claims Ct., 1982—. Author: Thire Party Practice in the United States Court of Claims or Two's Company, Three's A Crowd, 1976; contbr. articles to legal jours. Bd. advisors George Washington U. Nat. Law Ctr., 1991—. Mem. ABA (mem. coun. patent, trademark and copyright law sect. 1981-85), Internat. Bar Assn., Fed. Bar Assn., Va. Bar Assn., Va. State Bar, D.C. Bar, Fed. Cir. Bar Assn. (founder 1985, bd. dirs.), Bar Assn. D.C. (chmn. Ct. Appeals for Fed. Cir. Com., 1982-83, chmn. Patent, Trademark and Copyright Law sect. 1975-76, chmn. ct. of claims com. 1973-74, bd. dir. 1974-75, trustee, sec. rsch. found. 1980-81), Claims Ct. Bar Assn. (founder 1987, bd. dirs. 1987-90), ITC Trial Lawyers Assn. (founder 1984), U.S. C. of C. (chmn. patent, trademark and copyright coun. 1980-82), Am. Intellectual Property Law Assn., U.S. Trademark Assn., Patent Office Soc., Am. Arbitration Assn., Internat. Assn. Protection Indsl. Property, Univ. Club, City Club, Club at Franklin Sq. (bd. govs. 1990—), Congl. Country Club, Christian Legal Soc., Supreme Ct. Hist. Soc., Phi Gamma Delta, Delta Theta Phi. Presbyterian (elder 1980-82). Home: 6715 Wemberly Way Mc Lean VA 22101-1529 Office: Finnegan Henderson Farabow Garrett & Dunner 1300 I St NW Washington DC 20005-3314

HENDERSON, GARRY COUCH, information systems specialist; b. Brownwood, Tex., Oct. 23, 1935; s. Loyd Thomas and Oleta Colleen (Couch) H.; m. Jacqueline Sue Null, July 27, 1961; children: Teri Evan, Keri Maureen, Dari Colleen, Bari Kathleen. BS in Math., Sul Ross State U., 1960; MS in Oceanography, Tex. A & M U., 1962, PhD in Geophysics, 1964. Chief marine geophysicist Oceanonics, Inc., Morgan City, La., 1963-65; sr. rsch. scientist Gen. Dynamics, Ft. Worth, 1965-70, chief applied rsch., 1970-74, mgr. R & D programs, 1974-77; corp. dir. R & D Gen. Dynamics, St. Louis, 1977-81; dir. systems Stromberg-Carlson, Inc., Lake Mary, Fla., 1981-86; asst. v.p. systems effectiveness Timeplex, Inc., Woodcliff Lake, N.J., 1986-88, v.p. systems assurance, 1988-90, v.p. info. systems, 1990—; U.S. del. OAS, 1972, Internat. Union Geodesy and Geophysics, Lucerne, Switzerland, 1967; chmn. Symposium on Dynamic Gravimetry, Ft. Worth, 1969; vis. scientist NAS/NSF, 1968-70. Contbr. articles to profl. publs. Leader 4-H Club, Weatherford, Tex, 1974-77; v.p. programs Nat. Mgmt. Assn., Ft. Worth, 1972-73; counselor Boy Scouts Am., Ft. Worth, 1971-73; mem. Am. Assn. Sheriff's Posses, Weatherford, 1975-77. Staff sgr. USAF, 1954-60. Recipient Honor award Nat. Mgmt. Assn., 1970. Mem. IEEE, Soc. Info. Mgrs., Alpha Chi. Republican. Baptist. Office: Timeplex Inc 400 Chestnut Ridge Rd Westwood NJ 07675-7663

HENDERSON, HERBERT WAYNE, construction company executive; b. Youngstown, Ohio, Nov. 28, 1953; s. Phillip Clyde and Dorothy Louise (Mohler) H.; m. Eleanore Marie Flynn, Sept. 3, 1977; 1 child, Tyler Flynn. BBA, Kent State U., 1976; MBA, U. Pitts., 1989. Prodn. and inventory control mgr. Lubriquip Inc. div. Idex Corp., Cleve., 1977-82; plant mgr. Lubriquip Inc. div. Idex Corp., Pitts., 1982-90; materials mgr. Respironics Inc., Murrysville, Pa., 1990-91; pres. Deck Am. Corp. Inc., Pitts., 1991—. V.p. Peters Twp. Jaycees, McMurray, Pa., 1985-86, pres., 1987-88. Mem. Am. Mgmt. Assn., Am. Prodn. & Inventory Control Soc., Home Builders Assn. Met. Pitts., Peters Twp. C. of C. Republican. Roman Catholic. Home: 882 Bebout Rd Venetia PA 15367 Office: Deck Am Corp Inc 4017 Washington Rd Ste 340 McMurray PA 15317

HENDERSON, KAREN, policy analyst; b. Berne, Switzerland, July 7, 1954; (parents Am. citizens); d. Douglas and Dorothy Frances Henderson; 1 child, Joshua Peter. B. History, Reed Coll., 1977; MA in Law and Diplomacy, Tufts U., 1981, PhD, 1987. Asst. admissions Reed Coll., Portland, Oreg., 1977-78; asst. admissions and student affairs Fletcher Sch. Law & Diplomacy, 1981-83; fgn. policy legis. asst. Congressman Bill Richardson, Washington, 1990-91; legis. asst. Congressman Bill Lehman, Washington, 1991; presdl. mgmt. intern U.S. Nuclear Regulatory Commn., Washington, 1984-86, policy analyst, 1986-90, internat. policy analyst, 1991—. Rsch. grantee throughout grad. studies, 1978-87; Am. Polit. Sci. Fgn. Affairs Congl. fellow, 1990-91. Mem. Fletcher Sch. D.C. Alumni Orgn. (pres. 1986-89). Episcopalian. Office: US Nuclear Regulatory Commn Mail Stop 3-H-5 Washington DC 20555

HENDERSON, KAREN LECRAFT, judge; b. 1944. BA, Duke U., 1966; JD, U. N.C., 1969. Ptnr. Wright & Henderson, Chapel Hill, N.C., 1969-70, Sinkler, Gibbs & Simons, P.A., Columbia, S.C., 1983-86; asst. atty. gen. Columbia, 1973-78; sr. asst. atty. gen., dir. of spl. litigation sect., 1978-82, deputy atty. gen., dir. of criminal div., 1982; judge U.S. Dist. Ct. S.C., Columbia, 1986-90, U.S. Ct. Appeals (D.C. cir.), Washington, 1990—. Apptd. Dist. Ct. Adv. Com. Mem. ABA (litigation sect. and urban, state and local government law sect.), N.C. Bar Assn., S.C. Bar (government law sect., trial and appellate practice sect., fed. judges assn.). Office: US Ct Appeals DC Cir US Courthouse 3rd & Constitution Ave NW Washington DC 20001*

HENDERSON, KENNETH ATWOOD, investment counseling executive; b. Watertown, Mass., Oct. 18, 1905; s. Charles William and Anna Lyons (Atwood) H.; BS, Harvard U., 1926; m. Elizabeth Berry Marshall, June 10, 1944; 1 child, Caroline Marshall. With fgn. dept. Brown Bros. & Co., Boston, 1926-30; analyst Weil McKey & Co., Boston, 1931; salesman, engr. home and comml. heating dept. Standard Oil Co. N.J., Boston, 1932-36; investigator Raymond E. Bell, Inc., N.Y.C., 1936; analyst, editor Poor's, Babson Park, Wellesley, Mass., 1937; investment counsellor Cromwell & Cabot, Inc., Boston, 1937-42, 46-50; sr. vp. John P. Chase, Inc., Boston, 1950-74; pvt. practice investment counselling, Waban, Mass., 1975—; dir., treas. Henniker Crutch Co. Active investment, fin. coms. 2d Ch., Newton, Mass. Served to comdr. USNR, 1942-46. Fellow Harvard Travellers Club (hon.); mem. Boston Security Analysts Soc., Bond Analysts Soc. of Boston, Public Utility Analysts Boston, Am. Alpine Club (hon. treas., Angelo Heilprin award 1982), Can., London alpine clubs, Harvard Mountaineering Club, Explorers Club, Appalachian Mountain Club (hon.). Author: Handbook of American Mountaineering, 1942; New England Canoeing Guide, 1965, 68, 71; editor: Appalachia, 1947-55; contbr. articles Am. Alpine Jour., Appalachia, Alpine Jour., others. Home: 29 Agawam Rd Newton MA 02168-1302

HENDERSON, LOTHER SALOME, airline pilot, electrical engineer; b. Kingston, Pa., Jan. 2, 1952; s. Thomas S. and Evelyn M. (Henderson) H.; m. Karen R. Adams, Aug. 12, 1985; children: Thomas, Nicholas, Rebecca, Weston. BSEE, Case Western Res. U., 1973. Metallurgical technician ALCOA, New Kensington, Pa., 1969; jet fuel pump technician TRW, Cleve., 1970; engring. asst. GE, Cleve., 1971-73; commd. capt. USAF, 1973, fighter pilot F-4, 1973-81, ret., 1981; control engr. Corning Optical Wave Guide Plant, Wilmington, N.C., 1981-82; capt. US Air, Pitts., 1982—; engring. cons. G.A. Assoc., Sewickley, Pa., 1986—. Pianist, dir. Shaw AFB Gospel Choir, Sumter, S.C., 1979-81, Bibleway Mass Choir, Columbia, S.C., 1978-81; dir., adminstr. Social Actions Group, Columbia, 1979-81. Mem. Airline Pilots Assn. Methodist. Home: 2600 Fountain Hills Dr Wexford PA 15090 Office: US Air Greater Pitts Internat Airport Pittsburgh PA 15108

HENDERSON, RICHARD, retired toxicologist; b. Weston, Mass., Feb. 19, 1916; s. William Joseph and Nellie May (Kalloch) H.; m. Virginia Merrill Robinson, Oct. 5, 1942; 1 child, Ann Merrill. BS, MIT, 1938, PhD, 1948. Cert. Safety Profl. Asst. prof. Syracuse U., Syracuse, N.Y., 1947-51, assoc. prof., 1951-52; biochemist The Borden Co., N.Y.C., 1952-55; supr. Olin Mathieson Chem. Co., New Haven, 1955-58, rsch. assoc., 1958-62; dir. Environ. Hygiene & Toxicology Olin Co., New Haven, 1962-76, sr. scientist, 1976-81; teaching fellow MIT, Cambridge, Mass., 1938-41; rsch. asst. MIT, Cambridge, Mass., 1941-42, 46-47; cons. Health Scis., Osterville, Mass., 1981—. Inventor: 4 patents; contbr. articles to profl. jours. Chmn. Planning and Zoning Commn., Bethany, Conn., 1956-62. Major U.S. Army Q.M.C., 1942-45 PTO. Decorated Bronze Star. Recipient H.P. Hood fellowship MIT, Cambridge, Mass., 1946-47, Maurice R. Chamberland award, New Haven chpt. Am. Chem. Soc., 1978. Mem. MIT Club of Cape Cod (membership chmn. 1988-91). Home: 120 Smoko Valley Rd Box 975 Osterville MA 02655

HENDERSON, WILLIAM CHARLES, editor; b. Phila., Apr. 5, 1941; s. Francis Louis and Dorothy Price (Galloway) H. B.A., Hamilton Coll., 1963; postgrad., Harvard U., 1963, U. Pa., 1965-66. Assoc. editor Doubleday & Co., N.Y.C., 1972-73; pub. Pushcart Press, Wainscott, N.Y., 1972—; sr. editor Coward, McCann & Geohagan, Inc., N.Y.C., 1973-75; cons. editor Harper & Row Inc., 1976—; guest lectr. Harvard U., summer 1974, Sarah Lawrence Coll., U. Rochester, summers 1978, 87; lectr. Columbia U., 1978-80, Princeton U., 1984, 86, 87, Johns Hopkins U., 1989, Radcliffe Pub. Course, 1989; mem. nat. adv. bd. Center for the Book Library of Congress, 1979; pres. Pushcart Found. Author: His Son: A Child of the Fifties, 1981. The Kid That Could, 1990; editor, pub.: The Publish It Yourself Handbook, 1973, The Pushcart Prize: Best of the Small Presses, 1976—; editor: The Art of Literary Publishing, 1980, Rotten Reviews, 1986. Recipient Author award N.J. English Tchrs. Assn., 1972; Newsboy award Horatio Alger Soc., 1973; Carey-Thomas award, 1978. Mem. P.E.N. Home and Office: Pushcart Press PO Box 380 Wainscott NY 11975-0380

HENDLER, EDWIN, aerospace physiologist; b. Phila., Aug. 29, 1922; s. David and Elene (Kalman) H.; m. May Snyder, May 13, 1945; children: Lynn Karen Slotkin, Sandra Dee. BS, Pa. State U., 1943; MS, U. Pa., 1956, PhD, 1959. Physiologist Naval Air Material Ctr., Phila., 1946-52, head acceleration br., 1952-55; mgr. life scis. rsch. group Naval Air Engring. Ctr., Phila., 1956-74; head life scis. div. Naval Air Devel. Ctr., Warminster, Pa., 1975-81; cons. in field Cherry Hill, N.J., 1981—; mem. NAS-NRC Com. on Hearing, Bioacoustics and Biomechanics, Washington, 1964-81; project officer, advisor Air Standardization Coord. Com. Working Party 61-Aerospace Med. and Life Support Systems, Washington, 1965-80. Co-author: Unusual Environments and Human Behavior, 1963; contbr. chpts. to Physiological Problems in Space Exploration, 1964, Thermal Problems in Aerospace Medicine, 1968. Comdr. USNR. Recipient Paul Bert award Aerospace Physiol. Soc., 1973, Profl. Excellence award Life Scis. and Biomed. Engring. Br., 1988. Fellow Aerospace Med. Assn.; mem. Am. Physiol. Soc., Biophys. Soc., Sigma Xi. Home and Office: 8 Sandringham Pl Cherry Hill NJ 08003-1531

HENDLEY, EDITH DI PASQUALE, physiology and neuroscience educator; b. N.Y.C., Sept. 5, 1927; d. Michael and Rose (Parillo) Di Pasquale; m. Daniel Dees Hendley, Apr. 21, 1952; children: Jane Alice, Joyce Louise, Paul Daniel. AB, Hunter Coll. City N.Y., 1948; MS, Ohio State U., 1950; PhD, U. Ill., Chgo., 1954. Instr. U. Chgo., 1954-56; asst. lectr. U. Sheffield (Eng.), 1956-57; instr., rsch. assoc. Johns Hopkins U. Sch. Medicine, Balt., 1963-72; sr. investigator Friends Med. Sci. Rsch. Ctr., Balt., 1972-73; assoc. prof. U. Vt. Coll. Medicine, Burlington, 1973-83, prof., 1983—. Co-author 4 books; contbr. 49 papers to refereed jours. Rsch. grantee NIH, 1974—, NSF, 1986-89, Vt. affiliate Am. Heart Assn., 1982-83, The Sugar Assn. Inc., 1984-85. Mem. AAAS, Am. Physiol. Soc., Am. Soc. Pharmacology and Exptl. Therapeutics, Soc. for Neurosci. (exec. com., treas. Vt. chpt. 1978—), Assn. for Women in Sci. (treas. 1972-74, exec. com., long-range planning com. 1974-76). Home: 10 Highland Ter S Burlington VT 05403-7601 Office: Dept Physiology and Biophysics U Vt Coll Medicine Burlington VT 05405

HENDRICKSON, ALAN BRYCE, commercial banker; b. Glen Cove, N.Y., Dec. 9, 1945; s. Charles John and Adela Bromfield (Gunthel) H.; m. Jean Edith Peschenski, Nov. 25, 1967 (div. 1985); m. Stella M. Sarasy, Mar. 2, 1991; children—Michael A., Laura J. Student Wake Forest U., 1963-66; B.A. in Econs., C.W. Post Coll., 1966-67. Asst. v.p. Franklin Nat. Bank and European Am. Bank, N.Y.C., 1967-74; v.p. Mfrs. Hanover Trust Co., N.Y.C., 1974-85. Pres. Lynbrook chpt. Am. Cancer Soc., 1972-73, mem. theater com. Melville chpt. (N.Y.), 1975-80; coach Syosset Soccer Club (N.Y.), 1985-87; 1st v.p. Bank Leumi, 1985-87; exec. v.p., COO, CFO Canover, 1987—, treas., 1978; coach Syosset Little League, 1978-80; mem. adv. com. Mineola chpt. Am. Heart Assn., 1978-80. Mem. N.Y. State Soc. C.P.A.s, Syosset C. of C. (bd. dirs. 1975-78, treas. 1976-77). Republican. Episcopalian. Home: 12 Harmony Ct Syosset NY 11791 Office: Canover Industries Inc 57-65 Maspeth Ave Maspeth NY 11378

HENDRICKSON, CHRIS THOMPSON, civil engineering educator, researcher; b. Oakland, Calif., Mar. 31, 1950; s. Harold Thompson and E. Jean (Loomis) H.; m. Kathleen Devine, May 28, 1977; children: Andrew, Thomas, Peter. BS, MS, Stanford U., 1973; B of Philosophy, Oxford U., 1975; PhD, MIT, 1978. Asst. prof. Carnegie-Mellon U., Pitts., 1978-83, assoc. prof., 1983-87, prof. 1987—, acting head, 1989; assoc. dean Carnegie Inst. Tech., 1991—. Author: (with others): Transportation Investment and Pricing Principles, 1984, Project Management for Construction, 1989, Knowledge-based Process Planning for Construction and Manufacturing, 1989; contbr. articles to profl. publs. Recipient C.E. Ladd Research award Carnegie Inst. Tech., 1979; Rhodes scholar, 1973. Mem. ASCE, (com. chmn. 1983—, chmn. urban transp. div. 1989-90, Huber Rsch. award 1989), Am. Econ. Assn., Ops. Rsch. Soc. Am., Transp. Rsch. Bd. (com. chmn. 1989—), Phi Beta Kappa, Tau Beta Pi. Home: 6933 Rosewood St Pittsburgh PA 15208-2638 Office: Carnegie Mellon U Dept Civil Engring Pittsburgh PA 15213

HENDRICKSON, MARY ANGELA, political science educator; b. Fargo, N.D., Dec. 22, 1953; d. Roger R. and Loretta Joyce (Clark) Smith; m. John Erick Hendrickson, Aug. 20, 1983; 1 child, Erica. BS, Mankato (Minn.) State U., 1975, MA, 1978; PhD, U. Minn., 1987. Instr. U. Minn., Mpls., 1982-86; instr., asst. prof. Luther Coll., Decorah, Iowa, 1986-88; asst. prof. polit. sci. Wilson Coll., Chambersburg, Pa., 1988—; vis. summer scholar NYU, 1990; project dir. Commn. on Bicentennial U.S. Constn., 1991. Judge Pa. Bicentennial of Constn. Competition, 1991. Recipient Teaching Excellence award Sears, Roebuck and Co., 1991; grantee NSF, 1985, Am. Judicature Soc., 1985, U. Minn., 1985, NEH, 1989. Mem. Am. Polit. Sci. Assn., Pa. Polit. Sci. Assn., Nat. Women's Studies Assn. Democrat. Home: 241 College Ave Chambersburg PA 17201-1205 Office: Wilson Coll 1015 Philadelphia Ave Chambersburg PA 17201-1285

HENDRIX, LOREN ERVIN, chemical engineer; b. Muscatine, Iowa, Aug. 8, 1942; s. Walter Ervin and Bessie Elizabeth (Westbrook) H.; m. Betty Jo Walker, Aug. 12, 1966; children: Loren Jake, Sean Robert. BS in Math./Chem. Engring., U. Rochester, 1978. Cert. electroplater finisher. Machinist Schmarjie Tool Corp., Muscatine, 1965-67; tech. rep. Xerox Corp., Davenport, Iowa, 1967-69; chem. engring. tech. Xerox Corp., Webster, N.Y., 1970-81, chem. engr., 1981-86, sr. project engr., 1987—. Inventor selenium extrusion. Served with USAF, 1961-65. Mem. Am. Chem. Soc., Am. Electroplaters and Surface Finishers Soc. Methodist. Home: 1621 Hermance Rd Webster NY 14580-9331 Office: Xerox Corp 800 Phillips Rd Bldg 218 Webster NY 14580-9791

HENDRY, JEAN SHARON, psychopharmacologist; b. Hanover, Pa., June 2, 1947; d. Clarence Richard and Frances Lee (Manger) Shaver; m. Andrew Delaney Hendry, Jan. 17, 1970; 1 child, Robert Andrew. BA, Hunter Coll., 1976; MA, Princeton U., 1978; PhD, 1980. Rsch. asst. Hunter Coll., N.Y.C., 1974-75; asst. instr. Princeton U., Princeton, N.J., 1976-78; post doctoral fellow Med. Coll. Va., Richmond, 1979-82; psychology instr. U. Richmond, 1985-86, Pa. State U., Media, Pa., 1987-88; guest reviewer various psychological and pharmacological jours. Contbr. numerous articles to profl. jours. Active Nat. Trust for Historic Preservation, Colonial Williamsburg Found., World Wildlife Assn., Greenpeace, The Humane Soc. of the U.S. Mem. APA, Am. Psychol. Soc., Nat. Wildlife Fedn., Assn. princeton Grad. Alumni, Am. Horseshow Assn., Nature Conservancy, Nat. Audubon Soc., Sigma Xi.

HENICK, STEVEN TITMAN, business executive; b. N.Y.C., July 29, 1942; s. Bernard and Eva (Titman) H.; m. Bette Rosenbaum, Dec. 24, 1964; children: Richard Douglas, Jonathan David, Craig Lawrence, Sara Lynn. AB, Columbia U., 1964; MBA, Harvard U., 1971. With Procter & Gamble, Inc., various, 1971-78; mgr. advt. Procter & Gamble, Inc., Japan, 1979-81; v.p. Atari, Inc., Sunnyvale, Calif., 1982-83; v.p. client svcs. Williams Yurman ADvt., 1984; mgr. div. Tambrands, Inc., Lake Success, N.Y., 1985-86; v.p. Tambrands, Inc., Lake Success, 1987—; pres. Physicians Formula Cosmetics (subs. Tambrands Inc.), City of Industry, Calif., 1988-90, Actmedia Internat., 1990—. Served as capt. with USMCR, 1964-69, Vietnam. Mem. Delta Phi (Columbia U. chpt. pres. 1963-64). Club: Kobe (Japan). Office: ACTMEDIA Inc 301 Merritt 7 Norwalk CT 06856-5102

HENISCH, HEINZ KURT, physicist, photo-historian, educator, consultant; b. Neudek, Czechoslovakia, Apr. 21, 1922; came to U.S., 1963; s. Leo and Fanny (Soicher) H.; m. Bridget Ann Wilsher, Feb. 6, 1960. B.Sc., U. Reading, 1942, Ph.D., 1949, D.Sc., 1978. Lectr. physics U. Reading, Eng., 1948-63; prof. physics Pa. State U., University Park, 1963—, prof. history of photography, 1975-89, rsch. prof. history of photography, 1989—; cons. Energy conversion Devices, Troy, Mich., 1967—; mem. bd. dirs. Inst. for Amorphous Studies, Bloomfield Hills, Mich., 1982—. Author: Crystal Growth in Gels, 1970; (with B.A. Henisch) Chipmunk Portrait, 1970; Electroluminescence, 1962, Semiconductor Contacts, 1984, Crystals in Gels and Liesegang Rings, 1988, Periodic Precipitation, 1991. Editor: Materials Research Bull., 1965—, History of Photography, 1977-90. Fellow Phys. Soc. Gt. Britain, Royal Photog. Soc. Gt. Britain, Am. Phys. Soc., Photographic Hist. Soc. Am., Inst. Arts and Humanistic Studies. Office: Pa State U 221 b Arts Bldg University Park PA 16802

HENKEL, ARTHUR JOHN, JR., investment banker; b. Bklyn., Aug. 27, 1945; s. Arthur John and Catherine Rita (Burns) H.; AB, U. Conn., 1969; MBA, U. Chgo., 1971; m. Coralee S. Olicker, Sept. 27, 1981; children: Andrea Rae, Austin Olicker, Reid Baras, Kyra Leigh. USPHS trainee U. Chgo. Hosps. Clinics, 1969-71, adminstrv. asst. fiscal affairs, 1971; cons. Booz, Allen Hamilton, Inc., N.Y.C., 1972-74; asst. dir. ambulatory ops. New Eng. Med. Ctr. Hosp., Boston, 1974-75, dir. ambulatory care, 1975-77; assoc. mcpl. fin. dept. Kidder, Peabody and Co., Inc., N.Y C., 1977-78, asst. v.p., 1978-79, v.p., 1979-80, mng. officer health fin. group, 1980-87, dir., 1984-87, mng. dir. 1986-87; v.p. mcpl. fin. dept. Goldman, Sachs & Co., 1987—, instr. community health Tufts U. Sch. Medicine; mem. exec. com. alumni coun. U. Chgo. Program Hosp. Adminstrn., 1972-76; spl. teaching cons., fin. evaluation hosp. capital projects HEW, 1973. Chmn. investments com. Better Boys Found./Nat. Football League Players Assn. Awards Banquet, 1978, 80—. Recipient Mary Bachmeyer award U. Chgo., 1971; citation Commonwealth Mass., 1976.

HENKEN, BERNARD SAMUEL, clinical psychologist, speech pathologist; b. Everett, Mass., May 30, 1919; s. Issac Edward and Sarah B. (Shatzman) H.; m. Charlotte Popovsky, Dec. 20, 1953; children: Karen Beth, Donna Michele. Student, Boston Coll., 1938-41; BS, Harvard U., 1947; MS, Purdue U., 1950; D. Sci. in Psychology, Calvin Coolidge Coll., 1955. Lic. psychologist, cert. sch. psychologist, lic. speech pathologist, Mass.; diplomate Am. Assn. Clin. Counselors. Psychologist Carney Hosp., Boston, 1950-51; dir. speech pathology, psychologist Audiology Ctr., Lynn, Mass., 1951-56; psychologist, chief clin. counseling svcs. Brusch Med. Ctr., Cambridge, Mass., 1956-80; speech pathologist Mass. Gen. Hosp., Boston, 1951-52; speech pathologist, sch. psychologist Everett Pub. Schs., 1955-85; psychologist, clin. counselor North Shore Children's Hosp., Salem, Mass., 1966-74; psychologist Medford (Mass.) Pediatric Assocs., 1974—; prof. psychology Calvin Coolidge Coll., Boston, 1958-64; lectr. in psychology Lawrence Meml. Hosp., Medford, Mass., 1975-77; psychologist Alfano Med. Inst., Melrose, Mass., 1956-64. Contbr. articles to profl. jours. Cpl. M.C., U.S. Army, 1943-45, PTO. Fellow Nat. Assn. Counselors and Family Therapists (dir. 1973-76), Am. Psychol. Assn., Mass. Speech and Hearing Assn. (treas. 1957-59), Am. Assn. Clin. Counselors (pres. 1959-63), Mass. Sch. Psychologists Assn. (pres. 1972-74). Republican. Jewish. Home: 118 Waverly Ave Melrose MA 02176-4217 Office: Medford Pediatrics Assocs 116 Forest St Medford MA 02155-2598

HENLE, MARY, emeritus psychology educator; b. Cleve., July 14, 1913; d. Leo and Pearl (Hahn) H. A.B., Smith Coll., 1934, A.M., 1935; Ph.D., Bryn Mawr Coll., 1939; L.H.D. (hon.), New Sch. Social Research, 1983. Research assoc. Swarthmore Coll., Pa., 1939-41; instr. U. Del., Newark, 1941-42, Bryn Mawr Coll., Pa., 1942-44; mem. faculty Sarah Lawrence Coll., Bronxville, N.Y., 1944-46; from asst. prof. to assoc. prof. psychology New Sch. Social Research, N.Y.C., 1946-54, prof., 1954-83, prof. emeritus, 1983—; cons. Ednl. Services, Cambridge, Mass., 1965-67. Author: 1879 and All That, 1986; also articles, chpts. Editor books, including: Documents of Gestalt Psychology, 1961; Selected Papers of W. Köhler, 1971. J.S. Guggenheim Meml. Found. fellow, 1951-52, 60-61; research fellow Harvard U., Cambridge, 1963-64; sr. scholar Ednl. Services, Cambridge, 1964-65; vis. prof. Cornell U., fall 1981. Fellow Am. Psychol. Assn. (pres. div. 26 1971-72, pres. div. 24, 1974-75), AAAS; mem. EA. Psychol. Assn. (pres. 1981-82), Cheiron Soc. Democrat. Avocations: old houses; reading. Home: PO Box 404 Ridgefield CT 06877-0404

HENLEY, JOSEPH OLIVER, manufacturing company executive; b. Sikeston, Mo., June 25, 1949; s. Fred Louis and Bernice (Chilton) H. m. Jane Ann Rhodes, Aug. 21, 1971. BSBA, U. Mo., 1972; MBA, Mich. State U., 1973. Ops. analyst Midland-Ross, Inc., Cleve., 1974, prodn. control mgr., 1974-75; engring. systems mgr. Cameron-Waldron div., Somerset, N.J., 1976, prodn. control mgr., 1976-77; prodn. planning and mfg. systems mgr. ICM div. Massey Ferguson, Inc., Akron, Ohio, 1977-78; sr. audit specialist mfg. United Techs. Corp., Hartford, Conn., 1978-82; mfg. control systems mgr. UT Diesel Systems div., Hartford, Conn., 1983-84, materials mgr., 1983-84, internal cons., 1984-86; inventory mgr. Pratt & Whitney Aircraft div., Hartford, Conn., 1986-89, mgr. sychronous mfg., 1989—. With Army N.G., 1970-72. Mem. Nat. Assn. Purchasing Mgmt., Am. Prodn. and Inventory Control Soc., Assn. for Mfg. Excellence (N.E. region bd. dirs.), Beta Gamma Sigma, Sigma Iota Epsilon, Omicron Delta Epsilon. Presbyterian. Home: 25 Duncaster Rd Vernon Rockville CT 06066-4805 Office: Pratt & Whitney Aircraft Div 400 Main St East Hartford CT 06118-1873

HENN, FRITZ ALBERT, psychiatrist; b. Alden, Pa., Mar. 26, 1941; s. Fredrich and Luise (Kinin) H.; m. Suella, Aug. 1, 1964; children: Sarah, Stephen. BA, Wesleyan U., Middleton, Conn., 1963; PhD, Johns Hopkins U., 1967; MD, U. Va., 1971. Dir. rsch. tng. U. Iowa Hosps. and Clinics, Iowa City, 1975; asst. prof. U. Iowa, Coll. of Medicine, Iowa City, 1974-78, assoc. prof., 1978-81, prof. dept. psychiat., 1981; prof., chmn. SUNY, Stony Brook, 1982—; dir. L.I. Rsch. Inst., Stony Brook, 1982-83, Inst. of Mental Health Rsch., Stony Brook, 1983—; pres. Winter Conf. on Brain Rsch., 1990-92. Mem. editorial bd. Jour. Neurochemistry, 1980-90, Archives Gen. Psychiatry, 1983—. Cons. Project Dawn Justice Dept., 1973-74. Fellow Life Ins. Medicine Rsch. Fund, 1968-71, Falk fellow Am. Psychiat. Assn., 1972-74. Mem. AMA, AOA, Am. Coll. Psychiatrists, Am. Coll. Neuropsychopharmacology, Soc. for Neuro Sci., Psychiat. Rsch. Soc. (pres. 1992), Am. Soc. Neurochemistry, Sigma Xi. Office: SUNY Dept Psychiatry Stony Brook NY 11794-8101

HENNE, JAMES EARL, publisher; b. Phila., Sept. 30, 1947; s. Earl Franklin and Helen (Bietzel) H.; m. Kathleen frances Lalli, Jan. 4, 1969; children: Christina, Nicole. BS in Acctg., St. Joseph's U., 1973. Purchasing agt. Reliance Ins. Co., Phila., 1971-73; tech. editor Chilton Pub. Co., Radnor, Pa., 1973-78; mktg. mgr. Chilton Pub. Co./ABC Pub., Radnor, 1978-80, bus. mgr., 1980-83, regional sales mgr., 1983-85; pub. Capitol Cities/ABC Chilton Pub. Co., Radnor, 1985-89, group pub., 1989—. Lt. USAF, 1967-71. Mem. Am. Bus. Press, Bus. Publ. Assn., Bus. Profls. Advt. Assn., Soc. Auto. Engrs., Adcrafters, Detroit Athletic Club, Concord Country Club. Republican. Roman Catholic. Office: Capital Cities/ABC Chilton Way Radnor PA 19089

HENNELLY, EDMUND PAUL, lawyer, oil company executive; b. N.Y.C., Apr. 2, 1923; s. Edmund Patrick and Alice (Laccorn) H.; m. Josephine Kline; children: Patricia A. Anglin, Pamela J. Farley. BCE, Manhattan Coll., 1944; postgrad, Columbia U., 1944; JD, Fordham U., 1950. Bar: N.Y. 1950. Instr. Manhattan Coll., 1947-50; litigation assoc. Cravath, Swaine & Moore, 1950-51, sr. litigation assoc., 1953-54; asst. gen. counsel CIA, Washington, 1951-52; assoc. counsel Time, Inc., N.Y.C., 1954-56; asst. legis. cons. Mobil Oil Corp., N.Y.C., 1956-60, legis. cons., 1960-61, mgr. domestic govt. rels. dept., 1961-67, mgr. govt. rels. dept., 1967-73, gen. mgr. govt. rels. dept., 1974-78, gen. mgr. pub. affairs dept., 1978-86; pres., chief exec. officer Citroil Enterprises, N.Y.C., 1986—; bd. dirs. South Cay Trust; bd. dirs.,

mem. exec. com. Home Savs. Bank, N.Y.C., Bowery Savs. Bank, N.Y.C. Contbr. articles on engring. and law to profl. jours. Trustee, vice chmn. Daytop Village Found.; mem. adv. com. N.Y. State Legis. Com. on Higher Edn., Nassau County (N.Y.) Energy Commn., L.I. Citizens' Com. for Mass Transit, N.Y. State Def. Coun.; mem. White House Conf. on Natural Beauty, 1963; bd. dirs. Nat. Coun. on Aging; exec. com. Pub. Affairs Rsch. Coun. of Conf. Bd.; mem. Nassau County Econ. Devel. Planning Coun.; commr. nat. com. Commn. for UNESCO, 1982-85, head U.S. del. with personal rank of amb. 22d Gen. Conf., 1983, mem. internat. adv. panel, 1989—; mem. Pres.' Intelligence Transition Team, 1980-81; cons. Pres.'s Intelligence Oversight Bd.; trustee Austen Riggs Ctr., Pub. Affairs Found. Lt., USNR, 1943-46, PTO, ETO. Decorated Knight of Malta, Knight of Holy Sepulchre. Mem. ABA, Fed. Bar Assn., Assn. Bar City of N.Y., Acad. Polit. and Social Scis., Am. Good Govt. Soc. (trustee), Tax Coun. (bd. dirs.), Pub. Affairs Coun. (bd. dirs.), Freedom House (trustee), Am. Mgmt. Assn., Pi Sigma Epsilon, Delta Theta Phi, Army-Navy Club, Meadows Country Club, Sarasota Yacht Club, Explorers Club, Met. Club, Internat. Club, George Town Club, Capitol Hill Club, Knights of Malta, Knights Holy Sepulchre. Clubs: Army-Navy, Southward Ho Country, Babylon Yacht, Explorers, Met., Internat., George Town; Capitol Hill. Lodges: K.M., Knights Holy Sepulcher. Home: 84 Sequams Ln E West Islip NY 11795-4508 also: 3941 Hamilton Club Cir Sarasota FL 34242 Office: Citroil Enterprises 21 Argyle Sq Babylon NY 11702-2712

HENNESSEY, LISA IVY, promotions professional; b. Elizabeth, N.J., Feb. 1, 1959; d. Howard Seymour and Janet (Cohen) Shachtman; m. Patrick Hennessey, July 1, 1990. BS, Boston U., 1980. Dir. promotion Bus. Internat., N.Y.C., 1981—. Mem. Direct Mktg. Assn. Office: Bus Internat Corp 215 Park Ave S New York NY 10003-1603

HENNESSEY, RAYMOND FRANK, wholesale executive; b. Dover, N.H., Dec. 17, 1925; s. Raymond Joseph and Edith Margaret (Morrissette) H.; grad. high sch. Dover; m. July 23, 1949; children: Donald, Patricia, Raymond, Kathryn, Michael. With Nat. Bisquit Co., Dover, 1944-54; pres., chief exec. officer A. Lipson, Inc., Dover, 1954—; bd. dirs. Strafford Nat. Bank, Dover, Bank of N.H., Manchester; treas. Sta. WTSN, 1983—. Mem. Dover Sch. Bd., 1976-78; mayor pro tem City of Dover, 1978-82, mayor, 1982-84; rep. N.H. Gen. Ct., 1955-56, 80-84. Served with USN, 1942-45. Mem. Dover C. of C. (pres. 1975-76), Nat. Assn. Wholesale Grocers, Am. Legion, VFW, CAP. Democrat. Roman Catholic. Clubs: Moose (gov. 1974-75), K.C. (treas. 1978-80), Rotary (pres. 1976-77), Elks, Eagles. Avocation: boating. Home: 125 Silver St Dover NH 03820-3924 Office: A Lipson Inc 29 Interstate Dr Somersworth NH 03878-1210

HENNESSY, CHARLENE C., library director; b. Avoca, Pa., Apr. 26, 1928; d. Joseph P. and Mildred (Dever) Curley; m. F. D. Hennessy Jr., May 17, 1952; children: Jefferson D., Meg M., Bonnie E. BA, Marywood Coll., 1949; MS, Villanova U., 1977. Cert. pub. libr., N.Y., Pa. Children's libr. Bklyn. Pub. Libr., 1949-51; mem. army libr. svc. U.S. Army, Camp Kilmer, N.J., 1951-53; libr. Haverford (Pa.) Coll., 1954-55; asst. libr. Pa. RR, Phila., 1955-57; libr. Villanova (Pa.) U., 1957-59, 1982-87; libr. system coord. County of Delaware, Media, Pa., 1978-81; dir. Harcum Jr. Coll., Bryn Mawr, Pa., 1987—; cons. in field. Mem. coun. Lansdowne (Pa.) Borough, 1988—, mem. planning com., 1982-84. Mem. ALA, Pa. Libr. Assn., Del. County and Pa. State Lawyers' Wives (pres.). Republican. Roman Catholic. Office: Harcum Jr Coll Libr Montgomery Ave Bryn Mawr PA 19010-3403

HENNESSY, EDWARD LAWRENCE, JR., diversified aerospace/automotive products and engineered materials executive; b. Boston, Mar. 22, 1928; s. Edward Lawrence and Celina Mary (Doucette) H.; m. Ruth Frances Schilling, Aug. 18, 1951; children: Michael E., Elizabeth R. BS, Fairleigh Dickinson U., 1955; student, NYU. With Heublein, Inc., Hartford, Conn., 1965-72, v.p. fin., 1965-68, sr. v.p. adminstrn., fin., 1969-72; sr. v.p. fin. and adminstrn. United Techs. Corp., Hartford, 1972-77; chief fin. officer, group v.p. United Techs. Corp. (Systems and Equipment Group), 1977, exec. v.p., 1978-79; chmn., pres., chief exec. officer Allied Corp., Morris Township, N.J., from 1979; chmn., chief exec. officer Allied Signal Corp., Morristown, N.J., 1985—; bd. dirs. Nova Pharm. Corp., Martin Marietta Corp., Bank of N.Y., Union Tex. Petroleum Holdings, Inc. Trustee Cath. U. Am.; trustee Fairleigh Dickinson U., USCG Found. Served with USNR, 1949-55. Mem. Fin. Execs. Inst., Econ. Club N.Y. Roman Catholic. Clubs: Cat Cay (Bahamas); N.Y. Yacht; Ocean Reef, Anglers (Key Largo, Fla.). Office: Allied-Signal Inc 496 La Grandia Pl Ste 305 New York NY 10012 Office: Allied Signal Inc 101 Columbia Rd Morristown NJ 07960-4658*

HENNESSY, JOHN FRANCIS, III, consulting engineering company executive; b. N.Y.C., Nov. 27, 1955; s. John Francis Jr. and Barbara (McDonnell) H. AB, Kenyon Coll., 1977; BSME, Rensselaer Poly Inst., 1978; MS, MIT, 1988. Registered profl. engr., N.Y., N.J., Mass., Va., Nebr., Del., Calif. Project engr. Syska & Hennessy, N.Y.C., 1978-83; project mgr. Syska & Hennessy, San Francisco, 1983-86; v.p. Syska & Hennessy, L.A., 1986-87, Cambridge, Mass., 1987-88; sr. v.p. Syska & Hennessy, Cambridge, 1988-89, chmn., chief exec. office, 1989—; bd. dirs. N.Y. Bldg. Congress, N.Y.C., 1988—; co-chmn. Bldg. Industry Leadership Group, N.Y.C., 1988—; chmn. Times Square Subway Sta. Improvement Corp., N.Y.C., 1989—. Mem. USO of Met. N.Y.; mem. adv. bd. Salvation Army of N.Y.; mem. Bldg. Futures Coun. Sloan fellowship, 1987. Mem. ASHRAE, NSPE, ASME, Coun. on Tall Bldgs. and Urban Habitat, Univ. Club, Olympic Club, Union League Club (N.Y.C.), Met. Club (Washington), Lyford Cay Club (Nassau), Winged Foot Golf Club (Mamaroneck, N.Y.), Nat. Golf Links of Am., Princeton Club (N.Y.C.). Roman Catholic. Office: Syska & Hennessy 11 W 42d St New York NY 10036

HENNESSY, JOHN M., brokerage house executive; b. 1936. Vice chmn. CS First Boston Inc., until 1989, pres. CEO, 1989—; group pres., CEO Financiere Credit Suisse-First Boston, First Boston Corp., 1990—. Office: First Boston Inc Park Ave Pla 55 E 52nd St New York NY 10055-0002*

HENNIG, FREDERICK E., retail company executive; m. Margaret Jones; 4 children. With F.W. Woolworth Co., N.Y.C., 1949—, sr. v.p. worldwide mdse. ops., 1984-86, pres., chief operating officer, 1987—. Office: F W Woolworth Co 233 Broadway New York NY 10279-0001*

HENNIGAN, PATRICK JOHN, banker; b. Scranton, Pa., Apr. 17, 1945; s. Patrick Charles and Florence K. (Walsh) H. AB, Cath. U., 1967; MA, George Washington U., 1969, MPA, 1975; PhD, Syracuse U., 1978. Rsch. assoc. Welfare Planning Coun., Scranton, 1969-71; regional coord. Gov.'s Office State of Pa., Harrisburg, 1971-72; mgr. Ednl. Projects, Inc., Pitts., 1972-74; asst. prof. U. Va., Charlottesville, 1978-79, Columbia U., N.Y.C., 1979-82; asst. v.p. Morgan Guaranty Trust Co., N.Y.C., 1982-85; v.p., investment banker J.P. Morgan Securities, Inc., N.Y.C., 1985—; cons. Syracuse N.Y. Rsch. Corp., 1975-78. Contbr. articles to profl. jours. Mem. Am. Soc. Pub. Adminstrn. (coun. mem. 1982-84), Am. Irish Hist. Soc., Soc. Fellows of Syracuse U., N.Y. Athletic Club. Democrat. Roman Catholic. Club: N.Y. Athletic. Home: 106 Central Park S New York NY 10019-1563 Office: JP Morgan Securities Inc 60 Wall St New York NY 10260-0001

HENNIGAN, ROBERT DWYER, environmental science educator; b. Syracuse, N.Y., Sept. 21, 1925; s. John Joseph and Kathryn Roberta (Dwyer) H.; m. Virginia Frances Egan, May 6, 1950; children: Patricia, Robert, Joseph, Karen, Peter, William, Daniel, Christopher. BCE, Manhattan Coll., 1949; MA, Syracuse (N.Y.) U., 1964. Registered profl. engr., N.Y.; Diplomate Am. Acad. Environ. Engring. Engr. N.Y. State Dept. Health, Syracuse and Albany, 1949-60; asst. commr. N.Y. State Dept. Health, Albany, 1965-67; prin. engr. N.Y. State Office Local Grants, Albany, 1960-65; dir. State Univ. Water Resources Ctr., SUNY-ESF, 1967-70; exec. dir. Southeastern Water Supply Com., N.Y.C., 1970-75; prof. sch. environ. and resources mgmt. SUNY-Environ. Sci. and Forestry, Syracuse, 1970-75, dir., prof. grad. program in environ. scis., 1975-81, prof. sch. environ. and resource engring., 1981-86, chair environ. studies faculty, prof., 1986—; chmn. Onondaga County Water Quality Mgmt. Agy., 1987—, Onondaga Lake Adv. Com., 1987—, Onondaga County Environ. Mgmt. Coun., 1971-79; dir. Onondaga Lake Mgmt. Project, 1984-85; project mgr. Cen. N.Y. Water Quality Project, 1977-82; exec. sec. N.Y. Water Pollution Control Assn., 1970-79, 86—; trustee Onondaga County OLSI Landfill, 1988; cons. Atty. Gens. Office, 1991, Cayuga County, 1990-91, Cen. N.Y. Regional Planning and Devel. Bd., 1984-85, others. Mem. St. Mary's of the Lake Coun., 1973-78, 82-89, chmn. 1984-85, 85-86, lector, eucharistic min., chmn. fin. com., 1982—; pres. Onondaga County Citizens League, v.p. 1982-84, bd. dirs. 1980-82. With U.S. Army, 1943-46. Decorated Purple Heart, Bronze star; named Water Conservationist of Yr. N.Y. State Conservation Coun., Inc., Sears Foudn., Nat. Wildlife Soc., 1968; recipient Cert. of Appreciation Water Resources Commn. of State of N.Y., 1967, achievement award for Pub. Svc. Manhattan Coll. Alumni Soc., 1967, citation for outstanding svc. Temporary State Commn. on Water Resource Planning, 1964, outstanding performance award N.Y. State Office for Local Govt., 1962. Fellow ASCE, mem. Water Pollution Control Fedn. (task force on mem. assn./fedn. relationships, membership com. 1990—), N.Y. Water Pollution Control Assn. (pres. 1985-86, pres.-elect 1984-86, v.p. 1983-84, exec. sec. 1970-79, 86—, Bedell award 1980, Outstanding Leadership 1979), Am. Water Works Assn., Am. Water Resources Assn. (dir. N.Y. sect. 1982-84), Am. Soc. for Pub. Adminstrn., Upstate Freshwater Rsch. Inst. (chmn. 1982-84), Sigma Xi. Home: 3882 Highland Ave Skaneateles NY 13152-9355 Office: SUNY-ESF Bray Hall Syracuse NY 13210

HENNINGS, DOROTHY GRANT (MRS. GEORGE HENNINGS), educator; b. Paterson, N.J., Mar. 15, 1935; d. William Albert and Ethel Barbara (Moll) Grant; m. George Hennings, June 15, 1968. AB, Barnard Coll., 1956; MEd (NSF Acad. Yr. Inst. grantee), U. Va., 1959; EdD (Field Enterprise grantee), Columbia, 1965. Tchr., Pierrepont Elem. Sch., Rutherford, N.J., 1956-58, Thomas Jefferson Jr. High Sch., Fair Lawn, N.J., 1959-64; prof. edn. Kean Coll. of N.J., Union, 1965—. Recipient Edn. Press. award, 1974. Author citation N.J. Inst. Tech., Div. Continuing Edn., 1982. Mem. Nat. Coun. Tchrs. English, N.J. Reading Assn., Internat. Reading Assn. (Outstanding Tchr. Educator in Reading award 1992), Suburban Reading Coun., Textbook Authors Assn., Phi Beta Kappa, Phi Delta Kappa, Phi Kappa Phi, Kappa Delta Pi. Author: (with B. Grant) Teacher Moves, 1971; Content and Craft: Written Expression in the Elementary Sch., 1973; Smiles, Nods and Pauses: Activities to Enrich Children's Communication Skills, 1974; Mastering Classroom Communication: What Interaction Analysis Tells the Teacher, 1975; (with G. Hennings) Keep Earth Clean, Blue and Green: Environmental Activities for Young People, 1976; Words, Sounds, and Thoughts: More Activities to Enrich Children's Communication Skills, 1977; Communication in Action: Teaching the Language Arts, 1978, 4th edit., 1990; (with D. Russell) Listening Aids Through the Grades, 1979; (with G. Hennings) Today's Elementary Social Studies, 1980, 2d edit., 1989; Written Expression in the Language Arts, 1981; Teaching Communication and Reading Skills in the Content Areas, 1982; (with L. Fay) Star Show, 1989, Grand Tour, 1989, Previews, 1989, Reading with Meaning: Strategies for College Reading, 1990, Poets Journal, 1991, Beyond the Read Aloud: Learning to Read Ghrough Listening to and Reflecting on Literature, 1992; contbr. articles to Edn., The Record, Lang. Arts, Sci. Tchr., The Reading Tchr., Tchr. to Tchrs., Sci. and Children, Early Years, others. Home: 21 Flintlock Dr Warren NJ 07059-5014 Office: Kean Coll of NJ Morris Ave Union NJ 07083-7117

HENNINGSEN, VICTOR WILLIAM, JR., food company executive; b. N.Y.C., May 19, 1924; s. Victor William and Muriel Ann (Dillon) H.; m. Mary Florence Bemis Ludington, Aug. 27, 1949; children: Victor W., Christopher K., Mary Francis Henningsen Collins, Timothy F. B.S., U.S. Mcht. Marine Acad., 1945; B.A., Yale U., 1950. Salesman Henningsen Foods, Inc., N.Y.C., 1950-55, v.p., 1955-60, treas., 1960-62, pres., 1962-72; pres., chief exec. officer Henningsen Foods, Inc., White Plains, N.Y., 1972-91, chmn. bd., 1991—; chmn. Henningsen Foods, Ltd. U.K., Henningsen Van den Burg, Henningsen Nederlands B.V.; trustee Eastchester Savs. Bank, White Plains, N.Y.; bd. dirs. North Fork Bancorp, Southold Savs. Bank. Pres. United Fund of Pelham, N.Y., 1962; trustee Village of Pelham Manor, 1962-69, mayor, 1969-71; chmn. bd. Sweet Briar (Va.) Coll., 1979-84, New Rochelle (N.Y.) Hosp. Med. Ctr., 1991—. Mem. Poultry and Egg Inst. USA (bd. dirs.), Egg Products Mfrs. (chmn. 1980-82), Yale Club N.Y. (pres. 1966-68), Links Club (N.Y.C.). Republican. Roman Catholic. Home: 1045 Esplanade Pelham NY 10803-2905 Office: Henningsen Foods Inc 2 Corporate Park Dr White Plains NY 10604-3802

HENRICH, JEAN MACKAY, painter, sculptor, educator; b. Halifax, N.S., Can., Sept. 19, 1909; m. John William Henrich, 1943 (dec. 1944); 1 child, Margaret Person. Student, Art Inst. Chgo., 1929-31; BA, Antioch Coll., 1932; cert., U. Vienna, 1933; MA, U. Buffalo, 1954. Instr. sculpture Art Inst. Buffalo, 1938-43, 45-46; chmn. art dept. Buffalo Sem., 1946-79, artist-in-residence, 1979-89. One-woman shows at AAO Galleries, Buffalo, 1976, More-Rubin Gallery, Buffalo, 1979, Larkin House, Buffalo Seminary, 1986, 88, 89, 90, Adams Gallery, Dunkirk, N.Y., 1989; works include Geneva (N.Y.) Vets. Meml., 1939. Mem. Nat. League Am. Pen Women), Buffalo Soc. Artists, 20th Century Club. Unitarian. Home and Studio: 155 St James Pl Buffalo NY 14222

HENRICH, VICTOR EUGENE, physicist, educator; b. Detroit, Oct. 1, 1939; s. Victor Urban and Gladys Louise (Caldwell) H.; m. Janet Bolette Jensen, Dec. 9, 1967; children: Christopher Caldwell, Timothy Jensen. BSE, U. Mich., 1961, MS in Physics, 1962, PhD in Physics, 1967; MA (hon.), Yale U., 1983. Rsch. staff Lincoln Lab. MIT, Lexington, 1967-78; assoc. prof. physics Yale U., New Haven, 1978-83, prof., 1983—, Eugene Higgins prof. applied sci., 1991—; adv. bd. mem. Progress in Surface Sci., 1985—; panel for chem. physics Nat. Rsch. Coun., 1987-90. Contbr. articles to profl. jours. Mem. AAAS, Am. Phys. Soc., Am. Vacuum Soc., Materials Rsch. Soc., Catalysis Soc. New Eng., Conn. Acad. Sci. and Engring., Am. Ceramic Soc. Office: Yale U Dept Applied Physics PO Box 2157 New Haven CT 06520-2157

HENRIE, DAVID EUGENE, industrial chemist; b. Huntingdon, Pa., Dec. 20, 1940; s. Raymond Eugene and Charlotte Emily (Slagle) H.; m. Brigid Eileen Kenney, Feb. 8, 1973 (div. 1978); m. Mary Ellen McCarty, Aug. 8, 1981; children: Todd Ambrose, Tracey Ambrose, Tamra Ambrose. BS, Juniata Coll., 1962; PhD, Fla. State U., 1967. Rsch. assoc. MIT, Cambridge, 1968; chem. asst. prof. Juniata Coll., Huntingdon, Pa., 1968-72; environ. analyst Gilbert Assocs. Inc., Reading, Pa., 1972-73; lectr. in chemistry U. N.C., Greensboro, 1973-75; asst. prof. chemistry Loyola Coll., Balt., 1975-79, Bloomsburg (Pa.) State U., 1979-81; analytical chemist Conrail, Altoona, Pa., 1982—; chem. hygiene officer Conrail Tech. Svcs. Lab., Altoona, 1990-91, safety com. chmn., 1989-91; question writer med. coll. admission test Am. Coll. Testing; chem. usage com. chmn. Consolidated Rail Corp., Phila., 1990—. Author weekly newspaper column; contbr. articles to profl. pubs. Performer Easter Seal Telethon, Huntingdon, Pa., 1987. DuPont teaching fellow E.I. DuPont NeMours, 1963-64. Mem. Am. Chem. Soc., Benevolent and Protective Order of Elks. Episcopalian. Home: 1103 23rd Ave Altoona PA 16601-3058 Office: Conrail Tech Svcs Lab 2nd St Juniata Altoona PA 16603

HENRIKSEN, ANDERS FINN, ceramic manufacturing executive; b. Copenhagen, May 12, 1947; came to U.S. 1973; s. Ulf Finn and Lisbeth (Jensen) H.; m. Anne R. Oger (div. 1988); children: Alexandra, Thomas; m. Cheryl Anne Blanchette, 1989 (div. 1991). MSc in Chem. Engring., Tech. U. Denmark, Copenhagen, 1970; DSc, MIT, 1978. Teaching asst. MIT, Cambridge, 1978-80; cons. in ceramics, 1980-82; pres., chief exec. officer Ceramco Inc., Center Conway, N.H., 1982—. Mem. Am. Ceramic Soc., Am. Powder Metallurgy Inst., Am. Soc. Metals, Lions, Sigma Xi. Office: Ceramco Inc Rt 302 PO Box 300 Center Conway NH 03813

HENRIKSON, PAMELA SMITH, banker; b. Boston, Aug. 31, 1940; d. Everett Ware and Ruth Howe (Tyler) Smith; m. Alan K. Henrikson, June 17, 1965; children: Christopher Stevens, Katharine Tyler. BA, Smith Coll., 1962. Cert. tchr., Mass. Tchr. Springside Sch., Phila., 1962-64; tchr. The Winsor Sch., Boston, 1965-68, 70-78, dir. admissions, 1971-78; fin. aid officer Mt Vernon Coll., Washington, D.C., 1978-79; specialist not for profit BayBank Boston N.A., 1979-80; asst. v.p. Baybank Boston N.A., 1980-82, v.p., 1982-87, sr. v.p., 1987-91; exec. v.p. BayBank Boston/BayBank, 1991—. Mem. adv. com. The Schlesinger Libr., Radcliffe Coll., Cambridge, Mass. 1987-90;treas. Associated Grantmakers of Mass., Boston, 1983-86; bd. dirs. The Edn. Fund, Boston, 1983-88; fin. com. mem., corporator Harvard Community Health Plan, Brookline, Mass., 1987—; trustee Tenacre Country Day Sch., Wellesley, Mass., 1980-89, The Winsor Sch., Boston, 1987—, Episcopal Diocese of Mass., 1991—, Cambridge Community Found., 1991—, Smith Coll., 1992—; corporator Springfield (Mass.) Coll., 1981-87, Mt. Auburn Hosp., 1991—; bd. overseers Children's Hosp., 1991—. Recipient 1st place Essay contest, Jour. of Comml. Banking, 1987. Mem. Boston Estate Planning Coun. (exec. com.), Alumnae Assn. Smith Coll. (treas., chmn. fin. com. 1987-90), Christmas Cove Improvement Assn., The Vincent Club, Wellesley Country Club. Republican. Episcopalian. Office: BayBank 1414 Massachusetts Ave Cambridge MA 02138-3807

HENRIKSON, RAY CHARLES, anatomy educator; b. Worcester, Mass., May 22, 1937; s. Sigurd and Theresa (Edlin) H.; m. Katherine Pointer, Oct. 29, 1966; children: Charles A., Andrew J. BSc, U. Mass., 1959; MSc, Brown U., 1961; PhD, Boston U., 1966. Instr. Boston U. Med. Sch., 1966-67; scientist Commonwealth Sci. and Indsl. Rsch. Orgn., Australia, 1967-69; asst. prof. Columbia U., N.Y.C., 1969-76; assoc. prof. Albany (N.Y.) Med. Coll., 1976-89, prof., 1989—; mem. com. Nat. Bd. Med. Examiners, 1985-88. Author: Key Facts in Histology, 1986. Mem. Am. Assn. Anatomists, Am. Soc. Cell Biology, Assn. Devel. of Computer-Based Instrn. Systems. Office: Albany Med Coll Anatomy Dept Albany NY 12208

HENRY, CATHERINE THERESA, insurance company executive; b. N.Y.C., June 25, 1934; d. John Patrick and Bridie (Hartnett) H. Student, Queens Coll., 1960-63. With Equitable Life Assurance Soc., N.Y.C., 1952—, systems analyst, 1965-74, adminstrv. mgr., 1974-76, personnel mgr., 1976-80, asst. v.p., personnel officer, 1980-83, v.p., human resources officer, 1983-90, v.p. ins. svcs., 1990—. Exec. com. W. 89th St. Park Block Assn., N.Y.C., 1986—. Named to Acad. Women Achievers, YWCA, 1985. Mem. Am. Soc. Quality and Participation, Orgnl. Devel. Network, Orgnl. Devel. Network of Greater N.Y., N.Y. Human Resource Planners, Human Resource Planning Soc. (bd. dirs. 1990—). Office: Equitable Life Assurance 787 7th Ave New York NY 10019-6018

HENRY, KAREN SCHWAB, developmental editor; b. Phila., Oct. 4, 1954; d. Julius C. and Margaret (Ernst) Schwab; m. Thomas C. Henry, July 31, 1976; 1 xchild, Daniel I.S. Henry. BA, Oberlin (Ohio) Coll., 1975; MA, Tufts U., 1979, PhD, 1989. Adminstrv. dir. New Theatre Festival, Balt., 1976-77; editorial asst. Bedford Books, Boston, 1983-85, devel. editor, 1985—. playwright Boston Theatre Group, 1978—, adminstrv. dir., 1978—; author (opera) ASCONA, 1991, The Cell, 1988, (performance scores) The Burrow, The Companion, Ruth, The Cell, The Long Light: Voices of Aging, Crooked Eclipses and others. Fellowship Tufts U., 1978, Nat. Endowment for Arts, 1984, 86. Mem. MLA, Amnesty Internat., Mobilization for Survival, Phi Beta Kappa. Home: 26 Eastman St Dorchester MA 02125-2278 Office: Bedford Books of St Martin's Press 29 Winchester St Boston MA 02116-5328

HENRY, MARTHA VENNING, art gallery director, small business owner; b. Miami Beach, Fla., Feb. 13, 1950; d. George Howard Henry and Susan Marie (Venning) Etter. BA, Columbia U., 1976. Asst. Tambaran Gallery, N.Y.C., 1980-83; dir. Galerie Yves Arman, N.Y.C., 1983-84; cons. Parker & Parker Sculpture Ltd., N.Y.C., 1985; dir. Richard Green Gallery, N.Y.C., 1985-87; owner Martha Henry Fine Arts, N.Y.C., 1987-90; dir. traveling exhbns. New Eng. Ctr. for Contemporary Art, Brooklyn, Conn., 1988—; pres. Martha Henry, Inc., N.Y.C., 1990—; cons. Stark Gallery, N.Y.C., 1990-91. Author, editor exhbn. catalogs. Mem. NAFE, Am. Assn. Mus. (curators com.), Friends of Appraisers Assn. Am. Democrat. Office: 400 E 57th St New York NY 10022-3019

HENRY, PIERRE YVES, aerospace executive, writer, painter; b. Bonaventure, Que., Can., Apr. 2, 1932; s. J. Euclide and Aurélie (Forest) H.; m. June Briand, July 27, 1957; children: Michel, Nathalie. Visual Arts, Ecole des Beaux-Arts, Montreal, Can., 1954. Comml. artist Noranda Mines Ltd., Murdochville, Que., Can., 1954-60; editor Voyageur, Murdochville, Que., Can., 1960-65; coord. pub. rels. Noranda Mines Ltd., Toronto, Ont., Can., 1965-67, mgr. pub. rels., 1967-74; mgr. pub. rels. Pratt & Whitney Can., Longueuil, Que., 1974-77, dir. communications, 1977-82, v.p. communications, 1982—; bd. dirs. Internat. Aviation Mgmt. Tng. Inst., Montreal, Internat. Conf. Mus., Quebec City, Can., Vie des Arts, Montreal; chmn. Pub. Affairs Coun. Bd. of Can., 1988-91. Author: (book) Pays de Villages, 1987 (award of excellence, Que., 1988); initiator-coord. Art Exhibition Les Femmeuses, 1987-91; contbr. articles to profl. publs. Bd. dirs. Marsil Mus., Montreal, 1978-91, Orch. des Jeunes du Québec, Montreal, 1980-89; chmn. Les Petits Violons (Sch. of Violin), Montreal, 1987-90, Montebello (Que., Can.) Conf., 1988. Mem. Assn. Que. Mus. (hon.).

HENRY, WILLIAM ALOYSIUS, lawyer; b. Detroit, Aug. 9, 1956; s. John Michael and Margaret Ursula (O'Keefe) H.; m. Kyle Ann Kane, May 5, 1984; children: Alexander Daly, Kathleen Ross. AB cum laude, Harvard U., 1979; JD, Columbia U., 1984. Bar: D.C. 1984. Legis. asst. Rep. Bill Gradison, Washington, 1975-76, 77, 78, legis. dir., 1979-81; assoc. Squire, Sanders & Dempsey, Washington, 1984-90, Collier, Shannon, Rill & Scott, Washington, 1991—. Republican. Roman Catholic. Home: 4505 Conifer Ln Bethesda MD 20814-4009 Office: Collier Shannon Rill & Scott 3050 K St NW 1201 Pennsylvania Ave NW Washington DC 20007

HENSEL, JOHN CHARLES, physics educator; b. Pontiac, Mich., Dec. 5, 1930; s. Marion Lattig and Jessie Eileen (Miller) H.; m. Carolyn Olene Bahle, Apr. 17, 1958; children: Katherine, Thomas, Ann-Elizabeth, Caroline. BSE in Physics, U. Mich., 1952, MS in Physics, 1953, PhD in Physics, 1958. Mem. tech. staff Bell Labs. (AT&T), Murray Hill, N.J., 1958-89; disting. rsch. prof. physics N.J. Inst. Tech., Newark, 1990—. Editor: Proceedings of International Conference on Semiconductors, 1970; author: Electron-Hole Droplets in Semiconductors, 1977; contbr. over 80 articles to profl. jours.; patentee in field. Fellow Am. Phys. Soc.; mem. Sigma Xi. Home: 6 Hillcrest Ave Summit NJ 07901-2026 Office: NJ Inst Tech 161 Warren St Newark NJ 07102

HENSLEY, JOSEPH PAUL, podiatrist, pharmacist; b. Pittson, Pa., May 19, 1958; s. Clarence Woodfield and Mary Angela (Rossi) H.; m. Cherre Dawn Sholder, Nov. 25, 1989. BS in Pharmacy, U. Pitts., 1981; D of Podiatric Medicine, Pa. Coll. Podiatric Medicine, 1987. Pharmacist Thrift Drug, Pittston, 1981-82, Rite Aid, Kingston, Pa., 1982-83; surg. resident Podiatry Hosp. of Pitts., 1987-89; podiatrist Associated Foot and Ankle, York, Pa., 1989—. Contbr. papers and articles to profl. jours. Mem. Am. Coll. Foot Surgeons (assoc.), Am. Bd. Podiatric Surgeons (assoc.), Am. Podiatric Med. Assn., Pa. Podiatric Med. Assn., South Cen. Pa. Podiatric Med. Assn., U. Pitts. Alumni, Podaitry Hosp. Pitts. Alumni. Roman Catholic. Home: N-115 Camelot Arms York PA 17402

HENSON, WILLIAM L., agricultural economist, educator; b. Balt., Aug. 7, 1934; s. Lawson A. and Mattie K. (Ward) H.; m. Audrey E. Mills, Feb. 2, 1957; children: Cheryl, Elizabeth, Kathleen. BS, Md. State Coll., 1955; MS, Pa. State U., 1957, PhD, 1967. Egg inspector Commonwealth of Pa., Pitts., 1957-59; poultry inspector Am. Mktg. Svc. USDA, Fredericksburg, Pa., 1959-63; N.E. region poultry economist Econ. Rsch. Svc. USDA, University Park, 1967-84; lectr. econs. Pa. State U., University Park, 1968, asst. prof. dept. agrl. econs., 1968—, asst. to assoc. dean Coll. Agr., 1969-84; coord. grad. recruitment Coll. Agr., University Park, 1984—; asst. to dean Coll. Agr. Pa. State U., University Park, 1989—. Contbr. bulletins, articles and reports to publs. Recipient Presdl. Citation, Nat. Assn. Equal Opportunity Higher Edn., Washington, 1987. Mem. Am. Econ. Assn., Am. Agrl. Econ. Assn., Am. Poultry Sci. Assn., Minorities in Agrl., Natural Resources and Related Scis. (pub. rels. chair 1989-91, historian 1990-91, pres. 1991-92, Svc. award 1989). Roman Catholic. Home: 125 Norle St State College PA 16801-6957 Office: Pa State U 101 Agr Adminstrn Bldg University Park PA 16802

HENZE, HOWARD MARTIN, healthcare administrator; b. Albany, N.Y., July 6, 1947; s. Howard Martin Louis and Janet Wilma (Klotzke) H.; m. Carolyn Ann Wagner, May 17, 1981. BS, Rensselaer U., 1969; MPA, SUNY, Albany, 1976. Acct. analyst The Travelers, Albany, 1973-76; adminstrv. mgr. ambulatory svcs. Albany Med. Ctr., 1976-81; practice adminstrn. U. Pa. Med. Ctr., Phila., 1981-87; emergency adminstr. Atlantic City (N.J.) Med. Ctr., 1987-88; adminstrv. ambulatory svcs. Girard Med. Ctr., Phila., 1988-90; chief ops. officer Cataract Care Ctr., Johnstown, N.Y., 1990-91; bd. dirs. Soc. Ambulatory Care Profls. Am. Hosp. Assn., Chgo.,

1987-89; mem. Am. Coll. Healthcare Execs., Chgo., 1984; reviewer in field. Co-author: (with R. Rubright) Preconditions for Persuasion, Persuading Physicians, Disaster Planning, Hospital Adminstration Handbook, Editorial Board, Emergency Department Forms Manual; contbr. articles to profl. jours. Lt. USN, 1969-73. Mem. Mendellsohn Club Albany. Home: RR 3 Box 125 Gloversville NY 12078-9803

HERAGU, SUNDERESH SESHARANGA, industrial engineering educator; b. Hassan, Karnataka, India, June 28, 1959; came to U.S. 1988; s. Heragu Ramanuja Sesharanga and Seethamma Sesharanga Iyengar; m. Rita Sunderesh Narasimhan, June 18, 1989. BEng, U. Mysore, India, 1982; MBA, U. Sask., 1985; PhD, U. Man., 1988. Lectr. Adichunchanagiri Inst. Tech., Chikmagalur, India, 1982-83; asst. prof. SUNY, Plattsburgh, 1988-91; asst. prof. indsl. engring. Rensselaer Poly. Inst., Troy, N.Y., 1991—; lectr. in field; adj. prof. U. Man., 1989-92. Co-author: Design, Layout and Location of Facilities, 1993; contbr. articles to profl. jours. U. Man. grad. fellow, 1987-88. Mem. Inst. Mgmt. Sci., Inst. Indsl. Engrs., Prodn. and Ops. Mgmt. Soc. Hindu. Home: 22 Lori Dr Niskayuna NY 12309 Office: Rensselaer Poly Inst Decision Sci & Engring Troy NY 12180-3590

HERBER, ROLFE H., chemistry educator; b. Dortmund, Germany, Mar. 10, 1927; came to U.S., 1938; m. Rita J. Goldstein, June 27, 1954; children: Sharon, Karen, Sandra. BS, UCLA, 1949; PhD, Oreg. State U., 1952. Postdoctoral rsch. assoc. MIT, Cambridge, 1952-55; asst. prof. U. Ill., Urbana, 1955-59; assoc. prof., prof. I chemistry Rutgers U., New Brunswick, N.J., 1959, prof. II, 1977—; NSF sr. postdoctoral fellow Weizmann Inst., Rehovot, Israel, 1965-66; sr. scientist Centic des Etudes Nucleaires de Gienoble, Grenoble, France, 1974; vis. prof. Technion Inst. Tech., Haifa, Israel, 1981-82; cons. McGraw-Hill, Polaroid, Argus Chem., FMC Corp., also others. Author: Principles of Chemistry, 1960, Chemical Applications of Mossbauer Spectroscopy, 1968; also 3 others; contbr. over 200 articles to profl. jours. Grantee AEC, NSF, Petroleum Rsch. Fund, U.S.-Israel Binational Sci. Found. Fellow AAAS, Am. Phys. Soc. Office: Rutgers U Dept Chemistry PO Box 939 Piscataway NJ 08855-0939

HERBER, STEVEN CARLTON, physician; b. L.A., Aug. 25, 1960; s. Raymond and Marilyn Joyce (Dart) H.; m. Katherine Carol Jones, Apr. 23, 1989. BS, Pacific Union Coll., 1982; Dr.med., Loma Linda U., 1986. Diplomate Nat. Bd. Med. Examiners, 1987. Resident surgeon Med. Ctr. Loma Linda (Calif.) U., 1986-90; chief resident plastic surgery Yale U., New Haven, Conn., 1990—; researcher Dept. of Surgery, Loma Linda, CAlif., 1987-90. Contbr. articles to profl. jours. NIH grantee, 1988, MacPherson Soc. Clin. Sci. fellow, 1992; recipient Leadership award, AMA, 1991. Mem. Am. Med. Student Assn. (resident), San Bernardino County Med. Soc., Calif. Med. Assn. Republican. Adventist. Office: 44 Montoya Dr Branford CT 06405-2516

HERBERT, ANNE TIMBROOK, interior design executive; b. Elizabeth, N.J., May 13, 1934; d. Richard Elson and Marguerite Helen (Cawthorne) Timbrook; m. Norman Theodore Herbert, June 20, 1953 (div. Dec. 1980); children: Glenn, Jean, Janet. BFA, Syracuse U., 1955. Cert. interior design profl. Designer, draftsman Modern Kitchens of Syracuse, N.Y., 1955-57; designer, cons. Ouaquaga, N.Y., 1957-77; prin. Elson Assocs., Endwell, N.Y., 1977—; substitute tchr. in art, indsl. arts Jr. High and High Sch., Windsor, N.Y., 1968-69. Mem. Windsor Civic Club, 1960-70, pres., 1964; mem. Old Onaquaga Hist. Soc., Harpursville, N.Y., 1964—, pres., 1966-68, v.p. 1970-87; mem. Broome County Bicentennial Commn., Binghamton, N.Y., 1973-76; bd. dirs. Broome County Hist. Soc., Binghamton, 1974—. Mem. Am. Soc. Interior Designers (profl., bd. dirs., 1982-89, 92—, chpt. sec. 1984-85, Presdl. Citation for Disting. Svc. 1983), Univ. Singles, Inc. (pres. 1985-86, bd. dirs. 1983-90), Tau Sigma Delta, Phi Kappa Phi. Republican. Home: 3625 Leonard Dr Endwell NY 13760 Office: Elson Assocs 3625 Leonard Dr Endicott NY 13760-2411

HERBERT, APRIL HODGES, sculptor, freelance writer; b. N.Y.C., Apr. 30, 1934; d. Charles and Nora (Warndorfer) Hodges; m. Roy Arthur Herbert, July 4, 1953; children: Robin, Lauren, Michael. BA, Empire State Coll., SUNY, White Plains, 1967. Exhibited art works at Somerstown Gallery, Somers, N.Y., Creative Connections, Ridgefield, Conn.; one-woman shows include Stamford Sheraton Hotel, Conn., 1986, Hiram Halle Meml. Libr., Pound Ridge, N.Y., 1989; exhibited in juried shows at 39th and 42d Art of N.E. USA, Silvermine, Conn., 1988, FaberBirren Color Show, Stamford, 1990, Ridgefield Guild of Artists, Conn., 1991; 20 pvt. collections, 5 commd. works, others; author: The Tailgate Cookbook, 1970; contbr. articles to various mags. Mem. Vis. Arts Coun. Dalton Sch. Recipient Amidar award for sculpture 39th Art of the N.E. USA, Silvermine, Conn., 1988. Mem. Stamford Art Assn. (dir. 1988-90, Fred Kraus meml. award for sculpture 1989), Katonah Mus. Home: RR 2 Box 245 Pound Ridge NY 10576-9802

HERBERT, JAMES DALTON, psychology educator; b. Alice, Tex., June 20, 1962; s. Jim Dalton Herbert and Gracye Lee (Cates) H.; m. Diana Lee Nance, May 28, 1983; children: Aaron James, Sylvia Lee. BA, U. Tex., 1983; MA, U. N.C., Greensboro, 1986, PhD, 1989. Lic. psychologist, Pa. Rsch. asst. U. N.C., Greensboro, 1983-88, asst. dir. Psychology Clinic, 1987-88; psychology intern Beth Israel Med. Ctr., N.Y.C., 1988-89; asst. prof. psychiatry Med. Coll. Pa., Phila., 1989—, co-dir. Behavior Therapy clinic, 1989—. Contbr. articles to profl. jours. Rsch. grantee Sigma Xi, 1988. Mem. Am. Psychol. Assn. (Dissertation grantee 1988), Am. Psychol. Soc., Assn. for Advancement Behavior Therapy, Am. Assn. Applied and Preventive Psychology, Phila. Behavior Therapy Assn. (mem.-at-large 1990—, exec. bd.), Phi Beta Kappa, Psi Chi. Home: 219 Forrest Ave Narberth PA 19072 Office: Med Coll PA EPPI 3200 Henry Ave Philadelphia PA 19129-1187

HERBIG, GÜNTHER, conductor; b. Aussig, Germany, Nov. 30, 1931; s. Emil and Gisela (Hieke) H.; diploma Franz-Liszt-Hochschule, Weimar, Germany, 1956; m. Jutta Czapski, Oct. 30, 1958; children: Beate, Thomas. Mus. asst. Erfurt Theatre, 1956-57; condr. Deutsches Nat. Theatre, Weimar, 1957-62; prin. condr. Potsdam (Ger.) Theatre, 1962-66; condr. Berliner Sinfonie-Orchester, Berlin, 1966-72, chief condr., artistic dir., 1977-83; chief condr., artistic dir. Dresden (Ger.) Philharmonic Orchester, 1972-77; prin. guest condr. Dallas Symphony Orch., 1979-81; artistic advisor Toronto Symphony Orch., 1988, music dir., 1988—. Recipient Theodor Fontane Arts prize, 1964; German Dem. Republic Arts prize, 1970; Nat. prize German Dem. Republic, 1977. Roman Catholic. Office: Toronto Symphony, 60 Simcoe Ste C116, Toronto, ON Canada M5J 2H5*

HERBLOCK See BLOCK, HERBERT LAWRENCE

HERBST, MARIE ANTOINETTE, state senator; m. Paul Herbst. BA, Albany State Tchr.'s Coll.; Masters, Columbia U.; postgrad. secondary sch. adminstrn., U. Conn. Pub. sch. tchr. East Windsor, Conn.; mem., asst. majority leader Conn. State Senate from 35th Dist.; in 4th term as mayor Town of Vernon; chmn. pub. safety com.; asst. majority leader, 1989—; mem. fin., revenue, bonding com., 1989; mem. edn. com. Lector, Sacred Heart Ch.; past chmn. High Sch. CCD Sch.; past mem. Ladies of Sacred Heart; mem. Tri-Town Disabled Com., Vernon Town Council, 1975-79; past mem. Vernon Bd. Edn.; mem. Adult Edn. Adv. Commn., 1985; treas. Capitol Region Council of Govts., 1985. Mem. Internat. Edn. Assn., Nat. Edn. Assn., Conn. Edn. Assn., Phi Delta Kappa, Gamma Kappa Rho. Democrat. Roman Catholic. Home: 245 Brandy Hill Rd Vernon Rockville CT 06066-5609 Office: Legis Office Bldg Capitol Ave Hartford CT 06106-1706

HERBST, ROBERT LEROY, organization executive; b. Mpls., Oct. 5, 1935; s. Walter Peter and Bernice Mickey (Mikkelson) H.; m. Evelyn Clarice Elford, Sept. 22, 1956; children—Eric Elford, Peter Robert, Amy Jo. B.S. in Forest Mgmt, U. Minn., St. Paul, 1957. Dep. commnr. Minn. Conservation Dept., 1966-69; nat. exec. dir. Izaak Walton League Am., 1969-70; commr. natural resources State of Minn., 1971-77; asst. sec. fish, wildlife and parks Dept. Interior, Washington, 1977-81; sec. Dept. Interior, Jan. 20-26, 1981; exec. dir. Trout Unltd., 1981-90; pres. Lake Superior Ctr., Washington, 1990-92; Washington rep. TVA, Washington, 1992—; instr. U. Minn., 1954; mem. adv. faculty N. Am. Sch. Conservation, 1969-77; chmn. Gt. Lakes Fisheries Commn., 1978-80, steering com. Nat. Fishing Week, 1991; mem. U.S. Commn. UNESCO, 1978-79, Pres. Carter's Interagency Coun., 1978-80; co-chmn. Nat. Adv. Coun. Environ. Edn., 1989, chmn., 1990-92. Author: Careers in Environment, 1973, also articles. Mem. nat. bd. Boy Scouts Am., 1969-77; exec. bd. Viking council, 1975-76; mem. bd. House of Prayer Lutheran Ch., Richfield, Minn., 1969-77; bd. govs. African Inst. Econ. Edn. and Devel., 1980. Recipient Nat. Service award Izaak Walton League Am., 1971; Silver Beaver award Boy Scouts Am., 1977; Distinguished Service award U. Minn., 1969; named Pub. Adminstr. of Year in Minn. Am. Soc. Pub. Adminstrn., 1976. Mem. Natural Resource Coun. Am. (chmn. 1989—), Land Between Lakes Assn. (chmn. 1982—, trustee 1981—). Democrat. Office: TVA Ste 300 1 Massachusetts Ave NW Washington DC 20444

HERBST, WALTER JOSEPH, social security administrator; b. Albany, N.Y., Feb. 25, 1942; s. Walter C. and Marian (Renehan) H.; m. Elizabeth Rowen, Sept. 26, 1964; children: Michael W., Julianne, Jennifer R., Elizabeth M. Student, Mater Chrisi Sem., 1961; BBA, Marist Coll., 1963; postgrad., Cornell U., 1983-89. Claims rep. Social Security Adminstrn., N.Y.C. and N.J., 1963-66; field rep. Social Security Adminstrn., Spring Valley, N.Y., 1966-67; ops. supr. Social Security Adminstrn., Hackensack, N.J., 1967-68; staff devel. assoc. Social Security Adminstrn., N.Y.C., 1971-73; br. mgr. Social Security Adminstrn., Corning, N.Y., 1973-1986; dist. mgr. Social Security Adminstrn., Elmira, N.Y., 1986—; investment sales dir. Tax Facts, Buffalo, 1970; with First Investors Corp., N.Y.C., 1986-70; mem. Labor Rels. Cadre Soc. Security Adminstrn., 1983—. Mem. Salvation Army adv. bd., Corning, N.Y., 1982-85, planning commn., Horseheads, N.Y., 1976—; Coll. Ctr. of the Finger Lakes Adv. Bd.; bd. govs., Notre Dame High Sch., 1980-87, pres., 1984-86, v.p., 1982-84; bd. dirs Coun. of Community Svcs., co-founder, treas., 1974—; v.p. Little League, Horseheads N.Y., 1975—. Mem. Nat. Coun. Social Security Mgmt. Assn. (exec. com., treas. 1990—), N.Y. Regional Social Security Mgmt. Soc. (pres., v.p., treas. 1976-90), Soc. Fedn. Labor Rels. Profls. (Regional Commrs. Citation 1991), Rotary. Republican. Roman Catholic. Home: 415 S Main St Horseheads NY 14845-2448 Office: Social Security Adminstrn 333 E Water St Elmira NY 14901-3414

HERENDEEN, DAVID WARREN, music educator; b. Rochester, N.Y., Nov. 23, 1956; s. Robert Wood and Elsie Arthur (Smith) H.; m. Sara Bunn (div. 1986); 1 child, Fletcher Wood; m. Mary Louise Kemp, Nov. 24, 1988. MusB, Oberlin Coll., 1978, M Music Theater, 1979; postgrad., U. Ariz., 1986—. Apprentice Santa Fe Opera, 1979; resident baritone Mich. Opera, Detroit, 1979-80; teaching fellow Hartt Sch. Music, Hartford, Conn., 1980-81; resident Deutsche Oper Berlin, 1988-89; asst. prof. music Edinboro (Pa.) U., 1989—; performer, asst. to dir. in The Yellow Sound, Guggenheim Found., N.Y.C., 1981. Created role of Roderick Usher in world premier of Fall of the House of Usher, Hartt Opera Theater, 1980. Recipient German-Am. award German-Am. Soc., N.Y.C., 1988. Mem. Nat. Assn. Tchrs. Singing, Phi Mu Alpha (adviser 1990—). Presbyterian. Home: 118 W State St Albion PA 16401-1027 Office: Edinboro Univ Pa Heather Hall Edinboro PA 16444

HERENDEEN, WARREN RICHARD, English language educator, writer, consultant; b. Canandaigua, N.Y., July 3, 1934; s. John Edson and Florence Genevieve (Federkile) H. BA, Hobart Coll., 1957; MA, U. Chgo., 1958; PhD, U. Wis., 1965; MA, Columbia U., 1984, MEd, 1985, postgrad., 1985-91. Instr. English Carnegie-Mellon U., Pitts., 1958-59; teaching asst. U. Wis., Madison, 1959-63; instr. Georgetown U., Washington, 1963-65; instr., asst. prof. NYU, N.Y.C., 1965-72; asst. prof. humanities Eastman Sch. Music, U. Rochester, N.Y., 1972-73; asst. prof. English CUNY, N.Y.C., 1973-75; adminstr., prof. Mercy Coll., Dobbs Ferry, N.Y., 1975—; adj. prof. linguistics L.I. U., Westchester Campus, Dobbs Ferry, 1982—; reader coll. bd. essay tests and advanced placement, Princeton, N.J., 1989—; cons. CBS 60 Minutes, N.Y.C., 1982, PBS Firing Line, N.Y.C., 1984. Editor Jour. Hart Crane Newsletter, 1977-79, The Visionary Co.: A Mag. of the 20s, 1982-87, Jour. of Basic Writing, 1986—; contbr. articles to profl. jours. Active prison edn. programs. Recipient Disting. Scholar Cert., CUNY, N.Y.C., 1977, NEH award, NEH, Washington, 1980; rsch. grantee U. Wis., Georgetown U., NYU, 1961-72. Fellow U. Chgo.; mem. Phi Beta Kappa. Home: 7100 Boulevard E Guttenberg NJ 07093 Office: Mercy Coll 555 Broadway Dobbs Ferry NY 10522

HERINK, RICHIE, manufacturing company executive; b. Jersey City, Nov. 15, 1932; s. Reinhard and Anna (Golumb) H.; m. Nancy Gay Reck; children: Jennifer, Paul. ME, Stevens Inst. Tech., 1954; MS, Rensselaer Poly. Inst., 1957; EdD, Fairleigh Dickinson U., 1974; BA, Edison State U., 1976; BS, SUNY, 1976; PhD, Union Grad. Sch., 1979. Registered profl. engr., Vt., Mass. Staff engr. Western Electric Co., Kearney, N.J., 1957-67; systems analyst IBM Corp., White Plains, N.Y., 1967-76; mgr. IBM Corp., 1981-84, program mgr., 1976-81, 84—; workshop chmn. Nat. Rsch. Coun., Washington, 1986-87; mem. editorial bd., Internat. Jour. Tech. Mgmt., Milton Keynes, U.K., 1987-89, Jour. Engring. Tech. and Mgmt., Falls Church, Va., 1988-89. Patentee, transformer clamping device; author: College Level Statistics, 1965; editor: Psychotherapy Handbook. With U.S. Army, 1954-56. Recipient medallion for meritorious pub. svc., Econ. Devel. Coun. N.Y., 1977, medal for profl. accomplishment, U. Sofia, Bulgaria, 1988. Mem. Fairleigh Dickinson U. Doctoral Alumni Assn. (pres. 1981-85). Home: 78 Bingham Rd Ridgewood NJ 07450-2106 Office: IBM Corp 500 Columbus Ave Thornwood NY 10594-1900

HERKO, CARL HENRY, architecture writer; b. Buffalo, Mar. 18, 1955; s. Henry George and Jennie Helene (Panek) H. BA, SUNY Coll., Buffalo, 1977. Copy editor The Buffalo News, 1977-81, travel editor, 1981-84; editor Buffalo Mag. Buffalo News, 1985-91, architecture writer, 1992—. Recipient Media award N.Y. State Bar Assn., 1988. Roman Catholic. Home: 18 Arlington Pl Buffalo NY 14201-1302 Office: Buffalo News 1 News Plz Box 100 Buffalo NY 14240

HERMAN, ALLEN IAN, foundation administrator; b. Pitts., June 16, 1950; s. Harry W. and Ann (Burke) H.; m. Jacqueline Wadler, July 5, 1981; children: Zvi, Ari, Michal. BA, U. Pitts., 1972; MBA, U. Pa., 1974. Cancer coordinator Jamaica (N.Y.) Hosp., 1975-76; asst. adminstr. Health Sci. Ctr., SUNY, Bklyn., 1976-79, assoc. adminstr., 1979-83; chief exec. officer Nephrology Found. Bklyn., 1983—; lectr. SUNY Health Sci. Ctr. Health Related Professions, Bklyn., 1983—; mem. council ESRD Network #25, N.Y.C., 1980-88. Mem. editorial bd.: Jour. Greater N.Y. Med. Records Assn., 1984; contbr. articles to profl. jours. bd. dirs. Hebrew Acad. West Queens, Jackson Heights, N.Y., 1987—. Mem. Nat. Dialysis Assn. (bd. dirs. 1985-87, v.p. 1988, pres. 1989-90), Am. Coll. Healthcare Execs., Am. Hosp. Assn., Am. Pub. Health Assn., Nat. Renal Adminstrs. Assn., Wharton Health Care Alumni Assn. Democrat. Jewish. Office: Nephrology Found Bklyn 342 Flatbush Ave Brooklyn NY 11238-4973

HERMAN, BERNARD ALBERT, pharmaceutical company executive; b. Boston, Dec. 11, 1910; s. Michael and Celia Caroline (Pullman) H.; m. Haydée Irma Arevalo, May 14,1938; children: Kathleen Archer Barrow, Bradford Kent II. BA with high orations, Yale U., 1934. With R.H. Macy & Co., Inc., N.Y.C., 1934-41; ptnr. Eliot Restaurant Corp., Boston, 1946-52; chmn. bd., chief exec. officer, dir. Herman, Inc., Avon, Mass., 1950—; pres., chief exec. officer, dir. Archer Kent Stores, Avon, 1961—, Trade Winds Inn, Inc., Craigville, Mass., 1972—; ptnr. Kent Realty Co., Boston, 1972-87; trustee Bradford Realty Trust, Avon, 1950—, Archer Kent Realty Trust, Craigville, 1972—. Leader Boy Scouts Am., Newton Highlands, Mass., 1950-52; pres. Little League Baseball, Wellesley Hills, Mass., 1960-63; vestryman St. Paul's Episcopal Ch., Newton Highlands, 1952-55, St. Mary's Episcopal Ch., Newton Lower Falls, Mass., 1963-66. Served to Comdr. USN, 1941-46. Military scholar U.S. Army, 1930-34. Mem. Nat. Assn. Svc. Merchandisers, Nat. Assn. Drug Chains, Toiletry Merchandisers Assn. (chmn. bd. dirs. 1973-74), Yale Club of Boston, Harvard Club of Boston, Wardroom, Wellesley Country Club, Hundred Club of Mass., U.S. Navy League, Phi Beta Kappa. Republican. Lodge: Masons. Home: 57 Damien Rd Wellesley MA 02181-3415 Office: Herman Inc 7 New England Exec Pk # 6 Burlington MA 01803-5008

HERMAN, BETH WARSHOFSKY, sales and marketing executive; b. N.Y.C., Mar. 11, 1963; d. Fred and Carol Barbara (Masnik) Warshofsky; m. Arthur L. Herman, Aug. 9, 1987. AA, Fashion Inst. Tech., 1983; BA magna cum laude, CUNY, 1987. Sales cons. Frank Stella Ltd., N.Y.C., 1984-89; rsch. and spl. projects coord. Spence-Chapin, N.Y.C., 1987, social worker, 1988-89; dir. The Learning Annex, Washington, 1990-91; account exec. Computer Cons. Corp., Washington, 1991-92; dir. sales and mktg. The Bus. Source, 1992—; dir. mktg. Wordworks, Inc., 1992—. Author poems. Vol. Student Activities Office, Sewanee, Tenn., 1987-88, Bachuss, Sewanee, 1987-88; vol., advisor Women's Ctr., Sewanee, 1987-88.

HERMAN, BILL BRADLEY, real estate manager and developer; b. Passaic, N.J., Apr. 19, 1952; s. George and H. Lillian (Lissak) H.; m. Michelle Iris Glick, June 2, 1974: children: Aaron, Rikki. BA in Elem. Edn. magna cum laude, Farleigh Dickinson U., 1974. Cert. coach Rutgers Youth Sports Rsch. Coun. Maintenance mechanic Popular Svcs. Inc., Passaic, 1970-74; sales rep. McCormick & Co., Balt., 1974-75; tchr., kindergarten, 1st grade Saddle Brook (N.J.) Sch. System, 1975; account exec. Boyle Midway, Inc., Cranford, N.J., 1975-83; pres. and chief exec. officer G & S Mgmt., Inc., Clifton, N.J., 1983—. Sponsor Passaic Boys Club, 1981—; house chmn. Morristown (N.J.) Jewish Ctr., 1988—; coach Hanover (N.J.) Twp Youth Soccer, 1989, '90, Little League, 1990. Named Human Being of the Day, Z100 FM Radio, Secaucus, N.J., 1986; recipient KOUOD award, Morristown Jewish Ctr., 1989. Republican. Jewish. Home and Office: G&S Mgmt 1 Palm Ct Morris Plains NJ 07950-3267

HERMAN, BRUCE WHITNEY, artist, educator; b. Montclair, N.J., Jan. 13, 1953; s. William Chester and Ruth Lockwood (Raymond) H.; m. Margaret Scott Matthews, Nov. 15, 1973; children: Benjamin Scott, Sarah Elizabeth. BFA, Boston U., 1977, MFA cum laude, 1979. Art instr. The Beaver Country Day Sch., Chestnut Hill, Mass., 1980-83, The Waring Sch., Beverly, Mass., 1984-86; art instr. Gordon Coll., Wenham, Mass., 1984—, asst. prof. of art, 1986-88, chmn. art dept., 1988—; vis. lectr. Montserrat Coll. of Art, Beverly, 1987-88, Gordon Conwell-Theology Seminary, Hamilton, Mass., 1986-89; jury judge Rockport (Mass.) Art Assn., 1991; bd. dirs. Christians in the Visual Arts, Washington. Group exhbns. include Rose Art Mus., Brandeis U., 1982, exhbn. of religious art, St. Petersburg, USSR, 1992. Vestryman St. John's Episcopal Ch., Gloucester, Mass., 1985-88. Recipient Philip Guston prize Boston U., 1978, Smith Wesson award Springfield (Mass.) Art League, 1983. Mem. Coll. Art Assn. Home: 17 Walker St Gloucester MA 01930-1529 Office: Gordon College Grapevine Rd Wenham MA 01984-1701

HERMAN, DOROTHY, real estate broker; b. Bklyn., May 10, 1953; d. Joseph Edward and Louise (Dicerbo) D'Ambrosio; m. Jay Herman; 1 child, Christine. BA, Adelphia U., 1983. Cert. fin. planner. Mgr. Merrill Lynch Realty, L.I., N.Y., 1982-84, regional v.p., 1985-87, pres. L.I., 1988-90; co-owner, pres. Prudential L.I. Realty, 1990—; mem. faculty N.Y. Inst. Tech., 1988—. Contbr. weekly article to Newsday, 1990. Mem. Internat. Assn. of Fin. Planners (cert. fin. planner), L.I. Bd. Realtors, Columbia Soc. Real Estate Appraisers. Office: Prudential LI Realty 187 Main Pky W Plainview NY 11803-2807

HERMAN, ELLEN DORA, communications consultant, educator; b. N.Y.C., Mar. 1, 1950; d. Howard A. and Bernice (Weber) H. BA, George Washington U., 1971; MS, Boston U., 1973; MBA, NYU, 1986. Appointments sec. to Gov. Michael Dukakis Commonwealth of Mass., Boston, 1973-75; pvt. practice polit.and media cons. Boston and Washington, 1975-77; rev. officer, asst. to the sec. Dept. Treasury, Washington, 1977-79; account mgr. Press Brenner-Garth Assocs., N.Y.C., 1979-81; dir. internat. mktg. and corp. communications Am. Stock Exch., N.Y.C., 1981-86; v.p. Burson-Marsteller Pub. Rels., N.Y.C., 1986-87; asst. prof. Coll. Communication Boston U., 1987-90; cons. Strategic Communication Counseling, Cambridge, Mass., 1988—; lectr. mgmt. communication Harvard Bus. Sch., Boston, 1990—; cons. World Trade Ctr., Boston, 1988—, Toyota Auto, Osaka, Japan, 1989—, MBTA, Boston, 1989-91, NBC, GTECH, West Greenwich, R.I., 1991—. Mem. Gordon Ctr. for Pub. Policy of Brandeis U. Democrat. Jewish. Home: 61 Dana St Cambridge MA 02138-4310 Office: Harvard Bus Sch Soldiers Field Boston MA 02163

HERMAN, IRVING PHILIP, physics educator; b. Bklyn., Oct. 18, 1951; s. Nathan and Ida (Bresler) H.; m. Janet Pearl Kapstein, Aug. 21, 1977; children: Daniel Steven, Jonathan David. SB in Physics, MIT, 1972, PhD in Physics, 1977. Sr. physicist, sect. head Lawrence Livermore (Calif.) Nat. Lab., 1977-86; assoc. prof. applied physics Columbia U., N.Y.C., 1986—; mem. adv. bd. Interdisciplinary Laser Sci. Conf., 1985-89; co-organizer symposium on laser diagnostics and processing. Co-editor: Photon, Beam and Plasma Stimulated Chemical Processes at Surfaces, 1987; contbr. articles to profl. jours. Mem. IEEE Lasers and Electro-optics Soc., Materials Rsch. Soc., Am. Phys. Soc. Office: Columbia U Dept Applied Physics 202 SW Mudd New York NY 10027

HERMAN, JEFFREY ALAN, trade association executive, silversmith; b. Holyoke, Mass., May 17, 1959; s. Mark and Roslyn Marsha (Slavin) H.; m. Rebecca Nightingale, Oct. 16, 1988. BFA, Portland (Maine) Sch. Art, 1981. Designer, silversmith Gorham Mfg., Providence, 1981-83; silversmith Pilz Ltd., Providence, 1983-84; owner, operator restoration bus. Providence, 1984—; founder, dir. Soc. Am. Silversmiths, Cranston, R.I., 1989—. Mem. Design In Visual Arts (membership svcs. com.). Office: Soc Am Silversmiths PO Box 3599 Cranston RI 02910-0599

HERMAN, MAJA B. (MAYA B. HERMAN-SEKULICH), writer, poet, editor; b. Belgrade, Serbia, Yugoslavia, Feb. 17; came to U.S., 1980, naturalized, 1992; d. Bogomir Herman and Lily (Strauss) Tišma; m. Milosh Sekulich. MA, Belgrade U., 1977; PhD in Comparative Lit., Princeton U., 1986. Fulbright lectr. Rutgers U., New Brunswick, N.J., 1982-84; editor-in-chief Sappho Libr. Aquarius Pub. House, Belgrade, 1991—; cons. Novo Arts, N.Y.C., 1988-90; vis. lectr. Princeton (N.J.) U., 1985, 88; lectr., reader in field. Author: (poems) Camerography, 1990, Cartography, 1992, (essays) Literature of Transgression, 1986, rev. edit., 1992; editor/translator: Anxiety of Influence (H. Bloom) 1981, Cathedral (R. Carver) 1991, Myth and Structure (N. Frye) 1991; contbg. editor Night, 1990—; edited and translated intros. to 10 books; contbr. to scholarly jours. Princeton U. fellow, 1980-85, Fulbright fellow, 1982-84. Fellow AAUW; mem. PEN (Am. chpt., Serbian chpt.), Poetry Soc. Am. Home: 7 W 16th St Apt 3 New York NY 10011

HERMAN, MARIO LUIS, lawyer; b. Lima, Peru, Mar. 13, 1958; came to U.S., 1962; s. Mauricio Mario and Gloria (Campbell) H.; m. Kathleen Marie Hollenbeck, June 14, 1980; children: Damaris, Caroline, Felice. BA cum laude, Am. U., 1978; JD, Georgetown U., 1982. Bar: D.C. 1983. Assoc. Tedards and Jones, Washington, 1983-85, Jaeckle, Fleischmann, Washington, 1985-87, Murphy and Malone, Washington, 1988-89; ptnr. Tedards & Herman, Washington, 1989—, practice contingent antitrust bus. litigation, internat. trade, 1989—. Mem. ABA, Interam. Bar Assn., Ibero-Am. C. of C., Pi Sigma Alpha. Home: 9800 Summit Ave Kensington MD 20895-3733

HERMAN, ROBERT LEWIS, cork company executive; b. N.Y.C. July 16, 1927; s. Nat W. and Ruth (Stockton) H.; A.B., Columbia, 1948, B.S., 1949; m. Susan Marie Volper, Dec. 10, 1966; children: Candia Ruth, William Neal. V.p. Joseph Samuels & Sons, Inc., Whippany, N.J., 1953-62; pres. Dependable Cork Co., Inc., Morristown, N.J., 1962—; chmn. bd. Global Technology Systems. Co., Trevor, Wis., 1980—; bd. dirs. Concorco LDA, Lisbon, Portugal. Served to comdr. C.E. Corps, USNR, 1949-53. Mem. N.J. Mfrs. Assn., Naval Res. Assn., U.S. C. of C. Clubs: Navy League; Columbia U., Princeton (N.Y.C.). Inventor Corticiera natural cork wallcovering. Home: PO Box 1023 Morristown NJ 07962-1023 Office: PO Box 1102 Morristown NJ 07962-1102

HERMAN, SUSAN JANE, psychologist; b. Chgo.; m. Arthur Meinzer. PhD, U. Fla., Gainesville, 1970; Cert. in psychoanalysis, NYU, 1979. Psychologist Mount Carmel Guild, CMHC, Newark, 1970-72, Fairleigh Dickenson U. Clinic, Teaneck, N.J., 1972-73; pvt. practice Little Falls, N.J., 1972—; dir. psychol. svcs. Montclair State Coll., Upper Montclair, N.J., 1973—; supr. faculty Inst. Psychoanalysis of N.J., South Orange, 1982—; supr. Grad. Sch. Applied and Profl. Psychology, Piscataway, N.J., 1979—, Pace U. Grad. Sch. Psychology, N.Y.C., 1989—; clin. supr. dept. psychology Adelphi U., Garden City, N.Y., 1989—. Contbr. articles to

profl. jours. Mem. APA, N.J. Psychol. Assn., NYU Postdoctoral Grad. Assn. Office: Montclair State Coll Normal Ave Montclair NJ 07043-1607

HERMAN, WILLIAM JOHN, police chief; b. Millville, N.J., Jan. 18, 1942; s. Ellsworth Willard Herrmann and Frances (Compton) Hauser; m. Donna Jean (div. Feb. 1983); children: William John Jr., Kevin Andrew; m. Debbie Ann Kubiski; 1 child, Lyndsey Davis. AS, Cumberland County Coll., 1972; BA magna cum laude, Glasboro State Coll., 1974, MA, 1984; law enforcement exec. devel. course, FBI Acad., 1990. Cert. pub. mgr., N.J. Patrolman Millville Police Dept., Millville, N.J., 1965-72; sgt. Millville Police Dept., 1972-78, detective sgt., 1978-83, lt., 1983-86, capt., 1986-89, chief of police, 1989—; adj. faculty Camden County Coll., Blackwood, N.J., 1976-79, Cumberland County Coll., Vineland, N.J., 1984—. Author, editor: Police Policy Manual, 1987; author: (manual) Police Youth Week, 1976-89, (curriculum) Police Youth Week, 1976-89. Bd. dirs. Cumberland County Coll. Alumni, Millville, 1987. With USAF, 1960-64. Recipient Disting. Svc. award Millville Jaycees, 1988; named Outstanding Law Enfrcement Officer Millville Jaycees, 1985, Alumni of Month Cumberland County Coll., 1987. Mem. N.J. Patrolmen's Benevolent Assn. (pres. 1969-72), Patrolmen's Benevolent Assn. (silver life mem. local 213, Silver Life award 1986), Internat. Assn. Chiefs Police, N.J. Chiefs Police Assn., Am. Legion, USAF Non Commd. Officer Acad., Kiwanis, Elks. Republican. Methodist. Home: 28 Porreca Dr Millville NJ 08332-4840 Office: Millville Police Dept 18 S High St Millville NJ 08332-4244

HERMANN, JANE POMERANCE, ballet theatre executive; b. N.Y.C., Oct. 1, 1935; d. Robert Fulton and Sylvia (Forster) Pomerance; widowed; children: Elizabeth, John Robert, Hermann. BA, Barnard Coll., 1957. Audience developer Joffrey Ballet, N.Y.C., 1973-74, asst. gen. mgr., 1975-76; co-adminstr. Feld Ballet, N.Y.C., 1974-75; cons. City Ctr., N.Y.C., 1974-75; presentations dir. Met. Opera, N.Y.C., 1976-89; exec. dir. Am. Ballet Theatre, N.Y.C., from 1989, dir., 1990-92. Decorated knight Order of Lion Govt. of Finland; recipient Chevalier de Arts and Letters award, Govt. of France, 1988. Office: care Am Ballet Theatre 890 Broadway New York NY 10003-1211*

HERMANN, STEVEN ISTVAN, textile executive; b. Debrecen, Hungary, July 25, 1934; came to U.S., 1957.; s. Zoltan and Maria (Gacs) H.; m. Agnes S. Nadel, Oct. 17, 1958 (div. 1981); m. Elizabeth Takacs, Mar. 11, 1981; children: Roy, George. BS, U. Budapest, 1955. Architect N.Y. Firms, 1958-66; exec. Knitbrook Mills, N.Y.C., 1966-68; exec. v.p. Melena Knitting Co., E. Rutherford, N.J., 1968-69; pres., chief exec. officer Carnaby Mills, Inc., E. Rutherford, 1969-73, Korafab, Inc., N.Y.C., 1973-76; owner, pres. Texpro, Inc., East Rutherford, 1976-79; v.p. Meadows Knitting Corp., Kearny, N.J., 1979—, Safer Devel. & Mgmt. Co., Newark, 1989, Kuttner Prints Inc., 1988—, Safer Group of Cos., 1989—. Contbr. articles to profl. jours. Mem. Kampfe Lake Assn., Bloomingdale, N.J. Served to lt. Hungarian Army, 1952-56. Republican. Home: Kampfe Lake Bloomingdale NJ 07403 Office: Safer Group Cos 1875 Mccarter Hwy Newark NJ 07104-4211

HERMAN-SEKULICH, MAYA B. See HERMAN, MAJA B.

HERMESCH, ALAN L., public relations executive; b. Sabetha, Kans., Sept. 20, 1946; s. Albert and Eileen (Voet) H.; 1 child, Elisa. BS in Journalism, U. Kans., 1968; MA in Journalism, U. Mo., 1970. Media rep. Petersen Pub. Co., St. Louis, 1969-70; asst. advt. mgr. Stile-Craft Mfrs., Inc., St. Louis, 1971-72; laborer H.B. Deal Constrn. Co., St. Louis, 1972-73; pres. Lemoine Skinner Pub. Rels., St. Louis, 1975-77, Alan Hermesch Pub. Rels., St. Louis, 1977-79; info. officer Howard U., Washington, 1979-87, dir. pub. rels., 1987—; adj. inst. mass communications St. Louis Community Coll. Forest Park, 1975-79. Marymount U., Arlington, Va., 1990—. Mem. Fed. City Club, Nat. Press Club. Office: Howard U 2900 Van Ness St NW Washington DC 20008-1196

HERNANDEZ, ABISAIL (ABBY CAVADA), travel agent, entertainer; b. P.R., July 21, 1949; d. Ramon and Nelida (Torres) H. Student, Ramapo Coll., 1972. Social worker Bellevue Hosp., N.Y.C., 1969-70; asst. mgr. payroll pers. Doctors Hosp., N.Y.C., 1970-72; owner Fire and Earth Clothing Boutique, Yonkers, N.Y., 1972-80; singer, actor 5 Oaks, N.Y.C., 1987; travel agt. Escape Travel, Bronx, N.Y., 1992—. Singer, actor Kumhaja and Sera Sera, 1991 (Emmy award 1991). Republican. Home: 3130 Albany Crest Bronx NY 10463

HERNANDEZ, ENRIQUE, gynecologist, educator; b. Vega Baja, P.R., Oct. 25, 1951; s. Nathaniel and Ana Luisa (Lopez) H.; m. Marta Jimenez, May 29, 1971; children: David Enrique, Daniel Antonio. BS, U. P.R., Rio Piedras, 1973, MD, 1977. Diplomate Am. Bd. Med. Examiners, Am. Bd. Ob-Gyn, Am. Bd. Gynecol. Oncology. Resident in ob-gyn Johns Hopkins Hosp., Balt., 1977-81, fellow in gynecol. oncology, 1981-83; instr. ob-gyn Johns Hopkins U., Balt., 1981-82, asst. prof., 1982-83; chief gynecol. oncology service Tripler Army Med. Ctr., Honolulu, 1983-87, asst. dir. intern tng., 1984-87; assoc. prof. Med. Coll. Pa., Phila., 1987-89; prof. Med. Coll. Pa., 1989—; dir. div. gynecologic oncology Med. Coll. Pa., Phila., 1987—, prof., 1989—; pres. med. and dental staff Med. Coll. Hosps. Main Clin. Campus. Author: Manual of Gynecologic Oncology, 1989; contbr. articles to profl. jours. Maj. U.S. Army, 1983-87. Recipient Bristol award P.R. Med. Assn., 1977. Fellow ACS, Am. Coll. Ob-Gyns.; mem. Am. Soc. Clin. Oncology, Soc. Gynecologic Oncologists, Beta Beta Beta, Alpha Omega Alpha (pres. 1976-77 P.R. chpt.). Roman Catholic. Office: Med Coll Pa 3300 Henry Ave Philadelphia PA 19129-1191

HERNANDEZ, FRANK BERNARD, textiles manager; b. Habana, Cuba, Oct. 4, 1939; s. Manuel A. and Isabel (Bosque) H.; m. Isabel M. Milian, Feb. 8, 1957; children: Frank A., Doris I. Degree of Acct., Havana U., 1960. Gen. mgr. Perfect Thread Co., Valley Stream, N.Y., 1962—. Adminstrv. officer U.S. Power Squadron, Plum Beach br., Bklyn., 1990, exec. officer, 1991, comdr., 1992—. Recipient Leadership Devel. cert. U.S. Power Squadrons, 1991, Sr. Mem. Award for meritorious svc. U.S. Power Squadrons, 1991. Republican. Roman Catholic. Home: 9009 Seaview Ave Brooklyn NY 11236 Office: Perfect Thread Co 333 W Merric Rd Valley Stream NY 11582

HERNANDEZ, JACQUELINE CHARMAINE, lawyer; b. Trinidad, W.I., Nov. 1, 1960; came to U.S., 1975; d. Desmond and Jocelyn Virginia (Felix) H. BA, L.I. U., 1982; JD, NYU, 1985. Bar: N.Y. 1986, N.J. 1987, U.S. Dist. Ct. (so. and ea. dists.) N.Y. 1988. Assoc. Cooper and Kenny, N.Y.C., 1985-87, Semel, Boeckmann, Diamond, Schepp & Yuhas, N.Y.C., 1987-88, Wood, Williams, Rafalsky & Harris, N.Y.C., 1988-90, Cooper, Liebowitz, Royster & Wright, Elmsford, N.Y., 1990-92; ptnr. Cooper, Liebowitz Royster & Wright, Elmsford, N.Y., 1992—. Mem. Black Bar Assn. of Bronx County. Roman Catholic. Home: 25 Martine Ave Plz 25 PH 308 White Plains NY 10606 Office: Cooper Liebowitz Royster & Wright 3 W Main St Elmsford NY 10523-2414

HERNANDEZ, TOMAS CAPATAN, arts administrator; b. Manila, Nov. 5, 1946; came to U.S. 1967; s. Jose Fernandez and Angeles (Capatan) H. PhB in Philosophy and Lit., U. Santo Tomas, Manila, 1966; MA in Dramatic Art, U. Calif., Santa Barbara, 1968; PhD in Drama and Theatre, U. Hawaii, Honolulu, 1975. Asst. prof. Indo-Pacific lang. U. Hawaii at Manoa, Honolulu, 1975-79; vis. faculty theatre Ind. U., Bloomington, 1979-80; adj. faculty Eastman Sch. Music, Rochester, N.Y., 1980-81; freelance opera stage dir., 1981-82; assoc. prof. theatre Kans. State U., Manhattan, 1981-86; performing arts dir. Ariz. Commn. on Arts, Phoenix, 1986-91; dir., oper-mus. theater program NEA, Washington, 1991—. Fulbright travel grantee., 1967. Office: NEA 1100 Pennsylvania Ave NW Washington DC 20506-0005

HERNDON, JAMES HENRY, orthopaedic surgeon, educator; b. Los Angeles, Oct. 31, 1938; s. James Greene and Kathleen Theresa (Murphy) H.; m. Geraldine Grace Armiger, Feb. 26, 1971; children: Jennifer, Jonathan. BS, Loyola U., Los Angeles, 1961; MD, UCLA, 1965; MA, Brown U., 1979; MBA, Boston U., 1990. Diplomate Am. Bd. Orthopaedic Surgery. Intern Hosp. of U. Pa., 1965-66, resident in surgery, 1966-67; resident in orthopedics Children's Hosp.-Mass. Gen. Hosp. Boston, 1967-70; chief resident in orthopedics Mass. Gen. Hosp., 1970; asst. clin. prof. orthopaedic surgery Mich. State U., Grand Rapids, 1974-77, assoc. clin. prof., 1977-78; prof., chmn. dept. orthopaedics Brown U., Providence, 1979-88; surgeon-in-chief dept. orthopaedic surgery R.I. Hosp., Providence, 1979-88; silver prof., chmn. dept. Orthopaedic surgery U. Pitts., chief dept. orthopaedics and rehab. Presbyn. U. Hosp., Pitts., Montifiore U. Hosp.; site visitor Residency Rev. Commn., 1981—; examiner Am. Bd. Orthopaedic Surgery, Chgo., 1977—, pres., 1990-91. Reviewer Jour. Bone and Joint Surgery, 1975—; contbr. articles to profl. jours., chpts. to books; also author books. Trustee Meeting Street Sch., Providence, 1984-88, Harmarville Rehab. Hosp., Pitts., 1989—; mem. bd. govs. Arthritis Found., Providence, 1984-88, Pitts., 1989—. Served to maj. U.S. Army, 1971-73. Recipient Edith and Carl Lasky Meml. award UCLA Med. Sch., 1965, Bronze award Am. Congress Rehab. Medicine, 1972, clin. research award N.Y. Med. Soc., 1974. Fellow ACS, Am. Acad. Orthopaedic Surgeons; mem. Am. Orthopaedic Assn., Orthopaedic Research Soc., Am. Bd. Orthopedic Surgery (bd. dirs., pres. 1991-92), Residency Rev. Com. Orthopedic Surgery, Am. Soc. Surgery of Hand (chmn.). Clubs: Agawam Hunt (Providence), Hope (Providence), Longue Vue (Pitts.). Office: U Pitts Sch Medicine Rm M272 Scaife Hall Pittsburgh PA 15261

HERNON, RICHARD FRANCIS, engineer; b. N.Y.C., July 14, 1940; s. Francis Augusta and Mary Columba (Francis) H.; m. Susan Teresa Hartnett (dec. Jan. 1975); m. Jane Margaret Murphy, June 12, 1977; children: Robert Elizabeth, Richard Jr., Patrick. BCE, Rutgers U., 1962; MCE, N.J. Inst. Tech. (formerly Newark Coll. Engring.), 1969. Registered profl. engr., N.J. Constrn. engr. N.J. Dept. Transp., Trenton, 1964-74, fleet mgr., 1974-76; county engr. Hudson County, Jersey City, 1976-80; dir. engring. and planning N.J. Transit Waterfront Transp., Jersey City, 1980—. Pres. Rutgers Engring. Soc., New Brunswick, 1977, Island Heights (N.J.) Voters and Taxpayers, 1973-75; chmn. Island Heights Planning Bd., 1973-75. Served to 1st Lt. U.S. Army, 1962-64. Mem. ASCE. Roman Catholic. Home: 69 Hadley Ave Toms River NJ 08753-7769 Office: NJ Transit 2 Journal Sq Fl 8 Jersey City NJ 07306-4006

HERO, BARBARA FERRELL, art educator; b. L.A., Jan. 3, 1925; d. Paul C. and Lucile (Evans) Ferrell; children: Alfred O. III, Barbara Ann Hero Ruyle, Michelle Claire, David Evans. BA in Art, George Washington U., 1950; EdM in Math., Boston U., 1980. Art tchr. Marjory Webster Jr. Coll., Washington, 1953-54; printmaker, painter, 1948—; visiting artist lectr. U. Mass, Amherst, 1970's, Rochester (N.Y.) Inst. Tech., 1970's, U.S. Psychotronics Assn., Chgo., 1981-89; musical sound creator, Acoustic Brain Rsch., N.C., 1989. Exhibited in Carcoran Gallery of Art (Contemporary Am. Artist Series), 1950; paintings in collections: Chase Manhattan Bank, N.Y.C., 1960's, Miami (Fla.) Dade U., 1960's; contbr. articles to profl. jours. Mem. Math. Assn. Am., N.Y. Acad. Sci.

HEROLD, EDWARD WILLIAM, electrical engineer; b. N.Y.C., Oct. 15, 1907; s. Carl Frederick and Marie (Wollersheim) H.; m. Alexandra Dacis, Aug. 4, 1931; 1 dau., Linda Marlene Herold Johnson. B.S., U. Va., 1930; M.S., Poly. Inst. Bklyn., 1942, D.Sc. (hon.), 1961. Registered profl. engr., N.J. Research asst. Bell Telephone Labs., N.Y.C., 1924-26; engr. E.T. Cunningham Co., N.Y.C., 1927-29, RCA, Harrison, N.J., 1930-42; successively mem. tech. staff, dir. tube lab., dir. electronic research lab. RCA Labs., Princeton, N.J., 1942-59; v.p. research Varian Assos., Palo Alto, Calif., 1959-64; dir. tech. RCA Corp., Princeton, 1965-72; cons. electronics, mgmt. and patents, 1972—; bd. dirs. Inst. Radio Engrs., 1956-58, Engring. Found., 1975-78; chmn. bd. Palisades Inst., 1969-84; adv. council elec. engring. dept. Princeton U., 1957-71; cons. Dept. Def., 1950-76. Co-author: Color Television Picture Tubes, 1974; Author 50 tech. articles in field. Fellow IEEE (Founder's medal 1976); mem. Phi Beta Kappa, Sigma Xi. Address: 332 Riverside Dr E Princeton NJ 08540

HEROLD, RICHARD CARL, developmental biology educator; b. Butler, Pa., June 13, 1927; s. Carl Theodore and Charlotte Emma (Black) H. BS in Zoology, Pa. State U., 1950, MS in Zoology, 1951; PhD in Biology, U. Pa., Phila., 1961. Chemist Aeroprojects Inc., Westchester, Pa., 1953-57; jr. rsch. fellow Inst. Coop. Rsch., Phila., 1957-63; hon. rsch. fellow Univ. Coll., London, U.K., 1983-84; prof. devel. biology U. Pa., Phila., 1963—; dir. Swans Island Marine Lab., Minturn, Maine, 1966-89. Contbr. articles to profl. jours.; patentee in field. Founding mem. French Creek Assn., Chester Springs, Pa. Sigma Xi grantee NIH, Washington, 1986-91. Fellow Royal Hort. Soc., Royal Microscopical Soc.; mem. Electron Microscope Soc. Home: RR 1 Phoenixville PA 19460-9801

HERON, NYE BRIAN, art association administrator; b. Dublin, Ireland, June 25, 1952; came to U.S., 1973; s. Seamus Connolly and Maura (Sutton) H.; m. Kathleen Sheahan, June 30, 1980; children: Maura, Kara. Student, London U., 1970-72. Exec. dir. Irish Arts Ctr., N.Y.C., 1973—. Author: (plays) Siamsa, 1978, Donkey Hunting, 1989. Recipient Obie award, N.Y.C., 1987. Office: Irish Arts Ctr 553 W 51st St New York NY 10019-5019

HERPST, ROBERT DIX, lawyer, optical company executive, food executive; b. Teaneck, N.J., Jan. 23, 1947; s. Harold Dix and Anita Augusta (Adams) H.; children: Katherine Elizabeth, Lauren Gabriel; m. Theresa M. Jacobini, Oct. 24, 1987. BS, NYU, 1969; JD, Rutgers U., 1972. Bar: N.J., U.S. Supreme Ct. Assoc. Pitney, Hardin & Kipp, Morristown, N.J., 1972-77, BOC Group, Inc., Montvale, N.J., 1977-89; cons., 1989—; div. counsel BOC Group, Inc., Montvale, 1978-80, assoc. corp. counsel, 1980-82, corp. counsel, asst. sec., 1982-88, pres.; pres. Internat. Crystal Labs., Garfield, N.J., 1982-88, chmn. bd. dirs., 1988—; pres. NikeSyrena Corp., Warsaw, Poland, 1989—. Mem. ABA (internat. bus. law com., overseas equity and joint venture investment subcom. of corp., banking and bus. law sect.). Home: 13422 Palm Dr 1 Lincoln St Astatula FL 34705 Office: Internat Crystal Labs 11 Erie St Garfield NJ 07026-2307

HERR, PHILIP MICHAEL, lawyer; b. N.Y.C., June 22, 1955; s. Norman and Grace (Sporn) H.; m. Lorrie Wiener, Nov. 23, 1978; children: Gabrielle, Nicole, Adam. BS, BA magna cum laude, Long Island U., C.W. Post Ctr., 1977; JD, Ohio No. U., 1980. Bar: N.Y. 1981, U.S. Tax Ct. 1982. Tax staff Ernst & Whinney, N.Y.C., 1980-82; tax sr. Arthur Young & Co., N.Y.C., 1982-83; tax supr. Wiss & Co., Livingston, N.J., 1983-88; tax mgr. Spicer & Oppenheim, N.Y.C., 1988-90, Goldstein Golub Kessler & Co., N.Y.C., 1990—; adj. prof. bus. Ohio No. U., Ada, 1978-80, Fairleigh Dickinson U., Rutherford, N.J., 1983-86. Contbr. articles to profl. jours., chpt. to book. Mem. N.Y. Bar Assn., N.Y. Employee Benefits Group, Pi Gamma Mu. Jewish. Home: 8 Cross Ln Marlboro NJ 07746-1760 Office: Goldsten Golub Kessler & Co 1185 Ave Of The Americas New York NY 10036-2601

HERREGAT, GUY-GEORGES JACQUES, banker; b. Oostende, West Flanders, Belgium, July 22, 1939; came to U.S., 1966; s. Georges-Albert Maurice and Marie-Gerard S. (Elleboudt) H. Licence en philosophie, U. Louvain, 1961, licence en philosophie et lettres, 1964; postgrad., Yale U., 1966-67, PhD in Econs., 1972. Rsch. asst. U. Louvain (Belgium), 1964-66; rsch. assoc. Nat. Bur. Econ. Rsch., N.Y.C., 1967-72; internat. economist Brown Bros. Harriman & Co., N.Y.C., 1973-74; asst. v.p. Chem. Bank, N.Y.C., 1974-76; dep. chief economist European Am. Bank, N.Y.C., 1977-80; sr. advisor, sr. v.p. Societe Generale de Banque, N.Y.C., 1980-85; mgr. Banque Worms, N.Y.C., 1985-86; sr. v.p., dep. gen. mgr. Credit du Nord, N.Y.C., 1986—; cons. Am. Bankers Assn., N.Y.C., 1971, SEIDEIS-Futuribles, Paris, 1967-80, Ford Found., N.Y.C., 1972-73. Author: Managerial Profiles and Investment Patterns, 1972, (with others) The Diffusion of New Industrial Processes, 1974, THe Finances of the Performing Arts, 1974; contbr. articles to profl. jours. Yale U. fellow, 1966-67, Nat. Bur. Econ. Rsch. fellow, 1971-72; named Aspirant de Recherches Fonds National Belge de la Recherche Scientifique, 1967-72. Mem. Am. Econ. Assn., Acad. Polit. Sci., Yale Alumni Assn., Japan Soc., Inst. Internat. Bankers, Belgian-Am. C. of C. (bd. dirs. 1986—). Home: 30 E 81st St New York NY 10028-0222 also: 253 Atlantic Fire Island Pines NY 11782 also: 800 West Ave Miami Beach FL 33139 Office: Credit du Nord 520 Madison Ave New York NY 10022-4213

HERRELL, JAMES MILTON, psychologist; b. Austin, Tex., Feb. 17, 1943; s. James Ray and Georgia Maxine (Porter) H.; m. Ileana Collado, June 26, 1965; children: Christine, Robert. BA in Psychology, U. Tex., 1963; MA in Psychology, U. Md., 1965, PhD in Psychology, 1967; MPH, Johns Hopkins U., Balt., 1992. Lic. psychologist, Md., D.C.; cert. mental health adminstr. Dir. mental health Dept. Health, Montgomery County, Md., 1972-86; dir. spl. programs Dept. Addiction Victim and Mental Health Svcs., Montgomery County, Md.; chief exec. officer Psychol. Systems Internat., Potomac, Md., 1985—; part-time faculty St. Mary's U., San Antonio, 1968, Our Lady of the Lake Coll., San Antonio, 1968, U. Md., 1969-81, George Washington U., 1970-73, George Mason U., Fairfax, Va., 1979; cons. Pan Am. Health Orgn., Washington, 1980—, WHO, Geneva, 1989, USIA, Washington, 1985, Fundacion Convivir, Buenos Aires, 1989. Author: Drug Abuse Prevention, 1985; contbr. articles to profl. jours. Mem. Community Action Bd., Montgomery County, 1987—, Commn. for People with Disabilities, 1987—, Cancer Prevention Task Force, 1990—, Mental Health Adv. Com., 1972-85, Commn. on Aging, 1987—. Capt. U.S. Army, 1966-71. Decorated Bronze Star medal. Mem. APA, APHA, Assn. of Mental Health Adminstrs., Am. Coll. Health Care Execs., Md. Gerontol. Assn., Md. Psychol. Assn., Delta Omega. Home: 8717 Belmart Rd Rockville MD 20854-1610 Office: DAVMHS 401 Hungerford Dr Rockville MD 20850-4155

HERRERA, PAUL FREDRICK, accountant; b. Manilla, Philippines, Aug. 31, 1948; came to U.S., 1949 (parents Am. citizens); s. Raymond Mix and Emily Irene (Smith) H.; m. Valerie Ann Derryberry, June 24, 1982. BA, Washington U., 1970; M in Acctg., U. Ariz., 1977. CPA, Tex., N.Y. Sr. mgr. Price Waterhouse, Houston, 1976-86; ptnr. Deloitte & Touche (and predecessor firms), N.Y.C., 1986—. Capt. U.S. Army, 1970-75. Mem. Am. Inst. CPA's. Office: Deloitte & Touche 1 World Trade Ctr New York NY 10048

HERRESHOFF, HALSEY CHASE, architect; b. Providence, Sept. 6, 1933; s. A. Sidney DeWolf and Rebecca (Chase) H. BS, Webb Inst. Naval Architecture, 1955; MS, MIT, 1960. Registered profl. engr., Mass. Naval architect Bethlehem Steel Co., Quincy, Mass., 1960-63; instr. MIT, Cambridge, 1963-68; v.p. Herreshoff & Kerwin, Boston, 1963-83; pres. Herreshoff Designs, Boston, Bristol, R.I., 1972—, Halsey C. Herreshoff Inc., Bristol, 1967—, Herreshoff Marine Mus., Bristol, 1977—. Author: Sailing Handbook, 1980; designer boats and yachts, 1967—. Town councillor, Bristol, 1982-86; town adminstr., Bristol, 1986—; pres. Bristol Mus. Assn., 1980-82; crew mem., navigator Am.'s Cup Races, 1958, 74, 80, 83. Served to lt. USNR, 1955-59. Mem. Soc. Naval Architects Marine Engrs., Profl. Engrs. Soc. Republican. Episcopalian. Clubs: N.Y. Yacht, Bristol Yacht. Home: 125 Hope St Bristol RI 02809-2047 Office: Town of Bristol 10 Court St Bristol RI 02809-2208

HERRICK, ELBERT CHARLES, chemist, consultant; b. Joliet, Mont., Oct. 16, 1919; s. Charles Albert and Marie (Johnson) H.; m. Doris Christine Brock, June 1, 1962; children: David, Dennis, Douglas, Donna. BSChemE, Mont. State U., 1941; degree of ChemE, Princeton U., 1942; PhD in Organic Chemistry, MIT, 1949. Rsch. chemist Cen. Rsch. Dept. E.I. duPont de Nemours, 1949-54; assoc. rsch. chemist Houdry Process Corp., 1955-58; supr. chem. rsch. Climax Molybdenum Co., Mich., 1958-59; sr. rsch. chemist R&D div. Sun Oil Co., 1959-61; sr. rsch. chemist Textile Fibers div. Dow Chem. Co., 1962-64; cons. chemist and chem. engrs. pvt. practice, 1964-65; organic sect. head Great Lakes Rsch. Corp., 1965-67; dir. chem. rsch. Escambia Chem. Corp., 1967-69; sr. rsch. chemist Air Products and Chems., Inc., 1969-77; sr. chem. engr., scientist Tracor Jitco, Inc., 1977; environ. systems scientist The MITRE Corp., 1977-88; sr. staff specialist Dynamac Corp., 1988-89; pvt. practice Woodbine, Md., 1989—. Patentee in field; contbr. articles to profl. jours. Lt. USAF, 1942-45, ETO. Fellow Am. Inst. Chemists; mem. Am. Inst. Chem. Engrs., Am. Chem. Soc., N.Y. Acad. Scis., Sigma Xi, Tau Beta Pi, Phi Kappa Phi. Republican. Adventist. Home and Office: 2740 Florence Rd Woodbine MD 21797-7841

HERRICK, KRISTINE FORD, graphic design educator; b. Bryn Mawr, Pa., Feb. 7, 1947; d. Charles Burton and Leah (Bosler) Ford; m. Stephen Wickes Herrick, Oct. 11, 1969 (div. Apr. 1982); 1 child, Kristian Wickes; m. Lee M. Smith, June 6, 1987; 1 stepchild, Suzannah Stuart Smith. BS, Skidmore Coll., 1969; MFA, Temple U., 1983. Cert. art tchr., N.Y. Layout artist Capital Newspapers, Albany, N.Y., 1969-70; designer Slocum House Pub., Albany, N.Y., 1970; asst. art dir. Gen. Electric Co., Schenectady, N.Y., 1970-72; art dir. Kirkman 3 Advt., Albany, 1972-75; from instr. to asst. prof. Tyler Sch. Art Temple U., 1980-85; design cons. Springhouse (Pa.) Corp., 1983-85; asst. prof., program coordinator graphic design Coll. St. Rose, Albany, 1985—. Author: Trademarks, A History, 1982, Trademarks, An Evolution, 1983. V.p. Ctr. Sq. Assn., Albany, 1972—; founding mem. Historic Albany Assn., 1974—; bd. dirs. Berkshire Ballet Co., Albany, 1988—. Grantee for excellence in teaching Sears Roebuck Found., 1990. Mem. Am. Inst. of The Graphic Arts, Univ. and Coll. Designers Assn., Graphic Design Education Assn., Albany Area Advt. Club, The Creative Club, Am. Ctr. for Design. Office: Coll St Rose 432 Western Ave Albany NY 12203-1490

HERRICK, PETER, banker; b. White Plains, N.Y., Nov. 10, 1926; s. Harold and Alta (Lake) H.; m. Beatricia Bierau, Oct. 7, 1950; children: David, Wendy. AB, Williams Coll., 1950. With The Bank of N.Y., N.Y.C., 1951—; v.p. The Bank of N.Y., 1967-72, sr. v.p., 1973-79, exec. v.p., chief comml. banking officer, 1979-82, pres., chief operating officer, dir., 1982-90, vice chmn., 1990-92; bd. dirs. The Bank of N.Y. Co., Inc., HRE Properties; mem. Brit. N.Am. Com.; trustee N.Y. State Banking Bd. Bd. dirs. Better Bus. Bur. Met. N.Y.; trustee Hood Coll.; bd. govs. Hundred Yr. Assn. N.Y. Served with U.S. Army Air Corps, 1944-46; with USAF, 1950-51. Mem. N.Y. State Bankers Assn. (past bd. dirs., pres.), Shenorock Shore Club, Siwanoy Country Club. Office: Bank of NY 1 Wall St New York NY 10286-0001

HERRIDGE, PETER LAMONT, psychiatrist; b. N.Y.C., Sept. 4, 1951; s. Robert Troy and Irene (Klempner) H.; m. Deborah Ann Branigan, June 18, 1983; children: Justin Lamont, Matthew Troy. BS in Physics, Carnegie Mellon U., 1975; MD, Albert Einstien Coll., 1980. Diplomate Am. Bd. Psychiatry and Neurology. Resident psyciatry McLean Hosp. Harvard Med. Sch., Belmont, Mass., 1981-84; assoc. dir. neuropsyciatric evaluation unit Fair Oaks Hosp., Summit, N.J., 1986—; clin. fellow in psychiatry Harvard Med. Sch., Boston, 1984-86; clin. rsch. fellow Harvard Med. Sch., 1983, instr. psychiatry, 1984-86, asst. psychiatrist, 1984-86; chief resident for psychopharmacology McLean Hosp., 1983, sr. rsch. resident, 1983, psychiatrist-in-charge, 1984-86. Contbr. 12 articles to profl. jours. Mem. Am. Psychiatric Assn., Alpha Omega Alpha. Episcopalian. Office: Fair Oaks Hosp 19 Prospect St Summit NJ 07901-2442

HERRING, DAVID LAWRENCE, graphic artist; b. Bklyn., May 11, 1946; s. Sylvester Stephen and Helen (Chatterton) H. Grad. high sch., N.Y.C. Advt. artist The Christian Monitor, Boston, 1974-84, advt. art dir., 1984-87; sr. design artist World Monitor mag., Boston, 1987—. Sgt. U.S. Army, 1968-70, Vietnam. Home: 11 Byron Rd 482 Beacon St Apt 42 Ashland MA 01721 Office: World Monitor Mag 1 Norway St Boston MA 02115

HERRMANN, CYNTHIA CECILIA WIEBER, financial services system executive; b. Plainview, Tex., Dec. 17, 1951; d. Jerome John and Erma Cecilia (Mellgren) Wieber; m. Raymond Edward Herrmann, Sept. 7, 1991. BS, Pratt Inst., 1973; MBA, NYU, 1978. Data base systems programmer Western Electric, N.Y.C., 1973-75; sr. systems analyst Merrill Lynch, N.Y.C., 1975-77; sr. cons. Price Waterhouse, N.Y.C., 1977-78, mgr., 1979-81; project mgr. Morgan Stanley, N.Y.C., 1981-83; avp Info. Systems Planning Merrill Lynch, N.Y.C., 1983-84, v.p. Global Equities, 1985-87, v.p. Fgn. Exchange System, 1988-89; v.p., mgr. Inst. Sales Systems, N.Y.C., 1989—; project mgr. Share, 1977-82; mem. Securities Industry Assn., N.Y.C., 1981-85, Fin. Women Internat., 1992. Mem. Mus. Modern Art, Bklyn. Bot. Garden, Goddard Riverside Community Ctr., Berkshire Garden Ctr. Home: 115 E 9th St New York NY 10003 Office: Merrill Lynch World Financial Ctr S Tower New York NY 10080

HERRMANN, JOHN B., surgery educator; b. Cin., Nov. 21, 1932; s. Louis George and Marion (Bellows) H.; m. MaryJane Gaiser, Sept. 3, 1960; children: Christian L., Karen, Mark E. AB, Dartmouth Coll., 1954, cert. medicine, 1955; MD, Harvard U., 1957. Cert. Am. Bd. Surgery, N.B.M.E. Surg. intern Mass. Gen. Hosp., Boston, 1957-58, surg. resident, 1958-62; rsch. surgeon Walter Reed Army Inst. Rsch., Washington, 1962-64; asst. in

surgery Mass. Gen. Hosp., Boston, 1964-65; from. asst. prof. to assoc. prof. Georgetown U., Washington, 1965-72; prof. surgery U. Mass., Worcester, 1972—; chief of surgery Worcester City Hosp., 1972-83; vice chair surgery U. Mass. Med. Sch., Worcester, 1972—. Co-author: Case Studies in General Surgery, 1987; contbr. articles to profl. jours. Bd. dirs. local community group, Worcester, 1989—. Fellow Am. Coll. Surgeons; mem. Mass. Med. Soc., Worcester Dist. Med. Soc. (councilor 1988—), New Eng. Surg. Soc., New Eng. Soc. for Vascular Surgery (v.p. 1990-91), Soc. for Surg. Edn., Assn. Program Dirs. in Surgery, Assn. for Acad. Surgery. Office: U Mass Med Ctr 55 Lake Ave N Worcester MA 01655-0001

HERRMANN, KENNETH JOHN, JR., social work educator; b. Lackawanna, N.Y., Apr. 13, 1943; s. Kenneth John and Alice Jane (Gray) H.; m. Kathleen Wolf, Oct. 1969 (div. 1986); children: Kim-Eui, Gabe Sang-Koo, Mark Hoi-Duk, Rachele Hoi-Im, Ruth Myung-Hee. BA, Canisius Coll., 1972; MSW, SUNY, Buffalo, 1975. Tchr. St. Monica's Sch., Buffalo, 1963-67; sr. caseworker Erie County Child Welfare, Buffalo, 1969-73; family therapist Wyndham Lawn Home for Children, Lockport, N.Y., 1975-77; dir. children's svcs. Dept. Social Svc. County of Genesee (N.Y.), 1977-78; assoc. prof. social work SUNY, Brockport, 1978—; pvt. practice psychotherapy East Pembroke, N.Y., 1975—; adoption social worker Dillon Children's Svcs. Intercountry Adoption Program, 1982-84; internat. adoption social worker New Beginnings Child and Family Svcs., 1989—; dir. clin. svcs. 'Nam Era Svcs. Ctr., Batavia, N.Y., 1991—; mem. state bd. for social work N.Y. State Edn. Dept., 1984—; cons. UN Children's Fund, U.S. Senate, U.S. Congress; radio and TV appearances, lectr., cons. on children's rights, child abuse and neglect, fmaily violence. Author: I Hope My Daddy Dies, Mister, 1975, I'm Nobody's Child, 1982; author studies on internat. children's issues; contbr. articles to profl. jours. With U.S. Army, 1967-69. Mem. NASW, Def. for Children Internat., Vietnam Vets. Am., OURS, Bertha Capen Reynolds Soc. Home: 2614 E Main Rd East Pembroke NY 14056-0067 Office: SUNY Faculty Office Bldg Brockport NY 14420

HERRMANN, LACY BUNNELL, investment company executive, financial entrepreneur, venture capitalist; b. New Haven, May 12, 1929; s. James Joseph and Helen Georgia (Bunnell) H.; m. Elizabeth Ocumpaugh Beadle, May 23, 1953; children: Diana Parsons, Conrad Beadle. AB, Brown U., 1950; postgrad., London Sch. Econs., 1953-54; MBA, Harvard U., 1956. Asst. to purchasing mgr. and buyer Westinghouse Elec. Corp., Metuchen, N.J., 1956-60; asst. v.p. Douglas T. Johnston & Co., Inc., N.Y.C., 1960-66; v.p. Johnston Mut. Fund, Inc., N.Y.C., 1964-66; gen. ptnr. Tamarack Assocs., N.Y.C., 1966-84; chmn. bd., pres. Family Home Products, Inc., N.Y.C., 1972-84, Buxton's Country Shops, Jamesburg, N.J., 1973-86; pres., dir. STCM Mgmt. Co., Inc., N.Y.C., 1974—; founder, pres. STCM Corp., money market fund, N.Y.C., 1974-76; vice chmn. bd. trustees, v.p. Centennial Capital Cash Mgmt. Trust, N.Y.C. successor to STCM Corp., 1976-81; chmn. bd. trustees, pres. successor fund Capital Cash Mgmt. Trust, 1981—; pres., bd. dir. Incap Mgmt. Corp., 1982—; founder, chmn. bd. trustees, pres. Trinity Liquid Assets Trust, 1982-85, Oxford Cash Mgmt. Fund, 1982-88, Prime Cash Fund, 1982—, Cash Assets Trust, 1984—, Short Term Asset Res., 1984—, Hawaiian Tax-Free Trust, 1985—, Churchill Cash Res. Trust, 1985—, Tax Free Trust Ariz., 1986—, Tax Free Trust Oreg., 1986—, Tax Free Fund Colo., 1987—, Churchill Tax-Free Fund Ky., 1987—, Churchill Tax-Free Cash Fund, 1988—, Tax-Free Cash Asset Trust, 1988—, U.S. Treasuries Cash Assets Trust, 1988—, Cascades Cash Fund, 1989—, Narragansett Insured Tax Free Income Fund, 1992—, Tax Free Fund for Utah, 1992—, Saguaro Insured Tax Free Income Fund, 1992—; chmn., pres. Aquila Mgmt. Corp., 1983—, sponsor, adminstr. mut. funds; bd. dirs., v.p. Aquila Distbrs. Inc., 1981—, distbr. mut. funds; bd. dirs. Quest for Value Fund Investment Trust, Quest for Value Accumulation Trust, Quest Cash Res., Inc.; founder, chmn. bd. trustees, pres. N.Y. Localities Legal Obligations Cash Access Trust; chmn. Fiduciary Mgmt. Inc.; adviser Access, 1982—; organizer, bd. dir. and/or cons. to numerous small to medium sized corps. and orgns.; founding dir. mgmt. cons. firm merged with Towers, Perrin, Forster & Crosby; instr. Rutgers U., 1958-59; speaker various profl. investment orgns. Contbr. articles to profl. jours. Organizer, trustee endowed award Internat. div. Grad. Sch. Journalism, Columbia U., 1962—; trustee Meml. and Endowment Trust of St. Paul's Ch., Westfield, N.J., 1968—; mem. capital devel. com. St. Luke's Ch., Darien, Conn., 1978-85; mem. coll. scholarship fund com. St. Luke's Ch., Darien, Conn., 1976-85; trustee Brown U., 1990—. Lt. (j.g.) USN, 1951-54, Korea; lt. USNR ret. Mem. N.Y. Soc. Security Analysts, Harvard Bus. Sch. Club N.Y. (bd. dirs., officer, 1958-71), Assoc. Alumni Brown U. (bd. dirs. 1978-87, exec. com. 1980-85, pres. 1983-85), Harvard Club, N.Y. Athletic Club, Brown U. Club, N.Y.C. Club (bd. dirs. 1981-88), Brown U. of Fairfield Country Club (pres. 1977-82, bd. dirs. 1977—), Univ. Club (R.I.), Faculty Club Brown U. (Providence), Stratton Mountain Country Club (Vt.), Orleans Yacht Club (Mass.), Ariz. Club, Outrigger Canoe Club (Honolulu). Republican. Episcopalian. Home: 6 Whaling Rd Darien CT 06820-5930 Office: 380 Madison Ave New York NY 10017-2513

HERROLD, EDMUND MCMAHAN, internal medicine educator; b. N.Y.C., Feb. 22, 1949; s. Kenneth Frederick and Elizabeth (McMahan) H.; m. Ellen Jane Yamaguchi, Aug. 5, 1978; children: Kristin McMahan, Emily Jane. BS, Lehigh U., 1971; MD, PhD, Case Western Res. U., 1979. Diplomate Am. Bd. Internal Medicine, Bd. Cardiovascular Disease. Instr. medicine Case Western Res. U., Cleve., 1979-82; instr. medicine Cornell U. Med. Coll., N.Y.C., 1982-85, asst. prof. medicine, 1985-91, assoc. prof. medicine, 1991—; asst. attending physician N.Y. Hosp., N.Y.C., 1984-91, assoc. attending physician, 1991—; assoc. dir. nuclear cardiology, cardiology div., Cornell Med. Ctr., N.Y.C., 1991—. Contbr. articles to profl. jours. Recipient fellowship NSF, 1968, Samuel Haas Found., 1972-77. Fellow Am. Coll. Cardiology, Am. Heart Assn. (cardiovascular coun., Investigator 1985-88), N.Y. Cardiological Soc.; mem. IEEE, Am. Coll. Physicians, Am. Fedn. for Clin. Rsch., Soc. Nuclear Medicine. Home: 181 E 73d St 2A New York NY 10021 Office: NY Hosp Cornell Med Ctr 525 E 68th St New York NY 10021

HERRON, GEORGIA JOHNSON, educator; b. Washington, Nov. 19, 1924; d. Richard H.T. and Lucy Elizabeth (Lumpkins) Johnson; m. Oscar Smith Herron, Sr., Oct. 13, 1946; children—Carol, Smitty. B.S. in Edn., Miner Tchrs. Coll., Washington, 1946; M.A. in Edn., Trinity Coll., Washington, 1973. Tchr. pub. schs., Washington, 1946-76; team leader Tchr. Corps., 1974-75; instr. talented and gifted program Howard U., Washington, 1978-81, lectr. Sch. of Edn., 1979-81; sci. enrichment tchr. Shepherd Elem. Sch., Washington, 1981-84; curriculum developer Beers Model Sci. Lab., Washington, 1983—; guest lectr. Am. U., 1985, Trinity Coll., Washington, 1988; vol. sci. tchr. D.C. Pub. schs., 1976—; instr. elem. sci. U. D.C., 1987—, coord. vol. svcs., 1986—, vol. coord., instr. elem. sci. lab., 1990—; vol. instr. Audubon Naturalists Soc., 1983-91. Bd. dirs. Takoma Park Bapt. Tutorial Program, Washington, 1968; coordinator Green Guards, Washington, 1971-74. Named Tchr. of Yr., Sch. of Edn. Howard U., 1980, 81; recipient award for excellence in teaching sci. D.C. Joint Bd. Sci. and Engring. Edn., 1984. Mem. Nat. Sci. Tchrs. Am., D.C. Sci. Educators Assn. (Outstanding Sci. Educator of Yr. 1982), Audubon Naturalists Soc., Les Jolissantes Club, Young Ladies Club (Washington), Kiwanis (sec.), U. D.C. Alumni Assn. Democrat. Baptist. Home: 6514 7th St NW Washington DC 20012-2622

HERRON, THOMAS J., academic dean; b. Phila., Sept. 8, 1947; s. Thomas J. and Mary M. (Welsh) H. BA, St. Charles Sem., Overbrook, Pa., 1969; MDiv, 1973; SSL, Biblical Inst., Rome, 1979; STD, Gregorian U., Rome, 1986. Asst. pastor St. Albert the Great, Huntingdon Valley, Pa., 1973-76; tchr. Arch. Kennedy Highschool, Conshohocken, 1979-82; staff Congregation for the Doctrine of the Faith, Rome, 1982-88; academic dean St. Charles Sem., Overbrook, Pa., 1988—; chmn. Archdiocesan Med. Moral Com., Phila., 1989—, censor librorum Archdiocese of Phila., 1989—, chaplain Phila. Chpt. of Legatus, 1989—. Author: Most Probable Date of First Clement, 1987; editor: Catholic Priest as Moral Teacher, 1990; contbr. articles in profl. jours. Papal Chamberlain , Holy See, Vatican City, 1987; Prelate of Honor of His Holiness, Vatican City, 1991. Mem. Cath. Bibl. Assn., Cath. Theol. Soc., Assn. of Theol. Schools, Middles States Accrediting Agy. Roman Catholic. Home: 1000 E Wynnewood Rd Wynnewood PA 19096-3002

HERSCHBACH, DUDLEY ROBERT, chemistry educator; b. San Jose, Calif., June 18, 1932; s. Robert Dudley and Dorothy Edith (Beer) H.; m. Georgene Lee Botyos, Dec. 26, 1964; children: Lisa Marie, Brenda Michele. BS in Math., Stanford U., 1954, MS in Chemistry, 1955; AM in Physics, Harvard U., 1956, PhD in Chem. Physics, 1958; DSc (hon.), U. Toronto, 1977, Cornell Coll., 1988, Framingham State Coll., 1989, Adelphi U., 1990. Jr. fellow Harvard U., Cambridge, Mass., 1957-59, prof. chemistry, 1963-76, Frank B. Baird prof. sci., 1976—, mem. faculty council, 1980-83, master Currier House, 1981-86; asst. prof. U. Calif., Berkeley, 1959-61, assoc. prof., 1961-63; cons. editor W.H. Freeman lectr. Haverford Coll., 1962; Falk-Plaut lectr. Columbia, 1963; vis. prof. Gottingen (Germany) U., summer, 1963, U. Calif., Santa Cruz, 1972; Harvard lectr. Yale U., 1964; Debye lectr. Cornell U., 1966, Rollefson lectr. U. Calif., Berkeley, 1969, Reilly lectr. U. Notre Dame, 1969, Phillips lectr. U. Pitts., 1971; disting. vis. prof. U. Ariz., 1971, U. Tex., 1977, U. Utah, 1978, Gordon lectr. U. Toronto, 1971, Clark lectr. San Jose State U., 1979, Hill lectr., Duke U., 1988, Priestly lectr. Pa. State U., 1990, Kaufman lectr. U. Pa., 1990, Polanyi lectr. U. N.C., 1991, Dreyfus lectr. Dartmouth Coll., 1992. Assoc. editor: Jour Phys. Chemistry, 1980-88.. Guggenheim fellow U. Freiburg, Germany, 1968; vis. fellow Joint Inst. for Lab. Astrophysics U. Colo., 1969; Fairchild Disting. scholar Calif. Inst. Tech., 1976; Sloan fellow, 1959-63, Exxon Faculty fellow, 1980—; recipient pure chemistry award Am. Chem. Soc., 1965, Centenary medal, 1977, Pauling medal, 1978; Spiers medal Faraday Soc., 1976, Polanyi medal, 1981, Langmuir prize, 1983, Nobel Prize in Chemistry, 1986, Nat. Medal of Sci. 1991; named to Calif. Pub. Edn. Hall of Fame, 1987. Fellow Am. Phys Soc. (chmn. chem. physics div. 1971-72), Am. Acad. Arts and Scis.; mem. AAAS, Am. Chem. Soc., Nat. Acad. Scis., Royal Soc. Chemistry (fgn. hon. mem.), Am. Philos. Soc., Phi Beta Kappa (orator Harvard U. 1992), Sigma Xi. Office: Harvard U Dept Chemistry 12 Oxford St Cambridge MA 02138-2900

HERSCHITZ, ROMAN, scientist, researcher; b. Riga, Latvia, Sept. 3, 1954; s. Boruch and Selma (Schawel) H. BA, CUNY, 1977; MS, Cornell U., 1980, PhD, 1983. Prin. mem. tech. staff Gen. Electric Astro-Space Div., Princeton, N.J., 1983—; vis. lectr. Trenton (N.J.) State Coll., 1984-88, Rutgers U., New Brunswick, N.J., 1985. Inventor spacebased solar arrays; contbr. articles to profl. jours. Cornell U. scholar, 1978. Mem. AIAA, IEEE, Gen. Electric Engring. Excellence Com., Nat. Superconducting Consortium for Aerospace Applications, Ben Franklin Superconducting Consortium. Republican. Jewish. Home: 24-13 Ravens Crest Plainsboro NJ 08536 Office: Gen Electric Astro Space PO Box 800 Princeton NJ 08543-0800

HERSEY, JUDE SULLIVAN, social services administrator; b. Hartford, Conn., July 26, 1941; d. George Leonard and Cornelia (Hartnett) Sullivan; m. Donald Roger Hersey, Sept. 1, 1962; children: Reese Jeremy, Ashley Samantha. Liberal Arts Degree, Hartford Coll. for Women, 1961; student, U. Conn., 1985-90, Charter Oak Coll., 1990—. Benefits coord. First Conn. Bancorp., Hartford, 1978-79; personnel asst. Conn. Natural Gas Corp., Hartford, 1980; customer relations rep. Conn. Natural Gas Corp., 1980-85; victims' advocate/lobbyist Trauma Victims' Support Group Conn., Wethersfield, 1985—; community outreach coord. Trinity Coll., Hartford, 1988-89; community svc. faculty fellow dept. higher edn. State of Conn., Hartford, 1989-91; coord. New Britain (Conn.) Vol. Action Ctr., 1991-92, Conn. Safe Kids, 1992—; mem. community svc. adv. bd. Trinity Coll., Hartford, 1988-89; mem. community svc. fellowship adv. com., 1988-90; chairperson Community Svc. Fellowship Campus Contact Network, 1989-91; cons. Trauma Victims' Support Group, Wethersfield, 1985—; presenter Panelist Post-Trauma and Families: Assessing Needs and Facilitating Svc. Conf. Newington Childrens Hosp., 1986, Role of Friendship in Healing after Trauma Workshop, 1987, Social Problems and Legis. Solutions workshop, 1987, Legal Resources and Legis. Resources Workshop Post Coll. Bereavement Conf., Waterbury, 1988, How to Understand and Help Victims of Trauma workshop, 1989, Community Svc. and Fin. Aid, 1989, The Power Game, 1990; moderator in field; panelist, workshop leader Women in Leadership Confs. U. Conn., 1991; guest speaker on volunteerism Quinnipiac Coll., 1991; guest speaker Student Community Svc. Conn. Coun. on Higher Edn., 1991; model workshop presenter, panelist Beyond 1,000 Points of Light Conf. U. Mass., 1991, Don't Count Out the Mothers: Support for Trauma Victims and Their Families Workshop at Trauma and Victimization Conf. U. Conn., Vernon, 1991; sec. Family Community Leadership of Conn., bd. dirs.; active Hartford Hosp. Trauma Support Team After-Care Program. Author: Books for Victims of Trauma, 1985; editor: Campus/Community Connections Bull. and Newsletter, Branching Out ... It's Happening yearend summary. Mem. Conn. Alliance for Ins. Reform, Hartford, 1986-87, Victims' Svc. Coord. Coun., Hartford, 1987—; co-founder, pres. Trauma Victims' Support Group Conn., Hartford, 1986—; planner, coord. Earth Day, 1990 planning session and Conn. Campus Compact Meeting, 1989; moderator State Compacts Workshop for Campus Compact, Washington, 1989; planner, coord. Rally for your Good Works and the Good Earth; panelist Gov.'s Couns. on Vol. Action Conn. Vol. Leadership Conf., 1990, 91; coord. Robinson Humanitarian Svc. award ceremony, 1990; planner, coord. Make a World of Difference Conf., 1991; conducted mock-interviews for Cen. Conn. State U. Co-operative Edn. Program, 1990, 91; coord. tng. workshop series on community svc. program devel, 1990-91. Recipient citation for pub. svc. Conn. Gen. Assembly, 1987, Spirer-Robinson Pub. Svc. award U. Conn., 1987, Gov.'s Victim Svc. award State of Conn., 1988, Model Student Community Svc. Initiative Adminstrn. award U. Mass., 1991, Sticking Your Neck Out-Outstanding Community Svc. award The Giraffe Project, 1991. Mem. Nat. Soc. for Internships and Experiential Edn., Nat. Orgn. for Victim Assistance, Family Community Leadership Inst., Am. Assn. Vol. Adminstrs., Conn. Self-Help and Mut. Support Network. Home: 29 Dale Rd Wethersfield CT 06109-3329

HERSH, BARRY FRED, real estate developer, urban planner; b. N.Y.C., May 10, 1947; s. Philip and Ruth (Rubin) H.; m. Jeanne Marie Gasda, July 11, 1972; children: Alayne Sara, Michelle Heather. BA, CUNY, 1968; M of Urban Planning, NYU, 1972. Lic. real estate broker, N.Y. Dir. planning Chase Assocs., Syracuse, N.Y., 1973-77; prin. planner plan commn. Toledo-Lucas Co., 1977-81; housing planner Stamford (Conn.) Mayor's Devel. Office, 1981-82; exec. dir. Westhab, Inc., Hartsdale, N.Y., 1982-83; project mgr. Reynolds Metals Devel. Co., Orangeburg, N.Y., 1984—; adj. asst. prof. geography and urban planning U. Toledo, 1979-81, Cen. Conn. State U., New Britain, 1982; co-chmn. fin. Waterfront Ctr., Washington, 1986—; co-chmn. mktg. Rockland Econ. Devel. Corp.; instr. Grad. Builders Inst., 1988. Author: (with others) Toledo Harbor Area Plan, 1979 (Great Lakes Assn. award 1979); contbr. articles to profl. jours. Dir. Conn. Commuters, 1989—; mem. pres.'s coun. Dominican Coll., Orangeburg, 1987; active Trumbull (Conn.) Econ. Devel. Task Force, 1986, Rockland 2000 Planning Group, New City, N.Y., 1987, UN Habitat Group, 1991. Recipient Housing for Homeless award N.Y. State, Yonkers, 1983, Econ. Devel. award Rockland County Exec., 1986; fellow Columbia U., 1971. Mem. Am. Planning Assn., Nat. Assn. Office and Ind. Park Developers (Nalop Lit. award 1989), N.Y. State Builders Assn., Rockland Builders Assn. (chmn. comml. div.), Am. Inst. Cert. Planners (cert.), Nat. Assn. Corp. Real Estate Execs., Urban Land Inst., Regional Plan Assn. (Fairfield housing com. 1986). Jewish. Home: 188 Park Ln Trumbull CT 06611-2343 Office: Reynolds Metals Devel Co 17 Corporate Dr Orangeburg NY 10962-2615

HERSH, BERNARD, architect; b. Phila., Oct. 31, 1922; s. Israel and Anna (Levy) H.; m. Mildred Schwartzbard, Mar. 9, 1946; children: Joseph H., Mitchell E., Marian Hersh Press. BArch, U. Pa., 1948, MArch, 1948. Registered architect, N.J., N.Y., Pa., Fla.; lic. profl. planner. Prin. Bernard Hersh AIA, Fair Lawn, N.J., 1954—. Prin. works included Marathon Enterprises Facilities, East Rutherford, N.J., Norelco, Magnavox, Temple Beth Sholom, Fair Lawn, N.J., Country Club Towers, Clifton, N.J., also shopping ctrs., N.Y., Conn. and N.J. Mem. Fair Lawn Borough Coun., 1975—, mayor, 1982-83, 1984-85, dep. mayor, 1978-81, 1983-84; mem. Bergen County Transp. Coordinating Com., 1985. Cpl. USAAC, 1942-46. Recipient Key Man award Jaycees, Paterson, N.J., 1952; placed Prestigious Paris prize, Warren prize. Mem. AIA, N.J. Soc. Architects (bd. dir. 1969), Architects League No. N.J. (from treas. to pres. 1969, Vegliante award 1969), No. N.J. Interprofl. Coun. (pres. 1973-74), Nat. Coun. Archtl. Registration Bds. (cert.). Home and Office: 12-31 Jerome Pl Fair Lawn NJ 07410

HERSH, IRA PAUL, tax and financial planning consultant; b. Bklyn., July 14, 1948; s. Saul and Mildred (Leibowitz) Hershkowitz; m. Jan Bennett; children: Marcy Fay, Gregory Alexander, Carrie Elizabeth. BA, Queens Coll., 1969. Tax mgr. Wiss and Co., N.Y.C., 1970-77; contr. Assets Adminstrn. and Mgmt., Stamford, Conn., 1978-79; tax mgr. Exec. Monetary Mgmt., Inc., N.Y.C., 1980-84; pvt. practice tax and fin. planning, 1985—; pres. MacArthur Equities Ltd., 1985—. Mem. Rolling Hills Country Club. Home and Office: 20 Branch Brook Rd Wilton CT 06897-1520

HERSH, SHELDON PAUL, physician; b. Germany, Dec. 23, 1947; came to U.S., 1949; s. Fred and Sarah (Cytrin) H.; m. Helen Rosenbaum, Aug. 3, 1969; children: David, Joshua, Jennifer. BA, Yeshiva U., 1969; MD, N.Y. Med. Coll., 1978. Intern Brookdale Hosp. Med. Ctr., Bklyn., 1978-79; resident Manhattan Eye, Ear, and Throat Hosp., N.Y.C., 1979-82. Contbr. articles to profl. jours. Fellow Am. Acad. Otolaryngology; mem. Am. Rhinologic Soc., N.Y. State Med. Soc., Queens Med. Soc. Office: 110-11 72 Ave Forest Hills NY 11375

HERSH, STANLEY BLAIR, ophthalmologist; b. Pitts., Jan. 15, 1943. BS, Bethany Coll., 1964; MD, Chgo. Med. Sch., 1969. Diplomate Am. Bd. Ophthalmology. Resident in ophthalmology Yale-New Haven Hosp., New Haven, 1976; ophthalmologist Ophthalmic Surg. Assocs., Waterbury, Conn., 1976—; mem. staff in ophthalmology Waterbury Hosp., St. Mary's Hosp., Yale-New Haven Hosp., Waterbury, 1976—; clin. asst. prof. ophthalmology Yale-New Haven Hosp., New Haven, 1976—; cons. West Haven Vets. Hosp., West Haven, 1976—. Mem. AMA, Conn. State Med. Soc., New Haven County Med. Soc., Waterbury Med. Soc., Alpha Omega Alpha,. Office: Ophthalmic Surg Assocs 1201 W Main St Waterbury CT 06708

HERSHBERG, PHILIP ISAAC, physician, electrical engineer, investment advisor; b. Albany, N.Y., Aug. 5, 1935; s. Ben B. and Ann (Gewirtzman) H.; m. Elena Sue Simon, Dec. 25, 1958; children: Jeffrey Aaron, Janet Rose, Matthew Charles. BEE, Rensselaer Poly. Inst., 1957; M Engring., Yale U., 1958; MD, SUNY, Bklyn., 1966. Lic. physician, Mass., N.Y., Calif.; registered profl. engr., Mass., N.Y.; registered investment advisor SEC. Engr. Norden-Kitay Corp., Milford, Conn., 1957-58, ITT Labs., Nuley, N.J., 1958-59; rsch. assoc. Maimonides Med. Ctr., Bklyn., 1962-66; assoc. in medicine Brigham & Women's Hosp., Boston, 1968-73; rsch. assoc., asst. prof. Harvard U. Sch. Pub. Health, Boston, 1968-73; rsch. assoc. Lahey Clinic Found., 1967-75; asst. prof. Boston U. Sch. Medicine, 1973-81; dir. rsch. NEICO Co., Hopkinton, Mass., 1981-83; v.p. INVOCOM, Inc., Hopkinton, Mass., 1983-85; investment advisor Deermont Market Ctr., Wellesley, Mass., 1985—; pvt. practice medicine, Lynn, Mass., 1987—; assoc. med. dir. Worcester County Hosp., Boylston, Mass., 1990—. Contbr. articles to med. and tech. jours.; patentee in biomed. field. 1st lt. USAF, 1959-62; surgeon USPHS, 1966-67. Clarkson fellow SUNY, Potsdam, 1958, fellow Royal Coll. Health (Eng.), 1963. Mem. IEEE, Am. Coll. Preventive Medicine, B'nai B'rith (pres. Needham-Wellesley 1986-88, svc. award 1985). Home: 43 Harris Ave PO Box 332 Needham MA 02192 Office: Deermont Market Ctr 70 Walnut St Wellesley MA 02181-2100

HERSHCOPF, BERTA RUTH, psychotherapist, writer; b. N.Y.C., Oct. 1, 1924; d. Samuel and Marian (Gzinterman) Feinman; m. Jack Hershcopf, June 11, 1947; children: Shelley, Amy, David. AA, Morris Jr. Coll., Morristown, N.J., 1942; BA, Douglass Coll., 1944; cert., Postgrad. Ctr. for Mental Health, N.Y.C., 1973, N.Y. Med. Coll., N.Y.C., 1977. Dir. U.S.O., Nebr., Wyo., N.Y., 1944-46; psychiatric clin. counselor Long Island Jewish Hillside Med. Ctr., New Hyde Park, N.Y., 1974-75; counseling therapist Mt. Sinai Hosp., N.Y.C., 1977-78; asst. dir. Psychoanalytic Ctr., N.Y.C., 1980-82; pvt. practice N.Y.C., 1973—; dir. Am. Counseling and Psychotherapy Svcs., N.Y.C., 1981—; cons., workshop leader Women's Rsch. Project CUNY, N.Y.C., 1975-76; cons. Nat. Urban League, 1979; workshop leader Ctr. for Interpersonal Growth at Fordham U., N.Y.C., 1979-80. Mem. N.Y. State Assn. Practicing Psychotherapists (cert.), Am. Asn. for Counseling and Devel., Am. Mental Health Counselors Assn. Home and Office: 875 Park Ave New York NY 10021-0341

HERSHENSON, HERBERT MALCOLM, turbine components manufacturing company executive; b. Bklyn., Feb. 17, 1929; s. Louis Lerner and Rose (Gordon) H.; m. Barbara Ruth Freedman, Dec. 5, 1953 (dec. Oct. 1981); children: Linda, Judi, Paul; m. Rita Dunn, July 1, 1984. SB in Chemistry, MIT, 1949, PhD in Analytical Chemistry, 1952. Asst. prof. U. Kans., Lawrence, 1952, Wesleyan U., Middletown, Conn., 1952-55; lab. supr. Conn. Aircraft Nuclear Engine Lab., Pratt & Whitney Aircraft, Middletown, 1955-58; asst. mgr. materials engring. and rsch. labs. Pratt & Whitney Aircraft, East Hartford, Conn., 1960-77; asst. tech. dir. Baird Atomic, Inc., Cambridge, Mass., 1958-60; v.p. Turbine Components Corp., Branford, Conn., 1977—; pres. The Amity Group, investment advisers, Branford, 1984—; adj. assoc. prof. Rensselaer Poly. Inst., Hartford, Conn., 1956-58; bd. dirs. Bridgeways Communication Corp., Branford. Author 7 books; also articles. Mem. Amity Regional Bd. Edn., Woodbridge, Conn., 1973-83, chmn., 1980-83; pres. Amity Ednl. Found., 1988—; bd. dirs. Jewish Community Ctr., Greater New Haven, 1989—, treas., 1991-92, pres., 1992—; pres. Congregation Mishkan Israel, Hamden, Conn., 1990-92. Mem. Am. Chem. Soc., Am. Soc. for Quality Control, Sigma Xi. Office: Turbine Components Corp PO Box 801 Branford CT 06405

HERSHEY, ALFRED DAY, geneticist; b. Owosso, Mich., Dec. 4, 1908; s. Robert Day and Alma (Wilbur) H.; m. Harriet Davidson, Nov. 15, 1945; 1 son, Peter. B.S., Mich. State U., 1930, Ph.D. in Chemistry, 1934, D.M.S., 1970; D.Sc. (hon.), U. Chgo., 1967. Asst. bacteriologist Washington U. Sch. Medicine, St. Louis, 1934-36; instr. Washington U. Sch. Medicine, 1936-38, asst. prof., 1938-42, asso. prof., 1942-50; mem. staff, genetics research unit Carnegie Inst. of Washington, Cold Spring Harbor, N.Y., 1950-62; dir. Carnegie Inst. of Washington, 1962-74; ret., 1974. Contbr. articles to profl. jours. Recipient Nobel prize in Medicine (joint), 1969; Albert Lasker award Am. Pub. Health Assn., 1958; Kimber Genetics award Nat. Acad. Scis., 1965. Mem. Nat. Acad. Scis. Address: RD 1640 Moores Hill Rd Syosset NY 11791

HERSHEY, COLIN HARRY, management consultant; b. Everett, Pa., Aug. 31, 1935; s. Harry and Marjorie (Nycum) H.; m. Jacqueline Anderson, June 14, 1974; children: Barclay Harry, Marjorie Anderson. BSCE, Lehigh U., 1957; MBA, U. Pitts., 1967, postgrad., 1968. Registered profl. engr., Pa. Civil engr. contracting div. Dravo Corp., Pitts., 1957-59, cost engr., 1961-63; field engr. Army Corps Engrs., Pitts., 1958-61; mgr. mgmt. info. systems, atomic power div. Westinghouse Electric Co., Pitts., 1964-67; counselor Planning Dynamics, Inc., Pitts., 1968-70, v.p., 1970-72, pres., 1972-77, pres., chmn., 1977—; pres. Planware, Inc., Pitts., 1985-86. Author, editor: Strategic Planning Concepts, 1985; contbr. articles to profl. jours. Mem. Am. Mgmt. Assn. (adv. com. Strategic Mgmt. Program), Planning Forum, Duquesne Club, Alpha Tau Omega, Chi Epsilon. Office: Planning Dynamics Inc 135 Industry Dr Pittsburgh PA 15275-1035

HERSHEY, ROBERT LEWIS, mechanical engineer, management consultant; b. Chgo., Dec. 18, 1941; s. Maurice and Rose Beverly (Barrish) H. BSME summa cum laude, Tufts U., 1963; MSME, MIT, 1964; PhD in Engring., Cath. U. Am., 1973. Registered profl. engr., D.C., N.Y.; cert. mfg. engr. Engr. Bell Telephone Labs., Whippany, N.J., 1963-67; acoustics mgr. Weston Instruments, Inc., Poughkeepsie, N.Y., 1967-68; sr. scientist Bolt Beranek & Newman, Washington, 1968-71; acoustics program mgr. Booz Allen & Hamilton, Bethesda, Md., 1971-79; program v.p. Sci. Mgmt. Corp., Washington, 1979-80; div. v.p. AEA O'Donnell (formerly SMC O'Donnell), 1980-88; exec. engr., 1988—; sec. Engring. Registration Bd., D.C., 1987—, D.C. Profl. Coun., Washington, 1974; mem. coordinating com. on productivity Am. Assn. Engring. Socs., Washington, 1984-88. Author: How to Think With Numbers, 1982; contbr. articles to profl. jours.; patentee tempo enhancement device. Sci. policy analyst George Bush Presdl. Campaign, Washington, 1988; pres. Hamilton House Assn. Resident Tenants, Washington, 1988, 90—; mem. Joint Bd. on Sci. Engring. Edn., Washington, 1972-78. Recipient of the Design award Machinery Mag., 1963. Mem. ASME (chmn. Washington chpt. 1978-79), Nat. Energy Resources Assn., Mensa, Capital PC Users Group, Acoustical Soc. Am. (chmn. Washington chpt. 1982-83), D.C. Soc. Profl. Engrs. (pres. 1975-76, nat. dir. 1980-86, Young Engr. of Yr. 1974), D.C. Coun. Engring. and Archtl. Socs. (del. 1969—, pres. 1978-79, Pres.'s award 1989, Nat. Capitol award 1974), Soc. Mfg. Engrs. (chmn. Washington Robotics Internat. chpt. 1986-87), Washington Coal Club, MIT Club of Washington (pres. 1979-80), Washington Tufts U. Alumni Club (v.p. 1970-71), Tau Beta Pi (pres. Tufts student chpt. 1962-63,

v.p. Washington alumni chpt. 1988-89), Sigma Xi. Republican. Home: Apt 1033 1255 New Hampshire Ave NW Washington DC 20036-2328

HERSHFIELD, LOTTE CASSEL, writer, editor; b. Breslau, Germany, Jan. 20, 1931; came to U.S., 1946, naturalized, 1952; d. Isidor Lippman and Sabine (Leser) Cassel; m. Nathan Hershfield, Apr. 7, 1951; children—Leonie, Joel. A.A., McCoy Coll. Johns Hopkins U., 1951. Library asst. Enoch Pratt Free Library, Balt., 1948-51; copywriter, proof reader Jewish Times, Balt., 1947-48; copywriter, food editor Catholic Transcript, Hartford, Conn., 1970-86; personnel dir. adminstrv. office Mercyknoll, Inc., West Hartford, Conn., 1986—; library substitute West Hartford Pub. Schs., 1964-70; lectr. in field. Editor: Of Loaves and Fishes and Other Dishes, 1978, 2d edit., 1980. Contbr. articles to profl. jours., food section Hartford Courant, recipes in cookbooks. Mem. Arthritis Found. Conn. Democrat. Jewish. Lodge: Temple B'Nai Israel Sisterhood. Avocations: researching recipes; knitting; reading; writing; foreign traveling. Office: Mercyknoll Inc 243 Steele Rd West Hartford CT 06117-2741

HERSHMAN, CHRISTOPHER NOEL, clergyman, marriage and family therapist; b. Reading, Pa., Dec. 26, 1955; s. Raymond Robert Hershman and Gloria Mary (D'Agostino) Beamesderfer; m. Mary Ann Stolinas, May 3, 1980 (div. Aug. 1987); m. Patricia Jean Kentosh, May 12, 1990; 1 child, Alexander David. AAS, Reading Community Coll., 1975; BS, Kutztown (Pa.) U., 1977, MA, 1979; MDiv, Luth. Sem., Phila., 1984, M in Sacred Theology, 1988; DMin., Ea. Bapt., Phila., 1991. Ordained to ministry Evang. Luth. Ch. in Am., 1984. Counselor Luth. Home, Topton, Pa., 1976-79; addictions counselor Reading Hosp., 1979-80; pastor St. John's Evang. Luth. Ch., Fogelsville, Pa., 1984-92, St. James Evang. Luth. Ch., Allentown, Pa., 1992—; therapist Cath. Social Agy., Allentown, 1987-92, Assocs. for Growth and Recovery, Allentown, 1992—. Office: Regency Towers Ste 1B 1600 Lehigh Pkwy E Allentown PA 18103

HERSHMAN, JACK I., urologist; b. Bklyn., Oct. 7, 1955; s. Seymour and Sonia Elaine (Kamins) H.; m. Ingrid Gail Bernstein, Aug. 25, 1986; children: Melissa Paige, Jennifer Whitney. BA in Biology magna cum laude, U. Rochester, 1977; MD, Mt. Sinai Sch. Medicine, 1981. Diplomate Am. Bd. Urology. Resident in surgery Lenox Hill Hosp., N.Y.C., 1981-82; resident in urology Montefiore Med. Ctr., Bronx, N.Y., 1983-86; chief urology Phelps Meml. Hosp., North Tarrytown, N.Y., 1986—; attending urologist Dobbs Ferry (N.Y.) Hosp., 1986—, Westchester County Med. Ctr., Valhalle, N.Y., 1986—; clin. instr. urology N.Y. Hosp., N.Y.C., 1987—; chief section urology Phelps Meml. Hosp., North Tarrytown, 1990—. Fellow Am. Coll. Surgeons; mem. N.Y. State Med. Soc., Westchester County Med. Soc., Phi Beta Kappa. Office: 200 S Broadway Ste C Tarrytown NY 10591

HERSHMAN, JUDITH, advertising executive; b. Boston, Sept. 16, 1949; d. Max and Mollie (Cohen) H. BFA, Boston U., 1971. Pres., owner Hershman Advt. & Design, Foxboro, Mass., 1979—. Executed mural Kenmore Subway Sta., Boston, 1970. Mem. Women's Success Network, United C. of C., Creative Club of Boston. Home and Office: 41 Mechanic St Foxboro MA 02035-2027

HERSHOCK, HOWARD LESTER, safety professional; b. Willow Street, Pa., Sept. 3, 1919; s. John Chadwick and Ida Mae (Myers) H.; m. Anna L. Hall, Feb. 28, 1923 (div. Jan. 1959); children: Michael H., Jenelle C.; m. Katherine A. Rosbert, July 19, 1959; 1 child, Susan L. BS in Edn., Millersville U. Pa., 1941; MS in Edn., U. Pa., 1947. Indsl. arts tchr. Jr./Sr. High Sch., Elkridge, Md., 1941-42, Lansdowne, Pa., 1946-55; sales rep. DeWalt Div./AMF, Phila., 1955-60; sales supr./rep. Black & Decker, Towson, Md., 1961-79; safety assurance mgr. DeWalt Div./Black & Decker, Lancaster, Pa., 1980-81; cons. on power tool safety, Bryn Mawr, Pa., 1981—. With USN, 1942-45. Mem. Am. Soc. Safety Engrs., Nat. Safety Coun.

HERSHON, ROBERT MYLES, editor, publisher; b. Bklyn., May 28, 1936; s. Mark and Barbara (Pernick) H.; m. Donna Brook, Oct. 10, 1982; children: Jedediah, Elizabeth. BS, NYU, 1957. Editor, pub. Hanging Loose Press, N.Y.C., 1966—; communications dir. Grolier Inc., N.Y.C., 1971-75; exec. dir. Print Ctr., Inc., N.Y.C., 1976—; bd. advisors N.Y. Book Fair, N.Y.C., 1975-85. Author: (poetry) How to Ride on the Woodlawn Express, 1986, The Public Hug, 1980, A Blue Shovel, 1979, Rocks and Chairs, 1975. Creative Writing fellow Nat. Endowment for Arts, 1979, 90; recipient Richard Hugo prize Poetry N.W., 1988, Helen Bullis prize, 1990. Home: 231 Wyckoff St Brooklyn NY 11217-2208

HERSKOWITZ, MORTON STANLEY, psychiatrist; b. Trenton, N.J., May 23, 1918; s. Harry and Cecelia May (Krueger) H.; m. Frankie Kimmelman, 1946 (div. 1957); m. Karen Ann Tuttle, 1957; 1 child, Robin Ray. BA, Temple U., 1938; DO, Phila. Coll. Osteopathic Medicine, 1943. Diplomate Am. Osteo. Bd. Psychiatry. Analyst, trainee of Wilhelm Reich, 1949-52; pvt. practice psychiat. orgone therapy Phila., 1952—; clin. prof. psychiatry Phila. Coll. Osteopathic Medicine, 1966—. Author: Human Armoring, 1990. Home and Office: 2132 Pine St Philadelphia PA 19103-6580

HERSON, ARLENE RITA, television program host; b. N.Y.C.; d. Sam and Mollie (Friedman) Hornreich; m. Milton Herson, June 16, 1963; children: Michael, Karen. Student, Queens Coll., 1957, New Sch. for Social Research, N.Y.C., 1960. Exec. sec. Tex McCrary, Inc., N.Y.C., 1958-60; asst. to pres. Safire Pub. Relations, N.Y.C., 1960-62; columnist The Advisor, Inc., Middletown, N.J., 1974-78; producer, host The Arlene Herson Show, N.Y.C., 1978—; syndicated nationally on Tempo TV, 1988, Channel Am., 1989—; spokesperson Storer Cable TV, Monmouth County, 1989-91, Nutri/Systems, Monmouth and Ocean Counties, 1989-90, 92nd St. Y Benefit Com., Variety-The Children Charity; mem. Women's Project and Prodns., 1992. Dir. women's activities campaign for Sen. Jacob J. Javits, N.Y.C., 1968; bd. dirs. Monmouth (N.J.) Mus., 1982-86; com. mem. Children's Psychiatric Ctr., 1971-90, Monmouth Park Charity Fund, 1980-90; corp. exec. bd. Family and Children's Services, 1985-90; active Monmouth Ocean Devel. Council, 1981-90; life mem. Brandeis U. Library Fund, N.Y. chpt. Recipient CAPE award for best talk show on Cable TV Network, 1984-91, Woman of Achievement in Communications award Adv. Commn. on Status of women, 1986, Pub. and Leased Access award for best talk show Paragon Cable TV, N.Y.C., 1988, spl. resolution N.J. Assembly, 1988; featured Woman on the Move N.J. Bus. Jour., 1989; ACE; recipikent Willie award for outstanding svc. Will Rogers Inst., 1992. Mem. NAFE, NATAS, Nat. Acad. Cable Programming, Nat. Assn. Profl. Women, Women in Communications, Women in Cable, Am. Women in Radio and TV, Internat. Radio and TV Soc., Nat. Press Club, East River Tennis Club, Friars Club, Nat. Press Club.

HERTEL, SUZANNE MARIE, personnel administrator; b. Hastings, Neb., Aug. 8, 1937; d. Louis C. Hertel and W. Lenore (Cross) Budd. BA, Doane Coll., Crete, Neb., 1959; MSM, Union Theol. Sem., 1961; postgrad., U. Hartford, 1966, U. Conn., 1975; MA, Merrill Palmer Inst., 1977; EdD, Boston U., 1982. Music tchr. Pub. Sch., Wethersfield, Conn., 1962-63; serials libr. Hartford (Conn.)Sem. Found., 1963-64; elem. tchr. Pub. Sch., Glastonbury, Conn., 1965-79; asst. prof. Univ. Northern Iowa, Cedar Falls, Iowa, 1979-81; training mgr. Focus Research Systems Inc., W. Hartford, Conn., 1982-89; pers. adminstr. City of Hartford, 1989—. Recipient Maria Miller Stewart award, 1992. Mem. Am. Soc. Training and Devel., Am. Guild Organists. Democrat. Office: City of Hartford Mcpl Bldg 550 Main St Hartford CT 06103

HERTFELDER, ERIC KARL, non-profit organization administrator; b. Euclid, Ohio, Jan. 2, 1947; s. Karl Jacob and Evelyn Mae (Hoover) H.; m. Sarah Coonley Davies, Aug. 23, 1975. BA in English cum ladue, Brown U., 1969; MA in English, Columbia U., 1970; postgrad., Cornell U., 1974-76. Adminstr. R.I. Hist. Preservation Commn., Providence, 1971-74, exec. dir., 1976-84; exec. dir. Nat. Conf. of State Historic Preservation Officers, Washington, 1984—. Episcopalian. Office: Nat Conf State Historic Preservation Officers 444 N Capitol St NW # 332 Washington DC 20001-1512

HERTL, WILLIAM, chemist; b. Phila., July 2, 1932; m. Pamela Rider, Sept. 19, 1964; children: Julia, David. BS, U. Pa., 1954; PhD, Cambridge U., 1962. Shift analyst Atlantic Refining Co., Phila., 1958; postdoctoral fellow CIBA, A/G, Basel, Switzerland, 1962-63; sr. rsch. assoc. Corning (N.Y.), Inc., 1963—; prof. chemistry U. Andes, Merida, Venezuela, 1970-72; vis. scientist Cornell U., Ithaca, N.Y., 1987. Contbr. numerous articles to profl. jours.; patentee in field. Lt. (j.g.) USN, 1954-57. Mem. Am. Chem. Soc., Royal Soc. Chemistry, Am. Phys. Soc., Materials Rsch. Soc., Soc. for Applied Spectroscopy, Bohmische Phys. Soc. Office: Corning Inc Sullivan Park Corning NY 14830

HERTLER, WALTER RAYMOND, chemist; b. Phila., Apr. 10, 1933; s. Walter Mason and Emma (Muth) H.; m. Marilyn Jones, Oct. 14, 1961; children: Ann M., Russell W. BA, U. Pa., 1955; PhD, U. Ill., 1958. Chemist DuPont Co. Cen. Rsch., Wilmington, Del., 1958—. Contbr. articles to profl. jours.; patentee in field. Mem. Am. Chem. Soc. Office: DuPont Exptl Sta PO Box 80328 Wilmington DE 19880-0328

HERTZBERG, DANIEL, journalist; b. N.Y.C.. Degree, U. Chgo. Formerly with Buffalo Evening News, Newsday; with Wall St. Jour., N.Y.C., 1977—, now editor money and investing. Recipient Pulitzer Prize for explanatory journalism, 1988. Office: Wall St Jour 200 Liberty St New York NY 10281-1003

HERTZOG, DAVID RAY, surgeon; b. Elmira, N.Y., Feb. 1, 1952; s. Frank V. and Doreen (Bridges) H.; m. Ann W. White, Aug. 17, 1985; children: Sarah, Elizabeth. BA, Hamilton Coll., 1974; MD, Med. Coll. Pa., 1981. Diplomate Am. Bd. Surgery. Resident in surgery Med. Coll. Pa., 1981-86; pvt. practice Helene Fuld Meml. Ctr., Hamilton Hosp., Trenton, N.J., 1986—; surgeon Helene Fuld Med. Ctr., Hamilton Hosp., Mercer Med. Ctr., Trenton. Mem. Am. Coll. Surgeons. Office: Bldg 3 Ste F 3100 Princeton Pike Lawrenceville NJ 08648

HERVEY, ALBERT EUGENE, career officer; b. Hughes Springs, Tex., Aug. 14, 1939; s. Albert and Marguerite (Truitt) H.; m. Janis Ann Blauert, Aug. 10; div. 1990; children: Brian, Allison, Aaron. BA, Sam Houston State U., 1962; MS in Engring., U. Tex., 1975; postgrad., Nat. War Coll., 1982—. CPA, Md. Commd. 2d lt. U.S. Army, 1962, advanced through ranks to col., 1991; chief, master mobilization plan Dept. Def., Washington, 1983; sr. staff officer III Corps U.S. Army, Ft. Hood, Tex., 1983-86; comdr. USA Safety Ctr. Dept. Army, Washington, 1986-88; chief conv. forces analysis Joint Chief of Staff, The Pentagon, Washington, 1988-91; mgr. Cooper and Lybrand CPA's, Washington. Author: Electrical Generation Transmission and Distribution for Texas to the Year 2000, 1975, Airspace Control in Southwest Asia. Mosher Def. Inst. fellow, 1989-91. Fellow D.C. Soc. CPAs; mem. AICPA. Lutheran. Home: PO Box 46198 Washington DC 20050-6198

HERVEY, HOMER VAUGHAN, federal agency administrator; b. Texarkana, Tex., Sept. 27, 1936; s. Charles Ethelbert and Ambolyn (Vaughan) H.; m. Nancy McDonald, July 7, 1962; children: Nancy Vaughan, H.V. Jr. BS, Georgetown U., 1958, MA, 1962. Executive trainee Riggs Nat. Bank, Washington, 1958-61, U.S. Govt. Office of Edn., Washington, 1961-63; program officer Exec. Office of the Pres., Washington, 1963-73, Dept. of the Treasury, Washington, 1973-77, Fed. Preparedness Agy., Washington, 1977-79; program officer Fed. Emergency Mgmt. Agy., Washington, 1979-85, asst. assoc. dir., dir. ops., 1985—. Mem. exec. com. Georgetown U. Library, Washington, 1982—. Club: Chevy Chase. Office: Fed Emergency Mgmt Agy 500 C St SW Washington DC 20472-0002

HERWOOD, MARY CAROL, school administrator; b. Buffalo, May 23, 1931; d. Henry John and Anna Marie (Duffy) Kelleher; m. Ernest A. Herwood, May 26, 1962 (dec. Nov. 1982); children: Kelly Reilly, Patrick, Sheila. BS, D'Youville Coll., 1952; MEd, SUNY, Buffalo, 1970, PhD, 1980. Cert. sch. adminstr. and supr. Exec. sec. to v.p., gen. mgr. LoBlaw, Inc., Buffalo, 1960-65; grad. asst. acad. affairs SUNY, Buffalo, 1975-76; bus. tchr. Buffalo Pub. Schs., 1971-80, supr. of evaluation, 1980-85, supr. adminstrv. svcs., 1985—; bd. dirs. N.Y. Assn. Local Govt. Records Officers, 1990-91; pres. Cen. Office Educators Assn., 1991-92. Trustee St. Mary of the Lake Cath. Ch., Hamburg, N.Y., 1990—, parish coun. mem. 1990—, eucharistic min. 1985—, lector 1988—; chmn. adv. com. Sisters Hosp. Sch. Nursing, Buffalo; bd. dirs. Pinegrove Park Homeowners Assn. Mem. Brierwood Country Club. Democrat. Home: 17 Pinegrove Pk Hamburg NY 14075 Office: Buffalo Pub Schs 708 City Hall Buffalo NY 14202

HERZ, FRITZ, biochemist; b. Heilbronn, Wurttemberg, Germany, July 16, 1930; came to U.S., 1959; s. Ludwig and Ida Jella (Oppenheimer) H.; m. Vona Kern, May 8, 1966; children: Eric Nathan, Lisa Sonia. BA, Coll. Vicente Rocafuerte, Guayaquil, Ecuador, 1950; Chemist, Guayaquil U., 1954, PhD, 1955. Assoc. dept. head Inst. Nacional de Higiene, Guayaquil, 1955-57; Humboldt fellow Free U., Berlin, 1957-59; USPHS fellow Sinai Hosp., Balt., 1959-62, rsch. assoc., 1962-67, assoc. pediatric rsch. dir., 1967-73; asst. prof. pediatrics Johns Hopkins U., Balt., 1970-73; head tissue culture div. dept. pathology Montefiore Med. Ctr., Bronx, N.Y., 1973—; assoc. prof. pathology Albert Einstein Coll. Medicine, Bronx, 1973—. Contbr. articles to sci. jours.; reviewer sci. jours. NIH rsch. grantee, Bethesda, Md., 1989. Mem. Am. Soc. Biochemistry and Molecular Biology, Am. Chem. Soc. Democrat. Jewish. Home: 45 Dora Ln New Rochelle NY 10804-1005 Office: Montefiore Med Ctr 111 E 210th St Bronx NY 10467-2490

HERZ, PETER WILLIAM, advertising executive; b. N.Y.C., June 6, 1945; s. William Henry and Renate Maria (Reichman) H.; m. Jacqueline Susan Ritterman, May 30, 1947; children: Jordana S., Nicole L. BA, Syracuse U., 1969, MBA, 1971. Pres., founder Target Promotions, Inc., Stamford, Conn., 1976—, Sass, Inc., Stamford, 1982—; with Jornik div. Target Promotions; founder, pres. Jornik Co., Stamford, 1989—; cons. Nat. Computer Corp., Stamford, 1983-85. Author of software (2). Pfc. AUS, 1966-68. Mem. Specialty Advt. Assn. Internat., Specialty Advt. Assn. Greater N.Y. (bd. dirs. 1983-85), Specialty Advt. Assn. New Eng., Halloween Yacht Club, Jaguar Club New Eng. Democrat. Jewish. Office: Target Promotions Inc 441 Canal St Stamford CT 06902-5910

HERZBERG, SYDELLE SHULMAN, lawyer, accountant; b. N.Y.C., July 24, 1933; d. Hyman and Rose (Green) S.; m. Norman Joseph Herzberg, June 23, 1962; 1 child, Gilbert. BS, NYU, 1955; JD, Bklyn. Law Sch., 1957. Bar: N.Y. 1958; CPA, N.Y. Pub. acct. M. Sharlach & Co, N.Y.C., 1955-62; pvt. practice acctg. and law New Rochelle, N.Y., 1962—. Mem. bd. edn. Solomon Schechter Sch. of Westchester, White Plains, N.Y., 1975-78, bd. dirs. PTA, 1975-78; pres. PTA bd. Westchester Hebrew High Sch., Mamaroneck, N.Y., 1980-82; mem. budget adv. bd. City of New Rochelle, N.Y., 1975. Mem. AICPA, N.Y. State Soc. CPA, ABA, N.Y. State Bar Assn., Westchester Women's Bar Assn., Huguenot-Thomas Paine Hist. Assn. (treas. 1987—, trustee 1987—), LWV (pres. New Rochelle chpt. 1983-85, treas. Westchester chpt. 1989—, budget chair N.Y. 1989—, treas. N.Y. state 1991—). Jewish. Home: 46 Longvue Ave New Rochelle NY 10804-4119 Office: 519 Main St New Rochelle NY 10801-6334

HERZENBERG, JOHN ERIC, medical educator; b. Springfield, Mass., Apr. 13, 1955; s. Jerry S. and Helen (Chernaik) H.; m. Merrill S. Chaus, June 18, 1979. BA, MD, Boston U., 1979. Intern in gen. surgery Montefiore-Einstein Hosps., Bronx, N.Y., 1979-81; resident in orthopaedic surgery Duke U., Durham, N.C., 1981-85; fellow in pediatric orthopaedics Hosp. for Sick Children, Toronto, Ont., Can., 1985-86; instr. U. Mich., Ann Arbor, 1986-88, asst. prof., 1988-91; assoc. prof. U. Md., Balt., 1991—; co-dir. Md. Ctr. for Limb Lengthening & Reconstrn., Balt., 1991—. Mem. Am. Acad. Orthopaedic Surgeons, Assn. for Study of Application of Methods of Ilizarov, Assn. Bone and Joint Surgeons, Royal Coll. Surgeons, Can. Orthopaedic Assn., Pediatric Orthopaedic Soc. of North Am. Office: 2200 N Forest Park Ave Baltimore MD 21207

HERZFELD, JUDITH, biophysical chemistry educator; b. Guayaquil, Ecuador, Jan. 12, 1948; d. Wolfgang and Eva Hedwig (Rosenthal) Herzfeld; m. Robert Guy Griffin, Aug. 25, 1974; children: Sarah R., Rachel H. AB, Barnard Coll., 1967; PhD, MIT, 1972; MPP, Harvard U., 1973. Asst. prof. chemistry Amherst (Mass.) Coll., 1973-74; rsch. assoc. biophysics Harvard Med. Sch., Boston, 1974-75, lectr. biophysics, 1975-76, asst. prof. biophysics, 1976-83, assoc. prof. physiology and biophysics, 1983-85; assoc. prof. biophys. chemistry Brandeis U., Waltham, Mass., 1985-90, prof. biophys. chemistry, 1990—; peer reviewer jours. and granting agencies, 1973—. Contbr. articles to profl. jours.; author: Sense and Sensibility in Childbirth, 1985. Recipient Faculty Rsch. award Am. Cancer Soc., 1978-82; rsch. grantee NIH, 1976—, Am. Heart Assn., 1982-83, 85-88, Am. Diabetes Assn., 1978-79; recipient Faculty award for women NSF, 1991-96. Mem. AAAS, Am. Chem. Soc., Biophys. Soc., Am. Phys. Soc., Am. Soc. Biochemistry and Molecular Biology, N.Y. Acad. Scis., Protein Soc. Office: Brandeis U Dept Chemistry Waltham MA 02254-9110

HERZIG, BRUCE DAVID, computer programming analyst; b. Bklyn., Aug. 17, 1944; s. Samuel F. and Eleanor (Montrose) H.; m. Elaine Lefkowitz, June 15, 1968; children: Saralee, Heather, Melissa. BA, Gallaudet U., 1968. Systems programmer UNISYS, Roseville, Minn., 1968-71; math tchr., basketball coach Gov. Baxter State Sch. for Deaf, Portland, Maine, 1971-72; computer programmer U.S. Army War Coll., Carlisle, Pa., 1972-73; computer programming analyst U.S. Army-Pentagon, Washington, 1973—. Pres. Md. Sch. for Deaf-Parents, Tchrs., and Counselors Assn., Frederick, 1987-91, Nat. Racquetball Assn. Deaf, Rockville, Md., 1988-92; treas. Washington Jewish Soc. Deaf, 1980-84. Office: Nat Racquetball Assn Deaf 7532 Tarpley Dr Rockville MD 20855-2570

HERZIG, JULIE ESTHER, architect; b. N.Y.C., Jan. 23, 1951; d. Philip R. and Helene J. (Phillips) H.; m. Robert J. Desnick, Oct. 23, 1988; 1 child, Jonathan Phillips. BA, Mt. Holyoke Coll., 1973; BArch with honors, Pratt Inst., 1983. Draftsman Red Roof Design, N.Y.C., 1977-80; designer Phillips Janson Group, N.Y.C., 1983-84; pres. Herzig, Knechtel Assocs., N.Y.C., 1984-85, Herzig Design, N.Y.C., 1985—. Mt. Holyoke Coll. grantee, 1972. Mem. AIA, Mt. Holyoke Club.

HERZOG, DAVID PAUL, chemist; b. Detroit, Oct. 19, 1949; s. Hilary August and Katherine (Garczynski) H.; m. Kathleen Jean Shull, Mar. 18, 1972; children: Matthew, Gregory. BS in Biochemistry, Mich. State U., 1971; PhD in Microbiology, Notre Dame U., 1981. Asst. rsch. scientist Ames div. Miles Labs., Inc., Elkhart, Ind., 1971-72, from supr. to mgr., 1972-80; mgr. rsch. Micromedic System div. Rohm and Haas, Horsham, Pa., 1981-85; mgr. r & d ICN Micromedic Systems, Horsham, Pa., 1985-88; v.p. devel. Ohmicron Corp., Newtown, Pa., 1988-91, v.p. ops., 1991—. Contbr. articles to profl. jours. Cubmaster Boy Scouts of Am., Warrington, Pa., 1982-84; coach Warrington Athletic Assn., Warrington, 1983-91. Mem. Am. Assn. Clin. Chemists, Am. Soc. Microbiology, Am. Chem. Soc., Am. Water Works Assn., N.Y. Acad. Sci., Sigma Xi. Home: 999 Liberty Ln Warrington PA 18976-1745 Office: Ohmicron Corp 375 Pheasant Run Newtown PA 18940-3423

HERZOG, THOMAS NELSON, actuary; b. N.Y.C., Nov. 7, 1946; s. Alan George and Evelyn (Eisner) H.; m. Penny Wiggins McNeill, Dec. 24, 1945; children: Tracy, Steven. BS, Brown U., 1968; MA, U. Md., 1971, PhD, 1975. Assoc. Soc. Actuaries, Chgo., 1977—. Recipient Spl. Achievement award Sec./HUD, 1990, Acturial Edn. and Rsch. Fund Practitioners award, 1990. Mem. Am. Stat. Assn., Am. Risk and Ins. Assn. Office: HUD 451 7th St SW Washington DC 20410-8000

HESLIN, JO-ANN, dietician, nutritionist; b. Bayshore, N.Y., Feb. 16, 1946; d. Joseph and Anna (Hodl) Saufl; m. Joseph Heslin, Jan. 3, 1969; children: Kirsten, Karen. BS, SUNY, Oneonta, 1967; MA, NYU, 1970. Registered dietician, N.Y.; cert. home economist. Test kitchen assoc. Family Circle Mag., N.Y.C., 1967-69; pub. health nutritionist Nat. Dairy Coun., N.Y.C., 1969-70; asst. prof. Downstate Med. Ctr. SUNY, N.Y.C., 1970-75; cons., owner NRH Nutrition Cons., Valley Stream, N.Y., 1975—; Mem. editorial bds. Am. Baby Mag., N.Y.C., 1978—, Prevention Mag., Eamaus, Pa., 1984-86, Environ. Nutrition Newsletter, N.Y.C., 1985—, Childbirth Educator, N.Y.C., 1989-90. Author: No Nonsense Nutrition for Your Baby's First Year, 1980, Geriatric Nutrition, 1980, Nutrition for the Prime of Your Life, 1983, No Nonsense Nutrition for Kids, 1985, Megadoses: Vitamins as Drugs, 1985, Nutritional Care of the Older Adult, 1986, The Cholesterol Counter, 1988, 89, The Fat Counter, 1989, The Fat Attack Plan, 1990, The Diabetes Carbohydrate and Calorie Counter, 1991; contbr. numerous articles to profl. jours. Mem. Am. Dietetic Assn., Am. Home Econs. Assn., Home Economists In Business (Sec., com. chairs, 1986—, Am. Heart Assn. (cert. cardiovascular counselor), Am. Med. Writers Assn., Nat. Technical Resource, Pediatric Nutritionists. Office: NRH Nutrition Cons Inc 100 Rosedale Rd Valley Stream NY 11581-2802

HESLIN, JOHN THOMAS, entrepreneur, historic preservationist; b. Bklyn., Jan. 24, 1927; s. John Joseph and Edna (Young) H.; m. Cathleen Jane Hunter, June 24, 1950. AB, Duke U., 1952; MSc in Edn., Hofstra U., 1955; MDiv, Union Theol. Sem., 1990; postgrad., Art Students League, 1991. Supr. E.I. duPont de Nemours & Co., Inc., 1953; freelance editor, 1955-60; owner John T. Heslin Design Studio, 1960-66; pres. John T. Heslin & Co., Inc., 1966—; bd. dirs. Quilter's Corner, Inc.; career advisor Career Devel. Ctr., Duke U., 1992—. Author: A Consideration of the Condition of Creation, the Creator and Evil, 1990; author poetry. Fire chief Rockleigh (N.J.) Vol. Fire Dept., 1974-75; chmn. shade tree com. Borough of Rockleigh, 1975-80, marshall, 1975, historic adv. com., 1978-79; vice chmn. Rockleigh Bd. of Adjustment, 1977; chmn. Rockleigh Planning Bd., 1980; establishor Rockleigh Wildlife Preserve, 1977; co-founder, pres. N.J. Historic Homes Assn., 1977-79; founder, dir. Hopewell Found., 1981-84; chmn., bd. trustees Abram Demarest Homestead Restoration, 1981-84; trustee Cathleen Heslin Found., 1991—. With USN, 1944-46. Mem. N.J. State Vol. Fire Chiefs Assn., Duke U. Alumni Assn., Masons, Phi Beta Kappa, Mu Sigma. Episcopalian. Home: 5 Piermont Rd Rockleigh NJ 07647 Office: Old Haring Farm Rockleigh NJ 07647

HESS, CHARLES EDWARD, environmental horticulture educator; b. Paterson, N.J., Dec. 20, 1931; s. Cornelius W. M. and Alice (Debruyn) H.; children: Mary, Carol, Nancy, John, Peter; m. Eva G. Carroad, Feb. 14, 1981. BS, Rutgers U., 1953; MS, Cornell U., 1954, PhD, 1957; DAgr (hon.), Purdue U., 1983. Asst. prof. Purdue U., West Lafayette, Ind., 1958-61, assoc. prof., 1962-64, prof., 1965; research prof., dept. chmn. Rutgers U., New Brunswick, N.J., 1966, assoc. dean, dir. N.J. Agrl. Exptl. Sta., 1970, acting dean Coll. Agrl. and Environ. Sci., 1971, dean Cook Coll., 1972-75; dean Coll. Agr. and Environ. Scis., U. Calif.-Davis, 1975-89; assoc. dir. Calif. Agrl. Exptl. Sta., 1975-89; asst. sec. sci. and edn. USDA, Washington, 1989-91; prof. dept. environ. horticulture U. Calif., Davis, 1991—; cons. AID, 1965, Office Tech. Assessment, U.S. Congress, 1976—; chmn. study team world food and nutrition study Nat. Acad. Scis., 1976; mem. Calif. State Bd. of Food and Agri., 1984—, mem. Nat. Sci. Bd., 1982-88, vice chmn., 1984-88; co-chmn. Joint Council U.S. Dept. Agriculture, 1987—. Mem. West Lafayette Sch. Bd., Ind., 1963-65, sec., 1963, pres., 1964; mem. Gov.'s Commn. Blueprint for Agr., 1971-73. Served with AUS, 1956-58. Mem. AAAS (chmn. agriculture sect. 1989-90), Am. Soc. Hort. Sci. (pres. 1973), Internat. Plant Propagators Soc. (pres. 1973), Agrl. Research Inst., Phi Beta Kappa, Sigma Xi, Alpha Zeta. Office: U Calif Coll Agrl & Environ Scis Dept Environ Horticulture Davis CA 95616

HESS, CHARLES JAMES, educator; b. Bloomsburg, Pa., Jan. 7, 1950; s. Frease James and Doris May (Masteller) H.; m. Judith Ann Robbins, Mar. 31, 1973; children: Schelley Jo, Charlee Ann. BS in Edn., Bloomsburg (Pa.) U., 1971, MEd, 1982. Bus. tchr. Otselic Valley High Sch., South Otselic, N.Y., 1984-86; asst. prof. Broome Community Coll., Binghamton, N.Y., 1986-91, assoc. prof., 1991—. Mem. NEA, N.Y. State Assn. Two-Yr. Colls. Home: Rt 26 RD 1 Box 72 Johnson City NY 13790 Office: Broome Community Coll PO Box 1017 Binghamton NY 13902-1017

HESS, DONALD K., university administrator; b. Lititz, Pa., Nov. 18, 1930; m. Nancy Gordon, June 9, 1951; 1 child, Jennifer Lynn Hess Zannetos. BA, Franklin and Marshall Coll., 1952; MPA, Syracuse U., 1953. With AEC, Washington, 1953-58; asst. dir. Advanced Research Projects Agy., Dept. Def., Washington, 1958-66, OEO, Washington, 1966-70; dir. Peace Corps, Korea, 1970-72, Washington, 1972-74; v.p. campus affairs U. Rochester (N.Y.), 1974-83, v.p. adminstrn., 1983—. Trustee Assoc. Univs., Inc., Franklin and Marshall Coll.; bd. dirs. Rochester Gen. Hosp.; dir. Photographic Scis. Inc. Home: 2 Masters Cove Pittsford NY 14534-1072

HESS, GEOFFREY LAVERNE, accountant; b. Gettysburg, Pa., Dec. 20, 1949; s. Richard LaVerne and Beatrice Geraldine (Brown) H.; m. Cynthia

Jean Duvall, 1990; children: Chérie Ann, Laura Marie. BS in Acctg., Mt. St. Mary's Coll., 1976. CPA, Md., Pa. Acct. United Bldg. Corp., Germantown, Md., 1976-77; NAD resident auditor U.S. Army Corps Engrs., Balt., 1977-78; sr. acct., Councilor Buchanan and Mitchell, Bethesda, Md., 1979-80; internal auditor George Washington U., 1981; sr. acct. Buchanan and Co., Frederick, Md., 1981-82; acctg. mgr. PATS, Inc., Flight Refueling, Inc., Patrick Aircraft Tank Systems, Inc., 1983-85; contr. Annapolis Fed. Savs. Bank, 1985-88; mgmt. cons., 1988—. With USAF, 1968-72. Mem. AICPA, Md. Assn. CPAs, Internat. Platform Assn., Inst. Mgmt. Accts., Am. Legion. Republican. Mem. United Ch. of Christ. Home and Office: 1223 Cherrytown Rd Westminster MD 21158-1528

HESS, LAWRENCE EUGENE, JR., lawyer; b. Phila., Aug. 18, 1923; s. Lawrence Eugene and Charlotte (Engel) H.; m. Jane Strayer, June 11, 1949; children: Lawrence Edward, Charlotte Jane. Student, Princeton U., 1942-43; BS, U.S. Naval Acad., 1946; JD with honors, George Washington U., 1954. Bar: Pa. 1954, D.C. 1954, U.S. Supreme Ct. 1963. Commd. ensign USN, 1946, advanced through grades to lt. comdr., assigned to various ships and stas.; ret., 1966; house counsel Nat. Liberty Life Ins. Co., Valley Forge, Pa., 1966-67, Standard Computers, Inc., 1967-68; atty. Def. Pers. Support Ctr., Phila., 1968-69; counsel Am. Acceptance Corp., Phila., 1969-74; pvt. practice law Fort Washington, 1974—. Mem. editorial bd. George Washington U. Law Rev., 1952-53. Mem. Sch. Bd. Upper Dublin Sch. Dist., Montgomery County, Pa., 1981-85; chmn. bd. trustees Glenside (Pa.) United Meth. Ch., 1973-76, 89-91, trustee, 1987—, vice chmn. bd., 1988-89. Mem. ABA, Fed. Bar Assn., Pa. Bar Assn., Phila. Bar Assn., Montgomery Bar Assn., Comml. Law League Am., Judge Advs. Assn., Montgomery Trial Lawyers Assn., Navy League U.S., U.S. Naval Acad. Alumni Assn. Phila. (past. pres., bd. dirs.), The Ret. Officers Assn. (life, bd. dirs., pres. WG chpt. 1990-91), Am. Legion, Mil. Order World Wars, Army-Navy Country Club, Mfrs. Golf and Country Club, Masons. Republican. Home and Office: 515 Dreshertown Rd Fort Washington PA 19034-3022

HESS, P. GREGORY, lawyer; b. Wheeling, W.Va., Sept. 15, 1946; s. Philip Tilman and Virginia Lamberton (Jackson) H.; m. Susan Marion Kyff, Aug. 16, 1969; children: Philip Andrew, Peter Gregory, Michael Trevor, Aimee Suzanne. AB, Princeton U., 1968; JD, Yale U., 1971; LLM in Taxation, NYU, 1976. Bar: N.Y. 1972, Fla. 1976. Assoc. Breed, Abbott and Morgan, N.Y.C., 1971-73; ptnr. Williamson and Green, N.Y.C., 1973-76, Williamson and Hess, N.Y.C., 1976-80; of counsel Christy and Viener, N.Y.C., 1980, ptnr., 1980—; bd. dirs. Barr and Barr, Inc., N.Y.C. Trustee N.Y. Sch. for Deaf, White Plains, 1982—, pres., 1990—; trustee Princeton (N.J.) Campus Club, 1972—; bd. dirs. Greater Westchester Youth Orchs. Assn., Inc., Millwood, N.Y., 1986-91, chmn., 1988-91. Mem. Princeton Club N.Y., Whippoorwill Club, Inc. Home: 10 Garden Ridge 10 Garden Ridge Chappaqua NY 10514-3801 Office: Christy & Viener 620 5th Ave New York NY 10020-2402

HESSE, WILLIAM BLASS, real estate broker; b. N.Y.C., July 8, 1948; s. Stanley William and Elizabeth (Blass) H.; m. Eileen Weinberg, Mar. 25, 1972 (div. Apr. 1987); children: Stacy, Scott; m. Jennifer Nash, June 2, 1989. BA in Econs. with honors, Clark U., 1970. Lic. real estate broker, N.Y., Conn., N.J. Personal trust adminstr. Chase Manhattan Bank, N.Y.C., 1972-73; sales-leasing rep. Robert Martin Co., Elmsford, N.Y., 1972-75, dir. comml. leasing, 1975-77, mgr. condominium sales, 1977-78, asst. to chmn., 1978-82; pres. Robert Martin's Space Specialists, Inc., Elmsford, 1982—; retail shopping ctr. cons. Robert Martin Co., Elmsford, Value Properties, N.Y.C., Dilstan Realty, Scarsdale, N.Y. Contbr. numerous articles for publ. Bd. dirs. Tarrytown (N.Y.) C. of C., 1975-82; v.p., bd. dirs. YM-YWHA of Mid-Westchester, Scarsdale, N.Y., 1977—. Mem. Internat. Coun. Shopping Ctrs. Jewish. Office: Robert Martin's Space Specialists Inc 570 Taxter Rd Elmsford NY 10523-2311

HESSE, WILLIAM R., marketing and advertising executive; b. Dayton, Ohio, Jan. 19, 1914; s. Julius R. and Margaret (Reid) H.; m. Anne E., Vandervort, July 3, 1941; children: William R., Carol Anne, Mark Vandervort. AB, U. Cin., 1938. Supr. employment for men Procter & Gamble, Cin.; asst. to sales mgr. Procter & Gamble, 1937-46; v.p. Batten, Barton, Durstine & Osborn, Inc., Pitts. and N.Y.C., 1946-56; sr. v.p. Benton & Bowles, Inc., N.Y.C., 1956-58; exec. v.p. Benton & Bowles, Inc., 1958-61, pres., 1961-68, chief exec. officer, 1965-68; bd. dir., pres., chief exec. officer William R. Hesse Assocs., N.Y.C. and Greenwich, Conn., 1968-75; sr. v.p. Am. Assn. Advt. Agys., Washington, 1975-78, pres., chief exec. officer, 1978; chmn., pres. W.R. Hesse Assocs., Cons., Yarmouth Port, Mass., 1979—; sec., bd. dir. Advt. Coun.; bd. dir. Nat. Advt. Rev. Com., Advt. Rsch. Found., Traffic Audit Bur.; ptnr. Pacifica Park, Seattle. Mem. mgmt. com. YMCA; mem. adv. bd. Nat. Coffee Assn. Bd.; dirs. Urban League of N.Y. Served as lt. col. Inf. AUS, 1941-45. Recipient Putnam award Nat. Indsl. Advertisers Assn., 1949. Mem. Am. Mgmt. Assn., Am. Assn. Advt. Agys. (bd. dir.-at-large), Royal Soc. Arts (hon. corr.), N.Y. Athletic Club, Cummaquid Golf Club, The Beach Club. Home: 177 Mid Pine Dr Yarmouth Port MA 02675-1638 Office: WR Hesse Assocs Cons PO Box 399 Yarmouth Port MA 02675-0399

HESSINGER, CARL JOHN WILLIAM, lawyer; b. Allentown, Pa., Aug. 23, 1915; s. John J. Sr. and Mary B. (Notter) H.; m. Marguerite Kathryn Toland, June 10, 1950; children: Nancy K., Patricia A., Mariann, Holly A. LLB, U. Pa., 1940; BPh, Muhlenberg Coll., 1937. Bar: Pa. 1942, U.S. Supreme Ct. 1972. Pres. Allen Title Co., Allentown, 1942—; v.p. and counsel First Fed. Savings and Loan Assn. of Allentown, 1952-85; counsel, trustee Harry C. Trexler Found., Allentown, 1963—. Mem. Pa. Land Title Assn., Lehigh Country Club, Penquin Figure Skating Club, Phila. Skating and Humane Soc. Home: 1613 W Linden St Allentown PA 18102-4217 Office: 939 W Walnut St Allentown PA 18102-4864

HESTENES, ROBERTA RAE, college president, minister; b. Huntington Park, Calif., Aug. 5, 1939; d. Robert James and Besse Rae (Nipp) Louis; m. John D. Hestenes; children: Joan Hestenes Lehnen, Eric Magnus, Stephen Eastvold. BA, U. Calif., Santa Barbara; M in Divinity, Fuller Theol. Sem., 1979, D.Min., 1983. Ordained to ministry Presbyn. Ch., 1979. Dir. adult edn. and small group ministries United Presbyn. Ch., Seattle, 1967-74; assoc. in ministry LaCanada (Calif.) Presbyn. Ch., 1974-84; assoc. prof., dir. Christian Formation and Discipleship program Fuller Theol. Sem., Pasadena, Calif., 1975-87; bd. dirs., chmn. strategic planning com. World Vision U.S., 1980—; bd. dirs. World Vision Internat., 1982—, chmn. bd. dirs., 1985—; pres. Eastern Coll., St. Davids, Pa., 1987—; cons. numerous Presbyn. orgns.; minister Kenya, Australia, South Africa, Singapore, Hong Kong, South Korea, Philippines, Cen. am. Author: (books) Using the Bible in Groups, 1985, Discovering II Corinthians/Galatians, 1986, (taped courses) Building Christian Communicty Through Small Groups, 1985, Helping Christians Grow: Adult Formation and Discipleship in the Local Church, 1987; co-editor: Women and the Ministries of Christ, 1979; contbr. articles to profl. jours.;. Fellow Case Methods Inst.; mem. Am. Acad. Religion, Religious Edn. Assn., Nat. Assn. of Profs. of Christian Edn. Office: Ea Coll Office of the President 10 Fairview Dr Saint Davids PA 19087-3696

HESTER, KARLTON EDWARD, composer, performer, music educator; b. El Paso, Tex., Feb. 11, 1949; s. Webb and Clara (Briggs) H.; m. Bette Jean Hered; 1 child, Karlton William. MusB, U. Tex., El Paso, 1971; MusM, San Francisco State U., 1978; PhD in Composition, CUNY, 1990. Music dir. Eisenhower High Sch., Rialto, Calif., 1971-74, San Francisco and Oakland (Calif.) Pub. Schs., 1977-82, Contempory Jazz Art Movement, San Francisco and N.Y.C., 1977—; pres. Hesteria Records & Pub. Co., San Francisco and N.Y.C., 1981—; adj. prof. Bronx (N.Y.) Community Coll., 1985-88; adj. prof. Coll. of S.I., N.Y., 1988—, asst. prof., 1990-91; artist in residence N.Y. Found. for Arts, N.Y.C., 1984—; composer in residence Yard Dance Co., N.Y.C., 1986, Western Edition Cultural Ctr., San Francisco, 1980-81; asst. prof. Coll. S.I., N.Y., 1990-91, Cornell U., 1991—; dir. jazz ensembles Cornell U., Ithaca, N.Y., 1991—; composer in residence, music dir. Cazadero Music Camp, Berkeley, Calif., 1982. Producer, composer record albums. Mem. Rosicrucian Order, San Jose, Calif., 1980—. Recipient S.I. Community TV NOVA video award for a Children's Jazz Video; grantee Nat. Endowment for Arts, 1985, 89, New Eng. Coun. for Arts, 1986, S.I. Coun. for Arts, 1987, 90, 991; fellow Mellon Found., 1991—. Mem. ASCAP (popular and standard awards), Nat. Flute Assn., Am. Fedn. Musicians. Home: 705 Mitchell St Ithaca NY 14850-4932 Office: Cornell U Music Dept Lincoln Hall Ithaca NY 14853

HESTON, WILLIAM MAY, educational administrator; b. Toledo, Nov. 2, 1922; s. William May and Helen Marie (Lippstrew) H.; m. Marian Cannon Watt, June 17, 1950; children—Mary, Elizabeth, Katherine, Richard. B.Sc. cum laude with highest honors in Chemistry, Ohio State U., 1943; M.A., Princeton U., 1948, Ph.D. in Chemistry (LeRoy Wiley McKay advanced fellow in phys. chemistry 1949), 1949. With E.I. duPont de Nemours & Co., Inc., 1949-59; dir. office research Western Res. U., 1959-63, asso. chemistry, 1959-67, v.p. research, 1963-64, v.p. student svcs., 1964-66, vice provost, assoc. dean Faculty Arts and Scis., 1966-67; v.p. plans and programs Case Western Res. U., 1967-69; exec. dir. Mental Devel. Center, cons. for spl. programs, 1969; v.p. Hofstra U., 1969-73; exec. dir. Nassau Higher Edn. Consortium, 1973-75; exec. dir. L.I. Regional Adv. Council on Higher Edn., 1975-76, ind. cons., 1976—; assoc. provost N.Y. Inst. Tech., 1977-78; dir., dean Center for Natural Scis., 1978-88, prof. life scis., 1981-90, chmn. grad. program in clin. nutrition, 1983-90; Chmn. Cleve. Regional Com. Comprehensive Mental Health Planning Report, 1964-66; mem. adv. council Ohio Dept. Mental Hygiene and Correction, 1966-69; cons. grad. chemistry research facilities br. NSF, 1965-68, cons. sci. devel. program br., 1968-70; tech. cons. chemistry AID Govt. India, 1965; mem. program project com. Nat. Inst. Dental Research, NIH, 1964-68; spl. cons. Dental Research Inst. program, 1968-70; mem. Dental Research Inst. and spl. program adv. com., 1970-74; cons. to pharmacology-toxicology research program com. Nat. Inst. Gen. Med. Sci., NIH, 1976-81; mem. clin. cancer program project rev. subcom. Nat. Cancer Inst., 1981-88; cons. Engring. Research Group, Stanford Research Inst. Internat., 1981-84. Vice pres. Cleve. chpt. UNICEF, 1968-69; mem. 12th grade sci. adv. com. Cleve. Bd. Edn., 1967-69; mem. adv. council Natural Sci. Mus., Cleve., 1967-69; mem. health goals com. Cleve. Welfare Fedn., mem. community planning and devel. com., 1965-69, chmn. mental health planning com., 1966-69; mem. sci. adv. com. Nassau County Police Dept., 1969-72; edn. adv. com. Garden City Pub. Sch. System, 1974-75; mem. Garden City Bd. Edn., 1975-87, v.p., 1978-83, pres., 1983-87; research adv. group Nassau-Suffolk Regional Med. Program, 1974-75, pres. 1983-87; mem. Nassau County Manpower Adv. Council, 1974-75; sec. bd. trustees N.Y. Ocean Sci. Lab., 1969-72, vice chmn. trustees, 1972-74; trustee Cleve. Center Alcoholism, 1961-64, Mental Health Rehab. and Research, 1963-69, Vocat. Guidance and Rehab. Services, 1963-69, Laurel Sch., Cleve., 1967-69; chmn. bd. dirs. Nassau-Suffolk Community Health Edn. System, 1973-76; bd. dirs. Central Garden City Property Owners Assn., 1973-75; trustee L.I. Library Resources Council, 1975-78, AMD Research Found., 1977-78; bd. advs. Academic Financier; v.p. Garden City Hist. Soc., 1976-78, trustee, 1978-79; pres. Unitarian Universalist Ch. Cen. Nassau, 1989-91, pres. emeritus, 1991-92, treas., 1992—; trustee Metro N.Y. Dist. Unitarian-Universalist Assn., 1991—; Served with USNR, 1944-46. Fellow AAAS, Explorers Club; mem. N.Y. Acad. Pub. Edn., Hempstead C. of C. (participating dir. 1974-76), Phi Beta Kappa, Sigma Xi, Phi Lambda Upsilon, Phi Eta Sigma. Clubs: Cleveland Skating; Chapoquoit Yacht (West Falmouth, Mass.) (sec. 1969); Rowfant (Cleve.). Home: 47 Hilton Ave Garden City NY 11530

HETSKO, CYRIL FRANCIS, retired lawyer, corporation executive; b. Scranton, Pa., Oct. 4, 1911; s. John Andrew and Anna (Lesco) H.; m. Josephine G. Stein, Nov. 12, 1932; children: Jacqueline V. Hetsko Kaufer, Cyril M., Cynthia F. Hetsko Rainey, Jeffrey F. AB, Dickinson Coll., 1933; JD, U. Mich., 1936. Bar: Pa. 1937, N.Y. 1938, U.S. Supreme Ct. 1965. Assoc. Chadbourne, Parke, Whiteside & Wolff (name now Chadbourne & Parke), 1936-55, ptnr., 1955-64; gen. counsel Am. Brands, Inc., 1964-77, v.p., 1965-69, sr. v.p., 1969-77, also former dir.; former dir. Acme Visible Records, Inc., Acushnet Co., Am. Brands Export Corp., Am. Tobacco Internat. Corp., James B. Beam Distilling Co., James B. Beam Distilling Internat. Co., Duffy-Mott Co., Inc., Gallaher Ltd. (Gt. Britain), Master Lock Co., Master Lock Export, Inc., Swingline, Inc., Andrew Jergens Co., Sunshine Biscuits, Inc., Swingline Export Corp., Wilson Jones Co. Mem. ABA, Fed., N.Y. State bar assns., U.S. Trademark Assn. (dir. 1959-67, 68-72, 73-77, pres. 1965-66, hon. bd. chmn. 1966-67, mem. council past presidents 1977—), Explorers Club, Williams Club (N.Y.C.), Ridgewood (N.J.) Country Club, Order of Coif, Phi Beta Kappa, Phi Delta Theta, Delta Theta Phi. Republican. Presbyterian. Home: 714 Waverly Rd Ridgewood NJ 07450-1219

HETTICH, ARTHUR MATTHIAS, editor; b. Bklyn., May 5, 1925; s. Arthur M. and Elsa (Schaeffer) H.; m. Mary Elizabeth Fitz Randolph, Dec. 27, 1952; children: Michael, John, Elizabeth. B.A., Amherst Coll., 1949; M.S. in English, Columbia U., 1950. Editor Thomas Ashwell & Co., N.Y.C., 1950-52; asst. promotion dir. McCall Corp., N.Y.C., 1952-54; v.p. promotion dir. Family Circle, N.Y.C., 1954-66, v.p., editor-in-chief, 1968-88; pres. Family Circle, 1983-88; v.p., dir. pub. relations Cowles Communications, 1966-67; v.p., dir. mag. devel. mag. group N.Y. Times, 1988-89; pub. Insider Reports, 1991—. Author: Best of the Best, 1976, Four Star Kitchens, 1987; editor, pub.: The New York Suburbs, 1960. Served with USN, 1943-46. Mem. N.Y. Athletic Club, Shore Acres Yacht Club (Mamaroneck), Coveleigh Club (Rye). Home and Office: 606 Shore Acres Dr Mamaroneck NY 10543-4011

HETTRICK, WILLIAM EUGENE, music educator; b. Toledo, Nov. 15, 1939; s. William E., Jr. and Marian (Morse) H.; m. Jane Helen Schatkin, June 5, 1966. B.Mus., U. Mich., 1962, M.A., 1964, Ph.D., 1968. Asst. prof. music Hofstra U., 1968-75, assoc. prof., 1975-81, prof., 1981—; dir. Hofstra Collegium Musicum, 1969—. Editor: Gregor Aichinger: Cantiones Ecclesiasticae (1607), 1972, Bernhard Klingenstein: Rosetum Marianum (1604), 1977, Jour. Am. Mus. Instrument Soc., 1979-85, Musica Selecta, 1979—, Gregor Aichinger: The Vocal Concertos (2 vols.), 1986; mem. editorial bd. The American Recorder, 1979-89, Jour. Am. Mus. Instrument Soc., 1986—. Contbr. articles to profl. jours. Fulbright grantee, 1966-67; NEH stipend, 1971, NEH summer Inst., 1985, NEH Travel to Collections award, 1987. Mem. Am. Musicol. Soc., Am. Mus. Instrument Soc. (bd. govs. 1988—), Gesellschaft fuer Bayerische Musikgeschichte, Phi Beta Kappa. Home: 48-21 Glenwood St Little Neck NY 11362 Office: Hofstra U Hempstead NY 11550

HEUER, MARVIN ARTHUR, physician, science foundation executive; b. Mankato, Minn., Mar. 11, 1947; s. Marvin Ernst and Elaine Olive (Melahn) H.; m. Kathryn Ann Klejbuk, Nov. 28, 1975; children: David Walter, Michael Arthur. BA, Mankato State U., 1969; BS, U. Minn., Mpls., 1973, MD, 1973. Intership, resident family practice St. John's Hosp., St. Paul, 1973-74; ptnr. Family Med. Group practice Park Rapids (Minn.)/Walker Clin. LTD, 1974-80; assoc. med. dir. Smith Kline Beechman Corp., Phila., 1980-81, group dir. clin. rsch., 1981-82, acting v.p. world-wide ops., 1982-84, v.p., dir., 1990-92; v.p. med. affairs Ayerst Labs., Am. Homes Prodns., N.Y.C., 1984-87; v.p. R&D Wallace Labs., Cranbury, N.J., 1987-91; pres. Heuer Assocs., North Oaks, Minn., 1991—; physician Westview Clinic, West Saint Paul, Minn., 1991—; clin. asst. prof., Robert Wood Johnson Med. Sch., Dept of Family Med., New Brunswick, N.J.; mem. biotech. adv. bd. Mankato State U.; mem drug utilization rev. panel Dept. Health, Minn., 1992—. Contbr. 12 articles on drugs to profl. jours., tng. manual, Med. Monitors Guide 1983. Del. youth activities St. Matthews Luth. Ch., Moorestown, N.J., 1983-90, trustee 1983-92, alt. bd. mem. 1986; mem. property com. Incarnation Luth. Ch., St. Paul, 1992—. Fellow Am. Bd. Family Practice; mem. AMA, Am. Acad. Family Physicians, Minn. Med. Soc., Pharm. Mfrs. Assn (del. clin. safety 1985—), Minn. Acad. Family Practice (del.), Am. Coll. Cardiology, Am. Rheumatologic Assn. Republican. Home: 28 Nord Circle Rd Saint Paul MN 55127-6515 Office: Westview Clinic 156 Emerson Ave W Saint Paul MN 55118-2599

HEUMANN, PETER L., leasing company executive; b. N.Y.C., July 1, 1945; s. Peter and Alice Kathryn (Lovelace) H.; m. Rebecca Suzanne Gault, Dec. 20, 1969 (div. May 1991); children: David, Sarah, Leah, Joanathan. BS in Commerce, Washington & Lee U., 1967; MBA, U. Ill., 1969. Analyst Andersen Cons., Chgo., 1969-70, Gould Inc., Chgo., 1970-73; mgr. Gould Leasing Inc., Chgo., 1973-79; v.p. PHH Group, Balt., 1979-83; treas. The Scotsman Group, Inc., Balt., 1983—; guest lectr. MBA program Loyola Coll., Balt., 1988-89. Mem. Am. Assn. Equipment Lessors, The Planning Forum. Office: The Scotsman Group Inc 8211 Town Center Dr Baltimore MD 21236

HEUMAN-PERL, JOAN ALICE, nursing educator; b. Sonyea, N.Y., Aug. 12, 1950; d. Walter and Ruth (Levy) Heuman; 1 child, Caroline. BS, U. R.I., 1972; MS, SUNY, Buffalo, 1977; postgrad., U. Conn., 1990—. Psychiat. nurse E.J. Meyer Meml. Hosp., Buffalo, 1972-73; pub. health nurse Erie County Health Dept., Buffalo, 1973-76; instr. State Univ. Coll., Buffalo, 1977; nurse coord. Sunnyview Rehab. Ctr., Schenectady, 1977-80; clin. coord. Boston Vis. Nurse Assn., 1980-81; instr. Boston U., 1981-82; asst. prof. nursing Boston U., Providence, 1982-91; home care dir. nurses, adminstr. Lifetime Med. Home Care, Pawtucket, 1991—. Mem. ANA, APHA, Coun. on Computer Applications in Nursing, Am. Med. Informatics Assn., Sigma Theta Tau, Pi Lambda Theta.

HEWAT, WILLIAM BRIAN, marketing executive; b. Noranda, Que., Can., June 15, 1936; m. Anne Gibberd Whistock. BS in Elec. Engring., U. Western Ont., London, Ont., Can. Registered profl. engr., Can. Bell Can., Que., 1976-80, v.p. mktg., devel., 1980-83, exec. v.p. mktg., Ottawa, Can., 1983-93, pres., CEO, 1993—. Served to Sub-lt., Can. Navy, 1956-60. Mem. Mt. Stephen Club, Rideau Club. Office: Bell Can, 160 Elgin St Ste 1800, Ottawa, ON Canada K1G 3J4

HEWITT, BENJAMIN ATTMORE, psychologist; b. Westerly, R.I., Dec. 20, 1921; s. Benjamin Henry and Anne Mildred (Wangelin) H. BA, Yale U., 1943, MA, 1950, PhD, 1952. Lic. psychol., Conn. Pres. Psychol. Svcs., Inc., New Haven, Conn., 1958-70; rsch. assoc. Yale U., New Haven, 1960-68; cons. psychologist New Haven, 1969—; guest curator Work of Many Hands; Card Tables in Fed. Am. Yale U. Art Gallery, New Haven, 1981-82; furniture researcher, 1965—. Author: The Work of Many Hands: Card Tables in Federal America, 1982. With U.S. Army, 1943-46, PTO. Mem. APA, Conn. State Psychol. Assn. (coun. 1960-64, etics com. 1983-84), Friends of Am. Arts at Yale (sec. 1969-83, exec. com. 1969—). Office: PO Box 1538 Charlestown RI 02813-0907

HEWITT, DON S., television news producer; b. N.Y.C., Dec. 14, 1922; s. Ely S. and Frieda (Pike) H.; children: Jeffrey, Steven, Jill, Lisa; m. Marilyn Berger, Apr. 14, 1979. Student, N.Y. U., 1941; hon. degree, Brandeis U., 1990. War corr., World War II; producer 1st Kennedy-Nixon TV debate, 1960; exec. producer CBS Evening News with Walter Cronkite, 1960-65, 60 Minutes, 1968—. Recipient Paul White award Radio and TV News Dirs. Assn., 1987, Gold medal Internat. Radio and TV Soc., 1988, Gold Baton Columbia DuPont, 1988, Peabody award, 1989, Lowell Thomas Centennial award, 1992, 1st ann. Goldsmith award John F. Kennedy Sch. of Harvard U., 1992; named Broadcaster of Yr., Internat. Radio and TV Soc., 1980, to Hall of Fame, Acad. TV Arts and Scis., 1990.

HEWITT, ELINOR AMRAM, vocational educator; b. Oakland, Calif., Apr. 3, 1937; d. David Werner and Helen Louise (Newlin) Amram; m. Alan David Hewitt (div.); children: Diane, Paula, Laura, David. BA, Bryn Mawr Coll., 1958, MA, 1961; EdD, Temple U., 1986. Ednl. dir. Jewish Employment and Vocat. Svc., Phila., 1974-83; dir. rsch. and devel. Orleans Vocat. Ctr., Jewish Employment & Vocat. Svc., Phila., 1983-87; dir. Orleans Tech. Inst., Phila., 1987-91; dir. of rsch. Jewish Employment and Vocat. Svc., Phila., 1991—. Author: JTPA Assessment Manual, 1985; translator: Journals of Alexander Blok, 1973, Kierkegaard and Existential Philosophy, 1968. Chairperson adv. coun. for career and vocat. edn. Sch. Dist. Phila., 1991—; mem.-at-large S.E. Pa. Employer Adv. Coun., 1991—. Mem. Am. Vocat. Assn., Assn. Jewish Vocat. Svc. Profls., Pa. Assn. Pvt. Sch. Adminstrs. Home: 1873 Woodland Rd Abington PA 19001-3412 Office: Jewish Employment Vocat Svc 1845 Walnut St Philadelphia PA 19103

HEWITT, HARVEY JOHN, principal engineer; b. Three Mile Bay, N.Y., Dec. 24, 1934; s. John Christopher and Louise Mary (Merchant) H.; m. Rita Jane Benney, June 30, 1955; children: Kimberly Ann, David Wayne, John Richard. AAS with honors, SUNY, Canton, 1959; BS, U. Rochester, 1963. Rsch. technician Xerographic Rsch. dept. Xerox Corp., Rochester and Webster, N.Y., 1959-63; devel. engr. Photorecepter Devel. Area Xerox Corp., Webster, 1963-67, unit mgr., 1969-77, tech. specialist, 1969-79, sr. tech. specialist, 1979-84; photoreceptor program mgr. Xerographic Tech. Dept. Xerox Corp., Webster, 1967-69; project mgr. Alloy Photoreceptor Devel. Area Xerox Corp., Webster, 1984-88; technologist, prin. engr. Alloy Photoreceptor Mfg. Xerox Corp., Webster, 1989-91, plant mgr., 1991—; mem. adv. bd. Canton (N.Y.) Coll., 1970—; internat. cons. Xerox Alloy Photorecptors, Webster, 1980-91; sem. leader Diamond Rsch. Corp., Santa Barbara, Calif., 1989. Patentee in field. Elder Williamson (N.Y.) Presbyn. Ch., 1963-78; deacon Webster Bible Ch., 1985-90, mem. choir, 1982-89; vol., bd. dirs. Wayen County Rural Ministry, Williamson, 1963-72; fireman Pultneyville (N.Y.) Fire Dept., 1962-67; vol. ambulance Williamson Ambulance Corps., 1975-78. Republican. Home: 4309 Lake Rd Williamson NY 14589-9603 Office: Xerox Corp 800 Phillips Rd Webster NY 14580-9791

HEWSON, MARTIN GERARD, government official; b. Plattsburgh, N.Y., Jan. 1, 1929; s. Elmer Eduard and Hartie Maude (Martin) H.; m. Anne Rosalie Miner, Jan. 7, 1956; children: Martin G., Susan A., Thomas P., Eric C., Mickeyh M. Grad., U.S. Border Patrol Acad. Patrol inspector U.S. Border Patrol, El Paso, Tex., 1957-58, Brownsville, Tex., 1958-59, Richford, Vt., 1959-68; immigration inspector Immigration & Naturalization Dept., Pittsburg, N.H., 1968—. Chmn. U.C.V. Hosp. bd. dirs., Colebrook, N.H., 1973-88; pres. Indian Stream Med. Clinic, Colebrook, 1980-82; bd. dirs. Kerbs Meml. Hosp., St. Albans, Vt., 1967-68, others. With USAF, 1947-57. Named Outstanding Hosp. Trustee N.H. Hosp. Assn., 1985, Outstanding Performance Dept. of Justice, 1989. Mem. Lions, 45th Investment Club (v.p. 1985-86), K.C. (dep. grand knight 1987-92, grand knight 1992—). Republican. Roman Catholic. Home: Tatlayoko Acres RFD 1 PO Box 63 Pittsburg NH 03592-0063

HEY, JAMES CONRAD, marketing executive; b. Buffalo, Mar. 6, 1959; s. John Junior and Florence Clara (Truskey) H. BSChemE, Clarkson U., 1981; MBA in Gen. Mgmt., Harvard U., 1986. Product devel. engr. Procter & Gamble Inc., Cin., 1981-84; mktg. asst. Quaker Oats Co., Chgo., 1986-87, asst. product mgr., 1987-89; product mgr. Bristol-Myers Squibb Co.-Westwood Pharms., Buffalo, 1989-90; group product mgr. Bausch & Lomb, Inc., Rochester, N.Y., 1990-91; dir. mktg. personal products internat. div. Bausch & Lomb, Rochester, N.Y., 1991—. Tutor Cabrini Green Tutorial Program, Chgo., 1986-89. Office: Bausch & Lomb Inc 42 East Ave PO Box 743 Rochester NY 14603-0743

HEYDE, MARTHA BENNETT (MRS. ERNEST R. HEYDE), psychologist; b. New Bern, N.C., Jan. 31, 1920; d. George Spotswood and Katherine (McIntosh) Bennett; AB, Barnard Coll., 1941; MA, Columbia, 1949, PhD, 1959; m. Ernest R. Heyde, Aug. 17, 1946. Instr. psychol. founds. and services Tchrs. Coll., Columbia U., N.Y.C., 1953-60, research asst., career pattern study Horace Mann-Lincoln Inst., Tchrs. Coll. Columbia U., 1957-59, research assoc., 1960-70, cons., 1970-73. Mem. Barnard Coll. Alumnae Council, 1956-61, 69—, pres. class, 1956-61. Trustee, Barnard Coll., 1974-78, hon. vice-chmn. Barnard Coll. Centennial, 1987-89. Mem. Am. Psychol. Assn., Am. Personnel and Guidance Assn., Sigma Xi, Kappa Delta Pi, Pi Lambda Theta. Contbr. to research monograph The Vocational Maturity of Ninth Grade Boys, 1960, Floundering and Trial After High Sch, 1967; co-author: Vocational Maturity During the High School Years, 1979. Home: 140 Cabrini Blvd Apt 109 New York NY 10033-3434

HEYDEBRAND, WOLF VON, sociology educator; b. Kl. Tschunkawe, Germany, June 15, 1930; came to U.S., 1954; s. Georg Von and Sigrid Von (Waldersee) H.; m. Ruth Keiling, Sept. 1954 (div. 1973); 1 child, Gitry V.; m. Sarah Rosenfield, June 1974 (div. 1979); m. Elizabeth Robinson, Mar. 1987; children: Daniel Adam V., Sophia Ingrid V. M.A., U. Chgo., 1961, Ph.D., 1965. Asst. prof. sociology U. Chgo., 1964-67; assoc. prof. Washington U., St. Louis, 1967-71; prof. NYU, N.Y.C., 1973—; vis. assoc. prof. Columbia U., 1972-73; co-dir. Comparative Orgn. Research Program, U. Chgo., 1964-67; research assoc. Med. Care Research Ctr., St. Louis, 1967-71; co-prin. investigator Explorat's Health Service, N.Y.C., 1972-74. Author: Hospital Bureaucracy, 1973; (with others) Rationalizing Justice: The Political Economy of Federal District Courts, 1990; editor: Comparative Organizations, 1973; assoc. editor: Am. Jour. Sociology, 1964-67, Contemporary Sociology, 1972-74, Social Problems, 1981-84, Law and Soc. Rev., 1986—. Grantee NSF, 1964; grantee USPHS, 1967, Nat. Ctr. Health Service, 1972, Russell Sage Found., 1974-75. Mem. Am. Sociol. Assn. (pres. sect. orgns.

and occupations, 1987—), Ea. Sociol. Assn. (exec. council 1979-82), Law and Soc. Assn. (trustee), Internat. Sociol. Assn. Jewish. Office: NYU Dept Sociology 269 Mercer St Rm 411 New York NY 10003-6633

HEYER, JOHN HAJDU, college dean, conductor, musicologist; b. Altoona, Pa., Jan. 4, 1945; s. Joseph and Martha Elizabeth (Somerville) Hajdu; m. Sandra L. Heyer, 1973; children: John E., David J. MusB, DePauw U., 1966; MusM, U. Colo., 1970, PhD, 1973. Asst./assoc. prof. U. Calif., Santa Cruz, 1973-79, prof., dept. chmn., 1980-87; dean Coll. Fine Arts, Indiana (Pa.) U., 1987—; lectr. Carmel (Calif.) Bach Festival, 1980—. condr.: (recordings) Messe des Morts, Gilles, 1980, Motets, Lully, 1987; editor : (score) Messe des Morts, Gilles, 1984, (book) Studies on Lully, 1990. Pres. Rocky Ridge Music Found., 1989—. Mem. Am. Musicol. Soc. (council 1978-89, Noah Greenberg award 1980, 85). Office: Indiana U Pa Coll Fine Arts 110 Sprowls Hall Indiana PA 15701

HEYMAN, ANNETTE HELEN, radiologic technologist, retired; b. Springfield, Mass., Mar. 19, 1926; d. Leo and Flora Dorothy (Rubin) H. BS, U. Mass., 1947; cert. lab., x-ray tech., Ea. Sch. for Physicians Aides, 1949; MEd, Springfield Coll., 1964. Lic. radiologic tech., Mass.; registered med. asst. Med. asst. Dr. M. B. Fried, Springfield, 1947-48, Dr. Charles Furcolo, Springfield, 1949; chief x-ray tech. Western Mass. Hosp., Westfield, 1950-80, radiology dept. head, 1980-90; ret., 1990. Editor: Jour. Am. Registry of Med. Assts., 1981—. Mem., pres. B'Nai B'rith Young Women, Springfield, 1948-49, Nat. Coun. Jewish Jrs., Springfield, 1950-52. Mem. Am. Registry Radiologic Technologists, Am. Soc. Radiologic Technologists, Am. Registry Med. Assts. (life mem., bd. dirs. 1950—, sec. gen. 1961-81, exec. sec. 1981-86, exec. dir. 1986—), Mass. Soc. Radiologic Technologists (life mem., bd. dirs. Western dist. 1957), Mass. Employees Assn., Ret. State County & Mcpl. Employees Assn. (AFSCME retiree program 1991—), Springfield Coll. Alumni Assn., U. Mass. Alumni Assn., Temple Beth El and Sisterhood, B'Nai B'Rith Women (life mem., chpt. treas. 1981-88), Sigma Delta Tau (treas. 1946-47, alumni chpt. pres. 1956-60), Psi Tau Corp. (constrn. bldg. bd. 1947-58, 64-65), others. Home: 224 Westbrook Dr Springfield MA 01129

HEYN, WILLIAM CARVETH, real estate development company executive. BS, Northwestern U. Sales rep. Armstrong World Industries, Lancaster, Pa., 1937-40; sales mgr., later chmn. bd. dirs. Hanna Engrng. Works, Chgo., 1940-43; cons. Booz, Allen & Hamilton, Chgo., 1943-47; v.p. adminstrn. New Holland div. Sperry Rand, Holland, Pa., 1947-72; pres. Klein Chocolate Co., Elizabethtown, Pa., 1972-73, Libibs, Inc., Lancaster, 1960—; bd. dirs. Warfel Constrn. Co., Huth Engrs., Lancaster, Pa. Trustee, Franklin and Marshal Coll., Lancaster, Lancaster YWCA, Lancaster Free Pub. Library, Lancaster Symphony Assn. Mem. Lancaster C. of C., YMCA, Delta Tau Delta, Deru, Purplekey and Lynx Socs., Lancaster Country Club, Hamilton Club Lancaster, Birnam Wood Golf Club, Sailing Club Chesapeake, Pirates of Lancaster, Tucwan Club, Annapolis Yacht Club, Skytop Club. Republican. Home: 2609 Mondamin Farm Rd Lancaster PA 17601-5315

HEYS, JOHN RICHARD, research chemist; b. Dayton, Ohio, Oct. 15, 1947; s. George and Dorothy Estelle (Landefeld) H.; m. Anna Elizabeth Bury, June 28, 1975; 1 child, Stuart Landefeld. BA in Chemistry, DePauw U., 1969; PhD in Organic Chemistry, Stanford U., 1976. Rsch. assoc. Yale U., New Haven, 1976-77; assoc. chemist Midwest Rsch. Inst., Kansas City, Mo., 1977-79, sr. chemist, program mgr., 1979-83; sr. investigator SmithKline Beckman Corp. (later SmithKline Beecham Corp.), King of Prussia, Pa., 1983-87, asst. dir. synthetic chemistry, 1987-91; assoc. dir. synthetic chemistry, 1991—. Contbr. articles to tech. jours. With U.S. Army, 1969-71, Korea. Mem. AAAS, Am. Chem. Soc., Internat. Union Pure and Applied Chemistry, Internat. Isotope Soc. (pres. N.E. sect. 1988). Office: SmithKline Beecham Pharms PO Box 1539 King Of Prussia PA 19406-0939

HEYWARD, ANDREW JOHN, television producer; b. Roslyn, N.Y., Oct. 29, 1950; s. E.J.R. and Elisabeth Heyward; m. Jody Gaylin Heyward, May 23, 1976; children: David, Emily, Sarah. BA, Harvard U., 1972. Producer Sta. WNEW-TV News, N.Y.C., 1974-76; producer Sta. WCBS-TV News, N.Y.C., 1976-78, exec. producer, 1978-81; producer CBS Evening News CBS News, N.Y.C., 1981-84, sr. producer, 1984-87, exec. producer 48 Hours, 1987—. Mem. NATAS (Emmy award 1977-78, 84, 88, 89, 90). Office: CBS News 524 W 57th St New York NY 10019-2902

HEYWORTH, LAWRENCE, III, imaging systems manufacturing executive; b. Annapolis, Md., July 10, 1948; s. Lawrence Jr. and Jean (Holloway) H.; m. Marijo Oliver, Feb. 5, 1972; children: Marianne, Lawrence IV, Charlotte Cordes. BS, U.S. Naval Acad., 1970. Commd. ensign USN, 1984, advanced through grades to comdr., 1985; Caribbean country dir. Office Sec. Def., Washington, 1988-90; ret., 1990; mfg. supr. DuPont Imaging Systems, Towanda, Pa., 1990—. Coach Youth Soccer Orgn., Arlington, Va., 1989-90, Towanda, 1991. Recipient Superior Svc. award Dept. Def., 1990. Mem. U.S. Naval Inst. (bd. ddirs. 1979-80), Army-Navy Club. Republican. Episcopalian. Home: 305 York Ave Towanda PA 18848 Office: DuPont Imaging Systems RD 1 Box 15 Towanda PA 18848

HIBBARD, JOHN EUGENE, executive; b. Putnam, Conn., Mar. 27, 1936; s. J. Eugene and Sigrid Caroline (Nyholm) H.; m. Julia Mckain Lampkin, Mar. 30, 1959 (div. 1963); Bernice Arline Stoner, July 3, 1965; 1 child, Elizabeth Ann. BS, U. Conn., 1958. Tech., plant pest control USDA AG Rsch. Svc., Coral Gables, Fla., 1961-63; exec. dir. Conn. Forest & Park Assn. Inc., Middlefield, Conn., 1963—. Editor: (mag.) Conn. Woodlands, 1963-91, (guidebook) Conn. Walk Book, 9th-12th edit., 1972-78. Vice chmn. Bd. Selectman, Hebron, COnn., 1989-91, chmn. 1991—; chmn. Charter Commn., Hebron, 1987-88, Planning Zoning Commn., Hebron, 1976-81, Conservation Commn., Hebron, 1968-76. With U.S. Army, 1959-61. Mem. New Eng. Soc. Am. Foresters (chmn. 1986-87), Yankee Div. Soc. Am. Foresters. Democrat. Congregationalist. Home: 1072 Gilead St Hebron CT 06248-1111 Office: Conn Forest & Park Assn 16 Meriden Rd Rockfall CT 06481-2961

HIBBERT, JOCELYN CLARE, counselor, consultant; b. Barton-on-Sea, U.K., Sept. 12, 1963; d. Peter Glynn and Geraldine Ann (Williams) H. BS in Edn., U. Del., 1986; MS in Counseling, San Diego State U., 1988. Lic. guidance counselor K-12, Del.; lic. elem. and spl. edn. tchr., Del.; nat. cert. counselor; cert. ins. rehab. specialist. Spl. edn. tchr. Christina Sch. Dist., Newark, Del., 1987; guidance counselor San Diego (Calif.) City Schs., 1988; career advisor Univ. Calif. San Diego, La Jolla, 1988; grad. program advisor San Diego (Calif.) State Univ., 1987-89; vocat. cons. Delaware Valley Rehab. Svc., Wilmington, Del., 1989-90; sales cons. Victoria's Secret, Wilmington, 1990—; vocat. cons. Olsten Rehab., Wilmington, 1990—. Youth advisor Sr. High Youth Group, 1st Unitarian Ch., Wilmington, 1990—. Mem. AACD, Nat. Assn. Rehab. Profls. in Pvt. Sector, Nat. Rehab. Assn., First State Rehab. Counseling Assn. (sec. 1990, pres. 1991, past pres. 1992), Univ. Del. Alumni Assn., San Diego State Univ. Alumni Assn. Republican. Office: Upjohn Rehab Svcs 3535 Silverside Rd Wilmington DE 19810-4912

HIBBITTS, BERNARD JOHN, law educator; b. Halifax, N.S., Can., June 29, 1959; came to U.S., 1987; s. John Bernard and June Marie (Hilchey) H. BA, LLB, Dalhousie U., Halifax, 1980, 84; MA, Carleton U., Ottawa, Ont., 1981; BA, Oxford (Eng.) U., 1983; LLM, U. Toronto & Harvard Law Sch., 1986, 88; MA, Oxford (Eng.) U., 1989. Bar: N.S. 1987. Law clk. to Justice Gerald Le Dain Supreme Ct. Can., Ottawa, 1984; articled clk. McInnes, Cooper & Robertson, Halifax, 1986-87; vis. prof. law U. Pitts., 1988-89, asst. prof. law, 1989-92; assoc. prof. law, 1992—. Assoc. editor Harvard Internat. Law Jour., 1987-88; contbr. articles to profl. jours. Rhodes scholar, 1981; Knox fellow, 1987. Mem. ABA, Can. Bar Assn., Am. Soc. Legal History, Selden Soc. Anglican. Home: 5631 Northumberland St Apt 3 Pittsburgh PA 15217-1237 Office: U Pitts Sch Law 3900 Forbes Ave Pittsburgh PA 15260-0001

HICKEY, JAMES ALOYSIUS CARDINAL, archbishop; b. Midland, Mich., Oct. 11, 1920; s. James P. and Agnes (Ryan) H. J.C.D., Lateran U., Italy, 1950; S.T.D., Angelicum U., Italy, 1951; M.A., Mich. State U., 1962. Ordained priest Roman Catholic Ch., 1946; sec. to Bishop of Saginaw, 1951-60; rector St. Paul Sem., Saginaw, Mich., 1960-68; aux. bishop Saginaw, 1967-69; chmn. bishops' com. on Priestly Formation, 1968-69; rector N.Am. Coll., Rome, 1969-74; bishop of Cleve., 1974-80, archbishop of Washington, 1980—; chancellor Cath. U. Am., 1980—; elevated to cardinal, 1988; mem. Cen. Com. for 1975 Holy Year, 1973-75; chmn. Bishop's Com. Pastoral Rsch. and Practices, 1974-77, Bishop's Com. for Doctrine, 1979-82; chmn. bd. trustees Nat. Shrine of Immaculate Conception, 1980—; chmn. Bishops' Com. Human Values, 1984-87; chmn. Bishop's Com. on N.Am. Coll., 1988-92. Episcopal advisor to Serra Internat., 1981-88; Episcopal moderator Holy Childhood Assn., 1984—; chmn. Bishops' Com. on N.Am. Coll., 1988-91; mem. coun. for secretariat Synod of Bishops, 1991—. Address: Archdiocese Washington Archdiocesan Pastoral Ctr PO Box 29260 Washington DC 20017

HICKEY, KATE DONNELLY, college library director; b. Durham, N.C., Dec. 29, 1943; d. Frederick Stockham Jr. and Margaret Frances (Dougherty) Donnelly; m. Robert James Hickey Jr., Dec. 21, 1963; children: Robert James III, Marian Margaret. BA, Swarthmore Coll., 1966; MS Libr. Sci., Clarion U., 1982. Children's libr. Green Free Libr., Wellsboro, Pa., 1973-76; libr. U.S. Fish & Wildlife Svc., Wellsboro, 1976-83; reference libr. Williamsport (Pa.) Area Community Coll., 1983-84; dir. of the coll. libr. Pa. Coll. Tech. (formerly Williamsport Area Community Coll.), Williamsport, 1984—; elected sec. Interlibr. Delivery Svc. of Pa. Bd., State College, Pa., 1990—; chair, sec.-treas. Susquehanna Libr. Coop., Williamsport, 1986-90. Contbr. articles and book revs. to profl. pubs. Pres., bd. dirs. Mansfield (Pa.) Coop. Nursery Sch., 1969-73, Twin Tiers Regional Sci. Fair, Inc., Wellsboro, 1981-84. Mem. ALA, Pa. Libr. Assn. (elected sec. coll. and rsch. librs. bd. dirs. 1988-91), Coun. Pa. Libr. Networks (chairperson 1991—), BEta Phi Mu. Home: 403 W 8th Ave Williamsport PA 17701-7536 Office: Pa Coll Tech 1 College Ave Williamsport PA 17701

HICKEY, PATRICIA ALICE, surgical nurse coordinator; b. Keene, N.Y., June 22, 1935; d. John James and Daisy (Pratt) H. RN, St. Joseph's Hosp., 1955; BA, Mary Mount Manhattan Coll., 1983; MS, Fordham U., 1988. Staff nurse Placid Meml. Hosp., Lake Placid, N.Y., 1956-63; staff nurse Meml. Sloan Kettering Cancer Ctr., N.Y.C., 1963-68, head nurse, 1968, 1968-77, staff nurse, 1977-81, clin. specialist, 1981—; speaker in field. Contbr. articles to profl. jours. Vol. Legion of Mary Cath. Ch., N.Y., 1963-65, AIDS Counseling Behavior Modification, N.Y., 1986—, Health Internat. Nurses Conf., N.Y., 1990. Recipient Wholeness of Life award Greater N.Y. chpt. Hosp. Chaplains, Citizens award Keene Ctr. Sch. Honor Soc., 1991. Mem. AACD, Am. Operating Rm. Nurse Assn., Meml. Sloan Kettering Cancer Ctr. Nurses Assn. (pres. 1983-91), Fordham U. Alumni Assn., Mary Mount Manhattan Coll. Alumni Assn., St. Joseph's Hosp. Nursing Alumni Assn. Democrat. Roman Catholic. Home: 1233 York Ave Apt 12C New York NY 10021-6347 Office: Meml Sloan Kettering Cancer Ctr 1275 York Ave New York NY 10021-6094

HICKMAN, JANET S., college dean; b. Bklyn., Aug. 28, 1948; d. Richard and Frances J. (Falconer) Liberth; m. C. Kennedy Hickman, June 21, 1970; 1 child, Kennedy R. BSN cum laude, U. Bridgeport, 1970; MS, No. Ill. U., 1976; EdD, Temple U., 1987. RN, Ill., Ohio, Pa., Del., N.Y. Instr. St. Joseph Hosp., Joliet, Ill., Wright State U., Dayton, Ohio; asst. prof. Neumann Coll., Aston, Pa.; assoc. dean health professions Ea. Coll., St. Davids, Pa. Author: (with others) Nursing Theories, 3d edit., 1990, Mental Health and Psychiatric Nursing, 1992; contbr. articles to profl. jours. Mem. Nat. League for Nursing, Am. Assn. Colls. Nursing, Pa. Higher Edn. Nursing Schs. (sec.). Home: 1435 Clover Ln West Chester PA 19380-5906

HICKMAN, PETER JAMES, writer, editor, media-foreign affairs consultant; b. Dallas, May 28, 1931; s. Jesse Archibald and Ara America (Masterson) H.; m. Elida Lourdes Martin-Ulloa de H., June 19, 1967; children: Michael Anthony, Daniel Edward. BJ, U. Tex., 1957. Fgn. svc. officer U.S. Info. Agy., various locations, 1957-70; pub. affairs officer U.S. Govt. Agencies, Washington, 1970-83; internat. cons. Hickman Internat. Cons., Bethesda, Md., 1986-88; pub. affairs officer Agy. for Internat. Devel. and U.S. Dept. State, Washington, 1983-86; chief exec., mng. editor Interpress 77 S.A., Madrid, Washington, 1987-88; dir. communications Ctr. for Privatization, Washington, 1988-90; dir. internat. media and press divs. Theisen Communications, Inc., Washington, 1989—; corr. McGraw-Hill News Svc.; freelance journalist INSIGHT News and Features; cons. Am. C. of C., Argentina, AGORA Ctr. for Internat. Studies, Ctr. for Econ. Analysis Rosario, Co. Argentina de Construcciones and SADEI Media Group. Scoutmaster Boy Scouts Am., Bethesda, 1978—. Recipient Hon. award, U.S. Info. Agy., 1963, Citation, Gen. Svcs. Adminstrn., 1980. Mem. Fgn. Corrs. Assn. Argentina, Fgn. Corrs. Assn. Washington, Overseas Writers, Overseas Press Club Am., Washington Ind. Writers, USIA Alumni Assn., Diplomatic and Consular Officers Ret., Meridian House Internat., Internat. Coun. for Internat. Visitors, Internat. Visitors Info. Svc., Tex. State Soc., Soc. for Internat. Devel., Youth for Understanding Internat. Student Exchange, George Washington U. Club, Nat. Press Club (morning newsmakers com.), Ctr. for Fgn. Journalists (faculty), Am. Fgn. Svc. Assn. Republican. Home and Office: 6425 Hollins Dr Bethesda MD 20817-2347

HICKS, JANICE MARIE, physical chemistry educator; b. Balt., July 28, 1958; d. John Earl and Helen (Waytow) H. AB, Bryn Mawr (Pa.) Coll., 1980; MA, Columbia U., 1982, PhD, 1986. Postdoctoral fellow dept. chemistry and physics U. Pa., Phila., 1986-89; Clare Boothe Luce asst. prof. Georgetown U., Washington, 1989—. Author: (chpt.) Nonlinear Optics as A Probe of Surfaces and Interfaces, 1991; contbr. over 11 articles to profl. jours. Columbia U. fellow, 1986. Mem. Am. Chem. Soc., Am. Phys. Soc., Am. Geophys. Union, Assn. for Women in Sci., NSF (Presdl. Young Investigator 1991). Office: Dept Chemistry Georgetown U Washington DC 20057

HICKS, JOSEPH BRYAN, mental health counselor; b. Phila., Oct. 23, 1936; s. Edwin Joseph and Elizabeth (Bryan) H.; m. Nancy McCreary, Oct. 5, 1959 (div. 1973); children: Bryan, Lisa, Glen, Owen; m Marcia Ruth Morin, Dec. 24,1986. BA, Temple U., 1965, MEd, 1970. Cert. clin. mental health counselor. With sales dept. Borden Foods Co., Phila., 1960-65; rehab.counselor Bur. Vocat. Rehab. State of Pa., Rosemont, 1965-68; prevocat. evaluator Vanguard CareerGuidance Ctr., Valley Forge, Pa., 1968-69; rehab. counselor Vocat. Rehab. Svc. of Del., Kent and Suxxex Counties, 1969-83; counselor Div. Employment and Tng. State of Del., Wilmington, 1983-90; pvt. practice mental health counselor APR Counseling Assocs., Dover, Del., 1975—; instr. Del. Tech. and Community Coll., Dover, 1977-78; dir. Milton H. Erickson Inst. of Del., Dover, 1988—. Co-leader Moores Lake Environ. Assn., Dover, 1990. With U.S. Army, 1955-57. Mem. Am. Assn. Counseling and Devel., Am. Mental Health Counselors Assn., Del. Mental Health Counselors Assn., Anxiety Dosorders Assn. Am. Home and Office: 71 S Shore Dr Dover DE 19901-5736

HICKS, PAUL B., JR., retired petroleum company executive; b. Norfolk, Va., Oct. 3, 1925; s. Paul B. and Maerose (Rausch) H.; m. Lucile Green, Nov. 28, 1953; children: Paul Burton III, Peter David, Thomas Patrick. B.A., U. Va., 1950. Sales rep. Texaco Inc., 1953-57, dist. supr. merchandising, 1957-60; dist. sales mgr. Texaco Inc., Chgo., 1960-62; asst. div. sales mgr. Texaco Inc., 1962; mgr. merchandising Texaco Inc., N.Y.C., 1962; div. sales mgr. Texaco Inc., Columbus, Ohio, 1963-65; asst. to pres. Texaco Inc., N.Y.C., 1965-66; gen. mgr. sales dept. U.S. Texaco Inc., 1966-69; v.p. sales dept. Texaco Inc., U.S., 1969-72; v.p. worldwide sales Texaco Inc., 1972-75, v.p. pub. relations and personnel, 1975-77, v.p. pub. relations and advt., 1977-83; pres. Texaco Europe, 1983-90; sr. v.p. Texaco, Inc., 1986-90; retired, 1990. Mem. Winged Foot Golf Club (pres.), Greenwich Country Club, Farmington Country Club, Zeta Psi. Clubs: Winged Foot Golf (pres.), Greenwich Country, Farmington (Va.) Country. Home: 3 Cornelia Dr Greenwich CT 06830-3906

HICKS, WALTER JOSEPH, electrical engineer, consultant; b. Lawrence, Mass., Mar. 10, 1935; s. Walter Francis and Ethel Mary (Royds) H.; m. Faith Winfield McCrum, Apr. 4, 1959; children: Janet Lee, Walter David, Pamela Jean. BSEE, MIT, 1957, MSEE, 1957; PhD in Plasma Physics, N.Mex. State U., 1969. Elec. engr. Raytheon Co., Bedford, Mass., 1957-67; radar system engr., dept. mgr. Raytheon Co., 1970-74; tech. advisor Raytheon Co., Lowell, Mass., 1974-84; cons. engr. Raytheon Co., Bedford, 1984—; mem. sci. adv. bd. USAF, Washington, 1983. Patentee in field. Elder United Presbyn. Ch., Newton, Mass., 1978-82. Home: 7 Pinewood Rd Acton MA 01720-4409 Office: Raytheon Co Hartwell Rd Bedford MA 01730-2407

HIDEN, ROBERT BATTAILE, JR., lawyer; b. Boston, May 8, 1933; s. Robert Battaile Sr. and Clotilda (Waddell) H.; m. Ann Eliza McCracken, Mar. 27, 1956; children: Robert B. III, Elizabeth Patterson, John Hughes. BA, Princeton U., 1955; LLB, U. Va., 1960. Bar: N.Y. 1961, U.S. Ct. Appeals (2d cir.) 1974, U.S. Dist. Ct. (so. dist.) N.Y. 1975. Assoc. Sullivan & Cromwell, N.Y.C., 1960-67, ptnr., 1968—. Articles editor and contbr. U. Va. Law Rev., 1959-60; contbr., mem. bd. editors Futures Internat. Law Letter, 1987—. Trustee Hampton (Va.) U. and Hampton Inst., 1984—; commr. Larchmont Little League, N.Y., 1964-68; chmn. Larchmont Jr. Sailing Program, 1977-78; vestry, jr. warden St. John's Episc. Ch., Larchmont, 1982-86. Served to lt. (j.g.) USNR, 1955-57. Mem. ABA, N.Y. State Bar Assn., Assn. of Bar of City of N.Y., N.Y. County Bar Assn., Am. Judicature Soc., Raven Soc., Order of Coif, Omicron Delta Kappa. Democrat. Clubs: Larchmont U. (pres. 1976-77), Larchmont Yacht (trustee 1979-85, sec. 1990—); N.Y. Yacht (N.Y.C.); Scarsdale Golf (N.Y.). Home: 2 Walnut Ave Larchmont NY 10538-4232 Office: Sullivan & Cromwell 250 Park Ave New York NY 10177-0001 also: Sullivan & Cromwell 125 Broad St New York NY 10004

HIEMSTRA, JOHN E., executive; b. Oskaloosa, Iowa, June 21, 1928; s. Frank H. and Gertrude H. (DeKock) H.; m. Norma L. Franklin, Aug. 20, 1948; children: Carol, Ruth, Jean, Nancy. BA, Cen. U., 1952; EdD, Rtugers U., 1978; MDiv, New Brunswick Sem., 1955; DD, Cen. U., 1989. Ordained as min. of word. Min. First Reformed Ch., Waterloo, Iowa, 1955-59, Good Shepherd Ch., Westland, Mich., 1959-64; exec. min. Reformed Ch. Am., N.Y.C., 1964-72; communication dir. United Ministries, N.Y.C., 1972-79; exec. sec. Synod of N.Y., Tarrytown, 1979—; pres. Reformed Ch. Am., 1990-91; moderator Gen. Synod Ref. Ch. of Am., 1991-92; pres. N.Y. Coun. Chs., Syracuse, 1987-89; mem. N.Y.C. Ch. Coun., 1979—. Pres. Hudson Area Housing Agy., Tarrytown, 1985—, Spl. Ministries to Japanese, Bronx, 1986—. Named Man of Yr. Jaycees, Westland, 1963. Mem. Assn. Edn., Aircraft Owners and Pilots Assn., Classis of Rockland-Westchester, Rtugers Alumni Assn., New Brunswick Sem. Alumni Assn. Home: 4 Deerfield Ln West Nyack NY 10994 Office: Synod of NY 42 N Broadway Tarrytown NY 10591

HIGBIE, LESLIE WILSON, broadcaster, congressional staffer; b. Morris, Minn., Oct. 30, 1914; s. Edgar Creighton and Nellie May (Leslie) H.; m. Elizabeth Blood Rock, May 26, 1979. BS in Journalism, Univ. Ill., 1937; postgrad., George Washington U., Am. U. News broadcaster various radio stations, ea. U.S., 1938-47; correspondent Mut. Network Washington Bur., 1947-59; freelance writer and broadcaster various networks, Washington, 1959-64; spl. asst. Congressman William S. Moorhead, Pa., 1965-66; press sec. Sen. Eugene McCarthy, 1967-71; with U.S. Info. Agy. Voice of Am., Washington, 1971-76. Author: booklet on Gerontology Research, Nat. Inst. on Aging. Founding sponsor, exec. bd. mem. Taylor Run Citizens Assn., Alexandria, Va., 1954-57. Capt. USAAC, 1942-44, various overseas combat zones.

HIGBY, KATHLEEN ROSE, counseling agency executive, counselor, consultant; b. Providence, Sept. 12, 1950; d. Francis John and Edith Marie (Hilton) McCaffrey; m. Raymond F. Higby, June 20, 1972; children: Jodie Alexandra, Deanna Nicole, Kerri Kathleen. BA in Edn. and Psychology, U. R.I., 1968; MA in Agy. Counseling, R.I. Coll., 1983. Cert. clin. mental health counselor, chem. dependency clin. supr., alcohol and drug counselor; lic. mental health counselor, R.I. Tchr. Cranston (R.I.) Sch. Dept., 1972-74; counselor Warwick, R.I., 1983-85; sr. counselor Kent Ho., Warwick, R.I., 1985-87; clin. supr. Directions, West Warwick, 1987-89; group facilitator Codependency, S.D., 1989—; pres. Feeling and Healing Groups, Inc., Warwick, 1989—; cons., lectr., 1989—; lectr. codependency and couples, 1989—. Featured in documentary Adult Children of Alcoholics, WBZ-TV, Boston, 1989; pres. aux. R.I. Soc. Osteo. Physicians and Surgeons, 1987. Mem. AACD, R.I. Assn. Children of Alcoholics. Roman Catholic. Office: Feeling & Healing Groups 251 Pawtuxet Ave Warwick RI 02888-1900

HIGGINBOTHAM, A. LEON, JR., federal judge; b. Trenton, N.J., Feb. 25, 1928; m. Evelyn Brooks; children: Stephen, Karen, Kenneth, Nia. Student, Purdue U., 1944-46; BA, Antioch Coll., 1949; LLB, Yale U., 1952. Asst. dist. atty. Phila. County, 1953-54; ptnr. Norris, Green, Harris & Higginbotham, Phila., 1954-62; spl. dep. atty. gen. State of Pa., Harrisburg, 1956-62; commr. FTC, Washington, 1962-64; judge U.S. Dist. Ct. (ea. dist.) Pa., 1964-77, U.S. Ct. Appeals, Phila., 1977—; spl. hearing officer conscientious objectors U.S. Justice Dept., Washington, 1960-62; commr. Pa. Human Relations Commn., 1961-62. Office: US Ct Appeals 22613 US Courthouse 601 Market St Philadelphia PA 19106-1510

HIGGINBOTHAM, JOHN TAYLOR, lawyer; b. St. Louis, Feb. 10, 1947; s. Richard Cann and Jocelyn (Taylor) H.; m. Lauren Flint Totty, Aug. 9, 1975 (div. 1979). B.A., UCLA, 1969; J.D., Columbia U., 1972. Bar: N.Y. 1975, Calif. 1976. Assoc., Kirlin, Campbell & Keating, N.Y.C., 1972-74; atty. Nat. Bank of N.Am., N.Y.C., 1974-76; atty., dir. real estate Korvettes Inc., N.Y.C., 1979-82; assoc. Leon Katz, Bklyn., 1983-84; assoc. Finley, Kumble, Wagner, Heine, Underberg, Manley & Casey, N.Y.C., 1984-86; assoc. regional counsel HUD, N.Y.C., 1986-88, Sterling Securities, Inc., Manhasset, N.Y., 1989—. Editor: Safe Deposit Decisions and Practice, 1977—. Mem. NARAS, NATAS.

HIGGINS, BARBARA S., parent-child health nurse, educator; b. Waterville, Maine, July 5, 1955; d. Sherman and Eleanor (Winchenbach) Smith; m. Michael D. Higgins, June 23, 1979; children: Gregory M., Bennett P. BSN, U. So. Maine, Portland, 1977; MSN, U. Tex., Austin, 1983; MEd, U. Maine, 1982, PhD, 1989. Cert. Brazelton neonatal behavioral assessment scale. Pub. health nurse State of Maine, Bangor; nurse, labor and delivery Eastern Maine Med. Ctr., Bangor; assoc. prof. Husson Coll. Ea. Maine Med. Ctr., Bangor. Contbr. articles to profl. jours. Mem. NAACOG, Nat. Coun. on Family Rels., Sigma Theta Tau, Phi Kappa Phi.

HIGGINS, CRAIG STOCKTON, educator; b. Bklyn., Jan. 16, 1943; s. Russell Dwen and Emily Adele (Brockway) H.; m. Suzanne Parker, Sept. 11, 1965; children: Paige, Brooke. BA in English, Lafayette Coll., 1965; M in Hosp. Adminstrn., Duke U., 1970; MBA, Loyola Coll., Balt., 1975; PhD in Policy Scis., U. Md., 1985. Dir. planning Union Meml. Hosp., Balt., 1970-72, asst. dir., 1972-75; adminstr. The Johns Hopkins Children's Ctr., Balt., 1975-79; policy analyst, cons. The Nat. Ctr. of Health Svcs. Rsch., Rockville, Md., 1979-81; assoc. prof., chmn. Dept. Health Care Adminstrn., Stonehill Coll., North Easton, Mass., 1981—; cons. in field. Co-author: The Health Care Directory, 1988, 89; contbr. articles to profl. jours. Trustee Christ Congl. Ch., Brockton, Mass., 1985—, chmn. steering com.; pres., bd. dirs. Old Colony Hospice, Stoughton, Mass., 1985-91. With Med. Svc. Corps, U.S. Army, 1966-67, Vietnam. Mem. Am. Coll. Healthcare Execs. Home: 414 Center St South Easton MA 02375-1007 Office: Stonehill Coll Washington St North Easton MA 02357-0001

HIGGINS, DICK (RICHARD CARTER HIGGINS), multi-media writer, publisher, composer, artist; b. Cambridge, Eng., Mar. 15, 1938; came to U.S., 1939; s. Carter Chapin and Katharine (Bigelow) H.; m. Alison Knowles, May 31, 1960 (div. 1970); children: Hannah and Jessica (twins); m. Alison Knowles, 1984. Student, Yale U., 1957; BS in English, Columbia U., 1960; postgrad., Manhattan Sch. Printing, 1960-61; MA in English, NYU, 1977; studied with John Cage and Henry Cowell, 1958-59. Co-founder Happenings (Theater) movement, N.Y.C., 1958, Fluxus movement, N.Y.C., 1961; founder Something Else Press, N.Y.C., 1963-73; originator concept, developer (visual, mus. and lit. publs.) Intermedia, 1965; founder, operator Unpublished Edits., West Glover, Vt., 1972-85 (renamed Printed Editions, 1978, in operation until 1986); operator Something Else Gallery, 1966-69; tchr. Calif. Inst. Arts, 1970-71; mem. lit. panel N.Y. State Coun. on Arts, 1979-81; rsch. assoc. in visual arts, SUNY-Purchase, 1983-89; vis. Clark prof. in art Williams Coll., fall 1987, rsch. assoc. in history of art, 1989—. Author: What are legends, 1960, Jefferson's birthday/Postface, 1964, foew & ombwhnw, 1968, Die fabelhafte Geträume von Taifun-Willi, 1969, Computers for the arts, 1970, amigo, 1972, A book about love and war and death, 1972, The Ladder to the moon, 1973, For Eugene in Germany, 1973, City with all the angles, 1974, Modular Poems, 1975, classic plays, 1976,

Legends and Fishnets, 1986, Cat alley, 1977, The Epitaphs/Gli epitaphi, 1977, George Herbert's pattern poems: in their tradition, 1977, Everyone has sher Favorite (his or hers), 1977, The epickall quest of the brothers Dichtung and other outrages, 1977, A dialectic of centuries: notes towards a theory of the new arts, 1978, some recent snowflakes (and other things), 1979, of celebration of morning, 1980, Ten ways of looking at a bird, 1981, 26 mountains for viewing the sunset from, 1981, Selected early works, 1982, 1959/60, 1982, Art contemporain 10-20, 1983, Horizons: the poetics and theory of the intermedia, 1982 (Japanese edit. 1985), Intermedia, 1985, 2d edit., 1991, Poems, plain and fancy, 1986, Visible language, 1986, Pattern poems: a guide to an unknown literature, 1987, Fluxus: reception, 1991, The Journey, 1991, The Autobiography of the Moon, 1992; translator Novalis' Hymne an die Nacht, 1978, 2d edit., 1984, 3d edit., 1988, Czternascie tlumaczen telefonicznych dla Steve'a McCaffery, Poland, 1987; editor, annotator On the composition of images, sign and ideas by Giordano Bruno, 1991; musical works include first electronic opera Stacked Deck (with Richard Maxfield), 1958-59, Le petit cirque au fin du monde, un opéa arabasque, 1973, Piano Album: short pieces, 1962-84, 1980, Sonata for prepared piano, 1981, Variation on a natural theme, for orch., 1981, 1959/60, 1982, Song for any voice(s) and instrument(s), 1983, Sonata No. 2 for piano, 1983; author numerous plays, movies; ; editor: (with Wolf Vostell) Pop Architektur, 1969, Fantastic Architecture, 1971; 100 book inclusions; contbr. to numerous periodicals, 1962-89; author mimeo books, acting scripts, small multiples, buttons, postcards, pamphlets, booklets; films include A tiny movie, 1959, The flight of the Florence bird, 1960, The flaming city, 1961-62, The End, 1962, Invocation of canyons and boulders for Stan Brakhage, 1962, Plunk, 1962, For the dead, 1965, Scenario, 1968, Hank and Mary without apologies, 1969, Mysteries, 1969, Men & women and bells, 1970; videotapes include Gentle talk, 1977, A lecture on The Something Else Press and since, 1981, The flaming city, 1961-62, 81, Fluxus at Williams, 1987; radio performance pieces include Die fabelhafte Getraume von Taifun-Willi, 1970, City with all the angles, 1973, Scenes forgotten and otherwise remembered, 1985, Girlande für John, 1987, Five professionals whom you can trust, 1989, Three double helixes that aren't for sale, 1989; mus. publs. include Graphis 144, Wipeout for orchestra, Graphis 143, Softly for orchestra, 1967, Suggested by small swallows, 1973, Emmett Wiliams' ear/ L'orecchio di Emmett Williams, 1978; recordings include Telephone music, 1979, Eine zweite heutliche deutliche Sprache, 1972, Danger music 17, 1977, Plug: an acid novel, 1977, "glaslass" in Baobab, 1978, Poems and metapoems, 1983, Session with Bern Porter, 1983, Telephone translation #9, 1983, Bodies electric: arches and requiem for Wagner the criminal mayor, 1985, Glasslass, 1985, Constellations, 1986, Music by Dick Higgins, 1989; one or two-artist shows include Galerie Rene Block, Berlin, 1973, Centro de Arte y Communicacion, Buenos Aires, 1974, Galerie St. Petri, Lund, Sweden, 1974, Galerie Vehicule, Montreal, 1974, Museu de ArtContemporanea, Sao Paulo., Brazil, 1976, Galerie Ecart, Geneva, 1977, La Mamelle, San Francisco, 1977, Studio Morra, Naples, 1977, Galerie Inge Baecker, Bochum, 1978,82, C Space, N.Y.C., 1978, Galleri Sudurgata, Reykjavik, Iceland, Galerie Ars Viva, Berlin, 1982, Galerie A, Amsterdam, 1982, Emily Harvey Artworks, N.Y.C., 1986, 89, Art Gallery, San Diego State U., Calexico, Calif., 1987, Mid-Hudson Arts and Sci. Ctr., Poughkeepsie, N.Y., 1988, Emily Harvey artworks, N.Y, 1988, Galeria Potocka, Krakow, Poland, 1988; group exhbns. include Judson Gallery, N.Y.C., 1960, Fine Arts Gallery, U. B.C., 1969, Copenhagen Mus. Modern Art, 1972, Los Angeles Inst. of Contemporary Arts, 1978, Detroit Art Inst., 1979, Neuberger Mus., SUNY, Purchase, N.Y., 1981, Galerie Ars Viva, Berlin, 1982, Hayward Gallery, London, 1983, Staatsgalerie Stuttgart, 1984, Nexus Gallery, Phila., 1985, Mappin Art Gallery, Sheffield, Eng., 1986, Harlekin Art, Wiesbaden, 1987, Galleria Vivita 1, Florence, 1988, Stux Gallery, N.Y.C., others; represented in permanent collections and archives including Berlinische Galerie, Berlin, Gallery of Modern Art, Vienna, Austria, Sonja Henie-Niels Onstad Found., Oslo, Norway, Museu de Arte Contemporanea, Sao Paulo, Brazil, Museum of Modern Art, Copenhagen, Neue Staatsgalerie Stuttgart, Museo Vostell, Caceres, Spain, Jean Brown Archive, John Paul Getty Art Ctr., Los Angeles, Ruth and Marvin Sackner Archive of Visual Poetry, Miami Beach, Fla., Archiv Hanns Sohm, Neue Staatsgalerie Stuttgart; included in pvt. collections of Marcel Fleiss, Paris, Dr. Kenneth Friedman, N.Y.C., Emily Harvey, N.Y.C., Gil Williams, Binghamton, N.Y., Rene Block, Berlin, others; fluxus performances numerous locations U.S.A. and Europe. Ctr. for 20th Century Studies fellow U. Wis., Milw., 1977, DAAD fellow, Berlin, 1981-82, Banff (Alta., Can.) Centre fellow, fall 1990; N.Y. State Coun. on Arts grantee, 1968—, Collaborations grantee visual arts program N.Y. State Coun. on Arts, 1989—, Purchase Coll. grantee for pattern poetry projects, 1984-86, 88—; recipient Bill C. Davis Drama award for The Journey (1986-87), 1988—. Home: PO Box 27 Station Hill Rd Barrytown NY 12507

HIGGINS, JAMES BRUCE, international policy analyst; b. Hershey, Pa., Oct. 9, 1947; s. Donald Charles and Frances Jane (Sensor) H.; m. Christina Marie Johnson, Nov. 25, 1989. BS, U.S. Naval Acad., 1969. Commd. ensign USN, 1969, advanced through grades to comdr., 1984; mgmt. analyst Navy Manpower Analysis Ctr., Norfolk, Va., 1972-75; exec. asst. Naval Edn. and Tng. Ctr., Newport, R.I., 1979-80; ops. adviser Saudi Arabian Navy, Jubayl, 1984-85; internat. policy analyst, negotiator Sec. of Navy, Washington, 1988-90; ret., 1990; mgr. Japanese policy NASA Office Space Flight, Washington, 1990-92; chief internat. policy br. NASA Office of Space Systems Devel., Washington, 1992—. Mem. AIAA, Ret. Officers Assn., World Affairs Coun., Navy League. Home: 101 2d St NE Apt 1 Washington DC 20002

HIGGINS, JAMES HENRY, III, marketing executive; b. Providence, May 8, 1940; s. James Henry Jr. and Betty (Hall) H. AB, Brown U., 1962. Mem. faculty Gov. Dummer Acad., Byfield, Mass., 1964-66; rsch. assoc. Entelek Inc., 1966-69; mgr. sch. svcs. group Sterling Inst., 1969-72; vice pres. Vickerman and Schultz, Inc., Washington, 1985-87; sr. v.p. Complete Communications, Inc., Washington, 1987-90; dir. devel. The Brit. Consortium, Washington, 1990—; mktg. cons. Time Life Video, N.Y.C., 1972-73, Longman Group Ltd., Eng., 1973-74, McGraw-Hill Publs. Co., N.Y.C., 1975-85. Contbr. articles to boating publs. Mem. mgmt. com. A.S.K. Brown Mil. Collection, Brown U., 1990—. Mem. Am. Soc. Assn. Execs., Found. for Internat. Meetings (bd. dirs. 1987—), Mystic Seaport Mus. (yachting com. 1986—), Antique and Classic Boat Soc. (pres., v.p., bd. dirs. 1978—), Nat. Mus. for Women in the Arts (coun.), City Tavern Club, Agawam Hunt Club, Hope Club. Republican. Home: 2807 O St NW Washington DC 20007-3130 Office: The Brit Consortium 1133 15th St NW Washington DC 20005-2710

HIGGINS, JANE MARGARET, university administrator; b. Torrington, Conn., Jan. 10, 1954; d. Edward Corbet and Margaret Katherine (Vestali) H. BA, Ea. Conn. State U., 1976; MEd, U. Mo., 1978. Residence hall dir. Western Conn. State U., Danbury, 1977-80; asst. to assoc. dir. housing Cen. Conn. State U., New Britain, 1980-82, dir. residence life, 1982—. Contbr. articles to profl. jours. Asst. div. chair United Way, New Britain, 1985, div. chair edn., 1986; corporator New Britain Gen. Hosp., 1985—. Mem. N.E. Assn. Coll. and Univ. Housing Officers (chair women's issues com. 1989-91), Assn. Coll. and Univ. Housing Officers (chair energy com. 1985-87), Conn. Network of Housing Profls. (pres. 1991-92). Democrat. Roman Catholic. Office: Cen Conn State Univ 1615 Stanley St New Britain CT 06053-2439

HIGGINS, LINDA WESTAPAL, nursing educator; b. Pitts., Oct. 22, 1960; d. Lois Jean (Laird) Westapal; m. Colin Mark Higgins, Oct. 27, 1984; children: Maura C., Kyle D. BSN, Duquesne U., 1982; MSN, U. Pitts., 1987, postgrad., 1987—. RN, Pa. Staff nurse trauma unit Allegheny Gen. Hosp., Pitts., 1982-84; triage nurse Health Am., Pitts., 1984-86; teaching asst. U. Pitts., 1986-87; staff nurse ICU St. Clair Hosp., Pitts., 1987-88; nursing educator Carlow Coll., Pitts., 1988—; participated in blood pressure screening and blood sugar testing Medicine Shoppe, Pitts., 1986—. Contbr.: A New Approach to NCLEX-RN, 1989. Mem. Grad. Student Nurses Assn. U. Pitts., Sigma Theta Tau. Episcopalian. Office: Carlow Coll 3333 5th Ave Pittsburgh PA 15213-3165

HIGGINS, PETER THOMAS, government information management executive; b. Hackensack, N.J., Aug. 17, 1943; s. Joseph Alexander and Rita Barth (Buckley) H.; m. Kathleen Mary Melehan, June 6, 1970; 1 child, Kelton Charles. BS in Math., Marist Coll., 1967; MS in Math., Computer Sci., Stevens Inst. Tech., 1968. Front desk clk. Carlyle Hotel, N.Y.C., 1964-67; sci. programmer CIA, Washington, 1968-74, project engr., 1974-80, ops. engr. mgr., 1981-86; congl. fellow U.S. House of Reps., Washington, 1986-87, U.S. Senate, Washington, 1987; mgr. rsch. and devel. CIA, Washington, 1987-89, chief info. officer, 1989-92; dep. asst. dir. engring. FBI, Washington, 1992—; speaker in field. Local leader Jaycees, McLean, Va., 1970; vol. Dem. NAt. Conv., Atlantic City, N.J., 1964; Sunday sch. tchr. Holy Trinity Ch., Washington, 1983-91. Mem. Am. Polit. Sci. Assn. (Fgn. Affairs Congl. fellow 1986), Congl. Fellows Alumni Steering Com. Roman Catholic. Office: FBI Washington DC 20535

HIGGINS, ROBERT PRICE, zoologist; b. Denver, Oct. 8, 1932; s. Jay and Amy (Gates) H.; m. Gwendolyn Ailene Litherland, Aug. 15, 1954; children: Kent Eric, Scott Edwin (dec.), Kim Ailene. BA, U. Colo., 1956, MA, 1958; PhD, Duke U., 1961. Asst. prof., then assoc. prof. Wake Forest U., Winston-Salem, N.C., 1961-68; resident systematist Marine Biology Lab., Woods Hole, Mass., 1968; dir. Mediterranean Sorting Ctr. Smithsonian Inst., Kherreddine, Tunisia, 1969-71; dir. oceanography and limnology program Smithsonian Inst., Washington, 1971-74, sr. zoologist oceanographic sorting ctr., 1975-78, curator invertebrate zoology Nat. Mus. Natural History, 1978—; adj. prof. biology Western Caroline U., Cullowhee, N.C., 1989—; rsch. assoc. Baruch Inst. for Marine Biology and Coastal Rsch., Columbia, S.C., 1974—. Co-editor: Introduction to the Study of Meiofauna, 1988; editor proc. Internat. Symposium on Tardigrades, 1974; contbr. articles to profl. jours. Master sgt. USMCR, 1950-52. Grantee NSF, 1964, 68, NATO, 1988; James B. Duke fellow, 1959-61. Fellow AAAS, Explorer's Club; mem. Internat. Assn. Meiobenthologists (chmn. 1980-81), Am. Soc. Zoologists (chmn. div. invertebrate zoology 1969-70 , chmn. div. ecology 1975-76), Am. Microscopical Soc. (pres. 1979-80, assoc. editor 1966-69), Soc. Systematic Zoology (program officer 1967-68), Biol. Soc. Washington, Sigma Xi (pres. Wake Forest chpt. 1966-67). Republican. Presbyterian. Home: 2821 Oakton Manor Ct Oakton VA 22124-3014 Office: Nat Mus Natural History Smithsonian Inst Dept Invertebrate Zoology Washington DC 20560

HIGH, DANETTE COLLEEN, graphic designer; b. Balt., Apr. 21, 1964; d. David Lee Brown and Christine (Mason) H. BFA, Md. Inst. Coll. Art., 1986; postgrad., Parsons Sch. Design, Paris, France, 1987; MFA, Sch. Art Inst. Chgo., 1988. Graphics coord. Patuxent Pub. Co., Towson, Md., 1988-89; graphics coord. Balt. Messenger McCormick & Co., Inc., Towson, Md., 1990—; assoc. mem. multiple mgmt. bd. McCormick & Co., Inc., Sparks, Md., 1991. Named one of Outstanding Young Women of Am., 1988. Mem. Am. Inst. Graphic Arts, Macintosh Users Group. Office: McCormick & Co Inc 18 Loveton Circle Sparks MD 21152

HIGHLAND, HAROLD JOSEPH, computer scientist; b. N.Y.C., Apr. 26, 1917; s. Joseph Francis and Frances (Bernstein) H.; m. Esther Harris, June 16, 1940; 1 child, Joseph Harris. BS, CCNY, 1938, MS, 1939; PhD, NYU, 1942. Editor, pub. several consumer and trade publs., N.Y.; dean Arthur T. Roth Grad. Sch., dir. computer labs. L.I. U., 1958-66; prof. computer sci. SUNY, Farmingdale, 1978-80, Disting. prof., 1978-81, ret., 1981; prof. statistics and rsch. Hoftsra U., N.Y., 1968-70; adj. prof. computer sci. Hofstra U., 1974-75; Fulbright prof. computer sci. and ops. rsch. Helsinki (Finland) U. Tech., 1970-71; prof. computer sci. Nat. Tng. Ctr. U.S. Customs, 1971-73; mng. dir. Compulit Inc.; adviser Computer Security Tech. Com. of Chinese Computer Fedn., Beijing; chmn. internat. com. on info. security edn. and tng., mem. tech. com. on info. security Internat. Fedn. for Info. Prcoessing; mem. NATO Sci. Affairs Adv. Bd.; mem. Info. Security Rsch. Ctr., Queensland U. of Tech., Brisbane, Australia; pres. Virus Security Inst.; chmn. task force Implementation of ACM Internat. Plan; cons. to various govt. agys. in the U.S. and abroad. Author: Modelling and Simulation using GPSSII, 1971, Probability Models, 1972, Protecting Your Microcomputer System, 1984, Computer Virus Handbook, 1990; co-author (with Esther Harris Highland) CBASIC/CB86 With Graphics, and other; founding editor, editor-in-chief jour. Computers & Security, emeritus, 1990—; mem. editorial bd. Info. Systems Security, Virus Bull. (Eng.), Security Letter, Computer Law and Security Report (U.K.), SIGSAC Security, Audit and Control, CVIG News (Australia), Computer Fraud & Security Bulletin. Recipient DAR award in mil. law, 1938, Tremaine award for hist. rsch., 1938, Sci. Rsch. Soc. Annual award for profl. writing, 1963, Nat. Audio Visual Assn. Ednl. Film award, 1961; faculty fellow CCNY, 1938, Ford Found. fellow, 1964-65; IBM Computer grantee, 1962. Fellow Irish Computer Soc.; mem. ACM, AAAS, IEEE Computer Soc., N.Y. Acad. Sci., Info. Systems Security Assn., Computer Profls. Social Responsibility, Internat. Assn. Cryptographic Rsch., Soc. Basic Irreproducible Rsch. Home: 562 Croydon Rd Floral Park NY 11003-2814

HILBORN, ROBERT CLARENCE, physics educator; b. Norristown, Pa., June 24, 1943; s. Clarence Leonard and Dorothy Viola (Ditzler) H.; m. Shirley Ann Antosiewicz, June 27, 1970; children: Stephen, Kurt. BA, Lehigh U., 1966; MA, Amherst Coll., 1987; PhD, Harvard U., 1971. Postdoctoral rsch. assoc. SUNY, Stony Brook, 1971-73; asst. prof. physics Oberlin (Ohio) Coll., 1973-78, assoc. prof., 1978-84, prof., 1984-86; prof. Amherst (Mass.) Coll., 1986—; vis. assoc. prof. U. Calif., Santa Barbara, 1979-80; cons. Guilford Instruments, Oberlin, 1982-84; vis. lectr. Taiyuan (Shanxi, People's Republic of China) U. Tech., 1984; mem. steering com. Introductory Univ. Physics Project. Author: Chaos and Nonlinear Dynamics, 1992; contbr. over 20 articles to profl. jours. Mem. Am. Phys. Soc., Am. Assn. Physics Tchrs., Sigma Xi, Phi Beta Kappa. Home: 46 Rolling Ridge Rd Amherst MA 01002-1419 Office: Dept Physics Amherst Coll Amherst MA 01002

HILDEBRAND, DONALD ALLEN, electronics engineer; b. Colver, Pa., Feb. 17, 1937; s. John Clarence and Wilda Alida (Hill) H.; m. Edna Cora Farabaugh, Apr. 23, 1959; children: David Allen, Ann Marie. BSEE, U. of Pitts., 1960. Electronic engr. Rome (N.Y.) Lab., Griffiss AFB, 1960—. Patentee in field. Trustee Oriskany (N.Y.) Pub. Libr., 1978-89. Mem. IEEE. Home: 112 Manor Ln Oriskany NY 13424-9568 Office: Rome Lab/OCDE Griffiss AFB Rome NY 13441-5700

HILDEBRAND, FRANCIS BEGNAUD, mathematics educator; b. Washington, Pa., Sept. 1, 1915; s. Frank Alonzo and Inez (Patin) H.; m. Eleanor Maclaren Jenkins, Sept. 18, 1943; children—Susan Lee, Robert Craig, Jean Ellen. B.S., Washington and Jefferson Coll., 1936, M.A., 1938, Sc.D. (hon.), 1969; Ph.D., MIT, 1940. Mem. faculty MIT, Cambridge, 1938—, assoc. prof. math., 1950-67, prof., 1967-84, prof. emeritus, 1984—. Author: Advanced Calculus for Applications, 1949, 62, 76; Methods of Applied Mathematics, 1952, 65; Introduction to Numerical Analysis, 1956, 74; Finite-Difference Equations and Simulations, 1968. Mem. Am. Math. Soc., Math. Assn. Am., Sigma Xi, Phi Beta Kappa, Phi Delta Theta. Home: 7 Bucknell Rd Wellesley MA 02181-1201

HILDEBRAND, KRISTA WILLETT, architect; b. Syracuse, N.Y., Oct. 25, 1957; d. Donald Kline and Anne Sylvia (Loven) Willett; m. William Bennett Hildebrand II, June 20, 1987; 1 child, W. Bennett III. BArch, Syracuse U., 1980. Registered architect, N.Y. Jr. designer, draftsman Sargent, Webster, Crenshaw & Foley, Syracuse, 1980-81; intermediate designer, draftsman R.B.S.D., N.Y.C., 1981-83; intermediate designer Johanson Bennett, N.Y.C., 1983, Skidmore, Owings & Merrill, N.Y.C., 1984-87; project designer Spgainyc, N.Y.C., 1987-90; owner, architect K.W.H. Assocs., Rowayton, Conn., 1990—. Mem. AIA, Conn. Soc. Architects. Home and Office: 7 Burchard Ln Norwalk CT 06853-1103

HILDEBRANDT, FREDERICK DEAN, JR., management consultant; b. Upper Darby, Pa., Apr. 17, 1933; s. Frederick Dean and Ruth Taylor (Hart) H.; m. Marjorie Louise Smith, July 27, 1968; children: Frederick Dean III, Elizabeth Florence. AB magna cum laude, Dartmouth Coll., 1954, MS, 1955. Engr. Eastman Kodak Co., Rochester, N.Y., 1957-60; systems mgr. J.T. Baker Chem. Co., Phillipsburg, N.J., 1960-63; assoc. Booz, Allen & Hamilton Inc., N.Y.C., 1963-72, v.p., 1972-78; sr. v.p. Am. Ins. Assn., N.Y.C., 1978-81; v.p. Travelers Ins. Cos., Hartford, Conn., 1981-89; pres. Dean Hildebrandt & Assocs., Simsbury, Conn., 1989—; adminstr. Ins. Rsch. Coun., 1979, bd. dirs., 1982-88; vice chmn. bd. dirs. Workers Compensation Rsch. Inst., 1987-88. With U.S. Army, 1955-57. Mem. Inst. Mgmt. Cons. (cert. mgmt. cons.), Am. Soc. Assn. Execs., Phi Beta Kappa. Home: 38 Lincoln Ln Simsbury CT 06070-3014 Office: PO Box 1022 Simsbury CT 06070-7322

HILEY, PAUL CULVERWELL, physician, consulting gastroenterologist; b. Balt., Dec. 23, 1939; s. Eugene Walter Hiley and Frances Case Culverwell; m. Phyllis Anne Pfund, Apr. 13, 1963; children: Paul Jr., Christine, Mark, Carole, Stephen. BS, Wheaton Coll., 1960; MD, U. Md., 1964. Diplomate Am. Bd. Internal Medicine. Intern USPHS Hosp., Balt., 1964-65; resident in internal medicine USPHS Hosp., S.I., N.Y., 1965-68; fellow in Gastroenterology Mt. Sinai Hosp., N.Y.C., 1968-70; chief of Gastroenterology USPHS Hosp., S.I., 1970-71; mem. staff Kimball Med. Ctr., Lakewood, N.J., 1971—, chief Gastroenterology, 1977—, chief internal medicine, 1980-86, pres. med. staff, 1986-88; bd. trustees Kimball Med. Ctr., Lakewood, 1988-90; cons. in Gastroenterology Pt. Pleasant (N.J.) Hosp., 1973—. Lt. Comdr. USPHS, 1964-71. Fellow Am. Coll. Gastroenterology; mem. AMA, ACP, Am. Gastroenterologic Assn., Am. Soc. Gastrointestinal Endoscopy, N.J. Gastroenterologic Assn., N.J. Med. Soc. Republican. Methodist. Office: Lakewood Med Specialists 870 River Ave Lakewood NJ 08701

HILFSTEIN, ERNA, science historian, educator; b. Krakow, Poland; came to U.S., 1949, naturalized, 1954; d. Leon and Anna (Schornstein) Kluger; B.A., CCNY, 1967, M.A., 1971, Ph.D., City U. N.Y., 1978; m. Max Hilfstein; children: Leon, Simone Juliana. Tchr. secondary schs., N.Y.C., 1968-84, 86-92; collaborator Polish Acad. Scis., 1992—; vis. prof. Queens Coll., 1973; affiliate Grad. Sch./Univ. Center, City U. N.Y. NEH grantee, 1984-85; recipient Rector's medal U. N. Copernicus, Torun, 1989, Order of Merit medal Republic of Poland, 1990, Merit Silver medal. Mem. History Sci. Soc., Polish Inst. Arts and Scis. in Am., CUNY Acad. for the Humanities and Scis., Kósciuszko Found., United Fedn. of Tchrs. (chpt. chmn. 1978-84, 86-92, del. 1980-92). Democrat. Jewish. Author: Starowolski's Biographies of Copernicus, 1980; collaborator English version of Nicholas Copernicus Complete Works, vol. 1, 1972, vol. 2, 1978, vol. 3, 1985, vols. 2 & 3, 2d edit., 1992; contbr. articles and revs. to profl. jours. Editor: Science and History, 1978. Home: 1523 Dwight Pl Bronx NY 10465-1121

HILL, ANNE LYNN, corporate professional; b. Uniontown, Pa., Sept. 3, 1944; d. Robert Benjamin and Katherine Rebecca (Reynolds) Rankin; m. Howard Harry Hill, Aug. 23, 1964 (div. Dec. 1979); children: Jennifer Leigh, Carolyn Jeanne; m. Thomas A. Fessenden, Apr. 29, 1990. BS, U. Md., 1966. Elem. tchr. Prince George's County Bd. Edn., Upper Marlboro, Md., 1966-68; food service mgr. Bloomingdales, White Flint, Md., 1976-78; dist. mgr. ice cream parlors/restaurants Drug Fair, Inc., Alexandria, Va., 1978-80; dir. quality assurance and product devel. Marriott Corp., Washington, 1980-88, corp. procurement dir., 1988-90; v.p. food and beverage, 1990—. Mem. Roundtable for Women in Foodservice (Pacesetter award 1986), Nat. Assn. Female Execs., DAR. Republican. Presbyterian. Office: Marriott Corp 1 Marriott Dr Dept 817.63 Washington DC 20058

HILL, ARTHUR HENRY, wireless telecommunications services executive; b. Perth, Australia, Feb. 26, 1932; s. Clement Edward and Clara Hilder (Bestwick) H.; m. Julie Leotsinidis, July 4, 1959. BA, U. Western Australia, 1957; PhD, U. Minn., 1960. From lectr. to sr. lectr. U. Melbourne (Australia), 1961-63; asst. prof. U. Tex., Austin, 1964-66; asst. rep. Ford Found., Bangkok, Thailand, 1966-68, Manila, Philippines, 1968-72; dep. rep. UN Devel. Program, Western Pacific, 1972-74, Afghanistan, 1974-75; mktg. mgr. ITT, N.Y.C., 1975-82; v.p. CSP Internat., N.Y.C., 1982-85; gen. mgr. No. Bus. Info., N.Y.C., 1985-88; mgr. bus. planning AT&T, Basking Ridge, N.J., 1988—; cons. Hogg Found., Austin, 1965-66. Author: Europe's Wireless Revolution, 1991; contbr. articles to profl. jours. Home: 6 Pickle Brook Rd Bernardsville NJ 07924 Office: AT& T PCS 295 N Maple Ave Basking Ridge NJ 07920

HILL, BRICE EDWARD, construction executive; b. San Angelo, Tex., Aug. 24, 1951; s. James E. and Jenny (Garland) H.; m. Cathy Riney, Dec. 27, 1971; children: Heather, Shelby, James. BS in Bldg. Constrn., Tex. A&M U., 1973. Estimator J.W. Bateson, Dallas, 1973-74; estimator, engr. H.C. Beck, Dallas, 1974-76; sr. estimator Austin Comml., Dallas, 1976-78, chief estimator, 1979-80, v.p., chief estimator, 1980-81, v.p. ops., 1982-85; v.p. ops. Clark-Morris Co., Dallas, 1985-89; sr. v.p. ops. The George Hyman Constrn. Co., Bethesda, Md., 1989-91; exec. v.p. The George Hyman Constrn. Co., Bethesda, D, 1991—. Coach Bedford, Euless Soccer Assn., 1984-89, bd. dirs., registrar, 1988-90; vol. local Rep. candidates campaigns, Irving, Tex., 1978-81, Colleyville Tex., 1984—. Mem. Associated Builders and Contractors (bd. dirs. North Tex. chpt. 1977-79, 87-90, Metro Washington chpt. 1991—), Associated Gen. Contractors Am. Republican. Lutheran. Home: 851 Christensen Ct Great Falls VA 22066-1337

HILL, CLARA EDITH, psychology educator; b. Shivers, Miss., Sept. 13, 1948; d. Fletcher Von and Anna (Teich) H.; m. Jim Gormally, May 25, 1974; children: Kevin, Katherine. BA, So. Ill. U., 1970, MA, 1972, PhD, 1974. Lic. psychologist, Md. Asst. prof. dept. psychology U. Md., College Park, 1974-78, assoc. prof. dept. psychology, 1978-85, prof. dept. psychology, 85—. Author: Therapist Techniques and Client Outcomes, 1989; contbr. articles to profl. jours. Grantee NIMH, 1983-92. Mem. Soc. Psycotherapy Rsch. (pres. North Am. chpt., 1990); fellow Am. Psychol. Assn. Office: U Maryland Dept Psychology College Park MD 20742

HILL, DAVID LAWRENCE, research corporation executive; b. Boonville, Miss., Nov. 11, 1919; s. David Alexander and Mabel Clair (Brown) H.; B.S., Calif. Inst. Tech., 1942; Ph.D. (Socony Vacuum Co. fellow), Princeton U., 1951; m. Mary M. Shadow, Dec. 31, 1950; children—David A., Mary C., Robert L., John F., Cynthia A., Sandra E., James A. With U. Chgo. Metall. Lab. and Argonne Nat. Lab., 1942-46, assoc. physicist, group leader, 1944-46; asst. prof. physics Vanderbilt U., Nashville, 1949-52, assoc. prof., 1952-54; guest scholar Inst. Theoretical Physics, Copenhagen, summer 1950; cons. theoretical physics U. Calif., Los Alamos (N.Mex.) Sci. Lab., 1952-54, staff mem., 1954-58, group leader theoretical nuclear physics, 1955-58; mgmt. cons., 1958-60; pres. Phys. Sci. Corp., Fairfield, Conn., 1960-62, Nanosecond Systems, Inc., Fairfield, 1963-72, Particle Measurements, Inc., Southport, Conn., 1965-81, Harbor Research Corp., 1978—; chmn. bd. Integrated Total Systems, Inc., Hingham, Mass., 1968-81; pres. Southport Computers, Inc., Conn., 1973-81, Valutron N.V., Netherlands Antilles, 1980—; pres. Patent Enforcement Fund, Inc., Southport, Conn., 1990—; lectr. in field; sci. advisor to Vice Presdl. nominee, Senator Estes Kefauver, 1956; incorporator, exec. v.p. dir. Los Alamos Investment Corp., 1956-58; cons. physicist in field. Adv. com. on sci. and tech. of Adv. Council of Dem. Nat. Com., 1959-61. Fellow Am. Phys. Soc., AAAS; mem. IEEE, Fedn. Am. Scientists (nat. chmn. 1953-54), Sigma Xi. Contbr. articles to profl. jours. Office: Patent Enforcement Fund Inc PO Box L Southport CT 06490-0569

HILL, DAVID STEWART, education educator; b. Waterbury, Conn., July 22, 1947; s. Stewart M. and Leota Rose (Cronin) H.; m. Wilma Adele Hill, June 17, 1972; children: Bethanne, Stephen. BA, Allegheny Coll., 1969; MEd, Temple U., 1972, EdD, 1976. Asst. prof. SUNY, Binghamton; assoc. prof. Ohio State U., Columbus; assoc. prof. Keene (N.H.) State Coll., prof., chair edn. dept. Contbr. articles to profl. publs. Mem. Coun. Learning Disabilities (pres. 1990-91), New Eng. Ednl. Rsch. Orgn. (treas.), Epsilon Pi Tau. Home: 29 Grant St Keene NH 03431-3240 Office: Keene State Coll 132 Elliott Hall 229 Main Keene NH 03431-4183

HILL, ELIZABETH TREZISE, economics educator; b. DuBois, Pa., Mar. 26, 1936; d. William H. and Ethel L. (Lyons) Trezise; m. Richard A. Hill, May 30, 1958 (dec. Sept. 1981); children: Joan H. Smeltzer, David R. BSBA, Pa. State U., University Park, 1958; MA in Econs., U. Del., 1974; PhD in Econs., U. Md., 1985. Instr. in econs. Pa. State U., York, 1976-78; economist Pa. Milrite Coun., Harrisburg, 1982-84; asst. prof. econs. Pa. State U., Mont Alto, 1985—. Treas. Reinhardt Found., York, 1986—. Mem. Am. Econ. Assn., Ea. Econ. Assn., Nat. Assn. Bus. Economists, Pa. Econ. Assn. (bd.dirs. 1989—), Com. on Status of Women in Econs. Profession. Office: Pa State U Mont Alto Campus Mont Alto PA 17237

HILL, G. EUGENE, education educator; b. Canadian, Tex., Oct. 21, 1933; s. George Clarence and Mary Gladys (Young) H.; m. Glenda Gay Woodbridge, Dec. 31, 1972; children: Misha Kim, Robyn Annika. BS, West Tex. State U., 1955, MA, 1960; MA, U. Denver, 1962, EdD, 1964. Cert. life tchr., Tex.; cert. adminstr., N.Y. Tchr. Dumas (Tex.) Ind. Sch. Dist., 1955-58, Albuquerque City Schs., 1958-61; NDEA Title IV fellow U. Denver, 1961-64; asst. prof. Cen. Mo. State U., Warrensburg, 1964-66; assoc. prof. SUNY, Plattsburgh, 1966-68; assoc. prof., asst. dir. NDEA Title XI, Clarion, Pa., 1968-69; assoc. prof. Edinboro (Pa.) State Coll., 1969-70; prin., acting dir. Santiago (Chile) Coll., 1970-72; assoc. prof. Westminster Coll.,

New Wilmington, Pa., 1974—; seasonal naturalist Nat. Park Svc., Grand Canyon, Ariz., 1955-57, seasonal guide, Carlsbad Caverns, N.Mex., summers, 1961-63; cons. Cuyahoga Community Coll., Cleve., 1973-74, Mahoning County Bd. of Edn., Youngstown, OHio, 1980-82. Author video tape: Teaching Metrics, 1984. Mejor depotista Patrullas de Ski de Chile, Santiago, 1972; mission ambassador to Cen. Am. Western Pa. Conf. United Meth. Ch., 1990-91. Mem. Pa. Geog. Soc. (bd. dirs.), Kappa Delta Pi (counselor 1976—), Omicron Delta Kappa (advisor 1980—). Democrat. Home: 225 S New Castle St New Wilmington PA 16142-1432 Office: Westminster Coll Market St New Wilmington PA 16142

HILL, GORDON CHARLES, III, company executive; b. Springfield, Mass., Sept. 8, 1948; s. Gordon Charles and Sophia Catherine (Samsel) H.; m. Margaret Maria Thibeault, Mar. 20, 1949; children: Catherine Margaret, Gordon Charles, Nicholas John, Matthew David. BSBA, Am. Internat. Coll., Springfield, Mass., 1971. Cert. bldg. svc. exec.; cert. Weight Watchers instr. Mgr. Grace Food Svc., Springfield, 1971-74, Pappys Ent., Balt., 1974-78; account exec. Canteen Corp., Washington/Hartford, 1978-83; account rep. Paul Revere Ins. Co., New Haven, 1983-84; opts. mgr. Premier Maint., Inc., Milford, Conn., 1984-85; dir. ops. Premier Maint., Inc., 1985-86, v.p. ops., 1986—. Author/editor various tng. manuals, orientation manuals. Mem. Guilford (Conn.) 350th Birthday Com., 1988—; mem. Parish Coun., Guilford, 1989—; commr. E div. Guilford Soccer Club, 1990, F div., 1991; commr. Guilford Youth Basketball Midgets, 1991; mem. bus. adv. bd. Milford Mental Health, 1990-91. Mem. Nat. Recycling Coalition, Bldg. Svc. Contrs. Assn., Bldg. Svc. Contrs. Assn. Internat., Milford C. of C., 3928 Club (pres. 1986-89), Columbus Club (1st v.p. 1987-88), K.C. (grand knight 1988, coun. trustee 1989-91). Roman Catholic. Home: 519 W Lake Ave Guilford CT 06437-1312 Office: Premier Maint Inc 360 New Haven Ave # 392 Milford CT 06460-6666

HILL, HARRY EDWARD, III, manufacturing executive, management consultant; b. Phila., Aug. 1, 1948; s. Harry Edward Jr. and Mattie (Dillard) H.; m. Louise Lark; children: Harry Edward IV, Elisabeth Lark Hill. BA, Pa. State U., 1970; MBA, U. Mich., 1986. Sales rep. Scott Paper Co., N.Y.C., 1970-72; account exec. Shearson Am. Express, Phila., 1972-74; account mgr. Owens Corning Fiberglass, Hartford, Conn., 1974-76; sect. mgr. Owens Corning Fiberglass, Toledo, 1976-83; dist. mgr. Owens Corning Fiberglass, L.A., 1983-84; mng. ptnr. H.E. Hill & Co., Phila., 1984—; pres. Del. Car Co., Wilmington, 1987—; cons. Mexican Govt., Ann Arbor, Mich., 1984-86. Author: Business Plan Preparation, 1987. Board dirs. The West Hill Sch., Rosemont, Pa.; leader Boy Scouts Am., Hartford, 1974-76; mem. Rep. Party, Phila., 1968—. Mem. Phila. Mktg. Assn., Am. Assn. MBA's, U.S. Rowing Assn., Union League, Merion Cricket Club, Toledo Club, Merion Golf Club, Univ. Club, Whist Club, Masons. Home: 511 N Rose Ln Haverford PA 19041-1924 Office: Del Car Co 2d and Lombard Sts Wilmington DE 19899

HILL, JEFFERSON BORDEN, regulatory oversight officer, lawyer; b. Wilmington, Del., Nov. 5, 1941; s. Julian Werner and Mary Louisa (Butcher) H.; m. Gabrielle Marie Tourville, Mar. 19, 1976; children: Corinna Borden Hill, Lydia Richards Hill. BA, Harvard U., 1963, LLB, 1967. Bar: Del. 1967, D.C. 1972. Legis. asst. Congressman William V. Roth, Jr., Washington, 1967-70; attorney Antitrust div. U.S. Dept. Justice, Washington, 1970-76; asst. dir. Office of Policy Planning and Legis., Antitrust Div., U.S. Dept. Justice, Washington, 1976-77; br. chief Office Info. and Regulatory Affairs, Office Mgmt. Budget, Washington, 1977—; adj. prof. Georgetown U., Washington, 1987—. Mem. Met. Club. Republican. Home: 639 E Capitol St SE Washington DC 20003-1234 Office: Office Mgmt and Budget 17th and Pennsylvania Ave NW Washington DC 20503

HILL, LOWELL JAMES, human resource executive; b. Mpls., Feb. 7, 1945; s. James J. and Beryl (Lavaty) H.; m. Sherry Rae Hansen, Sept. 9, 1967; childen: Jason, Darren, Raegan, Kylie. BS in Bus., U. Minn., 1967, M.Indsl.Rels., 1969. Personnel supr. Monsanto Co., St. Louis, 1969-72; labor rels. supr. Monsanto Co., Ligonier, Ind., 1972-74; corp. mgr. employee rels. Emerson Elec., St. Louis, 1974-78; v.p. indsl. rels. Therm-O-Disc, Mansfield, Ohio, 1978-84; v.p. human resources E.L. Wiegand div. Emerson Elec., Pitts., 1984-87; corp. dir. employee rels. Havard Ind., Farmingdale, N.J., 1987—. Home: 660 White Ash Dr Langhorne PA 19047-8017 Office: Havard Ind Central Ave Farmingdale NJ 07727-1406

HILL, MARJORIE JEAN, psychologist, association executive; b. Bklyn., Aug. 8, 1956; d. Walter James and Laura Beulah (Cherry) H. AA, The Coll. of Staten Island, 1975; BA, Adelphi U., 1977, MA, 1979, PhD, 1981. Asst. dir. child psychiatry Kings County Hosp., Bklyn., 1981-88; internship coord., psychiatric edn. Lincoln Med. and Mental Health Ctr., Bronx, N.Y., 1988-90; dir. N.Y.C.'s Mayor's Office for the Lesbian & Gay Community, N.Y.C., 1990—; asst. prof. psychiatry N.Y. Med. Coll., Valhalla, 1988—; adj. faculty Coll. New Rochelle, 1988-91; adj. clin. assoc. Pace U., N.Y.C., 1989-91; adj. clin. prof. Yeshiva U., Bronx, N.Y., 1989—. Bd. dirs N.Y. Civil Liberties Union, N.Y.C., 1990, AIDS Films, N.Y.C., 1991—, Columbia County Youth Project, 1989—; mem. Black Leadership Commn. on AIDS, N.Y.C., 1991—; mem. N.Y.C. Fair Housing Task Force, 1990—. Recipient Community Organizer award WBAI N.Y.C. Learning Alliance, 1988, Community Svc. award Nat. Lesbian and Gay Health Found., 1988, Hall of Fame award Staten Island Community Coll., 1989, Community Svc. award Nat. Lesbian Conf., 1991, Bayard Rustin award Nat. Black Lesbian and Gay Leadership Forum, 1991. Mem. Am. Psychol. Assn., Assn. Women in Psychology (steering com. 1987), Am. Orthopsychiatric Assn., Assn. Black Psychologist (pres. 1988, treas. 1990, bd. mem., Nelson Mandela award 1990), N.Y.C. Task Force Against Sexual Abuse (award 1990), N.Y.C. Police Coun. on Lesbian and Gay Issues (co-chair). Office: Mayors Office Lesbian/Gay Community 52 Chambers St Rm 311 New York NY 10007-1222

HILL, PETER WAVERLY, lawyer; b. White River Junction, Vt., June 24, 1953; s. Richard Bert and Elaine Etta (Kimball) H.; m. Suzanne Miller, Nov. 21, 1983; 1 stepchild, Marshall Jackson Miller. BA in Philosophy and Govt., U. Ariz., 1975, JD, 1978. Bar: Ariz. 1978, U.S. Dist. Ct. (no. dist.) N.Y. 1979, N.Y. 1980, U.S. Ct. Appeals (2d cir.) 1982. Staff atty. Legal Aid Soc. Mid N.Y., Utica, 1978-79, Oneonta, 1979-83; assoc. Law Offices of Paternoster & O'Leary, Walton, N.Y., 1983-84; pvt. practice, Oneonta, 1985—; bd. dirs. OURS-Delaco Assn., Inc., Delhi, N.Y. Contbr. articles to profl. jours. Mem. N.Y. State com. Socialist Party, Syracuse; bd. dirs. Unitarian UniversalistSoc. of Oneonta. Mem. ABA, N.Y. State Bar Assn., Otsego County Bar Assn., Delaware County Bar Assn., Assn. Trial Lawyers Am., N.Y. State Trial Lawyers Assn., Nat. Lawyers Guild, Nat. Orgn. Social Security Claimants Reps. Unitarian Universalist. Home and Office: 384 Main St Oneonta NY 13820-1994

HILL, REBA DICKERSON, artist; b. Phila., Feb. 17, 1918; d. Evan Thomas and Reba Henrietta (Tyree) Dickerson; m. Harold Woodrow Hill, Mar. 15, 1940; children: Reba, Harold Jr., Allan. BS in Edn., Cheyney (Pa.) U., 1939; postgrad., Pendle Hill, 1938-39, Temple U., 1965, Barnes Found., Merion, Pa., 1945-47, U. Exeter, Eng., 1987, U. Pa. Tchr. Sch. Dist. Phila., 1950-68; faculty art dept. Cheyney U., 1969-72. Exhibited in group shows at Antioch U., Phila., 1983, Pavilion Gallery, N.J., 1983, N.J. State Mus., Trenton, N.J., 1983, Salmagundi Club, N.Y., 1985, Cork Gallery-Japan Am. Club Exhbn., Lincoln Ctr., N.Y., 1986, Kinkeleba Gallery, N.Y., 1986, Beaver Coll., Phila., 1986, Temple U. Law Sch., 1986, Nat. Arts Club, N.Y., 1986, U. Exeter, England, 1987, Esterhazy Palace, Eisenstadt, Austria, 1988, Afro-Am. Hist. and Cultural Mus., Phila., 1988, The Arnesen Gallery, Vail, Colo., 1989; represented by sidney Rothman The Gallery Barnegat LIght, N.J., DeVirgilis Designs, North Wales, Pa. Scholarship Humphreys Found., 1936-40. Mem. Phila. Water Color Club, (life, bd. dirs. 1992—), Sumi-e Soc. Am. Home: 207 E Cliveden St Philadelphia PA 19119-2312

HILL, ROBERT CHARLES, lawyer, foreign affairs policy adviser; b. Greenwich, Conn., Mar. 28, 1952; s. George Urho and Martha Ilona (Nyburn) H.; m. Mary Anne Carroll, May 13, 1972; children: Robert, Kristin, Jessica, David, Elizabeth, Michael. BA cum laude, CUNY, 1974; JD, Georgetown U., 1980. Bar: Va. 1980, U.S. Ct. Appeals (D.C. cir.) 1989, D.C., 1990. Tchr. The Heights Sch., Washington, 1977-79; dep. dir. presdl. correspondence The White House, Washington, 1981-83; spl. asst. to Asst. Sec. State Dept., Washington, 1983-87; dep. dir., counsel Office of Asylum Policy and Rev., U.S. Dept. Justice, Washington, 1987-89; assoc. Fragomen, Del Rey & Bernsen, P.C., Washington, 1989-91; ptnr. Graham & James, Washington, 1991—; mem. Commn. on Legal Immigration Reform, Washington, 1991. Mem. ABA, Am. Immigration Lawyers Assn. Republican. Roman Catholic. Office: Graham & James 2000 M St NW Ste 700 Washington DC 20036

HILL, RONALD PAUL, business educator; b. Chgo., Dec. 19, 1954; s. Edward W. and Dolores N. (Noble) H.; m. Noel Denise Porter, Sept. 8, 1984; children: Paul Armstrong, Phillip Jordan. BS, U. Md., 1976, MBA, 1978, PhD, 1984. Instr. U. Md., College Park, 1976-78, 80-83, George Washington U., Washington, 1978-80; asst. prof. Am. U., Washington, 1983-88, Cornell U., Ithaca, N.Y., 1988-89; assoc. prof. Villanova (Pa.) U., 1989—. Contbr. articles to profl. jours. Mem. Phi Kappa Phi, Phi Eta Sigma, Beta Gamma Sigma. Roman Catholic. Home: 124 Ivywood Ln Wayne PA 19087-2827 Office: Villanova U C&F Villanova PA 19085

HILL, THOMAS WILLIAM, JR., lawyer; b. N.Y.C., Dec. 25, 1924; s. Thomas William Sr. and Marion (Bond) H.; m. Elizabeth Rowe, June 18, 1949; children: Gretchen P., Catharine B., Thomas William III. BS, U. Pa., 1948; MBA, NYU, 1950; JD, Columbia U., 1953. Bar: N.Y. 1953, D.C. 1954, U.S. Supreme Ct. 1958, Fla. 1989; CPA, N.Y. Sr. tax acct. Hurdman & Cranstoun, 1949-50; asst. U.S. atty. So. Dist. N.Y., 1953-54; assoc. Cahill, Gordon, Reindel & Ohl, 1954-58; sr. ptnr. Spear & Hill, 1958-75; ptnr. Sidley & Austin, 1981-86; pres. Belco Petroleum Co., N.Y.C., 1962-63; legal adviser Sultanate of Oman, 1972-76; adj. prof. law U. Miami, 1986—. Contbr. articles to profl. jours. Vice chmn., pres., trustee Internat. Coll., Beirut, Lebanon, 1978-91. 1st lt. AUS, 1943-46. Decorated Bronze Star, Purple Heart, Medal of Oman (Sultanate of Oman), Order of Homayun (Iran). Mem. ABA, Assn. of Bar of City of N.Y., IBA, Racquet and Tennis Club (N.Y.C.), Winged Foot Golf Club, Woburn Golf Club (Eng.), Palm Beach Polo and Country Club, Phi Delta Phi, Kappa Sigma. Home: 2627 Muirfield Ct West Palm Beach FL 33414-7019

HILL, VALERIE CHARLOTTE, nurse; b. Shaftsbury, Vt., Dec. 2, 1932; d. William Henry Harrison and Angeline Margaret Stella (Fuller) Hill; m. Edward Joseph Klanit (dec. July 1984); 1 child, Joyce Ellen Klanit Artadi. Grad., The Mount Sinai Hosp. Sch. of Nursing, 1955. RN, N.Y. Staff nurse The Jack Martin Respiratory Ctr. of The Mt. Sinai Hosp., N.Y.C., 1955-57; v.p. Chauffeurs Unlimited, Inc., N.Y.C., 1957-77; staff nurse Rusk Inst., N.Y.C., 1957-58, Beth Israel Med. Ctr., N.Y.C., 1978-79; owner, mgr. Powers Fish Market, Inc., N.Y.C., 1977-84; tchr. Techs. for Creating, Albany, N.Y., 1983—; staff nurse Doctors Hosp., N.Y.C., 1984-86; pvt. duty nurse Personal Health Care Services, Albany, N.Y., 1987-88; nurse Albany Med. Ctr. Hosp., 1987—; real estate sales assoc. Century 21-Stanley Major Ltd., West Sand Lake, N.Y., 1988, Century-21 Home Towne Properties, Albany, 1989-92. Author numerous poems. Recipient Outstanding Service to Community award Mayor Koch City of N.Y., 1983. Mem. Alumnae Assn. Mt. Sinai Hosp. Sch. Nursing (various coms. 1965-77, bd. dirs. 1968). Democrat. Home: 70 2nd St Albany NY 12210-2517 Office: Albany Med Ctr Hosp 43 New Scotland Ave Albany NY 12208-3478

HILL, WILLIAM DAVID, judge; b. Trenton, N.J., June 4, 1928; s. Harry Russell and Mary Alice (Abrams) H.; m. Kathleen Patricia Johnson, June 19, 1954; children: W. David, Patricia Hill Grim, John, Thomas, Peter. BA, Rutgers U., 1950; LLB, Temple U., 1958. Bar: N.J. 1959, D.C. 1959, U.S. Supreme Ct. Claims adjustor Royal Globe Ins. Group, Trenton, 1954-57; claims supr. Aetna Ins. Co., Phila., 1957-58; law clk. N.J. Atty. Gen., Trenton, 1958-59, dep. atty. gen., 1959-61; referee form hearings N.J. Div. Workers Compensation, Camden, 1961-68, judge, 1968-76, supervising judge, 1976—; lecturer, panelist Inst. Continuing Legal Edn.; lecturer in field; participant moot ct. programs. County committeeman Dem. Party, Willingboro, N.J., 1961-62; counsel Planning Bd., Willingboro, 1970. 1st lt. U.S. Army, 1951-53. Decorated UN medal. Mem. Am. Judicature Soc., Soc. Wine Educators (charter), Am. Wine Soc. (wine judge) Le Soc du Cochon. Home: 6 Winterberry Ln Willingboro NJ 08046 Office: NJ Div Workers Compensation 518 Market St Camden NJ 08102

HILL, WILLIAM PLUMMER, retired steel company executive; b. Rehoboth Beach, Del., Mar. 30, 1908; s. Edward Samuel and Amanda (Boone) H.; m. Bertha Brittingham, Oct. 12, 1935; children: William P., John E., David G. BSMechE, U. Del., 1933; postgrad., Johns Hopkins U., 1937-52, Lehigh U., 1954. Registered profl. engr., Md., Ind., Pa. With Bethlehem Steel Co., Sparrows Point, Md., 1933-35, chief engr., 1947-48, asst. gen. mgr., 1948-53; asst. to v.p. ops. Bethlehem, Pa., 1953-58; v.p. engring. Nat. Steel Corp., Pitts., 1958-71, sr. v.p. tech., 1971-91; cons. Nat. Steel of Philipeans Nippon Steel Corp., Nippon Kokan Steel Corp., Kawasaki Steel Corp., Mexican Govt. Steel Plants, Internat. Exec. Svc. Corp. Contbr. articles to profl. jours.; patentee in field. Pres. Bethlehem Council Boy Scouts Am., 1958. Recipient Silver Beaver award Boy Scouts Am., 1970, Gt. Insignia in Gold award Fed. Pres. Austria, 1972. Fellow ASME; mem. Am. Iron and Steel Ins., Am. Iron and Steel Engrs. (past pres., chmn.), Am. Ordnance Assn., Am. Soc. Metal Engrs., Pa. Soc. Clubs: Dusquesne, Longue Vue (Pitts.); Saucon Valley (Bethlehem); Williams Country (Weirton, W.Va.); The Leash (N.Y.C.). Home: Edgewater Estates 56 Edgewater Dr Lewes DE 19958-9747

HILL, WINSLOW SMITH, infosystems specialist; b. Port Arthur, Tex., Sept. 11, 1925; s. Mark Lafayette and Bertha May (Smith) H.; m. Janet Bertha Round, June 14, 1947; children: Katherine Bertha, Martha Louise, Susan Beverly. BS, Tufts U., 1945, BSME, 1947. Asst. gen. mgr. Bethlehem Steel Corp., Bethlehem, Pa., 1947-81; pres. Computer Aid Inc., Bethlehem, 1981-87, Mgmt. Mentors Inc., Doylestown, Pa., 1987—; bd. dirs. Collgeate Mgmt. Systems Inc., Bethlehem. V.p., exec. bd. mem. Bucks County Boy Scouts Am., Doylestown, 1973—. Lt. (j.g.) USNR, 1943-46. Mem. Masons. Republican. Presbyterian. Home: 141 Shewell Ave Doylestown PA 18901-3724 Office: Mgmt Mentors Inc 350 S Main St Ste 211 Doylestown PA 18901-4873

HILLEBRAND, LAWRENCE JOHN, manufacturing executive; b. St. Louis, July 5, 1939; s. Jerry Waser and Ann (Boyd) H.; m. Kathleen Anne Kelly, Oct. 1, 1960; children: Stephen, Eric, Gregory, Kurt, Jason. BS in Aero Maintenance Engring., St. Louis, 1960; MS in Polit. Sci., Auburn U., 1972. Commdr. 2d lt. USAF, 1960, advanced through grades to col., 1980, ret., 1985; rsch. div. program mgr. LTV, Buffalo, 1985—; instr. SUNY, Buffalo, 1991—. Choir mem. St. Peter and Paul Ch. Mem. USAF Assn., Coun. Am. Mil., Nat. Contract Mgmt. Assn., Old Crows Assn. Roman Catholic. Home: 143 Cadman Dr Buffalo NY 14221-6963 Office: LTV Rsch Div PO Box 22 Buffalo NY 14220-0222

HILLER, DALE MURRAY, chemistry consultant; b. Chgo., Oct. 13, 1924; s. Cletus Murray and Anna (Keener) H.; m. Mary Aileen Garrett, June 29, 1952; children: Karen Ann, Margaret Ellen, Steven Richard, Eric David. BSEE, U. Nebr., 1947; AB in Chemistry, Miami U., Oxford, Ohio, 1948; PhD in Phys. Chemistry, Iowa State U., 1952. Rsch. assoc. E. I. duPont de Nemours & Co., Inc., Wilmington, Del., 1952-90; pvt. practice cons. Wilmington, 1990—. Contbr. articles to profl. publs.; patentee in field. Chmn. Del. Authority on Radiation Protection, Dover; mem. Rep. State Com., Wilmington, chmn. dist. com.; chmn. bd. dirs. World Federalist Asn., Washington. Master sgt. U.S. Army, 1943-46. Mem. Am. Chem. Soc., Phi Beta Kappa, Sigma Xi, Theta Chi, Omicron Delta Kappa. Episcopalian. Home and Office: 151 Oldbury Dr Wilmington DE 19808-1433

HILLERY, MARY JANE LARATO, producer, television host, editor, columnist, reserve army officer; b. Boston, Sept. 15, 1931; d. Donato and Porzia (Avellis) Larato; Asso. Sci. (scholar), Northeastern U., 1950; BS, U. Mass. Harvard Extension, 1962; grad. Command and Gen. Staff Coll., 1982; m. Thomas H. Hillery, Feb. 25, 1961; 1 son, Thomas H. Sales agt., linguist Pan Am. Airways, Boston, 1955-61; interpreter Internat. Conf. Fire Chiefs, Boston, 1966; tchr. Spanish, YWCA, Natick, Mass., 1966-67; community rels. cons., adv. bd. dirs., lectr. for migrant edn. project div. Mass. Dept. Community Affairs, Boston, 1967-69; editor-in-chief Sudbury (Mass.) Citizen, 1967-76; assoc. editor The Beacon, 1976-79, contbg. editor, 1979-83; area editorial adviser Beacon Pub. Co., Acton, Mass., 1970-80, editor, 1976-80; columnist Town Crier, 1987—; contbg. editor Towne Talk, 1975-79, Citizens' Forum, 1975-81; editor Spl. Forces Ann. History, 1990; dir. pub. affairs Mass. Dept. Environ. Quality Engring., 1981-83; producer, host TV interview show For the Record. Mem. Bus. Adv. Com., 1972-77, Sudbury Sch. Com., 1976-77; mem. Meml. Day Celebration Com., 1972—, master of ceremonies, 1973-92; mem. Sudbury Town Report, 1967-72, 85-88, chmn., 1969-72; chmn. Sudbury Vets. Adv. Com., 1986—; panelist Internat. Women's Year Symposium, 1975, Women in Politics, 1987, Women In Mil., 1987; mem. congl. 5th dist. Mass. nomination bd. USMA West Point, 1985—. Served with USN, 1950-54; lt. col. USAR; Persian Gulf, 1991; liaison officer U.S. Mil. Acad., 1976-89; pub. affairs officer 94th USAR Command, 1982-83, Office of Sec. of Def., The Pentagon, Washington, 1989—; mem. Congl. Nominating bd. USMA, 1985—; editor Hansconian, 1983-85. Decorated Meritorious Svc. medal 1985, Meritorious Service medal, Joint Svc. Achievement medal, 1991, Nat. Def. medal-Bronze Star, 1991, Outstanding Svc. award Sec. Def. Pub. Affairs, 1992; Named Editor of Year, Beacon Pub. Co., 1970; recipient medal of appreciation Internat. Order DeMolay, 1969, certificates of appreciation U.S. Def. Civil Preparedness Agency, 1975, Mass. Bicentennial Commn., 1976, Appreciation award U.S. Milit. Acad., 1976-86, Res. Officers Assn., 1986; citations Mass. State Senate, 1979, 82; Newswriting award Media Contest, Air Force Systems Command, 1984, Outstanding Svc. award Sec. Def. Pub. Affairs, 1991. Mem. Nat. Editorial Assn., Nat. Newspaper Assn., Nat. Press Club, New Eng. Press Assn., Bus. and Profl. Women's Club (1st v.p. 1973-74, pres. 1974-76, parliamentarian 1978-88, state bylaws com. 1977-78, 79-81, 1986-88, state legis. chmn. 1979-81, 86-88, State Polit. Action Com. Chmn., 1988-89, Woman of Yr. 1979, Woman of Achievement 1982), LWV (dir. 1964-68), Nat. League Am. Pen Women (exec. bd. Boston 1974-76, 78-88, pres. 1976-78, publicity chmn. 1979-80, chmn. bylaws com. 1979-80, 86-88, parliamentarian 1978-80, 82-88, auditor 1980-82, 84-88, 1st v.p. 1988-92), Res. Officers Assn. (life; state sec. 1978-79, pres. Boston chpt. 1986-88, army coun. rep. 1989-90, 92—, budget com., 1990-91, state publicity chmn. 1988-92, advisor editor 1991, Outstanding Svc. award 1978-79), Omega Sigma. Home: 66 Willow Rd Sudbury MA 01776-2663

HILLIER, JAMES, communications executive, researcher; b. Brantford, Ont., Can., Aug. 22, 1915; came to U.S., 1940; s. James Sr. and Ethel Anne (Cooke) H.; m. Florence Marjory Bell, Oct. 24, 1936; children: James Robert, William Wynship. BA, U. Toronto, Ont., Can., 1937, MA, 1938; PhD, U. Toronto, 1941, DSc (hon.), 1978; DSc (hon.), N.J. Inst. Tech., 1981. Rsch. asst. Banting Inst. U. Toronto Med. Sch., 1938-40; head electron microscope rsch. RCA Labs., Camden and Princeton, N.J., 1940-53; adminstrv. engr. corp. rsch. and engring. RCA Corp., Princeton, 1954-55; chief engr. comml. electronic products RCA Corp., Camden, 1955-57; gen. mgr. labs. RCA Corp., Princeton, 1957-58, v.p. labs., 1958-68; v.p. corp. rsch. and engring. RCA Corp., N.Y.C., 1968-69, exec. v.p. rsch. and engring., 1969-76, exec. v.p., sr. scientist, 1976-77, ret., 1977; dir. corp. rsch. Westinghouse Air Brake Co., Pitts. and Alexandria, Va., 1953-54; pres. Indsl. Reactor Labs., Princeton, 1964-65; mem. higher edn. study com. Gov.'s Office, State of N.J., 1963-64; mem. commerce tech. adv. bd. U.S. Dept. Commerce, Washington, 1964-70; chmn. adv. coun. dept. elect. engring. Princeton U., 1963-65; mem. adv. coun. Coll. Engring., Cornell U., Ithaca, N.Y., 1966—; mem. joint consultative com. U.S. AID/Egyptian Acad. Sci. Rsch. & Tech., Cairo, 1978-84. Co-author: Electron Optics and the Electron Microscope, 1945; co-contbr.: Medical Physics, 1944, vol. II, 1950, Colloidal Chemistry, vol. VI, 1946; contbr. Ency. Britannica, 1948. Inducted into Nat. Inventors Hall of Fame, 1980; recipient James Loudon Gold medal U. Toronto, 1937, Albert Lasker award APHA, 1960, Commonwealth award, 1980, Presdl. award Microbeam Analysis Soc., 1989. Fellow AAAS (chmn. nomination com. Sect. M 1965), IEEE (David Sarnoff award 1967, Founders medal 1981); Am. Phys. Soc. (mem. at large, governing bd. 1964-65); mem. Electron Microscope Soc. Am. (pres. 1944, Disting. Scientist award 1977), Indsl. Rsch. Inst. (bd. dirs. 1960-65, pres. 1964, Inst. medal 1975), Rotary (bd. dirs. 1988-91), Nassau Club, Sigma Xi. Home: 22 Arreton Rd Princeton NJ 08540

HILLIS, MADALYN LOUISE, not-for-profit association director, astrologer, futurist; b. Bklyn., June 23, 1951; d. Arthur and Agatha (Bartoletti) Botterio; m. Daniel Patrick Hillis, Sept. 6, 1971 (div. Aug. 1984); children: Mark Christopher, Katharine Zoe. BS, St. John's U., 1972. Fin. analyst Nat. Bank N.Am., N.Y.C., 1972-75; asst. dir. N.Y. State Chiropractic Assn., N.Y.C., 1975-77; vol. Nat. Coun. for Geocosmic Rsch., Ramsey, N.J., 1979-90, exec. dir., 1990—; cons. Astrascope Corp., Melrose, Mass., 1991—; cons., mgr. astrology product Malhotra and Assoc., Cranbury, N.J., 1992—. Editor Urania, 1986-87; author, editor Nat. Coun. for Geocosmic Rsch. Memberletter, 1986—; author Nat. Coun. for Geocosmic Rsch. Jour., 1991; monthly columnist Horoscope Guide, 1991-92. Pres. Village Sch. Parent Guild, Ridgewood, N.J., 1987-89; troop leader Girl Scouts U.S., 1991—; dir. yearbook Ramsey Jr. Football Assn., 1991—. Mem. NAFE, Astrological Soc. Princeton, Assn. for Astrological Networking. Office: Nat Coun for Geocosmic Rsch 105 Snyder Ave Ramsey NJ 07446

HILLMAN, CAROL BARBARA, communications executive; b. N.Y.C., Sept. 6, 1940; d. Joseph Hoppenfeld and Elsa (Spiegel) Hoppenfeld Resika; m. Howard D. Hillman, May 25, 1969. BA with honors, U. Wis., 1961; Fulbright scholar U. Lyon (France), 1961-62; MA, Cornell U., Ithaca, N.Y., 1966. Asst. editor Holt Rinehart & Winston, Pubs., 1965-66; staff assoc. pub. rels. Ea. Airlines, N.Y.C., 1966-74; pub. affairs mgr. Squibb Corp., N.Y.C., 1974-75; asst. dir. corp. pub. rels. Burlington Industries, N.Y.C., 1975-77, dir. corp. pub. rels., 1977-80, v.p. pub. rels., 1980-82; v.p. corp. communications Norton Co., Worcester, Mass., 1982-89, sr. cons. 1989-90; nat. dir. pub. rels. and communications Deloitte & Touche, Wilton, Conn., 1990-91; v.p. Univ. Rels. Boston U., 1991—; mem. Pub. Affairs Coun., Machinery & Allied Products Inst., 1982-89; mem. dep. policy com., agenda com. Mass. Bus. Roundtable, 1982-89; bd. dirs. Mass. Econ. Stabilization Trust, 1987—. Mem. Cornell Coun., Ithaca, 1981-85, pub. rels. com. 1981-88; mem. adv. coun. Coll. Human Ecology, Cornell U., Ithaca, 1982-84; mem. adv. bd. Ct. Apptd. Spl. Advocates, Worcester, 1983-87; voting mem. Wis. Union Trustees, U. Wis., Madison, 1982-90, trustee, 1990—; mem. Clark U. Assocs., Worcester, 1983-89; bd. dirs. Planned Parenthood League Mass., 1986-90; trustee Quinsigamond Community Coll., Worcester, 1987—. Cornell Grad. fellow Cornell U., 1962. Mem. Pub. Rels. Soc. Am., Women's Econ. Forum, Worcester C. of C. (bd. dirs. 1984-87), The Wisemen, Pub. Rels. Seminar (com. mem. 1981-89), Phi Beta Kappa, Phi Kappa Phi. Home: 299 Belknap Rd Framingham MA 01701-4716 Office: Boston U 143 Bay State Rd Boston MA 02215-1789

HILLMAN, JANICE LOUISE, computer graphics consultant; b. N.Y.C., May 30, 1951; d. Russell Lewis and Gloria (Napoli) H.;m. Leonard C. Shyles, June 5, 1977; children: Rebecca, Daniel. BSID, Ohio State U., 1981; MA, Purdue U., 1983. Prin. Info. Design Assocs., Downington, Pa., 1984—; instr., lectr. Md. Inst. Coll. Art, Balt., 1984-90, George Washington U., 1983-85, Smithsonian Instn., 1984, ACM Siggraph, 1984-88.

HILLMAN, LEON, electrical engineer; b. N.Y.C., July 31, 1921; s. Harry and Jennie (Gartenberg) H.; m. Rita Kathchen, July 18, 1948; children: David, Deborah. BEE, NYU, 1950. Registered profl. engr., N.J. Radio engr. Communication Devel. Co., Newark, 1940-42; head elec. sect. U.S. Army Engring. Lab., Ft. Monmouth, n.J., 1942-45; rsch. assoc. Elec. Engring. Dept., NYU, N.Y.C., 1946-51; v.p., chief engr. Prodn. Rsch. Corp., Thornwood, N.Y., 1951-56; pres. Automation Dynamics Corp., Northvale, N.J., 1957-71, ADCO Aerospace Inc., Closter, N.J., 1971—; electronics cons. Johnson Controls, Milw., 1949-69; lectr. in field. Contbr. articles to profl. jours. Chmn. United Jewish Appeal, Englewood, N.J., 1960, Demarest, N.J., 1978. Sgt. USAF, 1945-46. Named Hon. Citizen, State of Md., 1957. Mem. IEEE, Am. Phys. Soc., Sigma Xi, Eta Kappa Nu. Office: ADCO Aerospace Inc PO Box 748 Closter NJ 07624-0748

HILLMAN, RITA, investor; b. N.Y.C., May 16, 1912; d. Rudolf and Bertha (Goodman) Kanarek; m. Alex L. Hillman, Aug. 23, 1932 (dec. 1968); children: Richard Alan (dec.), Alex L. Student NYU, 1929-32. Mem. Met. Mus. Art (mem. vis. com. 20th century art dept.), Am. Friends Israel Mus. (exec. com.), Bklyn. Acad. Music (vice chmn.), Internat. Ctr. Photography (chmn.), Alex Hillman Family Found. (pres.). Home: 895 Park Ave New York NY 10021-0327 Office: 630 Fifth Ave New York NY 10111

HILLS, CARLA ANDERSON, federal official, lawyer; b. Los Angeles, Jan. 3, 1934; d. Carl H. and Edith (Hume) Anderson; m. Roderick Maltman

Hills, Sept. 27, 1958; children: Laura Hume, Roderick Maltman, Megan Elizabeth, Alison Macbeth. A.B. cum laude, Stanford U., 1955; student, St. Hilda's Coll., Oxford (Eng.) U., 1954; LL.B., Yale U., 1958; hon. degrees, Pepperdine U., 1975, Washington U., 1977, Mills Coll., 1977, Lake Forest Coll., 1978, Williams Coll., 1981. Bar: Calif. 1959, U.S. Supreme Ct. 1965. Asst. U.S. atty. civil div. Los Angeles, 1958-61; partner firm Munger, Tolles, Hills & Rickershauser, Los Angeles, 1962-74, Latham, Watkins & Hills, Washington, 1978-86, Weil, Gotshal & Manges, Washington, 1986-88; asst. atty. gen. civil div. Justice Dept., Washington, 1974-75; sec. HUD, 1975-77; U.S. trade rep. Exec. Office of the Pres., 1989—; dir. IBM, Corning Glass Works, Am. Airlines, Fed. Nat. Mortgage Assn., The Henley Group, Chevron Corp.; adj. prof. Sch. Law, UCLA, 1972; mem. Trilateral Commn., 1977-82, Am. Com. on East-West Accord, 1977-79, Internat. Found. for Cultural Cooperation and Devel., 1977-89, Fed. Acctg. Standards Adv. Council, 1978-80; bd. dirs. Internat. Exec. Service Corps.; mem. corrections task force Los Angeles County Sub-Regional; adv. bd. Calif. Council on Criminal Justice, 1969-71; mem. standing com. discipline U.S. Dist. Ct. for Central Calif., 1970-73; mem. Adminstrv. Conf. U.S., 1972-74; mem. exec. com. law and free soc. State Bar Calif., 1973; bd. councillors U. So. Calif. Law Center, 1972-74; trustee Pomona Coll., 1974-79, U. So. Calif., Brookings Instn.; mem. at large exec. com. Yale Law Sch., 1973-78; mem. com. on Law Sch. Yale Univ. Council; Gordon Grand fellow Yale U., 1978; mem. Sloan Commn. on Govt. and Higher Edn., 1977-79; mem. advisory com. Princeton U., Woodrow Wilson Sch. of Pub. and Internat. Affairs, 1977-80; trustee Am. Productivity and Quality Ctr., 1988—. Co-author: Federal Civil Practice, 1961; co-author, editor: Antitrust Adviser, 1971, 3d edit., 1985; contbg. editor: Legal Times, 1978—; mem. editorial bd.: Nat. Law Jour, 1978—. Trustee U. So. Calif., 1977-79, Norton Simon Mus. Art, Pasadena, Calif., 1976-80, Lawyers Com. for Civil Rights under Law, 1978-84; trustee Urban Inst., 1978-80, chmn., 1983-89; co-chmn. Alliance to Save Energy, 1977-89; vice chmn. adv. coun. on legal policy Am. Enterprise Inst., 1977-84; bd. visitors, exec. com. Stanford U. Law Sch., 1978-81; bd. dirs. Am. Coun. for Capital Formation, 1978-89; mem. adv. com. M.I.T.-Harvard U. Joint Ctr. for Urban Studies, 1978-82. Fellow Am. Bar Found.; mem. Los Angeles Women Lawyers Assn. (pres. 1964), ABA (chmn. publs. com. antitrust sect. 1972-74, council 1974, 77-84, chmn. 1982-83), Fed. Bar Assn. (pres. Los Angeles chpt. 1963), Los Angeles County Bar Assn. (mem. fed. rules and practice com. 1963-72, chmn. issues and survey 1963-72, chmn. sub-com. revision local rules for fed. cts. 1966-72, mem. jud. qualifications com. 1971-72), Am. Bar Inst. Clubs: Yale of So. Calif. (dir. 1972-74); Yale (Washington). Office: Exec Office of President US Trade Rep 600 17th St NW Washington DC 20506-0001*

HILSENRATH, LEE BETTY, mathematics educator; b. Bklyn., Dec. 6, 1934; d. Samuel and Gussie (Gelfand) Batch; m. Daniel Wallace Hilsenrath, Dec. 24, 1961; children: Joel Alan, Mark Harris. BA, Bklyn., 1956, MA, 1959. Cert. tchr. Math. tchr. John D. Wells Jr. High Sch., Bklyn., 1956; math. tchr. New Utrecht High Sch., Bklyn., 1956—, ret., 1991; dean of girls New Utrecht High Sch., 1972-85; student activities advisor New Utrecht High Sch., 1959-62; spl. edn. math. cons. New Utrecht High Sch. 1986-88. Mem. exec. bd. Coney Island chpt. Am. Parkinson's Disease Assn. Recipient Outstanding Profl. Svc. Tchr. award Bklyn. High Sch. div. Bd. Edn. N.Y.C., 1988, Bklyn. High Sch. Recognition Day award New Utrecht High Sch., 1989. Democrat. Jewish. Home: 945 E 15th St Brooklyn NY 11230-3703

HILTON, JOHN DAVID, business owner, infosystems specialist; b. Glastonbury, Conn., Apr. 20, 1958; s. John Chadwick and Carol Marion (Bickerstaffe) H. BS in Econs., Norwich U., 1980; BA in Geography, Fla. Atlantic U., 1983, MA in Econs., 1984. Instr. Vt. Coll., Montpelier, 1984; programmer Input-Output Computer Svcs., Waltham, Mass., 1984-86; systems analyst PSI, Internat., Inc., Fairfax, Va., 1986-87; project leader Vanguard Techs. Corp., Falls Church, Va., 1987-88; software engr. Synetics Corp., Wakefield, Mass., 1988-89; software specialist PSI, Internat., Inc., Fairfax, 1989—; owner, pres. JDH Assocs., Glastonbury, 1988—. 1st lt. USAF, 1980-81. Mem. Am. Econ. Assn., Ea. Econ. Assn., Assn. Computing Machinery, Nat. Assn. Accts. (bd. dirs. 1989-91), Inst. Mgmt. Accts. Republcian. Episcopalian. Office: JDH Assocs 240 Cedar Ridge Dr Glastonbury CT 06033-1836

HILTON, LEO, retired educator; b. Hoboken, N.J., Jan. 11, 1918; s. Sigmund and Betty (Marcus) Heitler; m. Geraldine Ettinger, Oct. 31, 1942; children: Susan, Melinda Butler. BS, St. John's U., 1938; MA, Columbia U., 1950, EdD, 1965. Tchr. Demarest High Sch., Hoboken, 1938-42; elem. tchr. Cedar Grove (N.J.) Bd. Edn., 1947-56; elem. prin. West Milford Twp. (N.J.) Bd. Edn., 1956-62, gen. supr., high sch. prin., 1962-65; prof., campus dir. William Paterson Coll., Wayne, N.J., 1965-88; prof. emeritus, cons., 1988—; cons. Urban Schs. Supts. of N.J., 1975—, Boy Scouts Am., 1972-75. Vol. Mayor's Task Force of Edn., Paterson, N.J., 1970-74; cons. Paterson Task Force on Poverty; chmn. State Commr.'s Adv. Com. on Ednl. Innovation, 1968-71. Recipient Human Rights award N.J. Edn. Assn., 1978. Mem. NEA, ASCD, N.J. Edn. Assn. (past local pres., county pres.), Am. Assn. Sch.Adminstrs., Paterson State Faculty Assn., Passaic County Coun. Ednl. Assns. (memexec. com.), Phi Delta Kappa. Jewish. Home: 310 Liberty St Apt 43 Little Ferry NJ 07643-1303

HILTON, W. EUGENE, computer consultant; b. Neptune, N.J., Oct. 31, 1945; s. Tom and Grace Minora (Morey) H.; m. Marjorie Ann Shipe, Feb. 15, 1970. AAS, Mercer County Community Coll., Trenton, N.J., 1968. Mgr. computer ops. Mercer County Community Coll., 1968-78; computer cons. Pinkerton Computer Cons., Warminster, Pa., 1978-79; mgr. R&L Data Ctrs., Bloomsbury, N.J., 1979-80; sr. cons. Pinkerton Computer Cons., Trevose, Pa., 1980—. With USMC, 1968-70, Vietnam. Office: Pinkerton Computer Cons 4 Neshaminy Interplex Ste 111 Trevose PA 19047

HILTZ, ARNOLD AUBREY, chemist; b. Sea View, Canada, July 31, 1924; came to the U.S., 1953; s. Aubrey Claremont and Fannie Mae (Bryanton) H.; m. Margery Jane Beer, July 17, 1946; children: Sharon Lynne, Deborah Jane. BS in Chemistry, Acadia U., Wolfville, Nova Scotia, 1947; PhD in Phys. Chemistry, McGill U., Montreal, Quebec, Canada, 1952. Ordained deacon, 1976, ordained priest, 1976. Rsch. scientific officer Def. Rsch. Bd. Canada, Quebec City, Canada, 1951-53; rsch. chemist Am. Viscose Corp., Phila., 1953-59, group leader, 1959-60; group leader Avisun Corp., Phila., 1960-65; rsch. chemist Borden Chem. Co., Phila., 1965-66; sr. scientist Gen. Electric Co., Phila., 1966-79, mgr. materials applications, 1979—; tutor math. and sci. Rose Tree Media (Pa.) Sch. Dist., 1958-74. Contbr. articles to profl. jours.; patentee in field. Sch. dir. Rose Tree Media Sch. Dist., 1969-74; bd. dirs., treas. Middletown (Pa.) Free Libr., 1964-69; bd. dirs. Sheepscot Island Co., MacMahan Island, Maine, 1983-85; docent Phila. Mus. Art, 1988—. Recipient Silver medal Gov.-Gen. Can. 1942, Canadian Overseas medal 1945, Frank J. Sensenbrenner fellow McGill U. 1949-51, inventor's medal GE 1984. Mem. Am. Chem. Soc. (sci. lectr. 1958—, chem. abstractor 1958-79). Republican. Episcopalian. Home: 524 Cedar Ln Swarthmore PA 19081-1105 Office: Gen Electric Co Goddard Blvd King Of Prussia PA 19406-2902

HILTZ, DAWN PAPP, shoe manufacturing executive; b. Norwalk, Conn. d. Frank Stephen and Elizabeth Madeline (Mola) Millard; m. Ellis Andrew Hiltz, Jr., Sept. 11, 1982. Student, Norwalk State Tech. Coll., Sacred Heart U., Am. Inst. Banking. Clk. Union Trust Co., Norwalk, 1978-82; asst. mgr. Matthew's, Westport, Conn., 1982; asst. to pres. ISP, Inc., Norwalk, 1982-86; asst. to pres. Pure Water Techs., Inc., Westport, 1986-89; asst. chmn., founder U. Brands (formerly Toddler U.), 1989—. Asst. to Chief exec. officer, chmn. Vol. Norwalk Seaport Assn., 1985, 86. Mem. NAFE, South Norwalk Boat Club Aux. (sec. 1989, 90). Republican. Roman Catholic. Avocations: skiing, scuba diving, photography. Home: 92 Barlow Plain Dr Fairfield CT 06430-5102 Office: U Brands 257 Riverside Ave Westport CT 06880-4806

HIMELFARB, RICHARD JAY, securities firm executive; b. Balt., Feb. 3, 1942; s. Jacob and Jennie (Willen) H.; m. Margaret Conn, Sept. 7, 1969; children: Elizabeth Jayne, Michael Ross. BA, Johns Hopkins U., 1962; LLB, Yale U., 1965. Bar: Md., 1965. Employed, then ptnr. Weinberg & Green, Balt., 1967-83; exec. v.p. Legg Mason, Inc., Balt., 1983—, also bd. dirs. Bd. dirs. Ctr. Stage, Inc., Balt., 1984—, Balt. Goodwill Industries, 1984—, Bryn Mawr Sch., 1991—; mem. com. Econ. Devel. Coun. Greater Balt., 1989—; pres. adv. coun. U. Md., Balt., 1990—. Capt. U.S. Army, 1965-67. Mem. Phi Beta Kappa. Home: 116 Taplow Rd Baltimore MD 21212-3312 Office: Legg Mason Wood Walker Inc 111 S Calvert St Baltimore MD 21202-6174

HIMELSTEIN, MONROE, surgeon; b. Lebanon, Conn., Jan. 18, 1924; s. Max A. and Dorothy J. (Malkin) H.; m. Faith Freedman, Apr. 26, 1953; children: Mary H. Cohn, Jane H. Sheehan. AB, Wesleyan U., Middletown, Conn., 1947; MD, Columbia U., 1951. Diplomate Am. Bd. Surgery, Nat. Bd. Med. Examiners. Intern Hartford (Conn.) Hosp., 1951-52, surgical resident, 1952-56, clin. asst. to sr. surgeon, 1956—; asst. clin. prof. Dartmouth Med. Sch., Hanover, N.H., 1984—; assoc. clin. prof. surgery U. Conn. Sch. of Medicine, Farmington, 1970—; cons. in surgery Inst. for Living, Hartford, 1977—, Rocky Hill Vet.'s Hosp., Rocky Hill, Conn., 1968—; bd. dirs. Capital Area Health Consortium, Hartford; chief of staff Hartford Hosp., 1986-89, bd. dirs. and exec. com., corporator; lectr. in field. Contbr. articles to profl. jours. Lt. (j.g.) USNR, 1943-46, PTO. Fellow Am. Coll. Surgeons; mem. Conn. Soc. Am. Bd. Surgeons, New Eng. Surgical Soc. (sr. mem.), AMA, Conn. Med. Soc., Hartford County Med. Assn. (bd. dirs. 1986—), Hartford Med. Soc. (chmn. bd. censors and adv. bd.). Jewish. Office: 85 Seymour St Hartford CT 06106

HIMELSTEIN, MORGAN YALE, English educator; b. Lebanon, Conn., Sept. 19, 1926; s. Max Abraham and Dorothy Judith (Malkin) H.; m. Libby June Rosenfeld, Dec. 21, 1958; children: Andrew Louis, Bruce Philip. BA, Wesleyan U., 1947; AM, Columbia U., 1948, PhD, 1958. Instr. English Univ. Rochester, N.Y., 1948-50, Adelphi Univ., Garden City, N.Y., 1957-60; asst. prof. English Adelphi Univ., Garden City, 1960-64, assoc. prof. English, 1964-68, dir. grad. studies in English, 1965-74, prof. in English, 1968—, summer chair in English, 1965-86; cons. various publs., 1970—, various opera theatres, 1980—. Author: Drama Was A Weapon, 1963, 1976; translator: La Grande Duchesse De Gerolstein, 1977, La Perichole, 1982, Orphee Aux Enfers, 1985, Die Fledermaus, 1990; contbr. articles to profl. jours. Trustee Garden City (N.Y.) Jewish Ctr., 1965—, pres., 1981-83. Cpl. U.S. Army, 1950-52. Recipient Winchester fellowship Wesleyan Univ., Middletown, Conn., 1948-49; honoree United Jewish Appeal, Garden City, 1978. Mem. Modern Lang. Assn., Wesleyan Alumni Schs. Com., Phi Beta Kappa. Home: 37 Maxwell Rd Garden City NY 11530-1844 Office: Adelphi Univ South Ave Garden City NY 11530

HINCKLEY, LYNN SCHELLIG, microbiologist; b. Poughkeepsie, N.Y., June 28, 1944; d. John Alfred and Hilda Louise (Russell) Schellig; m. Henry Pember, Apr. 15, 1967; children: John, Russell, Clark. BA, U. Conn., 1966. Rsch. asst. U. Conn., Storrs, 1966-67, microbiologist, dir. Conn. Mastitis Lab., 1977—; microbiologist Angell Meml. Animal Hosp., Boston, 1967-68, Pharm-House, Inc., Hope Valley, R.I., 1971-73. Contbr. articles to profl. jours. Mem. Nat. Mastitis Coun. (bd. dirs. 1990—), Nat. Conf. on Interstate Milk Shipments (com. chairperson 1989—), Am. Assn. Vet. Lab. Diagnosticians, Internat. Assn. Milk, Food and Environ. Sanitarians, Inc., Internat. Dairy Fedn. (expert group A7 1991—), N.E. Am. Soc. Microbiology, N.E. Dairy Practices Coun. (dir. task force 1991—), Conn. Mastitis Coun. (chairperson 1987—). Office: U Conn Diagnostic Testing 61 N Eagleville Road Ext # U-203 Storrs Mansfield CT 06269-3203

HINDERSINN, RAYMOND RICHARD, organic chemist, researcher; b. Central Falls, R.I., July 24, 1918; s. Richard R. and Rosalia E. (Aust) H.; m. Marion Alice McIntire, Aug. 20, 1944; 1 child, Kenneth Raymond. BS in Chemistry cum laude, Brown U., 1949; PhD in Organic Chemistry, U. Wis., 1954. Sr. rsch. chemist Hooker Electrochem. Corp., Niagara Falls, N.Y., 1954-56; supr. polymer rsch., polyurethane foams Hooker Chem. Corp., Grand Island, N.Y., 1956-66, supr. polymer applications and evaluation, 1967-70; rsch. coord. polyester rsch. program Hooker Chems. and Plastics Corp., Grand Island, 1970-73; sect. mgr. rsch. Hooker Chem. Corp., Grand Island, 1973-75; mgr. applications and testing Hooker Chems. & Plastics Corp., Grand Island, 1975-78, sr. scientist polymer rsch., 1978-81; tech. cons., 1981—; mem. Com. Fire Safety Aspects of Polymeric Materials Nat. Materials Adv. Bd., NAS. Contbr. articles to profl. jours.; over 50 patents in field of flame retardation. Mem. Am. Chem. Soc. (exec. com. Western N.Y. Sect., Schoellkopf medal, 1982), R.I. Honor Soc., Sigma Xi. Home and Office: 4288 Lower River Rd Youngstown NY 14174-9702

HINDMAN, EDWARD EVANS, meteorologist, educator; b. L.A., Sept. 26, 1942; s. Edward Evans and Josephine (Long) H.; m. Nancy Maxson, June 17, 1967 (div. June 1985); children: Kathryn, Andrew, Joseph. BSc, U. Utah, 1965; MSc, Colo. State U., 1967; PhD, U. Wash., 1975. Cert. cons. meteorologist; comml. pilot. Rsch. meteorologist Navy Weather Rsch. Facility, Norfolk, Va., 1967-71; fellow, rsch. meteorologist Naval Weapons Ctr., China Lake, Calif., 1971-79; rsch. assoc. Colo. State U., Ft. Collins, 1979-86; vis. assoc. prof. U.S. Naval Acad., Annapolis, Md., 1986-87, Drexel U., Phila., 1988; assoc. prof. of meteorology CCNY, N.Y.C., 1988—. Editor: Light Absorption By Aerosol Particles, 1982; contbr. articles to Jour. Applied Meteorology, Jour. Weather Modification, Jour. Atmospheric Ocean. Tech., Jour. Atmospheric Sci. Supt. Christ Luth. Kindergarten, Norfolk, 1970-71; mem. coun. Grace Luth. Ch., Ridgecrest, 1976-78; bd. dirs. Single Again, Prince of Peace Ch., Crofton, Md., 1987; treas. Cornerstone Luth. Ctr., N.Y.C., 1989-92. Named Disting. Alumnus, Luth. High Sch., L.A., 1977. Mem. Am. Meteorol. Soc. (program chair 1984, Maclewane award 1966), Weather Modification Assn. (trustee 1990-92, chair cert. bd. 1984-87), Soaring Soc. Am. (Gold Badge 1983), Explorers Club, Appalachian Mountain Club (resident naturalist 1987—). Office: CCNY EAS Dept 138th and Convent New York NY 10031

HINDMAN, MARGARET HORTON, college administrator; b. Salisbury, Md., Feb. 15, 1947; d. Herbert Elwood and Imogene (Caruthers) Horton; m. Don C. Hindman, Aug. 9, 1969; 1 child, Annemarie H. BA, Hood Coll., 1969; postgrad., Antioch Coll., 1974-77. Reporter Frederick (Md.) News-Post, 1969-72; counselor, project coord. Community Mental Health Svcs., Frederick, 1972-73; editor weekly newspaper Sentinel Newspapers, Gaithersburg, Md., 1973-74; writer, editor Nat. Clearinghouse for Alcohol Info., Gaithersburg, 1974-76; dir. pub. info. Hood Coll., Frederick, Md., 1976-79; publs. mgr. Nat. Clearinghouse for Alcohol Info., Rockville, Md., 1979-84; dir. communications Hood Coll., Frederick, 1984-89, assoc. v.p. communications, 1989—; freelance writer Balt. Sun, 1973-76, Nat. Inst. on Alcohol Abuse, Rockville, 1976-77. Contbr. articles to mags. and profl. jours. Mem. Md. Judicial Nominating Commn., 6th Dist., State of Md., Annapolis, 1986-88; alternate mem. Md. Water Quality Adv. Commn., Annapolis, 1991—. Recipient awards for mag. editing and direct mail Md. Press Women, 1984. Mem. Coun. for Advancement and Support of Edn., Ednl. Writers Assn. Office: Hood Coll Rosemont Ave Frederick MD 21701

HINDS, EDWARD ALLEN, physicist, educator; b. Cardiff, Wales, U.K., Sept. 8, 1949; came to U.S., 1975; s. Laurence and Ruth Cleeland (Shaw) H.; m. Ann Kathleen Carter; children: Victoria, Madeleine, Martin. BA with honors, Oxford U., 1971, PhD, 1974; MA (hon.), Yale U., 1989. Rsch. assoc. Columbia U., N.Y.C., 1975-76; rsch. assoc., lectr. Yale U., New Haven, 1976-77, asst. prof., 1977-81, assoc. prof., 1981-88, prof., 1988—; cons. Los Alamos (N.Mex.) Nat. Lab., 1979-84, Brookhaven Nat. Lab., L.I., 1985-86; vis. rsch. assoc. Oxford (Eng.) U., 1982, Serc vis. fellow, 1985-86. Contbr. articles to profl. jours. Named Alfred P. Sloan fellow Alfred P. Sloan Found., 1981, 85; recipient grants NSF, Washington, 1977-84, 83-92, 85-92, Nat. Inst. Standards and Tech., Gaithersburg, 1987-90. Office: Yale Univ Physics Dept 217 Prospect St New Haven CT 06520

HINDS, GLESTER SAMUEL, program specialist, tax consultant; b. N.Y.C., July 4, 1951; s. Glester Samuel and Kathryne Elizabeth (Ellison) H. BBA, Bernard M. Baruch Coll., 1973; MBA in Fin., Columbia U., 1975. Stock Broker, Ins. Broker, Notary. Staff acct. Peat Marwick Mitchell, N.Y.C., 1975-77; fin. analyst Citicorp, N.Y.C., 1977-79; sr. fin. analyst Am. Express, N.Y.C., 1979-80; owner, cons. Hinds Fin. Svcs., Long Island, N.Y., 1980-87; program specialist Calif. FTB, Manhasset, N.Y., 1987—; cons. Am. Entrepreneur's Assn., L.A., 1980-89; mem. Am. Soc. Notaries, Washington, 1986—. Editor: Financial Newsletter the H-Club, 1978-82; actor: On Camera TV Acting, 1986; contbr. articles to profl. jours. Founder Heritage Found., Washington, 1981, 82, Ronald Reagan Rep. Ctr., 1989; chman's com. U.S. Senatorial Bus. Adv., Bd., 1981, 82. Recipient Edward M. Paster Meml. award, Sigma Alpha award, Beta Gamma Sigma award, Beta Alpha Psi award, Bernard M. Baruch Coll., 1973. Mem. U.S. Olympic Soc., Rep. Presdl. Task force, 24K Club, USA Wrestling, Pro-Wrestling Hall of Fame (chmn.), U.S. Tennis Assn. Home: 31 Thomas St Coram NY 11727 Office: California Franchise Tax Bd 1129 Northern Blvd Manhasset NY 11030

HINELINE, PHILIP NEIL, psychologist; b. Rice Lake, Wis., May 29, 1940; s. Marion Asher and Edna (Conklin) H.; m. Catherine Virtue Almy. BA, Hamilton Coll., 1962; PhD, Harvard U., 1967. Exptl. psychologist Walter Reed Army Inst. of Rsch., Washington, 1966-69; lectr. Am. U., Washington, 1968-69; asst. prof. Temple U., Phila., 1969-72, assoc. prof., 1972-80, prof., 1980—; vis. rsch. prof. U. Sussex, Falmer, Eng., 1976-77. Assoc. editor Jour. of the Exptl. Analysis of Behavior, 1979-82, editor, 1983-87; contbr. articles to profl. jours. Capt. U.S. Army, 1964-69. Predoctoral fellow NIH, 1963-64; recipient James Soper Merrill award Hamilton Coll., 1962, Rsch. grant NIH, 1970-73, NSF, 1981-82, 90-92. Fellow APA, Am. Psychol. Soc.; mem. Assn. for Behavior Analysis (pres. 1990-91), Soc. for Behavior Analysis (pres. 1990-92), Soc. for Exptl. Analysis of Behaviors (bd. dirs. 1980-87, 89—, Assn. for Behavior Analysis, Psychonomic Soc., Sigma Xi. Home: 3020 Midvale Ave Philadelphia PA 19129-1028 Office: Temple U Philadelphia PA 19122

HINES, EDWARD JOSEPH, composer; b. North Bellmore, N.Y., Dec. 29, 1951; s. David Ermond and Katherine Rita (Bobersky) H. Student, Hartt Sch. of Music, Hartford, Conn., 1970-72; BA, Bennington Coll., 1981, MFA, 1983. Cert. instr. of music, Mass. Dir. Bennington (Vt.) July Program/Bennington Coll., 1981-84; ednl. cons. self-employed, Chgo., 1984, Cambridge, Mass., 1986-88; music pub. Edward Hines Music, Wendell, Mass., 1976—, composer, 1969—; music instr. Rowe, ERving, Sunderland Mass. Schs., 1988—; guest lectr. Turkish music, 1988—; composers' workshop participant Bennington Coll., 1979, 80. Composer, pub. of chamber music including Boxcars, 1989, Yeni Makam 1, 1992, Yeni Makam 2, 1992; contbr. articles to profl. jours. including Yeni Makam 1: New Sounds for Solo Bassoon Using Ancient Turkish Modes, 1992. Named Presser scholar Theodore Presser Pub., Bennington Coll., 1980; recipient Fulbright Rsch. grant, 1985-86, grant Amherst Arts Coun., 1989. Mem. Composer's Forum, BMI. Home and Office: W Main St Wendell MA 01379-9802

HINES, GEORGE LAWRENCE, surgeon; b. Bklyn., June 10, 1946; s. Frank and Ruth (Katzman) H.; m. Helene Anne Reitman, Aug. 23, 1969; children: Brian, Jennifer. BA, Boston U., 1969, MD, 1969. Diplomate Am. Bd. Gen. Surgery, Am. Bd. Thoracic Surgery, Am. Bd. Gen. Vascular Surgery. Intern Maimonides Med. Ctr., Bklyn., 1969-70; resident Sinai Hosp., Detroit, 1970-71; to chief resident L.I. Jewish Med. Ctr., N.Y.C., 1971-74; cardiothoracic resident NYU Med. Ctr., N.Y.C., 1974-76; attending physician Winthrop U. Hosp., Mineola, N.Y., 1976—; pvt. practice Mineola. Maj. U.S. Army Res., 1970-79. Fellow Am. Coll. Surgeons; mem. Am. Assn. for Thoracic Surgery, Soc. of Thoracic Surgeons, Internat. Soc. for Cardiovascular Surgery. Democrat. Jewish. Office: 173 Mineola Blvd Mineola NY 11501

HINES, HUBERT ORVILLE, data processing executive; b. Phoenix, Aug. 10, 1942; s. Hubert Otto Hines and Mary Alice Newberry Doyle; m. Hsio-Ying Cheng, June 17, 1972. AA, L.A. Pierce Coll., Woodland Hills, Calif., 1963; AB in Sociology, San Diego State Coll., 1969; postgrad., Nat. Ching Chi U., China, 1969-71; MA in Sociology, San Diego State U., 1974. Lic. security officer supr. Revenue officer U.S. IRS, San Diego, 1974-80; sr. computer specialist U.S. IRS, Washington, 1980—; corp. sec. ServCon, Inc., Washington, 1985-88; corp. treas. FinCon, Inc., Arlington, Va., 1985-89; v.p. Hancorp. Inc., Great Falls, Va., 1985-91; pres., chmn. bd. Propcon, Inc., Dover, Del., 1985-91. Assoc. editor The New Scholar jour., 1969. Pres. Timberlake Homeowners Assn., Great Falls, Va., 1991—; capt. IRS Volleyball Team 6, Washington, 1991—. With USN, 1963-65, USNR, 1965—. Mem. Naval Res. Assn. (life) (past chpt. pres.), Res. Officers Assn. (news editor), U.S. Navy League, Orgn. of Chinese Ams., Nat. Treasury Employees Union (steward 1991), Alpha Kappa Delta, Pi Sigma Alpha, Alpha Mu Gamma, Phi Kappa Phi. Republican. Roman Catholic. Home: 11113 Loran Rd Great Falls VA 22066

HINES, MARY ELIZABETH, academic administrator, philosophy educator; b. Bklyn., Aug. 27, 1937; d. John Patrick and Elizabeth Ellen Reynolds; m. Kenneth Dennis Hines, June 7, 1969; children: Sean, Kevin, Kathleen, Brendan. BA in Philosophy summa cum laude, St. Francis Coll., 1967; MA in Philosophy, Cath. U. Am., 1969, PhD in Philosophy, 1981. Elem. sch. tchr. Diocese Bklyn., 1957-67; prof. philosophy Catonsville (Md.) Community Coll., 1971—, assoc. dean, 1984—; part-time prof. philosophy U. Md., 1971-74, Cath. U., 1971-80, Coll. Notre Dame, Md., 1971—, Towson State U., 1983-84, Western Md. Coll., 1982-83, St. Mary's Sem. and U., 1981—. Book reviewer various philosophy texts, 1978—. Bd. govs. Hannah More Ctr., Reisterstown, Md., 1982-85; vol. Spl. Olympics. NDEA fellow, 1967-70, Am. Coun. on Edn. fellow, 1987; named Leader for the 80s, AAWCJC, 1982. Office: Catonsville Community Coll 800 S Rolling Rd Baltimore MD 21228-5317

HINGSON, ROBERT ANDREW, physician, educator, inventor, farmer; b. Anniston, Ala., Apr. 13, 1913; s. Robert A. and Elloree Elizabeth (Haynes) H.; m. Gussie Dickson, Mar. 2, 1940; children: Dickson James, Andrew Tobian, Roberta Ann, Ralph Waldo, Luke Lockhart. AB, U. Ala., 1935, postgrad., 1933-35, LHD (hon.), 1970; MD, Emory U., 1938; LHD, Monrovia (Liberia) Coll., 1962; LLD, William Jewell Coll., 1963, Eastern Bapt. Coll., 1963; LittD (hon.), Hardin-Simmons U., 1965; DSc (hon.), Thomas Jefferson U. Medicine, 1970. Commd. med. officer USPHS, 1938, advanced through grades to surgeon, med. officer various ships USCG and USN, 1939-40; fellow anesthesiology Mayo Clinic, Rochester, Minn., 1940-41; chief of dept. anesthesia, U.S. Marine Hosp. USPHS, Staten Island, N.Y., 1941-42; dir. rsch. and anesthesiology Lying-in Hosp., Jefferson Med. Coll., Phila., Pa. Hosp., 1943-45; dir., first prof. anesthesiology, U. Tenn., 1945-48; assoc. prof. obstetrics, anesthesiologist dept. obstetrics Johns Hopkins U., 1948-51; prof. anesthesia, founder dept. Case Western Res. U., 1951-68; prof. pub. health, anesthesiology and dental anesthesiology Magee Women's Hosp. U. Pitts. Sch. Medicine, 1968-73; cons. U.S. VA Hosp., Sunny Acres Hosp., Highland View Hosp., Met. Hosp., St. Anne's Hosp.; sr. cons. Amigos de Honduras Med. Service Mission; vis. prof. at univs. in New Guinea, New Zealand, Australia, S. Am., Asia, Africa, Europe, 1958-80; guest faculty numerous colls. and univs. Author: Control of Pain in Childbirth; co-author: Anesthesia for Obstetrics; co-editor: Pitkin's Conduction Anesthesia; contbr. articles to profl. jours., chpts. to books; developer clin. methods including hypospray, dermojet, Med-e-jet, continuous caudal and peridural analgesia; inventor; creator 12 med. motion pictures and video films with subjects relating to nerve block control of pain and other subjects in field. Trustee Religious Heritage Found., 1968; chmn. Polio Plus Program Rotary dist. 692, Ga.; pres. Edn. and Relief Found., World Fedn. Soc. Anesthesiologists, 1960-70; pres., founder Brother's Brother Found., med. dir., vaccination program Operation Brother's Brother, Liberia, 1962; dir. med. survey Cen. Am. nations, 1967; deacon local Bapt. ch.; dir. Bapt. World Alliance Interdenominational, Inter-Racial Med. Mission Survey of Aisa-Africa, 1958. Med dir. USPHS Res., 1951-78. Named Man of Yr. in Medicine Pitts. Acad. Medicine, 1974, 75, one of Ten Outstanding Young Men Am. U.S. Jaycees, 1947, Knight Grand Comdr. Humane Order African Redemption, 1962, Man of Distinction Pitts. Bapt. Assn., 1980, Man of Yr. Rotary of Ocilla, 1985, Humanitarian Svc. to Mankind award, 1989, Kiwanis humanitarian award, 1963; named to Gen. Francisco Morizan, 1968, Order Ruben Dario, 1968, Order Rodolfo Robles, 1974; recipient Service citation Costa Rica, 1967, service citation govts. of Nicaragua, Guatemala, Republic of Panama, El Salvador, Peru, Honduras, Dominican Republic, Haiti, Venezuela, Colombia, Cuba, Jamaica, Hadassah Service award Israel, 1968, Dahlberg Peace award Am. Bapt. Chs., 1977, Human Rights award UN Assn. Pitts., 1978, William O McQuiston Lectureship award Ill. Soc. Anesthesiologists, 1978, Paul Harris Fellowship award Rotary, 1978, Gaston Labat award Am. Soc. Regional Anesthesia, 1981, U.S. Pres.' award Internat. Volunteerism, 1987, Gov.'s Humanitarianism award, 1987, Gov. Clinton's Arkansas Travelers award, 1988, Rep. Presdl. Legion of Merit award, 1991; Hingson Day named in his honor, Oxford, Ala., 1985. Fellow Internat. Coll. Anesthesia, William Crawford Gorgas Med. Soc., Am. Soc. Anesthetists, Internat. Coll. Surgeons, Royal Coll. Surgeons (faculty anesthesiology), Am. Coll. Anesthesiology; mem. Coll. Physicians and Surgeons, Republic of Costa Rica (hon.), Internat. Research Soc. (v.p.), Am. Soc.

Anesthesiologists (bd. dirs. 1947-56), Rotary (internat. speaker), Sigma Xi, Pi Kappa Alpha. Home: PO Box 525 Ocilla GA 31774-0525 Office: Bros Bro Found 824 Grandview Ave Pittsburgh PA 15211-1442

HINITZ, BLYTHE SIMONE FARB, early childhood and elementary school educator; b. N.Y.C., Apr. 10, 1944; d. Max S. and Gertrude A. (Nachetowitz) Farb; m. Herman J. Hinitz, June 27, 1965. BA, Bklyn. Coll., 1965, MS, 1970; EdD, Temple U., 1977. Master tchr., tchr. N.Y. Bd. Edn., 1965-71; assoc. instr. child devel. C.C. of Phila., 1977-78; assoc. prof. early childhood edn. Trenton (N.J.) State Coll., 1978—; bd. dirs. Mercer County Child Devel. Program, Inc., 1982—. Author: Teaching Social Studies to the Young Child, 1992; co-editor: Bibliography of Selected Resources for the International Year of the Child, 1979; editor book rev. Jour. of Early Childhood Tchr. Edn., 1988—; contbr. chpts. to books, articles to profl. jours. Mem. Am. Ednl. Rsch. Assn., Nat. Assn. Edn. Young Children (tchr. edn. panel 1991—), Nat. Assn. Early Childhood Tchr. Educators (nat. treas. 1989—, bd. dirs.), Assn. Childhood Edn. Internat., World Orgn. Early Childhood Edn., Kappa Delta Pi (bd. dirs. Trenton alumni chpt. 1988—), Phi Delta Kappa (greater Trenton area chpt.). Home: PO Box 348 Feasterville PA 19053-0348 Office: Trenton State Coll Elem/Early Childhood Edn Dept Trenton NJ 08650-4700

HINKAL, SANFORD WAYNE, physicist; b. Williamsport, Pa., Aug. 11, 1944; s. Robert Lunger and Anna Matty (Nickles) H.; m. Kathy Lynne Boseck, Oct. 2, 1971; children: Robert, George. BS in Physics, Pa. State U., 1966. Mathematician NASA/Goddard Space Flight Ctr., Greenbelt, Md., 1966-67, 68-74; physicist space optics Optics Br. NASA/Goddard Space Flight Ctr., Greenbelt, 1974-80, aerospace engr. Optics Br., 1980-89, integration mgr. Space Sta. Freedom Flight Telerobotic Servicer Project, 1989-90, sci. instrument optical systems mgr. Hubble Space Telescope Project, 1991—. Contbr. articles to profl. jours. Sec. Kenmoor Middle Sch. PTA, Landover, Md., 1989-91. Mem. Optical Soc. Am. (pres. nat. capital sect. 1982-83), AIAA (sr.), Jaguar Owners Club (v.p. nation's capital chpt. 1974-80). Home: 9618 Wellington St Lanham Seabrook MD 20706-3654 Office: NASA/Goddard Space Flight Code 442 Greenbelt MD 20771

HINKEL, FREDERICK BRUCE, management consultant; b. N.Y.C., May 25, 1927; s. Frederick Bruce Hinkel; children: Wayne, Keith, Harold, Lynn, Scott. BS, Trinity Coll., Hartford, Conn., 1951; MBA, Hofstra U., 1962. Dist. mgr. N.Y. Telephone, 1966-75; dir. tng., cons. AT&T, 1976-86; mgmt. cons. New Providence, N.J., 1986—. Bd. dirs. Union County Psyhchiat. Clinic, Union, N.J., 1989—, Boy Scouts Am., Watchung Coun., 1989—; mem. Bd. of Adjustment, New Providence, 1988—. With CE, U.S. Army, 1945-46. Recipient Award of Merit, Boy Scouts Am., Union, 1990. Home and Office: Mgmt Performance Systems 15 Woodcrest Dr New Providence NJ 07974

HINKLE, PATRICIA MILLS, pharmacology educator; b. Glen Ridge, N.J., Oct. 12, 1943; d. Henry Hamilton and Margaret (Law) Mills; m. David Currier Hinkle, Oct. 26, 1968; children: Caroline, Daniel, Thomas. BA, Mt. Holyoke Coll., 1965; PhD, U. Calif., Berkeley, 1970. Postdoctoral fellow Harvard U., Boston, 1971-74; asst. prof. dept. pharmacology Med. Sch., U. Rochester, N.Y., 1975-81; assoc. prof. Med Sch., U. Rochester, N.Y., 1981-87; prof. Med. Sch., U. Rochester, N.Y., 1987—; mem. endocrinology study sect. NIH, 1987—. Mem. editorial bd. Endocrinology, 1984-87, editor., 1990. Predoctoral fellow NIH, 1967; postdoctoral fellow Am. Cancer Soc., 1970; Rsch. Career Devel. award NIH, 1982. Mem. Am. Soc. Biochemistry and Molecular Biology, Endocrine Soc., Am. Thyroid Assn., Am. Soc. Pharmacology and Exptl. Therapeutics, Phi Beta Kappa. Office: U Rochester Med Sch Dept Pharmacology Rochester NY 14642

HINNENKAMP, LAWRENCE F., tax specialist; b. Lynchburg, Va., Oct. 25, 1952; s. Frank Joseph and Mary Ann (Campion) H.; m. Antonia Genoese, June 23, 1990; 1 child, Rachel Mickina. BA in Bus. Adminstrn., Acct., Franklin and Marshall Coll., 1979; MBA, Owen Grad. Sch. Vanderbilt, Nashville, 1983; JD, Vanderbilt Sch. Law, 1983. Cpa, Tenn.; Bar: Pa., Tenn. Tax cons. Price Waterhouse, Nashville, 1983-87; tax mgr. Price Waterhouse, Kansas City, 1987-89; atty. Hartman Underhill & Brubaker, Lancaster, Pa., 1989-91; tax specialist Kuntz Lesher Siegrist & Martini, Lancaster, Pa., 1991—; adj. assoc. prof. taxation/bus. law Franklin and Marshall Coll., Lancaster, 1991—. Mgr. East Hempfield Cubs Midget Baseball Team, Lancaster, Pa., 1989—; trustee Found. Benefit of Hispanic People, Lancaster, Pa., 1990—; mem. Resurrection Sch. Bd. Edn., Lancaster, Pa., 1990—, Lancaster (Pa.) Cath. High Sch. Found. Bd., 1991—; pres., bd. dirs., Lancaster County Conservancy, Lancaster, Pa., 1991—. Mem. Lancaster Bar Assn., Pa. Bar Assn., Pa. Inst. CPA's, ABA, Tenn. Soc. CPA's, Lancaster County Estate Planning Coun., York County Estate Planning Coun., Lancaster Country Club. Office: Kuntz Lesher Siegrist & Martini 215 S Centerville Rd Lancaster PA 17603

HINSAHW, J. RAYMOND, surgeon educator; b. Butler, Okla., Oct. 8, 1923; s. J. Raymond and Lucille (Whitknack) H. BA, U. Okla., 1943, MD, 1946; PhD, Oxford U., 1951. Asst. prof. surgery U. Rochester, N.Y., 1957-63, assoc. prof. surgery, 1964-66, prof. surgery, 1967-89, prof. emeritus surgery, 1989—. Co-editor: Color Atlas of CO2 Laser Surgery, 1988. Pres. Upstate chpt. Med. Coll. Surgeons, Utica, 1973-74, Cen. N.Y. Surg. Soc., Syracuse, 1982-84. Lt. USN, 1943-45, 52-54. Recipient Rhodes scholarship, 1947, Albert K. Kaiser Medal of Honor, 1985, Founder's Soc. award Rochester Gen. Hosp. Found., 1986. Mem. Internat. Soc. for Laser Surgery and Medicine (exec. com. 1989—), Am. Soc. Laser Medicine and Surgery (program chmn. 1988-89), Soc. Univ. Surgeons, Rochester Acad. Medicine, N.Y. State Soc. Medicine (chmn. surg. sect. 1983), Cen. Surg. Assn., Am. Coll. Surgeons (bd. govs. 1981-87). Home: 748 Quaker Rd Scottsville NY 14546

HINSON, ROBERT WILLIAM, advertising executive, consultant; b. Neptune, N.J., Nov. 30, 1944; s. Herbert William and Bernice (Stadelhofer) H. AB in Econs. and Sociology, Boston Coll., 1966. Media planner Benton & Bowles, Inc., N.Y.C., 1968-70; v.p., assoc. media dir. SSC&B: Lintas Worldwide, N.Y.C., 1970-74, sr. v.p., dir. media ops., 1976-80; v.p., assoc. media dir. Foote Cone & Belding, Inc., L.A., 1974-76; exec. v.p., chmn. mgmt. com., chmn. ops. com., dir. media svcs. Rosenfeld, Sirowitz & Lawson, Inc., N.Y.C., 1980-85, exec. v.p., dir. mktg. and media svcs., chief adminstrv. officer, 1986-87; pres., chief exec. officer Hinson and Assocs., Inc., N.Y.C., 1987—; cons. in field. Author: Media Leverage, 1985. Media dir. Tuesday Team, Reagan-Bush '84 campaign, 1984; sustaining mem. Rep. Nat. Com.; mem. Ronald Reagan Presdl. Libr. Found., Monmouth County (N.J.) Rep. Orgn. Mem. Internat. Assn. TV, Arts and Scis., NATAS, Internat. Radio and TV Soc., Media Dirs. Industry Coun., Am. Assn. Advt. Agys. (media policy com. 1980-87), Am. Rsch. Found. (media com. coun. 1983-86), Boston Coll. Alumni Assn., Met. Opera Guild, Wagner Soc. N.Y., Monmouth County Hist. Soc., Nature Conservancy, Nat. Trust for Hist. Preservation, N.Y. Athletic Club, Deal (N.J.) Golf and Country Club, Coral Ridge Country Club (Fla.). Roman Catholic. Home: PO Box 33 Allenhurst NJ 07711-0033 also: 133 Pompano Beach Blvd Pompano Beach FL 33062

HINTERBUCHNER, CATHERINE N., rehabilitative medicine educator, physician; b. Greece, Nov. 22, 1926; m. Ladislav P. Hinterbuchner, Dec. 10, 1955. MD cum laude, Nat. & Kapodistriakon U., Athens, Greece, 1951. Intern St. Luke's Hosp., 1953-54; resident in internal medicine French Hosp., 1954-55; resident in internal medicine Kingsbrook Jewish Med. Ctr., 1955-56, fellow in phys. medicine and rehab., 1956-57; fellow in phys. medicine and rehab. N.Y. Med. Coll., 1956-57, N.Y. Med. Coll. and Met. Hosp. Ctr., 1959-60; acting cmn. dept. rehab. medicine N.Y. Med. Coll., Valhalla, 1970-71, prof., chmn. dept. rehab. medicine, 1971—; chief rehab. medicine, attending physician Met. Hosp. Ctr., N.Y.C., 1964—. Fellow ACP, N.Y. Acad. Medicine, Am. Acad. Phys. Medicine and Rehab.; mem. AMA, N.Y. State Med. Soc., N.Y.C. Med. Soc., Am. Congress Rehab. Medicine, N.Y. Acad. Scis.

HINTON, LESLIE FRANK, publishing executive; b. Bootle, Lancashire, Eng., Feb. 19, 1944; came to U.S., 1976, naturalized, 1985; s. Frank Arthur and Lilian Amy (Bruce) H.; m. Mary Christine Weadick, Mar. 30, 1968; children: Martin Frank, Thomas Adam, William Daniel, James Arthur, Jane Amy. Reporter Adelaide News, South Australia, 1960-65; desk editor Brit. United Press, London, 1965-66; reporter The Sun, London, 1966-69, 71-76; writer, editor Adelaide News, South Australia, 1969-70; U.S. corr. News Internat., N.Y.C., 1976-78; news editor The Star, N.Y.C., 1978-80, mng. editor, 1980-82; assoc. editor Boston Herald, 1982-85; editor-in-chief Star Mag., 1985-87; exec. v.p. Murdoch Mags., N.Y.C., 1987-90, pres., 1990-91; pres., chief exec. officer News Am. Pub., Inc., N.Y.C., 1991—. Office: News Am Pub Inc 1211 Ave Of The Americas New York NY 10036-8701

HINTZ, CHARLES BRADLEY, diversified financial executive; b. Chgo., Dec. 6, 1949; s. Charles Frank and Helen (Bernadette) H.; m. Kristine Ingrid Falsetta, July 23, 1980. BS, Purdue U., 1971; MS, U. So. Calif., 1976; MBA, U. Pa., 1978. Various treasury positions Standard Oil Co., of Calif., San Francisco, 1978-82; v.p., dir. treasury ops. The Northern Trust Co., Chgo., 1982-83, group v.p. corp. devel., 1983-84; v.p., treas. Anderson, Clayton & Co., Houston, 1984-86; prin. Morgan Stanley & Co., N.Y.C., 1986-91; treas. Morgan Stanley Group, N.Y.C., 1992—. Lt. comdr. USN, 1971-76. Mem. Fin. Execs. Inst., Nat. Assn. Corp. Treas. Club: Houston. Office: Morgan Stanley Group Inc 1251 Ave Of The Americas New York NY 10020-1104

HIPP, CLARE ARMITAGE, psychotherapist; b. Orange, N.J., Nov. 3, 1940; d. Robert Raymond and Helen (Olson) Armitage; m. Richard N. Hipp, Dec. 22, 1962; children: Robert, Susan, Todd. BA, Upsala Coll., 1962; MS, Western Conn. State U., 1991. Case aide social svc. Town of Newtown, Conn., 1981-82; mcpl. agt. for elderly Town of Newton, Conn., 1982-87; dir. sr. citizen outreach Cath. Family Svcs., Danbury, Conn., 1987—. Bd. dirs. Newtown Fund, 1982—, Salvation Army, Newtown, 1982—, Meals on Wheels, Newtown, 1982-87, Commn. on Aging, Newtown, 1987—. Mem. Am. Assn. Counseling and Devel. Home: 64 Taunton Hill Rd Newtown CT 06470-1771 Office: Cath Family Svcs 233 White St Danbury CT 06810-6892

HIRANO, MICHIO, neurologist; b. N.Y.C., Nov. 30, 1960; s. Asao and Keiko (Okubo) H. AB, Harvard U., 1982; MD, Albert Einstein, Bronx, N.Y., 1986. Diplomate Am. Bd. Psychiatry and Neurology. Med. intern Bronx Mcpl. Hosp., 1986-87; neurology resident Columbia-Presbyn. Hosp., N.Y.C., 1987-90, clin. asst. in neurology, 1990—; chief resident in neurology Columbia-Presbyn. Hosp., N.Y.C., 1989-90. Muscular Dystrophy Assn. fellow, 1990-92. Mem. Am. Acad. Neurology (jr.). Home: 75 Park Terrace E New York NY 10034 Office: NY Neurol Inst 710 W 168th St New York NY 10032

HIRAOKA, LESLIE SATOSHI, management science educator, real estate investor; b. Honolulu, June 18, 1941; s. George Yukio and Ellen Fusae (Shimokawa) H. Student, U. Hawaii, 1959-61; BS, U. Wash., 1963; MBA, Rutgers U., 1971; DSc Engring., MS, Columbia U., 1969, 64. Engr. Esso Rsch. & Engring. Co., Florham Park, N.J., 1968-71; program analyst U.S. Dept. Commerce, Washington, 1977-78; mgmt. sci. prof. Kean Coll., Union, N.J., 1971—; assoc. editor Engring. Mgmt. Jour., 1989—; founder mgmt. sci. program Kean Coll., Union, 1972; chmn. dept. mgmt. sci., 1975-77. Contbr. articles to profl. jours. Nat. adv. com. on rice U.S. Dept. Agrl., 1975-79. Recipient Shigeo Shingo prize Utah State U., Logan, 1989; Fed. Faculty fellow Am. Assembly of Collegiate Schs. of Bus.-Sears Roebuck, 1977-78. Mem. Am. Soc. Engring. Mgmt. Office: Kean College Dept Mgmt Sci Morris Ave Union NJ 07083-7131

HIRASUNA, THOMAS JYUN, biochemical engineer; b. Honolulu, Feb. 11, 1955; s. Masao and Pauline Tsuruko (Nakachi) H.; m. Jean Bartlett Hunter, Aug. 13, 1977; 1 child, Jeffrey Toshiro Hunter. SB, MIT, 1976; MS, Columbia U., 1983; PhD, Cornell U., 1991. Registered profl. engr., N.Y. Summer engr. Procter & Gamble, Cin., 1975; process engr. E.I. du Pont de Nemours, Seaford, Del., 1976-77; asst. chem. engr. Gen. Foods Corp., Tarrytown, N.Y., 1977-78, assoc. chem. engr., 1978-80, sr. chem. engr., 1980-84, project specialist, 1984-86; rsch. assoc. Cornell U., Ithaca, N.Y., 1986-91, postdoctoral assoc., 1991—. Patentee extruded protein product. Program com. chair Ithaca Community Childcare Ctr., 1991-92. Mem. Am. Inst. Chem. Engrs. (sec.-treas. food, pharm. and bioengring. div. 1991—, editor div. newsletter 1983-89), Am. Chem. Soc., Inst. Food Technologists, Am. Soc. Plant Physiologists, Am. Radio Relay League, Boston Computer Soc., Berkeley Macintosh Users Group, Tompkins County Amateur Radio Club, Cornell U. Amateur Radio Club (v.p. 1992—), Macintosh Users Group for Writers and Users of Macintosh Programs (publicity coord. 1991-92, newsletter editor 1992—). Home: 945 E State St Ithaca NY 14850 Office: Cornell U Sch Chem Engring Ithaca NY 14853

HIRES, WILLIAM LELAND, consultant; b. South Orange, N.J., July 5, 1918; s. Harrison Streeter and Christine B. (Leland) H.; m. Karen Reynolds Perrott, July 12, 1975; 1 dau., Jennifer Leland. BS, Haverford Coll., 1949; PhD, U. Pa., 1972. Asst. to dean of admissions, asst. dir of scholarships U. Pa., 1952-55; supr. psychol. svcs., spl. classes Office of Chester County (Pa.) Supt. of Pub. Schs., 1956-59; assoc. prof. West Chester Coll., 1960-61; adminstrv. asst. Office of Pres., asst. to sec. U. Pa., 1961-64; assoc. Edward N. Hay & Assocs., 1964-65; asst. supt. pub. schs. Chester County, 1966-68, pvt. cons., 1968-75; dir. diagnostic and consultative svc. Chester County Intermediate Unit, 1975-76, pvt. practice psychology, 1976-78; dir. pupil svcs. Upper Darby (Pa.) Sch. Dist., 1978-81; dean acad. studies Curtis Inst. Music, Phila., 1981-86; ptnr. Hires Assocs., Phila., 1987—. Mem. coun. U. Pa. Friends of Libr.; mem. exec. com. Haverford Coll. Libr. Assocs.; bd. dirs. Am. Ednl. Film and Video Ctr. With USMC, 1942-46, AUS, 1950-52; lt. col. AUS ret.; col. Pa. Army N.G. ret. Mem. AAAS, Am. Psychol. Assn., Soc. of Cin., Welcome Soc., Geneal. Soc. Pa. (bd. dirs.), Hist. Soc. Pa. (bd. dirs.), 1st Troop Phila. City Cavalry (hon.), Harvard Club, Phila. Club, Merion Cricket Club, Franklin Inn Club. Home: 106 Righters Mill Rd Penn Valley Narberth PA 19072

HIROOKA, SUEYUKI, electronics company executive; b. 1937. Pres. Sharp Electronics Corp., from 1985, chmn., 1992—. Office: Sharp Electronics Corp Sharp Plz Mahwah NJ 07430*

HIRREL, MICHAEL JOHN, lawyer; b. Buckroe Beach, Va., Oct. 13, 1951; s. Michael Ambrose and Evelyn Louise (Nuissl) H.; m. Mary Helen Ratchford, Apr. 16, 1984; 1 child, Shannon Maureen. BA magna cum laude, Boston Coll., Chestnut Hill, Mass., 1973; JD, George Washington U., 1977. Bar: D.C. 1977, U.S. Ct. Appeals (D.C. cir.) 1978, Fla., 1991. Atty. Hamel Park McCabe & Saunders, Washington, 1977-80, Arent, Fox, Kintner, Plotkin & Kahn, Washington, 1980-87, Davis, Graham & Stubbs, Washington, 1987-90; pvt. practice Washington, 1990—; speaker numerous convs. concerning Washington events, 1985, Internat. Radio and TV Soc. seminar, N.Y.C., 1989; organizer, moderator Davis, Graham & Stubbs/HDTV Conf., Washington, 1988, Las Vegas, 1989; mem. bus. and fin. panel HDTV Newsletter's Conf., N.Y.C., 1989, mem. fin. panel, Arlington, Va., 1990. Contbr.: Cablespeech, The Case for First Amendment Protaection, 1983, articles to profl. jours. Mem. ABA, Fed. Communications Bar Assn., D.C. Bar Assn., Fla. Bar Assn. (pub. utilities law com. 1992—). Democrat. Roman Catholic.

HIRSCH, ARTHUR ABRAHAM, chemist, educator; b. Vienna, Austria, Dec. 10, 1921; came to U.S., 1939; s. Morris L. and Anna (Hirsch) H.; m. Ruth Jaul, Apr. 10, 1949; 1 child, Steven N. BS, CCNY, 1946; MA, CUNY, 1956; PhD, NYU, 1960. Chief chemist Gen. Gummed Products, Linden, N.J., 1954-60, Skeist Labs., Newark, 1960-62; dir. R & D, Can. Tech. Tape, Inc., Montreal, Que., 1962-68; tech. dir. Standard Packaging Corp., Clifton, N.J., 1968-78, Arvey Corp., Cedar Grove, N.J., 1978-89; prin. scientist Hirsch & Assocs., Ft. Lee, N.J., 1989—; lectr. Wagner Coll., S.I., N.Y., 1957-59; adj. Prof. Bergen Community Coll., Pramus, N.J., 1989—, adj. prof. Stern Coll., N.Y., 1991—. Author: Flexible Food Packaging, 1991; contbg. author: Handbook of Adhesives, 1962, Ency. Packaging, 1986; numerous patents in packaging field. Rsch. grantee Nat. Rsch. Coun. Can., 1962-68, Def. Rsch. Bd. Can., 1963-68. Fellow Am. Inst. Chemists; mem. IEEE (sr.), TAPPI, Am. Chem. Soc. Home and Office: 2000 Linwood Ave Fort Lee NJ 07024-3086

HIRSCH, DANIEL, lawyer; b. Bklyn., Feb. 26, 1940; s. Burton and Lee (Roller) H.; m. Trina Lutter, July 15, 1965 (div.); children: Jessica Elyse, Jeremy Bram. BS, U. Pa., 1960; JD, Columbia U., 1963. Bar: N.Y. 1964. Assoc. Carter Ledyard & Milburn, N.Y.C., 1964-68; pvt. practice N.Y.C., 1968-74; ptnr. Jones, Hirsch, Connors & Bull, N.Y.C., 1974—; bd. dirs., Telemundo Group, Inc., Sorema, N.A. Lt. USNR, 1965-75. Mem. N.Y. State Bar Assn., Assn. of Bar of City of N.Y., Fedn. Ins. and Corp. Counsel, Univ. Club. Office: Jones Hirsch Connors & Bull 101 E 52d St New York NY 10022

HIRSCH, ELISABETH SCHIFF, education educator emeritus; b. Szombathely, Hungary, June 14, 1918; d. Edmund and Hilda (Schlesinger) Schiff; m. Julius E. Hirsch, Dec. 4, 1939; children: Naomi, Susan. BS, Columbia U., 1950; MA, New Sch. for Social Rsch., 1954; PhD, NYU, 1967. Cert. early childhood edn. Tchr. Beth Hayeled Sch. N.Y.C., 1948-51, Sch. for Young Profls., N.Y.C., 1951-52; tchr., dir. Young Israel of Sunnyside, N.Y.C., 1952-53, Jackson Heights Coop Nursery, N.Y.C., 1953-57; dir. Montefiore Nursery Sch., N.Y.C., 1957-59; tchr. Little Red Sch. House, N.Y.C., 1959-68; asst. prof. H. H. Lehman Coll., CUNY, N.Y.C., 1968-70; prof. The City Coll., CUNY, N.Y.C., 1970-88; pres. Early Childhood Edn. Coun., N.Y.C., 1973-76; mem. Tchr. Edn. Conf. Bd., Albany, N.Y., 1973-75; participant Longitudinal In-Depth Study N.Y. Dept. Edn., Albany, 1976-81; dir. Comprehensive Day-Care Tng. Program, CCNY, N.Y.C., 1977-81. Author, editor: The Block Book, 1974, 84; author: Problems of Early Childhood, 1983, (pamphlet) Transition Periods, 1974; contbr. articles to profl. jours. Bd. mem. Early Childhood Resource Ctr. N.Y. Pub. Libr., N.Y.C., 1980—. Mem. Nat. Assn. for Edn. Young Children, Assn. for Childhood Edn. Internat., Orgn. Mondiale pour l'Edn. Prescholaire. Jewish. Home: 235 Prospect Ave Hackensack NJ 07601-2510 Office: CCNY Convent Ave New York NY 10027-2604

HIRSCH, HARVEY STUART, psychiatrist; b. N.Y.C., Nov. 3, 1950; s. Leoanrd Samuel and Roberta Joan (Dreyer) H.; m. Linda Karen Green, Sept. 27, 1981; children: Daniel, Carly. BA, Columbia U., 1972; MD, Mt. Sinai Med. Sch., N.Y.C., 1976. Diplomate Am. Bd. Psychiatry and Neurology. Intern Mt. Sinai Hosp., N.Y.C., 1976, Attending physician, 1979—; clin. instr. Mt. Sinai Med. Sch., N.Y.C., 1979—; resident Mt. Sinai Hosp., N.Y.C., 1977-79. Mem. Am. Psychiat. Assn., Cum Laude Soc., Le Club (N.Y.C.), Phi Beta Kappa. Office: 3 E 80th St New York NY 10021-0117

HIRSCH, JOSEPH ALLEN, psychopharmacologist; b. N.Y.C., Aug. 30, 1950; s. Robert Theodore and Gertrude (Bernstein) H.; 1 child, Jason Mathew; m. Karen Weinberg, June, 1989. BS in Chemistry, Bklyn. Coll., 1972; BS in Pharmacy summa cum laude, Columbia U., 1975; PhD in Pharmacology, Downstate Med. Ctr., Bklyn., 1979; cert. in counseling, Postgrad. Ctr. Mental Health, 1989; postgrad., Psychotherapy Study Ctr., 1989-91; predoctoral in psychology, Pace U., 1990—. Lic. pharmacist; cert. counselor. Postdoctoral fellow MIT, Cambridge, Mass., 1979-81; rsch. assoc. Med. Coll. Cornell U., N.Y.C., 1981-83; asst. prof. St. John's U., Jamaica, N.Y., 1984-88; sr. editor McGraw Hill, N.Y.C., 1988-89; dir. profl. rels. Park Row Pubs., N.Y.C., 1989-91; assoc. prof. N.Y. Coll. Podiatric Medicine, N.Y.C., 1991-92; adj. asst. prof. then assoc. prof. L.I. U., Bklyn., 1984—; adj. asst. prof. Coll. of Dentistry, NYU, N.Y.C., 1989; adj. instr. in psychology Pace U., N.Y.C., 1991—. Freelance med. writer; contbr. articles to profl. jours. Recipient award Merck Sharp and Dohme, 1975. Mem. APA, AAAS, N.Y. Acad. Scis., Am. Orthopsychiat. Assn. Office: Pace U Dept Psychology 41 Park Row New York NY 10038-1502

HIRSCH, JUDD, actor; b. N.Y.C., Mar. 15, 1935; s. Joseph Sidney and Sally (Kitzis) H. B.S. in Physics, CCNY, 1960. Broadway appearances in Barefoot in the Park, 1966, Knock Knock, 1975 (Drama Desk award for best featured actor), Chapter Two, 1977-78, Talley's Folly, 1980, I'm Not Rappaport (Tony award for best actor in play 1986), 1985-86, Conversations with My Father (Tony award for best actor in play 1992), 1992; off-Broadway appearances in On the Necessity of Being Polygamous, 1963, Scuba Duba, 1967-69, King of the United States, 1972, Mystery Play, 1972, Hot L Baltimore, 1973, Prodigal, 1973, Knock Knock, 1975, Talley's Folly, 1979 (Obie award), The Seagull, 1983, I'm Not Rappaport, 1985, Conversations With My Father, Seattle, Broadway, 1991 (Tony award); regional appearances in Hough in Blazes, Annenberg Ctr., Phila., 1971, The Recruiting Officer, Harry Noon and Night, Line of Least Existence, Theater for Living Arts, Phila., 1989-70; stock and tour appearances in I'm Not Rappaport, nat. tour, 1978, Miss Reardon Drinks a Little, Palm Beach, Fla., 1972, Harvey, Chgo., 1971, Peterpat, Houston and Ft. Worth, 1970, A Thousand Clowns, Threepenny Opera, Fantastics, Woodstock, N.Y., 1964; TV appearances include The Keegans, 1975, Fear on Trial, 1975, Valentino, 1975, Medical Story, 1975, Delvecchio series, 1976-77, Rhoda, 1977, Taxi series, 1978-83 (Emmy award for best actor in a comedy series, 1981, 1983), Dear John series, 1988-92; TV movies include The Law, 1974, The Halloween That Almost Wasn't, 1979, Sooner or Later, 1979, Marriage is Alive and Well, 1980, First Steps, 1985, Brotherly Love, 1985, She Said No, 1990; films include King of the Gypsies, 1978, Ordinary People, 1980, Without a Trace, 1983, Teachers, 1984, The Goodbye People, 1984, Running on Empty, 1988. Mem. Acad. Motion Picture Arts and Scis., Acad. TV Arts and Scis., Screen Actors Guild, Actors Equity Assn., AFTRA. Office: care Morton L Leavy 11 E 44th St New York NY 10017-3608

HIRSCH, LARRY JOSEPH, retail executive, lawyer; b. Boston, July 1, 1938; s. Samuel and Anne (Rossman) H.; m. Kay Pollock, Mar. 16, 1974. BA, Syracuse U., 1962; JD, Suffolk U., Boston, 1968; grad. gemologist, Gem Inst. Am., Los Angeles, 1981. Bar: Mass. 1968, R.I. 1968, Fla. 1970.; cert. gemologist, Los Angeles, 1986. Mgr. Vality Dept. Store, Groton, Conn., 1962-63; asst. area dir. Am. Jewish Com., Miami, Fla., 1968-69; asst. city atty. City of Miami, Fla., 1969-71; atty Feuer & Feuer, Miami, Fla., 1971-74, Turano 7 Turano, Westerly, R.I., 1974—; asst. town solicitor Town of Westerly, R.I., 1975-76; pres. Westerly Jewelry Co. Inc., Westerly, R.I., 1978—; Mem. adv. bd. Fleet Bank, Westerly, 1984-90. Pres. Chariho-Westerly Animal Rescue League, 1976-89; bd. dirs. Community Hosp. of Westerly, 1985—, mem. adv. bd., 1984—; mem. Ctr. for the Arts, Westerly, 1984; v.p. Westerly Heart Assn., 1986; bd. dirs. Am. Heart Assn., Westerly, 1986—; mem. Charter Revision Comm., Westerly, 1985-89; bd. dirs. Joint Devel. Task Force, Westerly, 1988—, Animal Rescue League of So. R.I., 1988—. With U.S. Army, 1958-60. Larry Hirsch Day named in his honor, Town of Westerly, 1980; recipient Someone Spl. award, Channel 26 WTWS TV, New London, Conn., 1987; named Columbus Citizen of Yr., Golden Key Club, Westerly, 1989. Mem. Nat. Assn. Jewelry Appraisers, New Eng. Appraisers Assn., Am. Gem Soc., Gemological Inst. Am., Westerly Track Club (pres. 1976-89, bd. dirs.), Elks (Larry Hirsch Run 1980—), Fraternal Order Police. Office: Westerly Jewelry Co PO Box 324 Westerly RI 02891-0324

HIRSCH, MARTIN STANLEY, physician, researcher, educator; b. Cortland, N.Y., Apr. 16, 1939; s. Hans and Grete (Lipper) H.; m. Corinne Becker, Oct. 18, 1964; children: Tera Gretchen, Michael Edward. AB, Hamilton Coll., 1960; MD, Johns Hopkins U., 1964; MA, Harvard U., 1990. Diplomate Am. Bd. Internal Medicine, Am. Bd. Internal Medicine and Infectious Diseases. Intern in medicine U. Chgo. Clinics and Hosp., 1964-65, resident in medicine, 1965-66; fellow in virology Ctr. for Disease Control, Atlanta, 1966-68; fellow Nat. Inst. for Med. Rsch., London, 1968-69; fellow in infectious diseases Harvard U., Boston, 1969-71, asst. prof., 1971-76, assoc. prof., 1976-88, prof. medicine, 1988—; assoc. physician MGH, Boston, 1981-87; physician Mass. Gen. Hosp., Boston, 1988—; mem. sci. adv. bd. AM Found. for AIDS Rsch., 1987—; chmn. AIDS program adv. com. NIH, Bethesda, Md. Mem. editorial bd. New Eng. Jour. Medicine, 1990—; contbr. 98 chpts. to books and over 164 articles to profl. jours.; editor: Fields Virology, 1990. Surgeon USPHS, 1966-68. Fellow Infectious Disease Soc. Am.; mem. Am. Soc. Clin. Investigation, Am. Soc. Virology, Assn. Am. Physicians, Phi Beta Kappa, Alpha Omega Alpha. Home: 285 Franklin St Newton MA 02158-2302 Office: Mass Gen Hosp Fruit St Boston MA 02114-2620

HIRSCH, PAUL J., orthopedic surgeon, educator; b. Bklyn., Oct. 12, 1937; s. Morris M. and Dorothy (Wolitzer) H.; 1 child, Jeremy S. BA in English, Roanoke Coll., 1957; MD, U. Va., 1961. Diplomate Am. Bd. Orthopedic Surgery. Intern NYU-Bellevue Med. Ctr., N.Y.C., 1961-62, resident, 1964-68; chief orthopedic surgery Raritan Valley Hosp., Green Brook, N.J., 1969-71; pvt. practice orthopedic surgery Bridgewater, N.J., 1971—; active staff, chief orthopaedic svc. Somerset (N.J.) Med. Ctr.; cons. orthopedic surgery VA Hosp., Lyons, N.J.; courtesy staff Robert Wood Johnson U. Hosp., New Brunswick, N.J.; clin. asst. prof. orthopedic surgery Rutgers Med. Sch.,

1971-79; clin. instr. orthopedic surgery NYU-Bellevue Med. Ctr., 1969-79; clin. assoc. prof. orthopedic surgery N.J. Med. Sch., 1980—; chmn. N.J. Orthopaedic Symposium, 1976, 77, 78. Chmn. publs. com. Jour. Med. Soc. N.J. 1980-85; contbr. articles, editor profl. jours; mem. editorial bd. N.J. Medicine, Sportcare & Fitness. Trustee N.J. Found. Health Care Evaluation, 1978-80,Rutgers Prep. Sch., 1980-88, pres. bd. trustees, 1983-86; trustee, Somerset, County Coll.; bd. dirs. N.J. Med. Polit. Action Com., 1983—, sec.-treas. N.J. Com. for Quality Orthopaedic Care, 1986—; bd. trustees Orthopaedic Rsch. and Edn. Found., 1989—. With USAF, 1962-64. Mem. ACS, AMA, Am. Acad. Orthopedic Surgeons (bd. councilors 1982-88), Eastern Orthopedic Assn. (trustee 1981-84), N.J. Orthopedic Soc. (pres. 1979-80), Med. Soc. N.J. (chmn. orthopaedic sect. 1977-78, ho. of dels. 1976—, treas., 1982-86, 2d v.p. 1986-87, 1st v.p. 1987-88, pres. elect 1988-89, pres. 1989-90, trustee 1982-91), Somerset County Med. Soc., Acad. Medicine of N.J. (chmn. orthopaedic sect. 1975-78, trustee 1978-91, pres. elect 1982-83, pres. 1983-84), Am. Trauma Soc. (pres. cen. Jersey unit 1977-81), Internat. Soc. Orthopedic Surgery and Traumatology, N.J. Health Scis. Group (treas. 1982-83), N.J. Hosp. Assn. (trustee 1986-89), N.J. Assn. Med. Splty. Socs. (pres. 1979-80, dir. 1981-85), Ind. Sch. Chmn. Assn., Med. Inter-Ins. Exch. N.J. (bd. gov. 1987-90), N.J. State Med. Underwriters, Inc. (bd. dirs. 1990—, vice-chmn. bd. dirs. 1991—). Office: 720 US Hwy 202-206 Bridgewater NJ 08807

HIRSCH, RICHARD ARTHUR, mechanical engineer; b. N.Y.C., Jan. 2, 1925; s. Melvin Mordecai and Gertrude Matilda (Schwarz) H.; m. Carol Walter Sampson, June 18; children: Andrew Sampson, Patricia Ann. BAE, Rensselaer Poly. Inst., Troy, N.Y., 1945; MS in Applied Math., Brown U., Providence, 1950. Structural engr. Republic Aviation Corp., Farmingdale, N.Y., 1946-47; devel. engr. Swank, Inc., Attleboro, Mass., 1947-48; vibrations engr. Boeing Vertol, Morton, Pa., 1950-52; chief structures engr. AAI Corp., Balt., 1952-60; asst. tech. dir. Martin Marietta Corp., Balt., 1960-68; assoc. prof. U.S. Naval Acad., Annapolis, Md., 1968-82; prog. mgr. AAI Corp., Balt., 1982—. Contbr. articles to profl. jours. With USN, 1943-46. Fellow ASME (v.p. 1984-88, bd. govs. 1990-92); mem. NSPE, Soc. Engring. Edn. Home: 8220 Marcie Dr Baltimore MD 21208-1944 Office: AAI Corp PO Box 126 Cockeysville Hunt Valley MD 21030-0126

HIRSCH, ROBERT GEORGE, research and development director; b. Balt., Nov. 25, 1946; s. Henry G. and Teresa Marie (Potthast) H.; m. Kathleen Rodda, Nov. 27, 1970; children: Erik, Andrea. BS in Physics, U. Scranton, 1969; MA in Applied Physics, Harvard U., 1970; PhD in Physics, U. Va., 1974. Rsch. physicist, supr. DuPont Engring. Physics Lab., Wilmington, Del., 1974-78; asst. dir. engring. rsch. and devel. DuPont Engring., Wilmington, Del., 1978-79, sr. supr. materials rsch. and devel., 1979-81; cons. corp. planning DuPont, Wilmington, Del., 1981-84; mgr. market devel. DuPont Electronics, Wilmington, Del., 1984-85; lab. dir. electronics tech. DuPont Electronics, Research Triangle Park, N.C., 1985-88; site mgr. electronics devel. ctr. DuPont Electronics, Research Triangle Park, Del., 1988-89; dir. major acct. DuPont Electroncis, Research Triangle Park, Del., 1989-91; rsch. and devel. dir. DuPont Electronics, Wilmington, Del., 1991—; mem. bd. visitors Duke U., Durham, N.C., 1986—; mem. physics and math. bd. N.C. State U., Raleigh, 1986—; mem. industry adv. bd. N.C. A&T U., Greensboro, 1986-89; cons. in field. Contbr. articles to profl. jours. Dir. Lancachire Civic Assn.; Wilmington, 1974-79. Presdl. fellow U. Scranton, 1965-69, Woodrow Wilson fellow, 1970, U. Va. fellow, 1972-74; recipient NSF award, 1970-71. Mem. Am. Physical Soc., Am. Inst. Chem. Engrs., Internat. Soc. Hybrid Microcircuits, Internat. Electronics Packaging Soc., Alpha Sigma Nu, Sigma Pi Sigma. Home: 115 Chalfonte Ln Kennett Square PA 19348 Office: DuPont Co P13 Barley Mill Plaza Wilmington DE 19898

HIRSCHFELD, ABRAHAM JACOB, real estate developer, municipal official; b. Rymanov, Poland, Dec. 20, 1919; s. Simon and Sara (Simon) H.; m. Zipora Teicher, July 4, 1943; children: Rachel, Elie. PhD (hon.), Seminarius Lutherensus Espiscopus Americannus, 1961. Pres. Farlands Enterprises Inc., N.Y.C., 1956—, Radio City Parking, Inc., N.Y.C., 1959—, Vertical Club Corp., N.Y.C., 1980—, Hirschfeld Realty, N.Y.C., 1986—; ptnr. New York Penta Hotel, N.Y.C., 1983—; commr. City of Miami Beach, Fla., 1989—; organizer First Women's Bank; developer of the Chm. Bank Bldg.; builder Hirschfeld Theatre, 1988. Author Accidental Wedding, 1986. Mem. U.S. Electoral Coll., 1968-76, Pub. Devel. Corp., N.Y.C., 1970, Tri-State Regional Planning Commn., N.Y.C., 1979-82; treas. Dem. State Com., N.Y., 1972; pres. Dems. for Reagan, N.Y.C., 1980; trustee Fifth Ave. Synagogue, N.Y.C, 1982—, Daytop Found., N.Y.C., 1982; chair Keter Abraham Synagogue, Miami, 1987. Recipient Ben Gurion award State of Israel Bonds, 1975. Mem. Friar Club (N.Y.C.), High Ridge Country Club (Palm Beach, Fla.), Univ. Club. Democrat. Jewish. Office: Hirschfeld Realty 15 Penn Plaza Ste 150 New York NY 10001

HIRSCHFELD, ALBERT, artist; b. St. Louis, June 21, 1903; s. Isaac and Rebecca (Rothberg) H.; m. Florence Ruth Hobby, July 13, 1927; m. Dorothy Dolly Haas, May 8, 1943; 1 dau., Nina. Student, Nat. Acad., Art Students Leaque, County Council, London, Julienne's, Paris; DFA (hon.), U. Hartford, 1982, NYU, 1985, Brandeis U., 1989; LHD (hon.), Acad. of Art, 1984, CUNY, 1985, Brandeis U., 1989. theatre corr. in Moscow for N.Y. Herald Tribune, 1927. Sculptor one-man exhbns. include Newhouse Gallery, 1928, Waldorf Astoria, 1932, Morgan Gallery, 1936, Guy Mayer Gallery, 1942, John Heller Gallery, 1959, Hammer Gallery, 1967, Mus. City N.Y., 1973, Margo Feiden Gallery, 1973, Wako Galleries, Tokyo, 1975; theater caricaturist, N.Y. Times, 1925—; represented in permanent collections St. Louis Art Mus., Butler Inst. Am. Art, Whitney Mus. Am. Art, N.Y.C., Cleve. Art Mus., N.Y.C. Mus., N.Y. Pub. Library, Fogg Mus., Bklyn. Mus., Met. Mus. Art, Mus. Modern Art, Davenport Municipal Art Gallery, Mus. U. Wis., Lincoln Center Mus. Performing Arts, N.Y.C., murals in Fifth Ave. Playhouse, Am. Pavilion, World's Fair, Brussels, 1958; author: Manhattan Oases, 1932, Harlem, 1942; musical comedy Sweet Bye and Bye, 1946; The American Theatre, 1961, (with S.J. Perelman) Westward Ha, 1949, Show Business is No Business, 1951, Hirschfeld Folio, 1964, The World of Hirschfeld, 1970, (with Brooks Atkinson) The Lively Years, 1973, Rhythm folio 10 lithographs, Hirschfeld by Hirschfeld, 1979; The Entertainers, 1977, Art and Recollections from 8 Decades, 1991; U.S. postage stamps of comedians, 1991. Recipient Am. Specialist grant U.S. State Dept., 1960, Spl. Tony award for theatre caricature, 1974, Creative award Art Inst. Boston, 1976, City of N.Y. Arts and Culture award, 1979, Brooks Atkinson Tony award, 1984, Weissberger award Theatre Hall of Fame, 1985, New Eng. Theatre award, 1984, award of honor City of N.Y., 1979, League of N.Y. Theatres and Producers Theatre award, 1975, Life Achievement award Houston Film Festival, 1989, Edwin Booth award CUNY Graduate Sch. Mem. Illustrators Club (Hall of Fame 1986, Theater Hall of Fame 1990). Home: 122 E 95th St New York NY 10128-1705

HIRSCHHORN, KURT, pediatrics educator; b. Vienna, Austria, May 18, 1926; came to U.S., 1940, naturalized, 1945; s. Emanuel and Helen (Mayberger) H.; m. Rochelle Reibman, Dec. 20, 1952; children—Melanie D., Lisa R., Joel N. Student, U. Pitts., 1944; B.A., N.Y. U., 1950, M.D., 1954, M.S. (Bergquist fellow), 1958. Intern Bellevue Hosp., N.Y.C., 1954-55; resident Bellevue Hosp., 1955-56; fellow N.Y. U., 1956-57, U. Upsala, Sweden, 1957-58; instr. N.Y. U. Sch. Medicine, 1956-58, asst. prof., 1958-63, asso. prof., 1963-66; Arthur J. and Nellie Z. Cohen prof. genetics and pediatrics Mt. Sinai Sch. Medicine, City U. N.Y., 1966-76, Herbert H. Lehman prof., chmn. pediatrics, 1977—; adj. prof. biology N.Y. U., 1966-74; Established investigator Am. Heart Assn., 1960-65; career scientist N.Y.C. Health Research Council, 1965-75. Author numerous sci. publs.; Editor: (with Harry Harris) Advances in Human Genetics, 1969—; editorial bd. 16 sci. jours. Mem. council Village Community Sch., 1968-73, chmn., 1972-73. Served with AUS, 1944-47. Recipient Rudolph Virchow medal, 1974, Alumni Achievement award NYU Sch. Medicine, 1982. Fellow AAAS, Am. Acad. Pediatrics, N.Y. Acad. Medicine; mem. Inst. Medicineof the Nat. Acad. Scis., Am. Coll. Med. GeneticsAm. Soc. Clin. Investigation, Am. Assn. Physicians, Am. Pediatric Soc., Am. Soc. Human Genetics (pres. 1969, dir.), Pediatric Travel Club, Am. Assn. Immunologists, Harvey Soc. (v.p. 1979-80, pres. 1980-81, council 1981-84), Genetics Soc. Am., Environmental Mutagen Soc. (council 1969-76), Inst. for Soc. Ethics and Life Scis. dir. 1969-72), Am. Soc. Pediatric Chmn. (council 1983-86), Am. Cancer Soc. (coun. 1989—), Alpha Omega Alpha. Home: 29 Washington Sq W New York NY 10011-9128 Office: Mt Sinai Sch Medicine 1 Gustave L Levy Pl New York NY 10029-6504

HIRSCHLER, PHILIP, investment banker; b. N.Y.C., Nov. 1, 1955; s. Andre and Marion T. (Jason) H.; m. Carina Alberti, Feb. 2, 1989. BA, U. Va., 1977; MBA, Columbia U., 1979; JD, U. Pitts., 1982; LLM, Georgetown U., 1983. Bar: N.Y. 1983, D.C. 1983. Asst. to pres. T.H. Lehman & Co., Inc., N.Y.C., 1984-85; asst. treas. Rhone-Poulenc, Inc., Monmouth Jct, N.J., 1985-86; investment banker Avance Internat., N.Y.C., 1986-87; pres. Transnat. Cons., Ltd., N.Y.C., 1987-89; mng. dir. corp. fin. Minotaur Securities, Stamford, Conn., 1989-91; pres. Carphi Ltd., N.Y.C., 1991—. Mem. N.Y. Bar Assn., D.C. Bar Assn., ABA, Columbia Bus. Sch. Club, Order of barrister. Office: Carphi Ltd 257 Central Park W Apt 6A New York NY 10024-4109

HIRSCHMAN, ALBERT, histology and cell biology educator; b. N.Y.C., Oct. 20, 1921; s. Harry and Pauline (Stadler) H.; m. Mildred Laura Gottschall, July 18, 1943; children: Beverly, Sally Alice, Robert Steven. BS, CUNY, 1942; MS, Poly. U., 1946, PhD, 1952. Chem. technician Jewish Hosp. of Bklyn., 1942-43, sr. technician, 1943-47; instr. L.I. Coll. of Medicine, Bklyn., 1947-52; asst. prof. SUNY Health Sci. Ctr., Bklyn., 1952-62, assoc. prof. histology and cell biology, 1962—; cons., adj. prof. Touro Coll. Ctr. for Biomed. Edn., Dix Hills, N.Y., 1980—; vis. prof. Rockefeller U., N.Y.C., 1961-62, Hebrew U., Jerusalem, Israel, 1981-82. Contbr. over 30 sci. articles to profl. jours. Univ. devel. com. United Univ. Professions, Albany, N.Y., 1989—, governing bd., 1989—. Grantee NIH, 1955-73. Mem. AAAS, Am. Chem. Soc., N.Y. Acad. Scis., N.Y. Bone and Tooth Discussion Group (exec. dir. 1965—), Am. Assn. Anatomists. Office: SUNY Health Sci Ctr 450 Clarkson Ave Box 5 Brooklyn NY 11203

HIRSCHMAN, ALBERT OTTO, educator, political economist; b. Berlin, Apr. 7, 1915; s. Carl and Hedwig (Marcuse) H.; m. Sarah Chapiro, June 22, 1941; children: Catherine Jane, Elisabeth Nicole. Student, Sorbonne, H.E.C., London Sch. Econs., 1933-36; Dr. Econ. Sc., U. Trieste, 1938; LL.D. (hon.), Rutgers U., 1978; Rockefeller fellow, U. Calif.-Berkeley, 1941-43; D.Sc. (hon.), U. So. Calif., 1986. Economist Fed. Res. Bd., Washington, 1946-52; fin. adviser Nat. Planning Bd., Bogotá, Colombia, 1952-54; pvt. econ. cons. Bogotá, 1954-56; research prof. econs. Yale U., 1956-58; prof. internat. econ. relations Columbia U., 1958-64; prof. polit. economy Harvard U., 1964-74, Littauer prof. polit. economy, 1967-74; prof. Inst. for Advanced Study, Princeton, 1974-85, prof. emeritus, 1985—; fellow Ctr. Advanced Study Behavioral Scis., 1968-69; mem. Inst. for Advanced Study, 1972-73; fellow Wissenschaftskolleg zu Berlin, 1990-91. Author: National Power and the Structure of Foreign Trade, 1945, The Strategy of Economic Development, 1958, Journeys Toward Progress: Studies of Economic Policy-Making in Latin America, 1963, Development Projects Observed, 1967, Exit, Voice, and Loyalty: Responses to Decline in Firms, Organizations and States, 1970, A Bias for Hope: Essays on Development and Latin America, 1971, The Passions and the Interests: Political Arguments for Capitalism Before Its Triumph, 1977, Essays in Trespassing: Economics to Politics and Beyond, 1981, Shifting Involvements: Private Interest and Public Action, 1982, Getting Ahead Collectively: Grassroots Experiences in Latin America, 1984, Rival Views of Market Society and Other Recent Essays, 1986, The Rhetoric of Reaction: Perversity, Futility, Jeopardy, 1991; editor Latin American Issues-Essays and Comments, 1961; contbr. articles to profl. jours. Served with AUS, 1943-45. Recipient Frank E. Seidman Disting. award in polit. economy, 1980, Talcott Parsons prize for social sci., 1983, Kalman Silvert prize Latin Am. Studies Assn., 1986. Disting. fellow Am. Econ. Assn.; mem. NAS, Council Fgn. Relations, Am. Acad. Arts and Scis., Am. Philos. Soc.; fgn. mem. Brit. Acad., Accademia Nazionale dei Lincei (Rome). Address: Inst for Advanced Study Princeton NJ 08540

HIRSCHMAN, SHALOM ZARACH, physician; b. Troy, N.Y., Aug. 5, 1936; s. Meyer and Anne H.; m. Donna Tobi Adelman, July 11, 1965; children: Orin, Raquel. B.A., Yeshiva U., 1957; M.D., Albert Einstein Coll. Medicine, 1961; Ph.D. equivalent, NIH Grad. Sch., 1966. Intern medicine Mass. Gen. Hosp., Harvard Med. Sch., 1961-62, resident, 1962-63; research assoc. NIH, Nat. Insts. Arthritis, Metabolic and Digestive Diseases, 1963-65, sr. investigator, 1965-66; NIH fellow in medicine Columbia-Presbyn. Med. Center, N.Y.C., 1966-67; sr. investigator Nat. Cancer Inst., NIH, 1967-69; instr. medicine George Washington U. Sch. Medicine, 1963-65; assoc. prof. medicine, dir. div. infectious diseases Mt. Sinai Sch. Medicine, CUNY, N.Y.C., 1969-71; prof. medicine, dir. div. infectious diseases Mt. Sinai Sch. Medicine, CUNY, 1971—; attending physician Mt. Sinai Hosp., N.Y.C., 1971—; mem. merit rev. bd. VA, 1976-79; mem. virology and microbiology exec. bd. Am. Cancer Soc., 1981-86. Founder, trustee Touro Coll., Touro Law Sch., N.Y.C., 1970. Served with USPHS, 1963-69. NIH fellow, 1964; research grantee, 1970—. Fellow A.C.P., Am. Soc. Infectious Diseases, Am. Coll. Clin. Pharmacology, Royal Coll. Hygiene and Tropical Medicine; mem. Am. Biophys. Soc., Am. Soc. Microbiology, Soc. Gen. Virology, Am. Soc. Liver Diseases, Soc. Exptl. Biology and Medicine, Am. Soc. Clin. Investigation, Assn. Am. Physicians, Am. Fedn. Clin. Research, AAAS, N.Y. Acad. Scis. (chmn. microbiology sect. 1975), Harvey Soc. Office: Mt Sinai Med Ctr 1 Gustave L Levy Pl # 1090 New York NY 10029-6504

HIRSH, JAMES BAKER, education educator; b. Chgo., July 23, 1949; s. Bernard Louis and Regina (Baker) H.; m. Pat Moore, Dec. 1, 1974 (div. Mar. 1990); children: James E., Erin R. BA, U. Denver, 1971, MA, 1973, PhD, 1976. Dean continuing edn. Muhlenberg Coll., Allentown, Pa., 1976-86; project dir. Nat. Univ. Continuing Edn. Assn., Washington, 1986-87; dir. continuing edn. Delaware Valley Coll., Doylestown, Pa., 1987—; sec. Van Savn Ramsey & Van Houten, Chalfont, Pa., 1989-90; prin. Adult Edn. Mktg. Svcs., Quakertown, Pa., 1990—. Editor: Jour. H.E. Mgmt. Bd. dirs. Allentown Libr., 1986; v.p. Allentown Sch. Bd., 1986. Mem. Nat. Univ. Continuing Assn., Assn. Continuing Higher Edn. Democrat. Office: Delaware Valley Coll 700 E Butler Ave Doylestown PA 18901-2607

HIRSHFIELD, STUART, lawyer; b. N.Y.C., Dec. 31, 1941; s. William Louis and Anne (Frank) H.; m. Susanne Drucker, Jan. 22, 1967; children: Matthew S., Edward R. BA, Syracuse U., 1963, JD, 1966. Bar: N.Y. 1966, U.S. Dist. Ct. (so. and ea. dists.) N.Y. 1968, U.S. Ct. Appeals (2nd cir.) 1968. Assoc. Krauss & Krauss, N.Y.C., 1966-67; atty. N.Y. Cen. RR, N.Y.C., 1967-69; assoc. Blum, Haimoff, Gersen, Lipson & Szabad, N.Y.C., 1969; atty. CIT Fin., N.Y.C., 1970-72; assoc. Shea & Gould, N.Y.C., 1972-77, ptnr., 1977-88; ptnr.-in-charge of N.Y. bankruptcy practice Dewey Ballantine, N.Y.C., 1988—. Contbr. Asset Based Financing--A Transactional Guide, 1985. Assn. atty. Allenwood Civic Assn., Great Neck, N.Y., 1984; exec. com., bd. visitors Syracuse U. Coll. Law, 1991—. With USAR, 1966-72. Mem. ABA (com. on bankruptcy 1983—), N.Y. Bar Assn., Assn. of Bar of City of N.Y. (corp. reorgn. com. 1975-78, 82-85), Assn. Comml. Fin. Attys. (dir. 1970—), Rockefeller Ctr. Club. Office: Dewey Ballantine 1301 Ave Of The Americas New York NY 10019-6092

HIRSHLER, ERIC ERNEST, art historian; b. Ludwigshafen, Palatinate, Germany, May 8, 1924; came to U.S., 1938; s. Max and Helene (Riess) H.; m. Marilyn Nair, 1953; 1 child, Erica Eve Hirshler Clark. BA, Bowdoin Coll., 1945; MA, Yale U., 1946, PhD, 1951; postgrad., Columbia U., 1965-66. Lectr. Rutgers U., Newark, 1951-52; exec. asst. URO, N.Y.C., 1952-55; asst. dir. Leo Baeck Inst., N.Y.C., 1955-57; asst. editor UNESCO History of Mankind, New Haven and Paris, 1957-59; instr. Bklyn. Coll., 1957-59; asst. prof. to assoc. prof. Denison U., Granville, Ohio, 1959-69, prof., 1969-89, chmn. dept. art, 1967-72; chmn. dept. art history Carleton U., Ottawa, Can., 1972-74. Author, editor: Jews from Germany in the U.S., 1955; editorial bd. Sirmium, 1968-72.; contbr. articles to profl. jours. Exec. com. Granville Preservation Orgn., Granville, 1981-84. Grantee Lilley Found., 1978, NEH, 1985, Sirmium-Smithsonian Inst., 1969-72. Mem. Coll. Art Assn. Home: 36 Ware St Lewiston ME 04240-6214

HIRSHMAN, CAROL ANN, anesthesiology educator; b. Mont., Que., Can., Aug. 12, 1944; came to U.S., 1969; d. Philip and Susan (Lubert) Ditkofsky; m. John A. Hirshman, Jan. 31, 1970; 1 child, David. BSc, McGill U., Mont., 1965, MD, 1969. Instr. U. Colo. Med. Ctr., Denver, 1974, asst. prof., 1974-75; asst. prof. U. Oregn. Health Sci. Ctr., Portland, 1976-80, assoc. prof., 1980-84, prof., 1984-86; prof. Johns Hopkins Hosp., Balt., 1986—. Editor: Anesthesiology, 1986—; contbr. numerous articles to profl. jours. Recipient numerous NIH grants. Office: Johns Hopkins Sch Hygiene and Pub Health 615 N Wolfe St Rm 7006 Baltimore MD 21205-2104

HIRSON, DAVID, critic, playwright, writer; b. N.Y.C.; s. Roger O. and Alice (Thorsell) H. BA, Yale U., 1980; PhD, Oxford (Eng.) U., 1985. Author: (play) La Bête, 1991, (John Gassner Best New Am. Play award Outer Critics Circle, 1991, Special Best Play citation Best Plays 1990-91, 1991); translator: (opera) Gli Equívoci Nel Sembiàte, 1991; freelance critic and essayist L.A. Times Book Rev., The Times Lit. Supplement, London Rev. Books., others, 1983—. Recipient Marton prize for Best New Am. Playwright, Dramatists Guild, 1991, George Oppenheimer Best New Am. Playwright award N.Y. Newsday, 1991; nominee Best Play, Drama Desk, 1991, Hull-Warriner, 1991, Comedy of Yr. Lawrence Olivier award, 1992. Office: care Judy Daish Assocs Ltd, 83 Eastbourne Mews, London W2, England

HITCHCOCK, CHRISTOPHER BRIAN, computer and physical sciences research, development and systems executive; b. Albany, N.Y., Aug. 1, 1947; s. John Dayton and Patricia (Blake) H.; m. Kathryn Anne Fufte, Dec. 27, 1970; 1 child, Jonathan David. BS in Econs. and Acctg., St. John's U., Collegeville, Minn., 1969; MS with honors in Logistics Mgmt., USAF Inst. Tech., 1975. Cert. profl. contract mgr., logistician, profl. cost estimator/analyst. Commd. 2d lt. USAF, 1969, advanced through grades to capt., 1973; div. chief, dep. contracting, Hanscom AFB, Mass., 1977-79; sr. tech. rep. Analytical Systems Engring. Corp., Burlington, Mass., 1979-82, bus. devel. mgr., 1982-83, dir. contracts, 1983-84; sr. contracts mgr., Bolt Beranek and Newman, Inc., Cambridge, Mass., 1984-86, dir. contracts, 1986-92; dir. contracts and subcontracts The Cadmus Group, Inc., Waltham, Mass., 1992—; asst. to dep. base comdr., Henscom, AFB, 1989—; advanced through grade to lt. col. USAFR, 1991; speaker, moderator seminars in field. Decorated Air Force Commendation medal (2). Mem. Nat. Contract Mgmt. Assn. (chpt. pres.), Soc. Logistics Engrs., Order Daedalians, Armed Forces Communications and Electronics Assn., Soc. Cost Estimating and Analysis, Assn. Old Crows. Roman Catholic. Home: 49 Thomas St Belmont MA 02178-2438 Office: 135 Beaver St Waltham MA 02154

HITCHEN, ANN JONES, realtor; b. Granville, N.Y.; d. Edward Thomas and Mabel Eva (Skelly) Jones; m. Michael H. Hitchen, Feb. 9, 1962 (div. 1980); children: Tracey Hitchen Boyd, Jill M. Diploma, Hartwick Coll., 1960. Lic. realtor, N.Y. Legal sec., adminstrv. asst., account rep. GM, 1961-62; mgr. broker Thomas S. Nelson Real Estate, Granville, N.Y., 1969—, West Pawlet, Vt., 1969—. Mem. Nat. Assn. Realtors (cert. residential specialist), Realtors Nat. Mktg. Inst. (cert. residential broker), N.Y. State Assn. Realtors (grad. Realtors Inst., bd. dirs. 1980-84), N.Y. State Real Estate Appraisers, Washington County Bd. realtors (pres. 1979-81, bd. dirs. 1981—, Realtor of Yr. award 1983), Granville C. of C. Democrat. Office: Nelson Real Eatate 19 W Main St Granville NY 12832

HITE, WILLIAM KNOWLES, III, investment management company executive; b. Urbana, Ill., May 18, 1963; s. William K. Hite Jr. and Gayla Joe (Shafer) Thomas; m. Sandra Elaine Wrightsman, Dec. 19, 1986. BS in Acctg., Okla. State U., 1987. Staff to sr. acct. Coopers & Lybrand, Boston, 1987-90; asst. contr. TLP Leasing Programs, Inc., Boston, 1990-92, contr., 1992—. Republican. Home: 18 West St Marblehead MA 01945-1628

HITT, JOHN CHARLES, JR., university official; b. Houston, Dec. 7, 1940; s. John Charles and Mary W. (Green) H.; m. Martha Ann Halsted, Dec. 23, 1961; children: John Charles, Sharon Aileen. A.B. cum laude, Austin Coll., 1962; M.S. (Danforth fellow, NSF fellow), Tulane U., 1964, Ph.D. (Danforth fellow, NSF fellow), 1966. Cert. psychologist, Tex. Asst. prof. psychology Tulane U., 1966-69; assoc. prof. psychology Tex. Christian U., Ft. Worth, 1969-77; assoc. dean of univ. Tex. Christian U., 1972-77; v.p. Tex. Christian U. Research Found., 1974-77; dean Grad Sch. Tex. Christian U., 1975-77; v.p. acad. affairs Bradley U., Peoria, Ill., 1977-87; provost Bradley U., 1981-87; v.p. acad. affairs, prof. psychology U. Maine, Orono, 1987-92, interim pres., 1991-92; pres. U. Cen. Fla., Orlando, 1992—; bd. dirs. Quad Cities Grad. Study Ctr., 1985-87; bd. dirs. Seminar on Acad. Computing, 1985-88, chmn. bd. dirs., 1986-87. Mem. bd. co-editors: Psychological Research, 1973-76; contbr. articles in psychology and neuroscience to scholarly jours. Chmn. com. on social scis. Austin Coll. 125th Anniversary Commn., 1973-74; charter mem. Austin Coll. Bd. Edn. Visitors, 1976; Tex. Christian U. rep. Leadership Ft. Worth, 1973-74; program chmn. Forum Ft. Worth, 1976-77; mem. Tarrant County United Way Budget Com., 1975-77, Forward Ft. Worth, 1976-77; chmn. loaned exec. program Heart of Ill. United Way, 1979, chmn. edn. unit, 1980, bd. dirs. 1983-87; bd. dirs. Greater Peoria YMCA, 1980-84, SunBank; mem. community adv. council St. Francis Med. Ctr., Peoria, 1984-87; bd. dirs. Inst. Phys. Medicine and Rehab., Peoria, 1981-87, pres. bd. dirs., 1986-87; v.p. Penobscot Valley United Way, Bangor, Maine, 1989-92; trustee Bangor YWCA, 1991-92; vestry St. John's Episcopal Ch., Bangor, 1990-91; mem. Econ. Devel. Commn. Mid-Fla., Found. Orange County Pub. Schs., Fla. Info. Resource Network; bd. dirs. Orlando C. of C., Winter Park C. of C. Mem. Am. Psychol. Assn., Midwestern Psychol. Assn., Psychonomic Soc., Soc. for Neurosci., AAAS, Am. Assn. Higher Edn., Peoria Area C. of C. (bd. dirs. 1986-87), Greater Orlando C. of C., Winter Park C. of C., Sigma Xi, Alpha Chi, Psi Chi, Phi Kappa Phi. Democrat. Home: 2242 Westminster Terrace Oviedo FL 32765 Office: Pres Office U Cen Fla Box 25000 Orlando FL 32816

HITZ, WARREN HARDING, JR., technological education administrator; b. Hershey, Pa., Mar. 12, 1947; s. Warren Harding and Dorothy Arlene (Forney) H.; m. Elaine Carol Goddard, June 14, 1969; children: Kyle, Derek, Sharia, Malea, Seth. BS, Del. Valley Coll., 1969; MEd, Temple U., 1990. Mgr. Agway, Inc., 1969-72; dir. tech. edn. Milton Hershey Sch., Hershey, Pa., 1988—; football coach, Milton Hershey Sch., 1972-84, baseball coach, 1973-79. Coach baseball Penn Gardens Lions Club, Harrisburg, 1979-80, Lakeview Civic Club, Harrisburg, 1991; active Zion Evang. Luth. Ch., Harrisburg, 1985—. Mem. Am. Vocat. Assn., Pa. Vocat. Assn., Vocat. Adminstrs. Pa., Internat. Tech. Edn. Assn., Masons. Republican.

HIVELY, JANE STEWART WILCOX, music teacher, vocalist; b. Fall River, Mass., Aug. 29, 1952; d. Richard French and Jean (Ferguson) Wilcox; m. Jonathan Hively, July 18, 1987. MusB, Boston U., 1975; MusM, Schiller Coll., Strasbourg, France, 1976; postgrad., Guildhall Sch. Music & Drama, London, 1977. Singer Boston Lyric Opera, 1974, Strasbourg Opera, 1976; soloist Music Serving the Elderly, Newton, Mass., 1978-81, Old North Ch., Boston, 1980; voice tchr. Southeastern Mass. U., Dartmouth, 1980; pvt. practice voice tchr. Albany, N.H., 1987—; Dir. Yankee Doodle Opera, Conway, N.H., 1988; mus. dir. Resort Players, North Conway, N.H., 1989; lectr., career cons. Kennett High Sch., Conawy, 1985-87; dancer Leon Collins Tap Co., Boston, 1979. Author vocal instrn. book Singing is for the Birds, 1991; singer various cassette tapes. Mem. Rep. Presdl. Task Force, Washington, 1985—; mem. Conway Sch. Bd., 1989-90; mem. Rep. Nat. Com., Washington, 1989—. Recipient Cert. of Recognition, Rep. Nat. Com., 1991; Ada Draper Trust scholar, Boston U., 1975, Mascomet Ambassadors Club exch. scholar, 1970; Guildhall Sch. of Music and Drama grantee, 1977. Mem. Scottish Harp Soc. Am. Home and Office: Still Rd # 1160 Conway NH 03818

HIX, JAMES WILLIAM, sales executive; b. Tullahoma, Tenn., Oct. 8, 1947; s. Roy Newton and Alma (Zimmerman) H.; m. Carolyn Daves, Mar. 9, 1971; children: Tracey Leigh, Jeffrey Benjamin. BS in Biology, Memphis State U., 1974; MBA in Mgmt., Our Lady of the Lake U., 1988. Ter. rep. CIBA Pharm. Co., Jackson, Tenn., 1974-75, med. rep., 1975-78, profl. med. rep., 1978-83; hosp. rep. pharm. div. CIBA-Geigy, San Antonio, 1983-88; dist. mgr. CIBA-Geigy Pharm. Co., Dallas, 1988-89; mgr. hosp. planning and promotion CIBA-Geigy Pharm. Co., Summit, N.J., 1989-90, dir. inst. planning and promotion, 1990-91, dir sales planning and promotion, 1991—; bd. dirs. Epilepsy Found. of Bluebonnet Region, San Antonio, 1986-88; v.p. bd. dirs., 1987. Served with U.S. Army, 1966-69. Mem. Delta Mu Delta. Home: 11 Clearview Dr Long Valley NJ 07853

HLASTA, DENNIS JOHN, chemist; b. Youngstown, Ohio, July 13, 1953; s. Chester and Angeline (Slack) H.; m. Linda Lee, Aug. 16, 1975; children: Meredith, Erin, Margaret, Erik. BS, Ohio State U., 1975; MS, Yale Univ., 1977, M of Philosophy, 1978, PhD, 1979. Sr. rsch. chemist rsch. div. Sterling Winthrop Pharms., Rensselaer, N.Y., 1979-83; group leader Sterling Rsch. Group, Rensselaer, N.Y., 1983-90, rsch. leader, 1990—. Contbr. articles to profl. jours. Mem. AAAS, Am. Chem. Soc., Internat. Soc.

Heterocyclic Chemistry. Office: Sterling Winthrop Pharms 81 Columbia Tpke Rensselaer NY 12144-3411

HNATYSHYN, RAMON JOHN, governor general, commander in chief, lawyer; b. Saskatoon, Sask., Can., Mar. 16, 1934; s. John and Helen Constance (Pitts) H.; m. Karen Gerda Nygaard Andreasen, Jan. 9, 1960; children: John, Carl. BA, U. Sask., Can., 1954; LLB, U. Sask., 1956. Called to the bar, Sask., 1957, Ont., 1986; apptd. Queen's Counsel, Sask., 1973, Can., 1988. Pvt. practice, 1957-90; sr. ptnr. Gowling, Strathy & Henderson, Ottawa, Ont., Can., 1988-90; of counsel Hnatyshyn & Co., Saskatoon, 1974-90; mem. Parliament, Can., 1974-88; Minister of State for Sci. and Tech., 1979, Minister Energy, Mines, Resources, 1979-80; Minister Regulatory Affairs Govt. of Can., 1986, Minister Justice, Atty.-Gen., 1986-88, opposition house leader, 1984, govt. house leader, 1984-86; mem. Queen's Privy Coun. for Can., 1979— (pres. 1985-86), Gov. Gen., 1990—. Pres. Saskatoon Gallery and Conservatory Corp., 1974; campaign chmn. United Way, 1972; dir. United Community Funds, 1968-74. Named Chancellor and Prin. Companion of the Order of Can., Chancellor and Comdr. Order Mil. Merit, 1990; recipient St. Volodymyr medal award World Congress of Ukrainians, 1989. Mem. Saskatoon Bar Assn., Can. Bar Assn.; hon. life mem., Law Soc. Sask. Home and Office: Rideau Hall, 1 Sussex Dr, Ottawa, ON Canada K1A 0A1

HOADLEY, ROBERT BRUCE, wood science and technology educator; b. Waterbury, Conn., July 24, 1933; s. William Fremont and Esther (Anderson) H.; m. Barbara Anne Luskay, June 15, 1957; children: Susan Nelson, Lindsay Anne. BS in Forestry, U. Conn., 1955; MF in Wood Tech., Yale U., 1957, D. Forestry Wood Tech., 1962. Prof. wood sci. & tech. U. Mass., 1962—. Author: Understanding Wood, 1980, Identifying Wood, 1990, Holz Als Werkstoff, 1990; contbr. editor Fine Woodworking, 1991—. Mem. Forest Products Rsch. Soc., Soc. Wood Sci & Tech., Internat. Assn. Wood Anatomists. Office: Univ of Massachusetts Holdsworth Hall Wood Sci and Tech Amherst MA 01003

HOAGLAND, GLENN DANIEL, land conservationist; b. Morristown, N.J., Dec. 25, 1959; s. Kenneth Moore and Frances Louise (Schoch) H.; 1 child, Erin Marie. AA, Somerset County Coll., North Branch, N.J., 1980; B in Geography, SUNY, New Paltz, 1982; M in Rural Planning, U. Guelph (Ont., Can.), 1986. Intern Ulster County Devel. Corp., Kingston, N.Y., 1982; affordable housing cons. Rural Devel. Adv. Corp., Goshen, N.Y., 1984; Greenway planner Berkshire County Regional Planning Commn. Mass. Dept. Environ. Mgmt., Pittsfield, 1984-85; land preservation dir. Scenic Hudson, Inc., Poughkeepsie, N.Y., 1985-87; assoc. dir. Dutchess Land Conservancy, Inc., Bangall, N.Y., 1987-89; exec. dir. Dutchess Land Conservancy, Inc., Stanfordville, N.Y., 1989-91; dir. citizen action program Open Space Inst., Ossining, N.Y., 1991—; bd. mem. Wilderstein Preservation, Rhinecliff, N.Y., 1986-90. Mem. N.Y. State Regional Land Acquisition Adv. Com., Hudson Valley, 1990-91; mem. planning adv. com. Land Trust Alliance, Washington, 1991—; panelist, architecture planning and design program N.Y. State Coun. on the Arts, N.Y.C., 1991—. Democrat. Presbyterian. Home: 11 Park St Kingston NY 12401-5125 Office: Open Space Inst 145 Main St Rt 82 Ossining NY 10562

HOAGLAND, JIMMIE LEE, newspaper editor; b. Rock Hill, S.C., Jan. 22, 1940; s. Lee Roy and Edith Irene (Sullivan) H.; m. Elizabeth Becker, 1979; children—Laura Lee, Lily Hue, Lee Clayton. A.B. in Journalism, U. S.C., 1961; student, U. Aix-en-Provence, France, 1961-62. Reporter Evening Herald, Rock Hill, 1960; copy editor N.Y. Times Internat. Edit., Paris, France, 1964-66; reporter Washington Post, 1966-69, Africa corr., 1969-72, Middle East corr., 1972-75, Paris corr., 1975-77, fgn. editor, 1979-81, asst. mng. editor, 1981-86, assoc. editor, 1986—. Author: South Africa: Civilizations in Conflict, 1972. Mem. pres. adv. council U. S.C. Served with USAF, 1962-64. Recipient Pulitzer prize internat. report, 1970; Overseas Press Club award internat. reporting, 1977; Pulitzer prize for commentary, 1990; Ford Found. fellow Columbia U., 1968-69. Mem. Council on Fgn. Relations, Phi Beta Kappa, Pi Kappa Alpha. Office: 1150 15th St NW Washington DC 20005-2780

HOAGLAND, ROBERT EARL, direct mail fundraising executive; b. Abington, Pa., Apr. 24, 1951; s. George Wycoff and Emily Pearl (Willard) H.; m. Debra Louise Morgan, Mar. 16, 1973; children: Gwen Louise, Jennifer Emily, Jeffrey Earl. BA in Sociology, Bloomsburg (Pa.) U., 1974. Procurement coord. Suncom Industries, Sunbury, Pa., 1974-76; salesman Wickes Bldgs., Northumberland, Pa., 1977-78; tchr., parent coord. Northumberland County, Shamokin, Pa., 1978-80, dir. mktg., 1980-82; account exec. L.W. Robbins Assoc., Franklin, Mass., 1982-85, v.p., 1985-89, sr. v.p., chief oper. officer, 1990—; speaker at numerous direct mail fund raising seminars and workshops, 1991—. Elder St. Pauls United Ch. Christ, 1981-82; fund dir., steward Eliot Ch. United Ch. Christ, Newton, Mass., 1983-85; vice-chmn. fin. com. Franklin (Mass.) United Meth. Ch., 1987-91, chmn., 1992—, ministries chmn., 1989-92; corporator Mass. 4-H Found., 1988-91. Mem. Nat. Soc. Fund Raising Execs. (cert.), Assn. Direct Response Fund Raising Coun. (founder, bd. dirs. 1987-90, chmn. ethics com. 1988-90, mem. exec. com. 1990—, pres., chmn. 1991—). Republican. Office: LW Robbins Assoc 693 E Central St Franklin MA 02038-1349

HOAR, RICHARD MORGAN, toxicologist, consultant; b. Boston, Nov. 22, 1927; s. Carl Sherman and Ruth Dennis (Cole) H.; m. Rita Cecilia George, Aug. 27, 1949; 1 child, Andrew. BS, Dartmouth Coll., 1950; PhD, U. Kans., 1956. Assoc. prof. anatomy U. Cin. Coll. of Medicine, Cin., 1956-69; assoc. dir. toxicology Hoffmann-LaRoche, Nutley, N.J., 1969-85; sr. advisor Argus Rsch. Labs. Inc., Horsham, Pa., 1986—; cons. Argus Internat., Horsham, Pa., 1986—. Contbr. over 130 rsch. articles to profl. jours. Sci. advisor Am. Coun. on Sci. and Health, N.Y., 1988—. Cpl. U.S. Army, 1946-47. Mem. Teratology Soc. (treas. 1974-78, pres. 1980), Behavioral Teratology Soc. (pres. 1981), Am. Coll. Toxicology (pres. 1988-89). Office: Argus Rsch Lab Inc 905 Sheehy Dr Horsham PA 19044

HOAR, WILLIAM PATRICK, editor; b. Haverhill, Mass., Nov. 7, 1945; s. John Patrick and Helen Rose (Powers) H.; m. Louisa Miller, July 29, 1978; children: Meredith Miller Hoar, Emily Erin Hoar. AB, Bowdoin Coll., 1967. Contbg. editor Am. Opinion, Belmont, Mass., 1971-85; assoc. editor The Rev. of the News, Belmont, 1971-85; exec. editor, v.p. Conservative Digest, Washington, 1985-89, World Networks, 1989—; Washington corr. Southern Africa Spl. Dispatch, 1990-91, Newslink Africa, 1990-91; exec. dir. Second Decade Found., 1991—; editor World News Digest, Silver Spring, Md., 1991—; Washington editor New American, 1992—. Author: Architects of Conspiracy: An Intriguing History, 1984 (updated Japanese edit. 1991);l editor various jours. including Regions in Transition, 1990; contbr. articles to profl. jours. Mem. Bel Pre Civic Assn., Silver Spring, Md., 1985—, Nat. Trust for Historic Preservation. Staff sgt. U.S. Army, 1968-70. Decorated Army Commendation medal. Mem. White House Corres. Assn., Congl. Periodical Press Gallery, Soc., Profl. Journalists, Nat. Press Club, Am. Legion, Internat. Policy Forum (bd. govs.), Chi Psi. Home: 2916 Bluff Point Ln Silver Spring MD 20906-3043 Office: World News Digest 2916 Bluff Point Ln Silver Spring MD 20906-3043

HOARE, CAROL HREN, human resources educator; b. Harrisburg, Pa., July 23, 1940; d. Frank John and Mary Ann (Matesevac) Hren; m. Raymond R. Hoare, Feb. 8, 1964; children: Jennifer Rae, Raymond Robert. BS, Carlow Coll., 1962; MS, U. N.C., 1964; EdD, George Washington U., 1980. RN, Va. Asst. prof. in nursing Georgetown U., Washington, 1965-70; coordr. office community svcs. George Washington U., Washington, 1982-92, now prof., chmn. dept. human svcs., 1990—; pvt. practice, cons. Hoare Assocs., McLean, Va. Contbr. articles to profl. publs. Trustee, chair acad. affairs com. Carlow Coll. USPHS fellow. Mem. AACD, AAUP, Am. Assn. Adult and Continuing Edn., Phi Delta Kappa, Sigma Theta Tau. Home: 1556 Forest Villa Ln Mc Lean VA 22101-4130 Office: George Washington U Dept of Human Svcs T 605 Washington DC 20052

HOBAUGH, REGINA MARGARET, philosopher, educator; b. Phila., Sept. 13, 1945; d. Albin J. and Rose E. (DiNote) Mengis; m. John W. Hobaugh, Oct. 11, 1969; children: Julie, John. BA, Holy Family Coll., Phila., 1967; MA, U. Dayton, Ohio, 1969; PhD, Temple U., 1991. Instr. Holy Family Coll., Phila., 1969-72, lectr., 1972-83, asst. prof., 1983-91, assoc. prof., 1991—. Mem. Am. Cath. Philosophic Assn., Assn. of Profl. and Applied Ethics. Office: Holy Family Coll Grant & Frankford Aves Philadelphia PA 19114

HOBBS, J. TIMOTHY, SR., lawyer; b. Yakima, Wash., Sept. 23, 1941; s. Leonard M. and Virginia (Snider) H.; m. Barbara J. Hatfield, June 14, 1964; children: Amy Elizabeth, J. Timothy Jr. BA in Polit. Sci., U. Wash., 1964; JD, Am. U., 1968. Bar: D.C. 1969, U.S. Ct. Supreme Ct. 1973, U.S. Ct. Appeals (11th cir.) 1986, U.S. Ct. Appeals (5th cir.) 1989. Assoc. Mason Fenwick & Lawrence, Washington, 1969-76, ptnr., 1977-82, sr. ptnr., 1982-91; ptnr. Dykema, Gossett, Washington, 1991—. Author chpt. on copyright law, West's Federal Practice Manual, 1983. Pres. Arlington Outdoor Edn. Assn., 1990—. Mem. D.C. Bar (chmn. trademark com. 1982-84), U.S. Trademark Assn. Forums (speaker 1988), Washington Golf and Country Club. Home: 6135 Lee Hwy Arlington VA 22205-2134 Office: Dykema Gossett 1752 N St NW Washington DC 20036-2806

HOBBS, WILBUR EUGENE, social worker, consultant; b. Phila., Sept. 17, 1921; s. Irvin H. Hobbs and Ola Belle Stevens-Bryant; m. Rose Imogene Denny, Dec. 19, 1943; 1 child, Wilbur Eugene Jr. BS, West Chester U., 1943; MSW, U. Pa., 1951. Supr. Del. County Juvenile Court, Media, Pa., 1955-57; exec. dir. Sunnycrest Farm for Boys, Cheyney, Pa., 1957-61; supt. Pa. Youth Devel. Ctr., 1961-66; sr. cons. Greenleigh Assoc., Inc., N.Y.C., 1966-70; pres., founder Community Scis., Inc., Phila., 1970-74; commnr. dept. pub. welfare Children & Youth Pa., Phila., 1974-75; dep. sec. dept. pub. welfare southeastern region Pa. Children & Youth Pa., 1975-79; co-exec. dir. Crime Prevention Assn., Phila., 1979-81; deputy commr. dept. Human Svcs. City of Phila., 1981-83; ptnr. The Conservation Co., Phila, 1983-90; mgmt. cons. Hobbs and Assoc., Phila., 1990—; assoc. U. Pa. Sch. Social Work, Phila., 1978—; trustee Samuel S. Fels Fund, Phila., 1986—, Beaver Coll., Glenside, Pa., 1978-90; dir. Pa. Preservation Fund, Lancaster, 1990—, Phila. Citizens for Children and Youth, Phila., 1984—. Conbtr. articles to profl. jours. Dir. United Way of Southeastern Pa., Phila., 1951-89; dir. Urban League of Phila., 1980-89; pres. Frontiers Internat. Found., 1988—; chmn. Mayor's Exec. Commn. on Drug and Alcohol Programs, Phila., 1988—. Maj. U.S. Army, 1942-61. Recipient Humanitarian Gold Madalion Retarded Citizens, 1976, Leadership and Creative Svc. to Retarded Citizens award Temple U., Phila., 1979, Profl. Svc. award City of Phila., 1982, Disting. Alumni award West Chester U., Pa., 1988, Leadership award Urban League of Phila., 1988, All Pa. Coll. Disting. Alumni award, Washington, 1989, Bd. Leadership award Beaver Coll., Glenside, Pa., 1991. Mem. Coun. on Foundations, Assn. Black Foundation Execs., Phila. Club (pres. 1986-88), Assn. Black Social Workers, Acad. Certified Social Workers, Alpha Phi Alpha, Preservation Pa. (dir.). Lutheran. Home: 3436 W Coulter St Philadelphia PA 19129-1402 Office: PO Box 865 Frazer PA 19355-0917

HOBERMAN, CHUCK, mechanical engineer, inventor; b. Cambridge, Mass., Mar. 23, 1956; s. Norman and Mary Ann (Miller) H.; m. Carolyn Gray Cannon, Aug. 23, 1982. Student, Brown U., 1974-76; BFA in Sculpture, Cooper Union for Advancement of Art and Sci., 1979; MS in Mech. Engring., Columbia U., 1984. V.p. engring. Honeybee Robotics, N.Y.C., 1984-88; prin. Hoberman Assocs. Inc., N.Y.C., 1988—; adj. prof. architecture Columbia U., 1991—; cons. NASA Langley Rsch. Ctr. Hampton, Va., FTL Assocs., N.Y.C., Abrams Gentile Entertainment, N.Y.C., Johnson Camping Tent Corp., Binhamton, N.Y. Designs exhibited at Liberty Sci. Ctr., Jersey City, N.J., Cooper Union for Advancement of Art and Sci.; 7 patents in field. Design innovation grantee NEA, 1991; recipient IDEA90 Silver award Indsl. Design Soc. Am., 1990, Architecture, Planning, and Design Ind. Project award N.Y. State Coun. on Arts, 1991. Address: 472 Greenwich St New York NY 10013

HOBERMAN, MARY ANN, author; b. Stamford, Conn., Aug. 12, 1930; d. Milton and Dorothy (Miller) Freedman; m. Norman Hoberman, Feb. 4, 1951; children: Diane, Perry, Charles, Meg. BA, Smith Coll., 1951; MA, Yale U., 1984. With advt. dept. Gimbel's Dept. Store, N.Y.C., 1951-52; newspaper reporter Harrisburg, Pa., 1952; editor promotions N.Y. Graphic Soc., Greenwich, Conn., 1963-64; poetry cons.; lectr. in field; program coord. C.G. Jung Ctr., N.Y.C., 1981; adj. prof. Fairfield (Conn.) U., 1980-83; instr. Yale U., New Haven, 1989; founder, mem. The Pocket People, 1968-75; founder, performer Women's Voices, 1983—. Author: All My Shoes Come in Two's, 1957, How Do I Go?, 1958, Hello and Good-by, 1959, What Jim Knew, 1963, Not Enough Beds for the Babies, 1965, A Little Book of Little Beasts, The Raucous Auk, 1973, The Looking Book, 1973, Nuts to You and Nuts to Me, 1974, I Like Old Clothes, 1976, Bugs, 1976, A House Is a House for Me, 1978, Yellow Butter, Purple Jelly, Red Jam, Black Bread, 1981, The Cozy Book, 1982, Mr. and Mrs. Muddle, 1988, A Fine Fat Pig and Other Animal Poems, 1991, Fathers, Mothers, Sisters, Brothers, 1991. Bd. dirs. Greenwich Libr., 1988-91, Westchester Country Dance Soc., 1990—. Recipient Nat. Book award, 1984. Mem. Authors Guild. Home: 98 Hunting Ridge Rd Greenwich CT 06831-3134

HOBERMAN, SOLOMON, management consultant, volunteer; b. N.Y.C., Aug. 13, 1914; s. Isaac and Sarah (Lifschutz) H.; m. Dorothy F. Bergoffen, Apr. 13, 1947; children: James Lewis, Jane. BA, NYU, 1934. Examiner Mcpl. Civil Svc. Commn., N.Y.C., 1939-42; supervisory examiner N.Y.C. Dept. of Pers., 1946-54, dir. tng., 1954-59, dir. pers. rels., 1959-64, dept. pers. dir., 1964-65, pers. dir., chair civil svc. com., 1965-70; mgmt. cons. S. Hoberman, Mgmt. Cons., N.Y.C., 1970—. Editor, author: Practice of Management Development, 1989. Member Citizens Union, N.Y., 1980-91; trustee City Club of N.Y., 1975-91; dir. Foster Parents Plan, Warwick, R.I., 1965-91, Foster Parents Plan Internat., Warwick, 1972-88. Capt. USAF, 1942-46, ETO. Recipient Dist. Pub. Svc. award Nat. Civil Svc. League, 1969. Mem. Am. Soc. Polit. and Social Sci., Soc. for Pub. Adminstrn., Pub. Pers. Assn. (Charles E. Cushman Pub. Svc. award 1968), Coop. Work Experience Edn. Assn. (adv. com., S. Hoberman award 1989). Home and Office: 500 E 77th St New York NY 10162-0025

HOBSON, BUTCH, major league baseball team manager; b. Tuscaloosa, Ala., Aug. 17, 1951. Student, U. Ala. Player Boston Red Sox orgn., 1963-80, mgr. minor league teams, 1987-91; mgr. Boston Red Sox, 1992—; player Calif. Angels, 1981, N.Y. Yankees, 1982, N.Y. Yankee minor league team, 1982-85. Named. Internat. League Mgr. of Yr., 1991. Office: Boston Red Sox 24 Yawkey Way Boston MA 02215-3409*

HOBSON, JAMES RICHMOND, lawyer; b. Atlanta, Sept. 13, 1937; s. Richmond Pearson and Alice Chambers (Carey) H.; m. Nancy Hulbert Saussy, Nov. 29, 1963; children: Kathleen Hunter, Caroline Richmond, Susan Saussy. BA in English, Cornell U., 1959; MA in Govt., Georgetown U., 1963; JD, U. San Francisco, 1971. Bar: Calif. 1972, U.S. Ct. Appeals (9th cir.) 1972, U.S. Dist. Ct. (no. dist.) Calif. 1972, D.C., 1973, U.S. Ct. Appeals (D.C. cir.) 1973, U.S. Dist. Ct. D.C. 1973. Staff writer Charlotte (N.C.) Observer, 1963; researcher, writer Rep. Nat. Com., Washington, 1964-65; info. officer Hoover Instn., Stanford, Calif., 1966-72; atty., mgr. FCC, Washington, 1972-78; asst. v.p. GTE Svc. Corp., Washington, 1978-81; Washington counsel GTE Corp., Washington, 1982-91; v.p. Donelan, Cleary, Wood and Maser, P.C., Washington, 1991—. Editor mag. pieces for Med. Econs., 1965. Bd. dirs. Mid-Peninsula Citizens for Fair Housing, Palo Alto, Calif., 1971-72; sr. warden Immanuel Ch. of the Hill, Alexandria, Va., 1977, 90, jr. warden, 1976-88; mem. traffic and parking bd. City of Alexandria, 1980-82; mem. panel of arbitrators Am. Arbitration Assn.; vice chmn. adv. bd. Inst. for Conflict Analysis and Resolution, George Mason U., 1989—. Mem. ABA, Fed. Communications Bar Assn. (exec. com. 1984-87), Met. Club (Washington), Sigma Alpha Epsilon. Episcopalian. Home: 3613 Trinity Dr Alexandria VA 22304-1840 Office: Donelan Cleary Wood & Maser PC 1275 K St NW Washington DC 20005-4006

HOBSON, WILLIAM FREDERICK, state agency administrator, psychotherapist; b. Southington, Conn., July 8, 1951; s. Charles Foster Jr. and Catherine Agnes (Gura) H.; m. Eileen Anne Wylie, May 4, 1974; children: Maura, Sarah, Timothy. BA in Psychology, Bucknell U., 1973; MS in Guidance and Counseling, Cen. Conn. State U., 1975. Diagnostic counselor Conn. Correctional Inst., Somers, 1973-76, therapist sex offender program, 1977-84, dir. sex offender program, 1984—; social worker Conn. Dept. Children and Youth Svcs., Manchester, 1976-77; founder, clin. dir. Valley Counseling Assocs., Somers, 1982—. Contbr. articles to profl. jours. Guest talk show Breakaway, ABC, 1983, PBS, 1984, Sally Jessie Raphael Show, 1988. Mem. Assn. for Treatment of Sexual Abusers (clin.), Conn. Assn. for Treatment of Sexual Abusers (clin.). Office: Conn Correctional Inst Sex Offender Program PO Box 100 Somers CT 06071-0100 Office: Valley Counseling Assocs PO Box 160 Somers CT 06071-0160

HOCH, PEGGY MARIE, computer scientist; b. Balt., Dec. 2, 1959; d. Stanley Elijah Hoch, Jr. and Nancy Irene (Bishop) Austin. AA, Catonsville (Md.) Community, Coll., 1982; BS, Towson State U., 1987; MS, Johns Hopkins U., 1989. Lab. technician McCormick & Co., Hunt Valley, Md., 1980-84; computer scientist U.S. Army Concepts Analysis, Bethesda, Md., 1985-88; sr. assoc. programmer IBM Corp., Rockville, Md., 1989-91; computer programmer Nat. Oceanic and Atmospheric Adminstrn., Silver Spring, Md., 1991—. Author: (software) Design CDRLs for IBM/FAA, 1991. Recipient Nat. Computer Sci. award U.S. Achievement Acad., 1987, Computer Sci. award Towson (Md.) State U., Chemistry award Catonsville Community Coll., 1980. Mem. AIAA, Am. Assn. Artificial Intelligence, Johns Hopkins U. Alumni Assn. Home: 10551 # D2 Twin Rivers Rd Columbia MD 21044 Office: National Weather Svc 1325 E West Hwy Silver Spring MD 20910-3233

HOCHBERG, MARCIA GAIL, psychologist; b. Bklyn., July 4, 1957; d. Bernard and Joan Zinderman; m. Jody Alan Hochberg, June 8, 1980; children: Robert, Shane. BA, SUNY, Albany, 1978; PhD, SUNY, Stony Brook, 1985. Lic. psychologist, Pa., N.Y. Psychologist N.Y.C. Bd. Edn., 1982-85; postdoctoral fellow U. Wash., Seattle, 1986-87; psychologist Bryn Mawr Rehab. Hosp., Malvern, Pa., 1987—; researcher Stanley H. Kaplan Ednl. Ctr., N.Y.C., 1982-85. Mem. APA, Phila. Psychol. Soc., Phila. Neuropsychol. Soc. Office: Bryn Mawr Rehab Hosp 414 Paoli Pike Malvern PA 19355-3311

HOCHBERG, MARK S., cardiac surgeon; b. Providence, R.I., Nov. 26, 1947; s. Robert and Gertrude (Meth) H.; m. Faith Shapiro, June 6, 1976; children: Alyssa T., Asher R. BA, Brown U., 1969; MD, Harvard U., 1973; MD (Honoris Causa), Chongqing Sch. Med. Sci., China, 1987. Diplomate Am. Bd. Thoracic Surgery, Am. Bd. Surgery. Chief resident cardiothoracic surgery Mass. Gen. Hosp., Boston, 1980; clin. fellow in surgery Harvard Med. Sch., Boston, 1980; attending cardiac surgeon Newark Beth Israel Med. Ctr., 1981—, dir. cardiac surgery, 1988—; cons. cardiac surgeon Overlook Hosp., Summit, N.J., 1983—; asst. prof. surgery U. Medicine and Dentistry of N.J., Newark, 1981-87, assoc. prof. surgery, 1987—; chmn. grant rev. com. Am. Heart Assn., N.J. Affiliate, New Brunswick, 1986-88, bd. dirs., 1986—; bd. dirs., com. on med. affairs Corp. of Brown U., Providence, 1987—. Vice pres. Temple B'nai Jeshurun, Short Hills, 1988—. Lt. comdr. USPHS, 1975-77. Fellow ACS; mem. Soc. Thoracic Surgery, Am. Assn. Thoracic Surgery, Racquets Club, Alpha Omega Alpha. Home: 36 Stewart Rd Short Hills NJ 07078-1922 Office: Newark Beth Israel Med Ctr 201 Lyons Ave Newark NJ 07112-2094

HOCHBERG, MARTIN N., obstetrician/gnecologist; b. Bklyn., Oct. 22, 1937; s. Lew A. and Bess A. (Solovei) H.; m. Lois J. Robins, Mar. 5, 1967; children: Leigh Robert, Lauren K. BS, Union Coll., 1958; MD, N.Y. Med. Coll., 1963. Diplomate Am. Bd. Ob/Gyn. Intern Brookdale Hosp. Ctr., Bklyn., 1963-64, resident in ob./gyn., 1966-70; physician Obstetric and Gynecol. Assocs. of Ridgewood, N.J., 1970—; assoc. dir. dept. of Ob/Gyn, The Valley Hosp., Ridgewood, 1984-91. Lt. USN, 1964-66. Fellow Am. Coll. Ob/Gyn; mem. Am. Fertility Soc., Am. Assn. Gynecol. Laproscopists, N.J. Med. Soc., N.J. Ob/Gyn Soc., AMA. Office: Obstetric & Gynecol Assocs 550 N Maple Ave Ridgewood NJ 07450

HOCHBERG, RICHARD BARRY, obstetrics and gynecology educator, consultant; b. N.Y.C., May 18, 1938; s. Leo and Ida (Shapiro) H.; m. Alice Wofsy, Dec. 20, 1962 (div. 1978); children: Edward, James, Robert. BA, Alfred (N.Y.) U., 1960; postgrad., Poly. Inst. Bklyn., 1961-62; PhD, Hahnemann U., 1967; MA, Yale U., 1986. Rsch. assoc. Columbia U., N.Y.C., 1967-74, asst. prof., 1975-79; assoc. prof. Yale U., New Haven, Conn., 1980-84, prof., 1985—; cons. DuPont, Wilmington, Del., 1986—, Medi-Physics, Arlington Heights, Ill., 1988—. Editor: New Biology of Steroid Hormones, 1991; mem. editorial bd. Endocrinology, Steroids, Cancer Rsch., 1974-78, 86-89; inventor radio-halogenated estrogens, progesterone receptor ligands; contbr. numerous articles to profl. jours. NIH fellow, 1966, 67, grantee, 1976, 76-91, Am. Cancer Soc. grantee, 1978; recipient Alumnus of the Yr. award Hahnemann Med. Coll., 1976. Mem. AAAS, Endocrine Soc., Soc. for Gynecologic Investigation, Am. Soc. Biol. Chemistry and Molecular Biology. Office: Yale U Sch Medicine 333 Cedar St Dept Ob/Gyn New Haven CT 06510

HOCHBERG, RONALD MARK, lawyer; b. Bklyn., Apr. 3, 1955; s. Fred S. and Adele (Gunsberg) H.; m. Sharon A. Berg, Aug. 11, 1985; children: Rachel, Sarah. BA, Rutgers U., 1977; JD, Bklyn. Law Sch., 1980; LLM, U. Miami, 1982. Assoc. Klatsky & Klatsky, Red Bank, N.J., 1980-81, Fuerst, Singer & Yusem, Somerville, N.J., 1982-83, Law Offices of Steven Schanker, Melville, N.Y., 1983-86; ptnr. Schanker & Hochberg, Attys., Huntington, N.Y., 1986—; part-time prof. Adelphi U., Garden City, N.Y., 1984-89. Mem. ABA, N.Y. State Bar Assn., Estate and Tax Planning Coun. Office: Schanker & Hochberg 27 W Neck Rd Huntington NY 11743-2618

HOCHBRUECKNER, GEORGE J., congressman; b. L.I., N.Y., Sept. 20, 1938; m. Carol Ann Hochbrueckner; 4 children. Student, SUNY, Stony Brook, Hofstra U. Former engr. aerospace designer; mem. N.Y. State Assembly, Albany, 1974-84, 100th-102d Congresses from 1st N.Y. dist., 1987—. Served with USN. Democrat. Office: US Ho of Reps Washington DC 20515

HOCHMAN, MICHELE, counseling service executive, psychotherapist; b. Boston, Mar. 16, 1939; d. Charles and Ruth (Rosenthal) Gilman; m. B. Williams Hochman, June 19, 1959 (dec. 1984); 1 child, Jonathan Lee. BA, Rutgers Coll., 1960; MA, Rider Coll., 1983; PhD all but dissertation, Temple U., 1986. Nationally cert. counselor. Counselor Trenton (N.J.) Psychiatric Hosp., 1987-88, Community Guidance Ctr., Princeton, N.J., 1989-90; counselor, dir. Princeton Counseling Svcs., 1983—; clin. dir. St. Mary's Ctr. for Women, Trenton, N.J., 1992—; dir. Cen. Jersey Depressive Disorder Group, 1989—. Dir. PRIDE, Simmons Coll., 1982; vol. Princeton House, Meals on Wheels, Princeton Hub, Inc., Livingston Hosp., Princeton Profl. Roster; vol. therapist Ewing Edn. Ctr.; vol. substance abuse counselor Cath. Charities. Mem. Princeton Coll. Women's Club. Office: Princeton Counseling Svcs 34 Cedar Ln Princeton NJ 08540-5309

HOCHMAN, RONALD NORMAN, oncologist; b. Bklyn., Feb. 4, 1951; s. Aaron and Mary Blanche (Siegel) H.; m. Ruth Esther Margules, Aug. 19, 1973; children: Michael, Steven. AB, Princeton U., 1971; MD, Harvard U., 1975. Diplomate Am. Bd. Internal Medicine, Am. Bd. Med. Oncology. Intern, then resident in medicine Boston City Hosp., 1975-79; chief, div. hematology/oncology Mercy Cath. Med. Ctr., Phila., 1981-82; physician Sioux City (Iowa) Hematology-Oncology Assocs., 1982-84, Fallon Clinic, Worcester, Mass., 1984—. Contbr. articles to profl. jour. Mem. AMA, Am. Soc. Clin. Oncology, Am. Coll. Physicians. Office: Fallon Clinic 630 Plantation St Worcester MA 01505

HOCHREITER, JOSEPH CHRISTIAN, JR., engineering company executive; b. Bristol, Pa., Jan. 29, 1955; s. Joseph Christian and Mary Claire (Boyer) H.; m. Eileen Grace Wachtman, Aug. 31, 1984; 1 child, Erich. BA, Temple U., 1978; postgrad., Drexel U., 1983-85. Cert. ground water prof. Hydrologic tech. U.S. Geological Survey, Trenton, N.J., 1973-78, hydrologist, 1979-87; hydrologic mgr. Environ. Resources Mgt., Inc., Princeton, N.J., 1987-90, br. mgr., 1990-92, principal, 1991-92; v.p. Blasland, Bouck & Lee, Edison, N.J., 1992—; lectr. Pa. State U., Trevose, Pa., 1980-84. Author and co-author numerous reports, papers in related field; editorial bd. Jour. Ground Water, Columbus, Ohio, 1989—. Founder Bucks County Homeless Shelter, Levittown, Pa., 1985; bd. dirs. ARC, Langhorne, Pa., 1985-91, Human Growth Ctr., Holland, Pa., 1987—. Recipient Adult Vol. award Bucks County Courier Times, 1987. Mem. Am. Geophysical Union, Assn. Ground Water Scientists and Engrs., N.J. Acad. Sci., Geological Assn. N.J. Democrat. Home: 252 Hollow Branch Ln Yardley PA 19067 Office: Blasland Bouck & Lee Raritan Plz Fieldcrest Ave Edison NJ 08837

HOCHSTADT, JOY, biomedical research scientist, scientific and research director; b. N.Y.C., May 6, 1939; d. Julius Louis and Edith (Tabatchnick) H.; m. Harvey Leon Ozer, Feb. 3, 1960; 1 child, Juliane Natasha Hochstadt-Ozer. A.B. in Zoology, Barnard Coll., 1960; A.M. in Biologic Scis. (grad. fellow 1961-62), Stanford U., 1963; vis. fellow in tumor biology, Karolinska Inst., Stockholm, 1964-65; research fellow in biol. chemistry, Harvard U., 1965-66; Ph.D. in Microbiology, Georgetown U., 1968; postdoctoral fellow NIH, 1968-70. Diplomate Am. Bd. Clin. Chemistry. Instr. biology Coll. San Mateo, Calif., 1962-63; teaching asst. microbiology Georgetown Med. Sch., 1967-68; established investigator Am. Heart Assn.; lab. biochemistry Nat. Heart and Lung Inst., Bethesda, Md., 1970-72; sr. scientist Worcester Found. Exptl. Biology, Shrewsbury, Mass., 1972-76; adj. prof. biochemistry Central New Eng. Coll., Worcester, Mass., 1974-75; vis. prof. membrane research Weizmann Inst. Sci., Rehovot, Israel, 1976; vis. prof. biochemistry and biophysics U. R.I., Kingston, 1976-77; research prof. microbiology N.Y. Med. Coll., Valhalla, 1977-81; dir. Div. Clin. Biochemistry and Basic Research in Pathology, Cath. Med. Center, Queens, 1981-88; prof. clin. microbiology Cornell U. Med. Sch., 1986—; v.p., scientific dir. Hercon Labs. Corp. subs. Health Chem Corp., N.Y.C., 1988-90; sr. v.p. Biomed. Techs. div. Princeton Polymer Labs., Plainsboro, N.J., 1989—; dir. scientific devel. Maimonides Rsch. and Devel. Found., 1992—; predoctoral trainee USPHS, 1966-67, spl. trainee, 1973; investigator Am. Heart Assn., 1970-75; mem. NSF postdoctoral fellowship evaluation panel in biology NRC, 1975—; mem. postdoctoral fellowship evaluation panel NATO, 1978—; mem. cell biology study sect. NIH, 1979—, mem. biomed. scis. fellowship com., 1979—. Editorial bd. Jour. Bacteriology, 1975-80; contbr. research papers, methods articles and monographs to profl. lit. Mem. nat. policy com. Profl. Women's Caucus, 1970-73; mem. alumnae coun. Barnard Coll., 1975—, v.p. Class of 1960, 1990—; mem. com. revision biochemistry and biotech. subcom., in vitro methods subcom. U.S. Pharmacopeial Conv., 1990—. Cancer Internat. Rsch. Coop. Snell scholar, 1965; fellow USPHS, 1967-70; grantee NIH, 1973, NSF, 1978-80; travel award Am. Soc. Biol. Chemists, Stockholm, 1973, Hamburg, 1976, Am. Soc. Microbiology, Jerusalem, 1973. Fellow Am. Acad. Microbiology, Am. Inst. Chemists (profl. opportunities com., legis. com.), Nat. Acad. Clin. Biochemistry; mem. Am. Heart Assn. (basic sci. council), Am. Soc. Microbiology (status of women com. 1970-73, sec. physiology div. 1972-74, mem. divisional nominating com. 1973), Am. Soc. Biol. Chemists, Am. Assn. Clin. Chemists, AAAS, Am. Soc. Clin. Rsch., Am. Chem. Soc., Genetics Soc. Am., Harvey Soc., Am. Assn. Cancer Rsch., N.Y. Acad. Scis., Fedn. Am. Scientists, Assn. Women in Sci. (affirmative goals and actions com. 1973-75), Tissue Culture Assn. (Northeast planning com. 1986—), Am. Soc. for Cell Biology. Address: Saw Creek 1347 Cambridge Ct Bushkill PA 18324 Office: Princeton Polymer Labs 501 Plainsboro Rd Plainsboro NJ 08536 also: Maimonides R & D Found 979 48th St Brooklyn NY 11219

HOCHSTETLER, ALAN RAY, chemist; b. Nappanee, Ind., May 7, 1939; s. William M. and Mary Martha (Maust) H.; m. Gloria Marie Gallagher, June 10, 1972 (div. June 1979); m. Donna May Postpichal, July 18, 1981. BA in Chemistry, Goshen Coll., 1964; PhD in Organic Chemistry, Northwestern U., 1968. Instr. Northwestern U., Evanston, Ill., 1968-69; sr. rsch. chemist Givaudan-Roure Corp., Clifton, N.J., 1969—. Patentee in field; contbr. articles to profl. publs. Mem. Am. Chem. Soc. Methodist. Home: 157 Rutland Rd Glen Rock NJ 07452-1237 Office: Givaudan Corp 125 Delawanna Ave Clifton NJ 07014-1596

HOCHSTRASSER, JOHN MICHAEL, environmental engineer, industrial hygienist; b. Cin., July 19, 1938; s. Alvin Louis and Helen Augusta (Furst) H.; m. Wilma Ruth Reckman, Feb. 27, 1960; children: Ronald, Jennifer, Caroline. BSME, U. Cin., 1963, MS in Environ. Engring., 1972, PhD in Environ. Health, 1976. Registered profl. engr., Ohio, Ill., N.J.; diplomate Am. Acad. Environ. Engrs.; cert. indsl. hygienist Am. Bd. Indsl. Hygiene; registered occupational hygienist, Can.; lic. asbestos safety technician, N.J. Reliability and safety engr. GE Co., Evendale, Ohio, 1963-72; dir. environ. affairs G.D. Searle & Co., Skokie, Ill., 1975-78; dir. indsl. hygiene Tenneco Chems., Inc., Piscataway, N.J., 1978-83; project dir. Roy F. Weston, Inc., West Chester, Pa., 1983-85; dir. health and safety CH2M Hill, Inc., Parsippany, N.J., 1985-89; tech. dir. First Environ., Inc., Riverdale, N.J., 1989—. Mem. ASCE, NSPE, Am. Indsl. Hygiene Assn. (bd. dirs. 1987-90, chair ethics com. 1992-93), Am. Soc. Safety Engrs., Air and Waste Mgmt. Assn., Water Pollution Control Fedn., System Safety Soc., Inst. Environ. Scis., N.Y. Acad. Scis., Soc. for Risk Analysis. Home: 864 Shadow Ridge Rd Franklin Lakes NJ 07417-1516 Office: First Environment Inc 90 Riverdale Rd Riverdale NJ 07457-1707

HOCKEN, PETER DUDLEY, priest; b. Hove, Sussex, Eng., June 22, 1932; s. Robert and Enid Beatrice (Thorpe) H. Student, Oscott Coll., Birmingham, Eng., 1958-64; S.T.L., Accademia Alfonsiana, Rome, 1971; PhD, U. Birmingham, 1984. Ordained priest Roman Catholic Ch., 1964. Asst. priest St. Patrick's Ch., Corby, Eng., 1964-68; lectr. moral theology Oscott Coll., 1968-69, 71-76; mem., leader Mother of God Community, Gaithersburg, Md., 1976—; mem. editorial bd. One in Christ, Bedford, Eng., 1972—. Author: Streams of Renewal, 1986, One Lord One Spirit One Body, 1987; contbr. Dictionary of Pentecostal Charismatic Movements, 1988, also articles to numerous periodicals. Mem. Soc. for Pentecostal Studies (pres. 1985-86, exec. sec. 1988—). Home and Office: Mother of God Community 20501 Goshen Rd Gaithersburg MD 20879-4236

HOCKER, JOHN ROBERT, technical operations executive; b. Elwood, Ind., Aug. 11, 1935; s. Joseph Eugene and Helen Margaret (Benedict) H.; m. Barbara Siemers, Aug. 11, 1962; children: Constance Lynn, Guy Albert. BS in Engring., U.S. Mil. Acad., 1957; MS in Applied Math., U. Freiburg, Germany, 1965; M of Mil. Arts and Sci., U.S. Army Command and Gen. Staff Coll., 1971; student, French War Coll., Paris, 1976-78. Commd. 2d lt. U.S. Army, 1957, advanced through ranks to Col., 1978; co. comdr. 1st Calvalry Div. 1st Calvalry Div., Vietnam, 1966-67; assoc. prof. dept. math. U.S. Mil. Acad., West Point, N.Y., 1967-70; inspector Infantry Airborne/Spl Units for Mil Equipment Delivery Team, Phnom Penh, Cambodia, 1971-72; commdr. 1st Bn., 325th Airborne Infantry Bn., and 82nd Airborne div. U.S. Army, Fort Bragg, N.C., 1972-75; joint exercise dir. Orgn. of Joint Chief of Staff, Washington, 1975-76; policy dir. Hdqrs. U.S. European Command, Stuttgart, Germany, 1978-80; spl. asst. to Supreme Allied Comdr. Supreme Hdqrs. Allied Powers Europe, Belgium, 1980-82; chief of staff Def. Mobilization Systems Planning Activity, Washington, 1982-84; ret. U.S. Army, 1984; dir. bus. devel. Info. Systems Group Martin Marietta, Bethesda, Md., 1984-91, dir. tech. ops., 1991—. bd. dirs. Old Georgetown Village Homeowners Assn., North Bethesda, Md., 1990—. Decorated Bronze Star, Def. Superior Svc. Medal; Olmsted Found. scholar, 1963. Mem. AIAA, Am. Def. Preparedness Assn., Assn. U.S. Army, Armed Forces Communication Electronics Assn. (bd. dirs. Washington chpt. 1989—). Home: 5809 Tudor Ln Rockville MD 20852-2850 Office: Martin Marietta Corp 6801 Rockledge Dr Bethesda MD 20817-1836

HODDER, MICHAEL JOHN, numismatist; b. Hastings, Sussex, Great Britian, Aug. 21, 1946; came to U.S., 1957; s. Ernest George and Hilda Trevelyn (Brownfield) H.; m. Patricia Anne Mulvaney, Oct. 15, 1981; children: Anne Catherine and Margaret Mary (twins). AB, Seton Hall U., 1968; MA, NYU, 1971, CCNY, 1976; PhC, U. Calif., Berkeley, 1979. Head coin dept. Sotheby's, N.Y.C., 1980-83; pres. Spink & Son, N.Y.C., 1983-84; dir. rsch. Bowers & Merena Galleries, Wolfeboro, 1984-91; cons. Wolfeboro, 1992—. Author: The Norweb Collection, 1987, Encased Postage Stamps, 1989, Collector's Guide to Commemorative Coins, 1992. Mem. Am. Numismatic Assn. (historian 1991—), Am. Numismatic Soc., Numismatic Literary Guild.

HODESS, ARTHUR BART, cardiologist; b. N.Y.C., Jan. 15, 1950; s. Samuel and Dora (Rosenkrantz) H.; children: Joshua David, Jeremy Scott; m. S. Christina Ellsworth, Dec. 23, 1987; children: Jonathan Ellsworth, Jason Dorian. BA, Boston U., 1970; MD, Columbia U., 1974. Intern Hosp. of U. Pa., Phila., 1974-75, resident in medicine, 1975-77, fellow in cardiology, 1977-79; asst. instr. dept. medicine Hosp. U. of Pa., Phila., 1974-79; instr. physiology, dept. animal biology U. Pa., Sch. Veterinary Medicine, Phila., 1977-78; clin. assoc. dept. medicine U. Pa., Phila., 1979-81; attending cardiologist Brandywine Hosp., Coatesville, Pa., 1979—; dir. intensive care Brandywine Hosp., Coatesville, 1989—, chief of cardiology, 1990—, chmn. dept. medicine, 1991—; pres. Brandywine Valley Cardiology Assocs., Thorndale, Pa., 1991—. Contbr. articles to profl. jours. V.p. Chestnut Hollow Homeowners Assn., West Chester, Pa., 1990—; bd. dirs. Beth Israel Congregation, Coatesville, 1991—. Fellow Clin. Coun. Cardiology Am. Heart Assn. Fellow Am. Coll. Cardiology, Am. Coll. Chest Physicians; mem. ACP, Am. Soc. Echocardiography, Phila. Acad. Cardiology, Drinker Soc. for Critical Care in Phila., Cardiac Electrophysiology Group Soc. of Critical Care Medicine. Office: Brandywine Valley Cardio 3456 Lincoln Hwy Thorndale PA 19372-1006

HODGE, DAVID VAUGN, art gallery executive; b. Lower Marion Twp., Pa., Nov. 2, 1934; s. Dorthy Ann Oden; m. Ollie Mae Akins Joiner, July 25, 1955; children: Gary, Cheryl, Aaron, Kevin, Judine. Grad. high sch., Yonkers, N.Y., 1952; cert., Queensborough Community Coll., 1975, NYU, 1981. Pres. Am. Roots Art Gallery, St. Albans, N.Y., 1957—. Mem. Guy R. Brewer Dem. Club, Queens, N.Y., 1991. With USNR, 1952-55. Recipient Cert. of Appreciation Boy Scouts Am., 1990. Mem. NAACP, VFW, L.I. Black Artist Assn., Nat. Minority Bus. Coun., Cripus Attucks #60. Office: Am Roots Art Gallery 19317 Linden Blvd Jamaica NY 11412-3409

HODGES, KENNETH STUART, accountant; b. Bronx, N.Y., Nov. 2, 1955; s. Arthur Stuart and Arlene Marilyn (Hemme) H.; m. Diane Jean Lama, Aug. 20, 1977; children: Jonathan Stuart, Erika Jean. BBA, Iona Coll., 1977; MS in Adminstrn., Western Conn. State U., 1987. CPA, Conn. Staff acct. Coopers and Lybrand CPAs, Stamford, Conn., 1977-79; sr. acct. U.S. Surg. Corp., Norwalk, Conn., 1979-80; supr. accounts receivable Howmet Turbine Components, Greenwich, Conn., 1980-84; mgr. acctg. Guinness Import Co., Stamford, 1985-86; controller Fujitsu Imaging Systems Am., Danbury, Conn., 1986-90; dir. fin. Ultimate Data Systems, Wilton, Conn., 1990-91; controller Prentice Hall Legal & Fin. Svcs., N.Y.C., 1991—. Mem. Am. Inst. CPAs, Conn. Soc. CPAs. Republican.

HODGES, ROBERT H., JR., federal judge; b. 1944. BS, U. S.C., 1966, JD, 1969. Legis. aide to Sen. Strom Thurmond, 1969-71, legis. aide to Congressman Floyd Spence, 1971-77; v.p., gen. counsel First Nat. Bank of S.C., Columbia, 1977-85; exec. v.p., gen. counsel S.C. Bankers Assn., Columbia, 1985-86; with Quinn, Arndt & Manning, Columbia, 1986-90; judge U.S. Claims Ct., Washington, 1990—. With Air Force Guard USAF Guard Res., 1963-69. Mem. ABA, S.C. Bar, So. Assn. Bank Counsel, Richland County Bar Assn. Office: US Claims Ct 717 Madison Pl NW Washington DC 20005-1011*

HODGES, RONALD WILLIAM, entomologist; b. Lansing, Mich., Aug. 7, 1934; s. Lester Amos and Elma Johanna (Ahlstrom) H.; m. Elaine Rita Snyder, June 23, 1967; children: Steven Edward, Lawrence Bruce. BS, Mich. State U., 1956, MS, 1957; PhD, Cornell U., 1961. Rsch. entomologist Systematic Entomology Lab., ARS, U.S. Dept. Agr., Washington, 1962—; lab. chief Systematic Entomology Lab., ARS, U.S. Dept. Agr., Beltsville, Md., 1976-79; mng. dir. Wedge Entomol. Rsch. Found., Washington, 1984—. Author: Moths of America North of Mexico, 4 vols., 1971, 74, 78, 86; editor: Moths of America North of Mexico, 6 vols., 1984—; author, editor: Check List Lepidoptera, 1983. Mem. AAAS, Entomol. Soc. Am. (Thomas Say award 1990), Lepidopterists' Soc. (pres. 1975-76), Soc. Systematic Biology (sec. 1966-68), Md. Entomol. Soc., Entomol. Soc. Can., Washington Biologists Field Club (pres. 1976-79). Office: Nat Mus History MRC-168 Syst Entomology Lab USDA 10 and Constitution NW Washington DC 20560

HODGKINSON, VIRGINIA ANN, national voluntary association administrator; b. N.Y.C., May 14, 1941; d. Francis and Virginia Ann (Wilson) Dillmeier; m. Aref O. Fadil, Nov. 9, 1963 (div. 1979); Sharon, Randal (dec.), Heather; m. Harold L. Hodgkinson, Sept. 25, 1980; stepchildren: Ann, Edith, Christine. BA summa cum laude, Fairleigh Dickinson U., 1963, MA magna cum laude, 1964; postgrad., U. Ill., summer 1963; PhD, So. Ill. U., 1976. Tchr., researcher, 1963-67; assoc. prof. English lit. Beirut U. Coll., Lebanon, 1968-74, asst. dean acad. devel., 1972-74; cons. Resource Ctr. for Planned Change Am. Assn. State Colls. and Univs., 1976; exec. dir. Nat. Inst. Ind. Colls. and Univs., 1977-82; exec. dir. Nat. Ctr. for Charitable Stats., Washington, 1982—, v.p. rsch. ind. sector, 1983—; adj. prof. grad. pub. policy program Georgetown U., 1989—; mem. adv. com. Interlegal USA, Inc., 1991—, Metlife Resources, 1989—; mem. adv. coun. Ctr. for Study of Philanthropy CUNY; mem. Aspen Inst. Nonprofit Sector Rsch. Fund, 1991—; mem. doctoral fellowship adv. com. Ind. U. Ctr. on Philanthropy, 1990—, mem. editorial adv. com. 1991—; bd. dirs. First Nonprofit Ins. Co.; bd. trustees Fairleigh Dickinson U., 1989—. Assoc. editor Jour. of Nonprofit Mgmt. and Leadership, 1990—; co-author: The Nonprofit Almanac, 1992, Giving and Volunteering in the United States, 1988, 90; coeditor: The Future of the Nonprofit Sector, 1989, Faith and Philanthropy, 1990, The Non-profit Sector in a Global Community, 1991; contbr. articles to profl. jours. U. Ill. fellow, 1963, asst. doctoral fellow So. Ill. U., 1974-76. Mem. Phi Kappa Phi. Office: Ind Sector 1828 L St NW Ste # 1200 Washington DC 20036

HODGKINSON, WILLIAM JAMES, marketing company executive; b. Bklyn., July 31, 1939; s. William James and Augusta Anne (Botka) H.; A.B., Bucknell U., 1961; M.B.A., Columbia U., 1963; m. Virginia Evelyn Humphreys, Sept. 7, 1963; 1 dau., Elizabeth Anne. Mktg. research analyst Singer Co., N.Y.C., 1963-66; asst. adminstrn. Writing Paper div. Am. Paper Inst., N.Y.C., 1966-67; market research mgr. Diners Club, N.Y.C., 1967-68; with Dun & Bradstreet Cos., Inc., 1968—, mgmt. cons. William E. Hill Co. div., N.Y.C., 1971-73, mgr. fin. services group Donnelley Mktg. div., Stamford, Conn., 1973-86, v.p., 1987—. Bd. dirs. Bklyn. Pub. Library br., 1974-79, Enlightenment Together, Inc., 1971-76; research coordinator Presdl. Task Force on Improving Small Bus., 1969-70; v.p., trustee Montessori Sch. Bklyn., 1975-79; trustee Greens Farms Congl. Ch., 1983-85; co-chmn. Save Fairfield Com., 1984—. Served with U.S. Army, 1963. Grantee Columbia U., 1962-63; recipient Brotherhood award Bucknell U., 1960. Mem. Bank Mktg. Assn., Am. Mktg. Assn., Direct Mail Mktg. Assn., Phi Lambda Theta. Congregationalist. (bd. deacons 1971-78, pres. 1977-78). Club: Princeton of N.Y. Contbr. articles to profl. jours. Home: 4454 Black Rock Tpke Fairfield CT 06430-1802 Office: Donnelley Mktg div Dun & Bradstreet 1515 Summer St Stamford CT 06905-5111

HODGMAN, RICHARD MOREY, accountant, financial planner; b. Worcester, Mass., Aug. 23, 1949; s. Morey L. and Ruth V. (Menacher) H.; m. Arlene G. Wassel, May 12, 1973; children: Kenneth, Linda, Jennifer. BSBA, Georgetown U., 1971. CPA. Jr. staff Arthur Anderson & Co., Newark, 1971-72; semi-sr. staff M. Sternlieb & Co., Hackensack, N.J., 1972-73; sr. mgr. staff Rich, Baker, Rosenkrantz & Berman, Maplewood, N.J., 1973-78; owner Richard M. Hodgman CPA, Westwood, N.J., 1978—; bd. dirs. Heightened Independence and Progress Inc., Englewood. Treas., Borough of Emerson, N.J., 1981-86. Fellow AICPAs, N.J. Soc. CPAs; mem. K.C. (grand knight 1982-83, lt. 1988—). Office: RM Hodgman CPA 139 3D Ave Westwood NJ 07675

HODGSON, ROBERT ARNOLD, geologist, consultant, researcher; b. Orange, N.J., Sept. 22, 1924; s. Arnold Holmes and Eleanor Waidler (McConnell) H.; m. Lorna Erica Biberthaler, Mar. 24, 1948; 1 child, Cynthia Ellen Hodgson Clampitt. BA in Geology, Antioch Coll., 1950; MS in Geology, Brigham Young U., 1951, Yale U., 1957; PhD in Geology, Yale U., 1958. Field geologist Ohio Oil Co., Salt Lake City, 1951-54; sr. rsch. assoc. Gulf Oil Corp., Pitts., 1958-83; cons. pvt. practice, Jamestown, Pa., 1983—; adj. prof. Pa. State U., Sharon, 1988, Thiel Coll., Greenville, Pa., 1990. Contbr. articles to profl. jours. With USMC, 1943-46, PTO. Fellow AAAS, Geol. Soc. Am., Am. Congress on Surveying and Mapping, The Explorers Club; mem. N.Y. Acad. Scis., Sigma Xi. Home and Office: 403 Liberty St Jamestown PA 16134-9103

HODGSON, W(ALTER) JOHN B(ARRY), surgeon; b. Middlesborough, England, Sept. 17, 1939; came to U.S., 1975; s. Walter Aggett and Constance Lillian (Nelson) H.; m. Jean C. Morgan, Apr. 20, 1967; children: Sean, Russell, Miranda. MB, BS, Charing Cross Med. Sch., London, 1964; M of Surgery, London U., 1976. Rotating intern, resident London U., 1964-75; surgeon Bronx (N.Y.) VA Med. Ctr., 1975-78, asst. chief surg. service, 1977-82; pvt. practice specializing in surgery Mt. Sinai Hosp., N.Y.C., 1978-81; chief gastro-intestinal surgery Westchester Med. Ctr., Valhalla, N.Y., 1981—; prof. surgery N.Y. Med. Coll., Valhalla, 1987—, course organizer for laparoscopic surgery, 1990-92. Contbr. articles to profl. jours.; editor: Liver Tumors: Multidisciplinary Management, 1987; inventor cavitron surg. technique for livor tumor surgery. Organizer, coach Larchmont Jr. Soccer League, 1977; mem. Larchmont Rep. Com., 1985. Cavitron Co. grantee, 1978, Cavitron Lasersonics grantee, 1987. Fellow ACS, Am. Coll. Gastroneterology; mem. N.Y. Sur. Soc. for Acad. Surgery, Am. Assn. Clin. Anatomists. Episcopalian. Club: Larchmont Yacht. Office: NY Med Coll Dept Surgery Munger Pavilion Valhalla NY 10595

HODNETT, CHARLES NICHOLAS, toxicologist; b. Buffalo, Dec. 7, 1942; s. Charles Edward and Martha Elmira (Simonds) H.; m. Janet Marie Penrod, Feb. 4, 1967. BS in Chemistry, Baldwin-Wallace Coll., 1964; PhD in Pharmacology, U. Vt., 1974. Diplomate Am. Bd. Forensic Toxicology. Asst. chemist Cuyahoga County Coroner's Office, Cleve., 1964-69; toxicologist Project Crash, Burlington, Vt., 1972-73, Vt. State Med. Examiner, Burlington, 1973-74, Milwaukee County Med. Examiner, Milw., 1974-78; clin. asst. prof. N.Y. Med. Coll., Valhalla, 1978—; dir. toxicology and forensic science Westchester County Dept. Labs. and Rsch., Valhalla, 1978—; adj. asst. prof. Med. Coll. Wis., Milw., 1975-78; mem. toxicology adv. bd. SUNY-Purchase, 1983-89; mem. Westchester County Stop DWI Bd., White Plains, N.Y., 1982—, Westchester County Criminal Justice Adv. Bd., White Plains, 1989—; presenter at profl. confs. Contbr. articles to Jour. Forensic Scis., Jour. Anat. Toxicology. NDEA fellow, 1970-72. Fellow Am. Acad. Forensic Scis. (chair 1983-88); mem. Soc. Forensic Toxicologists (pres. 1989), N.Y. Acad. Sci., Internat. Assn. Forensic Toxicologists. Home: 115 Crescent Ave Rye NY 10580-2638 Office: Westchester County Dept Labs & Rsch 2 Dana Rd Valhalla NY 10595

HODNETT, JOHN PHILLIP, investment analyst; b. Providence, R.I., Apr. 23, 1962; s. Robert Michael and Barbara Ann (Major) H. BS, Northeastern U., 1985; MBA, Columbia U., 1991. CPA. With Arthur Andersen & Co., Boston, 1985-88; fin. cons. Shearson Lehman, Boston, 1988-89; acquisition analyst N.Y.C., 1989-90; sr. investment analyst Am. Mutual Ins. Co., Providence, 1991—; cons. Lila Delman Real Estate, Narragansett, R.I., 1989—. Assn. Corp. Growth fellow, 1991. Mem. Providence Soc. Fin. Analysts, Beta Gamma Sigma. Home: 51 Ocean Rd Wakefield RI 02882

HOEBER, FRANCIS WALTER, government official; b. Phila., Oct. 20, 1942; s. Johannes U. and Elfriede (Fischer) H.; m. Ditta Baron, July 1, 1967; children: Max, Julian. AB, Columbia U., 1965. Field examiner NLRB, San Francisco, 1968-69; field examiner NLRB, Phila., 1970-75, supervisory examiner, 1975-76, asst. to regional dir. Region 4, 1976—. Vice chmn. Com. of Seventy, Phila., 1988—; pres. Center City Residents Assn., Phila., 1983-84. Lt. (j.g.) USCGR, 1965-68.

HOEFLIN, RONALD KENT, newsletter publisher, philosopher, psychometrician; b. Richmond Heights, Mo., Feb. 23, 1944; s. William Eugene and Mary Elizabeth (Dell) H. Student, Calif. Inst. Tech., 1962-63, U. Calif., Berkeley, 1966-67, U. N.C., 1970-71; BA, U. Minn., 1968, Shimer Coll., 1974; MLS, Ind. U., 1970; MA, New Sch. Social Rsch., 1979, PhD, 1987. With various librs., 1969-85; publisher, editor Triple Nine Soc., N.Y.C., 1985-89; publisher, editor, founder Top One Percent Soc., N.Y.C., 1989—. Designer (intelligence tests) Mega Test, 1985, Titan Test, 1990. Mem. Am. Philos. Assn. (Fifth Ann. Rockefeller prize 1988), Mensa, Mega Soc. (founder 1982), Prometheus Soc. (founder 1982). Libertarian. Office: PO Box 539 New York NY 10101

HOEHN-SARIC, RUDOLF, psychiatrist; b. Graz, Austria, Feb. 5, 1929; came to U.S., 1959; s. Werner and Wilhelmine (Wiltschnig) H.-S.; m. Evanne Loh, Oct. 14, 1960; children: Christopher, Edward, Alexander. MD, U. Graz, 1954; diploma in psychiatry, McGill U., Montreal, Que., Can., 1959. Resident in psychiatry Allan Meml. Inst. and Verdun Protestant Hosp., Montreal, 1956-58; fellow in clin. pharmacology Sch. of Medicine Johns Hopkins U., Balt., 1958-59, mem. Phipps Psychotherapy Rsch. Unit, Sch. Medicine, 1962-74, instr. in psychiatry, 1962-64, asst. prof., 1964-71, assoc. prof., 1972-92; prof., 1992—; dir. psychiat. outpatient svcs. Johns Hopkins U., Balt., 1977—, dir. anxiety clinic, 1978—, co-dir. behavioral medicine clinic, 1977—; resident in neuropsychiatry U. Vienna, 1959-60; rsch. psychiatrist Springfield State Hosp., 1960-61; mem. editorial bd. Jour. Anxiety Disorders; cons. Embassy of Fed. Republic Germany, Washington. Contbr. articles to profl. publs. Grantee NIMH. Fellow Am. Psychiat. Assn., Am. Psychopathol. Assn.; mem. AAAS, Med.-Chirurgical Faculty Md., Soc. Biol. Pshcyiatry, Am. Psychosomatic Soc. Office: Johns Hopkins Hosp 115 Meyer Blvd Baltimore MD 21205

HOELZEMAN, RONALD GEORGE, electrical engineering educator; b. Pitts., Oct. 6, 1940; s. George and Grace (Reagle) H.; m. Bonnie Marie Hall, Aug. 16, 1974; 1 child, Barbara. BSEE, U. Pitts., 1964, MSEE, 1967, PhD, 1970. Engr. Westinghouse Electric Co., Pitts., 1964-67; teaching asst. U. Pitts., 1967-69, prof., 1970—, assoc. chmn. elec. engring. dept., 1980—; lectr. Am. U. Beirut, Lebanon, 1969-70. Recipient Outstanding Faculty award Dow Chem. Co., 1976. Fellow IEEE (v.p. edn. 1987-88, bd. dirs. 1985-88, Disting. Svc. award Computer Soc. 1987). Office: U Pitts Elec Engring Dept 348 BEH Pittsburgh PA 15261

HOENIGSWALD, HENRY MAX, linguist, educator; b. Breslau, Germany, Apr. 17, 1915; s. Richard and Gertrud (Grunwald) H.; m. Gabriele Schoepflich, Dec. 26, 1944; children: Frances Gertrude, Susan Ann. Student, U. Munich, 1932-33, U. Zurich, 1933-34, U. Padua, 1934-36; D.Litt., U. Florence, 1936, Perfezionamento, 1937; L.H.D. (hon.), Swarthmore Coll., 1981, U. Pa., 1988; M.A. (hon.), U. Pa., 1971. Staff mem. Istituto Studi Etruschi, Florence, 1936-38; lectr., research asst., instr. Yale U., 1939-42, 44-45; lectr., instr. Hartford Sem. Found., 1942-43, 45-46; lectr. Hunter Coll., 1942-43, 46; lectr. charge Army specialized tng. U. Pa., Phila., 1943-44, assoc. prof., 1948-59, prof. linguistics, 1959-85, prof. emeritus, 1985—, chmn. dept. linguistics, 1963-70, co-chmn., 1978-79, mem. Ctr. for Cultural Studies, 1987—, chmn. Caldwell Prize com., 1989-91; P-4 Fgn. Service Inst., Dept. State, 1946-47; asso. prof. U. Tex., 1947-48; sr. linguist Deccan Coll., India, 1955; Fulbright lectr., Kiel, summer 1968, Oxford U., 1976-77; corp. vis. com. fgn. lits. and linguistics MIT, 1968-74; chmn. overseers com. to visit dept. linguistics Harvard U., 1978-84; vis. assoc. prof. U. Mich., 1946, 52, Princeton U., 1959-60; vis. assoc. prof. Georgetown U., 1952-53, 54, Collitz prof., 1955; vis. prof. Yale U., 1961-62, U. Mich., 1968; mem. Seminar, Columbia U., 1965—; vis. staff mem., Leuven, 1986; fellow St. John's Coll., Oxford U., 1976-77; del. Comparative Linguistics Internat. Rsch. and Exchs. Bd., 1986—; cons. Etymological Dictionary of Old High German, 1980—; Poultney lectr. Johns Hopkins U., 1991; co-promotor, Leuven, 1992. Author: Spoken Hindustani, 1946-47, Language Change and Linguistic Reconstruction, 1960, Studies in Formal Historical Linguistics, 1973; Editor: Am. Oriental Series, 1954-58, The European Background of American Linguistics, 1979, (with L. Wiener) Biological Metaphor and Cladistic Classification, 1987, (with M.R. Key) General and American Ethnolinguistics, 1989; assoc. editor Indian Jour. Linguistics, 1977—; cons. editor Jour. History of Ideas, 1978—; adv. bd. Lang. and Style, 1968—, Diachronica, 1984—, Lynx, 1988—, Bryn Mawr Classical Rev., 1990—; mem. editorial bd. Oxford Internat. Ency. Linguistics, 1986-91. Am. Council Learned Socs. fellow, 1942-43, 44, Guggenheim fellow, 1950-51, Newberry Library fellow, 1956, NSF and Center Advanced Study Behavioral Scis. fellow, 1962-63, Faculty fellow Modern Langs. Coll. House, 1990-91; Festschrift in his honor, 1987. Corr. fellow British Acad.; mem. AAAS, NAS, Am. Philos. Soc. (rsch. com. 1972-84, libr. com. 1984—, chmn. 1988-91, membership com. class IV 1984-90, chmn. 1987-90, exec. com. 1988—, Henry Allen Moe prize 1991), Am. Acad. Arts and Sci., N.Y. Acad. Scis., Linguistic Soc. Am. (pres. 1958), Am. Oriental Soc. (editor 1954-58, pres. 1966-67), Philol. Soc. (London), Linguistic Soc. India, Societas Linguistica Europaea, Linguistics Assn. Gt. Britain, Internat. Soc. Hist. Linguistics, Indogermanische Gesellschaft, Am. Philol. Assn., Archaeol. Inst. Am., Società di linguistica italiana, Henry Sweet Soc., Studienkreis Geschichte der Sprachwissenschaft, N.Am. Assn. History of Lang. Scis. Home: 908 Westdale Ave Swarthmore PA 19081-1804 Office: U Pa 618 Williams Hall Philadelphia PA 19104-6305

HOEPER, BONNIE MAE, nurse; b. Wausau, Wis., July 29, 1940; d. Frederick Walter and Mae Alice (Hoeper) Schaumberger; children: Alan, Kimberly, Lynn. BS in Phys. Edn. magna cum laude, Springfield (Mass.)

Coll., 1963; AS in Nursing, Mohegan Community Coll., 1983. RN. Instr. phys. edn. Augustana Coll., Sioux Falls, S.D., 1963-65, Cutler Jr. High Sch., Groton, Conn., 1965-66; staff nurse Lawrence and Meml. Hosp., New London, Conn., 1983-84, 88-92, Stonington (Conn.) Vis. Nurses Assn., New London, Conn., 1984-87; staff nurse emergency rm. So. Maine Med. ctr., Biddeford, 1992—; instr. CPR Am. Heart Assn., Conn., 1983—, trainer CPR, 1984—. Supt. Sunday sch. Road Ch. Congl., Stonington, 1978-80, dir. Christian edn., 1980-81. Mem. Am. Assn. Critical Care Nurses. Home: PO Box 152 22 Federal St Wiscasset ME 04578

HOEPPER, CHARLES THOMAS, financial executive; b. Ridgewood, N.Y., Sept. 14, 1949; s. John Joseph and Rita (Griffin) H.; m. Noreen Graiani, May 21, 1977; children: Scott J., Laura E. BS in Acctg., U. Ill., 1971; MBA, St. John's U., 1978. CPA N.Y. Acctg. supr. Merrill Lynch & Co., N.Y.C., 1975-80; sr. auditor Ernst & Young, N.Y.C., 1978-80; sr. mgr. planning Continental Group Inc., Stamford, Conn., 1981-84; dir. fin. MCI, Ryebrook, N.Y., 1985—. Lt. USN, 1971-75. Mem. AICPA, NAA, NYSCPA. Roman Catholic. Office: MCI 5 International Dr Port Chester NY 10573-1058

HOERNER, GEORGE MILTON, JR., chemical engineering educator; b. Hershey, Pa., Feb. 12, 1929; s. George M. Sr. and Emma (Sutcliffe) H.; m. Margaret Dewart, June 22, 1957; children: Eric, Nancy. BSChemE, Lafayette Coll., 1951; MEd, U. Rochester, 1958; PhD, Lehigh U., 1963. Registered profl. engr., Pa. Process engr. to shift supr. E.I. duPont de Nemours, Paulin, N.J./Rochester, N.Y., 1951-57; asst. prof. Lafayette Coll., Easton, Pa., 1958-64, assoc. prof., 1964-76, prof., dept. head, 1976-91, prof. emeritus, 1991—; cons. Sun Oil Co., Marcus Heck, Pa., 1966-67, J.T. Baker Chem. Co., Phillipsburg, N.J., 1968-83. Bd. dirs., pres. Easton Area Sch. Bd., 1973-83, Colonial Northampton Sch. Bd., Nazareth, Pa., 1973-83. With U.S. Army, 1954-56. Sci. faculty fellow, NSF, Lehigh U., 1962-63. Fellow Am. Inst. Chem. Engrs.; mem. Instrument Soc. Am. (sr. mem.), Am. Soc. Engring. Edn., Nat. Soc. Profl. Engrs. Office: Dept Chem Engring Lafayette College Easton PA 18042

HOERSCH, ALICE L., college dean; b. Abington, Pa., Oct. 22, 1950; d. Albert Jr. and Alice Louise Johnson H. AB, Bryn Mawr Coll., 1972; MA, Johns Hopkins U., 1974, PhD, 1977. From asst. prof. to prof. of Geology La Salle U., Phila., 1977—, assoc. dean sch. arts and scis., 1986—; vis. lectr. Bryn Mawr (Pa.) Coll., 1980; cons. Office Atty. Gen., Harrisburg, Pa., 1988-89. Contbr. articles to profl. jours. Penrose Rsch. grantee Geol. Soc. Am., 1974; Gilman fellow Johns Hopkins U., 1972-77; recipient Emma Osborne award Bryn Mawr, 1972. Mem. AAAS, Geol. Soc. Am., Mineral. Soc. Am., Phila. Geol. Soc. (pres. 1986-88, sec.-treas. 1980-82), Nat. Assn. Geol. Tchrs., Am. Assn. Higher Edn. Office: La Salle U 1900 W Olney Ave Philadelphia PA 19141-1199

HOEXTER, ROLF, management and engineering consultant; b. Giessen, Germany, Sept. 30, 1927; came to U.S., 1940; s. Frederick and Anne (Kuhn) H.; m. Corinne Rosenfelder Katz, Dec. 25, 1955; children: Vivien, Michael F. B Aero. Engring., NYU, 1949, MME, 1951. Registered profl. engr., N.Y., N.J.; cert. mgmt. cons. Jr. engr. Am. Power Jet Co., Montclair, N.J., 1949; asst. sales engr. Eugene J. Brandt & Co., N.Y.C., 1949-50; sales engr. Chas. S. Wood & Co., Inc., N.Y.C., 1950-51; project engr. Curtiss Wright Corp., Wood Ridge, N.J., 1951-57; chief engr. Mosstype Corp., Waldwick, N.J., 1959-80; plant mgr. ThermaSol, Ltd., Leonia, N.J., 1981-82; v.p. mfg. and engring. The Nycal Co., Inc., South Hackensack, N.J., 1981-82; mgmt. and engring. cons. Milestone Mgmt. Group, Cranford, N.J., 1983-84; prin., sr. cons. East Hill Group, Englewood, 5, 1985—. Contbr. articles to profl. publs.; patentee air and oil separator, printing machinery. Pres., trustee Flat Rock Brook Nature Assn., Englewood, 1973-78, hon. trustee, 1991-92; trustee Dwight-Englewood Sch., 1976-82. With USAAF, 1946-47. Mem. ASME, Am. Soc. for Quality Control, Inst. Mgmt. Cons., N.Y. Pers. Computer Users Group, Stuyvesant Yacht Club (life), Chatham Yacht Club (Mass.).

HOF, LISELOTTE BERTHA, biochemist; b. Cologne, Germany, Jan. 1, 1937; came to U.S., 1967; d. Heinrich and Hedwig (Boemann) Hof; m. Peter B. Weber, Oct. 5, 1972. MS, U. Cologne, 1963, PhD, 1965. Postdoctoral fellow mental health rsch. inst. U. Mich., Ann Arbor, 1967-68; NIH postdoctoral fellow dept. pediatrics U. Chgo., 1968-70; asst. prof. dept. physiol. chemistry U. Bochum (Fed. Republic Germany), Germany, 1970-72; asst. prof. dept. biochemistry Albany (N.Y.) Med. Coll., 1972-78, assoc. prof. dept. biochemistry, 1978—; assoc. prof. biomed. sci. Sch. Pub. Health, SUNY, Albany, 1988—; women's liaison officer Albany Med. Coll., 1978—, v.p. faculty orgn., 1984-90, v.p. faculty senate, 1989—. Contbr. articles to profl. jours. V.p. faculty orgn. Albany Med. Coll., 1984-90, v.p. faculty senate, 1991—. Grantee Sigma Delta Epsilon, rsch. grantee NIH, 1977, 78, 88, Nat. Multiple Sclerosis Soc., 1983. Mem. AAAS, Am. Chem. Soc. (alternate councilor 1985-89, mem. exec. coun. ea. N.Y. chpt. 1985-88, pub. rels. chair Ea. N.Y. chpt. 1987-89), Am. Soc. Biochem. Molecular Biology, Am. Soc. Neurochemistry (Pub. affairs com. 1987-89), Soc. Complex Carbohydrates, N.Y. Acad. Sci., Assn. Women in Sci (co-pres. Albany chpt. 1991—). Office: Albany Med Coll A-10 47 New Scotland Ave Albany NY 12208-3412

HOFF, HENRY BAINBRIDGE, accountant; b. Rockville Centre, N.Y., Feb. 10, 1946; s. Arthur Bainbridge and Mary Augusta (Smith) H. BA, Yale U., 1967; JD, Fordham U., 1974. CPA, N.Y.; cert. genealogist. Sr. Arthur Young & Co., CPAs, N.Y.C., 1974-78; sr., mgr., ptnr. Reiner & Hoff, CPAs and predecessor firms, Darien, Conn., 1979—; Trustee Bd. Cert. Genealogists, Washington, 1980-89. Co-author: The Tangier Smith Family, 1978, Rubens et Ses Descendants, Vol. 4, 1985, The Roosevelt Family in America, 1990; editor The N.Y. Geneal. and Biog. Record, 1987—; contbr. geneal. articles to profl. jours. Sgt. U.S. Army, 1968-70, Vietnam. Fellow Am. Soc. Genealogists (pres. 1986-89); mem. AICPA, Conn. Soc. CPAs, N.Y. State Soc. CPAs, N.Y. Geneal. and Biog. Soc. (trustee 1985—), Descendants of Illegitimate Sons and Daus. of Kings of Britain (pres. 1988—), Koninklijk Nederlandsch Genootschap voor Geslacht en Wapenkunde (corr.). Episcopalian. Home: 67 Park Ave New York NY 10016-2557 Office: Reiner & Hoff CPAs 745 Boston Post Rd Darien CT 06820-4720

HOFF, PETER LEROY, architectural designer; b. Queens, N.Y., Oct. 15, 1940; s. Leroy Peter and Mary Louise (Taylor) H.; m. Patti L. Hoff, Nov. 17, 1968; children: Pamelia, Jeffrey, Phillip, Joseph, Robert. AA, Trenton Jr. Coll., 1958; BS, U. Md., 1960. Prodn. control analyst supr. Burroughs Crop., Plainfield, N.J., 1966-70; architectural estimator J.H. Buss Assocs., Plainfield, 1970-72; sr. estimator, project mgr. Gumina Bldg. and Constrn., New Brunswick, N.J., 1972-75; office mgr. Am. Sealcut Corp., West New York, N.J., 1975-77; sales engr. Standard Pipe Protection, Kearny, N.J., 1977-79; sr. chief archtl. engr. Capehorn, Inc., Paramus, N.J., 1979-81; sr. project mgr. W.F.C. Herbert Constrn. Co., N.Y.C., 1981-84; archtl. cons. Alexander Wolf and Son, Inc., N.Y.C., 1984-86; project dir., v.p. Corbel Constrn., N.Y.C., 1986-88; sr. estimator, cons. Crow Constrn., N.Y.C., 1988—; archtl. cons. Readington Twp. Planning Bd., Whitehouse Sta., N.Y., 1968-74. Served as staff sgt. U.S. Army, 1962-66. Home: 52 Mcclellan St Newark NJ 07114-2112

HOFF, SAMUEL BOYER, political science educator; b. Williamsport, Pa., June 7, 1957; s. Samuel Romberger and J. Mattie (Schultz) H.; m. Phyllis Rose Oliveto, Aug. 16, 1986. BA in Polit. Sci., Susquehanna U., 1979; MA in Polit. Sci., Am. U , 1981, SUNY, Stony Brook, 1983; PhD in Polit. Sci., SUNY, Stony Brook, 1987. Instr. SUNY, Stony Brook, 1982-86; asst. prof. SUNY, Geneseo, 1987-88; asst. prof. dept. history and polit. sci. Del. State Coll., Dover, 1989-92, assoc. prof. dept. history and polit. sci., 1992—; adj. instr. dept. social sci. N.Y. Inst. Tech., Old Westbury, N.Y., 1986; adj. asst. prof. Wittenberg U., Springfield, Ohio, 1987; vis. asst. prof. dept. govt. and politics Ohio Wesleyan U., Delaware, 1986-87; vis. asst. prof. Wichita (Kans.) State U., 1988-89; congl. intern U.S. Rep. Allen Ertel, Washington, 1978; mem. canvass staff Clean Water Action Project, Washington, 1980; rsch. asst. subcom. on human resources U.S. Ho. of Reps., Washington, 1980; asst. Senator Jacob Javits, Stony Brook, 1983-85. Contbr. articles to profl. jours. Committeeman Suffolk County Dems., L.I., 1984-86; presdl. candidate Dem. Party, 1988, Independent Party, 1992. Freedoms Found. scholar, 1990. Mem. Am. Polit. Sci. Assn., Acad. Polit. Sci., Nat. Social Sci. Assn., Northeastern Polit. Sci. Assn., Midwest Polit. Sci. Assn., Western Polit. Sci. Assn., So. Polit. Sci. Assn., Nat. Capital Area Polit. Sci. Assn., Pa. Polit. Sci. Assn., N.Y. Polit. Sci. Assn. Lutheran. Home: 31 Spruance Rd Dover DE 19901-4048 Office: Del State Coll Dept History Polit Science Dover DE 19901

HOFFERT, PAUL WASHINGTON, surgeon; b. N.Y.C., Feb. 22, 1923; s. Charles and Rose (Isaacs) H.; m. Rosolyn Sheiman, Apr. 20, 1947; children: Marvin Jay, Renée Beth, Deborah Susan. AB with honors, Columbia U., 1942; MD, cum laude, Yale U., 1945. Diplomate Am. Bd. Surgery, Am. Bd. Abdominal Surgery. Intern New Haven (Ct.) Hosp., 1945-46; fellow radiology Hosp. U. Pa., 1948-49; resident surgery VA Hosp., Bronx, N.Y., 1949-53; pvt. practice medicine specializing in gen. and vascular surgery, Yonkers, N.Y., 1953—; attending surgeon Yonkers Gen. Hosp., 1953—, chief of surgery, 1987—; sr. gen. and vascular surgeon St. Joseph's Hosp., 1953—; assoc. vascular surgeon Montefiore Hosp., 1965—; asst. prof. surgery Albert Einstein Coll., 1955—. Contbr. articles to profl. jours. Capt. U.S. Army Med. Corps, 1946-48. Recipient citation Am. Cancer Soc., 1960. Fellow Am. Coll. Surgeons (pres. Westchester, N.Y. chpt.), Am. Coll. Angiology N.Y. Acad. Medicine, Westchester Acad. Medicine (charter), Clin. Soc. N.Y. Diabetes Assn.; mem. N.Y. Surgical Soc., N.Y. Soc. Cardiovascular Surgery, Am. Zionist Orgn. (life) (past pres. Lincoln Park, Yonkers region), Phi Beta Kappa, Alpha Omega Alpha, Phi Delta Epsilon, Masons. Home: 1450 Flagler Dr Mamaroneck NY 10543-4605

HOFFMAN, ALAN JAY, lawyer; b. Phila., Aug. 31, 1948; s. Heinz Julius and Sylvia (Wise) H.; m. Judith Carol Greenberg, June 20, 1981; children: Jennifer, Lauren, Allison. BBA, Temple U., 1970; JD, Villanova U., 1973. Bar: Pa. 1973, U.S. Dist. Ct. (ea. dist.) Pa. 1973, U.S. Dist. Ct. Del. 1973, U.S. Ct. Appeals (3rd cir.) 1973, Del. 1977, U.S. Supreme Ct. 1984, D.C. 1990. Asst. U.S. atty. U.S. Dept. Justice, Wilmington, Del., 1973-78; ptnr. Dilworth, Paxson, Kalish & Kauffman, Phila., 1979—, mem. exec. mgmt. com., 1989-90, chmn. new bus. com., 1990-91; ptnr. Blank, Rome, Comisky and McCauley, Phila., 1992—; lectr. Widener Del. Law Sch., Wilmington, 1974. Co-editor, contbr. Villanova Law Review, 1972-73; contbr. articles to profl. jours. Bd. dirs. Men's Club Temple Adath Israel, Merion, Pa. 1987-88. Recipient Atty. Gen.'s Spl. Commendation U.S. Dept. Justice, Washington, 1977. Mem. ABA, Pa. Bar Assn., Fed. Bar Assn., Phila. Bar Assn., Del. Bar Assn., Assn. Trial Lawyers Am., Del. Trial Lawyers Assn., Pa. Trial Lawyers Asssn., White Manor Country Club (bd. dirs. 1988-90, admissions chmn. 1989—, 1st v.p. 1990—). Office: Blank Rome Comisky and McCauley 4 Penn Center Pla Philadelphia PA 19103

HOFFMAN, ALLAN STUART, lawyer; b. Boca Raton, Fla., Feb. 19, 1945; s. Elihu Bernard and Selma (Lewbel) H.; m. Karla Leigh Rakoff, Dec. 26, 1971; 1 child, Matthew Douglas. BSBA, Syracuse U., 1966; JD, U. Akron, 1969. Bar: Ohio 1969, U.S. Dist. Ct. (D.C. dist.) 1971, U.S. Ct. Appeals (D.C. cir.) 1971, U.S. Ct. Appeals (2d cir.) 1986, U.S. Supreme Ct. 1975. Pros. atty. antitrust div. U.S. Dept. Justice, Washington, 1969-73; assoc. Rowley & Scott, Washington, 1973-79, Seymour & Dudley, Washington, 1979-81; prin. Seymour, Seefried & Hoffman/Seymour & Hoffman, Washington, 1981-84; ptnr. Chapman, Duff & Paul/Rose, Schmidt, Chapman, Duff & Hasley, Washington, 1984-86; prin. Seymour & Hoffman, Chartered, Washington, 1986—. Mem. ABA (antitrust, litigation sects.). Home: 6921 Clifton Rd Clifton VA 22024-1525 Office: Seymour & Hoffman Chartered 4900 Massachusetts Ave NW Washington DC 20016-4358

HOFFMAN, ANNETTE KATHLEEN, college admissions counselor; b. Rochester, N.Y., Apr. 16, 1963; d. Norman Andrew and Mary Theresa (Cahill) H. BA in Sociology, SUNY, Oswego, 1985; MEd in Counseling, Suffolk U., 1989. Cert. guidance counselor, N.Y., Mass. Intern peer career counselor SUNY, Oswego, 1983-85; program coord. Leukemia Soc. Am., Rochester, N.Y., 1985-86; fellow, admissions asst. Suffolk U., Boston, 1987-89; admissions counselor Niagara U., Niagara Falls, N.Y., 1989—; mentor Career Beginnings Program, Boston, 1987-88. Vol. friend Compeer, Niagara Falls, 1991; bereavement counselor Niagara Hospice, Niagara Falls, 1991. Mem. Mental Health Assn. in Niagara County, AACD, Am. Sch. Counselors Assn., Coll. Student Pers. Assn. Roman Catholic. Home: 727 Cayuga St Apt 8 Lewiston NY 14092-1740

HOFFMAN, AUDREY IRIS, meeting planner; b. Troy, N.Y., Feb. 16, 1938; d. Sidney and Marica Joan (Rosengard) Sebelowitz; m. Harold Hoffman, Mar. 19, 1961; children: Brian, Lisa. BS in Elem. Edn., Russell Sage Coll., 1959, MS in Elem. Edn., 1961. Tchr. first grade Shenendehowa Cen. Sch., Elnora, N.Y., 1959-62; tchr. second grade Hebrew Acad., Albany, N.Y., 1968-81; meeting planner Audrey Hoffman Enterprises Inc., Albany, 1982—; exec. dir. Capital Speakers Bur., Albany,1 985-91. Mem. Albany-Colonie C. of C. (bd. dirs. 1987-91), Soc. Assn. Exec. of Upstate N.Y., Albany County Conv. & Visitors Bur., Meeting Cons. Network. Home and Office: 12 Prospect Ter Albany NY 12208-3010

HOFFMAN, DAN LAWRENCE, theatrical consultant, engineer; b. Reading, Pa., Oct. 15, 1946; s. Lawrence Bailey and Grace (Wegman) H.; m. Nellina Lombardo, Apr. 6, 1981; 1 child, Dylan Hildreth. BFA in Theater, Carnegie Mellon U., 1968. Tech. dir. Gutherie Theater, Mpls., 1968-71; instr. McGill U., Montreal, Quebec, 1971-75, Concordia U., Montreal, 1975-78; mgr. SGA Scenery, Bronx, N.Y., 1978-83; prin., v.p. Showtech Inc., Norwalk, Conn., 1983—; instr. theater dept. SUNY, Purchase. Mem. Illuminating Engring. Soc., U.S. Inst. for Theater Tech., Indsl. Computer Soc. Home: 2 Birch St Norwalk CT 06851-5106 Office: Showtech Inc PO Box 210 Norwalk CT 06856-0210

HOFFMAN, DAVID ALLEN, counselor, student affairs professional; b. Ft. Lauderdale, Fla., Apr. 10, 1962; s. Stanley Murray and Janet (Elwell) H. BA in Psychology, Eckerd Coll., St. Petersburg, Fla., 1984; MS in Counseling, Fla. State U., 1986; postgrad., U. Md., 1988—. Project tech. Psychol. and Family Cons., Tallahassee, Fla., 1985; mental health tech. Apalachee Community Mental Health Svcs., Tallahassee, 1985-86; group coord., mental health therapist Johns Hopkins Health System Francis Scott Key Med. Ctr., Balt., 1986-88; addictions therapist Johns Hopkins Health System Homewood Hosp., Balt., 1988-89; teaching asst. career devel. ctr. U. Md., College Park, 1990, evaluation cons. human rels. programs, 1990, rsch. cons. career devel. ctr., 1989-90, grad. asst. III counseling and personnel svcs., 1990-91, teaching asst. office of jud. programs, student honor coun., 1991—; doctoral intern Loyola Coll., Balt., 1991—; rsch. cons. Ctr. for Rsch. in Faith and Moral Devel. Candler Sch. Theology Emory U., Atlanta, 1991—. Active Baltimoreans United in Leadership Devel., 1988-90, Brown Meml. Park Ave. Presbyn. Ch., Balt., 1987—. Mem. AACD, Am. Coll. Pers. Assn., Assn. for Religious and Values Issues in Counseling, Nat. Assn. for Student Pers. Adminstrs., Omicron Delta Kappa. Democrat. Home: 406 Ridge Rd #11 Greenbelt MD 20770 Office: Counseling and Personnel U Md 3214 Benjamin Bldg College Park MD 20742

HOFFMAN, DAVID JOHN, physiologist; b. New London, Conn., Sept. 22, 1944; s. John Leslie and Margaret Amy (Stokes) H.; m. Suzanne Elizabeth O'Clair, Aug. 20, 1966; children: Michael David, James Stephen. BS, McGill U., 1966; PhD, U. Md., 1971. Instr. in genetics, embryology U. Md., College Park, 1968-71; postdoctoral fellow/NIH Oak Ridge Nat. Lab., Oak Ridge, Tenn., 1971-73; faculty, biology dept. Boston Coll., Newton, Mass., 1973-74; sr. staff physiologist Health Effects Rsch. Lab/U.S. EPA, Cin., 1974-76; rsch. physiologist Patuxent Wildlife Rsch. Ctr./USDI, Laurel, Md., 1976—. Mem. editorial bd. Archives of Environ. Contamination and Toxicology jour., 1986—, Jour. Toxicology and Environ. Health, 1989—, Environ. Toxicology and Chemistry, 1990—; contbr. chpts. to books, articles to profl. jours. Recipient dissertation fellowship U. Md., College Park, 1970, spl. achievement award USDI, 1990. Mem. Teratology Soc., Soc. Environ. Chemistry and Toxicology (editoral bd. 1990—), Soc. Exptl. Biology and Medicine, Soc. Toxicology, AAAS, Phi Sigma Soc. Home: 2622 Felter Ln Bowie MD 20715-2503 Office: Patuxent Wildlife Rsch Ctr USDI Laurel MD 20708

HOFFMAN, DAVID ROBERT, library director; b. Brownwood, Tex., Sept. 28, 1934; s. Albert W. and Adelaide (McKee) H. Student, Daniel Baker Coll., 1951-52; BA, Davis & Elkins Coll., 1954; MLS, Case Western Res. U., 1955. Adminstrv. asst. Wis. Free Libr. Commn., Madison, 1959-63; head info. svc. ALA, Chgo., 1963-66, asst. dir. internat. rels., 1966-68; coord., dep. state libr., state libr. Mont. State Libr., Helena, 1968-70; law cons. Oreg. State Libr., Salem, 1974; libr. manpower study dir. U. Wis., Madison, 1974-75; coord. interlibr. co. State Libr. of Pa., Harrisburg, 1975-81, dir. libr. svcs., 1981—, acting state libr., 1987-88; v.p. PALINET, Phiila., 1988-90. Editor Wis. Libr. Bull., 1959-63; contbr. articles to profl. jours. Mem. artistic policy com. Harrisburg Symphony Orch., 1988—; bd. dirs., sec. Market Sq. Concerts, Harrisburg, 1988—; sec., v.p. Harrisburg Civic Opera Assn., 1988-90; dir. Mid-Atlantic Preservation Svc., Bethlehem, Pa., 1985-90. With U.S. Army, 1957-59. Coun. on Libr. Resources fellow, 1969; recipient Sec.'s Commendation, Pa. Dept. of Edn., 1989. Mem. ALA (life, coun. 1970-71, nominating com. 1973, standards com. 1988—), Pa. Libr. Assn. (chair orgn. and by-laws com.). Democrat. Office: State Libr of Pa PO Box 1601 Harrisburg PA 17105-1601

HOFFMAN, DONALD BERTRAND, forensic toxicologist, educator, consultant; b. N.Y.C., May 3, 1939; s. David and Tillie (Miller) H. B.A. in Chemistry, NYU, 1959; M.A. in Chemistry, 1960, Ph.D. in Chemistry, Columbia U., 1967. Diplomate Am. Bd. Forensic Toxicology; cert. clin. toxicologist. Rsch. assoc. Jewish Chronic Disease Hosp., N.Y.C., 1967-68; NIMH postdoctoral fellow dept. psychiatry NYU Med. Ctr., 1968-69; sr. chemist Office Chief Med. Examiner, N.Y.C., 1969-87; rsch. scientist, 1987—; asst. prof. dept. forensic medicine, NYU Med. Ctr., 1977—; adj. asst. prof. John Jay Coll. Criminal Justice, N.Y.C., 1976—; mem. adv. bd. Fire Sci. Inst. John Jay Coll.; pvt. cons. in forensic toxicology; lectr. in field. Contbr. articles to profl. jours. Recipient Cert. Appreciation Victor Collymore Inst., N.Y.C. Fire Dept., 1981. Mem. Am. Acad. Forensic Scis., N.Y. Acad. Scis., Soc. Forensic Toxicologists (sec. 1975-76, charter mem.), Internat. Assn. Forensic Toxicologists, N.Y. Soc. Forensic Scis., Rsch. Soc. Sigma Xi, Soc. Med. Jurisprudence, Phi Beta Kappa. Jewish. Avocation: reading. Home: 1939 Grand Concourse Bronx NY 10453-4917 Office: Dept Toxicology Office of Chief Med Examiner 520 1st Ave New York NY 10016

HOFFMAN, E(ARL) KENNETH, educator; b. Rahway, N.J., Sept. 19, 1944; s. Earl Kenneth and Helen (Caikowski) H.; m. Candyce R. Jenkins, Apr. 27, 1970. BS, Fairleigh Dickinson U., 1966; MFA, NYU, 1968, MA, 1977, PhD, 1983. With WNET-TV Channel 13, N.Y.C., 1967-68; editor motion picture films W&W Films Inc., N.Y.C., 1971-72; assoc. prof. Seton Hall U., South Orange, N.J., 1972—; interim chmn. Seton Hall U., Dept. Communication, 1991. Author: Computer Graphics Applications, 1990; photographer (book) Legacy Through the Lens, 1987; writer/dir. (motion picture animation): Leaves in Space, 1976 (N.Y. Film Festival); cinematographer (motion picture): Treasures of the Past, 1974. Mem. Hist. Preservation Com., Morristown, N.J., 1991—. Lt. U.S. Army, 1968-70, Vietnam. 010N.J. Dept. Edn. grantee, 1984, 86. Mem. Assn. for Computing Machinery. Office: Seton Hall U 400 S Orange Ave South Orange NJ 07079

HOFFMAN, EDWARD MICHAEL, management and technology consultant, software developer, educator, author; b. Bklyn., Aug. 30, 1945. BS in Indsl. Adminstrn., New Haven Coll., 1967; MS in Computer Sci., Pratt Inst., 1973. Pres., chief exec. officer Dynamic Systems Resource, N.Y.C., 1973-85; chief operating officer Inference Tech. Corp., Greenwich, Conn., 1985-87; pres., chmn. Info. Tech. Mgmt., Inc., White Plains, N.Y., 1987—; asst. prof. CUNY, 1973-77; lectr. New Sch. Social Rsch., N.Y.C., 1975-92; cons. numerous cos., ical govts. and govtl. agys.; speaker numerous profl. seminars. Author (profl. seminars) Advanced Teleprocessing Network Configuration, Database Design and Package Selection, Corporate Data Modeling and Analysis.

HOFFMAN, JEFFREY MARC, motion picture director; b. Boston, Dec. 21, 1954; s. Harvey Hoffman and Ellaine (Quint) Rose; m. Elizabeth Guidry, Mar. 25, 1989. BFA, Syracuse U., 1977. Dir. photography Gov-Bud Prodns., L.A., 1978-88; freelance dir. photography ABC News, N.Y.C., 1980-85; dir. Nexus Network, N.Y.C. and L.A., 1991—; dir. photography film unit Los Angeles County Sheriff's Dept., L.A., 1985-87. Recipient Hatch silver award Boston Ad Club, 1989, Neba gold award, 1989, Clio nominee, 1989, 91. Mem. Internat. Alliance Theatrical Stage Employees and Technicians (dir. photography), Sigma Chi. Libertarian. Home: 146 Reade St New York NY 10013-3848

HOFFMAN, KARLA ANN, mathematics educator; b. Burlington, Vt., May 19, 1953; d. Donald Elwood and Lenora Mae (McElhiney) H. Student, W.Va. Wesleyan Coll., 1971-73; BS in Math., Towson State U., 1975; M Ednl. Adminstrn., U. Mass., 1986, cert. advanced grad. study, 1988. Tchr. math. Oxon Hill (Md.) High Sch., 1975-80; tchr. Harriet Tubman Mid. Sch., Portland, Oreg., 1980-84, chmn. dept., 1982-84; teaching and adminstrv. asst. grad. program ednl. adminstrn. U. Mass., Boston, 1984-88, instr. math. various programs, 1987-89; asst. prof. math. Calif. U. of Pa., 1989—; vis. cons. for mid. and high sch. math. tchrs. Boston Area Pub. Schs., 1986-89; instr. basic math. Curry Coll., Milton, Mass., 1988-89. Recipient Disting. Scholar award U. Mass., 1986. Mem. ASCD, Nat. Coun. Tchrs. Math., Pa. Coun. Tchrs. Math. Home: PO Box 175 Allison PA 15413-0175 Office: Math Dept Calif U Pa Allison PA 15413

HOFFMAN, LOWELL WILLIAM, psychologist; b. Mt. Pleasant, Pa., Aug. 18, 1954; s. William Floyd and Ruth (Hollingsworth) H.; m. Marie Therese Massabni, June 14, 1975; children: Robert Lowell, Karissa Marie. BA in Relgion, Bob Jones U., Greenville, S.C., 1975; MA in Religion, Westminster Theol. Sem., 1981; MS in Counseling and Human Rels., Villanova U., 1985; PhD in Clin. Psychology, Union Inst., 1990. Lic. psychologist, Pa. Counselor Profl. Counseling Ctr., Fort Washington, Pa., 1985-87; counselor, proprietor Brookhaven Ctr. for Counseling and Devel., Allentown, Pa., 1987-88, psychologist, proprietor, 1988—; psychologist Valley Ctr., Inc., Lansdale, Pa., 1988-89, Penn Found. for Mental Health, Sellersville, 1989—; cons. psychologist Parkland Family Health Ctr., Schnecksville, Pa., 1990—. Mem. Weisenberg Twp. Planning Commn., Lehigh County, Pa., 1991=92. Mem. Am. Psychol. Assn., Pa. Psychol. Assn., Christian Assn. for Psychol. Studies, Kappa Delta Pi (Xi Phi chpt.). Presbyterian. Home: RR 1 Box 608 Fogelsville PA 18051-9766 Office: Brookhaven Ctr Counseling and Devel 2 Windsor Plz Ste 60 Fogelsville PA 18051

HOFFMAN, MANDY LIPPMAN, realtor; b. Balt., Sept. 23, 1956; d. Eli Morton and Judith (Siegel) Lippman; m. Ira Eliot Hoffman, Dec. 17, 1988; 1 child, Lauren Samantha. BA in Communications, George Washington U., 1978; AAS in Interior Design, Parsons Sch. Design, N.Y.C., 1981. Asst. to advt. dir. Britches of Georgetowne, Washington, 1978; media planner and buyer Ted Bates Internat. Advt., N.Y.C., 1979-80; dir. Meredith Gallery, Balt., 1981-87; corp. art cons. Balt., 1988-91; realtor Shannon and Luchs Realtors, Washington, 1991—; exhbn. co-curator Norton Gallery Art, West Palm Beach, Fla., 1986; course coord. and moderator Jewish Community Ctr. Greater Washington, Rockville, 1989; residents assocs. program Smithsonian Instn., Washington, 1990. Chmn. affiliates Balt. Mus. Art, 1987-89; co-chmn. ann. spring forum James Renwick Alliance, 1990-91, membership chmn., 1991-92.

HOFFMAN, MARILYN FRIEDMAN, museum director. BA with Honors, Brown U., 1967, MA in Art History, 1971. Curator Fuller Art Mus., Brockton, Mass., 1971-73; acting dir. Fuller Art Mus., 1973-74; dir. Fuller Art Mus., Brockton, Mass., 1975-83; curator The Currier Gallery of Art, Manchester, N.H., 1984-87; dir. The Currier Gallery of Art, Manchester, 1988—; lectr. in field. Author numerous exhbn. catalogues, articles. Mem. Am. Assn. Mus.'s, Assn. Art Mus. Dirs., Coll. Art Assn. Office: Currier Gallery Art 192 Orange St Manchester NH 03104-4393

HOFFMAN, MERLE HOLLY, social psychologist, political activist, author; b. Phila., Mar. 6, 1946; d. Jack Rheins and Ruth (Dubow) H.; m. Martin Gold, June 30, 1979. BA magna cum laude in Psychology, Queens Coll., 1972; postgrad., CUNY, 1972-75. Founder, pres. Choices Women's Med. Ctr., Forest Hills, N.Y., 1971—; family planning cons. Health Ins. Plan, N.Y.C., 1973—; founder, pres. Ctr. for Comprehensive Breast Svcs., N.Y.C., 1979—, Merle Hoffman Enterprises, N.Y.C., 1986—; speaker, debator on women's rights and polit. issues; founder, pres. Nat. Liberty Com., 1981. Cons. editor Female Health Topics and Diagnostic Reporter, 1979-81; editor, pub. ednl. jour. On The Issues; contbr. articles in field to various publs.; producer documentary film Abortion A Different Light; founder N.Y. Pro-Choice Coalition; host cable TV series MH: On the Issues,

1986. Mem. Nat. Assn. Abortion Facilities (co-founder, pres. 1976-77), Nat. Abortion Fedn. (co-founder, sec. 1977-78), Phi Beta Kappa. Office: Choices Women's Med Ctr Inc 9777 Queens Blvd Flushing NY 11374

HOFFMAN, PAUL ROGER, aerospace executive; b. N.Y.C., May 10, 1934; s. Philip and Dorothy (Gossett) H.; m. Lynn Thompson; children: Lane, Spencer, Britton. BE, Yale U., 1955, MS, 1958, PhD, 1959. Market researcher Union Carbide, N.Y.C., 1959; dir. research and devel. Avco Systems, Wilmington, Mass., 1962-65; dir. Avco Space Systems, Lowell, Mass., 1965-70; v.p. Avco Systems, Wilmington, 1970-77; pres. Textron Splty. Materials, Lowell, 1977—. Served to 1st lt. USAF, 1959-62. Mem. AIAA, Am. Inst. Chemists. Clubs: Harvard, Yale, Longwood Cricket, Vesper. Home: 42 Fisher Ave Brookline MA 02146 Office: Textron Splty Materials 2 Industrial Ave Lowell MA 01851-5199

HOFFMAN, PETER IVAN, advertising professional; b. N.Y.C., Oct. 11, 1954; s. William and Florence Hoffman. Student, Sch. Visual Arts, 1977; BA in Communications, Queens Coll., 1975. Copywriter McCann-Erickson, N.Y.C., 1979-82; assoc. creative dir. J. Walter Thompson, N.Y.C., 1982; creative group head Ally Gargano/MCA Advt., N.Y.C., 1982-92; assoc. creative dir. Bozell Inc., Advt., 1992—; instr. Sch. Visual Arts, N.Y.C., 1981-84. Playwright: The Blueberry Season, Bachelors, The Hours Before Daylight; exhibited photography at Hudson River Gallery, 1990, Citibank-Hudson Valley Artists Series, 1992. Aux. police officer Queens, N.Y., 1973-75. Recipient Clio award, N.Y.C., 1980, 82, Show Merit award, N.Y.C., 1983, 84, 85, Amoth awards, 1980, 81, 83, Art Dirs. Club Am., 1981, 84, 85. Mem. Dramatists Guild Am., Author's League.

HOFFMAN, ROBERT PHILIP, internist; b. Bronx, N.Y., Dec. 10, 1945; s. A. Charles and Helen Gloria (Rosenberrg) H.; m. Patricia Mary Olbrych, Mar. 17, 1970; children: Matthew Evan, Elisa Michelle. BS, Union Coll., 1966; MD, Albany Med. Coll., 1970. Diplomate Am. Bd. Internal Medicine, Nat. Bd. Med. Examiners. Intern Albany (N.Y.) Med. Ctr. Hosp., 1970-71, resident, 1971-73; fellow Albany Med. Coll., 1973-75; lt. comdr. USN, Beaufort, S.C., 1975-77; physician Hampden County Med. Group, Springfield, Mass., 1977-79; clin. asst. prof. medicine Tufts U. Sch. Medicine, Springfield, 1979—; chmn. infection control Mercy Hosp., Springfield, 1981—; med. dir. Protocare of Mass., Springfield, 1985—; cons. infectious diseases Springfield Med. Assn., 1979—; clk. Springfield Med. Assocs. Protocare of West Mass., 1985—; med. dir., chmn. Med. Adv. Com., 1985—. Editor, reviewer: Handbook of Pharmacy, 1990. Med. adv. com. Holyoke (Mass.) UNA, 1988—; profl. adv. com. Rehab. Assocs., West Springfield, 1985-88; AIDS adv. program Longmeadow (Mass.) High Sch., 1985-89. Named Pipe orator Union Coll., 1966, Outstanding Sr., 1966. Mem. Infectious Disease Soc. of Am., Mass. Infectious Disease Soc., Am. Soc. for Microbiology, Am. Found. for Infectious Diseases, Am. Soc. for Internal Medicine, Amnesty Internat., Common Cause. Office: Springfield Med Assocs 2150 Main St Springfield MA 01104-3300

HOFFMAN, SAUL, plastic surgeon; b. Edmonton, Alta., Can., Feb. 17, 1931; came to U.S., 1964; s. Joseph and Gertrude (Caushansky) H.; m. Alice Hoffman, June 18, 1967; children: Daniel Paul, Jeffrey Michael. BS, U. Alta., 1951, MD, 1955. Pvt. practice N.Y.C., 1964—; clin. prof. Mt. Sinai Hosp.; chief plastic surgery div. Mt. Sinai-Beth Israel Hosp., 1982-88, Dr.'s Hosp., 1988—. Contbr. numerous articles to profl. jours. Fellow ACS; mem. Am. Assn. Plastic Surgeons, Am. Soc. Plastic and Reconstructive Surgeons. Home: 301 Hudson Ave Tenafly NJ 07670-1127 Office: 102 E 78th St New York NY 10021-0302

HOFFMAN, STEPHEN MAX, JR., bank executive; b. Phila., Dec. 7, 1949; s. Stephen Max Sr. and Ruth Mary (McDevitt) H.; m. Gloria Marie Palestini, Dec. 27, 1969; children: Stephen Max III, Mark Nicholas, Melissa Ann. BS in Fin., LaSalle U., 1972; postgrad., U. Wis., 1980-82. Asst. bank examiner Fed. Reserve Bank, Phila., 1972-77; bank examiner Fed. Reserve Bank, 1977-79, sr. bank examiner, 1979-87, examining officer, 1987-88, asst. v.p., 1988-89, v.p., 1989—. Staff sgt. U.S. Army, 1970-76. Roman Catholic. Office: Fed Res Bank 10 Independence Mall Philadelphia PA 19106-1574

HOFFMAN, TIMOTHY HERMAN, health care consultant; b. Chattanooga, Mar. 12, 1953; s. Francis Herman and Doris May (Radcliffe) H.; m. Joyce Harriet Miller, Sept. 2, 1978; children: Carolyn Joyce, Patrick Timothy. BS, U. Conn., 1978. Mental health aide Mansfield (Conn.) State Tng. Sch., 1975-78; sr. systems engr. Med. Ctr. Del., Wilmington, 1979-82; dir. mgmt. systems engring. Grad. Hosp., Phila., 1982-85; assoc. Laventhol and Horwath, Phila., 1985-87, mgr., 198-89; pres. Triad Assocs., Wilmington, 1989—; guest speaker numerous orgns. Bd. dirs. Lindamere Civic Assn., Wilmington, 1981-82, pres., 1982. Conn. State scholar, 1971. Mem. Hosp. Info. Mgmt. Systems Soc. (com. 1980-85, chair com. 1983-85), Del. Valley Hosp. Info. Mgmt. Systems Soc. (bd. dirs. 1980-88, pres. 1983-85), Hosp. Fin. Mgmt. Assn., Am. Mgmt. Assn. Home: 201 North Rd Wilmington DE 19809-3020

HOFFMAN, WAYNE LESLIE, JR., real estate agent; b. Belvidere, Ill., July 29, 1960; s. Wayne L. and Mary Jayne (Brentner) H.; m. Caitlin Anne Highton, Aug. 29, 1982; children: Hunter, Paige. BABA, Principia Coll., 1982. Lic. realtor, Md. Comml. real estate broker Spaulding & Slye, Bethesda, Md., 1982-86, Polinger Comml., Chevy Chase, Md., 1987-88; sr. leasing specialist West Group, Silver Spring, Md., 1988—. Mem. Nat. Assn. Realtors, Washington D.C. Assn. Realtors (Multi-million Dollar Leasing Club award 1988-91, Multi-million Dollar Sales Club award 1989), Washington Area Comml. Brokers Coun. Republican. Christian Scientist. Office: West Group 2221 Broadbirch Dr Silver Spring MD 20904

HOFFMAN, WILLIAM ALBERT, gastroenterologist; b. Yonkers, N.Y., Oct. 14, 1928; s. Sidney J. and Theresa (Ecker) H.; m. Joan Hoffman, July 3, 1949; children: David, Laurie, Erik, Andrew. BA, NYU, 1949; MD, SUNY, 1953. Diplomate Am. Bd. Internal Medicine, specialty bd. gastroenterology. Intern Boston City Hosp., 1953-56; resident New Haven Hosp., 1956-59; pvt. practice Fairfield, Conn., 1959—. Capt. USAF, 1953-55. Fellow ACP; mem. AMA, Am. Soc. Internal Medicine, Am. Gastroent. Soc., Am. Soc.. Gastroenterology, Conn. State Med. Soc., Fairfield County Med. Soc., Conn. State Soc. Gastroenterology, Alpha Omega Alpha. Office: Internal Medicine Assocs 1305 Post Rd Fairfield CT 06430

HOFFMANN, DIETRICH KARL, biochemist; b. Danzig, Germany, Dec. 10, 1924; came to U.S., 1957; s. Willy and Hella (von Jarchow) H.; m. Ilse Lemm, June 23, 1960; children: Peter W., Ralph W. BS, U. Kiel, Fed. Rep. Germany, 1952, MS in Chemistry, 1955; PhD, U. Munich, 1957. Rsch. fellow Max-Planck Inst. Biochemistry, Munich, 1955-57; vis. rsch. assoc. Sloan-Kettering Inst. for Cancer Rsch., N.Y.C., 1957-60, assoc., 1960-66, assoc. mem., 1966-69; mem. Am. Health Found., Valhalla, N.Y., 1970-80, assoc. dir., 1980—; mem. sci. adv. coun. div. cancer cause and prevention Nat. Cancer Inst., Bethesda, Md., 1981-84, 86-88; mem. expert panel Cosmetic Ingredient Rev., Washington, 1977—; mem. tech. adv. bd. smoking and health U.S. Surgeon Gen., Washington, 1979-88. Co-editor: Tobacco and Tobacco Smoke, 1967, Tobacco Carcinogenesis, 1986, (monograph) Tobacco-Specific N-Nitrosamines, 1991. Mem. Am. Assn. Cancer Rsch., Am. Chem. Soc., Am. Soc. Preventive Oncology, German Chem. Soc., Soc. Toxicology,, Steuben Soc. Am. (nat. coun. 1991). Lutheran. Home: 29 Holly Pl Larchmont NY 10538-1319 Office: Am Health Found 1 Dana Rd Valhalla NY 10595-1549

HOFFMANN, HEINZ KATL, painter, designer; b. Berlin, Dec. 10, 1918; came to U.S., 1956; married; children: Lutz, Regina, Bernd, Howard. Master degree, Master Sch. of Trade Art, Berlin, 1947. Pvt. practice Huntington, N.Y., 1957—. Mem. Berliner Club of L.I. (founder, pres. 1964-68), Ind. Profl. Painting Contractors Assn. of Am., Inc. (pres. 1982—, exec. dir. 1988). Office: PO Box 1759 Huntington NY 11743-0630

HOFFMANN, ILSE, research coordinator; b. Hamburg, Germany, July 1, 1934; came to U.S., 1958; d. Karl Hermann and Elly (Senkpiel) Lemm.; m. Dietrich Karl Hoffmann, June 23, 1960; children: Peter, Ralph. BS, Chemotechniker Coll., 1952. Teaching asst. Chemotechniker Coll., Hamburg, 1952-53; chem.-tech. asst. biochem. dept. U. Hamburg, 1953-58; rsch. asst. Sloan Kettering Inst. for Cancer Rsch., N.Y.C., 1958-65; rsch. coord. and sci. editor Am. Health Found., Valhalla, N.Y., 1975-85; spl. asst. to the pres., sci. editor Am. Health Found., Valhalla, 1985—. Contbr. articles to profl. jours. Mem. Steuben Soc. Am. (sec. nat. coun. 1981—), Soc. Nat. Shrine of the Bill of Rights (v.p. St. Paul's Eastchester Inc. 1983—). Republican. Lutheran. Office: Steuben Soc Am 6705 Fresh Pond Rd Ridgewood NY 11385

HOFFMANN, ROALD, chemist, educator; b. Zloczow, Poland, July 18, 1937; came to U.S., 1949, naturalized, 1955; s. Hillel and Clara (Rosen) Safran (stepson Paul Hoffmann); m. Eva Börjesson, Apr. 30, 1960; children: Hillel Jan, Ingrid Helena. BA, Columbia U., 1958; MA, Harvard U., 1960, PhD, 1962; D Tech. (hon.), Royal Inst. Tech., Stockholm, 1977; D.Sc. (hon.), Yale U., 1980, Columbia U., 1982, Hartford U., 1982, CUNY, 1983, U. P.R., 1983, U. Uruguay, 1984, U. La Plata, SUNY, Binghamton, 1985, Colgate U., Lehigh U., 1989, Carleton Coll., 1989, Ben Gurion Coll., 1989, U. of the Negev, 1989, U. Md., 1990, U. Athens, 1991, U. Thessaloniki, Greece, 1991, U. Ariz., 1991, U. Cen. Fla., 1991, Bar Ilan U., 1991; DSc (hon.), U. St. Petersburg, Russia, 1991, U. Barcelona, 1992. Jr. fellow Soc. Fellows Harvard, 1962-65; assoc. prof. Cornell U., Ithaca, N.Y., 1965-68; prof. Cornell U., 1968-74, John A. Newman prof. phys. sci., 1974—; U. Md., 1990. Author: (with R.B. Woodward) Conservation of Orbital Symmetry, 1970, Solids and Surfaces, 1988; author: (poetry) The Metamict State, 1987, Gaps and Verges, 1990. Recipient award in pure chemistry Am. Chem. Soc., 1969, Arthur C. Cope award, 1973, Fresenius award Phi Lambda Upsilon, 1969, Harrison Howe award Rochester sect. Am. Chem. Soc., 1970; ann. award Internat. Acad. Quantum Molecular Scis., 1970, Pauling award, 1974, Nobel prize in chemistry, 1981, inorganic chemistry award; Am. Chem. Soc., 1982, Nat. Medal of sci., 1983, Chem. Scis. award Nat. Acad. Sci., 1986, Priestley medal, 1990, N.N. Semenov Gold medal Acad. Scis. USSR. Mem. NAS (award in chem. scis. 1986), Am. Acad. Arts and Scis., Russian Acad. Scis. (Semenov Gold medal), Internat. Acad. Quantum Molecular Scis., Royal Soc. (fgn.), Indian Nat. Sci. Acad., Royal Swedish Acad. Scis., Finnish Acad. Arts and Letters, Acad. Scis. USSR.

HOFFMANN, WILLIAM FREDERICK, III, psychiatrist; b. N.Y.C., Oct. 26, 1940; s. William Frederick Jr. and Mary Angela (McDonnell) H.; m. Robin Lynn Zuckerman; children: William, Lisa, Keith. AB, Coll. of the Holy Cross, 1962; MD, Georgetown U., 1966. Diplomate Am. Bd. Psychiatry and Neurology. Physician Project Concern, Vietnam, 1969-71; pvt. practice in psychiatry N.Y.C., 1971-75, 78-84; resident in psychiatry St. Luke's Hosp., N.Y.C., 1975-78; unit chief Kings County Hosp., Bklyn., 1978-82; dir. behavioral scis. Family Practice Dept., Downstate Med. Ctr., Bklyn., 1981-83; chief, dept. psychiatry Newport (R.I.) Hosp., 1984-88; dir. Hoffmann Inst. for Psychotherapy, Middletown, R.I., 1988—; chief dept. of neuropsychiatry Carlton (Mass.) Meml. Hosp., 1991—; clin. asst. prof. psychiatry Brown U., Providence, 1986—. Contbr. articles to profl. jours. and lay publs. Member exec. com. Friends of Sakonnet, Portsmouth, R.I., 1988-90. Capt. U.S. Army, 1967-69, Vietnam. Mem. AMA, Am. Psychiat. Assn., R.I. Psychiat. Soc. (sec., treas. 1988—, pres. elect 1991—). Democrat. Roman Catholic. Home: 30 Ann Hutchinson Ct Portsmouth RI 02871-3815 Office: The Hoffmann Inst 294 Valley Rd Newport RI 02840-5273

HOFMEISTER, JANA MARIE, cardiologist. MD, SUNY Upstate Med. Ctr., Syracuse, 1976. Diplomate Am. Bd. Internal Medicine. Intern Albany (N.Y.) Med. Ctr., 1976-78, asst. resident, 1978-80, fellow div. cardiology, 1981-83; fellow div. cardiology Emory U., Atlanta, 1984; fellow coronary angioplasty and interventional cardiology Emory U. Hosp., 1985-86; presenter numerous cardiology confs. Contbr. numerous articles to profl. jours. Mem. AMA, Cardiac Soc. Upstate N.Y., N.Y. State Soc. Internal Medicine, Am. Soc. Cardiovascular Intervention, Syracuse Med. Alumni Assn. Home: 7 Reddy Ln Albany NY 12211-1697

HOFFNER, BRIAN KENT, slide production company executive, cartoonist; b. Lehighton, Pa., Apr. 10, 1961. BS in Telecommunications, Kutztown U., 1983. Audiovisual cons. Fuller Co., Allentown, Pa., 1983-84; media prodn. technician Lehigh County Community Coll., Schnecksville, Pa., 1984-89; asst. art dir. Wheeler Enterprises, Inc., Easton, Pa., 1989-90; v.p. Corp. Chrome, Inc., Allentown, 1990—. Author: Modeling and Acting, 1987, Resumes, Auditions and Camera Protocol, 1987. Republican. Lutheran. Office: Corp Chrome Inc 999 Postal Rd Allentown PA 18103-9338

HOFFNER, MARILYN, university administrator; b. N.Y.C., Nov. 16, 1929; d. Daniel and Elsie (Schulz) H.; B.F.A., Cooper Union; m. Albert Greenberg, May 29, 1949; children—Doren Roe, Peter Cooper. Art dir. Printers' Ink mag., N.Y.C., 1953-63; art dir. Print mag., N.Y.C., 1960-62; corp. art dir. Vision, Inc., Latin Am., 1963-75; dir. alumni relations Cooper Union, 1975-82, dir. devel., 1982—. Bd. dirs. Art Dirs. Club N.Y., 1973-75, 79-82, exec. sec., 1973-75, exec. treas., 1979-82; mem. Citizens Adv. Cultural Arts Com. Dutchess County, 1978-80. Named Alumnus of Yr., Cooper Union, 1968; recipient Gold medal Art Dirs. Club, 1979. Mem. Cooper Union Alumni Assn. (editor-in-chief 1971-74, 1st v.p. 1974-75), Council Advancement and Support of Edn., Type Dirs. Club (numerous awards), Nat. Arts Club (exhbn. com.). Contbg. editor Print mag., 1960-62, Art Direction, 1959-64, Graphics mag., 1959-82; designer mags., advt., books. Home: 51 5th Ave New York NY 10003-4320 Office: 41 Cooper Sq New York NY 10003-7136

HOFLAND, JOHN PIETER WILHELMUS, manufacturing executive; b. Roermond, Limburg, The Netherlands, Aug. 31, 1940; came to U.S., 1981; s. Jochem and Maria B. (Theelen) H.; m. Marijke Josephina Emilia Raymann, Aug. 1, 1962; children: Marianne A.H., Astrid P.E. Student, Akzo Pharma Mgmt. Tng. Program, The Netherlands, 1978-79. Cert. indsl. acct., The Netherlands. Location controller Intervet, Boxmeer, The Netherlands, 1968-70; group acct. Intervet Internat., Boxmeer, 1971, controller, 1973, sales mgr. South Am., 1980-81; v.p. Intervet Inc., Milsboro, Del., 1981—. Office: Intervet Inc PO Box 318 Millsboro DE 19966

HOFMANN, WILLIAM F., III, insurance executive; b. Syracuse, N.Y., Apr. 16, 1943; s. William F. and Cornelia (McLaughlin) H.; m. Marilyn Brainard, July 15, 1967; children: Heidi L., Kirsten A. BSBA, Boston U., 1966; MBA, Suffolk U., 1974. CLU, CPCU, cert. ins. counselor; lic. ins. adviser; accredited advisor in ins. Pres. Hofmann Ins. Agy., Inc., Belmont, Mass., 1978—. Contbr. articles to profl. jours. Mem. Town Meeting, Belmont, 1978—; v.p. Boston Children's Svc., 1980; trustee Plymouth Congl. Ch., 1989-92. With U.S. Army, 1965-71. Mem. Ind. Inst. Agts. Mass. (pres. 1987), Ind. Ins. Agts. Am. (state nat. dir.), Winchester Country Club, St. Georges Club, Heritage Club. Home: 223 Rutledge Rd Belmont MA 02178-2632

HOFSTETTER, EDWARD MAX, electrical engineer; b. N.Y.C., Nov. 17, 1932; s. Max and Maria (Heller) H.; m. Nancy Bennett, June 11, 1955; children: Christine, Karen. BS, MIT, 1955, MS, 1955, ScD, 1959. Asst. prof. MIT, Cambridge, Mass., 1959-63; staff mem. Lincoln Lab. MIT, Lexington, Mass., 1963—; cons. Tex. Instruments, Dallas, 1959-63. Contbr. articles to profl. jours.; patentee voice encoder and synthesizer. mem. IEEE, Sigma Xi. Home: 98 Wolf Rock Rd Carlisle MA 01741-1118 Office: MIT Lincoln Lab 204 Wood St Lexington MA 02173-6426

HOFSTETTER, ELEANORE OTTILIA, librarian; b. Camden, N.J., May 16, 1939; d. George and Anna O. (Kneissl) H. BS, Marywood Coll., 1961; MSLS, Drexel U., 1963; MA, U. Del., 1967. Instr. Trinity Coll., Burlington, Vt., 1961-62; reference libr. U. Del., Newark, 1963-66; assoc. libr. dir. Towson (Md.) State U., 1986—, acting libr. dir., 1989-92. Author: Twentieth Century German Novel, 1989, Newspapers in Maryland Libraries, 1977; contbr. articles to profl. jours. Mem. ALA, Md. Libr. Assn. Office: Towson State U Towson MD 21204

HOGAN, BRIAN JOSEPH, editor; b. Aberdeen, S.D., Apr. 11, 1943; s. Arthur James and Magdalena (Frison) H.; m. Jamie Isabelle Schwingel, June 21, 1987. BS in Aerospace and Mech. Engring., U. Ariz., 1965, BS in Geophysics-Geochemistry, 1968; MS in Journalism, U. Utah, 1972. Rsch. asst. U. Va. Rsch. Labs for Engring. Scis., Charlottesville, 1965-66; exploration geophysicist Anaconda Co., Tucson, 1968-71; assoc. editor Benwill Pub. Co., Brookline, Mass., 1973-74; asst. editor Design News, Boston, 1974-75; midwest editor Design News, Chgo., 1975-87; sr. editor Design News, Newton, Mass., 1987-89, mng. editor, 1989—. Author stage plays The Young O'Neil, 1983, Awakening, 1984. Precinct worker Cook County Rep. Com., Oak Park, Ill., 1986-87; interpreter Frank Lloyd Wright Home and Studio Found., Oak Park, 1981-87. Recipient numerous awards Am. Soc. Bus. Press Editors, Soc. Tech. Communication, Aviation Space Writers Assn. Mem. Am. Soc. Bus. Press Editors, Am. Hist. Print Collectors Soc. Republican. Roman Catholic. Office: Design News 275 Washington St Newton MA 02158-1611

HOGAN, CHARLES CARLTON, psychiatrist; b. Quincy, Ill., Oct. 5, 1921; s. Carlton Monta and Maryanne (Henley) H.; m. Nina Harriet Redman; children: Matthew P., Carlton H., Noelle N. Student, Bradley U., 1939-41, Ul Ill., 1941-42; MD, Columbia U., 1945, D Med. Sci., 1952. Diplomate Am. Bd. Psychiatry and Neurology. Intern Phila. Gen. Hosp., 1945-46; rsch. asst. neurology dept. Columbia U., N.Y.C., 1948-50, lectr. Ctr. for Psychoanalytic Tng., 1979—, psychoanalytic clinician Ctr. for Psychoanalytical Tng., 1948-52; resident N.Y. State Psychiatric Inst., N.Y.C., 1949-50; asst. physician Presbyn. Hosp., N.Y.C., 1951-54, asst. attending psychiatrist, 1954-60; asst. vis. psychiatrist Bronx (N.Y.) Mcpl. Hosp., 1960—; asst. clin. prof. psychiatry Albert Einstein Coll. Medicine, Bronx, 1960—; chmn. profl. adv. com. Riverdale Mental Health Clinic, Bronx, 1969-77; cons. Wiltwyck Sch. for Boys, Yorktown Heights, N.Y., 1971-77. Author: Psychosomatics and Inflammatory Disease of the Colon; editor Fear of Being Fat, 1985, Psychodynamic Technique in the Treatment of the Eating Disorders, 1992; contbr. articles to profl. publs., 12 chpts. to books on psychomatic disorders. Treas. Physicians for Social Responsibility, N.Y.C., 1968. Capt. U.S. Army, 1946-48. Fellow Am. Psychiat. Assn. (life); mem. AMA, Am. Psychoanalytic Assn. (life), N.Y. State Med. Assn., Am. Psychosomatic Soc., N.Y. Acad. Scis., Pan-Am. Med. Assn., Assn. for Psychoanalytic Medicine, World Mental Health Assn., Riverdale Yacht Club (bd. govs.), Undersea and Hyperbaric Med. Assn. Home: 6 Ploughmans Bush Bronx NY 10471-3541 Office: 8 E 96th St New York NY 10128-0820

HOGAN, DANIEL BOLTEN, management consultant; b. Lawrence, Mass., Sept. 20, 1943; s. Daniel Edward and Gisela (Bolten) H.; m. Jean Elizabeth Haley, Jan. 25, 1979; children: Matthew Pollard, Sarah Elizabeth, Haley Elizabeth. BA, Yale U., 1965; EdM, Boston U., 1971; JD, Harvard U., 1972, PhD, 1983. Lic. psychologist; bar: Mass., U.S. Dist. Ct. Mass. Rural community devel. worker U.S. Peace Corps, Butha-Buthe, Lesotho, 1967-69; mgmt. cons. Wayland, Mass., 1972-76; rsch. and teaching fellow Dept. Psychology and Social Rels., Harvard U., Cambridge, Mass., 1976-81; clin. fellow and instr. psychology Harvard Med. Sch., Boston, 1981-85; asst. in psychology McLean Hosp., Belmont, Mass., 1982-83, asst. psychologist, 1983, asst. attending psychologist, 1984-86; mgmt. cons. Weston, Mass., 1986-90; v.p. and dir. R & D McBer & Co., Boston, 1990; pres. The Apollo Group, Concord, Mass., 1991—; dir. Standex Internat. Corp., Salem, N.H.; sr. rsch. assoc. Nat. Ctr. for Study of Professions, Washington, 1976-83; mem. com. on use of human subjects in rsch. Harvard U. Faculty of Arts and Scis., 1980-81. Author: The Regulation of Psychotherapists: A Study in the Philosophy and Practice of Professional Regulation, vol. I, 1979, The Regulation of Psychotherapists: A Handbook of State Licensure Laws, vol. II, 1979, The Regulation of Psychotherapists: A Review of Malpractice Suits in the United States, vol. III, 1979, The Regulation of Psychotherapists: A Resource Bibliography, vol. IV, 1979; guest editor Law and Human Behavior, 1982-83, 87, cons. editor, 1985-91; contbr. articles to profl. jours., chpts. books. Trustee Cambridge Ctr. for Behavioral Studies, 1985-91; bd. dirs. New Eng. Tng. Inst., Stonington, Conn., 1976-78, Phillips Exeter Acad., Exeter, N.H., 1986-92, Community Change, Inc., Boston, 1972-79, adv. bd., 1979—. Maurice Falk Med. Fund. grantee, 1976-78. Fellow APA, Am. Psychol. Soc., Am. Orthopsychiatric Assn.; mem. Am. Psychology Law Soc. (dir. 1982-84), Internat. Assn. Applied Social Scientists (trustee 1976-79), Mass. Psychol. Assn. (bd. profl. affairs 1980-83), Mass. Bar Assn. Home: 229 Westford Rd Concord MA 01742-5232 Office: The Apollo Group 229 Westford Rd Concord MA 01742-5232

HOGAN, EDWARD ROBERT, financial services executive; b. Yonkers, N.Y., Mar. 21, 1939; s. John J. and Blanche (Corradi) H.; m. Linda Carroll, Sept. 25, 1959 (div. Oct. 1975); children: Linda Hogan Benya, Edward R. Jr., Barbara Hogan Comblo. Dist. mgr. New Eng. Life, Thornwood, N.Y., 1962-64; pres. Profl. Employment Svcs., Scarsdale, N.Y., 1964-66, Royal Transport & Distbn. Inc., Yonkers, N.Y., 1966-71; v.p. Fin. Ins. Group, N.Y.C., 1971-74, Franklin United Life Ins. Co., Garden City, N.Y., 1974-79; sr. v.p. Adv. Svcs. Corp., White Plains, N.Y., 1979-83; pres. Faculty Svcs. Corp., Wappingers Falls, N.Y., 1983—, FSC Adminstrv. Svcs. Corp., Wappingers Falls, N.Y., 1986—; registered prin. Cadaret, Grant & Co., Inc., Syracuse, N.Y., 1989—. Pres. Yonkers Young Rep. Orgn., 1960-64; v.p. Westchester County Young Reps., White Plains, 1961-63; candidate 1st Assembly Dist. State Assembly, Yonkers, 1962; Westchester County campaign dir. U.S. Sen. James L. Buckley, 1968. With USN, 1957-59. Mem. Nat. Tax Shelter Annuity Assn. Office: Faculty Svcs Corp PO Box 1635 Wappingers Falls NY 12590

HOGAN, GUY THEODORE, mathematics educator; b. LaBoca, Canal Zone, Republic of Panama, May 21, 1933; came to U.S., 1953; s. Leonard T. and Kathleen E. (Patrick) H.; m. Paula E. Tucker, Aug. 26, 1961; children: Kurt D., Sean M., Kahlil A. BA, Talladega Coll., 1957; MS, U. Chgo., 1959; PhD, Ohio State U., 1969; JD, Suffolk U., Boston, 1985. Asst. prof. math. Talladega (Ala.) Coll., 1959-61; asst. prof. Cen. State U., Wilberforce, Ohio, 1961-66; prof. SUNY, Oneonta, 1969-73; assoc. prof. U. Mass., Boston, 1973—; atty. Vol. Lawyers Project, Boston, 1986—. Contbr. articles to profl. publs. Sci. Faculty fellow NSF, Columbus, Ohio, 1967, Faculty Rsch. fellow SUNY, 1972, Summer Inst. fellow, NSF, Ithaca, N.Y., 1973. Mem. Am. Math. Soc., Omega Psi Phi, Beta Kappa Chi, Phi Delta Phi. Office: U Mass Harbor Campus Boston MA 02125

HOGAN, JAMES EDWARD, librarian; b. Worcester, Mass., Sept. 12, 1944; s. James Edward and Ann (Dombrosk) H.; m. Kathleen Berg; children: Pamela, Sarah Beth, Emily. BS, Worcester St. Coll., 1966; MA in History, U. Mass., 1968; MLS, Simmons Coll., 1974, ArtsD, 1983. Reference libr. U. Mass., Boston, 1974-75; asst. dir. libr. U. Lowell, Mass., 1975-77; asst. dir. libr. Holy Cross Coll., Worcester, Mass., 1977-86, dir. librs., 1986—. Vol. Peace Corps, Brazil, 1968-70. Mem. ALA, Assn. Coll. and Rsch. Librs., Cath. Libr. Assn., Appalachain Mountain Club, Beta Phi Mu. Roman Catholic. Home: 425 Howard St Northborough MA 01532-1032 Office: Holy Cross Coll Dinand Libr Worcester MA 01670

HOGAN, JOHN THOMAS, college counseling administrator; b. Pasadena, Calif., Oct. 26, 1943; s. Thomas Arnold and Cecelia Mae (Young) H.; m. Lorraine Frances Gersz, Oct. 9, 1971; children: Kathleen Anne, Maureen Regina, Ellen Mary. BA, St. John's Coll., Camarillo, Calif., 1966; postgrad., U. Calif., Riverside, 1967, LaVerne (Calif.) Coll., 1967-69; EdM, Boston U., 1973; PhD, U. Conn., 1980. Cert. tchr., Calif.; cert. guidance counselor, Conn. Social studies tchr. Pasadena Pub. Schs., 1968-70, Wuerzburg (Germany) Am. High Sch., 1970-73; sch. counselor Farmington (Conn.) Pub. Schs., 1973-75, career edn. cons., 1978-79; adminstv. grad. asst. U. Conn., Storrs, 1975-78; counseling cons. Regional Sch. Dist. 11, Chaplin, Conn., 1978-79; acting assoc. dir. Ctr. Personal Growth, U. Conn., Storrs, 1979-80; spl. lectr. Providence Coll. Grad. Sch., 1982—; dir. counseling/asst. dean student devel. Providence Coll., 1981—; mem. State Legis. Com. on Feasibility of Counselor Licensure, Providence, 1984-85; mem. sch. bd. St. Thomas Sch., Providence, 1983-85. Mem. Nat. Assn. Student Pers. Adminstrs. (exec. bd. R.I. 1991-92), Assn. Univ. and Coll. Counseling Ctr. Dirs., Am. Coll. Pers. Assn. (directorate mem. commn. on internat. student affairs 1983-87), Coll. Pers. Assn. R.I. (pres. 1986-87, exec. bd. 1981-88). Roman Catholic. Office: Providence Coll Student Devel Ctr Providence RI 02918

HOGAN, LINDA MARIE, management consultant; b. Balt., Dec. 8, 1955; d. James William and Corrine Jean (Griffith) Hogan; m. William Patrick Collins, Sept. 26, 1980; 1 child, Sarah Catherine. BSW in Social Welfare, SUNY, Albany, 1979; MS in Mgmt., Antioch U., 1988. Coord. systems devel. Living Resources Corp., Albany, 1977-83; pres. Tng. Dynamics, Albany, 1983—; sr. instrnl. design spealist GE Plastics, Pittsfield, Mass., 1989-90. Author: (tng. manuals) Platform Skills, 1990, Essentials of Dynamic Training, 1992, Effective Supervision, 1986, Management Development,

1986, High Performing Teams, 1991, Training for Trainers, 1987. Bd. dirs. N.Y. Spl. Olympics, Schenectady, 1984-86; leadership resource com. United Way of Northeastern N.Y., Albany, 1991—; mem. Clergy and Laity Concerned, N.Y.C., 1982—; mem. Habitat for Humanity, 1991—; com. mem. N.Y. State Assn. for Retarded Children, 1985-86. Recipient Capitol award Nat. Leadership Coun., Washington, 1991. Mem. ASTD (mem. exec. bd. Hudson Mohawk chpt.), Nat. Soc. Performance and Instrn., World Future Soc., Soc. for Accelerated Learning. Roman Catholic. Office: Tng Dynamics 488 Western Ave Albany NY 12203

HOGAN, LOIS SEKERAK, management consultant; b. Muncy, Pa., Nov. 20, 1948; d. Clarence R. and Fayetta (DeBord) Sekerak; m. Jeffrey Langdon, Oct. 17, 1976; children: Ross Daggett, Julianna Brett DeBord. BS, Kent State U., 1971; MA, Beacon Coll., 1983. Accedited pub. rels. practitioner. Copywriter Taylor-Jessop Advt., Akron, Ohio, 1971-73; asst. dir. advt. and pub. rels. Spaulding & Slye Corp., Boston, 1973-76; mktg. svcs. mgr. Spaulding & Co., Newton, Mass., 1976-79; dir. corp. communications The Capital Cos., Topsfield, Mass., 1985-87; counsel Jackson Jackson & Wagner, Exeter, N.H., 1987—. Contbg. editor PR Reporter. Named Career Girl of Yr., Bus. and Profl. Women's Assn., Akron, Ohio, 1972. Mem. Pub. Rels. Soc. Am. (treas. 1990-92), Orgn. Tranformation Assn. (bd. dirs. 1986-87), Orgn. Devel. Network. Mem. Soc. of Friends. Home: 74 Main St West Newbury MA 01985-1828 Office: Jackson Jackson & Wagner 14 Front St Exeter NH 03833-2747

HOGAN, THOMAS FRANCIS, federal judge; b. Washington, May 31, 1938; s. Bartholomew W. and Grace (Gloninger) H.; m. Martha Lou Wyrick, July 16, 1966; 1 son, Thomas Garth. A.B., Georgetown U., 1960, J.D., 1966; postgrad., George Washington U., 1960-62. Bar: Md. 1966, U.S. Dist. Ct. D.C. 1967, D.C. 1967, U.S. Ct. Appeals (D.C. cir.) 1972, U.S. Dist. Ct. Md. 1973, U.S. Supreme Ct. 1973. Law clk. to presiding judge U.S. Dist. Ct. D.C., 1966-67; counsel Nat. Commn. on Reform of Fed. Criminal Laws, Washington, 1967-68; ptnr. McCarthy & Wharton, Rockville, Md., 1968-75, Kenary, Tietz & Hogan, Rockville, 1975-81, Furey, Doolan, Abell & Hogan, Chevy Chase, Md., 1981-82; judge U.S. Dist. Ct. D.C., Washington, 1982—; asst. prof. Potomac Sch. Law, Washington, 1977-79; adj. prof. law Georgetown Law Ctr., 1985—. Pub. mem. Officer Evaluation Bd. U.S. Fgn. Service, 1973; chmn. Christ Child Inst. for Disturbed Children, 1975; bd. dirs. Providence Hosp., Washington, 1984-86. Recipient cert. recognition and appreciation for vol. services Montgomery County Govt., 1976; recipient cert. appreciation Christ Child Soc., 1976; St. Thomas More fellow Georgetown U. Law Ctr., 1965-66. Mem. ABA (Md. chmn. Drug Abuse Edn. Program, Young Lawyers sect. 1970-73, mem. Litigation sect.), Bar Assn. D.C. (mem. com. on D.C. cts.), Md. State Bar Assn. (Litigatin sect.), Montgomery County Bar Assn. (chmn. legal ethics com. 1973-74, lawyer referral service com. 1974-75, adminstrn. justice com. 1979-82, bd. govs. 1977-78), Nat. Inst. for Trial Advocacy Assocs., Def. Research Inst., Md. Assn. Def. Trial Counsel, Md. Trial Lawyers Assn., Georgetown U. Alumni Assn., Smithsonian Assocs., John Carroll Soc. Clubs: Barristers, Chevy Chase. Lodge: Knights of Malta.

HOGAN, THOMAS JOSEPH, media collection executive; b. Bklyn., Apr. 20, 1957; s. Michael and Joan (Ginnane) H.; m. Margaret Ann DeLiso, May 4, 1980. BA in Polit. Sci., Fordham U., 1976. Account exec. Hayt, Hayt & Landau Esqs., Great Neck, N.Y., 1977-78; office adminstr. Friesner & Salzman, Esqs., Great Neck, 1978-79; gen. mgr. SKO Inc., Glen Head, N.Y., 1979-86, SKO Brenner Am., Oceanside, N.Y., 1986-88; v.p., gen. mgr. Communications Credit & Recovery Corp., Westbury, N.Y., 1988—; cons. Only Natural Inc., Island Park, N.Y., 1987—, Enjoy Health Foods Inc., Bayside, N.Y., 1981-84. Office: Communications Credit & Recovery Corp 1025 Old Country Rd Westbury NY 11590-5257

HOGAN, WILLIAM T., university president; b. Lowell, Mass., Feb. 4, 1933; married, 1959; 3 children. B.S., Northeastern U., 1955; M.S., MIT, 1959; Ph.D. in M.E., Northeastern U., 1965. Mech. engr. Gen. Electric, 1955-56; mech. design engr. Redstone Arsenal, Ala., 1956-58; sr. scientist Avco Corp., 1961-63; sr. scientist Lowell Technol. Inst. (now U. Lowell (Mass.), 1963—, assoc. prof. mech. engring. to prof. and head dept. to dean engring., pres., 1981—. Office: U Lowell Office of Pres 1 University Ave Lowell MA 01854-2881*

HOGARTY, RICHARD ANTHONY, political scientist, educator; b. Princeton, N.J., Sept. 26, 1933; s. James Robert and Marie Frances (Piscurick) H.; m. Ann Woodward Jeffers, May 5, 1956; children: Margaret, Michael, Susan, Ann, Peter, Timothy. AB, Dartmouth Coll., 1955; MGA, U. Pa., 1960; PhD, Princeton U., 1965. Adminstrv. asst. U.S. Senate, Washington, 1960-61; rsch. asst. Princeton U., 1961-65; asst. prof. Rider Coll., Lawrenceville, N.J., 1965-68; asst. prof., assoc. prof. U. Mass., Boston, 1968-78, prof., 1978—; dir. Gov.'s Task Force on Migrant Labor, Trenton, N.J., 1967-68; cons. N.J. Dept. Community Affairs, Trenton, 1967-68, New Eng. Regional Commn., Boston, 1972, Boston Pub. Schs., 1976, City of Boston, 1977-78. Author (case studies): N.J. Farmers and Migrant Housing Rules, 1966, Delaware River Drought Emergency, 1970, The Endangered Metropolis, 1986, The Search for Massachusetts Chancellor, 1988, Searching for a U. Mass. President, 1991. Dir. Cranbury (N.J.) Housing Assocs., 1963-68, Citizens Coun. for Pub. Schs., Marblehead, Mass., 1969-72; vice-chmn. Dem. Town Com., Marblehead, 1970-80; sr. assoc. McCormack Inst. Pub. Affairs, Boston, 1988—. Lt. USMCR, 1955-57. Recipient William Addee Whitehead award N.J. Hist. Soc. 1967. Mem. ASPA, Am. Pol. Sci. Assn. Democrat. Roman Catholic. Home: 193 Green St Marblehead MA 01945-1511 Office: U Mass Boston MA

HOGBERG, CARL GUSTAV, retired steel company executive; b. Escanaba, Mich., July 19, 1913; s. Claus Emil and Anna C. (Franson) H.; BS in Metall. Engring., Mich. Coll. Mining and Tech., 1935, DEng (hon.) Mich. Tech. U., 1968; m. June Loraine Evans, June 10, 1935 (dec. Aug. 1991); children: David K., Janet H. (Mrs. Nicholas A. Matwiyoff). Blast-furnace apprentice South Chicago works, Carnegie-Ill. Steel Corp., 1935, various operating positions blast-furnace dept., 1935-39, sec. blast-furnace and coke-oven com., Pitts., 1939-41; asst. chmn. blast-furnace com. U.S. Steel Corp., Pitts., 1942-54, asst. to v.p. Mich. Limestone div., Detroit, 1955, asst. v.p., 1956, v.p., 1957-60, pres., 1960-63, v.p. raw materials service, parent co., 1964, pres. Orinoco Mining Co. subs., Caracas, Venezuela, 1965-70, v.p. internat. U.S. Steel Corp., 1970-73. Mem. AIME (J.E. Johnson, Jr. award 1945), Assn. Iron and Steel Engrs. (Kelly award 1950), Am. Iron and Steel Inst., Eastern Western States Blast Furnace and Coke Assns. Contbr. tech. articles trade publs. Home: Sherwood Oaks 100 Norman Dr Mars PA 16046-8203

HOGE, JAMES FULTON, JR., magazine editor; b. N.Y.C., Dec. 25, 1935; s. James Fulton and Virginia (McClamroch) H.; m. Alice Patterson Albright, June 2, 1962 (div. 1971); children: Alicia McClamroch, James Patrick, Robert Warren; m. Sharon King, Jan. 4, 1981. BA in Polit. Sci., Yale U., 1958; MA in Modern Am. and European History, U. Chgo., 1961; grad. Advanced Mgmt. Program, Harvard U., 1980. Fin. writer Chgo. Sun Times, 1958-62; fellow Am. Polit. Sci. Assn. Congl., 1962-63; Washington corr. Chgo. (Ill.) Sun-Times, 1963-65; city editor Chgo. Sun Times, 1965-67, mng. editor, 1967-68, exec. editor, 1968, editor, 1968-76; editor in chief Chgo. (Ill.) Sun-Times and Chgo. (Ill.) Daily News, 1976-78; exec. v.p., editor in chief Chgo. Sun Times, 1978-80, pub., 1980-84; chmn., pub. N.Y. Daily News, 1984-85, pub., pres., 1985-91; fellow Inst. Politics, John F. Kennedy Sch. Govt. Harvard U., Cambridge, Mass., 1991; sr. fellow Freedom Forum Media Studies Ctr., 1992; editor Fgn. Affairs Mag., N.Y.C., 1992—; mem. Pulitzer Prize Bd., N.Y.C., 1982-90, chmn. 1990-91; bd. govs. Columbia U. Mdia and Soc. Seminars, 1983—; mem. adv. bd. Ctr. for Fgn. Journalists, Overseas Devel. Coun., 1988—, Regional Plan Assn., 1988—; dir. N.Y.C. Partnership Found., 1992—; mem. vis. com. New Sch. for Social Rsch., 1991—; chmn. adv. bd. Queens Coll. Jour., 1988—; mem. program com. Ditchley Found. Recipient Pub. Service award U. Chgo., 1977, Am. Heritage award B'nai B'rith Anti Defamation League, 1981, Disting. Journalism award Better Govt. Assn., 1983, Civic Com. award Daily News, Anti Defamation League, 1985. Mem. Coun. Fgn. Rels., Am. Coun. on Germany, Soc. Profl. Journalists, Comml. Club, Century Assn., Sky Club, Pilgrims Club of U.S.

HOGENSEN, MARGARET HINER, librarian, consultant; b. Ottawa, Kans., Oct. 11, 1920; d. Hebron Henry and Nellie Evelyn (Godard) Hiner; widowed. BA, U. Wichita, 1942; BS in Library Sci., U. Denver, 1945. Circulation librarian Boise (Idaho) Pub. Library, 1945-49, Pomona (Calif.) Pub. Library, 1950-51; reference librarian WFIL-TV, Phila., 1963-69; rsch. dir. Concept Films, Washington, 1969-72; ind. researcher, cons. Greenbelt, Md., 1973—. Bd. dirs. Greenbelt Homes, Inc., 1977—, pres. 1983-88; past bd. dirs. Greenbelt Consumer Coop., Nat. Coop. Bank, Nat. Coop. Bus. Assn.; mem. Com. to Devel. Elderly Housing, Greenbelt, 1987—. Mem. Nat. Assn. Housing Coops (bd. dirs. 1986-87, 1990—). Democrat. Christian Scientist. Home: PO Box 218 Greenbelt MD 20768-0218

HOGG, JAMES HENRY, JR., education educator; b. Pleasantville, Pa., Aug. 15, 1926; s. James Henry and Carrie Ethel (Swan) H.; m. Elizabeth Beatrice George, Sept. 8, 1945 (dec. Feb. 1988); children: Carolyn Elizabeth, James Henry III. BA, Houghton Coll., 1951; MA, Allegheny Coll., 1961; EdD, Pa. State U., 1971. Cert. secondary tchr., Pa. Tchr. English and social studies Meadville (Pa.) Sr. High Sch., 1962-67; instr. in secondary edn. Pa. State U., University Park, 1968-71, asst. prof., 1971-77, assoc. prof., 1977—; trustee Houghton Coll., 1964-67; Pa. State Adv. Bd., Mid. States Assn. Colls. and Schs., 1984— (chairperson evaluation teams, 1983—). Contbr. articles to profl. jours. With U.S. Army, 1944-46, ETO. Named participant in 2d Inst. Am History Pa. State U., 1966, Assn. Tchr. Educators LaureATE, 1989; recipient cert. of appreciation U.S. House Reps. Page Sch., 1985. Mem. Nat. Assn. Tchr. Educators, Pa. Assn. Tchr. Educators, Phi Delta Kappa, Alpha Tau. Republican. Methodist. Home: 1729 Brodhead Rd Monaca PA 15061-2704

HOGUET, GEOFFREY ROBERT, investment banker; b. San Francisco, Oct. 8, 1950; s. Roland Henry and Gwendoline (de Rothschild) H.; m. Elizabeth Newell Beers, Dec. 1, 1980; 1 child, Max Roland. BS in Econs., U. Pa., 1972. Dep. mgr. Brown Bros. Harriman & Co., N.Y.C., 1975-83; pres. Hoguet & Keller Wittman & Co., N.Y.C., 1983-91; pres., chief exec. officer Creditanstalt Internat. Advisers, N.Y.C., 1991—; prin. Rothschildsche Forstverwaltung, Austria, 1972—, Otscherliftgesellschaft gmbh, Austria, 1972—; bd. dirs. Palmetto Preservation, Columbia, S.C., Ca New Europe Equity Ptnrs., Bermuda. Mem. River Club of N.Y., Racquet and Tennis Club of N.Y., Mashomack. Office: Creditanstalt Internat Advisers 245 Park Ave New York NY 10167-0002

HOHENADEL, JOHN HERMAN, retail food executive; b. Hillsboro, Wis., Dec. 5, 1950; s. Herman John and Mary Anne (Papas) H.; m. Janet Marie LaSota, July 14, 1979; children: Daniel, Michael, Richard. BS, West Chester (Pa.) U., 1973; M of Profl. Studies, Cornell U., 1979. Personnel asst. Acme Markets Inc., Phila., 1976-80, field personnel specialist, 1980-82, retail auditor, 1982-84; assoc. mgr. Acme Markets Inc., West Goshen, Pa., 1984-86; store supr. Acme Markets Inc., Sharon Hill, Pa., 1986-89, Yeadon, Pa., 1989-92, Devon, Pa., 1992—. Author: Equal Employment Opportunity Program for the Chain Store Retail Food Instry. Recipient Scholarship award Women's Club, 1965. Mem. Am. Mgmt. Assn. Republican. Roman Catholic. Home: 24 Dartmouth Cir Swarthmore PA 19081

HOHENDAHL, PETER UWE, comparative literature and German language and literature educator; b. Hamburg, Fed. Republic Germany, Mar. 17, 1936; came to U.S., 1964; s. Wilhelm and Emilie (Uelschen) H.; m. Iky Maria Zoetelief, July 2, 1965; children: Deborah, Gwendolyn. Student, U. Bern, Switzerland, 1955, U. Hamburg, 1955-57, 59-63; PhD, U. Hamburg, 1964; postgrad., U. Goettingen, Fed. Republic Germany, 1958. Asst. prof. Pa. State U., 1965-68; assoc. prof. Washington U., St. Louis, 1968-69, prof., 1970-77, head dept., 1972-77; prof. comparative and German lit. Cornell U., Ithaca, N.Y., 1977—; chmn. dept. German Cornell U., Ithaca, 1981-86, Schurman prof. German and comparative lit., 1985—; dir. Inst. for German Cultural Studies Cornell U., 1992—; Merton vis. prof. Berlin U., 1976; disting. vis. prof. Ohio State U., 1987. Author: Literaturkritik und Oeffentlichkeit, 1974, Der Europaeische Roman der Empfindsamkeit, 1977, The Institution of Criticism, 1982, Literarische Kultur im Zeitalter des Liberalismus, 1985, A History of German Literary Criticism, 1988, Building a National Literature, 1989, Reappraisals: Shifting Alignments in Postwar Critical Theory, 1991; mem. editorial bd.: Studies in 20th Century Lit., 1979—, German Quar., 1983-88. Fellow Harvard U., 1964-65, fellow Ctr. for Interdisciplinary Rsch., Bielefeld, 1981, 87, Guggenheim Found., 1983-84. Mem. MLA, Am. Assn. Tchrs. German, N.Am. Heine Soc. (exec. coun. 1982—, pres. 1986-90), Zeitschrift fuer Germanistik (bd. dirs. 1990—). Home: 81 Genung Rd Ithaca NY 14850-9602 Office: Cornell U Ithaca NY 14853

HOHN, JAMES SAMONTE, trust officer; b. N.Y.C., Nov. 9, 1946; s. Robert Oscar and Mary Elizabeth (Samonte) H.; m. Lucille Ann Maddalena, Sept. 7, 1975; children: Vincent, Nicholas, Mitchell. BA, CUNY, 1969; MBA, Fairleigh Dickinson U., 1982. With United Way of N.Y.C., 1973-75; dir. alumni fund Fairleigh Dickinson U., Rutherford, N.J., 1975-79; asst. dir. of devel. Internat. Ctr. for the Disabled, N.Y.C., 1979-81; dir. of devel. Girl Scouts, N.Y.C., 1981-82; exec. v.p. HCO Found., Orange, N.J., 1982-84; v.p. Maddalena Assocs., Chester, N.J., 1984-88, Compass Fin. Planning, Flanders, N.J., 1988-89, First Fidelity Bank, N.A. of N.J., Newark, 1989—; adminstr. Ohl Trust, Newark, 1989—, Talcott Fund, Newark, 1989—, Van Houten Fund, Newark, 1989—, Mills Found. Newark, 1989—; trustee William Limmer Found, Newark, 1991—; pres. Edn. Found. of the Chesters, N.J., 1991—. Mem. Chesterboro N.J. Bd. of Health, 1983-87; pres. Chester Bd. of Health, 1991-92; advisor Seton Hall U. Ctr. for Pub. Svc., West Orange, N.J., 1991—. Mem. Nat. Com. on Planned Giving, Coun. of N.J. Grantmakers, Chester Lions. Republican. Office: First Fidelity Bank NA NJ 765 Broad St Newark NJ 07102-3797

HOLABIRD, JEAN, artist; b. Boston, Dec. 3, 1946; d. John Augur Jr. and Donna Katharine (Smith) H. BA, Bennington Coll., 1969. guest lectr. Sch. Visual Arts, Parsons Sch., Cooper Union, Pratt Inst., N.Y.C., 1975-79; asst. printer Catherine Mosley Studio, N.Y.C., 1981-82; art editor St. Marks Poetry Project Newsletter, N.Y.C., 1987-90. Exhibited in group shows Inst. Allende, San Miguel, Mex., 1968, Noah Goldowsky Gallery, N.Y.C., 1976, Glass Gallery, N.Y.C., 1979, 87, Sarah Y. Rentschler Gallery, N.Y.C., 1978, 82, Neo Persona Gallery, N.Y.C., 1987, 89, 91. Recipient cert. of merit Vt. Coun. Arts, 1969. Democrat.

HOLAHAN, MARIE ELISHA, human development educator; b. Buffalo, N.Y., Aug. 6, 1959; d. James Alfred and Grace Louise (Hortage) Finn; m. Edward Charles Holahan, Jan. 7, 1984. BS in Elem. and Spl. Edn., U. Md., 1981, PhD in Human Devel., 1992. Cert. tchr., Md. 2nd grade tchr. Prince George's County Pub. Schs., Upper Marlboro, Md., 1984-87; grad. asst., rsch. asst. U. Md., College Park, 1987-89; prof. early childhood edn. Hood Coll., Frederick, Md., 1989-90; prof. human devel. and ednl. psychology Mt. St. Mary's Coll., Emmitsburg, Md., 1990—; program developer, parent educator House of Ruth, Washington, 1988, Dodge Park (Md.) Elem. Sch., 1988; parent educator Md. Coop. Extension Svc. at Cheverly (Md.)-Tuxedo Elem. Sch., 1989; co-speaker on parent edn., Bethesda, Md., 1988. Co-chmn. program com. Unitarian Fellowship of Frederick, 1990-91. Friend of the Coll. of Edn. scholar U. Md. Coll. Edn., 1989-90. Mem. Md. Assn. Tchr. Educators, Md. Consortium on Human Relationships in Edn., Md. Multicultural Coalition, Family Resource Coalition, Pi Lambda Theta. Home: 1595 Wise Ct Point of Rocks MD 21777 Office: Mt St Marys Coll Emmitsburg MD 21727

HOLBEN, RALPH ERDMAN, retired economist, consultant; b. Allentown, Pa., June 14, 1916; s. Ralph Penrose and Rhea Alice (Erdman) H.; m. Gudrun Hogseth, May 3, 1951. AB cum laude, Dartmouth Coll., 1939; MA, Columbia U., 1940, PhD, 1951; postgrad., Princeton (N.J.) U., 1940-41. Assoc. economist Office of Price Adminstrn., Washington, 1941-42; economist U.S. Dept. Treasury, Washington, 1945-47, Econ. Cooperation Adminstrn., Washington, 1949-50; with govt. agys. U.S. econ. assistance developing countries, 1951-79; econ. advisor Bank of Guatemala, 1959-60; econ. researcher Konjunctor Inst., Stockholm, 1947-48. Contbr. articles to profl. jours. With USN, 1943-45, PTO. Mem. Am. Econ. Assn., Am. Fgn. Svc. Assn., Sind Club (Pakistan), Princeton Club (N.Y.), U.S.S. Columbia Light Cruiser 56 Assn. Congregationalist.

HOLBROOK, BARBARA CARR SAN, advertising agency executive; b. Roanoke, Va.; d. Louis James and Eleanor (Brophy) San; m. John Pinckney Holbrook, May 29, 1956 (dec. 1989); children—David Carr, Priscilla Mann. B.A., U. N.C. Copywriter Doherty, Clifford, Steers, Shenfield, N.Y.C., 1954-56, Doyle, Dane, Bernbach, N.Y.C., 1956-58, Ogilvy & Mather, N.Y.C., 1958-59; copy group head Benton & Bowles, N.Y.C., 1959-70; v.p., assoc. creative dir. Grey Advt. Inc., N.Y.C., 1970-89, creative dir., 1989—. Bd. dirs. Nat. Assn. for Visually Handicapped. Named to Clio Hall of Fame, 1955; recipient Clio award, 1977, Hollywood Internat. Broadcast award, 1970, Andy award, 1970, 83, Grey Advt. Pres.'s award, 1985, 88, 91; Bus. Bldg. award Procter & Gamble, 1989, World Class Advt. award, 1990, Effie award, 1991. Democrat. Episcopalian. Office: Grey Advt Inc 777 3d Ave New York NY 10017

HOLBROOK, STEPHEN FULLER, management consultant; b. Westwood, N.J., Mar. 14, 1934; s. Joseph Carleton and Eleanor (Day) H.; m. Elaine Wilhovsky, Mar. 2, 1957; children: Julie Day, Martha Holbrook Ramsland, Holly Holbrook Nelson. B in Econs., Union Coll., 1956. Salesman mktg. mgmt. corp. new project devel. group Owens-Ill. Inc., Toledo, 1959-67; mktg. dir. Kepner-Tregoe, Princeton, N.J., 1967-70; chmn. bd. dirs., chief exec. officer Princeton Mgmt. Assocs. Inc., 1970—; mem. faculty Stonier Grad. Sch. Banking Am. Banking Assn., Washington, 1971—. Author: Effective Decision Making, Effective Planning, Effective Problem Solving and People Management, Rapid Reading for Busy People, 1991. Active Rep. Club, Montgomery Twp., 1970-77; twp. com., 1975-77; mem. planning bd., 1973-77; vice mayor, 1976-77. Lt. (j.g.) USNR, 1956-59. Mem. ASTD, Nat. Speakers Assn. (cert.), Christian Mgmt. Assn., Antique Auto Assn. Am. Nassau Racquet and Tennis Club. Mem. Evangelical Free Ch. Office: Princeton Mgmt Assocs 170 Township Line Rd Belle Mead NJ 08502-4103

HOLCH, ERIC SANFORD, artist; b. Andover, Mass., 1948; m. Betsy Holch; 2 children. BA in History, Hobart Coll., 1970; studied with Bruce Fabricant, 1970. With Kohler Co., Greenwich, Conn., 1971-85; now freelance artist, 1985. One man shows include Greene Gallery, Guilford, Conn., 1982, Portfolio Gallery, Stamford, 1983, 84, 88, D. Christian James Gallery, Summit, N.J., 1985, The Little Gallery Nantucket, 1986, 90, Martha Lincoln Gallery, Vero Beach, Fla., 1987, Gallery 39, Osaka, Japan, 1989-91; group exhbns. include Hurlburt Gallery, Greenwich, Conn., 1980, Munson Gallery, Chatham, Mass., 1983, Kenneth Taylor Gallery, Nantucket, 1983, Wenniger Gallery, Boston and Rockport, Mass., 1985, Gallery 39, Osaka, 1989, T.I.A.S., Tokyo, 1991, 92; exhibited in pvt. collections Champion Internat., Cheeseborough-Ponds. Home and Office: 49 Gerrish Ln New Canaan CT 06840-4116

HOLCOMB, GRANT, III, museum director; b. San Bernardino, Calif., Sept. 30, 1944. BA, UCLA, 1967; MA, U. Del., 1970, PhD, 1972. Asst. prof. Mt. Holyoke Coll., South Hadley, Mass., 1972-80, SUNY, Stony Brook, 1980-81; curator San Diego Mus. Art, 1981-83; assoc. dir. TimKen Art Gallery, San Diego, 1983-85; dir. Meml. Art Gallery, Rochester, N.Y., 1985—. Author: (exhibit catalogue) John Sloan, The Gloucester Years, 1980, Wake of the Ferry, 1984; contbr. articles to profl. jours. Bd. dirs. BOA edits., 1991—, Conv. Vis. Bur., 1990—. Kress fellow Nat. Gallery Art, 1972; Am. Council Learned Socs. grantee, 1980. Mem. Assn. Art Mus. Dirs., Arts for Greater Rochester (bd. dirs. 1985—), Aesthetic Edn. Inst. (bd. dirs. 1985—). Office: Meml Art Gallery 500 University Ave Rochester NY 14607-1484

HOLCOMBE, ANNA CALLUORI, art educator; b. Newark, Sept. 15, 1952; d. Anthony and Anna Felice (Pangaro) Calluori; m. Robert Everett Holcombe, Aug. 13, 1977; 1 child, Gabriele Calluori Holcombe. BA, Montclair State Coll., 1974; MFA, La. State U., 1977. Asst. prof. art Ill. Wesleyan U., Bloomington, 1979-84; assoc. prof. art SUNY, Brockport, 1984—; artist-in-residence Archie Bray Found., Helena, Mont., 1991, Watershed Ctr. for Ceramic Arts, 1988-92, pres.-elect, 1992—; bd. dirs. Empire State Crafts Alliance, 1986-89. Exhibited in one-person show at Meml. Art Gallery, 1991; group show at Faenza, Italy, 1989 (Gold medal 1989). Office: SUNY Dept Art and Art History Brockport NY 14420

HOLCOMBE, DOROTHY FREEMAN, writer, artist; b. Trenton, N.J., May 18, 1926; d. Allyne Maxwell and Mary Edythe (Dey) Freeman; m. Carl William Holcombe, Aug. 25, 1950; children: David, Daniel, Esther. BS in Art, Trenton State Coll., 1972; student, Moore Coll. Art, Phila. Author: (poems) Moments in Time, 1990; portrait painter (1st, 3d prize 1960-63); pub. poems, 1956-91 (2d, 4th prize). Violinist, Delaware Valley Philharm. Orch., Pa., 1953-70; mem. Levittown (Pa.) Artist Assn., 1956-60; mem. choir Mercer County Chorus, Trenton, 1951-52; mem. varioous youth orchs., Levittown and Trenton, 1956-59. Home: 219 Willow Dr Levittown PA 19054 also: Rt 849 W Newport PA 17074

HOLCOMBE, THOMAS CHARLES, technology executive; b. Birmingham, Ala., Jan. 21, 1948; s. William Collis and Bernell (Johnson) H.; m. Sandra L., Aug. 1, 1970; children: Tiffany, Sonya. BSChemE, Va. Polytechnic Inst., 1970; MBA in mgmt., Pace U., 1979, D of profl. studies, 1991. Registered profl. engr., N.Y. Product coord. Procter & Gamble Co., Cin., 1970-74; assoc. dir. tech. Union Carbide Corp., Tarrytown, N.Y., 1974-89; dir. tech. Dehydro-Tech Corp., East Hanover, N.J., 1989—. Patentee in field; contbr. articles to profl. jours. Mem. Am. Inst. Chem. Engrs., Water Pollution Control Fedn. Home: 376 Morris Ave Mountain Lakes NJ 07046-1653 Office: Dehydro-Tech Corp 6 Great Meadow Ln East Hanover NJ 07936-1703

HOLCOMBE, WILLIAM J., manufacturing company executive; b. 1925. V.p. De Laval Turbine Inc., 1961-72, pres., chief exec. office, 1965; group v.p. Transamerica Corp., 1972-75; chmn. bd. dirs. Teton Inc., 1976-86; chmn., CEO IMO Industries Inc., Trenton, N.J., from 1986, now chmn. Office: IMO Industries Inc 3450 Princeton Pike Trenton NJ 08648-1206*

HOLDEN, GARY, social work researcher; b. Springfield, Vt., Apr. 26, 1951; s. George and Helen H.; m. Kathleen M. Barker, Mar. 17, 1989. BA summa cum laude, U. Wash., 1984; MS, Columbia U., 1987, DSW with distinction, 1990. Rsch. asst. Ctr. for the Study of Relationships U. Wash., Seattle, 1982-83, Addictive Behaviors Rsch. Ctr. U. Wash., Seattle, 1983-84; asst. rsch. scientist, field placement N.Y. State Psychiat. Inst., N.Y.C., 1986-87; researcher Columbia U. Sch. Social Work, N.Y.C., 1987-89; lectr. NYU Sch. Social Work, N.Y.C., 1989-90; rsch. assoc. Mt. Sinai Sch. Medicine, N.Y.C., 1990-91, asst. prof., 1992—; adj. lectr./asst. prof. Columbia U. Sch. Social Wk., N.Y.C., 1989—; rsch. cons. Elmhurst Hosp., N.Y.C., 1991—. Peer reviewer Psychol. Reports, 1990—, Jour. Social Work and Health Care, 1990—; contbr. articles to profl. jours.; guest editor Jour. Social Work and Health Care, 1991. Leopold Schepp Found. scholar, 1985-87, Ednl. Opportunity Program scholar, 1984, U. Wash. Alumni Club scholar, 1983-84, Irene Hanan scholar, 1982-83; fellow NIMH Clin. Rsch., 1987-89, Marie Antoinette Cannon, 1985-86, U. Fla. Grad. Coun., 1984-85; grant support Nat. Inst. Allergic and Infectious Diseases, Nat. Coop. Inner-City Asthma Study, Nat. Inst. for Neurol. Disorders and Stroke, Minorities, Risk Factors and Stroke. Mem. NASW, Computer Use in Social Svcs. Network, Social Scis. Computing Assn., Phi Beta Kappa, Golden Key, Psi Chi, Chi Sigma Iota. Office: Mt Sinai Sch Medicine Dept Community Medicine 1 Gustave L Levy Pl New York NY 10029-6574

HOLDEN, JAMES STUART, federal judge; b. Bennington, Vt., Jan. 29, 1914; s. Edward Henry and Mary Anstiss (Thayer) H.; m. Helen Elizabeth Vetal, Mar. 3, 1941; children: Susan (Mrs. Spaeth), Peter Vetal, James Stuart. A.B., Dartmouth Coll., 1935, LL.D. (hon.), 1985; LL.B., Union U., 1938. Bar: Vt. 1938. Practice in Bennington, 1938-41, 46-48; state's atty. Bennington County, 1946-48; chmn. Vt. Pub. Service Commn., 1948-49; superior judge State, 1949-56; assoc. justice Supreme Ct. Vt., 1956-63, chief justice, 1963-72; U.S. dist. judge for Dist. of Vt., 1972-84, sr. U.S. dist. judge for, 1984—; Chmn. Vt. Statutory Revision Commn., 1957-62; chmn. provisional com. to establish Nat. Center for State Cts., 1971. Trustee Vt. State Library, 1959-69. Served to maj. 43d Inf. Div. AUS, 1941-46. Mem. 43d Inf. Div. Vets. Assn. (past comdr.), Am., Vt. bar assns., Conf. Chief Justices (vice chmn. 1969-70, chmn. 1971), Am. Judicature Soc., Inst. Jud. Administrn., Am. Law Inst. Protestant Episcopalian. Office: PO Box 818 North Bennington VT 05257-0818

HOLDEN, PETER DREW, engineering executive; b. Ossining, N.Y., Dec. 1, 1940; s. William Clarence Jr. and Florence (Dieckhoff) H.; m. Catherine Ann McCormack, Sept. 4, 1966; children: Peter Drew Jr., John David, Michael Justinian. BSME, Clarkson U., 1962; MSME, Cornell U., 1964. Registered profl. engr. Conn., La., Md., N.Y., Ohio, S.C. Engr. Ingersoll-Rand Co., Princeton, N.J., 1964-66; sr. staff engr. Exxon Corp., Florham Park, N.J., 1966-84; project engr. Syska and Hennessy, N.Y.C., 1984-87; dir. engring. Domino Sugar Corp., N.Y.C., 1987—. Patentee pneumatic saw. Proctor and Gamble fellow, 1962. Mem. ASME, NSPE, ASHRAE, Internat. Soc. Sugar Technologists. Republican. Congregationalist. Home: 9 Orchard Rd Chatham NJ 07928 Office: Domino Sugar Corp 1114 Avenue of the Americas New York NY 10036

HOLDEN, RAYMOND HENRY, clinical psychologist; b. Providence, Feb. 21, 1924; s. James Herbert and Martha (Sutcliffe) H. AB magna cum laude, Brown U., 1947; AM, Yale U., 1949; EdD, Boston U., 1960. Cert. psychologist R.I., Mass. Asst. in psychology Yale U., New Haven, 1947-48; dir. dept. psychology Meeting St. Sch., Providence, 1952-62; dir. child testing unit Brown U., Providence, 1957-70; dir. learning ctr. R.I. Coll., Providence, 1970-72, prof. dept. psychology, 1970-87; chief psychologist Vocat. Resources, Inc., Providence, 1965—, Tavares Pediatric Ctr., Providence, 1989—; vis. scientist Nat. Inst. Neurol. Disease and Strokes, NIH, Bethesda, Md., 1968-69; cons. Fuller Meml. Hosp., South Attelboro, Mass., 1977-85, Johnston (R.I.) Sch. Dept., 1977-91, Dartmouth (Mass.) Sch. Dept., 1986-87. Contbr. articles to profl. publs.; author test revs. Served as sgt. U.S. Army, 1943-46, PTO. Fellow Am. Psychol. Assn., Am. Orthopsychiatric Assn.; mem. Phi Beta Kappa, Sigma Xi, Phi Delta Kappa. Home: 9 Cambria Ct Pawtucket RI 02860-5117 Office: Vocat Resources Inc 100 Houghton St Providence RI 02904-1072

HOLDEN, RICK MARSHALL, computer consultant; b. Schenectady, N.Y., June 25, 1952; s. Wallace Alton and Doris Althea (Hover) H.; m. M. Andrea Anthony, Nov. 27, 1976; children: Jessica Lee, Katelyn Elizabeth, Emily Grace. BA, SUNY, Buffalo, 1974, MBA, 1980. Resident counselor Transitional Svcs. Inc., Buffalo, 1975, counselor, 1975-77, sr. counselor, 1977-81, program supr., 1981-83; planning officer Marine Midland Bank, Buffalo, 1983-85, project mgr., 1985-87, asst. v.p., mgr. tech. ctr., 1987-91; pres. Marshall Cons. Assocs., Amherst, N.Y., 1991—; ind. cons. in field, 1989—; panel speaker. Coach Amherst (N.Y.) Girls Softball League, 1989; asst. chmn. Parents Coun., Amherst, 1988. Mem. Am. Inst. Banking, We. N.Y. Cons. Assn. Home and Office: 5774 Kippen Dr East Amherst NY 14051-1971

HOLDEN, WILLIAM HOYT, JR., lawyer; b. Chgo.; s. William Hoyt and Bernice Elizabeth (McKenzie) H.; m. Mary Ann Kula, June 23, 1954 (div. June 1982); children: William, Christopher, Sarah, Peter. BS, U. Ill., 1954; JD, U. Md., Balt., 1965. Bar: Md. 1965, U.S. Supreme Ct. 1969. Assoc. Weinberg and Green, Balt., 1965-72, ptnr., 1973-83; sr. v.p. CRI, Inc., Rockville, Md., 1983-85; sr. advisor Legg Mason Wood Walker, Inc., Balt., 1985-86; pvt. practice Bethesda, Md., 1987—; pres., bd. dirs. Am. Franchise Consultants, Inc., Bethesda, 1987—; bd. dirs. Mid-Atlantic Title Closing, Inc. Capt. USNR, 1977, ret., 1982. Mem. Md. State Bar Assn., Order of Coif, Rotary. Republican. Office: 4400 E West Hwy Bethesda MD 20814-4524

HOLDER, ANNAMARIA JUDE MCGARVEY, educator; b. Jersey City, Aug. 14, 1964; d. Gary Lee and Andrea Maria (Rosko) McGarvey; m. Norman L. Holder, June 28, 1991. BA in Art Edn., Georgian Ct. Coll., 1986, postgrad. Cert. art instr., elem. classroom tchr., N.J. Art instr. Holy Family Sch., Lakewood, N.J., 1986—, 1st grade tchr., 1986-87, art dir., 1987—; tchr. adult art Jackson (N.J.) Community Sch., 1986-89; tchr. arts and crafts Ocean County Dept. Parks and Recreation, Lakewood, 1987. Decorating chmn. mid-winter ball St. Mary of the Lake Ch., Lakewood, 1988, 92, co-chmn., 1989, 90, 91, centennial com., 1989—, Cath. youth orgn. asst., 1986—. Recipient Geography Awareness award State of N.J., 1989, 91. Mem. ASCD, Nat. Cath. Educators Assn., Nat. Art Edn. Assn., Georgian Ct. Coll. Alumni Assn. Democrat. Home: 18 Central Ave Apt 1 Lakewood NJ 08701-3130 Office: Holy Family Sch E County Line Rd Lakewood NJ 08701

HOLDER, TIMOTHY SCOTT, fund raising executive; b. Elizabethton, Tenn., Jan. 30, 1955; s. John Bell Carden and Ida Ruth (Scott) H. BA, U. South, 1977; M in Pub. Adminstrn., Mid. Tenn. State U., 1979. So. fin. dir. Glenn for Pres., Washington, 1982-84; nat. staff mem. Mondale for Pres., 1984; dep. fin. chmn. Dem. Nat. Com., Washington, 1985-87; deputy fin. chair Gephardt for Pres., Washington, 1987-88; nat. staff mem. Dukakis for Pres., 1988; pres., founder The Holder So. Cos./CM Alliance, Washington, Nashville, 1984-90; dir. devel., mission planning The Episcopal Ch., New York, 1990—; bd. dirs. Protective Svc. Life Ins. Co., Jackson, Miss., 1987, 1988; bd. dirs. The Valladarer Found., Washington, 1987, 1988. Named one of Outstanding Young Men Am., 1983. Mem. St. Andrew's Soc., Sewandke Club, Phi Delta Phi, Kappa Epsilon. Democrat. Episcopalian. Home: The Cloister 321 E 43d St New York NY 10017 Office: The Episcopal Ch Ctr 815 2d Ave New York NY 10017 also: PO Box 1000 Elizabethton TN 37644-1000

HOLEMAN, GEORGE ROBERT, health physicist, consultant; b. Danville, Ky., Dec. 23, 1937; s. Ernest R. and Rosa Mae (Tuggle) H.; m. Pamela Reed, Sept. 5, 1959 (div. June 1984); children: David R., Heather L. Holeman. BA, Centre Coll. of Ky., 1960; AM, Harvard U., 1961. Health physicist, Knolls Atomic Power Lab. GE, Schenectady, N.Y., 1961-63; health physicist Yale U., New Haven, Conn., 1963-71; dir. health physics div. Yale U., 1971-86, lectr. in Pub. Health, 1963-85, lectr. in Epidemiology, 1985—, dir. radiation safety dept., 1986—; attending health physicist VA Med. Ctr., West Haven, 1976—; dir. Radionuclide Lab., Yale U. Cancer Ctr., 1974-77; cons. Environ. Evaluation Group, State of N.Mex., 1979-89; mem. ind. risk assessment team Gov.'s Office State of Conn., 1980-90. Contbr. 26 articles to profl. jours. Bd. dirs. Conn. Hazardous Waste Mgmt. Svc., 1983—, vice chmn., 1983—, acting chmn. and chief exec. officer, 1990-91. AEC health physics fellow, Harvard U., 1960-61, Brookhaven Nat. Lab., Upton, L.I., 1961; WHO fellow, Sweden, Fed. Rep. Germany, U.K., 1985; del. IRPA Congress, Health Physics Soc., West Berlin, 1983. Fellow APHA (governing coun. 1988-89), Am. Acad. Health Physics (diplomate, bd. dirs. 1988-90), Nat. Coun. on Radiation Protection (chair scientific com. 1985—); mem. Am. Assn. Physicists in Medicine (chair radiation protection com. 1980-85, mem. Sci. Coun. 1980-85), Health Physics Soc. (sec. 1980-82, bd. dirs. 1980-83). Office: Radiation Safety Dept Yale U 135 College St New Haven CT 06510-2411

HOLIAN, GAIL CONCA, English educator; b. Jersey City, Sept. 21, 1948; d. Samuel Joseph and Mariejoyee (Contey) Conca; m. John F. Holian, Dec. 26, 1970. BA, Georgian Court Coll., 1970; MA, St. Johns U., 1972; PhD in English Lit., Drew U., 1987. Instr. English Neptune Twp. (N.J.) Bd. Edn., 1971-80; adj. instr. English Ocean County Coll., Toms River, N.J., 1974-81; teaching fellow English NYU, N.Y.C., 1978-79; lectr. English Georgian Court Coll., Lakewood, N.J., 1978-80, asst. prof. English, 1980-88, assoc. prof., 1988, dir. writing program, 1982—, prof. English, 1992—; judge book rev. div. Ann. Creative Writing Awards, N.J. State Fedn. of Women's Clubs, 1988, N.J. State Ins. Women's Communicate with Confidence Speak-Off, 1988; pres. Holian and Assocs; cons. Lit. and Corp. Communications Svcs., Red Bank, N.J.; lectr. various confs. and assns. Contbr. articles to profl. jours. Vol. ARC, 1972-80; dir. media svcs. and publs. Found. for Rsch. in Optimal Living, Red Bank, N.J., 1984—; chairperson Instl. Integrity Self Study Group for Middle States Accreditation, Georgian Court Coll.; mem. steering com. Georgian Ct. Coll. Devel. Program, 1991—. Georgian Court Coll. grantee, 1968; recipient Nat. award Sears Roebuck Found., 1989, Found. for Higher Edn. Mem. MLA, Nat. Coun. Tchrs. English (judge Achievement Awards in Writing 1984), N.J. Coll. English Assn., Nat. Assn. State Dirs. (mem. tchr. edn. cert. evaluation team 1989), Inst. for Study of Psychology and Lit., Southeastern Medieval Assn., Medieval Acad. Am., Renaissance Soc. Am., Soroptomists (v.p. 1983-84), Sigma Tau Delta. Home: 65 Washington St Red Bank NJ 07701-1836

HOLIDAY, MARTHA, television producer, entertainer; Jazz stylist N.Y.C. night clubs; asst. fashion promotion, Simplicity Patterns Co., N.Y.C., 1956-57; hotel fashion dir., 1957—; staged fashion and jazz festivals, 1959-65; producer, singer, Newport, Monterey, Las Vegas, Stockholm, Nice; staged Salute to N.Y.C., hist. fashion pageant Operation Sail, July 4, 1976; producer, commentator cable TV The Martha Holiday Show, 1985—. Author: Fashion Show Techniques, 1959. Fashion editor: East, 1957; Fabulous Las Vegas, 1957-62. Mem. Town Tennis Club, West Side Tennis Club. Address: 119 E 83d St New York NY 10028

HOLIEN, KIM BERNARD, historian; b. Bad Cannstadt-Stuttgart, Fed. Republic of Germany, Mar. 10, 1948; (parents Am. citizens); s. Maurice Joel and Margaret Alice (Wild) H. BS, Bethel Coll., 1970; MA, George Mason U., 1984. With Dept. State, Washington, 1971-73; adjudicator GAO, Washington, 1975-76; with Nat. Archives, Washington, 1977-79; mil. historian Dept. Army, Washington, 1979—; historian Nat. Guard Bur., 1984; officer First North-South Brigade, Inc., 1974-84. Author: Battle at Ball's Bluff, 1985; asst. editor The Sharpshooter, 1976-79, 89; editor Clarion's Call, 1980-83, ann. rev. N.G. Bur., 1984. Recipient Letter of Commendation, Dept. State, 1971, Disting. Svc. award Va. div. Sons of Confederate Vets., 1980, Outstanding Svc. award, 1980, Outstanding Svc. award and Spl. Svc. award, 1981 (all Dept. Army), Comdr.-in-Chief's award Sons Confederate Vets., 1982, Comdr.'s award Sons Union Vets., 1982, cert. of achievement U.S. Army Ctr. Mil. History, 1984, Found. award Loudoun County Pub. Libr., 1989, also letters of commendation/appreciation Dept. Army, Sec. Def., 1983, spl. svc. award Chief of Mil. History, 1986, ofcl. commendation, 1988, letter of commendation Army Material Command, 1992. Mem. Am. Hist. Assn., Co. of Mil. Historians, D.C. Civil War Round Table (past pres.), Am. Mil. Inst., No. Va. Assn. of Historians (bd. dirs. 1979-81, 83-84), Alexandria Civil War Round Table (past pres.), Sons of Norway, Bethel Coll. Alumni Assn. (bd. dir.), Heritage of Honor (pres.), Friends of Ft. Ward (bd. dirs. 1990—). Lutheran.

HOLL, JANE ELLEN, army officer; b. Newark, Dec. 1, 1956; d. John Francis and Adel (Schwetz) Holl; m. David William Polomski, Feb. 9, 1985; children: Catherine, Adellyn. BA, Montclair State Coll., 1978; MS, U. So. Calif., L.A., 1985; AM, Stanford U., 1988, PhD, 1989. Commd. U.S. Army, 1978—, advanced through grades to maj.; tactical signal rep. U.S. Command Berlin to Allied Staff, Berlin, Ger., 1980-82; brigade signal officer U.S. Command Berlin, Berlin, Ger., 1981-82; sr. message officer The Office of the Army Chief of Staff, The Pentagon, Washington, 1983-84; co. comdr. Info. systems Command, Arlington Hall, Va., 1984-85; asst. prof. U.S. Mil. Acad., West Point, N.Y., 1989-90, assoc. prof. social sci., 1990—, dir. nat. security studies, 1990—. ROTC scholar, 1976-78; 21st Century Trust fellow, 1990, Coun. on Fgn. Rels. Internat. Affairs fellow, 1991. Fellow Inter-Univ. Seminar on Armed Forces and Soc.; mem. Coun. on Fgn. Rels., Armed Forces Communication-Electronics Assn., Am. Polit. Sci. Assn., Women in Internat. Security. Office: US Mil Acad Dept Social Scis West Point NY 10996

HOLLADAY, HARLAN, retired educator, artist; b. Greenville, Mo., Dec. 10, 1925; s. Franklin and Mae (Croy) H.; m. Elsie Ruffena Calbert, Jan. 27, 1950; children—Joan Adrian, Carol Lisa, Jeffrey Carl. B.S. in Edn, S.E. Mo. State Coll., 1949; student, Washington U., St. Louis, 1947-49; M.A., U. Iowa, 1951; Ph.D., Cornell U., 1966. Tchr. art, dir. art Poplar Bluff (Mo) pub. schs., 1951-53; tchr. art Des Moines High Sch., 1953-55; instr., then asst. prof. art U. Nev., 1955-58; teaching asso. Cornell U., 1958-59; asst. prof. drawing Cornell U. State Coll. Agr., 1959-60; mem. faculty St. Lawrence U., Canton, N.Y., 1961-91; prof. fine arts St. Lawrence U., 1966-91, prof. fine arts emeritus, 1991—, head dept. fine arts, 1966-71, Flint prof., 1967-91; ret., prof. emeritus, 1991—; tchr., artist-in-residence Am. Coll. Switzerland, Leysin, 1968-69. Paintings rep. several mus. and permanent collections. Served with AUS, 1944-46. Recipient prizes in nat. and regional exhbns. Mem. AAUP, Coll. Art Assn. Soc. Archtl. Historians, St. Lawrence County Hist. Assn., Renaissance Soc. Am. Unitarian-Universalist Ch. Home: 23 Judson St Canton NY 13617-1144

HOLLAND, BART KEITH, epidemiologist, biostatistician; b. N.Y.C., June 2, 1956; s. Stewart and Violette (Kanner) H.; m. Jean Marie Donahue, June 16, 1985; 1 child, Alicia Marie. MPH, Columbia U., 1977; MA, Princeton (N.J.) U., 1982, PhD, 1983. Asst. prof. U. Medicine & Dentistry of N.J., Newark, 1985—. Author: (chpt.) Mathematical Population Dynamics, 1991; contbr. numerous articles to med. jours. NIH/Ctr. for Disease Control grantee U. Medicine & Dentistry of N.J., 1987—. Mem. Soc. Math. Biology, Human Biology Coun., Population Assn. of Am., Sigma Xi. Office: U Medicine & Dentistry NJ 185 S Orange Ave Newark NJ 07103-2714

HOLLAND, DARRYL BOYD, foundation administrator; b. N.Y.C., May 24, 1953. Student, Columbia U., 1971-72. Computer specialist Leon Schekter, Esquire, N.Y.C., 1971-84, Stephen I. Soble's CPA Co., N.Y.C., 1984-90; dir. devel. Pacific Teddybears, U.S.A., N.Y.C., 1990—. Office: Pacific Teddybears USA Inc 3215 Arlington Ave Riverdale NY 10463-3326

HOLLAND, DENNIS J., sales and marketing executive; b. Buffalo, Apr. 20, 1949; s. Merton J. and Mary M. (Carroll) H.; m. Carolyn M. Jenkins, Oct. 23, 1976; children: John R., Michele N. BA in Bus., U. Iowa, 1972; MBA, Syracuse U., 1980. Sales rep. Kysor Indsl., Cleve., 1971-75; with sales mktg. Warflex Corp., Rome, N.Y., 1975-78; sales mgr. Welch Allyn, Skaneteles, N.Y., 1978-82; mgr. sales and mktg. Galileo Electro Optics, Sturbridge, Mass., 1982-86; dir. sales and mktg. Conax Buffalo Corp., 1986—. Mem. Rotary (bd. dirs. 1980-84). Republican. Roman Catholic. Home: 6651 N Campbell Ave Apt 134 Tucson AZ 85718-1361

HOLLAND, HUDSON, JR., merchant; b. Springfield, Mass., Aug. 7, 1939; s. Hudson and Christine (Fuller) H.; m. Sandra P. Ray, Sept. 7, 1963; children: Hudson III, John Fuller. BA, Williams Coll., 1961. V.p. J. L. Hudson Co., Detroit, 1961-80; pres. Nantucket (Mass.) House, Inc., 1980—. Trustee Hudson Webber Found., Detroit, 1965-92, Nantucket (Mass.) Cottage Hosp., 1982-92, Nantucket Hist. Assn., 1991-92. Mem. Fontinalis Club, Nantucket Yacht Club. Republican. Congregational. Home: Shear Pen Hill Cottage Nantucket MA 02554 Office: Nantucket House Inc 1 S Beach St Nantucket MA 02554-0368

HOLLAND, JAMES R., real estate corporation executive; b. St. Louis, Feb. 20, 1944; s. Randolph and Thelma (Robinson) H.; student Principia Coll., 1962-64; B.F.A., Ohio U., 1966; postgrad. U. Mo. Sch. Journalism, 1966; m. Helen M. Devine, Feb. 18, 1972; children—Danielle, James Randolph, Eric Marc. Photog. intern Nat. Geog. Soc., Washington, 1966, contract photographer for mag., 1967-68; film producer Christian Sci. Center, Boston, 1969-74; real estate developer, pres. Brownstone Properties, Inc., Boston, 1975-77; real estate broker Street & Co., Inc., Boston, 1978-82; pres. A Bit of Boston Real Estate, Inc., 1982—; photographs and films in permanent collections: Truman Library, Boston Public Library, Ohio, Mo. univs., others. Active Neighborhood Assn. Back Bay, 1972—, Boston Home and Property Owners Assn.; assoc. Boston Pub. Libr.; lifetime Friend of Beverly Hills (Calif.) Pub. Library, Dickerson Park Zoo, Mus. Ozarks History; mem. 10th Anniversary com. Boston U.'s Photographic Resource Ctr.; sponsor Babe Ruth Baseball League Team, 1992—. Recipient World Press Competition award, 1967, Newsweek/Bolex documentary film award, 1969, Indsl. Photography Film Competition award, 1970, Internat. Film and TV Festival of N.Y. bronze medal, 1971; named AAU Nat. Karate Champion, 1989; ranked 6th nationally in weapon's forms Reeves Sport Karate Ratings, 1989. Mem. Am. Soc. Mag. Photographers, Friends of Photography, Nat. Press Photographers (awards 1966, 67, 68), N.Am. Sport Karate Assn. (various awards). Author: The Amazon, 1971, Mr. Pops-Arthur Fiedler, 1972, Tanglewood (foreward Michael Tilson Thomas), 1973; contbr. Photojournalism-Principles and Practice (Clifton Edom), 2d edit., 1980; articles, photographs contbd. to various nat., internat. newspapers, mags., encys., video games, numerous textbooks; writer documentary film scripts; film work has appeared on NBC, ABC, CBS, PBS, BBC; producer limited edit. karate video tapes Twinkle Toes Videos. Office: A Bit of Boston Real Estate Inc 5 Brimmer St Boston MA 02108-1001

HOLLAND, JOSEPH R., state senator; b. Tacoma Park, Md., June 12, 1936; s. Joseph Robert and Catherine Virginia (Bresnahan) H.; m. Sally Anne Bowden, Sept. 13, 1958; children: Joseph, David, Steve, Gina, Mark, Colette, Cathy, Sarah, Douglas, Elizabeth. BS in Pub. Adminstrn., U. Md., 1960; postgrad., Rockland C.C., Suffern, N.Y., 1976-78. Bowling show personality Rockland Cable Vision, 1961-76; bowling show host Sta. WRKL, 1966-77; mgr. Brunswick Corp. New City (N.Y.) Bowl, 1965-67, 69; exec. asst. to chmn. Legislature Rockland County, N.Y., 1970-73, dep. clk., 1977-79, clk., 1979-88; owner Original Bike Shop, N.Y., 1974-79; tchr. adult edn. Bds. Coop. Ednl. Svcs., Westchester, N.Y., 1976; mem. N.Y. State Assembly, 1989-90, N.Y. State Senate, 1991—; sec. to bd. dirs. Rockland Employees' Fed. Credit Union, 1983-84; sports columnist Our Town Newspaper, 1975-77, Rockland County Times Newspaper, 1975-77; sports editor Stony Point Messenger; substitute tchr. Clarkstown Sch., Bds. Coop. Ednl. Svcs., Suffern Sch. Pres. United Way, 1985-87, v.p., 1973, chmn. govt. divsn., 1972, co-campaign chmn., 1987-88, bd. dirs., 1971-74, 1983—, tri-state bd. dirs., 1985-87, tri-state long range planning com., 1985-86, N.Y. State bd. dirs., 1987-89, N.Y. State long range planning com., 1987-88; founder, chmn. emeritus Rockland County Sports Hall of Fame, pres., 1973-75, 84-87, bd. dirs., 1973—; fin. chmn. Shatemuc dist. Boy Scouts Am., 1968, chmn. Bowl-a-thon coun., 1981—, chmn. dist. nominating com., 1982-88, coun. nominating com., 1982-88, chmn. New City/Bardonia Community enrollment SME drive, 1981-86, chmn. dist. community enrollment SME drive, 1987-88, chmn. troop 48, chmn. troop 313; mem. major fund raising com. Girl Scouts U.S., long term fund raising com. Rockland County coun., 1988-89; chmn. bowling chpt. Am. Heart Assn., 1983-85, chmn. pers. com. Orange, Rockland, and Sullivan chpt., 1982, chmn. nominating com. Rockland chpt., 1985, bd. dirs. Rockland chpt., 1985-87, bd. dirs. Orange, Rockland, and Sullivan chpt., 1980-85; sub-chmn. benefit Camp Jawonio, 1965-74; project coord. Rockland County Transp. Study for Sr. Citizens and Physically Handicapped, 1971-73; coord. Rockland County "Keep N.Y. State Clean", 1971-73, Rockland County Recycling Program, 1972-73, Rockland County for Met. Regional Coun. TV System, 1971-73; coord. pub. rels. Civil Def., 1971-73; treasurer O'Grady/Brown Scholarship Com., 1988, 89; bd. dirs. Geriatric Evaluation Svcs. Team, 1986; info. and records mgmt. com. N.Y. State Supreme and County Courts; active Rockland County EDP Adv. Com., 1970-74. Lt. USMC, 1960-63. Recipient First Ann. Humanitarian award Rockland County Assn. for Retarded Children, 1982, Co-King of Hearts award Rockland, Orange, and Sullivan chpt. Am. Heart Assn., 1985, Seventh Ann. Frank Lo Presti Community Svc. award Rockland County Vol. Firemen, 1985, Shatemuc Dist. award Boy Scouts Am., 1984, Shatemuc D.S.M., 1986, Shatemuc Dist. Award of Merit, 1988, Achievement award Nat. Assn. Counties, 1987; named hon. chmn. first ann. dinner Rockland County coun. Girl Scout U.S.; inducted to Rockland County Sports Hall of Records, 1981. Mem. NAACP (polit. action com. Nyack 1981—), SAR, Empire State Soc. of SAR, USMC League (P.I.O. officer 1982-84), U.S. Res. Officers Assn., Am. Legis. Exchange Coun., N.Y. State Assn. County Clks. (life, bd. dirs. 1981-83, 87, chmn. resolutions com. 1981-82, exec. com. 1982-83, jud. liaison com. 1983-86), Rockland County Hist. Soc., Rockland County Assessors' Assn., Rockland County Men's Bowling Assn. (bd. dirs. 1973—), Internat. Assn. Clks., Records, Election Ofcls., and Treas., Jaycees (v.p. 1968-69, chmn. voter registration drive 1968, chmn. pub. rels.), Rotary (hon., chmn. various coms. New City br.), Ancient Order Hibernians, Haverstraw Elks. Republican. Roman Catholic. Home: 9 Kent St New City NY 10956 Office: State Capitol Senate House Albany NY 12224 also: 150 Airport Exec Pk Spring Valley NY 10977

HOLLAND, LEO LAVERNE, construction equipment executive; b. Freeport, Ill., June 7, 1941; s. Laverne B. and Delores R. (Wilke) H.; m. Mary Ellen Sweeney, Nov. 27, 1965; children: Jennifer M., Brett L. BS, U. Wis., 1963; postgrad., Emory U., 1978. Factory svc. rep. John Deere Dubuque (Iowa) Works, 1963-66; field svc. rep. John Deere Co., Atlanta, 1966-67; ter. mgr. John Deere Indsl. Equipment Co., Balt., 1967-69, bus. mgr. advisor, 1969-71, div. retail fin. mgr., 1971-74, div. dealer fin. mgr., 1974-83, div. product support mgr., 1983—; chmn. Excellence Com., Balt., 1991—; mem. Warranty Study Group, Dubuque, 1991—; cons. Electronic Warranty, Dubuque, 1990—. Pres. Perring Pk. Community Assn., Balt., 1971-73; leader Balt. County 4-H Club, Cockeysville, Md., 1981—; mem. Md. 4-H All Stars, College Park, Md., 186—; mem. liturgy com. St. Francis Xavier Ch., Hunt Valley, Md., 1990—; v.p. Balt. County Fair Bd., Cockeysville, 1984-87. Mem. Equipment Maintenance Coun. (assoc., v.p. 1988-90, sec. 1990—, Richard M. Hwskins 1992), Optimist Club (bd. dirs. 1992). Office: John Deere Indsl Equipment Co 119 Lake Front Dr Cockeysville Hunt Valley MD 21030-2249

HOLLAND, ROBERT STEVENS, advertising executive, graphic designer; b. New Brunswick, N.J., Feb. 3, 1945; s. Ubert Cecil and Dorothy Teresa (Stevens) H.; m. Debra Ann Schlachman, June 21, 1969; children: David, Mairen. BFA, Md. Inst. Coll. Art, 1969. Asst. installationist The Balt. Mus. Art, 1969-72; art dir. Barton-Gillet, Balt., 1972-82; v.p., sr. art dir. Crowder Communications, Balt., 1982-84, ptnr., sr. art dir. R.S. Jensen, 1984-89; exec. art dir. William J. Kircher & Assocs., Washington, 1989-90; pres. Robert S. Holland Design, Ellicott City, Md., 1990—; bd. dirs. Advt. and Graphic Arts Soc. of Howard County. Mem. The Advt. and Graphic Arts Soc. Howard County (bd. dirs.), Am. Inst. Graphic Arts, Art Dirs. Club of Met. Washington, Printing Industries of Md. Democrat. Home: 2914 Evergreen Way Ellicott City MD 21042-1020

HOLLANDER, DAVID, obstetrician, gynecologist; b. N.Y.C., Dec. 11, 1952; s. Bernard and Ruth (Skolnick) H.; m. Phyllis Lake, June 13, 1976; children: Brian, Scott. BA, Tulane U., 1974; MD, Autonoma U. Guadalajara, Mex., 1978. Diplomate Am. Bd. Ob-Gyn, Am. Bd. Maternal and Fetal Medicine. Resident in ob-gyn Nassau County Med. Ctr., East Meadow, N.Y., 1980-84; fellow in maternal and fetal medicine U. Md., Balt., 1984-86; dir. maternal and fetal medicine St. Barnabas Med. Ctr., Livingston, N.J., 1986-90; cons. St. Barnabas Med. Ctr., Livingston, Md., 1986—; dir. maternal and fetal medicine Suburban Women's Physicians, Livingston, 1990—; cons. in maternal and fetal medicine St. Elizabeth Hosp., Elizabeth, N.J., 1987—, Elizabeth Gen. Med. Ctr., 1987—; mem. N.J. Maternal Child State. Contbr. articles to med. jours. Fellow Am. Coll. Ob-Gyn (N.J. adv. bd.), Soc. Perinatal Obstetricians. Office: Suburban Women's Physicians 316 Eisenhower Pky Livingston NJ 07039

HOLLANDER, HOWARD ROBERT, software engineering manager; b. N.Y.C., Oct. 1, 1952; s. Maxwell and Rhoda (Scheller) H.; m. Linda Robin Pike, May 24, 1975; children: Aileen Dara, Jonathan Lee. BEE, NYU, 1973; MS in Engring. Mgmt., Northeastern U., 1975. Software engr. GTE Sylvania Co., Boston, 1974-75; sr. engr. GTE Sylvania Co., Ogden, Utah, 1975-78; specialist engr. Boeing Aerospace Co., Ogden, 1978-82; engring. mgr. GE Aerospace Co., Syracuse, N.Y., 1982—; cons. U. Utah, Salt Lake City, 1980-82, Minimax Systems, Syracuse, 1982—, Eastern Communications, N.Y.C., 1983-86, The Combined Sch., 1989—; bd. dirs. LMN Pike Co., Syracuse. Contbr. articles to tech. publs. Treas. Congregation Brith Sholem, Ogden, 1980-82; bd. dirs. Temple Beth El, Syracuse, 1985—, treas., 1990-91, pres. Men's Club, 1991—; bd. dirs. Combined Sch., Syracuse, 1987—. Named. Hon. Ky. Col., 1987. Mem. Elfun Soc. (sec.), Navy League U.S., Mensa, Pompey Swim Club, Sundown Health Club, Eta Kappa Nu. Democrat. Jewish. Home: 615 Churchill Ct Fayetteville NY 13066-2535 Office: GE PO Box 4840 Syracuse NY 13221-4840

HOLLANDER, LAWRENCE JAY, marketing executive; b. Chgo., Feb. 15, 1940; s. Harry and Ann Blanche (Rovner) H.; m. Sallie Sue Mines, June 21, 1964; children: Marla, Amy, Rebecca. BSBA, Roosevelt U., 1963. Dir. Far East ops. Indsl. & Sci. Conf. Mgmt., Chgo., 1972-77; dir. mktg. Far East ops. Clapp & Poliak, Inc., N.Y.C., 1978-81; pres. Expoconsul Internat. Inc., Princeton, N.J., 1981—, EI Mktg., Inc., Princeton, 1987—, Ctr. for Tech. Concepts, Inc., Princeton, 1988-92, Expoconsul Mktg. Group, Inc., Princeton, 1992—. Bd. dirs. Congregation Beth Chaim, West Windsor, N.J., 1984, Jewish Community Ctr. of Delaware Valley, Ewing, N.J., 1987—, v.p., 1990—; bd. dirs. Jewish Fedn. Mercer and Buck Counties, N.J., Pa., 1988—, v.p., 1989-90. Mem. Nat. Assn. Exposition Mgrs., Am. Soc. Assn. Execs., Rotary Club of the Princeton Corridor (sec. 1990-91, sgt.-at-arms 1991-92, dir. 1992—). Republican. Jewish. Office: Expoconsul Internat Inc 500 College Rd E Princeton NJ 08540-6671

HOLLANDER, MILTON BERNARD, corporate executive; b. Bayonne, N.J., Nov. 29, 1928; s. Harry and Lena (Hutner) H.; m. Betty Ruth Grodberg, June 6, 1952; children—Eva Lynn, J. Steven, Aaron Phillip, Joel Daniel. BS, Purdue U., 1951; MS, MIT, 1953; PhD, Columbia U., 1959. Dir. engring. ctr. Am. Machine & Foundry Co., Springdale, Conn., 1956-67; v.p. tech. Am.-Standard, Inc., N.Y.C., 1967-72; chmn. sci. and tech. Gulf & Western Invention Devel. Corp., N.Y.C., 1974-85; v.p. sci. and tech. Gulf & Western

Industries, Inc., N.Y.C., 1972-85; ret., 1985; exec. v.p. Tech. Mgmt. Inc., Stamford, Conn., 1985—; chmn. bd., chief exec. officer Newport Electronics Inc., Stamford, 1989—; pres. Analog & Numeric Devices, Inc., Stamford, 1990—; cons. electronics lab. Columbia U., 1955-57; dir., tech. cons. Omega Engring. Inc., Stamford, Conn. Author tech. papers temperature measurement, metal cutting, instrumentation. Bd. dirs. Conn. Tech. Inst. Served with C.E. AUS, 1946-48, Korea. Recipient Outstanding Alumnus award Purdue U., 1972, Outstanding Mech. Engring. award, 1991; rsch. fellow MIT 1952-53; duPont rsch. fellow Columbia U., 1955-57; rsch. fellow Am. Soc. Tool and Mfg. Engrs., 1954-55; named Outstanding Young Man Am., 1965. Mem. ASME, Am. Welding Soc., Indsl. Research Inst. (bd. dirs.), Instrument Soc. Am., Soc. Mfg. Engrs., Sigma Xi. Office: Tech Mgmt Inc 3 Riverbend Ctr PO Box 4819 Stamford CT 06907-0819

HOLLDOBLER, BERTHOLD KARL, zoologist, educator; b. Erling-Andechs, Germany, June 25, 1936; came to U.S., 1973; s. Karl and Maria (Russmann) H.; m. Friederike Probst, Feb. 9, 1980; children: Jakob, Stefan, Sebastian. Dr. rer. nat., U. Wurzburg, 1965; Dr. habil., U. Frankfurt a.M., 1969. Prof. zoology U. Frankfurt a.M., 1971-72; prof. biology Harvard U., Cambridge, Mass., 1973-90, Alexander Agassiz prof. zoology, 1982-90; prof. U. Wurzburg, Federal Republic of Germany, 1989—; adj. prof. U. Ariz., Tucson; rsch. assoc. Harvard U. Author: (with Edward O. Wilson) The Ants, 1990 (Pulitzer Prize for General Nonfiction). John Simon Guggenheim fellow, 1980; recipient Sr. Scientist award Alexander von Humboldt Found., 1986-87, Gottfried Wilhelm Leibniz prize, 1989. Mem. Am. Acad. Sci., Deutsche Akademie der Naturforscher Leopoldina, Bayerische Akademie der Wissenschaften.

HOLLEMAN, PAMELA SMITH, manufacturing company executive; b. Chgo., Dec. 13, 1953; d. Sydney and Dorothy (Embick) Smith; m. Charles Coburn Holleman, May 3, 1980; children: Sydeny Caroline, Charles Coburn, Jr. BA magna cum laude, Rockford Coll., 1975; MA, U. Chgo., 1977; MBA, NYU, 1985. Fed. rep. U.S. Dept. Labor, Chgo., N.Y.C., 1977-81; contract adminstr. Andover (Mass.) Controls Corp., 1985-87, group contr., 1987-90; contracts mgr. Ingersoll-Rand Co., Nashua, N.H., 1990—. mem. choir Carlisle Congl. Ch. Talcott fellow U. Chgo., 1976. Mem. Beta Gamma Sigma. Home: 84 Rutland St Carlisle MA 01741-1213 Office: Ingersoll-Rand Co 150 Burke St Nashua NH 03060-4742

HOLLENBECK, ALBERT RUSSELL, psychology researcher; b. San Francisco, Apr. 6, 1948; s. Albert Russell and Mary Margaret (Allread) H.; m. Laura E Noble, Nov. 29, 1991. BS, U. Calif., Davis, 1970; PhD, U. Wash., 1976. Predoctoral assoc. U. Wash., Seattle, 1970-75; rsch. asst. Battelle Rsch. Ctrs., Seattle, 1974-75; staff fellow NIMH, Bethesda, Md., 1976-79; asst. prof. of psychology George Mason U., Fairfax, Va., 1978-86; sr. rsch. assoc., asst. dir. Am. Assn. Retired Persons Andrus Found., Washington, 1986—; guest researcher Nat. Cancer Inst., Bethesda, 1983-89; pvt. practice cons., Alexandria, Va., 1986—. Contbr. articles, revs. to profl. publs., chpts. to books. Grantee NSF, 1980, NIMH, 1984. Fellow Am. Psychol. Soc. (charter), Am. Orthopsychiat. Assn.; mem. AAAS, Am. Psychol. Assn., Soc. for Rsch. on Child Devel., Internat. Soc. for Study of Behavioral Devel., Internat. Soc. for Infant Studies, Eastern Psychol. Assn., Western Psychol. Assn., Calif. Scholarship Fedn. (life). Home: 5340 Holmes Run Pky Apt 1505 Alexandria VA 22304-2826 Office: AARP Andrus Found 601 E St NW Washington DC 20049-0002

HOLLENBERG, NORMAN KENNETH, medical educator; b. Winnipeg, Manitoba, Can., Oct. 9, 1936; came to U.S., 1965; BS in Medicine, U. Manitoba, 1960, PhD in Pharmacology, 1965; MS, Harvard U., 1976. Lic. Med. Mass. From rsch. assoc. to prof. Harvard U., Boston, 1965—. Assoc. editor: New England Jour. Medicine, 1975-89; editor of 14 books; contbr. over 400 articles to profl. jours. Isbister scholar, 1953-56, Adalstein Kristjamson Meml. travel scholar, 1961; recipient Govnrs. Gen. Gold medal, 1956, Prowse prize and medal Clin. Rsch., 1965, Royal Coll. Physicians Gold medal and prize, 1969. Mem. Am. Heart Assn., Am. Soc. Nephrology, Am. Soc. Pharm. Therapeutics, Am. Soc. Clin. Investigation, Hypertension Coun.

HOLLEYMAN, ROBERT WALKER, II, lawyer, business executive; b. New Orleans, Feb. 4, 1955; s. Robert Walker and Esta Rae (Sheffield) H. BA, Trinity U., 1976; JD, La. State U. Law Ctr., 1979. Bar: Tex. 1982, La. 1979. Law clk. U.S. dist. judge Jack M. Gordon U.S. Dist. Ct. (eas. dist.) La., New Orleans, 1979-81; atty. Margraves, Kennerly & Schueler, Houston, 1982; legis. dir., legis. asst. U.S. Senator Russell B. Long, Washington, 1982-86; sr. counsel Senate Com. on Commerce, Sci. and Transportation, Washington, 1987-90; managing dir. Bus. Software Alliance, Washington, 1990—. Mem. State Bar Tex., La. State Bar Assn. Office: Bus Software Alliance 1201 Pennsylvania Ave NW Washington DC 20004-2401

HOLLIDAY, RICHARD CARTER, business manager; b. Pitts., Nov. 27, 1938; s. Allen Preston and Mary Gertrude (Taylor) H.; m. Christine Grimstad, Sept. 2, 1961 (div. Sept. 1971); m. Ardis Stuart, Dec. 31, 1975; children: Margaret C., Richard Carter Jr. BA, Williams Coll., 1960; MBA, Harvard U., 1963. Sales rep. Harris Graphics Corp., Chgo., 1960-66; sales office mgr. Harris Graphics Corp., Westerly, R.I., 1966-69; v.p. sales Harris Graphics Corp., Westerly, 1969-77; v.p., gen. mgr. Harris Graphics Corp., Grapevine, Tex., 1977-82; v.p. mktg. Harris Graphics Corp., Westerly, 1982-83; chief exec. officer, comml. press div. Man Roland Inc., Somerset, N.J., 1983-91; pres. R. C. Holliday, Inc., Westerly, 1991—; bd. dirs. Sayers Printing, Inc., St. Louis. Commr. Westerly (R.I.) Housing Authority, 1968-72; dir. Westerly (R.I.) YMCA, 1968-76, 91—; commr. Planning and Zoning Bd., Argyle, Tex., 1980-82. Mem. Watch Hill Yacht Club (dir. 1968-76), Graphic Art Tech. Found. (dir. 1991—). Republican.

HOLLIN, MITCHELL LOUIS, investment fund administrator; b. Phila., Sept. 24, 1962; m. Cristy B. Bell, Oct. 21, 1989. BS, U. Pa., 1984, MBA, 1989. V.p. Pharmaco USA, Inc., Phila., 1984-87; assoc. Alan Patricof Associates, Radnor, Pa., 1988-90; v.p. Cedar Point Ptnrs. LP, Blue Bell, Pa., 1990—; chmn. Del. Valley Buyout Group, Phila.; bd. dirs. Del. Valley Venture Group, Phila. Office: Cedar Point Ptnrs 1767 Sentry Pky W Ste 200 Blue Bell PA 19422-2219

HOLLINGER, PAULA COLODNY, state senator; b. Washington, Dec. 30, 1940; d. Samuel and Ethel (Levy) Colodny; m. Paul Hollinger, Sept. 16, 1962; children: Ilene, Marcy, David. RN, Mt. Sinai Hosp., N.Y.C., 1961. Mem. Md. Ho. of Dels., 1978-86; mem. Md. Ho. of Dels. Md. State Senate, Annapolis, 1987—, chmn. health subcom. of econ. and environ. affairs com., 1987—; mem. Gov.'s Adv. Coun. on AIDS, senate chair, 1990—, adminstrv. exec., legis. rev. com., 1990—; mem. Joint Com. on Health Care Cost Containment, Gov.'s Task Force to Study Nursing Crisis; vice-chair health com. Nat. Conf. State Legis., 1990, chair, 1992, past chair sci. and resources tech. com., chair health com., 1992. Bd. dirs. Nat. Coun. Jewish Women, Safety First, 1990; past pres. Women Legislators of Md., 1986, 87, 88. Recipient Murry Guggenheim award, 1961, Edith Rosen Strauss award, 1987, Verda Welcome award for outstanding polit. achievements and pub. svc., 1989, Legislator of Yr. award Md. Nurse's Assn., 1984. Mem. B'nai B'rith Women, Chi Eta Phi. Office: Md State Senate Office Bldg State House Annapolis MD 21401-1991

HOLLINSHEAD, EARL DARNELL, JR., lawyer; b. Pitts., Aug. 1, 1927; s. Earl Darnell and Gertrude (Cahill) H.; m. Sylvia Antion, June 29, 1957; children: Barbara, Kim, Earl III, Susan. AB, Ohio U., 1948; LLB, U. Pitts., 1951. Bar: Pa. 1952, U.S. Ct. Mil. Appeals 1954, U.S. Dist. Ct. (we. dist.) Pa. 1955, U.S. Supreme Ct. 1956, U.S. Ct. Appeals (3d cir.) 1959, U.S. Dist. Ct. (ea. dist.) Ohio 1978. Sole practice Pitts., 1955-70; ptnr. Hollinshead and Mendelson, Pitts., 1970-89, Hollinshead, Mendelson, Bresnahan & Nixon, P.C., Pitts., 1991—; mem. Pitts. Estate Planning Council. Contbr. articles to profl. jours. Served to lt. USNR, 1951-55. Fellow Pa. Bar Found. (life); mem. Pa. Bar Assn. (chmn. real property div. 1983-85, real property, probate and trust sects. 1985-86), Allegheny County Bar Assn. (chmn. real property sect. 1975-76), Pa. Bar Inst. (lectr., planner, bd. dirs. 1988—), Am. Coll. Real Estate Lawyers. Home: 2535 Windgate Rd Bethel Park PA 15102-2730 Office: Hollinshead Mendelson Bresnahan & Nixon 230 Grant St Pittsburgh PA 15219-2105

HOLLIS, LINDA EARDLEY, urban planning consultant; b. Washington, Feb. 1, 1948; d. Edward Pixton and Margy (Anderson) Eardley; m. Daryl Joseph Hollis, July 18, 1970. BA, Pa. State U., University Park, 1968; M in Regional Planning, U. N.C., 1979. Planning analyst First-Citizens Bank, Raleigh, N.C., 1973-76; research assoc. ctr. for urban regional studies U. N.C., Chapel Hill, 1978-79; research assoc. The Osprey Co., Tallahassee, 1980-81, Patrick H. Hare Planning and Design, Washington, 1982-83; cons. Tischler & Assocs., Inc., Bethesda, Md., Washington and Falls Church, Va., 1983—; analyst dept. fiscal services Md. Gen. Assembly, Annapolis, 1988-89. Contbr. articles to profl. jours. Mem. North Washington Neighbors, Inc., 1987—. NEH grantee, 1980. Mem. Am. Planning Assn. (book reviewer 1980, div. for econ. devel. 1985—, nat. bd. dirs., regional rep. 1986-88, chmn. nat. state policy coordinating com. 1987-88, chair task force on women and minorities 1987-88), Washington Women in Planning (co-founder). Democrat. Home: 902 Aspen St NW Washington DC 20012-2512 Office: Tischler & Assocs Inc 4701 Sangamore Rd Ste 210N Bethesda MD 20816-2508

HOLLIS, PETER B., retail executive; b. Newton, Mass., 1943; married. B, U. Vt., 1965. With Bradlees div. Stop and Shop Inc.; sr. v.p. gen. merchandising Zayre Corp., 1971-82; exec. v.p. Fisher's Big Wheel Inc., New Castle, Pa., 1982, pres., 1984-86; former chief operating officer Ames Dept. Stores, Inc., Rocky Hill, Conn., pres., chief exec. officer, 1987-90. Office: Ames Dept Stores Inc 2418 Main St Rocky Hill CT 06067-2598

HOLLIS, ROY ESTES, clinical neuropsychologist; b. Cohasset, Mass., July 29, 1946; s. Leon Perley Hollis and Lillian May Abrahamsen; m. Dorothy Kathleen Gordon, Jan. 25, 1969 (div. June 1987); 1 child, Tracey Nicole. AB, Ea. Nazarene Coll., Quincy, Mass., 1968; MEd, Plymouth State Coll., 1972; PhD, Psychology, Boston Coll., 1976. Diplomate Am. Bd. Clin. Neuropsychology, Am. Bd. Profl. Psychology; lic. psychologist, Mass., N.H. Chmn. dept. social studies White Mts. Regional Sch. Dist., Whitefield, N.H., 1968-71; assoc. prof. edn. Ea. Nazarene Coll., 1971-78; dir. psychology Hampstead (N.H.) Hosp., 1978—; dir. Neuropsychology Assocs., East Hampstead, N.H., 1986—. Coach Pioneer League Girls Softball, Newburyport, Mass., 1989-90. Mem. APA, Soc. for Personality Assessment, Internat. Neuropsychol. Soc. Office: Hampstead Hosp East Rd Hampstead NH 03841-2228

HOLLIS, VIRGINIA WEARE, insurance executive; b. Manchester, Conn., July 19, 1948; d. Thomas Jr. and Alcester (Weare) H.; m. Peter Charles Walbert, Aug. 19, 1972 (div. Oct. 1988); 1 child, Katherine Hollis Walbert. BA, Allegheny Coll., 1970. Analyst Aetna Life and Casualty, Hartford, Conn., 1970-72, sr. analyst, 1972-74, mgr., 1974-78; mgr. CIGNA, Bloomfield, Conn., 1978-80, asst. dir., 1980-82, dir., 1982-85, asst. v.p., 1985-90, v.p., 1991—. Bd. dirs. FAVARH, Avon, Conn., 1987-90. Office: CIGNA A-140 Hartford CT 06152

HOLLOWAY, JAMES CURTIS, military officer; b. Lebanon, Ind., Nov. 6, 1951; s. William Curtis and Patricia Ann (Love) H.; m. Beverly Jean Rodgers, June 16, 1973; children: Cheryl Leigh, Gayle Lynn. BS, U.S. Naval Acad., 1973. Commd. ensign USN, 1973, advanced through grades to capt., 1992; div. officer USS Tautog, Pearl Harbor, Hawaii, 1974-77; tng. officer Nuclear Propulsion Tng. Unit, Windsor, Conn., 1977-79; engr. officer USS La Jolla, San Diego, 1979-82; material officer Staff of Commdr. Submarine Squadron Ten, New London, Conn., 1982-84; officer in charge Submarine NR-1, Groton, Conn., 1985-88; commanding officer USS Oklahoma City, Norfolk, Va., 1988-91; fellow Chief of Naval Ops. Strategic Studies Group, Newport, R.I., 1991—. Active Meth. Ch., Gales Ferry, Conn., 1979-88, Virginia Beach, Va., 1988-91. Recipient Vice adm. J.B. Stockdale award for inspirational leadership USN, 1990, Marjorie Sterrett Battleship Fund award USN, 1991. Mem. U.S. Naval Inst., U.S. Naval Acad. Alumni Assn.

HOLLOWAY, JAMES LEMUEL, III, foundation executive, retired naval officer; b. Charleston, S.C., Feb. 23, 1922; s. James Lemuel and Jean Gordon (Hagood) H.; m. Dabney Hix Rawlings, Dec. 14, 1942; children: Lucy Dabney Lyon, Jane Meredith. BSEE, Naval Acad., Annapolis, 1942. Cert. naval aviator, naval nuclear reactor operator. Commd. ensign USN, 1942, advanced through grades to adm., 1973, comdr. U.S. 7th fleet, 1971-73, vice chief naval ops., 1973-74, mem. Joint Chiefs of Staff, Dept. Def., 1974-78, chief naval ops., 1974-78, ret., 1978; pres. Coun. Am.-Flag Ship Operators, Washington, 1981-88, Naval Hist. Found., Washington, 1981—; expert witness Congl. Coms., 1978—; cons. Paine Webber, Washington, 1980-88; bd. dirs. U.S. Life Ins. Co., Washington, UNC Inc., Annapolis; chmn. spl. rev. group investigating Iranian hostage rescue, 1981; spl. envoy of v.p. Bush to Mid. East, 1986; commr. Presdl. Blue Ribbon Commn. on Def. Mgmt., 1985, Congl. Commn. on Mcht. Marine and Def., 1987-88, Presdl. Commn. on Longterm Integrated Strategy, 1987-88; U.S. rep. to South Pacific Commn., 1990—. Contbr. articles to mags. Trustee St. James Sch., Md., 1962—, pres., 1989—; bd. dirs. Olmsted Found., Washington, 1978—; mem. bd. advisors The Citadel, 1981-86; chmn. adv. bd. U.S. Naval Acad., 1983-91; chmn. Hist. Annapolis Found., Inc., 1981—. Decorated Bronze Star, Air Medals, Legion of Merit, D.F.C., Def. D.S.M. with two bronze oak leaf clusters, Navy D.S.M. with four bronze oak leaf clusters, Order of Rising Sun (Japan), Grand Cross (Fed. Republic Germany), Legion of Honor (France), others. Mem. Assn. Naval Aviation (chmn. 1985—), Met. Club (Washington gov. 1988—, pres. 1992), Brook Club (N.Y.C.), N.Y. Yacht Club (N.Y.C.), Md. Club (Balt.), Annapolis Yacht Club, Soc. Cin. Republican. Episcopalian. Home: 1694 Epping Farms Rd Annapolis MD 21401-6672 Office: Naval Hist Found Washington Navy Yard Bldg 57 Washington DC 20374

HOLLOWAY, JEFFREY JOHN, safety engineer; b. Perth Amboy, N.J., Oct. 31, 1948; s. Ferris James and Mary Ann (Kutzkir) H. BA, Rutgers U., 1988. Safety mgr. Cooperheat, Inc., Somerset, N.J., 1989—. Vol. Raritan Bay Med. Ctr., Perth Amboy, N.J., 1986-91. Mem. Am. Soc. Safety Engrs. Office: Cooperheat Inc Somerset NJ 08873

HOLLOWAY, LOVERTA RUTH, educator, writer; b. Pitts.; d. John Michael and Maybelle Loretta (O'Boyle) Imblum; m. John Wilson Holloway, July 10, 1948; children: John, Richard, Thomas, Bonnie, Robert, Jane, William, Michael, Matthew. AS, Camden County Coll., Blackwood, N.J., 1974; BA, Glassboro State Coll., 1976. Mem. chem. rsch. staff Carnegie Inst., Pitts., 1941-47; importer Loverta's Gifts, 1965-72, 76—; freelance writer, columnist. Author: A Journey of Love, 1991; author poems Am. Poetry Anthology, 1989. Mem. choir Camden Diocese of N.J., 1968—, auto harpist, song leader, lector, ch. music historian, children's Bible study leader, pro-life coord.; vol. numerous youth groups, scouting orgns. Recipient scholarship Glassboro State Coll., 1975. Mem. Nat. Right to Life, Writers Inst., Nat. Geographic Soc., Vols. of Am. Home: PO Box 35 533 Bowers Ave Runnemede NJ 08078

HOLLOWAY, RALPH LESLIE, anthropology educator; b. Phila., Feb. 6, 1935; s. Ralph L. and Marguerite (Grugan) H. BS in Geology, U. N.Mex., Albuquerque, 1959; PhD in Anthropology, U. Calif., Berkeley, 1964. Asst. prof. Columbia U., N.Y.C., 1964-69, assoc. prof., 1969-73, prof., 1973—. Editor: Primate Aggression, Territoriality and Xenophobia: A Comparative Perspective, 1974; contbr. numerous articles to profl. jours. Guggenheim Found. fellow, 1974; NSF grantee, 1984. Fellow AAAS, N.Y. Acad. Sci.; mem. Am. Anthrop. Assn., Am. Assn. Phys. Anthropologists, Soc. for Neurosci., Sigma Xi, Phi Beta Kappa. Office: Columbia U Dept of Anthropology New York NY 10027

HOLLOWAY, REID LOREN, communications-marketing-finance consultant; b. Buffalo, Apr. 16, 1953; s. Robert Lee and Aurelia (Muresan) H. BA, Colgate U., 1975; postgrad., NYU, 1980. Editor Harcourt Brace Jovanovich, N.Y.C., 1976-77; mgr. communications Sanford C. Bernstein & Co., N.Y.C., 1978-80; sr. corp. writer W.R. Grace & Co., N.Y.C., 1980-87; dir. communications, mktg. svcs. Edward S. Gordon Co., N.Y.C., 1987; cons. N.Y.C., 1988—. Appointee The Grace Commn., N.Y.C., Washington, 1982-85; mem. N.Y. Cares, 1987—. Mem. N.Y. Wednesday Pub. Rels. Group, Paris Health Club. Home and Office: 307 W 106th St New York NY 10025-3483

HOLLOWOOD, JAMES RICHARD, educational administrator, consultant; b. Durham, N.C., Jan. 16, 1943; s. James Richard Sr. and Gerre Helen (Bober) H.; m. Diane Elizabeth Garner (div. 1972); children: Tracy Antonia, Melissa Frances; m. Judith Arlene Blight; 1 child, James Glen. BS, U. Pitts., 1969, postgrad., 1970-73; EdD, Harvard U., 1979. Engring. technician Westinghouse Electric Corp., 1964-68; computer facility mgr. Burroughs Corp., 1968-70; planning and policy analyst Ofifce Instnl. Rsch. U. Pitts., 1970-73; policy analyst Mass. Bd. Higher Edn./Mass. Sec. Ednl. Affairs, 1973-74; mgmt. cons. Arthur D. Little, Inc., 1977-81; dir. corp. rels. Boston Coll., 1981-82; with ednl. products R & D Digital Equipment Corp., 1982-86; dir. assoc. programs, adminstrn. and fin. Beaver Country Day Sch., 1986—; exec. dir. Lexington Montessori Sch., 1990-91; cons. in field. Mem. First Ch. of Belmont. With USCG, 1960-64. Mem. Harvard Club of Boston and N.Y. Home: 31 Springfield St Belmont MA 02178-3754

HOLM, INGRID MARGARETA, psychiatric nurse; b. Bridgeton, N.J., Aug. 4, 1961; d. Carl Bierregaard and Ragnhild Margareta (Fornander) H. AA, Acad. of New Ch. Coll., 1981; BSN, Thomas Jefferson U., 1984. RN, Pa., N.J. Night charge nurse Med. Coll. Pa., Phila., 1984-90; field supr. Vis. Homemaker Home Health Aides Svcs. Gloucester County, Woodbury, N.J., 1985-91; nurse Adult Protective Svc. Unit Camden (N.J.) County Bd. Social Svcs., 1986—; psychiat. nurse Stienenger Ctr., Cherry Hill, N.J., 1985-86, Cen. Health Svcs., Phila., 1989—; instr. Vis. Homemaker Home Health Aide Svc. of Gloucester County, Woodbury, 1989. Active Am. Swedish Hist. Found. and Mus., Phila. 1967—. Mem. ANA, N.J. State Nursing Assn., New Sweden Co. Inc. (asst. to curator in preparation for royal visit 1988). Democrat. Mem. New Ch. of New Jerusalem. Office: Camden County Bd Social Svc 600 Market St Camden NJ 08101

HOLMAN, FREDERICK JOHN, landscape architect; b. Syracuse, N.Y., Feb. 18, 1947; s. Harvey John and Rena Mae (Kenyon) H.; m. Karen Elise Visconti, July 11, 1970. AAS, Paul Smiths (N.Y.) Coll., 1967; B Landscape Architecture, SUNY, Syracuse, 1970; BA, Syracuse U., 1970. Registered landscape architect, N.Y., Mass. Planner Urban Renewal Agy., Schenectady, N.Y., 1970-71, N.Y. Bur. of Planning, Schenectady, 1971-72; landscape technician Saratoga Assocs., Saratoga Springs, N.Y., 1972-75; prin. L.A. Partnership, Saratoga Springs, 1975-81; prin. Frederick J. Holman Assocs., Saratoga Springs, 1981-83, Rochester, N.Y., 1986-89, Buffalo, 1989—; sr. assoc. Reimann Buechner Partnership, Syracuse, 1983-86; guest critic SUNY, 1985; guest critic, lectr. SUNY, Buffalo, 1989-91; lectr. Fedn. Garden Club, N.Y., 1985-86. Illustrator, tech. editor: Reforestation of Arid Lands, 1977, 2d edit., 1986, 3d edit., 1988, (manual) Understanding Soil Conservation Techniques, 1991. Pres. Saratoga Springs Preservation Found., 1979-83; chmn. Saratoga Springs Planning Bd., 1980-83; bd. dirs. Buffalo Friends of Olmsted Parks, 1991-92. Mem. Am. Planning Assn., Am. Soc. Landscape Architects (chpt. pres. 1985-89, trustee 1991—, Svc. award 1989), N.Y. State Coun. Landscape Architects (pres. 1989-92), N.Y. Planning Fedn., Rotary (bd. dirs. Williamsville, N.Y. chpt. 1992—). Office: 5550 Main St Williamsville NY 14221

HOLMAN, MARGARET MEZOFF, fund raising consultant; b. Pitts., Mar. 6, 1951; d. Earl Robert and Margaret Joan (Miller) M.; m. Richard L. Holman, Nov. 3, 1973. BA in Journalism, U. Nebr., 1973. Dir. community rels. Monterey (Calif.) Peninsula Hosp., 1978-81; assoc. dir. devel. Barnard Coll., N.Y.C., 1982-83; acting dir. devel. CARE, Inc., N.Y.C., 1983-84; dir. devel. Am. Acad. Dramatic Arts, N.Y.C., 1984-86; sr. v.p. devel. and mktg. ASPCA, N.Y.C., 1986-91; pres. Holman Assocs., N.Y.C., 1991—. Mem. Nat. Soc. Fund Raising Execs. (v.p. career svcs. Greater N.Y. chpt. 1988), Women in Fin. Devel. (pres. 1990—). Office: Holman Assocs 145 W 67th St Apt 21K New York NY 10023-5935

HOLMBERG, R(OY) HOPKINS, healthcare executive; b. Oak Park, Ill., Apr. 11, 1939; s. Roy Harold and Katherine Doyle (Hopkins) H.; m. Judith Mary Vandell, Aug. 23, 1962; children: Beth Bonnet, Daniel Hopkins. AB in Philosophy, Dartmouth Coll., 1961; MHA, U. Minn., 1963. Adminstrv. resident Johns Hopkins Hosp., Balt., 1962-63; rsch. fellow U. Minn., Mpls., 1963-65; asst. exec. dir. Am. Rehab. Found., Mpls., 1965-69; sr. assoc. Harold F. Wise & Assocs., Washington, 1969-71; exec. dir. Boston-Brookline Health Resources Orgn., 1971-73; dir., prof. health mgmt. programs Boston U. Sch. Mgmt., 1973-84; exec. dir. Aga Khan Hosp., Nairobi, Kenya, 1984-89; prin. Red Pine, Newtonville, Mass., 1989—; prof. health mgmt. and policy U. N.H., 1991—; chmn. Assn. Univ. Programs in Health Adminstrn., Arlington, Va., 1982-83; mgmt. com. Health Adminstrn. Press, Ann Arbor, 1980-84; chmn. Mass. Bd. Registration Nursing Home Adminstrs., Boston, 1978-80; mem. Mass. Health Facilities Appeals Bd., Boston, 1972-80. Chmn. Dem.-Farmer Labor Party of Mpls., 1968-69. Mem. Am. Coll. Healthcare Execs., Mass. Pub. Health Assn. (treas. 1983-84), Muthaiga Country Club (Nairobi). Office: Redpine 24 Oak Cliff Rd Newton MA 02160-2325

HOLMES, BARBARA JEAN, real estate developer; b. Toronto, Ont., Can., Apr. 29, 1948; d. Campbell Carlisle and Phyllis (Saunders) H.; m. Robert M. Greene, Dec. 3, 1973 (div. 1977); 1 child, Bizia Catal. BA, U. Western Ont., London, 1970. Real estate saleswoman Menorca, Spain, 1972-74; owner Essential Alts., Rutland, 1978-83; pres. Star Enterprises, Rutland, 1984—; developer East Creek Ctr., 1986&; v.p. Hedgedale Enterprises, Inc., Toronto; franchise owner Taco Bell, 1991—. Founder, dir. East Creek Playhouse, Rutland, 1986-87; bd. dirs. Vt. Indsl. Devel. Authority, Montpelier, 1986-92. Mem. Women Bus. Owners Vt. (pres.), Smaller Bus. Assn. New Eng. (founding Vt. chpt.), Rutland Region C. of C., Rutland Indsl. Devel. Corp., UC Yacht Club (commodore 1987). Congregationalist. Office: Star Enterprises Inc PO Box 6069 Rutland VT 05702-6069

HOLMES, CHRISTOPHER FRANCIS, advertising agency executive; b. Boston, Dec. 3, 1959; s. William Burton and Marie F. (Crowley) H. BBA in Mktg., Suffolk U., 1984. Account exec. Ski Ad Internat. Inc., Boston, 1983-85, v.p., treas., 1985, pres., chief exec. officer, 1985—; chmn., pres., treas. Ski Ad Mktg. Group, Boston, 1989—; clk. Graphics Internat., Boston; advisor Ski Backs United S.A. Mem. Am. Mktg. Assn. Roman Catholic. Home and Office: Ski Ad Internat Inc 47 Candia St Weymouth MA 02189-1001

HOLMES, DAVID BRYAN, artist; b. Harrow, Eng., Aug. 8, 1936; s. Harold Percy and Ivy Ethel (Gregg) H.; student Twickenham Tech. Coll., Eng., 1954-57, Queen's U., Can., 1965-—, Harrow Sch. Art, Eng., London Sch. Art and Design, N.Y.C. Art Students League, 1971-72; m. Sigrid L. Frank. Compositor, typog. and graphic designer, Saint John, N.B., Can., 1960-64; free-lance artist, Kingston, Ont., Can., 1964—; instr. graphic arts, artistic anatomy, painting, illustration, etching and silverpoint drawing St. Lawrence Coll. Applied Arts and Tech., Kingston, 1968-74; one-man shows: Galerie Gauvreau, Montreal, Que., Can., 1969, 70, Wally F. Findlay Galleries Internat., N.Y.C., 1974, 76, 78, 80, 82, 83, 85, 87, 89, 90, 92, Chgo., 1977, 85, Beverly Hills, Calif., 1979, Palm Beach, Fla., 1981, 84, 86, 90, Agnes Etherington Art Centre, Queen's U., Kingston, 1967; group shows: Queen's U. Spring Exhbns., Kingston, 1964-72, Soc. Can. Artists Ann. Exhibition, 1968-71, Tom Thomson Gallery, Country Scenes Que., Montreal; represented in permanent collections in Europe and N.Am.; mem. Print and Drawing Council Can. Vice-pres., Kingston Arts Council, 1971-73. Served with Royal Marines, 1957-59. Mem. Soc. Can. Artists, N.Y. Art Students League, Internat. Soc. Artists of N.Y. Address: RR 3, Odessa, ON Canada K0H 2H0

HOLMES, DONALD DEAN, veterinarian; b. Mannford, Okla., Sept. 12, 1930; s. Raymond Kindred and Cornelia (Coonrod) H.; m. Mary Winton Whitaker, Aug. 28, 1955; children: Philip Dean, Carolyn Jean. DVM, Okla. State U., 1954, MS, 1962. Diplomate Am. Coll. Lab. Animal Medicine. Pvt. practice Norman, Okla., 1954-55; instr. Okla. State U., Stillwater, 1959-62, dir. Lab. Animal Resources, 1979-86, prof., 1979-86; chief vet. svcs. Civil Aeromed. Rsch. Inst., Oklahoma City, Okla., 1962-65; dir. U. Okla. Health Scis. Ctr., Oklahoma City, 1965-79; chief Vet. Med. Office Dept. Vet. Affairs, Washington, 1986—; chief Vet. Med. Unit, VA Hosp., Oklahoma City, 1965-79; assoc. prof. U. Okla. Coll. Medicine, Oklahoma City, 1965-79. Author: Clinical Laboratory Animal Medicine, 1984. Capt. U.S. Army, 1955-62. Scholar Okla. State U., 1948. Mem. AVMA, Am. Assn. Lab. Animal Sci., Am. Soc. Lab. Animal Practitioners, Nat. Assn. Fed. Veterinarians, Soc. Exptl. Biology and Medicine, Phi Kappa Phi, Sigma Xi. Democrat.

Methodist. Home: 2301 Jefferson Davis Hwy Arlington VA 22202-3820 Office: Dept Vets Affairs 810 Vermont Ave NW Washington DC 20420

HOLMES, MARILYN JANET, television producer, writer, management consultant; b. Paris, Apr. 14, 1934; d. Gerald Maurice and Denise Henriette (Schlesinger) Strauss; m. Henry Allen Holmes, July 25, 1959; children: Katherine Anne Holmes-Chuba, Gerald Allen. Diploma in European Civilization, U. Paris, 1955. Film officer U.S. Info. Agy., Washington, 1954-56; script writer Byron Films, Inc., Washington, 1958-59, prodn. mgr., 1956-58; exec. dir. St. Stephen's Sch. Bd., Rome, 1977-80; dir. family liaison office U.S. Dept. of State, Washington, 1980-82, TV producer, writer, 1985—; trainer amb. seminar Fgn. Svcs. Inst., Washington, 1987-91; crisis mgmt. cons. Overseas Security Adv. Coun., Washington, 1985-91. Producer, writer (video programs) Re-Entry, 1982 (Best Govt. Spl. award 1982), Crisis Management, 1985, AIDS, 1985, Security Overseas Seminar, 1990. Tutor Black Children's Program, Washington, 1957-59; doctor's helper Planned Parenthood, Washington, 1956-59; program dir. Am. Assn. Fg. Svc. Women, Washington, 1951-63; pres. Assn. Am. Women in Lisbon, Portugal, 1982-85. Democrat. Episcopalian. Home: 5027 Sedgewick St NW Washington DC 20016-1939 Office: US Dept of State DS/RM/SA Washington DC 20521

HOLMES, ROBERT RICHARD, chemistry educator; b. Chgo., Aug. 25, 1928; s. Robert W. and Charlotte (Stolpa) H.; m. Joan Marie Hickey, June 2, 1956; children: Mary Anne Jones, Kathryn Marie Webber, Robert Richard Holmes, Jr. BS, Ill. Inst. of Tech., Chgo., 1950; PhD, Purdue U., 1953. Assoc. prof. Carnegie Inst. Tech., Pitts., 1953-62; mem. tech. staff Bell Telephone Labs., Murray Hill, N.J., 1962-66; prof. U. Mass., Amherst, 1966—. Editor-in-chief: Phosphorus, Sulfur, Silicon and the Related Elements, 1987—; author 2 books in field; contbr. more than 200 articles to profl. jours. Recipient Faculty Fellowship award for Disting. Rsch. and Scholarship, U. Mass., Amherst, 1986; grantee NSF, NIH, ARO, others, 1954—. Mem. Am. Chem. Soc., Sigma Xi, Phi Lambda Upsilon. Roman Catholic. Home: 67 Aubinwood Rd Amherst MA 01002-1623 Office: U Mass Dept Chemistry Amherst MA 01003

HOLMES, WALTER JOHN, public relations consultant, author; b. N.Y.C., June 9, 1906; s. William Henry and Anna Katherine (McArdle) H.; m. Ellen Irene Jennings, Nov. 5, 1938 (dec. Sept. 1975); 1 child, Ellen Misita; m. Grace Ellen Pritchard, Dec. 8, 1990. Grad. high sch., N.Y.C. With adv. dept. N.Y. Morning World, N.Y.C., 1921-22; printing pressman Henleo Press, N.Y.C., 1922-31; chief radio announcer Sta. WBNX - Voice of Bronx, N.Y.C., 1932-47; v.p. Bronx C. of C., N.Y.C., 1947-54; pub. rels. asst. Compt. of City of N.Y., 1954-63, 66-70; pub. rels. dir. Empire State C. of C., Albany, N.Y., 1963-66; pub. rels. asst. to compt. Audit and Control State of N.Y., Albany, 1971-79; pvt. practice Albany, 1979—; mem. faculty Northeastern Inst. Commerce & Trade Execs. Yale U., 1957; pub. rels. asst. to N.Y.C. compt., 1966-70; acting pub. rels. dir. Schenectady (N.Y.) County Community Coll., 1979-81; pub. rels. cons. N.Y. State Tchrs. Retirement Systems, Albany, 1983-85, 85-87. Author: Essays & Poems of Walter J. Holmes, 1988. Publicity dir. Svc. Corps Retired Execs., Albany. Recipient Nat. Assn. Broadcasters award, 1945. Mem. Lions Club (pres. Bronx chpt. 1948-49, dist. gov. 1950-51), Lions Club (life, internat. counselor Albany chpt. 1963—, Melvin Jones fellow), N.Y. Press Club, Soc. of Silurians, Knights of Pythias, Elks (Troy bull. editor 1978, Disting. Citizens award 1985), Univ. Club, Adirondack Mt. Club. Democrat. Roman Catholic. Home and Office: 72 Pleasantview Ave Albany NY 12203-3215

HOLMES, WILLIAM JAMES, college president; s. William J. and Libbie (Stodola) H.; m. Joanne Prokop, Sept. 8, 1951; children: Mary, Ann, Sara. B.A., Iowa U., 1951, Ph.D. in English, 1962. Instr. English Iowa U., 1955-58; with Ohio U., 1958-70, asst. prof., 1962-65, assoc. prof., 1965-70; pres. Simmons Coll., Boston, 1970—. Contbr. articles to profl. jours. Served to capt. USAAF, 1945-49. Office: Simmons Coll 300 The Fenway Boston MA 02115

HOLMGRAIN, FLOYD HAROLD, JR., professional association administrator; b. Capiz, Philippines, Nov. 19, 1928; came to U.S., 1930; s. Floyd Harold and Lela Mae (Lockwood) H.; m. Marlene Joan Miller, Mar. 8, 1953; children: Floyd H. III, Randal E. BA, Chadron State Coll., 1949; MA, Stanford U., 1954; EdD, U. Nebr., 1960. Commd. 2d lt. USAF, 1951, advanced through grades to lt. col., 1969, ret., 1979; exec. dir. Nat. Acad. Opticianry, Bowie, Md., 1979—, Commn. on Opticians Accreditation, Bowie, 1979—. Recipient Beverly Myers Achievement award Nat. Acad. Opticianry, 1987. Mem. Rotary. Home: 12208 Lisborough Rd Bowie MD 20720-3544 Office: Nat Acad Opticianry Ste 112 10111 ML King Jr Hwy Bowie MD 20720

HOLMGREN, ADRIANA MCDONA, social worker; b. N.Y.C., June 2, 1943; d. Peter G. and Constance (Robinson) Wyckoff; m. Donald Burns, 1964 (div. 1971); children: Christopher, Timothy Sean; m. Ernest G. Holmgren, 1979. BA in Psychology, magna cum laude, Western Conn. State U., Danbury, 1983; MS, Western Conn. State U., 1985; MSW, Fordham U., 1985. Cert. social worker, Conn. Med. social worker St. Mary's Hosp., Waterbury, Conn., 1985-86, 88—; case mgr. State of Conn., Danbury, 1986-88. Mem. NASW, Am. Assn. Counseling & Devel., Psi Chi, Pi Gamma Mu. Office: St Mary's Hosp 56 Franklin St Waterbury CT 06706-1200

HOLMQUIST, BARTON, biophysicist, consultant, medical educator; b. L.A., Mar. 12, 1943; s. Caesar Holmquist; m. Janet Gene Goodwin (div. 1989); children: Kara, Brett. AA, L.A. Valley Coll., 1963; BA, U. Calif., Santa Barbara, 1965, PhD, 1968. Postdoctoral fellow Med. Sch. Harvard U., Boston, 1968-70, NIH tng. fellow Med. Sch., 1970-73, assoc. in biol. chemistry Med. Sch., 1971-87; assoc. prof. Med. Sch. Brigham & Womens Hosp., Boston, 1987—, assoc. staff mem., 1968—; vis. lectr. MIT, Cambridge, 1973; cons. Beckman Instruments, Fullerton, Calif., 1988—, BioNebraska, Lincoln, Nebr., 1989—. Inventor protease activation, device for kinetic analysis; contbr. numerous articles to profl. jours. Co-dir. Watch City Coffee House, Waltham, Mass., 1990—. Mem. AAAS, Am. Chem. Soc., Am. Soc. Biol. Chemists. Democrat. Home: 335 Prospect Hill Rd Waltham MA 02154 Office: Brigham & Womens Hosp 75 Francis St Boston MA 02115-6195

HOLMSTROM, FRANK ROSS, electrical engineering educator; b. Port Angeles, Wash., Dec. 28, 1936; s. Frank Gottfrid and Laura Estelle (Lofthus) H.; m. Lynda Lytle, June 21, 1961; children: Bret L., Cary Holmstrom Lytle. BSEE, U. Wash., 1958; MSEE, Stanford U., 1961, PhD in Elec. Engring., 1965. Rsch. asst. electronic labs. Stanford (Calif.) U., 1953-63; electronics engr. Electronics Rsch. Ctr., NASA, Washington and Cambridge, Mass., 1963-70; from asst. prof. to prof. elec. engring. U. Lowell (now U. Mass. at Lowell), 1970—. 1st lt. U.S. Army, 1963-65. Mem. AAAS, IEEE (sr.), Am. Soc. Engring. Edn., Phi Beta Kappa, Sigma Xi, Tau Beta Pi. Office: U Mass Lowell 1 University Ave Lowell MA 01854-2881

HOLMWOOD, JAMES MORLEY, insurance executive; b. Washington, Jan. 31, 1937; s. James Morley and Marie (Sandell) H.; m. Lillian Gilbreth (div. May 1971); children: James M. Jr., William Gilbreth (dec. May 1982), Amy Bunker, Michael Sandell; m. Sandra Parks, Sept. 30, 1982. BS in Indsl. Engring., Purdue U., 1961. With Exxon, various locations, 1961-71; pres. The Holmwood Corp., Wayne, Pa., 1971—. Mem. Million Dollar Round Table (life), Twenty Five Million Dollar Forum, Top of the Table, Union League of Phila., Merion Golf Club, Aronomink Golf Club. Republican. Office: The Holmwood Corp 987 Old Eagle School Rd Ste 713 Wayne PA 19087-1708

HOLRAN, BRUCE GRENVILLE, public relations director; b. Hackensack, N.J., May 24, 1934; m. Carolyn Tillou Holran, Sept. 9, 1961 (dec. 1971); m. Barbara Erb, Oct. 28, 1973; children: Jeffrey J., Holly Ann, Jill C., Peter T., Elizabeth D. AB, Colgate U., 1956. Asst. dir. pub. info. Colgate U., Hamilton, N.Y., 1956-60; alumni dir. Mt. Hermon (Mass.) Sch., 1960-62; dir. devel. Northfield Schs., East Northfield, Mass., 1962-64; dir. publ. rels. Clark U., Worcester, Mass., 1964-68, Franklin and Marchall Coll., Lancaster, Pa., 1968-86; dir. coll. rels. Elizabethtown (Pa.) Coll., 1986—. Editor: (mag.) F&M Today, 1982-86 (CASE award 1985). Bd. dirs. Manheim Twp. Sch. Bd., Neffsville, Pa., 1979-91, v.p. 1981-86, pres., 1986-90; bd. dirs. Intermediate Unit 13 Sch. Bd., Lancaster, 1979-91. 1st lt. USAR, 1957-62. Named Outstanding Men of Yr., Worcester Jaycees, 1968. Mem. Nat. Sch. Bd. Assn. (mem. fed. rels. network 1988-91), Internat. Assn. Bus. Communicators (past local chpt. officer 1981—), Coun. for Advancement and Support Edn. (past regional officer), Lancaster Cultural Coun. Republican. Presbyterian. Home: 1919 Rockford Ln Lancaster PA 17601-4921

HOLROYD, RICHARD ALLAN, researcher; b. Jamestown, N.Y., Dec. 31, 1930; s. Edmond W. and Effie I. (Carlson) H.; m. Dwana C. Holroyd, May 11, 1957; children: Thomas, Scott. BA, Wooster Coll., 1952; PhD, Rochester U., 1956. Asst. prof. UCLA, Jogjakarta, Indonesia, 1957-59; researcher Mellon Inst., Pitts., 1959-64, Atomics Internat., Canoga Park, Calif., 1964-69, Brookhaven Nat. Lab., Upton, N.Y., 1969—. Contbr. numerous articles to profl. jours. Mem. alumni bd. Coll. Wooster, 1990—. Recipient Humboldt award Germany, 1975. Office: Brookhaven Nat Lab Bldg 555 Upton NY 11973

HOLSINGER, VIRGINIA HARRIS, chemist; b. Washington, Mar. 13; d. Raymond Wilson and Elizabeth Blackstone (Riley) H. BS, Coll. of William and Mary, Williamsburg, Va., 1958; PhD, Ohio State U., 1980. Rsch. chemist Agrl. Rsch. Svc., Ea. Regional Rsch. Ctr., USDA, Washington, 1958-74; rsch. chemist Agrl. Rsch. Svc., ERRC, USDA, Wyndmoor, Pa., 1974—. Contbg. author publs. in field; contbr. articles to profl. jours. Recipient Col. Rohland Isker award R&D Assocs., Inc., San Antonio, 1983, award Fed. Lab. Consortium, 1986, also others. Mem. Am. Chem. Soc. (Disting. Svc. award 1986), Inst. of Food Techs. (chmn. dairy sect. 1990-91), Internat. Dairy Fedn., Am. Dairy Sci. Assn., Am. Cheese Soc., others. Episcopalian. Office: USDA-ARS-NAA-ERRC 600 E Mermaid Ln Philadelphia PA 19118-2598

HOLST, WILLEM, oil company executive; b. Yokohama, Japan, Dec. 22, 1911; came to U.S., 1924; s. Willem Nicolaas and Henriette (Hendrix) H.; m. Catherine Gabrielson (div. 1957); 1 child, Deirdre; m. Margaret Jennings, Nov. 14, 1959 (dec. Nov. 1986); m. Mary Katherine Davis, July 9, 1988. BChemE, MIT, 1932; postgrad., Harvard U., 1957. Mgr. tech. svc. Standard-Vacuum Oil Refinery, Pelembang, Indonesia, 1936-39; mgr. econ. coordination Standard Vacuum Oil Co., N.Y.C., 1946-56; v.p. Standard Vacuum Oil Co., White Plains, N.Y., 1957-61; v.p. and dir. long-range planning Esso Standard Ea. (subs. Exxon Corp.), N.Y.C., 1962-66; econ. cons. Pa., N.J., 1967—; pres. Princeton (N.J.) Total Return, Inc., 1988—; Mem. Aviation Gasoline Adv. Com., USA, 1943-45; vice-chmn. India Com. Bus. Coun. for Internat. Understanding, N.Y.C., 1966-68; cons. on India to Ford Found., N.Y.C., New Delhi, 1967-68; world food supply panel Pres.'s Sci. Adv. Com., Washington, 1967. Contbr. articles to profl. publs.; photographer: one-man exhibit on India, Mus. of Natural History, N.Y.C., 1967. Chmn. Tinicum (Pa.) Twp. Planning Commn., 1970-74. Mem. Coun. on Fgn. Rels., MIT Club of Princeton, Univ. Club, Harvard Club of Princeton, Exxon Annuitant Club, Sigma Alpha Epsilon, Tau Beta Pi. Home and Office: 36 Cameron Ct Princeton NJ 08540-3924

HOLT, BRENT MARION, human services administrator, psychologist; b. Faulkton, S.D., Aug. 7, 1953; s. Marion Albert and Dolores Joan (Strevel) H.; m. Peggy Ann Wagner, Aug. 10, 1985; children: Kathryn, Joseph, Alexis, Rani, Colby. BA, Huron Coll., 1975; MA, U. Minn., 1980. Asst. dir. admissions, alumni dir. Huron (S.D.) Coll., 1975-78; dir. counseling ctr. Hamline U., St. Paul, 1979-82; dean student svcs. Dakota Wesleyan U., Mitchell, 1982-85; assoc. sch. psychologist North Country Edn. Found., Gorham, N.H., 1985-87, Berlin (N.H.) Pub. Schs., 1988-90; psycho-ednl. specialist Lunenburg, Vt., 1987—; mgr. outpatient svcs. Founders Hall, St. Johnsbury, Vt., 1991—; faculty mem. Sch. for Lifelong Learning, U. System of N.H., Durham, 1987—. Bd. dirs. Dakota Wesleyan Presch., Mitchell, S.D., 1984-85. Named one of Outstanding Young Men Am., 1984. Mem. AACD, NASP, Nat. Assn. Alcoholism and Drug Abuse Counselors, N.H. Assn. Sch. Psychologist. Democrat. Episcopalian. Home: RR 1 Box 14 Lunenburg VT 05906-9702 Office: NE Vt Regional Hosp Founders Hall Hosp Dr Saint Johnsbury VT 05819

HOLT, HERBERT, psychiatrist; b. Vienna, Austria, Apr. 27, 1912; s. Leon and Cecilia (von Lempel) H.; Absolvent der Medizin, U. Vienna, 1937; Docteur en Medicine, U. Lausanne (Switzerland), 1938; m. Dolores Bolla di Osasco, July 14, 1961; children—Renata, Gerhard. Came to U.S., 1936, naturalized, 1941. Intern, Bellevue Hosp., N.Y.C., 1938-39, resident, 1939-41; practice medicine specializing in psychiatry and psychoanalysis, N.Y.C., 1951—; dean Westchester Inst., Rye, N.Y., 1970—; dir. N.Y. Inst. Existential Analysis, 1965—. Med. dir. Cathedral Counseling Service Cathedral Ch. St. John the Divine, N.Y.C., Actors Counseling Service, N.Y.C. Fellow Assn. for Applied Psychoanalysis (founding pres.), Am. Assn. for Social Psychiatry, Am. Soc. Psychoanalytic Physicians, Am. Ontoanalytic Assn., Am. Soc. Existential Psychiatry (pres. 1972—), Am. Acad. Psychoanalysis. Author: Free to Be Good or Bad, 1976; contbg. author Comprehensive Textbook of Psychiatry II, 1975. Editor: Jour. Modern Psychotherapy. Contbr. chpts. to textbooks, articles to profl. jours. Office: 185 E 85th St New York NY 10028-2140

HOLT, LINDA LEE, communications director; b. Trenton, N.J., Mar. 25, 1947; d. Jacob Garfield and Shirley Arlene (Wagner) B.; m. James Allen Holt, May 31, 1969; 1 child, Vanessa Sarada. BA cum laude, Rider Coll., 1971; postgrad., Calif. State U., Carson, 1991—. Cert. pub. mgr. Writer, editor Magee Pub., Bordentown, N.J., 1965-68; writer, critic The Trentonian, Trenton, 1968-76; communications dir. N.J. State Employees Assn., Trenton, 1976-78; writer N.J. Sch. Bds. Assn., Trenton, 1978-79; communications dir. N.J. Assn. Sch. Adminstrs., Trenton, 1979-80; dir. pub. rels. and pubs. Trenton State Coll., Ewing Township, N.J., 1980-86; dir. pubs. Assembly Majority Office, Trenton, 1986-90; dir. communications and coll. rels. Thomas Edison Coll., Trenton, 1990—; cons. Cable TV Network, Trenton, 1990—; presenter in field. Columnist New York Times, 1988, National Lampoon, 1989, 90; contbr. poetry to publs. Bd. dirs. Ewing Twp. C. of C., 1984-86, Ewing Twp. Bus. Enhancement Coun., 1985-86; mem. exec. com. Trenton Computer Festival, Ewing Twp., 1985-86; chair, com. mem. Thomas Edison State Coll. Recipient Women Helping Women award, Soroptimist, 1977, merit award N.J. Dept. Higher Edn., Trenton, 1985. Mem. Internat. Assn. Bus. Communicators, N.J. Communications-Advt. and Mktg. Assn., Jersey Shore Pub. Rels. Assn. (Jasper award 1984-86), Mensa. Presbyterian. Office: Thomas Edison State Coll 101 W State St Trenton NJ 08608-1101

HOLT, TIMOTHY ARTHUR, insurance company executive; b. Hartford, Conn., Mar. 16, 1953; s. Ralph and Elizabeth (Leonard) H.; m. Beverly Charney, Aug. 17, 1975; children: Melissa, Laura, Alexander. BA, U. Conn., 1975; MBA, Dartmouth Coll., 1977. Chartered fin. analyst. Securities analyst Aetna Life & Casualty Co., Hartford, 1977, investment officer, 1980, asst. v.p., 1983, v.p., 1987-89, v.p. fin., treas., 1989-91, v.p. portfolio mgmt., 1991—. Mem. investment com. Hartford U; corp. adv. bd. Nat. Head Start Assn. Edward Tuck scholar Dartmouth Coll. Tuck Sch., 1979. Mem. Phi Betta Kappa. Office: Aetna Life & Casualty Co City Pl Hartford CT 06156-9445

HOLTON, GERALD, physicist, science historian; b. Berlin, Germany, May 23, 1922; s. Emanuel and Regina (Rossmann) H.; m. Nina Rossfort, Sept. 12, 1947; children: Thomas, Stephan. Nat. certificate elec. engring., Sch. Tech., Oxford, Eng., 1940; B.A., Wesleyan U., 1941, M.A., 1942, D.H.L. (hon.), 1981; M.A., Harvard U., 1946, Ph.D., 1948; D.Sc. (hon.), Grinnell Coll., 1967, Kenyon Coll., 1977, Bates Coll., 1979; LL.D. (hon.), Duke U., 1981. Instr. Wesleyan U., 1941-42, Brown U., 1942-43; staff, officers radar course and OSRD Harvard, 1943-45, various faculty positions, 1945—; Mallinckrodt prof. physics and prof. history of sci.; exchange prof. Harvard-Leningrad U., 1962; vis. mem. Inst. Advanced Study, Princeton, 1964; fellow Center Advanced Study in Behavioral Scis., Stanford, 1975-76; vis. prof. M.I.T., 1976—; Herbert Spencer lectr. Oxford U., 1979; Jefferson lectr., 1981, John Simon Guggenheim fellow, 1980-81; mem. com. scholarly communications with People's Republic of China, NAS., 1970-71; mem. U.S. Nat. Commn. on UNESCO, 1975-80, U.S. Nat. Commn. of IUHPS, 1982-89, Council of Scholars, Libr. of Congress, 1980—, U.S. Nat. Commn. on Excellence in Edn., 1981-83; chmn. NSF, adv. com. for sci. and engring. edn., 1986-88; mem. com. on conduct of sci. NAS, 1989. Author: (with D.H.D. Roller) Foundations of Modern Physical Science, 1958, Science and the Modern Mind, 1958, Science and Culture, 1965, (with others) The Project Physics Course, 1970, 75, 81, The 20th Century Sciences: Studies in Intellectual Biography, 1971, Introduction to Concepts and Theories in Physical Science, 2d edit., 1985, Thematic Origins of Scientific Thought: Kepler to Einstein, 1973, 2d edit., 1988, The Scientific Imagination: Case Studies, 1978, (with others) Limits of Scientific Inquiry, 1979, Albert Einstein, Historical and Cultural Perspectives, 1982, The Advancement of Science, and its Burdens, 1986. Editor-in-chief: Daedalus, 1958-61; mem. editorial com., editorial adv. bd. The Collected Papers of Albert Einstein; contbr. articles to profl. jours. Trustee Wesleyan U., Boston Mus. Sci., Sci. Svc. Fellow AAAS (dir. 1967-71, George Sarton Meml. lectr. 1962), Am. Acad. Arts and Sci. (editor 1957-63, mem. exec. bd. 1970-78, coun. 1991—), Am. Phys. Soc. (chair divsn. history of physics 1992—), Académie Internationale d'Histoire des Scis. (v.p. 1981-89), Deutsche Akademie der Naturforscher-Leopoldina, Mass. Hist. Soc.; mem. Am. Inst. Physics (governing bd. 1968-74, Andrew Gemant award 1989), Am. Assn. Physics Tchrs. (Robert A. Millikan medal 1967, Oersted medal 1980), History Sci. Soc. (pres. 1982-84, George Sarton medal 1989), Soc. for History Tech., Soc. Social Studies Sci. (J.D. Bernal prize 1990), Fedn. Am. Scientists, Examiner Club, Phi Beta Kappa, Sigma Xi (McGovern medal 1985). Office: Harvard U Jefferson Phys Lab Cambridge MA 02138

HOLTON, SUSAN A, educator; b. Columbus, Ohio, Apr. 24, 1948; d. William C. and Mary (Floyd) H.; 1 child, Christopher L. Holton-Jablonski; m. Joe Snyders, Aug. 4, 1991. BS, Miami U., Oxford, Ohio, 1970; MA, Case Western Res. U., 1973, PhD, 1976. Dir. Gabriel Ames Assocs., Framingham, Mass., 1975—; asst. to pres., asst. prof. Bridgewater (Mass.) State Coll., 1984-88, dept. chair., assoc. prof., 1988-90, prof., 1990—, asst. to pres., 1991—; bd. dirs. Profl. Orgn. in Higher Edn.; coord. Mass. Faculty Devel. Consortium, 1988-90; chair., nominating com. Unitarian Universalis Assn., Boston, 1987-89; cons. Alban Inst., 1989—. Author: The Mad Madonna, 1987, Under the Influence of Life; contbr. articles to profl. jours. Dir. Ch. the Larger Fellowship, Boston, 1987—; founder FOCUS on Gifted and Talented, Framingham, Mass. Mem. Speech Communication Assn., Boston Area Assn. Psychol. Type (founder), N.E. Assn. Psychol. Type, AAUW, Ea. Communications Assn., Communications Assn. Mass., Alban Inst., AAUP, Am. Assn. for Higher Edn. Office: Bridgewater State Coll Presidents Office Bridgewater MA 02324

HOLTZ, ALIZA, medical communications executive, biologist; b. N.Y.C., Jan. 10, 1952; d. Itshak Jack and Gertrude Ruth (Beck) H. BA, Brandeis U., 1973; PhD in Biology, Boston U., 1980. Rsch. scientist N.Y. State Psychiat. Inst., N.Y.C., 1980-82; med. writer Revlon Health Care Group, Tuckahoe, N.Y., 1982; med. copywriter Rolf Werner Rosenthal Advt. Inc., N.Y.C., 1983; mgr. ednl. projects MED, Woodbridge, N.J., 1983-84; pres. Holtz Communications Inc., N.Y.C., 1985—; cons. numerous med. advt. agencies and pub. rels. firms, N.Y., N.J., Conn., 1981—; author, cons. Addison-Wesley Pub. Co., Reading, Mass., 1975-82. Author: Biology, 3d edit., 1981; author: (with others) High Risk Maternity Nursing, 1990; contbr. articles to profl. jours. 1st v.p. bd. dirs. Arts Interaction, N.Y.C., 1985-91. Mem. AAAS, Am. Museum of Natural History, Sigma Xi. Home: 275 Ft Washington Ave New York NY 10032-1203 Office: Holtz Communications Inc 275 Ft Washington Ave New York NY 10032-1203

HOLTZ, ITSHAK, artist; b. Skernevice, Poland, Dec. 14, 1925; came to U.S., 1950; s. Arie and Lisa (Golup) H.; m. Gertrude Ruth Beck, June 29, 1928; children: Aliza, Arie. Student, Jerusalem Art Acad., 1946-48, N.Y. Art Student's League, 1950-52, N.Y. Nat. Acad. Design, 1953-54; Diploma of Merit, U. De Le Art, Italy, 1982. One-man shows include NAD, Allied Artists, Audubon Artists, Internat. Art Show, Theodore Herzel Inst., Mus. Yeshiva U., N.Y.C.; represented in numerous pvt. collections in U.S., Can., Israel, Australia, and Europe. Recipicient gold medal Internat. Parliament for Safety and Peace, 1983, Oscar d'Italia, 1985. Mem. Students League of N.Y. (life), Art's Interaction N.Y. (Bd. Dirs. award 1989), Artists Equity N.Y. (Best in Show and Grumbacher Silver medal 1991). Home: 66 Ft Washington Ave New York NY 10032-4711 Office: Studio 118 E 28th St New York NY 10016-8413

HOLTZMAN, ARNOLD HAROLD, chemical company executive; b. Phila., May 11, 1932; s. William and Rae (Shapiro) H.; m. Phyllis Raskow, June 26, 1955; children: Rosalind Ann, Linda Susan, William Lewis. BS, Drexel Inst., 1954; MS, Lehigh U., 1956, PhD, 1957. Asst. metallurgist J. Bishop & Co., Malvern, Pa., 1954; with duPont Co., various locations, 1957—, rsch. mgr., dist. sales mgr. Polymer Intermediates dept., Wilmington, Del., 1973-76, mgr. new bus. programs, cen. rsch. and devel. dept., Wilmington, 1976-78, mgr. health products, 1980-81, dir. devel. div. cent. rsch. and devel. dept., 1982-89, cons., 1989—, pres. Action Games, Inc., 1988-89; bd. dir. Perceptive Systems, Inc., 1992—. Pres. Alzheimer's Associated Del. chpt. Recipient John Price Wetherill medal Franklin Inst., 1969. Fellow Am. Soc. Metals; mem. Sigma Xi. Patentee in processing of metals and non metals. Home and Office: 208 Stonecrop Rd Wilmington DE 19810-1320

HOLTZSCHUE, KARL BRESSEM, lawyer, author, educator; b. Wichita, Kans., Mar. 3, 1938; s. Bressem C. and Josephine E. (Landsittel) H.; m. Linda J. Gross, Oct. 24, 1959; children: Alison, Adam, Sara. AB, Dartmouth Coll., 1959; LLB, Columbia U., 1966. Bar: N.Y. 1967, U.S. Dist. Ct. (so. and ea. dists.) N.Y. 1968. Assoc. Webster & Sheffield, N.Y.C., 1966-73, ptnr., 1974-88; ptnr., head real estate dept. O'Melveny and Myers, N.Y.C., 1988-90; adj. prof. Law Sch. Fordham U., Bus. Sch. Columbia U., 1990—, Law Sch. Columbia U., 1991, Law Sch. U. Vermont, 1992—. Author: Real Estate Contracts, 1985, New York Practice Guide: Real Estate, Vol. 1 on Purchase and Sale, 1986, Real Estate Transactions: Purchase and Sale of Real Property, 1987; author: (with others) American Law of Real Property, 1991, Real Estate Development, 1991. Trustee Soc. St. Johnland, 1980-86; trustee Ensemble Studio Theatre, 1986-88, The Bridge, 1990, pres., 1992—; mem. coun. advisors Ticor Title Guarantee Co., 1988—. Lt. (j.g.) USN, 1959-62. Mem. ABA (com. on creditors rights in real estate financing 1i83-85, 87—, com. on fgn. investment in real estate 1987—, com. on legal opinions in real estate transactions 1990—), N.Y. State Bar Assn. (com. on real estate financing 1987—), Real Estate Bd. N.Y. (law com. 1980-90, co-chmn. 1989-90), Assn. Bar City of N.Y. (mem. com. on real property law 1977-80, chmn. 1987-90), Am. Coll. Real Estate Lawyers (mem. opinions com. 1989—, vice chair 1991—, TriBar opinions com. 1990—). Episcopalian. Home: Apt 3C 122 E 82d St New York NY 10028

HOLUB, CHARLES MICHAEL, construction executive; b. Balt., Oct. 12, 1948; s. Carl James and Pauline Francis (Lentz) H.; m. Mildred Kathleen Callahan, Jan. 3, 1970; children: Sean, Travis, Tyler. Student, U. Balt., 1966, U. Md., 1967-69. From laborer to pres. Potts & Callahan Inc., Balt., 1966—. Sgt. Spl. Force, USNG, 1966-72. Mem. Hillendale Country Club (bd. dirs., golf chmn.). Republican. Roman Catholic. Home: 15323 Falls Rd Sparks MD 21152 Office: Potts & Callahan Inc 500 W 29th St Baltimore MD 21211

HOLUB, EDWARD JOSEPH, II, emergency physician; b. Balt., Aug. 7, 1952; s. Edward Joseph and Helen Ruth (Brocklehurst) H.; m. Ann Louise Vizzi, Sept. 20, 1980; 1 child, Adria Vizzi Holub. BS in Biology, Loyola Coll., Balt., 1974; MD, Georgetown U., 1977. Diplomate Am. Bd. Emergency Medicine. Surgical resident Georgetown Hosp., Washington, 1977-79; emergency medicine resident Med. Coll. of Pa., Phila., 1979-80; emergency room staff physician Germantown Hosp., Phila., 1980-81, St. Mary Hosp., Langhorne, Pa., 1981—. Mem. com. Boy Scouts Am. Fellow Am. Coll. Emergency Physicians; mem. Wilderness Med. Soc., N.Y. Acad. of Sci. Office: Dept Emergency Medicine St Mary Hosp Langhorne-Newtown Rd Langhorne PA 19047

HOLVERSON, JOHN, art brokerage house executive, consultant, art appraiser; b. Marshfield, Wis., June 14, 1946. Student U. Iowa, 1965-66; BA, MacMurray Coll., 1967; MA, U. Iowa, 1971; postgrad. Attingham Summer Sch., 1982. Arranger collections Images of Women Photog. Exhbn., 1977, The Revolutionary McLellans, 1977, Miss Mary Cassatt: Impressionist from Pennsylvania, 1979, James Brooks: Paintings and Works on Paper, 1946-82, 83, Winslow Homer: The Charles Shipman Payson Collection, 1983, Maine Light: Temperas by Andrew Wyeth, 1983, Gaston LaChaise: A Retrospective, 1984, John Marin: The Maine Workd, 1985; summer intern Art Inst. Chgo., 1968-69; grad. asst. Mus. Art, U. Iowa, 1968-69, head grad. asst., 1969-70; curator Portland Mus. Art (Maine), 1970-73, editor monthly bull.,

1970, curator collections, 1973-81, acting dir., 1973-75, dir., 1975-87; founder J.H. Holverson Co., 1987—, also bd. dirs.; asst. dept. art MacMurray Coll., Jacksonville, Ill., 1963-65, 66-67. Mem. Am. Assn. Mus., Assn. Art Mus. Dirs., Soc. Preservation New Eng. Antiquities, Nat. Trust for State and Local Hist. Soc., Coll. Art Assn. Author: Rene Dubois and the Cathedrals of the Future, 1973; Fire Buckets and Bags in Portland, 1973; Antiques, 1974. Home: 292 Spring St Portland ME 04102-3714

HOLWAY, MICHAEL PAUL, air force officer; b. Waterville, Maine, May 1, 1955; s. Paul Snowman and Helen Louise (Walker) H.; m. Stephanie Ann Sutton, Mar. 21, 1986; children: Jennianne Lauranda, Ariel Lynne, Amanda Kristine. AS, U. Maine, 1976; BS, Thomas Coll., 1981, MBA, 1983. RN. Commd. 2nd lt. USAF, 1983, advanced through grades to capt., 1985; dir. personnel Mid-Maine Med. Ctr., Waterville, 1981-83; assoc. hosp. adminstr. USAF Hosp., Wurtsmith AFB, Mich., 1983-86, Warren AFB, Wyo., 1986-89; chief med. recruiting br. 3554th USAF Recruiting Squadron, Selfridge AFB, Mich., 1989-90; hosp. adminstr. 42nd Strategic Hosp., Loring AFB, Maine, 1990—; instr. bus. Alpena (Mich.) Community Coll., 1984-86, Laramie County (Wyo.) Community Coll., 1988-89, Chapman Coll., Cheyenne, Wyo., 1988-89, U. Maine, Presque Isle, 1991—. Supr., chmn. Wurtsmith Community Fed. Credit Union, Oscoda, Mich., 1985-86; mem. supervisory com. Warren Fed. Credit Union, Cheyenne, 1988-89. Mem. Am. Soc. Healthcare Human Resources Adminstrn., Air Force Assn., Am. Coll. Healthcare Execs., Mensa. Office: 42nd Strategic Hosp Loring AFB ME 04751

HOLZEMER, DAVID CHARLES, photographer; b. Columbus, Ohio, May 26, 1966; s. Michael and Judith Blair (Kannengerser) H. AS, Community Coll. Allegheny, Monroeville, Pa., 1990. Freelance photographer Community Coll. Allegheny County, Pitts., 1990—; electrician City Theater New Works Festival, Pitts., 1991; freelance photographer Single Parents Homemakers Group, Monroeville, 1992; part-time guitar instr. Community Coll. Allegheny County, 1991; photography tech. R.J. Lee Group, Inc., Monroeville, 1991—. Vol. photographer Greater Monroeville Arts Festival Coun., 1989—. Named Eagle Scout Boy Scouts Am., 1983, recipient Vigil Honors, 1987. Mem. Boyce Campus Music Ensemble (pres. 1988-89). Home: 4531 Old William Penn Hwy Monroeville PA 15146

HOLZER, HAROLD, public information officer, historian, writer; b. Bklyn., Feb. 5, 1949; s. Charles and Rose (Last) H.; m. Edith Spiegel, Feb. 27, 1971; children: Remy, Meg. BA, CUNY, Queens, 1969; diploma (hon.), Lincoln Meml. U., 1988, Lincoln Coll., 1992. Editor Manhattan Tribune, N.Y.C., 1969-73; dir. spl. projects Dept. Civic Affairs, City of N.Y., 1973-75; press sec. to Congresswoman Bella Abzug N.Y.C., 1973-77; communications specialist Sec. of State office, N.Y., 1978; dir. pub. affairs Sta. WNET (PBS), N.Y.C., 1978-84; v.p. pub. affairs Javits Conv. Ctr., N.Y.C., 1984-85; exec. v.p. pub. affairs Urban Devel. Corp., State of N.Y., 1985—. Co-author: The Lincoln Image, 1984, Changing Lincoln Image, 1985, The Confederate Image, 1987, The Lincoln Family Album, 1990, Lincoln on Democracy, 1990; contbr. more then 150 articles on Lincoln and the Civil War to popular mags., scholarly jours.; contbr. chpts. to books; columnist Antique Trader; contbg. editor: Americana Mag. 1991—; writer various pamphlets on Abraham Lincoln. Lectr. on Lincoln and Civil War before various historial groups; delivered keynote address at N.Y. State Mus. 125th anniv. display of Emancipation Proclamation, 1988; host, organizer Symposium on Emancipation Proclamation, 1986, co-organizer 2 traveling exhbns. on Lincoln and Civil War. Recipient Barondess/Lincoln award Civil War Round Table of N.Y., 1984, 91, George Washington medal Freedom Found. Valley Forge, 1988, Writer of Distinction award Internat. Reading Assn., 1989. Mem. Abraham Lincoln Assn. (bd. dirs. 1988-90, achievement award 1991), Lincoln Group of N.Y. (v.p. 1979-90, pres. 1990—, achievement award 1988), Lincoln Group Fla., Lincoln Group Ill., Lincoln Group Boston, N.Y. State Bd. for Hist. Preservation, 1983-85, N.Y. State Coun. for Humanities (bd. dirs. 1991—). Democrat. Jewish. Office: NY State Urban Devel Corp 1515 Broadway New York NY 10036-5702

HOLZMAN, FRANKLYN DUNN, economics educator; b. Bklyn., Dec. 31, 1918; s. Abraham and Mollie (Mandel) H.; m. Mathilda Sara Wiesman, Dec. 14, 1946; children—Thomas Ludwig, David Carl, Miriam Alexandra. B.A., U. N.C., 1940; M.A., Harvard, 1948, Ph.D., 1952. Economist Dept. Treasury, 1947-48, cons., 1949-52; research fellow Russian Research Center, Harvard, 1949-52, research asso., 1961—; prof. econs. U. Wash., 1952-61; prof. econs. Tufts U., mem. faculty Fletcher Sch. Law and Diplomacy, 1961—; vis. prof. U. Calif. at, Los Angeles, 1956, Stanford, 1957, Columbia, 1962, Mass. Inst. Tech., 1963; cons. U.S. Dept. Treasury, 1950, 51, UN, 1963-64, 89, U.S. ACDA, 1964-73, Joint Econ. Com. U.S. Congress, 1959, 73, 81, U.S. Commn. on Trade and Investment Policy, 1971, U.S. Dept. Commerce, 1972, 75-78; Stockholm Internat. Peace Research Inst., 1978. Author: Soviet Taxation: The Fiscal and Monetary Problems of a Planned Economy, 1955, Foreign Trade under Central Planning, 1974, Financial Checks on Soviet Defense Expenditures, 1975, International Trade Under Communism-Politics and Economics, 1976, Soviet Economy: Past, Present and Future, 1982, Economics of Soviet Bloc Trade and Finance, 1987. Served to staff sgt. USAAF, 1942-45. Winner Furth Internat. Ruble Convertibility Competition, 1990; honored by publ. Economic Adjustment and Reform in Eastern Europe and the Soviet Union: Essays in Honor of Franklyn D. Holzman, edited by Josef C. Brada, Ed. A. Hewett and Thomas Wolf, 1988. Mem. Am. Econ. Assn. (chmn. com. on US-USSR Confs., 1985-87), Am. Assn. Advancement of Slavic Studies (exec. com. 1964-65), Am. Assn. Study of Soviet-Type Economies (exec. com. 1966-67), Econometric Soc., Assn. for Comparative Econ. Studies (pres. 1976-77). Home: 33 Peacock Farm Rd Lexington MA 02173-6341

HOLZMAN, JACQUELIN, mayor. Councillor Richmond Ward, 1982-91; vice-chmn. phys. environment com. City of Ottawa, Ont., Can., 1982-85, dep. mayor, 1985-88, vice-chmn. policy, priorities and budgeting com., police svcs. bd., 1988-91, mayor, 1991—. Chmn. United Way Residential Campaign, 1970, Temple Israel Bldg. Com., 1972, Rehab. Inst. of Ottawa, 1970-75, Rehab. Inst. Housing Com., 1973-76, Jewish Social Svcs. Coun. of Ottawa, 1976-78, Ont. Coun. of Health Study on Psychiat. Aftercare, 1977-79, City of Ottawa Disabled Citizens Adv. Com., 1981, Ottawa Health Scis. Ctr., 1977-82, Adv. Com. on Rest Homes, Province of Ont., 1987-89; pres. Nat. Coun. of Jewish Women; bd. dirs. Kidney Found. of Ottawa Valley chpt., 1987—; vice-chmn. bd. trustees Superannuation Fund, 1988-91, Nat. Arts Ctr., 1991—, Civic Hosp., 1991—. Office: Office of the Mayor, 111 Sussex, Ottawa, ON Canada K1N 5A1

HOLZMAN, SEYMOUR, congressional staff official; b. Orange, N.J., Oct. 3, 1936; s. David and Sylvia (Miller) H.; m. Glenda Lou Ullman, May 29, 1960; children: Stewart Craig, Robert John (dec.). Student, NYU, 1958-61. Credit analyst Dunn & Bradstreet, East Orange, N.Y., 1961-63; office/warehouse mgr. Loucap Co., Inc., Hackensack, N.J., 1964; reporter, editor Bergen Evening Record, Hackensack, N.J., 1965-67; editor Scholastic Mags., Inc., N.Y.C., 1968-72, Ogden (Utah) Standard-Examiner, 1972-73; polit. editor Tampa (Fla.) Times, 1973-77; exec. asst. Fla. Sec. of State, Tallahassee, 1977-78; polit. cons. Tallahassee, 1979-82; staff dir. Congl. Subcom. on Health and Safety, Washington, 1983—. Mem. Fla. Adv. Coun. on Career Edn., Tallahassee, 1978-81, Planning and Zoning Bd., River Vale, N.J., 1969-71, Bd. of Edn., River Vale, 1971-72; pres. Glen Cove Homeowners Assn., Fairfax, Va., 1985-87; chmn. Econ. Devel. Com., River Vale, 1969. With U.S. Army, 1955-58. Office: Subcom on Health and Safety B345A RHOB Washington DC 20515

HOMER, IRVIN, education administrator, consultant; b. Trinidad and Tobago, Feb. 8, 1924; came to U.S., 1950; m. Mary Isabelle Jordan, Jan. 24, 1953; children: Norman, Valerie, Michael, Kurt. BA, Bklyn. Coll., 196l, MS in Edn., 1975, advanced diploma in edn. adminstrn., 1977. Cert. sch. adminstr., tchr. N-6, N.Y. Dir. regional opportunity ctr. CUNY, 1969-72; elem. tchr. N.Y.C. Bd. Edn., 196l-68, elem. tchr. trainer, 1968-69, funded coord. for alternative facilities/econ. devel. progrm, 1972-79, tchr. of adults, ctr. adminstr. aux. svcs. for high schs., 1983-90, edn. adminstr. adult learning ctr., 1986-91; adj. instr. Staten Island, York, and LaGuardia Community Colls., 1970-83. Supt. ch. sch. Holy Trinity Episcopal Ch., Hicksville, N.Y., 1986, vestryman, 1974-85, lay reader, 1977-91; mem. Literacy Bd., literacy vol., N.Y.C., 1972-77; leader Cub Scouts and Boy Scouts Am., Plainview, N.Y., 1978. NDEA scholar, 1965; recipient Outstanding Achievement award for community svc. Nat. Key Women Am., 1974. Mem. ASCD, Nat. Assn. Blacks in Vocat. Edn., Assn. Vocat. Edn. Adminstrs. N.Y. State, Am. Vocat. Assn., N.Y. State Occupational Edn. Assn., Bklyn. Coll. Alumni Assn., 100 Black Men Nassau/Suffolk Inc., Nat. Orgn. Black Coll. Alumni Inc., N.Y. Urban League.

HOMER, LOUIS DAVID, scientist; b. Washington, Mar. 21, 1935; s. David and Louise Berthe (Perreau) H.; m. Margie Winifred Parker, June 17, 1961; children: Margie Lou, David Louis, Mary Jane. AB, Columbia U., 1955; Phd, Med. Coll. of Va., 1962, MD, 1963. Assoc. prof. Emory U., Atlanta, 1963-67, Brown U., Providence, 1969-71; med. officer Naval Med. Rsch. Inst., Bethesda, Md., 1971—; statis. cons. Jour. Applied Physiology, Rockville, Md., 1979—. Contbr. numerous articles to profl. jours. Lt. comdr. USNR, 1967-69. Mem. AAAS, Am. Physiol. Soc., Soc. Math. Biology, Math. Assn. Am., Biometrics Soc. Office: Naval Med Rsch Inst Bethesda MD 20814

HOMER, PETER KEMP, hardware design engineer; b. Inglewood, Calif., Oct. 2, 1961; s. Stephen Bartlett Homer and Carol Spring (Lownes) Steele; m. Linda Jeanne Stahl, Apr. 6, 1990. BSME, Rensselaer Poly. Inst., 1983; MS in Aero. and Astron. Engring., Stanford U., 1984; postgrad., Westlawn Sch. Naval Architecture, 1988—. Engring. cons. W.F. Dowling, Inc., Southwest Harbor, Maine, 1983-84; structural design engr. Grumman Space Systems Div., Bethpage, N.Y., 1984-88; freelance machine designer PHX, Charlotte, N.C., 1988-90; hardware design engr. GE Astro Space Div., Princeton, N.J., 1990—; designer autonomous roving vehicle lab. Rensselaer Poly. Inst., 1981-82; lab. asst. dept. aeronautics and astronautics Stanford U., 1984. Patentee in field. Recipient Bausch & Lomb medal, 1979. Mem. AIAA, Aircraft Owners and Pilots Assn., U.S. Yacht Racing Union. Office: GE Astro-Space Div PO Box 800 M/S 410-2-A36 Princeton NJ 08543

HOMES, A. M., writer; b. Washington. BA, Sarah Lawrence Coll.; MFA, U. Iowa. Book reviewer Washington Post, Boston Globe, Miami Herald, Phila. Inquirer, 1991; art reviewer Art Forum, 1991; tchr writing program Columbia U., N.Y.C., 1991—. Author: (novel) Jack, 1989, (short story collection) The Safety of Objects, 1990; playwright: The Call-In Hour, 1981, The Coffin in the Living Room, 1986. Recipient Henfield Transatlantic Rev. award The Henfield Found., 1988; James Michener fellow U. Iowa, 1988-89; N.Y. Found. for Arts fellow, 1988; Helena Rubenstein fellow Whitney Mus., N.Y.C., 1988-89. Mem. PEN.

HONAN, JAMES PATRICK, professional educational program administrator; b. Suffern, N.Y., Jan. 13, 1956; s. Joseph A. and Catherine E. (McConnell) H.; m. Lisa J. Mars, Sept. 14, 1985. BA, Marist Coll., 1978; MA in Edn. and Human Devel., George Washington U., 1980, EdS, 1982; EdM, Harvard U., 1985, EdD, 1989. Instnl. rsch. coord. Office of Budgets Harvard U., Cambridge, Mass., 1983-87, project analyst fin. aid office, 1987-88; assoc. dir. programs in profl. edn. Harvard U., Cambridge, 1991—; dir. instl. and rsch. planning Lesley Coll., Cambridge, 1989-90, asst. to pres. for rsch. and planning rsch., 1990-91, exec. asst. to pres., 1991; teaching fellow Grad. Sch. Edn., Harvard U., 1984-89, lectr. Summer Sch., 1986—, lectr. Extension, 1991—. Contbr. articles to profl. jours. Member adv. bd. Plan for Social Excellence, Inc., Mt. Kisco, N.Y., 1990—; treas. Child Care Resource Ctr., Inc., Cambridge, 1991—. Office: Harvard U Grad Sch Edn Gutman Libr Rm 339 Cambridge MA 02138

HONIG, ALICE STERLING, psychologist; b. Bklyn., Apr. 19, 1929; d. William and Ida (Bender) Sterling; divorced, 1979; children: Lawrence Sterling, Madeleine Honig Lenski, Jonathan David. BA magna cum laude, Barnard Coll., 1950; MA, Columbia U., 1952; PhD, Syracuse U., 1975. Lic. psychologist, N.Y. Rsch. assoc. Upstate Med. Ctr., Syracuse, N.Y., 1962-64; family devel. rsch. program dir. Syracuse U., 1964-77, instr. child devel., 1969-71, asst. prof., 1971-75, assoc. prof., 1975-81, prof., 1981—. Author: Discipline, Cooperation and Compliance: an Annotated Bibliography, 1987, Parent Involvement in Early Childhood Education, 1979, Playtime Learning Games for Young Children, 1982, (with J.R. Lally) Infant Caregiving: A Design for Training, 1981, (with Wittmer) Infant/Toddler Caregiving: An Annotated Bibliography, 1982; editor: Risk Factors in Infancy, 1986, Early Parenting and Later Child Achievement, 1990, Optimizing Early Child Care and Education, 1990, (with D. Wittmer) Prosocial Devel. in Children: Caring, Helping and Cooperating, 1992; N.Am. editor: ECDC, 1983—; rsch. rev. editor: Young Children, 1980-87, Early Childhood Ednl. Rsch. Quarterly, 1985-89. Bd. dirs. Pioneer Women. Recipient Woman Achievement in Child Devel. award State of N.Y., 1983, award Sparrowgrass Poetry Forum, 1991; U.S. Office of Edn. Nat. fellow, 1969-71. Mem. APA, Soc. for Rsch. in Child Devel., Nat. Assn. for Edn. Young Children, Internat. Soc. for Study Behavioral Devel., Internat. Assn. for Infant Mental Health (pres.-elect. 1990—), Am. Ednl. Rsch. Assn., Am. Orthopsychiat. Assn., Jean Piaget Soc., World Assn. for Infant Psychiatry, Internat. Conf. on Infant Studies, Phi Beta Kappa. Jewish. Office: Syracuse U Coll for Human Devel 206 Slocum Ave Syracuse NY 13244-0001

HONIGMAN, HOWARD ARON, psychologist; b. Bklyn., Feb. 14, 1946; s. Max Raymond and Ethel (Cohen) H.; m. Joanne Edelson, July 15, 1973; children: Jacob Marc, Amy Ann. BA in Biology, Bklyn. Coll., 1966; MS in Psychology, Yeshiva U., 1977, PhD in Psychology, 1979. Lic. psychologist, N.Y. Psychology intern St. Vincent's Hosp., N.Y.C., 1975-76; staff psychologist Bklyn. Psychiat. Ctrs., Inc., 1977-88, clinic adminstr., 1988—; pvt. practice psychotherapist; lectr., supr. Bklyn. Inst. for Psychotherapy. Guest speaker East Midwood Jewish Ctr., Bklyn., 1991, Woodhull Hosp. Ctr., Bklyn., 1990, U. St. Thomas, Houston, 1989. Fellowship NIMH, 1972. Mem. APA, N.Y. Acad. Scis. Democrat. Jewish. Home: 1714 Ryder St Brooklyn NY 11234-4309 Office: 1714 Ryder St Brooklyn NY 11234-4309

HONTZ, ROBERT MILTON, JR., civil engineer; b. Pottsville, Pa., Apr. 24, 1943; s. Robert Milton and Marguerite Dettre (Brigham) H.; m. Carol Ann McCracken, Aug. 26, 1967 (div. Dec. 1990); children: Catherine Ann, Elizabeth Adele, Robert Milton III. BA in Liberal Arts, Elizabethtown Coll., 1966; BS in Civil Engring., Pa. State U., 1966, MS in Civil Engring., 1967. Registered profl. engr., N.J., Pa., Wyo. Engr. Exxon Rsch. and Engring. Co., Florham Park, N.J., 1967-70; project engr. Exxon Rsch. and Engring. Co., Florham Park, 1972-76; field engr. Esso Italiana Augusta (Italy) Refinery, 1970-71; project mgr. The Carter Mining Co., Gillette, Wyo., 1977-79; area mgr. Lagoven Refinery, Amuay, Venezuela, 1980-82; sect. head Exxon Rsch. and Engring. Co., Florham Park, N.J., 1982-84; asst. constrn. mgr. Rotterdam (Netherlands) Refinery Esso Nederland BV, 1984-86; constrn. advisor Western Div., Exxon Co. USA, Thousand Oaks, Calif., 1987-89; project mgr. Bayway Refinery, Exxon Co. USA, Linden, N.J., 1990—; chmn. oversight com. Tech. Survey Task Force Constrn. Industry Inst., Austin, 1990—. Baseball, basketball coach Tewksbury Twp. Recreation Program, Oldwick, N.J., 1987-91; dir. Albrook Montessori Sch., Basking Ridge, N.J., 1990-91. Named NSF trainee NSF, Pa. State U., 1966-67. Mem. Am. Soc. Civil Engrs., Washingtonville Rod & Gun Club, Chi Epsilon, Sigma Tau. Republican. Lutheran. Home: Rd 2 Box 492 Hoffmans Crossing Rd Califon NJ 07830 Office: Exxon Rsch & Engring Co PO Box 101 Florham Park NJ 07932-0101

HOOD, ALAN CONDIT, publishing executive; b. Orange, N.J., May 17, 1940; s. Alan Condit and Gail (Francisco) H.; m. Elizabeth Leiper Marshall, June 8, 1963 (div. Apr. 1984); children: Christopher, Abigail; m. Elizabeth Ann Rice, Aug. 4, 1984. BA, Williams Coll., 1962. Sales rep. G.P. Putnam's Sons, N.Y.C., 1962-64, Henry Regnery Co., Chgo., 1964-66; v.p. sales David McKay Co., Inc., N.Y.C., 1969-77; sales mgr., distbn. E.P. Dutton & Co., N.Y.C., 1977-78; mktg. and sales mgr. Stephen Greene Press, Brattleboro, Vt., 1978-81; proprietor Alan C. Hood, Book Svcs., Brattleboro, 1981-89; pres. Alan C. Hood & Co., Inc., Brattleboro, 1989—. Sgt. U.S. Army Intelligence Corps, 1966-69, Vietnam. Republican. Episcopalian. Home: 30 Country Hill Rd Brattleboro VT 05301-2509 Office: Alan C Hood and Co Inc 28 Birge St Brattleboro VT 05301-3206

HOOD, EDWARD EXUM, JR., electrical manufacturing company executive; b. Boonville, N.C., Sept. 15, 1930; s. Edward Exum and Nellie (Triplett) H.; m. Kay Transou, Dec. 30, 1950; children: Lisa Kay, Molly Ann. M.S. in Nuclear Engring., N.C. State U., 1953. Registered profl. engr., Ariz. Powerplant design engr. Gen. Electric Co., 1957-62, mgr. supersonic transport engine project, 1962-67, v.p., gen. mgr. comml. engine div., from 1968, v.p., group exec. internat. group, 1972-73, v.p., group exec., power generation group, 1973-77, sr. v.p., sector exec. tech. systems and materials sector, from 1977, vice-chmn., 1979—, now also exec. officer, bd. dirs. Served with USAF, 1952-56. Fellow AIAA; mem. Nat. Acad. Engring., Aerospace Industries Assn. (chmn. 1981). Home: Woods End Rd New Canaan CT 06840-4030 Office: GE 3135 Easton Tpke Fairfield CT 06431-0001*

HOOD, WILLIAM BOYD, JR., cardiologist; b. Sylacauga, Ala., Mar. 25, 1932; s. William Boyd and Katherine Elizabeth (Anderson) H.; m. Katherine Candace Todd, May 5, 1972; 1 son, Jefferson Boyce. B.S. summa cum laude, Davidson Coll., 1954; M.D., Harvard U., 1958. Intern Peter Bent Brigham Hosp., Boston, 1958-59, resident in internal medicine, 1959-60, 62-63; from asst. prof. to assoc. prof. medicine Harvard U., 1967-71; from assoc. prof. to prof. medicine Boston U., 1971-82; chief cardiology Boston City Hosp., 1973-82; prof. medicine U. Rochester (N.Y.), 1982—; head cardiology unit Strong Meml. Hosp., Rochester, 1982—; cons. NIH, 1975—. Mem. editorial bd.: New Eng. Jour. Medicine, 1974-81, Circulation, 1980-83, Circulation Research, 1982-89, Jour. Clin. Investigation, 1984-89; contbr. articles, revs. and editorials on cardiovascular physiology to profl. jours., chpts. to books. Served to capt. USAF, 1963-65. Research grantee NIH, 1971—; grantee Am. Heart Assn., 1971-76. Fellow ACP; mem. Am. Soc. Clin. Investigation, Assn. Am. Physicians, Am. Heart Assn., Am. Physiol. Soc., Assn. Profs. Cardiology (pres.-elect), Phi Beta Kappa, Alpha Omega Alpha. Office: U Rochester Cardiology Unit Box 679 601 Elmwood Ave Rochester NY 14642

HOOKER, DAVID ANDREW, educator; b. Kingston, Jamaica, Mar. 18, 1954; came to U.S., 1963; s. Desmond Ralph and Essie Myrna (Archbold) H.; m. Carol June Hutchins, Feb. 1, 1976; children: Sandra Michelle, Nathaniel Lee. BS, Andrews U., Berrien Springs, Mich., 1977, MA in Teaching, 1985; postgrad., U. Md., 1986—. Cert. tchr., Md., Ohio. Math. and sci. tchr. Eastern Shore Acad., Sudlersville, Md., 1977-84, Eastwood Jr. Acad., Columbus, Ohio, 1984-85; math. tchr. Takoma Acad., Takoma Park, Md., 1985—. Mem. Creation Rsch. Soc., Nat. Coun. Tchrs. of Math., Pathfinders (bd. dirs. 1980-81). Seventh-Day Adventist. Home: 6928 Shepherd St Hyattsville MD 20784-2534 Office: Takoma Acad 8120 Carroll Ave Silver Spring MD 20912-7397

HOOKER, MICHAEL KENNETH, college president; b. Richlands, Va., Aug. 24, 1945; s. Aaron Kenneth and Margaret (Smith) H.; m. Anna Hostettler, Dec. 22, 1966; 1 dau., Alexandra Christine. BA, U. N.C., 1969; MA, U. Mass., 1972, PhD, 1973; LittD (hon.), Drexel U., 1988. Asst. prof. Harvard U., Cambridge, Mass., 1973-75; asst. prof. philosophy Johns Hopkins U., Balt., 1975-77, asst. dean, 1977-78, assoc. dean, 1978-80, dean, 1980-82; pres. Bennington (Vt.) Coll., 1982-86, U. Md., Balt. County, 1986-92, U. Mass., Boston, 1992—; chmn. biotech. adv. com. Office Tech. Assessment, Washington, 1981-83; bd. dirs. Biotech. Devel. Corp., Inc., Interfacts, Columbia Bancorp, Inst. for Global Ethis; mem. adv. bd. Grace Ventures, Calif. Contbr. articles to philosophy jours.; editor: Descartes, 1978, Leibniz, 1982. Bd. govs. Nat. Aquarium; mem. adv. bd. Chesapeake Bay Outward Bound. Recipient Homewood award John Hopkins U., 1980, Chancellor's medal U. Mass., 1989; Woodrow Wilson fellow, 1972-73, Harvard U. faculty rsch. fellow, 1974. Mem. Leibniz Soc. (bd. dirs. 1979-83), Internat. Berkeley Soc. (v.p. 1978-79), Am. Philos. Assn. Soc. (chmn. com., bd. officers 1977-82). Home: 6304 Mossway Baltimore MD 21212-2218 Office: U Mass 250 Stuart St 12th Fl Boston MA 02116-5329

HOOP, RITA CAPORICCI, molecular biologist; b. Glendale, N.Y., Nov. 30, 1963; d. Rocco and Antonietta (Evangelista) Caporicci; m. Elmer Paul Hoop III, Dec. 27, 1986; children: Karen Elizabeth, Amanda Jane. BA in Biology, Cornell U., 1985; MS in Genetic Counseling, Ohio State U., 1987; postgrad., U. Pitts., 1992—. Presdl. fellow Ohio State U., Columbus, 1985-86, teaching asst. dept. genetics, 1986-87, rsch. asst. dept. molecular genetics, 1987; chief biorsch. svc. dept. clin. investigation Madigan Army Med. Ctr., Tacoma, 1988—; commd. 2d lt. U.S. Army, 1985, advanced through grades to capt.; project officer for clin. investigation, rsch. labs. Madigan Army Med. Ctr., Tacoma, 1988-92; grad. student researcher U. Pitts., 1992—; rsch. assoc. cell biology Cephalon, Inc., West Chester, 1991-92. Contbr. articles, abstracts to profl. publs. Mem. AAAS, Soc. Armed Forces Med. Lab. Scientists, N.Y. Acad. Scis., Sigma Xi. Home: 625 Churchill Ct Mars PA 16046

HOOPER, DONALD ROBERT, leasing company executive; b. Deer Island, N.B., Can., Apr. 17, 1935; came to U.S., 1954; s. Raymond Wendall and Norma (Doughty) H.; m. Peggy DeForest, June 28, 1958 (div. 1974); children: Diane Evelyn, John Gregory, Suzanne Carole, Donald Robert II; m. Susan Paula Amenta, May 22, 1987. BTh, Ea. Christian Inst., Orange, N.J., 1957; LLB, LaSalle U., Chgo., 1963; BS in Profl. Meteorology, U. Md. (Chaumont Air Base), 1964; DD (hon.), Univ. of West, Pasadena, Calif., 1978. Lic. real estate broker; cert. profl. supt. Chief exec. officer The Hooper Co., Somers, Conn., 1969—, Shopping Ctr. Svcs. Inc., Pasadena, Md., 1985—, Shopping Ctr. Svcs. Fla. Inc., St. Cloud, 1991, Shopping Ctr. Svcs. Del., Inc., Wilmington, Del., 1989—; dir. The Hooper Co., Somers, Conn., The Shopping Ctr. Svcs. Co., Somers. Author: Weather and Flight Patterns of Europe, 1963 (award 1963), Blueprint Reading, 1979, Weather of North Polar Regions, 1968. Mem. Rep. Nat. Com., Washington, 1990-91; mem. The Presdl. Trust, Washington, 1991-92; life mem. Air Force Aid Soc., Washington, 1957—. Sgt. USAF, 1956-67. Decorated Air Force Commendation medal; recipient Cert. of Recognition, Rep. Nat. Com., Washington, 1991. Fellow Am. Soc. Profl. Supts. (life, pres. 1980—, dir. 1980—); mem. Archaeol. Inst. Am., Somers Lions Club (dir. 1979-80), Woodland Rotary (dir. 1982-84). Mem. Ch. of God. Home: 56 Goodwin Dr Somers CT 06071-1922

HOOPER, JAMES BRYAN, management consultant; b. Newcastle, England, Apr. 7, 1941; came to the U.S., 1974; s. Stanley James and Edna Isobel (Smith) H.; m. Carol Melville, July 25, 1964; children: Katherine Jane, Caroline Emma. AS, Imperial Coll., London, 1960, BS, 1963. Various positions ending with sales mgr. ICI Fibres Div., Harrogate, England, 1963-74; group planning dir. Celanese Corp., Charlotte, N.C., 1974-77; dir. planning Celanese Fibers Mktg., N.Y.C., 1977-81; market devel. dir. Celanese Internat. Mktg., N.Y.C., 1981-84; dir. internat. mktg. Celanese Fibers Ops., N.Y.C., 1984-86; gen. mgr. mktg. Crown Textile Co., Jenkintown, Pa., 1986-87; sr. assoc. PXR Group, Rowayton, Conn., 1988-89; pres. Hooper & Assocs., Darien, Conn., 1990—. Home and Office: 29 Delafield Island Rd Darien CT 06820-6012

HOOPES, WALTER RONALD, chemical company executive; b. Darby, Pa., Aug. 3, 1933; s. Walter Theodore and Evelyn Grace (Phifer) H.; m. Joan Ruth Herr, Mar. 3, 1956; children: David, Robert, Susan, Bruce. BS in Indsl. Engring., Pa. State U., 1955; grad. cert., MIT, 1970. Mfg. supr., sales rep. E.I. duPont de Nemours & Co., Wilmington, Del., 1955-63; regional sales mgr. W.R. Grace & Co., Fullerton, Calif., 1963-68; product mgr. W.R. Grace & Co., Lexington, Mass., 1968-82; commercial mgr. W.R. Grace & Co., Mexico City, 1982-85; nat. sales mgr. W.R. Grace & Co., Lexington, Mass., 1985-86; v.p., gen. mgr. polymers ops. W.R. Grace & Co., Lexington, 1986—; vice chmn. Paper Synthetics div. Tech. Assn. Pulp & Paper Industry, Atlanta, 1981-82. Pres. Boston Guild for the Hard of Hearing, 1989-91. 1st lt. U.S. Army, 1955-57. Mem. TAPPI, Pi Kappa Phi. Home: 16 Cherry Ridge Rd Acton MA 01720-2206 Office: W R Grace & Co 55 Hayden Ave Lexington MA 02173-7999

HOOTON, BRUCE DUFF, editor, publisher; b. Waukegan, Ill., Dec. 11, 1928; s. Bruce Duff and Romine (Garrison) H.; 1 child, Harold Hart. Student Memphis Acad. Arts, 1946-47, Southwestern Coll., 1948-50, Harvard U., 1951-52. Editor, pub. Drawing mag., 1957-60; art critic, editor, N.Y. Herald Tribune, 1962-65; head N.Y. office Archives Am. Art, 1965-66; sr. editor ARTnews, 1968-69; exec. dir. Save Venice, N.Y.C., 1973-75; assoc. Lee Ault & Co., 1971—; editor, pub. Art/World, N.Y.C., 1976—. Editor: Mother and Child in Modern Art, 1964. Founder, v.p. Stravinsky-Diaghilev Found., N.Y.C., 1970-72; acting chmn. Venice Com., N.Y.C., 1969-70; bd. trustees Nassau County Mus. Art, N.Y.C., 1989—; founder, dir. Mfrs. Hanover Art-World Newspaper Art Critics Awards, 1983—; overseer Weir Farm Heritage Trust, Conn. Mem. Drawing Soc. N.Y.C. (founder, 1st pres. 1960—), Coffeehouse Club, Century Assn., Piping Rock Club. Republican.

Episcopalian. Home and Office: Art/World 55 Wheatley Rd Glen Head NY 11545-2907

HOOVER, DAVID CARLSON, lawyer; b. Waterville, Maine, Apr. 22, 1950; s. Jack Cauldwell and Mary Elizabeth (Donavan) H.; m. Kathleen Delia Powell, June 28, 1981; children: Maegan Elizabeth, Peter Daniel, Christian Shaw. BA, U. N.H., 1972; JD cum laude, Suffolk U., 1976. Bar: Mass. 1977, U.S. Dist. Ct. Mass. 1982, U.S. Supreme Ct. 1982, U.S. Ct. Appeals (1st cir.) 1983. Atty. advisor NOAA, Washington, 1976-79; gen. counsel Mass. Div. Marine Fisheries, Boston, 1979-83; spl. asst. atty. gen. Mass. Dept. Atty. Gen., Boston, 1980—; gen. counsel Mass. Dept. of Fisheries, Wildlife and Environ. Law Enforcement, Boston, 1983—; adminstrv. law judge Commonwealth of Mass., 1979—; lectr. Franklin Pierce Law Ctr., Concord, N.H., 1984. Contbr. articles to profl. jours. Active Cath. Youth Orgn., tchr., ch. lector. Recipient Am. Jurisprudence award Lawyers Cooperative Pub. Co. Mem. Mass. Bar Assn., Com. on Chemical Dependency, Atty. advisor to Mock-Trial Tournament, Law Related Edn. Com., Lawyers Concerned for Lawyers. Home: 808 Watertown St Newton MA 02165-2116 Office: Dept Fisheries Wildlife and Environ Law Enforcement 100 Cambridge St Rm 1901 Boston MA 02202-0001

HOOVER, EDDIE LEE, cardiothoracic surgeon, educator; b. Charlotte, N.C., Sept. 16, 1944; s. Arthur John and Geneva (Phifer) H. BA, U. N.C., 1965; MD, Duke U., 1969. Diplomate Nat. Bd. Med. Examiners, Am. Bds. Surgery and Thoracic Surgery. Intern Duke U., Durham, N.C., 1969-70, resident in gen. surgery, 1970-71; resident in gen. surgery N.Y. Hosp. Cornell U., N.Y.C., 1973-75, resident in cardiothoricic surgery, 1976-78; asst. prof. surgery Cornell U. Med. Ctr., N.Y.C., 1978-80; assoc. prof. surgery SUNY, Bklyn., 1980-87; prof. surgery Meharry Med. Coll., Nashville, 1987-90; prof., chmn. surgery SUNY, Buffalo, 1990—. Author surg. sci. manuscripts. Bd. mem. Urban League, Buffalo, 1991—. Lt. comdr. USN, 1971-73; PTO. Mem. Nat. Med. Assn. (pres. nat. surg. sect. Buffalo chpt. 1992—), Nat. Alumni Coun. Duke U. Med. Sch., Sigma Pi Boule. Home: 1217 Delaware Ave Buffalo NY 14209 Office: Erie County Med Ctr 462 Grider St Buffalo NY 14215

HOOVER, JACQUELINE SUE, banking officer; b. Pueblo, Colo., Feb. 19, 1966; d. Duane E. and Anna M. (Baier) H. BS, N.E. Mo. State U., 1988; MS, Colo. State U., 1990. Grad. teaching asst. Colo. State U., Ft. Collins, 1988-90; requirements analyst Citicorp/Citibank, Hunt Valley, Md., 1990—. Home: 4401 Silverbrook Ln Apt 203B Owings Mills MD 21117-4937 Office: Citibank 10751 Falls Rd Ste 300 Lutherville Timonium MD 21093-4520

HOOVER, JAMES BENTLEY, investment banker; b. Harrisburg, Pa., Jan. 22, 1955; s. James H. and Renalda G. (Gryalba) H.; m. Barbara J. Higgins, Sept. 29, 1979; children: Bradley, Court, Logan. BS, Elizabethtown Coll., 1975; MBA, Ind. U., 1977. V.p. Citicorp, N.Y.C., 1977-84; ptnr. Robertson, Stephens & Co., N.Y.C., 1984—; bd. dirs. Arbor Health Care Co., Lima, Ohio, U.S. Phys. Therapy, Inc., Houston; mem. spl. projects com. Meml. Sloan-Kettering, N.Y.C., 1985—. Home: 19 Dogwood Hl Glen Head NY 11545-3204 Office: 450 Park Ave New York NY 10022-2605

HOOVER, JOHN EDWARD, pharmacist, biomedical consultant; b. Middletown, Ohio, July 24, 1929; s. Lloyd Melangthon and Gertrude (Snider) H.; m. Marcia Lavanish, May 15, 1971; 1 child, Elizabeth A. BSc in Pharmacy, Ohio State U., 1952. Lic. pharmacist, Pa., Ohio. Community pharmacist various orgns. Middletown, 1954-58; profl. rep. Upjohn Co. and Merck Sharp & Dohme, Middletown, 1954-58; mgr. spl. svcs. Mack Pub. Co., Easton, Pa., 1960-66; dir. adminstrn. and communications Phila. Coll. Pharmacy and Sci., 1958-60, 66-78; cons. biomed. communications Swarthmore, Pa., 1956—; communications cons. to pres. Delmont Labs., Inc., Swarthmore, 1978—. Mng. editor Remington's Pharm. Scis., 1958—, Am. Jour. Pharmacy, 1966—; editor: Dispensing of Medication, 8th edit., 1976. Lt. U.S. Army, 1952-54, Korea. Mem. Am. Pharm. Assn., Am. Med. Writers Assn., Coun. Biology Editors, Drug Info. Assn., Am. Inst. History Pharmacy. Home and Office: 363 Riverview Rd Swarthmore PA 19081-1219

HOOVER, STEPHANIE ANN, advertising executive; b. Hershey, Pa., Oct. 31, 1960; d. Ernest Franklin and Marian Louise (Rearick) H.; m. Thomas Lee Stump, Feb. 5, 1988; 1 child, Christin Lee. Student, Harrisburg Area Community Coll, 1978-80. Owner Hoover's Janitorial Svc., Hershey, Pa., 1981-84; copywriter WHGB, Harrisburg, 1984-85, WSFM/WCMB, Harrisburg, 1985-86; free lance writer various publs. Cen. Pa. area, 1986—; mktg. dir. Capitol Area Transit, Harrisburg, 1987-91; pres., owner Your Prodn. House, Inc., Harrisburg, 1989—. Writer Bus. Month, 1986-87, Cen. Pa. Bus. Jour., 1988—; prodn. mgr. Homes by Owner, 1990-91; editor, writer, pub. The Communicator, 1991. Vol. ad agy. Older Am. Days Com., Harrisburg, 1991, South Cen. Pa. Food Bank, Harrisburg, 1991. Recipient Second Pl. award Pa. Songwriters Competition, 1982, Best Radio Commercial award Pa. Assn. Broadcasters, 1985. Mem. Pa. Soc. Assn. Execs. (communications com. 1990—). Democrat. Brethren. Office: Your Prodn House Inc 5806 Severna Pl Harrisburg PA 17111-4150

HOPF, FRANK RUDOLPH, dentist; b. N.Y.C., Sept. 1, 1920; s. Rudolph Aldridge and Jennie Victoria (Fusco) H.; B.S., Purdue U., 1942; postgrad. Middlesex U. Sch. Medicine, 1943-44; D.D.S., N.Y. U., 1953, postgrad., 1957-61; M.A., Columbia, 1953, M.P.H., 1955; m. Elsie Hedlund, Sept. 10, 1949; children—Christine, Frank, Victoria, William, Robert. Asst. dir. Bur. Dental Health, N.Y. State Dept. Health, Albany, 1956-57, regional dental dir., White Plains, 1967-90; pvt. practice dentistry specializing in periodontics, Rye, 1957—. Research asso. dept. periodontics, N.Y. U. Coll. Dentistry, 1958-61; clin. asst. prof. dept. periodontics N.J. Coll. Medicine and Dentistry, Jersey City, 1962-67; adj. asst. prof. dept. community dentistry Columbia Sch. Dental and Oral Surgery, N.Y.C., 1971-76; vis. prof. dept. preventive dentistry, Pitts. U. Sch. Dentistry, 1967-72. Pres., Country Ridge Home Owners Assn., Rye Brook, N.Y., 1960-62. Served with USNR, 1944-46. NIH grantee, 1957. Fellow Am. Public Health Assn., Am. Sch. Health Assn., N.Y. Acad. Dentistry, Am. Coll. Dentists; mem. ADA, N.Y. State Public Health Assn. (pres. 1970-72), Westchester Shore Dental Study Club (pres. 1960-61), Royal Soc. Health, North Eastern Soc. Periodontics, AAAS, Westchester Acad. Medicine, Am. Soc. Dentistry for Children, Federation Dentaire Internationale. Roman Catholic. KC (4 deg.). Club: Westchester Country (Rye, N.Y.). Contbr. articles to profl. publs. Home: 42 Rockinghorse Trl Rye Brook NY 10573-1038 Office: 175 Purchase St Rye NY 10580

HOPKINS, CHARLES PETER, II, lawyer; b. Elizabeth, N.J., June 16, 1953; s. Charles Peter Sr. and Josephine Ann (Battaglia) H.; m. Elizabeth Anna Altinger, Jan. 21, 1984; children: Courtney Alexandra, Ashley Elizabeth. AB summa cum laude, Boston Coll., 1975, JD, 1979; MBA, Rutgers U., 1987. Bar: N.J. 1979, U.S. Dist. Ct. N.J. 1979, U.S. Ct. Appeals (3d cir.) 1982, U.S. Supreme Ct. 1985, U.S. Tax Ct. 1988. Assoc. Gagliano, Tucci & Kennedy, West Long Branch, N.J., 1980; pvt. practice West Long Branch, 1980-81; assoc. Richard J. Sauerwein (formerly Sparks & Sauerwein), Shrewsbury, N.J., 1981-83, trial atty., 1983-87, sr. trial atty., 1987-90; mng. trial atty. Law Offices Charles Peter Hopkins II, Shrewsbury, 1990—; arbitrator U.S. Dist. Ct. N.J., 1985—, N.J. Civil arbitrator program, 1987—, Am. Arbitration Assn., 1991—. Mem. Def. Rsch. Inst., West Long Br. Sch. Bd., 1980-82. Mem. ABA, N.J. Bar Assn., Monmouth Bar Assn., N.J. Def. Assn., Def. Rsch. Inst., Phi Beta Kappa. Republican. Roman Catholic. Office: Shrewsbury Sq Office Ctr 655 Shrewsbury Ave Shrewsbury NJ 07702-4151

HOPKINS, ESTHER ARVILLA HARRISON, chemist, patent lawyer; b. Stamford, Conn., Sept. 18, 1926; d. George Burgess and Esther (Smalls) Harrison; m. John Payne Mitchell, Dec. 27, 1952 (div.); 1 child, Susan Weamah Emma; m. Thomas Ewell Hopkins, Jan. 20, 1959; 1 child, Thomas Ewell Jr. AB, Boston U., 1947; MS, Howard U., 1948, Yale U., 1962; PhD, Yale U., 1967; JD, Suffolk U., Boston, 1977. Bar: Mass. 1977. Instr. chemistry Va. State Coll., Petersburg, 1949-52; research chemist New Eng. Inst. Med. Research, Ridgefield, Conn., 1955-59, Am. Cyanamid Corp., Stamford, 1959-61; scientist Polaroid Corp., Cambridge, Mass., 1967-73, jr. patent atty., 1973-78, sr. project adminstr., 1979-86, tech. liaison mgr., 1986-88; dep. gen. counsel dept. environ. protection Commonwealth of Mass., Boston, 1989—. Contbr. articles to profl. jours. Trustee Boston U., 1985—, pres. Gen. Alumni Assn., 1985-87; bd. dirs. YMCA USA, Chgo.; clk. Clara Barton Camp for Girls with Diabetes Inc., North Oxford, Mass., 1985-90; clk. fin. com. Town of Framingham, Mass.; sec. Soc. Promoting Theol. Edn., Boston; bd. overseers Regional Lab. for Ednl. Improvement of the N.E. and The Islands, Andover, Mass.; mem. adv. com. MetroWest Health, Inc. Named Woman of Achievement, Mass. Fedn. Bus. and Profl. Women, 1979. Mem. Am. Chem. Soc. (chair com. profl. relations, chair northeastern sect. 1983), Phi Beta Kappa, Sigma Xi, Sigma Pi Sigma, Beta Kappa Chi, Alpha Kappa Alpha. Unitarian-Universalist. Home: 1550 Worcester Rd Framingham MA 01701-8968 Office: Dept Environ Protection Office of the Gen Counsel 1 Winter St Boston MA 02108-4747

HOPKINS, GAIL ETHEL, nursing systems director; b. White Plains, N.Y., July 23, 1941; d. Frank Howard and Ethel Mae (Braun) H. Nursing diploma, Westchester Sch. Nursing, 1962; BS, Iona Coll., 1982; postgrad., Pace U., 1991—. Charge nurse, emergency rm. White Plains (N.Y.) Hosp. Ctr., 1966-68, head nurse, emergency rm., 1968-74, staff nurse, operating rm., 1974-82, staff devel. educator, 1982-86, asst. dir. nursing med./surg./psychiat., 1987-91, dir. nursing systems, 1991—. Mem. Associated Operating Rm. Nursing. Home: 505 Central Ave White Plains NY 10606-1539 Office: White Plains Hosp Ctr Davis Ave White Plains NY 10601-4602

HOPKINS, JAMES ROY, psychology educator; b. Fieldale, Va., Dec. 7, 1944; s. Luther Edwin and Vergie Emma (Spencer) H. BA, U. Va., 1968; PhD, Harvard U., 1974. Asst. prof. Vassar Coll., Poughkeepsie, N.Y., 1974-79; assoc. prof. St. Mary's (Md.) Coll., 1980-85, prof., 1985—. Author: (textbook) Adolescence, 1983, co-author: (textbook) Psychology, 1987, 2d edit. 1990. Bd. dirs. St. Mary's Assn. Retarded Children, 1983-86. Mem. Am. Psychol. Assn., Soc. Rsch. in Child Devel., Soc. Rsch. in Adolescence, Soc. Psychol. Study Social Issues, Phi Beta Kappa, Sigma Xi, Psi Chi. Office: St Mary's Coll Saint Mary's City MD 20686

HOPKINS, JEANNE SULICK, accountant; b. Fair Lawn, N.J., Oct. 14, 1952; d. Peter and Margaret (McLaughlin) Sulick; m. Ronald T. Hopkins, Aug. 23, 1975. B.S., Syracuse U., 1974, M.B.A., 1975. With Price Waterhouse, Syracuse, 1975-83, staff acct., 1975-78, sr. acct., 1978-80, audit mgr., 1980-83; mgr. cost acctg. United Technologies/Carrier Corp., Syracuse, 1983-85; owner J.S. Hopkins & Co., CPA's, 1985-87, ptnr. Dannible & McKee, CPAs, 1987—; instr. in field. Mem. fund raising com. Syracuse Symphony Orch.; mem. Nat. Assn. Panhellenics. Mem. Am. Inst. C.P.A.s, Planning Execs. Inst., Hosp. Fin. Mgmt. Assn., N.Y. State Soc. C.P.A.s, Syracuse U. Alumni Assn., Delta Delta Delta. Club: Zonta. Office: Dannible & McKee 499 S Warren St Syracuse NY 13202-2609

HOPKINS, THOMAS DUVALL, economics educator; b. Spring Valley, Ill., Mar. 10, 1942; s. Joel Willis and Mildred (Duvall) H.; m. Jane Cole Eveleth, Apr. 20, 1968; children: Edward Eveleth, Catherine Chapin Hopkins. BA, Oberlin (Ohio) Coll., 1964; MA, Yale U., 1965, M of Philosophy, 1967, PhD, 1971. Asst. prof. econs. Bowdoin Coll., Brunswick, Maine, 1968-73; cons. Irwin Mgmt. Co., Inc., Columbus, Ind., 1973-75; asst. dir. Coun. on Wage and Price Stability, Washington, 1975-81, acting dir., 1981; dep. adminstr. Office of Mgmt. and Budget, Washington, 1981-84; assoc. prof. U. Md., College Park, 1984-87; assoc. prof. econs. Am. U., Washington, 1987-88; prof. econs., Arthur J. Gosnell prof. Rochester (N.Y.) Inst. Tech., 1988—; cons. Adminstrv. Conf. U.S., Washington, 1986-88, Office Tech. Assessment, U.S. Congress, Washington, 1987-89, Inst. Liberty and Democracy, Lima, Peru, 1986-91, U.S. Regulatory Info. Svc. Ctr., 1990-92, Congl. Budget Office, 1991; seminar leader Inst. Internat. Edn., Washington, 1987-88; mem. com. on tank vessel design marine bd. NRC, Washington, 1989-91; mem. com. on taxation, fin. and pricing Transp. Rsch. Bd. Co-author: Tanker Spills: Prevention by Design, 1991. Elder Presbyn. Ch., 1986—; deacon 3d Presbyn. Ch., Rochester, 1990—; mem. reunion gift com. Oberlin Coll., 1987-89; mem. coun. Eastman House, Rochester, 1991—. Woodrow Wilson Found. fellow, 1964. Fellow NSF; mem. Am. Econs. Assn., Nat. Economists Club, Assn. for Pub. Policy Analysis and Mgmt. Home: 215 Dorchester Rd Rochester NY 14610-1322 Office: Rochester Inst Tech CLA One Lomb Meml Dr Rochester NY 14623

HOPMAN, ELLEN EVERT, psychotherapist; b. Salzburg, Austria, July 31, 1952; came to U.S., 1954; d. Abraham Nathan and Marcia Elizabeth Evert; m. Albert Novelli, Jr., Jan. 14, 1973 (div. 1980). BS in Art Edn., Temple U., Phila., 1978; MEd in Mental Health Counseling, U. Mass., Amherst, 1990. Teaching Cert. Art tchr. Upper Darby Sch. Dist., Upper Darby, Pa., 1978-80; teaching asst. Temple U. Art Hist. Dept., Phila., 1980-82; health educator, master herbalist pvt. practice, Amherst, Belchertown, Mass., 1983—, psychotherapist, 1990—; environ. cons., Clean Water Action, Northampton, Mass., 1990-91. Author: Tree Medicine, Tree Magic, 1991; contbr. articles to profl. mags. Mem. AACD, Nat. Ctr. for Homeopathy, Nature Conservancy, Keltria (v.p.), Earth Spirit Community, Am. Herbalists Guild, N.E. Herb Assn. Democrat. Office: PO Box 219 Amherst MA 01004-0219

HOPP, MANFRED ERNST, chemical company executive; b. Ravensburg, Germany, Mar. 12, 1936; s. Ernst and Luise (Herbold) H.; m. Hede E.T. Sistig. BS in Chemistry, Tech. U., Karlsruhe, Fed. Republic Germany, 1957; MS in Chemistry, U. Munich, Fed. Republic Germany, 1961, Dr.rer.nat., 1962. Dir. research and devel. BASF Systems, Bedford, Mass., 1967-68; mgr. pigments application BASF AG, Ludwigshafen, Fed. Republic Germany, 1970-77; mgr. wood finishing dept. BASF F&L, Muenster, Fed. Republic Germany, 1978-80; gen. mgr. indsl. div. BASF F&L, Muenster, 1980-85; pres. Fritzsche Dodge & Olcott, N.Y.C., 1985-89; pres. comsumer products and life scis. div. BASF Corp., Parsippany, N.J., 1989. Lodge: Rotary. Home: 100 Cherry Hill Rd # Basf Parsippany NJ 07054-1106 Office: BASF Corp/Consumer Products & Life Scis Div 100 Cherry Hill Rd Parsippany NJ 07054-1146

HORAI, JOANN, psychologist; b. N.Y.C.; d. Charles J. and Stacia (Melnick) H. BA, U. Miami, Coral Gables, Fla., 1964, MS, 1968, PhD, 1970. Asst. prof. Hofstra U., Hempstead, N.Y., 1971-76; dir. Am. Psychol. Assn., Washington, 1976-89; organizational design cons. Washington, 1991—; pvt. practice quality and strategic planning cons., 1992—. Mem. Am. Soc. Assn. Execs., Am. Psychol. Assn.

HORAK, DONNA CHRISTINE, labor union administrator, director training; b. N.Y.C., July 14, 1947; d. Frank and Florence Elizabeth (Incledon) H.; m. Edwin Mendez (div. Nov., 1972); 1 child, Edwin Paul Mendez. BA, Marymount Coll., 1980. Accounts payable clk. Thomas Cook, Inc., N.Y.C., 1974-76; customer svc. rep. Rivera Eyewear Corp., N.Y.C., 1976-78; supr. registration Am. Mgmt. Assn., N.Y.C., 1978-84, tng. adminstr., 1984-86, program dir., 1988-89; tng. coord. Board of Edn., Long Island City, N.Y., 1987-87; tng. dir. PanSon Electronics, Inc., Greenpoint, N.Y., 1987-88; dir. tng. Local Union 74 Svc. Employees Internat. Union, Long Island City, 1989—. Chaplain aide Roosevelt Hosp., N.Y.C., 1978-82, Goldwater Hosp., Roosvelt Island, 1981-82, counselor, 1981-82; sec.-treas. Sodality of St. Catherine, N.Y.C., 1982-83; tchr. St. James Sunday Sch., Elmhurst, N.Y., 1971-72. Mem. ASTD. Episcopalian. Office: Local Union 74 SEIU 25-09 38th Ave Long Island City NY 11101

HORDON, ROBERT MARSHALL, geography educator; b. N.Y.C., July 10, 1936; s. Sidney and Betty (Flacks) H.; m. Sheila Feldman, Mar. 21, 1959; children: Laurence, Bruce. BA, Bklyn. Coll., 1959; MA, Columbia U., 1965, PhD, 1970. Instr. Rutgers U., New Brunswick, N.J., 1975—, asst. prof., 1970-76, assoc. prof., 1976—. Lt. (j.g.) USN, 1957-59. Mem. Am. Geog. Soc., Am. Water Resources Assn., Am. Inst. Hydrology, Am. Geophys. Union, Sigma Xi. Office: Rutgers U Dept Geography New Brunswick NJ 08903

HORE, JOHN EDWARD, commodity futures educator; b. Kingston-on-Thames, Surrey, Eng., Dec. 13, 1929; came to Can., 1954; s. Ernest and Doris Kathleen (Horton) H.; m. Diana King, May 3, 1958; children: Edward John Bruce, Celia Kathleen Hore Milne, Timothy Frank. B.A. with honors, King's Coll., Cambridge, Eng., 1952, M.A., 1957. Chartered fin. analyst. Asst. sales mgr. Borthwicks, London, 1952-54; security analyst Dominion Securities, Toronto, Ont., Can., 1955-57; asst. mktg. mgr. Rio Algom, Toronto, 1957-61; dir. Bell, Gouinlock & Co., Toronto, 1961-75; v.p., dir. futures Can. Securities Inst., Toronto, 1979—, seminar leader, 1980—; founding sec. Can. Nuclear Assn.; past v.p. Brit. Can. Trade Assn.; chmn. 1st Can. Internat. Futures Research Seminar, 1985, also editor Proc., 2 vols., 1986; speaker Can.-Am. Inst. Conf. on Fin. Svcs. at Detroit-Windsor, 1989, compliance seminar Futures Industry Assn. at Alexandria, Va., 1990; chmn. Can. Futures Conf., 1986; chmn. 3d, 4th, 5th and 6th Can. Internat. Futures Conf. and Research Seminars, 1987, 88, 89, 90 (mng. editor Selected Papers, 1988-91). Author: Trading on Canadian Futures Markets, 1984, 3rd edit., 1987, 4th edit., 1989; co-author: Association for Investment Management and Research Standards of Practice Handbook, 1982 (Pres. Reagan Citation 1984); co-editor: Canadian Securities Course, 1980—. Gov. Montcrest Sch., 1970-73; mem. Commodity Futures Adv. Bd., Ont., 1989—; apptd. mem. internat. com. Futures Industry Assn., Washington, 1988-91, rowing com. Upper Can. Coll., Toronto, 1982-86; pres. St. George's Soc. Toronto, 1978-80, chmn. edn. com., 1987. Served with Royal Army Ednl. Corps, 1948-49; Singapore. Mem. Toronto Soc. Fin. Analysts (bd. dirs. 1968-71), Assn. for Investment Mgmt. and Rsch. (formerly Fin. Analysts Fedn., bd. dirs. investment analysis standards 1974-85, emeritus 1985). Progressive Conservative. Anglican. Clubs: University (bd. dirs. 1980-83) (Toronto); Leander (assoc.) (Henley-on-Thames), Hurlingham, Royal Overseas League (hon. corr. sec. for Toronto) (London). Avocations: historical research, squash, choral music. Office: Can Securities Inst, 121 King St W, Toronto, ON Canada

HORGAN, DENNIS WILLIAM, computer scientist; b. N.Y.C., Oct. 22, 1963; s. Edward Joseph and Patricia Anne (Secor) H. BA, Georgetown U., 1985. Rsch. dir. Morningside Labs., Glen Rock, N.J., 1985—. Republican. Roman Catholic. Home: 12 Rock Rd Glen Rock NJ 07452-2024

HORGAN-AGUADO, JOSEPH PATRICK, writer; b. N.Y.C., Mar. 18, 1955; s. Charles Stanislaus Jr. and Anne (Burns) H.; m. Maria Haydee Aguado, Oct. 2, 1953; children: Rebecca Gabriella. Student, Plymouth State Coll., 1978-81. Med. records clk. New Rochelle (N.Y.) Hosp. Med. Ctr., 1974-75; div. head staff Camp Fatima, Gilmington, N.H., 1974-80; mem. door staff Hay Adams Hotel, Washington, 1983-85; actor Summer Nights Arena Theatre, New Rochelle, 1983; serials records technician Libr. and Info. Svcs. Dept. Internat. Brotherhood Teamsters, Washington, 1987—; freelance writer. Poetry included in anthology. Canvasser SANE/Freeze, 1983. Mem. Egalitarians Only Club (pres. 1989—), Friday's Smilin' Pint o' Guiness Club. Home: 7417 Carroll Ave Silver Spring MD 20912-5728 Office: Internat Brotherhood Teamsters 25 Louisiana Ave NW Washington DC 20001-2198

HORIGUCHI, ATSUKO, economist; b. Kobe, Japan, Mar. 13, 1962; came to U.S., 1980; d. Minoru and Reiko (Okumura) H. BA with honors, Johns Hopkins U., 1984; M. Pub. Policy, Harvard U., 1990. Teaching fellow Harvard U., Cambridge, Mass., summer 1983; program asst. SAIS Sch. Advanced Internat. Studies, Johns Hopkins U., Washington, 1984-85; fin. analyst Merrill Lynch Capital Markets, N.Y.C., 1985-86; rsch. analyst Merrill Lynch Japan, Tokyo, 1986-87, asst. to pres., 1987-88; intern World Bank, Washington, summer 1989; teaching fellow Harvard U., Cambridge, 1989-90; economist World Bank, Washington, 1990—. Mem. Amnesty Internat., 1992—. Named del. 21st Century Trust, London, 1990, Harvard-Stanford del. Berlin City Govt., 1989. Office: World Bank 1818 H St NW Washington DC 20433

HORINE, NELSON CHARLES, II, educator, educational administrator; b. Hagerstown, Md., June 12, 1947; s. Nelson Charles and Anna Lenore (Rupp) H.; m. Linnea May Henry, June 19, 1971; children: Matthew, Erik, Jeremy. BA, Edinboro State Coll., 1969; MEd, Loyola Coll., Balt., 1976; teaching cert., Towson State U., 1970; postgrad., U. Md., 1979—. Cert. gen. sci., biology, chemistry tchr., asst. prin., prin., Md. Tchr. phys. sci. Severna Park (Md.) Jr. High Sch., 1969-76; student affairs specialist Anne Arundel County Pub. Schs., Annapolis, Md., 1976-79; tchr. biology Glen Burnie (Md.) Sr. High Sch., 1979—, chmn. sci. dept., 1982—, asst. prin. summer sch. and evening high sch., 1983-85, prin., 1985—; vol. rsch. asst. Jug Bay Wetlands Sanctuary, Lothian, Md., 1987—; legis. reader EPA, 1988—; leadership dir. jr. high sch. program St. Mary's (Md.) Coll., 1978. Bd. dirs. March of Dimes, Balt., 1976-79, ARC, Balt., 1976-79, Am. Cancer Soc., Annapolis, 1976-79; project leader Cub Scout camping program Watchung (N.J.) Scout Camp, Boy Scouts Am., 1977, Cub Scouts committeeman, Severna Park, 1983-87. Named Sci. Tchr. of Yr., U.S. Naval Acad., 1987. Mem. Nat. Eagle Scout Assn. (Eagle Scout award 1963), Phi Delta Kappa, Beta Beta Beta, Alpha Sigma Nu. Democrat. Lutheran. Office: Glen Burnie Sr High Sch 7550 Baltimore-Annapolis Glen Burnie MD 21061

HORKA, ALFRED EDWARD, plastics company executive; b. Passaic, N.J., Feb. 26, 1921; s. Frank Walter and Anna (Haas) H.; m. Jean S. Lawton, Feb. 7, 1945; children: Douglas Lawton, Nancy Jean. BSChemE, Lehigh U., 1942. Project engr. Bakelite Corp., Bound Brook, N.J., 1945-48; sales engring. various cos., N.Y.C., 1948-56; sales mgr. New Eng. Tape Co., Hudson, Mass., 1956-59; founder, dir. pres. Plastic Extrusion & Engring. Co., Inc., Westborough, 1960—; indsl. panel adviser on modern plastics. Mem. adv. bd. Keene Tech. and Vocat. High Sch. Served to capt. USAAF, World War II. Paul Harris fellow Rotary Internat. Mem. Soc. Plastics Engrs. (sr. mem., dir. med. group, past chmn. med. products com.) Cen. Mass. Employers Assn. (dir.), Lehigh U. Alumni-Asa Packer Soc., Lehigh Tower Soc., U.S. Power Squadron (comdr. 1985-86, editor Rhumb Line), Worcester Found. Presbyterian. (elder, trustee). Clubs: Masons, Rotary (charter, past pres., sec. Westboro; past dist. sec., trustee), Hundred of Mass., Plaza (Worcester, Mass.). Home: 100 Ryder Rd North Falmouth MA 02556 Office: 170 Bartlett St Northborough MA 01532-2097

HORLICK, ALLAN, television broadcasting yearbook executive. Pres., gen. mgr. Sta. WRC-TV, Washington, 1987—. Office: Sta WRC-TV 4001 Nebraska Ave NW Washington DC 20016-2795

HORMOZI, FARROKH ZAD, economist, educator, consultant, researcher; b. Tehran, Iran, Jan. 16, 1937; came to U.S., 1964; s. Fatollah and Pouran (Varzi) H.; m. Nasrin Hakami, Sept. 1, 1966; children: Mandana, Mitra. MS in Math., Fairleigh Dickinson U., 1967; postgrad., NYU, 1967-71; MA in Econs., New Sch. for Social Rsch., 1978, PhD in Econs. with honors, 1980. Statistician Ministry Finance, Tehran, Iran, 1960-64; tchr. math. Franklin High Sch., N.Y.C., 1967-82, Hicksville (N.Y.) Pub. Sch., 1967-82; lectr., assoc. prof. Pace U., Pleasantville, N.Y., 1982-85, prof. econs., 1985-92, dept. chair, 1992—; cons. Amper Corp., N.Y.C., 1975-80; rsch. assoc. Rsch. Found., CCNY, 1978-85; prof. in residence IBM, N.Y.C., 1989, 90, 91. Contbr. articles to profl. jours. Speaker Unitarian Ch., N.Y.C., 1988, 89, IBM, La Haupe (Belgium) and N.Y.C., 1989, 90, 91 Dyson Soc. Fellows, N.Y.C., 1990, 91, NYU Grad. Sch. Arts, Bklyn. Poly. Inst. N.Y., Soc. Plastic Engrs., Armonk, N.Y., Internat. Tel. Co. Recipient Outstanding Teaching award Pace U., 1990. Fellow Soc. Fellows Pace U; mem. Am. Econ. Assn., Western Econ. Assn., Econometric Soc., Omicron Delta Epsilon. Democrat. Moslem. Home: 148 Washington Ave Plainview NY 11803-4020 Office: Pace U Bedford Rd Pleasantville NY 10570-1002

HORN, BARBARA RUTH, English language educator, writer; b. Hunnewell, Mo., Nov. 28, 1945; d. Frankie Lee and Naomi Ruth (Shumate) H. BA, U. Mo., 1967, MA, 1969; PhD, CUNY, 1977. Tchr. Trafalgar Sch. for Girls, Montreal, 1968-69; coadjutant Rutgers U., Jersey City, 1970-75; grad. fellow Queens Coll., CUNY, Flushing, N.Y., 1973-76; mem. faculty New Sch. for Social Rsch., N.Y.C., 1977—; prof. English Nassau Community Coll., SUNY, Garden City, 1976—. Contbr. essays to Nassau Rev., Iowa Woman, Esprit, Calyx, Belles Lettres, others. Vol., United Farm Workers Am., 1972-74; sec.-treas. Good Old Lower East Side Hist. Soc., 1982-83, pres., 1983-84. Mellon Found. fellow, 1989; NEH inst. participant, 1989. Mem. Soc. for Study of Midwestern Lit., Popular Culture Soc., Phi Beta Kappa. Home: PO Box 2047 New York NY 10009-8914 Office: SUNY Nassau Community Coll Stewart Ave Garden City NY 11530-2200

HORN, HENRY STAINKEN, biology educator; b. Phila., Nov. 12, 1941; s. Henry Eyster and Catherine Hedwig (Stainken) H.; m. Elizabeth Ruth Gates, Sept. 7, 1963; children: Jennifer Downing, Eric Bailey. AB, Harvard U., 1962; PhD, U. Washington, 1966. Asst. prof. biology Princeton (N.J.) U., 1966-71, assoc. prof., 1971-78, prof. biology, 1978-90, prof. ecology and evolutionary biology, 1990—, dir. program in environ. studies, 1991—. Author: The Adaptive Geometry of Tress, 1971. Bullard fellow, 1975, Nat. Sci. Found fellow, 1962-66. Fellow Am. Assn. for the Advancement Sci. Office: Princeton U Dept Biology Princeton NJ 08544

HORN, JANET, physician; b. Oak Ridge, Aug. 10, 1950; d. Harry and Molly (Rich) Horn; m. Alan R. Yuspeh, June 8, 1975. BA magna cum laude, Vanderbilt U., 1972; MS in Physiology and Biophysics, Georgetown U., 1973; MD, George Washington U., 1978. Diplomate Am. Bd. Internal Medicine, also sub-bd. Infectious Diseases; diplomate Am. Bd. Med. Examiners. Intern George Washington U. Hosp., Washington, 1978-79, resident in obstetrics and gynecology, 1979-81; resident in internal medicine Georgetown U., Washington, 1981-83; fellow in infectious diseases Johns Hopkins Hosp., Balt., 1983-85; mem. med. staff Georgetown U. Hosp., also Sibley Meml. Hosp., Washington, 1985-86, Johns Hopkins Hosp., 1986—, Sinai Hosp. of Balt., 1989—; asst. prof. medicine, div. infectious diseases Johns Hopkins U. Sch. Medicine, 1986—. Mem. editorial bd. Johns Hopkins Med. Grand Rounds, Am. Jour. Gynecologic Health; contbr. articles to profl. jours., chpts. to books. Bd. dirs. Chesapeake AIDS Found., 1989—; chair AIDS Coordinating and Adv. Coun. to Mayor, Balt., 1988—. Recipient Pearl M. Stetler Found. rsch. award Johns Hopkins U., 1987, Merck Found. clinician scientist rsch. award Johns Høpkins U., 1988. Mem. AAAS, ACP, Am. Soc. for Microbiology, Infectious Diseases Soc. Am., Johns Hopkins Med. and Surg. Assn., Phi Beta Kappa, Alpha Omega Alpha. Office: 5500 Newbury St Baltimore MD 21209-3652

HORN, JOHN CHISOLM, management consultant; b. N.Y.C., Jan. 16, 1915; s. William M. and Marguerite E. (Jacobs) H.; A.B., Cornell U., 1936, postgrad., 1937; LL.D., Susquehanna U., 1965; m. Solveig E. Wald, June 22, 1938; children: Phyllis Downing, John Chisolm, Stephen Lunde, Eric Laurens, Robert Gregg, Thomas Wald, Dorothy Traill, James Melchior. With John R. Wald Co., 1937-39; sec. Prismo Safety Corp., 1939-45, sec., treas., 1945-49, v.p., 1949-57, exec. v.p., 1957-62, pres., 1962-69; pres. John C. Horn Assocs., 1970—; pres. Prismo Universal Corp., 1969-70, vice chmn. bd., 1970—; asst. sec. Wald Industries, Inc., 1950-51, pres., 1951-69; exec. dir. Church Mgmt. Service, Inc., 1971—; dir. Long Siding Corp., Prismo France, Paris, Prismo Universal Ltd., Eng. cooperating cons. Tech. Diversification Services, 1972—; dir. Springfield Corp., Horn Co., Inc., 1989—. Dir. Huntingdon Bus. and Industry, Inc., 1958—; chmn. Indsl. Devel. Commn., 1959-60, area devel. chmn., 1960-62. Bd. dirs., vice chmn. Wald Found., 1954-63; mem. nat. council Boy Scouts Am., 1950—, nat. com. on cubbing, 1961-78, nat. com. exec. profl. tng., 1971—, exec. com Region III, 1961—, v.p. Juniata Valley council 1951-57, pres., 1957—; pres., bd. dirs. Huntingdon County United Fund, 1959-68; mem. indsl. and profl. council Pa. State U. Bd. dirs. Juniata Valley Schs., St. James Huntington Choir; pres. bd. dirs. Susquehanna U.; mem. bd. publ. Luth. Ch. Am., 1968-74. Recipient Silver Beaver, Lamb and Silver Antelope awards Boy Scouts Am., also Outstanding Civic Leader award, 1967. Mem. Army Ordnance Assn., NAM, AIM, Am. Mgmt. Assn., Am. Road Builders Assn., Internat. Bridge Tunnel and Toll Rd. Assn., Inst. Traffic Engrs., C. of C. (dir. 1955), Juniata Mountains Devel. Assn. (pres. 1956). Lutheran (home mission bd. Central Pa. Synod 1948—, com. on music and worship; synodical proposal com. 1957—, exec. bd. 1962-67, higher edn. com. 1967—). Home: Killmarnock Hall Alexandria PA 16611

HORN, LYLE WILLIAM, physiology educator, scientist; b. St. Paul, July 22, 1943; s. James Lyle and Julie Ann (Shermeta) H.; m. Jacqueline E. DeBaptiste, May 30, 1970. BS, U. Colo., 1966; PhD, Johns Hopkins U., 1973. Rsch. assoc. fluid mechanics Johns Hopkins U., Balt., 1973-74; asst. prof. U. Md. Sch. Medicine, Balt., 1974-81; assoc. prof. physiology Temple U. Sch. Medicine, Phila., 1982—. Referee various sci. jours.; contbr. articles to sci. jours. Founder, pres. Vols. Opposing Leakin Park Expressway, Inc., Balt., 1970. NIH grantee, 1976—. Mem. AAAS, Biophys. Soc., Soc. Gen. Physiologists. Office: Temple U Sch Medicine 3223 N Broad St Philadelphia PA 19140-5096

HORN, MARIAN BLANK, judge; b. N.Y.C., 1943; d. Werner P. and Mady R. Blank; m. Robert Jack Horn; children: Juli Marie, Carrie Charlotte, Rebecca Blank. Student, Barnard Coll., Columbia U.; student in law, Fordham U. Bar: N.Y. 1970, D.C. 1973, U.S. Supreme Ct. 1973. Asst. dist. atty. Bronx County, N.Y., 1969-72; assoc. Arent, Fox, Kintner, Plotkin & Kahn, 1972-73; project mgr. Am. U. Law Sch. study on alts. to conventional criminal adjudication U.S. Dept. Justice, 1973-75; litigation atty. Fed. Energy Adminstrn., 1975-76; sr. atty. office gen. counsel strategic petroleum res. br. Dept. Energy, 1976-79, dep. asst. gen. counsel for procurement and fin. incentives, 1979-81; dep. assoc. solicitor div. surface mining Dept. Interior, 1981-83, assoc. solicitor div. gen. law, 1983-85, prin. dep. solicitor, acting solicitor, 1985; judge U.S. Claims Ct., 1986—; adj. prof. law Washington Coll. Law, Am. U., 1973-76. Office: US Claims Ct 717 Madison Pl NW Washington DC 20005-1011*

HORN, MICHIEL STEVEN DANIEL, history educator; b. Baarn, The Netherlands, Sept. 3, 1939; arrived in Can., 1952, naturalized, 1958; s. Daniel and Antje Elisabeth (Reitsma) H.; m. Cornelia Schuh, Dec. 29, 1984; children: Daniel André, Patrick Benjamin. BA, U. B.C., 1963; MA, U. Toronto, 1965, PhD, 1969. Jr. officer Bank of Montreal, Victoria, B.C., Can., 1956-58; lectr. history Glendon Coll., York U., Toronto, Ont., Can., 1968-69, asst. prof., 1969-73, assoc. prof., 1973-82, prof., chmn. dept., 1982—; assoc. prin. Coll., 1978-81, dir. Can. Studies, 1986-89; acad. cons.-coord. Living and Learning in Retirement, 1976—. Editor, author: The Dirty Thirties, 1972; author: The League for Social Reconstruction, 1980, The Great Depression of the 1930s in Canada, 1984, Years of Despair, 1986; co-author: A Liberation Album, 1980, Canada, A Political and Social History, 1982; editor: A New Endeavor, 1986, Academic Freedom, 1987, The Depression in Canada, 1988; co-editor: Studies in Canadian Social History, 1974. Mem. North York Hist. Bd. and Local Archtl. Conservancy Adv. Com., 1977-80. Woodrow Wilson fellow 1963-64, Can. Coun. fellow/grantee, 1974-75, Social Sci. and Humanities Rsch. Coun. grantee, 1986-89, 90-91. Mem. York U. Faculty Assn. (chmn. 1972-73), Can. Assn. Univ. Tchrs. (exec. com. 1973-75, acad. freedom and tenure com. 1984-90), Ont. Confedn. Univ. Faculty Assns. (chmn. 1976-77), Massey Coll. Common Room Club, Glendon Squash Club (Toronto). Office: York U, 2275 Bayview Ave, Toronto, ON Canada M4N 3M6

HORN, RUSSELL EUGENE, JR., printing executive; b. York, Pa., Sept. 15, 1934; s. Russell Eugene and A. Eleanor (Baird) H.; m. Franziska Kathe Kastner; children: Silvia S., Russell E. III, Monika K., Ursula F., John D. Sgt. 1st class U.S. Army Security Agy., 1952-62; sales trainee, sales rep. Print-O-Stat, Inc., York, Pa., 1962-63; mgr. Print-O-Stat, Inc., York, 1970-73, exec. v.p., 1976-77, pres., 1977—; mgr. Print-O-Stat, Inc., Towson, Md., 1963-70; v.p. Print-O-Stat, Inc., Md., Del., 1973-76; bd. dirs. Pace Resources, Inc., office of pres., 1987—; bd. dirs. Buchart-Horn, Inc., and others; adv. bd. Dauphin Deposit Bank-York Region, 1984—; also officer, advisor, exec. various corps. Active various ednl., charitable activities. Mem. Mfg. Assn. York (Pa.), York Area C. of C., York Club of Printing House Craftsmen, Internat. Reprographics Assn., Eastern Regional Reprographics Assn. Home: 120 Leeds Rd York PA 17403-3814 Office: Print-O-Stat Inc 1011 W Market St York PA 17404-3411

HORNBLASS, ALBERT, ophthalmologist, ophthalmic plastic surgeon; b. N.Y.C., July 5, 1939; s. Maurice and Betty H.; m. Bernice Meriam Brooks, Dec. 23, 1973; children: David, Moshe, Elana. BA and B of Religious Edn., Yeshiva U., 1960; MD, U. Cin., 1964. Diplomate Nat. Bd. Med. Examiners, Am. Bd. Ophthalmology. Assoc. chief of ophthalmology Walter Reed Hosp., Washington, 1970-71; dir. ophthalmic, plastic and orbital surgery Manhattan Eye, Ear and Throat Hosp., N.Y.C., 1970—; clin. prof. ophthalmology SUNY Health Ctr., 1984—; chief of eye plastic surgery Lenox Hill Hosp., N.Y.C., 1972—. Author: Oculoplastic and Reconstructive Surgery Eyelids, Vol. I, 1988, Oculoplastice and Reconstructive Surgery Lacrimal System, Vol. II, 1990. Pres. Bd. Jewish Edn. of Greater N.Y., 1980-84; v.p. Jewish Braille Inst. of Am., N.Y., 1983; sec. Hebrew Immigrant Aid Soc., N.Y., 1980-88. Maj. U.S. Army, 1969-71, Vietnam. Decorated Bronze Star; recipient J. Eugene Chaplin Meml. Lectr. award, SUNY, N.Y.C., 1985, George Weinstein award/Lacrimal Gland Duct Cysts, N.Y. Ophthalmic Surgery Soc., 1986, cert. of award Am. Acad. Ophthalmology, San Fransico, 1982. Mem. Am. Soc. Ophthalmic Plastic and Reconstructive Surgery (pres.-elect 1992), Am. Israeli Ophthalmol. Soc. (pres. 1979—), Jerusalem Instn. for the Blind and Multicapped Children (pres. 1985), Am. Soc. Ocularists (bd. dirs. 1980—). Jewish. Office: 130 East 67th St New York NY 10021

HORNBLASS, BERNICE MIRIAM, interior designer, small business owner; b. N.Y.C., Sept. 12, 1951; d. Max and Sydell (Strickman) Brooks; m. Albert Hornblass, Dec. 23, 1973; children: David, Moshe, Elana. BA, Barnard Coll., Columbia U., 1973; MA, Tchrs. Coll., 1975; postgrad., NYU, 1976-79; cert. in interior design, Parsons Sch. Design, 1985-87. Cert. real estate salesman, N.J., N.Y. Tchr. CAlhoun Sch., N.Y.C., 1974-75; art therapist Carrier (N.J.) Clinic, 1976; with For Children Only, N.J., 1983-85; owner, mgr. Bernice-Hornblass-Interior Design, Englewood, N.J., 1987—. Exhibited in group shows N.J. Pub. Library, 1986, Jewish Community Ctr. on Palisade, 1986. Dir. sabbath community visitation program Meml. Slan-Kettering Meml. Hosp., N.Y.C., 1977—; mem. visitation program Englewood Hosp., 1986—; mem. program com. Amit-Am. Mizrachi Women, 1986-87. Recipient 10 yr. vol award Meml. Sloan-Kettering Hosp., 1987. Republican. Jewish. Home and Office: 156 Maple St Englewood NJ 07631-3630

HORNBY, DAVID BROCK, judge; b. Brandon, Manitoba, Can., Apr. 21, 1944; s. William Ralph Hornby and Retha Patricia (Fox) Sword; m. Helaine Cora Mandel, Oct. 9, 1946; children: Kirstin, Zachary. BA, U. Western Ont., 1965; JD, Harvard U., 1969. Bar: Va. 1973, Maine 1974, U.S. Supreme Ct. 1980. Law clk. U.S. Ct. Appeals, New Orleans, 1969-70; assoc. prof. U. Va. Sch. Law, Charlottesville, 1970-74; ptnr. Perkins, Thompson, Hinckley & Keddy, Portland, Maine, 1974-82; U.S. magistrate Dist. Maine, Portland, 1982-88; assoc. justice Maine Supreme Jud. Ct., Portland, 1988-90; judge U.S. Dist. Ct. Maine, 1990—. Contbr. articles to profl. jours.; editor, officer Harvard Law REv., 1967-69. Fellow Am. Bar Found.; mem. ABA, Am. Law Inst., Maine State Bar Assn., Maine Bar Found. (bd. trustees 1990—), Jud. Conf. of the U.S. (com. on ct. adminstrn. and case mgmt. 1990—), Cumberland County Bar Assn. Office: US Dist Judge US Courthouse 156 Federal St Portland ME 04101

HORNE, DOUGLAS STUART, truck company executive; b. Oak Park, Ill., Mar. 6, 1934; s. Douglas Simeon and Vesta Jean (Grice) H.; m. Diane Gail Brady, July 27, 1955 (div. Feb. 1984); children: Dale, Danette, Dana; m. Sandra Ann Hardig, Aug. 24, 1986. BS, Calif. State U., San Luis Obispo, 1959; MBA, Northwestern U., Evanston, Ill., 1980. Capt. U.S. Army, Ft. Devens, Mass., 1959-63; supr. indsl. relations Internat. Harvester Co., Chgo., 1963-72, asst. indsl. relations mgr., 1972-78, mgr. human resources, 1978-85; v.p. adminstrn. Mitsubishi Truck of Am., Inc., Bridgeport, N.J., 1985—; cons. in field. Republican. Roman Catholic. Home: 1002 Hillingham Cir Chadds Ford PA 19317-9254 Office: Mitsubishi Truck of Am Inc 100 Center Rd Bridgeport NJ 08014

HORNE, SCOTT JEFFREY, recycling company executive, lawyer; b. Bklyn., Jan. 5, 1955; s. Seymour M. Judie (Saffer) H.; m. Judith Theresa Stachniak, May 22, 1983. BA in Econs., Emory U., 1976; JD, John Marshall Law Sch., 1981. Bar: Ill. 1981, Md. 1982, Va. 1983, U.S. Ct. Appeals (4th cir.) 1983. Mem. sales and mgmt. staff AAA Brands Plastics Co., Atlanta, 1976-77; customer svc. rep. Davis Industries, Arlington, Va., 1977-78; asst. to pres. Davis Industries, Arlington, 1981, v.p., counsel, 1982-84; v.p., gen. counsel Prince Georges Scrap, Inc., College Park, Md., 1984—; also dir. Prince Georges Scrap, Inc., College Park, 1984-92; pres. Envi-Resource Mgmt. Group, Silver Spring, Md., 1992—; pvt. practice Silver Spring, 1992—. Mng. editor John Marshall Law Rev., 1981, assoc. lead articles editor, 1980. Bd. dirs., crusade chmn. Western Prince George's unit Am. Cancer Soc., 1987-90, pres., 1988-90; pres. Am. Cancer Soc. of Prince George County, 1990—; bd. dirs. Northwood Four Corner Civic Assn., 1988—. Mem. ABA, Inst. Scrap Recycling Industries (bd. dirs., pres. seaboard chpt. 1988-90, chmn. ad hoc regulatory com., 1992— chmn. environ. and legis. subcom. on state govt. matters 1990-92), Md. Recyclers Coalition (bd. dirs. 1991—), Ill. State Bar Assn., Md. State Bar Assn. Home: 107 Snowy Owl Dr Silver Spring MD 20901-1656 Office: Envi-Source Mgmt Group Inc 107 Snowy Owl Dr Silver Spring MD 20901-1656

HORNER, CARL MATTHEW, chemistry educator; b. Cicero, N.Y., June 4, 1930; s. Oscar Wendell and Gladys Cecilia (Horner) H. B.S., LeMoyne Coll., 1952; M.S., Syracuse U., 1958, Ph.D., 1965. Asst. prof. analytical chemistry SUNY-Oneonta, 1958-61, assoc. prof., 1961-64, prof., 1964—; coord. ann. instrumental chemistry workshops, 1986—. NSF CAUSE grantee, 1979-82; NSF CSIP grantee, 1986-88; Walter B. Ford Found. grantee, 1980, 83. Mem. Am. Chem. Soc., Soc. Applied Spectroscopy, AAAS, N.Y. Acad. Scis., Sigma Xi. Avocations: scuba diving, underwater photography. Achievements include: research in infrared spectroscopy and laboratory robotics. Home: 24 Suncrest Ter Oneonta NY 13820 Office: SUNY Phys Sci Bldg Oneonta NY 13820

HORNER, STEVEN MARK, insurance company executive, educator; b. Camden, N.J., June 26, 1951; s. Herbert H. and Evelyn (Lamberskie) H.; children: Steven M. Jr., Kelley-Anne. AA in Social Sci., Montgomery Community Coll., 1971; BA in Liberal Arts, Temple U., 1973. CPCU, CLU. Underwriter Harleysville (Pa.) Ins. Co., 1974-77, training coord., 1977-79, training mgr., 1979-82, asst. sec. training, 1982-88, asst. v.p. training, 1988—. Chmn. United Way, Harleysville, 1976-79. Recipient Outstanding Educator, Ins. Soc. Phila., 1985, 88, Merit award Nat. Assn. Mut. Ins. Cos., 1980. Mem. Soc. CPCUs (bd. dirs. 1990-92), Mut. Ins. Edn. Found. (bd. dirs. 1986-92), Soc. Ins. Trainers and Educators (v.p. 1983-87, 91-93), Assn. Quality and Participation. Office: Harleysville Ins Co 355 Maple Ave Harleysville PA 19438-2200

HORNSBY, JOAN RIGNEY, clinical psychologist; b. Waterbury, Conn., Feb. 3, 1940; d. John William and Anne (Norling) Rigney; m. James H. Hornsby, June 6, 1964; children: Alison Joan, Elizabeth Anne, Jennifer Ruth. AB magna cum laude, Harvard U., 1962; MS in Social Work, Columbia U., 1964; PhD in Psychology, Boston U., 1982. Lic. psychologist, Mass. Social worker Puerto Rican Govt. Agys., 1965-67; caseworker Family Svc. Assn., Fall River, Mass., 1969-71; social worker Children's Home, Fall River, Mass., 1971-77; clin. psychology trainee, teaching asst. Boston U. Sch. of Medicine Dept. Psychiatry, 1977-78; clin. psychology intern Bradley Hosp., Boston, 1978-79; psychologist Greater Fall River Mental Health Assn., 1979-83; dir. psychology dept. Corrigan Mental Health Ctr., Fall River, 1983-85, Family Svc. Assn. of Greater Fall River, Inc., 1985-88; field work supr. Boston Coll. Sch. Social Work, 1986-87; pvt. practice psychology Fall River, 1984—. Bd. dirs. Fall River Symphony Soc., 1990—; Friends Acad., n. Dartmouth, Mass., 1985-88; cellist Fall River Symphony, 1986—; vol. St. Luke's Episcopal Ch., Fall River, 1984—, vol. asst. organist. Mem. Am. Psychol. Assn. (clin. psychol. div. 12), S.E. Mass. Psychol. Assn., Mass. Psychol. Assn., Phi Beta Kappa. Democrat. Home and Office: 260 Lake Ave Fall River MA 02721-5407

HORNSTEIN, ALVIN SIDNEY, public relations company executive; b. Atlantic City, Nov. 15, 1926; s. Jack and Reba (Isenberg) H.; B.S. in Journalism, Temple U., 1950; m. Rita B. Reinheimer, Apr. 17, 1955; 1 child, Gary Ross. City editor Atlantic City Reporter, 1951-59; info. officer City of Phila., 1959-66, public info. dir., 1967-68, dir. tourism and public relations Conv. and Visitors Bur., 1968-77; dir. public relations Temple U. Health Scis. Center, 1977-78; dir. public relations, corp. communications MAACO Enterprises, King of Prussia, Pa., 1978—. Mem. adv. pub. affairs com. Manor Jr. Coll.; bd. dirs. Temple U. Entrepreneurial Inst. Served with U.S. Army, 1945-46. Recipient Discover Am. award, Discover Am. Travel Orgn., 1971, Chapel of Four Chaplains award. Mem. Phila. Public Relations Assn. (suburban pub. relations com.), Public Relations Soc. Am., Internat. Franchise Assn. (advt. and public relations mktg. seminar com., 2 Pub. Rels. awards), Am. Legion. Home: 1230 Greeby St Philadelphia PA 19111-5525 Office: Maaco Enterprises Inc King Of Prussia PA 19406

HOROSKO, MARIAN, education editor; b. Cleve., Aug. 4, 1927; d. Louis Senko and Marian Catherine (Gromand) H. Student, Cleve. Inst. of Music, 1936-43, Juillard Sch. Music, 1944-45, Sch. Am. Ballet, N.Y.C., 1944-51. Performer Ballet Russe de Monte Carlo, 1939, Met. Opera Ballet, 1951-54, N.Y.C. Ballet, 1954-62, (films) Eight By Eight, 1949, Prince Who Was A Thief, 1950, Royal Wedding, 1950, American in Paris, 1950 (broadway plays), Oklahoma, 1945-47, Along Fifth Avenue, 1948, Dance Me A Song, 1949; (staged classics) Buffalo Ballet; film curator: Dance Collection, Lincoln Ctr., 1960's; producer WNET, WNCN, 1961-77; author: Pas De Deux, 1982, Dancer's Survival Manual, 1986, Ballet Technique for Male Dancers, Martha Graham: Technique and Dance Evolution. Recipient first MEDART spl. recognition award, 1992. Home: 357 W 55th St New York NY 10019-4555 Office: Dance Mag 33 W 60th St New York NY 10023-7905

HOROSZEWICZ, JULIUSZ STANISLAW, cancer researcher, laboratory administrator; b. Warsaw, Poland, Jan. 4, 1931; came to U.S., 1961; s. Tytus Michal and Stefania (Domanska) H.; m. Hanna Urszula Kubik, Jan. 12, 1969; children: Nike Joanna, Peter Juliusz. D of Medicine summa cum laude, Acad. of Medicine, Lodz, Poland, 1954, DMSc, 1960. Teaching asst. dept. bacteriology Acad. of Medicine, Lodz, 1950-55, asst. prof., 1955-59, assoc. prof., 1959-61; cancer rsch. scientist Roswell Park Meml. Inst., Buffalo, 1962-64, sr. cancer rsch. scientist, 1964-67, assoc. cancer rsch. scientist, 1967-76, prin. cancer rsch. scientist, 1976-86; assoc. chief oncological urology rsch. N.Y. State Dept. Health, Roswell Park Meml. Inst. Div., Buffalo, 1986-88; dir. lab. of urol. rsch. Millard Fillmore Hosp., Buffalo, 1988—; dir. electron microscopy lab. viral oncology, 1963-66, dir. human fibroblast interferon program Roswell Park Meml. Inst., 1976-82; chmn. Pleuro-Pneumonia Like Organisms subcom. human cancer virus task force Nat. Cancer Inst., Bethesda, Md., 1963-64, mem. Nat. Prostatic Cancer Project working cadre, 1972-74; assoc. rsch. prof. microbiology SUNY, Buffalo, 1966—; rsch. prof. biology Canisius Coll., Buffalo, 1968—, Naigara U., Niagara Falls, N.Y., 1968—. Contbr. over 90 articles to profl. jours.; patentee on specific monoclonal antibody for diagnosis and treatment of human prostate cancer. Rockefeller Found. fellow, 1961-62; rsch. grantee Nat. Cancer Inst., 1979-82; named Citizen of Yr., Am.-Polish Eagle, Buffalo, 1967. Mem. AAAS, Am. Assn. Cancer Rsch., Am. Soc. Microbiology. Roman Catholic. Home: 2210 N Forest Rd Buffalo NY 14221-1346 Office: Millard Fillmore Hosp 3 Gates Cir Buffalo NY 14209-1194

HOROWITZ, DANIEL, history educator; b. New Haven, Mar. 23, 1938; s. William and Miriam (Botwinik) H.; m. Helen L. Lefkowitz, Aug. 18, 1963; children: Benjamin, Sarah Esther. BA, Yale U., 1960; PhD, Harvard U., 1967. Instr. history Wellesley (Mass.) Coll., 1966-67; instr., sr. tutor Harvard U., Cambridge, Mass., 1967-69, lectr. history, 1969-70; asst. prof. Am. studies Skidmore Coll., Saratoga Springs, N.Y., 1970-72; asst. prof. history Scripps Coll., Claremont, Calif., 1973-78, assoc. prof. history, 1978-86, Stephenson prof. history, 1986-88; prof. Am. studies and history Smith Coll., Northampton, Mass., 1989—; mem. nat. bd. cons. NEH, Washington, 1974-84. Author: Morality of Spending, 1984. Fellow Nat. Humanities Ctr., N.C., 1984-85, NEH, 1973. Mem. Am. Studies Assn., Orgn. Am. Historians, Am. Hist. Assn. Democrat. Jewish. Office: Smith Coll Wright Hall Northampton MA 01063

HOROWITZ, HUGH H., chemist; b. N.Y.C., Sept. 8, 1928; s. Max and Anna (Braksmayer) H.; m. Enid Garmise, Feb. 3, 1953; children: Amy A., Alan M., Lawrence S. BS, CUNY, 1949; MS, Columbia U., 1951, PhD, 1953. Chemist products rsch. div. Exxon Rsch. and Engring. Co., Linden, N.J., 1952-61, group leader fuel cell labs., 1961-66, 71-76, sr. rsch. assoc. corp. rsch. labs., 1966-71, 76-81; sr. rsch. assoc. corp. rsch. labs. Exxon Rsch. and Engring. Co., Annandale, N.J., 1985-86; sr. rsch. assoc. engring. tech. div. Exxon Rsch. and Engring. Co., Florham Park, N.J., 1981-85; sr. rsch. assoc. products rsch. div. Exxon Rsch. and Engring. Co., Linden, 1986—; presenter in field. Contbr. articles to profl. jours.; patentee in field. Mem. Am. Chem. Soc., Electrochem. Soc. (chmn. met. sect. 1982). Office: Exxon Rsch & Engring Co PO Box 51 Linden NJ 07036-0051

HOROWITZ, KENNETH LEE, insurance company executive, financial planner; b. Stockton, N.J., Oct. 4, 1941; s. Theodore and Charlotte (Levine) H.; m. Carolyn Katz Horowitz, July 19, 1967; children: Tobi Jill, Cori Lynn. BA, Rutgers U., 1963; MS in Fin. Svcs., Am. Coll., 1981, MS in Mgmt., 1985. CLU, chartered fin. cons.; registered health underwriter, registered fin. planner. Pilot, capt. USAF, Clovis, N.Mex., 1964-69; pilot, flight engr. Trans World Airlines, Jamaica, N.Y., 1969-70; agt. Mutual of Omaha, Succasunna, N.J., 1970-71, dist. mgr., 1971-74; gen. mgr. Mutual of Omaha, Cherry Hill, N.J., 1974-83; ops. officer Companion of N.Y., Rye, N.Y., 1984-86; div. mgr. Mutual of Omaha, Trevose, Pa., 1987—; moderator, bus. and advanced sales Life Underwriters Training Coun., Phila., 1988-90. Capt. USAF, 1964-69, Vietnam. Decorated 16 Air Medals, 2 Disting. Flying Crosses, USAF, 1966-67. Mem. Am. Soc. CLU's, Bucks County Estate Planning Coun., Bucks County Life Underwriters Assn., Ea. Gen. Agts. and Mgr. Assn. Home: 18 Olde Mill run Medford NJ 08055 Office: Mut of Omaha Co Ste 250 1210 Northbrook Dr Trevose PA 19053

HOROWITZ, KENNETH PAUL, lawyer; b. N.Y.C., May 6, 1956; s. Philip S. and Roslyn Horowitz. BA, SUNY, Brockport, 1977; MA, Georgetown U., 1984; JD, Bklyn. Law Sch., 1987. Bar: Conn. 1987, N.Y. 1988, U.S. Dist. Ct. (so. and ea. dists.) N.Y. 1988. Law libr. Burns Summit Rovins & Feldsman, N.Y.C., 1980-84; law clk. Dreyer and Traub, N.Y.C., 1985-87, assoc., 1987—. Chmn. bd. dirs., pres. 130 Hicks St. Owners Corp., Bklyn., 1986—. Mem. ABA, N.Y. State Bar Assn., Assn. of Bar of City of N.Y., N.Y. County Lawyers Assn. (com. on fed. cts.). Office: Dreyer and Traub 101 Park Ave New York NY 10178-0002

HORRELL, JEFFREY LANIER, library administrator; b. Carbondale, Ill., Sept. 19, 1952; s. C. William and Ettelye M. (Hanser) H. BA, Miami U., Oxford, Ohio, 1975; AM in Libr. Sci., U. Mich., 1976, MA, 1978. Libr. intern Nat. Gallery of Art, Washington, 1977; asst. libr. art and architecture U. Mich., Ann Arbor, 1977-80; libr. Sherman Art Libr./Dartmouth Coll. Libr., Hanover, N.H., 1981-86; Coun. Libr. Resources libr. mgmt. intern Syracuse (N.Y.) U. Libr., 1986-87, asst. to univ. libr. for planning, 1987-88, asst. univ. libr. pers., budget and planning, 1988-92; librn. Fine Arts Libr. Harvard Coll. Libr., Cambridge, 1992—; chair ARLIS/Mich, 1979-80, ARLIS/New Eng., 1982-83. Author: Treasures of the Hood Museum of Art, 1985; contbr. articles to profl. publs. Mem. ALA, Coll. Art Assn., Art Libr. Soc. N.Am. (pres. 1987-88), U. Mich. Sch. Librs. and Info. Studies Alumni Soc. (bd. dirs. 1991—). Office: Fine Arts Libr Fogg Art Mus 32 Quincy St Cambridge MA 02138

HORRIGAN, THOMAS H., physician; b. Waterbury, Conn., Feb. 21, 1926; s. Thomas Henry and Kethryn (Sullivan) H.; m. Rosemary Fitch, May 6, 1950; children: Christine, Kathleen, Kevin, Craig, Michael, Lisa. BS, Yale U., 1946; MD, NYU, 1949. Pvt. practice gen. medicine East Hartford, Conn., 1952-70; emergency physician St. Francis Hosp. and Med. Ctr., Hartford, 1970—; physician-in-chg. St. Francis Hosp. & Med. Ctr., 1975-80, acting dir. emergency med. dept., 1980-86, assoc. dir. emergency medicine, 1986—. Capt. U.S. Army, 1950-52. Fellow Am. Coll. Emergency Physicians; mem. Hartford County Med. Assn., Conn. Med. Soc., Hartford Med. Soc. Republican. Roman Catholic. Home: 22 Timberwood Rd West Hartford CT 06117-1458 Office: St Francis Hosp 114 Woodland St Hartford CT 06105-1200

HORROCKS, WILLIAM DEWITT, JR., chemistry educator; b. Orange, N.J., Dec. 7, 1934; s. William DeWitt and Lucille (Gutmann) H.; m. E. Joan Allan, June 15, 1963; 1 child, J. Allan H. BA, Wesleyan U., Middletown, Conn., 1956; PhD, MIT, 1960. Instr. chemistry Princeton (N.J.) U., 1960-63, asst. prof. chemistry, 1963-69; assoc. prof. chemistry Pa. State U., University Park, 1969-72, prof. chemistry, 1972--. Guggenheim fellow, 1974-75. Fellow AAAS; mem. Am. Chem. Soc., Biophysical Soc., Am. Soc. for Biochemistry and Molecular Biology. Office: Pa State U 152 Davey Lab Dept of Chemistry University Park PA 16802

HORSEMAN, ROY MERTZELL, retired security service executive; b. Queenstown, Md., June 12, 1935; s. Roy Mertzell and Anna Mary (Stuart) H.; m. Felicia Godoy, May 22, 1966 (dec. June 1968). BS, Clinton U., 1957; degree in criminology, Inst. Applied Sci., Chgo., 1969; LLB, Blackstone Law Sch. U. Chgo., 1970, JD, 1974. Registered internat. criminologist. Enlisted USMC, 1952, advanced through grades to col., served in Korea and Vietnam, ret., 1971; security cons. Brit. Consulate Gen., Phila., 1972-74; owner, operator Horseman Pvt. Security Svc., Phila., 1974-78; CEO, pres. Nat. Security Systems, Inc., Phila., 1976-79; columnist on security and safety, 1975-82. Founder Horseman Found., Phila., 1990—; active Ellis Island Centennial Found., N.Y.C., 1985. Decorated D.S.M., Navy Cross, Silver Star, Bronze Star with two gold stars, Purple Hearts; recipient Outstanding Citizen Achievement award U.S. Congress, 1976, 1000 Mile Runner award Marine Corps. Running Club, 1972. Mem. U.S. Naval Inst., Freedom Bell Soc., Internat. Assn. Universal Fingerprinting (life), Registered Internat.

Criminologists (life). Roman Catholic. Office: Horseman Found PO Box 1311 Philadelphia PA 19105-1311

HORSMAN, DAVID A. ELLIOTT, author, financial services executive, educator; b. Calvert County, Md., June 28, 1932; s. Alvin W. and Bessie L. (Elliott) H. Student, U. Chgo.; BA, San Francisco State U., 1964; MA, NYU, 1967, PhD, 1970; MDiv, Episc. Div. Sch., 1984. Fl. dir., stage mgr. WTOP-TV, Washington, 1959-61; TV writer/producer Insight, Nat. Coun. Chs., Washington, 1961-62; English master, dir. studies Searing Sch., N.Y.C., 1965-67; asst. prof. humanities Acad. Aeros., Flushing, N.Y., 1967-68; instr. humanities Rensselaer Poly. Inst., Troy, N.Y., 1969-70; assoc. prof., founder and coord. film sequence U. South Fla., Tampa, 1970-80; headmaster All Hallows Acad., Alexandria, Va., 1985-87; pres. Elliott Horsman & Assocs., 1988-89; fin. cons. Shearson Lehman Hutton, Inc., Balt., 1989-91; investment broker RAF Fin. Corp., Atlanta, 1991—; adj. prof. Union Grad. Sch., Yellow Springs, Ohio, 1976—. Author: The Liturgy as Communication, 1970, Introduction to Structural Description of Liturgical Dromena, 1979, (novel and screenplay) Pilgrims on Strange Strands, 1979. With U.S. Army, 1957-59. Recipient Founders Day award NYU, 1971. Mem. MLA, Nat. Soc. Hist. Preservation, Univ. Film Assn., Am. Film Inst., Internat. Platform Assn., Soc. Edn. in Film and TV, Alcuin Club. Episcopalian. Office: RAF Fin Corp 3399 Peachtree Rd NE Ste 1450 Atlanta GA 30326-1150

HORSNELL, MARGARET EILEEN, historian; b. St. Paul, Jan. 3, 1928; d. Kenneth George and Mary Elizabeth (Dowd) H. B.A., U. Minn., 1961, M.A., 1963, Ph.D. (Tozer Found. award 1966), 1967. Instr. history U. Minn., 1966-67; mem. faculty Am. Internat. Coll., Springfield, Mass., 1967—, assoc. prof. history, 1976-84, prof., 1984—, dept. chmn., 1987— . Recipient McKnight Found. award, 1968; alternate fellow AAUW, 1974-75; Am. Internat. Coll. summer grantee, 1970. Mem. Soc. History Edn., Inst. Early Am. History and Culture, So. Hist. Assn., Am. Legal Studies Assn., Phi Alpha Theta. Author: Spencer Roane: Judicial Advocate of Jeffersonian Principles, 1986; mem. editorial bd. This Constn., 1986-88; contbr. Encyclopedia of American Political Parties and Elections. Mem. adv. panel 500 Yrs. of Am. Clothing, 1989-92. Home: 15 Atwood Rd South Hadley MA 01075-1601 Office: Am Internat Coll 24 Lee Hall Springfield MA 01109

HORTON, ARTHUR MACNEILL, JR., neuropsychologist; b. Alexandria, Va., Jan. 21, 1947; s. Arthur MacNeill and Mary Alice (Carney) H.; m. Mary Whitesell, Jan. 31, 1976; children—Arthur MacNeill III, Frank Michael, John Patrick. B.A, U. Va., 1969, M.Ed., 1971, Ed.D., 1976. Diplomate in Clin. Psychology, Am. Bd. Neuropsychology and Behavior Therapy. Asst. prof. The Citadel, Charleston, S.C., 1976-77; dir. neuropsychology lab. VA Med. Ctr., Martinsburg, W.Va., 1977-82; coord. alcoholism program VA Med. Ctr., Balt., 1982-90; chief neuropsychology sect. VA Med. Ctr., Balt., 1985-90; instr. U. Va., 1974-75, W.Va. U., 1982, Johns Hopkins U., 1984; clin. asst. prof. psychiatry U. Md. Med. Sch., 1987-92; rsch. psychologist Treatment Rsch. Br. Nat. Inst. on Drug Abuse, 1990—. Mem. Am. Psychol. Assn., Internat. Neuropsychol. Soc., Assn. for Advancement of Behavior Therapy, Eastern Psychol. Assn., Md. Psychol. Assn. Roman Catholic. Office: Nat Inst on Drug Abuse 5600 Fishers Ln Rockville MD 20857-0001

HORTON, FRANK, congressman; b. Tex., Dec. 12, 1919; s. Frank and Mary (Hathcox) H.; m. Nancy Richmond, Dec. 14, 1980; children by previous marriage: Frank J., Steven W. BA, La. State U., 1941; LLB, Cornell U., 1947. Bar: N.Y. 1947. Assoc. Johnson, Reif & Mullan (and predecessor firm), Rochester, N.Y., 1947-52; ptnr. Johnson, Reif & Mullan (and predecessor firm), 1952-69; mem. 88th-102nd Congresses from 29th dist., 1963—; ranking minority mem. com. govt. ops., legis. and nat. security subcoms., post office and civil service com., exec. com. Ho. com. on coms., 1976—, mem. joint com. on atomic energy, 1975-77; mem. exec. bd. Congl. Arts Caucus; former exec. v.p., atty. Internat. Baseball League; participant U.S.-Can. Interparliamentary Conf., Ottawa, Ont., 1969, Washington, 1973; chmn. Commn. on Fed. Paperwork; co-chmn. Northeast-Midwest Congl. Coalition; mem. North Atlantic Assembly, 1981—; mem. Congl. Travel and Tourism Caucus. Congl. Steel Caucus, Congl. Human Rights Caucus, Congl. Post Caucus, Congl. Space Caucus, congl. adv. Pres's Commn. Nat. Agenda for Eighties; mem. Presdl. Adv. Commn. on Federalism; rep. of U.S. Ho. Reps. at dedication Israeli Knesset, 1966; others. Co-author: How to End the Draft-A Case for an All Volunteer Army, 1967, A Study of Urban Education in America, 1968, A Study of Air Safety, 1969; author: Election Reform: Remedy for an Impending Crisis, 1969, The Public's Right to Know, 1972, A Blueprint for Regulatory Reform, 1976. Mem. exec. com. Seneca dist. Otetiana council Boy Scouts Am., 1955—; pres. Rochester Community Baseball, Inc., 1957-62; councilman-at-large Rochester City Council, 1955-61; bd. visitors U.S. Naval Acad. Served to maj. AUS, 1941-46. Mem. ABA, N.Y. (exec. com. young lawyers sect. 1952), Rochester (sec. 1953-57), Fed., Western N.Y. (pres. 1956-57), D.C. bar assns., Res. Officers Assn. (past pres.), VFW, Am. Legion, Cornell Law Assn. (exec. com.), N.Y. Conservation Council, Order Coif, Phi Kappa Phi. Presbyterian (elder, trustee). Clubs: Jesters, Capitol Hill. Lodges: Masons (33 deg.); Shriners. Office: 2108 Rayburn Bldg Washington DC 20515

HORTON, JAMES WILLIAM, JR., retail food company official; b. Cambridge, N.Y., Aug. 22, 1959; .; s. James W. and L. Wilma (Bassett) H.; m. Pamela A. Legge, Mar. 5, 1988; children: Joseph, James W. III. BA in Labor Studies, Pa. State U., 1981; postgrad., Chapman U., Orange, Calif., 1991—. With P&C Foods, Inc., 1979—; co-mgr. Burlington, Vt., 1982-83; employee devel. specialist, field skills trainer Syracuse, N.Y., 1983-85, coord. labor rels., 1985-86, mgmt. devel. specialist, 1986-89, mgr. tng. and devel., 1989—; instr. Dale Carnegie and Assocs., Garden City, N.Y., 1990—; pres., owner Horton Assocs., Liverpool, N.Y., 1991—. Mem. ASTD (dir. food industry group 1991-92), Indsl. Rels. Rsch. Assn. Cen. N.Y. Office: P&C Foods Inc PO Box 4965 Syracuse NY 13221-4965

HORTON, JOSEPH JULIAN, JR., academic dean, educator; b. Memphis, Nov. 7, 1936; s. Joseph Julian and Nina (Williams) H.; m. Linda Anne Langley, May 30, 1964; children: Joseph Julian, Anne Adele, David Douglas. AA, Lon Morris Jr. Coll., 1955; BA, N.Mex. State U., 1958; MA, So. Meth. U., 1965, PhD, 1968; postgrad. Harvard U., 1970-71. Claims examiner Social Security Adminstrn., Kansas City, Mo., 1958-60, claims authorizer, 1960-61; with FDIC, Washington, 1967-71, fin. economist, 1967-69, coordinator merger analysis, 1969-71; prof., chmn. dept. econs. and bus. Slippery Rock State Coll. (Pa.), 1971-81; vis. fin. economist Fed. Home Loan Bank Bd., Washington, 1978-79; prof., chmn. commerce div. Bellarmine (Ky.) Coll., 1981-82, dean W. Fielding Rubel Sch. Bus., 1982-86; dean Sch. Mgmt. U. Scranton, Pa., 1986—; asst. prof. George Washington U., Washington, 1968-69, U. Md., College Park, 1969-70; pres. Pa. Conf. Economists, Congress of Polit. Economists, U.S.A. Bd. editors Eastern Econ. Jour.; contbr. to profl. jours. Recipient Cokesbury award So. Meth. U., 1965; NSF Grad. fellow, 1964-66, Ford Found. Dissertation fellow, 1966-67, Harvard U. Research fellow, 1970-71, Bank Adminstrn. Inst. Clarence Lichtfeldt fellow, 1981. Mem. Am. Econ. Assn., Am. Fin. Assn., N. Am. Econs. and Fin. Assn. (bd. dirs., v.p., pres.), Eastern Econ. Assn. (v.p.). Office: U Scranton Sch Mgmt Scranton PA 18510-4602

HORTON, MARTHA LOUISE, newspaper editor; b. Oneonta, N.Y., July 3, 1934; d. Ralph Daniel and Anna Leona (Kuhlman) Heim; m. Arrigo Raho, Jan. 22, 1965 (div. Jan. 1970); children: Marianna Raho, John Anthony Raho; m. Keith Willard, Oct. 16, 1976. BA, Pa. State U., 1956. Promotion asst. McGraw-Hill Pub. Co., N.Y.C., 1956-57; asst. editor The Am. Rev., Bologna, Italy, 1963-64; corr. Mc-Graw Hill World News, Milan, 1965; acct. exec. Spiro Assocs., Phila., 1966-68; pub. rels. mgr. Sonesta Hotels, Boston, 1968-72; dir. pub. rels. Marco Beach Hotel, Marco Island, Fla., 1972-76; dir. pub. rels. and publs. Elmira (N.Y.) Coll., 1976-80; sales assoc. Ambrose Real Estate, Elmira, 1985-88; editor-in-chief Chemung Valley Reporter, Horseheads, N.Y., 1989—. Contbr. articles to profl. jours. Bd. dirs. Arnot Art Mus., Elmira, 1991—. Recipient Gold Key award Am. Hotel and Motel Assn., 1972, Crystal Prism award Am. Advt. Fedn., 1980. Mem. LWV (dir. devel. N.Y. State bd. 1987-88), Pub. Rels. Soc. Am., Bus. and Profl. Women, Chemung County C. of C., Near Westside Neighborhood Assn., Torch Club, Kiwanis. Democrat. Congregationalist. Home: 412 W Clinton St Elmira NY 14901 Office: Chemung Valley Reporter 126 Main St Horseheads NY 14845

HORTON, MICHAEL, public affairs executive, information specialist; b. Montreal, Can., Mar. 10, 1918; s. Irving and Anne (Spector) H.; m. Lydia Franklin Wells, June 14, 1947; children: Hilary, Christopher, Lydia, Cleveland. BA, Bishop's U., Quebec, 1939; postgrad., Columbia U., 1940. News editor Sta. WMCA, N.Y.C., 1939-40; reporter Buffalo Evening News, 1940-41; news editor Washington-Times Herald, Washington, 1941-42; editor, columnist N.Y. Herald Tribune, Paris, 1946-52; chief French press br. Marshall Plan, Paris, 1952-53; dir. pub. rels. div. NBC, 1953-58; dir. info. CBS, N.Y.C., 1958-61; dir. pub. rels. div. CPC Internat., Zurich and Brussels, 1961-79; prin. Michael Horton Assocs., Brussels and Brunswick, Maine, 1979—. Author: (with others) Developing the Corporate Image, 1960. With MIS, 1942-46. Mem. Internat. Pub. Rels. Assn. (coun. mem. 1965—), Pub. Rels. Soc. Am., Nat. Press, Overseas Press. Unitarian. Home: 17 Cleaveland St Brunswick ME 04011-2109 Office: 17 Cleaveland St Brunswick ME 04011-2109

HORTON, PAUL CHESTER, psychiatrist; b. Cin., Jan. 29, 1942; s. Paul Chester Sr. and Elizabeth Pauline (Rice) H.; m. Mary Kathryn Kuphal, Sept. 11; children: Paul Andrey, Alexander Robert. BA, U. Minn., 1964; MD, &, 1968. Diplomate Am. Bd. Psychiatry and Neurology. Rotating intern U. Cin., 1969; resident in psychiatry Yale U., New Haven, 1972; staff psychiatrist Guidance Clinic of Camden County, West Collingswood, N.J., 1972-74, Milford (Conn.) Family and Child Guidance Clinic, 1974-77; mem. faculty Sch. Medicine Yale U., New Haven, 1974-76; pvt. practice Meriden, 1974—; cons. psychiatrist Child Guidance Clinic Cen. Conn., Meriden, 1980—; mem. faculty U. Conn. Sch. Medicine, Farmington, 1978-79; cons. Caring for Children, San Francisco, 1989—; reviewer Am. Jour. Psychiatry, 1980—, and others. Author: Solace, 1981, Solace, paperback edit. 1983, Solace, Japanese edit., 1985; sr. editor: The Solace Paradigm, 1988; contbr. articles to profl. jours. Big Brother Big Bros. Orgn., Mpls., 1964-68. Lt. comdr. USN, 1972-74. Mem. Am. Psychiat. Assn., Meriden Wallingford Med. Assn., Gridiron Club. Home: 570 Redstone Dr Cheshire CT 06410-1744 Office: 234 Hobart St Meriden CT 06450-4307

HORVATH, DANIEL C., computer service executive; b. Chgo., May 8, 1954; s. Frank and Katharnia (Hain) H.; m. Margaret Mauree Newsome, June 23, 1973; Cherie, Scott, Eric. MBA, Northeastern U., 1988. Mgr. Data Pathing, Inc., Cleveland, Mass., 1973-76; dist. mgr. Prime Computer, Natick, Mass., 1976-82; mgr. logistics Prime Computer, Natick, 1982-84; dir. customer svc. Apollo Computer, Chelmsford, Mass., 1984-89, Stratus Computer, Marlboro, Mass., 1989—. Office: Stratus Computer 55 Fairbanks Blvd Marlborough MA 01752-1298

HORVATH, RICHARD G(EORGE), finance company executive; b. Trenton, N.J., Feb. 22, 1933; s. Stephen John Sr. and Anna (Chlaupek) H.; m. Eleanor Barbara Maziekien, June 13, 1953; children: Richard G. Jr., Doreen A. BS in Bus. Mgmt., Fairleigh Dickinson U., 1955; MBA, Rutgers U., 1960. CLU. Various pos. Prudential, Newark, 1957-67; mgr. Prudential Ins. Co., Newark, 1967-69, assoc. gen. mgr., assoc. treas., 1969-71, gen. mgr., assoc. treas., 1971-73, gen. mgr., 1973-74, v.p. corp. svcs., 1974-78, v.p., 1978-84; v.p., head govt. health programs Prudential Ins. Co., Millville, N.J., 1984-87; sr. v.p. Prudential Asset Mgmt. Co., Florham Park, N.J., 1987—. Pres. Boys & Girls Clubs of Newark, 1979-80, chmn., 1980-81, The Mgmt. Inst., Glassboro, N.J., 1986-87; bd. trustees Newark Mus., 1982-92. With U.S. Army, 1955-57. Recipient Man and Boy award Boys & Girls CLubs of Newark, 1981; inducted into Garfield (N.J.) Hall of Fame, 1992. Mem. Fairleigh Dickinson U. Alumni Assn. (1st v.p. 1991—, bd. trustees). Office: Prudential Asset Mgmt Co 71 Hanover Rd Florham Park NJ 07932

HORVITZ, ABRAHAM, retired surgeon; b. Providence, Feb. 2, 1911; s. Jacob and Fannie (Krasnow) H.; m. Eleanor Feldman, Sept. 9, 1940; 1 child, Leslie Alan. AB, Brown U., 1932; MD, Columbia Med. Sch., 1936. Diplomate Am. Bd. Surgery. Intern Jewish Hosp. of Bklyn., 1937-39; resident in Pathology Harlem Hosp., N.Y.C., 1939-40; rsch. fellow Washington U. Med. Sch., St. Louis, 1940-41; resident in surgery Jewish Hosp. of Bklyn., 1941-42, 45-48; pvt. practice Providence, 1948-89; clin. asst. prof. surgery Brown U. Med. Sch., Providence, 1976—. Capt. U.S. Army, 1942-46, ETO. Fellow ACS; mem. AMA, Providence Surg. Soc., Providence Med. Assn., R.I. Med. Soc.

HORWITH, SUSAN KARDOS, banker; b. Allentown, Pa.; m. Brian K. Horwith. BS, Pa. State U., 1979; cert., Am. Inst. Banking, 1987; postgrad., Lubin Grad. Sch. Bus. Internal auditor investment banking and treasury Royal Bank Can., N.Y.C., 1985-87; unit head - personal banking Bank N.Y., N.Y.C., 1987-89, credit trainee, 1988-89, asst. treas., pvt. banker, 1989—. Named one of Outstanding Young Women Am., 1979. Mem. NAFE, Jr. League Bergen County (N.J.). Office: Bank NY 48 Wall St New York NY 10286

HORWITZ, ELEANOR CATHERINE, wildlife educator; b. N.Y.C., Dec. 21, 1941; d. Fritz and Hedwig E.F. (Kramer) Jahoda; m. Paul Horwitz, Aug. 15, 1964; children: Gregory Douglas, Catherine Helen, Laura Elizabeth. BA, Swarthmore Coll., 1962; MA, NYU, 1967; MS, Cornell U., 1969; postgrad., Oreg. State U., 1969-70. Sci. tchr. New Lincoln Sch., N.Y.C., 1962-67; coordinator outdoor edn. Lane County Int. Edn. Dist., Eugene, Oreg., 1969-70; staff writer Billerica (Mass.) Banner, 1971-72; instr., writer Mass. Audubon Soc., Lincoln, 1972-75; pub. use specialist U.S. Fish and Wildlife Service, Concord, Mass., 1975; staff writer Soc. Am. Foresters, Washington, 1975-76; chief info. and edn. Mass. Div. Fisheries and Wildlife, Westborough, 1977—; mem. Mass. Gov.'s Forestry Rev. Bd., Boston, 1976-77; mem. Sec.'s Adv. Group on Environ. Edn., exec. Office of Environ. Affairs, Commonwealth of Mass., 1988—; bd. dirs. Mass. Wildlife Fedn., 1986—, v.p., 1989—. Author: Clearcutting, A View from the Top, 1974; author, editor: Ways of Wildlife, 1977 (ACI Book award 1978); editor: (mag.) Massachusetts Wildlife, 1977—; contbr. articles to popular mags. Active Concord Natural Resources Commn., 1976-82, chmn. 1979-80; trustee Concord Land Conservation Trust, 1989—. Recipient R.E. Dimmick award Oreg. Wildlife Soc., 1970, citation Worcester County League Sportsmen's Clubs, 1987, citation Minuteman chpt. Ducks Unltd., 1987, Conservation award Mahor Fish & Game Assn., 1991; named Woman of Yr. N.E. County Quabloin Angles Assn., 1991. Mem. Outdoor Writers Am., New Eng. Outdoor Writers Assn. (membership sec. 1987-90, sec. 1990—), Am. Forestry Assn. (life), New Eng. Conservation Info. and Edn. Assn. (chmn. 1986-87, 90-91), Wildlife Soc. (prof. cert., chmn. edn. com. 1974-76, 84-87, nominating com. 1990-91, cert. of recognition 1978), Nashoba Sportsmen's Club (Acton, Mass.), Concord Rod and Gun Club, Maynard Rod and Gun Club (hon.). Mem. United Ch. of Christ. Office: Mass Div Fisheries and Wildlife Westboro MA 01881

HOSE, JOHN ROBERT, university administrator; b. N.Y.C., Aug. 31, 1940; s. Robert Haven and Anne (Runkle) H.; m. Janet Florence Rice, Aug. 1, 1970; children: John Daniel Haven, Jessica Susan Anne. BA, Middlebury Coll., 1962; MA, Columbia U., 1963, PhD, 1970. Exec. officer faculty senate CUNY, N.Y.C., 1970-75, asst. dean Queens Coll., 1975-80; exec. asst. to pres. U. N.H., Durham, 1980-83; exec. asst. to pres., assoc. v.p. univ. affairs Brandeis U., Waltham, Mass., 1983—; cons. Coun. Pres., New Eng. Land Grant Univs., Durham, 1980; mem. site visit team Mid. States Assn. Colls. and Sch., Washington, 1989. Mem. Elem. and Secondary Block Grant Adv. Com. for State of N.H., Concord, 1981-82; mem. Pub. Works Adv. Com., Durham, N.H., 1982-83, Zoning Bd. Adjustment, Durham, 1983. Office: Brandeis U 415 South St Waltham MA 02154-2700

HOSIE, JOHN JAMES, pharmacist, consultant; b. N.Y.C., Jan. 16, 1940; s. James Hill and Catherine (Duffy) H.; children: Daniel, Regina, Andrea, Valerie, Jacqueline. BS in Pharmacy, Fordham U., 1962. Pharmacist N.Y. Hosp., N.Y.C., 1962-63, Drug Fair, Hagerstown, Md., 1972-87; pharmacy mgr. Kent Drug Store, Binghamton, N.Y., 1965-72; pharmacist Peoples Drug Store, Waynesboro, Pa., 1987—; cons. pharmacist Mid-Atlantic Med. Health Care, Waynesboro, Pa., 1986—. Mem. Broome County Drug Abuse Coun., 1967-70. With U.S. Army, 1963-65. Mem. Pa. Pharm. Assn. (del. 1980—, regional bd. dirs. 1989—), South Cen. Pa. Pharmacists Assn. (pres. 1981), Met. Guild Pharmacists (exec. coun. 1975-85), VFW, Elks. Roman Catholic. Home: 833 Mountain View Rd Waynesboro PA 17268-1707 Office: Peoples Drug Store 40 S Broad St Waynesboro PA 17268-1611

HOSKIN, WILLIAM DICKEL, physician; b. Akron, Ohio, Jan. 24, 1920; s. Robert E. and Margaret (Dickel) H.; m. Lois Black, June 1, 1951; children: Mark, Ned, David. AB, Hiram Coll., 1942; MD, Western Res. U., 1947; MA in English, SUNY, Brockport, 1990. Intern, U.S. Naval Hosp., San Diego, 1951-52; practice medicine specializing in occupational medicine, 1954-83; instr. physics Hiram (Ohio) Coll., 1943; asst. supt. St. Luke's Hosp., Cleve., 1947-51; staff. physician Eastman Kodak Co., Rochester, 1954-69, asst. dir., 1969-70, med. dir. Kodak Park div., 1970-83; clin. assoc. preventive medicine and community health U. Rochester, 1974-75; mem. N.Y. State Senate Adv. Com. on Alcoholism, 1977-81. Contbr. articles to med. jours. and poetry to lit. jours.; mem. editorial bd. Hiram Poetry Rev. Pres. bd. trustees Norman Howard Sch.; bd. dirs. Park Ridge Chem. Dependency, 1979-83, Writers and Books, N.Y. State Literary Center; trustee Hiram Coll. Served as lt. USNR, 1951-54. Recipient Hiram Coll. Alumni Assn. Ann. award for Outstanding Achievement, 1972; Mrs. F. Ritter Shumway award for disting. vol. service in community health, 1980. Diplomate Am. Bd. Preventive Medicine. Fellow Am. Occupational Med. Assn., Am. Acad. Occupational Medicine, Am. Coll. Preventive Medicine, Garfield Soc.; mem. Indsl. Med. Assn. Upstate N.Y. (pres. 1969-70), Rochester Rehab. Center, Genesee Valley Heart Assn. (dir. 1965-76), N.Y. State Heart Assembly, Nat. Council Alcoholism, Health Assn. Rochester, Monroe County Learning Disabilities Assn. (bd. dirs. mental health chpt.), N.Y. State Bd. Profl. Med. Conduct, Rochester Poetry Soc. Club: U. Rochester Faculty. Home: 1563 East Ave Rochester NY 14610-1614

HOSLER, CHARLES LUTHER, JR., meteorologist, educator; b. Honey Brook, Pa., June 3, 1924; s. Charles Luther and Miriam Deichley (Stauffer) H.; m. Gladys Cheesbrough, 1947 (div.); children:Sharon Elizabeth, David Charles, Lynn Rebecca, Peter William; m. Anna R. Stahel, 1971. Student, Bucknell U., 1943-44, MIT, 1944-45; B.S., Pa. State U., 1947, M.S., 1948, Ph.D., 1951. Faculty Pa. State U., University Park, 1948—; prof. meteorology Pa. State U., 1960—, head dept., 1961-65, dean Coll. Earth and Mineral Scis., 1965-85, sr. v.p. rsch., dean Grad. Sch., 1985-92; Hydrographer Pa. Dept. Forests and Waters, 1949-59; meteorol. cons., 1950—, vis. prof. colls., lectr. civic and profl. groups; condr. daily TV weather program, 1957-67; spl. research microphysics of clouds; chmn. bd. atmospheric scis. and climate Nat. Acad. Scis., 1984-86; mem. Nat. Sci. Bd., 1985—; mem. nat. adv. com. on oceans and atmosphere.; chmn. bd. trustees Univ. Corp. for Atmospheric Research, Boulder, Colo., 1981-85. Contbr. articles to profl. jours. Served to lt. (j.g.) USNR, 1943-46; lt. comdr. Res. Fellow Am. Meteorol. Soc. (councilor, pres. 1976); mem. Nat. Acad. Engring., Am. Geophys. Union Am. Chem. Soc. (regional lectr. 1971-72), AAAS, Sigma Xi (pres. Pa. State U. 1958, nat. lectr. 1972), Tau Beta Pi. Home: 1229 Smithfield Cir State College PA 16801-6426 Office: Pa State U 617 Walker Bldg University Park PA 16802

HOSTETLER, JEFF W., professional football player; b. Johnstown, Pa., Apr. 22, 1961; m. Vicky Nehlen; children: Jason, Tyler, Justin. Attended, Pa. State U.; grad. in fin., W.Va. U. Cert. fin. planner. Player N.Y. Giants, 1984—; quarterback Superbowl XXV championship team, 1991. Named to Acad. All Am. Season, 1983-84. Address: care NY Giants Giants Stadium East Rutherford NJ 07073*

HOSTETTER, CARL FRANKLIN, computer scientist; b. Harrisburg, Pa., Aug. 6, 1965; s. Carl Eugene Hostetter and Patricia Ann (Hare) Hooker; m. Marilyn Ruth Kraut, Mar. 28, 1987. BS, Va. Tech. U., 1988. Electronics engr. NASA Goddard Space Flight Ctr., Greenbelt, Md., 1985—; chmn. Goddard conf. on space applications of artificial intelligence, Greenbelt, 1991-92. Editor jour. Vinyar Tengwar; contbr. articles to profl. publs. Roman Catholic. Home: 2509 Ambling Cir Crofton MD 21114 Office: NASA/GSFC Code 531.1 Greenbelt MD 20771

HOTCHIN, JOHN ELTON, health facility administrator, educator; b. Sutton-on-Sea, Eng., Apr. 7, 1921; came to U.S., 1952; s. Herbert Elton and Bessie (Thomas) H.; m. Peggy Britain, Sept. 21, 1951 (div. 1961); 1 child, Jennifer; m. Lois Mary Benson, Apr. 1, 1971; children: Shama, Tania. MD, London U., 1943, PhD, 1951, FRC Pathology, 1963. Rsch. scientist Nat. Inst. Med. Rsch., London, 1947-55; asst. prof. U. B.C., Vancouver, Can., 1955-57; asst. dir. Div. Sales and Rsch., Albany, N.Y., 1957-87, ret., 1987; rsch. scientist Dadley Observatory, Albany, 1962-70. Author: books; contbr. articles to profl. jours. Lt. Royal Navy, 1944-48. Home: 18 Daywood Rd Delmar NY 12054

HOTCHKISS, HENRY WASHINGTON, financial consultant; b. Meshed, Iran, Oct. 31, 1937; s. Henry and Mary Bell (Clark) H. BA, Bowdoin Coll., 1958. French tchr. Choate Sch., Wallingford, Conn., 1959-62; v.p. Chem. Bank, N.Y.C., 1962-80, v.p. Chem. Bank Internat. San Francisco, 1973-80; dir. corp. rels., mgr. Crédit Suisse, San Francisco, 1980-87, fin. cons., 1989—; dir. Indonesia-U.S. Bus. Seminar, Los Angeles, 1979. Assoc. bd. regents L.I. Coll. Hosp., 1969-71, pres., 1971, bd. regents, 1971-73, pres., bd. dirs. Gordonstown Am. Found, 1986—. Capt. USAR, 1958-69. Mem. Mayflower Soc., SAR, Soc. of the Cin., Heights Casino (bd. govs. Bklyn. chpt. 1971-73), New Eng. Soc. in City Bklyn. (v.p., dir. 1968-73), Explorers Club N.Y. (treas. no. Calif. chpt. 1984-86), St. Francis Yacht Club (San Francisco). Home: 80 Fort St Fairhaven MA 02719-2812

HOTZ, ROBERT BERGMANN, editor, publisher; b. Milw., May 29, 1914; s. Harry Phillip and Emma (Bergmann) H.; m. Joan Willison, Nov. 18, 1944; children: George, Michael, Robert Lee, Harry II. B.S., Northwestern U., 1936. Reporter, Paris edit. N.Y. Herald Tribune, 1936-37; reporter, editor Milw. Jour., 1938-41; news editor McGraw-Hill Pub. Co., Washington, 1946-49; dir. pub. relations Pratt & Whitney Aircraft, Hartford, Conn., 1950-52; editor Aviation Week and Space Tech. mag., N.Y.C., 1953-80; pub. Aviation Week and Space Tech. mag., 1976-80; editor Space Tech. Internat., 1958-80; editorial cons. McGraw-Hill, Inc., 1980-84. Author: With General Chennault, the Story of the Flying Tigers, 1943, Pratt and Whitney Aircraft Story, 1950, Both Sides of Suez, 1975, The Promise of the Space Age, 1980; editor: Way of a Fighter, Memoirs of Claire Lee Chennault, 1949. Mem. gen. adv. com. ACDA, 1982-92; mem. Presdl. Commn. on Shuttle Challenger Accident, 1986. Served from 2d lt. to maj. USAAF, 1942-46. Decorated Air medal with oak leaf cluster; recipient Airpower award Air Force Assn., 1958; Paul Tissandier diploma Fedn. Aeronautique Internationale, 1958; Press award Nat. Space Club, 1965; Strebig and Ball trophies Aviation/Space Writers Assn., 1972; Pub. Service award Am. Astronautical Soc., 1974; Lauren D. Lyman award Aviation/Space Writers Assn., 1974; 11th Crain award Am. Bus. Press Assn., 1978; Meritorious Service award Nat. Bus. Aircraft Assn., 1981. Mem. AIAA (Pendray Aerospace Lit. award 1981), 14th Air Force Assn., Royal Aero. Soc. (companion), Nat. Press Club, Caterpillar Club, RAF (London), Explorers Club (N.Y.C.). Home: Rams Horn Farm 9702 Mt Tabor Rd Middletown MD 21769-9523

HOU, SUI-HOI EDWIN, electrical and computer engineer, researcher; b. Hong Kong, Oct. 9, 1960; s. Sin-Tin William and Sau-Ching (Li) H.; m. Yuh-Lin Catherine Tang, Sept. 11, 1989; 1 child, Audrey Wen-Shi. BSEE and BSCompE magna cum laude, U. Mich., 1982; MS, Stanford U., 1984; PhD, Purdue U., 1989. Asst. prof. N.J. Inst. Tech., Newark, 1989—; cons. Siemens Corp. Rsch., Princeton, N.J., 1990. Mem. IEEE. Office: NJ Inst Tech Dept Elec and Computer Engring 323 Dr Martin Luther King Blvd Newark NJ 07102

HOUCHIN, JOHN FREDERICK, SR., human services administrator; b. Oak Park, Ill., Nov. 1, 1945; s. O. Boyd and Mary Ruth (Schroke) H.; m. Bette Louise Arnold, July 9, 1969; children: John Jr., David Locke. AA, Kemper Mil. Sch. & Coll., Boonville, Mo., 1966; BS, Ohio State U., 1968; EdD, U. Mass., 1987. Prog. dir. Cuyahoga County Assn. Retarded Citizens, Cleve., 1973-75; resdl. dir./asst. supt. Ohio Dept. Mental Health & Retardation, Broadview Devel. Ctr, Broadview Heights, Ohio, 1975-80; reg. mental retardation coordinator Mass. Dept. Mental Health, Region IV A, Watertown, Mass., 1980-83; dir. developmental svcs. Mass. Dept. Mental Health, Belchertown State Sch., 1983-86; asst. reg. dir. Conn. Dept. Retardation, Region 6, Waterford, 1986-91; chief executive officer G.B. Cooley Svcs. for Retarded Citizens, West Monroe, La., 1991—; lectr. in field. Contbr. book: Supported Employment Implementation, 1988. State adv. council Conn. Dept. Rehab. Svcs., Hartford, 1988-91. Capt. U.S. Army, 1969-72. Mem. Am. Assn. on Mental Retardation, Assn. for Persons with

Severe Handicaps, Internat. Platform Assn. Episcopalian. Office: GB Cooley Svcs 364 Cooley Rd West Monroe LA 71291-8800

HOUCK, LEWIS DANIEL, JR., management consultant; b. Cleve., July 9, 1932; s. Lewis Daniel and Mary Clark (Dowds) H.; A.B., Princeton U., 1955; M.B.A. with distinction, N.Y. U., 1964, Ph.D., 1971; m. Ellen Dorothy Thayer, Sept. 8, 1962 (div. 1975); children: Marianne Jennifer, Leland Daniel. Mgr. spl. research Young & Rubicam, Inc., N.Y.C., 1957-59; mktg. mgr. Selling Research, Inc., N.Y.C., 1959-62; ednl. projects mgr. Nat. Assn. Accts., N.Y.C., 1969-71; spl. cons. U.S. Dept. Agr., Washington, 1971-73; project leader nat. econ. analysis div. Econ. Research Service, 1973-79; pres. Houck Mktg. and Mgmt. Cons., Inc., 1979-85; pres. Houck & Assocs. Inc., Kensington, Md., 1986—; instr. N.Y.U. Grad. Sch. Bus. Adminstrn., 1966-69; trustee World U., 1982—, v.p., 1983-86. Served as 1st lt., AUS, 1955-56. Recipient Founders Day award N.Y.U. Grad. Sch. Bus. Adminstrn., 1971. Ford Found. fellow, 1964-66. Fellow Am. Biog. Inst. (Medal of Honor 1986), Internat. Biog. Assn. (hon. editorial adv. bd. 1981—); mem. Am. Acctg. Assn., Am. Econ. Assn., AIM, Am. Mktg. Assn., Am. Statis. Assn., AAAS, Acad. Polit. Sci., Am. Acad. Polit. and Social Sci., Internat. Platform Assn., Ind. Cons. Am., Internat. Council Small Bus. Episcopalian. Club: Princeton (Washington). Author: A Practical Guide to Budgetary and Management Control Systems, 1979. Home: 11111 Woodson Ave Kensington MD 20895-1608 Office: Houck & Assocs Inc PO Box 81 Kensington MD 20895-0081

HOUCK, WILLIAM WHITMAN, educator; b. Gloversville, N.Y., Oct. 26, 1936; s. Jay W. and Grace M. (Bridge) H.; m. Chardel A. Raux, Apr. 3, 1966; children: Jeffrey W., Joel W. BS, SUNY, Oswego, 1959, postgrad., 1960-73. Tchr. Oneida County BOCES, New Hartford, N.Y., 1959-91; exec. officer Pine Lake (N.Y.) Park and Campgroung, 1971—. Mem. N.Y. United Tchrs. Assn., Campground Owners N.Y. State, Masons, Shriners, Phi Delta Kappa. Republican. Roman Catholic. Home and Office: Pine Lake Pk & Campground HC01 Box 19A Caroga Lake NY 12032

HOUDE, EDWARD DONALD, fishery scientist; b. Attleboro, Mass., Sept. 4, 1941; s. Donald Wilfred and Helen Josephine (Hospit) H.; m. Sarah Ellen Libourel, Aug. 8, 1983; 1 child, Matthew Donald. BA, U. Mass., 1963; MS, Cornell U., 1965, PhD, 1968. Fishery scientist US Bur. Comml. Fisheries, Miami, Fla., 1968-70; from rsch. scientist to asst. assoc. and full prof. U. Miami, 1970-80; prof. U. Maryland, 1980; dir. biol. oceanography program Nat. Sci. Found., Washington, 1983-85. Office: U Md Chesapeake Biol Lab PO Box 38 Solomons MD 20688-0038

HOUGH, MARK TAYLOR, hospital executive; b. Providence, June 3, 1949; s. William Henry and Elinor Stewart (Taylor) H.; m. Nancy Gregg O'Brien, Sept. 15, 1973; children: Alden Gregg, Randall Sayles. BA, Muhlenberg Coll., 197l; MBA, Bryant Coll., 1974. Project assn. Hosp. Assn. R.I., Providence, 1972-74; asst. adminstr. Cranston (R.I.) Gen. Hosp., 1974-76; asst. corp. adminstr. St. Joseph Hosp., North Providence, R.I., 1976-79; v.p. Providence unit St. Joseph Hosp., South Providence, R.I., 1979-84; sr. v.p. Fatima unit St. Joseph Hosp., North Providence, 1984—; mem. R.I. Gov.'s Adv. Coun. on Cancer, 1987—; mem. faculty Salve Regina Coll., Newport, R.I., 1983—, Bryant Coll., Smithfield, R.I., 1985—. Mem. Am. Hosp. Assn., Cath. Hosp. Assn., Am. Coll. Health Care Execs. (cert., regent coun. 1986—), Health Care Mgmt. Assn. Mass., R.I. Health Care Mgmt. Assn. (bd. dirs., treas. 1983-85), Hosp. Assn. R.I., North Cen. C. of C. (bd. dirs. 1984—), Agawam Hunt Club (Rumford, R.I.), Sakonnet Golf Club (Little Compton, R.I.). Home: 243 Lincoln St Seekonk MA 02771-1715 Office: St Joseph Hosp 200 High Service Ave Providence RI 02904-5113

HOUGH-ROSS, RICHARD THOMAS, minister, religious organization administrator; b. Bellefonte, Pa., Jan. 5, 1951; s. Richard Thomas and Ruth Anne (Sumner) Ross; m. Patricia Jane Hough, Aug. 30, 1975; 1 child, Amelia Brynn. BS in Psychology, Pa. State U., 1972; MDiv, Andover Newton Theol. Sch., 1977. Ordained to ministry United Ch. of Christ, 1977. Pastor Highgate (Vt.) Meth. Ch., 1977-79, Peacham (Vt.) Congl. Ch., 1979-85; exec. v.p. The Norwich (Vt.) Ctr., 1985—. Mem. Bethel Bus. Assn., Rotary Club. Home: 124 Pleasant St Bethel VT 05032 Office: The Norwich Ctr Emerson Ct PO Box 710 Norwich VT 05055

HOUGHTON, AMORY, JR., congressman; b. Corning, N.Y., Aug. 7, 1926; m. Priscilla West, 1950; 4 children. BA, Harvard U., 1950, MA, 1952; hon. docotorate, Alfred U., 1963, Albion Coll., 1964, Cen. Coll., 1966, Clarkson Coll. Tech., 1968, Elmira Coll., 1982, Hartwick Coll., 1983, Houghton Coll., 1983. Exec. officer Corning Glass Works, 1951-86; mem. 100th-102nd Congresses from N.Y., 34th dist., 1987—; mem. Grace Commn., Bus. Council N.Y. State, Bus. Adv. Commn. for Gov. N.Y., Labor-Industry Coalition for Internat. Trade. Trustee Brookings Instn. Served with USMC, 1945-46. Mem. Corning C. of C. Republican. Lodge: Rotary. Office: US Ho of Reps 1217 Longworth Bldg Washington DC 20515*

HOUGHTON, JAMES RICHARDSON, glass manufacturing company executive; b. Corning, N.Y., Apr. 6, 1936; s. Amory and Laura (Richardson) H.; m. May Tuckerman Kinnicutt, June 30, 1962; children: James DeKay, Nina Bayard. AB, Harvard U., 1958, MBA, 1962. With Goldman, Sachs & Co., N.Y.C., 1959-61; v.p., European area mgr. Corning Glass Internat., Zurich, Switzerland, Brussels, Belgium, 1964-68; with Corning Glass Works (name changed to Corning Inc. 1989), 1962—, v.p., gen. mgr. consumer products div., 1968-71, vice chmn. bd., dir., chmn. exec. com., 1971-83, chmn. bd., chief exec. officer, 1983—; bd. dirs. Met. Life Ins. Co., J.P. Morgan Co. Inc., Dow Corning Corp., US-USSR Trade and Econ. Coun. Trustee Corning Inc. Found., Corning Mus. Glass, Pierpont Morgan Libr., N.Y.C., Bus. Coun. of N.Y. State, Met. Mus. Art; mem. Bus. Com. for Arts, N.Y.C., Coun. on Fgn. Rels., Trilateral Commn. Bus. Coun. With AUS, 1959-60. Mem. Bus. Roundtable. Episcopalian. Clubs: Corning Country; River, Harvard, Univ., Links (N.Y.C.); Brookline (Mass.) Country; Tarratine (Dark Harbor, Maine); Augusta (Ga.) Nat. Golf; Rolling Rock, Laurel Valley Golf (Ligonier, Pa.). Home: The Field 36 Spencer Hill Rd Corning NY 14830-9417 Office: Corning Inc Houghton Pk CB-09-8 Corning NY 14831

HOUGHTON, KATHARINE, actress; b. Hartford, Conn., Mar. 10, 1945; d. Ellsworth Strong and Marion Houghton (Hepburn) Grant. BA, Sarah Lawrence Coll., Bronxville, N.Y., 1965. Founding mem. Pilgrim Repertory Co. (Shakespeare touring co. sponsored by Ky. Arts Commn.), 1971-72, S.C. Arts Commn., 1972, Miss. Arts Commn., 1973, Conn. Arts Commn., St. Joseph Coll., 1974. Debut on Broadway stage in A Very Rich Woman, 1965; appeared in stage plays Charley's Aunt, New Orleans Repertory, 1966, The Front Page, Broadway, 1968, Ten O'Clock Scholar, Royal Poinciana Playhouse, Fla., 1969, The Private Ear/The Public Eye, Sullivan, Ill., 1969, Sabrina Fair, Ivoryton Playhouse, 1968, The Miracle Worker, Sullivan, Ill., A Scent of Flowers (Theatre World award), Off Broadway, 1969, Misalliance, Hartford Stage Co., 1970, The Taming of the Shrew, Actors Theatre, Louisville, 1970, Poor Richard, Tartuffe, 1970, Ring Around the Moon, Hartford Stage Co., 1970, Major Barbara, The Glass Menagerie, Actors Theatre of Louisville, 1971, Play It Again Sam, Actors Theatre of Louisville, 1971, Suddenly Last Summer, Ivanhoe, Chgo., 1973, The Prodigal Daughter, Kennedy Center, Washington, 1973, Bell, Book and Candle, Pensacola, Fla., 1974, The Rainmaker, Ind. Repertory Co., 1975, Spiders Web, Atlanta, 1977, Hedda Gabler, Nashville, 1978, Dear Liar, Dayton, Ohio, 1978, 13 Rue de L'Amour, Ind. Repertory Co., 1978, Antigone, Nashville, 1979, Uncle Vanya, Acad. Festival Theatre, Lake Forest, 1979, Forty Carats, Radford U. Theatre, Va., 1979, A Doll's House, St. Edward's U. Theatre, Tex., 1979, The Sea Gull, Pitts. Public Theatre, 1979, The Glass Menagerie, Pa. Stage Co., 1980, Taming of the Shrew, Pa. State Festival, 1980, Terra Nova, Actors Theatre of Louisville, 1980, The Merchant of Venice, South Coast Repertory, Costa Mesa, Calif., 1981, A Touch of the Poet, Yale Repertory Theatre, 1983, To Heaven in a Swing, Am. Place Theatre, N.Y.C., tour various theaters, 1983-85, Sally's Gone She's Left Her Name, Am. Festival Theatre, N.H., 1984-86, Vivat, Vivat Regina, Mad Woman of Chaillot, The Time of Your Life, Children of the Sun, Mirror Repertory Co., N.Y.C., 1985, A Bill of Divorcement, Westport Country Playhouse, Conn., 1985, One Slight Hitch, Charlotte Repertory Co., 1986, To Heaven in a Swing, Amherst Coll., Bowdoin Coll., 1986, and Bronson Alcott Centennial Celebration, 1988, The Hooded Eye, West Bank Downstairs Theatre Bar, 1987, Ivoryton Playhouse, 1987, Murder in the Cathedral, West Point Cadet Chapel, 1987, The Leaves of Vallombrosa, 1988, Our Town, Broadway, 1988-89, Love Letters, Ivoryton Playhouse, 1989, To Kill A Mockingbird, Paper Mill Playhouse, N.J., 1991; motion pictures include Guess Who's Coming to Dinner, 1967, The Gardener, 1972, Eyes of the Amaryllis, 1981, Mr. North, 1987, Billy Bathgate, 1990, Ethan Frome, 1992; TV series The Adams Chronicles, 1975; TV mini-series I'll Take Manhattan, 1986; appeared on TV in Legacy of Fear, 1974, The Color of Friendship, 1981, soap opera One Life to Live, 1989; toured in Sabrina Fair, 1975, The Mousetrap, Arms and the Man, Dear Liar, 1976, The Streets of New York, Westport, Conn., Guildford, N.H., Dennis, Mass., Denver, 1980; appeared in To True to Be Good, Acad. Festival Theatre, Lake Forest, Ill., 1977, Spingold Theatre, Waltham, Mass., 1977, Annenberg Center, Phila., 1977 ; author: (book) The Marry Month of May, 1988, (stage prodns.) Phone Play, 1988, Good Grief, 1988, Mortal Friends, 1988 (stage prodn. premiere 1988), The Lick Penny Lover, 1988; co-author: Two Beastly Tales, 1975; author: (play) To Heaven in a Swing, 1982, Merlin, 1984, Buddha, On the Shady Side, The Right Number (3 one-act plays), 1986; editor: MHG: A Biography, 1989, Buddha, 1988; screenplay The Heart of the Matter, 1989, Journey to Glasnost, 1990, Good Grief, 1991. Mem. Dramatists Guild.

HOULIHAN, WILLIAM JOSEPH, chemist; b. South Amboy, N.J., July 24, 1930; s. William John H. and Ann Elizabeth (Howley) Martin; m. Piroska Maria Bizony, June 13, 1959; children: Peter William, Michael Joseph, Anna Maria. BS, Seton Hall U., 1951; PhD, Rutgers U., 1955. Asst. prof. St. John's U., Jamaica, N.Y., 1956-57, Seton Hall U., South Orange, N.J., 1957-59; project leader Universal Oil Products, East Rutherford, N.J., 1959-62; group leader Sandoz Rsch. Inst., East Hanover, N.J., 1962-68, sect. head, 1968-75, sect. dir., 1975-89, dir. medicinal chemistry, 1989—; founder, co-chmn. Residential Sch. on Medicinal Chemistry, Madison N.J., 1987—; U.S. del. Internat. Union of Pure and Applied Chemistry, medicinal chemistry, 1982. Author, editor: Aldol Condensation, 1968, Platelet Activating Factor, 1990; editor: Indoles Vols. I-III, 1972, 79; patentee in field. Mem. Am. Chem. Soc. (chmn. North Jersey chpt. 1976). Roman Catholic. Home: 15 Raynold Rd Mountain Lakes NJ 07046-1610 Office: Sandoz Rsch Inst RR 10 East Hanover NJ 07936

HOULT, DAVID PARKS, mechanical engineering educator; b. Oxnard, Calif., Aug. 30, 1935; m. Zene Athans, May 10, 1986. BS, MIT, 1957; MS, Calif. Inst. Tech., 1958, PhD, 1962. Postdoctoral fellow Calif. Inst. Tech., Pasadena, 1962-63; prof. aero. engring. Pa. State U., State College, 1963-67; prof. mech. engring. MIT, Cambridge, Mass., 1967-74; sr. rsch. assoc. MIT, Cambridge, 1975—; mem. adv. bd. Pennzoil Co., Houston, 1988—. Author, editor: Oil on the Sea, 1969. Mem. Soc. Tribologist and Lubrication Engrs. Home: 9 Heard Rd Wayland MA 01778-2504 Office: MIT Dept Mech Engring Cambridge MA 02139

HOUPT, GROVER KREWSON, manufacturing company executive; b. Willow Grove, Pa., May 3, 1932; s. Horace L. and Daisy (Roberts) H.; m. Joan Kach, Aug. 21, 1954; children: Bryan, Jannine, Douglas. BSEE, Lehigh U., 1954; MSEE, Drexel U., 1960. Registered profl. engr., Pa. Engr. Fischer & Porter Co., Warminster, Pa., 1954-59; dir. R & D Automatic Timing & Controls Co., King of Prussia, Pa., 1959-80; v.p. Automatic Timing & Controls Co., King of Prussia, 1980-84, sr. v.p., 1984-91; cons. product devel., 1991—; dir. Automatic Timing and Controls Co., King of Prussia, 1980-91. Patentee in field. Mem. Am. Soc. Inventors (dir. 1981—), IEEE, ASME, Instrument Soc. of Am. Home: 759 Hedges Ln Wayne PA 19087-2003 Office: 759 Hedges Ln Wayne PA 19087

HOURIGAN, WILLIAM PATRICK, school administrator; b. Wilkes Barre, Pa., Oct. 10, 1944; s. John A. Jr. and Katharine (Mulcahy) H.; m. Linda Bonkiewicz, Oct. 6, 1973; children: Patrick, Erin. BS in Bus. Mgmt., C.W. Post Coll., 1967. Asst. treas. Wilkes-Barre Publ. Co., 1969-82; budget dir. N.Y. Dept. Corrections, N.Y.C., 1982-86; budget supr. N.Y. Human Resources Adminstrn., N.Y.C., 1986-87; bus. mgr. St. Bernard's Sch., N.Y.C., 1987—. Lt. USN, 1967-69. Mem. Lionel Collectors Club Am. (pres. 1979-80, 86-88, treas. 1989-91). Republican. Roman Catholic. Home: 387A Loop Rd Wilkes Barre PA 18707-9715 Office: St Bernard's Sch Inc 4 E 98th St New York NY 10029-6502

HOUSE, ANTOINETTE AIELLO (TONI HOUSE), public information officer; b. Washington, Jan. 5, 1943; d. Hugh Osgood and Mary (Aiello) H.; m. Eric Val Reuther, Feb. 17, 1961 (div. 1963); 1 child, Valerie Luise; m. Robert Whitewell Wilson, July 6, 1973 (div. Nov. 1989); m. William James Weller, May 6, 1990. Student, Wesleyan U., 1962-63, Am. Univ., 1963-66. Staff writer Washington Star, 1966-81, dep. picture editor, 1981; freelance writer Washington, 1982; pub. info. officer U.S. Supreme Ct., Washington, 1982—; chair Washington Star Reunion Com., 1982—; mem. faculty Inst. for Ct. Mgmt., Denver, 1985, 92; bd. dirs. Washington Press Club Found., 1985-90. Co-author: The Washington Sting, 1979. Mem. Journalists for Profl. Equality, Washington, 1971-75. Mem. Nat. Press Club (past pres., numerous offices), Nat. Inst. of Ct., Pub. Info. Coords. Office: US Supreme Ct Washington DC 20543

HOUSE, DOUGLAS WAYNE, sales and marketing executive; b. Charlotte, N.C., Nov. 8, 1955; s. Garland Bascomb and Ruth Neal (Swearingen) H. BA in Zoology, U. N.C., 1978. Shift mgr. Milliken and Co., Spartanburg, S.C., 1978-79; regional sales mgr. Organon Pharms., Charlotte, 1979-82; clin. chemistry specialist Abbott Labs., Chgo., 1982-84; account exec. Abbott Labs., Raleigh, N.C., 1984-86; nat. accounts mgr. Abbott Labs., Chgo., 1986-88; dist. mgr. Abbott Labs., Annapolis, Md., 1988-90; v.p. sales and mktg. Cambride Biotech Corp., Worcester, Mass., 1990—. Mem. Biomed. Mktg. Assn., Am. Soc. Microbiology. Republican. Methodist. Home: 9 Commonwealth Ave Apt 2 61 Manor Ave Wellesley MA 02181 Office: Cambridge Biotech Corp 365 Plantation St Worcester MA 01605

HOUSEPIAN, EDGAR MINAS, neurosurgery educator; b. N.Y.C., Mar. 18, 1928; s. Moses Minas and Makroulie (Ashjian) H; m. Marian Grace Lyon, Sept. 18, 1954; children: David Minas, Stephen Lyon, Jean Carleton Housepian. AB cum laude, Columbia U., 1949, MD, 1953. Intern in surgery U. Hosps. of Cleve., 1953-54, asst. resident in surgery, 1953-55; asst. resident in surgery Neurol. Inst., N.Y.C., 1955-56, asst. resident in neurol. surgery, 1956, asst. resident in neurology, 1957-58, sr. resident in neurol. surgery, 1958-59; asst. resident in neuropathology Columbia Presbyn. Med. Ctr., N.Y.C., 1956; asst. prof. Columbia U., N.Y.C., 1967-76, prof., 1976—; asst. neurol. surgeon Columbia Presbyn. Med. Ctr., N.Y.C., 1959-61, asst. attending neurol. surgeon, 1961-64, assoc. attending surgeon, 1964-75, attending surgeon, 1975—; asst. vis. neurol. surgeon Francis Delafield Hosp., N.Y., 1959-72; asst. attending neurol. surgeon N.Y. State Psychiat. Inst., 1962-80; attending neurol. surgeon VA Hosp., Bronx, 1962-69; cons. neurol. surgery U.S. Naval Hosp., St. Albans, N.Y., 1963-74, Englewood (N.J.) Hosp., 1964—, Greenwich (Conn.) Hosp., 1965—; mem. courtesy staff dept. surgery St. Luke's-Roosevelt Hosp. Ctr., N.Y., 1981—; guest lectr. Soviet Acad. of Sci., 1965; vis. prof. surg. neurology Edinburgh (Eng.) U., 1968; mem. search com. radiotherapy Columbia U., 1980-84, 88—, sec. staff com., 1962-68, mem. communicable disease and antibiotics com., 1966-75, mem. dean's ad hoc com. on nat. bds., 1974, mem. univ. senate exec. com., 1979-81, mem. fin. com. assn. of alumni of Physicians and Surgeons Coll., 1979—, mem. clin. rsch. adv. com. Cancer Rsch. Ctr., 1980—, mem. dean's adv. com. on continuing med. edn., 1987—, chmn. libr. and audiovisual com., 1972—, chmn. com. on human investigation, 1972—, mem. standing com. on edn., 1980—, chmn. credentials com., 1981—, active numerous other univ. coms.; mem. World Congress Ad Hoc TV Rev. Com., 1969; mem. claims rev. com. Med. Liability Mut. Ins. Co., 1978—; prin. investigator brain tumor chemotherapy sect., mem. comprehensive cancer sect. Nat. Cancer Inst., 1973-77; vis. prof. in surg. neurology Edinburgh U., 1968; vis. prof. Postgrad. Inst. Med. Edn. and Rsch., Chandigarh, India, 1981; guest lectr. Soviet Acad. Sci., 1965; active numerous other career related activities. Contbr. chpts. to books, articles to Jour. Neurosurgery, Jour. Neuropathology, Jour. Neuropathology and Exptl. Neurology, Jour. Nervous Mental Diseases, Perspectives in Neurol. Surgery, numerous others. Mem. med. adv. bd. Nat. Neurofibromatosis Found., 1978-81; mem. adv. com. Armenian Studies Program Columbia U., 1972-80; trustee Gulbekian Found., 1975-82. Served to lt. comdr. USNR, 1945-46, 1961-89. Donner Found. Rsch. fellow, 1956; Parkinson's Disease Found. Postdoctoral Rsch. fellow, 1959-61; Fulbright fellow, 1968; grantee Am. Cancer Soc., 1969-72, Nat. Cancer Inst., 1973-77. Fellow ACS; mem. AAAS, AMA, AAUP, Am. Acad. Neurol. Surgeons, Am. Assn. Neurol. Surgeons, Am. Epilepsy Soc., Am. Trauma Soc., Am. Pain Soc., N.Y. Acad. Sci., N.Y. County Med. Soc., N.Y. State Med. Soc., Internat. Soc. Rsch. in Stereoencephalotomy (charter), Assn. for Rsch. in Nervous and Mental Diseases, N.Y. Soc. Neurosurgery, Rsch. Soc. Neurol. Surgeons, N.Y. Neurol. Soc., Congress of Neurol. Soc., Soc. for Neurosci., N.Y. State Neurosurg. Soc., Internat. Assn. for the Study of Pain, Internat. Soc. on Disaster Medicine, Fulbright Alumni Assn., Internat. Brain Rsch. Orgn., World Fedn. Neuroscientists, Phi Beta Kappa, Sigma Xi. Office: Columbia U Coll Physicians & Surgeons 710 W 168th St New York NY 10032-2699

HOUSEWRIGHT, ARTEMIS SKEVAKIS, artist; b. Tampa, Fla., July 18, 1927; d. Paul Herakles and Evelyn Dorothy (Marshman) Skevakis; m. Rudolf A. Jegart, Mar. 12, 1952 (div. 1968); children: Rudi Artemis, Nike Chrysanche A.; m. Riley D. Housewright. AB, Fla. State U., 1949, MA, 1952. One man shows include Washington Fed. Savs. & Loan, Miami Beach, Fla., 1957, 59, 62, 68, Valdosta (Ga.) State Coll., 1968, LeMoyne Art Ctr., Tallahassee, 1968, Cosmos Club, Washington, 1976, Evelyn Walborsky Gallery, Tampa, 1979, Soc. Four Arts, Palm Beach (First prize, Purchase prize 1956, 57, 58), Tampa State Fair (First prize, Purchase prize 1955), others; exhibited in group shows at Sarasota (Fla.) Art Assn., 1957, 59 (Purchase prize), Miss. Art Assn., Jackson, 1957 (Purchase prize), numerous others; executed murals for Washington Fed. Savs. and Loan, Hollywood, Fla., 2d Nat. Fed. Savs. Bank, Washington, 1989, others. Episcopalian. Home and Studio: 147 Fairview Ave Frederick MD 21701

HOUTS, PETER STEVENS, social psychology educator; b. Great Neck, N.Y., Mar. 17, 1933; s. Thomas Cushing and Charlotte (Stevens) H.; m. Mary Davidoff, June 19, 1960; children: Thomas, David. BA, Antioch Coll., Yellow Springs, Ohio, 1955; PhD, U. Mich., 1963. Asst. prof. Goucher Coll., Towson, Md., 1963-65; postdoctoral fellow Med. Sch. Stanford U., Palo Alto, Calif., 1965-67; asst. prof. Coll. of Medicine Pa. State U., Hershey, 1967-70, assoc. prof. Coll. of Medicine, 1970—. Author: Case Studies in Primary Care, 1983, The Three Mile Island Crisis, 1988; editor: After the Turn On, What?, 1972; mem. editorial bd. Am. Jour. Cancer Edn., 1989—. Bd. dirs. Music at Gretna, Mt. Gretna, Pa.,1990—. With U.S. Army, 1957, USAR, 1957-63. Mem. APA, APHA, AAUP, Am. Psychol. Soc., Am. Soc. Clin. Oncology, Am. Assn. for Cancer Edn., Soc. Behavioral Medicine. Office: Pa State U Coll Medicine Dept Behavioral Sci Hershey PA 17033

HOVE, ANDREW CHRISTIAN, federal agency administrator; b. Minden, Nebr., Nov. 9, 1934; s. Andrew C. and Rosalie (Vopat) H.; m. Ellan Matzke, June 12, 1956; children: Catherine Breen, Peter, Nancy. BS, U. Nebr., 1956; postgrad., U. Wis., 1960-63. Chmn., chief exec. officer Minden Exec. Bank and Trust Co., 1960-90; vice chmn. FDIC, Washington, 1990—. Lt. USN, 1956-60. Office: FDIC 550 17th St NW Washington DC 20429-0002

HOVENGA, TRENT LAVERN, surgeon; b. Estherville, Iowa, July 29, 1958; s. LaVern Bernard and Jeradine Marian (Laidig) H.; m. Lisa Marie Borkowski, May 20, 1983; children: Bard Parker, Claire Marie. AB, Washington U., St. Louis, 1980; MD, U. Iowa, 1984. Commd. 2d lt. U.S. Army, 1980, advanced through grades to maj., 1990; gen. surgery resident Fitzsimons Army Med. Ctr., Aurora, Colo., 1984-89; staff surgeon Landstuhl (Germany) Army Regional Med. Ctr., 1989—. Mem. Assn. Mil. Surgeons U.S. Republican. Presbyterian. Home and Office: Box 501 APO AE 09180

HOVER, LEILA MESSING, medical librarian; b. Bklyn.; d. Herman Messing and Mildred (Klein) Wyte; m. John Gilbert Hover; children: Jeffrey J., Karen L. BS, SUNY, 1977; MLS, Rutgers U., 1978. Dir. libr. svcs. Holy Name Hosp., Teaneck, N.J., 1978-88; corp. libr. Physicians World Communications Group, Secaucus, N.J., 1988—; cons. libr. planning, 1981—. Mem. Med. Libr. Assn., Spl. Librs. Assn., Health Scis. Libr. Assn. N.J. (chairperson 1983-87, v.p. 1988-89, pres. 1989-90), Bergen-Passaic Health Scis. Libr. Consortium (chairperson 1979-80). Home: 2 Mountain Run Boonton NJ 07005-8710 Office: PW Communications Group 400 Plaza Dr Secaucus NJ 07094-3605

HOVERSLAND, ARTHUR STANLEY, science review administrator, animal physiologist; b. Hallock, Minn., Apr. 20, 1922; s. Andreas and Marie Josephine (Kolden) H.; m. Dorothy Helen Brist, Apr. 1, 1946; children: Beverly, Roger, Gordon, Paul, Carol. BS, Mont. State Coll., 1951, MS, 1958; PhD, Oreg. State U., 1970. Cert. profl. animal scientist. From instr. to assoc. prof. Mont. State Coll., Bozeman, 1951-67; rsch. assoc. U. Oreg. Med. Sch., Portland, 1967-70; from assoc. prof. to prof., chmn. Calif. State U., Fresno, 1970-78; health scientist adminstr. NIH, Bethesda, Md., 1978—; ad hoc reviewer USDA competitive grants, Washington D.C., 1988—; reviewer Small Ruminant Rsch. Jour., Amsterdam, The Netherlands, 1990—. Mem. Am. Soc. Animal Sci., Soc. for the Study of Reproduction, Soc. for the Study of Fertility, Assn. Registered Profl. Animal Scientists (bd. dirs. 1991—), Am. Physiol. Soc., N.Y. Acad. Sci. Office: NIH Div of Rsch Grants Bethesda MD 20892

HOVEY, ALAN EDWIN, JR., personnel executive; b. Burlington, Vt., Apr. 23, 1933; s. Alan Edwin and Jessie Miller (Emerson) H.; BSBA, U. Fla., 1956; postgrad. Cornell U. Law Sch.; m. Sue S. Weeks, Aug. 28, 1987; children: Alison Clair, Kimberly Ann, Christopher Owen, Adam Kimball. Civilian mgmt. anaylst Dept. Army, Orleans, France, 1958-60; with Century Housewares Co., 1961-80, dir. human resources, Buffalo, 1979; dir. personnel Everfast, Inc., Wilmington, Del., 1980-83; v.p. human Resources Mr. Goodbuys, Inc., Phila., 1983-91; dir. human resources The Salk Inst., GSD, Swiftwater, Pa., 1992—; mem. personnel policies forum Bur. Nat. Affairs, Inc., 1987-88; bd. dirs. Del. Valley Project with Industry, 1989—. Mem. East Aurora (N.Y.) Bd. Edn., 1976-80; chmn. Wilmington Gt. Am. Smokeout, Am. Cancer Soc. Served with AUS, 1956-58. Accredited Sr. Profl. Human Resources. Personnel Accreditation Inst. Mem. Greater Phila. C. of C. (chmn. retail coun. 1988-89), Am. Mgmt. Assn., Soc. Human Resource Mgmt. Republican. Unitarian. Home: 2741 Huntingdon Pike Huntingdon Valley PA 19006-5111 Office: The Salk Inst GSD PO Box 250 Swiftwater PA 18370

HOWARD, ANN HUBBARD, insurance agency executive; b. Dorchester, Md., July 2, 1938; d. Sherwood Marcus and Irene Meade (Cannon) Hubbard; m. Luke Vincent Howard Sr., Oct. 20, 1956; children: Annette H. Mitchell, Diana H. Johnson, Luke V. Jr., Peter Martin, Angela M., Joseph R. Grad. high sch., Easton, Md. Cert. health cons. Libr. aide Talbot County Bd. of Edn., Easton, 1973-74; advt. mgr. Talbot Banner Newspaper, Easton, 1974-77; regional mgr., account exec. Blue Cross-Blue Shield, Easton, 1977-87; agt. N.Y. Life Ins., Easton, 1987-88, Guardian Life Ins. Co., Easton, 1988—; pres., broker Ann H. Howard and Assocs. Inc., Easton, 1986—; owner Shorewoman Mag., 1980-83. Coord. Talbot County Health Fair, Easton, 1984-85. Mem. NAFE, Chesapeake Assn. Life Underwriters (pres. 1982-83), Md. State Assn. Life Underwriters (edn. coord., health chmn.), C. of C. (bd. dirs. 1973-86, pres. 1980, Businesswoman of Yr. award 1989). Democrat. Roman Catholic. Office: 3 Goldsboro St PO Box 2220 Easton MD 21601-2220

HOWARD, BARBARA VIVENTI, research foundation executive; b. East Orange, N.J., June 26, 1941; d. Louis and Angelina (DiBiase) Viventi; m. William James Howard, June 22, 1962; children: Laura, Sandra, Jeffrey. AB, Bryn Mawr Coll., 1963; PhD, U. Pa., 1968. Instr. U. N.C., Chapel Hill, 1968-70; asst. prof. George Washington U., Washington, 1970-73; asst. prof. Med. Coll. of Pa., Phila., 1973-76, assoc. prof. to vis. prof., 1976-91; scientist NIODIC-NIH, Phoenix, 1976-82; assoc. chief CONS-NIDDIC, NIH, Phoenix, 1982-88; dir. rsch. Medlantic Rsch. Found., Washington, 1988-90, pres., 1991—; chmn. Strong Heart Study Steering Com., Washington, 1988—; mem. nutrition study sect. NIH, Bethesda, Md., 1988-91. Editor: Insulin and the Cell Membrane, 1990, Lipoprotein Kinetics, 1982; assoc. editor:: Diabetes Care, 1990-91, Jour. Lipid Rsch., 1990—; contbr. over 100 articles to profl. jours. NIH grantee, 1988—. Fellow Am. Soc. Biochemistry and Molecular Biology; mem. Am. Diabetes Assn., Am. Fedn. Clin. Rsch., Am. Soc. for Clin. Nutrition, Internat. Study Group for Inplantable Insulin Delivery, Am. Heart Assn. (exec. com.), Bryn Mawr Club. Republican. Episcopalian. Home: 9120 Willow Gate Ln

Bethesda MD 20817-4107 Office: Medlantic Rsch Found 108 Irving St NW Washington DC 20010-2933

HOWARD, CECIL GERALD, management consultant, educator; b. Bareilly, India, Oct. 18, 1929; came to U.S., 1958; s. Edward Lawrence and Salome (Walters) H.; m. Surya Anamiah, Mar. 8, 1959; children: Salome, Susan. BA, Agra U., 1951; MBA, Ohio State U., 1960, PhD in Bus., 1965. Treas. Clara Swain Hosp., Bareilly, 1951-58; mgmt. trainee Warren-Teed Pharms., Inc., Columbus, Ohio, 1960-64; asst. prof. West Liberty (W.Va.) State Coll., 1964-66; assoc. prof. Ga. So. U., Statesboro, 1966-70, prof., 1970-74; assoc. prof. Howard U., Washington, 1975-84, prof., 1984—; employee devel. specialist NIH, Bethesda, Md., 1974-75. Contbr. over 30 articles to profl. jours. Am. Assembly of Collegiate Schs. of Bus.-Sears fellow, Bethesda, 1974-75. Mem. Acad. Mgmt., Acad. Internat. Bus., Assn. Mgmt., Acad. Internat. Mgmt. and Mktg. (div. chair). Republican. Methodist. Home: 806 Twin Oaks Dr Rockville MD 20854-2922

HOWARD, CLIFTON MERTON, psychiatrist; b. Quincy, Mass., Aug. 11, 1922; s. Clifton Merton and Ruth Gilkey (Heuderson); m. Margaret Carroll, June 16, 1951 (div. Aug. 1964); children: Kristen, Lauren, Siri; m. Susan D. Krex., May 30, 1965; children: Michael Scott, Jonathan, Robert. BS, Harvard U., 1944, MA, 1947; MD, Columbia U., 1963. Diplomate Am. Bd. Med. Examiners. Rsch. physicist Brookhaven Nat. Lab., 1947-48; founder Waveforms, Inc., 1951-53; pres., chief exec. officer Electronic Workshop, Inc., 1951-59, Sound Workshop, Inc. and E.W. Assocs., Inc., 1953-59; dir. evening Psychiat. Clinic, Mt. Carmel Guild, Union City, N.J., 1964-67; sr. psychiat. resident, drug rsch. svc. N.Y. State Psychiat. Inst., N.Y.C., 1965-66; asst. attending psychiatrist Vanderbilt Clinic, Columbia Presbyn. Med. Ctr., 1969-75; cons. in psychiatry Columbia Presbyn. Med. Ctr., 1969-75, assoc. attending psychiatrist, psychiat. drug rsch. unit, 1971-75; pvt. practice N.Y.C., 1967—, 1980—; instr. engring. dept., Harvard Coll., 1946; instr. physics dept. CCNY, 1948-50, NYU, 1948-54, psychiatry, Columbia Coll. of P&S, 1967-71, assoc. in psychiatry, 1971-75. Staff writer APPLE computer mag., 1982-85; co-founder S&H Software, Inc. designing and licensing software systems to Reader's Digest, D.C. Heath Co. and others. Lt. USNR, 1943-46, PTO. Mem. Am. Psychiat. Assn., Ams. of Armorial Ancestry, Ancient and Hon. Artillery Co. of Mass., Baronial Order of Magna Charta, Flagon and Trencher, Gen. Soc. Mayflower Descendants (surgeon gen. N.J. soc. 1978-84), Nat. Geneal. Soc., New Eng. Hist. and Geneal. Soc., Old Bridgewater Hist. Soc., Order of Founders and Patriots of Am., Order of the Crown of Charlemagne, Royal Bastard Soc., Soc. Descendants of Colonial Clergy, Soc. Ams. of Royal Descent, Soc. Colonial Wars and others. Home: 58 Van Orden Rd Harrington Park NJ 07640-1616 Office: 300 Central Park W Ste 1K New York NY 10024-1513

HOWARD, DAVID, academic program director, educator, fiction writer; b. Delaware, Ohio, Sept. 24, 1929; s. Dale David and Clarine (Morehouse) H. BA, Ohio Wesleyan U., 1953; student, Columbia U., 1961-62, 86, NYU, 1985-86. Lic. tchr., attendance coordinator, N.Y. News writer Australian Broadcasting Co., Sydney, 1955; editorial asst. N.Y. Times, N.Y.C., 1956-58; tchr. social studies N.Y.C. Bd. of Edn., 1958-82, hotel & shelter ednl. coordinator, 1982-89; asst. supr. N.Y.C. Truancy Patrol Teams, 1989—. Author: (book) Night Lights Went Out, 1966, Casa Alhambra, 1968. Reservist Fed. Emergency Mgmt. Agy., N.Y.C., 1980—. Served to lt. col. USAFR, 1953-75. Mem. Mystery Writers of Am., English Speaking Union. Republican. Protestant. N.Y.C. Anchor & Saber. Home: 324 E 61st St Apt 20 New York NY 10021-8709 Office: NYC Bd Edn Bur Attendance 110 Livingston St Brooklyn NY 11201-5065

HOWARD, DENNIS MARTIN, writer, producer, marketing executive; b. N.Y.C., Jan. 10, 1930; s. Stephen John and Nora Teresa (O'Connor) H. V.p., dir. mktg. The Zakin Co., N.Y.C., 1963-68; v.p., creative dir. Barickman Advt., N.Y.C., 1968-69; pres. D.M. Howard Co., Inc., Chatham, N.J., 1970-79, The Creative Dir., Chatham, 1980-90, Media 2000, Inc., Maspeth, N.Y., 1991—; cons. in advt., pub. rels., mktg. Writer, producer video. Recipient various editorial awards Cath. Press Assn., 1953-58, Best Print Ad Campaign award Advt. Club of N.J., 1975, Best TV Comml. award Advt. Club of N.J., 1975. Office: PO Box 110 Brookside NJ 07926-0110

HOWARD, GEORGE PRATT, airport trade association executive, economist; b. Altoona, Pa., July 1, 1930; s. George Charles and Margaret Elizabeth (Pratt) H.; m. Susan Pincus, Nov. 11, 1972; children: Constance, Catherine, Virginia. BA, U. Va., 1951; MBA, NYU, 1957. Assoc. dir. Mktg. Svcs. Co., Dun & Bradstreet, N.Y.C., 1958-61; dir. mktg. rsch. Ea. Airlines, N.Y.C., 1961-64; asst. dir. aviation Port Authority N.Y. and N.J., N.Y.C., 1964-89; pres. Airports Assn. Coun. Internat., Washington, 1989—. Editor: Airport Economic Planning, 1974. Pres. Brooklyn Heights Assn., Bklyn., 1972-74. 1st lt. USAF, 1952-55. Office: Airports Assn Coun Internat 1220 19th St NW Ste 200 Washington DC 20036-2446

HOWARD, GREGORY CHARLES, lawyer; b. Cambridge, Mass., Jan. 20, 1947; s. Robert L. and Nonamae (Lawlor) H.; m. Kathy Arlene Steinbacher, Oct. 1, 1983. Student Clarkson Coll., 1965-67; BS, Boston U., 1969; JD, New Eng. Sch. Law, 1975. Bar: Mass. 1975, U.S. Dist. Ct. Mass. 1975, U.S. Supreme Ct. 1979. Assoc. Carmen L. Durso, Boston, 1975-77, Norris Kozodoy & Krasnoo, Boston, 1977-79; sole practice, Boston, 1979-80, 86; ptnr. Hoff Ernstoff & Howard, Boston, 1980-86; pres. Gregory C. Howard, PC, Boston, 1986—. Home: 5 Eliot Ave Chestnut Hill MA 02167-1455 Office: 18 Tremont St Boston MA 02108-2301

HOWARD, HAROLD CHARLES, dean, strategic planner, consultant; b. Loogootee, Ind., Mar. 28, 1926; s. Rodolophus Henry and Grace Mae (Carroll) H.; m. Gladys Marie Richardson, Dec. 17, 1949; children: Mark Allen, Carol Joy. BA, No. Baptist Coll., 1962; MA, Loyola U., Chgo., 1963, PhD, 1965. Ordained to ministry Bapt. Ch., 1952. Asst. supt. Jerry McAuley Mission, N.Y.C., 1945-46; parish min. Cypress Ave. Bapt. Ch., N.Y.C., 1946-52; staff evangelist Bapt. Gen. Conf., Chgo., 1952-60; grad. study fellow Loyola U., Chgo., 1962-65; prof. history, exec. v.p., dean Ea. Coll., St. Davids, Pa., 1966-78, v.p. strategic planning, dean non-traditional edn., 1988—; prin. Howard Assocs., Radnor, Pa., 1978-88; dir. Am. Studies Inst., St. Davids, 1965-78; sr. cons. Main Event Mgmt. Corp., Sacramento, 1978-88; adv. bd. Franklin Fibre-Lamitex, Wilmington, Del., 1986—; cons. Model-Netics, Arthur Andersen, St. Charles, Ill., 1986-87; mgmt. tng. cons. AXA Corp., France, 1988-90. Officer Lower Merion Bapt. Ch., 1965—; active Univ. Planning Assoc., 1989—. Recipient Freedom Found. award, 1980; named Alumnus of Yr. Judson Coll. (formerly No. Bapt. Coll.), 1968. Mem. Phi Alpha Theta, Delta Mu Delta. Home: 51 Treaty Dr Wayne PA 19087-5510

HOWARD, JAMES JOSEPH, dentist; b. Tokyo, Feb. 13, 1950; came to U.S., 1950; s. Joseph John and Blanche Michaeline (Nowik) H.; m. Julie Suzanne Waith, Oct. 4, 1986; 1 stepchild, Adrian Richard Haskins; 1 child, Andrew James Howard. BA, Rutgers U., 1972; D.M.D., U. Pa., 1976. Dentist, major USAR, Short Gap, W.Va., 1972—; dentist assoc. Allen Dental Assocs., Cumberland, Md., 1978-80; pres., owner Howard Dental Group, Lavale, Md., 1980—; staff mem. Meml. Hosp., Cumberland, 1978-87, Sacred Heart Hosp., Cumberland, 1978—; profl. mem. adv. bd. Allegany County Bd. of Health. Mem. Jaycees, Cumberland, 1984-85. Capt. U.S. Army, 1976-78. Zeta Psi Clareth scholar U. Pa., 1973-74, grad. dental scholar U. Pa., 1973-74. Mem. ADA, Allegany-Garrett County Dental Soc. (pres. 1982, Past President's award 1983), Md. State Dental Assn., Amvets, VFW, Fraternal Order of Police, Eagles Aerie, Moose, Delta Sigma Delta. Republican. Roman Catholic. Office: Howard Dental Group 444 National Hwy Cumberland MD 21502-7197

HOWARD, JOAN ALICE, artist; b. N.Y.C., Apr. 28, 1929; d. John Volkman and Mary Alice Devlin; m. Robert Thornton Howard, June 26, 1949; children: Barbara Jo, Robert Thornton Jr., Gregory Lyon, Brian Devlin. Student, Hunter Coll., 1947-48, UCLA, 1967-68, Los Angeles Valley Coll., 1970-71. Dir., choreographer Acad. Dance, Floral Park and Forest Hills, N.Y., 1947-57; dir. dance. Cath. Parochial schs., N.Y.C., Bklyn., and Floral Park, N.Y., 1948-55; chmn. dept. dance Molloy Coll., 1958-67; artist sta. KNBC-TV, Los Angeles, 1967-74, NBC, N.Y.C., 1974-78, sta. WNBC-TV, N.Y.C., 1978-79; artistic dir. Brookville (N.Y.) Sch., 1980-85; dir. dance N.Y.C. YMCA, 1948; founder, dir. Queens-Nassau Regional Dance Theatre, 1950-55; choreographer Molloy Coll. Dance Theatre, 1959-67; cons. prenatal exercise, L.I., N.Y., 1980—; judge art show Westbury (N.Y.) Mural Project, 1979. One-woman shows include Dime Savs. Bank, Manhasset, N.Y., 1986-87, Ridgefield (Conn.) Guild Gallery, 1989-90, 91, Nardin Gallery Fine Arts, 1990, Chase Manhattan Bank, 1990-91, 92, Manhasset Libr. Gallery, 1990-91, Hutchinson Gallery L.I. U., 1991, Rose Gallery, Kent, Conn., 1991, Chelsea House, N.Y., 1991, Plandone Gallery, L.I., 1991, Sacco's, Ridgefield, 1991, Great Neck (N.Y.) Libr. Gallery, 1991, Chase Manhattan Bank, Cross River, N.Y., 1992; exhibited in group shows at Valley Ctr. Arts Gallery, L.A., 1968-72, Home Savs. & Loan Art Exhibits, L.A., 1969-70, Westwood Art Gallery, L.A., 1972, Onion Gallery, L.A., 1972, North Ridge Women's Ctr. Gallery, L.A., 1972, Great Neck (N.Y.) Ctr. Gallery, 1976, A&S Gallery, Manhasset, 1976, Gloria Vanderbilt Designers Showcase, 1978, Manhasset Libr. Gallery, 1985-89, Great Neck House Gallery, 1986-87, Hutchins Gallery C.W. Post Coll., L.I., 1986-90 (awards 1986, 87, 88, 89, 90), Dime Savs. Bank, Manhasset, N.Y., European Am. Bank, 1988, Nardin Fine Arts, Cross River, N.Y., 1989, Plandome Gallery, N.Y.C., 1990; exhibited in juried shows Nassau County Mus. Fine Arts, Roslyn, N.Y., 1985, Plandome Gallery, 1987-88, Great Neck House Gallery, 1986-89 (hon. mention), East Meadow Libr. Gallery, 1988, Freeport Gallery, 1988, Ridgefield Gallery, 1989, 91, Shelter Rock Gallery, 1989, rtRidgefield Gallery Portrait Show, 1989-90, Ridgefield Artists' Guild, 1989, Nardin Gallery, 1989, Hutchins Gallery L.I. U., 1991, Rose Gallery, Kent, Conn., 1991, Chelsea House Mus. Cultural Commn., 1991, Manhasset Gallery, 1990-91, Sacco, Ridgefield, 1991, Great Neck Libr. Gallery, 1991, Chase Manhattan Bank, Cross River, N.Y., 1992; choreographer contemporary ballet Crucifixion, 1960, Persephone, 1961, Cubes of Truth, 1962, Somewhere, 1965; appeared on radio show Coast to Coast on a Bus, 1939-47; Broadway prodn. Lady in the Dark, 1940-42; performed ballet in TV show Stars of Tomorrow, 1942, Sleeping Beauty, 1942. Dem. committeewoman, Glen Cove, N.Y., 1954-58. Recipient Del Rey Perpetual Race championship trophy, 1974, Little Sabot Perpetual Race trophy, 1972-74, So. Calif. Women's Sailing Conf. sabot championship, 1972-74, 1st Woman trophy Olympic Regatta, 1973. Mem. Dance Educators Am., Manhasset Art Assn., Women's Sailing Com. of U.S. Yacht Racing Union (fund raiser 1980-81), Am. Watercolor Soc. (aux.), Women's C. of C. L.A., Tri-County Artists Ridgefield Art Guild. Clubs: Calif. Yacht (Los Angeles) (Women's Perpetual Race trophy 1972-74), Sports Car of Am. Home and Office: 19 Autumn Rd South Salem NY 10590

HOWARD, JOSEFINA, restaurant owner; b. Habana, Cuba; came to U.S., 1940; d. Eduardo and Lina (Beceiro) Quiñones; children: Anthony, Stephen (dec.). Grad., N.Y. Sch. Interior Design, 1946; student, Peter Kump Cooking Sch., N.Y.C., 1979. Interior designer N.Y.C., 1946-58, Mexico City, 1958-78; owner LaFogata Restaurant, N.Y.C., 1980-83; co-owner, exec. chef Rosa Mexicano Restaurant, N.Y.C., 1984—. Home: 1063 1st Ave New York NY 10022-2903 Office: Rosa Mexicano 1063 1st Ave New York NY 10022-2903

HOWARD, JOSEPH CLEMENS, federal judge; b. Des Moines, Dec. 9, 1922; m. Gwendolyn Mae London, Dec. 1954; 1 son. B.A., U. Iowa, 1950; LL.B., Drake U., 1955, M.A., 1957, J.D., 1968; postgrad., Washington and Lee U., Northwestern U. Law Sch., U. Nev.; postgrad. hon. degree, Morgan State Coll., 1972. Bar: Md. Probation officer Supreme Bench Balt. City, 1958-60; mem. firm Howard and Hargrove, 1960-64; asst. state's atty., 1964-66, chief of trial sect., 1966-67, asst. city solicitor, 1967-68; spl. cons. dept. edn.; assoc. judge Supreme Bench of Balt. City, 1968-79; vis. prof. Grad. Sch. Nat. Coll. State Trial Judges, U. Nev., Reno, 1971; vis. lectr. Johns Hopkins U., Balt., 1971, 73; vis. prof. Nat. Coll. Dist. Attys., U. Houston, 1973; vis. lectr. Morgan State U., 1973-77; chief judge criminal ct. Supreme Bench of Balt. City, 1975-76; cons. communications dept. Nat. League Cities, 1978, Nat. Center for State Cts., 1978; chmn. exec. com. Md. Jud. Conf., 1977-78; judge U.S. Dist. Ct. Md., 1979—. Contbr. articles to legal jours. Mem. Mayor's Task Force on Community Relations, Balt.; chmn. Mayor's Task Force Juvenile Delinquency; bd. govs. Antioch Coll. Sch. Law, 1976-79; mem. Nat. Com. Black Elected Ofcls., 1972; mem. bd. govs. Citizens Planning and Housing Assn.; bd. dirs. Legal Aid Bur., Nat. Bar Found.; trustee Antioch Coll., 1974-75. Served with U.S. Army, 1944-47, PTO. Recipient Afro-Am. award, 1968; Police Community Relations award, 1971; Walter P. Carter award, 1971; Kappa Alpha Psi Achievement award, 1973; Benjamin Banneker Public Affairs award, 1975; Bicentennial Jud. award Black Am. Law Students Assn., 1976; Delta Sigma Theta Jud. award, 1977; Henry McNeill Turner Soc. award Bethel A.M.E. Ch., 1978; Man of Year award Nat. Assn. Negro Bus. and Profl. Women's Clubs, 1979; Women Behind the Community award, 1979; Spl. Jud. Service award Herbert M. Frisby Hist. Soc., 1980; Oustanding Alumni award Drake U., 1988. Mem. ABA, Nat. Bar Assn., World Assn. Judges, Monumental City Bar Assn., Phi Alpha Delta. Office: US Dist Ct 101 W Lombard St Baltimore MD 21201-2626*

HOWARD, JULIE DAY, social worker, therapist, consultant; b. Hartford, Conn., Jan. 11, 1949; d. James Leland and Sallie Day (Roberts) H.; m. Angelo John Lewis, June 23, 1985. M. of Human Svcs., Lincoln U., Oxford, Pa., 1984. Mental health asst. Belchertown (Mass.) State Sch., 1974-76, unit banker, coord. fair labor standards act, 1977-79, occupational therapist asst., 1979-80, rehab. counselor, 1980-81; case adv. Greater Trenton (N.J.) Community Mental Health Ctr., Inc., 1981-82, vocat. counselor, 1982-84, coord. vocat. svcs., 1984—; adj. therapist Family Svc. Princeton, N.J., 1990—; cons. Cath. Charities, Trenton, 1989; workshop presenter 13th ann. conf. Internat. Assn. Psychosocial Rehab. Svcs., Phila., 1988; program developer, group leader Nathan Azrin Job Club model, 1982-85. Author: Multicultural Communication: A Resource Guide for Helping Professionals, 1991. Mem. employment task force Human Svs. Adv. Coun. Mercer County, Trenton, 1985. Mem. Natural Resource Def. Coun., Greenpeace, Sierra Club. Home and Office: 27 Buttonwood St Lambertville NJ 08530-1644

HOWARD, KENNETH LEE, financial aid director, consultant; b. Washington, Jan. 5, 1945; s. Clyde E. and Gladys E. (Williams) H.; m. Ava Campbell, Nov. 22, 1972 (div. Dec. 1981). BA, Howard U., 1967. Grad. asst. Howard U., Washington, 1967-68, residence hall counselor, 1968-70; from fin. aid officer to dir. fin. aid office Washington (D.C.) Tech. Inst., 1970-73; dep. dir. fin. aid. office Fed. City Coll., Washington, 1973-76; dir. fin. aid office D.C. Tchrs. Coll., Washington, 1976-78; dep. dir. fin. aid office U. D.C., Washington, 1978-79, 79-83, acting dir. fin. aid office, 1979, 1984-89, acting dir. ctr. for fin. assistance, 1983-84, dir. fin. aid office, 1989—; Mem. by Congl. appt. Nat Belmont Guaranteed Student Loan Task Force, 1988. Contbr. articles to profl. jours. Recipient Dedicated Svc. cert. D.C. Pub. Schs., Washington, 1989, Appreciation cert. U.S. Drug Enforcement Adminstrn., 1991. Mem. Del.-D.C.-Md. Assn. Student Fin. Aid Adminstrs. (D.C. rep. 1975-78, pres. 1985-86, Outstanding Svc. 1988), Nat. Assn. Student Fin. Aid Adminstrs., Ea. Assn. of Student Fin. Aid Adminstrs. (Cert. Appreciation 1986, 91), Phi Delta Kappa (Cert. Recognition 1988). Republican. Roman Catholic. Home: 6018 Stevens Forest Rd Columbia MD 21045-3829 Office: U DC 4200 Connecticut Ave NW Bldg 39 Washington DC 20008-1174

HOWARD, MARGARET MARY, psychologist; b. Seattle, Aug. 13, 1957; d. Robert Hammen and Barbara Ann (Patten) H.; m. Thomas Louis Mirza, Sept. 30, 1990. BA, Western Wash. U., 1979; MA, So. Ill. U., 1983, PhD, 1988. Lic. psychologist, R.I. Coord. outpatient women's program Butler Hosp., Providence, 1987-89, 90—; with St. Joseph Hosp., Tacoma, Wash., 1989-90. Mem. R.I. Psychol. Assn., Am. Psychol. Assn., NOW. Office: Butler Hosp 345 Blackstone Blvd Providence RI 02906-7010

HOWARD, MEL, film producer, educator; b. Bklyn., Feb. 17, 1935. AB, Bklyn. Coll., 1955; student, Columbia U., N.Y.C., 1956. Assoc. dir. Am. Film Inst., 1967-69; head grad. div. Inst. Film & TV NYU, 1974-76; chmn. broadcast and film Boston U., 1990—. Assoc. exec. (films) Night of the Generals, Quackser Fortune Has A Cousin In The Bronx, Renaldo and Clara, Washington Affair, Snapshots (also dir.), The Chosen, The Goodbye People, Beat Street, He Makes Me Feel Like Dancing, Rented Lips, The Boost (theatre) Plough And The Stars, Raisin In The Sun (Broadway), Once There Was A Russian (Broadway); prodn. exec. (films) Twelve Chairs, Night Visitor, First Love, Ice, Switch, The Pawnbroker, Glen and Randa, The Swimmer, THe Happening, The Group, A Thousand Clowns, 5 Heartbeats; actor in films and theatre including leads in Hester Street and Snapshots; head european prodn. for UMC Pictures, Horizon Pictures, Sam Spiegel, Ely Landana. Fellow Sundance Inst.; mem. Actors Studio, Dirs. Unit. Office: Boston U Sch Communication 640 Commonwealth Ave Boston MA 02115

HOWARD, O.M. ZACK, biomedical researcher; b. Altus, Okla., Dec. 17, 1961; d. K.C. and Vernie V. (Roach) H.; m. James A. Turpin, June 9, 1990. BS, U. Okla., 1983; PhD, U. S.C., 1987. Rsch. asst. dept. chemistry U. Okla., Norman, 1981-83; teaching asst. dept. chemistry U. S.C., Columbia, 1983-84, grad. rsch. asst., 1984-87; postdoctoral fellow M.D. Anderson Cancer Ctr., Houston, 1987, project investigator, 1987-89; scientist I, Nat. Cancer Inst.-Frederick Cancer R&D Ctr. PRI/Dynacorp Co., Frederick, Md., 1989—. Contbr. articles to profl. jours.; inventor in field. Fellow M.D. Anderson Cancer Ctr., 1987. Mem. AAAS, Am. Assn. Cancer Rsch., N.Y. Acad. Sci., Golden Key, Phi Beta Kappa. Office: PRI/Dyncorp PO Box B Frederick MD 21702

HOWARD, PAUL LINDSAY, electrochemist, consultant; b. Hobbs, Md., Feb. 3, 1909; s. Charles and Olive Virginia (Collins) H.; m. Anna Elizabeth Clough, Dec. 27, 1932 (dec. Oct. 1981); children: Paul L., Carol Ann. AB, Western Md. Coll., 1929; MS, NYU, 1932; postgrad., Johns Hopkins U., 1932-33, NYU, 1933-34. Registered profl. engr., Washington. With Bell Telephone Lab., Kearny, N.J., 1930-32, E.S.B., Inc., Phila., 1935-42; head battery devel. Navy Dept., Washington, 1942-45; div. mgr. Burgess Battery Co., Antioch, Ill., 1945-47; v.p. electrochem. rsch. Graham Crowley & Assocs., Chgo., 1947-48; engr. missle battery devel. Nat. Bur. Standards, Washington, 1948-52; tech. dir. Yardney Electric Corp., N.Y.C., 1952-56, asst. v.p., 1956-61, v.p., dir., 1961-65; pres., chmn. bd. P.L. Howard Assocs., Greensboro, Md., 1965—. Patentee in field; contbr. articles to profl. jours. Mem. AIAA, Am. Def. Preparedness Assn. (life), Electrochem. Soc. (founder Washington-Balt. sect.), Am. Chem. Soc., Mason, Shriners. Home and Office: 208 Vaughn St Greensboro MD 21639

HOWARD, RICHARD CHARLES, audio visual executive; b. N.Y.C., May 13, 1929; s. Charles Stanley and Edna Mae (Deehan) H.; m. Anna Marie James, Oct. 29, 1958 (div. Jan. 1980); children: Wendy, Stanley, Ian. BSEd, SUNY, Oneonta, 1953; MS in Ednl. Adminstrn., U. Calif., San Francisco, 1963; EdS Inst. Tech., Syracuse U., 1971. Lifetime teaching cert., Calif. Tchr. various pub. schs., N.Y., N.J., 1953-64, Calif., 1953-64; asst. prof. edn., lab. sch. instr. Ea. Oreg. State Coll., 1965-67; asst. prof. edn., dir. audio visual W.Va. State Coll., 1967-68; asst. prof. edn. SUNY, Albany, 1968-69; lectr. in audio visual Syracuse (N.Y.) Univ., 1969-70; mgr. audio visual, to assoc. dir., to dir. audio visual Univ. R.I., Kingston, 1970—. Editor: (textbook) Reading In Instructional Technology, 1976. Commdr. Coast Guard Aux., Pt. Judith, R.I., 1980. With USN, 1946-48. Home: 23 Juniper Trail Narragansett RI 02882-2502 Office: U RI West Kingston RI 02881

HOWARD, RUFUS OLIVER, ophthalmologist; b. Knoxville, Tenn., June 30, 1929; s. Thomas Oliver and Mary Agnes (Smith) H.; m. Martha Grace Lang, Apr. 16, 1955; children: Amy, Thomas, Mary, Martha, Emily. BS, William and Mary Coll., 1949; SB, MIT, 1949, PhD, 1953; MD, Med. Coll. of Va., 1961. Diplomate Am. Bd. Ophthalmology. Researcher U.S. Army, Frederick, Md., 1952-54; rsch. chemist E.I. DuPont, Richmond, Va., 1954-57; student, intern Med. Coll. of Va., Richmond, 1957-62; resident ophthalmology Yale Med. Sch., New Haven, 1962-66, asst. prof., assoc. prof., 1967-74; ophthalmologist pvt. practice Grove Hill Med. Ctr., New Britain, Conn., 1974—; clin. prof. ophthalmologist Yale Med. Sch., New Haven, 1977—. Contbr. 75 articles to profl. jours. Mem. Am. Ophthal. Soc., Am. Acad. Ophthalmology, Conn. State Med. Soc., AMA. Presbyterian. Office: Grove Hill Med Ctr 300 Kensington Ave New Britain CT 06051-3916

HOWARD, RUSTIN RAY, corporate executive; b. Eugene, Oreg., Oct. 18, 1956; s. Ray L. and Dorothy V. (Johnson) H.; m. Maureen W. Howard, Dec. 17, 1979; children: Matthew, Aubrey, Danielle, Travis. BS, Brigham Young U., 1987; MBA, Cornell-Johnson Grad. Sch., Ithaca, N.Y., 1989. Missionary LDS Porto Alegre Mission, Rio Grande Do Sul, Brazil, 1976-78; ptnr. Solar Farms, Rupert, Idaho, 1979-87; analyst SROne Venture Capital, Ithaca, 1988-89; prin. H&H Techs., Ithaca, 1988-91; pres. Phyton Catalytic, Inc., Ithaca, 1990—, also bd. dirs., chief exec. officer, 1991—. Contbr.: International Mergers and Acquisitions, 1990. Leader Cub Scouts, Dryden, N.Y., 1989-91; pres. Young Men's Orgn., Rupert, 1983-86; mem. adv. bd. Tompkins County Trust Co., Cornell Biotech. Dept. Mem. Aircraft Owners and Pilots Assn., N.Y. Biotech. Assn. (legis. com.), JGSM Fingerlakes Club (bd. dirs. 1990—), Cornell Alumni Assn. (bd. dirs. 1991—). Republican. Mormon. Office: Phyton Catalytic Inc 95 Brown Rd Ithaca NY 14850-1247

HOWARD, STANLEY LOUIS, investment banker; b. New Kensington, Pa., Oct. 18, 1948; s. Stanley Joseph and Anne Irene (Mentecki) Hoderowski; m. Kathryn Lynn Franz, July 31, 1971 (div. Dec. 1981). BS, MIT, 1970; MBA, Harvard U., 1972. Sr. account exec. Cypherenetics Corp. div. ADP Network Svcs., N.Y.C., 1972-75; mgr. fin. systems IU Internat., Phila., 1975-76; v.p. Citibank, N.A., N.Y.C., 1976-81, Lehman Bros. Kuhn Loeb, N.Y.C., 1981-83; exec. v.p. Dean Witter Reynolds, Inc., N.Y.C., 1983-88; sr. v.p., dir. fin. Deutsche Bank Govt. Securities, Inc., N.Y.C., 1988-91; chief fin. officer Paresco, Inc., N.Y.C., 1991—. U.S. Sec. of Labor fellow, 1970. Republican. Roman Catholic. Home: 60 W 9th St New York NY 10011-8908 Office: Paresco Inc 51 Madison Ave New York NY 10010-1603

HOWARD, STEPHEN WRIGLEY, telecommunications executive; b. Buffalo, Sept. 7, 1940; '. Norman Wrigley and Vesta (Gow) H.; m. Eileen F. O'Neill (div. 1973); children: Elizabeth Anne, Amy Lindsay; m. Dimiti Ann Stegeman; 1 child, Sarah Winsome. BLS, Boston U., 1981. Underwriter Aetna Life & Casualty Co., Boston, 1963-66; mem. sales and mktg. staff New Eng. Telephone Co., Boston, 1966-82; mgr., cons. liaison AT&T, Morristown, N.J., 1983; ptnr. Howard Assocs., Lebanon, Maine, 1983—; adj. faculty, Boston U., 1982—; lectr., Software Inst., Andover, Mass., 1984-88. Author software. Mem. York County Citizens' Alliance, Lebanon, 1987—, Boston U. Alumnae Sch. Com., 1987—. Republican. Episcopalian.

HOWARD, VERNON ALFRED, philosophy educator; b. Skaargen, Denmark, Oct. 7, 1937; arrived in Can., 1943, came to U.S., 1945; s. Lars Alfred Jensen and Margaret Grace (Curll) Howard; m. Sonia Mora-Reyes, June 20, 1978 (div. 1982). BA, U. Maine, 1958; PhD, Ind. U., 1965. Assoc. prof. U. Western Ont., 1967-70; visiting prof. U. Pa., 1977-78; lectr. in edn. U. London, 1971-77; assoc. prof. Harvard U., 1978—, co-dir. philosophy of edn. rsch. ctr., 1983—; cons. corp. training Aetna Inst. Corp. Edn., Hartford, Conn., 1989-91. Author: Artistry: The Work of Artists, 1982, Thinking on Paper, 1986, Varieties of Thinking, 1990, Learning by all Means, 1992, Thinking Together, 1992. Recipient EXXON Edn. Found. grantee, 1983-86, Latsic Found. grantee, 1987-90; John Dewey fellow, 1981-82. Fellow Union Club St. John; mem. Harvard Club of Boston. Office: Harvard U Larsen Hall 506 Cambridge MA 02138

HOWARTH, WILLIAM LOUIS, education educator, writer; b. Mpls., Nov. 26, 1940; s. Nelson Oliver and Mary Watson (Prindiville) H.; m. Barbara Ann Brown, Aug. 16, 1963; children: Jennifer Lynn, Jeffrey Todd. BA, U. Ill., 1962; MA, U. Va., 1963, PhD, 1967. Instr. Princeton (N.J.) U., 1966-68, asst. prof., 1968-70, prof., 1970-73, assoc. prof., 1973-81, prof., 1981—. Author: The John McPhee Reader, 1976, The Book of Concord, 1982, Thoreau in the Mountains, 1982, Traveling the Trans-Canada, 1987; editor-in-chief Writings of Henry D. Thoreau, 1972-80. NEH fellow, 1977. Mem. MLA, Am. Studies Assn., Soc. Environ. Journalists, Coun. on Energy and Environ. Studies, Thoreau Soc. Am. (pres. 1976-78), Nat. Geographic Soc. (contract writer 1978—), Nat. Rural Studies Coun. (assoc., exec. com. Santa Fe coun.), Phi Beta Kappa. Office: Princeton U 22 Mccosh Cir Princeton NJ 08544-0001

HOWE, ANN CLARK, science educator; b. Richmond, Va.; d. William Baker and Louise (Graham) Clark; m. Charles Alfred Howe; children: Judith, Marjorie, David. MA, U. N.C., 1949; PhD, U. Tex., Austin, 1969. Prof. Syracuse (N.Y.) U., 1970-83; chair dept. math. and sci. edn. N.C. State U., Raleigh, 1983-89; chair dept. tchr. edn. U. Md., College Park, 1989—; cons. state and nat. edn. agys., 1975—; bd. dirs. Randolph-Macon Acad. Contbr. articles to profl. jours. Mem. AAAS (pres. edn. sect. 1978—), Nat. Assn. Rsch. in Sci. Teaching (pres., bd. dirs. 1980-84), Nat. Sci. Tchrs. Assn.

(bd. dirs.). Democrat. Unitarian-Universalist. Office: U Md 2311 Benjamin Bldg College Park MD 20742

HOWE, ARTHUR, journalist; b. Cleve. Grad. U. Pa., 1972. Formerly journalist with News Jour., Wilmington, Del., and other newspapers; former reporter The Phila. Inquirer, from 1979; now pres., pub. Montgomery Newspapers Inc., Fort Washington, Pa. Recipient Pulitzer Prize in Nat. Reporting, 1986. Office: Montgomery Newspapers PO Box 1628 Fort Washington PA 19034-8628

HOWE, GORDON, former professional hockey player, sports association executive; b. Saskatoon, Sask., Can., Mar. 31, 1928; came to U.S., 1944; s. Albert Clarence and Katherine (Schultz) H.; m. Colleen Janet Joffa, Apr. 15, 1953; children: Marty Gordon, Mark Steven, Cathleen Jill, Murray Albert. Student pub. schs., Can. Profl. hockey player with Detroit Red Wings Hockey Club (Nat. Hockey League), 1944-73, also past v.p.; with Houston Aeros (World Hockey Assn.), 1971-73, New Eng. Whalers (World Hockey Assn.), Hartford, Conn., 1977-78; dir. player devel. Hartford Whalers, NHL, 1980-82; spl. asst. to chmn., mng. ptnr. Hartford Whalers, 1982-92. Author: Gordie Howe, No. 9; (with Colleen Howe and Charles Wilkens) After the Applause, 1989. Recipient Order of Can. medal, 1971; named Canada's Athlete of Year, 1963; holder Hart Meml. Trophy, Art Ross Trophy, Lester Patrick Trophy; 12-time mem. NHL 1st All-Star Team; 9-time mem. NHL 2d All-Star Team; named Most Valuable Player and to 1st All-Star Team World Hockey Assn., 1974. Mem. Nat. League Hall of Fame, Mich. Sports Hall of Fame, Omaha Sports Hall of Fame. Congregationalist. Address: 6645 Peninsula Dr Traverse City MI 49684

HOWE, JAMES EVERETT, investment company executive; b. N.Y.C., Mar. 30, 1930; s. Ernest Joseph and Gladys Montgomery (Sills) H.; m. Judith DePuy Keating, May 9, 1959; children: James E., Jr., David K. BA, Williams Coll., 1952; MBA, Columbia U., 1954. Chartered fin. analyst. Statistician J.P. Morgan & Co., N.Y.C., 1956-59; investment research officer Morgan Guaranty Trust Co., N.Y.C., 1959-65; sr. analyst Tri-Continental Corp., N.Y.C., 1965-80; asst. v.p. J&W Seligman & Co., N.Y.C., 1980-81; chmn. investment com. Charles Edison Fund, East Orange, N.J., 1981—. Trustee Brook Found., N.Y.C., 1966-72, Charles Edison Fund, 1972—; bd. deacons Brick Presbyn. Ch., N.Y.C., 1963-66. 1st lt. USAF, 1954-56, ETO. Recipient Fin. award Wall St. Jour., 1954, award of Appreciation Thomas A. Edison Found., 1977. Mem. N.Y. Soc. Security Analysts, Inst. Chartered Fin. Analysts, Machinery Analyst of N.Y. (pres. 1967-68, charter mem.), Environ. Control Analysts of N.Y. (pres. 1975, charter mem.), Jamestown Soc. (charter), Genesee Valley Club (Rochester, N.Y.), Short Hills Club (N.J.), Alpha Kappa Psi (pres. 1953-54). Republican. Presbyterian. Home: 33 Keats Rd Short Hills NJ 07078-2913 Office: Charles Edison Fund 101 S Harrison St East Orange NJ 07018-1702

HOWE, RUSSELL WARREN, writer, journalist; b. London, Aug. 1, 1925; came to U.S., 1955; s. Selby Stanley and Eleanor Grace (Rushworth) H.; m. Naomi Parker-Thomson, May 15, 1964 (div. 1987); children: Desson Warren, Deirdre Warren, Russell Warren II; m. Yong-Ja Kim, Sept. 25, 1987. Lic.-ès-lettres, U. Sorbonne, 1948. Staff corr. Reuters, Paris, 1948-52; ind. writer France and Africa, 1952-55; staff corr. London Sunday Times, N.Y.C., 1955-57; ind. writer Africa, 1957-59; adviser to prime min. Govt. of Togo, West Africa, 1959-60; staff corr. Washington Post, Africa, 1960-65; ind. writer worldwide, 1965-68; staff corr. Christian Sci. Monitor, Africa, 1968-69, Baltimore Sun, Africa, 1969-71; media dir. Del. of European Community, Washington, 1972-75; ind. writer, Washington, 1972-82; def. corr. Washington Times, 1982-83, diplomatic corr., 1983-85; vis. prof. U. Dakar, Senegal, 1967-71; lectr. USIA, 1984-86. Author: The Light and the Shadows, 1952, Behold, the City, 1954, Theirs the Darkness, 1956, Black Star Rising, 1958, Black Africa: From Prehistory to the Eve of Colonial Rule, 1965, Black Africa: Colonial Rule and Modern Times, 1966, The African Revolution, 1968, Along the Afric Shore, 1975, Weapons: The International Game of Arms, Money and Diplomacy, 1980, Mata Hari--The True Story, 1986, The Koreans: Passion and Grace, 1988, Flight of the Cormorants, 1989, The Hunt for Tokyo Rose, 1990, Sleeping with the FBI, 1992; (with Sarah Hays Trott) The Power Peddlers, 1977. Sgt. RAF, 1943-46, ETO. Woodrow Wilson Internat. Ctr. scholar, Washington, 1972; Ford Found. fellow, 1965-66; recipient Bronze Venus Houston Internat. Film Festival, 1981, Mil. Affairs award World Watch Inst., 1990. Mem. Internat. Press Inst., Fgn. Corrs. Assn. (pres. 1987-89), PEN, Washington Ind. Writers, Inst. Journalists, Asia Soc., Japan-Am. Soc., Royal Commonwealth Soc., Smithsonian Assocs., Overseas Press Club, Sigma Delta Chi. Zen Buddhist. Home and Office: PO Box 32221 Washington DC 20007-0521

HOWE, WESLEY JACKSON, medical supplies company executive; b. Jersey City, June 7, 1921; s. Wesley Veith and Phyllis (Jackson) H.; m. Suzanne Rodrock, July 20, 1946; children: Marc Edward, Richard Douglas, Suzanne. ME, Stevens Inst. Tech., Hoboken, N.J., 1943, MS, 1953; DEng (hon.), Stevens Inst. Tech., 1981; LHD, U. N.J. Medicine & Dentistry (hon.), 1988. With Becton, Dickinson and Co., Rutherford, N.J., 1949—, group v.p., then exec. v.p., 1970-72, pres., chief exec. officer, dir., 1972-80, chmn. bd., 1980—, chief exec. officer, dir., 1980-89, pres., 1983-87; former dir. Ecolab Inc., Lukens, Inc; chmn. N.J. Mfrs. Ins. Co., N.J., Re-Ins. Co., N.J. Bus. and Industry. Chm. emeritus bd. trustees Stevens Inst. Tech. 1st lt. AUS, 1944-46, '51-52. Mem. N.J. C. of C. (dir.). Clubs: Arcola (N.J.) Country, Upper Montclair (N.J.) Country; University (N.Y.C.). Office: Becton Dickinson & Co 1 Becton Dr Franklin Lakes NJ 07417-1815

HOWELL, BARBARA FENNEMA, research chemist; b. Chgo., Dec. 18, 1924; d. Nick and Fern Alma (First) Fennema; m. Wilbur Alexander Howell, June 29, 1946; children: Susan Barbara, Gary Wilbur, Michael Owen. BA, U. Minn., 1946; MS, Kans. State U., 1949; PhD, U. Mo., 1964. Asst. prof. Kans. State Coll. of Emporia, 1964-69; postdoctoral fellow U. Mo., Rolla, 1969-71; rsch. chemist Nat. Inst. Standards and Tech., Gaithersburg, Md., 1971-87; materials engr. Naval Surface Warfare Ctr., Annapolis, Md., 1987—. Contbr. articles to profl. jour. Recipient Gordon award Chem. Soc. Washington, 1987. Mem. AAAS, Am. Chem. Soc. (councilor 1983-89, 92—). Democrat. Methodist. Office: Naval Surface Warfare Ctr Annapolis Detachment Code 2844 Annapolis MD 21402

HOWELL, BENJAMIN FRANKLIN, JR., geophysicist, educator; b. Princeton, N.J., June 12, 1917; s. Benjamin Franklin and Claire M. (Mead) H.; m. Constance M. Benson, June 30, 1943; children: Barbara Carolyn, Catherine Ann (dec.), Bonnie Andrea, James Benjamin. A.B., Princeton U., 1939; M.S., Calif. Inst. Tech., 1942, Ph. D., 1949. Research engr. div. war research U. Calif. at San Diego, 1942-45; geophysicist United Geophys. Co., 1946-49; faculty Pa. State U., 1949—, prof. geophysics, 1953—, head dept. geophysics and geochemistry, 1949-63; asst. dean Pa. State U. (Grad. Sch.), 1968-70, asso. dean, 1970-82, dean emeritus, 1982—; Chief cons. seismologist Vibratech Engrng. Co., Hazleton, Pa., 1955-69. Author: Introduction to Geophysics, 1959, Earth and Universe, 1972, Introduction to Seismological Reseach: History and Development, 1990; Editor: Contributions in Geophysics in Honor of Beno Gutenberg, 1958. Fellow Am. Geophys. Union (sec. sect. tectonophysics 1956-59, sect. seismology 1959-63), Geol. Soc. Am.; mem. soc. Exploration Geophysics, Seismol. Soc. Am. (pres. 1963-64), Phi Beta Kappa, Sigma Xi. Baptist. Home: 1143 Smithfield Cir State College PA 16801-6424 Office: 406 Deike Bldg University Park PA 16802

HOWELL, GLORIA LELLEN, playwright; b. Memphis, Aug. 27, 1948; d. Lyman Cummings and Frances (Thornton) H. Student, U. Tenn., Martin, 1966-67, 68-69, Memphis State U., 1967-68, 69-70. Writer free-lance TV L.A., 1976-78; mgr. Opera Singer Ruth Welting, 1979-88. Playwright: (musical) Another Night at the Opera, 1990; (dramas) Fama Sanctitatis, 1991, Better, 1991, Of the Sea and the South, 1992. Recipient New Eng. Playwright's award Valley Players, Waitsfield, Vt., 1991.

HOWELL, HARLEY THOMAS, lawyer; b. Chgo., June 5, 1937; s. Harley W. and Geneva (Engelmann) H.; m. Aliceann A. McLaughlin, Apr. 23, 1983; children by previous marriage: Shelley A. Young, Rebecca L. Ciociola, Emily S. A.B., Princeton U., 1959; J.D., Yale U., 1962. Bar: Md. 1962, U.S. Supreme Ct. 1966, D.C. 1972. Law clk. to chief judge U.S. Ct. Appeals (4th cir.) 1962-63; assoc. Semmes, Bowen & Semmes, Balt., 1966-72, ptnr., 1972—; mem. Gov.'s Commn. to Revise Annotated Code Md., 1975-85; mem. standing com. on rules of practice and procedure Ct. Appeals of Md., 1985—. Bd. dirs. Balt. Symphony Orch., 1975—, sec., 1986—; bd. dirs. Balt. Opera Co., 1991—; trustee Human Devel. at Sheppard Pratt, 1986—, Sheppard & Enoch Pratt Hosp., Towson, Md., 1991—. Served to capt. JAG Corps, U.S. Army, 1963-66. Decorated Army Commendation medal. Fellow Am. Coll. Trial Lawyers; mem. ABA, Md. State Bar Assn., Balt. City Bar Assn., D.C. Bar Assn., Fed. Bar Assn., Def. Rsch. Inst., Ctr. Club, Wine and Food Soc., Wranglers Law Club (Balt.). Democrat. Home: 1012 Chestnut Ridge Dr Lutherville Timonium MD 21093-1716 Office: Semmes Bowen & Semmes 250 W Pratt St Baltimore MD 21201-2423

HOWELL, RICHARD PAUL, SR., transportation engineer; b. Sarasota, Fla., Nov. 20, 1927; s. Paul Augustus and Mary Amanda (Snead) H.; m. Judith Kay Eshelman, Sept. 6, 1958; children: Richard Paul, Thomas Bradford, Robert Greggson, Mary Amanda. BS in Civil Engring., Mich. State U., 1949. Registered profl. engr., Ohio, Mass., R.I., Conn., N.Y., N.J., Pa., Del., D.C., Md. Track supr. to div. engr. Pa. R.R. and successor co. Penn Cen. R.R., 1949-71; chief R.R. engr. to v.p. Deleuw, Cather & Co., Washington, 1971—; tech. advisor to financing banks Eurotunnel, London, 1989-90; mem. Mich. State U. Alumni Engring. Coun., 1968-72; dep. gen. mgr. Northeast Corridor Rail Improvement Program, 1978-82. Contbr. articles on transp. to profl. publs. Dist. chmn. Md. gubernatorial campaign, 1967. Lt. USNR, 1945-46, Civil Engr. Corps Res. USNR. Recipient Toulmin medal Am. Soc. Mil. Engrs., 1979; named Railroader of Mo., Progressive Railroads, 1979. Mem. Am. Ry. Engring. Assn., Transp. Rsch. Bd., Camp Hill Jr. C. of C. (pres. 1961-62), Masons, Phi Delta Theta. Republican. Presbyterian. Home: 15205 Hannans Way Rockville MD 20853-1815 also: 27 South Terr Chautauqua NY 14722 Office: De Leuw Cather & Co 1133 15th St NW Washington DC 20005-2710

HOWELL, WILLIAM PAGE, real estate executive; b. Carnegie, Okla., July 27, 1952; s. Herman Glen and Muriel Joyce (Raby) H. BS, Southwestern U., Weatherford, Okla., 1975; MS, U. Okla., 1976. Chief exec. officer, pres. Howell Assocs., Norman, Okla., 1976-84; dir. Saudi Arabian Investment Corp., Dallas, London, 1984-87; dir. acquisitions Mitsui Fudosan (N.Y.) Inc., N.Y.C., 1987—; dir. adv. bd. Comml. Property News, N.Y.C., 1990—. Demographics coord. Dem. Nat. Com., Atlanta, 1976-77. Mem. Urban Land Inst., Assn. Fgn. Investors in U.S. Real Estate, Fedn. Internat. Adminstrs. de Bein Conseils Immobiliers, Japan Soc., N.Y. Real Estate Club. Home: 60 W 66th St Apt 30I New York NY 10023-6220

HOWELL-JONES, DAVID, editor, writer; b. Houston, Sept. 16, 1923; s. Charles Gordon and Mary Belle (Howell) Jones; m. Carolyn Walker Jones, Nov. 25, 1965. BA, Rice U., 1944; BS, Juilliard Sch. Music, 1949. Mem. editorial staff Columbia Ency., 1946-50; editor Columbia U. Press, N.Y.C., 1951-55; catalog editor Columbia Records, N.Y.C., 1956-58; chief editor U. Tex. Press, Austin, 1958-59; dir. Vanderbilt U. Press, Nashville, 1959-74; freelance editor, writer Washington, 1974—. Mem. Washington Book Pubs., Friday Morning Music Club (trustee Found. 1985—, chmn. internat. music competition 1989—). Democrat. Episcopalian. Home and Office: 4530 Connecticut Ave NW Washington DC 20008-4328

HOWELLS, WILLIAM DEAN, publishing company executive; b. Cambridge, Mass., Sept. 13, 1932; s. William White and Muriel Gurdon (Seabury) H.; m. Benitha Christina Lindeman, Dec. 29, 1962; children: Edward Stockmann, John Mead, Horace White, Rose Marie. AB, Harvard U., 1954; M Internat. Affairs, Columbia U., 1960. Intelligence analyst Dept. State, Washington, 1960-65; exec. asst. Am. Embassy, New Delhi, 1965-67; div. chief Dept. State, 1969-75; office dir. Sr. Exec. Svc., 1982-89; pres., pub. Howells House, Washington, 1990—. Author: India in Transition, 1976. Lt. USN, 1954-58, PTO. Recipient Superior Honor award Dept. of State, 1967, 82, 89, John Jacob Rogers award, 1989. Mem. Internat. Inst. Strategic Studies. Avocation: sailing. Office: Howells House PO Box 9546 Washington DC 20016-9546

HOWES, ALFRED S., business and insurance consultant; b. Troy, N.Y., Sept. 10, 1917; s. Alfred G. and Frances (Youngs) H.; m. Elizabeth Hoffner, Oct. 10, 1942; children: Wendy, Mary Lee, Constance Ellen. Student, Brown U., 1934-35, U. Ala., 1935-36, Syracuse U., 1943-44. Agt., advanced underwriting cons. for N.Y. and Vt. with Conn. Mut. Life Ins. Co.; owner bus. cons. co., 1946; pres. Employee Incentive Plans of Am., Inc.; chmn. bd. Utica Duxbak Corp., 1956-86; dir. Hyden, Inc., Outdoor Outfitters, 1960-86; pres., dir. Hyden, Inc. and Wood Realty Inc., 1970-80; bd. dirs. Emerson Plastics Corp., Insulating Shapes, Inc., Bering Trading Corp., Scotsmoor Co., Inc., Employee Incentive Plans, Inc., Killip Svcs., Inc., SVM Inc., Nursing Homes, Inc., Broad St. Realty Co., 1976-85, Smiley Bros., Inc., Mech. Tech., Inc., 1959-90, Pub. Gray Letter, Century Planning Co., Inc., Hurd Shoe Co., Wood & Hyde Co., McCormick Mgmt. Cons., 1981-89, Mohawk Valley Oil Co., Inc., AP Mew, Inc., Killip Laundering and Dry Cleaning Co. Inc., Utica Bulk Terminals Inc., Am. Paper Machinery Inc.; asst. purchasing agt. for neutral nations. Past sec., bd. dirs. N.Y.C. Estate Planning Council; bd. dirs. Placid's Parkas, Inc., 1956-82, Winchester Knitting Mills, Inc., 1960-75, J.A. Firsching & Son, Inc., 1976-85, Triple A Aircraft Corp.; mem. N.Y. State Temporary Commn. on Banking, Ins. and Fin. Services, 1983-84. Contbr. articles on taxes to profl. jours. Served with U.S. Army, ETO, 1943-46. Mem. Nat. Assn. Life Underwriters (pres. N.Y. chpt. 1965-66, life, pub. relations chmn. Million Dollar Round Table), N.Y. State Assn. Life Underwriters (chmn. com. to revise laws concerning decedents and their estates, pres. 1966-67), N.Y.C. Assn. Life Underwriters (bd. dirs., pres.), Am. Philatelic Soc., Assn. for Advanced Life Underwriting (pres. 1970-71). Clubs: Collectors, Brown (N.Y.C.); University (Albany); Fort Schuyler (Utica), Princeton (N.Y.C.), Ft. Orange (Albany). Home: 42 Fenimore Rd Scarsdale NY 10583-2252 Office: 7th Fl 488 Madison Ave New York NY 10022

HOWES, MICHAEL FRANK, chemical engineer; b. Balt., Jan. 24, 1951; s. Theodore Ignatius and Romaine (Kerr) H. BSChemE, Drexel U., 1986; MBA, Rutgers U., 1990. Chemist Dept. Def., Phila., 1982; asst. process engr. Occidental Chem. Co., Burlington, N.J., 1983; asst. rsch. scientist Mobil Cen. Rsch., Princeton, N.J., 1984; chief engr. Plastics Cons. & Mfg. Co., Camden, 1985-90; process engr. Huntsman Polypropylene, Woodbury, N.J., 1990—. V.p. Burlington County Young Reps., Mt. Holly, N.J., 1971-72; youth leader St. Paul's Ch., Pennsauken, N.J., 1981-83, com. chmn., mem. coun., 1982-83; selected for MBA Case Tournament Team, 1990. Mem. Soc. Mfg. Engrs., Am. Chem. Soc. Home: 310 S 4th St Woodbury Hgts NJ 08097-1315 Office: Huntsman Polypropylene PO Box 700 Woodbury NJ 08096-7770

HOWES, THEODORE CLARK, claims examiner; b. Ridgefield, Conn., Dec. 25, 1929; s. Robert Clark and Phyllis Evelyn (Greene) H.; m. Anne Christine Tourgee, Sept. 28, 1968. BS, Springfield (Mass.) Coll., 1956. Cert. tchr., Mass. Claims examiner Geico, Chevy Chase, Md., 1967-78, U.S. Dept. Labor, Washington, 1978—. Innovator in use of laser for mil. application. Sgt. USAF, 1948-52. Mem. Soc. Mayflower Descendants, Alden Kindred Am., Am. Legion. Republican. Congregationalist. Home: Fox Meadow Farm 17110 Bollinger School Rd Emmitsburg MD 21727-8721 Office: US Dept Labor 200 Constitution Ave NW Washington DC 20210-0002

HOWITT, ARNOLD MARTIN, university researcher, administrator, educator; b. N.Y.C., Jan. 6, 1947; s. Wilfred D. and Mildred (Wolch) H.; m. Maryalice Sloan; children: Matthew, Molly, Alexandra, Mark. BA, Columbia U., 1969; MA, Harvard U., 1971, PhD, 1976. Asst. prof. Brown U., Providence, 1974-76; asst. prof. Harvard U., Cambridge, Mass., 1976-80, assoc. prof., 1980-82, assoc. dir. Taubman Ctr. for State and Local Govt., Kennedy Sch. Govt., 1983—; cons. in field; part-time lectr. SUNY, 1984—. Author: Managing Federalism, 1984; co-author, editor: Perspectives on Management Capacity Building, 1986; contbr. articles to profl. jours. Office: Harvard U Kenndy Sch Govt 79 John F Kennedy St Cambridge MA 02138-5800

HOWITT, PAMELA TESLER, university dean, fundraiser; b. Providence, Apr. 10, 1955; d. Marvin Gerald and Marilyn (Schaffer) Tesler; m. Steven Samuel Howitt, Apr. 7, 1990. BFA, U. R.I., 1977; M in Profl. Studies, Pratt Inst., 1979. Dir. youth devel. programs Pratt Inst., Bklyn., 1979-80, dir. alumni resources, 1980-85; major gifts devel. officer Columbia U., N.Y.C., 1985-87; dir. devel. Columbia U./Columbia Presbyn. Med. Ctr., N.Y.C., 1987-89; asst. dean for devel. and external rels. Grad. Sch. Design Harvard U., Cambridge, Mass., 1989—; cons., fundraiser for various civic, polit., religious orgns. in N.Y., Mass. and R.I., 1979—. Author: (documentary) Coping with Death and Dying with Adolescents through Art Therapy. Mem. Nat. Soc. Fundraising Execs., Coun. for the Advancement and Support of Edn., Boston Soc. Architects, Univ. Club R.I., Harvard Club of Boston, Ledgemont Country Club. Office: Harvard U Grad Sch Design 48 Quincy St Cambridge MA 02138-3000

HOWLAND, RICHARD HUBBARD, architectural historian; b. Providence, Aug. 23, 1910; S. Carl Badger and Cora Augusta (Hubbard) H. A.B., Brown U., 1931, also hon. doctor's degree; A.M., Harvard U., 1933; Ph.D., Johns Hopkins U., 1946. Fellow Agora excavations, Athens, Greece, 1936-38; instr. Wellesley Coll., 1939-42; chief pictorial records sect. OSS, 1943-44; founder dept. history art Johns Hopkins, 1947, chmn. dept., 1947-56; pres. Nat. Trust for Historic Preservation, 1956-60; chmn. dept. civil history Smithsonian Instn., Washington, 1960-67; spl. asst. to sec. Smithsonian Instn., 1968-85; trustee Am. Sch. Classical Studies, Athens; founding mem. Am. Com. Internat. Commn. Historic Sites and Monuments. Author: (with Eleanor Spencer) Architecture of Baltimore, 1954, Greek Lamps and Their Survivals, 1958. Trustee, v.p. Sotterley Found., Accokeek Found., Inc.; trustee Irish Georgian Soc., Evergreen Found. Recipient O.E.B. award Queen Elizabeth, 1991; named Order of Geo I, Greece, Officer of Order of Brit. Empire, U.K., mem. U.S. Order of St. John of Jerusalem. Fellow Royal Soc. of the Arts, Phila. Athenaeum; mem. Fellows in Am. Studies, Soc. Archtl. Historians (founding mem.), English Speaking Union, Soc. Cincinnati (hon.), Md. Soc. Colonial Wars, Victorian Soc. in Am. (former pres.), Phi Gamma Delta. Clubs: Century Assn. (N.Y.C.), Knickerbocker (N.Y.C.); 14 West Hamilton Street (Balt.); 1925 F Street, Cosmos, Arts, Dacor-Bacon (Washington). Home: 3900 Cathedral Ave NW Apt 712A Washington DC 20016-5201

HOWLAND, RICHARD MOULTON, lawyer; b. Glen Cove, L.I., N.Y., Jan. 2, 1940; s. Richard Moulton and Natalie (Fuller) H.; m. Julie Rose Keschl, Sept. 28, 1974; children: Kimberly Merrill, Gillian Fuller. BA, Amherst Coll., 1961; JD, Columbia U., 1968. Bar: Mass. 1968. Assoc. firm Nutter, McLennen & Fish, Boston, 1968-69, DiMento & Sullivan, Boston, 1969-70; atty. for students U. Mass., Amherst, 1970-74; practice law, Amherst, 1974—; adj. prof. U. Mass., 1972-76; vis. lectr. Amherst Coll., 1983. Asst. moderator Town of Leverett, 1988, 89—; mem. Leverett Sch. Bldg. Com., 1988-89; trustee Art Inst. Boston, 1990—, Greenfield C. C. Found., 1991—; pres. Leverett PTO, 1981-85; pres. Interfaith Housing Corp., Amherst, 1984—; bd. dirs. Leverett Craftsmen and Artists, Inc., 1986—, treas. 1988-89, v.p. 1988-89, pres. 1989—; bd. dirs. Community Multisvc., Inc., Northampton, Mass., 1987—; trustee Wildwood Cemetery Assn. 1987—; bd. dirs., sec. Responsible Hospitality Inst., 1990—. Lt. (j.g.) USNR, 1961-65. Co-editor Mass. Lawyers Weekly, 1979—. Mem. ABA (chmn. profl. liability com. Gen. Practice Sect. 1987-90), Mass. Bar Assn. (chmn. com. on chem. dependency, Mass. Community Svc. award 1984), Franklin Bar Assn., Hampshire Bar Assn. (del. to Mass Bar Assn., sec., v.p. 1986), Assn. Trial Lawyers Am., Mass. Acad. Trial Lawyers, Amherst C. of C. (pres. 1985—), Skating Club (past v.p., treas. 1987—, Amherst). Democrat. Home: 112 Depot Rd Leverett MA 01054-9743 Office: 358 N Pleasant St Amherst MA 01002-1734

HOWLAND, ROBERT HERBERT, psychiatrist; b. St. Paul, Mar. 3, 1960; s. Herbert William and Helen Louise (Mortiz) H.; m. Donna Irene Fagan, June 18, 1982; children: Benjamin Norman, Timothy Robert, Matthew James. BS, Boston U., 1982; MD, U. Minn., 1986. Diplomate Nat. Bd. Med. Examiners, Am. Bd. Psychiatry and Neurology. Intern U. Pitts., 1986-87; resident Western Psychiat. Inst. and Clinic, Pitts., 1987-90, post-doctoral psychiatry rsch. fellow, 1989-90, asst. prof. psychiatry, 1991—; clin. psychiatrist VA Hosp., Pitts., 1988-90, Allegheny East Community Mental Health Ctr., Pitts., 1989-90. Author: (with others) The Biology of Depression, 1990, Schizophrenia and Amyotrophic Lateral Sclerosis, 1990, Anxiety Disorders, 1990, Pharmacotherapy of Dysthymia, 1991, Biological Studies of Dysthymia, 1991. Recipient Young Investigator award Nat. Alliance for Rsch. on Schizophrenia and Depression, 1991. Mem. AMA, Am. Psychiat. Assn. Republican. Roman Catholic. Office: Western Psychiat Inst 3811 Ohara St Pittsburgh PA 15213-2593

HOWLETT, D(ONALD) ROGER, art dealer, art historian; b. Syracuse, N.Y., Mar. 27, 1945; s. Donald Bliss and Dorothy Irene (Trautman) H. BA, Hamilton Coll., 1966; MA, SUNY, Cooperstown, 1967; postgrad., Yale U., 1968-69. Mem. curatorial dept. Garvan Coll., Yale U. Art Gallery, New Haven, 1967-68; mem. painting dept. Childs Gallery, Boston, 1970—, v.p., ptnr., 1972-83, pres., 1983—; pres. Childs Gallery, N.Y.C., 1983-91; councilor Emerson Gallery, Hamilton Coll., Clinton, N.Y., 1985—. Author: Sculpture of Donald De Lue, 1990, William Partridge Burpee, 1991; collections arranged: George Luks (author catalog), 1973-74, Molly Luce: Eight Decades f the American Scene (author catalog), 1983. Mem. Am. Assn. Mus., St. Botolph Club, Boston Athenaeum. Home and Office: Childs Gallery 169 Newbury St Boston MA 02116

HOWSE, W. FRANCES, academic administrator; b. Nashville, Aug. 20, 1947; s. Willie Frank and Betty Augusta (Davis) Lewis; children: Lynelle V., Allen, LaChelle L. BS with highest honors, Ten. State U., 1978; MA in Sociology, U. Pitts., 1980. Agy. liasion specialist Project Plan Allegheny Intermed. Unit, Pitts., 1980-81; instr. Careers, Inc., Pitts., 1982-83; coord., transfer svcs. La Roche Coll., Pitts., 1983-85; asst. dir. Homewood-Brushton Br. Community Coll. Allegheny, Pitts., 1985-86, asst. to v.p., exec. dean, 1986-89, dean, 1989—; Mem., bd. dirs. Homewood-Brushton Revitalization and Devel. Corp. Mem. Panel Am. Heritage, Nat. Conf. Christians and Jews, Pitts., 1984—, Nat. Coun. Negro Women, Pitts., 1988; chmn., bd. dirs. YouthBuild Pitts. Fellow Nat. Sci. Found., 1978-80. Mem. Nat. Coun. Resource Devel., East Liberty Arts Coun. (bd. dirs.). Democrat. Baptist. Office: CCAC Homewood Brushton Br 701 N Homewood Ave Pittsburgh PA 15208-1806

HOXIE, RALPH GORDON, author, educational administrator; b. Waterloo, Iowa, Mar. 18, 1919; s. Charles Ray and Ada May (Little) H.; m. Louise Lobitz, Dec. 23, 1953. BA, U. No. Iowa, 1940; MA, U. Wis., 1941; PhD, Columbia, 1950; LLD (hon.), Chung-ang U., 1965; LittD (hon.), D'Youville Coll., 1966; grad., Air War Coll., 1971; LHD (hon.), Gannon U., 1988, Wesley Coll., 1989, U. No. Iowa, 1990, Shepherd Coll., 1992. Roberts fellow Columbia, 1946-47, Roberts travelling fellow, 1947-48, asst. to provost, 1948-49; asst. prof. history, gen. editor Social Sci. Found.; asst. to chancellor U. Denver, 1950-53; project asso. Columbia Bicentennial History, 1953-54; dean Coll. Liberal Arts and Scis., L.I. U., 1954-55; acting dean C. W. Post Coll., 1954-55, dean, 1955-60, provost, 1960-62, pres., 1962-68; chancellor L.I. U., 1964-68, cons., 1968-69; pres. Center for Study of Presidency, 1969—; pub. mem. Fgn. Svc. officer selection bd. U.S. Dept. State; vis. lectr. U. Ala., U. Calif., Irvine, Columbia U., U. Colo., Colo. State U., U. Wyo., Chapman Coll., U. No. Colo., Colo. Coll., Gannon U., Gettysburg Coll., Heidelberg Coll., U. Kans., Muskingum Coll., Post Coll., St. Francis Coll. N.Y., USAF Acad., Naval War Coll., Nat. Archives, Nat. War Coll., Oglethorpe U., U. Pitts., U.Tex., El Paso, U. Wis., Northwestern U.; bd. govs. Banque Continentale br. Franklin Nat. Bank. Author: John W. Burgess, American Scholar, 1950, Command Decision and the Presidency, 1977, (with others) A History of The Faculty of Political Science, Columbia University, 1955, Organizing and Staffing the Presidency, 1980; editor: Frontiers for Freedom, 1952, The White House: Organization and Operations, 1971, The Presidency of the 1970's, 1973, The Presidency and Information Policy, 1981, The Presidency and National Security Policy, 1984 ; editor Presdl. Studies Quar., 1971—; contbg. author: (with others) Freedom and Authority in Our Time, 1953, The Coattailless Landslide, 1974, Power and the Presidency, 1976, Classics of the American Presidency, 1980, The Blessings of Liberty, 1987, Popular Images of American Presidents, 1988, Rating Game in American Politics, 1988, Science and Technology Advice to the President, Congress, and Judiciary, 1988, The American Presidency: Historical and Contemporary Perspectives, 1988, Points of View, 1988, The Presidency in Transition, 1989; contbr. articles to profl. jours. and encys. Bd. dirs. United Fund L.I., Bklyn. Inst. Arts and Scis., Tibetan Found., L.I. Council Alcoholism, Bklyn. chpt. A.R.C. Greater N.Y.; chmn., pres. bd. dirs. Am. Friends Chung-ang U.; pres. Pub. Mems. Assn. Fgn. Service; trustee Air Force Hist. Found., Kosciuszko Found. N.Y., Mackinac Coll., North Shore chpt. Am. Assn. UN, Downtown Bklyn. Assn., Council Higher

Ednl. Instns. N.Y.C.; mem. adv. bd. L. I. Air Res. Center; mem. adv. council Robert A. Taft Inst. Govt.; sec. Nassau County Commn. on Govt. Revision; co-chmn. Nassau-Suffolk Conf. Christians and Jews; dir., pres. Great-N.Y. Council Fgn. Students; bd. govs. Human Resources Ctr., N.Y. Korean Vets. Meml. Commn. Served from pvt. to capt. USAAF, 1942-46; brig. gen. USAF ret. Decorated Meritorious Service medal, Legion of Merit, numerous other medals; recipient Distinguished Service medal City N.Y., 1965; Paderewski Found. Man of Yr. award, 1966; Eloy Alfaro Internat. Found. Republic Panama Man of Year award, 1966; Alumni Achievement award U. No. Iowa; decorated Korean Cultural medal. Fellow Am. Studies Assn. Met. N.Y.; mem. Am. Hist. Assn., Internat. Assn. Univ. Pres., Am. Polit. Sci. Assn., Acad. of Polit. Sci., Navy League, Air Force Assn., Res. Officers Assn. (pres. Mitchel chpt.), V.F.W., Am. Legion, L.I. Assn. (dir.), Am. Polar Soc., Kappa Delta Pi, Pi Gamma Mu, Alpha Sigma Lambda, Delta Sigma Pi, Gamma Theta Upsilon. Republican. Episcopalian. Clubs: Century Assn., Met., Columbia Univ. Faculty House (N.Y.C.); Met. (Washington); Bklyn., Montauk (Bklyn.); Old Westbury Golf and Country and Mill River (hon.). Home: 10 Laurel Cove Rd Oyster Bay NY 11771-1920 Office: 208 E 75th St New York NY 10021

HOXTER, ALLEGRA BRANSON, radio news and freelance writer; b. Detroit, Jan. 2, 1934; d. Henry Clay and Anita (Coniglio) B.; m. Curtis Joseph Hoxter, Jan. 2, 1981. MusB, U. Mich., 1954; student, New Eng. Conservatory, 1954-55; MALS, U. Mich., 1958; student, Vienna (Austria) Acad. Music and Dramatic Arts, 1959-60. Fgn. corr. UPI, Vienna, 1960-64; editor, translator Austrian Consulate Gen., N.Y.C., 1965-67; writer, translator Curtis J. Hoxter, Inc., N.Y.C., 1967-68; radio, TV newswriter NBC, N.Y.C., 1968; radio news writer, editor Sta. WCBS, N.Y.C., 1968—; N.Y. Corr. Birmingham (Eng.) Evening Mail, 1974-81. Co-author: (hist. novel) Frontiers Aflame, 1987. Recipient Best Spot News award UPI, 1983. Mem. Writers Guild Am. East (pres. 1979-81, chmn. nat. council 1981-83), TV and Radio Working Press Assn. (sec. 1988—). Episcopal. Home: 34 Broadfield Rd New Rochelle NY 10804-2102 Office: Sta WCBS 51 W 52d St New York NY 10019

HOXTER, CURTIS JOSEPH, international economic adviser, public relations counselor; b. Marburg, Germany, July 20, 1922; s. Jacob and Hannah (Katzenstein) H.; AB, NYU, 1948, MA, 1950; m. Grace Lewis, Feb. 4, 1945 (dec.); children: Ronald Alan, Victoria Ann Finder, Audrey Theresa Strecker; m. 2d, Allegra Branson, Jan. 2, 1981. Staff contbr. AUFBAU-Reconstn., N.Y.C., 1939-40; feature writer, reporter L.I. Daily Press, 1940-42; editor, writer OWI, 1943-45; pub. info. officer Dept. State, 1945-47; info. cons. ECA, 1950-55; pub. rels. cons. various cos.; dir. pub. rels. Internat. C. of C., U.S. Coun. Internat. C. of C., 1948-53; freelance columnist Scripps-Howard Newspapers; exec. v.p. George Peabody and Assos., Inc., 1953-56; pres. Curtis J. Hoxter, Inc., internat. pub. rels. counsels and econ. and fin. advs. Adviser, U.S. Com. for UN Day; adv. on internat. econ. and fin. problems to govt. agys.; adv. U.S. Del. Disarmament Conf., London. with AUS, World War II. Decorated Comdr. Order of Merit of the Republic of Austria, 1991. Clubs: Met. (N.Y.C.), Overseas Press (N.Y.C.), Nat. Press, University (Washington), Bonnie Briar Country. Author weekly column Scripps-Howard papers, The Foreign Economic Scene; sr. advisor Internat. Economy mag.; contbr. and commentator articles to nat. mags. and newspapers. Office: 350 Lexington Ave New York NY 10016-0909

HOY, HAROLD JOSEPH, educator, management-marketing consultant; b. Pine Grove, Pa., Jan. 10, 1934; s. Harold Jefferson and Naomi E. (Fehr) H.; m. Z. Jane Brown, July 2, 1960; children: Kathryn Burgess, Elisabeth Wermuth, Suzanne, Kristen Shugrue. BS, Pa. State U., 1955; MBA, U. Hartford, 1973; postgrad., U. Conn., 1981, Pa. State U., 1990, U. Bradford, U.K., 1991. Gen. mgr. Montgomery Ward & Co., Chgo., 1955-67, D & L Stores, New Britain, Conn., 1967-81; prof. mgmt. Cen. Conn. State U., New Britain, 1974-79; prof. mktg. Pa. State U., Middletown, Pa., 1979—; pres. H.J. Hoy Assocs., Pine Grove, Pa., 1984—; founder, bd. dirs. Pa. State U. Small Bus. Devel. Ctr.; bd. dirs. U.S. Small Bus. Inst., Pa. State U., Harrisburg. Editorial reviewer various coll. book pubs. and acad. mgmt. and mktg. jours; contbr. articles to profl. jours. Active United Appeal, Harrisburg, Pa. 1st lt. Fin. Corps, U.S. Army, 1956-58, USAR, 1959-66. Mem. Am. Mktg. Assn., Acad. Mktg. Sci., Acad. Internat. Bus., Internat. Council for Sml. Bus., Masons, Elks. Home: 32 Mifflin St Pine Grove PA 17963-1432 Office: Pa State U Rt 230 Middletown PA 17057 also: PO Box 222 Marion CT 06444

HOYE, VINCENT JOSEPH, correctional education administrator, consultant; b. Boston, Sept. 15, 1933; s. Vincent Joseph and Eleanor Z. (Walsh) H.; m. Sheila Maloney, Aug. 20, 1960; children: Maura, Meeghan. AB in History and Govt., Stonehill Coll., North Eaton, Mass., 1958; MEd in Secondary Edn., Boston State U., 1981; C.A.G.S. in Edn. Adminstrn., U. Mass., Boston, 1983; C.A.G.S. in Occupational Edn., U. Mass., Amherst, 1991. Cert. sch. supt. grades K-12, prin., tchr., supt. dir. regional vocat.-tech., instr., Mass. Pres. Hoye Assocs., Boston, 1965-73; cons. New Eng. Lobster Systems, Boston, 1973—; instr. Tri County Regional Vocat./Tech., Franklin, Mass., 1979-85; vocat. coord. edn. div. Mass. Dept. Corrections, Boston, 1985-86, dept. dir., 1987, dir., 1988, supr., 1991—; supt. Va. Dept. Corrections Edn., Richmond, 1989; prin. Mass. Dept. Corrections, MCI Norfolk, 1990; mem. sch. com. Tri County Regional Vocat./Tech., 1986—; mem. standing com. div. Occupational Edn., Mass. Dept. Edn., Quincy, 1991, mem. vocat. planning Vocat. Edn. div. Va. Dept. Edn., Richmond, 1989; presenter confs. in field. Bd. dirs. North Attleboro CD, 1980-86; trustee North Attleboro Libr., 1981-85; mem. North Attleboro Dem. Town Com. Recipient Silver medal Mass. Humane Soc., Boston, 1947. Mem. Am. Assn. Sch. Adminstrs., Am. Correctional Assn., Correctional Edn. Assn. (state dir. 1988), Mass. Assn. Sch. Com. (chair energy com. 1987), Am. Vocat. Assn., Irish Cultural Assn., Mass. Bur. Pipefitters and Refrigeration Technicians, Pi Sigma Alpha, Pi Lambda Theta, Kappa Delta Pi. Democrat. Roman Catholic. Office: Mass Dept Corrections Edn Div 125 S Huntington Ave Jamaica Plain MA 02130-4798

HOYER, EDWARD JOSEPH, JR., librarian, editor; b. New Haven, Conn., Nov. 13, 1952; s. Edward Joseph and Lillian (Stannard) H.; m. Terri Kozlak, June 11, 1976; 1 child, Beth Ann Marie. BA, U. Conn., 1974; MLS, So. Conn. State U., 1978, MS, 1980. Cert. med. response technician I, Conn. Asst. periodicals libr. Hilton C. Buley Libr. So. Conn. State U., New Haven, 1977—. Editor, reporter (newsletter) The GrimFacts, 1991—; editor, contbr. (literary mag.) The Malcontent, 1991—. Part-time community svc. officer Glastonbury (Conn.) Police Dept., 1985—. Office: So Conn State U 501 Crescent St New Haven CT 06515

HOYER, JOHN RICHARD, pediatrician; b. Mpls., May 13, 1938; s. Ludolf Julius and Inez (Fuglesteen) H.; m. Carol E. Anderson, Aug. 20, 1983; children: Rolf William, John Steen. BA, Grinnell (Iowa) Coll., 1960; MD, Harvard U., 1964. Diplomate Am. Bd. Pediatrics. Intern in pediatrics U. Minn. Hosps., Mpls., 1964-65, resident in pediatrics, 1965-67, fellow in pediatric nephrology, 1970-73; med. researcher Phila.; asst. prof. pediatrics U. Minn., Mpls., 1973-74, Cornell Med. Coll., N.Y.C., 1974-76, Harvard Med. Sch., Boston, 1976-79; prof. pediatrics UCLA, 1979-83, U. Pa. Sch. Medicine, Phila., 1983—; vis. lectr. biol. chemistry Harvard Med. Coll., 1973-74; assoc. prof. medicine U. Pa., 1983-88, prof. medicine, 1988—; vis. scientist Dept. Medicine, U. Cambridge, 1989-90; established investigator Am. Heart Assn., 1974-79. Maj. U.S. Army, 1967-69. Mem. Phi Beta Kappa. Home: 9 Hathaway Cir Wynnewood PA 19096-1901 Office: Children's Hosp of Phila 34th St and Civic Ctr Blvd Philadelphia PA 19014

HOYER, LEON WILLIAM, physician, educator; b. Mpls., Mar. 6, 1936; s. Ludolf J. and Inez (Fuglesteen) H.; m. Diane Desmond Lawrence, Dec. 30, 1960; children: Helen Kristin, Sharon Anne, Erik William. AB, Harvard U., 1958; MD, U. Minn., 1962. Diplomate Am. Bd. Internal Medicine, Nat. Bd. Med. Examiners. Intern and asst. resident in medicine Presbyn. Hosp., N.Y.C., 1962-64; assoc. resident in medicine, fellow in hematology, asst. prof. medicine Strong Meml. Hosp.-U. Rochester Med. Ctr., 1966-70; prof. medicine, head hematology div. U. Conn. Sch. Medicine, Farmington, 1970-85, clin. prof. medicine, 1985—; dir. specialized ctr. for rsch. in transfusion medicine Holland Lab., ARC Blood Svcs., Rockville, Md., 1985—; adj. prof. genetics George Washington U., Washington, 1988—; chmn. med. and sci. adv. com. Nat. Hemophilia Found., N.Y.C., 1982-85; mem. hematology study sect. NIH, Bethesda, Md., 1976-80, 87-91. Editor: Factor VIII Inhibitors, 1984, Recombinant Technology in Hemostasis and Thrombosis, 1991; contbr. over 80 articles and 45 revs. to profl. publs., chpts. to books. Bd. dirs. Hartford (Conn.) chpt. ARC, 1976-78; mem. med. adv. com. Hartford County Lung Assn., 1973-76; mem. exec. com. coun. on thrombosis Am. Heart Assn., Dallas, 1981-83. Sr. surgeon USPHS, 1964-66. J. Macy Found. faculty scholar, 1978-79; recipient award for Excellence in Teaching, U. Conn. Alumni Assn., Murry Thelin Rsch. award Nat. Hemophilia Found., 1981; grantee Nat. Heart, Lung and Blood Inst., 1968—. Mem. Am. Soc. Hematology (chair publs. com. 1990—), Am. Soc. Clin. Investigation, Internat. Soc. Thrombosis and Hemostasis (sci. and standardization com. 1985-90). Home: 6 Bolling Ln Bethesda MD 20817-4004 Office: Holland Lab ARC 15601 Crabbs Branch Way Rockville MD 20855-2736

HOYER, PAUL JEAN, forensic pathologist; b. Chgo., Feb. 13, 1943; s. Ernest C. and Aviva Hoyer; m. Helen Leibowitz, Nov. 25, 1973; children: Rachel, Natalie, Sarah. BA in Chemistry, Reed coll., 1964; PhD in Chemistry, Northwestern U., 1968; MD, Jefferson Med. Coll., 1976. Rsch. chemist E I DuPont, Wilmington, Del., 1968-72; resident physician Jefferson Hosp., Phila., 1976-80; pathologist Einstein Med. Ctr., Phila., 1980-81, City of Phila., 1981—. Fellow Coll. Am. Pathologists, Am. Acad. Forensic Scis.; mem. Nat. Assn. Med. Examiners, Pa. Assn. Pathologists. Home: 2114 Spruce St Philadelphia PA 19103 Office: Office of Med Examiner 321 University Ave Philadelphia PA 19104

HOYER, PHYLLIS SCARBOROUGH, elementary school educator; b. Salisbury, Md., Oct. 14, 1938; d. Paul Daniel and Norma (Luettinger) Scarborough; m. Lawrence Cogswell Hoyer, July 8, 1961; children: Brian Lawrence, Andrew Scarborough. BS, Hood Coll., 1960; MEd, Towson State U., 1986; post grad., Hood Coll., U. Md. Cert. early childhood edn., home econs., Md. Tchr. Anne Arundel County Bd. of Edn., Annapolis, Md., 1960-61, Washington County Bd. of Edn., Hagerstown, Md., 1961-64, Frederick County Bd. of Edn., Md., 1972—; chairperson communication com., 1984-85; tchr. adv. com., 1977-80, 87-89; team leader, 1989-92; rep. kindergarten class, 1989-92. Instr. Frederick County YMCA, 1976-79; participating mem. Earthwatch, Orca Survey, 1989, Fiji Coral Communities, 1990, Canary Island Sea Life, 1992. Recipient Hon. Mention award Nat. Geographic Soc. Photography Contest, 1991. Mem. NEA, Md. State Tchrs. Assn., Frederick County Tchrs. Assn. (tchrs. rep. 1980-83), Nature Conservancy. Republican. Home: 8398 Cub Hunt Ct Walkersville MD 21793-9325 Office: Thurmont Elem Sch 805 E Main St Thurmont MD 21788-1798

HOYER, STENY HAMILTON, congressman; b. N.Y.C., June 14, 1939; s. Steen T. and Jean Baldwin (Slade) H.; m. Judith Elaine Pickett, June 17, 1961; children: Susan, Stefany, Anne. B.S., U. Md., 1963; LL.B., Georgetown U., 1966. Bar: Md. 1966. Exec. asst. to U.S. senator, 1962-66; mem. Haislip & Yewell, Marlow Heights, Md., 1966-69, Hoyer & Fannon, District Heights, Md., 1969-81; pvt. practice law, 1981—; mem 97th-102nd Congresses from 5th Md. dist., 1981—, mem. appropriations com., also Democratic steering and policy com.; chmn. House Dem. Caucus 97th-101st Congresses from 5th Md. dist., 1989—; co-chmn. Commn. on Security and Coop. in Europe; mem. Md. Senate, 1966-78, pres., 1975-78, chmn. Prince George's County del., mem. fin., joint budget and audit coms., 1968, chmn. joint commn. on intergovtl. cooperation, 1971. Mem. Md. Bd. Higher Edn., 1978-81; mem. Balt. Council Fgn. Relations; bd. visitors U. Md. Sch. Pub. Affairs. Mem. U. Md. Alumni Assn. (trustee), Phi Sigma Alpha, Omicron Delta Kappa, Delta Theta Phi, Sigma Chi. Home: 11822 Bishops Content Mitchellville MD 20716 Office: Longworth House Office Bldg Rm 1705 Washington DC 20515

HOYES, DONALD JAMES, publishing executive; b. Johnson City, N.Y., May 11, 1932; s. James and Edith (Mason) H.; m. Barbara Mae Westfall, June 5, 1953; children: Philip D., Susan D., Terry L, Thomas E., Donald J. Jr., Cynthia L. BS in Chemistry, SUNY, Binghamton, 1955; postgrad., U.S. Naval Postgrad. Sch., 1963-64; MS in Chemistry, U. Pa., 1967. Commd. ensign USN, 1956, advanced through grades to capt., 1977; comdg. officer Navy Combat Squadron, 1967-71; ops. officer USS Guadalcanal, Aircraft Carrier, 1971-74; assoc. chmn. math. dept. U.S. Naval Acad., Annapolis, Md., 1974-76, dean faculty/fin., 1976-77; dept. head Naval Intelligence, Suitland, Md., 1977-80; sr. engr. Vitro Corp., Silver Spring, Md., 1980-86; pres. Internat. Libr., Gaithersburg, Md., 1986—; pub. Internat. Libr., Gaithersburg, 1986—. Editor: Advertising Law Anthology, 1986-91, Insurance Law Anthology, 1986-91, Environmental Law Anthology, 1991. Mem. AAAS, Am. Chem. Soc., Am. Def. Preparedness Assn., Retired Officers Assn., Washington Book Pubs. Assn., Officers and Faculty Club. Methodist. Home: 604 Bay Green Dr Arnold MD 21012-2009 Office: Internat Libr 101 Lakeforest Blvd Ste 270 Gaithersburg MD 20877-2611

HOYLE, RANDY LOWELL, insurance executive; b. Jefferson, Iowa, Apr. 2, 1953; s. Lowell Eugene and Joyce Dwayne (Buntrock) H.; m. Barbara Jane Baird, May 18, 1975; 1 child, Valerie Jane. BS, No. Ill. U., Dekalb, 1975; MBA, Western Mich. U., 1989. With Hickman Bus. Products, Dekalb, 1969-75; underwriter Comml. Union Ins., Bloomington, Ill., 1975-78, territorial mgr., 1978-83, br. mgr., 1983-84; underwriting mgr. Foremost Ins. Co., Grand Rapids, Mich., 1984-86, asst. v.p. comml. underwriting div., 1986-91; v.p. ops. support GRE Ins. Group, N.Y.C., 1991—. Mem. Risk and Ins. Mgmt. Soc., Toastmasters. Republican. United Methodist. Office: GRE Ins Group 61 Broadway 33d Fl New York NY 10006

HOYT, EARL EDWARD, JR., industrial designer; b. Binghamton, N.Y., July 16, 1936; s. Earl Edward and Lea (LaRue) H.; m. Bernice Phillips Maseritz, Aug. 20, 1960; children: Earl Edward III, Justin Phillips. B with honors in Indsl. Design, Pratt Inst., 1960. Designer Donald Deskey Assocs., N.Y.C., 1960-65; pres. The Hoyt Group Inc., Franklin Lakes, N.J., 1965—; instr. Sch. Visual Arts, N.Y.C., Pratt Inst., Rutgers Sch. Package Engring.; lectr. in field. Awarded over 40 patents in field. Served with U.S. Army, 1954-56. Recipient awards archtl. design concept Am. Inst. Architects, 1964, Package Yr. Package Design Mag., 1970, Grand/Excellence in Design and Quality Soc. Plastic Industy, 1972, design Am. Inst. Graphic Artists Competition, 1st prize splty. design innovation-1st prize household products-1st prize communication excellence N.J. chpt. Packaging Inst. USA, 1979, package yr. Food and Drug Packaging Mag., 1978, 80, Jupiter Engring. excellence in design Western Plastics Exposition, 1980, package design excellence Clio, 1978, 81, 87, outstanding packaging achievement N.J. Packaging Execs. Club, 1982, 83, 86 (best of show/package yr.). Mem. Indsl. Designers Soc. Am. Republican. Home: 228 Hidden Pond Path Franklin Lakes NJ 07417-1615 Office: The Hoyt Group Inc PO Box 686 Franklin Lakes NJ 07417-0686

HOYT, ELLEN, artist, educator; b. Bklyn., Nov. 8, 1933; d. Martin and Estelle (Rabinowitz) Reiss; m. Jack Hoyt, July 1, 1954; children: Elyse, Laurence. Student, N.Y. State Tech. Coll., 1951. Tchr. art Kingsway Acad., Bklyn., 1963-77, Studio Dragonette, Bklyn., 1977-84, El Art Studio, Bklyn., 1984—; art cons. Salute to Israel Parade, N.Y.C., 1973-78; art juror All Communities Art, Bklyn., 1988-90; art demonstrator, lectr., 1985—. Exhibited in group shows Washington Square, N.Y.C., 1979—, Bklyn. Mus., 1981, 83, Met. Mus., N.Y.C., 1979, Stohr Mus., Nebr., 1985, Pa. State, 1986, Pan Am. Bldg., N.Y.C., 1991, Vista Hotel, N.Y.C., 1991; solo exhibits include Ethical Culture, N.Y.C., 1985, N.Y.C. Librs., 1980, 85, 86, 91, Belanthi Gallery, N.Y.C., 1982; permanent collections include FAB Steel Corp., L.A., Minigrip Ltd., N.Y.C., Gateway Nat. Park, N.Y.C. Active Sierra Club, N.Y.C., 1980—. Recipient Best in Show award Bklyn. Mus., 1983; scholar Washington Square Outdoor Art Exhibit, 1979. Mem. Am. Watercolor Soc., Nat. Arts League, Nat. Artists Profl. League, Bklyn. Watercolor Soc. (demonstrator 1970—, sec., historian 1978-91). Home and Studio: 1551 E 29th St Brooklyn NY 11229

HOYT, HENRY HAMILTON, JR., pharmaceutical and toiletry company executive; b. Orange, N.J., Aug. 10, 1927; s. Henry Hamilton and Anna Clark (Orcutt) H.; m. Muriel Virginia Christie, Feb. 5, 1960. A.B. cum laude, Princeton U., 1949. With Carter Wallace Inc., N.Y.C., 1950—, chmn. bd., chief exec. officer, 1975—. Bd. dirs. Deafness Rsch. Found., 1977—; trustee Pingry Sch., Hillside, N.J., 1970-78, pres. bd. dirs., 1972—. Served with Transp. Corps U.S. Army, 1946-47. Mem. Cosmetic, Toiletry and Fragrance Assn. (dir. 1965—, treas. 1966-76), Pharm. Mfrs. Assn. (dir. 1971-75), Proprietary Assn. (dir. 1970—). Episcopalian. Clubs: Univ., Met., Princeton of N.Y.; Baltusrol Golf (Springfield, N.J.); Oyster Harbors (Osterville, Mass.). Office: Carter-Wallace Inc 1345 Ave Of The Americas New York NY 10105-0099*

HOYT, JOHN WILLIAM, physician, health facility administrator, educator, consultant; b. Ashtabula, Ohio, July 3, 1945; m. Adaire L. Lisowski, Sept. 5, 1964; children: John Alexander, Julie Elizabeth, Lauren Meredith. BS, Baldwin Coll., 1967; MD, U. Cin., 1971. Intern Good Samaritan Hosp., Cin., 1971-72; resident in anesthesia Naval Regional Med. Ctr., Portsmouth, Va., 1972-74, fellow in critical care, 1975, dir. ICU dept. anesthesia, 1976-78; fellow in critical care U. Pitts., 1974-75, clin. assoc. prof. anesthesia and critical care medicine, 1984-88, clin. prof., 1988—; med. dir. med.-surg. ICU U. Va. Med. Ctr., Charlottesville, 1978-83, assoc. prof. anesthesia, 1982-83; head divsn. critical care medicine, dir. M/SICU St. Francis Med. Ctr., Pitts., 1983-89, chmn. dept critical care medicine, 1990—; med. dir. St. Francis Critical Care Transport, Pitts., 1985—; prof. dept. clin. pharmacy Duquesne U., Pitts., 1989—; adj. assoc. prof. dept. theology Duquesne U., Pitts., 1990—; cons. critical care edn. West Pa. Hosp., Pitts., 1989—. Author: Problems in Critical Care, 1991, Essentials of Surgical Critical Care, 1991, Critical Care Clinics of North America, 1992; editor: Critical Care Practice, 1991. Lt. comdr. USN, 1972-78. Fellow Am. Coll. Chest Physicians, Am. Coll. Critical Care Medicine; mem. Soc. Critical Care Medicine (coun.). Home: 3920 Shadowood Ct Allison Park PA 15101 Office: St Francis Med Ctr 45th St at Penn Ave Pittsburgh PA 15201

HOYTE, ROBERT MIKELL, chemistry educator; b. N.Y.C., Nov. 8, 1943; s. Albert Edward and Helen Ermine (Mikell) H.; m. Cheryl Patrice Browne, Nov. 21 1987; 1 child, Imara-Safi. BS cum laude, L.I. U., 1964; MS, Rutgers U., 1967, PhD, 1968. Asst. scientist Brookhaven Nat. Lab., Upton, N.Y., 1968-71; asst. chemistry prof. Medgar Evers Coll. CUNY, Bklyn., 1971-72; asst. prof. Coll. at Old Westbury (N.Y.) SUNY, 1972-74, assoc. prof., 1974-84, prof. Coll. at Old Westbury, 1984-90, disting. teaching prof. Coll. at Old Westbury, 1990—; vis. fellow Yale U. Sch. of Medicine, New Haven, 1980-81. Patentee in field; contbr. articles to profl. jours. Faculty grantee SUNY, 1976, NIH-Nat. Inst. Gen. Med. Scis. -Minority Access to Rsch. Careers faculty fellow, 1980, '90. Minority Biomed. Rsch. Support Program grantee Div. Rsch. Resources and Nat. Inst. Gen. Med. Scis., 1980—; travel grantee NRC, 1991. Mem. Am. Chem. Soc. (bd. dirs. local chpt. 1976-82, sec. local chpt. 1976-78, alt. councilor local chpt. 1983-84, edn. com. mem. local chpt. 1980, chmn. gen papers, div. chem. edn., 1981). Office: SUNY Coll at Old Westbury Chemistry Dept PO Box 210 Old Westbury NY 11568-0210

HOZACK, WILLIAM JAMES, orthopaedic surgeon, educator; b. Belfast, No. Ireland, Apr. 3, 1956; came to U.S., 1981; s. William James and Margaret Elizabeth (Malcomson) H.; m. Ann Dupuis, Aug. 27, 1977; children: James, Catherine, Bryan, Erin. BA cum laude, Harvard U., 1977; MD, McGill U., Montreal, Can., 1981. Diplomate Am. Bd. Orthopedic Surgery. Orthopaedic resident U. Pa., Phila., 1981-86; total joint fellow Jefferson Dept. Orthopaedics Rothman Inst., Phila., 1986-87; asst. prof. orthpaedics U. Miami, Fla., 1987-89; asst. prof. Jefferson Dept. Orthopaedics Rothman Inst., Phila., 1989—, dir. orthopaedic rsch., 1989—. Author: Complications of Total Hip Replacement, 1988; author, editor: The Hip, 1991; co-editor: (jour.) Seminars in Arthroplasty. Mem. AMA, Am. Acad. Orthopaedic Surgeons, Assn. for Arthritic Hip and Knee Surgery, Orthopaedic Rsch. Soc., Pa. Med. Soc., Orthopaedic Soc., Harvard Club of Phila., Phila. Cricket Club, Wissahickan Skating Club. Office: The Rothman Inst 800 Spruce St Philadelphia PA 19107

HRABOWSKI, FREEMAN ALPHONSA, III, university administrator; b. Birmingham, Ala., Aug. 13, 1950; s. Freeman A. II and Maggie (Geeter) H.; m. Jacqueline Coleman, Aug. 29, 1970; 1 child, Eric. BA, Hampton (Va.) Inst., 1970; MA, U. Ill., 1971, PhD, 1975. Asst. dean student svcs., vis. asst. prof. U. Ill., Champaign-Urbana, 1974-76; assoc. dean grad. studies Ala. A&M U., Normal, 1976-77; v.p. for acad. affairs, dean arts and scis. Coppin State Coll., Balt., 1977-87; exec. v.p. U. Md. Baltimore County, Balt., 1987-92, interim pres., 1992—, dir. Meyerhoff Scholarship program, 1989—. Mem. Md. Gov.'s Commn. on State Taxes and Tax Structure, Annapolis, 1990; co-chair Ptnrs. for Giving, Balt., 1990; chair Md. Humanities Coun., Balt., 1991; bd. dirs. U. Md. Med. System, Associated Cath. Charities, Balt.; v.p. bd. trustees Balt. City Life Mus. Recipient 20 Yr. Outstanding Alumnus award Hampton U., 1990. Mem. Phi Kappa Phi. Baptist. Home: 2709 Lawina Rd Baltimore MD 21216-1608 Office: U Md Baltimore County Baltimore MD 21228

HRINDA, JOHN JOSEPH, manufacturing executive; b. Pottsville, Pa., Apr. 26, 1951; s. John James and Dorthory (Slashinski) H.; m. Kathleen Joann Hrinda, June 10, 1972. AB, Harrisburg (Pa.) Area Community Coll., 1979; BBA, Pa. State U., 1983. Lab. technician Pa. State Dept. Environ. Resources, Harrisburg, 1970-72; press operator AMP Inc., Williamstown, Pa., 1972-73, product control scheduler, 1973-78; basic product mgr. AMP Inc., Harrisburg, Pa., 1978-79; plant supr. AMP Inc., Williamstown, Pa., 1979-82, quality supr., 1982-89, purchasing supr., 1989—; div. purchasing mgr. Goulds Pumps, Inc., Ashland, Pa., 1989—, mgr. mfg. and materials. Mem. Purchasing Mgmt. Assn., Mfg. Assn., Schuylkill County (chmn. 1990-91), KC (4 degree), Schuylkill County C. of C. Democrat. Roman Catholic. Office: Goulds Pumps Inc Ashland PA 17098

HRYCAK, PETER, mechanical engineer, educator; b. Przemysl, Poland, July 8, 1923; came to U.S., 1949, naturalized, 1956; s. Eugene and Ludmyla (Dobrzanska) H.; m. Rea Meta Limberg, June 13, 1949; children: Maria (dec.), Michael Paul, Orest W.T., Alexandra Martha. Student, U. Tubingen, Germany, 1946-48; B.S. with high distinction, U. Minn., 1954, M.S., 1955, Ph.D., 1960. Registered profl. engr., N.J. Adminstrv. asst. French Mil. Govt. in Germany, 1947-49; instr. mech. engring. U. Minn., Mpls., 1955-60; mem. tech. staff Bell Telephone Labs., Murray Hill, N.J., 1960-65; sr. project engr. Curtiss-Wright Corp., Woodridge, N.J., 1965; assoc. prof. mech. engring. N.J. Inst. Tech., 1965-68, prof., 1968—, dir. jet rsch. lab., 1966-92; Participant in Internat. Conf. on Engring. and Applied Sci. Contbr. articles to profl. jours.; one of original Telstar designers. Bd. dirs. Ukrainian Congress Com. Am., Mpls., 1956-60, Plast Camp, East Chatham, N.Y., 1963-68; v.p. Ukrainian Music Found., 1977-92. NASA grantee, 1967-68; NSF grantee, 1982-84. Mem. ASME, AIAA, AAUP, Inst. Environ. Scis. (sr.), Am. Soc. Engring. Edn., Ukrainian Engrs. Soc. Am. (pres. 1966-67), Am. Geophys. Union, Shevchenko Sci. Soc., Ukrainian Acad. Arts and Scis. in U.S.A., Am. Chem. Soc., Sigma Xi, Pi Tau Sigma, Tau Beta Pi. Home: 19 Roselle Ave Cranford NJ 07016-2532 Office: NJ Inst Tech 323 Martin Luther King Blvd Newark NJ 07102

HSIAO, GEORGE CHIA-CHÜ, mathematics educator; b. Shanghai, China, Sept. 9, 1934; came to U.S., 1960; m. Juliet C. Yeh, Sept. 7, 1963; children: Barbara, Jeffrey. BSCE, Nat. Taiwan U., Taipei, 1958; MSCE, Carnegie Inst. Tech., 1963; PhD in Math., Carnegie-Mellon U., 1969. Prof. Dept. Math. Scis., U. Del., Newark, 1977—; Gastprofessor, Mathematisches Institut A., U. Stuttgart, Germany, 1990; vis. prof. Dipartimento di Meccanica e Aeronautica, U. Degli Studi Di Roma, Rome, 1989, Dept. Math., U. Conecption, Chile, 1985; Gastprofessor Inst. for Math I. Free U. Berlin, 1979-80, 86, Fechbereich Mathematik, Technische Hochschule Darmstadt, West Germany, 1975-76, 83; lectr. Europe, China, S.Am., U.S. Co-author: Water Waves and Ship Hydrodynamics; adv. editor Math. Methods in the Applied Scis.; editorial adv. bd. Jour. Computational Mechanics; contbr. numerous articles to profl. jours. Fellowship Ctr. for Advanced Study U. Del., 1987-88; Alexander von Humboldt-Stiftung fellow, 1975-76, 83, 90. Mem. Am. Math. Soc., Soc. Indsl. and Applied Math., H-5 Panel of the Soc. of Naval Architects and Marine Engrs., Internat. Soc. for Intereaction of Mechanics and Math., Sigma Xi, Pi Mu Epsilon. Home: 54 S Fawn Dr Newark DE 19711-2545 Office: U Del Dept Math Scis Newark DE 19716

HSIN, VICTOR JUN-KUAN, transportation systems and telecommunications consultant; b. Hsin-Chu, Taiwan, Dec. 8, 1945; came to U.S., 1974; s. Chiang C. and T.M. (Shiao) H.; m. Alice C. Cheng, Dec. 31, 1976; children: Jeffrey, David. BS, Nat. Cheng-Kung U., Taiwan, 1968, MS, 1972; PhD, U. Tex., 1980. Researcher Metal Industries Rsch. Inst., Taipei, Taiwan, 1972-74; mem. tech. staff Bell Labs., Homdel, N.J., 1980-85; task leader GTE Corp., Vienna, Va., 1985-88; telecommunications and info. systems cons. The Mass. Inst. Tech. Rsch. Establishment, McLean, Va., 1989—; vice chmn. Govt. Open Systems Interconnection Profile Standards support group, 1990-

91; lectr. in computer sci., The Johns Hopkins U., Balt., 1990—. Editor Telecom Rev., 1991; contbr. articles to profl. jours. Chmn. Homdel Chinese Christian Ch., 1983. Lt. Republic of China Army, 1968-69. Mem. IEEE, Phi Kappa Phi.

HSU, CHARLES JUI-CHENG, manufacturing company executive, advertising agent; b. Taipei, Republic of China, Mar. 17, 1930; came to U.S., 1958; s. Neng-Tsai and (Kao-Yung) H. MA, Baylor U., 1965. Owner, mgr. Retaw Co., Flushing, N.Y., 1965—; pres. Retawmatic Corp., N.Y.C., 1968—. Patentee water or oil detecting devices field. Mem. Taiwan Mchts. Assn. Office: Retawmatic Corp 521 5th Ave New York NY 10175-0003 Other: 149-11A 41st Ave Flushing NY 11355

HSU, CHENG, decision sciences and engineering systems educator; b. Taipei, Republic of China, May 11, 1951; came to U.S., 1976; s. Chung-Yu and Te-Zeng (Yeh) H.; m. Ihsin Lydia Wu, Oct. 24, 1979; 1 child, Diana. BS in Indsl. Engring., Tunghai U., Taichung, Republic of China, 1973; MS, Ohio State U., 1978, PhD, 1983. Info. engr. China Tech. Cons., Inc., Taipei, 1975-76; grad. rsch. asst. Ohio State U., Columbus, 1977-80, grad. teaching assoc., 1980-82; asst. prof. decision scis. and engring. systems Rensselaer Poly. Inst., Troy, N.Y., 1982-88, assoc. prof., 1988—, dir. undergrad. programs, 1989-91; cons. Coopers and Lybrand, Albany, N.Y., 1988, Digital Equipment Corp., Nashua, N.H., 1991. Grantee GM, DEC, Johnson & Johnson, 1986-89, Aluminum Co. of Am., Digital Equipment Corp., GE, GM and IBM, 1986-92, AT&T, 1987, NATO, 1988, State of N.Y., 1988, NSF, 1991—. Mem. IEEE, ACM, Inst. Mgmt. Sci., Ops. Rsch. Soc. Am., Soc. Mfg. Engrs., Prodn. and Ops. Mgmt. Soc., N. Am. Chinese Bus. Educators Assn. (bd. dirs. 1988-90). Republican. Home: 5 Christine Ct Latham NY 12110-3734 Office: Rensselaer Poly Inst 5219 CII Troy NY 12180-3590

HSU, DONALD KUNG-HSING, university administrator; b. Shanghai, People's Republic China, Apr. 17, 1947; came to U.S., 1970; s. Kuo Chung and Ching Hwa (Yang) H.; m. Salome Yu-Ching Hsiao, Mar. 18, 1972; 1 child, Douglas. BS, Nat. Cheng King U., Tainan, Taiwan, 1969; PhD, Fordham U., 1975. Rsch. assoc. Princeton U., 1975, Columbia U., 1976; instr. chemistry N.J. Inst. Tech., Newark, 1977-78; v.p. TCK Industries Inc., Bklyn., 1977-81; instr. data processing NYU, N.Y.C., 1980-82; asst. prof. physics and computer sci. St. Peter's Coll., Jersey City, 1978-83; coord. computer sci. program Felician Coll., Lodi, N.J., 1983-88; tech. instr. Dun and Bradstreet, Basking Ridge, N.J., 1988; assoc. prof. Dominican Coll., Orangeburg, N.Y., 1988—, dir. bus. adminstrn., 1990—; mktg. cons. Otsubo Internat., Ft. Lee, N.J., 1984—; tech./project dir. computer grants Felician Coll., 1985-88. Contbr. articles to profl. jours. Sec., mem. exec. council Chinese Am. Acad. and Profl. Assn., N.Y.C., 1981-84. NASA fellow, 1975; NSF fellow, 1976, grantee, 1982-83. Mem. AAUP, IEEE (officer 1983-84), Assn. for Computing Machinery, Nat. Assn. Realtors, United Socs. of Engring. and Sci. of N.J. (pres. 1991—). Republican. Office: Dominican Coll Western Hwy Orangeburg NY 10962-2121

HSU, SAMUEL, music history educator, concert pianist; b. Shanghai, China, June 20, 1947; naturalized U.S. citizen, 1980; s. John and Dorothy (Wong) H.; B.S., Phila. Coll. Bible, 1969, B.Mus., 1969; Ph.D., U. Calif., Santa Barbara, 1972; postgrad. with Rosina Lhevinne (Pillsbury Found. grantee) Juilliard Sch. Music, 1972-76. Ordained deacon Presbyterian Ch., 1984, ordained elder, 1991. Instr. piano Westmont Coll., Montecito, Calif., 1971-72; instr. music history and piano Phila. Coll. Bible, 1972-74, asst. prof., 1974-76, assoc. prof., 1976-80, prof., 1980—, chmn. dept. piano, 1976—; Keyboardist Trenton Symphony Orch., 1983-84. instr. piano Csehy Summer Sch. Music, 1974—, bd. dirs., 1982—. Numerous solo and ensemble performance appearances including Kennedy Ctr., Washington, Phila. Acad. Music, Martin Luther King Chapel, Atlanta. Mem. Phila. Music Tchrs. Assn. (bd. dirs. 1976—, 2d v.p. 1980-82), Am. Musicol. Soc., Delta Epsilon Chi, Pi Kappa Lambda. Office: PO Box 2340 Philadelphia PA 19103-0340

HSUAN, HULBERT CHIEN-SHUAN, plasma physicist; b. Wu-gin, Jiangsu, China, Nov. 28, 1939; came to U.S., 1962; s. Tan Deng-Sue and Chung-Lieh (Liu) H.; m. Catherine Yuh-Ching Wang, Feb. 16, 1963; children: Abraham B., Bryan B. BSE, Nat. Taiwan U., Taipei, Republic of China, 1960; MSEE, U. Ill., 1963; PhD, Princeton U., 1967. Lic. elec. engr., Taiwan. From asst. prof. to prof. elec. engring. dept. U. Iowa, Iowa City, 1966-74; rsch. physicist Princeton Plasma Physics Lab. Princeton (N.J.) U., 1974-79, prin. rsch. physicist, 1979—; cons. scientist Danish Atomic Energy Nat. Lab., Roskilde, 1972, 73. Contbr. articles to Phys. Rev., Rev. Sci. Instrument, Physics of Fluids, Nuclear Fusion, other profl. publs. Fellow Am. Phys. Soc.; mem. IEEE (sr. mem., exec. com. plasma sci. and application com.), Sigma Xi, Eta Kappa Nu. Office: Princeton U Plasma Physics Lab PO Box 451 Princeton NJ 08543-0451

HU, JIMMY, corporate executive; b. Shanghai, China; s. Lee-Sung and Chow-Tze Hu; came to U.S., 1961, naturalized, 1974; B.Sc. in Elec. Engring., Dai-Dong U., China, 1955; M.Bus., Columbia U., 1967. Pres. Marine Works Inc., N.Y.C., 1966-71, UNI Enterprises Inc., N.Y.C., 1971—, Humaco Realty Corp., 1973-79, Kahu Mgmt. Corp., N.Y.C., 1973-78, Hu-Kron Realty Corp., N.Y.C., 1973-78, Hujim Realty Corp., N.Y.C., 1974—, Giant Trading Corp., 1974—, Ocean Supply Corp., N.Y.C., 1974—, KHCK Realty Corp., N.Y.C., 1974—, La Concha Catering and Restaurant Corp., N.Y.C., 1982-86. Mem. Soc. Naval Architects and Marine Engrs. Office: 437-439 3d Ave Brooklyn NY 11215

HU, JOSEPH CHI-PING, mortgage securities analyst; b. Taipei, Republic of China, Apr. 20, 1946; came to U.S., 1969; s. Shien-Teh and Pei-Hwa (Yu) H.; m. Linda M. Mei, Nov. 7, 1949; children: Justin, Brian. BA in Econs., Nat. Taiwan U., Republic of China, 1968; MA in Econs., U. N.Mex., 1971; PhD in Econs., Okla. State U., 1974. Asst. prof. dept. econs. U. Maine, Orono, 1974-75; assoc. planner Oklahoma City Planning Dept., 1975-77; economist Fed. Nat. Mortgage Assn., Washington, 1977-81; v.p. bond market rsch. dept. Salomon Bros. Inc., N.Y.C., 1981-85; sr. v.p., head mortgage research and strategy group E.F. Hutton, N.Y.C., 1985-86; exec. v.p., dir. mortgage research Shearson Lehman Hutton, N.Y.C., 1986-88; sr. v.p., Nomura Securities Internat., N.Y.C., 1988—. Author: Creative Study on Demographic Projection, 1980, Special Report on Housing and Mortgage-backed Securities, 1983, 84, 87, 88, 90-92; contbr. articles to profl. jours. Office: Nomura Securities Internat 180 Maiden Ln New York NY 10038-4925

HU, PING, writer, political activist; b. Beijing, Aug. 5, 1947; came to U.S., 1987; s. Datong Cai and Zhenqing Hu; m. Wan Li, Dec. 15, 1980; 1 child, Pan. MA, Beijing U., 1981; postgrad., Harvard U., 1987-88. Dep. chief editor Fertile Land mag., Beijing, 1979; dep. People's Congress of Haidian Dist., Beijing, 1980-83; editor Beijing Pub. House, 1983-85; researcher Beijing Acad. Social Scis., 1985-87; chief editor China Spring mag., N.Y., 1988-89; pres. China Spring Rsch., Inc., N.Y., 1988—; chmn. Chinese Alliance for Democracy, N.Y., 1988—. Author: On Freedom of Speech, 1979, Philosophical Reflections on Economic Reforms in China, 1985, Philosophical Notes, 1989, Give Me a Stand Point, 1989, Between Ideal and Reality, 1990. Mem. Chinese Scholars Polit. Sci. and Internat. Studies Inc. (pres. 1987-88). Office: China Spring Rsch Inc 74-14 Woodside Ave Elmhurst NY 11373

HUAMAN, DENNIS ERNEST, communications executive; b. N.Y.C., Dec. 26, 1941; s. Ernest and Cecelia (Medina) H.; m. Therese Carol Sutka, June 15, 1969; children: Marc, Elizabeth. BA, Fordham U., 1963, MA, 1968. Computer systems analyst U.S. Govt., Washington D.C., 1965-77; mgr. info. system security Gen. Elec. Space Systems Div., Phila., 1978-84; dir. secure product devel. Wang Labs., Lowell, Mass., 1984-87; mgr. GTE Secure Communications Div., Waltham, Mass., 1988—; lectr. American U.; speaker Secure Communications Computer Security Inst. Mem. ACM, IEEE, IEEE Computer Soc., Assn. Old Crows. Office: GTE 100 First Ave Waltham MA 02254

HUANG, ALICE SHIH-HOU, microbiology, molecular genetics educator; b. Nanchang, Kiangsi, China; came to U.S., 1949; d. Quentin K.Y. and Grace Betty (Soong) H.; m. David Baltimore, 1968. Student Wellesley Coll., 1957-59; BA, Johns Hopkins U., 1961, MA in Microbiology, 1963, PhD, 1966; MA (hon.), Harvard U., 1980; DSc (hon.) Wheaton Coll., 1982, Mt. Holyoke Coll., 1988, Med. Coll. Pa., 1991. Postdoctoral fellow Salk Inst. for Biol. Studies, San Diego, 1967; postdoctoral fellow dept. biology MIT, Cambridge, 1968-69, rsch. assoc., 1969-70; asst. prof. microbiology and molecular genetics Harvard U. Med. Sch., Boston, 1971-73, assoc. prof. microbiology and molecular genetics, 1973-78, prof., 1979-91; prof. microbiology in health sci. and tech. Harvard-MIT Program, 1979-91; dean for sci., prof. biology NYU, 1991—; sci. assoc. Channing Lab. and dept. med. microbiology Boston City Hosp., 1971-73; dir. labs. of infectious diseases Children's Hosp., Boston, 1979-89; vis. asst. prof. Academia Sinica, Nat. Taiwan U., Taipei, 1966, lectr., 1970; vis. assoc. prof. virology Rockefeller U., N.Y.C., 1975-76; Wellcome vis. prof. U. Miss., 1980. Assoc. editor Revs. of Infectious Diseases, 1978-89. Mem. editorial bd.: Intervirology, 1973-90, Archive of Virology, 1975-78, Jour. Virology, 1976—, Microbial Pathogenesis, 1985-90. Contbr. numerous articles to profl. jours. Recipient Research Career Devel. award USPHS., 1972-77, Eli Lilly award, 1977, award San Francisco Chinese Hosp., 1989; Alumni citation Nat. Cathedral Sch., Washington, 1978; John Hay Whitney Found. fellow, 1960-61, Burroughs Wellcome traveling fellow, 1979. Fellow Infectious Diseases Soc. Am.; mem. AAAS, Am. Soc. Microbiology (pres. 1988-89), Am. Soc. Biochemists and Molecular Biologists, Am. Soc. Virology, Am. Acad. Microbiology, Academia Sinica (Taiwan), Sigma Xi. Office: NYU 6 Washington Sq N New York NY 10003-6635

HUANG, JACOB CHEN-YA, physician, city official; b. Chia-Yi, Taiwan, Dec. 25, 1937; came to U.S., 1966, naturalized, 1974; s. Chang-Chiang and Agenes Cheng-Jen H.; m. Vivian Lin, Oct. 3, 1970; children—Phyllis, Albert, Edward. Intern, Taipei City Hosp., 1964-65, house officer in pediatrics, 1965-66; fellow in clin. pathology Albert Einstein Coll. Medicine-Lincoln Hosp., 1968-70; resident in family medicine Lutheran Med. Center, N.Y.C., 1970-71; clin. asso. prof. NYU, 1972-76; dist. health dir. N.Y.C., Dept. Health, 1971-76; med. dir. Paterson City (N.J.) Health Dept., 1977—; chmn. dept. family practice Dover (N.J.) Gen. Hosp. and Med. Center, 1980—; trustee N.J. Passaic PRO, 1987—; bd. dirs. ambulatory care adv. bd. Beth Israel Hosp., N.Y.C., 1972-76, community adv. bd. ambulatory services St. Vincent Med. Center, N.Y.C., 1972-76, COMED-IPA Inc., N.J., 1980—. Recipient Physician's Recognition award AMA, 1966, 69, 72—. Diplomate Am. Bd. Family Practice. Fellow Am. Coll. Preventive Medicine, Am. Acad. Family Physicians; mem. Am. Public Health Assn., Am. Chinese Med. Assn. N.J. (pres., founder), Chinese Am. Med. Soc. (bd. dirs.), Columbia U. Sch. Pub. Health Alumni Assn. (exec. bd. 1992—). Home: 3 Walnut Hill Dr Chester NJ 07930-3006 Office: Bartley Sq Rte 206 Flanders NJ 07836

HUANG, JOSEPH CHEN-HUAN, civil engineer; b. Nanking, China, Oct. 18, 1933; came to U.S., 1962, naturalized, 1972; M.S. in Structural Engring., Va. Poly. Inst. and State U., 1964; m. Elizabeth C. Huang, Sept. 3, 1966; children: Edith, Eleanor, Evelyn, Edna. Project engr. Green Assos., Inc., Balt., 1964-68; pres. Gen. Engring. Consultants, Inc., Balt., 1968—; chmn., chief exec. officer Highlights Corp., Towson, Md., 1976—. Mem. ASCE, Am. Concrete Inst., Nat. Soc. Profl. Engrs. Author: Prestressed Steel Structures; also tech. papers. Home: 3506 Templar Rd Randallstown MD 21133-2428 Office: 1248 E Joppa Rd Towson MD 21204 Office: 1045 Taylor Ave Towson MD 21204 Office: 825 N Hammonds Ferry Rd Ste B Linthicum Heights MD 21090-1350

HUANG, RU CHIH CHOW, molecular biology educator; b. Nanking, China, Apr. 2, 1932; came to U.S., 1954; d. I.K. and Djen (Tsao) Chow; m. P.C. Huang, June 10, 1956; children: Suber S., Suzanne S. BS, Nat. Taiwan U., Taipei, 1953; MS, Va. Polytech. Inst., 1956; PhD, Ohio State U., 1960. Postdoctoral fellow Calif. Tech. Inst., Pasadena, 1960-65; asst. prof. molecular biology Johns Hopkins U., Balt., 1965-71, assoc. prof., 1971-75, prof., 1975—; chmn. Gordon Rsch. Conf., 1980; chmn. bd. sci. counselors Nat. Inst. on Agint, NIH, Bethesda, Md., 1980-84; bd. dirs. Inst. Molecular Biology, Taiwan, 1987-88; mem. sci. adv. bd. Nat. Cancer Inst. Recipient Asian-Am. Scientist award NIH, NSF, 1985. Mem. Academia Sinica. Home: 4604 Kerneway Baltimore MD 21212-4715 Office: Johns Hopkins U Baltimore MD 21218

HUANG, SUEI-RONG, chemistry educator; b. Tainan, Taiwan, Republic of China, Jan. 1, 1932; came to U.S. 1957; s. Shou and Feng-ching (Wang) H.; m. Lily P.T. Chen, Jan. 30, 1965; children: Eric, Fritz, Jeffrey, Nina. BS, Nat. Taiwan U., 1954; MS, N.Mex. Highland U., 1960; PhD, Stevens Inst. Tech., 1964. Asst. prof. chemistry L.I. U., Bklyn., 1964-70, assoc. prof., 1970-76, prof. chemistry, 1976—; cons. Seiken Industry, Fukuoka, Japan, 1972—. Co-author: (lab manuals) General Chemistry, 1980, Organic and Biochemistry, 1980. Mem. Am. Chem. Soc., N.Y. Acad. Sci. Office: LI U Flatbush Ave Ext Brooklyn NY 11201

HUBAND, FRANK LOUIS, educational association executive; b. Washington, July 12, 1938; m. Carol Singer. BS, Cornell U., 1961, PhD, 1967; JD, Yale U., 1975. Bar: D.C. 1975, U.S. Patent Office, 1977; registered prof. engr., Tex. Asst. prof. elec. engring. and math. scis. Rice U., Houston, 1966-72; owner, pres. Engring. Systems, Houston, 1972-73; atty., advisor FEA, Washington, 1975-76; div. dir. NSF, Washington, 1976-90; exec. dir. Am. Soc. for Engring. Edn., Washington, 1990—; cons. Tex. Instrument, 1968-75; lectr. George Mason U., Fairfax, Va., George Washington U. Author: Protection of Computer Systems and Software, 1986. Mem. ABA, IEEE. Office: Am Soc for Engring Edn Ste 200 11 Dupont Cir NW Washington DC 20036-1207

HUBBARD, AMY NIX, advertising agency executive; b. Waterbury, Conn., May 26, 1949; d. George Cedric and Margaret (Gibbons) Nix. BA, U. Conn., 1971. Copywriter, account exec. Silverman Group, New Haven, 1974-79, Davidoff and Ptnrs., Westport, Conn., 1979-80; pres. Hubbard Advt., Branford, Conn., 1980—. Author: The ABC's of Advertising, 1979, (audio-visuals) Windpower: The Art of Sailing, 1980, Marketing of Intravenous Nursing Therapy, 1985. Mem. Arts Coun. of Great New Haven, 1984—, New Haven Symphony Aux., 1985—, Adirondack Conservancy, Elizabethtown, N.Y., 1983—, Beaux Arts Soc., N.Y.C. Recipient Printing Industry of Am. award, 1987. Mem. Conn. Art Dirs. Club (founder, bd. dirs. 1974—, Excellence award 1977, 78), Conn. Assn. Jungian Psychology, Grads. Club. Home: 13 Waterside Dr Guilford CT 06437-3102 Office: Hubbard Advt 150 W Main St Branford CT 06405-4031

HUBBARD, JOHN HAMAL, mathematician, educator; b. Barnstable, Mass., Oct. 7, 1945; s. Charles Joseph and Harriet (Bissell) H.; m. Barbara Ann Burke, June 23, 1974; children: Alexander, Eleanor, Judith, Diana. BA, Harvard U., 1967; PhD, U. Paris, 1973. Asst. prof. Harvard U., Cambridge, Mass., 1973-76; asst. prof. Cornell U., Ithaca, N.Y., 1976-79, assoc. prof., 1979-82, prof., 1982—; vis. prof. U. Paris XI, Orsay, France, 1976-77, 81-82, 89-90, MPI Mathematik, Bonn, Fed. Republic Germany, 1987-88. Co-author: (with B. West) Differential Equations, 1991; contbr. articles to profl. jours. Recipient Humboldt prize Humboldt Found., 1987. Mem. Am. Math. Soc. Home: 214 University Ave Ithaca NY 14850-3818 Office: Cornell U White Hall Ithaca NY 14853

HUBBARD, RICHMOND CHASE, psychiatrist; b. Saylesville, R.I., June 19, 1916; s. Carleton Waterbury and Katharine (Chase) H.; m. Jeanne Marie Pawloski, Sept. 12, 1965; children: David, Ruth, Brenda. AB in Social Sci., Antioch Coll., 1940; MD, U. Cin., 1946. Diplomate Am. Bd. Psychiatry and Neurology. Instr. social sci. Antioch Coll., Yellow Springs, Ohio, 1940-42; resident in psychiatry Elgin (Ill.) State Hosp., 1949-54; pvt. practice Bethel, Conn., 1954—. Capt. M.C., U.S. Army, 1942-49. Office: 233 Greenwood Ave Bethel CT 06801-2195

HUBBARD, RUTH, biology educator; b. Vienna, Austria, Mar. 3, 1924; came to U.S., 1938; d. Richard and Helene (Ehrlich) Hoffmann; m. Frank Twombly Hubbard, Dec. 26, 1942 (div. 1951); m. George Wald, June 11, 1958; children: Elijah, Deborah Hannah. AB, Radcliffe Coll., 1944, PhD, 1950; DSc (hon.), Macalester Coll., 1991, U. Toronto, Ont., Can., 1991; LHD (hon.), So. Ill. U., Edwardsville, 1991. Lab. technician Tenn. Pub. Health Service, Chattanooga, 1945-46; fellow U. Coll. Hosp. Med. Sch., London, 1948-49; Guggenheim fellow Carlsberg Lab., Copenhagen, Denmark, 1952-53; research fellow Harvard U., Cambridge, Mass., 1950-52, 54-58, research assoc., lectr., 1958-74, prof., 1974-90, prof. emerita, 1990—; vis. prof. M.I.T., Cambridge, 1972; cons. Boston Women's Healthbook Collective 1982—. Author: (with Margaret Randall) The Shape of Red: Insider/Outsider Reflections, 1988; author: The Politics of Women's Biology, 1990; editor: (book) Women Look at Biology Looking at Women, 1979, Genes and Gender II, 1979, Biological Woman-The Convenient Myth, 1982, Women's Nature: Rationalizations of Inequality, 1983; contbr. over 150 articles on sci. and women's issues to profl. and lay books and jours. Adv. coun. mem. Nat. Women's Health Network, Washington, 1980—; bd. dirs. Coun. Responsible Genetics, Boston, 1982—; mem. adv. bd. Boston Women's Fund, 1983-85; mem. adv. bd. Civil Liberties Union of Mass., 1990-91, bd. dirs., 1991—. Recipient Paul Karrer medal Swiss Chem. Soc., 1967, Peace and Freedom award Women's Internat. League for Peace and Freedom, 1985, Feminist Marathoner award Boston chpt. NOW, 1991, Disting. Svc. award Am. Inst. Biol. Sci., 1992. Mem. AAAS, Marine Biol. Lab. (trustee 1973-78, trustee emerita 1990—), Soc. Biol. Chemists, Nat. Women's Studies Assn., Phi Beta Kappa, Sigma Xi. Office: Harvard U Dept Biology 16 Divinity Ave Cambridge MA 02138-2097

HUBBARD, VAN SAXTON, career medical officer, pediatrics educator; b. Middletown, N.Y., Mar. 1, 1945; s. W. Saxton and M. Elizabeth (Van Fleet) H.; m. Linda Dell Rucker, May 21, 1974; children: Brian S., Kevin S. BS, Union Coll., Schenectady, N.Y., 1967; MD, Va. Commonwealth U., Richmond, 1974, PhD, 1974. Diplomate Nat. Bd. Med. Examiners, Am. Bd. Nutrition, Am. Bd. Pediatrics; lic. U.S. ind. user of radionucleotide, AEC; cert. of radionucleotide use in patients, AEC; med. lic. Minn., D.C. Commd. surgeon USPHS, 1976—, advanced through grades to med. dir., 1988; intern, then resident in pediatrics U. Minn. Hosps., Mpls., 1974-76; fellow, clin. assoc. pediatric metabolism br. NIH, Bethesda, Md., 1976-78, med. officer pediatric metabolism br., 1978-83, dir. nutrient metabolism program, 1983-90, dir. obesity, eating disorders and energy regulation program, 1983—, dir. clin. nutrition rsch. units program, 1983—; dir. and project officer U.S.-Japan coop. med. sci. program NIH, Bethesda, 1983—, dir. gastrointestinal digestion program, 1988-90; mem. staff pediatric dept. Nat. Naval Med. Ctr., Bethesda, 1979—; asst. rsch. prof. child health and devel. George Washington U., Washington, 1981-86, assoc. rsch. prof. child health and devel., 1986—; spl. govt. employee (expert) FDA, 1978-84; mem. human studies rev. com. USDA, 1986—, mem. policy adv. com., 1987—; mem. interagy. osteoporosis working group NHANES III, 1987—; mem. interagy. com. on human nutrition rsch., 1987-90; mem. fish oil test materials adv. com., 1987—; mem. Bethesda Campus Disaster Med. Assistance Team, 1987—, dep. chief med. officer, 1989-90, comdr., 1990—; mem. external rev. com. Ctr. Nutritional Scis., Va. Commonwealth U., 1988—. Asst. editor Am. Jour. for Clin. Nutrition, 1981-86; mem. editorial bd. Jour. Nutritional Biochemistry, 1989—, Jour. Parental and Enteral Nutrition, 1991—; reviewer various jours.; contbr. articles to profl. jours. Decorated USPHS Commendation medal; named Disting. Alumnus Sch. of Basic Health Scis., Va. Commonwealth U., 1989. Fellow Am. Acad. Pediatrics (mem. nutrition com. 1988—), Am. Coll. Nutrition; mem. Am. Inst. Nutrition, Am. Fedn. for Clin. Rsch., Am. Gastroent. Assn. (mem. rsch. com. 1988—, mem. animal rsch. task force 1989—), Am. Soc. for Clin. Nutrition (chmn. nominating com. 1987-88, mem. annual meeting program com. 1987-90, mem. continuing nutrition edn. com. 1987-90, mem. tellers com. 1990-92), Am. Soc. for Parenteral and Enteral Nutrition (mem. rsch. and data com. 1984—), Nat. Cystic Fibrosis Found. (mem. rsch. and rsch. tng. com. 1980-83, mem. conf. com. 1980-83), Cystic Fibrosis Found. (cons. ad hoc com. 1978, mem. med. program com. 1980—, trustee 1981-87), N.Y. Acad. Scis., N.Am. Assn. for Study Obesity, N.Am. Soc. Pediatric Gastroenterology and Nutrition, Soc. for Pediatric Rsch., Sigma Xi. Home: 5022 Acacia Ave Bethesda MD 20814-2890 Office: NIDDK NIH Westwood Bldg 3A18B Bethesda MD 20892

HUBBS, JOHN BREWSTER, computer systems analyst; b. Syracuse, N.Y., Mar. 6, 1941; s. Horace Newton and Mary Francis (Garni) H.; m. Jutta Margarit Gampp, Feb. 24, 1988; children: John Brewster, Lawrence Brewster. BSChemE, U. Colo., 1963; MBA, U. Colo., Denver, 1968. Engr. Martin Marietta, Denver, 1963-71; cons. in computer systems Denver, 1972-75; computer cons. Martin Marietta, Balt., 1976—. Founder Liberty Hill Homeowners Assn., Littleton, Colo., 1976; chmn. Bega-Littleton Sister City, Inc., 1986. Recipient A.E. Marshall award, Am. Inst. Chem. Engrs., 1963. Home: 6501 Laurel Dr Baltimore MD 21207-6328

HUBEL, DAVID HUNTER, physiologist, educator; b. Windsor, Ont., Can., Feb. 27, 1926; s. Jesse Hervey and Elsie (Hunter) H.; m. Shirley Ruth Izzard, June 20, 1953; children: Carl Andrew, Eric David, Paul Matthew. BSc, McGill U., 1947, MD, 1951, DSc (hon.), 1978; AM (hon.), Harvard U., 1962; DSc (hon.), U. Man., 1983; DHL (hon.), Johns Hopkins U., 1990. Intern Montreal Gen. Hosp., 1951-52; asst. resident neurology Montreal Neurol. Inst., 1952-53, fellow clin. neurophysiology, 1953-54; asst. resident neurology Johns Hopkins Hosp., 1954-55; sr. fellow neurol. scis. group Johns Hopkins U., 1958-59; faculty Harvard U. Med. Sch., 1959—, George Packer Berry prof. physiology, chmn. dept., 1967-68, George Packer Berry prof. neurobiology, 1968-82, John Franklin Enders univ. prof., 1982—; George H. Bishop lectr. exptl. neurology Washington U., St. Louis, 1964; Jessup lectr. biol. scis. Columbia, 1970; James Arthur lectr. Am. Mus. Natural History, 1972; Ferrier lectr. Royal Soc. London, 1972; Harvey lectr. Rockefeller U., 1976; Weizmann meml. lectr. Weizmann Inst. Sci., Rehovot, Israel, 1979; George Eastman prof. Oxford, Eng., 1991-92; Fenn lectr. 30th internat. congress Internat. Union Psychol. Sci., Vancouver, B.C., Can., 1986; researcher brain mechanisms in vision.; bd. syndics Harvard U. Press, 1979-83. Served with AUS, 1955-58. Recipient Trustees award Rsch. to Prevent Blindness, 1971, Lewis S. Rosenstiel award for disting. work in basic med. rsch., 1972, Karl Lashley prize Am. Philos. Soc., 1977, Louisa Gross Horwitz prize Columbia U., 1978, Dickson prize in medicine U. Pitts., 1979, Ledlie prize Harvard U., 1980, Nobel prize, 1981, Outstanding Sci. Leadership award Nat. Assn. for Biomed. Rsch., 1990, City of Medicine award, 1990; fellow Harvard Soc. Fellows, 1971—. Fellow Am. Acad. Arts and Scis.; mem. Nat. Acad. Sci., Am. Physiol. Soc. (Bowditch lectr. 1966), Deutsche Akademie der Naturforscher leopoldina, Soc. for Neurosci. (Grass lecture 1976), Assn. for Rsch. in Vision and Ophthalmology (Friedenwald award 1975), Johns Hopkins U. Soc. Scholars, Am. Philos. Soc. (Karl Spencer Lashley prize 1977), Royal Soc. London. Home: 98 Collins Rd Newton MA 02168-2235 Office: Harvard Med Sch Dept Neurobiology 220 Longwood Ave Boston MA 02115-5717

HUBER, BETTINA JULIA, sociologist; b. N.Y.C., Jan. 29, 1943; d. Wolfgang and Annita (Krahmer) H. BA, Oberlin Coll., 1965; MPhil, Yale U., 1968, PhD, 1973. Asst. prof. Univ. Calif., Santa Barbara, 1971-80; deputy exec. officer Am. Sociol. Assn., Washington, 1981-88; dir. rsch. Modern Lang. Assn., N.Y.C., 1988—. Author: (booklet) Embarking Upon a Career with an Undergraduate Sociology Major, 1982, (monograph) Employment Patterns in Sociology, 1985; contbr. articles to profl. jours. Mem. Am. Sociol. Assn., Soc. for the Study of Social Problems, Sociologists for Women in Soc. (chair publs. com. 1990—). Office: Modern Lang Assn 10 Astor Pl New York NY 10003-6935

HUBER, EUGENE ROBERT, theatre educator; b. Jamaica, N.Y., Nov. 21, 1947; s. Eugene George Huber and Evelyn Hazel (Henn) Wieser. BA in Drama, Hofstra U., 1969; MS in Speech and Drama Edn., C.W. Post Coll., 1971; PhD in Ednl. Theatre/Musical Theatre, NYU, 1990. Cert. secondary tchr. in English, Speech & Drama, Social Studies, N.Y. English tchr. Baldwin (N.Y.) Sr. High Sch., 1971-72; English tchr., drama dir. Jericho (N.Y.) Sr. High Sch., 1972-74, L.I. Luth. High Sch., Brookville, N.Y., 1976-82; adj. instr. Molloy Coll., Rockville Centre, N.Y., 1981-85; gen. mgr. NYU Summer Music Theatre, N.Y.C., 1982-84; assoc. prof. Kutztown (Pa.) U., 1986—; guest lectr. on mus. theatre and Stephen Sondheim; presenter Assn. for Theatre in Higher Edn. conf., Seattle, 1991. Author (original mus.) The Web, 1986 (semi-finalist Richard Rodgers Mus. Theatre award); dir. over 40 mus. prodns.; contbr. articles to profl. jours. Named one of Outstanding Young Men Am., 1977. Mem. AAUP, Assn. for Theatre in Higher Edn., Am. Soc. for Theatre Rsch., Am. Theatre Wing, N.Y. Shakespeare Soc., Sondheim Bias Soc. Home: 91 Lyons Rd Fleetwood PA 19522-9720 Office: Kutztown U Dept Speech and Theatre Kutztown PA 19530-1610

HUBER, IVAN, entomologist, educator, consultant; b. Zagreb, Croatia, Yugoslavia, Oct. 15, 1931; came to U.S., 1940; s. Francis and Irene (Deutsch) H.; m. Vivienne Hirchinson, Sept. 12, 1961; children: Jonathan, Mirella. AB, Cornell U., 1954; PhD, U. Kans., 1968. Instr. biology

Muhlenberg Coll., Allentown, Pa., 1966-68; asst. prof. biology Fairleigh Dickinson U., Madison, N.J., 1968-75; assoc. prof. Fairleigh Dickinson U., Madison, 1975-84, prof., 1984—; pres. Periplaneta, Inc. Boonton, N.J., 1977—. Sr. editor, contbg. author Cockroaches as Models for Neurobiology: Applications in Biomedical Research, 2 vols., 1990; contbr. articles to profl. jours. Mem. Entomol. Soc. Am., Soc. Systematic Zoology, Soc. for Study of Evolution, N.Y. Entomol. Soc. (treas. 1975-80). Office: Fairleigh Dickinson U Dept Biology Madison NJ 07940

HUBER, JACK TRAVIS, writer; b. San Antonio. MA, Columbia U., 1946, PhD, 1952. Prof. clin. psychology Adelphi U., Garden City, N.Y., 1955-67; prof. Hunter Coll., N.Y.C., 1967-89. Author: Through an Eastern Window, 1967, Report Writing in Psychology and Psychiatry, 1961; co-author: The Human Personality, 1976, Interviewing America's Top Interviewers, 1991. Home: 22 Trafton Ln Kittery ME 03904-5401

HUBER, JOAN JOYCE, financial planner, international speaker; b. Balt., Md., July 24, 1941; d. Anthony Frank and Mary (Wojciechowski) Grodzicki; children: René R. R. McFadden, Joseph R. Ries IV. Grad., Coll. Notre Dame, 1991. Cert. fin. planner. V.p. Pebsco, Balt., 1975-84; owner Fin. Planning Firm, Balt., 1984-88; v.p. Shearson Lehman Bros., Balt., 1988—. Trustee Md. State Retirement and Pension System, Balt., 1989—; mem. Md. Sister State Program, Balt., 1990—. Office: Shearson Lehman Bros 36 S Charles St Baltimore MD 21202

HUBER, RICHARD MILLER, writer, management training company executive; b. Ardmore, Pa., July 27, 1922; s. John Y. Jr. and Caroline (Miller) H.; divorced; children: Cintra Hutchinson Huber McGauley, Richard Miller Jr., Casilda Carter. BA, Princeton U., 1945; PhD, Yale U., 1953. Mem. faculty Princeton (N.J.) U., 1950-54; pres. Princeton Manor Constrn. Co., 1958-62; producer, moderator Sta. WHWH-AM-FM, Princeton, 1965-67; corr. Sta. WNET-TV, N.Y.C., 1967-68; dean Sch. Gen. Studies Hunter Coll., N.Y.C., 1971-77, exec. dir. div. continuing edn., 1977-82; asst. dir. TV and radio Nat. Endowment for the Humanities, Washington, 1983-84, spl. asst. to chmn., 1984-85; pres. Huber Assocs., Washington, 1985—; pres. Prodn.-in-Progress, Inc., Washington, 1986-89. Author: Big All The Way Through: The Life of Van Sandvoord Merle-Smith, 1952, The American Idea of Success, 1971, rev. edn., 1987, How Professors Play the Cat Guarding the Cream: Why We're Paying More and Getting Less in Higher Education, 1992; editor: (with Wheaton J. Lane) New Jersey Historical Series, 31 vols., 1965. Mem. Coun. of Friends, Princeton U. Libr. 2nd lt. USAAF, 1942-45, Italy. Decorated Air medal; award recipient N.J. Hist. Soc., Newark, 1965; recipient Award of Merit, Am. Assn. State and Local Historians, 1965, Author's award N.J. Assn. Tchrs. of English, 1965, Award of Recognition, N.J. Hist. Commn., Trenton, 1983. Mem. Soc. Am. Historians, Orgn. Am. Historians, Am. Hist. Assn., Issues Mgmt. Assn., Pretty Brook Tennis Club. Republican. Episcopalian. Office: Huber Assocs 2950 Van Ness St NW Apt 926 Washington DC 20008-1120

HUBERMAN, BENJAMIN, consultant; b. Havana, Cuba, Jan. 25, 1938; came to U.S., 1946; s. Henry and Marcella (Waisman) H.; m. Gisela Bialik, Oct. 13, 1963; children: Jonathan, Martin. AB, Columbia Coll., 1959; BS, Columbia U., 1960; diploma of Imperial Coll., U. London (Eng.), 1962. Sr. official Arms Control & Disarmament Agy., Washington, 1966-73, Nat. Security Coun., Washington, 1973-75; dir., policy evaluation Nuclear Regulatory Commn., Washington, 1975-77; sr. official Office Sci. and Tech. Policy, Washington, 1977-81; dep. sci. advisor to pres. White House, Washington, 1981; v.p. Cons. Internat. Group, Inc., Washington, 1982-88, pres., 1988-90; pres. Huberman Cons. Group, Washington, 1990—; bd. dirs. Zycad Corp., Menlo Park, Calif. Lt. USN, 1960-66. Fulbright scholar, London, 1960-61. Mem. Met. Club, Cosmos Club (Washington). Office: Huberman Cons Group 1090 Vermont Ave NW Washington DC 20005-4905

HUBICKI, DONALD EDWARD, state official; b. Troy, N.Y., Mar. 11, 1961; s. William and Dorothy Lucy (Tourajian) H.; m. Tracey Ann Welch, Oct. 15, 1988. BS, Rensselaer Poly. Inst., 1983, MS, 1988. Indsl. engr. Watervliet (N.Y.) Arsenal, Dept. Def., 1983-87; sr. elec. engr. Aluminum Co. Am., Massena, N.Y., 1987-89; mgr. fin. systems Empire Blue Cross-Blue Shield, Albany, N.Y., 1989-90; dir. transp. systems R & D N.Y. State Thruway Authority, Albany, 1990—. Bus. cons. Jr. Achievement, Albany, 1990. Mem. Project Mgmt. Inst., Albany Soc. Civil Engrs. Home: 10 Zelenke Dr Wynantskill NY 12198 Office: NY State Thruway Authority 200 Southern Blvd Albany NY 12209

HUBLER, JULIUS, artist; b. Granite City, Ill., Dec. 11, 1919; s. Voyle and Marie (Lewedag) H.; m. Loretta Lanter, Apr. 26, 1943; children: Stuart Alden, Ann Marlowe McClure. B.S., S.E. Mo. U., 1943; M.A., Ed.D., Columbia U., 1951. Sci. tchr. Wibaux High Sch., Mont., 1942-43, Ashton High Sch., Idaho, 1943-45; art instr. CCNY, 1946-48; prof. art SUNY-Buffalo, 1948-82; freelance artist Buffalo, 1982—; painter, graphic designer, sculptor, photographer. Exhibited in group shows Taipei Mus. Fine Arts, 1983-88, Internat. Miniature Print Biennial, 1989, Salon de Peinture et D'Estampe de Montreal, Que., Can., 1990, Albright-Knox Mus., Buffalo, 1991, Rodman Hall Nat. Exhbn. Ctr. St. Catharines, Ont., Can., 1991; author: Jour. Print World Lynd Ward, 1989. Mem. Western N.Y. Peace Ctr. Deans scholar; State U. Iowa grad. scholar, 1944; Arthur W. Dow scholar Columbia U., 1947; disting. service awardee U. Buffalo, 1958. Mem. AAUP (bd. dirs., pres. N.Y. state chpt. 1956-60), Soc. Am. Graphic Artists (Warren Mack Meml. purchase award 1962), NAD (assoc., Samuel F.B. Morse medal 1977, Anonymous prize 1980, Leo Meissner prize 1989), Amnesty Internat., Brit.-N.Am. Philatelic Assn., Buffalo Stamp Club, Helvetia Am. Club. Clubs: Buffalo Stamp, Helvetia Am. Address: 9855 Hollingson Rd Clarence NY 14031

HUBSMITH, ROBERT JAMES, surgeon; b. Passaic, N.J., Sept. 16, 1930; s. Edward A. and Gertrude Frances (Boffard) H.; m. Lois Abbey Landrie Husbmith, Set. 28, 1957; children: Robert J., Diance C., Edward J. BA, Cornell U., 1952; MD, Cornell U. Med. Coll., 1956. Cert. Am. Bd. Surgery, 1965, Am. Coll. Surgeons, 1967. Post grad. surgical St. Luke's Hosp., N.Y.C., 1956-58; residency Hackensach (N.J.) Hosp., 1961-64; surgeon pvt. practice, Butler, N.J., 1964—; instr. of surgery U. Med. and Dentistry of N.J., N.J. Med. Sch., Newark, 1991—; emeritus staff Chilton Meml. Hosp., Pompton Plains, N.J., 1991—; fire surgeon Kinnelon (N.J.) Col. Fire Dept., 1976—; pres. med.-dental staff Chilton Meml. Hosp., Pompton Plains, N.J., 1977. Bd. elders The Community Ch. of Smoke Rise, 1985-87, 90-92. Fellow ACS; mem. Soc. Surgeons of N.J., Kinnelon Jaycees. Home: 706 Orchard Rd Kinnelon NJ 07405 Office: 1395 Sate Hwy 23 Butler NJ 07405

HUCKABEE, CAROL BROOKS, psychologist; b. Marion, Ohio, Aug. 2, 1945; d. William Richard and Marjorie (Beal) Brooks; m. Roy M. Huckabee, Dec. 22, 1967; 1 child, Lear Elizabeth. BA, U. Colo., 1967; MS, NYU, 1982, PhD, 1985. Lic. psychologist, N.Y., Conn. Psychology intern Downstate Med. Ctr., Bklyn., 1982-84; staff psychologist Blythedale Children's Hosp., Valhalla, N.Y., 1984-86; dir. psychol. svcs. Arms Acres Hosp., Carmel, N.Y., 1986-88, cons., 1988-89; cons. psychologist Putnam Community Hosp., Carmel, 1988—; pvt. practice Brewster, N.Y., 1987—; sch. psychologist N.Y.C. Bd. Edn., 1984—. NIMH clin. tng. grantee, 1980-81, 81-82. Mem. Am. Psychol. Assn., N.Y. State Psychol. Assn., Conn. State Psychol. Assn. Democrat. Office: 155 Main St Brewster NY 10509-1435

HUCKINS, HAROLD AARON, chemical engineer; b. Cambridge, Mass., Nov. 28, 1924; s. Harold Aaron and Julia E. (Nugent) H.; m. Elizabeth L. Kearns, Nov. 15, 1952; children: Richard W., Robert M., Christopher N., Patricia A., Leslie K. BSChemE, Northeastern U., 1945; ASME, Lowell Inst., 1946; postgrad., Boston U., 1947-49, U. Pitts., 1950-52. Chem. process engr., asst. project mgr. Monsanto Chem. Co., Boston-Everett, Mass., 1945-49; sr. process engr., group leader Koppers Co. Chem. Div., Pitts., 1949-53; mgr. pilot plants, project mgr. Sci. Design Co., Inc., N.Y.C., 1953-66; v.p. tech. ops. Oxirane Chem. Co., Princeton, N.J., 1966-73; v.p. tech. assessment Halcon SD Group, N.Y.C., 1973-85; pres. Princeton Advanced Tech., Inc., 1985—; dir. Assn. Cons. Chemists & Chem. Engrs. div., N.Y.C., 1990-93, Materials Tech. Inst., St. Louis, 1976-85. Co-author: The Chemical Plant, 1966; contbr. articles to profl. jours. Fellow Am. Inst. Chem. Engrs. (dir. mgmt. div. 1981-82, dir. materials engring. sci. div. 1976-80, vice chmn. materials engring. and sci. div. 1990—, chmn. chem. tech. materials com. 1966-91, chmn. John Fritz medal commn. 1989); mem. Am. Soc. Materials, Am. Chem. Soc., Am. Ceramic Soc., Nat. Assn. Corrosion Engrs. (chmn. 1984), Mensa Internat. Office: Princeton Tech Inc 56 Finley Rd Princeton NJ 08540-7503

HUDAK, LINDA ELISE, illustrator, designer; b. Pompton Plains, N.J., Oct. 15, 1960; d. Peter and Carol (Komorowski) Hudak; m. Lawrence John Carnevale, May 19, 1990. BFA in Graphic Design, Rutgers U., 1983. Comml. artist IBM Corp., Franklin Lakes, N.J., 1982-83; graphic designer DuCair/Bioessence, North Bergen, N.J., 1984; illustration/designer/product designer Russ Berrie, Oakland, N.J., 1984—; prodn. artist The News, Wyckoff, N.J., 1991; owner, creative dir. LEH Graphic Design & Illustration, Oakland, 1990—. Illustrator children's books: Pipeline at Sportsman Ridge, 1982, Who Should I Be?, 1991; illustrator/author: Someone to Look Up To, 1990. Grand prize winner for mother's day display Svc. Merchandise and Chippenhook, 1989. Office: LEH Graphic Design PO Box 314 Oakland NJ 07436

HUDDLE, DAVID ROSS, English educator, writer; b. Ivanhoe, Va., July 11, 1942; s. Charles Richard and Mary Frances (Akers) H.; m. Marie Lindsey Massie; children: Elizabeth Ross, Mary Massie. BA Foreign Affairs, U. Va.; MA in English, Hollins Coll., 1969; MFA in Writing, Columbia U., 1971; D of Humanities (hon.), Shenandoah Coll., Winchester, Va., 1989. From instr. to assoc. prof. U. Vt., 1971-81, prof., 1982—; vis. prof. Middlebury Coll., 1981-82, faculty mem. Bread Loaf Sch. Middlebury Coll, 1979, 1985—, Bread Loaf Writers' Conf., 1983—; vis. writer U. Idaho, 1987, writer in residence, Ind. U., 1987; faculty mem. Tucson Writers' Conf., 1987-88; Judge AWP award series competition in short fiction, 1988, Hopwood Short Story contest, U. Mich., 1989; fiction panalist Nat. Endowment for the Arts Fellowship, 1990; writer, tchr. Highland Summer Conf. Radford U., Va., 1987, 1991. Author: A Dream with No Stump Roots in It, 1975, Paper Boy, 1979, Only the Little Bone, 1986, 88, Stopping by Home, 1988, The High Spirits: Stories of Men and Women, 1989, Intimates, 1992, The Nature of Yearning, 1992, The Writing Habit, 1992. Sgt. U.S. Army, Vietnam, 1964-67. Va. Ctr. for the Creative Arts fellow, 1976, William Raney Fellow in Prose, Bread Loaf Writiers' Conf., 1977, Nat. Endowment for the Arts Creative Writing fellow, 1978, Yaddo fellow, 1978, 1980; Recipient Lawrence Found. prize, 1979, James Wright prize, 1982. Mem. Assoc. Writing Programs, Authors Guild. Home: 34 N Williams St Burlington VT 05401-3304 Office: U Vt Dept English 308A Old Mill Burlington VT 05405

HUDDLE, ROBERT H., JR., thoracic surgeon; b. Elmira, N.Y., July 16, 1947; s. Robert H. and Ellen (Bird) H.; m. Kathleen J. Mullen, June 20, 1970; children: Christine, Katherine, Megan, Molly. BS, U. Notre Dame, 1969; MD, U. Buffalo, 1973. Diplomate Am. Bd. Gen. Surgery, Cardiothoracic Surgery. Resident in gen. surgery U. Rochester, N.Y., 1973-77, thoracic surgeon, 1977-79; pvt. practice Elmira, N.Y., 1979—. Fellow Am. Coll. Surgeons; mem. Soc. Thoracic Surgeons, Cen. N.Y. Surg. Soc., Upstate Thoracic Surg. Soc. Office: Elmira Surg Assn 304 Hoffman St Elmira NY 14905

HUDECHECK, ROSEMARY ANNE, music director, consultant; b. Phila., Nov. 5, 1949; d. Joseph James and Geraldine Marie (Rooney) H. MusB, Immaculata Coll., 1971; MusM, West Chester U. Pa., 1980; MA in Liturgical Studies, Cath. U. Am., 1989. Cert. music tchr., Pa. Music specialist Chester (Pa.)-Upland Sch. Dist., 1971-82; dir. Archdiocesan Boys Choir, Phila., 1975-87; assoc. dir. Cathedral Choir, Phila., 1975-82; music specialist Visitation Parish Cath. Sch., Norristown, Pa., 1984-87; dir. music and liturgy St. John the Baptist Cath. Community, Silver Spring, Md., 1987—, dir. children's choir, 1990—; music cons. Archdiocese Wilmington, Del., 1991; cantor Archdiocese Washington, 1987—. Vol. Shepherd's Table, Silver Spring, 1989—. Recipient Liturgy/Music award Pa. State Senate, 1985, Pa. Ho. of Reps., 1985. Mem. Nat. Assn. Pastoral Musicians, Dir. Music Ministries, Nat. Music Honor Soc., Pi Kappa Lambda. Democrat. Office: St John Bapt Cath Community 12319 New Hampshire Ave Silver Spring MD 20904-2998

HUDECKI, GREGORY EDWARD, dentist; b. Fort Bragg, N.C., June 21, 1946; s. Stephen Edward and Veronica Eileen (Kwolek) H.; m. JoAnne Agnes Dinino, July 27, 1968; children: James, Peter. BS, Niagara U., 1968; DDS, SUNY, Buffalo, 1972. Lic. DDS, N.Y. Dentist pvt. practice Buffalo, 1974—; pres. Apollonia Guild, Buffalo, 1985-86; mem. adv. bd. Western N.Y. Med. Waste Mgmt., Buffalo, 1990-91. Golf tournament chmn. Kids Escaping Drugs, 1986-91, chmn. 1991; basketball coach Mt. St. Joseph Acad., Buffalo, 1980-91; mem. adv. bd. Niagara U., 1988; chmn. bldg. com. St. Joseph Collegiate Inst., 1988, pres. bd. trustees, 1989; mem. bd. Erie Community Coll. Found., 1989—, Hospice Soc., 1991. Recipient Recognition award Alcoholism Svcs. of Western N.Y., Buffalo, 1990; named co-capt. Niagara U. Varsity Basketball Team, 1966-68, Man of Yr. St. Joseph Collegiate Inst. 1988, Coach of Yr. Mt. St. Joseph Acad., Buffalo, 1989. Fellow Am. Endontic Soc. (master 1990); mem. Am. Dental Soc., N.Y. State Dental Soc., Erie County Dental Soc., Am. Acad. Cosmetic Dentistry, Buffalo Zoological Soc. (profl. bd. 1988-91).

HUDIAK, DAVID MICHAEL, academic program administrator, lawyer, educator; b. Darby, Pa., June 27, 1953; s. Michael Paul and Sophie Marie (Glowaski) H.; m. Veronica Ann Barbone, Aug. 28, 1982; children: David Michael, Christopher Andrew. BA, Haverford Coll., 1975; JD, U. Pa., 1978. Bar: Pa. 1979, U.S. Dist. Ct. (ea. dist.) Pa. 1979, N.J. 1981, U.S. Dist. Ct. N.J. 1981. Assoc. Jerome H. Ellis, Phila., 1978-79, Berson, Fineman & Bernstein, Phila., 1979-80; sole practice Aldan, Pa., 1980-81; dir. tng. paralegal program PJA Sch., Upper Darby, Pa., 1982—, acting dir., 1983-89, dir., 1989—; v.p. The PJA Sch., Inc., 1989—, bd. dirs.; mem. staff Nat. Ctr. Ednl. Testing, Phila., 1982-87; instr. Villanova (Pa.) U., 1985. Mem. Havertown Choristers; active U. Pa. Light Opera Co., 1977-84. Mem. ABA, Pa. Bar Assn., Founders Club Haverford Coll. Office: PJA Sch 7900 W Chester Pike Upper Darby PA 19082-1992

HUDLEY, DONALD LEE, social worker; b. Washington, Dec. 14, 1946; s. Cornelius and Margaret (Black) H.; m. Beverly Smith, Nov. 30, 1968 (div. 1976); 1 child, Donald L. Jr.; m. Gwendolyn Wooden, Jan. 2, 1988. BA, Morris Coll., Sumter, S.C., 1969; MSW, Howard U., 1977. Lic. clin. social worker, Md. Drug abuse counselor Narcotic Treatment Adminstrn., Washington, 1970-73, Am. Tech. Asst. Corp., McLean, Va., 1973-75; addictions coord. Sheriff's Dept., Upper Marlboro, Md., 1975-77; dir. social svc. Environ. for Human Svc. of No. Va., Arlington, 1978-79; group home adminstr. Triangle Community Assn., Washington, 1977-78; adolescent social worker Devel. Svcs. Ctr., Washington, 1980-85; family counselor No. Va. Family Svcs., Falls Church, Va., 1978-80; contract therapist Family Svcs. of P.G. Co., Inc., Lanham, Md., 1982-83; sch. social worker D.C. Pub. Sch. System, Washington, 1985—. Mem. D.C. Pub. Sch. Crisis Intervention Team, 1990—. Mem. Coun. of Sch. Social Workers Metro Washington (treas. 1991—), Nat. Assn. Black Social Workers, Concerned Black Men, Am. Assn. Counseling and Devel., Kappa Alpha Psi. Democrat. Baptist. Home: 2112 Waterleaf Way Bowie MD 20721-2275

HUDRLIK, PAUL FREDERICK, chemistry educator; b. Portland, Oreg., May 10, 1941; s. Otto Louis and Claudia (Bergman) H.; m. Anne Marie Bachmann, Sept. 9, 1967; children: Janet, Carol. BS, Oreg. State U., 1963; MA, Columbia U., 1964, PhD, 1968. Postdoctoral fellow Stanford U., 1968-69; asst. prof. Rutgers U., New Brunswick, N.J., 1969-76; assoc. prof. Howard U., Washington, 1977-81, prof., 1981—. Author chpts. in books; contb. over 42 articles to profl. jours. Grantee NSF, and others. Mem. AAAS, Am. Chem. Soc., Royal Soc. Chemistry. Office: Howard U Dept of Chemistry Washington DC 20059

HUDSON, JOHN BALCH, chemical engineer, educator; b. Plymouth, Mass., Dec. 11, 1934; s. Harold Kenneth and Aurie Ninette (Balch) H.; m. Carol Jean Greenhill, July 6, 1957; children: Robert Brooks, David Kenneth, Jean Elizabeth. BChE, Rensselaer Poly. Inst., 1956, MS in Chemistry, 1958, PhD in Metallurgy, 1960. Phys. chemist Gen. Electric Co., Waterford, N.Y., 1956-57; phys. chemist rsch. Gen. Electric Co., Schenectady, N.Y., 1957-60; sr. rsch. staff Gen. Dynamics/Electronics, Rochester, N.Y., 1960-63; rsch. assoc. Rensselaer Poly. Inst., Troy, N.Y., 1963-65, asst. prof., 1965-67, assoc. prof., 1967-72, prof., 1972—; cons. Gen. Electric Co., Schenectady, 1963-66, NASA, Langley, Va., 1965-68, Watervleit (N.Y.) Arsenal, 1980-86, Leybold-Infilon Co., Syracuse, N.Y., 1985—. Contbr. articles to profl. jours.; author: Surface Science: An Introduction, 1991. NATO sr. postdoctoral fellow, 1972. Mem. Am. Vacuum Soc. (chmn. chpt. and div. com. 1982-84), AAAS, Materials Rsch. Soc., Saratoga Lake Sailing Club (commodore 1974). Home: 1180 Bellemead Ct Niskayuna NY 12309-2704 Office: Rensselaer Poly Inst Dept Materials Engring Troy NY 12180

HUDSON, STANTON HAROLD, JR., public relations executive, educator; b. Syracuse, N.Y., Jan. 28, 1951; s. Stanton Harold Sr. and Lucille (Shea) H. Cert. lang. and history, L'Univ. de Caen, France, 1970; BA in History/Polit. Sci., Canisius Coll., 1972; postgrad. law, SUNY, Buffalo, 1974-76. Legis. asst., asst. pub. rels. dir. Erie County Rep. Com., Buffalo, 1971-73; dir. pub. rels. and fin. Greater Niagara Frontier Coun. Boy Scouts Am., Buffalo, 1977-79; dir. pub. rels. Ellis Singer & Webb Advt., Buffalo, 1979-80; asst. v.p., mgr. mktg. communications M&T Bank, Buffalo, 1980-85; exec. dir. Shea's Ctr. for the Performing Arts, Buffalo, 1986; pres. Hudson Mktg. Communications, Buffalo, 1987-88; sr. dir. advt. and pub. rels. Blue Cross of Western N.Y., Inc., Buffalo, 1988-91; prin. Fredrickson & Hudson Assocs., Buffalo, 1991—; adj. prof. SUNY, Buffalo, 1987—. Editor employee newsletter M&T Bank Observer, 1981, 82 (Project PICA Grand award United Way of Buffalo and Erie County); mng. editor employee newsletter Blue Cross Ink, 1991 (Excalibur award Pub. Rels. Soc. Am. 1990). Bd. mem. and mem. mktg. com. Am. Lung Assn., Western N.Y., Buffalo, 1983—; bd. mem. Am. Lung Assn., N.Y. State, Albany, 1987—; chair pub. rels. and mktg. coms. greater Buffalo chpt. ARC, 1989—, bd. mem., 1991—; bd. mem., exec. com. Greater Buffalo Opera Co., 1991—. Mem. Pub. Rels. Soc. Am. (accredited pub. rels. practitioner, pres. Buffalo/Niagra chpt. 1990-91, treas. Northeast dist. 1992, mem. Pub. Policy com. PRSA 1992), Am. Mktg. Assn. (v.p. communications Buffalo/Niagara chpt. 1991-92), Western N.Y. Communications Steering Com. (chair 1991-92), Rotary (past dir.). Home: 839 Auburn Ave Buffalo NY 14222-1418 Office: Fredrickson & Hudson Assoc One Franklin PkN Buffalo NY 14202

HUEBNER, LAUREN JEANNE, medical products devices executive; b. San Francisco, Oct. 20, 1959; d. Gilbert Dolan and Phyllis Therese (Glynn) H.; m. Alexander Woodward Hartel, Mar. 16, 1988. BS, U. S.C., 1981. Med. sales rep. Codman & Shurtleff Inc. div. Johnson and Johnson, New Brunswick, N.J., 1982-88; territory sales mgr. St. Jude Med. Inc., St. Paul, 1988—. Vol. Devon (Pa.) Horse Show and Country Fair, 1988—. Republican. Roman Catholic. Home: 134 Lenape Dr Berwyn PA 19312-1847

HUEBSCH, MICHAEL CHRISTIE, investment professional; b. Stamford, Conn., Aug. 11, 1958; s. Ronald Elmer Huebsch and Lucy Beale (Smith) Rowan; m. Suzanne D'Harcourt Hooper, Sept. 23, 1989. BA in Polit. Sci., Trinity Coll., 1980; MBA in Fin., U. Pa., 1985. Asst. trust officer Bankers Trust Co., N.Y.C., 1981-83; v.p. The First Boston Corp., N.Y.C., 1985-89; ptnr., sr. portfolio mgr. Blackstone Fin. Mgmt., N.Y.C., 1989—. Republican. Episcopalian. Office: Blackstone Fin Mgmt 31st Fl 345 Park Ave New York NY 10154-0004

HUEY, J(OSEPH) WISTAR, III, import-export executive; b. Balt., Dec. 8, 1938; s. J. Wistar Jr. and Louisa Thompson (Macgill) H.; m. Rebecca MacRae Wilson, Feb. 2, 1963 (div. 1975); children: Cameron MacRae, Elizabeth Stewart, Rebecca Macgill, Joseph Wistar IV. BA, Johns Hopkins U., 1962. Underwriter emeritus Firemans Fund Ins. Co., Balt., 1962-70; v.p. comml. ins. Stump, Harvey & Cook, Inc., Balt., 1970-77; sr. account exec. Tonque Brooks & Co., Inc., Balt., 1977-85; v.p. comml. ins. Wye Ins., Inc., Balt., 1985-89; v.p. mktg. Ins., Inc., Balt., 1989-91; founder, CEO Chesapeake Antique & Classic Motorcars, Ltd., Balt., 1991—; cons., dir. Mortons Gourmet Wine Importers, Inc., Balt.; bd. dirs. Gaumer Enterprises, Balt., C.J. Dugan Real Estate, Balt.; chmn. bd. dirs. H.E.D. Telecons., Inc. Mem. Md. Hist. Soc., Bentley Drivers' Club, Highland Bagpipes. Home: 508 Greenwood Rd Ruxton MD 21204

HUEY, ROBERT DAVIS, accountant; b. Washington, Dec. 6, 1958; s. Harvey Lee and Roberta (Davis) H.; m. Susan Laura Barnes, Nov. 2, 1985. BS in Acctg., U. Del., 1981. CPA, Md. Auditor Coopers & Lybrand, Washington, 1981-83; ptnr. Huey & Assocs., P.C., Bethesda, Md., 1983—. Bd. dirs. Strategies to Elevate People, Greater Washington, 1988—, pres., 1990—. Mem. AICPA, Md. Inst. CPA's, D.C. CPA's. Presbyterian. Office: Huey and Assocs PC 4720 Montgomery Ln #802 Bethesda MD 20814

HUFF, JAMES FRANCIS, child welfare and school system administrator; b. Scranton, Pa., Sept. 13, 1939; s. Francis Joseph and Margaret (Bell) H.; m. Barbara Ann Haswell, Aug. 17, 1963; children: James, Jeffrey. BS, U. Scranton, 1962; MSW, Fordham U., 1964. Lic. social worker, Pa. Social worker Lackawanna County Children and Youth Svcs., Scranton, 1964-65; asst. supr. Cath. Social Svcs., Scranton, 1965-69; dir. social svcs. St. Michael's Sch., Tunkhannock, Pa., 1969-73, assoc. exec. dir., 1980-88, exec. dir., 1988—; exec. dir. Wyoming County Children & Youth Svcs./United Svcs. Agy., Tunkhannock, Pa., 1977-80; ctr. dir. Luzerne County Children and Youth Svcs./United Svcs. Agy., Wilkes Barre, Pa., 1974-77; practicum faculty Marywood Coll. Sch. Social Work, Scranton, 1985-88; peer reviewer Coun on Accreditation, N.Y.C., 1984—; mem. long range planning com. Cath. Charities USA, Washington, 1984-85. Mem. NASW, Acad. Cert. Social Workers, Am. Mgmt. Assn., Pa. Coun. Children's Svcs. (bd. dirs., treas., v.p. 1985-91, pres. 1991—). Office: St Michaels Sch PO Box 370 Tunkhannock PA 18657-0370

HUFFMAN, JAN, computer software engineer; b. Canton, Ill., June 29, 1943; s. Benny Lewis and Marguerite Bernita (Thrasher) H.; m. Nan Donovan (div. May 1991); children: Hallie, Heath, Amanda. BS, MIT, 1966. Mgr. engring. computer dept. Westinghouse Air Brake Co., Peoria, Ill., 1966-67; systems analyst Sis. of 3d Order of St. Francis, Peoria, Ill., 1967-69; sr. sect. mgr. McDonnell Douglas Auto Co., St. Louis, 1969-76; mktg. specialist Data Gen., Westboro, Mass., 1976-78, Prime Computer, Westboro, Mass., 1978-79; v.p. Absolut Software, Newton, Mass., 1979-89; software engr. Wang Labs., Lowell, Mass., 1989-91, PSDI, Cambridge, Mass., 1991—; speaker in field. Editor: (photo jour.) Tall Topix, 1990. Mem. Tall Clubs Internat. (editor 1990-91), Boston Beanstalk Tall Club (pres. 1991-92, treas. 1988-89). Home: 27 Indiana Terr Newton Upper Falls MA 02164-1314 Office: Project Software Devel Inc 20University Rd #200 University Rd Cambridge MA 02138

HUFTALEN, LISA FREEMAN, corporate executive, graphic designer; b. New Kensington, Pa., Feb. 24, 1953; d. Paul Eugene and Phyliss Maureen (Gravengaard) Freeman; m. Howard Benjamin Huftalen Jr., Sept. 13, 1987. Student, Iowa State U., 1971-75; BA in Graphics and Mktg., R.I. Coll., 1986. Visual merchandiser Army & Air Force Exch. Svc., Ft. Devens, Mass., 1978-81; art dir. Gro Com Group Pub., Barrington, R.I., 1981-82; mgr. advt. and mktg. svcs. Alumiline Corp., Lincoln, R.I., 1982-85; v.p., art dir. Gerald A. Schwarz & Assocs., Guilford, Conn., 1985-87; pres. L.E. Designers, Inc., Old Saybrook, Conn., 1987—, 1978—; graphic designer, vol. Save the Bay, Providence, 1982-87. Pres. River Colony Assn., Guilford, 1987-89. Mem. Old Saybrook C. of C. Republican. Congregationalist. Office: LE Designers Inc 900 Boston Post Rd Old Saybrook CT 06475-2136

HUG, JAMES EDWARD, religious organization administrator; b. Omaha, May 10, 1941; s. Edwin Joseph and Dorothy Ann (Spellecy) H. AB in Philosophy, Spring Hill Coll., 1965, MA in Philosophy, 1966; MA in Christian Spirituality, St. Louis U., 1973; PhD in Christian Ethics, U. Chgo., 1981. Ordained Jesuit priest, 1972. Instr. in philosophy Creighton U., Omaha, 1966-69; mem. editorial staff Theology Digest, 1969-73; lectr. in Christian spirituality St. Louis U., 1972-73; instr. in Christian ethics Jesuit Sch. Theology, Chgo., 1978-80; sr. fellow Woodstock Theol. Ctr., Washington, 1981-85; rsch. dir. Ctr. of Concern, Washington, 1986-88, exec. dir., 1989—; bd. dirs. Internat. Devel. Conf., Washington; cons. The Cath. Healthcare Assn. Author: Scripture Sharing on Bishops' Pastoral, 1987; co-author: Social Revelation: Profound Challenge for Christian Spirituality, 1987; editor, contbr.: Dimensions of the Healing Ministry, 1989; editor: Tracing the Spirit: Communities, Social Action..., 1983. Bd. dirs. Cen. Am. Refugee Ctr., Washington, 1983-85, Religious Task Force on Cen. Am., Washington, 1988—, U.S. Cath. Mission Assn., Washington, 1988—. Mem. Soc. Chirstian Ethics, Cath. Theol. Soc. Am. Office: Ctr of Concern 3700 13th St NE Washington DC 20017

HUGHES, EDWARD T., bishop; b. Lansdowne, Pa., Nov. 13, 1920. Student, St. Charles Sem., U. Pa. Ordained priest Roman Catholic Ch. 1947. Ordained titular bishop Segia and aux. bishop Phila., 1976-86; 2d bishop Diocese of Metuchen, N.J., 1986—. Office: Chancery Office PO Box 191 Metuchen NJ 08840-0191

HUGHES, GLENN D., social studies educator; b. Pitts., June 6, 1949; s. James Robert and Louise Ruth (Staib) H.; m. Susan Noreen May, Aug. 4, 1973. BA in Polit. Sci., Washington & Jefferson Coll., Pa., 1971; MS in Sec. Edn., Duquesne U., 1973. Gen. survey laborer R.M. Keddal & Assocs., Library, Pa., 1967-68; summer laborer Municipality of Bethel Park (Pa.), 1966-71; substitute tchr. Upper St. Clair Sch. Dist., Pitts., 1971-72; substitute tchr. Bethel Park Sch. Dist., 1971-72, tchr. social studies, 1972-91, head coach softball, 1982-91, asst. prin., 1991—; head softball coach Western Pa. Women's Fast-Pitch Softball, Pitts., 1985-90; dean of discipline Independence Middle Sch., Bethel Park, 1987-88. Co-author curriculum guides: Introduction to Social Studies, 1983, Social Studies for Seniors, 1991, Ancient World History, 1984. Recipient Nat. High Sch. Coaching award Scholastic Coach mag., 1988. Mem. Bethel Park Fedn. Tchrs. (exec. bd. del. 1989-91, bldg. rep. 1989-91). Republican. Lutheran. Office: Bethel Park Sr High Sch 309 Church Rd Bethel Park PA 15102-1695

HUGHES, JAMES SINCLAIR, electronic engineer; b. Woodbury, N.J., Oct. 3, 1934; s. James Sinclair and Mary Grace (Berkstresser) H.; m. Joanhanna Rebecca Rothman, Nov. 7, 1964 (dec. 1992); children: Kevin Michael, Shawn Patrick. BS in Physics, U. P.R., 1960, postgrad., 1960-62. Electronic engr. KSM Div. Omark Ind., Moorestown, N.J., 1968-73; physicist Nuclear Research Corp., Southampton, Pa., 1973; electronic engr. Scriptomatic, Inc., Phila., 1973-74, 76-81; optical engr. Geometric Data Corp., Wayne, Pa., 1974-76; subsubcontractor electronic design Ford Motor Co. EEC IV Tester, Pa., 1981—; pres. Arctinurus Co., Inc., Bellmawr, N.J., 1983—. Author: Works on the Star Particle Theory, 1974-92. Home: 20 Sullivan Ave Bellmawr NJ 08031-2332 Office: Arctinurus Co Inc PO Box 275 Bellmawr NJ 08099

HUGHES, PETER M., urologist; b. Glens Falls, N.Y., Apr. 26, 1952; s. Richard A. and Betty L. (Voelker) H.; m. Ann M. Poulos. MD, Autonomous U. Guadalajara, Mexico, 1978. Pvt. practice Glens Falls. Mem. Am. Urol. Assn. Office: 8 Harrison Ave Glens Falls NY 12801

HUGHES, PETER WILLIAM, surgeon; b. N.Y.C., Mar. 16, 1947; s. Timothy Joseph and Annastasia (Asimakes) H.; m. Diana Katherine Kaltsas, Dec. 9, 1973; children: Timothy William, Lauren Elena, Peter Ryan. BA, U. Va., 1968; MD, N.Y. Med. Coll., 1972. Diplomate Am. Bd. Orthopaedic Surgery. Intern St. Vincent's Hosp., N.Y.C., 1972-73; resident Met. and Flower and Fifth Ave. Hosp., N.Y.C., 1973-76; fellow Hosp. for Spl. Surgery, N.Y.C., 1976-77; Mem. sect. med. staff Stamford Hosp., Stamford, Conn., 1982-83; with sect. Stamford surg. com. Stamford Hosp., 1983-84; mem. exec. com. St. Joseph Hosp., Stamford, 1984-86; mem. sect. exec. com. St. Joseph Hosp., 1986-89, chief med. staff, 1989-91; team physician Darien (Conn.) High Sch., 1987—. Contbr. articles to Jour. Bone Joint Surgery, 1977, Clin. Orthopaedics and Related Rsch., 1977. Bd. dirs. Ch. Archangels, Stamford, 1984. Fellow Am. Acad. Orthopaedic Sugery, Am. Coll. Surgeons; mem. Stamford Med. Soc. (pres.-elect 1989). Office: Orthopaedic Assocs Stamford 90 Morgan St Stamford CT 06905-5402

HUGHES, SALLY PAGE, administrative secretary; b. Elizabeth, N.J.; d. Jeff and Irene (Miller) Page; m. July 31, 1954 (dec. Mar. 6, 1962); 1 child, Edward Joseph. Student, Kean Coll., Union, N.J., 1962-69, Upsala Coll., 1969-75. Sec., stenographer Vis. Nurse Assn., Plainfield, N.J., 1955-60, Kean Coll., Union, N.J., 1962-69; tchr. tng. program Upsala Coll., Urban Edn. Corps, East Orange, N.J., 1969-71; sec. to editor The Daily Jour., Elizabeth, N.J., 1971-75; prin. clk. Schering-Plough Corp., Union, 1976-80; unit sec. Elizabeth Multi-Svc. Ctr. Tng. Unit, Elizabeth, 1980-82; adminstrv. sec. Bd. of Edn., Elizabeth, 1982—. Author: (poetry) New Beginnings, 1991; composer: (song) On the Winning Side, 1991; co-writer (song) Where Shall I BE, 1991; soloist/poetess Channel 12 and CTN-Gospel Hour Music. T.V. Nationwide and Internat. Recipient Award of Merit, World of Poetry, 1991, Hon. Mention, Watermark Press, 1991; named Profl. Woman of Yr., Union County Club, Nat. Assn. Negro Bus. and Profl. Women's Club. Mem. NEA, Elizabeth Edn. Assn., N.J. Edn. Assn., Shiloh Bapt. Ch. Choir, Shiloh Bapt. Ch. Missionary Bd., Sun. Sch. Tchrs. Democrat. Baptist.

HUGHES, SARAH SHAVER, historian, educator; b. Alamogordo, N.Mex., Feb. 19, 1933; d. Frank Alvin Steffey and Margaret Amelia (Gibson) Shaver; m. Brady Alexander Hughes, Dec. 14, 1955; children: Danielle, Martha Zoe. BA, Sarah Lawrence Coll., 1954; MS, U. Wis., 1964; PhD, Coll. William and Mary, 1975. Teaching asst. Coll. William and Mary, Williamsburg, Va., 1967-68; instr. Christopher Newport Coll., Newport News, Va., 1972; adj. lectr. Thomas Nelson C.C., Hampton, Va., 1975-77; adj. instr., vis. lectr. Va. Wesleyan Coll., Norfolk, Va., 1970-73, 76; adj. instr., lectr. Hampton (Va.) U., 1965-67, 74-76, asst. prof., 1980-90; assoc. prof. history Shippensburg (Pa.) U., 1991—; cons. Ctr. Arts and Humanities, Hampton, 1970-81, Portsmouth (Va.) Pub. Libr., 1979-82, Nat. Park Svc., Washington, 1984-85, Nat. Endowment Humanities, 1991. Author: Surveyors and Statesmen, 1980; co-author: Lower Tidewater in Black and White, 1982; contbr. articles to profl. publs. Recipient Article award Berkshire Conf. Women Historians, 1979, History Scholar award Va. Social Sci. Assn., 1984; Fulbright fellow Am. Hist. Assn., 1982; Mellon rsch. fellow Va. Hist. Soc., 1989; resident fellow Va. Ctr. Humanities, Charlottesville, 1990. Mem. World History Assn. (exec. coun. 1984-85, 88), Am. Hist. Assn., Berkshire Conf. Women Historians, So. Assn. Women Historians, Orgn. Am. Historians, Inst. Early Am. History and Culture, Nat. Women's Studies Assn. Home: 609 E Orange St Shippensburg PA 17257-2143 Office: Shippensburg U Dept History/Philosophy Shippensburg PA 17257

HUGHES, SHARON MARY, trade association executive; b. Chgo., July 28, 1952; d. George Ingersoll and Rose Myrtle (Reed) H. BA in Polit. Sci. and Communications cum laude, Am. U., 1980, MS in Bus., Govt. Rels., 1985. Freelance photographer N.Y.C., 1972-76; advt. account exec. R.L. Newport and Co., N.Y.C., 1976-78; direct mail advt. mgr. John Wanamaker's, Phila., 1981-83; legis. intern U.S. Congressman James Florio, Washington, 1985; asst. dir. legis. affairs Nat. Food Processors Assn., Washington, 1985-87; mgr. govt. affairs Synthetic Organic Chem. Mfrs. Assn., Washington, 1987-89; exec. v.p. Nat. Coun. Agrl. Employers, Washington, 1989—; chmn. Ad Hoc Agrl. Labor Group, Washington, 1989—; sec.-treas. WISE Coalition, Washington, 1990—. Mem., sodalist Holy Rosary Ch. Sodality, Washington, 1989—. Mem. Women in Govt. Rels. (co-chair environ. task force 1988-89, agr. task force 1989-90, co-chair congrl. rels. com. 1992—), Am. Soc. Assn. Execs., Toastmasters. Democrat. Roman Catholic. Home: 909 G St SE Washington DC 20003-2819 Office: Nat Coun Agrl Employers 1735 I St NW Ste 704 Washington DC 20006-2402

HUGHES, THOMAS ALLEN, museum administrator; b. Rutland, Vt., Dec. 21, 1955; s. Hayden Allen and Jeanette Corrine (Burke) Hughes. B.A., Castleton State Coll., 1978; postgrad. U. Conn., 1978-79. Site mgr. Hubbardton Battle Mus., Vt., 1977-78, 80; interpretive programs asst. Washington's Hdqs., Newburgh, N.Y., 1980-84, historic site mgr. II, 1984—. Mem. Newburgh Hist. Soc., Mid-Atlantic Assn. Mus., Am. Assn. Mus. Home: PO Box 1185 Newburgh NY 12551-1185 Office: Washington's Hdqs 84 Liberty St PO Box # 1783 Newburgh NY 12551-1476

HUGHES, WILLIAM JOHN, congressman; b. Salem, N.J., Oct. 17, 1932; s. William W. and Pauline H.; m. Nancy L. Gibson; children: Nancy Lynne, Barbara Ann, Tama Beth, William John. AB, Rutgers U., 1955, JD, 1958; LHD (hon.), Mt. Vernon Coll., 1984, Glassboro State Coll., 1992. Bar: N.J. 1959. Ptnr. Loveland, Hughes & Garrett, Ocean City, N.J., 1968-78; 1st asst. pros. atty. Cape May County, N.J., 1960-70; mem. 94th-102d Congresses from 2d N.J. dist., 1974—; chmn. judiciary com. subcom. on intellectual property and jud. adminstrn., 1991—. Bd. govs. Shore Meml. Hosp., Sommers Point, N.J., 1972-76. Recipient Ann. Planning award Am. Planning Assn., 1979, Disting. Citizen award Atlantic Area coun. Boy Scouts Am., 1982, Legislator of Yr. award VFW, 1982, Pres.'s award Nat. Dist. Attys. Assn., 1982, Legis. Leadership award Nat. Assn. Chain Drug Stores, 1984, Humanitarian citiation Food Mktg. Chain Drug Stores and N.J. Food Council, 1984, Legis. award Nat. Assn. Police Orgns., 1984, Legis. Achievement award Fed. Law Enforcement Officers Assn., 1984, Man of Yr. award Girl Scouts Am., 1986, Legis. award N.J. Foster Parents Assn., 1986, Leo Fraser Super Achiever award Juvenile Diabetes Found., 1987, Arthur E. Armitage Sr. Disting. Alumni award Rutgers U., 1987, Disting. Info. Processing Pub. Service award Data Processing Mgmt. Assn., 1987; named Congressman of Yr., Nat. Assn. Police Orgns., 1986. Mem. ABA, N.J. Bar Assn., Ocean City Hist. Soc. (bd. dir. 1972-76), Ocean City C. of C. (bd. dir. 1960—), Exch. of Ocean City Club (pres. 1965-66, Nat. Big E. award 1965), Masons (master lodge, Worshipful Master 1969). Democrat. Episcopalian. Home: 1019 Wesley Rd Ocean City NJ 08226-4754 Office: US Ho of Reps 341 Cannon House Office Bldg Washington DC 20515

HUGHES, WILLIAM THOMAS, college administrator; b. Berwick, Pa., Nov. 13, 1940; s. William and Harriette (Runyan) H.; m. Kay M. Potter, Apr. 26, 1958; children: Debra R. (Hughes) Rock, Thomas M. BS in Secondary Edn., Bloomsburg U., 1963; MEd in Counseling, Shippensburg U., 1968. English tchr. Chambersburg (Pa.) Area Sch. Dist., 1963-68; counselor Waynesboro (Pa.) Area Sch. Dist., 1968-71; coord. Neighborhood Youth Corps, Dept. Labor, Franklin County, Pa., 1965-69; evening adminstr. Pa. State U. Continuing Edn., Mt. Alto, 1969-71; programs coord. div. undergrad. studies Pa. State U., Mt. Alto, 1971—. Bd. dirs. Waynesboro Area Sch. Dist., 1976-86, pres. bd. 1982; bd. dirs. Manito Dayt Treatment, Inc., Chambersburg, 1985—. Mem. Pa. Coll. Personnel Assn. (mem. 1st exec. bd. 1973, treas. 1980-87, pres. 1988-89, Outstanding Contribution award 1990), VFW, Elks. Republican. Mem. United Ch. of Christ. Office: Pa State U Mont Alto PA 17237-9799

HUGHS, RICHARD EARL, academic administrator; b. Rochester, N.Y., Jan. 2, 1936; s. Earl Leaman and Frances Rose H.; m. Gretchen Markwardt, Mar. 31, 1959; children—Mark Allen, Grant Evan. B.S. in Physics, U. Rochester, 1957; M.S. in Math, Purdue U., 1959, Ph.D., 1962. Systems analyst Sandia Corp., Albuquerque, 1962-64; asst. prof. Carleton Coll., 1964-66; pres. Math. Service Assos., Inc., Edwardsville, Ill., 1966-69; asso. prof. applied math. and info. systems So. Ill. U., 1966-69; sr. cons. Cresap, McCormick & Paget, Inc., 1968-70; assoc. dean Grad. Sch. Bus. Adminstr., NYU, 1970-77; dean Coll. Bus. Adminstrn., U. Nev., Reno, 1977-84; v.p. corp. affairs Sierra Pacific Resources, Reno, 1984-90; dean Sch. Bus. SUNY, Albany, 1990—; bd. dirs. Bonnel Fund, Inc.; bd. dirs., pres. Northeastern N.Y. Mgmt. Svcs. Corp.; bd. dirs., chmn. Citizens Pvt. Enterprise, 1986-89; com. on edn. C. of C. and Industry N.Y.C., 1970-74; adv. com. Medgar Evers Coll., CUNY, 1971-74; NSF rsch. fellow Purdue U., 1958-60. Mem. deferred compensation com. State of Nev., 1978-84, Nev. Gov.'s Commn. on Econ. Diversification, 1981-83, community liason com. IRS, 1991—; bd. dirs. Albany Bus. Maintenance Orgn. Mem. Assn. Corp. Growth, Western Assn. Collegiate Schs. Bus. (bd. dirs. 1977-84), Albany-Colonie Regional C. of C. (bd. dirs. 1991—), Rotary (bd. dirs. 1989-90), Sigma Xi, Beta Gamma Sigma. Office: Office of Dean Sch Bus SUNY Albany 1400 Washington Ave Albany NY 12222-0001

HUGO, FRANK TRIMBLE, kennel owner; b. Pitts., June 11, 1927; s. Ralph V. and Blanche Hugo; m. Norma Louise Hindmarsh, Jan. 14, 1949; children: Lesley, Victor, David, Elizabeth. Student, Bus. Training Coll., Pitts., 1950, NYU, 1963. Field engr. Fram Corp., Providence, 1956-59, dist. mgr., 1959-68, zone sales mgr., 1969-85; owner, operator Holly Creek Kennels, Marlton, N.J., 1981—. Mem. Bulldog Club of Am. (nat. councelor 1984-90), Bulldog Club of Phila. (show chmn. 1973-90). Republican. Office: Holly Creek Kennels RR 19 Marlton NJ 08053-9804

HUGUENIN, GEORGE RICHARD, business executive; b. East Stroudsburg, Pa., Nov. 6, 1937; s. George L. and Evelyn (Riday) H.; m. Ellen L. Moore, Jan. 4, 1975; 1 child, Paul Louis. SB, MIT, 1959; PhD, Harvard U., 1963. Asst. prof. Harvard U., Cambridge, 1963-67, sr. rsch. assoc., 1967-68; assoc. prof. U. Mass., Amherst, 1968-72, dir. five coll. radio astronomy observatory, 1970-83, prof., 1972-83; founder, pres. Millitech Corp., South Deerfield, Mass., 1982—; bd. trustees U. Mass., Boston, 1987-91. Co-author patent on object detection and location system, millimeter wave imaging device, contraband detection system; author millimeter wave locating, millimeter-wave imaging system; contbr. articles to profl. jours. Named Disting. Vis. Prof. Chalmers U. of Tech., Goteborg, Sweden, 1974; recipient So. New Eng. Entrepreneur of the Yr. award, 1991. Mem. IEEE (sr.), Am. Astron. Soc., Internat. Astron. Union, Internat. Sci. Radio Union, Assn. Old Crows. Office: Millitech Corp South Deerfield Rsch Pk South Deerfield MA 01373 Home: 3 Adams Ct South Deerfield MA 01373-9621

HUI, KOON-SEA, neuroscientist; b. Hong Kong, Sept. 21, 1948; came to U.S., 1976; s. Yuk-Tat and Kiu (Lau) H.; m. Maria Po-Ping Cheung, Aug. 27, 1974; children: Jacqueline, Electra Y. BSc with honors, Chinese U. of Hong Kong, 1971; MPhil, Hong Kong U., 1974; PhD, U. Sask., Saskatoon, Can., 1976. Demonstrator Chinese U. of Hong Kong, 1971-72; teaching asst. Hong Kong U., 1972-74; lab. scientist Sask. Govt., Saskatoon, 1974-76; rsch. scienitst Ctr. Neurochemistry, N.Y.C., 1976-83; lab. chief Nathan S. Kline Inst., Orangeburg, N.Y., 1983—; reviewer NSF, Washington, 1983—, Jour. Biol. Chemistry, Rockville, Md., 1989—; cons. Bioputa Ltd., Stevenage, Eng., 1988—; asst. rsch. prof. NYU, N.Y.C., 1980—. Contbr. chpts. to books. Mem. Affirmative Action Com., Orangeburg, 1987—. Grantee WHO, 1972, 80, BRSG, 1980, 88, NSF, 1979, NIH, 1978—, NIDA, 1991—. Mem. AAAS, Am. Soc. Biochemistry and Molecular Biology, Internat. Soc. Neurochemistry, Internat. Brain Rsch. Orgn., N.Y. Acad. Scis., Am. Soc. Neurochemistry, Hong Kong Soc. Neurosci. Office: Nathan S Kline Inst Orangeburg Rd Orangeburg NY 10962-2210

HUJAR, RANDAL JOSEPH, software company executive, consultant; b. L.A., May 28, 1959; s. Theodore Casmir and Josephine (Camin) H.; m. Kerrie Biancalana, Oct. 17, 1981; children: Tabitha, Allison, Colleen. BS in Fin. and Mktg., U. Santa Clara, 1981. Cons., programmer I.P. Sharp Assocs., Vienna, Austria, 1979-80; mktg. rep. Hewlett-Packard, Cupertino, Calif., 1981-83, mgr. internat. mktg., 1983-84; mgr. product line Hewlett-Packard, Roseville, Calif., 1985-86; dir. mktg. Ashton-Tate, East Hartford, Conn., 1986-88; mgr. product mktg. IBM, Milford, Conn., 1989-90; dir. 1-2-3 product line mktg. Lotus Devel. Corp., Cambridge, Mass., 1990-91; mng. ptnr., founder Lyriq Internat. Corp., Milford, Conn., 1991—. Contbr. articles to profl. jours. Com. mem. Boston Computer Mus., 1991—. Home: 64 Brookhaven Dr Glastonbury CT 06033

HUKILL, PETER BIGGS, pathologist; b. Lucerne, Switzerland, Feb. 3, 1927; s. George Raymond and Helen Naudain (Biggs) H.; m. Nancy Nelms, July 9, 1950 (div. 1969); 1 child, Anne Hukill Yeager. AB, Harvard U., 1947; MD, Yale U., 1953. Diplomate Am. Bd. Pathology. Intern Yale New Haven Hosp., 1953-54, resident, fellow, 1957-60; instr., asst. prof., then assoc. prof. pathology Yale U., New Haven, 1958-68; prof. pathology U. Ala., Birmingham, 1968-69, U. Conn., Farmington, Conn., 1969-77; clin. prof. U. Conn., Farmington, 1977—; dir. of labs. Charlotte Hungerford Hosp., Torrington, Conn., 1977—; assoc. clin. prof. Yale U., 1977—; cons. various Conn. hosps., 1977—; dir. Conn. Dermatopathology Lab., Torrington, 1977—. Contbr. articles to sci. jours. Capt. M.C. USAF, 1954-56. Fellow Am. Coll. Pathologists; mem. Am. Soc. Dermatopathology, Conn. Soc. Pathologists (pres. 1965-66). Office: Charlotte Hungerford Hosp 540 Litchfield St Torrington CT 06790

HULBERT, PHILLIP PHILLIP, public relations professional; b. Vandenburg, Calif., Feb. 16, 1962; s. Donald Ward and Yuette Hulbert. BA, Baylor U., 1984. Dir. communications United Way, Waco, Tex., 1984-85; pub. affairs officer Sec. of the Air Force, Office of Pub. Affairs, N.Y.C., 1985-89; account supr. Hill and Knowlton Pub. Rels., N.Y.C., 1989—. Mem. Big Apple Chapel, N.Y.C., 1988—. Capt. USAF, 1985-89, USAFR, 1989—. Republican. Office: Hill and Knowlton 420 Lexington Ave New York NY 10170-0002

HULL, DALLAS CARL, public relations professional; b. Bowling Green, Ohio, Aug. 3, 1949; s. Delbert Frank and Dana June (Sijan) H.; m. Catherine Lynn Krukar, July 8, 1978; children:Nuriel, Jonah. BA, Bowling Green State U., 1970, MA, 1971; postgrad., U. Mich., 1973-78, U. Tuebingen, Fed. Republic Germany, 1975-76. With Uetze (Fed. Republic Germany) Gymnasium, 1971-72; instr. DePaul U., 1973-79; pub. rels. cons., translator, 1979-88; dir., press officer Amnesty Internat., 1982-84; dist. sales and mktg. mgr. AS Technologies, 1984-85; pub. rels. specialist GE Plastics Media Svcs. Group, Pittsfield, Mass., 1985-86; account supr., dir. plastics publicity group SBN Pub. Rels., Seekonk, Mass., 1986-88; ptnr., dir. pub. rels. Allison, Hull and Malnati, Inc., Pittsfield, 1988—. Mem. Pub. Rels. Soc. Am. (Counselors Acad./ accredited). Office: Allison Hull & Malnati Inc 150 North St Ste 35 Pittsfield MA 01201-5102

HULL, DAVID STEWART, literary agency executive; b. Oshkosh, Wis., Mar. 21, 1938; s. Erastus Hewitt and Charlotte Anne (v. Kussowitz) H.; B.A. (gen. fellow 1960), Dartmouth Coll., 1960; postgrad. U. London, 1960-61. Story editor Universal Pictures-MCA, East Coast office, 1966-69; editor Coward McCann, Inc. N.Y.C., 1970-71; v.p. James Brown Assocs., Inc., N.Y.C., 1971-81; lit. agt. Peter Lampack Agy., N.Y.C., 1981-87; pres. Hull House Lit. Agy., Inc., 1987—. Vestryman, All Saints Episc. Ch., N.Y.C.; guest curator New-York Hist. Soc., 1986. Served to 2nd lt., USAR, 1961-62. Clubs: Coffee House, St. George's Soc. Author: Film in the Third Reich, 1969, 2nd edit., 1973; James Henry Cafferty, N.A., 1986. Hon. friend of Am. wing Met. Mus. Art, 1987—. Home and Office: 240 E 82d St New York NY 10028

HULL, JAMES CLARK, biology educator, plant ecologist; b. L.A., Nov. 29, 1945; s. William Clark and Georgia Dean (Calderwood) H.; m. Carol Ray, July 24, 1971; children: Brian William, Craig Clark. BA, U. Calif., Santa Barbara, 1968, PhD, 1974. Lectr. U. Calif., Santa Barbara, 1974-75; vis. asst. prof. Bishop's U., Lennoxville, Que., Can., 1975-76; prof. Towson (Md.) State U., 1976—; plant ecologist Smithsonian Instn., Edgewater, Md., 1981; vis. scholar Stanford U., Palo Alto, 1984-85. Contbr. articles to Am. Midland Naturalist, Acta Oecologia. Sgt. U.S. Army, 1969-71, Vietnam. NSF grantee, 1984; recipient Outstanding Faculty award Towson State U., 1990. Mem. Am. Inst. Biol. Scis., Ecol. Soc. Am., Sigma Xi. Office: Towson State U Dept Biol Scis Towson MD 21204

HULL, PHILIP GLASGOW, lawyer; b. St. Albans, Vt., Feb. 17, 1925; s. Charles Herman and Gladys Gertrude (Glasgow) H.; AB, Middlebury Coll., 1949; LLB (Ellis fellow, Kent scholar, Stone scholar), Columbia U., 1952; m. Gretchen Elizabeth Gaebelein, Oct. 24, 1952; children: Jeffrey R., Sanford D., Meredith Hull Smith. Bar: N.Y. 1952, Fla. 1977. Staff mem. sub-com. on adminstrn. internal revenue laws, com. on ways and means U.S. Ho. of Reps., Washington, 1951; assoc. firm Winthrop, Stimson, Putnam & Roberts, N.Y.C., 1952-63; ptnr., 1964—. Mem. Sch. Revenue Com., Cold Spring Harbor, N.Y., 1963-65; bd. dirs. Eagle Dock Found., Cold Spring Harbor, 1971-74, People's Symphony Concerts, N.Y.C., 1977—. L.I. Philharm, 1979-81, ; trustee Latin Am. Mission, Miami, Fl., 1969-79; elder Cen. Presbyn. Ch., Huntington, N.Y., 1958-78; mem. nat. missions bd. United Presbyn. Ch. U.S.A., 1967-73; trustee Madison Ave. Presbyn. Ch., N.Y.C., 1989—; mem. Lloyd Harbor Conservation Adv. Coun., 1973-77. Served with U.S. Army, 1943-46. Mem. N.Y. State Bar Assn., Fla. Bar Assn., Am. Coll. Trust and Estate Counsel, Christian Legal Soc. (dir. 1984—), Fellowship Christians in Univs. and Schs. (trustee 1983-90), Univ. Club N.Y.C. (bd. dirs. 1986-90), Downtown Athletic Club, Cold Spring Harbor Beach, Blue Key, Phi Beta Kappa. Office: Winthrop Stimson Putnam & Roberts One Battery Park Pla New York NY 10004-1490

HULL, RAYMOND WHITFORD, public relations executive; b. Cohoes, N.Y., Oct. 13, 1946; s. Raymond W. and J. Ruth (Barber) H. BS, Syracuse U., 1971. Spl. asst. to Gov. Nelson A. Rockefeller, Albany, N.Y., 1971; conf. asst. to commr. N.Y. State Dept. Environ. Conservation, Albany, 1971-74; exec. dir. Spl. Joint Legis. Commn. on Petroleum Distbn., Albany, 1974-75; asst. headmaster Hoosac Sch., Hoosick, N.Y., 1975-77; area coordinator N.Y. State Assembly, Albany, 1977-79; staff dir. N.Y. State Senate Com. on Energy, Albany, 1979-85; dir. pub. affairs Niagara Mohawk Power Corp., Albany, 1985-89; pub. affairs cons. Albany, 1990—. V.p. Rensselaer City Sch. Bd., N.Y., 1981-86; treas. bd. trustees Hoosac Sch., 1974-81, Rensselaer City Hist. Soc., 1980—; trustee Rensselaer County Hist. Soc., 1986—. Republican. Episcopalian. Clubs: Ft. Orange (Albany); SAR (N.Y.C.). Home: The Patroon Agts House 15 Forbes Ave Rensselaer NY 12144-1622

HULL, ROGER HAROLD, college president; b. N.Y.C., June 18, 1942; s. Max Harold and Magda Mary (Stern) H.; m. Anne Elizabeth Dyson, July 4, 1980; children: Roberto Franklin, Lincoln Macgregor. A.B. cum laude, Dartmouth Coll., 1964; LL.B., Yale U., 1967; LL.M., U. Va., 1972, S.J.D., 1974; LHD, Rockford Coll., 1988; LLD, Beloit Coll., 1992. Bar: N.Y. 1968. Assoc. firm White & Case, N.Y.C., 1967-71; spl. counsel to gov., Va., 1971-74; spl. asst. to chmn., dep. staff dir. Interagy. Task Force Law of Sea, NSC, 1974-76; v.p. devel. Syracuse U., N.Y., 1976-79, v.p. devel. and planning, 1979-81; pres. Beloit (Wis.) Coll., 1981-90, Union Coll., Schenectady, N.Y., 1990—; chancellor Union U., 1990—; mem. U.S. del. Law of Sea Conf., 1974-76; adj. prof. Syracuse Univ. Law Sch., 1976-81; bd. visitors Coll. William and Mary, Williamsburg, Va., 1970-74; mem. pub. instns. task force Assn. Gov. Bds., 1975. Author: The Irish Triangle, 1976; co-author: Law and Vietnam, 1968. Mem. ABA, Young Pres.' Orgn., Am. Soc. Internat. Law, Mohawk Country Club, Univ. Club. Office: Union Coll Schenectady NY 12308

HULSE, ROBERT DOUGLAS, high technology executive; b. Niagara Falls, N.Y., Aug. 16, 1943; s. Robert Edwin and Helen Louise (Kenny) H.; m. Nancy Louise Musser, Aug. 20, 1966 (div. 1986); children: Anne Warren, Robert Alexander; m. Karen Alice Karlberg, Dec. 31, 1987. AB, Princeton U., 1965; SMChemE, MIT, 1966, SM in Mgmt., 1968. Mgr. bus. analysis Halcon Internat. Inc., N.Y.C., 1968-73, dir. bus. planning, 1973-76; v.p., gen. mgr. Halcon Catalyst Industries, Little Ferry, N.J., 1976-82; v.p. planning & devel. Engelhard Industries, Iselin, N.J., 1982-84; pres., chief exec. officer Integrated Ionics Inc., Dayton, N.J., 1984-86, Sunstone Inc., Dayton, 1986-87; vice chmn. Princeton (N.J.) Entrepreneurial Resources, Princeton, N.J., 1988-90; pres., chief exec. officer SDTX Technologies, Inc., Princeton, 1989—; v.p. bus. devel. Enzon, Inc., South Plainfield, N.J., 1991—; cons. in field; dir. SDTX Technologies Inc., Princeton, 1989—; pres., dir. Captiva Technologies, Princeton, 1989—. Patentee in field. Dir. Gotham Light Opera Soc., N.Y.C., 1969-73; treas. Bloomingdale House of Music, N.Y.C., 1979-84. Named Univ. scholar Princeton U., 1961. Mem. The Union League Club, Doubles, Sigma Xi, Phi Beta Kappa. Republican. Episcopalian. Home: 706 Sayre Dr Princeton NJ 08540-5835 Office: Enzon Inc 40 Cragwood Rd South Plainfield NJ 07080-2480

HUMBER, RICHARD ALAN, microbiologist; b. San Francisco, May 9, 1947; s. Merrill Roy and Jeanette (Boynton) H.; m. Amy Doyle, June 19, 1977; children: Noel Andrew, Emily Rose. AB in Biol. Scis., Stanford U., 1969; MS in Botany, U. Wash., 1970, PhD in Botany, 1975. Postdoctoral fellow, faculty assoc. dept. entomology U. Maine, Orono, 1976-78; postdoctoral fellow dept. plant pathology Cornell U., Ithaca, N.Y., 1978-79; rsch. assoc. Boyce Thompson Inst., Ithaca, N.Y., 1979-82; adj. assoc. prof. dept. plant pathology Cornell U., Ithaca, N.Y., 1988—; mycologist, microbiologist USDA Agrl. Rsch. Svc., Ithaca, N.Y., 1982—. Mem. editorial bd. Mycologia, 1988-92, Jour. of Invertebrate Pathology, 1985-87; editor: (newsletter) Mycological Society of America, 1991-94. Recipient Steven Fox Meml. award Stanford U., 1969, Grad. Rsch. prize Mycological Soc. Am., 1975, Soc. for Evolutionary Protistology. Mem. Mycol. Soc. Am., Soc. for Invertebrate Pathology (chair jour. adv. com. 1986-87), Soc. for Evolutionary Protistology. Office: USDA Agrl Rsch Svc Soil & Nutrition Lab Tower Rd Ithaca NY 14853-0331

HUMBLE, ROBERTA MUDGE, technical communications educator; b. Westerly, R.I., Aug. 5, 1946; d. Robert Mitchell and Claire (Wordell) Mudge; m. John G. Humble, June 12, 1971 (div. June 1981). BA, U. R.I., 1968, MA, 1971. Instr. Community Coll. R.I., 1970-74, from asst. to assoc. prof., 1974-86, prof., 1986—; writing cons. R.I.N.G., providence, Textron, Inc., Providence, 1990, Mfg. Jewelers and Silversmiths, Providence, 1990, Talbot Treatment Ctr., Providence, 1991, AIPSO, Johnston, R.I., 1991. Author: Technical Victory, 1989, Oral Communications Manual, 1991. Mem. Rotary Club of North Kingstown (pres. 1991-92, Rotarian of Yr. 1990-91), Order of Fgn. Wars, R.I. Com. for Employer Support of the Guard and Reserve (exec.com., publs. editor, Person of Yr. 1991), Corvette Club of R.I. Office: Community Coll RI 400 East Ave Warwick RI 02886-1807

HUMER, PHILIP WILSON, information systems specialist; b. Carlisle, Pa., Nov. 8, 1932; s. Christian Philip and Corinne Barnett (Ramsay) H.; m. Margaret Dysart Barbour, Aug. 15, 1953 (div. Aug. 1978); children: Jean C.

Reardon, Kathleen A. Ries, Richard C. Humer; m. Felicia Forsythe Foulkes, June 20, 1981; stepchildren: Alice E. Foulkes-Garcia, Anne M. Foulkes. BS, Dickinson Coll., 1954; postgrad., Dickinson Sch. Law, Carlisle, Pa., 1954-55, U. Pitts., 1957-59; PhD, Pa. State U., 1964. Traffic engr. Pa. Dept. Hwys., Harrisburg, Pa., 1955-59; rsch. chemist Phillips Petroleum Co., Bartlesville, Okla., 1964-69; sr. rsch. chemist Pa. Indsl. Chem. Corp., Clairton, Pa., 1969-73, Hercules, Inc., Clairton, 1973-74; patent liaison FMC Corp., Middleport, N.Y., 1974-78, Princeton, N.J., 1978—. Mem. budget panel United Way, Princeton, 1990-91, campaign area chmn., 1985. Mem. Am. Chem. Soc., Phila. Patent Law Assn., AAAS. Republican. Presbyterian. Home: 8 Glenwood South Gate St Morrisville PA 19067-1022 Office: FMC Corp PO Box 8 Princeton NJ 08543-0008

HUMES, ROBERT ERNEST, pharmaceutical company executive; b. Erie, Pa., Sept. 30, 1943; s. Millard and Mildred Rosemary (Sabatino) H.; m. JoAnn Florence Malanka, May 29, 1965; children: Christine Marie, Robert Ernest Jr. BA, St. John's U., 1967; MBA, NYU, 1974. With Met. Life Ins. Co., N.Y.C., 1961-67; asst. to v.p. sales U.S. Life Ins. Co., N.Y.C., 1967-68; supr. ins. Bristol-Myers Co., N.Y.C., 1968-71; mgr. pers. planning Squibb Corp., N.Y.C., 1971-72, dir. pers. planning, 1972-75; exec. asst. to chmn. Squibb Corp., 1975-79; v.p. exec. asst. to chmn. Squibb Corp., N.Y.C., 1979-82; sr. v.p. human resources Squibb Corp., Princeton, 1982-89; sr. v.p. corp. resources and social responsibility Bristol-Myers Squibb Co. Pharmaceutical Group, Princeton, 1989-90. Chmn. Lawrence Twp. (N.J.) Mayor's Task Force on Pvt. Sector Initiatives, 1982; bd. dirs. Princeton chpt. ARC, chmn., 1990—; trustee United Way Princeton Area Communities; mem. Mercer County Pvt. Industry Coun.; mem. state corp. cabinet N.J. chpt. Am. Heart Assn., 1985-86. Mem. N.Y. Indsl. Rels. Assn. (pres. 1981-83), Greater Princeton Transp. Mgmt. Assn., Princeton C. of C. (bd. dirs.), Soc. for Human Resouce Mgmt. Home: 87 W Shore Dr Pennington NJ 08534-2009 Office: Squibb Corp PO Box 4000 Princeton NJ 08543-4000

HUMI, MAYER, mathematics educator; b. Baghdad, Iraq, Sept. 29, 1944; arrived in U.S., 1971; s. Joshua and Salima Mizrahi (Shulamit) H.; m. Carmella Zematch, Jan. 14, 1980; children: Michelle M., Joshua M. BSc, Hebrew U., Jerusalem, 1963, MSc, 1964; PhD, Weizmann Inst., Rehovot, Israel, 1969. Postdoctoral fellow Toronto U., Ont., Can., 1969-70, vis. asst. prof., 1970-71; prof. math. Worcester (Mass.) Poly. Inst., 1971—, Sinclair prof. math., 1988—; vis. asst. prof. Clark U., Worcester, 1973-74; vis. assoc. prof. Ga. Inst. Tech., Atlanta, 1978-79; cons. Worcester City Hall, 1975-77, Worcester Quality Food, 1980-82, Data Gen., Westboro, Mass., 1980-83. Author: Second Course on Differential Equations, 1988, Boundary Value Problems, 1991; contbr. articles to profl. publs. Grantee NSF, USAF, USN, U.S. Army, 1985—. Mem. Internat. Assn. Math. Physicists. Jewish. Office: Worcester Poly Inst 100 Institute Rd Worcester MA 01609-2276

HUMMEL, FRANKLIN, library assistant; b. Bristol, Conn., May 1, 1953. BA in Philosophy, Elon Coll., N.C., 1977. Libr. asst. South Portland (Maine) Pub. Libr., 1981-84, Boston Pub. Libr., 1984—; judge Lambda Literary Awards, Washington, 1991, 92. Mem. Gaylaxian Sci. Fiction Soc. (co-founder, pres. 1986-88), Gaylactic Network (founder, dir. 1987-91), Gaylaxians Internat. (founder, coord. 1991-92). Office: Gaylactic Network PO Box 1051 Back Bay Annex PO Box 127 Boston MA 02146

HUMPHREY, CHESTER BOWDEN, cardio-thoracic surgeon; b. Marblehead, Mass., July 29, 1939; s. Leonard Graves and Mary Louise (Bowden) H.; m. Joyce Claire Jazwinski, Mar. 20, 1971; 1 child, Andrew Bowden. BS, Dickinson Coll., 1961; MD, Temple U., 1965. Diplomate Am. Bd. Thoracic Surgery, Am. Bd. Surgery. Intern Hartford Hosp., 1965-66, resident in gen. surgery, 1966-71; resident in thoracic and cardiovascular surgery Naval Regional Med. Ctr., San Diego; cardio-thoracic surgeon Hartford (Conn.) Thoracic & Cardiovascular Group, 1976—. Adv. com. Town of West Hartford (Conn.) Paramedics, 1989—. Comdr. USN, 1970-76. Fellow Am. Coll. Surgeons, Am. Coll. Cardiology, Am. Coll. Chest Physicians; mem. Soc. for Thoracic Surgeons, Denton Cooley Surg. Soc., New England Soc. for Vascular Surgery. Office: Hartford Thoracic & Cardio- vascular Group 85 Seymour St Ste 325 Hartford CT 06106

HUMPHREY, GEORGE EDWARD, humanities educator; b. Weymouth, Mass., Aug. 24, 1949; s. Neal Vaughn and Georgia Elizabeth (Knaide) H.; m. Sytske Vreugdenhil, Aug. 30, 1969; children: Joost, Kaite. AB, Case Western Res. U., 1972; MA, Boston U., 1976, PhD, 1987; cert. mgmt. devel. program, Harvard U., 1991. Dir. theater Lake Cath. High Sch., Mentor, Ohio, 1972-74; teaching fellow Boston U., 1974-80; asst. prof. Mass. Coll. Pharmacy, Boston, 1980-87, assoc. prof., 1987—, chmn. liberal arts dept., 1984—. Editor: Pharmakon Jour., 1991; contbr. articles to profl. jours. Bd.dirs. The Brookline (Mass.) Music Sch., 1983-86; v.p. Brookline Found., 1981-89, pres., 1989-91. Mem. MLA (del. 1983-85), AAUP, Am. Assn. Colls. Pharmacy, Am. Assn. Higher Edn. Office: Mass Coll Pharmacy 179 Longwood Ave Boston MA 02115-5896

HUMPHREY, JAMES, screenwriter, poet; b. Sioux City, Iowa, Feb. 20, 1939; m. Norma Louise Van Vooren, Feb. 28, 1966; 1 child, Saroyan. BA/MA with honors, Brown U., 1977. Part-time tchr. Marshalltown (Iowa) Community Coll., 1967-68; tchr. Falmouth, 1970-71; part-time tchr. Harvard U., 1972, part-time rchr., 1973; part-time tchr. Kennebunk (Maine) High Sch., Merry Hill, N.C., 1974, Brown U., 1977, U. N.C., Providence, 1984, Lawrence Acad., 1985-87; tchr. Lawrence Acad., Independence, 1989, Harvard U., Cambridge, Mass. Author: (screenplays) Trying, 1989, A Fine Romance, 1990, Bye Bye Blackbird, 1991, The Long Way Home, 1991, Without the Consolation of Tears, 1992, Earth Angel, 1992, (poems) Argument for Love, 1970, The Re-Learning, 1976, After I'm Dead Will My Life Begin?, 1986, The Athlete, 1988; contbr. poems to prof. publs. Recipient Writer's award Carnegie Fund, 1978, Arts and Letters award Am. Acad. Inst. of Arts and Letters, 1976, Pen award Poets, Essayists and Novelists, 1976; candidate for Nobel prize in Lit., 1989. Home: 13 Nepperhan Ave Hastings On Hudson NY 10706-4014 Office: Poets Alive! Press 13 Nepperhan Ave Hastings On Hudson NY 10706-4014

HUMPHREY, ROSALIE ANNE, school counselor, educator, consultant; b. London, Eng., June 28, 1947; d. Noel Bertram and Ruth (Bowen) Seebe; m. Brian David Humphrey, Nov. 22, 1969; children: Joshua Noel, Rachel Ana. BA in Chemistry, W.Va. Wesleyan Coll., 1969; MEd in Sch. Counseling, U. Del., 1977. Cert. profl. counselor. Technologist Cornell U., Ithaca, N.Y., 1969-70; nuclear medicine technologist lab. Wilmington (Del) Med. Ctr., 1970-71; tchr. sci. Cecil County Pub. Sch., Elkton, Md., 1971-77, sch. counselor, 1977—; presenter in field. Editor, pub. chair MSCA Newsletter, 1978; contbr. articles to profl. jours. Grantee Md. State Dept. Edn., 1987-88; named Sch. Counselor of Yr., Md., 1991-92. Mem. Am. Sch. Counselor Assn. (v.p. so. region 1988-90, state assoc. chairperson 1989—, membership chair 1990, pres.-elect 1991-92, pres. 1992-93), Md. Assn. Counseling & Devel. (editor jour. 1986-89, conv. reporter 1988, 90-91). Office: Elkton High Sch 110 James St Elkton MD 21921-4900

HUMPHREY, SAMUEL STOCKWELL, former town official, physicist; b. Canton Center, Conn., Apr. 25, 1923; s. Harold William and A. Genevieve (Stockwell) H.; m. Mary Elizabeth Mills, Feb. 4, 1945; children: Warren Mills, Kenneth Stockwell, Marianne Ruth. BS, U. Conn., 1948; MA, Wesleyan U., Middletown, Conn., 1950; postgrad., U. Utah, 1961-63. Enlisted USAF, 1942, advanced through grades to lt. col., 1966, ret., 1971; physicist Wesleyan U., 1948-51; cons. physicist Canton, Conn., 1971-74; tchr. physics Canton (Conn.) High Schs., 1973-74, real estate broker, 1975—; first selectman Town of Canton, 1983-87, selectman, 1989-91; dir. Conn. Conf. of Municipalities, Conn. Interlocal Risk Mgmt. Agys. (CIRMA), 1987; bd. dirs. Sundown Ski Patrol, Inc.; mem. policy bd. and exec. com. Capitol Region Coun. of Govts., 1983-87; cons. physicist RCA, Burlington, Mass., 1971-74, Martin Marietta, Orlando, Fla., 1971-72; researcher in field. Author, editor numerous studies and reports. Trustee, treas. 1st Congl. Ch., Canton Ctr., 1972-85; chmn. Hist. Dist. Commn., Canton, 1972-80, Mcpl. Bd. Fin., Canton, 1975-83; justice of peace State of Conn., 1974—. Recipient numerous awards and decorations USAF and Philippines; Wesleyan U. fellow, 1948-50. Mem. Optical Soc. Am. (emeritus), Air Force Assn., Conn. Christmas Tree Growers Assn. (bd. dirs. 1984—, v.p. 1990, pres. 1992—), Hanscom Flying Club (Bedford, Mass., pres. 1955-59), Skiesta Club (pres. 1964-68), Sigma Xi (assoc.), Sigma Pi Sigma. Republican. Mem. United Ch. of Christ. Home: 96 Barbertown Rd Box 150 Canton Center CT 06020 Office: PO Box 150 Canton Center CT 06020-0150

HUMPHREY, WILLIAM ROLAND, aerospace company executive; b. Wilcoe, W.Va., Dec. 2, 1917; s. Church Gordon and Clarice (Booth) H.; student Harvard, 1937, Am. Mgmt. Assn., 1962-63; BS cum laude, U. Hartford, 1968, MBA magna cum laude, 1978; postgrad. Indsl. Coll. of Armed Forces, 1968-69; m. Alice E. Waters, June 30, 1956; children by previous marriage: Clarice Hilda, Margaret Helena, Stephen William. With N.Y., N.H. & H. R.R., 1937-50, traffic rep., Hartford, Conn., 1944-50; asst. traffic mgr. Billings & Spencer Co., Hartford, 1950-52; traffic mgr. Mattatuck Mfg. Co., Waterbury, Conn., 1952-56; traffic rep. Clipper Carloading Co., Chgo., 1957; traffic mgr. Kaman Aerospace Corp., Bloomfield, Conn., 1957—, dir. traffic, 1989—. Asst. dir. carrier agy. coordination and liaison Office Emergency Transp., 1964—; mem. Nat. Def. Exec. Res., 1954—; asst. dir. for resource mgmt. U.S. Dept. Transp., 1971—; adj. prof. dept. mktg. Austin Dunham Barney Sch. Bus. and Pub. Adminstrn., U. Hartford, 1974—; mem. DOD/NASA Traffic Logistics Interface Com., 1989—. Trustee East Hartford Inter-Ch. Housing Adminstrn., v.p., 1971—. Served with USCGR, 1940-44. Mem. Aerospace Industries Assn. (nat. vice chmn. traffic com. 1962-63), Nat. Indsl. Transp. League, New Eng. Shipper-Carrier Council, New Eng. Shippers Adv. Bd., Am. Soc. Traffic and Transp., Conn. Internat. Trade Assn., U.S. Naval Inst., Nat. Def. Transp. Assn., Am. Soc. Internat. Execs., Greater Hartford C. of C., Capitol Region Transp. Assn., Nat. Wildlife Fedn., Am. Mktg. Assn., Nat. Assn. Purchasing Mgmt. (life cert. purchasing mgr.), Charter Oak Shippers Assn., Am. Security Council (com. strikes in transp.), Internat. Platform Assn., Travelers' Century Club, Transp. Club, Conn. Quarter-century Traffic Club, City Club, Kiwanis, Delta Nu Alpha. Methodist (pres. ofcl. bd. 1965—, pres. bd. trustees). Home: 40 Mountain View Dr East Hartford CT 06108-2985 Office: Old Windsor Rd Bloomfield CT 06002

HUMPHREYS, ROBERT EDWARD, pharmacology and medical educator; b. N.Y.C., Dec. 24, 1942; s. Edward J. and Rosalie (Brown) H.; m. Barbara Kemp, June 15, 1968; children: David John, Daniel Mark. BS, Yale U., 1964, MD, 1970, PhD, 1969. Lic. physician, Mass. Intern U.S. Naval Hosp., Bethesda, Md., 1970-71, med. officer, 1971-73; research assoc. Harvard U., Cambridge, Mass., 1973-75; asst. prof. U. Mass. Med. Sch., Worcester, 1975-79, assoc. prof., 1979-86, prof., 1986—, dir. MD-PhD program, 1985—, chmn. immunology, 1987-89; interim chmn. pharmacology U. Mass. Med. Sch., 1992—. Contbr. numerous papers to med. jours. Am. Cancer Soc. fellow, 1976-79. Mem. Am. Assn. Immunologists, Am. Soc. Hematology. Home: 64 Alcott St Acton MA 01720 Office: U Mass Med Sch 55 Lake Ave Worcester MA 01655

HUMPHRIES, THOMAS JOEL, pharmaceutical company executive, educator; b. Worcester, Mass., Mar. 1, 1945; s. Joseph E.D. and Elizabeth A. (Grinkis) H.; m. Paula F. Callahan, June 26, 1971 (div. May 1990); children: Juliette, Joshua, Alicia. AB in Biology, Harvard U., 1966; MD, Tufts U., 1970. Diplomate Am. Bd. Internal Medicine, Am. Bd. Gastroenterology. Intern, resident in internal medicine Naval Regional Med. Ctr., Phila., 1970-74, fellow in gastroenterology, 1974-75; pvt. practice, Falmouth, Mass., 1978-81; group dir. Smith Kline & French, Phila., 1981-84; dir. R & D Merck Sharp & Dohme, West Point, Pa., 1984-90; v.p., chief med. officer Pharmakinetics Labs., Inc., Balt., 1990; v.p. R & D, Clin. Sci. Rsch. Internat., Balt., 1991-92; sr. v.p. med. affairs, chief med. officer Pharmaco-Clin. Sci. Rsch. Internat., Austin, 1992—; cons. to surgeon gen. USAF, 1984—; assoc. prof. Thomas Jefferson U., Phila., 1985—. Contbr. over 100 articles on internal medicine, gastroenterology and aerospace medicine to med. jours. Comdr. USN, 1966-78; col. M.C. USAFR. Recipient Physician's Recognition award AMA, 1976, 80, 83, 86, 89. Fellow ACP, Am. Coll. Gastroenterology; mem. Bockus Internat. Soc. Gastroenterology (trustee 1986—, sec. gen. 1991—), Harvard Club Md., Courtyard Tennis Club (Austin). Home: 9413 Bell Mountain Dr Austin TX 78730 Office: Pharmaco 4009 Banister Ln Austin TX 78704

HUNDLEY, GARRY WAYNE, risk management consultant; b. Chattanooga, Tenn., Jan. 8, 1951; s. Aryal Burton and Hazel Louise (Richards) H.; m. Judith Joan Whorpole; 1 child, Andrew James. BS, So. Tech. Inst., 1976. Chartered property casualty underwriter; assoc. of risk mgmt. Engr. Factory Mut. Engring., Atlanta, 1976-78; sr. cons. Factory Mut. Engring., Norwood, Mass., 1978-82; loss control mgr. Johnson and Johnson, Inc., New Brunswick, N.J., 1982-84, ins. mgr., 1984-88; risk mgr. Kraft, Inc., Glenview, Ill., 1988-89; asst. v.p., com. officer Crawford and Co., Atlanta, 1989—; nat. committeeman Risk and Ins. Mgmt. Soc., N.Y.C., 1987—; guest lectr. nat. and internat. confs., 1978—. Contbr. articles to profl. jours; editor: University Literary Magazine, 1973. Mem. Nat. Fire Protection Assn., Soc. Chartered Property Casualty Underwriters, Am. Soc. Safety Engrs., Soc. Fire Protection Engrs., Am. Mgmt. Assn., ALTA, Sports Car Club Am. Home: 305 Creekview Ter Alpharetta GA 30202-4697 Office: Crawford and Co PO Box 5047 5620 Glenridge Dr NE Atlanta GA 30302

HUNEKE, JOHN GEORGE, minister; b. Bklyn., Aug. 6, 1931; s. John Jacob and Adelaide (Peper) H. BA, Columbia U., 1953; MDiv, Luth. Theol. Sem., Phila., 1956; ThM, Harvard U., 1958. Ordained to ministry Luth. Ch., 1958. Asst. pastor Holy Trinity Luth. Ch., Bklyn., 1957-59; asst. to the pastor Trinity Luth. Ch., Middle Village, Queens, N.Y., 1959-60; pastor St. John's Luth. Ch., Greenpoint, Bklyn., 1960-73, Luth. Ch. of the Reformation, Bklyn., 1973—; instr. religion Wagner Coll., S.I., 1957-58; stewardship com. Met. N.Y. Synod Luth. Ch. Am., 1966-73. Author: Our Church 1867-1967, 1967. Bd. govs. Greenpoint Br. YMCA, Bklyn., 1963-73. Mem. Ordained Clergy Evang. Luth. Ch. Am. (Timotheans). Home: Ridgewood 6016 Palmetto St Queens NY 11385 Office: Luth Ch Reformation 105 Barbey St Brooklyn NY 11207

HUNGERFORD, GARY A., insurance executive, newspaper columnist; b. Bklyn., Apr. 20, 1948; s. Jean and Ann (Czarnikiewicz) H.; m. Eleanor Haragsim, Oct. 4, 1969. BBA cum laude, The Coll. of Ins., N.Y.C., 1974; MBA, The Coll. of Ins., 1978. CPCU. With Guardian Life Ins. Co., 1965-67, Providence Washington Ins. Co., 1967-68, The Atlantic Cos., 1968-74, Midland Ins. Co., 1974-76, Drake Ins. Co. of N.Y., 1976-78, Patricia Fleischman, Inc./Mead Reinsurance Corp., 1978-80, Vaughan & Hungerford Inc./Yorktown Indemnity Co., 1980-82, Tri-County Facilities, Ltd./Tri-County Facilities N.J., Inc., 1982-85; chmn., chief exec. officer Spl. Risk Facilities, Ltd., Lindenhurst, N.Y., 1985—, CompuPub. Svcs., Ltd., Lindenhurst, 1987—, Hungerford Arms Co., Ltd., Lindenhurst, 1983—; v.p., dir. Protective Ins. Agy., Ridgewood and Lindenhurst, N.Y., 1989—; columnist South Bays Newspaper, L.I. Columnist NYSRPA The Bullett, South Bays Newspaper, L.I.; columnist, editor, pub. Lindenhurst's Chamber News, 1990—; contbr. articles to local newspapers; sponsor U.S. Olympic Shooting Team. With U.S. Army, 1968-70. Mem. Soc. CPCU (N.Y.C. and L.I. chpts.), Soc. for Ins. Rsch., Casualty and Surety Soc. N.Y., Profl. Ins. Agts. N.Y., Profl. Ins. Wholesalers Assn., Coll. Ins. Alumni Assn., Coll. Ins. MBA Soc., Lindenhurst C. of C. (chmn.), Soc. Chartered Property and Casualty Underwriters, Nat. Assn. Desktop Publishers, L.I. Computer Assn., NRA (life, Inst. for Legis. Action, Polit. Victory Fund), Citizens' Com. for Right To Keep and Bear Arms (life, Citizen of Yr.), N.Y. State Rifle and Pistol Assn. (life), Northeastern Arms Collectors Assn., Lindenhurst Lions Club, Old Bethpage Rifle and Pistol Club, NRA Inst. Legis. Action, Nat. Assn. Federally Lic. Firearms Dealers, Second Amendment Found. (life), Lindenhurst C. of C. (chmn.). Republican. Office: Spl Risk Facilities Ltd 101 N Wellwood Ave Lindenhurst NY 11757-4005

HUNNICUTT, ANN SPROULE, retired dental hygienist; b. Norfolk, Va., July 18, 1930; d. Samuel Jackson and Alfreda (Jones) Sproule; m. Glen Charles Luff, Aug. 17, 1955 (div.); children—Susan Carol Luff-Chritton, David Gerrish Luff. A.A., Harcum Jr. Coll., 1950; cert. Thomas W. Evans Sch. Oral Hygien, U. Pa., 1953; B.S. with honors in Speech Pathology, Eastern N.Mex. U., 1968; postgrad. McGeorge Sch. Law, U. Pacific, 1973-77. Registered dental hygienist, Calif., Pa., Maine. Dental hygienist, 1967-88; owner, operator ind. dental hygiene practice, Santa Barbara, Calif., 1977-88; lectr. in field. Author: Be Your Own Boss, 1979; contbr. articles to profl. jours. Founder, 1st pres. Davis (Calif.) Soc. for Prevention of Cruelty to Animals, 1971. Recipient Humanitarian of Yr. award Sacramento Soc. for Prevention of Cruelty to Animals, 1974. Mem. Santa Barbara Dental Hygiene Assn. (pres. 1977, 78), Santa Barbara C. of C., Alumni U. Pa. Republican. Address: PO Box 602 Cape Neddick ME 03902-0602

HUNSINGER, DOYLE J., electronics executive; b. Hazelton, Pa., Nov. 12, 1947; s. Doyle J. and Doris Adele (Price) H.; m. Diane Barbara Trivigno, Oct. 12, 1968; children: Doyle III, Dana. BS in Mktg., Fairleigh Dickinson U., 1974. Various positions Sears, Roebuck & Co., Watchung, N.J., 1966-79; mdse. asst. Sears New York Group, Wayne, N.J., 1979-81; v.p., treas. CMF Key Services, Kenilworth, N.J., 1983-85; pres. CMF Bus. Supplies, South Plainfield, N.J., 1985—, DSI Delivery Systems, Inc., South Plainfield, N.J., 1987—, CMF Design Systems Inc., South Plainfield, 1987—, 701 Leasing Corp., South Plainfield, 1987—; mem. distbr. council Memorex Corp., Santa Clara, Calif., 1983-86. Committeeman Somerset County Rep. Orgn., Watchung, 1974—, mcpl. chmn. 1980; treas. Watchung Candidates Com., 1983—; cons. Union County (N.J.) Dist. 1 Adv. Bd., 1985—; capt. Watchung Fire Dept., 1980-83, trustee, 1988—; v.p., coach Watchung Little League baseball, 1982-83; scoring chmn. N.J. Synchronized Swimming, 1982-84; bd. dirs. Wilson Meml. Ch., Watchung, 1977-79, 83—, fin. chmn. 1984—. Served with USNG, 1967-74. Mem. Data Processing Mgrs. Assn. (bd. dirs. Cen. Jersey chpt.), N.J. Exempt Firemans Assn., Nat. Bus. Forms Assn., Union County C. of C., Cen. Jersey C. of C. Club: Watchung Fire (pres. 1979). Lodge: Optimists (sec. Watchung club 1975-76). Home: 701 Valley Rd Plainfield NJ 07060-6118 Office: CMF Bus Supplies Inc PO Box 339 South Plainfield NJ 07080-0339

HUNT, BERNICE, psychotherapist; b. Phila., June 15, 1920; d. Joseph Bernhardt and Sarah (Freedman) Herstein; m. David Kohn; children: Barbara Adler, Judith Wolman, Eugene Kohn; m. Morton Hunt, Sept. 10, 1971. Student, U. Wis.; MS, L.I. U. Cert. clin. mental health counselor. Children's sci. editor Coward-McCann Geohegan, N.Y.C., 1964-67; editor-in-chief Dandelion Press, N.Y.C., 1978-81; adj. prof. creative writing L.I. U., Southampton, N.Y., 1976-78. Author numerous books; contbr. articles to popular mags. Unitarian-Universalist.

HUNT, CHARLES BERNARD, budget analyst; b. Washington, Oct. 22, 1957; s. Robert and Edmonia C. (Boggs) H. BBA, Southeastern U., 1981. Mgr. Guest Services, Inc., Washington, 1982; purchasing agt. Carroll Manor, Inc., Washington, 1983; adminstr. PCA Internat., Hyattsville, Md., 1984; budget analyst/program analyst Exec. Office of Mayor/Budget Office, Washington, 1984-87; program analyst Met. Police Dept., Washington, 1987—. Juror, Superior Ct., Washington, 1984. Recipient Community award Martin Luther King Jr. Ctr. 1987. Avocations: tennis, swimming, writing. Home: 2115 Maryland Ave NE Washington DC 20002-3132 Office: 2106 38th St SE #210 Washington DC 20020

HUNT, DIANA DILGER, health care administrator; b. Ridgewood, N.J., Feb. 25, 1953; d. Daniel G. Dilger and Ruth M. Wheeler; m. Douglas Gordon Hunt, Nov. 1, 1987; children: Daniel Gordon, Kevin Douglas. BS, Quinnipiac Coll., 1975; MPA, L.I. U., 1992. Staff therapist Bergen Pines Hosp., Paramus, N.J., 1976-81; sr. occupational therapist Rockland Childrens Psychiatric Ctr., Orangeburg, N.Y., 1981-82; program dir. psychiatry Bergen Pines Hosp., Paramus, N.J., 1985-87, dir. occupational therapy, 1982-91; dir. rehab. svcs. Ramapo Ridge Hosp. of the Christian Health Care Ctr., Wyckoff, N.J., 1991—. Mem. Am. Occupational Therapy Assn., N.J. Occupational Therapy Assn. (award of merti), Profl. Health Adminstrn. Assn., Am. Coll. Healthcare Execs., Pi Alpha Alpha. Home: 8 Windsor Ter Mahwah NJ 07430-2815

HUNT, EARL STEPHEN, educational research analyst; b. Chattanooga, Nov. 28, 1948; s. Earl Gladstone Jr. and Mary Anne (Kyker) H.; m. Edeltraut Gilgan, Sept. 6, 1986. BA with honors, Emory and Henry Coll., 1971; MA, Am. U., 1973; PhD, U. Va., 1979. Instr. Fla. So. Coll., Lakeland, 1980-81; edn. cons., Nashville, N.Y.C., 1980-82; editor, cons., Washington, 1982-86; sr. rsch. analyst U.S. Dept. Edn., Washington, 1986—; mem. drug prevention task force U. S. Dept. Edn., Washinton, 1986-89; cons. U.S. Dept. Lab., Washington, 1990—, NSF, Washington, 1990—. Author: Drug Prevention Curricula: A Guide to Selection and Implementation, 1988; co-author: Classification of Instructional Programs, 1991; co-editor: The Apocalyptic Premise: Nuclear Arms Debated, 1982; also articles. Mem. Sangamore-Brooks Lane Citizens' Assn., Bethesda, Md., 1990—. Grantee USIA, 1982. Mem. Nat. Contract Mgmt. Assn., Am. Assn. for Higher Edn., Acad. Polit. Sci., Blue Key, Phi Delta Kappa, Alpha Phi Omega (life), Phi Gamma Mu. Methodist. Home: 5209 Sangamore Rd Bethesda MD 20816-2324 Office: US Dept Edn 555 New Jersey Ave NW Washington DC 20208-0002

HUNT, EVERETT CLAIR, engineering educator, researcher; b. Stamford, Conn., Dec. 28, 1928; s. Benjamin G. and Dorothy (Griffith) H.; m. Jay Kilby, July 12, 1952; children: Gerilyn, Scott, Erik. BS in Engring., U.S. Mcht. Marine Acad., 1951; MS in Engring., Rensselaer Inst. Tech., 1958; MS, Northeastern U., 1972; DSc, Eurotech., 1988. Registered profl. engr., Mass.; chartered engr., Eng. Engr. GE, Schenectady, N.Y., 1954-65; project mgr. GE, Lynn, Mass., 1965-66; cons. GE, Schenectady, 1966-67; engring. mgr. GE, Portland, Maine, 1967-69; mgr. quality control GE, Lynn, 1969-75; dir. Sun Shipbuilding, Chester, Pa., 1975-79; prof. U.S. Mcht. Marine Acad., Kings Point, N.Y., 1979-84; dir. rsch., prof. Webb Inst., Glen Cove, N.Y., 1984—; adj. prof. Widner Coll., Chester, Pa., 1978-79. Editor, author: Modern Marine Engineering, 1991; patentee forced circulation steam generator. Lt. USN, 1951-52, Korea. Recipient Bronze medal U.S. Dept. Transp., 1984. Fellow Inst. Marine Engrs.; mem. Inst. Indsl. Engrs. (sr.), Soc. Naval Architects and Marine Engrs., Pan-Am. Inst. Naval Engrs. Republican. Episcopalian. Home: PO Box 308 Warner NH 03278-9998 Office: Webb Inst Crescent Beach Rd Glen Cove NY 11542-1826

HUNT, FRANCIS HOWARD, retired navy laboratory official; b. Emporia, Kans., Apr. 12, 1919; s. Frederick Raymond and Mabel (Holmes) H.; B.A., Wesleyan U., 1941; m. Kathleen McLean, June 4, 1945; children—Deborah Mary, Laurie Jane, Peter Raymond. Supr. records Columbia U. div. War Research, New London, Conn., 1941-43, tech. editor, writer, 1943-44; with U.S. Navy Underwater Sound Lab., Fort Trumbull, New London, Conn., 1945-70, successively asst. to asst. tech. dir., 1945-47, staff asst. to tech. dir., head tech. info. div., 1947-60; assoc. tech. dir. for adminstrn., 1960-70; asso. dir. center operations Naval Underwater Systems Center, Newport, R.I., 1970-76. Mem. East Lyme Zoning Bd. of Appeals, 1956—; sec., 1960-78, chmn., 1978—; past mem. East Lyme Flood and Erosion Control Bd., Niantic (Conn.) Boy Scout Com., East Lyme Jr. High Sch. Planning Com.; mem. Conn. Fedn. Planning and Zoning Agencies. Bd. dirs. Niantic Public Library, 1962-83; bd. dirs. Child Guidance Clinic Southeastern Conn., 1959-62, East Lyme Nursing Assn., 1964-66; mem. East Lyme Republican Town Com., 1981-90; justice of peace, East Lyme, 1985—. Served with AUS, 1944-45. Decorated Purple Heart, Bronze Star Medal; recipient Outstanding mem. Town Commn. East Lyme C. of C., 1972, 81. Mem. Soc. Tech. Communications, Fed. Profl. Assn., Am. Def. Preparedness Assn., IEEE, Am. Mgmt. Assn. Conn., New London County (mem. adv. bd. 1968-70), Conn., Lebanon, Columbia hist. socs., Nat. Assn. Ret. Fed. Employees, Conn. Soc. Genealogists, Conn. Huguenot Soc. (pres. 1990—), Soc. Colonial Wars in Conn., Conn. Soc. SAR (mem. bd. mgrs. 1980-87, registrar 1984-87, Patriot medal 1987), Soc. of Cin. Congregationalist. Club: Lions (past pres.). Home: 6 Clark St Niantic CT 06357-2502

HUNT, HELEN, association executive; b. Dallas, Feb. 8, 1949; d. H.L. and Ruth (Ray) H.; m. Randy Kreiling (div. 1975); m. Harville Hendrix, Aug. 7, 1982. BA, So. Meth. U., 1971, MLA, 1975, MA, 1978. High sch. tchr. Dallas (Tex.) Ind. Schs., 1971-73; dir. Hunt Alternatives Fund, N.Y.C., 1980—; dir. Dallas (Tex.) Women's Fedn., 1983, 84, Women and Fedn. Corp. Philantropy, 1988-91; co-chair Nat. Network Women's Funds, 1984, 85; chair N.Y. Women's Fedn., N.Y.C., 1985-91. Commr. Mayor's Child Care Commn., N.Y.C., 1991. Mem. Women's Forum. Office: Hunt Alternatives Fund 1255 5th Ave Ste 2C New York NY 10029-4417

HUNT, HOWARD FRANCIS, psychologist, educator; b. Morgantown, W.Va., May 29, 1918; s. Harrison R. and Jane (Fisher) H.; m. Ida Altman, Aug. 16, 1941; children: Carol Ann Hunt Stark, William H., Steven C., John H. A.B., Mich. State Coll., 1940; Ph.D., U. Minn., 1943. Diplomate clin. psychology Am. Bd. Examiners Profl. Psychology. Instr. psychology U. Minn., 1943-44; asst. prof. psychology Stanford U., 1946-48; assoc. prof. U.

Chgo., 1948-54, prof., 1954, chmn. dept. psychology, 1955-62; chief psychiat. research (psychology) N.Y. State Psychiat. Inst., N.Y.C., 1962-77; prof. med. psychology Coll. Physicians and Surgeons, Columbia U., 1962-77; prof. psychology Columbia U., 1962-77; prof. psychology in psychiatry Cornell U. Med. Coll., N.Y.C., 1977-84; clin. prof. psychology in psychiatry Cornell U. Med. Coll., 1984—; attending psychologist N.Y. Hosp.-Cornell Med. Center, 1978-89; fellow (Center for Advanced Study in Behavioral Sci.), 1959-60; chmn. psychopharmacology rev. com. NIMH, 1958-61, mem., 1971-74, mem. bd. sci. counselors, 1961-65; mem. brain scis. com. Nat. Acad. Sci.-NRC, 1974-78; mem. N.Y. State Health Adv. Council, 1975-78. Contbr. articles to profl. publs.; editorial bd.: Jour. Psychiatry and the Law; editorial adviser on psychology: Ency. Brit., 1957—; editor: Dorsey Press Psychology Series, 1959-75, Jour. Abnormal Psychology, 1964-70. Bd. dirs. Founds. Fund for Research in Psychiatry, 1963-66; bd. dirs. Children's Village, Dobbs Ferry, N.Y., v.p., 1964-89. Served from ensign to lt. (j.g.) USNR, 1944-46. Recipient Salmon medal in psychiatry, 1978. Fellow AAAS, Am. Psychol. Assn., Eastern Psychol. Assn.; mem. Sigma Xi, Phi Kappa Phi, Kappa Sigma. Mem. Religious Soc. of Friends. Home: Ardsley Pk Irvington-on-Hudson NY 10533 Office: Cornell Med Ctr NY Hosp 21 Bloomingdale Rd White Plains NY 10605-1596

HUNT, JOHN MEACHAM, retired petroleum geochemist; b. Cleve., Dec. 1, 1918; s. Raymond Edward and Marguerite (Meacham) H.; m. Doris Press, Apr. 10, 1947 (div. June 1973); children: Randall Keith, Lawrence Lee; m. Phyllis Laking, Sept. 1, 1973. BA in Chemistry, Western Res. U., 1942; MS in Petroleum Chemistry, Pa. State U., 1943, PhD in Organic Chemistry, 1946. Instr. chemistry Pa. State U., University Park, 1947; rsch. chemist Jersey Prodn. Rsch. Co., 1948-55, head geochem. rsch., 1956-63; chmn. dept. chemistry and geology Woods Hole (Mass.) Oceanographic Inst., 1964-67, chmn. chemistry, 1967-74, sr. scientist, 1974-84, scientist emeritus, 1984—; chief scientist Red Sea Expdn., 1966, Black Sea Expdn., 1969; mem. U.S. del. petroleum geochemists to USSR oil fields and petroleum labs., 1962; vice chmn. workshop on inputs, fates and effects petroleum in marine environ. NAS, 1973, mem. U.S. nat. com. for geochemistry, 1974-76; chmn. Gordon Rsch. Conf. on Organic Geochemistry, 1976; Crosby lectr. dept. earth scis. MIT, 1981; mem. organizing com. 8th Internat. Congress on Organic Geochemistry, Moscow, 1977; lectr. numerous countries. Author: Petroleum Geochemistry and Geology; chmn. editorial bd. Organic Geochemistry, 1985-89; also over 100 articles. Recipient Karcher medal 3d Ann. Karcher Symposium, 1979. Mem. Am. Chem. Soc., Am. Assn. Petroleum Geologists (lectr. continuing edn. com. 1970-82, disting. lectr. 1964, assoc. editor Bull. 1964-85), Geochem. Soc. (Treibs medal 1982), European Assn. Organic Geochemists, Sigma Xi. Office: Woods Hole Oceanographic Inst Woods Hole MA 02543

HUNT, LAWRENCE JOHN, entrepreneur; b. Cleve., May 29, 1946; s. John Alexander and Jeanne Mildred (Morrison) H.; m. Edith Andrews, July 19, 1975; children: Laura Morrison, Gordon Andrews. BA, Colgate U., 1968; MBA, U. Chgo., 1974; postgrad., Tufts U., 1975. Licensed real estate sales, N.J. Auditor Gulf Oil Co., Linden, N.J., 1972; fin. analyst Chase Manhattan Bank, N.Y.C., 1975-77; pres. Hunt's Hut Inc., Roselle Park, N.J., 1977-83; prin. Metro Properties, Basking Ridge, N.J., 1983-90; account exec. Stuart James Investment Brokers, Iselin, N.J., 1990; pres. Seaboard Mktg. Inc., Raritan, N.J., 1990—; prin. Computer Pages N.J. Inc., Raritan, 1991—, Electronic Directories Inc., Raritan, 1991—. Pres. Liberty Corner Assn., Basking Ridge, 1985-86. With U.S. Army, 1968-71. Mem. Am. Legion, Jaguar Auto Group. Office: Seaboard Mktg Inc 91 E Somerset St Raritan NJ 08869-2117

HUNT, PATRICK JOHN, public relations executive; b. N.Y.C., May 15, 1935; s. John and Alice (Bradley) H.; m. Therese Maria Rolston; children: Mary Alice, Robert Barry. BA, St. Pius Coll., 1957; postgrad., Cath U. Am., 1958-61, Fordham U., 1964-65. Assoc. editor Lamp mag., Peekskill, N.Y., 1959-68; editor NCCJ, N.Y.C., 1968-69; dir. pub. info. SUNY, Stony Brook, 1969-74; dir. pub. rels. Carnegie-Mellon U., Pitts., 1974-76, U. Md., College Park, 1976-85; assoc. v.p. univ. and govt. rels. SUNY, Albany, 1985-90, asst. vice chancellor cen. adminstrn., 1990—; chmn. awards com. coun. univ. affairs and devel. SUNY, Albany, 1988; bd. dirs. Avila Inst. Gerontology, Hudson, N.Y. Mem. Pub. Rels. Soc. Am. (chmn. ednl. and cultural orgns. nat. sect. 1987—), Internat. Assn. Bus. Communicators, Prince George C. of C. (exec. bd. dirs. 1978-85). Democrat. Roman Catholic. Home: 2280 Nelson Dr Niskayuna NY 12309-3904 Office: SUNY N-120 University Plz Albany NY 12246-0001

HUNT, PETER TRUE, psychologist; b. Ithaca, N.Y., June 13, 1951; s. Gordon Ellsworth and Patricia (Rudd) H.; m. Sue Triplett, Nov. 9, 1989 (div.); m. Sarah Ivins, Sept. 22, 1990; 1 child, Ian. AB, Antioch Coll., 1974; PhD, Columbia U., 1979. Lic. psychologist, Conn. Psychologist Regional Dept. of Pediatrics, Waterbury, Conn., 1979-81, Newington (Conn.) Childrens Hosp., 1981—. Mem. Am. Psychol. Assn. Home: 426 Eastbury Hill Rd Glastonbury CT 06033-2062 Office: Newington Children's Hosp 181 E Cedar St Newington CT 06111-1500

HUNT, ROBERT CUSHMAN, anthropologist; b. Binghamton, N.Y., May 30, 1934; s. Robert Cushman and Fanny (Cassidy) H.; m. Muriel Eva Verbitsky, Sept. 21, 1960 (dec. Feb. 1980); 1 child, Melissa Gabriella; m. Irene J. Winter, Oct. 18, 1982. BA, Hamilton Coll., 1956; MA, U. Chgo., 1959; PhD, Northwestern U., 1965. Instr. Northwestern U., Evanston, Ill., 1964-65, asst. prof., 1965-66; asst. prof. U. Ill., Chgo., 1966-69; assoc. prof. Brandies U., Waltham, Mass., 1969-89, prof., 1989—; cons. ISAID, 1978, World Bank, 1982. Author: The Comparative Method, 1979; editor: Personalities in Culture, 1967; contbr. articles to profl. jours. NSF grantee, 1963-65, NIMH grantee, 1967-69, Tng. grantee, 1969-75, NSF grantee, 1990-92; Am. Coun. Learned Socs. fellow, 1975-76. Fellow Am. Anthrop. Assn., Royal Anthrop. Inst., AAAS; mem. Internat. Assn. Study Common Property, Soc. for Econ. Anthropology (pres. 1993). Office: Brandies U Dept Anthrop Waltham MA 02254

HUNT, RONALD DUNCAN, pathologist, veterinarian, educator; b. Los Angeles, Oct. 9, 1935; s. Charles H. and Margaret (Duncan) H. B.S., U. Calif.-Davis, 1957, D.V.M. with highest honors, 1959; student, UCLA, 1954-55. Research fellow pathology Harvard Med. Sch., 1963-64, research assoc. pathology, 1964-69, prin. assoc. pathology, 1969-72, assoc. prof. comparative pathology, 1972-77, prof. comparative pathology, 1977—; dir. Animal Resources Center Harvard Med. Sch., 1979-89; dir. New Eng. Regional Primate Research Center, Southborough, Mass., 1976—. Author: (with T.C. Jones) Veterinary Pathology, 1972, 5th edit., 1983, (with T.C. Jones and U. Mohr) Endocrine System, Respiratory System, Digestive System, Urinary System, Genital System; contbr. numerous articles on research on vet. pathology to profl. jours.; editorial bd.: Lab Animal Medicine, 1969—, Jour. Med. Primatology, 1977—, Internat. Life Scis. Inst, 1981—, Am. Jour. Vet. Research, 1978-80. Trustee Charles Louis Davis DVM Found., 1979—; exec. com. Tufts U. Sch. Vet. Medicine, 1979-82. Served with Vet. Corps U.S. Army, 1959-63. Mem. Am. Coll. Vet. Pathologists, AVMA, Internat. Acad. Pathology, Am. Soc. Exptl. Pathology, Am. Soc. Clin. Pathologists, Mass. Soc. Pathologists, Am. Assn. Lab. Animal Sci., New Eng. Soc. Pathologists, Internat. Primatological Soc., N.Y. Acad. Scis., Am. Assn. Accreditation of Lab. Animal Care (mem. exec. com. 1989).

HUNT, WILLIAM JOSEPH, JR., healthcare administrator; b. Phila., Aug. 8, 1950; s. William Joseph Sr. and Mary Hamilton (McBratney) H.; m. Charlene Ray Mayer, Aug. 18, 1973; children: Amy Michele, Kelly Colleen. AS, Hahnemann U., 1976, BS, 1979; MS, Houston Bapt. U., 1987. Mem. faculty physician asst. program Hahnemann U., Phila., 1976-79; clin. coord. physician asst. program King's Coll., Wilkes Barre, Pa., 1980-83; physician asst. Tunkhannock (Pa.) Med. Arts, 1979-83, USAF, Reese AFB, Tex., 1983-86; clinic adminstr. Geisinger Clinic and Med. Group, Scranton, Pa., 1986—; cons. Pa Med. Bd., Harrisburg, 1980-83; mem. adv. com. physician asst. program King's Coll., 1980-83, Hahnemann U., Phila., 1976—, mem. clin. faculty, 1979—. Mem. com. Rep. Party, Tunkhannock, 1983; sch. dir. Tunkhannock Area Sch. Dist., 1987—; chmn. Wyoming County C. of C., 1990—. 1st lt. USAF, 1968-72, 83-86, Vietnam. Fellow Am. Acad. Physician Assts. (legis. com 1982-86), Med. Group Mgmt. Assn., Pa. Soc. Physician Assts. (pres. 1981-83, bd. dirs. 1976-83, pres.'s adv. com. 1983—, Outstanding Svc. award 1983); mem. Soc. Air Force Physician Assts. (affiliate, legis. com. 1983-86), Wyo. County C. of C. (chmn.), Kiwanis, Masons. Episcopalian. Home: 59 Franklin Ave Tunkhannock PA 18657-1414 Office: Geisinger Med Group 125 Scranton Pocono Hwy Scranton PA 18505-2297

HUNT-CLERICI, CAROL ELIZABETH, academic personnel assistant; b. N.Y.C., Mar. 14, 1938; d. William Laubach and Mary Alice (Grace) Hunt; m. Francis Anthony Clerici, May 17, 1958; children: Francis Anthony Jr., David William, Paul Camilio. AB, Boston Coll., 1987, MA, 1990. Faculty pers. asst. academic v.p. office Boston Coll., Chestnut Hill, Mass., 1984—; psychol. counselor Summerhill House, Norwood, Mass., 1989—; vice chairperson staff adv. senate Boston Coll., Chestnut Hill, Mass., 1985-86, 90-91, chairperson, 1986-88. Rep. Walpole (Mass.) Town Meeting, 1977-82. Mem. APA (assoc.). Office: Boston Coll Asst VP Office 84 College Rd Chestnut Hill MA 02167-3838

HUNTER, ANNE KATHLEEN, medical association executive; b. Washington, Apr. 7, 1945; d. William Lucien and Genevieve (Milliken) Robey; m. Scott H. Hunter, Dec. 29, 1964; children: Jeffrey, Dean, Stacie. Student, Frostburg State U., 1963, Graceland Coll., 1965. Teaching asst. Prince George's County Schs., Md., 1980-87; exec. dir. Internat. Rett Syndrome Assn., Ft. Washington, Md., 1985—. Editor: Parent Idea Book, 1988, Educational and Therapeutic Intervention in Rett Syndrome, 1988, Bridges, 1992. Grantee Am. Legion Child Welfare Found., 1988, 90, 91, Mid-Atlantic Regional Human Genetics Network, 1991. Mem. Nat. Orgn. for Rare Disorders (v.p. 1991—).

HUNTER, KRISTIN EGGLESTON (MRS. JOHN I. LATTANY), writer, educator; b. Phila., Sept. 12, 1931; d. George Lorenzo and Mabel Lucretia (Monigault) Eggleston; m. Joseph E. Hunter, Feb. 29, 1952 (div. Jan. 1962); m. John I. Lattany, June 22, 1968; stepchildren: Leigh L. Norman, John I. Jr., Ramona, Andrew. BS, U. Pa., 1951. Sr. lectr. in English Univ. Pa., 1972—; writer in residence Emory Univ., 1979; lectr. Univ. Iowa, Haverford Coll., Univ. Ky., LaSalle Coll., Lincoln Univ., Nat. Coun. Tchrs. English, Libr. Assns. Conn., Mid-Atlantic States, No. Calif. and S.C., Alpha Kappa Alpha Sorority N.E. Regional Conv., and others. Author: God Bless The Child, 1964, The Landlord, 1966, The Soul Brothers and Sister Lou, 1968, Boss Cat, 1971, Guests in the Promised Land, 1973, The Survivors, 1975, The Lakestown Rebellion, 1978, Lou in the Limelight, 1981; contbr. short stories, poems, revs. and articles to jours. Recipient Univ. Wis. Children's Book Conf. Cheshire Cat Seal, 1970, Silver Slate-Pencil and Dolle Mina awards, The Netherlands, 1973, Chgo. Tribune Book World prize, 1973, Christopher award, 1974, Nat. Book award nomination, 1974, Drexel Univ. Children's Lit. award, 1981, N.J. State Coun. on the Arts Prose fellowship, 1981-82. Mem. PEN, Nat. Coun. Tchrs. English, Alpha Kappa Alpha. Office: U Pa Dept English Philadelphia PA 19104-6273

HUNTER, MARVIN THOMAS, plastic surgeon; b. Chattanooga, May 3, 1942; s. Marvin Thomas and Mildred Marie (Hackney) H.; m. Libby Leff, June 16, 1963 (div. 1976); children: Steven, Edward; m. Nancy Jean Zanzinger, Sept. 24, 1976; children: Adam, Mark. AB in Physics, Temple U., 1964; MD, Hahnemann U., 1968. Intern in surgery Hahnemann Hosp., Phila., 1968-69; resident in surgery Abington (Pa.) Hosp., 1969-70, 72-73; resident in plastic surgery Georgetown U., Washington, 1973-75; pvt. practice Plastic Surgery Assocs. Ltd., Doylestown, Pa., 1975—; chief plastic surgery, chmn. dept. surgery Doylestown Hosp., 1976—, Med. Coll. Hosp. Bucks County Campus, Warmininster, Pa., 1988—. Diplomate Am. Bd. Plastic Surgery. Maj., flight surgeon USAF, 1970-72. Mem. AMA, ACS, Pa. Med. Soc., Am. Soc. Plastic and Reconstructive Surgeons, Am. Soc. Aesthetic Plastic Surgern, N.E. Plastic Surgery Soc., Robert Ivy Soc., So. Med. Assn., Phila. Soc. Plastic Surgery, Internat. Microsurgery Soc., Bucks County Med. Soc. Office: Cosmetic Surgery Ctr Ste 2-3 S Atrium 301 S Main St Doylestown PA 18901 also: Plastic Surgery Assocs Ltd 205 Newtown Rd Ste 108 Warminster PA 18974

HUNTER, MATTHEW, public utility executive; b. Cumberland, R.I., Apr. 12, 1934; s. Matthew and Emily (Cottrell) H.; m. Elsie Louise Wellman, July 2, 1955; children: Diane L., Janice A., Cheryl L. Student, U. Maine, 1966-72; grad. exec. mgmt. program, U. Mich., 1978; grad. mktg. mgmt. program, Columbia U., 1985; grad. advanced mgmt. program, Bus. Sch. Harvard U., 1987. With Cen. Maine Power Co., Augusta, 1952—, various staff positions, 1952-72, purchasing agt., 1974-77, asst. to v.p., adminstrv. services, 1977-78, v.p. adminstrv. services, 1978-84, sr. v.p. customer services and div. ops., 1984—, exec. v.p., 1988-91, pres., chief exec. officer, 1991—; bd. dirs. Maine Yankee Atomic Power Co., Augusta, Cen. Maine Power Co. Bd. dirs. Maine Med. Ctr. Adv. Com. Mem. Electric Coun. New Eng. (bd. dirs.), Maine C. of C. and Industry (bd. dirs.). Republican. Home: 5 Nash St Augusta ME 04330 Office: Ctrl Maine Power Co Edison Dr Augusta ME 04336-0002

HUNTER, PAUL, artist; b. Paris, July 3, 1954; s. Raoul Hunter and Therese Amyot. BA, Laval U., Quebec, Can., 1977; MFA, Concordia U., Montreal, Can., 1979. One man shows include Tibor de Nagy Gallery, N.Y.C., 1987, 89, 90, Que. Mus., 1990, Musee Regional de Rimouski, Que., 1991, others; exhibited in group shows at Tibor de Nagy Gallery, 1990, 91, Springs Art Gallery, East Hampton, N.Y., 1990, Galerie Daniel, Montreal, 1990, Que. Mus., 1991, St.-Hyacinthe, Que., 1991, others; represented in permanent collections at Que. Mus., Butler Inst. Am. Art, Coca-Cola Co., Atlanta, Arthur Anderson and Co., Marsh & McClennan, Boston, Promise Found., N.Y.C. Home: 550 Riverside Dr Apt 52 New York NY 10027-3220

HUNTER, WILLIAM HARRY, III, foundation executive; b. Altoona, Pa., Mar. 29, 1952; s. William Harry and Kathryn Virginia (David) H.; m. Marsha Ann Berkey, Oct. 26, 1984; children: Adam Christian, Sara Renee, Matthew William. BA, Pa. State U., 1975. TV producer/dir. Altoona (Pa.) Area Sch. dist. KVQ-25-TV, 1976-77; IMU adminstr. So. Alleghenies Planning & Devel. Commn., Altoona, 1978-84; v.p. adminstrn. RPS Corp., Hollidaysburg, Pa., 1984-86; dir., fund grant devel. Cen. Pa. Med. Found., Altoona, 1986—. Bd. dirs. Altoona Family YMCA, 1989—; pres. St. Paul Luth. Ch., Altoona, 1990. Mem. Assn. for Healthcare Philanthropy. Lutheran. Office: Ctrl Pa Med Found 5th Fl 620 Howard Ave Altoona PA 16601-4899

HUNTER, WILLIAM SCHMIDT, engineering executive, environmental engineer; b. Bellwood, Pa., Mar. 24, 1931; =. William Franklin and Mary Mildred (Schmidt) H.; m. Barbara Ruth Crosland (dec. Mar. 1959); m. Sandra Lee Showalter, Aug. 26, 1961 (dec. Sept. 1991); children: Felicia Fawn, Clarissa Cay, Patricia Schmidt. BSME, Lehigh U., 1953. Registered profl. engr., Pa. Project engr. W.Va. Pulp & Paper Co., Tyrone, Pa., 1953-56; plant engr. W.Va. Pulp & Paper Co., Williamsburg, Pa., 1956-61; project engr. St. Regis Paper Co., DeFeriet, N.Y., 1961-62; plant engr. Ga. Pacific Corp., Lyons Falls, N.Y., 1962-67; sr. project engr. Allied Paper Co., Kalamazoo, Mich., 1967-69, Hammermill Paper Co., Erie, Pa., 1969-80; chief engr. Stora Papyrus Newton Falls, N.Y., 1980-81, v.p. engring., 1981-90, dir. environ. affairs, 1990—. Bd. dirs. Altoona (Pa.) Engring. Soc., 1955-58, Am. Cancer Soc., Lewis County, N.Y., 1965; vice chmn. Solid Waste Disposal Authority, St. Lawrence County, N.Y., 1992; com. chmn. Explorer Scouts, Williamsburg, Pa., 1959; councilman Williamsburg Borough Coun., 1961; pres., bd. trustees Edinboro (Pa.) Presbyn. Ch., 1978-79. Mem. ASME, TAPPI. Home: Rte 1 Box 63 Colby Ln Star Lake NY 13690 Office: Stora Papyrus Newton Falls Main St Newton Falls NY 13666

HUNTINGTON, PETER PERIT, cardiologist; b. Columbus, Ohio, Sept. 18, 1935; s. John W.P. Huntington and Mary Peters Larsen. MD, Ohio State U., 1961. Diplomate Am. Bd. Cardiovascular Disease. Intern Cin. Gen. Hosp., 1961-62, resident, 1962-65, fellowship in cardiovascular disease, 1964-65; dir. med. intensive care St. Joseph's Hosp., Syracuse, N.Y., 1990—. Maj. U.S. Army, 1965-68. Fellow Am. Coll. Cardiology. Avocations: skiing, gardening. Home: 150 Long Rd Tully NY 13159-9414 Office: 101 Union Ave Ste 607 Syracuse NY 13203-1780

HUNTINGTON, ROBERT HUBBARD, advertising agency executive; b. Sept. 28, 1937; s. Robert Hubbard and Katherine (Wolf) H.; m. Eleanor K. Gallagher, Mar. 18, 1961; children: Robert Hubbard III, Thomas Andrew, Elizabeth Gallagher. B.S., Cornell U., 1959; M.B.A., U. Pa., 1961. With Saatchi & Saatchi Compton Group Inc. (formerly Compton Advt., Inc.), N.Y.C., 1962-88, account handling, 1962-69, asst. treas., 1969-75, treas., sr. v.p., 1975-78, exec. v.p., chief adminstrv. officer, 1978-80, exec. v.p., chief operating officer, 1980-83, chmn., chief exec. officer, 1983-88; vice-chmn., chief operating officer, dir. DDB Needham Worldwide, Inc., N.Y.C., 1988—; bd. dirs. Omnicon Group, Inc. Served with U.S. Army, 1961. Clubs: University (N.Y.C.); Apawamis (Rye, N.Y.), Manursing Island (Rye, N.Y.). Office: DDB Needham Worldwide Inc 437 Madison Ave New York NY 10022-7001

HUNTOON, ROBERT BRIAN, chemist, food industry consultant; b. Braintree, Mass., Mar. 1, 1927; s. Benjamin Harrison and Helen Edna (Worden) H.; m. Joan Fairman Graham, Mar. 1, 1952; children: Brian Graham, Benjamin Robert, Elisabeth Ellen, Janet Lynne, Joelle. BS in Chemistry, Northeastern U., 1949, MS, 1961. Analytical chemist Mass. Dept. Public Health; microbiologist Met. Dist. Commn. Mass. Dept. Public Health, Boston, 1950-53; rsch. and devel. chemist Heveatex Corp., Melrose, Mass., 1953-56; with Gen. Foods Corp., 1956-70; acting quality control mgr. Gen. Foods Corp., Woburn, Mass., 1965-67; head group rsch. and devel. Gen. Foods Corp., Tarrytown, N.Y., 1967-70; dir. quality control U.S. Flavor div. Internat. Flavors & Fragrances, Teterboro, N.J., 1970-83, mgr. tech. svcs., 1983-87, mgr. product devel., 1987-89, cons., 1989—; ind. cons. product devel., 1989—. Contbr. articles on flavor and food quality control to profl. and co. publs.; patentee gelatin compositions and mfg. processes. Served with USCG, 1945-46. Mem. Essential Oils Assn. (com. mem.), Flavor and Extracts Mfg. Assn. (com. mem.), Am. Chem. Soc., Inst. Food Technologists, Internat. Platform Assn., Indsl. Mgmt. Club (v.p. 1967) (Woburn), Croton Yacht Club, Saugus River Yacht Club (treas. 1967-68). Republican. Lutheran. Office: 7 Scotland Hill Park Spring Valley NY 10977-5908

HUNTRESS, WESLEY THEODORE, JR., government executive; b. Washington, Apr. 11, 1942; s. Wesley Theodore and Elizabeth Agnes (Moran) H.; m. Roseann Albano, June 22, 1973; 1 child, Garret. BS, Brown U., 1964; PhD, Stanford U., 1968. Scientist Jet Propulsion Lab., Pasadena, Calif., 1968-88; dep. dir earth sci. NASA, Washington, 1988-90, dir. solar system exploration, 1990—. Home: NASA Code SL 600 Independence Ave Washington DC 20546

HUPPE, ALEX, public relations executive; b. Princeton, N.J., June 18, 1947; s. Bernard F. and Mary Lois (McMaster) H.; m. Lindsay Dearborn, Dec. 26, 1970 (div. 1990); m. Barbara C. Mulligan, Oct. 12, 1991. BA with honors, Harpur Coll., 1969; MA, U. Va., 1971. Prof. English Western Piedmont Community Coll., Morganton, N.C., 1971-79, asst. to pres., 1979-80; asst. dean Boston U., 1980-85; dir. news Dartmouth Coll., Hanover, N.H., 1985—; researcher Smith/Huppe Research, Boston, 1980-85. Co-author: Alaska National Communication Program, 1982. Chmn. bd. dirs. Celo Health and Edn. Corp., Burnsville, N.C., 1973-78. Mem. NATAS (New Eng. chpt. gov. 1983-87, Disting. Svc. award 1987), Pub. Rels. Soc. Am., Ivy League News Dirs. (sec. 1988-91). Office: Dartmouth Coll 23 S Main St Hanover NH 03755-2060

HURCOMBE, WENDY, small business owner; b. Edgware, Middlesex, Eng., Apr. 16, 1941; came to U.S., 1968; d. Ralph Hurcombe and Sheila (Vaughan-Jones) Locke. Retail Distbn. Cert., St. Martins Coll., London, 1960. Buyers clk. Dickins & Jones, London, 1958-60; personal sec. Shulton (Great Britain) Ltd., London, 1960-65, Black & Decker Ltd., Maidenhead, Eng., 1965-68; exec. sec. Cowles Communications, N.Y.C., 1968-71; exec. asst. to pres. Ted Bates Worldwide, N.Y.C., 1972-85, mgr. tng. and devel., 1985-87; pres., owner The Tickler File Co., N.Y.C., 1987—. Mem. NAFE, Am. Women's Econ. Devel.Corp., Nat. Assn. Profl. Organizers. Office: The Tickler File Co PO Box 289 New York NY 10113-0289

HURET, BARRY S., marketing professional; b. N.Y.C., May, 1938; s. Benjamin and Anna (Berko) H.; m. Marilynn Moskowitz, Feb. 1861; children: Abbey, Eric. BA with honors, Cornell U., 1961; MBA with distinction, N.Y. U., 1970. Asst. sales engr. Westinghouse Corp., Pitts., 1962-64; sales engr. MultiAmp Corp., Cranford, N.J., 1964-65; sales engr., regional mgr., nat. sales mgr. Gould, Inc., St. Paul, 1965-77; successively mktg. mgr., dir. mktg., dir. new bus. ventures, v.p. new bus. and govt. sales, dir. splty. product mktg. Exide Corp., Horsham, Pa., 1977-82; nat. sales mgr. battery sales div. Panasonic Indsl. Co., Secaucus, N.J., 1982-86, asst. gen. mgr. battery sales group, 1986—; bd. dirs. Mastushita Storage Battery Co. Am. Author: A User Friendly Guide to Selecting Rechargeable Batteries. Served to lt. U.S. Army, 1961-62. Recipient Hector Lazo Meml. Mktg. award NYU, 1970, Alumni Key, 1970. Mem. Cornell U. Alumni (v.p. class of '59), Electronic Industries Assn. (chmn. battery sect., accessory div.), Phi Beta Kappa. Home: 484 Kings Rd Yardley PA 19067

HUREWITZ, J(ACOB) C(OLEMAN), educator, author, consultant; b. Hartford, Conn., Nov. 11, 1914; s. Isaac S. and Ida (Aronson) H.; m. Miriam Freund, Mar. 29, 1946; children: Barbara Jean, Ruth Anne. BA, Trinity Coll., Hartford, 1936; MA, Columbia U., 1937, PhD, 1950; LittD, Trinity Coll., 1962; DHL, Gratz Coll., 1990. Sr. polit. analyst OSS, 1943-45, Dept. State, 1945-46; polit. adv. U.S. Cabinet Com. on Palestine, 1946; polit. affairs officer UN Secretariat, 1949-50; prof. Middle East polit. history Dropsie Coll., Phila., 1949-56; mem. faculty Grad. Sch. of Arts and Scis., Sch. Internat. Affairs, Columbia U., N.Y.C., 1950-84; prof. govt. Grad. Sch. of Arts and Scis., Sch. Internat. Affairs, Columbia U., 1958-84, prof. emeritus, 1985—; dir. Middle East Inst., 1971-84; vis. prof. polit. sci. Johns Hopkins Sch. Advanced Internat. Studies, 1956, Cornell U., 1970; cons. Carnegie Endowment for Internat. Peace, 1954, Rand Corp., 1962-71, Am. Council Learned Socs., 1963-64, Dept. State, 1966-71, Dept. Def., 1970-74, Stanford Research Inst., 1973-76, ABC News, 1979; founder, chmn. Univ. Seminar on the Middle East, Columbia U., 1971—; bd. research cons. Fgn. Policy Research Inst., Phila., 1972—, Inst. Fgn. Policy Analysis, Cambridge, Mass., 1976—; resident fellow Center for Advanced Studies in the Behavioral Scis., Stanford, Calif., 1962-63, Council on Fgn. Relations, N.Y.C., 1965-66; organizer, dir. internat. confs. on Middle East; participant Dartmouth Am.-Soviet Conf. XII, 1979. Author: The Struggle for Palestine, 1950, Middle East Dilemmas, 1953, Diplomacy in the Near and Middle East, 1956, Undergraduate Instruction on the Middle East in American Colleges and Universities, 1962, Middle East Politics: The Military Dimension, 1969, The Middle East and North Africa in World Politics: I, European Expansion 1535-1914, 1975, II, British-French Supremacy, 1914-1945, 1979; Editor and contbr.: Soviet-American Rivalry in the Middle East, 1969, Oil, the Arab-Israel Dispute and the Industrial World, 1976; Bd. editors: Middle East Jour, 1947-81, Orbis, 1974-91, Terrorism, 1977-81. Mem. adv. panel on tech. transfer to Middle East, Cong. Office of Tech. Assessment, 1982-84. Served with U.S. Army, 1942-43. Social Sci. Research Council grantee, 1946-48; Ford Found. fellow, 1954, 86-88; Guggenheim fellow, 1958-59; Am. Philos. Soc. grantee, 1960; Rockefeller Found. fellow, 1960-62; Ford Found. grantee, 1970; Exxon Edn. Found. grantee, 1981. Fellow Middle East Studies Assn. (founding fellow); mem. Am. Hist. Assn., Middle East Inst. Washington (gov. 1964—), Am. Polit. Sci. Assn., Acad. Polit. Sci., Council Fgn. Relations, Am. Inst. Iranian Studies (founding mem., 1st v.p. 1968-69), Internat. Inst. Strategic Studies, Inter-Univ. Seminar on Armed Forces and Soc. (founding mem.), Am. Research Ctr. in Egypt (gov.), Authors Guild, Phi Beta Kappa. also: 3 Hyatt Ln Westport CT 06880 Office: Columbia U Middle East Inst New York NY 10027

HURFORD, WILLIAM EDWARD, anesthesiologist; b. Pitts., Nov. 6, 1955; s. Walter Johnson and Antonie Marie (Stopchenko) H.; m. Lesley Gilbertson; 1 child, Peter William. AB, Dartmouth Coll., 1977; MD, U. Pa., 1981. Diplomate Am. Bd. Anesthesiology; cert. spl. qualifications in critical care medicine. Intern Mt. Auburn Hosp., Cambridge, Mass., 1981-82; clin. fellow medicine Harvard Med. Sch., Boston, 1981-82, clin. fellow anesthesia, 1982-86, instr. anesthesia, 1986-89; resident anesthesiology Mass. Gen. Hosp., Boston, 1982-84, fellow, 1984-86, asst. anesthesia, 1985-89, 90-91; asst. prof. anesthesia Harvard Med. Sch., Boston, 1990—; assoc. anesthetist Mass. Gen. Hosp., Boston, 1992—, med. dir. respiratory/surg. ICU, 1991—. Recipient Nat. Rsch. award, 1984. Mem. Am. Soc. Anesthesiologists, Internat. Anesthesia Rsch. Soc., Soc. Critical Care Medicine, Am. Thoracic Soc., Am. Coll. Chest Physicians, Am. Soc. Critical Care Anesthesiologists, Assn. Univ. Anesthesiologists, Mass. Med. Soc., Mass. Soc. Anesthesiologists. Office: Mass Gen Hosp Dept Anesthesia WH 5 Fruit St Boston MA 02114

HURLBURT, CHARLES ARTHUR, disability issues consultant; b. Middletown, Conn., Jan. 11, 1963; s. Charles Arthur Sr. and Mary Ann (Macca) H. AS in Human Svcs., Mitchell Coll., 1983; BS in Human Svcs., N.H. Coll., 1988; postgrad., So. Conn. State U., 1988—. Community living instr. Bethphage Luth. Svcs., Wethersfield, Conn., 1985-90; counselor disability issues Disability Counseling Svcs., Rocky Hill, Conn., 1988—; project coord. Ptnrs. in Policymaking Program U. Conn. Health Ctr., Farmington, 1990-91; conducted various presentations, 1989-91. Mem. AACD, Coun. Exceptional Children, Assn. Persons with Severe Handicaps, Conn. Coalition Families of Persons with Disabilities (bd. mem. 1989-91), Conn. Traumatic Brain Injury Assn., Middletown Com. Concerning People with Disabilities (co-chairperson 1990—). Democrat. Office: Disability Counseling Svcs 1800 Silas Deane Hwy Rocky Hill CT 06067-1331

HURLBUT, ROBERT HAROLD, health care services executive; b. Rochester, N.Y., Mar. 9, 1935; s. Harold Leroy and Martha Irene (Fincher) H.; m. Barbara Cox, June 14, 1958; children: Robert W., Christine A. Student, Coll. Hotel Adminstrn., Cornell U., 1953-56. Adminstr., dir. Pillars Nursing Home, Rochester, 1956—, Elmcrest Nursing Home, Churchville, N.Y., 1960—, Elm Manor Nursing Home, Canandaigua, N.Y., 1960—, Penfield Nursing Home, Rochester, 1963—, Avon (N.Y.) Nursing Home, 1964—, Newark (N.Y.) Nursing Home, 1965—, Lakeshore Nursing Home, Rochester, 1972—; bd. dirs. Marine Midland Bank; organizer, adminstrv. dir. Rohm Svcs. Corp., hdqrs. Rochester, 1964—; organizer, pres. Vari-Care Inc., hdqrs. Rochester, 1969—; commr. N.Y. State Incs. Fund; mem. nat. adv. bd. Rochester Inst. Tech. Sch. Hotel and Tourism Mgmt.; mem. Cornell U. Coun. Bd. trustees St. John Fisher Coll., Eastman Dental Ctr.; bd. dirs. Finger Lake Health Systems Agy.; mem. bd. mgrs. Strong Meml. Hosp.; mem. N.Y. State Sen. Lombardi's Task Force on Hosp. Alternate Care. Fellow Am. Coll. Health Care Adminstrs.; mem. N.Y. State Health Facilities Assn. (multi-facility com.), Rochester Area C. of C. (bd. trustees), Genesee Valley Club, Oak Hill, Cornell (Rochester), Lambda Chi Alpha. Home: 200 Sheldon Rd Honeoye Falls NY 14472-9316 Office: 277 Alexander St Rochester NY 14607

HURLEY, ANNE IRÈNE, medical illustrator; b. Red Bank, N.J., Nov. 20, 1958; d. John Robert and Jo Adriènne (Mellina) H.; m. Edward McCabe, Sept. 10, 1989. BA in Biol. Scis., Rutgers U., 1981; MA in Med. Illustration, U. Tex., Dallas, 1983. Biomed. illustrator, sculptor Rutgers U., New Brunswick, N.J., 1978-81; pvt. practice Dallas, 1982-87, Plainfield, Lakewood, N.J., 1988—. Illustrator: American Family Physician, 1982-83, A Woman's Decision, 1984, TMJ Internal Derangement and Arthrosis, 1985, Denny McKeown's Complete Guide to Midwest Gardening, 1985, Gardening in the South With Don Hastings, 1986-87, Orthopaedic Grand Rounds, 1987-88, A Teen Survival Guide, 1988; author, illustrator: The Development and Production of a Sculptural Restoration of Edaphosaurus Boanerges: A Documentation, 1983; represented in permanent exhibit So. Meth. U. Recipient cert. of merit Soc. of Illustrators, 1986. Mem. Assn. Med. Illustrators (hon. mention 1982, 1st place award in exhbn. 1983). Libertarian.

HURLEY, DEAN C., bank executive, lawyer; b. South Weymouth, Mass., Oct. 16, 1954; s. Dean C. and Neva (Richards) H. BS, Fairleigh Dickinson U., 1976, MBA, 1978; JD, N.Y. Law Sch., 1985. Bar: N.J. 1985, D.C. 1986. Asst. ops. mgr. Fieldcrest Mills, Inc., N.Y.C., 1976-77; spl. projects mgr. Citicorp Credit Svcs. Inc., N.Y.C., 1978-86; v.p., dir. fin. planning First Jersey Nat. Corp., Jersey City, 1986-88; v.p. asset strategies A/L. Mgmt. Dae Ichi Kangyo Bank div. The CIT Group, 1988—. Mem. Christian Ctr. Mem. Phi Delta Phi, Omicron Delta Epsilon. Republican. Home: 120 New Jersey Ave Lake Hopatcong NJ 07849-1503 Office: The CIT Group 650 Cit Dr Livingston NJ 07039-5703

HURLEY, JAMES J., priest, publisher; b. Spokane, Wash., Jan. 9, 1946; s. Alvin and Marjorie (Adams) H. BA in Philosophy, Don Bosco Coll., Newton, N.J., 1969; MA in English, Tulane U., 1972; MA in Theology, Pontifical Coll. Josephinum, Worthington, Ohio, 1976; MA in Journalism, Ohio State U., 1976. Ordained priest Roman Cath. Ch., 1976. Editor Salesian Bull., New Rochelle, N.Y., 1976-84, 85-88; cons. to gen. coun. Salesian Soc., Rome, 1984-85; pub. Don Bosco Multimedia, New Rochelle, 1988—. Mem. Nat. Coun. Cath. Evangelization (bd. dirs. 1990—). Home: 148 Main St New Rochelle NY 10801-5354 Office: Don Bosco Multimedia 475 North Ave New Rochelle NY 10801-3405

HURLEY, MICHAEL FRANCIS, addictions counselor; b. Worcester, Mass., Feb. 4, 1942; s. James Cornelius and Virginia Ruth (Madden) H.; m. Charlene Marie Bushee, Sept. 9, 1967 (div. Feb. 1986); children: Kara, Colin, Heather; m. Patricia Anne Tenanty, Mar. 15, 1990. BA, Holy Cross Coll., 1964. Analyst U.S. Govt., Washington, 1965-76; broker Draper Sears & Co., Boston, 1976-84; broker, pres. Hurley Property Mgmt., Rockville, Md., 1984-88; advocate City of Gaithersburg, Md., 1988—; program specialist Montgomery County Govt., Rockville, Md., 1989—; pvt. practice addictions counselor Sandy Spring, Md., 1989—; pres., bd. dirs. Ask for Help, Inc., Annapolis, Md., 1991—. Bd. dirs. Owners Condo Assn., Sandy Spring, 1992. Democrat. Roman Catholic. Home: 1017 Windrush Ln Sandy Spring MD 20860 Office: Montgomery County Addiction Svcs 1 Lawrence Ct Rockville MD 20850

HURLEY, STEVEN RAY, health program administrator; b. Tacoma Park, Md., July 10, 1947; s. Robert Warren and Stella Lavern (Burroughs) H.; m. Sharon Lynn Westfall, July 22, 1972; children: Samara Marie, Shannon Nicole. AS, Orange County Community Coll., Middletown, N.Y., 1969; BS, SUNY, New Paltz, 1970; MS, EdS, SUNY, Albany, 1974. Cert. guidance counseling. Probation officer Schoharie County Probation Dept., Schoharie, N.Y., 1974-79; investigator Office Profl. Med. Conduct, Albany, 1979, Office Health Systems Mgmt., Albany, 1979; sr. personnel adminstr. Office Mental Health, Albany, 1979-83; project dir. Office Mental Health, 1983-84; sr. pers. adminstr. N.Y. State Health Dept., Albany, 1984-89; health program adminstr., dir. staff ops. N.Y. State AIDS Inst., Albany, 1989—; instr. Gov.'s Office Employee Rels., Albany, 1984—. Founder, chmn. bd. dirs. Crisis Intervention Schoharie County, Schoharie, 1973-77; chmn. Zoning Bd. Appeals, Schoharie, 1973-83; mem. Schoharie County Dem. Com., 1979—, Schoharie Sch. Bd. Edn., 1989—; counselor Schoharie County Correctional Facility, 1987—. With USNR, 1964-71. Mem. Internat. Pers. Mgmt. Assn. (pres. 1987-88, Irv Handler Meml. award 1982), Orgn. Mgmt. Confidential Employees Assn. (adv. bd.), N.Y. State Sch. Bds. Assn., Am. Legion, Kiwanis. Democrat. Mem. Soc. of Friends. Home: RR 1 Box 174 Howes Cave NY 12092-9738 Office: NY State Dept Health AIDS Inst Rm # 359 Corning Tower Albany NY 12237-0658

HURLEY, WILLIAM JOSEPH, information systems executive; b. N.Y.C., June 14, 1939; s. William and Anna Rita (Hubschman) H.; m. Dorothy Ann Mellett, Sept. 23, 1961 (dec.); children: William, Terrianne, Barbara, Daniel; m. Marianne P. Jordan, Mar., 17, 1990. BBA, Pace U., 1968, MBA, 1973. Dir. info. system Gen. Foods Corp., White Plains, N.Y., 1973-79; dir. systems devel. Securities Industry Automation Corp., N.Y.C., 1979; dir. mgmt. info. systems Schering Plough Corp., Kenilworth, N.J., 1979-81, sr. dir. mgmt. info. systems, 1981-83, v.p. mgmt. info. service, 1983-88; v.p. world wide info. systems Technicon Corp., Tarrytown, N.Y., 1988-90; dir. info. systems Miles Inc., Tarrytown, 1990—. Pres. New City (N.Y.) Vol. Fire Engine Co. 1, 1979-81; commr. New City Fire Dist, 1983—. Served with USMC, 1956-59. Mem. Soc. Info. Mgmt., Assn. Systems Mgmt. (v.p. 1981), Am. Legion. Republican. Roman Catholic. Home: 10 Rugby Rd New City NY 10956-4029 Office: Miles Inc 511 Benedict Ave Tarrytown NY 10591-5005

HURNEY, LEE MAURICE, podiatrist; b. Flushing, N.Y., Jan. 13, 1950; s. Joseph Paul and Wilma (Berlitski) H.; m. Aug. 15, 1981; children: Evan, Christine. BS, St. John's U., Jamaica, N.Y., 1971; DPM, Ill. Coll. Podiatric Medicine, 1978. Diplomate Am. Bd. Podiatric Surgery. Pediatric physician West Haven (Conn.) Podiatry Assocs., P.C., 1979-89; prin. Lee M. Hurney, P.C., Branford, Conn., 1989—; surg. cons. West Haven VA Hosp., 1980-91; assoc. prof. N.Y. Coll. of Podiatric Medicine, N.Y.C., 1981-91, Coll. Podiatric Medicine, U. Iowa, Des Moines, 1985-91. Fellow Am. Coll. Foot Surgeons; mem. Am. Podiatric Med. Assn., Conn. Podiatric Med. Assn., New Haven County Podiatric Med. Assn. (pres. 1988-90), Rotary (sgt. at arms 1983-85). Office: 97 E Main St Branford CT 06405-3707

HURST, KENNETH LANDIS, physician, educator, health facility administrator; b. Lancaster, Pa., June 29, 1949; s. Lester Martin and Bertha (Landis) H.; m. Janice Marlene Martin, Aug. 1, 1970; children: Kristin Elisa, Jeremy Estel, Hans Erik. BA in Biology and Chemistry with honors, Messiah Coll., 1970; MD, U. Pa., 1975. Diplomate Nat. Bd. Med. Examiners, Am. Bd. Family Practice. Resident family practice program The Williamsport (Pa.) Hosp., 1975-78; clin. preceptor family practice residency program The Williamsport Hosp./Divine Providence Hosp., 1978-90, staff physician, 1978-90; physician co-founder, mem. Cornerstone Family Health, P.C., Williamsport, 1978-90; staff physician Lancaster Gen. Hosp./St. Joseph's Hosp. & Med. Ctr., 1990—; co. physician Armstrong World Industries, Inc., Lancaster, 1990—; asst. dir., asst. clin. prof. family practice program Lancaster Gen. Hosp., 1990—; physician mem. East Petersburg (Pa.) Family Health Ctr., Ltd., 1990—; med. dir. Hospice of Lancaster County, 1991—; med. dir. Community Home Care Svcs., Inc., Williamsport, 1987-90; founder, med. dir. St. Anthony's Free Med. Clinic, Williamsport, 1987-90. Contbr. chpt. Health Care for the Poor, 1990; editor, columnist Lycoming Medicine, 1981-90; columnist Lancaster Medicine, 1992—. Volunteer clin. asst. prof. dept. family practice and community health Temple U. Sch. Medicine; active med. missions Raleigh Fitkin Meml. Hosp., Manzini, Swaziland, 1975, Project Help, Pierre Payen, Haiti, 1983, 85, Med. Group Missions, San Jose Las Matas, Dominican Republic, 1991; founding pres. Physicians & Clergy Peace Initiative, Williamsport, 1986-89; hon. chmn. Lycoming County Cropwalk, Willamsport, 1987. Recipient Cert. of Appreciation, St. Anthony Free Med. Clinic, 1990, Williamsport Hosp. Family Practice/Cornerstone Family Health, P.C. residency, 1990. Fellow Am. Acad. Family Physicians, Pa. Acad. Family Physicians; mem. AMA., Am. Acad. Med. Ethics, Acad. Hospice Physicians, Family Rsch. Coun., Physicians for Social Responsibility, Mennonite Med. Assn., Lancaster County Med. Soc., Pa. Med. Soc., Christian Med. and Dental Soc. (state del. 1980-88, 92—, contbg. editor 1991—). Republican. Office: East Petersburg Family Health Ctr 2045 State St East Petersburg PA 17520-1216

HURST, MICHAEL WILLIAM, psychologist; b. Medford, Oreg., Dec. 9, 1947; s. William George and Betty Muriel (Stevens) H.; m. Patricia C. Scully, Aug. 22, 1970 (div. 1981); 1 child, Michelle P.; m. Renee Catherine Sancoff, Aug. 20, 1988; children: Rachel C., James M. BS, MIT, 1970; MEd, Boston U., 1972, EdD, 1974. Lic. psychologist, Mass., N.H.; cert. employee assistance profl. Rsch. assoc. Powell Assocs., Inc., Cambridge, Mass., 1970-72; rsch. and teaching fellow dept. counselor edn. Boston U., 1972-73, post-doctoral fellow and instr. dept. psychosomatic medicine, 1973-74, asst. prof. psychiatry, 1974-80, assoc. prof. psychiatry, 1980—; attending psychologist Univ. Hosp., Boston, 1978—; pres. Hurst Assocs., Inc., Boston, 1978-91; cons. to numerous orgns., 1978—; v.p. Am. PsychMgmt./Hurst Assocs., Inc., 1991—. Cons. editor: Behavioral Medicine, 1982-91; patentee in field; contbr. articles to profl. jours. Bd. dirs., treas. Mass. Spl. Needs Assn., Inc., Groton, 1973-76; bd. dirs., steering com. Mass. Psychol. Health Plan Inc., Groton, 1979-82; pres., v.p. Pine Acre Park Assn., Hampstead, N.H., 1982-85. Fellow Mass. Psychol. Assn.; mem. Am. Psychol. Assn., Am. Psychopathological Assn. (Morton Prince prize 1978), N.Y. Acad. Scis., Phi Delta Kappa, Delta Upsilon Alumni Assn. (bd. dirs. 1979-82). Republican. Episcopalian. Home: 3 Eastwood Dr Windham NH 03087-1638 Office: Hurst Assocs Inc 21 Custom House St Boston MA 02110-3525

HURST, ROBERT PHILIP, physics educator; b. Bozeman, Mont., May 30, 1930; s. John Wildedoor Hurst and Frances L. Stevens; m. Leslie Ann Hurst, Mar. 11, 1955 (dec. Sept. 1991); children: Kathleen, Frederick, Karl, William. BS, Mont. State U., 1952; MA, U. Tex., 1956, PhD, 1958. Jr. scientist GE Lab., Richland, Wash., 1952-54; postdoctoral fellow U. Tex., Austin, 1958, U. Wis., Madison, 1958-59, U. Ill., Urbana, 1959-60; asst. prof. U. Okla., Norman, 1960-62; asst. prof. physics SUNY, Buffalo, 1962-65, assoc. prof., 1965-68, prof., 1968—. Contbr. articles to sci. jours. Troop leader Boy Scouts Am., Amherst, N.Y., 1970—; deacon North Presbyn. Ch., Williamsville, N.Y., 1973-75, elder, 1980-83, trustee, 1985-89. Grantee Air Force Office Sci. Rsch., 1962-71. Mem. Am. Phys. Soc., N.Y. Acad. Scis. Democrat. Home: 241 Coronation Dr Buffalo NY 14226-1612 Office: SUNY Dept Physics Fronczak Hall Amherst NY 14260

HURT, STEPHEN WAYNE, psychology educator; b. Dallas, June 10, 1951; s. Thomas Wayne and Billie Margaret (Smith) H.; m. Valerie Lee Heim, Aug. 11, 1979; children: Kenneth Wayne, Jeremy Shepherd. BA, U. Tex., 1972; PhD, U. Chgo., 1978. Lic. psychologist, N.Y. Assoc. prof. psychology in psychiatry Cornell Med. Coll., White Plains, N.Y., 1979—; dir. acute Psychol. Svc., N.Y. Hosp.-Cornell Med. Coll./Westchester Div., White Plains, 1986—. Author: Psychological Assessment, Psychiatric DX, 1991. Leader Cub Scouts Am., White Plains, 1990. Mem. APA, N.Y. Acad. Scis., AAAS. Office: NYH-CMC-WD 21 Bloomingdale Rd White Plains NY 10605-1596

HURWITZ, ISRAEL SAMUEL, orthopedic surgeon; b. Boston, Feb. 22, 1930; s. Albert and Ada (Godinski) H.; m. Eleanor Phyllis Moran, Feb. 17, 1957; children: Amy Gutschenritter, Nancy Beth, Arthur Andrew. AB, Cornell U., 1952; MD, Tufts U., 1956. Diplomate Am. Bd. Orthopedic Surgery. Intern New Eng. Med. Ctr., 1957-58, resident in gen. surgery, 1958-60; resident in orthopedics Boston VA Hosp., 1960-63; pres. Orthopedic Asscs. of Marlboro, Mass., 1962—; bd. dirs. Marlborough Savs. Bank, Marlborough Hosp.; pres. Marlborough Hosp. Med. Staff, 1978-80. Bd. dirs. Mass. PRO, Waltham, 1988—. Capt. U.S. Army, 1958-60. Recipient Resident's prize Boston Orthopedic Club, 1962. Fellow Am. Acad. Orthopedic Surgeons (bd. councillors 1984-91); mem. Mass. Orthopedic Assn. (pres. 1988-89), New Eng. Orthopedic Soc., Boston Orthopedic Club, Middlesex West Med. Soc. (pres. 1983-85), Mass. Med. Soc. (exec. bd./alt. 1981—), Alpha Omega Alpha. Home: 15 Metacomet Way Sudbury MA 01776 Office: U5 Fremont St Marlborough MA 01752

HURWITZ, MARK HENRY, sales executive; b. Newark, Dec. 2, 1951; s. Murry L. and Elaine (Goldsmith) H.; m. Patricia B. Zeitler, Oct. 21, 1984; 1 child, Sarah Elizabeth. BA in Fine Arts Edn. cum laude, Kean Coll. N.J., 1974, MA in Fine Arts Edn. magna cum laude, 1982. Cert. tchr., N.J. Art tchr. Montgomery High Sch., Skillman, N.J., 1974-82; sales coord. Burger's Motorcycles, Three Bridges, N.J., 1982-85; acct. exec. Roger Wade Prodns., N.Y.C., 1985-88; v.p. sales Slide Systems, Inc., N.Y.C., 1988—. Editor monthly newsletter The Brigade Courier, 1987, quarterly The Express, 1988; freelance photographer The N.Y. Times Mag., 1979. Mem. Nat. Eagle Scout Assn., Co. of Mil. Historians, Brigade of the Am. Revolution (nat. bd. mem.-at-large 1979-82, 87-90, dir. pub. rels. 1976-87), 3d N.J. Regiment (comdr. 1990—, paymaster 1977-78), B'Nai B'rith. Democrat. Jewish. Home: 383 Jefferson Dr Hightstown NJ 08520-5316 Office: Slide Systems Inc 16 W 19th St Fl 6 New York NY 10011-4205

HURWITZ, SOL, business policy organization executive; b. Washington, Aug. 31, 1932; s. Morris Aaron and Rose (Honig) H.; m. Nina Deutch, May 3, 1959; children: Linda, Mark Aaron, Laura. BA, Harvard U., 1953, postgrad., 1955-56, advanced mgmt. program, 1977. Various communication and broadcasting positions Washington, 1956-60, N.Y.C., 1960-66; assoc. dir. info. Com. for Econ. Devel., N.Y.C., 1966-67, dir. info., 1967-72, v.p., 1972-80, sr. v.p., 1980-90, pres., trustee, 1990—; overseer Colby Coll., Waterville, Maine, 1980—; trustee Joint Coun. on Econ. Edn., N.Y.C., 1982—; dir. Pub. Edn. Fund Network, Washington. Contbr. articles to profl. jours. Trustee Bd. Edn., Rye, N.Y., 1970-76. With USN, 1953-55. Mem. Coun. on Fgn. Rels., Harvard Club N.Y.C., Manursing Island Club (Rye). Home: 800 Forest Ave Rye NY 10580 Office: Com for Econ Devel 477 Madison Ave New York NY 10022

HUSAR, EMILE, civil engineer, consultant; b. N.Y.C., Aug. 21, 1915; s. Elias and Tekla (Melech) H.; m. Lillian Semko, 1960; 1 child; 2 stepchildren. BCE, CCNY, 1938, MCE, 1940. Lic. profl. engr. and land surveyor, N.Y., N.J. Jr. engr. N.Y.C. Park Dept., 1940; jr. engr. def. constrn. Panama Canal, 1941; constrn. supt., designer, estimator gen. contractor, 1946-49; resident bldg. insp. N.Y.C. Bd. Edn., 1950; estimator bldgs. N.J. Turnpike, 1951; dir. pub. works, borough engr. sec. planning bd. bldg. insp. Leonia, N.J., 1952-64; chmn. bd. Stuyvesant Catering Corp., 1960-64; dir. pub. works, twp. engr. Twp. of Berkeley Heights, N.J., 1965-67; asst. city engr. East Orange, N.J., 1967-70; office and project engr. Clinton Bogert Assocs., Cons. Water & Sewer Engrs., 1970-76; borough engr., dir. pub. works Roselle, N.J., 1977; registered rep. First Investors Corp., 1967-69, Sage, N.J., 1969-76; pvt. practice as bldg. constrn. estimator and home inspection cons., 1976—; resident engr. Lawler, Matusky & Skelly, cons. engrs., N.Y.C., 1979-83, Singstad, Hurks & Assocs., 1984-85, RBA Group Engrs. & Planners, 1986-87, Shah Assocs. Cons. Engrs., 1987-88, Goodkind & O'Dea, Cons. Engrs., 1984, Massand Cons. Engrs., 1989-90. Pres. Ukranian Nat. Home of N.Y.C., 1956-62; conciliator N.J. Pub. Adv., 1981-84. 1st lt. C.E., U.S. Army, 1942-46. Recipient Presdl. citation for S.W. Pacific and Papuan Campaigns. Fellow ASCE; mem. Nat. Soc. Profl. Engrs., N.J. Soc. Profl. Engrs., 401 Investors Club (pres. 1965-75). Home and Office: 411 Charles Pl Leonia NJ 07605-1309

HUSBANDS, HUMPHREY OLIVER, economics educator; b. Barbados, Jan. 25, 1929; s. Leonard Bedford and Lenno Miriam (Small) H.; m. Waple Veronica Jemmott, Oct. 12, 1957; 1 child, Kaye Georgina. BBA summa cum laude, CUNY, 1974, MA in Econs., 1976, PhD in Econs., 1991. Clk. Merrill Lynch, N.Y.C., 1967-72; instr. Montclair State Coll., Upper Montclair, N.J., 1976-87; univ. fellow grad. sch. and univ. ctr. CUNY, N.Y.C., 1989-90; asst. prof. Black and Hispanic studies dept. Baruch Coll., CUNY, N.Y.C., 1991—. Contbr. articles to profl. jours. Lay reader, chalice minister Ch. of the Epiphany and St. Simon, Bklyn., 1982—; Montclair State Coll. rep. social scis. N.J Dept. Edn. Tchr. Certification Program, 1984. Robert C. Weaver Incentive scholar Baruch Coll. CUNY, 1974, Richter Grad. Sch. scholar Hunter Coll. CUNY, 1976. Mem. Beta Gamma Sigma. Democrat. Episcopalian. Home: 1176 E 46 St Brooklyn NY 11234 Office: Baruch Coll Black and Hispanic Studies Dept Box 285 17 Lexington Ave New York NY 10010

HUSON, GEORGE ROE, rocket propulsion engineer; b. Bklyn., Oct. 12, 1929; s. George R. and Lillian F. (Lomax) H.; m. Patsy Jane Edsall, Sept. 15, 1956; children: Gregory, Denise, Claire, Margaret. BChemE, Syracuse U., 1950; postgrad., Stuttgart Tech. Hochschule, Fed. Republic Germany, 1953-54; MChemE, NYU, 1956. Registered profl. Engr., N.J. Chem. engr. Mathieson Chem. Corp., Niagara Falls, N.Y., 1950-51; propellant rsch. engr. Bell Aircraft Corp., Niagara Falls, 1951-52; thruster analyst Reaction Motors, Inc., Denville, N.J., 1955-65; Apollo propulsion specialist Bellcomm Inc., Washington, 1965-67; spacecraft propulsion specialist Communications Satellite Corp., Clarksburg, Md., 1967-88; clean coal reviewer Tech. and Mgmt. Svc., Germantown, Md., 1988; propulsion cons. EUTELSAT, Paris, 1988-90; spacecraft cons. INTELSAT, Princeton, N.J., 1990—. Pres. Gaithersburg (Md.) High Sch. PTSA, 1976; referee Whetstone Swim Team, Gaithersburg, 1971-85. Fulbright scholar. Assoc. fellow AIAA (mem. tech. com. 1971-73, 81-83). Home: 19158 Roman Way Gaithersburg MD 20879-2038

HUSSAR, JOHN JAMES, computer imaging creator; b. Mt. Kisco, N.Y., Aug. 12, 1960; s. James August and Natalie Jean (McKissick) H. Student, Ithaca (N.Y.) Coll., 1978-80; BFA in Film Prodn., SUNY, Purchase, 1984. Writer/dir. No. Lights Entertainment, Ltd., N.Y.C., 1984-90; pres. Broadcast Imaging, Armonk, N.Y., 1990—; cons. Publication Technologies, Stamford, Conn., 1990-91. Writer/dir. (film) Forty Years from Hiroshima, 1985, Grandmothers House, 1986; author: The Pirates, 1987. Mem. Apple Programmer and Developers Assn. Office: Broadcast Imaging One Sunrise Dr Armonk NY 10504-1430

HUSSEIN, AHMED DIA, investment banker; b. Cairo, Egypt, May 28, 1941; came to U.S. 1966.; s. Ali Mohamed and Yemen Mostafa (El-Emawy) H.; m. Marjorie Battersby, May 20, 1977 (div. 1981); 1 child, Ali; m. Maha Anwar Nowailaty, Dec. 7, 1990; 1 child, Youmn. BEE, Cairo U., 1963; MSc, Am. U. Cairo, 1965; postgrad. diploma in stats., Cairo U., 1965; MSC in Math., Poly. Inst. N.Y., Bklyn., 1969; PhD in Elec. Engring., Poly. Inst. N.Y., 1969. Research assoc. Nat. Research Inst., Cairo, 1963-66; lectr. CUNY, 1966-70; sr. engr. IBM, East Fishkill, N.Y., 1969-70; asst. to assoc. prof. Am. U. Cairo, 1970-77; cons. engr. N.Y.C., 1977-79; account exec. Moseley Hallgarten, N.Y.C., 1979-80; v.p. L.F. Rothschild, N.Y.C., 1980-81; sr. v.p. Prudential Bache Securities, N.Y.C., 1981-86, Oppenheimer & Co., N.Y.C., 1986-87; v.p. Smith Barney, N.Y.C., 1987-89; sr. v.p. Shearson Lehman Hutton, Inc., N.Y.C., 1989—. Contbr. articles to profl. jours. Received Gold medal for social svcs. Cairo U., 1958; Fulbright scholar, 1965. Moslem. Office: Shearson Lehman Hutton One Penn Plz New York NY 10119

HUSSEY, PHILIP WILLIAM, JR., manufacturing company executive; b. N. Berwik, Maine, June 15, 1931; s. Philip William and Elizabeth (Taylor) H.; m. Martha Dewolf, Feb. 12, 1954; children: Timothy, Anne, Jonathan, Richard. AB, Colby Coll., Waterville, Maine, 1953, MA, 1983. Treas. Hussey Seating Co., N. Berwick, 1955-67, exec. v.p., 1963-67, pres., 1967—. Republican. Congregationalist. Office: Hussey Seating Co Dyer St North Berwick ME 03906

HUSZAR, GABOR BELA, obstetrician, gynecologist, andrologist; b. Budapest, Hungary, Nov. 3, 1938; m. Theresa Gal, July 20, 1966; children: Thomas, Andrew. MD, Med. Sch. Budapest, Hungary, 1963. Resident physician Univ. Budapest Sch. Medicine, Hungary, 1963-66; research fellow Retina Found., Boston, 1967-71; spl. research fellow Harvard Univ., Cambridge, Mass., 1971-74; asst. prof. dept. obstetrics, gynecology Yale Univ. Sch. Medicine, New Haven, 1974-80; dir. uterine physiol. lab. dept. obstetrics, and gynecology Yale Univ. Sch. Medicine, New Haven, 1978-86, assoc. prof., 1986-90, sr. rsch. scientist, 1991—; mem. reprodn. biology study sect. NIH, 1991, dir. sperm physiology lab., 1983—; cons. in field. Editor, contbr., author numerous articles in profl. jours, books; editor: The Physiology and Biochemistry of the Uterus, 1986. Patentee ob-gyn diagnostic instruments and fertility diagnostic procedures. Mem. editorial bd. Jour. andrology, Basic and Applied Myology, Hungarian Jour. Obstetrics and Gynecology, Mediterranean Jour. Gynaecology, Reproductive Technology Update. Grantee NIH, others. Mem. Am. Soc. Biol. Chemists, Soc. Gynecologic Investigation, Am Soc. Andrology, Am. Fertility Soc., Biophys. Soc., AAAS, Soc. Wine Educators (bd. dirs.). Democrat. Roman Catholic. Office: Yale U Sch Medicine Dept Ob-gyn 333 Cedar St New Haven CT 06510-3289

HUSZAR, MARTA JEAN, graphic designer; b. Boston, Nov. 17, 1953; d. Robert John and Jean Elizabeth (Robertson) H.; m. John Henry Morgan, July 21, 1979 (div. Mar. 1982, dec. Nov. 1983). Jr. cert. applied music, U. Hartford, 1971; BFA in Graphic Design, Phila. Coll. Art, 1976; postgrad., Fashion Inst. Tech., 1989-91, Yale U. Sch. Art, 1991—. Asst. art dir. Price Waterhouse & Co., N.Y.C., 1977-78; design dir. William H. Sadlier, Inc., N.Y.C., 1978-82; package and graphic designer The Schechter Group, Inc., N.Y.C., 1982; art dir. Bernard Hodes Advt., 1985-86; design cons. Marta Huszar Design, 1982—; design cons. Elle mag., 1988-91, Harper's Bazaar, 1990-91, Arista Records, Inc., Lippincott & Margulies, Inc.; intern Foca Co., summer 1992; milliner, hat designer, 1989—. Design cons.: Basic Dysrhythmias, 1988, biology book for Holt, Rheinhart. Home and Office: 265 College St Apt 8C New Haven CT 06510-2423

HUTCHENS, TIMOTHY RICE, magazine publishing company executive; b. N.Y.C., Feb. 24, 1938; s. John Kennedy and Katherine Reagan (Morris) H.; m. Mary Leonard Frederick Hutchens, Oct. 18, 1980; 1 child, Katherine. BA, Hamilton Coll., 1960. Reporter Holyoke (Mass.) Transcript-Telegram, 1960-61, Ariz. Republic, Phoenix, 1961-62, Hayward (Calif.) Daily Rev., 1963-64, N.Y. Herald Tribune, 1965-66; reporter, editor Washington Star, 1967-79; staff mem. U.S. Ho. Reps., Washington, 1979-81; exec. editor Pacific Stars and Stripes, Tokyo, 1981-84; ops. mgr. Insight Mag., Washington, 1984-88; gen. mgr. Annapolitan, Annapolis, Md., 1988—; mng. partner The Publick Enterprise newspaper, Annapolis, Md., 1991—. Organizer soup kitchens for homeless. Mem. Met. Washington Advt. Club. Democrat. Home: 6331 31st St NW Washington DC 20015 Office: Annapolitan 413 4th St Annapolis MD 21403

HUTCHENS, TRUDY PEARCE, editor; b. Arlington, Tex., Mar. 29, 1969; d. Theodore Delany and Mary (Leis) Pearce; m. Landon Ray Hutchens II, Nov. 24, 1990. Student, George Washington U., 1990-91. Editor, policy analyst Citizens For a Sound Economy, Washington, 1988-90; policy analyst Citizens For Congrl. Reform, Washington, 1990-91; asst. editor Family Voice Mag. Concerned Women For Am., Washington, 1991—. Author: Cleaning Up Congress, 1991; contbr. articles to newspapers nationwide. Asst. dir. Halpine Ch. Youth Ministry, Rockville, Md., 1989-91. Presdl. scholar Dallas Bapt. U., 1987, Nat. Right to Work Com. scholar, 1988.

Mem. County Reps. Club. Republican. Baptist. Home: 2310 Tenth St Apt 101 Arlington VA 22201 Office: Concerned Women For Am 370 L'Enfant Promenade # 800 Washington DC 20024

HUTCHESON, JANET REID, radiologist; b. N.Y.C., Feb. 21, 1934; d. John George and Ida Kauderer; m. Robert H. Hutcheson, Dec. 29, 1956; 1 child, Jonathan Edward; m. Eugene Streicher, Aug. 9, 1979. BA, Barnard Coll., N.Y.C., 1955; MD, U. Tenn., 1959. Intern St. Thomas Hosp., Nashville, 1961-62; resident in radiology Vanderbilt U., Nashville, 1962-65; instr. radiology Vanderbilt U., 1965-67, asst. prof. radiology, 1967-75; staff radiologist Group Health Assn., Washington, 1979-80, Drs. Prominski et al, Arlington, Va., 1980-85; pvt. practice specializing in radiology Washington, 1985-88; staff radiologist Laurel Beltsville Hosp., Laurel, Md., 1988—. Capt. USN, 1975-79. Democrat. Episcopalian. Home: 6521 Greentree Rd Bethesda MD 20817-3343 Office: 14201 Laurel Park Dr # 106 Laurel MD 20707-5297

HUTCHESON, ZENAS WILLARD, III, industry consultant; b. Andrews, Tex., May 17, 1953; s. Zenas Willard Jr. and Rosa Ellen (Oakley) H.; m. Susanne Brown Lilly, Feb. 20, 1982; children: Zenas W. IV, Henry David. BA in Chemistry, Dartmouth Coll., 1975; MBA, U. Chgo., 1979. Banking rep. Bank of N.Y., N.Y.C., 1975-78; cons. Bain & Co., London, 1979-81; ptnr. Daly, Hutcheson & Co., Boston, 1981-82; pres. Hutcheson & Co., Boston, 1982—; chmn. FFP Mgmt. Co. Mem. The Country Club (Brookline, Mass.), Sankaty Head Club (Nantucket, Mass.), Mpls. Club. Episcopalian. Office: Hutcheson & Co 196 Marlborough St Boston MA 02116-1822

HUTCHINS, DEXTER CARLETON, magazine editor, journalist; b. Crossett, Ark., Feb. 6, 1938; s. Burleigh Maurice and Lois Eleanor (Wilcoxon) H.; m. Judith Elaine Everett, Sept. 2, 1961; 1 child, Dana Carleton. BA, Pa. State U., 1961; postgrad., U. Pa., 1965-66. Reporter Phila. (Pa.) Inquirer, 1962-65; asst. fin. editor Bus. Week, N.Y.C., 1967-70; Washington corr. Bus. Week, Washington, 1970-77; gen. news editor Bus. Week, N.Y.C., 1977-78; Washington corr. Venture Mag., Washington, 1978-80; editorial dir. Scripps-Howard Bus. Jours., Houston, 1980-85; publisher Houston (Tex.) Bus. Jour., 1984-85; assoc. editor Fortune Mag., N.Y.C., 1985-87; mng. editor Fin. World Mag., N.Y.C., 1987-90, exec. editor, 1990—. Cpl. USMC, 1956-58. Mem. Antique Automobile Club Am. Presbyterian. Office: Fin World 1328 Broadway New York NY 10001-2121

HUTCHINS, GROVER MACGREGOR, pathologist, educator; b. Balt., Aug. 17, 1932; s. Grover and Elmore (Lawrence) H.; m. Loretta Helen Bajkowska, July 29, 1956; children: Diana, David, Sally. BA, Johns Hopkins U., 1957, MD, 1961. Intern, then resident Johns Hopkins Hosp., Balt., 1961-65, pathologist, 1967—, dir. autopsy pathology, 1976—; rsch. fellow Scripps Clinic and Rsch. Found., La Jolla, Calif., 1965-66; instr. in pathology Sch. Medicine, Johns Hopkins U., Balt., 1966-67, asst. prof., 1967-73, assoc. prof., 1973-83, prof. pathology, 1983—. Editor: Autopsy Performance & Reporting, 1990; contbr. articles to profl. publs., chpts. to books. Cpl. U.S. Army, 1952-54. Mem. Coll. Am. Pathologists (autopsy com. 1986—, advisor forensic pathology com. 1988—, chmn. autopsy com. 1991—, mem. commn. on anatomic pathology 1991—), Phi Beta Kappa, Alpha Epsilon Delta, Alpha Omega Alpha. Democrat. Episcopalian. Home: 1 Stratford Rd Baltimore MD 21218-1145 Office: Johns Hopkins Hosp Dept Pathology 600 N Wolfe St Baltimore MD 21205-2182

HUTCHINSON, B. THOMAS, ophthalmologist; b. Flatwoods, W.Va., Jan. 13, 1934; s. Bernard Mearns and Helen Louise (Buseman) H.; m. B. June Greene, Aug. 17, 1956; 1 child, Daniel. AB, W.Va. U., 1955, BA, 1956; MD, Harvard U., 1958. Diplomate Am. Bd. Ophthalmology, Nat. Bd. Examiners. Intern Pa. Hosp., Phila., 1958-59; ophthalmic fellow Howe Lab. of Ophthalmology Harvard Med. Sch., Boston, 1961-63; resident in ophthalmology Mass. Eye and Ear Infirmary, Boston, 1963-65, fellow in glaucoma, 1965-66; from asst. to assoc. prof. ophthalmology Harvard Med. Sch., Boston, 1965—; asst. clin. prof. Boston U., 1965-67; surgeon in ophthalmology Mass. Eye and Ear Infirmary, 1978—, assoc. chief of ophthalmology, 1985-90; cons. staff Mass. Gen. Hosp., 1965—; vis. prof. Pa. State Med. Ctr., 1977, U. Mich., 1977, W.Va. U., 1978, Med. Coll. Wis., 1978, Duke U., 1979, Wills Eye Hosp., 1979, 87, Med. Coll. Wis., 1980, Govt. Ophthalmic Coll. in Madras, India, 1981, U. Fla., 1982, W.Va. U. Sch. Medicine, 1982, Pacific Presbyn. Med. Ctr., 1987. Mem. editorial bd. AMA Archives of Ophthalmology, 1966-76, The Harvard Med. Sch. Health Letter, 1976—, Ophthalmology Alert, 1981-84; contbr. articles to profl. jours. Recipient Appleton Croft award W.Va. U. Sch. Medicine, 1956, Man of Vision award Nat. Soc. to Present Blindness, 1984, Lucien Howe medal, 1991. Fellow ACS; mem. AMA, Am. Acad. Ophthalmology (sec. for ophthalmic practice 1988—, pres.- elect 1992, chmn. Nat. Eye Care Project 1981—, Hon. award 1982), Am. Bd. Opthalmology (bd. dirs. 1988—, Lucien Howe medal 1991), Suffolk County Med. Soc., Mass. Med. Soc. (chmn. ophthalmology sect. 1977-78), New Eng. Ophthalmol. Soc. (profl. svc. rev. com. 1973-77, chmn. program com. 1981-83), Mass. Soc. of Eye Physicians and Surgeons (mem. exec. com. 1969—, treas. 1969-74, pres. 1978-79, councillor 1981-84), Assn. for Rsch. in Ophthalmology), Eye Study Club, Physicians Edn. Network, Ea. Mass. Profl. Standards Rev. Orgn., Phi Beta Kappa. Home: 69 Pigeon Hill Rd Weston MA 02193-1641 Office: Ophthalmic Cons of Boston 50 Staniford St Boston MA 02114-2517

HUTCHINSON, CHARLES MAXWELL, art gallery director; b. Melbourne, Victoria, Australia, Aug. 25, 1925; came to U.S., 1968; children: Rowan, Simone, Tanya. Degree in chem. enging., Royal Melbourne Inst. Tech., 1944. Dir., owner Max Hutchinson Gallery, N.Y.C., 1969-84, Sculpture Now, N.Y.C., 1973-78, Sculpture Fields, Kenoza Lake, N.Y., 1985—. Office: Sculpture Fields 12 Fulton Rd Kenoza Lake NY 12750

HUTCHINSON, GEORGE ALLEN, mathematician; b. Bklyn., Apr. 24, 1936; s. Henry Parks and Eleanor (Moore) H.; m. Carol Ann Occhiogrosso, Nov. 22, 1969; children: Daniel Allen, John Thomas, Andrew Moore. BA, Columbia U., 1958, PhD in Math., 1967. Teaching asst. Columbia U., N.Y.C., 1958-61; jr. mathematician U.S. Army Signal Corps R&D Lab., Ft. Monmouth, N.J., 1958-60; mem. tech. staff ITT Communications Systems Div., Paramus, N.J., 1962-63; asst. prof. Farleigh Dickinson U., Rutherford, N.J., 1964-65; rsch. mathematician NIH, Bethesda, Md., 1967—. Contbr. articles to Bull., Proceedings and Transactions of Am. Math. Soc., Jour. Algebra, Jour. Pure and Applied Algebra, Alegebra Universalis, Bull. of Math. Biophysics. Mem. Am. Math. Soc., Math. Assn. Am. Home: 1617 Rainbow Dr Silver Spring MD 20905-4144 Office: NIH Bldg 12A Rm 3045 Bethesda MD 20892

HUTCHINSON, MARTHA LUCLARE, pathologist; b. Alton, Ill., Oct. 26, 1941; d. Elmer Frank and LuClare (Hall) H.; m. Marshall Edward Kadin, June 15, 1980. BS, Iowa State U., 1963; PhD, Purdue U., 1970; MD, Case Western Res. U., 1974. Intern Cleve. Met. Gen. Hosp., 1974-75; resident U. Calif., San Francisco, 1975-77, U. Wash., Seattle, 1977-79; asst. prof. Purdue U., West Lafayette, Ind., 1970, U. Wash., Seattle, 1979-84; assoc. prof. pathology Tufts U., Boston, 1984—; dir. cytopathology New Eng. Med. Ctr. Hosps., Boston, 1984—. Co-investigator devel. and testing of automated devices to facilitate cytology (pathology) diagnosis, 1986—. NIH grantee, 1986, 89. Mem. AMA, Am. Soc. Clin. Pathology, Coll. Am. Pathologists, Internat. Soc. Analytical Cytology, Internat. Acad. Pathology, Am. Soc. Cytology, Internat. Soc. Analytical Cytology. Home: 103 Clinton Rd Brookline MA 02146-5812 Office: New Eng Med Ctr 750 Washington St Boston MA 02111-1533

HUTCHINSON, VIRGINIA NETTLES, librarian; b. Richmond, Va., Feb. 7, 1936; d. Joseph and Virginia (Davies) Nettles; m. John Michael Robin H., Oct. 3, 1959; children: Catherine Pierce, Peter Anthony. BA in English Lit., Mary Washington Coll., 1958. Librarian D.C. Pub. Library, Washington, 1958-59, 66-67; asst. to communications cons. Govt. Employees Ins. Co., Washington, 1973-78, librarian, 1978—. Mem. ALA, ASTD, Am. Mgmt. Assn., Soc. for Human Resources Mgmt., Spl. Librs. Assn., Book Discussion Group. Home: 113 Hesketh St Chevy Chase MD 20815 Office: Goodwin Learning Ctr GEICO Plz Washington DC 20076

HUTCHINSON, WILLIAM DAVID, judge; b. Minersville, Pa., June 20, 1932; s. Elmer E. and Elizabeth (Price) H.; m. Louise Meloney, 1957; children: Kathryn, William, Louise, Andrew. B.A. magna cum laude, Moravian Coll., 1954; J.D., Harvard U., 1957. Bar: Pa. Private practice law Pottsville, Pa., 1958-82; asst. dist. atty. Schuylkill County, Pa., 1963-69, solicitor, 1969-72; solicitor Blue Mountain Sch. Dist., Cressona, Pa., 1967-81; justice Pa. Supreme Ct., Harrisburg, 1982-87; judge U.S. Ct. Appeals (3d cir.), Pottsville, Pa., 1987—; chmn. Joint State Govt. Commn. Pa. Gen. Assembly, 1981; mem. Pa. Jud. Council, 1980-82; mem. Pomeroy Commn. on Unified Jud. System, 1980-82. Mem. Pa. Ho. of Reps., 1973-81, chmn. ethics com., 1981; mem. Blue Mountain Sch. Bd., 1963-66. Recipient John Amos Comenius award Moravian Coll., 1982. Mem. ABA, Pa. Bar Assn., Assn. Trial Lawyers Am., Pa. Trial Lawyers Assn., Am. Judicature Soc., Schuylkill County Bar Assn. (com. continuing legal edn.). Republican. Methodist. Office: US Ct Appeals 20614 US Courthouse 601 Market St Philadelphia PA 19106-1510 also: Chambers 410 W Market St Pottsville PA 17901*

HUTCHISON, JAMES ARTHUR, JR., engineering company executive; b. Gainesville, Mo., Oct. 25, 1917; s. James Arthur and Dora Ethel (James) H.; m. Imogene Cox, Dec. 5, 1946; children—Judith Lynn, Janet Gayle, James Arthur III. B.S. in Mech. Engring., Okla. State U., 1940; B.S. in Aero. Engring., Spartan Sch. Aeronautics, 1942; B.S. in Acctg., Okla. Sch. Accountancy, 1963. Registered profl. engr. Del., N.J., Md., V.I. Asst. chief engr. Spartan Aircraft Co., Tulsa, 1943-51; ptnr., owner H & H Engring. & Constrn. Co., Tulsa, 1951-68; sr. liaison engr. ILC Industries Inc. Apollo Astronaut Program, Dover, Del., 1968-72; v.p. Diamond State Engring. Inc., Dover, 1972-78; founder, chmn. bd. dirs. The JAED Corp., Smyrna, Del., 1978—. Chmn. bd. trustees 1st Baptist Ch., Dover, 1979-85. Recipient Gold Seal Del. Bd. Edn., 1974. Mem. Am. Inst. Steel Constrn., Am. Concrete Inst., Am. Soc. Heating Engrs., Central Del. Pilots Assn. (pres. 1977-78). Republican. Avocations: aircraft flight instruction. Office: The JAED Corp 19 Village Sq Smyrna DE 19977-1836

HUTCHISON, JAMES DONALD, state agency administrator; b. Columbus, Ohio, Nov. 15, 1932; s. Harold Warren and Valerie Helen (Jarnot) H.; m. Brenda Mae Ruth, Apr. 28, 1962; children: Caroline, Jamie, Adrianne, Shannon. Student, Niagara U., 1956-58, U. Buffalo, 1958-61. Technician Carborundum Co., Niagara Falls, N.Y., 1956-57; inspector Retail Credit Co., Atlanta, 1957-62; investigator N.Y. State Dept. Labor, Albany, 1962-88; adminstr., analyst N.Y. State Dept. Social Svcs., Albany, 1968—. Bd. mem. Lay Budget Com. East Green Bush Schs., N.Y., 1972-76; mem. Empire State Regatta Com., 1987-89. With USCG, 1950-53, U.S. Army, 1953-56. Mem. BPOE (esq. 1988-89), Elks (esq. 1988-89). Republican. Roman Catholic. Home: 258 Spring Ave Rensselaer NY 12144-3834

HUTCHISON-HALL, WILLIAM ELLSWORTH HENRY, IV, photographer, bank director; b. Jersey City, May 21, 1963; s. William Frederick and Mary Ruth (Hall) Ellinger; m. Andrea Lynn Bryant, May 28, 1988 (div. Nov. 1991); 1 child, Iain Henry William Bryant. Freelance photojournalist N.Y.C., 1978; trainee, assoc. R. Kovi & Co., Ltd., London, 1979-81; mng. dir. R. Kovi & Co., Ltd., Ottawa, Ont., Can., 1981-86, Berlin, 1986-87, N.Y.C., 1987-89; mng. dir. Hutchison Bros., Hall & Co., Ltd., London, 1990-92; also bd. dirs.; freelance comml. photographer Birmingham, Ala., 1991—; chmn. bd. dirs. Hutchison Bros., Hall & Co., Inc., 1990—; bd. dirs. Charlworth Devels., N.Y.C. Mem. Falkville (Ala.) Zoning Bd. Adjustment, 1988-89. Mem. Royal Photographic Soc. Gt. Britain, Am. Mgmt. Soc., Advt. Photographers Am., Internat. Platform Assn. Republican. Episcopalian. Home: 1321 17th Ave S #107 Birmingham AL 35205

HUTH, JOHN HARVEY, electronics executive; b. Bakersfield, Calif., Nov. 12, 1922; s. Harvey Frederick and Mabel Lucinda (Belcher) H.; m. Marietta Brown, Dec. 21, 1950 (dec. 1975); m. Doris Moss Bitz, Oct. 9, 1976; 1 stepchild, Debbie Leigh Bitz. BS, U. Calif., Berkeley, 1943; MS, Stanford U., 1947, PhD, 1950. Registered profl. engr. Ops. analyst Rand Corp., Santa Monica, Calif., 1950-64; with sr. exec. svc. Dept. of the Navy, Washington, 1964-86; sr. analyst VSE Corp., Indian Head, Md., 1986-88; sr. exec. PRC, Inc., Indian Head, 1988—; adj. prof. Cen. Mich. U., Washington, 1989—. Contbr. numerous articles to profl. jours. Lt. USN, 1945-46. Mem. U.S. Hovercraft Soc., Army-Navy Country Club. Office: PRC Inc 801 Strauss Ave N Indian Head MD 20640-1807 also: Ste 200 Crystal Pk2 Arlington VA 22202

HUTMAN, NORMA LOUISE, educator; b. Buffalo, Sept. 7, 1934; d. George A. and Florence (McLaughlin) H. BA, D'Youville Coll., 1956; MA, Western Res. U., 1957; lic., U. Madrid, 1960; PhD, U. Pitts., 1961. Instr. Chatham Coll., Pitts., 1957-61; asst. prof. Wilson Coll., Chambersburg, Pa., 1961-64; prof. Hartwick Coll., Oneonta, N.Y., 1964—. Author: A Dialogue with Time, 1962. Democrat. Episcopalian. Home: 540 Main St Oneonta NY 13820-2034 Office: Hartwick Coll Oneonta NY 13820

HUTSALIUK, YAREMA, public relations executive, military officer; b. N.Y.C., Aug. 5, 1960; s. Liuboslav and Renata (Kozicka) H. BA, Columbia U., 1982, M. Internat. Affairs, 1985. Media analyst Fleishman Hillard Pub. Rels., N.Y.C., 1987; account mgr. The Alexander Co. Pub. Rels., N.Y.C., 1988; account exec. Schlesinger Assocs. Pub. Rels., N.Y.C., 1988-90; pvt. practice N.Y.C., 1990—; pub. affairs officer USNG, 1990-92. Contbr. numerous articles on N.Y. N.G. in Desert Shield and Desert Storm. Counsel (pub. rels.) Councilman Enoch H. Williams, Bedford Stuyvesant, Bklyn., 1991, 27th Dist., N.Y.C. Decorated N.Y. State Mil. Commendation medal, Army Achievement medal. Mem. Bklyn. Soc. for Ethical Culture, Ft. Hamilton Officer's Club. Roman Catholic. Home: 316 W 88th St 2F New York NY 10024-2248 Office: HQ 1 BDE NYG State Armory 15074 6th Ave Whitestone NY 11357-1299

HUTSON, WILLIAM RICHARD, artist, educator; b. San Marcos, Tex., Sept. 6, 1936; s. Floyd Waymond and Mattie Lee (Edwards) H. Student, U. N.Mex., 1956-57, L.A. City Coll., 1958-59, L.A. Trade Tech. Coll., 1959, San Francisco Acad. of Art, 1960-61. Graphic artist Nat. Mus. of Art, Lagos, Nigeria, 1974-76; asst. prof. Ohio State Univ., Columbus, 1984-87; assoc. prof. Franklin and Marshall Coll., Lancaster, Pa., 1989—; guest speaker Met. Mus. of Art, N.Y.C., 1980, The Walters Art Gallery, Balt., 1990, Detroit Inst. Arts, 1991, U. de la Sorbonne Nouvelle, Paris, 1992; adj. lectr. Hunter Coll. of CUNY, 1979-83; juror/panelist Greater Columbus Arts Coun., 1991; juror Oglebay Inst./Stifel Fine Arts Ctr., Wheeling, W.Va., 1991; curator The Riffe Gallery, Columbus, 1991, Spaces Gallery, Cleve., 1991; vis. artist/instr. The Johns Hopkins U., Balt., 1989; vis. critic, Md. Inst. Coll. of Art, Balt., 1988; worldwide travel, study and ind. work. Numerous one-man shows including G.R. N'Namdi Gallery, Birmingham, Mich., 1991, James. E. Lewis Mus. Art, Morgan State U., Balt., 1990, Cone Univ. Ctr. Gallery, U. N.C., Charlotte, 1990, Calif. Afro-Am. Mus., L.A., 1988, Studio Mus. in Harlem, N.Y.C., 1987-88; exhibited in numerous group shows including Kenkeleba Gallery, N.Y.C., 1991, Bronx Mus. Art, 1989-90, Museo Civico d'Art Contemporanea di Gibellina, Palmero, Italy, 1989-90. Recipient Creative Artists Pub. Svc. Prog. award, N.Y.C., 1980, Cassandra Found. award, Chgo., 1972; grantee Nat. Endowment for Arts, Washington, 1974. Home: 355 W Chestnut St Apt 211 Lancaster PA 17603-3558 Office: Franklin and Marshall Coll Lancaster PA 17604-3003

HUTTON, ERNEST WATSON, JR., planning company executive; b. Ft. Myers, Fla., Oct. 25, 1944; s. Ernest Watson and Vera (Bowling) H.; m. Gretchen Bachrach, June 20, 1970; children: Elizabeth, Elinor. BA, Princeton U., 1966; BArch., U. Pa., 1968, MArch., M in City Planning, 1970. Sr. urban designer Jonathan Devel. Corp., Mpls., 1970-73, New Community Enterprises, Mpls., 1972-73, Arlen Realty & Devel. Corp., N.Y.C., 1973-74; sr. assoc. Llewelyn-Davies Assoc., N.Y.C., 1974-80; ptnr. Buckhurst Fish Hutton Katz Inc., N.Y.C., 1980-91, Buckhurst, Fish, Hutton, Katz & Jacquemart Inc., N.Y.C., 1992—. Author: (with others) Cultural Facilities in Mixed Use Development, 1986; prin. wks. include Pitts. Cultural Dist./CNG Tower/Benedum Ctr., 1980-87, Roanoke Vision Plan, 1980-86, Hartford Riverfront Recapture Plan, 1981-85, Knoxville Downtown Plan, 1987-89, rutland (Vt.) Downtown Plan, 1988-89, Charlotte Cultural Dist., 1991. Fellow Inst. Urban Design; mem. Am. Inst. Cert. Planners, Am. Planning Assn. (Nat. Planning award 1987), Urban Land Inst., Am. Inst. Cons. Planners, Am. Vaudeville Inc. (pres., bd. dirs.), Lucille Ball Comedy Festival (mng. prodr.), Cap and Gown Club (Princeton, N.J.). Home: 408 Pacific St Brooklyn NY 11217-2203 Office: Buckhurst Fish Hutton et al 72 5th Ave New York NY 10011-8004

HUTTON, HERBERT J., judge; b. 1937. AB, Lincoln U., 1959; JD, Temple U., 1962. With Housing and Home Fin. Agy., 1962-64; mem. firm Norris Brown & Hall, 1964-69, Norris, Wells & Neal, 1969-72, Norris & Wells, 1972-76, Simpkins & Tucker, 1977-88; hearing officer Bd. Revision Taxes, Phila., 1982-88; judge U.S. Dist. Ct. (ea. dist.) Pa., Phila., 1988—. Recipient Bd. Dirs. City Trusts' award, 1988. Mem. Phila Bar Assn. (Medal of Svc. 1982), Phila. Bar Found. (trustee), Fed. Judges Assn. Office: US Dist Ct 5118 US Courthouse 601 Market St Philadelphia PA 19106-1510*

HUTTON, JACK GOSSETT, JR., psychologist, educator; b. Denver, June 20, 1931; s. Jack Gossett and Margaretta Elizabeth (Lea) H.; student Colo. Coll., 1949-51; B.A., U. Denver, 1953, M.A., 1956; Ph.D., U. Conn., 1968. Asst. dir. div. ednl. measurement and research Assn. Am. Med. Colls., Washington, 1968-71; staff psychologist, profl. exams. div. Psychol. Corp., N.Y.C., 1971-73; ednl. psychologist, asso. prof. Coll. Dentistry, Howard U., Washington, 1973-79, ednl. psychologist, prof. Coll. Dentistry, 1979—; asso. prof. Sch. Edn., Howard U., 1973-77; vis. ednl. specialist Sch. Dentistry, W.Va. U., 1976-83; vis. scholar U. Mich., summer 1968; adj. asst. prof. Sch. Edn., Cath. U., 1969-71. Served with U.S. Army, 1956-58. Mem. Am. Psychol. Assn., Am. Edn. Research Assn., Nat. Council Measurement in Edn., Am. Assn. Dental Schs. (sec. sect. behavioral scis. 1975-76), Behavioral Scientists in Dental Research, AAUP, N.Y. Acad. Scis., Sigma Xi, Psi Chi, Phi Sigma. Contbr. articles to profl. jours. Home: PO Box 723 Saint Petersburg FL 33731-0723 Office: Howard U Coll Dentistry 600 W St NW Washington DC 20059-0001

HUTTON, WILLIAM MICHAEL, manufacturing company executive; b. Herrin, Ill., June 15, 1948; s. William T. and Violet (Childress) H.; m. Lois A. Piontkowski, Sept. 7, 1968; children: Cynthia L., Pamela. BS in Mgmt. Scis., So. Ill. U., 1972; MA in Ops. Mgmt., Vt. Coll. of Norwich U., 1991. Cert. foodservice profl. Mgr. machining ops. Ingersoll-Rand, Phillipsburg, N.J., 1973-83; mgr. of mfr. Bendix Aerospace Corp., Eatontown, N.J., 1983-84; v.p. ops. Follett Corp., Easton, Pa., 1984-87, pres., chief operating officer, 1988—; exec. in residence So. Ill. U., 1991—. Mem. adv. bd. coll. bus. and adminstrn., So. Ill. U., 1989—; chmn. adv. bd. Northampton Community Coll., 1991—; bd. dirs. Community Svcs. for Children, Bethlehem, 1989-91, Ben Franklin Inst., 1991—. Mem. So. Ill. U. Alumni Assn., Young Pres.'s Orgn. Republican. Roman Catholic. Home: 4640 Hillview Dr Nazareth PA 18064-8525 Office: Follett Corp PO Box D Easton PA 18044-2096

HUTTON, WINFIELD TRAVIS, management educator, management consultant; b. L.A., Aug. 17, 1935; s. Travis Calhoun and Frances (Gardemann) H. BS in Mgmt. summa cum laude, Ohio State U., 1956, MBA, 1957, PhD, 1959. Consumer economist Fed. Res. Bank Atlanta, 1959-62; prof. econs. Hunter Coll., CUNY, 1962-68; prof. European div. U. Md., 1968-79; prof. Troy State U.-Europe, Fed. Republic Germany, 1979—; cons. on mgmt., mktg. and econs. in Europe, 1968—. Author: (mgmt. computer simulations) City Finance, 1985, Simanage, 1989; author computer programs for rsch. stats.; contbr. articles to profl. jours. Lay reader St. Alban's Episcopal Ch., Kaiserslautern, Fed. Republic Germany, 1981-88. Mem. AAUP, Am. Mktg. Assn. (manuscript reviewer 1983—), Am. Econ. Assn., Beta Gamma Sigma. Home: Sooneckstrasse 4, D-6531 Trechtingshausen Federal Republic of Germany Office: Troy State U-Europe PSC-14 Box 4037 APO AE 09192

HUVOS, ANDREW, internist, cardiologist, educator; b. Budapest, Hungary, Apr. 23, 1930; came to U.S., 1950; s. Julian Gyula and Magdolna (Matyas) H.; m. Monique Chatriot, June 8, 1959; children: Christine, Anne, Philip. Student, Free U. Brussels, 1948-50, Harvard U., 1951; MD, Boston U., 1955. Diplomate Am. Bd. Internal Medicine, Am. Bd. Cardiovascular Disease. Resident in medicine Yale-New Haven Med. Ctr., 1955-59; fellow in cardiology Mass. Gen. Hosp., Boston, 1961-63; physician-in-charge cardiac catheterization lab. Univ. Hosp., Boston, 1963-70; chief cardiology Faulkner Hosp., Boston, 1970-74, chief medicine, 1974—; lectr. medicine Harvard Med. Sch., Boston, 1974-86; lectr. medicine and physiology Boston U. Sch. Medicine, 1976—; prof. medicine Tufts U. Sch. Medicine, Boston, 1985—; dir. Tufts Assoc. Health Plan, 1979-81. Contbr. articles to med. jours., chpts. to books. Chmn. bd. trustees Ecole Bilingue, Inc., Arlington, Mass., 1970-74; trustee Boston Med. Libr., 1981-85. Capt. M.C., U.S. Army, 1959-61. Recipient Excellence in Teaching award Boston U. Sch. Medicine, 1974; USPHS grantee, 1977-83. Fellow ACP, Am. Coll. Cardiology, Am. Coll. Chest Physicians (pres. New Eng. States chpt. 1981-83); mem. Am. Heart Assn. (fellow couns. clin. cardiology and circulation), Dorchester Med. Club, Roxbury Clin. Record Club, Alpha Omega Alpha. Presbyterian. Office: Faulkner Hosp Boston MA 02130

HUXSTER, HOWARD KNIGHT, psychiatrist; b. Balt., Dec. 25, 1924; s. Howard Leslie and May Eda (Knight) H.; m. Evelyn Rachel Intenzo, Aug. 16, 1961, (div. 1978); children: Peter Knight, Robert Hugh. Student, U. Pa., 1942-43, 46-47, various including U. Nebr., 1943-44, Drexel U., 1946-47; MD, Jefferson Med. Coll., 1952. Diplomate Am. Bd. Psychiatry and Neurology. Intern Walter Reed Army Med. Ctr., Washington, 1952-53; resident Norristown (Pa.) State Hosp., 1954-57; dir. Tri-County Mental Health Clinic, Norristown, Pa., 1958-61; psychiatric cons. Rehab. Ctr., U. Pa. Hosp., 1965-70; pvt. practice, Bala Cynwyd, Pa., 1961-70; dir. Phila. Psychoanalytic Clinic, 1970-80; pvt. practice Phila. and Newark, Del., 1970-88; psychiatrist Coatesville (Pa.) VA Med. Ctr., 1988—; cons. Bucks County Sch. Dist., 1960-70, U. Pa. Student Health Svcs., Phila., 1970-79. Fellow Am. Psychiatric Assn. (life); mem. Am. Psychoanalytic Assn., Internat. Psychoanalytical Assn., Phila. Psychoanalytic Soc. (sec. 1981-83), Phila. Psychoanalytic Inst., Del. Psychiatric Soc. Office: 111 N 49th St Philadelphia PA 19139-2718

HUYETT, DANIEL HENRY, III, federal judge; b. Reading, Pa., May 2, 1921; s. Daniel Henry, Jr. and Emma Alice (Moyer) H.; children: Cathy J. (Mrs. Tracy James Whitaker), Daniel B., Christina N. (Mrs. Harold G. Kelso III); m. Katrina H. King, Jan. 13, 1990. AB, U. Mich., 1942; JD, U. Pa., 1948. Bar: Pa. 1949. Practiced in Berks County, 1949-70; city solicitor Reading, 1952-56; U.S. dist. judge Eastern Dist. Pa., Reading, 1970—; lectr. Fed. Jud. Ctr., Washington, 1977, 78, 79; instr. Atty. Gen. Advocacy Inst., 1978-87; mem. subcom. supporting pers. ct. adminstrn. com. U.S. Jud. Conf., 1979-87, chmn. ad hoc ct. reporter study com., 1984-87, mem. adv. com. criminal rules, 1988-91. Mem. Pa. Labor Relations Bd., 1966-68, Pa. Pub. Utility Commn., 1968-70. Served as 1st lt. USAAF, World War II; capt. USAF Res. Mem. ABA, Pa. Bar Assn., Berks County Bar Assn., Am. Judicature Soc., Supreme Ct. Hist. Soc., Am. Law Inst. Home: 403 Green Ln Reading PA 19601-1009 Office: The Madison Bldg 400 Washington St Fl 5 Reading PA 19601-3908

HUYGHE, JACQUES MARCEL, manufacturing executive; b. Lille, Nord, France, Nov. 29, 1943; came to the U.S., 1981; s. Marcel and Jacqueline (Jeandaud) H.; m. Evelyne Vanackere, July 10, 1968; children: Julien, Jerome. B in Engring., Pub. Works, Paris, 1968; MS, Laval U., Quebec, 1976. Program mgr. Dept. Energy and Resources, Quebec, 1969-72; dep. gen. mgr. AeroPhoto, Inc., Quebec, 1972-76; gen. mgr. Quebec Mapping Co., 1976-79; v.p. U.S. ops. Matra Tech., Inc., Santa Clara, Calif., 1979-89; v.p. internat. mktg. Fairchild Def., Germantown, Md., 1990—. Contbr. articles to profl. jours. Mem. Armed Forces Communications and Electronics, Assn. Old Crows, Assn. for Unmanned Vehicles, Am. Soc. for Photogrammetry. Office: Fairchild Def 20301 Century Blvd Germantown MD 20874-1181

HUZINEC, MARY SUZANNE, reporter; b. McKeesport, Pa., Nov. 2, 1956; d. Andrew and Helen (Basarab) H.; m. William Haduch Jr., June 28, 1980 (div. 1984). BA in English Writing and Speech Communications, U. Pitts., 1978. Gen. assignment reporter Pitts. Press, 1978-79; arts and entertainment editor Beaver (Pa.) County Times, 1979-81; editorial asst. Life Mag., N.Y.C., 1981-82; TV news producer Sta. WPXI-TV, Pitts., 1982-85; reporter People Mag., N.Y.C., 1986—. Byzantine Catholic. Home: 404 W 51st St # 2B New York NY 10019-6509 Office: People Mag Rockefeller Ctr Time Life Bldg Rm 31-37E New York NY 10020

HWA, ERH-CHENG, economist; b. Chungking, China, Aug. 14, 1945; came to U.S., 1968; s. Ching-Hsiang and Lan-Chu (Liu) H.; m. Yu-Lin

Cheng; children: Candice Tien-Shing, Catherine Tien-Yi. BA, Nat. Taiwan U., Taipei, 1967; MA, Cornell U., 1971, PhD, 1973. Research assoc. Cornell U., Ithaca, N.Y., 1973-75, Nat. Bur. Econ. Research, N.Y.C., 1975-77; economist Internat. Monetary Fund, Washington, 1977-80; visiting prof. econs. Nat. Tsing-Hua U., Republic of China, 1987-88; economist, sr. economist, then prin. economist World Bank, Washington, 1980-87, 88—; econ. advisor Ministry Econs. Coun. Econ. Planning and Devel. Republic of China, 1987-88. Author: New Taiwan Dollar Appreciation and Structural Adjustment Policies, 1987; contbr. numerous articles to econs. jours. Lt. Republic of China Military Police, 1967-68. Grantee NSF, Washington, 1974-75. Mem. Am. Econ. Assn., Chinese Am. Profls. Assn. (v.p. metro. Washington chpt. 1983-84), Chinese Econ. Assn. North Am., Org. Chinese Ams., Chinese Community Ctr. Greater Metro. Washington Area, The Nat. Economists' Club. Office: World Bank 1818 H St NW Washington DC 20433-0002

HWANG, SAN-BAO, biophysicist, researcher; b. Kaohsiung, Taiwan, Republic of China, Sept. 8, 1946; came to U.S., 1970; s. Dunn and Jean (Hwang) Tsai; m. Shu-Chen Tsai, Aug. 30, 1970; children: Sandy, Michael. BS, Nat. Taiwan U., Taipei, 1969; PhD, U. Calif., Berkeley, 1976. Rsch. assoc. U. Calif., San Francisco, 1978-79; sr. rsch. biophysicist Merck Sharp and Dohme, Rahway, N.J., 1979-83, rsch. fellow, 1983-88, sr. rsch. fellow, 1988-91; dir. biochemistry CytoMed, Inc., Cambridge, Mass., 1991—; mem. U.S. adv. com. 4th Internat. Congress on platelet-activating factor. Contbr. articles to profl. jours. Mem. Biophysics Soc., Am. Soc. Biochemists & Molecular Biologists, N.Y. Acad. Sci., Soc. Chinese Bioscientists in Am. Home: 67 Canterbury Dr Scotch Plains NJ 07076-1508 Office: CytoMed Inc 840 Memorial Dr Cambridge MA 02139-3758

HYAMS, GERALD THEODORE, engineering executive; b. N.Y.C., Aug. 13, 1933; s. Ivor Isidore and Lilian Nessie (Goldberg) H.; m. Alice Ellen Cooperman, Dec. 28, 1952 (dec. Jan. 1988); children: Sheri Iris, Ian David, Julie Lyn; m. Sandra Judy Breitling, Oct. 9, 1988; 1 stepchild, Rommye M. Birnbaum. BSEE, Drexel Inst. Tech., 1963, MS in Engring. Mgmt., 1968. Cert. profl. engr. Sr. test engr. ITE Circuit Breaker Co., Phila., 1962-64; plant elec. engr. Triangle Pub's Inc., Phila., 1964-66; quality control engr. GE Co., Valley Forge, Pa., 1966-67; quality control mgr. Technitrol Corp., Phila., 1967-69; v.p. engring., mfg. AAPCO Inc., Pennsauken, N.J., 1969-72; staff elec. engr. City of Phila., 1972-83, chief elec. engr., 1983-87, engring. project mgr., 1987-90; sr. v.p., gen. mgr. Phila. Design Collaborative Inc., 1990—; adj. prof. elec. engring. Temple U., Phila., 1973-75; cons. in field. With USN, 1952-56. Mem. Am. Mgmt. Assn., Variety Club for Handicapped Children, Masons. Jewish. Home: 2001B Bainbridge St Philadelphia PA 19146 Office: Phila Design Collaborative 511 N Broad St Philadelphia PA 19123

HYATT-SMITH, ANN ROSE, non-profit organization executive, consultant; b. Portchester, N.Y., Sept. 25, 1953; d. David M. and Lenore (Moerschelle) Hyatt; m. Geoffrey D. Smith, June 24, 1984; children: Rachel Elana, Joshua Richard. BA in Lit., State U. Coll., Oneonta, N.Y., 1975; M in Profl. Studies, New Sch. for Social Research, 1986. Asst. to sec.-gen. Israel Interfaith Com., Jerusalem, 1977-79; field rep. United Jewish Appeal/ Fedn. Jewish Philanthropies, N.Y.C., 1979-81; asst. v.p. United Way of N.Y.C., 1981-83; dir. devel. Hebrew Arts Sch., Merkin Concert Hall, N.Y.C., 1983-84; asst. dir. devel. St. Vincent's Hosp. and Med. Ctr. N.Y., N.Y.C., 1984-86; program mgr. Bernd Brecher and Assocs., Inc., N.Y.C., 1986-88; pres. Hyatt Smith Assocs., White Plains, N.Y., 1988—; adj. faculty New Sch. for Social Research and Learning Alliance. V.p., treas. Village Ind. Dems., N.Y.C., 1985-86. Mem. Nat. Soc. Fund Raising Execs. (cert. fund raising exec.), Assn. Devel. Officers, Planned Giving Group of Greater N.Y., Assn. Healthcare Philanthropy. Jewish. Office: Hyatt Smith Assocs 20A Midland Ave White Plains NY 10606-2825

HYDE, HENRY BALDWIN, lawyer; b. Paris, Oct. 31, 1915; s. James Hazen and Martha (Leishman) H.; came to U.S., 1936; M.A., Cambridge (Eng.) U., 1936; LL.B., Harvard U., 1939; m. Marie de LaGrange, Apr. 1941; children—Lorna Hyde de Wangen, Isabel Hyde Jasinowski; m. Elizabeth Prokoff Piper, 1960. Admitted to N.Y. State bar, 1940, since practiced in N.Y.C.; mem. firm Goldstein, Shames & Hyde; and predecessor firms, 1953-78, Wormser, Kiely, Alessandroni, Hyde & McCann, 1978-90, Wormser, Kiely, Galef & Jacobs, 1990—; dir. Armand G. Erpf Fund. Bd. dirs. French Inst.-Alliance Francaise; hon. trustee Hosp. for Spl. Surgery, N.Y.C.; bd. dirs. William J. Donovan Found. Served with OSS, AUS, 1942-45. Decorated Bronze Star medal with oak leaf cluster, Croix de Guerre, Officier Legion d'Honneur. Mem. William J. Donovan Found., Council Fgn. Relations. Clubs: River (N.Y.C.); Travelers (Paris). Home: 565 Park Ave New York NY 10021-7344 Office: 711 3d Ave New York NY 10017

HYDE, HOWARD LAURENCE, lawyer; b. Boston, Sept. 4, 1957; s. Morris Morton and Evelyn Lee (Weinstein) H.; m. Nancy J. Paulu, May 18, 1985; 1 child, Emma Catherine. AB, Dartmouth Coll., 1979; JD, Harvard U., 1982. Bar: Mass. 1983, D.C. 1987, U.S. Dist. Ct. Mass. 1984, U.S. Ct. Appeals (1st. cir.) 1984. Jud. clk. Minn. Supreme Ct., St. Paul, 1982-83; assoc. Gaston Snow & Ely Bartlett, Boston, 1983-86; assoc. Arnold & Porter, Washington, 1986-91, spl. counsel, 1992—. Mem. ABA (Bus. law sect.). Office: Arnold & Porter 1200 New Hampshire Ave NW Washington DC 20036-6802

HYDRISKO, STANLEY JOSEPH, financial company executive; b. Windsor, Vt., Sept. 4, 1927; children: Rosemary, Robert. BS, U. Vt., 1951, postgrad., 1951-52. Cert. internal auditor, fraud examiner; chartered bank auditor. Bank examiner Fed. Reserve Bank, Boston, 1952-57; auditor Harvard Trust Co. (now Baybank Havard), Cambridge, Mass., 1957-70; asst. v.p. Baybanks Inc., Boston, 1970-80; sr. auditor 1st Am. Bank, Lake Worth, Fla., 1980-82; v.p. Cen. Fin. Corp., Randolph, Vt., 1982—. With U.S. Infantry, 1945-47. Home: RR 1 Box 165 Windsor VT 05089-9708 Office: Cen Fin Corp PO Box 191 Windsor VT 05089-0191

HYDZIK, MICHAEL JAMES, hotel executive, consultant; b. Elmira, N.Y., Nov. 4, 1950; s. William and Anna Ruth (Baker) H. AAS, Corning (N.Y.) Community Coll., 1970, SUNY, Delhi, 1975; BS, Lehigh U., 1975. Restaurant mgr. Holiday Inn, Horseheads, N.Y., 1974-76; banquet mgr. Am. Inn Town House, Rochester, N.Y., 1976-77; asst. food and beverage mgr. The Hotel Syracuse, Syracuse, N.Y., 1977-78; dir. catering The Am. Rochester, 1978-79; restaurant mgr. The Changing Scene, Rochester, 1979-81; dir. restaurants E.J. Delmonte Corp., Rochester, 1981-84; dir. food and beverage Sheraton U. Inn, Syracuse, 1984-86; exec. v.p. ops. The Thousand Islands Club, Alexandria Bay, N.Y., 1986-88; v.p. food and beverage The Lodge of Woodcliff, Fairport, N.Y., 1988-92; dir. food and beverage The Univ. Club of Rochester, 1992—. Mem. N.Y. State Wine & Grape Found., Penn-Yann, N.Y., Save the River, Clayton, N.Y. N.Y. State Wine Found. scholar, 1972. Mem. N.Y. State Restaurant Assn., Thousand Islands Club Yacht Club. Office: The Univ Club of Rochester 26 Broadway Rochester NY 14607

HYER, MICHAEL EDWARD, court reporting executive; b. Michigan City, Ind., Feb. 11, 1945; s. Frank Richard and Elizabeth Ann (Heise) H.; m. Renate Barbara Rimkus, Sept. 17, 1971; children: Mark Thomas, Sascha Frank. Student Russian lang., Syracuse U., 1965-66, 69-70. Court reporter N.Am. Reporting, Inc., Gaithersburg, Md., 1976-78; ct. reporting exec. StenoTech, Inc., Gaithersburg, 1978—; ct. reporter U.S. Ho. of Reps., Washington, 1976-78, U.S. Senate, Washington, 1976-78, Office of Presdl. Press Sec., 1978; cons./writer NIH, 1978—. Pubr./editor: NIH Recombinant DNA Adv. Com. Proceedings, 1978—, Psychosociological Characteristics of Alcoholism proceedings, 1986, 1st Conf. on Burns proceedings, 1984. Pres. Mill Creek Homeowners Assn., Rockville, Md., 1980-87, Magruder High Sch. Boosters Assn., Rockville, 1989; bd. dirs. Magruder High Sch. PTA, 1989—, others. With USAF, 1965-75. Decorated Air Force Commendation medal. Recipient Outstanding Vol. Svc. award, Montgomery County Pub. Schs., 1982, Magruder High Sch., 1987. Mem. AAAS, N.Y. Acad. Sci., Am. Med. Writers Assn., Am. Legion, Hastings Ctr., Internat. Platform Speakers Assn., Am. Pub. Health Assn. Republican. Methodist. Office: 36 N Summit Ave Gaithersburg MD 20877-2922

HYKEN, EDWARD JONATHAN, systems designer, consultant; b. St. Petersburg, Russia, July 26, 1967; came to U.S., 1982; s. Boris and Sophia Hyken. BS, Emory U., 1989. Rsch. asst. Carter Presdl. Ctr., Atlanta, 1986-89; staff cons. Andersen Cons., Milan and Nice, France, 1989-91; sr. cons. Andersen Cons., N.Y.C. and Sydney, Australia, 1991—. Mem. UJA, Sydney, 1991; resident adviser Residence Life-Emory U., Atlanta, 1987-89. Recipient Jerusalem fellowship, 1988. Home: PO Box 33252 Decatur GA 30033 Office: Andersen Cons 1345 6th Ave New York NY 10105

HYLA, JAMES FRANKLIN, rheumatologist, educator; b. Natick, Mass., Dec. 1, 1945; s. Walter John and Helen (Kipec) H.; m. Sharon Ann Frayer, June 21, 1969. BS in Engring. Physics, Cornell U., 1967; postgrad. in aeros. and astronautics, MIT, 1967-68; MD, U. Rochester, 1972. Diplomate Am. Bd. Internat. Medicine, Am. Bd. Rheumatology, Nat. Bd. Examiners. Med. intern Mary Imogene Bassett Hosp., Columbia U., Cooperstown, N.Y., 1972-73, resident in medicine, 1973-75; fellow in rheumatology U. Mich. Hosp., Ann Arbor, 1975-77; pvt. practice Syracuse, N.Y., 1977—; attending physician Community Gen. Hosp., Syracuse, 1977—, St. Joseph's Hosp., Syracuse, 1977—; attending physician Crouse Irving Meml. Hosp., Syracuse, 1977—, sec.-treas. med. starr, 1990-92; clin. assoc. prof. SUNY Health Sci. Ctr., Syracuse, 1978—; dir. Arthritis Ctr., St. Camillus Health and Rehab. Ctr., 1988—; mem. med. and sci. com., bd. dirs. Cen. N.Y. chpt. Arthritis Found., 1978—, v.p. devel. and fundraising, 1981-83. Contbr. articles to med. jours. Regional coord. Cornell Summer Job Network, Ithaca, N.Y., 1985—; mem. Cornell U. Coun., 1987-91; bd. dirs. Fedn. Cornell Clubs, 1984-88; regional dir. bd. Cornell Alumni Fedn., 1991—. Recipient nat. vol. svc. citation Arthritis Found., 1983. Fellow Am. Coll. Rheumatology; mem. ACP, Am. Soc. Internal Medicine, N.Y. State Med. Soc., Onondaga County Med. Sco., Cornell Club Cen. N.Y. (bd. govs. 1979—, corr. sec. 1981-82, v.p. 1982-83, pres. 1983-85, scholarship chmn. 1985—, treas. 1991—), Tau Beta Pi, Phi Eta Sigma. Democrat. Home: 118 Grenfell Rd Dewitt NY 13214-1624 Office: Rheumatology Assocs Cen NY 310 S Crouse Ave Syracuse NY 13210

HYLAND, THOMAS PATRICK, financial executive; b. Red Bank, N.J., July 27, 1964; s. Michael Joseph and Helen Patricia (Garland) H.; m. Linda Ann Weist, Mar. 28, 1987; children: Thomas Patrick Jr., Jason Michael. BS in Communications, Rutgers U., 1986, BA in English, 1986. Cert. stockbroker, ins. agt., mortgage broker. Clk. Food Circus Supermarkets, Inc., Hazlet, N.J., 1981-86; sr. fixed income securities specialist McLaughlin, Piven, & Vogel, Inc., N.Y.C., 1986-87; pres. TFS Securities, Inc., Lincroft, N.J., 1987—. Mem. Internat. Assn. Fin. Planners, Western Monmouth C. of C., Kiwanis Club (chmn. budget and fin. com. 1991). Roman Catholic. Home: 14 Miriam Pl Hazlet NJ 07730-2639 Office: TFS Securities Inc PO Box 487 437 Newman Springs Rd Lincroft NJ 07738

HYLE, JACK OTTO, orthomolecular psychologist; b. Allentown, Pa., Oct. 19, 1929; s. Lewis Calvin Hyle and Martha Elizabeth (Werft) Hart; m. Anna Louise LeCompte, July 29, 1950; children: Marsha, Jay, Bruce, Susan, Beth. BS in edn., Bob Jones U., 1959; M in edn., Temple U., 1961; PhD, Manahath Edn. Ctr., 1967; PMD, Fla. Inst. Tech., 1981. Toll switchman Bell Telephone Co., Harrisburg, Pa., 1950-56; tchr. math. Cen. Dauphin High Sch., Harrisburg, 1959-64; psychologist Narramore Found., Harrisburg, 1964-69; pvt. practice Harrisburg, 1969-89; instr. Pa. State U., 1963-64; prof. of behavioral medicine Fla. Inst. Tech., Melbourne, 1982-85. Contbr. to book, Out of Mighty Waters, 1982; pioneer Orthomolecular Procedure. Scoutmaster Boy Scouts Am., Altoona, Pa., 1947-55; commr. Boy Socuts Am., Harrisburg, Pa., 1960-61; Sunday sch. tchr.Grace Brethren Ch., Harrisburg, Pa., 1960-70. Served as sgt. USMC, 1947-50. Recipient Hon. Trophy Boy Scouts Am., 1954; named Eagle Scout, 1946. Mem. NEA (life), Internat. Acad. Preventive Medicine, Orthomolecular Med. Soc., Nat. Ctr. for Homeopathy, Occidental Inst. Rsch. Found. Republican. Home: 5840 Longview Rd Harrisburg PA 17112-3130

HYLTON, THOMAS JAMES, editorial writer; b. Reading, Pa., Dec. 20, 1948; s. William Harold and Mary Harriet (Kitzmiller) H.; m. Frances Wismer, Aug. 31, 1970. BA, Kutztown U. of Pa., 1970. Reporter, then copy editor The Mercury, Pottstown, Pa., 1970-86, editorial writer, 1986—. Co-founder, sec. Trees Inc., Pottstown, 1983; co-founder Old Pottstown Preservation Soc., 1984. Recipient Am. Planning Assn. award, 1988, 90, Edn. Writers Assn. award, 1989, 90, J. Richard Dew award Pa. Newspaper Pubs. Assn., 1989, Pulitzer prize Columbia U., 1990. Republican. Presbyterian. Home: 222 Chestnut St Pottstown PA 19464-5508 Office: Mercury Hanover & King Sts Pottstown PA 19464

HYMAN, ARNOLD, psychology educator, consulting psychologist; b. Bklyn., Mar. 15, 1931; s. Louis and Sadie (Levine) H.; m. Gertrude Lapidus, June 26, 1966; 1 child, Simeon. B.A., Bklyn. Coll., 1952, M.A., 1953; M.S., CCNY, 1961; Ph.D., U. Cin., 1966. Lic. psychologist, Conn. Tchr. mentally retarded, pub. elem. sch., N.Y.C., 1953-57; research asst. Columbia U., N.Y.C., 1958-61, research worker, 1963-67; research assoc. Bklyn. Jewish Hosp., 1968-71; asst. prof. psychology U. New Haven, 1971-74, assoc. prof., 1974, prof., 1984—; pvt. practice cons. psychology, New Haven, Conn., 1981—. Author teaching aid and book: Learning Statistics Empirically, 1972; also articles. Mem. Am. Psychol. Assn., AAAS, N.Y. Acad. Scis., Psychonomic Soc., NAACP, Sigma Xi. Jewish. Avocations: fishing; skiing; playing string bass; gardening. Home: 30 Bromley Ct Hamden CT 06514-1702 Office: U New Haven 300 Orange Ave W New Haven CT 06516

HYMAN, BRUCE MALCOLM, ophthalmologist; b. N.Y.C., May 22, 1943; s. Malcolm A. and Sylvia S. H.; A.B., Columbia U., 1964; M.D., N.Y. U., 1968. Intern in surgery Albert Einstein Coll. Medicine/Bronx Mcpl. Hosp., 1968-69; resident in ophthalmology Manhattan Eye, Ear and Throat Hosp., N.Y.C., 1971-74; pvt. practice medicine specializing in ophthalmology, N.Y.C., 1974—; tchr. attending surgeon Manhattan Eye, Ear and Throat Hosp., 1974—; med. cons. U.S. Seaplane Pilots Assn., 1975—, Health Ins. Plan Greater N.Y., 1977—; ophthalmologist to Hotel Trades Council, Hotel Assn. N.Y.C., 1974—; attending ophthalmologist Roosevelt Hosp., N.Y.C., 1979—, dir. adult outpatient ophthalmology, 1980—; police surgeon N.Y.C., 1977—, dep. chief police surgeon, 1978—; attending ophthalmologist Doctors Hosp., 1979—, Le Roy Hosp., 1979—, St. Luke's Hosp., 1980—; outpatient ophthalmologist N.Y. Hosp., 1975-77; clin. ophthalmologist Columbia Coll. Physicians and Surgeons, 1981—. Served with USPHS, 1969-71. Diplomate Am. Bd. Ophthalmology. Fellow ACS; mem. N.Y. State, N.Y. County med. socs., Am. Acad. Ophthalmology and Otolaryngology. Contbr. articles to profl. jours. Office: 133 E 64th St New York NY 10021

HYMAN, IRWIN A., psychologist; b. Neptune, N.J., Mar. 22, 1935; Henry Meltzer and Harriet (Greenitz) H.; m. Nada Pospishil (div.); children: Nadine, Deborah; m. Susan Brown, June 16, 1985; 1 child, Rachael. BA, U. Maine, 1957; MEd, Rutgers U., 1961, EdD, 1964. Lic. psychologist, N.J., Pa.; cert. sch. psychologist, N.J., Pa. Tchr. Millstone Twp. (N.J.) Schs., 1957-61; sch. psychologist Lawrence Twp. (N.J.) Schs., 1962-66; chief of clin. svcs. Tng. Sch. at Vineland, N.J., 1966-67; prof. spl. edn., chief clin. psychologist Keane Coll., Union, N.J., 1967-68; prof. sch. psychology Temple U., Phila., 1968—, dir. Nat. Ctr. for Study of Corporal Punishment, 1977—; cons. sch. psychologist Pennington (N.J.) Sch., 1986—; cons. childrens mag., 1986-89; tech. specialist Chinese Univs. Project, World Bank, 1987; cons. ACLU, 1977—, U.S. Ho. Reps., Washington, 1990, U.S. Senate, Washington, 1984. Author: Reading Writing and the Hickory Stick, 1990; co-editor: Corporal Punishment in American Education, 1979, School Consultation; cons. editor Sch. Psychology Review, 1985-87; contbr. articles to profl. jours. Recipient Dorothy Hughes Meml. award NYU, 1982. Fellow Am. Psychol. Assn. (pres. div. 16 1977-78, Disting Svc. to Sch. 1986), Internat Soc. for Rsch. on Aggression; mem. Nat. Assn. for Advancement of Sci., Soc. for Traumatic Stress Studies, Coun. for Exceptional Children, Am. Ednl. Rsch. Assn., Phi Delta Kappa. Democrat. Jewish. Office: Temple U 255 RHA 255 Rita Philadelphia PA 19122

HYMAN, ISABELLE, fine arts educator; b. N.Y.C., Apr. 19, 1930; d. Benjamin Joseph and Rachel (Tandick) Miller; m. Jerome E. Hyman, July 1, 1960. B.A., Vassar, 1951; M.A., Columbia U., 1955; M.A., Inst. Fine Arts, NYU, 1966, Ph.D., 1968. Instr. fine arts NYU, N.Y.C., 1963-68, lectr., 1968-69, asst. prof., 1969-71, assoc. prof., 1971-80, prof., 1980—; Robert Sterling Clark vis. prof. art history Williams Coll., fall 1991. Author: 15th Century Florentine Studies, 1977; co-author: Architecture: Prehistory to Post-Modernism, 1986. Editor: Brunelleschi in Perspective, 1974. Contbr. articles to profl. jours. Villa I Tatti fellow, 1972-73; Guggenheim fellow, 1988-89. Fellow Pierpont Morgan Library; mem. Coll. Art Assn. (bd. dirs. 1982-86), Soc. Archtl. Historians, Renaissance Soc. Am., Grolier Club. Office: NYU Fine Arts Dept 303 Main St New York NY 10044-0065

HYMAN, LAURA, business executive; b. Providence, June 11, 1927; d. Morris and Hilda (Sugarman) Ackerman; m. Donald Kerwin, Sept. 18, 1949 (div. 1953); m. Richard K. Hyman, Apr. 12, 1957; children: Howard, Melissa. BFA, RISD, Providence, 1948. Office mgr. Colonial Mortgagee, Huntington, N.Y., 1958-64; sr. libr. asst. Cold Spring Harbor (N.Y.) Lab., 1973-87, asst. to dir. librs./mktg., 1987-88, adminstr., bus. mgr. librs./pub. affairs, 1988—. One-woman shows include East River Savs. Bank, Huntington, N.Y., 1982, Union Savs. Bank, Huntington, 1988, Cold Spring Harbor Lab., 1988, 89, 91; group shows North Country Village, L.I., 1981, Huntington Twp. Art League, 1985, 86, 87, 89, 90, Guild Hall, East Hampton, 1989, 91. Committeewoman Huntington (N.Y.) Dem. Com., 1988-89. Mem. Spl. Librs. Assn. (assoc. editor 1987-88). Office: Cold Spring Harbor Lab Bungtown Rd Cold Spring Harbor NY 11724-2209

HYMAN, LAWRENCE ROBERT, psychiatrist; b. Amsterdam, N.Y., Dec. 7, 1940; s. Morris Arthur and Bertha (Berkman) H.; m. Lois Armstrong Wilson, June 27, 1978; children: Elyse Michelle, Michael Louis, Joshua William. BA, Ohio Wesleyan U., 1963; MD, Chgo. Med. Sch., 1968. Intern then resident U. Wis., Madison, 1968-72; guest worker NIH, Bethesda, Md., 1973-76; asst. prof. Johns Hopkins Sch. Medicine, Balt., 1976-78; resident George Washington U., Washington, 1978-80; asst. clin. prof. U. Md., Balt., 1981-84; pvt. practice Columbia, Md., 1981—; active staff dept. psychiatry Howard County Gen. Hosp., Columbia, Md., 1981—; chief exec. officer Orchard Hill Treatment Ctr. for Chem. Dependency, Columbia, 1987—; dir. div. addictions Howard County Gen. Hosp., Columbia, Md., 1991—; cons. Family Therapy Inst., Rockville, Md., others. Contbg. editor Gould Med. Dictionary, 1979; contbr. articles to profl. jours. Adv. bd. Nat. Kidney Found., Balt., 1971. Maj. M.C., AUS, 1972-76. Recipient USPHS Rsch. Career Devel. award, 1977; NIH fellow, 1972; NIH grantee. Mem. Am. Psychiat. Assn., Md. Psychiat. Soc., Med. and Chirurgical Faculty State of Md., Howard County Med. Soc., Am. Orthopsychiat. Assn. Home: 3681 Folly Quarter Rd Ellicott City MD 21042-1452 Office: 201 11055 Little Patuxent Pky Columbia MD 21044

HYMAN, MARY BLOOM, science education programs coordinator; m. Sigmund M. Hyman, 1947; children: Carol Ann Hyman Williams, Nancy Louise. BS, Goucher Coll., 1971; MS, Johns Hopkins U., 1977. Asst. dir. Edn. Md. Sci. Ctr., Balt., 1976-81, dir. edn., 1981-90; coord. sci. edn. programs Loyola Coll., Balt., 1990—; trustee Goucher Coll. Mem. quantitative literacy com. Md. State Dept. Edn., edn. outreach adv. panel Smithsonian Inst.; mem. Nat. Urban League Preschool Sci. Collaborative. Recipient Disting. Women award Gov.'s Office, Annapolis, Md., 1981; Meritorious Svc. award Johns Hopkins U., 1983; Outstanding Svc. to Sci. Edn. award. Assn. Sci. Dept. Chairmen of Balt. County Pub. Schs., 1989. Mem. Fund for Ednl. Excellence (bd. dirs.), Md. Assn. Sci. Tchrs. (bd. dirs.), Women in Math/Sci. Task Force Md. State Dept Edn., Phi Beta Kappa, Phi Delta Kappa. Home: 10815 Longacre Ln Stevenson MD 21153

HYMAN, WILLIAM, career counseling consultant, radio communicator; b. Neptune, NJ, Nov. 1, 1958; s. Jack Anthony and Evelyn (Epstein) H. Phila. Coll. Tech.; BA, Muhlenberg Coll., Allentown, Pa., 1980; MA, Ohio State U., 1982. Assoc. dir. Phila. Coll. Textile, 1987—; radio host Sta. WPEN and WMGK, Phila., 1990—; dir. Jewish Employment Vocat. Svcs., 1991—; career cons. Peterson's, Princeton, N.J., 1991. Asst. to treas. George Burell for Phila. City Coun., 1987; fund raiser George Burell for Mayor, Phila., 1991; bd. mem. Hillel of Greater Phila., 1991. Mem. Speechweavers-Toastmasters (pres. 1990—), Middle Atlantic Placement Assn., Fairmount Bus. and Neighbors Assn. Democrat. Jewish. Home: 835 N Newkirk St Philadelphia PA 19130-1707 Office: Jewish Employment Vocat Svc 1845 Walnut St Philadelphia PA 19103-4728

HYMES, WILLIAM RUSSELL, lawyer, public official; b. Booth, W.Va., Mar. 22, 1927; s. James Russell and Nannie Beatrice (Matthews) H.; m. Dorothy Jean Smith, June 27, 1953; children: Suzanne E. Ader, Colleen A. Frazier, Janette R. Reda. BA, W.Va. Wesleyan Coll., 1950; JD, U. Balt., 1959. Bar: Md. 1959, U.S. Dist. Ct. Md. 1959, U.S. Supreme Ct. 1965. Sr. clk. Gen. Motors, Chevrolet div., Balt., 1950-59; supt. of claims State Farm Mutual Automotive Ins. Co., Wayne, N.J., 1959-63; ptnr. Hymes, Sadler, Williams & Hanson, Ellicott City, Md., 1963-79; state's atty., elected ofcl. Howard County, Ellicott City, 1979—. Mem. Plumbing Code Adv. Com., Ellicott City, 1979-83. With USN, 1944-46. Named Citizen of Yr., Rotary Club, Elkridge, Md., 1983. Mem. Md. State Bar Assn., Nat. Dist. Attys. Assn., Md. State's Atty's Assn. (pres., sec., treas. 1980-89), Howard County Bar Assn. (pres., sec., treas. 1983-86) State's Attys. Assn. (pres. 1987-89), Howard County Citizen's Assn. (sec. 1970-72), Inns of Ct. (bencher), Am. Legion, VFW, Masonic Lodge, Lions Club (3rd b.p. 1985-90). Democrat. Presbyterian. Home: 3109 Hearthstone Rd Ellicott City MD 21042-2403 Office: States Atty Howard County Ct House 8360 Court Ave Ellicott City MD 21043

HYMOFF, EDWARD, editor, author, news, broadcasting and publishing company executive, corporate and university public affairs officer; b. Boston, Oct. 12, 1924; s. Gustave and Gertrude E. (Kravetsky) H.; divorced; children: Jennifer, Yves K. BS in Journalism, Boston U., 1949; MA, Columbia U., 1950. Reporter, city desk asst. N.Y. World Telegram and Sun, 1951; bur. chief, sr. war corr. Internat. News Svc., Korea and Indochina, 1951-54; news editor, mgr. NBC News, N.Y.C., 1954-58; spl. corr. CBS News, USSR and Eastern Europe, 1958-59; dir. news and pub. affairs radio sta. WMGM, N.Y.C., 1959; aero. sci. tech. and pub. affairs/pub. policy accounts rep. Carl Byoir & Assos., N.Y.C., 1959-63; mng. dir. Vietnam Mil. Histories Pub. Co., Atlantic Highlands, N.J., Hong Kong, Vietnam, 1966-69; assoc. editor THINK, IBM Corp., Armonk, N.Y., 1969-71; exec. editor NBC-TV News, 1974-75; dir. communications/pub. affairs Corp. for Pub. Broadcasting, Washington, 1977-80; mgr. editorial services Arthur D. Little, Inc., Cambridge, Mass., 1981-86; v.p. corp. communications and mktg. Nat. Security Inst., Westborough, Mass., 1986-88, 89—; assoc. adminstr. external affairs Internat. Space U., Boston, 1988-89; bd. dirs. Universal Satellite Corp., 1981—; trustee Inst. Conflict Mgmt., 1983-89; cons. USIA, 1957-58, Dept. Def., 1964-66, LWV Edn. Fund for Presdl. debates, TV producer Nat. Sci. Bd., NSF, 1980; TV documentaries and pub. affairs producer Nat. Ednl. TV Network, 1964-66; pub. relations cons. aerospace industries, 1963-66. Author: (with Martin Caidin) The Mission, 1964; author: The Kennedy Courage, 1965, International Troubleshooter for Peace, 1965, Guidance and Control of Spacecraft, 1966, 1st Marine Division in Vietnam, 1967, 1st Air Cavalry Division in Vietnam, 1967, 1st Marine Aircraft Wing in Vietnam, 1968, 4th Infantry Division in Vietnam, 1968, The OSS in World War II, 1972, rev. edit. 1986; (with Bill Cantor) Fire: Prevention, Protection, Escape, 1984; author over 1000 mag. articles. Served with AUS, OSS,World War II. Recipient Non-Fiction Writing award Aviation/Space Writers Assn., 1965, 78, Distinguished Alumni Achievement award for journalism Boston U., 1966, Apollo Achievement award NASA, 1971. Mem. Internat. Inst. Strategic Studies, Co. Mil. Historians, Authors Guild, Writers Guild Am. East, Am. Soc. Journalists and Authors, Aviation/Space Writers Assn., Radio-TV News Dirs. Assn., Vets. of the OSS (asst. sec. 1978-81, mem. exec. com. 1981—), Soc. Profl. Journalists, Overseas Press Club, Nat. Press Club. Home and Office: PO Box 129 Belmont MA 02178-0002

HYNDMAN, ARNOLD GENE, biology educator; b. L.A., Oct. 16, 1952; s. Joseph Eugene and Inez Eloise (Streets) H.; m. Juliet Masculino, Aug. 12, 1978; children: Aaron, Jason, Joseph, Adam. AB, Princeton U., 1974; PhD, UCLA, 1978. Lectr. UCLA, 1978-79; NIH postdoctoral fellow Ohio State U., Columbus, 1978-80; postdoctoral researcher U. Calif., San Diego, 1979-81; asst. prof. Rutgers U., New Brunswick, N.J., 1981-90, dir., 1983-90, assoc. prof., 1990—, assoc. provost, 1990—; cons. Chautauqua Program, 1989-90, NSF, 1988-91, NIMH, 1987-88. NSF rsch. grantee, 1988. Mem. Soc. Neurosci. (chair com. 1984-87). Office: Rutgers U Office of Provost 18 Bishop Pl New Brunswick NJ 08901-1103

HYNES, RICHARD OLDING, biology educator; b. Nairobi, Kenya, Africa, Nov. 29, 1944; s. Hugh Bernard Noel and Mary Elizabeth (Hinks) H.; m. Fleur Marshall, July 29, 1966; children: Hugh Jonathan, Colin Anthony. BA with honors, U. Cambridge, Eng., 1966, MA, 1970; PhD,

MIT, 1971. Asst. prof. biology MIT, Cambridge, 1975-78, assoc. prof., 1978-83, prof. Dept. Biology, 1983—, assoc. head Dept. Biology, 1985-89, head, 1989-91, dir. Ctr. for Cancer Rsch., 1991—; investigator Howard Hughes Med. Inst., Bethesda, Md., 1988—. Author: Fibronectins, 1990; editor Tumor Cell Surfaces and Malignancy, 1979, Surfaces of Normal and Malignant Cells, 1979; contbr. articles to profl. jours. Guggenheim Found. fellow, 1982. Fellow AAAS, Royal Soc. London; mem. Am. Soc. Cell Biology, Soc. for Devel. Biology. Office: MIT Ctr for Cancer Rsch Cambridge MA 02139

HYRICK, MARIE LYNNÉ, sales representative, nurse; b. Buffalo, Nov. 22, 1954; d. Robert Michael and Elza Carolyn (Zorich) H. BSN, U. Buffalo, 1976. RN, N.Y. Staff nurse Deaconess Hosp., Buffalo, 1976-80, asst. head nurse outpatient dept., 1980-82; pharm. sales rep. Merrell Dow Pharms., Cin., 1982—. Vol. usher Shea's Performing Arts Ctr., Buffalo, 1978—. Mem. U. Buffalo Alumni Assn. Democrat. Roman Catholic. Home: 41 Amana Pl Buffalo NY 14224-3050

HYTIER, ADRIENNE DORIS, French educator; d. Jean and Katharine Hytier Matson. B.A. summa cum laude, Barnard Coll., 1952; M.A., Columbia U., 1953, Ph.D., 1958. Instr. French Vassar Coll., 1959-61, asst. prof., 1961-66, assoc. prof., 1966-70; prof. French Vassar Coll., Poughkeepsie, N.Y., 1970—, Lichtenstein Dale prof. French, 1974—; vis. assoc. prof. Columbia U., 1966, U. Calif., 1968-69. Editor for French lit.: The 18th Century: A Current Bibliography since 1970, 17 vols., Two Years of French Foreign Policy: Vichy 1940-42, 1958, 2d edit., 1974, Les Dépêches diplomatiques du Comte de Gobineau en Perse, 1959, La Guerre, 1975, 4th edit., 1991; contbr. revs. and articles in field. Decorated chevalier des Palmes Académiques, 1974; fellow Guggenheim Found., 1967-68. Mem. MLA, Am. Assn. Tchrs. French, Am. Soc. 18th Century Studies, NE Soc. for 18th Century Studies, Mid. Atlantic Soc. 18th Century Studies, Internat. Soc. 18th Century Studies, Phi Beta Kappa. Home: 71 Raymond Ave Poughkeepsie NY 12601-6106 Office: Vassar Coll PO Box 372 Poughkeepsie NY 12601-0372

IACONA, LYNN ANN, lawyer; b. Queens, N.Y., May 14, 1958; d. Anthony Andrew and Florence Mary (Procelli) I.; m. Mark Elliott Goidell, Aug. 25, 1985; 1 child, Kimberly Ann. BA, Bucknell U., 1980; JD, Hofstra U., 1983. Bar: N.Y. Staff atty. Legal Aid Soc. Nassau County, Mineola, N.Y., 1983-85; assoc. atty. Law Offices of Robert R. Serpe, Huntington, N.Y., 1985-88; staff atty. Town Atty's Office Town of Babylon, Lindenhurst, N.Y., 1988-89; dep. town atty. Town of Babylon, Lindenhurst, N.Y., 1989-91; staff atty. Town of Babylon, Lindenhurst, 1991-92; counsel Town of Babylon Sanitation Commn. 1988-89, Ethics Bd., 1988-92. Background singer: (gospel rock album) Rebekah Ward, 1978. Committeewoman Suffolk County, N.Y., Dem. Com., 1990—. Named to Outstanding Young Women of Am., 1988, Criminal Law fellow Hofstra U., Hempstead, N.Y., 1981, 82; recipient scholarships N.Y. State Regents, 1976, Port Washington (N.Y.) Singers, 1976. Mem. ABA, N.Y. State Bar Assn., Suffolk County Bar Assn., Mortar Bd., Phi Mu, others. Roman Catholic. Home: 9 Shaw Ave Babylon NY 11702-2323

IACONIANNI, FRANK JOSEPH, research chemist; b. Phila., Oct. 12, 1954; s Guido Felice Iaconianni and Annina (Cavalieri) Di Liberato; m. Catherine Elizabeth Black, June 14, 1991. BS, Drexel U., 1977, PhD, 1984. Chemist Franklin Rsch. Ctr., Norristown, Pa., 1980-89; sr. chemist Sun Chem. Corp., Carlstadt, N.J., 1989-91; sr. analytical chemist Phila. Naval Shipyard, 1991—; cons. Franklin Rsch. Ctr., Norristown, 1978-80, Drexel U., Phila., 1979-82. Patentee in field; contbr. articles to profl. jours. Mem. Am. Chem. Soc., Phi Lambda Upsilon Chem. Soc. (treas. 1976-79). Home: 188 Cowbell Ln Willow Grove PA 19090 Office: Phila Naval Shipyard Code 134 1 Bldg 121 Philadelphia PA 19112

IADANZA, EUGENE ANTHONY, lawyer; b. Tokyo, Dec. 11, 1948; s. Igino J. and Josephine C. (Cantasano) I.; m. Diane E. Brannan, Aug. 12, 1972 (div. May 1988); children: Kimberly J., Jeremy I. BA, Monmouth Coll., 1970; JD, Georgetown U., 1973. Bar: N.J. 1973, U.S. Dist. Ct. N.J. 1973, U.S. Ct. Appeals (3rd cir.) 1973. Assoc. Gagliano, Tucci & Kennedy, Long Branch, N.J., 1973-80; ptnr. Tucci, Iadanza & Reisner, West Long Branch, N.J., 1980—; staff atty. City of Long Branch, 1982-90, Long Branch C. of C., 1984—, Eatontown Bd. Edn., 1978—, Shrewsbury Planning Bd., 1981—, Rumson Planning Bd., 1983—; twp. atty. Twp of Holmdel, 1989-91; borough atty. Borough of Keansburg, 1989—, mcpl. prosecutor Holmdel Twp., 1980-91, Borough of Tinton Falls, 1976-77, borough atty., 1982. Mem. Long Branch Fire Dept., 1975—; alumni pres. Monmouth Coll., 1978-80, ann. fund. chmn. 1989-90; city chmn. Long Branch Reps., 1980-84. Mem. ABA, N.J. Bar Assn., Monmouth County Bar Assn. (chmn. legis. com. 1986-91), Rep. Nat. Lawyers Assn., Long Branch Exchange Club, Rotary. Roman Catholic. Home: 691 Buttonwood Ave Long Branch NJ 07740-5855 Office: Tucci Iadanza & Reisner 1090 Broadway West Long Branch NJ 07764-1303

IADEROSA, GINA MARIE, public relations executive; b. Cleve., May 24, 1960; d. Gregory A. and Jo-Ann Marie (Stangato) I. BA, John Carroll U., 1982. Sales asst. IBM, Cleve., 1981-83; publs. editor Sherman & Assocs., Warren, Ohio, 1983-84; communications editor Macmillan Pub. Co., N.Y.C., 1984-86; asst. dir. pub. rels. Cartier, Inc., N.Y.C., 1986-87; dir. pub. rels. Carlos Falchi, Inc., N.Y.C., 1987-89, Paloma Picasso, N.Y.C., 1989-91; cons. N.Y.C., 1991—. Editor: (newsletter) Internat. Assn. of Bus. Communicators. Bd. dirs. Am. Suicide Found., 1991—; vol. Meml. Sloan Kettering Cancer Ctr., N.Y.C., 1991—.

IAFE, WILLIAM, real estate and construction company official; b. Bklyn., Nov. 3, 1955; s. William J. and Sylvia F. (Hertgen) I.; m. Linda M. Holder, July 28, 1984; children: Christina, William. BE, Cooper Union, 1977; MBA, NYU, 1991. Lic. profl. engr., N.Y., N.J.; lic. profl. planner, N.J. Constrn. engr. Walsh Constrn. Co., Trumbull, Conn., 1978-82; project mgr. U.S. Army C.E., N.Y.C., 1983; project dir. Olympia & York, New Brunswick, N.Y.C., N.J., 1983—. Home: 60 Monroe Ave Edison NJ 08820-3619 Office: 237 Park Ave New York NY 10017-3142 Office: Olympia & York 760 Hwy 18 East Brunswick NJ 08816

IANNI, JERRY GIROLAMO, mathematician; b. Englewood, N.J., Nov. 28, 1970; s. Vincent and Frances (Denaro) I. AA, Rockland Community Coll., Suffern, N.Y., 1985; BA, SUNY, Albany, 1988; BS, Ramapo Coll. N.J., Mahwah, 1989; BA, Jersey City State Coll., 1989; MS, Stevens Inst. Tech., 1992. Math. tutor Rockland Community Coll., Suffern, N.Y., 1985, Ramapo Coll. N.J., Mahwah, N.J., 1988-89; free lance musician Leonia, N.J., 1989—; teaching asst. Stevens Inst. Tech., Hoboken, N.J., 1989-91; clarinetist/bass clarinetist Jersey City State Coll. Symphony of Winds & Percussion, 1987—, Jersey City State Coll. Community Orch., 1987—; adj. prof. Bergen Community Coll., Paramus, N.J., 1991—. Composer: Reflections, 1988, Sequentia, 1988, Introduction and Rondo, 1989, The Gothic Knights' March, 1991. Recipient Gold Ribbon Cert., Rockland County Music Tchrs. Guild, 1985; Manhattan Sch. of Music scholar, 1985, Coors Vets. Meml. scholar, 1986; recipient spl. award Friends of Music & Art of Hudson County, 1989. Mem. Am. Fedn. Musicians.

IANNONE, BARTHOLOMEW CHARLES, English educator; b. N.Y.C., May 3, 1945; s. Carmine and Raffaella (Napolitano) I. BA in English, Fordham U., 1967, MA in English, 1969; studies with Katherine Sergara, studies with Allan Jones. Elem. tchr. N.Y.C. Bd. Edn., 1968-72, per diem tchr., 1972-73, 85—, high sch. English tchr., 1973-78; real estate agt. Landith Realty, N.Y.C., 1979-81; bill collector Nat. Mag. Co., N.Y.C., 1982-83; parochial tchr. N.Y. Cath. Archdiocese, N.Y.C., 1984-85; actor, writer, producer theater and video N.Y.C., 1963—; actor, writer, producer, mgr. in theater, video and cable TV, N.Y.C., 1978—. Author: Classic Profiles, 1980; (plays) Vampire of Transylvania, Royal Family of Hollywood, Pheasant Under Glass, Every Inch a Lady, The Roman and The Slavegirl, A Valentine for Viola, Quest for the Dinosaurs, The Beautiful People; (films) Virginia Woolfe, The Bloomsbury Circle, Serpico, String City, Women of Today, Fools Paradise; actor, producer cable TV, (videos) Classic Profiles, Bear Liar, Pheasant Under Glass. Broadcaster WFUV-Radio, N.Y.C., 1964-65, MCTV, N.Y.C., 1988—; singer St. Kilian Choir, 1989—. Mem. KC. Republican. Roman Catholic. Office: NYC Bd Edn 110 Livingston St New York NY 11735

IANNOTTI, JOSEPH PATRICK, orthopedic surgeon; b. N.Y.C., Dec. 16, 1954; s. Frank Thomas and Victoria (Artuso) I.; m. Cindy Baskind, July 12, 1975; 1 child, Matthew. BS, Fordham U., 1975; MD, Northwestern U., 1979; PhD in Cell Biology, U. Pa., 1987. Resident in orthopedic surgery U. Pa., Phila., 1979-83, chief resident, 1983-84, asst. prof. orthopedic surgery, 1984—; chief of shoulder svc. Hosp. of U. Pa., Phila., 1988—. Author, editor: Rotator Cuff Disorders, 1992; editor: Orthopaedic Knowledge Update, 1992, Basic Science Orthopaedics, 1992; contbr. to profl. publs. NIH postdoctoral fellow U. Pa., 1980-81; recipient Career Devel. award NIH, 1984-89, DeForest Willard award U. Pa., 1984; N.Am. travel fellow Am. Orthopaedic Assn., 1985, Am. Brit. Can. fellow, 1992. Fellow Am. Acad. Orthopaedic Surgeons; mem. Orthopaedic Rsch. Soc., Am. Shoulder and Elbow Surgeons, Acad. Orthopaedic Soc., Pa. Orthopaedic Sco. Office: Hosp of Univ Pa 3400 Spruce St Philadelphia PA 19104

IANNUZZI, DANIEL ANDREW, publishing and broadcasting executive; b. Montreal, Que., Can., Feb. 24, 1934; s. Andre Daniele and Maria Rosa (Pons) I.; m. Beryl Kirkwood, May 1956 (div. 1970); children: Derek, Doreen; m. Elena Caprile, June 20, 1971; 1 child, Michael. Student of Journalism, Sir George William Coll., Montreal, 1952; student, Sch. of Graphic Arts, Montreal, 1953; hon. academician, Tiberina Acad., Rome, 1977. Editor, publisher, founder Corriere Canadese Italian newspaper, Toronto, Can., 1954-72; exec. producer City TV, Toronto, 1972-79; pres., exec. producer, founder CFMT-TV Multilingual TV, Toronto, 1979-88; chmn., pub. Daisons Corp., Toronto, 1979—; pres., chief exec. officer World TV Network, Toronto, 1988—; pres., chief exec. officer Multi Media Capital Corp., Toronto, 1989—. Recipient Order of Ont., 1989, Order of Can., 1990, award of excellence Gov. Can., 1986, Order Republic Italy Gov. Italy, 1987; named Can. Family Man B'nai B'rith, 1977. Mem. Multilingual Media Assn. (hon. pres. 1989), Knights of Malta (knight commdr.), Albany Club, Primrose Club. Progressive Conservative. Roman CAtholic. Home: One Benvenuto Pl Ste 727, Toronto, ON Canada M4V 2L1 Office: MultiMedia Capital Corp, 1100 Caledonia Rd, Toronto, ON Canada M6A 2W5

IANNUZZI, JOHN NICHOLAS, lawyer, author, educator; b. N.Y.C., May 31, 1935; s. Nicholas Peter and Grace Margaret (Russo) I.; m. Carmen Maria Barrios, Aug. 1979; children: Dana Alejandra, Christina Maria, Nicholas Peter II, Alessandro Luke; children from previous marriage: Andrea Marguerite, Maria Teresa. BS, Fordham U., 1956; JD, N.Y. Law Sch., 1962. Bar: N.Y., U.S. Dist. Ct. (so. and ea. dists.) N.Y. 1964, U.S. Dist. Ct. (no. and we. dists.) N.Y. 1965, U.S. Ct. Appeals (2d cir.) 1965, U.S. Supreme Ct. 1971, U.S. Dist. Ct. Conn. 1978, U.S. Tax Ct. 1978, U.S. Ct. Appeals (5th and 11th cirs.) 1982, U.S. Ct. Appeals (4th cir.) 1988. Assoc. Law Offices of H.H. Lipsig, N.Y.C., 1962, Law Offices of Aaron J. Broder, N.Y.C., 1963; ptnr. Iannuzzi & Iannuzzi, N.Y.C., 1963—; adj. assoc. prof. trial advocacy Fordham U. Law Sch. Author: (fiction) What's Happening, 1963, Part 35, 1970, Sicilian Defense, 1974, Courthouse, 1977, J.T., 1984, (non-fiction) Cross-Examination: The Mosaic Art, 1984, Trial Strategy and Psychology, 1992. Mem. ABA, N.Y. County Bar Assn., N.Y. Criminal Bar Assn., Columbian Lawyers Assn., Lipizzan Internat. Fedn. (pres.). Roman Catholic. Home: 118 Via Settembre, 9 Roma Italy Office: Iannuzzi & Iannuzzi 233 Broadway New York NY 10279-0001 also: 775 Park Ave Huntington NY 11743 also: 345 Franklin St San Francisco CA 94102 also: Advokatunburo Schumacher, Harneggstrasse FH, 8001 Zurich Switzerland also: 1253 Phillips Sq, Montreal, PQ Canada also: 120 Adelaide St W, Toronto, ON Canada H3B 3G3

IASILLO, PETER, concrete company executive, village mayor; b. Port Chester, N.Y., Feb. 27, 1929; s. Casper and Catherine (Sileo) I.; m. Gloria Sementini, Oct. 14, 1950; children—Peter, Katherine, Judy. Cert. in art Parsons Sch. Design, 1947; cert. in math. Norwalk State Tech., 1953, Wright Tech. Inst., 1954. Design draftsman Aerotec Industries, Greenwich, Conn., 1956-59; chief draftsman nuclear div. UOP Instruments, Greenwich, 1959-62, sr. nuclear designer, 1962-70; pres. Maguire Bros. Brush Co., Port Chester, 1970-86; mktg. dir. Bryam Concrete Co., Port Chester, 1986—; mayor Village of Port Chester, 1980—. Mem. staffs State Senator J. Pisani, Albany, N.Y., 1978-81, Assemblyman John Perone, Albany, 1978-84; v.p. Don Bosco Community Ctr., 1973-74; trustee Village of Port Chester, 1970-80. Recipient numerous pub. service and athletic awards, 1978—. Mem. Nat. League Cities, Westchester County Village Ofcls. Assn. (exec. bd. 1980—, pres. 1982-83), N.Y. State Conf. Mayors (exec. bd. 1984—), Indsl. Mgmt. Club (pres. 1966-67), Am. Legion. Republican. Roman Catholic. Lodge: Rotary (exec. bd. 1974-77). Home: 7 Fairview Pl Port Chester NY 10573-4896 Office: Bryam Concrete Co 21 Townsend St Port Chester NY 10573-4309

IATESTA, JOHN MICHAEL, lawyer; b. Orange, N.J., Dec. 29, 1944; s. Thomas Anthony and Marie Monica I.; m. Paulina Clare Pascuzzi, July 11, 1971. BS magna cum laude, Seton Hall U., 1967, JD cum laude, 1976; MS, Fordham U., 1968; LLM in Corp. Law, NYU, 1986. Bar: N.J. 1976, U.S. Dist. Ct. N.J. 1976, U.S. Ct. Appeals (3d cir.) 1981, N.Y. 1982, U.S. Supreme Ct. 1985. Law sec. to presiding judge appellate div. Superior Ct. N.J., Trenton, 1976-77; assoc. Wilentz, Goldman & Spitzer, Woodbridge, N.J., 1977-81, D'Alessandro, Sussman & Jacovino, Florham Park, N.J., 1981-83; corp. counsel Rhone-Poulenc Inc., Monmouth Junction, N.J., 1983—. Recipient Book prize Tchrs. Coll. Columbia U., 1967. Mem. ABA, N.J. Bar Assn., Am. Corp. Counsel Assn., Order of the Cross & Crescent, Delta Epsilon Sigma, Kappa Delta Pi. Office: Rhone-Poulenc Inc Black Horse Ln Monmouth Junction NJ 08852

IATRIDES, JOHN ORESTES, educator; b. Salonica, Greece, Oct. 30, 1932; came to U.S., 1950, naturalized, 1967; s. Orestes John and Froso (Valassi) I.; m. Nancy M. Lonnroth, June 29, 1963. BA, Ohio Wesleyan U., 1953; MA, U. Mich., 1954; MSS, Inst. Social Studies, Hague, 1960; PhD, Clark U., 1962. Info. officer Prime Minister's Office, Athens, Greece, 1956-58; mem. faculty So. Conn. State U., New Haven, 1962—, prof. polit. sci., 1968—, chmn. dept., 1966-86; vis. prof. polit. sci. Yale U., 1975, Harvard U., 1979, Princeton U., 1989. Author: Balkan Triangle, 1968, Revolt in Athens: Greece's Communist Second Round, 1944-45, 1970, Ambassador MacVeagh Reports, Greece, 1933-47, 1980; editor: Greece in the 1940s, 1981, Greek American Relations, A Critical Review, 1981, Studies in the History of the Greek Civil War, 1945-49, 1987; mem. editorial bd. jour. Modern Greek Studies, 1983—; contbr. articles to profl. jours. Am. review editor Balkan Studies, 1968—. Served to 2d lt. Hellenic Nat. Def. Gen. Staff, Athens, 1955-56. Mem. Soc. Historians Am. Fgn. Rels. Assn., Internat. d'Etudes du Sud-est European, Am. Polit. Sci. Assn., Modern Greek Studies Assn. Home: 470 Radmere Rd Cheshire CT 06410-3212

IATROPOULOS, MICHAEL JOHN, management executive; b. Athens, Greece, Nov. 8, 1938; came to U.S. 1966; s. John Michael and Marina (Yancoglu) I.; m. Barbara Jeanne McNeil, Aug. 27, 1966; children: John Michael, Mary Ellen. AB, Athens Coll., Greece, 1958; MD, U. Tuebingen, Ger., 1964; Dr.Med.Sc., U. Tuebingen, 1965. Research assoc./resident Div. Biomed. Sci., Brown U., Providence, 1966-67; resident dept. internal medicine U. Cologne, Ger., 1967-68; instr. pathology div. biomed. sci. Brown U., 1968-70; resident dept. pathology U. Mo., Columbia, 1970-71; spl. fellow toxicology CEPT Albany (N.Y.) Med. Coll., 1972-74; asst. prof. ICES Albany Med. Coll., Alamogordo, N.Mex., 1974-77; assoc. prof., dep. dir. ICES Albany med. Coll., 1977-78; dept. head MRD Am. Cyanamid Co., Pearl River, N.Y., 1978-89; head regulatory pathology Am. Health Found., Valhalla, N.Y., 1989—; pres. Labpath Mgmt., Inc., Suffern, N.Y., 1989—; assoc. prof. pathology N.Y. Med. Coll., N.Y., 1989—. Author: New Anticancer Drugs, 1983, Gastrointestinal Toxicology, 1986, Carcinogenicity, 1988, Toxicokinetics and New Drug Development, 1989; assoc. editor Jour. Toxicologic Pathology, 1981-83, editorial bd., 1983—. Mem. Soc. Toxicology, Soc. Toxicologic Pathologists (councillor 1981-86), Internat. Fedn. Soc. Toxicologic Pathologists (sec.-gen. 1989—). Home and Office: 6 Bruce Ct Suffern NY 10901-3310

IBA, BARBARA JEAN YOUNG, government agency administrator; b. Ellwood City, Pa., Oct. 18, 1937; d. Robert Harold and Ellen Lucille (Newton) Young; R.N., Presbyn.-Univ. Hosp., Pitts., 1958; student Bethany (W.Va.) Coll., 1958-59; B.S. in Nursing, U. Pitts., 1961; postgrad. Am. U., 1980; m. Edward Toshikatsu Iba, Oct. 23, 1965; children—Jennifer Emi, Robert Yoshio. Staff nurse Presbyn.-Univ. Hosp., 1958-59, Bethany Coll., 1958-59; nursing instr. Presbyn.-Univ. Hosp., 1959-64; nurse, population genetic researcher Nat. Inst. Dental Research, NIH, Bethesda, Md., 1964-74, equal opportunity coordinator, 1974-80, acting fed. women's program mgr., 1980-84, fed. women's program mgr., 1984-88; mgr. program employment of person with disabilities Pub. Health Svc., Rockville, Md., 1988—; chief of staff Equal Opportunity Evaluation Task Force, 1979-80; mem. Woodside Child Care Program Task Force, Silver Spring, Md., 1973-79; vice chmn. NIH Child Care Program Adv. Coms., 1973-74. Chmn., Parents of Preschoolers, Inc., 1974-75; mental retardation adv., Washington. Fed. nurse trainee, 1960; mem. ann. conf. planning com. Fed. Govt.-wide Perspectives on Employment of Persons with Disabilities, 1987—. Recipient Equal Opportunity Achievement award Nat. Inst. Dental Research, 1978; Dir.'s award NIH, 1980. Mem. Women's Equity Action League, Federally Employed Women, Kensington Bus. and Profl. Women (1st v.p. 1985-86). Home: 8716 Milford Ave Silver Spring MD 20910-5031 Office: Pub Health Svcs Parklawn Bldg Rockville MD 20857

IBACH, DOUGLAS THEODORE, minister; b. Pottstown, Pa., July 23, 1925; s. Hiram Christian and Esther (Fry) I.; B.S. in Edn., Temple U., 1950, postgrad. Sch. Theology, 1950-52; M.Div., Louisville Presbyn. Theol. Sem., 1954; m. Marion Elizabeth Torok, Sept. 2, 1950; children—Susan Kay, Marilyn Lee, Douglas Theodore, Grace Louise. Ordained to ministry Presbyn. Ch., 1953; pastor, Pewee Valley, Ky., 1952-55, West Nottingham Presbyn. Ch., Colora, Md., 1955-61, Irwin, Pa., 1961-67, Knox Presbyn. Ch., Falls Church, Va., 1967-72, United Christian Parish Reston (Va.), 1972-87; exec. dir. Camping Assn. of the Presbyteries of Northwestern Pa., Mercer, Pa., 1986-90; pastor Pulaski (Pa.) Presbyn. Ch., 1990—. Youth ministry cons. Nat. Capital Union Presbytery, 1967-86; ecumenical officer Nat. Capital Presbytery, chmn. stewardship com., 1986—; mem. ecumenical relations com. Synod of Virginias, also mem. Interfaith Conf. of Metro Washington; bd. dirs. Reston Inter-Faith, Inc.; dir. Presbyn. Internat. Affairs Seminars. adv. bd. Christmas Internat. House; mem. ch. devel. and redevel. com., Christian edn. com. Lake Erie Presbytery, stated supply Pulaski (Pa.) Presbyterian Ch.; sec. New Wilmington Mininsterium; exec. dir. Camping Assn. of Presbyteries of No. Pa., 1986-90. With USNR, 1943-44. Mem. Council Chs. Greater Washington (pres., chmn. instl. ministry commn.), Piedmont Synod U.P. Ch. (dir. youth, camping), Acad. Parish Clergy Assn. Presbyn. Christian Educators, Fairfax County Council Chs. (pres.), Com. 100 Fairfax County, Mercer Fun Club (bd. dirs.). Home: RR 1 Box 584 New Wilmington PA 16142-9546 Office: Pulaski Presbyn Ch Liberty St and Shenango Ave Pulaski PA 16143

ICAHN, CARL C., arbitrator, options specialist, corporation executive; b. Queens, N.Y., 1936; m. Liba Icahn; 2 children. B.A., Princeton U., 1957; postgrad., NYU Sch. Medicine. Apprentice broker Dreyfus Corp., N.Y.C., 1960-63; options mgr. Tessel, Patrick & Co., N.Y.C., 1963-64, Gruntal & Co., 1964-68; chmn., pres. Icahn & Co., N.Y.C., 1968—; chmn., chief exec. officer ACF Industries Inc., Earth City, Mo., 1984—, also bd. dirs.; chmn., bd. dirs., pres., chief exec. officer Trans World Airlines Inc., N.Y.C., 1986—; chmn., bd. dirs. Bayswater Realty & Capital Corp. Office: Icahn & Co Inc 100 S Bedford Rd Mount Kisco NY 10549-3443 also: ACF Industries Inc 3301 Rider Trail S Earth City MO 63045 also: TWA Inc 605 3rd Ave New York NY 01058*

IEVOLI, RICHARD JOSEPH, psychologist; b. N.Y.C., Oct. 15, 1946; s. Joseph John and Josephine Marie (De Cillis) I.; 1 child, Melody. BA, Kean Coll., 1974; MA, U. Md., 1977; PhD, Temple U., 1983. Lic. psychologist, Pa. Adjunct faculty Rutgers U., Camden, N.J., 1981-84, Villanova U., Phila., 1984—; instr. Med. Coll. Pa., Phila., 1984-86; psychologist Phila. State Hosp., 1986-87, So. Home for Children, Phila, 1987; attending psychologist Phila. Psychiat. Ctr., 1985—; adjunct supervising psychologist Ea. State Sch. and Hosp., Trevose, Pa., 1986—; sr. psychologist Cath. Social Svcs., Phila., 1988—; attending psychologist Westmeade Ctr., Wyndmoor, Pa., 1990—; dir. Bala Psychol. Assocs., Bala Cynwyd, Pa., 1983—; consulting psychologist Hosp. of Phila. Coll. Osteopathic Medicine, Phila., 1987-88; cons.-nuclear access Stanard & Assocs., Chgo., 1990—. Assoc. Human Svcs. Ctr. Phila. Soc. of Clin. Psychologists, 1988. Mem. APA, Pa. Psychol. Assn., Phila. Soc. Clin. Psychologists, Assn. for Advancement Psychology. Roman Catholic. Home: 633 Launfall Rd Plymouth Meeting PA 19462-2115 Office: Bala Psychol Assocs GSB Bldg Bala Cynwyd PA 19004

IFKOVIC, EDWARD JOSEPH, English language educator; b. North Branford, Conn., June 16, 1943; s. Anthony Joseph and Anna Eva (Farkash) I. BS, So. Conn. State U., 1965; MA, U. N.C., Chapel Hill, 1966; PhD, U. Mass., 1972. Tchr. Branford (Conn.) High Sch., 1966-69; prof. English Tunxis Community Coll., Farmington, Conn., 1972—; lectr. USIA, Washington, 1985—. Author: Anna Marinkovich, 1981 Yugoslavs in America, 1977, Dream Street: American Movies, 1979; author anthology: American Letter, 1979. Recipient Excellence in Teaching award, Tunxis Community Coll., 1991. Mem. MLA, Multi-Ethnic Lit. Soc. of Am. (chair 1974-76). Home: 462 Broadview Ter Hartford CT 06106-3803 Office: Tunxis Community Coll Farmington CT 06032

IGNATIADIS, VARVARA, infosystems specialist; b. Athens, Greece, Sept. 2, 1955; came to U.S., 1980; d. Michael and Magdalini (Mouratidou) Avgidis; m. Panayiotis A. Ignatiadis, July 26, 1979. AAS with honors, La Guardia Community Coll., 1982; BBA, Baruch Coll., 1987; MBA, Pace U., 1992. Programmer/analyst Res. Mgmt. Fund., N.Y.C., 1982-84, A.C.I., N.Y.C., 1984-85, Swissre N.A., N.Y.C., 1985-88; sr. programmer/analyst Merrill Lynch, N.Y.C., 1988—; facultative project mgr. Munich Am. Reinsurance, 1989. Mem. Greek Club (pres. 1981-82). Greek Orthodox.

IH, CHARLES CHUNG SEN, electrical engineering educator, researcher; b. Hankow, Hupei, China, May 15, 1933; came to U.S., 1958; s. Young H. and Moon-Hua (Lee) I.; m. Donna M. Chou, Sept. 15, 1959; children: Ronald, Bennet. BSEE, Nat. Taiwan U., Taipei, 1956; MSEE, Lehigh U., 1959; PhD in Physics, U. Pa., 1966. Engr. Sperry Rand Univac (now Unisys), Blue Bell, Pa., 1959-63; mem. tech. staff RCA Labs (now SRI East), Princeton, N.J., 1966-70; sr. physicist, dir. CBS Labs., Stamford, Conn., 1971-75; prof. elec. engring. U. Del., Newark, 1975—; cons. Robotic Vision Systems, Inc., Haupauge, N.Y., 1984-86, ISC Def. System, Lancaster, Pa., 1985-87, E.I. Du Pont de Nemours & Co., Wilmington, Del., 1986-88, Holometrix, Inc., Cambridge, Mass., 1987—. Contbr. articles to sci. jours.; patentee on holographic scanner, archival color image storage, holographic optical head, high speed fiber communication. Bd. dirs. Chinese Am. Community Ctr., Hockessin, Del., 1987—. Rsch. grantee NSF, 1983-86, Innovative Sci. and Tech. Office, 1987-92, NIH, 1989-92. Mem. IEEE, Optical Soc. Am. Office: U Del Dept Elec Engring Newark DE 19716

ILCHMAN, ALICE STONE, college president, former government official; b. Cin., Apr. 18, 1935; d. Donald Crawford and Alice Kathryn (Biermann) Stone; m. Warren Frederick Ilchman, June 11, 1960; children: Frederick Andrew Crawford, Alice Sarah. BA, Mt. Holyoke Coll., 1957; MPA, Maxwell Sch. Citizenship, Syracuse U., 1958; PhD, London Sch. Econs., 1965; LHD, Mt. Holyoke Coll., 1982, Franklin and Marshall Coll., 1983. Asst. to pres., mem. faculty Berkshire Community Coll., 1961-64; lectr., asst. prof. Ctr. for South and Southeast Asia Studies U. Calif.-Berkeley, 1965-73; prof. econs. and edn., dean Wellesley (Mass.) Coll., 1973-78; asst. sec. edn. and cultural affairs Dept. State, 1978; asso. dir. edn. and cultural affairs Internat. Communication Agy., 1978-81; advisor to sec. Smithsonian Instn., 1981; pres. Sarah Lawrence Coll., Bronxville, N.Y., 1981—; intern, asst. to Sen. John F. Kennedy, 1957; dir. Peace Corps Tng. Program for India, 1965-66; chmn. com. on women's employment NAS; bd. dirs . J & W Seligman Cos. Author: The New Men of Knowledge and the New States, 1968, (with W.F. Ilchman) Education and Employment in India, The Policy Nexus, 1976. Trustee Mt. Holyoke Coll., 1970-80, Mass. Found. for Humanities and Pub. Policy, 1974-77, East-West Center, Honolulu., 1978-81 Expt. in Internat. Living, The Markle Found., The Rockefeller Found., The U. of Cape Town, South Africa, Corp. Adv. Bd.; mem. Smithsonian Council, Yonkers Emergency Fin. Control Bd., 1982-88, Am. Ditchley Found. Program Com., Internat. Research and Exchange Bd., Com. for Econ. Devel.; bd. dirs. N.Y. Telephone Co. Mem. Nat. Acad. Pub. Adminstrn., NOW Legal Def. Edn. Fund, Coun. Fgn. Rels., Cosmpolitan Club (N.Y.C.), Century Assn. (N.Y.C.), Bronxville Field Club. Home: 935 Kimball Ave Bronxville NY 10708-5507 Office: Sarah Lawrence Coll Office of the President Bronxville NY 10708

ILCHMAN, WARREN FREDERICK, university administrator, political science educator; b. Denver, Sept. 6, 1933; s. Frederick Warren and Imogene (Trovinger) I.; m. Alice Crawford Stone, June 11, 1960; children: Frederick Andrew Crawford, Alice Sarah Crawford. B.A., Brown U., 1955; Ph.D., U. Cambridge, Eng., 1959. Asst. prof. Ctr. Devel. Econs. Williams Coll., Williamstown, Mass., 1960-64; from asst. prof. to prof. polit. sci. U. Calif., Berkeley, 1965-73, dir. Ctr. South and Southeast Asian Studies, 1970-73; vis. prof., research assoc. Ctr. Population Studies, Harvard U., Cambridge, Mass., 1973-74; prof. polit. sci. and econs., dean arts and scis. Grad. Sch., Boston U., 1974-76; program adviser internat. div. Ford Found., N.Y.C., 1976-80; v.p. for research and grad. studies SUNY, Albany, 1980-83, provost Nelson A. Rockefeller Coll. Pub. Affairs and Policy, 1983-87, dir. Rockefeller Inst. Govt., 1983-87, exec. v.p., 1987-90; pres. Pratt Inst., Bklyn., 1990—. Author: Professional Diplomacy in the U.S, 1961, New Men of Knowledge and the Developing Nations, 1966, Professionals as Agents of Change, 1968, The Political Economy of Change, 1969 (translated into French, Spanish, Japanese, Hindi and Arabic), Political Economy of Development, 1972, Comparative Public Administration and The Conventional Wisdom, 1973, Policy Sciences and Population, 1975, Education and Employment: The Policy Nexus, 1976, New York in the Year 2000, 1986, Caring and Coping, 1986. Marshall scholar U.K.; recipient Harbison prize Danforth Found., 1969. Mem. Am. Soc. Pub. Adminstrn. (Burchfield award 1965), Asia Soc., Am. Polit. Sci. Assn., Assn. Asian Studies, Nat. Acad. Pub. Adminstrn., Cosmos Club, Univ. Club, Bronxville Field Club, Phi Beta Kappa. Episcopalian. Home: 935 Kimball Ave Bronxville NY 10708-5507 Office: Pratt Inst 200 Willoughby Ave Brooklyn NY 11205-3899

ILIFF, NICHOLAS TAYLOR, oculoplastic surgeon, educator; b. Balt., Jan. 19, 1947; s. Charles Edwin and Elizabeth Jackson (Haines) I.; m. Paula Rebecca Bender, May 27, 1972; children: Nicholas Taylor Jr., Benjamin William. BA, Williams Coll., 1968; MD, Johns Hopkins U., 1972. Diplomate Am. Bd. Ophthalmology. Asst. prof. ophthalmology Johns Hopkins Sch. Medicine, Balt., 1979-86, asst. prof. plastic surgery, 1985-86, assoc. prof. ophthalmology and plastic surgery, 1987—; bd. dirs. div. oculoplastic surgery Wilmer Inst. of Johns Hopkins U. Sch. Medicine, Balt. Co-author: Oculoplastic Surgery, 1979. Fellow Am. Acad. Ophthalmology; mem. AMA, Med. and Chirurgical Faculty Md., Balt. City Med. Soc., Am. Ophthal. Soc., Annapolis Yacht Club, Md. Club. Office: Maumanee 127 Wilmer Inst 600 N Wofe St Baltimore MD 21287-9218

ILIFF, WARREN JACKSON, ophthalmologist; b. Balt., July 23, 1944; s. Charles Edwin and Elizabeth Jackson (Haines) I.; m. Sarah Harris MacDonald, May 29, 1971; children: Marshall Jackson, Frances Jane. BA, Williams Coll., 1966; MD, Johns Hopkins U., 1970. Intern Johns Hopkins U., Balt., 1970-71, fellow in ophthalmic pathology, 1971-72; resident in ophthalmology Johns Hopkins-Wilmer Eye Inst., Balt., 1972-75; pvt. practice Balt., 1975—; assoc. prof. ophthalmology Johns Hopkins U., 1984—. Author: Orthoplastic Surgery, 1978; contbr. articles on ophthalmology to profl. jours., chpts. to books. Mem. Am. Acad. Ophthalmology (honor award 1983), Am. Ophthal. Soc. Office: 14 W Mt Vernon Pl Baltimore MD 21201

ILLUZZI, VINCENT, state senator, lawyer; b. Montpelier, Vt., Sept. 17, 1953; s. Vincent and Angela (Piscetelli) I. BA cum laude, St. Michael's Coll. Vt., 1975; JD, Vt. Law Sch., 1978. Bar: Vt. Dep. state atty. Essex and Orleans Counties, Vt., 1979-80; mem. Vt. Senate, Montpelier, 1981—, asst. minority leader, 1985-88, 91-92. Mem. Gov.'s Com. on Children and Youth, 1972-76, Gov.'s Com. on Adminstrn. of Justice, 1973-77; student mem. Vt. State Bd. Edn., 1973-77. Republican. Roman Catholic. Office: Vt State Senate State Capitol Montpelier VT 05602

IMAMSHAH, NORMAN DAVID, computer company executive, contractor; b. Chaguanas, Trinidad, W.I., Dec. 23, 1942; came to U.S., 1966; s. Clifford Macaulay and Thelma Viola (Hart) I.; m. Lynne Elizabeth Harrison, Apr. 23, 1984; children: Nicole Marie, Clifford Harrison, Brandon Michael. BA with gen. honors, U. W.I., Trinidad, 1966; MBA in Quantitative Analysis, Cornell U., 1968. CPA, Md.; lic. home improvement subcontractor, Md. Mgmt. sci. analyst United Brands, Inc., Boston, 1968-70; corp. fin. analyst Agway, Inc., Dewitt, N.Y., 1970; ops. rsch. analyst Bristol Labs., Syracuse, N.Y., 1970-72; mgr. sales analysis Burger King Corp., Miami, Fla., 1972-76; mgr. mktg. MIS Cordis Dow Corp., Miami, Fla., 1976-78; dir. MIS planning and analysis Holiday Inns, Memphis, 1978-79; mgr. computer svcs. Cordis Dow Corp., Miami, 1979-81; dir. computing svcs. Montgomery Coll., Rockville, Md., 1981-92; dir. computing and info. tech. U. Vt., Burlington, 1992—; adj. prof. Fla. Internat. U., Miami, 1974-77, Nova U., Ft. Lauderdale, Fla., 1981. Govt. Nat. scholar, Trinidad, 1963-66; Ford Found. scholar Internat. Inst. Edn., 1966-68. Home: 176 Lost Nation Rd Essex Junction VT 05452-2426 Office: U Vt 238 Waterman Bldg Burlington VT 05405-0160

IMBER, BARRY, manufacturing executive; b. Jersey City, N.J., 1945. LLD (hon.), Acad. Scienza, Rome, 1982. V.p., purchasing, advt., legal Western Bed Products, Bronx, N.Y., 1972—; gen. mgr. Randall Wire div. Western Bed Products, Bronx, 1974—, dir., gen. mgr. Chapel Hill div.; bd. dirs. Sentry-Western Coatings, East Stroudsburg, Pa.; ptnr., trustee Geosafe Chem. Rsch. Found., East Stroudsburg, 1990—; mem. Environmentality Group, Greenwich, Conn. Co-inventor new generation of ingestible, environmentally beneficial solvents, surfactants and coatings; inventor optosonic plasma process of phoresolaser coating; author of the theory of atomic structured isostatic constant orientational axial migration-negative ionic force. Recipient Value Analysis award Purchasing Mag., 1989, 90, 92. Mem. Nat. Assn. Purchase Mgmt. Office: Western Bed Products 444 Tiffany St Bronx NY 10474-6716

IMBER, JONATHAN, artist; b. Baldwin, N.Y., Oct. 1, 1950; s. Harold and Helen (Lerner) I. BFA, Cornell U., 1972, MFA, 1977. Instr. Boston Mus. Sch., 1987—; vis. artist Radcliffe Coll., Cambridge, Mass., 1986—, Sch. Visual Arts, N.Y.C., 1990—; vis. com. Provincetown (Mass.) Fine Arts Work Ctr., 1987—. Exhibited in group shows, including Nielsen Gallery, 1980, 81, 83, 85, 87, 89, 92, Munroe Gallery, 1983, 84, 87, 90, Fogg Mus., Mus. Fine Arts, also others. Recipient awards in visual arts Nat. Endowment for Arts, Rockefeller Found., Equitable Corp, engelhard award, 1984; fellow Mass. Found. for Arts, 1985, Nat. Endowment for Arts, 1987.

IMBERT, RICHARD CONRAD, insurance company executive, real estate developer; b. N.Y.C., Jan. 30, 1941; s. Henry A. and Patricia (Boyer) I.; m. Diane B. Thackray, Aug. 28, 1958; children: Peter, Cynthia, Elise. Grad. high sch., Amityville, N.Y. Underwriter Ins. Co. N.Am., Hempstead, N.Y., 1961-64; sales exec. Ashby Lee Biedler, Inc., N.Y.C., 1964-67, pres., 1967-74; pres. Fisher-Biedler, Inc., Amityville, 1974-85, Am. Profl. Agy., Inc., Amityville, 1974—, R.C.I. Industries Inc., Amityville, 1980—, IMP Properties, Inc., Amityville, 1975—; v.p. L.I. Polymers, Hauppauge, N.Y., 1988; dir., chmn. bd. Polymerix, Inc., N.J., 1990—; ptnr. Sheraton Hotel, Hauppauge. Chmn. bishop's appeal com. St. Martin of Tours Roman Cath. Ch., Amityville, 1985, trustee, 1987-90, bishop's coun of stewarts, 1990; mem. Rep. Senatorial Inner Circle, Pres. Adv. Com. Mem. Fisher Island (Fla.) Club, Southward Ho Country Club (West Islip, N.Y.). Republican. Office: RCI Industries Inc 95 Broadway Amityville NY 11701-2718

IMBRIANI, ROBERT PETER, SR., executive; b. N.Y.C., Dec. 9, 1948; s. Michael Rocco and Mary (Schiavone) I.; m. Edna Graterole, Jan. 15, 1970 (div. Oct. 1975); m. Doreen Ray, Nov. 30, 1975; children: Robert Peter Jr., Brian Albert. AS in Aero. Engring., Acad. Aero., 1970; MBA in Internat. Trade & Bus., NYU, 1971. Warehouse supr. Kay Bee Foods, Richard Hill, N.Y., 1963-67; warehouse, dist. mgr. Rene D. Lyonn Imports, Richard Hill, N.Y., 1967-69; v.p., dir. The Myers Group (U.S.) Inc., Jamaica, N.Y., 1969—; instr. World Trade Inst., N.Y.C., 1980—, SUNY at Plattsburgh, 1991—. Contbr. articles to profl. jours. Religious instr. Holy Trinity Ch., Valley Stream, N.Y., 1988—; asst. coach Valley Stream Baseball League, 1989—. Sgt. inf. N.Y. Nat. Guard, 1970-76. Mem. JFK Internat. Airport C. of C., JFK Internat. Airport Customs Bur. Assn. Republican. Roman Catholic. Office: The Myers Group (US) Inc 14909 183rd St Jamaica NY 11413-4042

IMMONEN, GERALD MATTHEW, artist; b. Detroit, Apr. 16, 1936. Cert., Cooper Union, N.Y.C., 1958; BFA, Yale U., 1960, MFA, 1962. Prof. art R.I. Sch. Design, Providence, 1963—. Exhibitions include Smithsonian Inst., Washington, 1965-67, Yale U., New Haven, 1967, Smith Coll. Mus. of Art, Northampton, Mass., 1975, Museum of Art, R.I. Sch. Design, 1981, Charles Cowles Gallery, N.Y.C., 1984, 86, Forum/Zurich Art Fair, Switzerland, 1984, Art in Embassy Program, 1989—; public collections include Met. Mus. Art, N.Y.C., Memphis Brooks Mus. Art, Chase Manhattan Bank, N.Y.C. Recipient Alice Kimball Traveling fellow, 1960; R.I. State Coun. on the Arts grantee, 1984; recipient John Frazier Award for Excellence in tEaching, R.I. Sch. design, 1990. Home: 19 Creighton St Providence RI 02906-1518 Office: RI Sch of Design 2 College St Providence RI 02903-2707

IMMORDINO, PETER ANTHONY, surgeon; b. N.Y.C., Mar. 11, 1937; s. Santo and Aida Maria Elena (Florentino) I.; m. Susan Marie Mally, Feb. 20, 1971; children: Mary Helen, Timothy Santo, Nora Elizabeth, Margaret Cecilia. AB magna cum laude, NYU, 1958; MD, Columbia U., 1962. Diplomate Am. Bd. Surgery. Intern Roosevelt Hosp., N.Y.C., 1962-63, resident, 1963-64; resident surgery Lenox Hill Hosp., N.Y.C., 1966-68, chief resident surgery, 1968-69; resident pediatric surgery Tufts New Eng. Med. Ctr., Boston, 1969-71, instr. surgery, 1970-71; instr. surgery N.Y. Med. Coll., N.Y.C., 1971-72; pvt. practice surgery Gen. Surgery Assocs. New London, Conn., 1972—; clin. instr. surgery U. Conn. Coll. Medicine, Farmington, 1990—. Mem. Physicians for Social Responsibility, New Haven, 1982, Internat. Physicians for Prevention Nuclear War, Boston, 1985. Lt., M.C., USNR, 1964-66. Mem. AMA, ACS, Am. Acad. Pediatrics, Phi Beta Kappa, Beta Lambda Sigma, Delta Phi Alpha. Home: 351B Boston Post Rd East Lyme CT 06333 Office: Gen Surgery Assocs New London PC 359 Montauk Ave Ste 2C New London CT 06320

IMONDI, DEBORAH ANN, investment manager; b. Providence, R.I., Sept. 26, 1952; d. David Joseph and Doris Regina (Aldrich) Guay; m. Dennis Joseph Imondi, Oct. 26, 1974. BA in Econs., U. R.I., 1982, MBA, 1986. Trust officer, econonomist R.I. Hosp. Trust Nat. Bank, Providence, 1970-84; v.p. adminstrn. Van Liew Capital, Providence, 1984-88; v.p. ops. Textron Investment Mgmt. Co., Providence, 1988—. V.p. R.I. Spl. Olympics, 1989—; treas. Leadership R.I.; v.p. bd. dirs. R.I. 4-H Club Found., 1980—, New Eng. Fellowship for Rehab. Alternatives, Providence, 1988—, R.I. Rape Crisis, 1992—. Office: Textron Investment Mgmt Co 40 Westminster St Providence RI 02903-2525

IMPERATO, F. NICHOLAS, publishing executive; b. Jersey City, Nov. 16, 1944; s. Nicholas Floyd and Helen Carmella (Bardino) I.; m. Patricia Sheila Mclaughlin, Oct. 31, 1970; children: Nicole, Michael. BA in English, Lynchburg U., 1968. Sales mgr. Dunhill of Phila., 1968-71; account exec. Xerox Learning Systems, Ft. Washington, Pa., 1971-72; sales mgr. Applied Learning Corp., King of Prussia, Pa., 1972-74; sr. mktg. rep. Bowne Time Sharing, Phila., 1974-75; pres. Strafford-Harwen, Bala Cynwyd, Pa., 1975-78; br. mgr. Mead Data Cen., Phila., 1978-85; pres. Profl. Info. Corp., King of Prussia, 1985—. Bd. dirs., pres. Lower Merion (Pa.) Soc., 1985—. Lt. (j.g.) USN, 1966-72. Mem. Porsche Club Am. (pres.). Republican. Roman Catholic. Office: Profl Info Corp Nat Law Network 112 Long Rd King Of Prussia PA 19406-3030

IMPERATO, PASCAL JAMES, physician, health administrator, author, editor, medical educator; b. N.Y.C., Jan. 13, 1937; s. James Anthony and Madalynne Marguerite (Insante) I.; m. Eleanor Anne Maiella, June 4, 1977; children: Alison Madalynne, Gavin Humbert, Austin Clement. B.S., St. John's U., 1958, D.Sc. (hon.), 1977; M.D., SUNY, Downstate Med. Ctr., 1962; M.P.H. and Tropical Medicine, Tulane U., 1966. Diplomate: Am. Bd. Preventive Medicine, Nat. Bd. Med. Examiners. Fgn. fellow Assn. Am. Med. Colls., Kenya, Tanzania, Uganda, 1961; intern dept. internal medicine L.I. Coll. Hosp., 1962-63, resident dept. medicine, 1963-65; fgn. rsch. fellow Tulane Univ.-U. del Valle, Cali, Colombia, 1965; N.Y. Acad. Medicine/Glorney Raisebeck fellow Tulane U., New Orleans, 1965-66; med. epidemiologist smallpox eradication-measles control program Ctrs. Disease Control/USPHS, Mali, 1966-72; dir. Bur. Infectious Disease Control, N.Y.C. Dept. Health, 1972-74, prin. epidemiologist, dir. immunization program, 1972-74, 1st dep. commr., 1974-77, dir. pub. health residency tng. program, 1974-77; chmn. N.Y.C. Swine Influenza Immunization Task Force, 1976-77; med. cons. Africa Bur., U.S. AID, 1974; commr. health N.Y.C., 1977-78; chmn. N.Y.C. Bd. Health, 1977-78; chmn. bd. N.Y.C. Health and Hosps. Corp., 1977-78; chmn. exec. com. N.Y.C. Health Systems Agy., 1977-78; acting health services adminstr. N.Y.C., 1977-78; clin. instr. dept. medicine Cornell U. Med. Coll., N.Y.C., 1972-74, asst. clin. prof., 1974-78, asst. clin. prof. dept. pub. health, 1974-77, assoc. clin. prof., 1977-78, adj. prof., 1979—; clin. assoc. prof. dept. preventive medicine & community health SUNY Health Sci. Ctr. at Bklyn., 1974-77, lectr., 1977-78, prof. and chmn., 1978—; mem. staff N.Y. Hosp., 1972-78, L.I. Coll. Hosp., 1973—, State Univ. Hosp., 1978—, Kings County Hosp., 1978—; lectr. dept. community medicine Mt. Sinai Sch. Medicine, CUNY, 1974—, dept. health adminstrn. Columbia U. Sch. Pub. Health, 1982—; cons. N.Y. State Edn. Dept., 1982-87, Nat. Acad. Scis., 1985, dept. community health svcs. and ambulatory care Brookdale Hosp. Med. Ctr., 1987—, program for appropriate tech. in health U.S. AID, 1985-89; med. dir. rsch. devel. and Epidemiology Island Program Rev. Orgn., 1991—. Author: Doctor in The Land of the Lion, 1964, (with Osa Johnson) Last Adventure, 1966, Bwana Doctor, 1967, The Treatment and Control of Infectious Diseases in Man, 1974, The Cultural Heritage of Africa, 1974, A Wind in Africa, 1975, What To Do About the Flu, 1976, African Folk Medicine, 1977, Historical Dictionary of Mali, 1977, 2d edit., 1986, Dogon Cliff Dwellers: The Art of Mali's Mountain People, 1978, Medical Detective, 1979, (with wife) Mali: A Handbook of Historical Statistics, 1982, The Administration of a Public Health Agency, 1983, Buffoons, Queens and Wooden Horsemen, 1983, (with Greg Mitchell) Acceptable Risks, 1985, (with Robert I. Goler) Early American Medicine, 1987, Arthur Donaldson Smith and the Exploration of Lake Rudolf, 1987, Acquired Immunodeficiency Syndrome: Current Issues and Scientific Studies, 1989, Mali: A Search for Direction, 1989, (with wife) They Married Adventure: The Wandering Lives of Martin and Osa Johnson, 1992; contbr. articles to profl. jours.; cons. editor: N.Y. State Jour. Medicine, 1983, dep. editor, 1983-86, editor, 1986—; editor Jour. Community Health, 1985—; editorial bd. Explorers Jour., 1979-88, The Am. Jour. of Chinese Medicine, 1985—; mem. med. adv. bd. The Med. Herald, 1992—. Bd. dirs. Pub. Health Rsch. Inst., 1977-78, Community Coun. Greater N.Y., 1977-78, Med. Health and Rsch. Assn., 1977-78, N.Y. Heart Assn., 1983-84, Greater N.Y. Hosp. Assn., 1977-78, Milton Helpern Library Legal Medicine, 1977-89, hon. trustee, 1989—; trustee Martin and Osa Johnson Safari Mus., 1964—; mem. adv. bd. Physicians for Social Responsibility, 1983—; mem. N.Y. State Bd. Medicine, 1985—, vice chair, 1990—; mem. Bd. Zoning and Appeals Village of Plandome Heights, N.Y., 1986-90; trust Plandome Heights, 1990-92; mem. sci. adv. bd. Explorers Club, 1988—; chair N.Y.C. Met. Area Task Force on Syphilis, 1990-91; mem. Bd. Regents L.I. Coll. Hosp., 1992—. Served to lt. comdr. USPHS, 1966-69. Recipient Meritorious Honor award and medal Dept. State, 1971, US AID Meritorious Honor award and medal, 1970, Outstanding Alumnus award Tulane U., 1978, Delta Omega Nat. Merit award, 1978, Frank Babbot award SUNY, 1980, Disting. Alumni Achievement award, and medal SUNY, 1987, Spl. Service award for smallpox eradication USPHS, 1987; Fulbright scholar, North Yemen, 1985. Fellow ACP, Royal Soc. Tropical Medicine and Hygiene, Royal African Soc., Am. Coll. Epidemiology, Am. Coll. Preventive Medicine; mem. Am. Soc. Tropical Medicine and Hygiene, N.Y. Soc. Tropical Medicine (v.p. 1976-77, pres. 1989-90), Kings County Med. Soc., Tanzania Soc., Med. Soc. State N.Y., East African Wildlife Soc., African Studies Assn., Author's Guild, Explorers Club, Delta Omega, Alpha Omega Alpha. Roman Catholic. Office: Box 43 450 Clarkson Ave Brooklyn NY 11203

IMPOCO, LAURA JO, early childhood elementary special education educator, counselor; b. Springfield, Mass., Sept. 29, 1967; d. Joseph F. Jr. and Joanne M. (Morrisino) I. BS in Early Childhood, Springfield Coll., 1989, MEd in Rehab., 1990, cert. of advanced study, 1992. Cert. elem.tchr., Mass., Office for Children Presch. Infant Toddler Dir. II. Pre-kindergarten tchr. Kindercare, Springfield, 1987; counselor Habilitation Ctr. for the Handicapped, Boca Raton, Fla., 1990; dir. HeadStart, Springfield, 1990-91. Pres. grad. class Springfield Coll., 1992. Mem. AACD, Nat. Rehab. Assn., Nat. Rehab Counseling Assn., Orton Dyslexia Soc., Nat. Assn. for the Edn. Young Children. Roman Catholic. Home: 44 N Circle Dr East Longmeadow MA 01028-1345

IMRE, PAUL DAVID, mental health administrator; b. N.Y.C., May 30, 1925; s. Maximilian and Bluma (Datz) I.; B.S., U. Ill.-Urbana, 1950; M.A., N.Y. U., 1951; M.P.H., Johns Hopkins U., 1963; m. Jo Ellen Varner, Aug. 16, 1956; children—David Maximilian, Robert Bruce. Extern City Hosp., Welfare Island, N.Y., 1951-52; intern Springfield State Hosp., Sykesville, Md., 1952-53; chief psychologist Cherokee Mental Health Inst., Iowa, 1953-54; staff and chief psychologist Spring Grove State Hosp., Catonsville, Md., 1954-62; research assoc. Johns Hopkins U., 1964-72; dir. mental health ctr. Balt. County Dept. Health, Catonsville, 1970-88 ; cons. Md. State Dept. Health and Mental Hygiene, 1954-70, Children's Guild of Md., 1962-70, Jewish Child and Family Service, Balt., 1957-62; pvt. practice psychology, Columbia, Md. and Balt., 1951—. Served with inf., AUS, 1943-46; ETO. Research grantee; cert. psychologist, Md. Mem. Md. Psychol. Assn. (pres. div. II 1982-83, cert. of recognition 1978), Am. Psychol. Assn., Am. Pub. Health Assn. Club: Johns Hopkins (Balt.). Home: 10418 Green Mountain Cir Columbia MD 21044-2456

IMREY, FRANCES GLORIA, writer; b. N.Y.C., Feb. 21, 1927; d. Ference Imrey and Sara Ellen Walsh; m. Pietro Sisto Santucci, June 29, 1949 (div. Dec. 1981); children: Robert M., Joan M. Ramo, James, Thomas, Laura Ann, Diana Ellen, Joseph, Richard A. BA, Trinity Coll., Washington, 1974. Med. technologist NIH, Bethesda, Md., 1947-50; ghost writer for various M.D.'s Washington, 1950-61; pvt. investigator Bethesda, 1980-81; pres. Francesca, Silver Spring, Md., 1990—. Contbr. articles to med. jours. Fund raiser Montgomery Co-Med. Soc., Rockville, Md., 1960-65, The Christ Child Soc., Washington, 1970. Office: Francesca 3444 Midvale Ave Philadelphia PA 19129

INADA, KENNETH KAMEO, philosophy educator; b. Honolulu, May 7, 1923; s. Asajiro (Morimoto) I.; m. Masako Onmori, Mar. 23, 1953; 1 child, Ernest Yasuo. BA, U. Hawaii, 1949; MA, U. Chgo., 1951; PhD, U. Toyko, 1960. Asst. prof. U. Hawaii, Honolulu, 1960-65, assoc. prof., 1965-69; assoc. prof. SUNY, Buffalo, 1969-71, prof., 1971-92, disting. svc. prof., 1992—. Co-editor: (collective essays) Buddhism and American Thinkers, 1984; series editor SUNY Press, 1983-90. Sgt. U.S. Army, 1943-45, ETO. Overseas Tng. fellow Ford Found., 1956-60, sr. fellow Am. Inst. of Indian Studies, 1966-67; recipient Cultural award Janpanese Assn. for the Promotion of Buddhism, 1990. Mem. Am. Philos. Assn., Soc. for Asian and Comparative Philosophy, Internat. Soc. for Chinese Philosophy, Assn. Asian Studies. Home: 30 Hidden Rdg Common Buffalo NY 14221-5762 Office: SUNY Dept of Philosophy 658 Baldy Hall Amherst NY 14260

INDURSKY, ARTHUR, lawyer; b. Bklyn., Jan. 1, 1943; s. David and Anne (Levine) I.; m. Deanne Fiedler, Mar. 26, 1967; 1 child, Blake. BBA, CCNY, 1964; JD, Bklyn. Law Sch., 1967. Bar: N.Y., 1968. Entertainment counsel Columbia Pictures, N.Y.C., 1969-72; mng. ptnr. Grubman Indursky Schindler & Goldstein P.C., N.Y.C., 1973—; law firm specializes in music and recording industry; moderator Canadian Recording Industry, 1986; speaker Disting. Alumni Series, Bklyn. Law Sch. 1987-89; lectr. Copyright Soc., N.Y., 1988. Recipient 1st Ann. Alumni Achievement award, Bklyn. Law Sch., 1992. Office: Grubman Indursky Schindler & Goldstein PC 152 W 57th St New York NY 10019-3301

INDUSI, JOSEPH PAUL, research administrator, mathematician; b. Ossining, N.Y., Apr. 12, 1942; s. Joseph John and Anna Theresa (Santella) I.; m. Karen Ann Sabo, Nov. 19, 1978; 1 child, Joseph Lawrence. BS in Elec. Engring., U. Bridgeport, 1965; MS in Applied Math., SUNY, Stony Brook, 1969, PhD in Applied Math., 1971. Systems cons. Burndy Corp., Norwalk, Conn., 1972-73; mathematician Brookhaven Nat. Lab., Upton, N.Y., 1973—, dep. div. head, Tech. Support Orgn., 1983-86, div. head, Tech. Support Orgn., 1986—, assoc. chmn., Dept. Nuclear Energy, 1990—. Contbg. author encyclopedia, 1987; contbr. articles to profl. jours. NSF traineeship, SUNY at Stony Brook, 1965-68. Mem. Inst. Nuclear Materials Mgmt. (exec. com. 1991-93, chmn. long range planning com. 1990-91). Office: Brookhaven Nat Lab 29 Cornell Ave Upton NY 11973-9999

INFANTOLINO, PHILIP LOUIS, cardiologist; b. Newark, N.J., Mar. 23, 1942; s. Jospeh and Mary (Testa) I.; m. Alberta Barrauo, June 3, 1956; children: Joseph, Dena. BA, Rutgers U., 1964; MD, N.J. Coll. Medicine, 1968. Diplomate Am. Bd. Cardiology. Intern Harlem Hosp., N.Y.C., 1968-69, resident in medicine, 1969-71, resident in cardiology, 1971-73; assoc. chief of staff Point Pleasant (N.J.) Hosp., 1991—, sec. med. staff, 1989-91, trustee, 1989—. Fellow Am. Coll. Cardiology; mem. AMA. Roman Catholic. Office: 2640 Hwy 70 Manasquan NJ 08736

INFUSINO, JEFFREY SCOTT, management consultant; b. Newark, Mar. 7, 1950; s. Thomas Phillip and Estelle (Balsam) I.; m. Randi Beth Diamond, Nov. 8, 1981. BSEE, MIT, 1973, BS in Mgmt., 1973; MBA, U. Chgo., 1976. Div. asst. No. Trust Co., Chgo.; prin. A.T. Kearney, Chgo., 1976-83; ptnr., mgmt. cons. KPMG Peat Marwick, N.Y.C., 1983—. Office: KPMG Peat Marwick 345 Park Ave New York NY 10154-0004

ING, SAMUEL WEI, physicist; b. Shanghai, China, Sept. 26, 1932; came to U.S., 1950; m. Mabel K. Yang, June 25, 1958; children: Julie Ing Stern, Bonnie, Emilie Ing Slaughter, Polly. BS, MIT, 1953, MS, 1954, DSc, 1959. Asst. prof. Bucknell U., Lewisburg, Pa., 1959-60; physicist GE Co., Syracuse, N.Y., 1960-64; sr. scientist Xerox Corp., Webster, N.Y., 1964-70; prin. scientist Xerox Corp., Webster, 1970-77, sect. mgr., 1977-80, lab. mgr., 1980-85, dir., 1985-87, tech. mgr., 1987—. Contbr. articles to profl. jours.; patentee in field. Recipient Achievement award Chinese-Am. Engrs. and Scientists Assn. So. Calif., 1990. Fellow Am. Inst. Chemists, Soc. for Imaging Sci. and Tech. (conf. v.p. 1986-88, bd. dir. 1986-89); mem. Sigma Xi. Office: Xerox Corp Phillips Rd Webster NY 14580-9710

INGAGLIO, DIEGO AUGUSTUS, dentist; b. Phila., Dec. 4, 1922; s. Salvatore and Maria Concetta (Giordano) I.; D.D.S., U. Pa., 1947; m. Geraldine Jean Capizzi, July 11, 1948; children: Marie, Francene. With Phila. Mouth Hygiene Dept., 1947-50; asst. clin. dir. Emerson R. Sausser Med. Dental Clinic, Jefferson Hosp., Phila., 1950-51; pvt. practice dentistry, Drexel Hill, Pa., 1953—; staff Suburban Gen. Hosp., Norristown. Mem. Congressional Adv Bd. Editor-in-chief U. Pa. Dental Jour., 1945-47. With AUS, 1943-45, 51-53. Pres. mature adults Resurrection Ch., Marmora, N.J. Fellow Acad. Gen. Dentistry, Acad. Dentistry Internat., Royal Soc. Health; mem. ADA, AAAS, Pa. Dental Assn., Chester-Delaware County Dental Assn., Am. Internat., Philadelphia County Socs. Clin. Hypnosis, Nat. Space Inst., Phila. Physhodontontic Soc. (past pres.), Royal Soc. Hygiene, Am. Assn. Ret. Persons, Nat. Assn. Federally Lic. Firearms Dealers, Nat. Rifle Assn., Omicron Kappa Upsilon, Psi Omega. Address: 670 Breckley Ave Marmora NJ 08223

INGBAR, MARY LEE, economist; b. N.Y.C., May 18, 1926; d. Lee Adam Gimbel and Edward C. and Ruth (Prince) Mack; m. Sidney H. Ingbar, May 28, 1950; children: David H., Eric E., Jonathan. SB in Econs. cum laude, Radcliffe Coll., 1946, AM in Econs., 1948, PhD in Econs., 1953; MPH cum laude, Harvard, 1956. Corrector dept. econs. Harvard U., 1949-50, Tufts U., 1949; rsch. assoc. Grad. Sch. Pub. Adminstrn. Harvard U., Cambridge, Mass., 1961-66; assoc. prof. health econs. in residence U. Calif., San Francisco, 1972-75; prin. rsch. assoc. in preventive and social medicine Harvard Med. Sch., Boston, 1976-80; prof. family and community medicine U. Mass. Med. Sch., Worcester, 1977-82, prin. rsch. assoc. in social medicine and health policy, 1980-85, prin. assoc. in social medicine and health policy, 1985—; prin. rsch. assoc. in medicine, Beth Israel Hosp., Boston, 1976-88; vis. prof. health econs. The Amos Tuck Sch. of Bus. Adminstrn. at Dartmouth Coll. and Dartmouth Med. Sch., 1976-77; project dir. Innovative Methods of Pricing Ambulatory Care Treatment for Patients with Hypertension/U.S. Dept. Health Human Svcs. grant, 1980-82; cons. various cos. including WaterTest Corp., Manchester, N.H., 1982-88, Software Craftsmen, Inc., Boston, 1982-84; bd. dirs. WaterTest Corp.; lectr. in field, others. Editorial bd. Medical Care Jour., 1977-79; contbr. chpts. to books, articles to profl. jours. Overseer Peter Bent Brigham Hosp., 1976-84; trustee Brigham and Women's Hosp., 1984-86. Fellow APHA (chmn. med. care sect. 1978-79, governing coun. 1974-76, 85-88, 91—); mem. AAAS, Am. Assn. Med. Systems and Informatics, Am. Econ. Assn., Am. Hosp. Assn., Assn. Health Svcs. Rsch., Mass. Pub. Health Assn., Ops. Rsch. Soc. Am. Home and Office: 305 Dudley St Brookline MA 02146-5935

INGELS, JACK EDWARD, horticulture educator; b. Indpls., Mar. 28, 1942; s. Carl Eugene and Mary Louise (Fultz) I. BS, Purdue U., 1964; MS, Rutgers U., 1966; postgrad., Ball State U., 1968-70. Rsch. asst. Rutgers U., New Brunswick, N.J., 1964-66; prof. SUNY, Cobleskill, 1966-89, disting. teaching prof., 1990—; hort. cons. J.C. Penney Corp., N.Y.C., 1966-69; landscape designer, 1966—; hort. and/or landscape cons. numerous small cos., 1970—; pres. J. Ingels Assoc., 1991—. Author: Landscaping: Principles and Practices, 4th edit., 1991, Ornamental Horticulture: Principles and Practices, 1985. Chmn. Cobleskill Restoration and Devel., Inc., 1991—, bd. dirs., 1988—; mem. Schoharie County Coun. on Arts, Cobleskill, Albany Inst. of History and Art. Mem. Associated Landscape Contractors Am., Northeastern N.Y. Nursery Assn., Genesee-Finger Lakes Nursery Assn., Univ. Club (Albany, N.Y.), Moose, Elks. Home: Jay Ridge Apts Cobleskill NY 12043 Office: SUNY Cobleskill NY 12043

INGENTHRON, KAREN BARBARA, housing administrator; b. Phila., Apr. 16, 1945; d. Walter William and Doris Shafer (Fehnel) I.; m. Edward Kerrigan Prescott, Aug. 7, 1970 (div. 1974); m. Al Lewis, Oct. 19, 1985. BA with honors, U. Calif., Berkeley, 1967; postgrad., CUNY, 1988—. Leading actress Berkeley Repertory Theatre, 1967-77; artist-in-residence Playmakers Repertory Theatre, Chapel Hill, N.C., 1982, 84-85; peer counselor SAG/AFL-CIO, N.Y.C., 1983; artist-in-residence Stagewest, Springfield, Mass., 1986; assoc. dir. Eastside Improvement Soc., N.Y.C., 1987—; freelance acting coach, Calif. and N.Y., 1969—; voice tchr. Berkeley Repertory Theatre, 1970-76; masseuse Gross Sch., L.A., 1981; dir., dramaturg 52d St. Project, N.Y.C., 1991. Playwright (play) Loopty-Loo, 1986, Soul-Line, 1989, Dance With Me, 1990. Writer Coun. on Econ. Priorities, N.Y.C., 1989—, 20/20 Vision, N.Y.C., 1990—. Violet Richardson Ward fellow, 1966; named Black Belt, Tae Kwon Do Karate, 1981. Mem. SAG, AFTRA, AAUW, NOW, Nat. Arbor Found., Actor's Equity, Gnostic Ctr. Office: Eastside Improvement Soc 150 E 62d St New York NY 10021

INGERMAN, PETER ZILAHY, systems consultant; b. N.Y.C., Dec. 9, 1934; s. Charles Stryker and Ernestine (Leigh) I.; AB, U. Pa., 1958, MS in Elec. Engring., 1963; PhD, Greenwich U., 1991; m. Carol Mary Pasquale, Dec. 19, 1970 (div. May 1980). CLU; cert. data processor, computer programmer, systems profl., emergency med. technician. Rsch. investigator U. Pa., Phila., 1958-63; tech. dir. programming research, Westinghouse, Balt., 1963-65; mgr. RCA, Cherry Hill, N.J., 1965-71, staff 1971-72; sr. staff cons., Equitable Life Assurance Soc. of U.S., N.Y.C., 1972-77; ind. cons., 1977—; adj. prof. computer sci. Pratt Inst. Tech., 1968-73; mem. working groups Internat. Fedn. Info. Processing, 1962—; rep. Conf. Data Systems Langs., 1967-71, Am. Nat. Standards Inst., 1960-69. Bd. dirs. Phila. Health Plan, Inc., 1975-77, Crossroads Runaway Program, Inc., 1981-82, Willingboro Emergency Squad, 1986-89, Compliance, Inc., 1989—, Providence House, 1991—. Fellow Brit. Computer Soc.; mem. IEEE (Sr.), AAAS, Assn. Computing Machinery, N.J. Acad. Scis., Data Processing Mgmt. Assn., Bus. Forms Mgmt. Assn., Mensa, Am. Cryptogram Assn., Brit. Engring. Coun. (chartered engr.), Am. Guild Organists, Triple Nine Soc., Sigma Xi (life), Upsilon Pi Epsilon. Author: A Syntax-Oriented Translator, 1966, Russian transl., 1969; contbr. papers to pubs.; patentee electronic circuits. Office: 40 Needlepoint Ln Willingboro NJ 08046-1997

INGERSOLL, EARL GEORGE, English educator, researcher; b. Spencerport, N.Y., May 6, 1938; s. Earl Datan and Rose (Neth) I.; m. Mary Kathleen Cosgrove, June 17, 1960; children: Jeffrey E., Timothy E. BA, U. Rochester, 1960; MA, Syracuse U., 1963; PhD, U. Wis., 1971. Prof. SUNY, Brockport, 1964—. Author: Representations of Science and Technology in British Literature Since 1880, 1992; editor: Margaret Atwood: Conversations, 1990, Conversations with May Sarton, 1991; co-editor: The Post-Confessionals, 1989. Mem. Modern Lang. Assn., Coll. English Assn., N.Y. Coll. English Assn., D.H. Lawrence Soc., Soc. for Literature and Sci. Home: 173 Dewey St Churchville NY 14428-9344 Office: SUNY Coll Brockport NY 14420

INGERSOLL, WILLIAM BOLEY, lawyer, real estate developer; b. Washington, Sept. 21, 1938; s. William Brown and Loraine (Boley) I.; m. Carolyn Grace Potter, Sept. 8, 1963; children: William Brett, Courtney Lynn, Wayne Brandon, Dana Lee. BS, Brigham Young U., 1964; JD, Cath. U. Am., 1968. Bar: Va. 1968, D.C. 1969. Atty. Office of Corp. Counsel D.C., 1967-69; atty. Office Gen. Counsel, HUD, 1969-70; ptnr. Fried, Klewans, Ingersoll & Bloch, Washington, 1970-72; pres. Ingersoll and Bloch Chartered, Washington, 1972—; mng. ptnr. JC Assocs. Real Estate Devel., Washington, 1973—; gen. counsel Am. Resort and Residential Devel. Assn.; lectr. in field; Bd. dirs. Nat. Timesharing Coun., 1981—; mem. Garrison Presdl. Commn., 1984; mem. bd. adv. J. Ruben Clark Law Sch., 1987—, chmn. 1991—. Mem. ABA, Fed. Bar Assn., D.C. Bar Assn., Va. Bar Assn., Va. Assn. Trial Lawyers, Land Devel. Inst. (vice chmn.), Brigham Young U. Alumni Assn. (bd. dir. 1984—), Order of Coif, Univ. Club Washington. Coeditor-in-chief of Land Devel. Law Reporter, Land Trends, 1973—. Mormon. Co-editor-in-chief Law Reporter and Land Trends, 1973—, Time Sharing Law Reporter, 1980—, The Digest of State Land Sales, 1976—, D.C. Real Estate Reporter, 1982—, Real Estate Opportunity Report, 1986. Contbr. in field. Mem. nat. adv. com. Inside Real Estate, 1985—. Home: 713 Potomac Knolls Dr Mc Lean VA 22102-1421

INGIS, GAIL, interior designer, educator, writer; b. U.S., Nov. 1, 1935; d. Bernard and Claire Gerber; children: Linda, Richard, Paul. student in bus. Bklyn. Coll., 1953; grad. in interior architecture and design N.Y. Sch. Interior Design, 1973, B.F.A., 1980; postgrad. Pratt Inst., N.J. Inst. Tech., Parsons Sch. of Design. Prin. Ingis Design Assoc., Woodcliff Lake, N.J., 1970—; interior designer The Design Store, locations in Washington, Md., N.J., 1977-78; prof. Kean Coll., Union, N.J., 1977-80, The King's Coll., Briarcliff Manor, N.Y., 1980-82, N.Y. Sch. Interior Design, 1980-82; mem. design staff Bloomingdale's, N.Y.C., 1981-82; founder, prin. Interior Design Inst. (merged with Berkeley Coll. Bus.), Woodcliff Lake, N.J., 1982—, chmn. interior design dept., 1988-91; head interior designer, office adminstr. Africa Inland Mission, Pearl River, N.Y., 1991—; founder D'Image Inc., Saddle River, N.J., 1986. Troop leader Girl Scouts U.S., N.Y.C. and Woodcliff Lake, 1964-69. Mem. Am. Soc. Interior Designers (admissions com. N.J. chpt. 1978, edn. chmn. 1978-86, co-chmn. pro-licensing com. 1984-86, com. legis. for interior designers 1988—, bd. dirs. 1985-87, service awards 1978, 83-86), AIA profl. affiliate, Inst. Bus. Designers, U.S. Profl. Tennis Assn. (cert. tennis instr.), Illuminating Engring. Soc. N.Am., Interior Design Educators Council. Club: Altrusa. Home: 121 A S Maple St Park Ridge NJ 07656 Office: 135 Crooked Hill Rd Pearl River NY 10965-1147

INGLE, MARCUS DAVID, development management professional; b. Des Moines, Apr. 15, 1943; s. Robert Thomas and Marie (Hayden) I.; m. Diana Lee Johnson, Aug. 26, 1967; children: Aric, Aaron, Danika. BA, U. Calif., 1965; MPA, U. Wash., 1967; MPhil, Syracuse U., 1975, PhD in Social Sci., 1977. Intern internat. devel. U.S. Agy. for Internat. Devel., Washington; pub. adminstrn. advisor U.S. Agy. for Internat. Devel., Thailand, Guatemala and Vietnam, 1967-73; v.p. Practical Concepts, Inc., Washington, 1978-81; internat. mgmt. specialist Devel. Project Mgmt. Ctr. USDA, Washington, 1981-83; dir. Internat. Devel. Mgmt. Ctr. U. Md. System, College Park, 1983—; sr. advisor Caribbean Agrl. Inst., Trinidad, 1983-88; sr. trainer Oreg. State U., Eugene, 1985; program mgr. Thailand Affected Village, Bangkok, 1987—. Author: Microcomputers in Development, 1986; contbr. articles to profl. jours. Bd. dirs. West Hillandale Swim Club, Silver Spring, Md., 1987-89. Mem. Am. Soc. Pub. Adminstrn. (chair 1991-92), Internat. Comparative Adminstrn. (elected to exec. bd. 1983-85, 89—), Am. Youth Ballet Guild (elected pres. 1990-91). Office: U Md System Internat Devel Mgmt Ctr 2349 Computer & Space Sci College Park MD 20742-2445

INGRAHAM, JOHN WRIGHT, banker; b. Evanston, Ill., Nov. 10, 1930; s. Harold Gillette and Mildred (Wright) I.; m. Barbara Gaye Barker, Nov. 8, 1967; children—Kimberly, Elizabeth, Scott. A.B., Harvard U., 1952, M.B.A., 1957; postgrad., NYU Grad. Sch. Bus., 1963-68. Jr. lending positions Citicorp, N.Y.C., 1957-66, sr. lending positions, 1966-70, head instl. recovery mgmt., 1970-78, dep. chmn., credit policy com., 1979—, sr. v.p. oversight N.Am lending, 1979-84, sr. v.p. oversight Latin Am. lending, 1985-88, sr. v.p. oversight global pvt. bank lending and investing, 1988—; bd. dirs. Sprague Techs., Inc., Greenwich, Conn.; past bd. dirs. Ark. Best Corp., Ft. Smith; chmn. audit com. Presto Industries, Houston, 1986-88; vice chmn. bd. Penn Cen. Corp., Cin., 1978-84, chmn. fin. com., 1982-91, past bd. dirs.; rep. banking industry before coms. and hearings U.S. Ho. Reps., U.S. Senate, 1976-78. Trustee Noble and Greenough Sch., Dedham, Mass., 1987—; mem. bus. adv. coun. to dean Grad. Sch. Bus., U. Ark., Fayetteville, 1985—; mem. com. for Asian rsch. Harvard U. Fairbank Ctr., Cambridge, Mass. Lt. USN, 1952-55, Korea. Mem. Fin. Acctg. Standards Bd. (mem. task forces 1974-81), Robert Morris Assocs. (bd. dirs. 1972-75, Disting. Svc. award 1978), Union Club, Rockaway Hunting Club, Gulfstream Bath and Tennis Club, Quogue (N.Y.) Field Club, Ocean Club, Harvard Club Boston. Republican. Christian Scientist. Home: 950 Park Ave New York NY 10028-0320 Office: Citicorp 399 Park Ave New York NY 10043-0001

INGRAHAM, SAMUEL COOKE, III, health care executive; b. Phila., Sept. 2, 1939; s. Samuel Cooke II and Florence (Develin) I.; m. Judith Ann Bosanec, Sept. 12, 1964; children: Janet Ann, Susan Elizabeth. BS in Pharmacy with Honors, Phila. Coll. Pharmacy and Sci., 1962, MS in Hosp. Pharmacy Adminstrn., 1963; MS in Environ. Health, U. Cin., 1969. Registered pharmacist, Pa. Commd. officer USPHS, 1963—, advanced through grades to pharmacist dir., 1989—; dep. dir., sr. program analyst Program Mgmt. Office Office of Device Evaluation, FDA, Rockville, Md., 1989—; mem., former chmn., program chmn. N.E. Fed. Med. Region Pharmacy Subcom., 1975—; pres. various appointment bds. USPHS, 1980—. Mem. Am. Pharm. Assn., Assn. Mil. Surgeons U.S., Commd. Officers' Assn., Rho Chi. Roman Catholic. Office: FDA Office Device Evaluation Program Mgmt Office HFZ-405 1390 Piccard Dr Rockville MD 20850

INLANDER, CHARLES BENNETT, consumer advocacy executive; b. Chgo., Dec. 6, 1946; s. Herbert Nathan and Elizabeth (Lederer) I.; m. Dale Francena Jacobsen, May 19, 1979; 1 child, Amy Francena. BA in Govt. and Pub. Adminstrn., Am. U., 1969. Asst. dir. alumni rels. Am. U., Washington, 1970, dir. alumni rels., 1970-71, asst. dir. devel., 1971-72; exec. Pa. Assn. for Retarded Citizens, Harrisburg, 1973-76; exec. dir. Inst. for Rsch. and Devel. in Retardation, Harrisburg, 1976-78; fed. ct. master D.C. Govt., Washington, 1978-82; pres. The People's Med. Soc., Allentown, Pa., 1983—; lectr. Sch. Medicine, Yale U., New Haven, Conn., 1985—; cons. numerous orgns., 1970—. Author: Take This Book to the Hospital, 1985, 91, Medicine on Trial, 1988 (Am. Nursing Book of Yr. 1989), Medicare Made Easy, 1991; contbr. articles to profl. jours. Bd. dirs. Civil Justice Found., Washington, 1985—, Nat. League for Health Care, N.Y.C., 1989—, Lehigh Valley Bus. Conf. on Health Care, Bethlehem, Pa., 1984-92; pres. Harrisburg Pa. Human Rels. Coun., 1975-78; chairperson Gov.'s Task Force on Protection and Advocacy, Harrisburg, 1976. Mem. ACLU (pres. Cen. Pa. chpt. 1975-78), Am. Soc. Assn. Execs., Omicron Delta Kappa. Democrat. Jewish. Office: Peoples Med Soc 462 Walnut St Allentown PA 18102

INMAN, DANIEL JOHN, mechanical engineer, educator; b. Shawano, Wis., May 10, 1947; s. Glen and Wilma (Sidebotham) I.; m. Catherine Little, Sept. 18, 1982; children: Jennifer W., Angela W., Daniel J. BS, Grand Valley State, Allendale, Mich., 1970; MAT, Mich. State U., 1975, PhD, 1980. Instr. physics Grand Rapids (Mich.) Ednl. Park, 1970-76; technical staff Bell Labs., Whippany, N.J., 1978; rsch. asst. Mich. State U., East Lansing, 1976-79, 79-80, instr., 1978-79; prof. SUNY, Buffalo, 1980; chmn. U. Buffalo, 1989—; dir. Mech. Systems Lab., Buffalo, 1984; adj. prof. Brown U., Providence, 1986; cons. Kistler Instrument Corp., Amherst, N.Y., 1985. Author: Vibration: Control Stability and Measurement, 1988, 90; assoc. editor ASME Vibration, Acoustics, Stress and Reliability in Design, 1984—, ASME Jour. Applied Mechanics, SEM Jour. of Theoretical and Exptl. Modal Analysis, 1986, Mechanics of Structures and Machines; tech. editor ASME Jour. Vibration and Acoustics. Presdl. Young Investigator NSF, 1984-89. Fellow ASME (chair Buffalo sect. 1986-87), AIAA (assoc.); mem. IEEE (Control Systems Soc.), Am. Acad. Mechanics, Soc. Indsl. and Applied Math., Am. Helicopter Soc. Home: 1 Blue Ridge Ct Getzville NY 14068-1192 Office: SUNY AB Dept Mech and Aero Engring Buffalo NY 14260

INMAN, JOHN KEITH, chemist; b. St. Louis, May 21, 1928; s. Chelsea O. and Dorothy Caroline (Keith) I.; m. Nancy Jeanne Jaques, Apr. 24, 1954; children: Nancy Jeanne, Louise Anne, Keith Griscom. BS, Calif. Inst. Tech., 1950; PhD, Harvard U., 1956. Rsch. group leader Mich. Dept. of Health, Lansing, 1956-60; dir. biochemistry Ortho Pharm. Corp., Raritan, N.J., 1960-63; postdoctoral fellow Johns Hopkins U., Balt., 1963-65; chief bioorganic chemistry sect., Lab. Immunology Nat. Inst. Allergy and Infectious Diseases/NIH, Bethesda, Md., 1965—. Author: (chpt.) Theoretical Immunology, 1978, The Peptides, vol. 3, 1981. Overseer Bethesda Friends Meeting, 1991—. Mem. Am. Chem. Soc., Am. Assn. Immunologists, Sigma Xi. Mem. Soc. of Friends. Home: 9200 Wadsworth Dr Bethesda MD 20817-2412 Office: Nat Inst Allergy Infectious Diseases/NIH Bldg # 10 Rm 11N 311 Bethesda MD 20892

INNIS, YVONNE PHYLLIS-JEAN, nurse, insurance company administrator; b. Sanicholas, Aruba, Netherlands Antilles, Mar. 10, 1948; came to U.S., 1975.; d. William Conrad and Ruby Marion (Edwards) I. BS in Human Services, N.H. Coll., 1984; MS in Urban Studies, So. Conn. State U., 1986; Lic. Practical Nurse, John Radcliffe Sch. of Nursing, Oxford, Eng., 1969; MALS, Wesleyan U., 1990. Asst. charge nurse Churchill Hosp., Oxford, Eng., 1971-75; claims reviewer Aetna Life and Casualty, Hartford, Conn., 1975-77; lic. processor Hartford Steam Boiler, 1977-79, supr. claim services, 1979-82, mktg. asst., 1982-87, 88, exec. asst., 1988—. Mem. Wadsworth Atheneum, Hartford, 1986—; sec. town com. A Conn. Party, 1992—. Mem. Internat. Platform Assn. Anglican. Home: 10 Frederick St Hartford CT 06105-4561 Office: Hartford Steam Boiler Inspection and Ins Co One State St Hartford CT 06012-3001

INSINGA, JOANNE THERESA, owner; b. Bklyn., Dec. 9, 1954; d. Lawrence Daniel and Marie Theresa (Lorenzo) Melore; m. John Michael Insinga, May 30, 1976; children: Janice, James. Student, SUNY Coll. at Old Westbury, L.I., N.Y., 1977-79, SUNY-Farmingdale, L.I., N.Y., 1977-79, Nassau County Community Coll., L.I., N.Y., 1977-79. Sr. stenographer N.Y. State Dept. of Audit and Control, N.Y.C., 1972-77, SUNY Coll. at Old Westbury, L.I., 1977-79; calligraphy tchr. Town of Hempstead Svcs. for Aging, L.I., 1988—; calligrapher, owner Fine Calligraphy Co., L.I., 1991—; instr. in field; freelance party planning cons. in field. Author: Fine Jewelry: Made from Glazed Paper and Things, 1991, Let's "Address" Your Envelopes, 1992, A Party to Remember, 1992. Cultural arts chairperson Seaford Harbor Sch. PTA, L.I., 1986—, legis. chairperson, 1989—; exec. bd. mem. Com. for Handicapped Accessibility, L.I., 1989—; instr. Homemaker's Coun. of Nassau County, L.I., 1987—; leader Girl Scouts of Nassau County, L.I., 1985-87; cub scout den mother Boy Scouts of Am., L.I., 1986-89. Recipient citation Nassau County Exec. Thomas S. Gulotta, 1990, svc. pin Nat. Congress Parents and Tchrs., 1992. Mem. Island Scribes (instr. 1988—), Homemakers Coun. of Nassau County (instr. 1987—). Office: Fine Calligraphy 2350 Pine St Seaford NY 11783

INTERRANTE, LEONARD VINCENT, chemistry educator; b. Bklyn., Apr. 6, 1939; s. Leonard and Mildred (Esposito) I.; m. Vita Louise MacFarland, Aug. 29, 1959; children: Victoria Lynn, John Alan. AB, U. Calif., Riverside, 1960; PhD, U. Ill., 1964. NSF postdoctoral fellow U. Coll. London, 1963-64; asst. prof. U. Calif., 1964-68; rsch. chemist Gen. Electric Corp., Schenectady, N.Y., 1968-85; prof. chemistry Rensselaer Polytechnic Inst., Troy, N.Y., 1985—; editor Chemistry of Materials Am. Chem. Soc., 1988—; cons. AKZO Chems., Dobbs Ferry, N.Y., 1987—, Allied-Signal Corp., Morristown, N.J., 1990—, Butterworths-Heinemann Publs., Boston, 1990. Editor ACS Sympos Ser. No. 5, 1974, MRS Sympos Vol. No. 204, 1991; contbr. arti cles to profl. jours. Fellow AAAS; mem. Am. Chem. Soc., Materials Rsch. Soc., Am. Ceramic Soc. Democrat. Office: Rensselaer Poly Inst Dept Chemistry Troy NY 12180-3590

INTINTOLO, JOHN AUGUSTINE, engineer; b. Phila., July 10, 1962; s. John Joseph and Lorraine Elizabeth (Watts) I.; m. Melissa Lee Ussery, Oct. 26, 1991. BS Aero. Engring., U.S. Naval Acad., 1984; M.Eng. in Systems Engring., Va. Inst. Tech., 1992. First level mgr. Patrol Squadron Eight, Brunswick, Maine, 1986-87, COMSEC material mgr., 1987-88, second level mgr., 1988-89; commd. ensign USN, 1984, advanced through grades to lt., 1988; asst. ops. officer Patrol Squadron Eight, Keflavik, Iceland, 1989-90; program engr. Naval Air Systems Command, Washington, 1990-91, asst. program mgr. flight tng. systems, 1991—. Decorated Navy Achievement medal. Mem. AIAA, Soc. Automotive Engrs. (assoc.), Tau Beta Pi. Republican. Home: 5802 Larpin Ln Alexandria VA 22310-1223 Office: Naval Air Systems Command Washington DC 20361-1205

INTRATOR, ORNA, statistician, educator; b. Tel Aviv, Dec. 1, 1960; came to U.S., 1986; d. Uri and Esther Kroch; m. Nathan Intrator; 1 child. BSc, Tel Aviv U., 1986; ScM, Brown U., 1988, PhD, 1991. Teaching asst. Brown U., Providence, 1986-90, rsch. asst., 1990-91, vis. asst. prof., 1991—. Mem. Biometric Soc. (Eastern N.Am. Region), Am. Math. Soc., Am. Statis. Soc., Sigma Chi. Office: Brown U Box F Providence RI 02912

INTRAVIA, JOHN ANDREW, gastroenterologist; b. N.Y.C., July 28, 1950; s. Lawrence and Irene (Bisagni) I.; m. Margaret Irene Ryan, June 14, 1975; children: John Thomas, Marissa Kathryn. BS, Georgetown U., 1971; MD, St. Louis U., 1975. Diplomate Am. Bd. Internal Medicine in internal medicine and gastroenterology, Nat. Bd. Med. Examiners. Intern St. Vincent's Hosp. and Med. Ctr., N.Y.C., 1975-76, resident in internal medicine, 1976-78; fellow gastroenterology U. Conn.-Farmington and affiliated hosps., 1978-80; pvt. practice gastroenterology Middletown, Conn., 1980—. Mem. AMA, ACP, Am. Soc. Internal Medicine, Conn. State Med. Soc., Middlesex County Med. Assn. (pres. 1990-92), Alpha Omega Alpha. Roman Catholic. Office: 85 Church St Middletown CT 06457

INTRILIGATOR, MARC STEVEN, lawyer; b. Oceanside, N.Y., July 14, 1952; s. Alan and Sally (Jacobs) I.; m. Roxann Kathleen Hoff, Aug. 28, 1977; children: Seth Adam, Joshua Ross, Daniel Benjamin. BA, SUNY, Binghamton, 1974; JD, Boston U., 1977. Bar: N.Y. 1978. Assoc. Dreyer and Traub, N.Y.C., 1977-83, ptnr., 1984—. Projects editor: Boston U. law rev., 1976-77. Trustee, v.p. Croton Jewish Ctr. Mem. ABA, Assn. of Bar of City of N.Y., Highlands Country Club, Tau Epsilon Phi. Office: Dreyer & Traub 101 Park Ave New York NY 10178-0002

INZINGA, JACQUELINE MARIE, counselor; b. Rochester, N.Y., Feb. 26, 1967; d. Bradley Richard and Connie Marie (Casciani) Gisel; m. Christopher R. Inzinga, Oct. 5, 1991. BS in Criminology & Criminal Justice, Niagara U., 1989, MS in Sch. Counseling, 1991. Cert. sch. counselor, N.Y. Residence counselor Women's Place, Rochester, 1990—; job counselor Bd. Coop. Edn. Svcs. #1, Fairport, N.Y., 1990—. Mem. AACD, Am. Rehab. Counseling Assn., Pub. Offender Counselors Assn. Democrat. Roman Catholic. Home: 206 Cornhill Pl Rochester NY 14608

IOLI, JAMES PETER, podiatrist; b. N.Y.C., Mar. 13, 1951; s. Fredrick and Dolores (Domino) I.; m. Debbie Lyn Wood, Aug. 2, 1975; 1 child, Jennifer Lyn. BS in Biology, SUNY, Albany, 1973; D. of Podiatric Medicine, Ohio Coll. Podiatric Medicine, 1978. Diplomate Am. Bd. Podiatric Surgery, Am. Bd. Podiatric Orthopedics. Resident Cen. New England Podiatry Residency Program, Fitchburg, Mass., 1978-80; pvt. practice Fitchburg, 1980-82; podiatrist Mass. Gen. Hosp., Boston, 1982-86; pvt. practice Stoughton, Mass., 1986—; mem. attending staff Braintree (Mass.) Hosp., 1982—, Goddard Meml. Hosp., 1986—; cons. examiner Mass. Bd. Registration Podiatry, 1980-88. Contbr. articles to profl. jours. Fellow Am. Coll. Foot Orthopedists; mem. Am. Podiatric Med. Assn., Am. Coll. Foot Surgeons, Am. Coll. Podopediatrics (pres. 1990-92), Am. Soc. Podiatric Medicine, Mass. Podiatric Med. Soc. (edn. com. 1983-88). Office: 907 Sumner St Ste M-209 Stoughton MA 02072

IOVENKO, MICHAEL, lawyer; b. N.Y.C., Jan. 19, 1930; s. Michael James and Ludmila (Tenchova) I.; m. Sarah Montague Bingham, Dec. 3, 1965 (div. Nov. 1976); children: Christopher, William; 1 stepchild, Barry B. Ellsworth; m. Nancy R. Newhouse, Mar. 6, 1983. BA, Dartmouth Coll., 1951; JD, Columbia U., 1954. Asst. gen. sec. World Univ. Service, Geneva, 1955-58; assoc., then ptnr. Putney, Twombly, Hall & Hirson, N.Y.C., 1959-70; U.S. del. Gen. Assembly UN, N.Y.C., 1967; dep. supt., gen. counsel N.Y. State Banking Dept., N.Y.C., 1971-72; ptnr. LeBoeuf, Lamb, Leiby & MacRae, N.Y.C., 1972-85, Hughes Hubbard & Reed, N.Y.C., 1986-89, Breed, Abbott & Morgan, N.Y.C., 1989—. Contbr. articles to profl. jours. Pres., bd. dirs. N.Y. State Council Family Child Care Agys., 1981-85; bd. dirs., v.p. Berkshire Farm Ctr. for Youth, Canaan, N.Y.; pres. Legal Aid, N.Y.C. Mem. ABA, N.Y. State Bar Assn. (ho. of dels. 1984-88, chair banking law com. 1986-90), Assn. of Bar City of N.Y. (exec. com.), Midday Club, Century Club. Democrat. Home: 154 W 88th St New York NY 10024-2429 Office: Breed Abbott & Morgan One Citicorp Ctr New York NY 10022

IRANI, SANDS KENYON, gastroenterologist; b. Marion, Ohio, Jan. 8, 1942; s. Ardeshir Behram Irani and Gwendolen (Mouser) Gay; m. Maureen O'Laughlin, June 8, 1968; children: Kristin, Lauren. BA, U. of the South, 1963; MD, George Washington U., 1968. Diplomate gastroenterology Am. Bd. Internal Medicine. Intern Boston VA Hosp., 1968-69; resident internal medicine George Washington Hosp., VA Hosp., Washington, 1971-73; fellow gastroenterology George Washington Hosp., Washington, 1973-75; pvt. practice gastroenterology and internal medicine Trujillo, O'Kieffe & Irani, MD, Washington, 1975-84, Washington Clinic Med. Ctr., 1984—; clin. prof. medicine George Washington U. Sch. Medicine, Washington, 1989—; assoc. clin. prof. medicine Georgetown U. Sch. Medicine, Washington, 1989—; cons. gastroenterology NIH, Bethesda, Md., 1975—. Lt. USN, 1969-71. Fellow ACP, Am. Coll. Gastroenterology; mem. Am. Soc. for Gastrointestinal Endoscopy, Md. Soc. for Gastrointestinal Endoscopy (treas. 1985-87, v.p. 1987-89). Roman Catholic. Home: 9425 Locust Hill Rd Bethesda MD 20814 Office: Washington Clinic 5401 Western Ave NW Washington DC 20015

IRETON-HEWITT, JOHN HOWARD, corporate executive; b. N.Y.C., Oct. 7, 1937; s. Charles Joseph and Barbara R. (Read) I-H.; children: Erin, Robert, John. BA, Calif. State U., L.A., 1967; MA, U. Redlands, 1985. Various pos. Pharmaseal Labs. div. Am. Hosp. Supply Corp., various cities, 1959-71; product mgr. Avon Products, Pasadena, Calif., 1971-72; from indsl. relations mgr. to gen. mgr. Fleetwood Enterprises, Riverside, Calif., 1972-77; div. mgr. Skyline Corp., Redlands, Calif., 1978-84; gen. mgr. DeRose Industries, Pa., 1984-87; pres., chief exec. officer Burlington Homes, Oxford, Maine, 1987—. Author: New Product Design and Development for Mobile Homes, 1985. State committeeman Rep. Cen. Com., Augusta, Maine, 1989—. Mem. Mfg. Housing Assn. Maine (bd. dirs. 1987—). Office: Burlington Homes New Eng PO Box 263 Oxford ME 04270-0263

IRISH, MARILYN ELEANOR, entrepreneur, executive food service; b. St Louis, Feb. 28, 1943; d. Clarence Fredrick and Doris Eleanor (Lawrence) Jeffers; m. Thomas Frederic Irish, May 30, 1970; children: Erik, Jon. MusB in Edn., Drake U., 1965. Elem. music tchr. Windsor Elementary Sch., DesMoines, 1965-66; vocal, instrumental tchr. Old Mission Jr. High Sch., Shawnee Mission, Kans., 1966-67; tchr., Music, Humanities Bitburg Am. Sch. Fine Arts, Fed. Rep. Germany, 1967-69; music tchr. Syracuse (N.Y.) Levin Jr. High, 1969-70; mktg. exec. IBM Data Processing, Syracuse, 1970-71; entertainer Hyatt & Hilton Hotels, Cherry Hill, N.J., 1972-80; founder Irish Contractors, West Berlin, N.J., 1983—; cons., designer Connoisseur Restaurant Foodcarts and Amenities, West Berlin, 1987—; cons. Sheraton Hotels, Boston, 1986—. Dir. German, Am. Music Festival, Frankfurt, Fed. Rep. Germany, 1968; mem. Geographical Soc. Phila., Acad. Music. Named All-State Accompanist, Iowa All-State Music Festival, Des Moines, 1960, Master Accomanist, Andrew White Opera Baritone, Des Moines, 1962-65. Republican. Home: 6 Cedar Ct West Berlin NJ 08091 Office: Connoisseur Irish Contractors PO Box 1820 Atlantic City NJ 08404-1820

IRONS, ALDEN HATHEWAY, federal agency official; b. Boston, Nov. 3, 1939; s. Richard Kendall and Audrey Priscilla (Radcliffe) I.; m. Judith Ann Lisle, July 21, 1962; children: Catherine Irons Olson, Stephen Hatheway, Richard Kendall. BA, Harvard Coll., 1961. Joined Fgn. Svc. Dept. State, 1962; officer Am. Embasy, Bamako, Mali, 1962-64; consular officer Am. Embassy, Oslo, 1964-67; internat. rels. officer Dept. State, Washington, 1967-72; labor and polit. officer Am. Embassy, Helsinki, Finland, 1972-76; polit. sect. chief Am. Embassy, Port-au-Prince, Haiti, 1976-78; internat. rels. officer African Bur., Dept. State, Washington, 1978-83; dep. prin. officer, labor officer U.S. Consulate Gen., Casablanca, Morocco, 1983-86; officer Internat. Orgns. Bur., Dept. State, Washington, 1986-88; advisor worker rights Dept. State, Washington, 1988—. Mem. vestry St. Dunstan's Episcopal Ch., McLean, Va., 1989-92, sr. warden 1991-92. Mem. Indsl. Rels.

Rsch. Assn. (Washington chpt.), Harvard Club (Washington chpt.). Episcopalian. Office: Dept State S/IL Washington DC 20520-7538

IRVINE, HORACE HILLS, II, manufacturing company executive; b. St. Paul, June 1, 1937; s. Thomas Edward and Sally (Ordway) I.; children from previous marriage: Horace III, Julia, Kathryn; m. Andrea Pennig, July 30, 1977; children: Kevin, John, Catherine, Andrew, Mary. AB, Princeton U., 1959; postgrad., Harvard U. Grad. Sch., 1966. Fouder, pres., treas., chmn., chief exec. officer Hadco Corp., Salem, N.H., 1966-79, chmn., chief exec. officer, 1976-86, chmn. bd., 1986—. Pres., bd. dirs. exec. com. Nat. Inst. Music Theater, Washington, 1976-79; bd. dirs. Ordway Music Theatre, St. Paul, 1985—; trustee Boston Lyric Opera Co., Boston, 1989, chmn., 1990—; mem. adv. bd. Am. Repertory Theatre, Cambridge, 1989; bd. overseers New Eng. Conservatory, 1990—. Mem. Inst. Interconnecting and Packaging Electronic Cirs. (bd. dirs. 1980-84), Harvard Club, Lanam Club, Union Boat Club, White Bear Yacht Club, Ocean Reef Club, Princeton Club of N.Y., Sankaty Golf and Beach Club. Home: 20 Louisburg Sq Boston MA 02108-1203 Office: Hadco Corp 10 Manor Pky Salem NH 03079-4871

IRVINE, JOHN MICHAEL, statistician, consultant; b. Washington, Mar. 2, 1954; s. Robert Klink and Mary Byrne (Newlon) Irvine; m. Sharian Lewitt, Oct. 21, 1978. BA, Pomona Coll., 1976; MPhil, Yale U., 1978, PhD, 1982; MA, Georgetown U., 1986. Rsch. fellow U.S. Census Bur., Washington, 1980-82; sr. analyst CIA, Washington, 1982-89; rsch. scientist Environ. Rsch. Inst. Mich., Arlington, Va., 1989—; lectr. Albertus Magnus Coll., New Haven, 1978-79, So. Conn. State Coll., New Haven, 1978-80; cons. Astra Pharms., Framingham, Mass., 1978-80, Consumers Union, Mt. Vernon, N.Y., 1978-80; pres. Arundel Coop., Inc., Washington, 1982-84. Contbr. sci. papers, articles to profl. jours. Mem. Am. Statis. Assn., Washington Statis. Soc., Builders of the Adytum, Nat. Capital Skating Club, Phi Beta Kappa, Sigma Xi, Pi Mu Epsilon. Office: ERIM 1101 Wilson Blvd Arlington VA 22209-2248

IRVINE, PETER BENNINGTON, fund raiser, lawyer; b. Chattanooga, June 8, 1951; s. James Bennington and Susan (Chambliss) I.; m. Angela Cowan, Mar. 5, 1983; stepchildren: John Clark Rumble, Laura Rumble O'Connell. BA, U. Tenn., 1974, JD, 1979; postgrad., Bread Loaf Sch. of English, 1981-82. Bar: Tenn. 1979, Pa. 1983. Assoc. Chambliss, Bahner, Crutchfield, Gaston & Irvine, Chattanooga, 1979-81; copy editor Chattanooga Times, 1981-82; grant writer, researcher Seton Hill Coll., Greensburg, Pa., 1983-86, dir. devel., 1986-89; assoc. dir. planned giving U. Pitts., 1989-92, dir. planned giving, 1992—. Bd. dirs. Calliope: the Pitts. Folk Music Soc., 1991—, sec., 1992—. Mem. Nat. Soc. Fundraising Execs., Pitts. Planned Giving Coun. (pres. 1992—), Pitts. Estate Planning Coun. Episcopalian. Home: 235 Foxhurst Dr Pittsburgh PA 15238-1817 Office: U Pitts 500 Craig Hall Pittsburgh PA 15260

IRVINE, REED JOHN, media critic, corporation executive; b. Salt Lake City, Sept. 29, 1922; s. William John and Edna Jessup (May) I.; m. Kay Araki, Aug. 14, 1948; 1 son, Donald. A.B., U. Utah, 1942; postgrad., U. Colo., 1943-44, U. Wash., 1949; B.Litt., Oxford U., Eng., 1951. With Gen. Hdqrs. of Allied Occupation of Japan, Tokyo, 1946-48; economist bd. govs. Fed. Res. System, Washington, 1951-63, adviser internat. fin., 1963-77; chmn. bd. Accuracy in Media, Inc., Washington, 1971—; editor AIM Report; syndicated columnist, radio commentator; chmn. Accuracy in Academia, 1985—. Author: Media Mischief and Misdeeds, 1984; co-author: (with Cliff Kincaid) Profiles of Deception, 1990. Dir. Council Def. of Freedom, Washington, 1970—. Served with USNR, 1942-43, USMC, 1943-46, PTO; to capt. USMCR, 1944-46. Recipient George Washington medal Freedom Found., 1980, Ethics in Journalism award World Media Assn., 1987. Mem. Phi Beta Kappa. Mem. LDS Ch. Office: 1275 K St NW Washington DC 20005-4006

IRVING, A. MARSHALL, marine engineer; b. Waterbury, Md., Apr. 10, 1929; s. Walter Reid and Gertrude Elizabeth (Bennett) I.; m. Arline Doris Timmermann, July 19, 1952; children: Marshall Reid, William Anderson, Laurie Anne, Pamela Leigh. BS in Marine Engring., U.S. Merchant Marine Acad., Kings Point, N.Y., 1951; MS in Mgmt. Engring., L.I. U., 1969. Registered profl. engr. N.Y. Marine engr. U.S. Lines Co., N.Y.C., 1951-52; design engr. Sikorsky Aircraft, Bridgeport, Conn., 1953; project engr. to quality control engr. mgr. Dayton T. Brown Inc., Bohemia, N.Y., 1953-72; main engines officer USS Intrepid, N.Y.C., 1954-56; gen. mgr. Cougar Inc., Chgo., 1972-73; adminstrv. law judge N.Y. State Dept. Environ. Conservation, Stony Brook, 1973-89; litigation cons. Mineola, N.Y., 1983—; subcom. chmn. and sec. Am. Nat. Stds. Inst. Z90, N.Y.C., 1968—; dir., sec. Snell Meml. Found., St. James, N.Y., 1983-92. Designer prototype weapons delivery system for naval aircraft, 1968. Dir. Setauket Neighborhood House, 1975—. Lt. cdr. USNR, 1973. Lt. comdr. USN, 1973. Mem. ASTM, NSPE, Am. Soc. Safety Engrs. Republican. Episcopalian. Home: 48 Mud Rd Setauket NY 11733-2233 Office: Inter-City Testing 167 Willis Ave Mineola NY 11501-2621

IRVING, GEORGE WASHINGTON, JR., health science association administrator; b. Caribou, Maine, Nov. 20, 1910; s. George Washington Sr. and Adelaide Louise (Butman) I.; m. Frances Catherine Connell, June 4, 1938; children: George Washington III, Mary Constance Fitzpatrick. BS, George Washington U., 1933, MA, 1935, PhD, 1939; postgrad., USDA Grad. Sch., 1933-35, U. Ill., 1937. Rsch. fellow George Washington U. Med. Sch., 1935-38; rsch. fellow Med. Coll. Cornell U., N.Y.C., 1938-39; asst. in chemistry Rockefeller Inst. Med. Rsch., N.Y.C., 1939-42; head protein rsch. USDA, New Orleans, 1942-44; div. head USDA, Beltsville, Md., 1944-47; asst. chief Bur. of Chemistry USDA, Washington, 1947-54, br. chief agrl. mktg. svc., 1954, dep. adminstr. agrl. rsch. svc., 1954-64, assoc. adminstr. agrl. rsch. svc., 1964-65, adminstr. agrl. rsch. svc., 1965-71; rsch. assoc. Fed. Am. Soc. Exptl. Biology, Bethesda, Md., 1972—; lectr. in antibiotics USDA Grad. Sch., Washington, 1946-52; lectr. in biochemistry George Washington U. Med. Sch., 1947-53; exec. v.p. Agrl. Rsch. Inst., Bethesda, 1982-84; v.p. Internat. Life Sci. Inst., Washington, 1985-87; freelance cons. in field; v.p., mem. grad. coun. George Wash. U., 1956, mem. governing bd., 1959-60; chmn. sci. adv. bd. Sugar Rsch. Found., N.Y., 1967-71; lectr. in field; trustee Nutrition Found., N.Y., 1965-84, chmn. bd., 1983-84; mem. food additives com. NRC, 1985—. Contbr., co-contbr. numerous articles to profl. jours. and books; patentee in field. Witness U.S. Congress, Washington, 1947-71; vol. sci. tchr. D.C. Pub. Schs., 1990—; primary lectr. 1st Internat. Congress of Food Sci. and Tech., Lincoln, 1962, 3 Congress, Washington, 1970. Fellow AAAS (v.p., chair agr. sect. 1962, mem. at large 1963-67), Wash. Acad. Sci. (del rep. Inst. Food Tech. 1946—, Phys. Scis. award 1946, pres. 1955), Alpha Chi Sigma (pres. Washington chpt. 1948-49, assoc. editor nat. mag. Indpls. 1970-84, Svc. award 1968, Man of Yr. 1975); mem. Am. Chem. Soc. (cons. 1978—), Chem. Soc. Wash. (pres. 1953, Svc. award 1973), Am. Soc. Biochemistry and Molecular Biology, Am. Inst., Chemists, Toastmasters, Cosmos Club (pres. 1974-75), Sigma Xi, Tau Kappa Epsilon. Republican. Roman Catholic. Home and Office: 4601 N Park Ave Bethesda MD 20815-4519

IRVING, GEORGE WASHINGTON, III, research director, veterinarian, military officer; b. N.Y.C., Apr. 25, 1940; s. George Washington Jr. and Frances (Connell) I.; m. Alice Marie Graves, Dec. 21, 1968; 1 child, George Washington IV. BS, U. Md., 1962; DVM, Purdue U., 1965; MS, Tex. A&M U., 1970. Diplomate Am. Coll. Lab. Animal Medicine, Am. Coll. Vet. Preventive Medicine. Commd. 1st lt. USAF, 1966, advanced through ranks to col., 1984; base veterinarian Niagara Falls Internat. Airport, N.Y., 1966, 388th Tactical Fighter Wing, Korat, Thailand, 1966-67; base veterinarian Wilford Hall USAF Med. Ctr., Lackland AFB, Tex., 1968; asst. chief vet. edn. br. USAF Sch. Aerospace Medicine, San Antonio, 1970-75; chief div. lab. animal medicine Armed Forces Inst. Pathology, Washington, 1976-79; grad. Armed Forces Staff Coll., 1975-76, Air War Coll., 1977; program mgr. Air Force Office Sci. Rsch., Bolling AFB, D.C., 1979-82, dir. life sci., 1982-83; USAF liaison U.S. Army Med. R & D Command, Ft. Detrick, Md., 1983-84, dir. med. chem. def. rsch. program, 1984-87; cons. to surgeon gen. USAF, Washington, 1983—; dir. Armed Forces Radiobiology Rsch. Inst., Bethesda, Md., 1987-91; chief of staff human systems ctr. Brooks Air Force Base, Tex., 1991—; instr. grad. rsch. program NIH, Bethesda, 1976-85; merit rev. VA, Washington, 1978-84; cons. Stunkard, Miller Assocs., Bowie, Md., 1976-79. Editor: Selected Topics in Laboratory Animal Medicine, 15 vols., 1971-75; contbr. articles to jours. and chpts. to books. Vice-minister Secular Franciscan Order, Holy Name Province, 1989-91. Decorated Legion of Merit, Def. Superior Svc. medal. Fellow Aerospace Med. Assn.; mem. AVMA, Assn. Mil. Surgeons of U.S. (McCallam award 1988), D.C. Vet. Med. Assn. (pres. 1982), Am. Assn. for Lab. Animal Sci. (pres. nat. capital area br. 1981-82), Brooks AFB Rod and Gun Club (pres. 1973-74). Republican. Roman Catholic. Office: Human Systems Ctr Brooks AFB (HSC/CS) San Antonio TX 78235

IRVING, GITTE NIELSEN, educator; b. Copenhagen, Nov. 5, 1954; came to U.S., 1976; d. Sven Aage and Aase (Espersen) Nielsen; m. Richard Frederick Irving, June 5, 1976; children: Erik Christian, Emilie Jessica. BA, U. Iceland, Reykjavik, 1976; MEd, Lesley Coll., 1977. Cert. elem. tchr., spl. edn. tchr., Mass.; cert. by Mass. Gen. Hosp. in use of Orton-Gillingham strategies for remediation of dyslexia, 1989. Spl. edn. aide Brookline (Mass.) Pub. Schs., 1977-78; spl. edn. tchr. Ashland (Mass.) Pub. Schs., 1978-81, Greater Lawrence Ednl. Collaborative, Andover, Mass., 1981-82; owner, dir. Comprehensive Academics, Inc., Winchester, Mass., 1983—; guest columnist Winchester Star, 1986; mem. com. early edn. planning Winchester Pub. Schs., 1986, com. missions and social concerns United Meth. Ch., Winchester, 1987, co-chair, 1988-91, adv. coun. Spl. Edn. Parents, Winchester, 1985—; mem. com. on sch. configurations, subcom. to Sch. Com., Winchester, 1991-92. Editor spl. edn. presch. newsletter, 1985-86; guest columnist Winchester STar, 1986. V.p. Neighborhood Coop. Nursery Sch., Winchester, 1989, 88-90; mem. com. on sch. utilization, subcom. to sch. com., Winchester, 1991-92. Home: 12 Stone Ave Winchester MA 01890-1332 Office: Comprehensive Acads 573 Main St Winchester MA 01890-2900

IRVING, ROBERT CHURCHILL, quality assurance professional, manufacturing company executive; b. Waltham, Mass., Sept. 15, 1928; s. Frederick Charles and Emily Alvina (Churchill) I.; A.S., Franklin Inst. of Boston, 1965; cert. of profl. achievement Northeastern U., 1975; children—Robert F., John W. Sr. draftsman Mason-Neilan, Boston, 1948-54; mgr. design services Kinney Vacuum Co., Gen. Signal Corp., Boston, 1955-69; mgr. engring. svcs. Sturtevant div. Westinghouse Electric Corp., Hyde Park, Mass., 1969-81, supr. quality assurance, 1981-84; mgr. engring. svcs. Am. Davidson, Inc., Hyde Park, Mass., 1984-87, mgr. quality control, 1987-89, mgr. quality assurance Howden Sirocco, Inc., 1989—. Served with U.S. Army, 1946-48. Mem. Am. Def. Preparedness Assn., Am. Soc. for Quality Control (sr.), Am. Security Council, Am. Legion. Home: 11 Linda Ave Brockton MA 02401-3129 Office: One Westinghouse Pla Hyde Park MA 02136

IRVING, TERRY (EDWARD B. IRVING, III), television producer; b. Bryn Mawr, Pa., Dec. 3, 1951; s. Edward Burroughs Jr. and Marion (Kirk) I.; m. Ellen Clifford, Sept. 12, 1981; children: Margaret Yunger, Megan McNeil. BA, Haverford (Pa.) Coll., 1973. Motorcycle courier ABC News, Washington, 1973-74, desk asst. Good Morning Am., 1974-75, assoc. producer, 1977-81, producer, 1981-82, producer The Last Word, 1982, producer Nightline, 1982-90; producer Weekend News, Washington, 1990—. Mem. NATAS (Emmy award 1985, 87, 89, 90). Quaker. Office: ABC News 1717 Desales St NW Washington DC 20036-4407

IRWIN, BYRON, management consultant; b. Pottstown, Pa., June 25, 1941; s. Ronald and Gertrude (Gilbert) I.; m. Mila Dunbar, Apr. 4, 1984; children: Bart, Mark, Mila, Erik. BA, Drew U., 1966; MBA, George Washington U., 1968. Assoc. dir. Thomas Jefferson U. Hosp., Phila., 1971-78; pres., chief exec. officer United Health Svcs., Binghamton, N.Y., 1978-83, Alta BAtes Corp., Berkeley, Calif., 1983-84; dir. APM, N.Y.C., 1984—; mem. adv. bd. Liberty Mut. Ins. Co., 1978-83, Binghamton SUNY Grad. Mgmt. Coun., 1978-83; speaker in field, 1980—. Contbr. numerous articles to profl. jours. Gov. appointee, chmn. code com. N.Y. State Hosp. Rev and Planning Coun., Albany, N.Y., 1978-83; mem. adv. coun. Bd. Coop. Edn. Svc., Binghamton, 1978-83. Rsch. grantee Hartford Found., 1981-82. Mem. Am. Coll. Healthcare Execs., Am. Hosp. Assn., Am. Mgmt. Assn., Hosp. Assn. N.Y. (bd. dirs.). Office: APM Inc 810 7th Ave New York NY 10019-5818

IRWIN, JUDITH WESTPHAL, language educator; b. Kenosha, Wis., Jan. 25, 1949; d. Carl Wells and Beulah (Kessler) Westphal; 1 child, Christina. BA, Ill.Wesleyan U., 1970; MS, PhD, U. Wis. Tchr. 7th grade Dundee (Ill.) Pub. Schs., 1973-75; asst. prof. edn. Purdue U., West Lafayette, Ind., 1978-82; assoc. prof. Loyola U., Chgo., 1982-87; prof. U. Conn., Storrs, 1987—; conductor numerous lang./writing/comprehension workshops. Author: Teaching Reading Comprehension Processes, 1986, 2d revised edit., 1991; co-author: Promoting Active Reading Comprehension Strategies, 1989; editor: Understanding and Teaching Cohesion Comprehension, 1986; co-editor: Reading/Writing Connections: Learning from Research; contbr. articles to profl. jours. Mem. Instructional Reading Assn., Nat. Coun. Rsch. in English. Office: U Conn Dept Edn Storrs CT 06268

IRWIN, MARTIN, psychiatrist; b. N.Y.C., Oct. 15, 1949. BA, Cornell U., 1967; MD, U. Pa., 1971. Resident in psychiatry U. Chgo., 1975-79, fellow in child psychiatry, 1977-79; dir. psychiat. in-patient unit Children's Meml. Hosp., Chgo., 1979-82; dir. child neuropsychiatry in-patient unit, dir. tng. Tulane U. Med. Ctr., New Orleans, 1982-84; chief children's in-patient unit, dir. med. student edn. Badley Hosp./Brown U., Providence, 1984-88; dir. div. child and adolescent psychiatry, assoc. prof. SUNY Health Sci. Ctr., Syracuse, 1988—. Author: Psychiatric Hospitalization of Children, 1982; contbr. articles to profl. jours. Mem. Am. Psychiat. Assn., Am. Acad. Child Psychiatry, Soc. for Biol. Psychiatry, Profs. Child Psychiatry. Office: SUNY Health Sci Ctr 750 E Adams St Syracuse NY 13210-2306

IRWIN, RICHARD STEPHEN, physician, scientist, educator; b. New London, Conn., Nov. 15, 1942; s. Harold H. and Sylvia Rowena (Hendel) I.; m. Diane Hazel Northrop, June 21, 1969; children: Rachel Helen, Sara Beth, Catherine Jamie, Rebecca Susan. BS, Tufts U., 1964, MD, 1968. Diplomate Am. Bd. Med. Examiners, Am. Bd. Internal Medicine, Am. Bd. Pulmonary Disease; spl. cert. in critical care medicine. Intern Tufts New Eng. Med. Ctr., Boston, 1968-69, jr. asst. resident in medicine, 1969-70; fellow in pulmonary disease Columbia-Presbyn. Hosp., N.Y.C., 1970-72, 1970-72; dir. med. ICU R.I. Hosp., Providence, 1974-79; asst. prof. medicine Brown U., Providence, 1974-79; assoc. prof. medicine U. Mass. Med. Sch., Worcester, 1979-82, prof. medicine, 1982—; dir. pulmonary and critical care medicine U. Mass. Med. Ctr., Worcester, 1979—; dir. Respiratory Care Dept., U. Mass. Med. Ctr., Worcester, 1979—, Pulmonary Nursing Svc., 1989—, Pulmonary Rehab., 1986—, Asthma Self-Mgmt. Program, 1990—. Author textbook chpts.; co-editor: (textbook) Intensive Care Medicine, Jour. Intensive Care Medicine, 1986—; contbr. numerous articles to profl. jours. Maj. USAF, 1972-74. Fellow Am. Coll. Physicians, Am. Coll. Chest Physicians (gov. Mass. chpt.); mem. Am. Thoracic Soc. (ea. sect. pres. 1980-81), Nat. Assn. Med. Dirs. Respiratory Care. Office: U Ma Med Ctr 55 Lake Ave N Worcester MA 01655-0001

ISAAC, RAEL JEAN, writer; b. N.Y.C., June 17, 1933; d. Judah M. and Fannie S. Isaacs; m. Erich Isaac, June 17, 1956; children: Gamaliel, Gideon, Raphael, David. BA summa cum laude, Barnard Coll., 1954; MA, Johns Hopkins U., 1956; PhD, CUNY, 1972. Author: Adopting a Child Today, 1965, Israel Divided, 1976, Parties and Politics of Israel, 1981, Coercive Utopians (with Erich Isaac), 1983, Madness in the Streets (with Virginia Armat), 1990. Fulbright scholar, 1955.

ISAACMAN, STEVEN, finance executive; b. Phila., June 16, 1930; s. Irving and Sylvia (Kamp) I.; m. May 27, 1952; children: Richard, Ilene Schaefer, Lisa Oswald. BS, Drexel U., 1952. Pub. acct., 1952-56; asst. controller Strick Trailers, Fairess Hills, Pa., 1956-68; chief acct. Permaneer Corp., St. Louis, 1968-72; cons. Phila., 1972-76; dir. fin. Angelo Bros. Co., Phila., 1976—. Officer Rhawnhurst Townwatch, Phila, 1988—, pres. 1991; trustee Nat. Found. for Ilietis and Colitis, Phila., 1989; pres. Phila. Sch. Ad Hoc Com., 1965; mem. 2nd Dist. Action Coun., Phila., 1988-89. Named Man of Yr. Brith Sholom Sports, Phila., 1976; recipient Townwatch award Phila. Police Dept., 1986. Mem. Nat. Assn. Accts., Controllers Coun., Brith Sholom. Democrat. Jewish. Home: 1213 Wellington St Philadelphia PA 19111-4226 Office: Angelo Bros Co 12401 Mcnulty Rd Philadelphia PA 19154-1099

ISAACS, ARNOLD ROBINSON, writer, political science educator; b. N.Y.C., Feb. 6, 1941; s. Harold Robert and Viola (Robinson) I.; m. Kathleen Muir Taylor, Nov. 23, 1962; children: Jennifer, Katherine, Robert. BA, Harvard U., 1961. Assoc. editor Current, N.Y.C., 1961-62; successively reporter, corr., editor Balt. Sun, 1962-81; instr. polit. sci. Towson (Md.) State U., 1983—; writer, 1981—. Author: Without Honor: Defeat in Vietnam and Cambodia, 1983; co-author: Pawns of War, 1987; contbr. articles to newspapers and mags. Mem. Nat. Book Critics Circle. Home: 1788 Chesapeake Pl Pasadena MD 21122-5803 Office: Towson State U Polit Sci Dept Towson MD 21204

ISAACS, SUSAN, novelist, screenwriter; b. Bklyn., Dec. 7, 1943; d. Morton and Helen (Asher) I.; m. Elkan Abramowitz, Aug. 11, 1968; children: Andrew, Elizabeth. Student, Queens Coll., 1965; LittD (hon.), Dowling Coll., 1988. From editorial asst. to sr. editor Seventeen mag., N.Y.C., 1965-70; freelance writer, 1970-76, author, 1976—, book reviewer, 1980—, screenwriter, 1984—. Author: Compromising Positions, 1978, Close Relations, 1980, Almost Paradise, 1984, Shining Through, 1988, Magic Hour, 1991; screenwriter Compromising Positions, 1985; screenwriter, co-producer Hello Again, 1987. Trustee Queens Coll. Found., North Shore Child & Family Guidance Assn. Mem. Mystery Writers Am., Nat. Book Critics Circle, PEN, Poets and Writers, Internat. Assn. Crime Writers. Jewish.

ISAACSON, EDITH LIPSIG, civic leader; b. N.Y.C., Jan. 18, 1920; d. I.A. and Bertha (Evans) Lipsig; m. Selian Hebald; children: Anne Mandelbaum, Selian Jr.; m. William J. Isaacson. Student, Radcliffe Coll., 1936-39, 41; LLB, St. Lawrence U., 1943. Pres. Forest Knolls Corp., N.Y.C., 1960—, Norman Homes Corp., N.Y.C., 1968—; cataloguer Nat. Collection Fine Arts, Smithsonian Instn., 1969-72. Author biographies Am. artists; writer club handbooks. Fellow Pierpont Morgan Library, N.Y.C.; mem. Carnegie Council Ethics Internat. Affairs, founders com. Am. Symphony Orch., N.Y., 1962; nat. sec. Women's Am. Orgn. Rehab. through Tng., 1950; trustee Allergy Found. Am. Mem. Radcliffe Coll. Alumni Assn. (chmn. clubs 1966). Clubs: Harvard (N.Y.C.), Cosmopolitan (N.Y.C.) (bd. govs. 1987—); Radcliffe (pres. Washington chpt. 1969) (pres. N.Y. chpt. 1959, 63, bd. sponsors 1974).

ISAACSON, MELVIN STUART, library director; b. N.Y.C., Apr. 12, 1949; s. Max and Ida (Savitsky) I.; m. Shelley Allyn Thielle, Apr. 3, 1976; 1 child, Scott Brandon. BA in English, Bklyn. Coll., 1972; MLS, Pratt Inst., 1973. Cataloger Yeshiva Univ., N.Y.C., 1973-76, John Jay Coll. of Criminal Justice, N.Y.C., 1976-77; head cataloger Pace Univ., N.Y.C., 1977-81; head of original monographs cataloging Columbia Univ., N.Y.C., 1982-87; head of cataloging Columbia Univ., Health Sci. Libr., N.Y.C., 1987; libr. dir. Pace Univ., N.Y.C., 1988—. Mem. ALA, Archons of Collophon, N.Y. Tech. Svcs. Librs. (sec., treas. 1983-84, membership/social chair 1984-85), Westchester Acad. Libr. Dirs. Orgn., Beta Phi Mu. Home: 1415 Milford Ter Teaneck NJ 07666-2248 Office: Pace U Henry Birnbaum Libr Pace Plz New York NY 10038

ISAACSON, NORMAN HARRY, physician, educator; b. N.Y.C., Apr. 9, 1922; s. Louis and Pauline (Sanders) I.; m. Estelle Ettman, June 29, 1947; children: Paul (dec.), Dale, Lee. BA, NYU, 1941, MD, 1944. Intern Jewish Hosp. Bklyn., 1944-45, asst. resident in pathology, 1945-46; surg. resident George Washington U. Med. Ctr., Washington, 1948-52; clin. prof. surgery George Washington U. Med. Sch., Washington, 1952—. Author text chpts.; contbr. over 60 articles to profl. jours. Fellow Am. Coll. Surgeons, Internat. Coll. Proctology; mem. AMA, D.C. Med. Soc., Internat. Coll. Surgeons, Soc. Am. Gastrointestinal Endoscopic Surgeons, Jacobi Med. Soc., Washington Acad. Surgery. Democrat. Jewish. Home: 7138 River Rd Bethesda MD 20817 Office: Surg Assocs 2440 M St NW Ste 706 Washington DC 20037

ISAACSON, ROBERT WILLIAM, marketing executive; b. Waltham, Mass., Sept. 3, 1942; s. Arthur Einar and Marion Eleanor (Lobdell) I.; m. Joan Patricia Mac Farlane, June 18, 1967; children: Robert Eric, David William. BS, Northeastern U., 1965; MBA, U. Mass., 1966. Mktg. analyst W.R. Grace, Cambridge, Mass., 1967-71; planning mgr. Dymo Industries, Randolph, Mass., 1971-74; mktg. mgr. Esselte Meto, Randolph, 1974-81; ptnr. Alpha Assocs., Wellesley Hills, Mass., 1981-88; corp. mktg. dir. Unifirst Corp., Wilmington, Mass., 1988—. Contbr. articles to profl. jours. With USAR, 1966-74. Mem. Am. Mktg. Assn., Inst. Indsl. Launderers, Lakes Region Environ. Assn., Trout Unltd. Office: Unifirst Corp 68 Jonspin Rd Wilmington MA 01887

ISBY, DAVID CARPENTER, lawyer; b. Flushing, N.Y., Nov. 3, 1953; s. Joseph and Peggy (Carpenter) I. BA, Columbia U., 1975; JD, NYU, 1978. Editor Simulations Publs., Inc., N.Y.C., 1970-79; pvt. practice law Bklyn., 1979-81; legis. asst. U.S. Congress, Washington, 1981-84; researcher Reagan '84 Campaign, Washington, 1984-85; sr. staff mem. BDM Internat., McLean, Va., 1985-92; sr. staff mem. arms control Sparta Inc., McLean, 1992—; dir. Com. for a Free Afghanistan, Inc., Washington, 1981—, Inst. Rsch. on Small Arms, Washington, 1988—. Author: Weapons and Tactics of the Soviet Army, 1981, Armies of NATO's Central Front, 1985, Russia's War in Afghanistan, 1986, War in a Distant Country, 1989. Recipient Charles Roberts award Simulation Industry, 1978, 79. Mem. Internat. Inst. Strategic Studies. Republican. Home: 32-25 88th St Flushing NY 11369 Office: Sparta Inc 7926 Jones Branch Dr Mc Lean VA 22102-3303

ISDANER, LAWRENCE ARTHUR, accountant; b. Phila., June 6, 1934; s. Irving and Frances (Ford) I.; m. Audrey Goldstein, Apr. 4, 1957; children: Scott Alan, Bart Matthew. BS, U. Pa., 1956. CPA, Pa. Mng. ptnr. Isdaner & Co., CPAs, Bala Cynwyd, Pa., 1967—; spl. adviser to bd. dirs., United Valley Bank, Phila., 1988—. Author: Army Industrial Fund and Cost Accounting Manual, 1958. Bd. dirs. Golden Slipper Club, Phila., 1974—, pres., 1977, Athletic Trauma Rsch. Fund, Bala Cynwyd, 1985—, Inst. for Arts in Edn.; internat. bd. dirs. Pop Warner Little Scholars, Phila, 1992—. With U.S. Army, 1957-59. Mem. AICPA, Pa. Inst. CPAs, Germantown Cricket Club, Desert Mountain Club, Kiwanis. Home: 1720 Balsam Ln Villanova PA 19085-1802 Office: Isdaner & Co 100 Presidential Blvd Bala Cynwyd PA 19004-1108

ISDELL, CHARLES JAMES, airport administrator, film commissioner; b. Phila., July 11, 1950; s. Charles J. and Catherine R. (Heffernan) I.; children: Brian C., Kevin J. BA, Temple U., 1972, MEd, 1986. Adminstrv. dir. Procurement Dept., Phila., 1980-87, Office of City Rep., Phila., 1987-89, Phila. Internat. Airport, 1989—; acting dir. Phila. Film Office, 1990—. Choreographer dances including Duchamps Celebration, 1987, JFK Tribute, 1989. Tutor, Phila. Literacy Commn., 1989-90; vol. Phila. Com. for the Homeless, 1985-86; mem. com. on arts and entertainment AFL/CIO, Phila., 1991—. Mem. Phila. Dance Alliance (pres. bd. 1989—).

ISELIN, JOHN JAY, university president; b. Greenville, S.C., Dec. 8, 1933; s. William Jay and Fannie Harrington (Humphreys) I.; m. Josephine Lea Barnes, Sept. 8, 1956; children: William Jay II, Benjamin Barnes, Josephine Lea, Fannie Humphreys, Alison Jay. AB, Harvard U., 1956, PhD, 1965; B.A., Corpus Christi Coll., U. Cambridge, Eng., 1958, M.A., 1963; hon. degree, Adelphi U., L.I. U., Lander Coll. Rsch. fellow Brookings Inst., Washington, 1960-61; sr. writer Congl. Quar., Washington, 1961; corr.-editor Newsweek mag., 1962-65, sr. editor nat. affairs, 1965-69; v.p., pub. Harper & Row Publs. Inc., N.Y.C., 1969-71; pres., trustee Ednl. Broadcasting Corp., Channel 13, sta. WNET, N.Y.C., 1971-87; pres. The Cooper Union for the Advancement of Sci. and Art, N.Y.C., 1988—. Bd. overseers Harvard U., 1970-76; chmn. Ea. Ednl. Network, 1978-80; mem. Am. Friends of U. Cambridge; mem. adv. bd. Yale U. Sch. Mgmt., Lower Manhattan Cultural Commn.; trustee Nat. Geog. Soc., Josiah Macy Jr. Found., Ventures in Edn., Waterford Inst. Recipient Disting. Citizen award trustees SUNY. Mem. Coun. on Fgn. Rels., Metropolitan Club (Washington), Century Club. Home: 153 W 12th St New York NY 10011-8201 Office: The Cooper Union Cooper Sq New York NY 10003-7102

ISELIN, SALLY CARY, writer; b. Nahant, Mass., June 16, 1915; d. Charles Pelham and Edith Goddard (Roelker) Curtis; m. Lewis Iselin, June 14, 1935 (dec.); children: Edith Byron, Sarah Morrison. Student, Harvard U., 1933. Editorial asst. sports and fgn. news depts. Newsweek mag., N.Y.C., 1942-45; soc. and non-fiction editor Town & Country Mag., N.Y.C.,

1945-48; reporter, researcher Life Mag., N.Y.C., 1948-50; writer-contact CBS, N.Y.C., 1951; fashion editor Women's Home Companion, N.Y.C., 1956; freelance writer. Fund raiser Planned Parenthood, 1935—, Robert Kennedy for Senate, 1964. Democrat. Episcopalian. Clubs: Colony, Fashion Group. Home: Belfast Rd Camden ME 04843

ISENBERG, STEVEN LAWRENCE, newspaper executive; b. Detroit, Oct. 19, 1940; s. A.G. Jerry and Lucille (Potaschnik) I.; m. Barbara Lee Levy, Nov. 26, 1967; 1 child, Christopher Michael. BA in English, U. Calif., Berkeley, 1962; BA in English Lang. and Lit., U. Oxford, Eng., 1964, MA, 1966; JD, Yale U., 1976. Bar: N.Y. 1976. Asst. to dir. Bur. Budget, N.Y.C., 1967-68; chief staff, asst. to mayor Office of Mayor, N.Y.C., 1969-73; litigator Breed, Abbott and Morgan, N.Y.C., 1976-82; asst. to pub. Newsday, L.I., N.Y., 1982-83; pub., chief exec. officer So. Conn. Newspapers, Stamford, 1983-86; assoc. pub. Newsday, N.Y. Newsday, N.Y.C., 1986-90; pub. Sports, inc., N.Y.C., 1987-88; exec. v.p. mktg. L.A. Times, 1991—. Mem. staff presdl. campaigns Robert F. Kennedy, 1968, John V. Lindsay, 1972; pres. adv. bd. to Coll. Letters and Scis., U. Calif., Berkeley. Mem. Coun. Fgn. Affairs, Yale Club, Century Assn. Democrat. Jewish. Home: 151 Central Pk W Apt 3N New York NY 10023-1514 Office: LA Times Times Mirror Sq Los Angeles CA 90053

ISENHOWER, WILLIAM DAVID, JR., otolaryngologist; b. Newton, N.C., Mar. 24, 1958; s. William David and Rebecca (Troutman) I.; m. Lynn Bollinger, July 12, 1980; children: Matthew, Jason. BS, Davidson Coll., 1980; MD, U. N.C., 1984. Commd. 2nd lt. U.S. Army, 1980, advanced through grades to maj., 1990—; staff otolaryngologist U.S. Army, Frankfurt, Germany, 1989—; instr. ACLS, advanced trauma life support. Pres. Trinity Luth. Ch., Frankfurt, 1992. Fellow ACS, Am. Acad. Otolaryngology/Head and Neck Surgery; mem. AMA, Am. Acad. Facial Plastic and Reconstructive Surgery. Republican. Home and Office: 97th Gen Hosp Box 17 Unit 25717 APO AE 09242

ISERI, OSCAR AKIO, pathology educator; b. Thomas, Wash., Aug. 23, 1927; s. Matt Matahichi and Kisa (Okuna) I.; m. Anna Mae Ashton, July 1, 1961; children: David A., Kimi Ann, Lori Jean. BS, Antioch Coll., Yellow Springs, Ohio, 1952; MD, Harvard U., 1956. Diplomate Am. Bd. Pathology, Nat. Bd. Med. Examiners. Med. intern King County Hosp., Seattle, 1956-57; asst. resident in medicine U. Wash., Seattle, 1957-58, trainee exptl. pathology, 1958-61, rsch. instr., 1961-62; from asst. to assoc. pathologist Mallory Inst. Pathology, Boston, 1964-74; asst. prof. pathology Tufts U. Sch. Medicine, Boston, 1964-70, assoc. prof., 1970-74; prof. U. Md. Sch. Medicine, Balt., 1974—; mem. staff VA Med Ctr, Balt.; asst. vis. physician in pathology Boston City Hosp., 1965-69, assoc. vis. physician, 1969-74; lectr. in field Harvard Med. Sch., Boston, 1965-74; mem. nutrition com. Mass. Heart Assn., Boston, 1968-69. Contbr. numerous articles and abstracts to med. jours. Staff sgt. U.S. Army, 1946-48. Fellow Mass. Med. Soc.; mem. Electron Microscopy Soc. Am., Am. Soc. Study of Liver Diseases, Internat. Acad. Pathology (U.S.-Can. div.), Am. Assn. Pathologists. Office: VA Med Ctr 3900 Loch Raven Blvd Baltimore MD 21218-2108

ISKRZYCKI, THOMAS JOHN, protective services official; b. Bayonne, N.J., July 22, 1944; s. John Joseph and Lorraine Teresa (Rec) I.; m. Kathaleen Kandy Dortch, Aug. 20, 1966; 1 child, Thomas Drew. AAS, Brookdale Coll., 1978. Mail carrier U.S. Post Office, Linden, N.J., 1963-65; state trooper N.J. State Police, Div. Hdqrs., West Trenton, 1964—; chmn. Nat. Troopers Coalition, Albany, N.Y., 1980-89. Mem. N.J. SEED, Trenton, 1991—. Mem. Nat. Law Enforcement Coun., Internat. Assn. Chiefs of Police, State Troopers Fraternal Assn. N.J. (pres. 1970—, legis. agt. 1988—), N.J. Soc. Assn. Execs., N.Y./N.J. Crime Clinic, Govs. Com. to Deter Crime, Govs. Pub. Safety & Health Coalition, Govs. Pub. Safety Coalition, Rutgers U. Labor Alumni Assn., Brookdale Coll. Alumni Assn. Office: State Troopers Fraternal 2519 Hwy 35 Bldg A Manasquan NJ 08736-1901

ISLAM, MUHAMMAD AZADUL, physicist, educator; b. Bogra, Bangladesh, Dec. 23, 1951; came to U.S., 1975; s. Muhammad Mohsin Ali and Amena Khatun; m. Aziza Gole Afroz, July 24, 1987. BSc with honors, Dhaka U., Bangladesh, 1974; MS, U. Ala., 1977; MPhil, Columbia U., 1979, PhD, 1981. Teaching asst. U. Ala., Tuscaloosa, 1975-77; faculty fellow, then head teaching asst. Columbia U., N.Y.C., 1977-79; grad. rsch. asst. Columbia Radiation Labs., N.Y.C., 1979-81; postdoctoral fellow U. Colo., Boulder, 1981-83; lectr. San Diego State U., 1983-85; asst. prof. SUNY, Potsdam, 1985-89, assoc. prof. physics, 1989—. Contbr. articles to profl. publs. Mem. AAAS, United Univ. Profs., N.Y. State United Tchrs., Am. Fedn. Tchrs., Islamic Soc. North Am. (trustee Potsdam chpt. 1990—), N.Y. Acad. Scis., Am. Phys. Soc., Sigma Xi, Sigma Pi Sigma. Home: 6 Poplar St Potsdam NY 13676-2113 Office: SUNY Dept Physics Potsdam NY 13676

ISLAN, GREGORY DEFONTAINE, cable television executive; b. Stamford, Conn., Aug. 23, 1947; s. Alfred Falk and Audrey (deFontaine) I.; m. Anne Martense Sneath, May 26, 1984; children: Lydia deFontaine, Abigail Sneath, William Wade. AB, Gettysburg Coll., 1970; MBA, U. Va., 1980. Asst. dir. pub. relations Salisbury (Md.) State Coll., 1974-78; v.p., gen. mgr. Satellite Cablevision, Inc. (div. Capital Cities Corp.), Greenwood, Ind., 1980-82; v.p. corp. devel. United Video Mgmt., Inc., Greenwich, Conn., 1982-88; v.p. mergers and acquisitions Daniels and Assocs., N.Y.C., 1988-91; prin. Riverside Cable Mgmt., Greenwich, Conn., 1991—. Trustee, City Hall Mus. and Cultural Ctr., Salisbury, 1976-78. Served with the U.S. Army, 1971-74, Viet Nam. Mem. U. Va. Club (officer Fairfield/Westchester chpt. 1984—), Gettysburg Coll. Club (pres. Fairfield/Westchester chpt. 1987-91), Riverside Yacht Club. Episcopalian. Home: 103 Summit Rd Riverside CT 06878-2106 Office: Riverside Cable Mgmt PO Box 187 Old Greenwich CT 06870-0187

ISLER, NORMAN JOHN, aircraft engine company administrator, consultant; b. Passaic, N.J., May 8, 1929; s. John and Irene Agnes (Good) I.; m. Margaret Jane Evans, Feb. 18, 1955; children: David, Barbara, Ann, Beth. BME, Clarkson U., Potsdam, N.Y., 1951; M in Engring. Mgmt., Northeastern U., 1966. Registered profl. engr., N.Y. Mgr. evaluation engring. GE Small Aircraft Engine Dept., Lynn, Mass., 1958-70, mgr. quality control, 1970-72; mgr. Metroliner program GE Transp. Systems Div., Erie, Pa., 1972-77; mgr. locomotive design GE Transportation Systems Div., Erie, Pa., 1977-80; mgr. tech. requirements GE Small Aircraft Engine Dept., Lynn, 1980-87, mgr. product support engring., 1987-89, mgr. engine program, 1989—. Contbr. articles to profl. jours.; patentee in field. Pres. Topsfield (Mass.) Hist. Soc., 1989—; mem. Topsfield Pers. Bd., 1991; mem. Topsfield Historic Dist. Commn., 1989—; trustee Wellman Trust. 1st lt. U.S. Army, 1951-53, Korea. Decorated Army Commendation medal. Mem. ASME. Roman Catholic. Home: 135 Perkins Row Topsfield MA 01983-1909

ISMAIL, ZAFAR ABU MOHAMED, physics educator, researcher, consultant; b. Keymore, India, Oct. 9, 1930; came to U.S., 1982; s. Abulkhair Mohamed and Zakiya Yusuf; m. Syeda Fazila Akhtar Bokhari, Aug. 21, 1965; children: Atif Zafar, Khurram Zafar, Faiza N. Zafar, Mona S. Zafar. MSc, Panjab U., Lahore, Pakistan, 1952, MA, 1954; BA with Honours, Cambridge (Eng.) U., 1958; DPhil in Elem. Particle Physics, Oxford (Eng.) U., 1964. Tchr. St. Mary's High Sch., Sukkur, Pakistan, 1952-53; instr. Mumtaz Coll., Khairpur Mirs, Pakistan, 1954-56; lectr., sr. lectr. Sind U., Hyderabad, Pakistan, 1958-65, assoc. prof., 1965-71, prof., 1971-72; prof. Tripoli (Libya) U., 1972-82; prof. physics Daemen Coll., Amherst, N.Y., 1983—; pres. B-Z Enterprises, Buffalo, 1988—; cons. Morris & Lee Inc., Buffalo, 1991—. Contbr. numerous articles on high energy nuclear physics to sci. jours. Scholar Pakistan Ministry Edn., 1953; fellow Colombo PLan, 1960. Mem. Am. Phys. Soc., Am. Assn. Physics Tchrs., Inst. Physics U.K. Republican. Home: 64 Northington Dr East Amherst NY 14051-1717 Office: Daemen Coll 4380 Main St Buffalo NY 14226-3592

ISO-AHOLA, SEPPO ENSIO, educator; b. Saarijärvi, Finland, Nov. 11, 1948; came to U.S., 1971; s. Aaro Matti and Sylvi (Ruuska) I.; m. Leena Riitta Koskela, Sept. 2, 1973; children: Vikke, Ville, Vertti, Viola. BS, U. Jyväsklä, 1971, MS, 1972; MS, U. Ill., 1973, PhD, 1976. Asst. prof. U. Iowa, Iowa City, 1976-80, assoc. prof. U. Iowa, 1980-81, U. Md., College Park, 1981-84; prof. U. Md., 1984—, dept. chmn., 1989—. Author: Social Psychology of Leisure and Recreation, 1980, Psychology of Sports, 1986; editor: Jour. Leisure Rsch. Lt. Finland Army, 1968-69. Recipient Charles Brighbill award, U. Ill., 1987. Mem. Am. Psychol. Assn., Nat. Recreation & Park Assn. (recipient Theodore and Franklin Roosevelt award for Excellence in Recreation & Park Rsch. 1987). Office: U Md Coll Health Human Performance College Park MD 20742

ISQUITH, FRED TAYLOR, lawyer; b. N.Y.C., June 6, 1947; s. Stanley and Rita (Hoskwith) I.; m. Susan Nora Goldberg, May 23, 1976: children: Fred, Rebecca. BA, Brooklyn Coll. of CUNY, 1968; JD, Columbia U., 1971. Bar: N.Y. 1972, D.C. 1976, U.S. Dist. Ct. (so., ea. and no. dists.) N.Y. 1975, U.S. Dist. Ct. (we. dist.) Mich. 1992, U.S. Ct. Appeals (2d cir.) 1975, U.S. Ct. Appeals (8th cir.) 1985, U.S. Ct. Appeals (3d cir.) 1986, U.S. Ct. Appeals (4th cir.) 1990, U.S. Supreme Ct. 1983. Assoc. Fulbright & Jaworski, N.Y.C., 1971-75, Kaye Scholer et al, N.Y.C., 1975-80; ptnr. Wolf Haldenstein Adler Freeman & Herz, N.Y.C., 1980—; bd. dirs. 103 East 84th St. Corp., N.Y.C., Sheinkopf Communications, Ltd. Mem. ABA, N.Y. State Bar Assn. (coms. on securities and legis.), D.C. Bar Assn., Assn. of Bar of City of N.Y., Bklyn. Bar Assn. (civil practice law and rules com., legis. com. and fed. ct. coms.), Columbia Club. Office: Wolf Haldenstein Adler Freeman & Herz 270 Madison Ave New York NY 10016-0601

ISRAEL, BERNARD MEYER, pharmacist; b. Berlin, N.H., Nov. 28, 1929; s. Reuben and Gertrude (Evans) I.; m. Joan Ruth Schay, Feb. 7, 1954; children: Deborah Lynn, Aaron Saul, Andrea Schay, Joshua Jay. BS in Pharmacy, Columbia U., 1951, MS in Pharmacy, 1953; PhD in Pharmacy, U. Wis., 1961. RPh, N.H., N.Y., Calif., Fla. Postdoctoral rsch. fellow Rutgers U., New Brunswick, N.J., 1961-65; group leader White Labs. div. Schering Corp., Kenilworth, N.J., 1965-69; sect. head Smith Miller and Patch, Cooper Labs. Inc., New Brunswick, 1969-74; rsch. assoc. Block Drug Co., Inc., Jersey City, N.J., 1974—. Gabbai Congregation Ahavas Achim, New Brunswick, Highland Park, N.J., 1965—. Cpl. U.S. Army, 1953-55. Recipient Diekman award Columbia U., 1951, Alumni Silver medal, 1951; Isaac Plaut fellow, 1951-53. Mem. AAAS, Am. Pharm. Assn., Am. Chem. Soc., Sigma Xi, Rho Chi, Alpha Zeta Omega. Jewish. Home: 256 Handy St New Brunswick NJ 08901-2944 Office: Block Drug Co Inc 257 Cornelison Ave Jersey City NJ 07302-3113

ISRAEL, FRED L(EWIS), history educator; b. N.Y.C., Feb. 8, 1934; s. Jack C. and Evelyn (Wallach) I. BS, CCNY, 1955; MA, Columbia U., 1956, PhD, 1959. From asst. prof. to assoc. prof. dept. history CCNY, N.Y.C., 1955-73, prof., 1973—. Author: Nevada's Key Pittman, 1963; editor: (with Arthur Schlesinger Jr.) History of American Presidential Elections, 4 vols., 1971, Justices of the U.S. Supreme Court, 4 vols., 1969, (with Arthur Schlesinger Jr.) Running for President, 2 vols., 1993. Recipient Louis Knott Koontz Meml. award Am. Hist. Assn., 1962, Scribe's award ABA, 1970; pvt. audience with Pope Paul VI, The Vatican, 1968; Danforth Found. assoc., 1967-69. Office: CCNY Dept History New York NY 10031

ISRAEL, IRA M., psychiatrist; b. Bklyn., May 27, 1919; s. Charles and Bertha (Zerman) I.; m. Muriel Miller, Oct. 26, 1948; children: Roy, Charles. BA, U. Pa., 1939; MD, Middlesex U., 1943. Diplomate Am. Bd. Psychiatry and Neurology. Intern Israel Zion Hosp., Bklyn., 1943; resdient Elmhurst (N.Y.) Hosp. Mt. Sinai Hosp. Svcs., 1963-66; instr. psychiatry Mt. Sinai Med. Sch., N.Y.C., 1966-71; dir. psychiatry Cen. Gen. Hosp., Plainview, N.Y., 1984-90; pvt. practice, Plainview, 1948—. Lt. (sr. grade) USPHS, 1944-46, capt. U.S. Army, 1952-53. Fellow Am. Psychiat. Assn.; mem. N.Y. State Med. Soc., Nassau County Psychiat. Soc., Nassau County Med. Soc. Office: 700 Old Country Rd Plainview NY 11803-4932

ISRAEL, JACOB SAMUEL, anesthesiologist, educator; b. N.Y.C., Mar. 23, 1926; s. Flora (Shapiro) I.; m. Alice Jacobson, June 16, 1946 (div. 1973); children: Robert, Janet Rauscher, John; m. Judith Ohn, Apr. 17, 1985. BA, Columbia Coll., 1946; MD, NYU, 1949. Intern Lincoln Hosp., Bronx, N.Y., 1950-51; asst. prof. anesthesiology SUNY, Syracuse, 1954-75, dir. respiratory therapy, 1968-73; prof. clin. anesthesiology Columbia Presbyn. Hosp., N.Y.C., 1975-80; prof. anesthesiology Albert Einstein Coll. Medicine, Bronx, N.Y., 1980—; dir. anesthesiology Montefiore Affiliated North Cen. Bronx Hosp., 1990—. Editor: The Recovery Room, 1988; contbr. articles to profl. jours.; author: (with others) Anesthesiology for Medical Students, 1991. Pres. Sakier Charity Found., N.Y.C., 1989—. Comdr. USNR, 1944-54, 88—. Recipient Centrum award Cen. N.Y. Respiratory Care, 1974. Mem. N.Y. State Soc. Anesthesiologists (dist. dir. 1983-91, Cert. Appreciation 1990), Am. Soc. Anesthesiologists (del. 1988-91, rep. armed svcs. com. 1990—, appointee nat. bd. respiratory care 1990—, appointee bd. med. advisors assn. respiratory care 1984-90). Home: 65 Severn St Scarsdale NY 10583-6848 Office: North Ctrl Bronx Hosp 3424 Kossuth Ave Bronx NY 10467-2489

ISRAEL, LESLEY LOWE, political consultant; b. Phila., July 21, 1938; d. Herman Albert and Florence (Segal) Lowe; m. Fred Israel, Dec. 18, 1960; children: Herman Allen, Sanford Lawrence. BA, Smith Coll., 1959. Dir. media advance Humphrey for Pres., Washington, 1967-68, dir. politic. intelligence, 1972; dir. scheduling Bayh for Pres., Washington, 1971; spl. asst. Jackson for Pres., Washington, 1975-76; coordinator nat. labor Kennedy for Pres., Washington, 1979-80; sr. v.p. The Kamber Group, Washington, 1981-87; pres., chief exec. officer Politics, Inc., Washington, 1987—; bd. dirs. The Kamber Group, Washington. Pres. Jewish Community Ctr. of Greater Washington, Rockville, Md., 1981-83; bd. mgrs. Adas Israel Synagogue, 1981-83; mem. Dem. Charter Commn., 1982-83, Dem. Del. Selection Commn., 1983-84, Dem. Site Selection Com., 1989-90, 90—, Nat. Dem. Club, 1986—; chair Washington Regional Bd., ADL, 1991—; mem. Nat. Commn. ADL, 1991—; chair Washington Bd. Friends of Tel Aviv U. Recipient Spl. Service award Jewish Community Ctr., 1984; named one of 100 Most Powerful Women, Washingtonian mag., 1990. Jewish. Home: PO Box 69 Royal Oak MD 21662-0069 Office: Politics Inc 1920 L St NW Washington DC 20036-5004

ISRAEL, LYNNE CHARLENE, occupational therapist; b. Los Angeles, Mar. 20, 1946; d. Wayne Edwin and Evelyn Elizabeth (Firnhaber) Thomsen; m. Barry John Israel, June 22, 1968; children: Alison, Ashley, Brenna. BS, San Jose State U., 1968. SIPT cert. by Sensory Integration Internat. Occupational therapist Rehab. Services of Columbus, Ga., 1969, Good Samitarian Hosp., Balt., 1970-72; o.t. Nat. Naval Med. Ctr., Bethesda, Md., 1972-74, Fairfax County Pub. Schs., Va., 1975-77; pvt. practice o.t. Washington, 1977—; cons. occupational therapy D.C. Community Services, 1985—, United Cerebral Palsy, 1983-87. Mem. Wash. Ind. Svcs. for Ednl. Resources, Am. O.T. Assn., D.C. O.T. Assn. Democrat. Home and Office: 1979 Biltmore St NW Washington DC 20009-1509

ISRAEL, ROBERT ALLAN, statistician; b. N.Y.C., Mar. 30, 1933; s. John J. and Ray (Sladkus) I.; m. Barbara Diane Johnston, Jan. 26, 1953; children: John, Richard, Deborah, Pamela, James, Michael. BA, Hofstra Coll., 1954; MS, Columbia U., 1957. Med. analyst Md. State Health Dept., Balt., 1959-63, chief div. statis. rsch., 1963-66; chief mortality stats. br. Nat. Ctr. for Health Stats., Washington, 1966-68, dir. div. vital stats., 1968-72, assoc. dir. for ops., 1972-75, dep. dir., 1975-92, assoc. dir. for internat. stats., 1992—; head WHO collaborating ctr. for disease classification for North Am., 1975—. Co-author: The Methods and Materials of Demography, 1973. Recipient Superior Svc. award U.S. Pub. Health Svc., 1972, 79, scholarship N.Y. State Bd. Regents, 1950-54, fellowship U.S. Public Health Svc., 1956-58, Special Recognition award Asst. Sec. for Health. Fellow Am Pub. Health Assn. (stats. sect. award, 1986), Am. Statis. Assn.; mem. Internat. Epidemiology Assn. Office: Nat Ctr for Health Stats 6525 Belcrest Rd Hyattsville MD 20782-2003

ISRAELS, MICHAEL JOZEF, lawyer; b. N.Y.C., Sept. 27, 1949; s. Carlos Lindner and Ruth Lucille (Goldstein) I.; m. Maija-Sarmite Jansons, Aug. 31, 1980; children: Aleksandrs Lehman, Peter Carlos. A.B. magna cum laude, Amherst Coll., 1972; J.D., Harvard U., 1975. Bar: N.Y. 1976, U.S. Dist. Ct. (so. and ea. dists.) N.Y. 1976, D.C. 1977, N.J. 1980, U.S. Dist. Ct. N.J. 1980. Assoc. Shearman & Sterling, N.Y.C., 1975-79; sole practice, N.Y.C., 1979-81; ptnr. Courter, Kobert, Laufer & Pease, P.A., Hackettstown, N.J., 1981-83, Fitzpatrick & Israels, Bayonne and Secaucus, N.J., 1983-87, 89—; sr. ptnr. Waters, McPherson, McNeill, Fitzpatrick, P.A., Secaucus, N.J., 1987-89; gen. counsel Kearny (N.J.) Mcpl. Port Authority, 1985—, Jersey City Mcpl. Port Authority, 1986—; Kearny Mcpl. Utilities Authority, 1988—; mem. N.J. Debt. Mgmt. Adv. Com., 1986—; cons. U.S./USSR Trade Council, N.Y.C., 1979, Council on Religion and Internat. Affairs, N.Y.C., 1980. Author: (with Moore, Thomson and Linsky) Report of the New England Conference on Conflicts Between Media and Law, 1977. Contbr. articles to legal jours. Bd. dirs. Community Tax Aid, Inc., N.Y.C., 1976-82, Am. Jewish Com., N.Y.C., 1980-88 , Anti-Defamation League N.J., Livingston, 1981—, U.S. Assn. Internat. Migration, 1988—; mem. religious sch. com. Temple Emanu-El, N.Y.C., 1972-84. Mem. ABA (gov. Law Student div. 1974-75), Assn. Bar City N.Y., N.J. Bar Assn. Democrat. Clubs: Met. Opera, Harvard (N.Y.C.). Home: PO Box 22 Tranquility NJ 07879-0022 Office: Fitzpatrick & Israels 400 Plaza Dr Secaucus NJ 07094-3605

ISRAELSKY, BRAD RICHARD, pharmacist; b. Bklyn., July 11, 1955; s. Irving Harold and Janice (Weinisch) I.; m. Roberta Lynn Schwartz, June 24, 1984; children: Erica, Evan. BSc, Phila. Coll. Pharmacy, 1978. Registered pharmacist, N.J., Pa., Fla. Pharmacist Rite Aid Corp., Phila., 1978-82, The Mill Pharmacy, Mt. Laurel, N.J., 1982-85, Woodcrest Pharmacy, Cherry Hill, N.J., 1985-87; pharmacy mgr. The Rx Place, Stratford, N.J., 1987—. Mem. N.J. Pharm. Assn., Am. Pharm. Assn. Democrat. Jewish. Home: 425 Hialeah Dr Cherry Hill NJ 08002

ISSELBACHER, KURT JULIUS, physician, educator; b. Wirges, Germany, Sept. 12, 1925; came to U.S., 1936, naturalized, 1945; s. Albert and Flori (Strauss) I.; m. Rhoda Solin, June 22, 1955; children: Lisa, Karen, Jody, Eric. AB, Harvard U., 1946, MD cum laude, 1950. Intern, then resident Mass. Gen. Hosp., Boston, 1950-53; investigator NIH, 1953-56; chief gastrointestinal unit Mass. Gen. Hosp., 1957-89, chmn. com. rsch., 1967, dir. Cancer Ctr., 1987—; prof. medicine Harvard Med. Sch., 1966—, chmn. exec. com. depts. medicine, 1968—, Mallinckrodt prof. medicine, 1972—, chmn. univ. cancer com., 1972-87; mem. governing bd. NRC, 1987-90. Editor-in-chief: (Harrison) Principles of Internal Medicine, 1976, 91—. Recipient award for disting. achievement in nutrition Bristol-Myers Squibb, 1991. Fellow ACP, Am. Acad. Arts and Scis.; mem. Nat. Acad. Scis. (chmn. food and nutrition bd. 1983-88, mem. exec. com., mem. coun. 1987-90), Assn. Am. Physicians (pres. 1977-78). Home: 20 Nobscot Rd Newton MA 02159-1323 Office: Mass Gen Hosp 32 Fruit St Boston MA 02114-2698

ISSEROFF, HADAR, molecular parasitologist; b. Newark, Dec. 24, 1938; s. Bar Kochba and Batia (Pushinsky) I.; m. Eileen Cynthia Reifler, Sept. 3, 1960; children: Raanan, Chari. BS in Biology, Bklyn. Coll., 1960; MS, Purdue U., 1963, PhD, 1966. Postdoctoral fellow Rice U., Houston, 1965-68; asst. prof. SUNY, Buffalo, 1968-72; assoc. prof. SUNY, 1973-78, prof., 1978—; vis. assoc. prof. Sackler Sch. Medicine, Tel-Aviv, 1975; vis. scientist Dept. Molecular & Cell Biology, Roswell Park Meml. Inst., Buffalo, 1983, vis. prof., scientist, 1990—; cons. U.S. Dept. Agr. Reviewer Jour. Parasitology, John Wiley & Sons; contbr. articles to profl. jours., chpts. to books. NIH postdoctoral fellow, Dept. HEW-NIH, 1966-68; NIH grantee, 1972-75, 76-79, 81-83; recipient Pres. Award for Scholarship and Creativity SUNY, 1987. Fellow AAAS; mem. Am. Physiol. Soc., Am. Soc. Parasitologists, Am. Soc. Zoologists. Jewish. Office: SUNY 1300 Elmwood Ave Buffalo NY 14222-1095

ISSEROW, SAUL, metallurgist; b. Berlin, Mar. 8, 1922; came to U.S., 1924; s. Samuel and Feiga (Donchin) I.; m. Rachelle A. Rosenberg, Sept. 5, 1954; children: Faye Landes, Miriam. BA, Bklyn. Coll., 1941; MS, Pa. State U., 1945, PhD, 1950. Assoc. chemist Armour Rsch. Found., Chgo., 1949-52; mgr. Nuclear Metals Inc., Concord, Mass., 1952-70; devel. dept. head Tyco Labs., Waltham, Mass., 1970-71; metall. Army Material Tech. Lab., Watertown, Mass., 1971—. Contbr. chpts. in books and articles to profl. jours. Pres. Young Israel of Brookline (Mass.) Synagogue, 1961-63. Mem. ASTM, Am. Chem. Soc., Am. Soc. for Metals (com. for internat. materials rev. 1985—), Am. Powder Metallurgy Inst., Nat. Assn. of Corrosion Engrs., Sigma Xi, Phi Lambda Upsilon, Pi Mu Epsilon. Home: 41 Brentwood Ave Newton MA 02159-1739 Office: Army Materials Tech Lab 405 Arsenal St Watertown MA 02172-2775

ISSLER, HARRY, lawyer; b. Cologne, Germany, Nov. 14, 1935; came to U.S., 1937; s. Max and Fanny (Grunbaum) I.; m. Doris Helen Lukow, June 1, 1958; children: Adriane P. Schorr, M. Valerie, Stephanie L. BS, U. Wis., 1955; JD, Cornell U., 1958. Bar: N.Y. 1958, U.S. Supreme Ct. 1962, U.S. Ct. Mil. Appeals 1967, U.S. Dist. Ct. (so. and ea. dists.) N.Y. 1960, U.S. Customs Ct. 1964, U.S. Tax Ct. 1964; cert. specialist in civil trial advocacy Nat. Bo. Trial Advocacy. Assoc. Wing & Wing, N.Y.C., 1958-60, Fuchsberg & Fuchsberg, N.Y.C., 1960-62; ptnr. Issler & Fein, N.Y.C., 1963-68, Shaw, Issler & Rosenberg, N.Y.C., 1968-70; pvt. practice N.Y.C., 1970-79; sr. ptnr. Issler & Schrage, P.C., N.Y.C., 1979—; arbitrator Civil Ct., N.Y. County, 1979-91; hearing officer N.Y. State Tax Appeals, 1975-77, Supreme Ct. of N.Y., N.Y. County Med. Malpractice Panel, 1980-91; judge advocate N.Y. State. Served with U.S. Army, 1958-59, N.Y. Army N.G., 1963-88, ret. brig. gen., 1988. Ford Found. scholar, 1951-55. Mem. N.Y. State Bar Assn., Assn. of Bar of City N.Y., Am. Trial Lawyers Assn., N.Y. State Trial Lawyers Assn., 42d Infantry Div. Officers Club (N.Y.C., pres. 1979-80), Officers Club (U.S. Mcht. Marine Acad.), 42d Infantry Rainbow Div. Assn. (pres. 1989), Phi Alpha Delta, Pi Lambda Phi (Omega chpt., pres. 1953-54). Home: 1365 York Ave New York NY 10021-4029

ISTRICO, RICHARD ARTHUR, physician; b. Bklyn., Oct. 18, 1951; s. Arthur Ralph and Gloria Rose (Petrocelli) I.; m. Candace P. Conforti, July 20, 1974; children: Jonathan Richard, Daniel Robert. BS, Pace U., 1973; DO, Phila. Coll. Osteo. Medicine, 1978. Chief intern Interboro Hosp., 1978-79; resident in family practice Baptist Med. Ctr., 1979-80, chmn. utilization review com., 1981-82, mem. pharmacy formulary com., 1981-82; panel physician N.Y. State Athletic Commn., 1981—; team physician USA/ABF Olympics Com., Colorado Springs, Colo., 1981—; med. dir. N.Y. Golden Gloves, 1986—, N.Y. Met. Am. Boxing Fedn., 1988, Golden Hoops. Basketball Tournament, 1986—; attending physician Deepdale Hosp., Little Neck, N.Y., 1980—, Parkway Hosp., Forest Hills, N.Y., 1989—; active mortality and morbidity com. Deepdale Hosp., Little Neck, 1990—. Mem. AMA, Am. Osteo. Assn. (bd. cert.), Am. Coll. Sports Medicine, Am. Osteo. Acad. Sport Medicine, Am. Coll. Gen. Practitioners (cert.), Fla. Osteo. Med. Soc., Beta Beta Beta. Republican. Roman Catholic. Office: 158-01 Crossbay Blvd Howard Beach NY 11414

ISWARA, KADIRAWEL, gastroenterologist; b. Kalmanai, Sri-Lanka, Dec. 1, 1944; came to U.S., 1970; s. Periyathamby Kadirawelpillai and Grace Rasanayagam; m. Geetha Somanader, Dec. 15, 1976; children: Shalini, Sanjeevan. MBBS, U. Ceylon, Sri-Lanka, 1968. Bd. cert. internal medicine, gastroenterology. Intern in medicine Coney Island Hosp., Bklyn., 1970-71, resient in medicine, 1971-72; resient in medicine Vets. Hosp., Bronx, N.Y., 1972-73; fellow in gastroenterology Maimonides Med. Ctr., Bklyn., 1973-76, assoc. dir. gastroenterology, 1976-80, attending gastroenterologist, 1976—; staff gastroenterologist St. Vincent Med. Ctr., Staten Island, N.Y., 1980—, Baylay Seton Hosp., Staten Island, 1980—; clin. asst. prof. medicine Health Sci. Ctr. Downstate SUNY, Bklyn., 1976—. Contbr. articles to profl. jours. Pres. Assn. of Tamil in USA, 1983-84. Lt. col. USAR, 1991, Saudi Arabia. Decorated Nat. Def. medal, Army Commendation medal, N.Y. State Cross medal N.Y. State. Fellow ACP, Am. Coll. Gastroenterology, Am. Coll. Internat. Physicians (pres. N.Y.-N.J. chpt. 1990-92); mem. Am. Gastroenterology Assn., Am. Liver Found., Ilietis Colitis Foun. Methodist. Office: 2560 Ocean Ave Brooklyn NY 11229

ISZARD, CALVIN OSCAR, JR., television production executive, county freeholder; b. Millville, N.J., Nov. 20, 1943; s. Calvin Oscar Sr. Iszard and Margaret N. (Gardella) Pedulla; m. Nancy A. Jesuele, June 27, 1967 (div. 1973); m. Judith Ann Koons, Sept. 26, 1975; children: Barbara, Lisa, Jonathan. BA, Glassboro (N.J.) State U., 1966; MA, Glassboro (N.J.) State Coll., 1968. Cert. fine arts and secondary English tchr., Pa. Adminstrv. asst. Tri-state Instructional Broadcasting, Phila., 1968-69; news producer, newscaster sch. dist. radio and TV Sta. WHYY-TV-12, Phila., 1969-70; producer, dir. N.J. Pub. Network, Trenton, 1970-75, exec. producer, 1975-80; program mgr. Sta. WWAC-TV, Atlantic City, 1980-81; pres. Original Video, Inc., Trenton, 1981-84; facilities mgr. Bell Atlantic Corp. TV, Phila., 1984—; producer broadcast, corporate and home video programs, 1970-84; performer, narrator various freelance corp. prodns., N.Y.C. and Phila., 1981-85. Dir. Painting With Pat Witt, 1984; host, producer TV series Atlantic

City Tonight, 1981; exec. producer nat. PBS series Shepherd's Pie, 1975. Mem. coun. East Windsor (N.J.) Mcpl. Govt., 1988-91, dep. mayor, 1989-90; mem. adv. bd. East Windsor Community Edn. Adv. Coun., 1986-90; Rep. candidate for N.J. Gen. Assembly, 1989; elected Mercer County Freeholder, 1992-95. U. Pa. grantee, 1966; Ea. Ednl. Network grantee, 1975; recipient Best TV News Feature award Nat. Press Club, 1981, Achievement of Excellence award Bell Atlantic, 1991. Mem. Internat. TV Assn., N.J. Cable User's Assn. (pres. 1985-90). Republican. Methodist. Office: Bell Atlantic Corp TV 1 Pky Philadelphia PA 19102-1515

ITZKOWITZ, MURRAY, health facility administrator; b. N.Y.C., Apr. 29, 1928; s. Jack and Gussie (Schmeir) I.; m. Phyllis Mervis; children: David, Steven, Jacob. BS, CCNY, 1948; MSW, Columbia U., 1952. Cert. social worker. Case worker Community Svc. Soc., N.Y.C., 1954-55; social worker Youth House for Boys, N.Y.C., 1955-57; social work supr. Jewish Child Case Assn., N.Y.C., 1957-59; adminstr. Jewish Bd. of Guardians, N.Y.C., 1959-68; exec. dir. Abbott House, Irvington, N.Y., 1968-69, The Bridge, Inc., N.Y.C., 1969—; chmn. Fedn. of MH, MR & AS, N.Y.C., 1990—; mem. N.Y. State Mental Health Planning Coun., 1992. Cpl. U.S. Army Med. Svc. Corp., 1952-54. Life Fellow Am. Orthopsychiatric Assn.; mem. World Assn. Psychosocial Rehab. U.S. (pres.), World Assn. Psychosocial Rehab. (treas.). Office: The Bridge Inc 248 W 108th St New York NY 10025

IULIUCCI, JOHN DOMENIC, toxicologist; b. Camden, N.J., June 11, 1942; s. Louis Domenic and Carmella Antoinette (Maise) I.; m. Linda Ann Lawrence, Aug. 26, 1967; children: Michele, Marianne, Louis. BS in Pharmacy, Temple U., 1967, MS in Pharmacology, 1970, PhD in Pharmacology, 1973. Diplomate Am. Bd. Toxicology. Sr. scientist Warner Lambert, Morris Plains, N.J., 1972-75; supr. toxicology Adria Labs., Wilmington, Del., 1975-77; mgr. safety evaluation Adria Labs., Plain City, Ohio, 1977-84; dir. toxicology and pharmacology Centocor Inc., Malvern, Pa., 1984—. Mem. Soc. Toxicology, Am. Coll. Toxicology, Teratology, Soc. Office: Centocor 200 Great Valley Pky Malvern PA 19355-1339

IVANHOE, HERMAN, dentist; b. Russia, Aug. 18, 1908; came to U.S., 1912, naturalized, 1930; s. Samuel and Rose (Kelmenson) I.; B.S., Columbia, 1929, D.D.S., 1931; LL.D. (hon.), Chosun U., Korea, 1979; m. Lynn Rugof, Mar. 6, 1943; children—Eliot Richard, Cindy Beth. Practice gen. dentistry, Bklyn., 1931—; acting attending in charge dept. dentistry Maimonides Hosp., Bklyn., 1959; mem. staff Caledonia, Samaritan, Community hosps.; guest of Chilean Govt. to help dental profession, 1968; cons. orthodontics Edn. Alliance N.Y.; hon. dean Sch. Dentistry, Chosun U., Korea, 1973; mem. orthodontic panel N.Y.C. Bd. Health. Served with USAAF, 1943-46. Recipient Conspicuous Alumni Service medal Columbia U., 1974, commendation State Dept.-AID. Fellow Internat. Coll. Dentistry, Am. Coll. Dentists; mem. Am. Soc. Study Orthodontics (cert.), Am. Dentists for Fgn. Service (founder, bd. dirs, Presdl. citation), ADA (life), Assn. Dental Alumni Columbia (pres. 1966-67, recipient meritorious award 1972), Pierre Fauchard Acad. Club: B'nai B'rith (pres. Jordan lodge). Contbr. to profl. publs. Introduced topical fluoridation program Carribbean area, 1974—. Established over 2500 dental clinics in 50 fgn. indigent countries; active promoting dental practice fgn. countries; equipped 11 fgn. dental schs., Korea, Peru, Honduras, Uruguay, Chile, Ecuador, China, Egypt, Philippines, Israel, Bolivia. Home: 1151 E 7th St Brooklyn NY 11230-4007 Office: 619 Church Ave Brooklyn NY 11218

IVANIER, ISIN, manufacturing company executive; b. Vijnita, Romania, Apr. 9, 1906; s. Jacob and Perl (Weintraub) I.; m. Fancia Herling; children: Paul, Sydney. Grad., Technion, Haifa, Israel, 1982; DSc (hon.). Chmn., dir. Ivaco, Inc.; dir. Atlantic Steel Co., Canron Inc., Nat. Wire Products Industries, Inc.; bd. dirs. Fla. Wire and Cable Co., Docap Corp., 1985, Wright's Canadian Ropes Ltd., Bakermet Inc. Decorated Order of Can. Club: Montefiore. Office: Ivaco Inc, 770 Rue Sherbrooke St W, Montreal, PQ Canada H3A 1G1

IVANOVITCH, MICHAEL STEVO, economist; b. Cetinje, Yugoslavia, Sept. 9, 1939; m. Elena Maria Balsinde, Apr. 11, 1987; children: Alexandra, Nicholas, Alexander. Diploma in Law, U. Belgrade, Yugoslavia, 1961; MBA, Columbia U., 1972, M of Philosophy, 1976, PhD, 1977. Rsch. assoc. Columbia U. Inst. on Western Europe, N.Y.C., 1977-78; prof. Columbia U. Grad. Sch. Bus., N.Y.C., 1978-88; internat. economist Fed. Res. Bank of N.Y., N.Y.C., 1978-79; prin. adminstr., sr. economist Orgn. for Econ. Cooperation and Devel., Paris, 1979-89; pres. MSI Global, Inc., N.Y.C. and Paris, 1989—; adj. prof. Columbia U.; advisor Credit Lyonnais, Paris, 1989—, Euroforum, Madrid, 1989—, Dai-Ichi Life Ins. Co., Tokyo and London, 1989—, Kuwait Investment Office, London, 1989—, The Yasuda Life Ins. Co., London and Tokyo, 1990—, The Meiji Life Ins. Co, Tokyo, 1991—. Democrat. Russian Orthodox. Home: 22 Crystal St New Canaan CT 06840 Office: MSI Global Inc 340 W 57th St New York NY 10019-3706

IVERSEN, NICHOLAS DRAKE, public relations executive; b. Des Moines, Dec. 25, 1951; s. Robert William and Mary P. (Drake) I.; m. Anne C. Fretz, Sept. 15, 1979; children: Kristin, Patrick. BA, Columbia U., 1973, MFA, 1979. Editor Columbia U. Law Sch., N.Y.C., 1978-82; editor Kinney Shoe Corp., N.Y.C., 1982-86, pub. rels. various, 1986-89, internal communications mgr., 1989—. Author: Recordmakers and Recordbreakers, 1977. Winner Hope Plumly award in fiction Columbia U. Sch. of the Arts, 1979. Charter mem. The Planetary Soc., 1981—. Office: Kinney Shoe Corp 233 Broadway New York NY 10279-0001 Office: Kinney Shoe Corp 233 Broadway New York NY 10279-0001

IVES, ANSON BRADLEY, lawyer; b. Jacksonville, Fla., Sept. 8, 1964; s. William Maner and Sue (Howe) I. BA, U. N.C., 1986, JD, 1989. Bar: Va. Assoc. Hunton and Williams, Richmond, Va., 1989-91, N.Y.C., 1991—. Bd. dirs. William Byrd Community House, Richmond, 1990. Morehead scholar U. N.C., 1986. Mem. ABA, Va. Bar Assn. Republican. Episcopalian. Office: Hunton and Williams 200 Park Ave New York NY 10166-0136

IVES, JEANETTE ROUTH, health facility administrator; b. Portland, Maine, Mar. 15, 1950; d. Richard G. and Justina (Dimillo) I. Diploma, Mercy Hosp. Sch. Nursing, Portland, Maine, 1971; BSN, Westbrook Coll., 1986; MS, Boston U., 1987. Adminstr. Mercy Hosp., Portland, Maine, 1984-88; dir. nursing support svcs. Mass. Gen. Hosp., Boston, 1988—. Mem. AONE, Mass. Orgn. Nursing Execs., Sigma Theta Tau. Home: 11 Main St Charlestown MA 02129-3759 Office: Mass Gen Hosp 32 Fruit St Boston MA 02114

IVESON, WILLIAM EDWARD, elementary school teacher; b. Port Jefferson, N.Y., Feb. 13, 1940; s. Robert Joseph and Helen (Droste) I. BS in Elem. Edn., SUNY, Brockport, 1963; MEd, U. Washington, 1970. Cert. tchr. K-6, social studies 7-12, N.Y. Tchr. grade 6 Hilton (N.Y.) Cen. Sch., 1963-64, tchr. grade 5, 1966-67, social studies tchr., grade 6, 1967-69, '70—; exchange tchr. grades 5-6, Lara Primary Sch., Lara, Victoria, Australia, 1980-81, social studies tchr. grade 6, 1981—. Vol. Brockport (N.Y.) Vol. Fire Dept., 1958-76. With USNR, 1964-66, Vietnam. Participant Tri-Univ Project, U. Wash., Seattle, 1969-70, Asian Geographic. Inst. Nat. Dept. Edn., Syracuse, N.Y., 1968. Mem. Rochester Coun. for Social Studies (adv. bd. 1982—), N.Y. State Coun. for Social Studies (Outstanding Social Sci. Tchr. 1984), Nat. Coun. Geographic Edn., N.Y. Geographic Alliance (tchr. cons., adv. bd. 1991—), Internat. Teaching Fellowship Assn., Found. for Internat. Edn., Am. Fedn. Tchrs., N.Y. State United Tchrs., Phi Delta Kappa. Home: 169 Hill Rd Hilton NY 14468 Office: Hilton Ctrl Sch 200 West Ave Hilton NY 14468

IVEY, ALLEN EUGENE, psychologist, educator. AB with distinction, Stanford U., 1955; Fulbright scholar, U. Copenhagen, Denmark, 1955-56; EdD, Harvard U., 1959. Cert. Am. Bd. Profl. Psychology. Prof. psychology Boston U., Bucknell U., Colo. State U., U. Hawaii, 1968-91; disting. univ. prof. U. Mass., Amherst, 1991—; Fulbright lectr. Flinders U., Australia, 1981-82. Contbr. over 200 articles to jours., chpts. to books, and books (19 books translated into 14 langs.). Named Counselor Educator of Yr. Am. Mental Health Counseling Assn., 1990. Mem. APA, AACD (profl. devel. award 1992), ACES (publ. award 1991). Baptist. Home: 2 Cranberry Ln Amherst MA 01002-2802 Office: U Mass Amherst MA 01003

IVEY, HENRY FRANKLIN, physicist; b. Augusta, Ga., June 16, 1921; s. Henry Franklin and Minnie Lee (Lively) I.; m. Sylvia Berg, July 18, 1948; children—Lisa Anne, Stephen David. A.B. summa cum laude, U. Ga., 1940; M.S. in Physics, 1941; Ph.D., M.I.T., 1944. Mem. staff radiation lab. M.I.T., 1942-45; with lamp div. Westinghouse Electric Corp., Bloomfield, N.J., 1947-63; mem. staff research and devel. center Westinghouse Electric Corp., Pitts., 1963-75; adv. scientist tech. assessment Westinghouse Electric Corp., 1978-86; ret. Westinghouse Electric Corp., Pitts., 1986. Author: Electroluminescence and Related Effects, 1963. Recipient cert. of appreciation OSRD, 1945. Fellow IEEE; mem. Am. Phys. Soc., Optical Soc. Am., Soc. Info. Display, AAAS, Electrochem. Soc. (hon.), Internat. Assn. Jazz Record Collectors, Phi Beta Kappa, Sigma Xi, Phi Kappa Phi, Pi Mu Epsilon, Sigma Pi Sigma.

IVEY, MARY BRADFORD, counselor; b. Bemidji, Minn., May 27, 1941; d. Rupert William and Florence V. (Jenson) Bradford; m. Thomas William Bohn, June 20, 1941 (div.); children: Elizabeth Ann, Kathryn Marie; m. Allen Eugene Ivey, Aug. 2, 1982. BA, Gustavus Adolphus, 1963; MS, U. Wis., Madison, 1969; EdD, U. Mass., 1978. Cert. counselor. Counselor Amherst (Mass.) Pub. Schs., 1976—; vis. prof. Flinders U., Adelaide, Australia, 1982, Keene (N.H.) State Coll., 1988, U. Mass., Amherst, 1991; lectr. and workshop presenter in field. Co-author four books; contbr. articles to profl. jours. Named Exemplary Guidance Program Top Ten in Country Christi McAuliff Conf., Va. Tech. U., 1988. Mem. AACD, Mass. Sch. Counseling Assn., Franklin-Hampshire Counseling Assn. Democrat. Lutheran. Home: 2 Cranberry Ln Amherst MA 01002-2802 Office: Amherst Schs Amherst MA 01002

IVINS, STEVEN DAVID, editor; b. Phila., Feb. 17, 1937; s. Charles Max and Edith Ann (Levy) I.; m. Nancy Sanger, Oct. 11, 1974 (div. 1991); children: Mark, Carol, Julie. BS in Econs., U. Pa., 1959, LLB, 1962; LLM, George Washington U., 1969. Bar: Pa. 1962, D.C. 1974. Staff atty. Machinery & Allied Products Inst., Washington, 1964-66, IRS, Washington, 1967-70; atty., adviser Commerce Dept., Washington, 1970-72; assoc. editor Kiplinger Tax Letter, Washington, 1972-75, editor, 1975—. Author: Office of International Operations, 1964, Accumulated Earnings Tax, 1967. Mem. Arlington (Va.) Sch. Bd., 1989—, Six-Year Planning Coms., Arlington Schs., 1985-86; pres. County Council of PTA, Arlington, 1988-89, Big Bros. of No. Va., 1967-69. Recipient Outstanding Citizen award, Arlington Sch. Bd., 1988; named Big Brother of Yr., No. Va. Big Bros., 1966. Mem. ABA, Nat. Sch. Bds. Assn., D.C. Bar Assn., Fed. Bar Assn., Arlington C. of C., Masons. Hebrew. Office: Kiplinger Washington Editors 1729 H St NW Washington DC 20006-3904

IZZI, JOHN DONALD, educator, author; b. Providence, Dec. 31, 1931; s. Joseph and Elizabeth (Kinney) I.; B.A., Providence Coll., 1953; M.Ed., R.I. Coll., 1965; postgrad. (NSF grantee), U. Vt., 1959, 60, 63, Seton Hall U., 1961, Yale U., 1966, Boston U., 1968-70; m. Patricia Margaret Crowley, Aug. 27, 1979; children: John, Matthew, Jessica; children by previous marriage: Kathleen, Donna, James. Tchr. various schs., R.I., 1955-62; head math. dept. Seekonk (Mass.) High Sch., 1966-67; state supr. math. Mass. Dept. Edn., 1967-68; tchr. Pilgrim High Sch., Warwick, R.I., 1962-66, head math, dept., 1968-72; head math. dept. Toll Gate High Sch., Warwick, 1972-88; coord. secondary sch. R.I. Hosp., 1988-89; tchr. math. and sci. Westport (Mass.) High Sch., 1989-91, math adviser, biology/sci. tchr.; adj. faculty Bristol C. C., Mass., 1992—; pres. Smallstate Co., Warwick, 1975—; prin. Warwick Adult Edn., 1987-88; extension lectr. U. R.I., 1976—; math. coach Toll Gate Acad. Decathlon State Champions, 1985, New Eng. Math League Div. Champions, 1989-90; dir. Prep Inst., Warwick, Math. Edn. Service, Providence, 1965-66, Toll Gate Metrication Project, Warwick, 1972-73; creator 1st federally funded sch. metrication project in U.S. 1972, Izzi Metric Slide Chart, 1974, Izzi Decimal System, 1974; dir. Smallstate Math. Inst., Warwick, 1989-90, Smallstate Scholarship Svc., Warwick, 1991—; advisor Am. Security Council, 1973-79; metrication cons. Nat. Council Tchrs. Math., 1973—, computer software reviewer, 1981—; adj. faculty Community Coll. R.I., 1981—, Bristol Community Coll., Mass., 1992—. Mem. Mass. Gov.'s Hwy. Safety Act Com., 1967-68. Served with U.S. Army, 1953-55. Recipient Distinguished Achievement award Ednl. Press Assn. Am., 1974; named Best Math. Tchr. in Am. Ky. Ednl. TV, 1990. Mem. NEA, Am. Fedn. Tchrs., Nat. Council Tchrs. Math., Assn. Supervision and Curriculum Devel., Am. Assn. Sch. Adminstrs. Metric Assn., Assn. Tchrs. Math. in New Eng., New Eng. Regional Metric Assn. (edn. commr. 1976-80), Mass. Dept. Edn. Assn. (v.p. 1967-68). Textbook reviewer AAAS, 1968-74; book reviewer Phi Delta Kappan, 1974-76. Author: Metrication, American Style, 1974, Looking at the Metric System, 1977, Adult Metric Guide, 1977, Basic Metric Competency Test, 1977, My Irish, Voices of America, 1991; editorial adviser New Eng. Math. Jour., 1982-85; contbr. articles to various publs. Home: 243 Greenwood Ave Warwick RI 02886-2015 Office: PO Box 8796 Warwick RI 02888-0796

IZZO, RICHARD S., biochemist; b. Queens, N.Y., Feb. 21, 1951; s. Silvio and Mary (Boniti) I.; m. Jo-Anne Longhitano, Mar. 24, 1974; children: Amanda Jean, Jayne Anne. BS, SUNY, Stony Brook, 1973; MS, L.I. U., 1977. Rsch. asst. Nassau County Med. ctr., E. Meadow, N.Y., 1974-77; chemist Mercy Hosp., Rockville Ctr., N.Y., 1977-79; rsch. biochemist Nassau County Med. Ctr., E. Meadow, 1979—. Contbr. articles to profl. jours. Mem. N.Y. Acad. Sci. Republican. Roman Catholic. Home: 2 Sussex Ln Lake Grove NY 11755-2537

JABBOUR, JOSEPH MITCHELL, plastic surgeon; b. Bklyn., May 23, 1950; s. Joseph Mitchell and Elizabeth Kathryn (Condron) J.; m. Louise Vincenti, May 29, 1972; children: Suzanne, Michelle. BS, Fordham U., 1972; MD, NYU, 1976. Diplomate Am. Bd. Plastic Surgery, Am. Bd. Surgery. Intern St. Vincent's Hosp., N.Y.C., 1976-77, surgery asst., 1977-81; plastic surgery resident NYU Med. Ctr., N.Y.C., 1981-83, microsurgery fellow, 1983-84; surgery attending physician St. Vincent's Hosp., N.Y.C., 1984—, Manhattan Eye, Ear and Throat Hosp., N.Y.C., 1984—. Fellow ACS; mem. Am. Soc. Plastic and Reconstructive Surgery, Am. Lipoplasty Soc. Roman Catholic. Office: 20 Fifth Ave New York NY 10011

JABLON, PAUL CHRISTOPHER, science educator; b. Queens, N.Y., Mar. 1, 1949; s. Rudolph P.S. and Edna C. (Walz) J.; m. Martha Weinberger, July 31, 1988. BS in Biology, Manhattan Coll., 1970; PhD in Sci. Edn., NYU, 1989. Cert. tchr., N.Y. Tchr. sci. and video Haaren High Sch., N.Y.C., 1970-73; dist. coord. Project City Sci. NYU, 1974-77; sci. dept. coord. Middle Coll. High Sch., L.I. City, N.Y., 1977-86; co-dir. The Bongo Program La Guardia Community Coll., Long Island City, N.Y., 1978-89; sci. staff developer Office of Alternative High Schs., N.Y.C., 1989-90; asst. prof. Sch. Edn., Bklyn. Coll., 1990—; chairperson N.Y.C. Alliance for Sci., 1991—; curriculum writer Engring. Concepts Curriculum Project, 1975-76. Founding editor Adaptation, 1978-80; contbr. articles to profl. jours. Advisor Jr. Acad. Sci., 1977-83; exec. bd. Greenwich Village Coalition Against Nuclear Arms, N.Y.C., 1988—; elected Dem. County Com., N.Y.C., 1980-90. Mem. N.Y. Biology Tchrs. Assn. (pres. 1980-81, Lifetime Achievement award 1985), Nat. Assn. of Sci. Tech. and Soc., Elem. Sch. Sci. Assn. (exec. bd. 1991—), Nat. Sci. Tchrs. Assn., Sci. Coun. of N.Y.C. (exec. bd. 1980-82), N.E. Region of Am. Educators of Tchrs. of Sci. (bd. dirs. 1992—). Home: 11 Charlton St New York NY 10014 Office: Sch Edn Bklyn Coll Bedford Ave & Ave H Brooklyn NY 11210

JABLONER, HAROLD, chemist; b. N.Y.C., Oct. 25, 1937; s. Matthew and Gussie (Wagner) J.; m. Sheila Annette Krautman, Nov. 18, 1962 (div. 1989); children: Paula R., Matthew L., Amy B. BS, CUNY, 1957; PhD, Poly. Inst. of N.Y., Bklyn., 1963. Rsch. chemist Hercules Powder Co., 1963-68; sr. rsch. chemist Hercules Inc., 1968-71, rsch. scientist, 1971-78, rsch. assoc., 1978-84, sr. rsch. assoc., 1984-89, disting. scientist, 1989—; disting. scientist Hercules Inc., Wilmington, Del., 1989—. Patentee in polymer chemistry. Office: Hercules Inc 16 Annesway Landenberg PA 19350

JABLONS, JOEL SIMEON, sales agency executive; b. N.Y.C., Nov. 26, 1920; s. Abraham and Ruth (Taylor) J.; m. Thelma Karpel, Feb. 12, 1956; children: Jerome D., Daniel A. BS, NYU, 1942; postgrad., Columbia U., 1947-48. Account exec. Sterling Advt. Agy., N.Y.C., 1946-48; advt. dir. Teena Paige Inc., N.Y.C., 1948-52; v.p. Mark, Simeon, Renard Advt. Agy., N.Y.C., 1952-59, Alan Berni, indsl. design, N.Y.C., 1959-61; v.p. mktg. All State Properties, N.Y.C. and Lauderhill, Fla., 1961-66, Schine Enterprises, N.Y.C., 1966-68; exec. v.p. Fashion Tress, Wig City, N.Y.C., 1968-69; pres. Saxon Securities, N.Y.C., 1969-74, The Tee Jay Co., Woodmere, N.Y., 1974—. Capt. USAAF, 1942-46, ETO. Republican. Jewish. Home: 313 Woodmere Blvd Woodmere NY 11598-2033 Office: The Tee Jay Co 313 Woodmere Blvd Woodmere NY 11598-2033

JABLONSKI, DANIEL GARY, physicist, electrical engineering educator; b. Washington, Nov. 15, 1954; s. Frank Edward and Dorothy Elaine (Condor) J.; m. Elizabeth Jan Trimble, Oct. 2, 1982; 1 child, Matthew. BSEE, MIT, 1976, MSEE, 1977; PhD in Physics, Cambridge U., 1982. Registered profl. engr., Md. Rsch. physicist Naval Surface Weapons Ctr., White Oak, Md., 1981-86; adj. prof. Capitol Coll., Laurel, Md., 1985—; rsch. physicist Supercomputing Rsch. Ctr., Bowie, Md., 1986-91; physicist, elec. engr. Applied Physics Lab. Johns Hopkins U., Laurel, Md., 1991—; Mem. MIT Edn. Coun., 1988—. Contbr. articles to profl. jours.; patentee in field. Mem. IEEE (sr., editorial bd., 1981—), Am. Phys. Soc., Eta Kappa Nu. Home: 12220 Somersworth Dr Silver Spring MD 20902-1563 Office: Johns Hopkins U Applied Physics Lab Johns Hopkins Rd Laurel MD 20723-6099

JABLONSKY, STEPHEN, music educator; b. N.Y.C., Dec. 5, 1941; s. Benjamin and Adelaide (Robinson) J.; m. Roberta Nusim, Aug. 29, 1965. BA, CCNY, 1962; postgrad., Harvard U., 1962-63; MA, NYU, 1964, PhD, 1973; postgrad., Bridgeport U., 1982-83. Cert. music tchr., N.Y. Music tchr. N.Y.C. Bd. Edn., 1965-68; asst. dir. Lake Bryn Mawr Camp, Honesdale, Pa., 1968-70; assoc. prof. CCNY, N.Y., 1964—; cons. Lifetime Learning Systems, Fairfield, Conn., 1978-90; conducting fellow Nat. Orchestral Assn., N.Y.C., 1973-76; bd. dirs. Musigraphics, Inc., Easton, Conn., 1975-80; profl. artist/graphic designer, 1968-92. Contbr. articles to profl. jours. NEA fellow, 1975, N.Y. State Regents Teaching fellow, 1962. Mem. AAUP, ASCAP, Internat. Trumpet Guild, Stamford Art Assn., New Canaan Soc. for the Arts, Profl. Staff Congress, Phi Mu Alpha, Alpha Epsilon Pi. Home: PO Box 305 Easton CT 06612-0305 Office: CCNY 138th St and Convent Ave New York NY 10031

JACEY, CHARLES FREDERICK, JR., accounting company executive, consultant; b. Staten Island, N.Y., Feb. 16, 1936; s. Charles Frederick and Marie A. (Coakley) J.; m. Arlene Theresa Biele, Jan 14, 1984: children: Lauren, David, Curtis, Jonathan, Samantha. BBA, Pace U., 1957. CPA. Mem. audit staff Coopers & Lybrand, N.Y.C., 1957-69, ptnr., 1969, mng. ptnr. N.Y. metro region, 1976-87, vice chmn., 1982—. Trustee, treas. Police Athletic League, N.Y.C., 1980—; trustee, chmn. fin. com. Pace U., N.Y.C., 1984—. Mem. Baltusrol Golf Club, Bd. Rm. Club. Office: Coopers & Lybrand 1301 Ave of the Americas New York NY 10019-6022

JACKIW, ROMAN, physicist; b. Lublinec, Poland, Nov. 8, 1939; came to U.S., 1949; s. Nicholas and Zenobia (Kostyk) J.; m. So-Young Pi, Sept. 4, 1981; children: Stefan Pi, Simone Ahlborn, Nicholas. BA, Swarthmore Coll., 1961; PhD, Cornell U., 1966. Jr. fellow Harvard Soc. of Fellows, Cambridge, Mass., 1966-69; asst., assoc. to prof. MIT, Cambridge, 1969—; vis. prof. Rockefeller U., N.Y.C., 1977-78, U. Calif., L.A., Santa Barbara, 1980, Columbia U., N.Y.C., 1989-90. Contbr. over 150 articles to profl. jours. Alfred P. Sloan fellow Sloan Found., 1969-71, J.S. Guggenheim fellow Guggenheim Found., 1977-78. Fellow Am. Acad. of Arts and Scis. Office: MIT 6-320 Cambridge MA 02139

JACKMAN, HENRY NEWTON ROWELL, Canadian provincial official; b. Toronto, Ont., Can., June 10, 1932; s. Henry Rutherford Jackman and Mary Rowell J. m. Maruja Trinidad, Aug. 14, 1964; children: Henry, Duncan, Maria Victoria, Consuelo, Trinity. BA, U. Toronto, 1953; LLB, attended London Sch. Econs; hon. LLD, U. of Windsor., 1956. Exec. asst. to mem. Ho. of Commons, 1959-61; formerly pres. Can. & Fgn. Securities Co. Ltd., Can. No. Prairie Lands. Co. Ltd.; formerly chmn. bd. Empire Life Ins. Co., Nat Trust Co., Nat. Trustco Ltd., others;; dir. numerous cos., Lt. Gov. of Ont., 1991—. pres. Empire Club Can., 1971-72, Albany Club, 1982-84, Can. Opera Co., 1984-86, Ballet Opera House, 1986-89; former chmn., Atlantic Council of Can. hon. lt.-col., Gov. Gen's House Guards. Office: Office of the Lt Gov, Main Parliament Bldg, Toronto, ON Canada M7A 1A1*

JACKSON, BENJAMIN TAYLOR, surgeon, educator, medical facility administrator; b. Jacksonville, Fla., Apr. 28, 1929; s. Julian Harold and Helen Louise (Blasingame) J.; m. Alda Jean Davis, June 18, 1953; children: Benjamin Taylor Jr., Jean Leigh, Kimberly Louise, Jillian Davis. MD, Duke U., 1954; MS, Brown U., 1982. Diplomate Am. Bd. Surgery. Instr. Med. Coll. of Va., Richmond, 1963-64; asst. prof. Sch. of Medicine Boston U., 1964-67, assoc. prof. Sch. of Medicine, 1967-75, prof. Sch. of Medicine, 1975-80; vis. surgeon U. Hosp., Boston, 1975-80; prof. Brown U. Sch. Medicine, Providence, 1980—; chief surg. svc. VA Med. Ctr., Providence, 1980—. Contbr. articles to profl. jours. Capt. U.S. Army, 1955-57. Mem. ACS, Soc. Univ. Surgeons, Soc. for Gynecologic Investigation. Methodist. Home: 11 October Ln Weston MA 02193-1724 Office: VA Med Ctr Davis Pk Providence RI 02908

JACKSON, BERNICE HAMMOND, cultural organization administrator; b. Washington, Jan. 29, 1918; d. William Madison and Isabelle (Robinson) Hammond; m. Albert Oscar Lewis, Oct. 7, 1945 (div. 1950) 1 child, Albert Oscar Jr.; m. Frederick Jackson, Apr. 20, 1952; 1 child, Frederick Bernard. Student, Howard U., 1936-39, 41-45, Carnegie Hall, N.Y.C., 1949-51, Luigi Modern Dance, N.Y.C., 1951. Founder, dir. Hammond Dance Studios, Washington, 1939-43, Bernice Hammond Sch. of Dance, Washington, 1944-52, N.E. Acad. Dance, Washington, 1952—; founding pres. Assn. for the Preservation and Presentation of the Arts Inc., Washington, 1964—; soloist Nat. Negro Opera Co., Washington, 1949-51; founder Ballet Africana Americana, Washington, 1949; originator Negro May Dance Festival, Washington, 1952. Composer, choreographer (children's ballet) Hokus Pokus, The Magic Goodwill Pixie, 1957; author, composer (musical operetta) Bye Gone Days, 1974; pub. (storybook) Hokus Pokus, The Magic Goodwill Pixie, 1981. Co-chairperson City-wide Youth Prodn. for Commrs. Youth Coun., Constn. Hall, Washington, 1963; chairperson Reopening of the Frederick Douglass Home, Dept. Interior, Washington, 1972; bd. dirs., Phyllis Wheatley YWCA; pres. citizens bd. Chamberlain Career Ctr., 1990. Recipient Svc. in the Performing Arts award Gamma Phi Delta, 1966, Outstanding award Hammond Dancers Washington Pan-Hellenic Coun., 1972, Outstanding Community Svc. award Kappa Alpha Psi, 1977, Cert. of Appreciation 1st Ann. Mayor's Art award, 1981. Mem. Nat. Assn. Colored Womens Club, Howard U. Women's Club (life). Baptist. Home: 3022 14th St NE Washington DC 20017 Office: Assn Preservation and Presentation of Arts Inc 2011 Benning Rd NE Washington DC 20002

JACKSON, BYRON HADEN, religion educator; b. Lexington, Va., Dec. 25, 1943; s. Jack Lee and Lillian Vaden (Snyder) J.; m. Beverly Diane Fortson, Aug. 29, 1967; 1 child, Rachel Lynn. BA, Randolph-Macon Coll., Ashland, Va., 1966; MDiv, Union Theol. Sem., Richmond, Va., 1971; EdD, Columbia U., 1980. Asst. pastor First Presbyn. Ch., Rocky Mount, N.C., 1968-70; assoc. pastor Harvey Browne Meml. Presbyn. Ch., Louisville, 1974-78; staff assoc. Gen. Assembly Mission Bd., Atlanta, 1978-83; coord. Gen. Assembly Coun., Atlanta, 1983-86; asst. prof. Pitts. Theol. Sem., 1986-91, assoc. prof., 1991—; trustee Presbyn. Sch. Christian Edn., Richmond, 1974-80. Mem. ASCD, Assn. Presbyn. Ch. Educators, Religious Edn. Assn., Assn. Theol. Field Edn. (rsch. coord. 1989-91). Democrat. Office: Pitts Theol Sem 616 N Highland Ave Pittsburgh PA 15206-2596

JACKSON, CHARLES NEASON, II, trade association administrator; b. Richmond, Va., Mar. 16, 1931; s. Miles and Thelma (Manning) J.; m. Marlene Costello Mills, Jan. 31, 1959; children: Renata, Andrea, Charles III. BS, Va. Union U., 1958; MBA, Temple U., 1962; MS, Southeastern U., 1976. Spl. agt. IRS, Phila., 1961-66; sr. auditor USAID/Nigeria, Lagos, 1967-69; v.p. Nat. Urban Coalition, Washington, 1969-81; pvt. practice cons. Washington, 1981-91; dir. fin. Soc. Am. Foresters, Bethesda, Md., 1991—. Trustee Media Assocs., Washington, 1973-80, Washington Hosp. Ctr., 1975-85; treas. Vols. in Tech. Assistance, Washington, 1974-79. With USAF, 1951-55, Korea. Recipient Outstanding award Nat. Urban Coalition, 1975, Appreciation award Wash. Hosp. Ctr., 1985. Mem. Am. Soc. Assn. Execs., Nat. Soc. Pub. Accts. Roman Catholic. Office: Soc Am Foresters 5400 Grosvenor Ln Bethesda MD 20814

JACKSON, DONALD KENNETH, transportation company executive; b. Castor, Alta., Can., Apr. 6, 1944; children: Andrea, Sara. BA, U. Alta., 1965; MBA, U. Western Ont., London, Can., 1967. Pres. Tricil Ltd., Calgary, Alta., 1973-76, chmn., 1976-87; group v.p. Trimac Ltd., Calgary, 1976-77, also bd. dirs.; asst. to pres. John Labatt, Ont., 1988-89; pres., chief exec. officer Laidlaw Inc., Burlington, Ont., 1989—, also bd. dirs.; bd. dirs. Derlan Industries, ADT Ltd., Attwoods Pl., The Pub. Policy Forum. Past chmn. Canadian Coun., Young Pres.'s Orgn. Mem. Nat. Tank Truck Assn. (past chmn.), Nat. Truck Leasing Assn. (past pres.). Office: Laidlaw Inc, 3221 N Service Rd PO Box 5028, Burlington, ON Canada L7R 3Y8

JACKSON, DONALD RICHARD, marketing professional; b. N.Y.C., Oct. 7, 1938; s. Roger W. and Anita (Leopardi) J.; m. Dvora Sesskin, Oct. 1, 1960 (div. June 1970); children: Hadley Drew, Edwinna Toby; m. Andra Paley, Mar. 15, 1971 (div. Mar. 1985); children: Rebecca, Lexis; m. Betts Chilton Saunders, July 3, 1986. BA, MA, Adelphi U., 1960. Mgmt. trainee Doubleday & Co., Garden City, N.Y., 1965-67; promotion dir. Decker Communications, Inc., N.Y.C., 1967-69; pres. The Jackson-Hill Group, N.Y.C., 1969-70; dir. of dir. mktg. Am. Internat. Group, N.Y.C., 1970-73; v.p. advt. SAI Group, Inc., Cherry Hill, N.J., 1973-74; pres. Don Jackson & Assocs., Cherry Hill, 1974-84; mktg. officer Continental Am. Life, Newark, Del., 1984-86; pres. Don Jackson Cons., Middletown, Del., 1986-89; chmn. The Jackson Cons. Group, Ltd., 1989—; cons. Comml. Travelers Mut. Ins. Co., Utica, N.Y., 1986-91, Union Labor Life Ins. Co., 1989—, Capitol Holding Corp./Direct Response Group, 1991-92, Mut. Benefit Life Ins. Co., 1990-91, New Eng. Bus. Svcs., 1990-91, Amoco Oil Corp., 1990—, NAFE, 1991—, Starmount Life Ins. Co., 1992—. Author: 151 Secrets of Insurance Direct Marketing Practices Revealed, 1989, Telemarketing C.A.M.P., 1988, Winning, Insurance Direct Marketing for Agents and Brokers, 1991; editor newsletter Inside Fin. Svcs. Mktg., 1989—; contbr. articles to profl. jours. Lt. comdr. USN, 1960-65. Mem. Direct Mktg. Assn. (chmn. fin., Direct Mktg. Ins. Coun., mem. Fin. Svcs. Coun., ins. exec. of yr.), Phila. Direct Mktg. Assn. Republican. Roman Catholic. Office: PO Box 246 Middletown DE 19709-0246

JACKSON, DWAYNE ADRIAN, insurance company executive; b. N.Y.C., Aug. 3, 1955; s. George Earl and Ina Elizabeth (Stockton) J.; m. Cheryl Denise Robinson; children: David, Courtney. BA, Westfield State U., 1977. CLU. Insur. adjuster Crawford & Co., Springfield, Mass., 1977-79; funding analyst Mass. Mutual Life, Springfield, 1979-82, benefits mgr., 1982-84, fin. reporting mgr., 1984-86, fin. acctg. dir., 1986-91, 2nd v.p., 1991—; bd. chmn. minority adv. group Mass. Mutual Life Ins., Springfield, 1991. Bd. dirs. W.W. Johnson Life Ctr., Springfield, 1984; mentor I Have a Dream Found., Springfield, 1989. Democrat. Episcopalian. Office: Mass Mutual Life Ins Co 1295 State St Springfield MA 01111-0001

JACKSON, ETHEL NOLAND, molecular geneticist; b. Geneva, N.Y., Apr. 27, 1944; d. Lloyd H. and Ethel May (Beare) Noland; m. David Archer Jackson, June 17, 1966; 1 child, Holly Bunting. BA, Harvard U., 1966; PhD, Stanford U., 1973. Postdoctoral fellow Med. Sch. U. Mich., Ann Arbor, 1972-74, asst. prof. microbiology Med. Sch., 1974-81; rsch. dir. molecular genetics div. Genex Co., Gaithersburg, Md., 1981-85, exec. dir. rsch. ops., 1985; rsch. supr. E.I. du Pont de Nemours & Co., Wilmington, Del., 1987-90, rsch. mgr., 1990—. Contbr. articles to profl. jours. Mem. AAAS, Am. Soc. Microbiology, Genetics Soc. Am. Home: 298 Old Kennett Rd Kennett Square PA 19348-2725 Office: EI du Pont de Nemours & Co Exptl Sta 228/211 Wilmington DE 19880-0228

JACKSON, FRED, oil executive; b. Transylvania, Minor, July 21, 1952; s. Fred Sr. and Marie J.; children: Tawanna, Tanecia. Internat. Degree of Master/Mates Pilots, Md. U., 1959. With Internat. Mktg. Corp., Phila., 1982—. Contbr. articles to jours. Republican. Home and Office: 8407 Williams Ave Philadelphia PA 19150-1920

JACKSON, HARRY ALLEN, naval architect, marine engineer; b. Saginaw, Mich., Dec. 7, 1916; s. Allen D. and Ina Ruth (Lorimer) J.; m. Mary Rebecca McElroy, Apr. 15, 1944; children: Harry Allen Jr., Lisle Ann. BS, U. Mich., 1940. Profl. engr., N.H., Wash., Conn. Commd. capt. U.S. Navy, 1935, naval architect, 1941-69, ret., 1969; pvt. practice in engring. Groton, Conn., 1969—; dir. SEA Inc., San Diego, Calif., 1978—; sr. lectr. MIT, Cambridge, Mass., 1971—. Author: (textbook) Submarine Design Notes, 1982; contbr. tech. papers to profl. jours. Fellow Soc. Naval Architects and Marine Engrs., Royal Inst. Naval Architects; mem. Am. Soc. Naval Engrs. (hon. Harold E. Saundes award 1980). Home and Office: 17 Birch Ln Groton CT 06340-6003

JACKSON, HERMOINE PRESTINE, psychologist; b. Wilmington, Del., Mar. 11, 1945; d. Herman Preston and Ella Brooks (Roane) Jackson. BA, Elizabethtown (Pa.) Coll., 1967; MA, Ohio State U., 1979, PhD, 1991. Tchr. Wilmington (Del.) pub. sch. sys., 1967-68, Phila. Pub. Sch. Sys., 1968-74; psychologist Midland (Mich.) Hosp., 1979-81, Cen. Mich. U., Mt. Pleasant, 1979-81, West Seneca (N.Y.) Devel. Ctr., 1981-90, N.Y. State Div. for Youth Buffalo Residential Ctr., 1990—; mem. admissions/discharge com. St. Augustine Ctr., Buffalo, 1983—. Co-author test manual: Manual of Assessment Instruments for the MR/DD Population, 1978. Task force mem. Youth Planning Com., Buffalo, 1989. Named Outstanding Instr., Cen. Mich. U., 1981. Mem. Am. Psychol. Assn., Am. Assn. on Mental Retardation, Psychol. Assn. Western N.Y., Coalition of 100 Black Women (corres. sec. 1988—). Home: 1 Norwalk Ave Buffalo NY 14216-2819 Office: NY State Div for Youth 485 Best St Buffalo NY 14208-2493

JACKSON, HOWARD LEE, architect; b. Verdun, France, June 6, 1957; came to U.S., 1957; s. Johnny and Zeola (Cole) J.; m. Karen Alease Colbert, Aug. 5, 1983; 1 child, Chantelle Celia. BArch, Hampton U., 1981. Running back Balt. Colts (NFL), 1981-82, Washington Feds. (U.S. Football League), 1982-83; salesman Vorwerk USA, Balt., 1983-84, 84 Lumber, Balt., 1984-85; grad. architect, tng. supr. Ryland Group, Inc., Columbia, Md., 1985-91; architect Regional Bldg. Systems, Columbia, Md., 1991—. Facilitator Black Student Achievement of Howard County (Md.), Pub. Sch. System, 1987—; elder Knox Presbyn. Ch.; mem. Evangelism and Mission Com. to Balt., Presbytery; cubmaster Boy Scouts Am., Balt.; Harambee Bd. Balt. Presbytery; strategy team mem. Baltimorians United in Leadership Devel. Democrat. Home: 1004 N Central Ave Baltimore MD 21202-5502 Office: Regional Bldg Systems 5560 Sterrett Pl Columbia MD 21044-2608

JACKSON, JAMES MONTGOMERY, actuary, consultant; b. Rochester, N.Y., Oct. 27, 1950; s. J. Edward and Suzanne (Montgomery) J.; m. Christine S. Fitch, Feb. 13, 1981 (div. May 1991); children: Dael L., J. Bradford. Student, Lafayette Coll., 1968-70; BS, SUNY, Albany, 1971; MBA, Boston U., 1985. Actuarial trainee Kwasha Lipton, Englewood CLiffs, N.J., 1972-74; asst. actuary Kwusha Lipton, Englewood CLiffs, N.J., 1974-75, actuary, 1976-77; cons. A.S. Hansen Inc., Boston, 1977-80; sr. actuarial mgr. A.S. Hansen Inc., White Plains, N.Y., 1980-83, mgr. support facility, 1983-87; prin. Mercer-Meidinger-Hansen, White Plains, N.Y., 1987-88; mng. v.p. Noble Lowndes, Roseland, N.J., 1988—. Mem. Am. Acad. Actuaries, Soc. Actuaries (assoc.). Home: PO Box 333 Oldwick NJ 08858-0333

JACKSON, JAMES ROBERT, meeting planner; b. Kearny, N.J., July 9, 1922; s. Robert and Ethel (Fine) J.; m. Shirley Newill, Jan. 6, 1951; children—Todd, Lauren. B.A., Lafayette Coll., 1943. Dir. manpower Colonial Life Ins. Co., East Orange, N.J., 1956-62; dir. brokerage Manhattan Life Ins. Co., N.Y.C., 1962-68; regional mgr Mchts. Life Ins. Co., Buffalo, N.Y., 1968-73; asst. v.p. Am. Eagle Life Ins. Co., Morristown, N.J., 1973-78; v.p. Buck Hill Inn, Buck Hill Falls, Pa., 1978-81; pres. Total Conf. Planning, Inc., Maplewood, N.J., 1981—, James R. Jackson & Assocs., Inc., Maplewood, 1981—. Trustee, Peddie Sch., Hightstown, N.J., 1947-77, pres., mem. alumni bd., 1948—. Del. Homeowners Assn.; trustee Burlington County Community Coll. Found., 1990-91. Served with USNR, 1943-46, ETO, PTO, 1951-52, Korea. Mem. Life Underwriters Assn., Sales Execs. Club N.J. (bd. govs.), Meeting Planners Internat., Assn. Indep. Meeting Planners, Meeting Consultants Network. Presbyterian. Club: Maplewood (Trustee 1958-60).

JACKSON, JIMMY JOE, litigation consultant; b. Fabens, Tex., Nov. 27, 1947; s. Andrew Donald and W. Lucille (Briley) J.; m. Susan F. Robertson, Aug. 25, 1968; children: Robert R., Ruth A. BS in Mgmt., MIT, 1970, MS in Mgmt., 1974; MBA in Fin., So. Ill. U., 1973. Ptnr. Arthur Andersen & Co., S.C., N.Y.C., 1974-91; litigation cons. self-employed Monmouth Junction, N.J., 1991—. Capt. USAF, 1970-73. Mem. Am. Statis. Assn. Baptist. Home: 14 Zev Ct Monmouth Junction NJ 08852-9772 Office: 14 Zev Ct Monmouth Junction NJ 08852-9772

JACKSON, JOHN EARNEST, television producer; b. Jackson, Tenn., Mar. 26, 1941; s. Robert Hampton and Rosie Mae (Jackson) Reid; m. Lillian Hudson, Apr. 14, 1971 (div. Nov. 1971). Communication dir. minority recruitment U.S. Peace Corps, Washington, 1969-73; pres. JEJ Prodns., Inc., Washington, 1973-77, WAQT Prodns., Inc., N.Y.C., 1977—. Producer TV programs including: Annual Rhythm and Blues Awards TV Special, Best of Rhythm and Blues, Black College Scoreboard, Jive Time Players, Diary, Kickin' It, The Ebony Affair. Vol. Peace Corps, so. India, 1966-68. Office: WAQT Prodns Inc PO Box 6540 Yorkville Sta New York NY 10128

JACKSON, KAREN LOUISE, educator; b. Queens, N.Y., Apr. 6, 1949; d. Eugene Lester and Jean Louise (Gantt) Jones; m. John Michael Jackson, Oct. 1, 1969; children: Pamela, Lamont, John V. Student, Coll. New Rochelle, 1988-90. Home attendant Bronxdale Home Svcs., Bronx, N.Y., 1980-81; daycare tchr. East Tremont Daycare Ctr., Bronx, 1981-91; supr., tchr. Lancaster (Pa.) Daycare Ctr., 1991—; adv. com. Pub. Sch. 72, Bronx, 1990-91; presenter workshops. Contbr. articles to profl. jours. Bd. dirs. Throggs Neck Daycare Ctr., Bronx, 1978-79, chair parents com., 1979-80; lic. pastor King's Temple, Lancaster, 1991—. Home: 1139 Wabank Rd Lancaster PA 17603

JACKSON, MARTIN FREDRIC, photo-illustrator; b. N.Y.C., Oct. 21, 1946; s. Walter Herbert Jackson and Frances (Prewett) Conley; m. Barbara Ann Gelman, Sept. 16, 1971. BA, L.I. U., 1970; postgrad., U. Hull, York, Eng., 1971. Staff photographer Photo Media, N.Y.C., 1973-76, Wagner Internat. Time Life, N.Y.C., 1976-79; staff photographer Bantam Books and Sunset Books Roband, Charlton, and Barvin Publs., N.Y.C., 1979-82; author, photographer N.Y.C., 1982-85; pres./owner Jackson Photography and Design, Phila., 1985—; art dirs. Delaware Valley Mag., Langhorn, Pa., 1990-91; pres./owner Jackson Investment Group, N.Y.C., 1991—. Creator and photographer: Plain Jane Works Out, 1983; photographer: 30 Days to a More Beautiful Bottom, 1982, How to Books, 1970-79; contbr. photographs to profl. jours. Recipient Creativity/Gold Photographs 1991, 55th Gold for Excellence 1991, 7 Gold awards for Art Direction 1991, 1 silver award for photography 1991, 3 Design Excellence awards 1991. Mem. Am. Soc. of Mag. Photographers, Art Dirs. Club of Phila., Nikon Profl. Photographers, Kodak Profl. Photographers, Film and Drama Club (pres. 1968-70). Office: Jackson Photography Design 320 Catharine St Philadelphia PA 19147

JACKSON, PATRICIA LEE (MRS. CLIFFORD L. JACKSON), psychologist; b. N.Y.C.; d. Albert George and Lisbeth P. (Lee) Scharf; B.A., Barnard Coll.; M.A., Ph.D., Tchrs. Coll. Columbia U.; m. Clifford L. Jackson. Dir. psychol. testing R. H. Macy & Co., Inc., 1941-49; employment dir. Alexander's Dept. Stores, Inc., Bronx, N.Y., 1949-52; asst. prof. psychology Hunter Coll., N.Y.C., 1951-66, assoc. prof., 1966-77, coordinator of counseling services, 1959-71; research dir. Klein Inst. for Aptitude Testing, Inc., N.Y.C., 1953-59, asst. v.p., 1957-59; pvt. practice in psychotherapy, 1964—. Trustee Alfred Adler Inst.; v.p. bd. trustees Ch. of Healing Christ (Emmet Fox Ch.), N.Y.C. Mem. AAAS, Am. Assn. Counseling & Devel., Am. Psychol. Assn., Am. Statis. Assn., Am. Group Psychotherapy Assn., N.Y. Soc. Clin. Psychologists. Author articles in field. Home: 129 E 35th St New York NY 10016-3884

JACKSON, PATRICK JOHN, public relations counsel; b. Grand Rapids, Mich., Sept. 5, 1932; s. Ira William and Edythe Jane (Minnema) J.; m. Isobel W. Parke, Oct. 4, 1974; children: Richard, Kevin, Pamela, Roberta, Jennie. Student, Kenyon Coll., 1950-53; M.Ed., Antioch U., 1979. Dir. sports publicity Kenyon Coll., 1951-52; reporter Grand Rapids Press, 1953-54; advt. dir. Beckley (W.Va.) newspapers Corp., 1954-55; v.p. Jackson, King & Griffith, Waynesboro, Va., 1956-59; account exec. Ruder & Finn, N.Y.C., 1958; sr. counsel, co-founder Jackson, Jackson & Wagner, Exeter, N.H., 1959—; editor PR Reporter, 1976—, Who's Who in Pub. Relations, 1976—, Channels, 1982—; adj. prof. public relations Boston U. Sch. Public Communication, 1973-82; vis. prof. Universidad de Sagrado Corazon, 1990. Editor: N.H. Conservation Directory, 1970-80; co-author: Public Relations Practices: Managerial Case Studies and Problems, 1990. Chmn. Strafford-Rockingham Regional Coun., 1977-78; chmn. Southeastern N.H. Regional Planning Commn., 1976-77; mem. Gov.'s Com. on N.H. Future, 1978-79; co-founder, legis. agt. Environ. Coalition, 1972-83; mem. Gov.'s Com. on Forest Resources, 1981-82; founder, lobbyist Statewide Program of Action to Conserve our Environment, 1968—; founder Environ. Found., 1975; dir. Granite State Pub. Radio; mng. trustee Richmond Realty Trust, 1973—; trustee Antioch U., 1981-88, First Amendment Congress, 1980—; chmn. N.H. Agr. Task Force; convenor N.Am. Pub. Rels. Coun., 1980—; founder, chmn. Epping Planning Bd., 1967-72; pres. Seacoast Region Assn., 1978-82; bd. dirs. N.H. Social Welfare Coun., 1982-85, Youth Communication, Inc., 1985—; mem. bd. vis. Def. Info. Sch., 1986—, chmn., 1989—; trustee Internat. Bus. Communicators Found., 1991—; mem. pub. rels. adv. bd. Ferris State U., 1988—. Recipient Communicator of Yr. award Glassboro State U., 1980, Arthur W. Page award U. Tex. 1984, Vern C. Shrantz award Ball State U., 1982, Gold Anvil award, 1986, Learning & Liberty award, 1987. Fellow Pub. Rels. Soc. Am. (pres. New Eng. chpt. 1974-75, nat. dir. 1976-77, nat. sec. 1978, nat. pres.-elect 1979, pres. 1980, Lincoln award for pub. svc. 1978); mem. Am. Assn. Pub. Opinion Rsch., Nat. Sch. Pub. Rels. Assn., Orgn. Devel. Network, Portsmouth Athanaeum, Delta Kappa Epsilon. Quaker. Home: Tributary Farm Epping NH 03042 Office: Jackson Jackson Wagner 14 Front St Exeter NH 03833-2747

JACKSON, RICHARD SEYMOUR, retired broadcast executive; b. Bklyn., Dec. 16, 1915; s. G. Harry and Mae Vera (Clark) J.; m. Mary French Mathes; children: Richard S. Jr., Mary French Jackson Werbe, James M. AB, Dartmouth Coll., 1939. Salesmen E.T. Sullebarger Co., N.Y.C., 1939-40; exec. trainee Aetna Ins. Co., Hartford, Conn., 1940-42; freelance cartoonist, 1946-47; comic artist, asst. editor King Features Syndicate, 1947-48; dir. spl. events Sta. WAVE-TV, Louisville, 1949-51; asst. radio, TV dir. J.M. Mathes Advt. Agy., N.Y.C., 1951-57, v.p. radio and TV dept., 1957-59; pub. radio sales Robert L. Jennings Assocs., Inc., N.Y.C., 1959-60; producer Jerry Johnston Assocs., N.Y.C., 1960-62; prin. WBEC, Inc., Pittsfield, Mass., 1961-81; chmn. nat. nominating com. AP Radio-TV Assn., 1963. Active trust com. Pittsfield Nat. Bank (merged with the Bank of Boston), 1966-84, also bd. dirs., 1964-84, mem. discount com., 1964-74, 80-84, chmn. adv. com., 1975-80, chmn. audit com., 1975-80; trustee South Mountain Assn., 1968—, v.p., 1977—, pres., 1975-76; bd. dirs. Berkshire chpt. Rec. for the Blind, 1980—, nat. orgn. bd. 1986-87, chmn. bd. 1984-89, chmn. fin. com. 1982-84; mem. various Mass. and Greenwich (Conn.) civic orgns. in the past. Served to lt. USN, 1942-45. Receipient of the Grasshopper award Commonwealth of Mass., 1973. Mem. Pittsfield Club, York Golf and Tennis Club, Dartmouth Club (Berkshire County chpt., v.p. 1963-64, sec. 1986-87, chmn. enrollment com. 1962-66), Lenox Club, Augmenticus Yacht Club, York Harbor Reading Rm. Republican. Episcopalian. Home: 777 West St Pittsfield MA 01201-5726 also: PO Box 78 Starboard Ln York Harbor ME 03911

JACKSON, ROBERT RUSSELL, financial officer; b. Warren, Pa., Apr. 30, 1953; s. Russell H. and Alberta (Ristau) J.; m. Cheryl A. Raffaele, Nov. 30, 1974; children: Nicole Dawn, Shawn Robert. BS in Fin. and Econs., Gannon U., 1974; MBA, Chatman Coll., 1983. Fin. analyst United Refining Co., Warren, Pa., 1975-76; div. acctg. mgr. United Refining Co., Warren, 1976-79, staff acct., 1979-80; mgr., gen. acctg. Bristol-Myers, Syracuse, N.Y., 1980-82; mgr., cost acctg. Bristol-Myers, Syracuse, 1982-84, mgr., fin. planning, 1984-86; corp. contr. Zippo Mfg. Co., Bradford, Pa., 1986-90; chief fin. officer Zippo Mfg. Co., Bradford, 1990—; also bd. dirs. Zippo Mfg. Co. dir. YMCA, Bradford, 1989, treas., 1990-91; co-dir. Walk Am.-March of Dimes, 1989. Mem. Nat. Assn. Accts. (dir. 1976-78, 82-83). Lutheran. Office: Zippo Mfg Co 33 Barbour St Bradford PA 16701-1998

JACKSON, ROBERT SCOTT, artist; b. Newburyport, Mass., Apr. 30, 1946; s. Pauline (Mackie) Jensen; m. Catherine Mary Chaisson, Oct. 26, 1968; children: Matthew, Bryan. Studies with, R.H. Ives Gammell, Williamstown, Mass., 1969, Robert Douglas Hunter, Boston, Sidney Willis, Bennington, N.H.; grad. with honors, Vester George Sch. Art, Boston, 1970. Artist Newburyport, 1968—; owner, dir. Mid. Gallery, Newburyport, 1970-75; ptnr., dir. Jackson-Wetherbee Gallery, Newburyport, 1984-87; instr. Studio of Robert Scott Jackson, West Newbury, Mass., 1975—; guest lectr. Phillips Exeter (N.H.) Acad., 1978. Artist approximately 1200 paintings; one-man show Churchill Gallery, 1991; represented in permanent collections at R.H. Love Gallery, Chgo., Sherburne Gallery, Nantucket, Mass., Wilson Gallery, Nantucket, Pierce Gallery, Portsmouth, N.H. Mem. Citizen's Adv. Bd., Newburyport, 1974. Recipient Silver medal Jordan Marsh Annual Show, Boston, Gold medal-best of show Ogunquit (Maine) Art Ctr., Grumbacher award Ogunquit Art Ctr., Best of Show award Ellsworth Gallery, Conn., Guild of Boston Artists award Northshore Art Assn.; recipient award Nat. Acad. Galleries, N.Y.C., Worcester (Mass.) Art Mus., Fed. Res. Bank, Boston, Allied Artist, N.Y.C., Churchill's Fine Arts, Cape Cod, Mass., Churchill's Gallery, Newburyport. Mem. North Shore Art Assn. (Gloucester, Mass., Guild of Boston Artist prize 1975, 90), Copley Soc. (Copley master, art com. 1984, John Singleton Copley award 1977, 7 other awards through 1989), Acad. Artists, Salmagundi Club, Nat. Exchange Club. Roman Catholic. Office: Studio of Robert Scott Jackson PO Box 125 83 Main St West Newbury MA 01985

JACKSON, SHEILA CATHRYN, storyteller; b. Wichita Falls, Tex., July 12, 1952; d. Fred Mervin and Mary Jean (Freeland) J. BA, Eckerd Coll., 1974; MA, Okla. State U., 1978. Freelance story analyst Warner Bros., N.Y.C., 1985-86, Lightyear Entertainment, N.Y.C., 1988-89, Columbia Pictures, 1989-92. Performed original stories in programs including Mohegan Storytelling Festival, 1990, 91, Home for Contemporary Theatre and Art, N.Y.C., 1990, Cooper Square Theatre, N.Y.C., 1990, 91, Broome St. Theatre, N.Y.C., 1991, Manhattan Class Co., Nat Horne Theatre, N.Y.C., 1991, Sam Houston Regional Libr. & Rsch. Ctr., Liberty, Tex., 1991, Cornelia St. Cafe/Theatre Downstairs, N.Y.C., 1988, 92; sole writer, performer The Aunt Betty Stories, Vortex Repertory Co., Austin, Tex., 1991, La MaMa La Galleria, N.Y.C., 1991, 92. Treas. Arts Coaliton of Ind. Democrats, N.Y.C., 1992. Grantee Poets & Writers, Inc. through The James Irvine Found., Lannan Found., Lila Wallace-Readers Digest Found., N.Y.C., 1992. Mem. AFTRA, SAG, Nat. Assn. Preservation and Perpetuation of Storytelling, Tejas Storytelling Assn., Dramatists Guild, The Playwrights Ctr., N.Y. Storytelling Ctr. Home: FDR Sta PO Box 7554 New York NY 10150

JACKSON, STANLEY WEBBER, psychiatrist, medical historian; b. Montreal, Que., Can., Nov. 17, 1920; came to U.S., 1952; s. Clarence Stanley and Ada D. (Webber) J.; m. Joan Katherine Currie, Aug. 12, 1946. BCom, McGill U., 194l, MD, CM, 1950; MA, Yale U., 1975. Diplomate Am. Bd. Psychiatry and Neurology. Gen. med. intern Royal Victoria Hosp., Montreal, 1950-5l; resident in psychiatry Provincial Mental Hosp, Essondale, B.C., Can., 195l-52; resident in psychiatry Pinel Hosp., Seattle, 1952-54, staff psychiatrist, acting med. dir., 1954-57; diploma San Francisco Psychoanalytic Inst., 1962, Seattle Psychoanalytic Tng. Ctr., 1962; pvt. practice Seattle, 1957-64; rsch. fellow Yale U., New Haven, 1964-66, asst. prof., assoc. prof. psychiatry and history of medicine, 1966-75, prof., 1975—, exec. dir. Yale Psychiat. Inst., 1987-89. Author: Melancholia and Depression: From Hippocratic Times to Modern Times, 1986; editor: (with William Pargeter) Observations on Maniacal Disorders, 1988, Jour. of History of Medicine and Allied Scis., 1992—; contbr. numerous articles to book revs. to med. jours., chpts. to books. Flying officer RCAF, 194l-45, ETO, PTO. Fellow Am. Psychiat. Assn. (life); mem. Am. Assn. for History Medicine, Am. Hist. Assn. Home: 72 Downs Rd Bethany CT 06524 Office: Yale U Sect History of Med 333 Cedar St New Haven CT 06510

JACKSON, THOMAS CLYDE, public relations executive, writer, editor; b. Ayer, Mass., Sept. 13, 1949; s. Wallace Renton and Helen Frances (Suitor) J.; m. Betsy Alice Percoski, Apr. 7, 1973; children: Emma Elizabeth, Abigail Wallis. Student, U. Md., 1967-70; BA, U. Conn., 1972; MBA, U. New Haven, 1987. Recipient Citation for Excellence award AP, 1976, 77. Editor: Nuclear Waste Mgmt., 1981, Public Information Handbook, 2d edit.; co-editor: Coast Alert, 1981; author: (with others) Public Information, 1989, 92. Vestry mem. St. Paul's Episcopal Ch., New Haven, 1986-89; founding pres. New Haven Land Trust, 1984-87; bd. dirs., sec. St. Thomas's Day Sch., New Haven, 1986-88, Fair Haven Hist. Preservation Soc., New Haven, 1988—; mem. New Haven Bd. Edn., chmn. adminstrn./fin. com., 1990—; mem. mktg. com. New Haven Symphony. Mem. Am. Water Works Assn. (com. chmn. 1985—), Pub. Rels. Soc. (v.p. So. Conn. chpt. 1991—, chmn. utilities sect. 1989-90, mem. Nat. Accreditation Bd.), Am. Mgmt. Assn., Greater New Haven C. of C. (chmn. environ. issues com.). Democrat. Home: 334 Front St New Haven CT 06513-3223 Office: Regional Water Authority 90 Sargent Dr New Haven CT 06511-5966

JACKSON, VELMA LOUISE, lawyer; b. Sewickley, Pa., Aug. 2, 1945; d. Matthew Edward and Sarah Frances (Carter) J. BS, Duquesne U., 1968; MEd, U. Pitts., 1977; JD, U. Cin., 1982. Bar: W.Va. 1985, Pa. 1986. Chemist Calgon Corp., Pitts., 1969-70; mgr. lab. svcs. Polytech Inc., Cleve., 1970-76; engr. Procter & Gamble Co., Cin., 1976-79; v.p. F.U.T.U.R.E. Assocs., Sewickley, 1982—; law clk., jud. asst. Orphans Ct. div. Ct. Common Pleas, Pitts., 1985-89; pvt. practice Pitts., 1989—; environ. cons. Creative Mgmt. Systems, Detroit, 1979-81; tech. writer O.H. Materials Inc., Findlay, Ohio, 1980-81; instr. bus. law Carlow Coll., Pitts., 1986—; bd. dirs. Sentinel Fin. Svcs. Inc. Writer poetry; contbr. articles to profl. jours.; developed cut plant preservative, 1975. Bd. dirs. Sewickley Community Ctr., 1983-89, 91—, Group Against Smog and Pollution, Pitts., 1987—; treas. Quaker Valley Dist. Dems., 1984—, commr. Police Civil Svcs. Commn., Sewickley, 1986—; invitee Citizen Amb. Project to India, Republic of China and USSR Internat. Amb. Programs Inc., Spokane, Wash., 1987-88. Mem. ABA, AAUW, Nat. Assn. Colored Women's Club (local pres. 1985-87, state 1st v.p. 1988—), Nat. Assn. Negro Bus. and Profl. Women, Pa. Bar Assn., W.Va. Bar Assn., African Ams. for Self-Determination (co-founder), Am. Biographical Inst. Rsch. Assn. (mem. adv. coun.), Internat. Biographical Ctr., Delta Sigma Theta. Baptist. Home: 339 Little St Sewickley PA 15143-1468

JACKSON, WILLIE LEE, guidance counselor; b. Waynesboro, Ga., Apr. 1, 1945; s. J.D. and Annabell (Holmes) J. BA, Hope Coll., Holland, Mich., 1969; MA, Princeton Sem., 1971; EdM, Rutgers U., 1975; MA, Columbia U., 1989. Dorm counselor Rutgers Coll., New Brunswick, N.J., 1971-74; coll. counselor Livinston Coll., New Brunswick, 1974-83; high sch. counselor N.Y.C. Bd. Edn., 1988—. Mem. AACD. Home: 2790 Broadway # 125 New York NY 10025-2843

JACOB, GARY STEVEN, real estate developer; b. N.Y.C., Nov. 4, 1949; s. Ernest Leo and Anne Sylvia (Lewis) J.; m. Linda Ann Ivanhoe, Aug. 17, 1969; children: Adam, Michael, Alissa. ScB in Applied Math. magna cum laude, Brown U., 1971; MBA, Harvard U., 1973. Asst. to pres. Glenwood Mgmt. Corp., New Hyde Park, N.Y., 1973-75, v.p., 1975-81, exec. v.p., 1981—. Mem. Real Estate Bd. N.Y., Associated Owners and Builders Greater N.Y. (bd. dirs. 1983—), Rent Stabilization Assn. N.Y. (v.p. 1983—, lectr. at seminars 1987—), East Mid-Manhattan C. of C., West Side C. of C. Clubs: Harvard Bus. Sch. (N.Y.C.); Rolling Hills Country (Wilton, Conn.). Office: Glenwood Mgmt Corp 1200 Union Tpke New Hyde Park NY 11040-1708

JACOB, JOHN EDWARD, social service agency executive; b. Trout, La., Dec. 16, 1934; s. Emory and Claudia (Sadler) J.; m. Barbara Singleton, Mar. 28, 1959; 1 child, Sheryl Renee. BA, Howard U., 1957, MSW, 1963; LHD (hon.), Old Dominion U., 1983, Fisk U., 1984; LLD (hon.), LaFayette Coll., 1985, Tuskegee U., 1986, Cen. State U., 1986, Fla. Internat. U., 1988, Dominican Coll., 1988, Howard U., 1990; LHD (hon.), Morris Brown U., 1991, So. Ill. U., Boston Coll. Caseworker, then child welfare casework supr. Balt. Dept. Public Welfare, 1960-65; mem. staff Washington Urban League, 1965-70, acting exec. dir., 1968-70; dir. community orgn.-tng. Eastern region Nat. Urban League, 1970; exec. dir. San Diego Urban League, 1970-75; pres. Washington Urban League, 1975-79; exec. v.p. Nat. Urban League, N.Y.C., 1979-81, pres., chief exec. officer, 1982—; field work instr. Howard U. Sch. Social Work, 1963-65, lectr., 1967-69, chmn. bd.; cons.,

lectr. in field; bd. dirs. Local Initiative Support Corp., Bennett Coll., Nat. Westminster Banco, Anheuser Busch Cos., Nat. Park Found., Bennett Coll., N.Y. Tel. Co., Continental Corp., Coca-Cola Enterprises Inc. Author weekly column To Be Equal, 1982. Vice chmn. bd. trustees Howard U., 1971-78, chmn. 1988-91, chmn. emeritus 1991—; mem. jud. nominating commn. U.S. Dist. Ct. and U.S. Cir. Ct., Washington, 1978; bd. overseers U. Calif., San Diego, 1974-75; bd. dirs. NCCJ, 1983-88, Eisenhower Found., 1984-86, Ind. Sector, 1984-89, Jr. Achievement, 1985-91; chmn. Citizens' Commn. on AIDS for N.Y.C. and No. N.J., 1985. With AUS, 1957-58. Recipient Whitney M. Young Meml. award Washington Urban League, 1979, United Way Am. profl. leadership award, Public Service award United Black Fund Washington, 1979, Achievement award Eastern province Kappa Alpha Psi, 1976, Outstanding Community Service award Howard U. Sch. Social Work Alumni Assn., 1979, Spl. Citation Atlanta Club, Howard U. Alumni Assn., 1980, Hudson L. Lavell Social Action award, Phi Beta Sigma, 1982, Exemplary Servcie award, Alumni Club L.I. Howard U., 1983, Achievement award, Zeta Phi Beta, 1984, Blackbook's Bus. & Profl. award, Dollars and Sense mag., 1985, Nat. Kappaman Achievement award Durham Alumni Chpt., Kappa Alpha Psi, 1984, Bayard Rustin Humanitarian award, 1989, Lifetime Achievement award St. Louis chpt. NAACP, 1991, Equal Justice award Nat. Bar Assn., 1991. Mem. Nat. Assn. Social Workers, Acad. Cert. Social Workers. Democrat. Episcopalian. Office: 500 E 62d St New York NY 10021-8309

JACOB, SHIRLEY ANN, counselor; b. Weymouth, Mass., Nov. 3, 1949; d. John Robert and Dorothy Elizabeth (Shirley) Sheehan; m. Michael Jacob, Oct. 15, 1983. BS in Edn., Bridgewater State Coll., 1971; MEd in Health, Plymouth State Coll., 1981. Cert. tchr., health educator, counselor, N.H. Tchr. 1st grade Weymouth (Mass.) Pub. Schs., 1971-79; tchr. 1st and 2d grades Wentworth (N.H.) Elem. Sch., 1979-81; tchr. 2d grade Campton (N.H.) Elem. Sch., 1981-84; sch. counselor Inter-Lakes Elem. Sch., Meredith, N.H., 1984—; trainer N.H. Comprehensive Guidance and Counseling Program, Concord, 1990-91. Mem. ACA, N.H. Sch. Counselors Assn., N.H. Assn. for Counseling and Devel. Office: Inter-Lakes Elem Sch 21 Laker Ln Meredith NH 03253

JACOBEY, JOHN ARTHUR, III, surgeon, educator; b. Albuquerque, Oct. 27, 1929; s. John Arthur Jr. and Zelma Mae (Wolfe) Jacobey Mann; m. Linda Caldwell Fox Cabot, June 13, 1981. AB, Dartmouth Coll., 1951; postgrad., U. Colo., 1951-53; MD, Harvard U., 1956. Diplomate Am. Bd. Surgery, Am. Bd. Thoracic Surgery. Intern Jefferson Davis Hosp., Baylor U., Houston, 1956-57; resident Boston City Hosp., 1957-58, Dartmouth Med. Ctr., Hanover, N.H., 1958-59, Peter Bent Brigham Hosp., 1962-63, St. Mary's Hosp., London, 1963-64, Baylor Affiliated Hosp., Houston, 1964-65; rsch. fellow Harvard Med. Sch., 1959-62; pvt. practice medicine specializing in cardiovascular and thoracic surgery Denver, 1965-71, 72-76; staff surgeon Cheyenne (Wyo.) VA Med. Ctr., 1971-72; asst. prof. clin. surgery SUNY, Stony Brook, 1977-83; pvt. practice medicine specializing in cardiovascular and thoracic surgery Dover, N.J., 1984-89; clin. instr. surgery U. Colo., Denver, 1965-69; clin. assoc. prof. surgery U. Medicine and Dentistry N.J., Robert Wood Johnson Med. Sch., New Brunswick, 1984—. Prin. investigator, author publs. on synchronous assisted circulation, superior mediastinal exploration. Lay reader, chalice bearer Episcopal Ch., Manhasset, N.Y., 1976-83, Mountain Lakes, N.J., 1984-90, Westfield, N.J., 1990—. Fellow Am. Coll. Chest Physicians; mem. AMA, Soc. Thoracic Surgeons, Am. Thoracic Soc., N.J. Soc. Thoracic Surgeons, N.Y. Soc. Thoracic Surgery, N.J. Acad. Medicine, Am. Heart Assn., N.J. Med. Soc., Mass. Med. Soc., Harvard Club (Boston), Univ. Club (Denver). Republican.

JACOBOWITZ, HENRY GEORGE, marketing executive; b. Huntington, N.Y., Jan. 19, 1958; s. Marvin Leonard and Ellen (Lysanski) J. BS, U. Hartford, 1981, MBA, 1982. Account coord. Stone & Adler Inc., N.Y.C., 1983-84; mktg. mgr. Jan Stuart Co., N.Y.C., 1984-86; dir. sales Gruene, Inc., Beverly Hills, Calif., 1986-88; account exec. Merchandising Workshop, Inc., N.Y.C., 1988-92, Font & Vaamonde Advt., N.Y.C., 1992—.

JACOBS, ALICIA MELVINA, account executive; b. Newark, June 24, 1955; d. Alvin and Melvina (McKinney) J. BA, Oberlin Coll., 1977. Caseworker Essex County Welfare Bd., Newark, 1977-78; sr. audit analyst N.J. Blue Cross, Newark, 1978-80; fin. analyst N.Y. State Office of the Spl. Cont., N.Y.C., 1980-81; account exec. Fortune Temporary Personnel, N.Y.C., 1981-84; sales mgr. Wall St. Temporary, N.Y.C., 1984-85; account exec. Maxwell Macmillan, N.Y.C., 1985-90, Newark, 1990—. Fund-raising chmn. The Africa Project, N.Y.C., 1989—; sec. We Are Family, Newark, 1989—; mentor, tutor Welcome Bapt. Ch., Newark, 1991—; vol. Scott-Krueger Cultural Ctr., Newark, 1991—. Recipient Heroine award Montclair (N.J.) High Sch., 1990, Participant award Madison Ave. Sch., Newark. Mem. NAACP, N.J. Law Librs. Assn., Coalition of 100 Black Women. Home: 289-91 Ogden St Orange NJ 07050-3226

JACOBS, BARBARA FRANK, risk management consultant; b. Mt. Kisco, N.Y., June 17, 1942; d. Howard and Mary (Brown) F.; m. Stewart M. Jacobs, Aug. 30, 1964 (div. 1979). BA, U. Rochester, 1963; MS, Queens Coll., 1970. Tchr. various schs., Eastchester, Scarsdale, Harrison, N.Y., 1963-64, 67-74; editor, coll. textbook dept. David McKay Co., N.Y.C., 1964-65; hosp. adminstr. Downstate Med. Ctr., N.Y.C., 1965-67; programmer Anistics, N.Y.C., 1975-77, project mgr., 1978-82, asst. v.p., 1982-83, v.p., 1983—; systems analyst Blue Cross/Blue Shield, N.Y.C., 1977-78; dir. mgmt. decision lab. NYU Sch. Bus., 1990-92. Editor: The Past Recaptured, 1975. Mem. Am. Mgmt. Assn. Republican. Jewish. Avocations: classical piano playing, jewelry making, bridge, tennis. Home: 4 Field End Ln Eastchester NY 10709-1110 Office: Anistice 220 E 42d St New York NY 10017

JACOBS, CARL HENRY, biomaterials engineer; b. Lewisburg, Pa., Jan. 29, 1948; s. Robert M. and Shirley (Kaplan) J.; m. Anita Issacson, June 28, 1970; children: Eliezer Louis, Abraham Robert. BSME, U. Vt., 1970, MS, 1972, PhD, 1974. Asst. prof. Ga. Inst. Tech., Atlanta, 1974-79; group leader Howmedica, Groton, Conn., 1979-83; dir. rsch. labs. Zimmer, Warsaw, Ind., 1983-89; v.p. mfg. ops. Orthomet, Mpls., 1989-91; dir. quality assurance Osteonics, Allendale, N.J., 1991—. Mem. ASME, ASTM, Orthopaedic Rsch. Soc., N.Y. Acad. Scis. Home: 1504 Jefferson St Teaneck NJ 07666 Office: Osteonics 59 Rt 17 Allendale NJ 07401-1677

JACOBS, CHARLES M., healthcare consultant, software executive; b. N.Y.C., May 28, 1933; s. Lawrence L. and Estelle (Siegle) J.; m. Susan Weagly, Aug. 26, 1979; children: Emily, Jessica. AB, U. Chgo., 1953, JD, 1956; postgrad., U. London, 1958-59. Bar: Ill., N.Y., D.C. Asst. prof., Bigelow fellow U. Chgo. Law Sch., 1957, 59-60; assoc. Paul, Weiss, Rifkind, Wharton & Garrison, N.Y.C., 1961-62; prin. David Sage Cons., N.Y.C., 1963-67; v.p. Aspen Systems Corp., Pitts., 1968-70; assoc. dir. Joint Commn. on Accreditation of Health Care Orgns., Chgo., 1970-75; pres., chief exec. officer InterQual Inc., Marlborough, Mass., 1976—; pres., chief exec. officer MediQual Systems, Inc., Westboro, Mass., 1980-87, chmn. bd., 1987-91; dir., cons. in field, 1991—; lectr. in field. Co-author: Measuring the Quality of Medical Care, 1976, ISD - A Criteria and Review System, 1978—, Surgery Indications Monitoring Procedure, 1982—. Recipient Founder's awar Am. Coll. Utilization Rev. and Quality Assurance Physicians, 1986. Mem. Nat. Health Lawyers Assn., Am. Soc. Hosp. Attys., Am. Assn. of Pref. Prov. Orgns. (bd. dirs. 1988—, bd. dirs. Found. 1990—, editorial bd. 1990—), Amnesty Internat., Friends of Oxford Acad. Office: InterQual Inc 293 Boston Post Rd Marlborough MA 01752-3601

JACOBS, CHRISTOPHER HARRY, marketing consultant; b. Newport, Shropshire, Eng., Apr. 17, 1948; came to U.S., 1985; s. Harry George and Florence (Ward) J.; m. Nancy Post, June 7, 1990. BA in Bus. Administrn., Poly. Wolverhampton, Wolverhampton, Eng., 1969. Analyst, programmer Stafford County Coun., Eng., 1968-69; mgr. retail systems Centre-File Ltd., London, 1969-74; project mgr. Univac Svcs. AG, Sajarevo, Yugoslavia, 1974-76; tech. mgr. Univac Internat. Div., London, Eng., 1976-79; mgr. mktg. support Sperry Univac, London, Eng., 1979-84; dir. mktg. Sperry Internat. Div., Phila., Pa., 1985-86; dir. mkt. strategy Unisys Corp., Blue Bell, Pa., 1987-88; v.p. product strategy Unisys Corp., Pa., 1988-89; prin. Jacobs Internat., Phila., 1989—. Contbr. articles to profl. jours. Office: Jacobs Internat 616 W Upsal St Philadelphia PA 19119-3626

JACOBS, DAVID MICHAEL, history educator, UFO researcher; b. L.A., Aug. 10, 1942; s. Jack Jacobs and Ethel (Raskin) Shinder; m. Irene Diana Schultz, Nov. 9, 1963; children: Evan, Alexander. BA, UCLA, 1966; MA, U. Wis., 1968, PhD, 1973. Asst. prof. history U. Nebr., Lincoln, 1974-75; asst. prof. history Temple U., Phila., 1975-81, assoc. prof., 1981—. Mem. editorial bd. Jour. of UFO Studies; assoc. editor Jour. of Sci. Exploration; author: The UFO Controversy in America, 1975, Secret Life, 1992; contbr. more than 25 articles to profl. jours. Recipient Nat. Abduction Rsch. grant, 1991. Mem. Soc. for Sci. Exploration (councilor 1986-88), Intruders Found. (bd.d irs.), Orgn. of Am. Historians. Office: Temple U Dept of History Philadelphia PA 19122

JACOBS, DONALD WARREN, dentist; b. Waynesburg, Pa., Apr. 6, 1932; s. Donald Ray and Nellie Fayette (Church) J.; m. Diane Jeanette Marshall, June 28, 1958; children: Donald Marshall, Carol Anne Jacobs Nagle. BS, Waynesburg Coll., 1953; DDS, U. Pitts., 1961. Pvt. practice York, Pa., 1963—. Author: Implant Materials, 1961, Esthetic Dentistry, 1970. Lt. (j.g.) USN, 1953-57; lt. Dental Corps USN, 1958-63. Recipient Presidential Achievement award Pres. of U.S., Washington, 1980. Fellow Acad. Gen. Dentistry, Internat. Coll. Dentists, Am. Coll. Dentists, Royal Soc. Health, Pierre Fauchard Acad.; mem. ADA, Pa. Dental Assn. (del. chmn. coms. 1972-83), York County Dental Soc. (pres.), Fifth Dist. Dental Soc. (pres.), York C. of C., Tall Cedars of Lebanon, Masons, Shriners, Delta Sigma Phi, Psi Omega. Republican. Presbyterian. Home: 1265 Detwiler Dr York PA 17404-1107 Office: 2801 N George St York PA 17402-1000

JACOBS, ELEANOR ALICE, retired clinical psychologist, educator; b. Royal Oak, Mich., Dec. 25, 1923; d. Roy Dana and Alice Ann (Keaton) J. B.A., U. Buffalo, 1949, M.A., 1952, Ph.D., 1955. Clin. psychologist VA Hosp., Buffalo, 1954-83; EEO counelor VA Hosp., 1962-79, chief psychology service, 1979-83; clin. prof. SUNY, Buffalo, 1950-83; speaker on psychology to community orgns. and clubs, 1952—; Mem. adult devel. and aging com. NICHD, HEW, 1971-75. Researcher for publs. on hyperbaric medicine, hyperoxygenation effect on cognitive functions in aged. Recipient Outstanding Superior Performance award Buffalo VA Hosp., 1958, Spl. Recognition award SUNY, Buffalo, Spl. Recognition award SUNY, 1971; W.L. McKnight award Miami Heart Inst., 1972; Adminstrs. commendation VA, 1974; Dirs. commendation VA Med. Center, Buffalo, 1978; Disting. Alumni award SUNY, Buffalo, 1983; named Woman of Yr. Bus. and Profl. Women's Clubs, Buffalo, 1973. Mem. Am. Psychol. Assn., Eastern Psychol. Assn., N.Y. State Psychol. Assn., Am. Group Psychotherapy Assn., Am. Soc. Group Psychotherapy and Psychodrama, Psychol. Assn. Western N.Y. (Disting. Achievement award 1976), Group Psychotherapy Assn. Western N.Y., Undersea Med. Soc., Sigma Xi. Home: 221 Pleasant Ave N, Ridgeway, ON Canada L0S 1N0

JACOBS, ELI S., computer equipment company executive, professional baseball team executive; b. Cambridge, Mass.. Grad., Yale U., 1959, Yale Law Sch., 1964. Chmn. bd. Memorex-Telex, Balt. Orioles, 1989—; pvt. practice E S Jacobs & Co, N.Y.C.; bd. dirs. Times Mirror Co. With AUS. Office: E S Jacobs & Co Seagram Bldg 18th Fl 375 Park Ave New York NY 10152*

JACOBS, EUGENE GARDNER, psychiatrist, psychoanalyst, educator; b. Providence, Jan. 3, 1926; s. E. Gardner and Edna Jacobs; m. Alice L. Smith, Apr. 12, 1951 (div. 1980); children: Susan, Nancy, John, Peter; m. Mary A. Maher, Dec. 20, 1988. AB, Yale U., 1948; MD, U. Pa., 1952. Diplomate Am. Bd. Psychiatry and Neurology. Intern Pa. Hosp., Phila., 1952-53; resident Neurol. Inst. N.Y., N.Y.C., 1953-54; rsch. fellow Columbia U., N.Y.C., 1954-55; resident N.Y. State Psychiat. Inst., Columbia Presbyn. Hosp., N.Y.C., 1955-58; staff psychiatrist Inst. of Pa. Hosp., Phila., 1958-62, sr. attending psychiatrist, 1974—; chief psychiatrist Student Health Svc., Temple U., Phila., 1973-77; chief dept. psychiatry Phila. Naval Hosp., 1981-85; assoc. clin. prof. Hahnemann U., Phila., 1981—; pvt. practice Phila., 1958—. Mem. Drs. Symphony Orch., Phila., 1982—. Capt. USNR. Fellow Am. Psychiat. Assn. (life); mem. AMA, Phila. Assn. for Psychoanalysis, Am. Psychoanalytic Assn., Phila. Psychiat. Soc. Home: 5400 Wissahickon Ave Philadelphia PA 19144-5223 Office: 111 N 49th St Philadelphia PA 19139-2718

JACOBS, FLORA GILL, museum director; b. Washington, Dec. 22, 1918; d. Morris Hilliard and Dora (Seidenman) G.; m. Ephraim Jacobs, Sept. 8, 1940; 1 child, Amanda Bolling. Student, George Washington U., 1936-40. Asst. editor woman's/fashion pages Washington Times-Herald, Washington, 1940-42, editor woman's/fashion pages, 1942-43; founder, dir. Washington Doll's House and Toy Mus., Washington, 1975—. Author: A History of Dolls' Houses, 1953, rev. edit., 1965, Dolls' Houses in America, 1975, Victorian Dolls' Houses, 1967, four juvenile books. Recipient Crystal award Internat. Guild Miniature Artisans 1991. Mem. Mystery Writers of Am., Author's Guild, Children's Book Guild of Washington (past pres.), Nat. Press Club, Newswoman's Club. Democrat. Home: 16 W Kirke St Chevy Chase MD 20815-4246 Office: Washington Dolls House & Toy Mus 5236 44th St NW Washington DC 20015-2182

JACOBS, JACK EDMOND, computer company executive; b. Jersey City, N.J., Dec. 24, 1948; s. Benjamin and Shirley (Goldstein) J.; m. Katherine Marie Sheeler, Aug. 26, 1978; children: Caitlin, Daniel, Sarah, Ariel. BS, E. Stroudsburg U., 1970; MS, U. Maine, 1978. Pres. Jacobs Computer Svcs., Closter, N.J., 1981—, Software House of N.J., Hillsdale, N.J., 1982-89; v.p. Applied Systems Tech., Park Ridge, N.J., 1985—. Founder, bd. dirs. United for Life, Closter, N.J., 1991. Office: Jacobs Computer Svcs 330 Demarest Ave Closter NJ 07624-2514

JACOBS, JANE BRAND, lawyer; b. N.Y.C., Sept. 20, 1940; d. Alexander Byron and Katherine (Brammer) Brand; divorced; 1 child, Alexander Byron. BA, Swarthmore Coll., 1962; LLB magna cum laude, Columbia U., 1965. Assoc. Patterson, Belknap, Webb & Tyler, N.Y.C., 1965-70, 72, ptnr., 1973—; assoc. Graham & James, San Francisco, 1971. Sec., exec. com. Family Dynamics, Inc., N.Y.C., 1989. Mem. State Bar Calif., N.Y. State Bar, Assn. Bar City N.Y. (lectures and continuing edn. com. 1985-88, 89—), Rockefeller Ctr. Club, N.Y. Lawn Bowling Club (v.p. 1992—). Democrat. Episcopalian. Home: 160 W End Ave Apt 19D New York NY 10023-5601 Office: Patterson Belknap Webb & Tyler 30 Rockefeller Ctr New York NY 10112-0002

JACOBS, JEFFREY LEE, lawyer; b. Boston, Jan. 20, 1951; s. Philip and Millicent T. (Katz) J.; m. Deborah R. Rath, June 7, 1981; children: Alison, Hannah. BA, U. Pa., 1973; MPA, U. So. Calif., 1979; JD, Pace U., 1985. Bar: Conn. 1985, N.Y. 1988. Asst. to comptroller gen. U.S. Gen. Acctg. Office, Washington, 1976-80; sr. rsch. assoc. Nat. Acad. Pub. Adminstrn., Washington, 1980-83; dir. of seminars Prentice Hall, Clifton, N.J., 1985-87; pres. TV Edn. Network, Inc., N.Y.C., 1987—; lectr. Ga. Tax Inst., Ohio Fed. Tax Inst. Co-author: GAO: Government Accountability, 1979; producer, writer TV series The CPA Report, 1988-91; producer, writer radio series Legal Practice Alert, 1990—. Mem. ABA (taxation sect.). Home: 16 Janson Dr Westport CT 06880-2568 Office: TV Edn Network 1270 Ave of the Americas New York NY 10020-1700

JACOBS, JEREMY M., diversified holding company executive, hockey team owner; m. Margaret Jane Davis; 6 children. DHL (hon.), Canisius Coll. Chmn., c.e.o. Del. North Cos., Buffalo, NY; former owner Cin. Royals Basketball team; owner, gov. Boston Bruins, NHL, 1975—; owner Boston Garden, 1975—. active with United Way, NCCJ. Office: Del North Cos 1 Del North Plz 438 Main St Buffalo NY 14202*

JACOBS, JOHN WILLIAM, psychiatrist; b. Washington, Dec. 27, 1943; s. Arthur Theodore and Marcia Alexandria (Fox) J.; m. Peri Pike; 1 child, Seth Jordan; m. Vivian F. Diller, Jan. 11, 1986; children: Jordana, Gideon. BA, Brandeis U., 1965; MD, Albert Einstein Coll. Medicine, 1969. Resident in psychiatry Albert Einstein Coll. Medicine, Bronx, N.Y., 1970-73; fellow in liaison psychiatry Montefiore Med. Ctr., Bronx, 1973-75, dir. outpatient dept., 1977-82; dir. psychiat. residency tng. Montefiore Med. Ctr., 1982-87; dir. postgrad. psychotherapy tng. program Albert Einstein Coll. Medicine, 1987-91; pvt. practice, N.Y.C., 1973—. Author: Fatherhood and Divorce, 1986; contbr. articles to profl. jours. Fellow Am. Orthopsychiat. Assn.; mem. Am. Psychiat. Assn., Soc. for Liaison Psychiatry, Am. Family Therapists Assn. Office: 40 E 89th St Apt 7F New York NY 10128-1220

JACOBS, JOSEPH JAMES, lawyer, communications company executive; b. Toronto, Ont., Can., Mar. 18, 1925; came to U.S., 1925; s. Sidney and Hildred Veronica (Greenberg) J.; m. Carole Evelyn Bent, Jan. 22, 1946 (div. 1972); children—Carole Lynn Urgenson, Joseph James III; m. Edna Mae Meincke, Jan. 5, 1973. J.D., Tulane U., 1950. Bar: La. 1950, N.Y. 1951, U.S. Dist. Ct. (so. dist.) N.Y. 1953, U.S. Ct. Mil. Appeals 1953, U.S. Ct. Appeals (2d cir.) 1977, U.S. Ct. Appeals (D.C. cir.) 1980. Assoc. Proskauer, Rose, Goetz & Mendelsohn, N.Y.C., 1950-53; asst. gen. counsel, asst. to pres. Am. Broadcasting Co., N.Y.C., 1954-60; gen. atty. Metromedia, Inc., N.Y.C., 1960-61; dir. program and talent negotiations United Artists TV, Inc., 1961-66; atty. United Artists Corp., N.Y.C., 1966-69; v.p., counsel United Artists Broadcasting, Inc., N.Y.C., 1969-71; gen. atty. ITT World Communications Inc., N.Y.C., 1972-74; v.p., legal dir. ITT Communications Ops. and Info. Services Group (formerly U.S. Telephone & Telegraph Corp.), N.Y.C. and Secaucus, N.J., 1974-83, ITT Communications and Info. Services, Inc., Secaucus, 1983-87; v.p., gen. counsel U.S. Transmission Systems, Inc., Secaucus, 1984-87, ITT World Communications Inc., Secaucus, 1984-87; of counsel Seyfarth, Shaw, Fairweathr & Geraldson, N.Y.C., 1988-89; v.p., gen. counsel Graphic Scanning Corp., Englewood, N.J., 1989-91; v.p., gen. counsel Ram/BSE, L.P., Woodbridge, N.J., 1992—. Bd. editors Tulane Law Rev., 1949, asst. editor-in-chief, 1950. Served with parachute inf. U.S. Army, 1943-46, ETO, PTO, to maj. USAFR ret. Mem. Assn. Bar City of N.Y., Fed. Bar Assn., Order of Coif. Republican. Jewish. Home: 572 Sanderling Ct Secaucus NJ 07094-2220 Office: Ram/BSE LP 10 Woodbridge Center Dr Woodbridge NJ 07095

JACOBS, LAURENCE STANTON, physician, educator; b. Boston, Mar. 24, 1940; s. David W. and Sylvia Dorothea (Berenson) J.; m. Katherine Elizabeth Meyerand, Mar. 24, 1963; children: Karen Emily, Pamela Susan. AB magna cum laude, Harvard U., 1960; MD, U. Rochester, 1965. Diplomate Am. Bd. Internal. Medicine. Intern Barnes Hosp., St. Louis, 1965, resident, 1966-67; research fellow Washington U. Med. Sch., St. Louis, 1967-68, 70-72, asst. prof., 1972-77; assoc. prof. U. Rochester, 1977-82, prof., 1982—, dir. Clin. Research Ctr., 1977-91; assoc. dean Sch. Medicine and Dentistry U. Rochester, N.Y., 1990—; dir. residency edn. Strong Meml. Hosp., 1990—; researcher in field; chmn. merit rev. bd. in endocrinology VA, Washington, 1983-86; mem. study sect. NIH, 1987-91. Contbr. articles to profl. publs., chpts. to books. Served to lt. comdr. USPHS, 1968-70. Mem. Assn. Clin. Research Ctr. Dirs. (treas., bd. dirs., pres.-elect, pres. 1987-89), Endocrine Soc. (sci. program com. 1983-85), Am. Fedn. for Clin. Research, Am. Soc. for Clin. Investigation, Internat. Soc. for Neuroendocrinology, N.Y. Acad. Scis., Alpha Omega Alpha. Office: U Rochester Sch Medicine PO Box 601 601 Elmwood Ave Rochester NY 14642

JACOBS, MARIAN BECKMANN, corporate professional; b. Teaneck, N.J., Dec. 20, 1935; d. Frederick J. and Marguerite J. (Thoma) Beckmann; BA cum laude (Grace Potter Rice fellow), Barnard Coll., 1957; MA (Columbia scholar, Quincy Ward Boese fellow, James Furman Kemp fellow), Columbia, 1959, PhD, 1963; m. Warren R. Jacobs Jr., Sept. 5, 1959 (dec.); children: Laura Diane, Anita Michelle; m. 2d, Donald H. Norman, Jan. 9, 1975 (dec.). Research asst. mineralogy dept. Columbia, N.Y.C., 1960-63; research asso. Lamont-Doherty Geol. Obs. of Columbia, Palisades, N.Y., 1963—; asst. prof. oceanography Ramapo Coll. of N.J., Mahwah, 1974-76; sr. analyst market and industry research for polymers and spl. chems. ARCO Chem. Co., Inc. subs. Atlantic Richfield Co., 1976-89; mgr. bus. and devel. Environ. and Engring Cons. Svcs. Dunn Geosci. Corp. (name changed to Dunn Corp. Environ. & Engring. Cons. Svcs.), Parsippany, N.J., 1989—. NSF grantee, 1965-66, 66-67, 69-71, 71-72, 72-73. Mem. Soc. Plastic Engrs., AAAS, Mineral Soc. Am., Geol. Soc. Am., Phi Beta Kappa, Sigma Xi. Contbr. articles to profl. jours. Research X-ray diffractions and fluorescence studies deep-sea sediments and particulate matter in sea water. Home: PO Box 572 7 Robin Rd Mahwah NJ 07430 Office: Dunn Corp Environ & Engring Consulting Svcs 35 Waterview Blvd Parsippany NJ 07054-1111

JACOBS, MICHAEL AARON, orthopedic surgeon; b. Newark, Oct. 30, 1953; s. Abraham and Minna (Stolar) J.; m. Margaret Berta Bandomir, Oct. 2, 1984; children: Joshua, Benjamin, Matthew. BS, Bowdoin Coll., 1975; MD, Columbia U., 1979. Intern gen. surgery Hosp. U. Pa., Phila., 1979-80; resident gen. surgery Bryn Mawr (Pa.) Hosp., 1980-81; resident orthopedic surgery Combined Harvard Program, Boston, 1981-85; fellow Johns Hopkins U., Balt., 1985-86, asst. prof. Sch. Medicine, 1986-90; pvt. practice Clin. Assocs., P.A., Balt., 1991—. Editorial assoc. Jour. Arthroplasty, 1991—; editorial bd. Jour. Orthopaedic Tech., 1991—. Fellow Am. Acad. Orthopaedic Surgery; mem. Internat. Soc. Orthopaedic Surgery and Traumatology, Assn. Arthritic Hip and Knee Surgery, Md. Orthopaedic Soc., Md. Soc. Rheumatic Diseases. Office: 5601 Loch Raven Blvd Baltimore MD 21239

JACOBS, RICHARD MICHAEL, educator, consultant; b. Chgo., May 8, 1955; s. Robert Walter and Mary Frances (White) J. BS, Villanova U., 1976; MA, Cath. Theol. Union, 1983, Maryknoll Sch. Theology, 1982; MDiv, Cath. Theol. Union, 1982; MA, U. Tulsa, 1984, PhD, 1990. Cert. tchr., adminstr., supt., Okla. Instr. Mendel Cath. Prep., Chgo., 1976-78, 82, St. Ignatius Coll. Prep., Chgo., 1981; instr. Cascia Hall Prep. Sch., Tulsa, 1983-85, dir., 1985-90; prof. Govs. State U., 1990, Villanova (Pa.) U., 1991—. Contbr. articles to profl. jours. Bd. dirs. Cascia Hall Prep. Sch., Inc., 1986, Denmar, Inc., Tulsa, 1989. Mem. ASCD, Am. Edn. Rsch. Assn., Augustinian Secondary Edn. Assn., Nat. Assn. Secondary Sch. Prins., Nat. Cath. Edn. Assn., Nat. Mid. Sch. Assn., North Ctrl. Assn. Colls. and Secondary Schs., Am. Mgmt. Assn., Assn. Mgmt., U. Coun. Edn. Adminstr., Phi Delta Kappa, Kappa Delta Pi (treas. 1988-89, pres.-elect 1989-90, pres. 1990). Home: Austin Hall Villanova PA 19085 Office: Villanova U Dept Ednl Adminstrn Villanova PA 19085

JACOBS, RICHARD MOSS, consulting engineer; b. N.Y.C., Jan. 19, 1925; s. Joseph and Rhoda E. (Levine) J.; m. Esther Rosalyn Siegal, Dec. 19, 1948; children: George Howard, Miriam Wendy, Robert Allan. BS in Indsl. Engring., Syracuse U., 1949, MS in Indsl. Engring., 1952. Registered profl. engr., N.J., Calif., cert. safety profl., quality engr., reliability engr. Mgr. reliability engring. RCA, Moorestown, N.J., 1951-59; mgr. reliabity, quality control, safety Sylvania Electric, Waltham, Mass., 1959-63; asst. dir. reliability Westinghouse Electric Co., Pitts., 1963-69; prof. indsl. engring. N.J. Inst. Tech., Newark, 1969-77; pres. Cons. Services Inst., Inc., Livingston, N.J., 1970—; mem. faculty Syracuse U., Villanova U., Drexel U., Boston U., Air Force Inst. Tech.; past internat. sec. reliability com. Internat. Electrotech. Commn., U.S. chief del., chmn. Formal Design Rev., Com., 1969—. Mem. editorial rev. bd. Reliability Transactions IEEE, Microelectronics and Reliability. Served with USN, 1943-46. Fellow Am. Soc. Quality Control, Israel Soc. for Quality Assurance; mem. IEEE (former sec. reliability group), ANSI, ASME, ASTM, Am. Soc. Safety Engrs. (chmn. safety engring. and risk analysis div. 1991-92). Democrat. Jewish. Office: Cons Svcs Inst Inc 651 W Mt Pleasant Ave Livingston NJ 07039-1609

JACOBS, RITA DIANE, English educator; b. N.Y.C., May 12, 1946; d. Morris M. and Charlotte (Bleier) J. BA, Queens Coll., N.Y.C., 1967; MA, U. Pa., 1968, PhD, 1974. Instr. to prof. English Montclair State Coll., Upper Montclair, N.J., 1971—; exec. asst. to pres. and chancellor Coll. of S.I. and CUNY, 1979-80; vis. assoc. prof. NYU, 1981; bd. dirs. Nat. Asian Am. Theatre Co., 1988—; cons. in field. Editorial and rsch. coord.: A Day in the Life of America, 1986, A Day in the Life of Japan, 1985; contbr. articles to profl. jours. Writer Bill Bradley for U.S. Senate campaign, N.J., 1990; active Woodstock Guild. Rockefeller Found. fellow, 1974-76, Am. Coun. on Edn. fellow, 1979-80. Mem. Columbia U. Am. Civilization Seminar (chair 1982-84), Lotos Club. Office: Montclair State Coll Upper Montclair NJ 07043

JACOBS, ROBERT ALAN, rabbi, institute administrator; b. Bklyn., Aug. 29, 1948; s. David R. and Jane (Heller) J.; m. Sylvia M. Guenzburger, June 14, 1970; children: Laurence, Stephanie. BA, NYU, 1970; MA in Hebrew Letters, Hebrew Union Coll., 1973. Ordained rabbi, 1975. Rabbi Temple Beth El, Salinas, Calif., 1975-79; asst. rabbi Temple Emanuel of Great Neck, N.Y., 1979-82; rabbi Temple Emanuel of Long Beach, N.Y., 1982-89; dep. dir. Leo Baeck Inst., N.Y.C., 1989, exec. dir., 1990—; rabbi Congregation

Agudas Achim, Livingston Manor, N.Y., 1990—. Mem. Assn. Reform Zionists Am. (life, nat. bd. dirs. 1989—), Cen. Conf. Am. Rabbis, N.Y. Bd. Rabbis (life, bd. govs. 1987—). Office: Leo Baeck Inst Inc 129 E 73d St New York NY 10021

JACOBSEN, GLENN MICHAEL, social work educator, administrator; b. Oelwein, Iowa, July 29, 1946; s. Glenn William and Jean Marie (Roske) J.; m. Barbara Elaine Marsh; children: Erich, Dain, Amy. BGS, U. Iowa, 1973, MSW, 1974, PhD, 1984. Exec. dir. Willow Creek Neighborhood Ctr., Iowa City, Iowa, 1975-77; instr. U. Iowa, Iowa City, 1978-81; asst. prof. U. Iowa, 1981-87; assoc. prof., chairperson Niagara University, N.Y., 1987-91; assoc. prof., program dir. BSW Del. State Coll., Cover, 1991—; cons. People's Place II, Milford, Del., Del. Adolescent Program, Wilmington, Niagara County Family Violence Project, 1990-91, Mid-Eastern Iowa Mental Health Ctr., Iowa City, 1983-84, Voluntary Action Coun., West Liberty, Iowa, 1979-83, Iowa Dept. Human Svcs., Tama (Iowa) County Mental Health Ctr., Wheatland Involvement Ctr., others; program chair Rural Mental Health Symposium, Dubuque, Iowa, Issues in Rural Human Svcs., Iowa City; co-chair program devel. com., chair edn. com. rural social svcs. adv. com. N.Y. State Dept. Social Svcs., Albany, 1989-91; exec. com., treas., registrar 15th Nat. Inst. on Social Work and Human Svcs. in Rural Areas, SUNY, Fredonia, N.Y., 1989-90; planning com. rural human svcs. N.Y. State Dept. Social Svcs., Ithaca, N.Y., 1988-89; Iowa steering com., Kansas State U., 1987, others. Co-editor: (juried proceedings) 23rd Ann. Conf. N.Y. State Social Work Edn. Assn., 1991, 15th Nat. Inst. on Social work in Rural Areas, 1991, others; guest editor Human Svcs. in the Rural Environment, 1991; reviewer book chptrs.; contbr. articles to juried proceedings and scholarly jours. Bd. dirs. Cedar County Coordinated Child Care, Tipton, Iowa, 1977-78, Willow Creek Neighborhood Ctr., Iowa City, 1983-85; co-founder N.Y. Rural Human Svcs. Coalition, 1988-91, steering com. recipient Meritorious Svc. award U. Mo., 1986. Mem. Assn. on Community Orgn. and Social Adminstrn. (co-chair), Nat. Assn. Social Workers (bd. dirs., rural social work task force 1983-85, planning com. Iowa chptr. 1979, project dir. N.Y. chptr. 1990), N.Y. State Social Work Edn. Assn. (registrar, conf. planning com., treas. 1987—), Am. Pub. Welfare Assn. (steering com., chair svc. delivery track central states conf. 1979).

JACOBSEN, JULIA MILLS, educational administrator; b. Princeton, N.J., July 26, 1923; d. Alan Balch and Mary (Handlan) Mills; m. Lawrence Jacobsen, Sept. 7, 1945; children: John Lawrence, Mary Mills Brintnall. AB, Sweet Briar (Va.) Coll., 1945. Tchr, dir. alumnae and devel. Holton-Arms Sch., Wshington, 1954-62; pres. Baker, Jacobsen and Sanders, Inc., Washington, 1962-65; exec. v.p. Edutech, Inc., Washington, 1965-67; dir. govt. rels. and sponsored programs Sweet Briar Coll., 1967-90; spl. asst. rsch./contracts and grants Washington office U. So. Calif., 1979-82; v.p., dir. Assn. Affiliated Coll. and Univ. Offices, 1978—; mem. Va. State adv. coun. Community Svc. and Continuing Edn., 1977-80; mem. R&D adv. com. Va. Coun. Higher Edn., 1972-80; pres. Coll.-Univ. Resource Inst., 1982-88, chmn. bd. dirs., 1989—; cons. in field. Contbr. articles to profl. jours. Councilwoman Town of Bethany Beach, Del, 1984—; mem. D.C. Med. Care Adv. Coun., 1973-76; mem. pub. rels. adv. bd. USO, 1978-84; bd. dirs. Vis. Nurse Assn., Washington, 1970-86, pres., 1973-77; appointed by pres. to Nat. Adv. Coun. on Edn. Professions Devel., treas., acting chmn., 1973-76; bd. dirs. Found. for Advancement of Culture and Edn. Indian River Sch. Dist., Del., 1991—. Mem. Nat. Coun. Univ. Rsch. Adminstrs. (exec. com. 1973-78), Soc. Rsch. Adminstrs. (bd. dirs. 1985-91), Coun. Advancement and Support Edn., Jr. League Washington, Sulgrave Club, Fed. City Club, U. Women's Club (London). Republican. Episcopalian. Home: Box 263 97 3d St Bethany Beach DE 19930 Office: 1001 Connecticut Ave NW Ste 901 Washington DC 20036-5504

JACOBSEN, LINDA STALLARD, college dean; b. Noble, Ill., Apr. 17, 1948; d. Silven Leo and Rhoda Rosalee (Rutger) S.; m. James R. Jacobsen, 1968 (div.); m. Richard L. Simmons, 1982. BA, So. Ill. U., 1970, MA, 1975, PhD, 1981. Assoc. prof., asst. to acad. dean MacCormac Jr. Coll., Chgo., 1976-79; dean students MacCormac Jr. Coll., Berkeley, Ill., 1980-83, Thames Valley State Tech. Coll., Norwich, Conn., 1983—; founding mem., bd. dirs. Consortium for Women's Career Devel. and Tng., New London, Conn., 1986-90, pres. bd. dirs., 1988-90; collaborative mem. Coordinated Edn. and Tng. Opportunities Collaborative, New London County, Conn., 1988—. Author paper presentations at profl. confs. Sex equity grantee Conn. State Dept. Edn., 1984-86, gender equity grantee, 1989-94, CETO grantee, 1989-91, Tech-Prep grantee, 1991-94. Mem. Am. Assn. Women in Community and Jr. Colls., Nat. Coun. Student Devel., Conn. Coll. Pers. Assn. Office: Thames Valley State Tech Coll 574 New London Tpke Norwich CT 06360-6598

JACOBSEN, ROBERT THOMAS, precious metal refinery executive; b. N.Y.C., Apr. 7, 1937; s. Ole and Thelma (Holby) J.; m. Arlene Joan Pettersen, July 9, 1960 (div. Jan. 1982); m. Elaine Rochelle Parritt, Jan. 16, 1986; children: Cheryl Denise, Eric Alan. BA in Chemistry, U. Rochester, 1958; MS in Teaching, Columbia U., 1960; PhD in Chemistry, Clarkson U., 1966. High sch. tchr. Lakeland Sch. Dist. #1, Mohegan Lake, N.Y., 1959-62; postdoctoral assoc. Cornell U., Ithaca, N.Y., 1965-67; sr. scientist Sprague Electric Co., North Adams, Mass., 1967-76, engring. mgr., 1976-80; tech. dir. Sabin Metal Corp., Scottsville, N.Y., 1980-88, v.p., 1986—; prof. Williams Coll., Williamstown, Mass., 1969-79, North Adams State Coll., 1975-77. Contbr. articles to profl. jours.; patentee in field. Mem., chmn. Williamstown Sch. Bd., 1972-80. Mem. Internat. Precious Metal Inst. (environ. com. 1986-91), Am. Chem. Soc., Am. Inst. Chem. Engrs., N.Y. Acad. Scis., Mass. Assn. Sch. Coms. (life, bd. mem., pres. 1975-80), Sigma Xi. Office: Sabin Metal Corp 1647 Wheatland Center Rd Scottsville NY 14546-9723

JACOBSEN, THEODORE H. (TED H. JACOBSEN), labor union official, educator; b. N.Y.C., July 27, 1933. BS, Fordham U., 1955; postgrad., Hunter Coll., 1957-80, NYU, 1957-80, Columbia U., 1957-80. Cert. high sch. English tchr., N.Y.C. Tchr. English, N.Y.C. Bd. Edn. (on leave), 1957-86; sec. coun., editor Labor News and Trade Union Handbook, N.Y.C. Cen. Labor Coun., AFL-CIO, N.Y.C., 1986—; mem. exec. bd. Jewish Labor Com., N.Y.C., 1977—, Workers Def. League, N.Y.C., 1986—, Am. Labor ORT, N.Y.C., 1986—; regional v.p. Union Label and Svc. Trades Dept., N.Y., 1980—; mem. adv. bd. Harry Van Arsdale Jr. Coll. Labor Studies, Empire State Coll., N.Y.C., 1986—; mem. adv. coun. for occupation edn. N.Y.C. Bd. Edn., 1986—, vice-chmn., 1989—. Mem. Community Bd. 8, Manhattan, 1987—; mem. nat. adv. coun. Social Dems. USA, Washington, 1987—; mem. exec. bd. Workman's Circle Home-Geriatric Ctr., 1986-89, treas., 1989—; sec. Robert F. Wagner Labor Archives, NYU, 1986—; bd. dirs. Cath. Cath. Interracial Coun., 1987—, United Way of N.Y., 1988—, campaign labor chmn., 1989—; bd. dirs. Coun. on Environ., N.Y.C., 1988—; mem. Transition Ctr. Bd. Advisors, N.Y.C. Bd. Edn., 1991—, Svc. Area Planning Group, 1991—; trustee ARC, 1991—; mem. adv. bd. Vocat. Edn. Leadership Program Fordham U., 1988-91; exec. bd. Friends of A. Philip Randolph Campus High Sch. at City Coll., 1990—; mem. Naval War Coll. Found., 1989—; mem. N.Y. State coastal mgmt. adv. com. N.Y. Harbor Maritime Industry, 1988—; charter mem. Battle of Normandy Found., 1988—; chmn. N.Y. Trade Union Coun. for Histadrut, 1992—. Recipient Cope awards N.Y. State United Tchrs., 1975, 78, Best Newsletter award, 1974, 75, 79, 80, 81, spl. award educators chpt. Jewish Labor Com., 1986, Roberto Clemente award Nat. Assn. for Puerto Rican Civil Rights, 1988, 75th Anniversary Cert. of Appreciation, U.S. Dept. Labor, 1988, Hurricane Hugo Disaster Relief citation ARC, 1990, Disting. Svc. award Italian Hosp. Soc., 1991, 80th Anniversary Exemplar award NAACP, N.Y. br. 1991, Good Scout award Greater N.Y. Couns. Boy Scouts Am., 1992; named Man of the Yr. Jewish Heritage Com. & Educators chpt., 1990, Educator of Yr. Assn. Tchrs. of N.Y., 1986. Mem. AFTRA, NATAS, NAACP (golden life heritage mem.), United Fedn. Tchrs. (editor newsletter chpt. chmn. 1974-86, mem. P.M. staff 1973—, Eli Trachtenberg award 1966, 74, 77, 81, Albert Lee Smallheiser citation 1976), Jewish Tchrs. Assn., Cath. Tchrs. Assn., Internat. Labor Communications Assn., Coalition Labor Union Women, Black Trade Unionists Leadership Com. (man of yr. 1992), Italian-Am. Studies Com., Jewish Heritage Com., Irish-Am. Heritage Mus. (charter), Yiddish Sons Erin (hon.), U.S. Naval Inst., Internat. Platform Assn., B'nai B'rith (teamsters lodge 2201, trustee 1989—). Office: NYC Cen Labor Coun AFL-CIO 386 Park Ave S New York NY 10016-8804

JACOBSON, BARRY STEPHEN, lawyer, administrative judge; b. Bklyn., Mar. 30, 1955; s. Morris and Sally (Ballaban) J. Cert. in drama, Sch. of Performing Arts, N.Y.C., 1973; BA, CUNY, 1977, MA, 1980; JD, Bklyn. Sch. Law, 1980. Bar: N.Y., 1981, U.S. Dist. Ct. (ea. and so. dists.) N.Y. 1981, U.S. Dist. Ct. (we. and no. dists.) N.Y., 1988, U.S. Dist. Ct. D.C., 1988, U.S. Ct. Appeals (2d cir.) 1981, U.S. Ct. Appeals (fed. and D.C. cirs.) 1988, U.S. Supreme Ct. 1984, U.S. Ct. Claims, 1985, U.S. Tax Ct. 1988 and others. Sole practice Bklyn., 1981; asst. corp. counsel N.Y.C. Law Dept., Bklyn., 1981-84; asst. dist. atty. Borough of Queens, Kew Gardens, N.Y., 1984-85; judge adminstrv. law N.Y. Dept. Motor Vehicles, Bklyn., 1985-86, 87—; assoc. counsel N.Y. State Dept. Health, N.Y.C., 1986; arbitrator N.Y.C. Small Claims Ct., 1986—; gen. counsel Amersfort Flatlands Devel. Corp., Bklyn., 1981-82; arbitrator N.Y.C. Civil Ct. 1987—; adminstrv. law judge N.Y.C. Parking Violators Bur., 1987—; mem. Indigent Defenders Appeal Panel, 1988—; sr. adminstrv. law judge N.Y.C. Parking Violation Bur., 1989—; leader Nat. Jud. Coll., N.Y. Mem. Roosevelt Dem. Party, Bklyn., 1984—, mem. adv. bd., 1989—, treas., 1990—; active Kings Hwy. Dem. Party, Bklyn., 1982—, Dem. com. 1986—; active King's County Young Dems., 1985-86; gen. counsel Bklyn. Coll. Hillel, Bklyn. Coll. Student Govts., 1980—, also advisor; treas. local div. dept. mtr. vehicles pub. employees fedn. AFL-CIO; coun. ldr. div. #255 Pub. Employee's Fedn., 1989—, conv. del. 1989, 90, 91; chmn. Bklyn. Traffic Employee Assistance Prog., 1989—. Named one of Outstanding Young Men Am., 1983, 85, 86, 87, 88. Mem. ABA (judicial sect., spl. const. judges traffic cts. com.), Am. Judges Assn. (hwy. safety com.), Bklyn. Bar Found. (trustee, bd. dirs.), Am. Arbitration Assn. (forums 1988—), Am. Judicature Soc., Assn. Adminstrv. Law Judges (pres.), N.Y. State Dept. Motor Vehicles (v.p.), N.Y. State Adminstrv. Law Judges Assn. (pres. bd. dirs. parking violation com., v.p.), N.Y. State Bar Assn. (pres. for DMV, spl. com. juvenile justice, adminstrv. law jud. coms., jud. adminstrn. com.), Bklyn. Bar Assn. (family ct. com., chmn. young lawyers sect., trustee 1991, chmn. adminstrn. law com.), N.Y. County Lawyers Assn. (family Ct. Com.), Bklyn. Coll. Alumni Assn. (gen. counsel student govt. affiliate 1983—, bd. dirs. 1985—), Jaycees, B'nai B'rith, Hillel (bd. dirs. 1983—, gen. counsel 1987—), many others. Jewish. Home: 3232 Shore Pky Apt 6H Brooklyn NY 11235-4427 Office: NY State Dept Motor Vehicles 350 Livingston St 4th Fl Brooklyn NY 11217

JACOBSON, GILBERT H., lawyer; b. Memphis, Feb. 6, 1956; s. Irvin and Edith (Shainberg) J.; m. Shauna Brown, Aug. 23, 1983; children: Yisroel, Esther, Nechama, Mordechai. BBA, Memphis State U., 1980; JD, Touro Coll. Sch. Law, Huntington, N.Y., 1983. Bar: N.Y. 1984, Tenn. 1985, Colo. 1986. Tax cons. Rooney, Pace, Inc., N.Y.C., 1983-84; chief fin. officer Denton Mills, Inc., New Albany, Miss., 1984-85; endowment cons. Coun. of Jewish Fedns., N.Y.C., 1986-90; assoc. dir. endowment devel. Coun. of Jewish Fedns., 1990-92, assoc. dir. planned giving and found. rels., 1992—. Contbr. articles to profl. jours. Founding pres. Torah Community Project, Denver, 1985-86; officer Congregation Adas Israel, Passaic, N.J., 1987—. Mem. Am. jewish Community Orgn. Personnel, N.Y. State Bar Assn. Office: Coun of Jewish Fedns 730 Broadway New York NY 10003-9511

JACOBSON, HAROLD, physical chemist, pharmaceutical executive; b. N.Y.C., Jan. 15, 1929; s. Aaron and Lillie (Berman) J.; m. Charlotte Schindler, May 20, 1952 (dec. Nov. 1970); children: Eric M., David G.; m. Joyce Reznick, Feb. 11, 1973; 1 child, Michael L. BS, CCNY, 1950; PhD, Poly Inst Bklyn., 1959. Chemist Good Housekeeping Mag., N.Y.C., 1950-52, Nat. Bur. Standards, Washington, 1952-55, Nat. Cash Register Co., Dayton, Ohio, 1959-61; mem. tech. staff Bell Telephone Labs., Murray Hill, N.J., 1961-63; sr. scientist, analyst R & D E.R. Squibb & Sons, New Brunswick, N.J., 1963-77, dept. head quality control, 1977-87; dir. regulatory affairs Bristol-Myers Squibb, Princeton, N.J., 1987—; adj. prof. Middlesex County Coll., Edison, N.J., 1967-70; chmn. Packaging Group Conf., New Brunswick, 1990; lectr. various tech. mtgs. Author: (with others) Pharmaceutical Dosage Form: Tablets, 1980, 2d edit., 1989, Analysis of Antibiotics, 1985; contbr. articles to profl. sci. jours. Mem. Am. Assn. Pharm. Scientists (chmn., bd. dirs. N.E. Ann. Mtg. Group 1978-81), Am. Chem. Soc., N.Y. Acad. Sci., Parenteral Drug Assn. Office: Bristol-Myers Squibb Rt 206 & Province Line Rd Princeton NJ 08543

JACOBSON, I. BERNARD, ferry company administrator; b. Newark, Oct. 27, 1933; s. Abram V. and Jean M. (Balis) J.; m. Vivien Elaine Fromer, Dec. 25, 1958 (div. 1984); children: Michael Alan, Karin Elizabeth; m. Jeanne Sillay, Dec. 28, 1985. BS in Engring., U.S. Coast Guard Acad., 1958; MS in Mgmt. with distinction, U.S. Naval Postgrad. Sch., Monterey, Calif., 1965. Lic. capt. vessels of 100 tons or less, U.S. Coast Guard. Commd. ensign U.S. Coast Guard, 1958, advanced through grades to comdr., 1972, ret., 1977; sr. cons. Enviro Control, Rockville, Md., 1977-78; sr. assoc. Booz, Allen & Hamilton Inc., Bethesda, Md., 1978-81, Temple, Barker & Sloane Inc., Lexington, Mass., 1982-88; gen. mgr. North Ferry Co. Inc., Shelter Island, N.Y., 1988—, Shelter Island Hts. Property Owners Corp., 1988—; co-chair sub. com. on ferry ops. Transp. Rsch. Bd., Washington, 1975-90. Contbr. articles to profl. jours. Decorated Coast Guard Commendation medal (2). Mem. Nat. Assn. Passenger Vessel Owners (rsch. com. 1991—), Lions (bd. dirs. 1992). Home: PO Box 613 Shelter Island Heights NY 11965-0613 Office: North Ferry Co Inc PO Box 589 Shelter Island Heights NY 11965-0589

JACOBSON, LAWRENCE SEYMOUR, television executive producer; b. Waterbury, Conn.; m. Alice Bernhard; children: Marlo, Amy. BA, U. Conn. Exec. producer Jim Ameche Prodns.; exec. east coast prodn. Am. Internat. Pictures, 1977-80; pres. Grosso-Jacobson Entertainment Corp., N.Y.C., 1980—;. Assoc. producer Children's Theatre WNBC, N.Y.C., 1961, Emmy Awards NBC, 1962, Connie Francis Spl. ABC, 1963; exec. producer Jim Ameche Prodns., 1963-65, Carlton Fredricks Program ABC, 1966-67, Water World, 1971-75, The Racers, 1974-79 (creator), Miss Am. Teenager Pageant, 1977-79, Daytime Star, 1979, Comeback, 1979-80, Baker's Dozen, 1981-82, Night Heat, 1983-88 (Gemini award Best Dramatic TV series 1986, 87, TV Guide award Most Popular program, Can., 1986, 87), Trackdown, 1984, Hot Shots, 1985, Out of the Darkness, 1985 (Christopher award), Diamonds, 1985-87, Gunfighters, 1987, Cop Talk, 1989, True Blue, 1989-90, Family for Joe, 1989-90, Counterstrike USA, 1990—, Top Cops, 1990—, Bellevue Emergency, 1991, Secret Service, 1992, Gangsters, 1992, Police File, 1992. Mem. N.Y.C. Film, Theatre and Broadcasting Adv. Coun. (mayor's 1983-90). Office: Grosso-Jacobson Entertainment 767 3d Ave New York NY 10017-2023 also: 8981 Sunset Blvd Los Angeles CA 90069

JACOBSON, LESTER CHARLES JOHN, linguist; b. Rugby, N.D., June 24, 1963; s. Leonard June and Carol (Schmaltz) J. Zertifikat, Goethe Institut, 1984; postgrad., Universitat Trier, 1985-86; BA, U. N.D., 1987; MA, U. Pitts., 1989. Lang. instr. U. N.D., Grand Forks, 1986-87; mng. editor U. Pitts. Jour., 1989; lang. instr. The Lang. Ctr., Pitts., 1989; vis. lectr. U. Lodz, Poland, 1990; doctoral student U. Pitts., 1989—; freelance translator, 1987—. Contbr. articles to profl. jours. Andrew Mellon fellow U. Pitts., 1991, Fgn. Lang. and Area Studies fellow U. Pitts., 1987, 88, 90; Presdl. scholar for study abroad U. N.D., 1985, Nat. Merit scholar, 1981; grantee Internat. Rsch. and Exchs. Bd., 1991, 92. Mem. Phi Sigma Iota Fgn. Lang. Honor Soc., Am. Assn. for Advancement Slavic Studies, Linguistic Soc. Am., MLA, Am. Assn. Tchrs. Slavic and East European Langs. Office: U Pitts Slavic Langs 1417 CL Pittsburgh PA 15260

JACOBSON, LOUIS MARTIN, state and local tax executive; b. Paterson, N.J., Sept. 1, 1935; s. Jacob Isidore and Vera (Rubin) J.; m. Sherry Kershnar, Sept. 1, 1962; children: Nancy Alyse, Pamela Sue, Steven Rory. BBA, CCNY, 1960; MA, Bklyn. Coll., 1965. Employment interviewer N.Y. State Dept. of Labor, Bklyn., 1960-62; tchr. N.Y.C. Bd. of Edn., Bklyn., 1962-67; early childhood program specialist N.Y.C. Dept. Human Resources, 1967-69; sr. human rights specialist N.Y.C. Dept. Human Rights, 1969; dep. commr. N.Y.C. Dept. Ports & Terminals, 1970-73; asst. adminstr. N.Y.C. Dept. Fin., 1973-74; dep. commr. N.Y. State Dept. Taxation & Fin., Albany, 1975-81, exec. dep. commr., 1981-83; dir. state and local taxes Ernst & Young, N.Y.C., 1983—. Co-editor (newsletter) State & Local Tax Report, 1983—. With U.S. Army, 1954-56, ETO. Mem. N.Y. State Bus. Coun. (chmn. tax subcom.), N.Y.C. C. of C. and Industry (chmn. subcom.), NYU State Tax Forum (co-founder), City Club of N.Y., Nanuet Black and Gold Club (pres., Svc. to Youth award 1991), Pearl River Elks. Home: 4 Crabapple Ln Nanuet NY 10954-3614 Office: Ernst & Young 277 Park Ave New York NY 10172-0003

JACOBSON, MELVIN JOSEPH, applied mathematician, acoustician, educator; b. Providence, Nov. 25, 1928; s. Charles and Rose (Chusmir) J.; m. Dorothy Troup, June 8, 1952 (div. Aug. 1985); children—Deborah Lynn, Donald Bruce; m. Corinne Ribner, Dec. 21, 1986. A.B., Brown U., 1950; M.S., Carnegie Inst. Tech., 1952, Ph.D., 1954. Instr. Carnegie Inst. Tech., Pitts., 1953-54; mem. tech. staff Bell Telephone Labs., Whippany, N.J., 1954-56; asst. prof. math. Rensselaer Poly. Inst., Troy, N.Y., 1956-58; assoc. prof. Rensselaer Poly. Inst., 1958-63, prof., 1963-90, prof. emeritus, 1991—; prin. investigator and cons. Office Naval Rsch. Contracts, 1957-93; contract Unisys. Corp., 1985-88; prin. investigator NSF grant, 1962-67; contract Inst. for Naval Oceanography, 1987-91, NASA, 1988-91, U.S. Mil. Acad. (for U.S. Army Atmospheric Scis. Lab.), West Point, N.Y., 1989-91; vis. prof. Rosenstiel Sch. Marine and Atmospheric Scis., U. Miami, Fla., 1963-64, adj. prof., 1969-72; cons. to industry, NRC. Contbr. articles to numerous publs. Fellow Acoustical Soc. Am.; mem. AAUP, Soc. for Indsl. and Applied Math., Sigma Xi, Phi Kappa Phi, Pi Mu Epsilon. Home: 1 Lisa Ln Troy NY 12180-6818

JACOBSON, MURRAY M., chemical engineer; b. Boston, Jan. 2, 1915; s. Robert H. and Charlotte (Moses) J.; m. Madelyn Ruth Marder, June 28, 1962; 1 child, Richard. BS, Tufts U., 1935. Engr. GE, Lynn, Mass., 1940; chem. engr. Watertown (Mass.) Arsenal Labs., 1940-54, chief chem. metallurgy lab., 1955-56, chief materials scis. lab., 1957-62; dep. chief materials engring. div. Army Materials Rsch. Agy., Watertown, 1963-66; chief prototype lab. Army Materials and Mechanics Rsch. ctr., Watertown, 1967-69, chief materials test div., 1970-74; tech. mgr. Jacon Industries, Boston, 1975-90, materials engring. cons., 1975—; mem. Com. on Corrosion, U.S. War Adv. Com., 1942-45; invited panelist Nat. Acad. Scis., 1976-79. Recipient Cert. of Commendation U.S. War Dept., 1945. Mem. ASM, Am. Chem. Soc., Nat. Assn. Corrosion Engrs. (Boston chpt. chmn. 1954-55). Home: 285 Clark Rd Brookline MA 02146-5823

JACOBSON, RICHARD KALMAN, aerospace transportation executive; b. Birmingham, Ala., May 30, 1920; s. John and Sophie (Coplan) J.; m. Alois Reilly, 1943 (div. 1945); m. Ethel Davies, Feb. 25, 1946; children: John, Jeremy, Mary Ann. BS, Samford U., 1948; MS, MIT, 1952. Commd. 2d lt. USAF, 1942, advanced through grades to col., 1958, ret., 1964; sr. dir. McDonnell Douglas Astro. Co., Huntington Beach, Calif., 1964-69, program dir. launch vehicle program, 1969-74, dir. space programs, 1974-80; v.p., gen. mgr. McDonnell Douglas Tech. Svcs. Co., Huntsville, Ala., 1980-84; v.p. bus. devel. McDonnell Douglas Astro. Co., St. Louis, 1984-87; pres., chief exec. officer SPACEHAB, Inc., Washington, 1987-91, chmn. exec. com., also bd. dirs. Decorated Legion of Merit, Disting. Flying Cross, Air medals, Croix de Guerre; recipient Award for Industry Excellence Washington Space Bus. Roundtable, 1991; named Entrepreneur of Yr. nominee, 1991. Mem. AIAA (sr.), Air Force Assn., Am. Contract Bridge League (life master), Huntsville Country Club, Internat. Town & Country Club, Order of Daedalians, Masons, Scottish Rite, Shriners, Elks. Home: 12 Northampton Huntsville AL 35801 Office: SPACEHAB Inc 600 Maryland Ave SW Ste 530 Washington DC 20024

JACOBSON, STEPHEN LOUIS, educational administration educator; b. N.Y.C., June 25, 1948; s. Leo and Anne J.; m. Anita B. Greber-Jacobson; children: Kim, Carrie, Joshua. BA, Bklyn. Coll., 1969; MA, Brooklyn Coll., 1975; MS, SUNY, New Paltz, 1978; PhD, Cornell U., 1986. Spl. edn. tchr. N.Y.C. Bd. of Edn., Bklyn., 1970-78, Renaissance Project, Ellenville, N.Y., 1978-82; rsch. asst. Cornell U., Ithaca, N.Y., 1982-86; asst. prof. ednl. adminstrn. SUNY, Buffalo, 1986—. Author: Educational Leadership in an Age of Reform, 1990; contbr. articles to profl. jours. Office: SUNY 471 Baldy Hall Buffalo NY 14260

JACOBUS, MARTIN KARL, sales executive; b. St. Louis, Oct. 4, 1951; s. Fred D. and Patty L. (Brown) J.; m Jennifer P. Jacobus, Jan. 18, 1973; children: Jason, Seth, Tyler, Cole. BS in Edn., U. Tenn., 1974; MS in Edn., So. Ill. U., 1977, postgrad., 1978-80. Tchr., coach Sparta (Ill.) High Sch., 1974-78, athletic dir., 1978-81; customer svc. rep. World Color Press, Mt. Vernon, Ill., 1981-84; sales exec. World Color Press, N.Y.C., 1984-86, mgr. sales planning, 1986-87, dir. mktg., 1987-89, v.p. mktg., 1989-90, v.p. sales, 1990—. Mem. Gravure Assn. Am. Republican. Lutheran. Office: World Color Press Inc 600 3d Ave New York NY 10016

JACOBY, ALBERTA PETRIE, television producer; b. Worthington, Minn., Sept. 1, 1911; d. Stelle S. and Blanche (Petrie) Smith; m. Kenneth Haycraft (div. 1937); m. Thomas Fair Neblett (div. 1941); m. Oscar Altman (div. 1949); m. Irving Jacoby (dec. 1985); children: Clair, Sara, Peter, Leslie, Tamar, Oren. BS summa cum laude, U. Minn., 1936, M, Yale U., 1967. Reporter Mpls. Star, 1935-36; prof. golfer Women's Tour, 1937-39; writer U.S. Dept. Justice, Washington, 1940-41, U.S. Office War Info., Washington, 1942-44; assoc. dir. communications USPHS, Washington, 1945-48; dir. communications NIMH, Washington, 1949-51; exec. dir. communications Mental Health Film Bd., N.Y.C., 1952—; asst. prof. communications Yale U., New Haven, 1967—; ind. tv producer New Haven, 1975—; cons. Nat. Conf. Social Workers, Am. Psychiat. Assn., Pres. Com. on Handicapped, Group for Advancement of Psychiatry. Producer 25 films on mental health, 1954— (Golden Eagle, cert. excellence). Mem. Yale Club, Mid Ocean Club, Phi Beta Kappa. Home: 1 Moose Hill Rd Guilford CT 06437-2358

JACOBY, HENRY DONNAN, economist, educator; b. Dallas, June 25, 1935; s. Henry Harris and Margaret Cameron (Miller) J.; m. Martha Hughes Jacoby, Apr. 4, 1959; children—Daniel Donnan, Caroline Hughes. B.S. in Mech. Engring, U. Tex., Austin, 1957; Ph.D. in Econ, Harvard U., 1967. Systems analyst Tudor Engring. Co., San Francisco, 1959-61; economist Harvard Devel. Adv. Service, Argentina Project, 1963-65; asst. prof. dept. econs. Harvard U., Cambridge, Mass., 1965-69; assoc. prof. polit. economy John F. Kennedy Sch. Govt., 1969-73; prof. mgmt. MIT, Cambridge, 1973—, William. F. Pounds prof. mgmt., 1991—, chmn. faculty, 1988-91; dir. Center for Energy Policy Research, 1978-83; vis. scholar London Bus. Sch., 1983-84; chmn. Mass. Gov.'s Emergy Energy Tech. Adv. Com., 1973-74; mem. Nat. Petroleum Coun., 1975-83. Author: (with F.S. Brooman) Macroeconomics, 1970, (with R. Dorfman and H.A. Thomas, Jr.) Models for Managing Regional Water Quality, 1973, (with J.D. Steinbruner) Clearing The Air, 1973, Analysis of Investment in Electric Power, 1979, (with R. deLucia) Energy Planning for Developing Countries, 1982, (with R.L. Gordon and M.B. Zimmerman) Energy: Markets and Regulation, 1987. Served with USN, 1957-59. Mem. Am. Econ. Assn., Tau Beta Pi. Democrat. Episcopalian. Office: MIT Sloan Sch of Mgmt 50 Memorial Dr Cambridge MA 02142-1347

JACOBY, JEFF, journalist, commentator; b. Cleve., Feb. 10, 1959; s. Mark and Arlene Fay (Winograd) J. Student, Hebrew U., Jerusalem, 1977; BA with distinction, George Washington U., 1979; JD cum laude, Boston U., 1983. Bar: Ohio 1983. Atty. Baker and Hostetler, Cleve., 1983-84; exec. dir. Mass. Civic Interest Coun., Boston, 1984-85; asst. to pres. Boston U., 1985-87; chief editorial writer Boston Herald, 1987—; columnist Lowell (Mass.) Sun, 1985-86; polit. analyst Sta. WBUR-FM Nat. Pub. Radio, Boston, 1987—; talk show host Sta. WBZ, Boston, 1990—; commentator Opinion Page, Monitor Channel, Boston, 1991-92. Program host New Eng. cable news Talk of New Eng., 1992—; contbr. columns to various newspapers. Exec. com. Cuyahoga County Rep. Party, Cleve., 1983-84; dep. campaign mgr. Ray Shamie for U.S. Senate, Boston, 1984; dir. rsch. Mass. Rep. Party, Boston, 1987; active Brookline (Mass.) Rep. Town Com., 1984-88, Coun. on Pub. Renewal, Brookline, 1986-87. Jewish. Home: 431 Washington St #6 Brookline MA 02146 Office: Boston Herald 1 Herald Sq Boston MA 02106

JACOBY, JOHN BURTNER, university development officer; b. Flint, Mich., Dec. 9, 1943; s. George Alonzo and Ruth Bookwalter (Burtner) J.; m. Victoria Ann Dowling, June 21, 1968 (div. 1985); children: Peter, David; m. Patricia Burton Carpenter, Nov. 23, 1985; stepchildren: Bradford Carpenter, Scott Carpenter. AB, Amherst Coll., 1966; AM, Stanford U., 1971, PhD, 1971. Asst. prof. So. Meth. U., Dallas, 1971-78; devel. officer Amherst (Mass.) Coll., 1979-87, MIT, Cambridge, Mass., 1987—. Office: MIT 77 Massachusetts Ave Rm 10-277 Cambridge MA 02139

JACOBY, MONTE HERRMANN, foundation administrator; b. Alton, Ill., May 23, 1931; s. Philip William and Ruth Mae (Herrmann) J.; m. Nancy Ann Horn, Oct. 16, 1954; 1 child, William Arthur. B.A., DePauw U., 1953.

Employment mgr. Olin Corp., East Alton, Ill., 1953-62, dir. univ. relations, Stamford, Conn., 1962-74, dir. ednl. and charitable trust, 1974-81, dir. external pub. relations, 1981-86, exec. dir. The Deafness Found., 1987; industry v.p. Coll. Placement Council, Bethlehem, Pa., 1972; mem. minority edn. com. NRC, 1975-78; mem. industry adv. com. Ind. Coll. Funds Am., N.Y.C., 1980-83. Author papers in field. Mem. corp. adv. com. Opportunities Industrialization Ctr., Stamford, 1975-76; mem. vol. staffing com. U.S. Navy Dept., Washington, 1972; chmn. devel. com., trustee Xavier U. La., New Orleans; pres. bd. dirs. Boys Town Ill., Grafton, 1965; bd. dirs. Yerwood Youth Ctr., Stamford, 1970, Boys Clubs Am., Stamford, 1970, Nat. Alliance Bus., Washington, 1978, Liberation House, drug treatment ctr., Stamford. Recipient Disting. Service award Alton Jaycees, 1965; Chancellor's Merit award Atlanta U. Ctr., 1972. Mem. So. Coll. Placement Assn. (life mem.; industry v.p. 1973), Am. Soc. Engring. Edn., Am. Sociol. Soc., Coop. Edn. Assn., U.S. C. of C. (edn. com. 1978-79), Conn. Engring. and Tech. Soc. (exec. com. 1978), Sigma Alpha Epsilon. Republican. Presbyterian. Club: Woodway Country (Darien, Conn.). Avocations: travel, water sports, youth work. Home: 350 Hycliff Ter Stamford CT 06902-2022 Office: Deafness Rsch Found 9 E 38th St New York NY 10016-0003

JACOBY, TAMAR, journalist, author; b. N.Y.C., Nov. 28, 1954; d. Irving and Alberta (Smith) J. Grad., UN Internat. Sch., N.Y.C., 1972; BA, Yale U., 1976. Writer, editor Hudson Rsch. Europe, Paris, 1976-77; editorial staff N.Y. Rev. Books, 1977-81; dep. editor Op-Ed Page N.Y. Times, 1981-87; sr. writer Newsweek, N.Y.C., 1987-89, justice editor, 1988-89; lectr. Yale U., New Haven, Conn., 1986-90; instr. The New Sch. for Social Rsch., N.Y.C., 1991. Author articles for Fgn. Affairs, The New Republic, Times Lit. Supplement, The Washington Monthly, others. Fellow Nat. Endowment for the Humanitites, 1992, Alicia Patterson journalism fellow, 1990. Mem. Coun. Fgn. Rels., Helsinki Watch. Home: 7 Gracie Sq New York NY 10028-8030

JACOLOW, MELVIN F., business owner, corporate executive; b. N.Y.C., Dec. 1, 1934; s. Solomon and Gertrude Mildred (Sussman) J.; m. Marie Eisenberg, June 7, 1959; children: Susan, Steven. BA, NYU, 1956; MA, Columbia U., 1957; postgrad., Pace U., 1968. Editor Great Am. Press, N.Y.C., 1957-61, McGraw-Hill, Inc., N.Y.C., 196-269; dir. publs. Am. Waterworks Assn., N.Y.C., 1969-72; creative and promotion mgr. med. edn. div. CIBA-GEIGY Corp., Summit, N.J., 1972-76; pres. Melvin F. Jacolow Assocs., Aberdeen, N.J., 1976—. Staff sgt. USAR, 1959-65. Home and Office: 88 Oxford Ln Matawan NJ 07747-2153

JACQUART, PHILLIP GORDON, field service manager; b. Ironwood, Mich., Mar. 14, 1937; s. Gordon Everett and Gertrude Sylvia (Risku) J.; m. Joanne DeYoung, May 8, 1959 (div. 1986); children: Kendall, Kathy, Robert; m. Patricia Ann Richard, Mar. 25, 1989. Grad. high sch., Ironwood, Mich. Field svc. rep. RCA Svc. Co., Theatre & Indsl. Svc., South Plainfield, N.J., 1969-88; eastern regional mgr. field svcs. Nat. Cinema Svc. Corp., Southbridge, Mass., 1988—. With USN, 1955-59. Mem. Soc. Motion Picture & TV Engrs., Found. Motion Picture Pioneers Inc. Home: 44 Dennison Hill Rd Southbridge MA 01550-3812

JACQUET, YASUKO FILBY, pharmacologist, researcher; b. San Francisco; d. Atow and Fude (Okumura) Matsuoka; m. Royston Herbert Filby, Apr. 27, 1958 (div. 1962); 1 child, Mariko Filby; m. Herve Jacquet, May 26, 1969. B.A., State U. Iowa, Iowa City, 1953; Ph.D., Ind. U., 1962. Research fellow Yale U., New Haven, Conn., 1963-65; staff fellow NIMH, Bethesda, Md., 1965-66; research scientist N.Y. State, N.Y.C., 1966—; vis. scientist Nat. Inst. Med. Research, Mill Hill, London, 1977, Pharmacology Inst., Uppsala, Sweden, 1979, Columbia U., Coll. Physicians and Surgeons, N.Y.C., 1983. Contbr. numerous articles on the mechanism of opiate action and pain pathways in the central nervous system to scientific jours. Mem. Soc. Neurosci., Am. Soc. Pharmacology, Exptl. Therapeutics, Internat. Narcotics Research Conf., Sigma Xi. Home: 200 California Rd Apt 22 Bronxville NY 10708-4427 Office: Nathan Kline Inst Psychiat Rsch Orangeburg NY 10962

JACQUETTE, DALE, philosophy educator; b. Sheboygan, Wis., Apr. 19, 1953; s. Matt A. and Mabel M. (Sass) J.; m. Tina M Traas, Aug. 14, 1976. BA in Philosophy, Oberlin Coll., 1975; MA in Philosophy, Brown U., 1981, PhD in Philosophy, 1983. Vis. prof. Philosophy Franklin & Marshall Coll., Lancaster, Pa., 1983-85, U. Nebr., Lincoln, 1985-86; assoc. prof. Pa. State U., University Park, 1986—. Author (book) Meinongian Logic, 1992; contbr. articles to profl. jours. Rsch. fellow NEH, Bloomington, Ind., 1984, Alexander von Humboldt-Stiftung U., Mannheim, Germany, 1989-90. Mem. Am. Philos. Assn., Soc. for Exact Philosophy, Am. Soc. for Aesthetics, Hume Soc., Internat. Wittgenstein Assn., Internat. Soc. for the Study of Argumentation, Internat. Schopenhauer-Vereinigung. Office: Pa State U Dept Philosophy 246 Sparks Bldg University Park PA 16802

JACQUIN, JILL, employee assistance counselor; b. Orange, N.J., Dec. 6, 1959; d. John Maxwell and Edith (Caffarra) J. B, Northeastern Bible Coll., Essex Fells, N.J., 1982; M Counseling cum laude, Montclair State Coll., 1991. Cert. employee assistance profl.; cert. alcoholism counselor. Operator, tchr. Trans World Radio, Bonaire, Netherlands Antilles, 1982-83; employee U.S. Postal Svc., Pompton Lakes, N.J., 1984—, employee assistance counselor, 1989—; addictions awareness coord. Silk City Youth Svcs., Paterson, N.J., 1990—; substance awareness coord.lor Morris Coun. on Alcoholism, Denville, N.J., 1989—; Essex County EAP counselor, Cedar Grove, N.J., 1989-91; pvt. cons., contractor G&J Addictions Inc., Cedar Grove, N.J., 1991; high sch. addictions cons. County Alcoholism Edn. Programs, 1980-91. Author: The Grapevine, 1989. Mem. adv. bd. Morris Coun. on Alcoholism, 1991. Mem. Nat. Employee Assistance Profls., Nat. Assn. Counselors in Career and Devel., Compulsive Gamblers Assn., Assn. Rehab./Addiction Counselors, N.J. Counselors Assn. Home: 463 Preakness Ave Apt 19A Paterson NJ 07502-1129 Office: US Postal Svc 2d Fl 205 Jefferson St Perth Amboy NJ 08861-9998

JACQUINET, DAMIEN JEAN, corporate executive; b. St. Quentin, France, Apr. 24, 1962; came to U.S., 1984; s. Albert Paul and Colette (Goubet) J. MBA, Ecole Superieure Libre des Sciences commerciales Appliqées, Paris, 1984. Pres. Publicite-Support-Info., Paris, 1982-84; comml. attache French Embassy, N.Y.C., 1984-85; div. mgr. FrancoSteel/DAVAL, N.Y.C., 1985-87; founder, pres. Nida-Core, N.Y.C., 1987—; pres. Eureka-Xelux, 1990—, Aero-Laminates, 1991—. Author: GSP Paris, 1983, Chinaware Market in the USA, 1985. Office: Nida Core PO Box 1571 New York NY 10013-0869

JACULLO, JEAN LOUISE, retail executive; b. Hackensack, N.J., Mar. 16, 1950; d. Peter James and Ines (Rapuzzi) J. BS with honors, U. Del., 1972. Asst. buyer, group mgr., dept. mgr. Bamberger's, Newark, 1972-79, buyer, 1979-84; merchandise mgr. Bamberger's, Rockaway, N.J., 1983-84; merchandise adminstr. corp. buying R.H. Macy, N.Y.C., 1984-85, v.p. merchandising, 1985-91, group v.p., 1991—. Vol. N.Y. Cares, N.Y.C., 1990-91; mem. Met. Mus., Mus. Modern Art, N.Y.C. Mem. Fashion Group, Career Links.

JAECKEL, JAMES CARL, computer services specialist, consultant, educator; b. Montery, Calif., Aug. 10, 1944; s. Harold Richard and Isabelle June (Kennedy) J.; m. Linda Margret Rothmund, June 22, 1968 (div. Feb. 1984); m. Patricia VanderLinden, Feb. 20, 1986; children: Chad, Tamera, Todd. BA, Glassboro (N.J.) State Coll., 1968; MA, Jersey City State Coll., 1972; postgrad., Rutgers U., 1972-76. Cert. tchr., supr., N.J. Tchr. Wayne (N.J.) Bd. Edn., 1968-83, mgr. computer svcs., 1986—; dir. svcs. N.A.M.E., Wayne, 1983—; adj. prof. William Peterson Coll., Wayne, 1989-91; sr. ptnr. Vanell Group, Sparta, N.J., 1983—; cons. for edn. Apple Computer Co., Edison, N.J., 1989—; dir. World History Computer Lab., Woodrow Wilson Found., Princeton, N.J., 1991. Republican. Unitarian. Home: 30 Ridge Rd Sparta NJ 07871-2602 Office: NAME Fallon Ctr Wayne NJ 07470

JAFFE, AUSTIN JAY, business administration educator; b. Chgo., Aug. 15, 1952; s. Aaron and Shirley (Davis) J.; m. Lynn Laiken, June 12, 1977; children: Alexander M., Roxanne L. BS in Fin., U. Ill., 1974, MS in Fin., 1975, PhD in Fin., 1978. Fellow Coll. Bus. Adminstrn., U. Ill., Urbana, 1974-75; asst. prof. fin. and real estate Coll. Bus. Adminstrn., U. Oreg., Eugene, 1977-80; vis. asst. prof. Coll. Bus. Adminstrn., Pa. State U., University Park, 1980-81, assoc. prof., 1981-87; rsch dir. Inst. for Real Estate Studies, 1985—; prof. Coll. Bus. Adminstrn., Pa. State U., University Park, 1987—; Philip H. Sieg prof. bus. adminstrn. Pa. State U., University Park, 1991—; vis. prof. dept. real estate econs. Royal Inst. Tech., Stockholm, 1987-88; vis. scholar U. Amsterdam, 1991; pres. JS & Assocs., State College, Pa., 1987—; advisor and cons. on real estate; external examiner U. Nairobi, 1988, 89. Author: Fundamentals of Real Estate Investment (2d edit.), 1989, Complete Real Estate Investment Handbook, 4th edit. 1988, Analyzing Real Estate Decisions Using Lotus 1-2-3, 1985, Real Estate Investment Decision Making, 1982, Property Management in Real Estate Investment Decision Making, 1979; functional editor: Interfaces, 1987-88; co-editor Jour. Real Estate Lit., 1991—; spl. editor: Research in Law and Economics, 1987; mem. editorial rev. bd. Am. Real Estate and Urban Econ. Assn., 1984-87, Jour. of Managerial Issues, 1988—, Jour. of Property Valuation and Investment, 1989—, Jour. Real Estate Rsch., 1986—, Rsch. in Real Estate, 1988; developer computer software Real Estate Invest Templates, 1987, 88, 91; contbr. articles to profl., internat. and acad. jours. Rsch. grantee Swedish Inst., 1987, S.W. Council for Bldg. Rsch./S.W. Fedn. Rental Property Owners, 1988; Homer Hoyt Advanced Studies Inst. fellow, 1988—. Mem. Am. Real Estate and Urban Econs. Assn. (bd. dirs. 1984-86, 89-91, 2d v.p. 1992), Am. Real Estate Soc., Am. Fin. Assn., Am. Inst. Real Estate Appraisers, Am. Law and Econ. Assn., European Fin. Assn., European Network Housing Rsch., Internat. Sociol. Assn., Nat. Teaching Faculties, Fin. Mgmt. Assn., Appraisal Inst., Urban Land Inst., Soc. Real Estate Appraisers, Beta Gamma Sigma. Jewish. Home: 505 W Nittany Ave State College PA 16801-4059 Office: Pa State U Smeal Coll Bus Adminstrn University Park PA 16802

JAFFE, BERNARD MICHAEL, surgeon; b. N.Y.C.; s. Abner I. and Sylvia (Rothman) J.; m. Marlene Lambert, June 4, 1961; children: Mark Allen, Debra Lynn. B.A., U. Rochester, 1961; M.D., NYU, 1964. Diplomate Am. Bd. Surgery. Asst. prof. surgery Washington U., St. Louis, 1971-75; assoc. prof. Washington U., 1975-77, prof., 1977-79; prof., chmn. dept. surgery SUNY Health Sci. Ctr. at Bklyn., 1979-92; prof. surgery, chief div. surgery Tulane Univ. Med. Ctr., New Orleans, 1992—. Author: (with Behrman) Methods of Hormone Radioimmunoassay, 1980; editor in chief Surgical Rounds, 1989—. Served to lt. col. USAF, 1972-74. James IV traveling surg. fellow. Mem. ACS, Assn. Acad. Surgery (pres. 1978-79), Soc. Univ. Surgeons (sec. 1979-82pres. 1983-84), Am. Surg. Assn., Am. Bd. Surgery (exec. com. 1987-88, rep. to Am. Bd. Med. Specialists 1986-89), Soc. Clin. Surgery, Surg. Biol. Club I (sec. 1982-85), Am. Soc. Clin. Investigation, Soc. Surgery Alimentary Tract (pres. 1987-88), Halsted Soc., Phi Beta Kappa, Alpha Omega Alpha. Office: Tulane U Med Ctr 1430 Tulane Ave New Orleans LA 70112

JAFFE, ELIZABETH LATIMER (BETSY JAFFE), career consultant; b. Washington, Nov. 22, 1935; d. Julian Lane and Virginia Ross (Gillen) Latimer; m. Morton Irving Jaffe, June 16, 1962. BA, Antioch Coll., 1958; MBA, U.Conn., 1963; EdD, Columbia U., 1985. Buyer G. Fox Co., Hartford, Conn., 1963-70, Gimbels, Macys, N.Y.C., 1971-76; dir. corp. bd. resource and ops. Catalyst, N.Y.C., 1977-82; pres., founder Career Continuum, N.Y.C., 1982—; adj. faculty New Sch. Grad. Mgmt. Author: Altered Ambitions, 1991; contbr. articles to profl. jours. Mem. Am. Soc. Tng. and Devel. (bd. dirs. N.Y.C. 1979-84, 85-88, 92—, chmn. 1986-87; nat. exec. com. 1980-82, 86-87, womens network outstanding achievement award nat. 1984), Am. Assn. Counseling and Devel., Internat. Alliance (bd. dirs. 1991—), Acad. Mgmt., Harvard Bus. Sch. Club, Kappa Delta Pi, Beta Gamma Sigma. Avocations: travel; film; photography.

JAFFE, ERIC ALLEN, physician, educator, researcher; b. N.Y.C., Apr. 7, 1942; s. Robert Irving and Ruth (Stern) J.; m. Barbara Ruth Little, Feb. 25, 1971; children: Matthew, Alison. Student, Cornell U., 1959-62; MD, SUNY, Bklyn., 1966. Intern then resident Kings County Hosp., Bklyn., 1966-68; resident N.Y. Hosp., N.Y.C., 1968-70, fellow dept. hematology, 1970-72; instr. medicine Cornell U. Med. Coll., N.Y.C., 1972-73, asst. prof., 1973-77, assoc. prof., 1977-82, prof., 1982—. Editor: The Biology of Endothelial Cells, 1984. Recipient Young Scientist award Passano Found., Balt., 1977. Mem. Am. Soc. Clin. Investigation, Assn. Am. Physicians. Office: Cornell U Med Coll 1300 York Ave New York NY 10021-4896

JAFFE, IRMA BLUMENTHAL, art educator; b. New Orleans; d. Harry and Estelle (Blumenthal) Levy; m. Donald Korshak, July 15, 1935 (div. 1941); 1 child, Yvonne; m. Samuel B. Jaffe, June 12, 1941. BS, Columbia U., 1958, MA, 1960, PhD, 1966. Researcher, curator Whitney Mus. Am. Art, N.Y.C., 1963-66; asst. prof. art Fordham U., Bronx, N.Y., 1966-68, assoc. prof., 1968-70, prof., 1970—; cons. Md. Ctr. Public Broadcasting, 1984-85. Author: Joseph Stella, 1970, John Trumbull: Patriot of the American Revolution, 1975, John Trumbull's Declaration of Independence, 1976, The Sculpture of Leonard Baskin, 1980; co-author: Selections from the Permanent Collection of the Arkansas Art Center, 1983; contbg. author: Genius of American Painting, 1973, The American Revolution and Eighteenth Century Culture, 1986, Art of the Western World, 1989; editor: (with R. Wittkower) Baroque Art The Jesuit Contribution, 1972, The Italian Presence in American Art 1860-1920, 1st vol., 1989, 2d vol., 1992; mem. editorial bd. Am. Art Jour., 1981—; contbg. editor Art News jour., 1983—; contbr. articles to profl. jours. Chmn. grants application bd. Musician's Emergency Fund, N.Y.C., 1985—. Recipient Owl award Columbia U., Virgilliana medal Instituto della Enciclopedia Italiana; NEH fellow, 1973-74; grantee in field. Mem. Am. Soc. for 18th Century Studies, Am. Studies Assn., Coll. Art Assn., Phi Beta Kappa. Avocation: tennis. Home: 880 5th Ave New York NY 10021-4951 Office: Fordham U Bronx NY 10458

JAFFE, MARK CHARLES, retirement counselor; b. N.Y.C., Oct. 6, 1960; s. Bernard S. and Ruth M. (Perilla) J. Student, U. Edinburgh, 1980-81; BA in Polit. Sci. magna cum laude, U. Pa., Phila., 1982; postgrad., U. Conn. Sch. Law, 1983-86. Cert. financial planner, 1991. Page U.S. Senate, Washington, 1977; market rsch. analyst Rsch. in Perspective, Inc., N.Y.C., 1978-81; law clk. Nathan & Eistenstein, P.C., Bloomfield, Conn., 1984-85, Zeisler & Zeisler, P.C., Bridgeport, Conn., 1985; fin. planner Am. Fin. Cons., Westport, Conn., 1988-91; retirement counselor Retirement Counseling Assocs., Westport, 1991—; adj. lect. U. Bridgeport, 1989. Vol. law clk. Conn. Legal Svcs., Inc., Norwalk, 1984. Mem. Internat. Bd. of Standards and Practices for Cert. Fin. Planners, Internat. Assn. Fin. Planning, Penn-Edinburg Exch. Soc., U. Pa. Alumni Assn., U. Conn. Law Sch. Alumni Assn., Appalachian Mountain Club. Republican. Jewish. Home: 11 Spriteview Ave Westport CT 06880 Office: Retirement Counseling Assoc PO Box 169 495 Post Road E Westport CT 06881

JAFFE, MARK M., lawyer; b. Paterson, N.J., Sept. 18, 1941; s. Irving and Bertha (Margolis) J.; m. June A. Fisher, June 19, 1977. BS in Econs., U. Pa., 1962; JD, Columbia U., 1965. Bar: N.J. 1965, La. 1968, N.Y. 1970, U.S. Dist. Ct. (ea. dist.) N.Y., U.S. Ct. Mil. Appeals, U.S. Ct. Appeals (2d and 5th cirs.), U.S. Dist. Ct. N.J., U.S. Supreme Ct. Assoc. Hill, Betts & Nash, N.Y.C., 1969-72, ptnr., 1972—. Lt. USCG, 1965-68. Mem. ABA, N.J. Bar Assn., La. Bar Assn., Assn. of Bar of City of N.Y., Am. Judicature Soc., Maritime Law Soc. Home: 377 Rector Pl New York NY 10280-1432 Office: Hill Betts & Nash 1 World Trade Ctr Ste 5215 New York NY 10048-0499

JAFFE, MICHAEL, material scientist; b. N.Y.C., May 10, 1942; s. Arthur and Martha (Bronfin) J.; m. Kathleen L. Coughlin, Aug. 11, 1973; children: Sean Benjamin, Joshua Brian. BA in Chemistry, Cornell U., 1963; PhD in Chemistry, Rensselaer Poly. Inst., 1967. Rsch. supr. Celanese Rsch. Co., Summit, N.J., 1974-78, rsch. mgr., 1981-82, sr. rsch. assoc., 1982-89; group leader Fiber Industries Inc., Charlotte, N.C., 1978-81; rsch. fellow Hoechst Celanese Rsch. Div., Summit, 1989—. Editor jour. Polymers for Advanced Techs. Mem. Am. Chem. Soc. (chmn. polymer materials, sci. and engring. div. 1991). Office: Hoechst Celanese Rsch Div 86 Morris Ave Summit NJ 07901-3900

JAFFE, MORRY, computer programmer; b. N.Y.C., Oct. 10, 1940; s. Isaac and Molly (Wolf) J.; m. Lou Bronusa, Nov. 2, 1990. BS in Physics, CCNY, 1962, PhD in Physics, 1971; cert. in programming, CUNY, 1982; MA in Physics, Boston U., 1964. Lab. helper N.Y.C. Dept. Air Resources, 1973-78; asst. transit mgmt. analyst Manhattan & Bronx Surface Transit Operating Authority, N.Y.C., 1978-82; cons. Group 88, N.Y.C., 1984-90, AGS, N.Y.C., 1990. Recipient cert. of appreciation EPA, 1978. Home: 65 Park Ter E New York NY 10034-1447

JAFFE, PAUL LAWRENCE, lawyer; b. Phila., June 24, 1928; s. Albert L. and Elsie (Pelser) J.; children: Marc David, Richard Alan, Peter Edward. B.A., Dickinson Coll., 1947; J.D., U. Pa., 1950. Bar: Pa. Assoc. Wolf, Block, Schorr and Solis-Cohen, Phila., 1950-57; sole practice Phila., 1957-59; mng. ptnr. Mesirov, Gelman, Jaffe, Cramer and Jamieson (and predecessors), 1959—; bd. dirs. Regent Nat. Bank. Pres. Reform Congregation Keneseth Israel, 1974-77; trustee Fedn. Jewish Agys. Phila.; trustee Moss Rehab. Hosp., pres., 1977-80, chmn. bd., 1980-84, hon. chmn. bd., 1984—; trustee, mem. exec. com. Union Am. Hebrew Congregations; chmn. United Law Network, 1987-89. Mem. ABA, Pa. Bar Assn., Phila. Bar Assn., Am. Coll. Real Estate Lawyers, Union League, Lawyers Phila., Loveladies Tennis. Clubs: Pyramid, Union League, Lawyers Phila., Loveladies Tennis. Home: 272 S 2nd St Philadelphia PA 19106-3905 Office: 1735 Market St Fl 38 Philadelphia PA 19103-7501

JAFFE, STANLEY RICHARD, film producer, director; b. N.Y.C., July 31, 1940; s. Leo and Dora (Bressler) J.; m. Melinda Long; children—Bobby, Betsy, Katie, Alexander. B.S. in Econs, Wharton Sch., U. Pa., 1962. With Seven Arts Asso. Corp., 1962-67, exec. asst. to pres., 1964; dir. E. Coast programming Seven Arts TV, 1963-64, dir. programming, 1965-67; pres., chief corp. officer Paramount Pictures Corp., 1969-70; pres. corp., also pres. Paramount TV, 1970-71; pres. Jaffilms, Inc., 1971; exec. v.p. worldwide prodn. Columbia Pictures Corp., 1975-76; pres., chief operating officer Paramount Communications, N.Y.C., 1991—. Creator, writer, asso. producer: The Professionals, 1963; exec. producer series for syndication Johnny Cypher, 1965-67; producer: films Goodbye, Columbus, 1968, Bad Company, 1971, Bad News Bears, 1974, Kramer vs. Kramer, 1979 (Oscar award best picture Acad. Motion Picture Arts and Scis., Di Donatello award 1979), Taps, 1981, Without a Trace, 1983, Fatal Attraction, 1987, The Accused, 1988, Black Rain, 1989; exec. producer: film Man on a Swing, 1973, Racing with the Moon, 1984, Firstborn, 1984. Mem. Acad. Motion Picture Arts and Scis. Club: Variety (N.Y.C.).

JAFFE, STEVEN, librarian; b. N.Y.C., Sept. 7, 1928; s. Aaron and Rose (Levine) J.; m. Louise M. Jaffe, Aug. 26, 1962 (div. Dec. 1974); 1 child, Aaron L.; m. Rae R. Jaffe, Dec. 26, 1976; stepchildren: Claudia L. Finneran, Lauren A. Finneran. BA, Yeshiva Coll., 1952; MA in History, Columbia U., 1953, MLS, 1958. Reference librarian Pollack Library Yeshiva U., N.Y.C., 1958-60; librarian U.S. Naval Applied Sci. Lab., Bklyn., 1960-70; corp. librarian Consol. Edison Co., N.Y.C., 1970—. Mem. Spl. Libraries Assn. (pres. N.Y. chapter 1974-75), U.S. Naval Inst., Navy League, Civil War Round Table of N.Y. Club: Edison Camera (pres. 1974-76). Home: 67-15 102d St Forest Hills NY 11375 Office: Consol Edison Co 4 Irving Pl Rm 1650S New York NY 10003-3502

JAFFE, WILLIAM A., management consultant, educator; b. Philipsburg, Pa., June 21, 1938; s. Reuben and Freda (Azen) J.; m. Honora F. Aronow, Feb. 12, 1967; children: Matthew, Robin. BA in Journalism, Pa. State U., 1960; MS in Mgmt., U. Ill., 1962. Lectr., field rep. Gen. Electric, N.Y.C., 1960-61; adminstr. RCA Corp., N.Y.C., 1962-69; v.p., prin. Towers Perrin, Cleve., also Washington, 1969-90; prin., practice leader Alexander & Alexander Cons. Group, Washington, 1990—; adj. assoc. prof. George Washington U., Washington, 1990—. Contbr. articles to mags. Pres. Temple Beth Ami, Rockville, Md., 1984-86; v.p. adminstrn. Nat. Capital Area coun. Boy Scouts Am., 1988—; mem. exec. bd. UJA Fedn. Washington, chmn. pers. com., 1991—. Recipient Svc. to Pa. State award Pa. State U., 1991. Mem. Mt. Nittany Conservance (v.p. 1988—), Assn. Cons. Mgmt. Engrs. (com. chair 1982-84), Pa. State U. Alumni Assn. (exec. bd. 1978-90), Lion's Paw Alumni Assn. (pres. 1986-88), Phi Sigma Delta (v.p. housing corp. 1991—). Home: 9305 Sprinklewood Ln Potomac MD 20854

JAFFESON, RICHARD CHARLES, association administrator; b. Rochester, N.Y., May 6, 1947; s. Simon and Molly (Schulman) J. BA cum laude, U. Akron, Ohio, 1969; MA, U. Akron, 1971; postgrad., U. Cin., 1971-72. Sr. environ. planner Md.-Nat. Capital Park Planning Commn., Silver Spring, Md., 1972-78; coordinator council progs. Am. Planning Assn., Washington, 1978-82; dir. sci. and tech. Ctr. for Profl. Devel., U. Md., College Park, 1982-90; dir. edn. RBA, 1990—; mem. Nat. Employment Commn., Chevy Chase, Md., 1990-92; ind. rsch. supr. Smithsonian Instn., Bombay Nat. Hist. Soc., 1973-76. Creator/editor: Capital Capsule mo. bull., 1983-88; creator/producer: Event and Employment Recording, weekly tape, 1984-92; exec. editor: Capital Comments newsletter, 1985-86; contbr. articles to profl. jours. Mem. Am. Planning Assn. (chpt. v.p. 1978-80, 84-86), Assn. Am. Geographers (pres. 1976-77, mgr. award fund 1982—), Am. Econ. Devel. Coun. (dir. basic econ. devel. course 1984-90, bd. regents 1989-91), Am. Inst. Cert. Planners. Home: PO Box 15282 Bethesda MD 20825-5282

JAFOLIS, STEPHEN NICHOLAS, safety consultant; b. Manchester, N.H., Sept. 6, 1950; s. Spiro T. and Helen A. Jafolis; m. Marietta Vissaracou, July 16, 1978; 1 child, Helen. BSEE, Northeastern U., Boston, 1973. Cert. safety profl. Mem. tech. staff Lockheed-Sanders, Nashua, N.H., 1968-76; sr. safety cons. Wausau Ins. Cos., Burlington, Mass., 1976—. Mem. Am. Soc. Safety Engrs. Home: 42 Trull Brook Ln Tewksbury MA 01876-1052 Office: Wausau Ins Cos 25 Mall Rd Burlington MA 01803-4100

JAGEN, EDWARD JOSEPH, writer, child safety educator, criminal investigator; b. Chgo., July 22, 1949; s. William Ernest Jagen and Katherine (Morris) Donaldson; m. Marie Schneider, May 29, 1967 (div. July 1973); m. Linda Mae Forte, Nov. 29, 1976; 1 child, Dawn. DD (hon.), Universal Life U., 1988, PhD in Religious Philosophy, 1989. Cert. U.S. Dist. Ct. expert for internat. terrorism, drugs, child abuse. Police officer Vice Squad Met. Police, Washington, 1969-70; spl. agt. undercover Anti-terrorist Squad Fed. Task Force, Washington, 1970-74; spl. agt. undercover Fed. Task Force Organized Crime and Racketeering, Washington, 1974-79; spl. investigator Security Info. Br. Police Dept., Washington, 1979-84; pres. Two Eagles Internat., Washington, 1984—; chmn., co-founder Nat. Missing Child Search Soc. Inc., Kensington, Md., 1984-88; writer White Feather & Co. Pub., Solomons, Md., 1990—; creator Good Knight Child Safety Awareness Program, Solomons, 1991—; child safety educator Good Knight Campaign for Protection, 1991—; cons. child abuse prevention ChildHelp USA, Washington and Calif., 1990. Author: A Good Knight Story, 1990, The Quest of the Junior Blue Knights, 1990 (Gabriel award 1990); producer (audio cassette) A Good Knight Story, 1990, (video) Good Knight Child Safety Ednl. Video, 1991. Sgt. U.S. Army, 1966-69. Recipient Investigative Svcs. award Met. Police, 1974, Silver Star for Bravery award Nat. Assn. Chiefs of Police, 1983, Gov's. citation Gov. Md., 1990, For the Love of a Child award Childhelp U.S.A., 1990, Knighthood, 1991, Gov.'s Vol. of Yr. award for pub. safety, 1992, Diamond award United to Serve Am., 1992, commendations Gov. Tex., 1992, L.A. County Bd. Suprs., 1991, commendation in Congl. Record, U.S. Congress, 1991; Good Knight Child Safety Awareness Program month proclaimed by mayors of Washington, 1991, Farmington, N.Mex., 1991, by execs. Prince George's County, Md., 1991, Montgomery County, Md., 1991. Mem. NRA, Internat. Assn. Chiefs of Police, Fraternal Order Police. Home: PO Box 354 Solomons MD 20688 Office: Good Knight Campaign for Protection PO Box 507 Kensington MD 20895

JAGT, JACK, trading company executive; b. New Amsterdam, Drenthe, The Netherlands, Sept. 15, 1942; arrived in Can., 1950; s. Arend and Nancy (Haan) J.; m. Mary Patricia Start, Mar. 22, 1969; children: Gregory Aren, Derek Alan. BA, Calvin Coll., 1969. Client svc. exec. A.C. Nielsen & Co., Toronto, Ont., Can., 1969-73; plant mgr. Jerr Mfg. Inc., Coopersville, Mich., 1973-74; stats. svcs. mgr. Atty Gen. Ont., Toronto, 1974-75; dir. stats. Rubber Assn. Can., Toronto, 1975-79; v.p. trading H.A. Astlett & Co. Can., Toronto, 1979-83, 87-89, pres., 1989—; also, bd. dirs.; pres. H.A. Astlett & Co., N.Y.C., 1984-86. Bd. dirs. Christian Reformed Ch., Christian Reformed Ch. Extension Fund, Clarkson Christian Reformed Ch.; bd. dirs. Work Rsch. Found. Mem. Rubber Assn. N.Y., Rubber Assn. Singapore, Bd. Trade Toronto. Home: 781 Fletcher Valley Dr, Mississauga, ON Canada L5J 2X4 Office: H A Astlett & Co Inc, 8 King St E Ste 1908, Toronto, ON Canada M5C 1B5

JAGTIANI, JULAPA RUNGKASIRI, financial educator; b. Bangkok, Dec. 28, 1957; came to the U.S., 1980; d. Sathien and Apa (Arunin) Rungkasiri; m. Anil R. Jagtiani, Dec. 31, 1990. BBA in Acctg., Thammasat U., Bangkok, 1979; MBA in Fin., NYU, 1982, MPhil, 1986, PhD in Fin. and Internat. Fin., 1989. Instr. in internat. fin. NYU, 1989; asst. prof. fin. U. Calgary, Alberta, Canada, 1989-90, Syracuse (N.Y.) U., 1990—. Contbr. articles to profl. jours. Rockefeller Found. fellow, 1980-85; Alberta Energy Co. grantee, 1990. Mem. Am. Fin. Assn., Am. Econ. Assn., Fin. Mgmt. Assn., So. Fin. Assn. Home: 127 Greyrock Pl Apt 906 Stamford CT 06901-3108 Office: Syracuse U Sch Mgmt 900 S Crouse Ave Syracuse NY 13244

JAGUS, ROSEMARY, biochemistry educator; b. Swanwick, Derbyshire, U.K., Feb. 1, 1950; came to U.S., 1977; d. Alojzy and Joan (Bailey) J.; m. Dermot Cooper, Aug. 8, 1980 (div. Mar. 1984). BSc, U. Coll. of North Wales, Bangor, 1971; PhD, U. Coll. London, 1976. Bursar Imperial Cancer Rsch. Fund, London, 1971-74; postdoctoral fellow U. Sussex, Falmer, U.K., 1974-77; vis. scientist NIH, Bethesda, Md., 1977-83; asst. prof. Sch. of Medicine U. Pitts., 1983-90; assoc. prof. Ctr. Marine Biotech. U. Md., Balt., 1990—. NIH grantee, 1983—, 84-89, NSF grantee, 1991—. Mem. AAAS, Am. Soc. Biol. Chemistry and Molecular Biology, NIH Alumni Assn. Roman Catholic. Office: U Md Ctr Marine Biotech 600 E Lombard St Baltimore MD 21202-4073

JAIN, ASH, environmental consultant; b. New Delhi, Sept. 14, 1950; came to U.S., 1973; s. Gian C. and Prakash V.J.; m. Sangya Jain; children: Rahul, Anish. BS with honors, Indian Inst. Tech., Bombay, 1973; MS, Kans. State U., 1975; MBA, Rutgers U., 1986. Sr. process specialist Stork-Bowen Engring., Finderne, N.J., 1975-78; sr. process engr. Lederle Labs. (div. Am. Cyanamid), Bound Brook, N.J., 1978-87; corp. mgr. environ. engring. Sterling Drug (subs. Eastman Kodak), N.Y.C., 1987-91; program dir. Environ. Resources Mgmt., Inc., Ewing, N.J., 1991—; environ. update conf. faculty Pharm. Mfrs. Assn., Charleston, S.C., 1990, Grand Rapids, Mich., 1991. Contbr. articles to profl. jours. Co. coord. United Way, N.J., 1974-75; active Boy Scouts Am., N.J., 1990. Merit scholar Govt. India, 1969-71. Mem. Am. Inst. Chem. Engrs., Phi Lambda Upsilon. Jainism. Home: 891 Ardsley Ln Bridgewater NJ 08807 Office: Environ. Resources Mgmt Inc 300 Phillips Blvd Ste 200 Ewing NJ 08618

JAKAB, IRENE, psychiatrist; b. Oradea, Rumania; came to U.S., 1961, naturalized, 1966; d. Odon and Rosa A. (Riedl) J. MD, Ferencz József U., Kolozsvar, Hungary, 1944; lic. in psychology, pedagogy, philosophy cum laude, Hungarian U., Cluj, Rumania, 1947; PhD summa cum laude, Pazmany Peter U., Budapest, 1948; Dr honoris causa, U. Besançon, France, 1982. Diplomate Am. Bd. Psychiatry. Rotating intern Ferencz József U., 1943-44; resident in psychiatry Univ. Hosp., Kolozsvar, 1944-47, resident in neurology, 1947-50; resident internal medicine Univ. Hosp. for Internal Medicine, Pécs, Hungary, 1950-51; chief physician Univ. Hosp. for Neurology and Psychiatry, Pécs, 1951-59; staff neuropathol. rsch. lab. Neurol. Univ. Clinic, Zurich, 1959-61; sect. chief Kans. Neurol. Inst., Topeka, 1961-63; dir. rsch. and edn., 1966; resident psychiatry Topeka State Hosp., 1963-66; asst. psychiatrist McLean Hosp., Belmont, Mass., 1966-67; assoc. psychiatrist McLean Hosp., 1967-74; prof. psychiatry U. Pitts. Med. Sch., 1974-89, prof. emerita, 1989—, co-dir. med. student edn. in psychiatry, 1981-89; dir. John Merck Program, 1974-81; mem. faculty dept. psychiatry Med. Sch., Pecs, 1951-59; asst. Univ. Hosp. Neurology, Zurich, 1959-61; assoc. psychiatry Harvard U., Boston, 1966-69, asst. prof. psychiatry, 1969-74, program dir. grad course mental retardation, 1970-87; lectr. psychiatry, 1974—. Author: Dessins et Peintures des Aliénés, 1956, Zeichnungen und Gemälde der Geisteskranken, 1956; editor: Psychiatry and Art, 1968, Art Interpretation and Art Therapy, 1969, Conscious and Unconscious Expressive Art, 1971, Transcultural Aspects of Psychiatric Art, 1975; co-editor: Dynamische Psychiatrie, 1974; editorial bd.: Confinia Psychiatrica, 1975-81; contbr. articles to profl. jours. Recipient 1st prize Benjamin Rush Gold medal award for sci. exhibit, 1980, Bronze Chris plaque Columbus Film Festival, 1980, Leadership award Am. Assn. on Mental Deficiency, 1980; Menninger Sch. Psychiatry fellow, Topeka, 1963-66. Mem. AMA, Am. Psychol. Assn., Am. Psychiat. Assn., Société Medico Psychologique de Paris, Internat. Rorschach Soc., N.Y. Acad. Scis., Internat. Soc. Psychopathology of Expression (v.p. 1959—), Am. Soc. Psychopathology of Expression (chmn. 1965—, Ernst Kris Gold Medal award 1988), Royal Soc. of Medicine (affiliate), Internat. Soc. Child Psychiatry and Allied Professions, Internat. Assn. Knowledge Engrs. (v.p. for medicine), Deutschsprachige Gesellschaft für Psychopathologie des Ausdruckes (hon.), Deutschsprachige Gesellschaft fur Psychopathologie des Ausdrucks (Prinzhorn prize 1967). Home and Office: 74 Lawton St Brookline MA 02146-2501

JAKLITSCH, DONALD JOHN, chemical engineer, consultant; b. Bklyn., Dec. 25, 1947; s. Ernest John and Mary Ann (Rupp) J.; m. N. Chapin, 1971 (div. 1975); children: Maizy, Zoie; m. Marie Theresa Bostic, Apr. 18, 1988. BA, SUNY, New Paltz, 1970; MS, U. Lowell, 1986, DEng, 1990. Chemist U.S. Army Material and Mechanic Rsch. Ctr., Watertown, Mass., 1982-84, chem. engr., 1984-88; chem. engr. U.S. Army Materials Tech. Lab., Watertown, 1988-91, U.S. Army Missile Command, Redstone Arsenal, Ala., 1991—; chmn. civilian welfare coun. U.S. Army Materials Tech. Lab., Watertown, 1988-89; reviewer K-15 com. ASME, 1990. Contbr. articles to profl. jours. Recipient tech. commendation Dept. Army, 1989, 90, 91. Mem. Soc. for Advancement Material and Process Engring., Am. Soc. for Composites, Indsl. Computing Soc. (charter). Home: 153 Cedar Ln New Market AL 35761 Office: US Army Missile Command Attn AMSMI-RD-ST-CM/ D Jaklitsch Redstone Arsenal AL 35898-5247

JAKOBE, VIRGINIA ELLIS, retired educator; b. Molino, Mo., Sept. 10, 1922; d. Clyde William and Lucy (Baker) Ellis; m. Henry George Jakobe Sr., Feb. 23, 1963; 1 child, Henry George. BS, NE Mo. State U., 1946; MA, Columbia U., 1960. Cert. elem. art tchr., Mo., N.Y. Tchr. Ellis Sch., Molino, 1941-43; tchr. art and English Marceline Sch., Mo., 1943-44; remedial tchr. Berkley Sch., Mo., 1944-46; tchr. elem. art Maplewood Sch., Mo., 1946-54, Univ. City Schs., Mo., 1954-63, Saranac Lake (N.Y.) Cent. Schs., 1970-90. Editor Show Me Art, 1962-64; originator The Children's Art Exhibit Saranac Lake Cen. Sch., 1970—. Pres. Saranac Lake/N.Y. PTA., 1968-69, St. Louis County Art Tchrs. Assn., 1954-55. Mem. N.Y. State Art Tchrs. Assn., Paint and Palette Artists Assn., Delta Kappa Gamma (sec.). Republican. Episcopalian. Home: 12 Rockledge Rd Saranac Lake NY 12983-1928

JALBERT, NORMAN WILLIAM, rubber distribution and manufacturing executive; b. Providence, R.I., Mar. 3, 1943; s. Raymond A. and Eva Marie (Autote) J.; m. Margaret Mary McPhail, Jan. 29, 1966; children: Michelle M., Elizabeth A., Crhistopher R. BS, Providence Coll., 1965; MBA, Bryant Coll., 1975. Mktg. rep. Atlantic-Richfield, Springfield, Mass., 1968-70; customer rep. Acushnet Co., New Bedford, Mass., 1970-72; sales person J. Royal Co., Barrington, R.I., 1972-89, pres., 1989—. Pres. St. Brendan Sch. PTA, East Providence, 1978-79, v.p., 1980-82. 1st lt. U.S. Army, 1965-67, Korea. Decorated Army Commendation medal, Armed Forces Exptl. medal. Roman Catholic. Home: 68 Monmouth Dr Riverside RI 02915-1468 Office: J Royal Co Inc 40 Bay Spring Ave Barrington RI 02806-1302

JALLER, MICHAEL M., orthopaedic surgeon; b. Zurich, Switzerland, Feb. 25, 1924; came to U.S., 1926; s. Arthur and Anna (Eliash) J.; m. Helen F. Cowan, June 24, 1944; children: David, Daniel, Amy. BA, NYU, 1944; MD, U. Lausanne (Switzerland), 1952. Diplomate Am. Bd. Orthopaedic Surgery. V.p. A. Jaller & Co. Inc., N.Y.C., 1944-61; intern Waterbury (Conn.) Gen. Hosp., 1952-53; surg. resident Bridgeport (Conn.) Gen. Hosp., 1953-54; orthopedic resident U. Hosp. of Cin., Cin. Gen. Hosp., 1954-57; instr. orthopaedic surgery U. Hosp., Cin., 1954-57, chief resident in orthosurgery, 1956-57; rsch. fellow in biophysics Weitzmann Inst., Rehovoth, Israel, 1965; chief cons. VA Hosp., Washington, 1966-71; pres. Greater Washington Orthopaedic Group, Silver Spring, Md., 1967—; bd. dirs. Rotocast Plastics Inc. Pres. Silver Spring Jewish Ctr., Silver Spring, 1984-91. With U.S. Army, 1942-46. Fellow ACS, Am. Acad. Orthopaedic Surgery, Royal Soc. Health, Washington Art League, Selby Bay Yacht Club. Republican. Office: Greater Washington Orthopaedic Group 2101 Medical Park Dr Silver Spring MD 20902

JALONGO, MARY RENCK, educator; b. Pitts., Jan. 30, 1950; d. Herbert Hanson and Felicia Ann (Gemmellaro) Renck; m. Frank Severio Jalongo, Aug. 13, 1977. BA in English, U. Detroit/Mercy Coll., 1971; MAT, Oakland U., 1972; PhD, U. Toledo, 1978. Tchr. Capac (Mich.) Local Sch., 1971-72, Cloverleaf Local Sch. Dist., 1972-75; grad. asst. U. Toledo, 1975-78, instr., 1977-78; asst. prof. Ind. U. of Pa., 1978-82, assoc. prof., 1982-85, prof. profl. studies in edn., 1985—; lectr. in field; conductor seminars in field; cons. in field. Author: Young Children and Picture Books, 1988, The Role of the Teacher in the 21st Century: An Insider's View, 1991, Developing Children's Listening Skills, 1991, Early Childhood Language Arts, 1992; contbr. articles to profl. jours., chpts. to books. Recipient nat. award Am. Assn. Higher Edn., 1985, Ednl. Press Assn. Am., 1988, 91, Pa. Outstanding Young Woman award, 1983, others; named Disting. Prof. Ind. U. Pa., 1991-92. Home: 654 College Lodge Rd Indiana PA 15701 Office: Ind U Pa 312 Davis Hall Indiana PA 15705

JAMES, ANTHONY SEPTIMUS, business executive; b. Spanish Town, Jamaica, Jan. 4, 1951; s. Lester Augustus and Edna Mae (Anderson) J.; m. Janise A. Bolling, Aug., 1973 (div. 1978); 1 child, Anthony Johann; m. Beverly E. Wright, Sept. 19, 1980; children: Marcus Mosiah, Toni Nicole. BS, Long Island U., 1974; MBA, NYU, 1980; postgrad., U. Pa., 1990—. Sr. acct. CPC Internat., Englewood Cliffs, N.J., 1974-76; sr. budget analyst Sperry Hutchinson Co., N.Y.C., 1976-77; mgr. Avon Products, Inc., N.Y.C., 1977-80; fin. controller Hi-Lo Food Stores, Kingston, Jamaica, 1981-82, Nat. Sugar Co. Ltd., Kingston, 1982-84; cons. Am. Internat. Group Inc., N.Y.C., 1984-89, dir., 1989-91; pres. A.S. James & Assocs. Co. Ltd., N.J., 1991—; tchr. St. Jago High Sch., Spanish Town, 1969-71. Active Rep. Nat. Com., 1987—. Mem. Caribbean Assn. Burlington (founding 1990, ex officio 1990—). Episcopalian. Home and Office: 17 Thornleigh Pl Willingboro NJ 08046

JAMES, G. ROBERT, business executive, corporate development consultant; b. Bartholoma, Federal Republic of Germany, Jan. 21, 1961; came to U.S., 1975; s. Edward and Ingeburg Marianne (Krause) J.; m. Connie Ann Lawhon, Apr. 19, 1986; 1 child, Emily Elizabeth. BA in Psychology, Columbus Coll., 1984, MBA in Mktg./Fin., 1987. Account exec. MRI Internat., Columbus, Ga., 1985-86; mgr. investor rels. Burnham Svc. Corp., Columbus, 1986-88; prin. Communications Mgmt. Assocs., Columbus, 1988-90; v.p. The Brown Corp., Balt., 1990-91; pres. The Solomon Group, Bel Air, Md., 1991—; bd. dirs. Morgan Pierce Internat., Balt., 1991—. Editor: (medical book) Weight Training in Pre-Pubescents, 1985; contbr. articles to profl. jours. Mem. Columbus Youth Soccer Assn., 1982-86. Finalist fgn. studies Rotary, Columbus, 1984; Goethe Inst. scholar, Columbus, 1979; recipient commendation Rep. of Namibia, 1991. Mem. Young Entrepreneurs Orgn., Turnaround Mgmt. Assn. Office: The Solomon Group 101 S Main St Ste 200 Bel Air MD 21014

JAMES, GARY DOUGLAS, biological anthropologist, educator, researcher; b. Norwich, Conn., Dec. 6, 1954; s. Godfrey Merchant and Joan (McIllwaine) J.; m. Kathleen Louise Wilson, July 28, 1979. BA, Wake Forest U., 1976; MA, Pa. State U., 1980, PhD, 1984. Part-time instr. Pa. State U., University Park, 1982-84; postdoctoral fellow Med. Coll. Cornell U., N.Y.C., 1984-86, asst. prof. physiology and biophysics, 1986-91, asst. prof. physiology in medicine, 1986-91, assoc. rsch. prof. of physiology in medicine, 1991—, assoc. rsch. prof. of physiology and biophysics, 1991—. Contbr. chpt. to book, articles to profl. jours. Recipient New Investigator Rsch. award NIH, 1986; NIH postdoctoral trainee, 1984. Fellow Human Biology Council; mem. Am. Assn. Phys. Anthropologists, Soc. Study Social Biology, Soc. Behavioral Medicine, Am. Soc. Hypertension, Lambda Alpha. Lutheran. Office: Cornell U Med Coll Cardiovascular Ctr 520 E 70th St New York NY 10021-4896

JAMES, HAROLD, history educator; b. Bedford, Eng., Jan. 19, 1956; came to U.S., 1986; m. Marzenna Kowalik, 1991. BA, Cambridge U., Eng., 1978, PhD, 1982. Fellow Peterhouse Coll., Cambridge U., 1978-86; asst. lectr. Cambridge U., 1985-86; asst. prof. history Princeton (N.J.) U., 1986-91, assoc. prof., 1991—. Author: The German Slump, 1986, A German Identity, 1989; editor: Banking in Interwar Europe, 1991; editorial bd. Hist. Jour., 1991—, Contemporary European History, 1991—. Office: Princeton U History Dept Princeton NJ 08544

JAMES, JUDITH VOGEL, newspaper executive; b. Wrentham, Mass., May 13, 1937; d. Frank Chafee and Charlis V.; m. Stevenson Munro, Apr. 25, 1959 (dec. Apr. 1970); children: Mark Stevenson, Eric Burton, Katherine Charlis, Stevenson Jr.; m. Howard Anthony James Jr., Jan. 1, 1972; children: Jonathan Howard Chafee, Paul Cooper. BS, U. N.H., 1960. Sec. Westbrook (Maine) C. of C., 1961; newspaper advt. saleswoman, reporter Westbrook American, 1962-65; pub. Westbrook Guide; co-owner, pub. Twin-Town Shopper, Norway and South Paris, Maine, 1965-66, Northland News, Berlin, N.H., 1966-73; co-owner, pub. Berlin Reporter, 1967-70, owner, pub., 1970—; v.p. James Newspapers, Norway, 1976—; mem. earth connection project team U. Maine, 1989-91. Interviewer Ctr. Vol. Action, Portland, Maine, 1988-90. Office: The Berlin Reporter PO Box 38 151 Main St Berlin NH 03570

JAMES, MICHAEL ANDREW, lawyer; b. Indpls., June 8, 1953; s. Joseph Schell and Dorothy Agnes (Meth) J. BA, U. Va., 1975; JD, Yale U., 1978. Bar: N.Y. 1979. Assoc. Chadbourne & Parke, N.Y.C., 1978-80; assoc. Zimet, Haines & Friedman, N.Y.C., 1980-85, ptnr., 1986—. Mem. ABA, Assn. Bar City N.Y., Phi Beta Kappa. Democrat. Roman Catholic. Office: Zimet Haines & Friedman 460 Park Ave New York NY 10022-1906

JAMES, MILTON GARNET, economist; b. Guyana, Jan. 27, 1937; came to U.S., 1969, naturalized, 1976; s. Reginald Nathaniel and Caroline Elizabeth J.; m. Joyce Fernandes, July 31, 1960; children: Caroline, Jacqueline, Milton Garnet, Michael, Mark. BS, U. London, 1964, PhD, 1973; MBA, St. John's U., N.Y., 1972. Instr. econs. Baruch Coll., CUNY, 1972-74; asst. prof. mktg. Ramapo Coll. N.J., 1974-77; cons. econs., N.Y.C., 1978—. Chmn. Guyanese Community Coun., U.S., 1976—. Recipient Pub. Svc. award Guyanese Community Coun., 1982. Mem. Am. Econs. Assn., Caribbean Studies Assn., Masons. Episcopalian. Research in econ. devel., econometric forecasting, monetary and fiscal policies. Home: 649 E 23d St Brooklyn NY 11210-1127 Office: Bd Edn 65 Court St Brooklyn NY 11201-4954

JAMES, ROBERT LEO, advertising agency executive; b. N.Y.C., Sept. 23, 1936; s. Leo Francis and Mildred Virginia (Schaffa) J.; m. Anne Krapp, Feb. 2, 1968; children: Robert Leo, Victoria, Jeffrey. A.B., Colgate U., 1958; M.B.A., Columbia U., 1961. Field researcher Farm Jour., Inc., Cleve., 1956-57; salesman Procter and Gamble Co., Schenectady, 1958-59; office head sales mgr. Procter and Gamble Co., Syracuse, N.Y., 1959-60; product mgr. household products, brand mktg. and new product devel. Colgate Palmolive Co., N.Y.C., 1961-64; account exec. Ogilvy and Mather, Inc., N.Y.C., 1964; account supr Ogilvy and Mather, Inc., 1965-66, v.p., account supr., 1967-69; sr. v.p., mgmt. service dir. Marschalk Co., Inc., N.Y.C., 1968, dir., 1969—, exec. v.p., 1970, gen. mgr., 1971, pres., 1974, chmn. bd., chief exec. officer, 1975-80; vice chmn. Interpub. Group of Cos., Inc., 1980—, also dir.; vice chmn. McCann-Erickson Worldwide, 1981-85, chmn. bd., pres., 1985—; adj. asso. prof. mktg. Fordham U., 1968-69; dir. Broadlands Farm (thoroughbred horses.). Mem. nat. svc. coun. Colgate U.; trustee Fordham Prep. Sch., 1977-83, South Street Seaport Mus.; bd. dirs. March of Dimes, N.Y.C.s; mem. alumni bd. Columbia U. Grad. Sch. Bus.; chmn. 4As. Mem. Am. Assn. Advt. Agys. (vice chmn., bd. dirs. advt. coun.), Young Pres. Orgn. Internat., Greenwich Power Squadron, Columbia Bus. Sch. Alumni Assn. (bd. dirs.), N.Y. Yacht Club (trustee), Clove Valley Rod and Gun Club (bd. dirs.), Indian Harbor Yacht Club (bd. dirs.), NY40 Assn. (chmn.), River Club, Delta Kappa Epsilon. Home: 68 W Brother Dr Greenwich CT 06830-6751 Office: McCann-Erickson Worldwide 750 3rd Ave New York NY 10017-2703

JAMES, ROBYN LEONARD, private foundation executive; b. Greencastle, Ind., July 20, 1953; s. Robert Gene and Daisy Elizabeth (Stepp) L.; m. Anthony Oliver James, Aug. 25, 1979 (div. 1986). English major, U. N.C., 1973; AA, Kings Coll., Durham, N.C., 1974; student, U. Pa., 1984-85. Adminstrn. asst. Health Scis. Libr. U. N.C., 1975-77; sec. to asst. state libr. State Libr., Raleigh, N.C., 1978; asst. grants adminstrn. N.C. Dept. Cultural Resources, Raleigh, N.C., 1978-79; tech. sec. Sch. Veterinary Med. U. Pa., 1979-80; program asst. Middle East Center U. Pa., 1980-82; program adminstr., fiscal coord. Middle East Rsch. Inst. U. Pa., 1982-86; adminstr. Assoc. Middle East Rsch., Phila., 1986-88; asst. sec. treas. and chief fin. officer Hitachi Found., Washington, 1988—; budget dir. Nat. Com. to Internationalize Edn. Through Satellites, Phila., 1982-88; loan com. mem. Del. Valley Community Reinvestment Fund, Phila., 1990—. Steering com. mem. Interfaith Coalition ME Peace, Washington, 1990—, Am. Arab Anti-Discrimination Com. 1989-90; tutor Mayor's Program Literacy, Phila., 1985-88. Mem. Coun. Founds., Neighborhood Funders Group, Women Corp. Philanthropy, Nat. Congress Community Econ. Devel. Office: Hitachi Found 1509 22d St NW Washington DC 20037-1073

JAMES, SHARPE, mayor; b. Jacksonville, Fla., Feb. 20, 1936; m. Mary Mattison; 3 children. Grad., Montclair State Coll.; M, Springfield Coll. Former mem. faculty Essex County Coll., Newark, from 1968, then prof.; mayor City of Newark, 1986—. mem. Newark City Council, 1970-86. Served with AUS. Office: City Hall 920 Broad St Newark NJ 07102-2609*

JAMES, WILLIAM HALL, former state official, educator; b. North Providence, R.I., July 20, 1910; s. John William and May (Hall) J.; m. Virginia Stowell, June 24, 1950, 1 child, Hillery Stowell. Student, U. Lausanne, 1928-29; B. Phil., Brown U., 1933; MA, Yale U., 1946, PhD, 1953; LLD, U. New Haven, 1976. Tchr. New Canaan (Conn.) Bd. Edn., 1933-36; teaching prin. Easton (Conn.) Bd. Edn., 1936-42, 46-47, supervising prin., 1947-53, supt. schs., 1953-58; supt. schs. Branford (Conn.) Bd. Edn., 1958-66; staff Commn. Higher Edn., Hartford, Conn., 1966-77; dir. accreditation and scholarships Commn. Higher Edn., Hartford, 1966-77; ret., 1977; cons. Greater New Haven State Tech. Coll., 1977-78, Conn. Commn. Higher Edn., 1980-81; adj. prof. history So. Conn. State Coll., New Haven, 1947-49, adj. prof. econs. and labor-mgmt. rels, 1981—, adj. prof. labor-mgmt. rels.; adj. prof. internat. rels., Eurasian affairs and history Western Conn. State Coll., Danbury, 1949-58; adj. prof. ednl. adminstrn. U. Bridgeport (Conn.), 1958; adj. prof. econs. and indsl. rels. U. New Haven, West Haven, Conn., 1979—, adj. prof. indsl. rels; adj. prof. labor-mgmt. rels., mgmt. Teikyo Post U., Waterbury, Conn., 1988—; lectr. in field. Author: The Monetarists and the Current Crisis, 1975. Mem. North Branford (Conn.) Commn. Econ. Devel., 1980—, chmn., 1981—; mem. PTA. Maj. USAAF, 1942-46. Recipient Disting. Friend of Greater New Haven State Tech. Coll. award, 1984. Mem. SAR, NEA, Conn. Edn. Assn., Conn. Assn. Pub. Sch. Supts., Conn. Assn. Advancement Sch. Adminstrn., Am. Assn. Sch. Adminstrs., Yale Post-Doctoral Seminar Group (pres. 1968-69), Conn. State Employees Assn., Conn. Coun. Higher Edn. (treas. 1971-77), Am. Assn. Higher Edn., Royal Can. Geog. Soc., Numerical Control Soc., Rotary North Branford, Conn. (sec.-treas. Schoolmaster's U.S. 1965-69), Am. Legion (post comdr. Easton 1948-49), Exchange Club. Home: 373 Reeds Gap Rd Northford CT 06472-1106

JAMESON, JAY MARSHALL, financial executive; b. Coatesville, Pa., Dec. 30, 1943; s. Delmar K. and Hagar A. (Heston) J. B.A. in Bus., Parsons Coll., 1966; m. Barbara Vukmanic, Jan. 14, 1977; children: Jacqueline, Jay M., John and Ann Marie (twins). Acct., Johnston, Young & Ofria, CPA's, Bala Cynwyd, Pa., 1967-69; acct. Yaverbaum & Co., CPA's, Harrisburg, Pa., 1969-70; chief acct. Polyclinic Med. Ctr., Harrisburg, 1970-79; v.p. fin. Horsham Hosp., Ambler, Pa., 1979-84; pres. Jameson and Co., Gwynedd, Pa., 1984—. With USAR, 1966-72. Mem. C. of C. (small Bus. coun., bd. dirs.), Hosp. Fin. Mgmt. Assn., Med. Group Mgmt. Assn., Nat. Staff Network. Lodge: Rotary (Norristown, bd. dirs.). Home: 604 Brookwood Ln North Wales PA 19454-2420 Office: Jameson & Co PO Box 1 Gwynedd PA 19436-0001

JAMESON, PAUL VLADIMIR, surgeon; b. Kikinda, Vojvodina, Yugoslavia, July 14, 1929; came to U.S., 1962; s. Vladimir D. and Olga (Nikolic) Jakovljevic; m. Mary Elizabeth White, Nov. 15, 1969; children: Joshua, Hannah, Rachel. MD, Belgrade (Yugoslavia) U., 1952. Diplomate Am. Bd. Gen. Surgery, Am. Bd. Thoracic Surgery; lic. physician, Mass. Resident surgery U. Ljubljana, Yugoslavia, 1955-59; fellow in heart surgery Guy's Hosp., London, 1959-60; resident surgery Dartmouth Med. Sch., Hanover, N.H., 1963-66; resident thoracic surgery Boston City Hosp., 1966-68; thoracic surgeon Thoracic Assocs., Stoughton, Mass., 1968-72; pres. Thoracic Surgeons, Inc., Brockton, Mass., 1972—; chief thoracic surgery Cardinal Cushing Hosp., Brockton, Mass., 1985—; thoracic surgeon Goddard Hosp., Stoughton, Mass., 1968—, Norwood (Mass.) Hosp., 1987—, Southwood Hosp., Norfolk, Mass., 1987—. Contbr. articles to profl. jours. Fellow ACS, Am. Coll. Chest Physicians. Republican. Episcopalian. Office: Thoracic Surgeons Inc 830 Oak St Brockton MA 02401

JAMISON, JUDITH, dancer; b. Phila., 1944; d. John J. Student, Fisk U., Phila., Phila. Dance Acad. (now U. of Arts); studied with, Anthony Tudor, John Hines, Delores Brown, John Jones, Joan Kerr, Madame Swaboda. vis. disting. prof. Univ. of Arts. N.Y. dance debut in Agnes DeMille's "The Four Marys", 1965; dancer, Alvin Ailey Am. Dance Theater, N.Y.C., 1965-80, touring U.S., Europe, Asia, S. Am., Africa, dancer, choreographer, 1980—, guest assoc. artistic dir. 30th ann. tour, named artistic dir. dance and theater Ailey Am. Dance Ctr., 1990—; guest appearances with Harkness Ballet, Am. Ballet Theatre, San Francisco Ballet, Dallas Ballet; starring role created for her in Joseph's Legend (John Neumeier), Vienna Opera, Le Spectre de la Rose (Maurice Bejart), Brussels, Paris, N.Y.C.; star Broadway show Sophisticated Ladies, 1980; now with Maurice Hines Dance Sch., N.Y.C.; founder Jamison Project; choreographer Divining for Alvin Ailey Am. Dance Theatre, works for Maurice Bejart, Dancers Unltd. Dallas, Washington Ballet, Jennifer Muller/The Works, Alvin Ailey Repertory Ensemble, Ballet Nuevo Mundo de Caracas, also for opera Boito's Mefistofele for Opera Co. Phila.; subject of PBS spl. The Dancemaker; subject of book Aspects of a Dancer. Recipient Disting. Service award Mayor of N.Y.C., 1982; recipient Disting. Service award Harvard U., 1982, Key to City of N.Y., 1976. Address: Am Dance Theater care Alvin Ailey 1515 Broadway New York NY 10036*

JAMISON, STEVEN R., construction company executive; b. York, Pa., Nov. 2, 1951; s. Frayer R. and Vivian L. (Hoover) J.; children from previous marriage: Joshua Steven, Alicia Marie; m. Elizabeth C. Winemiller, June 5, 1989; 1 child, Andrew Steven. AS in Engring., York Coll. of Pa., 1981, BS in Engring. Mgmt., 1985. Timekeeper R. S. Noonan, Inc., York, 1970-74, estimator, 1974-82, chief estimator, 1982-86; dir. estimating/purchasing H. H. Hogg, Inc., York, 1986-87; project coord. Robert A. Kinsley, Inc., York, 1987-89; dir. of pre-constrn. H. B. Alexander & Sons, Inc., Harrisburg, Pa., 1989-90; v.p. H. B. Alexander & Sons, Inc., Harrisburg, 1990-92, pres., 1992—. Bldg. com. Strand Capitol Performing Arts Ctr. Mem. Constrn. Mgmt. Assn. Am. (quality mgmt. com.), Rotary. Methodist. Home: 107 Buchanan Dr York PA 17402-4802

JANAVEY, HARRY WILLIAM, advertising agency executive; b. Miami, Fla., Feb. 3, 1959; m. Susan Lynn Schneyman, May 17, 1982; children: Michael, Sarah. BBA, Pace U., 1981. Dir. acctg. svcs. Sawdon & Bess Advt., N.Y.C., 1981-85; divisional contr. Foote, Cone & Belding Advt., N.Y.C., 1986; v.p. fin. WCRS Inc., N.Y.C., 1987-89; v.p., contr. Dellafemina, McNamee, WCRS Inc., N.Y.C., 1989; sr. v.p., chief fin. officer Geer, DuBois Inc., N.Y.C., 1990—. Mem. N.Y. Credit Fin. Mgmt. Assn., N.Y. Assn. Advt. Fin. Profls. Office: Geer DuBois Inc 114 5th Ave New York NY 10011-5604

JANBAZIAN, MOVSES BOQHOS, charitable organization executive; b. Ainjar, Bekaa, Lebanon, July 26, 1945; s. Boghos M. and Agnes (Andonian) J.; m. Louisa Youmushakian, Sept. 30, 1978; children: Vahak Boghos, Ani Agnes. BA, Haigazian Coll., Beirut, Lebanon, 1968; M.Christian Edn., Near East Sch. Theology, Beirut, Lebanon, 1971. Ordained to ministry United Ch. of Christ, 1984. Dir. social action com. Union of Armenian Evang. Chs. Near East, Beirut, 1971-73; pastor Igreja Cen. Evangelica Armenia, Sao Paulo, Brazil, 1973-80; field dir. Armenian Missionary Assn. Am., Paramus, N.J., 1980-87, exec. dir., 1987—. Editor AMAA News; contbr. articles to profl. jours. Bd. trustees Stephen Philibosian Found., Haigazian Univ. Coll.; hon. mem. Children's Fund of Rep. of Armenia; mem. United Armenian Fund; mem. Com. on Cultural Res. with Armenians Abroad of the Rep. of Armenia. Mem. Armenian Evang. World Coun. Office: Armenian Missionary Assn 140 Forest Ave Paramus NJ 07652-5326

JANCU, PAUL, financial investment company executive; b. Braila, Romania, Feb. 13, 1926; came to U.S., 1953; s. Israel and Otilia (Weiss) J.; children: Robert, Alisa. BBA, Pace U., 1957; MBA, NYU, 1960. Investment banker Ira Haupt & Co., N.Y.C., 1957-63; adminstrv. mng. dir. L.F. Rothschild & Co., N.Y.C., 1963-87; co-chief exec. officer Marine Midland Capital Markets Corp., N.Y.C., 1988—; mem. adv. bd. N.Y. State Fiscal Reform Coun., N.Y.C., 1987-89; coun. mem. N.Y. State Debt Policy Bd., N.Y.C., 1979-87; speaker in field; guest lectr. Pace U., N.Y.C., 1990-91. Mem. Orgn. for Rehab. & Tng. (nat. bd. mem.), Internat. Bridge Tunnel & Turnpike Assn., Govt. Fin. Officers Am., NYU Money Marketeers, Mcpl. Forum N.Y., N.Y.C. City Club.

JANCUK, WILMA ANN, chemical engineer; b. Cleve., Nov. 15, 1944; d. Andrew L. and Josephine (Yushkiwicz) Diskant; m. Richard J. Jancuk, Oct. 28, 1967 (div. 1979); 1 child, David. B.Chem.Engring., Ohio State U., 1967; MS in Chem. Engring., IIT, Chgo., 1973; MS in Environ. Engring., IIT, 1975. Registered profl. engr., Ill., N.J.; cert. indsl. hygienist, safety profl., hazardous materials mgr. Student engr. Allied Chem. Co., Syracuse, N.Y., 1966; engr. Goodyear Tire & Rubber Co., Akron, Ohio, 1967-69; devel. engr. Western Elec. Co., Chgo., 1969-75; sr. engr. AT&T, Princeton, N.J., 1975-88, sr. staff engr., 1988—; cons. in field; chmn. conf.symposium HazMat, Atlantic City, 1984-85. Contbr. articles to profl. jours. Del. People to People Citizen Ambassador Prog., 1989. Recipient Tech. Achievement award, AT&T, 1972, 87, Tribute to Women in Industry award, YWCA, 1987. Mem. Am. Soc. Safety Engrs., Am. Indsl. Hygiene Assn., ACS, Inst. Hazardous Matls., PrinCen Bridge Club. Republican. Roman Catholic. Home: 11 Hart Ave Hopewell NJ 08525-1405 Office: AT&T PO Box 900 Princeton NJ 08544-0001

JANDL, RICHARD LOWE, management consultant; b. Racine, Wis., June 12, 1924; s. Otto and Edith (Lowe) J.; m. Donna Rae Kennedy, Aug. 23, 1946 (div. 1981); children: Rae, William, James; m. Joyce Elinor Arlington, Nov. 6, 1981. BA in Econs., U. Wis., 1950; postgrad., Harvard Bus. Sch., 1962-63. Gen. mgr. Tung Sol Electric, Newark, N.J., 1947-60; v.p. mktg. and sales Sola Electric, Elk Grove, Ill., 1960-63; v.p. mktg. Interlake, Chgo., 1963-67; group mgr., corp. dir. mktg. United Shoe Machinery, Boston, 1967-70; exec. dir. New Eng. Aquarium, Boston, 1970-74; dir. North Am. opers., chief exec. officer Velco Corp., N.Y.C., 1974-75; chief exec. officer Union Hosp., Lynn, Mass., 1975-78; v.p. McKenna, Jandl & Assocs., Inc., Lynnfield, Mass., 1978-91; lectr. Harvard Bus. Sch., Babson Coll., Boston U.; cons., speaker in field. Contbr. articles in field. Mem. fin. com. Town of Lynnfield, chmn. S.O.S.; trustee Fuller Pond Village. 2d lt. U.S. Army, 1943-46, ETO. Recipient health and safety award Town of Lynnfield. Home: 9 Fox Run Middleton MA 01949-2378 Office: Jandl Assocs Inc 50 Salem St Lynnfield MA 01940

JANELLE, LOUISE CECILE, school guidance counselor, school social worker; b. Manchester, N.H., Sept. 9, 1949; d. Jerome Paul and Claire Marguerite (Lemire) J.; m. R. Wayne Hoitt, Aug. 28, 1975; children: Melanie Janelle Hoitt, John Janelle Hoitt. BA in Social Svc., U. N.H., 1972; MEd in Sch. Counseling, Notre Dame Coll., 1991. Counselor Youth Devel. Ctr., Manchester, 1974-76, Port House, Portsmouth, N.H., 1976-78; floral designer C&C Flowers, Rochester, N.H., 1978-82; owner, mgr. All Season's Flowers, Manchester, 1982-88; ednl. asst. City of Manchester Schs., Manchester, 1988-90; home/sch. coord. Chandler Sch., Manchester, 1990—. Mem. AACD, N.H. Sch. Counselor Assn. (bd. dirs. 1989-91), New Eng. Assn. for Specialists in Group Work, Am. Sch. Counselor Assn., Rockingham Herb Soc. Roman Catholic. Home: 437 Patten Hill Rd Candia NH 03034-2526

JANES, G(EORGE) SARGENT, physicist; b. Bklyn., Apr. 12, 1927; s. Warham W. and George Sargent (Leubuscher) J.; m. Ann P. Brown, June 29, 1952; children: William, Thomas, Catherine, George, Susan. BA, Cornell U., 1949; PhD, MIT, 1953. Mem. research staff nuclear sci. div. Indsl. Coop, MIT, 1953-56; prin. research scientist Avco Everett Research Lab., Everett, Mass., 1956-74; v.p. isotope research Avco Everett Research Lab., 1974-82, dir. laser isotope research program, 1974-81, dir. dye laser tech., 1983-87; v.p. research Jersey Nuclear Avco Isotopes, Inc.; vis. scientist, rsch. affiliate, mem. adv. com. MIT Regional Laser Ctr., 1981—; assoc. Woods Hole Oceanographic Inst., 1983; physics and med. applications of lasers cons. Lincoln, Mass., 1987—; bd. dirs. Valley Pond Corp., Lincoln, Mass. Contbr. articles to profl. jours. Mem. Lincoln Bd. Assessors. Fellow Am. Phys. Soc., AIAA (assoc.); mem. AAAS, Sigma Xi. Club: Appalachian Mountain (past governing council). Home and Office: 34 Conant Rd Lincoln MA 01773-3900

JANES, ROBERT JAMES, retired state government official; b. Wethersfield, Conn., Nov. 10, 1925; s. James Fox and Eleanor (McKee) J.; m. Julia Griffiths, Feb. 22, 1952; children: Elizabeth Janes Nesbitt, Heidi Janes Patinkin. AB, Brown U., 1947. Marine state agt. Aetna Life and Casualty Co., Hartford, Conn., 1947-61; v.p. Ins. Underwriters, Inc., Providence, 1961-83; exec. v.p. Morton Smith, Inc., Providence, 1983-88; dir. dept. bus. regulation State of R.I., Providence, 1988-90; ret., 1990; mem. R.I. Senate, 1974-83; chmn. Barrington Sch. Com., 1962-74. Ensign USNR, 1944-46. Mem. University Club Providence. Republican. Episcopalian.

JANES, WILLIAM SARGENT, real estate corporation executive; b. Cambridge, Mass., Mar. 24, 1953; s. G. Sargent and Ann (Brown) J.; m. Alice Maxine Rowley, June 19, 1982; children: Pack Sargent, Maxine Cotton. BA, Bowdoin Coll., 1976. Sr. sales cons. coldwell Banker, Washington, 1976-84; ptnr. Lincoln Property Co., Washington, 1984-89; pres. Rock Creek Ptnrs., Inc., an affiliate of Keystone Inc., Washington, 1990—. Mem. Urban Land Inst., Soc. Indsl. Realtors, Nat. Assn. Indsl. and Office Pks., Cathedral Coll. of Laity (devel. com.), Decade Soc. Home: PO Box 1204 Middleburg VA 22117 Office: Rock Creek Ptnrs Inc 1133 Connecticut Ave NW Washington DC 20036-4305

JANEWAY, ELIOT, economist; b. N.Y.C., Jan. 1, 1913; s. Meyer Joseph and Fanny (Siff) J.; m. Elizabeth Hall, Oct. 29, 1938; children—Michael, William. Ed., Cornell, 1932; grad. student, London Sch. Econs. Former adviser to U.S. presidents; former bus. editor Time mag., N.Y.C., former adviser to editor-in-chief; former cons. bus. trends Newsweek mag.; econ. adviser numerous industries; pub. Janeway Letter; pres., dir. Janeway Pub. & Research Corp., N.Y.C.; chmn., chief exec. officer Classic Rarities Inc., N.Y.C.; chmn. Classic Rarities, Inc. Author: The Struggle for Survival, 1951, reissue, 1968, The Economics of Crisis, 1968, What Shall I Do With My Money?, 1970, You and Your Money, 1972, Musings on Money, 1976, Prescriptions for Prosperity, 1983; contbg. writer to Commonweal, Barron's, N.Y. Times; contbr. numerous publs. Berkeley fellow Yale U. Address: 15 E 80th St New York NY 10021*

JANI, SUSHMA NIRANJAN, child and adolescent psychiatrist; b. Gwalior, Madhya, Pradesh, India, Sept. 26, 1959; came to U.S., 1983; d. Kirty Ambalal and Purnima Kirty (Bhatt) Dave; m. Niranjan Natwerlal Jani, Mar. 30, 1983; chidlren: Suni Jani, Raja Jani. Inter Sci., Mithibai Coll., Bombay, India; MB;BS, B.J. Med. Coll., Ahmedabad, India; MD in Adult Psychiatry, Ind. U., 1984; MD in Child Psychiatry, Johns Hopkins U., 1987. Diplomate Am. Bd. Psychiatry and Neurology, sub-bd. Child Psychiatry. Child psychiatrist Johns Hopkins Univ. Hosp., Balt.; asst. clin. prof., dir. child & adolescent psychiatry U. Md., Balt.; chief cons. psychiatrist Balt. Detention Ctr., 1988-89, cons. psychiatrist Vets. Hosp., Indpls., 1986-87. Vol. Radha-Krishna Leprosy Camp, Bombay, 1981-83. Mem. AMA, Am. Acad. Child & Adolescent Psychiatry, Am. Psychiatry Assn., Md. Psychiat. Soc., Columbia Assn., India Assn. Hindu. Home: 10485 Owen Brown Rd Columbia MD 21044 Office: U Md Hosp 630 W Fayette St Baltimore MD 21201

JANICE, BARBARA, medical illustrator; b. Bklyn., Jan. 25, 1949; d. Irving and Blanche (Lass) Rothman; 1 child, Stacey-Alissa. BS in Biology, L.I. U., 1971; studied with Susan Moscowitz, John Broccoli. Staff illustrator Courier-Life Pubs., Bklyn., 1975-78, The Village Voice, N.Y.C., 1978-80; art dir., dept. anatomy SUNY Health Sci. Ctr., Bklyn., 1989-91; freelance illustrator Walt Disney Prodns., N.Y.C., 1990—, Orlando, Fla., 1990—; illustrator EuroDisney, Orlando, N.Y.C., 1991—; dir. Barbara Janice Graphics, N.Y.C. and Fla., 1980—; guest speaker Pratt Sch. Art & Design, Bklyn., 1991. Illustrator: Current Operative Urology, 6th edit., 1989, A Historical Profile of the Children's Medical Center, 1990, The Day the Alphabet Was Born, 1991; represented in permanent collections SUNY Health Sci. Ctr. Vol. artist Coalition for the Homeless, N.Y.C., 1985. Recipient 1st place N.Y. Art Critics award, 1984, other awards for illustrations, 1990-91. Mem. Assn. Med. Illustrators, Soc. Illustrators (1st place 34th ann. exhbn. 1991, 2d place 33d ann. exhbn. 1990), Graphic Artists Guild (profl. rep.). Jewish. Home: 10100 Reflections Blvd W # 204 Sunrise FL 33351 Office: Walt Disney Prodns 4575 N University Dr Fort Lauderdale FL 33351

JANICKI, THOMAS N., management consultant; b. Sewickley, Pa., Dec. 1, 1952; s. Edmund N. and Mildred (Farkasovsky) J. BS in Math., Carnegie-Mellon U., 1974; MBA, U. Pitts., 1980. Strategic planner PPG Industries, Pitts., 1974-80; owner Retail Convenience Stores, Pitts., 1980-87; pres. Effective Mgmt. Group, Warrendale, Pa., 1987—; mem. adv. coun. Pa. Power Regional Adv. Coun., New Castle, 1991. Pres. Cranberry (Pa.) C. of C., 1989-90; chairperson Cranberry Chamber Women's Abuse Shelter Holiday Collection Fund, Butler County, Pa., 1990. Mem. ASTD (Pitts. chpt.), Cranberry C. of C. (bd. dirs. 1991—, Outstanding Svc. award 1991), Sigma Tau Gamma (bd. dirs. 1992—). Republican. Roman Catholic. Office: Effective Mgmt Group 10 Warrendale Bayne Rd Warrendale PA 15086-7556

JANJIGIAN, ALBERT SARKIS, management consultant; b. Cambridge, Mass., Apr. 20, 1946; s. Albert Arakel and Mary Victoria (Ohannessian) J.; m. Susan Ellerin, Aug. 8, 1982; 1 child, Adam. BA, Bowdoin Coll., 1968; MS in Acctg., Northeastern U., 1970. Pres., founder Detectronics, Inc., Watertown, Mass., 1971-75; v.p. distbn. Aritech Corp., U.S. (merged with Detectronics, Inc.), Framingham, Mass., 1975-80, v.p., gen. mgr., 1980-85; pres. Arrowhead Techs./Arrowhead Distbn., Inc., Medway, Mass., 1985-88; pres., chief exec. officer Cerberus Techs., Inc., Medway, 1987-88; chmn. STAT Resources, Inc., Brookline, Mass., 1988—. Contbg. author: Museum, Archive & Library Security, 1983. Mem. Am. Soc. Profl. Security, Security Industry Assn. (pres. 1982-86, sec. 1989—), Associated Locksmiths of Am. Office: STAT Resources Inc 822 Boylston St Chestnut Hill MA 02167-2504

JANKLOW, LINDA LEROY, civic worker, volunteer; b. L.A., Apr. 17, 1938; d. Mervyn LeRoy and Doris (Warner) Vidor; m. Morton Lloyd Janklow, Nov. 27, 1960; children: Angela Janklow Harrington, Lucas Warner. BA, Smith Coll., 1959. Vice chmn., mem. exec. com., bd. dirs. Lincoln Ctr. Theater, N.Y.C., 1979-91, chmn., 1991—. V.p., treas. Vidor Found., N.Y.C., 1978—; chmn. ArtsConnection, N.Y.C., 1979—; founding trustee, mem. exec. com., chmn. collection com. Am. Mus. of Moving Image, N.Y.C., 1979—; mem. adv. coun. Tisch Sch. Arts, NYU, 1980-91; mem. adv. bd. Guggenheim Mus., N.Y.C., 1986-91; pres., chief exec. officer Janklow Found., N.Y.C., 1988—; trustee Nat. Coun. for Families and TV, L.A., 1989—; bd. dirs. The New 42d St., N.Y.C., 1990—. Office: Lincoln Center Theatre 150 W 65th St New York NY 10023-6903

JANKOWSKI, THEODORE ANDREW, artist; b. New Brunswick, N.J., Dec. 14, 1946; s. Theodore Andrew and Lois (Amarescu) J.; m. Rebecca Buck, July 23, 1983; 1 child, Tito Henry. Student, McMurrough Sch. Art, Indialantic, Fla., 1956-58, 74-75, R.I. Sch. Design, 1972, Cape Sch. of Art, Provincetown, Mass., 1975-76, 79-87, Cen. Fla. U., 1976-77. Solo exhbns. include Eye of Horus Gallery, Provincetown, 1985; group shows include Provincetown Art Assn. Mus., 1984, Bethlehem (Pa.) City Hall, 1988, Michael Ingbar Gallery, N.Y.C., 1988, 91; represented in permanent collections State Mus. at Palace of Peter the Gt., Leningrad, USSR, Mishkan Olemanut Mus. Art, Israel, CIGNA Mus., Phila., Johns Hopkins U., Balt., Holyoke (Mass.) Mus. Art., McGill U., Montreal, Que., Can., others. Mem. Copley Soc. Boston. Home: 1937 Ravenwood Dr Bethlehem PA 18018-1534

JANNOTTI, GENE, telecommunications professional; b. Newburgh, N.Y., Oct. 10, 1946; s. Pellegrino and Anne J.; m. Lisette Tremblay, Oct. 12, 1975. BS in Math., Siena Coll., 1968; MA in Math., St. John's U., 1970; MS in Bus. Policy, Columbia U., 1981. Cert. systems profl. Asst. programmer N.Y. Telephone, N.Y.C., 1971-72, computer ops. mgr., 1973-80, staff mgr., 1980-84; programmer Bell Labs., Greensboro, N.C., 1972-73; dist. mgr. Bell Communications Rsch., Piscataway, N.J., 1984-87; staff dir. NYNEX Corp. Communications, N.Y.C., 1987-89, NYNEX Videoteleconferencing, N.Y.C., 1989-91; dir. ops. NYNEX Computer Ops., Pearl River, N.Y., 1991; dir. NYNEX Software Devel., N.Y.C., 1992—. Capt. U.S. Army Res., 1968-74. Mem. Data Processing Mgmt. Assn. (bd. dirs. N.Y. chpt. 1980-84, exec. v.p. 1984), Germania Corinthian Union. Roman Catholic. Home: Llewellyn Park West Orange NJ 07052 Office: NYNEX Rm 942 1166 Ave of Americas New York NY 10036

JANOSKO, RUDOLPH E. M., psychiatrist; b. Munhall, Pa., Apr. 30, 1930; s. Rudolph E. and Anne (Gerek) J.; m. Audrey M. Nemeth, May 18, 1932; children: Beth, Gwen, Ellen. BS, U. Pitts., 1952, MD, 1956. Cert. in psychiatry Am. Bd. Psychiatry and Neurology. Intern Easton (Pa.) Hosp., 1956-57; resident in psychiatry U. Pitts., 1957-59, 61-62; instr. psychiatry U. Pitts. Sch. Medicine, 1962-65; lectr. U. Pitts. Dept. Spl. Edn., Grad. Sch., 1966-70; clin. asst. prof. psychiatry U. Pitts. Sch. Medicine, 1965-75; mem. attending staff Presbyn.-Univ. Hosp., Pitts., 1962—; faculty Pitts. Psychoanalytic Inst., 1970—; clin. assoc. prof. psychiatry U. Pitts. Sch. Medicine, 1975—; tng. and supervising analyst Am. Psychoanalytic Assn., Pitts. Psychoanalytic Inst., 1979—; pres. Pitts. Psychoanalytic Ctr., 1981-83; dir. Pitts. Psychoanalytic Inst., 1985-86; med. dir. Family Svcs. of Western Pa., Pitts., 1988—; cons. Greater Pitts. Guild for Blind, Bridgeville, Pa., 1964—, Social Security Adminstrn., HHS, Pitts., 1979—. Author in field. Capt. USAF, 1959-61. Recipient Meritorious Distinction award Greater Pitts. Guild for Blind, 1967, Outstanding Tchr. award Western Psychiat. Inst., 1981. Fellow Am Psychiat. Assn.; mem. Am. Psychoanalytic Assn., Pitts. Acad. Medicine, Pitts. Psychoanalytic Soc. (pres. 1983-85), AMA. Republican. Roman Catholic. Home: 2534 Mt Royal Rd Pittsburgh PA 15217-2542 Office: 161 N Dithridge St Pittsburgh PA 15213-2646

JANOW, CHRIS, mechanical engineer; b. N.Y.C., Apr. 22, 1953; s. John and Angie (Bizzios) J. BME, CCNY, 1975, MME, 1980. Mech. engr. Fuze Devel. and Engr. Directorate, Picatinny Arsenal, N.J., 1975-80; mech. engr. nuclear and fuze div. Large Caliber Weapons System Lab, Picatinny Arsenal, 1980-84; mech. engr. fuze div. Armament Engring. Directorate, Picatinny Arsenal, 1984-85; systems engr. battlefield mgmt. br., fire control div. Fire Support Armaments Ctr., Picatinny Arsenal, 1985-87; program mgmt. engr. AUS Office of Product Mgr. for Fuzes, Picatinny Arsenal, 1987-88; gen. engr. and assoc. product mgr. for close combat AUS Office of Product Mgr. for Fuzes, 1988—; exec. sec. Fuze Engring. Standardization Working Group, Picatinny Arsenal, 1983-85; tech. cons. AUS Fuze Safety Rev. Bd., 1987—. Author and editor: Guide for Fuze Safety Presentations, 1988, Fuze Development Guide, 1990, Fuze Acquisition Guide, 1991. Vice-pres. Greek Orthodox Youth of Am., St. Spyridon Ch., N.Y.C., 1974-75. Mem. ASME, Assn. U.S. Army, Picatinny Officers Club, Pi Tau Sigma. Greek Orthodox. Home: 20 Jefferson St Apt E1 Hackensack NJ 07601 Office: Office of Product Mgr Fuzes Attn: AMCPM FZ Picatinny Arsenal NJ 07806-5000

JANOWITZ, HENRY DAVID, physician, researcher, medical educator; b. Paterson, N.J., Mar. 23, 1915; s. Sam and Rose (Meyers) J.; m. Adeline R. Tintner, Oct. 31, 1942; children: Mary Rebecca, Anne Francis. B.A., Columbia U., 1935, M.D., 1939; M.S., U. Ill., 1949. Intern Mt. Sinai Hosp., N.Y.C., 1939-41; resident in medicine Mt. Sinai Hosp., 1947-48; practice medicine specializing in gastroenterology N.Y.C., 1956—; head div. gastroenterology Mt. Sinai Hosp., 1958-83, attending physician gastroenterology, 1961-85, now cons. in gastroenterology, 1985—, clin. prof. medicine, 1967-85; emeritus clin. prof. medicine, 1985—; mem. Am. Bd. Gastroenterology, 1966-70; chmn. program project com., div. arthritis and metabolism NIH, 1969-70. Author: (with D.A. Dreiling and C.V. Perrier) Pancreatic Inflammatory Disease, 1965; Inflammatory Bowel Disease: A Personal View, 1985, Your Gut Feelings, 1987; contbr. 300 articles to profl. jours.; editorial bd.: Proceedings of Soc. for Exptl. Biology and Medicine, 1974-86, Am. Jour. Physiol, 1970-74, Jour. Chronic Diseases, 1966-88. Founder Ileitis and Colitis Found. Am. Served to maj. U.S. Army, 1942-46. Recipient Jacobi medal Mt. Sinai Sch. Medicine, N.Y.C., 1974. Mem. Am. Soc. Clin. Investigation, Assn. Am. Physicians, Am. Phys. Soc., Am. Gastroent. Assn. (pres. 1972-73, Friedenwald medal 1973), N.Y. Gastroent. Assn. (pres. 1968-69). Office: 1075 Park Ave New York NY 10128-1003

JANSKY, JEANNETTE JEFFERSON, learning disabilities specialist; b. Urbana, Ill., Nov. 27, 1927; d. Bernard Levi and Irma Nicholson (Williams) Jefferson; m. Curtis Moreau Jansky, Aug. 14, 1949 (div. 1976); 1 child, Matthew Jefferson. BS, U. Ill., Urbana, 1949; MS in Pre-Clinical Psychology, CCNY, 1960; PhD in Edn. Psychology, Columbia U., 1970. Speech therapist Blythedale Convalescent Home, Valhalla, N.Y., 1950-51; clinician Lang. Disorder Clinic Columbia-Presbyn. Med. Ctr., N.Y.C., 1951-57, 65-72, dir. Lang. Disorder Clinic, 1972-74, dir. de Hirsch Robinson Reading Clinic, 1974—; pvt. practice learning disabilities specialist, N.Y.C., 1951—; mem. adv. bd. Fisher-Landau Found., N.Y.C., 1986—. Author (with K. de Hirsch): Predicting Reading Failure, 1966, Preventing Reading Failure, 1972; contbr. chpt. to books; assoc. editor Annals Dyslexia, Towson, Md., 1981—. Recipient N.Y. State award Orton Soc., 1977; grantee Health Research Council N.Y., 1966, Babies Hosp. Fund, 1966, Bienecke Found., 1974, 82. Fellow Am. Orthopsychiat. Assn.; mem. Am. Psychol. Assn., Internat. Reading Assn., Orton-Dyslexia Soc., Sigma Xi. Democrat. Presbyterian. Clubs: Cosmopolitan (N.Y.C.); Columbia U. Faculty (N.Y.C.). Home: 120 E 89th St New York NY 10128-1516 Office: 51 E 73d St New York NY 10021

JANTSCH, ROBERT CRAIG, massage therapist; b. Pitts., Dec. 28, 1953; s. Albert Joseph and Ruby Rowene (Double) J. Diploma, Boulder Sch. Massage Therapy, Colo., 1981. Massage therapist The Rivers Club, Pitts., 1986-89; dir. Pitts. Sch. Massage Therapy, 1987—; pvt. practice Pitts., 1981—. Mem. Am. Massage Therapy Assn. (chair We. Pa. unit 1987-90, nat. del. 1990,'91, '92), Associated Bodywork and Massage Profls. Home: 1032 Flemington St Pittsburgh PA 15217

JANUZZI, JAMES LOUIS, physician, internist, gastroenterologist; b. N.Y.C., Feb. 2, 1941; s. Fred and Alexandra (Calogera) J.; m. Louise Marie Carini, June 27, 1964; children: Marisa, James, Louis. AB, St. Peter's Coll., 1962; MD, N.Y. Meml. Coll., 1966. Diplomat of Am. Bd. Internal Medicine and Gastroenterology. pres. med. staff St. Vincent's Hosp., N.Y.C., 1989-91. Bd. trustees St. Vincent;s Hosp., N.Y.C., 1989—. Capt. U.S. Army, 1968-70. Office: 29 Washington Sq W New York NY 10011

JANZ, MILLI, cultural association executive; b. N.Y.C., Apr. 10; d. Samuel Gelfer; m. Abraham Janz; children: Burton, Stephen, Daniel. Student, NYU. Writer Culture Cues newspaper; exec. dir. Am. Community Cultural Ctr. Assn., N.Y.C.; tchr., dir. Theater for Young People, N.Y.C. Trustee Pequannock Twp. Pub. Libr. Mem. Dramatists Guild, Authors League. Home and Office: 19 Foothills Dr Pompton Plains NJ 07444-1033

JARCHO, SAUL WALLENSTEIN, retired physician, medical historian; b. N.Y.C., Oct. 25, 1906; s. Julius and Susanna (Wallenstein) J.; m. Irma Seijo, Oct. 24, 1948; children: Thomas, Andrew. AB magna cum laude, Harvard U., 1925; MA, Columbia U., 1926, MD, 1930. Diplomate Am. Bd. Internal Medicine. Asst. house surgeon N.Y. Lying-in Hosp., 1930; intern, house physician Mt. Sinai Hosp., N.Y.C., 1931-33, asst. in pathology, 1933-34, in charge cardiovascular rsch., 1945-51, adj. physician, 1940-48, assoc. attending physician, 1951-70; staff mem. Sch. Tropical Medicine, San Juan, P.R., 1930, 38, 41; asst., instr. pathology Johns Hopkins U., Balt., 1934-36; instr., assoc. in pathology Coll. Physicians and Surgeons, Columbia U., N.Y.C., 1936-42; mem., chmn. history medicine study sect. NIH, 1959-63, mem. history life scis. study sect., 1974-76; mem. Armed Forces Med. Libr. Adv. Group, 1954-56, cons. 1973-78; bd. regents Nat. Libr. Medicine, 1961-65, mem. index medicus com., cons., 1975-88. Author: The Concept of Heart Failure from Avicenna to Albertini, 1980; translator: The Clinical Consultations of Giambattista Morgagni, 1985, Clinical Consultations and Letters by Ippolito Francesco Albertini, Francesco Torti, and other Physicians, 1989; editor: Human Palaeopathology, 1966; cons. editor in chief, editor Trans. and Studies of Coll. Physicians of Phila., 1979-83; contbr. numerous articles, book revs. to profl. jours. From capt. to lt. col. AUS, 1942-46. Fellow AAAS, Am. Pub. Health Assn., N.Y. Acad. Medicine (editor bull. 1967-77, acad. plaque 1979); mem. AMA, Am. Coll. Physicians (life), Am. Assn. Pathologists and Bacteriologists, Am. Assn. for History Medicine (William Welch medal 1963, pres. 1968-70, Lifetime Achievement award 1988), Am. Soc. for Tropical Medicine, Soc. Med. Cons. to Armed Forces, History Sci. Soc., Harvey Soc. (life), Phi Beta Kappa. Home: 11 W 69th St New York NY 10023-4742

JARECKI, HENRY GEORGE, financial executive; b. Stettin, Germany, Apr. 15, 1933; s. Max Jarecki and Gerda Kunstmann; m. Gloria Friedland, 1957; children: Andrew, Thomas, Eugene, Nicholas. MD, U. Heidelberg, Germany, 1957. Diplomate Am. Bd. Psychiatry and Neurology. Dir. Mocatta Metals Corp., N.Y.C., 1970-89, Mocatta & Goldsmid Ltd., London, 1973-89, Mocatta Hong Kong Ltd., 1975-89, Cerro Metals (U.K.) Ltd., London, 1989—; chmn. Brody, White & Co. Inc., N.Y.C., 1971—, Guana Island Hotel Corp., British Virgin Islands, 1975—, Falconwood Corp., N.Y.C., 1976—; asst. prof., lectr. dept. psychiatry Sch. Medicine Yale U., New Haven; gov. BVI Community Coll., British Virgin Islands, 1989—. Author: Modern Psychiatric Treatment, 1971; contbr. articles to profl. jours. Trustee Am. Mus. Natural History, 1991—; bd. dirs. Botanic Soc. Brit. V.I., 1986—, Rural Voice Inc., Washington, 1987—, Am. Hepatitis Assn., 1988, Internat. Liaison Com., Food Corps Progs. Mem. Nat. Futures Assn. (bd. dirs.), Am. Psychiat. Assn. (Presdl. Commendation 1984). Office: Falconwood Corp 4 World Trade Ctr 5th Fl New York NY 10048

JARECKI, JANIS MARIE, speech-language pathology educator; b. Butler, Pa., Dec. 24, 1955; d. Edward Henry and Margaret (Druga) J. BS, Allegheny Coll., 1978; MS, Clarion U. of Pa., 1981; postgrad., Kent (Ohio) State U. Lic. speech-lang. pathologist, Pa., Ohio. Speech-lang. pathologist Sagamore Hills (Ohio) Child Psychiat. Hosp., 1981, Mercy Hosp. Pitts., 1984-85, Kent State U., 1985-87; asst. prof. Clarion U. of Pa., 1987—. Mem. Am. Speech-Lang. and Hearing Assn., Assn. Pa. State Coll. and Univ. Faculties, Internat. Affairs Assn., Pa. Speech and Hearing Assn. Republican. Byzantine Cath. Office: Clarion U Pa Dept Speech Pathology and Audiology 117 Davis Hall Clarion PA 16214

JARON, DOV, biomedical engineer, educator; b. Tel Aviv, Oct. 29, 1935; came to U.S., 1958, naturalized, 1972; s. Meir and Sara (Levit) Yarovsky; m. Brooke E. Boberg, Sept. 16, 1978; children: Shulamit, Tamara. B.S. magna cum laude, U. Denver, 1961; Ph.D., U. Pa., 1967. Sr. research asso. Maimonides Med. Center, Bklyn., 1967-70; dir. surg. research Sinai Hosp. of Detroit, 1970-73; asso. prof. elec. engring. U. R.I., Kingston, 1973-77; prof. U. R.I., 1977-79, coordinator biomed. engring., 1973-79; dir. Biomed. Engring. and Sci. Inst., prof. biomed. engring. and sci. Drexel U., Phila., 1979—; vis. prof. elec. engring. Rutgers U., New Brunswick, N.J., 1968-73; adj. prof. biomed. engring. Wayne State U., 1971-73; adj. prof. physiology Temple U. Sch. medicine, 1980—; adj. prof. radiology Jefferson Med. Coll., 1983—; dir. Div. Biol. and Critical Systems, NSF, 1991—. Contbr. articles to sci. jours. NSF, NIH, Office Naval Research, pvt. founds. research grantee. Fellow IEEE, Am. Inst. for Med. and Biol. Engring.; mem. AAAS, AAUP, Biomed. Engring. Soc., Am. Soc. for Engring. Edn., Assn. for Advancement Med. Instrumentation, Internat. Soc. Artificial Organs, Am. Soc. for Artificial Internal Organs, Biophys. Soc., N.Y. Acad. Scis., Engring. in Medicine and Biology of IEEE (pres. 1986-87), Sigma Xi, Tau Beta Pi, Eta Kappa Nu. Home: 2957 Tilden St NW Washington DC 20008-1150 Office: NSF Div Biol and Critical Systems 1800 G St NW Washington DC 20550-0002

JAROS, ROBERT JAMES, data processing executive; b. Port Reading, N.J., June 30, 1939; s. Michael and Marian (Kurta) J.; m. Margaret Efthin, May 19, 1974; children: Marian Reilly, Jennifer, Christina,. Student, Rutgers U., 1957-65. With Prudential Ins. Co., Newark, 1957-77; sr. systems analyst, project leader Ins. Svcs. Office, N.Y.C., 1977-81; project mgr. Shearson Lehman Bros. Inc., N.Y.C., 1981-88; cons. G & J Assocs., Middletown, N.J., 1988—. Mem., past chmn. Middletown Twp. Transp. Com., 1988—; mem., past pres. Rolling Knolls Civic Soc.; mem. U.S. Power Squadron, Watchung Power Squadron; Rep. County committeeman, Monmouth County, 1989—. With USAR, 1962-68. Fellow Life Mgmt Inst. Soc. of Greater N.Y.; mem. Am. Soc. CLU's, Am. Legion. Greek Orthodox. Home: 12 Jocarda Dr Middletown NJ 07748-3337

JAROSLAWICZ, DAVID, lawyer; b. Paris, Jan. 19, 1947; came to U.S., 1948; s. Moses and Mina (Etner) J.; m. Rena Nadoff, Feb. 3, 1987. BA, NYU, 1968; JD, Bklyn. Law Sch., 1971, LLM, 1974. Bar: N.Y. 1972, Calif.

1972, Fla. 1978, U.S. Supreme Ct. 1986. Pvt. practice N.Y.C., 1978—. Office: 150 William St New York NY 10038-2603

JARRETT, RICHARD STEVEN, marketing professional; b. N.Y.C., Dec. 21, 1955; s. Paul Seymour and Beverly (Bernhardt) J.; m. Kathleen Crank, May 24, 1992. BS, Cornell U., 1977; M of Mgmt., Northwestern U., 1987. Asst. personnel mgr. Amstar Corp., N.Y.C., 1977-80, Phila., 1980-81; personnel mgr. Frito-Lay, Atlanta, 1981-83, Wooster, Ohio, 1983-85; asst. product mgr. Chesebrough-Pond's Inc., Greenwich, Conn., 1987-90; product mgr. James River Corp., Norwalk, Conn., 1990—.

JARRETT, RUTH, financial officer; b. Bklyn., Feb. 11, 1942; d. Ernest David and Joyce (Litzky) Kurnow; m. Jeffrey Edward Jarrett, June 16, 1963; children: Michael Philip, Debra Lynn, Daniel Mark. BS in Edn., N.Y.U., 1963; MS in Acctg., U. R.I., 1980. Survey analyst Soc. of the Plastics Industry, N.Y.C., 1963-81; cons. Technic, INc., Cranston, R.I., 1981; fiscal mgr. Univ. R.I. Found., Kingston, R.I., 1981-88; chief fin. officer Univ. R.I. Found., Kingston, 1988—. Pres. elect Jewish Community Coun., Kingston, 1991—. Recipient Founder's Day award N.Y.U., 1963. Mem. Assn. Profl. & Acad. Univ. Women, Triangle Club, South County Hadassah (treas. 1989-91), Beta Alpha Psi. Office: U RI Found 21 Davis Hall Kingston RI 02881

JARUDI, NABEEL IZZAT, ophthalmologist, educator; b. Beirut, Aug. 4, 1941; came to U.S., 1987; s. Izzat Chafik and Nadia Saad (Anouti) J.; m. Mona Nizar Turk, June 13, 1976; children: Lama, Jarudi. BS, Am. U. Beirut, 1962, MD, 1966. Diplomate Am. Bd. Ophthalmology. Intern Am. U. Beirut, 1966-69, resident, 1969-70, clin. assoc. prof., 1972-87; chief resident U. Mo., Columbia, 1970-71; fellow U. Iowa Med. Ctr., Iowa City, 1971-72; chief ophthalmology Brockton/West Roxbury VA Med. Ctr., 1987—; ophthalmologist Brigham & Women's Hosp., Boston, 1988—; clin. instr. ophthalmology Harvard Med. Sch., Boston, 1989—; ophthalmologist New Eng. Eye Cons., Peabody, Mass., 1988—. Fellow ACS, Am. Acad. Ophthalmology. Office: New Eng Eye Cons 39 Cross St # 102 Peabody MA 01960

JARVIK, ROBERT, biomedical research scientist; b. Midland, Mich., May 11, 1946; m. Marilyn vos Savant, 1987. BA, Syracuse U., 1968, DSc (hon.), 1983; MA, NYU, 1971; MD, U. Utah, 1976; Dr sc (hon.), Hahnemann U., 1985. Rsch. asst. Div. Artificial Organs U. Utah, Salt Lake City, 1971-76, asst. dir. exptl. labs. Div. Artificial Organs, 1976-82, asst. rsch. prof. surgery, 1979-87; pres. Symbion, Inc., Salt Lake City, 1981-87, Jarvik Rsch., Inc., N.Y.C., 1987—; mem. nat. selection panel NASA Tchr. in Space Project, Washington, 1985. Sect. editor Internat. Jour. Artificial Organs, 1979-88; inventor repeating hemostatic clip instruments and cartridges, total artificial hearts powered by electrohydraulic energy; patentee in field. Named Inventor of Yr. Intellectual Property Owners, 1983, named John W. Hyatt award Soc. Plastics Engrs., 1983; recipient Golden Plate Am. Acad. Achievement, 1983, Gold Heart award Utah Heart Assn., 1983. Mem. Am. Soc. Artificial Internal Organs.

JARVIS, EDWARD CURTIS, manufacturing and distribution company executive, international business consultant; b. Malden, Mass., Jan. 6, 1951; s. John Albert and Shirley Ann (Fronduto) J.; m. Nancy Jean Cotoia, June 24, 1973; 1 child, Ryan Edward. BA in History and Psychology, Bridgewater State Coll., 1972; postgrad., Salem State Coll., 1973-74; exec. MBA, Suffolk U., 1983. Mfg. and personnel mgr. Cape Dory Yachts, Tanton, Mass., 1974-77; plant mgr. Am. Alumninum Inc., Malden, 1977-80; mgr. human resources Prime Computer, Natick, Mass., 1980-81; orgn. and manpower rep., systems cons. aircraft engine bus. group GE, Lynn, Mass., 1981-83; mgr. profl. compensation and human resources systems Gen. Electric Co., Lynn, Mass., 1983-84; dir. human resources U.S. ops. Scitex Am. Corp., Bedford, Mass., 1984-85; corp. dir. worldwide human resource planning Scitex Corp. Ltd., Herzlia, Israel, 1985-86; corp. v.p., corp. dir. human resources Towle Mfg. Co., Burlington, Mass., 1986-88; exec. v.p., gen. mgr. Demakes Enterprises, Lynn, Mass., 1988-89, chief exec. officer, 1989—; internat. bus. cons. Bd. dirs. Lynn Bus./Edn. Found., 1990—. Mem. Am. Compensation Assn., Am. Soc. Personnel Adminstrn., New Eng. Human Resources Mgmt. Group, Rte. 128 Internat. Personnel Group, Nat. Hon. Soc., Bus Adminstrn., Beach Club, Swampscott Yacht Club. Roman Catholic. Home: 90 Farragut Rd Swampscott MA 01907-1949 Office: Demakes Enterprises Inc 37 Waterhill St Lynn MA 01905-2134

JARVIS, WILLIAM HYDE, aerospace engineer, researcher; b. Detroit, Mar. 26, 1964; s. Daniel Gene and Sarah Jene (Hyde) J.; m. Julie M. Jarvis. BS in Aerospace Engring., U. Toronto, Can., 1987; MS in Aerospace Engring., Embry Riddle Aero. U., 1989; M in Engring. Mgmt., George Washington U., 1991, postgrad. in Ops. Rsch., 1991—. Lab. instr. Embry Riddle Aero. Div., Daytona Beach, Fla., 1987-89; aerospace engr. Naval Surface Warfare Ctr., Indian Head, Md., 1989—. Mem. AIAA, Ops. Rsch. Soc. of Am., Lambda Chi Alpha. Home: 12216M Eagles Nest Ct Germantown MD 20874-2571 Office: Naval Surface Warfare Ctr Indian Head MD 20640

JASINSKI, ARNOLD ROBERT, pharmacist; b. Chester, Pa., Apr. 10, 1933; s. Matthew and Pauline (Nicgorski) J.; m. Helen Mary, Nov. 9, 1957; children: Mary, Sandra, Robert, Joseph. BS in Pharmacy, Phila. Coll. Pharmacy & Sci., 1954. Retail pharmacist various retail stores, Chester, Pa., 1954-56; hosp. pharmacist Delaware Hosp., Wilmington, 1956-57; analytical chemist E. DuPont, N.J., 1959-61; retail pharmacist City Pharmacy of Elkton (Md.) Inc., 1961-67, owner, pharmacist, 1967—. With USN, 1957-59. Mem. Nat. Assn. Retail Pharmacists, Md. Pharm. Assn., Am. Pharm. Assn., Am. Consultant Pharmacist, Nat. C.of C., Alumni Assn. Phila. Coll. Pharm. Sci. Office: City Pharmacy of Elkton Inc 723 N Bridge St Elkton MD 21921-5398

JASINSKI, JERRY, chemistry educator; b. Newport, N.H., July 28, 1940; s. Victor and Ann P. (Piotrowski) J.; m. Jacquelin A. Sargeant, Aug. 20, 1966; children: Jana L., John M., Jennifer A. BA in Chemistry, U. N.H., 1964, MS for Tchrs. of Chemistry, 1968; M in Natural Sci., Worchester Poly. Inst., 1968; PhD, U. Wyo., 1974. Chemistry and physics tchr. Middleburg (N.Y.) Cen. Sch., 1964-65; physics tchr. Stevens High Sch., Claremont, N.H., 1965-68; chemistry and physics tchr. Springfield (Vt.) High Sch., 1968-70, 75-78; teaching asst. chemistry dept. U. Wyo., Laramie, 1970-73; fellow Los Alamos Scientific Lab., 1973-74; postdoct. chemistry dept. U. Va., Charlottesville, 1974-75; from asst. prof. to prof. chemistry Keene (N.H.) State Coll., 1978—; vis. fellow U. Copenhagen, summer 1972; cons. Chem. Environ. and Nuclear Resource Svcs., Springfield, 1975—. Contbr. articles to profl. jours. including Jour. Coordination Chemistry, Jour. Am. Chem. Soc., Jour. Organic Chemistry; presenter in field. NSF grantee, 1989—, NIH grantee, 1990—; recipient numerous grants for rsch., 1984—. Fellow Am. Inst. Chemists; mem. AAAS, Am. Chem. Soc., Am. Crystallographic Soc., Am. Phys. Soc., Am. Assn. Physics Tchrs., Health Physics Soc., New England Inst. Chemists (treas. 1988—), KC, Sigma Xi. Republican. Roman Catholic. Home: 12 Orchard Ln Springfield VT 05156-2203 Office: Keene State Coll Chemistry Dept 229 Main St Keene NH 03431-4101

JASKOL, EARL, manufacturing executive; b. Pitts., Feb. 22, 1943; s. Norman and Sylvia (Krall) J.; m. Elaine Shien, Dec. 25, 1968; children: Dana Lynn, Matthew Alan. BS in Econs., U. Pa., 1965; MBA, Drexel U., 1970; postgrad., N.J. Inst. Tech., 1974-76. Various mfg. pos. Uniroyal, Phila., Joliet, Ill., 1965-70, Clorox Co., Jersey City, 1970-73; plant supt. J.L. Prescott & Co., Paterson, N.J., 1973-76, Ferdinand Gutmann & Co., Bklyn., 1976-79; plant mgr. Flock Industries, Inc., Phillipsburg, N.J., 1979-80; pres. J&J Flock Products, Inc., Easton, Pa., 1980—, Filmtech Corp., Easton, 1985—. Mem. Inst. Indsl. Engrs., Nat. Fedn. Ind. Bus. (guardian). Office: J&J Flock Products Inc PO Box 2005 Easton PA 18044-2005

JASLOW, HOWARD, engineer; b. Bklyn., Jan. 5, 1935; s. Louis and Myrtle (Schneider) J.; m. Barbara Theodora Karney, June 9, 1956; children—Amy Lisa, Russell Todd, Kenneth Mark, Wayne Harris, Melinda Kay. B. Aero. Engring., Poly. Inst. Bklyn., 1956; M.S. in Physics, Adelphi U., 1963. Engr., N.Am. Aviation, Los Angeles, 1956-58; engr. Republic Aviation, Farmingdale, N.Y., 1958-61; chief engr. Colt Firearms, Jericho, N.Y., 1961-72; project engr. Oceanics Inc., Plainview, N.Y., 1972-76; mgr. research and devel. Gould Inc., Melville, N.Y., 1976-82; sr. research engr. Norden Systems, Melville, 1983-84; dir. engring. ILC Data Device Corp., Bohemia, N.Y., 1984-87; sr. staff scientist Digital Signal Corp., Bohemia, 1987-91; pres. Innovative Algorithms, Smithtown, N.Y., 1991—. Contbr. articles in fields of aerodynamics and motion simulation to profl. jours.; patentee ammunition. Mem. AIAA, AAAS, N.Y. Acad. Scis. Home: 23 Neil Dr Smithtown NY 11787-1597 Office: Innovative Algorithms 23 Neil Dr Smithtown NY 11787-1597

JASPEN, NATHAN, educational statistics educator; b. N.Y.C., Oct. 21, 1917; s. Jacob J. and Sarah (Kantor) J.; m. Helen G. Shulman, June 11, 1944; children: David, Robert, Sandra Hughes, Daniel, Richard. B.S., CCNY, 1942; M.A., George Washington U., 1944; Ph.D., Pa. State U., 1949. Occupational analyst USES, Washington, 1942-47; rsch. fellow Pa. State U., 1947-49, asso. prof., 1949-52; dir. stats. automation Nat. League Nursing, N.Y.C., 1952-59; also cons.; asso. prof. NYU, 1959-62, prof. ednl. stats., 1962-82, prof. emeritus, 1982—, chmn. dept. ednl. stats., 1963-80, chmn. dept. math., sci. and statis. edn., 1980-82; cons. Am. Pub. Health Assn., USPHS, Bd. Coop. Edn. Services, Westchester, Bd. Jewish Edn. N.Y. Contbr. articles to profl. jours. Fellow AAAS, Am. Psychol. Assn.; mem. AAUP, Am. Ednl. Research Assn., Am. Statis. Assn., Assn. Computing Machinery, Inst. Math. Stats., Math. Assn. Am., Psychometric Soc., Sigma Xi, Pi Mu Epsilon, Psi Chi. Home: 200 Winston Dr Cliffside Park NJ 07010-3234

JASPER, SEYMOUR, lawyer; b. N.Y.C., May 15, 1919; s. Louis and Gussie (Levitch) J.; m. Geulah Eidelsberg, Nov. 24, 1940 (dec.); children: Michael, Ronald, Jeffrey, Idylia; m. Barbara Gray, Feb. 11, 1975. BS, NYU, 1939; JD, Columbia U., 1956. Bar: N.Y. 1956. Assoc. Young, Kaplan & Edelstein, N.Y.C., 1956-59; ptnr. Jasper, Sandler & Lipsay, N.Y.C., 1959-62; sole practice N.Y.C., 1962—. Served with USN. Mem. Assn. of Bar of City of N.Y. (estate planning, probate), N.Y. State Bar Assn. Office: 18 E 48th St New York NY 10017-1014

JASPERSEN, FREDERICK ZARR, economist; b. Phila., Sept. 23, 1938; s. Frederick Franklin and Jean Lorraine (Zarr) J.; m. Margie C. Trainor, Oct. 10, 1965. B.A. in Internat. Relations, Dartmouth Coll., 1961; M.A. Peace Corps fellow, Ind. U., 1965, Ph.D. in Econs., 1969. Mem. Peace Corps, Colombia, 1961-63; teaching asst. fellow Ind. U., Bloomington, 1964-65; Harvard U. econ. advisor Ministry Fin., Chile, 1968-69; economist Standard Oil N.J., N.Y.C., 1969-70, Am. Embassy Brazil, 1970-71; sr. economist World Bank, Washington, 1978-86, lead economist macroecon. adjustment policy and growth, 1987—; lectr. econs. Chile, Brazil, Ind. U. Contbr. author: World Development Report, 1981, Adjustment Experience and Growth Prospects of the Semi-Industrial Countries, 1981. V.p. Sidwell Friends Sch. Alumni Assn., 1978-80. Ford Found. Latin Am. teaching fellow Fletcher Sch., Tufts U., 1967-68. Mem. Am. Econ. Assn. Clubs: Dartmouth (Washington); Georgetown, U. Yates. Home: 5013 Randall Ln Bethesda MD 20816-1917 Office: 1818 H St NW Washington DC 20433-0002

JASS, HERMAN EARL, chemist consultant; b. Chgo., Mar. 30, 1918; s. Jacob and Bess (Gastwirth) J.; m. Alaine Florence Pabich, July 27, 1947; children: Daniel Keith, Diane Clare Ketelhut. BS with honors, U. Ill., 1939; MS in Chemistry, Northwestern U., 1950, PhD in Biochemistry, 1953. Rsch. chemist People's Gas Co., Chgo., 1940; chief biochemist Helene Curtis Inc., Chgo., 1941-51; group leader Armour Pharm. Co., Chgo., 1953-55; assoc. rsch. dir. Revlon, Inc., N.Y.C., 1955-64; v.p. R & D Carter Product, Div. C-W, Cranbury, N.J., 1964-76; pharm. cons. self-employed, Skillman, N.J., 1976—; columnist Cosmetics & Toiletries Mag., Wheaton, Ill., 1978—. Patentee in field; contbr. tech. articles to profl. jours. Pres. George Washington Coun. Boy Scouts, Pennington, N.J., 1970-73; v.p. Assn. for Improvement Montgomery Twp., N.J., 1986—. Recipient CIBS award Cosmetic, Toiletry & Fragrance Assn., 1978. Fellow AAAS, Soc. Cosmetic Chemists; mem. Am. Chem. Soc., Dermal Clin. Evaluation Soc. (pres 1985-87), Regulatory & Profls. Soc., Sigma Xi. Home and Office: 29 Platz Dr Skillman NJ 08558-1814

JASTROW, WERNER, police officer; b. Berlin, Apr. 26, 1934; came to U.S., 1952; s. Alfred and Dorothea Meta (Frankenstein) J.; m. Marlene Carol Youngelson, July 22, 1956; children: Kathryn Helen, Barbara Louise, John Steven. Owner, mgr. Dover (N.J.) Cabinet Shop Inc., 1956-63, J. & P. Bldg. Co., Dover and Boonton, N.J., 1957-69, Golden Age Home, Boonton, 1963-69; lt. Office Morris County Sheriff, Morristown, N.J., 1969—. Committeeman Morris County Republican Com., 1964-89. Mem. Masons. Jewish. Home: 325 Monroe St Boonton NJ 07005-2165 Office: Morris County Sheriff CN 900 Morristown NJ 07960-0900

JAY, MICHAEL ELIOT, radiologist; b. Bklyn., Nov. 29, 1949; s. Leon and Ruth (Zucker) J.; m. Susan C. Champagne. BS with honors, SUNY, Stonybrook, 1971; MD, Georgetown U., 1975. Diplomate Am. Bd. Radiology. Rotating internship Nassau County Med. Ctr., East Meadow, N.Y., 1975-76, resident in diagnostic radiology, 1976-79; fellow in cardiovascular radiology Brigham Woman's Hosp., Boston, 1979-80, staff radiologist, 1980-91; assoc. chief dept. radiology West Roxbury (Mass.) VA Med. Complex, 1980-91; instr. radiology Harvard Med. Sch., Boston, 1980-86, asst. clin. prof. radiology, 1986—; lectr. in field. Editorial bd.: Jour. Cardiovascular Medicine, 1985-86, Primary Cardiology, 1986-87, Choices in Cardiology, 1987—; contbr. articles to profl. jours. Mem. New England Cardiovascular Interventional Radiology Soc., Radiology Soc. N. Am. Jewish. Office: VA Med Ctr Vfw Hwy Revere MA 02151-2553

JAYCOX, ROBERT PETER, director of student aid; b. Englewood, N.J., Apr. 15, 1931; s. Edwin Kenneth and Lillian Weipert (Ackhurst) J.; m. Jean Hamilton, Aug. 13, 1955; children: Peter H., Linda A. BA, Colgate U., 1953, MAT, 1957. Tchr. social studies Chatham (N.J.) High Sch., 1957-58; asst. dir. admissions Colgate U., Hamilton, N.Y., 1958-59, asst. dir. admissions and student aid, 1959-60, dir. of student aid, 1960—; cons. N.Y. Higher Edn. Svcs. Corp., Albany, N.Y., 1972-80; cons. in field; chpt. advisor Alpha Tau Omega, Hamilton, 1958-72. Contbg. author: 50 College Admissions Directors Speak to Parents, 1988; contbr. articles to profl. jours. Member vestry St. Thomas Episcopal Ch., Hamilton, 1969-75; chmn. Village of Hamilton Rep. Caucus, 1972-77; commr. Village of Hamilton Mcpl. Utilities Commn., 1985—. With USAF, 1951-54, U.S. Army, 1953-55. Mem. Nat. Assn. Student Fin. Aid Adminstrs., N.Y. State Fin. Aid Adminstrs. Assn. (chartered, sec., treas. 1959-69, v.p. 1970, 25 Yr. Svc. award 1985), Eastern Assn. Student Aid Adminstrs. (chartered, sec., treas. 1971-73, v.p. 1974-75). Home: 33 Madison St Hamilton NY 13346-1105 Office: Colgate U 13 Oak Dr Hamilton NY 13346-1338

JAYNE, CYNTHIA ELIZABETH, psychologist; b. Pensacola, Fla., June 5, 1953; d. Gordon Howland and Joan (Rockwood) J. AB, Vassar Coll., 1974; MA, SUNY, Buffalo, 1978, PhD, 1983. Lic. psychologist, Pa. Instr. dept. psychiatry Temple U. Sch. Medicine, Phila., 1982-84, asst. prof., 1984-85, asst. dir. outpatient services, asst. dir. residency tng., 1982-85, clin. asst. prof., 1985—; pvt. practice psychology Phila., 1985—. Contbr. articles to profl. jours. Soc. for Sci. Study Sex scholar, 1981; Sigma Xi grantee, 1981, Kinsey Inst. Dissertation award, 1983. Mem. Am. Psychol. Assn., Ea. Psychol. Assn., Soc. for Sci. Study Sex (bd. dirs. 1984-86). Office: 1209 Locust St Philadelphia PA 19107-5409

JAYSON, JEFFREY ARTHUR, television director and producer; b. Beloit, Wis., June 13, 1949; s. Herman Louis and Beverly Mae (Zimbler) J.; m. Lorene Ann Goodman, Aug. 15, 1984. BS, Marquette U., 1970; MA, U. Wis., 1972. Asst. broadcast dir. Allied Stores Mktg., N.Y.C., 1973-74; reporter Sta. WRKL/WINS Radio, N.Y.C., 1974-76, AP, N.Y.C., 1976-78, Vis News, London, 1978-79; prodr. ABC-News, N.Y.C., 1979-86; dir., prodr. Good Morning Am., N.Y.C., 1986—. Recipient Best Reporting award AP,1974, 75, 76, Teddy award Outdoor Writers, 1992. Mem. AFTRA, Dirs. Guild Am., Writers Guild Am. Office: Good Morning Am 1965 Broadway New York NY 10023

JEAS, WILLIAM C., electronics and aerospace executive; b. Worcester, Mass., June 9, 1938; m. Irene M. Merkle, June 18, 1961; 1 child, Dean W. BS, U.S. Naval Acad., 1961; MBA, Air Force Inst. Tech., 1970. Commd. 2d lt. U.S. Air Force, 1961, advanced through grades to col., 1980, ret., 1986; served various assignments in R & D, engring. & prodn., 1961-85; chief operating officer, v.p. mktg. TE Products, Inc., Framingham, Mass., 1986—; bd. dirs., TE Consulting, Inc., Comtec, Inc. Mem. IEEE (sr. mem.), AIAA, SPIE, Armed Forces Communications Electronics Assn., U.S. Naval Acad. Alumni Assn., Air Force Assn. Home: 87 Wesson Ter Northborough MA 01532-1955

JEDRUCH, JACEK, nuclear engineer; b. Warsaw, Poland, Feb. 22, 1927; came to U.S., 1951, naturalized, 1957; s. Alexander and Anna (Borsuk) J.; m. Eva Christina Hoffman, Apr. 15, 1972. BSME, Northeastern U., 1956; MS in Nuclear Engring., MIT, 1958; PhD in Nuclear Engring., Pa. State U., State College, 1966. Metall. analyst Acme Type Metals Co., Everett, Mass., 1952-53; engr. trainee H.B. Smith Co., Westfield, Mass., 1953-56; rsch. asst. Columbia Nat. Co., Cambridge, Mass., 1957; scientist Westinghouse Electric Co., Pitts., 1957-65, fellow scientist, 1966-82; pvt. practice cons. Pitts., 1983-84; prin. engr. Ebasco Svcs. Inc., N.Y.C., 1985-89; sr. prin. engr. Ebasco Svcs. Inc., 1990—; adj. assoc. prof. applied physics and nuclear engring. Columbia U., N.Y.C., 1989. Author: Constitutions, Elections and Legislatures of Poland, 1493-1977, 1982, Nuclear Engineering Data Bases, Standards, and Numerical Analysis, 1985. Served with Polish Army, 1944-46, with British Army 1946-48. Kosciuszko Found. grantee, N.Y.C., 1982. Mem. ASME, Am. Nuclear Soc., Internat. Commn. for History of Rep. and Parliamentary Instns. Republican. Roman Catholic. Club: MIT of Western Pa. (Pitts.) (treas. 1978-82). Home: 21 Nassau Dr Summit NJ 07901-1715 Office: Ebasco Svcs Inc 2 World Trade Ctr New York NY 10048-0203

JEE, JUSTIN SOONHO, U.S. government official; b. Pusan, Korea, June 29, 1951; came to U.S., 1976; s. Hanwoong and Boksoo (Park) J.; m. Ahyung Lee, May 2, 1976. BS, U. Korea, 1976; BS in Acctg., U. Minn., 1980; MBA, San Diego State U., 1984. CPA, Minn., Va.; cert. mgmt. acct. Tax acct. Midway Nat. Bank, St. Paul, 1981-83; fin. analyst Medical, Inc., Inver Grove Heights, Minn., 1984-87; sr. acct. Internat. Trade Adminstrn., Import Adminstrn., U.S. Dept. Commerce, Washington, 1987-90; sr. bus. devel. specialist Minority Bus. Devel. Agy., U.S. Dept. Commerce, Washington, 1990—; cons. Bus. Devel. Ctr., San Diego, 1984. Mem. Am. Inst. CPA's, Minn. Soc. CPA's, Inst. Cert. Mgmt. Accts. (cert.), D.C. Inst. CPA's. Home: 13804 Foggy Hills Ct Clifton VA 22024-2407 Office: US Dept Commerce Minority Bus Devel Agy Rm 5099C 14th St & Constitution Ave Washington DC 20230

JEFFERS, GENE, public relations professional; b. Canton, Ohio, Oct. 30, 1948; s. Eugene Leroy, Jr. and Ann Elizabeth (Eberhart) J.; m. Carol Saile, Aug. 21, 1971; children: Jessica Ann, Jane Elizabeth. BA in Psychology, U. Md., 1971, MA in Journalism/Pub. Rels., 1983. Mgr., retail Sun Radio, Washington, 1971-72; mgr., photo studio Vicar Photography, Silver Spring, Md., 1972-73; freelance photojournalist Washington, 1973-78; staff photographer ARC, Washington, 1978-82, spl. projects asst., 1982-83, asst. dir. pub. affairs, 1983-85, media rels. assoc., 1985-87, mgr. media rels., 1986-88; v.p. pub. affairs Nat. Assn. Broadcasters, Washington, 1988—. Recipient Gold "Cindy" award Indsl. Photography, 1981. Mem. Pub. Rels. Soc. Am. (Silver Anvil award 1987). Home: 9710 Wightman Rd Gaithersburg MD 20879-1253 Office: Nat Assn of Broadcasters 1771 N St NW Washington DC 20036-2805

JEFFORDS, JAMES MERRILL, senator; b. Rutland, Vt., May 11, 1934; s. Olin Merrill and Marion (Hausman) J.; m. Elizabeth Daley; children: Leonard Olin, Laura Louise. BS, Yale U., 1956; LLB, Harvard U., 1962. Bar: Vt. 1962. Law clk. to Judge Ernest Gibson Vt. Dist., 1962; ptnr. firm Bishop, Crowley & Jeffords, Rutland, 1963-66, Kenney, Carbine & Jeffords, Rutland, 1966-69; atty. gen. State of Vt., 1969-72; ptnr. firm George E. Rice, Jr. and James M. Jeffords, 1973-74; mem. 94th-100th Congresses from Vt., mem. agr. com., ranking minority mem. edn. and labor com., chmn. environ. study conf., 1978-79, a founder Congl. solar coalition, mem. Congl. tourism caucus, mem. Nat. Commn. on Employment and Unemployment Stats., U.S. senator from Vt., 1989—, mem. Senate environment and pub. works com., labor and human resources com., fgn. rels. com., vets. affairs com., ranking minority mem. on Nr. Ea. and South Asian affairs subcom., mem. terrorism, narcotics and internat. ops. subcom., western hemisphere and peace corps affairs subcom.; ranking minority mem. Senate labor subcom.; mem. environment and pub. works com., vet. affairs com., spl. com. on aging; mem. New Eng. Congl. Caucus, N.E.-Midwest Econ. Advancement Coalition; town agt. Shrewsbury, 1964-68, zoning adminstr., 1966-68, zoning adminstr., 1966-68; mem. Jud. Selection Bd., 1967-68; chmn. Hwy. Dept. Investigating Com., 1968; mem. Vt. Senate, 1967-68. With USNR, 1956-59; capt. Res. (ret.). Mem. Am. Bar Assn., Vt. Bar Assn., Rutland County Bar Assn., Am. Judicature Soc. (dir. 1973-76), VFW. Republican. Congregationalist (trustee). Lodges: Lions, Elks. Office: US Senate 530 Dirksen Bldg Washington DC 20510-4503

JEFFREY, CHARLES CAHILL, physician; b. LaJunta, Colo., Mar. 3, 1944; s. George Bernard and Mildred (Measurac) J. BA, So. Conn. State U., 1967; MPH, Yale U., 1969; MD, Case Western Res. U., 1975. Diplomate Am. Bd. Anesthesiology. Instr. health and PE, asst. gymnastics coach So. Conn. State U., New Haven, 1970-71; grad. asst. med. edn. Med. Sch. Case Western Res. U., Cleve., 1972-73; intern medicine Mt. Sinai Hosp., Cleve., 1975-76; resident anesthesia Mass. Gen. Hosp., Boston, 1976-79, asst. anesthetist, 1979-80, 81—; dir. intensive care Mt. Auburn Hosp., Boston, 1980-81; fellow Harvard U. Med. Sch., 1976-79, instr. anesthesia, 1979—. Trainer U.S. team Gymnastcis-World Championships, Bulgaria, 1974. Named Disting. Alumnus So. Conn. State U., 1991. Mem. Am. Soc. Anesthesiologists, Mass. Soc. Anesthesiologists, Harvard Mus. Assn. Office: Mass Gen Hosp Fruit St Boston MA 02114

JEKOT, EDWARD JOSEPH, SR., government career service professional; b. Enfield, Conn., Aug. 5, 1939; s. Walter Albert and Frances Elizabeth (Olechney) J.; m. Marilyn Jean Bateman, May 30, 1964; children: Darlene, Frances, Edward Jr., Wayne. BA, U. of Conn., 1962; postgrad., U. of Okla., 1973. Cert. comml. lender, cert. credit adminstr. Officer in charge Western Mass. U.S. SBA, Holyoke, 1968-72; br. mgr. U.S. SBA, Milw., 1972-73; asst. dist. dir. U.S. SBA, Chgo., 1973-75, Hartford, Conn., 1975-89; procurement ctr. rep. U.S. SBA, Newport, R.I., 1989—; adj. prof. U. of Hartford, 1981—; instr. Asnuntuck C.C., Enfield, 1982-84, program mgr. Conn. Small Bus. Devel. Ctr., Hartford, 1982-89; internat. trade officer Conn. World Trade Ctr. Assn., Hartford, 1985-88; cons. R.I. Dept. Econ. Devel. Fed. Procurement Office/Task Force, Providence, 1985-88; bd. dirs. Conn. Correctional Industries, Hartford, 1980-86. Contbr. articles on small bus. mgmt. topics to mags. and newspapers. Rep. Greater Hartford Leadership, C. of C., 1983, Capitol Region Council of Govt., Hartford, 1979-87, Conn. Rural Devel. Initiative Com., Eastern/Western, Conn., 1988; mem. Recreational Park, Somers, Conn., 1978, 91; chmn., founder Enfield Taxpayers Assn. Inc., 1977. Recipient Quality Performance award U.S. SBA, 1974, 77, Spl. Achievement award, 1980, Mgrs. Merit Performance award, 1985, Superior Performance award, 1990, 91, Small Bus., Advocats award Conn. Small Bus. Fedn., 1985. Mem. Nat. Contract Mgrs. Assn., Pol.ish Nat. HOme Assn. Inc. (pres 1985-87), KC, N.Am. Fishing Club (charter), Ducks Unltd., Nat. Wild Turkey Fedn., Fed. Execs. Bd. Home: 421 Hall HIll Rd Somers CT 06071 Office: US SBA Naval Undersea Warefare Ctr Bldg 11 Newport RI 02841

JELALIAN, ALBERT V., electrical engineer; b. Bridgewater, Mass., June 30, 1933; s. Siragan and Zarouhi (Tanelian) J.; m. Mary B. Karoghlanian; children: Alan H., Leslie K. BSEE, Northeastern U., 1957. Reg. profl. engr., Mass. Engr. Raytheon Co., Lexington, Mass., 1957-81; asst. labs. mgr. Raytheon Co., Sudbury, Mass., 1981-86, 91—; asst. dir. Raytheon Co., Sudbury, 1986-91. Inventor: holds ten patents relating to aviation safety and military products; contbr. articles to profl. jours; published book on laser radar systems, 1992. Recipient Recognition award NASA, Washington, 1974, Group Achievement award, 1975. Mem. AIAA, IEEE, Infrared Info. Symposium (nat. chmn. vice chmn. active systems 1989-91, nat. chmn., 1991—). Republican. Armenian Orthodox. Home: 3 Reeves Rd Bedford MA 01730-1334 Office: Raytheon Co 528 Boston Post Rd Sudbury MA 01776-3375

JELASKO, MICHAEL JOSEPH, insurance company executive; b. Derby, Conn., Dec. 30, 1949; s. Michael J. and Helen Lena (Telep) J.; m. Lois Agnes Haggerty, Apr. 26, 1975; children: Deborah E., Lisa M., Karl E., Elizabeth M. Student, South Conn. State U., 1967-68; ABAS, South Cen.

Community Coll., New Haven, Conn., 1968-70. CLU Am. Coll., Bryn Mawr, Pa., 1987; chartered fin. cons. Am. Coll., 1987. Spl. agt. John Hancock Cos., Hamden, Conn., 1974-76; sales supr. John Hancock Cos., Hamden, 1976-80, sales mgr., 1980-83; v.p. Coordinated Benefits, Inc., Madison, Conn., 1983-85; pres., treas. Coordinated Benefits, Inc., Milford, Conn., 1985—; v.p. Karl, Inc., 1985-89, pres., treas., 1989—. Mem. Dem. Town com., Orange, Conn. Staff sgt. USAR, 1970-78. Recipient Pres.'s Cabinet award John Hancock Cos., 1984, 86, 88, Pres. Hon. Club award John Hancock Cos., 1979, 80, 83, 85, 87, Pres.' Honor Coun. award Prin. Mut. Life 1986, 87, 88. Mem. New Haven Life Underwriters Assn. (bd. dirs.), New Haven County Sheriff's Assn., New Haven CLUs Assn. (bd. dirs.), Million Dollar Round Table (life and qualifying mem.), Quinnipiak Club (New Haven), Milford Yacht Club, Racebrook Country Club (Orange), Pres's. Honor Club (Boston), Pres. Club. Democrat. Roman Catholic. Home: 557 Broadview Rd Orange CT 06477-2168 Office: PO Box 111 Milford CT 06460-0111

JELENIK, OTTO JOHN, Canadian government minister; b. Prague, Czechoslovakia, May 20, 1940; arrived in Can., 1951; s. Henry and Jarmila (Zizka) J.; m. Leata Mary Bennett, Aug. 17, 1974; children: Misha, Jamie. Educated, Swiss Alpine Bus. Coll. Formerly profl. figure skater, then founder, operator mfg. bus. Oakville, Ont.; mem. Can. Parliament, 1972-84; min. of state for fitness and amateur sport Can. Govt., 1984-88, min. of supply and svcs., receiver gen., min. responsible for Stats. Can. and Royal Can. Mint, 1988-89, min. of nat. revenue, 1989—, also vice-chmn. com. on cultural affairs & nat. identity; former Opposition spokesperson on small bus., held numerous cabinet positions including Consumer and Corp. Affairs critic; former TV sports commentator. Gold medalist (with sister Maria) at World Pairs Figure Skating Championships, Prague, 1962; elected to Can.'s Sports Hall of Fame. Progressive Conservative. Office: Min Nat Revenue, House of Commons, Rm 133 East Block, Ottawa, ON Canada K1A 0A6

JELLOWS, TRACY PATRICK, software engineer; b. Quincy, Mass., Oct. 15, 1951; d. Henry David and Dorothy Margret (Joyce) J. BS in Physics, Bridgewater (Mass.) State Coll., 1981; postgrad., U. Mass., Boston, 1982. Support specialist Standard Software Inc., Randolph, Mass., 1982-83; sr. support supr. Lotus Devel. Corp., Cambridge, Mass., 1983, software engr., 1984-85, sr. software engr., 1985-89; prin. engr. 1-2-3 Graphics Lotus Devel. Corp., 1989-90; prin. engr. Edsun Labs., Waltham, Mass., 1990-91; prin. engr., cons. Saturn Software, Brockton, Mass., 1991—. Mem. IEEE, Assn. Computing Machinery, Boston Computer Soc. Democrat. Roman Catholic. Home: 9 Toby Rd Brockton MA 02402-1947

JEN, FRANK CHIFENG, finance and management educator; b. Shanghai, China, May 15, 1931; came to U.S., 1957; s. Seybold E. and Susan (Lin) J.; m. Daisy Chi, Aug. 26, 1962; children: Amy K., Wendy K., Edward K. B.S., N. Central Coll., 1959; M.B.A., U. Wis., 1960, Ph.D., 1963. Asst. prof. finance SUNY, Buffalo, 1964-66, assoc. prof., 1966-68, prof., 1968—, Mfrs. & Traders Trust Co.'s prof. banking and finance, chmn. dept. finance, 1967-70, chmn. dept. operating analysis, 1970-77, dir. advanced comml. lending and credit analysis program, 1977—; vis. prof. Nat. Center for Indsl. Mgmt. Devel. at Dalian, China, 1980-91; co-dir. China-M.B.A. program SUNY-Buffalo 1984-91; chmn. MBA program SUNY-Buffalo, 1992—. Mem. Am. Fin. Assn., Am. Econ. Assn., Soc. Econ. and Fin. Mgmt. in China (pres. 1985-88), Pi Gamma Mu, Beta Gamma Sigma. Home: 287 Forestview Dr Buffalo NY 14221-1439 Office: SUNY Buffalo Sch Mgmt Jacobs Ctr Amherst NY 14260

JENIFER, FRANKLYN GREEN, academic administrator; married; 3 children. Grad., postgrad., Howard U., 1965; D in plant virology, U. Md., 1970. Prof. biology, assoc. provost, dept. chmn., chmn. univ. senate Rugters U., N.J., 1970-79; vice chancellor N.J. Dept. Higher Edn., 1979, Mass. Dept. Higher Edn., 1986; chancellor Mass. Bd. of Regents Pub. Higher Edn. System Office, Boston, until 1990; pres. Howard U., Washington, 1990—. Office: Howard U Office of Pres 2400 6th St NW Washington DC 20059-9997*

JENKINS, ADELBERT HOWARD, psychology educator; b. St. Louis, Dec. 10, 1934; s. Herbert Crawford and Helen Alma (Howard) J.; m. Betty Jo Lanier, July 5, 1969; 1 child, Christopher Lanier. BA, Antioch Coll., Yellow Springs, Ohio, 1957; MA, U. Mich., 1958, PhD, 1963. Lic. psychologist, N.Y. USPHS postdoctoral fellow Albert Einstein Coll. Medicine, Bronx, N.Y., 1962-64, from asst. instr. to instr., 1964-67; asst. prof. clin. psychology NYU Med. Ctr., N.Y.C., 1967-71; assoc. prof. psychology Faculty Arts and Sci. NYU, 1971—; tng. cons. N.Y. VA Hosp., N.Y.C., 1974—, Bronx VA Hosp., 1975—; M.L. King-Rosa Parks vis. prof. dept. psychology U. Mich., 1987. Author: Psychology of the Afro-American, 1982; contbr. articles to profl. jours. Mem. bd. deacons Riverside Ch., N.Y.C., 1989-90, mem. edn. commn., 1990-92. Ford Found. grantee, 1976, 80; recipient M.L. King Jr. award N.Y. Soc. Clin. Psychologists, 1984. Fellow APA, Soc. for Personality Assessment; mem. Assn. Black Psychologists (chair N.Y.C. chpt. 1970, Scholar of Yr. 1983), N.Y. State Psychol. Assn., Ea. Psychol. Assn., Nat. Register Health Svc. Providers Psychology. Office: NYU 715 Broadway New York NY 10003-6806

JENKINS, ANTHONY CHARLES, correspondent; b. London, Apr. 13, 1956; came to U.S., 1986; s. Victor Silverstein and Anne Elizabeth Jenkins de Blanes. BA, Durham U., 1978. Sr. account exec. Internat. Mktg., London, 1980-82; Nicaragua corr. Guardian Newspaper, London, 1982-85, sr. corr. Central Am. and Caribbean, 1985-86; U.S. corr. Expresso, Lisbon, Portugal, 1986—. Author: Nicaragua and the U.S.A. Years of Conflict, 1989, Nicaragua A Decade of Rebellion, 1991; contbr. articles to profl. jours. Pres. Durham Students' Union, 1978-79; gen. sec. Fgn. Corr. Assn., Nicaragua, 1984-86. Recipient Gazeta Prize, Journalists' Assn., Portugal, 1988. Home and Office: Expresso 40 Macdougal St New York NY 10012-2939

JENKINS, JANE AMY, actuarial analyst; b. Camden, N.J., Aug. 10, 1965; d. William Edward and Olga (Matyas) Rapp; m. Scott Jason Jenkins, July 1, 1989. BS in Math., St. Joseph's U., 1987. Actuarial student Milliman and Robertson, Radnor, Pa., 2987-88; actuarial analyst O'Sullivan Assocs., Voorhees, N.J., 1988—. Mem. Nat. Math. Frat. Republican. Roman Catholic. Home: 57 Picadilly Cir Marlton NJ 08053-4235 Office: O'Sullian Assocs 1307 White Horse Rd Ste 500 Voorhees NJ 08043-2176

JENKINS, KENNETH VINCENT, literature educator, writer; b. Elizabeth, N.J.; s. Thomas Augustus and Rebecca Meredith (Williams) J.; children: Roderick, Howard, Rebecca, Leah. AB, MA, Columbia Coll.; postgrad., Columbia U. Tchr. South Side Sr. High Sch., Rockville Centre, N.Y., 1953-72, chmn. dept. English, 1965-72; prof. Afro-Am. lit. Nassau Community Coll., Garden City, N.Y., 1972—, chmn. Afro Am. studies dept., 1975—, supr. adj. faculty, 1974-82; cons. in English, N.Y. State Dept. Edn., Albany, 1965-72; mem. Regents Question Com. in English, Albany, 1966-71. Author: Last Day in Church, 1955, Teaching African Literature, 1960; contbr. revs., poems to profl. publs. Chairman bd. dirs., founder Target Youth Ctrs., Inc., 1973-76, African-am. Book Ctr., 1982—; mem. nat. bd. Pacifica Found., 1973-79, chmn., 1975-76, pres., 1976-78; bd. dirs. Sta. WBAI-FM, N.Y.C., 1972-85, Nassau County Youth Bd., 1976—, chmn., 1978—; mem. N.Y. Gov.'s Commn. on Youth, 1984—, Morningside Players Theatre, N.Y.C., 1987—; bd. dirs. L.I. Community Found., 1989—, N.Y. State Youth Support, Inc., 1990—. Pennington grantee, 1953, community, county, state awards, M.L. King award Celebration Com. Nassau County, 1990; mem. bd. Schombrug Ctr., N.Y.C., 1990—. Mem. Afro-Am. Inst., Assn. Study of Afro-Am. Life and History, Mensa, Phi Delta Kappa. Office: Nassau Community Coll Garden New York NY 11530

JENKINS, ROBERT NESBIT, real estate executive; b. Glen Ridge, N.J., May 28, 1951; s. George Pollock and Marian (O'Brien) J.; m. Heidi Lynn Gage, May 17, 1986. BA, Colo. Coll., 1973; MBA, Columbia U., 1980. With Trammell Crow Co., Dallas, 1973-78; v.p. Eastdil Realty Inc., N.Y.C., 1980-83, Am. Realty Capital, N.Y.C., 1983-85, Cornerstone Capital Inc., N.Y.C., 1985-86, Pocantico Devel. Assocs. Inc., N.Y.C., 1986-89, Met. Life Ins. Co., N.Y.C., 1989—. Trustee Blair Acad., Blairstown, N.J., 1987—; elder Brick Presbyn. Ch., N.Y.C., 1991—. Mem. Racquet and Tennis Club. Republican. Office: Metro Life Ins Co 200 Park Ave 1 Madison Ave New York NY 10166

JENKINS, WARDELL LEWIS, telecommunications administrator; b. Washington, Dec. 18, 1940; s. James Lewis and Leitha Beatrice (Gamble) J.; m. Johnella Tolliver, Nov. 24, 1962; children: Antoine Lewis, Shawn Kimberly. Grad., Cardoza High Sch., Washington, 1955-58; postgrad., Washington Tech. Inst., 1974-77, Fed. City Coll., Washington, 1980-82. Telecommunications operator U.S. Dept. State, Washington, 1963-85, communication mgr., 1985—, also chief systems & network control, 1989—; participant Strategic Arms Limitation talks, Helsinki, 1970, Presdl. Econ. Conf., Ottawa, Can., 1981. Mem. Fairfield Knolls Civic Assn., District Heights, Md. Sgt. USAF, 1958-62. Mem. Am. Legion, Non-Commd. Officers Assn., Am. Assn. Retired Persons, Armed Forces Communications & Electronic Assn., Parents of Alumni-Marquette U. Roman Catholic. Home: 7311 Walker Mill Rd Southern Maryland Facility MD 20743 Office: US Dept State 321 C St NW Washington DC 20520

JENKS, BRENDA, educator; b. Newport, Vt., Oct. 15, 1943; d. Martin and Elizabeth (Cargill) Gray; m. William A. Jenks; children: William H., Sharon A. Cert., Maine Med. Sch. Nursing, 1964; BS, U. Vt., 1977, MEd, 1991. RN; cert. sch. nurs, cert. profl. tchr. in health occupations and spl. edn.; cert. cardiopulmonary resuscitation instr. Staff nurse Rehab. Ctr. MCHV, Burlington, Vt., Santa Monica (Calif.) Hosp.; instr. Fanny Allen Sch. Practical Nursing, Winooski, Vt.; sch. nurse Mt. Mansfield Union High Sch., Jericho, Vt.; health careers tchr. Essex Junction (Vt.) Sch. Dist. Recipient award for Outstanding Vocat. Program for State of Vt., 1991. Mem. NEA, Am. Vocat. Assn., Vt. Vocat. Assn., Essex Junction Tchrs. Assn., Vt. Tchrs. Assn., vocat. Indsl. Clubs Am. (chpt. advisor). Home: 12 Vale Dr Essex Junction VT 05452-4340

JENKS, GEORGE MERRITT, retired librarian; b. Purcell, Okla., Aug. 1, 1929; s. Darrell C. and Muriel Helena (Denison) J.; m. Zoya Elaine Hochstein, Mar. 2, 1957; children: Darrell Allan, Mark Denison, Andrew Leslie. BA, U. Okla., 1949, MA, 1951, MLS, 1959; postgrad., UCLA, 1954-56. Reports officer CIA, Washington, 1956-57; instr. fgn. langs. N.Mex. State U., Las Cruces, 1957-58; librarian I Queens Borough Pub. Library, Jamaica, N.Y., 1959-60; cataloger head acquisitions Calif. State U., Northridge, 1960-63; asst., then acting libr. U. Tasmania, Hobart, Australia, 1963-66; chief tech. svcs., univ. libr. Coll. Devel. Libr., Bucknell U., Lewisburg, Pa., 1966-91, ret., 1991; lectr. Immaculate Heart Coll., Los Angeles, 1961-63, Hobart Tech. Coll., Tasmania, Australia, 1964-66. Contbr. articles to profl. jours. Pres. Ry. Hist. Soc., Lewisburg, 1971; mem. planning commn. City of Lewisburg, 1984-87. Served with USMC, 1951-53, Korea. Decorated Purple Heart. Mem. ALA, Pa. Library Assn., AAUP. Democrat. Lodge: Kiwanis (pres. Lewisburg chpt. 1970). Home: 202 N 2d St Lewisburg PA 17837

JENNER, EDWARD LEVANT, chemical researcher; b. Pontiac, Mich., Mar. 27, 1918; s. Roy C. and Alice E. (Marsh) Jenner; m. Dorothy Ilean Ragla, July 3, 1942; chilren: Charles A., Edward W., Margaret A. AB, Lake Forest (Ill.) Coll., 1939; MS, U. Mich., 1940, PhD, 1942. Rsch. chemist Nat. Def. Rsch. Commn., Ann Arbor, Mich., 1941-45; rsch. chemist Du-Pont, Wilmington, Del., 1945-82, ret., 1982; rsch. chemist U. Calif., Berkeley, 1961-62. Contbr. articles to profl. jours. Fellow AAAS; mem. Am. Chem. Soc. Home: 107 Lands End Rd Wilmington DE 19807-2519

JENNIK, SUSAN MARIE, non-profit organization executive, lawyer; b. Milw., Dec. 27, 1952; d. Francis John and Rosemary Ann (Stefaniak) J.; m. Richard Douglas Hollander, Oct. 11, 1975 (div. 1983); 1 child, Michael Jennik Hollander. BS, U. Wis., Kenosha, 1978; JD, NYU, 1981. Bar: N.Y. 1982. Assoc. atty. Hall, Clifton & Schwartz, N.Y.C., 1981-84; asst. atty. gen. N.Y. State Dept. Law, N.Y.C., 1984-85; regional organizer Teamsters for a Dem. Union, Bklyn., 1985-89; dir. women's project Assn. for Union Democracy, Bklyn., 1985-89, exec. dir., 1989—. Contbr. articles to profl. jours. Bd. dirs. North Star Community Funding Bd., N.Y.C., 1987-90, L.I. Ctr. for Workers Rights, Amityville, N.Y., 1989—. Root-Tilden scholar, 1978-81; recipient Pub. Svc. award NYU Sch. Law Alumni Assn., 1990. Mem. Nat. Employment Lawyers Assn., Nat. Lawyers Guild. Office: Assn for Union Democracy 500 State St Brooklyn NY 11217

JENNINGS, ALFRED HIGSON, JR., educator, actor, singer; b. Danbury, Conn., Dec. 24, 1959; s. Alfred Higson and Linda (Keating) J. BS, U. Conn., 1982, MMus, 1984. Cert. profl. educator, Conn. Teaching asst., choral dept. U. Conn., Storrs, 1982-84; tchr. music Danbury Pub. Schs., 1985—; asst. condr. Concert Choir/Chamber Singers, U. Conn., 1982-84, asst. dir. Annual Elizabethan Christmas Dinner Concert, 1983; musical dir. for theatrical prodns. Danbury High Sch., 1985-88; bariton soloist St. Mathew Episcopal Ch. Choir, Wilton, Conn., 1986—. Vocal dir. plays The Sound of Music, 1986, Camelot, 1988, Annie, 1990, others; actor in plays Godspell, 1985, South Pacific, 1987, Oklahoma!, 1988, You're a Good Man, Charlie Brown, 1988, Into the Woods, 1991, others. Named Tchr. of Yr., South St. Elem. Sch., 1990; recipient Project Redesign grant Danbury Pub. Schs., 1991-92. Mem. NEA, Musicals at Richter, Inc. (sec. 1987-88, v.p. 1988-89, program editor 1991-92), Am. Choral Dirs. Assn., Music Educators Nat. Conf. Home: 8 Cipolla Ln Brookfield CT 06804 Office: Danbury Pub Schs 1 School Ridge Rd Danbury CT 06811-5254

JENNINGS, BRUCE, research institute director; b. Ft. Wayne, Ind., Apr. 27, 1949; s. Hugh Jack and Margaret Evangeline (Wisman) J.; m. Margaret Ann Machulis, May 26, 1972; 1 child, Andrew. AB, Yale U., 1971; MA, Princeton U., 1973. Instrn. asst. Princeton (N.J.) U., 1974-75; asst. prof. Stockton State Coll., Pomona, N.J., 1975-80; rsch. assoc. Hastings Ctr., Briarcliff Manor, N.Y., 1980-83, assoc., 1983-91, exec. dir., 1991—; adj. prof. Vassar Coll., Poughkeepsie, N.Y., 1989; cons. U.S. Senate Com. on Ethics, Washington, 1980, U.S. Army Ethics Task Force, Indpls., 1983; treas., bd. dirs. Am. Health Decisions, Denver, 1988—; mem. ethics com. N.Y. Hosp./Cornell Med. Ctr., N.Y.C., 1989—. Co-author: Ethics of Legislative Life, 1985, Congress and the Media, 1985, New Choices, New Responsibilities, 1990; edtior of books; contbr. articles to profl. jours. Advisor Josephson Inst. Ethics, Marina del Rey, Calif., 1990—; mem. task force Episcopal Diocese N.Y., N.Y.C., 1992—; chair Westchester Fair Campaign Com., White Plains, N.Y., 1991—. Griffin Meml. scholar Yale U., 1967-71. Mem. Am. Polit. Sci. Assn., Columbia Seminar Social Thought (assoc.), Assn. Pub. Policy and Mgmt., Conf. Polit. Thought, Conf. Polit. Thought, Yale Club N.Y., Yale Westchester Alumni Assn. (v.p. 1991—). Democrat. Episcopalian. Office: Hastings Ctr 255 Elm Rd Briarcliff Manor NY 10510

JENNINGS, CAROL, marketing executive; b. Marion, Ohio, Oct. 2, 1945; d. Richard P. and Mary (LeMaster) J.; m. John Putnam Merrill Jr., Jan. 3, 1981. BA, Miami U., Oxford, Ohio, 1967. News editor Penton Pub. Inc., Cleve., 1967-69; pub. rels. exec. Cen. Nat. Bank, Cleve., 1969-71; dir. pub. rels. New Eng. Conservatory of Music, Boston, 1971-74, Bklyn. Acad. Music, N.Y.C., 1974-75; account exec., supr. Hill and Knowlton, N.Y.C., 1975-81, from v.p. to mng. dir., 1981-87; sr. v.p., gen. mgr. Hill, Hilliday, Connors, Cosmopolus, Boston, 1987, Hill and Knowlton, Boston, 1987-90; dir. corp. communications Bain and Co., Boston, 1991—. Office: Bain and Co 2 Copley Pl Boston MA 02117

JENNINGS, CHARLES RICHARD, sales and marketing executive; b. East Liverpool, Ohio, July 18, 1941; s. Robert Thomas and Helen Dell (Miller) J.; m. Sylvia Jean Hunt, Nov. 15, 1969; children: Brent, Brad. Student, Ohio State U., 1959, Ohio No. U., 1960. Dist. supr. Marrud Inc., Norwood, Mass., 1961-65; sales rep. Scott Paper Co., Cleve., 1965-69; dist. mgr. Menly and James Labs., Phila., 1969-71; mgr. merchandising K'nS Dept. Stores, Millersburg, Pa., 1971-72; dist. supr. Keystone Drug, Lebanon, Pa., 1972-75; buyer, merchandiser Laneco Inc. div. Wetterau, Inc., Easton, Pa., 1975-85; dir. retail merchandising corp. Alco Health Svcs., Phila., 1985-90; v.p. northeastern region Coats Distbrs. Inc., Dunn, N.C. and Wilkes-Barre, Pa., 1990—. Fellow Drug Salesman Assn. Pa. (Man of Yr. 1985). Republican. Presbyterian. Home: 461 Dewberry Ave Bethlehem PA 18017-4720 Office: Coats Distbrs Inc Hwy 421 W Dunn NC 28334 also: Coats Distbrs Inc 1 Alta Rd Wilkes Barre PA 18702

JENNINGS, DONALD EDWARD, physicist; b. New Rochelle, N.Y., May 30, 1948; s. John Nugent and Margareta Regina (Nebel) J.; m. Jeanne Graham, May 30, 1970; children: Emily Elizabeth, Elyse Anne. BS, No. Ariz. U., 1970; PhD, U. Tenn., 1974. Rsch. assoc. physics dept. U. Tenn., Knoxville, 1974-76; resident rsch. assoc. planetary systems br. NAS/NRC, NASA Goddard Space Flight Ctr., Greenbelt, Md., 1976-77, space scientist, 1977—; astronomy tchr. U. Md., College Park, 1990—; investigator SKIRT Space Shuttle Experiment, 1991; instrument scientist Cassini mission to Saturn CIRS, 1990—; investigator various study programs on planets, sun and stars. Co-author: Exploration of the Solar System, 1991; contbr. articles to profl. publs.; patentee in field. Vol. local elem. schs. NDEA fellow, 1971-74; NSF trainee, 1970-71. Office: NASA Goddard Space Flight Ctr Code 693 Greenbelt MD 20771

JENNINGS, DONALD ERB, psychologist; b. Chattanooga, July 2, 1939; s. James Robert Jennings and Nell (Erb) Allen; m. Nancy Sue Sells, Feb. 18, 1965; children: Nicole, Beth, Susan. BS, Livingston U., 1964; MEd, U. Tenn., 1968; D.Ed., U. Pa., 1979. Lic. psychologist, Pa. Rehab. psychologist Moccasin Bend Psychiat., 1964-65; rehab. counselor State of Tenn., 1965-66, Commonwealth of Pa., 1966-67; cons. psychologist rehab. unit Pa. Hosp., 1967-69, Nazareth Mental Health Ctr., 1969-72; psychologist Hahnemann Med. Coll. and Hosp., Phila. Prison System, 1980-82; v.p., psychologist Edn. & Vocat. Guidance Consultants, Inc., 1967-81; dir. psychology sect. NE Outpatient and Rehab. Ctr., 1985-87; instr. psychology St. Joseph's U., Phila., 1967—; pvt. practice psychologist Phila., 1967—; cons. Cooper St. Pain Group, 1980-85, pain clinic South Phila. Orthopedic Assocs., 1982-83; presenter in field. Contbr. articles to profl. jours. Mem. Am. Psychol. Assn., Pa. Psychol. Assn. (chair impaired psychologist program, ethics com.), Phila. Soc. Clin. Psychologists, Am. Assn. for the Advancement Psychology, Am. Orthopsychiat. Assn., Am. Psychology-Law Soc., Nat. Acad. Forensic Scientists, Nat. Assn. Rehab. Profls. in Pvt. Sector, Nat. Rehab. Assn., Nat. Forensic Ctr., Internat. Rehab. Inst., Nat. Head Injury Found. (profl.), Am. Bd. Profl. Disability Evaluators, Am. Bd. Med. Psychotherapists. Home: 27 Galena Ct Southampton PA 18966-1125 Office: 826 Bustleton Pike Unit 109 Langhorne PA 19053-6057

JENNINGS, FREDERIC BEACH, JR., economist, consultant; b. Boston, Dec. 29, 1945; s. Frederic Beach III and Ellen (Osgood) J.; m. Lucille Candace Giglio, Aug. 15, 1975; 1 child, Frederic Beach V. BA magna cum laude, Harvard U., 1968; MA in Econs., Stanford U., 1980, PhD in Econs., 1985. Jr. medicare acct. Blue Cross-Blue Shield, Boston, 1968-69; ind. rsch. fellow Inst. Humane Studies, Menlo Park, Calif., 1969-71, 77-78; asst. mgr. Globe Bag Co., South Boston, 1972-73; rsch. asst. Charles River Assocs., Cambridge, Mass., 1973-74; rsch. and teaching fellow Stanford (Calif.) Dept. Econs., 1974-79; instr. econs. Tufts U., Medford, Mass., 1979-83; asst. prof. Bentley Coll., Waltham, Mass., 1985-87; sr. econ. cons. The Mac Rsch. Group, Cambridge, 1987-88, Charles River Assocs., Boston, 1988-91; sr. mgr. econ. analysis group office of fed. tax svcs. Arthur Andersen & Co., Washington, 1991—; chmn., rep. Stanford Grad. Student Coun., 1974-76; senator Stanford Student Seante, 1975-76; co-pres. Associated Students Stanford U., 1976-77; founder Stanford Grad. Students Assn., 1978-79, The Bentley Participants, Waltham, 1986-87, Full circle Discussion Group Tufts U., Medford, 1981-84; resident assoc. Residential Edn., Stanford, 1978-79. Author: Democracy in Disarray, 1978, (paper) Value, Exchange and Profit, 1966, (essays) Academy, Society and Personal Growth, 1983, Whither Our Education?, 1983. Mem. Am. Econ. Assn., Cliometrics Soc., Indsl. Orgn. Soc., Western Econ. Assn., Atlantic Econ. Soc., Harvard Travellers Club. Home: 199 Argilla Rd Ipswich MA 01938-2615 Office: Arthur Andersen & Co 1666 K St NW Washington DC 20005

JENNINGS, JOHN ROBERT ROGERS, lawyer; b. Toronto, Ont., Can., July 10, 1937; s. Robert Douglas and Mary Adelaide (Rogers) J.; m. Eyton Margaret Embury, Apr. 4, 1964; children: Evan, Simon. BA with honors, U. Toronto, 1959; LLB, York U., Toronto, 1962. Bar: Ont. 1964. Articled to P.B.C. Pepper, Queen's Counsel, Toronto, 1962-63; ptnr. Jennings, Clute, Lovatt & Jones, Toronto, 1964-72, Kingsmill, Jennings, Toronto, 1972-91; Queens Counsel Province of Ont., 1976—; judge Gen. div. Ont. Ct. of Justice, Toronto, 1991—. Chmn., mem. adv. bd. Windsor (Ont.)-Essex Mediation Ctr. Pilot Project, 1981-84. Capt. Queen's Own Rifles of Can., 1957, ret. Fellow Am. Coll. Trial Lawyers; mem. Can. Bar Assn. (pres. 1989-90), CBAnet, Inc. (pres. 1989-90), The Advocates' Soc. (pres. 1987), County of York Law Assn. (pres. 1976), Toronto Golf Club, Badminton and Racquet Club (Toronto), Rideau Club (Ottawa). Office: Court House, 361 University Ave, Toronto, ON Canada M5G 1X9

JENNINGS, RALPH MERWIN, broadcasting executive; b. N.Y.C., Mar. 26, 1938; s. Wesley B. and Nan M. (Alderman) J.; m. Paula A. Tadlock, July 28, 1982; children: Alma Nan, Matthew. BA, Coll. Wooster, 1963; MA, NYU, 1966, PhD, 1968. Ops. dir., producer Sta. WRVR-FM, N.Y.C., 1962-63; producer, dir. Sta. KSLH-FM, St Louis, 1963-64; coord. Hunter Coll. TV Ctr., N.Y.C., 1964-66; gen. mgr. Sta. WFUV-FM, N.Y.C., 1985—; dep. dir. Office Communication United Ch. Christ, N.Y.C., 1967-80; communicaitons cons. N.Y.C., 1980—; cons. on communications policy U.S. Cath. Conf.; mem. exec. com. Ea. Pub. Radio. V.p., bd. dirs. John Milton Soc. for the Blind, N.Y.C., 1978—; bd. dirs. Counsel of Chs. for N.Y.C. Mem. United Ch. Christ. Office: Fordham U Sta WFUV-FM Bronx NY 10458

JENNINGS, ROBERT LEE, aircraft maintenance executive; b. N.Y.C., May 6, 1946; s. Leo William and Ruth Helen (Fehrenbach) J.; m. Francine Marie DiPietro, May 30, 1976; children: David Robert, Robert Michael. Grad., Teterboro (N.J.) Sch. Aeros., 1971. Line serviceman Atlantic Aviation Corp., Teterboro, 1970-74; instr. Teterboro Sch. Aeros., 1972-73; supr. aircraft maintenance Dart & Kraft, Inc., Teterboro, 1974-84; pres., chief exec. officer Big A Flying Club, Inc., 1974—; chief of maintenance Am. Standard, Inc., 1984-87; bd. dir. maintenance Damin Jet Inc., 1987-89, aircraft maint. Am. Bus. Jet, Inc., 1989-90, Brunswick Air Svc., 1985-87, Jet Air Internat., aircraft maintenance Seagull Aricraft Corp. With USN, 1964-69; Vietnam. Mem. Profl. Aircraft Maintenance Assn., Nat. Bus. Aircraft Assn., Am. Inst. Econ. Rsch., Les Amis du Vin, German Wine Society. Republican. Roman Catholic. Home: RR 6 Box 339 Newton NJ 07860-9240 Office: 333 Industrial Ave Teterboro NJ 07608-1022

JENNINGS, ROGER LEE, manufacturing company executive; b. N.Y.C., June 14, 1940; s. Asa Will and Irene (Mackedon) J.; m. Susan Martens, Aug. 9, 1969; children: Ryan Kent, Carey Leigh, Erin Elizabeth, Andrew Regan. BA, Ohio Wesleyan U., 1962; MBA, U. Pa., 1968. Mgmt. cons. Coopers & Lybrand, N.Y.C., 1968-74; treas., contr. Finch Pruyn & Co., Inc., Glens Falls, N.Y., 1974-79; pres. Finch Pruyn Sales, Inc., Glens Falls, 1978-79, R. Jennings Mfg. Co., Inc., Glens Falls, 1979—; bd. dirs. CEN, Albany, N.Y. Contbr. articles on screen printing and high voltage substas. to profl. jours.; numerous patents in screen printing field. Bd. dirs. Adirondack Regional C. of C., Glens Falls, 1978; Rep. committeeman, 1991—. Republican. Congregationalist. Office: 8 Glen St Glens Falls NY 12801-4438

JENNISON, PETER SAXE, publishing executive; b. Swanton, Vt., July 2, 1922; s. Clark Saxe and Louise (Warren) J.; m. Jane Dryden Lowe, May 11, 1946; 1 child, Andrew Clark. BA, Middlebury Coll., 1947. News editor Publishers Weekly, N.Y.C., 1947-52; deputy dir. Am. Book Publ. Coun., N.Y.C., 1952-64; exec. dir. Nat. Book Com., N.Y.C., 1964-71; founder, chmn. The Countryman Press, Woodstock, Vt., 1973—; cons. Dept. of State, Washington, 1961, Franklin Book Programs, N.Y.C., 1962-63. Author: The Mimosa Smokers, 1959, The Governor, 1963, The History of Woodstock, Vermont, 1985, The Roadside History of Vermont, 1989. Trustee Vt. Hist. Soc., Montpelier, 1984-90, Norman Williams Libr., Woodstock, 1981—. Sgt. AUS, OSS, 1943-46. Mem. Rotary (pres. Woodstock 1981-82), St. Botolph Club. Democrat. Episcopalian. Home: Happy Valley Rd Taftsville VT 05073 Office: The Countryman Press Maxham Meadow Woodstock VT 05091

JENSEN, CHARLES PATRICK, stockbroker; b. N.Y.C., Oct. 23, 1931; s. Charles Frederick and Charlotte (Johnston) J.; m. Mignon Jean Kniskern, Apr. 1, 1956 (div. 1977); children: Karen, Susan; m. Wakliria Lucia Von Randow, Nov. 3, 1980; 1 child, Caroline. BA magna cum laude, CCNY, 1963. Stockbroker, chief tech. analyst MKI Securities Corp., N.Y.C., 1964-91, equities trader, 1984-91. Editor: (newsletter) Technical Trends of Market. Served with U.S. Army, 1953-55. Mem. Phi Beta Kappa. Republican. Roman Catholic. Office: MKI Securities Corp 61 Broadway New York NY 10006-2704

JENSEN, DAVID WARREN, aerospace engineer, educator; b. LaChappelle, France, Jan. 23, 1956; came to U.S., 1958; s. Warren Edgar and Verla B. (Muir) J.; m. GayLynn Brady, June 27, 1980; children: Joshua, Brady,

Mark, Lisa. BS cum laude, Brigham Young U., 1980; SM, MIT, 1981, PhD, 1986. Engring. aid Bur. Reclamation, Provo, Utah, 1978-79; research asst. MIT, Cambridge, Mass., 1980-86; asst. prof. aerospace engring. Pa. State U., University Park, 1986-91, assoc. prof., 1991—. Pres. MIT Grad. Student Coun., Cambridge, 1983-84. Recipient Spl. Achievement award Bur. Reclamation, Provo, 1978; USN-Am. Soc. for Engring. Edn. summer faculty research fellow, 1987, Air Force Office Sci. Rsch.-Universal Energy Systems, 1988. Mem. AAUP, AIAA, ASCE, Am. Soc. Engring. Edn., Am. Soc. Composites, Soc. Engring. Sci., Soc. Photo-Optical Instrumentation Engrs., Phi Kappa Phi, Tau Beta Pi, Sigma Xi. Republican. Mormon. Avocations: camping, horses, basketball, computers, racquetball. Home: 1011 Crabapple Dr State College PA 16801-4253 Office: Pa State U 233 Hammond Bldg University Park PA 16802

JENSEN, HELENE WICKSTROM, nutritionist, educator; b. Carthage, Mo., Mar. 3, 1929; d. Frank Emil and Lois (Stroup) Wickstrom; m. Robert Gordon Jensen, Dec. 20, 1947; children: Gordon Lee, Jeffrey Alan. BS, U. Mo., 1951; MS, U. Conn., 1983. Registered dietitian. Dietitian-in-charge U. Mo., Columbia, 1952-56; therapeutic dietitian Windham Community Meml. Hosp., Willimantic, Conn., 1967, dir. food service, 1967-72; dir. sch. lunch program Windham Pub. Schs., Willimantic, 1963-66; lectr. U. Conn., Storrs, 1972-78, leader ednl. outreach program, 1979—. Recipient award Met. Life Ins. Co., 1985, Czajowski Nutrition award U. Conn., 1989, Disting. Alumna award U. Conn. Agr. and Natural Resources Alumni Assn., 1989. Mem. Am. Dietetic Assn. (presenter), Am. Sch. Food Svc. Assn. (exec. bd. 1989-91, presenter), Soc. Nutrition Edn., Conn. Sch. Food Svc. Assn. (com. mem.), Conn. Nutrition Coun. (presenter), Conn. Dietetic Assn. (presenter, Dietitian of Yr. 1987), Phi Kappa Phi, Gamma Sigma Delta. Home: 186 Chaffeeville Rd Storrs Mansfield CT 06268-2637 Office: U Conn U-17 Nutritional Scis Storrs CT 06268

JENSEN, KATHERINE KEMP, insurance company executive; b. Canandaigua, N.Y., July 22, 1955; d. Harry Frederick and Charlotte Ruth (Doebereiner) Kemp; m. Fred E. Jensen, Mar. 7, 1987; stepchildren: Brett, Stacey, Marceil. BA, Siena Coll., 1976. Cert. property and casualty ins. instr. Dir. local programs N.Y. State Assembly, Albany, 1976-77; assoc. realtor Grad. Realtor Inst. LaLonde Realty, Inc., Fairport, N.Y., 1978-81; ops. unit mgr. Allstate Ins. Co., Rochester, N.Y., 1981-84; adminstrv. svcs. mgr. Allstate Ins. Co., Rochester, 1984-88; market sales mgr. Allstate Ins. Co., Jamestown, 1988—. Chmn. N.Y. State Teen Age Reps., 1973-74; mem. N.Y. State Rep. Platform Com., 1974; mem. Perinton Rep. Com., 1978-88, chmn., 1985-88; mem. Zoning Bd. Appeals, Perinton, N.Y., 1981-88, chmn., 1985-88. Recipient Mary Ann award N.Y. State Reps., 1974. Mem. Am. Mgmt. Assn., Western Pa. Paint Horse Club, Chautauqua Region Life Underwriters, Jamestown Area C. of C., Empire State Paint Horse Club (pres. 1986-87). Home: RR 1 Columbus PA 16405-9801 Office: Allstate Ins Co 560 W 3d St Jamestown NY 14701

JENSEN, PHILIP BAILEY, urologist; b. Kingston-on-Thames, Surrey, Eng., Apr. 10, 1922; s. Axel P.C. and Mabel (Bailey) J.; m. D. Patricia Riley, Nov. 28, 1953; children: Frances, Charles, Richard. MB, BS, London U., 1952. Diplomate Am. Bd. Urology. House physician Middlesex Hosp., London, 1952-53, Cen. Middlesex Hosp., London, 1953, Royal No. Hosp., London, 1953-54; resident Greenwich (Conn.) Hosp., 1954-56, Columbia Presbyn. Med. Ctr., N.Y.C., 1956-59; pvt. practice Greenwich, 1959-75, Sharon, Conn., 1976—; attending physician Greenwich (Conn.) Hosp., 1959-75, United Hosp., Port Chester, N.Y., 1961-75, New Milford (Conn.) Hosp., 1977—, Sharon (Conn.) Hosp., 1976—; instr. urology Coll. Physicians and Surgeons, Columbia U., N.Y.C., 1959-75. Lt. Royal Naval Vol. Res., 1941-46. Fellow ACS. Home: 59 Hilltop Rd Sharon CT 06069 Office: Assoc NW Urology PC Hospital Hill Rd Sharon CT 06069

JENSEN, ROBERT GRANVILLE, academic dean, geography educator; b. Seattle, June 16, 1935; s. John Granville and Eva Phillips (Watson) J.; m. Nansie Jean Gilfillan, June 8, 1957; children: Carolyn, Maryann, Paul. BS, Oreg. State U., 1957; MA, U. Wash., Seattle, 1962, PhD, 1964. Acting asst. prof. Portland (Oreg.) State U., summer 1963; from asst. prof. to assoc. prof. geography Syracuse (N.Y.) U., 1964-78, prof., 1979—, chmn. dept., 1973—, interim dean Grad. Sch., 1989-90, dean Grad. Sch., 1990—, dir. Soviet and East European Studies, 1968-75; del. Soviet-Am. Seminar on Cities, Moscow, 1975. Contbr., editor: (with Shabad and Wright) Soviet Natural Resources in the World Economy, 1983 (Geog. Soc. Chgo. award 1984, named one of outstanding acad. books, Choice 1984-85); assoc. editor Soviet Geography, 1983-87; co-editor Soviet Economy, 1984-88; contbr. articles to profl. jours. Mem. Commr.'s Doctoral Coun. N.Y. State Dept. Edn., 1989-92. Served to 1st lt. USMC, 1957-60. Fgn. Area fellow to USSR Am. Council Learned Socs., 1965-66; Fulbright-Hays faculty research fellow to USSR, 1970-71; Sr. Exchange scholar Internat. Research and Exchanges Bd., 1970-71; NSF grantee, 1977-80. Mem. Am. Assn. Advancement of Slavic Studies, Am. Geog. Soc., Assn. Am. Geographers (chmn. splty. group 1980-81, 83-84). Democrat. Home: 304 Scott Ave Syracuse NY 13224-1726 Office: Syracuse U Office of Dean Grad Sch Bowne Hall Ste 303 Syracuse NY 13244-1200

JENSEN, SOREN STISTRUP, mathematics educator; b. Aalborg, Denmark, Jan. 12, 1956; came to U.S., 1981; s. Johannes and Lilly (Christensen) J.; m. Pauline Quek Hwang, Jan. 5, 1985; children: Sine, Elizabeth, Natasha. Cand. Scient. in Math., Physics, Aalborg U., 1980; PhD in Math., U. Md., 1985. Rsch. fellow Aalborg (Denmark) U., 1980-83; rsch. asst., then faculty rsch. asst. Inst. Phys. Sci. and Tech., U. Md., College Park, 1982-85; asst. prof. math. U. Md., Balt., 1985-92, assoc. prof. math., 1992—; vis. asst. prof. to assoc. prof. math. Rutgers U., New Brunswick, N.J., 1991. Contbr. articles to profl. jours. Grantee, Fulbright Found., 1981, Office Naval Rsch., 1987—; award recipient Office Sci. Rsch., USAF, 1988, NSF, 1990. Mem. Am. Math. Soc., Soc. for INdsl. and Applied Math. (referee Jour. Numerical Analysis 1988—, NSF 1989, Jour. Computational Physics, Numerische Math. 1990—, Comms. on Pure and Applied Math. 1991, Math. and Computer Modelling 1991). Home: 11818 Snow Patch Way Columbia MD 21044-4414 Office: U Md Dept Math Baltimore MD 21228

JENSEN, SUSAN ANN, advertising executive; b. Ashton, Idaho, Oct. 30, 1946; d. Orville Arnold and Irma Hazel (Kortesoja) Jensen; m. Paul Singer, Oct. 1, 1983. BA, U. Oreg., 1971; MBA, U. Wash., 1974. Dir. research Cole Weber, Seattle, 1972-75, v.p., 1975-79; v.p. Ogilvy Mather, N.Y.C., 1979-84; sr. v.p. Rapp Collins, N.Y.C., 1984-87, Wells, Rich, Greene, N.Y.C., 1987-89; ptnr. Jensen & Singer, N.Y.C., 1989—. Mem. Direct Mktg. Assn. Republican. Mem. Unitarian Ch. Home: 170 E 88th St New York NY 10128-2204

JENSON, PAULINE MARIE, speech and hearing educator; b. Orange, N.J., Mar. 7, 1927; m. Bernard A. Jenson, Aug. 22, 1948; 1 child, Mark J. BS, Trenton State Coll., 1948; MA, Columbia U., 1950, PhD, 1969. Lic. speech pathologist and audiologist, N.J. English, history tchr. Bordentown (N.J.) High Sch., 1948-49; teacher of the deaf Lexington Sch. for Deaf, N.Y.C., 1950-51, N.J. Sch. for Deaf, West Trenton, 1951-56, 58-61, St. Mary's Sch. for Deaf, Buffalo, 1956-58; speech pathologist Hunterdon Med. Ctr., Flemington, N.J., 1959-60, dir. speech and hearing, 1960-62; asst. prof. Trenton (N.J.) State Coll., 1962-65; instr., lectr. Teacher's Coll., Columbia U., N.Y.C., 1966-69; prof. dept. speech pathology and audiology Trenton (N.J.) State Coll., 1970—, dept. chairperson, 1991—; cons. Universal Films & Visual Arts, N.Y.C., 1968-70, State Agys. & Schs. for Handicapped, N.J., N.Y., 1976—; evaluator Coun. on Edn. of Deaf, Washington, 1979-83. Author: (with others) Speech for the Deaf Child, 1971; inventor cueing system for deaf speakers, 1976; editor: (info. booklets) Topics, Princeton, N.J., 1980-86. Help line vol. N.J. Assn. for Children with Hearing Impairments, Princeton, 1973—; co-author, cons. Senate Bills on Deafness, Trenton, 1979—; commr. Legislative Commn. to Study Svcs. for Hearing Impaired Children, Trenton, 1988-90. Recipient post masters scholarship U.S. Office Edn., Teacher's Coll., Columbia, U., 1965; grant N.J. Dept. Edn., 1973. Mem. N.J. Assn. for Children with Hearing Impairment (founder, exec. dir. 1973—), N.J. Speech Lang. and Hearing Assn. (life mem., Disting. Svc. award 1985), Am. Speech Lang. and Hearing Assn. (cert.), Cen. Jersey Speech and Hearing Assn. Office: Trenton State Coll Hillwood Lakes Trenton NJ 08625-4700

JENSSEN, PAUL HAROLD, controller; b. Mossapequa Park, N.Y., Apr. 30, 1956; s. Richard and Dorothy J.; m. Debra Esernio, Dec. 29, 1979; children: Brian, Mark. BS in Acctg., Albany U., 1978; MBA with honors, Columbia U., 1987. CPA, N.Y. Mgr. Touche Ross & Co., N.Y.C., 1978-84; controller AP, N.Y.C., 1984—. Home: 23 Searingtown Rd Searingtown NY 11507 Office: AP 50 Rockefeller Plz New York NY 10020

JEON, BANG NAM, economist, researcher; b. Masan, Korea, Sept. 20, 1954; came to U.S., 1981; s. Soong Il and Kap Sun (Park) H.; m. Kyong Ae Shin, Aug. 8, 1981; children: Tae Whan, Mee Jung, Mee Young. BA, Seoul (Korea) Nat. U., 1977; MA, Ind. U., 1983, PhD, 1987. Economist Korea Exch. Bank, Seoul, 1977-81; cons. Hudson Inst., Indpls., 1986; asst. prof. econs. Rose-Hulman Inst. Tech., Terre Haute, Ind., 1987-88, Drexel U., Phila., 1988—; vis. rsch. fellow Ind. U., Bloomington, 1988. Author: Factoring Financing, 1981. Dai-Han Ins. Group fellow, 1974-77; recipient Henry M. Oliver Meml. award Ind. U., 1987. Mem. Am. Econ. Assn., Am. Fin. Assn., Western Econ. Assn., Midwest Econ. Assn., Pa. Econ. Assn. Presbyterian. Home: 3835 Mary St Drexel Hill PA 19026-2819 Office: Drexel U 32d and Market St Philadelphia PA 19104

JEPPSON, BUCKLEY CARLOS, publisher; b. Monticello, Utah, June 26, 1948; s. Thomas Charles and Claire (Hyde) J.; m. Marie Diane Fansler, Sept. 12, 1970; 1 child, Olivia Marie. BA, Calif. State U., Long Beach, 1972, MA, 1974. Asst. prof. Weber State U., Ogden, Utah, 1974-79; editorial dir. Gibbs Smith, Pub., Layton, Utah, 1980-90; pub. Preservation Press, Washington, 1990—. State coord. Amnesty Internat., Salt Lake City, 1987-90. Democrat. Mormon. Home: PO Box 65361 Washington DC 20035-5361 Office: Nat Trust Historic Preservation 1785 Massachusetts Ave NW Washington DC 20036-2117

JEPPSON, JOHN, corporate professional, director; b. Worcester, Mass., Dec. 10, 1916; s. George Nathaniel and Selma Ulrika (Swanstrom) J.; m. Julie Armstrong, June 6, 1939 (div. 1946); children: John III, Julie Jeppson Stout; m. Marianne Jenner Shellabarger, Jan. 15, 1947; children: Eric Shellabarger, Ingrid Georgia Selma Jeppson Mach. Student, Deerfield Acad., 1934; B, Amherst Coll., 1938, DSc, 1963; MBA, Harvard U., 1940; LLD, Clark U., 1968. Dir., chmn. Norton Co., Worcester, 1940-85; chmn. bd. Guaranty Bank & Trust Co., Worcester, 1973-87, Crompton & Knowles Corp., N.Y.C., 1965-87, Kennecott Copper Corp., N.Y.C., 1972-77; dir. The Foxboro (Mass.) Co., 1966-88. Pres. Am. Antiquarian Soc., 1977-87; chmn. trustee emeritus Clark U.; dir. Worcester County Music Assn.; hon. trustee Worcester Art Mus. Lt. comdr. USN, 1942-45. Recipient Isaiah Thomas award for distinguished community svc. Worcester Advt. Club, 1977. Mem. Worcester Fire Soc., Worcester County Music Assn. (pres., bd. dirs.), St. Wulstan's Soc., Amherst U. Alumni Assn.

JEPSEN, JANE BARRY, educator; b. Hartford, Conn., Sept. 14, 1934; d. Richard Joseph and Mary Eleanor (Mahoney) Barry; m. Donald Allen Jepsen, July 2, 1960; children: Donald Jr., Anders B., Mary Lou, Laura L. BA, St. Joseph Coll., West Hartford, 1956; MA, U. Hartford, 1960; CAS, Wesleyan U., Middletown, Conn., 1980. Secondary tchr. City of Hartford, 1956-61; prof. U. Hartford, 1972—. Author: How to Say It, The Art of Public Speaking, 1983, 2d edit., 1991. Mem. nat. bd. Nat. Fedn. Rep. Women, 1986-90, mem. exec. com., 1990-92, chmn. pub. rels., 1992-94; state pres. Conn. Fedn. Rep. Women, 1986-90; mem. Conn. Rep. Cen. Com., 1986-90, state chmn. liaison com., 1986-90; mem. Windsor Rep. Town Com., 1970—; pres. Windsor Rep. Women's Club, 1971; justice of peace, 1972—; del. state congl. and senatorial convs., co-capt. Windsor 3d dist.; fundraiser, recruiter Am. Heart Assn., 1976—. Named Windsor Rep. of Yr., 1991; recipient citation Conn. Legislature, 1991, proclamation plaque Windsor Town Coun., 1991. Mem. Eugene O'Neill Theatre Assn., Neptune Park Beach Assn. (past bd. govs.), St. Joseph Coll. Alumni Assn. (bd. dirs. 1983-88). Home: 495 Palisado Ave Windsor CT 06095-2033

JEPSEN-LOZANO, LISA, marketing and public relations executive; b. Pitts., June 7, 1952; d. Elwood Maris and Kathryn Elaine (Beiersdorfer) J.; m. Miguel Angel Lozano, Sept. 10, 1975; children: Gloria Darin, Marisa Mae. AB, Middlebury (Vt.) Coll., 1974. Asst. pubs. editor Allegheny Gen. Hosp., Pitts., 1977-78; mgr. employee communications Equibank, Pitts., 1978-79, mgr. communications, 1979-81, banking officer, mgr. exec. offices, 1981-83, asst. v.p. community & govt., 1983-84; dir. mktg. Deloitte & Touche, Pitts., 1984—. Trustee Arsenal Family and Children Ctr. Pitts., 1985—, chmn. of bd., 1989-92; trustee Soc. for Contemporary Crafts, Pitts., 1985-91, pres., 1986-88; trustee Western Pa. chpt. Leukemia Soc. Am., 1985—, Found. for California U. Pa., 1987—; mem. governing com. Three Rivers Art Festival, Pitts., 1985—. Mem. Pub. Relations Soc. Am., Am. Mktg. Assn., Rivers Club. Unitarian Universalist. Office: Deloitte & Touche Two Oliver Plz Pittsburgh PA 15222

JERGE, DALE ROBERT, loss control specialist, industrial hygienist; b. Buffalo, Oct. 15, 1951; s. Herbert L. and Ruth R. (Maxson) J.; m. Susan B. Rinaldo, Jan. 22, 1983; 1 child, Nicholas D. AAS, Erie Community Coll., Amherst, N.Y., 1972; BA in Sociology, SUNY, Buffalo, 1974, MS in Social Scis., 1976, postgrad., 1988—. Cert. occupational health and safety technologist; cert. hazardous materials supr.; cert. indsl. pulmonary technologist; cert. safety and security dir.; cert. occupational hearing conservationist. Loss control specialist Twin Fair, Buffalo, 1975-79; indsl. hygienist Continental Ins. Tech. Svcs., Buffalo, 1979—; adj. prof. Niagara County Community Coll., Lockport, N.Y., 1989—. Mem. APHA, Am. Soc. Safety Engrs., Am. Insl. Hygiene Assn., World Safety Orgn. (affiliate mem., cert. safety and security profl., cert. hazardous materials supr.), Coun. for Accreditation in Occupational Hearing Conservation (cert.). Office: CTEK 50 Lakefront Blvd Buffalo NY 14202-4301

JERIS, JOHN STRATIS, environmental engineering educator; b. Boston, June 6, 1930; s. Stratis Jeris and Marian Zadelis; m. Helen Marie Jones, Oct. 12, 1958; children: Joanne Marie, Paul Stratis. BSCE, MIT, 1953, MS in Sanitary Engring., 1954, ScD in Sanitary Engring., 1962. Registered profl. engr., N.Y., D.C., N.J. Project engr. Stearns & Wheler, Cons. Engrs., Cazenovia, N.Y., 1956-59; rsch. asst. MIT, Boston, 1959-62; lab. dir., prof. civil engring., environ. engring. and sci. grad. program Manhattan Coll., Riverdale, N.Y., 1962—, dir. environ. engring. and sci. grad. program, 1966-78, 87—; v.p. R & D, Ecolotrol, Inc., Westbury, N.Y., 1970—; tech. dir. N.Y. State Tech. Svc. Program, 1967-70; environ. commr. City of Yonkers, N.Y., 1974—; cons. G. Heileman Brewing Co., Union Carbide, Superior Fibres, Inc., others, 1963—; investigator Fed. Water Pollution Control Adminstrn., 1964-70, Nassau County Dept. Pub. Works, 1972-81, 1979-82, 1983-85, Nat. Oceanic and Atmospheric Agy., 1974, U.S. EPA, 1979-81, N.Y. State Energy R & D Authority, 1983-85; pres.'s adv. com. N.Y. Ocean Scis. Lab., 1971—, pres.'s coun., 1971-76; sludge mgmt. adv. com. Westchester County, N.Y., 1979-81; citizens adv. com. Indsl. Waste Pretreatment Program, Westchester County, 1981-84. Contbg. editor Water and Wastes Engring. Editorial Adv. Bd., 1969-73, 1979-81; contbr. over 80 articles in field. With U.S. Army C.E., 1954-56. Named Outstanding Educator Am., 1971; recipient Progress in Engring. award Com. on Engring. Progress, 1970, Kenneth Allen Meml. award N.Y. Water Pollution Control Assn., 1975, John Chester Brigham Svc. award, 1976, Thomas R. Camp medal Water Pollution Control Fedn., 1979, De La Salle medal, 1985. Mem. ASCE (chmn. 1964, exec. com. sanitary engring. group met. sect.), Am. Chem. Soc. (Water, Air and Waste Chemistry div.), Am. Waterworks Assn., N.Y. Water Pollution Control Assn. (chmn. tech. program 1971-75, program com. 1972—, chmn. student com. 1975-87, mem., 1987—, dir. Lower Hudson Valley sect. 1982-85, dir. Met. sect. 1988-91, Chpt. Award of Merit 1992), Assn. Environ. Engring. Profs., Internat. Assn. on Water Pollution Rsch. and Control, Sigma Xi (pres. Manhattan chpt. 1978). Home: 57 Pietro Dr Yonkers NY 10710 Office: Manhattan Coll Manhattan Coll Pky Riverdale NY 10471

JERMANSKY, GARY, trust manager; b. Kings, N.Y., Sept. 25, 1960; s. Harvey and Pearl J.; m. Irene Yuen, June 25, 1986. BS, Pace U., 1989. Benefit adminstr. Banker's Trust, N.Y.C., 1981-84; internal auditor Price Waterhouse, N.Y.C., 1984; unit head for pension trust accts. U.S. Trust Co., N.Y.C., 1984-88; sect. head for pub. funds Bank of N.Y., N.Y.C., 1988-90; trust dept. mgr. Custodial Trust Co., Princeton, N.J., 1990—. Home: 25 Schaeffer Ln Freehold NJ 07728-2808

JEROME, JAMES ALEXANDER, Canadian federal justice; b. Kingston, Ont., Can., Mar. 4, 1933; s. Joseph Leonard and Phyllis (Devlin) J.; m. Barry Karen Hodgins, June 7, 1958; children: Mary Louise, William Paul, James Leonard, Joseph Alexander (dec.), Megan Phyllis. B.A., U. Toronto, 1954; LL.B., Osgoode Hall, 1958. Bar: Ont. Alderman City of Sudbury, Ont., 1966-67; MP Ho. of Commons, Ottawa, Can., 1968—, parliamentary sec. to pres. Privy Coun., speaker, 1974, 79, mem. Privy Coun., 1981—; assoc. chief justice Fed. Ct. Can., 1980—. Roman Catholic. Office: Fed Ct Can, Kent & Wellington Sts, Ottawa, ON Canada K1A 0H9

JERROLD, S. HARRISON, physician; b. Bklyn., Apr. 20, 1934; s. Harry Jerrold and Lillie Silverblatt; married, June 23, 1963; children: Stacey, Michelle. BS, Franklin and Marshall Coll., 1954; MD, St. Louis U., 1958. Diplomte Am. Bd. Ophthalmology. Resident in ophthalmology Bronx VA Hosp., 1959-62; pvt. practice Edison, N.J., 1962—. Fellow Am. Acad. Ophthalmology. Office: Tower Bldg Tower Bldg 7 Hwy 27 at Parsonage Rd #101 Edison NJ 08820

JESHURAN, WINSTON RAJADURAL, anesthesiologist; b. Manipay, Ceylon, Nov. 30, 1939; s. S.R. and C.T. (Christina) Rajadurai; m. Cynthia S. Jeshuran, Dec. 29, 1969; children: Brian, Winston Jr. MD, Faculty of Medicine, Ceylon, 1966. Diplomate Am. Bd. Anesthesiology. Intern Misericordia-Fordham, 1969-70, resident in internal medicine, 1970-71; resident in anesthesiology St. Luke's Med. Ctr.; attending anesthesiologist Meriden (Conn.)-Wallingford Hosp., 1973-85; dir. dept. anesthesiology Vets. Meml. Med. Ctr., Meriden, 1985—; bd. govs. Vets. Meml. Med. Ctr., Meriden, 1990—. Inventor fiberoptic tube T-piece, 1991. Lt. col. USMC, 1991, Saudia Arabia. Fellow Am. Coll. Anesthesiologists; mem. Am. Coll. Surgeons and Physicians, Am. Soc. Anesthesiologists, Conn. State Med. Soc., Conn. State Soc. Anesthesiologists, New Haven County Med. Assn. Home: 615 Riverside Dr Cheshire CT 06410 Office: Veterans Meml Med Ctr 391 Broad St Meriden CT 06450

JESPERSEN, NEIL DAVID, analytical chemist, educator; b. Bklyn., Mar. 5, 1946; s. Jack William Eric and Evelyn Lillian (Nelson) J.; m. Marilyn Josephine Zak, Apr. 25, 1970; children: Lisa Marie, Kristen Marie. BS, Washington & Lee U., 1967; PhD, Pa. State U., 1971. Asst. prof. U. Tex., Austin, 1971-77; assoc. prof. St. John's U., Jamaica, N.Y., 1977—. Editor: Biochemical & Clinical Applications of Thermal Analysis, 1982; author chpts. in books; contbr. over 20 articles to profl. jours. Grantee Rsch. Corp., 1983, Fenem Inc., 1990. Mem. Am. Chem. Soc. (chmn. N.Y. chpt. 1991—), Eastern Analytical Symposium (chmn. Somerset, N.J. chpt.), Sigma Xi. Office: St Johns U Grand Central & Utopia Pky Jamaica NY 11439

JESSEE, S. LEE, environmental protection specialist; b. Roanoke, Va., Jan. 5, 1954; d. Carl William and Shirley Lee (Davidson) L. Student, Va. Poly. Inst. & State U., 1972-74; AAS in Mech. Engring., New River C.C., Dublin, Va., 1976; BA, Trinity Coll., Washington, 1990. Cert. engring. technologist; cert. hazardous substance incident response mgr. Site planner Long, Brown & Assocs., Fairfax, Va., 1976-77, Patton, Harris, Rust & Assocs., Fairfax, 1977-79; engr. SCS Engrs., Reston, Va., 1979-84; environ. protection specialist, head environ. program dept., Naval Med. Command of Nat. Capital Region, Bethesda, Md., 1984-89; environ. protection specialist Farmers Home Adminstrn., Washington, 1989-90, U.S. Dept. Energy, Washington, 1990—; agy. rep. geog. info. systems subcom. Natural Resources & Environ. subcom.; mem. site-specific conceptual design com. Super Conducting Super Collider, Dept. Energy; subteam head Tiger Team Environ., Stanford Linear Accelerator Ctr., 1991. Naval on-scene comdr. Montgomery (Md.) County Local Emergency Planning & Response Com.; mem. budget com. Pulaski (Va.) County United Way, 1976. Mem. Internat. Assn. for Impact Assessment, Met. Washington Fed. Safety Coun., Hazardous Materials Control Rsch. Inst., Smithsonian Instn. Resident Assoc. Program. Office: US Dept Energy Code EH-252 1000 Independence Ave SW Washington DC 20585

JESSUP, WILLIAM MCCLELLAN, JR., arts educator, photographer, videographer, graphic designer; b. Balt., May 12, 1928; s. William M. Sr. and Gladys (Jones) J.; married, 1956. BS, Coppin State Coll., 1951; MA, NYU, 1960. Tchr. N.Y. State Tng. Sch. for Girls, N.Y.C., 1953-55, Balt. City Pub. Schs., 1955-80; instr. Upward Bound, Johns Hopkins U., Balt., 1965-68; cons. Nat. Forum for Black Pub. Adminstrs., 1988-89. Crew mem. Sam Davis Jr. Documentary film prodn., Phila.; cameraman Sta. WBAL-TV North Star. Bd. dirs. Cloisters Childrens Mus., Balt., 1987—. Pvt. with U.S. Army, 1951-53. Mem. Md. Art Coun. Democrat. Baptist. Home: 1904 Chelsea Rd Baltimore MD 21216-2410

JESTER, ROBERTS CHARLES, JR., engineering services company executive; b. Atlanta, July 12, 1917; s. Roberts Charles and Lynwood (Waters) J.; children: Rita (Mrs. Charles B. Jones, Jr.), Carol (Mrs. John M. Sisk, Jr.), Janelle (Mrs. Michael C. Patty). B.S., U. Ga., 1940; grad., Advanced Mgmt. Program, Harvard, 1957. Chief clk. Ga. R.R., 1936-40; project mgr. Mich. Design & Engring. Co., 1941-42; partner Allstate Engring. Service Co., Dayton, Ohio, 1943-45; pres. Allstates Engring. Co., 1945—; chmn., chief exec. officer Allstates Engring. Co. Inc., Allstates Design & Devel. Co. Inc., Trenton, N.J., 1954-89; pres., treas. Pennco Enterprises Inc., Trenton, 1956—; dir. N.J. Nat. Bank. Bd. dirs., vice chmn. Greater Trenton Symphony Assn.; bd. dirs. George Washington council Boy Scouts Am.; bd. govs. Hamilton Hosp.; mem. lay adv. bd. St. Francis Hosp.; trustee YMCA, Trenton. Mem. Greater Trenton C. of C. (bd. dirs.), Masons, Shriners, Engrs. Club, Trenton Country Club (past pres.), Met. Club N.Y.C., Little Egg Harbor Yacht Club. Republican. Presbyterian. Office: Pennco Enterprises Inc 367 Pennington Ave Trenton NJ 08618-3697

JETER, CLIFTON B., JR., finance executive; b. Martinsville, Va., Feb. 22, 1944. BA, Howard U.; MBA, Am. U.; postgrad. advanced mgmt. program, Harvard U. CPA, Md. Mgr. adv. serv. div. Wolf and Co., CPA's; chief fin. officer John F. Kennedy Ctr. for Performing Arts, Washington, 1977—. Mem. AICPA, Nat. Assn. Accts. (bd. dirs.), Md. Assn. CPA's, D.C. Inst. CPA's, Am. Mgmt. Assn., Nat. Black MBA Assn., Nat. Assn. Black Accts., Washington Bd. of Trade. Office: JF Kennedy Ctr 2700 F St NW Washington DC 20566-0002

JETER, MICHAEL, actor. Stage appearances: Grand Hotel (Tony award 1990), Only Kidding, The Boy Next Door, Greater Tuna, Cloud Nine, G.R. Point (Theatre World award), Alice, Accidental Death of an Anarchist, Once in a Lifetime, Zoo Story; films include Soup For One, Zelig, Hair, Dead Bang, Just Like in the Movies, Tango and Cash, The Fisher King, 1991; TV series Evening Shade (Emmy award supporting actor, 1992); episodes of Designing Women, Lou Grant, One Life to Live and others. Office: care Writers & Artists Agy 19 W 44th St Rm 1000 New York NY 10036-6095

JEWELEWICZ, RAPHAEL, obstetrician/gynecologist, educator; b. Nowogrodek, Poland, Dec. 26, 1932; came to U.S., 1963; s. Chaim and Chaia (Tawricki) J.; m. Ronnie Oved, July 3, 1955; children: Rachel, Dov, Daniel, Dory. MD, Hebrew U., Jerusalem, 1961. Cert. Am. Bd. Ob-gyn. 1971, 89, reproductive endocrinology, 1973. Intern Hadassah Hebrew U. Hosp., Jerusalem; resident NYU Med. Ctr., Bellevue Hosp., N.Y.C.; assoc. prof. ob-gyn. Columbia U., N.Y.C., 1975—; bd. dirs. div. reproductive endocrinology Columbia U. Coll. Physicians and Surgeons, N.Y.C. Author: Clinical Aspects of Cervical Incompetence, 1989, The Menstrual Cycle: Physiology, Reproductive Disorders and Infertility, 1992; editor ob-gyn. investigation; mem. editorial bd. several sci. jours.; contbr. over 100 articles to profl. jours. Mem. Am. Coll. Ob-gyn., Am. Coll. Surgeons, Am. Fertility Soc., Am. Gynecol. & Obstet. Soc., N.Y. Obstet. Soc., N.Y. Gynecol. Soc. (sec. 1992—), Soc. for Gynecol. Investigation, Soc. for Study Reproduction. Jewish. Home: Church St Alpine NJ 07620 Office: Columbia Presbyn Med Ctr 630 W 168th St New York NY 10032

JEWELL, GEORGE BENSON, lawyer, educator, minister; b. Evanston, Ill., Mar. 26, 1944; s. Benson Murray and Ellen Louise (Mahle) J.; m. Pamela Elaine Peterson, Aug. 12, 1967; children: Jeffrey Benson, Brian Edward. BA, Beloit (Wis.) Coll., 1966; MDiv, Gordon-Conwell Theol. Sem., 1978; JD, Washington U., St. Louis, 1971. Bar: Ill. 1971, Mo. 1972, Mass. 1990, U.S. Dist. Ct. (ea. dist.) Mo. 1973, U.S. Dist. Ct. Mass. 1991. Trust adminstr. Ill. Nat. Bank, Springfield, 1971; corp. atty. Ralston Purina Co., St. Louis, 1971-75; assoc. pastor Westminster Presbyn. Ch., Bluefield, W.Va., 1978-81; sr. pastor Westminster Presbyn. Ch., Cape Girardeau, Mo., 1981-

86, Evang. Free Ch., Cape Girardeau, 1986-88; pvt. practice Cape Girardeau, 1988-89; coll. counsel, dir. gift planning, adj. assoc. prof. bus. law Gordon Coll., Wenham, Mass., 1989—; mem. pres.'s adv. coun. Gordon Coll., 1990—; instr. in bus. law S.E. Mo. State U., Cape Girardeau, 1986; cons. Stone, McGhee, Feuchtenberger & Barringer, Bluefield, 1980-81; mng. editor Washington University Law Quarterly. Deacon Cen. Presbyn. Ch., St. Louis, 1974-75; scoutmaster Appalachian coun. Cub Scouts Am., Bluefield, 1979; mem. bd. advisors Sta. KUGT, Cape Girardeau, 1988; baccalaureate speaker Cen. High Sch., Cape Girardeau, 1988; bd. dirs. Young Life of Cape Girardeau, 1987-88. Mem. Nat. Assn. Coll. and Univ. Attys. (ad hoc com. on income devel. 1990-91, ad hoc com. svcs. small colls. 1991-92), Boston Bar Assn. (Coll. and Univ. com., estate planning Com.), Planned Giving Group of New Eng., Christian Legal Soc., Mo. Bar Assn. (franchise tax subcom. corp. law and bus. orgn. coms.), Evang. Free Ch. Ministerial Assn., Manchester Athletic Club, Sigma Alpha Epsilon. Home: 45 Old Cart Rd South Hamilton MA 01982-2516 Office: Gordon Coll 255 Grapevine Rd Wenham MA 01984-1895

JEWETT, FRANK SNIFFEN, psychiatrist; b. Greenwich, Conn., Jan. 11, 1932; s. Freeborn Garrettson and Beatrice (Sniffen) J.; m. Constance Comly, June 16, 1956 (div. 1966); children: Ellen, Hilary; m. Marguerite Thomas, May 17, 1981. AB, Yale U., 1953; MD, Columbia U., 1957, postgrad., 1959-61. Diplomate Am. Bd. Psychiatry and Neurology. Pvt. practice N.Y.C., 1963—; intern U. Chgo., 1957-58; resident N.Y. Psychiat. Inst., 1958-61; sr. rsch. scientist N.Y. Psychiat. Inst., N.Y.C., 1963-67; staff psychiatrist Phelps Meml. Hosp., North Tarrytown, N.Y., 1967-71, sr. attending psychiatrist, 1971-77, dir. psychiatry, 1977-80; assoc. attending psychiat. Harlem Hosp., N.Y.C., 1982—; asst. clin. prof. psychiatry, Columbia U., N.Y.C., 1974—, project dir. rsch. program issues of ethics and values in health care, 1978-82. Mem. N.Y. Dem. County Com., N.Y.C., 1986—; cons. in psychiatry Peace Corps, N.Y.C., 1963-68. Capt. U.S. Army, 1959-61, ETO. Mem. Am. Psychiat. Assn., Yale, Century. Episcopalian. Home and Office: 26 E 93d St New York NY 10128

JEWETT, JOHN PERSINGER, electronics executive, lawyer; b. Yakima, Wash., July 26, 1943; s. John Persinger and Rosemary (Koontz) J.; m. Isabel Jean Goodman, June 18, 1966; children: Jonathan Goodman, Todd Andrew, Christopher Matthew. BA, Trinity Coll., 1965; JD, U. Conn., 1968; LLM, London Sch. Econs., 1969. Bar: Conn. 1968, U.S. Dist. Ct. Conn. 1969, Pa. 1979. Assoc. Tyler, Cooper, Grant, Bowerman & Keefe, New Haven, 1969-71; mktg. administr. Computer Div. RCA, Marlboro, Mass., 1971-72; asst. gen. counsel Sperry Univac, Blue Bell, Pa., 1972-79; assoc. corp. counsel Data Gen. Corp., Westboro, Mass., 1979-81; v.p., gen. counsel Apollo Computer Inc., Chelmsford, Mass., 1981-86; v.p. fin. and administrn., chief fin. officer and treas. Bitstream Inc., Cambridge, Mass., 1986-89; pres. Blue Point Techs., Inc., Nashua, N.H., 1989-91; chmn., chief exec. officer Calidus Systems, Waltham, Mass., 1991—; mem. Selden Soc., 1986-75. Mem. exec. bd. Algonquin Coun. Boy Scouts Am., Framingham, Mass., 1980—, pres. 1986-88; mem. exec. bd. Metrowest United Way, Framingham, 1988—. Recipient Silver Beaver, Silver Antelope and Disting. Eagle, Boy Scouts Am., 1986, 90, 92. Mem. ABA, Nat. Eagle Scout Assn. (life), Nashawtuc Country Club (Concord, Mass.). Democrat. Episcopalian. Home: 52 Witherell Dr Sudbury MA 01776-1248 Office: Calidus Systems 1601 Trapelo Rd Waltham MA 02154

JEWETT, TRUDA CLEEVES, social welfare administrator; b. Boston, May 14, 1931; d. John B.M. and Jere Finch (Schell) Cleeves; m. C. Lincoln Jewett, Mar. 6, 1954; children: Lisa, Laura. Student, George Washington U., 1957-59; EdM, Harvard U., 1983. Exec. dir. Coro Found., N.Y.C., 1979-82; asst. exec. dir. Children's Aid Soc., N.Y.C., 1982—; Trustee Kimball Union Acad., Meriden, N.H., 1985—, Outward Bound, N.Y.C., 1988—, Am. Farm Sch., Thessalonika, Greece, 1985—; chmn. bd. dirs. Nat. Theatre of the Real, Chester, Conn., 1991—. Mem. Harvard Club N.Y., Explorers Club, Cosmopolitan Club N.Y.C., Harvard Alumni Assn. (chair 1989—). Republican. Episcopalian. Office: Childrens Aid Soc 105 E 22d St New York NY 10010

JEZL, BARBARA ANN, chemist, automation consultant; b. Pitts., June 7, 1947; d. James L. and Elizabeth (Bannister) J. BS in Chemistry, U. Del., 1969, PhD in Organic Chemistry, 1974. Jr. chemist Am. Cyanamid, Pearl River, N.Y., 1969-70; NSF postdoctoral assoc. U. Cin., 1974-76; inst. application specialist E.I. DuPont de Nemours & Co., Wilmington, Del., 1976-79, mem. computing staff, 1979-84, staff specialist, 1985—. Author: Science, 1990; contbr. articles to profl. jours. Bd. dirs. Unitarian-Universalist Fellowship of Newark, 1981-85, pres., chmn. bd., 1986-87, rep. Delaware Valley Area Coun., Phila., 1983-85, v.p. Fellowship of Newark, 1984-85. Mem. AAAS, IEEE, Am. Chem. Soc., Assn. for Computing Machinery, Macintosh Sci. and Tech. Assn. (bd. dirs., co-chmn. tech. adv. com. 1990—), Sigma Xi. Home: 5448 W Pinehurst Dr Wilmington DE 19808-2619 Office: EI duPont de Nemours & Co Exptl Sta PO Box 80320 Wilmington DE 19880-0320

JICHA, HENRY LOUIS, JR., securities analyst, consultant; b. N.Y.C., June 25, 1928; s. Henry Louis Sr. and Pauline Blanche (Sobisek) J.; m. Jeanette Anne McIntyre, Feb. 25, 1951; children: Henry, Douglas, Jeanette. BA, Columbia U., 1948, MA in Geology, 1951, PhD in Econ. Geology, 1952. Geologist U.S. Geol. Survey, 1948-49, N.Mex. Bur. Mines and Mineral Resources, Socorro, 1951-56; asst. prof. geology Colo. Sch. of Mines, Golden, 1957-58; security analyst Baker, Weeks & Co., N.Y.C., 1958-61; editor, analyst Value Lines Investment Survey, N.Y.C., 1961-62; analyst, mgr. N.Y. Rsch. Cts. and Co., N.Y.C., 1962-68; analyst Neuberger, Loeb, N.Y.C., 1968-71, Jessup & Lamont, N.Y.C., 1971-74, Bache (name changed to Prudential Inc.), N.Y.C., 1974-83; sr. v.p., dir., dir. rsch. Wood Gundy Inc., N.Y.C., 1983-90; cons. HLJ Cons., Ardsley, N.Y., 1990—. Contbr. articles to profl. jours. Mem. N.Y. Soc. Security Analysts, Chartered Fin. Analysts, Environ. Control Analysts of N.Y. (pres. N.Y.C. chpt. 1981, 82). Home and Office: 12 Western Dr Ardsley NY 10502-1913

JILLETTE, ARTHUR GEORGE, JR., school system administrator; b. Malden, Mass., May 1, 1937; s. Arthur George and Esther Harriett (Peachey) J.; m. Janet Downs White, June 20, 1960 (div. 1973); 1 child, Joseph Arthur; m. Beatrice Miriam Ellis, May 3, 1975; children: Grace Schultz, Andrew Hopkins, Timothy Hopkins. BS, Boston U., 1960, MRE, 1964; cert. in audio communicative disability, NYU, 1967. Cert. tchr., N.H., community coll. administr., Calif. Assoc. rsch. scientist NYU Deafness Rsch. Ctr., N.Y.C., 1965-67; cons. spl. edn. N.H. Dept. Edn., Concord, 1967-74, 85-88, acting dir. spl. edn., 1974-75; dir. planning and devel. N.H. Div. Vocat. Rehab., Concord, 1975-79; dean spl. svcs. N.H. Tech. Coll., Claremont, 1979-83, dean students, 1983-85; dir. spl. svcs. Sch. Adminstrv. Unit #43, Newport, N.H., 1988-91, asst. supt. schs., 1991—; dir. Lake Sunapee Mediation Program, Newport, 1990—, N.H. Mediation Assn., Concord, 1986-87, Bancroft Products, Concord, 1976-79; pres., dir. Sullivan County Rehab. Ctr., Claremont, 1980-83. Editor: Denominational Work With the Deaf, 1966. Moderator Town of Goshen, N.H., 1980—, planning bd. chmn., 1985-89, zoning bd. chmn., 1986-89. Social and Rehab. Svcs. fellow U.S. Dept. Edn., 1964-65. Mem. Nat. Stereoptican Assn., Nat. Assn. Watch and Clock Collectors, Boston Computer Soc., Elks, Odd Fellows, Masons. Democrat. Mem. Soc. of Friends. Home: HCR 66 Box 181 Goshen NH 03752-7705 Office: Sch Adminstrv Unit #43 15 Sunapee St Newport NH 03773

JINDRAK, KAREL FRANCIS, pathologist, researcher, educator; b. Merin, Czechoslovakia, Mar. 29, 1926; came to U.S., 1967; s. Frantisek and Marie (Vetesnik) J.; m. Heda Kult, Jan. 6, 1951; 1 child, Heda. MD, Charles U. Med. Sch., Prague, Czechoslovakia, 1950, PhD, 1963. Diplomate Am. Bd. Anatomic and Clinical Pathology. Asst. prof. pathology Charles U. Med. Sch., 1956-65; pathologist Rsch. Inst. for Pharmacy and Biochemistry, Prague, 1965-67; researcher U. Hawaii, Honolulu, 1967-68; resident in pathology Mt. Sinai Hosp., N.Y.C., 1969-71; attending pathologist Meth. Hosp., Bklyn., 1971—; dir. dept. pathology Czechoslovakian Hosp., Vietnam, 1957-60; clin. asst. prof. pathology SUNY, Bklyn., 1973—. Co-author: (with Alicata J.E. Jindrak) Angiostrongylosis in the Pacific and Southeast Asia, 1970, (with H. Jindrak) Sing, Clean Your Brain, and Stay Sound and Sane, 1986. Capt. M.C., Czechoslovakian Army, 1951-56. Recipient Spl. award Czechoslovakian Ministry Health, 1951. Fellow Am. Coll. Pathologists. Office: Meth Hosp 506 6th St Brooklyn NY 11215-3645

JINNETT, ROBERT JEFFERSON, lawyer; b. Birmingham, Ala., May 9, 1949; s. Bryan Floyd Jr. and Elizabeth Coleman (Borders) J.; m. Doreen S. Ziff, Aug. 2, 1975; children: Brynn Leigh, Maren Alexandra. BA, Harvard U., 1971; JD, Cornell U., 1975. Bar: N.Y. 1976, U.S. Dist. Ct. (no. dist.) N.Y. 1976, U.S. Dist. Ct. (so. dist.) N.Y. 1978, U.S. Dist. Ct. (ea. dist.) N.Y. 1979, U.S. Supreme Ct. 1988. Law clk. N.Y. State Ct. Appeals, Albany, 1975-77; assoc. Rogers & Wells, N.Y.C., 1977-82; assoc. LeBoeuf, Lamb, Leiby & MacRae, N.Y.C., 1983-85, ptnr., 1986—. Contbg. author: High Tech Real Estate, 1985, The Commercial Real Estate Tenant's Handbook, 1987; contbr. articles to profl. jours. Bd. dirs. The Nat. Found. For Rsch. in Blood Diseases, Inc. Recipient 3d nat. prize Nathan Burkan Meml. Competition, ASCAP, 1974; DAAD fellow U. Heidelberg, Germany, 1971-72. Mem. Nat. Assn. Corp. Dirs. (v.p. N.Y. chpt.), Jamestowne Soc. (gov. N.Y. chpt.), Soc. of War of 1812, S.R. (bd. mgrs. 1991—), Soc. Colonial Wars. Episcopalian. Office: LeBoeuf Lamb Leiby & MacRae 520 Madison Ave New York NY 10022-4213

JOFFROY-BLACK, FLORENCE HELENE, international sales and marketing executive; b. Paris, Apr. 23, 1965; came to U.S., 1985; d. Claude Roland Louis and Michele (Lavieuville) Joffroy; m. Scott Hilliard Black, Mar. 4, 1988. BSBA in Mktg., U. Hartford, West Hartford, Conn., 1986, MBA in Mktg. and Fin., 1988. Adminstr. Colombo, Inc., Andover, Mass., 1989-90, internat. sales and mktg. mgr., 1990—. Mem. NAFE, Am. Mktg. Assn. (award 1988), Am. Mgmt. Assn., Alliance Francaise. Home: 94 Mill Pond North Andover MA 01845-2902 Office: Colombo Inc 3 Riverside Dr Andover MA 01810

JOGLEKAR, PRAFULLA NARAYAN, information systems management professional; b. Dhulia, India, May 12, 1947; s. Narayan D. and Nirmala N. (Parchure) J.; m. Suvarna P. Lagu, Oct. 15, 1951; children: Aditya, Ajinkya. BSc, Nagpur (India) U., 1966; MBA, Indian Inst. Mgmt., Ahmedabad, India, 1968; MS, U. Pa., 1972, PhD, 1978; postgrad., U. Rochester, U. Minn., Ind. U. Staff analyst Dept. Atomic Energy, Bombay, India, 1968-69; systems analyst Voltas (PVT) Ltd., Bombay, 1969-70; mgmt. research analyst U. Pa., Phila., 1970-72; from instr. to full prof. La Salle U., Phila., 1972-87, chmn. mgmt. dept., 1973-77, 79-82, dir. applied research ctr., 1979-85, Lindback prof. bus. adminstrn., 1987-89, Lindback prof. prodn. and ops. mgmt., 1991—; mgmt. cons. various pvt. firms, govt. agys., nonprofit orgns., Phila., 1972—; expert witness fed. court, Montreal, Can., 1985. Contbr. articles to profl. jours. and confs.; editor Varta, Indian Students Assn., Phila., 1975-76. Pres. Marathi Mandal, Phila., 1980-81; mem. People to People Systems Engring. Delegation, Peoples Republic China, 1986. Nat. Merit scholar Govt. of India, Nagpur and Ahmedabad, 1962-68, D.C.M. scholar Indian Inst. Mgmt., Ahmedabad, 1968; grantee La Salle U., 1980, 82, 87. Mem. Inst. Mgmt. Scis., Am. Mgmt. Assn., Nonprofit Mgmt. Assn. (bd. dirs. 1985-90). Hindu. Home: 202 Lenape Ave Philadelphia PA 19126-1432 Office: La Salle U 20th and Olney Sts Philadelphia PA 19141

JOHANSEN, JOSEPHINE LILLIESTA, mathematics educator; b. Atlanta, Oct. 24, 1953; d. Charles J. and Ondine K. (Kennedy) O'Donnell; m. Eric Luther Johansen Sr.; children: Jennifer L., Eric L. Jr. BS in Math., Rutgers U., 1975; MS in Math., Drexel U., 1987. Math. tchr. Camden (N.J.) High Sch., 1977-79; math. tchr. adult div. Camden County Vocat. Sch., Gloucester Township, N.J., 1980-81; instr. math. Camden County Coll., Camden, Blackwood, N.J., 1981-88, Rutgers U., Camden, 1988—. Mem. Feed Homeless, Project Interaction, Camden, 1988—. Episcopalian. Home: 112 Paradise Dr Voorhees NJ 08043-4924 Office: Rutgers U 5th & Penn Sts Camden NJ 08102

JOHANSEN, LAWRENCE ANDREW, actuary; b. N.Y.C., May 15, 1950; s. Hans Andrew and Mildred Evelyn (Livingston) J.; m. Carolyn Ann Virgili, June 6, 1970; children: Karen, Alyssa. BS, U. Buffalo, 1971. Mgr. rsch. and valuation dept. N.Y. Tchrs. Retirement System, Albany, 1981-84, asst. to the actuary, 1984-89, actuary, 1989—; advisor Govtl. Acctg. Standards Bd., Norwalk, Conn., 1987—. V.p. 1st Luth. Ch., Albany, 1981-83, 90-92, treas., 1977-79, 85-87; bd. dirs. Good Samaritan Luth. Home, Albany, 1984-86, Good Samaritan Nursing Home, Albany, 1984-86. Mem. Am. Acad. Actuaries (pension acctg. com. 1988—), Am. Soc. Pension Actuaries, Conf. Actuaries in Pub. Practice, Joint Bd. Enrollment Actuaries, Soc. Actuaries (assoc.), Adirondack Actuaries Club (v.p., pres. 1983-88). Office: NY State Tchrs Retirement 10 Corporate Woods Dr Albany NY 12211-2395

JOHANSON, WILLIAM GARY, new business development executive, consultant; b. Duluth, Minn., Nov. 19, 1946; s. William Reinold and Ellen Edna (Cameron) J.; m. Frances Shirely Lee, June 7, 1969; children: Jennifer, Janine, Jeannette, William C. BS, U. Minn., Duluth, 1968; BSME, U. Minn., Mpls., 1969; MAS, U. Del., 1975. Registered profl. engr., Del. Engr., supr., venture mgr. E.I. DuPont Co., Wilmington, Del., 1972—. Patentee centrifuge rotors. Comdr. U.S. Navy, 1969-72. Mem. Soc. Mfg. Engrs. (sr.), Res. Officers Assn. (pres. 1989-90). Presbyterian. Home: 16 Bridleshire Rd Newark DE 19711 Office: EI DuPont Brandywine Bldg Wilmington DE 19898

JOHARI, HAMID, mechanical engineering educator; b. Tehran, Iran, Sept. 13, 1961; came t U.S. 1978; s. Mohammad and Parirash (Hosseini) J. BS, Calif. Inst. Tech., 1983; MS, U. Wash., 1985, PhD, 1989. Postdoctoral rsch. fellow U. Wash., Seattle, 1989; asst. prof. mech. engring. Worcester (Mass.) Poly. Inst., 1989—. Marsh fellow, U. Wash., 1983-85. Mem. AIAA (assoc. mem.), ASME (assoc. mem.), Am. Phys. Soc. Office: Worcester Poly Inst 100 Institute Rd Worcester MA 01609-2276

JOHN, FRANK HERBERT, JR., real estate investor, marketing representative; b. Georgetown, Guyana, Mar. 4, 1961; s. Frank Herbert Clement John and Doris Marian Schofield Jones; m. Barbara Jean Stewart, June 2, 1989; 1 child, Andre Nicholas John. BBA, Howard U., 1984. Systems engr. intern IBM, N.Y.C., 1983; account rep. IBM, Washington, 1984—; owner FHJ Properties, Washington, 1989—. Assoc. editor ATSIS Jour., 1982. Bd. dirs. Concerned Black Men, Washington, 1989—, chmn. internat. awareness program, 1990—. Mem. Delta Sigma Pi, Beta Gamma Sigma. Baptist. Home: 8521 Ritchboro Rd Forestville MD 20747 Office: FHJ Properties PO Box 34685 Washington DC 20043

JOHN, JOBY, marketing educator; b. Trivandrum, Kerala, India, Aug. 2, 1957; came to U.S., 1983; s. John Mattamala and Sarah (Mathew) Chacko; m. Rajeshri Vora, July 12, 1987. BS in Pharm. (hon.), Birla Inst. Tech. and Sci., Rajasthan, India, 1978; MBA, U. Madras, India, 1980; PhD in Mktg., Okla. State U., 1987. Spl. projects asst. India Tobacco Co., 1980; profl. svc. officer Pfizer, India, 1981; product mgr. Salequip (Finolex), Bombay, 1982; instr. mktg. Okla. State U., Stillwater, 1984-86; asst. prof. Bentley Coll., Waltham, Mass., 1986—. Contbr. articles to profl. jour. Health Care Mktg., jours. including Jour. Profl. Svcs, Jour. Mktg. Edn., Psychol. Reports, Healthcare Mgmt. Rev. Mem. Am. Mktg. Assn., Assn. Consumer Rsch., Am. Acad. Advt., Acad. Mktg. Sci., Acad. Internat. Bus. Home: 70 Oak Hill Rd Needham MA 02192-4049 Office: Bentley Coll 175 Forest St Waltham MA 02154-4705

JOHN, ROBERT MCCLINTOCK, lawyer; b. Phila., May 21, 1947; s. Lewis Timothy and Marie (McClintock) J.; m. Barbara Ann Weand, May 10, 1975; children: Jennifer, Ryan. BA, Villanova U., 1969, JD, 1972. Bar: Pa. 1972, U.S. Dist. Ct. (ea. dist.) Pa. 1973. Atty. Schneider, Nixon & John, Hatboro, Pa., 1972-74, ptnr., 1975—. Scoutmaster Boy Scouts Am., Hatboro, 1972—, long range planning com. 1979; lectr. and student loan com. Hatboro-Horsham High Sch., 1972—; mgr. Little League, Horsham, Pa., 1985—; referee Hatboro-Horsham (Pa.) Youth Basketball Assn., 1990-91. Recipient award Hatboro-Horsham Sch. Bd., 1979, medal Hatboro YMCA Triathlon, 1983, Silver Beaver award Boy Scouts Am., 1981, Scoutmaster's award of Merit, 1989, Nat. God. and Svc. award, 1991. Mem. ABA, Pa. Bar Assn., Montgomery County Bar Assn., Pa. Trial Lawyers Assn., Greater Hatboro C. of C. (pres. 1983, Honored Citizen Svc. to Youth award 1984), Navy League (sec. southeastern Pa. coun. 1975-88, pres. 1989, S.E. Pa. Coun. Svc. to Youth and Community award 1990, Willow Grove naval Air Sta. svc. award 1986), Rotary (pres. 1984, Dist. Gov.'s Outstanding Pres.'s award 1984). Republican. Roman Catholic. Home: 83 Home Rd Hatboro PA 19040-1830 Office: Schneider Nixon & John 76 Byberry Ave # 698 Hatboro PA 19040-3419

JOHNOPOLOS, STEPHEN GARY, public relations executive; b. Chgo., Jan. 3, 1950; s. Alexander and Anna (Poncher) J. BS, De Paul U., 1973. Cons., writer music, advt., pub. rels. Saxton, Pa., 1972-83; program coord., grantsman Huntingdon County Commrs., Huntingdon, Pa., 1983-85; human svcs. dir. Huntingdon County Commrs., 1985-87; program dir., grantsman Employment & Tng., Inc., Huntingdon, 1988; pub. rels.-devel. coord. So. Alleghenies Planning and Devel. Commn., Altoona, Pa., 1989—; lectr. and seminar speaker in field. Author: Proposals and Grants: A Comprehensive Curriculum, 1987, One Branch, 1988, Writing Proposals That Sell, 1988. Bd. dirs. Allegheny Ballet Co.; pres. Tussey Mountain Sch. Dist., Saxton, 1984-85, Weatherization, Inc., Huntingdon, 1987, Employment and Tng. Inc., Huntingdon, 1987; pres. Mental Health/Mental Retardation Citizens Adv. Bd., 1990-91. Recipient Past Pres. award of appreciation Weatherization Bd. Dirs., 1988, Tussey Mountain Sch. Dist., 1985, Tussey Mountain Jaycees, 1978, Poetry Award of Merit, 1989, Golden Poety award, 1989, Silver Poet award, 1990. Mem. State Coll. Area Musician's Assn. Home: 2 Elm St Wood PA 16694-9999 Office: So Alleghenies Pl-Devel Com 541 58th St Altoona PA 16602

JOHNS, JOHN RICHARDS, utility professional; b. New Haven, May 10, 1952; s. Edwin Richards and Gwendolyn Karen (Waldner) J. Student, Western Conn. State Coll., 1972-74, So. Conn. State Coll., 1977-78. Telephone operator Conn. Light and Power Co., Bethel and Norwalk, 1976-78; customer svc. rep. Northeast Utilities, Stamford, Conn., 1978-81; meters and svc. dispatcher Northeast Utilities, Madison, Conn., 1981—; temp. cons. Northeast Utilities, Madison and Rocky Hill, Conn., 1987—. Com. mem. West Haven Constl. Bi-Centennial Commn., 1987—; mem. combined clubs West Haven, Inc., West Haven Armed Forces Day Com. Mem. Conn. Soc. Genealogists, New Eng. Hist. Genealogical Soc., West Haven Hist. Soc., New Haven Colony Hist. Soc., Annawon Fellowcraft Club (pres. 1988-89), George Allen Club, Philosophic Lodge of Rsch., Tex. Lodge of Rsch., St. Albans Lodge of Rsch., Quatro Coronati Lodge of London, Philalethes Soc., Swenson Swedish Inst., Masons (lodge master 1992), Shriners. Democrat. Home: 53 Center St West Haven CT 06516-3805 Office: NE Utilities New Rd Madison CT 06443-2507

JOHNS, MICHAEL DOUGLAS, speechwriter; b. Allentown, Pa., Sept. 8, 1964; s. Glenn Franklyn and Nancy Louise (Hummel) J. Student, Cambridge (Eng.) U., 1984; BBA in Econs., U. Miami, 1986. Reporter Human Events Mag., Washington, 1983; fellow Congressman Don Ritter, Washington, 1984; asst. editor Policy Rev. Mag., Washington, 1986-88; fgn. policy analyst The Heritage Found., Washington, 1988-91; spl. asst. to pres. Drew U., Madison, N.J., 1991-92; speechwriter to Pres. of U.S. The White House, Washington, 1992—. Author: U.S. and Africa Statistical Handbook, 1991; contbg. author: The Third Generation, 1987; contbg. editor USSR Monitor, The Heritage Found., 1989-91; contbr. articles to profl. jours. Recipient Shell Oil Co.'s Century III Leadership award, 1981, Svc. award Kiwanis, 1982, cert. appreciation Spl. Olympics, 1983. Mem. Iron Arrow Honor Soc., Young Smithsonian Benefactors Soc., Lambda Chi Alpha. Republican. Lutheran. Office: The White House OEOB Rm 122 Washington DC 20500

JOHNS, MICHAEL MARIEB EDWARD, otolaryngologist, university dean; b. Detroit, Jan. 27, 1942; s. Trina Lou DelCampo; children: Christina, Michael. BS, Wayne State U., 1964, Grad. Biol. Sci., 1965; MD with distinction, U. Mich., 1969. Diplomate Am. Bd. Otolaryngology. Intern Univ. Hosp., Ann Arbor, Mich., 1969-70, resident in otolaryngology, 1971-75; resident in gen. surgery St. Joseph's Mercy Hosp., Ann Arbor, 1970-71; asst. prof. U. Va. Med. Ctr., Charlottesville, 1977-79, assoc. prof., 1979-82, prof., 1982-84; prof. Johns Hopkins U. Sch. Medicine, Balt., 1984—, dean med. faculty, v.p. medicine, 1990—; mem. Greater Balt. Com., 1991—; co-chmn. Md. Sci. Week Blue Ribbon Panel, Balt., 1992—. Co-author: Head and Neck Cancer, 1990; contbr. articles to profl. jours. Grantee Robert Wood Johnson Found., 1992. Mem. The Center Club. Office: Johns Hopkins U Sch Medicine 720 Rutland Ave Baltimore MD 21205-2196

JOHNS, WARREN LEROI, lawyer; b. Nevada, Iowa, June 9, 1929; s. Varner Jay and Ruby Charlene (Morrison) J.; m. Elaine C. Magnuson, July 24, 1955 (div. June 1983); children: Richard Warren, Lynn Cherie Johns Pence; m. Ruth Page Scott, Sept. 29, 1985. BA, La Sierra U., 1950; MA, Andrews U., 1951; JD, U. So. Calif., 1958. Bar: Calif. 1959, U.S. Dist. Ct. (cen. dist.) Calif. 1959,U.S. Supreme Ct. 1963, Md. 1976, D.C. 1976, U.S. Dist. Ct. Md. 1976, U.S. Dist. Ct. D.C. 1976, U.S. Tax Ct. 1976, U.S. Ct. Appeals (4th cir.) 1976, U.S. Ct. Appeals (10th cir.) 1977, U.S. Ct. Customs and Patent Appeals 1979. Gen. counsel So. Calif. Conf. Seventh-day Adventists, Glendale, 1959-63, Pacific Union Conf. Seventh-day Adventists, Glendale and Sacramento, 1964-69; pvt. practice Sacramento, 1969-75; gen. counsel Gen. Conf. Seventh-day Adventists, Washington, 1975-92, trustee; pvt. practice Silver Spring, Md., 1992—; spl. counsel to gen. conf., mem. adv. bd. Ctr. for Ch./State Studies, De Paul U. Coll. Law, Chgo., 1987—. Author: Dateline Sunday USA, 1967; founding editor JD, 1978-92. Chmn. bd. dirs., pres. Sacramento Area Econ. Opportunity Coun., 1974. Recipient Frank Yost award Ch. State Coun., Glendale, 1972, Alumnus of Achievement award Andrews U., 1981. Mem. ABA (vice-chmn. com. on torts, nonprofit, charitable and religious orgns., sect. of tort and ins. practice 1990-91), Am. Judicature Soc., Assn. Trial Lawyers Am., Nat. Health Lawyers Assn., Internat. Religious Liberty Assn. (trustee, v.p.),. Democrat. Office: 12501 Old Columbia Pike Silver Spring MD 20904-6600

JOHNSEN, WALTER CRAIG, venture capitalist; b. N.Y.C., Dec. 15, 1950; s. Walter S. Johnsen and Therese L. Nissen; m. Wendy Ann Wilding Davies, July 14, 1990. BS, Cornell U., 1973, MS in Eng., 1974; MBA, Columbia U., 1978. Gen. ptnr. First Century Partnerships, N.Y.C., 1981-85; v.p. Smith Barney, Harris Upham Venture Corp., 1978-85; mng. ptnr. Johnsen Securities, N.Y.C., 1985—; bd. dirs.Columbian Bus. Sch., Marshall Products, Inc., Lincolnshire, Ill., Marine Med. Corp., San Diego, Buffalo Med. Specialties, Clearwater, Fla., N.J. Mem. St. Francis Yacht Club, Cornell Club, Westhampton Yacht Squadron, Mill Reef Club. Office: Johnsen Securities 224 E 49th St New York NY 10017

JOHNSON, ADDIE COLLINS, educator, former dietitian; b. Evansville, Ind., Feb. 28; d. Stewart and Willa (Shamell) Collins; m. John Q. Johnson, Sept. 6, 1958 (dec. Aug. 1991); 1 child, Parker. BS, Howard U., 1956; MEd, Framingham State Coll., Mass., 1967. Registered dietitian, Mass. Dietitian Boston Lying-In Hosp., 1957-61; dietitian Diet Heart Study, Harvard U. Sch. Pub. Health, Boston, 1962-63; tchr. Foxboro (Mass.) Pub. Sch., 1967—; dietitian Sch. Medicine Boston U., 1975-77, Westinghouse Health Systems, Boston; faculty Dept. Nursing Boston State Coll., 1979-82; nutrition cons. Head Start program Westinghouse Sch., Boston, 1979-82; instr. Dept. Nursing U. Mass., 1981—, Bridgewater State Coll., Mass., 1982—; mem. state adv. council Dept. Edn. Bur. Nutrition Edn., 1981-83. Bd. dirs. Norfolk-Bristol County Home Health Assn., Walpole, Mass., 1975-78; presenter Nat. Social Studies Assn., Boston, 1984-85; instr./trainer health services edn. ARC, 1987—. Mem. Am. Dietetic Assn., Am. Home Econs. Assn., Eastern Mass. Home Econs. Assn. (bd. dirs. 1978), Mass. Tchrs. Assn. (higher edn. com. 1984-87), Soc. Nutrition Edn., AAUW, NAACP (life), Delta Kappa Gamma (journalist Iowa chpt. 1986-88, membership chmn. 1988-92), Delta Sigma Theta. Home: 92 Morse St Sharon MA 02067-2719 Office: Foxboro Mechanic St Foxboro MA 02035-2028

JOHNSON, ALBERT LLEWELLYN, II, software engineer; b. Pitts., Aug. 29, 1960; s. Albert L. Sr. and Ann O. Johnson; m. Michele J. Green, May 2, 1987; children: Sarah, Albert III. BS, Carnegie-Mellon U., 1983, MS, 1989. Cert. computer programmer, mgmt tech. change. Programmer Merck & Co., Pitts., 1983-85; program adminstr. Software Engring. Inst., Pitts., 1985-88, mem. tech. staff, 1988-91; sr. analyst Corning (N.Y.), Inc., 1991—. Mem. IEEE Computer Soc., Assn. Computing Machinery. Office: Corning Inc W Pulteney St Corning NY 14831

JOHNSON, ALEXANDER CHESTER, educational administrator; b. Rochester, N.Y., Nov. 18, 1932; s. Peter and Stefania (Firko) J.; m. Virginia A. Gardinier, Dec. 27, 1958; children: Alexander Joseph, William, Christopher, Daniel, Peter. BS, SUNY, Blackport, 1954, MS, 1958; postgrad., U. Rochester, 1964, John Fisher Coll., 1989-91. Cert. ednl. adminstr. From tchr. to vice prin. City Sch. Dist., Rochester, 1957-64, prin., 1964-90. Dir. Project Head Start, Rochester, 1964-65; chmn. Parish Coun. St. Thomas Apostle Sch., Rochester, 1974-76. Sgt. U.S. Army, 1955-57, Korea. Mem.

Sch. Adminstrs. N.Y. State (chmn. Reg. 11, 1984), Rochester Real Estate Bd. Republican. Roman Catholic. Home: 227 Belcoda Dr Rochester NY 14617-2948

JOHNSON, ALVIN DONNEL, human resources executive; b. Burlington, N.J., Jan. 10, 1940; s. Julius Alexander and Lessie (Covington) J.; m. Lawon Patricia Hinton, Aug. 23, 1969; 1 child, Donnel Wesley. BA in Econs., Howard U., 1966; MBA in Mgmt., Rutgers U., 1973. Passenger svc. agt. Am. Airlines, N.Y.C., 1966-67; sr. employee adminstr. Ethicon Inc. (J&J), Somerville, N.J., 1967-76; mgr. personnel adminstrn. Bristol-Myers Co., N.Y.C., 1977-88; v.p. human resources ABB Simcon/NC, Bloomfield, N.J., 1989—; cons. Dunn & Sons Maintenance Corp., Plainfield, N.J., 1977—; mem. Edges Group Inc., N.Y.C., 1970—. Chmn. com. bd. dirs. Freehold Area YMCA, Freehold, N.J., 1984—; bd. dirs. Buffalo (N.Y.) Urban League, 1979-81; bd. trustees Family Counseling Svc. Somerset County, Greenbrook, N.J., 1975-78; pres. Frontiers Internat. Inc., Plainfield, 1973-75. Mem. N.Y. Urban League, Friends of Distinction (treas. 1982-86, sec. 1989-91). Home: 50 Pheasant Run Freehold NJ 07728-7765

JOHNSON, BARRY LEIGH, telecommunications engineer; b. Northampton, Mass., Jan. 18, 1947; s. Carlton L. and Elisabeth S. (Zschiesche) J.; m. Lisa Beryl Shulgold Johnson, Oct. 20. 1985; children: Taryn Johnson, Carlyn Johnson. BS in Elec. Engring., Northeastern U., 1970; MS in Elec. Engring., Stanford U., 1972. Tech. staff AT&T Bell Labs., North Andover, Mass., 1970—. Mem. Tau Beta Pi, Eta Kappa Nu, Phi Kappa Phi. Office: AT&T 1600 Osgood St North Andover MA 01845

JOHNSON, BENJAMIN LEIBOLD, education training and management analyst; b. Norborne, Mo., Nov. 23, 1950; s. Murrell Faxton and Chlora Pauline (Naylor) J. BA, Central Mo. State U., 1971, BS, 1974, MS, 1976; MPA, U. Okla., 1988. Tchr., Raytown and Independence (Mo.) Public Schs., 1974-76; with Wayne Regan, Inc., Realtors, Shawnee, Kans., 1976; tchr., chmn. dept. social studies, English, French, Breckenridge (Mo.) Pub. Schs., 1979-80; career intern edn. specialist Ft. Sill, Okla., 1980-82, tng. analyst/edn. specialist, 1982-85; edn. specialist/instr. U.S. Army Engrs. Sch., Fort Belvoir, Va., 1985-88; mgmt. analyst, dep. chief of staff plans and programs, directorate of manpower and orgn. hdqrs. U.S. Air Force Office Spl. Investigations, Bolling AFB, D.C., 1988—. dept. chmn. social studies, English and French, also edn. specialist. Served with USNR, 1976-79. Mem. Assn. Am. Geographers, Nat. Soc. for Performance and Instruction, Am. Acad. Polit. and Social Scis., Am. Soc. for Pub. Adminstrn., Project Mgmt. Inst., Naval Enlisted Res. Assn., Assn. Supervision and Curriculum Devel., Masons, Scottish Rite, Order DeMolay. Home: 7528 Republic Ct Apt 204 Alexandria VA 22306-7528

JOHNSON, BRIAN, psychiatrist, psychoanalyst; b. Oceanside, N.Y., Jan. 22, 1952; s. Lauren Theodore and Virginia Loretta (Mutter) J.; m. Letitia Upton. BS, Columbia U., 1972; MD, N.Y. Med. Coll., Valhalla, 1976; Cand. in sychoanalysis, Boston Psychoanalytic Inst., 1980-89. Diplomate Am. Bd. Psychiatry. Intern Hoplem Hosp., 1976-77; resident Met. Hosp., N.Y.C., 1977-78; resident in psychiatry Cambridge (Mass.) Hosp., 1978-81; pvt. practice Newtonville, Mass., 1981—; clin. instr. Harvard Med. Sch., Boston. Contbr. articles to profl. jours. Mem. Am. Med. Soc. for Addictions, Am. Psychiatric Assn., Am. Psychoanalytic Assn., Mass. Psychiatric Soc., Boston Psychoanalytic Soc. Home and Office: 5 Park Pl Newton MA 02160-1910

JOHNSON, BRIAN ROBERT, musician, writer; b. Meadville, Pa., Aug. 8, 1960; s. Robert Frederick and Lillian Yvonne (Ciprich) J.; m. Carole Ann Harrison, Feb. 14, 1984. Grad. high sch., Conneaut Lake, Pa., 1978. Musician Rampage, Conneaut Lake, 1982-84, Abandoned Refrigerators, Greenville, Pa., 1984-85, The Fridges, Greenville, 1985-87, Wax Coloniels, Greenville, 1985-89; writer Bent Mag., Greenville, 1989; musician Illuminatus, Sharon, Pa., 1990—; editor They Won't Stay Dead! Mag., 1989; writer Secrets, Greenville, 1991; publisher Cellar Productions, Greenville, 1992—. Albums include: Illuminatus! Illuminatus!, 1991, 1992; producer Wax Coloniels, 1988-90; movie reviewer: TrashoRama, 1991; author numerous poems. Active animal rights and anti-censorship. Recipient 1st pl. award Pitts. Rock Challenge, 1990. Home: 11 Werner Rd Greenville PA 16125 Office: Cellar Productions 11 Werner Rd Greenville PA 16125

JOHNSON, BRUCE EDWARD, distribution company executive; b. Hempstead, N.Y., Dec. 29, 1959; s. William David and Diane Kathryn (Ryan) J.; m. Lee Luise Wurster, July 18, 1981. B in Acctg., Dowling Coll., 1980; MBA in Fin., U. So. Calif., 1983. Facility controller ElectroSound Group, Sun Valley, Calif., 1980-84; corp. controller, chief acctg. officer ElectroSound Group, Hauppauge, N.Y., 1984-86; v.p. fin., chief fin. officer Syscomm Internat. Corp. (previously Info. Tech. Services, Inc.), Hauppauge, 1986—, also bd. dirs.; ind. fin. cons., Ridge, N.Y., 1985—; acctg. internship instr. Dowling Coll., Oakdale, N.Y., 1984—. V.p. Ridge Vol. Fire Dept., 1985. Mem. Nat. Assn. Accts., U. So. Calif. Alumni Assn., Dowling Coll. Alumni Assn. Republican. Office: Syscomm Internat Corp 275 Marcus Blvd Ste F Hauppauge NY 11788-2022

JOHNSON, BRUCE LYNN, record producer, entertainer; b. Phila., Jan. 22, 1969; s. Bruce Lynn Johnson and Maxine Inez (Walker) Robinson. Student, Community Coll. of Air Force, 1987-88. Producer, chief exec. officer Legion of Rap Prodns., Phila., 1988—; with custodial svcs. Thomas Jefferson U., 1989-91; engring. intern Third Story Rec., Phila., 1990-91; producer 2 Tuff Prodns., Phila., 1990—; freelance producer Phila., 1990—; instr. in instruments Fresco and Miz Entertainment, Phila., 1990-91; prodn. cons. for Phila.-based band Flexx, 2 Tuff Prodns., 1991—; promotions cons. Nu X Perience Sound Co., Phila., 1991—. Producer, artist (12 inch album) Hip Hop Buddy, 1990, (cassette) L.O.R. Goes Underground, 1991; mem. Phila.-based band Earth Tribe. Mem. Union 1199/AFSCME, Phila., 1989. With USAF, 1986-88. Mem. Broadcast Music Inc. Home: 5343 Girard Ave Philadelphia PA 19131

JOHNSON, BRUCE MARVIN, English language educator; b. Chgo., Apr. 29, 1933; s. George A. and Elsie L. (Clausing) J.; m. Jean C. Kruger, June 29, 1957; 1 son, Abram. A.B., U. Chgo., 1952; B.A., Northwestern U., 1954, M.A., 1955, Ph.D., 1959. Instr. English U. Mich., 1958-62; asst. prof. English U. Rochester, N.Y., 1962-68, assoc. prof., 1968-76, prof., 1976—, chmn. dept. English, 1981-84. Author: Conrad's Models of Mind, 1971, True Correspondence: A Phenomenology of Thomas Hardy's Novels, 1983. Sr. fellow NEH, 1974-75; fellow Guggenheim Found., 1977-78. Mem. MLA. Democrat. Home: 16 Kirklees Rd Pittsford NY 14534-1556 Office: U Rochester Dept English Rochester NY 14627

JOHNSON, CALVIN, JR., college administrator; b. Balt., Oct. 31, 1951; s. Calvin and Corine (Emerson) J.; m. Ann Mary Braun, Mar. 9, 1975; children: Laura Ellen, Julie Beth, Joseph William. AA, Community Coll. of Balt., 1972; BS, SUNY, Stony Brook, 1974, MS, 1977; PhD, U. Md., 1985. Reg. respiratory therapist. Respiratory therapy tech. Sinai Hosp., Balt., 1971-72; sr. respiratory therapy tech. Southside Hosp., Bay Shore, N.Y., 1973-74; dir. respiratory therapy dept. U. Md. Hosp., Balt., 1974-75; respiratory therapist J.T. Mather Hosp., Port Jefferson, N.Y., 1975-77; ednl. dir. Respiratory Therapy Svcs., Inc., Balt., 1977-78; asst. prof., clin. coord. Community Coll. Balt., 1978-79, asst. prof., program coord., 1979-83, assoc. prof., dept. chmn., 1983-86; assoc. dean natural and health scis. Westchester Community Coll., Valhalla, N.Y., 1986—; staff adv. com. mem. Manpower Distbn. Project, Nat. Health Coun., 1973-76; profl. edn. and tng. cons. Am. Lung Assn. Md., Timonium, 1975-86; adv. coun. health careers/occupations Dunbar High Sch., Balt., 1983-84; mem. health occupations adv. coun. Balt. City Pub. Schs., 1985-86; lectr. in field. Researcher, author: Auto Body Work and Your Health, 1984; co-author: Advanced Respiratory Therapy, 1984, 2d edit. 1985; author book/lecture: Contributions of Blacks to Science, 1987, 2d edit. 1990; contbr. articles to profl. jours. Bd. dirs. Bolton Hill Nursery Sch., Balt., 1981-83; pres. PTO of Mt. Washington Elem. Sch., Balt., 1985-86; mgr. Little League Baseball, Elmsford, 1987-90; trustee Bd. of Edn., Elmsford, 1989—; bd. dirs. Westchester County Emergency Med. Svcs. Coun., Inc., Valhalla; mem. parent coun. Alexander Hamilton High Sch., Elmsford. Recipient Award of Excellence, Sch. Allied Health Professions, SUNY, Stony Brook, 1974, Bronze award, United Way, White Plains, 1987, 88, 91, others. Mem. Am. Assn. for Respiratory Care, Am. Soc. Allied Health Professions, Coun. on Allied Health Edn. of SUNY, Nat. Coun. for Occupational Edn., Allied Health Assn. N.Y. State. Office: Westchester Community Coll 75 Grasslands Rd Valhalla NY 10595-1636

JOHNSON, CARL EARLD, bank executive; b. N.Y.C., Dec. 3, 1936; s. Francis Alexander and Gwendolyn Vera (Trotman) J.; m. Mozelle Baker, June 6, 1961; children: Brian A., Carla D. BS, CCNY, 1958; MBA, CUNY, 1963. Mgr. spl. projects Mobil Oil Corp., N.Y.C., 1981-85; dir. compliance Campbell Soup Co., Camden, N.J., 1985-90; v.p. United Jersey Bank, Princeton, N.J., 1991—. Bd. dirs. West Windsor Zone Adjustment, Princeton Junction, N.J., 1984-89. Mem. Nat. Urban Affairs Coun., EDGES Group Inc., Soc. Human Resources in Mgmt., Inst. Mgmt. Cons. Office: Princeton Employee Rels Cons Inc PO Box 2981 Princeton NJ 08543-2981

JOHNSON, CARLA RAE, sculptor, art educator; b. East Chicago, Ind., Mar. 9, 1947; d. Carl Einor and Ruth Elizabeth (Steele) J. BS, Ball State U., 1969; MA, U. Iowa, 1974, MFA, 1975. Lectr. SUNY, Plattsburgh, 1975-76, Miss. State U., Starkville, 1977-80; adj. lectr. contemporary sculpture Westchester art workshop Westchester Community Coll., White Plains, N.Y., 1985—; adj. lectr. ceramics/sculpture Kingsborough Community Coll., Bklyn., 1986—. Sculptor (sculpture installation) Gray Matters, 1990. Pollock-Krasner fellow Pollock-Krasner Found., N.Y.C., 1990. Mem. Internat. Sculpture Ctr., Women's Caucus for Art, Soho 20 Artists (pres. 1988-89, chmn. bd. 1989-90, vice chair 1990—).

JOHNSON, CHARLES E., JR., paper company executive; b. Boston, Jan. 9, 1955; s. Charles E. and Sandra M. (Cimemo) J.; m. Darlene McConaghy, Oct. 1, 1983; children: Charles E., Christopher Andrew. BA in Polit. Sci., Tufts U., 1977; MBA, Suffolk U., 1979. Sales rep. Westvaco Corp., N.Y.C., 1979-81, Chgo., 1981-83; product mgr. Westvaco Corp., N.Y.C., 1983-86; gen. mgr. Westvaco Can. Ltd., Toronto, Ont., 1987—. Mem. Can. Paper Box Mfg. Assn. Office: Westvaco Can Ltd, 5915 Airport Rd Ste 712, Mississauga, ON Canada L6T 3S2

JOHNSON, CHARLES MICHAEL, college official; b. Seoul, Oct. 13, 1965; s. Michael Thayer and Chung Ja (Im) J. BA, U. Conn., 1988. Rsch. assoc. U. Conn. Found., Storrs, 1988; supr. J.C. Penney Catalog, Manchester, Conn., 1988-90; dir. rsch. Barnard Coll., N.Y.C., 1990—. Mem. Am. Prospect Rsch. Assn., Zeta Psi. Republican. Home: 47 Crestwood Ave Tuckahoe NY 10707 Office: Barnard Coll 3009 Broadway New York NY 10027-6598

JOHNSON, CHARLES PATRICK, financial executive; b. Bridgeport, Conn., Jan. 3, 1961; s. Frank Bruen and Millie Ann (Costa) J. BS in Bus. Mgmt., U. Bridgeport, 1983; BS in Acctg., Sacred Heart U., 1987, MBA in Acctg. and Fin., 1989. Promotion analyst James River Corp., Norwalk, Conn., 1984-85, fin. analyst, 1985-87; acct. Peat Marwick Main & Co., Ft. Lauderdale, Fla., 1987; contr. Inline Plastics Corp., Milford, Conn., 1988-91, chief fin. officer, 1991—. Republican. Roman Catholic. Office: Inline Plastics Corp 40 Seemans Ln Milford CT 06460-4358

JOHNSON, CINDY SWAN, consulting psychologist; b. Sayre, Pa., Sept. 5, 1959; d. Harry Alfred and Phyllis Jean (Blauvelt) Swan; m. Brent Martin Johnson, July 28, 1984; children: Elizabeth May, Matthew Brent. MS, U. Oreg., 1983; BS, SUNY, Cortland, 1991. Cert. sch. psychologist, N.Y. Employment interviewer Harrah's Casino, Reno, Nev., 1983-84; coord. Washoe Assn. for Retarded Citizens, Reno, 1984-86; sch. psychologist Elmira (N.Y.) City Sch. Dist., 1986-89; pvt. practice N.Y.C., 1989—. Member, bd. dirs. Valley Montessori Sch., Big Flats, N.Y., 1989—. Mem. Nat. Assn. Sch. Psychologists, N.Y. Assn. Sch. Psychologists, Chemung Assn. for Retarded Citizens. Methodist. Home: 494 Ridge Rd Horseheads NY 14845-1533

JOHNSON, CIRI DIANE, graphic design firm owner; b. Ann Arbor, Mich., Aug. 19, 1956; d. Paul Christian and Genevieve Ruth (Shanklin) J. Student, U. Ariz., 1974-76, U. Oreg., 1976-78; BFA, San Francisco Art Inst., 1980; MA, NYU, 1982. Artist asst. Lucio Pozzi, N.Y.C., 1983-85; editor, art dir. New Observations Mag., N.Y.C., 1985-91; owner Ciri Johnson Design, Bklyn., 1991—; asst. tchr. Parson's Sch. Design, N.Y.C., 1985-86; instr. NYU, 1982. Prin. works published in The National Poetry Magazine of Lower East Side, 1988-90; designed promotional piece for Elisa Monte Dance Co. chosen for reproduction in 1991 Artist's Market. Mem. Resources for Women, Small Bus. Svc. Bur., Tucson Ad Club. Democrat.

JOHNSON, CURTISS SHERMAN, writer, former publishing executive; b. Meriden, Conn., Apr. 7, 1899; s. Sherman Foster and Adele (Curtiss) J.; B.S., Wesleyan U., 1921; m. Mary Lawton, Sept. 12, 1922 (dec. 1968); children: Curtiss Sherman, Dorothy L. (Mrs. Robert Pollitt) (dec.); m. Barbara Burleigh, Nov. 1968. Advt. mgr. Manning Bowman & Co., Meriden, 1921-26; v.p. The Silex Co., Hartford, Conn., 1927-28; rep. Curtis Publishing Co., Phila., 1928-32; pres. Curtiss Johnson Publs., Deep River, Conn., 1946-60; v.p. Deep River Nat. Bank; dir. Deep River Savs. Bank. Mem. Conn. Flood Control and Water Policy Commn., Hartford, 1954; mem. staff Gov. of Conn., 1940-46; mem. Conn. Safety Commn. Dir. emeritus Middlesex Hosp.; trustee Henry Whitfield State Mus.; chmn. emeritus Conn. River Mus. Served as lt., inf. U.S. Army, World War I; maj. Conn. State Guard, World War II. Mem. Conn. Editorial Assn. (pres. 1941-43). Author: Three Quarters of a Century, 1949; Politics and a Belly-Full, 1962; The Indomitable R. H. Macy, 1964; America's First Lady Boss, 1965; Deadline, 1969; Raymond E. Baldwin, Connecticut Statesman, 1972; History of Pratt-Read Corporation, 1976. Home: 163 Essex Meadows Essex CT 06426-1523

JOHNSON, DARYL DIANE, oil painter; b. N.Y.C., Aug. 28, 1953; d. Wilbur Henry and Dorothy (Hinton) J.; m. C. Roth Benson, May 8, 1982; 1 child: Sven Hardy Benson. BFA, Hope Coll., 1975; postgrad., U. Cin., 1976, Art Student's League, N.Y.C., 1978, Vt. Studio Sch., Johnson, 1988. Paintings in permanent collections of: Aetna Ins. Co., Hartford, Conn., Delta Airlines, Boston, Gen. Electric, Greenwich (Conn.) Hosp., Mariott Hotels, N.Y.C. and St. Louis, Pepsico, Purchase, N.Y., WMUR-TV, Manchester, N.H. One-man shows: Bell Gallery, Stamford, Conn., 1983, Cityarts Gallery, New Haven, 1987, Hatfield Gallery, Manchester, 1989, McGowan Gallery, Concord, N.H., 1990. Author commd. works Mary Immaculate Hosp., 1983, mural "New Hampshire Triptych" WMUR-TV, 1992. Recipient painting award Conn. Painters and Sculptors Show, Stamford Mus., 1981. Mem. N.H. Art Assn. (in juried shows recipient 1st prize 1989, 90, Miriam Sawyer award 1989, Connor award 1990), Found. for Community of Artists, Boston Visual Arts Union, Candia Jr. Woman's Club. Home and Office: 173 Merrill Rd Candia NH 03034

JOHNSON, DAVID BLACKWELL, safety engineer; b. Annapolis, MD, June 16, 1954; s. Charles McCoy and Jane (Ingling) J.; m. Jacalyn Benjamin, Aug. 7, 1976; children: Sarah Ingling, Jeffrey Blackwell, Kevin Berington. BA, Drew U., 1976; postgrad., NYU, 1976-78. Cert. safety profl. Am. Bd. Cert. Safety Profls. Rsch. assoc. NYU Med. Ctr., 1978-79; safety engr., indsl. hygienist Burroughs Corp., Plainfield, N.J., 1979-80; mgr. safety and indsl. hygiene Unisys Corp., Plainfield, 1980-81; corp. supr. hazardous materials Revlon, Inc., Edison, N.J., 1981-82; mgr. safety and health Revlon, Inc., 1982-84; mgr. indsl. hygiene and safety Celanese Engring. Resins, Inc., Chatham, N.J., 1984-87; corp. dir. environ., health and safety affairs Hoechst Celanese Corp., Somerville, N.J., 1987—; bd. dirs., Celanese Emergency Brigade Tng. Ctr., Rock Hill, S.C., 1987—. Adviser safety com., City of Summit, N.J., 1985. Mem. Am. Indsl. Hygiene Assn. (treas. N.J. sect. 1984-85), Am. Soc. Safety Engrs., Nat. Safety Mgmt. Assn., Am. Pub. Health Assn., Kiwanis. Episcopalian. Home: 25 Waldron Ave Summit NJ 07901-2805 Office: Hoechst Celanese Corp Rt 202-206 Somerville NJ 08876-1258

JOHNSON, DAVID EMANUEL, program manager; b. Boston, Sept. 11, 1937; s. Robert Herbert and Alice (McGoings) J.; m. Carolyn Yvonne Matthews, July 6, 1968; 1 child, Lawan Marcella. Student, CCNY, 1955-56, USAF Engring. Tech. Sch., 1956-64. Customer engr. trainee to systems assurance rep. IBM, Balt., 1964-78, field mgr., 1978-80; systems support mgr. IBM, Gaithersburg, Md., 1980-82; equal opportunity programs mgr. IBM, Washington, 1982-83, quality mgr., 1983-84, br. mgr., 1984-86; br. mgr. IBM, Balt., 1986-90, program mgr. community and external programs, 1990—; pres., founder Johnson Cons. Group, Inc., Balt., 1992—; mem. adv. bd. City Pub. Schs., Urban League Info. Processing Tng. Ctr., Balt.; mem. pres.'s adv. coun., found. bd. Bowie State U.; mem. Investing in Balt. Com.; working with Myerhoff scholars program UMBC, Md. Bd. dirs. Found. for Youth Impact, Balt.; mem. Mayor's Youth Leadership Inst., Balt., Citizen's Adv. Bd. Hickey Training Sch., Md.; founder Project Road-Map (adult mentoring-youth program), Balt.; working with dept. juvenile svcs. mentoring program Boot-Camp After Care Programs Across State of Md. Home: 339 Beaumont Ave Baltimore MD 21228-3013 Office: IBM 9 State Cir Annapolis MD 21401-1903

JOHNSON, DAVID SIMONDS, meteorologist; b. Porterville, Calif., June 29, 1924; s. Frank David and Wanda (Simonds) J.; m. Margaret T. McFarland, Nov. 29, 1974 (dec. Dec. 1987). Student, U. Calif.-Berkeley, 1942-43, Reed Coll., 1943-44, Harvard U., 1945; AB, UCLA, 1948, MA, 1949. Meteorol. aide U.S. Weather Bur., Boise, Idaho, 1946-47; rsch. asst. to asst. meteorologist UCLA, 1947-52; assoc. meteorologist Pineapple Rsch. Inst., Honolulu, 1952-56; with U.S. Weather Bur., 1956-65, dir. Nat. Weather Satellite Ctr., 1964-65; dir. Nat. Environ. Satellite Ctr. Environ. Sci. Svcs. Adminstrn., Washington, 1965-70, Nat. Environ. Satellite Svc. NOAA, 1970-80; asst. adminstr. for satellites NOAA, 1980-82; spl. asst. to pres. Univ. Corp. for Atmospheric Rsch., Washington, 1982-83, also cons.; pres. Damar Internat., 1984-86; sr. program officer NAS-NRC, 1986—; mem. working group II com. space rsch. Internat. Coun. Sci. Unions, 1965-69; chmn. panel neutral atmosphere, 1966-69; mem. working group VI com. space rsch., 1965-78; mem. panel edn. and manpower com. atmospheric scis. NAS, 1967-69; mem. Gov. Md. Sci. Resources adv. bd., 1963-67; exec. com. panel on satellites World Meteorol. Orgn., 1973-82, cons. to sec.-gen., 1982-86. Co-author: Studies of the Structure of the Atmosphere over the Eastern Pacific Ocean in Summer, 1961. With USAAF, 1943-46. Recipient Gold medal Dept. Commerce, 1965, Satellite Silver medal, 1985; Exceptional Svc. NASA, 1966, award Nat. Civil Svc. League, 1974, William T. Pecora award, 1978, Presdl. Meritorious Svc. award, 1980. Bellow Am. Meteorol. Soc. (pres. 1974, councilor 1963-65, 68-70, 73-76, 81-83, exec. com. 1969-70, 73-75, 81-83, planning commn. 1989—, chmn. com. atmospheric measurements 1965-68, Brooks award 1982), AIAA (assoc.), Am. Geophys. Union, Am. Astronautical Soc. (bd. dirs. 1988—, exec. com. 1988-92, Achievement award 1982); mem. AAAS, Internat. Acad. Astronautics, Cosmos Club (Washington), Sigma Xi. Mem. United Ch. of Christ. Home: 1133 Lake Heron Dr # 3A Annapolis MD 21403-3518 Office: NAS/NRC 2101 Constitution Ave NW Washington DC 20418-0001

JOHNSON, DAVID WILLIS, food products executive; b. Tumut, New South Wales, Australia, Aug. 7, 1932; came to U.S., 1976; s. Alfred Ernest and Eileen Melba (Burt) J.; m. Sylvia Raymonde Wells, Mar. 12, 1966; children: David Ashley Lawrence, Justin Christopher Kendall, Harley Alistair Kent. BS in Econs., U. Sydney, Australia, 1954, diploma in Edn., 1955; MBA, U. Chgo., 1958. Mgmt. trainee Colgate-Palmolive, Sydney, 1959-60, product mgr., 1961, asst. to mng. dir., 1962, brands mgr., 1963, gen. products mgr., 1964-65; asst. gen. mgr., mktg. dir. Colgate-Palmolive, Johannesburg, Republic of South Africa, 1966, chmn., mng. dir., 1967-72; pres. Warner-Lambert/Parke Davis Asia, Hong Kong, 1973-76; pres. personal products div. Warner-Lambert Co., Morris Plains, N.J., 1977, pres. Am. Chicle Div., 1978; exec. v.p., gen mgr. Entenmann's div. Warner-Lambert Co., Bay Shore, N.Y., 1979; pres. specialty foods group Warner-Lambert Co., Morris Plains, 1980-81, v.p., 1980-82; pres., chief exec. officer Entenmann's div. Warner-Lambert Co., Bay Shore, 1982; v.p. Gen. Foods Corp., White Plains, N.Y., 1982-87; pres., chief exec. officer Entemann's, Inc., Bay Shore, 1982-87; chmn., pres., chief exec. officer Gerber Products Co., Fremont, Mich., 1987-89, chmn., chief exec. officer, 1989-90; pres., chief exec. officer Campbell Soup Co., Camden, N.J., 1990—; also bd. dirs. Gerber Products Co., Fremont, Mich.; bd. dirs. CIGNA Corp., Colgate-Palmolive Co. Mem. Am. Bakers Assn. (past bd. dirs.), Am. Mgmt. Assn. Office: Campbell Soup Co World Hdqrs Campbell Pl Camden NJ 08103-1702

JOHNSON, DEANE FRANK, communications company executive; b. Des Moines, Sept. 2, 1918; s. Frank Joseph and Alma Odessa J.; m. Anne McDonnell, Nov. 9, 1968; 1 son, Deane Frank. A.B., Stanford, 1939, J.D., 1942. Bar: bar. Mem. firm O'Melveny & Myers, 1942-49, partner, 1949-81, mng. partner, 1977-81; pres. Warner Communications, Inc., N.Y.C., from 1980; also dir. Warner Communications, Inc. Trustee Am. Film Inst, Calif. Inst. Tech; mem. bd. mgrs. Meml. Sloan Kettering Cancer Ctr.; bd. dirs. Am. Mus. of The Moving Image, ARC, Boy Scouts Am., Actors Fund. Mem. Am. Bar Assn., Order Coif. Episcopalian. Clubs: Los Angeles Country (Los Angeles), Calif. (Los Angeles); The Links (N.Y.C.); Shinnecock Hills Golf, Nat. Golf Links (Southampton, L.I.); Lyford Cay (Bahamas); Mt. Kenya Safari. Office: Warner Communications Inc 75 Rockefeller Pla New York NY 10019

JOHNSON, DON ROBERT, religious organization leader, administrator; b. Salina, Kans., Oct. 8, 1942; s. Ben Henry and Bertha Lucile (Armstrong) J.; m. Judith Mae Skelton, Apr. 12, 1980; children: Jennifer, Monica, Anaise, Rebekah. AA, S.W. Bapt. Coll., 1962; BA, East Tex. Bapt. Coll., 1964; MDiv, Midwestern Theol. Sem., 1968; postgrad., U. Iowa, 1969-70. Ordained to ministry So. Bapt. Conv., 1966, United Meth. Ch., 1970. Pastor various Meth. chs., Iowa, 1968-74, Calvary United Meth. Ch., Waterloo, Iowa, 1974-82; chaplain Stephens Coll., Columbia, Mo., 1982-86; sr. leader N.Y. Soc. for Ethical Culture, N.Y.C., 1986—; dir. Metzger Price Fund, N.Y.C., 1987—; advisor Ctr. for Urban Well-Being, Carmel, Calif., 1988—; speaker. Contbr. articles to jours. Chmn. multi-cultural com. Mid Mo. Assn. of Colls. and Univs., Columbia, 1984-86; pres. Neighborhood Housing Svcs., Inc., Waterloo, Iowa, 1978-82; chmn. People's Community Health Clinic, Waterloo, 1978-80. Mem. Nat. Leaders Coun., Am. Ethical Union (cert.), Internat. Humanist and Ethical Union. Office: Ethical Culture Soc 2 W 64th St New York NY 10023-7104

JOHNSON, DOROTHY SUTHERLAND, school guidance counselor; b. Phila., Sept. 28, 1951; d. Robert Archibald and Lillian Mae (Armstrong) Sutherland; m. Maurice Hugo Johnson, Feb. 26, 1985. BS in Edn., Temple U., 1972; MA, Villanova U., 1976. Cert. elementary tchr and guidance counselor Pa. Tchr. Sch. Dist. of Phila., 1972-85; guidance counselor Sch. dist. of Phila., 1985-91, Colonial Sch. Dist., New Castle, Del., 1991—. Recipient Ruth W. Hayre Community Svc. award Sch. Dist. of Phila., 1988. Mem. ASCD, ACA, Pa. Sch. Counselors Assn. (exec. bd. 1987-89), Del. Sch. Counselors Assn., Am. Sch. Counselors Assn., Phi Delta Kappa. Home: 7 Evans Dr Landenberg PA 19350-9393 Office: Castle Hills Elem Sch Moores Ln New Castle DE 19720

JOHNSON, EDWARD ERIC, publishing company executive; b. Nyack, N.Y., Jan. 14, 1944; s. Andrew Gunnar and Marie (Bach) J.; m. Susan Marie Payne, Sept. 9, 1972; 1 child, Kerstin Ann. BS, Rensselaer Poly. Inst., 1966; MBA, Stanford U., 1968. Cons. McKinsey & Co., Inc., San Francisco, 1968-74; dir. Office Fed. Drug Mgmt., Exec. Office of Pres., Washington, 1974-77; v.p. ops. Am. Can Internat., Greenwich, Conn., 1977-84; v.p. planning and devel. Times Mirror Co., Los Angeles, 1984-88, group v.p., 1988—. Republican. Congregationalist. Home: 4418 Oakwood Ave La Canada Flintridge CA 91011-3414 Office: The Times Mirror Co Times Mirror Sq Los Angeles CA 90012-3816

JOHNSON, EDWARD FULLER, investment banker, consultant; b. Princeton, N.J., Sept. 14, 1921; s. Rankin and Kate Gilbert (Fuller) J.; m. Joan Van Alstyne, Apr. 1, 1950; children: Susan, Keats, Kate, Kimball, David, Edward; m. 2d, Zoë Van Antwerp Wells, June 10, 1988. ME, Cornell U., 1946. With J.G. White Constrn. Co., Venezuela, 1947-48, George S. Armstrong, Mgmt. Cons. Engrs., N.Y.C., 1948-50; ptnr. Van Alstyne Noel Co., N.Y.C., 1952-61; dir. Johnson Redbook Service, Prescott, Ball & Turben, N.Y.C., 1970-90, Johnson Redbook Svc., Lynch Jones & Ryan, N.Y.C., 1991—; cons. to diversified industries; mem. polymers panel Nat. Acad. Scis., 1980-82. Chmn. No. Valley Red Cross Fund Dr., Englewood, N.J., 1964-65; councilman, Englewood, 1967-70; chmn. bd. dirs. Englewood Community Chest, 1976-78; pres. Bayhead (N.J.) Rep. Club; mayor, Bayhead, 1992—. Capt. USAF, World War II, Korea. Decorated Air medal with 2 oak leaf clusters. Mem. N.Y. Analysts Soc., Apparel and Textile Analysts Group (pres. 1987-88), Chem. Analysts Group, Merchandising Analyst Group (pres. 1986-87), Home Furnishing Analysts Group, Englewood Club, Bayhead Yacht Club, Mantoloking Yacht Club, Bond Club, Cornell Club. Presbyterian. Home: 821 East Ave Bay Head NJ

08742 Office: Johnson Redbook Svc 15th Fl 345 Hudson St New York NY 10014

JOHNSON, EDWARD MICHAEL, molecular biologist, educator; b. Kenosha, Wis., Apr. 9, 1945; s. Edward and Mary Margaret (Pratch) J.; m. Elizabeth Buckingham Childs, June 14, 1969; 1 son, Nathaniel Livingston. B.A., Pomona Coll., 1967; Ph.D., Yale U., 1971. Postdoctoral fellow Rockefeller U., N.Y.C., 1971-73, asst. prof. molecular biology, 1975-81, assoc. prof., 1981—; research assoc. Sloan-Kettering Cancer Ctr., N.Y.C., 1973-75; adj. assoc. prof. Cornell U. Grad. Sch. Med. Sci., N.Y.C., 1981—; prof. molecular pathology Mt. Sinai Med. Sch., 1984—. Contbr. numerous articles to sci. publs. Jane Coffin Childs fellow in molecular biology, 1971; Leukemia Soc. Am. Spl. Fellow, 1974; recipient Faculty Rsch. award Am. Cancer Soc. Mem. Am. Soc. Biolchem. and Molecular Biology, Am. Soc. for Pharmacology and Exptl. Therapeutics, Am. Soc. for Cell Biology, N.Y. Acad. Scis., AAAS. Home: 531 E 88th St Apt 4B New York NY 10128-7756 Office: Mt Sinai Sch Medicine 1 Gustave L Levy Pl # 1194 New York NY 10029-6504

JOHNSON, EUGENE CLARE, data processing company executive; b. Whitehall, Wis., Nov. 19, 1940; s. Paul Reuben and Clara Theresa (Severson) J.; m. Livia Ann Baynes, Sept. 23, 1967; children: Andrew Paul, Anthony Alexander. Student, Madison Coll., 1959, Pasadena Coll., 1961, Purdue U., 1962, Harvard U., 1974. Vol. Peace Corps, Chile, 1962-64; acct. Am. Ins. Underwriters, N.Y.C., 1964-66; advanceman to Pres. Richard M. Nixon N.Y.C., 1966-68; asst. treas. Bristol-Myers Co., N.Y.C., 1968-69; spl. asst. to Gov. Nelson Rockefeller N.Y.C., 1969-77; mgr. advanced systems div. U.S. Postal Service, Washington, 1971-80; with govt. relations dept. ITT, Washington, 1980-85; exec. v.p., chief operating officer TCom Systems, Inc., Washington, 1985-88; v.p. market devel. Diversified Data and Communications Inc., Washington, 1988-90; pres., chief exec. officer Bus. Mail Express, Inc., Washington, 1990—; founder Electronic Funds Trnasfer Assocs., Washington, 1977. Patentee performance analyzer. Sr. advisor Reagan Presdl. Transition Team, 1980; presdl. appointee U.S. Archtl. and Transp. Barriers Compliance Bd., 1988—; pres., chief exec. officer Alliance Families for Christian Values., 1990—. Mem. Washington Tennis Patrons Assn. Club: Kenwood Golf and Country (Bethesda, Md.) (chmn. bd. dirs. 1987). Home: 5719 Newington Rd Bethesda MD 20816-1281 Office: Bus Mail Express Inc 1211 Connecticut Ave NW 888 17th St NW Washington DC 20036

JOHNSON, EUGENE JOSEPH, art historian, educator; b. Memphis, May 22, 1937; s. Eugene J. and Mary Elizabeth (Thornton) J.; m. Leslie Griffiths Nicholson, Oct. 30, 1965; children: Eugene IV, Nicholson Griffiths. BA, Williams Coll., 1959; MA, NYU, 1963, PhD, 1970. Asst. prof. U. Tenn., Knoxville, 1965; asst. prof. Williams Coll., Williamstown, Mass., 1965-73, assoc. prof., 1973-80, prof., 1980—, chmn. dept. art, 1977-80, 90-91; vis. prof. art Cooper Union, N.Y.C., 1980, Rhodes Coll., Memphis, 1988,. Author: S. Andrea in Mantua, 1975, Charles Moore, 1986, Memphis, An Architectural Guide, 1990. Me. Soc. Archtl. Historians, Mass. Hist. Commn. Office: Williams Coll Dept Art Williamstown MA 01267

JOHNSON, FRANCIS, chemistry and pharmacology educator; b. Bristol, Eng., Mar. 12, 1930; s. Francis and Ada (Waterworth) J.; m. Beatrice Wordie, Feb. 26, 1955 (div.); m. Marta Maureen Lawson, Dec. 23, 1989; children: Michael, Laura, Francis. BSc, Glasgow U., 1951, PhD, 1954. Postdoctoral fellow Boston (Mass.) Univ., 1954-57; rsch. scientist Dow Chem. Co., Wayland, Mass., 1957-74; prof. dept. pharmacology SUNY, Stony Brook, 1974—; dir. rsch. Ganes Chems., Inc., Carlstadt, N.J., 1990—. Patentee in field; contbr. over 100 articles to profl. jours. Mem. AAAS, Am. Chem. Soc., N.Y. Acad. Sci., The Chem. Soc. (U.K.), Royal Soc. Arts (U.K.). Home: 18 Coraway Rd East Setauket NY 11733-2266 Office: SUNY Dept Chemistry Stony Brook NY 11794-3400

JOHNSON, FRANKLIN KEVIN, science teacher, consultant, medical researcher; b. Chgo., Apr. 21, 1954; s. Harlan G. and Delores Mae (Jackson) J.; m. Edna Cala, Apr. 19, 1984. BA, Monmouth Coll., Ill., 1976; MS, U. Ill., 1983. Cert. secondary sch. sci. tchr., Ill., N.J., Pa. Sci. tchr. Monmouth Pub. Schs., 1976-81; chemistry tchr. Clifton (Ill.) Regional Schs., 1983-84; biology tchr. Moore Cath. High Sch., Staten Island, N.Y., 1984-85; clin rsch. assoc. Oxford Rsch. Internat. Corp., Clifton, N.J., 1985-86; biology tchr. and coach Princeton (N.J.) Regional Schs., 1986-88; honors biology tchr. and coach Higland Park (N.J.) Bd. Edn., 1988-91; med. rsch. assoc. Knoll Pharms. BASF unit, Whippany, N.J., 1991—; part time sci. instr. Jointure for Community Adult Edn., Bound Brook, N.J., 1991—; pharm. cons. Oxford Rsch. Internat. Corp., Clifton, N.J., 1987-89, Ortho Bio Tech. Unit Johnson & Johnson Advanced Health Care, N. Brunswick, N.J., 1989; adj. instr. in biology Raritan Valley Community Coll., North Branch, N.J., 1988—. Vol. Dem. Orgn., Monmouth, 1972. Mem. N.J. Edn. Assn., N.J. Biology Tchrs. Assn., Med. Writers Assn., Drug Info. Assn., Am. Heart Assn. Lutheran. Office: Knoll Pharms BASF Unit 30 N Jefferson Rd Whippany NJ 07981-1045

JOHNSON, GERARD G., apparel company executive; b. Evanston, Ill., Feb. 13, 1941; s. Gerard Burkhardt and Alice (Griffin) J.; m. Jean Hill, Aug. 16, 1967; children—Matthew, Sarah, Christopher. S.B., U.S. Naval Acad., Annapolis, 1963; M.B.A., Harvard U., Boston, 1969, D.B.A., 1972. Asst. prof., instr. Harvard Bus. Sch., Boston, 1969-75; dir. indsl. engring. Electric Boat-Gen. Dynamics, Groton, Conn., 1975-77; cons. self-employed, Old Saybrook, Conn., 1977-78; asst. treas. The Continental Group Inc., Stamford, Conn., 1978-82; v.p., treas. Gen. Instrument Corp., N.Y.C., 1982-85, v.p. fin., chief fin. officer, 1985-88; v.p. fin., chief fin. officer VF Corp., Wyomissing, Pa., 1988—; instr. Internat. Tchrs. Program, Fountainbleau, France, 1973. Creative cons. annual editions Readings in Business, 1973-74. Vice pres. Liberty Corner Assn., N.J., 1984-85; bd. dirs. Berks County 4-H. Lt. USN, 1963-67. Baker scholar Harvard Bus. Sch., 1969. Mem. Century Club (Harvard Bus. Sch.), Fin. Execs. Inst. Roman Catholic. Office: VF Corp 1047 N Park Rd Reading PA 19610-1339

JOHNSON, GREGORY PAUL, marketing, business and rehabilitation consultant; b. Altoona, Pa., June 12, 1954; s. Richard Paul and Vada (Panos) J.; m. Linda Marie Karl, Oct. 18, 1980; children: Selina, Adam, Tara. AS, Monroe Community Coll., 1974; BA, Cornell U., 1976. Bd. cert. clin. assoc. Am. Acad. Pain Mgmt., bd. cert. ins. rehab. specialist Bd. for Rehab. Cert. Owner Johnson Enterprises, Harrisburg, Pa., 1979—; rehab. specialist Cen. Rehab. Assn., King of Prussia, Pa., 1980-87; rehab. supr. Cen. Rehab. Assn., Harrisburg, 1987-88; owner Susquehanna Rehab. Svcs., Harrisburg, 1988—. Mem. AACD, Am. Rehab. Assn., Nat. Rehab. Assn. (job placement div.), Nat. Assn. Rehab. Profls. in Pvt. Sector, Nat. Assn. Self Employed, Vocat. Evaluations and Work Adjustment Assn., Harrisburg Claims Assn., Network Bus. Opportunity Entrepreneurs. Mem. Christian Ch. Home and Office: Johnson Enterprises 265 Brindle Rd Mechanicsburg PA 17055-9771

JOHNSON, HAROLD ARTHUR, manufacturing company executive; b. Warren, Pa., May 17, 1924; s. Oscar William and Alvina Victoria (Nelson) J.; B.S. in Indsl. Engring., Pa. State U., 1950; m. Alice Meredith Jones, June 15, 1955; children—Mark, Thomas. Draftsman, Pa. Furnace and Iron Co., Warren 1941-43, engr., 1950-52, chief engr., 1952-61, sales and engring. mgr., 1961-63, sec.-treas., 1963-68, v.p., 1968-72, also dir.; exec. v.p., dir. Allegheny Valve Co., Allegheny Coupling Co., Warren, 1972-82, pres., treas., 1982—, also dir.; exec. v.p. Rand Machine Products, Inc., Jamestown, N.Y., 1972—, also dir. Active Warren County Sch. Authorities, 1961—, chmn., 1980—; chmn. Warren County Hosp. Authority, 1971—; exec. com. Boy Scouts Am., 1973—, pres. 1986-87; former treas. Trinity Episcopalian Ch.; sr. warden, vestryman, trustee Erie (Pa.) Diocese, 1975-81 ; bd. dirs., pres., treas. DeFrees Family Fund. Served with AUS, 1943-46. Decorated Bronze Star. Mem. ASME, Truck Trailer Mfrs. Assn. (tank conf. engring. com., chmn. 1961-62), C. of C., Am. Legion (past officer), Tau Beta Pi, Phi Kappa Phi, Phi Eta Sigma, Phi Sigma Kappa. Republican. Clubs: Conewango, Conewango Valley Country, Rotary, Masons, Shriners, Grotto. Contbr. articles in field to profl. jours. Home: 103 Memorial Dr Warren PA 16365-4111 Office: 419 3d Ave Warren PA 16365

JOHNSON, HAYNES BONNER, journalist, author; b. N.Y.C., July 9, 1931; s. Malcolm Malone and Ludie (Adams) J.; m. Julia Ann Erwin, Sept. 21, 1954 (div.); children—Katherine Adams, David Malone, Stephen Holmes, Sarah Brooks, Elizabeth Haynes. B.J., U. Mo., 1952; M.S., U. Wis., 1956. Reporter Wilmington (Del.) News-Jour., 1956- 57; with Washington Star, 1957-69; nat. corr. Washington Post, 1969-73, asst. mng. editor, 1973-77, columnist, 1977—; Ferris prof. journalism and pub. affairs Princeton U., 1975-78; TV commentator P.B.S. Washington Week in Rev.; lectr. in field. Author: Dusk at the Mountain, 1963, The Bay of Pigs, 1964, (with Bernard M. Gwertzman) Fulbright: the Dissenter, 1968, (with George C. Wilson) Army in Anguish, 1972, (with Nick Kotz) The Unions, 1972, (with Richard Harwood) Lyndon, 1973, The Working White House, 1975, In The Absence of Power, 1980, (with Howard Simons) The Landing, 1986, Sleepwalking Through History, 1991; editor: The Fall of a President, 1974. Served to 1st lt. AUS, 1952-55. Recipient Pub. Svc. prize and Grand award for reporting Washington Newspaper Guild, 1962, 68, Interpretive Reporting award, 1965, Nat. Reporting award, 1968, Pulitzer prize for nat. reporting, 1966, Headliners award for nat. reporting, 1968, Sigma Delta Chi gen. reporting award, 1969; fellow in communications Duke U., 1973-74. Mem. Nat. Acad. Pub. Adminstrn. Clubs: Gridiron (Washington); Nassau (Princeton); Fed. City (Washington). Office: Washington Post Co 1150 15th St NW Washington DC 20071

JOHNSON, HORTON ANTON, pathologist; b. Cheyenne, Wyo., Nov. 12, 1926; s. Horton Antonius and Katharine Mary (Tidball) J.; m. Caryl Abell Daly, Nov. 20, 1970; children by previous marriage: Katherine, Kristin, Margaret, Ann, Gregory, Marjorie. AB, Colo. Coll., 1949; MD, Columbia U., 1953. Diplomate: Am. Bd. Pathology. Intern Univ. Hosp., Ann Arbor, Mich., 1953-54; resident in pathology Univ. Hosp., 1954-57, Pondville Cancer Hosp., Walpole, Mass., 1957-58; scientist Brookhaven Nat. Lab., 1958-60, 63-70; asst. prof. pathology U. Utah, 1960-63; prof. pathology SUNY, Stony Brook, 1970-72, Ind. U., 1972-75; prof., chmn. dept. pathology Tulane U., New Orleans, 1975-84; prof. pathology Columbia U., N.Y.C., 1984-91; dir. pathology St. Luke's-Roosevelt Hosp. Ctr., N.Y.C., 1984-91. Served with USNR, 1944-46. Recipient Lederle Med. Faculty award, 1961. Fellow Coll. Am. Pathologists; mem. Am. Assn. Pathologists, Internat. Acad. Pathology, Biophys. Soc., Radiation Research Soc., N.Y. Acad. Scis., Assn. Clin. Scientists, Soc. Health and Human Values, Phi Beta Kappa, Alpha Omega Alpha. Home: 39 North Cove Rd Old Saybrook CT 06475-3118 Office: Three Lincoln Center Plz Ste 28G New York NY 10023-7613

JOHNSON, J. ALBERT, lawyer; b. Medford, Mass., Feb. 23, 1933; s. John A. and Helen (Devane) J.; m. Suzanne Conley. BA, Northeastern U., 1952; LLB, Boston Coll., 1956, JD, 1969. Bar: Mass., U. S. Dist. Ct. Mass., U.S. Ct. Claims, U.S. Ct. Appeals (1st, 2d, 4th, 5th, 8th and 9th cirs.), U.S. Ct. Mil. Appeals, U.S. Supreme Ct. Teller, clk. Newton Waltham (Mass.) Bank, 1946-50; sound engr. DeMambro Radio Corp., Boston, 1950-52; spl. asst. Registrar Motor Vehicles, Boston, 1951—; assoc. Badger, Pratt, Doyle & Badger, Boston, 1957-58, Lee Bailey, Boston, 1960—; sr. ptnr. Johnson, Mee & May, Boston, 1980—; pvt. practice Boston, San Francisco, L.A., Washington; legal officer, pros. atty. Town of Hingham Police Dept.; vis. lectr. U. Tenn., U. Mich., U. Wis., Albany State U., North Adams State Coll., Ill. State U., Boston Coll.; counsel Commonwealth Mass., Registry Motor Vehicles; advisor Dept. Pub. Safety, Commonwealth Mass.; master and hearings officer Mass. Superior Ct.; dir. Enstrom Helicopter Corp., Menominee, Mich., Advocate Airways Inc., Plymouth, Mass.; vis. lectr. U. Tenn., U. Mich., U. Wis., Ill. State U., Boston Coll., Albany State U. Law Sch. Mem. commn., counsel Commonwealth Mass., Gov.'s Hwy. Safety Bur.; past committeeman Old Colony coun. Boy Scouts Am.; mem. Comm. on Codification of Laws, Commonwealth of Mass.; bd. dirs. Old St. Mary's Paulist Ctr., Paulist Fathers, San Francisco, Carney Hosp., Boston, Interactive Scis. Corp., Boston, Papa Gino's of Am., Inc., Fla. Symphonic Pops Orch. With USMC. Fellow Am. Judicature Soc.; mem. ABA, Am. Trial Lawyers Assn., Mass. Bar Assn., Mass. Trial Lawyers Assn., Ancient and Honorable Artillery Co. Mass., Mass. Chiefs Police Assn., Boston Coll. Law Sch. Alumni Assn., Aircraft Owners and Pilots Assn., Air Traffic Controllers Orgn., Helicopter Assn. Am., New Eng. Chiefs Police Assn., Registry of Motor Vehicles Inspectors Assn., Ancient and Hon. Artillery Co. Mass., USMC League, Am. Legion, Mil. Order Fgn. Wars. Home: Apt 1K Charles River Pk 8 Whittier Pl Boston MA 02114-1499

JOHNSON, J. CHESTER, financial executive, government consultant, poet; b. Chattanooga, Sept. 28, 1944; m. Freda Stern; children: Juliet Christina, Guilbert Roland. Student, Harvard U., 1962-65; BSE, U. Ark., 1967. Sr. analyst Moody's Investors Svc., 1968-71; head pub. fin. rsch. and adv. group The Morgan Bank, 1972-77; dep. asst. sec. U.S. Treasury Dept., Washington, 1977-78; pres., prin. Govt. Fin. Assocs., Inc., N.Y.C., 1979—; bd. dirs., chair fin. com. N.Y. State Environ. Facilities Corp., 1991—; chmn. Fed. Task Force to create Nat. Devel. Bank; chmn. Fed. Inter-agy. Task Force for Improvement Govtl. Fin. Reporting; chmn. Fund to Assure Pub. Infrastructure Fin., Nat. Infrastructure Bond Coalition, 1988-91; interviewed on pub. fin. Cable News Network, ABC Morning News Feature, PBS News Roundup, NBC Nightly News, others. Author: (poetry) OH America!, January 12th, 1967, 2d edit., 1975, Shorts: For Fun, Not for Instruction, 1985, It's A Long Way Home, An American Sequence, 1985, Shorts: On Reaching Forty, 1985; co-author: Original Disclosure Guidelines for Securities' Offerings by State and Local Governments, 1976, The Future of Boston's Capital Plant, 1980, Mayor's Financial Management Handbook, 1985; contbr. articles to profl. jours. Recipient Young So. Poets award, Internat. Poets award. Mem. Nat. Assn. Ind. Pub. Fin. Advisors (pres. 1989-91), Nat. Soc. Mcpl. Analysts, Nat. Fedn. Mcpl. Analysts (Disting. Lifetime Contbn. award 1988). Office: Govt Fin Assocs Inc 71 Broadway Ste 1301 New York NY 10006-2601

JOHNSON, JAMES GORDON, career consultant; b. Roanoke, Va., Aug. 30, 1929; s. Gordon E. and Louise (Wright) J.; m. Barbara Bell, Sept. 11, 1955; children: Richard, Karen, David. BS, U. Va., 1951; MBA, U. Pa., 1955. Cert. career devel. counselor. V.p. Snelling & Snelling, Inc., Paoli, Pa., 1969-74, Bernard Haldane Assocs., Phila., 1974-80; v.p. Haven Scott Assocs., King of Prussia, Pa., 1980-91, chmn., chief exec. officer, 1991—. Pres. Paoli Civic Assn., 1971-72. Lt. U.S. Army, 1951-53, Korea. Mem. Nat. Assn. Career Devel. Cons. (pres. 1987-89). Home: 405 Hilltop Rd Paoli PA 19301-1212 Office: Haven Scott Assocs 200 N Warner Rd Norristown PA 19406

JOHNSON, JAY FRANCIS, design engineer; b. Fort Riley, Kans., May 10, 1934; s. Hibbert Omstead and Kathryn Joan (McNeil) J.; m. Patricia Ann Scavio, Oct. 12, 1957; children: Christine, Steven, Julie, Geraldine, Teresa, Daniel, Matthew, David. Student, Creighton U., 1952-53, U. Nebr., 1968-70. Cert. steamfitter apprentice. Supr. J.J. Hanigan, Omaha, 1964-67; mech. supt. Martig Plumbing and Heating, Omaha, 1967-70; pipe support supt. Jelco Inc., Brownsville, Nebr., 1970-75; lead engr. Bechtel Corp., Russellville, Ark., 1975-77; engring. supr. W.B.G., Hanford, Wash., 1977-78; lead engr. Ebasco Services, Inc., Olympia, Wash., 1978-81; asst. to mgr. Ebasco Services, Inc., New Orleans, 1981-82; area mgr. Ebasco Constructors, Inc., Bay City, Tex., 1982-87; chief field engr. Ebasco Constructors, Inc., Glenn Rose, Tex., 1987-89; prin. engr., task lead Ebasco Svcs. Inc., Knoxville, Tenn., 1989-90; engring. coord. Ebasco Constructors Inc., New Orleans, 1991—; engring. cons. Ebasco Svcs. Inc., Seoul, Republic of South Korea, 1990-91; facilities inspector USMC, Overland Park, Kans., 1975; instr. Grays Harbor Coll., Elma, Wash., 1980-81. Judge Voters Commn., Omaha, 1955-70; commr. Boy Scouts Am., Omaha, 1960-65; pres. C.C.D., Grandview, Wash., 1979. With USMC, 1955-80. Recipient Freedom award Freedoms Found., 1955, Ak Sar Ben award Knights of Ak Sar Ben, 1968, Master Pistol award NRA, 1968, Pistol award 9th Marine Corps Dist., 1969; named admiral Gt. Navy of State of Nebr., 1972. Mem. ASME (affiliate, chmn. Olympia chpt. 1980-81), De Cordova Club, Marine Corps League. Democrat. Roman Catholic. Home: 229 Dunleith Dr Box 2515 Destrehan LA 70047 Office: Ebasco Constructors Two World Trade Ctr New York NY 10048-0752

JOHNSON, JEAN ELAINE, nurse, psychologist; b. Wilsey, Kans., Mar. 11, 1925; d. William H. and Rosa L. (Welty) Irwin. B.S., Kans. State U., 1948; M.S. in Nursing, Yale U., 1965; M.S., U. Wis., 1969, Ph.D., 1971. Instr. nursing Iowa, Kans. and Colo., 1948-58; staff nurse Swedish Hosp., Englewood, Colo., 1958-60; in-svc. edn. coord. Gen. Rose Hosp., Denver, 1960-63; rsch. asst. Yale U., New Haven, 1965-67; assoc. prof. nursing Wayne State U., Detroit, 1971-74, prof., 1974-79; dir. Ctr. for Health Rsch., 1974-79; prof. nursing, assoc. dir. oncology nursing Cancer Ctr., U. Rochester, 1979—; Rosenstadt prof. health rsch. Faculty Nursing U. Toronto, 1985. Contbg. author: Handbook of Psychology and Health, vol. 4, 1975; contbr. articles to profl. jours. Recipient Bd. Govs. Faculty Recognition award Wayne State U., 1975, award for disting. contbn. to nursing sci. Am. Nurses Found. and Am. Nurses Assn. Coun. for Nurse Researchers, 1983, Grad. Teaching award U. Rochester, 1991, Disting. Researcher award Oncology Nursing Soc., 1992; grantee NIH, 1972. Fellow AAAS, Acad. for Behavioral Medicine Rsch.; mem. Inst. Medicine of NAS (com. on patient injury compensation 1976-77, membership com. 1981-86, governing coun. 1987-89), ANA (chmn. coun. for nurse researchers 1976-78, mem. commn. for rsch. 1978-82), Am. Psychol. Assn., Sigma Xi, Omicron Nu, Phi Kappa Phi. Home: 1412 East Ave Rochester NY 14610-1619 Office: U Rochester Cancer Ctr 601 Elmwood Ave Rochester NY 14642-9999

JOHNSON, JERE MACY, printing company executive; b. Meriden, Conn., Nov. 1, 1954; s. Foster Macy and Polly Jane (Eggleston) J.; m. Elizabeth Carroll Schleck, Dec. 10, 1954; children: Colin Macy, Christopher Carroll, Conor Sherman. Student, Tufts U., 1977. Mktg. rep. Procter & Gamble, Boston, 1977-78; sales rep. Miller-Johnson, Meriden, Conn., 1978-86; sales mgr. Miller-Johnson, 1986-88, pres., also dir., 1988—; bd. dirs. Meriden Trust, 1986—. Mem. community relations com. Meriden Wallingford Hosp., 1987—, bd. govs., 1986—. Mem. Printing Industry of Conn., Printing Industry of Am., Graphic Arts Tech. Found., Meriden C. of C. (dir. 1988—), Rotary (bd. dirs. 1986—, pres. 1988-89). Republican. Congregationalist. Home: 384 Race Hill Rd Madison CT 06443-1665 Office: Miller Johnson Inc 476 Pratt St Meriden CT 06450-3430

JOHNSON, JEROME EDWIN, financial executive; b. Phila., Aug. 16, 1942; s. Lorne Ernest and Helen Wyndworth (Redelmeier) J.; m. Esther V. Lento, Jan. 15, 1966; children: Carl Albert, David Lorne. BSBA, Rider Coll., 1967; MBA in Investments, NYU, 1968. CPA, N.J. Analyst, supr. profit analysis Philco-Ford Corp., Blue Bell, Pa., 1968-75, mgr. fin. analysis, 1975-77; asst. group contr. Proctor Silex div. SCM Corp., King of Prussia, Pa., 1977-83; dir. fin. Franklin Computer, Pennsauken, N.J., 1983-84; dir. fin. planning Decision Industries, Horsham, Pa., 1984-86, asst. corp. contr., 1986-88; contr., chief fin. officer Decision Data Products Co., Horsham, 1988-91; corp. treas. Decision Data Inc., Horsham, 1991—. Vice pres. Birchwood Community Assn., Cinnaminson, N.J., 1978. Mem. AICPA. Office: Decision Data Inc 410 Horsham Rd Horsham PA 19044

JOHNSON, JOAN MARIE, educator; b. Hamilton, N.Y., Aug. 17, 1954; d. John H. and Genevieve (Zombek) J. AAS in Restaurant Mgmt., SUNY, Morrisville, 1974; BS in Hotel, Restaurant & Tourism, Rochester Inst. Tech., 1976, MBA, 1982; D, Syracuse U., 1991. Mgr., concessions Ogden Food Svc., Albany, N.Y., 1976; mgr. Rochester (N.Y.) Inst. Tech. Food Svc., 1976-81; dean, assoc. prof. SUNY, Sch. Hospitality, Health & Food Tech., Morrisville, 1981—; EdD; pres. Madison County Tourism Com. Inc., N.Y., 1990—; chmn. strategic planning com. Nat. Asns. Coll.-Univ. Food Svcs., Lansing, Mich., 1990—, pres. region I, 1985-87, chmn. edn. region I, 1983-85. Contbr. articles to profl. jours. Recipient Sarah Margaret Gillam award. Office: SUNY Sch Hospitality Morrisville NY 13408

JOHNSON, JOHN LOWELL, research physicist; b. Butte, Mont., Mar. 18, 1926; s. Lowell Wallace and Esther (Thornwall) J.; m. Barbara Marion Hynds, June 30, 1951; children: Lowell John, Lesley Jean Johnson Gelb, Jennifer Ruth. BS, Mont. State U., 1949; MS, Yale U., 1951, PhD, 1954. Rsch. asst. Yale U., New Haven, 1949-54; sr. scientist atomic power dept. Westinghouse, Pitts., 1954-64; fellow engr. Westinghouse Rsch. Labs., Pitts., 1964-68, adv. scientist, 1968-79; cons. scientist Westinghouse R & D Ctr., Pitts., 1979-85; mem. vis. rsch. staff Princeton (N.J.) U., 1955-68, vis. rsch. physicist, 1968-71, vis. prin. rsch. physicist, 1971-85, prin. rsch. physicist, 1985—; vis. scientist Culham (Eng.) Lab., Los Alamos (N.Mex.) Sci. Lab., Max Planck Inst. for Plasma Physics, Garching, Germany, Australian Nat. U.; vis. prof. Nagoya (Japan) U., 1987; logistics supr. 9th Internat. Atomic Energy Agy. Internat. Conf. on Plasma Physics and Controlled Nuclear Fusion Rsch., 1982, 13th, 1990; conf. presenter in field. Contbr. over 100 articles to physics jours. Scoutmaster troop 88 George Washington coun. Boy Scouts Am., 1971-87; mem. Princeton Com. on Alcohol and Drug Abuse, 1985-86. With USN, 1944-46. Recipient Silver Beaver award Boy Scouts Am., 1978. Fellow Am. Phys. Soc. (sec.-treas. div. plasma physics 1974-78, organizer meetings and Sherwood confs.); mem. Sigma Xi (sec., treas., v.p., pres. Princeton chpt. 1981-88). Methodist. Office: Princeton U Plasma Physics Lab PO Box 451 Princeton NJ 08543-0451

JOHNSON, JONAS TALMADGE, educator; b. Ravenna, Ohio, Jan. 3, 1947; s. J. Norman and K. Alice (Harkarader) J.; m. Janis, Dec. 22, 1968; children: Olin T., Rurik C., Ivar N. MD, SUNY, Syracuse, 1972; postgrad., Dartmouth Coll., 1965-68, U. W.Va., 1972-74. Asst. prof. U. Pitts., 1979-84, assoc. prof., 1984-87, prof., 1987—, vice chmn., 1982-89; active staff Montefiore Hosp., Pitts., 1987—; cons. VA Med. Ctr. Pitts., 1979-80, Children's Hosp. Pitts., 1980-89; bd. dirs. Head & Neck Oncology and Immunology, Pitts., 1986—. Editor: Antibiotic Therapy in Head and Neck Surgery, 1987; co-editor: Tracheotomy, 1985, Instructional Courses, vol. 1, 1988, Instructional Courses, vol. II, 1989; editor Am. Jour. of Otolaryngology; contbr. articles to profl. jours. Mjr. USAF, 1977-79. Recipient Honor award, Am. Acad. Otolaryngology, 1982, Merit award, Clin. Rsch., Am. Acad. Ophthalmology/Otolaryngology, 1976, Ben Shuster award, Am. Acad. Facial Plastic/Reconstructive Surgery, 1976. Fellow Soc. Head and Neck Surgery, Am. Soc. Head and Neck Surgery, Am. Laryngological, Rhinological and Otological Soc., Am. Diopter and Decibel Soc., Am. Bronchoesophagologic Soc., Am. Coll. Surgeons. Office: Eye and Ear Inst 203 Lothrop St Ste 500 Pittsburgh PA 15213-2588

JOHNSON, JOSEPH EDWARD, microcomputer sales and services executive; b. Mt. Holly, N.J., Apr. 30, 1932; s. James Edward and Christine DeKalb (Hatcher) J. BEE with high honors, Rutgers U., 1954; postgrad., Cornell U. Engr. Bell Telephone Labs., Inc., Whippany, N.J., 1955-64, Holmdel, N.J., 1972-82; engr. Bellcomm., Inc., Washington, 1964-72; v.p. Bit Processing, Inc., Lawrenceville, N.J., 1982—. Editor: (mag.) Rutgers Engineer, 1953 (Gold R award 1954). Recipient NASA Apollo Achievement award. Mem. AIAA, World Future Soc., Tau Beta Pi, Eta Kappa Nu. Republican. Episcopalian. Home: 33 Linden Dr Spring Lake NJ 07762-2159 Office: Bit Processing Inc Quakerbridge Executive Ctr Ste 305 Lawrenceville NJ 08648

JOHNSON, JUDITH LYNN, psychologist; b. Washington, June 15, 1955; d. James K. and Mary Ellen (Brugge) J.; m. William G. McCown, June 16, 1984. BS, James Madison U., Harrisonburg, Va., 1977; MA, George Mason U., Fairfax, Va., 1980; PhD, Loyola U. of Chgo., 1989. Lic. psychologist, Pa. Rsch. psychologist VA Med. Ctr., New Orleans, 1988-89; neuropsychologist Neurologic Group of Bucks/Montgomery County, North Wales, Pa., 1989-91; asst. prof. psychology Villanova (Pa.) U., 1991—; adj. prof. div. mental health svcs. Hahnemann U., 1991. Contbr. articles to profl. jours.; co-editor books. Office: Villanova U Tolantine Hall Villanova PA 19038

JOHNSON, KATHARYN PRICE (MRS. EDWARD F. JOHNSON), civic worker; b. Smyrna, Del., Mar. 24, 1897; d. Lewis M. and Jennie Cairl (Smithers) Price; grad. Centenary Coll., 1915; student Goucher Coll., 1915-18; m. Edward F. Johnson, Nov. 16, 1920; children—Edward A., Jane Cairl Johnson Kent. With Liberty Loan Com. for Md. and Liberty Loan Assn. of Balt., 1918-20; pres. Women's Guild Hitchcock Meml. Ch., 1930-32; dir. Scarsdale Woman's Club, 1933-36; dir. White Plains Thrift Shop, 1930-43, pres, 1936-43; mem. exec. com. Scarsdale Community Fund, 1934-38; active Scarsdale council Girl Scouts, 1937-53, commr., 1939-41, now hon. mem. Scarsdale-Hartsdale council, 1953-69; mem. region 2 com. Girl Scouts U.S.A., 1942-56, mem. nat. bd., exec. com., 1947-55, chmn. orgn. and mgmt. dept., 1952-55, mem. nat. field com., 1943-55, mem. equipment service com. 1956-69, mem. internat. com., 1956-60, mem. meml. gifts com., 1974-81; mem. Bd. Edn., Scarsdale, N.Y., 1943-46; disaster chmn. Scarsdale chpt. ARC, 1942-45; mem. Commn. Human Rights, 1958-69, Commn. Status of Women, 1957-69; rep. World Assn. Girl Guides and Girl Scouts to UN, 1957-71, mem. NGO com. on UNICEF, 1965-72, sec., 1968-70; participant World Confs., World Assn. Girl Guides and Girl Scouts, Greece, 1960,

Denmark, 1963, Japan, 1966, Finland, 1969, Can., 1972, Eng., 1975, Iran, 1978, World Conf., U.S., 1984. Recipient Juliette Low World Friendship medal Girl Scouts USA, 1984. Mem. Nat. Council Women U.S., Scarsdale Hist. Soc., Olave-Baden-Powell Soc. (founder), Pi Beta Phi. Republican. Presbyterian. Clubs: Scarsdale Woman's (life), Scarsdale Golf, Nat. Women's Republican; Shenorock Shore. Home: 165 Brewster Rd Scarsdale NY 10583-2021

JOHNSON, LAVERN OSCAR, accountant; b. Denver, Dec. 26, 1935; s. Oscar E. and Helen (Nelson) J.; m. Phyllis Jean Parker, June 20, 1959 (div. May, 1973); m. Maureen Gail Wrobel, Nov. 18, 1975. BS in Bus. Adminstrn., U. Denver, 1958. CPA, N.Y. Staff mem. Price Waterhouse, Denver, 1956-66; ptnr. Main Hurdman, N.Y.C., 1966-87, KPMG Peat Marwick, Montvale, N.J., 1987-91; dir. KPMG Peat Marwick, N.Y.C., 1991—. Mem. AICPA (acctg. stds. exec. com. 1977-79, continuing profl. edn. exec. com. 1980-86, bd. examiners 1990—). Office: KPMG Peat Marwick 767 5th Ave New York NY 10153-0002

JOHNSON, LEO FRANCIS, physicist; b. White Plains, N.Y., Nov. 6, 1928; s. Leo Frederick and Marion (Walker) J.; m. Barbara Harman, Feb. 10, 1962; children: David, Kathleen, Mark, Christopher. BA, U. Vt., Burlington, 1951; MA, Syracuse U., 1955, PhD, 1959. Test engr. GE, Schenectady, N.Y., 1951-53; rsch. asst. Syracuse (N.Y.) U., 1954-59; mem. tech. staff AT&T Bell Labs., Murray Hill, N.J., 1959-86; pvt. practice cons. Bedminster, N.J., 1986—; cons. Amoco Laser Co., Naperville, Ill., 1987-89, Amoco Rsch. Ctr., Naperville, 1989—; rsch. assoc. U. Cen. Fla., Orlando, 1990-91. Contbr. articles to profl. publs.; patentee in field. Mem. St. Brigid Sch. Bd. Edn., Peapack, N.J., 1971-72; mem. Bedminster Sch. Bd. Edn., 1978-85; mem. Twp. Com., Bedminster, 1989—; mem. Bedminster Planning Bd., 1991—. Fellow Am. Phys. Soc., Sigma Xi. Republican. Home and Office: 150 Riverwood Ave Bedminster NJ 07921-2509

JOHNSON, LEO GORDON, architect; b. Philipsburg, Pa., Jan. 25, 1933; s. Michael and Anna (Vaselinkie) J. B.Archl. Engring., Pa. State U. 1958; M.Arch., Cath. U., 1962. Registered profl. architect D.C., Md., Va., W.Va. Architect, assoc. Edwin Weihe & Assocs., Washington, 1960-71; architect, owner Leo Gordon Johnson Assoc./Architects, Planners, Washington, 1971—. Mem. AIA. Office: Leo Gordon Johnson Assocs 1255 Hampshire Ave NW Washington DC 20036

JOHNSON, LLOYD HARLIN, aerospace engineer, consultant; b. Granite, Okla., May 15, 1928; s. Olie Pope Johnson; m. Mary Frances Maddox, Dec. 27, 1959; children: Amanda, Julian, Wendell. Registered aero. engr., Tex. Chief aero heating U.S. Army Missile Command, Huntsville, Ala., 1961-65; phys. scientist CIA, Washington, 1965-73; aerospace engr. AVCO/Rockwell Internat., Beltsville, Md., 1973-79, USN, Washington, 1979—; v.p. Va. Res. Officers Assn., Washington, 1989. Contbr. articles to profl. jours. Lt. col. USAFR. Recipient Exec. award Fairfax Youth Club, 1975. Fellow AIAA (assoc., editor Ala. sect. newsletter 1963-65, Schilling award 1965). Republican. Presbyterian.

JOHNSON, MARIJO ANNE, arts administrator, producer; b. Battle Creek, Mich., July 21, 1935; d. Earl Marshall Mason and Marietta (Scott) Johnson; 1 child, Randolph M. Student, Chgo. Mus. Coll., 1953-55, Roosevelt U., 1958-62; B in Music Edn., Pace U., 1982. Cert. U.S. SBA, The Workshop in Bus. Opportunities, Inc. Album liner coordinator Mercury Record Corp., Chgo., 1963-67; supr., artists and repertoire adminstr. CBS Records, N.Y.C., 1967-72; music assoc. N.Y. State Council on Arts, N.Y.C., 1972-73; exec. adminstr. N.Y. Jazz Repertory Co., Inc., 1973-75; exec. dir. Consortium of Jazz Orgns. and Artists, Inc., N.Y.C., 1976-81; spl. projects asst. Uniworld Group, Inc., N.Y.C., 1982-86; pres. Marijo Johnson Arts Mgmt., N.Y.C., 1986—; music panelist N.Y. State Coun. on Arts, N.Y.C., 1973-75; faculty contractor Bennington Coll. Summer Jazz Project, Vt., 1976; advisor Soundscape Performance Ctr., N.Y.C., 1980-81, Universal Symphony Orch., N.Y.C., 1981-86; bd. dirs. Festival on the River, N.Y.C., 1971-72. Sect. editor Jazz Mag., 1979; columnist Jazz Spotlite News, 1982. Tchr. Literacy Vols. N.Y., N.Y.C., 1983; active Park West Village Tenant's Assn., 1982—; chmn. Pan African Resource Com., 1984-85. NEA grantee, Washington, 1976-77, 78-79; Ford Found. grantee, N.Y.C., 1979, Community Service Soc. grantee, N.Y.C., 1986. Mem. Minority Women Entrepreneurs' Network (chmn. 1986-87), Assn. Performing Arts Presenters. Office: Marijo Johnson Arts Mgmt 784 Columbus Ave Apt 14M New York NY 10025-5914

JOHNSON, MAURICE JOSEPH, press photographers gallery administrator; b. Englewood, N.J., Sept. 9, 1919; s. Maurice L. and Mary Louise (McQuillan) J.; m. Rolanda Stoneback, Sept. 24, 1966; children: Keith Erik, Maureen Elizabeth. Grad., Mineola (N.Y.) High Sch., 1936. With photo dept. Internat. Tel. & Tel., N.Y.C., 1937-41; photographer Internat. News Photos, Washington, 1941-53, bur. mgr., 1953-55; photographer UPI, Washington, 1955-70; supt. Press Photographers Gallery of U.S. Senate, Washington, 1970—. Recipient George Polk award L.I. U. Mem. Nat. Press Club. Home: 3804 Raymond St Chevy Chase MD 20815 Office: US Senate S-317 US Captiol Washington DC 20510

JOHNSON, NANCY LEE, congresswoman; b. Chgo., Jan. 5, 1935; d. Noble Wishard and Gertrude Reid (Smith) Lee; m. Theodore H. Johnson, July 16, 1958; children—Lindsey Lee, Althea Anne, Caroline Reid. B.A., Radcliffe Coll., 1957; postgrad., U. London, 1957-58. Vice chmn. Charter Commn. New Britain, Conn., 1976-77; mem. Conn. Senate from 6th dist., 1977-82, 98th-102nd Congresses from 6th Dist. Conn., Washington, 1983—. Lectr. Am. art New Britain Mus. Am. Art, 1968-71; pres. Friends of Library, New Britain Pub. Library, 1973-76; pres. Radcliffe Club No. Conn., 1973-75; bd. dirs., pres. Sheldon Community Guidance Clinic, 1974-75; dir. religious edn. Unitarian Universalist Soc. New Britain, 1967-72, pres., 1973-75; bd. dirs. New Britain Symphony Soc., 1975-77, Plainville Group Home, 1975-76, United Way New Britain, 1976-79. Recipient Outstanding Vol. award United Way, 1976; English Speaking Union grantee, 1958-59. Republican. Home: 141 S Mountain St New Britain CT 06052-1511 Office: 227 Cannon Washington DC 20515*

JOHNSON, NEIL RICHARD, psychiatrist; b. Jamestown, N.Y., May 4, 1945; s. Gilbert Lofton and Bernice Winoma (Harrison) J. AB, U. Rochester, 1967; MD, U. Pitts., 1971. Diplomate, Am. Bd. Psychiatry and Neurology. Intern N.Y. Med. Coll., Met. Hosp., 1971-72; resident Mass. Gen. Hosp., Boston, 1972-75; pvt. practice, Boston, 1975—; clin. assoc. dept. psychiatry Mass. Gen. Hosp., Boston, 1975—; assoc. med. dir., Human Resource Inst., Brookline, Mass., 1975-84; clin. assoc., dept. psychiatry, Cambridge (Mass.) City Hosp., 1984-85; chief of psychiatry, Cen. Hosp., Somerville, Mass., 1984-85; staff psychiatrist, Westwood (Mass.) Lodge Hosp., 1985—, Jackson Brook Inst., Portland, Maine, 1985; disability evaluations cons., Mass. Med. Evaluations, Chestnut Hill, 1985-88. Mem. AMA, Am. Psychiat. Assn., Mass. Psychiat. Assn., Mass. Med. Soc. Democrat. Home and Office: 14 Turning Mill Rd Lexington MA 02173-1318

JOHNSON, NORMA HOLLOWAY, federal judge; b. Lake Charles, La.. B.S., D.C. Tchrs. Coll., 1955; J.D., Georgetown U., 1962. Bar: D.C. 1962, U.S. Supreme Ct. 1967. Pvt. practice law Washington, 1963; atty. Dept. Justice, Washington, 1963-67; asst. corp. counsel D.C., 1967-70; judge D.C. Superior Ct., 1970-80, U.S. Dist. Ct. (D.C. dist.), Washington, 1980—; Bd. dirs. Nat. Children's Center, Washington, National Street Law Inst. Mem. Am. Bar Assn., Nat. Bar Assn., D.C. Bar, Nat. Council Juvenile Ct. Judges, Am. Judicature Soc. (dir.), Nat. Assn. Women Judges (dir.). Office: US Dist Ct US Courthouse 3rd & Constitution Ave NW Washington DC 20001*

JOHNSON, NORMAN JEREMY E., research and development scientist; b. Columbia, S.C., Dec. 12, 1935; s. Norman John and Aili (Kolehmainen) J.; m. Katherine Purcell Adams, July 29, 1967; children: Christopher Blair, Stephen Robert, Daniel Norman, Sarah Kathrine. BS in Elec. Engring., U. Mich., 1957, BS in Engring. Math., 1957, MS in Astronomy, 1964, PhD in Astronomy, 1971. Project mgr. Barnes Engring., Stamford, Conn., 1960-63; assoc. astronomer Inst. Sci. & Tech., Maui, Hawaii, 1969; teaching fellow U. Mich., Ann Arbor, 1970-71; sr. scientist Block Engring., Cambridge, Mass., 1972-78; chief scientist Block Engring., Cambridge, 1978-85; chief scientist (SPI) Thermo Electron Corp. R&D Ctr., Waltham, Mass., 1985-89; pres. Specialty Instruments, Bedford, Mass., 1989—; cons. Specialty Instruments, Bedford, 1989—. Contbr. 13 articles to profl. jours. Named Trainee NASA, 1964. Mem. IEEE, Optical Soc. Am., Internat. Soc. for Optical Engring., Am. Astron. Soc., Am. Soc. for Programmetry and Remote Sensing, Sigma Xi, Eta Kappa Nu. Office: Specialty Instruments 19 Crosby Dr Bedford MA 01730-1419

JOHNSON, OMOTUNDE EVAN GEORGE, economist; b. Freetown, Sierra Leone, Mar. 27, 1941; came to U.S., 1961; s. Evan George and Elizabeth O. (Allen) J.; m. Octavia Olayemi John, Oct. 30 1965; children: Olatunde Cheryl, Omoyemi Evan, Olubayo Darryl. BA, UCLA, 1965, MA, 1967, PhD, 1970. Lectr. in econs. Calif. State U., Long Beach, 1967-69; lectr. U. Sierra Leone, Freetown, 1969-73; vis. asst. prof. U. Mich., Ann Arbor, 1973-74; economist IMF, Washington, 1974-79, sr. economist, dep. div. chief, 1979-92, advisor, 1992—; resident rep. IMF, Ghana, 1987-90. Contbr. numerous articles to profl. jours. Mem. AAAS, Am. Econ. Assn., U.S. Chess Fedn., Royal Econ. Soc. of U.K., Nat. Symphony Orch. Assn. Episcopalian. Home: 6117 Tammy Dr Alexandria VA 22310-1524 Office: IMF 700 19th St NW Washington DC 20431-0002

JOHNSON, PAUL WILLIAM, government relations professional; b. San Francisco, Jan. 29, 1958; s. Donald William Johnson and Alice (Coleman) King; m. Lisa Marie Foehr, Apr. 9, 1983; children: Nicole Diane, Garrett William. BA in History and Econs., U. Calif., Santa Barbara, 1980. Chief of staff for Rep. Gene Chappie U.S. Congress, Washington, 1980-84; sr. lobbyist A&K Assocs., Inc., Washington, 1984-85; ptnr., sr. v.p. Fleishman-Hillard, Inc., Washington, 1985—. Bd. dirs. Nat. Kidney Found., N.Y.C., 1990—; mem. Dem. Congl. Campaign Com., Washington, 1986—, Dem. Leadership Conf., Washington, 1989—. Mem. Am. League Lobbyists, Rep. Inner Circle, Capitol Hill Club, Sigma Chi. Republican. Office: Fleishman-Hillard Inc 1301 Connecticut Ave NW Washington DC 20036

JOHNSON, PHYLLIS MARIE, charitable organization executive; b. Providence; d. Anthony and Philomina Emma (DeCubellis) Macchia; m. Joseph Formato, Sept. 14, 1957 (dec. 1966); children: Christopher Joseph, Keira Noelle; m. Thomas Johnson, Apr. 18, 1980. AB, Brown U., 1956; MS, So. Conn. State U., 1979. Reporter Cheshire (Conn.) Herald, 1967-75; asst. program coord. Conn. Am. Bicentennial Commn., Hartford, 1975-78; sr. v.p. United Way Capital Area, Hartford, 1979-89; pres., chief profl. officer United Way Metrowest, Framingham, Mass., 1989—; mem. nat. profl. adv. com., United Way Am., Alexandria, Va., 1983-89. Recipient various communication award from local press orgns. and United Way Am. Mem. Rotary. Office: United Way Metrowest 276 Union Ave Framingham MA 01701-6394

JOHNSON, RAYMOND ARD, psychiatrist, educator; b. Lewistown, Pa., Nov. 22, 1942; s. Raymond Ard and Elsie Clara (Sowers) J.; m. Susan R. Andrulonis, Sept. 4, 1969 (div. Aug. 1985); 1 child, Hilary; m. Caroll Janet Krause, Oct. 26, 1985. BS in Speech Therapy, Bloomsburg State U., 1965; MD, Temple U., 1972. Diplomate Am. Bd. Psychiatry and Neurology. Speech therapist Montgomery County Sch. System, 1965-68; intern in internal medicine Hahnemann U., Phila., 1972-73, resident in psychiatry, 1977-80, now asst. clin. instr.; emergency room physician, admitter. Atlanta Emergency Physicians Group, Riverdale, Fla., 1975-77; pvt. practice Penn Valley, Pa., 1980—; dir. addictive svcs. Guiffre Med. Ctr., Phila., 1980-81, program dir. substance abuse unit Fairmount Inst., Phila., 1981-87, Horsham Clinic, Ambler, Pa., 1987-89; med. dir. Malvern (Pa.) Inst., 1989—; psychiat. cons. Impaired Physicians Com., Lemoyne, Pa., 1988-89, Camden (N.J.) Diocese, 1988-89; bd. dirs. Starting Point, Collingswood, N.J.; speaker in field; mem. complimentary med. staff Northwestern Psychiat. Inst.; exec. mem. Coun. for Compulsive Gambling; assoc. med. dir. addiction svcs. Northwestern Inst. Psychiatry., 1991. Contbr. articles to med. jours. Lt. comdr. M.C., USN, 1973-75. Mem. AMA, Am. Psychiat. Assn. (Falk fellow 1980), Am. Soc. Addictive Medicine (cert.), Am. Med. Soc. on Alcoholism and Other Drug Dependencies (cert.), Pa. Psychiat. Assn. Republican. Home and Office: 1201 Greentree Ln Narberth PA 19072-1219

JOHNSON, RHODA ANN BROWN, dog breeder; b. Narberth, Pa., Mar. 25, 1938; d. Lewis Sarle and Daisy (Adams) Brown; m. Larry C. Johnson, June 16, 1956; children: William Lewis, Richard Lawrence. AB, Douglass Coll., New Brunswick, N.J., 1966; MS, Rutgers U., 1969. Teaching asst. Rutgers U., New Brunswick, 1969-72; instr. biology Georgian Ct. Coll., Lakewood, N.J., 1973-74; instr. biology Trenton (N.J.) State Coll., 1974-75, coadjutant prof. biology, 1978-82; sci. tchr. Stuart Country Day Sch., Princeton, 1975-80; founder, owner, dir. Gold-Rush Kennels, Princeton, 1973—. Contbr. articles to profl. publs. Recipient #1 Golden Retriever Top Champion award, numerous other awards. Mem. Golden Retriever Club Am., Garden State Golden Retriever Club (sec. 1975-78). Home: 1040 Mercer Rd Princeton NJ 08540-4809 Office: Gold Rush Kennels 1040 Mercer Rd Princeton NJ 08540-4809

JOHNSON, RICHARD EARLES, economic council executive; b. Evanston, Ill., Oct. 5, 1920; s. Earle Freeman and Elizabeth Dale (Oberteuffer) J.; m. Patricia Rose Brown, July 14, 1954; children: Richard F., Elizabeth C. BA, Harvard U., 1942; MA, Georgetown U., 1954. Various positions U.S. Fgn. Svc., Dept. of State, 1947-80; pres. U.S. Yugoslav Econ. Coun., Washington, 1983—. Lt. comdr. USN, 1942-46, PTO. Home: 3218 Klingle Rd NW Washington DC 20008-3403 Office: US Yugoslav Econ Coun Ste 303 1901 N Fort Myer Dr Arlington VA 22209

JOHNSON, RICHARD FREDERICK, psychologist, researcher, educator; b. Boston, July 11, 1943; s. Frederick and Alice Hilda (Kullen) J.; m. Sharyn Lois Doyle, Sept. 11, 1965; children: Wendy Kullen, Adam Bruns. BA with honors, Northeastern U., 1966; MA in Psychology, Brandeis U., 1968, PhD, 1970. Lic. psychologist, Mass. Rsch. psychologist Medfield (Mass.) Found., 1972-76; rsch. psychologist Human Factors and Physiology Group U.S. Army Natick R&D Labs., 1976-83; rsch. psychologist, acting chief Mil. Performance and Neurosci. div. U.S. Army Rsch. Inst. Environ. Medicine, Natick, 1983—; mem. faculty Medfield State Hosp., 1974-76; sr. lectr. psychology Northeastern U., 1971-76, 84—; cons. in field. Editorial cons. Psychosomatic Medicine, 1987—, Exercise and Sport Sciences Reviews, 1985—, Jour. Consulting and Clinical Psychology, 1973-83; corr. assoc. commentator The Behavioral And Brain Scis., 1978—; contbr. over 80 articles to profl. jours., book chpts., tech. reports. Capt. Med. Svc. Corps U.S. Army, 1970-72, with Res., 1966-74. Recipient Milton H. Erickson Sci. Excellence award Am. Soc. Clin. Hypnosis, 1977; grantee Nat. Inst. Mental Health, 1972-76; fellow Brandeis U. 1967-70. Fellow Am. Psychol. Assn. (chmn. conv. program div. gen. psychology 1974-75), Am. Psychol. Soc.; mem. AAAS, Aerospace Med. Assn.,Human Factors Soc., Soc. Applied Exptl. Engring. Psychologists, Sigma Xi (chmn. program com., 1989-90, pres.-elect 1990, pres. 1991). Office: US Army Rsch Inst Environ Medicine Mil Performance & Neurosci Div Natick MA 01760-5007

JOHNSON, ROBERT EUGENE, physiologist; b. Conrad, Mont., Apr. 8, 1911; s. Arthur D. and Florence May (Disbrow) J.; m. Margaret Hunter, Jan. 11, 1935; children: Thomas Arthur, Charles William, Katherine Helen (dec.). B.S. in Chemistry, U. Wash., 1931; B.A. in Physiology (Rhodes scholar), U. Oxford, Eng., 1934, D.Phil. in Biochemistry, 1935; M.D., Harvard U., 1941. Research asst. advancing to asst. prof. indsl. physiology Harvard Fatigue Lab., 1935-46; expert cons. QMC 3, AUS, 1941-46; dir. U.S. Army Med. Nutrition Lab., Chgo., 1946-49; prof. physiology U. Ill. at Urbana, 1949-73, head dept., 1949-60, dir. univ. honors program, 1959-67, acting dean Grad. Coll., 1952-53; prof. biology Knox Coll., Galesburg, Ill., 1973-79; coordinator Knox Coll.-Rush U. Med. Program, 1973-79; sci. cons. Presbyn.-St. Luke's Hosp., Chgo., 1973-83; pres. Horn of the Moon Enterprises, Montpelier, Vt., 1980—; vis. prof. physiology U. Vt., 1983—. Co-author: Metabolic Methods, 1951, Physiological Measurements of Metabolic Functions in Man, 1963; author: Sir John Richardson, 1976; also articles in profl. jours. NSF Sr. Postdoctoral Research fellow, 1957-58; Guggenheim Meml. Found. fellow, 1964-65. Mem. Am. Soc. Clin. Investigation, Am. Physiol. Soc., Nutrition Today, History of Sci. Soc., Phi Beta Kappa, Sigma Xi. Home and office: 5 E Terrace South Burlington VT 05403

JOHNSON, RONALD BRYAN, controller; b. Greenfield, Mass., Apr. 25, 1948; s. Robert and Elizabeth (Winsky) J.; m. Diane Elizabeth MacDonald, Mar. 25, 1972; children: Erica E., Kirsten M. BS in Bus. Adminstrn., Northeastern U., 1971; MBA, U. Conn., 1975. CPA, N.H., CMA, CFE; cert. fraud examiner, mgmt. acct. Spl. agt. IRS Intelligence Div., Hartford, Conn., 1971-77; ops. analyst IRS Criminal Investigation Div., Washington, 1977-79; chief CID staff IRS Criminal Investigation Div., Andover, Mass., 1979-85; tax mgr. Lawrence B. Martin, CPA, Manchester, N.H., 1985-86; controller Ronco, Inc., Manchester, 1986-89; cons., prin. Bedford, N.H., 1989-90; controller Dean's Floor Covering Ctr., Manchester, N.H., 1990—. Mem. AICPA, Nat. Assn. Accts., Nat. Assn. Cert. Fraud Examiners (cert.). Home: 28 Blackbird Dr Bedford NH 03110-4400 Office: Dean's Fl Covering Ctr 159 Frontage Rd Manchester NH 03103-6013

JOHNSON, RUTH, small business owner; b. Kane, Pa., Apr. 1, 1937; d. Emil T. and Alice Mary (Mitchell) J. BS, Pa. State U., 1959; postgrad., Northwestern U., 1962, Stanford U., 1964. Speech pathologist McKean County Pub. Schs., Smethport, Pa., 1959-62, San Francisco Pub. Schs., 1963, Palo Alto (Calif.) Unified Sch. Dist., 1964-66; founder Phonic Ear Inc., Petaluma, Calif., 1964-74, Phonic Ear Ltd., Can., Phonic Ear Internat. A/S, Denmark, Phonic Ear GmbH, Fed. Republic Germany; navigator Ketch Phonic Ear, 1974-84; pres., owner, communications cons. Protocol Internat. Ltd., State College, Pa., 1984—; founder Phonic Ear Gmbh, Germany. Patentee speech therapy tools and auditory tng. systems for hearing-speech-lang. impaired. Founder scholarship funds Kane (Pa.) High Sch., Pa. State U. Soc. Disting. Alumni. Mem. Assn. Image Cons. Internat., Kappa Kappa Gamma. Home and Office: Protocol Internat Ltd 1644 Woodledge Cir State College PA 16803-1875

JOHNSON, SHERRI LYNN, animal scientist; b. Youngstown, Ohio, Sept. 26, 1956; d. J.B. and Jean (Haseley) J. BS in Animal Sci., Rutgers U., 1978, MS in Animal Sci., 1982. Toxicology lab. tech. Product Safety Labs., East Brunswick, N.J., 1978-82; toxicology supr. Ciba-Geigy Pharm., Summit, N.J., 1982-84; report writer Ciba-Geigy Pharm., 1984-85; submissions writer/project ldr. toxicology Am. Cyanamid, Pearl River, N.Y., 1985-88; project coordinator ops. and devel. Am. Cyanamid, 1989—. Mem. Drug Info. Assn. Office: Am Cyanamid Co Middletown Rd Pearl River NY 08837

JOHNSON, STEVEN NELSON, financial software firm executive; b. Plattsburgh, N.Y., July 11, 1953; s. Corydon Marshall and Ruth Leigh (Hazelwood) J.; m. Katharine Carlyle Bennett, Oct. 23, 1982; children: Nelson Bennett, Marshall Fitch. BA, U. Va., 1975, MBA, 1981. Sales rep. The Stanley Works, New Britain, Conn., 1976-79; asst. to group v.p. Burlington Industries, N.Y.C., 1981-82, dir. internat. mktg., 1982-84; mkt. mgr. Gordon Haskett & Co., Stamford, Conn., 1984-86, dir. mktg., 1986—; cons. U. Miami (Fla.), 1989-90, Mitchell Wolfson Sr. Found., Miami, 1989—, United Meth. Ch. Bd. Gen. Pensions, Evanston, Ill., 1990—. Co-designer Global Inv. Software, 1989-91. Usher 1st Prsbyn. Ch. New Canaan (Conn.), 1988; contbr. Community Nursery Sch. Wilton (Conn.), 1989; mem. Wilton Hist. Soc., 1989-91; sponsor Harvest Ball Am. Cancer Soc., Wilton, 1989, 90; fundraiser Darden ann. giving campaign U. Va., 1991. Award Burlington Industries, N.Y.C., 1982. Mem. Colonnade Soc. U. Va. Alumni Assn., Darden Sch. Sponsors, TILKA (life). Republican. Congregationalist. Home: 92 Ruscoe Rd Wilton CT 06897-1424 Office: Gordon Haskett & Co 5 High Ridge Pk Stamford CT 06905-1326

JOHNSON, SUE BETH, accountant; b. Tylertown, Miss., Oct. 10, 1953; d. M. Elton and Edith K. (Rice) Waring; m. David M. Johnson, June 11, 1977; children: Christina, Lucas. BA in Chemistry/Math., Millsaps Coll., 1975; MS in Math., U. Miss., 1981, M Acctg., 1986. CPA, Miss. Sales auditor Gayfer's Dept. Store, Jackson, Miss., 1975; lab. technician Med. Ctr. U. Miss., Jackson, 1976-77; lab. asst. Pharmacy Sch. U. Miss., University, 1979-80, grad. asst. dept. math., 1980-81, sr. rsch. technician dept. biology, 1983-85, grad. asst. dept. acctg., 1985-86; mfg. cost acct. Eastman Kodak Co., Kingsport, Tenn., 1987-90; acct. Ciba-Geigy Corp., Newport, Del., 1991—. Mem. AICPA, NAFE, Beta Alpha Psi. Home: 733 Gateway Rd Hockessin DE 19707-9543 Office: Ciba Geigy Corp 205 S James St Newport DE 19804

JOHNSON, TERRY LEE, retail executive; b. Jamestown, N.Y., Nov. 6, 1950; s. Stanley R. and Elaine G. (Seaberg) J.; m. Sharmane K. Heinz, Apr. 7, 1972; children: Tara Lynn, Erik Richard. AAS in Ophthalmic Dispensing, Erie Community Coll., Buffalo, 1975. Optician Sterling Optical Corp., Jamestown, 1975-76; optician, mgr. Sterling Optical Corp., Utica, N.Y., 1976-80, dist. mgr., 1980-90; pres. Forty Vision Corp., Fayetteville, N.Y., 1990—; sec. Eastview Vision Corp., Victor, N.Y., 1990—; pres. Vision Ptnrs. Ltd., Canandaigua, N.Y., 1991—; sec. Northern Vision Corp., Watertown, N.Y., 1991—; mem. Franchise Steering Com., N.Y.C., 1992—. With U.S. Army, 1970-73. Fellow Nat. Acad. Opticianry; m. Am. Legion (adjutant 1984, 85, 86, vice comdr. 1987, 88, comdr. 1989, fin. officer 1990, 91). Office: Vision Ptnrs Ltd 5 Bristol St Ste # 5 Canandaigua NY 14424

JOHNSON, THOMAS BUCKLEY, citizen organization executive, consultant; b. Lewiston, Maine, Apr. 29, 1955; s. Donald Melvin and Mary Elizabeth (Twitchell) J. BA in Am. Studies, Am. U., 1979; MA in New Eng. Studies, U. Maine, 1990. Self employed restoration contractor Bridgton, Maine, 1979-82; historic interpreter Nat. Pk. Svc., Washington, 1982-85; curator Bridgton (Maine) Hist. Soc., 1985-90; exec. dir. Maine Citizens for Hist. Preservation, Portland, Maine, 1990—; bd. dirs. Maine Community Cultural Alliance, Augusta; adv. bd. mem. Statewide Preservation Planning For Maine, Augusta, 1990—; curatorial cons. Bridgton (Maine) Hist. Soc., 1990—. Contbr. articles to profl. jours. Mem. steering com. Bridgton (Maine) Revitalization Commn., 1986-89; trustee Lake Region Ctr. for Handicapped Individuals, Bridgton, 1986-88. Named Elizabeth Perkins fellow Old York (Maine) Hist. Soc., 1989. Mem. Am. Assn. for State and Local History, Nat. Trust for Hist. Preservation (Project Prepare fellow, Boston, 1989-90), Soc. for the Preservation of New Eng. Antiquities, Phi Kappa Phi. Home: RR 1 Box 1260 Bridgton ME 04009-9773 Office: Maine Citizens for Historic Preservation 165 State St # 1198 Portland ME 04101-3797

JOHNSON, THOMAS FRANCIS, allergist; b. Lewiston, Maine, July 29, 1942; d. Thomas Francis and Winifred Emma (Flaherty) J.; m. Carleen G. Tombarello; children: Christopher, Thomas III, Jennifer Lynn, Tiffany Kira. Student Loyola Coll., Montreal, Can., 1959-60; M.D., U. Toronto, 1966. Diplomate Am. Bd. Internal Medicine, Am. Bd. Allergy and Immunology. Intern, St. Vincent Hosp., Worcester, 1966-67; resident Mayo Clinic, Rochester, Minn., 1967-69, 71-73, SUNY-Buffalo, 1973-75; organizer, founder New Eng. Allergy and Immunology, P.C., North Andover, Mass., 1975, pres., owner, 1975—; organizer, founder New England Allergy and Immunology Lab., Inc., North Andover, 1973, pres., owner, 1984—. Served to maj. USAF, 1969-71. Teagle Found. scholar, 1962-66. Fellow Am. Coll. Allergists, Am. Assn. Cert. Allergists, Am. Assn. Clin. Immunologists and Allergists; mem. AMA, Am. Acad. Allergy and Immunology, Mass. Med. Soc. Home: 34 Samoset Dr Salem NH 03079 Office: New England Allergy & Immunology PC 555 Turnpike St North Andover MA 01845-5923

JOHNSON, THOMAS STEPHEN, banker; b. Racine, Wis., Nov. 19, 1940; s. H. Norman and Jane Agnes (McAvoy) J.; m. Margaret Ann Werner, Apr. 18, 1970; children: Thomas Philip, Scott Michael, Margaret Ann. AB in Econs., Trinity Coll., 1962; MBA, Harvard U., 1964. Instr. Grad. Bus. Sch. Ateneo de Manila U., Philippines, 1964-66; spl. asst. to contr. U.S. Dept. Def., Washington, 1966-69; with Chem. Bank, N.Y.C., 1969-89, pres., dir., 1983-89; pres., dir. Manufacturers Hanover Trust Co., Mfrs. Hanover Corp., N.Y.C., 1989-91; resigned Mfrs. Hanover Trust Co., Mfrs. Hanover Corp., N.Y.C., 1991; bd. dirs. Pan Atlantic Inc., R.R. Donnelly & Sons, Inc., Prudential Ins. Co. Board dirs. Union Theol. Sem., Inst. Internat. Edn.; trustee Trinity Coll., Asia Soc.; v.p., bd. dirs. Cancer Rsch. Inst., Channel 13-WNET. Mem. The Group of 30, Coun. on Fgn. Rels., Econs. Club N.Y., Montclair Golf Club, Palm Beach Polo and Country Club, Harvard Bus. Club N.Y.C., River Club N.Y.C., The Links N.Y.C., Chgo. Club. Democrat. Roman Catholic. Office: 270 Park Ave New York NY 10017-2014

JOHNSON, THRUSTON CHARLES, violinist; b. Louisville, July 19, 1914; s. C. T. and Lorena (Stewart) J.; m. Evelyn Steil. Studies with Carl

Flesch, London, Belgium, 1937-38; studies with Ivan Galamian, N.Y.C.; grad., N.Y. Coll. of Music, 1951; B, Manhattan Sch. Music, 1953, M, 1963; cert. specialist in music edn., Columbia U., 1963. Cert. tchr., N.Y. Mem. Stokowski Tour N.Am., S.Am., 1940-41, All-Am. Orch. Tours, N. and S.Am., 1940-41; 1st violinist Pitts. Symphony Orch., 1944; asst. concertmaster, soloist, 1st violinist Radio City Music Hall, 1944; 1st violinist Chgo. Symphony Orch., 1945-48; concertmaster Kansas City Philharm. Orch., 1948-50; tours with NBC Opera TV Co., Boston Pops Orch., 1958—; soloist Carnegie Recital Hall, N.Y.C., 1976-88; guest prof. Cosmopolitan Sch. Music, Chgo., 1951, N.Y. Coll. Music, 1957, Vermont State U., 1958; assoc. prof. Augustana Coll., Sioux Falls, S.D., 1959; founder Chgo. Artists Trio, 1945; chmn. string dept. Kans. City Conservatory of Music, 1948-50; performing staff Inst. Humanistic Studies, Aspen, Colo., 1950. Feature writer Musical Leader, 1945-48; contbr. articles to Hist. Soc. Ky., The Filson Club, Louisville; producer, narrator, host "Records from Abroad", Sta. WABF-FM (now Sta. WNCN-FM), N.Y.C., 1950-59; radio violin recitals Sta. Sta. WNYC-FM and Sta. WFUV-FM, 1950-62; violin soloist with Kansas City Philharmonic Orch., 1948-50, Fort Wayne Philharmonic Orch., 1951, Naumberg Symphony Orch., N.Y.C., 1959, Chgo. Civic Orch., 1935; soloist Town Hall, N.Y.C., 1939; solo recitals UN Sch., N.Y.C., 1965-76; prodr., narrator, soloist Children's Series recs. Ambassador records, 1950-59; violin recital RCA closed Cir. TV, World's Fair, N.Y.C., 1963; violin recitals in Louisville, 1938, Jacksonville, Fla., 1930-33, Kansas City, Chgo., 1935-48, Carnegie Hall, N.Y.C., 1987; recording rare works of violin and piano lit. Internat. Festival Series Archives. With USAAF. WWII. Recipient Kodaly award Hungarian Govt., 1982; named to Hon. Order Ky. Colonels. Mem. Phi Delta Kappa. Home: 600 W 116th St # 121 New York NY 10027-7010

JOHNSON, TIMOTHY ANDREW, cartoonist, producer; b. Oceanside, N.Y., July 16, 1968; s. Thomas Morton and Joan Claudette (Karst) J. Pres. Tim Johnson Prodns., Oceanside, N.Y., 1988—. Author: (greeting card line) Happy Holidays, 1990; (cartoon book) Private Arthur, 1990-91; co-producer (with Tom Gill) (prints) The Lone Ranger, 1991. Vol. campaign poster Dean Skelos, state senator, Rockville Center, N.Y., 1986.

JOHNSON, TRACEY DENISE, writer, actress; b. Phila., May 20, 1966; d. Grady and Addie (Ruth) Flood; m. Joseph Johnson, Sept. 26, 1987; children: Kanishra, Latasha, Jermere. BA, Temple U., 1990. Pub. rels. dir. Jazz 90.1 FM, WRTI, Phila., 1989-90; writer, actress, 1990—. Author: How to Survive in LA, 1990; screenwriter: (TV movie) Misguided Deception, 1990; playwright: When the Drugs Move In, 1990; lyricist: My Girlfriends' Boyfriend, 1990, others; author poetry and articles published in various newspapers and jours.; actress Rocky V, 1990; actress in comml. American House Sub, Inc., 1990. Recipient Fitness award, 1984, Scholarship award, 1984, Sci. award, 1983. Mem. Song Writers Guild of Am., Ice Skating Inst. of Am. Democrat. Pentecostal. Home and Office: 8218 Michener Ave Philadelphia PA 19150-1704

JOHNSON, WALTER, human service agency executive; b. Bayonne, N.J., Aug. 2, 1939; s. Walter J. and Ann M. (Kulaga) J.; m. D. Elaine Smith, June 24, 1961 (div. 1969); children: Mark Walter, Cheryl Ann Monteleone; m. Maureen Catherine Mantin, Dec. 13, 1969 (dec.); 1 child, Julie Elisa. BBA, Pace U., 1964. Fin. asst. N.Y. World-Telegram & Sun, N.Y.C., 1958-66; asst. controller Christ Hosp., Jersey City, 1966-73; dir. fin. United Way of Cen. Jersey, Milltown, N.J., 1973-84; exec. dir. Family and Children's Service, Long Branch, N.J., 1984—; mem. State Adv. Bd. for Probation, Trenton, N.J., 1983-87, Human Service Adv. Council, Freehold, N.J., 1985—, Youth Service Commn., Freehold, 1985—, chmn., 1982. Counselor Vols. in Probation, Freehold, 1974—; v.p. Citizens of Fairview Civic Assn., Middletown, 1975; mem. Juvenile Conf. Com., Middletown, 1984—, chmn. adv. coun., 1985; bd. dirs. Hyacinth Found. AIDS Project, 1989—, treas., 1990—. Named Outstanding Vol. Monmouth County Family Ct., 1984. Mem. Am. Mgmt. Assn., Long Branch C. of C. (bd. dirs.). Roman Catholic. Office: Family and Children's Svc 191 Bath Ave Long Branch NJ 07740-6134

JOHNSON, WALTER HARRY, language professional, educator; b. Camden, N.J., Sept. 28, 1938; s. George Paul and Dorothy Lucy (Abrams) J.; m. Gretchen Marie McKeon, Aug. 20, 1966; children: Kevin, Danica, Maura, Nathaniel. BS in English, St. Joseph's U., Phila., 1960; MA in English, Villanova U., 1966; MA in Children's Lit., Simmons Coll., 1984. English and religion tchr. Camden (N.J.) Catholic High Sch., 1960-62; English and religion tchr. Cathedral High Sch., Trenton, N.J., 1962-68, English dept. chmn., 1967-68; prof. English and speech Cumberland County Coll., Vineland, N.J., 1968—; composition instr. Trenton (N.J.) Jr. Coll., 1965-67; lectr. St. Mary Magdalen Ch., Millville, N.J., 1971-81, Sacred Heart Ch., Vineland, 1982—. Contbr. articles to profl. jours. Dir. Little Theatre of Vineland, 1972-77; mem. Police Community Rels. Bd., Vineland, 1990—. Named Director of the Year Little Theatre of Vineland, 1973, 1974. Mem. Nat. Edn. Assn. Nat. Coun. Tchr. of English, N.J. Edn. Assn., N.J. Coun. of Tchrs. of English, Assembly of Literature for Adolescents, Found. for Children's Literature. Democrat. Roman Catholic. Home: 46 Boxwood Dr Vineland NJ 08360-2936 Office: Cumberland County Coll College Dr Vineland NJ 08360-7456

JOHNSON, WALTER HENRY, III, aviation executive; b. White Plains, N.Y., May 15, 1948; s. Walter Henry Jr. and Marcelle (Rheaume) J.; m. Tracy Tennant, Dec. 28, 1968 (div. 1979); children: Dustin McCarthy, Wallis Tennant; m. Leslie Rodgers Kehoe, Mar. 1, 1980; children: Allison Rodges, Peter Fitzgerald, Meril Dean. BA, Kings Coll., N.Y.C., 1970. Dist. sales mgr. Overseas Nat. Airways, N.Y.C., 1973-76, v.p. sales, 1976-78; asst. gen. mgr. Bahamas Air, Nassau, Bahamas, 1978-81; gen. mgr. Flying Tiger Line, N.Y.C., 1981-82; exec. v.p., chief ops. officer Nat. Airlines, N.Y.C., 1982-86; pres. Dallister Aviation, Norwalk, Conn., 1986-89. Republican. Episcopalian. Home: 12 Sturges Ridge Rd Wilton CT 06897-3229 Office: Dallister Aviation 3010 Westchester Ave Purchase NY 10577-2524

JOHNSON, WALTER ROLAND, metallurgist, consultant; b. Boston, Feb. 10, 1927; s. Gustave Hjalmar and Gertrude Dagmar (Peterson) J.; m. Janet L. Campbell, Mar. 31, 1962; children: Meryl Ann, Leah Kathryn, Christa Helen. BS in Metall. Engring., MIT, 1958. Registered profl. engr., Mass. Instr. MIT, Cambridge, Mass., 1950-58; metallurgist Raytheon Co., Missile Systems Div., Andover, Mass., 1958-69; chmn. QUBE Resources Profl. Cons., Gloucester, Mass., 1969—. With USAAF, 1944-46. Mem. Am. Soc. for Metals Internat. (chmn. Boston chpt. 1975-76). Republican. Home and Office: 35 Norseman Ave Gloucester MA 01930-1026

JOHNSON, WILLIAM ALEXANDER, clergyman, philosophy educator; b. Bklyn., Aug. 20, 1934; s. Charles Raphael and Ruth Augusta (Anderson) J.; m. Carol Genevieve Lundquist, June 11, 1955; children—Karin Ruth, Karl William, Krister Frederick. B.A., Queens Coll., City U. N.Y., 1953; B.D. (Univ. fellow, Morrow Meml. fellow, Daniel Delaplaine fellow), Union Theol. Sem., 1956; Teol. Kand., Lund U., 1957, Teol. Lic., 1958, Teologie Doktor, 1962; M.A., Columbia U., 1958, Ph.D. (Univ. fellow, Rockefeller Bros. fellow), 1959. Ordained deacon Meth. Ch., 1955, priest Episcopal Ch., 1968. Profl. baseball player N.Y. Giants, 1949-51; dir. Boys Club, Salvation Army, Jamaica, N.Y., 1952-54; minister Mt. Hope and Teabo Meth. chs., Wharton, N.J., 1954-56; elder Meth. Ch., 1956; minister Immanuel and Union Meth. chs., Bklyn., 1957-59; asst. in instrn. Columbia U., N.Y.C., 1957, Union Theol. Sem., N.Y.C., 1958; instr., asst. prof. religion Trinity Coll., Hartford, Conn., 1959-63; lectr. philosophy and theology Hartford Sem. Found., 1961-62; assoc. prof. religion, chmn. dept. religion Drew U., Madison, N.J., 1963-66; research prof. religion NYU, N.Y.C., 1966; vis. lectr. Union Theol. Sem., N.Y.C., 1966; vis. prof. religion Princeton (N.J.) U., 1966-68; prof., chmn. dept. religion Manhattanville Coll., Purchase, N.Y., 1967-71; vis. prof. Christian ethics Gen. Theol. Sem., N.Y.C., 1970; Albert V. Danielsen prof. Christian thought, prof. philosophy and history of ideas Brandeis U., Waltham, Mass., 1971—; canon residentiary Cathedral Ch. of St. John The Divine, N.Y.C., 1973—; vis. prof. Protestant theology N.Am. Coll., Vatican City, 1969-75, Bryn Mawr Coll., 1976, U. Strasbourg, France; vis. scholar MIT, Cambridge, 1974-75; vis. prof., Tokyo, Japan, Stockholm, Sweden, 1979, U. Gothenburg, 1979; examining chaplain Diocese of the Arctic, 1982; prof. nr. Ea. and Jewish studies Brandeis U., 1988. Author: The Philosophy of Religion of Anders Nygren, 1958, Christopher Polhem: The Father of Swedish Technology, 1963, Nature and the Supernatural in the Theology of Horace Bushnell, 1963, On Religion: A Study of Theological Method in Schleiermacher and Nygren, 1964, Problems in Christian Ethics, 1965, (with Nels F.S. Ferré) Swedish Contributions to Modern Theology, 1966, The Search for Transcendence, 1974, The Christian Way of Death, 1974, Invitation to Theology, 1979, Philosophy and the Gospel, 1979, (with Moorhead Kennedy) Christianity and Terrorism, 1986, O Boundless Salvation, 1987; debut as Popolo in Aida Met. Opera, 1989; contbr. articles to profl. jours.; lectr., Europe, Asia, Africa, South Am., Australia, Caribbean., Arctic. Democratic committeeman Hartford, 1960-63; mem. exec. com. Am. Friends Service Com., Coll. Div., 1966-70; bd. dirs. Queens Coll. CUNY. Recipient David F. Swenson-Kierkegaard Meml. award, 1964, Harbison award for Tchr. of Yr. Danforth Found., 1965; named Outstanding Young Man in Am. Jr. C. of C., 1964; Disting. Alumnus Queens Coll., 1980; Scandinavian-Am. Found. fellow, 1956, 85; Fulbright scholar U. Copenhagen, 1957-58; Dempster Grad. fellow Meth. Ch., 1958; Am. Philos. Soc. fellow, 1971, 85. vis. rsch. fellow Princeton, 1972; Guggenheim fellow for study in Rome, Italy, 1972; NSF grantee, 1978; Rockefeller fellow Aspen Inst., 1978, fellow Aspen Inst., Jerusalem, 1982; Nat. Endowment Humanities grantee, 1978, 86; grantee Arthur Vining Davis Found., 1981; grantee Trinity Ch. of N.Y.C., 1982, 84; grantee Tauber Inst. Study of European Jewry. Mem. Am. Acad. Religion, Asia Soc., Japan Soc., Scandinavian-Am. Heritage Soc., Am. Philos. Assn., Danforth Assos., Soc. for Sci. Study Religion, Soc. for Religion in Higher Edn. (Kent fellow 1959), Soc. Anglican Theologians, Vasa Order Am., Am. Soc. Christian Ethics, Swedish Pioneer Hist. Soc., Soc. for Scandinavian Study, Willa Cather Pioneer Meml. Found., Authors Guild, Episcopal Churchmen for S.Africa, New Haven Theol. Group, Westchester Inst. Psychiatry and Psychoanalysis (dir.), Ecumenical Found. for Christian Ministry, English Speaking Union, Ch. Soc. for Coll. Work, Columbia University Club, Met. Opera Club, The Pilgrims, The Coffee House, Lotos Club, Century Club, Explorer's Club, Phi Beta Kappa, Pi Gamma Mu, Phi Sigma Tau. Home: 27 Fox Meadow Rd Scarsdale NY 10583-2903 also: 44 Pascal Ave Rockport ME 04856 Office: Brandeis U Rabb Grad Ctr Waltham MA 02154

JOHNSON, WILLIAM DOUGLAS, obstetrician-gynecologist; b. Greensboro, N.C., Nov. 25, 1928; s. Ruben Edgar and Lillie Belle (Jones) J.; m. Susan Allibone Budd, Aug. 23, 1952; children: Thomas Allibone, William Douglas Jr., Ann Chandlee. BA, Davidson Coll., 1949; MD, U. Pa., 1953. Diplomate Am. Bd. Ob.-Gyn. Intern Walter Reed Army Hosp., 1953-54; resident Presbyn. Hosp., Phila., 1956-59; pvt. practice, Wilmington, Del., 1960—; sr. attending physician Med. Ctr. Del. and St. Francis Hosp., Wilmington, 1960—; asst. prof. ob-gyn. Thomas Jefferson U. Sch. Medicine, Phila., 1970—. Capt. USAF, 1953-56. Fellow Am. Fertility Soc., Am. Coll. Ob-Gyn.; mem. Obstet. Soc. Del.(pres. 1986-88), Obstet. Soc. Phila., Wilmington (Del.) Country Club, Pinehurst (N.C.) Country Club. Republican. Episcopalian. Office: 2323 Pennsylvania Ave Wilmington DE 19806-1332

JOHNSON, WILLIAM JOSEPH, stockbroker; b. Cleve., Apr. 10, 1941; s. Robert David and Ann (Sercely) J.; m. Joan Donna Anshutz, June 18, 1966; children: Donna, Jennifer. BA, Ohio State U., 1966; postgrad., NYU, 1971-75. Account exec. Merrill Lynch, N.Y.C., 1966-73, Cyrus J. Lawrence, N.Y.C., 1973-77; v.p. Kuhn Loeb, N.Y.C., 1977-78, Donaldson Lufkin and Jenrette, N.Y.C., 1978—. Served with USNR, 1961-63. Named Outstanding Broker, Reg. Rep mag., Newport Beach, Calif., 1986. Roman Catholic. Home: 14 Green Hill Rd Madison NJ 07940-2526

JOHNSON, WILLIAM R., state supreme court justice; b. Oct. 21, 1930; married; 2 children. Student, Dartmouth Coll., Harvard U. Pvt. practice law Hanover; state senator N.H. Gen. Assembly, Concord, state rep.; judge N.H. Superior Ct., Concord, 1969-85, N.H. Supreme Ct., Concord, 1985—; instr. law Dartmouth Coll., Hanover. Office: NH Supreme Ct Noble Dr Concord NH 03301-6179

JOHNSSON, HILLARY CRUTE, soloist, opera singer; b. N.Y.C., Apr. 12, 1959; d. Samuel and Helena A. (Barker) Johnson; m. Reginald Crute, Sept. 11, 1989. Student, Am. Inst. Music, Graz, Austria, 1978, 79; BFA, CCNY, 1979; student, Mozarteum, Salzburg, Austria, 1981, Met. Opera Young Artists Program, N.Y.C., 1984-87. Opera singer Opera Ebony, Opera North, Phila., 1982, Memphis Opera, 1986, Little Orch. Soc., N.Y.C., 1987, Opera Orch. N.Y., N.Y.C., 1987, N.J. State Opera, Newark, 1984, N.J. Lyric Opera Co., Trenton, 1985, El Paso (Tex.) Symphony Orch., 1987, Chgo. Symphony, 1986, 87, Met. Opera Co., N.Y.C., 1985—; adjudicator: Leontyne Price Vocal Arts Competition, 1991. Recorded: (Am. opera) Eventide, Joseph Fennimore. Recipient awards Liederkranz Found., N.Y.C., 1983, Sullivan Found., N.Y.C., 1983, Leontyne Price Vocal Arts award, Negro Bus. and Profl. Women, Washington, 1988, 1st Pl. award Amato Opera Assn., N.Y.C., 1984. Mem. Am. Guild Mus. Artists. Democrat. Office: Met Opera House Lincoln Ctr New York NY 10023

JOHNSTON, BARRY HASLER, social services administrator; b. Crossett, Ark., Aug. 26, 1954; s. Kenneth and Marian (Richelderffer) J.; m. Lois M. De Hart, Aug. 12, 1978. BA, Eisenhower Coll., 1976; MS, Shippensburg U., 1978; postgrad., Temple U., 1985. Tchr. Crystal Run Sch., Fallsburg, N.Y., 1977-78; casework coord. Pa. Assn. for the Blind, Pottsville, 1978-79; vocat. counselor Creative Health Systems, Pottstown, Pa., 1979-81; vocat. specialist ARBOR, Inc., Phila., 1981-82; project dir. JEVS, Inc., Phila., 1982-85, Rural Opportunities, Inc., West Chester, Pa., 1985-87; dir. devel. Assn. for Retarded Citizens, West Chester, Pa., 1987—; cons. Programs for Exceptional People, Phila., 1990—, Main Line Ednl. Svcs., Rosemont, Pa., 1990—; conv. speaker ARC of the U.S., Arlington, Tex., 1989. Bd. dirs. 100 Centre Ave. Homeowners Assn., Jeffersonville, Pa., 1985-87, Chester County Migrant Ministries, West Chester, 1986-87. Recipient Campaign Vol. award United Way of Chester County, 1990, Appalachian Trail award Keystone Trails Assn., 1984. Mem. Internat. Mgmt. Coun. (program chmn. 1991—), Appalachian Trail Conf., Appalachian Mountain Club, League of Am. Wheelmen. Home: 421 Centre Ave Norristown PA 19403-3222 Office: Assn for Retarded Citizens 24 S New St West Chester PA 19382-2986

JOHNSTON, CARLA BROOKS, public policy and management consultant; b. Rochester, N.Y., Apr. 2, 1940; d. James Ovid Brooks and Helen (Porschet) Brooks Casety; m. Frederick L. Johnston, Jr., Dec. 30, 1961 (div. Dec. 1983); children—Frederick L., III, J. Elise. B.A., Coll. of Wooster, Ohio, 1961; M.A., Andover Newton Theol. Sch., Mass., 1966. Funding and devel. coordinator Mayor Ralph's Office, Somerville, Mass., 1970-73; exec. dir., budget analyst MBTA Adv. Bd. (pub. transport legis. of 79 mayors), Boston, 1973-76; exec. dir. Met. Area Planning Council, Boston, 1977-79; dep. exec. dir. Union of Concerned Scis., Cambridge, Mass., 1979-81; founder, pres. New Century Policies, cons. firm, 1981—. Author: Reversing the Nuclear Arms Race, 1985, Election Coverage: Blueprint for Broadcasters, 1991 (translated into Russian, distbn. by Moscow U.), International Television Co-Production, 1992. Editor: Under the Interstate, 1975. Dir. film City Roots, 1975; dir. project/video for Eastern Europeans on media role in elections, 1991. Elected mem. Dem. State Com., Mass., 1984-88, Dem. Nat. Platform com., San Francisco, 1984; selected Dem. Drafting com., Washington, 1984; founding mem. Nat. Freeze Voter, Fort Worth, 1983; candidate for U.S. Ho. of Reps. from 8th dist. Mass., 1986. Scholarships to India, 1961, to Germany, 1956; first peace fellow Radcliffe, Bunting Inst., 1983-84, Loeb fellow Harvard, 1973-74. Mem. Cambridge Ctr. Adult Edn. (pres. 1983-85). Avocations: travel; walking; camping; cooking. Office: New Century Policies PO Box 964 Boston MA 02103

JOHNSTON, DAVID RITCHEY, construction company executive; b. Highland Park, Ill., Nov. 7, 1950; Sherman and Vivian (Ritchey) J. BS, So. Ill. U., 1976. Owner Survival Systems Constrn., Bath, Maine, 1976-77; cons. Nat. Rec. and Parks Assn., Rosslyn, Va., 1977-78, Planning Research Corp., McLean, Va., 1978-79; v.p. Potomac Energy Group, Alexandria, Va., 1979-83; pres. Passive Solar Industries Council, Alexandria, Va., 1981-83, Lightworks Constrn., Inc., Bethesda, Md., 1983—; bd. dirs. Whole Systems Design, Inc., Lorton, Va., Potomac Energy Group, Inc., Bus. Crafters, New Alternative in Pub., Retailing & Advt. Author: Technical Solar Field Guide, 1979; exec. producer (film) Sunbuilders, 1980. Pres. Cabin John (Md.) Citizens Assn., 1986; bd. dirs. Renewable Energy Inst., 1982-83, STAR Found., Portland, Maine, 1979-89. Named to Remodeling Industry Hall of Fame, 1989. Mem. Nat. Assn. Remodeling Industry (bd. dirs.), Entrepreneurs Group of Washington, D.C. (pres.), Excellence Group, Bus. Crafters (bd. dirs. 1991—), New Age Pubs. and Retailers Assn. Home: 8029 Riverside Dr Cabin John MD 20818-1628 Office: Lightworks Constrn 5110 Ridgefield Rd Ste 402 Bethesda MD 20816-3346

JOHNSTON, EDWARD JOSEPH, professional hockey team executive; b. Montreal, Que., Can., Nov. 24, 1935; m. Diane Johnston; 3 children. Former profl. hockey goaltender NHL with Boston Bruins, Toronto Maple Leafs, St. Louis Blues, Chgo. Blackhawks; coach N.B. Hawks, Am. Hockey League, 1978-79, Chgo. Black Hawks, NHL, 1979; coach Pitts. Penguins, NHL, 1980-83, gen. mgr., 1983-89; v.p., gen. mgr. Hartford Whalers, 1989—. Office: Hartford Whalers 1 Civic Center Plz Hartford CT 06103-1504*

JOHNSTON, FRANK C., psychologist; b. West Hartford, Conn., June 21, 1955; s. Frank C. and Chris (Butler) J.; m. Susan H. Leffert, July 26, 1981. BA, Fairfield U., 1977; MEd, Columbia U., 1979, MA, 1979; PhD, SUNY, Albany, 1984. Sch. psychologist bd. coop. ednl. svcs. Herkimer, N.Y., 1979-80; intern Counseling Ctr., SUNY, Buffalo, 1983-84; psychologist Family Svc. Rochester, N.Y., 1985-87, Child and Youth div. Rochester Mental Health Ctr., 1988; pvt. practice Rochester, 1988—; cons. Brockport (N.Y.) Day Care Ctr., 1989-90, Learning Devel. Ctr., Rochester Inst. Tech., 1989—. Mem. APA, N.Y. State Psychol. Assn., Genesee Valley Psychol. Assn. (mem. legal legis. com. 1988-90, mem. ins. com. 1990—, chmn. ins. com. 1990), Rochester Area Assn. Clin. Psychologists, Nat. Register Health Svc. Providers in Psychology. Office: 16 Goodman St N Ste 111 Rochester NY 14607-1554

JOHNSTON, GERALD SAMUEL, physician, educator; b. Johnstown, Pa., Aug. 4, 1930; s. Florence Gerald and Lorna Freda (Lawhead) J.; m. Dorothy Anna Jones, June 18, 1956; children: Joy Johnston Biciocchi, Jill A. Verna, Jana S. Moritzkat, Gerald S. Jr., Amy L. Tapparo, Douglas S. BS, U. Pitts., 1952, MD, 1956. Diplomate Am. Bd. Internal Medicine, Am. Bd. Nuclear Medicine. Intern Walter Reed Gen. Hosp., Washington, 1956-57; resident in internal medicine Brooke Gen. Hosp., San Antonio, 1958-61; commd. med. officer U.S. Army, 1955-71, advanced through grades to col., 1971; capt. USPHS, 1971-82; surgeon 358 Gen. dispensary, Seoul, Korea, 1961-62; chief nuclear medicine Walter Reed Gen. Hosp., Washington, Md., 1963-69, Letterman Gen. Hosp., San Francisco, 1969-71, NIH, Bethesda, Md., 1971-82; acting chmn. dept. radiology U. Md., Balt., 1989-92, prof. medicine, radiology and oncology, 1982—. Author two books; contbr. over 170 articles to profl. jours. Decorated Legion of Merit, 1970. Fellow ACP, Am. Coll. Radiology; mem. AMA, AAUP, Am. Coll. Nuclear Medicine, Soc. Nuclear Medicine, Soc. of Chmn. of Acad. Radiology Depts. Republican. Office: U Md Hosp 22 S Greene St Baltimore MD 21201-1544

JOHNSTON, GORDON ROBERT, chemist, educator; b. Portland, Oreg., July 13, 1928; s. Earl Gordon and Catherine Cecilia (Bieker) J.; m. Elizabeth Mary Ann Lane, Aug. 6, 1960; children: Catherine, Therese, William, Dennis. BS, U. Portland, 1950, MS, 1952; PhD, U. Ill., 1956. Rsch. chemist Dow Chem. Co., Midland, Mich., 1956-58; rsch. assoc. U. Oreg. Med. Sch., Portland, 1958-60; rsch. chemist Crown Zellerbach Corp., Camas, Wash., 1960-62, Aerojet-Gen. Corp., Azusa, Calif., 1962-63; postdoctoral fellow Calif. Inst. Tech., Pasadena, 1963-64; prof. San Diego Coll. for Women, 1964-66, Pa. State U., Monaca, 1966—; cons. Pa. Right to Know Law, Beaver, 1986—. Active sch. bd. Beaver, 1971-76, 1985-89; candidate U.S. Ho. of Reps., Pa., 1988, 90. Mem. Am. Chem. Soc., Sigma Xi. Republican. Roman Catholic. Home: 1709 10th Ave Beaver PA 15009-1347 Office: Pa State U Beaver Campus Monaca PA 15061-2799

JOHNSTON, JAMES CANNON, financial executive; b. Ogden, Utah, May 6, 1955; s. Peter Budge and Charlotte (Cannon) J.; m. Mary Theresa Hazen, June 5, 1979; children: Rachel, Peter, Matthew, David, Anne, Samuel. AB, Princeton U., 1979; MBA, U. Chgo., 1981. Fin. analyst Cummins Engine Co., Inc., Columbus, Ind., 1981-85; dir. fin. Cadec Systems, Inc., Londonderry, N.H., 1985-86; owner Johnston Co., Manchester, N.H., 1986—; part-time chief fin. officer Biomat Corp., Belmont, Mass., 1988-89, Aurora Tech., Waltham, Mass., 1990—, Alder Rsch. Ctr., Woburn, Mass., 1990—, Timeslips Corp., Essex, Mass., 1991—, Union Machine Co., Peabody, Mass., 1991—; mem. bd. advisors CFO mag. Mem. alumni schs. com. Princeton U. Mem. Licensing Execs. Soc., Am. Arbitration Assn. (panel mem.), U. N.H. Small Bus. Devel. Network (profl. advisor). Mem. LDS Ch. Office: 355 W Mitchell St Manchester NH 03103-7351

JOHNSTON, JOSEPHINE ROSE, chemist; b. Cranston, R.I., Aug. 9, 1926; d. Robert and Rose (Varca) Forte; m. Howard Robert Johnson, Mar. 7, 1949; 1 child, Kevin Howard. Student, Carnegie Inst., 1945-47; BS, Mich. State U., 1972, MA, 1973; postgrad., MIT, 1973—. Med. technologist South Nassau Community Hosp., Rockville Centre, N.Y., 1947-50; med. technologist Mich. State U., East Lansing, 1950-53, faculty specialist, 1966-76; dept. pathology Albany (N.Y.) Med. Ctr., 1953-54; med. lab. supr. Bulova Watch Co., Jackson Heights, N.Y., 1954-57; sr. chemistry technologist Mid Island Hosp., Bethpage, N.Y., 1958-66; sr. rsch. assoc. Uniformed Svcs. Univ., Bethesda, Md., 1976-78; asst. to chmn. dept. physiology Uniformed Svcs. Univ., Bethesda, 1978-82, assoc. to chmn., 1982—. Contbr. articles in field to profl. jours. Cons. Danzines Found., Lauderdale, Fla. Mem. Analytical Chem. Soc., Data and Electronic Soc., Internat. Platform Assn. Lutheran. Office: 6813 Woodville Rd Mount Airy MD 21771-7611

JOHNSTON, VIRGINIA ANNE, musician, teacher; b. Kansas City, Mo., Oct. 9, 1966; d. Michael Joseph and Mary Catherine (Bennett) J. MusB, Syracuse U., 1988; MusM, Boston U., 1991. Tchr. Benedictine Acad., Elizabeth, N.J., 1988-89; tchr., coach N.J. Youth Symphony, Summit, 1988-89, 91—; data entry operator Beneficial Nat. Bank, Bedminster, N.J., 1990, 91; pvt. instr. clarinet and saxophone N.J., 1988—; adminstrv. asst. Philharmonic Orch. N.J., Warren, 1992—. Author, composer Introduction and Variation, 1988; composer over 20 orch. and chamber compositions, 1985—; clarinetist Aspen (Colo.) Music Festival, 1987, 88, Vista Winds, Boston, 1989-90; composer, clarinetist Coll. Chamber Ensemble N.J., Montclair, 1988-90; founding mem., performer Triad Arts Ensemble, Bedminster, N.J., 1992—. Finalist Young Composers grant ASCAP, 1989, 90, 91; Hon. Mention, Billboard Song Contest, 1990, 1st place Concerto Competition, Syracuse U., 1987, 88. Mem. Broadcast Music Inc., Am. Music Ctr., Internat. Clarinet Soc. (semi-finalist Young Artists Clarinet Concerto Competition 1989), Composers Guild N.J., Phi Kappa Phi, Sigma Alpha Iota (v.p. 1987-88), Phi Kappa Lambda.

JOHNSTONE, D. BRUCE, university administrator; b. Mpls., Jan. 13, 1941; s. D. Bruce and Florence Morton (Elliott) J.; m. Gail Eberhardt, July 30, 1965; children—Duncan Bruce, Cameron. B.A., Harvard U., 1963, M.A.T., 1964; Ph.D., U. Minn., 1969. Tchr. econs. and history Westport, Conn., 1964-65; asst. dir. U. Minn. Center for Econ. Edn., 1966-69; adminstrv. asst. to Sen. Walter F. Mondale, 1969-71; project specialist Ford Found., 1971-72; exec. asst. to pres. U. Pa., 1972-77, assoc. prof. edn., 1976-79, v.p. for adminstrn., 1977-79; pres. State U. Coll. at Buffalo, 1979-88; chancellor SUNY System Office, Albany, 1988—. Author: New Patterns for College Lending, 1973, Sharing the Costs of Higher Education, 1986; contbr. articles to profl. jours. Bd. dirs. The Coll. Bd., Am. Coun. on Edn., Nat. Faculty Exch., N.Y. Higher Edn. Svcs. Corp., Job Tng. Partnership Coun. N.Y. State, N.Y. State Martin Luther King, Jr. Inst. for Non-Violence; mem. N.Y. State Coun. on Econ. Edn. Mem. Am. Assn. Higher Edn., St. Andrew's Soc., Harvard-Radcliffe of Ea. N.Y. Club, Cosmos Club. Democrat. Episcopalian. Home: SUNY Plz South Tower Albany NY 12246 Office: SUNY System State University Plz Albany NY 12246

JOHNSTONE, MONICA CAROLYN, writer, educator; b. Phila., Aug. 23, 1959; d. Parland Richard and Constance Mary (McLaughlin) J. BA, U. Calif., Berkeley, 1981, MA, 1983, PhD, 1987. Lectr. U. Calif., Berkeley, 1987-88; asst. prof. Loyola Coll. Md., Balt., 1988—; faculty advisor Loyola Coll. Martial Arts Club, Balt., 1988—, Speech and Debate Club, 1990, student play prodns., 1990-91; instr. Assumption U., Bangkok, Thailand, 1991. Musician: California Band, 1977-81. Recipient Levi Strauss Found. scholarship, 1977-81, Charles Mills Gayley fellowship, 1982, 83, Wollenberg grant, 1983, 84, Prytanean Hon. Soc., 1986, Humanities Rsch. fellowship U. Calif., 1986, I.C.A. Grad. Student Teaching award, 1987, Loyola Faculty Devel. Summer Rsch. grant, 1989; named Club Advisor of Yr., 1990. Fellow Order of the Golden Bear (warden 1986-87); mem. Speech Communication Assn., Modern Lang. Assn., Rhetoric Soc. Am., Nat. Coll. Tchrs. of English,

Clan Johnstone in Am. Democrat. Office: Loyola Coll Writing & Media 4501 N Charles St Baltimore MD 21210-2601

JOHNSTONE, PHILIP MACLAREN, lawyer; b. Sharon, Conn., Mar. 24, 1961; s. Rodney Stuart and Frances Louise (Davis) J.; m. Elizabeth Laird McGovern, Sept. 10, 1988. BA in Econs. magna cum laude, Duke U., 1983; JD, U. Pa., 1986. Bar: Mass. 1986, Conn. 1987, U.S. Dist. Ct. Conn. 1988. Assoc. Greenberg, Parenteau & Geraghty, P.C., New London, Conn., 1992—; bd. dirs. J Boats, Inc., Newport, R.I., 1987—. Bd. dirs. United Way of Wilton, 1991. Mem. ABA, Mass. Bar Assn., Conn. Bar Assn., Wadawanuck Club (admissions com. 1989-91, tennis com. 1989-90). Republican. Episcopalian.

JOHNSTON-O'CONNOR, ELIZABETH J., marketing research consultant; b. Waterbury, Conn., Sept. 13, 1952; d. William Smithwick and Catherine (McElligott) Johnston; m. Daniel Johnston O'Connor, June 21, 1980; children: Kelly Elizabeth, Catherine Arlene, James Patrick, William Daniel. BA, St. Bonaventure U., 1974; MA in Psychology, U. Rochester, N.Y., 1978, PhD, 1981. Cons. Xerox Corp., Rochester, 1978-79; mktg. scientist Life Ins. Mktg. and Rsch. Group, Hartford, Conn., 1980-88; pres. Johnston O'Connor Rsch., Newtown, Conn., 1984—. Author: Management Dynamics, 1982, Personal Selling, 1984. Mem. Am. Mktg. Assn. (bd. dirs. Conn. chpt. 1985-88, Mktg. Maverick award 1988), Am. Psychol. Assn. Office: Johnston O'Connor Rsch 5 Saw Mill Ridge Rd Newtown CT 06470-1422

JOLLEY, JOHN KENNETH, researcher; b. N.Y.C., Dec. 4, 1945; s. Willie Lee and Bertha (Holloway) J.; m. Linda Lowery, Sept. 21, 1968 (div. 1975); 1 child, Erica Nichole; m. Jena Oliva York, Aug. 4, 1979; children: Janelle York, Jonathan Lloyd. BS in Sociology, N.C. Agrl. & Tech. State U., Greensboro, 1968; M of Social Welfare, U. Wis., 1971; cert. tng. program design and evaluation, U. Pitts., 1976, cert. tng. small bus. mgmt., acctg., fin, 1980. Cert. nat. investigator, 1988. Survey rsch. coord. community devel. project Ctr. for Instl. Devel. and Rsch., Greensboro, N.C., 1972; researcher Washington U., St. Louis, 1973; rsch. assoc., lectr. Inst. for Urban Rsch. Howard U., Washington, 1974-75; rsch. asst. D.C. Pub. Sch. System, Washington, 1976-77; program analyst Dept. Employment Svcs., Pitts., 1979; rsch. asst. Consad Rsch. Corp., Pitts., 1980-81; operation rsch. analyst Met. Police Dept., Washington, 1981-88; asst. lottery oper. officer D.C. Lottery & Charitable Games Control Bd., Washington, 1988; data mgr. Howard U. Coll. Md., Washington, 1991—; asst. prof. dept. sociology and social svcs. N.C. Agrl. & Tech. State U., Greensboro, 1971-72; program analyst Community Rels. Social Devel. Commn., Milw., 1970-71; student counselor, supr. Upward Bound N.C. Agrl. and Tech. State U., Greensboro, summer, 1968; substitute tchr. Greensboro Pub. Sch. System, 1969; pub. rels. specialist and supr. Dept. Parks, Recreation and Cultural Affairs, N.Y.C., summer, 1964-71, Dept. Recreation, Goldsboro, N.C., summer, 1962-63; lectr. and cons. in field. Youth counselor supr. Give Youth a Chance, Milw., 1969-71; program developer, palnning advisor Wis. Upper Mich. Senate the Luth. Ch. in Am., Milw., 1969-71; chmn. evaluation and rsch. program com. Met. YMCA, Pitts., 1979-81; bd. dirs Greensboro Assn. Poor People, 1971-72, Greensboro Day Care Ctr., 1971-72; bd. dirs. Washington Regional United Way, 1988—; awards com. local chpt. NASW, St. louis, 1973; pres. search com. George Warren Brown Sch. Social Work, 1973-74. Child Welfare grantee NIH, 1969; recipient Cert. Recognition for Vol. Work award Met. Program Com. YMCA, 1980. Mem. Nat. Conf. on Social Welfare, Nat. Planners Assn., Data Mgmt. Assoc. Clin. Pharmacology. Democrat. Congregationalist. Home: 623 Buchann St NE Washington DC 20017 Office: Howard U 2112 Georgia Ave NW Washington DC 20059

JOLLYMORE, NICHOLAS JOHN, lawyer, educator; b. Duluth, Minn., Nov. 9, 1946; s. John Welcome and Elizabeth Ruth (Maki) J. BA, U. Minn., 1968, MA, 1970; JD, Fordham U., 1978; LLM, NYU, 1992. Bar: N.Y. 1979. Reporter United Press Internat., Newark and Trenton, N.J., 1971-75; assoc. Rogers & Wells, N.Y.C., 1978-83; assoc. counsel Simon & Schuster, Inc., N.Y.C., 1983-84; assoc. gen. counsel Time Inc., N.Y.C., 1984—; adj. assoc. prof. sch. law Fordham U., 1981—. Contbr. articles to profl. jours. Mem. Assn. of Bar of City of N.Y., Copyright Soc. U.S. Democrat. Home: 56 W 11th St Apt SRE New York NY 10011 Office: Time Warner Inc 1271 Ave of the Americas New York NY 10020

JOLSON, LOIS ROCHELLE, association executive, human resources specialist; b. N.Y.C., Jan. 7, 1959; d. Kenneth and Pearl (Zable) J. BA in Fine Art, Queens Coll., CUNY, 1979; MS, N.Y. Inst. Tech., 1985. Cert. sr. profl. in human resources. Pres. Jimmy Connors Internat. Fan Club, Forest Hills, N.Y., 1977-83; pers. asst. 3D/Internat., N.Y.C., 1979-81; supr. Poly Gram Corp., N.Y.C., 1981-85; mgr. Equitable Life Assurance Soc., N.Y.C., 1985-90; mgr. human resources N.Y. Hosp., N.Y.C., 1990—; pres. Colm Wilkinson Appreciation Soc., Forest Hills, 1989—. Editor, author newsletter Born to Sing, 1989—. Mem. Am. Compensation Assn., Nat. Assn. Fan Clubs. Office: Colm Wilkinson Appreciation Soc PO Box 543 Forest Hills NY 11375

JONAS, GILBERT, public relations and fund raising executive; b. Bklyn., July 22, 1930; s. Harry and Mitzi (Rosenstein) J.; BA, Stanford U., 1951; grad. cert. Chinese studies Columbia U., 1953, MA in Internat. Affairs, 1955; m. Barbara L. Selby, Sept. 1953 (div. Nov. 1961); 1 child, Susan; m. P. Joyce Theise, Dec. 27, 1964; children: Jillian, Stephanie. Pub. rels. counsel African Independence movements and East Asian govts., 1955-67; exec. sec. Am. Friends of Vietnam, N.Y.C., 1956-57; v.p. Harold L. Oram Inc., N.Y.C., 1958-61; exec. sec. Am. Med. Ctr. for Burma, N.Y.C., 1959-61; Far East cons., acting dir. Far East, Peace Corps, Washington, 1961; pres., owner Gilbert Jonas Co., Inc., N.Y.C., 1962—. Dir. pub. info. N.Y. Youth for Stevenson, 1956; mem. exec. com. N.Y. Com. for Dem. Voters, 1959-62; pres. Reform Ind. Dem. of N.Y., 1958-59; mem. civil rights staff Nat. Citizens for Kennedy-Johnson, 1960; devel. counsel NAACP, 1965—, life mem.; mem. steering com. N.Y. Citizens for Humphrey-Muskie, 1968; nat. coord. Charles Evers for Gov. Miss., 1971; co-founder N.Y.C. Reform Movement, Dem. party, 1958-63; bd. dirs. Am. Com. on Africa, 1955-59, League Indsl. Democracy, 1972—; nat. coord. Holy Land Conservation Fund, 1977-82. Served with AUS, 1953-55. Recipient Annual Freedom award Miss. NAACP, 1970, Annual Humanitarian award Manhattan NAACP, 1989. Mem. Overseas Press Club, Phi Beta Kappa, Sigma Delta Chi. Home: 215 E 80th St New York NY 10021-0531 Office: 150 E 58th St New York NY 10022

JONASON, PAULINE MARIE, art educator, retired; b. N.Y.C., Jan. 26, 1928; d. Mario Gabriel and Concetta Virginia (Ruggio) Barbara; m. Charles Raymond Jonason, July 8, 1950; children: Raymond Charles (dec.), Ruthellen Harris, Randall Paul. BA in Edn., Queens Coll., 1948; postgrad., Columbia U., 1949; MA in Edn., CCNY, 1950; postgrad., Adelphi U., 1960. Opaquer Paramount Pictures Famous Studios, N.Y.C., 1944; teen-age program dir. Queens YWCA, Flushing, N.Y., 1948; art tchr. Hicksville (N.Y.) Jr. High Sch., 1949-52, Woodland Elem. Sch., Hicksville, 1955-61; art tchr. Hicksville Sr. High Sch., 1961-84, chmn. art dept., 1970-84, sr. class advisor, 1981-84, ret., 1984; artist North Merrick, N.Y., 1984—. Actress in sch. plays, 1972, 74, 76. Mem. NEA, AARP, Nat. Mus. Women in the Arts, Nat. Geog. Soc., Met. Mus. Art, Am. Mus. Natural History, Tri-County Tchrs. Retirement Coun., Hicksville Classroom Tchrs. Assn., Earth Watch. Home: 978 Little Whaleneck Rd Merrick NY 11566-1223

JONASSEN, GAYLORD D., manufacturing executive, new products and market development; b. East Orange, N.J., Oct. 13, 1932; s. Jonas M. and Alma M. (Stelter) J.; B.S. in M.E., Ariz. State U., 1960; m. Shirley Ann Christophel, June 15, 1956; children—Glenn, Brenda, Devel. engr. Motorola Semiconductor, Phoenix, 1956-60; plant and facilities research and devel. engr. Western Electric, N.Y.C., 1960-65; new products mgr. Deutsch Relays, Long Island, N.Y., 1965-67; new product mktg./sales mgr. Kinemotive Corp., Farmingdale, N.Y., 1967-69; div. mgr. Atlantic Sci. Corp., Plainview, N.Y., 1969-70; exec. v.p., tech. dir. Telecommunications Industries, Inc., Copaigue, N.Y., 1970-73; founder, pres., Internat. Protein Industries, Inc., Hauppauge, 1973-84, chmn. bd., 1973-84; mgmt. cons. Gaylord Jonassen Assocs., 1984-85; systems engring. project mgr. Norden Systems, 1985-91; Gaylord D. Jonassen Assocs., 1991—. Served with U.S. Navy, 1950-54. Recipient Disting. Achievement award, Coll. Engring. and Applied Sci., Ariz. State U., 1982; ASTM fellow, 1958. Mem. L.I. Assn. Commerce and Industry. Baptist (deacon). Patentee in field. Contbr. articles to various publs. Home: 9 Wood Ln Smithtown NY 11787-4931 Office: 75 Maxess Rd Melville NY 11747-3182

JONES, ALEX S., reporter; b. Greeneville, Tenn., Nov. 19, 1946; m. Susan E. Tifft, Sept. 21, 1985. BA, Washington and Lee U., 1968. Editor Greeneville (Tenn.) Sun, 1978-83; bus. reporter N.Y. Times, from 1983, press reporter. Author: (with Susan E. Tifft) The Patriarch: The Rise and Fall of the Bingham Dynasty, 1991. Recipient Pulitzer prize for specialized reporting, 1987; Nieman fellow, 1981-82. Home: 225 W 86th St Apt 309 New York NY 10024 Office: The New York Times 229 W 43d St New York NY 10036-3913

JONES, BARBARA PENDLETON, psychologist, educator; b. Atlanta, Apr. 2, 1947; d. Eugene Banks Jr. and Barbara Lee (Murlin) P.; m. Boisfeuillet Jones Jr., Sept. 13, 1969; children: Lindsay Pendleton, Theodore Boisfeuillet. BA, Wellesley Coll., 1968; MA, Boston U., 1974, PhD, 1977; grad., Balt.-Washington Inst. of Psychoanalysis, 1992. Diplomate Am. Bd. Profl. Psychology, Am. Bd. Clin. Neuropsychology. Staff psychologist dept. psychology and neurology McLean Hosp., Belmont, Mass., 1976-80; instr. psychology dept. psychiatry McLean Hosp. Harvard Med. Sch., Boston, 1977-88; asst. clin. prof. dept. psychiatry and behavioral scis. George Washington U., Washington, 1980—; pvt. practice psychologist Washington, 1981—; neuropsychologist NIMH, Bethesda, Md., 1985—; asst. clin. prof. psychiatry Georgetown U., Washington, 1989—; bd. dirs. Am. Acad. Bd. Cert. Psychologists. Contbr. articles to profl. jours. Recipient Lewis B. Hill award Balt. Washington Inst., Laurel, 1989. Mem. APA, Internat. Neuropsychol. Soc. (Phillip M. Rennick award 1977), Am. Psychoanalytic Assn. Home: 4331 Forest Ln NW Washington DC 20007-1137 Office: 4601 Connecticut Ave NW Ste 20 Washington DC 20008-5715

JONES, BARCLAY GIBBS, regional economics researcher; b. Camden, N.J., June 3, 1925; s. Barclay Gibbs Jones and Kathryn (Prince) Preston; m. Anne Van Syckel Tompkins, June 8, 1957; children: Barclay Gibbs, Louise Tompkins. BA, U. Pa., 1948, BArch, 1951; MRP, U. N.C., 1955, PhD, 1961. Registered architect, N.C. Community planner Citizens Coun. on City Planning, Phila., 1951; from instr. to asst. prof. Dept. City Regional planning U. Calif. at Berkeley, 1956-61; from assoc. prof. to prof. Dept. City Regional Planning Cornell U., 1961—; program dir. Cornell Inst. for Social and Econ. Rsch., 1983—; exec. com. mem. Nat. Ctr. for Earthquake Engring. Rsch., Buffalo, 1989-91, rsch. com. mem. 1991—. Editor Protecting Historic Architecture and Museum Collections from Natural Disasters, 1986; contbr. articles to profl. jours. Bd. mem. Archtl. Rsch. Ctrs. Consortium, Inc., 1980—; chair Ithaca (City) Landmarks Preservation Commn., N.Y., 1984—; pres. Historic Ithaca and Tompkins County, Inc., 1979-81, bd. mem. 1975-81; bd. mem. Nat. Preservation Inst., Inc., 1984—; with U.S. Army, 1943-46. Decorated Purple Heart; recipient Pub. Svc. award Nat. Park Svc., U.S. Dept. Interior, 1988; fellow U.S. Internat. Coun. on Monuments and Sites, 1986. Mem. AIA, AAAS, AAUP, Am. Inst. Cert. Planners, Am. Planning Assn., Am. Statis. Assn., Earthquake Engring. Rsch. Inst., Nat. Trust Historic Preservation, N.E. Regional Sci. Assn. (pres 1975-76, 87-88), Am. Econ. Assn., Regional Sci. Assn. (coun. 1976-80, pres. 1983, archivist 1984—), Soc. Archtl. Historians, Urban Regional Info. Systems Assn. (pres. 1966-69), Phi Kappa Phi. Republican. Episcopalian. Home: 502 Turner Pl Ithaca NY 14850-5630 Office: Cornell U 106 W Sibley Hall Ithaca NY 14853

JONES, BENJAMIN JOSEPH, government association executive, lawyer; b. Campbellsville, Ky., Jan. 10, 1951; s. Davis and Clara (Pyles) J.; m. Karen Greene, Aug. 24, 1974 (div. Apr. 1984); 1 child, Matthew Harper. BA, U. Ky., 1974, JD, 1979. Bar: Ky. Researcher Coun. of State Govts., Lexington, Ky., 1974-76; dir. law and justice Coun. of State Govts., Lexington, 1986-90; dir. Washington office Coun. of State Govts., Washington, 1990—; cons. Coun. of State Govts., Lexington, 1976-83; atty. pvt. practice Lexington, 1979-86; city atty. Cynthiana, Ky., 1981-83, Hazard, Ky., 1984-86; dir. Washington office Coun. of State Govts., Washington, 1990—; cons. in field. Contbr. articles to profl. jours. Grantee U.S. Dept. Transp., 1987-91, U.S. Dept. Justice, 1987-91. Republican. Office: Coun of State Govts 444 E Capitol St NW Washington DC 20001-1512

JONES, BILL, newspaper publishing executive; b. Durham, N.C., Dec. 24, 1949; s. Crawford and Lucille (Kennedy) J.; m. Grace M. Dillard, Oct. 28, 1972; children: Yolanda G., Terrance D. BS, Va. State U., 1972; MBA, U. Alaska, 1973; real estate cert., Lee Inst., New Haven, Conn., 1981. Asst. dir. Town of Milford (Conn.) Parks and Recreation, 1978-80; dir. Town of Madison (Conn.) Beaches, Park and Recreation, 1980-86; dist. circulation mgr. Newspaper, New Haven, Conn., 1986—; notary pub. State of Conn., Hartford, 1980—. Chmn. Coalition of Concerned Citizens, New Haven, 1980—; deacon United House of Prayer for All People, 1980—. Capt. U.S. Air Force, 1973-78. Mem. Masons. Home: 231 Clifton St New Haven CT 06513-3319

JONES, BRIAN JOSEPH, sociology educator; b. Phila., Aug. 3, 1950; s. Francis Joseph and Dolores Helen (Daley) J.; m. Suzanne Maria Hufnal, Aug. 18, 1972; children: Megan, Christopher. BA, MA, U. Pa., 1972, PhD, 1979. Prof. sociology Villanova (Pa.) U., 1976—. Author: Social Problems, 1988; also numerous articles. Recipient Lindback Teaching award Villanova U., 1979. Mem. Am. Sociol. Assn., Soc. for Study Social Problems, Phi Beta Kappa. Democrat. Roman Catholic. Office: Villanova U Sociology Dept Villanova PA 19085

JONES, CLYDE ADAM, art educator, artist; b. Cobleskill, N.Y., Nov. 10, 1924; s. Lester L. and Myra (Karker) J.; BFA, Syracuse U., 1948, MA, 1954; EdD, Pa. State U., 1961. Tchr. art North High Sch., Binghamton, N.Y., 1948-49, 1950-56; instr. ceramics Jr. League of Binghamton, 1950-53; guest instr. ceramics Rehab. Guild, Saranac Lake, N.Y., 1951-54; asst. prof. art edn. Edinboro (Pa.) State Coll., 1956-58; instr. Creative Arts Workshop, Cornell U., Ithaca, N.Y., summer, 1958; asst. prof. child devel. U. Conn., Storrs, 1961-66, asst. dean Sch. Home Econs. and Family Studies, 1976-79, trustee Syracuse U. Libr. Assocs., 1970, assoc. prof. human devel. and family rels., 1966—; prof. emeritus, 1985—; cons. Head Start program, Conn., 1965-66. Mem. Gov.'s Commn. on Status of Women, 1965-67; bd. dirs. Greater Mansfield Arts Coun., 1986—, mem. adv. bd., 1989—; mem. governing bd. Nat. Assn. for Creative Children and Adults, 1986—. With AUS, 1943-45. Mem. Conn. Assn. for Edn. of Young Children (v.p. 1970-72), New Eng. Assn. for Edn. of Young Children (publs. com. 1980—, editor newsletter 1963-65), Hartford Assn. for Edn. of Young Children (pres. 1967-69), Nat. Assn. for Edn. of Young Children, Soc. for Rsch. in Child Devel., Nat. Soc. for Study of Edn., Nat. Art Edn. Assn. (rsch. trainee 1965), Internat. soc. for Edn. thru Art, Assn. for Childhood Edn. Internat., Conn. Home Econs. Assn. (del., dir. 1978-82, newletter editor 1984—), Am. Home Econs. Assn., Phi Delta Kappa. One man shows: Rehab. Guild, Saranac Lake, N.Y., Windham Hosp., Willimantic, Conn., Art Bldg, Pa. State U., Student Union U. Conn.; group shows include: Roberson Meml., Binghamton, N.Y., Erie (Pa.) Art Mus., Munson-Williams-Proctor Inst., Utica, N.Y., Mus. of Fine Arts, Syracuse, Norwich (Conn.) Art Mus., Schoharie County Arts Coun., Albany Inst. of History and Art, Essex (Conn.)) Art Assn.; illustrations for history volumes of Sch. of Home Econs. and Family Studies and Sch. of Nursing, U. Conn. Home: 52 Storrs Heights Rd Storrs Mansfield CT 06268-2322 Office: U Conn Sch Family Studies Storrs CT 06268

JONES, CYNTHIA CLARKE, artist; b. Bklyn., Aug. 12, 1938; d. Arthur Ottio and Emma (Gibbs) Clarke; m. Robert H. Jones. Apr. 21, 1968 (div. Sept. 1977); 1 child, Kim Marie. Student, Bklyn. Mus., 1954-57, Art Career Sch., 1958, Hunter Coll., N.Y.C., 1963-65. One woman shows include Queens Borough Pub. Libr., Jamaica, N.Y., 1986, Baruch Coll., 1972; exhibited in group shows Queens Coun. on Arts Exhibit at Gertz Dept. Store, 1972, Queens Coll. Arts Festival, 1972, Dist. Coun. 37, First Art Exhbn., 1972, Artist Equity Group Shows Union Carbide, 1975, 77, Queensborough Community Coll. Invitational Show at Holocaust Resource Ctr., 1985, Pen and Brush, 1990, AQA Gallery, 1990, AQA at Chung Cheng Gallery at St. Johns U., 1987-90, Lowenstein Libr. Gallery Fordham U., 1989, Arlington Arts Ctr., 1991, Pursuit of Peace Ceres Gallery, 1991; designer cover Rsch. Papers Stats. Dept. Bernard M. Baruch Coll., 1973; works reprinted in Locally Speaking Local 384 newsletter. Donator work to MUSE Gallery, 1990, to Hale House Ctr., Inc.; active Women's Caucus for Art. Recipient Joseph Grumbacher Co. award, 1958, Scholastic Art award and key, 1957, Fine Arts award Queensboro Soc., 1973, Oustanding Painting award, 1973, France Lieber Meml. award Nat. Assn. Women Artists, Inc., 1992, two certs. of merit Latham Found., 1956-58; scholar Latham Found., 1958. Mem. Artists Equity Assn., Inc. N.Y., Alliance of Queens Artists, Coll. Art Assn., Queens Coun. on Arts, Ind. Arts Assn., Arlington Arts Ctr. Va., Queensboro Coll. Art Gallery (assoc.), Nat. Assn. Women Artists. Office: 11332 Mayville St Jamaica NY 11412-2410

JONES, DALE EDWIN, lawyer; b. Rahway, N.J., Oct. 22, 1948; s. Horatio Gates and Audrey Irma (Morgan) J.; m. Karen Anne Woodhall, June 19, 1971 (div. 1985); children: Sharon, Michael, Stephan; m. Maria D. Noto, Aug. 2, 1987 (div. 1989); m. Joan E. DiTullo, Oct. 18, 1991. BA, Rutgers U., 1970, JD, 1973. Bar: N.J. 1973, U.S. Dist. Ct. N.J. 1973, U.S. Supreme Ct., 1977, N.Y. 1983; cert. criminal trial atty. N.J. Supreme Ct. First asst. dep. pub. defender Office of Pub. Defender, Newark, 1974-84, dep. pub. defender in charge capital litigation, 1984-87, asst. pub. defender, 1987—; mem. model jury charge com., N.J. Supreme Ct. criminal practice com., Trenton, 1983-87—, com. media rels., 1987—. Mem. ACLU, NAACP, ACDL-N.J., Greenpeace, Nat. Assn. Criminal Def. Lawyers, Amnesty Internat. Democrat. Office: Pub Defender Office R J Hughes Justice Complex CN-850 Trenton NJ 08625

JONES, DALLAS WILLIAMS, company executive; b. Malad, Idaho, Sept. 11, 1941; s. Lester T. Jones and Lillith Ione Williams Tuck; m. Sandra Lee Schenk, July 30, 1964; children: Timothy, Melinda, Benjamin, Deborah, Michael, Brent, Jennifer. BS in Acctg., Brigham Young U., 1965; M. Bus., Washington U., 1967. Asst. to pres. Edison Bros. Stores, Inc., St. Louis, 1967-72; v.p. United Sporting Goods, L.A., 1972-77; pres., ptnr. Sabre Products, Inc., Van Nuys, Calif., 1977-80; pres. Electronic Systems Products div. Bell & Howell, 1980-81; gen. mgr. Heat Extractor Corp., St. Johnsville, N.Y., 1981-82; pres., ptnr. Zorcom Ent., Inc., Utica, N.Y., 1982-86; founde,r pres. Trim-A-Lawn Corp., Utica, N.Y., 1986—; chmn. bd. Electronic Kits Internat., Irvine, Calif., 1975—; chmn. Zorcom Ent., Inc., Utica, 1986—. Bishop Mormon Ch., Sherman Oaks, Calif., 1977-81, stake presidency (1st counselor), Syracuse, N.Y., 1983—; dist. chmn. Boy Scouts Am., Utica, 1987-89. MBA scholar award Washington U., 1967. Republican. Home: 3 White Pine Rd New Hartford NY 13413 Office: Trim-A-Lawn Corp 419 Mandeville St Utica NY 13502

JONES, DAVID GALBRAITH, psychologist; b. Newburyport, Mass., Feb. 28, 1938; s. Alvah Wesley and Barbara Louise (Galbraith) J. BA, U. Mass., Boston, 1969; AM, Boston U., 1970, PhD, 1977. Designated forensic psychologist, Mass. Psychologist Depot, Inc., Scituate, Mass., 1973-76, Coastal Community Counseling Ctr., Hingham, Mass., 1982-86, Westborough (Mass.) State Hosp., 1988—; supervising psychologist Boston City Hosp., 1974-86, Problems in Living Inst., Lynn, Mass., 1978-79; adult psychotherapist South Shore Counseling Assocs., Hanover, Mass., 1977-82; psychodiagnostician Gender Identity Svc., Boston, 1978-81; pvt. practice Hingham and Westborough, 1982—; forensic psychologist Bridgewater (Mass.) State Hosp., 1986-88. Contbr. articles to profl. jours. With USN, 1955-65. NIMH fellow, 1972. Mem. APA, AAAS, Philological Soc. London. Office: Westborough State Hosp Lyman St Westborough MA 01581-1419

JONES, DEREK CHARLES, economics educator; b. Middlesbrough, Yorkshire, Eng., June 7, 1946; s. David Charles Jones and Mary Gent; m. Carole Marshall Gilmartin, Nov. 23, 1973; children: Christopher, Trevor. MSc with distinction, London Sch. Econs., 1969; BA with 1st class honours, Newcastle-upon-Tyne (Eng.) U., 1968; MA, Cornell U., 1970, PhD, 1974. Instr. Cornell U., Ithaca, N.Y., 1971; instr. econs. Hamilton Coll., Clinton, N.Y., 1972-73, asst. prof., 1973-78, assoc. prof., 1978-84, prof., 1984—, chmn. dept., 1978-83, 87—; assoc. fellow program on participation and labor mgmt. Cornell U., 1978—, James L. Ferguson prof., 1987—; vis. fellow European U. Inst., Warwick, Eng., 1983, Florence, Italy, 1984, Arbetslivcentrum Stockholm, 1988, 90; vis. fellow Sofia U., 1989, 90 ; rsch. fellow Warwick U., 1976-77, Manchester (Eng.) U., 1984-85; U.K. corr. Econ. Analysis and Workers' Mgmt., 1975-78; Am. corr. Econ. Analysis and Workers' Mgmt., 1978—, Economia Publica, 1986—; organizer colloquia and confs.; presenter in field at over 40 instns.; cons. World Bank, 1984-86, Brookings Instn., 1989, Internat. Labor Orgn., also others. Editor: (with Jan Svejnar) Participatory and Self-Managed Firms, 1982; co-series editor Advances in the Economic Analysis of Participatory and Labor Mannaged Firms, Vol. 1, 1985, Vol. 2, 1987, Vol. 3, 1988, Vol. 4, 1992; bd. editors Econ. Analysis and Workers' Mgmt., 1985—, Econ. and Indsl. Democracy, 1987-90, 90—; referee profl. jours.; contbr. numerous articles and book revs. to profl. jours., chpts. to books. Grantee NSF, 1983-86, 87-90, 91—, Leverhulme Found., 1980-82, Arbetsmiljfonden, 1990-91, others; Hallsworth fellow, 1984-85, German Marshall Fund rsch. fellow, 1983, other fellowships. Mem. AAUP (faculty compensation com. Hamilton chpt. 1978-80, chmn. 1978-80). Democrat. Home: RR 4 Box 394 Clinton NY 13323-9349 Office: Hamilton Coll Dept Econs Clinton NY 13323

JONES, DIONNE JUANITA, educational administrator, researcher, consultant; b. Georgetown, Guyana, Sept. 14, 1945; came to U.S., 1970; d. Henry Hamilton and Beryl Marjorie (Williams) J.; children—Marcus Anthony, Dustin Troy, Dayton Lance. B.S. Howard U., 1974, M.S.W., 1976, PhD, 1987. Cert. tchr., Washington. Lectr., Putney Coll., London, 1968-70; instr. Walter Reed Med. Ctr., Washington, 1971-73; research assoc. Mental Health Ctr., Washington, 1976-78; publ. specialist Inst. Urban Affairs, Washington, 1978-79; research cons. M.Battle Assocs. and L.S.C., Washington, 1979-81; coordinator edn. and tng. Howard U. Hosp., Washington, 1982-84, sr. research assoc., Nat. Urban League, 1986—, adj. prof., Howard U., 1988—. Co-author: Higher Education and High Risk Students: Future Trends, 1990; author (with others) Mental Health: A Challenge to the Black Community, 1978; editor: Teenage Pregnancy: Developing Strategies for Change in the 21st Century, 1989, Prescriptions and Policies: The Social Well-being of African Americans in the 1990s, 1990; assoc. editor Black Caucus Jour., 1977-79, The Urban League Rev., 1986-88; editor Urban Research Rev., 1977-79, The Urban League Rev., 1988—. Mem. adv. bd. dirs. St. Gabriel's Ch., Washington, 1977-78, tchr. Sunday Sch., 1977-79; mem. Ladies Guild, Trinity Episcopal Ch., Washington; speaker area high schs., Washington, 1978-79; mem. parents adv. com. YMCA, Washington, 1989—. Mem. Am. Ednl. Rsch. Assn., Am. Psychol. Assn., Am. Evaluation Assn. (editorial bd.), Ea. Evaluation Rsch. Assn. (exec. bd.), Assn. Social and Behavioral Scientists (mem. editorial bd., exec. com.), Phi Beta Kappa. Democrat. Home: 705 Hillsboro Dr Silver Spring MD 20902-3218 Office: Nat Urban League 1111 14th St NW Ste 600 Washington DC 20005-5699

JONES, E. STEWART, JR., lawyer; b. Troy, N.Y., Dec. 4, 1941; s. E. Stewart and Louise (Farley) J.; m. Constance M., Dec. 28, 1968; children: Christopher, Brady, Erin. BA, Williams Coll., 1963; JD, Albany Law Sch., 1966. Bar: N.Y. 1966, U.S. Dist. Ct. (no. dist.) N.Y. 1966, U.S. Supreme Ct. 1970, U.S. Ct. Appeals (2d cir.) 1976, U.S. Dist. Ct. (we. dist.) N.Y. 1987, U.S. Claims Ct. 1991; cert. specialist in civil and criminal trial advocacy. Asst. dist. atty. Rensselaer County (N.Y.), 1968-70, spl. prosecutor, 1974; ptnr. E. Stewart Jones, Troy, 1974—; lectr. in field; mem. com. on profl. standards of 3d jud. dept. State of N.Y., 1977-80, mem. 3d jud. screening com., Albany county; mem. merit selection panel for selection and ppointment of U.S. magistrate for No. Dist. N.Y., 1981, 91; bd. dirs. The Univ. Found. at Albany, trustee Troy Savs. Bank. Contbr. numerous articles to profl. jours. Bd. trustees The Albany Acad., Albany Law Sch.; active Nat. Alumni Coun. Albany Law Sch.; mem. N.Y. State Jud. Screening Com. Albany County. With USNG. Fellow Am. Bar Found., Am. Inns Ct., Internat. Acad. Trial Lawyers, Am. Bd. Criminal Trial Lawyers, Am. Coll. Trial Lawyers, Inner Circle of Advs., Roscoe Pound Assn., Am. Bd. Profl. Liability Attys. (diplomate); mem. N.Y. State Bar Assn. (Outstanding Practitioner award 1980, mem. continuing edn. com. 1977-78, mem. exec. com. of criminal justice sect. 1977-90, mem. exec. com. trial lawyers sect. 1981—, mem. spl. com. med. malpractice, other coms.), N.Y. State Trial Lawyers Assn. (bd. dirs. 1982-91, dir. emeritus 1991), Capital Dist. Trial Lawyers Assn. (bd. dir. 1973-76), ABA (numerous coms.) Calif. Attys. for Criminal Justice, Practising Law Inst., Am. Judicature Soc. (sustaining), Rensselaer County Bar Assn., Am. Soc. Law and Medicine, ACLU, N.Y. Civil Liberties Union, Lawyer to Lawyer Consultation (panel), Albany County Bar Assn.,

N.Y. State Defenders Assn., Am. Arbitration Assn. (nat. panel of arbitrators), Dispute Resolutions, Inc. (nat. panel of arbitrators), Fed. Bar Coun., Upstate Trial Attys. Assn., Inc., Nat. Bd. Trial Advocacy (diplomate), Nat. Assn. Criminal Def. Lawyers, N.Y. State Assn. Criminal Def. Lawyers, Am. Bd. Trial Advocates (advocate), Inst. for Injury Reduction (founder), Trial Lawyers for Pub. Justice (founder), Civil Justice Found. (founding sponsor), Schuyler Meadows Club, Troy Country Club, Troy Club, Steuben Athletic Club, Ft. Orange Club, Wychmere Harbor Club, Stone Horse Yacht Club (Harwich Port, Mass.), Equinox Country Club (Manchester, Vt.), Williams Club (N.Y.C.). Home: 46 Schuyler Rd Albany NY 12211-1447 Office: 28 2d St Troy NY 12181

JONES, EDWARD ALLEN, manufacturing engineer; b. Piqua, Ohio, Nov. 28, 1946; s. Thomas Loya and Bessie Faith (Coffman) J.; m. Angeliki Athanasiou, Oct. 4, 1969; children: Faith H., Thomas A. BSME, Union Coll., 1978, postgrad., 1985—. Toolmaker GE, Schenectady, N.Y., 1970-74; foreman GE, Schenectady, 1974-75, instr., 1976-78, project engr., 1978-84, mfg. engr., 1984—; exec. officer Advance Base Functional Component, Albany, 1988—; cons. to GE. Author: Reactor Equipment Cost Estimating Manual, 1989. Co-provider Family Care Home for Adults, Schenectady, 1972—. With USN, 1966-70. Mem. Soc. Mfg. Engrs., Naval Enlisted Res. Assn. (v.p. 1984-85), GE Apprentice Alumni Assn. Eastern Orthodox Ch. Office: GE 600 Liberty St Schenectady NY 12305-2160

JONES, ELIN DENISE, public relations professional, writer; b. Orangeburg, S.C., Oct. 25, 1955; d. Oscar Jr. and Johnsie Elizabeth (Jefferson) J. BS in English and Biology, Mary Washington Coll., 1977; MS in Pub. Rels. Adminstrn., Am. U., 1979. Pub. rels. cons. Flair Internat., Washington, 1980-83; fashion editor Washington Living Mag., Washington, 1983-87; head pub. info. office D.C. Pub. Libr., Washington, 1985-88; chief of community affairs D.C. Dept. of Corrections, Washington, 1988-91; columnist Washington View Mag., 1989-91. Editor newsletter Whats up D.O.C., 1988—; contbr. articles to profl. jours., mags. including People, Essence and The Washington Post. Mem. Internat. Tng. Communications (1st v.p. 1989), Am. Correctional Assn., Toastmasters (pres. 1989, treas. 1989). Roman Catholic.

JONES, FRANCIS THOMAS, chemistry educator; b. Pottsville, Pa., Oct. 19, 1933; s. Francis Thomas and Marion Amelia (Kagel) J.; m. Nuran, Jan. 3, 1981; children: Anne Celal, Marian Frances. BS, Pa. State U., 1955; PhD, Poly. Inst. Bklyn., 1960; M.Engring., Stevens Inst. Tech., 1975. Postdoctoral GEC fellow The Univ., Cookridge Labs., Leeds, Eng., 1960-62; faculty participant Oak Ridge (Tenn.) Nat. Lab., 1965; rsch. scientist Union Carbide Nuclear Co., Tuxedo, N.Y., 1962-64; from asst. to prof. Stevens Inst. Tech., Hoboken, N.J., 1964-71, dept. head chemistry and chem. engring., 1979-90, prof. chemistry, 1971—; faculty sec. Stevens Inst. Tech., 1971-79. Contbr. articles to profl. jours.; inventor in field. Organist, choir dir. Trinity Episcopal Ch., Cliffside Park, N.J., 1990—. Recipient Trinity award Episcopal Ch., 1991. Mem. Am. Chem. Soc. Home: 692 Stewart St Ridgefield NJ 07657-1915 Office: Stevens Inst Tech Castle Point on the Hudson Hoboken NJ 07030

JONES, FRED RICHARD, financial executive; b. Springfield, Mo., Nov. 7, 1947; s. Gene Butler and Florence Edith (Hardin) Jones; m. Nancy Elizabeth Albers, July 15, 1978; children: Elizabeth Hardin, Peter Albers, Gregory Wood. BS in Computer Sci., U. Mo., Rolla, 1969; MBA in Fin., Stanford U., 1973. Systems analyst Chemagro Corp., Kansas City, Mo., 1969-71; asst. v.p. 1st Nat. Bank of Chgo., 1973-78; v.p. leasing CMI Corp., Troy, Mich., 1978-79; asst. treas. Penn Cen. Corp., N.Y.C., 1979-84; dir. treas. fin. svcs. Combustion Engring., Inc., Stamford, Conn., 1984-85, asst. treas., 1985-86, treas., 1986-89, v.p., treas., 1989-90; pres. ABB Fin. Svcs. Inc., Stamford, 1990-92; sr. v.p., CFO Joy Technologies, Pitts., 1992—; mem. adv. bd. Allendale Ins., Providence, 1989-82. Bd. dirs. Sr. Ctrs. of Met. Chgo., 1974-76; mem. stewardship com. Noroton Presbyn. Ch., Darien, Conn., 1989-91, elder, 1990-92. Mem. Nat. Assn. Corp. Treas., Fairchester Treas. Group (pres. 1989-91), Fin. Execs. Inst. (corp. fin. com.), Lake Club (New Canaan, Conn.), Sprite Island Yacht Club (Norwalk, Conn.). Republican. Presbyterian. Home: 620 Pine Rd Sewickley PA 15143 Office: Joy Techs Inc 301 Grant St Pittsburgh PA 15219-1490

JONES, GENE STANLEY, special events producer, casting specialist; b. N.Y.C., May 17, 1951; s. Stanley L. and Gladys Jones. BA with honors, U. Mich., 1972. TV sportcaster Channel 3, Mich., 1973-75; producer commls. Sta. WIQB-FM, Ann Arbor, 1975-78; stage entertainer A&A Prodns., 1974-80; talent coord. Variety Arts Ctr., Los Angeles, 1978-80; pres. Internat. Jugglers Assn., N.Y.C. and L.A., 1980-83; creative dir. Royal Entertainment, N.Y.C., 1983—, pres., 1986—; ofcl. judge Guinness Book World Records, N.Y.C., 1991—, assoc. editor, 1986—; dir. Mime/Jugglers Network, N.Y.C., 1984—; exec. producer Corporate Theatrics. 1991—. Author: (poetry) I Hate To Read Book, 1975, Sunday's Mail, 1988; contbg. author: The Book of Sports Lists, 1981, 2d edit., 1984; contbg. editor Guinness Book of Sports Records; contbr. articles to Jugglers World mag.; assoc. producer The Silent Treatment, N.Y.C., 1987. Mich. Council for Arts research grantee, 1978. Mem. Screen Actors Guild, Am. Fedn. TV and Radio Artists, Internat. Jugglers Assn. (hon. bd. dirs. 1983-84), Internat. Spl. Events Soc., Internat. Soc. Meeting Planners. Democrat. Office: Royal Entertainment PO Box 383 New York NY 10040-0383

JONES, GEORGE BRYAN, psychologist; b. Scotia, Calif., June 8, 1947; s. George Bryan and Jennie Mildred (Wise) J.; m. Cynthia Louise Chester, Aug. 14, 1976; children: Carrie Beth, Christian Bryan. BS, Pa. State U., 1969; MA, Temple U., 1976, MEd, 1986, PhD, 1987. Lic. psychologist, Pa. Faculty mem. dept. psychiatry Med. Coll. Pa., Phila., 1988-89; commd. lt. comdr. USPHS, 1990—; adj. faculty Dept. Counseling Psychology Temple U., Phila., 1987-89; cons. spl. projects Naval Mil. Pers. Command, Washington, 1982-90; governing bd. mem. Intercommunity Action, Inc., Cmmunity Mental Health/Mental Retardation Ctr., Phila., 1985-90. Coun. mem. Epiphany Luth. Ch., Phila., 1985-90. Comdr. USNR, 1969-90. Mem. AACD, Am. Psychol. Assn. (assoc.), Pa. Psychol. Assn. (assoc.), Naval Res. Assn., Assn. Mil. Surgeons of the U.S., Res. Officer Assn., Commd. Officer Assn. of USPHS. Republican. Home: 264 Fountain St Philadelphia PA 19128-4508 Office: NIMH USPHS 5600 Fishers Ln Rockville MD 20857-0001

JONES, HOWARD WILLIAM, marketing administrator; b. Chgo., July 19, 1935; s. William Robert and Mary Elizabeth (Hills) J.; m. Arlene Adella Farnham, Aug. 3, 1957; children: Jeffrey Randall, Steven Earl, Christopher William, Marjorie Lynn. BSME, Ariz. State U., 1959. Engr., quality/process control GE Co., Schenectady, N.Y., 1959-62; engr., systems devel. Airesearch Mfg. Co., Phoenix, 1962-67; engr., applications/sales Caterpillar, Phoenix, 1967-71, Piscataway, N.J., 1971-77; mgr. project engring. Cummins Cogeneration Co., N.Y.C., 1977-80; product mgr. Sundstrand Corp., Rockford, Ill., 1980-89; mktg. mgr. Mechanical Tech. Inc., Latham, N.Y., 1989—. Chmn. Raritan Twp. Mcpl. Utility Authority, Flemington, N.J., 1979-80; v.p. Tempe Jaycees, Ariz., 1963-64. Mem. AIAA, Soc. Automotive Engrs. (met. sec. chmn. 1978-79, sect. bd. dirs. 1979-82). Home: 2 Timberland Dr East Greenbush NY 12061-9700

JONES, HUGH ALAN, lawyer; b. Danville, Pa., July 22, 1950; s. John B. and Dorothy (Kessler) J.; m. Alessandra M. Chango, May 29, 1982. BA, U. Pa., 1972; JD, Widener U., 1990. Bar: Pa. 1990. Chief clk. Northumberland County, Sunbury, Pa., 1979-80; dist. adminstr. Pa. Dept. Revenue, Sunbury, 1980-89; legal intern Pa. Office Atty. Gen., Norristown, 1989-90; assoc. Carpenter, Diehl, Kivko & Wilkison, Sunbury, 1991—. Mem. Rep. State Com. Pa., Harrisburg, 1979-92; trustee Mt. Carmel (Pa.) Pub. Libr., 1981—, pres., 1991—; sec. Northumberland County Hist. Soc., 1980-86. Mem. ABA, Pa. Bar Assn., Northumberland County Bar Assn., Masons, Lions. Episcopalian. Home: 216 S Hickory St Mount Carmel PA 17851-0301 Office: Carpenter Diehl & Kivko 1070 Market St Sunbury PA 17801-0743

JONES, JAMES R., former congressman, lawyer; b. Muskogee, Okla., May 5, 1939; m. Olivia Barclay, 1968; children—Geoffrey Gardner, Adam Winston. A.B. in Journalism and Govt, U. Okla., 1961; LL.B., Georgetown U., 1964. Bar: Okla. 1964, D.C. 1964. Legis. asst. to Congressman Ed Edmondson, 1961-64; spl. asst. to Pres. Lyndon Johnson, 1965-69; mem. 93d-99th congresses from 1st Dist. Okla., 1973-87; chmn. budget com. 97th and 98th Congress; chmn. social security subcom. 99th Congress; ptnr. Dickstein, Shapiro & Morin, Washington, 1987-89; chmn. bd., chief exec. officer Am. Stock Exch., N.Y.C., 1989—; mem. adv. coun. on Social Security. Chmn. Am. Bus. Conf. Served as capt. CIC AUS, 1964-65. Mem. Okla. Bar Assn., D.C. Bar Assn., Am. Legion, Tulsa C. of C. Democrat. Club: Rotarian. Home: 544 E 86th St New York NY 10028-7536 Office: Am Stock Exch 86 Trinity Pl New York NY 10006-1818

JONES, JAMES THOMAS, JR., tobacco company executive; b. Beverly Manor, Va., June 14, 1946; s. James Thomas and Irene Celestine (Baldwin) J.; m. Vionia Ann Fisher, July 5, 1966; children: James T. III, Vionia Jr., Veronica. Field sales rep. R.J. Reynolds Tobacco Co., Camden, N.J., 1973-76; asst. div. mgr. R.J. Reynolds Tobacco Co., Phila., 1976-80; div. mgr. R.J. Reynolds Tobacco Co., Newark, 1980-84; regional tng. and devel. mgr. R.J. Reynolds Tobacco Co., N.Y.C., 1984-88; nat. trade rels. mgr., minority markets R.J. Reynolds Tobacco Co., Winston-Salem, N.C., 1988-90; chain accounts mgr. R.J. Reynolds Tobacco Co., Edison, N.J., 1990—; cons., Sioux IndianTribe, Marty, S.D., 1989—. Mem. Internat. Platform Assn., S.C. Legis. Black Caucus, S.C. Legis. Corp. Roundtable. Republican. Baptist. Home: 80 Highland Ridge Rd Freehold NJ 07728-8288 Office: RJ Reynolds Tobacco Co 400 Raritan Center Pky Raritan Ctr Edison NJ 08837

JONES, JANET MARIE, mental health professional; b. Balt., Oct. 25, 1958; d. Clinton and Phyllis Jean (Dillard) J. BA in Psychology, U. Md., 1980; MA in Clin. Psychology, Towson State U., 1983. Cert. profl. counselor; cert. community support specialist. Mental health technician NIMH, Bethesda, Md., 1984-85; mental health counselor II Liberty Community Mental Health Ctr., Balt., 1986-87; case mgr. specialized case mgmt. program Balt. Mental Health Systems, 1988-90, asst. program dir., clin. supr., 1990—. Mem. AACD, Md. State Bd. Profl. Counselors. Office: Specialized Case Mgmt 2523 Gwynns Falls Pky Baltimore MD 21216

JONES, JEAN ELIZABETH MAKINI, mediator, educator, toll collector; b. N.Y.C., Feb. 7, 1959; d. Benjamin DeWitt and Eara Jean (Reynolds) J.; (widowed); children: Rael-Robert Carlyle, Avery-Robert Amon. AB in Psychology, Douglass Coll., 1975; cert. in mgmt., SUNY, Albany, 1988. Cert. tchr., N.Y. Counselor U. Settlement House, N.Y.C., 1969-71; mgr. Neilson Dining Svcs., New Brunswick, N.J., 1972-75; program dir. YWCA, Rochester, N.Y., 1975-76, dir. city programs, 1976-77; educator Urban League, Rochester, 1977-78; mediator Am. Arbitration Assn., Rochester and N.Y.C., 1978—; tchr. N.Y.C. Bd. of Edn., 1979-81; mgr. St. Christophers Homes, L.I., 1984; toll collector N.Y. State Thruway Authority, Albany, 1984—; tchr. poetry Poets in Pub. Svc., N.Y.C., 1991—. Author: Travelin on Faith/Travelin on Credit, 1982, Veiled Truths: No Resume at My Funeral, 1992; editor poetry Shooting Star Rev., 1985. Mem. Harlem Writer's Guild. Office: English Eloquence Opt Opp PO Box 23144 Hollis NY 11423

JONES, JENNIFER CAROLYN, research psychologist; b. Northampton, Mass., Apr. 9, 1961; d. Owen Craven and Beverly Jean (Schmidt) J. Student, U. Mass., 1979-80; BA with honors, SUNY, Stony Brook, 1984; PhD, SUNY, Albany, 1990. Asst. prof. dept. psychiatry U. Pa., Phila., 1990—; workshop leader Dept. Vets. Affairs, Coco Beach, Fla., 1990; statis. cons., clin. cons. U. Ark. for Med. Scis., Little Rock, 1991. Co-editor column The Behavior Therapist, 1990—; contbr. articles to profl. jours. Mem. APA (div. 12), Assn. for Advancement Behavior Therapy. Democrat. Office: Ctr Psychotherapy Rsch 3600 Market St Philadelphia PA 19104

JONES, JOSEPH HAYWARD, lawyer; b. Shamokin, Pa., July 9, 1924; s. Joseph H. and Anna Elizabeth (Lippiatt) J.; m. Grace Loretta Hicks, Mar. 17, 1951; children: Elizabeth Christie, Joseph H. Jr., Gregory H. BA, Ursinus Coll., 1947, LLD (hon.), 1987; JD, Dickinson Sch. Law, Carlisle, Pa., 1950; LLM, NYU, 1954. Bar: Pa. 1950, U.S. Supreme Ct. 1959. Ptnr. Williamson, Friedberg & Jones, Pottsville, Pa., 1950—; bd. dirs. Meridian Bancorp, Meridian Bank, Meridian Asset Mgmt., Inc., St. Jude Polymer Corp.; mem. Pa. Judicial Reform Commn., 1987. Past pres. Appalachian Trail coun. Boy Scouts Am., Hawk Mountain coun. Boy Scouts Am.; sec., past pres. Schuylkill Econ. Devel. Corp.; pres. Pottsville Area Devel. Corp., 1986; bd. dirs. Salvation Army, Pa. Lawyers Trust Account Bd., 1989—. Lt. (j.g.) USN, 1942-45, PTO. Recipient Silver Beaver award Boy Scouts Am., Disting. Citizen award Pa. State U., Schuylkill, 1987, Citizen of Yr. award St. David's Soc. Schuylkill and Carbon Counties; named Young Man of Yr., Pottsville Area Jaycees, Vol. of Yr., So. Schuylkill United Fund, 1972. Mem. Pa. Bar Assn. (pres. 1987-88, chmn. task force legal svcs. to poor), Pa. Bar Found. (pres.), Masons (33 deg.), Lions (past pres.). Home: 2100 Mahantongo St Pottsville PA 17901-3112 Office: Williamson Friedberg & Jones One Norwegian Pla Pottsville PA 17901

JONES, LARRY MARTIN, surgeon; b. Marion, Ind., July 5, 1952; s. Norman Harvey and helen Louise (Stanley) J.; m. Donna Suzanne Leddy, June 10, 1979; children: Erin Beth, Ashley Brooke, Adam Michael. AB in Zoology, Ind. U., 1974, MD, 1977. Diplomate Am. Bd. Surgery. Intern Miami Valley Hosp., Dayton, 1977-78, resident in gen. surgery, 1978-82; gen. surgeon R.K Finley Jr. & S.F. Miller MD's Inc., Dayton, 1982-87; dir. trauma ctr. The Mercy Hosp. Pitts., Pitts., 1987—, dir. burn unit, 1991—. Author (book chpt.) Clinical Medicine, 1988; contbr. articles to profl. jours. Fellow ACS; mem. ACP Execs., Am. Trauma Soc., Washington County Med. Soc., Ea. Assn. for the Surgery of Trauma, Pa. Soc. of Critical Care Medicine, Pa. State Med. Assn., Internat. Coll. Surgeons, Am. Acad. Med. Dirs., Pitts. Surg. Soc. Home: 117 Old Oak Rd McMurray PA 15317 Office: The Mercy Hosp of Pitts 1400 Locust St Pittsburgh PA 15219

JONES, LAURA ELLEN, trade association executive, consultant; b. Bklyn., Nov. 24, 1944; d. Louis and Eva (Kushner) J. BA, CUNY, 1966. Sec. to bd. Soc. Plastics, N.Y.C., 1970-77; program dir. Am. Assn. Exporters and Importers, N.Y.C., 1978-86; dep. dir. Internat. Footwear Assn., N.Y.C., 1986-89; exec. dir. U.S. Assn. Importers Textile and Apparel, N.Y.C., 1989—; mem. industry trade adv. com. Fashion Inst. Tech., N.Y.C., 1991—. Recipient achievement award Fashion Inst. Tech., 1991. Mem. Women in Internat. Trade (pres. N.Y.C. chpt. 1988-90), Orgn. Women in Internat. Trade (nat. sec. 1990—). Office: US Assn Importers Textiles and Apparel 17 W 17th St New York NY 10011-5510

JONES, LAURIE LYNN, magazine editor; b. Kerrville, Tex., Sept. 2, 1947; d. Charles Clinton and Jean Laurie (Davidson) J.; m. C. Frederick Childs, June 26, 1976; children: Charles Newell (Clancy), Cyrus Trevor; 1 stepchild, Ariel Childs. B.A., U. Tex., 1969. Asst. to dir. coll. admissions Columbia U., N.Y.C., 1969-70; asst. to dir. Office Alumni-Columbia U., N.Y.C., 1970-71; asst. advt. mgr. Book World, 1971-72, Washington Post-Chgo. Tribune, 1971-72; editorial asst. N.Y. Mag., N.Y.C., 1972-74, asst. editor, 1974, sr. editor, 1974-76, mng. editor, 1976—. Mem. Am. Soc. Mag. Editors, Women in Coummunication, Advt. Women N.Y. Republican. Methodist. Home: 40 Great Jones St New York NY 10012-1115 also: 62 Giles Hill Rd Redding Ridge CT 06876 Office: NY Mag 755 2d Ave New York NY 10017-5906

JONES, LAWRENCE TUNNICLIFFE, lawyer; b. Mineola, N.Y., Jan. 20, 1950; s. Carroll Hudson Tunnicliffe and Florence Virginia (Greene) J. BA, U. Va., 1972; JD, U. Richmond, 1975. Bar: Va. 1975, D.C. 1976, N.Y. 1976, U.S. Dist. Ct. (ea. and so. dist.) N.Y. 1976, U.S. Supreme Ct. 1986. Bus. mgr. law review U. Richmond, Va., 1974-75; ptnr. Carroll Hudson Tunnicliffe Jones and Lawrence Tunnicliffe Jones Attys. at law, Mineola, 1976—. Trustee Nassau County Hist. Soc., 1976—, pres., 1983-89; bd. dirs. Friends of Hist. St. George's Ch., Hempstead, N.Y., 1982—, v.p., 1990-92, pres., 1992—; bd. dirs. St. Mary's Devel. Fund, Garden City, N.Y., 1983-89, pres., 1987-89; pres. coun. Cathedral Sch. St. Paul Alumni Fund, Inc., Garden City, 1984—; bd. govs. Cathedral Sch. St. Mary, Garden City, 1983-86. Mem. ABA, Va. State Bar Assn., N.Y. State Bar Assn., Nassau County Bar Assn., Nassau County Tax and Estate Planning Coun., Univ. Club (N.Y.C.), Univ. Club (L.I., pres. 1986-87, bd. dirs. 1983-86, 89—), Garden City Golf Club, Mineola-Garden City Rotary (dir. 1991—). Episcopalian. Home: 158 Cathedral Ave Hempstead NY 11550-1140 Office: Jones & Jones 286 Old Country Rd Mineola NY 11501-4108

JONES, LEON, lawyer, educator; b. Vincent, Ark., Dec. 26, 1936; s. Lander Corbin and Una Bell (Lewis) J.; m. Bobbie Jean Washington, Dec. 23, 1965 (div. Dec. 1986); children: Stephanie Ruth, Gloria Jean. BS, U. Ark., Pine Bluff, 1963; EdD, U. Mass., 1971; JD, Cath. U. Am., 1981; PhD in Alternative Medicine (hon.), Colombo (Sri Lanka) Gen. Hosp., 1986. Bar: Pa. 1985, D.C. 1986, U.S. Dist. Ct. D.C. 1986, U.S. Ct. Appeals (D.C. cir. ct.) 1986. Lectr. sch. edn. U. Mass., Amherst, 1969-70, asst. dir. Nat. Leadership Tng. Inst., 1970-71; coord. rsch. and evaluation Gov.'s State U., Park Forest South, Ill., 1971-72, acting assoc. dean coll. human learning and devel., 1972; asst. to v.p. acad. affairs Howard U., Washington, 1972-74, dir. Sch. Edn.'s ctr. for rsch. and devel., 1974-76, prof. Sch. Edn., 1973—; mem. office of majority whip U.S. Ho. Reps., Washington, 1974—; pvt. practice law Washington, 1986—; proposal reader U.S. Dept. Edn., Washington, 1985-86; rsch. bd. advisors The Am. Biog. Inst., Raleigh, N.C., 1984-88; speaker in field. Author: From Brown to Boston: Desegregation in Education 1954-74, 1979; contbr. articles to profl. jours. Mem-at-large Howard U. faculty Senate, 1990—, mem. rules com., 1990, chmn. faculty Senate's promotion and tenure com., 1988-90, edn. appt. promotions and tenure com., 1991—. Rsch. grantee Ford Found., N.Y.C., 1976. Mem. ABA, AAUP, ACLU, Bar Assn. D.C., Assn. Trial Lawyers Am., Nat. Inst. Trial Advocacy, Phi Kappa Phi. Mem. Baha'i Faith. Home: 917 Snure Rd Silver Spring MD 20901-1028

JONES, LORNA D., mental health administrator; b. Boston, Dec. 23, 1947; d. William Mattox and Myrtle Jane (Webb) Alston; m. Benjamin E. Jones, Aug. 7, 1976; 1 child, Kiah Shani. BA, U Mass., 1969; MEd, Northeastern U., 1972. Med. case worker dept. health and hosps. Boston City Hosp. Emergency Svcs., 1969-73, exec. officer, adminstrv. asst., 1973-77; pres. Boston Youth Motivation, Inc., 1973-75; adminstrv. asst. dept. nursing Mass. Rehab. Hosp., Boston, 1977-78; coord./community support prog. Brockton (Mass.) Area Multi-Svcs., Inc., 1978-80; dir. rehab. svc. unit Dorchester (Mass.) Counseling Ctr., 1980-81, asst. dir., 1981-82, pres., chief exec. officer, 1982—. Trustee Mental Health Corps. of Mass.; adv. bd. Dorchester Substance Abuse Tng. Project; bd. dirs. Mass. Coun. Human Svc. Providers; adv. com. United Way of Mass. Bay; mem. Northeast Children's Mental Health Task Force, Nat. Forum for Black Pub. Adminstrs., others. Mem. Women in Politics, 100 Black Women (Boston chpt.). Office: Dorchester Counseling Ctr 622 Washington St Dorchester MA 02124

JONES, LOWELL ROBERT, safety and industrial hygiene consultant; b. Hazleton, Pa., Mar. 18, 1931; s. Robert Franklin and Aleath Louise (Fritz) J.; m. Joanne Marie Iorio, Aug. 4, 1961; children: Deborah Lee, Robert Lowell, John G. Lally. AS, Harrisburg (Pa.) Area Coll., 1981. Assessor Luzerne County Commrs., Wilkes-Barre, Pa., 1950-56; weighmaster Honeybrook Mines, Inc., Hazleton, 1956-60; dispatcher Capitol Trailways, Harrisburg, 1960-68; safety dir. Hempt Bros., Inc., Camp Hill, Pa., 1968-78, York (Pa.) Stone & Supply Co., 1978-80; dir. safety and indsl. hygiene High Industries, Inc., Lancaster, Pa., 1980—; substance abuse cons. High Industries, Inc., 1985—. Mem. Internat. Loss Control Mgmt. (master), Internat. Loss Control Hazardous Waster Mgrs. (sr.), Am. Soc. Safety Engrs. (pres. 1979-80), Am. Indsl. Hygiene Assn., Lancaster Safety Coun. (pres. 1985-86, 88-89), Indian River Yacht Club, Lehigh Valley Cub, Masons. Republican. Home: 21 Valleybrook Dr Lancaster PA 17601-4612 Office: High Industries Inc 1853 William Penn Way 10008 Lancaster PA 17605-0008

JONES, MARK LOGAN, education association executive, educator; b. Provo, Utah, Dec. 16, 1950; s. Edward Evans and Doris (Logan) J. BS, Ea. Mont. Coll., 1975; postgrad. in labor relati, Cornell U.; postgrad., SUNY, Buffalo. Narcotics detective Yellowstone County Sheriff's Dept., Billings, Mont., 1972-74; math tchr. Billings (Mont.) Pub. Schs., 1975-87; rep. Nat. Edn. Assn. of N.Y., Buffalo, Jamestown, 1987-91, Nat. Edn. Assn. Alaska, Anchorage, 1991—. Photographs featured in 1991 N.Y. Art Rev. and Am. Artist. Committeeman Yellowstone Dem. Party, Billings, 1984-87; exec. com. Dem. Cen. Com., Billings, 1985-87; bd. dirs. Billings Community Ctr., 1975-87; concert chmn. Billings Community Concert Assn., 1980-87; bd. dirs. Chautauqua County Arts Coun. With U.S. Army, 1970-72. Recipient Distinguished Svc. award, Billins Edn. Assn., 1985, Mont. Edn. Assn., 1987. Mem. Billings Edn. Assn. (bd. dirs. 1980-82, negotiator 1981-87, pres. 1982-87), Mont. Edn. Assn. (bd. dirs. 1982-87), Ea. Mont. Coll. Tchr. Edn. Project, Accreditation Reviewer Team Mont. Office Pub. Edn., Big Sky Orchard, Masonic, Scottish Rite. Home: PO Box 102904 Anchorage AK 99510-2904 Office: Nat Edn Assn Alaska 1411 W 33d Ave Anchorage AK

JONES, MERRIS LEE, JR., computer consultant; b. Newark, Del., Aug. 17, 1964; s. Merris Lee and Louise (Stanley) J. BA, Rutgers U., 1987; MS, Drexel U., 1992. Computer cons. Amtrak, Washington, 1976-78; computer staff Rutgers U., New Brunswick, N.J., 1983-84; computer operator Chase Manhattan Bank, Wilmington, Del., 1987-89; teaching asst. U. Del., Newark, 1989-90, grad. fellow, 1990-91; software engr. Jones Labs., Newark, 1989-91; computer cons. Integrated Sci. Technologies, Newark. Mem. IEEE, Am. Math. Soc., Am. Computer Soc., Alpha Phi Omega. Home: 3 Glen Ridge Ave Salem NJ 08079-1804

JONES, MOLLY MUFICH, labor relations and training consultant; b. Helena, Mont., Aug. 13, 1949; d. William Peter and Thelma A. (Tomcheck) Mufich; m. Lawrence T. Jones, June 25, 1977 (div. May, 1987). BA, U. Mont., 1971; MEd, Boston U., 1977. Office mgr. Harvard Law Sch., Cambridge, Mass., 1971-77; dir. inst. rels. Am. Productivity Ctr., Houston, 1979-82; program mgr. John Gray Inst., Beaumont, Tex., 1982-85; dir. human resources Ceramicus, Phila., 1985-86; ptnr. Accord Assocs., Phila., 1986—; mem. Prevailing Wage Bd. for Gov. Pa., Harrisburg, 1980-90. Mem. ASTD (exec. bd. mem. Quality Work Life/Employee Involvement network), LWV, Indsl. Rels. Rsch. Assn., Soc. for Human Resource Mgmt. Home: 9009 Vernon View Dr Alexandria VA 22308-2844 Office: Accord Assocs 117 S 17th St Ste 402 1 Bala Plz Ste 321 Philadelphia PA 19103

JONES, OWEN J(OHN), III, laser sales executive; b. Harrisburg, Pa., Oct. 12, 1949; s. Owen J. Jr. and Tamea Ann (Mixell) J.; m. Penny A. Henson, 1982. BS in Chemistry, Lehigh U., 1971, MBA, 1972. Sales engr. Enthone, Inc., New Haven, 1973-78, UPA Tech., Syosset, N.Y., 1979-80; sales engr., sales mgr. Allied Corp./Apollo Lasers, Chatsworth, Calif., 1981-82; sales mgr. Lumonics Marking Corp., Camarillo, Calif., 1982-89; v.p. sales and mktg. A-B Lasers Inc., 1989—. Mem. Laser Inst. Am., Am. Electroplaters and Surface Finishers Soc., Am. Soc. Metallurgists. Republican.

JONES, PATRICIA ELSIE, small business owner, children's book author; b. New Bedford, Mass., Apr. 4, 1949; d. Kenneth John and Allaire (Re) Whelan; m. Douglas Allen Jones, Feb. 4, 1967; children: Michele, John, Allen, Kenneth. Cert. travel agt. Travel agt. Fields & Cusick Travel, Warwick, R.I., 1980-83; owner, mechanic Warren (R.I.) Bike and Craft Shop, Inc., 1983—; travel agt. Travel Concepts, Taunton, Mass., 1986-88. Author: From the Beginning, 1990, Ending the Line on Litter, 1990, Water Down the Drain, 1991. Sunday Sch. tchr., youth group tchr. Baptist Temple Ch., Fall River, Mass. Republican. Home: 59 Lazywood Ln Swansea MA 02777 Office: Warren Bike & Craft Shop Inc 365 Child St Warren RI 02885

JONES, RAYMOND MOYLAN, strategy and public policy educator; b. Phila., Dec. 28, 1942; s. Raymond and Elizabeth (Shaw) J.; m. Barbara Ann Donaghue, May 22, 1965; children: Andrea Marie, Audra Marie. BS, U.S. Mil. Acad., 1964; MBA, Harvard U., 1971; JD, U. Tex., 1973. Bar: Tex. 1973. Commd. 2d lt. U.S. Army, 1964, advanced through grades to capt., 1966, ret., 1969; legal asst. to chmn. Occidental Petroleum Corp., L.A., 1973-75; pres. Oxy Metal Industries Internat., Geneva, 1975-77, Occidental Resource Recovery Corp., Irvine, Calif., 1978-81; v.p. Hooker Chem. Corp., Houston, 1977-78; pvt. practice cons. Austin and Irvine, 1981-86; lectr. Calif. State U., Long Beach, 1986, U. Md., College Park, 1986-90, Loyola Coll., Balt., 1990—. Contbr. articles, book rev. to profl. publs. Mem. Friends of Austin Symphony Orch., 1981-82; fin. cons. St. Stephen's Episc. Ch., Austin, 1981-83; mem. Ludwig Von Mises Inst., Burlingame, Calif., 1987—, Intercoll. Studies Inst., Bryn Mawr, Pa., 1987—; mgmt. con. ARC, Balt., 1988—. U. Md. grantee, 1987. Mem. Am. Econ. Assn., Acad. Internat. Bus., Strategic Mgmt. Soc., Acad. Mgmt., State Bar Tex., Harvard Club. Roman Catholic. Home: 305 Kerneway Baltimore MD 21212-4714 Office: Loyola Coll in Md Sellinger Sch Bus Mgmt Baltimore MD 21210-2699

JONES, RETHA SIMMONS, educator, business executive; b. Frankfort, Ohio, Oct. 18, 1945; d. Virgil and Hallie (Brewer) Simmons; m. Atlas Mordecai Jones, Jr., July 18, 1970; 1 child, Heidi Udele. BS, Ohio U., 1968;

MS, Cleve. State U., 1973; postgrad., Temple U., 1985—; cert. in human behavior, U. So. Calif., 1972. Libr. Adena High Sch., Frankfort, 1968-69; tchr. Frankfort Elem. Sch., 1969-70, Mercer Elem. Sch., Shaker Heights, Ohio, 1970-79, William Henry Mid. Sch., Dover, Del., 1980-89; propr., pres. Twice As Nice, Inc., Dover, Del., 1987—; workshop innovator Ohio Dept. English, 1973-79. Named Tchr. of Yr., Capital Sch. Dist., 1988; ALA scholar, 1970. Mem. NEA, Del. Edn. Assn. (workshop innovator 1985—), Capital Educators Assn. (v.p. 1987-88), NAFE, Cen. Del. Bus. Assn., Alphabetts (pres. 1983-86), Links (sec. Dover 1987-89), Phi Delta Kappa. Home: 812 Monroe Ter Dover DE 19901-4118 Office: Twice As Nice Inc 31 W Loockerman St Dover DE 19901

JONES, RICHARD ALLEN, horse breeder, educator; b. Freeport, Pa., Aug. 16, 1931; s. Paul Alfred and Nettie Minerva (Shearer) J.; B.A., Roberts Wesleyan Coll., 1953; MDiv, Asbury Sem., 1957; M.A., SUNY, Buffalo, 1971; M.S., Fredonia State Coll., 1971; m. Ruth B. Kelley, Aug. 1, 1953; children—Jonathan Dwight, Suzanne Ruth, Stephen Kent, Gregory Scott. Tchr., Lower Burrell, Pa., 1957, Rushford, N.Y., 1960, Gowanda, N.Y., 1961, Pine Valley, South Dayton, N.Y., 1962-92; ordained to ministry, Free Meth. Ch., 1957; minister, Salamanca, N.Y., 1957-59, Belfast, N.Y., 1959-61, South Dayton, 1961-66; pres. Eagleview Enterprises, South Dayton, 1980—; owner Eagleview Farm, 1971—. County committeeman Conservative Party, 1982; mem. Orchard Park Presbyn. Ch.; founder, chair Chautauqua County Reading Task Force. Mem. Assn. Arabian Horses (dir.), Chautauqua County Reading Assn. (pres., founder), Internat. Platform Assn., Assn. Supervision and Curriculum Devel., N.Y. Reading Assn., Pine Valley Tchrs. Assn. (pres.), Western N.Y. Arabian Assn., Internat. Arabian Assn., U.S. Dressage Assn., Western N.Y. Dressage Assn. Address: Cottage Rd South Dayton NY 14138

JONES, ROBERT LEE, accountant; b. Cheverly, Md., July 12, 1944; s. Bernard C. and Winifred (Brookman) J.; m. Martha Beth Frazier, Dec. 30, 1972; 1 child, Brenda. BS, U. Md., 1967. Ptnr., shareholder Hariton, Mancuso & Jones, P.C., Washington, 1967—; pres. Washington Estate Planning Coun., 1986; mem. IRS Info. Reporting Program Adv. Com., Washington, 1991-92; speaker in field. Contbr. articles to profl. jours. Mem. exec. com. fundraiser Leukemia Soc. Am., Washington, 1990-91. Mem. AICPA (coun. mem. 1990-91, chmn. tax forms com. 1990-91, exec. com. tax div. 1991-92, W-4 Altman award), D.C. Inst. CPA's (bd. mem. 1987-92, pres. 1991-92), Md. Assn. CPA's, Assn. Practicing CPA's. Office: Hariton Mancuso & Jones 1101 17th St Ste 1100 Washington DC 20036

JONES, R(ONALD) CONRAD, toxicologist, public health researcher; b. Warrensburg, Mo., Nov. 6, 1944; s. (Ronald) Conrad and Elizabeth (Herzog) J.; m. Lisa S. Garych, Apr. 27, 1991. BS, U. Wis., Stevens Point, 1971; MS, Albany Med. Coll., 1978; PhD with highest honors, Rutgers U., 1987. Biol. and med. scis. prof. Hudson Valley Community Coll., Troy, N.Y., 1977-78; corp. rsch. toxicologist General Foods Corp., Tarrytown, N.Y., 1979-83; cancer rsch. scientist/nutritional toxicologist American Health Foundation, Valhalla, N.Y., 1985-89; sr. staff environ. toxicologist Westchester County Health Dept., Hawthorne, N.Y., 1989—. Patentee inhibition of formations of food borne mutagens/carcinogens; contbr. articles to scientific publs. Mem. Soc. Toxicology (Nat., Mid-Atlantic chpts.), Am. Assn. Cancer Rsch., Internat. Soc. Regulatory Toxicology & Pharmacology, N.Y. Acad. Sci., NRDC/EDF/CPSC/CSPI/ USPIRG/Greenpeace, Nat. Coalition Against Misuse of Pesticides. Office: Westchester County Health Dept 19 Bradhurst Ave Hawthorne NY 10582

JONES, ROSS, publishing company executive; b. N.Y.C., June 21, 1942; s. A. Ross and Eleanor (Brennon) J.; m. Katherine Cody, June 2, 1972; children: Brennon, Kasey. BA, Brown U., 1965; MBA, Columbia U., 1970; AMP, Harvard U., 1988. Dep. mgr. Brown Bros. Harriman & Co., N.Y.C., 1970-77; v.p. treas. Readers Digest Assn., Inc., Pleasantville, N.Y., 1977—; Bd. dirs. N. Am. Reinsurance Co., N.Y.C., CML Group, Inc. Acton, Mass., 59 Wall St. Fund, N.Y.C. 1st lt. U.S. Army, 1966-69, Vietnam. 1st lt. Us. Army, 1966-69, Vietnam. Home: 157 Stone Rd Bedford NY 10506 Office: Reader's Digest Rd Pleasantville NY 10570

JONES, ROXANNE HARPER, state legislator; b. N.C., May 3, 1928; d. Gilford and Mary (Bruton) Harper; m. James H. Jones, 1957 (dec.); children: Patricia Hill, Wanda Crews. Student pub. schs. Bd. dirs. Pa. Minority Bus. Devel. Authority, Pa. Legis. Black Caucus, 1985—, Pa. Intra-Govtl. Long Term Care Coun.; minority chmn. urban affairs and housing com., mem. pub. health and welfare com., community and econ. devel. com., aging and youth com. Pa. State Senate, 1985—. Recipient Nat. Welfare Rights Orgn. Leadership award Nat. Welfare Rights Orgn., 1972, Woman of Yr. award Zeta Phi Beta, 1985, Achievement cert. Nat. Coun. Negro Women, 1985. Bd. dirs. Ams. for Democratic Action; co-chmn. Coalition Concerned Citizens; exec. dir. Phila. Citizens in Action; mem. Allegheny West Found. Mem. Apolstolic Ch. Home: 2330 W Allegheny Ave Philadelphia PA 19132-1422 Office: Pa State Senate State Capitol Harrisburg PA 17120

JONES, SALLY DAVIESS PICKRELL, writer; b. St. Louis, June 4, 1923; d. Claude Dildine and Marie Daviess (Pittman) Pickrell; m. Charles William Jones, Sept. 2, 1943; 1 son, Matthew Charles. Student, Mills Coll., Oakland, Calif., 1941-43, U. Calif.-Berkeley, 1944, Columbia, 1955-58. Author: (novel) The Lights Burn Blue, 1947. Mem. UN Women's Guild, Fgn. Policy Assn., Nat. Coun. Women, Asia Soc., English-Speaking Union, Met. Mus. Art, Internat. Platform Assn., Women's Internat. Forum. Episcopalian. Address: 311 E 58th St New York NY 10022

JONES, SANDRA LAVERN, librarian; b. Washington, Jan. 2, 1948; d. Julius Ellis and Evelyn Augusta (Best) Moon; m. Ronald Edwin Jones, Dec. 14, 1985. BA, Fed. City Coll., 1975; MS, U. D.C., 1978, MA in Adminstrn. and Supervision, 1992. Adminstrv. specialist Immigration and Naturalization Svc., Washington, 1975-79; archivist Nat. Archives and Record Svc., Washington, 1980-82; libr. D.C. Pub. Schs., 1983—; cons. D.C. Transp. Pub. Space Project, 1982-83. Vol. libr. Lorton (Va.) Reformatory Youth Ctr., 1979-80; co-founder Neighborhood Watch Program, Washington, 1981, community coord., 1987--; v.p. 6th Dist. Adv. Coun., 1982-83; historian East Washington Park Citizens Assn., 1982-84, editor, 1982-83. Recipient Grass Roots award D.C. Fedn. Civic Assns., 1983. Mem. ALA, D.C. Libr. Assn. (program coord. 1986). Democrat. Methodist. Office: Prince Georges County Pub Schs Carmody Hills Elem Sch 401 Jadeleaf Ave Capital Heights MD 20743-2573

JONES, SHELDON ATWELL, lawyer; b. Melrose, Mass., Apr. 20, 1938; s. Sheldon Atwell and Hannah Margaret (Andrews) J.; m. Priscilla Ann Hatch, Sept. 10, 1966; children: Sarah Percy, Abigail Atwell. BA, Yale U., 1959; LLB, Harvard U., 1965. Bar: Mass. 1965, U.S. Dist. Ct. Mass. 1967. Assoc. Gaston, Snow, Motley & Holt, Boston, 1965-72; ptnr. Gaston Snow & Ely Bartlett, Boston, 1972-87, Dechert Price & Rhoads, Boston, 1987—; sec. H&Q Healthcare Investors, Boston, 1987—. Lt. (j.g.) USN, 1959-62. Mem. ABA (chmn. subcom. on investment cos. 1980-86, state regulation of securities com.), Mass. Bar Assn., Boston Bar Assn., Yale Club, Harvard Club. Congregationalist. Home: 70 Indian Spring Rd Concord MA 01742-5512 Office: Dechert Price & Rhoads Ten Post Office Sq S 12th Fl Boston MA 02109

JONES, SUSAN DORFMAN, writer; b. N.Y.C., Oct. 4, 1939; d. Joseph and Sarah (Sorrin) Dorfman; m. William Harry Jones, Sept. 18, 1960; children: Jeffrey Scott, Eric David, Timothy Mark. BA, Syracuse U., 1961. Pres., owner Antiques Corp. Am., 1972-77; communications officer Riggs Bank, Washington, 1978-81; mgr. publs. Potomac Electric Power Co., Washington, 1981-82; sr. mgr. corp. communications MCI Corp., Washington, 1982-83; dir. corp. communications Sears World Trade, Washington, 1983-85; dir. corp. communications and govt. rels. Oxford Devel. Corp., Bethesda, Md., 1985-87; communications expert pub. health svc./health and human svcs. U.S. Alchohol, Drug Abuse, Mental Health Adminstrn., Rockville, Md., 1989—; free-lance writer, cons., Washington, 1975—; radio personality Sta. 4KQ, Brisbane, Australia, 1962; adj. prof. communications Am. U., Washington, 1978-82. Author, editor, project mgr. corp. ann. reports; writer sch. bd. candidates and home rule campaign speeches, Washington, 1970-76. Treas. D.C. Recreation Dept., 1973-79; bd. dirs. Murch Elem. Sch., Washington, 1969, 73. Recipient 1st pl. award for columns N.Y. Press Assn., 1961, Gold Quill award Internat. Assn. Bus. Communicators, 1980. Mem. Internat. Assn. Bus. Communicators (treas. 1981), Nat. Assn. Bank Women, Women in Telecommunications, Nat. Press Club, Pub. Rels. Soc. Am. Democrat. Jewish. Home and Office: 3777 Oliver St NW 3777 Oliver St NW Washington DC 20015

JONES, THOMAS MAXFIELD, college administrator; b. Fall River, Mass., Feb. 28, 1938; s. Thomas Cole and Carolyn (Maxfield) J.; m. Elaine Starke Jones, June 4, 1960; children: Thomas S., Kimberly M., David H., Christopher C., Sarah W. BA, Bowdoin Coll., 1960; MA. Teaching, Brown U., 1961. Br. mgr. Pawtucket (R.I.) Inst. for Savs., 1964-68; dean admissions and records Roger Williams Coll., Bristol, R.I., 1968-72; registrar Miami (Fla.)-Dade Community Coll., 1972-73; registrar, dir. inst. rsch. North Adams (Mass.) State Coll., 1973-78, acting pres., 1991, v.p. adminstrn. and fin., 1978—. Corporator North Adams Regional Hosp., North Adams Hoosal Savs. Bank, North Adams State Coll. Found. Capt. U.S. Army, 1960-64. Democrat. Home: 53 E Quincy St North Adams MA 01247-4307 Office: North Adams State Coll Church St North Adams MA 01247-4100

JONES, THOMAS WRIGHT, educator; b. Riverside, Calif., Oct. 3, 1947; s. Thomas Wright and Elizabeth Margaret (Leach) J.; m. Julie Kay Guker, Dec. 26, 1969; 1 child, Thomas Wright Jr. BA, U. South Fla., 1969; MA, George Peabody Coll. for Tchrs., 1973; PhD, U. Pitts., 1978. Cert. spl. edn., mental retardation, hearing impaired. Tchr. Dade County Pub. Schs., Miami, Fla., 1969-73; edn. specialist Mid-Atlantic North Regional Deaf-Blind Ctr., Bronx, 1973-75; asst. prof. Tex. Tech. U., Lubbock, 1978-81; asst. prof., assoc. prof., prof. Gallaudet U., Washington, 1981—; cons. programs for children with multiple disabilities, 1975—. Contbr. articles to profl. jours. Clk. Universalist Nat. Meml. Ch., Washington, 1990—. Personnel Preparation grantee, U.S. Dept. Edn., 1981, 83, 84, 87, 90. Mem. Convs. Am. Instrs. Deaf, Assn. Persons Severe Handicaps, Coun. Exceptional Children, Alexander Graham Bell Assn. Deaf, Assn. Coll. Educators in Hearing Impairment. Home: 9232 Arlington Blvd Fairfax VA 22031-2505 Office: Gallaudet U Dept Edn 800 Florida Ave NE Washington DC 20002-3660

JONES, WALLACE JUDE, school business adminstrator; b. Johnstown, Pa., Oct. 28, 1942; s. Charles Plummer and Jeanette (Wirick) J.; m. Mary Ann Leckey; 1 child, Todd Patrick. Student, U. Pitts., 1961-62. Registered sch. bus. adminstrn., Pa. Br. mgr. Dial Consumer Discount Corp., Allentown, Pa., 1965-72; bus. mgr., mem. bd. sec. Westmont Hilltop Sch. Dist., Johnstown, Pa., 1972-83; bus. adminstr. Waynesboro (Pa.) Area Sch. Dist., 1983—; trustee Pa. Sch. Dist. Liquid Asset Fund, Pottstown, 1982—; bd. dirs. Sch. Dist. Ins. Consortium, 1991—. Sec. Waynesboro Area Tax Bd., 1982—, Westmont Hilltops Schs. Authority, Johnstown, 1972-83; treas. Westmont Hilltop Recreation Commn., Johntown, 1979-83. U.S. Army, 1962-65. Mem. Pa. Assn. Sch. Bus. Ofcls. (Gary E. Resser Meml. award 1987), Assn. Sch. Bus. Ofcl. Internat. Republican. Roman Catholic. Home: 6332 Fairway Dr W Fayetteville PA 17222-9648 Office: Waynesboro Area Sch Dist PO Box 72 210 Clayton Ave Waynesboro PA 17268

JONES, WILLIAM CHARLES, computer science educator; b. Chgo., Feb. 2, 1944; s. William Charles and Ersa Jones; m. Virginia Kay Reedquist, Sept. 3, 1967; 1 child, Catherine Anne. BA in Math., S.W. Mo. State U., 1965; PhD in Math., Purdue U., 1969; MS in Computer Sci., Rensselaer Poly. Inst., 1989. Computer sci. prof. Cen. Conn. State Univ., New Britain, 1969-91. Author: (books) Pascal Problem Solving, 1986, Modula-2 Problem Solving, 1987, Data Structures, 1989. Mem. Math. Assn. of Am. Home: 275 Carlton St New Britain CT 06053-2445 Office: Ctrl Conn State U 1615 Stanley St New Britain CT 06053-2439

JONES-SHOEMAKER, CYNTHIA CAVENAUGH, early childhood educator, university administrator; b. Washington, Feb. 13, 1938; d. Robert LaTourrette and Herta (Wilson) Cavenaugh; m. Roger H. Jones, July 4, 1958 (div. Dec. 1984); children: Roger C., Michael, Steve, Allison; m. Douglas Shoemaker, Oct. 1989. BS, Cornell U., 1959; MEd, U. Md., 1974, PhD, 1981. Prof. and dir. day care and preschool adminstr. Trinity Coll., Washington, 1974-84; asst. to dean Catholic U., Washington, 1982; program dir. Montgomery Coll., Rockville, Md., 1983; exec. dir. Early Childhood Edn. Adminstrn. Inst., Rockville, 1975—; assoc. dir. George Washington U., Washington, 1984—; adj. prof. Trinity Coll., Washington, 1974-78, Webster Coll., St. Louis, 1982, George Mason U., Fairfax, Va., 1989-92; cons. Md. State Dept. Edn., 1982, Leesburg Child Devel. Ctr., 1982, GE, 1980, OEO, Mpls., 1971, U.S. Dept. Health, Edn. and Welfare, 1971. Speaker at numerous meetings, conferences, and workshops; research papers in field; contbr. articles to profl. jours. Elder Rockville Presbyn. Ch.; chmn. Tri-County Staff Devel. Consortium, Charles County, St. Mary's County and Calvert County, Md., 1987-89; vol. Aide Program Ritechie Pk. Elem. Sch., 1969-70; mem. Md. Coun. Staff Com. for Recognition of Excellence in Staff Devel., 1987-88, conf. chmn., 1990-91; active No. Va. Profl. Devel. Coun., 1986-88, bd. advisors YWCA preschs., 1984-86, Rockville Day Care Assn., 1972-74, Md. Community Coordinated Child Care Com., 1969-76. Grantee Md. State Dept. Edn., 1988, 89, U.S. Small Bus. Adminstrn., 1983, 84; recipient Nat. award for outstanding svc. Parent Coop. Preschs. Internat., Washington, 1970. Mem. Nat. Assn. for the Edn. of Young Children, Assn. for Supervision and Curriculum Devel., Assn. for Childhood Edn. Internat., Parent Cooperative Preschools Internat. (pres. 1971-72, 1st v.p. 1968-72, legis. chmn. 1973-76). Republican. Presbyterian. Home: 1370 Canterbury Way Rockville MD 20854-6104

JONSSON, KJARTAN A., consulting company executive, engineer; b. Saudarkroki, Skagafyrdi, Iceland, Oct. 19, 1940; came to U.S., 1969; s. Jon Sigvladi Nikodemusson and Anna Fridriksdottir; m. Beverly Rose Cherry; children: Vanessa Joy, Valeree Anna, Kristjana Elisabeth, Erika Gabrielle. Diploma, Polytechnik, Denmark, 1966; MS, Wash. U., St. Louis, 1972. Registered profl. engr., Md., N.H., N.Y., Maine, Vt.; lic. engr., Iceland, Denmark, Norway, Sweden, Germany. Ptnr. Forenade VVS Konsulter, Stockholm, Sweden, 1966-69; assoc. prof. Wash. U., St. Louis, 1970-72; assoc. L. McLeod Assocs., Towson, Md., 1972-74; cons. Gen. Electric Co., Schenectady, N.Y., 1974-75; pres., owner Sun Econ, Inc., Ballston Lake, N.Y., 1975-77, Energy and Value Cons., P.C., Scotia, N.Y., 1975—; owner, pres., and CEO Air Purification, Inc., Scotia, 1989—; cons. Greater N.Y.C. Hosps. Assn., 1984—, N.Y. State Food Mchts. Assn., Yonkers, 1978-84, Health Care, Comml. and Indsl. Facilities; owner, founder Air Purification, Inc., 1989—. Author: Environmental Systems for Medical Clinics, 1972; contbr. more than 250 articles to profl. mags.; 83 patents in field. Mem. NSPE, AIA (assoc.), ASHRAE, Assn. Energy Engrs., (profl. cert. energy mgr., environ. engrs. and mgrs. inst.), Am. Hosp. Assn., N.Y. State Soc. Profl. Engrs., Nat. Fire Protection Assn., Schenectady Profl. Engrs. Soc. (v.p. 1989-90, pres. 1990—), Schenectady C. of C. (dir. 1983-85), Rotary (Paul Harris fellow 1987, dir. Schenectady chpt. 1984-87). Republican. Lutheran. Home: 239 Stage Rd Ballston Lake NY 12019-2612 Office: Energy & Value Cons PC 491 Saratoga Rd Scotia NY 12302 also: Air Purification Inc 491 Saratoga Rd Scotia NY 12302

JOOS, FELIPE MIGUEL, mechanical engineer; b. Montevideo, Uruguay, Sept. 4, 1952; came to U.S., 1973; s. Carlos Jose and Alma Elena (Gieschen) J.; m. Caroline Rose Crocker, Aug. 28, 1982; children: Carolina Lucia, Catrina Aneliese, Celina Maria. BS in Applied Sci. and Engring., Calif. Inst. Tech., 1976; MSME, MIT, 1978, PhDME, 1982. Cert. engr., Uruguay. Engr. Ingenieros Consultores Latinoamericanos Limitada, Montevideo, Uruguay, 1978-79; mech. engr. research and devel. div. Gen. Electric Corp., Schenectady, N.Y., 1982-85; project engr. Creare, Inc., Hanover, N.H., 1985-87; sr. engr. Eastman Kodak Co., Rochester, N.Y., 1987—; indsl. fellow Ctr. for Interfacial Engring., U. Minn., Mpls., 1991-92. Contbr. articles to profl. jours. Mem. ASME, Am. Inst. Chem. Engrs., Soc. Hispanic Profl. Engrs. (v.p. 1989-90, treas. 1990—, treas. Eastern Tech. and Career Conf. 1991), Tau Beta Pi. Home: 478 Stone Rd Pittsford NY 14534-2856 Office: Eastman Kodak Co Kodak Park Rm 228 Rochester NY 14650-0001

JORDAN, ALBERT ROBERT, cinematographer; b. Norristown, Pa., Dec. 27, 1945; s. Albert James Jordan and Josephine (Claire) Zelinski. AA, L.A. City Coll., 1973; BA, Calif. State U., L.A., 1975. Pub. Echo, Atchfala, La., 1975-77; freelance photographer Phila., 1977—; judge Monitor Awards, N.Y.C., 1987-90. With U.S. Army, 1965-67, Vietnam. Home and Office: 739 Chain St Norristown PA 19401-3713

JORDAN, AMY BETH, media studies educator, consultant; b. Worcester, Mass., Nov. 23, 1961; d. Dennis Edward and Linda Kay (Hansen) J.; m. John M. Spandorfer, Aug. 17, 1986; 1 child, David Jordan. BA in Communication, Muhlenberg Coll., 1983; MA in Communications, U. Pa., 1986, PhD in Communications, 1990. Researcher Rodale Press, Emmaus, Pa., 1983-84; instr. media studies Widener U., Chester, Pa., 1989-90, asst. prof., coord. media studies, 1990—; cons. Media Perspectives, Marlton, N.J., 1990—. Contbr. chpt. to book. Workshop leader Please Touch Mus., Phila., 1990, Children's House, Pottstown, Pa., 1990. Scholar U. Pa., 1984-89. Mem. Speech Communication Assn., Internat. Communication Assn. Home: 315 Conway Ave Narberth PA 19072-2102 Office: Widener U Dept Media Studies Chester PA 19013

JORDAN, ANDREW STEPHEN, electronic materials scientist; b. Mezökövesd, Hungary, May 1, 1936; came to U.S., 1957; s. Geza and Lenke (Szegö) J.; m. Priscilla Theisz, June 28, 1968; children: Daniel R., William B. BS, Pa. State U., 1959; PhD, U. Pa., 1965. Engr. Philco Corp., Landsdale, Pa., 1959-62; sr. engr. Westinghouse R & D Ctr., Pitts., 1962; mem. tech. staff AT&T Bell Labs., Murray Hill, N.J., 1965-84, supr., 1984-91, disting. mem. tech. staff, 1991—; mem. editorial bd. Jour. Materials Sci.: Materials in Electronics, 1989—. Contbr. articles to sci. jours., chpts. to books.; patentee in field. Mem. Materials Rsch. Soc., Am. Assn. Crystal Growth (mem. exec. com. 1987—). Office: AT&T Bell Labs Mountain Ave New Providence NJ 07974-2005

JORDAN, ANGEL GONI, electrical and computer engineering educator; b. Pamplona, Spain, Sept. 19, 1930; came to U.S., 1956, naturalized, 1966; s. Hilario and Perpetua (Goni) J.; m. Nieves Alfonso Cuartero, July 8, 1956; children: Xavier, Edward, Arthur. M.S., U. Zaragoza, Spain, 1952, Carnegie Inst. Tech., 1959; Ph.D., Carnegie Inst. Tech., 1959; Dr. h.c., Poly. U. Madrid, Spain, 1985. With Naval Ordnance Lab., Madrid, 1952-56; instr. elec. engring. Carnegie-Mellon U., 1956-58, asst. prof. elec. engring., 1959-62, assoc. prof., 1962-65, prof., 1965-90, univ. prof., 1990—, U.A. and Helen Whitaker prof., 1972-80, head dept., 1969-79; dean engineering Carnegie-Mellon U. (Carnegie Inst. Tech.), 1979-83; provost Carnegie-Mellon U., 1983-91; rsch. fellow Mellon Inst. Indsl. Rsch., 1958-59; cons. to industry; bd. dirs. Calif. Micro Devices, Inc., Enterprise Corp., Allegheny Heart Inst., Keithley Inst., Inc., Magnascreen Corp. Contbr. articles to profl. jours. Dir. Pitts. High Tech. Council, 1983—; bd. dirs. Pa. Sci. and Engring. Found, 1981-83. Recipient Enterprise award Pitts. Bus. Times, 1985; NATO sr. scientist fellow, 1976; Fulbright Disting. scholar, 1988; named Edn. Man of the Yr., Pitts., 1987. Fellow IEEE, AAAS; mem. Am. Phys. Soc., Am. Soc. Engring. Edn., Nat. Acad. Engring., Sigma Xi, Eta Kappa Nu, Phi Kappa Phi, Tau Beta Pi. Home: 5874 Aylesboro Ave Pittsburgh PA 15217-1446 Office: Carnegie-Mellon U Wean Hall 4618 Pittsburgh PA 15213

JORDAN, DAVID, electrical engineering educator; b. Ambler, Pa., Nov. 2, 1940; s. Arthur Harold and Mary Corona (Schoff) J.; m. Carol Elizabeth Mowen, July 28, 1961; 1 child, Catherine Elizabeth. BEE, Cornell U., 1963, MS, 1964, PhD, 1970. Registered profl. engr., Conn. Engring. asst. Mpls. Honeywell Inc., Phila., 1959-60; grad. asst./instr. Cornell U., Ithaca, N.Y., 1968-70; prof. elec. engring. U. Conn., Storrs, 1970—; cons. Conn. Innovations, Inc., Rocky Hill, 1980—. Contbr. articles to profl. jours. Chmn. Bd. Edn., Willington, Conn., 1987—, Planning and Zoning Commn., Willington, 1977-85. Lt. USAF, 1964-67. Mem. IEEE (sr. mem.), AAUP (chpt. pres. 1987-88), Am. Soc. Engring. Edn., Sigma Xi, Phi Kappa Phi, Eta Kappa Nu, Tau Beta Pi. Republican. Congregationalist. Office: ESE Dept of U Conn 260 Glenbrook Rd Storrs Mansfield CT 06269-3157

JORDAN, GEORGE E., art critic, historian, antique dealer; b. Ky., Oct. 29, 1940; s. William Ransom and Allie (Wells) J.; m. Casandra Springer, 1964 (div. 1972). B.F.A., Ringling Sch. Art, 1964; postgrad., East Tenn. State U., 1967. Curator Reece Mus., Johnson City, Tenn., 1966-68; bd. dirs. Huntsville Art League and Mus. Assn., Ala., 1969; curator, registrar New Orleans Mus. Art, 1970-72; art critic Times-Picayune, New Orleans, 1976-80; critic, free lance writer, 1980—; instr. art history and painting New Orleans Acad. Fine Arts, 1985—; specialist on artists who worked in La. 1780—. Contbg. editor Art and Auction mag., 1981-83; contbr. La. !Paintins 19th Cnetury, The William Groves Collection, 1971, Cncycl. of New Orleans Artists. Mem. steering com. WYES-TV Pub. TV Art Auction, New Orleans, 1985. Avocations: music, theatre. Home and Office: 1 Riverside Ave Westport CT 06880-4214

JORDAN, JOHN LESTER, artist, educator; b. Houston, Dec. 21, 1944; s. Jesse Peavy and Catherine Myrtle (Sheffield) J.; m. Irena Veronika Lawicki (sep.); 1 child, Najel Solomon. Student, U. Houston, 1963-65, St. Thomas U., 1974. Artist Hurlock Real Estate Co., Houston, 1963-65; salesman-designer Dennis Sleep Shop, Houston, 1967-71; dir. Jerusalem Jewels, Denver, 1979-84, Hawaii, 1985; art rep. Whitney-Morse Art Group, Saugerties, N.Y., 1988-90; tchr. Onteora Sch. Dist., Woodstock, N.Y., 1988-91; dir. Gaudeamus-Jordan, Woodstock, 1985—; producer Paramour Prodns., Woodstock, 1990—. Host, producer: (tv show) Ramble On, 1990—; sculpture. Master of ceremonies Hiroshima to Now, Catskill Alliance, Woodstock, 1990; asst. organizer for Catskill Alliance for Peace, Woodstock, 1990; mem. The Green Party, Woodstock, 1990-91; contbr. Family of Woodstock, 1990-91. With USAF, 1965-67. Mem. Woodstock Guild, Woodstock Artists Assn. Home: PO Box 1050 Woodstock NY 12498-0961

JORDAN, JOHN MICHAEL, economist, researcher; b. Mountain View, Calif., Aug. 20, 1963; s. Robert R. and Joanne (Zaccore) J. BA, George Wash. U., 1985. Intern indsl. dept. AFL-CIO, Washington, 1986-87, cons. indsl. dept., 1987-88; asst. to regional dir. No. Am. regional office Internat. Union of Food and Allied Orgns., Washington, 1988-89; rsch. dir. Sheet Metal Workers Internat. Assn., Washington, 1989—. Contbr. articles to profl. jours. Mem. Indsl. Rels. Rsch. Assn. Office: Sheet Metal Internat Assn 1750 New York Ave NW Washington DC 20006

JORDAN, JOHN PATRICK, government agency executive, research scientist, educator; b. Salt Lake City, Apr. 23, 1934; s. Herbert Spencer and Madalene (Driscoll) J.; m. Thelma Marie Marsh, Sept. 4, 1954; children: Sharon Ann, Dennis Patrick, Jeffrey Terrance, Kevin Brian, Maureen Kathleen, Shaun Timothy, Kelly Christopher, John Clancy. BS in Animal Sci., U. Calif., Davis, 1955, PhD in Comparative Biochemistry, 1963; postdoctoral tng. Inst. Ednl. Mgmt., Harvard U., 1974; HHD (hon.), Lincoln U., Mo., 1990. NIH predoctoral fellow U. Calif., Davis, 1959-62; asst. prof. chemistry Oklahoma City U., 1962-65, assoc. prof., 1965-68; assoc. prof. biochemistry Colo. State U., 1968-71, prof., 1971-83, assoc. dean Coll. Natural Scis., 1968-72, dir. univ.-wide core curriculum in biology, 1968-73, dir. Univ./Agrl. Expt. Sta., 1972-83; exec. dir. Inst. Agr., 1982-83; dir. Coop. Extension Svc., 1983; adminstr. Coop. State Rsch. Svc. U.S. Dept. Agr., 1983—; cons. NASA (Manned Orbiting Rsch. Lab., Lunar Receiving Lab.), NIH, NSF, Dept. Def.; Ency. Brit., several univs.; rep. Joint Coun. for Food and Agrl. Scis., 1980—; co-chmn. Western Regional Agrl. Rsch. Planning Com., 1975-78; mem. Nat. Expt. Sta. Com. on Agrl. Rsch. Policy and Orgn., 1977-78, chmn., 1979; pioneer in agrl. rsch. adminstrn., ednl. innovation and effects of proposed space capsule environs. on metabolism of animals. Pres. St. Patrick's Sch. Bd., Oklahoma City, 1966-68, St. Joseph's Sch. Bd., Ft. Collins, 1970-76; dep. chief of staff 95th div. (tng.) USAR, 1963-65; mobilization designee Office of Chief of Rsch. and Devel., U.S. Army, 1965-77, ret. res., 1977. Served to 1st lt. 101st Airborne Div. RA, 1955-58. Recipient Bond award Am. Oil Chemists Soc., 1967, Gustav Ohaus award Nat. Sci. Tchrs. Assn., 1972, Disting. Svc. award USDA, 1986, U.S. Presdl. Rank award, 1988. Fellow AAAS, Am. Inst. Chemists; mem. Biochem. Soc., Am. Physiol. Soc., Aerospace Med. Assn., Soc. Exptl. Biology and Medicine, Am. Inst. Biol. Sci. (chmn. nat. com. pub. policy 1979-83, pres. 1989—), Sigma Xi, Phi Beta Kappa. Office: Coop State Rsch Svc US Dept Agr Rm 305-A Washington DC 20250

JORDAN, JUDITH VICTORIA, clinical psychologist, educator; b. Milw., July 28, 1943; d. Claus and Charlotte (Backus) J.; m. William M. Redpath, Aug. 11, 1973. AB, Brown U., 1965; MA, Harvard U., 1968, PhD, 1973. Diplomate Am. Bd. Profl. Psychology. Psychologist Human Relations Service, Wellesley, Mass., 1971-73; assoc. psychologist McLean Hosp., Belmont, Mass., 1978—, dir. women's studies program, asst. dir. tng. in psychology, 1982-91, dir. tng. in psychology, 1991; asst. dir. tng. in psychology Mclean Hosp., 1982-91, dir. tng. in psychology, 1991; vis. scholar Stone Ctr. Wel-

lesley Coll., 1985—; asst. prof. psychiatry Harvard Med. Sch., 1988—; cons. in field. Author: Empathy and Self Boundries, 1984, Women's Growth in Connection, 1991, (with others) The Self in Relation, 1986; editor, author: Relational Self in Women. Mem. Am. Psychol. Assn., Mass. Psychol. Assn. (bd. dirs. 1983-85), Phi Beta Kappa. Office: McLean Hosp 115 Mill St Belmont MA 02178-1048

JORDAN, KATHLEEN ANNE FINN, researcher; b. N.Y.C., Dec. 13, 1940; d. Cornelius Patrick and Ellen (Finn) J. MA in Internat. Edn. and Polit. Sci., Mich. State U., 1972, PhD, 1981. Cert. counselor. Overseas educator Rome, Israel, Iran, 1970-78; teaching asst., adminstr. Mich. State U., East Lansing, 1978-81, researcher, 1991—; adminstr. profl. counseling George Washington U., Washington, 1980-88; program coord. ACPA Nat. Conf., Washington, 1987-89; mgmt. cons. in field, 1989—, cross cultural researcher, 1988—; cons. vs. Ho. of Reps., Washington, 1982. Author: (play) The Whoosh Factor, 1987; contbr. articles to profl. jours. Vol. Whitman Walker Clinic, Washington, 1988—. Democrat. Home and Office: 2828 Connecticut Ave NW Washington DC 20008-1536

JORDAN, KATHLEEN SMITH, psychotherapist; b. Syracuse, N.Y., Nov. 9, 1949; d. William Patrick and Agnes (Kelly) Smith; m. David G. Massey (div. Dec. 1985); 1 child, Erin Massey. BA in Social Sci., Mich. State U., 1971; MEd in Counseling, Northeastrn U., 1974; PhD in Counseling, Fla. State U., 1978. Counseling psychologist St. Joseph's U., Phila., 1978-80; mgmt. cons. AT&T Bell Labs., Holmdel, N.J., 1980-86, Concord, Mass., 1986—; counselor Endicott Coll., Beverly, Mass., 1990—; founding dir. Allergy Alternatives, Concord, 1990—; instr. Concord Carlise Community Edn., 1988—. Recipient 2d Pl. award New Woman New Bus. Contest, 1991. Mem. Am. Assn. Counseling and Devel. Office: Allergy Alternatives PO Box 241 Concord MA 01742-0002

JORDAN, PETER FRIEDRICH, aeronautical researcher; b. Hamborn, Rhein, Germany, June 13, 1911; came to U.S., 1953; Otto and Therese (Erdmenger) J.; m. Elisabeth A. K. Lehmann, Oct. 26, 1936; children: Elke, Grete, Hans, Frauke. D rer nat., U. Göttingen, Germany, 1937. Staff mem. Aerodynamische Versuchsanstalt, Göttingen, Germany, 1937-45; prin. sci. officer Royal Aeronautical Establishment, Farnborough, Eng., 1946-53; from staff mem. to head structural dynamics Martin-Marietta, Balt., 1953-62, prin. rsch. scientist, 1962-76; rsch. scientist Air Force Office Sci. Rsch., Washington, 1976. Contbr. numerous articles to sci. and profl. jours. Fellow AIAA (assoc. fellow). Home: 800 Southerly Rd Apt 1114 Baltimore MD 21204-8410

JORDAN, THERESA JOAN, psychologist, educator; b. Irvington, N.J., Sept. 17, 1949; d. Ernest Anthony and Helen Joan (Debski) Balazs. BA, NYU, 1971, MA, 1972, PhD, 1979. Lic. psychologist, N.Y., N.J. Grad. fellow Nat. Inst. Occupational Safety and Health, N.Y.C., 1971-74; rsch. asst., rsch. coord. Project City Sci. NYU, 1974-79, assoc. dir. for rsch. Ctr. for Devel. Studies, 1979-82; asst. prof. medicine N.J. Med. Sch., Newark, 1982—; dir. Ctr. for Med. Info. N.J. Med. Sch., Newark, 1989—; cons. Ctrs. for Disease Control, Atlanta, 1990; speaker Am. Lung Assn., N.Y., 1990, Am. Thoracic Soc., N.Y., 1990. Contbr. articles to profl. jours. Mem. U.S. Icelandic Demonstration Team. Mem. APA, Soc. for Med. Decision-Making, Eastern Ednl. Rsch. Assn. (2d v.p. 1985-87). Office: NJ Med Sch Med Info Ctr 185 S Orange Ave Newark NJ 07103-2714

JORDON, DEBORAH ELIZABETH, lawyer; b. Pitts., June 24, 1951; d. Joseph Mitchell and Marjorie Odessa (Glaude) J. BA, Brown U., 1972; JD, Yale U., 1975. Bar: Pa. 1975, N.Y. 1978, U.S. Dist. Ct. (ea. and so. dists.) N.Y., 1978. Law clk. to presiding justice U.S. Dist. Ct. (ea. dist.) Pa., Phila., 1975-77; assoc. Paul, Weiss, Rifkind, Wharton & Garrison, N.Y.C., 1977-79; asst. to mayor City of N.Y., 1979-82; counsel to pres. CCNY, 1982-84; sr. atty. NBC, N.Y.C., 1984-87, asst. gen. atty., 1987-88, gen. atty., 1988-89, sr. gen. atty., 1989—; v.p. NBC Internat. Ltd.; bd. dirs. NBC Europe, Inc.; chmn. bd. dirs. Harlem Legal Svcs., Inc., N.Y.C.; bd. dirs. Met. Assistance Corp., N.Y.C. Bd. dirs. N.Y.C. Sports Commn., Bennett Coll., Greensboro, N.C., 1985—, Lifelong Learning Program, N.Y. 1981-82, Marymount Manhattan Coll., N.Y.C., 1984-87. Named Achiever in Industry Harlem YMCA, N.Y.C., 1988. Mem. Phi Beta Kappa. Roman Catholic. Home: 200 W 79th St New York NY 10024-6212 Office: NBC Inc 30 Rockefeller Plz New York NY 10112

JORGENSEN, JUDITH STRONG, public relations executive; b. Los Angeles, May 9, 1959; d. James Knox and Mary Elizabeth (Leonard) Strong; m. Gregory Arnold Jorgensen, Apr. 25, 1987. AB in Comparative Lit., Occidental Coll., 1981; MS in Journalism, Northwestern U., 1982. With Harcourt Brace Jovanovich, N.Y.C., 1983-84, Esquire Mag. Group Inc., N.Y.C., 1984-87; mgr. pub. rels. Esquire Mag., N.Y.C., 1987; group mgr. pub. relations Hearst Mags., N.Y.C., 1987-88; mgr. publicity Condé Nast Publs. Inc., N.Y.C., 1988-89; dir. communications Mag. Pubs. of Am., N.Y.C., 1989—. Mem. Pub. Rels. Soc. Am., N.Y. Women in Communications, N.Y. Jr. League. Office: Mag Pubs of Am 575 Lexington Ave New York NY 10022-6102

JORGENSON, WILLIAM LLOYD, food industry consultant; b. Phila., Dec. 12, 1942; s. James Koefred and Mary Jane (Stewart) J.; m. B. Joan Emshoff, Mar. 25, 1967 (div. 1977); children: Susan, Todd William. BA, Colgate U., Hamilton, N.Y., 1965; grad., Oslo U., 1965. Group product mgr. Colgate-Palmolive, Sydney, Australia, 1965-69; mktg. dir. Quaker Oats, Chgo., 1969-72; mng. dir. Quaker Oats, Caracus, Venezuela, 1972-74; v.p. Latin Am. Quaker Oats, Chgo., 1974-81; chief operating officer, pres. Terson Co., Chgo., 1981-84; chief exec. officer, pres. Fanny Farmer, Boston, 1984-87; sr. prin. The Hale Group, Boston, 1987—; bd. dirs. Xytronyx, San Diego, 1982—. Author: Corporate Profiles, 1975. Office: The Hale Group 8 Cherry St Danvers MA 01923-2808

JOSEPH, BERNARD MICHEL, marketing executive; b. Brussels, Belgium, Sept. 7, 1962; came to U.S., 1989; s. Jean and Anne-Marie (Petit) J.; m. Pascale A. Leribaux, Oct. 11, 1961. Student, Solvay Bus. Sch., Brussels, 1983-84, MBA, 1987; degree in advt., Belgian Mktg. Mgmt. Assn., Brussels, 1987. Product mgr. Joseph & Co., Brussels, 1987-88; internat. sales mgr. UCI Trading, Inc., Elmsford, N.Y., 1989-90; mgr. U.S. ops. Tradinvest Alliance, Inc., Cambridge, Mass., 1990-91; internat. mktg. mgr. IME Computers, Brighton, Mass., 1991—; bd. dirs. TCBY Franchising Stores, Porchester-Mamaroneck, N.Y., Joseph & Co., Brussels. Chief Boy Scouts, Brussels, 1985-86. With Belgian Army, 1988-89. Mem. Internat. Trade Com. of The Sbane. Home: 16 Kidder Ave Somerville MA 02144 Office: IME Computers 1340 Soldiers Field Rd Brighton MA 02135

JOSEPH, GREGORY PAUL, lawyer; b. Mpls., Jan. 18, 1951; s. George Phillip and Josephine Sheha (Nofel) J.; m. Barbara Joseph, Jan. 19, 1979. BA summa cum laude, U. Minn., 1972, JD cum laude, 1975. Bar: Minn. 1975, N.Y. 1979, U.S. Dist. Ct. Minn. 1975, U.S. Dist. Ct. (so. and ea. dist.) N.Y. 1979, U.S. Ct. Appeals (8th cir.) 1976, U.S. Ct. Appeals (2d cir.) 1979, U.S. Ct. Appeals (D.C. cir.) 1980, U.S. Supreme Ct. 1983, U.S. Tax Ct. 1987, U.S. Ct. Appeals (7th cir.) 1989. Pvt. practice Mpls., 1975-79; assoc. Fried, Frank, Harris, Shriver & Jacobson, N.Y.C., 1979-82, ptnr., 1982—; asst. U.S. spl. prosecutor, N.Y.C., Washington, 1981-82. Author: Modern Visual Evidence, 1984, Sanctions: The Federal Law of Litigation Abuse, 1989, Civil RICO: A Definitive Guide, 1992; co-author: Evidence in America, 1987; editor: Emerging Problems Under the Federal Rules of Evidence, 1983, reporter 2d edit., 1991; co-editor: Sanctions: Rule 11 and Other Powers, 1986, 2d rev. edit., 1988; contbr. articles to profl. jours. Fellow Am. Bar Found.; mem. ABA (coun. mem. 1992—, chmn. various coms. 1985—), Am. Law Inst., N.Y. State Bar Assn. (chmn. trial evidence com. 1988—), Minn. State Bar Assn., N.Y. County Lawyers Assn., Assn. Bar City of N.Y. Home: 40 E 88th St Apt 7C New York NY 10128-1176 Office: Fried Frank Harris Shriver & Jacobson One New York Pla New York NY 10004

JOSEPH, J. JONATHAN, interior designer; b. Gloucester, Mass., Jan. 14, 1932; s. George Stephen and Maryann (Lattof) J.; cert. Vesper George Sch. Art, Boston, 1952; student theater design Boston Conservatory Music, 1951. Assoc. designer Reva Lewitt, Boston, 1952-67; owner interior design bus., Boston, 1967—; cons. in fine arts; spl. research 19th century glass in Am., also Tiffany glass; exhibited Tiffany glass collection Mus. Fine Art, Boston, 1965, Worcester (Mass.) Art Mus., 1968. Important decorating works include: restoration of Plaza Hotel, N.Y.C., Ronald Reagan Presdl. Libr., Simi Valley, Calif., 1991. Recipient award Internat. V'Soske Rug Design. Mem. Am. Soc. Interior Designers (chmn. bd. New Eng. chpt. 1965-66, chpt. v.p. 1969-71, pres. 1971-72, bd. dirs. 1986-87), Nat. Early Am. Glass Club (1st v.p. 1967-69), Appraisers Assn. Am., Mus. Fine Arts Boston. Author: Jane Peterson, An American Artist, 1981; co-curator: (exhbn.) Jane Peterson: An Impression, Hickory (N.C.) Mus. of Art, 1987; contbr. revs. and articles to profl. publs. Address: PO Box 1220 Back Bay Annex Boston MA 02117

JOSEPH, RICHARD S., cardiologist; b. N.Y.C., Mar. 27, 1937; s. Charles Irving and Lillian (Horowitz) J.; m. Frances B. Rappaport, Jan. 27, 1963; children: Lauryl, James, Alisa, Jennifer. BA magna cum laude, Hofstra Coll., 1958; MD, Albert Einstein U., 1962. Intern U. Utah Affiliated Hosp., Salt Lake City, 1962-63; resident in chest medicine Bronx Mcpl. Hosp., Bronx, N.Y., 1963-64; resident internal medicine Mt. Sinai Hosp., N.Y.C., 1966-68; fellow in cardiology Nassau County Med. Ctr., East Meadow, N.Y., 1968-69; pvt. practice cardiology Huntington (N.Y.) Hosp., 1969—, chief cardiology, 1981-90, attending cardiology, 1973—; cons. in cardiology Kings Pk. (N.Y.) Hosp., 1971—; electro cardiographer Huntington (N.Y.) Hosp., 1971—; co-dir. cardiac stress lab Huntington (N.Y.) Hosp., 1975—; dir. Huntington (N.Y.) Cardiac Rehab., 1977—. Contbr. articles to profl. jours. Speaker med. adv. bd. Suffolk County Heart Assn., Blue Point, N.Y., 1971-73; speaker med. dir. Huntington (N.Y.) YMCA, 1973-77. Lt. USN, 1964-66. Recipient Pres. prize Hofstra Coll., Uniondale, N.Y., 1954; named Valedictorian Hofstra Coll., Uniondale, N.Y., 1958. Fellow Am. Coll. Cardiology; mem. Alpha Omega Alpha. Hebrew. Office: 205 E Main St Huntington NY 11743

JOSEPH, RODNEY RANDY, artist; b. Providence, July 13, 1945; s. Sidney Wilson and Philomena Joseph; m. Rumiko Antoinette Joseph, Jan. 29, 1971; children: Randy P., Reiner Scott. Student, Sch. Practical Art, Boston, 1964-67, Boston Conservatory Music, 1972-73. With Joseph Art Studio, Plymouth, Mass., 1973-76; arbitrator Better Bus. Bur., Fair Haven, Mass., 1977-79; producer Cape 11-Cable, Yarmouth, Mass., 1980-81; pres. Creative Life for Humanitary Arts Soc., Plymouth, 1992—; pres. Creative Life Inc., Plymouth, 1976-92; program designer Office for Children of Boston, Plymouth, 1978-79. Produced children's video: Captain Randy and Scott Terrific Adventures. Designed programs & campaigned for revitalization policies, talent laws. Recognized by Pres. Reagan Pvt. Sector Initiatives, 1982. Mem. Boston Social Libr. (life). Republican. Home: 558 Wareham Rd Plymouth MA 02360

JOSEPH, SAMMY WILLIAM, microbiologist, educator, researcher, consultant; b. Jacksonville, Fla., Oct. 10, 1934; s. William Tony and Zahara (Abraham) J.; m. Marianne Gertrude Cotte, Aug. 12, 1967; children: Jeffrey Keith, Jennifer Michelle. BSA, U. Fla., 1956; MS, St. John's U., N.Y.C., 1964, PhD, 1970. Commd. ensign USN, 1956, advanced through grades to capt., 1977; microbiologist U.S. Naval Med. Sch., Bethesda, Md., 1957-58, 62-67, St. Albans (N.Y.) Naval Hosp., 1958-62, Naval Med. Rsch. Unit, Jakarta, Indonesia, 1970-73; comdg. officer Navy unit USN, Ft. Detrick, Frederick, Md., 1973-75; dep. chmn. microbiology dept. Naval Med. Rsch. Inst., Bethesda, 1975-79; dir. infectious diseases rsch. program U.S. Naval Med. R & D, Bethesda, 1979-81; ret. USN, 1981; chmn. dept. microbiology U. Md., 1981-89, prof., 1989—; specialty advisor Bur. Medicine and Surgery USN, Washington, 1974-80; U.S.-Egypt Joint Working Group on Health Cooperation, Washington, 1979-81; vis. scientist Office Naval Rsch., London, 1977; chmn. proposal rev. panel for Program for Sci. and Tech. Cooperation, AID, Washington, 1985-88; sci. adv. bd. Dept. Natural Resources, Energy Adminstrn., Md. Power Plant Rsch. Program, Balt., 1987-91. Contbr. articles to Internat. Jour. Systematic Bacteriology, Infection and Immunity, Applied and Environ. Microbiology, Jour. Bacteriology, Sci. V.p. Mill Creek Civic Assn., Derwood, Md., 1978. Decorated Legion of Merit; recipient USN contract fellowship, 1967-70. Fellow Am. Acad. Microbiology, Am. Soc. Microbiology (selection com. Burroughs Wellcome vis. professorships in microbiology 1983, 85, 88, 89, 90, chmn. subcom. on gram negative, facultatively anaerobic fermentative rods 1986-88); mem. AAAS, Assn. Mil. Surgeons U.S., N.Y. Acad. Sci., Smithsonian Inst., Sigma Xi, Sigma Circle, Omicron Delta Kappa. Methodist. Home: 5914 Granby Rd Rockville MD 20855-1419 Office: U Md Dept Microbiology College Park MD 20742-0001

JOSEPH, SHARON JEAN, psychologist; b. Elkins, W.Va., Feb. 28, 1950; d. Paul James and Wilda Lee (Gum) J. BA, Wheeling (W.Va.) Jesuit Coll., 1972; MA, Duquesne U., 1977, PhD, 1985. Adjunctive therapist Appalachian Mental Health Ctr., Elkins, 1972-74, dir. partial hosp. program, 1974-76; acad. grad. asst. dept. psychology Duquesne U., Pitts., 1977-79; team leader partial hosp. unit Centerville Clinics, Fredericktown, Pa., 1980-81; sr. therapist S.W. Mental Health/Mental Retardation Ctrs. St. Johns Hosp., Pitts., 1981-83; pvt. practice Pitts., 1983—; cons. Carnegie-Mellon U., Pitts., 1984—; clin. psychologist Greater Pitts. Rehab. Hosp., 1988—, dir. psychology, 1990—. Active YMCA, Elkins, Washington, Pa., 1972-80, Recycling Group, Elkins, 1972-76. Mem. Greater Pitts. Psychology Assn. (chair publs. com. 1988-89), Am. Psychol. Assn., Pa. Psychol. Assn., Soc. for Personality Assessment, Western Pa. Group Psychotherapy Assn., Soc. Personality Assessment. Home: 215 Orange St Monroeville PA 15146-4128 Office: Med Ctr East 211 N Whitfield St Ste 392 Pittsburgh PA 15206-3031

JOSEPH, STEPHEN LAURENCE, lawyer; b. Manchester, Eng., June 24, 1954; came to U.S., 1978; s. Edward Joseph and Joyce (Gandz) Isaacs; m. Simone Hana Uzan, May 22, 1987; 1 child, Edward Jacob. BA in Eng. Law with honors, South Bank Polytech., London, Eng., 1977; LLM in Internat. Law, U. Va., 1979. Bar: D.C. 1980, Md. 1991. Assoc. Nossaman, Krueger & Marsh, Washington, 1979-82; ptnr. Myron H. Nordquist P.C., Washington, 1982; assoc. Duncan, Allen & Mitchell, Washington, 1983, Herrick & Smith, Washington, 1984; ptnr. Kline & Joseph, Washington, 1987—; cons. law of the sea interpretation project, 1979-82, UN, 1980; guest lectr. George Washington U. Sch. of Law, 1981; pres. Skytrans, Inc., 1983—. Office: Kline & Joseph 1776 K St NW Ste 210 Washington DC 20006-2304

JOSEPH, SUSAN B., lawyer; b. N.Y.C., June 1, 1958. BS in Econ. and Bus. Mgmt., Ramapo Coll. of N.J., 1981; JD cum laude, Seton Hall U., 1985. Bar: N.J. 1985, U.S. Dist. Ct. N.J. 1985, N.Y. 1988, U.S. Dist. Ct. (so. and ea. dist.) N.Y. 1991. Legal asst. Prudential Ins. Co. Am., Newark, 1982-85; assoc. Fox & Fox, Newark, 1985-86, Elkes, Maybruch & Weiss, P.A., Freehold, N.J., 1986-87; asst. counsel N.Am. Reins. Corp., N.Y.C., 1987-90; assoc. Mark D. Lefkowitz, Esq., 1991; mgr. GRE Ins. Group, Princeton, N.J., 1991—. Vol. campaign Bill Bradley for Senate, 1984, 90; vol. Starlight Found., N.Y.C., 1988—. Mem. ABA, N.J. State Bar Assn. (sect. on entertainment and arts law, newsletter editor 1992—), Am. Philatelic Soc., The Strollers (provisional). Home: 747 Valley St Apt 3K Maplewood NJ 07040-2663

JOSEPHS, JESS J., physicist, educator; b. N.Y.C., Jan. 4, 1917; s. Jacob I. and Mollie (Barouch) J.; m. Margaret Milroy Lewis, June 22, 1962; children: John Lewis III (stepson), Kenneth, Nancy Lewis (stepdau.), David. AB, NYU, 1938, MSc, 1940, PhD, 1943. Instr. phys. chemistry Northwestern U., 1946-47; asst. prof. phys. scis. U. Chgo., 1947-50; asst. prof. physics Boston U., 1950-56; asst. dir. upper Atmosphere Physics Lab., Boston U., 1951-54; prof. physics Smith Coll., 1956—, chmn. physics dept., 1977—, prof. emeritus of physics, 1986—; staff cons. Lincoln Labs., Mass. Inst. Tech., 1956-59, Mitre Corp., 1960-62. Author: The Physics of Musical Sound, 1967; contbr. to Ency. Physics, 1967, 73, 85. Bd. overseers Williston Northampton Sch., 1970-73. Served with USNR, 1943-46. Mem. Am. Phys. Soc., Am. Assn. Physics Tchrs., Acoustical Soc. Am., Audio Engring. Soc., Sigma Xi, Phi Lambda Upsilon. Home: 3300 Darby Rd # C1004 Haverford PA 19041-1061

JOSEPHS, MELVIN JAY, professional society administrator; b. N.Y.C., Apr. 26, 1926; married, 1948. BSc, Rutgers U., 1950, MSc, 1952, PhD in Plant Physiology and Botany, 1954. Plant physiologist Dow Chem. Co., Midland, Mich., 1954-60; assoc. editor Chem. and Engring. News Am. Chem. Soc., 1960-66; mng. editor Environ. Sci. and Tech., 1966-70, Chem. and Engring. News, 1970-73; asst. dir. Prodn. and Program Mgmt. Nat. Tech. Info. Svc., U.S. Dept. Commerce, Washington, 1973-76; chief Toxicology Data Bank, Nat. Libr. Med. HEW, Washington, 1976-78; asst. dir. Nat. Tech. Info. Svc. Office Govt. Agy. Support Dept. Commerce, Washington, 1978-86; exec. dir. Am. Soc. Plant Physiologists, Rockville, Md., 1986—. Mem. Am. Chem. Soc., Cosmos Club, Nat. Press Club, Sigma Xi. Office: Am Soc Plant Physiologists 15501 Monona Dr Rockville MD 20855-2768

JOSEPHSON, ALAN SAMUEL, medical educator; b. Bronx, N.Y., Nov. 30, 1930; s. Max and Mildred (Berk) J.; m. Adeline Goldberg, Dec. 24, 1955; children: Michelle, Neil, Debra. AB, NYU, 1952, MD, 1956. Diplomate Am. Bd. Medicine, Allergy and Immunology, Diagnostic Lab. Immunology. Intern III med. div. Bellevue Hosp., N.Y.C., 1956-57, med. resident, 1957-58, chief med. resident, 1960-61; USPHS trainee NYU, 1958-60; instr. Coll. of Medicine U. Cin., 1961-63; asst. prof. SUNY, N.Y.C., 1963-67, assoc. prof., 1967-75; prof. SUNY Downstate Med. Ctr., Bklyn., 1975—; dir. div. allergy and immunology SUNY, Bklyn., 1970—. Fellow ACP, Am. Acad. Allergy and Immunology. Office: SUNY 450 Clarkson Ave # 50 Brooklyn NY 11203-2098

JOSEPHSON, WILLIAM HOWARD, lawyer; b. Newark, Mar. 22, 1934; s. Maurice and Gertrude (Brooks) J. A.B., U. Chgo., 1952; J.D., Columbia, 1955; commoner, St. Antony's Coll., Oxford (Eng.) U., 1958-59. Bar: N.Y. 1956, D.C. 1966, U.S. Supreme Ct. 1959. Assoc. Paul, Weiss, Rifkind, Wharton & Garrison, N.Y.C., 1955-58, Joseph L. Rauh, Jr., Washington, 1959; Far East regional counsel ICA, 1959-61; spl. asst. to dir. Peace Corps, 1961-62, dep. gen. counsel, 1961-63, gen. counsel, 1963-66; asso. Fried, Frank, Harris, Shriver & Jacobson, N.Y.C., 1966-67; ptnr. Fried, Frank, Harris, Shriver & Jacobson, 1968—; spl. counsel N.Y.C. Human Resources Adminstrn., 1966-67, City Univ. Constrn. Fund, 1967—, N.Y.C. Bd. Edn., 1968-71, N.Y.C. Employees' Retirement System, 1975-86; Nat. Dem. vice presdl. campaign coord., 1972; pres. Peace Corps Inst., 1980—; mem. N.Y. State Gov. Task Force Pension and Investment, 1987-89, N.Y. State Hist. Records Adv. Bd., 1990—. Bd. editors: Columbia Law Rev, 1953-55. Recipient William A. Jump award exemplary achievement pub. adminstrn., 1965; Disting. Service award and Valerie Kantor awards Mex. Am. Legal Def. and Edn. Fund, 1980, 81. Mem. Assn. Bar City N.Y. (spl. com. on Congl. ethics 1968-70), Council on Fgn. Relations. Jewish. Home: 58 S Oxford St Brooklyn NY 11217-1305 Office: Fried Frank Harris Shriver & Jacobson 1 New York Plz New York NY 10004

JOSLYN, CATHERINE RUTH, art educator, artist; b. Cleve., May 18, 1950; d. Richard Owen and Mary Ellen (See) Joslyn. BA, Colby Coll., 1972; MFA, Ind. U., 1977. Owner Woven Images, Kansas City, 1973-77; vis. artist Kansas City (Mo.) Art Inst., 1978-79; asst. prof. Clarion (Pa.) U., 1979-85; dir. Clarion Festival of Arts, 1984-86; founding dir. univ. honors program Clarion (Pa.) U., 1986-88, assoc. prof. art, 1986-90, prof. art, 1991—; Commonwealth speaker Pa. Humanities Coun., Phila., 1991; cons. art educator, 1973—; exhibited art internationally; lectr. internationally. Contbr. articles to Macmillan Dictionary of Art and profl. jours. Ch. elder First Presbyn., Clarion, 1988-91; tutor Clarion County Literacy Program, 1987-88. Grantee Pa. Coun. on the Arts, 1985, Clarion U. Found., 1980-89, Clarion U. Coll. Arts and Scis., 1989, 90, 91. Mem. Surface Design Assn. (bd. dirs, N.E. regional rep. 1982-87, 91), Coll. Art Assn., Nat. Mus. Women in Arts. Office: Clarion U Dept Art Clarion PA 16214

JOSOVITZ, MICHAEL S., podiatrist; b. Lakewood, N.J., Jan. 19, 1961; s. Herman and Florence J. BS in Biochemistry, Albright Coll., 1983; D of Podiatric Medicine, Pa. Coll. Podiatric Medicine, 1987. Residency James C. Giuffre Med. Ctr., Phila., 1987-88; preceptorship Family Footcare Group, Monticello, N.Y., 1989-90; podiatrist pvt. practice Manhawkin, N.J., 1990—. Assoc. mem. Am. Podiatric Med. Assn., N.J. Podiatric Med. Soc. Home: 1065 Mulberry Pl Toms River NJ 08753-5246 Office: 568 E Bay Ave Manahawkin NJ 08050-3340

JOST, WESLEY WILLIAM, automotive executive; b. Bklyn., Sept. 3, 1930; s. Wesley W. and Virginia Ruth (Holton) J.; m. Barbara J. Herbert, Aug. 29, 1954; children: Polly, Penny, Peggy, Perry, Peter, Philip, Patrick, Pamela, Paul. Grad high sch., Manasquan, N.J. Enlisted U.S. Army, 1951; owner Jost Garage, Inc., Wall, N.J., 1953—; retired U.S. Army, 1959; owner Ziebart Auto Ctr., Wall, 1970—, Ryder Truck Rental, Inc., Wall, 1980—, Jost Auto Sales, Wall, 1986—; mgr. Sea Coast Chevrolet Truck Ctr., Wall, 1986-89. Editor: Spray Dust Mag., 1964-65. Member Cong. Chris Smith Congl. Club, Washington, 1985—, Allaire Airport Adv. Com., Wall, 1985—, Wall Twp. Govt. Body, 1987—, Newark Internat. Airport Adv. Commn.; chmn. Wall Twp. Pub. Works, 1987-89; mayor Twp. of Wall, 1988, 89, dep. mayor, 1990, 91, 92. Recipient Disting. Achievement award Internat. Franchise Assn., 1975, Award #1, Ziebart Dealer in Nation, 1975. Mem. Wall C. of C. (Golden Osprey award 1985), VFW (Belmar, N.J. chpt., quarter master 1956-60, Plaque 1960), Am. Legion, Air Force Assn., 200 Club (Monmouth County). Home: 113 Ocean Ave Belmar NJ 07719-2081 Office: Ziebart 1726 Hwy 35 Belmar NJ 07719-3440

JOTCHAM, THOMAS DENIS, marketing communications consultant; b. Llandudno, Wales, Feb. 21, 1918; s. George James and Marion (Brand) J.; m. Margaret Jean Thirlwell, Aug. 10, 1940; children: Patricia, Douglas, Joy, Candace (dec.). Student, Lower Can. Coll., 1929-36, McGill U., 1937-39. Sales rep. Montreal Lithographing Co., Ltd., Montreal, 1945-47; sales mgr. Wesco Waterpaints Can., Ltd., Montreal, 1947-48; advt. mgr. Pepsi-Cola Co. Can., Ltd., Montreal, 1948-52, mgr., 1952-54; asst. advt. mgr. Reader's Digest Assn., Ltd., Montreal, 1954-56; mgr., v.p. Foster Advt. Ltd., Montreal, 1956-73, exec. v.p., 1973-75, pres., 1977-81; vice chmn. Foster Advt. Ltd., Toronto, 1981-83, Sherwood Communications Group Ltd., Toronto, 1981-83; mem. coun. Montreal Bd. Trade, 1973-75, v.p., 1977-78, pres., 1979, hon. chmn., 1980-81. Bd. dirs. Grace Dart Hosp., 1973-83, pres., 1979-83; bd. dirs. Can. Coun. Christians and Jews, 1978-81, Les Grands Ballets Canadien, 1976-77; pres. Venetion Condominium, Inc., pres. 1984, 88—. Maj. Can. Army, 1940-45. Recipient ACA Gold medal, 1978; charter recipient McGill Mgmt. Achievement award, 1981. Fellow Inst. Can. Advt. (pres. 1976-77); mem. Can. Advt. and Sales Assn. (pres. 1960-61), Advt. and Sales Execs. Club (pres. 1956-58), Advt. and Sales Assocs. Montreal (pres. 1948-49), Advt. Agy Coun Que. (pres. 1975-76), Can.-S. African Soc. (bd. dirs. 1980-89, chmn. 1983-86), Internat. Swimming Hall of Fame (bd. dirs. 1990—), Mount Stephen Club (pres. 1967-68), St. James Club (com. chmn. 1979-81), Royal Montreal Golf Club, Ontario Club, Thistle Curling Club (pres. 1977-78), Ft. Lauderdale Golf and Country Club (dir. 1990—), Coral Ridge Yacht Club, Psi Upsilon. Home and Office: 1 Las Olas Cir Apt 1101 Fort Lauderdale FL 33316-1635

JOUKOWSKY, ARTEMIS A. W., private investor; b. Shanghai, China, Dec. 26, 1930; s. Artemis M.W. and Helen (Skvorzov) J.; m. Martha Content Sharp, June 9, 1956; children: Nina Lydia Koprulu, Artemis W. III, Michael A. AB, Brown U., 1955, LLD (hon.), 1985. Dep. to dir. Am. Internat. Underwriters, Milan, 1960-66, dep. to regional dir. for Europe, 1963-66, dir. Italian div., 1963-65; regional v.p. for Middle East, North Africa Am. Internat. Underwriters, Beirut, 1966-72; pres., regional dir. S.E. Asia Am. Internat. Underwriters, Hong Kong, 1972-74; v.p. Am. Internat. Underwriters, N.Y.C., 1974-77; mng. dir. Middle East Assurance and Reinsurance Co., Beirut, 1966-72; dir. Tam Sigorta, Istanbul, Turkey, 1967-72, Union Atlantique de Reassurance SA, Brussels, 1979-88, European Am. Underwriters, Vienna, Austria, 1979-87; dir., shareholder's rep. AIG Joint Ventures with Govt. Agencies, N.Y.C., 1979-87, pres. socialist countries div. and spl. world markets div., 1977-87. Founder, chmn. Brown U. Sports Found., 1983—; trustee Brown U., Providence, R.I., 1985—, vice chancellor 1988—; mem. adv. com. Inst. for Internat. Studies, 1981—, Ctr. for the Study Fin. Markets and Insts., 1987—, Ctr. for Old World Archaeology and Art, 1981—; mem. bd. govs. John Carter Brown Libr., 1988—; trustee Lawrenceville Sch., N.J., 1984—; mem. vis. com. Boston Mus. Fine Arts, 1985—; dir. Clear Pool Camp, 1976—; co-founder Am. Sch. Milan, 1962, bd. govs., 1961-65, pres. 1963-64, fin. com. 1962-65. Mem. U.S. C. of C. (gov. Hong Kong chpt.), U.S.-USSR Trade and Econ. Coun. (tourist and travel com. 1974-77), Hungarian-Am. Trade and Econ. Coun. (vce chmn. 1984-87), Exploreer's Club (N.Y.C.), India House (N.Y.C.), Hong Kong Club (life), Brown Club (N.Y.C.), Larchmont (N.Y.) Yacht Club, St. Croix Yacht Club (U.S. V.I.) Univ. Club (Providence), Hope Club (Providence). Office: Brown U 5 Benevolent St Providence RI 02912-0001

JOURNEY, DREXEL DAHLKE, lawyer; b. Westfield, Wis., Feb. 23, 1926; s. Clarence Earl and Verna L. Gilmore (Dahlke) Journey Gilmore; m. Vergene Harriet Sandsmark, Oct. 24, 1952; 1 child, Ann Marie. BBA, U. Wis., 1950, LLB, 1952; LLM, George Washington U., 1957. Bar: Wis. 1952, U.S. Dist. Ct. (we. dist.) Wis. 1953, U.S. Supreme Ct. 1955, U.S. Ct. Appeals (4th cir.) 1960, U.S. Ct. Appeals (5th cir.) 1961, U.S. Ct. Appeals (D.C. cir.) 1965, U.S. Ct. Appeals (7th and 9th cirs.) 1967, U.S. Ct. Appeals (1st cir.) 1969, D.C. 1970, U.S. Dist. Ct. D.C. 1970, U.S. Ct. Appeals (2d, 3d, 6th, 8th and 10th cirs.) 1976, U.S. Ct. Appeals (11th cir.) 1981. Counsel FPC, Washington, 1952-66, asst. gen. counsel, 1966-70, dep. gen. counsel, 1970-74, gen. counsel, 1974-77; ptnr. Schiff, Hardin & Waite, Washington, 1977—; mem. mediation program, U.S. Dist. Ct. (D.C. cir.), 1989—, early neutral evaluation program, 1989—; mem. case evaluation program D.C. Superior Ct., 1991—. Author: Corporate Law and Practice, 1975; contbr. articles to profl. jours. Pres. Am. U. Park Citizens Assn., Washington, 1970-72; trustee Lincoln-Wesmoreland Housing Project, Washington, 1978-79. Served with Mcht. Marine Res. USNR, 1944-46, USNG, 1948-50. Knapp scholar U. Wis., 1952. Mem. ABA, Fed. Bar Assn., Fed. Energy Bar Assn., Nat. Lawyers Club, Internat. Club Washington, The Army and Navy Club, Phi Kappa Phi, Phi Eta Sigma, Theta Delta Chi. Republican. Congregationalist. Clubs: Internat. of Washington, Army and Navy. Lodge: Masons. Home: 4540 Windom Pl NW Washington DC 20016-2452 Office: Schiff Hardin & Waite 1101 Connecticut Ave NW Washington DC 20036-4303

JOVANCICEVIC, VLADIMIR, chemist; b. Belgrad, Yugoslavia, Dec. 14, 1947; came to U.S. 1984; s. Gvozden and Milunka (Bosnjakovic) J.; m. Nadezda Prvulovic, July 4, 1969; 1 child, Ana. BSc, U. Belgrad, 1972, MSc, 1976; PhD, U. Paris VI, 1980. Rsch. chemist Inst. Tech. Scis., Belgrad, 1975-78; rsch. engr. Electricite de France, Les Renardiaires, 1980-81; rsch. assoc. Centre National de Rech. Scientifique, Paris, 1981-82; sr. rsch. engr. Sasilor-Sollac, Thionville, France, 1982-84; sr. rsch. assoc. Tex. A&M U., College Station, 1984-87; sr. rsch. chemist W. R. Grace & Co., Columbia, Md., 1987—. Contbr. articles to profl. jours.; patentee in field. Mem. Am. Chem. Soc., Electrochem. Soc., Nat. Assn. Corrosion Engrs. Office: W R Grace & Co 7379 State Rt 32 Columbia MD 21044-4098

JOY, PATRICK FRANCIS, mechanical engineer; b. Woodbury, N.J., Mar. 21, 1943; s. Patrick Francis and Mary Imelda (Corcoran) J.; m. Leona Helene Jurska, July 1, 1967; 1 child, Kevin. BSME, Drexel U., 1966, MSME, 1969. Registered profl. engr., N.J. Sr. engr. Advanced Tech. Labs., RCA, Camden, N.J., 1966-76; sr. rsch. engr. Exxon Rsch. Co., Linden, N.J., 1977-79; mgr. R & D, Exxon Enterprises, Inc., Florham Park, N.J., 1979-81; sr. staff engr. Exxon Rsch. and Engring. Co., Florham Park, 1981-83; prin. engr. Astro Space div. GE, Princeton, N.J., 1983-86; unit mgr. GE, Princeton, 1986—. Contbr. articles to profl. jours.; inventor thermally controlled lasers, color filter for low light camera, fibrous air solar eollector. Mem. New Providence (N.J.) Bd. Edn., 1981-83; v.p. St. Ignatius Home and Sch. Assn., 1987-89, treas., 1988-91; chmn. Capital Accounts com. St. Ignatius Capital Fund Drive, 1991—; chmn. class endowment fund Drexel U., 1990-91. Fellow AIAA (assoc.); mem. GE Elfun Soc., A.J. Drexel Soc. Office: GE Astro Space Div PO Box 800 Princeton NJ 08543-0800

JOY, ROBERT JOHN THOMAS, medical history educator; b. South Kingstown, R.I., Apr. 5, 1929; s. Angelo Francois and Mary Frances (Egan) J.; m. Beverly June Boxer, July 5, 1952 (div. May 1984); children: Robert L.F., Lisa; m. Janet Lillian Brady, July 12, 1985. BS, U. R.I., 1950; MD, Yale U., 1954; MA, Harvard U., 1965; cert., Armed Forces Staff Coll., 1968. Intern, resident Walter Reed Army Med. Ctr., Washington, 1954-58; asst. dir. environ. medicine U.S.A. Med. Rsch. Lab., Fort Knox, Ky., 1959-61; comdr. U.S.A. Rsch. Inst. for Environ. Medicine, Natick, Mass., 1961-62; chief comdr. U.S.A. Med. Rsch. Team, Saigon, Vietnam, 1965-66; chief med. rsch. div. Office of Surgeon Gen., U.S. Army, Washington, 1968-69; dep. med. and life scis. Office of Dir. Def. Rsch. and Engring., Washington, 1969-71; dep. dir., dir. Walter Reed Inst. Rsch., Washington, 1971-76; prof. mil. medicine Uniformed Svcs. U. Health Scis., Washington, 1976-81, prof., chmn. med. history, 1981—; v.p. Gorgas Meml. Inst., Washington, 1979-81; hon. faculty Indsl. Coll. Armed Forces, Washington, 1990. Editor Jour. History Medicine and Allied Scis., 1983-87; contbr. articles to jours. in field; editor monographs on mil. medicine. Col. U.S. Army, 1954-81, Vietnam. Decorated Disting. Svc. medal; recipient John Shaw Billings award Am. Mil. Surgeons of U.S., 1966, William P. Clements award Uniformed Svcs. U. Health Scis., 1980. Fellow ACP, Coll. Physicians Phila; mem. Am. Assn. History Medicine (William Osler medal 1954, coun. 1979-81), Am. Physiol. Soc., Osler Soc. (bd. govs. 1986-89). Home: 5821 Highland Dr Bethesda MD 20815-5531 Office: Uniformed Svcs U Dept Med History 4301 Jones Bridge Rd Bethesda MD 20814-4799

JOYCE, ANNE RAINE, editor, director of publications; b. South Bend, Ind., Oct. 2, 1942; d. James Agee and Marjorie Elizabeth (Gilstrap) Raine; m. Glenn Russell Joyce, Aug. 19, 1962; 1 child, Adam Russell. AB, Cen. Meth. Coll., 1962; MA in French, U. Mo., 1966; MA in Linguistics, U. Iowa, 1979. Cert. tchr., Mo. Tchr. Centralia (Mo.) High Sch., 1962-64; instr. Coe Coll., Cedar Rapids, Iowa, 1978-79, Georgetown U., Washington, 1980-83; asst. editor Am.-Arab Affairs, Washington, 1983-84; editor, dir. publs. Mid. East Policy, Washington, 1984—; gen. sec. Mid. East Policy Coun., 1991—. Mem. edn. com. Fairfax County (Va.) PTA Bd., 1986-88. U.S. Dept. Def. fellow, 1964-66; recipient Recognition award Am.-Arab Affairs Coun., 1988, Disting. Alumni award. Cen. Meth. Coll., 1990. Mem. Middle East Studies Assn., LWV (fin. chair Fairfax county chpt. 1981—). Home: 6916 Tulsa Ct Alexandria VA 22307-1730 Office: Middle East Policy Coun 1730 M St NW # 512 Washington DC 20036-4505

JOYCE, CHARLES VINCENT, III, bank executive, accountant; b. Evansville, Ind., Jan. 19, 1942; s. Charles V. II and Anna (Blanford) J.; m. Marion Joan Gough, Dec. 26, 1959; children: Joan M. Joyce Catterton, John C., Janet T. AA in Bus. Adminstrn., Montgomery Coll., Takoma Park, Md., 1967; BSBA magna cum laude, U. Md., 1969. CPA, Md. Sr. auditor Price Waterhouse, Washington, 1969-75; dir. fin. acctg. Fed. Home Loan Mortgage Corp., Washington, 1975-76; dir. loan adminstrn. Student Loan Mktg. Assn., Washington, 1976-82; dir. internal audit Nat. Corp. for Housing Ptnrships., Washington, 1982-85; v.p. Am. Security Bank, N.A., Washington, 1985—. Past pres., treas. Rolling Terrace PTA, Takoma Park, Rolling Terrace Civic Assn., Takoma Park; past dir., treas., coach Langley Park (Md.) Boys and Girls Clubs; chmn. fin. com. St. Camillus Cath. Ch., 1984—. Recipient scholarship awards Beta Alpha Psi, 1969, Delta Sigma Pi, 1969. Mem. AICPA, Md. Assn. CPAs (auditing standards com. 1982-92), KC (grand knight 1982-83). Republican. Roman Catholic. Home: 616 Quaint Acres Dr Silver Spring MD 20904

JOYCE, GLENN RUSSELL, physicist; b. St. Louis, June 24, 1939; s. M.G. and Myra E. (Russell) J.; m. Anne Raine, Aug. 19, 1962; 1 child, Adam. BA, Cen. Meth. Coll., 1961; MS, U. Mo., 1963, PhD, 1966. Prof. U. Iowa, Iowa City, 1966-80; sr. rsch. physicist Naval Rsch. Lab., Washington, 1980—. Contbr. over 90 articles to profl. jours. Fulbright fellow, Germany, 1968. Fellow Am. Phys. Soc. Office: Naval Rsch Lab Washington DC 20375

JOYCE, JOHN JOSEPH, English educator; b. Buffalo, N.Y., Aug. 1, 1930; s. Leo A. and Margaret Louise (Edgar) J.; m. Carole J. King, Aug. 22, 1970; children: Stephen Leo, Patrick John. BA, Canisius Coll., 1952, MA, 1960; PhD, SUNY, Binghamton, 1977. Insur. agt. Employers Mutuals, Fireman's Fund, Buffalo, 1954-59; tchr. Lackawanna (N.Y.) Sr. High Sch., 1959-65; prof. Nazareth Coll. Rochester, N.Y., 1965—; chmn. English dept. Nazareth Coll., Rochester, 1980-87. Contbr. articles to profl. jours. Sgt. major U.S. Army Infantry, 1952-54, Korea. Recipient Disting. Teaching award, Nazareth Coll. Alumni, Rochester, 1990. Mem. MLA, Coll. English Assn. (exec. dir. 1984—, Disting. Svc. award 1991), N.Y. Coll. English Assn. (newsletter editor 1978-84, bd. dirs., v.p. 1979—), Nat. Coun. Tchrs. of English, Conf. Coll. Tchrs. of English, English Coalition (organizing com. 1985-87). Roman Catholic. Office: Nazareth Coll Rochester Rochester NY 14618

JOYCE, ROSEMARY ALEXANDRIA, anthropology educator; b. Lackawanna, N.Y., Apr. 7, 1956; d. Thomas Robert and Joanne Hannah (Poth) J.; m. Russell Nicholas Sheptak, Jan. 7, 1984. BA, Cornell U., 1978; PhD, U. Ill., 1985. Instr. Jackson (Mich.) Community Coll., 1983; lectr. U. Ill., Urbana, 1984-85; asst. curator Peabody Mus., Harvard U., Cambridge, Mass., 1985-86, asst. dir., 1986-89; asst. prof. anthropology Harvard U., Cambridge, Mass., 1989-91, assoc. prof. anthropology, 1991—. Author: Cerro Palenque, 1991; contbr. articles to profl. jours. NSF grantee, 1989, NEH grantee, 1985, 86; Fulbright fellow, 1981-82. Mem. Soc. for Am. Archaeology, Am. Anthropol. Assn., New Eng. Mus. Office: Harvard U Peabody Mus 11 Divinity Ave Cambridge MA 02138-2096

JOYCE, WILLIAM B., physicist; b. Columbus, Ohio, Oct. 17, 1932; s. William J. Jr. and Louise (Beeler) J.; m. Alice Barker, June 21, 1958; children: Ann, John, Wendy, William. B in Engring. Physics, Cornell U., 1955; PhD, Ohio State U., 1966. Mgr. advanced tech. Accuray Corp., Columbus, 1963-66; mem. tech. staff AT&T Bell Labs., Murray Hill, N.J., 1966-82, disting. mem. tech. staff, 1982-88, fellow, 1988—. Contbr. articles to profl. jours. Lt. (j.g.) USN, 1955-58. Office: AT&T Bell Labs 600 Mountain Ave Rm 2350D New Providence NJ 07974-2010

JOYE, DONALD DAVID, chemical engineering educator; b. N.Y.C., Feb. 23, 1946; s. Elwood E. and Grace M. (Raso) J.; m. Claudia Tindall, June 28, 1969; children: Colin, Gavin, Christopher. BS in Engring., Princeton U., 1967; MS, Lehigh U., 1969, PhD, 1972. Lic. patent agt. Asst. prof. Lafayette Coll., Easton, Pa., 1972-75; sr. process engr. Sherwin-Williams Chems., Toledo, 1976-77; vis. asst. prof. Lehigh U., Bethlehem, Pa., 1977-79; patent agt. minerals and chems. div. Engelhard Corp., Metro Park, N.J., 1979-81; assst. prof. chem. engring. Villanova (Pa.) U., 1981-87, assoc. prof., 1987—; cons. to various orgsn.; fellow Naval Med. Rsch. Inst., Bethesda, Md., 1988—. Contbr. articles to profl. jours. Pres. Chester County (Pa.) Home Schoolers Assn., 1987—. Mem. Am. Inst. Chem. Engrs., Water Pollution Control Fedn., Am. Soc. for Engring. Edn. (fellow 1988—), Soc. Rheology. Evangelical. Office: Villanova U Dept Chem Engring Villanova PA 19085

JOYNER, SUZANNE DIMASCIO, marketing executive; b. Phila., Dec. 2, 1942; d. Placido L. and Lillian G. (Smith) Mosca; m. Richard DiMascio, Dec. 26, 1963 (div. Nov. 1976); children: Christopher, Jeffrey; m. James H. Joyner III, Jan. 1, 1980; children: James IV, Gordon, Christopher, Richard, Jeffrey. RN; cert. nurse specialist in gerontology. Dir. nursing North Pa. Convalescent Home, Lansdale, 1976-78; clin. research assoc. Pharmacia, Piscataway, N.J., 1978-80, product mgr., 1980-85, sr. product mgr., 1985-86, group product dir., 1986-88; mktg. exec. Wyeth Ayers Internat. Co., Phila., 1988—, sr. product mgr., 1988—. cons. nursing, 1977-79; cons. Thane Assocs., 1983-86. Author: (manual) Debrisan for Wound Care, 1977. Republican. Roman Catholic. Avocations: walking, swimming, aerobics. Home: 26 Solebury Mountain Rd New Hope PA 18938-1113 Office: Wyeth Internat Co 150 Rodor Chester Rd Radnor PA 19101

JUBELIRER, ROBERT C., lawyer, state senator; b. Altoona, Pa., Feb. 9, 1937; s. Samuel H. and Darothy (Brett) J.; 4 children. Grad., Pa. State U., Dickinson Sch. Law. Bar: Pa. Mem. Pa. Senate, 1974—, majority leader, 1981-84, pres. pro tem, 1984—. Chmn. Blair County Multiple Sclerosis Soc.; bd. dirs. Allegheny chpt. Nat. Multiple Sclerosis Soc.; mem. adv. coun. Hollidaysburg Vets. Home; past hon. chmn. Tuckahoe dist. Penns Woods coun. Boy Scouts Am.; hon. chmn. Jr. Achievement. Recipient 1st Freedom of Info. Day award Am. Sch. Counselors Assn., Miracle Mile Disting. Svc. award Pa. Rural Electric Assn., 1988, State Guardian of Sml. Bus. award Pa. chpt. Nat. Fedn. Ind. Bus., Disting. Svc. award Nat. Constable Assn., 1990, Fulton County Human Svcs. Coun. award for Leadership on Rural Health Issues, 1991; named Legislator of Yr., one of ten Outstanding Legislators of Yr. Nat. Rep. Legislators, Assn., 1985. Mem. Pa. Bar Assn., Blair County Bar Assn., Rotary, Masons. Office: Pk View Ctr PO Box 2023 Twelve Sheraton Dr Altoona PA 16603-2023

JUCEAM, ELEANOR PAM, behavioral sciences educator; b. Bklyn., June 24, 1936; d. Simon and Berta (Field) Pam; m. Robert Emanuel Juceam, May 24, 1970; children: Daniel James, Jacquelyn Brooke, Gregory Andrew. B.A., Brandeis U., 1958; M.A., NYU, 1960, NYU, 1963; Ph.D., NYU, 1969. Exec. asst. to pres. Queensboro Community Coll., CUNY, 1969-72, assoc. dean coll., 1969-72, dir. spl. programs CUNY, 1972-73, univ. dir. spl. programs, 1978-79; dept. chmn., prof. behavioral scis. Hostos Community Coll., CUNY, 1981—; mem. pres. coun. Brandeis U., Waltham, Mass., 1972—. Recipient Founders Day award NYU, 1969. Mem. City U. Women's Coalition, NOW. Jewish. Home: 106 Hemlock Rd Manhasset NY 11030-1214 Office: Hostos Community Coll Dept Behavioral Social Scis 500 Grand Concourse Bronx NY 10451-5323

JUDD, JACOB, history educator; b. N.Y.C., July 16, 1929; s. Harry and Ida (Nadelman) Judlowitz; m. Irene H. Nadelman, Apr. 29, 1951; children: Karen, Les. AB, NYU, 1950, MA, 1953, PhD, 1959. Instr. NYU, 1956-58; lectr. Hunter Coll., N.Y., 1958-63; asst. prof. Lehman Coll./CUNY, 1963-69, assoc. prof., 1969-77, prof., 1978—, chmn. dept. history, 1985-88, 89—, acting dean of arts and humanities, 1988-89; lectr. in field; hist. rsch. cons. Hist. Hudson Valley (formerly Sleepy Hollow Restorations), 1968-88, others. Editor: The Loyalist Americans: A Focus on Greater New York, 1975, The Revolutionary War Memoir and Selected Correspondence of Philip Van Cortlandt, Vol. I, 1976, Correspondence of the Van Cortlandt Family of Cortlandt Manor, 1748-1800, Vol. 11, 1977, Vol. III, 1978, Vol. IV, 1981; co-editor: Business Enterprise in Early New York, 1979, An Emerging Independent American Economy 1815-1875, 1980, Am. Industrialization, Economic Expansion and the Law, 1981, others; contbr. articles to profl. jours. Recipient Tomahawk award Westchester County Hist. Soc., 1984, NEH grant, 1976-77, N.Y. State Bicentennial Grant, 1976. Mem. Am. Hist. Assn., Orgn. Am. Historians, N.Y. Hist. Soc., Urban History Group, Conf. on N.Y. History, Soc. for Historians of Early Republic, Labor History Soc., others. Office: CCNY Lehman Coll 250 Bedford Park Blvd W Bronx NY 10468-1589

JUDD, RICHARD LOUIS, executive dean; b. Bridgeport, Conn., Mar. 22, 1937; s. Wilbur Franklin and Priscilla (Nagy) J.; m. Nancy Ruth Fox, Nov. 30, 1963; children: Sarah, Jonathan. BS with honors, Cen. Conn. State U., 1959; MA, Ohio State U., 1961; PhD, U. Conn., 1971. Instr. psychology Cen. Conn. State U., New Britain, 1964-68, assoc. dean, 1968-69, dean student affairs, 1969-82, exec. dean, prof. emergency med. scis., 1982—; vis. exec. Am. Coun. Edn., USDA, 1981; bd. dirs. Reflexite Corp. Sr. author: First Responder, 1981, 88 2d edition, Geriatric Emergencies, 1986. Commr. New Britain Police Dept., 1981-89; dir. emergency ops. command City of New Britain, 1982—; campaign chmn. United Community Svcs., New Britain, 1987-88, pres., 1990—, Verdienstkreuz, Fed. Republic of Germany, 1990. Demi fellow, 1970; named Citizen of Yr., 1990. Home: 119 Ten Acre Rd New Britain CT 06052-1531 Office: Cen Conn State U 1615 Stanley St New Britain CT 06053-2439

JUDGE, DAVID ALLEN, facilities manager; b. Stamford, Conn., Aug. 17, 1964; s. James Vincent and Mary Helen (Madagan) J. Diploma in elec. tech., J.M. Wright Tech., Stamford, 1982. Electrician Drinkwater Bros., Stamford, 1979-83, City Elec., Stamford, 1983-85; facilities mgr. Benenson Capital Co., Stamford, 1985—. Vol. fire fighter, Glenbrook Fire Dept., New Hope Fire Co., Stamford, Ct., 1983—, EMT, FFI. Mem. Nat. Fire Protection Assn., Am. Inst. Plant Engrs., Assn. Energy Engrs., Bldg. Owners Mng. Assn., Soc. Real Property Adminstrs. Roman Catholic. Office: Benenson Capital Co 1600 Summer St Stamford CT 06905-5125

JUDGE, EDWARD HENRY, history educator; b. Detroit, June 7, 1945; s. Henry Frank and Edna Bernice (Lipon) J.; m. Susan Page Gundry, Aug. 21, 1970; children: John, Stephen, Matthew, Christopher. BA, U. Detroit, 1967; MA, U. Mich., 1969, PhD, 1975. Materials coord. Fisher Body/Div. Gen. Motors, Detroit, 1965-68, 70; quality control inspector Ford Motor Co., Ypsilanti, Mich., 1969-70; teaching fellow, grad. student U. Mich., Ann Arbor, 1967-75; lectr. U. Mich. Residential Coll., Ann Arbor, 1975-76; USSR Exch. Scholar Internat. Rsch. Exchs., Leningrad/Moscow, 1976-77; asst. prof. history SUNY, Plattsburgh, 1977-78; asst. prof. history Le Moyne Coll., Syracuse, N.Y., 1978-82, assoc. prof. history, 1982-92, prof. history, 1992—, chmn., dept. history, 1988—; human rels. instr. N.Y. Air Nat. Guard, Syracuse, 1979-91, affirmative actions officer, 1979-91. Author: Plehve: Repression and Reform in Russia, 1983; Easter in Kishinev; Anatomy of Pogram, 1992, Modernization and Revolution, 1992. Mem. presenting team Worldwide Marriage Encounter, Syracuse, 1987—; coun. mem. Holy Cross Parish, DeWitt, N.Y., 1985—; lay minister Cath. Diocese of Syracuse, 1987—; bd. dirs. Parents of Retarded Adults and Youths, 1990—. Lt. col. Air N.G. 1991. Recipient First Books award Am. Hist. Assn., Washington, 1981, NEH rsch. travel grants, Paris, 1986, Leningrad, 1990; NEH summer seminar grantee Cornell U., 1986. Mem. Am. Assn. Advancement of Slavic Studies, Cen. N.Y. Assn. Russian Historians, Down Syndrome Assn. Cen. N.Y. Democrat. Office: Le Moyne Coll Dept History Syracuse NY 13214

JUDSON, ARNOLD SIDNEY, management consultant; b. Brockton, Mass., Mar. 29, 1927; s. Moses Joel and Fanny (Becker) J.; m. June Brenner, June 19, 1949; children: Pamela F., Jill E. BS in Chem. Engring., MIT, 1947, MS in Orgnl. Behavior, 1948. Prodn. foreman U.S. Rubber Co., Providence, 1948-50; personnel mgr., mfg. mgr., then dir. tng. and devel. Polaroid Corp., Cambridge, Mass., 1950-62; mgmt. cons. The Emerson Cons., Ltd., London, 1962-66; sr. mgmt. cons. Arthur D.Little, Inc., Cambridge, 1966-76; dir., mgmt. cons. The Berwick Group, Inc., Boston, 1976-81; pres., chief exec. officer Gray-Judson-Howard, Inc., Cambridge, 1981-90; chmn. Gray-Judson-Howard, Inc., 1990—. Author: A Manager's Guide to Making Changes, 1966, Making Strategy Happen, 1990, Changing Behavior in Organizations, 1991; contbr. articles to bus. publs.; composer orchestral and chamber music. Vice chmn. bd. dirs., Greater Boston Rehab. Svcs., Watertown, 1984-91. With USN, 1945-46. Mem. Univ. Club Boston. Home: 220 Marlborough St Boston MA 02116-1771 Office: Gray Judson Howard Inc 101 Main St Cambridge MA 02142-1519

JUDY, DAVID WILLIAM, radio reading service executive; b. Annapolis, Md., June 26, 1960; s. William Raines and Marion Faith (Diegelmann) J.; m. Lee Ann Villemaire, apr. 19, 1986 (div. Oct. 1988); m. Mary Honore O'Connell, Nov. 10, 1990. BA in Theatre Arts, U. Hartford, 1983. Adminstrv. coord. Conn. Radio Info. System, Wethersfield, 1984-85; news reporter/producer Sta. WASR-AM/Sta. WLKZ-FM, Wolfeboro, N.H., 1985; news anchor/reporter Sta. WMMW-AM, Meriden, Conn., 1986; vacation/relief newsman Sta. WJMJ-FM, Bloomfield, Conn., 1986—; exec. dir. Conn. Radio Info. System, Wethersfield, 1986—. Mem. Assn. Radio Reading Svcs. (treas. 1990—, bd. dirs. 1989-90), Univ. Club Hartford, Lions Club Windsor. Office: Conn Radio Info System 589 Jordan Ln Wethersfield CT 06109-1041

JUGENHEIMER, DONALD WAYNE, advertising and communications educator, university administrator; b. Manhattan, Kans., Sept. 22, 1943; s. Robert William and Mabel Clara (Hobert) J.; m. Bonnie Jeanne Scamehorn, Aug. 30, 1970 (dec. 1983); 1 child, Beth Carrie; m. Kaleen B. Brown, July 25, 1987. BS in Advt., U. Ill.-Urbana, 1965, MS in Advt., 1968, PhD in Communications, 1972. Advt. copywriter Fillman & Assocs, Champaign, Ill., 1963-64, 66; media buyer Leo Burnett Co., Chgo., 1965-66; asst., assoc. prof. U. Kans., Lawrence, 1971-80, prof. journalism, dir. grad. studies and rsch., 1980-85; Manship prof. journalism La. State U., Baton Rouge, 1985-87; prof., chmn. dept. communications and speech Fairleigh Dickinson U., Teaneck, N.J., 1987-89, 92—, dean coll. liberal arts, 1989-92; adv. cons. U.S. Army, Fort Sheridan, Ill., 1981-90, Am. Airlines, 1989-91, IBM Corp., 1989—; cons. editor Grid Publ., Columbus, Ohio, 1974-84; grad. and rsch. dir. U. Kans., 1978-84, adv. chmn., 1974-78. Author: Advertising Media Sourcebook and Workbook, 1975, 3d edit., 1989, Strategic Advertising Decisions, 1976, Basic Advertising, 1979, 2d edit., 1991, Advertising Media, 1980, Problems and Practices in Advertising Research, 1982, Advertising Media: Strategy and Tactics, 1992; bd. editors Jour. Advt., 1985-89. Subscription mgr. Jour. of Advt., 1971-74, bus. mgr., 1974-79; chmn. U. Div. United Fund, Lawrence, 1971-72; pres. Sch.-Community Relations Council, Lawrence, 1974-75. Recipient Hope Teaching award U. Kans, 1977, 78 Kellogg Nat. fellow W.K. Kellogg Found., 1984-88; named Outstanding Young Men in Am. Nat. Jaycees, 1978. Mem. AAUP, Am. Acad. Advt. (pres. 1984-86), Assn. For Edn. in Journalism (head advertising div. 1977-78), Kappa Tau Alpha, Alpha Delta Sigma. Presbyterian. Home: 35 Windsor Ter Mahwah NJ 07430-2814 Office: Fairleigh Dickinson U Dept Communications & Speech Teaneck NJ 07666

JUHASE, KIM STEVEN, lawyer; b. Bronx, N.Y., Oct. 17, 1953; s. Jonah and Dorothy Ann (Pytell) J.; m. Kathleen Ann McGowan, Aug. 4, 1984. BA, SUNY, Albany, 1974; JD, Bklyn. Law Sch., 1977. Bar: N.Y. 1978, N.J. 1992. Asst. corp. counsel City of N.Y., 1977-79; assoc. Weinstein, Chayt & Bard, Bklyn., 1979-80, Law Office Morris Kimmel, N.Y.C., 1980-82; pvt. practice, N.Y.C., 1982—. Editor-in-chief Corp. Counsel Reporter, 1978-79, Bklyn. Barrister, 1979-80; contbr. articles to profl. jours. Pres. parish counsel Roman Cath. Ch. Assumption of Blessed Virgin Mary, Bklyn., 1981-91. Mem. N.Y. State Bar Assn. (exec. editor N.Y. Internat. Law Rev. 1988—, chmn. affirmative action subcom. Civil Practice Law and Rules com. 1992—), Soc. for Am. Baseball Rsch., KC, Masons. Republican. Home: 38 Whitney Rd Short Hills NJ 07078 Office: 350 Broadway New York NY 10013

JUHRE, HAROLD WILLIAM, JR., retired state official; b. Buffalo, June 19, 1932; s. Harold William and Marie Augusta (Eichhorn) J.; m. Jean Argyle Campbell, May 25, 1963 (div. Sept. 1981); children: Alexandra Campbell, Michael Rittenhouse. BS in Polit. Sci., Wesleyan U., Middletown, Conn., 1954; MPA, Syracuse U., 1957. Dir. rsch. N.Y. State Div. Housing and Community Renewal, N.Y.C., 1962; with N.Y. State Div. Budget, Albany, 1957-92, pub. fin. assoc., prin. and asst. chief budget examiner, 1965-68, dep. chief budget examiner, 1968-92; guest lectr. Union Coll., Schenectady, Syracuse (N.Y.) U., SUNY, Albany, Russell Sage Coll., Troy, N.Y. Ind. candidate for Albany City Coun., 1967; bd. dirs. local chpt. ACLU, Albany, 1991—, Albany Bridge to Moscow, East-West Bridges for Peace, 1990—. With U.S. Army, 1954-56. Fellow State Acad. for Pub. Adminstrn. (exec. dir. 1986-90, cert. of appreciation 1990); mem. Am. Soc. for Pub. Adminstrn. (coun. Empire State Capital chpt. 1987-92, Disting. Svc. award 1990), Am. Assn. for Budget and Program Analysis, UN Assn. USA (bd. dirs. Capital Area chpt. 1992—), Torch, Club Internat. Democrat. Unitarian. Home: 13 Main St Albany NY 12203-1418

JUKES, TERENCE DOUGLAS, marketing professional; b. St. Catharines, Ont., Can., Nov. 25, 1952; came to U.S., 1990; B of Commerce in Bus., U. Guelph, Ont., 1976; MBA, York U., Toronto, Ont., 1977. Pres. Misco N. Am.; bd. dirs. Misco Can. Inc., Misco Inc. (U.S.A.). Mem. Direct Mktg. Assn., Can. Direct Mktg. Assn. Office: Misco Inc Computer Supplies One Misco Plz Holmdel NJ 07733

JULIAN, IDA, college foundation administrator; b. Phila., Apr. 12, 1945; d. Henry Stephen and Naomi (Filemyr) Meller; m. Edward A. Cahill, II; children: Melanie, Donald. AA, Bucks County Coll., Newtown, Pa., 1981; student, Thomas Edison State Coll., Trenton, N.J., 1990—. Pres. Cybis Porcelains, Trenton, 1969-87; fin. advisor Prudential Bache, Princeton, N.J., 1987-89; v.p. Thomas Edison State Coll. Found., 1990—. Bd. dirs. Salvation Army, Trenton, 1980-91, Am. Cancer Soc., Mercer County, N.J., 1991, Am. Boychoir Sch., Princeton, N.J., 1986-90, George Washington coun. Boy Scouts Am., 1988—; mem. adv. bd. Helene Fuld Med. Ctr., Trenton, 1983—; pres. Mercer County Community Coll. Found., Trenton, 1984-90; bd. dirs. YWCA, Trenton, 1983—, v.p., 1990. Mem. Nat. Soc. Fund Raising Execs., Mercer County C. of C., Princeton C. of C., Zonta, Rotary. Home: 5 Applewood Dr Hopewell NJ 08525-2117 Office: Thomas Edison State Coll Found 101 W State St Trenton NJ 08608-1101

JUMP, BERNARD, JR., economics educator; b. Dayton, Ohio, Mar. 9, 1938; s. Bernard and Elin S. (Peterson) J.; m. Elizabeth Gay Ferguson, Aug. 22, 1959; children: Eric Christopher, Edie. BBA, U. Cin., 1960; MA in Econs., Ohio State U., 1962, PhD in Econs., 1964. Asst. prof. econs. Ball State U., Muncie, Ind., 1964-65; economist Esso Standard Eastern Inc., N.Y.C., 1965-66; assoc. prof., chmn. dept. econs. Hollins Coll., 1966-74; NSF postdoctoral fellow in urban econs. Maxwell Sch., Syracuse U., N.Y., 1970-71, vis. prof. in pub. adminstrn. and econs., 1974-76, prof. pub. adminstrn., 1976—, sr. research assoc., met. studies program, 1976—, dir. master pub. adminstrn. program, 1976-79; chmn. dept. pub. adminstrn. Maxwell Sch., Syracuse U., 1979—, assoc. dean, 1984—; fellow in systems analysis NASA, 1969; fellow Acad. for Contemporary Problems, 1975-79; cons. in field. Co-editor Public Employment and State and Local Government Finances, 1980; contbr. articles to profl. publs., chpts. to books, monographs. NDEA fellow, 1961-64. Mem. Nat. Tax Assn. (mem. intergovtl. fiscal relations com. 1975—, mem. property taxation com. 1971-74,

bd. dirs. 1986-89), Am. Soc. Pub. Adminstrn., Govt. Fin. Officers Assn., Assn. for Pub. Policy Analysis and Mgmt., Am. Econs. Assn., N.Y. State Govt. Fin. Officers Assn. (gov.), Beta Gamma Sigma. Home: 8300 Salt Springs Rd Manlius NY 13104-9759 Office: Syracuse U Maxwell Sch Dept Pub Adminstrn 205 Maxwell Hall Syracuse NY 13244-1090

JUNE, JOAN YVONNE, minority affairs administrator; b. Hawkinsville, Ga.; d. David Lewis and Essie (Sanders) Scott; m. Gilbert Charles June; 1 child, Athena Danielle. BS in Adminstrn., Mercy Coll., 1983; MS Edn in Guidance and Counseling, CUNY, 1991. Asst. dir. Office of Minority Affairs N.Y. Med. Coll., Valhalla, 1985—. Mem. AACD, Assn. Multicultural Counseling and Devel., N.Y. State Assn. Counseling and Devel., Assn. Multiculture Counseling and Devel., Assn. Am. Med. Colls., Am. Mgmt. Assn., Nat. Assn. Med. Minority Educators Inc. (N.E. region chairperson bud. and fin. com. 1988-90), bd. dirs. 1988-90, mem. award com. 1987-90, conf. mgmt. team 1990, nat. chairperson budget and fin. com. 1991-92, bd. dris. and conf. mgmt. team).

JUNEAU, PIERRE, broadcasting company executive; b. Verdun, Que., Can., Oct. 17, 1922; s. Laurent Edmond and Marguerite (Angrignon) J.; m. Fernande Martin, Mar. 17, 1947; children: Andre, Martin, Isabelle. BA, College Sainte-Marie, Montreal, 1944; postgrad. in philosophy, Sorbonne, Paris, 1949; lic. in philosophy, Inst. Cath., Paris, 1949; PhD (hon.), York U., Toronto, 1972, LLD (hon.), 1973; PhD (hon.), Trent U., Peterborough, Ont., 1981, LLD (hon.), 1987; PhD (hon.), Moncton (New Brunswick, Can.) U., 1988. With Nat. Film Bd. Can., 1949-66; dist. rep., asst. regional supr. of Que., chief internat. distbn. Nat. Film Bd. Can., Montreal, 1951; asst. head European office Nat. Film Bd. Can., London, 1952-54; sec. Nat. Film Bd. Can., Montreal, 1954-64, sr. asst. to commr. and dir. French Lang. prodn., 1964-66; vice chmn. Bd. Broadcast Govs., Ottawa, 1966-68; chmn. Can. Radio-TV Commn., Ottawa, 1968-75; minister communications Govt. Can., Ottawa, 1975, adviser to Prime Min., 1975; chmn. Nat. Capital Commn., 1976-78; under sec. state Govt. Can., 1978-80, dep. min. communications, 1980-82; pres. CBC, Ottawa, 1982-89; vis. prof. U. Montreal, 1989—; co-founder Cité libre, periodical, 1949; co-founder, 1st pres. La Fedn. des Mouvements de Jeunesse au Que., early 1950's; bd. dirs. Electromome Ltd., Sta. CISM Radio. Co-founder Montreal Internat. Film Festival, 1950's, pres., 1959-68; former sec., former bd. dirs. Albert-Prevost Psychiat. Inst., Montreal, 1960s; former chmn. bd. Ecole nouvelle St.-Germain; co-founder, bd. dirs. Institut Canadien d'Education des Adultes; bd. dirs. Nat. Arts Centre. Decorated officer Order Can. Mem. Royal Soc. Can., Club of Rome. Office: U Montreal, Dept Communications, Montreal, PQ Canada R3C 2H1

JUNGALWALA, FIROZE BAMANSHAW, neuroscientist, neurochemist, educator; b. Surat, Gujarat, India, Aug. 28, 1936; came to U.S., 1964; s. Bamanshaw Dadabhai and Tehmina B. (Chiniwala) J.; m. Khorshed Firoze Wadia, Mar. 17, 1968; children: Ferzin, Jehanjir. BSc with honors, Gujarat U., Ahmedabad, 1956, MSc, 1958; PhD, Indian Inst. Sci., Bangalore, 1963. Postdoctoral fellow U. Wis., Madison, 1964-66; rsch. assoc. Washington U. Med. Sch., St. Louis, 1966-68; vis. fellow Cambridge (Eng.) U., 1968-71; asst. biochemist Eunice Kennedy Shriver Ctr., Waltham, Mass., 1971-75, assoc. biochemist, 1975-79, sr. biochemist, 1979—; from asst. to assoc. to sr. biochemist Mass. Gen. Hosp., Boston, 1972—; assoc. prof. Harvard Med. Sch., Boston, 1989—. Assoc. editor Jour. Lipid Rsch., Boston, 1981-83, mem. editorial bd., 1983-86; mem. rev. com. NIH, Bethesda, Md., 1985-89, 91—; contbr. over 100 articles to sci. jours. Founder, pres. Zoroastrian Assn. Greater Boston Area, 1980-86. Nat. Multiple Sclerosis Soc. rsch. fellow, N.Y., 1968-70; recipient rsch. grants NIH, 1971—, Rsch. Career Devel. award, 1975-80. Mem. AAAS, Internat. Soc. Neurochemistry, Am. Soc. Biol. Chemistry and Molecular Biology, Am. Neurochem. Soc. Office: Eunice Kennedy Shriver Ctr 200 Trapelo Rd Waltham MA 02154-6332

JUNGMANN, FREDERICK ARTHUR, non-profit organization consultant; b. St. Louis, Nov. 28, 1936; s. Harold Leon and Minnette Selma (Brunswick) J. Student, U. Vt., 1954-58; postgrad., New Sch. for Social Research, N.Y.C., 1958-60, NYU, 1969-72. Assoc. dir. personnel Mt. Sinai Hosp. and Med. Ctr., N.Y.C., 1961-65, Thomson, McKinnon, Inc., N.Y.C., 1966-69; dir. personnel and mgmt. devel. Baker, Weeks & Co., Inc., N.Y.C., 1969-75; founder, pres., exec. dir. Jobs for Youth-Boston Inc., 1976-81, chief exec. officer, 1983-86; elected four succesive terms town moderator Truro, Mass., 1976-80, cons., 1981-85; pres. Lymphoma Found. of Am., Inc., West Palm Beach, Fla., 1988-91; adv. bd. Lymphoma Found. Am., Inc., Washington, 1991—; exec. dir. Ctr. for Coastal Studies, Inc., Provincetown, Mass., 1984-86, bd. dirs. 1982-; co-founder, bd. dirs., Nat. Youth Employment Coalition, Inc., N.Y.C., 1979-86; founder, bd. dirs. Jobs for Youth-Chicago, Inc., 1979-81. Host classical music program on WOMR (local pub. radio sta.). Informal advisor Royal Jubilee and Prince's Trusts, London, 1984-90; mem. U. Vt. Alumni Career Counselling Svc. Network; bd. dirs. Castle Hill Ctr. for Arts, Truro, 1985-87; bd. dirs. exec. com. Nat. Coalition for Cancer Survivorship, Inc., Washington, 1988—. Recipient Lewis Hine award Nat. Child Labor Com., 1985, first recipient annual Frederick Jungmann award for community svc. Ctr. for Coastal Studies, Inc., 1991. Mem. Mass. Businessman's Assn. Home: Pleasant Point Rd Box 583 South Wellfleet MA 02663

JURECIC, ROBERT LOUIS, sales executive; b. Cleve., Jan. 17, 1950; s. Louis and Mollie E. (Drobnic) J.; m. Beverly J. Robison, Aug. 16, 1975; children: Dean, Sean. Student, Lakeland Coll., Mentor, Ohio, 1970-72. Lighting buyer Forest City Materials, Cleve., 1970-75; sales mgr. consumer div. Keystone Lighting, Bristol, Pa., 1975-80; gen. sales mgr. Keene Consumer Products, Union, N.J., 1980-84; v.p. Liteway div. USI Lighting, Bristol, 1984—. Mem. Am. Mgmt. Assn. Office: Liteway PO Box 700 Bristol PA 19007-0700

JURICK, MARILYN LOU (LYN JURICK), marketing professional; b. N.Y.C., Apr. 14, 1929; d. Samuel and Beatrice (Goodman) Robins; m. Robert Herbert Jurick, Oct. 21, 1951; children: Susan Lee, Jeffrey Steven. BA, Cazenovia Coll., 1947-49. Sec. FALA Direct Mktg., N.Y.C., 1978-80; sec., treas. FALA Direct Mktg., L.I., N.Y., 1980—, FALA Direct of Fla., 1983—; bd. dirs. Fleet Bank, L.I. Founding pres., bd. mem. Ronald McDonald House of L.I.; hon. dir. Five Towns United Way; trustee L.I. Jewish Med. Ctr. Recipient Humanitarian award Five Towns United Way, 1986, 1st Vol. of the Yr. award Assn. for the Help of Retarded Children, 1965; named Woman of the Week, Nassau Herald, 1966, Woman of the Yr., 1978, 1st Vol. and Outstanding Fund Raiser, Nat. Soc. Fund Raising Execs., 1990. Republican. Home: 1357 Boxwood Dr E Hewlett Harbor Long Island NY 11557 Office: FALA Direct Mktg Inc 70 Marcus Dr Melville NY 11747-4210

JURIN, ERIC WILLIAM, roofing contracting company executive; b. Sellersville, Pa., May 12, 1952; s. Ivan Frank and Margaret Carolyn (Merritt) J.; m. Kathleen Mary O'Shaughnessy, Oct. 14, 1972; children: Christopher J., Courtney. Student, Springfield (Mass.) Coll., 1970-71. Owner, mgr. Eric W. Jurin Roofing Svcs., Green Lane, Pa., 1972—. Mem. Upper Bucks C. of C., Nat. Roofing Contractors Assn., Humanist Soc., Gt. Dane Club Am., Gt. Dane Club Raritan Valley.

JURKEVICH, GAYANA, Spanish educator, consultant; b. Montreal, Que., Can., Apr. 24, 1953; came to U.S., 1953; d. Igor and Marianna (Pospielovsky) J. AB, Mt. Holyoke Coll., 1974; MA, U. Minn., 1977; PhD, NYU, 1987. With pers. mgmt. U.S. Dept. of State, Washington, 1977-81; rsch. fellow NYU, 1983-86; asst. prof. Barch Coll. CUNY, 1987—; actress, dir., voice-overs; mem. grant rev. panel-comparative lit. CUNY, 1990-91, mem. grant rev. panel Spanish lit., 1991-92. Author: The Elusive Self: Archetypal Approaches to the Novels of Miguel de Unamuno, 1991; contbr. articles in Hispanic Rev., Comparative Lit., MLN, Hispania, ALEC, Revista Hispánica Moderna. Recipient Publ. award Program for Cultural Cooperation Spanish Ministry of Culture U.S.'s Univs., 1990. Mem. Modern Lang. Assn., Am. Assn. Tchrs. Spanish and Portugese, Phi Kappa Phi. Home: 60 Plaza St E # 6N Brooklyn NY 11238-5040

JUSKO, WILLIAM JOSEPH, pharmaceutical scientist, educator; b. Salamanca, N.Y., Oct. 26, 1942; s. Joseph Chester and Pauline Helen (Wrona) J.; m. Laura Jean Gillett, May 30, 1964; children: Suzanne, Marjorie, Katherine. BS in Pharmacy, SUNY, Buffalo, 1965, PhD, 1970; Doctor Honoris Causa, Med. Acad. of Cracow, Poland, 1987. Rsch. pharmacologist VA Hosp., Boston, 1969-72; asst. prof. Boston U. Sch. Medicine, 1970-72; asst. prof. SUNY, Buffalo, 1972-74, assoc. prof., 1974-77, prof., 1977—; dir. Clin. Pharmacokinetics Lab., Buffalo, 1972-81; vis. scientist Mario Negri Inst. for Pharmacology, Milan, 1978-79; cons. Wyeth Labs., Radnor, Pa., 1976—, various other cos., 1980—. Editor: (book) Applied Pharmacokinetics, 1980, 2d rev. edit., 1992; contbr. numerous rsch. articles to profl. jours. Recipient Rorer award Am. Coll. Gastroenterology, Toronto, Can., 1980. Fellow AAAS, Am. Assn. Pharm. Sci., Am. Coll. Clin. Pharmacology (Russell Miller award 1988), Am. Coll. Clin. Pharmacy (Disting. Svc. award 1989); mem. Am. Soc. Clin. Pharm. Therapy (Rawls-Palmer award 1987). Office: SUNY Dept Pharmaceutics Buffalo NY 14260

JUSSIM, ESTELLE, historian and critic, visual arts and photography; b. N.Y.C., Mar. 18, 1927; d. Boris and Manya (Glusker) J. BA, Queens Coll., 1947; MS, Columbia U., 1963, D Libr. Sci. in Media, 1970; PhD, Linköping (Sweden) U., 1990. Free-lance graphic designer N.Y.C., 1948-60; teaching asst. Columbia U., N.Y.C., 1963-64; asst. prof. Hampshire Coll., Amherst, Mass., 1969-72; prof. visual communication, film, photography, graphic arts history Simmons Coll., Boston, 1972—. Author: Slave to Beauty, 1981, Frederic Remington, The Camera and the Old West, 1984, Landscape as Photograph, 1985, Visual Communication and the Graphic Arts, 1985, Stopping Time, 1989, The Eternal Moment, 1990; author of numerous articles and essays. Trustee Visual Studies Workshop, Rochester, N.Y., 1980—. Doctoral fellow Columbia U., 1966-69, Guggenheim fellow, 1982-83. Felllow German Soc. for Photography (hon.), Am. Soc. for History Photography (hon.); mem. Soc. for Photog. Edn. Home: PO Box 132 Granby MA 01033-0132

JUST, MARION REBECCA, political scientist, educator; b. Bklyn., Feb. 6, 1943; d. Harold M. and Pauline (Kessler) Brown; m. Harold A. Just, Mar. 21, 1964; children: Sara, Marjorie, Thomas. BA, Barnard Coll., 1963; MA, Johns Hopkins U., 1965; PhD, Columbia U., 1969. Asst. prof. Wellesley (Mass.) Coll., 1970-76, assoc. prof., 1976-82, chmn. dept. polit. sci., 1982-85, prof., 1982—; rsch. fellow Ctr. for Press, Politics and Pub. Policy, Kennedy Sch., Harvard U., Cambridge, Mass., 1988; vis. scholar dept. polit. sci. MIT, Cambridge, 1989, vis. rsch. assoc. Ctr. for Internat. Studies. Co-author: Coping in a Troubled Society, 1974, Common Knowledge: News and the Construction of Political Understanding, 1992; contbr.: Controversial Issues in Presidential Selection, 1991; contbr. articles to profl. jours. Grantee Spencer Found., 1988-90, SLoan Found., 1987, NSF, 1992. Mem. Am. Polit. Sci. Assn. (chair polit. communication sect. 1991—), AAUP (nat. coun. 1989—), Am. Assn. Pub. Opinion Rsch., Northeastern Polit. Sci. Assn. (pres. 1983-84), New England Polit. Sci. Assn. (pres. 1990-91). Office: Wellesley Coll Dept Polit Sci Pendleton E Wellesley MA 02181

JUTILA, SIMO ANTERO, manufacturing executive; b. Tampere, Finland, Jan. 13, 1957; came to U.S., 1990; s. Pekka Eero Antero and Raili Terttu Marjatta (Pitkänen) J.; m. Riitta Leena Sohlman, Nov. 24, 1978; 1 child, Jani. MSc in Engring., Tampere U. Tech., 1983; MSc in Mgmt., Calif. Am. U., Escondido, 1990. Mgr. prodn. devel. United Paper Mills Ltd./Jylhävaara Engring. Works, Valkeakoski, Finland, 1983-85; gen. mgr. United Paper Mills Ltd./Jylhavaara Refiner Plate Factory, Valkeakoski, Finland, 1985-86, Ahlstrom Screen Plate Works, Varkaus, Finland, 1987-89; pres. Ahlstrom Screen Plates, Inc., Glens Falls, N.Y., 1990-91; v.p. Ahlstrom Process Equipment, Inc., Glens Falls, 1992—. Lt. arty. Finnish armed forces, 1982-83. Mem. Cen. Assn. for Engrs. with MSc in Engring. (bd. dirs. Helsinki unit 1987-89). Office: Ahlstrom Process Equipment Murray St Glens Falls NY 12801

JUTRAS, THOMAS HENRY, JR., mechanical engineer; b. Providence, R.I., Feb. 27, 1968; s. Thomas Henry and Joan Henriette (Ricci) J. BSME, Worcester Poly. Inst., 1990. Design engr. United Technologies Hamilton Standard, Windsor Locks, Conn., 1990-91; fire protection engr. EPM, Inc., Framingham, Mass., 1992—. Mem. AIAA, ASME, Soc. Fire Protection Engrs. Roman Catholic. Home: Apt A 18 Somerset St Worcester MA 01609-2110 Office: EPM Inc 759 Concord Rd Framingham MA

KABACK, STUART MARK, chemist; b. Elizabeth, N.J., June 12, 1934; s. Robert and Regina (Hausman) K.; m. Marilyn Feldman, Dec. 25, 1955; children: Robin Naomi Kaback McGowan, Gilbert Paul. AB, Columbia Coll., 1955; MA, Columbia U., 1956, PhD, 1960. Chemist Esso Rsch. & Engring. Co., Linden, N.J., 1960-68; sr. rsch. chemist Exxon Rsch. & Engring. Co., Linden, 1968-76, rsch. assoc., 1976-85, sr. rsch. assoc., 1985-90, sci. advisor, 1990—; mem. adv. panel Maxwell Communications, 1988—. Mem. editorial adv. bd. Jour. Chem. Info. Computer Sci., 1974-76, Chemtech, 1985-86, Online Inc. Database mag., 1982—; mem. adv. com. Derwent Publs., 1974—; contbr. articles to mags. and profl. jours.; patentee in field. Pres. Temple Beth-El, 1981-82, 91—. mem. adv. panel Maxwell Communications, 1988—; chair patent task force Am. Petroleum Inst., 1980-90. Mem. Am. Chem. Soc. (chem. info. div., asst. sec. 1970-71, treas. 1971-72), Patent Info. Users Group (liaison to PDG 1989—), Chem. Structure Assn. Home: 222 Denman Rd Cranford NJ 07016-2933 Office: Exxon Rsch & Engring Co PO Box 121 Linden NJ 07036-0121

KABAK, DOUGLAS THOMAS, lawyer; b. Elizabeth, N.J., Nov. 19, 1957; s. Aaron and Marilyn Virginia (Johnson) K.; m. Elisabeth Wiggin McDuffie, Oct. 21, 1989; 1 child, Matthew Thomas McDuffie Kabak. BA, Rutgers U., 1979, MBA, 1990; JD, Seton Hall U., 1982; postgrad., U. Exeter, Eng., 1980. Bar. N.J. 1982, U.S. Dist. Ct. N.J. 1982. Law clk. Superior Ct. N.J., Elizabeth, 1982-83; assoc. Z. Lance Samay, Morristown, N.J., 1983-86; asst. dep. pub. defender Office Pub. Defender, Elizabeth, 1986—; legal rep. St. Joseph's the Carpenter Bd. Edn., Roselle, N.J., 1985-87. Dir. St. Joseph the Carpenter Cath. Youth Orgn., Roselle, 1986-88, coach, 1981-86. Mem. ABA, N.J. Bar Assn., Union County Bar Assn., KC. Roman Catholic. Home: 16 Indian Spring Rd Cranford NJ 07016-1616 Office: Pub Defender Office 3d Fl 65 Jefferson Ave Elizabeth NJ 07201-2425

KABAK, IRWIN WILLIAM, industrial engineer; b. N.Y.C., May 21, 1936; s. Harry and Clara (Slomin) K.; m. Gertrude Katzowitz, Sept. 7, 1957; children: Michele Lori, Cindy Robin. B in Indsl. Engring., NYU, 1956, M in Indsl. Engring., 1958, PhD, 1964. Registered profl. engr., Calif., Fla., N.Y., N.J., Pa. Cost control analyst Mergenthaler Linotype, Bklyn., 1956-57; ops. rsch. engr. Esso Rsch. and Engring. Co., Linden, N.J., 1957-58; mem. tech. staff, specialist Bell Telephone Labs., Holmdel, N.J., 1958-65; prof. ops. rsch. Sch. Bus. NYU, 1965—; pres. Modelmetrics, Inc., Edison, N.J., 1967—; bd. dirs. N.J. Automobile Full Ins. Underwriting Assn., 1988-91, Stat-a-Matrix, 1985—, Taxtronics, Inc., 1969-71, Hardboard Fabricators Inc., 1970-71; adj. asst. prof. NYU, 1963-65; lectr. Am. Mgmt. Assn., 1966-69. Contbr. articles to profl. jours. Bd. dirs. sch. evaluation Edison Sch. System, 1965; active Rent Control Bd., Edison, 1991. Mem. Ops. Rsch. Soc. Am. (mem. edn. com. 1988-91), Inst. Indsl. Engrs. (life), Inst. Mgmt. Scis., N.Y. Stock Exch. (panel arbitrators 1991—), NYU Alumni Assn. (bd. dirs.). Democrat. Jewish. Home: 109 Stephenville Pky Edison NJ 08820-2610

KABALA, EDWARD JOHN, lawyer, corporation executive; b. Phila., Mar. 21, 1942; s. Stan and Margaret (Toner) K.; m. Gail L., Dec. 28, 1963; children: Courtenay, Paxson. BS, Pa. State U., 1964; JD, Duquesne U., 1970. Bar: Pa. 1970, U.S. Dist. Ct. (we. dist.) Pa., 3d cir. 1970, U.S. Tax Ct. 1970. Indsl. engr. Allegheny Ludlum Steel Co., 1964-67; sr. indsl. engr. Titanium Metals Corp. Am., 1967-68; patent engr. U.S. Steel Corp., 1969, atty., 1970; atty. Houston, Cooper, Speer and German, Pitts., 1970-73; pres. Kabala & Geeseman and predecessor firm, Pitts., 1973—; pres. P.F.G. Leasing Co., K&G Cons., Ltd.; counsel Allegheny Med. Soc.; author, lectr. pensions, estate planning, taxation, fin. planning health care law various univs. and profl. orgns. of physicians, attys., accts., dentists, 1976—. Author: Defending Your Practice in a Blue Sheild Audit, 1992. Mem. ABA (sect. of taxation com. on closely held corps. and com. on profl. service corps., sect. of bus. banking and corp. law com. on employee benefits), Pa. Bar Assn., Allegheny County Bar Assn., Am. Acad. Hosp. Attys. Home: 18 Forest Glen Dr Pittsburgh PA 15228-1513 Office: The Waterfront 200 Forest Ave Pittsburgh PA 15202-1938

KABAT, ELVIN ABRAHAM, immunochemist, biochemist, educator; b. N.Y.C., Sept. 1, 1914; s. Harris and Doreen (Otis) K.; m. Sally Lennick, Nov. 28, 1942; children: Jonathan, Geoffrey, David. B.S., CCNY, 1932; M.A., Columbia U., 1934, Ph.D., 1937; LL.D. (hon.), U. Glasgow, 1976; Doctoral degree (hon.), U. Orleans (France); Ph.D. (hon.), Weizmann Inst. Sci., Rehovot, Israel; DSc honoris causa, Columbia U., 1987. Lab. asst. immunochemistry Presbyn. Hosp., 1933-37; Rockefeller Found. fellow Inst. Phys. Chemistry, Upsala, Sweden, 1937-38; instr. pathology Cornell U., 1938-41; mem. faculty Columbia U., N.Y.C., 1941—; asst. prof. bacteriology Columbia U., 1946-48, assoc. prof., 1948-52, prof. microbiology, 1952-85, prof. human genetics and devel., 1969-85, Higgins prof. microbiology, 1984-85, Higgins prof. emeritus microbiology, 1985—; mem. adv. panel on immunology WHO, 1965—; lectr. 25th Michael Heidelberger Lecture, Coll. Physicians and Surgeons, Columbia U., 1986; 10th anniversary lectr. Metchnikoff Immunology Bldg. Inst. Pasteur, Paris; expert cons. Nat. Cancer Inst., 1975-82, Nat. Inst. Allergy and Infectious Disease, 1983-88, NIH, Office of Dir., 1989—; Alexander S. Wiener lectr. N.Y. Blood Center, 1979. Author: (with M.M. Mayer) Experimental Immunochemistry, 1948, 2d edition, 1961, Blood Group Substances, Their Chemistry and Immunochemistry, 1956, Structural Concepts in Immunology and Immunochemistry, 1968, 2d edit., 1976, (with T.T. Wu and H. Bilofsky) Variable Regions of Immunoglobulin Chains, 1976, Sequences of Immunoglobulin Chains, (with others) Sequences of Proteins of Immunological Interest, 1983, 4th edit., 1987, 5th edit., 1991 (with T.T. Wu, M. Reid-Miller, H.M. Perry and K.S. Gottesman).; mem. editorial bd.: Jour. Immunology, 1961-76, Transplantation Bull, 1957-60. Recipient numerous awards including: Ann. Research award City of Hope, 1974, award Center for Immunology, State U. N.Y., Buffalo, 1976, Louisa Gross Horwitz award Columbia U., 1977, R.E. Dyer lectr. award NIH, 1979, Townsend Harris medal CCNY, 1980, Philip Levine award Am. Soc. Clin. Pathology, 1982, award for excellence Grad. Faculties Alumni Columbia U., 1982, Disting. Svc. award Columbia U. Coll. Physicians and Surgeons, 1988, Dickson Prize for Medicine U. Pitts, 1986, Academy medal, N.Y. Acad. Medicine, 1989, Nat. Medal of Sci. 1991; named Pierre Grabar Lectr. Societe Francaise d'Immunologie and German Soc. of Immunology; Fogarty scholar NIH, 1974-75. Fellow AAAS, Am. Acad. Allergy (hon.); mem. NAS, Am. Acad. Arts and Scis., Am. Assn. Immunologists (past pres.), Am. Soc. Biol. Chemists, Am. Chem. Soc., Harvey Soc. (pres. 1976-77), Am. Soc. Microbiology, Internat. Assn. Allergists, Soc. Française d'Allergie (hon.), Biochem. Soc. (Eng.), Assn. for Research in Nervous and Mental Diseases, AAUP, Assn. de Microbiologists de Langue Francaise, Société de Biologie, Société de Immunologie (hon.), Japanese Electrophoresis Soc. (hon.), Phi Beta Kappa, Sigma Xi. Home: 70 Haven Ave New York NY 10032-2600 Office: Columbia U Coll Physicians and Surgeons Dept Microbiology 701 W 168th St New York NY 10032-2704

KABELA, FRANK, JR., broadcast executive; b. Hackensack, N.J., July 31, 1938; s. Frank Sr. and Margaret Louise (Erlinger) K.; m. Patricia Ann Bors, Apr. 22, 1961; children: Elisabeth Ann, David John. AB, Rutgers U., 1960. Reporter Bergen Evening Record, Hackensack, N.J., 1960-61; editor Johnson & Johnson, New Brunswick, N.J., 1962-63; pub., gen. mgr. Sentinel Pub. Co., East Brunswick, N.J., 1963-66; pres. Kabela & Dragoset, Inc., Princeton, N.J., 1966-69; exec. v.p. Greater Media, Inc., New Brunswick, 1969-71; pres., chief operating officer Greater Media, Inc., East New Brunswick, N.J., 1981—; co-owner Princeton Ptnrs., 1971; pres. The Kabela Co., Phoenix, Ariz., 1974-81. With U.S. Army, 1961, USAR, 1961-67. Office: Greater Media Inc 2 Kennedy Blvd East Brunswick NJ 08816-1248

KACHELE, ANDREW REYNOLDS, mining company executive; b. Bridgeport, Conn., Mar. 16, 1947; s. Andrew Martin and Elizabeth Jennings (Reynolds) K.; m. Karen Regina Soltesz, Sept. 6, 1969; children: Fredrick Ryan, Clayton Douglas. BA in Econs., Yale U., 1969. Purchasing mgr. Avco-Lycoming, Stratford, Conn., 1969-81; dir. purchasing Chandler Evans Corp., West Hartford, Conn., 1981-85; gen. mgr. corp. purchasing and adminstrn. Unimin Corp., New Canaan, Conn., 1985—. Nominee 1st selectman Town of Trumbull, Conn., 1975, mem. bd. fin., 1971-77; mem. bd. fin. Town of Easton, Conn., 1988—; vice chmn. Easton Reps., 1986-88. Home: 85 Kachele St Bridgeport CT 06611 Office: Unimin Corp 258 Elm St New Canaan CT 06840-5328

KACHUCK, BEATRICE, education educator; b. Bklyn., Jan. 3, 1926; d. Joseph and Lydia (Greenberg) K.; children: Paul Alan Levy, Dan David Levy. BA, Bklyn. Coll., 1948; MA, NYU, 1955, PhD, 1972; student, Bank St. Coll., 1948. Cert. elem. tchr., N.Y. Tchr., dir. Day Care Ctrs., Nursery Schs., N.Y.C., 1945-50, 53-55; tchr. Baldwin Plainview (N.Y.) Pub. Schs., 1959-64; reading specialist Lawrence Pub. Schs., Cedarhurst, N.Y., 1964-68; prof. CUNY, Bklyn., 1968—; presenter in field. Contbr. articles to profl. jours. Grantee Nat. Inst. Edn., faculty rsch. CUNY. Mem. APA, Am. Ednl. Rsch. Assn., Assn. for Women in Psychology, Internat. Reading Assn., Nat. Reading Conf., Nat. Women's Studies Assn., Project on Study Gender and Edn. Office: CUNY Bklyn Coll Brooklyn NY 11210

KACSER, CLAUDE, physics educator; b. 1934. BA, Oxford U., 1955, MA, PhD in Physics, 1959. Research fellow physics Magdalen Coll., Oxford U., 1958-59, 61-62; instr. Princeton U., 1959-61; asst. prof. Columbia U., 1962-64; asst. prof. U. Md., College Park, 1964-67, assoc. prof. physics, 1967—. Author: Special Theory of Relativity, 1967; contbr. articles to profl. jours. Mem. Am. Assn. Physics Tchrs. Office: U Md Dept Physics College Park MD 20742-4111

KACZMARSKI, MICHAEL JOHN, controller, company executive; b. Pitts., June 29, 1953; s. Richard T. and Audrey A. (Picard) K.; m. Beverly Ann Baker, Nov. 30, 1974; 1 child, Nathan. BS in Acctg., Pa. State U., 1974; MBA, Duquesne U., 1989. CPA, Pa. Mem. audit staff Touche Ross & Co., Pitts., 1974-77, sr. staff mem., 1977-79; mgr. acctg. Ketchum Communications, Inc., Pitts., 1979-81, asst. contr., 1981-84, contr., 1984-85, v.p., contr., 1985-88, sr. v.p., contr., 1988—. Mem. AICPA, Pa. Inst. CPAs., Fin. Execs. Inst., Rivers Club. Home: 2075 Southwell Dr Library PA 15129-8850 Office: Ketchum Communications Inc 6 PPG Pl Pittsburgh PA 15222-5406

KADABA, MURALI PARTHSARATHY, motion research scientist, technology and business consultant; b. Bangalore, Mysore, India, Jan. 16, 1949; came to U.S., 1970; s. Parthasarathy R. and Sharada (Belur) K.; m. Jean Holland, Mar. 30, 1979; 1 child, John P. Breckinridge Kadaba. BS, Bangalore U., 1969; MS, U. Cin., 1972; PhD, U. Ky., 1978; MBA, Columbia U., 1991. Chief motion analysis lab. Helen Hayes Hosp., West Haverstraw, N.Y., 1979—; cons. Childrens Hosp., Richmond, Va., 1988-89; staff mem./cons. Shriner's Hosp., Houston, 1990—; tech. cons. Univ. Complutense Sch. Nursing and Phys. Therapy, Madrid, 1991—. Bd. assoc. editors Jour. Orthopaedic Rsch., 1991—; editorial cons. Jour. Biomechanics. Rsch. grantee Paralyzed Vets. Am., 1985, NIH, 1985-88, Richmond Cerebral Palsy Ctr. award, 1992. Mem. IEEE, Orthopaedic Rsch. Soc. Office: Helen Hayes Hosp Rt 9W West Haverstraw NY 10993

KADISH, LORI GAIL, clinical psychologist; b. Newark, Mar. 6, 1962; d. Gerald Bernard and Marlene (Brodsky) K. BA in Psychology, Emory U., 1984; MS in Clin. Psychology, Fla. Inst. Tech., 1987, PsyD in Clin. Psychology, 1988. Lic. psychologist, N.J., N.Y., Fla.; cert. addiction specialist. Tutor Dekalb County Juvenile Detention Ctr., Atlanta, 1982-83; edn. counselor, interviewer Planned Parenthood, Atlanta, 1983; crisis intervention counselor Helpline, Atlanta, 1982-84; therapist Brevard Community Mental Health Ctr., Melbourne, Fla., 1984-86; therapist adolescent-adult psychiat. unit Wuesthoff Meml. Hosp., Rockledge, Fla., 1986-87; psychology intern South Oaks Hosp., Amityville, N.Y., 1987-88; staff clin. psychlogist, team leader Fair Oaks Hosp., Summit, N.J., 1988—; pvt. practice clin. psychology, Summit, 1990—, Livingston, 1992—; presenter in field. Vol. recreational and occupational therapist asst. St. Barnabas Hosp., Livingston, N.J., 1983; vol. psychiat. nurse asst. Muhlenberg Hosp., Plainfield, N.J., 1983. Mem. APA, Ea. Psychol. Assn., N.Y. State Psychol. Assn., N.J. Psychol. Assn., Fla. Psychol. Assn., Soc. Psychologists in Addictive Behaviors, Assn. for Advancement Behavior Therapy, Bergen County Assn. Lic. Psychologists. Office: Fair Oaks Hosp 19 Prospect St Summit NJ 07901-2442

KADY, MICHAEL STANLEY, manufacturing company executive; b. Ft. Wayne, Ind., June 10, 1949; s. Frank A. and Vera B. (Highley) K.; m. Linda S. McSherry, Jan. 23, 1971; children: Aaron A., Bradley C. BSME, Purdue U., 1972; MBA, Butler U., 1975. Registered profl. engr., Ind. Mfg. engr. chain div. FMC, Indpls., 1972-75, prodn. planning supr., 1975-76, prodn. mgr., 1976-78; planning analyst Cooper Industries, Inc., Houston, 1978-80,

controller Portable Rig div., Dallas, 1980-82, dir. fin. Demco div., Oklahoma City, 1982-85; plant mgr. Nicholson/Cooper Steel, Greenville, Miss., 1985-87; gen. mgr. Cooper Hardware & Components Operation, Beacon Falls, Conn., 1987—; assoc. faculty mem. Ind. U./Purdue U., Indpls., 1975-77. Bd. dirs. United Way of Naugatuck and Beacon Falls. Mem. Mensa. Office: Cooper Hardware & Components Operation PO Box 157 Beacon Falls CT 06403-0157

KAEL, PAULINE, film critic, author; b. Petaluma, Calif., June 19, 1919; d. Isaac Paul and Judith (Friedman) K.; 1 child, Gina James. Student, U. Calif., Berkeley, 1936-40; LLD (hon.), Georgetown U., 1972; D. Arts and Letters (hon.), Columbia Coll., Chgo., 1972; LittD (hon.), Smith Coll., 1973, Allegheny Coll., 1979; LHD (hon.), Kalamazoo Coll., 1973, Reed Coll., 1975, Haverford Coll., 1975; DFA (hon.), Sch. Visual Arts, N.Y.C., 1980. Movie critic New Yorker mag., 1968-91. Author: I Lost it at the Movies, 1965, Kiss Kiss Bang Bang, 1968, Going Steady, 1970, Deeper into Movies, 1973 (Nat. Book award 1974), Reeling, 1976, When the Lights Go Down, 1980, 5001 Nights at the Movies, 1982, enlarged edit., 1991, Taking It All In, 1984, State of the Art, 1985, Hooked, 1989, Movie Love, 1991; contbg. author: The Citizen Kane Book, 1971; contbr. to numerous other mags. Recipient George Polk Meml. award, 1970, Front Page award Newswomen's Club N.Y., 1974, 83; Guggenheim fellow, 1964. Mem. Phi Beta Kappa (hon.). Office: New Yorker 20 W 43d St New York NY 10036-7400

KAFKA, MARIAN STERN, neuroscientist; b. Richmond, Va., Mar. 30, 1927; d. Henry Sycle and Adele (Lewit) Stern; m. John S. Kafka, Oct. 3, 1952; children: David Egon, Paul Henry, Alexander Charles. AB in Zoology, Conn. Coll., 1948; PhD in Physiology, U. Chgo., 1952. Rsch. asst. dept. physiol. chemistry Emory U. Sch. Medicine, Atlanta, 1952-53; rsch. assoc. Ill. Neuropsychiat. Inst., U. Ill. Sch. Medicine, Chgo., 1953-54; rsch. asst. dept. internal medicine Yale U. Sch. Medicine, New Haven, 1954-57; USPHS postdoctoral fellow endocrinology br. Nat. Heart, Lung and Blood Inst. NIH, Bethesda, Md., 1965-68, physiologist hypertention-endocrine br., 1968-74; physiologist sect. biochemistry and pharmacology Biol. Psychiatry Br. NIH, Bethesda, 1974-82; physiologist Clin. Neurosci. Br. NIMH, Bethesda, 1982-86; exec. sec. neurobehavioral rsch. rev. subcom., neuroscis. rsch. rev. com. NIMH, Rockville, Md., 1986, exec. sec. cellular neurobiology & psychopharmacology com., 1986-90; chief clin. rev. br. div. extramural activities NIMH, Rockville, 1990—. Contbr. articles, revs. to sci. publs. Recipient Adminstr.'s award for Meritorious Achievement, ADAMHA, 1989; Marie J. Mergler fellow in physiology, 1950. Mem. AAAS, Am. Physiol. Soc. (mem. pub. affairs and pub. info. com. 1974-79, chair pub. info. com. 1980-84, centennial com. 1979-85), Soc. for Neurosci., Endocrine Soc., Biophys. Soc., Internat. Soc. Chronobiology, Fedn. Am. Soc. for Exptl. Biology (pub. info. com. 1977-82), Phi Beta Kappa, Sigma Xi. Home: 7834 Aberdeen Rd Bethesda MD 20814-1102 Office: NIMH Parklawn Bldg 5600 Fishers Ln Rm 902C Rockville MD 20857-0001

KAGAN, JULIA LEE, magazine editor; b. Nurnberg, Fed. Republic Germany, Nov. 25, 1948; d. Saul and Elizabeth J. (Koblenzer) K. A.B., Bryn Mawr Coll., 1970. Researcher Look Mag., N.Y.C., 1970-71; editorial asst., asst. editor McCall's Mag., N.Y.C., 1971-74, assoc. editor, 1974-78, sr. editor, 1978-79; articles editor Working Woman mag., N.Y.C., 1979-85, exec. editor, 1985-88; editor Psychology Today, 1988-90; sr. editor McCalls, 1990-91; contbg. editor Working Woman, 1991—; vis. J. Stewart Riley prof. journalism Ind. U., 1991-93. Co-author: Manworks: A Guide to Style, 1980; contbg. author: The Working Woman Success Book, 1981, The Working Woman Report, 1984; editor-in-chief Lamaze Parents' Mag., 1992—. Pres. Appleby Found., N.Y.C., 1982-84; bd. dirs. Women's Counseling Project, N.Y.C., 1983—; chmn. selection com. Alumnae Assn. Bryn Mawr Coll. Recipient 2d Ann. Advt. Journalism award Compton Advt., 1983. Mem. Am. Soc. Mag. Editors, Am. Soc. Pub. Opinion Researchers. Club: Princeton (N.Y.C.). Home: 523 W 121st St Apt 42 New York NY 10027-5901

KAHALAS, HARVEY, business educator; b. Boston, Dec. 3, 1941; s. James and Betty (Bonfeld) K.; m. Dianne Barbara Levine, Sept. 2, 1963; children: Wendy Elizabeth, Stacy Michele. BS, Boston U., 1965; MBA, U. Mich., 1966; PhD, U. Mass., 1971. Data processing coordinator Ford Motor Co., Wayne, Mich., 1963-66; lectr. Salem (Mass.) State Coll., 1966-68; asst. prof. bus. Worcester (Mass.) Polytech. Inst., 1970-72; asst. prof. Va. Polytech. Inst., Blacksburg, 1972-75, assoc. prof., 1975-77; assoc. prof. SUNY, Albany, 1977-79, assoc. dean, 1979-81, prof., 1979-89, dean, 1981-87; pres. HKE Inc., 1987—; prof. U. Mass., Lowell, 1989—; dean, 1989—; cons. Aspen Inst. for Humanistic Studies/Fund for Corp. Initiatives, N.Y.C., 1980—, Gen. Electric, Schenectady, N.Y., 1981-85, Gen. Motors, Tarrytown, N.Y., 1987-89. Contbr. articles to profl. jours. Bd. dirs. Fund for Corp. Initiatives, N.Y.C., 1980—, Nat. Found. Ileitis and Colitis, Albany, 1982—, Blue Cross Northeastern N.Y., Albany, 1983—, Capital Dist. Bus. Rev., Albany, 1984—. Named Disting. Alumni, U. Mass., 1982, Disting. Lectr. USIA, 1985, Am. Participant USIA, 1989, Fulbright Coun., 1988. Mem. Acad. Mgmt. (treas. 1971-73, mem. exec. com.), Human Resource Planning Soc. (hon.), Human Resource Systems Profls. (hon.), Beta Gamma Sigma, Delta Tau Kappa. Home: 500 Stratton Pl Delmar NY 12054-2729 Office: U Mass Coll Mgmt 1 University Ave 1 University Ave Lowell MA 01854

KAHAN, MARLENE, professional association executive; b. Bronx, N.Y., June 10, 1952; d. Meyer and Ruth (Baroth) Schmulewitz. BA in Psychology, CUNY, 1973. Tchr. elem. sch., Bronx, 1974-75; asst. to pres. Mag. Pubs. Am., N.Y.C., 1976-83; asst. dir. Am. Soc. Mag. Editors, N.Y.C., 1983-90, exec. dir., 1990—. Recipient Gold Key award PR News, 1991. Mem. Women in Communications (program com. N.Y.C. 1991, 92). Office: Am Soc Mag Editors 575 Lexington Ave New York NY 10022-6102

KAHL, ALFRED LOUIS, JR., business administration educator; b. Michigan City, Ind., Oct. 4, 1932; s. Alfred Louis and Marion Carr (Wheeler) K.; m. Lola Latini, Dec. 3, 1955; children—Karen, Kevin. B.Sc., Phoenix U., 1957; B.A., U. Md., 1960; diploma Indsl. Coll. Armed Forces, 1961; M.B.A., U. Pitts., 1962; Ph.D., U. Fla., 1969. Cert. data processor Data Processing Mgmt. Assn.; profl. adminstr. Inst. Chartered Secs. and Adminstrs. in Can. Asst. prof. banking and fin. U. Ga., Athens, 1965-70; prof. commerce U. Tunis (Tunisia), 1970-72; prof., chmn. dept. bus. administrn. Mankato State U. (Minn.), 1972-74; assoc. prof. adminstrn. U. Ottawa (Ont., Can.), 1974—, vice chmn. dept. bus. adminstrn., 1976-78, chmn., 1979, asst. dean, 1991—; cons. in field. Author: (with A. Belkaoui) Corporate Financial Disclosure in Canada, 1978; (with E. Brigham and W. Rentz) Canadian Financial Management: Theory and Practice, 1983; (with J. Riggs and W. Rentz) Essentials of Engineering Economics, 1983; editor: (with others) International Business: The Canadian Way, 1980, rev. edit., 1983; (with M. Crener and B. Dasah) Introduction to Management: A Canadian Perspective, 1981, Process of Management: A Canadian Perspective, 1981; (with W. Rentz) Cases, Readings and Exercises in Canadian Financial Management Theory and Practice, 1983; (with others) Engineering Economics, 1986; (with E. Brigham and W. Rentz, W. Rentz and L. Gapenski) Canadian Financial Management, 2d. edit., 1987, 3rd edit., 1991; contbr. numerous articles to profl. jours. Fulbright sr. fellow, Burundi, 1977. Fellow Fin. Analysts Fedn.; mem. Acad. Internat. Bus., Acad. Mgmt., Adminstrv. Scis. Assn. Can., Am. Acctg. Assn., Am. Econ. Assn., Am. Fin. Assn., Am. Inst. for Decision Scis., Can. Acad. Acctg. Assn., Fin. Mgmt. Assn., Inst. Indsl. Engrs., Internat. Inst. Forecasters, Micro-Computer Investors Assn., Montreal Soc. Fin. Analysts, Nat. Assn. Bus. Economists, Strategic Mgmt. Soc., Inst. Mgmt. Scis., Beta Gamma Sigma, Alpha Iota Delta, Phi Kappa Phi. Home: 163 Craig Henry Dr, Ottawa, ON Canada K2G 3Z8 Office: U Ottawa, Faculty Adminstrn, Ottawa, ON Canada K1N 6N5

KAHLENBERG, JEANNETTE DAWSON, civic organization executive; b. Chgo., May 22, 1931; d. Horace and Frances Jeannette (Ledlie) Dawson; m. Richard Walter Kahlenberg, Sept. 3, 1955; children: Joy Kahlenberg Fallon, Trudi Kahlenberg Picciano, Richard Dawson. BA, Wellesley Coll., Wellesley, Mass., 1953; MA, Union Theol. Sem.-Columbia U., 1956. Dir. Christian edn. The Presbyterian Ch., Madison, N.J., 1955-56; dir. fin. devel. LWV of Minn., St. Paul, 1978-80; cons. fin. devel. Nat. Bd. YWCA of U.S.A., N.Y.C., 1981-84; v.p. adminstrn. China Inst. in Am., N.Y.C., 1984-86; exec. dir. Citizens Union of City of N.Y., 1986—. Co-author: What's the Score in Minnesota, Equal Opportunity for Girls in Athletics, 1979; editor (newsletter) Citizens Union Reports, 1986—. Mem. sch. bd. White Bear Lake (Minn.) Area Schs., 1975-80, Spl. Vocat. Tech. Sch. Dist., NE Suburban St. Paul, 1978-80; trustee United Theol. Sem. of the Twin Cities, New Brighton, Minn., 1975-80; local pres. state bd. dirs. LWV, Minn., 1973-79. Presbyterian. Home: 480 Fairway Rd Ridgewood NJ 07450-3412 Office: Citizens Union of the City of NY 198 Broadway New York NY 10038-2515

KAHN, ALAN EDWIN, lawyer; b. N.Y.C., Aug. 9, 1929; s. Joseph and Harriet Rose (Rubel) K.; m. Regina Wolf, Aug. 7, 1960 (div. Jan. 1978); 1 child, Jolie Galen; m. Patricia Ann Dugan, June 4, 1978. BBA, CCNY, 1950; JD, Bklyn. Law Sch., 1956. Bar: N.Y. 1956, U.S. Dist. Ct. (so. and ea. dists.) N.Y. 1978, U.S. Tax Ct. 1978; CPA, N.Y. Staff asst. Feinberg, Jacobs & Furman, N.Y.C., 1956-57; sole practice N.Y.C., 1957—; tax cons. to various nonprofit orgns., N.Y.C., 1977—. Cons. Vol. Lawyers for the Arts, N.Y.C., 1978—. Sgt. U.S. Army, 1951-52. Mem. N.Y. State Bar Assn., Assn. Trial Lawyers Am. (mem. com. 1990—), N.Y. State Trial Lawyers Assn. (chmn. subcom. on legis. estate and trusts 1979, speaker bd. 1990—, mem. com. 1991—), N.Y. County Lawyers Assn. (taxation corps. and partnerships 1988—), Assn. Trial Lawyers City N.Y., Jewish Lawyers Guild, N.Y. State Soc. CPAs, Odd Fellows (grand adv. bd. N.Y. chpt. 1979-80, gen. counsel grand lodge 1989—), Nat. Sculpture Soc., Mchts. Club (bd. govs., asst. sec., sec. and gov. 1992—). Democrat. Home: 370 1st Ave New York NY 10010-4923 Office: 299 Broadway New York NY 10007-1901

KAHN, CARL RONALD, research laboratory administrator; b. Louisville, Jan. 14, 1944; s. David L. and Reva W. (Waldman) K.; m. Susan Becker; children: Stacy, Jeffrey. BA, U. Louisville, 1964, MD, 1968, MS, 1984; MA (hon.), Harvard U., 1984; DSc (honoris causa), U. Louisville, 1984, U. Paris-Pierre and Marie Curie, 1990. Diplomate Am. Bd. Internal Medicine, Am. Bd. Endocrinology and Metabolism. Intern and resident in ward medicine Barnes Hosp., St. Louis, 1968-70; clin. assoc., sr. clin. assoc., clin. endocrinology br. Nat. Inst. Arthritis, Metabolism and Digestive Diseases, NIH, Bethesda, Md., 1970-73; sr. investigator Diabetes Br. NIH, Bethesda, Md., 1973-78, chief diabetes br., 1979-81; rsch. dir Joslin Diabetes Ctr., Boston, 1981—; assoc. prof. Harvard Med. Sch., Boston, 1981-84, prof. medicine, 1984—, Mary K. Iacocca prof. medicine, 1986—; lectr. symposia, meetings, thesis supr., course dir. and devel. numerous med. instns.; admitting and attending physician NIH Clin. Ctr., 1972-81; physician Brigham and Women's Hosp., Boston, 1981, chief div. Diabetes and Metabolism, 1981; assoc. staff Endocrinology/Internal Medicine, New Eng. Deaconess Hospital, Boston, 1982, active staff, 1986; clin. assoc. prof. medicine, Uniformed Svcs. U. Health Scis, Bethesda, Md., 1979-81; vis. scientist Centre de Moleculaire, Centre National de la Recherche Scientifique, Gif-sur-Yvette, France, 1979-80; adj. prof. genetics George Washington U., 1980-81; overseas vis. prof. Royal Melbourne Hosp., Australia, 1985—; vis. prof. Royal Postgrad. Hosp., London, 1985—; Rosemary Sarver vis. prof. in endocrinology and metabolism, The Hosp. of the Good Samaritan, L.A., 1985. Author or co-author over 399 publications in field; mem. editorial bds. Jour. Clin. Endocrinology and Metabolism, 1977-80, Diabetes, 1977-84, Am. Jour. Medicine, 1979-84, Jour. Clin. Investigation, 1979-84, Jour. Receptor Rsch., 1980-83, Hormone and Metabolic Rsch., 1980-83, Endocrinology, 1981-85, Jour. Biol. Chemistry, 1983-88, Diabetes and Metabolism Revs., 1984, Receptor, 1989—; exec. editor Trends in Endocrinology and Metabolism, 1989—. Mem. Nat. Diabetes Adv. Bd., 1981-85, co-chmn. rsch. com., 1982-85. Recipient David Rumbough Meml award for Sci. Achievement Juvenile Diabetes Found., 1977, CIBA-Geigy Drew award for biochem. rsch., 1981, Mary Jane Kugel award Juvenile Diabetes Found., 1982, AFCR award for Outstanding Clin. Rsch. under Age 40, 1983, Sol Berson Meml. lectureship NIH, 1983, Hehnemann Lectr. in Pharmacology U. Calif.,1984, Pfizer Biomed. Rsch. award, Pfizer inc., 1986, Cristobal Diaz award Internat. Diabetes Fedn., 1988, others. Mem. Am. Acad. Arts & Scis., Am. Fedn. Clin. Rsch. (award for outstanding clin. rsch. under age 40 1983), The Endocrine Soc. (Edwin B. Astwood lectr. 1987), Am. Diabetes Assn. (Eli Lilly award for rsch. 1980, Otto Brandman award N.J. affiliate 1989, Elliott P. Joslion medal Mass. affiliate), Am. Soc. Clin. Investigation (nat. coun. 1986—, pres. elect 1987-88, pres. 1988-89), Am. Soc. Biol. Chemistry, Assn. Am. Physicians, Sigma Xi, Alpha Epsilon Delta, Phi Kappa Phi, Alpha Omega Alpha. Office: Joslin Diabetes Ctr One Joslin Pl Boston MA 02215

KAHN, CAROLE, journalist; b. N.Y.C., Feb. 17, 1937; d. Saul and Mae (Sheweloff) K. BA, Bklyn. Coll., 1957; MS in Journalism, Columbia U., 1960. Feature writer Conn. Sun. Herald, Bridgeport, 1962-68; investigative reporter Hartford Times, 1968-70, Boston Herald Traveler, 1970; co-anchor, assoc. producer Conn. Pub. TV, Hartford, 1970-71; dir. info. City of N.Y., BPSSA Sr. Programs, 1973-74; dir. broadcast film Consumers Union, Mt. Vernon, N.Y., 1974-77; co-producer, writer Buyline: Betty Furness, WNBC-TV, N.Y.C., 1977-80; econ./fin. producer NBC News, N.Y.C., 1980—. Producer/writer ednl. film: The Six Billion $ Sell, 1976 (Learning AV award 1976), Kicking Tires is Not Enough, 1976; script editor, reporter documentary: War Called Peace, 1980. Pres. 522 Apts. Corp., N.Y.C., 1983-85, bd. dirs., 1982. Corp. for Pub. Broadcasting career fellow, 1970; recipient Peabody award for Buyline: Betty Furness, Regents U. Ga., 1977, Emmy award Nat. Acad. TV Arts and Scis., 1977, 78, 79, Wilbur award Religious Pub. Rels. Coun., 1990, CPA award for Chinese Econs., N.Y. State Soc. CPAs, 1990. Office: NBC News 30 Rockefeller Plz New York NY 10112-0002

KAHN, DANIEL GERALD, stockbroker; b. N.Y.C., Jan. 11, 1955; s. Hugo and Margaret (Darmstadter) K.; m. Shira Lynne Orenstein, July 8, 1984; 1 child, Yael. BA, Cornell U., 1976; MBA, NYU, 1978. Salesperson Rodar Textile Corp., N.Y.C., 1976-84; stockbroker Dean Witter Reynolds Co., N.Y.C., 1985—. Active Jewish Big Bros. program, N.Y.C., 1977-82; vol. visitor to elderly Dorot, N.Y.C., 1985; campaign worker Liz Holtzman for Senate, N.Y.C., 1980. Democrat. Office: Dean Witter Reynolds 900 3d Ave New York NY 10022

KAHN, DORIS CHILTON, dentist; b. N.Y.C., Aug. 11, 1928; d. B. Bernard and Bertha (Wareck) Chilton; m. Stuart Lipman Kahn, Aug. 26, 1951; children: Richard, Paul, James. AB, Hunter Coll., 1947; DDS, NYU, 1951. Lic. dentist, N.Y., N.J. Pvt. practice dentistry Higland Park, N.J., 1951-85; instr. NYU Coll. Dentistry, 1951-53. Bd. trustees YMHA, Highland Park, 1977-83, Anshe Emeth Meml. Temple, New Brunswick, N.J., 1983—; pres. Jewish Hist. Soc. Cen. N.J., 1988-92. Home: 132 N 8th Ave Highland Park NJ 08904-2918

KAHN, ELY JACQUES, JR., writer; b. N.Y.C., Dec. 4, 1916; s. Ely Jacques and Elsie Plaut Mayer; m. Virginia Rice, 1945 (div. 1969); children: Ely Jacques III, Joseph Plaut, Hamilton Rice; m. Eleanor Munro, 1969; stepchildren: David T.M. Frankfurter, Alexander M. Frankfurter. Grad., Horace Mann Sch., 1933; A.B., Harvard U., 1937; LL.D. (hon.), Marlboro Coll., 1986. Writer, reporter N.Y.C., 1937—; adj. prof. writing Columbia, 1974-75, 81-82. Author: The Army Life, 1942, G. I. Jungle, 1943, McNair: Educator of an Army, 1945, The Voice, 1947, Who, Me? 1949, The Peculiar War, 1952, The Merry Partners, 1955, The Big Drink, 1960, A Reporter Here and There, 1961, The Stragglers, 1962, The World of Swope, 1965, A Reporter in Micronesia, 1966, The Separated People, 1968, Harvard: Through Change and Through Storm, 1969, The First Decade, 1972, (with Joseph P. Kahn) The Boston Underground Gourmet, 1972, Fraud, 1973, The American People, 1974, The China Hands, 1975 (Sidney Hillman prize), Georgia: From Rabun Gap to Tybee Light, 1978, About The New Yorker and Me, 1979, Far-flung and Footloose, 1980, Jock: The Life and Times of John Hay Whitney, 1981, The Staffs of Life, 1985, The Problem Solvers, 1986, Year of Change: More About The New Yorker and Me, 1988, Supermarketer to the World, 1991; contbr.: The New Yorker, other nat. mags. Bd. dirs. Assn. Harvard Alumni, 1969-72. Served with AUS, 1941-45. Recipient Legion of Merit award, Disting. Achievement award Horace Mann Sch., 1981. Mem. Authors Guild Am., Authors League Am., PEN (exec. com. 1976-79), Soc. Am. Historians, Harvard Club (N.Y.C.), Century Assn., Phi Beta Kappa, Kappa Alpha Tau. Home: 1095 Park Ave New York NY 10128-1154 also: Truro MA 02666 Office: The New Yorker 20 W 43d St New York NY 10036

KAHN, FAITH-HOPE, nurse, adminstrator, writer; b. N.Y.C., Apr. 25, 1921; d. Leon and Hazel (Cook) Green; RN, Beth Israel Med. Center, N.Y.C., 1942; student N.Y. U., 1943; m. Edward Kahn, May 29, 1942; children: Ellen Leora, Faith Hope II, Paula Amy. First scrub operating room Beth Israel Hosp., N.Y.C., 1942; supr., operating room Hunts Point Gen. Hosp., 1942; gynecol. reconstrn. procedures researcher Phoenixville (Pa.) Gen. Hosp., 1943, Sydenham Hosp., N.Y.C., 1945; supr. ARC Disaster Field Hosp., Queens, N.Y., 1950-51; adminstr., mgr. team coordinator Dr. Edward Kahn, FACOG, Queens Village, N.Y., 1945—. Inventor, publicity chmn. Girl Scouts U.S.A., 1953; exec. dir. publicity Woodhull Schs., 1956-60, pres., 1961-62; exec. dir. publicity N.Y. Dept. Parks Figure Skating, 1956-70; exec. dir. publicity and applied arts St. John's Hosp., Smithtown, N.Y., 1965-66; state advisor N.Y., U.S. Congressional Adv. Bd., Washington, 1981—; nat. adv. bd. Am. Security Council, 1978—; founder Am. Security Found.; bd. trustees, Am. Police Hall of Fame and Mus., 1983—; mem. Republican Presdl. Task Force, 1986, Statue of Liberty and Ellis Island Centennial Commn., N.Y., 1986—. Recipient citation ARC, 1951, Am. Law Enforcement Officers Assn., Bronze medal Am. Security Council Ednl. Found., 1978, spl. recognition award Center Internat. Security Studies, 1979, Meml. Plate, Patriots of Am. Bicentennial, 1976, Great Seal of U.S.A. Plate, cert. Am. Sons Liberty, 1987, Good Smaritan award, 1987, Justice award Cross of Knights, 1987 Knights of Justice award, 1987; named Knight Chevalier Venerable Order of Michael the Archangel, 1987. Fellow, World Lit. Acad. (life), Acad. Nat. Law Enforcement (hon.); mem. Am. Acad. Ambulatory Nursing Adminstrn., Nurses Assn., Nat. League Nursing, Am. Coll. Obstetricians and Gynecologists, Nat. Assn. Physicians' Nurses, Nat. Critical Care Inst., Assn. Operating Room Nurses, AAAS, Nat. Assn. Female Execs., N.Y. Acad. Scis., Am. Police Acad. (cert. appreciation 1979, 83), Am. Fedn. Police, The Retired Officers Assn., Internat. Platform Assn., Security and Intelligence Found. (cert. appreciation 1986), Internat. Intelligence and Orgnd. Crime Investigators Assn., Smithtown Hist. Soc., Nat. Audubon Soc., NRA. Clubs: Tiyospaye, Paul Revere, Sterlingshire Woman's. Author, editor: The Easy Driving Way for Automatic and the Standard Shift, 1954; (with Edward Kahn) The Pelvic Examination, Outline and Guide for Residents, Internes and Students, 1954; (with Edward Kahn) Traction Hysterosalpingography for Uterine Lesions, 1949; contbr. articles profl. and lay jours. Home and Office: 21316 85th Ave Hollis Hills NY 11427-1324

KAHN, FRED A., federal agency adminstrator; b. Wiesbaden, Fed. Republic of Germany, Dec. 19, 1932; came to U.S., 1952, naturalized, 1953; s. Max and Selma (Grünebaum) K.; m. Rita Mei-Yu Chow, Dec. 19, 1963; 1 child, Anna Rosa. BA with honors, U. Md., 1960; MA, Johns Hopkins U., 1963; cert., Harvard U., 1972. Guide, demonstrator U.S. pavilion Brussels World's Fair, U.S. Dept. State, 1958; editorial asst. Am. Polit. Sci. Assn., Washington, 1960; program officer African Am. Inst., Washington, 1961-62; teaching fellow Howard U., Washington, 1963-64; editor John F. Holman Co., 1964-65; program specialist U.S. Office Econ. Opportunity, Washington, 1965-66; adminstrv. aide Covington and Burling (law firm), Washington, 1966-67; program specialist U.S. Office Econ. Opportunity, Washington, 1967-69; from program specialist to program analyst U.S. Dept. Labor, Washington, 1969-72; sr. labor economist U.S. Dept. Labor, 1972-83, sr. contract compliance advisor, 1983-87, sr. closeout specialist, 1987—; freelance writer, Washington; instr. in field. Author: War and Remembrance, An Eyewitness Account, 1988, Freddy Kahn's Story, 1989; editorial bd. Pub. Adminstrn. Rev., 1976-78, The Bureaucrat, 1973-76; editor-in-chief Nat. Capital Area-Am. Soc. Pub. Adminstrn., 1972-75; contbr. articles to profl. jours. Elected nat. bd. dirs. Soc. Govt. Economists, Washington, 1976-77; capt. Nat. Youth Soccer Champion of Belgium, 1948/Daring Club de Verviers; asst. coll. sec., Am. Friends Svc. Com., 1956, counsellor, 1959; with Coll. Unit, N.H. State, 1957. With U.S. Army, 1953-55. Woodrow Wilson fellow Nat. Woodrow Wilson Fellowship Found., 1960-61, teaching fellow Howard U., 1963-64; Johns Hopkins scholar Johns Hopkins U., 1961-62; recipient awards for Outstanding Achievement, U.S. Dept. Labor, 1972, 79, 1988, 1991. Mem. Am. Econ. Assn., Am. Soc. for Pub. Adminstrn. (nat. coun. mem. 1975-78, vol. steering com. sect. Am. women in pub. adminstrn.), Jewish Holocaust Survivors, Friends Greater Washington, Nat. Economists Club, Bethesda Sport and Health Club, Johns Hopkins Alumni Assn., Am. Legion, VFW, Jewish War Vets., Fedn. des Lycees et Athenees de Belgique (nat. sec. Fedn. Belgian Students 1951-52, two journalism awards 1959), Pi Delta Epsilon, Sigma Delta Chi, Pi Sigma Alpha (pres. 1959-60), Alpha Phi Omega. Republican. Jewish. Home: 4512 W Virginia Ave Bethesda MD 20814-4612

KAHN, JAMES STANLEY, marketing executive; b. Reading, Pa., Nov. 13, 1947; s. Harold Lee and Anna Emily (Mademann) K.; m. Pamela Dorothy Palka, Aug. 22, 1981; children: Brian Christopher, Stephen James, Stephanie Lynn. BS, Millersville U., 1971; grad. mgmt. program, Pa. State U., 1978. CPCU. Underwriter Aetna Casualty & Surety, Reading, Pa., 1972-77, Gt. Am. Ins. Co., Lancaster, Pa., 1977-78; mgr. Wotiz-Josephs Inc., Allentown, Pa., 1978-80; pvt. practice Reading, Pa., 1980-81; account mgr. Palley-Simon Assocs., Jenkintown, Pa., 1981-84, Flanigan, O'Hara & Gentry, Horsham, Pa., 1984-85; underwriting mgr. McCay Corp., Bordentown, N.J., 1985-86; mgr. mktg. Auld & Co., Trenton, N.J., 1986-89; account exec. Marsh & McLennan Cos., Inc., Camp Hill, Pa., 1989-92, Feinerman Group, Harrisbury, Pa., 1992—. Designer data gathering forms, 1977. V.p. Montrose Manor Civic Orgn., Shillington, Pa., 1976-77, pres. 1977-79. Served with USAF, 1965-69. Recipient Outstanding Acad. Achievement award, Ins. Soc. Phila., 1988. Mem. Mercer County Ind. Ins. Agts. Am. (treas. 1988-89), Lions (v.p. 1979-80). Republican. Lutheran. Home: RD 6 Box 522 Lebanon PA 17042 Office: Marsh & McLennan Inc 100 Pine St Ste 500 Harrisburg PA 17101

KAHN, JENETTE SARAH, publishing company executive; b. Altoona, Pa., May 16, 1947; d. Benjamin and Rosalind (Aronson) K. BA cum laude, Radcliffe Coll, 1968. Co-founder, editor Kids mag., Cambridge, Mass., 1970-73; creator, editor Dynamite mag., 1973-74; pub., editor Smash mag., 1974-76; pub. DC Comics, N.Y.C., 1976-81; pres., pub. DC Comics, from 1981, now pres., editor-in-chief. Jr. council Mus. Modern Art, 1975-81; active Big Sisters and Big Brothers, from 1978; mem. nat. adv. coun. Nat. Network of Runaways and Youth Svcs.; pres. Wonder Woman Found. Grantee Kress Found., 1969. Office: DC Comics 1325 Ave of the Americas New York NY 10019*

KAHN, LAURENCE HOWARD, human resource consultant; b. Boston, May 6, 1943; s. David and Florance (Shief) K.; m. Barbara Polakoff, July 1, 1979; 1 child, Jonathan Benjamin. BS, Northeastern U., Boston, 1967; EdD, U. Mass., 1974. Tchr. Newton (Mass.) Pub. Schs., 1967-70; rsch. asst. Nat. Adv. Coun. on Vocat. Edn., Washington, 1973-74; project dir. Applied Mgmt. Scis., Silver Spring, Md., 1974-75; orgn. cons. Insight, Inc., Pottstown, Pa., 1975-78; mgr. manpower and orgnl. planning ARA Svcs., Inc., Phila., 1978-79; dir. human resource devel. Smithkline Beckman Corp., Phila., 1979-87; pres. L H Kahn, Lafayette Hill, Pa., 1987—; editorial bd. Ctr. for Creative Leadership, Greensboro, N.C., 1979—, adj. staff, 1987—. Dir. Met. Hosp., Phila., 1987-89. Mem. ASTD, Phila. Human Resource Planning Group (chmn. program com. 1989, chmn. outreach com. 1990, chmn. nominating com. 1991).

KAHN, LESLIE RUTH, service executive; b. N.Y.C., Jan. 15, 1947; d. Murrey and Florence (Marine) Kahn; child from previous marriage: Steven Craig Ringelheim. AAS, N.Y. Tech. Coll., N.Y.C., 1972; BA, CUNY, 1981. Adminstr. coll. dentistry NYU, N.Y.C., 1967-71; dental hygienist Dr. Steven S. Baron, DDS, Rego Park, N.Y., 1974-79; office mgr. Dr. Jerome Levine, DDS, N.Y.C., 1973-74; dental hygienist Dr. Steven S. Baron, DDS, Rego Park, N.Y., 1974-78; pres. Craig Med. and Dental Pers. Agy., Inc., N.Y.C., 1980—; adj. lectr. CUNY Med. Assts. Sch., 1981, Greater N.Y. Dental Meeting, 1980-86; cons. in field. Contbr. articles to profl. jours. Recipient Academic Excellence award Health Edn. Mem. N.Y. State Dental Hygiene Soc. (hons.), Fla. State Dental Hygienist Soc., Fla. Dental Soc. Office: Craig Med Dental Agy 11 Middle Neck Rd Great Neck NY 11021

KAHN, LUDWIG WERNER, educator; b. Berlin, Germany, Oct. 18, 1910; came to U.S., 1936, naturalized, 1943; s. Bernhard and Dora (Frishberg) K.; m. Tatyana Uffner, July 12, 1941; children—Andrée S., Miriam. Student, U. Berlin, 1928-30, 31-33, U. Paris, 1931; M.A., U. London, 1936; Ph.D., U. Berne, 1934. Staff mem. Warburg Inst., London, 1934-36; asst. lectr. Univ. Coll., U. London, 1935-36; instr. U. Rochester, 1936-40, Bryn Mawr Coll., 1940-42; editor Strategic Index of Latin Am., 1942-43; instr. Vassar Coll., 1942-45, asst. prof., 1945-47; asst. prof. Coll. City N.Y., 1947-53, asso. prof., 1953-62, prof., 1963-67, chmn. dept. Germanic and Slavic langs., 1961-67; prof. Columbia, 1967—, Gebhard prof. Germanic langs. and lits., 1973-79,

Gebhard prof. emeritus, 1979—; dir. Deutsches Haus, 1973-79; vis. prof. Yale Grad. Sch., 1968, 79, Tech. U., Stuttgart, Germany, 1959-60, Grad. Center, City U. N.Y., 1971. Author: Shakespeares Sonette in Deutschland, 1935, Social Ideals in German Literature, 1939, Literatur und Glaubenskrise, 1964; contbr. numerous articles to profl. jours.; Asso. editor: Germanic Rev, 1967-89. Mem. regional selection com. Woodrow Wilson Found., 1962-66; mem. Fulbright Screening Com., 1971-73. Decorated grand cross 1st class Fed. Republic of Germany).; Sr. Fulbright lectr.; Faculty fellow Fund Advancement Edn., 1951-52; Guggenheim fellow, 1969-70; Fulbright research fellow, 1959-60, 69-70. Mem. Modern Lang. Assn. (sect. chmn. 1955), AAUP, Am. Assn. Tchrs. German, Germanistic Soc. Am. (dir. 1968-89). Home: 9 Atherstone Rd Scarsdale NY 10583-6607

KAHN, MARK BENNET, vascular surgeon, educator; b. Harrisburg, Pa., Feb. 11, 1957; s. Hyman Richard and Sara (Margolis) K. BA, Oberlin Coll., 1979; MD, Jefferson Med. Coll., 1983. Diplomate Am. Bd. Gen. Surgery; cert. vascular surgeon. Resident in gen. surgery U. Pitts., 1983-85; chief resident N.J. Med. Sch., Newark, 1985-87, 87-88; staff surgeon J.L. McClellan Meml. Vets. Hosp., Little Rock, 1988-90; resident vascular surgery U. Ark. Med. Scis., Little Rock, 1988-90; asst. prof. surgery & attending surgeon Med. Coll. Pa., Phila., 1990—; staff surgeon, co-dir. vascular lab. Phila. VA Med. Ctr., attending surgeon Jeanes Hosp., Fox Chase Cancer Ctr.; presenter in field; researcher in field. Contbr. articles to profl. jours. Mem. AMA, Am. Coll. Surgeons (assoc.), Pa. Med. Soc., Phila. County Med. Soc. Office: Vascular Surg Assocs 3300 Henry Ave Philadelphia PA 19129-1191

KAHN, PETER C., biochemist, educator; b. N.Y.C., Mar. 20, 1940; s. Victor Ferdinand and Diana Freda (Rubin) K.; m. Jennifer Bronwen Nielsen, Dec. 17, 1966; children: Bronwen, Rebecca. BA, Harvard U., 1961; PhD, Columbia U., 1972. Chemistry master Abeokuta Grammar Sch., Abeokuta, Nigeria, 1961-63; rsch. assoc. Columbia U., N.Y.C., 1972-75; rsch. assoc. Albert Einstein Coll. Medicine, Bronx, N.Y., 1975-76, instr., 1976; asst. prof. Rutgers U., New Brunswick, N.J., 1976-81, assoc. prof., 1981—; vis. scientist Yale U., New Haven, 1987-88, Centre Nat. de Recherche Scientifique, Paris, 1988, 89; vis. prof. Univ. René Descartes, Paris, 1992. Contbr. numerous articles to profl. jours. and seminars. Mem. N.J. Agent Orange Commn., Trenton, N.J., 1981-91; bd. trustees Unitarian Soc. of New Brunswick (N.J.), 1985-88; bd. dirs. Morningside Gardens Nursery-Kindergarten, N.Y.C., 1972-77. Grantee NIH postdoctoral fellowship, 1974-75. Mem. AAAS, Am. Chem. Soc., Assn. Ofcl. Analytical Chemists, N.Y. Acad. Sci. Office: Rutgers U Lipman Dr Lipman Hall New Brunswick NJ 08903

KAHN, RICHARD PAUL, investment executive; b. Phila., Mar. 10, 1926; s. Charles and Ruth (Goldberger) K.; children: Joanne Ruth, Richard Douglas, Stephen Robert; m. Keke Belber, Mar. 27, 1988. BS in Engring., Pa. State U., 1949. News broadcaster Sta. KDRO, Sedalia, Mo., 1946; chem. engr. St. Regis Paper Co., Kalamazoo, Mich., 1949-50; chief engr. Reiss Assocs., Inc., Newton, Mass., 1950-55; pres. BoMyte Co., Silverdale, Pa., 1956-61; v.p. Belding Heminway Co., New Britain, Pa., 1961-66; specialist Phila. Stock Exchange, 1967-81; gen. ptnr. Dayton, Kahn, Heppe, Hancock & Co., Phila., 1981-90; pres. Gibraltar Fund, Inc., 1983-90, also bd. dirs.; sr. investment advisor Prudential Securities, 1990—. Sr. pilot CAP, 1968-; pres. North Penn Squadron, Inc., 1977—. Served with USAAF, 1944-45. Mem. Acad. Natural Scis., Soaring Soc. Am., Phila. Glider Council, Aircraft Owners and Pilots Assn., Bucks County Aviation Assn., Pa. State U. Alumni Assn., U.S. Amateur Ballroom Dancers Assn. (pres. chpt. 612 1991—). Republican. Jewish. Office: 1516 Locust St Philadelphia PA 99102

KAHN, ROBIN PHOEBE, artist; b. N.Y.C., Jan. 17, 1961; m. Kirby A. Gookin, Sept. 1, 1986. BA, Columbia U., 1982; MFA, Pratt Inst., 1985. Fine artist; co-founder, spl. issue mag. editor SOS Internat. One-woman shows include White Room, White Columns, N.Y., 1990, Sophia Ungers, Koln, Real Art Ways, Hartford, Conn., 1991, Roy Boyd, L.A., 1992; group exhbns. include Andrea Rosen Gallery, N.Y., 1991, Massimo Audiello Gallery, N.Y., 1991, Lino Silverstein, Barcelona, 1991, Simon Watson, N.Y., 1991, Galerie Sophia Ungers, 1991, Simon Watson, N.Y., 1991, Tom Cugliania, N.Y., 1990, Fernando Alcolea, N.Y., 1991, Galerie Antoine Candau, Paris, 1990, Galerie Sophia Ungers, Koln, 1990, Marta Cervera Gallery, N.Y., 1989. Co-founder Agencia de Viaje, Spain, 1992. Grantee Nat. Endowment for Arts, 1989, Art Matters, Inc., 1988. Home: 114 Mercer St New York NY 10012-5214 Studio: 135 Plymouth St Brooklyn NY

KAHNE, HILDA, economics educator; b. Milford, Conn., Apr. 27, 1922; d. Joseph and Sarah (Rostow) Rosenbaum; m. Merton Kahne, Oct. 1956; children: David, Daniel, Joseph. BA, U. Wis., 1943; MA, Harvard U., PhD, 1953. Asst. prof. Wellesley (Mass.) Coll., 1948-58; asst. dean Radcliffe Inst., Cambridge, Mass., 1966-77; prof. econs. Wheaton Coll., Norton, Mass., 1977—. Author: Part-time Work: New Perspectives for Older Workers and Women, 1985: co-editor: Women's Work and Women's Lives: Continuing Struggle Around the World, 1992; contbr. articles to profl. jours. Office: Wheaton Coll Norton MA 02766

KAIDEN, RICHARD LOUIS, ophthalmologist; b. Bklyn., Feb. 2, 1941; s. Murray and Lillian (Rosenthal) K.; m. Arlene, Sept. 5, 1964; children: Jonathan, Douglas, Amy. BA, Cornell U., 1962; MD, Albert Einstein, 1966. Diplomate Am. Bd. Ophthalmology. Ophthalmologist Dr. Soll & Kaiden, P.A., Westwood, N.J., 1971-75, Westwood Ophthalmology Assocs., P.A., 1975—; bd. trustees Pascack Valley Hosp., Westwood, 1980, 81, pres. gen. active staff, 1980, 81; team ophthalmologist N.J. Giants, N.J. Nets, N.J. Knights, 1984—. Capt. U.S. Army, 1966-67. Mem. Am. Acad. Ophthalmology, Am. Bd. Ophthalmology, Am. Coll. Surgeons, Bergen County Med. Soc., AMA. Office: Westwood Ophthalmology Asso 10 Irvington St Westwood NJ 07675-1792

KAILIAN, ARAM HARRY, architect; b. Phila., Oct. 23, 1949; s. Harry G. and Louise (Haledjian) Caily; m. Kathryn I. Zakian, May 27, 1973; children: Arsine K., Aram E. BS, Temple U., 1973; student, Tyler Sch. Fine Art, Phila., 1967-69, Drexel U., 1970-71. Project architect Kuljian Corp., Phila., 1970-73, Urban Engrs. Inc., Phila., 1973-76; project designer Wm. F. Lotz Designers, Horsham, Pa., 1976-78; prin./architect Clyde H. Goff & Assocs./A.H. Kailian, Architects, Interior Design, Constrn. Mgmt., Bala Cynwyd, Pa., 1982—, Kailian Assocs., Bryn Mawr, Pa., 1978—. Contbr. articles to profl. jours. Mem. Dem. Nationalities Coun., Washington, 1976—, Nat. Rep. Heritage Groups Coun., 1976—; bd. dirs. Armenian Nat. Com. Am., 1983-89. Mem. AIA, Pa. Soc. Architects, Am. Arbitration Assn., Nat. Acad. Conciliators, Nat. Trust for Historic Preservation, Acad. Polit. Sci. Democrat. Armenian Orthodox. Office: Clyde H Goff & Assocs/AH Kailian Architect City Line Ave GSB Bldg 102 Bala Cynwyd PA 19004

KAINEN, PAUL CHESTER, mathematician; b. Washington, July 31, 1943; s. Jacob and Bertha (Friedman) K. BA, George Wash. U., 1966; PhD, Cornell U., 1970. Assoc. prof. Dept. of Math. and Statistics Case Western Res. U., Cleve., 1970-77; mem. tech. staff Bell Telephone Labs., Holmdel, N.J., 1977-81, The Analytic Scis. Corp., Reston, Va., 1983-88; cons. Laser Arts, N.Y.C., 1981-83, Indsl. Math, Washington, 1988—. Author: (with others) The Four Color Problem, 1977. Mem. Soc. for Indsl. and Applied Math., Internat. Neural Network Soc. Office: Indsl Math 3044 N St NW Washington DC 20007-3424

KAISER, DIANE, sculptor, art educator; b. Bklyn., May 27, 1946; d. Emil and Etta (Lazell) K.; m. Melvyn S. Berger, Dec. 25, 1977; 1 child, Elisabeth Joanna. B.A. summa cum laude, Brandeis U., 1968; M.F.A., Columbia U., 1970. Picture editor Art Ency., The Greystone Corp., N.Y.C., 1968; chmn. art dept. The Chapin Sch., N.Y.C., 1970-79; instr. art Northfield Mt. Hermon Sch., Mass., 1979-80; lectr. art Smith Coll., Northampton, Mass., 1980-83; supr. art St. Hilda's and St. Hugh's Sch., N.Y.C., 1983-87; asst. prof. art Elms Coll., Chicopee, Mass., 1990—; reviewer art Daily Hampshire Gazette, Northampton, 1980. One-man shows include Mus. Fine Arts, Springfield, 1981, 14 Sculptors Gallery, N.Y.C., 1985, 86, Mus. Fine Arts, Springfield, 1989; exhibited in group shows at Mus. Modern Art Lending Gallery, 1977, Aldrich Mus. Contemporary Art, Ridgefield, Conn., 1975, Chesterwood, Stockbridge, Mass., 1986, 87, Stamford Mus. and Nature Ctr., 1988; prin. works include Bradley Palmer State Park, 1992. Brandeis U. scholar, 1968; MacDowell Colony fellow, 1973; Committee for the Visual Arts grantee, 1977, Amherst Arts Lottery grantee, 1990, 91.

KAISER, HARVEY HAROLD, university administrator, architect; b. Bklyn., July 8, 1936; s. Jerome and Ray (Tobak) K.; m. Linda Jean Pembroke, Sept. 24, 1960; children: Sven-Erik, Robert P., Christina R. B in Architecture, Rensselaer Poly. Inst., 1959; M in Architecture, Syracuse U., 1965, PhD in Social Sci., 1974. Registered architect. Assoc. ptnr. Sargent, Webster, et al, Syracuse, N.Y., 1962-70; assoc. prof. Syracuse U., 1970—, asst. v.p., 1972-75, v.p., 1975-85, sr. v.p., 1985—; cons. U.S. Dept. of State, Washington, 1984, U.S. Dept. of Justice, Washington, 1980—, Cornell U., 1980—, McGill U., 1980—, Mass. Bd. of Regents, 1980—. Author: The Building of Cities, 1978, Great Camps of the Adirondacks, 1982, Managing Facilities More Effectively, 1980, Facilities Audit Workbook, 1982, Crumbling Academe, 1984, The Facilities Managers Reference, 1989, Planning and Managing Higher Education Facilities, 1989. Bd. dirs. Russel Sage Coll., Troy, N.Y., 1978—, Fisk U., Nashville, Tenn., 1985-86, Profl. Med. Conduct Bd., N.Y., 1980-85, Lake Placid (N.Y.) Ctr. for Arts, 1989—; project dir. Onondaga County Conv. Ctr., Syracuse, 1988—. Capt. USAR, 1960-68. Recipient fellowship Rensselaer Poly. Inst., 1959, Am. Scandinavian Fedn., 1960, Nat. Endowment for Arts, 1979, 84, N.Y. State Coun. on Arts, 1980. Mem. Syracuse Stage (bd. dirs. 1984—), Consol. Industries (bd. dirs. 1988—), Univ. Hill Corp. (bd. dirs. 1980—), Lightworks (bd. dirs. 1988—), Assn. Governing Bds., Assn. Phys. Plant Adminstrs., Am. Inst. Architects. Office: Syracuse U Skytop Office Bldg Syracuse NY 13244

KAISER, JILL ADLER, small business owner; b. N.Y.C., Mar. 4, 1948; d. Victor and Bernice (Lustgarten) Adler; m. Louis P. Kaiser, June 24, 1973; children: Lauren, Scott. BA, Barnard Coll., 1968; MBA, NYU, 1970. Econ. analyst Fed. Res. Bank N.Y., N.Y.C., 1970-71; fin. analyst Celanese Corp., N.Y.C., 1971-73; asst. to v.p. Nat. Bur. of Econ. Rsch., New Haven, Conn., 1973-76; owner, pres. Mgmt. Bookkeeping & Acctg., Orange, Conn., 1978—. Mem. Entrepreneurial Woman's Network (treas. 1987-89, sec. 1989-90, pres. 1990-91). Office: Mgmt Bookkeeping & Acctg PO Box 1011 Orange CT 06477

KAISER, ROBERT, chemical engineer, consultant; b. Strasbourg, France, June 22, 1934; came to U.S., 1942; s. Bruno and Julie (Wolf) K.; m. Madeleine Marie Butty, June 1, 1970; children: Pierre Joseph, Martine Louise. SB, MIT, 1956, SM, 1957, ScD, 1962. Registered profl. engr., Mass. Rsch. engr. M.W. Kellogg Co., Piscataway, N.J., 1961-66; sr. staff scientist Space Systems div. Avco Corp., Lowell, Mass., 1966-70, area mgr., 1970-74; v.p. Bruno Kaiser Corp., N.Y.C., 1970—, Hi-Seas Industries Inc., N.Y.C., 1982—; pres. Entropic Systems, Inc., Winchester, Mass., 1985—, Argos Assocs., Inc., Winchester, 1977—; vis. scientist Materials Systems Lab., MIT, Cambridge, 1982-85; bd. dirs. Bruno Kaiser Corp., Hi-Seas Industries, Inc., Argos Assocs., Inc., Entropic Systems, Inc. Patentee in field. Capt. U.S. Army Res., 1961-62. Recipient invention award NASA, 1970, 75. Mem. Am. Chem. Soc., Am. Inst. Chem. Engrs., Inst. Environ. Scis. Home: 12 Glengarry St Winchester MA 01890-2512

KAISER, SAAMIR, lawyer; b. London, Oct. 17, 1964; s. Mustapha Kaiser and Laila (Fernandes) Ahmed; m. Ruth Ann Chinitz, Aug. 25, 1991. BA in Polit. Sci. and Internat. Rels., George Washington U., 1985; JD cum laude, U. Mich., 1990; cert., Harvard U., 1991. Bar: Md. 1991. Staff atty. Resolution Trust Corp., Washington, 1990-91; assoc. Inter. Trade Cons., Washington, 1991—; pro bono advisor Com. for Internat. Human Rights, Washington, 1990—. Founder, mng. editor newsletter for the William O. Douglas Law Soc., 1989-90. Recipient Am. Jurisprudence award Lawyer's Co-op Pub. Co., 1990. Mem. ABA, Fed. Bar Assn., Md. State Bar Assn., Am. Inst. Banking, Am. Inn of Ct. (Prettyman-Leventhal chpt.), ACLU (legis. watch Lansing, Mich. chpt. 1988-90), George Washington U. club. Home: 3714 N Rosser St Apt 104 Alexandria VA 22311-3759 Office: Internat Trade Cons 2020 Pennsylvania Ave NW Ste 160 Washington DC 20006

KAISER, SETH ALAN, chiropractor, physical therapist; b. Buffalo, June 26, 1956; s. Samuel and Beatrice Merle (Lippa) K.; m. Kim Marie Matynka, Aug. 31, 1990. Student, Canisius Coll., 1976; BS, Daemen Coll., 1979; D Chiropractic, Can. Meml. Chiropractic Coll., 1988. Lic. phys. therapist, N.Y.; lic. chiropractic, N.Y. Recreation counselor Erie County Parks & Recreation Dept., Buffalo, 1974; phlebotomist Millard Fillmore Hosp., Buffalo, 1974-78, phys. therapist, 1982-84; phys. therapist Furgala's Nursing Home, Lancaster, N.Y., 1980-81, Deaconess Hosp., Buffalo, 1981-82; pvt. practice phys. therapy Buffalo, 1982-84; phys. therapist Hamlin Terr. Nursing Home, Buffalo, 1984-85; phys. therapist assoc. Kaiser Phys. Therapy & Fitness, Williamsville, N.Y., 1984—; chiropractor Kaiser Chiropractic & Therapy, East Aurora, N.Y., 1990—; cons. Lothlorien Therapeutic Riding Ctr., East Aurora, N.Y., 1989-90. Vice-chmn. Bike-WNY, Buffalo, 1991—. Mem. Physiotherapist Assn. N.Y. State (pres. 1988—), N.Y. State Chiropractic Assn., Kiwanis, Elma. Jewish. Home and Office: Kaiser Chiropractic 538 Oakwood Ave East Aurora NY 14052-2304

KAISH, MORTON, painter, educator; b. Newark, Jan. 8, 1927; s. Morris and Sophie (Furman) K.; m. Luise H. Meyers, Aug. 15, 1948; 1 dau., Melissa. B.F.A., Syracuse U., 1949; postgrad., Academie de la Grande Chaumiere, Paris, 1951, Istituto d' Arte, Florence, Italy, 1952, Accademia delle Belle Arti, Rome, 1957. Vis. critic Parsons Sch. Design, N.Y.C., 1966-70, Phila. Coll. Art, 1983; mem. faculty Art Students League, N.Y.C., 1974—; guest critic Sch. Visual Arts, N.Y.C., 1967; vis. prof. Queens Coll., Flushing, N.Y., 1979; vis. artist U. Wash., Seattle, 1979; fellow MacDowell Colony, 1976; artist-in-residence Dartmouth Coll., 1974, U. Haifa, Israel, 1985; prof. Fashion Inst. Tech., SUNY, N.Y.C., 1973—; vis. artist Susquehanna U., 1985; dir. Carl Fischer Mus. Instrument Co., 1964-70; vis. artist Columbia U., N.Y.C., 1986, Boston U., 1987. One-man shows include Manhattanville Coll., Purchase, N.Y., 1955, Rochester (N.Y.) Meml. Art Gallery, 1955, Guild Hall, Easthampton, L.I., 1969, U.S. Info. Service, Rome, 1973, Dartmouth ,Coll., Hanover, N.H., 1974, Staempfli Gallery, N.Y.C., 1964, 67, 71, 73, 79, 83, 86, 89, Osborne Gallery, Rochester, N.Y., 1989, Century Assn., N.Y., 1989; group shows Mus. Galleria 11 Torcoliere, Rome, 1957, Barone Gallery, N.Y.C., 1959, Art Inst. Chgo., 1964, Sheldon Meml. Art Gallery, Lincoln, Nebr., 1964, U. Nebr., Lincoln, 1964, Krannert Art Mus., U. Ill., Urbana, 1965, 68, Herron Mus. Art, Indpls., 1965, Mary Washington Coll., Fredericksburg, Va., 1965, Am. Acad. Arts and Letters, N.Y.C., 1966, Pa. Acad. Fine Arts, Phila., 1966, Ark. Art Ctr., Little Rock, 1966, Whitney Mus. Am. Art, N.Y.C., 1966, Finch Coll. Mus. Art, N.Y.C., 1966, N.J. State Mus., Trenton, 1966, Krannert Art Mus., 1968, Kent (Ohio) State U., 1970, U.S. Info. Service, Rome, 1972, New Sch. Social Research, N.Y.C., 1973, Child Hassam Purchase Fund Exhbn., N.Y.C., 1973; invitational exhbns. Child Hassam Purchase Fund, 1975, Am. Acad. Arts and Letters, 1975, Drawings U.S.A., 1975, Minn. Mus. Art, St. Paul, 1975, Springfield Art Mus., 1975, Springfield Mus. Art, Mo., 1975, Galerie Brusberg, Berlin, W.Ger., 1980, Taft Mus., Cin., 1981, NAD, N.Y.C., 1983, 85, 89, 91; represented in permanent collections Whitney Mus. Am. Art, N.Y.C., Bklyn. Mus., Nat. Mus. Art, Smithsonian Instn., Washington, Guild Hall, Easthampton, N.Y., Williams Coll., Williamstown. Mass., Syracuse U., N.Y., Swarthmore Coll., Indpls. Mus. Art, U. Mich. Mus. Art., Guilford Coll., Greensboro, N.C. Recipient SUNY Rsch. Found. award, 1983, Gervasi award, 1985, William Ward Ranger Fund purchase award, 1983, 85, Benjamin Altman prize, 1989, Andrew Carnegie prize, 1992, Disting. Alumni award for Achievement in the Visual Arts Syracuse U., 1989; faculty exch. scholar SUNY, 1987. Mem. Century Assn., NAD (coun. mem., William A. Paton prize 1983), Artists' Choice Mus. (bd. artists), Artists' Fellowship (trustee). Address: 610 W End Ave New York NY 10024

KAITA, ROBERT, physicist, consultant; b. Tokyo, Japan, Sept. 2, 1952; came to U.S., 1957; s. Reiichi and Midori (Kokita) K.; m. Chiu-Tze Lin, Apr. 19, 1980; 1 child, Courtney Lin. BS, SUNY, 1973; PhD, Rutgers U., 1978. Rsch. assoc. Princeton (N.J.) U., 1978-80, rsch. staff, 1980-84, rsch. physicist, 1984-90, prin. rsch. physicist, 1990—; cons. Internat. Thermonuclear Exptl. Reactor, Garching, Fed. Republic of Germany, 1990—; co-prin. investigator Princeton Beta Experiment-Modification. Acad. adv. Found. for Thought and Ethics, Richardson, Tex., 1990—. N.Y. State Regents scholar, 1969-73, C.V. Starr Found. scholar, 1969-73. Mem. Am. Phys. Soc., AAAS, Sigma Xi. Democrat. Baptist. Home: 27 LeValley Dr Manalapan NJ 07726-9802 Office: Princeton U Plasma Physics Lab PO Box 451 Princeton NJ 08543-0451

KAJI, AKIRA, microbiology educator; b. Tokyo, Jan. 13, 1930; came to U.S., 1954; s. Kiichi and Chiyo (Hanai) K.; m. Hideko Katayama, July 22, 1955; children: Kenneth, Eugene, Naomi, Amy. BS, Tokyo U., 1953; PhD, Johns Hopkins U., 1958; MS (hon.), U. Pa., 1973. Rsch. fellow Johns Hopkins Hosp., Balt., 1958-59; guest investigator Rockefeller U., N.Y.C., 1959; rsch. assoc. microbiology Vanderbilt Med. Sch., Nashville, 1959-62; vis. scientist Oak Ridge (Tenn.) Nat. Lab., 1962-63; assoc. U. Pa. Med. Sch., Phila., 1963-64, asst. prof. microbiology, 1964-67, assoc. prof., 1967-72, prof., 1972—; permanent mem. bd. sci. councilors Nat. Eye Inst., Bethesda, Md., 1987-92; prof., chair Tokyo U. Faculty Pharm. Scis., 1972-73; vis. prof. Kyoto U. Virus Rsch. Inst., 1985. Contbr. over 160 articles to profl. jours. Recipient Fulbright-Smith-Mundt award, 1954, Helen Hay Whitney award, 1964-69, John Simmon Guggenheim award, 1972-73, Fogarty Internat. Sr. award, 1985-86. Mem. Am. Soc. Biol. Chemistry and Molecular Biology, Am. Soc. Cell Biology, Am. Soc. Microbiology, Am. Soc. Chemistry. Office: U Pa Sch Medicine Dept Microbiology 258 Johnson Pavilion Philadelphia PA 19104-6076

KAJI, HIDEKO KATAYAMA, pharmacologist; b. Tokyo, Jan. 1, 1932; came to U.S., 1954; d. Sakae and Tsuneko (Matsuda) Katayama; m. Akira Kaji, Aug. 23, 1958; children: Kenneth, Eugene, Naomi, Amy. BS, Tokyo Coll. Pharmacy, 1954; MS, U. Nebr., 1956; PhD, Purdue U., 1958. Vis. scientist Oak Ridge (Tenn.) Nat. Lab., 1962-63; assoc. U. Pa., Phila., 1963-64; rsch. assoc. The Inst. Cancer Rsch., Phila., 1965-66, asst. mem., 1966-76; vis. mem. Max Planck Inst. Molek. Gen., Berlin, 1972-73, Nat. Inst. Med. Rsch., London, 1973; assoc. prof. Jefferson Med. Coll., Phila., 1976-82; vis. prof. Wistar Inst., Phila., 1984-85; prof. molecular and devel. biology, oncogenisis, drug devel. Jefferson Med. Coll., Phila., 1983—; cons. Nippon Paint Co., Ltd., Tokyo, 1990—, Coatesville (Pa.) VA Hosp., 1982-84. Contbr. articles to profl. jours. Fellow NIH (bd. dirs. 1986-89); mem. Am. Soc. Biochemistry and Molecular Biology, Am. Soc. Pharmacol. and Exptl. Therapeutics, Am. Soc. Microbiology, Sigma Xi. Home: 334 Fillmore St Philadelphia PA 19111-2129 Office: Jefferson Med Coll 1020 Locust St Philadelphia PA 19107-6799

KAJOR, MICHAEL STEVEN, electrical engineer; b. Paterson, N.J., Jan. 10, 1950; s. Alexander and Antoinette (Grasso) K. Student, RCA, N.Y.C., 1969-71; BSEE in Power Systems, N.J. Inst. Tech., 1975, MSEE in Biomed. Engring., 1978. Theoretical analyst, simulations engr. ITT Def. Communication Systems, Nutley, N.J., 1978-80; elec. engr., physicist Ardec U.S. Army, Dover, N.J., 1980—; adj. prof. N.J. Inst. Tech., 1988. Co-author: Selforganization of Communication Nets, 1981. Exempt fireman City of Riverdale, 1973-85; active Smithsonian Instn., Union Concerned Scientists, Physicians Against Nuclear War, Conservation Internat., Amnesty Internat., Nat. Resources Def. Coun.; mem. Rep. Nat. Com. Recipient cert. for phys. achievement USMC, 1966, cert. U.S. Army, 1984, 87, cert. of recognition Dem. Jajority Action Fund, 1988, Walking for Hungry award CROP, 1986, Excellence in Edn. award St. Joseph's Indian Sch., 1989, cert. of appreciation Native Am. Rights Fund, 1989. Mem. AAAS, AIAA, ASPCA, NRA, IEEE, KC (grand knight 1986-88, Cert. of Merit Marian coun. 1989), ASM Internat., Am. Nuclear Soc., Am. Chem. Soc., Internat. Soc. Optical Engring., Nat. Soc. Profl. Engrs., Nat. Fedn. Fed. Employees, Internat. Soc. Pharm. Engrs., N.Y. Acad. Scis., Soc. Am. Mil. Engrs., Internat. Soc. Hybrid Microelectronics, Soc. for Imaging Sci. & Tech., Nat. Fire Protection Assn., Nat. Parks and Conservation Assn., Conservation Internat., Audubon Soc., Wilderness Soc., Futuristic Soc., William Penn Assn., Jacques Cousteau Soc., Nat. Geographic Soc., Order of the Engr., Better World Soc., World Wildlife Fund, Common Cause, Nat. Arbor Day Found., Am. Forestry Assn., The Nature Conservancy, N.Y. Zool. Soc., Sierra Club, Arthur Murray Club (Bronze cert. 1990, grad. 1990), Engring. Soc. Detroit, ASM Internat., IPA, SID, ASA, AIIM, Sigma Xi (chpt. pres. 1990-91), Tau Beta Pi, Eta Kappa Nu, Tau Kappa Epsilon (Kappa-Eta chpt.). Home: 6 Munn Ave Riverdale NJ 07457-1138 Office: Ardec US Army Picatinny Arsenal Bldg 95N Dover NJ 07806-5000

KAKU, MICHIO, theoretical nuclear physicist; b. San Jose, Calif., Jan. 24, 1947; s. Toshio and Hideko (Maruyama) K. BA, Harvard U., 1968; PhD, U. Calif.-Berkeley, 1972. Rsch. assoc. Princeton U., N.J., 1972-73; assoc. prof. CCNY and Grad. Ctr., 1973-83, prof., 1983—; vis. prof. NYU, 1988, Inst. for Advanced Studies at Princeton U., 1990. Author: Nuclear Power: Both Sides, 1983; Beyond Einstein, the Cosmic Search for the Unified Field Theory, 1986, Introduction to Superstrings, 1988, Strings, Conformal Fields, and Topology, 1991, Quarks, Symmetries, and Strings, 1991, Quantum Field Theory: A Modern Introduction, 1992; contbr. 60 articles to profl. jours. Fellow AAAS, Am. Phys. Soc. Avocations: nuclear arms control, nuclear power. Office: CCNY Physics Dept 138th St at Convent Ave New York NY 10031

KAKU, RYUZABURO, precision instruments manufacturing company executive; b. Okazaki, Japan, May 19, 1926; m. Akiko Kaku, Mar. 7, 1934; children—Naoko, Toshiro. B., Kyushu U., Japan, 1954. Gen. mgr. fin. acctg. div. Canon Inc., Tokyo, 1968—, gen. mgr. fin. and acctg. div, pers. adminstrn. div., 1970—, appointed mng. dir., gen. mgr. of fin. and acctg. div. and bus. infor. processing div., 1970—, mng. dir. corp. planning and fin., acctg., 1977—, pres. and rep. dir., 1977—, chmn., 1989—. Recipient The Honour of the Legion d Honneur, Medal of Honour with Blue Ribbon. Mem. Bus. Machine Makers Assn. (adviser 1988), Japan Assn. Corp. Execs. (vice chmn. 1989), Japan Camera Industry Assn. (chmn. 1989), Tokyo C. of C. Office: Canon Inc, 2-7-1 Nishi-Shinjuku 2-chome, Shinjuku-ku, Tokyo 160, Japan also: Canon USA Inc 1 Canon Plz Lake Success NY 11042*

KALABINSKI, JACEK MICHAL, journalist; b. Warsaw, Poland, Sept. 11, 1938; came to U.S., 1983; s. Waclaw Michal and Maria Janina (Lipinska) K.; m. Barbara Halina Rybicka, Sept. 13, 1973; 1 child, Marta. Student, U. Warsaw, 1955-59; MA in Journalism, Warsaw U., 1961. Fgn. editor CAF Newsphotos, Warsaw, 1964-66; news editor Sztandar Mlodych, Warsaw, 1966-68; news writer, editor Polish Nat. Radio, Warsaw, 1968-73, commentator, 1973-81; fgn. affairs commentator Tygodnik Mazowsze, Warsaw, 1981-83; vis. fellow Yale U., New Haven, 1983-84; sr. corr. Radio Free Europe, N.Y.C. and Washington, 1984-90; corr. Gazeta Wyborcza, Washington, 1990—; pres. Polish Journalists Assn., Warsaw, 1980-83. Author: Iran--A New Power?, 1975. Profl. journalism fellow Stanford U., 1978-79; recipient Best Commentary award Fgn. Press Club, Warsaw, 1977. Home and Office: 6003 Coral Sea Ave Rockville MD 20851

KALAN, GEORGE RICHARD, venture capitalist; b. Cleve., Dec. 13, 1944; s. Edward George and Betty Virginia (Triska) K.; m. Cheryl Ann Fine, Aug. 27, 1976; children: Gavin Richard, Jonathan Edward. BEE, Case Inst. Tech., 1966; MEE, MIT, 1968; MBA, Harvard U., 1978. Project mgr., engr. Charles Stark Draper Lab. (formerly MIT Instrumentation Lab.), Cambridge, 1968-76; mgmt. cons. Booz, Allen & Hamilton, Inc., Sao Paulo, Brazil and N.Y.C., 1978-81; pres. Kalan Sutton McGraw, Inc., Short Hills, N.J., 1981-85; pres., mng. gen. ptnr. Orien Ventures, Inc./Orien Ptnrs., L.P./Orien Ventures Ptnrs. L.P., Westport, Conn., 1985—; bd. dirs. Rosh Intelligent Systems, Inc., Needham, Mass., Phys. Optics Corp., Torrance, Calif., Inst. for Clin. Applications Inc., Brookline, Mass. Recipient MIT Cert. Commendation for contbn. to design and devel. of Apollo lunar module autopilot, 1969, Apollo Achievement award, NASA, 1969, Presdl. Medal Freedom for participation in Apollo 13 mission rescue operation, 1970. Home: 72 Good Hill Rd Weston CT 06883-2820 Office: Orien Ventures Inc 315 Post Rd W Westport CT 06880-4739

KALAS, FRANK JOSEPH, JR., naval officer; b. Stafford Spring, Conn., Dec. 31, 1943; s. Frank Joseph and Margaret Mary (LaPanne) K.; m. Minh Tran, June 24, 1972; children: Jennifer Ann, Joanne Catherine. BBA, U. N.Mex., 1966; MS, U. Ark., London, Eng., 1974. Sr. auditor Knox & Scott, CPAs, Albuquerque, 1963-66; commd. officer USN, 1967, advanced through grades to capt.; dir. fin. mgmt. office Naval Sea Systems Command, Washington, 1988—. Author: Food Service Operations and Contracting, 1987. Decorated Meritorious Svc. medal. Mem. Soc. Logistics Engrs. (pres. 1979-80), Profl. Picture Framer's Assn. (cert.), Am. Soc. Mil. Comptrs. (Outstanding Mem. award 1985), Nat. Amateur Press Assn. Roman Catholic. Office: Naval Sea Systems Command 2211 Jefferson Davis Hwy Arlington VA 22202-3744

KALBERER, DOLLETTA ANN, educator; b. Queens, N.Y., June 10, 1951; d. Charles Anthony and Janet Margaret (Lloyd) Whitford; m. William Arthur Kalberer, Sept. 4, 1952; children: Bonnie Jeannine, Lorie Ann. BS in Edn., Wagner Coll., 1973; MA in Spl. Edn., Hofstra U., 1978. Cert. elem. and spl. edn. tchr., N.Y. Substitute tchr. Patchogue-Medford Sch. Dist., N.Y., 1973-74; spl. edn. tchr. Bklyn. Devel. Ctr., N.Y., 1974-82, Bernard Fineson Devel. Ctr., Howard Beach, N.Y., 1982-89, Mill Neck (N.Y.) Manor Sch. for the Deaf, 1989—. Arthur Pense Meml. scholar, 1977. Mem. Hillcrest Civic Assn., Bklyn. Long Island Alumni (pres. 1977-79), PTA, Luth. Women's Club, Alpha Omicron Pi (v.p. 1972-73),. Republican. Lutheran. Home: 356 Carnation Ave Floral Park NY 11001-3438 Office: Mill Neck Manor Sch for the Deaf Frost Mill Rd Mill Neck NY 11765-1100

KALDIS, GUY CONSTANTINE, social studies educator, art dealer; b. N.Y.C., Aug. 1, 1937; s. Aristodimos and Laurie Elaine (Eglington) K., m. Marguerite Lois Belisle, Sept. 13, 1958 (div. Mar. 1979); children: Jason Alexander, Xanthe Ruth, Timothy Andrew. Cert. secondary tchr., N.Y. Tchr. Farmingdale (N.Y.) Pub. Schs., 1960-62, Smithtown (N.Y.), 1962-64, Oceanside (N.Y.) Pub. Schs., 1964-66, Tarrytown (N.Y.) Pub. Schs., 1966—; art dealer Kaldisart, N.Y.C.. Pres. Community Relations Council of Islip, N.Y., 1965-66, Interfaith Council For Action, Ossining, N.Y., 1971-72; vice-chmn. Ossining Town Dems., 1972-76; chmn. Dem. Com., Ossining, 1975-76. Mem. Westchester Council for Social Studies (sec. 1978-80), N.Y. Council For Social Studies. Democrat. Unitarian. Home: 1 Tavano Rd Ossining NY 10562-3105 Office: Sleepy Hollow High Sch 210 N Broadway Tarrytown NY 10591-2624

KALELKAR, ASHOK SATISH, consulting company executive; b. Ahmedabad, India, June 10, 1943; came to U.S., 1960; s. Satish Dattatrey and Chandan (Parekh) K.; m. Joanne Bottiglieri, June 21, 1969 (div. Sept. 1983); children: Dorian, Jessie, Milan. BS in Math., George Wash. U., 1963; SBME, SMME, MIT, 1964, postgrad., 1966; PhD in Engring., Brown U., 1969. Sr. scientist Factory Mut. Rsch. Co., Norwood, Mass., 1969-71; staff Arthur D. Little Inc., Cambridge, Mass., 1971-76, sr. staff, 1976-80, v.p., 1980-85, sr. v.p., 1985; bd. dirs. Opinion Rsch. Co., Princeton, N.J., Cambridge (U.K.) Cons., Arthur D. Little Enterprises; chmn. bd. dirs. Program Systems Mgmt. Co., Cambridge. Contbr. articles to profl. jours. Mem. Soc. for Risk Mgmt., Combustion Inst., Ops. Research Soc. Am. Unitarian. Office: Arthur D Little Inc 25 Acorn Pk Cambridge MA 02140-2301

KALER, ERIC WILLIAM, chemical engineer, educator; b. Burlington, Vt., Sept. 23, 1956; s. Ronald Maurice and Mary Elizabeth (Kindred) K.; m. Karen Fults, Dec. 30, 1979. BS, Calif. Inst. Tech., 1978; PhD, U. Minn., 1982. Asst. prof. chem. engring. U. Wash., Seattle, 1982-87, assoc. prof., 1987-89; assoc. prof. chem. engring. U. Del., Newark, 1989-91, prof., 1991—; cons. Shell Devel. Co., 1983-90, BP Am., 1987-88, Kodak, 1988—, DuPont, 1988—. Conbr. numerous articles to profl. jours. Elder Andrew Riverside Presbyn. Ch., Mpls., 1980-82, Northminster Presbyn. Ch., Seattle, 1984-88. Named Presdl. Young Investigator NSF, Washington D.C., 1984; Presdl. Scholar Dept. Edn., Washington, 1978. Mem. Am. Chem. Soc., Am. Inst. Chem. Engring., Am. Crystollographic Assn. Republican. Lodge: Masons. Home: 24 Nightingale Cir Newark DE 19711-3776 Office: U of Del Dept Chem Engring Newark DE 19716

KALES, PAUL ALBERT, engineering educator; b. Boston, Dec. 8, 1937; s. Maurice H. and Eleanor (Kopp) K.; m. Judith Freund, Feb. 27, 1977. BS, Northeastern U., Boston, 1960, MS, 1965. Registered profl. engr., Mass. Engr. GE Co., Lynn, Mass., 1960-64; sr. engr. Avco Corp., Wilmington, Mass., 1964-68, Raytheon Co., Wayland, Mass., 1968-82, C.S. Draper Lab., Cambridge, Mass., 1982-85; assoc. prof. indsl. tech. U. Lowell, 1985—; cons., trainer Statis. Process Control and Reliability/Maintainability Engring. Contbr. articles to profl. jours. Originator and com. mem. Mass. State Quality Awards Com., Lowell, 1990, 91. Mem. NSPE, Profl. Engrs. in Edn., Mass. Soc. Profl. Engrs., Nat. Assn. Indsl. Tech., Am. Soc. Quality Control. Democrat. Jewish. Office: U Lowell One University Ave Lowell MA 01854

KALICHARRAN, JUDITH, real estate company executive; b. Ponce, P.R., Feb. 1, 1955; d. Jose Elias and Placida (Olmeda) Cintron; m. Ramesh Dalchan Kalicharran, Dec. 4, 1974; children: Jagdesh Ramdial, Nadesh Ramdial, Romanee Ramdial. AS, St. John's U., Jamaica, N.Y., 1984, BS, 1985, MA in Govt. and Politics, 1987. With R.D. Kali Realy Corp., Jamaica, 1980—, Arcel Driving Sch., Inc., Jamaica, 1980—, Kali Travel, Ltd., Jamaica, 1980—; paralegal intern Dean, Falanga & Rose Law Firm, L.I., 1985; intern Ombudsman program Dept. State N.Y., 1987. Contbr. poetry to profl. pubs. Home: 87-26 169th St Jamaica NY 11432

KALIN, JESSE GENE, philosophy educator; b. Lompoc, Calif., May 2, 1940; s. Rey Frederick and Esther Ida (Robison) K.; m. Virginia Mae Beckwith, Dec. 22, 1962; 1 child, Mary. BA, Stanford U., 1962; PhD, U. Calif., Berkeley, 1969. From instr. to asst. prof. SUNY, Buffalo, 1967-71; from asst. to assoc. prof. Vassar Coll., Poughkeepsie, N.Y., 1971-82, prof., 1982—. Assoc. editor Philosophy & Literature, 1977—; contbr. articles to profl. jours. Office: Vassar Coll PO Box 379 Poughkeepsie NY 12601-0618

KALINOSKI, HENRY THOMAS, research chemist; b. Phila., Dec. 26, 1957; s. Henry Francis and Vivian Marie (Sullivan) K.; m. Margaret Ann Cistone, Mar. 26, 1984; one child, Adrielle Arienne. BS, Phila. Coll. Textiles and Sci., 1979; MS, Lehigh U., 1981, PhD, 1984. Post-doctoral fellow U. Wash., Richland, 1984-85; Hanford rsch. fellow Pacific N.W. Labs., Richland, 1985-86; rsch. scientist Battelle Meml. Inst., Pacific N.W. Labs., Richland, 1986-87; sr. rsch. scientist, supr. analytical chemistry, mass spectrometry, chromatography, and spectroscopy Unilever Rsch. U.S., Edgewater, N.J., 1987—. Contbr. articles on applications of analytical chemistry, chromatography and mass spectrometry to profl. jours. Mem. Am. Chem. Soc., Am. Soc. Mass Spectrometry. Home: 278 Carentan Rd Hopatcong NJ 07843-1856 Office: Unilever Rsch US 45 River Rd Edgewater NJ 07020-1075

KALIPOLITES, JUNE TURNER, rehabilitation professional; b. Grasmere, N.H., Aug. 10, 1932; d. Louis O. and Edith Mae (Allen) Turner; m. Nicholas G. Kalipolites, Feb. 12, 1955; children: George, Stephanie, Athena. AA, Hesser Coll., Manchester, N.H., 1977; BS, U. N.H., 1980; Degree in Rehab. Adminstrn. and Svcs., So. Ill. U., Carbondale, 1982; EdD in Endl. Leadership, Vanderbilt U., 1992. Cert. rehab. counselor. Office mgr. Harris Upham and Co., Inc., Manchester; mgr. Amuskeag Bank & Trust Co.; rehab. counselor Div. Vocat. Rehab., Nashua, N.H.; rsch. asst. So. Ill. U.; rehab. cons. N.H. Div. Vocat. Rehab., Concord. Author: Profile of Women in Rehabilitation Administration: A Common Theme, 1992, Projects with Industry: A Unique Concept for Providing Rehabilitation Services to Persons with Severe Disabilities, 1982. LaVerne Noyes scholar. Mem. NAFE, AACD, Am. Rehab. Counseling Assn., Nat. Rehab. Counseling Assn. (bd. dirs. 1986-87), Nat. Rehab. Adminstr. Assn. (nat. bd. dirs. 1983-87, 92-93), N.E. Rehab. Counseling Assn. (pres. 1987, bd. dirs. 1977—), N.J. Rehab. Assn. (bd. dirs. 1977—, treas. 1978, 89-92), Rho Sigma Chi, Chi Sigma Iota. Democrat. Greek Orthodox. Home: 668 Lake Ave Manchester NH 03103-3538 Office: NH Div Vocat Rehab 78 Regional Dr Concord NH 03301-8508

KALISHER, SHEILA LYNN, invention company executive; b. Detroit, July 12, 1944; d. Jack Allyn and Beatrice Sybil (Rosenfeld) Cohen; m. Lester Kalisher, May 8, 1966; children: Aaron James, Lisa Jineen. Student, U. Mich, 1962-63; BA, Wayne State U., 1967. Cert. secondary tchr. Tchr. English Virginia Beach (Va.) Sch. System, 1968-69; pres., chief exec. officer A.L.L.'S. WELL & CO., Livingston, N.J., 1986—. Patentee in field. Mem. Women's Am. Orgn. Rehab. Through Tng. (v.p. 1981-82), Nat. Soc. Inventors (sec. pub. rels. 1987—), Welcome Wagon Club (pres. Livingston chpt. 1980-81). Home and Office: 94 N Rockledge Dr Livingston NJ 07039-1121

KALKHOF, THOMAS CORRIGAN, physician; b. Wellsville, N.Y., Aug. 12, 1919; s. Arthur Albert and Evelyn (Corrigan) K.; m. Mary E. Jones, Mar. 3, 1946 (dec. 1955); children: Thomas E., Susan A., Mark A., Patricia D.; m. 2d Constance N. McCarthy, Apr. 19, 1958; children: Christopher J., Constance M., Craig Alan. B.S., Gannon U., 1943; M.D., Marquette U., 1946. Intern, resident St. Vincent's Hosp., Erie, Pa., 1946-47; pvt. practice nutritional problems, continued breast cancer rehab. and mammography, thermography, gen. geriatrics and psychosomatic medicine Erie, 1947—; med. dir. Twinbrook Med. Ctr., 1960-84; dir. Iroquois Med. Centre, Erie; staff mem. St. Vincent's Health Ctr., Hamot Med. Ctr., Erie; pres., dir. Small Hosp. Cons., Inc., Erie, 1954—. Past chmn. Pa. Bd. Accreditation Nursing Homes and Related Facilities; past pres. Cath. Social Svcs., Erie; past pres. Erie County Ind. Coun. on Aging.; bd. dirs. Cath. Charities USA Commn. on Aging. With M.C., AUS, 1943-44. Fellow Am. Coll. Health Care Adminstrs., Am. Geriatric Soc., Am. Acad. Family Physicians, Acad. Psychosomatic Medicine; mem. AMA, Pa. Health Care Assn. (past pres.) Acad. Psychomatic Medicine (past pres.), Pa. Acad. Family Physicians (past pres. Erie chpt.), Assn. Physicians in Chronic Disease Facilities (past pres.), Am. Soc. Clin. Hypnosis, Pa., Erie County Med. Socs., Nat. Geriatric Soc. (pres.), Soc. Prospective Medicine, Pa. Thoracic Soc., Ind. Coun. on Aging (past pres.), KC (4 deg.). Republican. Roman Catholic. Home: 3749 E Lake Rd Erie PA 16511-1346 Office: 4401 Iroquois Ave PO Box 7265 Erie PA 16510

KALKSTEIN, LAURENCE SAUL, geography educator; b. Bklyn., Jan. 29, 1948; s. Herman Benjamin and Anne (Friedman) K.; m. Rhona Jeanne Finkel, June 13, 1971; 1 child, Adam. BA, Rutgers U., 1969; MA, La. State U., 1972, PhD, 1974. Asst. prof. UCLA, 1973-75; asst. prof. geography U. Del., Newark, 1975-81, assoc. prof., 1981-88, prof., 1988—; vis. scientist NOAA, Washington, 1982-83, EPA, Washington, 1989-90; cons. E.I. Du Pont de Nemours & Co., Wilmington, Del., 1988—, Salt River Project, Phoenix, 1988—. Editor: Global Climate Change, 1991; also numerous articles; developer weather stress index. Recipient Excellence in Teaching award U. Del., 1980; grantee EPA, 1985—, U.S. Geol. Survey, 1988-90, Salt River Project, 1988—, Environ. Can., 1990—. Mem. Am. Meteorol. Soc., Assn. Am. Geographers, World Meterol. Orgn. (rapporteur). Office: U Del Dept Geography Newark DE 19716

KALLEY, GORDON STEWART, industrial engineering educator; b. Windham, Conn., Dec. 4, 1953; s. Alexander and Dorothy (Madden) K.; m. Wendi Lee Griffiths, Oct. 21, 1978; 1 child, Cassandra. BSBA, U. N.H., 1977; BS in Indsl. Engring., N.J. Inst. Tech., 1981, MS in Indsl. Engring., 1985. Staff cons. Modern Human Resources, Bridgewater, N.J., 1980-85; asst. prof. of indsl. engring. N.J. Inst. Tech., Newark, 1981—. Mem. Inst. Indsl. Engrs. (sec. 1990—), N.Y. Acad. Scis. (advisor 1990—), Soc. Mfg. Engrs. (sec. 1991—). Home: 2 Beekman Rd Bridgewater NJ 08807-2602 *Died June 7, 1992.*

KALLINA, EMANUEL JOHN, II, lawyer; b. Balt., Dec. 18, 1948; s. Robert Wooding and Elanor Lee (Stinson) K.; m. Anne M. Vik, Jan. 16, 1982; children: James E. (dec.), Deborah A., Kristine L., Abigail M. BA in English, Bowdoin Coll., Brunswick, Maine, 1970; JD, U. Md., 1973; LLM in Taxation, NYU, 1974. Bar: Md. 1974, D.C. 1977. Law clk. Hon. R. Dorsey Watkins, U.S. Dist. Judge, Balt., 1974-75; assoc. McKenney, Thomsen & Burke, Balt., 1975-77; pvt. practice law Balt., 1977-78; ptnr. Niles, Barton & Wilmer, Balt., 1978-82; pres., atty. Kallina, Levinson & Burns, Balt., 1982-85, Kallina & Assocs., Balt., 1985—; real estate broker Kallina Realty Associs., Balt., 1985—; life ins. agt. Balt., 1990—; series 22 securities lic. agt., Balt., 1987—. Contbr. articles to profl. jours.; frequent speaker in field. Bd. dirs. Nat. Com. on Planned Giving, 1993—; house ch. leader Grace Fellowship Ch., Balt., 1989. Mem. ABA, Md. Bar Assn., Balt. Assn. Tax Counsel (pres. 1981-82), Chesapeake Planned Giving Coun. (co-founder, del. 1991, bd. dirs. 1991—), IRS Study Group, Pres.'s Club Gettysburg Coll., Pres.'s Club Hood Coll. Republican. Office: Kallina & Assocs 6507 York Rd Baltimore MD 21212-2115

KALLIR, JOHN, advertising agency executive; b. Vienna, Austria, Apr. 23, 1923; came to U.S., 1939; s. Otto and Francisca (Countess zu Löwenstein) K.; m. Joyce Rubin, Apr. 16, 1949; children—Jane Katherine, Barbara Sue. B.S., Manhattan Coll., 1943; M.A., Columbia U., 1950. Research librarian S.B. Penick & Co., Jersey City, N.J., 1946; editor E.R. Squibb & Sons, Bklyn., N.Y., 1947-49; copywriter Paul Klemtner & Co., Newark, 1950-51; acct. exec., v.p. William D. Mc Adams, N.Y.C., 1952-61; founder, pres. Kallir, Philips, Ross, N.Y.C., 1962-85; chmn. bd. Kallir, Philips, Ross, 1986—; v.p. Galerie St. Etienne, N.Y.C.; ptnr. Grandma Moses Properties, N.Y.C. Dist. leader Dem. Town Com., Greenburgh, N.Y., 1968-81; mem. Planning Bd., Greenburgh, N.Y., 1982-87; bd. dirs. Greenburgh Nature Ctr. Served to cpl. U.S. Army, 1943-46. Mem. Med. Advt. Agy. Assn. (bd. dirs.), Pharm. Advt. Council, N.Y. Acad. Scis., AAAS, Am. Hist. Assn. Democrat. Office: Kallir Philips Ross Inc 333 E 38th St New York NY 10016-2745

KALLOS, BRUCE OLIVER, business executive; b. Ridgefield, Conn., Apr. 5, 1935; s. A. Oliver and Helen Elizabeth (Keeler) K.; m. Lee Spaulding Masselman, Sept. 26, 1956; children: Jay, Wendy, Tracey. BSME, BS in Indsl Adminstrn., Yale U., 1956. Registered profl. engr., Del. Engr. E.I. Du Pont, Seaford, Del., 1956-62, planner, 1962-81; fin. advisor Wilmington, Del., 1981-86, bus. strategist, 1987—. V.p. U.S. Jaycees, Tulsa, 1963-64; pres. Del. Jaycees, Dover, Del., 1962-63; chmn. investment com. State of Del. Employees Pension Fund, Dover, 1983—, trustee State of Del. pension fund, 1981—. Mem. Council Instl. Investors (treas. 1985—), Nat. Assn. State Investment Officers (bd. dirs. 1986—), Internat. Jaycees (life senator). Republican. Episcopalian. Home: 903 Barley Mill Rd Wilmington DE 19807-2803

KALMAN, THOMAS IVAN, chemistry educator, researcher; b. Budapest, Hungary, Jan. 20, 1936; came to U.S., 1963; s. George and Edith (Ban) K.; m. Marietta Sophia Szeben, Jan. 25, 1963; children: Rob P., Nicolette C. Diploma in chem. engring., Tech. U., Budapest, 1959; PhD, SUNY, Buffalo, 1968. Asst. prof. Sch. of Pharmacy SUNY, Buffalo, 1970-75, assoc. prof. Sch. of Pharmacy, 1975—; vis. assoc. prof. Sch. of Medicine Yale U., New Haven, 1975-76; mem. sci. adv. com. Am. Cancer Soc., Atlanta, 1990—; mem. spl. rev. com. Nat. Inst. Allergy and Infectious Diseases/NIH, Bethesda, 1990—. Co-editor: New Approaches to the Design of Antineoplastic Agents, 1982; editor: Drug Action and Design: Mechanism Based Enzyme Inhibitors, 1979; contbr. articles to profl. jours. NIH fellow, 1966-67, 67-69, Career Devel. award, 1971-76. Fellow Am. Inst. Chemistry; mem. AAAS, Am. Assn. Cancer Rsch., Am. Chem. Soc., N.Y. Acad. Scis., Sigma Xi, Rho Chi. Office: SUNY Dept Med Chemistry 457 Cooke Hall Buffalo NY 14260

KALMUS, ELLIN, art historian, educator; b. N.Y.C.; d. Victor and Mata (Heineman) Roudin; m. Murray L. Silberstein, Oct. 6, 1949 (dec. 1968); children: James, Barbara Silberstein Keezell, John; m. Allan H. Kalmus, May 16, 1969. BA cum laude, Vassar Coll., 1946. Asst. dept. publs. and exhbns. Mus. Modern Art, N.Y.C., 1946-49; asst. tchr. Mus. Modern Art, 1950; lectr. Riverdale Country Sch., N.Y.C., 1970—, Dalton,Trinity, Columbia Grammar, Birch Wathen Schs., N.Y.C., 1971-83, Fifth Ave. Presbyn. Ch., St. James Episcopal Ch., N.Y.C., 1982-83; lectr. pvt. groups N.Y.C., 1975—; mem. vis. com. photographs and slide libr. Met. Mus. Art, N.Y.C., 1978—, lectr., 1986, 87; mem. teaching staff Ethical Culture Sch. for Adult Edn., New Sch. for Social Rsch., 1980-81; Paris lectr. Friends of Vieilles Maisons Francaises, 1988; series lectr. Darien Community Assn., 1988-92, London Lectr. Arts Club of London, 1990. Trustee, head edn. com. Riverdale Country Sch., N.Y.C., 1978-84. Pierpont Morgan Libr. fellow, 1986, Frick Collection fellow, 1992. Mem. Phi Beta Kappa, Cosmopolitan Club, Sunningdale Club (Scarsdale, N.Y.). Home: 125 E 72d St New York NY 10021-4299

KALOUDIS, GEORGE STERGIOU, educator; b. Kos, Dodecanese, Greece, Jan. 3, 1952; came to U.S., 1975; s. Stergos Antoniou and Valsamina (Hatzimihalis) K.; m. Penelope Thornton, June 6, 1975; children: Stergos Kaloudis, Naomi Kaloudis. BA, Panteios Sch. Polit. Sci., Athens, 1974; MA, Calif. State U., Fullerton, 1976; PhD, Kans. U., 1981. Instr. Bunker Hill Community Coll., Boston, 1983-84, Daniel Webster Coll., Nashua, N.H., 1983-88; asst. prof. Rivier Coll., Nashua, 1988—, dir. history and polit. sci., 1991—; Author: The Role of the U.N. in Cyprus from 1964-79, 1991. Coach Merrimack (N.H.) Youth Assn., 1989-90; active Earth Day com. Rivier Coll., 1990, minority recruitment task force, 1990, chair bicentennial com., 1988—; advisor state/local polit. campaigns. With Greek Navy, 1981-82. Mem. Am. Polit. Sci. Assn., Dodecanese Soc., Pi Sigma Alpha. Greek Orthodox. Home: 31 Woodland Dr Merrimack NH 03054-3217 Office: Rivier Coll 429 Main St Nashua NH 03060-5033

KALSNER, STANLEY, educator, pharmacologist, physiologist; b. N.Y.C., Aug. 21, 1936; s. William Louis and Sadie (Feldman) K.; m. Jenny Book, Aug. 4, 1963; children—Lydia, Pamela, Louisa. AB, NYU, 1958; postgrad., SUNY Downstate Med. Ctr., 1959-62; PhD, U. Man., Can., 1966; postgrad., Cambridge (Eng.) U., 1966-67. Asst. prof. pharmacology U. Ottawa, Ont., Can., 1967-72, assoc. prof., 1972-77, prof., 1977-85; prof., chmn. dept. physiology Med. Sch. CUNY, 1985—; med. rsch. scientist on heart disease and blood vessel function; sci. referee Med. Rsch. Coun. Can., Can. Heart Found. Editor, contbr. chpts. to books, articles to jours.; asso. editor Can. Jour. Physiology and Pharmacology, until 1985; mem. editorial bd.: Jour. Autonomic Pharmacology, Blood Vessels. USPHS fellow, 1960-67; Med. Rsch. Coun.-NRC and Ont. Heart Found. grantee; Am. Heart Assn. grantee, 1987—. Mem. AAAS, AAUP, Can. Pharmacology Soc., Am. Soc. Pharmacology and Therapeutics. Home: 21 Hillcrest Rd Suffern NY 10901-6834 Office: CUNY Med Sch 138th St and Convent Ave New York NY 10031

KALSOW, CAROLYN MARIE, ocular immunologist; b. Elgin, Ill., July 9, 1943; d. Arnold W. and Marie E. (Wolff) K.; m. Richard W. Krause, July 25, 1981; children: Jeffrey Hutchison, Paul Krause, Michael Hutchison, John Krause, Carolyn Krause. BS, Iowa State U., 1965; MA, U. Tex., Galveston, 1967; PhD, U. Louisville, 1970. Dir. clin. ocular micro. ophthalmology U. Louisville, 1974-81, instr., asst. prof., assoc. prof. ophthalmology, 1971-81; adj. assoc. prof. biology Hope Coll., Holland, Mich., 1981-85; sr. scientist ophthamology U. Rochester, N.Y., 1986—; vis. asst. prof. med. sch. U. South Fla., Tampa, 1972; mem. visual sci. A-1 study sect. NEI, NIH, PHS, Washington, 1982-86. Contbr. articles to Int. Arch. All. Appl. Immunology, Invest. Ophthalmol. Visual Scis., Jour. Immunology, World Uveitis Symposium, Ocular Immunology Today. Mem., various offices Luth. Ch.-Mo. Synod, Louisville, 1967-81, Holland, Mich., 1981-85, Mendon, N.Y., 1985—. Recipient Disting. Alumna award Elgin (Ill.) Community Coll., 1975. Mem. AAAS, Am. Assn. Immunology, European Pineal Study Group, Assn. Rsch. Visual Ophthalmology, Internat. Soc. Eye Rsch., Phi Kappa Phi, Sigma Xi. Home: 15 Fountainbleau Mendon NY 14506-9740 Office: U Rochester Sch Med/Dental Dept Ophthalmology PO Box 314 Rochester NY 14642-0001

KALTENBACH, JANE COUFFER, zoology educator; b. Chgo., Dec. 21, 1922; d. Robert William and Frances Jane (Rayner) C.; m. John Paul Kaltenbach, 1946; m. Robert Leslie Townsend, Aug. 30, 1966. BS, Beloit Coll., 1944; MA, U. Wis., 1946; PhD, U. Iowa, 1950. Asst. zoology U. Wis., Madison, 1944-47, assoc. zoology, 1950-53; asst. zoology U. Iowa, Iowa City, 1947-50; Am. Cancer Soc. fellow Wenner-Grens Inst., Stockholm, 1953-56; asst. prof. zoology Northwestern U., Evanston, Ill., 1956-58; asst. prof., then assoc. prof. zoology Mt. Holyoke Coll., South Hadley, Mass., 1958-70, prof. biology, 1970—. Contbr. articles to profl. publs. Grantee Northwestern U. Grad. Sch., 1957, 58, NSF, 1960-63, Mt. Holyoke Coll., 1966-91, Rsch. Corp., 1987-90. Fellow AAAS; mem. Am. Soc. Zoologists, Am. Soc. Anatomists, Soc. Devel. Biology, Corp. Marine Biol. Lab., Soc. Biology and Medicine, Phi Beta Kappa. Home: 139 Cold Hill Rd Granby MA 01033-9705 Office: Mt Holyoke Coll Dept Biol Scis South Hadley MA 01075

KALTOFEN, ERICH, computer science, scholar; b. Linz, Austria, Dec. 21, 1955. MS, Rensselaer Poly. Inst., 1979, PhD, 1982. Lectr. U. Del., Newark, 1981-82; asst. prof. U. Toronto, 1982-84; asst. prof. dept. computer sci. Rensselaer Poly. Inst., Troy, N.Y., 1984-88, assoc. prof., 1988-91; prof. Rensselaer Poly. Inst., Troyu, N.Y., 1992—. Editor: Computers and Mathematics, 1989, Computational Algebraic Complexity, 1990, Applicable Algebra in Engineering Communication and Computing, vol. 1, 1991; assoc. editor SIAM Jour. Computation, 1988-91; mem. editorial bd. Jour. Symbolic Computation, 1987. Recipient IBM Faculty Devel. award, 1985. Mem. Assn. for Computing Machinery, Soc. Indsl. and Applied Math., Am. Auto Assn., SIGSAM (vice chmn. 1988-90). Office: Rensselaer Poly Inst Troy NY 12180

KALTSOS, ANGELO JOHN, electronics executive, educator, photographer; b. Boston, Aug. 19, 1930; s. John Angelo and Rita Thomas (Goudas) K.; m. Verna Kay Wilson, June 30, 1952 (dec. Jan. 1973); children: Pamela, Elaine, Gregory, Stephanie, Lenora, Demetra, Dana. Student, Mass. Radio and TV Sch., Boston, 1955-57, Harvard Coll. Extension, 1964, Boston State Coll., 1965-67, U. N.M., 1976, Fitchburg State Coll., 1977. Clk. U.S. Postal Svc., Boston, 1954-57; electronic rsch. technician Crosley div. Avco, Cin., 1957; electronic technician Raytheon Mfg. Co., Waltham, Mass., 1957-63; educator Cambridge (Mass.) Sch. Dept., 1961-81; ind. ethnology rsch. N.Mex., 1969—; mgr. Pampas, Inc., Boston, 1987-90; bd. dirs. Expansion Dance Co., Boston; cons. 5 P.I.E., Albuquerque, 1976—, Indian Tribal Group, N.Mex.; lectr. S.W. Indian Culture in Boston, Cambridge area, 1990—; pres., treas. Spartan Enterprises, Inc., 1965-69. Author: Southwest Indian, 1986; one-man photo exhibits: Christmas Tree Gallery, Manteo, N.C., 1977, The 4th St. Photo Gallery, N.Y.C., 1980, Cambride Rindge and Latin Sch., Mass., 1981, Jay's, Cambridge, Mass., 1983, Here Today Gallery, Boston, 1984, Andover (Maine) Town Hall, 1984, 86, Piedmont Art Assn., Martinsville, Va., 1985-86, Cambalache Gallery, Boston, 1986-87, The 4th St. Gallery, N.Y.C., 1990; contbg. journalist in field. Chmn. No Thank Q Hydro Quebec, Andover, Maine, 1988-91, coord., 1991; regional and media coord. N.E. Alliance to Protect James Bay, 1990-91; mem. senate faculty Cambridge Sch. Dept., 1980-81; sec. New Eng. Model Car Assn. of Raceways, 1966-69; coord. No Thank Q Hydro-Quebec, Dryden, Maine, 1991—; exec. bd. dirs., mem. adv. bd. N.E. Alliance to Protect James Bay, 1991—, treas; educator Cambridge (Mass.) Adult Ctr., 1990—, Paulist Ctr., Boston, 1991. Mem. Appalachian Mountain Club. Greek Orthodox. Home: 10 Lesley Ave Somerville MA 02144-2607

KALUGIN, LLOYD, college administrator; b. Jersey City, Mar. 25, 1926; s. David and Rose (Fleischer) K.; m. Elaine Elkind, Dec. 24, 1947; children: Vicki, Craig. BS, L.I. U., 1950; MA, NYU, 1951, 1951; EdD, Rutgers U., 1975. Instr. L.I. U., N.Y.C., 1950-51; asst. buyer May Co., N.Y.C., 1951-52, Bond Clothes, N.Y.C., 1952-53; buyer Meyer Bros., Paterson, N.J., 1953-56; store mgr. Robert Hall Clothes, N.J., 1956-62, Franklin Simon, Eatontown, N.J., 1962-68; prof. Middlesex County Coll., Edison, N.J., 1968-72, chmn. dept., 1972-74, dir. coop. edn., 1974—. With U.S. Army, 1944-46, ETO. Home: 9B Molly Pitcher Ct Cranbury NJ 08512-4625 Office: Middlesex County Coll 155 Mill Rd Edison NJ 08837-3675

KAMAN, CHARLES HURON, diversified technologies corporation executive; b. Washington, June 15, 1919; s. Charles W. and Mabel (Davis) K.; m. Helen Sylvander, Oct. 20, 1945 (div.); children: Charles William II, Cathleen, Steven Wardner; m. Roberta C. Hallock, Sept. 1, 1971. BS in Aero. Engring. magna cum laude, Cath. U. Am., 1940; DSc (hon.), U. Colo., 1984, U. Hartford, 1985; LLD (hon.), U. Conn., 1985. With Hamilton Standard Propellers div. United Aircraft Corp., East Hartford, Conn., 1940-45; pres. Kaman Corp., Bloomfield, Conn., 1945-90, chmn. bd., 1945—, chief exec. officer, 1986—; chmn. Vertical Lift Aircraft council of Aerospace Industries Assn., 1964, Helicopter council, 1954; former mem. The World Affairs Ctr. Honors adv. bd. Bd. govs. Cath. U. Am.; bd. dirs. Inst. of Living; founder, pres., bd. dirs. Fidelco Guide Dog Found., Inc.; founder, Am. Leadership Forum, U. Hartford; former trustee Western New England Coll.; former mem. Catholic U. bd. govs.; past corporator Health Care Facilities Planning Council of Greater Hartford; past indsl. com. mem. Greater Hartford YMCA. Recipient Disting. Service award Conn. Jr. C. of C., 1953, Engr. of Year award Conn. Soc. of Profl. Engrs. inc., 1961, Alumni Achievement award Cath. U. Am., 1961, Outstanding Young Man of Yr. award Hartford Jr. C. of C., 1948, Assoc. award Navy Helicopter Assn., 1975, Nat. Human Relations award Nat. Conf. of Christian and Jews, 1987, The Fleet Adm. Chester W. Nimitz award Navy League of the U.S., 1986. Fellow Am. Helicopter Soc. (pres. 1958, dir. 1959-61, Dr. Alexander Klemin award 1981), AIAA; mem. Conn. Bus. and Industry Assn. (dir., exec. com.), Nat. Acad. Engring., Conn. Soc. Profl. Engrs., Aviation Hall of Fame (charter), Navy Helicopter Assn. (hon.), Newcomen Soc. Am. 1983, Navy League of U.S. (nat. adv. coun.), Pi Tau Sigma (hon.), Beta Gamma Sigma, Am. Helicopter Soc., Conn. Acad. Sci. and Engring., Conn. Aero. Hist. Assn. Office: Kaman Corp 1322 Blue Hills Ave Bloomfield CT 06002-1303*

KAMARCK, LAWRENCE NORBERT, playwright; b. Canton, N.Y., June 6, 1927; s. Martin and Frances Kamarck; m. Caroline Langmaid (div. Nov. 1970); children: Jonathan, Matthew, Mitchell, Valerie; m. Catherine Rich, Nov. 5, 1970. BA, Harvard U.; MFA, Yale U. Author: Dinosaur, 1969 (Edgar Allen Poe award 1969), Bell Ringer, 1970 (N.Y. Times 10 Best Chillers), Informed Sources, 1979; playwright: The Keeping of Philip, 1984 (CBS Dramatists Guild award). Mem. Dramatists Guild, Authors Guild. Home: PO Box 304 Woodstown NJ 08098

KAMEEN, JOHN PAUL, newspaper publisher; b. Carbondale, Pa., June 2, 1941; s. Joseph Charles and Mary Veronica (O'Neill) K.; m. Carole Helen McCusker, Nov. 8, 1969; 1 child, Patricia. BS in Electronics, U. Scranton, 1963, postgrad., 1964-65. Publisher The Forest City (Pa.) News, 1967—; sec. Greater Forest City (Pa.) Industry, Inc., 1968—; bd. dirs. Community Bancorp, Inc., Forest City, 1978—. Contbr. numerous articles on hunting to mags. and pubs. Mem. Forest City Rep. Com., 1968-78; councilman Forest City Borough, 1974-78; pres. Susquehanna County Rep. C Club, 1991-92. Recipient Community Betterment award, Pa. C. of C., Harrisburg, 1970, Cert. of Nat. Merit, US Dept. HUD, Washington, 1982. Mem. Pa. Newspaper Pubs. Assn. (bd. dirs. 1980-84). Roman Catholic. Office: The Forest City News 636 Main St Forest City PA 18421-9602

KAMEN, GARY PAUL, physiologist, educator; b. Boston; s. Hyman and Beatrice (Shain) K.; m. Roberta Jane Kamen. BS, U. Mass., 1974, PhD, 1980. Postdoctoral fellow St. Louis U. Sch. Medicine, 1979-80; asst. prof. Ind. U., Bloomington, 1980-84, assoc. prof., 1984-88; assoc. prof. Boston U., 1988—; reviewer for numerous profl. jours.; grant reviewer Dept. Vets. Affairs, NIH, AAHPERD Rsch. Consortium; editorial assoc. Cts., Health Sci. and the Law, Insight into Cts. Contbr. chpts. to Contbns. of Physical Activity to Human Well-Being, 1986, Current Clinics in Sports Medicine, 1990, Computer-Aided Electromyography and Expert Systems, 1989; contbr. articles to European Jour. Applied Physiology, Rsch. Quarterly for Exercise and Sport, Am. Jour. Phys. Medicine, Am. Jour. Clin. Nutrition, Jour. Sports Medicine and Phys. Fitness, Ergonomics, Jour. Motor Behavior, Medicine and Sci. in Sports and Exercise, Am. Corrective Therapy Jour., Perceptual and Motor Skills. Recipient Nat. Rsch. Svc. award NIH, 1986; USPHS grantee, Spencer Found. grantee, Lilly Endowment grantee, Nat. Inst. Aging grantee. Fellow Am. Coll. Sports Medicine, AAHPERD; mem. Am. Physiol. Soc., Soc. for Neurosci., Internat. Soc. Biomechanics, Gerontol. Soc. Am., Internat. Soc. Electrophysiol. Kinesiology, AAAS, North Am. Soc. for Psychology Sport and Phys. Activity, Am. Running and Fitness Assn., Internat. Brain Rsch. Orgn., Nat. Strength and Conditioning Assn., Fedn. Am. Socs. Experimental Biology, Sigma Xi. Office: Boston U 635 Commonwealth Ave Boston MA 02215-1610

KAMEN, MILTON, business consultant; b. N.Y.C., Jan. 1, 1921; s. Paul and Miriam (Berger) Kaminsky; m. Renee Weiss, June 27, 1948; children: Peggy, Michael. Student, Cornell U., 1938-39; BA, Columbia Coll., 1940, postgrad., 1941-42; LLD (hon.), London Inst. Rsch., 1973. V.p. advt. and sales M. Udell & Co., N.Y.C., 1948-55, pres., 1955-68; copywriter, producer Kamen Assocs., N.Y.C., 1969-77; dir. MRK Publs., N.Y.C., 1977—, 7E Assocs., N.Y.C., 1990—; pres. Gramercy Park Clothes, N.Y.C., 1968-80. Author: The Grandparents Book, 1977, The Secret Record Book, 1990; contbr. articles to mags. Bd. dirs. Holyland Registry, Tel Aviv, Israel, 1982—, Nursing Home Vis. Svc., West Palm Beach, Fla., 1989—, ComputerKids Edn. Ctr., Hartford, Conn., 1990—. Named to Textile Hall of Fame, Am. Arbitration Assn., 1957, Award for Svc., 1947-63. Mem. Columbia Coll. Alumni Assn. (bd. dirs. 1966-70), Princeton Club, Beta Gamma Sigma (hon.). Office: 7E Assocs 301 E 66th St New York NY 10021

KAMEN-KAYE, MAURICE, consulting geologist; b. London, Aug. 17, 1905; s. Aaron and Hanna (Gold) Kaye; m. Dorothy Allers, Dec. 27, 1938. BS, Royal Coll. of Sci., London, 1926, Royal Sch. of Mines, London, 1929. Petroleum geologist Caracas Petroleum Corp., Venezuela, 1930-40, chief geologist, 1941-50; cons. geologist Can., U.S.A., 1950-54; rsch. geologist Conorada Petroleum Corp., N.Y.C., Tulsa, 1955-68; cons. geologist Cambridge, Mass., 1968—. Co-author: China, Stratigraphy, Paleogeography and Tectonics, 1991; contbr. more than 20 papers to profl. publs. Mem. Geol. Soc. Am., Am. Assn. Petroleum Geologists, Soc. Exploration Geophysicists. Home and Office: 1 Waterhouse St # 5 Somerville MA 02144-1715

KAMENY, NAT, advertising agency executive; b. N.Y.C., Nov. 6, 1923; s. Michel and Bessie (Sunshine) K.; m. Ruth Zatal, Mar. 27, 1943; children: Ellen, Leslie, Debra. Student, CCNY, 1941-42, 46-47. Propr. Camenard Studios (profl. photographers), 1945; founder, chmn. KSW & G, Inc. (advt.), N.Y.C., 1946-78; pres. Israel Communications, Inc. (pub. relations), 1969-78, Kameny Comm., Inc., 1978-89; chmn. Venet Advt., 1989—; pres. Primary Systems Corp. Past pres. Jewish Fedn. Bergen County; vice chmn., nat. commr., nat. exec. com., nat. planning com., nat. mktg. com. Anti-Defamation League; chmn. Internat. Ctr. for Holocaust Studies; sec. N.Am. Jewish Students Appeal; v.p. Jewish Telegraphic Agy.; founder, trustee Israel Hosp. Fund; mem. exec. com. Jewish Found. for Christian Rescuers; asst. to mayor, Bergenfield, N.J., 1960-62, indsl. commr., Bergenfield, 1960-64; vice chmn. Bergenfield Planning Bd., 1960-67; chmn. Bergen County Dem. Campaign Com., 1960-61. Mem. League Advt. Agys. (pres. 1962-63), Overseas Press Club. Lodge: B'nai B'rith. Address: 85 Thames Blvd Bergenfield NJ 07621 Office: 245 5th Ave New York NY 10016-8728

KAMERAS, DAVID HOWARD, writer, small business owner; b. Washington, June 3, 1952; s. Boris Morris and Tillie (Block) K.; m. Beth Joan Anderson, Aug. 12, 1985; 1 child, Robin Alena. BA in Am. Studies, Coe Coll., 1974; postgrad., U. Mo., 1974, Iowa State U., 1976-78; MA in Journalism, U. Iowa, 1978. Editor Engring. Svcs. and Publs., Inc., Gaithersburg, Md., 1974; writer Gail Industries, Cedar Rapids, Iowa, 1975-76, Norand Corp., Cedar Rapids, 1976-78; product info. specialist Penril Corp., Rockville, Md., 1978-79; asst. press sec. U.S. Senator John Culver, Washington, 1979-81; writer, editor Libr. of Congress, Washington, 1981-82; press staff asst. U.S. Senator Paul Sarbanes, Washington, 1982-83; press sec. U.S. Rep. Tim Valentine, Washington, 1983-84; pub. affairs coord. Transp. Inst., Camp Springs, Md., 1984—; owner Kameras Intruments, Garrett Park, Md., 1972—. Vol. McCarthy Presdl. Campaign, Bethesda, Md., 1968, Ribicoff Senate Campaign, Norwalk, Conn., 1968; county del. Udall Presdl. Campaign, Cedar Rapids, 1976. Mem. Nat. Def. Transp. Assn., U.S. Naval Inst., Navy League of the U.S., Office and Profl. Employees Internat. Union. Home: 313 Ellsworth Dr Silver Spring MD 20910-4221 Office: Kameras Instruments PO Box 399 Garrett Park MD 20896-0399

KAMERMAN, JACK B., sociology educator, researcher, writer; b. Bklyn., Dec. 15, 1940; s. Jacob and Fanny (Goldman) K.; m. Constance Lynn Munro, June 3, 1979; children: William Lewis, David Munro. BA, CUNY, 1962; PhD, NYU, 1979. Instr. U. Minn., Mpls., 1965-68, Adelphi U., Garden City, N.Y., 1968-73, William Paterson Coll., Wayne, N.J., 1973-76; assoc. prof. sociology Kean Coll. N.J., Union, 1978—; mem. com. on suicide prevention N.Y.C. Police Dept., 1991—; presenter in field to profl. meetings and confs.; manuscript reviewer Greenwood Press, Prentice-Hall, Holt, Rinehart, Winston, F.E. Peacock, Harper & Row, Random House, Duxbury Press, Hamilton Pubs., 1973—. Author: Death in the Midst of Life: Social and Cultural Influences on Death, Grief, and Mourning, 1988; co-editor: Performers and Performances: The Social Organization of Artistic Work, 1983; columnist, contbg. editor Twin Citian Mag., 1966-68; contbr. numerous articles and revs. on sociology of death and music to profl. jours. Grantee NEH, 1988, rsch. grantee Henry Murray Ctr. for Study of Lives, Radcliffe Coll., 1990. Mem. Am. Sociol. Assn., Assn. Death Edn. and Counseling (cert. death educator), Am. Assn. Suicidology, Acad. Criminal Justice Scis., Condrs. Guild, Boston Soc. for Gerontologic Psychiatry. Office: Kean Coll NJ Dept Sociology and Social Work Union NJ 07083

KAMIKAWA, ALDEN TANEMITSU, trade association executive; b. Fresno, Calif., Dec. 18, 1940; s. Thomas Taneichi and Miyeko Lorene (Kawamoto) K.; BA, San Francisco State U., 1963, MS, 1968. Vol., Peace Corps, Colombia, 1963-65; counselor U.S. War on Poverty Program, Job Corps, 1965-66; vocat. rehab. counselor Calif. Dept. Rehab., San Jose, 1968-71; assoc. dir. manpower devel. and tng. dept. Nat. Assn. Home Builders, Washington, 1971-81, dir. ops., manpower devel. and tng. div., 1982-83; v.p., sec. Home Builders Inst., Washington, 1984—. Participant Pres.'s Jobs-for-Vets. Nat. Com.; mem. adv. com. Job Corps, Dept. Labor, Washington; bd. dirs. Peace Corps Friends of Colombia. Mem. Am. Rehab. Counseling Assn., Am. Soc. Assn. Execs., Am. Assn. for Counseling and Devel., Am. Vocat. Assn., Japanese Am. Citizens League. Assoc. producer film: Build a Better Life. Home: 1721 P St NW Washington DC 20036-1342 also: 8 Bridge Rd Middlesex Beach DE 19709 Office: Home Builders Inst 15th and M Sts NW Washington DC 20005

KAMIN, AMY ROSE, cosmetic services-manufacturing company executive; b. Pitts., July 22, 1960; d. Marvin and Hannah (Honig) K.; m. Neil Sadick, Sept. 19, 1987. BA in Communications, Chatham Coll., 1982. Profl. magician and ventriloquist, Pitts., 1972-82; art dir. day camp Chatham Coll., Pitts., 1975-78; prodn. asst. Stas. KDKA-TV and WTAE-TV, Pitts., 1979-81; with Fashion Office, Gimbels Dept. Store, Pitts., 1980-81, exec. trainee, group mgr., asst. buyer, buyer, 1981-85; retail exec. Lord & Taylor, N.Y.C., 1985-88; mdse. councilor Macys N.E., N.Y.C., 1989; founder, pres. ARK Industries, Inc., N.Y.C., 1989—. Vol. bus. and profl. div. United Jewish Appeal, Pitts., N.Y.C., 1978, mem. power breakfast com., 1991-92; former vol. Jr. League, Pitts.; v.p., bd. dirs. B'nai B'rith Hillel, Pitts., 1982-84; coll. fair recruiter Chatham Colls., N.Y.C., 1992; bd. dirs. bus. and profl. div. United Jewish Appeal, 1992. Mem. Montefiore Hosp. Soc., Cosmetic, Toiletry and Fragrance Assn.; Nat. Coun. Jewish Women.

KAMINKER, PAUL ANDRE, sales and marketing executive; b. Paris, June 9, 1933; came to U.S., 1946; s. Georges and Cornelia Marie (Kampers) K.; m. Betty J. Adams, Mar. 7, 1954 (div. Feb. 1983); children: Michele, Nancy; m. Arlene Feinberg, May 2, 1986. Student, Walter Hervey Jr. Coll., 1952, Hofstra U., 1954-55. Sales rep. Gen. Mills, N.Y.C., 1954-60, Kendall Co., N.Y.C., 1960-62; nat. sales mgr. Smith Lee Co., Inc., Oneida, N.Y., 1962-68; gen. sales mgr. Standard Package Corp., Union, N.J., 1968-71; dir. sales Plastics, Inc., St. Paul, 1971-75; pres. P&K Mktg. Assocs. Inc., Tampa, 1975-87; v.p. sales and mktg. Atlantic Cheinco Corp., Burlington, N.J., 1987-90, First Phillips Mfg. Corp., Acton, Mass., 1990—. Dist. staff Little League Baseball, N.J., Tampa, Fla., 1960-85; radio reader Sta. WUSF Radio Reading Svc., Tampa, 1982-87. With U.S. Army, 1952-53. Recipient 25 Yr. Plaque Little League Baseball, 1985, 5 Yr. Plaque WUSF Radio Reading Svc., 1987. Republican. Office: First Phillips Mfg Corp 1 Acton Pl Acton MA 01720

KAMINS, BARRY MICHAEL, lawyer; b. Bklyn., Oct. 3, 1943; s. Abe and Evelyn Bertha (Goffen) K.; m. Fern Louise Kamins, Mar. 30, 1968; 1 child, Allyson. BA, Columbia U., 1965; JD, Rutgers U., 1968. Bar: N.Y. 1969, U.S. Dist. Ct. (ea. dist.) N.Y. 1973, (so. dist.) N.Y. 1973, U.S. Supreme Ct. 1974. Asst. dist. atty., 1969-73; dep. chief Criminal Ct. Bur., 1971-73; ptnr. Flamhaft, Levy Kamins & Hirsch; mem. grievance com. 2d and 11th Jud. Dist.; adj. asst. prof. in criminal law N.Y. Tech. Coll.; apptd. spl. prosecutor, Kings County, 1990-91. Mem. ABA, N.Y. State Bar Assn., Bklyn. Bar Assn. (v.p.), Kings County Criminal Bar Assn. (past pres.), Nat. Dist. Attys. Assn., Assn. of Bar of City of N.Y. (mem. jud. com.). Author: The Social Studies Student Investigates the Criminal Justice System, 1978, New York Search and Seizure, 1991; numerous articles in criminal law. Office: 16 Court St Brooklyn NY 11241-0004

KAMINSKI, LINDA J., academic affairs executive; b. Easton, Pa., Jan. 31, 1950; d. George J. and Dorothy (Almeida) Joseph; m. Daniel J. Fineran, Aug. 7, 1971 (div. 1981); 1 child, Kimberly; m. Gerald T. Kaminski, July 30, 1988. BS in Music Edn., Mansfield U., 1971; MA in Edn., George Washington U., 1975; EdD in Higher Edn. Adminstrn., Coll. William & Mary, 1979; MS in Counseling, U. Nebr., Omaha, 1982. Music tchr. Honolulu Sch. System, 1971-72, Hampton (Va.) Sch. System, 1973-79; div. chmn. Coll. St. Mary, Omaha, 1981-83, asst. dean acad. affairs, 1979-83; campus mgr. Met. Community Coll., Omaha, 1983-87, asst. to v.p. edn. svcs., 1984-87; v.p. acad. affairs Westmoreland County Community Coll., Youngwood, Pa., 1987—. Bd. dirs. Westmoreland County Choral Soc. Mem. Nat. Coun. Instl. Adminstrs., Pa. Coun. Internat. Edn., Pa. Assn. of Two Yr. Colls., Western Pa. Higher Edn. Coun. (bd. dirs. 1991—), Rotary (bd. dirs. 1989—). Home: 118 Franklin Dr Greensburg PA 15601-1305 Office: Westmoreland Community Coll Youngwood PA 15697

KAMINSTEIN, PHILIP, psychiatrist; b. N.Y.C., Feb. 3, 1928; s. Isidor and Frances (Lance) K.; children: Paul Kellogg, James Kellogg. BA, Columbia U., 1947, MA, 1948; MD, SUNY, Bklyn., 1952. Diplomate Am. Bd. Psychiatry and Neurology. Resident in psychiatry Bklyn. State Hosp., 1953-54, sr. resident in psychiatry, 1956-59; asst. chief psychiatrist VA Med. Ctr., Coral Gables, Fla., 1959-60; dir. psychiat. tng. and edn. Spring Grove State Hosp., Balt., 1960-61; vis. psychiatrist Queens Gen. Hosp., Jamaica, N.Y., 1961-65; attending psychiatrist Morrisania City Hosp., Bronx, N.Y., 1965-67, Bellevue Psychiat. Hosp., N.Y.C., 1967-70; pvt. practice, Forest Hills, N.Y., 1962—; cons. psychiatrist Cath. Med. Ctr., Queens, 1986—; attending psychiatrist Parkway Hosp., 1991—. Hon. police surg. N.Y.C. Police Dept., 1975—. Capt. USAF, 1954-56. Fellow Am. Psychiat. Assn. (life), N.Y. Acad. Medicine; mem. Am. Soc. Psychoanalytic Physicians. Office: 110-20-71 Ave #405 Forest Hills NY 11375

KAMIS, EDWARD JOSEPH, general contractor; b. Detroit, Aug. 31, 1927; s. John Victor and Frances (Kozma) K.; m. Diana Repoli, Nov. 18, 1950; children: Edward Jr., Joanne, Michael Anthony. BS, U. Conn., 1953. With acctg. dept. Conn. Light & Power Co., Berlin, 1953-55; office mgr. All Time Mfg., New Britain, Conn., 1955-58; computer analyst Pratt & Whitney Aircraft, East Hartford, Conn., 1958-76; chief exec. officer Kamis Assocs., Glastonbury, Conn., 1976—. Pres. South Glastonbury Bus. Assn., 1976-81, Conn. Morgan Horse Assn., 1966; treas., dir. Assn. for Planned Growth, Glastonbury, 1989—; pres., dir. South Mill Village Assn., Glastonbury, 1986—; chmn., dir. Olde Towne Tourism Dist., Conn., 1986-92. Sgt. U.S. Army, 1946-49. Republican. Home: Hi-Gait Farms Rd South Glastonbury CT 06073-2212

KAMKE, PAUL BURTON, accountant, small business owner; b. Mt. Vernon, N.Y., Apr. 5, 1959; s. Burton Harris and Katherine Eleanor (Hatfield) K.; m. Gail Foster, Sept. 22, 1990; 1 child, Kristyn Leigh, July 25, 1991. BS in Commerce, U. Va., 1981. CPA, N.Y. Staff acct. Peat Marwick Mitchell, Stamford, Conn., 1981-83; sr. acct. Main Hurdman, Stamford, 1983-85; with Citicorp, Harrison, N.Y., 1985-86; owner Paul B. Kamke, CPAs, N.Y.C., 1986—; host nat. radio call-in show Ask the CPA, 1991; guest host radio talk shows Sta. WABC, N.Y.C., 1991, Sta. WOR, N.Y.C., 1992; mem. roundtable Sonny Bloch Radio Shows, N.Y.C., 1987—. Mem. Met. Real Estate and Investors Assn. (bd. dirs. Garwood, N.Y. chpt. 1989—), N.Y. State Soc. CPA's, Beta Gamma Sigma. Office: 420 Lexington Ave New York NY 10170-0002

KAMM, ROGER DALE, biomedical engineer, educator; b. Ashland, Wis., Oct. 10, 1950; s. Rudolph Wilhelm and Betty Jane (White) K.; m. Judith Mary Brown, Sept. 1, 1974; 1 child, Peter Martin. BS, Northwestern U., 1972; SM, MIT, 1977, PhD, 1977. Lectr. MIT, Cambridge, 1977-78, asst. prof., 1978-81, assoc. prof., 1981-87, prof. mech. engring., 1987—. Contbr. over 60 articles to profl. jours. Mem. ASME, Am. Physiol. Soc., Biomed. Engring. Soc. (sr. mem., chair awards com. 1989-91), Assn. Rsch. in Vision and Opthalmology. Home: 31 Nonesuch Weston MA 02193 Office: MIT 77 Massachusetts Ave Rm 3-260 Cambridge MA 02139-4307

KAMMERMAN, ARTHUR CHARLES CYRIL, communications consultant; b. London, Apr. 17, 1915; came to U.S., 1918; s. Arthur Augustus and Gladys Nelson (Ratcliffe) K.; m. Helen Julie Henderson, Dec. 26, 1939; children: Julie Madeleine Kammerman Hogenauer, Peggy Joan Kammerman Grashof, Charles Henderson. AB in English with honors, Rutgers U., 1937. Asst. mgr. Vick Chem. Co., N.Y.C., 1937-42; v.p., creative supr. Batten, Barton, Durstine & Osborn, Inc., N.Y.C., 1942-70; v.p., dir. Henderson Constrn. Co., 1962-76; v.p. advt. and pub. rels. Coun. for Aid to Edn., N.Y.C., 1971-86; communications cons., 1986—; bd. dirs. Federated Purchaser, Inc., Kenilworth, N.J., chmn., 1975—. Author: Highlights of the History of the Episcopal Church in Westfield, 1983. Vestryman St. Paul's Episcopal Ch., 1960-66, sec., 1986-91; bd. govs., chmn. Schs. Nursing and Allied Health, Muhlenberg Regional Med. Ctr., Plainfield, N.J., 1964—; trustee Westminster Choir Coll., Princeton, N.J., 1963-66; trustee Westfield (N.J.) United Fund, 1946-67, pres. 1959-60; bd. dirs. Union County Planned Parenthood, Plainfield, 1965-72, pres., 1968-72; mem. Union County Rep. Com., 1946-56; bd. dirs. Lambda Chi Alpha Ednl. Found., 1956-78, dir. emeritus, 1990. Recipient 1931 award for outstanding svc. Rutgers U., 1947. Mem. Rutgers U. Alumni Assn. (pres. 1960), Phi Beta Kappa, Alpha Delta Sigma, Beta Gamma Delta. Home and Office: 1 Stanley Oval Westfield NJ 07090-2424

KAMOWITZ, HERBERT MEYER, mathematics educator; b. Bklyn., Dec. 31, 1931; s. William and Sylvia (Abelson) K.; m. Elaine Heyman, Dec. 24, 1955; children: David Louis, Sylvia Jean, Anne Lisa. BS, CCNY, 1952; MS in Math., Brown U., 1954, PhD in Math., 1960. Sr. staff scientist Avco Corp., Wilmington, Mass., 1957-66; assoc. prof., math. U. Mass., Boston, 1966-70, prof., math., 1970—; vis. scientist Weizmann Inst. of Sci., Rehovot, Israel, 1973, 80. Contbr. articles to profl. jours. Mem. Am. Math. Soc. Office: U Mass Dept Math Boston MA 02125-3393

KAMPF, CINDY ALISE, public relations executive; b. Honolulu, Aug. 14, 1961; d. Joel and Isobel Linda (Cohen) K. BA, Muhlenberg Coll., Allentown, Pa., 1983; grad., Syracuse U., 1983-85. Project mgr. Hemming and Gilman, Inc., N.Y.C., 1985-86; asst. account exec. Dorf & Stanton Communications, Inc., N.Y.C., 1986-87; spl. events coord. Dorf & Stanton Communications, Inc., 1987-88; account exec. Keyes Martin Pub. Rels., Springfield, N.J., 1988-90; ind. pub. rels. cons. Cin-Sational Events and Publicity, West Orange, N.Y., 1990—; pub. rels. cons. various orgns., 1985—. Area chmn. Hands Across Am., N.J., 1986; mem. young profls. com., bd. mgrs. Cancer Care of N.J.; fundraiser spl. events Am. Indian Coll. Fund. Mem. Pub. Rels. Soc. Am., Pro Bono, Muhlenberg Metro Alumni Assn., Newhouse Alumni Assn. Home and Office: 44 Hart Dr West Orange NJ 07052-1113

KAMPITS, EVA IDA, academic dean; b. Budapest, Hungary, Feb. 22, 1946; came to U.S., 1951; d. Ernest Michael and Ilona (Gondi) K.; m. Dan Catalin Stefanescu, Aug. 4, 1979; children: Andreea N., Cristina F. Cert., U. Innsbruck, Austria, 1963; BA, Harvard U., 1968; MA, Boston Coll., 1971, PhD, 1977. Instr. freshman seminars MIT, Cambridge, Mass., 1973-80, freshman advisor, 1975-80, sophomore advisor, 1976-80, adminstrv. officer Artificial Intelligence Lab., 1967-78, asst. to dir. Lab. for Computer Sci., 1977-80, rsch. affiliate Media Lab., 1987-88; acad. dean Pine Manor Coll., Chestnut Hill, Mass., 1980—; chmn., trustee NERComp (bd. editors NERComp Jour.); mem. NEARnet; vice chair Gov.'s Coun. on Ednl. Tech.; steering com. Mass. Telecomputing Coalition. Mem. Modern Lang. Assn., Soc. for the Advancement of Scandinavian Study, South Atlantic Modern Lang. Assn., Assn. for Computing Machinery. Republican. Roman Catholic. Office: Pine Manor Coll 400 Heath St Chestnut Hill MA 02167-2332

KAMPOURIS, EMMANUEL ANDREW, corporate executive; b. Alexandria, Egypt, Dec. 14, 1934; came to U.S., 1979; s. Andrew George and Euridice Anne (Caralli) K.; m. Myrto Stellatos, July 4, 1959 (dec.); children: Andrew, Alexander. Student, King's Sch., Bruton, Somerset, U.K., 1953; M.A. in Law, Oxford U., 1957; cert. in ceramic tech., North Staffordshire Coll. of Tech., U.K., 1962. Plant mgr., dir. "KEREM", Athens, Greece, 1962-64; dir. "HELLENIT", Athens, Greece, 1962-65; mng. dir. Ideal Standard, Athens, 1966-79; v.p., group exec. internat. and export Am. Standard Inc., New Brunswick, N.J., 1979-84; sr. v.p. bldg. products Am. Standard Inc., New Brunswick, 1984-89; pres., chief exec. officer Am. Standard Inc., N.Y.C., 1989—; bd. dirs. Ideal Refractories SAI, Athens, Ideal Standard Mexico, Am. Standard Sanitaryware (Thailand) Ltd., INCESA, San Jose, Costa Rica, Hoxan Corp., Sapporo, Japan. Bd. dirs. Greek Mgmt. Assn., Athens, 1975-77, Fedn. of Greek Industries, Athens. Mem. Young Pres. Orgn., Chief Execs. Orgn., Econ. Club of N.Y., Oxford Union, Oxford Law Soc., Am. Hellenic C. of C. (gen. sec. 1975-79), Chemists Club, Laurel Valley Golf Club. Greek Orthodox. Clubs: Spring Brook Country (Morristown, N.J.); Quogue Field, Quogue Beach (L.I., N.Y.). Office: Am Standard Inc 1114 Ave Of The Americas New York NY 10036-7703 also: Am Standard Inc 1 Centennial Plz Piscataway NJ 08855-6820*

KAMUDA, KAREN BILSBURY, assistant editor, publisher; b. Milford, Mass., Sept. 12, 1939; d. Ernest Joseph and Marjorie Patten (Harris) Bilsbury; m. Edward Stephen Kamuda, July 11, 1987; children: Wesley Richard, Michelle. Graphologist, pvt. practice, 1960-69; ins. broker Loyal Protective Life, 1970-77; entertainer, producer self-employed, 1969-87; sec. Titanic Hist. Soc., Indian Orchard, Mass., 1987—; asst. editor The Titanic Commutator, Indian Orchard, 1987—; pub., owner 7C's Press, Springfield, Mass., 1991—. Mem. Soc. Am. Magicians, Titanic Hist. Soc. (sec. 1987—). Office: 7C's Press PO Box 90035 Springfield MA 01139-2118

KANARKOWSKI, EDWARD JOSEPH, data processing company executive; b. Jersey City, May 5, 1947; s. Joseph Anthony and Lillian Dorothy (Pietrowicz) K.; m. Carol Ann Miller, Sept. 14, 1969; children: Edward, Kelly, Paul, Karen, Kevin. BA, St. Peter Coll., 1969; grad., U.S. Army Command and Gen. Staff Coll., Ft. Leavenworth, Kans., 1985. Corp. communications cons. N.J., 1973-75; staff writer Daily and Sunday Register, Shrewsbury, N.J., 1975-77; corp. staff writer ADP, Roseland, N.J., 1977; dir. corp. communications ADP, Roseland, 1983-88, v.p. corp. communication, 1988—; adj. vis. prof. communications St. Peter's Coll., 1985—; corp. career adv. grad. sch. bus. Rutgers U., N.J. Capt. U.S. Army, 1971-73, maj. N.G. Decorated Army Commendation medal (3); named Hon. Ky. Col. Commonwealth of Ky., 1988. Mem. Internat. Assn. Bus. Communicators, Meeting Planners Internat., 3d U.S. Inf. Div. Assn., N.J. Mil. Acad. (assoc.). Roman Catholic. Home: 132 Yellowbank Rd Toms River NJ 08753-3167 Office: One ADP Blvd Roseland NJ 07068

KANAROWSKI, STANLEY MARTIN, chemist, chemical engineer, government official; b. Beausejour, Man., Can., Dec. 12, 1912; came to U.S., 1923, naturalized, 1928; s. Joseph and Caroline Kanarowski; m. Pearl Lewus, Aug. 8, 1936 (dec.); children: Stanley Martin Jr., Janice Ellen, Nancy Carol Kanarowski Cioffari. BS, U. Toledo, 1934; postgrad., Ohio State U., 1938-42, U. Akron, 1943-47, NYU, 1954, Xavier U., 1969, U. Wis., U. Mich., U. Ill., U. Mo. Chemist, chief chemist Ohio Dept. Liquor Control, Columbus, 1936-42; sr. cons. chemist Nebr. Ordnance Plant Firestone Tire and Rubber Co., Fremont, 1942-43; asst. dir. corp. gen. lab., chief factory product, chem. engr., rsch. and devel. compounding engr. Firestone Tire and Rubber Co., Akron, Ohio, 1943-49; lab. dir., asst. rsch. and devel. mgr. Fremont (Ohio) Rubber Co., 1949-52; rsch. and devel. chem. engr. Glass Fibers, Inc., Waterville, Ohio, 1952-53; chief rsch. and devel. chemist-engr., mgr. quality control Dairypak Butler, Inc., Toledo, 1953-60; chief chemist No. Ohio Region Lab. Liquor Control Enforcement Div. State of Ohio, Cleve., 1960-62; rsch. and devel. chemist-engr. Consol Paper Co., Monroe, Mich., 1962-63; chemist City of Toledo, 1963-64; project engr., head chemist investigations sect. Ohio River Div. U.S. Army Engr. Div. C.E., 1964-69; project leader, prin. investigator U.S. Army Constrn. Engring. Rsch. Lab., Champaign, Ill., 1969-86; ret. U.S. Army Constrn. Engring. Rsch. Lab., 1986. Mem. U. Ill. Symphony Orch., 1970-86, Montgomery Coll. Symphony Orch., 1987—. Recipient Army-Navy E award, 1943. Mem. Am. Inst. Chem. Engrs., Am. Chem. Soc. (mem. rubber div. 1954—), Am. Def. Preparedness Assn. Address: 1329 Excaliber Ln Sandy Spring MD 20860

KANDEL, NELSON ROBERT, lawyer; b. Balt., Sept. 15, 1929; m. Brigitte Kleemaier, Feb. 28, 1957; children: Katrin, Christopher, Peter. BA, U. Md., 1951, LLB, 1954. Bar: Md. 1954, U.S. Supreme Ct. 1964, D.C. 1980. Prin. law firm, Balt., 1957—. With U.S. Army. Mem. ABA, Md. Bar Assn., Balt. Bar Assn. Democrat. Lutheran. Office: 100 Light St Baltimore MD 21202-1004

KANDEL, PAUL DAVID, internist; b. Middletown, N.Y., Feb. 27, 1944; s. Morris and Beatrice Althea (Abramson) K.; m. Linda Beck, Dec. 5, 1970; children: Bree, David. BA in Biologic Scis., SUNY, Buffalo, 1965; MD, U. Bologna, 1970. Diplomate Am. Bd. Internal Medicine. Intern internal medicine Northern Westchester Hosp., Mt. Kisco, N.Y., 1971-72, resident internal medicine, 1972-73; resident internal medicine U. Buffalo Sch. Medicine, 1973-74; pvt. practice internal medicine, 1974—; intern Northern Westchester Hosp. Ctr., Mt. Kisco, 1971; resident Northern Westchester Hosp. Ctr., Mt. Kisco, N.Y., 1972-73, attending physician, 1974—; resident SUNY Med. Sch. Hosps., Buffalo, 1974; v.p. med. staff Northern Westchester Hosp., 1981-83, med. med. bd., 1986-89, editor newsletter. Police surgeon Mt. Kisco Police Dept., 1985-89. Fellow Soc. for Vascular Medicine

and Biology; mem. Am. Soc. Internal Medicine, ACP. Office: 101 S Bedford Rd Mount Kisco NY 10549-3439

KANDER, JOHN HAROLD, composer; b. Kansas City, Mo., Mar. 18, 1927; s. Harold S. and Berenice (Aaron) K. BA, Oberlin Coll., 1951, D (hon.), 1988; MA, Columbia U., 1953. Composer for theatrical prodns. (with James and William Goldman) A Family Affair, 1961, (with Fred Ebb) Flora, the Red Menace, 1964, Cabaret (Tony award), 1966 (N.Y. Drama Critic's Circle award), The Happy Time, 1967, Zorba, 1968, 70 Girls 70, 1971, Chicago, 1975, The Act, 1977, Woman of the Year, 1981 (Tony award), The Rink, 1984, Kiss of the Spider Woman, 1990, And the world Goes Round, 1991; for films Something for Everyone, 1969, Cabaret, 1972, Funny Lady, 1975, A Matter of Time, French Postcards, Lucky Lady, 1976, New York, New York, 1977, Kramer vs. Kramer, 1980, Still of the Night, 1982, Blue Skies Again, 1982, Places in the Heart, 1984, Billy Bathgate, 1991; for TV spl. Liza with a Z, (Liza Minnelli), 1974 (Emmy award), Gypsy in My Soul (Shirley MacLaine), Goldie and Liza Together (Goldie Hawn and Liza Minnelli), Baryshnikov on Broadway, An Early Frost, 1985, Liza in London. Mem. Dramatists Guild., Nat. Inst. Music Theatre, Songwriters Hall of Fame. Address: care Dramatists Guild 234 W 44th St New York NY 10036

KANDL, MARK DAVID DORN, computer consultant, computer programmer; b. Elizabeth, N.J., July 24, 1968; s. Morris and Edith Eugenia (Dorn) K. B in Arts and Sci., Stanford U., 1991. Cons. Stanford (Calif.) U., 1986-87; asst. product mgr. BASF Corp., Parsippany, N.J., 1987, tech. mktg. specialist, 1988, programmer, 1989; system designer AMS Computech, Munich, Germany, 1990; owner Internat. Computer Cons., Elizabeth, N.J., 1991—. Advising assoc. Stanford U., 1988-89. Nat. Merit scholar Nat. Merit Scholarship Corp., 1986, Rotary scholar Rotary Found., Elizabeth, N.J., 1986, N.J. Disting. scholar N.J. Dept. Edn., 1986; fellow of the Euromanagers Forum '91, Euromanagers Forum, Brussels, 1991. Home: 128 DeHart Pl Elizabeth NJ 07202 Office: Internat Computer Consult Box 318 Elizabeth NJ 07207

KANDOR, JOSEPH ROBERT, education educator; b. Clairton, Pa., Jan. 23, 1960; s. John M. and Susan (Ronyak) K.; m. Janice A. Kugel, Jan. 24, 1960; children: Ronalee, Sundae. BS in Edn., Slippery Rock U., 1960; MEd, U. Pitts., 1963; EdD, SUNY, Buffalo, 1970. Cert. sch. counselor, N.Y. Tchr. phys. edn. Versailles Elem. Sch., McKeesport, Pa., 1960-63; sch. counselor Geneva (Ohio) Sch. Dist., 1963-66, Sweet Home Sch. Dist., Buffalo, 1966-69; prof., chair dept. counselor edn. SUNY, Brockport, 1970—; cons., evaluator Oak Orchard Health Ctr., Brockport, 1985-86; co-chair Greece (N.Y.) Sch. Dist. Counseling Bd., 1988-90; rep. Coun. Accreditation of Counseling and Related Ednl. Programs, 1988—; evaluator Liberty Partnerships Program, Rochester, N.Y., 1988-90. Contbr. articles to profl. jours.; exec. producer video series: Going to College, 1986. Mem. AMECD (treas. 1980-82, chair CACREP 1988—, Arthur A. Hitchcock award 1991, Award for Disting. Profl. Svc.), ACD, Monroe County Counselors Assn. (Outstanding Counselor Educator award 1988), Assn. Counselor Edn. and Supervision (Profl. Svc. award North Atlantic region 1990, SUNY-Buffalo Sch. of Edn. Dist. Alumni award 1992), Chi Sigma Iota (pres. 1988-89). Office: SUNY Brockport 119 Faculty Brockport NY 14420

KANDRAVY, JOHN, lawyer; b. Passaic, N.J., May 9, 1935; s. Frank and Anna (Chan) K.; m. Alice E. Sullivan, Feb. 17, 1962; children: Elizabeth Ann, Katherine Ann. BA, Wesleyan U., Middletown, Conn., 1957; JD, Columbia U., 1960. Bar: N.J. 1960, D.C. 1969, U.S. Supreme Ct. 1973, N.Y. 1982. Assoc. Shanley & Fisher, Newark, 1961-67, ptnr., 1968-80; ptnr. Shanley & Fisher, Morristown, N.J., 1980—. Mem. Gov.'s Mgmt. Commn., State of N.J., 1970; chmn. Planning Bd., Ridgewood, N.J., 1981-85, Zoning Bd. Adjustment, 1979-81; mem. bd. advisors Coll. Bus. Adminstrn., Fairleigh Dickinson U., 1983-87, chmn. bd. advisors, 1985-86; mem. Soc. of Valley Hosp., Ridgewood; chmn. bd. trustees Cen. Bergen Community Mental Health Ctr., N.J., 1970-73; bd. trustees Palisades Counseling Ctr., Rutherford, 1968-81, The Forum Sch., Waldwick, N.J., 1987—, The Forum Sch. Found., Waldwick, 1978—, The Valley Hosp., Ridgewood, 1992—. Edward John Noble Found.grantee, 1957-60. Mem. ABA, N.J. Bar Assn., Essex County Bar Assn., D.C. Bar Assn., Morris County Bar Assn., Essex Club (gov. 1976-85), Wesleyan U. Alumni Assn. (chmn. 1981-83), Indian Trail Club (Franklin Lakes, N.J.), Ridgewood Country Club, Morristown Club. Republican. Presbyterian. Home: 56 Monte Vista Ave Ridgewood NJ 07450-2428 Office: Shanley & Fisher 131 Madison Ave Morristown NJ 07960-6097

KANDUTSCH, ANDREW AUGUST, biochemist; b. Kennan, Wis., Oct. 10, 1926; s. Hugo and Marie (Yauch) K.; m. Nancy Thulin, Sept. 13, 1952; children: Mark, Carl. BA, Ripon Coll., 1950; MS, U. Wis., 1952, PhD, 1954. Rsch. asst. U. Wis., Madison, 1951-54; rsch. assoc. Jackson Lab., Bar Harbor, Maine, 1954-57, staff scientist, 1957-64, sr. staff scientist, 1964-91, assoc. dir. rsch., 1981-84, dir. rsch., 1988-91, emeritus sr. staff scientist, 1992; rsch. fellow Harvard U., Cambridge, Mass., 1962-63. Contbr. over 130 articles and revs. to profl. publs. Staff sgt. U.S. Army, 1944-46. Mem. Am. Soc. Biochemistry and Molecular Biology. Democrat. Office: Jackson Lab Bar Harbor ME 04609

KANE, CHARLES FAIRWEATHER, JR., investment executive; b. Cleve., Aug. 12, 1950; s. Charles Fairweather and Elizabeth (Gould) K.; m. Anne Webster Eldridge, Mar. 9, 1956. Student, Dickinson Coll., 1968-70; BS, Babson Coll., 1973. Mgmt. trainee Shawmu County Bank, Cambridge, Mass., 1974-75; investment exec. Reynolds Securities, Boston, 1975-78, Kidder Peabody and Co., Boston, 1978-86; v.p. Tucker Anthony and R.L. Day, Boston, 1986—; bd. dirs., v.p. Motor Car Co. of New England, Boston. Bd. overseers Boys and Girls Clubs Boston, 1983-85; trustee, mem. adv. coun. Trustees of Reservations, Essex, Mass., 1987—. Mem. Ducks Unltd. (sr. v.p., bd. dirs.), Ducks Unltd. Can. (bd. dirs. 1991—), Union Club Boston (bd. govs. 1990—, capt. 1990—), Duxbury Yacht Club (bd. dirs. 1990—), Union Boat Club (capt. 1990—). Home: PO Box 241 251 Harrison St Duxbury MA 02331-0241 Office: Tucker Anthony & R L Day One Beacon St Boston MA 02134

KANE, GEOFFREY PETER, physician; b. Boston, Mar. 2, 1944; s. Arthur Roland and Helen Frances (Hood) K.; m. Suzanne Hope Milo, June 15, 1969; children: Sarah Britton, David Milo. BS, Boston Coll., 1966; MD, Yale U., 1971, MPH, 1979. Diplomate Am. Bd. Internal Medicine; cert. in addiction medicine. Intern, resident in social internal medicine Montefiore Med. Ctr., Bronx, N.Y., 1971-74; internist, coord. rsch./tng. in alcoholism unit Martin Luther King Jr. Health Ctr., Bronx, N.Y., 1974-78; sr. physician Exxon Rsch. & Enging. Co., Linden, N.J., 1978-84; dir. health svcs. spl. programs Empire Blue Cross/Blue Shield, N.Y.C., 1984-88; med. dir. adult chem. dependency svcs. Brookside Hosp., Nashua, N.H., 1988—; adj. faculty Antioch New Eng. Grad. Sch., Keene, N.H., 1991—; assoc. mem. nat. adv. com. Work in Am. Inst., 1984-85. Author: Inner-City Alcoholism, 1981; contbr. chpt. to book, articles to profl. jours. Co. surgeon Poningoe Engine and Hose Co., Rye, N.Y., 1984-88; trustee Community Health Law Project, East Orange, N.J., 1982-88. Mem. APHA, Am. Coll. Occupational Medicine, Am. Soc. Addiction Medicine, N.Y. Acad. Scis., Authors Guild. Office: Brookside Hosp 29 Northwest Blvd Nashua NH 03063

KANE, HOWARD JAY, franchising executive; b. Neptune, N.J., May 16, 1947; s. William H. and Sara (Horowitz) K.; m. Alix Rich, Feb. 1, 1979; 1 child, Jennifer. AA, Manhattan Community Coll., N.Y.C., 1967; BA, L.I. U., 1970; JD, Bklyn. Law Sch., 1974. Asst. to dean adminstrn. Manhattan Community Coll., 1970-71; v.p. mktg. Galleria Mobili, N.Y.C., 1973-76; contract specialist Brookhaven Nat. Labs., Upton, N.Y., 1976-78; counsel Standard Brands, Inc., N.Y.C., 1978-83, Standard Brands Inc., 1979-83; dir. legal and bus. affairs Suffolk Mktg. Inc., Smithtown, N.Y., 1983-88; pres., chief operating officer Deerfield Communications Corp., N.Y.C., 1988-90, also bd. dirs.; exec. v.p. Reciprocal Merchandising Svcs., N.Y.C., 1990-91; regional dir. Jani King of N.Y., 1991-92; nat. dir. franchise devel. Pudgie's Famous Chicken Ltd., Woodbury, N.Y., 1992—, Pudgie's Famous Chicken, Ltd., Woodbury, N.Y., 1992—; cons. Broadway play Stardust, N.Y.C., 1988-92; producer records and cassettes, 1986—. L.I. U. community scholar, 1968-70. Mem. ABA (del. ABA Ho. of Dels. 1972-74), Am. Traders Assn., Direct Mktg. Assn. Office: Pudgie's Famous Chicken Ltd 7600 Jericho Tpke Woodbury NY 11797

KANE, JACQUELINE JONES, retired guidance counselor; b. Balt., Nov. 9, 1917; d. George and Lucinda (Maddox) Jones; m. Philip Gough Kane, June 14, 1941; children: Jacqueline Anne, Philip Gough Jr., Katherine Maddox Kane-Smith. BS in Edn., Morgan State U., 1945; MS in Ednl. Counseling, CCNY, 1969; postgrad. Cert. guidance counselor, N.Y.; qualified lay profl. leader Luth. Ch. Elem. tchr. Balt. Pub. Schs., 1940-44; elem. tchr. N.Y.C. Pub. Schs., 1949-68, guidance counselor, 1969-78; coord. Coll. Opportunity Edn. Program, N.Y.C., 1969-71; counselor Bklyn. Coll. Outreach Program, 1972-73; reading programmer Program for Pregnant Teen Girls, N.Y.C., 1970; program developer Programs for Paraprofls., N.Y.C., 1970. Participant ad hoc sessions Voters Rights Bill, 1982, ad hoc com. state scholarships for needy students in pvt. coll., N.Y., 1969; membership chmn., mem. multicultural affairs com. N.Y. Synod, Evang. Luth. Ch. Am.; tchr. Sunday Sch., Summer Bible Sch., Sunday Nursery Sch.; pres. ch. coun., mem. ann. conf. and assembly planning com., multi-cultural commn., edn. com., regional participation and nat. multi-cultural comm. Recipient award St. John's Evang. Luth. Ch.; co-recipient (with Philip Kane) plaques Alpha Kappa Alpha for service to students at Lehman Coll., 1986, Assn. of Black Women in Higher Edn., 1988; named Woman of the Yr. Luth. Social Svcs. of Met. N.Y., 1991. Mem. United Fedn. Tchrs., Assn. Black Women in Higher Edn. (award), NAACP (life), Urban League, Alpha Kappa Alpha. (historian 1979-82, award Xi Xi chpt.). Home: 631 Commonwealth Ave Bronx NY 10473

KANE, JAY BRASSLER, banker; b. Bklyn., June 4, 1931; s. Arthur Ferris and Margaret (Brassler) K.; grad. Poly. Prep. Sch., 1949; A.B.; Columbia, 1953, postgrad. Sch. Bus., 1954; M.B.A., N.Y. U., 1961; m. Marian Albertson, Oct. 15, 1960; children: Lisa Ferris, James Brassler. With Met. Life Ins. Co., N.Y.C., 1954-55; with Bankers Trust Co., N.Y.C., 1955—, asst. v.p., 1965-68, v.p., 1968-88; v.p. BT Brokerage Corp., 1988-90; dir. pub. funds Frank Russell Trust Co., N.Y.C., 1990—; also mgr. corp. pension funds, mktg. dir. trust services. Speaker Am. Bankers Assn.; lectr. New Sch. for Social Research. Mem. N.Y. Soc. Security Analysts, Fin. Analysts Fedn., Am. Pension Conf. Clubs: Riverside (Conn.) Yacht; N.Y. Yacht. Contbr. articles to profl. jours. Home: Hilton Heath Cos Cob CT 06807 Office: 712 Fifth Ave New York NY 10019

KANE, JEFFREY, academic dean; b. N.Y.C., Sept. 18, 1952; s. Arthur and Roslyn (Becker) K.; m. Jane Eve Suib, June 9, 1974; children: Gabriel Saul, Emily Ruth, Jesse Adam. BA, Queens Coll., 1974; MA, Adelphi U., 1975; PhD, NYU, 1982. Tchr. Rudolph Steiner Mid. Sch., N.Y.C., 1975-78; adj. lectr. edn. Adelphi U., Garden City, N.Y., 1979-80, lectr., 1979-80, asst. prof., 1980-86, asst. provost, 1986-87, assoc. provost, 1987-88, acting dean sch. edn., 1988-89, dean, 1989—. Author: Beyond Empiricism: Michael Polanyi Reconsidered, 1984, In Fear of Freedom, 1984; editor Holistic Edn. Rev., 1991. Grantee Myrin Inst. Adult Edn., Roothbert Fund. Mem. Am. Assn. Colls. Tchr. Edn., Am. Ednl. Rsch. Assn., Assn. Tchr. Educators, Am. Ednl. Studies Assn., Mid. Atlantic State Philosophy Edn. Soc., Philosophy Edn. Soc., Soc. Ednl. Reconstrn. Office: Adelphi U Sch Edn PO Box 701 Garden City NY 11530-0701

KANE, JOSEPH CHARLES, management consultant; b. Jackson, Wyo., July 9, 1935; s. Maxwell J. and Ethel M. (Read) K.; A.B., Rutgers U., 1957; M.B.A., U. Pa., 1963; Ph.D., Harvard U., 1974; m. Janet Allis, Aug. 28, 1982. With Gen. Motors Corp., Detroit, 1957-61; cons. McKinsey & Co., Phila., 1961-63; prin. Joseph Kane Assocs., N.Y.C., 1963-70; cons. Cambridge Consulting Group, Lexington, Mass., 1970—, prin., 1970—; pres. CMA Products, Stoneham, Mass., 1982—, High Tech Leasing Corp., N.Y.C., 1982—; pres. Charles River Advisors, 1988; lectr. Purdue U., SUNY. Mem. Am. Mgmt. Assn., Nat. Assn. Mgmt. Consultants. Author: To Merge? Why, Why Not, 1972; Small Business: Characteristics of the Successful Entrepreneur, 1982; The Negotiation Process in the Successful Merger Buyout, 1982. Office: Cambridge Cons Group 33 Bedford St Ste 11 Lexington MA 02173-4430

KANE, MARCIA SUSAN, bank executive; b. N.Y.C., June 4, 1959; d. Howard Eugene and Sydell (Friedman) K. Cert. fin. planning, NYU, 1980, BA in Communications, 1986. Pension specialist Union Dime Savs. Bank, N.Y.C., 1978-81; money market specialist Goldome (formerly Union Dime Savs. Bank), N.Y.C., 1981-82; customer svc. unit mgr. Citibank, N.A., N.Y.C., 1982-85, keogh product mgr., 1986-87, shareholder communications mgr., 1988-89, asst. v.p., tax shelter conversion mgr., 1990—. Author: (with others) Critical Reading-Level G, 1980. Bd. dirs. Forest Hills Owners Corp., N.Y.C., 1991-92. Mem. N.Y. Bus. and Profl. Women's Club. Office: Citibank Nat Ops Div 6300 8th Ave Brooklyn NY 11220-4791

KANE, MARGARET BRASSLER, sculptor; b. East Orange, N.J., May 25, 1909; d. Hans and Mathilde (Trumpler) Brassler; m. Arthur Ferris Kane, June 11, 1930; children: Jay Brassler, Gregory Ferris. Student, Packer Collegiate Inst., 1920-26, Syracuse U., 1927, Art Students League, 1927-29, N.Y. Coll. Music, 1928-29, John Hovannes Studio, 1932-34; PhD (hon.), Colo. State Christian Coll., 1973. head craftsman sculpture, arts and skills unit ARC, Halloran Gen. Hosp., N.Y., 1942-43; jury mem. Bklyn. Mus., 1948, Am. Machine & Foundry Co., 1957; com. mem. An Am. Group, Inc. Work exhibited at Jacques Seligmann Gallery, N.Y., Whitney Ann. Exhbns., all Sculptors Guild Mus. and Outdoor Shows, Nat. Sculpture Soc. Ann. Bas-Relief Exhbn., 1938, Whitney Mus. Sculpture Festival, 1940, Bklyn. Mus. Sculptors Guild, 1938, Bklyn. Soc. Artists, 1942, Lawrence (Mass.) Art Mus., 1938, N.Y. World's Fair, 1939, Sculptors Guild World's Fair Exhbn., 1940, Robinson Gallery, N.Y., 1939, Traveling Mus. and Instns., 1938, Lyman Allyn Mus., 1939, Met. Mus., Internat. Exhbns., 1940, 1949, Roosevelt Field Art Ctr., N.Y.C., 1957, Phila. Mus., N.Y. Archtl. League, Nat. Acad., Penn. Acad., Chgo. Art Inst., Am. Fedn. Arts, Riverside Mus., Montclair Mus., Grand Cen. Art Galleries, Lever House, N.Y.C., 1959-81, Rye (N.Y.) Library, 1962, Lever House Sculptors Guild Ann. Exhbn., 1973-81, N.Y. Bot. Garden, 1981, Sculptors Guild 50th Anniversary Exhbn., Lever House, 1987-90, 1st Bi-Coastal exhibits San Francisco, Collection Donald Trump, 1988, Collection Rene Anselmo, 1991, Shidoni Galleries, Santa Fe, N.Mex., 1989, Am. Sculpture, Hofstra Mus., 1990; nat. tour. Am. sculpture by EducArt Projects Inc., 1992; also exhbns. of nat. scope, 1938—; solo sculpture exhbn., Friends Greenwich (Conn.) Library, 1962; executed plaque for Burro Monument, Fairplay, Colo.; exhibited N.Y. Bank for Savs., 1968, Mattatuck Mus., Con., 1967, Lamont Gallery, N.H., 1967, Phila. Art Alliance Exhibition Sculpture of the American Scene, 1987, Am. References (Artists) Chicago, 1989—; executed: 18 foot carving in limewood depicting History of Man; reprodns. in Contemporary Stone Sculpture, 1970, Contemporary American Sculptures, Am. References, Chgo., 1989—; contbr. articles to mags.; feature article in Greenwich (Conn.) Time, 1990. Recipient Anna Hyatt Huntington award, 1942; Am. Artists Profl. League and Montclair Art Assn. Awards, 1943; 1st Henry O. Avery Prize, 1944; Sculpture Prize Bklyn. Soc. Artists, Bklyn. Mus., 1946; John Rogers Award, 1951; Lawrence Hyder Prize, 1952, 54; David H. Zell Meml. Award, 1954, 63; hon. mention U.S. Maritime Commn., 1941 and; A.C.A. Gallery Competition, 1944; Med. of honor for sculpture Nat. Assn. Women Artists, 1951; Med. of honor for sculpture Nat. Acad. Galleries, N.Y.; prize for carved sculpture, 1955; animal sculpture, 1956; 1st award for sculpture Greenwich Art Soc., 1958, 60; 1st award for sculpture Annual New Eng. Exhbns., Silvermine, Conn. Fellow Internat. Inst. Arts and Letters (life); mem. Nat. Assn. Women Artists (2nd v.p. 1943-44), Nat. League Am. Pen Women, Inc. (OWL award for The Arts 1991), The Pen and Brush (emeritus 1992), Artists Coun. U.S.A., Bklyn. Soc. Artists, Greenwich Soc. Artists (mem. coun.), Internat. Sculpture Ctr., Internat. Soc. Artists (charter), Sculptors Guild, Inc. (sec. to exec. bd. 1942-45, chmn. exhbn. com. 1942, 44), Silvermine Guild Artists, Nat. Trust for Hist. Preservation. Home and Studio: 30 Strickland Rd Cos Cob CT 06807-2729

KANE, MICHAEL JOEL, physician; b. Erie, Pa., July 2, 1951. BS, U.S. Naval Acad., 1973; MD, N.J. Med. Sch., 1983. Diplomate Am. Bd. Internal Medicine. Attending physician Jefferson Med. Coll., Phila., 1988-91, Med. Ctr. at Princeton, N.J., 1991—. Fellow ACP, Acad. Medicine of N.J., Am. Soc. Clin. Oncology, Am. Assn. Cancer Rsch., Oncology Soc. N.J., Med. Soc. N.J. Office: Med Ctr at Princeton 253 Witherspoon St Princeton NJ 08540

KANE, PETER GERARD, technology manager; b. Bklyn., Oct. 8, 1962; s. John McAllister and Pauline Philomena (Flynn) K. BS in Fin. and Internat. Bus., NYU, 1986. Bus. systems analyst Merrill Lynch & Co., N.Y.C., 1986-88; v.p., mgr. image technol. Barclays Bank PLC, N.Y.C., 1988—; v.p., dir. User Net-File Net Internat. User Group, Cosa Mesa, Calif., 1988—; founding mem. SMART-FS Image SIG, N.Y.C., 1990-92. State chmn. N.J. Young Reps., 1985-86; vice chmn. Substandard Housing Bd., Summit, N.J., 1984-87. Mem. Assn. for Info. and Image Mgmt. Republican. Roman Catholic. Home: 5 Sheridan Rd Summit NJ 07901

KANE, RACQUEL ELONA, advertising executive; b. Jersey City, Aug. 29, 1932; d. Jack and Ruth (Baumann) Sheps; m. Richard Kane, Oct. 7, 1950 (dec. Oct. 1987); children: Brandi, Cindi. Student, CCNY, 1949-51. Pres., chief exec. officer Marden-Kane, N.Y.C., 1987—. Pres. Assn. Help for Retarded Children, 1968-74. Mem. Friar's Club. Jewish.

KANE, STANLEY BRUCE, food products executive; b. N.Y.C., June 5, 1920; s. Jacob and Anna (Epstein) K.; m. Janet Marilyn Haas, May 23, 1948; children: Katherine, Betsy, Priscilla. Student, NYU, 1938-39. With Kane-Miller Corp., N.Y.C., 1938—, chmn. bd., 1959-77, pres., chief exec. officer, 1977—, also bd. dirs. Served with USAAF, 1942-45. Home: 539 Norsota Way Sarasota FL 34242-1029 Office: Kane-Miller Corp 555 White Plains Rd Tarrytown NY 10591-5109

KANE, WALTER REILLY, physicist, researcher; b. Ithaca, N.Y., Nov. 3, 1926; s. Paul Vincent and Lillian Mary (Reilly) K.; m. Margaret Gunn, Aug. 21, 1953; 1 child Katherine Skiff. BS, Stanford U., 1949; MS, U. Washington, 1951; PhD, Harvard U., 1959. Physicist Nat. Bur. Standards, Washington, 1951-52; staff mem. Los Alamos (N.Mex.) Nat. Lab., 1952-55; physicist AVCO Mfg. Co., Everett, Mass., 1956-57, Brookhaven Nat. Lab., Upton, N.Y., 1958—. With U.S. Army, 1944-46. Recipient predoctoral fellowship NSF, 1954-56, John Tyndell fellowship, Harvard U., 1957-58. Fellow Am. Phys. Soc.; mem. Inst. Nuclear Materials Mgmt. Office: Brookhaven Nat Lab Bldg 197C Upton NY 11973

KANEGSBERG, HENRY S., business consultant; b. Newark, June 13, 1945; s. Jule W. Kanegsberg and Miriam (Bach) Steigman. BS, Ithaca Coll., 1967; MBA, NYU, 1969. With RCA Corp., N.Y.C., 1969-78; v.p. fin. and adminstrn. NBC News, N.Y.C., 1979-82, NBC Ops. and Tech. Svcs., N.Y.C., 1982-84; v.p. fin. RCA Records, N.Y.C., 1984-86; v.p. fin. and ops. NBC, N.Y.C., 1986-89; sr. v.p. fin. and adminstrn. Random House, N.Y.C., 1989-90; pres. ExecuSystems, Inc., Teaneck, N.J., 1991—. Chair community bd. St. Luke's Roosevelt Hosp. Ctr., N.Y.C., 1989—. Mem. N.Y.C. Club. Home: 1 Lincoln Square Plz New York NY 10023-7129 Office: ExecuSystems Inc 141 Lees Ave Teaneck NJ 07666-3857

KANG, EDWARD PAOTAI, biochemist, consultant; b. Chung King, China, Aug. 11, 1942; came to U.S., 1961, naturalized, 1977; s. Kang Wai and Kang Ying-Yee Poon m. Nancy Kiang, July 12, 1970; 1 child, Melissa N. B.S., U. So. Calif., 1966; M.S., Howard U., 1969, Ph.D., 1973; postgrad., U. Md. Pharmacy Sch., 1969-71. Biochemistry investigator Inst. for Med. Rsch., James F. Mitchell Found., Washington, 1972-73; rsch. assoc. ARC Blood Svcs. Labs., Bethesda, Md., 1973-80; sr. scientist, mgr. rsch. and devel. Electro-Nucleonic Inc., Columbia, Md., 1980-86; dir. infectious diseases div. United Biomedical, Inc., Lake Success, N.Y., 1986-87, dir. clin. studies, 1987-90; pres. E.P. Kang Cons., Garden City, 1991—; instr. Coll. Pharmacy, Howard U., 1971, lectr. chemistry dept., 1972. Contbr. articles to profl. jours. First aid instr. ARC Safety Svcs., Montgomery County, Md., 1974-86. Recipient Disting. Alumnus award Howard U. Grad. Sch., 1982. Fellow Am. Inst. Chemists, Nat. Acad. Clin. Biochemistry; mem. Am. Chem. Soc., Assn. Clin. Biochemistry (UK), Nat. Acad. Clin. Biochemists, Internat. Soc. Thrombosis and Haemostasis, Internat. Soc. Blood Transfusion, Am. Assn. Blood Banks, N.Y. Acad. Scis., AAAS, Am. Assn. Clin. Chemistry, Am. Soc. Microbiology, Biochem. Soc. London, Sigma Xi, Rho Chi. Baptist. Office: PO Box 117 Garden City NY 11530-0117

KANIA, ANTOINETTE MARY, college library administrator; b. Elizabeth, N.J., Apr. 18, 1943; d. Anthony and Catherine (Katrenych) K.; m. John C. Kuzma, Jan. 30, 1965 (div. 1982); 1 child, Melissa; m. Hendrik Edelman, Mar. 14, 1986; stepchildren: Stijn, Mark, Kees. BA, Douglass Coll., 1965; MLS, Rutgers U., 1969, EdD, 1984. Tchr. Russian, English Boonton (N.J.) High Sch., 1965-67; head allied health libr. Essex County Coll., Newark, 1967-76; dir. learning resources Somerset County Coll. (now Raritan Valley Community Coll.), Somerville, N.J., 1976-85; dean of librs. Suffolk Community Coll., Selden, N.Y., 1985—; libr. cons. Mid. States Accreditation Assn., Phila., 1979—, Atlantic Community Coll., Mays Landing, N.J., 1986, Burlington County Coll., Pemberton, N.J., 1989, California U. of Pa., 1989, Md. Higher Edn. Commn., Balt., 1989, Balt.'s Internat. Culinary Coll., 1990, Art Libr. Soc. N.Am., Tucson, 1990—, Dundalk (Md.) Community Coll., 1990, Wilmington (Del.) Coll., 1991. Author: (with others) Off Campus Library Services, 1991; compiler: (bibliography) ERIC Document Service, 1988; contbr. articles to profl. jours. Mem. Am. Assn. Women in Community Colls., ALA, Assn. Coll. & Rsch. Librs. (exec. bd. sec. Met. N.Y. chpt. 1991-92), Assn. of Dirs. of Two-Yr. Coll. Librs. of N.J. (pres. 1982-83), L.I. Coun. Acad. Libr. Dirs., N.J. Libr. Assn., N.Y. Librs. Assn., Suffolk County Libr. Assn., SUNY Librarians Assn. Home: 750 Columbus Ave Apt 9L New York NY 10025 Office: Suffolk Community Coll 533 College Rd Selden NY 11784-2851

KANIECKI, THADDEUS JOHN, chemist; b. Bklyn., Mar. 24, 1931; s. Walter and Marianne (Napolska) K.; m. Florence Florek, Aug. 27, 1955; children: Marianne, Walter, John. BA, NYU, 1953, MS, 1955, PhD, 1960. Rsch. chemist Lever Bros. Co., Edgewater, N.J., 1960-68; rsch. mgr. Armour-Dial, Chgo., 1968-72; sect. mgr. Am. Cyanamid Co., Clifton, N.J., 1972-74; rsch. dir. Clenesco div. Stauffer Chem. Co., Westport, Conn., 1974-88; tech. dir. Diamond Chem. Co., Lyndhurst, N.J., 1988—. Fairfield Chem. Co. rsch. fellow, 1954-56. Mem. Met. Dairy Tech. Soc. (pres. 1986-87). Home: 2 Van Allen Pl Pompton Plains NJ 07444-1510

KANJORSKI, PAUL EDMUND, congressman, lawyer; b. Nanticoke, Pa., Apr. 2, 1937; s. A. Peter and Wanda (Nedbalski) K.; m. Nancy Marie Hickerson, Nov. 22, 1962; 1 child, Nancy Marie. Student, Temple U., 1961, Dickinson Sch. Law, 1965. Bar: Pa. Ptnr. Kanjorski & Kanjorski, Wilkes-Barre, Pa., 1966-84; mem. 99th-102d Congresses from 11th Pa. dist., 1985—. Acting solicitor City of Nanticoke, 1969-81; Pa. Workmen's Compensation referee, 1972-80; bd. dirs. Wyoming San. Authority, Wilkes-Barre, 1972-84; trustee Wilkes U. Mem. Wilkes-Barre Law Library Assn. Democrat. Roman Catholic. Office: 424 Cannon Washington DC 20515

KANN, PETER ROBERT, journalist, business reporting and services company executive; b. N.Y.C., Dec. 13, 1942; s. Robert A. and Marie (Breuer) K.; m. Francesca Mayer, Apr. 12, 1969 (dec. 1983); m. Karen Elliott House, 1984; children: Hillary Francesca, Petra Elliott, Jason Elliott. BA, Harvard U., 1964. With The Wall St. Jour., 1964—; journalist N.Y.C., 1964-67, Vietnam, 1967-68, Hong Kong, 1968-75; pub., editor Asian edit., 1976-79, assoc. pub., 1979-88; formerly asst. to chmn. and mem. exec. com. Dow Jones & Co., 1986-89, pres. internat. and mag. groups, 1986-89, also chmn. bd. dirs.; pub. Wall St. Jour., 1989—; pres. Dow Jones & Co., N.Y.C., 1989-91, chmn., chief exec. officer, 1991—; dir. Group Expansion, Paris, 1987—; chmn. bd. Far Ea. Econ. Rev., 1987-89; elected mem. Pulitzer Prize Bd., 1987—. Trustee Asia Soc., 1989—, Inst. for Advanced Study, Princeton, 1990—. Recipient Pulitzer prize for internat. reporting, 1972. Club: Spee (Cambridge, Mass.). Office: Dow Jones & Co Inc 200 Liberty St New York NY 10281

KANNEL, WILLIAM BERNARD, cardiovascular epidemiologist; b. Bklyn., Dec. 13, 1923; s. Joseph M. and Sarah M. (Golden) K.; m. Rita R. Lefkowitz, May 29, 1943; children: Linda J. Kannel Isaacson, Steven Michael, Patricia M. Kannel Hoffman, Forrest S. M.D., Ga. Med. Coll., 1949; M.P.H., Harvard U., 1959; Dr. Medicine (hon.), U. Gothenburg, 1985. Intern, resident internal medicine S.I. Pub. Health Hosp., 1949-50, 53-56; asst. Peter Brent Brigham Hosp., 1956-63; assoc. dir. Framingham (Mass.) Heart Study, Nat. Heart and Lung Inst., 1950-53, 56-67, dir., 1967-79; cons. Framingham Union Hosp., Cushing Hosp.; assoc. medicine Boston U. Med. Sch.; assoc. preventive medicine Harvard U. Med. Sch.; prof. medicine and Pub. Health, vis. physician, chief preventive medicine and epidemiology sect., rsch. fellow Ctr. Health and Advanced Policy Studies Boston U. Sch.

Medicine; med. dir. USPHS, 1949-79; chief med. adv. bd. to NASA, 1981-84. Mem. editorial bd. Am. Heart Jour., Jour. Cardiopulmonary Rehab., Primary Cardiology, Jour. Clin. Epidemiology, Hypertension; contbr. articles to med. jours. Mem. scientific adv. bd. USAF, 1977-78. Served with U.S. Army, 1943-46, AUS, 1949-79. Recipient Gairdner Found. award, 1976, Einthoven award Leiden U., Netherlands, 1973, Francis medal U. Mich. Med. Sch., 1975, Polish Copernicus award, 1977, Dana award, 1972, 86, Soc. Prospective Medicine award, 1979, J.D. Bruce Meml. medal ACP, 1982, Rsch. in Hypertension award Nat. Conf. on Cholesterol and Hypertension, 1991, named Arvilla Berger lectr., N.Y. Cardiological Soc., 1988, Disitng. Lectr. of Yr., Bosotn U., 1988. Fellow Am. Coll. Cardiology, Am. Coll. Epidemiology, Am. Coll. Preventive Medicine (hon.), Am. Heart Assn. (fellow council epidemiology, former chmn. council epidemiology), Am. Coll. Physicians; mem. Assn. Commd. Officers USPHS, Alpha Omega Alpha. Home: 30 Eliot St Natick MA 01760-6058 Office: Boston U Med Ctr Sect Epidemiology and Preventive Medicine B612 Univ Hosp 88 E Newton St Boston MA 02118 also: Boston U Framingham Heart Study S Thurber St Framingham MA 01701

KANNER, LAWRENCE THEODORE, principal; b. N.Y.C., Dec. 17, 1929; s. Morris Joseph and Celia (Tannenstock) K.; m. Ruth Cecelia Behr., Apr. 5, 1952; children: Michael David, Ellen Gabrielle. BA, Bklyn. Coll., 1951; Cert. of Advanced Study, Queens Coll., 1965; EdD, Rutgers U., 1974. Cert. sch. adminstr., secondary sch. prin., sch. dist. adminstr., N.Y., N.J., Mass. Instr. dept. of edn. Queen's (N.Y.) Coll., 1964-65; tchr. core subjects L.I. City High Sch., Queens, 1951-54, tchr. social studies, 1954-62, coord. coop. edn., 1962-64, dir. prep program, 1965-66, dir. oper. talent search, 1966-67; prin. Grover Cleveland Jr. High Sch., Caldwell, N.J., 1967-75, Roth High Sch., Henrietta, N.Y., 1975-87; prin. Rush-Henrietta Sr. High Sch., Henrietta, 1987-92, retired, 1992. Editor: (with others) The Middle School, 1972; contbr. articles to profl. jours. Pres. Pittsford (N.Y.) Vol. Ambulance, 1985; mem. com. Boy Scouts Explorer Post, Pittsford, 1981-86. Fellow Inst. for the Devel. of Ednl. Activities (sr.); mem. Adminstrs. Assn. of Rush-Henrietta (pres. 1986-87), Phi Delta Kappa.

KANNRY, SYBIL, psychotherapist, consultant, b. Tulsa, Okla., Oct. 1, 1931; d. Julius and Celia Bertha (Triger) Zeligson; children: Jeffrey Alan Shames, Erica Leslie Shames, Jonathan Adam Shames. Student U. Colo., 1949-51; BA, U. Okla., 1953; MSW, NYU, 1974. Diplomate in Clin. Social Work; cert. clin. social worker, N.Y., addiction counselor, employee assistance profl., alcoholism counselor, N.Y. Tchr. piano, Tulsa, 1956-61; psychiatric social worker Essex County Hosp., Cedar Grove, N.J., 1974-75, Rockland Psychiat. Ctr., Spring Valley, N.Y., 1975, adult team supr., 1975-78, adult team supr., Haverstraw, N.Y., 1978, clinic supr., Orangeburg, N.Y., 1978-83, clinic dir., Yonkers, N.Y., 1983-84; founder, dir. Indsl. Counseling Assocs., South Nyack, N.Y., 1982-84, Ctr. for Corp. and Community Counseling, South Nyack, 1984—; founder, pres. Tulsa Assn. for Childbirth Edn., 1957-59. Fellow Soc. Clin. Social Work Psychotherapists; mem. Am. Assn. Marriage and Family Therapy (clin. mem.), N.Y. Milton H. Erickson Soc. for Psychotherapy and Hypnosis, Nat. Assn. Social Workers, Am. Orthopsychiat. Assn., Acad. Cert. Social Workers, Employee Assistance Profl. Assn., Soc. Clin. and Exptl. Hypnosis. Home and Office: 2 Clinton Ave Nyack NY 10960-4716

KANOFSKY, ALVIN SHELDON, physics educator; b. Phila., July 5, 1939; s. Philip and Mollie (Edelstein) K.; m. Toby Blum Levine, June 9, 1963; children: Robert, Nathan. BA, U. Pa., 1961, MS, 1962, PhD, 1966. Rsch. asst. Johnson Found. Med. Physics, Phila., 1957-59, physics dept. U. Pa., 1960-66; faculty Lehigh U., Bethlehem, Pa., 1967—, prof. physics, 1976—, dir. Lehigh Accelerator Lab., 1985—; pres. R&D Co., 1969—. Contbr. articles to profl. jours. Fellow Am. Phys. Soc.; mem. AAAS, AAUP, Soc. Photo-Optical Intrumentation Engrs., Bethlehem C. of C., Sigma Xi. Jewish. Lodge: Rotary. Avocations: hiking, jogging, biking, piano, tennis. Office: Lehigh U Physics Dept Bldg 16 Bethlehem PA 18015

KANOVITZ, HOWARD, painter; b. Fall River, Mass., Feb. 9, 1929; s. Meyer Julius and Dora (Rems) K. BS, Providence Coll., 1949; postgrad., R.I. Sch. Design, 1949-51, NYU, 1959-61. Instr. Bklyn. Coll., 1962-64, Pratt Inst., 1964-66; prof. Southhampton Coll., 1977-78, Sch. Visual Arts, N.Y.C., 1981-85. Artist, painter exhibited Tibor de Nagy Gallery, 1956, Stable Gallery, 1962, Jewish Mus., 1966, Waddell Gallery, 1969; one man shows include U.S. and Europe, Stefanotty Gallery, N.Y.C., 1975, Galerie Jöllenbeck, Cologne, 1977, Gallerie Bridgehampton, L.I., N.Y., 1977, Akademie der Kunste, Berlin, 1979, Kestner Gesellschaft, Hannover, 1979, Alex Rosenberg Gallery, 1982, Inge Baecker Gallery, 1987, 88, 91, Cologne, 1987, Marlborough Gallery, 1988, 90, Hokin-Kaufman Gallery, Chgo., 1989; group exhibits include Whitney Mus., N.Y.C., 1972, Berlin Nat. Gallery, 1976, Guild Hall, East Hampton, L.I., 1976, Dokumenta 6, Kassel, 1977, Alex Rosenberg Gallery, 1978, Louise Himmelfarb Gallery, Watermill, L.I., 1979, Los Angeles Mus. Contemporary Art, 1984, Indpls. Mus. Art, 1985, Ludwig Mus., Cologne, 1988, Parrish Art Mus., Southampton, L.I., 1988, Fla. Internat. U., Miami, 1989, Met. Mus., N.Y.C., 1991, Weatherspoon Art Gallery, Greensboro, N.C., 1991. Studio: 463 Broome St New York NY 10013

KANSKY, LAWRENCE JOSEPH, JR., podiatrist; b. N.Y.C., June 14, 1957; s. Lawrence Joseph Sr. and Marilyn (Moore) K.; m. Irene Diane Lucas, Sept. 10, 1983; children: Christine, Jessica. BS, U. Scranton, 1979; D Podiatric Medicine, Pa. Coll. Podiatric Medicine, 1983. Diplomate Am. Bd. Podiatric Surgery. Resident in foot surgery Nesbitt Meml. Hosp., Kingston, Pa., 1983-84; podiatrist Nat. Health Svc. Corp., Freeland, Pa., 1984-88; pvt. practice Hazleton, Pa., 1988—; bd. dirs. United Penn Bank, West Hazelton, Pa. Fellow Am. Coll. Foot Surgeons; mem. Am. Podiatric Med. Assn., Luzerne County Podiatric Med. Assn. (pres. 1987). Roman Catholic. Office: 943 N Church St Hazleton PA 18201-1839

KANTER, ANN RAWSON, consulate public affairs officer; b. Leicester, Eng., May 14, 1938; came to U.S., 1966; d. William Ernest and Helen Milton Chalmers (Hay) Rawson; m. Donald L. Kanter, Aug. 13, 1966; children: James, Sarah. BA, Leeds U., Eng., 1959; MA, U. Soc. Calif., 1979. Analyst Imperial Chem. Industries, London, 1960-64; researcher Smith Warden, London, 1964-66; project leader Diagnostics Rsch. Inc., Donald L. Kanter, Inc., L.A., 1972-81; researcher Northern Ireland Indsl. Devel. Bd., Boston, 1982-86; vice consul British Consulate Gen., Boston, 1986—; sec. Marshall Scholarship Com., 1986—. Contbg. editor: (book) The Cynical Americans, 1989. Bd. dirs. Care, County Hosp., L.A., 1972; v.p. U. So. Calif. Faculty Wives, 1974; vice chmn. Ann Banning Assistance League of So. Calif., 1976-80. Mem. Faculty Wives Club Boston U., English Speaking Union, Old North Bridge Hounds Hunt Club. Home: 91 Somerset St Belmont MA 02178-2005

KANTER, KENNETH R., electronic company executive; b. N.Y.C., Apr. 9, 1935; s. Harry and Lillian (Berger) K.; m. Winnie Kanter, Sept. 7, 1957; children: Beth M. Kanter Foley, Andrew D., Karen A. Kanter Zeigher. BME, Poly. Inst. Bklyn., 1956; MSME, Columbia U., 1960; cert. The Exec. Program, U. Va., 1982. Sr. engr. Ford Instrument Co., L.I., N.Y., 1956-64; div. program mgr. Fairchild Camera, Syosset, N.Y., 1964-77; v.p. ops. Simmonds Precision - MCD, Cedar Knolls, N.J., 1977-84; pres. BTR-Russell Plastics Tech. Co., Lindenhurst, N.Y., 1984-87; v.p., gen mgr. M/A-COM, MPD, Hauppauge, N.Y., 1987-91; v.p. ops. North Atlantic Industries, Hauppauge, N.Y., 1988-92; pres., chief exec. officer Levitt Indsl. Textile Co., 1992—. Contbr. articles to mags. Pres. Little League Baseball, Merrick, N.Y., 1973-78; dir. Merrick Basketball League, 1976-79; pres. Temple Beth Am., 1987-88, chmn. bd. dirs., 1988-90. Home: 1888 Stanley Dr Merrick NY 11566-5116

KANTER, LORNA JOAN, artist; b. Passaic, N.J., Apr. 10, 1931; d. Nathan Michael and Sadye (Ludwig) Teninbaum; m. Leon Stein (div.); children: Gail Ellen, Gary Steven; m. Max Julius Kanter, Dec. 21, 1970; stepson, Jason Mark. Grad., Am. Art Sch., 1962; student, Pratt Graphic Art Ctr., 1963, Art Students League, 1977, 78, 79 80. guest tv appearances Joe Franklin Shows, N.Y.C., 1985, 89, N.Y. Art Cable, N.Y.C., 1986-90, The Tom Sullivan Show, Clifton, N.J., 1987; radio guest The Barry Farber Show, N.Y.C., 1986. One-woman shows include Montclair State Coll., N.J., 1981, Wayne Cultural Ctr., N.J., 1982, Salmagundi Club, N.Y.C., 1984, Cartier, N.Y.C., 1986; group exhbns. include J. Richards Gallery, N.J., 1983, 85, Nathans Gallery, N.J., 1984-86, Gallery Gaffney, Palm Springs, Calif., 1985, Wyckoff Gallery, Inc., N.J., 1986, Gallery Madison 90, N.Y.C., 1981-90, Select Ethan Allen Galleries, USA, Germany, Japan, 1988-90, Bergdorf Goodman Nena's Choice Gallery, N.Y.C., 1981-90, Bergen Community Mus., Somerset Community Mus., Jersey City Mus., Montclair Art Mus.; represented in permanent collections including The White House, Reagan Libr., USS Intrepid Mus., Doulas MacArthur USO, Hilton Hotels. Recipient scholarships Am. Art Sch., 1959-62, Pratt Graphic Art Ctr., 1963, Art Students League, 1977-80, Green Ribbon award Nat. Arts Club, 1964, Artist of Yr. award Beaux Arts Soc., Inc., 1984, citation for patriotic art Nat. Mil. Order of the Purple Heart, 1985, award winner Am. Artist Mag., 1988-89, and others. Mem. Am. Soc. for Psychical Rsch., N.Y. Artists Equity Inc., Beaux Arts, Inc. Home and Office: 24 Janice Ter Clifton NJ 07013-4214

KANTHAL, JEFFREY MICHAEL, service company executive; b. Bronx, Jan. 9, 1946; s. Theo and Senta (Berney) K.; m. Janice A. Weiner, May 21, 1972 (div. Jan. 1990); children: Darren, Marissa, Craig. BS in Bus. Mgmt., CCNY, 1973. Credit clk. Gen. Foam Corp., N.Y.C., 1963-73; rte. supv. Marlow Candy Co., Bronx, 1973-75; pres. JJD Vending Inc., Valley Cottage, N.Y., 1975-84; pres., chief exec. officer Inv. Svc. Specialities Inc., Hicksville, N.Y., 1984—. Bd. dirs. Nyack Little League, Valley Cottage, 1988-89; speaker various high schs., 1990—. Mem. NASE, B'nai B'rith. Jewish. Home: 1087 Grand Blvd Westbury NY 11590 Office: Inv Svc Specialities Inc PO Box 42 Hicksville NY 11802

KANTOUNIS, STRATOS GEORGE, surgeon; b. N.Y.C., Dec. 2, 1931; s. George Stratos and Liberty (Tsarnas) K.; m. Joan Amanda Schuman, Dec. 8, 1956; children: Lizabeth Ann, Stratos Jeffrey. BS, CCNY, 1954; MD, SUNY, Bklyn., 1958. Diplomate Am. Bd. Surgery. Intern Bellevue Hosp., N.Y.C., 1958-59, resident surgery, 1959-61; resident surgery Manhattan VA Hosp., N.Y.C., 1962-64; chief gen. surgery South Nassau Community Hosp., Oceanside, N.Y., 1980-91, pres. med. staff, 1988-90, attending gen. surgeon, 1967—. Capt., M.C. U.S. Army, 1964-67. Fellow ACS, Nassau Acad. Medicine; mem. AMA, Hellenic Med. Soc., Nassau Surg. Soc. (v.p.). Republican. Greek Orthodox. Office: 2 Lincoln Ave Rockville Centre NY 11570

KANY, JUDY C(ASPERSON), state senator; b. June 29, 1937; d. Helmer C. and Florence P. Casperson; m. Robert Kany, Aug. 16, 1958; children: Kristin, Geoffrey, Daniel. BBA, U. Mich., 1959; MPA, U. Maine-Orono, 1976. Mem. Maine Ho. Reps., 1975-82, Maine Senate, 1982—, chmn. Maine's Adv. Commn. on Radioactive Waste, 1981-87, Joint Standing Com. Legal Affairs, Joint Standing Com. on State Govt., 1982-86, Joint Standing Com. Energy and Natural Resources, 1983-84, 89-90, Joint Standing Com. Banking and Ins., 1991-92, com. Maine Lakes, 1990-92; mem. Commn. on Maine's Future, 1976, 87-89; mayor Waterville, Maine, 1988-89. Democrat. Home: PO Box 508 Belgrade Lakes ME 04918-0508 Office: Maine State Senate State Capitol Bldg Augusta ME 04330

KANZER, LARRY, locksmith owner, food service director; b. Albany, N.Y., June 13, 1942; s. Sanford and Beatrice Helen (Strick) K.; m. Ginger Sherman, July 13, 1966 (div. 1985); 1 child, Glen Harris; m. Lynn Karen Trost, June 2, 1985. A.A.S. in Culinary Arts, N.Y.C. Community Coll., 1962; Cert. Food Service supr. Auburn U., 1982-83; Master Locksmith, Foley Belsaw Inst., 1985. Food beverage controller Longchamps Restaurants, N.Y.C., 1962-65; dir. food service Laurelcrest Prep Sch., Bristol, Conn., 1965-69; owner, operator Anze's Place Restaurant, Nashua, N.H., 1969-73; dir. food service Servend-Seilers, Waltham, Mass., 1973-76, Service Systems, Cambridge, Mass., 1976-78, ARA Services, White Plains, N.Y., 1978-88; owner Lots of Lock, Etc., 1988—. Com. chmn. Cub Scouts Am., Nashua, 1977-80; umpire Little League, Nashua, 1978-81. Served to sgt. USMCR, 1963-69. Recipient Otto Klitgord Meml. award N.Y.C. Community Coll., Bklyn., 1962, Student Govt. Service award, 1962; Cert. of Merit Jewish War Vets. of U.S., Bronx, N.Y., 1982, Cert. and Publ. Locksmith Ledger, Nat. Locksmith. Democrat. Avocations: gunsmithing; clock repair, woodworking; antiques; gardening. Office: Lots of Lock Etc Locksmith Shop Rick-Ba Plz Rt 739 Lords Valley PA 18428

KANZER, MARK, retired psychoanalyst; b. N.Y.C., Dec. 6, 1908; s. Edward M. and Susan Kanzer; m. Viva Schatia, June 3, 1938; children: Paul Mark, Alan Mark. BS, Yale U., 1928; MD, U. Berlin, 1934. Med. cert. Resident neurology Mt. Sinai Hosp., N.Y.C., 1937-38; resident psychiatry Bellevue Hosp., N.Y.C., 1938-40; editorial bd. Jour. of the Am. Psychoanalytic Assn., N.Y.C., 1954-71; dir. div. psychoanalytyic edn. SUNY, N.Y.C., 1960-70; dir. emeritus div. psychoanalytic edn. SUNY, N.Y.C.; Freud lectr. 34th Freud Anniversary, Freud and Oedipus N.Y. Psychoanalytic Inst. and Soc. Co-author: Freud and his Self-Analysis, Freud and his Patients, 1984, The Psychoanalytic Study of the Child, 1988. Mental health ednl. activities Westchester County, White Plains, N.Y., 1951-88; councillor N.Y.C. chpt. United Jewish Appeal. Major AUS, 1940-46. Recipient Community Mental Health award Mental Health Assn. Westchester County, 1985; Freud fellow Yale U., Cornell U. Mem. Am. Psychiat. Assn. (councillor-at-large 1971-74), Am. Psychoanalytic Assn. Home: 168 Sunny Ridge Rd Harrison NY 10528-1912

KANZLER, WALTER WILHELM, biology educator; b. Jersey City, Sept. 17, 1938; s. George Hess and Martha (Strasser) K. BA, Montclair State Coll., 1960, MA, 1963; MA, Marshall U., 1964; PhD, U. Cin., 1972. Cert. counselor, N.J. Instr. biology Union City (N.J.) High Schs., 1960-65; asst. prof. Trenton State Coll., 1965-66; instr. biology Wagner Coll., S.I., N.Y., 1966-72, asst. prof., 1972-76, assoc. prof., 1976-84, prof., 1984—; adj. prof. St. John's U., S.I., 1989, St. Peter's Coll., Jersey City, 1990—; cons. Scientist's Ctr. Animal Welfare, Washington, 1981—. Author: Phermones and Trail Making in Ants. fellow NASA, 1969-70, NSF, U. Calif., 1971. Mem. AAAS, Nat. Wildlife Fedn., Animal Behavior Soc., Sigma Xi, Beta Beta Beta. Home: 376 New York Ave Jersey City NJ 07307-1105 Office: Wagner Coll Biology Dept 631 Howard Ave Staten Island NY 10301-4495

KAO, RACE LI-CHAN, medical educator; b. Chungking, China, Dec. 1, 1943; came to U.S., 1967, naturalized, 1980; s. Yu-Ho and Tsing (Tsou) K.; m. Lidia Wei Liu, Aug. 18, 1969; children—Elizabeth, Grace. B.S., Nat. Taiwan U., 1965; M.S., U. Ill., 1971, Ph.D., 1972. Rsch. assoc. U. Ill., Urbana, 1972, Pa. State U., Hershey, 1972-75, asst. prof. physiology, 1976-77; asst. prof. surgery, physiology, biophysics U. Tex. Med. Br., Galveston, 1977-82, dir. cardiothoracic research, 1977-82; assoc. prof. surgery Washington U., St. Louis, 1982-83; dir. surg. rsch. Allegheny-Singer Rsch. Inst., Pitts., 1983-92; prof. surgery Med. Coll. Pa., Phila., 1988-92; C.H. Long prof. surgery East Tenn. State U., Johnson City, 1992—; reviewer, cons. Nat. Heart, Blood and Lung Inst., NIH, 1984—. Contbr. numerous articles in field to profl. jours. Pres., U. Tex. Chinese Assn., 1980. Served with ROTC, Repub. of China, 1965-66. Nat. Taiwan U. Univ. scholar, 1962-65; grantee NIH, 1979—, Tex. Heart Assn., 1979-80, Upjohn Co., 1977-79, Pa. Heart Assn., 1986-89, Mo. Heart Assn., 1982-83. Mem. Coun. on Circulation Am. Heart Assn. Mem. Am. Physiol. Soc., Internat. Soc. Heart Rsch., Am. Soc. Artificial Internal Organs, Am. Inst. Biol. Sci., Nat. Soc. Med. Rsch., N.Y. Acad. Sci., AAAS, Nutrition Today Soc. Home: 4 Blackberry Ct Johnson City TN 37604 Office: East Tenn State U Dept Surgery JH Quillen Coll Medicine Johnson City TN 37614-0575

KAPADIA, MEHERNOSH MINOCHEHER, senior quality engineer; b. Bombay, India, Feb. 14, 1960; came to U.S., 1982; s. Minocheher G. and Baimai (Sarkari) K.; m. Monaz C. Desai, Jan. 7, 1986; 1 child, Sanaya Mehernosh. BE, U. Bombay, Bombay, India, 1981; MS, Pa. State U., 1983; MBA, St. Joseph's U., 1990. Cert. quality engr. Grad. rsch. asst. Pa. State U., University Pk., 1982-83, rsch. engr., 1983; engr. ATT Microelectronic Lightwave, Reading, Pa., 1984-85, planning engr., 1985-88, quality engr., 1988-91, sr. quality engr., 1991—; lectr. local chpt. Am. Soc. Quality Control Engrs., Reading, 1990; instr. quality courses, Reading, 1990—. Contbr. articles to profl. jours. Mem. Am. Soc. Quality Control. Home: 457 S Wyomissing Ave Shillington PA 19607 Office: Lightwave Quality Engring 2525 N 12th St Dept 2320 Reading PA 19612

KAPATKIN, FRED, accountant, lawyer; b. Bklyn., Sept. 22, 1927; s. Herman and Pearl (Rosner) K.; m. Selma Levy; children: Keith B., Amy Sue. Student, Bklyn. Coll., 1943-45; BBA in Acctg., CCNY, N.Y.C., 1949; JD, Bklyn. Law Sch., 1953. Bar: N.Y. 1954; CPA, N.Y. Assoc. acct., legal cons. Bernstein & Freedman, N.Y.C., 1963-69, 1970-78; chief fin. officer, contr. W.A. Di Giacomo Assoc., N.Y.C., 1969-70, Lehr Assocs., N.Y.C., 1978-85; acct., legal cons. Fred Kapatkin, CPA, N.Y. Met. area, 1985—; adj. prof. acctg. N.Y. Inst. Tech., 1976-78. With USMC, 1945-47. Mem. YMHA, Am. Assn. Ret. Persons. Home: 4024 Demont Rd Seaford NY 11783-1427 Office: 226A Post Ave Westbury NY 11590-3094

KAPCZYNSKI, HELMUT HERMANN, surgical instrument company executive; b. Berlin, Fed. Republic of Germany, June 18, 1946; s. Franz and Dora (Rautenberg) K.; m. Susan Gillespie (div. Aug. 1985); children: Jennifer, Amy; m. Colleen Neff, Apr. 21, 1990. Degree in social work, Acad. of Social Work, Berlin, 1971. Gen. mgr. China Books and Periodicals, N.Y.C. and Chgo., 1971-81; v.p. Misdom-Frank Corp., N.Y.C., 1981-86; pres. K-Medic Inc., Leonia, N.J., 1986—; pres. Toulaine Owners Corp., N.Y.C., 1989—. Office: K-Medic Inc 117 Ft Lee Rd Leonia NJ 07605-2216

KAPIKIAN, ALBERT ZAVEN, physician, epidemiologist; b. N.Y.C., May 9, 1930; s. Zareh Kaloust and Baizar (Bazikian) K.; m. Catherine Firth Andrews, Feb. 27, 1960; children: Albert Kaloust, Thomas Firth, Gregory Baird. BS, Queens Coll., 1952; MD, Cornell U., 1956; postgrad., Johns Hopkins U. Sch. Hygiene and Pub. Health, 1961-62. Intern Meadowbrook Hosp., Hempstead, N.Y., 1956-57; commd. med. officer USPHS, 1957, advanced through grades to med. dir., capt., ret., 1988; with USPHS Civil Svc., 1988-90, USPHS Sr. Exec. Svc., 1990—; with epidemiology sect. Lab. Infectious Diseases, Nat. Inst. Allergy and Infectious Diseases, NIH, Bethesda, Md., 1957—, head epidemiology sect., 1967—; rsch. prof. child health and devel. George Washington U. Sch. Medicine and Health Svcs., 1977—; temporary advisor WHO, 1980-88, 91. Contbr. articles to profl. jours. Recipient Meritorious Svc. medal USPHS, 1970, 74, Disting. Svc. medal USPHS, 1983; Disting. Alumnus award Queens Coll., 1974, Stitt award Assn. Mil. Surgeons, 1974, Kabakjian award Armenian Students Assn. Am., 1974, 87. Mem. AAAS, Infectious Diseases Soc. Am., Am. Epidemiol. Soc., Am. Pub. Health Assn., Soc. Epidemiol. Rsch., Am. Soc. Microbiology (Behring Diagnostics award, 1987). Mem. Armenian Apostolic Ch. Home: 11201 Marcliff Rd Rockville MD 20852-3631 Office: NIH Bethesda MD 20892

KAPILEVICH, MENDEL BERKOVICH, mathematician; b. Ukraine, USSR, Mar. 1, 1923; came to U.S., 1988; s. Berka Mendelevich and Alexandra Leibovna (Khazanova) K.; m. Khana Leibovna Kaplan, Jan. 29, 1961; children: Boris Mendelevich, Liliya Mendelevna. Student, U. Moscow, 1945-49, PhD, 1957; degree in mech. engring., MAI, Moscow, 1948. Rsch. assoc. Cen. Aero-Hydrodynamical Inst., Moscow, 1948-53; sr. lectr. in math., chmn., head math. dept. Moscow Evening Metall. Inst., 1953-87, ret. Author: (in Russian) Linear Differential Equations of Mathematical Physics, 1964, Eng. edit., 1967, German edit., 1967; contbr. numerous articles to profl. publs. Recipient medal Pres. of Supreme Soviet, 1984, Vet. of Labor, USSR. Mem. Am. Math. Soc., Soc. for Indsl. and Applied Math. (orthogonal polynomials and spl. functions activity group). Home: 40 Wallingford Rd Apt 553 Brighton MA 02135-4745

KAPLAN, ALBERT, investment company executive; b. Gouverneur, N.Y., Apr. 20, 1932; s. Sol and Esther (Chodosh) K. BA, St. Lawrence U., 1954. DuPont, Glore Forgan, Ltd.; Mng. dir. duPont, Clore Forgan, Ltd., London, 1960-70, Ylore Forgan, Ltd., Luxembourg, 1970-80; Middle East rep. Dominick & Dominick, Inc., Jerusalem, 1980-85; pres. Albert Kaplan & Co., Ltd., Paris, 1986-91; sr. v.p. Paine Webber, Inc., N.Y.C., 1991-92. Mem. Masons. Jewish. Home and office: 301 W 53d St New York NY 10019

KAPLAN, ALLEN STANFORD, rabbi; b. Chgo., Mar. 26, 1939; s. Nathan and Belle Sarah (Levin) K.; m. Jane Gruber, July 22, 1967; children: Walter H., Sarah N., David J. BA, U. Cin., 1960; BHL, MAHL, Hebrew U. Coll.-Jewish Inst. Religion, 1965; DD, N.Y., 1990. Ordained rabbi, 1965. Rabbi Temple Beth Sholom, N.Y.C., 1970-78; assoc. dir. N.Y. Bd. Rabbis, N.Y.C., 1978-82; assoc. dir. N.Y. Fedn. Reform Synagogues, N.Y.C., 1982-91, dir., 1991—; v.p., bd. dirs. JACS Found., N.Y.C.; advisor on religious matters Gay Men's Health Crisis, N.Y.C., 1988—. Contbr. articles to profl. jours. Comdr. USNR, 1980—. Mem. Cen. Conf. Am. Rabbis, Internat. Psychology Assn., Naval Res. Assn., Assn. N.Y. Reform Rabbis (treas. N.Y.C. chpt. 1987—). Home: 445 E 86th St New York NY 10028-6433 Office: Union Am Hebrew Congregations 838 5th Ave New York NY 10021-7064

KAPLAN, ANDREW R., computer consultant; b. Newark, Mar. 15, 1957; s. Howard and Beth (Raphael) K.; m. Karen Mendel, Sept. 19, 1987. BA, Dickinson Coll., 1979; MBA, Fordham U., 1984. Mktg. asst. Home Box Office, N.Y.C., 1979-80, fin. analyst, 1981-82, 84-88; bus. mgr. The Movie Channel, N.Y.C., 1982-83; pres., founder A.R.K. Enterprises, Inc., Stamford, Ct., 1988—. Chmn. Corp. Vol. in Action, 1989-91. Mem. Ind. Computer Cons. Assn., Nat. Assn. TV Arts & Scis., Stamford C. of C. Jewish. Office: A R K Enterprises Harbour Sq 700 Canal St Stamford CT 06902-5921

KAPLAN, BARNARD ALAN, Ophthalmologist; b. N.Y.C., Dec. 6, 1949; s. Herbert Wilbur and Blanche (Darf) K.; m. Amy Mann, Sept. 11, 1976; children: Sarah, Naomi. BA, U. Pa., 1970, MD, 1974. Diplomate Am. Bd. Ophthalmology. Ophthalmologist Eye Assocs. P.A., Cherry Hill, N.J., 1979—; bd. trustees PRO of N.J., Voorhees, 1983—; mem. exec. com. Summit Surg. Ctr., Voorhees, 1990—. Fellow Am. Acad. Ophthalmology (bd. govs. N.J. chpt. 1990—); mem. AMA, Med. Soc. N.J., Camden County Med. Soc., Jewish Men's Clubs (v.p. 1990—). Office: Eye Assocs PA Rte 70 East Gate Dr Voorhees NJ 08034

KAPLAN, BERNARD JOSEPH, surgeon; b. New Britain, Conn., Jan. 14, 1918; m. Samuel L. and Ethel (Marcus) D.; m. Hattie Kuniansky, Apr. 9, 1946; children: Sheryl Lynn, Robin Lee. BS, Muhlenberg Coll., 1941; MD, U. Vt., 1949; MSc in Proctology, U. Minn., 1955. Diplomate Am. Bd. Colon and Rectal Surgery, Nat. Bd. Med. Examiners. Intern St. Francis Hosp., Hartford, Ct., 1949-50; resident in gen. surgery U.S. VA Hosp., Newington, Ct., 1950-53; fellow colon and rectal surgery U. Minn. Hosp., Mpls., 1953-55; practice medicine specializing in colon and rectal surgery Hartford, 1955-88; attending surgeon St. Francis and Mt. Sinai Hosps., Hartford, 1955—; asst. clin. prof. surgery U. Conn. Med. Sch., Farmington, Conn., 1974-85, assoc. clin. prof. surgery, 1986—; clin. investigator pharm. cos.; vis. surgeon Dempsey Hosp., Farmington, 1973—; program dir. colon and rectal surgery St. Francis Hosp., 1985-88. Contbr. articles to med. and profl. jours. Pres. Hartford unit Am. Cancer Soc., 1970-72, Conn. div. 1977-79, bd. dirs., 1981-89. Recipient C. Graham Eddy endoscopic award Biologic Photographic Assn., 1968, med. edn. award, 1970; bronze award and nat. divisional award Am. Cancer Soc., 1983, cert. of merit Conn. div., 1989. Fellow ACS, Internat. Coll. Surgeons, Am. Soc. Colon and Rectal Surgeons (v.p. 1986-87, Hermance plaque 1961, N.Y. Soc. Colon and Rectal Surgeons award 1969), North Eastern Soc. Colon and Rectal Surgeons (pres. 1979-81), New Eng. Soc. Colon and Rectal Surgeons (past pres.), Soc. Am. Gastrointestinal Endoscopic Surgeons; mem. AMA, Conn. Med. Soc., Hartford County Med. Assn. (bd. dirs. 1969-71), Pilot's Point Yacht Club (commodore 1982-83, 88-90). Republican. Jewish. Home: 138 Captains Dr #ain S Westbrook CT 06498-1811 Office: 929 Boston Post Rd Ste 214 Old Saybrook CT 06475-2143

KAPLAN, CAROL OLIVE, television news anchor, producer, educator; b. Rochester, N.Y., Jan. 18, 1961; d. Robert Philip and Diane Olive (Neides) K. BA in English and Communication, SUNY, Buffalo, 1982; MA in Journalism, The Am. U., 1983. Anchor, reporter Sta. WICZ-TV, Binghamton, N.Y., 1983-85; anchor Sta. WCJB-TV, Gainesville, Fla., 1985-88; anchor, exec. producer Sta. KOMU-TV, Columbia, Mo., 1988-90; instr. U. Mo., Columbia, 1988-90; anchor, environ. reporter Sta. WGRZ-TV, Buffalo, 1990—; asst. prof. broadcast journalism Canisius Coll., Buffalo, 1991—. Mem. Investigative Reporters and Editors (judge 1989). Home: 224 Greengage Cir East Amherst NY 14051-1342 Office: Sta WGRZ-TV 259 Delaware Ave Buffalo NY 14202-2055

KAPLAN, EDITH FREUND, neuropsychologist; b. N.Y.C., Feb. 16, 1924; d. Benjamin and Minnie (Surkes) Freund; divorced; 1 child, Michael Paul. BA, Bklyn. Coll., 1949; MA, Clark U., 1952, PhD, 1968. Rsch. psychologist VA Med. Ctr., Boston, 1958-76; dir. neuropsychol. svcs. VA

Med. Ctr., 1976-87; neuropsychology cons. World Health Orgn., Aging Project, Geneva, Switzerland, 1980-84; sr. neuropsychologist Framingham (Mass.) Heart Study, 1976-90; neuropsychology cons. Franciscan Children's Hosp., Brighton, Mass., 1985—; neuropsychologist Risk Mgmt. Found., Cambridge, Mass., 1986-91; sr. neuropsychologist Forest Manor Head Injury Ctr., Middleboro, Mass., 1982-91; affiliate prof. psychology Clark U., Worcester, Mass., 1977—; assoc. prof. neurology, psychiatry Boston U. Sch. Medicine, 1980—; bd. dirs. Boston Neuropsychol. Found., Boston, 1984—; mem. adv. bd. Nat. Head Injury Found., Boston, 1982-90 (Recognition of Outstanding Svc. 1982). Co-author: Assessment of Aphasia, 1983; co-author: of tests Boston Naming Test, 1983, Calif. Verbal Learning Test, 1987, WAIS-R As A Neuropsychol. Instrument, 1991. Recipient Disting. Svc. award Mass. Speech Hearing Soc., 1977, Ezra Saul Psychol. Svc. award Mass. Psychol. Assn., 1984. Fellow Am. Psychol. Assn. (div. 40 pres. 1987); mem. Am. Bd. Clin. Neuropsychology (bd. dirs. 1981-87), Acad. Aphasia (governing bd. 1971-74), Internat. Neuropsychol. Soc. (pres. 1980), Internat. Neuropsychology Aymposium, World Fedn. Neurology Rsch. Aphasia Group. Office: Boston U Sch Medicine 85 E Newton St # 957M Roxbury MA 02118-2337

KAPLAN, EDNA ENGELMAN, public relations executive; b. Haifa, Israel, Dec. 29, 1948; came to U.S., 1957; d. Symcha and Judith (Warsawer) Engelman; m. Donald M. Kaplan, Apr. 3, 1976; children: Jonathan Howard, Scott Andrew. BA in Psychology cum laude, Bklyn. Coll., 1970; MS in Communications, Boston U., 1988. Rsch. asst. Downstate Med. Ctr., Bklyn., 1973-76; rsch. assoc. Am. Insts. for Rsch., Cambridge, Mass., 1976-79; cons. Boston, 1980-87; acct. staff Nicolazzo and Assocs., Boston, 1987-88; pres. KOGS Communication, Marblehead, Mass., 1989—; bd. dirs. Tower Sch. Parents Assn. Author: Practice Made Perfect: The Physician's Guide to Communication and Marketing, 1990; co-author book chpt.; contbr. articles to newspapers. Bd. dirs. Jewish Community Ctr. North Shore, 1980—, coms. chmn., 1982-89, officer, exec. com., 1982-87. Recipient New Leadership award Jewish Welfare Bd., 1983, Pres.'s award Jewish Community Ctr., Marblehead, 1986, Dean's Alumni award Boston U., Coll. Communication, 1988. Mem. Pub. Rels. Soc. Am., Jewish Community Ctr. North Shore, Corinthian Yacht Club. Home: 20 Lehman Rd Marblehead MA 01945-2028 Office: KOGS Communication PO Box 603 Marblehead MA 01945-0603

KAPLAN, FRED, English literature educator; b. Bronx, N.Y., Nov. 4, 1937; s. Isaac and Bessie (Zwirn) K.; m. Gloria Taplin, June 6, 1959 (div.); children: Benjamin, Noah, Julia. BA, Bklyn. Coll., 1959; MA, Columbia U., 1961, PhD, 1966. Instr. Lawrence U., Appleton, Wis., 1962-64; asst. prof. Calif. State U., L.A., 1964-67; assoc. prof. to full prof. English Queens Coll.-CUNY, Flushing, 1967-90; Disting. prof. English Queens Coll. & Grad. Ctr. CUNY, N.Y.C., 1990—; vis. prof. Bar-Ilan U., Israel, 1987, U. Paris, 1985-86; Fulbright prof. U. Copenhagen, 1972-73. Author: Miracles of Rare Device, 1972, Dickens and Mesmerism, 1975, Sentimentality in Victorian Literature, 1987, Thomas Carlyle, A Biography, 1983, Charles Dickens: A Biography, 1988, Henry James, The Imagination of Genius, A Biography, 1992; editor Dickens Studies Ann., 1980—. Fellow Guggenheim Found., 1977-78, Huntington Libr., 1981-82, NEH, 1983, Nat. Humanities Ctr., 1985-86, Rockefeller Found., 1990. Mem. MLA, Dickens Soc. Am. (pres. 1990-91). Home: 151 Bergen St Brooklyn NY 11217-2209 Office: Queens Coll CUNY Dept English Flushing NY 11367

KAPLAN, FREDERIC CLARK, artist, writer; b. Phila., Jan. 2, 1948; s. Milford Earl and Ethel (Morrine) K.; m. Bettie Francis Knox, May 1, 1970 (div. June 1984); m. Alice Elizabeth Overton, Oct. 15, 1984. Student, Pa. Acad. Fine Art, 1967-69, Phila. Coll. Art, 1981. Pub. Arts Objectively, Phila., 1974-76; freelance artist Phila., 1977-83; dir. mktg. Lawrence Factor, Inc., Miami, Fla., 1983-84; dir. spl. projects Herder's Cutlery, Inc., Malvern, Pa., 1984-87; freelance artist Folcroft, Pa., 1987—; editor Kane Communications, Inc., Upper Darby, Pa., 1988-89; editor, art editor Pen-Del Fed-Fax, Greenville, Del., 1989-90; cons. Lawrence Factor, Inc., Miami, 1985—; art reviewer Art Matters, Phila., 1990—. Author, artist: Frederic C. Kaplan: A Collection of Drawings, 1971; represented by Goforth Rittenhouse Galleries, Phila., 1991—. Recipient merit award Am. Artist Mag., 1978. Office: Kaplan Illustration & Design PO Box 83 Folcroft PA 19032-0083

KAPLAN, GEORGE HARRY, astronomer; b. Hagerstown, Md., Apr. 24, 1948; s. Abner Jacob and Katharine (Bowser) K.; m. Carol Zyskowski, Aug. 12, 1972. BS, U. Md., 1969, MS, 1976, PhD, 1985. Rsch. asst. U. Md., College Park, 1967-71; tchr. sci. Balt. City Pub. Schs., 1969-71; astronomer U.S. Naval Obs., Washington, 1971—. Contbr. articles to profl. jours. Recipient James M. Gilliss award, U.S. Naval Obs. Mem. AAAS, Am. Astron Soc., Internat. Astron. Union (working group on reference systems, lectr. summer sch. Malaysia 1990), Phi Beta Kappa, Sigma Xi. Lutheran. Office: US Naval Obs 34th & Massachusetts Ave NW Washington DC 20392-5100

KAPLAN, HARLEY LANCE, financial planner; b. Far Rockaway, N.Y., Sept. 26, 1961; s. Norman and Evelyn (Goz) K. BBA, Boston U., 1983. Cert. fin. planner. Interior designer United Electric Co., Boston, 1979-82; internat. cons. Etibank, Ankara, Turkey, 1982-83; fin. planner Cigna Corp., Boston, 1983-89; registered investment advisor, prin. Beta Industries, Boston, 1989—; dir. Starlite Enterprises, N. Reading, Mass., Kitco Corp., Stow. Bd. dirs. Jewish Meml. Hosp., Roxbury, Mass. Recipient Citizenship award Sch. Dist. Town of Woodmere, N.Y., 1979, Top Coll. Fighter award N.Am. Karate Fedn., 1981. Mem. Internat. Assn. Fin. Planning, Coll. Fin. Planning (registry lic. practitioners), Boston U. Downtown Alumni (bd. dirs. 1987—), Mensa, Rotary, Samba-Karate Club (instr. 1984—). Democrat. Jewish. Home: 68 Maple St Sherborn MA 01770

KAPLAN, HAROLD PAUL, physician, health science facility administrator; b. N.Y.C., Jan. 22, 1939; s. David Benjamin and Sophie (Cohen) K.; m. Barbara Anne Sundstrom, Mar. 28, 1962; children: Todd, Jonathan, Robin, Scott. BS, Tufts U., 1959; MD, Yale U., 1963. Diplomate Am. Bd. Internal Medicine. Physician Internal Medicine Assocs., Meriden, Conn., 1970—; v.p. Internal Medicine Assocs., Meriden, 1974—, med. dir., mng. ptnr., 1985—; chief of gastroenterology Meriden-Wallingford (Conn.) Hosp., 1976-91, chief of medicine, 1980-82, corporator, 1984—; chief of medicine WWII Vets. Meml. Hosp., 1977-79; corporator Vets. Meml. Med. Ctr., 1991—; bd. dirs. Healthworks, Ltd., Wallingford. Contbr. articles to profl. jours. Pres. Alliance for Edn. of North Haven, Conn., 1974-86, So. Conn. Swim League, 1978-83; chmn. ofcls. tech. com. Conn. Swimming, 1981-85; mem. parents coun. exec. com. Bowdoin Coll., 1988-91. Fellow ACP; mem. Am. Gastroent. Assn., Am. Soc. Gastrointestinal Endoscopy, Am. Soc. Internal Medicine, Farms Country Club of Wallingford (bd. govs. 1981-86). Republican. Office: Internal Medicine Assocs 116 Cook Ave Meriden CT 06450-5540

KAPLAN, HARRIET, audiologist, educator; b. N.Y.C., Oct. 26, 1934; d. Adolph and Bertha (Dershewitz) Feder; m. Irwin Kaplan, Aug. 25, 1956; children: Noel Harold, Michele Karen. BA in Speech Pathology, Bklyn. Coll., 1955; MS in Audiology, Pa. State U., 1957; PhD in Speech and Hearing Sci., U. Md., 1974. Cert. clin. competence in audiology. Teaching asst., dept. speech and hearing sci. Univ. Md., College Park, 1971-73; asst. prof., dept. speech pathology/audiology Cath. Univ., Washington, 1974-78; part time lectr., dept. audiology/speech pathology Cath. Univ., 1978-80; part time lectr., dept. speech and hearing sci. Univ. Md., College Park, 1980-81; asst. prof., dept. audiology/speech Gallaudet Univ., Washington, 1981-86, assoc. prof., dept. audiology/speech, 1986-90, prof., dept. audiology/speech, 1990—. Author: Audiometric Interpretation: A Manual of Basic Audiometry, 2d edit., 1993, Audiometric Interpretation: Site of Lesion Testing, 1983, Speechreading, An Aid to Understanding, 1985; contbr. chpts. to books and articles to profl. jours. Grantee Gallaudet Rsch. Inst., 1982-83, 83, 87, Gallaudet Univ. Presdl. award, 1985-86, AARP Andrus Found., 1986. Jewish. Office: Gallaudet U 800 Florida Ave NE Washington DC 20002-3660

KAPLAN, JAMES LEE, airline company executive; b. N.Y.C., Apr. 29, 1939; s. Daniel Boaz and Sally (Saklad) Kaplan Tabenken. B in Chemistry, U. Maine, 1962, student Sch. Law, 1965-67; MS in Bus., Husson Coll., 1984. Ops. mgr. Bangor (Maine) Broadcasting, 1971-73; cargo sr. mgr. Airlift Internat., Inc., Miami, Fla., 1973-74; cargo ops. mgr. Varig Airlines, Rio De Janeiro, Brazil, 1974-79; regional mgr. sales svc. Braniff Internat. Airways, N.Y.C. and Miami, Fla., 1980-82; v.p. M.W. Gwinn Co., Bangor, 1982-84; dir. Arrow Airways, Miami, 1984; cargo svc. mgr. Servair, Inc., Jamaica, N.Y., 1985-86; dir. passenger svcs. Five Star Airlines, Boston, 1987-88; v.p. ops., chief oper. officer Lineas Aereas Latur, Mexico City, 1988-89; pres., chief exec. officer Falcon Air, Inc., Miami, 1989—; v.p. Milcon Internat., Ft. Lauderdale, Fla., 1992—; cons. David Bluth and Assoc., N.Y.C., 1984-87. Mem. Community Planning Com., Bangor, 1972, Bangor on Ice; mem. Pres. Club Rep. Nat. Com. Mem. Aircraft Owners and Pilots Assn., Res. Officers Assn. U.S., Air Force Assn., Jaycees (dir., v.p. Bangor chpt. 1971-72), U. Maine Alumni Assn., Husson Coll. Alumni Assn., Centurion Club, Wings Club, Am. Fedn. Police. Home: 187 Clyde Rd Bangor ME 04401-3401 Office: Falcon Air 19 W Flagler St Ste 207 Miami FL 33130

KAPLAN, JOAN DAVIDSON, pharmaceutical company executive; b. Middletown, N.Y., Dec. 3, 1943; d. A. Martin and Zelda (Feldsher) Davidson; m. Joel David Kaplan, Mar. 7, 1963; children: Howard, Shana. RN, Beth Israel Hosp. Sch. Nursing, N.Y.C., 1964; BS, SUNY, 1982. RN, N.Y. Nurse various hosps., N.Y.C., 1964-75; with Biostat, Bronx, 1975-77; med. rep. Abbott Labs., North Chicago, Ill., 1977-80, hosp. sales rep., 1980-85, dist. sales mgr., 1985-88, nat. account exec., 1988—. Author: Handbook for the Business Traveler, 1991. Home: 46 Diane Dr New City NY 10956

KAPLAN, JONATHAN HARRIS, management consultant, health care and infosystems specialist; b. N.Y.C., Apr. 29, 1957; s. Bernard and Arlene (Lavender) K.; m. Lorraine Caryl Weiss, Aug. 6, 1983; children: Alexandra Lindsay, Elizabeth Sydney. AB, Cornell U., 1979; MPH, U. Pitts., 1980. Cert. data processor, mgmt. cons., systems profl. Statistician Nat. Ctr. Health Stats., Hyattsville, Md., 1980; assoc. installation dir. Shared Med. Systems, N.Y.C., 1981, installation dir., 1981-82; cons. Ernst & Young, N.Y.C., 1982-83, sr. cons., 1984, supr., 1985, mgr., 1985-86, sr. mgr., 1986-90, ptnr., 1990—; adj. prof. health care adminstrn. Baruch Coll., CUNY. Speaker in field. USPHS grantee for achievement in pub. health studies, Washington, 1979, 80, Westinghouse Sci. award, Shared Med. Systems Field Svc. award. Mem. Am. Coll. Healthcare Execs., Am. Assn. Healthcare Cons., Am. Assn. Med. Informatics, Am. Hosp. Assn., Inst. Mgmt. Cons., IBM User Group (ECHO), Healthcare Info. and Mgmt. Systems Soc., Inst. Mgmt. Cons., Healthcare Fin. Mgmt. Assn., N.Y. Acad. Scis., Inst. Cert. Computer Profls., Met. Healthcare Adminstrs. Assn., Cornell U. Alumni Assn., N.Y. Acad. Sci., Pelham Country Club. Office: Ernst & Young 277 Park Ave New York NY 10172-2099

KAPLAN, LEE MICHAEL, neuroscientist, physician, educator; b. N.Y.C., July 1, 1954; s. Bernard and Arlene (Lavender) K. AB, Harvard U., 1974; MD, PhD, Einstein Med. Sch., 1981. Diplomate Am. Bd. Internal Medicine, 1984; subspecialty Gastroenterology, 1987. Medicine intern Mass. Gen. Hosp. Harvard Med. Sch., Boston, 1981-82, asst. prof. medicine, neurosci., cell biology, 1982-84, fellow, 1984-87; instr. in medicine Harvard Med. Sch., 1987-88, asst. prof. neurosci., cell biology, 1988—; asst. physician Mass. Gen. Hosp., 1988—; sr. fellow Cannon Soc., Harvard Med. Sch., 1990—; assoc. Dunster House, Harvard U., 1983—; scientific adv. bd. mem. PeptiMed, Inc., Cambridge, 1991—. Editor Einstein Quarterly Journal of Biology and Medicine, 1981-91. Recipient Pettis Meml. award AMA, Chgo., 1981; named Krancer Rsch. scholar Nat. Found. for Ileitis and Colitis, N.Y.C., 1987, Stuart Rsch. scholar Am. Gastroenterol. Assn., Thorofare, N.J., 1987. Fellow Am. Coll. Gastroenterology; mem. Am. Coll. Physicians, Am. Fedn. Clin. Rsch., Am. Gastroent. Assn., Am. Assn. for Study of Liver Diseases, Am. Soc. Microbiology, Alpha Omega Alpha. Jewish. Home: 19 W Cedar St Boston MA 02108 Office: Mass Gen Hosp GI Unit Jackson 7 Jackson 8 Boston MA 02114

KAPLAN, LEONARD L., pharmaceutical company executive; b. N.Y.C., Oct. 10, 1928; s. Morris and Minnie (Barer) K.; m. Susan E. Orent, June 30, 1968; children: Robert, Marc. BS in Pharmacy, Ohio State U., 1952; MBA, CUNY, 1963; PhD, NYU, 1968. Registered pharmacist, N.Y., Ohio. Research scientist Sterling Research Inst., Renssalaer, N.Y., 1956-59; mgr. research Vicks Chem. Co., Mt. Vernon, N.Y., 1959-69; mgr. research Johnson & Johnson Research Ctr., New Brunswick, N.J., 1969-75, dir. research, 1975-82; v.p. research Ortho Pharm. Corp. Advanced Care, Raritan, N.J., 1982-89; v.p. rsch. Sterling Drug, 1989—; cons. Rutger U. Sci. and Engring. Research Ctr., Piscataway, N.J., 1986-87. Contbr. articles to profl. jours; patentee in field. Pres. New Brunswick Bus. & Profl. Assn., 1977-80. Served to lt. USMC, 1952-54. Recipient Merck Sci. award Ohio State U., 1955, Outstanding Scholar award NYU, 1968, Outstanding Achievement award Advanced Care Products, 1985. Fellow N.Y. Acad. Scis., Sigma Xi; mem. Am. Pharm. Assn., Soc. Cosmetic Chemists, Am. Assn. Clin. Chemistry. Home: 1 Minuteman Ct East Brunswick NJ 08816

KAPLAN, MADELINE, law firm administrator; b. N.Y.C., June 20, 1944; d. Leo and Ethel (Finkelstein) Kahn; m. Theodore Norman Kaplan, Nov. 14, 1982. AS, Fashion Inst. Tech., N.Y.C., 1964; BA in English Lit. summa cum laude, CUNY, 1982; MBA, Baruch Coll., 1990. Free-lance fashion illustrator N.Y.C., 1965-73; legal asst. Krause Hirsch & Gross, Esquires, N.Y.C., 1973-80; mgr. communications Stroock & Stroock & Lavan Esquires, N.Y.C., 1980-86; dir. adminstrn. Cooper Cohen Singer & Ecker Esquires, N.Y.C., 1986-87, Donovan Leisure Newton & Irvine Esquires, N.Y.C., 1987—. Contbr. articles to profl. jours. Founder, pres. Knolls chpt. of Women's Am. Orgn. Rehab. Through Tng., Riverdale, N.Y., 1979-82, v.p. edn., Manhattan region, 1982-83. Mem. Assn. Legal Adminstrs., Am. Soc. Tng. and Devel., Soc. Human Resources Mgmt., Sigma Iota Epsilon (life).

KAPLAN, MELVIN HYMAN, medical educator; b. Malden, Mass., Dec. 23, 1920; s. Harry and Rena (Chernoff) K. A.B., Harvard U., 1942, M.D., 1952. Intern Boston City Hosp., 1952; research fellow medicine House of Good Samaritan, Boston; also asst. bacteriology and immunology Harvard Med. Sch., 1953; research assoc. medicine, instr., also established investigator Am. Heart Assn., 1954-57, assoc. bacteriology and immunology, 1957-58; practice medicine, specializing in rheumatology and clin. immunology Cleve., 1958—; asst. prof. medicine Sch. Medicine Western Res. U., 1958-60, assoc. prof., 1960-65, prof., 1965—, dir. div. immunology and rheumatology, 1974-82; acting chmn. lab. medicine U. Mass., 1974-79; assoc. physician Cleve. Met. Gen. Hosp., 1958-62, physician, 1962-74; Cons. allergy and immunology study sect. USPHS, 1964-69; asso. mem. com. streptococcal diseases Armed Forces Epidemiological Bd., 1956-70; temp. adviser WHO Study Cardiomyopathies in Africa, 1965; mem. merit review bd. VA, 1972—; mem. med. adv. bd. Arthritis Found., New Eng. Lupus Found. Assoc. editor: Jour. Lab. and Clin. Medicine, 1963-68, Jour. Clin. and Exptl. Immunology, 1965-71; Contbr. articles to profl. jours. Served with AUS, 1942-46. Recipient Research Career award USPHS, 1964. Mem. Am. Soc. Clin. Investigation, Am. Rheumatism Assn., Am. Assn. Immunologists. Home: 1500 Worcester Rd Apt 605E Framingham MA 01701-8967 Office: 55 Lake Ave N Worcester MA 01655-0001

KAPLAN, MICHAEL LEWIS BERNARD, lawyer; b. Bklyn., June 27, 1934; s. Hymen and Pearl (Goldenberg) K.; m. Harriet S. Goldman, Apr. 8, 1965; 1 child, Elizabeth Anne. AB, Brown U., 1955; JD, U. Va., 1958. Bar: N.Y. 1958, N.J. 1990. With The Mut. Life Ins. Co. of N.Y., N.Y.C., 1961-91, assoc. gen. counsel, 1976-83, v.p., ins. counsel, 1984, v.p., chief counsel individual fin. svcs., 1985-89, v.p. chief counsel human resources and corp. affairs, 1989-91; dep. gen. counsel Blue Cross and Blue Shield of N.J., Newark, 1991—; v.p. law, sec. MONY Realty Investors, Mass., 1989-90. With U.S. Army, 1958-60. Mem. ABA, Assn. Life Ins. Counsel, Am. Corp. Counsel Assn. Home: 1500 Palisade Ave Apt 11F Fort Lee NJ 07024-5318 Office: Blue Cross and Blue Shield 33 Washington St Newark NJ 07102

KAPLAN, MITCHELL ALAN, sociologist, researcher; b. Bklyn., Jan. 26, 1954; s. Murray Robert and Claire (Meshnick) K. BA in Sociology and Psychology cum laude, L.I. U., 1976; MA in Sociology, New Sch. for Social Rsch., 1979; PhD in Sociology, CUNY, 1987. Rsch. fellow Narcotic and Drug Rsch. Inc., N.Y.C., 1986-89, cons., 1989-90; cons. Am. Found. for AIDS Rsch., N.Y.C., 1989-90; rsch. scientist Rsch. & Tng. Inst. Nat. Ctr. for Disability Svcs., Albertson, N.Y., 1991—; evaluation cons. office rsch. and ednl. assessment Bklyn. divsn. N.Y.C. Bd. Edn., 1992—. Co-author: (chpt.) Days with Drug Distribution Which Drugs? How Many Transactions? With What Returns? 1990. Bd. dirs. Greater N.Y. chpt. Dystonia Med. Rsch. Found., Oakland Gardens, N.Y., 1989-91. Nat. Inst. on Drug Abuse fellow, 1986-89. Mem. APHA, Nat. Rehab. Assn., Soc. for Disability Studies, N.Y. Acad. Scis., Am. Sociol. Assn., N.Y. State Sociol. Assn., Am. World Health Assn., Am. Assn. Sex Educators, Counselors and Therapists, Am. Assn. for Pub. Opinion Rsch., Nat. Rehab. Counseling Assn., Nat. Rehab. Assn. (job placement div. 1991), Pi Gamma Mu, Psi Chi, Phi Theta Kappa. Democrat. Jewish. Home: 2560 Batchelder St Brooklyn NY 11235-1555 Office: Nat Ctr Disability Svcs 201 I U Willets Rd Albertson NY 11507-1599

KAPLAN, PHILIP LARRY, psychologist; b. Bklyn., Oct. 7, 1950; s. Benjamin and Ida (Spector) K.; m. Iris M. Saltiel, Apr. 20, 1986; children: Samantha, Benjamin. BA, CCNY, 1974; MA, Case WEstern U., 1977, PhD, 1984. Lic. psychologist, N.J. Psychologist U. Med. and Dentistry of N.J.-Com. Mental Health Ctr., Piscataway, N.J., 1978-84; dir. Family Crisis Intervention Unit, New Brunswick, N.J., 1984-88; psychologist pvt. practice, North Brunswick, N.J., 1984—; cons. Damon House, New Brunswick, 1989—, N.J. Assn. Correction, New Brunswick, 1979-89; clin. supr. Rutgers U. Grad. Sch. Applied Profl. Psychology, 1988—. Mem. Youth Svcs. Commn., Middlesex County, N.J., 1984-90. Mem. Am. Psychol. Assn., N.J. Psychol. Assn. Office: 1224 How Ln North Brunswick NJ 08902-1720

KAPLAN, RONALD V., financial executive; b. N.Y.C., Oct. 23, 1930; s. Morris and Ethel (Glass) K.; B.BA, N.Y. U., 1951; MBA in Acctg., Columbia, CUNY, 1956; m. Bette Wise, June 27, 1954; children: Bruce, Jerry, Michael. Acct. Ernst & Young, CPAs, N.Y.C., 1954-66; treas., chief fin. officer Gen. Hose & Coupling Co., Caldwell, N.J., 1966-68; v.p., treas., chief fin. officer Midland Capital Corp., N.Y.C., 1968-82; v.p., treas., chief fin. officer Belding Heminway Co. Inc., 1982—. CPA, N.Y. Chmn. bd. pres. Flight Svcs., Inc., Ft. Lauderdale, Fla., 1977-81. Mem. AICPA, N.Y. State Soc. CPAs, K.P., Beta Gamma Sigma. Home: 21 Tammy Ter Wayne NJ 07470-2519 Office: Belding Heminway Co Inc 1430 Broadway New York NY 10018-3308

KAPLAN, STEVEN MARK, accountant; b. Bklyn., June 22, 1952; s. Irwin and Ruth (Lieberman) K.; m. Susan Lynn Rosenberg, Nov. 19, 1972; children: Eric, Corey, Shannon. BS in Acctg., Bklyn. Coll., 1973. CPA, N.Y. Staff acct. Morris Sherwood & May, N.Y.C., 1973-74; sr. acct. Slater & Slater, Rockville Centre, N.Y., 1974-75; ptnr. Kaplan and Roberts CPA, East Rockaway, N.Y., 1975—. Treas. Temple Beth Am, Merrick, N.Y., 1989—, Merrick-North Merrick Little League, 1990—, v.p., 1989; bd. dirs. Merrick-North Merrick Police Athletic League, 1984-88. Mem. AICPA, N.Y. State Soc. CPA's, Nat. Soc. Pub. Accts. Office: Kaplan & Roberts 345 Atlantic Ave East Rockaway NY 11518-1429

KAPLAN, SUSAN, lawyer. BA summa cum laude, Hofstra U., 1971; JD, Columbia U., 1974. Bar: N.Y. 1975, U.S. Dist. Ct. (so. and ea. dists.) N.Y. 1975. Assoc. Patterson Belknap & Webb, N.Y.C., 1974-76; asst. dist. atty. Nassau County, N.Y., 1976-81; asst. chief prosecution Office Profl. Discipline, State of N.Y., 1981-83; dep. dir. prosecution Office Profl. Discipline State of N.Y., 1983-85; pvt. practice N.Y.C., 1985—; mem. adv. bd. Employee Assistance Program Health Care Network, 1988—; lectr. in field. Contbr. articles to profl. jours. Mem. adminstrv. bd. Soc. Meml. Sloan-Kettering Cancer Ctr., 1975-78; mem. adv. coun. Nassau County Boy Scouts Am., 1977-87, v.p., 1981-84; sec., bd. dirs. Harkness Ballet Found., 1980-86. Assoc. fellow N.Y. Acad. Medicine 1990-91, fellow 1992—. Mem. N.Y. State Bar Assn. (com. on pub. health 1975-78, com. on profl. discipline 1983-90, com. on health law 1985-88, com. to confer with state med. soc. 1985—, vice chair 1986-87, chair 1987—). Office: 165 W End Ave Apt 27P New York NY 10023-5536

KAPLAN, SUSAN ROBIN, lawyer; b. Providence, Aug. 7, 1954; d. Leonard and Beverly (Olswäng) K. BA in Urban Studies magna cum laude, Mount Holyoke Coll., 1976; Masters in City and Regional Planning, Rutgers U., 1979, JD, 1980. Bar: N.J. 1980, U.S. Dist. Ct. N.J. 1980. Litigation assoc. Hannoch Weisman, Roseland, N.J., 1980-84; assoc. counsel K. Hovnanian Co. of N.J., Inc., Red Bank, 1984-85; asst. corp. counsel Lanidex Corp., Parsippany, N.J., 1985-88; exec. v.p. Mt. Hope Properties, Inc., Dover, N.J., 1988-90; of counsel Hutt & Berkow, P.C., Woodbridge, N.J., 1989—. Mem. ABA, N.J. State Bar Assn. (sec., bd. dirs., land use law sect. 1989-90, vice chair 1991-92, chair 1992).

KAPLAN, THEODORE NORMAN, insurance company executive; b. Newburgh, N.Y., July 23, 1935; s. Edward and Bella (Kesten) K.; m. Madeline Kahn, Nov. 14, 1982; children: Garrett, Judith. BS in Acctg., Syracuse U., 1957. CLU. Ins. sales Aetna Life, N.Y.C., 1959-67, Bankers Life, N.Y.C., 1967-73, Conn. Mut., N.Y.C., 1973-77; benefits cons. Theodore N. Kaplan Assocs., Inc., N.Y.C., 1977—. Mem. Life Underwriters Assn., Million Dollar Round Table (life and qualifying mem.). Office: Theodore N Kaplan Assoc Inc 515 Madison Ave New York NY 10022-5403

KAPLIN, WILLIAM ALBERT, lawyer, educator, consultant; b. Saratoga Springs, N.Y., May 11, 1942; s. Albert W. and Joan M. (Benton) K.; m. Margaret Ann Downey, June 19, 1965 (div.); children: Colleen Michele, Keith William; m. Barbara Ann Mosebrook, Aug. 11, 1979; stepchildren: Lynn Susan Fennell, Carole Ann Fennell. AB in Polit. Sci., U. Rochester, 1964; JD, Cornell U., 1967. Bar: D.C. 1968, U.S. Ct. Appeals (D.C. cir.) 1969, U.S. Supreme Ct. 1972. Jud. clk. U.S. Ct. Appeals (D.C. cir.), Washington, 1967-68; atty. HEW, Washington, 1968-70; asst. and assoc. prof. law Cath. U. Am., Washington, 1970-78, prof., 1978—, dir. law and pub. policy program, 1984-85; vis. assoc. prof. law Cornell U., Ithaca, N.Y., 1975; vis. prof. law Wake Forest U., Winston-Salem, N.C., 1990-91; disting. vis. scholar Inst. for Higher Edn. Law and Governance, U. Houston, 1991; vis. scholar Inst. Ednl. Leadership, Washington, 1976-77; mem. nat. adv. bd. Ctr. for Constl. Studies, 1979-90, Notre Dame, South Bend, Ind., Mercer U., Macon, Ga.; mem. nat. adv. coun. J.M. Dawson Inst. Ch.-State Studies, 1991—, Baylor U., Waco, Tex.; lectr., presenter, workshop leader various orgns. Author: The Law of Higher Education, 1978 (Borden award Am. Coun. Edn. 1979), 2d edit., 1985; co-author: State, School and Family, 1973, 2d edit., 1979, The Law of Higher Education: 1985-90 Update, 1991; editor-in-chief Cornell Law Rev., 1966-67; editor Jour. Coll. and Univ. Law, 1976-80; mem. editorial bd. Synthesis: Law & Policy in Higher Education, 1989—; contbr. numerous articles and monographs to legal publs. Mem. edn. appeal bd. U.S. Dept. Edn., 1977-82; elder Grace Presbyn. Ch., Lanham, Md., 1980—. NEH fellow 1982. Mem. ABA, Nat. Assn. Coll. and Univ. Attys. (fellow 1990), Am. Assn. Higher Edn., Order of Coif, Phi Kappa Phi. Democrat. Office: Cath U Sch Law Washington DC 20064

KAPOOR, SHEELA, physician; b. Multan, Punjab, India, Aug. 28, 1940; came to U.S., 1962; d. A. N. and Ishwardevi (Kakkar) Pattney; m. Kedar N. Kapoor; children: Nidhi, Alok. Student, Mahila Vidalaya Coll., Lucknow, India, 1955-57; B in Medicine and Surgery, King George Med. Coll., 1962. Intern Gandhi Meml. Hosp., Lucknow, India, 1962-63; resident I Worcester City Hosp., 1966-67; resident II Bklyn. Cumberland Med. Ctr., 1967-68; pediatrician rebound children and youth program Children's Hosp., Phila., 1973-74; pediatrician Jefferson Children & Youth Program, Phila., 1974-75, S.E. Phila. Neighborhood Health Ctr. affiliate Pa. Hosp., 1975-76, Health Dist. #6, 1976-79; pvt. practice Haddonfield, N.J., 1979-86; physician New Lisbon (N.J.) Devel. Ctr., 1982—; part-time pediatrician Atlantic County Health Dept., Mayslanding, N.J., 1975-82; pediatrician comprehensive approach to community health program Jewish Hosp., Bklyn., 1971-73; pediatrician comprehensive child care program Brookdale Hosp., Bklyn., 1970-71. Fellow Am. Acad. Pediatrics; mem. Gloucester County Med. Soc., N.J. Med. Soc. Hindu.

KAPOTES, CHARLES NICHOLAS, psychologist; b. Bklyn., Mar. 25, 1927; s. Nicholas Constantine and Anna (Papatheodore) K.; m. Despina Joakimides, Mar. 4, 1956; children: James Charles, Nicholas Stephen, Alexandra. BA, St. John's U., 1950; PhD, NYU, 1955. Lic. psychologist, N.Y.; Diplomate Am. Bd. Med. Psychotherapists. Social investigator N.Y. Welfare Dept., Bklyn., 1954-55; clin. psychologist Payne Whitney Cornell Med. Ctr., N.Y.C., 1955-57; instr. Cornell U. Med. Coll., N.Y.C., 1955-57, NYU Inst. Phys. Med. and Rehab., N.Y.C., 1957, VA, N.Y.C., 1957-58; psychol. cons. Family Cons. Svc., Episcopal Diocese, Queens, N.Y., 1973-88; chief psychologist North Nassau Mental Health Ctr., Manhasset, N.Y., 1972-78; clin. psychologist N.Y. Mental Health Svcs., Bayshore, N.Y., 1990—, Bleuler

Psychotherapy Ctr., Forest Hills, N.Y., 1957—; clin. child psychologist St. Mary's Hosp. for Children, Bayside, N.Y., 1959—; cons. and psychologist in bilingual field. With USNR, 1945-46. Founder's Day scholar NYU, 1955; Children's Asthma Found. grantee, 1965-66. Mem. APA, N.Y. State Psychol. Assn., Queens County Psychol. Assn., N.Y. Acad. Scis., Archeol. Inst. Am., Greek Am. Behavioral Scis. Inst. Home and Office: 111 Executive Dr New Hyde Park NY 11040-1015

KAPP, ROBERT WESLEY, JR., toxicologist, consultant; b. Point Pleasant, N.J., Jan. 31, 1945; s. Robert W. Sr. and Renee Lehman (Stickland) K.; m. Beverly Ann Hodnett; children: Robert III, Sheri Lynn, Bonney Lea. AB, Syracuse U., 1967; MS, U. Mo., 1968, George Washington U., 1974; PhD, George Washington U., 1979. Med. technologist Group Health Assn., Washington, 1970-73; staff scientist Hazleton Labs. Am., Vienna, Va., 1973-78; sr. scientist, mgr. Hazelton Labs. Am., Vienna, Va., 1978-79; from assoc. dir. to dir. div. toxicology Exxon Corp., East Millstone, N.J., 1979-89; pres., chief exec. officer Biotox, Inc., Belle Mead, N.J., 1989—; mem. safety com. U. Med. and Dental Schs. N.J., 1986—; cons. EPA Genetic Toxicology Program, Washington, 1979-86, Nat. Toxicology Program Bd. Sci. Counselors, McLean, Va., 1982—; vis. faculty U. Tex. Cancer Ctr., Galveston, 1982—; adj. prof. dept. epidemiology U. Tex. Med. Br., Galveston, 1985—. Author, editor: (tng. manual) Clinical Cytogenetics, 1972, rev. edit., 1979; author: (with others) Single Cell Monitoring Systems, 1984; editor: (workshop manual) Clinical Diagnostics, 1971-80; contbr. articles to profl. jours. Mem. environ commn. Montgomery Twp., Belle Mead, 1984-89, mem. health commn., 1988-90; mem. gov's. commn. on animal testing State of N.J., Trenton, 1988-89; chmn. budget com. Princeton (N.J.) Area United Way, 1986-89. With USN, 1968-72, Vietnam. Named Outstanding Young Man in Am., Jaycees, 1977. Mem. ASTM (com. chmn. 1989—), Am. Coll. Toxicology, N.Y. Acad. Scis., Soc. Toxicology (placement com. 1984-86), Environ. Mutagen Soc. (counselor 1974-78). Republican. Methodist. Home: 52 Hoagland Dr Belle Mead NJ 08502-5501 Office: Biotex PO Box 1317 Belle Mead NJ 08502

KAPR, JOHN ROBERT, operations executive; b. Dumont, N.J., Dec. 15, 1954; s. Charles Frank and Gertrude (Baird) K.; m. Karen Marie Hansen, May 22, 1976; children: Kristin, Jennifer, Jon. AAS, Bergen Community Coll., 1976. Parts specifier Volvo of Am., Rockleigh, N.J., 1976-77; parts technical specialist BMW of N.Am., Inc., Montvale, N.J., 1977-78, dist. parts mgr., 1978-81, depot mgr., 1981-84; parts distbn. mgr. BMW of N.Am., Inc., Mount Olive, N.J., 1984-90; v.p. ops. Transeuro Group Inc., Edison, N.J., 1990-91; pres. Ka-Pro Builders, Midland Park, N.J., 1991—. Mem. Coun. of Logistics Mgmt., Internat. Material Mgmt. Soc., Mount Olive C. of C., Morris County C. of C., NRA, Am. Motorcyclist Assn., Sports Car Club Am., Internat. Motor Sports Assn. Presbyterian. Club: 200 of Warren County. Home: 2 Cherry Ln Blairstown NJ 07825-9326

KAPRAL, CHARLES ANTHONY, systems analyst; b. Luzerne, Pa., Nov. 3, 1944; s. Samuel Kapral and Hermina (Jenny) Britz; m. Marie Andrea Lazar, Jan. 9, 1971. Tech. cert., RCA Inst., 1970. Engring. assoc. Western Elec., 1970-75; systems analyst Fedders Corp., 1976-83, Culbro Corp., 1983-86; sr. project analyst Wakefern Food Corp., 1986—. Sgt. USAF, 1963-67. Recipient Cert. Honor Am. Lunar Soc., 1991. Mem. Am. Lunar Soc., Assn. of Luner and Planet Obs., Am. Astron. Assn. Home: 6601 Hana Rd Edison NJ 08817

KAPUS, JOSEPHINE DISTEFANO, title searcher; b. Flushing, N.Y., Aug. 22, 1928; d. Joseph and Rose (LoSchiavo) DiStefano; m. Robert Francis Kapus, Sept. 23, 1959. Student, NYU, 1946-49. Sec. NYU, 1946-49; stenographer FBI, N.Y.C., 1949-51; adminstrv. asst. Indonesian Consulate Gen., N.Y.C., 1951-53; exec. sec. B. Altman and Co., N.Y.C., 1953-58; legal sec. various law firms, New London, Conn., 1959-65; recorder Atlantic Community Coll., Mays Landing, N.J., 1966-69; free-lance title searcher Atlantic and Cape May Counties, N.J., 1978—; Researcher Hamilton Twp. Hist. Soc. Author: The Proud American—The Story of a Mays Landing Hotel, 1982 (cert. of recognition Hamilton Twp., resolution Bd. Chosen Freeholders, Atlantic County, N.J.), Mr. Northfield, 1989, (monographs) Miss Lizzie Price on Early Northfield, 1976, The Churches of Northfield, 1978, Forgotten Pastures, 1984 (cert. Atlantic City Rescue Mission); contbr. numerous stories and articles to local and nat. mags. Mem. Northfield Pub. Library Assn., 1973-83. Recipient Cert. of Achievement plaque, Northfield, 1983. Mem. Nat. Writers Club, Mystery Writers Am., Atlantic County Title Searchers Assn., Atlantic County Hist. Soc. (pres. 1992—), Cape May County Hist. Soc., Northfield Pub. Libr. Assn. (pres. 1982-83), Monoco Canoe Club (Brick Twp., N.J.). Republican. Baptist. Home: 113 Davis Ave Northfield NJ 08225-2242

KARABOTS, JOSEPH WILLIAM, engineering executive; b. Hartford, Conn., Dec. 5, 1956; s. William and Lucy (Makris) K. BS in Geology and Geophysics, U. Conn., 1981. Rsch. asst. NSF, Aleutian Islands, Alaska, 1981-82; sr. and gen. field engr. Schlumberger Ltd., various cities, 1982-87; sr. engr. Vitro Corp., Newport, North London, R.I., Conn, 1987-89; dir. bus. devel. Briggs Assocs., Cumberland, R.I., 1989—. Vol. Spl. Olympics, Providence, 1984—, Providence Waterfront Festival, 1990—, R.I. Dept. Econ. Devel.-Internat. Rels., 1991—. Recipient Citizens award City of Hartford, 1977. Mem. Providence C. of C. (amb. 1989—, mem. fedn. environ. task force 1991—, chmn. tech. com.), Trade Club, Toastmasters Internat. (sec. 1991—). Greek Orthodox. Office: Briggs Assocs Inc 527 Pound Rd Cumberland RI 02864-2710

KARACSONY, ATTILA TIBOR, marketing professional; b. Budapest, Hungary, July 31, 1954; came to U.S., 1956; s. Ignac and Eva (Suss) K. BS in Journalism, Syracuse U., 1977. Mgr. mktg. Coopers & Lybrand, Parsippany, N.J., 1988—. Editor N.J. Emerging Bus. Svcs. Rev., 1989, N.J. High Tech. Newsletter, 1990; mem. editorial adv. bd. Morris County Mag., 1991. Chmn. Newark Mus. Coun. Mem. Assn. Acctg. Mktg. Execs. (exec. sec.), N.J. Biosci. Assn. Republican. Roman Catholic. Office: Coopers & Lybrand 1 Sylvan Way Parsippany NJ 07054-3805

KARADIMOS, JAMES D., podiatrist; b. Kearny, N.J., Nov. 5, 1960; s. Evan and Katherine K. BS, Albright Coll., 1983; D of Podiatric Medicine, Ohio Coll. Podiatric Medicine, 1987. Med. staff Worcester (Mass.) City Hosp., St. Vincent Hosp., Worcester, U. Mass. Med. Ctr. Office: Assoc Foot Specialists 22 Summer St Westborough MA 21581

KARAHALIS, JOHN, psychologist; b. ELmhurst, N.Y., June 27, 1955; s. Eraclis and Ann (Arabagis) K.; m. Patricia Cunningham, Aug. 25, 1979; children: Maryanne Patricia, John Connell. AA, St. John's U., 1975, BA in Psychology, 1977, MS, 1979, profl. diploma, 1981. Cert. sch. psychologist N.Y. Mental hygiene therapist Westchester Devel. Svcs., Tarrytown, N.Y., 1978-79; asst. mgr. group home A.H.R.C., N.Y.C., 1979; dir. community residence F.P.R.O., Bklyn., 1979-80; sch. psychologist United Cerebral Palsy, Roosevelt, N.Y., 1980-83; staff psychologist L.I. Devel. Ctr., Melville, N.Y., 1983-85, Pilgram Psychiat. Ctr., West Brentwood, N.Y., 1985—; dir., behavorial svcs. A.B.L.E. Inc., Commuk, N.Y., 1986—; cons. B.O.C.E.S., Westbury, N.Y., 1990—, cons., sch. psychologist Patchoque/Medford Sch. Dist., Patchogue, N.Y., 1987-88; master instr. behavior tng. Office Mental Health, Albany, N.Y., 1990—; presenter in field. Mem. Am. Psychol. Assn., Nassau County Psychol. Assn. Democrat. Greek Orthodox. Office: Pilgrim Psychiat Ctr Box A West Brentwood NY 11717

KARAM, DAOUD BOUTROS, physiatrist; b. Ain Kabou, Lebanon, Aug. 4, 1934; came to U.S., 1962; s. Boutros D. and Najla (Maluf) K.; m. Barbara M. Rudolph, Oct. 8, 1966; children: Lisa C., Mina Y. MD, St. Joseph U., Beirut, 1962. Asst. attending Long Island Jewish/Queens Hosp. Ctr. Affiliation, Jamaica, N.Y., 1969-73; internship Queens Hosp. Ctr., Jamaica, N.Y., 1962-63; residency N.Y. Med. Coll. Physical Medicine and Rehabilitation, 1963066; fellowship Rehabilitation Inst. Montreal, 1966-69; residency Mt. Sinai, Elmhurst, N.Y., 1969-70; assoc. attending Long Island Jewish/Queens Hosp. Ctr. Affiliation, Jamaica, N.Y., 1973-79; dir. rehab. medicine Coler Meml. Hosp., N.Y.C., 1980-87; med. dir. Orthopedic and Rehab. Diagnostic and Treatment Ctr., Jamaica, 1987-92, Island Orthopedic and Sport Medicine, Massapequa, N.Y., 1992—; instr. SUNY, Stony Brook, 1971-73, asst. prof., 1973-79; asst. prof. N.Y. Med. Coll., N.Y.C., 1980—. Contbr. articles to profl. jours. Fellow Am. Acad. Phys. Medicine and Rehab.; mem. AMA, N.Y. Soc. Phys. Medicine and Rehab. (pres. 1987-88, chmn. exec. com. 1988-89). Republican. Maronite. Home: 12 Tower Ct Syosset NY 11791-3623 Office: Island Orthopedic and Sport Medicine 660 Broadway Massapequa NY 11758

KARAMCHANDANI, BALRAM CHETANDAS, food company executive; b. Karachi, Pakistan, Aug. 2, 1944; s. Chetandas J. and Devi C. Karamchandani; m. Kamini Ramchand Tulsiani, Mar. 3, 1972; children: Prashant, Ashish, Kunal. B MechE, U. Baroda, India, 1967, postgrad., 1968; MS in Indsl. Engring., U. Ark., 1970; MBA, Kent State U., 1980. Indsl. engr. Day & Zimmerman, Texarkana, Tex., 1970-74, Morton Frozen Foods, Russellville, Ark., 1974-75; mgr. indsl. engring. Morton Frozen Foods, Crozet, Va., 1975-77; mgr. indsl. engring. Stouffer Frozen Foods, Solon, Ohio, 1977-79, asst. plant mgr., 1979-81, dir. indsl. engring. and prodn. planning, 1981-89; v.p. mfg. svc. Nestlé Chocolate and Confectionery Co., Columbus, Ohio, 1989-92; v.p. ops. Nestlé Dairy Systems, Columbus, 1992—. Mem. Am. Inst. Indsl. Engrs. (sr., bd. dirs. 1970-74). Republican. Hindu. Home: 7315 Penneyroyal Pl Dublin OH 43017 Office: Nestlé Dairy Systems 17th and Joyce Ave Columbus OH 43216

KARBEN, SHELLEY VALERIE, educator; b. Mt. Vernon, N.Y., Dec. 1, 1944; d. Sidney and Helen (Minskoff) Gross; children: Ryan Scott, Lori Jennifer. BS, 1966; MA, NYU, 1971. Cert. tchr. spl. edn., N.Y. Tchr. kindergarten and elem. East Ramapo Cen. Sch. Dist., Spring Valley, N.Y., 1966—, tchr. learning disabilities, tchr. emotionally handicapped, tchr. mentally handicapped, tchr. learning disabilities resource room; cons. Jewish Day Schs, Yeshivas Schs., Hebrew Schs. for Spl Edn., 1969—; dir. summer spl. edn. program Yeshiva. Mem. Profl. Cons. Staff, N.Y. State Sen. Commn. on Child Abuse, Albany, 1974; mem. Commn. of Ethnic Studies, Westchester County, 1975-76; exec. com. Dem. Party, Town of Ramapo, N.Y., 1985—, mem. task force affordable housing, 1991, mem. bd. assessment rev., 1988; mem. Hebrew Programs for The Disabled, Nat. Commn. on Torah Edn., Yeshiva U., 1974-76, Fleetwood Synagogue Sisterhood, Mt. Vernon, N.Y., pres., 1976-77; pres. Hillcrest Civic Assn., 1990—. Mem. Assn. for Children with Learning Disabilities, Coun. for Exceptional Children, Assn. for Supervision and Curriculum Devel., B'nai Brith (pres. Mt. Vernon 1975-77). Jewish.

KARCH, JOSEPH MICHAEL, safety engineer, consultant; b. Elizabeth, N.J., Apr. 27, 1942; s. Joseph Karch and Rose (Bartone) Morphy; m. Carol Lee Rotella, Oct. 6, 1968; children: Joseph Michael Jr., Kevin, Chris. BA, Kean Coll. N.J., 1975; MA, NYU, 1978, postgrad., 1987—. Emergency med. coord. Roosevelt Hosp., N.Y.C., 1971-73; mgr. loss control Essex Chem. Co., Clifton, N.J., 1973-78; sr. cons., asst. v.p. Marsh & McLennan P.C., Cedar Knolls, N.J., 1978-86; dir. engring. AIG Risk Mgmt., N.Y.C., 1986—; mem. tech. com. ISO, N.Y.C., 1988—; seminar speaker. Mem. Emergency Ambulance Unit, Union, N.J., 1965-71; coach Boy's Club, Union, 1966-67, City League, Rahway, N.J., 1978-85; leader Boy Scouts Am., Rahway, 1979-86. With USMC, 1960-64. Grantee U.S. Govt., 1972, NYU, 1977. Mem. Am. Soc. Safety Engrs. (profl.), Am. Indsl. Hygiene Assn., Nat. Solid Waste Mgmt. Assn. (tech. com. 1989—). Office: AIG Risk Mgmt New York NY 10000

KARCHMER, CLIFFORD LEROY, research administrator; b. Memphis, July 16, 1946; s. I. Gilbert and Poppy (Hamer) K.; m. Barbara Donohue, Jan. 17, 1970; children: Alise Hamer, Adam Berg, Andrew Robert. BA, Princeton U., 1968; MA, U. Wis., 1971; MPA, Harvard U., 1973. Spl. investigator Pa. Crime Commn., St. Davids, 1969-72; program dir. Mass. Commn. on Crime Justice, Boston, 1973-76; dir. Mass. Organized Crime Coun., Boston, 1976-77; rsch. scientist Battelle Mem. Inst. (HARC), Seattle and Washington, 1977-1986; assoc. dir. Police Exec. Rsch. Forum, Washington, 1986—; adj. prof. Am. U., Washington, 1981—; founding ptnr. Nat. Inst. Econ. Crime, Vienna, Va., 1985—. Contbg. editor Firehouse Mag., 1978—; contbr. articles to profl. jours. Mem. St. John's Men's Club. Jewish. Office: Police Exec Rsch Forum 2300 "M" St, NW Washington DC 20037

KARDAS, GERALD EUGENE, management consultant; b. Lackawanna, N.Y., Dec. 9, 1949; s. Henry and Dolores Marie (Jarnot) K.; m. Janice Ellen Kleeman (div. 1982); 1 child, Ellen Hayward; m. Carol Lynn Tetreault, June 8, 1985; 1 child, Kristen Carrie-Lynn. BS in Aero. and Astronautical Engring., MIT, 1971; MSME, George Washington U., 1973; MS in Mgmt., Rensselaer Poly. Inst., 1982. Engr. Northrop Corp., Hawthorne, Calif., 1970, George Washington U./NASA, Hampton, Va., 1971-73; engr. United Techs. Corp./Pratt and Whitney Aircraft, East Hartford, Conn., 1973-76, sr. engr., 1979-81; project mgr. chem. systems div. United Techs. Corp., Sunnyvale, Calif., 1976-79; mgr. tech. planning Combustion Engring., Stamford, Conn., 1981-88; v.p. mktg. AMDATA/Combustion Engring., Windsor, Conn., 1988-90; sr. mgr. mgmt. cons. Black & Decker Corp., Berlin, Conn., 1990—. Author: (NASA tech. report) Externally Blown Flaps, 1973. Mem. condominium bd. Farmington Woods Condominiums, Avon, Conn., 1985-88, mem. covenants com., 1988-91. Mem. AIAA (sr. mem., Conn. chmn. 1989-90), Assn. for Mfg. Excellence. Home: 9 Sweetbriar Ln Avon CT 06001-4536

KARDON, PETER FRANKLIN, foundation executive; b. N.Y.C., May 5, 1949; s. Leonard and Annette (Rappaport) K. AB, Dartmouth Coll., 1970; MA, U. Chgo., 1975, PhD, 1984. Asst. to exec. dir. MLA of Am., N.Y.C., 1980-84; acad. affairs assoc. Office of Chancellor, NYU, N.Y.C., 1984-86, dir. acad. projects, 1986-88; dir. planning John Simon Guggenheim Meml. Found., N.Y.C., 1988—, dir. Latin Am. program, 1991—; adj. prof. medieval and Renaissance studies NYU, N.Y.C., 1986—. Reynolds scholar Dartmouth Coll., 1970-71; Fulbright-Hayes fellow, 1973-74, Georges Lurcy fellow, 1976-77, Whiting fellow U. Chgo., 1978-79. Office: JS Guggenheim Meml Found 90 Park Ave New York NY 10016-1302

KARDOS, MEL D., lawyer; b. Phila., Feb. 6, 1947; s. Julius S. and Rose (Klein) K.; m. Ellen D. Kleinman, Mar. 1, 1984; children: Lindsay Dara, Matthew Daniel. BS, Temple U., 1970; MEd, Trenton State Coll., 1972; JD, U. Balt., 1975. Bar: Pa. 1975, N.J. 1975, U.S. Dist. Ct. (ea. dist.) Pa. 1975, U.S. Dist. Ct. N.J. 1975, U.S. Supreme Ct. 1984. Asst. pub. defender Bucks County, Doylestown, Pa., 1975-80; ptnr. Kardos & Lynch, Newtown, Pa., 1980, Kardos & Heley, Newtown, 1980-87, Kardos, Rickles and Sellers, Newtown, 1988-; adj. prof. Temple U., Phila., 1987. Mem. ABA, Bucks County Bar Assn., Assn. Trial Lawyers Am., Soc. for Am. Baseball Research. Democrat. Office: Kardos Rickles Sellers & Heley 626 S State St Newtown PA 18940-1561 also: 194 S Broad St Trenton NJ 08608

KARDYS, JOSEPH ANTHONY, chemist; b. Chicopee, Mass., Jan. 11, 1925; s. Frank and Sophia (Gell) K.; m. Dorothea Ella Sweeney; children: Jan Lynne, Edward Joseph, Gary John. BS, U. Cen. Conn., 1948; MS in Organic Chemistry, Rensselaer Polytech. Inst., 1950. Instr. Rensselaer Polytech. Inst., Troy, N.Y., 1948-50; chief chemist vitamin A organic prodn. lab. Pfizer, Inc., Groton, Conn., 1950-75, sr. devel. chemist chem. div., 1975—. Holder numerous patents in field. Mem. Polit. Action Com., Pfizer, Inc., 1975—. Mem. Am. Chem. Soc., Catalyst Soc. Am., Soc. Chemists and Engrs. Ea. Conn. Democrat. Roman Catholic. Clubs: Shennecossett Yacht (treas. 1960-62), Great Books of New London County (discussion leader 1955-65). Home: 75 Rope Ferry Rd Waterford CT 06385-2617 Office: Pfizer Inc Eastern Point Roads Groton CT 06340

KAREL, MARTIN LEWIS, mathematician, educator; b. Balt., Mar. 15, 1944; s. Leonard and Charlotte Ruth (Lockman) K.; m. Karin Jean Johnson, June 18, 1972; children: Irene Samantha, Alexander Johnson, Benjamin Runar. BA, John's Hopkins U., 1966; MA, U. Chgo., 1967, PhD, 1972. Asst. Inst. for Advanced Study, Princeton, N.J., 1972-73, mem., 1973-74; asst. prof. math. U. N.C., Chapel Hill, 1974-80; asst. prof. math. Rutgers U., Camden, N.J., 1980-83, assoc. prof. math., 1983—. NSF rsch. grantee, 1974-80, 81-85. Mem. Am. Math. Soc. Democrat. Jewish. Home: 104 Country Club Dr Wilmington DE 19803-2918 Office: Rutgers U Dept Math Scis CCAS Camden NJ 08102

KARELSEN, FRANK EPHRAIM, III, lawyer; b. N.Y.C., Feb. 24, 1927; s. Frank Ephraim and Sophie (Van Raalte) K.; m. Marjorie Weinstock, Oct. 9, 1954 (div. 1958); 1 child, Franklin; m. Ursula Steiner, June 24, 1960; children: Juliet, Eva. BA, Columbia Coll., 1947; JD, Yale U., 1950. Bar: N.Y. 1950. Sec. to assoc. judge Stanley H. Fuld N.Y. State Ct. Appeals, 1950-51; assoc. to sr. ptnr. Kurzman Karelsen & Frank, N.Y.C., 1951—. Chmn., bd. govs. Ethical Culture Schs., N.Y.C., 1986-89; pres. Alumni Fedn. of Columbia U., N.Y.C., 1971-73, Ramapo Anchorage Camp for Emotionally Disturbed Children, N.Y.C., 1983-86; chmn. Citizens Adv. Com. Housing and Devel. Adminstrn., N.Y.C., 1979-87, N.Y. State Bar Com. on Coops. and Condominiums, N.Y.C., 1980-86; spl. asst. to Gov. Adlai E. Stevenson, N.Y.C., 1952-56; spl. asst. to Sen. Hubert H. Humphrey, N.Y.C., 1960-68. Office: Kurzman Karelsen & Frank 230 Park Ave New York NY 10169-0005

KAREN, LINDA TRICARICO, fashion designer; b. Bklyn., June 8, 1961; d. John William and Phyllis Jean (D'Addario) T. Student, Bucks County Community Coll., 1978-79; AAS, Fashion Inst. Tech., 1992. Retail mgr. Canadians, Brooks, Casual Corner, 1980-83; coord. sales and design Sure Snap Corp., N.Y.C., 1983-84; asst. designer E.S. Sutton Inc., N.Y.C., 1984-86; designer Good 'N Plenty Inc., N.Y.C., 1986-90; designer, merchandiser Leonard A. Feinberg, Inc., N.Y.C., 1991—; free-lance illustrator, designer. Contbr. fashion trend reports, Milan, Italy, 1984, Rome, 1985, Milan and Florence, Italy, 1986, London and Paris, 1987, Montreal, Can., 1988. Mem. Fashion Soc., NAFE. Democrat. Roman Catholic. Home: 316 Berry Rd Monroe NY 10950

KARESH, JAMES WINKER, ophthamologist, educator; b. Chgo., June 29, 1948. BA, Case Western Res. U., 1970, MA, 1973, MS, 1973; MD, U. Md., 1979. Diplomate Am. Bd. Ophthalmology; cert. Am. Soc. Ophthalmic Plastic and Reconstructive Surgery. Intern Children's Hosp. Nat. Med. Ctr., Washington, 1979-80; resident in ophthalmology U. Md. Hosp., Balt., 1980-83; fellow U. Ill. Eye and Ear Inst.-Michael Reese Hosp., Chgo., 1983-84; lectr. U. Ill., Chgo., 1983-84; asst. prof. U. Md., Balt., 1984-91, asst. clin. prof., 1991—; asst. prof. Johns Hopkins U., Balt., 1991—; mem. peer rev. com. med. and chirurgical faculty of state of Md., Balt., 1987—. Contbr. articles on ophthalmology and ophthalmic plastic and reconstructive surgery to profl. jours., chpts. to books; author 1 book. Recipient Honor award Am. Acad. Ophthalmology, 1989. Mem. Md. Soc. Eye Physicians and Surgeons (bd. dirs., treas., newsletter editor 1985—). Office: Krieger Eye Inst Sinai Hosp Balt 2411 W Belvedere Baltimore MD 21215

KARIN, GLORIA SUSAN, education educator; b. Bklyn., Dec. 16, 1941; d. Martin and Estelle (Kelban) Berkowitz; m. Steven Norman Karin, Nov. 21, 1964; children: Janice Michelle, Lori Felicia, Marcy Lynn. BA, Queens Coll., 1962, MS in Edn., 1964; postgrad., St. John's U., 1964-66; EdD, Columbia U., 1971. Tchr. Meadow Lawn Elem. Sch., East Meadow, N.Y., 1962-63, Pub. Sch. 88 Q, Ridgewood, N.Y., 1963-66; guidance cons., tchr. Cert. Tutoring Svc., Flushing, N.Y., 1966-73; adj. asst. prof. C.W. Post Ctr., L.I. Univ., Greenvale, N.Y., 1972-76; instr. Pa. Bus. Inst., Pottstown, Pa., 1986-88; adj. prof. psychology Mount Saint Mary Coll., Newburgh, N.Y., 1989-90, asst. prof. psychology, 1990-91; adj. instr. Reading (Pa.) Area Community Coll., 1978, Marist Coll., Poughkeepsie, N.Y., 1989—, Ulster County Community Coll., Stone Ridge, N.Y., 1991—; presenter workshops to convs. and sch. groups. Pres. exec. bd. Earl Elem. Sch. PTO, Boyertown, Pa.; bd. dirs. Cornerstone of the Arts, Inc., Pottstown; treas. exec. bd. Jewish Women's League, Pottstown; publicity chair Woodstock Jewish Congregation, Woodstock. Mem. AACD, N.Y. State Assn. for Counseling and Devel., Assn. for Counselor Edn. and Supervision, Pa. Assn. for Counselor Edn. and Supervision (sec.-treas. 1980-83, author Newsnotes column in Of Current Interest 1979-80), Am. Sch. Counselors Assn., N.Y. Sch. Counselors Assn., North Atlantic Region Assn. for Counselor Edn. and Supervision, Phi Beta Kappa, Pi Lambda Theta, Kappa Delta Pi. Democrat. Jewish. Home: PO Box 5 Woodstock NY 12498-0005

KARIN, STEVEN NORMAN, principal; b. Bklyn., Apr. 18, 1941; s. Mike and Edith K.; m. Gloria Susan Berkowitz, Nov. 21, 1964; children: Janice Michelle, Lori Felicia, Marcy Lynn. BA, Bklyn. Coll., 1962, MA, 1966; cert., Hofstra U., 1974; EdD, Nova U., 1985. Cert. tchr., N.Y. Tchr. math. Sewanhaka High Sch., Floral Park, N.Y., 1962-76; math. coord. Gates-Chili Cen. Sch. Dist., Rochester, N.Y., 1976-77; asst. prin. Pottstown (Pa.) Sr. High Sch., 1977-84, asst. athletic dir., 1984-88; asst. prin. Pottstown Jr. High Sch., 1984-88; prin. Onteora Jr.-Sr. High Sch., Boiceville, N.Y., 1988—; chmn. Dist. K-12 Math Com., Pottstown, 1980-85; pres. No. Chesmont Jr. High Sch. League, Pottstown, 1985-86. NSF scholar, 1971-72. Mem. Nat. Assn. Secondary Prins., Nat. Coun. Tchrs. Maths., Assn. for Supervision and Curriculum Devel., Assn. Maths. Tchrs. N.Y. State, N.Y. State Assn. for Supervision and Curriculum Devel. Jewish. Home: PO Box 5 Woodstock NY 12498-0005

KARINCH, MARYANN, public relations executive; b. Lebanon, Pa., Jan. 5, 1953; d. Karl George and Ann Marie (Rudy) K.; m. Robert Richard Graul, July 13, 1990. BA in Speech, Drama, Cath. U. Am., 1974, MA in Drama, 1979. Exec. asst. Nat. Coun. Agrl. Employers, Washington, 1974-78; mng. dir. New Playwrights Theatre, Washington, 1979-81; devel. dir. Capital Children's Mus., Washington, 1981-83; freelance writer, pub. rels. cons. Washington, 1983-88; dir. communications Computer and Bus. Equipment Mfrs. Assn., Washington, 1988—. Author: (with others) Technology 2001, 1991; contbr. articles to profl. jours. Office: Computer and Bus Equipment Mfrs Assn 311 1st St NW Washington DC 20001

KARL, ERIC ALAN, financial analyst; b. Niskayuna, N.Y., Dec. 18, 1956; s. Ludwig L. and Anne E. (Roark) K. BA, Hamilton Coll., 1978; MA in Indsl. Relations, U. Warwick, Coventry, Eng., 1979. Fin. analyst Gen. Electric Plastics, Pittsfield, Mass.; fin. analyst Bergen ops. Gen. Electric Plastics, Zoom, The Netherlands; fin. analyst Gen. Electric Plastics, Mt. Vernon, Ind., 1980-83, Gen. Electric Capital, Stamford, Conn., 1983-87; mgr. customer fin. Gen. Electric Co., Fairfield, Conn., 1987-89; mgr. portfolio analysis GE Capital, Stamford, Conn., 1989-90; dir. investments Sumitomo Corp. of Am., N.Y.C., 1990—; bd. dirs. Phoenixcor Inc., 1992—. Exec. advisor Jr. Achievement, Stamford, 1984-85. Mem. Am. Assn. Equipment Lessors. Republican. Methodist. Lodge: Lions (local bd. dirs. 1984-86). Office: Sumitomo Corp Am 345 Park Ave New York NY 10154-0004

KARL, KURT ERSKINE, economist; b. Eugene, Oreg., July 23, 1952; s. Emil William and Margaret Ann (McClymonds) K.; m. Ida Louise Green, May 27, 1988; children: Zoe Thandiwe, Julia Louise. BA with honors, U. Oreg., 1974; MSc, London Sch. Econs., 1975; PhD, Princeton (N.J.) U., 1992. Rsch. assoc. Birkbeck Coll., London, 1975-77; statistician Cen. Stats. Office, Mbabane, Swaziland, 1977-80; dir. long term svc. Wharton Econometrics, Phila., 1981-86; cons. WEFA Group, Bala Cynwyd, Pa., 1986-90, sr. dir., U.S. short-term svc., 1990—. Author: (with others) Third Five Year Development Plan-Swaziland, 1976, Report on Population Development-Swaziland. Mem. Am. Econ. Assn., Nat. Assn. Bus. Economists, Phi Beta Kappa. Office: WEFA Group 401 E City Ave Bala Cynwyd PA 19004-1122

KARL, LEO EMIL, JR., automotive executive; b. New Canaan, Conn., Apr. 18, 1929; s. Leo E. and Rose L. (Kelley) K.; m. Katherine M. Horan, Aug. 22, 1959; children: Leo, Stephen, Joseph, Katherine, Mary, Elizabeth, Christopher, Sara, John, Robert. BBA, Fairfield U., 1951. Office mgr., sec. Karl Chevrolet Co., New Canaan, 1951-57, pres., dealer, 1957—; corporator New Canaan Savs. Bank, 1961-82; bd. dirs. Union Trust Co., New Canaan. Mem. New Canaan Bd. Social Services, 1961-81, chmn., 1981—; trustee St. Aloysius Ch., New Canaan, 1971—. Served as cpl. U.S. Army, 1952-54. Mem. New Canaan c. of C. (bd. dirs. 1981-84, Outstanding Citizen award 1987). Democrat. Roman Catholic. Lodges: KC, Lions. Home: 175 Silvermine Rd New Canaan CT 06840-4909 Office: The Karl Chevrolet Co PO Box 1146 261 Elm St New Canaan CT 06840

KARLAN, ANDREW WARREN (DREW KARLAN), pharmaceutical company executive; b. N.Y.C., May 2, 1944; s. Laurence Jack and Isabelle (Kerner) K.; m. Rosalyn Silverberg, Mar. 1, 1969; children: Mara Lisa, Adam Jason. B.A. in Biology, Hofstra U., Hempstead, N.Y., 1967; M.S. in Biology, Adelphi U., Garden City N.Y., 1972; M.B.A. in Pharm. Mktg., Fairleigh Dickinson U., Teaneck, N.J., 1982. Rsch. assoc. Worthington Biochem. Corp., Freehold, N.J., 1972-73; supr. E.R. Squibb & Sons, Inc., New Brunswick, N.J., 1973-79, sect. head, 1979-82, asst. mgr. of investigational data, 1982-88, regulatory mgr. , 1988-89, sr. regulatory mgr., 1989-91; dir. regulatory affairs Roberts Pharm. Corp., Eatontown, N.J. Publicity chmn.

Howell Jewish Community Ctr., (N.J.), 1977—, pres. Men's Club; vice chmn. United Way-Squibb, New Brunswick, 1982; chmn. Jewish com. on Scouting, dist. vice chmn.; cubmaster Monmouth Council Boy Scouts Am., Monmouth County N.J., 1983—. 1st lt. U.S. Army, 1969-71, LTC USAR. 1967—. Mem. Res. Officers Assn., Parental Drug Assn., Regulatory Affairs Profl. Soc., Drug Info. Assn., Delta Mu Delta. Home: 121 Sargent Rd Freehold NJ 07728-2842 Office: Roberts Pharm Corp Dept Pub Affairs Eatontown NJ 07724

KARLAN, LUANN FLORIO, medical management and research consultant; b. Bklyn., Oct. 20, 1954; d. F. Anthony and Barbara Ann (Fehlker) Florio. Student, CUNY, Bklyn., 1972-77; student, Columbia U., 1974, 75, Pace U., 1977. Cert. tchr. pvt. vocat. schs., N.Y. Rsch. assoc. animal studies dept. urology Meml. Sloan-Kettering Cancer Ctr., N.Y.C., 1977-79; dir. fin. Med. Practice Adminstrn., N.Y.C., 1979-85; clin. trials coord. pharm. industry N.Y.C., 1985-87; regional dir. Dorex, Inc., Orange, Calif., 1988—; pres., owner Venturemedicus, Inc., N.Y.C., 1987—; cons. sci. adv. Bar Ilan U., Ramat Gan, Israel and N.Y.C., 1987-90; cons. Camille and Henry Dreyfus Found., 1988-90; cons. to gen. counsel Columbia Presbyn. Med. Ctr., N.Y.C., 1988-90. Instr. Handicapped Riders, New Eng., 1987—; bd. govs. Dressage Found., 1990—. Social Sci. scholar Bklyn. Coll. Sch. Social Scis., CUNY, 1975-77. Mem. U.S. Dressage Fedn. (del. region 8 1989, editor newsletter, dist. rep. 1990—), Nat. Mus. for Women in the Arts (charter), Women's Internat. Yachting Assn. (charter), Sch. Am. Ballet (assoc.), Art Students League N.Y. Office: Venturemedicus Inc Ste 212 27 W 72th St New York NY 10023

KARLE, JEROME, research physicist; b. N.Y.C., June 18, 1918; married, 1942; 3 children. B.S., CCNY, 1937; A.M., Harvard U., 1938; M.S., U. Mich., 1942, Ph.D. in Phys. Chemistry, 1943. Rsch. assoc. Manhattan project, Chgo., 1943-44, U.S. Navy Project, Mich., 1944-46; head electron diffraction sect. Naval Rsch. Lab., Washington, 1946-58, head diffraction br., 1958-68, now head lab. for structure matter, 1968—; mem. NRC, 1954-56, 67-75, 78-87; chmn. U.S. Nat. Com. for Crystallography, 1973-75. Recipient Nobel prize in chemistry, 1985. Fellow Am. Phys. Soc.; mem. NAS (chairperson chemistry sect. 1988-91), AAAS, Am. Chem. Soc., Am. Math. Soc., Crystallograph Assn. (treas. 1950-52, pres. 1972), Internat. Union Crystallography (mem. exec. com. 1978-87, pres. 1981-84). Office: US Naval Rsch Lab Structure Matter Code 6030 Washington DC 20375

KARLSON, KARL EUGENE, surgeon; b. Worcester, Mass., July 20, 1920; s. Karl Johann and Mabel Cecelia (Fisher) K.; m. Gloria E. Anderson, June 24, 1947; children—Karl, Peter, Nancy, Steven, James, Matthew. Student, Bethel Coll., 1938-39; B.S., U. Minn., 1943, M.D., 1944, Ph.D., 1952. Diplomate: Am. Bd. Surgery. Intern U. Minn., Mpls., 1944-45; resident in surgery U. Minn., 1947-51; mem. faculty dept. surgery Downstate Med. Center SUNY, Bklyn., 1951-71; prof. surgery Downstate Med. Center SUNY, 1959-71; prof. med. sci. Brown U., Providence, 1971-90, prof. emeritus, 1990—; surgeon-in-charge thoracic and cardiovascular surgery R.I. Hosp., Providence, 1971-85; cons. in surgery Miriam Hosp., R.I. Hosp., VA Hosp.; adj. prof. biomed. engring. U. R.I. Contbr. chpts. to med. books, articles to med. jours. Served with USN, 1945-46, 54-56. NIH fellow, 1950-51. Mem. Am. Surg. Assn., Soc. Univ. Surgeons, Soc. Clin. Surgery, Am. Assn. Thoracic Surgery, A.C.S., Soc. Thoracic Surgeons, Soc. Vascular Surgery, Am. Coll. Cardiology, Internat. Cardiovascular Soc., Soc. Internat. de Chirugie. Home: 252 Bowen St Providence RI 02906-2240

KARMELIN, MICHAEL ALLEN, financial executive; b. Bronx, N.Y., Feb. 26, 1947; s. Samuel and Fannie (Levine) K.; m. Risa G. Kaplan, Apr. 2, 1966. BBA, Baruch Coll. CUNY, 1972; MBA, NYU, 1979. CPA, N.Y. Staff acct. Allied Chem. Corp., N.Y.C., 1965-69; consol. acct. Avco Corp., Greenwich, Conn., 1969-72, supr. consol. acctg., 1972-73, subs. asst. controller, 1973, mgr. consol. plans and forecasts, 1973-75, mgr. planning, 1975-78, dir. fin. planning and analysis, 1979-85, sr. dir. long-range fin. planning and auditing Avco Systems div., Wilmington, Mass., 1985, v.p., corp. staff, GRP mgr. corp. real estate Merrill Lynch & Co., N.Y.C., 1985—. Mem. The Planning Forum, Inst. Mgmt. Accts. Home: 7 Ilana Ln New City NY 10956-1014 Office: Merrill Lynch & Co World Fin Ctr South Tower New York NY 10080

KARNOW, STANLEY, journalist, writer; b. N.Y.C., Feb. 4, 1925; s. Harry and Henriette (Koeppel) K.; m. Claude Sarraute, July 15, 1948 (div. 1955); m. Annette Kline, Apr. 21, 1959; children: Curtis Edward, Catherine Anne, Michael Franklin. B.A., Harvard U., 1947; student, U. Paris, France, 1948-49; Inst. d'Etudes politiques, U. Paris, Paris, 1949-50. Corr. Time mag., Paris, 1950-57; bur. chief North Africa Time-Life, 1958-59, Hong Kong, 1959-62; spl. corr. London Observer, 1961-65, Time, Inc., 1962-63; Far East corr. Sat. Eve. Post, 1963-65; Far East corr. Washington Post, 1965-71, diplomatic corr., 1971-72; spl. corr. NBC News, 1973-75; assoc. editor The New Republic, 1973-75; columnist King Features, 1975-88, Le Point, Paris, 1976-83, Newsweek Internat., 1977-81; editor Internat. Writers Service, 1976-86; chief corr. PBS series Vietnam: A Television History, 1983; chief corr., narrator PBS Series The U.S. and the Philippines: In Our Image, 1989. Author: Southeast Asia, 1963, Mao and China: From Revolution to Revolution, 1972, Vietnam: A History, 1983 (Emmy, Dupont, Polk Peabody awards 1984), In Our Image: America's Empire in the Philippines, 1989 (Pulitzer Prize for History 1990); co-author: Asian Americans in Transition, 1992; also articles, TV scripts. Served with USAAF, 1943-46. Recipient citation Overseas Press Club, 1966, Ann. award for best newspaper interpretation of fgn. affairs, 1968, Pulitzer prize for history, 1990; fellow Inst. Politics John F. Kennedy Sch. Govt.; Neiman fellow Harvard U., 1957-58, East Asian-Research Ctr. fellow, 1970-71. Mem. Coun. Fgn. Rels., Asia Soc., Soc. Am. Historians, Signet Soc., Century Assn., PEN Am. Ctr. Club, Chek-O Club (Hong Kong). Home: 10850 Spring Knolls Dr Rockville MD 20854-1550

KAROFF, RICHARD MARTIN, stockbroker; b. Boston, Nov. 24, 1929; s. George Karoff; m. Barbara Joy Fagg, Jan. 29, 1955 (div. June 1973); children: David, Paul, John. AB in Econs., U. Mich., 1951. Stockbroker Paine Webber, Boston, 1955—. Dir. exec. com. New Eng. Hosp. DBA, Boston, 1961—; chair fin. com. Dimock Community Health Ctr. Lt. USN, 1952-55, Korea. Office: Paine Webber Inc 265 Franklin St Boston MA 02136

KAROL, JOHN JACOB, JR., producer, filmmaker; b. Mt. Kisco, N.Y., Apr. 1, 1935; s. John J. and Ann (Hale) K.; m. Georgina P. Forbes, Oct. 1963, (div. 1977); 2 children: Angelisse F., Christopher H.; m. Portia L. Fitzhugh, June 21, 1980; 1 child, Fitzhugh B. BA, Williams Coll., 1958; LLB, Yale U., 1962. Assoc. Lord, Day & Lord, N.Y.C., 1962-64; parliamentary draftsman Atty. Gens. Chambers, Zomba, Malawi, Africa, 1964-67; deputy commr., gen. counsel State of Vermont Dept. of Taxes, Montpelier, Vt., 1967-69; producer, filmmaker Apertura, Orford, N.H., 1969—. Prodns. include (film) Coolidge: A Life for Our Time, 1992, Brush Dance, 1985, Ben's Mill, 1982 (Acad. award nomination 1982, Golden Eagle award 1982), Main Street, 1979, A Place in Time, 1977 (Golden Eagle award 1977), Settling In, 1974, A Better Chance, 1969, (video) Photographing with Fred Picker, 1991, Printing With Fred Picker, 1990 (Golden Eagle award 1990), Ben's Water Tub, 1990, (multimedia) Life and Taxes, 1982, Is It Fair?, 1979, Working Places, 1975, Countdown, 1972, ...So Goes Vermont, 1971. Dir. Inherit N.H., Concord, 1984-90; trustee Upper Valley Land Trust, Norwich, Vt., 1987-90, mem. exec. bd. St. Martin's Ch., Fairlee, Vt., 1976-79, jr. warden, 1978. Mem. Soc. Motion Picture and TV Engrs., Century Assn. N.Y.C., Tavern (Boston). Home and Office: Apertura Main St Orford NH 03777

KAROL, REUBEN HIRSH, civil engineer, sculptor; b. Toms River, N.J., Aug. 25, 1922; s. Joel Benjamin and Molly K.; m. Sylvia Gross, Sept. 3, 1943; children: Diane, Leslee, Michael. B.S. in Civil Engring., Rutgers U., 1947, M.S., 1949. Lic. profl. engr., N.J. Asst. prof. civil engring. Rutgers U., New Brunswick, N.J., 1947-51, dir. Rutgers Ctr. Continung Engring. Studies, 1967-85, prof. civil engring., 1980-85; prof. emeritus Rutgers U., 1985—; cons. engr. chem. grouting, design engr. Standard Oil Devel. Co., Linden, 1951-56; dir. Engring. Chem. Research Ctr. Am. Cyanamic Co., Princeton, 1956-67; pres. Karol-Warner, Inc., mfr. sci. instruments, 1952-85. Author four coll. texts including Chemical Grouting, 2d edit., 1990; contbr. numerous articles to profl. jours.; U.S. and fgn. patentee in field; exhibited wood sculpture in 9 one-man shows, 7 group shows; commd. wood sculpture, Busch Student Ctr., outdoor concrete sculpture Civil Engring. Lab., Rutgers U.; represented in permanent collections in galleries in N.J., Pa., Fla. Served to 1st lt. Signal Corps U.S. Army, 1943-46. Mem. ASCE (chmn. grouting com. 1976-82 Robert Ridgway award), ASTM (chmn. grouting com. 1979—, Outstanding Achievement award), Am. Soc. Engring. Edn., Nat. Soc. Profl. Engrs. Home and Office: 536 Sayre Dr Princeton NJ 08540-5851

KAROW, CHARLES STANLEY, computer consultant; b. Detroit, Aug. 9, 1954; s. Stanley Eugene and Juliette (Seelye) K. BSEE magna cum laude, Vanderbilt U., 1975. Registered profl. engr., Md. Project engr. IIT Rsch. Inst., Annapolis, Md., 1976-79; electronic engr. Nat. Telecommuinications and Info. Adminstr., Dept. Commerce, Washington, 1979-87; pres. Karow Assocs., Inc., Balt., 1987—. Contbr. numerous articles to nat. and internat. jours.; author, developer numerous software applications for nat. and internat. use, 1977—. Treas. Butcher's Hill Assn., Balt., 1982, v.p., 1983. Mem. IEEE, Ind. Computer Cons. Assn. Home and Office: 2208 E Baltimore St Baltimore MD 21231-2001

KARP, ABRAHAM JOSEPH, historian, rabbi, educator; b. Indura, Poland, Apr. 5, 1921; came to U.S., 1930, naturalized, 1930; s. Aaron and Rachel (Schor) K.; m. Deborah Burstein, June 17, 1945; children:Hillel J., David J. BA magna cum laude, Yeshiva U., 1942; Rabbi, Jewish Theol. Sem. of Am., 1945, MHL, 1949, DD, 1971; DHL (hon.), Gratz Coll., 1985. Rsch. prof. Jewish Theol. Sem. Am.; rabbi Beth Shalom Synagogue, Kansas City, Mo., 1951-56; Rabbi Beth El, Rochester, N.Y., 1956-72; prof. history and religious studies U. Rochester, 1972-91, Philip S. Bernstein prof. Jewish studies, 1976-91; vis. prof. Dartmouth, 1967, Hebrew U., Jerusalem, 1970, Jewish Theol. Sem. Am., 1967-71, 75-76; corr. mem. Inst. Contemporary Jewry, Hebrew U., 1973—. Author: The Jewish Way of Life, 1962, The United Synagogue of America-A History, 1963, The Jewish Experience in America, 1971, Golden Door to America, 1976, To Give Life, 1980, The Jewish Way of Life and Thought, 1981, Hayyei Haruah shel Yahadut Amerika (Hebrew, in Israel), 1984, Haven and Home: A History of the Jews in America, 1985, From the Ends of the Earth: Judaic Treasures of the Library of Congress, 1991; editor: Conservative Judaism-The Legacy of Solomon Schechter, 1965, Beginnings-Early American Judaica, 1976, Yeshiva Mus., From the Ends of the Earth; translator: Five from the Holocaust, 1975; contbg. author: Jewish Art and Civilization, 1972; mem. editorial bd. Midstream; curator exhbn. From the Ends of the Earth: Judaic Treasures of the Library of Congress, 1991, Mordecai Manuel Noah: The First American Jew, 1987. Mem. Am. Jewish Hist. Soc. (pres., chmn. publs. com., Lee M. Friedman medal 1976), President's Historians Circle Jerusalem, Rabbinical Assembly, Assn. Jewish Studies, Conf. on Jewish Social Studies (v.p.), Phi Beta Kappa. Home: 3333 Henry Hudson Pky Apt 22E Bronx NY 10463-3227

KARP, ALLEN, motion picture company executive; b. Toronto, Ont., Can., Sept. 18, 1940; s. David and Mollie (Newman) K.; m. Sharon Silver, May 23, 1961; children: Debra Anne, Amy Lynn, Melanie Claire. LLB, U. Toronto, 1964; LLM, York U., Can., 1975. Bar: Ont. 1966. With Goodman and Carr, 1966-70, sr. ptnr., 1970-86; with Cineplex Odeon Corp., Toronto, 1986-90, pres., CFO, 1990—, also bd. dirs.; bd. dirs. Plitt Theatre, Inc., RKO Century Warner Theatres, Inc. Co-chmn. Laskin Chair Endowment, Hebrew U. of Jerusalem; dir. Toronto chpt. Weizman Inst. for Sci. Office: Cineplex Odeon Corp, 1303 Yonge St 3d Fl S, Toronto, ON Canada M4T 2Y9*

KARP, HOWARD M., physician, osteopath; b. Paterson, N.J., Jan. 11, 1941; s. Max and Bertha (Schwartz) K.; m. Linda Dreishdoon, Dec. 24, 1967; children: Bryan, Sean. BA, Rutgers U., 1961; DO, Kirksville (Mo.) Coll. Osteo. Medicine, 1969. Diplomate Am. Bd. Internal Medicine. Physician Atlantic Med. Renal Inst., Northfield, N.J., 1974—; pres. med. staff Shore Meml. Hosp., Somers Pt. N.J., 1981, chmn. dept. medicine, 1988-94.

KARP, PETER SIMON, marketing executive; b. New City, N.Y., Dec. 9, 1935; s. Joseph Bernard and Esther (Wexler) K.; m. Mona Leea Pecheux; children: Matthew Henry, Mark Andrew. BA, Hobart Coll., 1954; MFA, Columbia U., 1957. Reseacher Bur. Advt., Am. Newspaper Pubs. Assn., N.Y.C., 1954-56; media dir. Smith, Hage & Knudsen, Inc., N.Y.C., 1957-59; media and research dir. CAG Advt., Inc., N.Y.C., 1960-62; exec. v.p. Bennett-Chaiken, Inc., N.Y.C., 1963-66; pres., founder Bus. Sci. Internat., N.Y.C., 1967—; mng. dir. The Concept Testing Inst., N.Y.C., 1972—; chair, chief exec. officer Pimi. Inc., N.Y.C., 1986—; dir. Office of the Future Panel, N.Y.C., 1976—; co-dir. The Genesis Group, N.Y.C., 1983—. Co-author: Customer Satisfaction: How to Maximize, Measure and Market your Company's Ultimate Product, 1989, Competing on Value, 1991; creator BSI Tech. Value Assessments, 1989-90; editor BSI Newsletter, 1976—. Pollster Ken Keating Campaign, State of New York, 1964; vol. Grand Cen. YMCA, N.Y.C., 1964-82. Fellow Inst. Dirs. (London); mem. Am. Mktg. Assn., Advt. Research Found., Artificial Intelligence Assn., N.Y. Acad. Sci. Jewish. Club: Palisades Tennis. Home: 157 Tweed Blvd Nyack NY 10960-4900

KARPA, JAY NORMAN, surgeon; b. Feb. 6, 1935; s. Isador and Dora (Wiener) K.; m. Elizabeth Jane Karpa, Nov. 24, 1960; children: Debra Lynn, Michael David, Lisa Michelle, Jonathan Saul. BS, Johns Hopkins U., 1955; MD, U. Md., 1958. Diplomate Am. Bd. Surgery. Intern Sinai Hosp., Balt., 1958-59, resident, 1959-64; pvt. practice gen. surgery Balt., 1964—; mem. active staff gen. surgery Balt. County Gen. Hosp., Randallstown, Md., 1965—, Sinai Hosp., Balt., 1964—; chief surgery North Charles Gen. Hosp., Balt., 1983-85; cons. disability determination Social Security Adminstrn., Balt., 1980-82. Fellow ACS; mem. Balt. Acad. Surgery. Office: 1700 Reistertown Rd Ste 217 Baltimore MD 21208

KARPE, RICHARD, judge; b. N.Y.C., June 5, 1929; s. Jacob and Fay (Scher) K.; m. Linda M. Weber, Aug. 15, 1965; children: Steven M., David E., Joanne. AB, Syracuse U., 1950; MBA, NYU, 1961; JD, Columbia U., 1953. Bar: N.Y. 1953. Asst. trial counsel Waterfront Commn., N.Y.C., 1956-62; adminstrv. law judge N.Y. State Dept. Labor, N.Y.C., 1962-91, Social Security Adminstrn., N.Y.C., 1991—. Sgt. U.S. Army, 1953-55. Office: Social Security Adminstrn 26 Federal Plz New York NY 10278

KARPEL, RICHARD LESLIE, biochemistry researcher and educator; b. N.Y.C., May 31, 1944; s. Louis and Mollie (Schaffer) K.; m. Madeline Ann Blatt, June 6, 1968; 1 child, Emily Miriam. Student The Cooper Union, 1961-63; B.A., Queens Coll., 1965; Ph.D., Brandeis U., 1970. Postdoctoral fellow, research assoc. Princeton U., N.J., 1970-76; asst. prof. U. Md.-Balt. County, Catonsville, 1976-81, assoc. prof. biochemistry, 1981—. Contbr. articles to profl. jours. Mem. Howard County Sci. Adv. Com., Md., 1984. Research grantee NIH, 1977-81, 83-87, Am. Cancer Soc., 1977-79, 83-84, 88-91, Am. Heart Assn., 1979-80; sr. assoc. NRC, 1982-83. Mem. Am. Soc. for Biochemistry and Molecular Biology, Am. Chem. Soc., AAAS, Sigma Xi. Office: U Md Balt County Dept Chemistry & Biochemistry Baltimore MD 21228

KARPEN, MARIAN JOAN, financial executive; b. Detroit, June 16, 1944; d. Cass John and Mary (Jagiello) K. BA, Vassar Coll., 1966; postgrad. Sorbonne, Paris, N.Y. U. Grad. Sch. Bus., 1974-77. New Eng. corr. Women's Wear Daily, Fairchild Publs.-Capital Cities Communications, 1966-68, Paris fashion editor, TV and radio commentator Capital Cities Network, 1968-69; fashion editor Boston Herald Traveler, 1969-71; nat. syndicated newspaper columnist and photojournalist Queen Features Syndicate, N.Y.C., 1971-73; account exec. Blyth Eastman Dillon, N.Y.C., 1973-75, Oppenheimer, N.Y.C., 1975-76; v.p., mcpl. bond coordinator Faulkner Dawkins & Sullivan (merged Shearson Hayden Stone), N.Y.C., 1976-77; mgr. retail mcpl. bond dept. Warburg Paribas Becker-A.G. Becker (merger Becker Paribas into Merrill Lynch), N.Y.C., 1977-79, sr. v.p. and prin., 1977-84; sr. v.p., ltd. ptnr. Bear Stearns & Co., 1984-87, assoc. dir., 1987-90; pres., prin. The EuroEast Group, Inc., N.Y.C., 1990—; Hambrecht & Quist, 1992—; lectr. fin. seminars, 1978—; mem. bus. adv. council U.S. Rep. Senate. Founder WorkTalk, St. John the Martyr Ch., N.Y.C., 1992, creator newsletter "The WorkTalk Times"; mem. benefit com. March of Dimes, 1983; mem. Torchlight Ball com. Internat. Games for Disabled, 1984, other benefit coms.; friend vol. Whitney Mus. Am. Art. Recipient Superior Prodn. award Becker Paribas, 1983. Mem. Nat. Assn. Securities Dealers (registered rep.), N.Y. Stock Exchange (registered rep.), N.Y.C. Women's Econ. Roundtable, Am. Soc. Profl. and Exec. Women, AAUW, U.S. Figure Skating Assn., Fishing Club of Am. (angler's honor roll), English Speaking Union, Vassar Club N.Y. (bd. dirs., mem. exec. com.), Skating Club (N.Y.C. and Boston). Past editorial bd. Retirement Planning Strategist; contbr. articles and photographs to newspapers and mags. Office: EuroEast Group Inc 233 E 69th St New York NY 10021 also: Hambrecht & Quist 230 Park Ave New York NY 10169

KARPINSKI, KENNETH LEE, computer software administrator; b. Pitts., Nov. 4, 1947; s. Frank Joseph and Rita Edna (Kelly) K.; m. Suzanne E. Landry, July 4, 1987. BA in Journalism and Communications, Point Park Coll., Pitts., 1971. Master control dir. WQED TV, Pitts., 1966-67; prodn. dir. WEEP AM/FM Radio, Pitts., 1967-70; air talent WJPA AM/FM Radio, Washington, Pa., 1970-71; program dir. WDVE FM Radio, Pitts., 1971-76; prodn. dir. WMJX FM Radio, Miami, Fla., 1976-77; ops. mgr. Synatrak Film & Sound, Hollywood, Fla., 1977-78; program dir. WAXY FM Radio, Ft. Lauderdale, Fla., 1978-89, WFYR FM Radio, Chgo., 1989; project mgr. Radio Computing Svcs., Scarsdale, N.Y., 1989—; mktg. cons. WAXY-FM Radio, 1989-90. Author: (instrn. manual) Selector Version 12, 1990. Recipient Addy award Am. Advt. Fedn., 1979, 81. Home: 2901 Village Dr Brewster NY 10509 Office: Radio Computing Svcs 2 Overhill Rd Ste 100 Scarsdale NY 10583

KARPINSKI, RICHARD HENRY STEPHEN, plastic surgeon; b. N.C., Dec. 7, 1945; s. Henry Stephen and Beatrice Dolores (Luczycki) K.; m. Kristina Nordling, Nov. 3, 1973; 1 child, Stefan Gottfrid. BS in Biology with honors, St. Joseph's U., 1967; MD, Harvard Med. Sch., 1971. Diplomate Am. Bd. Surgery, Am. Bd. Plastic Surgery. Intern in surgery Boston City Hosp., 1971-72, resident in surgery, 1972-73; resident in surgery New Eng. Deaconess Hosp., 1973-77; resident in reconstructive plastic surgery NYU Med. Ctr., 1979-81; teaching fellow in anatomy Harvard U., 1974; tutor in surgery U. Aberdeen (Scotland), 1974; instr. in anatomy Harvard U., 1976; clin. fellow in surgery Harvard U., 1976; clin. instr. in surgery Creighton U., 1977; clin. instr. in plastic surgery NYU, 1979; instr. in plastic surgery Columbia P&S, 1981; mem. credentials com. St. Luke's/Roosevelt Hosp., 1990—, ambulatory surgery com., 1988—, infection control com., 1988-89. Presenter in field of plastic surgery, 1978—. Trustee Med. Liability Mutual Ins. Co., N.Y.C., 1992. Maj. USAF, 1977-79. Fellow Am. Coll. Surgeons; mem. Am. Soc. Plastic and Reconstructive Surgeons, N.Y. County Med. Soc. (workers' compensation com. 1983—), Med. Soc. N.Y. Office: 38 E 72d St New York NY 10021

KARSEN, SONJA PETRA, Spanish educator emeritus; b. Berlin, Apr. 11, 1919; came to U.S., 1938, naturalized, 1945; d. Fritz and Erna (Heidermann) K. Titulo de Bachiller, 1937; B.A., Carleton Coll., 1939; M.A. (scholar in French), Bryn Mawr Coll., 1941; Ph.D., Columbia U., 1950. Instr. Spanish Lake Erie Coll., Painesville, Ohio, 1943-45; instr. modern langs. U. P.R., 1945-46; instr. Spanish Syracuse U., 1947-50, Bklyn. Coll., 1950-51; asst. to dep. dir. gen. UNESCO, 1951-52, Latin Am. Desk, tech. assistance dept., 1952-53, mem. tech. assistance mission Costa Rica, 1954; asst. prof. Spanish Sweet Briar Coll., Va., 1955-57; assoc. prof., chmn. dept. Romance langs. Skidmore Coll., Saratoga Springs, N.Y., 1957-61, chmn. dept. modern langs. and lits., 1961-79, prof. Spanish, 1961-87, prof. emerita, 1987; cons. Hudson-Mohawk Assn. Colls. and Univs., 1990; Faculty rsch. lectr. Skidmore Coll., 1963; Fulbright lectr. Free U., Berlin, 1968; mem. adv. and nominating com. Books Abroad, 1965-67. Author: Guillermo Valencia, Colombian Poet, 1951, Educational Development in Costa Rica with UNESCO's Technical Assistance, 1951-54, Jaime Torres Bodet: A Poet in a Changing World, 1963, Selected Poems of Jaime Torres Bodet, 1964, Versos y prosas de Jaime Torres Bodet, 1966, Jaime Torres Bodet, 1971, Ensayos de Literatura E Historia Iberoamericana/Essays on Iberoamerican Literature and History, 1988, Papers on Foreign Languages, Literature and Culture, 1982-87, 88; translator: The Role of the Americas in History (Leopoldo Zea), 1991; editor Lang. Assn. Bull., 1980-83; mem. editorial adv. bd. Modern Lang. Studies; contbr. articles to profl. jours. Decorated chevalier dans l'Ordre des Palmes Academiques, 1964; recipient Leadership award N.Y. State Assn. Fgn. Lang. Tchrs., 1973, 76, 78, Nat. Disting. Leadership award, 1979, Disting. Service award, 1983, 86, Capital Dist. Fgn. Language Disting. Service award, 1987; recipient Spanish Heritage award, 1981, Alumni Achievement award Carleton Coll., 1982; exchange student auspices Inst. Internat. Ednl. at Carleton Coll., 1938-39; Buenos Aires Conv. grantee for research in Colombia, 1946-47; faculty research grantee Skidmore Coll., summer 1959, 61, 63, 64, 67, 69, 70, 73, ad hoc faculty grantee, 71, 78, 85. Mem. Am. Assn. Tchrs. Spanish and Portuguese, Nat. Assn. Self-Instructional Lang. Programs (v.p. 1981-82,pres. 1982-83), AAUW, AAUP, MLA (del. assembly 1976-78, Mildenberger medal selection com 1984-86), El Ateneo Doctor Jaime Torres Bodet (founding mem.), Nat. Geog. Soc., Instituto Internacional de Literatura Iberoamericana, Asociacion Internacional de Hispanistas, UN Assn. U.S.A., Am. Soc. French Acad. Palms, Fulbright Alumni, Phi Sigma Iota, Sigma Delta Pi. Home: 1755 York Ave Apt 37A New York NY 10128-6808

KASAKOVE, SUSAN, interior designer; b. Newark, N.J., Nov. 11, 1938. BFA, U. Buffalo, 1958, Hunter Coll., 1960; postgrad., N.Y. Sch. of Interior Design, 1960-64, New Sch. for Social Rsch., 1967-68, Pratt Inst., 1968-69. Asst. interior designer Rodgers Assocs., N.Y.C., 1964-66; interior designer Walter Dorwin Teague Assocs., N.Y.C., 1966-70; sr. interior designer N.Y. State Facilities Devel. Corp., N.Y.C., 1970—. Interior designs include projects for Eli Lilly & Co., Bank of Bermuda, Quaker Oats Corp., N.Y. State Office of Mental Health, N.Y. State Office of Mental Retardation, Cattaraugus County, Warren County. Reading tutor Vols. for Children's Svcs., N.Y.C., 1976-82; chair Friends of White Plains (N.Y.) Symphony, 1981-83; vol. dept. Asian Studies Met. Mus. Art, N.Y.C., 1988—, vol. guide edn. dept., 1978—; Rep. treas. 11th Ward, Yonkers, N.Y., 1979-81. Recipient Outstanding Svc. to Sch. award Rockland County (N.Y.) Lions Club, 1955. Home: 793 Palmer Rd Apt 3F Bronxville NY 10708-3305 Office: NY State Facilities Devel Corp 909 3d Ave New York NY 10022

KASCH, RICK DARREL, hotel chain executive; b. Norfolk, Nebr., May 23, 1950; s. Albert Darrel and Phyllis Lorraine (Pederson) K.; m. Mary Elizabeth, May 20, 1972 (Aug. 1980); 1 child, Abigail; m. Colleen Bannon, Apr. 5, 1986; children: Caitlin, Patrick. BS in Acctg., U. S.D., 1972. Sr. acct. Arthur Andersen and Co., Kansas City, Mo., 1972-77; ptnr. JW Meara and Co., Kansas City, 1977-79; chief fin. officer Integra Corp., Dallas, 1979-84, Johnson Enterprises, Oklahoma City, 1984-85; pres. Pk. Ste. Corp., Dallas, 1985-87; v.p. ITT Sheraton Corp., Boston, 1987—. Mem. AICPA. Office: Sheraton Corp 60 State St Boston MA 02109-1803

KASDON, SOLOMON CHARLES, physician, educator; b. N.Y.C., Dec. 19, 1912; s. David and Sarah (Mirkikn) K.; m. Muriel E. Cohen, Dec. 26, 1943; children: Madeline A., Louisa B. Kasdon Ellias. BS, Yale U., 1933, MS, 1934, MD, 1938. Diplomate Am. Bd. Ob-Gyn. Intern Yale -New Haven Hosp., 1938-39, D.C. Gen. Hosp., Washington, 1939; asst. resident U. Chgo. Clinics, 1941-42; chief resident Henrotin Hosp., Chgo., 1942-43; resident Carney Hosp., Boston, 1944; from instr. to prof. medicine Tufts U., Boston, 1943-85, prof. emeritus, 1985—; instr. Boston U., 1950-56, Harvard U., Boston, 1951-85; pres. Med. Rsch. Found. Boston, Inc., 1951—, chief of staff Booth Meml. Hosp., Brookline, Mass., 1953-63; chief ob-gyn. Waltham (Mass.) Hosp., 1956-60. Author: Atlas of Insitu Cancer of the Cervix, Diagnosis and Treatment of Insitu Cancer of Cervix; (with others) Ovarian Hormones, Cytology; contbr. 76 articles to profl. jours. on enzymes, cytology. Pres. Boston Investment Assocs., 1958-60. Lt. comdr. USNR, 1943-47. Fellow ACS, Am. Coll. Ob-Gyn.; mem. St. Botolph Club, Yale Club Boston, Harvard Club Boston, Cohasset Yacht Club. Home: 88 Beach St Cohasset MA 02025-1422

KASINDORF, BLANCHE ROBINS, educational administrator; b. N.Y.C., May 18, 1925; d. Samuel David and Anna (Block) Robins; B.A., Hunter Coll., 1944; M.A., N.Y.U., 1948; postgrad. Cornell U., 1946-50; m. David Kasindorf, July 1, 1960. Tchr. pub. schs., Bklyn., 1945-56; instr. Bklyn. Coll., 1956-57; asst. in research for Puerto Rican Study Ford Found. and N.Y.C. Bd. Edn., 1956-57; asst. prin. N.Y.C. Pub. Schs., 1957-59; research assoc. ednl. program rsch. and stats. N.Y.C. Bd. Edn., 1959-63, coordinator spl. edn. liaison div. child welfare for Bur. Curriculum Research, 1963-64; jr. prin., integration coordinator Bklyn. Sch. Dist. 44, 1964-65; prin. Pub. Sch. 7-8, Bklyn., 1965-87; cons. to numerous social agys. Mem. NEA, Council

Exceptional Children, N.Y.C. Elementary Sch. Prins., Council Supervisory Assns. Contbr. to profl. publs.; also editor instructional materials. Home: 1655 Flatbush Ave Brooklyn NY 11210-3276

KASKY, RITA, fund raising executive; b. N.Y.C., July 10, 1940; d. Richard and Alice (Kirschner) K. BA, U. Conn., 1962. Advt. sales rep. Am. Baby mag., N.Y.C., 1968-71; field rep. United Jewish Appeal, N.Y.C., 1972-74; dir. nat. fund raising Nat. Coun. Jewish Women, N.Y.C., 1974-78; exec. dir. Asthma and Allergy Found. Am., N.Y.C., 1978-82; dir. chpts. div. Cancer Care, Inc., N.Y.C., 1982-86; dir. devel. and pub. rels. Am. Diabetes Assn., N.Y.C., 1987-89; assoc. dir. Brandeis U., N.Y.C., 1989—. Mem. Women in Fin. Devel., Nat. Soc. Fund Raising Execs., Exec. Women in Human Svcs. Home: 788 Columbus Ave New York NY 10025-5951

KASLOW, RICHARD ALAN, epidemiologist; b. Omaha, Mar. 1, 1943; s. Benjamin E. and Sophia (Handler) K.; m. Leanne Penelope Davidson, July 18, 1970; children: Jessica, Daniel. BA, Yale U., 1965; MD, Harvard U., 1969, MPH, 1976. Intern, then resident Mt. Sinai Hosp., N.Y.C., 1969-71; med. epidemiologist Ctrs. for Disease Control, Atlanta, 1971-73, chief arthritis, 1976-79; resident U. Calif., San Francisco, 1973-74; fellow in infectious diseases Children's-Beth Israel Hosp., Boston, 1974-76; chief epidemiology and biometry sect. Inst. Allergy & Infectious Diseases, NIH, Bethesda, Md., 1979-88, chief epidemiology and biometry br., 1988—; adj. prof. health-care scis. Geroge Washington U., Washington, 1988—; adj. prof. preventive medicine/biometrics USUSH, Bethesda, 1988—. Editor: Epidemiology of AIDS, 1989; contbr. articles to profl. jours. Reader Washington Ear, Silver Spring, Md., 1990—; mem. troop com. Boy Scouts Am., Chevy Chase, Md., 1989-90; active various civic orgns. Capt. USPHS, 1971—. Fellow ACP, Infectious Diseases Soc. Am., Am. Coll. Epidemiology; mem. Am. Epidemiologic Soc., Soc. for Epidemiologic Rsch., others. Office: Nat Inst Allergy Infectious Diseases NIH Solar 3A24 Bethesda MD 20892

KASLUSKY, ANNE, chemical engineer; b. Birmingham, U.K., Dec. 13, 1948; came to U.S., 1963, naturalized, 1969; d. Richard and June (Catcheside) Smith; m. David Holt, 1970 (div. 1982); children: Jennifer Anne, Stephen Richard; m. Stan Kaslusky, July 23, 1989. BSChemE, Newark Coll. Engring., 1973; MSChemE, Imperial Coll. Sci. and Tech., London, 1977; MBA, Fairleigh Dickinson U., 1987. Instr. Newark Coll. of Engring., 1977-79; staff product specialist Hoechst Celanese Corp., Summit, N.J., 1979—. Contbr. articles to profl. jours.; patentee in field. Asst. treas. 1st Bapt. Ch., Westfield, N.J. Mem. Soc. Plastics Engring., Am. Inst. Chem. Engrs. (com. mem.), Tau Beta Pi, Omega Chi Epsilon, Omicron Delta Kappa. Democrat. Am. Baptist. Home: 151 Effingham Pl Westfield NJ 07090-3925 Office: Hoechst Celanese Corp 86 Morris Ave Summit NJ 07901-3900

KASNOWSKI, CHESTER NELSON, artist, educator; b. Perth Amboy, N.J., Jan. 23, 1944. BFA, Dayton Art Inst., 1971; MFA, Tulane U., 1973. Curator New Orleans Mus. Art, 1971-74; tchr. So. Vt. Art Ctr., Manchester, 1981—. One man show includes Bertha Undang Gallery, N.Y.C., 1984, 85, 87, 91; group exhbitions at Dartmouth Coll., 1978, Robert Hall Fleming Mus., 1981, Franklin Furnace, 1982, 84, Bertha Undang Galley, 1983, Hand Gallery, 1985; permanent collections Bklyn. Mus., Franklin Furnace, Solomon R. Guggenheim Mus., stedelijk Mus., Tate Gallery, Whitney Mus. of Am. Art. Grantee Nat. Endowment Arts, 1974, 78. Mem. Coll. Art Assn. Home and Studio: PO Box 1 Weston VT 05161

KASPAR, ANNE PAMELA, investment adviser; b. N.Y.C., Mar. 26, 1960; d. Henry F. and Caroline (Schuster) K. BA, Wells Coll., 1982. Asst. acct. exec. Alden Pub. Rels., N.Y.C., 1982-84; acct. exec. Hill, Knowlton, Inc., N.Y.C., 1984-86; sr. v.p. Lehman Bros., Inc., N.Y.C., 1986-88; corp. mktg. assoc. Oppenheimer & Co., Inc., N.Y.C., 1988-89; v.p. investments Bear, Stearns, Co., N.Y.C., 1989-90; investment advisor, v.p. First Albany Corp., N.Y.C., 1990—. Mem. Nat. Rep. Com., N.Y.C., 1989-91. Mem. Met. Mus. Art. Home: 118 E 91st St Apt 5B New York NY 10128-1689 Office: First Albany Corp 71 Broadway New York NY 10006-2601

KASPER, HORST MANFRED, lawyer; b. Dusseldorf, Germany, June 3, 1939; s. Rudolf Ferdinand and Lilli Helene (Krieger) K.; 1 child, Olaf Jan. Diplom-Chemiker, U. Bonn., 1963, Dr. rer. nat., 1965; J.D., Seton Hall U., 1978. Bar admittee: N.J. 1978, U.S. Patent Office, 1977. Mem. staff Lincoln Lab., M.I.T., Lexington, 1967-69; mem. tech. staff Bell Telephone Labs., Murray Hill, N.J., 1970-76; asso. Kirschstein, Kirschstein, Ottinger & Frank, N.Y.C., 1976-77; patent atty. Allied Chem. Corp., Morristown, N.J., 1977-79; sole practice, Warren, N.J., 1980-83; with Kasper and Weick, Warren, 1983-85, Kasper and Laughlin, 1985—. Mem. ABA, N.J. Bar Assn., Internat. Patent and Trademark Assn., Am. Patent Law Assn., N.J. Patent Law Assn., Am. Chem. Soc., Electrochem. Soc., Am. Phys. Soc., AAAS, N.Y. Acad. Scis. Contbr. numerous articles to profl. jours.; patentee semicondr. field.

KASPIN, JEFFREY MARC, floor covering professional; b. Bklyn., May 30, 1948; s. Seymour and Frances (Babad) K.; m. Susan Jane Engel, Apr. 17, 1977; children: Jodi-Anne, Stacey, Melanie. BA, Am. U., 1970. Cert. tchr., Va.; cert. archtl. carpet rep.; cert. tech. carpet rep. Tchr. Fairfax (Va.) Sch. System, 1970-72; exec. v.p. sales and mktg. Atlantic Distbrs., S.I., 1972-88; sales and ter. mgr. Norman D. Lifton Co., Mt. Vernon, N.Y., 1988-89; mgr. customer svc. Norman D. Lifton Co., Yonkers, N.Y., 1990—; gen. mgr. Western Carpet Distbrs., Bklyn., 1989-90; sales and ter. mgr. Columbus (Ga.) Carpet Mills, 1990; floor convering cons. to architects, contractors, builders, retailers, publs.; floor covering profl. speaker, 1984-90. Vol. Spl. Olympics, Washington, 1968-69; bd. dirs. Country Swim Club, East Brunswick, N.J., 1982—; fundraising chmn. Am. Cancer Soc., Middlesex County, N.J., 1984-86; trustee Temple B'nai Shalom, East Brunswick, 1986-89; v.p. U.S. Jaycees, 1978-85. Mem. L.I. Carpet Club, Nat. Assn. Floor Covering Distbrs., N.J. Carpet Club. Office: Norman D Lifton Co Inc 15 Wells Ave Yonkers NY 10701-2753

KASPRENSKI, MATTHEW ANTHONY, physician; b. Elizabeth, N.J., Feb. 17, 1932; s. Matthew Joseph and Josephine Elizabeth (Murzinski) K.; m. Rosemarie Damweber, Jan. 7, 1956; children: Matthew L., Maria L., Lisa A., Michael D., Kara J., Krista S. BA, St. Vincent Coll., Latrobe, Pa., 1953; MD, Hahnemann U., Phila., 1957. Diplomate Am. Bd. Family Practice. Intern Sacred Heart Hosp., Allentown, Pa., 1957-58; pvt. practice family medicine Whitehall, Pa., 1960-91; med. dir. employee health Lehigh Valley Health Network, Allentown, 1991—. Capt., U.S. Army, 1958-59, Germany. Mem. AMA, Am. Acad. Family Practice, Pa. Med. Soc., Lehigh County Med. Soc. Office: Lehigh Valley Hosp PO Box 689 1200 S Cedar Crest Blvd Allentown PA 18105-1556

KASPRZAK, KENNETH EUGENE, environmentalist; b. Buffalo, N.Y., Feb. 6, 1953; s. Eugene Jerome and Rose Pauline Kasprzak; m. Roseann Marie Yannotti, Jan. 19, 1980; children: Karl Eugene, Nicholas Thomas, Madaleine Rose. BA, U. Buffalo, 1975. Environ. pollution analyst Starks Assocs., Inc., Buffalo, 1974-77; environ. lab./waste water plant supr. Evans Chemetics/Div. of WR Grace, Waterloo, N.Y., 1978-80; environ. compliance safety analyst Spaulding Fibre Co., Inc., Tonawanda, N.Y., 1980-86; coord. indsl. health svcs. Great Lakes Carbon Corp., Niagara Falls, N.Y., 1986; dir. environ. health and safety SUNY, Geneseo, 1986—. Asst. coach Town of Clarence (N.Y.) Baseball Assn., 1987-92, umpire, 1990-92. Mem. Nat. Fire Protection Assn., Am. Soc. Safety Engrs., Inst. Hazardous Materials Mgmt., SUNY Environ. Safety and Health Assn. Office: SUNY Coll at Geneseo Geneseo NY 14454-1457

KASS, R. ROBERT, jewelry business executive; b. Chgo., Mar. 28, 1925; s. Joseph J. and Betty (Rose) K.; m. Geraldine Natalie Rothberg, Oct. 19, 1947; children: Stephanie, Leslie, Laura. BA, Washington Sq. Coll., 1947. Sales rep. David Grad Co., N.Y.C., 1947-48; exec. Paramount Corp., N.Y.C., 1948-67; registered rep. Francis I. DuPont & Co., N.Y.C., 1967-70; exec. v.p. Ronnie Jewelry Inc., Pawtucket, R.I., 1970-71; pres., chief exec. officer KassCo, Inc., Barrington, R.I., 1971—. Committeeman Rep. Town Com., Barrington, 1973-74. With USMCR, 1943-45; PTO. Mem. Mfg. Jewelers Sales Assn. Am. (dir. 1982-87), Internat. Jewelry Trade Assn. Am. (chmn. 1989), Mfg. Jewelers & Silversmiths of Am. (legis. committeeman 1986-89), Fashion Jewelry Assn. Am., Costume Jewelry Salesmen's Assn., providence Jewelers Club, Masons, Shriner. Home and Office: KassCo Inc 21 New Meadow Rd Barrington RI 02806-3721

KASS, WILLIAM ALAN, lawyer; b. Bklyn., May 6, 1932; s. Joseph B. and Sarah Kass; m. Joanne S. Schenker, Mar. 27, 1957; children: Thomas, Deborah. AB, Dartmouth Coll., 1954; LLB, Yale U., 1959; postgrad., N.Y.U. Bar: N.Y. 1960, Fla. 1978, U.S. Dist. Ct. (so. dist.) N.Y., U.S. Ct. Appeals (2d cir.). Assoc. Olwine, Connelly, Chase, O'Donnell & Weyher, N.Y.C., 1959-63; ptnr. Kass, Goodkind, Wechsler, Labaton, N.Y.C., 1963-84, Kantor, Davidoff, Wolfe, Rabbino & Kass, N.Y.C., 1984—; lectr. Am. Mgmt. Assn., Conn., N.Y. Editor, Yale Law Jour., 1958-59. Mem. Tournament Com. Met. Golf Assn., N.Y.C., 1980—; dir. Juvenile Diabetes Found. Lt. (j.g.) USNR, 1954-56. Recipient Roote Tilden Law Scholarship, Chgo. U. Nat. Law Scholarship. Mem. Sunningdale Country Club, Phi Beta Kappa. Home: 1120 Park Ave New York NY 10128 Office: Kantor Davidoff et al 51 E 42nd St New York NY 10017

KASSAPOGLOU, CHRISTOS, aeronautical engineer; b. Athens, Nov. 27, 1959; came to U.S., 1978; s. George and Dia (Alexis) K. BS, MIT, 1982, MS in Aeros. and Astronautics, MSME, 1984. Stress analyst Beech Aircraft Corp., Wichita, Kans., 1984-87; structures researcher Sikorsky Aircraft, Stratford, Conn., 1987—; seminar speaker on cert. of civil composite aircraft in Milan (Italy), Toronto, and Ottawa (Can.), Advance Tech. Svcs. Internat., Wichita, 1987—. Recipient Salisbury Webb award MIT, 1982, R. DuPont fellow, 1983. Mem. AIAA, Am. Helicopter Soc. Office: Sikorsky Aircraft MS S314A2 6900 Main St Stratford CT 06497-1361

KASSEBAUM, JOHN PHILIP, lawyer; b. Kansas City, Mo., Oct. 24, 1932; s. Leonard Charles and Helen Nancy (Horn) K.; m. Nancy Josephine Landon, June 8, 1955; children: John Philip, Richard L., William A., Linda J. Johnson m. Llewellyn Hood Sinkler, Aug. 4, 1979; stepchildren: G. Dana, J. Marshall, Huger II., Llewellyn H. Sinkler. AB, U. Kans., 1953; JD, U. Mich., 1956. Bar: Kans. 1956, N.Y. 1979, U.S. Ct. Appeals (2d, 4th, 10th, D.C. cirs.), U.S. Tax Ct., 1976, U.S. Supreme Ct., 1971. Ptnr. Kassebaum & Johnson, N.Y.C. and Wichita, 1970—; spl. asst. atty. gen. Kans., 1970. Chmn. Gov.'s Adv. Commn. Kans. Instl. Mgmt., 1961-69; chmn. bd. dirs. Skowhegan (Maine) Sch. Painting and Sculpture; bd. dirs., pres. Carolina Art Assn. and Gibbes Art Gallery, Charleston, S.C.; pres. Spoleto Festival U.S.A., Charleston; treas. Am. Arts Alliance, Washington; curator of ceramics Spencer Mus. Art, U. Kans., 1960—; bd. dirs. Nat. Inst. for Music Theater. Mem. ABA, Assn. of Bar of City of N.Y., Assn. Trial Lawyers Am., Kans. Trial Lawyers Assn., Kans. Assn. Def. Counsel, Fedn. Ins. Counsel, Yeaman Hall Club (pres. Charleston). Republican. Episcopalian. Author: Kassebaum Collection, Vol. I, 1981. Home: 59 Meeting St Charleston SC 29401-2508 Office: 575 Madison Ave New York NY 10022-2511 also: 125 N Market St Wichita KS 67202

KASSEES, JOANNE MASSAD, counselor, program director; b. Wilmington, Del., Mar. 28, 1951; d. Massad Jacob and Nijmeh K. B Arts and Scis., U. Del., 1973; MS in Edn. Counseling, Youngstown State U., 1978. Nat. bd. cert. counselor, cert. family life educator. Pvt. practice counselor Wilmington, 1979-83; program dir. Delawareans United to Prevent Child Abuse, Wilmington, 1982—; cons. proposal review Nat. Ctr. on Child Abuse and Neglect, Washington, 1985—; with Office of Juvenile Justice and Delinquency Prevention, 1991—. Author: (with others) All In My Family, 1985, Educators' Guide to Child Abuse Prevention, 1986; developer: (program) Adolescent Sexual Abuse Prevention Project, 1985. Bd. dirs. ch. newspaper Communion, Wilmington, 1980-86; vestry mem. Trinity Episcopal Parish, Wilmington, 1989-91. Recipient Commrs. award U.S. Dept. Health and Human Svcs., Chgo., 1985, Annual award Del. Coun. on Crime and Justice, Wilmington, 1990, Cert. of Appreciation, U.S. Dept. Justice, Washington, 1991; named Outstanding Young Individual, Wilmington (Del.) Jaycees, 1986. Mem. AACD, Internat. Soc. for Prevention of Child Abuse and Neglect, Assn. for Religious and Value Issues in Counseling, Assn. for Specialists in Group Work, Nat. Coun. on Family Relations, Christian Assn. for Psychol. Studies. Office: Delawareans United Prevent Child Abuse 124 Cedar Dr Wilmington DE 19804-2242

KASSINGER, THEODORE WILLIAM, lawyer; b. Atlanta, Jan. 26, 1953; s. Edward Theodore and Sarah Mell (Laurent) K.; m. Ruth Lynn Good, Oct. 13, 1984; children: Anna Laurent, Austen Elizabeth. BLA, U. Ga., 1975, JD, 1978. Bar: Ga. 1978, D.C. 1986. Atty.-advisor U.S. Internat. Trade Commn., Washington, 1978-80; atty., advisor U.S. Dept. State, Washington, 1980-81; internat. trade counsel com. on fin. U.S. Senate, Washington, 1981-85; ptnr. Vinson & Elkins, Washington, 1990—. Co-author: U.S. Regulation of International Trade, 1987, Basic Documents in International Economic Law, 1989. Mem. ABA, Coun. Fgn. Rels., Am. Soc. Internat. Law (group chair 1985-87). Republican. Roman Catholic. Office: Vinson & Elkins 1455 Pennsylvania Ave NW Washington DC 20004-1008

KASSOF, ALLEN H., foundation administrator; b. N.Y.C., Dec. 17, 1930; s. Morris and Sophia B. Kassof; m. Arianne Scholz, 1953; children: Andrea, Arlen, Anita. BA, Rutgers U., 1952; AM, Harvard U., 1954, PhD, 1960. Asst. prof. Smith Coll., Northampton, Mass., 1957-60; asst. prof. Princeton (N.J.) U., 1961-65, assoc. prof., asst. dean coll., 1965-68; exec. dir. Internat. Rsch. and Exchs. Bd., N.Y.C. and Princeton, 1968-92; dir. N.Y. Project on Ethnic Rels. in Eastern Europe, Carnegie Corp. N.Y., Princeton, 1991—; cons. conf. security and cooperation, Europe, Hamburg, Germany, Budapest, Hungary, 1980, 85; mem. pres. com. fgn. lang., Wash., 1978-79; mem. U.S. task force, Romania, Bucharest, 1990—. Mem. Am. Assn. Advancement Slavic Studies, Coun. Fgn. Rels. Home: 949 Mercer Rd Princeton NJ 08540-4823 Office: Project on Ethnic Rels One Palmer Sq Princeton NJ 08542-3718

KASSOFF, HAL, state highway administrator; b. N.Y.C., June 13, 1943; s. Stanley and Vera (Jaffe) K.; m. Lori E. Dolinko, June 26, 1965; children: Debra, Jason. BSCE, City U. of N.Y., 1965; MS in Transp., Northwestern U., Chgo., 1966. Hwy. engr. and project mgr. Fed. Hwy. Adminstrn., Washington, 1966-72; project mgr. Md. Dept. Transp., College Park, 1972-73; regional mgr. Md. Dept. Transp., Silver Spring, 1973-78; dir. office of planning and preliminary engring. Md. State Hwy. Adminstrn., Balt., 1978-84, administr., 1984—. Recipient Charles Mathias award for Outstanding Pub. Adminstrn. Am. Soc. for Pub. Adminstrn., 1987, Community Transp. award Inst. of Traffic Engrs., Washington, 1987, Spl. Commendation award U.S. Dept. Transp., 1988, Engr. of Yr. award NSPE (Balt. chpt.) 1987. Mem. ASCE, Am. Assn. State Hwy. and Transp. Ofcls. Inst. Transp. Engrs. Office: MD State Hwy Adminstrn 707 N Calvert St Baltimore MD 21202

KASTEN, WILLIAM ARTHUR, coast guard officer; b. Wausau, Wis., Sept. 24, 1956; s. William Jud and Willowene Dot (Atkeson) K. BS in Polit. Sci., U. Wis., 1979. Legis. asst. State Senator's Office, Madison, Wis., 1979-82; state rep. Wis. Legislature, Madison, 1983-87; pres. From Wisconsin With Love, Inc., Mosinee, 1987-88; chief of staff State Senator's Office, Madison, 1988-89; asst. historian U.S. Coast Guard/Exxon Valdez Oilspill, Anchorage, 1989-90; congl. projects coordination officer planning staff USCG Hdqrs., Washington, 1990-92; asst. ops. officer USCGC SWEETGUM (WLB 309), Mobile, Ala., 1992—. Mem. resolutions com. Wis. Rep. Party, 1983-85, chmn. rules com., 1984. With USN, 1974-76. Recipient Achievement medal USCG, 1990, 92. Mem. U.S. Naval Acad. Alumni Assn., U.S. Naval Inst. Home: # 28-900 Downtowner Blvd Mobile AL 36609 Office: USCGC SWEETGUM (WLB 309) USCG Base S Broad St Mobile AL 36615

KASTENHOLZ, JAMES PETER, management consultant; b. Yorkers, N.Y., Sept. 30, 1963; s. Joseph Bernard and Louise Elaine (Rau) K. Cert., London Sch. of Econs., Eng., 1984; BS, U. Colo., 1985; MBA, Duke U., 1990. Comml. underwriter Crum & Forster Comml. Ins., N.Y.C., 1986-88; mgmt. cons. Coopers & Lybrand, N.Y.C., 1990—. Mem. Inst. Mgmt. Cons. Democrat. Home: 126 W 11th St #64 New York NY 10011 Office: Coopers and Lybrand 1301 Ave of the Americas New York NY 10019

KASTER, LEWIS ROSS, lawyer, writer; b. N.Y.C., Apr. 14, 1932; s. Benjamin Charles and Lillian (Sherman) K.; m. Carol Goodz, Sept. 1, 1966; children; Stephanie Blair, Rachel Lauren. BS magna cum laude, Syracuse U., 1951; LLB, Columbia U., 1954. Bar: N.Y. 1954, U.S. Ct. Mil. Appeals 1955, U.S. Tax Ct., U.S. Ct. Appeals (2d cir.) 1975. Faculty asst. to dean Columbia Law Sch., N.Y.C., 1952-54, 58, lectr.-in-law, 1982-89, 92—; law assoc. Roberts & Holland, N.Y.C., 1958-66; ptnr. Robinson Silverman Pearce Aronsohn & Berman, N.Y.C., 1966-74, Trubin Sillcocks Edelman & Knapp, N.Y.C., 1974-81; mng. ptnr. Carro Spanbock Kaster & Cuiffo, N.Y.C., 1981-90, counsel, 1990—; lectr.-in-law Am. Law Inst./Am. Bar Inst., Phila., Practicing Law Inst., N.Y.C. Editor: jour. of taxation; contbr. articles to real estate jours. Dir. Forest Hills (N.Y.) Gardens Corp., 1974. Capt. JAGC, U.S. Army, 1955-58. Harlan Fiske Stone scholar 1952-54, James Kent scholar 1954. Mem. ABA (tax sect., real estate tax problems com. chmn. 1973-75, spl. advisor 1975-76), N.Y. State Bar Assn. (mem. exec. com. 1977-78), Assn. of Bar of City of N.Y., Am. Coll. Real Estate Lawyers (chair partnership com., 1988-91, mem. planning com. 1990, gov. 1991-94), Beta Sigma Gamma, Beta Alpha Psi. Jewish. Office: Carro Spanbock Kaster & Cuiffo 1345 Avenue of Americas New York NY 10105-0099

KASZUBOWSKI, MARTIN JOHN, aerospace engineer; b. Walled Lake, Mich., May 5, 1960; s. Raymond August Kaszubowski and Monica Genevieve Sutter; m. Natalie Ann Brothers, May 13, 1988. BS in Aerospace Engring., U. Mich., 1982. Assoc. engr. Gen. Dynamics, Troy, Mich., 1983-84; software engr. McDonnell Douglas, Houston, 1984-86; project engr. PRC, Inc., Hampton, Va., 1986-89; group engr. CTA, Inc., Newport News, 1989-91; sr. program officer Nat. Rsch. Coun., Washington, 1991—. Contbr. articles to profl. jours. Mem. AIAA, Am. Astron. Soc. Office: Nat Rsch Coun 2101 Constitution Ave NW Washington DC 20418

KATCHER, PHILIP MARTIN, insurance consultant; b. Bklyn., Dec. 20, 1944; s. Arnold B. and Shirley Y. (Haber) K.; m. Karyn S. Nathanson, Oct. 19, 1968; children: Tamra Dawn, Todd Bryan. Pres. Northcliffe Agy., Inc., Cleve., 1977-81; regional v.p. Beneficial Ins. Group, Peapack, N.J., 1981-85; pres. Northcliffe Agy., Inc., Long Valley, N.J., 1985—. Office: The Northcliffe Agy Inc PO Box 412 Long Valley NJ 07853-0412

KATES, SUSAN PRENTKY, industrial consultant; b. Providence; d. Joseph and Henrietta Prentky; m. Steven Michael Kates, Nov. 4, 1970; children: Jacqueline, Daniel. BA, Russell Sage Coll., 1965; MA, Columbia U., 1968, Seton Hall U., 1972. Dir. pers. Poly. Inst. of Bklyn., 1968-70; counseling psychologist B'nai B'rith Career and Counseling Svcs., Union, N.J., 1970-84; exec. recruiter S.K. Assocs., Union, 1978—; indsl. cons. Career Cons., Inc., Union, 1976—. Mem. Am. Psychol. Assn., N.J. Assn. Sch. Psychologist, Am. Pers. and Guidance Assn. Home: 77 Nottingham Rd Fair Lawn NJ 07410-3614 Office: Career Cons 1767 Morris Ave Union NJ 07083-3511

KATHE, BARBARA ANN, college dean, English and American literature educator; b. Norwich, Conn., Feb. 7, 1931; d. Arthur Paul and Adelaide Ann (Cyr) K. BA, St. Joseph Coll., West Hartford, Conn., 1964, MA, 1967; PhD, Drew U., 1979. Asst. prof. English St. Joseph Coll., 1979-81, assoc. prof., 1981-87, 1981-87, chair dept. English, 1981-87, chair humanities div., 1985-87, dean Grad. Sch., 1987-91, acad. dean, 1991—; vis. faculty fellow Yale U., 1980-91; vis. scholar Columbia U., 1981-82; adj. assoc. prof. Assumption Coll., Worcester, Mass., 1981-82, Columbia U., N.Y.C., summers 1980-85; Fulbright scholar U. Iceland, Reykjavik, 1982-83; cons., lectr. counseling dept. St. Joseph Coll., 1980—; cons. Scandinavian Soc. Conn., West Hartford, 1990—, Harvard Inst. Edn. Mgmt., 1991. Author poetry, personal essays and acad. articles. Cons. Vets. Affairs Human Rights Commn., West Haven, 1976—. NEH grantee, 1980, 85-88. Mem. Am. Assn. Higher Edn., Assn. Acad. Deans. Home: 42 Timberline Rd PO Box 1056 New Hartford CT 06057 Office: St Joseph Coll 1678 Asylum Ave West Hartford CT 06117-2700

KATHENES, BRIAN G., management consultant; b. Jersey City, N.J., Feb. 27, 1956; s. Gunnar H. and Peggy (McCabe) K.; m. Nancy Arnot, Aug. 29, 1987; 1 child, Tyler. BSChemE, N.J. Inst. Tech., 1978. Supr. Estee Lauder, Inc., Melville, N.Y., 1977-80; dir. Halston Fragrances, Dayton, N.J., 1980-84; mktg., sales dir. R.G. Pfeiffer, Orange, N.J., 1984-88; pres. Progressive Bus. Concepts, West Trenton, N.J., 1984—; tng. cons. AT&T, Basking Ridge, N.J., 1989-91, Andersen Cons., Stamford, Conn., 1989-91, Nabisco Biscuit, Hanover, N.J., 1990-91; trainer Internat. Soc. Appraisers, Chgo., 1988-91; mktg. cons. prog. seminar, 1989. Bd. dirs. N.J. Spl. Olympics, 1986-88; cons. Jr. Achievement, Princeton, N.J., 1978, 81, Muscular Dystrophy Assn., EatonTown, N.J., 1984-91; instr. Am. Heart Assn., New Brunswick, N.J., 1978-91, N.J. Dept. Health, Trenton, 1978-91. Mem. Internat. Soc. of Appraisers (dir. communications 1989-91, Outstanding Marketer of Yr. award 1989, Computer Contbr. award 1988), N.J. Appraisers (pres. 1990-91), ASTD (edn. com. 1989-91), N.J. Dept. of Health (tng. coord. 1978-91, Outstanding Inst. award 1980). Office: Progressive Bus Concepts PO Box 77296 Trenton NJ 08628-6296

KATIMS, JASON ALEXANDER, playwright; b. Bklyn., Dec. 10, 1960; s. Robert Harold and Ruth Sandra (Ohsie) K.; m. Kathleen Ann Castillo, Nov. 8, 1986. BA, Queens Coll., 1984. Playwright: Catch!, 1988, The Man Who Couldn't Dance, 1989, Men in Pits, 1990, Driving Lessons, 1991. Recipient Alumni award for excellence in writing Queens Coll., 1984. Mem. Circle Repertory Playwrights Lab., Dramatists Guild. Democrat. Jewish. Home: 491 4th St Brooklyn NY 11215

KATKIN, EDWARD SAMUEL, psychology educator; b. N.Y.C., Aug. 15, 1937; s. Nathan and Rosalind (Davis) K.; m. Felice Lapin, Aug. 10, 1958 (dec. 1961); m. 2d Wendy Sue Freedman, Feb. 3, 1963; children: Kenneth, Elizabeth. B.A., CCNY, 1958; Ph.D., Duke U., 1963. Asst. prof. SUNY, Buffalo, 1963-66, assoc. prof., 1966-70, prof. dept. psychology, 1970-86 (chmn. 1980-86); prof. dept. psychology SUNY, Stony Brook, 1986—, chmn. dept. psychology, 1986-92. Fellow Am. Psychol. Assn.; mem. Soc. Psychophysiol. Research (pres. 1983-84), Am. Psychosomatic Soc., N.Y. Acad. Sci. Home: 11 Bayview Ave East Setauket NY 11733-3903 Office: SUNY Dept Psychology Stony Brook NY 11794

KATOH, ARTHUR KOW, medical researcher; b. Honolulu, Aug. 24, 1933; s. Herman S. and Hide (Koizumi) K.; m. Aug. 16, 1963; children: Ara K., Austin K., Ann K. BA, Syracuse U., 1954; MS, U. Ill., 1956, PhD, 1960; MPH, U. Pitts., 1986. Rsch. assoc. U. Ill., Urbana, 1961-62; asst. prof. biology U. Toledo, Ohio, 1962-63; rsch. assoc. Argonne (Ill.) Nat. Lab., 1963-66; dir. cancer rsch. lab. Mercy Hosp., Pitts., 1966-74, chief div. nuclear pathology and oncology, 1974—. Contbr. articles to profl. jours. Recipient grants for numerous founds. and agys. including Leukemia Found., Elsa U. Pardee Found., NIH, Atomic Energy Commn. Office: Mercy Hosp 1400 Locust St Pittsburgh PA 15228

KATOPIS, ANTHONY, telecommunications engineer; b. Athens, Greece, Dec. 22, 1944; came to U.S., 1969, 82; s. Christos and Hariclia (Economidou) K.; m. Anastasia Pepelasi, July 31, 1969; children: Hariclia, Sophia. Diploma elec. engr., Nat. Tech. U., Athens, 1967; MA, Princeton U., 1971, PhD in Elec. Engr., 1972. Engr. Greek Telecom, Athens, 1968-69, subsect. chief, 1973-82; sr. engr. Intelsat, Washington, 1982—; lectr. Nat. Tech. U., Athens, 1976-82; adj. prof. U. Md., College Park, 1984. Contbr. articles to profl jours. Mem. Greek Chamber of Tech. Greek Orthodox. Home: 4610 Roxbury Dr Bethesda MD 20814-4040 Office: Intelsat 3400 Internat Dr NW Washington DC 20008

KATTER, NAFE EDMUND, academic administrator, dramatic arts educator; b. Saginaw, Mich., Oct. 26, 1926; s. Nafe Webb and Meta Edna (Blohm) K. AB, U. Mich., 1949, AM, 1951, PhD, 1963. Teaching fellow U. Mich., Ann Arbor, 1950-53; asst. prof. Northern Iowa U., Cedar Falls, 1956-57; asst. prof. U. Conn., Storrs, 1958-63, assoc. prof., 1963-70, prof., 1970—, assoc. dept. head, head acting program, 1985—. Performer Hartford Stage Co., 1980-85, Company One, Hartford, 1989—, Mansfield Hist. Soc., Mansfield Center, Conn., 1990. Mem. AAUP, Actor's Equity Assn., Phi Kappa Phi. Lutheran. Home: PO Box 126 Storrs Mansfield CT 06268-0126 Office: U Conn Dept Dramatic Arts 802 Bolton Rd Storrs Mansfield CT 06268

KATZ, ABRAHAM, retired foreign service officer; b. Bklyn., Dec. 4, 1926; s. Alexander and Zina (Rabinowitz) K.; children: Tamar, Jonathan, Naomi. B.A. cum laude, Bklyn. Coll., 1948; M.I.A., Columbia U., 1950; Ph.D., Harvard U., 1968. Commd. fgn. service officer Dept. State, 1951; 1st sec. U.S. missions to NATO, OECD, Paris, 1959-64; counselor Am. Embassy, Moscow, 1964-66; dir. office of OECD European Communities and

Atlantic Polit. Econ. Affairs, Washington, 1967-74; dep. chief of mission OECD, Paris, 1974-78; dep. asst. sec. for internat. econ. policy and research Dept. Commerce, Washington, 1978-80; asst. sec. internat. econ. policy Dept. Commerce, 1980-81; U.S. rep., ambassador OECD, Paris, 1981-84; pres. U.S. Coun. Internat. Bus., 1984—. Author: The Politics of Economic Reform in the Soviet Union, 1972. Decorated grand officier Ordre National du Merite (France). Mem. Am. Polit. Sci. Assn., Assn. Advancement Slavic Studies, Am. Fgn. Svc. Assn., Am. Assn. Comparative Econ. Studies, Coun. on Fgn. Rels., Cosmos Club, Harvard Club, Century Assn., B'nai Brith. Office: US Coun Internat Bus 1212 6th Ave New York NY 10036-1602

KATZ, ALIX MARTHA, respiratory care practitioner; b. Newark, Dec. 7, 1948; d. Leo F. and Anne (Chase) K. AS, Passaic County Community Coll., Paterson, N.J., 1982. Cert. respiratory therapy technician. Staff respiratory therapist Hosp. Ctr. at Orange, N.J., 1979-82; home care respiratory practitioner Homed Convalescent Equipment, Mountain Lakes, N.J., 1982-85; clin. respiratory supr. Elizabeth (N.J.) Gen. Med. Ctr., 1985-86; dir. respiratory therapy Paramed. Specialities, Inc., Fairfield, N.J., 1986-88; respiratory therapist Ultra-Care Health Care Svcs., East Orange, N.J., 1988—. Drug and Hosp. Union scholar, 1980. Mem. Am. Assn. for Respiratory Care, Nat. Soc. Cardio-Pulmonary Technologists, Respiratory Therapy Hist. Soc., Methaphys. Ctr. N.J. Democrat. Jewish. Home: 115453 Old Short Hills Rd West Orange NJ 07052-1015

KATZ, ARNOLD MARTIN, insurance brokerage firm executive; b. Schenectady, N.Y., Mar. 22, 1940; s. David and Minna Katz; m. Marsha Katz, Sept. 4, 1969; 1 child, Sharon. BS in Pub. Relations, Boston U., 1962. Cert. life underwriter, Pa. Sales rep. Mass. Gen. Life Ins. Co., Hartford, Conn., 1964-66, sr. sales rep., 1966-67, asst. mgr., 1967; mgr. Phila., 1967-72; v.p. Boston, 1972-76; pres. Brokerage Concepts, Inc., Phila., 1977—; chmn. bd. dirs. Brokers Svc. Inc., N.Y.; pres. BCI Holdings Inc., Atlantic Adminstrs., Waltham, Mass., Group Source, Phila., Am. Ind. Life Ins. Co. Contbr. articles to profl. jours. Bd. dirs. Moss Rehab. Hosp., Phila., 1985—, Police Athletic League, Phila., 1986—; exec. com. Einstein Hosp., Phila., 1987—; v.p. Belmont Hosp. 1987—. Served to maj. U.S. Army, 1962-73. Mem. Life Underwriter Assn., CLU (bd. dirs. Phila. chpt.). Jewish. Office: Brokerage Concepts Inc 651 Allendale Rd King Of Prussia PA 19406-1438

KATZ, BERNARD, psychiatrist; b. Cin., July 26, 1936; s. Harry and Mildred (Davidorf) K.; m. Barbara Strauss Rosenbaum, June 4, 1965; children: Matthew Strauss, Emily Carrie. BA with honors, Ohio U., 1958; MA, U. Chgo., 1960; MD, U. Louisville, 1967. Diplomate Am. Bd. Psychiatry and Neurology. Intern U. Wis. Hosp., Madison, 1967-68; resident Mass. Mental Health Ctr., Boston, 1968-71; chief psychiatry USPHS Hosp., Brighton, Mass., 1971-73; founding med. dir. Westwood (Mass.) Lodge Hosp., 1973-83; psychiatrist in chief Human Resource Inst., Brookline, Mass., 1983—; sr. mental health cons. dept. correction Commonwealth of Mass., 1985—; chief psychiat. cons. U.S. Dept. Army, Boston, 1969—; assoc. clin. prof. Boston U., 1974—; clin. instr. Harvard Med. Sch., Boston, 1983—. Psychiat. advisor Senate Commonwealth of Mass. Lt. comdr. USPHS, 1968-71. Fellow Am. Psychiat. Assn.; mem. Mass. Psychiat. Soc. (pres. 1984, treas. 1979-84). Jewish. Office: Human Resource Inst 227 Babcock St Brookline MA 02146-3199

KATZ, CANDACE KAUFMAN, federal agency administrator; b. Hartford, Conn., May 14, 1947; d. Harold and Violet (Web) Kaufman; m. Hadrian R. Katz, Apr. 1, 1977; children: Gwendlyn Rebecca, Jonathan Harold. AB magna cum laude, Radcliffe Coll., 1969; MA, Harvard U., 1970, PhD, 1976; JD, Georgetown U., 1982. Asst. prof. English Northeastern U., Boston, 1975-77; atty. U.S. Dept. HHS, Washington, 1981-82; program officer div. pub. programs NEH, Washington, 1982-89, dep. to dir. div. pub. programs, 1990—. Woodrow Wilson fellow, 1969, Grad. Prize fellow Harvard U., 1969-73. Mem. MLA, South Atlantic MLA, Bar of D.C., Phi Beta Kappa. Home: 1324 Lancia Dr McLean VA 22102 Office: NEH 1100 Pennsylvania Ave NW Washington DC 20506

KATZ, DANIEL ROGER, conservation executive; b. Cin., Nov. 7, 1961; s. Simon Daniel and Harriett (Rosensweet) K. Cert., Nat. Chengchi U., Taipei, Taiwan, 1981; BA, Ohio State U., Columbus, 1983; cert., Cen. China U. Sci. & Tech., Wulnan, People's Republic of China, 1984. China program coord. Shearman & Sterling, N.Y.C., 1984-85; exec. dir. Rainforest Alliance, N.Y.C., 1986—; bd. dirs. World Parks Endowment, N.Y.C.; mem. adv. bd. Earth Love Fund, London, 1991—, Rainforest Conservancy, Princeton, N.J., 1991—, New Forest Project, Washington, 1991—. Featured in (book) The Road to Extrema, 1991. Recipient fellowship Ohio State U.-Provence of Hubei, People's Republic of China, 1983, Kellogg Nat. fellowship, 1989-92, Jinlu award Ohio State U., 1983. Mem. Explorers Club. Office: Rainforest Alliance 270 Lafayette St Ste 512 New York NY 10012

KATZ, HILDA, artist; b. June 2, 1909; d. Max and Lina (Schwartz) K. Student, Nat. Acad. Design; student (3 awards; New Sch. Social Research scholarship), 1940-41. Author: (under pen name Hulda Weber) poems including numerous anthologies, spl. ltd. edit., 1987-88; anthologies include The Bloom, 1984-85, 87, Perfume and Fragrance, 1988, 89, Lightning & Rainbows, 1989, 90; contbr.: numerous poems, short stories to books and mags. including Humpty Dumpty's Mag. (publ. for children); contbr. commemorative poetry to mus. and govt. including Pres. Ronald W. Reagan, 1985, Pres. Chaim Herzog of Israel, 1987, series of poems in N.Y. State Mus. of Albany, 1987, 89, Yad Vashem Meml. Archives, Jerusalem, 1987, Mus. of Jewish Heritage, 1988, 89, Jewish Theol. Sem. of Am., 1989, Ft. Lewis Coll. Found., 1990, Jewish Nat. and Univ. Libr., Jerusalem, 1990, The Simon Wiesenthal Ctr., U.S.A., 1990, U.S. Holocaust Meml., Washington, 1991, Libr. Congress, Washington, 1991; one-woman exhbns. include Bowdoin Coll. Art Mus., 1951, Calif. State Library, 1953, Print Club Albany, N.Y., 1955, U. Maine, 1955, 58, Jewish Mus., 1956, Pa. State Tchrs. Coll., 1956, Massillon Mus., 1957, Ball State Tchrs. Coll., 1957, Springfield (Mass.) Art Mus., 1957, Miami Beach (Fla.) Art Ctr., Richmond (Ind.) Art Assn., 1959, Old State Capitol Mus. La., other exhbns. include: Corcoran Bienniale Library of Congress, Am. in the War Exhbn, N.Y. State Mus. of Albany, 1989, Jewish Theol. Sem. of Am., 1989, 26 mus., Am. Drawing anns. at: Albany Inst., Nat. Acad. Design, Conn. Acad. Fine Arts, Bklyn. Mus., Delgado Mus., Art-U.S.A., 1959, Congress for Jewish Culture, Met. Mus. Art., Springfield (Mo.) Art Mus., Children's Mus. Hartford, Conn., Miniature Printers, Peoria (Ill.) Art Ctr., Pa. Acad. Fine Arts, Originale Contemporate Graphic Internat., France, Bezalel Nat. Mus., Israel, Venice (Italy) Bienniale, Royal Etchers and Painters Exchange Exhibit, Eng., Bat Yam Mus., Israel, Paris, France, 1958, 59, Am.-Italian Print Exchange, numerous libraries, artists socs., invitational exhbns. include, Rome, Turin, Venice, Florence, Naples (all Italy), Nat. Academe Muse, France, Israel, USIA exhbns. in, Europe, S. Am., Asia, Africa; represented spl. collections, U.S. Nat. Mus., 1965, U. Maine, 1965, Library of Congress, 1965-71, Met. Mus. Art, 1965-66, 80, Nat. Gallery Art, 1966, Nat. Collection Fine Arts, 1966-71, 78, Nat. Air and Space Mus., 1970, N.Y. Pub. Library, 1971, 78, U.S. Mus. History and Tech., 1972, Naval Mus., 1972, Ft. Lewis Coll., Durango, Colo., 1980-81, Boston Pub. Library, 1980-81, Israel Nat. Mus., Jerusalem, 1980-81, State Mus. Albany, N.Y., 1980, N.Y. State Mus. Archives, Albany, 1979-89; also represented in permanent collections U.S. Nat. Mus., U. Maine, Libr. of Congress, Met. Mus. Art, Nat. Coll. Fine Arts, D.C., Nat. Gallery Art, D.C., Nat. Air and Space Mus., D.C., N.Y. Pub. Libr., Nat. Mus. History and Tech., Bklyn. Mus., New Britain Mus. Am. Art, Mus. of City of N.Y., Jewish Mus. of N.Y., N.Y. State Mus. of Albany, Israel Mus., Jerusalem, Boston Pub. Libr., Ft. Lewis Coll. Art Mus., Colo., Balt. Mus. Art, Franklin D. Roosevelt, Fogg Mus., Harvard, Santa Barbara (Calif.) Art Mus., Syracuse U., Colorado Springs Fine Arts Ctr., Pennell Collection, Am. Artists Group Prize at Samuel Golden Coll., U. Minn., Calif. State Library, Pa. State Library, Bezalel Nat. Mus., Archives Am. Art Smithsonian Instn. (art and poetry), 1979-92, Washington, Archives and State Mus. Albany, N.Y. (120 works), Newark Pub. Library, Addison Gallery Am. Art, Bat Yam Municipal Mus., Safed Mus., Israel, Pa. State Tchrs. Coll., Richmond Art Assn., Peoria (Ill.) Art Ctr., Boston Pub. Library, St. Margaret Mary Sch. Art, Musee Nat. d'Art Modern, Yad Vashem Meml. Archives, Jerusalem (poetry), 1987, N.Y. State Mus. and Archives; spl. collections paintings, drawings and prints acquired by 19 nat. and internat. mus./archives including U.S. Nat. Mus., Washington, 1965, Univ. Maine Art, 1965, Libr. Congress, Washington, 1965, 71, Met. Mus. N.Y., 1965, 80, Nat. Coll. Fine Arts, 1966, 71, 78, Nat. Gallery Art, 1966, Nat. Air & Space Mus., 1966, N.Y. Pub. Libr., 1971, 78, Nat. Mus. History/Tech., 1971, Bklyn. Mus. Art, 1978, Mus. City N.Y., 1978, Jewish Mus. N.Y., 1979, N.Y. State Mus. Albany, N.Y., 1979-90, Israel Mus., 1980, Ft. Lewis Coll. Mus., 1980, Smithsonian, 1979, Yad Vashem Meml. Mus./Archives, 1987, Mus. Jewish Heritage, N.Y., 1989, Jewish Theological Seminary Am., 1989, Jewish Nat. & Univ. Libr., Israel, 1990. Represented as artist and poet: Miss. Art Assn. Internat. Water Color Club award 1947, 51, New Haven Paint and Clay Club, purchase award Peoria Art Ctr. 1950, Print Club Albany 1962, also Library of Congress, U. Minn., Calif. State Library, Met. Mus. Art, Pa. State Tchrs. Coll., Art Assn. Richmond, Ind., N.Y. Pub. Library, Newark Pub. Library, St. Margaret Mary Sch. Art Coll., landscape award Soc. Miniature Painters, Gravers and Sculpture, James Joyce award Poetry Soc. Am. 1975; presented spl. commemoration to Yad Vashem Meml. Hist. Site, Jerusalem, 1987; named Dau. of Mark Twain 1970; life fellow Met. Mus. Art; named to Exec. and Profl. Hall of Fame (plaque of honor 1966). Recipient World Order of Narrative Poets; named Membro Honoris Causa dell'Accademia di Scienze, Letteri, Arti Classe Accademica "Nobel", Milan, 1974, 75, Classe Storia Letter-Atura Americana, Milan, 1978, Exec. and Profl. Hall of Fame-Life, 1966; named A Daughter of Mark Twain, 1970; Met. Mus. fellow, 1966. Fellow Internat. Acad. Poets (founder 1977); mem. Soc. Am. Graphic Artists (group prize 1950), Print Club Albany (N.Y.), Boston Printmakers (award 1955), Washington Printmakers (exhbns.), Conn. Acad. Fine Arts, Am. Color Print Soc., Audubon Artists (group exhbns., award 1944), Phila. Water Color Club (group exhbns.), Nat. Assn. Women Artists (award 1945, 47), Print Council Am., Hunterdon Art Center, Internat. Platform Assn., Poetry Soc. Am., Artists Equity N.Y., Authors Guild, Inc., Accademia Di Scienze, Lettere, Arti-Milano, Italy (Consigliere, named hon. mem. as artist 1974, author/poet 1975, Nobel designate 1978); Academia Di Scienze. Lettere, Arti, Classe. Office: 915 W End Ave Apt 5D New York NY 10025-3503

KATZ, JEFFREY HARVEY, lawyer, mayor; b. Newark, Apr. 16, 1947; s. Jack and Beatrice (Weinstock) K.; m. Sharon R. Davis, Nov. 7, 1971; children: Stacey, Justin. B of Engring, Stevens Inst. Tech., 1970; JD, Seton Hall U., 1981. Bar: N.J. 1981, U.S. Dist. Ct. N.J. 1981, U.S. Ct. Appeals (3d cir.) 1984, U.S. Supreme Ct. 1985. Engr. RKO Gen., Sta. WOR-AM-FM-TV, N.Y.C., 1967-70; mgr., engr. Pub. Svc. Electric & Gas Co., Newark, 1977, mgr. telecommunications systems, 1977—; mgr. telecommunications advanced tech. Pub. Svc. Electric & Gas Co., 1990—; prosecutor Twp. of Springfield, N.J., 1982-85, mem. governing body, 1985—, mem. bd. health, 1986-87, 90-92, mem. planning bd., commr. pub. safety, 1988—, mayor, 1988, 89, dep. mayor, 1992—; mem. Downtown Redevel. Com., Springfield, N.J., 1990—; chmn. adv. com. Mcpl. Cable TV, Springfield, 1974-76. Trustee Stevens Inst. Tech., Hoboken, N.J., 1971-74, mem. presdl. search and selection com., 1974-75; lt. Police Res., Springfield, 1968—; mem. Gov.'s Mgmt. Improvement Program, Trenton, N.J., 1982-83; mem. local govt. affairs adv. com. N.J. Assembly, 1989-91; mem. recreation com., 1990—. Named One of Outstanding Young Men of Am., U.S. Jaycees, 1971-73, Citizen of Yr. Springfield B'nai B'rith, 1976, Citizen of Yr. Policeman's Benevolent Assn. Local, 1976, Springfield, 1985; recipient award for 25 continuous yrs. of pub. svc. N.J. Bldrs. Assn., 1989, Silver Life Card award Policemen's Benevolent Assn. Local 76, 1991. Mem. ABA, IEEE, Soc. Cable TV Engrs., N.J. State Bar Assn., Union County Bar Assn., Internat. Platform Assn., Jewish War Vets. of U.S. Republican. Jewish. Office: 182 Meisel Ave Springfield NJ 07081-1830

KATZ, JEFFREY OWEN, software company executive; b. Queens, N.Y., Apr. 6, 1950; s. Nathan and Rosalyn (Anker) K. BA, SUNY, Stony Brook, 1973; PhD, U. Lancaster, Eng., 1983. Computer cons. U. Lancaster, Eng., 1975-76; mathematician/programmer Brain Rsch. Labs., N.Y.C., 1986; design engr., programmer Heart Map, Inc., N.Y.C., 1986-87; computer cons. Am. Soc. for Psychical Rsch., N.Y.C., 1986-90; pres. Sci. Cons. Svcs., Inc., Selden, N.Y., 1989—; v.p. Datatek Inc., Mass., 1991—. Contbr. articles to profl. jours.; referee Brit. Jour. Math. Psychology, 1983-84, Brit. Jour. Psychology, 1984; author computer programs. Vol., lectr. Union of Concerned Scientists, 1983, Animals in Distress, 1991. SUNY grad. fellow, 1973; MENSA grantee, 1974. Mem. Am. Soc. Psychical Rsch., Brit. Psychol. Soc., Mensa. Home: 20 Stagecoach Rd Selden NY 11784-1528 Office: Sci Cons Svcs Inc 20 Stagecoach Rd Selden NY 11784-1528

KATZ, JERROLD PINYA, management consultant; b. Winnipeg, Man., Can., June 11, 1939; came to U.S., 1969; s. Lionel Isaac and Minnie (Bordoditsky) K.; m. Brenda Rochelle Moss, Aug. 23, 1967; children: Rena, Shira, Ariella, Lev. B Comm. with honours, U. Man., 1968; MBA, Columbia U., 1972, PhD, 1974. Instr. bus. Columbia U., N.Y.C., 1970-73; cons. Procter & Gamble, Cin., 1974-75; prof. Simmons Coll., Boston, 1975-80; cons. Northwest Industries, Chgo., 1980-81; prof. Babson Coll., Wellesley, Mass., 1982-85; mgr. Coopers & Lybrand, Boston, 1981-88; prin. Noble Bus. Decisions, Newton, Mass., 1988—. Contbr. articles to profl. jours. Mem. ABA, Appraisal Soc. Am., Am. Assn. Pub. Opinion Rsch., Am. Econ. Assn., Am. Fin. Assn., Am. Mktg. Assn., Am. Prodn. and Inventory Control Soc., Am. Sociol. Assn., Am. Stat. Assn., Assn. Computing Machinery, Assn. Consumer Rsch., Decision Scis. Inst., Inst. Mgmt. Scis., Planning Forum, Columbia Bus. Club (treas. 1987-88,m pres. 1989-91). Jewish. Home: 155 Eastbourne Rd Newton MA 02159-1605 Office: Noble Bus Decisions 155 Eastbourne Rd Newton MA 02159-1605

KATZ, JERRY, podiatrist; b. N.Y.C., May 29, 1961; s. David and Eva (Duell) K.; m. Susan Jane Siegel, July 18, 1986; 1 child, Rachel Paige. BA in Biology, CUNY, 1983; D Podiatric Medicine, Ill. Coll. Podiatric Medicine, 1987. Diplomate Am. Bd. Podiatric Surgery. Lab. asst. dept. pathology Sch. Medicine, NYU, N.Y.C., 1979-80; rsch. asst. Beth Israel Med. Ctr., Mt. Sinai Sch. Medicine, N.Y.C., 1981-83, animal technician, 1983, rsch. asst. dept. ophthalmology, 1984; mem. staff Wheaton (Md.) Podiatry Assocs., 1989-90; pvt. practice podiatry Randallstown, Md., 1990—; mem. staff Liberty Med. Ctr., Inc., Balt. County Gen. Hosp., Montgomery Gen. Hosp. Contbr. articles to profl. publs. Mem. Am. Podiatric Med. Assn. (vice chmn. 1987-90, liaison to prodiatry polit. action com. 1987-89), Md. Podiatric Med. Assn. Jewish. Office: 5310 Old Court Rd Randallstown MD 21133

KATZ, JOSE, cardiologist, theoretical physicist; b. Havana, Cuba, June 6, 1944; s. Lipa and Victoria (Masson) K.; m. Anke Ebsen; children: Susan, David, Rachel, Hannah. BS, U. Ill., 1963, MS, 1964, PhD, 1967; MD, F.U., Berlin, 1980. Rsch. assoc. physicist U. Hamburg, Fed. Republic Germany, 1967-69; instr. physics Purdue U., Lafayette, Ind., 1969-71; asst. prof. physics Free U. of Berlin, West Berlin, Fed. Republic Germany, 1971-74; prof. physics F.U., West Berlin, Fed. Republic Germany, 1974-82; resident in internal medicine Cleve. Met. Gen. Hosp., Mt. Sinai Med. Ctr., Cleve., 1982-85; cardiology fellow Southwestern Med. Sch., Dallas, 1985-88; asst. prof. medicine and radiology Columbia U., Coll. of Physicians and Surgeons, N.Y.C., 1988—; co-dir. cardiovascular magnetic resonance Columbia U. Coll. of Physicians and Surgeons, Presbyn. Hosp., N.Y.C., 1988—. Contbr. articles to profl. jours., chpts. to books. Fellow ACP, Am. Coll. Cardiology, Am. Coll. Chest Physicians, Am. Coll. Angiology, Am. Heart Assn. (coun. clin. cardiology, coun. on cardiovascular radiology, coun. on basic scis.), Soc. Magnetic Resonance Imaging, Soc. Magnetic Resonance in Medicine; mem. AMA, Radiol. Soc. N.Am., Soc. Nuclear Medicine, N.Am. Soc. Cardiac Imaging, Sigma Xi, Phi Kappa Phi, Sigma Tau, Pi Mu Epsilon, Tau Beta Pi. Office: Columbia U Div Cardiology 630 W 168th St New York NY 10032

KATZ, JULIAN, gastroenterologist, educator; b. N.Y.C., Apr. 3, 1937; s. Abraham M. and Fay (Sher) K.; m. Sheila Moriber, Aug. 18, 1963; children—Jonathan Peter, Sara Katherine. A.B., Columbia U., 1958; M.D., U. Chgo., 1962. Diplomate: Am. Bd. Internal Medicine. Intern U. Chgo. Hosps., 1962-63; resident in medicine Duke U., 1963-65; fellow in gastroenterology Yale U., 1965-67; practice medicine specializing in gastroenterology, internal medicine and geriatrics Phila., 1969—; prof. medicine, lectr. in physiology and biochemistry Med. Coll. Pa., 1970—; prof. medicine Jefferson Med. Coll., 1988—; also lectr. local and nat. groups; chief clin. gastroenterology Med. Coll. Pa. Editor profl. jours.; Contbr. articles to profl. jours. and books. Served with USN, 1967-69. Fellow ACP, Am. Coll. Gastroenterology; mem. Am. Soc. Gastrointestinal Endoscopy, Am. Soc. Study Liver Disease, Am. Gastroenterological Assn., others. Home: 701 Dodds Ln Gladwyne PA 19035-1516 Office: Gastrointestinal Specialists 2 Bala Pla Bala Cynwyd PA 19004

KATZ, LEONARD WILLIAM, management consultant; b. N.Y.C., May 3, 1938; s. Melville James and Ruth (Seidman) K.; m. Betsy Park, June 30, 1962; children: Stephen G., Debra S. AB, Dartmouth Coll., 1960; MBA, Amos Tuck, 1961; D of Bus. Adminstrn., George Washington U., 1972. Assoc. prof. George Washington U., Washington, 1965-75; dir. of consulting Am. Hosp. Supply Co., Elmsford, N.Y., 1975-77; v.p. Whittaker Med. Systems, Chgo., 1977-79; mgr. midwest health care Deloitte Haskins & Sells, Chgo., 1979-82; mgr. in charge healthcare practice Grant Thornton & Co., Chgo., 1982-84; sr. cons. Arthur D. Little, Inc., Cambridge, Mass., 1984-90; pres. Katz & Assocs., Sudbury, Mass., 1990—. Author (chpt. in book) Cases in Healthcare Financial Management, 1984; contbr. articles to profl. jours. Chmn. Health Ctr. Task Force, City of Bowie, Md., 1970-72; mem. Sudbury Indsl. Devel. Commn., 1989—, Sudbury Long Range Planning Com., 1991—. Capt. U.S. Army, 1961-64. Mem. Inst. of Mgmt. Cons. (cert. mgmt. cons., bd. dirs. 1983-84), Healthcare Fin. Mgmt. Assn. (Follmer Bronze Merit award 1988), New Eng. Assn. Ind. Healthcare Cons. (pres. 1991—), Med. Group Mgmt. Assn. Office: Katz & Assocs 40 Shadow Oak Dr Sudbury MA 01776-3164

KATZ, LOIS ANNE, internist, nephrologist; b. Rockville Centre, N.Y., Dec. 1, 1941; d. Irvin Martin and Frances (Berenstein) Fradkin; m. Arthur A. Katz, Aug. 18, 1962; children: David, Brian. BA, Wellesley Coll., 1962; MD, NYU, 1966. Diplomate Am. Bd. Internal Medicine, Am. Bd. Nephrology. Intern medicine Bellevue Hosp., NYU, N.Y.C., 1966-67, resident medicine, 1967-68; sr. resident medicine N.Y. Hosp., N.Y.C., 1968-69; chief resident medicine N.Y. VA Med. Ctr., N.Y.C., 1969-70, fellow nephrology, 1970-71, staff physician, 1970-74, assoc. chief nephrology, 1974—, assoc. chief of staff ambulatory care, 1980—; asst. prof. clin. medicine NYU Sch. Medicine, N.Y.C., 1974-79, assoc. prof., 1979—. Blood dr. chmn. Beth Emeth Synagogue, Larchmont, N.Y.; alumna admission rep. Wellesley-in-Westchester, N.Y.; bd. mem. Women's Med. Assn., N.Y.C., 1986-92. Fellow ACP; mem. Am. Soc. Nephrology, Am. Med. Women's Assn., Soc. Gen. Internal Medicine, Women in Nephrology (treas. 1985-89), Am. Soc. Hypertension, Sigma Xi, Alpha Omega Alpha. Jewish. Office: Dept Vets Affairs Med Ctr 423 E 23d St New York NY 10010

KATZ, MARVIN, federal judge; b. 1930. B.A., U. Pa., 1951; LL.B., Yale U., 1954. Pvt. practice law, 1954-77; asst. commnr. IRS, 1977-81; assoc. Mesirov, Gelman, Jaffe, Cramer & Jamieson, Phila., 1981-83; judge U.S. Dist. Ct. (ea. dist.) Pa., Phila., 1983—. Office: US Courthouse Independence Mall W #13613 601 Market St Philadelphia PA 19106-1510*

KATZ, MICHAEL ALAN, investments company executive; b. New York City, June 21, 1963; s. Ivan F. and Marcia (Botnik) K. BS, Univ. Fla., 1985. V.p. D.H. Blair, N.Y.C., 1987—. Office: D H Blair 44 Wall St New York NY 10005 Home: 150 E 61 St New York NY 10021

KATZ, MORTON NORRIS, lawyer; b. Hartford, Conn., May 15, 1919; s. Abraham Albert and Ida Edith (Farber) K.; m. Shirley Grace Dinerstein, Nov. 29, 1964; children: Rachel Anne, Naomi Phyllis. BS, U. Conn., 1939; MS, Iowa State Coll., 1942; JD, U. Conn., 1951. Bar: Conn. 1951, U.S. Dist. Ct. Conn. 1952, U.S. Supreme Ct. 1956, U.S. Ct. Mil. Appeals 1956. Pvt. practice Hartford, 1951-55; pntr. Fauliso & Katz, Hartford, Farmington, Avon, Conn., 1955—; Mem. Conn. Pub. Transp. Commn., Hartford, 1982—. Contbr. articles to profl. jours. Mem. Dem. Town Com., Avon, 1967—. Col. U.S. Army, 1940-72. Decorated Legion of Merit. Mem. ABA, Conn. Bar Assn., Elks (exalted ruler Hartford Lodge 1968-69), Masons (dist. dep. Grand Lodge of Conn. 1984-86) Order Eastern Star (worthy grand parton 1986-87, gen. grand chpt. chmn. appeals and grievances com. 1991—). Democrat. Office: Fauliso & Katz PO Box 558 Avon CT 06001-0558

KATZ, NORMAN, manufacturing company executive; b. Zwickau, Germany, Apr. 10, 1925; came to U.S., 1940; naturalized, 1944; s. Paul and Dora (Ungar) K.; m. children: Ira and Stephen (twins); m. Sandra Dale Hendricks, Dec. 22, 1988. BA in Econs., Columbia U., 1943. Exec. v.p. John Weitz Jrs., Inc., N.Y.C., 1947-52; pres. Norman Katz, Inc., N.Y.C., 1952-58, At Home Wear, Inc., N.Y.C., 1959-75, I. Appel Corp., N.Y.C., 1976—; instr. econs. CCNY, 1947-51. Trade chmn. Fedn. Jewish Philanthropies, 1957-71. Served with AUS, 1943-46. Recipient Torch Liberty award Anti Defamation League, 1987, Femmy Intimate Apparel Industry award, 1988. Mem. Am. Apparel Mfrs. Assn. (vice-chmn. intimate apparel coun. 1989-90, chmn. 1991, bd. dirs. 1992). Clubs: Saugatuck Harbor Yacht (Westport, Conn.), Harrow U.S.A. (N.Y.C.). Home: 160 E 38th St New York NY 10016-2651 also: Timberlake Estate Jackson TN 38305 Office: I Appel Corp 136 Madison Ave New York NY 10016-6711

KATZ, RICHARD ALAN, scientist, mathematician; b. Providence, Oct. 14, 1950; s. Nathan and Lena (Stepak) K.; m. April Lee Pomeroy, Aug. 28, 1976; 1 child, Robert Jereme. BS in Math., U. R.I., 1972; PhD in Applied Math., Brown U., 1991. Prin. analyst, group mgr. Analysis & Tech., Inc., North Stonington, Conn., 1972-80; prin. analyst, project leader Sonalysts, Inc., Waterford, Conn., 1980-86; sr. prin. scientist ORI, Inc., Rockville, Md., 1986-89; sr. tech. adminstrv. staff mem. Naval Underwater Systems Ctr., Dept. Navy, Newport, R.I., 1989—; adj. faculty mem. Rensselaer Poly. Inst., HGC Affiliate, Hartford, Conn. and Troy, N.Y., 1989—; colleague Ctr. for Fluid Mechanics, Turbulence and Computation div. applied math. Brown U., Providence, 1989—; lectr. in field. Contbr. over 50 articles to profl. publs. Mem. AAAS, Am. Math. Soc., Am. Phys. Soc., Soc. for Indsl. and Applied Math., Acoustical Soc. Am., N.Y. Acad. Scis., Sigma Xi. Home: 11 Winthrop Dr East Lyme CT 06333-1033 Office: Naval Underwater Systems Ctr Dept Navy Code 821 Bldg 679 Newport RI 02841

KATZ, RICHARD JON, marketing and advertising company executive; b. Bklyn., Feb. 26, 1932; s. Irving Paul and Lillian Katz; A.A.S., Bklyn. Coll., 1960; m. Helene Borow, June 7, 1953; children—Robin Lee, Juli Beth, Jennifer Sue. Pres., creative dir. Katz, Jacobs & Douglas Advt., N.Y.C., 1960-75; pres., creative dir., KNL Advt., N.Y.C., 1975-78, Ric Katz & Assos. Inc., N.Y.C., 1978—; pres., chief exec. officer Rams Mktg. Inc., N.Y.C., 1978—; pres., creative dir. The Ramstar Group Advt., 1986—; pres., chief exec. officer Pinnacle Mktg. & Resources, Inc., 1990; lectr. Fashion Inst. Tech., NYU. Trustee inst. geriatric care New Sch. for Research, Hunter, N.Y, The Parker Jew. Inst. geriatric care. Served with USAF, 1951-55. Recipient awards for creativity, graphics, design and mktg. Mem. Am. Mgmt. Assn., President's Club, Antrium Club, Glen Heads Country Club. Author: Professional Guidelines for Effective Advertising. Office: 110 E 59th St New York NY 10022

KATZ, ROBERT MATHIAS, marketing professional; b. N.Y.C., Apr. 15, 1949; s. Irving and Elaine (Gross) K.; m. Florence L. Vago, Nov. 22, 1972; children: Laura M.; Alison M. BBA in Statistics, Baruch Coll., 1967-71, MBA in Statistics, 1971-74. Teaching asst. SEEK/Baruch Coll., N.Y.C., 1970-72; rsch. analyst Market Statistics, N.Y.C., 1972-73, sr. rsch. assoc., 1974-75, assoc. dir. rsch., 1976-77, mgr., 1978-79, v.p., 1980-84, sr. v.p., 1984-92, pres., 1992—; presenter Am. Mgmt. Assn., 1982-83, Advt. Rsch. Found. Show, 1985, Sales and Mktg. Mgmt. Show, 1986, 88, 89, 91. Contbr. articles to profl. jours. Mem. Am. Mgmt. Assn., Am. Mktg. Assn., Am. Statistical Assn. Home: 73-59 196 St Fresh Meadows NY 11366 Office: Market Stats 633 3rd Ave New York NY 10017-6706

KATZ, ROBERT NATHAN, ceramic engineer; b. Williamsport, Pa., Sept. 2, 1939; s. Louis and Rose Bernice (Golbitz) K.; S.B., M.I.T., 1961, Ph.D., 1969; M.S., U. Mich., 1963; children—Pamela Lynn, Jonathan Adam; m. Barbara Kurn Rubin, June 15, 1986. Research asst. U. Mich., 1961-62; metallurgist Army Materials Research Agy., Watertown, Mass., 1962-65; ceramic engr. Army Materials Tech. Lab., Watertown, Mass., 1965-70, chief ceramics research div., 1970-87, chief materials technologist, 1987-89; assoc. prof. mech. engring. Worcester (Mass.) Poly. Inst., 1990-91, Norton prof. materials sci. and engring., 1990-91, Norton rsch. prof., 1991—; chief materials technologist Army Materials Tech. Lab., Watertown, Mass., 1991—; liaison mem. various coms. Nat. Materials Adv. Bd.; participant Nat. Acad. Sci. Naval Studies Bd., Future Carreir Tech. Study, 1990-91; external examiner Bd. Grad. Studies, U. Cambridge (Eng.), 1979; cons. Dept. Def., Dept. Energy, Congl. Office of Tech. Assessment; mem. U.S. del. NATO Com. on Challenges of Modern Soc., 1974; mem. organizing com., lectr. NATO Advanced Study Inst. Nitrogen Ceramics, 1976, 81. Trustee, Temple

Israel of Natick, 1979-80. Recipient tech. writing award Dept. Army, 1981. Fellow Am. Ceramic Soc.; mem. Nat. Inst. Ceramic Engrs., New Eng. Ceramic Soc. (F.H. Norton award 1978), Am. Soc. Metals, Sigma Xi. Editor: Ceramics for High Performance Applications, 1974, Vol. II, 1978, Vol. III, 1983. Mem. editorial bd. Internat. Jour. High Tech. Ceramics, 1984-89, Jour. European Ceramic Soc., 1989—. Contbr. articles to tech. publs. Home: 1731 Beacon St #1403 Brookline MA 02146 Office: US Army Materials Tech Lab Watertown MA 02172

KATZ, SHELDON, mechanical technology educator; b. Bklyn., Nov. 26, 1934; s. Nathan and Esther (Cohen) K.; m. Esther Rubin, Nov. 23, 1960 (separated); children: Neal Steven, Donald Brian. BME, CCNY, 1963; MS in Engring. Tech., Rochester Inst. Tech., 1970. Draftsman, designer Royal Switchboard Co., Bklyn., 1957-61; project engr. Esso Rsch. and Engring. Co., Linden, N.J., 1963-64; sr. engr. Electronics div. Gen. Dynamics, Rochester, N.Y., 1964-69; prof. mech. tech. SUNY, Canton, 1969—; chmn. St. Lawrence Internat. chpt. Soc. Mfg. Engrs., 1970-79. Mem. Grasse River Players, Canton, 1974-86, North Country Pub. Radio, Canton, 1978—. With U.S. Army, 1955-57. Mem. Inst. Indsl. Engrs., United Univ. Profs. (grantee 1985), Tau Beta Pi, Pi Tau Sigma. Jewish. Home: 118 Leroy St Apt D3 Potsdam NY 13676 Office: SUNY Coll Tech Canton NY 13617

KATZBERG, JANE MICHAELS, health care administrator, consultant; b. Bklyn., Apr. 17, 1940; d. David Donn and Shirley (Ingram) Michaels; m. Mitchell Ronald Katzberg, Jan. 19, 1959; children: Michael Loren, Todd Alexander. BS, Adelphi U., 1961; M of Profl. Studies in Health Care Adminstrn., L.I. U., 1975. Cert. home economist, tchr., N.Y. Mgr. quality assurance Suffolk Physicians, Central Islip, N.Y., 1979-81; dir. quality assurance Community Hosp. of Glen Cove, N.Y., 1982-84; dir. intermediate care facilities program United Cerebral Palsy, Commack, N.Y., 1985-86; dir. svcs. for handicapped Town of Huntington, L.I., N.Y., 1986—; pres., cons. Images, Dix Hills, N.Y., 1985-88; lectr. in field. Mem. Citizens Adv. Com. for Handicapped, Town of Huntington, 1985-86; pres. Howell Rd. Sch. PTA, North Valley Stream, N.Y., 1973; meeting rep. N.Y. State Advocate for Disabled, 1986—; mem. div. dirs. Community Resource Dept., 1986-89, mem. div. dirs. human svcs., 1989—; facilitator for Nat. Orgn. Disability award for Town of Huntington, N.Y. State Eleanor Roosevelt award for Town Huntington. Acad. scholar C.W. Post Coll., Greenvale, N.Y., 1974. Mem. Assn. Local Govt. Advocates for Disabled. Republican. Jewish. Home: 81 Buttonwood Dr Huntington Station NY 11746-4804 Office: Town of Huntington Svcs for Handicapped 100 Main St Huntington NY 11743-6904

KATZENBACH, JOHN STRONG MINER, author; b. Princeton, N.J., June 23, 1950; s. Nicholas deB. and Lydia Phelps (Stokes) K.; m. Madeleine Helena Blais, May 10, 1980; children: Nicholas, Justine. BA, Bard Coll., 1972. Author: In the Heat of the Summer, 1982, First Born, 1984, The Traveler, 1987, Day of Reckoning, 1989, Just Cause, 1992. Mem. Internat. Assn. Crimewriters, Mystery Writer's of Am., PEN Internat.

KATZENSTEIN, GARY JAY, infosystems/organizational behavior specialist; b. N.Y.C., May 11, 1956. ScB in Computer Sci., Brown U., 1978; MS in Computer Sci., UCLA, 1983, MBA, 1983; postgrad., Carnegie-Mellon U., 1991—. Cons. Sigma Systems, L.A., 1980-83; writer, researcher Becker and Hayes, L.A., 1982-83; mgr., instr. Princeton Rev., N.Y.C., 1985-91. Author: Funny Business, 1989. Scholar Henry Luce Found., 1983-84, Grumman Aerospace, 1974-78; fellow ARCO Found., 1981-82, R.C. Baker Found., 1982-83, William Larimer fellow, 1991—.

KATZMAN, RANDI MICHELE, social worker; b. N.Y.C., Mar. 13, 1964; d. Bert and Selma (Levine) A. BA in Psychology, Hofstra U., 1985; MSEd in Counseling, Hunter Coll., 1991. Caseworker Thomas Jefferson HFA, Bklyn., 1985-87; social worker N.Y. Found. for Sr. Citizens, N.Y.C., 1987-91, Sephardic Home For the Aged, Bklyn., 1991—; therapeutic aid Samuel Schulman Rehab. Inst., Bklyn., 1983-85. Mem. AACD, Phi Beta Kappa, Psi Chi. Democrat. Jewish. Home: 1755 E 13th St 939 E 85th St Brooklyn NY 11229 Office: Sephardic Home for the Aged 2266 Cropsey Ave Brooklyn NY 11214-5797

KATZMANN, GARY STEPHEN, lawyer; b. N.Y.C., Apr. 22, 1953; s. John and Sylvia (Butner) K. AB summa cum laude, Columbia U., 1973; MLitt, Oxford U., 1976; MPPM, JD, Yale U., 1979. Bar: Mass. 1982, U.S. Dist. Ct. Mass. 1983, U.S. Ct. Appeals (1st cir.) 1983, D.C.. 1984, U.S. Ct. Appeals (2d cir.) 1987, N.Y. 1990, U.S. Ct. Appeals (fed. cir.) 1991. Law clk. to judge U.S. Dist. Ct. (so. dist.) N.Y., N.Y.C., 1979-80, U.S. Ct. Appeals (1st cir.), Boston, 1980-81; research assoc. ctr. criminal justice Law Sch. Harvard U., Cambridge, Mass., 1981-83; asst. U.S. atty., chief appellate atty., dep. chief criminal div., chief legal counsel U.S. Atty.'s Office, Mass., 1983—; lectr. Harvard U. Law Sch, 1990—. Author: Inside the Criminal Process, 1991; editor Yale U. Law Jour. Mem. ABA, Phi Beta Kappa. Office: US Attys Office 1107 JW McCormack POCH Boston MA 02109

KATZMANN, ROBERT ALLEN, legal educator, non-profit association executive, political scientist; b. N.Y.C., Apr. 22, 1953; s. John and Sylvia Edith (Butner) K. AB summa cum laude, Columbia U., 1973; MA in Govt., Harvard U., 1975, PhD in Govt., 1978; JD, Yale U., 1980. Bar: Mass. 1982, U.S. Ct. Appeals (1st cir.) 1983, D.C. 1984, U.S. Dist. Ct. Mass. 1984. Law clk. to judge U.S. Ct. Appeals (1st cir.), Concord, N.H., 1980-81; rsch. assoc. Brookings Instn., Washington, 1981-85, fellow, 1985—; adj. prof. law, pub. policy Georgetown U., Washington, 1984-92; William J. Walsh prof. govt., prof. law, 1992—; pres. Governance Inst., Washington, 1986—; vis. prof. polit. sci. UCLA, Washington program, 1990—; vis. chair, Wayne Morse prof. law and politics U. Oreg., 1992; cons. Fed. Cts. Study Com., 1990; vice chair Com. on govt. Ops. and Separation of Powers. Author: Regulatory Bureaucracy: The Federal Trade Commission and Antitrust Policy, 1980, Institutional Disability, 1986; co-editor: Managing Appeals in Federal Courts, 1988; editor: Judges and Legislators, 1988; article and book editor Yale U. Law Jour., 1979-80. Mem. ABA (adminstrv. law sect. 1991—), Am. Judicature Soc. (bd. dirs.), Am. Polit. Sci. Assn., Assn. Pub. Policy Analysis and Mgmt., Phi Beta Kappa. Home: 3028 Porter St NW # 304 Washington DC 20008-3292 Office: Brookings Instn Govtl Studies Program 1775 Massachusetts Ave NW Washington DC 20036-2188

KATZOWITZ, LAUREN, philanthropic and non-profit consultant. BS in Comparative Lit. with honors, Brandeis U., 1970; MS with honors, Columbia U., 1971. With, Newsweek mag., then Phila. Bull.; free-lance writer, editor, cons., until 1975; cons. Ford Found., 1972-75; mgr. PBS programs Exxon Corp., 1978-81, Great Performances, Live From Lincoln Ctr., Dance in America, NOVA, The MacNeil/Lehrer Report; communications mgr. Exxon Rsch. and Engring. Co., 1981-84; regional liaison Europe and Africa, Exxon Corp., 1984-86; exec. dir. Found. Svc., 1986—; pres. LK Consulting, 1986—. Pres. Bronx Ednl. Svcs.; trustee Women's Action Alliance, Am. Friends of Inst. Internat. d'Etudes Musicales, St. Maximin, France, B'nai B'rith Hillel/Jewish Assn. for College Youth. Named one of 12 Women to Watch in the Eighties, Ladies' Home Jour., 1979. Regional Finalist Pres.'s Commn. on White House fellow, 1984. Office: LK Consulting 505 E 79th St New York NY 10021-0709

KATZPER, MEYER, analyst; b. Ramat-Gan, Israel, July 31, 1936; came to U.S., 1937; s. Moses and Lillian (Gincenberg) K.; m. Linda Beryl Schwartz, Aug. 19, 1973; children: Moshe Ariel, Margalit Ahuva, David Evan. BA, BRE, Yeshiva U., 1957; PhD, NYU, 1967. Asst. prof. L.I. U., N.Y.C., 1966-67; sr. rsch. scientist Nat. Biomed. Rsch. Found., Silver Spring, Md., 1967-70; asst. prof. SUNY, Plattsburgh, 1970-73; tech. assoc. Ocean Data Systems, Inc., Rockville, Md., 1974-76; assoc. prof. George Washington U. Med. Sch., Washington, 1978-84; ind. cons. systems and info. analysis Rockville, Md., 1976-89; sr. staff fellow Ctr. for Drug Evaluation and Rsch., FDA, Rockville, 1989—. Author: Fortran Programming Through Examples, 1973; co-author: Modeling and Simulation of Alcohol Utilization, 1976; (with others) Brain Oxygen Supply and Electrical Act, 1969; author: (monograph) Modeling of Long Term Care, 1980; editor: Social and Environmental Analysis, 1970. Dir. Beth Sholom Beth Hamedrash Series, Rockville, 1977-78; faculty advisor Hillel, Plattsburgh, 1972-73; faculty Lehrhaus, Washington, 1975-76. NSF fellow, 1958; Miner Inst. Environ. grantee SUNY, 1972.

KAUFFMAN, ANDREW JOHN, political specialist, writer; b. Phila., Nov. 27, 1920; s. Reginald Wright and Ruth (Hammitt) K.; m. Elizabeth Conant, Sept. 12, 1943 (div. Oct. 1959); m. Daphne S. Ennis, Mar. 21, 1977. BA, Harvard U., 1943. Polit. specialist U.S. Dept. State, Washington, 1943-56; fgn. svc. officer U.S. Dept. State, various posts, 1956-70; corp. dir. Gen. Plywood, Louisville, Springfield, Ky., Mass, 1966-68; writer Washington, 1971—; bd. dirs. Video Communications, Springfield. Editor: (textbook) Mountaineering for Beginners, 1978; co-author: The Guiding Spirit, 1983. Mem. Am. Alpine Club (bd. dirs. 1983-86, v.p. 1988, Angelo Halprin award 1988), Appalachian Mountain Club, Potomac-Appalachian Trail Club (hon., mountaineering sect.). Democrat. Home: 2800 Woodley Rd NW Washington DC 20008

KAUFFMAN, BRUCE WILLIAM, lawyer, former state supreme court justice; b. Atlantic City, Dec. 1, 1934; s. Joseph Bernard and Lilyan (Abraham) K.; m. Carol Jackson, June 15, 1991; children from previous marriage: Bradley Leonard, Marjorie Beth, Robert Andrew, Laurie Ann, Christine Lynne. BA, U. Pa., 1956; LLB, Yale U., 1959. Bar: N.J. 1960, Pa. 1961, D.C. 1982, U.S. Supreme Ct. 1965. Law clk. to judge N.J. Superior Ct., Trenton, 1959-60; assoc. Dilworth, Paxson, Kalish, Levy & Dilks, Phila., 1960-65, ptnr., 1966-80, chmn. litigation dept., 1975-80; justice Supreme Ct. of Pa., 1980-82; chmn., sr. ptnr. Dilworth, Paxson, Kalish & Kauffman, Phila., 1982—; apptd. to Jud. Inquiry and Rev. Bd., 1984-89, chmn., 1988; mem. com. of censors U.S. Dist. Ct., Ea. Pa., 1976-80; del. Pa. Constl. Conv., 1967-68; chmn. Montgomery County Govt. Study Commn., 1973-74; mem. Civil Svc. Commn., Lower Merion Twp., 1978-80, 82-91, chmn., 1985-91; mem. adv. com. to U.S. Commn. on Civil Rights, 1985—; pres. Merion Park Civic Assn., 1966-68; mem. Nat. Adv. Coun. for Quality; trustee U. of the Arts, Phila. Bd. dirs. Alzheimer's Disease and Related Disorders Assns., Inc; mem. Supreme Ct. Hist. Soc.; mem. Phila. Spl. Investigation Com., 1985-86; mem. exec. com. Cen. Phila. Devel. Ctr., 1989—; trustee Nat. Constn. Ctr., 1988—. Fellow Am. Coll. Trial Lawyers, Am. Law Inst., Internat. Acad. Trial Lawyers, Am. Bar Found., Phila. Bar Found. (pres. 1982-84); mem. Am., Pa. Bar Assn., Phila. Bar Assn. (ho. of dels.), Atlantic City Bar Assn., Am. Judicature Soc., Juristic Soc., Lawyers' Club Phila., Yale Law Sch. Assn. (v.p. 1985), Pa. Soc., USCG Aux., Union League Club, Locust Club, Order of Coif, Pi Sigma Alpha, Phi Gamma Mu, Phi Beta Kappa. Office: Dilworth Paxson Kalish Ste 3200 1735 Market St Philadelphia PA 19103

KAUFFMAN, JEFFREY MICHAEL, psychotherapist; b. Phila., Dec. 29, 1942; s. Raymond and Florence (Packer) K.; m. Hilda Kauffman; 1 child, Daniel. MA, New Sch. for Social Rsch., 1977; MSS, Bryn Mawr Sch. of Social Work, 1985; postgrad., Inst. for Psychoanalytic, Phila. Cert. profl. death counselor. Psychotherapist Life Guidance Svc., Broomall, Pa., 1976-88; dir. Ctr. for the Care of Community Insts., Bala Cynwyd, Pa., 1988—, Grief Counseling and Support Svcs., Bala Cynwyd, 1988—; bereavement cons. various groups in Phila. area including Families of Murder Victims, MADD, Assn. for Ind. Growth; tng. cons. other Phila. groups including Temple U., Phila. Corp. on Aging. Contbr. articles to profl. jours. Mem. adv. bd. Job Corps., Phila. br., 1988—; bd. dirs. Families of Murder Victims, Phila, 1989—. Recipient Svc. award Leukemia Soc. Southeastern Pa., 1988. Mem. NASW, Assn. for Death Edn. and Counseling (pres. Del.-Pa. chpt. 1989—), Pa. Soc. for Clin. Social Work, (program chmn. 1991—). Office: Ctr Care Community Instns PO Box 2232 Bala Cynwyd PA 19004-6232

KAUFFMAN, LEON A., internist, educator; b. Phila., July 26, 1934; s. Isadore and Clara (Kenig) K.; B.A., Temple U., 1957, M.D., 1961; m. Rita Aurora B. Young, Apr. 2, 1969; children—Christopher I., Chandler S. Intern, Einstein Med. Center, Phila., 1961-62, resident in pathology, 1962-63; resident in internal medicine Hahnemann Med. Coll. and Hosp., Phila., 1963-65, fellow in pulmonary physiology and chest diseases, 1965-66; sr. instr. medicine Hahnemann U. Med. Sch., 1966-70, asst. prof., 1970-77, assoc. prof., 1977—, dir. pulmonary function lab., 1968-70, dir. respiratory intensive care unit, 1969-73, pulmonary cons. to shock and trauma unit, 1970-80; asst. dir. div. pulmonary medicine, 1970-73; pulmonary cons. U.S. Naval Hosp., 1973-77; med. dir. respiratory therapy St. Agnes Med. Center, Phila., 1973-78, assoc. attending in medicine; chmn. div. pulmonary medicine Met. Hosp., Phila., 1974-83, dir. Sch. Respiratory Therapy Tech., 1978-83; chmn. sub com. on sterilization of respiratory therapy equipment Am. Lung Assn. of Phila., 1975-81. Past mem. adv. com. Sch. Respiratory Therapy, Community Coll. Phila. Diplomate Am. Bd. Internal Medicine, subsplty. Bd. Pulmonary Disease. Fellow Am. Coll. Chest Physicians, Phila. Coll. Physicians; mem. Laennec Soc. Phila. (pres. 1975-76, exec. com. 1972-78), AMA, Pa. Med. Soc., Phila. County Med. Soc. (com. chronic respiratory disease and air pollution), Am. Thoracic Soc., A.C.P., Am. Acad. Med. Dirs. Respiratory Therapy, Phila. Drinker Soc. Critical Care Medicine, N.Y. Acad. Scis. Contbr. articles to profl. jours. Office: 1930 Pine St Philadelphia PA 19103-6626

KAUFFMAN, LUKE EDWARD, minister; b. Hummelstown, Pa., Dec. 19, 1941; s. Jeremiah Martin and Mary Elizabeth (Kreider) K.; m. Sandra Jean Garber, Aug. 1, 1964; children: Kurt Alan, Kent David, Kristen Lyn. AA, Hershey (Pa.) Jr. Coll., 1961; BA, Grace Coll., Winona Lake, Ind., 1963; MDiv, Grace Theol. Sem., Winona Lake, Ind., 1966; DMin, Luther Rice Sem., Jacksonville, Fla., 1989. Ordained to ministry Fellowship of Grace Brethren Chs., 1969. Pastor Grace Brethren Ch., Beaverton, Oreg., 1966-69; sr. pastor Grace Brethren Ch., Myerstown, Pa., 1969—; founder Grace Christian Sch., Myerstown, 1974; trustee Brethren Missionary Herald Co. Winona Lake 1974-77; pres. Grace Brethren Home Mission Coun., 1982—, Grace Brethren Investment Found. 1982—, Northern Atlantic Dist. Mission Bd. of Fellowship of Grace Brethren Chs.; speaker Grace Brethren Hour (radio) 1976-88, The Message of Grace (TV) 1983-88; dir. Grace Christian Sch. Myerstown 1974—; founder, dir. Grace Community, Inc. (retirement community) 1987—. Author: Eldership Church, 1978, Church Planting Principles and Policies That Produce, 1989. Chaplain Pa. State Senate 1983. Mem. Pa. Counseling Ctr (v.p. 1970-76). Republican. Home: 613 Hilltop Rd Myerstown PA 17067-1746 Office: Grace Brethren Ch 430 E Lincoln Ave Myerstown PA 17067-2297

KAUFMAN, CHARLES, physics educator; b. Bklyn., June 4, 1937; s. Irving and Lillian (Greenbaum) K.; m. Carol DeAcutis, June 12, 1967; children: Eleanor DeAcutis Kaufman, Amelia DeAcutis Kaufman. BS, U. Wis., 1956; MS, Pa. State U., 1959, PhD, 1963. Instr. Pa. State U., University Park, 1963-64; from asst. prof. to prof. physics U. R.I., Kingston, 1964—; physicist USN, Newport, R.I., 1969-71; vis. asst. prof. physics U. Wis., Madison, 1965-66; cons. physicist Raytheon Co., Newport, R.I., 1978-83; gast vortragender U. Vienna, Austria, 1971-72; sr. visitor U. Cambridge, Eng., 1985-86. ASEE/ONR fellow, 1991, 92. Mem. AAUP, AAAS, Am. Physical Soc., Acoustical Soc. of Am., N.Y. Acad. Scis. Office: U RI Physics Dept East Hall Kingston RI 02881

KAUFMAN, DAVID JOSEPH, lawyer; b. Harrisburg, Pa., Apr. 7, 1931; s. S. Herbert and Bessie (Claster) K.; m. Virginia Stern, Aug. 30, 1959; children: David J. Jr., James H. BS in Econs. cum laude, Franklin and Marshall Coll., 1952; JD cum laude, U. Pa., 1955. Bar: Pa. 1955. First assoc., then ptnr. Wolf, Block, Schorr & Solis-Cohen, Phila., 1957—; chmn., exec. com., 1979, 83. Bd. dirs. Abington (Pa.) Mem. Hosp., 1981—; pres. Congregation Rodeph Shalom, Phila., 1983-86. Served with U.S. Army, 1955-57. FEllow Am. Coll. Trust and Estate Counsel; mem. ABA, Pa. Bar Assn. (chmn. real property, probate and trust sect. 1986-87), Phila. Bar Assn. (chmn. probate sect. 1977). Republican. Home: 2191 Paper Mill Rd Huntingdon Valley PA 19006-5817 Office: Wolf Block Schorr & Solis-Cohen 1200 Packard Bldg Philadelphia PA 19102

KAUFMAN, DONALD SAUL, advertising agency executive; b. Bronx, N.Y., Apr. 18, 1945; s. Maurice A. and Sarah (Greenspan) K.; m. Susan Marcus, June 15, 1980; children: Jenny, Maia. BS, SUNY, New Paltz, N.Y., 1969, MA, 1973. Copy chief Doremus & Co., N.Y.C., 1980-82; sr. writer Muir, Cornelius, Moore, Inc., N.Y.C, 1982-84; pres. Absolutely Write, Inc., Valhalla, N.Y., 1984—. Editor IBM U.S. Mktg. Announcements, 1990-92; scriptwriter AT&T, 1990-92; creative dir. The Guide-IBM PC, 1983, 84 (Andy award 1984). Pub. Relations com. for Mayor of Mt. Vernon, N.Y., 1986—; bd. dirs. So. Westchester YM & YWHA, 1985—. Recipient CLIO award, 1987, Pro-Comm award Bus./Profl. Advt. Assn., 1986, Andy award of Distinction Advt. Club of N.Y., 1985, Bronze award Internat. Film and TV Assn., 1983. Mem. Advt. Club of Westchester. Democrat. Office: Absolutely Write Inc 465 Columbus Ave Valhalla NY 10595-1336

KAUFMAN, HARRY, retail executive; b. Altoona, Pa., July 16, 1937; s. Nathan and Ethel (Ritchin) K.; m. Margaret Anne Weiss; children: Ira, David. BBA, U. Pitts., 1959, M.Bus. Retailing, 1960. Owner, chief exec. officer Kaufman Stores & Wedding World Stores, Altoona, Pa., 1970—, Kaufman's Real Estate & Devel., Altoona, 1980—; developer The Kaufman Gallery, Altoona, 1987. Chmn. Pa. Retailers Polit. Action Com., 1987—; nat. bd. dirs. Union of Am. Hebrew Congregations-N.Am., 1987—; pres. Temple Beth Israel, Altoona, 1977-79; bd. dirs. Jewish Meml. Ctr., Altoona, 1989—; pres. Greater Altoona Econ. Devel. Corp., 1991—; mem. Sesquicentennial Com., Altoona, 1989; vice chmn. Altoona Redevel. Authority, 1989—; bd. dirs. Am. Heart Assn., Altoona, 1988-89. Named Retailer of the Yr., Pa. Retailers Assn., 1987. Mem. Pa. Retailers Assn. (v.p. 1986—), Kiwanis. Home: 3509 Baker Blvd Altoona PA 16602-1827 Office: Kaufman Stores 1301 11th Ave Altoona PA 16601-3301

KAUFMAN, IRVING N., transportation executive; b. N.Y.C., Jan. 21, 1924; s. Samuel and Maru (Jagorda) K.; m. Ruth Lillian Soicher, Sept. 12, 1948 (div. 1987); children: Richard B., John S., Joan E. BEE, CCNY, 1950. Div. dir. Airborne Instruments Lab., Deer Park, N.Y., 1950-66; group v.p. Gen. Instrument Corp., Hicksville, N.Y., 1966-71; pres. Page Communications Engrs., Inc., Vienna, Va., 1971-75; pres., chief exec. officer Communication Corp. of Am., Washington, 1975-77; pres. Loral Electronic Systems, Inc., Yonkers, N.Y., 1977-85; corp. sr. v.p. Loral Corp., Yonkers, 1977-85; pres., chmn. Sino Am. Transport, Inc., Washington, 1985—. Served with U.S. Army, 1942-45, ETO. Mem. IEEE, Assn. Old Crows, Assn. Unmanned Vehicles, U.S. Naval Inst., Am. Friends Chung-Ang U., Inc. (bd. dirs. 1982—), Nat. Mil. Family Assn. (bd. advisors 1986—). Republican. Club: Internat. (Washington). Home: 2510 Virginia Ave NW Washington DC 20037-1904 Office: Sino Am Transport Chennault Bldg 1049 30th St NW Washington DC 20007-3823

KAUFMAN, JESS, communication, financial and marketing consultant; b. Bklyn., June 12, 1920; s. Samuel and Alice (Simon) K.; B.S., N.Y.U., 1949, also postgrad.; m. Selma Helen Bruckner, June 20, 1948; children—Steven, David, Susan. Staff tax dept. G.A. Saxton & Co., N.Y.C., 1938-41; chief acct. 3d Naval Dist., 1943-46; comptroller, asst. treas. Hytron div. CBS, N.Y.C., 1946-48; v.p. mktg. Executone, Inc., Long Island City, N.Y., 1948-81; cons. Weinrich-Zitzmann-Whitehead Inc. Fin. Services, 1981-84; pres. Kaufman Assocs. Internat., cons. firm, 1981—; chmn. bd., chief exec. officer Express Telecom Inc., 1983-84; fin. cons. , Stratford, Conn., 1985-88; dir. sr. observer program Nass Am. Community Coll., Garden City, N.Y., 1989—; guest lectr. Grad. Sch. Pub. Health, N.Y.U., Grad. Sch. Pub. Health, Columbia U., N.Y.C., Grad. Sch. Pub. Health, Yale U., New Haven, Conn., Army Surgeon Gen. Inst. for Research, Washington, Sch. of Architecture, Stanford (Calif.) U., Am. Hosp. Assn. Inst. on Elec. and Mech. Engring. Design for Hosps., Chgo.; cons. communications and med. electronics AID, industry interface Exec. Br. of U.S. Govt.; participant Nat. Conf. on Internat. Econ. and Social Devel., Washington, HEW Confs. on biology and engring. in medicine, White House Conf. on Health; vis. lectr. hosp. communication systems and health care to various hosp. assns. Participant Gov.'s Conf. on Aging, State of N.Y.; bd. dirs. Producers Council, Inc., Washington. Served with USN, 1941-43. Decorated Purple Heart; elected to Student Hall of Fame, N.Y.U. Fellow Am. Pub. Health Assn., AAAS, Royal Soc. of Health; mem. Assn. of Mil. Surgeons of U.S., Internat. Hosp. Fedn., Am. Hosp. Assn., AMA, Fgn. Policy Assn., Am. Mgmt. Assn., Pub. Health Assn. of N.Y., Alpha Phi Sigma, N.Y.U. Alumni Assn. (mem. fund campaign com.). Contbr. articles on hosp. communications to profl. publs. Home: 220 Loines Ave PO Box 702 Merrick NY 11566

KAUFMAN, JOE, writer, illustrator; b. Bridgeport, Conn., May 21, 1911; s. Morris and Goldie (Haimowitz) K.; m. Evalyn Darrow, Feb. 23, 1957; children: Marshall, Arthur. Author/illustrator: How Things Work, 1971, The Human Body, 1975, Earth and Space, 1978, Creepy, Crawly Creatures, 1985, numerous mags. including Colliers, The Saturday Evening Post, Fortune, Sports Illustrated, TV networks. Recipient Art Dirs. Club medal, 1948, Nat. Sci. Tchrs. Assn. Children's Sci. Book award, 1973, Gold award, Silver award Art Dirs. Club. Mem. Soc. Illustrators, Authors Guild. Address: 18 W 70th St New York NY 10023

KAUFMAN, JOHN ROBERT, marketing and information management consultant; b. New Cumberland, Pa., Dec. 13, 1931; s. Jean Coulsen and Mercedes Katherine (Beshore) K.; m. Antoinette Anna Dolores Falcone, Apr. 30, 1988. AB, Pa. State U., 1953; MBA, U. Pa., 1955. V.p. N.W. Ayer & Son, Inc., Phila., 1965-80; pres. HBS, Inc. (Help Bus. Services, Inc.), Swarthmore, Pa., 1980—, Swarthmore Bus. Dist. Authority, 1991—. Pres. Swarthmore Bus. Dist. Authority, 1991—. Capt. USNR, ret. Mem. Am. Mktg. Assn. (nat. v.p., publisher 1975-80), Am. Mktg. Assn. (pres. Phila. chpt. 1968), Parlin Bd. Govs. (chmn. 1982-84), Soc. Competitor Intelligence Profls. Club: University (N.Y.C.). Lodge: Rotary (local pres. 1985). Home: 112 Park Ave Swarthmore PA 19081-1799 Office: HBS Inc Hbs Bldg 110 Swarthmore PA 19081

KAUFMAN, JUDITH, psychologist, educator; b. N.Y.C., Sept. 10, 1942; d. Nathan and Dorothy (Pattick) H.; m. Sheldon E. Kaufman, Nov. 1, 1964. BBA in Indsl. Psychology, CCNY, 1963, MS in Sch. Psychology, 1965; PhD in Ednl. Psychology, Yeshiva U., 1970. Lic. sch. psychologist, N.Y., psychologist, N.Y. Social worker Jewish Family Svc., N.Y.C., 1964-65; tchr. elem. sch. N.Y.C. Bd. Edn., 1965-66, psychologist in tng., 1966-67; asst. prof. psychology U. Bridgeport (Conn.), 1970-73; cons. affective edn. Model Learning Disabilities System, State College, Pa., 1973-76; assoc. prof. psychology Ferkauf Grad. Sch. Yeshiva U., N.Y.C., 1976-83, Ferkauf-Silverstein prof. psychology, program dir., 1983-88; dean of students Fairleigh Dickinson U., Rutherford, N.J., 1988-89; prof. Fairleigh Dickinson U., Rutherford, 1989—, v.p. pres. student affairs, 1989—; cons. Pub. Edn. Assn., 1982-88, Greenwich Assn. Retarded Citizens, 1983-88, Norwalk Assn. Retarded Citizens, 1983-88, pediatric AIDS project AECOM, 1985-89, dept. pediatrics Albert Einstein Coll. Medicine, 1986-88, N.Y.C. Bd. Edn., 1988-90, others. Author: (with others) Psychological Aspects of Gynecology and Obstetrics, 1978, Screening for Handicapped or Gifted, 1986, Standards and Evaluation in the Education and Training of Professional Psychologists, 1987, Testing Adolescents, 1987; contbr. articles to profl. jours. Mem. allocation panel United Way, Bergen County, 1991. Faculty rsch. grantee U. Bridgeport, 1971-72. Mem. Nat. Assn. Student Pers. Adminstrs. (adv. bd. region II, teleconferencing chair 1990-91), Am. Assn. Ind. Coll. and U. N.J. (subcom. on human diversity conf.), Am. Psychol. Assn. (various coms.), Nat. Assn. Sch. Psychologists (treas. 1982-84, N.E. regional dir. 1985-87, founder and dir. children's fund 1985-89), N.Y. State Psychol. Assn. (bd. dirs. 1977-79, pres. sch. div. 1977-79, chair awards com. 1982-83), Sch. Psychology Educators Coun. N.Y. State, Rotary, others. Home: 680 W End Ave New York NY 10025-6815 Office: Fairleigh Dickinson U 1000 River Rd Teaneck NJ 07666-1914

KAUFMAN, ROBERT MAX, lawyer; b. Vienna, Austria, Nov. 17, 1929; came to U.S., 1939, naturalized, 1945; s. Paul M. and Bertha (Hirsch) K.; m. Sheila Seymour Kelley. B.A. with honors, Bklyn. Coll., 1951; M.A., NYU, 1954; J.D. magna cum laude, Bklyn. Law Sch., 1957. Bar: N.Y. 1957, U.S. Supreme Ct. 1961. Successively jr. economist, economist, sr. economist N.Y. State Div. Housing, 1953-57; atty. antitrust div. U.S. Dept. Justice, 1957-58; legis. asst. to U.S. Senator Jacob K. Javits, 1958-61; assoc. Proskauer Rose Goetz & Mendelsohn, N.Y.C., 1961-69, ptnr., 1969—; chmn. bd. Pirelli Cable Corp., Pirelli Armstrong Tire Corp.; bd. dirs. Haseg (S.A.); mem. N.Y. State Legis. Adv. Com. on Election Law, 1973-74; chmn. adv. com. N.Y. State Bd. Elections, 1974-78; chmn. N.Y. State Bd. Pub. Disclosure, 1981-82, U.S. Army Chief of Staff's Spl. Commn. on Honor System, 1988-89, N.Y. Chief Judge's Com. on Availability of Legal Svcs., 1988-90; referee Commn. on Jud. Conduct; chmn. Fund for Modern Cts. Co-author: Congress and the Public Trust, 1970, Disorder in the Court, 1973 ; co-gen.-editor: Matthew Bender Treatise on Health Care Law, 4 vols. Bd. dirs., mem. exec. com. Lawrence M. Gelb Found., Inc., Vols. of Legal Svc., N.Y. Lawyers in the Pub. Interest; bd. dirs., sec. Community Action for Legal Svcs., Inc., 1976-78; dir., mem. exec. com. Legal Aid Soc., 1985-90; mem. platform com. N.Y. Rep. State Com., 1974; mem. jud. selection adv. coms. Senator Javits, 1972-80, and Senator Moynahan, 1977—; mem. distbn. com.

N.Y. Community Trust; bd. dirs. N.Y. Community Funds, James Found.; others. With U.S. Army, 1957-58. Fellow Am. Bar Found., N.Y. State Bar Found.; mem. ABA, Assn. of Bar of City N.Y. (pres. 1986-88, past chmn. com. on 2d Century; past chmn. exec. com., past chmn. com. profl. responsibility, past chmn. spl. com. on campaign expenditures, past chmn. com. civil rights, past vice chmn. com. grievances, chmn. delegation to state bar ho. dels.), N.Y. State Bar Assn. (ho. of dels. 1978, 86-90), N.Y. County Lawyers Assn. (past chmn. com. on civil rights), Am. Law Inst., Assn. Bar Fund (v.p.). Office: Proskauer Rose Goetz & Mendelsohn 1585 Broadway New York NY 10036-8200

KAUFMAN, STEPHEN E., lawyer; b. N.Y.C., Feb. 16, 1932; s. Herbert and Gertrude Kaufman; m. Marina Pinto, June 22, 1967; children: Andrew H. and Douglas P. BA, Williams Coll., 1953; LLB, Columbia U., 1957. Bar: N.Y. 1958, U.S. Ct. Appeals (2d cir.) 1958, U.S. Dist. Ct. (so. and ea. dists.) N.Y. 1960, U.S. Supreme Ct. 1963. Asst. U.S. Atty. U.S. Attys. Office, So. Dist., N.Y., 1964-69, chief of criminal div., 1964-69; pres. Stephen E. Kaufman, P.C., N.Y.C., 1976—; bd. dirs. Shearson High Yield Fund Inc., Shearson Govt. and Agys. Inc., Shearson Daily Dividend Inc., and other Shearson Funds. Fellow Am. Coll. Trial Lawyers; mem. ABA, N.Y. State Bar Assn., Assn. of Bar of City of N.Y. Office: 277 Park Ave New York NY 10172-0003

KAUFMANN, HENRY MARK, mortgage banker; b. Basel, Switzerland, May 23, 1929; came to U.S. 1940; s. Ferdinand and Carola (Levy) K.; m. Barbara Lurie, Dec. 23, 1961; children: Frederic, Nancy. Student, Univ. Geneva, Switzerland, 1948; BA in Economics, Oberlin Coll., 1951; JD, Harvard U., 1954. Bar: N.Y. 1957, U.S. Ct. Appeals 1960, U.S. Supreme Ct. 1960, U.S. Tax Ct. 1974. V.p. Pearce Mayer & Greer, N.Y.C., 1958-70, I.F.C. Capital Resources, N.Y.C., 1970-75, Smith Barney Real Estate Corp., N.Y.C., 1975-80; pres., chmn. Henry Kaufmann Assocs., Larchmont, N.Y., 1980—. With Mil. Intelligence Europe 1955-57. Mem. New Rochelle Bar Assn., N.Y. Bar Assn., New York County Lawyers Assn., Harvard Club. Home: 64 Greentree Dr Scarsdale NY 10583-7029 Office: Henry Kaufmann Assocs 2 East Ave Larchmont NY 10538-2419

KAUFMANN, MARK STEINER, banker; b. N.Y.C., Dec. 3, 1932; s. Milton L. and Elsa S. (Steiner) K.; B.S. cum laude in Bus. Adminstrn., Lehigh U., 1953; m. Carole Richard, June 16, 1957; children—Jon Richard, Susan Helen. Vice pres., dir. mktg. Standard Fin. Corp., N.Y.C., 1958-64; sr. v.p., dir. Milberg Factors, Inc., N.Y.C., 1964-73; dir. corp. devel. Chase Manhattan Bank, N.Y.C., 1973-87, sr. v.p., 1987—, dir. strategic planning, 1989—; chmn. Lower Manhattan Cultural Council, Wall St. Planning Group; co-chmn. banking div. UJA/Fedn. Past treas. bd. trustees Calhoun Sch., N.Y.C.; trustee Temple Israel, N.Y.C.; mem. bus. adv. coun. Lehigh U. Served as 1st lt. USAF, 1953-55. Recipient Human Relations award Anti-Defamation League, 1973, Human Relations award Am. Jewish Com., 1987. Mem. Am. Arbitration Assn., Old Oaks Country Club, Beta Gamma Sigma, Lambda Mu Sigma, Pi Gamma Mu, Omicron Delta Kappa. Home: 124 W 79th St New York NY 10024-6446 Office: Chase Manhattan Bank 1 Chase Manhattan Plz New York NY 10081-0001

KAUFMANN, MICHAEL MYRON, safety engineer; b. Bklyn., Oct. 14, 1940; s. Bernard and Betty (Lifland) K.; m. Frances Hymans, June 9, 1962; children: Stephanie, Alan. BSME, Worcester Poly. Inst., 1962; postgrad., Sacramento (Calif.) State Coll, 1963-64, Hofstra U., 1966-67, N.Y. Inst. Fluid Power, 1982. Registered profl. engr., N.Y., Calif.; cert. safety profl. Engr. trainee E.W. Bliss Co., div. Gulf & Western, Canton, Ohio, 1962-65; plant mgr. Revere Survival Products, Deer Park, N.Y., 1965-77; mgr. maint. and engring. The Vitarine Co., div. West Chems., Springfield Gardens, N.Y., 1977-78; dir. engring. Revere Supply Co., Inc., N.Y.C., 1978-80; dir. ops. Sci. Ind., Inc., Bohemia, N.Y., 1980-81; dir. engring. Hydrodyne Ind., Inc., Hauppauge, N.Y., 1981-83; sr. design engr. Aircraft Porous Media, Inc., Glen Cove, N.Y., 1983-88; mgr. applications engring. Pall Indsl. Hydraulics Corp., East Hills, N.Y., 1988-89; cons. Tech. Med. Forensic Cons., W. Hempsatead, N.Y., 1989—. Patentee in field. Vol. Boy Scouts Am., Nassau County, 1948—; rep. Nassau Com. for Camping, East Meadow, N.Y., 198-85. 1st lt. Signa Corps, U.S. Army, 1962-64. Recipient Excellence in Machine Design, Machinery Mag., 1962, Silver Beaver, Boy Scouts Am., 1988. Mem. ASME (safety com.), ASTM (F-13 com.), Am. Soc. Safety Engrs., Systems Safety Soc., Family Morot Home Assn., Acad. Model Aeros., Nassau Good Sam Club (corr. sec. 1979-85), Masons (master 1973-74). Office: Kaufmann Cons Co 140 S Park Dr Massapequa Park NY 11762-1025

KAUFMANN, THOMAS DACOSTA, art history educator; b. N.Y.C., May 7, 1948; s. Richard Kohns and Manette Rodrigues (DaCosta) K.; m. Virginia Burns Roehrig, June 1, 1974; 1 child, Catharine Roehrig. BA, MA, Yale U., 1970; MPhil, Warburg Inst. of London, Eng., 1972; PhD, Harvard U., 1977. Asst. prof. art and archaeology Princeton U, N.J., 1977-83; assoc. prof. Princeton U, 1983-89; prof. Princeton U., 1989—; vis. prof. U. Pa., 1980; symposium organizer Princeton U. Art Mus., U. Calif. Art Mus., Santa Barbara, 1982, 89, 90; guest curator Princeton U. Art Mus., 1982, 88; cons. J.P. Getty Ctr., Malibu, Santa Monica, Calif., 1985, 86, 88, 89, 90; adviser collection inventory Art Inst. Chgo., 1988; selector various fellowships, 1985—. Author: Variations on Imperial Theme, 1978 (award ACLS Soc. Sci. Rsch. Coun. 1977-78), Drawings from the Holy Roman Empire, 1982, Art and Architecture in Central Europe, 1983, School of Prague, 1988 (Mitchell prize 1988), Central European Drawings, 1989, The Mastery of Nature, 1992; contbr. articles, book chpts. to profl. publs. Adviser, negotiator Internat. Rsch. Exch. Bd./Am. Coun. Learned Socs.-Polish Acad. Scis. agreements, 1982—, Internat. Rsch. Exch. Bd./Am. Coun. Learned Socs. Czechoslovak Acad. agreements, 1985—. Marshall Allison fellow, 1970; fellow David E. Finley Nat. Gallery of Art, Washington, 1974-77, Am. Coun. Learned Socs., 1982; sr. fellow Alexander von Humboldt Stiftung, Berlin and Munich, 1985-86, 89-90; grantee NEA, NEH. Mem. Coll. Art Assn., Renaissance Soc. Am. Home: 39 Princeton Ave Princeton NJ 08540-5255

KAUNE, CHARLES ROBERT, career counselor, marketing representative; b. Muskogee, Okla., Oct. 4, 1943; s. Elizabeth (Hartson) K.; m. Hannelore Hoppe, Dec. 20, 1980; children: Lore, Walter. AB, Utica Coll., N.Y., 1967; student teaching, Colgate U., Hamilton, N.Y., 1968; MA, Marywood Coll., Scranton, Pa., 1978. Counseling. English tchr. Vernon-Verona-Sherrill High Sch., Vernon, N.Y., 1967-68; employment interviewer N.Y.S. Dept. of Labor, Binghamton, N.Y., 1972-76, employment counselor, 1976-89; supervising counselor N.Y.S. Dept. of Labor, Syracuse, N.Y., 1989-91, assoc. mktg. rep., 1991—; career counselor, 1st Brigade. 98th Div. U.S.A.R., Schenectady, N.Y., 1989—. Recipient Vocat. Rehab. Ednl. grant, Syracuse U., N.Y., 1987. Mem. Nat. Bd. for Cert. Counselors, N.Y.S. Assn. Employment Counselors, Nat. Employment Counselor Assn., Military Educator and Counselors Assn. Republican. Roman Catholic. Home: 3169 Reston Dr Baldwinsville NY 13027-1700 Office: NYS Community Svcs Regional Office 677 S Salina St Syracuse NY 13202-3532

KAUNITZ, HANS, physician, pathologist; b. Vienna, Austria, Oct. 20, 1905; came to U.S., 1941; s. Arpad and Elsa (Hohenberg) K.; m. Esther Beckwith, Apr. 7, 1943. MD, U. Vienna, Austria, 1930. Lic. physician, N.Y. Supervising physician Vienna U. Hosp., 1932-38; assoc. prof. of medicine U. of Phillipines, Manila, 1938-40; from asst. prof. to clin. prof. Columbia U., N.Y.C., 1956-75. Contbr. numerous articles to profl. jours., sci. papers to meetings, confs. Recipient Presidential Merit medal Pres. of Phillipines, Presidential Hon. medal, Austria, 1961. Mem. Pirquet Soc. (Disting. Mem. award 1970), Am. Oil Chem. Soc. (Achievement award 1971, Alton Bailley medal 1981, Hans Kaunitz Student award 1988). Home: 152 E 94th St New York NY 10128-2510 Office: Columbia U Dept Pathology 630 W 16th St New York NY 10032

KAURENE, BRUCE RICHARD, health care computer software executive; b. Phila., Feb. 22, 1955. BSBA, Pa. State U., 1976. Programmer, analyst Eastman Kodak, Rochester, N.Y., 1976-78; project mgr. E. I. duPont, Wilmington, Del., 1978-84; sr. dir. Erisco, Inc., N.Y.C., 1984—; instr. U. Del., Wilmington, 1979-84. Office: Erisco Inc 1700 Broadway New York NY 10019-5905

KAUTH, BENJAMIN, podiatric consultant; b. N.Y.C., Oct. 20, 1913; m. Bertha Locke. Student, CCNY, 1935-38; D in Podiatric Medicine, N.Y. Coll. Podiatric Medicine, 1939, postgrad., 1944-45; postgrad., CCNY; HHD (hon.), N.Y. Coll. Podiatric Medicine, 1981. Pvt. practice N.Y.C., 1939-78; podiatric cons., 1978—; co-chief podiatry staff St. Clare's Hosp., N.Y.C.; chief of staff podiatry Jewish Home and Hosp. for Aged, Village Nursing Home of St. Vincents Hosp.; mem. staff French Polyclinic; chief podiatry panel 1199 Nat. Fund; coord. podiatry panel 32 B-J Health Ctr.; mem. med. panel Med. Malpractice Bronx County; trustee, mem. exec. coun. N.Y. Coll. Podiatric Medicine; cons. Podiatrist Local 1199 Health Fund, Equitable Life Assurance Co., various other third-party insurers, pub. rels. firms. Editorial asst. N.Y. Podiatrist Del. to Nat. Conv.; contbr. articles to profl. jours. Bd. dirs. Adams Sch. for Retarded Children, Am. Jewish Distbn. Com. Mem. Am. Coll. Foot Surgeons (assoc.), Am. Podiatric Med. Assn. (pub. affairs com., editorial asst.), Podiatry Soc. of the State N.Y. (spl. asst. to pres., editorial asst. annual meeting), N.Y. County Podiatry Soc. (sec., exec. bd.), Fair Harbor Yacht Club (sec.), Friars. Home and Office: 302 W 12th St New York NY 10014-1945

KAUZMANN, WALTER JOSEPH, chemistry educator; b. Mt. Vernon, N.Y., Aug. 18, 1916; s. Albert and Julia Maria (Kahle) K.; m. Elizabeth Alice Flagler, Apr. 1, 1951; children: Charles Peter, Eric Flagler, Katherine Elizabeth Julia Kauzmann Pacala. B.A., Cornell U., 1937; Ph.D., Princeton U., 1940; PhD (hon.), U. Stockholm, 1992. Westinghouse research fellow Westinghouse Mfg. Co., E. Pittsburgh, Pa., 1940-42; mem. staff Explosives Research Lab., Bruceton, Pa., 1942-44, Los Alamos Lab., 1944-46; asst. prof. Princeton U., 1946-51, asso. prof., 1951-60, prof. chemistry, 1960-82, chmn. dept., 1964-68, David B. Jones prof. chemistry, 1963-82, chmn. biochem. sci. dept., 1980-81; vis. scientist Atlantic Research Lab., NRC Can., 1983; vis. lectr. Kyoto U., 1974; vis. prof. U. Ibadan, 1975. Author: Quantum Chemistry, 1957, Kinetic Theory of Gases, 1966, Thermal Properties of Matter, 1967, (with D. Eisenberg) Structure and Properties of Water, 1969. Jr. fellow Soc. Fellows, Harvard, 1942; Guggenheim fellow, 1957, 74-75; Recipient Linderstrom-Lang medal, 1966. Fellow AAAS, Am. Acad. Arts and Scis., Am. Phss. Soc.; mem. Nat. Acad. Scis., Am. Soc. Biochemistry and Molecular Biology, Am. Geophys. Union, Am. Chem. Soc., Fedn. Am. Scientists, Astron. Soc. Pacific, Royal Astron. Soc. Can., Math. Assn. Am., Sigma Xi. Office: 301 N Harrison St Ste 152 Princeton NJ 08540-3512

KAWAJA, KALEEM ULLAH, electrical engineer; b. Kunpur, India, Mar. 5, 1941; came to U.S. 1969; s. Hakeem U. and Anees Kawaja; m. Tahoora Kawaja, Feb. 8, 1975; children: Mona Kaleem, Omar Kaleem. BSEE, Indian Inst. Tech., 1963; MS in Engring. Mgmt., Bklyn. Poly. Inst., 1973. Registered profl. engr., N.Y., Md., Tex. Sr. engr. Ebasco Svcs., N.Y.C., 1969-74; project mgr. Brown & Root, Inc., Houston, 1974-80; supervising engr. Bechtel Corp., Gaithersburg, Md., 1980-85; project mgr. Bendix Corp., Columbia, Md., 1985-89; engring. mgr. NASA, Greenbelt, Md., 1989—. Editor The AIM jour.; contbr. articles to profl. jours. Mem. Asian Am. Adv. Group, NASA/Goddard Space Flight Ctr., Greenbelt, 1991—; pres. Assn. of Indian Muslims of Am., Washington, 1989-91; mem. Rep. Nat. Com. Recipient Honor award NASA, 1992, Mgmt. Recognition award, 1991, Hind Rattan Jewel of India award Non-Resident Indians Welfare Soc., New Delhi, 1991. Mem. ASME. Home: 11649 Masters Run Ellicott City MD 21043

KAWAJA, TERENCE GERARD, investment banker; b. Chandler, Que., Can., Dec. 19, 1962; came to U.S., 1989; s. Donald John and Mary Catherine (McCormack) K. BA, U. Western Ont., London, Can., 1985; JD, Osgoode Hall Law Sch., Toronto, Can., 1989; MBA, York U., Toronto, 1989. Fin. analyst Royal Trust Corp., Toronto, 1986-87; assoc. McCarthy & McCarthy, Toronto, 1988; assoc. Salomon Bros. Inc., N.Y.C., 1989-92, v.p., 1992—. Pres. Osgoode Hall Progressive Conservative Club, Toronto, 1987-89, Progressive Conservative Assn., Toronto, 1985-86. Mem. Can. Soc. N.Y., Met. Club (N.Y.C.), Can. Club N.Y., Albany Club of Toronto. Office: Salomon Bros Inc 7 World Trade Center New York NY 10048

KAWANO, JAMES CONRAD, marketing consultant. Student, U. Calif., Berkeley, 1972-73; PharmD, U. Calif., San Francisco, 1978; postgrad., U. Pa., 1986—. Registered pharmacist, Calif., Pa. Clin. pharmacist Med. Coll. Pa. and Hosp., Phila., 1978-82; med. devel. coord. E.R. Squibb and Sons, U.S., Princeton, N.J., 1982-84; mktg. rsch. supr. E.R. Squibb and Sons, U.S., Princeton, 1984-85, mktg. rsch. mgr., 1985-86; mgr. strategic planning and bus. analysis Squibb U.S., Princeton, 1986-87, bus. devel. mgr., 1987-88; mgr. product planning worldwide bus. devel. Squibb Pharms. Group, Princeton, 1988-89; mgr. product planning pravastatin, worldwide strategic product planning Bristol-Myers Squibb Pharm. Group, Princeton, 1989-90; sr. product planning mgr., strategic product planning Bristol-Myers Squibb Pharm. Group, 1990-91; cons. pharm. mktg. devel. Narberth, Pa., 1991—. Patentee in field. Mem. Am. Soc. Hosp. Pharmacists, Pa. Soc. Hosp. Pharmacists, Calif. Pharmacists Assn.

KAWASHIMA, TAKESHI, artist; b. Takamatsu, Japan, Jan. 13, 1930; came to U.S., 1963; s. Tsuneichi and Mizue (Tada) K.; m. Junko Kuruma, Feb. 5, 1973; 1 child from previous marriage, Kokoro. Student Musashino Art U., Tokyo, 1951-56, Art Students League, N.Y.C., 1965-66. One man shows include Nantenshi Gallery, Tokyo, 1984, Mitsukoshi Dept. Hall, Takamatsu City, 1987, Gallery Internat. 57, N.Y.C., 1988, Nantenshi Gallery, Tokyo, 1989, Takamatsu City Mus. of Art, 1989, Yamaso Art Gallery, Kyoto, Japan, 1990, Ryoko Art Gallery, Kyoto, 1991, Magna Gallery N.Y.C., 1992; exhibited in group shows at Bergen Mus. Art and Sci., N.J., 1983, Sande Webster Gallery, Phila., 1983, Mus. Modern Art, Guuma, Japan, 1984, Fire House Gallery of Nassau Community Coll., Garden City, N.Y., 1985, Gallery Internat. 57, N.Y.C., 1988, Gallery Internat. 52, N.Y.C.; works represented in collections at The Mus. Modern Art, N.Y.C., 1965, Chase Manhattan Bank, N.A., N.Y.C., 1966, SUNY, Postdam, 1970, 73, Kyoto Nat. Mus. of Art, 1976, Ohara Mus. Art, Kurashiki, Japan, 1984, 87, Tokyo Met. Mus. Art, Kushiro Uoichiba Corp., Hokkaido, Japan, Takamatsu Mcpl. Mus. Art, 1987, Tokushima Mus., 1986, 87, Ohara Mus. Art, Kurashiki City, 1989, Toyama Prefectural Mus. of Art, Toyama-ken, 1989; Daniel Schnakenberg scholar, 1965; Bd. of Control scholar, 1966; recipient Silvermine award, 1967. Home: 11 Mercer St 2 F New York NY 10013

KAWATA, PAUL AKIO, health association administrator; b. Salt Lake City, July 24; s. William and Miyeko (Hashima) K. BA, U. Pacific; MA, Antioch U., Seattle. Mem. mayor's staff City of Seattle, 1980-85; exec. dir. Nat. AIDS Network, Washington, 1986-89, Nat. Minority AIDS Coun., Washington, 1989—; cons. WHO, Geneva. Co-author: Everything You Wanted to Know About AIDS. Named hon. citizen City of New Orleans, 1987; recipient Michael Hirsh award Body Positive, N.Y.C., 1990. Mem. Internat. AIDS Orgn. (bd. dirs.), JACL. Democrat. Office: Nat Minority AIDS Coun 300 I St NE 4th Fl Washington DC 20002

KAWULA, JOHN MICHAEL, professional society administrator; b. Passaic, N.J., Apr. 6, 1947; s. Stanley Michael and Catherine (Petryshyn) K.; m. Jean Marie Wiecke, Dec. 1, 1979; children: John Jr., Melissa, Michael, Gregory, Sean. BA, Fairleigh Dickinson U., Teaneck, N.J., 1969; postgrad., U. Wis., 1988. Pub. rels. mgr. The Record, Hackensack, N.J., 1969-72; mgr. pub. rels. and rsch. The Paterson News, Hackensack, N.J., 1972-74; dir. pub. rels. Point Purchase Advt. Inst., N.Y.C., 1974-78; chief exec. officer, pres. Point Purchase Advt. Inst., Englewood, N.J., 1981—, organizer, bd. dirs. Japan divs., 1985; organizer, bd. dirs. Europe divs. Point Purchase Advt. Inst., 1989; v.p. Donaldson Mktg., South Hackensack, N.J., 1978-81; bd. dirs., mem. adv. com. Waukesa Coll., 1987; organizer Can. Task Force, 1990, European Task Force, 1991; speaker and lectr. in field. Author: (books) Newspaper In The Classroom, 1972, Responding to AIDS in Your Business, 1990, POP and the Environment--What We Can Do, 1990, AIDS: An Employee Guideline, 1991; contbg. edit. (book) Handbook of Sales Promotion, 1983; pub. Newspaper, Mags. POPAI News, 1981; producer Video Tapes Consumer Behavior Drug Stores, 1985, Consumer Behavior Drug Stores and Supermarkets, 1987, 88, Careers in POP Video, 1988, Advertising Video, 1988, Career in Marketing, 1989, Careers in Marketing, 1989, Careers in Creativity, 1990; contbr. editor Marketing Communications, 1981-83. Coach Ridgewood Baseball, Basketball Assn., 1978-84, 89—; leader Boyscouts Am., Ridgewood, 1975-83; mem. Freedom to Advertise Coalition, Washington. Recipient Award of Excellence Assn. Trends Mag., 1987, 88, 89, 90, European PLU Oscar award, 1988, Recognition citation HHS, 1990, citation Adam Walsh Children's Fund. Mem. Am. Soc. Assn. Execs. (Gold Cir. award 1985, Award Excellence 1990), N.J. Soc. Assn. Execs. (Communications Merit Award 1990), N.Y. Soc. Assn. Execs., Sales Execs. Club of N.Y. Roman Catholic. Office: Point Purchase Advt Inst 66 N Van Brunt St Englewood NJ 07631-3461

KAY, HELEN (MRS. HERBERT J. GOLDFRANK), writer; b. N.Y.C., Oct. 27, 1912; d. Hyman and Tessie (Herman) Colodny; m. Herbert John Goldfrank, Dec. 25, 1933; children: Lewis Robert, Deborah, Joan. Student public schs. Washington, writer workshops N.Y.U., Bank St. Coll. Editorial research Time mag., N.Y.C., 1936, Fortune mag., 1937, Labor Press, SMCWA News, 1943-44, CIO News, 1945. Bd. dirs. Learning to Read Through the Arts at the Guggenheim, 1980. Mem. Authors League, PEN, Soc. Children's Book Writers. Author: Apple Pie For Lewis, 1951, Snow Birthday, 1955, One Mitten Lewis, 1955, City Springtime, 1957, A Pony for the Winter, 1959, Lincoln, A Big Man, 1958, Abe Lincoln's Hobby, 1961, How Smart Are Animals, 1963, The Secrets of the Dolphin, 1964, A Stocking for a Kitten, 1965, Picasso's World of Children, 1965, reprinted, 1977, An Egg is for Wishing, 1966, Man and Mastiff, 1967, Apes, 1970, The Staff of the Shepherd, 1983, The First Teddy Bear, 1985; many others. Address: 375 Nannyhagen Rd Thornwood NY 10594

KAY, MARGARET J., psychologist; b. Washington, Apr. 16, 1951; d. Joseph Allen and Joan (Auchter) Brown; m. Jeffrey Edward Kay, Nov. 24, 1984; children: Meghan Joan, Jennifer Elizabeth. BA, Ind. (Pa.) U., 1973; MS, U. Waterloo, Ontario, Canada, 1977. Licensed Psychologist. Cert. Sch. Psychologist. Diplomate Am. Bd. Med. Psychotherapists. Research asst. Dept. Air Force, Washington, 1973; mgmt. trainee Hamilton Bank, Lancaster, Pa., 1973-74; psychologist Reality Home Svcs. for Children, Waterloo, Ontario, Canada, 1976-77; chief psychologist, v.p. Pan Am Corp., Hershey, Pa., 1977-81; psychologist, owner Lancaster (Pa.) Psychol. Svcs., 1981—; cons. in field. Author: Parent Power: Understanding Right To Education Laws, 1980. Sec. Lancaster LD Pvt. Sch. Project, 1988—. Recipient Cert. of Appreciation Lancaster Assn. for Children & Adults with Learning Disabilities, 1985. Mem. Am. Psychol. Assn., Orton Dyslexia Soc., Pa. Psychol. Assn. Republican. Roman Catholic. Home: 600 Randolph Dr Lititz PA 17543-9091 Office: 2818 Lititz Pike Lititz PA 17543-9375

KAY, ROBERT WILLIAM ANTHONY, consultant; b. London, Oct. 3, 1952; came to U.S., 1987; s. Fred and Marjorie Hayes (Grime) K.; m. Dorothy Joyce Raw, July 19, 1980; children: Alexandra Louise, Lucinda Elizabeth. MA in Math., Oxford U., 1974, math. (hon.), 1976. Asst. v.p. Citibank N.A., London, 1974-77; v.p. Chase Manhattan Bank N.A., London, 1977-87; pres. Morgan Stanley Trust Co., Jersey City, N.J., 1987-90, Global Securties Cons. Svcs., New Providence, N.J., 1991—; exec. dir. Cedel, Luxembourg, 1985-87; dir. Internat. Ops. Assn., N.Y.C., 1985-87, Chase Manhattan Trustees Ltd., 1986-87. Home: 44 Cayuga Way Short Hills NJ 07078-1249 Office: Global Securities Cons Svcs 139 South St New Providence NJ 07974-1945

KAYAR, SUSAN RENNIE, physiologist; b. Highland, Ill., May 17, 1953; d. Sedat Arif and Ruth Annalea (Houseman) K. BS, U. Miami, Fla., 1974, PhD, 1978. Rsch. asst. Everglades Nat. Park, Flamingo, Fla., 1978-79; rsch. assoc. U. Colo., Boulder, 1979-81; rsch. fellow U. Colo., Denver, 1981-84, U. Bern, Switzerland, 1984-89; instr. U. Medicine & Dentistry of N.J., Piscataway, 1989-90; physiologist Naval Med. Rsch. Inst., Bethesda, Md., 1990—. Contbr. numerous articles to profl. jours. Maytag fellow U. Miami, 1974-77, Fogarty Found. fellow Swiss NSF, 1984-85; Nat. Merit scholar U. Miami, 1971-74; NRC/NIH grantee, 1981-84, Am. Heart Assn. grantee, 1989-90. Mem. Am. Soc. Zoologists, Am. Physiol. Soc., Microcirculatory Soc., Internat. Soc. Oxygen Transport to Tissue, Capital Hiking Club. Office: Nat Naval Med Ctr Diving Biomed Tech Naval Med Rsch Inst Bethesda MD 20889-5055

KAYE, JANET MIRIAM, psychologist; b. New Haven, Mar. 2, 1937; d. Al and Rose (Marcus) Sovitsky; m. Donald Kaye, June 26, 1955; children: Kenneth, Karen, Kendra, Keith. BS, NYU, 1958, MA, 1960; PhD, Med. Coll. of Pa., 1980. Clin. instr. Med Coll. of Pa., Phila., 1980-82, asst. prof., 1982-86, assoc. prof., 1986—. Contbr. articles to profl. jours. Mem. Am. Assn. Cancer Edn., APA, Am. Soc. Clin. Hypnosis, Soc. Health & Human Values, Gerontol. Soc. of Am., Am. Soc. Psychiat. Oncology, Coll. of Physicians of Pa., Internat. Soc. Exptl. Hypnosis. Office: Med Coll PA 3300 Henry Ave Philadelphia PA 19129-1191

KAYE, NANCY WEBER, cell biology consultant; b. Englewood, N.J., Sept. 14, 1929; d. William Oscar and Edith Rebecca (Sanders) Weber; m. Gordon Israel Kaye, June 4, 1956; children: Jacqueline Elizabeth, Vivienne Rebecca. BA, Swarthmore Coll., 1951; MA, Hunter Coll., 1954; AM, Columbia U., 1958, PhD, 1960. Rsch. worker in anatomy Columbia U., N.Y.C., 1962-67, rsch. worker in ophthalmology, 1967-70, rsch. assoc. in ophthalmology, 1973-76; rsch. assoc. in ophthalmology Albany (N.Y.) Med. Coll., 1976-79, rsch. assoc. in anatomy and medicine, 1979-82, asst. prof. in anatomy, 1982-89, rsch. cons. in medicine, 1990—. Contbr. articles to profl. jours. Named postdoctoral fellow NIH, Columbia U., 1960-61. Mem. AAAS, AAUW (Jean Lennox Kimmel fellow 1959-60), Am. Soc. for Cell Biology, Am. Assn. Anatomists, Assn. for Rsch. in Vision & Ophthalmology, N.Y. Acad. Sci., Sigma Xi. Home: 212 Pinewoods Ave Troy NY 12180-7244 Office: Albany Med Coll 47 New Scotland Ave Albany NY 12208-3412

KAYE, NEIL SCOTT, psychiatrist; b. Albany, N.Y., June 1, 1958; s. Jesse J. and Shirley Mae (Poskanzer K.; m. Susan M. Donnelly, July 2, 1988. BA, Skidmore Coll., 1980; MD, Albany Med. Coll., 1984. Diplomate Nat. Bd. Med. Examiners, Am. Bd. Psychiatry and Neurology; lic. med. practitioner, N.Y., Mass., Del.; bd. cert. geriatric psychiatry, 1991. Rotating intern Albany (N.Y.) Med. Ctr. Hosp., 1985, resident dept. psychiatry, 1986-87; with crisis unit coverage Capital Dist. Psychiat. Ctr., Albany, 1986-87; forensic fellow dept. psychiatry Syracuse U.-SUNY Upstate, 1987-88; asst. prof. psychiatry sch. medicine U. Mass., Worcester, 1988-90; evening admissions & continuing treatment unit psychiatrist Worcester State Hosp., 1988-90; dir. consultation and liaison psychiatry Med. Ctr. Del., Christiana Hosp., Wilmington, 1990-92; spl. guest instr. Widener U. Sch. Law, 1991—; asst. prof. dept. psychiatry Thomas Jefferson Sch. Medicine, 1991—; chmn. credentials com. Worcester State Hosp., Worcester; cons. psychiatrist State of N.Y., Auburn (N.Y.) Prison, 1987-88; weekend ward coverage VA Hosp., Albany, 1987-88, supr. jail social worker Rensselaer County Jail, Forenic Svc., Rensselaer County Mental Health Dept., 1987-88; supr. social workers, medication mgmt. for the clinic, Social Security and Disability evalutions, child custody Rensselaer County Mental Health Dept., Unified Svcs., Rensselaer, N.Y., 1987-88; lectr., presenter. Contbr. articles to profl. jours. Rowing referee U.S. Rowing Assn., 1987—; founder and co-chmn. Empire State Regatta, Albany, 1984-87; mem. Downtown Redevel. Commn., Albany, 1984-90, Riverfront Devel. Commn., Albany, 1984-90; at-large mem. bd. dirs. Albany Med. Coll. Aluni Assn., 1985—; vol. driver, attendant, EMT, Saratoga Emergency Corps, 1978-80; house counselor Skidmore Coll, 1979, residence asst., 1980; dir. Camp Shelley Day Camp, New Scotland, N.Y., 1977-82; adv. com. Schaffer Libr. Health Scis., 1981-87. Recipient Mayor's Proclamation for Community Svc., Albany, 1985, Tricentennial Proclamation, Albany, 1986; named Rappeport Fellow nominee, 1987. Mem. AMA (Physicians Recognition award for Continuing Med. Edn.), Am. Psychiat. Assn., N.Y. State Med. Soc., Mass. Med. Soc., Nat. Assn. Sports Ofcls., Am. Acad. Forensic Scis. (com. on ethics 1990—, award for best paper by a forensic fellow 1989), Am. Acad. Psychiatry and the Law (com. on AAPL/APA rels. 1988—, com. on ethics 1988—), Assn. Am. Med. Colls. (faculty 1988—), N.Y. Acad. Scis., Internat. Wine and Food Soc., Am. Acad. Psychiat. Adminstrs., Assn. Compulsive Therapy, Am. Assn. Geriatric. Home: 3 Hayloft Ct Limestone Hills Wilmington DE 19808 Office: Med Ctr Del Dept Psychiatry Dir Consultation and Liaison Psychiatry Wilmington DE 19899 also: Allied Psychiat Svcs 1601 Concord Pike Ste 92-100 Wilmington DE 19803

KAYE, WALTER, financial executive; b. Bklyn., Aug. 22, 1927; s. Jack and Ida (Shapiro) K.; m. Bernice Glatzer, May 6, 1952; children: Steven Mark, Russell Stuart. Student, CCNY, 1950-53; postgrad. (fellow), N.Y. Inst. Credit, 1956. Credit mgr., treas. A. Steinam Co., Inc., N.Y.C., 1951-68; v.p. Ambassador Factors Corp., N.Y.C., 1968-74; sr. v.p. Congress Factors Corp., N.Y.C., 1974-84; pres., chief exec. officer Mcht. Factors Corp.,

N.Y.C., 1985—. Served with U.S. Army, 1944-46. Recipient Yitzak Rabin award B'nai B'rith, 1982; recipient Plaque Manhattan Credit, 1979. Mem. N.Y. Inst. Credit, N.Y. Credit and Fin. Mgmt., Nat. Comml. Fin. Assn., Manhattan Credit (pres. 1978-79) Empire Credit (pres. 1971-74), The Financemen's Group Club, 475 Club. Home: 61 Bramblebrook Rd Ardsley NY 10502-2233 Office: Mcht Factors Corp 1450 Broadway New York NY 10018-2201

KAYHART, MARION, biology educator; b. Kinnelon, N.J., Sept. 14, 1926; d. Lawrence and Beatrice (Ackerman) K. BA, Drew U., 1947; MA, U. Pa., 1949, PhD, 1954. Lab. instr. Drew U., Madison, N.J., 1947-48; instr. biology Roanoke Coll., Salem, Va., 1949-51; asst. prof. biology Roanoke Coll., Salem, 1951-52; asst. instr. U. Pa., Phila., 1952-53, rsch. asst., 1953-54; chair of dept. Cedar Crest Coll., Allentown, Pa., 1954-87, from. asst. prof. to full prof., 1954—; faculty rep. bds. of trustees Cedar Crest Coll., Allentown, 1968-72. Bd. trustees Allentown Osto. Med. Ctr., 1976-86. Recipient Alumnae Assn. award for excellence in teaching Cedar Crest Coll. Alumnae Assn., 1984, Alumnae Achievement award in sci. Drew U., 1970. Mem. AAAS, Am. Genetic Soc., Nat. Biology Tchrs. Assn., Nat. Scis. Tchrs. Assn. Democrat. Office: Cedar Crest Coll Dept Biology 100 College Dr Allentown PA 18104-6196

KAYLOR, JEFFERSON DANIEL, JR., electronics executive; b. Birmingham, Ala., Dec. 10, 1947; s. Jefferson Daniel and Mary Charlye (Montague) K.; m. Terry Frances Hill, June 13, 1970; children: Christopher Robert, Laure Danielle. BS, USN Acad., 1970; MBA, Fla. Inst. Tech., 1981, MS, 1983. Sr. electronic systems engr. E-Systems, Garland, Tex., 1977-79; sr. staff engr. Sperry, Clearwater, Fla., 1979-83; program mgr. Amecom div. Litton Systems, College Park, Md., 1983-85, program dir., 1985-87, dir. advanced systems programs, 1989—; v.p. ops. Micro-Tel div. Adams-Russell, Hunt Valley, Md., 1987-88, div. mgr., 1988-89; cons. and lectr. in field. Lt. USN, 1970-77. Mem. Armed Forces Communicaitons and Electronics Assn., USN Res. (captain selectee 1992), Naval Res. Assn., Navy League, Assn. Old Crows (pres. club 1981-82). Republican. Methodist. Home: 4040 Firefly Way Ellicott City MD 21042 Office: Litton Systems Amecom Div 5115 Calvert Rd College Park MD 20740

KAYSER, KENNETH WAYNE, lawyer; b. N.Y.C., Apr. 28, 1947; s. William Gilbert and Joan Phyliss (Bach) K.; m. Linda Calcote, Apr. 13, 1968; 1 child, Christopher R. BA, Syracuse U., 1969; JD, Seton Hall, 1977. Bar: N.J. 1977, U.S. Dist. Ct. N.J. 1977, U.S. Cir. Ct. (3d cir.) 1988, U.S. Ct. Internat. Trade 1990. Asst. prosecutor Essex County Prosecutor's Office, Newark, 1978-82; assoc. Brach, Eichler, Rosenberg, Silver, Bernstein & Hammer, Roseland, N.J., 1982-83; sole practice West Orange, N.J., 1983-84, Roseland, 1984—. Mem. ABA, N.J. State Bar Assn., Essex County Bar Assn., Assn. Criminal Def. Lawyers N.J. Democrat. Office: 354 Eisenhower Pky Livingston NJ 07039-1023

KAZAN, BASIL GIBRAN, religious music composer; b. Jditah-Chtaura, Lebanon, May 16, 1914; came to U.S., 1957; s. Economos Girgeos and Tamam (Shehadey) K.; m. Viola Habeeb, Aug. 16, 1970. BA, Patriarchal Lycee, Damascus, Syria, 1935; diploma in theology, U. Athens, 1956. Prof. St. John's Seminary, Khonchara, Lebanon, 1939-43, Oriental Coll., Zahle, Lebanon, 1943-45, Am. U., Beirut, Lebanon, 1945-47; sec. to Patriarch Alexandros of Antioch, Damascus, 1947-50; pastor, theology student U. Athens, 1950-56; pastor various chs. in U.S.A., 1957-64; bookstore owner, operator Beirut, 1964-67; composer Antiochan Archdiocese N.Am., Englewood, N.J., 1967—; profl. cantor St. Mary's Orthodox Ch., Bklyn., 1967—; prof., translator Berlitz Sch. and Translation Service, N.Y.C., 1970-80; adviser Consulate Gen. of Lebanon, N.Y.C., 1973-80; prof. Byzantine Chant St. Vladimir's Sem., Crestwood, N.Y. 1975-77; asst. examiner Bd. Edn., Bklyn., 1974—; asked to come from Lebanon in 1966 by Primate of Antiochan Orthodox Christian Archdiocese of N.Am. for Byzantine Music Project in English, producing nine vols. to date. Composer music and words Soyo Anthem Syrian Orthodox Youth Orgn., 1986; composed and translated numerous religious verses and svcs. Active Rep. Nat. Com., 1984—. Recipient decoration from Patriarch Alexandros' Golden Jubilee, 1954; presented Highest Antonian Gold Medal of Merit on 25th year of work on Byzantine Music Project, By His Eminence Metropolitan Philip, 1992. Home: 265 87th St Brooklyn NY 11209-4911

KAZARIAN, PAUL, electrical appliance company executive; b. 1955. Grad., Columbia U., 1980. With Goldman Sschs & Co., 1980-87; pntr. Japonica Ptnrs., 1987—; chmn. bd. Sunbeam-Oster Co., Inc., Providence. Office: Sunbeam-Oster Co Inc 1 Citizens Plz 6th Fl Providence RI 02903*

KAZEE, PAUL MICHAEL, not-for-profit administrator; b. Lansing, Mich., Jan. 23, 1956; s. Paul Warren and Arlene Mary (Wrobel) K.; m. Sui Ten Lin Ng, Oct. 7, 1989. AS, Lansing Community Coll., 1982; BFA, NYU, 1987; DDiv (hon.), Universal Life Ch., Modesto, Calif., 1989. Apprentice electrician GM Oldsmobile, Lansing, 1976-80; handicapper svcs. asst. Lansing Community Coll., 1981-82; gen. mgr. Pla. Cinema Corp., N.Y.C., 1983-85; dir. office svcs. Citizens Com. for N.Y.C., 1986—; dramatic arts instr. East Lansing (Mich.) Arts Workshop, 1979-80. Author video Handle w/Care, 1988; dir. film ...And You're So Special?, 1989 (works in progress recognition award 1988, artistic achievement honor Paris 1990); music critic Bklyn. Excelior, 1992—. Candidate Lansing Sch. Bd., 1977; exec. bd. dirs. local UAW, Lansing, 1978-79. Democrat. Office: Citizens Com for NYC 3 W 29th St Fl 6 New York NY 10001-4598

KAZEM, ISMAIL, radiation oncologist, educator, health science facility administrator; b. Cairo, Feb. 28, 1931; came to U.S., 1966; s. Mohamed and Khadiga A. (Abou-Hadid) K.; m. Barbara Jean Whitelock; children: Farid, Mohamed, Karen, Ramsey. MB, ChB, Ain Shams U., Cairo, 1955; diploma in radiotherapy, Royal Coll. Radiologists, London, 1960. Diplomate Am. Bd. Nuclear Medicine, Am. Bd. Radiology. Rotating intern Demerdach U. Hosp., Cairo, 1955-56; clin. demonstrator radiology dept. Ein Shams U. Faculty Medicine, 1956-59; trainee Meyerstein Inst. Radiotherapy, Middlesex Hosp., London, 1959, 60; IAEA fellow Strahlen Klinik, Czerny Krankenhaus, U. Heidelberg (Fed. Republic Germany), 1959; sr. registrar dept. radiotherapy St. Bartholomew's Hosp., London, 1960-61; lectr., then asst. prof. radiation therapy U. Alexandria (Egypt), 1962-65; sr. researcher Inst. Nuclear Medicine, German Cancer Rsch. Ctr., Heidelberg, 1965-66; instr., then asst. prof. radiology Hahnemann Med. Coll. and Hosp., Phila., 1966-70; prof., chmn. dept. radiation therapy and nuclear medicine Sint Radboud Acad. Hosp., Cath. U., Nijmegen, The Netherlands, 1970-83; dir. dept. radiation therapy and Regional Cancer Ctr. Mercer Med. Ctr., Trenton, N.J., 1983—; clin. prof. radiation oncology Temple U., Phila., 1985-91; clin. prof. radiology U. Medicine and Dentistry N.J., Camden; mem. courtesy staff Helen Fuld Med. Ctr., Trenton; mem. cons. staff Freehold (N.J.) Area Hosp.; presenter in field to sci. meetings. Author: (poetry) An Anthology of My Own Thing, 1975, Reflections and Definitions, 1978, Conversations with My Thoughts, 1992, Introduction to Oncology (in Dutch), 1983; mem. editorial bd. N.J. Medicine; editor Mercer County Medicine. Mem. exec. com. Mercer County unit Am. Cancer Soc.; mem. pilot project task force for breast cancer screening in Mercer County, N.J. Dept. Health, Trenton, also mem. reaction group licensure reform project; mem. adv. coun. N.J. Office Pub. Guardian for Elderly. WHO fellow, 1963. Fellow Royal Soc. Medicine (London), Royal Coll. Radiologists (London), Acad. Medicine, N.J.; mem. AMA, Am. Coll. Nuclear Medicine (charter), Soc. Nuclear Medicine, Am. Coll. Radiology, Am. Soc. for Therapeutic Radiology and Oncology, Netherlands Soc. Radiotherapy, European Soc. Therapeutic Radiology and Oncology, Am. Assn. Cancer Edn., Am. Soc. Clin. Oncology, Pan Am. Med. Assn., World Med. Assn. (assoc.), Am. Endocurietherapy Soc., Pa. Med. Soc., N.J. Med. Soc., N.Y. Acad. Scis., also others. Office: Mercer Med Ctr 446 Bellevue Ave # 1658 Trenton NJ 08618-4597

KAZEMI, ABBAS ASHTIANI, economics educator, researcher; b. Tehran, Iran, Dec. 6, 1956; came to U.S., 1977; s. Reza and Marhamat (Kazemi) K. BS, Nat. U. Iran, 1976; MA, SUNY, Stony Brook, 1982, PhD, 1987. Prof. Bucknell U., Lewisburg, Pa., 1983-84, R.I. Coll., Providence, 1984—. Contbr. articles to profl. jours. SUNY scholar, 1980-85. Mem. Am. Econ. Assn., Econometric Soc. Am., Southwestern Soc. Economists, Rotary. Moslem. Office: RI Coll 600 Mt Pleasant Ave Providence RI 02908-1924

KE, GANG, political economy educator; b. Beijing, China, Oct. 30, 1950; came to U.S., 1984; s. Cheng Ke and Xianlu Li; m. Meng Zhang, Jan. 30, 1984; 1 child, Jessica Judith. BA, Jilin U., 1982; MA, U. Toledo, 1987; PhD, U. Colo., 1988, U. Md., 1992. Assoc. researcher Chinese Acad. of Social Scis., Beijing, 1982-84; vis. scholar U. Toledo, Ohio, 1984-87; grad. fellow U. Colo., Boulder, 1987-88; grad. fellow U. Md., College Park, 1989-90, teaching asst., 1990-92; pres. Orient Exchange, Inc., College Park. Contbr. articles to profl. jours. Exec. dir. The Alliance of Chinese Patriots, Washington, 1989; pres. com. of Chinese Corrs., College Park, 1989—; dir. theoretical rsch. dept. Ind. Fedn. Chinese Students and Scholars in USA, Washington, 1990. Mem. Am. Polit. Sci. Assn., Polit. Sci. Assn. Chinese Student and Scholars in USA, Chinese Philosophy Assn. Office: Com Chinese Correspondence 3402 Tulane Dr Hyattsville MD 20783

KEAGLE, DOUGLAS LEE, physician; b. Elizabeth, N.J., June 9, 1946; s. LeRoy Curtis and Jane Alice (Beckman) K.; m. Donna Theresa Cocola, Sept. 28, 1974; children: Danielle, Dyana, Dana, Douglas. BA, Northeastern U., 1969; DO, Phila. Coll., 1973. Diplomate Am. Bd. Internal Medicine. Intern Fitzgerald Mercy Hosp., Darby, Pa., 1973-74; resident internal medicine Mercy Cath. Med. Ctr., Darby, Pa., 1974-76; assoc. attending physician Huntington Gen. Hosp. and Faulkner Hosp., Jamaica Plain, Mass., 1976-77; staff physician Sacred Heart Gen. Hosp., Chester, Pa., 1977-78; attending physician Mercy Cath. Med. Ctr., Darby, 1978—, Riddle Meml. Hosp., Media, Pa., 1978—. Mem. AMA, Am. Coll. Physicians, Pa. Med. Soc., Delaware County Med. Soc. Republican. Home: 3440 Goshen Rd Newtown Square PA 19073-3424 Office: 1 N Belfield Ave Havertown PA 19083-4928

KEAGLE, SUSAN JANE, academic administrator, educator; b. Corning, N.Y., June 27, 1940; d. Charles Roger and Mary Catherine (Lesky) K. AA, Corning (N.Y.) Community Coll., 1960; BS, Elmira Coll., 1966; MS in Edn., Ind. U., 1973. Tchr. elem. grades City of Elmira (N.Y.) Sch. System, 1965-66; asst. dean students, residence hall dir. SUNY, Oneonta, 1966-71, assoc. dean for residence life, 1971-88, assoc. v.p. residence life and housing, 1988—. Mem. Accomodations and Welfare Officers of Gt. Britain (hon.), Nat. Assn. Student Pers. Adminstrs. (profl. affiliate), United Univ. Profs., Coll. Student Pers. Assn. of N.Y. State, SUNY Housing Adminstrs., Oneonta Faculty Assn. Democrat. Roman Catholic. Office: SUNY 118 Netzer Adminstrn Oneonta NY 13820

KEAGLE, WILLIAM ALOYSIUS, JR., utility executive; b. Balt., June 22, 1952; s. William Aloysius and Mary Magdalen (Goeller) K.; m. Diana Irene Cyr, June 15, 1974; children: Sara Marie, Lee Hyun Jung. BSEE, Northeastern U., Boston, 1975; M. of Engring. Adminstrn., George Washington U., 1989. Registered profl. engr., Md. Engr. Balt. Gas & Elec. Co., 1975-81, sr. engr., 1981-86, gen. supr. spl. engring. and tests, 1986-92, gen. supr. billing metering, 1992—. Block capt. Dunmore Community Assn., Catonsville, Md., 1989—; mem. electronic tech. com. Me. State Dept. Edn., Balt., 1988. Recipient For God and Youth award Office of Youth Ministry, Balt. Archdiocese of Roman Cath. Ch., 1981. Mem. IEEE (sr., co-chmn. host com. power industry computer applications conf. 1991), IEEE Power Engring. Soc. (chmn. 1985-86), Md. Soc. Profl. Engrs., Tau Beta Pi. Democrat. Roman Catholic. Office: Balt Gas & Elec Co PO Box 1475 ETF/RBC Baltimore MD 21203

KEAMY, DONALD GEORGE, otolaryngologist, plastic surgeon; b. Lawrence, Mass., Sept. 23, 1930; s. Mitchell Fadoul and Wadie (Freije) K.; m. R. Yvonne Hajjar, Sept. 12, 1957; children: Cheryl, Jean, Donald Jr. AB, MIT, 1953; MD, Tufts U., 1957. Practitioner pvt. practice, Lawrence, Mass., 1964—. Fellow Am. Coll. Surgery, Am. Acad. Facial Plastic and Reconstructive Surgery, Am. Bd. Cosmetic Surgery, Am. Bd. Otolaryngology; mem. New England Otolaryngology Surgery, Am. Acad. Cosmetic Surgeons. Office: 101 Amesbury St Lawrence MA 01840

KEAN, JOHN VAUGHAN, lawyer; b. Providence, Mar. 12, 1917; s. Otho Vaughan and Mary (Duell) K.; AB cum laude, Harvard U., 1938, JD, 1941. Bar: R.I. 1942. With Edwards & Angell, Providence, 1941—, ptnr., 1954-87; of counsel, 1987—. bd. dir., sec. The Robbins Co., Attleboro, Mass. Chmn. Downtown Providence YMCA, 1964-67. Bd. dirs. Greater Providence YMCA, 1964-76. Capt. AUS, 1943-46, 50-52, brig. gen. Decorated Legion of Merit. Mem. ABA, R.I. Bar Assn., N.G. Assn., Res. Officers Assn., Assn. U.S. Army, R.I. Army N.G. (brig. gen. 1964-72). Episcopalian. Clubs: Harvard R.I. (pres. 1964-66), Agawam Hunt, Hope, Providence Art, Turks Head; Army and Navy (Washington); Sakonnet Golf (Little Compton, R.I.). Home: 518 W Main Rd Little Compton RI 02837-1121 Office: Edwards & Angell 2700 Hospital Trust Tower Providence RI 02903-4706

KEAN, THOMAS H., academic administrator, former governor; b. N.Y.C., Apr. 21, 1935; m. Deborah Bye; children: Thomas, Reed, Alexandra. A.B., Princeton; M.A., Columbia. Tchr. history and govt.; mem. N.J. Assembly, 1967-77, speaker, 1972, minority leader, 1974; acting gov., 1973, gov., 1981-89; pres. Drew U., Madison, N.J., 1990—; bd. dirs. Beneficial Corp. Address: Office of Pres Drew U Madison NJ 07940*

KEANE, MARY ELIZABETH, accountant, healthcare executive; b. Boston, June 19, 1953; d. William Joseph and Olga Anne (Galasti) K. BS, Boston Coll., 1975; MBA, U. Pa., 1986. CPA, N.J. Sr. acct. Mobil Oil Corp., N.Y.C., 1975-84; bus. analyst Johnson Matthey, West Chester, Pa., 1986-88; asst. contr. Commodore Internat. Ltd., West Chester, 1988-90; chief fin. officer HAPSCO Group, Inc., Harrisburg, Pa., 1990—. Mem. Beta Gamma Sigma. Republican. Roman Catholic. Home: 297 Fox Run Exton PA 19341-2119

KEARNEY, JOHN PETERS, English educator; b. Buffalo, June 7, 1940; s. Norman Loyola and Dorothy (Peters) K.; m. Carol Jean Walker, Dec. 23, 1968; children: Roberta Jean, Anthony Allen, Brian Leigh, Jeffrey Reynold, David Bennett, Barbara Ellen. BA, Benedictine Coll., Atchison, Kans., 1962; MA, U. Mich., 1963; PhD, U. Wis., Madison, 1968. Asst. prof. English Wis. State U., Superior, 1967-68, Seattle U., 1968-71; prof., chmn. Lebanon Valley Coll., Annville, Pa., 1971—. Alt. del. to Dem. Nat. Conv., Chgo., 1968. NEH fellow, 1986. Mem. MLA, Northeast MLA, Nat. Coun. Tchrs. English. Roman Catholic. Home: 318 Reigerts Ln Annville PA 17003-2110 Office: Lebanon Valley Coll Annville PA 17003

KEARNEY, RICHARD CRAIG, political scientist, consultant, educator; b. Memphis, Mar. 17, 1946; s. Walter D. and Katherine (Day) K.; m. Mary Jane Howland (div. 1982); 1 child, Nicole; m. Kathy S. Morgan, Jan. 16, 1949; 1 child, Joel Morgan. BS, Miss. State U., 1968, M in Pub. Adminstrn., 1974; PhD, U. Okla., 1977. Instr. U. Coll. Asmara, Ethiopia, 1972-73; asst. prof. polit. sci. U. No. Iowa, Cedar Falls, 1977-78; prof. U. S.C., Columbia, 1983-90; prof., head pub. adminstrv. program U. Conn., Storrs, 1990—, dir. Inst. Pub. and Urban Affairs, 1990—; pres. Richard Kearney & Assocs., Columbia, 1983-90, Storrs, 1990—; vis. prof. pub. adminstrn. U. Catolica Madre y Maestra, Dominican Republic, 1984-85; panelist NSF, 1990—. Author: Administration and Management, 1974, Labor Relations in the Public Sector, 1984, 92, Resurgence of the States, 1986, State and Local Government, 1990, 92; co-editor: Pub. Pers. Mgmts., 1983, 89; editor: Rev. Pub. Pers. Administrn., 1982—. Precinct chmn. Dem. Orgn., Lexington County, S.C., 1979-81. Served as lt. (j.g.) USNR, 1968-71. Grantee Faculty Rsch. U.S.C., 1983, U. Conn., 1991; Fulbright fellow U. Mauritius, Reduit, 1987-88. Mem. Southwestern Polit. Sci. Assn., Am. Soc. for Pub. Adminstrn. (mem. coun. 1984, 86-87), Am. Polit. Sci. Assn., Midwest Polit. Sci. Assn., S.C. Polit. Sci. Assn. (Best Profl. Paper 1986). Democrat. Office: U Conn MPA Program U-106 Storrs CT 06269

KEARNS, DAVID TODD, federal agency administrator; b. Rochester, N.Y., Aug. 11, 1930; s. Wilfrid M. and Margaret May (Todd) K.; m. Shirley Virginia Cox, June 1954; children—Katherine, Elizabeth, Anne, Susan, David Todd, Andrew. B.S., U. Rochester, 1952. With IBM, 1954-71, v.p. mktg. ops., data processing div., until 1971; with Xerox Corp., Stamford, Conn., 1971-91; group v.p. for info. systems Xerox Corp., 1972-75; group v.p. charge Rank Xerox and Fuji Xerox, 1975-77, exec. v.p. internat. ops., 1977; pres., chief exec. officer Xerox Corp., 1977-85, also dir., pres., chief operating officer, 1977-82, pres., chief exec. officer, 1982-85, chmn., chief exec. officer, 1985-90, chmn., 1990-91, also chmn. exec. com.; ret., 1991; dep. sec. edn. U.S. Dept. Edn., Washington, 1991—; bd. dirs. Rank Xerox Ltd., Time Warner, Inc., Fuji Xerox, Chase Manhattan Corp., Dayton Hudson Corp., Ryder Systems; chmn. Tri-State United Way; bd. trustees Ford Found. Bd. visitors Grad. Sch. Bus., Duke U.; bd. dirs. U. Rochester; trustee Nat. Urban League, Ford Found.; chmn. United Way Tri State; mem. Pres' Edn. Policy Adv. Com. With USNR, 1952-54. Mem. Am. Philos. Assn., Bus. Roundtable, Coun. on Fgn. Rels. Office: US Dept Edn 400 Maryland Ave SW Ste 4015 Washington DC 20202-0002

KEARNS, WILLIAM STANLEY, architectural designer; b. Chgo., Jan. 1, 1941; s. John Wallace and Martha (King) K.; m. Julia Tedesco Valentine, June 22, 1985 (div. 1987). AB, Princeton U., 1962; postgrad., U. Va., 1963-64, Columbia U., 1967-72. Archtl. designer/draftsman Nicholas Satterlee, Washington, 1965-67, Philip Johnson/J. Burgee, N.Y.C., 1967-70, Carson, Lundin & Thorson, N.Y.C., 1970-71, Richard Meier & Assocs., N.Y.C., 1972; archtl. designer/project architect Arthur Cotton Moore, Washington, 1974-75; project architect Meyers & D'Aleo, Balt., 1976-78, Peter Marino, 1983-84; prin. Billymark, N.Y.C., Miami Beach, 1984—; assoc. Novecento Corp., Genoa, Italy and Miami; lectr. in field. Recipient award FAAIA, Genoa, Italy, 1991. Mem. AIA (assoc.), Archtl. Club Miami, Nassau Club. Democrat. Episcopalian.

KEARSE, AMALYA LYLE, federal judge; b. Vauxhall, N.J., June 11, 1937; d. Robert Freeman and Myra Lyle (Smith) K. B.A., Wellesley Coll., 1959; J.D. cum laude, U. Mich., 1962. Bar: N.Y. 1963, U.S. Supreme Ct. 1967. Assoc. Hughes Hubbard & Reed, N.Y.C., 1962-69; ptnr. Hughes Hubbard & Reed, 1969-79; judge U.S. Ct. Appeals (2d cir.), 1979—; lectr. evidence N.Y. U. Law Sch., 1968-69. Author: Bridge Conventions Complete, 1975, 3d edit., 1990, Bridge at Your Fingertips, 1980; translator, editor: Bridge Analysis, 1979; editor: Ofcl. Ency. of Bridge, 3d edit, 1976; mem. editorial bd. Charles Goren, 1974—. Bd. dirs. NAACP Legal Def. and Endl. Fund, 1977-79; bd. dirs. Nat. Urban League, 1978-79; trustee N.Y.C. YWCA, 1976-79, Am. Contract Bridge League Nat. Laws Commn., 1975—; mem. Pres.'s Com. on Selection of Fed. Jud. Officers, 1977-78. Named Women's Pairs Bridge Champion Nat. div., 1971, 72, World div., 1986, Nat. Women's Teams Bridge Champion, 1987, 9o, 91. Mem. ABA, Assn. of Bar of City of N.Y., Am. Law Inst., Lawyers Com. for Civil Rights Under Law (mem. exec. com. 1970-79). Office: US Ct Appeals US Courthouse Foley Sq New York NY 10007-1501

KEAT, JAMES ELDRED, aerospace engineer; b. New Cumberland, Pa., Apr. 3, 1932; s. James Eldred and Elizabeth L. (Tritt) K. AB, Dickinson Coll., 1955; BSEE with honors, Case Inst. Tech., 1955; MS, Pa. State U., 1960; PhD, MIT, 1983. Assoc. engr. Glenn L. Martin Co., Balt., 1955-57; sr. engr. Fairchild Stratos Corp., Hagerstown, Md., 1957-63, Westinghouse Aerospace Div., Balt., 1963-72; systems analyst Computer Scis. Corp., Silver Spring, Md., 1972-77; cons. engr. Computer Scis. Corp., Greenbelt, Md., 1990—; Draper fellow MIT, Cambridge, 1978-83; engr. Draper Lab., Cambridge, 1983-85; sr. scientist Photon Rsch. Assocs., Cambridge, 1985-89. Contbr. articles to profl. jours. Mem. AIAA, IEEE. Republican. Methodist. Home: 5913 Cherrywood Ter Greenbelt MD 20770-3143 Office: Computer Scis Corp 10110 Aerospace Rd Lanham Seabrook MD 20706-2276

KEAT, JAMES SUSSMAN, newspaper editor, reporter; b. N.Y.C., Dec. 25, 1929; s. Harold Edward and Ida (Sussman) K.; m. Betty Yurina, Dec. 24, 1955 (div. 1983); m. Christine Louise Swan Thompson, June 14, 1986; 1 stepchild, Christine Rene Thompson. AB, Brown U., 1951; MS, Columbia U., 1952. Reporter N.Y. Herald Tribune, 1952-53; reporter, fgn. corr., editor Balt. Sun, 1956—. Pulitzer Traveling fellow, 1953, Ford Found. fellow, 1953-56. Mem. Nat. Press Club, Soc. Profl. Journalists, Hamilton St. Club. Home: 1001 Riverside Ave Baltimore MD 21230-4133 Office: Balt Sun 501 N Calvert St Baltimore MD 21278-0001

KEATING, RICHARD JOSEPH, public relations administrator, educator; b. L.I. City, N.Y.; s. Michael Joseph and Anna Marie (McKeen) K.; m. June Margaret Rowan, July 13, 1962; children: Michael, Catherine, June, Joseph. BA, U. Dayton, Ohio, 1953; MS, Hofstra U., 1958; PhD, St. John's U., Jamaica, N.Y., 1963. Asst. prin. McArthur High Sch., Levittown, N.Y., 1961-63; dir. secondary edn. Dunkirk (N.Y.) Pub. Schs., 1963-65; spl. project officer U.S. Office of Edn., Washington, 1965-68; dir. instructional svcs. U.S. Dept. of Interior, Washington, 1968-71; staff dir. U.S. Congress Task Force, Washington, 1971-72; asst. to U.S. senator U.S. Senate, Washington, 1972-74; dir. congl. affairs Coastal Zone Mgmt. Program, Washington, 1974-78, Nat. Oceanic and Atmospheric Adminstrn., Washington, 1978-82; dir. external rels. satellite program Nat. Oceanic and Atmospheric Adminstrn., Suitland, Md., 1982-88; dir. pub. rels. Thomson-CSF, Inc., Arlington, Va., 1988—. Author: (guide) Exhibitor's Guide, 1990, (booklet) Thomson-Streamlined for the 90's, 1991; scriptwriter (video) Thomson-A Success Story, 1991. Mem. Am. Def. Preparedness Assn., Navy League-Air Force Assn. Home: 9204 Ethan Ct Laurel MD 20708-2501 Office: Thomson-CSF Inc 2231 Crystal Dr Ste 814 Arlington VA 22202-3739

KEATING, TIMOTHY JAMES, academic administrator, Spanish educator; b. Elgin, Ill., Oct. 6, 1946; s. John Richard and Doris Anna (Fischer) K.; m. Jayne Annette Stefani, Aug. 17, 1968; children: Ruth Johanna, Jacob Michael. BA, Gonzaga U., 1968; MA, SUNY, Albany, 1971, PhD, 1981. Instr. Spanish Hartwick Coll., Oneonta, N.Y., 1971-75, asst. prof. Spanish, 1975-81; assoc. prof. Spanish Hartwick Coll., Oneonta, 1981-91, prof. Spanish, 1991—, asst. dean spl. programs, 1985-87, assoc. dean, 1987—, acting provost, 1988-89, assoc. dean for acad. affairs, 1987—; evaluator programs abroad Commn. on Higher Edn. Mid. States, Phila., 1983—. Translator: (book, poetry) Six Cuban Poets, 1983. Pres. bd. dirs. Modern Dance Artists, Oneonta, 1990—; commr. Zoning Bd. Appeals, Oneonta, 1989—; mem. internat. adv. bd. Batuz Found., Washington, 1991. NDEA Title IV Grad. fellow U.S. Govt., SUNY, Albany, 1968-71. Mem. MLA, Am. Assn. Tchrs. Spanish and Portuguese. Home: 74 Elm St Oneonta NY 13820-1533 Office: Hartwick Coll Oyaron Hill Oneonta NY 13820

KEATS, WILLIAM FRANK, tax accountant, financial planner; b. Nyack, N.Y., Mar. 11, 1941; s. Philip Louis and Sylvia (Werner) K.; m. Kathleen Scarlett Martin, Aug. 1, 1965; children: David, Jennifer. BSBA in Acctg., Nichols Coll., 1963; CFP, Adelphi U., 1985; postgrad., Hofstra U., 1986-91. Enrolled agt. Acct. Mobil Oil Corp., N.Y.C., 1964-66; tax acct. Phelps Dodge Corp., N.Y.C., 1966-69; auditor Greenberg & Levy CPAs, N.Y.C., 1969; acct. supr. Metco, Westbury, N.Y., 1969-70; acct. Nassau County, Mineola, N.Y., 1970-91; prin. Keats Tax & Acctg., Merrick, N.Y., 1970-92. Trustee Suburban Temple, Wantagh, N.Y., 1991; chmn. bd. South Shore Planning Coun., Dry Rock Cafe, Wantagh, 1990-92. Mem. Internat. Assn. Fin. Planning, Nat. Assn. Tax Profls., N.Y. Soc. Ind. Accts. (v.p. 1988-92). Home and Office: 64 Roydon Dr E Merrick NY 11566-1423

KEBEL, KEITH NELSEN, information management executive; b. N.Y.C., Oct. 14, 1946; s. Herbert F. and Adelaide D. (Nelsen) K.; m. Mary E. Antonelli, June 8, 1974; children: Lisa, Laura, Michelle. BS, U. Pitts., 1968; MBA, CUNY, 1976. Analyst Exxon, Florham Park, N.J., 1970-75, dir. fin. planning system, 1979-82, dir. computer tech., 1982-85; mgr. MIS Exxon, Bangkok, Thailand, 1975-77; mgr. internat. systems Exxon, N.Y.C., 1977-79; dir. mfg. systems Pfizer, N.Y.C., 1985-88; dir. corp. systems Bristol-Myers Squibb, East Brunswick, N.J., 1988-90; v.p. info. svcs. Bristol-Myers Squibb, Princeton, N.J., 1990—. Office: Bristol-Myers Squibb Rte 206 & Province Line Rd Princeton NJ 08540

KEDDIE, ROLAND THOMAS, physician, hospital administrator, lawyer; b. Altoona, Pa., Oct. 21, 1928; s. John Barkeley and Jessie E. (Keddie) Isenberg; B.S. cum laude, U. Pitts., 1956, M.D., 1957, J.D., 1970; m. Suzanne M. Seno, Feb. 6, 1978; 1 dau., Dawn Michelle; children by previous marriage: Roland, Thomas, Francis, Robert, Michael, Karen, Andrew, Rosemary. Intern St. Josephs Hosp., Pitts., 1958; practice medicine specializing in emergency medicine and family practice; admitted to Pa. bar, 1970; medico legal cons., 1970—; med. dir. Westmoreland Manor, Greensburg, Pa., 1971; dir. emergency dept. Connemaugh Valley Meml. Hosp., Johnston, Pa., 1976-77, Shadyside Hosp., Pitts., 1978-80, chmn. dept. emergency services McKeesport (Pa.) Hosp., 1980-83, also dir. emergency medicine residency program; pres. EmergiCenters Inc., 1983—; chmn. dept. family practice St. Clair Hosp., Pitts., 1990—; pres. Emergency Med. Services Inst.,

1982-85; adj. prof. Sch. Nursing, U. Pitts. Served with USN, 1946-47, 50-52. Diplomate Am. Bd. Family Practice. Mem. Am. Coll. Emergency Physicians (life, bd. dirs. Pa. chpt. 1977-81, 83-86, v.p. 1980-81, pres. 1985-86), Pa. Med. Soc., Hosp. Assn. Pa. (mem. profl. practice com. 1981-82), Allegheny County Bar Assn., AMA (Physicians Recognition award 1974, 77, 80), Allegheny County Med. Soc., Pa. Emergency Health Services Council (dir. 1980), Soc. Tchrs. Emergency Medicine, Beta Beta Beta. Roman Catholic. Home: 332 Meadowcrest Dr Cecil PA 15321-9711 Office: Charters Valley Med Ctr Bridgeville PA 15017

KEEFE, EDWARD FRANCIS, gynecologist, educator; b. N.Y.C., June 11, 1910; s. Edward Francis and Ellen (DeForest) K.; m. Harriette Malley, June 28, 1952 (dec. 1990); 1 child, Mart Maria. BS, CCNY, 1931; MD, Cornell U., 1935. Internship St. Luke's Hosp., N.Y.C., 1936, St. Luke's Hosp. and St. John's Hosp., Bklyn., 1936-38; asst. resident Meml. Hosp., N.Y.C., 1938-39, Sloane Hosp. for Women, N.Y.C., 1939-40; mem. attending staff St. Vincents Hosp., N.Y.C., 1940-75; adj. prof. N.Y. Med. Coll., Valhalla, 1991—; pres. Forest Industries Inc., Linacre Labs., Greenwich, Conn., 1971—. Inventor Ovulindex thermometer. Passed asst. surgeon USPHS, 1942-46. Decorated Knight Sovereign Military Order of Malta. Fellow Am. Coll. Obstetricians and Gynecologists. Roman Catholic.

KEEFE, WILLIAM LEE, accountant, consultant; b. Pawtucket, R.I., Apr. 3, 1937; s. Henry and Irene C. Keefe; m. Patricia Ann Keefe, Aug. 1, 1965; children: Kathleen, Brian, Stephen. BBA, Bryant Coll., 1967; postgrad., Babson Coll., 1968-69. Registered profl. acct., R.I. From jr. acct. to supervising acct. State of R.I., 1960-88; pvt. practice acctg. cons. Cumberland, R.I., 1988—; cons. Small Bus. Devel. Ctr., R.I., 1988—, Occupational Industrialization Corp. of R.I., 1988-89, Nat. Edn. Assn. of R.I., 1988-92; cons. substance abuse Mental Health Mental Retardation, R.I., 1990-91. With U.S. Army, 1956-58.

KEEGAN, JOHN ALOYSIUS, JR., periodontist; b. Troy, N.Y., Jan. 2, 1941; s. John Aloysius and Mary (Miccio) K.; children: Bridget, John III, Matthew; m. Mary Pat VanDenBurg, July 26, 1985. BS, Albany Coll. Pharmacy, 1961; DDS, Georgetown U., 1966, MS, 1968. Resident in periodontics VA Hosp., Washington, 1968; pharmacist Donnelly & Hanna, Troy, N.Y., 1961-62; pvt. practice dentist Washington, 1966-68; periodontist Queern & Williams, DDS, P.C., Schenectady, N.Y., 1970-71, Keegan & Collins, DDS, P.C., Troy, N.Y., 1971—; dir. regional bd. Key Bank N.Y., Albany, N.Y., 1984-91. Dir. Troy (N.Y.) Boys Club, 1982—. Capt. USAF, 1968-70. Decorated Bronze star USAF, 1970; named Outstanding Young Men of Am., 1972, Hall of Fame, Troy (N.Y.) Boys Club, 1991. Mem. ADA, Am. Acad. Periodontics, N.Y. State Soc. Periodontists (dir. 1985—), Upper N.Y. Soc. Periodontists (pres. 1983-85), Troy Dental Study Club (pres. 1981), Troy Boys Club (pres. 1984-86), Country Club Troy (dir. 1991). Republican. Roman Catholic. Home: 26 Timberwick Dr Clifton Park NY 12065 Office: Keegan & Collins DDS PC 2119 Burdett Ave Troy NY 12180

KEEGAN, ROBERT HENRY, marketing executive, consultant; b. Bronxville, N.Y., Jan. 31, 1944; s. Albert F. and Ruth H. (Hamilton) K.; m. Joyce Ann Meyer, Dec. 14, 1968; children: Gary R., Karen S., David M. BS, BSEE, Ind. Inst. Tech., 1967; MS, U. Dayton, 1972. Elec. engr. Collins Radio Co., Cedar Rapids, Iowa, 1964-68; project mgr. Flight Dynamics Lab. USAF, Wright-Patterson AFB, Ohio, 1969-74; program mgr. Mead Corp., Dayton, Ohio, 1974-79; ptnr. Specifications & Svcs., Newtown, Conn., 1980—; tech. advisor Pitney Bowes, Norwalk, Conn., 1979-80; mem. adj. faculty Western Conn. State U., Danbury, 1982—. Author: Cost Estimating for the Electronics Industries, 1982; contbr. numerous articles to profl. jours. Legislator Newtown Legis. Coun., 1988-90; chmn. bd. Western Conn. coun. Camp Fire, Danbury, 1984—; trustee United Way of No. Fairfield County, Danbury, 1988-90; mem. math adv. coun. Newtown Pub. Schs., 1989—. Mem. IEEE, Am. Assn. Univ. Profs. Republican. Mem. Congregational Ch. Office: Specifications & Svcs 20 Washbrook Rd Newtown CT 06470-2603

KEELER See WALSH, KEITH KEELER

KEELER, JOHN MONTGOMERY, lawyer; b. Binghamton, N.Y., July 5, 1933; s. Charles Addison and Esther (Montgomery) K.; m. Jacqueline Ann Covert, Nov. 5, 1955 (div. Feb. 1978); children: Gregory C., Matthew M., Ann E.; m. Marcella McPherson, July 23, 1978. AB, Hamilton Coll., 1955; LLB, Cornell Law Sch., 1961. Bar: N.Y., 1961, Fla., 1987. Spl. agt. trainee Glens Falls (N.Y.) Ins. Co., 1955-56; assoc. Hinman, Howard & Kattell, Binghamton, 1961-68, ptnr., 1969—, mng. ptnr., 1982—; bd. dirs. N.Y. State Electric and Gas Corp., Binghamton, Security Mutual Life Ins. Co., Binghamton. Pres. Broome County United Way, Binghamton, 1982-84; bd. dirs. United Way of N.Y. State, Albany, 1989—, The Hoyt Found., Binghamton, 1987—. With U.S. Army, 1956-68. Mem. ABA, Broome County Bar Assn. (pres. 1987-88), N.Y. State Bar Assn., Binghamton Club, Binghamton Country Club, Live Wire Club, Order of Coif. Republican. Episcopalian. Home: 14 Campbell Road Ct Binghamton NY 13905-4302 Office: Hinman Howard & Kattell 700 Security Mutual Bldg 80 Exchange St Binghamton NY 13901-3406

KEELER, WILLIAM HENRY, archbishop; b. San Antonio, Mar. 4, 1931; s. Thomas Love and Margaret T. (Conway) K. BA, St. Charles Sem., Phila., 1952; STL, Pontifical Gregorian U., Rome, 1956, JCD, 1961; DD (hon.), Lebanon Valley Coll, Pa., 1984, Gettysburg Coll., 1986, Susquehanna U., 1989; LHD (hon.), Mt. St. Mary's Coll., 1985. Ordained priest Roman Catholic Ch., 1955, consecrated bishop, 1979. Sec. diocesan tribunal Diocese of Harrisburg, Pa., 1956-58, defender of the bond, 1961-66, vice-chancellor, 1965-69, chancellor, 1969-79, aux. bishop and vicar gen., 1979-83, bishop of Harrisburg, 1984-89; archbishop of Balt., 1989—; chmn. Md. Cath. Conf., 1989—; co-chmn. Pa. Conf. Inter-Ch. Cooperation, 1981-89; pres. Pa. Cath. Conf., 1983-89; chmn. com. ecumenical and inter-religious affairs Nat. Conf. Cath. Bishops, 1984-87, mem., 1987—, Episcopal moderator for Cath.-Jewish Rels., 1988—, sec., 1988-89, v.p., 1989—; mem. Internat. Joint Com. for Cath.-Orthodox Theol. Dialogue, 1986—. Mem. Interreligious Forum Greater Harrisburg, 1969-89; mem. exec. bd. Keystone Area coun. Boy Scouts Am., 1979-89. Recipient Gold medal Pope John XXIII, 1961; named papal chamberlain Pope Paul VI, 1965; prelate of honor Pope Paul VI, 1970; recipient John Baum Humanitarian award Dauphin County unit Am. Cancer Soc., 1984, Anti-Defamation League Americanism award, 1985, De Tocqueville Soc. award, 1988, Disting. Eagle Boy Scouts Am., 1990. Mem. Canon Law Soc. Am., Am. Cath. Hist. Soc.

KEELEY, TIMOTHY W., social studies educator, consultant; b. Saratoga Springs, N.Y., Mar. 3, 1949; s. William Joseph and Anna Katherine (Hvizdak) K.; m. Gale A. McAllister, Feb. 19, 1971; children: Damien S., Katie M., Brian M. BA, SUNY, 1971, MA, 1975; cert. of labor, Cornell U., 1979. Cert. Social Studies Educator. Tchr. Shenendehowa Schs., Clifton Park, N.Y., 1971—; Am. Fedn. Tchrs. del. Shenendehowa Tchrs., Clifton Park, 1979-93, New York State United Tchrs., 1986-93; pres. Scotia-Glenville (N.Y.) Bd. Edn., 1987-91, mem. 1982-93. Chmn. First Reformed Dutch Fair, Scotia, 1983-84; pres. Scotia Jr. High PTA, 1987-89. Nat. Endowment for Humanities fellow, 1987; Freedoms Found. fellow, 1984, 90; Taft Found. fellow 1979; lifetime mem. N.Y. State PTA, 1989—. Mem. Nat. Coun. Social Studies, Capital Dist. Coun. Social Studies (newsletter editor 1985-87), N.Y. State Coun. Social Studies, N.Y. State Sch. Bds. Assn. Republican. Home: 408 S Reynolds St Scotia NY 12302-1602 Office: Shenendehowa High Sch 970 Rte 146 Clifton Park NY 12065-3688

KEELEY, WAYNE JOSEPH, film and video production company executive, law educator; b. Yonkers, N.Y., Nov. 9, 1956; s. Joseph Thomas and Lucille (Sansone) K. BA, Fordham U., 1978; JD, St. John's U., Jamaica, N.Y., 1981. Bar: N.Y. 1982. Assoc. Wilson, Elser, Moskowitz, Edelman & Dicker, N.Y.C., 1981-85; pres., chief exec. officer, chmn. bd. dirs. Bennu Prodns., Inc., N.Y.C., 1985—; sr. v.p. Sunbird Advt., N.Y.C., 1985-86, The Bennu Found., N.Y.C., 1987—; prof. law Baruch Coll, N.Y.C., 1987—. Producer, author (video) Interview Techniques, 1985, Preparing For The Job Interview, 1987, Crack Down, 1987, Say No To Strangers, 1990, Icy Death, 1991, Point of No Return, 1991, Evolution's End?, 1991; contbr. articles to law periodicals, revs. Active Assn. for a Better N.Y., N.Y.C.; dir. Sea Scouts, N.Y.C., 1978. Mem. ABA, N.Y. State Bar Assn., Am. Film Inst., Assn. Ind. Video and Filmakers. Roman Catholic. Office: Bennu Prodns Inc 171 Madison Ave New York NY 10016-5110

KEEM, MICHAEL DENNIS, veterinarian; b. Buffalo, July 29, 1950; s. Sanford Joseph and Clara C. (Chmiel) K.; m. Mary Beth Fix, June 1, 1973; children: Chelsey, Erin, Daniel, Ryan. BS, Niagara U., 1972; MS, U. Wyo., 1974; DVM, Cornell U., 1979. Assoc. veterinarian Spink Vet. Assn., Attica, N.Y., 1979-80; assoc. veterinarian Cheektowaga (N.Y.) Vet. Hosp., 1980-1984, vet., owner, pres., 1985—; vet., owner, pres. Amclare Vet. Hosp., P.C., Williamsville, N.Y., 1987—; ptnr. Greater Buffalo Vet. Emergency Svcs., P.C., 1985—. Com. chmn. pack 601 Boy Scouts Am., 1989-91, Webelos den leader, 1991-92, asst. scoutmaster, 1992—. Mem. AVMA, Animal Birth Control Soc. (bd. dirs. 1981—), N.Y. State Vet. Med. Soc., Am. Animal Hosp. Assn., Western N.Y. Vet. Med. Assn. (pres. elect 1988, pres. 1989, past pres. 1990, bd. dirs. 1991—), Niagara Frontier Vet. Soc. (bd. dirs. 1986—), Buffalo Acad. Vet. Medicine, Phi Kappa Phi, Phi Zeta. Republican. Roman Catholic. Office: Cheektowaga Vet Hosp PC 957 Dick Rd Buffalo NY 14225-3598 also: Amclare Vet Hosp PC 895 Hopkins Rd Williamsville NY 14221

KEEN, ARNOLD RALPH, research scientist; b. Newton, W.Va., Oct. 4, 1918; s. Robert Looney and Eva Ethel (Helmic) K.; m. Shirley Eloise Harless, Mar. 11, 1944. BSBA, W.Va. U., 1941; BS in Chemistry, U. Del., 1947, MSME, 1956. Registered profl. engr. Various positions du Pont Co. Engring Dept., Wilmington, Del., 1941-77; pres., dir. rsch. Hydronic Rsch. Found., Landenberg, Pa., 1983—. Inventor in field. Dir. So. Co. Med. Ctr., West Grove, Pa., 1960-75, pres., bd. dirs., 1975-79; supr Twp. Govt., Chester County, Pa., 1979-80, auditor, 1986-88. Mem. AAAS, N.Y. Acad. Scis., Masons, Royal Arch Masons. Democrat.

KEEN, JAMES PARKER, public issue educator; b. Harrisburg, Pa., May 21, 1946; s. Robert Donald and M. Enid (Parker) K.; m. Cheryl Hollmann, Mar. 29, 1975; 1 child, Justin Hollmann. BA, Haverford (Pa.) Coll., 1968; EdD, Harvard U., 1979. Tchr., adminstr. Phila. Pub. Schs., 1968-73; coord./com. on internat. studies Harvard U., Cambridge, 1974-81; prof. edn. Lesley Coll. Grad. Sch., Cambridge, 1981-88; instr. Harvard Div. Sch., Cambridge, 1982-85; co-dir. N.J. Govs. Sch. Pub. Issues, West Long Branch, N.J., 1982—; exec. dir., bd. overseers Govs. Sch. N.J., West Long Branch, 1985—; co-incumbant, Millicent Fenwick Professorship Monmouth Coll., West Long Branch, 1988—; cons. Lilly Endowment, Indpls., 1990—, Govs. Sch. of Fla., New Coll., Sarasota, 1988-90, Chinook Learning Community, Seattle, 1991—; bd. dirs. Nat. Conf. of Govs. Sch., Frankfort, Ky.; chair learning theory group Nat. Soc. for Internships and Experiantial Edn., Raleigh, N.C., 1989—. Guest editor Systems Rsch., 1986; contbr. articles to profl. jours. Coun. mem. Commrs. Adv. Coun. on Gifted Edn., Trenton, N.J., 1989—, Cen. N.J. Urban Schs. Improvement Coun., Monmouth County, N.J., 1988—; adv. mem. on acad. alliances, Trenton, 1989—; edn. task force Monmouth Ocean Devel. Coun., Wall, N.J., 1990—. Grantee Lilly Endowment, 1990—, G.R. Dodge Found., 1983-84, Internat. Ctr. for Integrative Studies, 1981, Pres. Venture Fund, Harvard U., 1979, 80; recipient Award Ella Lyman Cabot Trust, 1979, 80. Mem. Soc. for Values in Higher Edn., Coun. for the Advancement of Citizenship, Am. Assn. of Higher Edn., Internat. Ctr. for Integrative Studies, Nat. Conf. on Youth Leadership. Mem. Soc. of Friends. Home: 580 Cedar Ave West Long Branch NJ 07764-1757 Office: Monmouth Coll West Long Branch NJ 07764

KEENAN, ANTHONY HAROLD BRIAN, gift company executive; b. Toronto, Ont., Can., June 13, 1940; s. Harold Joseph and Ann Elizabeth (McGowan) K.; m. Marilyn Elaine Stanley, Aug. 29, 1964; children: Karen, Kevin, Sean. V.p. O.E. McIntyre Ltd., Montreal, Que., Can., 1965-72; gen. mgr. Xerox Edn. Group, Toronto, 1972-75; pres. Leisure Books Ltd., Montreal, 1975-82; exec. v.p. World Book Ency., Chgo., 1982-86; pres., chief exec. officer Regal Greetings & Gifts, Inc., Toronto, 1986—; bd. dirs. CML Industries, Toronto, PDL Can. Ltd., Que., Jay Norris Can. Ltd., Montreal; speaker numerous mktg. groups, 1970—. Chmn. direct response United Way, Toronto, 1988-89, com. mem. promotional programs, 1991. Lt. Can. Army, 1959-65. Recipient Vic Perry award United Way, 1991. Mem. Can. Direct Mktg. Assn. (chmn. 1978-79, Marketer of Yr. 1976), Direct Mktg. Club Toronto (pres. 1975-77), Royal Can. Mil. Inst., Arty. Officers Assn., Can. Club Chgo., Can. Racing Drivers Assn., Toronto Bd. Trade. Roman Catholic. Home: 25 Beaufort Hills Rd, Richmond Hill, ON Canada L4E 2N2 Office: Regal Greetings & Gifts Inc, 939 Eglinton Ave E, Toronto, ON Canada M4G 2L6

KEENAN, E(DMUND) TERRENCE, financial consultant; b. Bklyn., Jan. 12, 1965; s. Thomas Michael and Marlene (Franca) K. Assoc. in Bus. Adminstrn., Morris County Coll., Randolph, N.J., 1985; student, U. Md., 1985-86; B in Fin., Stocton Coll., Pomona, N.J., 1987. Fin. cons. Wheatfirst Butcher & Singer, Ocean City, N.J., 1988—; founder The Ice Cream Univ., Stone Harbor, N.J., 1988—; pres., chief exec. officer T.K. Keenan Co. Inc., Ocean City, 1989—. Author: Strategic Job Search, 1990. Republican. Roman Catholic. Home: PO Box 1155 Ocean City NJ 08226-7155 Office: Wheatfirst Butcher & Singer 801 Central Ave Ocean City NJ 08226

KEENAN, ELIZABETH LOUISE, librarian; b. Worcester, Mass., June 23, 1932; d. Thomas Joseph Keenan and Dorothy Gordon Hunt Corwin. BA, Clark U., Worcester, Mass., 1954; MLS, Simmons Coll., Boston, 1959; BMus, Northwestern U., Evanston, Ill., 1971; MMus, Am. Conservatory Music, Chgo., 1973. Serials cataloger Widener Libr., Harvard U., Cambridge, Mass., 1954-59; ref. librarian Countway Med. Libr., Harvard U., Cambridge, Mass., 1959-61; readers svcs. librarian Downstate Med. Ctr., SUNY, Bklyn., 1961-64, Am. Dental Assn., Chgo., 1964-67; head asst. Hild Reg. Libr., Chgo. Pub. Libr., 1967-74; librarian II music sect. Chgo. Pub. Libr., 1975-81; readers svcs. librarian Wheaton Coll., Norton, Mass., 1981-86; dir. Regis Coll. Libr., Weston, Mass., 1986—; cons. Boston Latin Acad., 1989—, Deutsche Schulverein, Walpole, Mass.,1990—. Contbr. articles to profl. jours. Mem. ALA, Assn. Coll. and Rsch. Librs., Cath. Libr. Assn., Mass. Libr. Assn., Med. Libr. Assn. (Ida and George Eliot award 1967), New Eng. Libr. Assn., Nat. Assn. Tchrs. of Singing, Delta Phi Alpha, Mu Phi Epsilon. Episcopalian. Home: 27 Holden St Attleboro MA 02703-1717 Office: Regis Coll Libr 235 Wellesley St Weston MA 02193-1505

KEENAN, GERALD JOHN, fleet manager; b. Wigan, Lancashire, Eng., Dec. 26, 1927; came to U.S., 1930; s. John and Margaret Mary (Lowe) K.; m. Margaret Josephine Petras, May 24, 1952; children: Thomas, Barbara. Payroll clk. Breeze Corp., Newark, 1944-46; IBM operator Prudential Ins. Co., Newark and Jacksonville, Fla., 1947-57; fleet mgr. GAB Bus. Svcs. Inc., N.Y.C. and Parsippany, N.J., 1958—. With U.S. Army, 1946-47. Mem. Nat. Assn. Fleet Adminstrs. (hon.). Republican. Roman Catholic. Home: 45 Oakwood Ave Livingston NJ 07039-4139 Office: GAB Bus Svcs Inc 9 Campus Dr Parsippany NJ 07054-4408

KEENAN, JAMES AUGUSTINE, JR., academic administrator, consultant; b. Waterbury, Conn., Apr. 29, 1932; s. James A. and Anna (Harmon) K.; m. Mary Louise Crane, Sept. 7, 1957; children: John, Anne, Patricia, James III. BS, Holy Cross Coll., 1954; LLB, Georgetown U., 1957. Bar: Conn. 1957, D.C. 1957, U.S. Ct. Appeals (D.C. cir.), 1957, U.S. Supreme Ct. 1960. Spl. agt. FBI, Washington, 1957-63; dir. annual giving Holy Cross Coll., Worcester, Mass., 1962-69; v.p. U. St. Thomas, St. Paul, 1969-83, Coll. St. Catherine, St. Paul, 1983-85, Mass. Eye and Ear Infirmary, Boston, 1985-89, Emmanuel Coll., Boston, 1989—; pres. Keenan & Assocs., Lowell, Mass., 1989—; cons. Fund for Theol. Edn., Princeton, N.J., 1982-84, Cretin-Derham High Sch., St. Paul, 1983-85, Nat. Cath. Ednl. Assn., Washington, 1989—. Trustee Pollard Meml. Libr., Lowell, 1990—, Minn. Mus. Art, St. Paul, 1980-85; bd. dirs. Acad. Notre Dame, Tyngsboro, Mass., 1989—. Mem. Nat. Assn. Hosp. Devel., Coun. of the Advancement and Support of Edn., Holy Cross Alumni Assn. (mem. alumni senate), Holy Cross Club of Minn. (pres. 1974-80). Roman Catholic. Home: 56 Avenue A Lowell MA 01851-4707 Office: Emmanuel Coll 400 The Fenway Boston MA 02115

KEENAN, JAMES JOSEPH, organizational consultant, educator; b. N.Y.C., Oct. 13, 1931; s. James Joseph and Genevieve Agnes (Commerford) K.; m. Elizabeth Leontine Myers, Feb. 7, 1960; children: James Joseph III, Thomas J., Elizabeth M., Patrick J., Michael J.J. BA, Manhattan Coll., 1953; MA, Fordham U., 1955; PhD, Columbia U., 1964. Lic. psychologist, Conn. Sr. rsch. scientist Inst. for Rsch. in Human Devel., Phila., 1956-57; mng. scientist Dunlap and Assocs., Darien, Conn., 1957-70; prin. exec. Keenan Assocs., Wilton, Conn., 1970—; prof. Grad. Sch. Communications, Bus. Sch., Fairfield (Conn.) U., 1970—; orgn. cons. GE, IBM, Xerox, Mastercard, Peat Marwick Mitchell, GTE, Westinghouse, Douglas Aircraft, 3M, Atari, Apple, 1957—; chmn. bd. sci. advisors Muzak Corp. Author: USAF Handbook for Human Performance Development, 1965, U.S. Navy Handbook for Human Performance Development, 1967, Human Performance and Communication Systems, 1981, The Communications Generalist, 1989. Comdr. USN, 1954-57. Mem. APA (various offices), Internat. Communication Assn., Human Factors Soc. Am., New Eng. Psychol. Assn. Office: 117 Cavalry Rd Wilton CT 06897-3636

KEENAN, JOHN FONTAINE, federal judge; b. N.Y.C., Nov. 23, 1929; s. John Joseph and Veronica (Fontaine) K.; m. Diane R. Nicholson, Oct. 6, 1956; 1 child, Marie Patricia. BBA, Manhattan Coll., N.Y., 1951; LLD (hon.), Manhattan Coll., 1989; LLB, Fordham U., 1954; LLD (hon.), Mt. St. Vincent Coll., 1989. Bar: N.Y. 1954, U.S. Dist. Ct. (so. dist.) N.Y. 1970. From asst. dist. atty. to chief asst. dist. atty. N.Y. County Dist. Atty.'s Office, 1956-76; spl. prosecutor, dep. atty. gen. City of N.Y., 1976-79; chmn. bd., pres. N.Y.C. Off-Track Betting Corp., 1979-82; criminal justice coord. City of N.Y., 1982-83; judge U.S. Dist. Ct. So. Dist. N.Y., N.Y.C., 1983—; chief asst. dist. atty. Queens County Dist. Atty.'s Office, N.Y., 1973; adj. prof. John Jay Coll. Criminal Justice, N.Y.C., 1979-83. Contbr. articles to law jours. Chmn. Daytop Village, Inc., N.Y.C., 1981-83. Served with U.S. Army, 1954-56. Recipient Frank S. Hogan award Citizens Com. Control of Crime in N.Y., 1975; cert. of recognition Patrolmen's Benevolent Assn., 1976; 1st Ann. Hogan-Morgenthau Assocs. award N.Y. County Dist. Atty.'s Office, 1976, Medal of Achievement, 1992; Excellence award N.Y. State Bar Assn., 1978, award N.Y. Criminal Bar Assn., 1979, Disting. Faculty award Nat. Coll. Dist. Attys., 1978, Louis J. Lefkowitz award Fordham Urban Law Jour., 1983. Mem. N.Y. State Bar Assn. (criminal justice exec. com. 1980—), Assn. Bar City of N.Y. (criminal justice council 1982—), Nat. Dist. Attys. Assn., N.Y. State Dist. Attys. Assn. Republican. Roman Catholic. Clubs: Amackassin (Yonkers, N.Y.); Skytop (Pa.); Merchants (N.Y.C.). Office: US Dist Ct US Courthouse 40 Foley Sq Rm 234 New York NY 10007-1502

KEENAN, KATHLEEN GLORIA, public relations professional; b. Honolulu, Apr. 4, 1955; d. Paul Conrad and Diana (Toner) K. BA cum laude, Cath. U., Washington, 1977. Writer, producer and asst. programming WGMS Radio, Rockville, Md., 1980-83; sr. account exec. Hartz/Meek Internat., Washington, 1983-85; dir. pub. relations Wyndham Bristol Hotel, Washington, 1985-86, The Sheraton Grand on Capitol Hill, Washington, 1986-88, The Sheraton Carlton, Washington, 1988—. Contbr. monthly articles to Ovation Mag., 1981-83. Mem. Hotel Pub. Relations Profls. Republican. Roman Catholic. Home: 4201 Cathedral Ave NW #407E Washington DC 20016 Office: The Sheraton Carlton 923 16th & K Sts NW Washington DC 20006

KEENAN, ROBERT J., non-profit organization administrator, educator; b. Rockville Centre, N.Y., Dec. 21, 1956; s. Robert A. and Barbara (White) K.; m. Ivette Malave, Feb. 6, 1982. BA, St. John's U., 1979; MSW, Adelphi U., 1985. Cert. social worker. Social worker Mill Neck (N.Y.) Manor Sch. Deaf, 1980-86; instr. Hofstra U., Hempstead, N.Y., 1987-90; assoc. prof. Dowling Coll., Oakdale, N.Y., 1990—; exec. dir. Lutheran Friends of the Deaf, Mill Neck, N.Y., 1986—; cons., trainer No. Ill. U., Dekalb, 1989. Nassau Dem. committeeman, del., Mineola, N.Y., 1982-87. Recipient commendation U.S. Post Office, 1987, Cert. of Excellence City of N.Y., 1989, Vol. award Nassau County, N.Y., 1989. Mem. NASW (del. 1989-92), Nat. Rehab. Assn., Conf. Ednl. Adminstrs. Serving Deaf, Nat. Rehab. Adminstrs. Assn., Assn. Persons in Supported Employment, N.Y. State Assn. Rehab. Facilities, N.Y. State Assn. Educators of the Deaf, Rotary. Democrat. Roman Catholic. Home: 15 Fairfield Ln Huntington Station NY 11746-2022 Office: Luth Friends of the Deaf PO Box 193 Mill Neck NY 11765-0193

KEENE, CHARLES THORNTON, communications executive; b. Middletown, Conn., Apr. 29, 1945; s. Philip and Virginia (Thornton) K. Student, U. Freiburg, 1965-66; BA with honors, U. Va., 1967; MA, Northwestern U., 1968. Pub. info. specialist USAF, 1968-73; communications specialist Conn. Mutual Life Ins. Co., Hartford, Conn., 1974-78; sr. communications specialist CIBA-Geigy Corp., Ardsley, N.Y., 1978-80, mgr. external communications, 1980-86, mgr. environ. communications, 1986—. Board dirs. Ferry Stoops, Inc., Hastings-on-Hudson, N.Y., 1987-91; selection com. mem. Am. Field Svc. chpt., Hastings-on-Hudson, 1987-89, bd. dis., 1989—, pres. 1990—; bd. dirs. The Gallery at Hastings-on-Hudson, 1991—; mem. Hastings-on-Hudson Conservation Commn., 1991—. Mem. Pub. Rels. Soc. Am. (pres. 1983, v.p. 1982, treas. 1980-81, program co-chair 1991), Westchester/Fairfield chpt. Hastings House Coop. Assn. (bd. dirs. 1990—). Democrat. Methodist. Home: 765 N Broadway Hastings On Hudson NY 10706 Office: CIBA-GEIGY Corp 444 Saw Mill River Rd Ardsley NY 10502-2600

KEENE, CHRISTOPHER, conductor, author, librettist, musician; b. Berkeley, Calif., Dec. 21, 1946; s. James Phillip and Yvonne San Jule Yvette (Cyr) K.; m. Sara Frances Rhodes, Dec. 21, 1967; children: Anthony Alexander, Nicholas Patrick. Ed., U. Calif. at Berkeley, 1963-67. Aast. condr. San Francisco Opera, 1966, San Diego Opera, 1967; mem. conducting staff N.Y.C. Opera, 1969—, music dir., 1982-86, gen. dir., 1989—; music dir. Festival of Two Worlds, Europe, dir., Am.; founder, music dir. L.I. Philharm., 1979-90; music dir. Syracuse (N.Y.) Symphony Orch., 1975-84; music dir., pres. Artpark Buffalo Philharm., 1974-89. Guest condr. Spoleto Festival, 1968, 69, 71, music dir., 1977; mus. dir., Am. Ballet Co., 1969-70; with Santa Fe Opera, 1971, Covent Garden, 1973, N.Y.C. Opera, 1970 (Julius Rudel award), Met. Opera, 1971, Chgo. Symphony, 1976, Berlin Opera, 1976; numerous guest appearances opera cos., maj. symphony orchs., 1972—; mus. dir., pres. Artpark, 1975-89, Syracuse Symphony Orch., 1975-84, L.I. Philharmonic, 1979-89; condr. world premiere Rasputin (Reise), The Most Important Man (Menotti), 1971, Yerma (Villa-Lobos), 1971; condr. N.Y. premiere X, The Life and Times of Malcom X (Davis), Of Mice and Men (Floyd), Akhnaten (Glass); condr. soundtrack Altered States; composer: ballet The Consort, 1970; author: libretto Duchess of Malfi; translator others; works presented include by Roger Sessions, Keith Jarrett, William Schuman, Joseph Schwantner, Michael Tippett, Stephen Douglas, John Corigliano, David Diamond; recs. include Diamonds 5th Symphony, soundtrack for film Altered States. Recipient Ditson Condr.'s award Columbia U., 1991. Office: NYC Opera 20 Lincoln Ctr New York NY 10023

KEENE, MICHELLE LASALLE, government official; b. Darby, Pa., Oct. 22, 1965; d. Herbert George Jr. and Glenna (Lasalle) K. BA magna cum laude, Bowdoin Coll., 1987; MA in Law and Diplomacy, Tufts U., 1990. Intern secretariat UN, N.Y.C., summer 1989; researcher Fletcher Sch., Budapest, Hungary, summer 1989; researcher, cons. Ctr. Environ. Mgmt, Tufts U., Medford, Mass., 1989-90; internat. environ. program mgr. EPA, Washington, 1990—. Vol. coord. Vols. for Indigents, Phila., 1987-88; vol. Nationalities Svcs. Ctr., Phila., 1987-88. Recipient Presdl. Mgmt. Intern, U.S. Office of Personell and Mgmt., 1990. Office: US EPA 401 M St SW A-106 Washington DC 20460

KEENE, PAUL FARWELL, artist; b. Phila., Aug. 24, 1920; s. Paul F. and Josephine B. (Hebron) K.; m. Laura A. Mitchell, Dec. 24, 1944; children: Paul Jacques, Lydia Burr. BFA, Temple U., 1947, BS in Edn., 1947, MFA, 1948; postgrad., Acad. Julien, Paris, 1949-51. Prof. Phila. Coll. of Art, 1956-68, program chmn., 1960-65, chmn. painting dept., 1967-68; prof. Bucks County Community Coll., Newtown, Pa., 1968-85. One man shows include Afro Am. Mus., Phila., 1991, James A. Michener Art Mus., Doylestown, Pa., 1991; recipient Van Der Zee award Brandywine Workshop, 1990; Whitney Found. fellow, 1952-54. 2d lt. USAAF, 1941-45. Home and Studio: 2843 Bristol Rd Warrington PA 19876

KEENEY, PHILIP GREGORY, food technology consultant, former educator; b. Caldwell, N.J., Feb. 28, 1925; s. Mark H. and Eleanor (McCollough) K.; m. Elsie E. Bamesberger, Nov. 9, 1957; 1 child, Philip G. II. BS, U. Nebr., 1949; MS, Ohio State U., 1953; PhD, Pa. State U., 1955. Asst. mgr. Tri-County Dairy, Winthrop, Minn., 1949-51; asst. prof. Pa. State U., University Park, 1955-62, assoc. prof., 1962-66, prof. food sci., 1966-85, prof.

emeritus, 1985—; cons. State College, Pa., 1985—; bd. dirs. Germantown Mfg. Co., Broomall, Pa. Contbr. over 150 articles to profl. jours. 1st lt. U.S. Army, 1943-45, PTO. Fellow AAAS; mem. Inst. Food Technologists, Am. Dairy Sci. Assn., Am. Chem. Soc., Sigma Xi, Gamma Sigma Delta, Phi Tau Sigma. Home: 1449 Curtin St State College PA 16803-3020

KEESEE, PATRICIA HARTFORD, volunteer; b. Nashville, Jan. 29, 1928; d. William Donald and Mary Carolyn (Gwyn) Hartford; m. Thomas Woodfin Keesee Jr., June 26, 1953; children: Thomas Woodfin III, Anne Hartford Keesee Niemann; 1 stepson: Allen P.K. Keesee. BA in English, Radcliff Coll., 1950; BA in Environ. Scis., SUNY, Purchase, 1977. Lab. asst. Rockefeller U. (formerly Rockefeller Inst. Med. Rsch.), N.Y.C., 1951-54. Pres. Fed. Conservationists of Westchester County, Purchase, 1985-87; mem. Women's Coun. of N.Y. Botan. Garden, Bronx, 1982—, Wetlands Commn., Bedford, N.Y., 1988—, Conservation Bd. Town of Bedford, 1978-88, Westchester County Environ. Mgmt. Commn., 1979-88; trustee Lower Hudson Chpt. Nature Conservancy, Katonah, N.Y., 1980-90, 91—, chmn., 1983-86; vice-chmn. N.Y. State Bd. Nature Conservancy, Albany, 1986-88, trustee, 1983-91; chmn. Byram com. Nature Conservancy, Bedford, 1978-81. Mem. N.Y. Acad. Scis., Garden Club Am. (conservation com. 1983-85, vice chmn. conservation com. 1985-87, bd. dirs. 1989-91, vice chmn. scholarship com. 1991—). Episcopalian. Home: Sarles St RD # 3 Mount Kisco NY 10549-2812

KEETON, KATHY MERLE, publisher; b. Republic of South Africa, Feb. 17, 1939; d. Keith and Queenie K.; m. Jan. 17, 1988. Student, Royal Ballet Sch., London. Vice chmn. vice chmn., chief operating officer, N.Y.C., 1969—; Pres. Omni mag., N.Y.C., 1978—; pres. Longevity Mag., Compute Mag. Author: (with Yvonne Baskin) Woman of Tomorrow, 1985, Longevity: The Science of Staying Young, 1992; exec. producer TV program Omni: Visions of Tomorrow, The New Frontier. Active Fund for the Aging (City Meals on Wheels), Corp. Blood Drive, Nat. Coalition Against Censorship. Recipient Publisher of Yr. citation, Outstanding Woman in Publishing award March of Dimes, Unity of the City of N.Y. award Mayor Dinkins. Mem. AIAA, Amateur Astronomers Assn., Am. Space Found., Robotics Internat. SME, Space Generation Found., L-5 Soc. Office: Omni Mag 1965 Broadway New York NY 10023-5904

KEFALIDES, NICHOLAS ALEXANDER, physician, educator; b. Alexandroupolis, Greece, Jan. 17, 1927; came to U.S., 1947, naturalized; s. Athanasios and Alexandra (Aematidou) K.; m. Eugenia Georgia Kutsunis, Nov. 24, 1949; children—Alexandra Jane, Patricia Ann, Paul Thomas. B.A., Augustana Coll., Rock Island, Ill., 1951; B.S., Univ. Ill.-Chgo., 1953, M.S. in Biochemistry, 1956, M.D., 1956, Ph.D. in Biochemistry, 1965; M.S. (hon.), U. Pa., 1971; doctorate (hon.) U. Reims, France, 1987. Asst prof medicine, Univ Ill. Coll Medicine, Chgo., 1964-65; asst prof medicine, U. Chgo., 1965-69, assoc prof medicine, 1969-70; assoc prof medicine and biochemistry, U. Pa., Phila., 1970-74, prof medicine, 1974—, prof. biochemistry and biophysics, 1975—. Contbr. chpts. to books, articles to profl. jours. Served as surgeon USPHS, 1957-60.; Recipient Borden Research Found. award, 1956; Guggenheim fellow, 1977. Mem. AAAS, Am. Assn. Pathologists, Am. Soc. Clin. Investigation, Am. Soc. Biol. Chemists, Am. Soc. Cell Biology. Achievement includes the discovery of Collagen type IV in basemant membranes. Office: Connective Tissue Rsch Inst 3624 Market St Philadelphia PA 19104-2611

KEGELES, LAWRENCE STEVEN, physician, physicist; b. Madison, Wis., Feb. 9, 1947; s. Gerson and Bertha (Webber) K.; m. Wendy Carol Winer, Aug. 10, 1987; 1 child, Laura Rosalyn. AB, Princeton (N.J.) U., 1969; PhD, U. Pa., 1974; MD, Mt. Sinai Sch. Medicine, 1991. Rsch. assoc. U. Pa., Phila., 1974-76, U. Alta., Edmonton, Can., 1976-78, Stevens Inst. Tech., Hoboken, N.J., 1978-81; mem. tech. staff AT&T Bell Labs., Murray Hill, N.J., 1981-87; resident Columbia Presbyn. Hosp., N.Y.C., 1991—. Contbr. articles to profl. jours. Mem. N.Y. Acad. Scis., Phi Beta Kappa, Alpha Omega Alpha, Sigma Xi. Home: 127 W 96th St Apt 13D New York NY 10025-6430

KEGELES, S. STEPHEN, behavioral science educator; b. Manchester, N.H., June 2, 1925; s. Alex and Jennie (Wilder) K.; m. Jane Ainsworth, Jan. 3, 1948; children: Susan, Martha, Nancy, Robert, Dorothy. BA, Drake U., 1949; MA, Boston U., 1951, PhD, 1955. Rsch. psychologist Boston Psychopathic Hosp., 1950-52, USPHS, Washington, 1954-56; chief social psychol. studies sect. Div. Pub. Health and Resources, USPHS, 1957-62, chief social studies br., 1960-62; rsch. assoc., lectr. U. Mich., 1962-65, assoc. prof. pub. health, asst. dir. pub. health practice, 1965-66, co-dir., doctoral tng. program in pub. health adminstrn., 1966-69, prof. dept. behavioral scis. and community health, 1969—; sr. rsch. scientist Ctr. for the Environ. and Man, Inc., Hartford, Conn., 1970-71; assoc. dir. Conn. Cancer Control Rsch. Unit at Yale, 1986-89; head, behavioral scis., 1986-89; expert cons. WHO, 1969-79; tech. advisor surgeon gens. adv. com.; adv. com. Conn. State Dept. Health Svcs. Contbr. articles to profl. jours., chpts. to books. With USN, 1943-45. Recipient Disting. Sr. Sci. award Behavioral Scientists in Dental Rsch., 1988, numerous grants from various orgns. Fellow Acad. Behavioral Medicine Rsch.; mem. Internat. Assn. Dental Rsch., Am. Assn. Dental Rsch., Am. Pub. Health Assn., Am. Psychol. Assn. Home: 114 N Main St West Hartford CT 06107-1209 Office: U Conn Health Ctr Dept Behavioral Scis Farmington CT 06032

KEGELMAN, MATTHEW ROLAND, research chemist; b. Mahopac, N.Y., June 24, 1928; s. Orlando and Muriel (Brown) K.; m. Mary Joan Connelly, Oct. 12, 1953; children: John P., Matthew F., Jerome T., Joseph E., Thomas A., Mary F., Christine M., Bernadette A., James W., Daniel G. BS, Fordham U., 1948, MS, 1949, PhD, 1952. Rsch. chemist DuPont Co., Wilmington, Del., 1953-63, sr. rsch. chemist, 1964-72, rsch. assoc., 1962-78, sr. rsch. assoc., 1978—. Contbr. articles to profl. jours.; patentee in field. Mem. AAAS, Am. Chem. Soc., Sigma Xi. Republican. Roman Catholic. Home: 204 N Pembrey Dr Wilmington DE 19803-2005

KEGGI, JULIA QUARLES, society executive; b. Evanston, Ill., Jan. 24, 1935; d. Joseph Very and Mary Louise (Fronheiser) Quarles; m. Kristaps Juris Keggi, July 27, 1957; children: Catherine Keggi Hunter, Mara Walden, Caroline Saunders. BA, Smith Coll., 1956. Co-chair campaign for mus. Mattatuck Mus. and Hist. Soc., Waterbury, Conn., 1985-86; mem. bldg. com. Mattatuck Mus., Waterbury, 1986-87; pres. Mattatuck Mus. and Hist. Soc., Waterbury, 1990—. Deaconness Middlebury (Conn.) Congl. Ch., 1972-74; mem. Middlebury (Conn.) Rep. Town Com., 1974-75; state team capt. Conn. Women's Golf Assn., 1980-82; pres. Middlebury (Conn.) Garden Club, 1986-88. Mem. County Club Waterbury (chmn. 1971, 72, 73, 74, 77, 78, 80, 83, green com. 1990—), Highfield Club. Republican. Home: 1321 Whittemore Rd Middlebury CT 06762

KEGLEY, JOHN FRANKLIN, educator, psychotherapist; b. Evanston, Ill., Mar. 6, 1944; s. Charles William and Elizabeth Euphemia (Meck) K.; m. Mary Frances Gardner, Dec. 28, 1966; children: Carolynn Elizabeth, Geoffrey Gardner. BA, Gettysburg Coll., Pa., 1966; MA, George Washington U., Washington, 1969, EdS, 1970, EDD, 1973. Counselor, tchr. D.C. Pub. Schs., Washington, 1966-72; lectr. in edn. Va, Polytechnic Inst. & SU, Reston, Va., 1974-79; community coord. Montgomery County Pub. Schs., Rockville, Md., 1972-79, supr. of spl. svcs., 1979-81, pupil personnel worker, 1981—; mental health counselor pvt. practice, Rockville, Md., 1979—; cons. Girl Scouts of Am., Bethesda, Md., 1973; bd. dirs. Child Care Ctr., Rockville, Md., 1972; speaker WDCA-TV Newsprobe, Washington, 1982; bd. dirs. The C.W. Kegley Lectureship in Political Philosophy, Bakersfield, Calif., 1986—. Founder: Gateway Alternative Sch., 1978; supr. Kaps I-V Keeping All Pupil in Sch., 1973-78; grantsman, supr. Richmond Montgomery Intergroup Rels. Project, 1975; supr. Inward, Outward, Upward 1976; contbr. articles to profl. jours. Recipient The Harry E. Detwiler Meml. award in counseling, The George Washington U., 1977. Mem. Am. Assn. for Counseling and Devel., Am. Mental Health Counselors Assn., Internat. Assn. Pupil Pers. Workers, Assn. for Counseling Edn. and Supervision, Phi Delta Kappa, Phi Delta Theta. Lutheran. Home: 9604 Napoleon Way Gaithersburg MD 20879-2160 Office: Interagence & Alternative Programs 4910 Macon Rd Rockville MD 20852-2228

KEHOE, L. PAUL, state legislator; b. Carthage, N.Y., May 21, 1938; s. Leo A. and Mildred (Piddock) K.; B.A., Syracuse U., 1959, LL.D., 1962; m. Elizabeth M. Weber, 1963; children—L. Paul, John Michael, Patrick Lewis. Admitted to N.Y. bar, 1962; practice law, Wolcott, N.Y.; dist. atty. Wayne County, N.Y., 1967-71; mem. N.Y. Assembly, 1979-80; mem. N.Y. State Senate, 1981—. Served with AUS, 1962-63. Mem. ABA, Wayne County Bar Assn., N.Y. State Bar Assn. Republican. Clubs: Rotary, Elks. Office: 50 E Main St Wolcott NY 14590 also: NY State Senate State Capitol Albany NY 12247

KEICHER, WILLIAM EUGENE, electrical engineer; b. Pitts., Dec. 28, 1947; s. William John and Gina Rina (Magrini) K.; m. Barbara Marie Gurgacz, Aug. 12, 1972; children: Lisa Ann, Kathy Marie, William Michael. BSEE, Carnegie-Mellon U., 1969, MSEE, 1970, PhD in Elec. Engring., 1974. Sr. elec. engr. CBS Labs., Stamford, Conn., 1974-75; mem. tech. staff Lincoln Lab., MIT, Lexington, Mass., 1975-83, asst. group leader, 1983-85, group leader, 1985—; cons. Sci. and Engring. Support Group for Strategic Def. Initiative, Arlington, Va., 1988; co-chair for numerous confs. in field. Editor: Millimeter Wave Technology, 1982; contbr. articles to profl. publs.; patentee spatial filter system. Capt. U.S. Army, 1974. Mem. IEEE (sr.), Optical Soc. Am., Assn. Old Crows. Roman Catholic. Home: 6 Winn Valley Dr Burlington MA 01803-4727 Office: MIT Lincoln Lab 244 Wood St Rm 270L Lexington MA 02173-6499

KEILHOLTZ, PATRICIA DIANE, art director; b. Balt., Oct. 29, 1950; d. John Joseph and Phyllis Elaine (Fromm) Strucko; m. William LeRoy Keilholtz, Feb. 22, 1975. AA, Catonsville Community Coll., 1972. Typesetter Knight Press, Balt., 1969-70; copywriter Montgomery Ward, Balt., 1970-72, layout artist, 1972-75; mech. artist Ray Thompson & Assocs., Balt., 1975-78, Alpha Graphics, Balt., 1978, Eisner and Assocs., Balt., 1978-80; art dir. Noble Steed & Assocs., Inc., Balt., 1980—; tchr. Md. Inst. Coll. Art., Balt., 1989, Catonsville Community Coll., Balt., 1989, 90. Recipient Best in Balt. award Advt. Assn. Balt., 1986, Desi award Graphic Design U.S.A., 1986, 87, silver award Health Care Mktg., 1988, 89, Flashes of Brilliance competition Bronze award Acad. for Health Svcs. Mktg., 1992. Democrat. Office: Foxleigh Bldg 2330 W Joppa Rd Lutherville Timonium MD 21093-4609

KEILLOR, GARRISON EDWARD, writer, radio host, storyteller; b. Anoka, Minn., Aug. 7, 1942; s. John P. and Grace R. (Denham) K. B.A., U. Minn., 1966. Author: Happy to be Here, 1982, Lake Wobegon Days, 1985, Leaving Home, 1987, We Are Still Married: Stories and Letters, 1989, (novel) WLT: A Radio Romance, 1991; creator: radio shows A Prairie Home Companion, Garrison Keillor's American Radio Company; contbns. articles to mags. (New Yorker, Harpers). Recipient Grammy award for best non-mus. recording Lake Wobegon Days, 1987, Ace award, 1988, Best Mus. and Entertainment Host awards, 1988, 89, medal for spoken lang. Am. Acad. and Inst. Arts and Letters, 1990. Democrat. Plymouth Brethren. Address: Am Radio Co 80 Eighth Ave Ste 1210 New York NY 10011

KEIM, PETER DE GRAAF, hospitality industry consultant; b. N.Y.C., Feb. 7, 1941; s. W. Franklin and Dorothy Elizabeth (DeGraaf) K.; m. Judith Ann Schott, Apr. 24, 1965; children: Andrew Franklin, Steven Whitfield. BS in Hotel Adminstrn., Cornell U., 1969; MBA, Drexel U., 1972. Asst. mgr. Dorado (P.R.) Beach Hotel, 1965-66; cons. Laventhol & Horwath, Phila., 1969-72; cons., mgr. Laventhol & Horwath, Kansas City, Mo., 1972-75; prin. Laventhol & Horwath, Boston, 1975-78, sr. prin., 1978-88; assoc. prof. U. N.H., Durham, 1988-89; pres. The Keim Co. Inc., Durham, 1988—; mem. adv. bd. Boston U. Sch. Hotel Restaurant Mgmt., 1980-87, New Eng. Ctr. Continuing Edn., Durham, 1989—. Co-author: Ethics in Accounting, 1992. Mem. parish com. 1st Parish Cohasset, Mass., 1981. With U.S. Army, 1962-65. Mem. Am. Hotel Motel Assn. (allied mem.), Internat. Soc. Hospitality Cons. (charter mem.), Internat. Inst. Quality Ethics in Svc. and Tourism (treas. bd. dirs. 1991), Cornell Soc. Hotelmen (pres. New Eng. chpt. 1982-84), Cornell Real Estate Coun. Republican. Home and Office: 8 Cold Spring Rd Durham NH 03824-4302

KEIMIG, SCOTT DAVID, environmental administrator; b. Omaha, Oct. 13, 1953; s. Justinian A. and Joyce Arlene (Wagelie) K.; m. Deborah Gellerman. BS, St. Ambrose U., 1975; MS, U. Iowa, 1978, PhD, 1982. Cert. indsl. hygienist. Rsch. asst. U. Iowa, Iowa City, 1977-82; staff scientist Brookhaven Nat. Lab., Upton, N.Y., 1982-84; sr. scientist Fredrick (Md.) Cancer Rsch. Lab., 1984-89; dir. environ. Cath. U. Am., Washington, 1989—. Contbr. articles to profl. jours. Recipient First Young Alumnus award St. Ambrose U., 1987. Mem. Chesapeake Indsl. Hygiene Assn. (pres. 1989-90). Office: Cath U Am Dept Environment and Safety Washington DC 20064

KEISER, HENRY BRUCE, lawyer, publisher; b. N.Y.C., Oct. 26, 1927; s. Leo and Jessie (Liebeskind) K.; m. Jessie E. Weeks, July 12, 1953; children: Betsy Cordelia Keiser Smith, Matthew Roderick. BA with honors in Econs., U. Mich., 1947; JD cum laude, Harvard U., 1950. Bar: N.Y. 1950, D.C. 1955, Fla. 1956, U.S. Supreme Ct. 1954. Trial atty. CAB, Washington, 1950-51; head counsel alcoholic beverages sect. OPS, 1951-52; legal asst. to Judge Eugene Black U.S. Tax Ct., 1953-56; pvt. practice law Washington, 1956—; founder, chmn. bd., pres. Fed. Pubs., Inc., 1959-85; chmn. bd. dirs. Gene Galasso Assocs., Inc., Washington, 1963—, Empire Carriages, London, 1984—, Lion Worldwide, London, 1985—, U.S. Telemktg., Inc., Atlanta, 1986—, The Arkhon Corp., Cherry Hill, N.J., 1983—, pres., 1991—; founder, chmn. bd. Crown Eagle Communications Ltd., London, 1978-84; chmn. bd., pres. Keiser Enterprises, Inc., Washington, 1985—, Phila. Inst., 1986—; chmn. sec. adv. com. on constrn. contract document reform HUD, 1983-85; bd. dirs. Nat. Bank Commerce, 1983-84; mem. adv. cabinet Southeastern U., 1965-75; judge, bd. contract appeals AEC, 1965-75; profl. lectr. Dept. Agr., 1960-77, George Washington U., 1961-79, U. San Francisco, 1965-82, Coll. William and Mary, 1966-75, Calif. Inst. Tech., 1967-72, U. So. Calif., 1973-74, U. Denver, 1975-85, Air Force Inst. Tech., 1975-76, U. Santa Clara, 1975-81. Trustee Touro Coll., 1979—. 1st lt. Judge Adv. Gen. Corps, USAF, 1952-53; maj. Res. (ret.). Lord of Tuxford (hereditary), Nottinghamshire, Eng. Fellow ABA (pub. contracts sect., coun. 1972-75, Disting. Svc. award 1987), Am. Bar Found., Nat. Contract Mgmt. Assn.; mem. N.Y. Bar Assn., Fla. Bar Assn., D.C. Bar Assn. (bd. dirs. 1965-66, chmn. adminstrv. law sect. 1964-65), Cosmos Club, Nat. Press Club, Army-Navy Club, Crockford's Club (London). Jewish. Home: 7200 Armat Dr Bethesda MD 20817-2108 Office: 2828 Pennsylvania Ave NW Washington DC 20007-3719

KEISTER, DONALD LEE, biochemist; b. Beckley, W.Va., Dec. 10, 1933; s. Roy Howard and W. Myrtle (Neel) K.; m. Joyce Elizabeth Diggs, Jan. 17, 1937; children: Alan Hamilton, Julie Eileen, Cristyn Ann. BS, W.Va. Wesleyan Coll., 1954; MS, U. Md., 1956, PhD, 1959. Rsch. assoc. Johns Hopkins U., Balt., 1959-61, Rsch. Inst. Advanced Study, Balt., 1961-62; investigator, sr. investigator Charles F. Kettering Rsch. Lab., Yellow Springs, Ohio, 1962-84; rsch. leader USDA Agrl. Rsch. Svc. Nitrogen Fixation & Soybean Genetics Lab., Beltsville, Md., 1984-90, USDA Agrl. Rsch. Svc., Soybean & Alfalfa Rsch. Lab., Beltsville, 1990—; sr. scientist U.S. Dept. of State, U.S. Sci. Tech. Inst., 1984-91; speaker in field. Editor: The Rhizosphere and Plant Growth, 1991; contbr. over 100 scientific papers to profl. jours. and books. Grantee NSF, U.S. Dept. Agrl.; fellow Nat. Found., 1959-61. Mem. Am. Soc. Microbiology, Am. Soc. Biochemistry Molecular Biology, Am. Soc. Plant Physiologists. Home: 12408 Silverbirch Ln Laurel MD 20708-2556 Office: USDA Agrl Rsch Svc Bldg 011 HH-19 BARC-W Beltsville MD 20705-2350

KEITER, DALE H., management consultant; b. Boston, July 20, 1952; s. Irving Jules and Barbara June (Caplan) K.; m. Gale Coren, Sept. 7.; children: Laura, Jonathan. AB, Clark U., Worcester, Mass., 1974; MA, New Sch. for Social Rsch., N.Y.C., 1976; PhD, NYU, 1981. Cons. Key Assocs., N.Y.C., 1979-81; corp. psychologist Rohrer, Hibler, Replogle, Detroit, 1981-85; pres. Mgmt. Affiliates, Greenwich, Conn., 1985—.

KEITH, BARRY HAROLD, environmental scientist; b. Northbridge, Mass., Sept. 16, 1954; s. Harold and Louise Thobia (Hansen) K.; m. Pamela Jean Clemons, May 16, 1981; stepchildren: Shanti, Leif. BS, U. N.H., 1976, MS, 1982. Registered profl. forester, Maine, N.H.; cert. wildlife biologist. Wildlife biologist U.S. Army C.E., Franklin, N.H., 1976-77, 78; terrestrial ecologist Wilbur Smith & Assocs., Inc., Concord, N.H., 1977; sr. ecologist BCI Geonetics, Inc., Laconia, N.H., 1977-78; ind. consulting ecologist Laconia, 1978-79; wetlands project mgr. N.H. Extension Svc., Conway, 1979-80; environ. scientist B.H. Keith Assocs., Freedom, N.H., 1980—; cons., U.S. Am. Internat. Devel., Washington, 1987—. Contbr. articles to environ. pubs. Mem. Freedom (N.H.) Conservation Commn., 1988—. Mem. Wildlife Soc. (bull. editorial referee 1983), Soc. Wetland Scientists, Soc. Ecol. Restoratin and Mgmt., Soc. Am. Foresters, N.H. Assn. Wetland Scientists, Ducks Unlimited (chmn. 1985—, Disting. Svc. award), Soc. for Protection of N.H. Forests, Freedom Club. Republican. Office: BH Keith Assocs Elm St Freedom NH 03836

KEITH, DENNIS DALTON, chemist; b. Hartford, Conn., July 11, 1943; s. Roy Leon and Angeline (Panesis) K.; m. Jo-Linda Leib, Jan. 30, 1966; children: Tanya Hope, Emily Nicole. BS, Bates Coll., 1966; MS, Yale U., 1967, MPhil, 1968, PhD, 1969. Postdoctoral fellow Harvard U., Cambridge, Mass., 1969-71; sr. scientist Hoffmann-La Roche Inc., Nutley, N.J., 1971-76; rsch. fellow Hoffman-La Roche Inc., Nutley, N.J., 1976-81, rsch. group chief, 1981-83, rsch. sect. chief, 1983-85, dir. anti-infective chemistry, 1985-91, sr. dir. medicinal chemistry, 1991—. Office: Hoffmann-La Roche Inc Kingland Ave Nutley NJ 07110

KEITH, QUENTIN GANGEWERE, English educator, retired military officer, editor; b. Bethlehem, Pa., Aug. 14, 1919; s. Stanley Raymond and Estelle Naomi (Gangewere) K.; m. Pamela Margaret Havlicek, May 14, 1944 (dec. 1945); m. Sylvia E. Phillips Nov. 29, 1945 (dec. 1991); children: Jennifer Estelle, Vaughn Phillips Montaigne (dec. 1990). BA, Lehigh (Pa.) U., 1940; postgrad., U. Paris, 1945; BA with honors, Cambridge (Eng.) U., 1947, MA, 1952. Commd. 2d lt. U.S. Army, 1940, advanced through grades to col., 1972, ret., 1979; instr. humanities Rutgers U., N.J., 1948-51; mem. faculty, dir. devel. Monmouth (N.J.) Coll., 1955-59, assoc. prof. English, 1959-83; emeritus prof. English Monmouth (N.J.) Coll., SD, 1983—; dir. Keith Library, Red Bank, N.J., 1985—; rare book cons. Guggenheim Libr., Monmouth Coll., 1959—; mem. cons. faculty Command and Gen. Staff Coll., Ft. Leavenworth, Kans., 1974-80. Author: Skyline Stories, 1954, A Short History of Communications, 1955; editor: The Army Wife, The Air Force Wife, 1952; editor Brit. Schs. & Univs. Quar., 1954-58; contbr. editor: Columbia Ency., 2d edit., 1947-48, Columbia-Lippincott Gazetteer, 1947-48. Founder English Speaking Union U.S., Monmouth County, 1958, br. pres., 1971-74, regional dir., Washington, 1973-75. Decorated Legion of Merit, Bronze Star, Croix-de-Guerre (France), Normandy Arrowhead. Mem. Am. Soc. for Eighteenth Century Studies, Coun. Am.'s Mil. Past, Am. Mil. Inst., Army & Navy Club, Army & Navy Club (London). Anglican. Office: Keith Libr 217 W Front St Red Bank NJ 07701-1162

KELE, ROGER ALAN, microbiologist; b. Waterbury, Conn., Jan. 24, 1943; s. Alan E. and Lillian S. (Dancsak) K.; m. Anne Frances Schackner, July 2, 1972; children: Kirsten Debra, Marc Jonathan. AB, Clark U., 1964; MA, Harvard U., 1966; PhD, U. Wis., 1970. Rsch. microbiologist Lederle Labs., Pearl River, N.Y., 1970—. Mem. Soc. Indsl. Microbiology. Office: Lederle Labs 100-625 Middletown Rd Pearl River NY 10965-2611

KELEJIAN, HARRY HERAND, economics educator; b. N.Y.C., July 12, 1937; s. Jack Shavarsh and Sally Surpoohe (Vartanian) K.; m. Irene Mary Negosh (div. Dec. 1986); children: David, Douglas, Melinda. BA, Hofstra U., 1962; MA, U. Wis., 1966, PhD, 1968. Asst. prof. econs. Princeton (N.J.) U., 1968-71; assoc. prof. econs. NYU, N.Y.C., 1971-74; prof. econs. U. Md., College Park, 1974—; cons. AT&T Communications, Bedminster, N.J., 1989-90. Author: Introduction to Econometrics, 1989; contbr. numerous articles to profl. jours. With U.S. Army, 1954-56. Mem. Am. Econ. Assn., Econometric Soc. Home: 3917 Commander Dr College Heights Estates Hyattsville MD 20782 Office: U Md Dept Econs College Park MD 20742

KELETI, GEORG, microbiologist, researcher; b. Michalovce, East Slovakia, Czechoslovakia, May 30, 1925; s. Louis and Lilly (Silberstein) K.; m. Martha Helene Maxian, July 28, 1956; children: Eva, Daniel. Degree in pharmacy, Comenius U., Bratislava, Czechoslovakia, 1950, PhD in Microbiology, 1952; candidate of sci. in biology, Acad. Scis., Bratislava, 1961; cert., Continuing Edn. Physicians, Bratislava, 1963. Asst. prof. microbiology Comenius U., 1950-53, prof.'s asst., 1953-63, assoc. prof., 1963-68; sr. fellow Max-Planck Inst., Freiburg, Fed. Republic of Germany, 1968-70; asst. resident prof. U. Pitts., 1970-79, assoc. prof., 1979—; sr. scientist Bactex Pitts., 1986-87; cons. in field. Author: Handbook of Micromethods for the Biological Sciences, 1974; contbr. articles to profl. jours. Patentee Anti-tumor process using a Brucella Abortus preparation, 1989. Served to 1st lt. Czech. Army, 1951-54. Mem. Am. Soc. Microbiology, Allegheny Soc. Microbiology. Home: 5831 Nicholson St Pittsburgh PA 15217-2309

KELLAR, JEFF FREDERICK, sculptor; b. Washington, Sept. 25, 1949; s. Harold Charles and Deynard Elizabeth (Collins) K.; m. Judy Ann La Brasca, May 29, 1971; 1 child, Anne. BA in English/Film Making, U. Pa., 1971; postgrad., Pa. Acad. Fine Arts, Fleisher Meml. Art Inst. Instr. Haystack Mtn. Sch. of Crafts, Deer Isle, Maine, 1987; artist in residence U. So. Maine Sculpture Dept., 1987. Exhibited in group shows at Joan Whitney Payson Gallery Art, 1985, Bowdoin Mus. Art, 1986, Barridoff Galleries, Portland, Maine, 1988, 90, Farnsworth Mus., 1989, Portland Mus. Art, 1988, 90, 91; one-man shows include Barridoff Galleries, 1989, Gallery Camino Real, Boca Raton, Fla., 1991; contbr. revs. and articles to profl. jours. Apptd. to Maine Arts Commn., 1988-90, Gov.'s Adv. Bd., 1988. Recipient Maine Times Design award, 1987, First prize Washington Craft Show, 1984, First prize Phila. Mus. of Art, 1983, Daphne award, 1981, Honorable mention Kenyon Film Festival, 1971. Home: PO Box 4770 Portland ME 04112-4770

KELLEHER, PHILIP CONBOY, medical scientist; b. New Rochelle, N.Y., July 23, 1928; s. Hugh Joseph and Winifred Mary (Conboy) K.; m. Virginia Frances Rago, Apr. 16, 1955 (div. July 1977); children: Philip Francis, Kathleen Ann, Patrick David Conboy. BS, Georgetown U., 1950, MD, 1954. Diplomate Am. Bd. Internal Medicine. Resident in internal medicine SUNY Upstate Med. Ctr., Syracuse, 1955-58; fellow in biochemistry Sch. Medicine Harvard U., Boston, 1960-63; asst. in medicine Mass. Gen. Hosp., Boston, 1961-63; from instr. to assoc. prof. Sch. Medicine U. Vt., Burlington, 1963—; vis. scientist Sir William Dunn Sch. Pathology, Oxford, Eng., 1979-80. Contbr. articles to profl. publs. Mem. tech. adv. com. Lake Champlain Mgmt. Conf., Vt. and N.Y., 1991. Capt. U.S. Army, 1958-60. Grantee NIH, 1991—, Nat. Found. for Ileitis and Colitis, 1991—, also NIH, Am. Cancer Soc., March of Dimes Birth Defect Found. Mem. Soc. for Oncodevelopmental Biology and Medicine, Am. Soc. Cancer Rsch., Trout Unltd. (nat. bd. dirs. 1988—, v.p. cen. Vt. chpt. 1987—), Lake Champlain Walleye Assn. Democrat. Home: 60 Manor Woods S Burlington VT 05403-7117 Office: U Vt C 313 Given Bldg Burlington VT 05405

KELLEHER, WILLIAM GORDON, data processing company executive; b. Beverly, Mass., June 11, 1942; s. Francis P. and Elizabeth (Pope) K.; m. Rosalie Pittari, Dec. 26, 1970; children: David, Lisa. BEE, Rensselaer Poly. Inst., 1966; M.Engring. Mgmt., Northeastern U., Boston, 1970. Quality engr. Honeywell Inc., Brighton, Mass., 1966-70, quality mgr., 1970-74; assoc. project dir. Honeywell Inc., Waltham, Mass., 1974-77; dir. design assurance Data Gen., Westboro, Mass., 1977-81, dir. new products, 1982, dir. corp. quality, 1982-83; plant mgr. Data Gen., Southboro, Mass., 1984-87; dir. ops. Data Gen., Westboro, 1987-91; cons., 1991—; ptnr. Thomas Group, Inc., Bedford, 1992—. Unit commr. Boy Scouts Am., Bedford, Mass., 1982—. Mem. Metro West C. of C. (dir. 1985-89). Home: 22 Pine St Bedford MA 01730-2818

KELLER, DIANE JOY, medical marketing consultant; b. Phila., June 15, 1959; d. Edward Medwin and Jane Ida (Wirth) Rech; m. George A. Keller, Sept. 19, 1981; 1 child, Christine Marie. BS, Pa. State U., 1980. RN. Pharm. sales rep. E.R. Squibb & Sons, 1982-87; dir. mktg. Shaffer Cardiovascular Assocs., 1987-89; owner Med. Mktg. Cons. Ltd., 1989—.

KELLER, JAMES LEROY, human resources executive, educator; b. Dallastown, Pa., June 16, 1947; s. Robert L. and Margaret M. (Wilson) K.; m. Jody L. Spigle, Apr. 22, 1978; children: Matthew W., Sadie W. BS, West Chester (Pa.) U., 1969; MEd, U. Ariz., 1970; EdD, Temple U., 1975. Tchr. elem. Friends Select Sch., Phila., 1971-72; cons. Rsch. for Better Schs., Phila., 1971-73; chief prevention and tng. dept. Gov. Com. on Drug and

Alcohol Abuse, Harrisburg, Pa., 1973-76; exec. dir. Commonwealth Prevention Alliance, Harrisburg, 1976-78; instr. Med. Coll. of Pa., Phila., 1976-78; dir. human svcs. York (Pa.) County Govt., 1978-86; pres. Keller Resources Inc., York, 1986—; instr. Pa. State U., York, 1985—; chmn. mktg. com. Community Transit, Inc., York, 1989—. Author: Career Focus, 1989, Human Resource Essentials, 1991. Mem. York 2000 (vice chmn. 1986—). Mem. Soc. of Friends. Home: 131 Edgewood Dr York PA 17403-3605 Office: Keller Resources Inc 1215 E Market St York PA 17403-5800

KELLER, JOHN RICHARD, insurance company executive; b. Harrisburg, Pa., June 1, 1924; s. Frank Landis and Clemens (Benchoff) K.; m. Janice Marie Taylor, Sept. 1, 1946; children: David Richard, Robert Alan, Nancy Marie. BS in Econs., Franklin and Marshall Coll., 1950. Crewchief traffic survey Pa. Dept. Highways, Harrisburg, 1950-52; underwriter Retailers Mutual Ins. Co., Harrisburg, 1952-57, asst. sec.-treas., 1957, sec.-treas., 1957-69; ptnr. City Ins. Agy., Harrisburg, 1957-69; pres., chief exec. officer Yorktowne Mutual Ins. Co., York, Pa., 1975-86, chmn. bd., 1986—; past mem. bd. dirs. Mut. Svc. Orgn. Trustee, deacon Augsburg Luth. Sch., 1959-70, Lakeside Luth. Ch., Harrisburg, 1970-80. Mem. Nat. Assn. Mut. Ins. Cos., Pa. Assn. Mut. Ins. Cos. (pres. 1982-83, bd. dirs. 1971-75), York Area C. of C., Am. Legion, Franklin and Marshall Coll. Alumni Assn., Sparks Club (co-chmn. edn. com. 1963), Embers Club (pres. 1974), Masons, Shriners. Republican. Home: 130 Yellow Breeches Dr Camp Hill PA 17011-8341

KELLER, KEVIN JOHN, sales executive; b. Commack, N.Y., June 1957; s. Robert and Mary Keller; m. Irene Jean Damiano, Oct. 1984; children: Sara, Matthew. BS, SUNY, Oswego, 1979, MS, 1981. Sales trainee U.S. Steel-Alside, Garden City, N.Y., 1981; salesperson U.S. Steel-Alside, New Brunswick, N.J., 1981-82; div. sales staff Alside Inc., Clifton, N.J., 1983-87, sales mgr., 1988-91; residential field sales devel. Allied Bldg. Products, Inc., East Rutherford, N.J., 1991—. Treas. bd. trustees Bald Eagle Village Homeowners Assn., West Milford, N.J., 1988-91. Mem. Nat. Assn. Remodeling Industry (sec. bd. dirs. 1989-91, treas. bd. dirs. 1991—). Republican. Roman Catholic.

KELLER, MARGARET GILMER, English educator; b. Harrisburg, Pa., July 11, 1922; d. Charles Greenawalt and Mary Ellen (Sullivan) Gilmer; m. George Henry Keller III, July 13, 1940; children: Mary Ellen, Margaret Marie, George Henry. AB, Trinity Coll., 1933, AM, Columbia U., 1934; cert. 1942, cert. State Tchrs. Coll., Bloomsburg, Pa., 1934; Acting chmn. history dept., Trinity Coll., Washington, 1935-36, chmn. classical dept., Convent Sacred Heart, 1936-37, Steelton (Pa.) High Sch., 1937-41; adj. prof. English dept. Rutgers U., 1946—, mem. dean's adv. com. U. Coll., 1968, also advisor to women's clubs U. Coll.; chmn. classical dept., Glen Rock (N.J.) High Sch., 1956-59, chmn. fgn. lang. dept, 1959—. Active Am. Cancer Soc., Community Chest ARC, Girl Scouts U.S.A.; mem. nominating bd. Ridgewood (N.J.) Nursing Service, 1959-60; Republican county committeeman; trustee Trinity Coll. (life), 1963-67, 1974—, chmn. 75th Anniversary Fund, 1974-75. Honored by Rutgers U., 1953, 61, 65, 71, 82, 87, Newman Province of N.J., 1963, Nat. Jaycees, 1973, Middle States Assn. Comm. on Secondary Schs., 1970, 74; recipient Robert Ax citation Glen Rock High Sch., 1971, Case Inst., 1976, Alumnae Service award Trinity Coll., 1977, 87, Pres.'s medal, 1982; named Outstanding Tchr. of Yr., Rutgers U., Newark, 1982, Disting. Prof. of Yr., 1988-89. Mem. NEA, N.J. Edn. Assn., Am. Classical Soc., AAUW (former dir.), Archeol. Inst. Am., MLA, Suprs. Assn. N.J. (sec. 1973-76), Am., N.J., Mid-Atlantic States classical socs., AAUP, Chaplain's Aid Assn., Trinity Coll. Alumnae Assn. (nat. pres. 1963-67, recipient Nat. Achievement award, 1987), Rutgers Alumni Assn. (hon., advisor), Phi Chi Theta (hon.), Alpha Sigma Lambda (hon., advisor). Clubs: Newman (adviser Rutgers U.), Univ. Coll. Women (hon. Rutgers U.), Coll. Home: 200 Phelps Rd Ridgewood NJ 07450-1419 Office: Rutgers U New Brunswick NJ 08901

KELLER, MARK, medical educator; b. Austria, Feb. 21, 1907; came to U.S., 1913; s. Judah and Hannah (Fortgang) K.; m. Sarah Vivienne Hirsh, Dec. 30, 1930; 1 child, Ita Naomi. Med. editor med. sch. NYU, 1933-40; documentalist lab. applied physiology Yale U., New Haven, Conn., 1941-60; editor Internat. Bibliography of Studies on Alcohol, New Haven, Conn., 1966-82; lectr. applied physiology Yale U., New Haven, Conn., 1960-62; prof. documentation Rutgers U., New Brunswick, N.J., 1962-77; vis. prof. Ctr. Alcohol Studies Rutgers U., Piscataway, N.J., 1983—; assoc. prof. seminar on drugs and soc. Columbia U., N.Y.C., 1974—; adj. prof. Brandeis U., Waltham, Mass., 1980-82; adv. bd. grad. libr. sch. Rutgers U., 1970-74; chmn. adv. bd. Addiction Studies Found., Jerusalem, 1984—; dir. Alcohol Rsch. Documentation, New Brunswick, 1984—. Author: The Alcohol Language, 1958, CAAAL Manual, 1965, Dictionary of Words About Alcohol, 1982; editorial bd. Med. Communications, 1978-80; contbr. Ency. Americana, 1954, Ency. Judaica, 1971, Ency. Britannica, 1974-87, Ency. of Bioethics, 1978; editor Jour. of Studies on Alcohol, 1959-77; contbr. numerous articles to profl. jours. Recipient Jellinek Meml. award Jellinek Meml. Found., 1977. mem. AAAS, Am. Med. Writers Assn. (Hammond award for disting. med. journalism 1976), APHA, Brit. Soc. for Study Addiction, Coun. Biology Editors, Am. Pub. Health Assn. Jewish. Home: 125 Stedman St Brookline MA 02146-3008 Office: Rutgers U Ctr Alcohol Studies Smithers Hall Piscataway NJ 08855

KELLER, NANCY JOAN, education educator. BA in Edn., SUNY, Fredonia, 1964, MS in Edn., 1966; EdD in Reading and Lang. Arts, SUNY, Buffalo, 1973. Elem. tchr. Brocton (N.Y.) Cen. Schs., 1964-65, Fredonia Cen. Schs., 1968-69; elem. tchr., supr. Fredonia Campus Sch., SUNY, 1966-68; instr. edn. SUNY, Fredonia, 1966-68; doctoral resident, instr. summer sch. SUNY, Buffalo, 1972-73; dir. Boorody Meml. Reading Ctr., Dunkirk, N.Y., 1973-75; dir. model comprehensive svc. Dunkirk Pub. Schs., 1975-76; prof. edn., dir. tchr. licensure Bemidji (Minn.) State U., 1976-87; prof. edn., dir. reading programs SUNY, Oneonta, 1987—; cons. numerous pub. schs., Minn., N.Y., 1976—; workshop presenter various pub. schs. and colls., Minn., N.Y., 1976—. Co-author: Parents and Children Reading Together, Enrichment Activities for the Home; choreographer pub. TV documentary Together and Apart. Mem. outreach com., pastor and parish adv. bd. 1st United Meth. Ch., Bemidji, 1977-87, mem. ch.-campus outreach com., 1989-91; instr. dance community edn. and B.S.U. non-credit, Bemidji, 1977-87; mem. Minn. Adv. Bd. for Arts; invited to be a judge ballet competition Minn. chpt. Nat. Soc. Arts and Letters, 1990. Mem. NEA, Internat. Reading Assn. (conf. presenter 1976—), N.Y. State Reading Assn., Catskill Area Reading Coun., United Univ. Profs. State U. Coll. Oneonta Faculty Assn. Home: 135 East St Oneonta NY 13820-1321 Office: SUNY Reading Ctr Alumni Hall Oneonta NY 13820

KELLER, PEARL JOSEPHSON, sports organization executive, writer; b. Holyoke, Mass., Dec. 19, 1923; d. Israel and Lorena (Gan) Josephson; m. Seymour Paul Keller, Dec. 18, 1949; children: Jan Keller Schultz, David, Richard, Lisa. Student, Oberlin Coll., 1941-42; MusB, Yale U., 1947; cert. in teaching, Perkins Inst., Watertown, Mass., 1948; postgrad., Tex. Christian U., 1948-49. Exec. dir. Women's All-Star Assn., Chappaqua, N.Y., 1971—. Mem. Bowling Writers Assn. Am. (1st v.p. 1972-92, pres. 1992—), Nat. Women Bowling Writers (life, past pres.), Women's Internat. Bowling Congress (bd. dirs. 1984—), World Bowling Writers, Met. Bowling Writers (sec. 1970—). Democrat. Jewish. Home and Office: 29 Garey Dr Chappaqua NY 10514

KELLER, RUDOLF, electrochemist, electrometallurgist; b. Winterthur, Switzerland, Dec. 27, 1933; came to U.S., 1961; s. Heinrich and Elsa (Kron) K.; m. Elisabeth Langhard, Sept. 1, 1962; children: Andrea Katharina, Eva Susanna. Dr.sc.nat., Swiss Fed. Inst. Tech., Zurich, 1960. Electrochemist Stanford Rsch. Inst., South Pasadena, Calif., 1961-63; mem. tech. staff Rocketdyne, Canoga Park, Calif., 1963-70; scientific expert Swiss Aluminium Ltd., Neuhausen, Switzerland, 1970-77; group leader Argonne (Ill.) Nat. Lab., 1977-79; staff mem. Alcoa Labs., Alcoa Center, Pa., 1979-83; propr. EMEC Consultants, Export, Pa., 1984—; cons. EG&G Idaho, Dept. Energy, 1983-85, Battelle Pacific N.W. Labs., 1985-88; rsch. assoc. Carnegie Mellon U., 1988—; sr. vis. lectr. Post Coll. Profl. Edn., CMU, 1990—. Contbr. numerous articles to profl. jours.; patentee in field. Mem. Internat. Soc. Electrochemistry (treas. 1980-83), The Electrochem. Soc. (sect. chmn. 1986-87), The Minerals, Metals and Materials Soc. (exec. com. of sect. 1984-87), Am. Chem. Soc., Space Studies Inst. (sr.). Home and Office: EMEC Consultants RD 3 Roundtop Rd Export PA 15632-9803 Also: Lab at Schreiber Indsl Dist New Kensington PA 15068

KELLER, THOMAS WALTER, II, sales executive; b. York, Pa., Apr. 30, 1952; s. Thomas Walter I and Mary Catherine (Breen) K.; m. Lynn Rebecca Robinson, Apr. 7, 1973; children: Brian Thomas, Adam Thomas. Cert. radiologic tech., Med. Field Service Sch., Ft. Sam Houston, Tex., 1972; BS in Bus. Mgmt., York Coll., 1980. Radiologic technologist Dewitt Army Hosp., Ft. Belvoir, Va., 1972-74; spl. procedures technologist York (Pa.) Hosp., 1974-83; account mgr. Thomson-CGR Med. Corp., Malvern, Pa., 1983-87, Philips Med. Systems, Plymouth Meeting, Pa., 1987—. Asst. scoutleader Boy Scouts Am., York, 1975—. Mem. Am. Soc. Radiologic Technologists, Pa. Soc. Radiologic Technologists. Republican. Lutheran. Home: 783 Priority Rd York PA 17404-2455 Office: Philips Med Systems 5170 Campus Dr Plymouth Meeting PA 19462-1134

KELLEY, ALBERT JOSEPH, federal agency official; b. Boston, July 27, 1924; s. Albert Joseph and Josephine Christine (Sullivan) K.; m. Virginia Marie Riley, June 7, 1945 (dec. Aug. 1988); children: Mark, Shaun, David; m. JoAnn Veronica Palmer, Dec. 14, 1991. BS, U.S. Naval Acad., 1945; BSEE, MIT, 1948, ScD, 1956; postgrad., U. Minn., 1954, Carnegie-Mellon U., 1974. Commd. ensign USN, 1945, advanced through grades to comdr., 1961; carrier pilot USN, Korea, 1950-51; exptl. test pilot Naval Air Test Ctr. USN, 1951-53, program engr. F-4 aircraft Bur. Aeros., 1956-58, mgr. Eagle missile program Bur. Weapons, 1958-60; mgr. Agena program NASA, 1960-61, dir. electronics and control, 1961-64, dep. dir. Electronics Research Ctr., 1964-67; dean sch. mgmt. Boston Coll., 1967-77; pres. Arthur D. Little program Systems Mgmt. Co., Cambridge, Mass., 1977-85, chmn., 1985-88; sr. group v.p. Arthur D. Little Inc., Cambridge, Mass., 1985-88; sr. v.p. strategic planning United Techs. Corp., Hartford, Conn., 1988-90; dep. under sec. of def. internat. programs Pentagon, Washington, 1990—; chmn. Bd. Econ. Advisors Commonwealth of Mass., 1970-74; chmn. bd. dirs. Arthur D. Little Valuation Inc., 1985-86; corp. mem. C.S. Draper Lab. Corp., Cambridge, 1975-90; cons. The White House; mem. NRC Space Applications Bd., 1976-82. Author: Venture Capital, 1977, New Dimensions of Project Management, 1982; contbr. articles to profl. jours. Trustee Milton (Mass.) Acad., 1975-83; bd. dirs. Mass. Bus. Devel. Corp., Boston, 1969-78, Mass. Tech. Devel. Corp., Boston, 1979-82, Am. Assembly Collegiate Schs. Bus., 1970-76. Recipient Exceptional Svc. medal NASA, 1967. Fellow IEEE, AIAA (assoc.); mem. Internat. Acad. Astronautics, Armed Forces Communications and Electronics Assn. (v.p. 1962-65), Algonquin Club, Army Navy Country Club, Wollaston Golf Club, Milton-Hoosic Club, Sigma Xi, Tau Beta Pi. Home: 1501 Highwood Dr Arlington VA 22207-4702 Office: Pentagon DUSD (IP) Rm 3E1082 Washington DC 20301

KELLEY, ALOYSIUS PAUL, university president, priest; b. Carlisle, Pa., Oct. 4, 1929; s. Aloysius Paul and Teresa (Barron) K. A.B., St. Louis U., 1955, M.A., 1956, Ph.L., 1956; S.T.L., U. Innsbruck, Austria, 1963; Ph.D., U. Pa., 1968; LL.D. (hon.), Sacred Heart U., 1985. Joined S.J., 1949; ordained priest Roman Catholic Ch., 1962; chmn. dept. classics Georgetown U., 1969-71, asst. acad. v.p., 1971-72, acting acad. v.p., 1972-74, exec. v.p. for acad. affairs and provost, 1974-79; pres. Fairfield (Conn.) U., 1979—. Trustee Georgetown Prep. Sch., 1969-72, Loyola Coll., Balt., 1971-75, Scranton U., 1974-80, Bridgeport Area C. of C., 1979-82, St. Joseph's U., Phila., 1980-86, Georgetown U., 1982-88, 89—, Conn. Grand Opera, 1980—, John Carroll U., 1987—; mem. D.C. Commn. Postsecondary Edn., 1974-79; vice chmn. Conn. Conf. Ind. Colls., 1980-81, chmn. 1981-83. Fulbright-Hayes fellow, 1971. Mem. Am. Philol. Assn., Am. Assn. Univ. Adminstrs., Am. Assn. Higher Edn., Algonquin Club (Bridgeport, Conn.), Patterson Club. Democrat. Clubs: Algonquin, Patterson. Home and Office: Fairfield U Fairfield CT 06430

KELLEY, DAVID CHARLES, television news producer; b. Washington, Aug. 5, 1957; s. Albert J. and Virginia M. (Riley) K.; m. Catherine A. Sherry, May 30, 1987. BA, Dartmouth Coll., 1979. Producer ABC News, N.Y.C., 1989—, assoc. producer, 1983-86, field producer, 1985-86, segment producer, 1986-89; segment producer long-form programming unit ABC News, 1988-89. Producer (TV programs) Prime Time Live, 1989—, Beyond the Shuttle, ABC, 1988; assoc. producer (TV programs) OurWorld, 1986-87, Jennings/Koppel Reports, 1987, ABC Spl. Reports, 1983-85. Mem. Dirs. Guild Am. Office: ABC News 147 Columbus Ave New York NY 10023

KELLEY, EDWARD ALLEN, publisher; b. Clinton, Mass., June 28, 1927; s. Edward Francis Kelley and Lillian Marion (Keigwin) French; m. Margaret Jordan Talbott, Feb. 24, 1962; children: Catherine, Edward, Michael. BA, Trinity Coll., Hartford, Conn., 1950; STM, Gen. Theol. Sem., N.Y.C., 1953. Mgr. bookstore Morehouse-Barlow Co. Inc., N.Y.C., 1957-61, v.p., editorial dir., 1961-74; sr. v.p. Oxford U. Press, N.Y.C., 1974-83; pres. Kelley Assocs., Ridgefield, Conn., 1983-87; pres., pub. Morehouse Pub. Co., Ridgefield, 1988—. Editor The Episcopal Ch. Ann., 1967-74, 87—. With USNR, 1945-47, World War II. Democrat. Episcopalian. Home: 345 North St Ridgefield CT 06877-2514 Office: Morehouse Pub Co 871 Ethan Allen Hwy Ste 204 Ridgefield CT 06877-2801

KELLEY, GEORGE EDWARD, engineering management systems consultant; b. Providence, Oct. 28, 1940; s. George and Grace Emily (Conley) K.; m. Carlotta Marie DiMaio, Aug. 3, 1963; children: Jacqueline G., George A., James E. BSME, U. R.I., 1963, MBA, 1972. Project engr. Grinnell Corp., Providence, 1962-71; mktg. engr. Hartwell Co., East Providence, R.I., 1971-72; asst. to pres. for bus. planning ITT Grinnell Indsl. Piping Co., Kernersville, N.C., 1972-73; from sr. mgmt. systems engr. to asst. mgr. mgmt. systems div. Stone and Webster Engring. Corp., Boston, 1973-90, sr. supr. project control, 1990—; dir. S and W Fed. Credit Union, Boston, 1989—. Trustee Greenville (R.I.) Pub. Libr., 1990—. Mem. ASME, Project Mgmt. Inst. Home: 6 Apple Seed Dr Greenville RI 02828-1102 Office: Stone and Webster Engring Co 245 Summer St Boston MA 02107

KELLEY, JOHN GARY, information systems executive; b. Victorville, Calif., Feb. 13, 1954; s. Varney Wilson and Marie Elizabeth (Bixler) K.; m. Cheryl Lynn Dalton, Mar. 18, 1978; children: Samantha Lynn, Robert Scott. Grad. high sch., San Antonio. Computer ops. supr. Western Pub.-Datapage, St. Louis, 1985-86; div. tech. mgr. Computer Assocs. Internat., Inc., Pitts., 1986-90; cons. mgr. Omega Systems, Inc., Pitts., 1990-91; prin., cons. Data Ctr. Automation Svcs., Mt. Lebanon, Pa., 1990—; instr., dir. support svcs. Protech Profl. Tech. Svcs., Monroeville, Pa., 1991—. Author: Programming REXX, SAA Procedural Language, 1991, Using MVS/TSO and ISPF, 1991. Performer Uptown Mt. Lebanon, 1990. With USAF, 1974-85. Deocrated Commendation medal. Mem. Smithsonian Instn. (assoc.), Am. Mensa. Methodist. Home: 383 Jayson Ave Pittsburgh PA 15228-1213 Office: ProTech Profl Tech Svcs 1 Monroeville Ctr Ste 470 Monroeville PA 15146-2144

KELLEY, KATHRYN, psychologist, educator; b. Tulsa; d. Lawrence J. and Johnnie A. Kelley; married; 2 children. BA in Psychology, U. Okla.; MS in Social-Personality Psychology, Purdue U., PhD in Psychology. Asst. prof. psychology Marquette U., Milw., 1977-78, U. Wis.-Milw., 1978-79; asst. prof. psychology SUNY-Albany, 1979-85, assoc. prof., 1985—, dir. indsl. and organizational psychology, 1987-90. Author or editor: An Introduction to Personality: Research, Theory, and Applications, 1981, Alternative Approaches to the Study of Sexual Behavior Education, 1986, Females, Males and Sexuality Education, 1987, Exploring Human Sexuality, 1992, Issues, Theory, and Research in Industrial/Organizational Psychology Education, 1992. Bur. Indian Affairs higher edn. fellow, 1974-77. Mem. Am. Psychol. Assn., Eastern Psychol. Assn., Soc. Sci. Study of Sex, Soc. Exptl. Social Psychology, Am. Psychol. Soc. Office: SUNY Albany NY 12222

KELLEY, ROYDEN KRUEGER, food company executive; b. Elkhart, Ind., June 8, 1911; s. Chester R. and Carrie B. (Krueger) K.; m. Grace K. Baumgart, June 12, 1937; 1 child, Charles Keith. Student, Wabash Coll., 1933; grad. advanced mgmt. program, Harvard U., 1953; LHD, Clinton Coll., 1974. Chmn. Nabisco Foods, Ltd., 1954-56; exec. v.p. Dromedary Co., div. Nat. Biscuit Co., 1956-57, pres., 1957-58, v.p. parent co., 1958—; chmn. Nabisco-Astra Nutrition Products, Inc., 1970-74. Mem. nat. paraprofl. pers. com. Boy Scouts Am.; nat. adv. com. White House Conf. on Children, 1970; bd. dirs. Jr. Achievement. With AUS, 1943-46, PTO. Mem. Beta Theta Pi. Republican. Presbyterian. Home: RR 1 Box 1950 Montpelier VT 05602-9717 Office: SCORE Small Bus Adminstrn Federal Bldg State St Montpelier VT 05602

KELLEY, THOMAS FRANCIS, entrepreneur, biomedical manufacturing executive; b. Melrose, Mass., Mar. 23, 1932; s. Thomas F. and Anna D. (Coughlan) K.; m. Irene W. Gesiak, Aug. 11, 1956; children: Steven E., Kenneth J., Richard T. AB, Boston U., 1954, MA, 1955; PhD, Brown U., 1959. Rsch. assoc. Bio Rsch. Inst., Inc., Cambridge, Mass., 1959-68; dir., advanced devel. Instrumentation Lab., Inc., Lexington, Mass., 1968-82; cons. Norfolk Assocs., Inc., Canton, Mass., 1982-84; pres. Statspin Technologies, Norwood, Mass., 1984—; bd. dirs. AMDEV, Inc., Danvers, Mass., 1982-84, BioNostics, Inc., Acton, Mass., 1983—; invited speaker to nat. and internat. biomed. mktg. confs. Patentee in field. Founder Canton (Mass.) Men's Hockey League, 1973. Mem. Am. Assn. for Clin. Chemistry, Am. Soc. Clin. Pathology (assoc.). Office: Statspin Technologies 85 Morse St Norwood MA

KELLGREN, JOHN, chemist; b. N.Y.C., Dec. 26, 1940; s. Otto and Edith (Johnson) Kjellgren; m. Joanne Selmasska, Apr. 17, 1971; children: Carl, Eric. BS, Rutgers U., 1962; PhD, Columbia U., 1967; MBA, U. New Haven, 1978, MS in Indsl. Engring., 1984. Rsch. scientist Uniroyal Inc., Wayne, N.J., 1967-84; tech. supt. Uniroyal Inc., Middlebury, Conn., 1967-84; process chemist Rhein Chemie Corp., Trenton, N.J., 1985—. Fellow Am. Inst. Chemists; mem. Am. Chem. Soc., mem. Royal Inst. Chemists (fgn.), Phi Beta Kappa, Delta Phi Alpha, Pi Mu Epsilon, Phi Lambda Upsilon, Sigma Xi. Office: Rhein Chemie Corp 1008 Whitehead Road Ext Trenton NJ 08638-2495 Home: 78 Terrapin Ln Trenton NJ 08619-1364

KELLNER, DOUGLAS ERNEST, financial executive; b. Buffalo, Oct. 4, 1956; s. Ernest Carl Jr. and Joan (Herman) K.; m. Barbara Ellen Crissman, Nov. 17, 1984; 1 child, Amanda Ellen. BS summa cum laude, Pa. State U., 1978. CPA, N.Y. Staff acct. Ernst and Whinney, Buffalo, 1978-79, advanced staff acct., 1979-80, sr. acct., 1980-81, audit supr., 1981-84; corp. controller Faller, Klenk and Quinlan, Inc., Buffalo, 1984-86, v.p. fin. and adminstrn., 1986-87; v.p. fin. and adminstrn. Healy-Schutte and Co., Buffalo, 1987-88, sr. v.p., chief fin. officer, 1988-90; mng. ptnr., chief fin. officer Schutte & Co., Buffalo, 1990—; lectr. Niagara Frontier Industry and Edn. Coun., Buffalo, 1988—, bd. dirs., 1990—. Committeeman Tonawanda (N.Y.) Rep. Com., 1988—; alumni Leadership Buffalo, 1988—; sect. chmn. communications div. United Way, 1990. Mem. AICPA, N.Y. State Soc. CPA's, Am. Mgmt. Assn., Pa. State U. Alumni Club Western N.Y. (pres. 1982-90), Buffalo Jr. C. of C. (pres. 1982-85), Buffalo Area C. of C. (bd. dirs. 1982-85), Saturn Club, Park Country Club, Rotary. Presbyterian. Home: 128 Louvaine Dr Buffalo NY 14223-2744 Office: Schutte & Co 1207 Delaware Ave Buffalo NY 14209-1401

KELLOGG, MARION SCHUYLER, electric company executive, retired; b. Rochester, N.Y., June 15, 1920; d. Howard Schuyler and Stella Julia (Dengler) K. AB in Math. and Physics, Manhattanville Coll., 1942, LHD (hon.), 1981; MS in Physics, Brown U., 1944; LLD (hon.), St. Lawrence U., 1975, Babson Coll., 1976; DSc (hon.), Russell Sage Coll., 1976. Instr. physics Brown U., Providence, 1942-44; engr. asst. GE, Schenectady, N.Y., 1944-45, employee rels. specialist lab., 1945-49; mgr. tech. and supervisory pers. flight propulsion GE, Lynn, Mass., 1949-51; mgr. employee rels. flight propulsion GE, Cinn., 1951-58; cons. mgmt. devel. HQ staff GE, N.Y.C., 1958-70, cons. mktg. HQ staff, 1970-74; v.p. corp. cons. svcs. GE, Fairfield, Conn., 1974-83, ret., 1983; bd. dirs. Citytrust Bancorp, Bridgeport, Conn. Author: What to do About Performance Appraisal, 1965, Closing Performance Gap, 1967, Putting Management Theories to Work, 1968, Talking With Employees, 1969, Career Management, 1972; contbr. articles to profl. jours. Fellow Internat. Acad. of Mgmt.; mem. N.Y. Acad. Sci., Sigma Xi.

KELLY, DANIEL MARTIN, stockbroker; b. N.Y.C., Nov. 29, 1906; s. Daniel Kelly and Cecilia Martin Bull; m. Helen Kemp, July, 1934; children: Daniel, Andrew, William, Ellen. BS, NYU, 1934, MA, 1939; PhD (hon.), St. Joseph's Coll., Bklyn., 1992. Ptnr. Salomon Bros.-Hutzler, N.Y.C., 1940-70; cons. Swiss Re Advisors, N.Y.C., 1972—; dir. Swiss Reins. Cos. of N.Am. Trustee St. Joseph's Coll., Bklyn., 1941-91. Mem. N.Y. Futures Exchange, Boston Stock Exchange. Roman Catholic. Office: Swiss Re Advisors 200 Park Ave New York NY 10166

KELLY, DAVID HILARY, classicist, educator; b. Phila., Sept. 23, 1929; s. Joseph H. and Hannah (Maloney) K.; m. Elizabeth Winn, Aug. 15, 1970 (dec. 1991); children: Joseph, Christine, Karen. BA, Cath. U., 1952; MA, U. Pa., 1954, PhD, 1958. Tchr. West Cath. High Sch. and LaSalle High Sch., Phila., 1952-61; prof. LaSalle U., Phila., 1961-70; prof. classics Montclair State Coll., Upper Montclair, N.J., 1970—. Contbr. articles and revs. to scholarly publs. Mem. Classical Assn. Atlantic States (pres. 1977-78), Am. Philol. Assn. Roman Catholic. Office: Montclair State Coll Valley Rd Montclair NJ 07042-2709

KELLY, DAVID MICHAEL, poet, creative writing educator; b. Grand Rapids, Mich., June 23, 1938; s. Earl Peter and Margaret (Weisel) K.; m. Sylvia Hayden Neahr, Aug. 12, 1960; children: Jordan, Colette, Willow Esodie. BA in Journalism, Mich. State U., 1961, MA in Composition Literature, 1962; MFA in Creative Writing, U. Iowa, 1966. English instr. Univ. Wis.-Stout, Menomonie, Wis., 1962-65; teaching asst. Univ. Iowa, Iowa City, 1965-66; remedial composition specialist Ea. Iowa Community Coll., Muscatines, 1966-67; dir. creative writing, assoc. prof. English SUNY, Geneseo, 1967—; poetry panelist judge N.Y. State Coun. on Arts, N.Y.C., 1980-81; presenter in field. Author: (poetry books) Instructions for Viewing a Solar Eclipse, 1972, Filming Assasination, 1979 (Elliston Found. award 1980); contbg. editor: The Push Cart Awards Antology, Wainscott, N.Y., 1988—, AISLING, San Francisco, 1974-80. Named Atlantic Young Poet, Atlantic Monthly Mag., Boston, 1967; recipient Creative Arts Pub. Svc. awards N.Y. State Coun. Arts, N.Y.C., 1974, 79, Poetry fellowship Nat. Endowment for Arts, 1976, 92, N.Y. Found., 1989. Fellow N.Y. Foudn. Arts (poetry award 1989); mem. Poetry Soc. Am. Home: PO Box 53 Geneseo NY 14454-0053 Office: State Univ Coll Geneseo NY 14454

KELLY, EILEEN ANNE, accountant; b. New Haven, July 25, 1965; d. James Daniel Jr. and Helen Dympna (Byrne) K. BS in Health Svcs. Adminstrn., Providence Coll., 1987; MBA in Acctg., U. Conn., 1989. Acct. Dollarwise Fin. Svcs., New Haven, 1987-89, Bruce E. Carusillo, CPA, Woodbury, Conn., 1990, S. M. Esposito & Co., Woodbridge, Conn., 1990—; cons. Hydro-Flex, Inc., Naugatuck, Conn., 1987—, Conn. SBA, 1990. Recipient Small Bus. Devel. Achievement award Conn. Small Bus. Adminstrn., 1989. Mem. Conn. Soc. CPAs. Roman Catholic. Home: 15 Tuttle Ct Bethany CT 06524-3027

KELLY, H. VINCENT, psychiatrist, educator; b. Bklyn., July 13, 1933; s. Harold Vincent and Anna Dolores (Rocco) K.; m. Catherine Elizabeth O'Connor, Dec. 29, 1956; children: Christopher, Jeffrey, Vivian, Carole, Justin. BS in Biology, Georgetown U., 1955, MD, 1959. Diplomate Am. Bd. Psychiatry and Neurology. Resident in psychiatry Georgetown Hosp., Washington, 1964-66; chief psychiatrist area C, CMHC DC Govt., Washington, 1966-71; clin. dir. Community Mental Health Ctr. D.C. Govt., Washington, 1971-80; consulting psychiatrist North Community Mental Health Ctr. D.C. Govt., Washington, 1981—; clin. assoc. prof. Georgetown dept. psychiatry, Washington, 1984—. Contbr. articles to profl. jours. Bd. dirs. Potomac (Md.) Community Theatre, 1989-91. Lt. USN, 1959-64. Fellow Am. Psychiat. Assn.; mem. Washington Psychiat. Soc., Am. Family Therapy Assn. (charter mem.). Republican. Roman Catholic. Home and Office: 6813 Newbold Dr Bethesda MD 20817-2224

KELLY, JAMES ANTHONY, priest; b. Worcester, Mass., Apr. 22, 1949; s. James and Elisabeth (Allen) K. BA in Philosophy and Govt., Harvard Coll., 1971; PhD in Philosophy, CUNY, 1979. ordained priest Roman Cath. Ch., 1982. Dir. Riverside Study Ctr., N.Y.C., 1977-79; procurator Prelature of Opus Dei, Rome, 1984-88; vicar USA region Prelature of Opus Dei, New Rochelle, N.Y., 1988—. Home and Office: 99 Overlook Circle New Rochelle NY 10804

KELLY, JAMES MCGIRR, federal judge. BS, Wharton Sch., 1951; JD, Temple U., 1957. Law clk. to judge U.S. Ct. Common Pleas, Phila., 1957-58; asst. dist. atty. Phila. County, 1958-60; asst. atty. U.S. Dist. Ct. (ea. dist.)

Pa., Phila., 1960-62; master jury selection bd. U.S. Ct. Common Pleas, Phila., 1962-64; judge U.S. Dist. Ct. (ea. dist.) Pa., Phila., 1983—; pvt. practice law Phila., 1962-83; spl. asst. atty. gen. Commonwealth of Pa., 1965. Mem. Pa. Pub. Utility Commn., 1966-77. Served with USN, 1951-53. Office: US Courthouse Independence Mall W #8614 601 Market St Philadelphia PA 19106-1510*

KELLY, JAMES PATRICK, real estate executive; b. N.Y.C., Sept. 19, 1952; s. James Francis and Marie Theresa (Clancy) K.; m. Renee Ann Beech, Aug. 31, 1980; children: James, Erin, Ryan. BBA, Temple U., 1976. Lic. real estate broker, Pa. Sr. appraiser Equitable Life Assurance Co., Pitts., 1977-81; sr. real estate fin. rep. Westinghouse Credit Corp., Pitts., 1981-84; v.p. Am. Equity Corp., Pitts., 1984-86; pres. Keystone Realty Group, Pitts., 1987—, also bd. dirs.; bd. dirs. KMP Mgmt. Inc., Pitts., Apt. Connection Ltd., Pitts. Bd. mem. Bethel Ch. League, Bethel Park, Pa., 1992, St. Valentine's Baseball Assn., Bethel Park, 1992; mgr. Youth Baseball, Bethel Park, 1991-92. Recipient Cert. award Am. Inst. Appraisers, 1980, 82. Mem. Internat. Coun. Shopping Ctrs., Nat. Assn. Ind. and Office Pks., Steel Town Corvette Club. Republican. Catholic. Office: Keystone Realty Group 1910 Cochran Rd Ste 405 Pittsburgh PA 15220

KELLY, JAMES THOMAS, manufacturing company president, consultant; b. Newburgh, N.Y., May 16, 1942; s. Thomas J. and Catherine (Kearney) K.; m. Patricia K. Kelly, Dec. 12, 1970; children: Elizabeth, Sean. BS, U. Notre Dame, Ind., 1964. Asst. to mng. ptnr. Haskins & Sells, N.Y., 1964-70; founding officer Unimin Corp., New Canaan, Conn., 1970-77; exec. v.p. & dir. Usinor Industries, N.Y.C., 1977-83; pres. & dir. Chariot Group, Inc., N.Y., 1984—; The Chariot Group, Inc., N.Y.C.; pres., cons. Jepsco Ltd., Mountainside, N.J., 1983—. Home: 35 Geoffrey Ct Chatham NJ 07928-1449 Office: The Chariot Group Inc 45 Rockefeller Plz New York NY 10111-0002

KELLY, JOYCE MARIE, conservation organization director, policy analyst; b. Mpls., July 28, 1940; d. Christian J. and Marie H. (Marshik) Cremers; m. C. Christopher Kelly, Oct. 9, 1965. BA, U. Minn., 1962; MA, Johns Hopkins U., 1964. Sr. staff analyst to asst. sec. Dept. Interior, Washington, 1977-81; chief wilderness, recreation, cultural programs Bur. Land Mgmt., Washington, 1981-85; dep. dir. drinking water program EPA, Washington, 1985-87; pres. Defenders of Wildlife, Washington, 1987-88; exec. dir. Wildlife Habitat Enhancement Coun., Silver Spring, Md., 1988—. Contbr. articles to profl. jours. Trustee Northland Coll., Ashland, Wis., 1987—; v.p. Howard County Conservancy, Ellicott City, Md., 1990—; bd. dirs. Alliance for Environ. Edn., Washington, 1990—, Ptnrs. in Parks, 1988—. Recipient regional Stephen Mather award Nat. Parks and Conservation Assn., 1985. Roman Catholic. Office: Wildlife Habitat Enhancement 1010 Wayne Ave Silver Spring MD 20910

KELLY, KATHLEEN MARY, illustrator, writer, graphic designer; b. Waterbury, Conn., Dec. 8, 1964; d. Thomas Joseph and Elsa Anne (Mrazik) K.; adopted d. Priscilla Adomaitis K. BFA in Illustration, Paier Coll. Art, 1986. Owner Kelly Art Studios, Manchester, Conn., 1987—; graphic designer Davidoff White Good Inc., Westport, Conn., 1989-90, Printwood Innovations, Stamford, Conn., 1990-91; freelancer Kirchoff/Wohlberg, Madison, Conn., 1991-92, Young Assocs., Westport, 1990—, Everett Studios, White Plains, N.Y., 1991—, The Mind's Eye, Stamford, 1988-91. Author, illustrator: River Friends, 1988; illustrator Modern Critical Views of Henry David Thoreau, 1987, Thomas Hardy, 1987, A Small Pleasure, 1988, Sisters, Long Ago, 1990, One Ghost, Too Many!, 1991; illustrator, product designer The Especially Yours Collection, 1992. Mem. Soc. Childrens Book Writers and Illustrators. Roman Catholic. Office: 158 Forest St Ste # 708 Manchester CT 06040

KELLY, KEITH JOHN, journalist; b. Bklyn., Sept. 10, 1954; s. John Joseph and Virginia (O'Connell). Student, SUNY, Stony Brook, 1972-74; BA in English Lit., SUNY, Oneonta, 1976. Reporter Smithtown News, L.I., N.Y., 1976-77; asst. editor McGraw-Hill, Inc., N.Y.C., 1977-79, chief editor, 1986-87; bur. chief Mag. Week, N.Y.C., 1989-91, editorial dir., 1991-92; chief editor Folio: First Day, editor-at-large Pub. News and Folio Cowles Bus. Media, N.Y.C., 1992—. Freelance journalist; spl. corr. The Irish Press, Dublin, Ireland; v.p., exec. editor Mag. Week, 1990. Mem. Nat. Writers Union, Soc. Profl. Journalists. Democratic. Roman Catholic. Home: 198 Avenue A Apt 5B New York NY 10009-3401 Office: Cowles Bus Media 232 Madison Ave New York NY 10016

KELLY, L. THOMAS, magazine publisher, museum director; b. Erie, Pa., Oct. 12, 1945; s. Harry James and Anna (Lassman) K.; m. Kathryn N. Kelly, Sept. 3, 1966; children—Sean Thomas, Allison Erin. B.S. in Mgmt. Sci., U. Rochester, 1967, M.B.A. in Fin., 1968. Cons. Ernst & Ernst, N.Y. C., 1968-72; bus. mgr. Natural History mag. Am. Mus. Natural History, N.Y. C., 1972-76; pub. Natural History mag. Am. Mus. Natural History, N.Y.C., 1982—, asst. mus. dir., 1985—; v.p. fin. Nuestro Publ., 1976-77; mag. group controller N.Y. Times Corp., N.Y.C., 1978-80; dir. ops. Inside Sports/Newsweek, N.Y.C., 1980-82. Office: Am Mus Natural History Central Pk W & 79th St New York NY 10024

KELLY, LYNN C., marketing consultant; b. Putnam, Conn., Oct. 23, 1947. BA, U. Conn., 1969; MBA, U. Hartford, 1979. From cons., account mgmt. to adminstr. planning and control Aetna Life and Casualty, Hartford, Conn., 1969-79; dir. mktg. strategy Aetna Ins. Co., Hartford, 1979-82; dir. mktg. rsch. and communications Cigna Corp., Bloomfield, Conn., 1982-85; dir. mktg. svcs. Travelers Cos., Hartford, 1985-87; pres. Mktg. Leverage, Inc., Glastonbury, Conn., 1987—. Chair strategic planning com. Town of Glastonbury, 1988-90. Mem. Am. Mktg. Assn., Bus. and Profl. Women (Glastonbury chpt.), Greater Hartford C. of C. (bd. dirs., chair membership com. 1988-90), Glastonbury C. of C. (bd. dirs. 1st v.p. 1990—), Hartford Women's Network (chair issues com., mem. steering com. 1979-82), 43d Aviation Flying Club, Glastonbury Hills Golf Club. Office: Mktg Leverage Inc 85 Commerce St Glastonbury CT 06033

KELLY, MARGUERITE LELONG, writer; b. New Orleans, June 26, 1932; d. Charles A. and Alice (Richardson) Lelong; m. Thomas V. Kelly; children: Katherine, Michael, Marguerite, Helen. Syndicated columnist Tribune Media Svcs., Orlando, Fla., 1979—. Author: The Mother's Almanac, 1975, rev. edit., 1991, Mother's Almanac II, 1989. Bd. dirs. Friendship House, Washington, 1959-69; trustee D.C. Pub. Libr., 1983—. Democrat. Roman Catholic. Office: PO Box 15310 Washington DC 20003

KELLY, MICHAEL GEORGE, machine manufacturing company executive; b. Gardner, Mass., Nov. 23, 1959; s. Thomas Patrick and Margaret Ann (McCormick) K.; m. Sharon Marie Garlitz, May 11, 1985; children: Erin Kathleen, Ann Morgan. BSME, MS, MIT, 1983; MBA, Harvard U., 1990. Staff engr. C.S. Draper Lab., Inc., Cambridge, Mass., 1982-83, 86-88; field engr. Schlumberger Wireline Svcs., Aberdeen, Scotland, 1983-85, sr. field engr., 1985-86; mgr. bus. devel. John Brown Inc., West Warwick, R.I., 1990-91, v.p. bus. devel., 1991—; pres. Mediclean Tech., Inc., West Warwick, 1991—, also bd. dirs. Patentee in field. C.S. Draper fellow, 1982-83. Mem. ASME, Pi Tau Sigma, Delta Tau Delta. Office: John Brown Inc 1600 Division Rd West Warwick RI 02893

KELLY, PAUL CHARLES, JR., wholesale distribution executive; b. Boston, Nov. 9, 1948; s. Paul Charles Sr. and Marion Agnes (McCarthy) K.; m. Jean Marie McDonell, Aug. 21, 1976; children: Kristy Ann, Paula Marie, Shannon Jean. Assoc., Johnson and Wales Coll., 1968; BBA, Ft. Lauderdale U., 1970, MBA, 1971. Sales mgr. Superior Fence Co., Canton, Mass., 1971-79; ops. mgr. Marshalls, Woburn, Mass., 1979-86, G Fox, South Windsor, Conn., 1986-88; dir., distbr. Dry Goods, Aston, Pa., 1988-89; gen. mgr. Svc. Mdse., Montgomery, N.Y., 1990—. Republican. Roman Catholic. Home: 186 Hummingbird Ct Montgomery NY 12549

KELLY, PAUL KNOX, investment banker; b. Boston, Feb. 18, 1940; s. Thomas Joseph and Rita Patricia Kelly; m. Nancy Lee Belden, July 17, 1978; 1 child, 3 stepchildren. A.B. in English, U. Pa., 1962; M.B.A. in Fin, Wharton Sch., 1964. Investment analyst bond dept. Prudential Ins. Co. Am., 1964-65; asst. treas. Comml. Credit Co., 1965-68; v.p. First Boston Corp., N.Y.C., 1968-75; ptnr., mem. mgmt. com., dir. Prescott, Ball & Turben, Cleve., 1975-77; sr. v.p., dir. Butcher & Singer, Inc., 1977-78; exec. v.p., mem. exec. com., dir. Blyth Eastman Dillon & Co., N.Y.C., 1978-80; mng. dir. Merrill Lynch White Weld Capital Markets Group, N.Y.C., 1980-82; exec. v.p., dir. Dean Witter Reynolds, Inc., 1982-84; pres., dir. Quadrex Securities Corp., 1984-85, Peers & Co., N.Y.C., 1985-90; pres., bd. dirs. PH II, Inc., Westport, Conn., 1988—, Knox & Co., N.Y.C., 1992—; pres. bd. dirs. Knox & Co., N.Y.C.; bd. dirs. THT, Inc., Hydrox Corp., Ltd., N.Z. Mem. Union Club (Cleve.), Chagrin Valley Hunt Club, Princeton Club (N.Y.C.), Marco Polo Club. Home: 30 Edgewater Hillside Westport CT 06880-6101 Office: PH II Inc 16 Wilton Rd Westport CT 06880-3108

KELLY, R. (RICHARD) DENNIS, software engineer; b. Pitts., July 7, 1945; s. Richard Elliot and Anna Elizabeth (Finsinger) K.; M. Nicole J. Cook, Oct. 31, 1966 (div. Dec. 1980); children: Erin M., Morgen A.R.; m. Lili J. Byrer, Oct. 14, 1984. BA, Carnegie Tech. Inst., 1967. Safety and software engr. Westinghouse Electric, Pitts., 1966—. Office: Westinghouse Electric PO Box 355 Pittsburgh PA 15230-0355

KELLY, ROBERT EMMETT, telecommunicaitons operations manager; b. Cambridge, Mass., Feb. 6, 1952; s. Charles Patrick and Patricia Anne (McCormack) K.; m. Ann Marie McDonough, June 1, 1991. Student, St. Michael's Coll., Winooski, Vt., 1969-71. Owner, operator REKording, Everett, Mass., 1976—; asst. staff mgr. New Eng. Telephone Co., Boston, 1985-88, ops. mgr. svcs. provisioning, 1991—; mem. tech. staff Bell Communications Rsch., Piscataway, N.J., 1988-91. Vol. Cambridge coun. Boy Scouts Am., 1972—. Mem. Audio Engring. Soc. Roman Catholic. Home: 22 Hillside Ave S-1 Everett MA 02149-3914 Office: New Eng Telephone Co RM 1240 185 Franklin St Boston MA 02107

KELLY, ROBERT F., district judge; b. 1935. BS, Villanova U., 1957; LLB, Temple U., 1960. Pvt. practice law Media, Pa., 1961-62, 64-76, Chester, Pa., 1962-64; law clk. to Hon. Francis J. Catania Ct. Common Pleas, Delaware County, Pa., 1964-72; prothonotary Delaware County, 1972-76; former judge Ct. Commnon Pleas 32d Jud. Dist. Pa.; judge U.S. Dist. Ct. (ea. dist.) Pa., Phila., 1987—; lectr. law Villanova U. Law Sch. Voluntary defender Delaware County, 1962; chmn. Delaware County Rep. Exec. Com., 1972-76. Mem. ABA, Am. Judicature Soc., Pa. Bar Assn., Pa. Trial Judges Assn., Delaware County Bar Assn., Delaware County Field and Stream Assn., Greater Phila. Dahlia Soc. Office: US Dist Ct 11613 US Courthouse 601 Market St Philadelphia PA 19106

KELLY, ROBERT LYNN, advertising agency executive; b. Chgo., Oct. 25, 1939; s. Carl Robert and Annabel Pauline (Lindsay) K.; m. Maria Graciela Gonzalez, Oct. 26, 1963; children: Albert E., Elizabeth A. BA, Gettysburg Coll., 1961. Dir. pub. info. Oxnard AFB, Calif., 1961-64; with Armstrong Cork Co., Lancaster, Pa., 1964-67; owner Bob Kelly Advt., Quito, Ecuador, 1967-70; partner, writer, account exec., mgr. Ibold & Kelly Advt., Lancaster, 1970-72; founder, pres. Kelly Advt., Inc., Lancaster, 1972-84; pres. Kelly Michener Inc., Lancaster, Pa., 1984—; guest lectr. F & M Coll., and Millersville U., 1971—; lectr. Lancaster Community Gallery, 1977 . Active various civic orgns.; bd. dirs. Lancaster Community Gallery, 1978-89, v.p., 1983-89; mem. campaign coms., Lancaster County Rep. orgns., 1973-75; bd. dirs. Rockford Plantation, 1979-89, v.p., 1988-89; v.p. Let's Lifebelt Lancaster, 1984-85. Served with USAF, 1961-64. Mem. Nat. Advt. Agy. Network (nat. chmn. 1984), Am. Assn. Advt. Agys. (chmn. regional bd. govs. 1989-90), Lancaster Advt. Agy. Council (sec. 1987—). N.G. Assn. U.S., Sales and Mktg. Execs. Episcopalian. Clubs: Hamilton; Lancaster Tennis and Yacht (bd. dirs., v.p. 1986-87, commodore 1988-89). Contbr. articles to profl. jours. Home: 1112 Wheatland Ave Lancaster PA 17603-2543 Office: Kelly Michener Inc 416 W Marion St Lancaster PA 17603-3417

KELLY, SHARON PRATT, mayor; b. Washington, Jan. 30, 1944; d. Carlisle and Mildred (Petticord) Pratt; m. Arrington Dixon (div.); children: Aimee Arrington, Drew Arrington; m. James Kelly III, Dec. 7, 1991. BA, Howard U., 1965, JD, 1968. Bar: D.C. 1970, U.S. Dist. Ct. D.C. 1970, U.S. Ct. Appeals (D.C. cir.) 1970, U.S. Tax Ct. 1970. Assoc. Pratt & Queen, P.C., Washington, 1971-76; lawyer, prof. Antioch Sch. Law, Washington, 1972-76; assoc. gen. counsel Potomac Electric and Power Co., Washington, 1976-79, dir. consumer affairs, 1979-83, v.p. consumer affairs, 1983-86, v.p. pub. policy, 1986-89; elected mayor Washington, D.C., 1990. Chmn. Ea. regional caucus Dem. Nat. Com., Washington, 1976-85, treas., 1985-89; nat. committeeperson D.C. State Com., Washington, 1977—. Recipient Disting. Svc. award Fedn. Women's Clubs, 1986, Nat. Assn. Black Women Attys., 1987, 88, Presdl. award NAACP, 1983, Disting. Leadership award United Nego Coll. Fund, 1985. Mem. Women's Rsch. and Ednl. Inst. (bd. dirs. 1986-88), D.C. Unified Bar, D.C. Bar Assn., Links Club, Jack & Jill Club. Home: 8227 W Beach Terr NW Washington DC 20012 Office: Office of Mayor D C Bldg Washington DC 20004*

KELLY, WINFIELD M., state official; b. Prince George's County, Md., Sept. 2, 1935; s. Winfield M. Sr. and Margaret (Gwinn) K.; m. Barbara Doolittle; seven children. Chmn. bd. dirs., chief exec. officer Dimensions Health Corp.; sec. of state State of Md., Annapolis, 1987—. Roman Catholic. Office: Sec of State's Office 16 Francis St Jeffrey Bldg Annapolis MD 21401*

KELMAN, EDWARD MICHAEL, lawyer; b. N.Y., Aug. 29, 1943; s. Jack H. and Evelyn (Karp) K.; m. Judith Ann Edelstein, June 28, 1970; children: Matthews S., Joshua K. AB, Cornell U., 1965; JD, NYU, 1968. Bar: N.Y. 1969, Conn. 1972. Asst dist. atty. N.Y. County Dist. Atty.'s Office, 1968-71; assoc. Glazer & Wechsler, Stamford, Conn., 1971-72, Squadron, Gartenberg, Elenoff & Plesent, N.Y., 1972-73; sr. atty. CBS Records, CBS, Inc., N.Y., 1973-76; asst. gen. atty. CBS Pub., CBS, Inc., N.Y., 1976-77; v.p. law Chappell Music Co., N.Y., 1977-80; of counsel Law Offices of Michael Sukin, N.Y., 1980-82; v.p. bus. affairs and acquisitions Thorn EMI Video & TV, N.Y., 1982-83; pvt. practice entertainment and media law N.Y., 1983—. Vice chmn. Mayor's TV & Film Commn., Stamford, 1986—; cons. First Night Entertainment Com., Stamford, 1990. Recipient Spl. award Rec. Ind. Assn. Am., 1975. Mem. Assn. of Bar of City of N.Y. (entertainment law com.), Conn. Bar Assn., Nat. Acad. Popular Music, Cornell Club of Fairfield County, Cornell Club of N.Y., Friars Club. Office: 747 3rd Ave New York NY 10017-2803

KELMAN, GARY ALLEN, educator; b. Bridgeport, Conn., Sept. 26, 1951; s. Norman M. and Sarah G. (Galprien) K.; m. Joyce Rose Vozzo, June 20, 1976; children: Lauren, Kevin. BS, Cen. Conn. State U., 1973; MA, Fairfield U., 1978; postgrad., Wesleyan U., 1982, Cen. Conn. State U., 1983. Cert. secondary edn., solar installation, media specialist, vocat. sch. adminstrn. Physics instr. J.M. Wright RVTS, Stamford, Conn., 1973-85; related dept. head Bullard-Havens RVTS, Bridgeport, Conn., 1985—; athletic dir. Bullard-Havens RVTS, 1987, adult edn. supr., 1989; energy auditor Energy Cost Cutters, Westport, Conn., 1981-83; carpenter Jim Moran Constrn., Stratford, Conn., 1985, Kaesman Carpenter-Contractor, Easton, Conn., 1988; mem., com. chair New Eng. Assn. Schs. & Colls., Mass., 1983; athletic steering chmn. div. vo-tech. schs. State of Conn., 1988—. Co-author: Energy Auditing, 1984, Safety Curriculum, 1985, Nuclear Energy Curriculum, 1991. Polit. action chmn. State Vocat. Fedn. Tchrs., Berlin, Conn., 1985; fundraising mem. Bridgeport Lions Club, 1984; mem. Bridgeport Democratic Town Com., 1986. Named to Tchr. in Space Program NASA, 1985. Mem. NSTA, Nat. Honor Soc. (hon. mem. Bullard-Haven chpt.), Conn. ASCD, Conn. Sci. Tchrs. Assn., Conn. Sci. Suprs. Assn., Nat. Sci. Suprs. Assn., Conn. Assn. Physics Tchrs. Home: 56 Round Hill Terrace Milford CT 06460-1837 Office: Bullard Havens RVTS 500 Palisade Ave Bridgeport CT 06610-3499

KELSO, JOHN GLOVER, SR., recycling company executive; b. Birmingham, U.K., Jan. 10, 1932; s. A. Donald and Florence (Merwin) K.; m. Patricia Ann Wilson, Aug. 16, 1958; children: Alexandra Helen Kelso Johnson, John G. Jr. BA, Harvard U., 1953; postgrad., Northwestrn U., 1981. Registered profl. engr., Mass. Gen. mgr. Norton Casale, S.A., Mendoza, Argentina, 1961-62; mng. dir. Norton, S.A., Sao Paulo, Brazil, 1963-68; v.p. Latin Am. region Norton Internat., Inc., Worcester, Mass., 1967-68; v.p., gen. mgr. Coated Abrasives Div. Norton Co., Troy, N.Y., 1969-76; pres. pipe and plastics group Certainteed Inc., Valley Forge, Pa., 1976-79; v.p. ops. NYPRO, Inc., Clinton, Mass., 1979-83; pres. Clipper Abrasives, Inc., Marshfield, Mass., 1984-85; v.p. mfg. Sippican, Inc., Marion, Mass., 1986-88; pres. ENT Med. Devices, Inc., Wareham, Mass., 1989-90; exec. v.p. Jet-A-Way, Inc., Boston, 1990—. Inventee in field; contbr. articles to profl. jours. Lt. USNR, 1952-63. Mem. Coated Abrasive Mfrs. Inst. (pres. 1974-75). Home: PO Box 251 Marshfield Hills MA 02051-0251 Office: Jet-A-Way Inc 47 Kemble St Roxbury MA 02119-2807

KEMELHOR, ROBERT E(LIAS), mechanical engineer; b. N.Y.C., May 19, 1919; m. Shirley P. Tennen; children: Judith Ellen, Joel Martin, Barry Alan. Student Pre-Law, Bklyn. Coll., 1936-38; BS in Mech. Engring., George Washington U., 1949. Registered profl. engr., Washington. Sr. draftsman Bur. Ships Navy Dept., Washington, 1940-43, design engr. Bur. Ordnance, 1943-46, sr. engr. head weapon launching sect. Bur. Aeros., 1946-53; chief engr. design, devel. prodn. McLean Devel. Labs., Copiague, N.Y., 1953-58; dir. rsch. and devel. Pesco Products div. Borg-Warner Corp., Bedford, Ohio, 1958; with applied physics lab. Johns Hopkins U., Laurel, Md., 1958—; program mgr. John Hopkins U., Laurel, 1982-85, chief engr. tech. svcs. dept., 1986-91; pvt. practice cons. Bethesda, 1991—. Numerous patents in field; contbr. articles to profl. jours. U.S. del. Internat. Standards Orgn. Subcom., Mfg. Automation. Fellow AIAA (assoc.); mem. Am. Astronautics Inst. (sr. mem.), Soc. Mfg. Engrs. (sr. mem., chmn. Washington chpt. No. 48), Sigma Tau, Tau Beta Pi. Home: 6211 Redwing Ct Bethesda MD 20817-5914

KEMENYFFY, STEVEN, artist, art educator; b. Budapest, Hungary, Aug. 18, 1943; came to U.S., 1945; s. Joseph and Elizabeth (Gosztony) K.; m. Susan Berenice Hale, Oct. 5, 1968; 1 child, Maya. BA, Augustana Coll., Rock Island, Ill., 1965; MA, U. Iowa, 1966, MFA, 1967. Instr. U. Iowa, Iowa City, 1966-67, U. Wis., Whitewater, 1967-69; prof. ceramics Edinboro U. of Pa., 1969—; lectr., workshop presenter; vis. lectr. Renwick Gallery of the Nat. Mus. of Am. Art, Smithsonian Instn., Washington, 1991, Fusion, Toronto, Can., 1991, Walnut Creek (Calif.) Civic Arts Edn., 1991, Potter-supply Lucky Lambo, Bussum, Holland, 1990, C.L.A.Y., Phoenix Coll., 1990, Lucia Bittencourt Studio, San Paulo, Brazil, 1989, Nat. Ceramics '88, Wellington, New Zealand, 1988, Internat. Exptl. Ceramic Studio, Kecskemet, Hungary, 1989; co-owner Swift Creek Pottery & Press, McKean, Pa. Exhibited in group shows at Cin. Art Mus., 1987, Craftsmen Potters Assn., London, 1987, New Zealand Soc. Potters, Inc., Wellington, 1988, NCECA, Kansas City, Mo., 1989, John Michael Kohler Art Ctr., Sheboygan, Wis., 1990, Craftsman's Gallery, Cleve., 1991, West Chester (Pa.) U., 1992, Claytrade, Portland, Oreg., 1992.; represented in permanent collections at Smithsonian Instn., Washington, Kaiser Permanente Med. Ctr., Irvine, Calif., Everson Mus. Art, Syracuse, N.Y., Rohm and Haas, Phila., McBrier Properties Group, Erie, Pa., Ubukata Industries Co., Inc., Nagoya, Japan. Home: 4570 Old State Rd Mc Kean PA 16426-2239 Office: Edinboro U Pa Edinboro PA 16412

KEMLER, R(OBERT) MICHAEL, lawyer; b. Boston, Oct. 25, 1945; s. Charles and Evelyn (Jaffe) K.; m. Deborah Glaser, Aug. 20, 1970 (div. 1980); 1 child, Matthew Alex Kemler Nelson. AB, U. Pa., 1967; JD, Boston Coll., 1970; LLM, U. Pa. (partial fellowship-grad. law student), 1972; postgrad., U. Oxford, Eng., 1970-71. Guest lectr. forensic psychology Hosp. U. Pa., Phila., 1972; atty. law reform health law and Medicaid Community Legal Svcs., Phila., 1973-79; lectr. health law Villanova (Pa.) U., 1980; atty. Pub. Interest Law Ctr. of Phila., 1979-80; asst. regional atty. Office of Civil Rights, U.S. Dept. Health & Human Svcs., Phila., 1980-82; asst. dep. pub. advocate N.J. Dept. Pub. Advocates, Trenton, N.J., 1982-87; assoc. litigation dept. Duane, Morris & Heckscher, Phila., 1987-88; of counsel Monaghan & Gold, Phila., 1990—; cons. legal medicine Wood Inst., Coll. Physicians of Phila., 1990—; lectr. in field; apptd. mediator U.S. Dist. Ct. (ea. dist.) Pa., 1992—. Author: A Handbook on the Medicaid Boycott and Antitrust, 1981, Mock Medicine Malpractice Trial, U. Pa. Medical Sch., 1989; contbr. articles to profl. jours. Bd. dirs. Pa. Pro Musica, Phila., 1990—; bass II Mendelssohn Club of Phila., 1990; asst. mgr. Pa. Ballet, Phila., 1985-88. Nat. Legal Svc. Corp. rsch. fellow, 1981, U. Pa. Law Sch. fellow, 1972. Mem. Phila. Bar Assn. (Medico-legal com. 1989-91). Democrat. Home: 2016 Addison St Philadelphia PA 19146-1307 Office: Monaghan & Gold of Counsel 1411 Walnut St #200 Philadelphia PA 19102

KEMMERER, KATHLEEN MARY, English educator; b. Wilkes-Barre, Pa., May 19, 1952; d. S. Edgar and Mary (Sullivan) Nulton; m. Eugene G. Kemmerer, July 19, 1975; children: Mary, Laurie, Timothy, Elizabeth. BA magna cum laude, Coll. Misericordia, Dallas, 1974; MA, U. Scranton, 1988; postgrad., Fordham U., 1988—. Sec. tchr. Dallas (Pa.) Schs., 1974-78; editor/writer Blue Cross of Northeastern Pa., Wilkes-Barre, Pa., 1978-80; adj. prof. English Coll. Misericordia, Dallas, 1985-88; adj. prof. communications and English U. Scranton, 1989-90; asst. prof. English Wilkes U., Wilkes-Barre, Pa., 1990—; lectr. in field. Editor: A History of the Descendnts of Benjamin Spaulding, 1988; author poetry. Fordham U. presdl. scholar, 1988-89, Coll. Misericordia scholar, 1970-74. Mem. Am. Soc. for 18th Century Studies, N.E. Am. Soc. for 18th Cen. Studies (travel grant 1989), E. Cen. Soc. 18th Cen. Studies (Grad. Student prize 1989), Fordham U. Grad. Student Assn., MLA, Coll. Lang. Assn., Johnson Soc. of Cen. Region, Kappa Gamma Pi (pres. 1980-88). Home: 346 Harris Hill Rd Shavertown PA 18708-9684 Office: Wilkes U Wilkes Barre PA 18766

KEMMERER, PETER REAM, financial executive; b. N.Y.C., Dec. 20, 1942; s. Mahlon Sistie and Colette Noel (Fitch) K.; m. Lillian Reilly, Sept. 15, 1990. BBA, Georgetown U., 1966; MBA, Am. U., 1970; MA, New Sch., 1975. Analyst corp. planning Otis Elevator Co., N.Y.C., 1971-74; mgr. fin. and adminstrn. bus. equipment div. SCM Corp., N.Y.C., 1975-80; pres. Mesa Verde, Inc., Princeton, N.J., 1980—, also bd. dirs.; mng. ptnr. Jezel-Bezel Ptnrs., Princeton, 1980—. Roman Catholic. Club: Princeton (N.Y.C.). Office: Mesa Verde Inc 344 Nassau St Princeton NJ 08540-4615

KEMP, EUGENE THOMAS, veterinarian; b. MacDonough, N.Y., Mar. 22, 1930; s. Oswald Milton and Almira Dorothy (Allen) K.; m. Ruth Emer Stoll, Sept. 29, 1951 (dec. Sept. 1977); 1 child, William Allen; m. Margaret Atenna Rowland, Dec. 27, 1980. BS, Cornell U., 1951, DVM, 1957. Sr. ptnr. Day Hollow Animal Clinic, Owego, N.Y., 1957—. Contbr. articles to profl. jours. Bd. dirs. 1st Ch. of Nazarene, Owego, 1991; v.p. Tioga County Bd. Health, 1988-91; mem. Owego-Apalachin Bd. Edn., 1961-71; mem. Broome-Tioga Bd. Coop. Edn. Svcs., Binghamton, N.Y., 1969-83, pres., 1971-76; founding pres. Broome-Tioga Coun. Sch. Bd. Pres., 1973. Mem. So. Tier Vet. Med. Assn. (pres.-elect. 1991—), Am. Vet. Med. Assn., N.Y. State Vet. Med. Assn., Kiwanis (pres. Owego chpt. 1968). Republican. Home and Office: 345 Day Hollow Rd Owego NY 13827-5307

KEMP, EVAN J(ENNINGS), JR., federal official; b. N.Y.C., May 5, 1937; s. Evan Jennings Kemp and Francesca Butler (Moore) Bliss; m. Jane McMaster Copeland, Sept. 19, 1970. BA, Washington & Lee U., 1959; LLB, U. Va., 1964; LLD (hon.), Nova U., 1990. Atty. Office of Chief Counsel IRS, Washington, 1964-67; atty. div. corp. fin. and corp. regulation SEC, Washington, 1967-80; exec. dir. Disability Rights Ctr., Washington, 1980-87; commr. EEOC, Washington, 1987-90, chmn., 1990—; lectr. Cath. U. Law Sch., Washington, 1980-87. Contbr. numerous articles to profl. jours.; TV appearances. Active civil rights of disabled people. Mem. Omicron Delta Kappa. Republican. Roman Catholic. Office: US EEOC 1801 L St NW 10th Fl Washington DC 20507

KEMP, JACK FRENCH, secretary of housing and urban development of U.S., former congressman; b. L.A., July 13, 1935; m. Joanne Main; children: Jeffrey, Jennifer, Judith, James. B.A., Occidental Coll., 1957; postgrad., Long Beach State U., Calif. Western U. Spl. asst. to gov. Calif., 1967; spl. asst. to chmn. Republican Nat. Com., 1969; mem. 92d-100th congresses from 31st N.Y. Dist., 1971-89; sec. Dept. of Housing and Urban Development, 1989—; profl. football player for 13 years; pub. relations officer Marine Midland Bank, Buffalo; candidate for Rep. Presdl. nomination, 1987-88. Mem. Pres.'s Council on Phys. Fitness and Sports; mem. exec. com. player pension bd. NFL. Recipient Disting. Service award N.Y. State Jaycees; Outstanding Citizen award Buffalo Evening News, 1965, 74. Mem. Nat. Assn. Broadcasters, Engrs. and Technicians, Buffalo Area C. of C., Sierra Club, Am. Football League Players Assn. (co-founder, pres. 1965-70). Republican. Office: HUD Office Sec 451 7th St SW Washington DC 20410-0002*

KEMP, THERESA ANNE, defense systems contract administrator; b. Washington, July 5, 1956; d. Francis Edward and Mary Frances (Healey) K. BA, U. Calif., Irvine, 1980. Adminstr. asst. Palmer Bros., Inc., Washington, 1980-82; contract mgmt. rep. Westinghouse Electric Corp., Balt., 1982-85; subcontract adminstr. The Boeing Co., Seattle, 1985-88; contract adminstr. IBM, Gaithersburg, Md., 1988—. Active Nat. Pub. Radio. Mem. Nat. Contracts Mgmt. Assn., Nature Conservancy. Republican. Home: 18616 Pier Point Pl Gaithersburg MD 20879

KEMP, THOMAS JAY, librarian; b. Nashua, N.H.; s. Willard Henry and Eleanor Frances (Huse) K.; m. Vi Tuong Lam; children: Andrew Thomas, Sarah Eleanor. BA, Brigham Young U., 1973, MLS, 1974; cert. photographic preservation, Rochester Inst. Tech., 1979. Office supr., history div. Lee Library, Brigham Young U., Provo, Utah, 1971-74; local history and genealogy librarian Ferguson Library, Stamford, Conn., 1974-81; grant reviewer NEH, Washington, 1978-84; ref. librarian Sacred Heart U., Fairfield, Conn., 1980-82; head librarian Weed Meml. Library, Springdale, Conn., 1981-82, Turn of River Library, Stamford, Conn., 1982-86; asst. dir. Pequot Library, Southport, Conn., 1986-89; libr. dir. Hist. Soc. Pa., Phila., 1989—; tchr. Office of Continuing Edn., Stamford, 1975-80; lectr. in field; called to testify U.S. Senate hearings on the new archivist of U.S., 1986. Author: Office of Patriarch to the Church in The Church of Jesus Christ of Latter-day Saints, 1981, Stamford, Connecticut 1872 City Directory, 1981, Connecticut Periodical Index, 1981-86, Genealogies in the Ferguson Library, 1982, Connecticut Researcher's Handbook, 1982, Connecticut Biography and Portrait Index, 1985—, Genealogies in Connecticut Libraries and Historical Societies, 1985, Kemp Family of County Cavan, Ireland, 1985, Inexpensive Items for Building Your Genealogical Library, 1977, Home Study Courses of Interest to Genealogists and Local Historians, 1986, Kemp Bibliography, 1986, Kemp Family Records, 1986, Kemp Family Passport Records, 1986, Vital Records Handbook, 1988, Connecticut Divorces Granted by Resolve of the General Assemby of the State of Connecticut, 1988, Connecticut Changes of Name Granted by Resolve of the General Assembly of the State of Connecicut, 1988, Darien Connecticut, 1989 Vital Records: An Index to Birth, Engagement, Marriage and Death Announcements, 1990, Litchfield County, Connecticut Obituary Announcements 1989, 1990, New Canaan, Connecticut 1989 Vital Records: An Index to Birth, Engagement, Marriage and Death Announcements, 1990, International Vital Records Handbook, 1990, Connecticut Historians and Genealogists 1890-1990, 1991; editor: Connecticut Ancestry, 1987-89, Richmond Family News Jour., 1971-76, Gradalis Review, 1973-74; local history and genealogy collection Thomas Jay Kemp Genealogy and Local History Collection Darien Libr., 1989; contbr. articles to profl. jours. Missionary to Colo.-N.Mex. Mission, Denver, 1968-70; bd. dirs. Pa. Ctr. for the Book, 1990-91. With USN, 1965-71. Recipient Hattie M. Knight award NYU, 1974, Merit award Conn. League Hist. Socs., 1983. Mem. Assn. for Bibliography of History, New Eng. Libr. Assn. (bibliography com. 1979-80), Conn. Libr. Assn. (hon. mention, Librarian of the Yr, 1987), Orgn. Am. Historians U.S. newspaper project, 1977), Am. Libr. Assn., (ref. svcs. div., chmn. history sect. 1989-90, chmn. nominations com., 1984, chmn. program com. 1983, pre-conf. planning com. 1981, genealogy com. 1978-82, local history com. 1986—), Coun. of Nat. Libr. Info. Assns. (chmn. 1989-90), New Eng. Archivists, N.H. Libr. Assn., N.Y. Geneal. and Biog. Soc., Geneal. Soc. Pa. (pubs. com. 1989—, acquisitions com. 1989—), Libr. Assn. (U.K.), Libr. Assn. of Ireland, Soc. Am. Archivists, Am. Soc. Indexers (pres. 1987-88), Assn. Profl. Genealogists (exec. v.p. 1988-90, trustee 1990—), Middlesex Geneal. Soc. (Darien, Conn., bd. dirs. 1984-89, trustee 1989—), Gen. Soc. Mayflower Descendants (bd. assts. Conn. 1983), SAR, Order of Founders and Patriots, Phi Alph Theta. Office: Hist Soc of Pa 1300 Locust St Philadelphia PA 19107-5699

KEMPA, GERALD, manufacturing company executive; b. Chgo., Sept. 24, 1934; s. Stanley John and Mary (Michalek) K.; m. Annette Marie Valentino, Sept. 3, 1960; children: Gerald, Amanda, Leslie Anne. BS, No. Ill. U., 1958, MS, 1960. Sales rep. Adams Corp. divsn. Beatrice Foods, N.Y.C., 1960-63, regional sales mgr., 1963-65; v.p. mktg. Adams Corp. divsn. Beatrice Foods, Beloit, Wis., 1965-70; pres. Treat Potato Chip Co. divsn. Beatrice Foods, Riverhead, N.Y., 1970-74, Beatrice Frosted Foods divsn. Beatrice Foods, L.I. City, N.Y., 1974-80; v.p. sales and mktg. Carey-McFall Corp., Montgomery, Pa., 1981-86, sr. v.p., 1986—, also bd. dirs. Mem. Am. Window Coverings Mfrs. Assn. (trustee 1986-88). Roman Catholic. Home: 60 Foxcroft Ln Manhasset NY 11030-3721 Office: Carey McFall Corp 104 W 40th St # Conc New York NY 10018-3617

KEMPIN, LINDA JEANNE, marketing professional; b. Chgo., June 5, 1951; d. Emil August and Margaret Mary (Pierorazio) K. Student, U. Ill., Chgo., 1969-71; BFA, No. Ill. U., 1974; MBA, Keller Grad. Sch. of Mgmt., Chgo., 1985. Layout editor, asst. prod. mgr. The No. Star, DeKalb, 1972-74; advt. and promotional dir. Group Travel Enterprises, Chgo., 1973-74; design asst. 3M/Nat. Advt., Chgo., 1974; assoc. art dir. R.R. Donnelley & Sons Co., Chgo., 1975-79; communications cons. Saga Communications Group, Greenwich, Conn., 1979-81; sr. project mgr. PCS Reports Ltd., Oak Brook, Ill., 1981; account supr. Tassani Advt., Chgo., 1982-85; dir. mktg. and corp. affairs The Ayco Corp., Albany, N.Y., 1986—; Co-author mo. col. "Money Matters" in Homestyle mag., 1990—. Co-author monthly Money Matters column Homestyle mag., 1990—. Pub. rels. chmn. Vanguard of the Albany Symphony Orch., 1988; v.p., publicity chmn. Southeast Lakeview Assn., Chgo., 1976-78; speaker United Way N.Y. State, Syracuse, 1988, Am. Soc. on Aging Conf., Washington, 1989; mem. Vanguard/Albany Symphony Orch. Mem. Hudson Valley Writers Guild, Bus. and Profl. Women, Am. Ctr. for Design, Am. Mgmt. Assn., Pub. Rels. Soc. Am., Steuben Athletic Club. Mem. Hudson Valley Writers Guild, Bus. and Profl. Women, Am. Ctr. for Design, Am. Mgmt. Assn., Pub. Rels. Soc. Am., Steuben Athletic Club. Office: The Ayco Corp One Wall St Albany NY 12205-3894

KEMPKES, MICHAEL ALAN, electrical engineer; b. Lincoln, Nebr., Oct. 31, 1960; s. George Thomas and Kathryn Sue (Milne) K.; m. Julie Elise Johnson, Sept. 26, 1987. BSEE, Rose-Hulman Inst. Tech., 1982; MBA, Northea. U., 1985. Design engr. McDonnel Douglas Corp., St. Louis, 1981; dir. bus. devel. ARE, Inc., Bedford, Mass., 1987—. Capt. USAF, 1981-87. Mem. IEEE, Air Force Assn., Eta Kappa Nu (treas. 1981-82). Home: 10 Shannon Cir Westford MA 01886-3942 Office: Applied Rsch Engring Inc 3 Preston Ct Bedford MA 01730-2319

KEMPNER, ROBERT MAX WASILII, lawyer, political scientist; b. Freiburg, Germany, Oct. 17, 1899; came to U.S., 1939, naturalized; s. Walter K. and Lydia (Rabinowitsch) K.; m. Ruth Hahn (Benedicta Maria); children: Lucian Walter, André Franklin. Student of law, polit. sci., pub. adminstrn., criminology, Univs. of Berlin, Breslau, Freiburg (Germany); student polit. sci., pub. adminstrn., criminology (Dr. of Law and Pub. Adminstrn.); PhD (hon.), U. Osnabrück. Prof. e.H. Senate Berlin; asst. to state atty. Berlin, 1926, judge mcpl. ct., 1927; superior govt. counselor chief legal adviser of Prussian police system of 76,000 men; (recommended suppression of Nazi party and prosecution of Hitler for high treason, fired and expatriated by Hitler), Ministry of Interior, Berlin; judge civil service tribunal Ministry of Interior, 1928-33; lectr. German Acad. Politics Sch. Social Work, Police Inst., Berlin, 1926-33; counselor internat. law and migration problems, 1934-35; Pres. and prof. polit. sci. Fiorenza Coll., Florence, Italy, and Nice, France, 1936-39; research asso. and asst. Inst. Local and State Govt., U. Pa. (research on machinery of European dictatorships under Carnegie and Carl Schurz grants), 1939-42; expert to Fed. courts, espionage and fgn. agt. trials; expert cons. Dept. Justice, OSS and to sec. of War on legal, polit., police and intelligence techniques of European dictatorships and fgn. orgns. in, 1942-45; U.S. staff prosecutor in Nuremberg trials against Goering, Frick et al; research dir. U.S. prosecution, 1945-46; dep. U.S. chief of counsel for war crimes, chief prosecutor of German Reich cabinet mems., state secs. and diplomats investigation of Holocaust, 1946-49; expert cons. in internat. law; atty. indemnification matters and prosecution of war criminals, 1951—; cons. Reichstag fire trial, 1960; cons. to Israel Govt. in Eichmann case, 1961; vis. prof. Erlangen; lectr. schs., colls., univs. and pvt. orgns. Author several books, primarily on Germany, 1931—, The Judgment in The Wilhelmstrassen Case, 1950, German Police Administration, 1953, Eichmann and Accomplices, 1961, SS Under Crossexamination, 1964, 86, The Warren Report in German Language, 1964, Edith Stein and Anne Frank-Two of Hundred thousand, 1968, The Third Reich under Crossexamination, 1969, The Murder of 35,000 Berlin Jews, 1971, American Courts in Germany, 1971, The Missed Hitler Stop, 1983, Memoirs: Prosecutor of an Epoch, 1983, The Kempner Bibliography, 1987; contbr. to profl. jours. Decorated German Grand Cross of Merit with star Fed. Republic Germany, Cross of Polonia Restituta.; recipient medal with Star and Schulterband, Fed. Republic Germany; medal Charles U., Prague, Carl von Ossietzky medal, Wilhelm Leuschner medal; named hon. prof. emeritus Senate Berlin. Fellow U. Jerusalem.; Mem. Am. Polit. Sci. Assn., Am. Soc. for Internat. Law, German Bar. Home: 112 Lansdowne Ct Lansdowne PA 19050-2349 Office: Feuerbachstrasse 21, 6 Frankfurt am Main Germany

KENDALL, DONALD MCINTOSH, food products company executive; b. Sequim, Wash., Mar. 16, 1921; s. Carroll C. and Charlotte (McIntosh) K.; m. Sigrid Ruedt von Collenberg, Dec. 22, 1965; children—Donna Lee Kendall Warren, Edward McDonnell, Donald McIntosh, Kent Collenberg. Student, Western Ky. State Coll., 1941-42; LL.D., Stetson U., 1971. Spl. field rep. Pepsi-Cola Co., 1947-48, mgr. fountain sales, 1948-49, br. plant mgr. fountain sales, 1949-50, spl. rep., 1950-52, v.p. nat. accounts fountain sales, 1952-57; pres. Pepsi Cola Internat., 1953-63, Pepsi-Cola Co. (merger with Frito-Lay 1965), 1963-65; pres., chief exec. officer PepsiCo, Inc., 1965—, chmn. bd., chief exec. officer, 1971-86, chmn. exec. com., 1986—, also bd. dirs.; bd. dirs. Pan Am. Airways, Atlantic Richfield, Investors Diversified Services Mut. Fund Group; chmn. NOVA Pharm., Lorimar-Telepictures, Nat. Alliance Businessmen, 1969-70, dir., 1970-78. Chmn. Nat. Center for Resource Recovery, Inc. 1970-76, bd. dirs., 1976—; chmn. Emergency Com. for Am. Trade, 1969-76, mem., 1976—; bd. dirs. U.S.-USSR Trade and Econ. Council; chmn. Am. Ballet Theatre Found., 1973-77, chmn. exec. com., 1977-83. Served to lt. AC, USNR, 1942-47. Mem. Internat. C. of C. (trustee council), C. of C. U.S. (dir., vice-chmn. 1980-81, chmn. 1981-82), Blind Brook Club, Lyford Cay Club, River Club, Round Hill Club, Links. Office: Pepsico Inc Office of Pres Purchase NY 10577*

KENDALL, DONALD RODERICK, JR., investment banking; b. Northampton, Mass., May 10, 1952; s. Donald and Phyllis A. Kendall; m. Diane Stone, July 10, 1976; children: Corinne J., Lincoln R. BA, Hamilton Coll., 1974; MBA, Ames Tuck Sch. Bus., 1976. Acct. Arthur Anderson & Co., Boston, 1975; prin. Morgan Stanley & Co., Inc., N.Y.C., 1976-83; pres. Kendall & Co., Inc., N.Y.C., 1983-85; mng. dir. Drexel Burnham Lambert Incorp., N.Y.C., 1984-90; pres. Drexel Leasing Co., N.Y.C., 1984-90; mng. dir. Kendall Capital Ptnrs., L.P., N.Y.C., 1990-92, First Boston Corp., N.Y.C., 1992—. Mem. Prospect Park Alliance, Bklyn. Office: First Boston Corp Park Avenue Plz New York NY 10055

KENDALL, HENRY WAY, physicist; b. Boston, Dec. 9, 1926; s. Henry P. and Evelyn Louise (Way) K. BA, Amherst Coll., 1950; PhD in Nuclear Physics, MIT, 1955; DSc (hon.), Amherst Coll., 1975. NSF fellow MIT, Cambridge, 1954-56, from asst. to assoc. prof., 1961-67, prof. physics, 1967—; rsch. assoc. High Energy Lab. Stanford U., 1956-57, lectr. physics, 1957-58, asst. prof., 1958-61. Recipient Nobel prize in physics, 1990. Fellow AAAS, Am. Acad. Arts Scis., Am. Phys. Soc. (co-recipient Panofsky prize 1989). Office: MIT Dept Physics Cambridge MA 02139*

KENDALL, LEIGH WAKEFIELD, surgeon; b. Brattleboro, Vt., Mar. 8, 1937; s. Irwin Samuel and Laura Eliza (Walbridge) K.; m. Grace Eleanor Fullarton, July 1, 1961; children: William Leigh, Bradley Edward. AB, U. Pa., Phila., 1959; D of Medicine, U. Vt., 1963; MS, U. Ill., Chgo., 1965. Diplomate Bd. Med. Examiners, Am. Bd. Surgery. Intern then resident surgery U. Ill. Hosp., Chgo., 1963-69; rsch. fellow Am. Cancer Soc., Chgo., 1964-65; clin. fellow Am. Cancer Soc., 1968-69; staff surgeon USN Hosp., Great Lakes, Ill., 1969; surgeon USN Hosp. Ships, Vietnam, 1969-70; pvt. practice Lancaster, Pa., 1971—; instr. surgery U. Ill. Hosp., Chgo., 1968-69; active staff St. Joseph Hosp., Lancaster, 1971—, sect. chief gen. surgery, 1981-88, chmn. dept. surgery, 1989—; mem. courtesy staff Lancaster Gen. Hosp., 1971—; cons. surgery Franklin and Marshall Coll., Lancaster, Masonic Homes, Elizabethtown, Pa. Lt. comdr. USNR M.C., 1959-71, Vietnam. Decorated 1st Class Mil. Honor medal Republic of Vietnam. Fellow ACS, Internat. Coll. Surgeons; mem. AMA, Pa. Med. Soc., Pa. Oncologic Soc., Warren H. Cole Soc., Royal Soc. Medicine (Eng.), Ripon Soc., Intrepids Club, Sigma Nu. Republican. Episcopalian. Home: 1314 Quarry Ln Lancaster PA 17603-2424 Office: 822 Marietta Ave Lancaster PA 17603-3239

KENDRICK, JAMES EARL, computer consulting and information services company executive; b. Indpls., Sept. 12, 1940; s. John William and Mable E. (Coleman) K.; m. Carrie L. Fair, July 19, 1969; children: Carrie F., Leslie F., John F. BA, Butler U., 1963; postgrad., Ind. U., 1963-65. Exec. dir. Knox County Econ. Opportunity Council, Barbourville, Ky., 1965-66; rsch. scientist N.Y. U., 1967-68; mgr. Volt Info. Scis., Washington, 1968-71, Nat. Urban Coalition, 1972-74; pres. Kendrick & Co., Washington, 1974-91, sr. v.p., 1992—. Mem. Fellowship Merry Christians. Recipient Rural Service award OEO, 1968; citation Washington chpt. Am. Soc. Tng. and Devel., 1971; named one of Outstanding Young Men of Am., 1974. Mem. Inst. Mgmt. Consultants (bd. dirs. Washington chpt.), CEO Club, Air Traffic Contrs. Assn., Soc. Profl. Mgmt. Cons., Sigma Delta Chi. Author: Community Energy Workbook, 1974; National Urban Agenda Survey, 1974; (video) Americans on the Move, 1984; (software) Help for PC DOS, 1985; contbr. articles to profl. jours. and newsletters. Presbyterian (elder). Home: 1412 Dale Dr Silver Spring MD 20910-1501 Office: Kendrick & Co 1025 Connecticut Ave NW Ste 700 Washington DC 20036-5405

KENEALY, MATTHEW H., III, hydrogeologist; b. Stamford, Conn., Apr. 4, 1956; s. Matthew Henry Jr. and Jeanne (Wagstaff) K.; m. Cynthia Ann Johnson, June 19, 1982; children: Matthew, Kathryn. BS, Allegheny Coll., 1978. Cert. profl. geologist. Staff geologist Todd Giddings & Assoc., Inc., Clarion, Pa., 1978-80, br. mgr., 1980-85, br. mgr., sr. hydrogeologist, 1985-87; assoc., sr. hydrogeologist Blazosky Assocs. Inc., State College, Pa., 1987—; Participant profl. confs. Mem. Am. Inst. Profl. Geologists, Assn. Ground Water Scientists and Engrs. Home: 613 E Irvin Ave State College PA 16801-6606 Office: Blazosky Assocs Inc 205 E Beaver Ave Ste 201 State College PA 16801-4902

KENIG, M(ARVIN) JERRY, academic dean; b. Phila., Sept. 20, 1936; s. Abraham Nathan and Lillian Irene (Augenstein) K.; m. Rochelle Iris Naiburg, Aug. 20, 1959; children: Neil Steven, Melissa Helene Kenig Harvey. BSME, Drexel U., 1959, MSME, 1963; MA, Princeton U., 1963, PhD, 1965. Registered profl. engr., Pa., Mich. Engring. trainee Naval Air Exptl. Sta., Phila., 1955-56, Naval Air Material Ctr., Phila., 1957, Westinghouse Electric Co., Lester, Pa., 1958-59; prof. mech. engring. Drexel U., Phila., 1960-83, various adminstrv. positions, 1970-75, asst. to pres., 1975-83; chmn. mech. engring. dept. Western Mich. U., Kalamazoo, 1983-88; dean engring. U. New Haven, West Haven, Conn., 1989—; cons. in field. Contbr. articles to profl. publs. Active various civic orgns. 1st lt. USAR, 1959-60. Recipient numerous awards. Mem. NSPE, AAAS, ASME, Am. Soc. Engring. Educators, Am. Def. Preparedness Assn., Am. Acad. Mechanics, Pi Tau Sigma, Tau Beta Pi, Phi Kappa Phi, Sigma Xi. Office: U New Haven 300 Orange Ave West Haven CT 06516-1999

KENNAN, ELIZABETH TOPHAM, college president; b. Phila., Feb. 25, 1938; d. Frank and Henrietta (Jackson) Topham; m. Michael Burns, 1986; 1 child, Frank Alexander Kennan. BA summa cum laude, Mt. Holyoke Coll., 1960; MA, St. Hilda's Coll. Oxford U., Eng., 1962; PhD, U. Wash., 1966; LHD (hon.), Trinity Coll., Washington, 1978, Amherst Coll., 1980, St. Mary's Coll., 1982, Oberlin Coll., 1983; LLD (hon.), Smith Coll., 1984; LittD (hon.), Cath. U. Am., 1985, U. Mass., 1988. Asst. prof. history Cath. U. Am., Washington, 1966-70, assoc. prof., 1970-78, dir. mediaeval and Byzantine studies program, 1970-78, dir. program in early Christian humanism, 1974-78; pres. Mt. Holyoke Coll., South Hadley, Mass., 1978—; lectr. in field; dir. NYNEX Corp., White Plains, N.Y., N.E. Utilities, Hartford, Conn., Berkshire Life Ins. Co., Pittsfield, Mass., Ky. Home Mut. Life Ins. Co., Louisville, Shawmut Bank, Boston; cons. to various colls.; pres. Five Colls., Inc., 1985—; dir. Coun. on Libr. Resources, 1982—; mem. Indo-U.S. Subcommn. of Am. Secretariat. Translator, author: (with John D. Anderson) On Consideration (St. Bernard of Clairvaux), 1976; contbr. articles to profl. publs. Mem. Dana Found., Higher Edn. Program Commn., 1986—; trustee U. Notre Dame, South Bend, Ind. Named Tchr. of Yr., Cath. U. Am., 1977; Marshall scholar, 1960; Woodrow Wilson fellow, 1962. Mem. Mediaeval Acad. Am. (coun. 1984-86), Coun. on Fgn. Rels., Phi Beta Kappa. Home: Pres' House Mt Holyoke Coll South Hadley MA 01075 Office: Mt Holyoke Coll Office of the President South Hadley MA 01075

KENNAN, JOAN ELISABETH, foundation executive; b. Highland Park, Ill., Apr. 24, 1936; d. George Frost and Annelise (Sorenson) K.; m. Kevin F.X. Delany, Feb. 9, 1991; children: Brandon Trowbridge Griggs, Barklie Kennan Griggs. BA, Conn. Coll., 1959; student, Sorbonne U., Paris, 1954-55; cert., Am. U., Washington, 1984-85. Senate staffer U.S. Senate office of Nancy Landon Kassebaum, Washington, 1986-87; exec. dir. Arcana Found., Washington, 1987—. Office: Arcana Found Ste 1000 901 15th St NW Washington DC 20005

KENNEDY, ANTHONY MCLEOD, U.S. Supreme Court justice; b. Sacramento, July 23, 1936. AB, Stanford U., 1958; student, London Sch. Econs.; LLB, Harvard U., 1961; JD (hon.), U. Pacific, 1988, U. Santa Clara, 1988. Bar: Calif. 1962, U.S. Tax Ct. 1971. Former ptnr. Evans, Jackson & Kennedy; prof. constl. law McGeorge Sch. Law, U. of Pacific, 1965-88; judge U.S. Ct. Appeals (9th cir.), Sacramento, 1976-88; justice U.S. Supreme Ct., Washington, 1988—; mem. bd. student advisors Harvard Faculty, 1960-61. Fellow Am. Bar Found. (hon.), Am. Coll. Trial Lawyers (hon.); mem. ABA, Sacramento County Bar Assn., State Bar Calif., Phi Beta Kappa. Office: US Supreme Ct Washington DC 20543

KENNEDY, CHESTER RALPH, JR., former state official, art director; b. Middleboro, Mass., Apr. 22, 1926; s. Chester Ralph and Mary Carmen (Mello) K.; m. Barbara Ann Partridge, June 27, 1953; children: Karen Brooke, Scott Douglas. BFA, Mass. Coll. Art, 1951; postgrad., New Eng. Adult Edn. Inst., 1959, Boston U., 1966, Brandies U., 1985. Supr. pub. health edn. Mass. Dept. Pub. Health, Boston, 1953-56, coordinator health edn., 1956-74, asst. dir. health edn., 1974-81, dir. health edn., 1981-84, dist. health officer, 1984-89; ret., 1989; asst. art dir. Barchét Studios, Middleboro, 1949-59, art dir., co-owner, Sherborn, Mass., 1959—; cons. USPHS, Assn. State and Territorial Health Officers; lectr., instr. Harvard, Boston U., Mass. Coll.; mem. Acad. Master Plan Adv. Commn., Mass. State Coll. System; exhibit chmn. 22nd World Health Assembly. Editor: Commonwealth of Mass. Secretarial Reference Manual, 1969; designer blue ribbon exhibit New Eng. Hosp. Assembly, 1969; designer five pvt. homes. Pres. Reach Out, Inc., 1970-74, bd. dirs., 1974—; bd. dirs. Greater Framingham Mental Health Assn., 1974-76; elected to Sherborn Bd. Health, 1974-86; mem. Solid Waste Recovery Tech. Com., 1975-84; co-chair Coalition Organinzed for Health Edn. in Schs., 1989. With USN, 1944-46. Recipient Boy Scouts Am. Organizer award 1941; Commonwealth Mass. Disting. Svc. citation 1971, Health Edn. citation New Eng. Consortium Health Edn. Assn., 1975, Coalition Organized for Health Edn. in Schs. citation, 1989; Reach Out award, 1977, Southeastern Assn. Health Bds. award, 1989, Michael Dukakis Gov.'s award, 1989, Mass. Dept. Pub. Health award, 1989. Mem. New Eng. Health Edn. Assn. (pres. 1971-72), Mass. Health Coun., New Eng. Health Promotion Coun., Soc. Pub. Health Edn., Mass. Audubon Soc., Mass. Archeol. Soc., Mass. Coll. Art Alumni (pres. 1968-72), Assn. Mass. State Colls. Alumni (pres. 1973-75), Mass. Pub. Health Assn. (health edn. chmn. 1974-76, 25 yr. award 1986, Paul Revere award 1990), Mass. Health Officers Assn. (emeritus, Curtis M. Hillard award 1989, exec. sec. 1992—), Mass. Assn. Health Bds. (hon., exec. bd. 1990—), New Eng. Pub. Health Assn. (pres. 1984-85, Ira Hiscock award 1980, 25 yr. award 1989, pres. com. pub. health mus. in Mass. 1991—). Home: 178 Washington St Sherborn MA 01770-1022 Office: Barchét Studios 178 Washington St Sherborn MA 01770-1022

KENNEDY, DAVID MICHAEL, sales and marketing executive; b. Easton, Pa., Aug. 24, 1951; s. Paul G. and Claire Ann (Weidaw) K.; m. Elizabeth R. Rienzo, May 13, 1972; children: David M. Jr. (dec.), Kevin Scott. BSBA, Villanova (Pa.) U., 1973. Sales rep. 3M Co., St. Paul, 1977-80; sales mgr. Franklin Printers Supply Co., Phila., 1980-86; regional and nat. sales mgr. W.R. Grace & Co., Lexington, Mass., 1986-89; v.p. sales and mktg. DYC Supply Co., Ft. Lee, N.J., 1989—. Member adv. bd. Lehigh County Vocat. Tech. Mem. IBFI (past mem. tech. and prodn. mgmt. com.), Lehigh Valley Club Printing House Craftsmen (1st v.p. 1990-91, pres. 1991—), KC. Democrat. Roman Catholic. Home: 3727 Pheasant Hill Dr Allentown PA 18104-9685 Office: DYC Supply Co 222 Brg Pla S Fort Lee NJ 07024

KENNEDY, DAVID WOODFORD, writer; b. New Rochelle, N.Y., July 6, 1941; s. Andrew William and Elizabeth (Pratt) K.; m. Carol Stokes, Apr. 20, 1965 (div.); 1 child, Shauna Ewing; m. Barbara Knispel, Oct. 4, 1985. BA, Grinnell (Iowa) Coll., 1963; LLB, Washington and Lee U., Lexington, Va., 1966; MBA, Wagner Coll., Staten Island, N.Y., 1978. Assoc. editor McGraw-Hill, N.Y.C., 1975-77; editor Harcourt Brace Jovanovich, N.Y.C., 1977-78; writer N.Y.C., 1978—; adj. prof. Lab. Inst. Merchandising, N.Y.C., 1987—. Author: Condominium and Cooperative Apartment Buyers and Sellers Guide, 1984, 86, Money Making Money, 1987, Insurance: How Much Do You Need, 1987, Perfectly Legal, 1983-87. With U.S. Army, 1966-68. Mem. Am. Soc. Journalists and Authors (pres. 1988-89), N.Y. Fin. Writers Assn. Inc. Home and Office: 422 E 81st St New York NY 10028-5878

KENNEDY, DAVIS LEE, newspaper editor, publisher; b. Elkins, W.Va., Aug. 21, 1938; s. John A. and Bruce (Lee) K.; m. Heningham George; children: Bruce Lee, Scott Lyons, Heningham Lyons. BA magna cum laude, Harvard U., 1960, MBA, 1966. Bus. editor Virginian Pilot, Norfolk, 1966-67, with advt. dept., 1967-69; fin. advt. mgr. Balt. Sun, 1969-70, mktg. and advt. promotion mgr., 1970-76; gen. mgr. Alexandria (Va.) Port Packet, 1977-79; editor, pub. Gazette Newspapers, Gaithersburg, Md., 1980—. Bd. dirs. Nat. Chamber Orchestra, 1989—, Davis and Elkins Coll., 1989—. Mem. Chevy Chase Country Club, Met. Club, Green Spring Valley Hunt Club. Episcopalian. Home: 10 Quincy St Chevy Chase MD 20815 Office: Gazette Newspapers PO Box 6006 Gaithersburg MD 20884-6006

KENNEDY, EDWARD MOORE, senator; b. Boston, Feb. 22, 1932; s. Joseph Patrick and Rose (Fitzgerald) K.; m. Joan Kennedy (div.); children: Kara Anne, Edward Moore, Patrick Joseph; m. Victoria Anne Reggie, 1992. A.B., Harvard U., 1956; postgrad., Internat. Law Sch., The Hague, Netherlands, 1958; LL.B., U. Va., 1959. Bar: Mass. 1959, U.S. Supreme Ct. 1963. Asst. dist. atty. Suffolk County, Mass., 1961-62; U.S. senator from Mass., 1962—, chmn. judiciary com., 1979-81, ranking Dem. mem. labor and human resources com., 1981—, also mem. armed service, joint econ., labor and human resources (chmn. full com., chmn. subcom. on health 1971-80) and judiciary coms. Author: Decisions for a Decade, 1968, In Critical Condition: The Crisis in America's Health Care, 1972, Our Day and Generation, 1979, (with Mark O. Hatfield) Freeze: How You Can Help Prevent Nuclear War, 1979. Pres. Joseph P. Kennedy, Jr. Found., from 1961; trustee Children's Hosp. Med. Ctr., Boston, John F. Kennedy Library, Boston Symphony (emeritus), John F. Kennedy Ctr. for Performing Arts, Robert F. Kennedy Meml. Found., Boston Coll., Mass. Gen. Hosp. Served with AUS, 1951-53. Decorated knight comdr. Order of Phoenix (Greece), grande croce Al Merito della Republica Italiana (Italy), Order el Sol (Peru); named One of 10 Outstanding Young Men, U.S. Jaycees, 1967; recipient meritorious svc. citation U.S. Com. for Refugees and Am. Immigration and Citizenship Coun., Solidarity award Nat. Conf. on Soviet Jewry, award Nat. Mil. Family Assn., 1985, Homeric award Chian Fedn., Scopus award Am. Friends Hebrew U., Hubert H. Humphrey award Leadership Conf. on Civil Rights, others. Mem. Tech. Assessment Bd., Congl. Friends of Ireland, Biomed. Ethics Bd., Arms Control Observer Group, Commn. on the Bicentennial of the U.S. Constitution, Martin Luther King Jr. Fed. Holiday Commn., NAACP. Office: US Senate 315 Russell Senate Bldg Washington DC 20510*

KENNEDY, ELLEN WOODMAN, educator; b. Laconia, N.H., June 23, 1950; d. Arthur Stone and Rosemary (Jackson) Woodman; m. Thomas Daniel Kennedy, July 27, 1974 (dec. Aug. 1988); children: Susan Elaine, Margaret Ann. BE, Keene State Coll., 1973; MS, So. Conn. State U., 1982. Cert. tchr., N.H., Conn. Tchr. home econs. Cen. High Sch., Manchester, N.H., 1974-75, High and Middle Schs., West Haven, Conn., 1975-83; adult edn. tchr. Derry (N.H.) Adult Edn., 1974—; freelance clothing decorator. Author: New England Saturday Night Suppers, 1988. Mem. ASCD, NAFE, Am. Home Econs. Assn., N.H. Home Econs. Assn., Am. Quilters Assn. Republican. Congregationalist. Home and Office: 452 Mammoth Rd Londonderry NH 03053

KENNEDY, HARRIET FORTE, museum administrator; b. Cambridge, Mass., 1939; d. Dalton H. and Ruby M. (Scott) Forte; divorced; children: Dana, Justin. Cert. in arts adminstrn., Harvard U., 1974; BA in Art His-

tory cum laude, Northeastern U., 1977. Asst. registrar Mus. Fine Arts, Boston, 1968-73; asst. dir., registrar Mus. Nat. Ctr. Afro-Am. Artists, Boston, 1973—, curator, 1980—; prof. art history Mass. Coll. of Art, Boston, 1980-83, Northeastern U., Boston, 1979-80, Simmons Coll., Boston, 1989-90. Compiler art book: Bessie Smith, 1988, also various catalogues. Mem. Medford (Mass.) Fair Housing Commn., 1985—; mem. Medford Arts Coun., 1970's. Mem. Am. Assn. Mus./Internat. Coun. Mus. (mus. partnership 1983), Afro-Am. Mus. Assn. (past sec., past parliamentarian), Nat. Conf. Artists, Cambridge Art Assn. (past bd. dirs.). Home: 12 Sharon St Medford MA 02155-6718 Office: Afro-Am Artists Inc 300 Walnut Ave Roxbury MA 02119-1369

KENNEDY, JAMES HARRINGTON, editor, publisher; b. Lawrence, Mass., Feb. 20, 1924; s. James H. and Margaret Helen (Hyde) K.; m. Sheila Conway, July 1, 1950; children: Kathleen, Brian, Kevin, Gail, Patricia, Maureen, Constance. BS, Lowell Textile Inst., 1948; MS, MIT, 1950. Mgmt. trainee Chicopee Mfg. Corp., Manchester, N.H., 1950-51; mng. editor Textile World McGraw Hill Pub. Co., Greenville, S.C., 1951-54; dir. communications Bruce Payne & Assocs., Westport, Conn., 1954-58; pres. James H. Kennedy & Co., Westport, 1958-70; editor, pub. Cons. News, Fitzwilliam, N.H., 1970—, Exec. Recruiter News, 1980—. Founder Fitzwilliam Conservation Corp., pres., 1970-72; chmn. Fitzwilliam Sq. Dances, 1970-80; mem. Fitzwilliam Planning Bd., 1970-72; trustee Am. Liquid Trust, Greenwich, Conn., 1975-78. Served to capt., inf. AUS, 1942-46. Mem. Fitzwilliam Hist. Soc., Acad. Mgmt., N.Y. Bus. Press Editors, Phi Psi. Republican. Roman Catholic. Clubs: Fitzwilliam Swimming (pres. 1978-84), Nat. Press. Address: Templeton Turnpike Fitzwilliam NH 03447

KENNEDY, JOHN WILLIAM, manufacturing company executive; b. Summit, N.J., May 20, 1956; s. William John and Jean Mary (Krutisia) K.; m. Cecelia Marie Hamrock, Dec. 26, 1981. BS with honors, North Adams State Coll., 1978; MBA with honors, Columbia Pacific U., 1987, BS in Indsl. Engring., 1988. Cert. tchr., N.J. Tchr. Mountainside (N.J.) Sch. Dist., 1979-82, Chatham (N.J.) Boro Sch. Dist., 1982-83; plant mgr. The Chatham Club Recreation Ctr., 1982-85; ops. mgr. Coleman Equipment, Inc., Irvington, N.J., 1985-91; project mgr. automated sorting systems div. Sandvik Process Systems, Totowa, N.J., 1991—; plant mgr., ops. mgr., cons., Madison (N.J.) Community Pool., 1971-87. Co-patentee, vacuum lifter, air logic weightless circuit; contbr. tech. articles to trade publs. Active Denville (N.J.) area Boy Scouts Am., 1984—, chmn. dist. advancement com., 1990—; mem. area com. Spl. Olympics, Flanders, N.J., 1987—, event dir., Morris, Sussex and Warren counties, 1988—. Named Eagle Scout Boy Scouts Am., 1970. Mem. Am. Mgmt. Assn., Inst. Indsl. Engring., Internat. Platform Assn. Republican. Roman Catholic. Home: 2 Burnet Rd Madison NJ 07940-1206 Office: Sandvik Seamco Systems 29 Commerce Way Totowa NJ 07512-1154

KENNEDY, JOSEPH PATRICK, II, congressman; b. Brighton, Mass., Sept. 24, 1952; s. Robert F. and Ethel (Skakel) Kennedy; m. Sheila Rauch, 1979 (div.); 2 children: Joseph P. III, Matthew. Grad., U. Mass., Boston, 1976. Chmn. Citizens' Energy Corp.; mem. 100th-102nd Congress from 8th Mass. dist., 1986—; mem. com. on banking, fin. and urban affairs, com. on vets.' affairs, select com. on aging 100th-101st Congress from 8th Mass. dist. Active Can. Robert F. Kennedy Meml. Democrat. Office: Ho of Reps Office House Mems Washington DC 20515*

KENNEDY, MAY GRABBE, congressional staff member; b. Jacksonville, Fla., July 19, 1951; d. William Eugene and May (Haverty) G. BA cum laude, Ga. State U., 1974, MA, 1978, PhD, 1982. Rsch. assoc. Yale U., New Haven, 1979-80; grad. rsch. asst. Ga. State U., Atlanta, 1981-82; asst. prof. dept. psychology Mercer U., Macon, Ga., 1982-88; congl. fellow APA, Washington, 1988-89; cons. NIMH, Rockville, Md., 1990, Planned Parenthood Fedn. of Am., Washington, 1989; profl. staff Select Com. on Children, Youth and Families, U.S. Congress, Washington, 1990—; cons. Med. Ctr. of Cen. Ga., Macon, 1985-89; researcher Macon/Bibb County Pub. Schs., 1982-85. Contbr. articles to profl. jours. Mem. Infant Mortality Coalition, Macon; charter mem. Cen. Georgians for Cen. Am., Macon. Congl. Sci. fellow APA, 1988. Mem. APA (coord. Com. on Women, div. 27 1989-91, reg. coord. S.E. div. 27, 1985-87), Am. Psychol. Soc., southeastern Psychol. Assn.

KENNEDY, ROBERT DELMONT, petrochemical company executive; b. Pitts., Nov. 8, 1932; s. Thomas Reed and Lois (Smith) K.; m. Sally Duff, Jan. 28, 1956; children: Robert Boyd, Kathleen Tyson, Thomas Alexander, Melissa Kristine. BSMechE, Cornell U., 1955. With Union Carbide Corp., 1955—; various positions with Nat. Carbon div., 1957-77, pres. Linde Div., N.Y.C., 1977-82, sr. v.p. corp., 1981, exec. v.p., 1982, pres., chief oper. officer chemicals and plastics, 1985-86, pres., chief exec. officer Union Carbide Corp., Apr., 1986—, chmn., chief exec. officer, Dec., 1986—. Past mem. bd. govs. Internat. Sch. Geneva; chmn. bd. trustees, New Hampton Sch.; moderator program humanistic studies Aspen, 1979—, bd. trustees; chmn. Inroads, Inc. Recipient Internat. Palladium medal Societe de Chime Industrielle, 1991. Fellow Am. Inst. Chemists (hon.); mem. Chem. Mfrs. Assn. (chmn. bd. 1989-90, former chmn. exec. com.). Office: Union Carbide Corp 38C Grove St Ridgefield CT 06877-4657

KENNEDY, ROBERT SPAYDE, engineering educator; b. Augusta, Kans., Dec. 9, 1933; s. Kirk Randel and Marene Lucile (Spayde) K.; m. Eleanor Emma Stagliola, June 27, 1981; children: Carole Lesley, Nancy Allison, Nina Margret. BSEE, U. Kans., 1955; MSEE, MIT, 1957, DSc in EE, 1963. Instr. engring. MIT, Cambridge, 1958-63, asst. prof., 1963-67, assoc. prof., 1967-74, prof., 1974—; Dir. MIT Communication Forum, 1986-88; housemaster MacGregor House, MIT, 1985-91. Author: Fading Dispersive Communication Channels, 1968; contbr. numerous articles to jours. in field. Lt. USNR, 1955-57. Fellow IEEE (pres. info. theory group 1976-77). Home: 3 Green St Eastport ME 04631-1315 Office: MIT Dept of Elec Engring Rm 35-211 Cambridge MA 02139

KENNEDY, THOMAS PATRICK, financial executive; b. N.Y.C., Oct. 13, 1932; s. Andrew Francis and Marie P. (Scullen) K.; m. Mary P. Drennan, Jan. 14, 1956 (dec.); children: Thomas Patrick, Kevin M., Michael J., Mary P., Deborah A. BS, St. Peter's Coll., 1958; postgrad., Seton Hall U., 1959. Accountant, Haskins & Sells, CPAs, N.Y.C., 1953-54, 55-57; staff Emerson Radio & TV, N.Y.C., 1957-58; various exec. positions CBS, N.Y.C., 1958-67; with Ford Found., N.Y.C., 1967; dir. fin. Pub. Broadcasting Lab., N.Y.C., 1967-69; with Children's TV Workshop (Sesame St.), N.Y.C., 1969-80, v.p. fin. and adminstrn., 1969-78, treas. 1969-78, sr. v.p., 1978-80; exec. dir. Ctr. Non-Broadcast TV, 1980-85; pres. Tomken Mgmt., Ltd., 1980—, chmn. bd., 1983—; chmn. bd., chief exec. officer Effie Techs. Inc., 1984—; v.p., corp. fin. Jersey Capital Mkts Group, Inc., 1987-88; chief exec. officer, chmn. bd. Corp. Strategies Group, Inc., 1988-89; v.p. Vantage Securities, Inc. (coventure with Whitehall Fin. Group), 1991—; cons. in field; bd. advisers Franciscan Communication Ctr.; bd. dirs., exec. dir. Ctr. for Non-Broadcast TV, 1980-85. With C.E., U.S. Army, 1954-55. Mem. Fin. Exec. Inst., Internat. Radio and TV Soc., Inst. Broadcast Fin. Mgmt., Nat. Assn. Accountants, Internat. Broadcast Inst., Internat. Inst. Communication, Internat. Assn. Fin. Execs., Am. Assn. Ind. Investors. Roman Catholic. Home: 7004 Blvd E 3-21 F Guttenberg NJ 07093 Office: Ste 2D 150 Ocean Lane Dr Miami FL 33149-1416

KENNEDY, TRAVER HALL, high technology consultant; b. Evanston, Ill., Mar. 1, 1952; s. Traver Hall Tomberlin and Martha (Cory) Kennedy; m. M. Deborah Reis, June 26, 1976 (div. Dec. 1988); children: Kathryn Rose, Graham Stevens, Elizabeth Van Der Veer. AB, Bowdoin Coll., 1975; postgrad., MIT, 1986. Staff worker Headstart, Brunswick, Maine, 1975-77; pres., chief exec. officer MacBeans Audio & Video, Brunswick, 1977-85; dir. bus. devel. Coastal Computer Ctrs., Brunswick, 1985-88; chief mktg. officer, corp. v.p., bd. dirs. Computerland Maine and Third Wave Systems, Brunswick, 1988-89; co-founder Ainslee Assocs., Portland, Maine, 1989—; chmn. Maine Digital Rec., Inc., Brunswick, 1983-84; pres. Delta Sigma Corp., Brunswick, 1982-85. Contbr. to mag. Bd. dirs. Maine Festival, Inc., Portland, 1981-82; mem. fin. com. Tom Andrews for Congress, 1990. Mem. Assn. Systems Mgrs. Democrat. Office: Ainslee Assocs 290 Baxter Blvd Portland ME 04101-1620

KENNEDY, VERONICA MARY SYLVIA, English educator; b. London, June 11, 1930; came to the U.S., 1957; d. George Langton and Eveline Mary (White) Wilson; m. William Henry Joseph Kennedy, Oct. 9, 1965; 1 child, Francesca Mary Sylvia. BA, St. Hilda's Coll., Oxford U., Eng., 1951; MA, Oxford U., 1955, London U., 1955. Teaching asst. U. Wash., Seattle, 1954; asst. mistress English high sch. England, 1955-57; teaching asst. U. Calif., Berkeley, 1957-58; instr. English Coll. Notre Dame, Belmont, Calif., 1958-62, Elmira (N.Y.) Coll., 1962-64; lectr. English CUNY, 1964-65; asst. prof. English St. John's U., Jamaica, N.Y., 1965—; editorial bd. mem. Studies in Medievalism, Holland, Mich., 1982—. Contbr. numerous articles, poems, reviews, stories, and puzzles to profl. jours. Recipient various scholarships; Fulbright travel grantee, 1954. Mem. N.E. MLA, Sci. Fiction Rsch. Assn., N.Y. Browning Soc., Studies in Medievalism. Roman Catholic.

KENNEDY, WARREN CHARLES, mechanical engineer; b. Pitts., Dec. 25, 1941; s. Charles Edward and Seda Emma (Shalamunec) K.; m. Karen Lucille Rothaupt, Aug. 20, 1988. BSME, U. Pitts., 1964; MSME, Carnegie Mellon U., Pitts., 1966; PhD, Carnegie Mellon U., 1972. Sr. engr. Westinghouse Rsch. Lab., Pitts., 1969-75; asst. prof. mech. engring. Gannon U., Erie, Pa., 1976-81; vis. assoc. prof. mech. engring. Union Coll., Schenectady, N.Y., 1981-85; adj. assoc. prof. Rensselaer Poly. Inst., Troy, N.Y., 1985-89; prin. engr. Elec. Boat div. Gen. Dynamics, Groton, Conn., 1989-92; with J I L Systems Inc., Groton, 1992—. Contbr. articles to profl. jours.; patentee in field.

KENNEDY, WILLIAM BURTON, university administrator; b. Detroit, Apr. 24, 1928; s. Walter John and Theresa Elizabeth (Burton) K.; m. Irene Mary Armstrong, June 20, 1959; children: Patrick Leo, Brian Francis, Kevin Michael. AB in History magna cum laude, U. Bridgeport, 1953; AM in Am. Civilization, U. Pa., 1954; postgrad., columbia U., 1954-57. Mem. editorial staff Bridgeport (Conn.) Post Pub. Co., 1953-54; dir. alumni rels. U. Bridgeport, 1954-65, spl. asst. to chancellor for spl. events, 1965-67, instr. history, 1955-64; asst. to pres., asst. prof. history Sacred Heart U., Fairfield, Conn., 1967-77, assoc. prof. history, cons. govt. rels., 1977-80, assoc. v.p. pub. affairs, 1980-83, v.p. pub. affairs, 1983—. Mem. Conn. Conf. Ind. Colls., Coun. Advancement and Support of Edn., Algonquin Club Bridgeport, Bridgeport Regional Bus. Coun., Lions. Roman Catholic. Office: Sacred Heart U 5151 Park Ave Fairfield CT 06432-1000

KENNEDY, WILLIAM JAMES, pharmaceutical company executive; b. Troy, N.Y., Dec. 4, 1944; s. James Francis and Marjorie (Albrecht) K.; m. Mary Monika Silasz, July 22, 1967; children: Susan M., John R., Morgan E. BS, Siena Coll., Loudonville, N.Y., 1966; MA, Clark U., Worcester, Mass., 1969; PhD, SUNY, Buffalo, 1975. Assoc. dir. drug regulatory affairs Pfizer Pharms., N.Y.C., 1977-80; asst. dir. drug regulatory affairs Berlex Labs., Morristown, N.J., 1980-81; dir. drug regulatory affairs Kali Pharma, Elizabeth, N.J., 1981-82, GD Searle & Co., Skokie, Ill., 1982-86; v.p. drug regulatory affairs ICI Pharms. Group, Wilmington, Del., 1986—; cons. various pharm. cos., 1981-86. Contbr. articles to profl. jours. and chpts. to books. NIH fellow, 1971-75. Mem. Pharm. Mfrs. Assn. (chmn. drug regulatory affairs com. 1991), Del. Valley Regulatory Affairs Forum (chmn. 1988), Nat. Acad. Sci. Home: 116 Marcella Rd Wilmington DE 19803-3411 Office: ICI Pharms Group Concord Pike & New Murphy Wilmington DE 19897

KENNEDY, WILLIAM THOMAS, accountant; b. Pottsville, Pa., Oct. 27, 1938; s. Francis J. and Madeline R. (Sheridan) K.; m. Marilyn T. McLaughlin, Sept. 28, 1963; children: Maureen, Tracey, Christine, Scott. BS, Mt. St. Mary's Coll., Emmitsburg, Mo., 1960. CPA. Ptnr. Ernst & Young, N.Y.C., 1961—; Trustee N.Y. Med. Coll. Valhalla, 1990—; dean's adv. com. Rutgers Grad. Sch. Mgmt., Newark, 1985-87. Mem. AICPA, N.Y. State Soc. CPAs, N.Y. Athletic Club, Spring Brook Country Club. Roman Catholic. Office: Ernst & Young 277 Park Ave New York NY 10172-0003

KENNELLY, BARBARA B., congresswoman; b. Hartford, Conn., July 10, 1936; d. John Moran and Barbara (Leary) Bailey; m. James J. Kennelly, Sept. 26, 1959; children: Eleanor Bride, Barbara Leary, Louise Moran, John Bailey. BA in Econs, Trinity Coll., Washington, 1958; grad., Harvard-Radcliffe Sch. Bus. Adminstrn., 1959; M.A. in Govt, Trinity Coll., Hartford, 1971. Mem. Hartford Ct. of Common Council, 1975-79; sec. of state State of Conn., Hartford, 1979-83; mem. 98th-102nd Congresses from 1st Dist. Conn., Hartford, 1982—. Trustee Trinity Coll., Hartford, Conn.; previously active in numerous civic, polit., and govt. orgns. in Greater Hartford, Conn. Democrat. Roman Catholic. Office: 204 Cannon House Office Bldg Washington DC 20515*

KENNEVAN, WALTER JAMES, educator; b. N.Y.C., Aug. 29, 1912; s. David Patrick and Ellen Kathleen (Grogan) K.; m. Marguerite Roberta Stevens, Oct. 12, 1940; children: JoEllen Kennevan Berlin, Steven. BS in Commerce, Catholic U. Am., 1938, MS in Commerce, 1940, M Fiscal Adminstrn., 1943. Mgmt. supr. Nat. Capital Housing Authority, Washington, 1942-48; asst. comptroller Bur. Ordnance U.S. Dept. Navy, Washington, 1948-57; dir. computer systems Office of Navy Comptroller Washington, 1957-69; prof. info. sci. Am. U., Washington, 1969-77, prof. emeritus, 1977—; cons. NIH, Washington, 1964-65, U.S. Dept. State, Washington, 1964-65, U.S. Civil Svc. Commn., Washington, 1964-65. Author: Management and Computer Systems, 1973; contbr. articles to numerous publs. Mem. Cen. Suffrage Com. D.C., 1946-47, Vets. of the Battle of the Bulge. Staff sgt. U.S. Army, 1943-46, ETO. Mem. Soc. Info. Mgmt. (nat. sec. 1975), Acad. Mgmt., Assn. Systems Mgmt., Ancient Order of Hibernians, Kenwood Country Club. Democrat. Roman Catholic. Home: 5218 Marlyn Dr Bethesda MD 20816-1947

KENNEY, DONNA DENISE, accountant; b. Bklyn., Oct. 4, 1960; d. Donald and Sherry Sheila (Nedol) Yules; m. Eugene L. Kenney, Jr., May 31, 1981; children: Kyle Asher, Graham Stewart. BBA in Bus. Mgmt., Adelphi U., 1981, MBA with distinction, 1989. CPA, N.Y. Jr. acct. Claude A. Isaac, Pub. Acct., Freeport, N.Y., 1987; grad. asst. dept. acctg. and law Adelphi U., Garden City, N.Y., 1984-89; sr. acct. Kreitzman Barragato and Kreitzman, CPAs, Smithtown, N.Y., 1989-91, Kreitzman and Kreitzman, CPAs, Smithtown, 1992—. Mem. N.Y. State Soc. CPAs (com. mem. acctg. and auditing Suffolk chpt. 1991—, award of honor 1989), Delta Mu Delta, Eta Chi Alpha. Office: Kreitzman and Kreitzman 9 Brooksite Dr Smithtown NY 11787-3400

KENNEY, JOHN MICHEL, architect; b. N.Y.C., Oct. 22, 1938; s. John Peter and Madeline Loretta (Fuller) K.; m. Karin Suominen, Aug. 20, 1989; children: John Michel, James Brian, Dion Patrick. AAS, Orange County Community Coll., 1966; student, Columbia U., 1969. Registered architect, N.Y., N.J., Conn., Pa., Del. V.p., ptnr., dir. health facilities Perkins & Will Architects, White Plains, N.Y., 1968-81; pres. Architecture for Health Sci. and Commerce, P.C., White Plains, 1981—. Vice chmn. Orange County Dem. Coms., N.Y., 1968; chmn. Dem. Com., Middletown, N.Y., 1966-68; co-chmn. Robert Kennedy Presdl. Election Primary, Orange/Sullivan County, 1968. Mem. Nat. Coun. of Archtl. Registration Bds., N.Y. Soc. Hosp. Planning, Am. Assn. Hosp. Planners, N.Y. Acad. Scis. Democrat. Office: AHSC Architects 777 Old Saw Mill River Rd Tarrytown NY 10591-6700

KENNY, ROBERT MARTIN, human resources executive, consultant. BA in Eng./Psychology, NYU, 1972, MBA in Organizational Devel., 1987; postgrad., Saybrook Inst., 1991—. Sr. employee rels. counselor, mgmt. trainee Fed. Res. Bank, N.Y.C., 1972-73; human resources adminstr. Internat. Ctr. for Integrative Studies, N.Y.C., 1973-85; nat. human resources adminstr. The Door-A Ctr. of Alternatives, and Adolescent Health Ctr., N.Y.C., 1985-87, dir. human resources, 1988—; mgr. human resource planning Citibank, N.Y.C., 1987-88; cons. in field, 1986—. Pres. bd. dirs. West 13th St. Owners N.Y.C., 1979-84; active nat. election campaigns, N.Y.C., 1972—. Regents scholar N.Y. State Bd. Regents, 1968; Christopher Connell scholar Cathedral Coll., 1968. Mem. APA, ASTD, Assn. Humanistic Psychology, Met. Assn. Applied Psychology, Soc. Human Resource Mgmt., Organizational Devel. Network, Beta Gamma Sigma. Office: The Door A Ctr Alternatives 121 Ave of The Americas 3d Fl New York NY 10013-1510

KENNY, SHIRLEY STRUM, college administrator; b. Tyler, Tex., Aug. 28, 1934; d. Marcus Leon and Florence (Golenternek) S.; m. Robert Wayne Kenny July 22, 1956; children: David Jack, Joel Strum, Daniel Clark, Jonathan Matthew, Sarah Elizabeth. BA, BJ, U. Tex., 1955; MA, U. Minn., 1957; PhD, U. Chgo., 1964; LHD (hon.), U. Rochester, 1988. Chair English dept. U. Md., College Park, 1973-79, provost Arts and Humanities, 1979-85; pres. CUNY Queens Coll., Flushing, 1985—; bd. dirs. Toys 'R' Us, Chem. Bank Regional Adv. Bd. Author: The Conscious Lovers, 1968, The Plays of Richard Steele, 1971, The Performers and Their Plays, 1982, The Works of George Farquhar, 2 vols.,1988; editor: British Theatre and the Other Arts, 1984; contbr. numerous articles to profl. jours. Bd. dirs. Carnegie Found. for the Advancement of Teaching, Goodwill of Greater N.Y., Seagrams Scholarship; mem. com. Regional Plan Assn. N.Y. Recipient Disting. Alumnus award U. Chgo. Club Washington, 1980, Svc. and Leadership award N.Y. Urban League, 1988; named Outstanding Woman, U. Md., 1983, Outstanding Alumnus, U. Tex. Coll. Communication, 1989. Mem. Am. Handel Soc., MLA, Am. Soc. for Theatre Rsch., Am. Soc. for 18th Century Studies, Bibliog. Soc. Va., Sigma Alpha Iota. Office: CUNY Queens Coll 65-30 Kissena Blvd Flushing NY 11367

KENSINGER, RICHARD GERALD, social worker, psychotherapist; b. Smock, Pa., Nov. 17, 1947; s. Richard Lincoln and Elizabeth Ann (Cvengros) K.; m. Paula Leskovic, June 19, 1972; children: Mindi Cecile, Bradley Richard. BA, Calif. (Pa.) State U., 1969; MSW, W. Va. U., 1976. Lic. social worker, Pa. Psychotherapist Mon Valley Mental Health, Monessen, Pa., 1976-77; clin. supr. Altoona (Pa.) Hosp. Ctr. Mental Health Svc., 1977—. Staff sgt. USAF, 1969-73. Mem. Nat. Assn. Social Workers. Republican. Roman Catholic. Office: Altoona Hosp CMHS 620 Howard Ave Altoona PA 16601-4899

KENT, ALLEN, library and information sciences educator; b. N.Y.C., Oct. 24, 1921; s. Samuel and Anna (Begun) K.; m. Rosalind Kossoff, Jan. 24, 1943; children: Merryl Frances Kent Samuels, Emily Beth Kent Yeager, Jacqueline Diane Kent Maryak, Carolyn May Kent Hall. B.S. in Chemistry, CCNY, 1942. Sci. editor Intersci. Pubs., 1946-51; research assoc. Ctr. Internat. Studies, MIT, 1951-53; prin. documentation engr. Battelle Meml. Inst., Columbus, Ohio, 1953-55; asso. dir. Ctr. for Documentation and Communication Research; prof. library sci. Western Res. U., Cleve., 1955-63; dir. office communications programs, chmn. interdisciplinary doctoral program info. sci., prof. info. sci., edn. and computer sci. U. Pitts., 1963-76; Univ. Disting. Service prof. library and info. sci. and assoc. dean U. Pitts. Sch. Library and Info. Sci., 1976-91, interim dean, 1985-86, prof. emeritus, 1992; mem. mgmt. info. com. Health and Welfare Assn. Allegheny County, Pa., 1972-80; dir. Marcel Dekker, Inc., N.Y., 1978—. Author: (with others) Machine Literature Searching, 1956, (with J. W. Perry) Documentation and Information Retrieval, 1957, Tools for Machine Literature Searching, 1958, Centralized Information Services, 1958, Mechanized Information Retrieval, 1962, 2d edit., 1966; also fgn. transls. Specialized Information Centers, 1965; Information Analysis and Retrieval, 1971, Resource Sharing in Libraries, 1977, On-Line Revolution in Libraries, 1978, Structure and Governance of Library Networks, 1979, Use of Library Materials, 1979, Information Technology, 1982; editor, co-editor numerous books in field; exec. editor: Ency. Library and Info. Sci, 1968—, Ency. Computer Sci. and Tech, 1972—, Ency. Microcomputers, 1984—, Ency. of Telecommunications, 1988—. Chmn. bd. Interuniv. Communications Council Inc., 1971-74. Served with USAAF, 1942-46. Recipient Info. Tech. Merit award Eastman Kodak Co., 1968. Fellow AAAS; mem. Assn. Computing Machinery, ALA, Am. Soc. Info. Sci. (Award of Merit 1977, Award for Best Info. Sci. Book of Yr. 1980, Pioneer in Info. Sci. 1987), Acad. Sr. Profls. Eckerd Coll., Cosmos Club. Home: Cochran Hall 911 1500 Cochran Rd Pittsburgh PA 15243-1061 Office: U Pitts Sch Libr and Info Sci Pittsburgh PA 15260

KENT, DONALD PAUL, community organization development executive; b. Manhasset, N.Y., Aug. 10, 1954; s. Louis and Ruth (Dreier) K.; m. Ellen Goosenberg, Sept. 9, 1990. BA in Internat. Rels., Beloit Coll., 1977; MA in Higher Edn. Adminstrn., Columbia U., 1983. Asst. dean of students Manhattan Coll., Riverdale, N.Y., 1979-80; asst. dir. Earl Hall Columbia U., N.Y.C., 1980-84; nat. dir. orgns. Statue of Liberty-Ellis Island Found., N.Y.C., 1985-86; asst. dir. endowment devel. Coun. Jewish Fedn., N.Y.C., 1987-88, assoc. dir. endowment devel., 1988-89, dir. endowment devel., 1989-92; asst. exec. dir. Coun. Jewish Fedns., N.Y.C., 1992—; commr. UAHC Eisner Inst. Commn., Great Barrington, Mass., 1989—; mem. exec. bd. Planned Giving Group of Greater N.Y., N.Y.C., 1991—; membership com. mem. Nat. Com. on Planned Giving, Indpls., 1992—. Editor newsletter The Endowment Review, 1990—. Chmn. tenth yr. reunion Beloit (Wis.) Coll., 1987.

KENT, GORDON DONALD, research electrical engineer; b. Pittsfield, Mass., Oct. 1, 1920; s. Rockwell II and Kathleen (Whiting) K.; m. Phyllis A. Kennedy, Dec. 13, 1956 (div. 1986); 1 child, David G. BS in Engring., U. Wis., 1947; MS in Engring., Stanford U., 1950, PhD in Engring., 1953. Rsch. asst. Stanford (Calif.) U., 1948-52; rsch. engr. Inst. Advanced Studies, Princeton, N.J., 1952-53; rsch. fellow Harvard U., Cambridge, Mass., 1953-57; assoc. prof. Syracuse (N.Y.) U., 1957-63, prof., 1963-86; rsch. engr. Dielectric Labs. Inc., Cazenovia, N.Y., 1986-90; proprietor GDK Products, Cazenovia, 1991—; cons. Sperry, L.I., N.Y., 1954-55, GE, Syracuse, 1960-66, Brit. Petroleum-Am., Cleve., 1988; guest prof. Eidgenösiche Technische Hochschüle, Zurich, 1964. Contbr. articles to profl. jours.; patentee in field. Sgt. U.S. Army, 1941-45. Home and Office: 1995 Stanley Rd Cazenovia NY 13035-9314

KENT, HOWARD LEES, obstetrician, gynecologist; b. Norristown, Pa., Nov. 27, 1930; s. Howard Linnaeus and Margaret (Cairns) K.; m. Margaret Louise Hermanutz, Oct. 17, 1959; children: Howard Lees Jr., Lisanne, Margaret, Kristyn. AB in Zoology, U. Pa., 1952; MD, Hahnemann U., 1958. Diplomate Am. Bd. Ob-Gyn. Pvt. practice Hammonton, N.J., 1964-81; assoc. prof. Thomas Jefferson U., Phila., 1982—. Author: (with others) Vaginitis/Vaginosis, 1991; editor: Proceedings-Obstetrical Society of Philadelphia, 1980-82; contbr. articles to profl. jours. Fellow Internat. Soc. for Study of Vulvar Disease, Royal Soc. Medicine, Am. Coll. Ob-gyn. (key contact), Am. Coll. Surgeons, Coll. Physicians of Phila. (libr. com. 1980-89), Obstet. Soc. Phila. (asst. sec. 1978-81); mem. N.J. Ob-gyn. Soc., Vesper Club, U. Pa. Alumni. Republican.

KENT, IRWIN I., consulting actuary; b. Bayonne, N.J., May 15, 1923; s. John and Bessie (Handelman) K.; m. Marian Kavrell, Nov. 28, 1948; 1 child, Kenneth Alan. BS, U. Iowa, 1942; postgrad., U. N.Mex., 1942-43, Calif. Inst. Tech., 1943-44, U. Mich., 1946-47. Cons. actuary, v.p. Pension Planning Co., N.Y.C., 1947-61; cons. actuary, pres. Actuarial Svcs., Inc., Union, N.J., 1961-86; v.p. Alexander & Alexander Cons. Group, Inc., Lyndurst, N.J., 1986-91, Kent Cons., Lyndhurst, 1991—; cons. actuary; lectr. in field. Commr. Twp. of Cranford, N.J., 1961-69, 72. 1st lt. USAF, 1943-46. Fellow Conf. Actuaries in Pub. Practice (pres. 1989-90); mem. Am. Acad. Actuaries, Soc. Actuaries, Enrolled Actuaries Meeting Com. (chmn. 1986-87). Republican. Home: 46 Lenhome Dr Cranford NJ 07016-2953 Office: Alexander & Alexander Cons Group Inc 125 Chubb Ave Fl 2D Lyndhurst NJ 07071-3504

KENT, JEANNE YVONNE, artist; b. Lawrence, Mass., Feb. 6, 1947; d. Gerard George and Cecile Fecteau Galarneau; m. Martin Joseph Kent, Dec. 4, 1971; 1 child, Nicole Michelle. Student, Lowell State Tchr.'s Coll., 1966-68, Northeastern U., 1970-73; BFA, Mass. Coll. Art, 1989. Resident asst., slide lectr. Elderhostel Mass. Coll. Art, Boston, 1988; slide lectr. Weymouth North High Sch., East Weymouth, Mass., 1990; instr. art Lee Wards Arts and Crafts Store, Quincy, Mass., 1990. Exhibited in group shows at Mass. Coll. Art, Boston, 1988-89, Rubin O'Barry's Coffee Shop, Jamaica Plain, Mass., 1989, Arts in the Pks., Boston, 1989, Brookline (Mass.) Art Soc., 1989-90, Boston Visual Artist's Union, 1990, Arnold Arboretum of Harvard U., Jamaica Plain, 1992; author poetry. Recipient Silver medal World of Poetry, 1989, Intergenerational Poetry hon. mention award West Roxbury Pub. Libr., 1989, 4th Pl. award (painting) Dedham Arts and Crafts Fair, 1990; poems named the Best Poems of the 90's, Nat. Libr. Poetry. Mem. Mass. Indoor Tennis Assn., West Roxbury Art Assn., Dedham Art Assn., Dedham Racquetime Athletic Club. Home: 5 Eastland Rd Jamaica Plain MA 02130

KENT, KENNETH MITCHELL, medicine educator; b. Tifton, Ga., July 19, 1938; s. Joseph and Allene (Mitchell) K.; m. Diane Chapman, Dec. 1969 (div. 1984); children: Mark, Laura; m. Carolyn Jane Ewels, Dec. 21, 1984; children: Elizabeth, Christopher, Stephen. BS, Emory U., 1960, MS, 1964, MD, 1965, PhD, 1970. Diplomate Am. Bd. Internal Medicine, Am. Bd. Cardiology. Intern Grady Meml. Hosp., Atlanta, 1967-68; resident Emory U. Affiliated Hosps., Atlanta, 1968-69; commd. surgeon USPHS, 1969, advanced through grades to med. dir., 1979; from sr. investigator to div. chief USPHS, NIH, Bethesda, Md., 1969-81; assoc. prof. medicine Georgetown U. Med. Ctr., Washington, 1981-90; chmn. circulatory devices panel FDA, Washington, 1988-90. Contbr. over 150 articles to med. jours. NIH grantee, 1987. Fellow Am. Coll. Cardiology, Soc. Cardiac Angiography. Office: Washington Cardiology Ctr 110 Irving St Ste 4B14 Washington DC 20010

KENT, ROBERT JOHN, marine biologist; b. N.Y.C., May 20, 1948; s. Stanley Paul and Mary Katherine (Ladany) K. BA, SUNY, Buffalo, 1970; MA in Environ. Studies, SUNY, Stony Brook, 1984. Instr. Butler County Community Coll., Butler, Pa., 1975-78; coop. extension agt., 4-H natural resources specialist Cornell Coop. Extension, Riverhead, N.Y., 1978-89; sea grant program coord. N.Y. Sea Grant, Riverhead, 1989—. Contbr. articles to profl. publs. Recipient Epsilon Sigma Phi Outstanding Team Achievement award, 1992, Outstanding Marine Edn. Program award Coastal Extension Profls., Ithaca, 1984, 86, Outstanding Program Achievement award Cornell U., 1986, State Early Career award Epsilon Sigma Phi, 1988. Mem. Coop. Extension 4-H Agts (spl. svc. award 1981), Ukrainian Nat. Assn., Ecol. Soc. Am., Nat. Marine Educators Assn., The Koscoiuszko Found. Episcopalian. Office: New York Sea Grant 39 Sound Ave Riverhead NY 11901-1114

KENYON, CHARLES LINCOLN, instrument company executive; b. Providence, Jan. 8, 1933; s. Albert Greene and Bernice Gertrude (Stairs) K.; m. Marilyn Anne Broden, June 2, 1957; children: Lisa Anne, David Broden. BA, Brown U., 1958; postgrad., U. R.I., 1960-61. Sales engr. Baldwin-Lima-Hamilton Electronics, Waltham, Mass., 1961-63, A.S.E.A. Corp., Armonk, N.Y., 1963-67; v.p. mktg. Digital Applications, Inc., N.Y.C., 1967-70; ptnr. LDE, Inc., White Plains, N.Y., 1970-78; cons. Concept Group, Old Greenwich, Conn., 1978-82; dir. research and devel. Biomatic Inc., Cranford, N.J., 1982-86; chief exec. officer Airwave Ltd., Newport, 1988—. Contbr. articles to tech. jours.; inventor bio-screen, 1987; patentee in field. Served to sgt. U.S. Army, 1953-55, Korea. Home: 14 Caswell Ave Newport RI 02840-1818

KENYON, REGAN CLAIR, research foundation executive; b. St. Louis, Jan. 31, 1949; s. Robert Clair and Nina Naoma (Giesler) K.; m. Mary Margaret Quinlan, June 2, 1979; children: Regan Clair Jr., Moriah Quinlan. BA, U. Mo., 1969, MEd, 1973; EdD, Harvard U., 1983. Tchr. Ferguson-Florissant R-2 Sch. Dist., Mo., 1971074; prin. Manor Sch., St. Croix, Virgin Islands, 1974-77; head of upper sch. Country Day Sch., St. Croix, Virgin Islands, 1977-78; exec. asst. U.S. Dept. Edn., Washington, 1978-80; adminstrv. asst. Harvard U., Cambridge, Mass., 1980-81; cons. to pres. MA Higher Edn. Assistance Corp., Boston, 1981-83; exec. dir. Secondary Sch. Admission Test Bd., Princeton, N.J., 1983-92; pres. Princeton (N.J.) Inst. for Ednl. Rsch., 1987—; cons. fed. and state govt. foundations, Washington, 1979—; dir. The Edn. Fund, Boston, N.J., 1983-88; trustee Georgine Learning Ctr., Trenton, N.J., 1986-87; founder, pres. Princeton Inst. Ednl. Rsch., Princeton, N.J., 1987—; sec. Internat. Task Force, Princeton, N.J., 1990—. contbr. articles to profl. jours.; inventor, editor in field. Mem. N.J. State Bd. Edn., Trenton, N.J., 1987-91, Nat. State Bds. Edn., Washington, 1987-91, Audit Com. N.J. State Bd. Edn., Trenton, N.J., 1989-91, Resolutions Com. Nat. State Bds., Washington, 1989. Fellow Edn. Policy for George Washington U. Inst. for Ednl. Leadership, Washington, 1978-79, U. Mo., St. Louis, 1969-71, Harvard U., 1982; Gustav Harris scholar Harvard U., 1980-83; recipient Horace Mann Prof. Contbr. citation U.S. Dept. Edn., Washington, 1980. Mem. Am. Ednl. Rsch. Assn., Inst. for Ednl. Leadership, Ednl. Excellence Network, Harvard Club, Nassau Club, Phi Delta Kappa. Roman Catholic. Home: 5 Cedar Brook Terr Princeton NJ 08540 Office: Secondary Sch Admission Test Bd 12 Stockton St Princeton NJ 08540

KENYON, ROGER ALAN, small business owner; b. Wagner, S.D., Mar. 15, 1953; s. Robert Lee and Virginia Marie (Homcho) K.; m. Patricia Maureen Sullivan, May 30, 1981. BA, Gonzaga U., 1975; PhD, U. Ottawa, Ont., Can., 1981; JCD, St. Paul U., Ottawa, 1983. Cert. elem. sch. tchr. Assoc. dir. Tribunal Cath. Archdiocese of Seattle, 1977-86; pres. eduTec, Lynwood, Wash., 1987—. Author: Existential Structures, 1976, Macintosh Introductory Programming, 1988; contbr. articles to profl. jours.; author several ednl. programs. Mem. Internat. Reading Assn., Nat. Sci. Tchrs. Assn., Apple Profl. Developers Assn., Nat. Coun. Tchrs. of Maths.

KEOCHAKIAN, SIMON V., psychologist, educator; b. Madison, Maine, May 13, 1935; s. Vartan S. and Mariam M. (Manoogian) Karchakian; m. Joan Gail Bennett, Aug. 25, 1956; children: Stephen, Gregory, Geoffrey. BS, Springfield Coll., 1958, MS, 1961; EdD, U. Mass., 1970. Lic. psychologist and guidance counselor, Mass.; cert. expressive therapist. Assoc. dir. clin. svcs. Ctr. Counseling and Academic Devel. U. Mass., Amherst, 1960—, assoc. prof. sch. edn., 1971—, dir. continuing edn. for psychologists, 1989—; vis. lectr. Lesley Coll., Cambridge, Mass., 1979; Fulbright Sr. lectr. Coun. for Internat. Exch. of Scholars, Armenia, 1982. Co-author: Access Policy and Procedure and the Law in Higher Education, 1978. Pres. Amherst chpt. SEIU Local 509 ALF-CIO, 1991—. Mem. Am. Assn. Applied and Preventive Psychology, Nat. Expressive Therapy Assn. (life). Home: 174 West st Amherst MA 01002 Office: U Mass Berkshire House Amherst MA 01003

KEOGH, PATRICK JAMES, real estate developer, lawyer; b. N.Y.C., Jan. 27, 1944; s. John and Annie Kavanagh K.; m. Amber Caroline Forrest, Feb. 5, 1966 (div. May 1986); children: Matthew, Erin. BS, Manhattan Coll., 1965; JD, Georgetown U., 1971. Bar: Va. 1971. Program analyst Pub. Bldgs. Svc., GSA, Washington, 1966-74; econ. analysis dir. Office of Info. Resource Mgmt., GSA, Washington, 1976-85; bd. chmn. First Fed. Credit Union, Washington, 1982-86; program mgr. OIRM, GSA, Washington, 1985-87, PBS, GSA, Washington, 1987-92. Author: Asset Backed Financing, 1988; contbr. various articles to profl. periodicals. Roman Catholic. Home: 6337 Georgetown Pike McLean VA 22101 Office: GSA 18th & F Sts NW Washington DC 20405

KEOHANE, NANNERL OVERHOLSER, college president, political scientist; b. Blytheville, Ark., Sept. 18, 1940; d. James Arthur and Grace (McSpadden) Overholser; m. Patrick Henry III, Sept. 16, 1962 (div. May 1969); 1 child, Stephan; m. Robert Owen Keohane, Dec. 18, 1970; children: Sarah, Jonathan, Nathaniel. BA, Wellesley Coll., 1961, Oxford U., Eng., 1963; PhD, Yale U., 1967. Faculty Swarthmore Coll., Pa., 1967-73, Stanford U., Calif., 1973-81; fellow Ctr.for Advanced Study in the Behavioral Scis. Stanford U., 1978-79, 87-88; pres., prof. polit. sci. Wellesley (Mass.) Coll., 1981—; bd. dirs. State St. Boston Corp., IBM. Author: Philosophy and the State in France: The Renaissance to the Enlightenment, 1980; co-editor: Feminist Theory: A Critique of Ideology, 1982. Trustee WGBH Ednl. TV Found., 1981—, Colonial Williamsburg Found., 1988—; bd. dirs. Carnegie Found. for Advancement of Teaching, 1986—; bd. trustees Ctr. for Advanced Study Behavioral Scis., Stanford U., 1991—. Marshall scholar, 1961-63; AAUW dissertation fellow; fellow Am. Acad. Arts and Scis. Mem. Council on Fgn. Relations, Phi Beta Kappa, Cosmopolitan Club (N.Y.C.), Saturday Club (Boston), Comml. Club (Boston), Algonquin Club. Democrat. Office: Wellesley Coll Office of Pres Wellesley MA 02181-8201

KEON, THOMAS PETER, pediatric anesthesiologist, educator; b. Detroit, June 1, 1936; s. Peter Francis and Mary Irene (McCool) K.; m. Janice Kathleen Lahue, Aug. 18, 1962; children: Peter, Elizabeth, Timothy. BS, St. Patrick's Coll., Ottawa, Ont., Can., 1959, MD, 1965. Diplomate Am. Bd. Anesthesiology, Royal Coll. Physicians and Surgeons. Intern Cooper Hosp., Camden, N.J., 1965-66; resident in anesthesia U. of Ottawa/Ottawa (Ont.) Civic Hosp.; fellow in pediatric anesthesia and critical care medicine The Children's Hosp. of Phila.; pvt. practice Almonte, Ont., 1966-71; dir. ICU Children's Hosp. Ea. Ont., Ottawa, 1975-78; assoc. prof. anesthesia U. Pa. Sch. Medicine, Phila., 1979—; anesthesiologist Children's Hosp. Phila., 1979—. Contbr. articles on anesthesiology to profl. jours., chpts. to books. Mem. AMA, Am. Soc. Anesthesiology, Am. Acad. Pediatrics. Office: Childrens Hosp Phila 34th St Civic Ctr Blvd Philadelphia PA 19104

KEONJIAN, EDWARD, engineering consultant; b. Tiflis, Georgia, Russia, Aug. 14, 1909; s. Mkrtich and Satenik K.; m. Virginia Megerian (dec. 1969); 1 child, Edward Jr. MS, PhD, Leningrad Inst. Elec. Engring., USSR, 1932, PhD, 1932. Electronics rsch. engr. Leningrad, 1932-40; assoc. prof. Inst. Elec. Engring., Leningrad, 1940-42; lectr. CCNY, N.Y.C., 1949-51; devel. engr. GE, Syracuse, N.Y., 1951-58; staff scientist ARMA div. ARMA div. American Bosch, Garden City, N.Y., 1958-64; sect. chief failure analysis Grumman Aircraft, Bethpage, N.Y., 1964-72; vis. prof. Cairo (Egypt) U., 1972-74; cons. engr. Great Neck, N.Y., 1974—. Co-author, editor 5 engring. texts; contbr. articles to profl. jours.; patentee in field. Disting. fellow Electronic Industry Assn., 1963; grantee NSF, 1970-72. Fellow IEEE (live mem. com. 1966—); mem. Explorers Club. Home: 40 Stoner Ave Great Neck NY 11021-2116

KERAMAS, JAMES GEORGE, engineering educator; b. Athens, Attica, Greece, Oct. 13, 1928; came to U.S., 1955; s. George Anthony and Irene (Poulios) K.; m. Virginia Krea, June 23, 1952; children: George, Renita Keramas Johnson. BSME, Athens Poly. Inst., Greece, 1950, MSME, 1952; MEd in Occupational Edn., Fitchburg State Coll., 1978; EdD in Occupational Edn., U. Mass., 1990. Lic. engr. Mass.; cert. vocat. edn. instr., Mass. Design engr. Simplex Wire & Cable Co., Cambridge, Mass., 1955-60; sr. project engr. W.R. Grace Co., Woburn, Mass., 1960-62; dir. engring. Fibersearch Corp., Lawrence, Mass., 1962-63; pres. Alliance Engrs. & Rsch. Corp., Woburn, Mass., 1963-71; dir. rsch. Crompton and Knowles Corp., Agawan, Mass., 1971-73; sr. cons. engr. Foster-Miller Assocs., Waltham, Mass., 1973-76, Teledyne Corp., Woburn, Mass., 1976-77; assoc. prof. Daniel Webster Coll., Nashua, N.H., 1975-77, Middlesex Community Coll., Bedford, Mass., 1976-85; prof. U. Lowell, Mass., 1984—; cons. Concord Control, Inc., Boston, 1981-86, Abrasive Products Inc., Braintree, Mass., 1983—. Author: Curriculum Development for High Technology Programs, 1990; patentee High Pile Machine, Rechargeable Battery, Shrink Wrap Machine. Supt. Sun. Sch. Greek Orthodox Ch., Woburn, 1980-85. Lt. Greek Royal Navy, 1953-55. Fellow IEEE; mem. Masons (past master), Am. Hellenic Assn. (named Industrialist 1967). Office: U Lowell One University Ave Lowell MA 01854

KERBEL, ROBERT NORTON, social service agency administrator; b. Atlantic City, May 28, 1931; s. Jules and Mamie (Feinstein) K.; m. Ruth Ptashkin, Nov. 13, 1955; children: Paul, Steven, Deborah. BA, U. Pa., 1953; MSW, Bryn Mawr Coll., 1958. Lic. social worker, Del. Dir. Jewish Fedn. South Broward, Hollywood, Fla., 1972-75, Allied Jewish Fedn. Denver, 1975-77; asst. internat. dir. B'nai B'rith Youth Orgn., Washington, 1977-83; asst. dir. Jewish Fedn. Del., Wilmington, 1983-85, exec. v.p., 1985—. Mem. NCCJ, Wilmington, 1983—; bd. dirs. Leadership Del., Wilmington, 1984—, People to People, Wilmington, 1984—. Recipient best pub. rels. award Coun. Jewish Fedns., 1990, Nat. Assn. Fund Raising Execs., Del., 1990. Mem. NASW, Acad. Cert. Social Workers, Assn. Jewish Community Orgn. Profls. (nat. bd. dirs. 1962—), Conf. Jewish Communal Svc., Del. Assn. Non Profit Orgns. (bd. dirs. 1985—), United Way Execs. (bd. dirs. Wilmington 1985—). Home: 2510 Fairlee Rd Wilmington DE 19810-3506 Office: Jewish Fedn Del 101 Garden Of Eden Rd Wilmington DE 19803-1511

KERN, DANIEL EDMUND, economist, educator; b. Rockland, Maine, Feb. 6, 1965; s. Edmund Robert and Sandra Beverly (Mullins) K. BA in Polit. Sci., Plymouth State Coll., 1988; MA in econs., Northeastern U., Boston, 1988-90. Teaching asst. Northeastern U., 1988-90; with Workers' Compensation Rsch. Inst., Cambridge, Mass., 1990-91. Mem. Pi Gamma Mu, Omicron Delta Epsilon. Home: 15 Pine Grove Rd Exeter NH 03833-4718

KERN, FRANK NORTON, lawyer; b. Waymansville, Ind., Feb. 19, 1920; s. Frank W. and Irene (Everdon) K.; m. Minnetta Louise Wooden, Apr. 9, 1944; children—Cynthia Jennifer, Candace. B.A., Ohio Wesleyan U., 1941; M.B.A. with distinction, Harvard, 1943, LL.B. cum laude, 1948. Bar: Ohio 1948, Pa. 1953, N.Y. 1956, D.C. 197. Practiced in Cleve., 1948-51, N.Y.C., 1956—; assoc. firm Squire, Sanders & Dempsey, Cleve., 1948-51; tax atty. U.S. Steel Corp., Pitts., 1951-54; ptnr. charge tax dept. Reid & Priest, N.Y.C., 1955-80. Mem. Ohio Wesleyan U. Assocs. and Investment Com., 1962—. Sr. warden Christ's Ch., Rye, N.Y., 1986—. Served to lt. with USNR, 1943-46. Mem. ABA, Inter-Am. Bar Assn., Phi Beta Kappa. Republican. Episcopalian. Clubs: Met. (Washington); Apawamis (Rye); Sky, Recess (N.Y.). Contbr. articles to profl. jours. Home: 16 Puritan Rd Rye NY 10580-1931

KERN, WERNER, chemist; b. Basel, Switzerland, Mar. 18, 1925; came to U.S. 1948; s. Karl and Josephine (Voelker) K.; m. Mildred C. Patti, Nov. 20, 1955; children: Jeffrey K., Vanessa A., Peter R. Cert. Chemistry, U. Basel, 1944; Dipl. Langs., Polyglot Sch. of Langs., Montreux, Switzerland, 1947; BA in Chemistry, Rutgers U., 1955. Chemist Hoffman-LaRoche, Basel, 1942-48; rsch. chemist Hoffman-LaRoche, Nutley, N.J., 1948-55; chief chemist Nuclear Corp. of Am., Denville, N.J., 1958-59; scientist Solid State div. RCA, Somerville, N.J., 1959-64; fellow tech. staff RCA Labs., Princeton, N.J., 1964-87; pres. Werner Kern Assocs., E. Windsor, N.J., 1987—; sr. scientist Lam Rsch. Corp., San Diego and Fremont, Calif., 1988-92; tech. cons. Teltech, Inc., Mpls., 1988—; lectr. Am. Vacuum Soc., 1981—. Co-author, editor: Thin Film Processes, 1978, Thin Film Processes II, 1991; author/editor: Silicon Wafer Cleaning Technology, 1992; contbr. articles to profl. jours. Recipient Cert. of Recognition, NASA, 1981, Cert. of Achievement, Soc. for Tech. Communications, 1986. Fellow Electrochem. Soc. (chmn. Dielectrics div. 1982-84, advisor solid state div. 1985-87, Callinan award 1971); mem. Am. Vacuum Soc., Sigma Xi. Home and Office: 439 Probasco Rd East Windsor NJ 08520-5518

KERNAGHAN, JOHN THOMAS, optician, educator, laboratory administrator; b. Drexel Hill, Pa., July 20, 1953; s. Frank John Jr. and Ernestine Elizabeth (Sapp) K.; m. Celeste DeMatteo, Apr. 28, 1979 (div. Mar. 1982); m. Nancy Lee Jones, Mar. 2, 1985. Student, Pa. State U., Media, 1971-74. Diplomate Am. Bd. Opticianry. Apprentice optician Drs. Sternberg and Zaslow, Phila., 1975-79; retail mgr. State Optical Co., Phila., 1979-87, finish lab. mgr., 1981-86; asst. retail mgr. Lens Crafters, Springfield, Pa., 1987-89, lab. mgr., 1989-91; lab. mgr. Lens Crafters, Phila., 1991—. Committeman Yeadon (Pa.) Republican Party, 1971-75. Fellow Nat. Acad. Opticians. Episcopalian. Home: 3269 Aramingo Ave Philadelphia PA 19134

KERNAN, BARBARA DESIND, senior government executive; b. N.Y.C., Jan. 11, 1939; d. Philip and Anne (Feuer) Desind; m. Joseph E. Kernan, Feb. 14, 1973. BA cum laude, Smith Coll., 1960; postgrad. Oxford U., 1963; MA, Harvard U., 1963; postgrad. in edn. policy George Washington U., 1980. Editor Harvard Law Sch., 1960-62; tchr. English, Newton High Sch. (Mass.), 1962-63; editor Allyn & Bacon Pubs., Boston, 1963-64; edn. assoc. Upward Bound, Edn. Assocs., Inc., Washington, 1965-68; edn. program specialist Title I, Elem. and Secondary Edn. Act, U.S. Office Edn., 1969-73; fellow Am. Polit. Sci. Assn., Senator William Proxmire and Congressman Alphonzo Bell, 1973-74; spl. asst. to dep. commr. for elem. and secondary edn. and dir. dissemination, sch. finance and analysis, U.S. Office Edn., 1975-77, chief program analysis br. div. edn. for disadvantaged, 1977-79; chief grant program coordination staff Office Dep. Commr. for Ednl. Resources, 1979-80; chief priority concerns staff Office Asst. Sec. Mgmt., U.S. Dept. Edn., Washington, 1980-81; dir. div. orgnl. devel. and analysis Office of Dep. Undersec. for Mgmt., 1981-86; Sr. Exec. Svc. candidate on spl. project to improve status of women Sec. Transp., Washington, 1983-84; inducted Sr. Exec. Svc., 1986; assoc. adminstr. for adminstrn. Nat. Hwy. Traffic Safety Adminstrn., U.S. Dept. Transp., 1986—, career devel. leader to presdl. mgmt. interns, 1989-91. Recipient awards U.S. Office Edn., 1969, 71, 77, U.S. Dept. Edn., 1981-86, U.S. Dept. Transp., 1991, Small Agy. Coun., 1990; scholarships U. Mich., 1956-58, Smith Coll., 1958-60, Harvard U., 1962-63; Am. Polit. Sci. Assn. fellow, 1973-74; Sr. Exec. fellow John F. Kennedy Sch. Govt. Harvard U., 1983.

KERNER, DANIELLA, artist, educator; b. Tel-Aviv, Israel, May 24, 1952; d. David and Miriam (Hmelnitsky) K. BFA, Sir George Williams U., Montreal, Can., 1974; MFA, Temple U., 1977. Lectr. Moore Coll. Art, Phila., 1976-78; instr. Tyler Sch. Art, Phila., 1975-85, asst. prof., 1985—; dir. art workshops Tyler Sch. Art, 1983—. Sculptor The Water Gap, 1976; author: (video tape) Al Cast in Color, 1988. Bd. mem. Friends of Bezalel Acad. Phila chpt., 1982—. Recipient Johnson Matthey Platinum Jewerly Design award, 1981; Crafts-in-the-Pk. grantee Nat. Pk. Svc., 1976. Mem. Soc. N.Am. Goldsmiths (NEA rsch. grant 1988). Jewish. Office: Tyler Sch Art Beech and Penrose Aves Philadelphia PA 19126

KERNER, FRED, book publisher, writer; b. Montreal, Can., Feb. 15, 1921; s. Sam and Vera (Goldman) K.; m. Jean Elizabeth Somerville, July 17, 1945 (div. Apr. 1951); 1 son, Jon Fredrik; m. Sally Dee Stouten, May 18, 1959; children: David, Diane. BA, Sir George Williams U. (now Concordia U.), Montreal, 1942. Asst. sports editor Montreal Gazette, 1942-44; news editor Can. Press, Montreal, Toronto, N.Y.C., 1944-50; asst. night city editor A.P., N.Y.C., 1950-57; editor Hawthorn Books, Inc., N.Y.C., 1957-58, pres., 1965-68; exec. editor Crest-Premier Books, Hall House, Fawcett World Libr., N.Y.C., 1958-63; editor-in-chief Crest-Premier Books, Fawcett World Libr., N.Y.C., 1963-65; pres. Centaur House, Inc. (pubs.), 1964-80, Paramount Securities Corp., 1965-67, Veritas Internat. Pubs., 1976—, Publishing Projects, Inc., 1967—, Communications Unltd., 1968—; editorial dir. book and ednl. divs. Reader's Digest, Can., 1969-75; v.p., pub. dir. Harlequin Enterprises Ltd., 1975-83, editor emeritus, sr. cons. editor, 1984—; v.p. Publitex Internat. Corp. (pubs.), 1968-75; pres. Athabaska House, 1975-77; dir. Nat. Mint, Inc.; panelist various profl. confs.; chmn. Internat. Affairs Conf. Coll. Editors, 1965; drama festival adjudicator, 1940-48; Broadway theatrical script cons., 1948-56; mem. nat. com. Am. Newspaper Guild, 1949-54, Wire Svc. Guild, 1954-57. Author: (with Leonid Kotkin) Eat, Think and be Slender, 1954, (with Walter M. Germain) The Magic Power of Your Mind, 1956, (with Joyce Brothers) Ten Days to a Successful Memory, 1957, Stress and Your Heart, 1961; pseudonym Frederick Kerr: Watch Your Weight Go Down, 1962, (with Walter M. Germain) Secrets of Your Supraconscious, 1965, (with David Goodman) What's Best for Your Child and You, 1966, (with Jesse Reid) Buy High, Sell Higher, 1966; (pseudonym M.H. Thaler) It's Fun to Fondue, 1968, (with Ion Grumeza) Nadia, 1977, Careers in Writing, 1985, Mad About Fondue, 1986, (with Andrew Willman) Prospering Through the Coming Depression, 1988, Home Emergency Handbook and First-Aid Guide, 1990; contbg. author: Successful Writers and How They Work, 1958, Words on Paper, 1960, Overseas Press Club Cookbook, 1964, The Seniors' Guide to Life in the Slow Lane, 1986, The Writer's Essential Desk Reference, 1991, Lifetime: A Treasury of Uncommon Wisdoms, 1992, Chambers's Ency.; books transl. into French, German, Japanese, Portuguese, Spanish and Italian; editor: Love is a Man's Affair, 1958, Treasury of Lincoln Quotations, 1965, The Canadian Writer's Guide, 9th edit., 1985, 10th edit., 1988, 11th edit., 1992, Selling Your Short Fiction, 1992. Mem. local sch. bd., N.Y.C., 1968-69; chmn. sch. com. Westmount High Sch., 1970-72; mem. sch. com. Roslyn Sch., 1973; chmn. publs. com. Edward R. Murrow Meml. Fund; judge Dr. William Henry Drummond Nat. Poetry Contest; trustee Gibson Lit. Awards, C.A.A. Lit. Awards, Benson & Hedges Lit. Awards, CA&B Student Creative Writing Awards; bd. govs. Concordia U., 1975-79; hon. life mem. Can. Book Pubs. Coun.; founding mem. exec. com. Pub. Lending Rights Commn., 1986-89, vice chmn., 1988-89; founding dir. Toronto Book and Mag. Fair, bd. dirs., 1990—. Winner of 2 internat. awards for advertorial writing, 1990. Fellow Can. Copyright Inst. (vice chmn.), Acad. Can. Writers (vice chmn., bd. govs. 1986—); mem. European Acad. Arts, Scis. and Humanities, Orgn. Can. Authors and Pubs. (founding dir.), Can. Authors Assn. (v.p. 1972-80, founding dir. Lit. Luncheons, pres. Montreal br. 1974-75, nat. pres. 1982-83, hon. life, chmn. editorial adv. com. Can. Author and Bookman 1978—, chmn. grievance com. 1983—, pub. com. 1986-92), Periodical Writers' Assn. Can. (chmn. grievance com. 1991—), Can. Writers' Found. (bd. govs. 1982—), Mystery Writers Am., Writers' Union Can. (chmn. grievance com. 1990—), Soc. Profl. Journalists Pres.' Club, Book and Periodical Coun. (bd. govs. 1983—), Nat. Speakers Assn., Authors Guild, Authors League Am., Internat. P.E.N., Nat. Speakers Assn., Am. Acad. Polit. aial Sci., Can. Assn. Restoration of Lost Positives (pres.), Can. Soc. for the Preservation of the Natural Bowtie (pres.), Can. Book Pubs. Counc. (hon. life), Sir George Williams U. Alumni Assn. (founding pres. N.Y.C. br., exec. com. 1970-75, pres. 1971-73), Sigma Delta Chi. Clubs: Advt., Deadline, Overseas Press, Dutch Treat (N.Y.C.); Toronto Press; Author's (London). Home: 25 Farmview Crescent, Willowdale, ON Canada M2J 1G5 Office: 55014 Fairview Mall, Willowdale, ON Canada M2J 5B9

KERNEY, THOMAS LINCOLN, II, investments and real estate professional; b. Princeton, N.J., Dec. 16, 1950; s. James Jr. and Elsie (Regan) K. BA in Journalism, Tex. Christian U., 1973. With Peyton Assocs., Princeton. Trustee James Kerney Found., Princeton, 1983—, sec., 1992—; trustee Trenton Area Soup Kitchen, 1985-87, Princeton Edn. Ctr. at Blairstown, 1987-89, Princeton Child Devel. Inst., 1988—, N.J. State Mus., 1988—, Morven, Princeton, 1989-91, Princeton Small Animal Rescue LEague, 1991—. Mem. Nassau Club, Bedens Brook Club. Roman Catholic. Home: 42 Fackler Rd Princeton NJ 08540

KERNS, ED, administrator; b. Richmond, Va., Feb. 22, 1945; s. Edward J. and Joy (Burgess) K.; m. Ardith Talbott, Oct. 15, 1983; 1 child, Whitney. BFA, Richmond Profl. Inst., 1967; MFA, Md. Inst., 1969. Tchr., art Bentley Sch., N.Y.C., 1970-72; head art dept. Baldwin Sch., N.Y.C., 1972-74, Friends Sem., N.Y.C., 1974-79; assoc. prof., head art dept. Lafayette Coll., Easton, Pa., 1980-86, prof. art, head art dept., 1986-88, Eugene H. Clapp prof. humanities in art dept., 1988—. One person exhbns. include Rosa Esman Gallery, N.Y.C., 1974-87, William Patterson Coll., Ben Shahn Galleries, Wayne, N.J., 1989, Cedar Crest Coll., Allentown, Pa., 1986, Painted Bride Arts Ctr., Phila., 1984, Pa. Acad. Fine Arts, Morris Gallery, Phila., 1982. Van Wickle Gallery, Easton, 1980, Suzette Schochet Gallery, Newport, R.I., 1977, Abe Sachs Gallery, N.Y.C., 1972, 74. Group shows include Villanova (Pa.) Art Gallery, 1989, Rosa Esman Gallery, 1975-77, 79-88, Wilson Gallery, Bethlehem, Pa., 1976, 87, Lafayette Coll., 1984, Lafayette & Muhlenberg Coll., 1984, Karl Sterner Gallery, Easton. 1984, Md. Inst., 1981, 83, Commodities Corp., Princeton, N.J., 1982, Albright Coll., 1982, Chgo. Art Expo., 1982, Randolph Macon Coll., 1981, Museo civico e gallerie d'arte e d'arte moderna, Udine, Itaaly, 1980, Goddard-Riverside Gallery, N.Y.C., 1979, many others. Office: Lafayette Coll 205 Williams Ctr Easton PA 18042-6570

KERNS, PAULA IRENE, social services administrator; b. Lonaconing, Md., Nov. 6, 1950; d. George Peter and Naomi Aleda (Wade) Grove; m. William Price Brand, Sept. 2, 1972 (div. Dec. 1982); children: Paula Leigh, Meghan Naomi; m. Richard Anthony Kerns, Sept. 15, 1990. Student, Allegany Community Coll., Cumberland, Md., 1981-82. Sec. Columbia Gas of Md., Cumberland, 1969-72, G.A. Brown & Son, Inc., Fairmont, W.Va., 1973-75; asst. to exec. dir. County United Way, Inc., Cumberland, 1982-85, acting exec. dir., 1986, exec. dir., 1987—; bd. dirs. Health Service Found., Cumberland, 1982-87. Sec. Frostburg Rep. Club, 1985-86. Mem. Cumberland Lions. Methodist. Home: 7 Seldom Seen Rd Lonaconing MD 21539 Office: County United Way Inc 111 S George St PO Box 307 Cumberland MD 21502

KERPCHAR, MICHAEL, engineer, business owner, researcher; b. Passaic, N.J., June 19, 1924; s. Peter Kerpchar and Veronica Warholack; m. Jennie S. Hallock, Apr. 12, 1953; 1 child, Lorraine. Grad. high sch., Clifton, N.J., MSEE Equivalent. Sect. head to dir. astronautics lab. Kearfott Co., Little Falls, N.J., 1950-62; mgr. systems engring. spacecraft systems RCA, Princeton, N.J., 1962-64; rsch. scientist Nortronics, Palos Verdes, Calif., 1964-66; mgr. advanced program Gourdine Systems, Livingston, N.J., 1966-67; chief underwriter systems Kollsman Instrument, Elmhurst, N.Y., 1967-69; v.p. engring. dept. Ocean Metrics, Fairfield, N.J., 1969-73; mgr. advanced program Harris Corp., Syosset, N.Y., 1974-76; dir. advanced program

Dewey Electronics, Paramus, N.J., 1976-79; prin. scientist The Kerpchar Co., Lake Hiawatha, N.J., 1979—; devel. new products Kerpchar Co., 1992—. Contbr. articles to profl. jours. Mem. AIAA, SPIE, Old Crows, IEEE (sr.). Republican. Roman Catholic. Home: 17 Nokomis Ave Lake Hiawatha NJ 07034-2505

KERR, ARNOLD D., civil engineering educator; b. Suwalki, Poland, Mar. 9, 1928; came to U.S. 1954; s. Osher and Riva (Kremer) Kierszkowski; m. Berta Borgenicht, Aug. 28, 1966; children: Regina J., Orin S. Dipl.Ing., Tech. U. Munich, 1952; MS, Northwestern U., 1956, PhD, 1958. Design engr. Hazelet & Erdal Cons. Engrs., Chgo., 1955; asst. rsch. scientist Inst. Math. Scis., NYU, N.Y.C., 1958-59; asst. prof. aeronautics NYU, N.Y.C., 1959-61, assoc. prof., 1961-66, prof., 1966-73; vis. prof. civil engring. Princeton (N.J.) U., 1973-78; prof. civil engring. U. Del., Newark, 1978—; cons. in field; fellow Ctr. for Advanced Study, U. Del., 1989-90; mem. NAS/NRC Com. on Cooperation with USSR on Ice Mechanics, 1991-92. Contbr. over 100 articles to profl. jours.; editor: Railroad Track Mechanics and Technology, 1978; co-editor: Productivity in U.S. Railroads, 1980. Bd. dirs. Westover Hill Woods Assn., Wilmington, 1983—. Fellow Ctr. for Advanced Study, U. Del., 1989-90. Mem. ASME, Am. Rwy. Engring. Assn. (chair sub-com. 1991—), Internat. Soc. for Interaction of Mechanics and Math., Inst. for R.R. Engring. (pres. 1980—). Office: U Del DuPont Hall Newark DE 19716

KERR, DONALD MACLEAN, JR., physicist; b. Phila., Apr. 8, 1939; s. Donald MacLean and Harriet (Fell) K.; m. Alison Richards Kyle, June 10, 1961; 1 dau., Margot Kyle. B.E.E. (Nat. Merit scholar), Cornell U., 1963, M.S., 1964, Ph.D. (Ford Found. fellow, 1964-65, James Clerk Maxwell fellow 1965-66), 1966. Staff Los Alamos Nat. Lab., 1966-76, group leader, 1971-72, asst. div. leader, 1972-73, asst. to dir., 1973-75, alt. div. leader, 1975-76; dep. mgr. Nev. ops. office Dept. Energy, Las Vegas, 1976-77; acting asst. sec. def. programs Dept. Energy, Washington, 1978; dep. asst. sec. def. programs Dept. Energy, 1977-79, dep. asst. sec. energy tech., 1979; dir Los Alamos Nat. Lab., 1979-85; sr. v.p. EG&G, Inc., Wellesley, Mass., 1985-88, exec. v.p., 1988-89, pres., 1989—; mem. Navajo Sci. Com., 1974-77; mem. sci. adv. panel U.S. Army, 1975-78; mem. engring. adv. bd. U. Nev., Las Vegas, 1976-78, Cornell U., 1985—; chmn. com. R&D Internat. Energy Agy., 1979-85; mem. nat. security adv. coun. SRI Internat., 1980-89; mem. adv. bd. U. Alaska Geophys. Inst., 1980-85; mem. sci. adv. group Joint Strategic Planning Staff, 1981-91; mem. adv. com. Naval Rsch., 1982-85; mem. corp. Draper Lab., 1982—; mem. adv. bd. Georgetown U. Ctr. Strategic Internat. Studies, 1981-87; bd. dirs. Mirage Systems, Sunnyvale, Calif., Resources for the Future, Washington. Published research on plasma physics, microwave electronics, ionospheric physics, energy and nat. security. Trustee New Eng. Aquarium, 1989—. Fellow AAAS; mem. Am. Phys. Soc., Am. Geophys. Union, Nat. Assn. Mfrs. (bd. dirs. 1986—), Southwestern Assn. Indian Affairs, World Affairs Coun. Boston (bd. dirs. 1988—), Atlantic Coun. (bd. dirs. 1991—), Sigma Xi, Tau Beta Pi, Eta Kappa Nu. Clubs: Cosmos (Washington); Algonquin (Boston). Office: EG&G Inc 45 William St Wellesley MA 02181-4004

KERR, FRANK JOHN, astronomer, educator; b. St. Albans, Eng., Jan. 8, 1918; s. Frank Robison and Myrtle Constance (McMeekin) K.; m. Maureen Parnell, Jan. 7, 1966; children: Gillian Wheeler (dec.), Ian Kerr, Robin Lowry. B.Sc., U. Melbourne, Australia, 1938, M.Sc., 1940, D.Sc., 1962; M.S., Harvard U., 1951. Rsch. scholar U. Melbourne, 1939-40; mem. staff radiophysics lab. Commonwealth Sci. and Indsl. Rsch. Orgn., Sydney, Australia, 1940-68; vis. prof. U. Md., 1966-68, prof., 1968-87, prof. emeritus, 1987—, dir. astronomy program, 1973-78, acting provost div. math. phys. scis. and engring., 1978-79, provost, 1979-85; vis. scientist Leiden U., 1957; vis. prof. U. Tex., 1964, U. Tokyo, 1967; Mem. NSF Adv. Panel Astronomy, 1969-72, chmn., 1971-72. Co-editor: Procs. Internat. Astron. Union Symposia, 1963, 73; Contbr. numerous articles to profl. jours. Trustee Assoc. Univs., Inc., 1981-84; dir. Univs. Space Rsch. Assn. Astronomy Program, 1984-. Fulbright travel grantee, 1950-51; Leverhulme fellow, 1967; NSF research grantee, 1967-83; Guggenheim fellow, 1974-75. Mem. Internat. Astron. Union (pres. commn. 33 1976-79), Am. Astron. Soc. (councillor 1972-75, v.p. 1980-82). Club: Cosmos (Washington). Home: 12601 Davan Dr Silver Spring MD 20904-3504 Office: U Md Astronomy Dept College Park MD 20742

KERR, JOHN WELLINGTON, English educator; b. Gouverneur, N.Y., Dec. 4, 1950; s. Grant Wellington and Junedeen (Bullock) K. BS, SUNY, Geneseo, 1973; MS, SUNY, Potsdam, 1981; postgrad., SUNY, Albany, 1991—. Elem. tchr. Lawnwood Elem. Sch., Ft. Pierce, Fla., 1973-74, Clifton-Fine Cen. Sch., Star Lake, N.Y., 1974-76; cons. South Western Bell Telephone, Houston, 1976-79; English prof. SUNY, Canton, N.Y., 1979-82, Cobleskill, N.Y., 1982—. Home: 14 Smt St Richmondville NY 12149 Office: SUNY Cobleskill Cobleskill NY 12043

KERR, PAMELA MARIANNE, counselor; b. Phila., Aug. 21, 1953; d. Charles Henry and Doro (Maier) K.; m. Christopher Lynden Roach, Apr. 9, 1977; children: NcKinsey Lynden Kerr, JaQuinley Maier Kerr. AB in Art History, Smith Coll., 1975; MA in Counseling, Rider Coll., 1979. Counselor basic studies div. Burlington County Coll., Pemberton, N.J., 1979; mng. editor Charles Kerr Enterprises Inc., New Hope, Pa., 1980-85; crisis counselor Woman Space, Trenton, N.J., 1986-89; counseling cons. Women's Crisis Svcs., Flemington, N.J., 1986-89; pvt. practice Stockton, N.J., 1989—; founder, dir., counselor Open Door Counseling and Ednl. Svcs., Flemington, 1990-91; group facilitator Career Svcs. and Life Planning Ctr., Flemington, 1986-90; project coord. N.J. Coalition for Battered Women, Trenton, 1989. Author: A Model Framework for Children's Programs in Battered Women's Shelters, 1989; editor: Lords Locator: Map Guides to America's Finest Restaurants, 1980-82. Active Ad Hoc Com. to Gov.'s Adv. Coun. , Trenton, 1989. Mem. N.J. Coalition for Battered Women, Internat. Network Agsint Incest and Child Sexual Abuse, Am. Assn. for Counseling and Devel., N.J. Assn. for Counseling and Devel.

KERR, ROBERT BENJAMIN, merger and acquisition company executive; b. Pitts., Jan. 26, 1943; s. Robert P. and Ella (Pell) K.; m. Marilyn Lee Whitcomb, Dec. 18, 1965; children: Kristen, Brian, Kathryn. BA, BSME, Pa. State U., 1965; MBA, Wayne State U., 1971. CPA, N.J. Sales engr. Union Carbide Corp., N.Y.C., 1965-71, Tenn. Alloys Corp., Chattanooga, 1971-74; v.p. sales Shieldalloy Corp., Newfield, N.J., 1974-86; pres. Everingham & Kerr, Inc., Haddon Heights, N.J., 1986—. Bd. dirs. Millville (N.J.) Pub. Libr., 19822—. lst lt. U.S. Army, 1965-67. Mem. AICPA, Inst. Bus. Appraisers. Homem: 608 Quail Dr Millville NJ 08332 Office: 115 White Horse Pike Haddon Heights NJ 08035-1909

KERR, THEODORE WILLIAM, JR., entomology educator; b. Patterson, N.J., Nov. 20, 1912; s. Theodore William and Daisy Abt (Henshaw) K.; m. Grace Marie Grimes, July 2, 1938. BS, U. Mass., 1936; PhD, Cornell U., 1941. Rsch. asst. Cornell U., Ithaca, N.Y., 1937-42; sr. scientist Uniroyal Corp., Bethany, Conn., 1942-46; rsch. prof. U. R.I., Kingston, 1946-76, rsch. prof. emeritus, 1976—. Contbr. articles to profl. jours. Mem. Entomol. Soc. Am., Masons (32 degree), Sigma Xi, Phi Kappa Phi. Home: 42 Clara Ln Narragansett RI 02882-1443

KERR, THOMAS HENDERSON, III, electrical engineer, researcher; b. Washington, Nov. 9, 1945; s. Thomas Henderson Jr. and Norma Elaine (McAllister) K.; m. Aniece Ragland, July 5, 1975; children: Thomas Henderson IV, Stephen McAllister Pearson. BSEE magna cum laude, Howard U., 1967; MSEE, U. Iowa, 1969, PhD, 1971. Control engr. R & D Ctr. GE, Schenectady, N.Y., 1971-73; mem. tech. staff The Analytic Sci. Corp., Reading, Mass., 1973-79; sr. analyst systems engr. Intermetrics Inc., Cambridge, Mass., 1979-86; with tech. staff Lincoln Lab. MIT, Lexington, 1986—; cons. Nat. Security Indsl. Assn., Boston, 1979-86; instr. Northeastern U., Boston, 1990—. Contbr. over 100 articles to profl. publs. Math. tutor Civic Ctr., Schenectady, 1971, Union Coll., Schenectady, 1972-73, Union Meth. Ch., Boston, 1973-74. Recipient NSF traineeship, 1968-70. Mem. IEEE (sr., chmn. control systems sect. Boston, 1990—), IEEE Aerospace and Electronic Systems (M. Barry Carlton award 1988), AIAA (sr.), Inst. Nav., Am. Def. Preparedness Assn., Math. Assn. Am., Sigma Xi, Tau Beta Pi, Pi Mu Epsilon, Sigma Pi Sigma, Eta Kappa Nu. Methodist. Home: 11 Paul Revere Rd Lexington MA 02173-6632

KERRY, JOHN FORBES, senator; b. Denver, Dec. 11, 1943; s. Richard John and Rosemary (Forbes) K.; m. Julia Stimson Thorne, May 22, 1970; children: Alexandra, Vanessa. B.A., Yale U., 1966; J.D., Boston Coll., 1976. Bar: Mass. 1976. Nat. coordinator Vietnam Vets. Against The War, 1969-71; asst. dist. atty. Middlesex (Mass.) County, 1976-79; ptnr. firm Kerry & Sragow, Boston, 1979-82; lt. gov. State of Mass., 1983-85; U.S. senator from Mass., 1985—. Author: The New Soldier, 1971. Democratic candidate for Congress from 5th Mass. Dist., 1972; bd. vistors Walsh Sch. Fgn. Service, Georgetown U. Served to lt. (j.g.) USNR, 1966-69. Decorated Silver Star; decorated Bronze Star with oak leaf cluster, Purple Hearts (3). Roman Catholic. Office: US Senate 362 Russell Senate Bldg Washington DC 20510*

KERSTEN, CHRISTIAN GEORGE, university administrator; b. Paris, Jan. 11, 1949; s. Henry George and Elisabeth (Reiter) K.; m. Mary Menasche, May 29, 1970 (div. 1983); children: Michael Kenneth, James Alexander; m. Mary Louise Coleman, Jan. 5, 1985; 1 child, Hilary Coleman. BA, L.I. U., 1971; postgrad., NYU, 1974-76. Dir. ann. giving Manhattan Coll., Riverdale, N.Y., 1972-73; assoc. dir. alumni fedn. NYU, N.Y.C., 1973-76; assoc. dir. devel. Clark U., Worcester, Mass., 1976-80; assoc. dir. univ. devel. Tufts U., Medford, Mass., 1980-83; asst. chancellor univ. devel. U. Calif., Santa Barbara, 1983-87; dir. devel. Norman Rockwell Mus., Stockbridge, Mass., 1987-88; v.p. for univ. advancement SUNY, Albany, 1988—. Dir. Mohawk Hudson Community Found., Albany, 1988-91. Recipient Grand Award for Improvement Coun. for Advancement and Support of Edn./U.S. Steel, 1981, Gold Medal for fundraising publs., 1986. Mem. Coun. for Advancement and Support of Edn., Nat. Soc. Fundraising Execs. Democrat. Unitarian-Universalist. Home: Whippoorwill Hill Rd RD 1 Box 397 Hillsdale NY 12529 Office: SUNY-Albany 1400 Washington Ave #231 Albany NY 12222

KERSTETTER-HULL, JOANNE RITA, financial counseling executive; b. Washington, Oct. 5, 1952; d. Dale David and Patricia Claire (Chisholm) Kerstetter; m. Albert J. Hull, Jr., Jan. 1, 1983; children: Jessica Lynn, Ashley, Jason. BA, U. Md., 1974, MS, 1979. Pres. Consumter Credit Counseling Svc. Greater Washington, Inc., Washington, 1976—; commr. State of Md., Dept. Licensing & Regulation, Balt., 1978-85; Dir. Nat. Found. Consumer Credit, Silver Spring, Md., 1985—, treas., 1988-90; dir. Internat. Credit Assn. Greater Washington, Silver Spring, 1989—; elected 3d vice chmn. Internal Credit Assn., 1991—. Mem. NAFE, Consumer Edn. & Info. Assn. Va., Assn. Fin. Counseling & Planning Edn., Greater Washington Soc. Assn. Execs.

KERWIN, CORNELIUS MARTIN, dean, public affairs educator; b. Waterbury, Conn., Apr. 10, 1949; s. Daniel Vincent and Mary Catherine (Shea) K.; m. Ann D. Londe, Sept. 3, 1972; children: Michael Barnett, Alex Daniel. BA, Am. U., 1971; MA, U. R.I., 1972; PhD, Johns Hopkins U., 1978. Program asst. Johns Hopkins U., Balt., 1972-75; instr. Washington Semister Program, 1975-78; program dir. Sch of Govt. and Pub. Adminstrn., Washington, 1978-80, asst. prof., 1980-84, assoc. prof., 1984-88; acting dean sch. pub. affairs Am. U., Washington, 1988-89, dean sch. pub. affairs, prof., 1989—; cons. IBM, Corp., Rockville, Md., 1984—, U.S. Fed. Energy Regulatory Commn., Washington, 1983-88, U.S. EPA, Washington, 1988—, and others. Contbr. book chpts., conf. papers, and articles to profl. jours. Regional finalist White House Fellowship Competition, 1980. Mem. Nat. Assn. Schs. Pub. Affairs and Adminstrn. (commn. on peer rev. and accreditation 1990—), Am. Soc. Pub. Adminstrn. (bd. dirs. nat. capital area chpt. 1990—, chmn. sect. on pub. law and adminstrn. 1991—), Am. Polit. Sci. Assn., Smithsonian Assocs. Office: Am U Sch Pub Affairs 4400 Massachusetts Ave NW Washington DC 20016-8001

KESLER, LARRY DEAN, automotive company executive; b. Nyssa, Oreg., Dec. 26, 1944; s. Vibert L. Kesler and Fern G. LaVoie; m. Marlene Morgan, Aug. 21, 1968; children: Stephanie, Steven, Andrew, Jarom, Megan. BS in Econs. magna cum laude, U. Utah, 1969; MBA, U. Pa., 1971. Fin. analyst GM, Detroit, 1971-75; asst. comptr. Inland div. GMC, Dayton, Ohio, 1975-79; instr. acctg. dept. Sinclair Community Coll., Dayton, 1977-79; dir. and fin. mgr. Inlan Industria de Components Mecanicos Ltd., Ponte de Sor, Portugal, 1979-82; asst. comptr. Harrison div. GM, Lockport, N.Y., 1982-84, dir. strategic planning and systems devel., 1985-86, dir. program mgmt. and new ventures, 1987, gen. dir. sales and materials mgmt., 1987-88, gen. dir. internat. bus. unit, 1989-91, gen. dir. internat. bus. unit, sales and materials mgmt., 1991—; bd. dirs. Diavia, Molinella, Italy, DELFA, Cua, Venezuela, Calsonic Harrison Corp., Utsynomia, Japan. Vice chmn. and dir. campaign United Way, Ea. Niagara County, N.Y., 1991; dir. Lewiston Trail Boy Scouts Am. Vice chmn. and dir. campaign United Way, Ea. Niagara County, N.Y., 1991. Mem. Ea. Niagara County C. of C. (long range planning com. 1989-91). Mem. LDS Ch. Office: Harrison Div GM 200 Upper Mountain Rd Lockport NY 14094-1896

KESSEL, KATHY L., marketing professional; b. Rochdale, Mass., June 13, 1951; d. Norman James and Theresa I. (Dumas) LaPlante; m. McKeen C. Kessel, June 6, 1970 (div. 1977); 1 child, Melynne C. BS in Mech. Engring., U. N.H., 1975; MS in Mgmt. of Tech., MIT, 1988. Mfg. engr. Tex. Instruments, Attleboro, Mass., 1976-78, project mgr., 1978-80; software engr. Automatix, Billerica, Mass., 1980-83, product mgr., 1983-87; mktg. mgr. ICAD, Cambridge, Mass., 1988-92, dir. mktg., 1992—. Home: 92C Commonwealth Ave 3 Griffin Circle Wayland MA 01778

KESSELMAN, BRUCE ALAN, financial executive, consultant; b. Vineland, N.J., Sept. 11, 1951; s. Frederick Alexander and Ann (Leiderman) K.; m. Paula Jean Farkas, Jan. 22, 1984; children: Joshua, Heather. BA in Russian with distinctions, Rutgers U., 1973. CLU. Ins. agent Home Life of N.Y., New Brunswick, N.J., 1973-75; sales mgr. Home Life of N.Y., Green Village, N.J., 1975-77; field mgr. Home Life of N.Y., Madison, N.J., 1977-79; dir. tng. Home Life of N.Y., N.Y.C., 1979-81; regional coord. E.F. Hutton & Co., N.Y.C., 1981-83; v.p. sales Money Mktg. U.S.A., N.Y.C., 1983-85; exec. v.p. mktg. Money Mktg. U.S.A., N.Y.C., 1986-89, 1985-86; pres., mng. dir. Money Mktg. U.S.A., Matawan, N.J., 1989—, also bd. dirs. V.p Edison (N.J.) Jaycees, 1979-81. Mem. Middlesex-Somerset Assn. Life Underwriters (bd. dirs. 1973-79), Am. Soc. CLU's and Chartered Fin. Cons., Ins. Brokers Assn. N.J., Am. Soc. Computer Cons., Alpha Epsilon Pi (regional gov. N.J.-N.Y. chpt. 1974-81). Republican. Jewish. Home: 88 Pendleton Pl Old Bridge NJ 08857-2846 Office: Money Mktg USA One Money Pla PO Box 377 Matawan NJ 07747-0377

KESSINGER, TOM G., college president; b. Paterson, N.J., Mar. 24, 1941; s. Harold Caldwell and Ann (Prodehl) K.; m. Varyam K. Chawla, June 26, 1962; children: William C., Colin C. BA, Haverford Coll., 1965; AM, U. Chgo., 1967, PhD, 1972; MLitt (hon.), U. Pa., 1975. Asst. prof. U. Va., Charlottesville, 1970-73; assoc. prof. U. Pa., Phila., 1973-77; program officer Ford Found., New Delhi, India, 1977-79; rep. Jakarta, Indonesia, 1979-81; rep. S.E. Asia Ford Found., Jakarta, 1981-87; rep. India, New Delhi Ford Found., New Delhi, India, 1987-88; pres. Haverford (Pa.) Coll., 1988—. Author: Vilyatpur 1848-1968, 1974. Woodrow Wilson fellow, 1965, fellow Danforth Found., 1965, Nat. Def. Fgn. Lang., 1965. Democrat. Mem. Soc. of Friends. Home: 1 College Cir Haverford PA 19041-1311 Office: Office Pres Haverford Coll 370 Lancaster Ave Haverford PA 19041-1392

KESSLER, ALAN LEE, company executive; b. N.Y.C., Aug. 21, 1950; s. William Ned and Naomi (Ehrenreich) K.; m. Marian Eve Merer, Dec. 1, 1950 (div. Aug., 1989); 1 child, Ingrid Beth. Grad. high sch., Oceanside, N.Y. Mgr. Ea. Camera, Port Washington, N.Y., 1973, EPD Color Labs., Hempstead, N.Y., 1974; tech. rep. Nikon, Inc., Garden City, N.Y., 1974-75, product mgr., 1975-79; product mgr. AIC Photo, Carle Place, N.Y., 1979-80; dir. sales/mktg. AIC Photo, 1980-87; pres. Phoenix Corp. of Am., Oceanside, 1987—. Recipient Best on L.I. award L.I. Advt. Coun., 1984. Mem. Photographic Mfrs. & Distbr. Assn. (bd. dirs. 1984—). Democrat. Jewish. Office: Phoenix Corp of Am 112 Mott St Oceanside NY 11572-5823

KESSLER, FREDERICK MELVYN, acoustical engineer; b. Bklyn., May 15, 1932; s. Abraham and Freida (Lurie) K.; m. Joan Miriam Keiles, May 2, 1954; children: Fran, Andrew, Rachel. BSME, CCNY, 1954; MSME, Rutgers U., 1967, PhDEE, 1971. Jr. test engr. Curtiss Wright Corp., Woodbridge, N.J., 1954-55; sr. mech. engr. U.S. Navy David Taylor Model Basin, Washington, 1959-61; rsch. engr. Ingersoll Rand Co., Princeton, N.J., 1961-70; cons., v.p. Lewis S. Gooodfriend & Assoc., Morristown, N.J., 1971-73; ptnr. Dames & Moore, Cranford, N.J., 1973-83; pres. FMK Tech., Inc., Bound Brook, N.J., 1983—; instr. Rutgers U., New Brunswick, N.J., 1968-71. Co-author: (with M. Crocker) Noise and Noise Control, 1982; contbr. articles to profl. jours.; patentee high pressure fluid gun, stress measuring device, muffler. Active N.J. Noise Control Coun., Trenton, 1971-80; former mem. Environ. Commn., Bridgewater Twp. Lt. (j.g.) USN, 1956-59. Fellow Acoustical Soc. Am. (asst. editor 1979-82); mem. Inst. Noise Control Engring. (pres. 1988, v.p. tech. affairs, cons. editor), Sigma Xi. Office: FMK Tech Inc PO Box 168 Bound Brook NJ 08805-0168

KESSLER, HAROLD DAVID, police chief; b. York, Pa., Nov. 18, 1945; s. Harold Thomas and Lorraine Hilda (Patterson) K.; m. Carol Ann Zimmerman, Sept. 2, 1967; children: Michelle R., Lisa L. Diploma, Pa. State Police Acad., 1971, FBI Nat. Acad., 1977; AS, York Coll. Pa., 1973. Patrolman Springettsbury Twp. Police Dept., York, 1968-72, sgt., 1972-80, chief police, 1980—. Budget chmn. York-Adams Drug and Alcohol Coun., 1982-86. Named Officer of Yr., Optimist Club, Suburban York, 1971, East York, Pa., 1975, Outstanding Young Law Officer, Northeastern Jaycees, Manchester, Pa., 1981. Mem. Internat. Chiefs Police Assn., Pa. Chiefs Police Assn., Cen. Pa. Chiefs Police Assn., York County Chiefs Police Assn. (pres. 1983-84), FBI Nat. Acad. Assn., NRA, Fraternal Order Police, Masons, Shriners. Home: 3330 Harrowgate Rd York PA 17402-4333 Office: Springettsbury Twp PD 1501 Mt Zion Rd York PA 17402

KESSLER, PETE WILLIAM, dentist; b. Paterson, N.J., Feb. 21, 1949; s. Martin and Bernice S. Kessler; m. Sue E. George, Nov. 2, 1988; children: Kasey Martin, Kelly George. BA, Peabody Conservatory of Music, 1971; BS, U. Md., 1976, MS, 1978, DDS, 1982. Bassist, musician Roberta Flack, Alexandria, Va., 1970-73, Atlantic Records, N.Y.C., 1970-75; pvt. practice Balt., 1982—. Office: 4801 Ritchie Hwy Baltimore MD 21225

KESSLER, RICHARD JOHN, professional staff member; b. Oneida, N.Y., Apr. 11, 1948; s. Richard John Kessler and Mary Alice (Starr) Day; m. Pamela Mary Jameson Cox, June 18, 1978; children: Tristan, Catriona, Nicholas, Duncan. BA, Colgate U., 1970; MA, Tufts. U., 1974, M.A.L.D., 1976, PhD, 1986. Fellow Ctr. for Strategic and Internat. Studies, Washington, 1980-84; sr. assoc. Carnegie Endowment for Internat. Peace, Washington, 1985-88; profl. staff mem. fgn. rels. com. U.S. Senate, Washington, 1989—; vis. prof. Am. U., Washington, 1988. Author: Rebellion and Repression in the Philippines, 1989; co-author: The Critical Link: Energy and National Security in the 1980's. Mem. vestry St. John's Episcopal Ch., Chevy Chase, Md., 1991. Sgt. U.S. Army, 1970-73, Vietnam. Decorated Bronze star, Army Commendation medal, Vietnam Cross of Gallantry; Rotary Internat. Grad. fellow, 1978; Nat. Merit scholar, 1966. Democrat. Office: US Senate Fgn Rels Washington DC 20510

KESSLER, SIDNEY H., history educator; b. N.Y.C., Mar. 14, 1926; s. Benjamin I. and Bessie (Weber) K.; divorced; children: Perry Sean, Sybil Bess. BA cum laude, Montclair State Coll., 1948; MA in History, Columbia U., 1950; MLS, Pratt Inst., 1953; Cert. Judaic Studies, Gratz Coll., 1975. High sch. tchr. Logan County High Sch., Sterling, Colo., 1948-49; caseworker N.Y.C. Dept. Welfare, 1951-52; libr. Bklyn. Pub. Libr., 1953-54, Suffern (N.Y.) High Sch., 1954-55, The Rhodes Sch., N.Y.C., 1955-57; instr. history Glassboro (N.J.) State Coll., 1958-63, asst. prof., 1963-65, assoc. prof., 1965-78, prof., 1978-91, prof. emeritus of history, 1991, chmn. dept., 1977-79; in-svc. tng. leader, Bridgeton (N.J.) Pub. Schs., 1972-73; adult edn. cons. Margate (N.J.) Jewish Ctr., 1973; tchr. adult inst. Temple Beth El, Cherry Hill, N.J., 1974; adj. prof. extension div. Gratz Coll., Phila., 1975. Contbr. articles to profl. jours. and books. With U.S. Army, 1944-46. Recipient N.Y. State War Svc. scholarship, 1957, Merit award Sch. Liberal Arts, Glassboro State Coll., 1985-86; named to Legion of Honor, Chapel of Four Chaplains, Phila, 1984; grantee Sch. Liberal Arts, Glassboro State Coll., 1979, 80, 87, 88. Mem. Nat. Coun. Holocaust Educators, Am. Legion, Phi Alpha Theta, Kappa Delta Pi. Jewish. Home: 141-C Stonybrook Apts Woodbury NJ 08096

KESSLER, WALLACE FRANK, school director, tour developer; b. Mar. 22, 1938; m. Susan Carol Morse, June 20, 1969 (div. Nov. 1972). BA, U. Vt., Burlington, 1959, postgrad., 1963. Cert. secondary tchr., Vt. Founder, cultural program tchr. Cutler Acad., Craftsbury, Vt., 1959-63; founder outdoor program, English dept. The Stowe (Vt.) Sch., 1963-66; asst. to headmaster, tchr. Pine Ridge Sch., Williston, Vt., 1967-71; dean of students Middlesex Coll., Stowe, 1966; founder, operator Itrospect Sch. for Boys, Stowe, 1972-85; headmaster Vt. Land and Sea Sch., Springfield, 1985-86; mgr. Tauck Tours, Westport, Conn., 1987-89; founder, Walrus Tours Youth World Camps, Balt., 1986—; scis. selection com. Vt. Acad. Arts, Montpelier, 1966-68. Home: PO Box 1044 Stowe VT 05672-1044 Office: Youth World Camps 10 Old Bridge Rd West Palm Beach FL 33415-2523

KESTEN, RONALD E., restaurant equipment manufacturing executive; b. Pitts., July 3, 1942; s. Einer R. and Pauline (Yuhas) K.; m. Sue Ann Klingensmith, Feb. 15, 1969; children: Lauren Beth, Dana Ann, Ronald Daniel. Student, U. Pitts., 1961-63. Draftsman Ralph Underwood Co., Pitts., 1960-61; draftsman/salesperson Curran-Taylor, Inc., Clairton, Pa., 1961-64; gen. mgr. Curran-Taylor, Inc., McMurray, Pa., 1966-78; exec. Kesten & Egerman Co., Pitts., 1978-88; sales rep. H-Mak, Inc., Pitts., 1988-89; factory rep. Mordell-Pekter & Assocs., Flourtown, Pa., 1989-90; sales mgr. MTS Sales & Svc., Bethel Park, Pa., 1990-91; owner Kesten & Assocs., McMurray, 1991—. With U.S. Army, 1964-66. Mem. Pitts. Exec. Assn. (pres.), Peters Twp. C. of C. (pres.), North Strabane/84 C. of C. (pres.). Republican. Roman Catholic. Office: Kesten & Assocs 3107 Washington Rd # 19 McMurray PA 15317-3157

KESTENBAUM, STUART JON, arts admininstrator, writer; b. Newark, May 12, 1951; s. Milton Lewis and Annette (Weiss) K.; m. Susan B. Webster, Aug. 19, 1979; children: Isaac, Samuel. BA, Hamilton Coll., Clinton, N.Y., 1973. Exec. dir. Children's Mus. Greater Portland, Cape Elizabeth, ME, 1977-80; assoc. ME Arts Commn., Augusta, ME, 1980-85, asst. dir., 1985-88; exec. dir. Haystack Mt. Sch. Crafts, Deer Isle, ME, 1988—; chmn. ME Alliance for Arts Edn., Portland, ME, 1988-90; panelist Nat. Endowment for the Arts, Washington, 1989—; cons. ME Arts Spon. Assn., Augusta, 1989—. Author: Pilgrimage (poems), 1990; contbr. articles to profl. jours. Office: Haystack Mt Sch of Crafts PO Box 518 Deer Isle ME 04627-0518

KESTENBAUM, WILLIAM WOLF, research scientist; b. Vienna, Austria, Sept. 20, 1921; came to U.S., 1938; s. Alfred and Ada (Berger) K.; m. Sylvia Kall, Sept. 14, 1944; 1 child, Peter J. B Mech. Engring., CCNY, 1944; MEE, NYU, 1952; PhD, Bklyn. Poly. Inst., 1961. Engr. Western Electric, Kearny, N.J., 1944-47; sr. rsch. sect. head Sperry, Great Neck, N.Y., 1947-71; cons. AIL, Dear Park, N.Y., 1971-75; prof. Bklyn. Poly. Inst., 1972-79; lectr. Hofstra U., Hempstead, N.Y., 1970-72; chief scientist, chief engr. Polyflon, New Rochelle, N.Y., 1975-79; chief scientist Republic Electronics, Hauppauge, N.Y., 1979-89; pres. WWK Cons., Lido Beach, N.Y., 1989—; cons. N.Y, N.J., Fla., 1960—. Contbr. articles to profl. jours. Pres. B'nai B'rith, Long Beach, N.Y., 1980-82; mem. bd. Am. Heart Assn., Long Beach, 1983-84; v.p. Civic Assn., Lido Beach, 1984-87. With USN, 1944-46. Mem. Old Crows. Home and Office: WWK Cons 295 Lido Blvd Long Beach NY 11561-5004

KESTER, MARY MARTHA IRENE, interior designer; b. Phila., July 6, 1913; d. Charles Wells and Martha Irene (Davis) K. Cert., Moore Coll. Art, Phila., 1935. Draftsman Gen. Electric Co., Phila., 1937-43, USMC Women's Res., Arlington, Va., 1943-45, W. Stanleigh Krewson, Phila., 1945-47, RCA Corp., Camden, Cherry Hill, N.J., 1951-72; draftsman, instr. Moore Coll. Art, 1947-51; draftsman, designer Kester Assocs., Lumberton, N.J., 1951—. Republican. Presbyterian. Home and Office: 9 Church St Lumberton NJ 08048-1218

KESTERMAN, FRANK RAYMOND, investment banker; b. N.Y.C., May 5, 1937; s. Francis Anthony and Marion Catherine (Curth) K.; m. Iris Joan Jacobs, Mar. 21, 1964; children: Lezlie Ann, Noel John-Francis, Amanda. BS, U.S. Mcht. Marine Acad., King's Point, N.Y., 1959; MBA, Am. U., 1968; postgrad. advanced internat. studies, Johns Hopkins U., 1974-75; cert. advanced comml. banking, U. Va., 1982. CPA, Md. Ensign USN,

1959, advanced through grades to lt. (j.g.), 1961; nuclear power engr. USN, Vallejo, Calif., 1961-66; asst. to dir. research U.S. Maritime Adminstrn., Washington, 1967-72; pres. Internat. Services Corp., Washington, 1972-76; v.p. Shipbuilders Council Am., Washington, 1976-80, R.I. Hosp. Trust Nat. Bank, Providence, 1981-86; sr. v.p. 1st Oxford Corp., Washington, 1987-90; mgr. govt. guaranteed debt fin. mgt. svc. credit adminstrn. U.S. Dept. Treas., Washington, 1991—; advisor acquisitions P.R. Maritime Shipping Authority, San Juan, 1972-75; dep. dir. UN Port Project, Muscat, Oman, 1973-75; cons. on ship fin. World Bank, The Philippines, 1974, on port projects, Mex. and Panama, 1980. Adv. editor: Jour. Maritime Law and Commerce, 1972-87; contbr. articles to profl. jours. Bd. dirs. USMMA Found., 1990-92. Mem. AICPA, Md. Assn. CPAs, D.C. Inst. CPAs, Assn. Govt. Accts., Washington Savoyards Ltd. (treas. 1991—). Home: 4 Winterberry Ct Bethesda MD 20817-4846 Office: Dept of Treasury 401 14th St SWRm 500 Washington DC 20227

KESTY, ROBERT EDWARD, chemical manufacturing company executive; b. Camden, N.J., Dec. 11, 1941; s. Edward Adam and Helen Dorothy (Maciejko) Krzysztanowicz; m. Louise Marie Kesty, June 12, 1976; children: Nicole Christina, Alicia Anne, Christopher Edward. Student, Purdue U., 1960-63. Tech. rep. E.F. Houghton & Co., Phila., 1963-67; rsch. chemist H. Miller Corp., Phila., 1968-72; owner, founder R.E. Kesty Inc., Medford, N.J., 1977—; cons. Air Products and Chems. Inc., Middlesex, N.J., 1973; tech. advisor EPA, Indpls., 1974-76. Contbr. articles to profl. jours.; patentee in field. Recipient Franklin and Marshall Alumni award Franklin & Marshall Coll., 1959; recipient Hearst Trophy William Randolph Hearst Found., 1959. Mem. Nat. Assn. of Corrosion Engrs., South Jersey C. of C. Roman Catholic. Home: 1 Country Club Dr Medford NJ 08055 Office: RE Kesty Inc PO Box 342 Medford NJ 08055-0342

KETCHEN, GAVIN LEO, career officer; b. Caldwell, N.J., July 7, 1962; s. Leo Melvin and Evelyn Beryl (Gavin) K.; m. Deborah Anne Eyman, May 12, 1984; children: William Gavin, Michael David. B of Tech. in Mechanical Engring., U. Dayton, 1984; M of Aviation Sci., Embry Riddle Aero. U., 1989. Commd. 2d lt. USAF, 1984, advanced through grades to capt. Mem. AIAA, Air Force Assn., Order of Daedalions. Republican. Episcopalian.

KETCHUM, JAMES ROE, curator; b. Rochester, N.Y., Mar. 15, 1939; s. George Roe and Mary Louise (Frantz) K.; m. Barbara M. Van Ness, Aug. 18, 1962; children: John Van Ness, Sarah Graham, Timothy Roe, Chester Arthur. A.B., Colgate U., 1960; postgrad., Georgetown U., 1960-61, George Washington U., 1961-62. Staff historian Dept. Interior, Washington, 1960-62; registrar The White House, Washington, 1962-63; curator The White House, 1963-70, U.S. Senate, Washington, 1970—. Editor: The White House: An Historic Guide, 1962-70; contbr. numerous articles to profl. jours. and encys. Mem. Com. Preservation of White House, 1964-70; trustee U.S. Capitol Hist. Soc., 1971-79; alt. mem. Fed. Council Arts and Humanities, 1974—; trustee Woodrow Wilson Birthplace Found., 1980—. Member Am. Assn. Museums, City Mus. Washington, Nat. Trust Historic Preservation, Theta Chi. Office: US Senate Commn Art US Capitol Bldg Rm S-411 Washington DC 20510-7102

KETCHUM, WILLIAM CLARENCE, JR., lawyer, author; b. Columbia, Mo., Mar. 29, 1931; s. William C. and Mildred Ann (Roberts) K.; m. Erica Stoller; children: Rachel, Aaron. B.A., Union Coll., 1953; J.D., Columbia U., 1956. Bar: N.Y. 1960. Atty. Kriendler & Kriendler, N.Y.C., 1956, Martin, Clearwater & Bell, N.Y.C., 1960-65, R.S. Lane, N.Y.C., 1965-69; law sec. to Judge Lane of Civil Court, New York County N.Y.C., 1969-76; instr. course on Am. antiques New Sch., N.Y.C., 1970-87; instr. antiques course Hunter Coll., N.Y.C., 1978-79; mem. faculty NYU, 1984—, Folk Art Inst., 1987—, Marymount Coll., Tarrytown, N.Y., 1987—; guest curator Mus. Am. Folk Art, N.Y.C., 1974—, curator spl. projects, 1985—; guest curator Nassau County Fine Arts Mus., 1980; curator Female Folk Artists U.S., Japan, 1988-89, Am. Bd. Games Katonah (N.Y.) Mus. Art, 1992; guest speaker Seminar on Early Am. Life, Pa. Farm Mus., Lancaster, 1974; guest lectr. Flemington Hist. Soc., 1975-76, antiques seminar N.Y.U., 1973-75, 78-79, 81-84, New Haven Hist. Soc., 1975, Shelburne (Vt.) Mus., 1976, 78, St. Mary's of the Woods Coll., Terre Haute, Ind., 1976-78, Cooper-Hewitt Mus., 1978, Nassau County Fine Arts Mus., 1980, Mus. Am. Folk Art, 1978-84, Peale Mus., Balt., 1984, Del. Art Mus., 1985, N.Y. State Mus., 1985, Seattle Art Mus., 1986-87, Jacksonville (Fla.) Mus. of Art, 1987, Marymount Coll., 1987-92, Hiram (Ohio) Coll., 1988, Triton Mus., Santa Clara, Calif., 1988, Chautauqua (N.Y.) Inst., 1989, Art & Culture Ctr. Hollywood, Fla., 1990, Philbrook Mus. Art, Tulsa, 1991; cons. antique series Time-Life, Inc., 1976-78; series cons. Knopf Collectors' Guides to Am. Antiques, 1982-84; guest speaker Smithsonian Instn., 1976, Mercer Mus., 1977, Hancock Shaker Mus., 1977. Author: Early Potters and Potteries of New York, 1970, second ed. 1987; The Pottery and Porcelain Collectors Handbook, 1971; American Basketry and Woodenware, 1974; American Bottles, 1975; American Hooked Rugs, 1976; A Catalog of American Antiques, 1977, rev., 1990; The Family Treasury of Antiques, 1978; Catalog of American Collectibles, 1979, rev., 1990; Western Memorabilia, 1980; Auction, 1980; Collecting American Craft Antiques, 1980; Toys; Furniture 2, 1981; The Catalog of World Antiques, 1981; The Book of Boxes, 1982; Chests, Cupboards, Desks and Other Pieces, 1982, A Guide to Bottle Collecting, 1985; Am. Folk Art of the Twentieth Century, 1983; Pottery and Porcelain, 1983; Collecting Toys for Fun & Profit, 1985; Collecting 40's and 50's Collectibles for Fun and Profit, 1985; Sports Collectibles for Fun and Profit, 1985; All American, Folk Arts and Crafts, 1986; American Country Pottery, 1987, Making a Living in Antiques, 1990, Holiday Collectables, 1990, American Redware, 1990, Am. Stoneware, 1991, Country Wreaths and Baskets, 1991, Collecting the West, 1992; contbg. author: The American Sporting Collectibles Handbook, 1982, Is It Genuine, 1986; also articles to profl. jours. Served to lt., USNR, 1956-60. Recipient Ambassador of Honor award English Speaking Union, 1984. Mem. N.Y.C. Bar Assn. (mem. com. uniform state laws 1972-76, mem. art com. 1976-78), N.Y. State Bar Assn., N.Y. State Hist. Soc. Home: 241 Grace Church St Rye NY 10580-4211

KETO, C. TSEHLOANE, historian; b. Matatiele, South Africa, Feb. 23, 1941; came to U.S. 1968; s. Victor Lentsoe and Catherine Naniwe (Mazibu) Tsehloane; children: Lefa Victor, Lefanyana James. BA, U. South Africa, Pretoria, 1963; MA, Am. U., Washington, 1966; PhD, Georgetown U., Washington, 1972. Instr. Lincoln U., Oxford, Pa., 1969-70, Elizabethtown (Pa.) Coll., 1970; asst. prof. U. Kans., Lawrence, 1970-73; assoc. prof. Temple U., Phila., 1973-91, prof., 1991—, dir. Inst. of African and African-Am. Affairs, 1985-92, dir. grad. program African-Am. Studies, 1990—; pres. Keto Assocs., Inc., Blackwood, N.J., 1989—. Author: Aftermath of the Jameson Raid, 1980, American South African Relations, 1985, Africa Centered Perspective of History, 1989, rev. edit., 1991. Active Amnesty Internat.; mem. Concerned African Ams. Glaucester Twonship. Mem. Am. Hist. Assn., African Studies Assn., African Heritage Studies Assn. (bd. dirs. 1988—), Nat. Coun. for Black Studies, So. Africa Rsch. Assn. (membership sec. 1976-80), Orgn. South Africans (publicity sec. 1987-89). Episcopalian. Home: PO Box 1490 Laurel Springs NJ 08021 Office: Temple U Broad and Montgomery Sts Philadelphia PA 19122

KETTEN, DARLENE R., marine scientist; b. St. Louis, Oct. 21, 1947; d. Angus L. and Lorraine E. (Rolling) K. BA in Biology and French, Washington U., 1971; MS, MIT, 1979; PhD, Johns Hopkins U., 1984. Lectr. biology Suffolk U., Boston, 1975-78; lectr. psychology Goucher Coll., Balt., 1983-84; asst. prof. biol. scis. Towson State U., Balt., 1980-84; postdoctoral fellow MIT, Cambridge, Mass., 1984-87; rsch. fellow Mass. Eye and Ear Infirmary, Boston, 1985-87, rsch. assoc., 1987—; rsch. assoc. Harvard U., 1987-88; instr. dept. otology and laryngology Harvard Med. Sch., 1988—; mem. cultural affairs com. Johns Hopkins U., selection com. Gilman Lectureship; bd. assocs. Bermuda Biol. Sta. Contbr. numerous articles to profl. jours. Fellow NIH, 1980-81, NSF, 1982-84, Smithsonian Instn., 1982-84. Mem. AAAS, Soc. Neuroscis., Acoustical Soc. Am., Animal Behavior Soc., Marine Mammology Soc., Assn. for Research in Otolaryngology, Internat. Soc. for Stereology, Biometric Soc., Sigma Xi. Office: Cochlear Implant Rsch Lab Mass Eye and Ear Infirmary Dept Otolaryngology 243 Charles St Boston MA 02114

KETTINGER, DAVID JOHN, advertising consultant; b. Abington, Pa., Feb. 21, 1954; s. Ralph Joseph and Mary Elizabeth (Reilly) K. Student, Villanova U., 1973-75. Disc jockey Sta. WBUX-Radio, Doylestown, Pa., 1975-77; disc jockey, researcher Sta. WPST-Radio, Trenton, N.J., 1977-80; disc jockey, pub. rels. dir. Sta. WKHI-FM, Ocean City, Md., 1980-81; ops. dir., program dir. Sta. WWTR-WETT-Radio, Ocean City, Md., 1981-82; advt. cons. sales dept., producer Agy. Voice Overs, Ocean City, 1983-89; asst. sales mgr., 1989-90; sales mgr. Stas. WWTR and WETT, Ocean City, 1990-91, sales mgr., disk jockey, 1991—; disc jockey Sta. WQHQ-FM, Salisbury, Md., 1990-91; part-time air announcer, comml. producer, copywriter United Artist Cable TV of Ea. Shore, 1991—. Vol. fireman Weldon Fire Co. (mem. fire prevention and publicity coms.), 1972-81; active Muscular Dystrophy Assn., Ocean City Power Squadron. Republican. Roman Catholic. Home: 2820 Plover Dr # 13 Ocean City MD 21842-5438 Office: Sta WWTR-FM/WETT-AM 5700 Coastal Hwy Ocean City MD 21842-3190

KETTLEWELL, JAMES K., art historian, educator; b. Chgo., July 27, 1930; s. John Kenneth and Audrey Genevieve (Harness) K.; m. Lucy Jepson Cadou, Apr. 1952 (div. 1974); children: John Jepson, Chloe Hart; m. Jane Walenta Rehl, Sept. 1987. AB, Harvard Coll., 1952; AM, Harvard U., 1953. Teaching fellow Harvard Coll., Cambridge, Mass., 1952-53; curator Mus. Art of Ogunquit (Maine), 1953; lectr. U. Toronto, Ont., 1955-57; prof. art history Skidmore Coll., Saratoga Springs, N.Y., 1957—, dir. art history, 1990—; curator The Hyde Collection, Glens Falls, N.Y., 1967-80; cons. N.Y. State Coun. on arts, 1962-65, Hudson Valley Commn., 1962-70; dir. Gallery Assn. N.Y. State., 1970-78; trustee Saratoga County Hist. Soc. Author: Catalogue of the Hyde Collection, 1981, Saratoga Springs, An Architectural History, 1991. Office: Skidmore Coll North Broadway Saratoga Springs NY 12866

KEYES, CAROL RUTH, early childhood educator; b. Bklyn., May 24, 1935; d. Mortimer and Hana (Manberg) Fogel; m. Gordon Keyes, June 29, 1958; children: Alexander, Madelyn, Theodore. BA in Psychology, Hunter Coll., CUNY, 1957; MS in Edn., Queens Coll., CUNY, 1971; PhD in Child Devel. Early Childhood Edn., Union Inst., 1980; postgrad., Hofstra U., 1978. Cert. elem. tchr., N.Y. Dir., child study ctrs. Pace U., N.Y.C., 1985-89, chmn., dept. early childhood, 1985-87; dir., child care Hofstra U., Hempstead, N.Y., 1976-82; assoc. prof. early childhood Pace U., White Plains, N.Y., 1990—; cons. in field. Author: Early Childhood Adminstrn., Helping Children Grow: The Adult's Role; co-editor spl. issue Early Childhood Rsch. Quar., 1991. Mem. Nat. Assn. for Edn. Young Children, Nat. Coalition for Campus Child Care (past pres.), N.Y. State Assn. Early Childhood Tchr. Educators, Nat. Assn. Early Childhood Tchr. Educators, Orgn. Mondiale pour l'Education Prescolaire. Office: Pace U 78 N Broadway White Plains NY 10603-3796

KEYES, DAVID ELLIOT, mechanical engineering educator; b. Bklyn., Dec. 4, 1956; s. Elliot Fuller and Edna (Corsini) K.; married; 2 children. BSME, Princeton U., 1978; MS, Harvard U., 1979, PhD, 1984. Rsch. assoc. Yale U., Dept. Computer Sci., New Haven, Conn., 1984-85; asst. prof. Yale U., Dept. Mechanical Engring., New Haven, 1986-90; assoc. prof. Yale U., Dept. Mechanical Engring., 1990—; vis. scientist Inst. Computer Applications in Sci. and Engring., Hampton, Va., 1990. Editor: Domain Decomposition Methods in Partial Differential Equations, 1991; contbr. articles to profl. jours. Named Presdl. Young Investigator, NSF, Washington, 1989. Mem. Am. Soc. Mechanical Engrs., AIAA (coun. mem. 1991—), Soc. Indsl. and Applied Math. (sec. 1991—), The Combustion Inst., Tau Beta Pi, Sigma Xi, Phi Beta Kappa. Office: Yale U Dept Mechanical Engr PO Box 2159 New Haven CT 06520-2159

KEYMER, DAVID KING, university vice provost; b. Lakewood, Ohio, Apr. 30, 1936; s. John Lyman and Miriam Virginia (Ray) K.; m. Esther Ann Bendik, Dec. 26, 1964; 1 child, Jeremy Bendik Keymer. BA in Polit. Sci., Hiram (Ohio) Coll., 1958; MA in History, NYU, 1967; MPhil in History, Yale U., 1971, PhD in History, 1977. Tchr. Spanish and history Olmsted Falls (Ohio) Sch. Dist., 1959-64; tchr. history Harrison (N.Y.) Sch. Dist., 1965-69; lectr. in history Wells Coll., Aurora, N.Y., 1971-78; dir. spl. programs SUNY Inst. Tech., Utica, 1978-79, asst. dean grad. studies and continuing edn., 1979-83, asst. to v.p. acad. affairs, 1983-84, dean of students, 1984-92; vice provost for student affairs Calif. State U., Stanislaus, 1992—; adj. faculty SUNY Inst. Tech., 1978—; adj. faculty assoc. Empire State Coll., Utica, 1980-89. Vice-pres. N.Y. State Assn. for Retarded Children, Inc., Delmar, 1984-92; pres. Assn. for Retarded Citizens, Utica, 1985-88. Yale grad. fellow, 1970-71; Coun. for European and Comparative Studies rsch. grantee, 1969-70, NDEA grantee, 1967-70; Martha Holden Jennings teaching scholar, 1963-65. Mem. Coun. Student Affairs Officers of SUNY (sec. 1990—), Coll. Student Pers. Assn., Nat. Assn. Student Pers. Adminstrs. Office: SUNY Inst Tech PO Box 3050 Utica NY 13504-3050

KEYS, MARSHALL THEODORE, information network professional; b. Ann Arbor, Mich., Mar. 19, 1945; s. Theodore Crawford and Margery (Soenksen) K.; m. Sandra Bailey, Dec. 28, 1966; children: Emily, David. BA, Rutgers U., 1966; MA, Vanderbilt U., 1969, PhD, 1976; MS in Libr. Sci., U. N.C., 1977. English instr. Millsaps Coll., Jackson, Miss., 1970-74; asst. reference libr. Hampden-Sydney (Va.) Coll., 1974-75; info. specialist EPA, Research Triangle Park, N.C., 1976-77; sr. reference libr. U. Miss., Oxford, 1977-79; libr. dir. Curry Coll., Milton, Mass., 1979-86, acad. dean, 1986-89; dir. Nelinet, Inc., Newton, Mass., 1985—, chmn., 1988-89, exec. dir., 1989—; exec. com. OCLC Users Coun., Columbus, Ohio, 1990-91; speaker at libr. and pub. orgns.; network adv. com. Libr. Congress. Columnist Nelinet Liaison, 1989—. Mem. ALA, Assn. Coll. and Rsch. Librs. Episcopalian. Home: 300 Reedsdale Rd Milton MA 02186-3930 Office: Nelinet Inc 2 Newton Executive Park Newton MA 02162-1434

KEYS, PAUL ROSS, human services management educator; b. St. Louis, Mar. 21, 1940; s. Charles and Josie (Jones) K.; m. Marva Shegog, May 7, 1963; children: Michael, Roderick, Pamela. BS, St. Louis U., 1963, MSW, 1971; PhD, U. Wis., Milw., 1983. Exec. dir. Champaign (Ill.) Urban League, 1969; deputy dir. Concentrated Employment Program, St. Louis, 1971; asst. dir. Legis. Nat. Assn. of Social Workers, Washington, 1971-74; exec. dir. Community Svcs. Coun. Columbia, Mo., 1974-76; dir. Broward County (Fla.) Dept. of Human Svcs., 1976-78; deputy adminstr. Community Svcs. Div. State of Wis., 1978-81; adj. prof. pub. adminstrn. PACE U., White Plains, N.Y., 1984—; faculty doctoral program CUNY, 1987—; fellow Ctr. Social Adminstrn, Hunter Coll., N.Y.C., 1985—. Author: New Management in Human Services, 1988; founding editor Jour. of Multicultural Social Work, 1989—; contbr. articles to profl. jours. Sec. Nat. Network for Social Work Mgrs., Washington, 1989. Cpt. USAF, 1963-69. Recipient Martin Luther King fellowship, 1970, Commendation Resolution, Mo. Gen. Assembly, 1976, Fulbright Rsch. fellowship, Tokyo, 1990-91. Mem. NASW (exec. com. 1988), ASPA (exec. com. 1988—), Omega Psi Phi (Community Svc. award 1977). Home: 90 Waterbury Pky Cortlandt Manor NY 10566 Office: Hunter Coll Sch of SW 129 E 79th St New York NY 10021-0367

KEYSER, DAVID RICHARD, aerospace engineer, consultant; b. Ft. Wayne, Ind., Dec. 5, 1941; s. Richard Joseph and Nadine Della (Mueller) K.; m. Martha McKee, June 6, 1965 (div. Feb. 1991); children: Wendy, Orion; m. Eleanor Kinsley, May 1992. BSME, Swarthmore (Pa.) Coll., 1963; MSME, U. Pa., 1965; PhD, Eurotech Rsch. U., Hilo, Hawaii, 1991. Registered profl. engr., Calif. Mech. engr. Naval Boiler & Turbine Lab., Phila., 1965-81; aerospace engr. Naval Air Devel. Ctr., Warminster, Pa., 1981—; cons. TelTech Inc., Mpls., 1987—. Contbg. author: Fluid Meters, 6th edit., 1971; inventor fluidic accelerometer and fluidic igniter. Mem. ASME (vice chair rsch. com. fluid meters 1976-86, 90—, chair fluid control systems 1983-88, chair subcom. of flow measurement com. 1981-91, exec. com. fluid power systems and tech. div. 1989—, bd. dirs., bd. vice chair performance test codes 1991—, contbg. author Jour. Measurements, Codes and Standards 1977-81). Mem. Religious Soc. of Friends. Home: PO Box 1426 Southampton PA 18966-0827 Office: Naval Air WARPARG Ctr 6013 Warminster PA 18974

KEYSERLING, MARY DUBLIN, economist, consultant; b. N.Y.C., May 25, 1910; d. Louis J. and Augusta Dublin; m. Leon H. Keyserling, Oct. 4, 1940 (dec.). BA, Barnard Coll., 1930; postgrad., London Sch. Econs., 1931-32; PhD, Columbia U., 1933; LLD (hon.), Bryant Coll., 1967; hon., Women's Med. Coll. Pa., 1968. Rsch. staff mem. Com. on Costs of Med. Care, Washington, 1930-31; adminstrv. asst. State Charities Aid Assn., N.Y.C., 1931; prof. econs. Sarah Lawrence Coll., Bronxville, N.Y., 1933-38; exec. dir. Nat. Consumers League, N.Y.C., 1938-40; coord. hearings Com. on Nat. Def. Migration Ho. of Reps., Washington, 1941; chief rsch. and stats. div., personal asst. to Mrs. Eleanor Roosevelt Office Civilian Def., Washington, 1942-43; chief liberated areas div. Fgn. Econ. Adminstrn., Washington, 1943-45; dir. internat. econ. analysis div. U.S. Dept. Commerce, Washington, 1946-53; assoc. dir. Conf. on Econ. Progress, Washington, 1953-63, 69-88; assoc. dir. and cons. economist; cons. economist, U.S. and overseas, 1953-63, Washington, 1969—; congl. testifier to mems. of Congress; dir. Women's Bur., U.S. Dept. Labor, 1964-69; exec. vice chmn. Interdepartmental Com. of Status of Women, Washington, 1964-69. Author: Windows on Day Care, 1972, N.Y.C. Child Care Programs, 1973, also numerous book chpts., more than 1500 articles, speeches and pamphlets. V.p. United Neighborhood Ctrs. Am., Washington; exec. dir. Project Action for Children and Youth; mem. adv. commn. on child devel. NAS, 1972-76; mem. various bds. Nat. Consumers League, Clearing House of Women's Issues (past pres.), Nat. Health Security Coun., Nat. Child Day Care Assn. (past pres.), others; trustee Internat. Overseas Edn. Recipient Medal of Distinction Barnard Coll., 1980, Ann. award Am. Med. Women's Assn., Leadership for Freedom award Roosevelt U., Disting. Svc. award 100th Anniversary Nat. Conf., Nat. Conf. on Social Welfare, others; named one of 25th Most Influencial Couples in U.S. Ladies Jour.; postdoctoral rsch. fellow Columbia U. Grad. Sch., 1933-34. Mem. Am. Econ. Assn., Women's Nat. Dem. Club (pres. 1963-64), Phi Beta Kappa. Home and Office: 2101 Connecticut Ave NW Washington DC 20008-1728

KEZER, PAULINE RYDER, state legislator; b. Boston, Feb. 4, 1942; d. Paul Washington and Madeline (Farmer) Ryder; m. Kenneth Ronald Kezer, Sept. 23, 1962; children—Anne Elizabeth, Pamela Lynne, Cynthia Karen. B.Psychology, Colby Coll., 1963; postgrad. Central Conn. State Coll., 1978, 83. Tutor sci. and humanities New Britain Schs. Teenage Parent Program, New Britain Conn., 1964-78; mem. Conn. Ho. of Reps., Hartford, 1979—, asst. minority leader, 1981-84, asst. majority leader, 1985-86; Sec. State Conn., 1991—; bd. dirs. New Eng. Caucus Women Legislators, 1983-84, chmn., 1985-86; pres. Conn. Order Women Legislators, Hartford, 1981-82; mem. adv. com. Central Conn. State U. Polit. Inst., New Britain, 1983-84; mem. adv. bd. Colonial Bank, Plainville, Conn., 1980-85. Camp dir. Girl Scout Council, 1972-81, assoc. chair, 1975-78, v.p., 1979-85, nat. bd. dirs., 1984—; pres., v.p., treas., bd. dirs. YWCA, New Britain, 1971-79; chmn., sec. Inland Wetlands Com., 1972-79; mem. Republican Town Com., Plainville, 1977-84; exec. bd. Eastern region Council State Govts.; vol. New Britain Cancer Soc., 1980-85; bd. dirs. Collaboration for Conn.'s Children, 1985—; mem. adv. bd. Tunxis Community Coll., 1984—; mem. nat. rev. team Project Hometown Am., 1986; ; hon. chair Conn. Citizen Bee, 1992; vice chair Conn. Rep. Party, 1987-89. Recipient Thanks Badge and Conn. Yankee award Conn. Yankee Girl Scout council, Farmington, 1982, 79; named Outstanding Citizen, Jaycees, Plainville, Conn., 1980; Outstanding Vol., New Britain YWCA, 1978; Legislator of Yr., Conn. Valley Girl Scout council, Hartford, 1984; recipient Women Helping Women award Soroptomists, Hartford, 1984—; Harvard U. Inst. Politics fellow, 1990, Am. Leadership Forum fellow, 1991-92. Mem. Nat. Order Women Legislators (legis. chair 1986), Women Execs. in State Govt., Conn. Fedn. Rep. Women (2d v.p. 1992—), Ea. Region Coun. State Govts. (exec. bd. 1991-92), Nat. Assn. Secs. of State (exec. bd. 1991-92, Alpha Delta Pi. Republican. Episcopalian (vestryman St. Mark's Ch. 1991—). Club: Newcomers (pres. 1965-67) (New Britain). Office: Office of the Sec of State State Capitol Hartford CT 06106

KHAIRULLAH, ZAHID YAHYA, management sciences and marketing educator, consultant; b. Bombay, India, Sept. 29, 1945; came to U.S., 1972; s. Yahya Gulamhusein Dawoodbhoy and Sugra Abdulhusein Abdulcarim (Batliwala) K.; m. Durriya Haider Cassumji, May 1971; children: Nazifah, Firhana, Sakhiba. B Tech. in Metall. Engring., Indian Inst. Tech., Bombay, 1971; MS in Mech. Engring., SUNY-Buffalo, 1974, MBA in Mgmt. Sci., 1977, PhD in Mgmt., 1982. Jr. officer M/S Spl. Steels, Ltd., Bombay, 1971-72; design engr. M/S Secure Enterprises, Buffalo, 1974-77; asst. prof. mgmt. scis. St. Bonaventure U., N.Y., 1977-82, assoc. prof., chmn. depts. mgmt. sci. and mktg., 1982-85, 01—; prof., mgmt. scis. and mktg. depts., 1982—; dean Sch. Bus. Adminstrn., 1987-90; chmn. dept. mgmt. scis., 1991-92; rsch. assoc. SUNY-Buffalo, 1979; cons. in field; lectr. various colls. and univs. Contbr. articles to profl. jours. Active So. Tier West Econ. Devel. Task Force, 1982-83, So. Tier West Community Devel. Com. 1988-91. Fellow Acad. Mktg. Sci., Inst. Mktg. Mgmt.; mem. Am. Inst. Decision Scis., Inst. Mgmt. Scis., Islamic Soc. So. Tier (exec. com. 1982—, treas. 1982-89, 91—), Am. Soc. Ops. Rsch., Am. Prodn. Inventory Control Soc. (cert., v.p. edn., seminars 1984-85, pres. 1985-87, bd. dirs. Pa.-N.Y. chpt. 1984-91), Beta Gamma Sigma (life), Delta Mu Delta (life). Home: 2316 Sheldon Dr Allegany NY 14706-9651 Office: St Bonaventure U Sch Bus Adminstrn Saint Bonaventure NY 14778

KHAN, AL-SAMEEN TEWFIK, electrical engineering educator; b. San Fernando, Trinidad, July 7, 1961; came to U.S., 1979; s. Mohamed Azim and Homida Khan; m. Crystal Ann Killen, Dec. 28, 1980; children: Timigen Jewfik, Hillary Alesha. BS in Physics and Math., Del. State Coll., 1983; MSEE, U. Va., 1986; postgrad., U. Del., 1989—. Engr. Tex. Instruments, Dallas, 1987; instr. Del. State Coll., Dover, 1988—. Mem. IEEE, Alpha Kappa Mu, Alpha Chi. Office: Del State Coll Dover DE 19901

KHAN, JAMIL AKBER, manufacturing company executive; b. Hyderabad, Pakistan, Mar. 17, 1952; came to U.S., 1979, naturalized, 1981; s. Mehboob Khan and Shamin (Akhter) Ghori; m. Tahira Bano, Feb. 27, 1981; children: Farooq Jamil, Omar Jamil. BSc, U. Sind, Hyderabad, 1971, MSc, 1974; PhD, U. London, 1979; MBA, U. New Haven, 1986. Chartered chemist. Asst. prof. D.J. Coll., Karachi, Pakistan, 1974-76; demonstrator Univ. Coll. London, 1976-79; rsch. assoc. Duke U., Durham, N.C., 1979-81; rsch. chemist Uniroyal, Inc., Middlebury, Conn., 1981-84, rsch. scientist, 1984, specialist, product/market devel., 1984-86; mgr. market devel. Montedison USA Inc., 1986-87; product mgr. Ausimont, 1987—; mgr. sales and mktg., bus. mgr. Enimont, 1990—; cons. in field. Editor: Physical Chemistry, 1977; contbr. articles to internat. jours.; inventor in field. Fellow Am. Inst. Chemists; mem. Am. Chem. Soc., Royal Soc. Chemistry (Eng.), UNESCO-Internat. Orgn. for Coop. and Devel., Sigma Xi. Avocations: jogging, photography, tennis, reading. Home: 575 Bensel Dr Landing NJ 07850-1922 Office: 1211 Ave Of The Americas New York NY 10036-8701

KHAN, SHAHRUKH RAFI, economist, educator; b. Abgotagad, Pakistan, Oct. 4, 1952; s. M. Rafi and Nazli (Rafi) K.; m. Stephanie Bunker, May 17, 1980; children: Sophia Bunker-Khan, Lila Bunker-Khan. BS with honors, London Sch. Econs., 1973; MA in Devel. Econ., Williams Coll., 1976; PhD in Econs., U. Mich., 1983. Sect. head, pub. policy Pakistan Inst. of Devel. Econs., Islamabad, Pakistan, 1983-87; lectr. SUNY, Oneonta, N.Y., 1987-88; asst. prof. Vassar Coll., Poughkeepsie, N.Y., 1988—; cons. UNESCO, 1984-86, World Bank, 1988-89, U.S. Aid, 1988—. Author: Profit and Loss Sharing, 1987, Higher Education and Employment Opportunities, 1988; contbr. over 44 articles to profl. jours. Recipient 2d prize Nat. Bank Coun. Pakistan, 1989. Home and Office: Vassar Coll Box 284 Poughkeepsie NY 12601

KHARE, MOHAN, chemist; b. Varanasi, India, May 15, 1942; came to U.S., 1967, naturalized, 1971; s. Dwarka Nath and Rampyari Devi Khare Srivastava; m. Meena K., Nov. 20, 1973; 1 child, Rohit. BSc, Banaras Hindu U., 1961, MSc, 1963, PhD, 1967. Rsch. assoc. U. Md., College Park, 1967-69, Oreg. State U., Corvallis, 1969-70; sr. rsch. assoc. Cornell U., Ithaca, N.Y., 1970-78; analytical specialist Hydroscience Inc., (subsidiary of Dow Chem. Co.), Knoxville, Tenn., 1978-80; tech. specialist IT Enviroscience subs. IT Corp., Knoxville, 1980-82; rsch. prof. chemistry U. Nev., Las Vegas, 1982-84, mgr. organic div. quality assurance lab. under coop. agreement with EPA, 1982-84; mgr. organic analysis lab. Environ. Monitoring Svcs. Rockwell Internat., Thousand Oaks, Calif., 1984-85; dir. environ. analytical lab. EA Engring, Sci., and Tech., Inc., Sparks, Md., 1985-87; sr. v.p. Recra Environ., Inc., Columbia, Md., 1987-88; pres., chief exec. officer Envirosystems, Inc., Columbia, 1989—. Contbr. articles to profl. jours. including protocols and standard oper. procedures for hazardous waste analytical program. Mem. AAAS, Am. Chem. Soc., Am. Soc. Mass Spectrometry. Home: 10189 Maxine St Ellicott City MD 21042-6316 Office: Envirosystems Inc 9200 Rumsey Rd Ste 102B Columbia MD 21045-1934

KHATIB, GHASSAN, science historian, mechanical engineer; b. Doha, Qatar, Apr. 23, 1962; came to U.S., 1984; s. Kassem Mohammad and Shamma (Issa) K.; m. Nada Fouad El-Debs. B in Engring., Am. U., Beirut, Lebanon, 1984; MSME, Columbia U., 1986; MA, Cornell U., 1989, PhD, 1991. Dir. Midhold (Ltd.) Inc.; mng. dir. Intext Trading Ltd. Mem. Lebanese Engring. Syndicate, ASME, Internat. Soc. for History of Sci., British Soc. for History of Sci., AAAS. Moslem. Home: 278 Beacon St Apt 12 Somerville MA 02143-3548

KHAYAT, AZEEZ VICTOR, psychiatrist; b. N.Y.C., Aug. 13, 1933; s. Victor Azeez and Clotilde (Habesch) K.; m. Waltraud Ahlswede K.; m. July 6, 1965; children: Astrid Helen, Alexandra Frances, Victor Rudolph. BBA, Am. U. of Beirut, 1951; MD, Bachelor Surgery, Bachelor Art in Obstetrics, U. Ireland, Dublin, 1958. Diplomate Am. Bd. Psychiatry and Neurology. Intern Med. Sch. Wash. U., St. Louis, 1959-60; resident Med. Sch. Wash. U., Washington, 1960-62; chief of svc. Saint Elizabeths Hosp., Washington, 1964-71; sr. attending physician Wash. Hosp. Ctr., Washington, 1971—; psychiat. cons. NIH, 1971-73, Washington Clinic Med. Ctr., 1971-83. Author: (med. jour.) The Vietnam Syndrome, 1965. Comdr. USN, 1962-64. Decorated Purple Heart. Mem. AMA, Am. Psychiat. Assn., Assn. of Mil. Surgeons of the U.S., Wash. Psychiat. Soc. (pub. info. com. 1981-86), Med. Soc. of D.C., Kenwood Golf and Country Club, Rotary Internat., KC. Republican. Roman Catholic. Home: 11024 Stanmore Dr Rockville MD 20854-1525 Office: 5454 Wisconsin Ave Ste 1435 Bethesda MD 20815-6950

KHAZEH, KHASHAYAR (KASHI KHAZEH), finance educator; b. Tehran, Iran, Oct. 27, 1948; came to U.S., 1973, naturalized, 1984; s. Manouchehr and Parvindokht (Tajbakhsh) K.; m. Melinda Ann Brawley, Oct. 29, 1978; 1 child, Keemia Leigh. BS, Nat. U. of Iran, 1972; BS with honors, U. Tenn., 1976; MBA, Mankato (Minn.) State U., 1978; MA, U. Tenn., 1981, PhD, 1985; post doctoral studies, U. Md., 1987. Asst. controller, then mgr. Shiraz Indsl. Group, Tehran, 1968-72; dir. mktg. Farmoj Co., Tehran, 1978; instr. U. Tenn., Knoxville, 1983-85; asst. prof. fin. Salisbury (Md.) State U., 1985-91, assoc. prof. fin., 1991—. Contbr. articles to profl. jours. 2nd lt. Iranian Army, 1972-73. Mem. Am. Econs. Assn., Ea. Fin. Assn., Midwest Fin. Assn., Fin. Mgmt. Assn. (faculty advisor local student chpt. 1988—, Outstanding Faculty award 1990, Disting. Faculty award 1991). Home: 3 York Dr Salisbury MD 21801-9479

KHAZEI, AMIR MOSHEN, surgeon, oncologist; b. Teheran, Iran, July 21, 1928; came to U.S., 1957; s. Abol Khasem and Esmat (Khaligh-Azam) K.; m. Carmeline Victoria Grace Picardi; children: Alan, Darla, Mia and Lance (twins). BS, U. Lausanne, Switzerland, 1952, MD and Cert. d'Etudes Medicale, 1957. Diplomate Mass. Bd. Medicine, N.H. Bd. Medicine; qualified Am. Bd. Surgery. Intern Mercy Hosp., Pitts., 1957-58, resident in gen. surgery, 1957-62; fellow in surgery Leahy Clinic Found., Boston, 1962-63, assoc. staff mem. surgery and chemotherapy, 1963-67, assoc. dir. surg. rsch. lab., 1967-68; attending surgeon VA Hosp., Manchester, N.H., 1968-70; staff surgeon Cath. Med. Ctr./Elliot Hosp., Manchester, 1971—; pres., chmn. exec. com. of med. staff Cath. Med. Ctr., 1981-82. Mem. editorial bd. Living With Cancer; co-author book; contbr. articles to profl. jours. Mem. bd. Incorporator Cath. Med. Ctr., 1981—, trustee, 1981-90, Fidelity Health Alliance Bd., Manchester, 1991—; pres. N.H. div. Am. Cancer Soc., 1977-79, nat. del. dir., 1982-91. Recipient St. George medal Am. Cancer Soc., 1982, Golden Apple award Cath. Med. Ctr., 1990, Med. Staff award N.H. Hosp. Assn., 1990. Fellow Am. Coll. Angiology, Internat. Coll. Angiology, Inter-Am. Coll. Physicians and Surgeons; mem. AMA, Am. Fed. Clin. Rsch., N.H. Med. Soc. (pres., chmn. exec. com. 1986-87), N.Y. Acad. Scis., Orgn. State Med. Assn. Pres.'s (life), Transplantation Soc., Hillsborough County Med. Soc. (pres. 1981-82), Am. Assn. for Cancer Edn. Office: 88 McGregor St Ste # 304 Manchester NH 03102

KHORANA, HAR GOBIND, chemist, educator; b. Raipur, India, Jan. 9, 1922; s. Shri Ganpat Rai and Shrimati Krishna (Devi) K.; m. Esther Elizabeth Sibler, 1952; children: Julia, Emilie, Dave Roy. BS, Punjab U., 1943, MS, 1945; PhD, Liverpool (Eng.) U., 1948; DSc, U. Chgo., 1967. Head organic chemistry group B.C. Rsch. Coun., 1952-60; vis. prof. Rockefeller Inst., N.Y.C., 1958—; prof. co-dir. Inst. Enzyme Rsch. U. Wis., Madison, 1960-70, prof. dept. biochemistry, 1962-70, Conrad A. Elvehjem prof. life scis., 1964-70; Alfred P. Sloan prof. biology and chemistry MIT, Cambridge, 1970—; vis. prof. Stanford U., 1964; mem. adv. bd. Biopolymers; researcher chem. methods for synthesis of nucleotides, coenzymes and nucleic acids, elucidation on the genetic code, lab. synthesis of genes, biol. membrane and light-transducing pigments. Author: Some Recent Developments in the Chemistry of Phosphate Esters of Biological Interests, 1961; mem. editorial bd.: Jour. Am. Chem. Soc, 1963—; contbr. numerous articles to profl. jours. Recipient Merck award Chem. Inst. Can., 1958, Gold medal Profl. Inst. Pub. Service Can., 1960, Dannie-Heinneman Preiz Göttingen, Germany, 1967, Remsen award Johns Hopkins U., 1968, Am. Chem. Soc. award for creative work in synthetic organic chemistry, 1968, Louisa Gross Horwitz prize, 1968, Lasker Found. award for basic med. research, 1968, Nobel prize in medicine, 1968; elected to Deutsche Akademie der Naturforscher Leopoldina HalleSaale, Germany, 1968; Overseas fellow Churchill Coll., Cambridge, Eng., 1967. Fellow Chem. Inst. Can., Am. Acad. Arts and Scis.; mem. NAS. Office: MIT Rm 180511 Dept Biology and Chemistry Cambridge MA 02139

KIANG, ROBERT L., mechanical engineer, researcher; b. Chung King, China, Nov. 30, 1939; came to U.S., 1962; s. Johnson C. and C.C. (Huang) K.; m. Ming Deng; 1 child, Jennifer. BS, Taiwan U., Taipei, 1961; MS, Stanford U., 1964, PhD, 1969. Staff scientist SRI Internat., Menlo Park, Calif., 1963-87; project engr. David Taylor Rsch. Ctr., Annapolis, Md., 1987—; part-time prof. San Jose State U., Calif., 1982-84; vis. prof. U.S. Naval Acad., Annapolis, 1990-91. Mem. ASME. Home: 408 Hartman Dr Severna Park MD 21146-2049 Office: David Taylor Rsch Ctr Code 2721 Annapolis MD 21402

KIBBE, JAMES WILLIAM, real estate broker; b. Bound Brook, N.J., Oct. 5, 1926; s. Orlando A. and Anna Rose (Tomb) K.; m. Bettie Brooks Dailey, June 11, 1949; children: James William Jr., Linda Jean. BS, U. Md., 1951. Real Estate salesman Eig & Mc Keever, Silver Spring, Md., 1955-57, Weaver Bros, Inc., Chevy Chase Bldg. (Md.), 1957-70, asst. v.p. sales, leasing dept., 1970-72, sales mgr., 1972-73, v.p. sales mgr., 1973-82, sr. v.p., sales mgr., 1983-89; sr. v.p. dir. sales, The Michael Co., 1989—; lectr, in field; chmn. Brokers and Salesmen's council, 1968-69. Served with USNR, 1944-46. Mem. Soc. Indsl. and Office Realtors (pres. Md. and D.C. chpt. 1985-86, nat. bd. dirs. 1988-90), Nat. Assn. Realtors, D.C. Assn. Realtors, Montgomery County Bd. Realtors, Md. Assn. Realtors, Washington Bd. Trade, Washington Builders Assn., Nat. Assn. Indsl. and Office Parks (bd. dirs. 1987), Nat. Inst. Real Estate Brokers (state chmn. 1968-70), New Am. Network (adv. bd. dirs. 1986—, adv. bd. chmn. 1991—). Republican. Methodist. Club: Sandy Spring Lions (pres. 1965-66). Home: 1000 Ashland Dr Ashton MD 20861-9718 Office: The Michael Co 9658 Baltimore Ave College Park MD 20740-1346

KIDALOWSKI, RAYMOND JOHN, financial planner, accountant; b. Schenectady, NY, Apr. 16, 1946; s. Raymond Joseph and Mary Agnes (McGinn) K.; m. Laurel Marie Keppler, Apr. 26, 1981; children: Stefan Matthew, Nicholas Raymond. BA, SUNY, 1967; BBA, Pace U., 1972. CPA, N.Y. Acct. Mann Judd Landau, N.Y.C., 1973-79; treas., contr. York Rsch. Corp., Stamford, Conn., 1979-81; mgr. Arthur Place & Co., CPA, P.C., Albany, N.Y., 1981-83; treas., contr. The AYCO Corp., Albany, 1983-88; fin. planning pension specialist Northwestern Mut. Life, Albany, 1988—; employee benefits cons. for various cos., 1989—; seminar presenter exec. devel. programs Suffolk U., Boston, 1991—, Russell Sage Coll., Albany, 1991—. Contbr. articles to mags. Pres. sch. bd. St. Thomas Sch., Delmar, N.Y., 1991. Lt. U.S. Army, 1968-80, Vietnam. Mem. AICPA (fin. planning div.), Nat. Assn. Life Underwriters, N.Y. State Soc. CPAs (com. head). Office: Northwestern Mut Life 951 Albany-Shaker Rd Latham NY 12110

KIDAWA, ANTHONY STANLEY, podiatrist educator; b. Phila., Apr. 1, 1942; s. Felicia H. (Kopczynski) K.; m. Nancy A. Skokowski, Sept. 20, 1969; children: Kevin, Lori. BS, Villanova U., Pa., 1964; D of Podiatric Med., Pa. Coll. Podiatric Medicine, Phila., 1969. Podiatric cons. We. Jersey Hosp. Central Div., Camden, N.J., 1970-72; active staff Girard Med. Ctr., Phila., 1971—; courtesy admit staff John F. Kennedy Memorial Hosp., Turnersville, N.J., 1973—; from chmn. dept. med. to section chief Pa. Coll. of Podiatric Med., Phila., 1976—; rotating dir. Foot Health Ctr., Phila., 1981-83; nat. speaker panel Hoechst-Roussel Pharm. Co., Sommerville, N.J., 1987—; dir. pres. Clindialab, Inc., Phila., 1984—; editoral cons. Current Podiatric Med. Publ., N.Y.C., 1982-85; contbg. editor Year Book of Podistric Med., Chgo., 1984, Podiatry Tracts, Phila., 1987; manuscript rev. Pan Jour. of Am. Podiatric Med., Bethesda, 1989—. Researcher Clinical Angiology Nerve Block Study, 1984 (Bronze award 1985; author: Articles & Abstract Periph Circulation, 1984; co-author film Toenail Burr Tech., 1987. Organizer Clindialab, Inc., Phila, 1989—; judge Lions Club Miss Am. Prelim, Glassboro, N.J., 1990. Research Grantee Collagen Corp, Phila, 1985, Leggs Corp., 1986, Aris-Isotoner Corp., 1987, Becton-Dickenson Corp, 1988, Zimmer Corp, 1989. Fellow Am. Soc. Podiatric Med.; Mem. Alumni Assn. Pa. Coll. Podiatric Med. (pres. 1973). Roman Catholic. Home: 2028 Chapel Ave W Cherry Hill NJ 08002-2014 Office: PA Coll Podiatric Med 810 Race St Philadelphia PA 19107-2406

KIDDER, C. ROBERT, battery manufacturing company executive; b. 1943. BSIE, U. Mich., 1966; MS, Iowa State U., 1968. With Ford Motor Co., Detroit, 1968-69, McKinsey & Co., N.Y.C., 1972-78, Dart Industries, 1978-80, Duracell Europe, 1980-81; with Duracell Internat. Inc., 1981—, pres., CEO, from 1988, now chmn., CEO, also bd. dirs. With USN, 1969-72. Office: Duracell Inc Berkshire Blvd Bethel CT 06801-1001*

KIDECKEL, DAVID ARTHUR, anthropologist; b. Detroit, Jan. 12, 1948; s. Ben and Ida (Saltzman) K.; m. Liza A. LaRose, Mar. 2, 1969 (div. Jan. 1973); 1 child, Mimi; m. Judith Marie Bernadotte, July 21, 1978; children; Zachary, Caitlin. BA, Wayne State U., 1969; PhD, U. Mass., 1979. Asst./assoc. prof. anthropology Cen. Conn. State U., New Britain, 1977-88, prof., chmn. dept., 1988—; vis. prof. anthropology and East European studies Yale U., New Haven, 1983. Editor: Anthropology Quar., vol. 3, 1982; co-editor Anthropology of East Europe Rev., 1988—; author: Solitude of Collectivism; contbr. articles and revs. to profl. jours. Asst. coach West Hartford (Conn.) Dragons Youth Soccer Club, 1990—. U.S. Dept. Edn. grantee, 1989-91; Fulbright Hayes grantee U.S. Dept. Edn., Romania, 1975-76; Am. Coun. Learned Socs. travel grantee, Zagreb, Yugoslavia, 1988. Fellow Am. Anthrop. Assn.; mem. AAUP, Soc. Anthropology of Europe (program chair 1991-92), Am. Ethnol. Soc., Soc. Romanian Studies, East European Anthropology Group (mem. exec.bd. 1985-91, chairperson 1987-90), Phi Beta Kappa, Alpha Kappa Delta. Office: Cen Conn State U Dept Anthropology Diloreto Hall New Britain CT 06050

KIEFER, J. RICHARD, JR., corporate executive; b. Phila., Mar. 3, 1928; m. Gwendolen Clara Watkins, June 20, 1953; children David Richard, Linda Lauretta, Nancy Ellen, Carol Gwen. BS in Chem. Engring., Drexel U., 1950; postgrad., Temple U. With McCloskey Corp., Phila., 1947-89, with rsch. and devel., with customer product evaluation dept., v.p. community, industry and regulatory affairs. Mem. Phila. Opera Guild, Met. Opera Guild, Olney Symphony Assn., Pa. Ballet Assn., Zool. Soc. Phila., Franklin Inst., Friends of Independence Nat. Hist. Park, N.E. Phila. Cultural Coun., Meml. Soc. Greater Phila. (past pres., treas., bd. dirs.), Friends of Pennypack Park. Mem. Phila. Paint and Coatings Assn. (past pres., bd. dirs.), Phila. Soc. Coatings Tech. (past pres., bd. dirs., by-laws com. chmn., handbook editor, tech. com., Liberty Bell awards), Fed. Soc. Coatings Tech. (past coun., bd. dirs., exec. com., Trigg award), Am. Chem. Soc., N.E. High Sch. Alumni Assn., Soc. Gallows Birds, Rotary (sec., bd. dirs.), Masons, Alpha Phi Omega, Zeta Theta. Home: 1027 Loney St Philadelphia PA 19111-2624

KIEFFER, STEPHEN AARON, radiologist, educator; b. Mpls., Dec. 20, 1935; s. Julius Hyman and Anita Elaine (Brudnick) K.; m. Cyrile Frada Kaplan, Dec. 21, 1958; children—Alisa, Mitchell, Stuart, Paula. B.A. summa cum laude, U. Minn., 1956, B.S., 1957, M.D., 1959. Diplomate: Am. Bd. Radiology. Intern Wadsworth VA Hosp., Los Angeles, 1959-60; resident in radiology U. Minn. Hosps., Mpls., 1960-62, 64-65; NIH fellow in neuroradiology, 1966-68; instr. U. Minn. Med. Sch., Mpls., 1966-67; asst. prof. U. Minn. Med. Sch., 1967-68, asso. prof., 1968-72, prof., 1972-74; chief radiology service Mpls. VA Hosp., 1968-74; prof., chmn. dept. radiology SUNY-Health Sci. Ctr., Syracuse, 1974—, chmn. governing bd. clin. practice mgmt. plan, 1985-88; v.p., mem. med. bd., mem. med. exec. com. Univ. Hosp., 1988—; cons. Syracuse VA Med. Center, Crouse-Irving-Meml. Hosp. Co-author: Introduction to Neuroradiology, 1972; co-editor: An Atlas of Cross-sectional Anatomy, 1979; contbr. numerous articles to profl. jours., also chpts. to books; editorial adv. bd.: Radiology, 1980-85, assoc. editor, 1986, cons. to editor, 1987—; cons. to editorial bd. Am. Jour. Neuroradiology, 1980—; assoc. editor: Yearbook of Radiology, 1981-86; editorial bd. RadioGraphics, 1987—. Chmn. tech. adv. subcom. on computed tomography Cen. N.Y. Health Systems Agy., 1979-80; mem. tech. adv. com. on computed tomography N.Y. State Office Health Systems Mgmt., 1981; bd. dirs. Syracuse Jewish Fedn., 1975-81, 90—, v.p., 1990—; bd. dirs. Academic Health Profls. Ins. Assn., 1991—. Capt. M.C. U.S. Army, 1962-64. Nat. Heart Inst. trainee, 1961-62; Nat. Inst. Neurol. Diseases and Blindness fellow, 1966; James Picker Found. scholar, 1966-68. Fellow Am. Coll. Radiology (councilor 1986—); mem. Am. Roentgen Ray Soc. (publs. com. 1979-84), Am. Soc. Neuroradiology (pres. 1978-79), AMA, Assn. Univ. Radiologists (program com. 1985-86), Cen. N.Y. Radiol. Soc. (chmn. program com. 1979-82), Med. Soc. State of N.Y., Minn. Radiol. Soc. (sec. 1974), Neurosurg. Soc. Am., Onondaga County Med. Soc., Radiol. Soc. N.Am. (refresher course com. 1977-82, program com. 1984-91), Soc. Chairmen Acad. Radiology Depts., N.Y. State Radiol. Soc. (v.p. 1985-86, pres. 1987-88), Acad. Health Profls. Ins. Assn. (bd. dirs. 1991—), Eastern Neuroradiological Soc. (pres. 1991—), Phi Beta Kappa, Alpha Omega Alpha. Jewish. Home: 503 Standish Dr Syracuse NY 13224-2015 Office: 750 E Adams St Syracuse NY 13210-2306

KIELY, DAN RAY, lawyer, banking and real estate development executive; b. Ft. Sill, Okla., Jan. 2, 1944; s. William Robert and Leona Maxine (Ross) K.; BA in Psychology, U. Colo., 1966, JD, Stanford U., 1969; children: Jefferson Ray, Matthew Ray. Bar: Colo 1969, D.C. 1970, Va. 1973. Assoc. firm Holme, Roberts and Owen, Denver, 1969-70; pres. DeRand Equity Group, Arlington, Va., 1973-89; pres., chmn. bd. Bankwest Corp. and related banks, Denver.; pres., dir. United Gibralter Corp. Del., Inc., Unocam, Inc., 1987—; ptnr. Starlin & Kiely, P.C., 1989—; trustee DeRand Real Estate Investment Trust, 1974—; chmn. Pace Holdings, Inc., Washington, 1988—, Washington Capital Corp., 1989—; speaker, lectr. in field. Deacon, McLean (Va.) Bapt. Ch., 1977-80. Served as officer, USAR, 1969-73. Decorated Legion of Merit; cert. property mgr. Mem. ABA, Nat. Bd. Realtors, Inst. Real Estate Mgmt., Nat. Assn. Rev. Appraisers, Internat. Coun. Shopping Ctrs., Nat. Assn. Real Estate Investment Trusts, D.C. Bar Assn., Va. Bar Assn., Colo. Indsl. Bankers Assn. (bd. dirs. 1985-87), The Internat. Inst (cert. valuer). Home: 10 Vista Gardens Trail Apt 204 Vero Beach FL 32962-1779 Office: 1038 31st St NW Washington DC 20007

KIELY, MICHAEL HUGHES, journalist; b. Long Beach, Calif., Nov. 4, 1944; s. John Roche and Margaret Lee K.; m. Maria Pascher, Feb. 8, 1975; children: Inmay Pascher, Yung Kwang John, Kotun Cartha. BA, U. Redlands, 1967; MA, NYU, 1987. Programmer analyst Bechtel Corp., San Francisco, 1970-72; overseas missionary Unification Ch., 1975-82; fgn. corr. The News World, 1975-82; journalist The News World and N.Y.C. Tribune, 1982-91; pres. Global Atlantic, 1988—; systems editor N.Y.C. Tribune, 1988-89, exec. asst. to editor-in-chief, dir. resource devel., 1989—. Chmn. 1800 Blessed Family Assn. of Unification Ch., N.Y.C., 1986-89; bd. dirs. Nat. Inst. for Rehab. Engring., Butler, N.J., 1987—; chmn. bd. Greenwich Village Neighborhood Sch., N.Y.C., 1987-89; elder Nat. Hdqrs. Ch. of the Unification Ch., 1988—. Mem. Mensa, East Side Conservative Club, N.Y. Press Club, Rotary Club of Chestnut Ridge. Republican. Mem. Unification Ch. Home: 30 Spring Hill Terr Chestnut Ridge NY 10677

KIEPPER, JAMES JULIUS, educator; b. Syracuse, N.Y., Oct. 29, 1933; s. John Carl and Sarah Esther (McFadden) K.; m. Ulrike Manuela Ruffert, June 2, 1984. BA magna cum laude, N.Eng. Coll., 1958; MA, SUNY, Albany, 1962, MA in Polit. Sci., 1970. College intern St. Paul's Sch., Concord, N.H., 1959-60; tchr. Columbia High Sch., Greenbush, N.Y., 1959-64; univ. prof. SUNY, Albany, 1964—; cons. NSF, Union Coll., Schenectady, N.Y., 1965-66, Title III Planning Project, Albany, 1968-69; cons., exec. dir. Tchr. Edn. Conf. Bd., Albany, 1978—. Spl. asst. Romney for Pres. Com., Concord, N.H., 1968, Rockefeller for Pres., Albany, 1968; assoc. Presidential Mission to Latin Am., 1969. Mem. Assn. Tchr. Educators (v.p. 1980-81), Univ. Club of Albany, Internat. Order Odd Fellows, Masons, Phi Delta Kappa (pres. 1966-68). Republican. Episcopalian. Office: SUNY 1400 Washington ED 246 Albany NY 12222

KIERNAN, HENRY GERARD, humanities administrator; b. Bklyn., Jan. 3, 1951; s. Edward Henry and Mary Theresa (Doherty) K.; m. Jane Marie Plavac, June 23, 1973; children: Jennifer, Nicole, Sean. BA, Glassboro State U., 1972; MA, NYU, 1975; MEd, Rutgers U., 1977, EdD, 1992. Cert. prin., N.J.; cert. supr., N.J.; cert. tchr. Asst. prin. Pinelands Regional High Sch., Tuckerton, N.J., 1973-80;, 1980-85; supr. humanities So. Regional High Sch., Manahawkin, N.J., 1985—; adj. prof. Glassboro State coll., Burlington County Coll. Contbr. articles to profl. jours. Mem. ASCD, Nat. Coun. Tchrs. English, Internat. Reading Assn., N.J. Assn. Sch. Adminstrs., Pinelands Adminstrs. Union (pres.), Rutgers Leadership Devel. Inst. Office: 600 N Main St Manahawkin NJ 08050-3093

KIERNAN, JOHN EDWARD, financial analyst; b. Bronx, N.Y., Feb. 16, 1967; s. Thomas J. and Carol Anne (Farley) K. BA, St. Vincent Coll., Latrobe, Pa., 1989; postgrad., U. Va., 1991—. Fin. analyst Smith Barney, Harris Upham & Co. Inc., N.Y.C., 1989-90; sr. fin. analyst Primerica Corp., N.Y.C., 1990-91. Trained vol. Voluntary Income Tax Assistance Program, Latrobe, 1985-89; mem. dist. com. Greater N.Y. coun. Boy Scouts Am., 1989-90; mem. steering com. Street Project, Inc., N.Y.C., 1989-91. Mem. Nat. Assn. Accts., Am. Mgmt. Assn. Republican. Roman Catholic. Home: 2106 Arlington Blvd # 22 Charlottesville VA 22903-1537

KIERNAN, MICHAEL JAMES, investment executive; b. Bronx, Dec. 18, 1963; s. James Francis and Kathleen Marie (Hunt) K. BA in Econs., Rutgers Coll., New Brunswick, N.J., 1986; postgrad., Northwestern U., Chgo., 1990. Portfolio mgr. UBS Asset Mgmt. Inc., N.Y.C., 1987—. Recipient Mktg. award, Craft Yarn Assn., 1990. Mem. Am. Bankers Assn. Roman Catholic. Office: UBS Asset Mgmt 1211 Ave of the Americas 1211 Ave Of The Americas New York NY 10036

KIERNIESKY, NICHOLAS CHARLES, psychology educator; b. Fort Jackson, S.C., Dec. 28, 1943; s. Charles and Olga Kierniesky; m. Diane Maria Morris, May 30, 1970; children: David, Stephen. BA, LaSalle Coll., 1966; MS, Villanova (Pa.) U., 1968; PhD, Tulane U., 1972. Asst. prof. Mt. St. Mary's Coll., Emmitsburg, Md., 1971-76, assoc. prof. psychology, 1977-82, prof., 1983—, chair of psychology, 1980—. Contbr. articles to profl. jours.; presenter at confs. Bd. dirs. Torch Club, Gettysburg, Pa., 1990-91, Little League, Gettysburg, 1986-90. Mem. APA, Am. Psychol. Soc. (charter), Ea. Psychol. Assn., N.Y. Acad. Scis., Sigma Xi, Alpha Epsilon, Psi Chi. Democrat. Office: Mount Saint Marys Coll Dept Psychology Coad Sci Bldg Emmitsburg MD 21727

KIGER, PATRICK JOSEPH, writer; b. McKeesport, Pa., Aug. 16, 1957; s. Jerome Bonaparte and Mae (Lyons) K.; m. Martha Pearson, July 20, 1991. BA in Journalism, Pa. State U., 1979. Freelance writer Pitts., 1979-81; staff writer Pitts. Mag., 1981-83, assoc. editor, 1984; mag. writer Pitts. Press., 1984-86; gen. assignment reporter Orange County Register, Santa Ana, Calif., 1986-89; sr. writer Balt. Mag., 1989—. Contbr. numerous articles to publs. Vol. Pitts. Literacy, 1983-84, Moveable Feast, Balt., 1991—. Recipient 1st Pl. award Column Writing Pitts. Press Club, 1986, 1st Pl. award Investigative Reporting, 1986, 1st Pl. award Best Series Orange County Press Club, 1988, 2nd Pl. award Best Writing Calif. Newspaper Pubs., 1988. Mem. Md. Soc. Profl. Journalists (1st Pl. award Gen. Reporting 1991), Investigative Reporters & Editors. Office: Balt Mag 16 S Calvert St Baltimore MD 21202

KILBORN, GARY LEE, utilities company executive; b. Buffalo, N.Y., Aug. 1, 1947; s. Leland William and Doris Mildred (Schultz) K.; m. Janice Jane Boll, Aug. 2, 1969; children: Derek, Jennifer. AAS in Civil Tech., Erie Community Coll., Buffalo, 1968. Designer Niagara-Mohawk Power Co., Buffalo, 1968-74, audit clk., 1974-81, mem. theft of svc. staff, 1981-83, mem. customer svc. staff, 1983-88, designer, 1988—; owner Western N.Y. Dance Championships, West Seneca, 1990—. Treas. Krakowiacy Polish Folk Dancers, West Seneca, 1983-89; pres. Grace Luth. Ch., Buffalo, 1988-89, 92, treas., 1975-85, 91; pres. Luth. Brotherhood Brn., Buffalo, 1987-88, treas., 1984-86. Recipient Outstanding Svc. award Designer, 1989, Niagara Frontier Folk Arts Coun., 1988, Friends of the Night People, 1988, Krakowiacy Polish Folk Dancers, 1991, Care Ptnr. award Luth. Svc. Soc., 1988-91. Republican. Home: 83 Pinewood Dr West Seneca NY 14224 Office: Niagara-Mohawk Power Corp 535 Washington St Buffalo NY 14203

KILBURN, DONALD C., publishing company executive; b. Atlanta, Mar. 16, 1956; s. William R. and Jean K. BA, Coll. of Wooster, 1979; postgrad., Wharton Sch. Bus., 1986. Mgr. Gulf Coast Svcs., Cleve., 1979-83; pres. Ginn Press/Simon & Schuster, Boston, 1983—. Bd. dirs. Newton (Mass.) Needham Mental Health, 1988—, Riverside Clinic, Norwood, Mass., 1990—. Mem. AMA, Am. Assn. Pubs. Office: Ginn Press 160 Gould St Needham MA 02194-2300

KILBURN, PENELOPE WHITE, data processing executive; b. Freeport, N.Y., June 25, 1940; d. William Prescott and Marian (Churchill) White; m. Edwin Allen Kilburn, Feb. 7, 1964; children: Penelope Allen, Nancy Kitchen. BA, Barnard Coll., 1962. Elem. sch. tchr. Holmdel (N.J.) Bd. Edn., 1975-78; tech. writer Continental Data Ctr., Neptune, N.J., 1983-86; with Johnson & Higgins, N.Y.C., 1986-89; asst. v.p., 1989-91; v.p. Johnson & Higgins, N.Y.C., 1991—. Active mem. Jr. League, Monmouth County, 1973-80, sustaining mem., 1980—; chmn. St. Georges refugee com., Rumson, N.J., 1981-83; mem. St. Georges By the River Altar Guild, Rumson. Mem. Soc. for Tech. Communication. Episcopalian. Office: Johnson & Higgins 125 Broad St Newark NJ 07104-3916

KILLEEN, MELISSA HELEN, retail executive; b. Binghamton, N.Y., Oct. 28, 1955; d. Louis Merrow and Frances (Gerhauser) K.; m. Howard Scott Landsman, Aug. 7, 1982; 1 child, Lee Francis. BFA cum laude, Syracuse U., 1976; Cert. in sculpture, Johnson Atelier Tech. Sch., 1978. Craft coord. Hand Crafts Gallery, Haddonfield, N.J., 1976-77; asst. dept. chairperson Johnson Atelier, Princeton, N.J., 1976-79; mgr. Richard Kagan Gallery, Phila., 1978-79; dir., owner The Gallery at 401, Magnolia, N.J., 1979-81; dir. Landsman Gallery, Cherry Hill, N.J., 1982—. Coord. Com. to Benefit the Children/Phila. Art Show, 1981-91, Nat. Coun. Jewish Women Art Show, Camden, N.J., 1992—. Mem. Am. Soc. Appraisers (sec. 1989-90, pub. rels. chair 1989-93, 2d v.p. 1992—). Home: PO Box 926 Cherry Hill NJ 08003-0926 Office: Landsman Gallery 401 White Horse Pike S Magnolia NJ 08049-1094

KILLHOUR, WILLIAM GHERKY, paper company executive; b. Phila., June 2, 1925; s. William Brelsford and Jean (Gherky) K.; AB in Econs., U. Pa., 1947; m. Josephine Quarrier Greenwood, July 12, 1947; children: Daphne S. (Mrs. John David Polys), William Brelsford II, Jean Gherky (Mrs. David Akers), Gilson Engel. Salesman, Quaker City Paper Co., York, Pa., 1947-50; co-founder W.B. Killhour & Sons, Inc., Phila., 1950, salesman, treas., mgr. printing paper div., 1950-61, pres., 1961-84; v.p. sales Killhour Comml. Paper Co., 1984—; mem. Paper Distbn. Coun. of U.S., 1977-81; past mem. mcht. adv. com. Sorg Paper Co., Scott Paper Co., Howard Paper Mills, Kimberly Clark. Pres., Stafford Sch. PTA, 1959; advisor Savannah Coll. of Arts and Designs. Served from ensign to lt. (j.g.) USNR, 1944-46; PTO. Mem. U.S. Rowing Assn. (cert., past chmn. Master's com., coach 1991) Paper Trade Assn. Phila. (pres. 1966), Nat. Paper Trade Assn. (regional dir. 1974—, mem. indsl. paper com. 1972-73, nat. treas. 1977-78, nat. v.p. 1978-80, pres. 1980-81), Susquenhanna Litho Club (pres. 1970), Jr. Execs. Club Graphic Arts of Phila. (dir. 1955-60), St. Andrews Soc. Phila., York Club Printing House Craftsmen, Fearing Family Orgn., Mayflower Soc., Merion Cricket Club, Palmetto Rowing Club (founder, pres., head coach Hilton Head, S.C.), Philadelphia Racquet Club (chmn. squash racquets com. 1972-82), Country of York, Undine Barge Club, Spanish Wells Golf Club (Hilton Head, S.C.), Masons. Nat. age group champion double sculls, 1982, 85, 91, nat. single sculls champion, 1985, world single sculls champion, 1990, Can. Henley single sculls champion, 1985, world 8-oar crew champion, Toronto, 1985, world 4-oar crew champion, 1985, 87, 90, 91, world double sculls bronze, 1985, world double sculls champion, 1990, 91,

nat. 8-oar crew age group champion, 1986, 88, 89, 90, nat. 4-oar crew age group champion, 1987, 88, 89, 90, 91, Nat. Quad champion, 1991, single scull winner Head of Chattahoochie Regatta, Atlanta 88, and numerous others.

KILMAIN, WILLIAM HENRY, trade association executive; b. Newton, Mass., Sept. 4, 1936; s. Edward Thomas and Christine Agnus (Degnan) K.; m. Nancy Ellen Scammon, July 4, 1959; 1 child, Stephen. BS, Northeastern U., 1959. CPCU, Mass. Underwriter Mass. Automobile and Workers Compensation Burs., Boston, 1959-60; underwriter, sr. underwriter, then spl. agt. Hartford Ins. Group, Boston, 1960-68; spl. agt. Ins. Co. N.Am., Boston, 1968-70; adminstr., corp. sec. Mass. Automobile Rating Bur., Boston, 1970-72; exec. dir. Ind. Ins. Agts. Mass., Boston, 1972—; dir., officer, chmn. Ins. Inst., Northeastern U., Boston, 1983-87; trustee Ins. Libr. Boston, 1988—. With U.S. Army, 1959-73. Mem. CPCU (bd. dirs., officer, pres. Boston chpt. 1981-86), Ins. Agt. Assn. Execs. (past officer), Am. Soc. Assn. Execs., New Eng. Soc. Assn. Execs., Meeting Planners Internat. Office: Ind Ins Agts Mass 11 Beacon St Boston MA 02108-3002

KILMANN, RALPH HERMAN, business educator; b. N.Y.C., Oct. 5, 1946; s. Martin Herbert and Lilli (Loeb) K.; m. Ines Colon, May 28, 1988; children: Catherine Mary, Christopher Martin, Arlette Martin. BS, Carnegie Mellon U., 1970; MS, Carnegie-Mellon U., 1970; PhD, UCLA, 1972. Instr. U. Pitts. Katz Grad. Sch. Bus., 1972, asst. prof., 1972-75, assoc. prof., 1975-79, prof., 1979—, George H. Love prof. orgn. and mgmt., 1991—, coord. orgnl. studies group, 1981-84, 86-89, dir. program in corp. culture, 1983—; pres. Organizational Design Cons., Pitts., 1975—. Author: Social Systems Design: Normative Theory and the MAPS Design Technology, 1977, Beyond the Quick Fix: Managing Five Tracks to Organizational Success, 1984, Managing Beyond the Quick Fix: A Completely Integrated Program for Creating and Maintaining Organizational Success, 1989, Escaping the Quick Fix Trap: How to Make Organizational Improvements That Really Last, 1989, Workbook for Implementing the Five Tracks: Vols. I and II, 1991, Logistics Manual for Implementing the Five Tracks: Planning and Organizing Workshop Sessions, 1991, Logistics Manual for Implementing the Five Tracks: Planning and Organizing Workshop Sessions, 1992; co-author: Methodological Approaches to Social Science: Integrating Divergent Concepts and Theories, 1978, Corporate Tragedies: Product Tampering, Sabotage and Other Catastrophes, 1984, The Management of Organization Design: Vols. I and II, 1976, Producing Useful Knowledge for Organizations, 1983, Gaining Control of the Corporate Culture, 1985, Corporate Transformation: Revitalizing Organizations for a Competitive World, 1988, Making Organizations Competitive: Enhancing Networks and Relationships Across Traditional Boundaries, 1991; mem. editorial bd. Jour. Mgmt., 1983-86, Acad. Mgmt. Exec., 1987-90, Jour. Organizational Change Mgmt., 1988—; developed Kilmann Insight Test, Learning Climate Questionnaire, Thomas-Kilmann Conflict-Mode Instrument in Ednl. Testing Svc., MAPS Design Tech. for Social Systems Design, Kilmann-Saxton Culture-Gap Survey; contbr. chpts. to books, articles to profl. jours. Mem. Eastern Acad. Mgmt. (treas. 1975-76, dir. 1983-86), Am. Psychol. Assn., Inst. Mgmt. Scis. (1st prize Nat. Coll. Planning competition 1976), Beta Gamma Sigma, Sigma Xi. Home: 165 Millview Dr Pittsburgh PA 15238-1625 Office: U Pitts Jos M Katz Grad Sch Bus Roberto Clemente Dr Pittsburgh PA 15260

KILMARTIN, JOSEPH FRANCIS, JR., business executive, consultant; b. New Haven, Mar. 11, 1924; s. Joseph Francis and Lauretta M. (Collins) K.; student St. Thomas Sem., 1944; BA, Holy Cross Coll., 1947; m. Gloria M. Schaffer, June 26, 1954; children: Joanne, Diane. Prodn. mgr. A.C. Gilbert Co., New Haven, 1947-49; profl. performer Broadway show Small Wonder, also TV shows Your Hit Parade, Philco Playhouse, Armstrong Circle Theatre, 1949-50; producer NBC-TV, N.Y.C., 1950-53; v.p. sales Cellomatic Corp., N.Y.C., 1953-59; sr. v.p. Transfilm Inc., N.Y.C., 1959-62, MPO Videotronics, N.Y.C., 1962-66; pres. Bus. Programs Inc., Larchmont, N.Y., 1966-75, Greenwich, Conn., 1975—; lectr. in field, cons. Mexican Dept. Agrarian Affairs and Colonization, 1974—. Active fund-raising Community Chest, 1947-49, ARC, 1947-49, Boy Scouts Am., 1958-66, United Fund, 1970-73; mem. Congl. Adv. Bd., Presdl. Task Force, Atlantic Coun., Conn. Venture Group; bd. dirs. Lee County Arts Coun.; mem. exec. com. Lee County Rep. Party Coun. Recipient medal of excellence Mexican Agrarian Affairs and Colonization Dept., 1976; Golden Medallion award in bus. communication Miami Internat. Film Festival, 1978. Mem. Am. Mgmt. Assn., TV Execs. Soc., Pres.'s Assn. Republican. Clubs: Larchmont (N.Y.) Yacht Club, Westchester Country Club, Univ. Club (N.Y.C.), Carolina Trace Country Club. Home: 241 Lakeview Dr Sanford NC 27330-8349 Office: 87 Greenwich Ave Greenwich CT 06830

KILTS, DOUGLAS WALTER, insurance broker; b. Cooperstown, N.Y., Oct. 11, 1946; s. Donald W. Kilts and Irene J. (Borst) Snyder; m. Dawn F. Busfield, Sept. 14, 1968; 1 child, Caitlin Pramer. AB in French, Middlebury (Vt.) Coll., 1968; MPA, Cornell U., 1972; MBA, NYU, 1977; AAS in Nursing, L.I. Coll., 1984. Staff broker Marsh & McLennan Cos., Inc., N.Y.C., 1969-70, 72-78, asst. v.p., 1978-81, v.p., 1981-90, sr. v.p., 1990—; staff nurse emergency dept. Beth Israel Hosp., 1984—. Treas. 35 Pierrepoint St. Owners, Bklyn., 1979-90. Mem. Emergency Nurses Assn., Phi Beta Kappa, Beta Gamma Sigma. Democrat. Unitarian. Home: 35 Pierrepont St Brooklyn Heights NY 11201-3360 Office: Marsh & McLennan 1221 Avenue of Americas New York NY 10036

KIM, BRIAN HYUNG, banking executive; b. Lansing, Mich., Aug. 5, 1965; s. Tai Sung and Okjin (Kim) K. BSEE, U. Mich., 1986; MBA, U. Pa., 1990. Cons. Arthur Andersen & Co., Chgo., 1986-88; mgr. Citicorp/Citibank, N.Y.C., 1990—. Tutor Cabrini Green Vols., Chgo., 1987. Angel scholar U. Mich., 1985. Republican. Office: Citicorp 399 Park Ave New York NY 10043-0001

KIM, DAVID SANG CHUL, seminary president, publishing executive; b. Seoul, Korea, Nov. 9, 1915; came to U.S., 1959; m. Eui Hong Kang, Jan. 6, 1942; children: Sook Hee, Sung Soo, Hyun Soo, Young Soo, Joon Soo. BA in English Lit., Chosen Christian Coll., Seoul, 1939; postgrad., U. Wales, 1954-55, Western Conservative Bapt. Sem., 1959-61, U. Oreg., 1962-63; MA, U. Oreg., 1965; postgrad., Pacific Sch. Religion, Berkeley, Calif., 1965-66; PhD, Columbia Pacific U., 1988. Mem. staff Chosen Rubber Industry Assn., Seoul, 1939-45; fin asst. U.S. Mil. Govt., Kunsan City, Korea, 1945-48; govt. official Ministry of Fin., Ministry of Social Affairs and Health, Ministry of Fgn. Affairs Govt. of Republic of Korea, Seoul, 1948-59; charter mem. Unification Ch., Seoul, 1954; 1st missionary to Eng., 1954-55; missionary, evangelist Unification Ch., U.S., 1959-70; supr. counseling Clearfield Job Corps Ctr., Clearfield, Utah, 1966-70; founder, pres., owner The Cornerstone Press (name change to Rose of Sharon Press), 1978; charter mem., pres., trustee World Relief Friendship Found., Inc. (now Internat. Relief Friendship Found., Inc.), 1974—; pres. Internat. One World Crusade Inc., 1975—; pres. Unification Theol. Sem., 1975—; charter mem., trustee Nat. Coun. Chs. and Social Action, 1976—; advisor, fin. supporter Global Congress of World Religions, Inc., 1978—; charter mem. Internat. Religious Found., Inc., 1982—; v.p. Unification Thought Inst., 1989; founder, pres. Global Edn. Rsch. and Devel. Fund, Inc., 1981—. Author: Individual Preparation for His Coming Kingdom: Interpretation of the Principle, 1964; Victory Over Communism and the Role of Religion, 1972; editor: (book series) Day of Hope in Review, Part I-1972-74, 1974, Part 2-1974-75, 1975, Part 3, Vol. 1-1976-1981, 1981. Office: Unification Theol Sem 10 Dock Rd Barrytown NY 12507-5000

KIM, HEEMONG, art director; b. Seoul, Korea, Mar. 7, 1957; came to U.S., 1977; s. Chung Up and Byong Rye Kim; m. Haewon Moon, July 9, 1983; children: Bosung, Wusung. BA, R.I. Coll., Providence, 1980; MS in Communication Design, Pratt Inst., 1983. Asst. art dir. The Direct Mktg. Group, Inc., N.Y.C., 1983-85; art dir. Chaffee Case & Ptnrs., Providence, 1986-91, HEEMONG KIM, Art Direction, Providence, 1991—; asst. prof. R.I. Coll., 1985—. Home: 100 Wyndham Ave Providence RI 02908 Office: RI Coll Art Dept 600 Mt Pleasant Ave Providence RI 02908-1924

KIM, HYONG SOK, electrical engineering educator; b. Seoul, Apr. 13, 1962; s. Hung Min and Kwang Soon K.; m. Sang Weon Gang, July 7, 1990; 1 child, Justine Sung-Hae Kim. B Engring., McGill U., 1984; MASc, U. Toronto, 1987, PhD, 1990. Asst. coord. No. Telecom., Toronto, Ont., Can., 1989, lectr., 1990; asst. prof. Carnegie Mellon U., Pitts., 1990—. Contbr. articles to profl. jours. Recipient fellowships Nat. Sci. and Engring. Rsch. Coun., Toronto, 1984-88, Univ. Toronto Mary Beatty fellowships, 1989. Mem. IEEE, Assn. for Computing Machinery. Office: Carnegie Mellon U Dept ECE Pittsburgh PA 15213

KIM, IH CHIN, pediatrician; b. Seoul, Korea, Aug. 6, 1925; s. Young Whan and Young Ho (Cho) K.; came to U.S., 1953, naturalized, 1965; MD, Seoul Nat. U., 1950; student Yon Sei U., 1944-46; postgrad. U. Pa., 1954-55; m. Helen Fern Wagner, Mar. 15, 1957; children: Catherine Joy Kim Smith, Stephen Thomas. Intern, Transp. Hosps., Seoul and Pusan, Korea, 1950-51; resident in pediatrics Pusan Children's Charity Hosp., 1951-53, Children's Hosp. Phila., 1953-55, fellow in pediatric gastroenterology, 1955-58, research assoc., 1958-67, med. staff, 1963-67; practice medicine, specializing in pediatrics, Easton, Pa., 1965—, Phillipsburg, N.J., 1971—; staff dept. pediatrics Hahnemann Med. Coll. and Hosp., Phila., 1967—, Easton Hosp., 1965—, Warren Hosp., Phillipsburg, N.J., 1966—, chief dept. pediatrics, 1978—; clin. asst. prof. pediatrics Hahnemann Med. Coll., Phila., 1971—. Diplomate Am. Bd. Pediatrics. Fellow Am. Acad. Pediatrics; mem. AMA. Presbyterian. Club: Country of Northampton County. Contbr. articles to med. jours. Address: 6 Ivy Court Easton PA 18042 Office: 985 Belvidere Rd Phillipsburg NJ 08865

KIM, JAI SOO, physics educator; b. Taegu, Korea, Nov. 1, 1925; came to U.S., 1958, naturalized, 1963; s. Wan Sup and Chanam (Whang) K.; m. Hai Kyou Kim, Nov. 2, 1952; children: Kami, Tomi, Kihyun, Himi. B.Sc. in Physics, Seoul Nat. U., Korea, 1949; M.S. in Physics, U. Sask., Can., 1957, Ph.D., 1958. Asst. prof. physics Clarkson Coll. Tech., Potsdam, N.Y., 1958-59; asst. prof. physics U. Idaho, Moscow, 1959-62, assoc. prof., 1962-65, prof., 1965-67; prof. atmospheric sci. and physics SUNY, Albany, 1967—, chmn. dept. atmospheric sci., 1969-76, rep. Univ. Corp. for Atmospheric Research, 1970-76; cons. Korean Studies Program SUNY, Stony Brook, 1983-85; vis. prof. Advanced Inst. Sci. and Tech., Seoul, Korea, 1983; cons. U.S. Army Research Office, 1978-79, Battelle Meml. Inst., 1978-81, Environ. One Corp., 1978-84, N.Y. State Environ. Conservation Dept., 1976-82, Norlite Corp., 1982-84, Korean Antarctic Program, 1988—. Contbr. articles to profl. jours. Mem. Am. Inst. Physics, Am. Geophys. Union, Sigma Xi. Home: 33 Folmsbee Dr Albany NY 12204-1205 Office: 1400 Washington Ave Albany NY 12222-0001

KIM, KATHLEEN, psychiatrist; b. Balt., Jan. 23, 1958; d. Martin and Christine Kim. BA, Brown U., Providence, 1979; MD, Brown U., 1983; MPH, Harvard U., Boston, 1983. Diplomate Am. Bd. Psychiatry and Neurology. Intern Norwalk (Conn.) Hosp., 1983-84; residency Yale U. Sch. of Medicine, Dept. of Psychiatry, New Haven, 1984-87; dir. Psychiat. Ambulatory Svcs., Yale/New Haven Hosp., 1987—. Office: Yale/New Haven Hosp Partial Hosp Program 425 George St New Haven CT 06511

KIM, KI HOON, economist, educator; b. Taegu City, South Korea, Jan. 23, 1933; came to the U.S., 1957; s. Yoon Sung and Ha Hyang (Kwon) K.; m. Soo Wha Chai, June 6, 1964; children: Albert Sung-Chan, Noel Mi-Hye. BA, Seoul Nat. U., 1956; MRE, N.Y. Theol. Sem., 1960; MA, Clark U., 1962; PhD, U. Conn., 1968. Bank clk. Bank of Korea, Seoul, 1956-57; grad. asst. U. Conn., Storrs, 1963-67; asst. prof. Cen. Conn. State U., New Britain, 1967-72, assoc. prof., 1972-81, prof., 1981—; mem. exec. com. World Univ. Svc., Geneva, 1959-60; cons. Stanley Works, New Britain, 1987-88; dir. Korean studies Cen. Conn. State U., 1989-90, dir. Inst. for Asian and Am. Studies, 1990—; fellow Yale U., 1982-83; columnist The Korea Ctrl. Daily/N.Y., 1991-92. Contbr. articles to profl. jours. Spl. advisor to mayor, New Britain, 1982-89, water commr., 1984-90; chmn. New Britain-Atsugi Sister City Com., 1989—. With Korean Air Force, 1956-57; founding mem. Greater Hartford Korean Sch., 1985-87. Devel. fellow Inst. Internat. Edn., 1965-67; recipient Spl. award Conn. World Trade Assn., 1987, Cert. Appreciation SBA, 1987, Plaque Appreciation Han Nam U., 1988, Alumni Assn., 1985, 86, 88. Mem. Am. Econ. Assn., AAUP, Korean-Am. U. Profs. Assn. (regional conf. dir. East 1990—), Korean-Am. Econ. Assn., Korean-Am. Soc. Conn. (bd. dirs. 1987-90), Greater Hartford C. of C., Omicron Delta Epsilon. Congregationalist. Home: 497 Commonwealth Ave New Britain CT 06053-2407 Office: Cen Conn State U 1615 Stanley St New Britain CT 06053-2439

KIM, MYUNGHEE, psychiatrist, child psychiatrist, psychoanalyst; b. Pusan, Korea, Nov. 8, 1932; came to U.S. 1959; d. Too Soo and Boo Sil (Kim) K.; m. Peter Riemann, June 28, 1962; children: Kim, Hannah. MD, Seoul Nat. U., Korea, 1959; Psychoanalyst, NYU, 1981. Intern Hackensack (N.J.) Hosp., 1959-60; resident in psychiatry Grassland Hosp., Valhalla, N.Y., 1960-62, Bronx Mcpl. Med. Ctr., 1962-63; staff psychiatrist Roosevelt Hosp., N.Y.C., 1964-65; fellow in child psychiatry Union County Psychiat. Clinic, Plainfield, N.J., 1968-70; child psychiatrist Child Guidance and Family Svc., Orange, N.J., 1970-72; pvt. practice child and adult psychiatry, psychoanalysis Springfield, N.J., 1972—; cons. Headstart Nursery Sch., Orange, 1971-72; faculty in psychiatry Bergen Pane Hosp., Paramus, N.J., 1977-83; instr. psychiatry N.J. Med. Sch., Newark, 1988—; clin. asst. prof. UMDNJ-Robert W. Johnson Med. Sch., 1991—. Editor N.J. Psychoanalytic Soc. Bull., 1989—; contbr. articles to profl. jours. Mem. Am. Psychoanalytic Assn., Internat. Psychoanalytic Assn., Pychoanalytic Assn. N.Y., Am. Psychiatric Assn., N.J. Psychoanalytic Soc., Seoul Psychoanalytic Study Group. Home and Office: 272 Short Hills Ave Springfield NJ 07081-1029

KIM, OSCAR, chemical research scientist; b. Seoul, Korea, May 23, 1934; came to U.S., 1963; s. Young B. and Doo-up Kim; m. Young C. Oh, May 3, 1963; children: Andrew, Gilbert, Patricia. BS, Seoul Nat. U., 1961; MS, Tex. Christian U., 1965; PhD, NYU, 1972, postgrad., 1973. Rsch. chemist Inmont Corp., Clifton, N.J., 1965-67; sr. rsch. chemist Norda Inc., East Hanover, N.J., 1967-68; rsch. scientist Schering A.G. Pharm., Harriman, N.Y., 1974-84; pres. Chemtest Labs., Elmwood Park, N.J., 1984—; adj. asst. prof. Fordham U., Bronx, N.Y., 1973-74. Contbr. articles to profl. jours. V.p. Korean Assn. of N.Y., 1968-72. Rsch. fellow NSF, 1970-72, Petroleum Rsch. Found., 1963-65. Mem. ASTM, Am. Chem. Soc. Engring. Assn., Am. (pres. 1974-75, Korean scientist), Am. Coun. Ind. Labs., Assn. Ofcl. Analytical Chemists. Home: 113 Bergen Ave Waldwick NJ 07463-2110 Office: ChemTest Labs 101 Midland Ave Elmwood Park NJ 07407-2414

KIM, PAN SOO, import/export company executive; b. Kwang-Ju, South Korea, Oct. 1, 1947; came to U.S., 1981; s. Young Tae and Yang Lyae (Chun) K.; m. Shin Ae Chang, Oct. 19, 1975; children: Young Kyong, Yong Han, Warrick Junsuk. BA, Seong-Kyun-Kwan U., 1972. Sales mgr. Union Steel Mfg. Co. Ltd., Seoul, South Korea, 1972-81, Kukje-ICC Corp., East Rutherford, N.J., 1981-84; office mgr. Kukje-ICC Corp., Houston, 1984-85, Union Steel Am. Co., Houston, 1985-87; gen. mgr. Union Steel Mfg. Co. Ltd., Seoul, 1987-88; pres. Union Steel Am. Inc., Teaneck, N.J., 1988—. Dir. Korean Sch. Houston, 1986-87. Home: 408 Birchtree Ln Northvale NJ 07647 Office: Union Steel Am Inc 500 Frank W Burr Blvd Teaneck NJ 07666

KIM, PO (PO-HYUN KIM), artist; s. Jae-Ho and Sun-Yoo K.; m. Sylvia Wald. MFA, U. Ill., 1957. Prof., chmn. dept. art Chosun U., Kwangju, Korea, 1946-55; instr. NYU, N.Y.C., 1962-63. Solo exhbns. include Gallery Modern Art Internat., Baldham-Munich, Germany, 1980, others U.S. and abroad; group shows include Bklyn. Mus. Art, Indpls. Mus. Art, 1978; represented in permanent collections Chgo. Art Inst., Solomon R. Guggenheim Mus., N.Y.C. Home: 417 Lafayette St New York NY 10003

KIM, SEONG-JUN, anesthesiologist; b. Seoul, Republic of Korea, Feb. 16, 1937; came to U.S., 1965; s. Man-Bong and Duk-Hee (Kang) K.; m. Jung-Joong Yoon, July 3, 1965; children: Andrew, Caroline, Jennifer, Patricia. MD, Seoul Nat. U., 1961. Diplomate Am. Bd. Pediatrics, Am. Bd. Anesthesiology. Intern Seoul Nat. U. Hosp., 1961-62, French Hosp., N.Y.C., 1965-66; pediatric resident Wyckoff Heights Hosp., Bklyn., 1966-68; pediatric clinic fellow Down State Med. Ctr., Bklyn., 1968-69, anesthesia resident, 1969-71; med. staff Phelps Meml. Hosp. Ctr., North Tarrytown, N.Y., 1971-84, dir. anesthesia dept., 1984-91, sr. attending anesthesia dept., 1991—. Med. officer Army of Republic of Korea, 1962-65. Fellow Am. Coll. Anesthesiologists; mem. AMA, Am. Soc. Anesthesiologists, Internat. Soc. Anesthesiologists. Home: 53 Cottonwood Ln Briarcliff Manor NY 10510

KIM, SYNJA P., corporate business planner; b. Seoul, Republic of Korea; came to U.S., 1967; d. Byung Jae and Jung-D (Kim) Park; m. Sang Joo Kim, Dec. 4, 1976. BS in Acctg., Va. Commonwealth U., 1971; MBA in Fin. and Multinat. Mgmt., U. Pa., 1986. Jr. analyst Am. Fgn. Ins. Assn., N.Y.C., 1971; internal auditor Ethan Allen, Inc., Danbury, Conn., 1972-74, sr. acct., 1975-77; sr. acct. Carolina Power & Light Co., Raleigh, N.C., 1978-79, fin. analyst, 1980-82, sr. fin. analyst, 1983-87; mgr. budget planning and fin. analysis Internat. Life and Group, CIGNA Worldwide, Phila., 1987-89; mgr. bus. planning CIGNA Internat. Fin. Svcs., Phila., 1989, dir. bus. planning, 1989—; pres. Inst. Korean-Am. Studies, 1986—; instr. Korean-Am. Lang. Sch., Rsch. Triangle Park, N.C., 1979-81; guest speaker Raleigh C. of C., 1982; program coordinator Nat. Coun. for Internat. Visitors Ctr., Rsch. Triangle Park, N.C., 1984-87; bd. dirs. Signex, Inc., 1991—. Mem. Nat. Assn. Accts. Republican. Office: CIGNA Internat Fin Svcs Two Liberty Pl 55th Fl 1601 Chestnut St PO Box 7716 Philadelphia PA 19192

KIM, THERESA KI-JA, theatre arts educator; b. Seoul, Korea, Feb. 12, 1933; came to U.S., 1966; d. Chung-sang and Kwang-su Kim; children: Charlotte Ok-ju Lee, Christina Young-ju Lee, Thomas Chool-il Lee. BA, Sookmyung Womens U., Seoul, 1956; student, Wroxton (Eng.) Coll., 1968; MA, Fairleigh Dickinson U., 1969; PhD, NYU, 1988. Adj. instr. Bklyn. Coll., CUNY, 1975-76, adj. asst. prof., 1978-89, adj. assoc. prof., 1988-89; instr. Fairleigh Dickinson U., Rutherford, N.J., 1975-76; vis. assoc. prof. U. Iowa, Iowa City, 1989-90, Trinity Coll., Hartford, Conn., 1990; asst. prof. theatre arts SUNY, Stony Brook, 1991—; founder, artistic dir. Asian Ctr. for Performing Arts, N.Y.C., 1977-84, 91—, Asian Theatre of Bklyn. Coll., 1979-85; founding mem. Stage 7 Matrix, N.Y.C., 1973-75; project dir., tour mgr. The Asia Soc. Performing Arts Program, N.Y.C., 1977, 81. Translator: Korean Pongsan Masked Dance-Drama, 1976, 91; dir. The Bacchae, 1985; producer The Tale of Yangban, 1974. Workshop grantee Nat. Acad. Arts, Taiwan, Republic of China, 1984, 88, Seoul Acad. Arts, Seoul, 1988; travel grantee U.S.-Japan Friendship Commn., Japan, 1980. Mem. Assn. Theatre in Higher Edn., Asian Studies Assn., Am. Lit. Translators Assn. Buddhist. Home: 692 E 42d St Brooklyn NY 11203 Office: SUNY Stony Brook NY 11794

KIM, UNSUP, university director, educator; b. Seoul, June 29, 1934; s. Changsik and Gong K.; m. Myungsoon Kang, Jan. 5, 1963. Premed., Seoul Nat. U., 1955, MD, 1959. Diplomate Am. Bd. Surgery. Resident surgery Capital Army Hosp., Seoul, 1959-63; staff surgeon First KOKA Surg. Hosp., Republic of Korea, 1964-65; resident surgery Mt. Sinai Med. Ctr., N.Y.C., 1967-72, clin. asst. surgury, 1972-74, asst. attending, 1974-77, assoc. attending, 1977-83, attending, 1983—, prof. surgery Sch. Medicine, 1974—; dir. surgery Elmhurst (N.Y.) Hosp. Ctr., 1975—; chief of surgery Capital Army Hops., 1967; asst. attending Mt. Sinai Svcs.-City Hsop. Ctr., Elmhurst, 1972-75. Decorated Bronze Star medal, (2) Silver Star medals. Fellow Am. Coll. Surgeons; mem. Am. Coll. Gastroenterology, Assn. Acad. Surgery, Queens Med. Soc., Soc. Surgery Alimentary Tract, N.Y. Surg. Soc., Collegium Internationale Chirurgiae Digestive, Internat. Coll. Surgeons. Office: Elmhurst Hosp Ctr Rm C5-3 79-01 Broadway Elmhurst NY 11373

KIM, WILLA, costume designer; b. L.A.; d. Shoon Kwan and Nora Kim; m. William Pene Du Bois. Costume designer Goodtime Charley (Tony award nomination), 1974-75, Dancin (Tony award nomination), 1977-78, Sophisticated Ladies, 1980-81 (Tony award 1980-81), Song and Dance, 1985-86 (Tony award), Legs Diamond, 1988-89, Will Rogers at the Follies, 1991 (Tony award). Recipient Asian Woman of Achievement award Asian Am. Profl. Women, 1983. Recipient Obie award, 1964-65, Drama Desk award, 1969, 70, 71, 72, Maharam award, 1971, 72, Emmy award, 1981, Tony award, 1980-81, 90-91. Democrat. Home: 250 W 82nd St New York NY 10024-5421

KIM, YOUNG HO, orthodontist; b. Seoul, Korea, Oct. 17, 1927; came to U.S., 1952, naturalized, 1962; s. Woo Hyun and Doo Keum (Park) K.; m. Mazie Ann Lim, May 19, 1956; children: Stuart K., Jonathan C. D.D.S., Seoul Nat. U., 1949; M.S., U. Rochester, 1958; D.M.D., Tufts U., 1960. Diplomate Am. Bd. Orthodontists.Jonathan C. Specialist in orthodontics, Weston, Mass., 1964—; instr. Harvard Dental Sch., 1960-65; assoc. prof. Boston U. Grad. Sch. Dentistry, 1967-70; vis. clin. prof. Yonsei U. Coll. Dentistry, 1972; cons. VA Hosp., West Roxbury, Mass., 1974-83; assoc. clin. prof. Tufts U. Sch. Dental Medicine, 1981—. Chmn. bd. trustees Myung Hwee Won Found., 1976-86; pres. North Atlantic Component of The Angle Soc. Orthodontists, 1989-90; pres. Multiloop Edgewise Arch-Wire Technic and Rsch. Found., 1991—. Mem. ADA, Am. Assn. Orthodontists, Mass. Dental Soc., Angle Soc. Orthodontists, Omicron Kappa Upsilon. Home: 154 Summer St Weston MA 02193-2476 Office: 30 Colpitts Rd Weston MA 02193

KIMATIAN, STEPHEN H., broadcasting executive, lawyer, writer; b. N.Y.C., Oct. 19, 1941; s. Eli P. and Lucille (Ourganian) K.; m. Janet G. Serabian, June 21, 1964; children: Stephen, Ellen. AB, Princeton U., 1963; JD, Cornell U., 1966. Bar: N.Y. 1966, Md. 1978. Assoc. O'Donnell & Schwartz, N.Y.C., 1967-70; dir. employee and labor rels. Westinghouse Broadcasting Learning and Leisure Time Co., 1970-75; exec. adminstr. Sta. WJZ-TV, Balt., 1975-76, v.p., gen. mgr., 1976-78, area vice chmn., 1978-79; practice law, 1979-80; ptr. Hooper Kiefer & Cornell, 1981-84; exec. dir. Md. Pub. TV, 1984-86; pres., gen. mgr. Sta. WKBW-TV, Queen City Broadcasting, Inc., Buffalo, 1986—; former trustee U.S. Bankruptcy Ct., Dist. Md.; health claims arbitrator, State of Md.; sec. Westinghouse Broadcasting Co., Inc.; dir. Wyman Park Med. Systems. Bd. dirs., vice chmn. Balt. Urban League; chmn. bd. Balt. Broadcast Skills Bank; bd. dirs. Balt. area coun. Boy Scouts Am. (Silver Beaver award), Health and Welfare Coun. Cen. Md., Balt. Goodwill Industries, NCCJ; chmn. bd. trustees Community Coll. Balt.; judge Md. Humanities Journalism Awards Com.; pres. Md. Pub. Broadcasting Found.; bd. dirs. Sudden Infant Death Syndrome, Inst. of U. Md. Sch. Medicine, Internat. U. Consortium for Telecommunications; mem. Mayor's Coordinating Com. on Criminal Justice; trustee Children's Hosp. Buffalo; mem. bd. dirs. Buffalo Urban League, Buffalo Philharm. Orch.; bd. regents Canisius Coll.; bd. dirs. Children's Hosp. of Buffalo, Shea's Theatre Blue Ribbon Com. Named Man of Yr. Exec. Women Internat. Mem. Bar Assn. City of Balt. (exec. coun.), Eastern Ednl. Network (trustee), Southern Ednl. Communications Assn., Variety Club (exec. com., devel. bd. St. Columban Ctr., named Man of Yr.). Armenian Orthodox. Office: WKBW-TV PO Box 726 Derby NY 14047

KIMBELL, CHARLES WILLIAM, III, health care executive; b. Utica, N.Y., May 7, 1943; s. Charles William and Florence (Starr) K.; m. Beverly Carol Moore, Nov. 22, 1969. BA in Human Rels., Salem Coll., 1966. Dist. exec. to dir. exploring Nassau County Coun. Boy Scouts Am., Roslyn, N.Y., 1966-73; exec. dir. Five Towns United Way, Woodmere, N.Y., 1973-78; dir. devel. Franklin Gen. Hosp., Valley Stream, N.Y., 1978-84; dir. resource devel./pub. rels. St. John's Episcopal Hosp., Far Rockaway, N.Y., 1984-87; dir. resource devel. Episc. Health Svcs., Inc., 1987-91; v.p. planned giving and devel. Masonic Charity Found., Wallingford, Conn., 1991—. Chmn. bd. dirs. Five Towns United Way, 1978-90; bd. dirs., pres. Rockaway Devel. & Revitalization Corp., 1984-91; mem. vestry Trinity-St. John's Episc. Ch., Hewlett, N.Y., 1983-88, St. Mark's Episcopal Ch., Islip, N.Y.; mem. U.S. Coast Guard Aux. Flotilla; gen. chmn. Episc. Charities of L.I. Appeal, 1991. Recipient Silver Beaver award Boy Scouts Am., 1983, Bishop Cross Disting. to Diocese of L.I., 1991. Mem. Nat. Assn. Hosp. Devel. (region III cabinet mem.), Nat. Soc. Fund Raising Execs. (past pres. L.I. chpt., Outstanding Fund Raising Exec. 1991), Rockaway C. of C. (bd. dirs. 1985-87). Republican. Club: Cedarhurst Yacht, South Bay Cruising. Lodge: Kiwanis (bd. dirs. 1967-87). Home: 129 S Penataquit Ave Bay Shore NY 11706-8834 Office: Masonic Charity Found Conn PO Box 70 Wallingford CT 06492

KIMBER, WILLIAM JOHN, cardiologist; b. Glen Ridge, N.J., Nov. 10, 1931; s. William Francis and Jean Miriam (Hogg) K.; m. Patricia Mary Moynihan, Aug. 11, 1956 (div. 1981); children: Katherine Anne, James Robert, David Patrick, John Michael; m. m. Ann Chubbuck, Dec. 5, 1981. BA, Cornell U., 1954; MD, U. Pa., 1960. Diplomate Am. Bd. Internal Medicine, Am. Bd. Cardiology. Intern Mountainside Hosp., Montclair, N.J., 1960-61; resident in medicine Mayo Clinic, Rochester, Minn., 1962-65, fellow in cardiology, 1965-67; assoc. in cardiology Geisinger Med. Ctr. Clinic, Danville, Pa., 1968—, dir. cardiac catheterization lab., 1974—, asst. dir. dept. cardiology, 1986—, dir. Cardiovascular Sch. Tech., 1991—;

clin. prof. medicine Pa. State U., Hershey, 1984-88, Jefferson Med. Coll., Phila., 1989—. Fellow Am. Coll. Cardiology; mem. Am. Heart Assn. (chpt. pres. 1974-75, v.p. Pa. affiliate 1979, Disting. Svc. award 1975, Merit Svc. medal 1979). Office: Geisinger Med Ctr N Academy Ave Danville PA 17822

KIMBERLAND, KENDALL GRAHAM, association executive; b. Charleston, W.Va., Oct. 15, 1907; s. Henry Maynard and Angie Mary (Graham) K.; m. Louise Fuller Hosford, July 6, 1936; children: Virginia Fuller Kimberland, Ann Graham Kimberland, Margaret Hosford Kimberland. AB, Columbia U., 1929, AM, 1935; postgrad., Princeton U., Concordia U., Montreal U., NYU, Montreal. Comml./internat loan officer The Chase Manhattan Bank N.A., N.Y.C., 1929-73; ret.; dir. Habib Am. Bank, N.Y.C.; adj. prof. Hudson Coll., Jersey City, 1935-37, Am. Inst. Banking, Jersey City, 1937-39, N.Y. Inst. Fin., N.Y.C., 1968-70, Upsala Coll., East Orange, 1970-71, Bloomfield Coll., 1978-79, Montclair State Coll., 1981-82; chmn. bd. African Ponderosa, Ltd., Nairobi; econ. cons. Indsl. Devel. Bank Afghanistan, 1973; mgmt. cons. Indsl. & Comml. Devel. Corp., Nairobi, 1973-74; devel. economist Min. of Planning, Govt. of Laos, 1974; sr. econ. advisor Min. Fin., Fiji, 1976-78. Del. for refugee relief Am. Friends Svc. Com., Phila., 1942-45. Mem. SAR, SCORE, AAUP, Assn. for Internat. Devel., Dunworkin Club of Montclair. Democrat. Religious Soc. of Friends. Home: 25 Lincoln St Glen Ridge NJ 07028-1204

KIMBERLY, ROBERT PARKER, medical educator; b. New Haven, July 29, 1946; s. John Taylor and Beatrice Eileen (Branch) K.; m. Susan Johnson Alesbury, June 17, 1972; children: Christopher, Taylor, Sarah, Michael, Thomas. AB, Princeton (N.J.) U., 1968; MA, New Coll., Oxford, Eng., 1970; MD, Harvard U., 1973. Diplomate Am. Bd. Internal Medicine. Fellow ARB, NIAMDDK, NIH, Bethesda, Md., 1975-77; fellow Hosp. Spl. Surgery-Cornell Med. Ctr., N.Y.C., 1977-79, asst. prof., 1979-84, assoc. prof., 1984-91, prof., 1991—; Andrew Mellon Found. tchr., scientist, 1980. Contbr. numerous articles to profl. jours. Lt. comdr. USPHS, 1975-77. Rhodes Trust scholar, 1968. Fellow ACP, Am. Coll. Rheumatology (pres. N.E. chpt. 1990-91); mem. N.Y. Rheumatism Assn. (pres. N.Y.C. chpt. 1992-93), Am. Assn. Immunologists, Am. Soc. Clin. Investigation. Office: Hosp Spl Surgery Cornell Med Ctr 535 E 70th St New York NY 10021-4872

KIMELBERG, HAROLD KEITH, neuroscience researcher, educator; b. Hertford, Eng., Dec. 5, 1941; came to U.S., 1963; s. Maurice and Sarah (Cohen) K. BSc in Zoology, U. London, 1963; PhD in Biochemistry, SUNY, Buffalo, 1968. Sr. cancer rsch. scientist dept. neurosurgery Roswell Park Meml. Inst., Albany, N.Y., 1970-74; asst. rsch. prof. dept. biochemistry Roswell Park Div. SUNY, Albany, 1973-74; assoc. prof. biochemistry, rsch. assoc. prof. neurosurgery Albany Med. Coll., 1974-80, rsch. prof. neurosurgery, prof. pharmacology, toxicology and biochemistry, 1980—; prof. Sch. Pub. Health Scis. SUNY, Albany, 1988—; adj. prof. biology SUNY, Albany, 1980—. Editorial bd.: Glia, Jour. Neurochemistry, Jour. Cerebral Blood Flow & Metabolism; contbr. articles to Scientific American, Science, Nature, Jour. Neurosci. Fulbright fellow; grantee NIH. Mem. Nat. Inst. Health (nls study sect. Bethesda, Md. chpt. 1991—). Office: Albany Med Coll Div Neurosurgery A-60 47 New Scotland Ave Albany NY 12208-3412

KIMMEL, ALLAN JEFFREY, psychology educator; b. Balt., June 14, 1952; s. Donald and Helen M. (Hertzbach) K. BA in Psychology, U. Md., 1974; MA in Social Psychology, Temple U., 1978, PhD in Social Psychology, 1983. Asst. prof., dir. human resources cert. program Moravian, Bethlehem, Pa., 1982-86; assoc. prof. psychology Fitchburg (Mass.) State Coll., 1986—; jour. referee AIDS Edn. & Prevention, 1990—. Author: Ethics of Human Subjects Research, 1981, Ethics & Values in Applied Social Research, 1988; contbr. numerous articles to profl. jours. Recipient Ruth Butler Achievement award Fitchburg State Coll., 1987, medal, 1989. Mem. Am. Psychol. Soc. (chartered), Internat. AIDS Soc., Soc. Psychol. Study of Social Issues, Soc. for Advancement Social Psychology (regional chair steering com. 1986-91), New Eng. Psychol. Soc., Eastern Psychol. Assn. Democrat. Office: Fitchburg State Coll 160 Pearl St Fitchburg MA 01420-2697

KIMMEL, PAUL ROBERT, financial director; b. Balt., Sept. 7, 1947; s. Walter William and Lisette Marie Elizabeth (Hazenzahl) K.; m. Cynthia Ann Bowers, Nov. 17, 1984; children: Elliott Paul, Charlotte Lisette Marie. BS in Engring. summa cum laude, Case Inst. Tech., 1969; MBA, Harvard Sch. Bus. Adminstrn., 1975. CPA. Mfg. mgr. Procter & Gamble Co., Cin., 1969-73; sr. acct. Arthur Andersen & Co., Boston, 1975-78; dir. mfg. and control Brilliant Seafood Co., Boston, 1978-79; sr. analyst Am. Cyanamid Co., Wayne, N.J., 1979-81; plant controller Shulton Inc., Mays Landing, N.J., 1981-83; mgr. acctg. and systems Am. Cyanamid Co. Med. Internat. Div., Wayne, N.J., 1983-85; dir. corp. acctg. Hartz Mountain Corp., Harrison, N.J., 1985-86; v.p. Citibank/Citicorp, N.Y.C., 1986-89; controller Airwick Industries, Wayne, N.J., 1989-90; dir. acctg. devel. Reckitt & Colman Inc., Wayne, N.J., 1990—. Mem. Am. Inst. CPA's, N.J. Soc. CPS's, Inst. Mgmt. Acct., Confrerie de la Chaine des Rotisseurs, Harvard Club of N.Y.C., Harvard Club of N.J., Harvard Bus. Sch. Club of N.Y., Packanack Lake Country Club. Republican. Lutheran. Home: 15 Lake Dr E Packanack Lake NJ 07470-4323 Office: Reckitt & Colman Inc 1655 Valley Rd PO Box 943 Wayne NJ 07474-0943

KIMMEL, PETER SCOTT, facility management executive; b. N.Y.C., May 19, 1947; s. Seymour and Florence (Steiner) K.; children: Daniel Landay Kimmel, Adam Lorence Kimmel. BA, Knox Coll., Galesburg, Ill., 1968; M in Arch., U. Calif., 1972. Environ. psych. Westinghouse Elect. Corp., Pitts., 1972-76; visiting lectr. Carnegie-Mellon U., Pitts., 1976; facility prog./planner Built Environ. coord., Toronto, Ontario, Can., 1976-77; cons. FTC, Washington, 1978-79, Equal Employment Opportunity Commn., Washington, 1979; sr. realty spl. Gen. Svcs. Adminstrn., Washington, 1979-87; prin. Facility Solutions, Inc., Washington, 1987-88; pres. Peter S. Kimmel & Assocs., Bethesda, Md., 1988—; hon. adv. bd. Gralla Publ. Nat. Conf., N.Y.C., 1984-86, AEC Expo Conf., 1987-88; speaker Bldgs. Conf., 1989, 90, Office Planning Users Group, 1989, 92, Internat. Facility Mgmt. Assn. Conf., 1985, 90, 92, AEC Systems Japan, 1989, AEC Ssytems U.S., 1983, 84, 85, 87, 89, 91, 92, AEC Expo, 1987, 88, Gralla Publ., 1984, 86, AIA, 1985; mem. continuing edn. faculty George Washington U., Washington, 1992. Inventor, patentee Modular Lighting System, 1980; contbg. editor Micro CAD News, 1989, 90, 91, Facilities Design and Mgmt., 1991, 92, Design Net, 1992; contbr. articles to Archtl. Tech., 1986, AT-Japan, 1986-87, Bldgs., 1987, Micro CAD News, 1989, 90, 91, Facilities Design Mgmt., 1989, 91, 92, Design Net, 1992, Bldgs & Grounds Maint., 1988, Jour. of Internat. Facility Mgmt. Assn., 1988, 91. Recipient Design Excellence award, Indsl. Design Mag., 1976. Mem. AIA, Internat. Facility Mgmt. Assn. (Disting. Svc. award 1985, Chpt. of Yr. 1985, Disting. Author award, 1987), Internat. Facility Mgmt. Assn. Chpt. (pres. 1984-86, treas. 1986-87), Bannockburn Community Club (bd. dirs. 1981-82). Office: Peter S Kimmel & Assocs The Kenwood Bldg 5272 River Rd Ste 400 Bethesda MD 20816-1405

KIMMEL, ROBERT IRVING, communication systems design consultant, former state government official; b. Uniontown, Pa., Jan. 28, 1922; s. Andrew Filson and Dorothy Jean (Walker) K.; student Bucknell U., Lewisburg, Pa., 1940-41, 43-44, Washington U., St. Louis, 1942, Pa. State U., 1972; children—Donna Jean, Robert Filson, LuAnna Pat, Kevin Normaine, Gregory Paul. Self-employed entertainer, 1944; mgr. Cassiday Theaters, Midland, Mich., 1945-56; engring. illustrator Dow Chem. Co., Midland, 1956-59; engring. mgr. Radio Communications Co., Bloomsburg, Pa., 1959-64; chief electronics Pa. State Police, Harrisburg, 1964-74, dir. communications div., 1974-79; chmn. Pa. Law Enforcement Telecommunications Planning Com., 1976-79; design cons. Communications Systems Design Assocs., Harrisburg, 1979—; v.p. Partnership, Inc., 1980—; mgr. Paxton Herald and Paxton Herald West newspapers, 1981—; cons., lectr. in field. Mem. task force Cultural Center, Harrisburg, 1975-76; head coach Lakevue Midget Baseball Assn., 1976-78; pres. council St. Mark's Lutheran Ch., Harrisburg, 1975-79; bd. dirs. Harrisburg Performing Arts Co., 79, Emergency Health Services Fedn., 1984-86; v.p., bd. dirs. Am. Lung Assn. Cen. Pa., 1987—, treas., 1989—; bd. dirs. Am. Lung Assn. Pa., 1988—; instr. Dancers Workshop, 1979—; sec.-treas. Susquehanna Valley Assn., 1984—; co-chmn. customer adv. coun. U.S. Postal Svc., 1991—. Served with USAF, 1942-43. Recipient various pub. service awards, certs. of merit. Fellow Radio Club Am.; mem. Assn. Pub.-Safety Communications Officers (pres. 1978-79), Pa. Chiefs Police Assn. (life; chmn. frequency adv. com. 1967-79), Engrs. Soc. Pa. (pres. 1978-79), Nat. Assn. Dance and Affiliated Artists (past v.p.), Greater Harrisburg Arts Council (dir.), Internat. Platform Assn. Author papers in field. Developer vehicle location system, elec. security systems. Home: 880 Scenery Pl Harrisburg PA 17109-5323 Office: 101 Lincoln St Harrisburg PA 17112-2599

KIMURA, KIMI TAKEUCHI, social worker, educator; b. Kyoto, Japan, Apr. 13, 1936; came to U.S., 1954; d. Kinzo Fujiwara and Miyo Takeuchi; divorced; 1 child, Fumi Kimura Inouye. BA, Doshisha Women's Coll., Kyoto, 1938; postgrad., Columbia U., 1955-56; MFA, Boston U., 1957. Cert. secondary English tchr., interpreter, Japan. Rsch. assco. South Manchurian RR Rsch., Toyko, 1936-41; travel cons. SITA Internat. Travel, N.Y.C., 1957-58; vis. prof. Howard U., Washington, 1958-59; overseas adv. Japan Pubs. Assn., Tokyo, 1959-68; asst. cultural attache Embassy of Japan, Washington, 1962-66; sr. rsch. assoc. Columbia U., N.Y.C., 1973-76; case worker Lenox Hill Neighborhood Assn., N.Y.C., 1977-87; trade negotiator, various bus. firms, Tokyo, N.Y.C., 1945—; dir. social work Japan/Am. Assn., N.Y.C., 1983-84; cons. Nat. Theatre of Japan, Tokyo, 1966-73; fundraiser The Vol. Coun. of Philharmonic- Symphony Soc. N.Y. Inc., 1986—. Contbr. numerous features articles to jours.; producer various plays, 1957. Campaign worker, Dem. Party, N.Y.C., 1976-78. Recipient Translation award, Nat. Sci. Found., Washington, 1973-76, Older Am. Act, Title III, Washington, 1977—. Mem. Am. Ednl. Theatre (officer 1972-73, Citation 1973), N.Y. Philharmonic (assoc. mem., Citation 1989). Home: 350 65th St Apt 12A Brooklyn NY 11220-4942 Office: Lenox Hill Neighborhood 331 E 70th St New York NY 10021-8698

KINCADE, WILLIAM HADLEY, policy analyst; b. Cleve., June 21, 1939; s. Gerard Majella Jr. and Hildegarde Lorraine (Hadley) K.; m. Susan Eleanor Mollenauer, Oct. 27, 1962; children: Jennifer Lee, Susan Hadley. BA, Princeton U., 1961; cert., Def. Lang. Inst., 1965; MA, Am. U., 1969, PhD, 1980. Commd. officer USN, 1962, advanced through grades to lt. comdr., 1971, transferred to Res., 1970; editor, newsman AP, Albany, N.Y., 1970-71; profl. staff cons. Arms Control and Fgn. Policy Caucus, Washington, 1972-75; staff dir. joint com. def. prodn. U.S. Congress., Washington, 1975-77; sr. assoc. Carnegie Endowment for Internat. Peace, Washington, 1977-86; exec. dir. Arms Control Assn., Washington, 1977-84; dir., spl. projects Access: A Security Info. Svc., Washington, 1986-88; assoc. prof. The Am. U., Washington, 1989—; sr. rsch. assoc. Internat. Inst. for Strategic Studies, London, 1982; adj. prof. Georgetown U., Washington, 1983-89; prin. researcher Kincade Assocs., 1985—. Co-editor: Negotiating Security, 1979, Nuclear Proliferation in 1980s. Bd. dirs. Nat. Security in Nuclear Age. Nat. Def. Edn. Act fellow Am. U., Washington, 1971-73. Mem. Internat. Studies Assn. , Internat. Inst. Strategic Studies, Can. Ctr. for Arms Control and Disarmament (council advisors 1985—). Democrat. Home: McLean Gardens A169 3710 39th St NW Washington DC 20016-5517 Office: The Am U Sch Internt Svc 4400 Massachusetts Ave NW Washington DC 20016-8001

KINCAID, STEVEN RANDALL, marketing professional; b. Oklahoma City, July 19, 1953; s. William Calvin Hoover and Mary Elizabeth (Cochran) K.; m. Bernadette Mary Frances Girasek, Jan. 12, 1985. BA, Okla. State U., 1975; MA, U. Ill., 1977, PhD, 1980. Rsch. analyst Gen. Foods Corp., White Plains, N.Y., 1980-82; rsch. assoc. Opinion Rsch. Corp., Princeton, N.J., 1982-85, rsch. dir., 1985-86, rsch. exec., 1986-87, account exec., 1989-91; cons. John Hancock Life Ins. Co., Boston, 1987-88, dir. rsch., 1988-89; dir. rsch. Prudential Ins. Co., Newark, 1991—. Named Eagle Scout Boy Scouts Am., 1968. Mem. Am. Assn. Pub. Opinion Research, Am. Polit. Sci. Assn., Applied Polit. Sci. Study Group. (charter), Phi Kappa Phi. Democrat. Methodist. Office: Prudential Ins Co 213 Washington St Newark NJ 07102-2917

KINCH, DALPHINE NORA, counseling psychologist; b. Easton, Md., Mar. 2, 1953; d. William S. and Christina Elizabeth (Frierson) Brown. BS in Psychology, Morgan U., Balt., 1975; MS in Counseling Psychology, Loyola Coll., Balt., 1981; PhD in Counseling Psychology, Howard U., Washington, 1991. Nat. cert. counselor; cert. prof. counselor Md. Juvenile counselor Juvenile Svcs. Adminstrn., Balt., 1976-84; fed. probation officer U.S. Dept. Probation, Balt., 1984-87; predoctoral intern Crownsville (Md.) Hosp. Ctr., 1988-89; psychologist assoc. Rosewood Hosp. Ctr., Owings Mills, Md., 1989; psychologist/therapist Total Health Care, Inc., Balt., 1989; counseling psychologist VA, Balt., 1987—. Mem. APA, Am. Assn. Counseling and Devel., Internat. Assn. of Addictions and Offender Counselors, Alpha Kappa Alpha. Baptist. Home: PO Box 70095 Baltimore MD 21237 Office: VA Rm 214A 31 Hopkins Plaza Baltimore MD 21201

KINDRED, GEORGE CHARLES, lithography executive; b. Bklyn., Nov. 20, 1898; s. Robert C. and Caroline (Hoag) K.; spl. courses, Columbia and N.Y. U.; m. Dorothy Estabrook, Mar. 10, 1928; children—George Estabrook, John MacGregor. Buyer, W. R. Grace and Co., 1919-23; western sales mgr. Snyder and Black, 1923-28; pres. Kindred, MacLean and Co., 1928-59; pres. Underhill, Inv., Inc., 1959—. Served in U.S. Army World War I, USCG Aux., World War II. Fellow Graphic Arts Tech. Found.; mem. A.I.M., St. Andrews Soc., Point Purchase Advt. Inst. (founder, past pres.), Lithographers Nat. Assn. (past treas., dir.), Met. Lithographers Assn. (past pres.), Lithographic Tech. Found. (past treas., dir.), English-Speaking Union, Am. Legion, U.S. Power Squadrons. Episcopalian (vestryman). Clubs: Lotos (N.Y.C.); Fox Meadow Tennis; Saugatuck Harbor Yacht (Westport, Conn.); Sanderling (Siesta Key, Fla.). Home: 4822 Ocean Blvd Siesta Key Sarasota FL 34242 Office: 338nod Hl Rd Wilton CT 06897

KING, ALEXANDER HARVEY, materials science educator, academic administrator; b. Mitcham, Eng., July 1, 1954; came to U.S., 1979; s. Neil Mair and Dora (Morris) K.; m. Christine Elizabeth Dring, July 9, 1977; children: Benjamin Mair, Gavin Alexander. B in Metallurgy, Sheffield U., 1975; DPhil, Oxford U., 1979. Chartered engr., U.K. Harwell EMR fellow Oxford (Eng.) Univ., 1979; postdoctoral assoc. MIT, Cambridge, Mass., 1979-81; asst. prof. SUNY, Stony Brook, N.Y., 1981-84; assoc. prof. SUNY, Stony Brook, 1984-90, prof., 1990—, assoc. vice provost for grad. studies, 1987-89, vice provost for grad. studies, 1989—; founding mem. Open Mind, Stony Brook, 1990. Editor: Interface Migration and Control of Microstructure, 1986, Structure/Property Relationships for Interfaces, 1991; contbr. articles to profl. jours. Recipient Rsch. Initiation grant The Engring. Found., 1982, Rsch. grants NSF, 1983-86, 86-89, 89-91, Rsch. grants Army Rsch. Office, 1986, 87. Mem. Metall. Soc., Am. Soc. for Materials, Materials Rsch. Soc., Am. Phys. Soc., Electron Microscope Soc. Am., Inst. of Materials (U.K.). Office: SUNY Stony Brook NY 11794

KING, BERNARD DAVID, cardiologist, pharmaceutical company executive; b. Lima, Ohio, Feb. 4, 1949; s. David Bernard and Edith Hedwig (Schimmens) K.; m. Kathleen Marek, Nov. 11, 1984; children: Matthew, Meaghan, Hillary. BS cum laude, U. Notre Dame, Ind., 1970; MD cum laude, Ohio State U., Columubus, 1973. Intern in medicine Riverside Meth. Hosp., Columbus, Ohio, 1973-74; sr. resident in medicine Riverside Meth. Hosps., Columbus, 1978-79; resident in pathology The Ohio State Univ. Hosps., Columbus, 1977-78; fellow in cardiology Mt. Sinai Med. Ctr., N.Y.C., 1979-81; asst. prof. medicine N.Y. Med. Coll., Valhalla, 1981-86, asst. prof. physiology, 1984—; dir. cardiology tng. program Westchester County Med. Ctr., Valhalla, 1983-86; dir. clin. cardiovascular investigation Smith Kline & French Labs., Phila., 1986-89; med. dir. ConvaTec div. Squibb Co., Princeton, N.J., 1989-90; v.p. med. and regulatory affairs Worldwide Convatec div. Bristol-Myers Squibb, Princeton, N.J., 1990—; mem. com. for protection of human subjects, N.Y. Med. Coll., Valhalla, 1982-86, faculty senate, 1984-86. Contbr. articles to sci. jours. Served as capt. USAF, 1974-77. Grantee Am. Heart Assn., 1985-87. Fellow ACP, Am. Coll. Cardiology, N.Y. Cardiol. Soc., Soc. For Cardiac Angiography; mem. Am. Fedn. Clin. Research. Roman Catholic. Home: 237 Norsam Dr Langhorne PA 19047-8504 Office: Convatec CN 5254 Princeton NJ 08543

KING, CHARLES THOMAS, retired educator; b. Coatsville, Pa., July 19, 1911; s. John Henry and Estella (Orr) K. m. Dorothy Eckman, Nov. 30, 1933; children: Marilyn Mae, Kenneth Alan, Donald Edwin. BS, West Chester State Coll., 1932; EdM, Temple U., 1944; EdD, Rutgers U., 1957. Tchr. West Pottsgrove Twp. Sch., Stowe, Pa., 1933-35; tchr. Haverford Twp. Sch., Havertown, Pa., 1935-38, dir. elem. health and phys. edn., 1938-42; prin. Llanerch Sch., Havertown, Pa., 1942-45; supervising prin. West Pottsgrove Twp. Sch., Stowe, Pa., 1945-47; prin. Glenwood and Short Hills Schs., Millburn, N.J., 1947-51, asst. to supt., 1951-59, asst. supt., 1959-62, supt., 1962-74; mem. state adv. council on Handicapped 1968-72; mem. state cert. appeals com., 1972-74. Pres. Millburn Community Coun., 1954-56; bd. dirs. Millburn Pub. Libr., 1962-74; chmn. N.J. Coun. Econ. Edn., 1972-74; deacon Congl. Ch., 1963-66. Mem. Essex County Supts. Roundtable (chmn. 1965-66), West Chester State Coll. Alumni Assn. (chpt. pres. 1981-83, Disting. Alumni award 1982), Milburn Coaches Assn. (Man of Yr. award 1989), Rotary (pres. 1957-58, Paul Harris fellow 1986, Svc. Above Self plaque 1989), Phi Delta Kappa (chpt. pres. 1959-60, emeritus 1974). Home: 115 Hobart Ave Short Hills NJ 07078-2057

KING, CYNTHIA REMINGTON, nurse; b. Rochester, N.Y., Dec. 9, 1956; d. John Andrew and Martha (Remington) King. BS in Biology and Psychol, Trinity Coll., Hartford, Ct., 1978; BSN, Creighton U., 1983; MS in Nursing, U. Nebr., Omaha, 1987; postgrad., U. Rochester, 1990—. cert. Medical Office Mgmt. Med. asst. Center for the Health Sciences, Los Angeles, 1979-80; office mgr. Eric A. Lewis, M.D., Inc., Beverly Hills, Calif., 1980-82; staff nurse level III U. Nebr. Med. Ctr., Omaha, 1983-87; supr. of oncology Archbishop Bergan Mercy Hosp., Omaha, Nebr., 1987-88; nurse mgr. bone marrow transplant unit Strong Meml. Hosp., Rochester, N.Y., 1988-90; clin. faculty Sch. Nursing, U. Rochester; cons., educator Spl. Care Cons., Rochester, N.Y. Contbr. articles to profl. jours., chpts. to books. Bd. dirs. Leukemia Soc. Am., 1990—, Am. Cancer Soc., 1987-89. Mem. AACCN, Oncology Nursing Soc. (nominating com. 1987-89, chmn. 1988-89, mem. fall inst. com., chair-elect 1990-91, chair 1991—), Coun. Nursing Mid. Mgrs., Sigma Theta Tau. Home: 180 Clovercrest Dr Rochester NY 14618-3220

KING, EDMUND LUDWIG, retired educator; b. St. Louis, Jan. 1, 1914; s. William Frederick B. Seifert and Lydia (Ludwig) King; m. Willard Mae Fahrenkamp, Jan. 29, 1951. BA, U. Tex., 1933, MA, 1934, PhD, 1949. Instr., asst. prof. modern langs. Miss. State Coll., 1936-41; instr. English U. Tex., Austin, 1946; instr. Spanish Princeton (N.J.) U., 1946-50, asst. prof. Spanish, 1950-57, assoc. prof., 1957-66, prof. Spanish, 1966—, Cardenter prof. Spanish, 1982—; chmn. romance langs. Princeton U., 1966-72, corp. pres. Internat. Inst. in Spain, Boston, Madrid, 1975-82, resident dir. 1982-83. Author: Becquer: From Painter to Poet, 1953; translator: The Structure of Spanish History, 1953; editor: El Humo Dormido, 1991; cons. American Heritage Larousse Spanish Dictionary, 1986. Maj. U.S. Army, 1941-46. Mem. MLA, Hispanic Soc. Am. (corr.), Internat. Inst. in Spain (hon. dir.). Democrat. Episcopalian. Home: 171 Western Way Princeton NJ 08540-7207 Office: Dept Romance Langs Princeton U Princeton NJ 08544

KING, EMMETT ALONZO, III, business executive, insurance consultant; b. Norfolk, Va., June 9, 1942; s. Emmett S. and Mary Lee (Sutton) K.; m. Yvonne J. Bullock, Apr. 5, 1965 (div. 1979); children: Andre, Jacqueline; m. Yvonne Levelle Kier, Oct. 19, 1980; stepchildren: Richard, Roland. Student, Mary-Hardin-Baylor Coll., 1967, Coll. of Ins., 1971. Benefits rep. EBS Mgmt. Cons., Inc., N.Y.C., 1968; sr. group adminstr. group ins. sales office Conn. Gen. Life Ins. Co., N.Y.C., 1968-70; successively group adminstr., account exec., asst. v.p., v.p., mgr. employee benefits dept. Bayly, Martin & Fay, Inc., N.Y.C., 1971-83; sr. cons. Graycliffe Associates, Inc., N.Y.C., 1983-84; account exec. Hartford Ins. Co., N.Y.C., 1984-86; nat. account exec., sr. cons. GAB Bus. Services, Inc., Parsippany, 1986-88; dir. mktg. Total Plan Adminstrs., Inc. (subs. Blue Cross and Blue Shield N.J. Inc.), Cranford, N.J., 1988—; vis. lectr. Princeton U.; vis. prof. Dillard U.; mem. Nat. Urban League Black Exec. Exch. Program; 3-time judge Ala. Jr. Miss Program; hon. trooper Ala. State. Charter mem. Tri-W Black Families, Inc., 1979-82. With Army Security Agy., U.S. Army, 1961-67. Mem. Nat. Ins. Industry Assn. (charter), 100 Black Men Inc., Am. Spl. Risks Assn., Group Ins. Assn. Greater N.Y. (charter), Self Ins. Inst. Am., N.Y.C. C. of C. (bus group on health), Greater Newark C. of C., N.Y. Bus. Alliance Inc. (charter), First Tues. Group (founder 1982—), The New Yorkers Club (charter 1990). Office: Total Plan Adminstrs Inc 65 Jackson Dr Cranford NJ 07016-3516

KING, HIRAM BRONSON, oil company executive; b. N.Y.C., Aug. 24, 1931; s. Rodger and Mary Coolidge. Student, Georgetown U., Washington, 1955-59. Cert. tchr., Fla. Pvt. tutor Fieldston Sch., Riverdale, N.Y., 1958-59; instr. Morris County Tchrs. Assn., Morristown, N.J., 1968-78; sales rep. Sponsored Chase Manhattan Bank, N.Y.C., 1985—. Instr. safety ARC, N.Y.C., 1956-65. With USAF, 1951-55. Mem. Nat. Council Social Studies, Delta Phi Epsilon. Republican. Episcopalian. Home: PO Box 397 Pocomoke City MD 21851-0397 Office: The Chase Manhattan Bank NA 1 Chase Manhattan Plz New York NY 10081-0001

KING, JAMES B., university administrator; b. Ludlow, Mass., Mar. 27, 1935; married; 5 children. B.A., Am. Internat. Coll., 1960. Tchr. Ludlow Jr. High Sch., 1961-62; investigator fraudulent securities Securities div. Dept. Public Utilities, Mass., 1963-64, supr. investigators, 1964-65; jr. community action technician, sr. community technician, asso. commr. Commonwealth Service Corps, 1965; dir. Holyoke Program for Aging, 1966-67; spl. asst. Office Senator Edward M. Kennedy, Boston, 1967-75; fellow J.F. Kennedy Sch. Govt., Harvard U., 1972-73; dir. mktg. and community affairs Mass. Bay Transp. Authority, Boston; spl. asst. to Pres. for pers. The White House, Washington, 1977; chmn. Nat. Transp. Safety Bd., Washington, 1978-82; assoc. v.p. dept. govt. and community affairs Harvard U., 1982-83; sr. v.p. for pub. affairs Northeastern U., Boston; chief staff U.S. Senator John J. Kerry, Boston, 1991—. Past chair Mass. Aero. Commn.

KING, JAMES EDWARD, museum director; b. Escanaba, Mich., July 23, 1940; s. G. Willard and Grace (Magee) K.; m. Frances Bartos, Jan. 15, 1973; 1 child, Scott E. BS, Alma Coll., 1962; MS, U. N.Mex., 1964; PhD, U. Ariz., 1972. Lab asst. in biology Alma Coll., Mich., 1960-62; rsch. asst. dept. biology U. N.Mex., Albuquerque, 1962-64; teaching asst. dept. botany and plant pathology Mich. State U., East Lansing, 1964-66; plant industry inspector Mich. Dept. Agriculture, Lansing, 1966-68; rsch. asst. dept. geochronology U. Ariz., Tucson, 1968-71, rsch. assoc. dept. geoscis., 1971-72; assoc. curator paleobotany Ill. State Mus., Springfield, 1972-78, head sci. sects. and full curator, 1978-85, asst. dir. for sci., 1985-87; adj. assoc. prof. dept. geology U. Ill., Urbana, 1979-88; dir. Carnegie Mus. Natural History, Pitts., 1987—; adj. prof. biology Sangamon State U., Springfield, Ill., 1983-87; adj. rsch. scientist Hunt Inst. Bot. Documentation, Carnegie Mellon U., Pitts., 1988—; adj. prof. dept. geology and planetary sci., U. Pitts., 1988—; vis. scientist in residence Alma (Mich.) Coll., 1985; served on grad. coms. at So. Ill. U., Case Western Res. U., S.W. Mo. State U., U. Ill. Author sci. papers on topics related to geology and paleobotany; mem. editorial bd. Jour. Archaeol. Sci., 1980-87. Mem. adv. com. Ctr. for Environ. and Occupational Health, U. Pitts. Fellow Ill. State Acad. Sci. (pres. 1981-82); mem. AAAS, Am. Assn. Mus. (program com.), Am. Quaternary Assn. (treas., exec. com. 1976-84), Am. Assn. Stratigraphic Palynologists, Assn. Sci. Mus. Dirs. (v.p. 1992—), Assn. Systematics Collections (v.p. 1989-91, pres. 1991—), Ecol. Soc. Am., Mid-Atlantic Assn. Mus., Sigma Xi (pres. Springfield chpt. 1985-86). Office: Carnegie Mus Natural History 4400 Forbes Ave Pittsburgh PA 15213-4080

KING, JOHN ALLISON, waste industry executive, chemical engineer; b. Washington, Oct. 19, 1935; s. James Richmond and Margaret (Allison) K.; married, 1970 (div. 1982); children: Sonja Denise, Sabrina Eugenia. B in Chem. Engring., Bklyn. Poly. Inst., 1957; DHL (hon.), Filmore Inst., 1973. Engr., chemist Socony Mobil Oil Co., Bklyn., 1953-56; night supt. J.T. Baker Chem. Co., Phillipsburg, N.J., 1956-58; chem. engring. editor McGraw-Hill, N.Y.C., 1958-63; engr. Vitro Engring., Silver Spring, Md., 1963-65; exec. deNora Engrs., Milan, Italy, 1966-68; pres. Sci. Communications Inc., Washington, 1968-78; exec. EPA, Washington, 1978-81; Washington dir. Laidlaw Inc., Washington, 1981-92; bd. dirs. Hazardous Waste Treatment Coun., pres., 1988-89, chmn. bd., 1989-90; pres. bd. dirs. Environ. Bus. Assn., Nat. Assn. Environ. Mgmt., bd. dirs., 1992—; adj. prof. environ mgmt. U. Md., pres. Nat. Assn. Environ. Safety Health Prof. Author 5 profl. books; contbr. articles to profl. publs. Bd. dirs. Keyes Ferry Acres Citizens, Harpers Ferry, W.Va., 1988. Mem. Am. Inst. Chem. Engrs. (session chmn.), Am. Chem. Soc., Blue Ridge Country Club, Moose, Alpha Chi Sigma.

KING, JOHN PAUL, defense electronics development company executive; b. Lubbock, Tex., Aug. 23, 1941; s. John Gustus and Joe Dorothy (Reese) K.; m. Susan J. Anderson, Aug. 21, 1976 (div. June 1991); 1 child, John Herbert. BSEE, Tex. Tech. Coll., Lubbock, 1964; MSEE, U. Santa Clara, 1971. Sr. engr. GTE Sylvania, Inc., Mountain View, Calif., 1967-71, ESL, Inc., Sunnyvale, Calif., 1971-75; sr. v.p., dir. Signal Sci., Inc., Santa Clara, Calif., 1975—. Patentee in field. Cubmaster Ellicott City (Md.) area Boy Scouts Am., 1987, troop com. chmn., 1988—. Capt. U.S. Army, 1964-67. Sr. mem. IEEE. Office: Signal Sci Inc 1334 Ashton Rd Hanover MD 21076-3119

KING, JOHN STUART, geology educator; b. Buffalo, N.Y., Nov. 12, 1927; s. Roy J. and Ramona (Lane) K. BA, U. Buffalo, 1955, MA, 1957; PhD, U. Wyo., 1963. Rsch. engr. Carborundum, Niagara Falls, N.Y., 1959-60; asst. prof. geology SUNY, Buffalo, 1963-65, assoc. prof. geology, 1965-68, prof. geology, 1968—, chmn., dept. geology, 1967-71, dir. geology field camp, 1968—; cons. Electrominerals Div., Carborundum, Niagara Falls, 1963-66. Recipient Chancellor's award for Excellence in Teaching, SUNY Cen., Albany, N.Y., 1983. Fellow Geol. Soc. of Am.; mem. Am. Assn. Petroleum Geologists. Republican. Home: 35 Shepard Ave Buffalo NY 14217-1913

KING, KATHERINE CHUNGHO, pediatrician; b. Beijing, People's Republic of China, Aug. 27, 1937; came to U.S., 1955; d. Ginpoh Yeh and Wen Ying (Hsu) King; m. Peter A.J. Adam (wid. June 1980); m. Louis H. Li, June 8, 1985. BA, Meredith Coll., 1957; MD, Bowman Gray Sch. Medicine, 1962. Diplomate Nat. Bd. Med. Examiners, Am. Bd. Pediatrics, Am. Bd. Neonatal-Perinatal Medicine. Resident in pediatrics Cleve. Metro Gen. Hosp./Case Western Res. U., 1962-66; instr. of pediatrics Case Western Res. U., Cleve., 1969-71, asst. prof. to assoc. prof. pediatrics, 1971-85, assoc. prof. reproductive biology, 1979-85; assoc. prof. pediatrics Albert Einstein Coll. of Medicine, N.Y.C., 1989—; co-dir. Perinatal Clin. Rsch. Ctr. Cleve. Metro Gen. Hosp., 1969-85, dir. div. neonatology, 1981-85; staff neonatologist Schneider Children's Hosp., New Hyde Park, N.Y., 1985—. Contbr. articles to profl. jours. Recipient grants for Devel. of Glucose Control, Diabetics Assn. of Greater Cleve., 1968-70, Disordered Fetal Metabolism, NIH, 1983-88, GIP Responses of Newborns, Ross Labs., 1983, Perinatal Outreach, Fan Fox and Leslie R. Samuel Found., N.Y., 1990. Fellow Am. Acad. Pediatrics, Am. Coll. Nutrition; mem. Am. Fedn. Clin. Rsch., Soc. Pediatric Rsch., Ea. Soc. Pediatric Rsch., Am. Diabetes Assn. Home: 19 Gramatan Ct Bronxville NY 10708-3015 Office: Schnieder Children's Hosp New Hyde Park NY 11042

KING, KATHLEEN MARIE, public administrator, management consultant executive; b. Hartford, Conn.; d. Perry and Marie Caesar (Williams) K. BA, U. Hartford, 1972, MPA, 1981. Acct. specialist IBM Corp., Hartford, Conn., 1974-79; cons. Plan B, Inc., Hartford, Conn., 1979-80; chief exec. officer, pres. Inst. for Mgmt. Planning and Devel., Bloomfield, Conn., 1981—; instr. St. Joseph Coll., West Hartford, Conn., 1982-85; adj. faculty Tunxis Community Coll., Farmington, Conn., 1982-85, Greater Hartford Community Coll., 1982-85; dir. Women's Commn., City of Hartford, 1986—; cons. City of Hartford, 1989—, Conn. Black Women's Edn. and Rsch. Found., Hartford, 1989. Chair WVIT-30 Community Adv. Bd., West Hartford, 1986-90; Dem. committeeperson, Bloomfield, Conn., 1985—; dir. Conn. Black Women's Edn. and Rsch. Found., 1983-88; dir. communications Middlesex United Way, Middletown, Conn., 1985-86. Recipient Achievement award Weaver High Sch., Hartford, 1990, Leadership Achievement award Greater Hartford Community Coll., 1991. Mem. Am. Soc. Pub. Adminstrn., ASTD, Am. Indian Archaeol. Inst. Episcopalian. Home: 9 Darby St Bloomfield CT 06002-3607

KING, LARRY L., playwright, actor; b. Putnam, Tex., Jan. 1, 1929; s. Clyde Clayton and Cora Lee (Clark) K.; m. Jeanne Casey, Nov. 25, 1950 (div. Nov. 1964); children: Alexandria, Kerri Lee, Bradley Clayton; m. Rosemarie Courmaris, Feb. 20, 1965 (dec.); m. Barbara Sue Blaine, May 6, 1978; children: Lindsay Allison, Blaine Carlton. Student, Tex. Tech U., 1949-50. Oil field worker El Paso Natural Gas Co., Jal, N.Mex. and Midland, Tex., 1943-45; reporter Hobbs (N.Mex.) Daily Flare, 1949, Midland Reporter-Telegram, 1950-52, Odessa (Tex.) Am., 1952-54; adminstrv. asst. U.S. Congress, Washington, 1954-64; freelance writer Washington, 1964—; pres. Texhouse Corp., Washington, 1979—; Ferris prof. journalism and polit. sci. Princeton (N.J.) U., 1973-75; Disting. Lyndon B. Johnson lectr. Southwest Tex. State University, 1991. Author: (books) The One-Eyed Man, 1966, ...And Other Dirty Stories, 1968, Confessions of a White Racist, 1971, The Old Man and Lesser Mortals, 1974, Wheeling and Dealing, 1978, Of Outlaws, Con Men, Whores, Politicians and Other Artists, 1980, The Whorehouse Papers, 1981, That Terrible Night Santa Got Lost in the Woods, 1981, None But a Blockhead: On Being a Writer, 1986, Warning: Writer At Work, 1986, Because of Lozo Brown, 1988, (plays) The Best Little Whorehouse in Texas, 1978, The Kingfish, 1979, The Night Hank Williams Died, 1986, The Golden Shadows Old West Museum, 1987, Christmas: 1933, 1987; also numerous articles; starred in: The Best Little Whorehouse in Texas (on Broadway), 1979, The Night Hank Williams Died (off Broadway), 1989; contbg. editor Harper's 1967-71, New Times, 1974-77, Tex. Monthly, 1973-78, Tex. Observer, 1964-74. Sgt. AUS, 1946-49. Recipient Stanley Walker Journalism award Tex. Inst. of Letters, 1972, Tony award League of N.Y. Theatres and Producers, 1978-79, Mary Goldwater award Theatre Lobby, 1988, Helen Hayes award, 1989; elected to Tex. Walk of Stars, 1988; Nieman fellow Harvard U., 1969-70, Duke U. fellow, 1975-76. Mem. Authors Guild, PEN, Writers Guild Am. East, Actors Equity Assn., Nat. Acad. TV Arts and Scis. (Emmy award 1981), Nat. Writers Union, Screenwriters Guild East, Dramatists Guild, Actor's Equity, Sandhills Club (Monahans, Tex.), Pelican Club (Odessa), Mystic Knights of the Sea. Democrat.

KING, LAWRENCE WAYNE, purchasing executive, procurement manager, electrical engineer; b. Washington, Oct. 8, 1940; s. Clarence W. and Luella (Brown) K.; m. K. Lynn Kralovec, May 9, 1964 (div. Jan 1979); 1 child, Wayne A.; m. Marcia L. Mason, June 15, 1985; 1 child, Jayme M.; stepchildren: Edward Fogarsi, Mark Fogarsi, Rick Fogarsi. BSEE, Drexel U., 1963; MSEE, U. Pa., 1970. Registered profl. engr., Del. Co-op engr. Delmarva Power, Wilmington, Del., 1960-62; engr. Hercules, Inc., Wilmington, 1963-65, sr. engr., 1965-68, engring. specialist, 1968-74, buyer I, 1974-78; project engr. Hercules, Inc., Magna, Utah, 1978-80; plant engr. Hercules, Inc., Harbor Beach, Mich., 1980-86; purchasing sect. mgr. Hercules, Inc., Wilmington, 1986-91, procurement mgr., 1991—. Prodn. mgr. musical comedies including Mame, Carousel, Kismet, South Pacific, Oklahoma, for local theater cos. Mem. IEEE (textile industry com. 1973-80, conf. com. 1976-78, sec. 1978-80, sec.-treas. Del. Bay sect. 1963-78, dance com.), Del. Soc. Profl. Engrs., Rotary (treas., bd. dirs. Caesar Rodney club 1990-91, sgt.-at-arms 1989-90, pres.-elect 1991-92, pres. Harbor Beach club 1985-86, chmn. festival com. 1984-85). Home: 2115 Brandywood Dr Wilmington DE 19810-2434 Office: Hercules Inc 1313 N Market St Wilmington DE 19894-0001

KING, LLEWELLYN WILLINGS, publisher, lecturer, journalist; b. Bulawayo, Zimbabwe, Oct. 6, 1939; came to U.S., 1963; s. Herbert Willings and Dorothy Ann (Hooper) K. Student, Churchill Coll., 1951-55. City editor The Citizen, Harare, Zimbabwe, 1958-60; sub-editor Ind. TV News, London, 1960-61, Sunday Mirror, London, 1961-63; copy editor N.Y. Herald Tribune, N.Y.C., 1963-64; pres. Sovereign Assocs., N.Y.C., 1964-66; editor wire desk Washington Daily News, 1966-69; asst. editor Washington Post, 1969-70; reporter McGraw Hill, Washington, 1970-73; chmn. King Pub. Group, Washington, 1973—; founder Women NOW mag., N.Y.C., 1965; pres. Washington-Balt. Newspaper Guild, 1967-69, 70. Contbr. articles to profl. jours. Mem. Aircraft Owners and Pilots Assn., Soc. Profl. Journalists, Nat. Press, Royal Commonwealth. Office: King Pub Group 627 National Press Bldg Washington DC 20045

KING, MARCIA JONES, potter, physicist; b. Oak Park, Ill., May 17, 1934; d. Walter Leland Jones and Florence W. (Dull) Anderson; m. James Craig King, Nov., 1953 (div. 1966); 1 child, James Craig King, Jr. BS, Johns Hopkins U., 1960, PhD, 1969. Elec. engr. Electronic Communications, Inc., Timonium, Md., 1959-63; research assoc. theoretical particle physics Syracuse (N.Y.) U., 1969-72; asst. editor The Physical Rev. Brookhaven Nat. Lab., Upton, N.Y., 1972-74; physicist Argonne (Ill.) Nat. Lab., 1974-78; pvt. practice potter and physicist Syracuse, N.Y., 1978—. Contbr. articles to profl. jours.; exhibiter pots throughout cen. N.Y. Mem. AAAS, Am. Physical Soc., Syracuse Ceramic Guild (pres. 1982-84), Phi Beta Kappa, Sigma Xi. Democrat. Home and Office: 228 Buckingham Ave Syracuse NY 13210-3024

KING, MARGARET CAROLYN, assistant dean; b. Gloversville, N.Y., Sept. 8, 1943; d. Arthur Robert and Margaret Peryl (Whipple) K. BA, Ursinus Coll., Collegeville, Pa., 1965; MS, SUNY, Albany, 1970, EdD, 1984. Cert. in secondary edn., N.J. Tchr. Toms River (N.J.) High Sch., 1965-69; counselor, coord. acad. advising Ocean County Coll., Toms River, 1970-80; grad. asst., office of the pres. SUNY, Albany, 1980-81, asst. to dean of grad. studies, 1981-82; dir. counseling Schenectady County Community Coll., Schenectady, N.Y., 1982-84, asst. dean for student devel., 1984—; cons. on acad. advising; mem. faculty ACT Summer Inst. on Acad. Advising, Iowa City, 1986—. Contbr. chpt. to books, articles to profl. jours. Pres. Schenectady County Coun. on Arts, 1990—; mem. exec. bd. Human Svcs. Planning Coun., Schenectady, 1989—; vol. usher capt. Proctor's Theatre, 1986—. Recipient award for excellence in profl. svc. Schenectady County Community Coll. Found., 1989, SUNY Chancellor's Award for Excellence in Profl. Svc., 1990. Mem. Nat. Acad. Advising Assn. (pres. 1991—, Svc. award 1990). Democrat. Office: Schenectady County Community Coll 78 Washington Ave Schenectady NY 12305-2294

KING, MAXWELL E. P., newspaper editor; married; two children. Grad., Harvard U., 1967. Began journalism career at Louisville Courier-Journal, Providence Journal; City Hall reporter Phila. Inquirer, 1972-74, city editor, from 1974, then various newsroom mgmt. positions, including asst. mng. editor, assoc. mng. editor, v.p. consumer mktg. and distbn., 1987-88, sr. v.p. div., 1988-90, editor, exec. v.p., 1990—; staff writer Forbes Mag., N.Y.C., 1977-78. Office: Phila Inquirer 400 N Broad St Philadelphia PA 19103*

KING, MICHAEL JAMES, podiatric surgeon; b. Sandusky, Ohio, Oct. 17, 1957; s. James Everett and Nola Jean (potts) K.; m. Laura Ann Novak, June 4, 1983; children: Lindsay, Christopher. BS, Baldwin-Wallace Coll., 1979; D of Podiatric Medicine, Ohio Coll. Podiatric Medicine, 1983. Diplomate Am. Bd. Podiatric Surgery. Surg. resident Toledo Riverside Hosp., 1983-85; podiatric surgeon pvt. practice Howell, N.J., 1985-87; podiatric surgeon Foot Care Assocs., Inc., Fall River, Mass., 1987—; 2d v.p. Mass. Podiatric Med. Soc., Boston, 1991-92. Author: (book chpts.) Infectious Diseases of the Lower Extremity, 1990. Recipient 1st Place for Papers Written, Am. Coll. Foot Surgeons, 1985. Fellow Am. Coll. Foot Surgeons. Office: Foot Care Assocs Inc 235 Hanover St Fall River MA 02720-5246

KING, PAMELA ANN, artisan; b. Cleve., Sept. 3, 1951; d. Kenneth Everett and Elaine Martha (Burrell) K. French interpreter Trans World Airlines, Boston, 1974-79; artisan The Glass Menagerie, Newton, N.H., 1979-91, Archtl. Art Glass Studio, Haverhill, Mass., 1991—. Major works include commns. for City Pl., Lafayette Pl., Copley Pl., City Transp. Bldg., all Boston. Home and Office: 63 Webster St Haverhill MA 01830-5927

KING, PETER J., lawyer; b. Stowe Township, Pa., June 15, 1938; s. Peter and Mary (Dugan) K.; m. Dolly J. Mauro, Apr. 23, 1960; children: Linda, Carole, Ronald. BA, Duquesne U., 1960, JD, 1963. Bar: Pa. 1963, U.S. Dist. Ct. (we. dist.) Pa. 1963, U.S. Supreme Ct. 1967. Ptnr. Tucker & Arensberg, Pitts., 1964-80; sole practice Pitts., 1980-85; ptnr. King & Kulik, Pitts., 1986-91, King & King, Pitts., 1991—. Editor-in-chief Duquesne U. Law Rev., 1962. Solicitor Montour Sch. Dist., McKees Rocks, Pa., 1969-88. Irishman of Yr. award Knights of Equity, 1980. Mem. Allegheny County Bar Assn. (various offices), Duquesne U. Law Alumni Assn. (officer 1968—, pres. 1989—), Duquesne U. Alumni Assn. (bd. dirs. 1970-82). Democrat. Roman Catholic. Lodge: Italian Sons and Daus. Am. (past. pres. Morningside club). Home: 1441 Duffield St Pittsburgh PA 15206-1320 Office: King & King 20 Chatham Sq Pittsburgh PA 15219

KING, PHILIP GORDON, public relations consultant; b. Ely, Minn., Apr. 11, 1922; s. Herbert Sidney and Ruth Marie (Trimble) K.; m. Onriette Lebron, Feb. 23, 1957; children: Gordon Rivard, Philip David, Bernardine Victoria. A in Bus., Ely Jr. Coll., 1942; BS, Northwestern U., 1948, MA, 1950; postgrad. Columbia U., 1950-51. Tech. dir. Columbia U. Theater, 1950-51, Houston (Tex.) Playhouse, 1951-52, Civic Light Opera, Grand Rapids, Mich., 1952-54; editor/publicist CBS/TV Network, L.A., 1954-60; v.p. Pat McDermott Co., N.Y.C., 1960-62; pub. info. dir. Sta. WCBS-TV, N.Y.C., 1962-65; pub. rels. cons. NEA, N.Y.C., 1965-68, dir. press, radio and TV rels., Washington, 1968-72, pub. info. mgr., 1972-83; pres. King Communications, Washington, 1983-88, Warren, Vt., 1988—; grad. lectr. CCNY, 1962-64; pub. rels. cons. NEA, Washington, 1983-88, Prentice Hall Inc., Englewood, Cliffs, N.J., 1984, Assn. Supervision and Curriculum Devel., 1984-88, Phi Delta Kappa Internat., 1984-89, Green Mountain Cultural Ctr., 1988—, Internat. TV and Film Festival N.Y., 1988—, League of Vt. Writers, 1989—. Capt. U.S. Army, 1942-46, ETO. Mem. NEA, Am. Assn. Pub. Rels. Execs., Edn. Writers Assn. Democrat. Presbyterian.

KING, RICHARD EUGENE, soil scientist; b. Norfolk, Va., Dec. 27, 1948; s. Richard Allen and Dorothy Marietta (Brinkley) K.; m. Carol Janet Maiden, Oct. 7, 1972 (separated June 1990); 1 child, Andrew Lee. BS in Agrl. Econs., Pa. State U., 1971. Soil conservationist USDA Soil Conservation Service, West Chester, Pa., 1971-73; specialist soil and water mgmt. Yerkes Assocs. Inc., Bryn Mawr, Pa., 1973-82; ptnr. Momenee-King Assocs., Ardmore, Pa., 1982-86, Bryn Mawr, 1986-89; ptnr. King Environ., Strafford, Pa., 1989-90, King of Prussia, Pa., 1990—. Served with USAR, 1972-78. Mem. Pa. Assn. Profl. Soil Scientists (cert.), Am. Registry Cert. Profl. Agronomy, Crops and Soils (cert.), Soil Sci. Soc. Am., Am. Soc. Agronomy, Geol. Soc. Am., Soil Conservation Soc. Am., Am. Planning Assn. (environ. adv. bd. 1983—). Republican.

KING, STEPHEN EDWIN, novelist; b. Portland, Maine, Sept. 21, 1947; s. Donald and Nellie Ruth (Pillsbury) K.; m. Tabitha Jane Spruce, Jan. 2, 1971; children: Naomi Rachel, Joseph Hillstrom, Owen Phillip. B.S., U. Maine, 1970. Tchr. English Hampden (Maine) Acad., 1971-73; writer in residence U. Maine at Orono, 1978-79. Novels include Carrie, 1974, Salem's Lot, 1975, The Shining, 1976, The Stand, 1978, Firestarter, 1980, Danse Macabre, 1981, Cujo, 1981, Different Seasons, 1982, The Dark Tower: The Gunslinger, 1982, Christine, 1983, Pet Semetary, 1983, The Talisman, Cycle of the Werewolf, 1985, Skeleton Crew, 1986, The Eyes of the Dragon, 1987, Misery, 1987, The Dark Tower: The Drawing of the Three, 1987, The Tommyknockers, 1987, The Dark Half, 1989, The Stand, 1990, Four Past Midnight, 1990, The Dark Tower III: The Waste Lands, 1991, Needful Things, 1991, Gerald's Game, 1992; short story collection Night Shift, 1978; author numerous other short stories; (as Richard Bachman) Rage, 1977, The Long Walk, 1979, Roadwork, 1981, The Running Man, 1982, Thinner, 1984; author numerous short story screenplays; writer, creator TV program "Stephen King's Golden Years", 1991. Mem. Author's Guild Am., Screen Artists Guild, Screen Writers of Am., Writer's Guild. Democrat.

KING, STEVEN, financial services consultant; b. Queens, N.Y., June 1, 1960; s. Arthur Chris and Catherine Anne (Butcher) K.; m. Donna L. Mielenz; 1 child, Rachel Lynn. Grad. high sch., Farmingdale, N.Y. Mgr. Alarmingly Safe and Sound, Huntington, N.Y., 1983-84; sr. electronics technician Continental Instruments, Westbury, N.Y., 1984-86; owner Regal Products, Hollis Park, N.Y., 1986—; registered rep. First Investors Corp., N.Y.C., 1987-90; pres., owner First Funding Corp. of LI, Melville, N.Y., 1988-90; gen. agt. Franklin United Life Ins., 1992—; ind. agt., mortgage cons. Bankers Security Life and N.Am. Benefit Assn., 1990—. Local campaign worker Rudolph Guilliani for Mayor of N.Y.C., 1989; mem. Rep. Nat. Com., 1990, legis. adv. campaign for Sen. Frank Padavan, 1990. Mem. Lions Club Internat., Sea Cliff, N.Y. Republican. Roman Catholic. Office: 88-73 193st Hollis Park Gardens NY 11423

KING, TAMMY LYNN, actress, model; b. Greenville, Ky., Aug. 12, 1964; d. William Loyd and Reva Jane (Heltsley) K. Diploma, Am. Inst. Modeling, 1985; BFA, BS, Freed-Hardeman U., 1986. Freelance model and actress N.Y., Miss. and Tenn., 1978-92; recruiter, instr. Am. Inst. Modeling, Jackson, Tenn., 1986-87; pub. rels., recruiter Peters Performing Arts Camp, N.Y.C., 1987; administrv. asst. Lehman Bros., N.Y.C., 1988-91; instr. Barbizon Modeling Sch., N.Y.C., 1991-92; house model, prodn. asst. Torino Jrs., N.Y.C., 1991-92; judge, coach various pageants, Tenn., Miss., N.Y., 1986-92; exec. dir. Miss So. N.Y. Scholarship Program, 1991, 92. Organizer Easter party Catherine St. Shelter, N.Y.C., 1991, Christmas party Abum Respit Ctr., Bklyn., 1991, Easter party 1992. Named Female Vocal winner Mid-South Fair Youth Talent Contest, Memphis, 1985, Miss. Fayette County Egg Festival, Tenn., 1985, first runner-up runway modeling S.E. Models Conv., 1986, first runner-up talent Modeling Assn. Am. Internat., 1987, first runner-up Miss USO, 1992; semifinalist Miss N.Y. USA, 1990; recipient U.S. Nat. Speech and Drama awards, 1982-83, U.S. Nat. Band award, 1980-83, Svc. award HRA Vol. Svcs., 1992. Republican. Mem. Ch. of Christ. Home: 1409 York Ave #4 New York NY 10021 Office: Torino Jrs 12A Fl 462 7th Ave New York NY 10018

KING, THOMAS, physician, physiology educator; b. Shanghai, China, June 1, 1934; came to U.S., 1965; s. Tung Ming and Yen Vee (Sung) K.; m. Amy Penn, July 15, 1959; children: Susan, Caroline. MB, Ch.B., U. Edinburgh, Scotland, 1959, MD, 1963. Asst. prof. medicine Cornell U. Med. Ctr., N.Y.C., 1970-73, assoc. prof. medicine, 1973-82, acting chief div. pulmonary and critical care medicine, 1982-85, 91—. Recipient Pulmonary Acad. award Nat. Heart & Lung Inst., 1972-77. Fellow Royal Coll. Physicians London, Am. Coll. Chest Physicians; mem. N.Y. Trudeau Soc. (pres. 1978-79), Chinese-Am. Med. Soc. (pres. 1984-85), Am. Thoracic Soc., Med. Rsch. Soc. of U.K., Am. Fedn. Clin. Rsch., Am. Physiology Soc. Office: Cornell U Med Ctr 520 E 70th St # 505 New York NY 10021-4896

KING, THOMAS L., diversified manufacturing company executive; b. 1930. AB, Harvard U., 1953, MBA, 1959. With Ferris & Co., 1959-62; asst. to pres. Mgmt. Systems Corp., 1962-63; with Standex Internat. Corp., 1963—, succesively v.p., treas. from 1974, also mem. exec. com., 1974-79, sr. v.p., treas., 1979-83, exec. v.p., then pres., treas., 1983-85, pres., CEO, 1985—, also bd. dirs. Lt. USN, 1953-56. Office: Standex Internat Corp 6 Manor Pky Salem NH 03079-2897*

KING, THOMAS LAWRENCE, librarian, library science educator; b. Medina, Ohio, Feb. 21, 1953; s. Thomas and Mozella (Watkins) K.; m. Toni Carol Denton; 1 child, Maria Louise. BA in Geography, U. Akron, 1979; MA in Geography, U. Colo., 1983; MLS, U. Pitts., 1986. Grad. asst., urban studies dept. Univ. Akron, Ohio, 1978; grad. fellow (NSF) Univ. Colo., Boulder, 1979; grad. libr. asst. Univ. Colo., Earth Scis. Libr., Boulder, 1982; grad. asst., Grad. Sch. Sch. Libr. and Info. Sci., 1983; grad. libr. asst. Univ. Pitts., Sch. of Libr. and Info. Sci., Pitts., 1984-85; reference libr. Libr. of Congress, Geography & Map div., Washington, 1987-88; sci. reference, maps libr., earth scis. bibliography SUNY, Binghamton, 1989—, asst. libr./asst. prof., 1988—. Contbr. chpt. to book. Participant First Annual Heart Run/Walk, Am. Heart Assn., Broome County, N.Y., 1990. Mem. ALA (map and geography round table, assn. of coll. and rsch. librs./bibliographic instrn. sect., black caucus, sci. and tech. round table), SUNY Librs. Assn. (libr. instrn. com., comparison of sci. librs. com.), Spl. Librs. Assn. (geography and map div., sci. and tech. div.), N.Y. Libr. Assn. Home: PO Box 1705 Binghamton NY 13902-1705 Office: SUNY Binghamton PO Box 6012 Binghamton NY 13902-6012

KING, WILLIAM DOUGLAS, technical services executive; b. Balt., Nov. 21, 1941; s. James and Mary Jane (Molloy) K.; m. Maribeth McDermott, July 22, 1977; children: Douglas J. McDonald, Collin J. McDonald, William D. Jr. BS, U. N.C., 1964; MBA, Harvard U., 1969. With McKinsey & Co., Inc., Los Angeles, 1969-73, Kaufman & Broad, Los Angeles, 1973-74, Davis Pacific Corp., Santa Monica, Calif., 1974-76, Rapid Am. Corp., N.Y.C., 1976-79, Internat. Tech. Corp., Torrance, Calif., 1979-90, JWP, Inc., Purchase, N.Y., 1990—; bd. advisors Essroc Corp. Trustee Chadwick Sch., Palos Verdes Peninsula, Calif., 1982—. Served as capt. USMC, 1964-67, Vietnam. Mem. World Pres. Orgn., Chief Execs. Orgn. Republican. Episcopalian. Clubs: Links, Harvard (N.Y.C.); California, Los Angeles Country. Office: JWP Inc 2975 Westchester Ave Purchase NY 10577-2518

KING, WILLIAM PATRICK, college official; b. S.I., N.Y., Dec. 2, 1962; s. Martin Joseph and Rose Florence (Fagan) K. BBA, Loyola Coll., Balt., 1985, MBA, 1988. Designated ofcl. fgn. student authorization/advisement INS. Asst. dir. events adminstrn. Loyola Coll., 1984-85; admissions counselor Capitol Coll., Laurel, Md., 1985-87, coord. admissions, 1987-88, dir. admissions, 1988—; salesman I. Magnin, Kensington, Md., 1985-87; guest lectr. Nat. Assn. Home-Based Bus., Balt., 1990—. Designer brochures. Bd. dirs. Clary's Forest II Condominium Assn., Columbia, Md., 1990—; vol. 1st Generation Coll. Bound, Laurel, 1991—. Recipient svc. award Loyola Coll., 1985, Dedicated Svc. award Capitol Coll., 1990. Mem. Nat. Assn. Coll. Admissions Counselors, Nat. Assn. Fgn. Student Advisors, Dirs. Admission for Md. Ind. Colls. and Univs. Assn., Potomac and Chesapeake Assn. Coll. Admissions Counselors. Roman Catholic. Home: 11520 Little Patuxent Pkwy Apt 304 Columbia MD 21044 Office: Capitol Coll 11301 Springfield Rd Laurel MD 20708-9759

KING, YVONNE MARCELLA, education and reading educator; b. Phila., Aug. 25, 1939; d. Wallace and Bella (Crew) Frye. BA, West Chester U., Pa., 1960; MA, U. Calif., Sacramento, 1969; EdD, U. Ga., Athens, 1981. Tchr. Washington, Sacramento, Levittown, Pa., 1960-72; reading coord. Franklin Sch. Dist., Franklin, Mass., 1972-75; reading tchr. Hilsman Middle Sch. Adult Edn., Athens, Ga., 1976-79; assistantship U. Ga., Athens, Ga., 1979-81; coll. instr. Elizabeth City State U., Elizabeth City, N.C., 1981-86; tcr. Millersville U., Millersville, Pa., 1986—; adv. Minority Recruitment Task Force, Millersville, Pa., 1989-91; adv. bd. mem. Nat. Coun. for Accreditation of Tchr. Edn., Newark, 1990-91. Contbr. articles to profl. jours. Adv. bd. Project forward LEAP, Lancaster, Pa., 1988-91; adv. tutoring program, Urban League Guild, Lancaster, Pa., 1989-90. Named Tchr. of Yr., Elizabeth City State U., N.C., 1984. Mem. Lancaster Lebanon Reading Coun., Coll. Reading Assn., Urban League Lancaster County, N.C. Reading Coun. Episcopalian. Home: 466 Dohner Dr Lancaster PA 17602-3374 Office: Stayer Hall Rm 223 Millersville U Millersville PA 17551

KINGHAM, RICHARD FRANK, lawyer; b. Lafayette, Ind., Aug. 2, 1946; s. James R. and Loretta C. (Hoenigke) K.; m. Justine Frances McClung, July 6, 1968; 1 child, Richard Patterson. BA, George Washington U., 1968; JD, U. Va., 1973. Bar: D.C. 1973, U.S. Dist. Ct. D.C. 1974, U.S. Ct. Appeals (D.C. cir.) 1974, U.S. Ct. Appeals (8th cir.) 1977, U.S. Supreme Ct. 1977, U.S. Ct. Appeals (5th cir.) 1980. Editorial asst. Washington Star, 1964-68, 69-70; assoc. Covington & Burling, Washington, 1973-81, ptnr., 1981—; lectr. law U. Va., Charlottesville, 1977-90; mem. com. issues and priorities new vaccine devel. Inst. Medicine, NAS, 1983-86, Nat. Adv. Allergy and Infectious Diseases Coun. NIH, 1988—, adv. bd. World Pharms. Report. Articles editor U. Va. law rev., 1972-73; contbr. articles to profl. jours. Served with U.S. Army, 1968-69. Mem. ABA, Food and Drug Law Inst., Food Law Group (U.K.), Soc. Vertebrate Paleontology, Order of Coif. Republican. Episcopalian. Home: 49 Oakley St, London SW3 5HA, England also: Rte 1 Box 198 Detroit Lakes MN 56501 Office: Acheson House, 46 Hertford St, London W1Y 7TF, England also: Covington & Burling 1201 Pennsylvania Ave NW PO Box 7566 Washington DC 20044

KINGSBURY, CHARLES HERBERT, retired firefighter; b. New London, Conn., Nov. 4, 1932; s. Fred Burton and Viola C. (Curtis) K.; m. Joanne Sylvia DuBois, May 5, 1956; children: Kathleen Anne, Patice Anne, Kimberly Anne, Colette Anne, Tammy Anne. Grad. high sch., Northampton, Mass. Profl. fire fighter. From firefighter to lt. City of New Britain, Conn., 1967-91; ret., 1991. Bldg. com. New Fire House, City of New Britain, Conn., 1983. With USN, 1950-54. Recipient Ofcl. Recognition, Mayor City of New Britain, 1991, Mayor Donald J. Defronzo, 1991; recipient awards for saving lives, 1972, 74. Mem. VFW, Internat. Assn. Fire Fighters, Ancient Order of Hibernians, Elks City of New Britain. Home: 189 Miami Ave Newington CT 06111-3965

KINGSBURY, HERBERT BRENNEIS, engineering educator; b. Pitts., Feb. 15, 1934; s. Herbert Fletcher and Barbara (Brenneis) K.; m. Ellen Fish, Feb. 17, 1989; children from previous marriage: Hester B., Rachel M., Herbert M. BS, U. Conn., 1958; MS, U. Pa., 1961, PhD, 1964. Scientist Dyna Structures Inc., Phila., 1961-63; engr. GE, Phila., 1963-65; asst. prof. Pa. State U., State College, 1965-68; assoc. prof., then prof. dept. mech. engring. U. Del., Newark, 1968—; engring. cons., 1965—. Contbr. articles to profl. jours., chpts. to books. Chmn. Del. chpt. Sierra Club, 1975-80. Mem. AAUP, ASME, Am. Soc. Engring. Edn., Am. Acad. Mechanics, Am. Soc. Biomechanics, Del. Soc. Profl. Engrs., Sigma Xi, Tau Beta Pi, Pi Tau

Sigma. Home: 443 Lincoln Ave Portsmouth NH 03801-5121 Office: U Del Dept Mech Engring Newark DE 19716

KINGSLEY, DARWIN PEARL, III, sports association executive; b. N.Y.C., Sept. 15, 1927; s. Darwin Pearl Jr. and Heywood (Butler) K.; m. Margaret Jane Cotton, Aug. 26, 1950; children: Peter B., E. Anne Kingsley Musgrove, James D., Elizabeth Jane. BA, Yale U., 1950; EdM, Harvard U., 1958. Tchr., adminstr. Fay Sch., Southborough, Mass., 1950-65; asst. headmaster Episcopal Acad., Merion Station, Pa., 1965-74; exec. dir. U.S. Squash Racquets Assn., Bala-Cynwyd, Pa., 1974-91, mng. dir., 1991—; sec., U.S. Squash Racquets Assn., 1965-71, v.p., 1971-73, pres. 1973-75. Editor U.S. Squash Racquets Assn. yearbook; contbr. articles to profl. jours. Sgt. U.S. Air Corps, 1944-45. Mem. Rotary (pres. Marlborough, Mass. 1961, pres. Bala-Cynwyd 1971). Republican. Home: 117 Elmwood Ave Narberth PA 19072-2409 Office: US Squash Racquets Assn 23 Cynwyd Rd PO Box 1216 Bala Cynwyd PA 19004

KINGSLEY, SARAH DU BOIS, magazine production executive; b. Evanston, Ill., June 23, 1958; d. Samuel Seton Maitland and Saranne (Borda) Du Bois; m. Robert Logan Kingsley, June 14, 1980; children: Sarah Borda, Robert. Student, Denison U., 1976-78. Prodn. asst. Sci. 80-Sci. 84, Washington, 1980-84; prodn. editor Psychology Today Mag., Washington, 1984—; prodn. mgr. air and space Smithsonian Instn., Washington, 1986—. Bd. dirs. Huntington Terrace Community Assn., Bethesda, Md., 1988—. Republican. Episcopalian. Home: 5431 Lincoln St Bethesda MD 20817-3761 Office: Smithsonian Instn 370 Lenfant Pla SW Washington DC 20024

KINGSTON, NEAL MARTIN, educational testing company executive; b. Yonkers, N.Y., Sept. 28, 1951; s. Louis Robert and Sylvia Lee (Brown) K.; m. Maxine Beth Gottlieb, May 23, 1982; 1 child, Laura Beth Helen. AA, Westchester Community Coll., Valhalla, N.Y., 1972; BA, SUNY, Stony Brook, 1974; MEd, Columbia U., 1977, MPhil, 1983, PhD, 1983. Sci. tchr. Yonkers Bd. Edn., 1974-76; assoc. measurement statistician Ednl. Testing Svc., Princeton, N.J., 1978-81, sr. measurement statistician, 1983-88, dir. grad. record exams. rsch. and test devel., 1988-90, exec. dir. workplace assessment and tng., 1990-91; dir. selection rsch. Los Angeles County Dept. Pers., L.A., 1981-82; pres. Measured Progress, Inc., Hopewell, N.J., 1991—; adj. faculty Calif. Sch. Profl. Psychology, L.A., 1982, Rutgers U., New Brunswick, N.J., 1984-85. Contbr. articles to profl. jours. Active Bd. Edn. Franklin Twp., N.J., 1985, Environ. Commn., East Ammell, N.J., 1990. Mem. APA (div. membership chair 1988), Am. Psychol. Soc., Am. Ednl. Rsch. Assn., Nat. Coun. Measurement in Edn. (program chair 1989), Psychometric Soc., Soc. Applied Learning and Tech., Soc. Indsl. and Orgnl. Psychology. Home: 46 Mountain Rd Hopewell NJ 08525-2505 Office: Measured Progress Inc 46 Mountain Rd Hopewell NJ 08525-2505

KINIGAKIS, PANAGIOTIS, research scientist, engineer, author; b. Chanea, Greece, July 11, 1949; s. John and Evangelia (Vozinakis) K.; m. Kalliopi Paleologos, July 31, 1977; children: Evangelia, Maria Anna. BS, Superior Agrl. Sch., Athens, Greece, 1971, MS, 1973; MS in Food Sci., Rutgers U., 1979. Packaging devel. specialist Am. Cyanamid Co., Clifton, N.J., 1979-81; sr. packaging engr. Warner Lambert Co., Morris Plains, N.J., 1981-83; tech. services supr. M&M Mars Inc., Hackettstown, N.J., 1983-87; packaging engring. mgr. Gen. Foods Corp., White Plains, N.Y., 1987—; agrl. engr. Food Agrl. Orgn. div. of UN, Chanea, 1975-77. Patentee pkg. equipment and mfg. systems; contbr. articles to profl. jours. Advisor Greek Orthodox Youth Assn., Randolph, N.J., 1986, Hamilton, N.J., 1990. Mem. Inst. Food Tech., Tech. Assn. Pulp and Paper Industry, Inst. Packaging Profls. Greek Orthodox. Home: 65 Amherst Way Princeton Junction NJ 08550-1836 Office: Gen Foods USA 555 S Broadway Tarrytown NY 10591-6399

KINN, JOHN MATTHIAS, association executive, consultant; b. N.Y.C., July 25, 1925; s. John M. and Marie A. (Bremme) K.; m. Gloria Anita Thomas, Dec. 26, 1953; children: Robert A., Ian M., Laurel K. B.S. in Elec. Engring., U. Mo., 1949. Cert. assn. exec. Sr. engr. Western Electric Co., N.Y.C., 1950-53; group chief Bell Telephone Labs., Whippany, N.J., 1953-55; assoc. editor Electronics mag., McGraw-Hill, N.Y.C., 1955-59; engring. editor IBM Jour., N.Y.C., 1959-61, mgr. sci. info., 1961-65; dir. edn. IEEE, N.Y.C., 1965-79, cons., 1979-80; v.p. engring. Electronic Industries Assn., Washington, 1980—; mem. exec. com. U.S. Nat. Com. Internat. Electrotech. Commn., 1984—; U.S. del. Internat. Electrotech. Commn. Coun. Contbr. articles to various books and mags., 1983—. Chairman com. on semiconductor tech. Internat. Electrotech. Commn., 1989—; chmn. adv. com. on electronics and telecommunications IEC, chmn. com. on surface mounting tech. With USN, 1943-46, PTO. Mem. IEEE (sr.), Am. Soc. Assn. Execs., Am. Soc. Tng. Dirs., AAAS. Office: Electronic Industries Assn 2001 Pennsylvania Ave NW Washington DC 20006-1813

KINNEAR, JAMES WESLEY, III, petroleum company executive; b. Pitts., Mar. 21, 1928; s. James Wesley and Susan (Jenkins) K.; m. Mary Tullis, June 17, 1950; children: Robin Wood (Mrs. David Bruce Anderson), Susan, James Wesley IV, William M. BS with distinction, U.S. Naval Acad., 1950. With Texaco, Inc., 1954—; sales mgr. Texaco, Inc., Hawaii, 1959-63; div. sales mgr. Texaco, Inc., L.A., 1963-64; asst. to vice chmn. bd. dirs. Texaco, Inc., N.Y.C., 1964-65, asst. to chmn. bd. dirs., gen. mgr. marine dept., 1965, v.p. supply and distbn., 1966-70, sr. v.p. strategic planning, 1970-71, sr. v.p. worldwide refining, petrochems., supply and distbn., 1971-72, sr. v.p. world wide mktg., also in charge internat. marine ops. and petrochems., 1972-76, sr. v.p. internat. marine and aviation sales petrochem. dept., marine dept., mktg. and refining in Europe, 1976-78, dir., 1977—, exec. v.p., 1978-83; pres. Texaco USA Texaco, Inc., 1982-84; vice chmn. bd. dirs. Texaco, Inc., White Plains, 1983-86, pres., chief exec. officer, 1987—; bd. dirs. Corning Inc., Asarco Inc. Trustee St. Paul's Sch., Concord, N.H. Served to lt. comdr. USNR, 1950-54. Mem. Am. Petroleum Inst. (bd. dirs.), Nat. Petroleum Coun. (bd. dirs.), Bus. Coun. of N.Y. (bd. dirs.), Bus. Round Table, Bus. Coun., U.S. Naval Inst., Round Hill Club (Greenwich, Conn.), Verbank Hunting Club, Brook Club (N.Y.C), Iron City Fishing (Parry Sound, Ont.), Augusta Club (Ga.), Nat. Golf Club. Episcopalian. Home: 149 Taconic Rd Greenwich CT 06831-3113 Office: Texaco Inc 2000 Westchester Ave White Plains NY 10650-0001

KINNEY, ARTHUR FREDERICK, literary history educator; b. Cortland, N.Y., Sept. 5, 1933; s. Arthur F. and Gladys (Mudge) K. BA magna cum laude, Syracuse U., 1955; MS, Columbia U., 1956; PhD, U. Mich., 1963. Instr. Yale U., New Haven, Conn., 1963-66; asst. prof. U. Mass., Amherst, 1966-69, assoc. prof., 1969-73, prof., 1973-85, Copeland Prof., 1985—; keynote speaker nat. and internat. confs. in field. Author more than 20 books, including: Humanist Poetics, 1986, Continental Humanist Poetics, 1989, John Skelton: Priest as Poet, 1988; editor: Renaissance Historicism, 1987, Elizabethan Backgrounds, 1974, revised edit. 1990, Rogues, Vagabonds, and Sturdy Beggars, 1973, 2nd edit. 1990; editor English Literary Renaissance jour., (book series) Twayne English Authors Series-Renaissance, Massachusetts Studies in Early Modern Culture; editorial bd. several jours.; editorial cons. in field. With AUS, 1956-58. Recipient Disting. Teaching award U. Mass., 1990, Chancellor's medal, 1985, Univ. Rsch. fellowship, 1976; Sr. NEH Fellow, 1973-74, '77-78, Sr. Huntington Libr. Fellow, 1973-74, '78, '83, Sr. Folger Shakespeare Libr. Fellow, 1974, '90, '92. Mem. Modern Lang. Assn. (pres. Coun. of Editors of Learned Jours., 1971-73, 78-81), Shakespeare Assn. Am., Renaissance Soc. Am. (coun. mem.), Renaissance English Text Soc. (pres. 1985—), Sixteenth-Century Studies Conf. Home: 25 Hunters Hill Cir Amherst MA 01002-3116 Office: English Dept U Mass Amherst Amherst MA 01003

KINNIBURGH, ALAN JAMES, molecular biologist, educator; b. Elmhurst, Ill., Oct. 3, 1951; s. Theodore and Elizabeth (Pitcarin) K. BS, U. Ill., 1973; PhD, U. Chgo., 1977. Rsch. assoc. U. Wis., Madison, 1977-82; asst. prof. Roswell Park Cancer Inst., Buffalo, 1982-87, assoc. prof., 1987-91, prof., head Lab. of Molecular Diagnostics, 1991—; mem. adv. bd. Assn. for Rsch./Childhood Cancer, Buffalo, 1990—; mem. hematology rev. bd. VA, Washington, 1990—. Recipient Louis Pasteur award U. Ill., 1973. Mem. AAAS, Am. Assn. Microbiology, Am. Assn. Cancer Rsch., N.Y. Acad. Sci. Office: Roswell Park Cancer Inst Elm and Carlton Sts Buffalo NY 14263

KINSELLA, DANIEL JOHN, electrical engineer; b. Rochester, N.Y., Dec. 14, 1952; s. John Joseph and Lucille Kate (Taylor) K. BSEE, Rensselaer Poly. Inst., 1975, MSEE, 1976. Gen. radio telephone lic. FCC. Elec. design engr. Harris Corp., Rochester, N.Y., 1976-77; sr. elec. design engr. Raytheon Co., Sudbury, Mass., 1977-84; sr. field applications engr. Monolithic Memories, Inc., Framingham, Mass., 1984-86, dist. sales mgr., 1986-87; sr. field application engr. Advanced Micro Devices, Burlington, Mass., 1987-88; field applications engr. WSI, Stow, Mass., 1988—. Mem. Boston Computer Soc., Mensa. Home and Office: 210 Barton Rd Stow MA 01775

KINSELLA, JOHN DEGAN, lawyer; b. Syracuse, N.Y., Mar. 6, 1941; s. Edward M. and Genevieve L. (Degan) K.; m. Natalie C. Miguel, June 27, 1964; children: Edward J., John M. BS in Acctg., Syracuse U., 1964, JD, 1970. Bar: N.Y. 1971. Assoc. counsel U.S. Small Bus. Adminstrn., Syracuse, 1971-73; asst. dist. atty. Onondaga County, Syracuse, 1973-77, chief asst. dist. atty., 1978; lawyer Melvin Law Firm, P.C., Syracuse, 1979—; election commr. Onandaga County, 1979—; del. 5th Jud. Dist. Conv., Syracuse, 1976—. Mem. N.Y. Rep. State Com., Albany, 1991—. Roman Catholic. Office: Melvin Law Firm PC 6834 Buckley Rd North Syracuse NY 13212

KINSELLA, MARCO ANTONIO, secondary educator; b. Mexico City, Mex., Aug. 26, 1954; came to U.S., 1959; s. Richard and Conchita (Harper) K.; m. Joy Nalini Zavala, July 9, 1983; 1 child, Liana Shalini. BS, Allentown Coll., 1977; MS, Cen. Conn. State U., 1982; postgrad., U. Conn., 1985—. Educator State Dept. Edn., Hartford, Conn., 1990—; instr. math and sci. State of Conn. Dept. Edn., New Britain, 1978—; adj. faculty mem. dept. math. Cen. Conn. State U., New Britain, 1986—. Treas. League of United Latin Am. Citizens, Hartford, 1985; mentor U. Conn. Mentor Program, Hartford, 1985. Mem. Am. Biol. Assn., Am. Chem. Assn. Democrat. Roman Catholic. Home: 153 Worthington Rd Glastonbury CT 06033 Office: 104 Webster St Hartford CT 06114-1252

KINSEY, JAMES ANDREW, ophthalmologist, physician, educator; b. Binghamton, N.Y., Oct. 18, 1945; s. Ernest Schroeder and Pauline (Gunsalus) K.; m. Kathleen Ann Bloomer, Aug. 23, 1970; children: Jennifer Lynn, Sherryn Michelle, Megan Anne. BA, Syracuse U., 1967; MD, SUNY, Syracuse, 1971. Diplomate Am. Bd. Ophthalmology. Intern St. Mary's Hosp., Rochester, N.Y., 1971-72; resident in ophthalmology SUNY Upstate Med. Ctr., Syracuse, 1974-77; ophthalmologist, physician Eye Cons. Syracuse, P.C., 1977—; assoc. clin. prof. ophthalmology SUNY, Syracuse, 1980—. Lt. comdr. M.C. USN, 1972-74. Fellow Am. Acad. Ophthalmology; mem. AMA, N.Y. State Med. Soc., N.Y. State Ophthalmology Soc., Onondaga County Med. Soc. Home: 5105 Balmoral Dr Fayetteville NY 13066 Office: Eye Cons Syracuse PC 1101 Erie Blvd E Syracuse NY 13210

KINSLEY, MICHAEL E., magazine editor; b. Detroit, Mar. 9, 1951; s. George and Lillian (Margolis) K. AB, Harvard U., 1972, JD, 1977; postgrad., Magdalen Coll., Oxford U., Eng., 1972-74. Bar: D.C. Mng. editor The Washington Monthly, 1975; mng. editor The New Republic, Washington, 1976-79, editor, 1985-89, sr. editor, 1989—; editor Harper's Mag., N.Y.C., 1981-83; Am. Survey editor The Economist, London, Eng., 1988-89; contbg. writer Time mag., 1987—; co-host CNN Crossfire, 1989—. Office: New Republic 1220 19th St NW Washington DC 20036-2405

KINSMAN, DAVID BAILEY, association administrator; b. Northampton, Mass., Dec. 17, 1953; s. Donald Markham and Helen Katharine (Bailey) K.; m. Sharon Christine Goldener, Dec. 16, 1988; 1 child, Ross Thomas. BA, U. Mass., 1976. Assoc. dir. pub. rels. and communications Charnas, Inc., Manchester, Conn., 1979-82; exec. asst. to sec. of state Govt. of Conn., Hartford, 1982, communication dir. speaker of house, 1983; asst. dir. mem. affairs AIA, Washington, 1983-85; dir. pub. affairs Eye Bank Assn. Am., Washington, 1985-87; mgr. program support and devel. Pub. Affairs Coun./Found. for Pub. Affairs, Washington, 1987—. Contbr. chpts. to books. Mem. Pub. Rels. Soc. Am. (accredited, bd. dirs. Nat. Capital chpt. 1990—, President's citation 1991), Am. Soc. Assn. Execs. Office: Pub Affairs Coun 1019 19th St NW # 200 Washington DC 20036

KINSMAN, DONALD MARKHAM, animal scientist, educator; b. Framingham, Mass., May 20, 1923; s. Joshua Starr and Florence Ruby (Markham) K.; m. Helen Katherine Bailey, Aug. 28, 1949; children: Elizabeth, David, Martha. BS, U. Mass., 1949; MS, U. N.H., 1951; PhD, Okla. State U., 1964. Instr. U. N.H., Durham, 1949-51, U. Vt., Burlington, 1951-52; farm mgr. U. Mass., Amherst, 1952-56; prof. U. Conn., Storrs, 1956-88, prof. emeritus, 1988—; pres., treas. Kin-Tec Enterprises, Inc., Storrs, 1988—; mem. meat inspection evaluation team NAS-USDA, 1989-91; mem. organic food standards bd. USDA, 1992—; pres. New Eng. Livestock Conservation, Inc., 1970-82. Editor: International Meat Science Dictionary, 1978, International Sausage Book, 1981, International Directory of Meat Scientists, 1985; contbr. more than 100 articles to profl. jours. Treas. Mansfield Retirement Community, Storrs, 1975—. Cpl. USMC, 1942-46, PTO. Danforth fellow, 1980. Fellow Am. Soc. Animal Sci. (Disting. Tchr. award 1990, Internat. award 1992); mem. Am. Meat Sci. Assn. (past bd. dirs., pres. 1978, Signal Svc. award 1975, Disting. Tchr. award 1981, R.C. Pollock award 1988), Coun. for Agrl. Sci. and Tech., Alpha Gamma Rho. Republican. Congregationalist. Home: 45 Moulton Rd Storrs Mansfield CT 06268-1317 Office: U Conn Dept Animal Sci Storrs CT 06269-4040

KINSMAN, FRANK WILLIAM, mechanical engineering educator, company executive; b. Elmira, N.Y., July 28, 1925; s. Richard Ellard and Helen (McCann) K.; m. Elizabeth Ann George, Jan. 12, 1952; children: Robert, Susan, Andy, Tom, Ted. BME with distinction, Cornell U., 1949, PhD in Mech. Engring., 1955; MS in EM, Stanford U., 1950. Registered profl. engr., N.Y. Rsch. engr. Bell Telephone Labs., Murray Hill, N.J., 1953-58, Gleason Gear Works, Rochester, N.Y., 1958-60; cons. engr. Fairport, N.Y., 1960-63; pres. Inter-mec, Fairport, 1962—; prof. mech. tech. Monroe Community Coll., Rochester, 1963—; cons. IBM, Endicott, N.Y., 1961. Contbr. articles on gear design, stress analysis and geology to profl. jours.; patentee push button telephones, undersea telephone cable systems, pneumatic machinery. With AUS, 1943-46, ETO. Recipient Disting. Prof. award Monroe Community Coll., 1983. Mem. Am. Soc. for Metals, Mid-Town Tennis Club. Republican. Unitarian. Home: 151 Bluhm Rd Fairport NY 14450-9561 Office: Monroe Community Coll 1000 E Henrietta Rd Rochester NY 14623 also: Inter-Mec PO Box 444 Fairport NY 14450

KINSTLINGER, JACK, engineering executive, consultant; b. Antwerp, Belgium, Mar. 2, 1931; came to U.S., 1939; s. Joseph and Rose (Lichtblau) K.; m. Marilyn Wiseman, July 16, 1967; children: Michael, Jeremy. BS in Civil Engring., Rensselaer Polytechnic Inst., 1952; MS in Civil Engring., MIT, 1954. Registered profl. engr., N.Y., Pa., Wash., N.H., Colo., Del., Mass. Assoc. Tippetts, Abbett, McCarthy, Stratton, N.Y.C., 1957-68; dep. sec. Pa. Dept. Transp., Harrisburg, 1968-75; state hwy. dir. State of Colo., Denver, 1975-82; v.p. Daniel-Mann-Johnson-Mendenhall, Denver, 1982-84; pres., chmn. bd. dirs. KCI Techs., Inc., Balt., 1984—. Bd. dirs. Am. Jewish Com., Balt., 1986—, Balt. Jewish Coun.;mem. adv. bd. Nat. Aquarium Balt., 1986—; dir. design div. Am. Roads and Transp. Builders Assn., Washington, 1987—, Nat. Soc. Profl. Engrs., Balt., 1987—. Served to lt. (j.g.) Civil Engring. Corps, USN, 1954-57. Fellow ASCE; mem. Am. Inst. Cert. Planners, Engring. Soc. Balt., Greater Balt. Com., Greater Washington Bd. Trade, Am. Acad. Scis. (transp. bd., chmn. transp. com.), Am. Cons. Engrs. Coun., Md. C. of C. (bd. dirs.). Office: KCI Techs Inc 1020 Cromwell Bridge Rd Baltimore MD 21204-3396

KINZEY, WARREN GLENFORD, anthropology educator; b. Orange, N.J., Oct. 31, 1935; s. Warren Parry and Mildred Irene (Hazzard) K.; m. Trilby Taylor, Mar. 24, 1957 (div. 1977); children: Claudia, Andrea, Monica; m. Julianne L. Kelly, Apr. 16, 1983. BA, U. Minn., 1956, MA, 1958; postgrad., U. Chgo., 1957-60; PhD, U. Calif., Berkeley, 1964. Asst. prof. U. Calif., Davis, 1963-70; assoc. prof. CCNY and Grad. Sch., 1970-83, prof., 1983—; asst. research anatomist Nat. Ctr. Primate Biology, U. Calif. Davis, 1964-65, planning officer regional med. program Sch. Medicine, 1967-68; chmn. Dept. Anthropology CCNY, 1984-87, dir. Program in Community Health Edn., 1987-88; program dir. phys. anthropology NSF, Washington, 1988-90. Editor: Evolution of Human Behavior: Primate Models, 1987; contbr. articles to profl. jours. Research grantee NIH, 1965, 82, Wenner-Gren Found. grantee, 1965, 71, NSF grantee, 1980, 81, 88, 89, 91, World Wildlife Fund grantee, 1986, Earthwatch grantee, 1975-77, 80, 83. Fellow Am. Anthrop. Assn. (program editor biol. anthropology 1983-87), Am. Assn. Physical Anthropologists (assoc. editor jour. 1986-90), Am. Soc. Primatologists (cons. editor jour. 1984—), N.Y. Acad. Scis. (chair anthropology sect. 1987-88), Am. Assn. Anatomists. Unitarian. Home: 185 Riverview Ave Tarrytown NY 10591 Office: CUNY City Coll Dept of Anthropology Convent Ave New York NY 10031-9198

KIPPEL, GARY M., psychologist; b. Bklyn.; s. Philip and Florence (Wiederlight) K.; m. Ronnie G. Spilka, July 27, 1977. BA, Bklyn. Coll., 1963; MA, Queens Coll., 1964; PhD, NYU, 1973. Cert. psychologist, N.Y.; lic. tchr.; cert. adminstr. and supr. Research asst. Ctr. for Urban Edn., Inst. Child Devel. and Exptl. Edn., N.Y.C., 1965-67; tchr. P.S. 219, Bklyn., 1967-69; research asst. Hdqrs. N.Y.C. Bd. Edn., Bklyn., 1969-73, research assoc., 1974-77, asst. dir. edn. research, 1978-90; chief adminstr. for test devel. and tech. support Office of Recruitment, Pers. Assessment and Licensing, 1990—; adj. assoc. prof. ednl. psychology NYU, N.Y.C., 1971, 80; adj. assoc. prof. mgmt. Pace U., N.Y.C., 1978—. Contbr. articles to profl. jours., chpts. to books. V.p. E. Midwood Jewish Ctr., Bklyn., 1989—; chmn. bd. edn. Rabbi Harry Halpern Day Sch., Bklyn., 1987-90. Univ. Scholar Queens Coll., 1964. Mem. Am. Psychological Assn., Nat. Coun. Measurement in Edn., Am. Ednl. Research Assn., Soc. Indsl. and Organizational Psychology. Office: NYC Bd Edn 65 Court St Brooklyn NY 11201-4954

KIPPING, HANS F., dermatologist; b. Chgo., Jan. 8, 1924; s. Johaanes and Johannah (Rauch) K.; m. Rosemary New, Jan. 3, 1928; children—Susan, John, David. M.D., U. Buffalo, 1947. Intern, Buffalo Gen. Hosp., N.Y., 1947-48, resident in indsl. medicine, Millard Fillmore Hosp., Buffalo, 1948-49; resident in dermatology E.J. Meyer Meml. Hosp., Buffalo, 1953-56; practice medicine specializing in dermatology, Buffalo, 1956—; clin. prof. dermatology SUNY-Buffalo; attending dermatologist Erie County Health Care Ctr., 1979; dermatologist Buffalo Gen. Hosp., cons. dermatology Roswell Park Meml. Inst., 1980—; cons., lectr. in field. Contbr. articles, research studies to profl. jours. Served to capt. USAF, 1950-52. Fellow Am. Soc. Dermatopathology; mem. Assn. Profs. Dermatology, AMA, Soc. Investigative Dermatology, Am. Acad. Dermatology, Dermatology Found., Toronto Dermatology Soc., Buffalo-Rochester Dermatology Soc. (pres. 1962-63), N.Y. State Dermatology Soc. (pres. 1974-75). Republican. Methodist. Club: Youngstown Yacht. Home: 192 Castlebrook Ln Buffalo NY 14221-4475 Office: 4444 Main St Buffalo NY 14226-4420

KIRBY, BRUCE ROBERT WILLIAM, product designer; b. Ottawa, Ont., Can., Jan. 2, 1929; came to U.S. 1965; s. David Pattee and Eileen F.M. (Bruce) K.; m. Margo Alma, June 1, 1956; children: Margo Janice, Kelly June. Sr. matriculation, Lisgar Coll. Inst., Ottawa, Ont., 1948. Reporter Ottawa Jour., 1949-56; editor Montreal (Que.) Star, 1956-65, Yacht Racing Mag., Norwalk, Ct., 1965-75; yacht designer Rowayton, Ct., 1969—. Designer Laser sailboat, Am.'s Cup contenders Canada I and II, 1983, 87. Mem. N.Y. Yacht Club (model com.), Noroton Yacht Club (Conn., bd. dirs. 1985-86). Avocations: yacht racing, three olympic games, two nat. championships and Admir al's Cup. Home: 213 Rowayton Ave Norwalk CT 06853-1240

KIRCHHAUSEN, TOMAS, scientist; b. Lima, Peru, Feb. 23, 1952; came to U.S., 1978; s. Kurt and Mimi (Luwisch) K. PhD, 1977. Assoc. prof. Harvard U., Boston, 1986—. Office: Harvard Med Sch Dept Anatomy & Cell Biology 220 Longwood Ave Boston MA 02115-5717

KIRCHMAN, CHARLES VINCENT, lawyer; b. Washington, June 28, 1935; s. Floyd Vincent and Dorothy Johanna (Johnson) K.; m. Erika Ottilie Knoeppel, July 4, 1959; children: Mark C., Eric H., Charles E. BA, U. Md., 1959; JD, George Washington U., 1962. Bar: DC 1962, Md. 1970. Security specialist Adj. Gen.'s Office, U.S. Army, 1962-64; sole practice, Washington, 1964-70, Wheaton, Md., 1970-73; ptnr. Andrews & Schick, Waldorf, Md., 1973-77; sole practice, Wheaton, Md., 1977—. Mem. adv. bd. Immigration Reform Law Inst. Served with AUS, 1953-56. Mem. Am. Trial Lawyers Assn., D.C. Bar Assn., Md. Bar Assn., Charles County Bar Assn., Am. Arbitration Assn. (nat. panel), Md. Hist. Soc. Democrat. Club: Manor Country. Home: 14801 Notley Rd Silver Spring MD 20905-5837 Office: 11141 Georgia Ave Wheaton MD 20902

KIRCHNER, THOMAS, pharmacologist; b. Phila., June 7, 1952; s. John Michael and Barbara Katherine (Margerum) K.; m. Kathleen Marie Tait, May 11, 1972; children: Jennifer Kathleen, Meghan Marie, Kathleen Marie. BS in Biology, Ursinus Coll., 1973. Biologist Wyeth Labs., Radnor, Pa., 1973-82; assoc. pharmacologist Smith Kline & French Labs., Phila., 1982-83; sr. assoc. scientist RW Johnson Pharm. Rsch. Inst., Raritan, N.J., 1983—. Contbr. articles to jours. Mem. N.Y. Acad. Scis., Physiol. Soc. Phila. Internat. Soc. Immunopharmacology, Mid Atlantic Pharmacology Soc. Republican. Methodist. Office: RW Johnson Pharm Rsch Inst Rte 202 Raritan NJ 08869

KIRIKOS, NICK, engineer, consultant; b. Boston, Oct. 7, 1916; s. James Nicholas and Zoe J. (Serelis) K.; m. Janet Olive Wood, Sept. 9, 1984. Grad. high sch., Franklin, Mass. Engr. Wrought Iron Kitchen Equipment, Boston, 1939-52; chief engr. Thompson-Winchester, Boston, 1952-59; owner, food facilities cons. Norwood, Mass., 1960—. Contbr. articles to profl. jours. Sgt. U.S. Air Force, 1941-46, PTO. Mem. VFW (sec.), Am. Legion (past comdr.). Republican. Greek Orthodox. Home and Office: 4 Harvey Rd Attleboro MA 02703-4313

KIRK, ALEXANDER, artist; b. Tucson, Sept. 30, 1948; s. Edward B. and Nadia Kirk. Student, Sch. Visual Arts, 1969-70, SUNY, 1982—. Pres., dir. Art-O-Rama Gallery, New Rochelle, 1968-72; prodn. mgr., photographer, color pressman Web Co. Press, Mt. Vernon, N.Y., 1971-77; dir. Kirk Studio, Eastchester, N.Y., 1972-76; printer, artist, art dealer Kirk's Art Gallery, N.Y.C., 1977-79; dir. Kirk Merchandising Svc., Patterson, N.Y., 1977-79, Art-Vall Gallery, New Rochelle, N.Y., 1979—. Tchr., master martial arts. Democrat. Episcopalian. Home and Office: Art-Vall Gallery 73 Rodman Oval New Rochelle NY 10805-3012

KIRK, DAVID SHELBY, computer consultant; b. Little Rock, Feb. 4, 1941; s. Oliver Richard and Ruby Geraldine (Morgan) K.; m. Linda Jane Christian, Nov. 23, 1960; 1 child, Robert David. BA in Liberal Studies, SUNY, Brockport, 1981. Project leader Able, Inc., Hartford, Conn., 1965-66; systems engr. Burroughs Corp., Syracuse, N.Y., 1966-68; supr. tech. planning Carrier Air Conditioning, Syracuse, 1968-70; dir. tng. computer systems div. RCA, Syracuse, 1970-71; mgr. tech. support Mutual of N.Y., Syracuse, 1971-78, dir. devel. ctr., 1978-85, dir. mgmt. info. systems, 1985-89; cons. David Kirk Assocs., Cicero, N.Y., 1989—. Author: Cobol II Power Programming Desk Reference, 1991, The MVS Primer, 1992. Staff sgt. USAF, 1960-65. Mem. Assn. for Computing Machinery (program com. 1991—). Episcopalian. Home: 5961 Farrington Rd Cicero NY 13039-9068

KIRK, DAVID STARR, real estate consultant; b. Greenwich, Conn., Oct. 25, 1943; m. Peggy (O'Connor) Kirk; children: Nathaniel, Garrett, Anne. BA, U. Pa., 1965, MBA, 1967. Acct. exec. Laudauer Assocs., N.Y.C., 1968-71; v.p., sr. v.p., prin., bd. dirs. Boston Fin. Group, 1971—. Mem. Am. Inst. Real Estate Appraisers (various offices), Am. Soc. Real Estate Counselors (various offices), Urban Land Inst. Home: 28 Mt Vernon St Boston MA 02108-1402 Office: Boston Fin Group 101 Arch St Boston MA 02110-1103

KIRK, DONALD JAMES, consultant, accounting educator; b. Cleve., Nov. 28, 1932; s. John James and Helen Anna (Pilskaln) K.; m. Tara Collins, May 30, 1975; children: J. Alexander, Bruce D.; stepchildren: John Needham, Elizabeth Needham. B.A., Yale U., 1959; M.B.A., NYU, 1961; LL.D. (hon.), Lycoming Coll., 1979. Acct. Price Waterhouse & Co., N.Y.C., London and Washington, 1959-73; partner Price Waterhouse & Co., 1967-73; mem. Fin. Acctg. Standards Bd., Stamford, Conn., 1973-77, chmn., 1978-86; prof. acctg. Columbia U. Grad. Sch. of Bus., 1987—; dir. Gen. Re Corp., 1987—; trustee Fidelity Group Mut. Funds, 1987—. Officer, bd. dirs. Urban League of Southwestern Fairfield County, Conn., 1971-77; mem. Greenwich (Conn.) Rep. Town Meeting, 1971-77, Greenwich Bd. of Estimate and Taxation, 1977-89; bd. dirs. Nat. Arts Stabilization Fund, 1983—; bd. overseers NYU Schs. Bus., 1985-89; trustee The Greenwich Hosp. Assn.,

1989—, Greenwich Found. for Community Gifts, 1991—. Aviator USN, 1953-57. Recipient Alumni Achievement award NYU Grad. Sch. Bus. Adminstrn., 1980. Mem. AICPA (governing coun. 1987-90, Gold medal award for disting. svc.), Am. Acctg. Assn., Fin. Execs. Inst. (bd. dirs. N.Y.C. 1990—), Yale Alumni Assn. of Greenwich (bd. dirs. 1988—), Stanwich Club (past pres.), Yale Club N.Y.C. Office: Columbia U Grad Sch Bus 602 Uris Hall New York NY 10027

KIRK, HAROLD MARK, music educator; b. Vincennes, Ind., Oct. 28, 1950; s. Harold William and Betty Jane (Hankins) K.; m. Kari Ellen Gleim, Oct. 26, 1986; children: Kelsey Elizabeth, Ian Philip. B in Music Edn., Berklee Coll. of Music, 1972; MusM in Composition, U. Ill., 1985. Jazz musician, 1962—, composer and arranger, 1970—; asst. prof. Rutgers U., New Brunswick, N.J., 1986—; pres. Tuckle Day Music, Inc., North Brunswick, N.J., 1990—. Composer, arranger numerous compositions. Music area coord. N.J. Teen Arts Assn., New Brunswick, 1989, 90, 91; career day counselor Boy Scouts Am./Eagle Scouts, New Brunswick, 1990. With U.S. Army, 1972-78. N.J. Summerfest grantee, 1990. Mem. AAUP, Am. Fed. Musicians Local 802, Coll. Music Soc., Am. Legion. Lutheran. Home: 424 Hamilton St # 424B Somerset NJ 08873-2193 Office: Rutgers U Mason Grass Sch of the Arts New Brunswick NJ 08901

KIRKNER, JAMES NORMAN, social services financial executive, realtor; b. Abington, Pa., Feb. 14, 1935; s. Atlee Anderson and Kathryn (Norcom) K.; m. Darlene Joyce Frankenfield, Nov. 27, 1954; children: Keith, David, Kenneth. Cert. in fin., U. Pa., 1959; BS, Pacific Western U., 1984. Cert. residential specialist, residential brokerage mgr.; grad. Realtors' Inst., Real Estate Nat. Mktg. Inst. Office mgr. LaTouraine Coffee Co., Phila., 1954-62; bus. mgr. Christ's Mission, Sea Cliff, N.Y., 1962-64; contr. Monarch Foods div. Consol. Foods, Phila., 1964-69, Jacobs Music Stores, Phila., 1969-70; v.p. Glenside (Pa.) Bond and Mortgage Co., 1970-78; pres. Century 21 Kirkner Assocs., Horsham, Pa., 1978—; dir. fin. Lakeside Youth Svc., Willow Grove, Pa., 1989—; pres. Suburban Multiple Listing Svc., Oreland, Pa., 1985-86; bd. dirs. Inter-County Abstract Ltd., Ft. Washington, Pa. Bd. dirs. Lakeside Youth Svc., 1965-89, chmn. bd., 1985-86. With USN, 1952-54. Mem. Pa. Assn. Realtors (bd. dirs. 1981-86), East Montgomery Bd. Realtors (pres. 1984, Realtor of Yr. award 1985, Disting. Svc. award 1986), Kiwanis (pres. Jenkintown, Pa. 1989-90, Disting. Pres. award 1991). Republican. Baptist. Office: Lakeside Youth Svc PO Box L Willow Grove PA 19090-0918

KIRKPATRICK, FRANCIS H(UBBARD), JR., scientific research company director, consultant; b. Laurel Hill, N.C., Nov. 7, 1943; s. Francis Hubbard and Jean Orr (Murray) K.; m. Cornelia Ewart Goodreds, Aug. 30, 1969; 1 child, Adam Bane. BA in Physics, Harvard Coll., 1964; PhD in Biophysics, Stanford U., 1970. Registered U.S. patent agent, 1991. Postdoctoral intern Biophysics Program, Wash. State U., Pullman, 1969-71; postdoctoral fellow dept. radiation biology and biophysics U. Rochester (N.Y.) Sch. Medicine, 1972-74, asst. prof. dept. radiation biology and biophysics, 1974-80; lab. mgr. Pall Corp., Glen Cove, N.Y., 1980-82, mgr. biotech. rsch., 1982-84; tech. dir. FMC BioProducts, Rockland, Maine, 1984—; cons. Nalge Corp., 1977-80; mem. spl. study sect. NIH, 1977, 79; mem. Genetics Small Bus. Innovative Rsch. Spl. Study Sect., 1988—; lectr. in field. Contbr. articles to sci. jours.; patentee in field. Pres. South-East Area Coalition, Rochester, 1977; mem. fin. com. 1st Universalist Ch., Rockland. Recipient Rsch. Career Devel. award NIH, 1975-80; competitive fellow NIH, 1967, 72; grantee NIH, 1974-80, U.S. Dept. Energy, 1975-80. Mem. Biophys. Soc., Optical Soc. Am., Am. Soc. Cell Biology, Am. Chem. Soc., Am. Soc. Biochemistry and Molecular Biology. Home: Woods Rd Owls Head ME 04854 Office: FMC BioProducts 191 Thomaston St Rockland ME 04841-2129

KIRKWOOD, JAMES MACE, pharmaceutical company executive; b. Chgo., Sept. 19, 1942; s. Robert Charles and Helen Maxine (Butler) K.; m. Anne Naylor, June 21, 1963 (dec. Oct. 1972); m. Nancy Lynne Sleesman, Oct. 4, 1986; 1 child: Jocelyn Anne. BS in Pharmacy, U. Pitts., 1965; D in Pharmacy (hon.), U. Md., 1981. Lic. pharmacist Pa., Md., Del., Va., N.J., W.Va., Maine; cert. analyst Walter V. Clarke Activity Vector Analysis. Pharmacy, store mgr. Sun Drug Co., Greensburg, Pa., 1966-72; owner Profl. Bldg. Pharmacy, Greensburg, 1972-74; pharmacy area supr. Keystone Stores, Lebanon, Pa., 1974-76; dir. profl. placement Rite Aid, Balt., 1976-80; pharmacy dist. mgr. Grand Union Corp., Elwood Park, N.J., 1980-81; dir. pharmacy ops. White Shield Stores, Camp Hill, Pa., 1981-85; from pharmacy supr. to corp. supr. 3d party ops. Rite Aid, N.J., Pa., 1985-89; dir. profl. pers. Rite Aid, Harrisburg, Pa., 1989—; adj. instr. U. Pitts. Sch. Pharmacy, 1989-92; cons. Rivercrest Ctr., Mont Clar, Pa., 1982-92, Hanover (Pa.) Surgicare Ctr., 1992. Mem. Am. Soc. Cons. Pharmacists, Cen. Pa. Pitts. Club (pres. 1990-92), U. Pa. Alumni Assn. (mem. strategic planning com.), U. Pitts. Alumni Coun., Pa. Pharmacy Assn., N.Y. Skyliners, Reading Buccaneer Alumni Assn., Capitol Area Pharmacy Assn., Lions, Rotary, Westshoremen Alumni Assn. Republican. Lutheran. Home: 394 Rising Sun Rd Millersburg PA 17061

KIRKYLA, VIKTORAS ANTANAS, engineering executive, consultant; b. Kaunas, Lithuania, Apr. 4, 1940; came to U.S., 1950; s. Antanas and Henrika (Buika) K.; m. Irena Marija Petniunas, Sept. 7, 1963; children: Kristina, Andrius, Laura. BCE, CCNY, 1963. Registered profl. engr., N.Y., N.J., Oreg. Civil engr. Calif. Div. of Hwys., San Francisco, 1963-66; project engr. DeLeuw, Cather & Assocs., N.Y.C., 1966-68; dept. head, project mgr. Parsons Brinckerhoff, N.Y.C., 1968-87; founder, mng. prin. Kirkyla & Remeza Cons. Engrs., N.Y.C., 1987—, also bd. dirs.; cons. Govt. of Lithuania, N.Y.C., 1990—. Co-author: Standard Handbook for Civil Engineers, 1974, 2d and 3d edits., 1978. Scoutmaster Lithuanian Boy Scouts, N.Y.C., 1966-78; instr. Pitco-Engr. Tng., N.Y.C., 1983-86; dir. Lithuanian Cultural Ctr., N.Y.C., 1983-86. Cpl. USMCR, 1961-66. Mem. Am. Rd. and Tunnel Builders Assn., Assn. for Advancement Baltic Studies (conf. coord., fundraiser 1963-78). Roman Catholic. Office: Kirkyla & Remeza 650 First Ave New York NY 10016

KIRMSE, SISTER ANNE-MARIE ROSE, nun, educator, researcher; b. Bklyn., Sept. 23, 1941; d. Frank Joseph Sr. and Anna (Keck) K. BA in English cum laude, St. Francis Coll., 1972; MA in Theology with honors, Providence Coll., 1975; PhD in Theology, Fordham U., 1989. Joined Sisters of St. Dominic, Roman Cath. Ch., 1960; cert. elem. tchr., N.Y. Tchr. elem. sch. Diocese Bklyn., 1962-73; instr. adult edn. Diocese Rockville Centre, N.Y., 1974—; dir. religious edn. St. Anthony Padua Parish, East Northport, N.Y., 1975-83; dir. spiritual programs Diocese of Rockville Centre, 1979—; demonstration tchr. Paulist Press, N.Y.C., 1968-70; cons. Elem. Sch. Catechetical Assocs., Bklyn., 1971-73; mem. adj. faculty grad. program Sem. Immaculate Conception, Huntington, N.Y., 1979-80; adj. instr. Molloy Coll., Rockville Centre, 1985, St. Joseph's Coll., Patchogue, N.Y., 1990-91; asst. to Rev. Avery Dulles, Fordham U., Bronx, 1988—, rsch. assoc. Laurence J. McGinley chair in religion and soc., 1989—. Recipient Dominican scholarship Providence (R.I.) Coll., 1973, Kerygma award Diocese Rockville Centre, 1980, Presdl. scholarship Fordham U., 1988; McGinley fellow Fordham U., 1988. Mem. L.I. Women's Ordination Conf. Democrat. Roman Catholic. Office: Fordham U Keating Hall 322 Laurence J McGinley Chair in Religion and Soc Bronx NY 10458

KIRNAN, JEAN POWELL, psychology educator; b. Short Hills, N.J., Mar. 30, 1956; d. Bernard MacDonald and Marie (Harrity) Powell; m. John Vincent Kirnan, Aug. 23, 1980; children: Tarah, Katelyn, Patrick. BA in Psychology cum laude, Immaculate Coll., 1978; MA, Fordham U., 1980, PhD in Psychometrics, 1986. Rsch. analyst Prudential Ins. Co. Am., Newark, 1981-86; asst. prof. Psychology Trenton (N.J.) State Coll., 1986—. Contbr. articles to profl. jours. Mem. APA (Divs. 5 and 14 human resources cons.). Office: Trenton State Coll Hillwood Lakes CN 4700 Trenton NJ 08650-4700

KIRSCH, DAVID ALAN, marketing professional; b. N.Y.C., Feb. 2, 1933; s. Morris and Bertha Kirsch; m. Paula Ann Ehrlich, Nov. 12, 1957; children: Deborah, Kayla, Harlan, Andrew. BA cum laude, Amherst Coll., 1954; JD, U. Chgo., 1957. Pres. No-Cal Corp., N.Y.C., 1968-80; ptnr. Metzger/Kirsch Assn., N.Y.C., 1981-85; pres. Tomsun Foods, Greenfield, Mass., 1985-89; chief oper. officer Kozy Shack Foods, Inc., Mineola, N.Y., 1990—; adj. prof. mgmt. Hofstra U., Hempstead, N.Y., 1988—. Dir., v.p. Calorie Control Coun., Atlanta, 1968-80; trustee Village of Kensington, Great Neck, N.Y., 1975-80. Home: 55 Beverly Rd Great Neck NY 11021

KIRSCH, KAREN JILL, direct mail marketing professional; b. Nassau, N.Y., Aug. 6, 1957; d. Louis and Joyce (Frey) Zeitchek; m. Herbert Kirsch, Nov. 21, 1981; 1 child, Jennifer Lynn. BA, Queens Coll., 1979; MA, St. Johns Coll., 1982. Sales asst. R.L. Polk Co., N.Y.C., 1981-83; pres., chief exec. officer Best Mailing Lists, Inc., N.Y.C., 1984—. Named INC 500 Co., 1989. Mem. Direct Mktg. Assn. Republican. Office: Best Mailing Lists Inc 38 W 32d St New York NY 10001

KIRSCH, LAURENCE STEPHEN, lawyer; b. Washington, July 20, 1957; s. Ben and Bertha (Gomberg) K.; m. Celia Goldman, Aug. 19, 1979; children: Rachel Miriam, Max David. BAS, MS, U. Pa., 1979; JD, Harvard U., 1982. Bar: D.C. 1982, U.S. Ct. Appeals (3d cir.) 1983, U.S. Dist. Ct. D.C. 1985, U.S. Ct. Appeals (D.C. cir.) 1985, U.S. Supreme Ct. 1987; registered environ. assessor, Calif. 1988. Law clk. to presiding judge Pa. Dist. Ct., Phila., 1982-83; vis. asst. prof. law U. Bridgeport (Conn.) Law Sch., 1983-84; assoc. Cadwalader, Wickersham & Taft, Washington, 1984-90, ptnr., 1991—; chmn. steering coms. Superfund. Editor-in-chief Indoor Pollution Law Report, 1987-91; contbr. articles to profl. jours. Mem. ABA, Fed. Bar Assn., AAAS, Air Pollution Control Assn. (indoor air quality com.), Environ. Law Inst., Nat. Inst. Bldg. Scis. (indoor air quality com.), Am. Soc. Testing and Measurement (indoor air quality com.), Phi Beta Kappa. Home: 7212 Longwood Dr Bethesda MD 20817 Office: Cadwalader Wickersham & Taft 1333 New Hampshire Ave NW Washington DC 20036-1511

KIRSCH, WILLIAM JOSEPH, lawyer; b. Mineola, N.Y., July 26, 1956; s. Anthony A. and Rita H. (Dias) K. BA, U. N.C., 1978; JD, UCLA, 1981; diploma Europe Inst., U. Amsterdam, 1982. Bar: D.C. 1982, N.Y. 1984. Cons. Internat. Inst. Communications, London, 1982; atty., mem. fed.-state joint bd. staff FCC, Washington, 1983-86, spl. counsel internatl policy, 1986-88, dep. asst. bur. chief internat., 1988—. James M. Johnston scholar, 1974-78, Western Univs. scholar, 1978-81, Netherlands Found. scholar, 1981-82. Mem. N.Y. State Bar Assn., D.C. Bar, Phi Beta Kappa. Roman Catholic. Home: 1211 S Eads St Apt 211 Arlington VA 22202 Office: FCC 1919 M St NW Rm 534 Washington DC 20554

KIRSCHBAUM, JOEL JEROME, chemist; b. N.Y.C., Nov. 23, 1935; s. Louis and Paula (Rosenblum) K.; m. Marilyn Marie Johnson, June 25, 1960; children: Amy Beth, Fredric Johnson. BS, CCNY, 1957; MS, U. Conn., 1960; PhD, Rutgers U., 1963. Chemist Bristol-Myers Squibb, New Brunswick, N.J., 1964—; bd. dirs. Inst. Motivated Behavior, Belle Mead, N.J., 1971—; edit. bd. Jour. Pharm. Biomed. Analysis, Oxford, Eng., 1984—. Contbr. articles to profl. jours. Mem. Am. Chem. Soc., Am. Assn. Pharm. Sci., Am. Soc. Biochemistry Molecular Biology. Jewish. Home: 10 Hiland Dr Belle Mead NJ 08502-3225 Office: Bristol-Myers Squibb 1 Squibb Dr New Brunswick NJ 08901-0191

KIRSCHBERG, REVA GODLOVE, museum director; b. Kansas City, Mo., Nov. 22, 1921; d. Walter and Hazel (Davidson) Godlove; m. Richard H. Holstein, Jan. 9, 1943 (dec. 1945); 1 child, Nancy Holstein Mantell; m. Alan Kirschberg, May 20, 1956; 1 child, Ann Kirschberg Holland. BA, U. Tex., 1941; MEd, U. Houston, 1948. Dir. Congregation Emnanu-El Mus., N.Y.C., 1985—; coord. collection catalog A Temple Treasury: The Judaica Collection of Congregation Emanu-El of City of N.Y., 1989. Office: Congregation Emanu El 1 E 65th St New York NY 10021-6501

KIRSCHENBAUM, LOUIS JEAN, chemistry educator; b. Washington, Apr. 17, 1943; s. Abraham Isaac and Ruth (Kraut) K.; m. Susan Schulman, Sept. 15, 1943; children: Jay, Cynthia. BS in Chemistry, Howard U., 1965; MS in Chemistry, Brandeis U., 1967, PhD in Chemistry, 1968. Lectr. Brandeis U., Waltham, Mass., 1968-69; postdoctoral fellow Naval Ordnance Lab., White Oak, Md., 1969-70; asst. prof. chemistry U. R.I., Kingston, 1970-76, assoc. prof., 1976-83, prof., 1983—; vis. assoc. prof. Ben Gurion U., Beersheva, Israel, 1978-79; vis. scientist, Nat. Cancer Inst., NIH, 1991-92. Author: Introduction to Quantitative Chemical Analysis, 1972; also over 50 articles. Pres. Jewish Community Coun. South County. Grantee Petroleum Rsch. Fund, 1972, 85-89, NATO Collaborative Grants Program, 1982-88. Mem. Am. Chem. Soc. (com. for project SEED 1984—, alt. counselor 1990—, grantee 1986), Phi Beta Kappa, Sigma Xi, Phi Kappa Phi, Beta Kappa Chi. Home: 1783 South Rd Kingston RI 02881-1775 Office: U RI Dept Chemistry Kingston RI 02881

KIRSCHNER, RONALD ALLEN, osteopathic plastic surgeon, otolaryngologist, educator; b. N.Y.C., Jan. 18, 1942; s. Hyman C. and Eleanor (Pinkus) K.; m. Olivia Barbara Schlesinger, June 27, 1964; children: Andrew Scott, Julie Renee. AB, NYU, 1962; DO, Phila. Coll. Osteo. Medicine, 1966, MS in Otolaryngology, 1972. Diplomate Am. Osteo. Bd. Otolaryngology. Intern Le Roy Hosp., N.Y.C., 1966-67; resident Grandview Hosp., Dayton, Ohio, 1967-68; resident Phila. Coll. Osteo. Medicine, 1970-72, asst. prof., 1972-74, assoc. prof., 1974-76, clin. assoc. prof., 1976-85, clin. prof., 1985-90, prof., chmn. dept. otolaryngology, bronchoesophagology and facial plastic surgery, 1990-92, dir. emerging tech., 1992—; dir. neurosensory unit, 1973-76; NIH fellow Armed Forces Inst. Pathology, Washington, 1971; practice medicine specializing in plastic, otolaryngology and laser surgery, Bala Cynwyd, Pa., 1976—; attending physician Grad. Hosp., 1991—; attending physician, cons. Presbyn.-U. Pa. Med. Ctr., 1987—, Hosp. of Phila. Coll. Osteo. Medicine, chmn. laser and endoscopy com., 1987-89, 91—, mem. exec. com., 1990-92; attending physician Suburban Gen. Hosp., chief ear, nose and throat and plastic surgery, 1976—, chmn. div. surgery, 1983-89, exec. com., 1983-89; attending physician, cons. Del. Valley Med. Ctr., 1985—; v.p., chief med. adv. Courtlandt Group, 1979-85, exec. v.p., 1985-86, also dir. rsch. and edn., 1986; otolaryngologist Pa. Hearing Assn., 1986—; preceptor Xanar Laser Div., Johnson & Johnson, 1982; design cons. Pilling, Inc., 1982-87, Inframed Inc., 1985—, Sigma Dynamics Inc., Rhein Med., Inc., 1988—; otologic cons. Nat. Childrens' Hearing Aid Bank; pres. Kirschner Design Group, Inc., 1987—; bd. dirs. KDG-Rotem U.S.A., Pa. Acad. Cosmetic Surgery; dir. head and neck YAG laser protocol Cooper Lasersonics, 1983-88; chmn. med. symposium Internat. Conf. on Applied Laser Electro Optics, 1986, 87, 91; session chair Medtech '89, Freie Univ., Berlin, 1989; vis. prof. internat. sch. for quantam electronics Etore Majorana Nato, Erice, Sicily, 1990; cons. Bur. Vocat. Rehab., Imunodiagnostics Lab., Allergy Mgmt. Systems Inc.; dir. 1st World Congress on Cosmetic Laser Surgery, 1992. Served with M.C., USN, 1968-70; lt. comdr. Res. Recipient award for disting. teaching Lindbach Found., 1973, Legion of Honor, Chapel of Four Chaplains, 1982; Survivor of Yr. award, 1984; named Disting. Practitioner Am. Acads. of Practice. Fellow Pan Am. Allergy Assn., Phila. Acad. Facial Plastic Surgery, Phila. Laryngologic Soc., Phila. Coll. Physicians, Am. Soc. Lasers in Medicine and Surgery, Am. Auditory Soc., Am. Acad. Otolaryngology-Head and Neck Surgery, Soc. Ear, Nose, and Throat Advances in Children, Am. Acad. Facial Plastic Surgery (assoc.), Soc. Photo Optical Engrs., Osteo. Coll. Ophthalmology and Otorhinolaryngology, Osteo. Coll. Otorhinolaryngology and Ophtalmology, Am. Acad. Cosmetic Surgery; mem. Am. Osteo. Assn. (editorial cons. Jour. 1977—, editorial referee 1980—), Pa. Med. Soc., Pa. Acad. Otolaryngology, Pa. Acad. Cosmetic Surgery (bd. dirs. 1990—), Internat. Soc. Cosmetic Plastic Surgeons (bd. dirs.), Philadelphia County Osteo. Med. Assn. (chair laser com.), Centurian Club of Deafness Rsch. Found., Internat. Assn. Logopedics and Phoniatrics, Midwestern Biolaser Inst., Inst. for Applied Laser Surgery (pres.), Pa. Osteo. Med. Assn. (chmn. com. otolaryngology 1984-88, 90—, chmn. com. promotion of rsch. 1985-88), Am. Acad. Osteopathy, Survivors Club of Phila. Coll. Osteo. Medicine (pres. 1981-82), Internat. Soc. for Optical Engring., AAAS, AMA, Acad. Surgical Rsch., N.Y. Acad. Scis., Am. Soc. Liposuction Surgery, Laser Assn. Am. (sec. 1985-88), Laser and Electro Optics Mfrs. Assn., Am. Assn. Advancement Med. Instrumentation, Am. Soc. Cosmetic Surgeons, Pa. Hearing Aid Soc. (otologist), Pan Am. Assn. Otolaryngology and Bronchoesophagology, Pa. Acad. Opthalmology and Otolaryngology, Pa. Osteo. Med. Soc., Del Valley Tinnitus Assn. (chmn. com. otolaryngology 1984-88, 90—, cd.), Laser Inst. Am. (sr. Outstanding Svc. award 1986, chmn. lasers 1987-89, bd. dirs. 1989—, dir., chmn. com. on biology and medicine 1989—), Pa. Acad. Cosmetic Surgery (bd. dir.), Am. Acad. Cosmetic Laser Surgery (bd. dirs. 1991—), Pa. Med. Soc., Montgomery County Med. Soc., Sigma Xi, Sigma Chi, Lambda Omicron Gamma (pres. 1981-82, Disting. Service award Caduceus chpt. 1982), Variety Club, NYU Club, Vesper Club, Pickwick Club of Phila., Masons, Shriners. Jewish. Med. editor Med. Portfolio, 1980-85; guest editor Surg. Clinics of N.Am., 1984; monthly columnist Photonics Spectra, 1987-91; contbg. editor Photonics Spectra, 1988—; mem. editorial bd. Pa. Osteo. Med. Jour., Laurin Publs., 1987—, Laser Applications; contbr. articles to med. jours., chpts. in med. texts; developer various med. instruments. Office: 2 Bala Cynwyd Pla Ste 17il Bala Cynwyd PA 19004

KIRSCHSTEIN, RUTH LILLIAN, physician; b. Bklyn., Oct. 12, 1926; d. Julius and Elizabeth (Berm) K.; m. Alan S. Rabson, June 11, 1950; 1 child, Arnold. B.A. magna cum laude, L.I. U., 1947; M.D., Tulane U., 1951; D.Sc. (hon.), Mt. Sinai Sch. Medicine, 1984; LL.D. (hon.), Atlanta U., 1985; DSc (hon.), Med. Coll. Ohio, 1986; LHD (hon.), L.I. Univ., 1991. Intern Kings County Hosp., Bklyn., 1951-52; resident pathology VA Hosp., Atlanta, Providence Hosp., Detroit, Clin. Ctr., NIH, Bethesda, Md., 1952-57; fellow Nat. Heart Inst. Tulane U., 1953-54; mem. staff NIH, Bethesda, 1957-72, 74—; asst. dir. div. biologics standards NIH, 1971-72; dep. dir. Bur. Biologics, FDA, 1972-73, dep. assoc. commr. sci., 1973-74; dir. Nat. Inst. Gen. Med. Scis., 1974—, acting assoc. dir. women's health, 1990-91; mem. Found. Advanced Edn. Scis.; chmn. grants peer rev. study team NIH; mem. Inst. Medicine, NAS, 1982—; co-chair, sec. Spl. Emphasis Oversight Com. on Sci. and Tech., 1989—; co-chair PHS Coordinating Com. on Women's Health Issues, 1990—; mem. Office of Tech. Assessment Adv. Com. on Basic Rsch., 1989—. Recipient Superior Service award HEW, 1971, 78, Presdl. Meritorious Exec. award, 1980, Presdl. Disting. Exec. Rank award, 1985. Mem. AMA (Dr. Nathan Davis award 1990), Am. Assn. Immunologists, Am. Assn. Pathologists, Am. Soc. Microbiology, Am. Acad. Arts and Scis. Home: 6 West Dr Bethesda MD 20814-1510 Office: Nat Inst Gen Med Scis 5333 Westbard Ave Bethesda MD 20892-0001

KIRSH, M. ELI, scientist, philosopher, writer; b. Balt., Mar. 21, 1950; s. Marton Charles and Frances Ida (Rosenberg) K. BA, Johns Hopkins U., 1972; MA, Hunter Coll., 1981; MPhil, CUNY, 1983, PhD, 1986. Rsch. asst. Linton Bionetics, Frederick, Md., 1972, Johns Hopkins Hosp., Balt., 1973-74, Johns Hopkins U., Balt., 1974-76; grad. teaching asst. U. Mo., Columbia, 1976-78; adj. lectr. CUNY, 1978-82; lab. scientist U. Md., Balt., 1984-85, postdoctoral scientist, 1985. Artist; photographer; contbr. articles to profl. jours. Mem. Sherlock Holmes Soc. Office: PO Box 91181 Washington DC 20090-1810

KIRSHNER, JACOB, physician; b. N.Y.C., Jan. 9, 1927; s. Philip and Irene (Walzer) K.; m. Sylvia Ann Shyken, Aug. 19, 1956; children: Daniel, Miriam, Eli, Ruth. BS magna cum laude, CCNY, 1945; AM, Columbia U., 1947; MD, SUNY, 1951. Diplomate Am. Bd. Internal Medicine. Rotating inter Mt. Sinai Hosp., N.Y.C., 1951-52, asst. resident internal medicine, 1953-54; jr. asst. resident Montefiore Hosp., Bronx, N.Y., 1952-53; sr. resident VA Hosp., Bronx, 1954-55, fellow cardiology, asst. chief cardiac sect. dept. medicine, 1955-57; cons. medicine dept. medicine South Amboy (N.J.) Meml. Hosp., 1957—; sr. attending physician dept. medicine St. Peter's Med. Ctr., New Brunswick, N.J., 1957—; clin. asst. prof. Coll. Medicine & Dentistry N.J. Robert Wood Johnson Med. Sch, New Brunswick, 1971-82, clin. assoc. prof., 1982—; mem. exec. com. med. dental staff St. Peters Med. Ctr., New Brunswick, 1962—, sec.-treas., 1985-86, v.p., 1987-88, pres., 1989-90. V.p. Congregation Anshe Emeth of South River, 1971-72, pres., 1972-75; v.p. Jewish Fedn. Raritan Valley, 1976-78, pres., 1978-80; life mem. bd. dirs. Jewish Fedn. Greater Middlesex County, 1985—; chmn. local com. State of Israel Bonds; mem. State Bd. Jewish Nat. Fund; co-chmn. Jewish Community Rels. Coun. Middlesex County, 1985-87; mem. exec. com. Nat. Jewish Community Rels. Adv. Coun., 1986-89, 90—, co-chmn. strategy com. World Jewry and Internat. Human Rights, 1990—. With USN, 1945-46. Recipient David Ben Gurion award State of Israel Bonds, 1976, Samuel I. Hoddeson Humanitarian award Jewish Fedn. Raritan Valley, 1981, Presdl. award Jewish Fedn. Greater Middlesex County, 1988. Mem. Med. Soc. N.J., Middlesex County Med. Soc., Alpha Omega Alpha. Home: 53 Ferris St South River NJ 08882-1829 Office: Old-Bridge-Sayreville Med Group 53 Main St Sayreville NJ 08872-1594

KIRSHNER, ROBERT, astrophysicist, educator; b. Long Branch, N.J., Aug. 15, 1949; s. D.R. and Virginia (Klarman) K.; m. Lucy Rand Herman, June 15, 1970; children: Rebecca Rand K., Matthew Klarman K. AB, Harvard Coll., 1970; PhD, Calif. Inst. Tech., 1975. Research assoc. Kitt Peak Nat. Observatory, Tucson, 1974-76; asst. prof. astronomy U. Mich., Ann Arbor, 1976-80, assoc. prof. astronomy, 1980-82, prof. astronomy, 1982-85; dir. McGraw-Hill Observatory, 1980-85; prof. astronomy Harvard U., Cambridge, Mass., 1985—, chmn. astronomy dept., 1990—; vis. com. Mt. Wilson and Las Campanas Observatory, Pasadena, 1986-89, Space Telescope Sci. Inst., 1988-89; chmn. observatory vis. com. Associated Univs. for Rsch. in Astronomy, Washington, 1983-86, bd. dirs., exec. com., 1989—; mem. sci. adv. com. Nat. New Tech. Telescope, Tucson, 1983-84, Com. on Space Astronomy and Astrophysics, 1982-85, Space Telescope Users Com., 1990—; Marc Aaronson Meml. lectr. U. Ariz., 1989; Grubb Parson lectr. U. of Durham, 1990; Delphasus lectr. U. Calif., Santa Cruz. Contbr. over 180 articles to scientific jours. and mags. including Nat. Geographic, Nat. History, Scientific Am. NSF fellow, 1970, Alfred P. Sloan Found. fellow, 1979. Fellow Am. Phys. Soc., Am. Acad. Arts and Scis.; mem. Am. Astron. Soc. (councilor 1986-88), Internat. Astron. Union, Astron. Soc. Pacific. Home: 174 Walden St Concord MA 01742-3623 Office: Ctr for Astrophysics MS-19 60 Garden St Cambridge MA 02138-1596

KISE, JAMES NELSON, architect, urban planner; b. Trenton, May 2, 1937; s. Charles Richard and Gladys May (Doll) K.; m. Rachel Bok, Dec. 20, 1958 (div.); children: Jefferson Bok, Charles Curtis; m. Sarah Ludlow Ogden Smith, June 15, 1974; children: Laura Ludlow Susanna, Anthony Lawrence Triplett. BArch, U. Pa., 1959, MArch, 1963, M in City Planning, 1964; postgrad., U. Rome, 1959-60. Registered architect, Pa. New town planner Harvard-MIT Joint Ctr. of Urban Studies Ciudad Guayana Project, Caracas, Venezuela, 1961-62; ctr. city planner Phila. City Planning Commn., 1962-66; project dir. Wallace McHarg Roberts & Todd, Phila., 1966-67; dir. urban design ctr. Nat. Urban Coalition (formerly Urban Am., Inc.), Washington, 1967-70; ptnr. Kise Franks & Straw (formerly David Crane & Ptnrs.), Phila., 1970—; lectr. U. Pa., 1962-67; adj. instr. urban design Drexel U., 1974-76; dir. Curtis Pub. Co., 1970-75. work includes master plans for Schukill River Park, Phila., 1965, Downtown Harrisburg, Pa., 1975, Sadat City, Egypt, 1977, Acad. Ctr. for Performing Arts, 1981, Atlantic City Master Plan, 1986, South Broad St. Design, Phila., 1991. Bd. dirs. Settlement Music Sch., 1963-83, Phila. Mus. Art, 1975—, Ebenezer Maxwell Mansion, 1980—, Cen. Phila. Devel. Corp., 1989—, The Found. for Architecture, 1991—, Fleisher Art Meml., 1970—, pres., 1982—; bd. dirs. Washington Community Sch. Music, 1967-70, pres. bd., 1968-70. Mem. Am. Inst. Planners, Am. Inst. Architects, Racquet Club, Phila. Cricket Club, Tau Sigma Delta. Democrat. Episcopalian. Home: Lane's End 3031 School House Ln Philadelphia PA 19144-5431 Office: 219 N Broad St Philadelphia PA 19107-1511

KISELICA, WINIFRED THERESA, religious education administrator; b. Elizabeth, N.J., Jan. 22, 1929; d. Patrick and Margaret (McNamara) Smyth; m. Otto Rudolph Kiselica, Sept. 4, 1954; children: John, Mark, Mary, Patricia, Matthew. BA in English and BS in Edn., Kean Coll., 1973, postgrad. in theology. Cert. tchr. English, K-12, religious studies. Substitute tchr. various schs., N.J., 1969-73; dir. religious edn. St. Joseph's Parish, Roselle, N.J., 1973—. Roman Catholic.

KISELIK, PAUL HOWARD, manufacturing executive; b. Newark, Nov. 29, 1937; s. Jerome W. and Rose (Ramo) K.; m. Teri Nimaroff, Sept 6, 1959; children: Daniel, Jonathan. BS in Indsl. Engring., Lehigh U., 1960; MS in Mgmt. Engring., N.J. Inst. Tech., 1965. Registered profl. engr., N.J., Pa. V.p. Nimrow Carton Co., Elizabeth, N.J., 1961-71; pres., chief exec. officer Sebro Packaging Corp., South Hackensack, N.J., 1971—; pres., chief exec. officer Rayart Folding Box Co., South Hackensack, 1971—, Lane Graphics, South Hackensack, 1984—; sr. ptnr. Green St. Assn., South Hackensack, 1979—. Author: Equity Financing of a Small Business, 1965. Lt. U.S. Army, 1960-61. Mem. TAPPI, Newtonian Soc., Morristown-Beard Sch. Alumni Assn. (v.p. 1979-81), Asa Packer Soc., Tau Beta Pi, Alpha Pi Mu. Office: Sebro Packaging Corp 280 Green St South Hackensack NJ 07606-1428

KISH, GEORGE FRANKLIN, thoracic and cardiovascular surgeon; b. Toledo, Ohio, Mar. 30, 1944; s. George F. and Ann (Kucharski) K.; m. Joann Mata Kish, Mar. 16, 1968; children: Jeremy, Nathan. BS, Ohio State U., 1966, MD, 1970. Surg. intern George Washington U. Med. Ctr., 1970-71, surg. resident, 1971-74, surg. rsch. fellow, 1974-75, chief surg. resident, 1975-76, thoracic and cardiovascular surgery resident, 1976-78; asst. prof. surgery W.Va. U. Med. Ctr., Morgantown, 1978-80; cardiovascular surgeon D'Angelo Clinic, Erie, Pa., 1980—; chief cardiovascular surgery Hamot Med. Ctr., Erie, 1982—. Contbg. author International Trends in General Thoracic Surgery, Vol. 7, 1991; contbr. articles to profl. jours. Dr. I.S. Grisoff fellow cardiovascular surgery George Washington U., 1974-75; affiliate rsch. grantee Am. Heart Assn., W.Va. Med. Ctr., 1979. Fellow ACS, Internat. Soc. Cardiovascular Surgeons, Soc. Thoracic Surgeons, Am. Coll. Cardiology, Am. Coll. Chest Physicians, Southeastern Surg. Congress, Internat. Coll. Angiology. Home: 218 Frontier Dr Erie PA 16505 Office: D'Angelo Clinic 104 E 2d St Erie PA 16507

KISIEL, HENRY FRANCIS, JR., vocational rehabilitation administrator, educator; b. Worcester, Mass., June 1, 1950; s. Henry Francis Sr. and Clara Bernice (Kotonski) K.; m. Patricia Ada Grana, Sept. 21, 1974; children: Kaitlin, Colin. BA in Sociology cum laude, Assumption Coll., 1972, MA in Rehab. Counseling, 1974, cert. advanced grad. studies, 1974. Counselor vocat. rehab. Conn. Dept. Mental Retardation, Pomfret, 1973-76; supr. vocat. rehab. Conn. Dept. Mental Health, Middletown, 1976-78; sr. counselor Conn. Dept. Edn., Meriden, 1978-83; lectr. So. Conn. State U., New Haven, 1980—, South Cen. Community Colll., New Haven, 1989—; chief vocat. rehab. Conn. Workers' Compensation Commn., Middletown, 1983—. Grad. fellow U.S. Rehab. Svc. Adminstrn., 1972. Mem. Am. Assn. Coll. and Univ. Profs., Congress of Conn. Community Colls. Democrat. Roman Catholic. Office: Div Workers Rehab 230 Main Street Ext Middletown CT 06457-4406

KISIELOWSKI, EUGENE, engineering executive; b. Leczowka, Tarnopol, Poland, May 30, 1932; arrived in U.S., 1959; s. Wladyslaw and Helena (Berezanko) K.; m. Rosemary Booth, July 31, 1957; children: Richard Julian, Helen Teresa, Eugene Stephen. BSME, Huddersfield (Eng.) Tech. Coll, 1955; MSc in Aero. Engring., Coll. Aeronautics, Cranfield, Eng., 1972. Aero. engr. Avro Aircraft Co., Malton, Ont., Can., 1957-59; asst. project engr. Kellett Aircraft Corp., Willow Grove, Pa., 1959-60; sr. analytical engr. Plasecki Aircraft Corp., Phila., 1960-61; supr. II Vertol div. Boeing Co., Ridley Park, Pa., 1961-65; dir. aero. engring. Dynascis. Corp., Blue Bell, Pa., 1965-71; pres., chief exec. officer United Terex, Inc., Fairview Village, Pa., 1971—. Contbr. articles to profl. publs. Vol. various local polit. campaigns. Mem. AIAA, Am. Helicopter Soc., Cranfield Students Soc. Republican. Home: 3020 Oak Dr Norristown PA 19401-1543 Office: United Terex Inc 2579 Industry Ln Fairviewvill PA 19403

KISNAD, HITEN VITHAL, psychiatrist; b. Bombay, India, Feb. 4, 1958; came to U.S., 1982; s. Vithal Harkisandas and Madhukanta (Machwala) K. Pre-med., Mithibai Coll. of Arts, Bombay, India, 1976; MBBS, Topiwala Nat. Med. Coll., 1980. Diplomate Am. Bd. Psychiatry and Neurology (psychiatry), Am. Bd. Psychiatry and Neurology (child and adolescent psychiatry). Intern B.Y.L. Nair Hosp., Bombay, India, 1981-82; resident B.Y.L. Nair Hosp., Bombay, 1982, U. Tex. Med. Branch, Galveston, Tex., 1983; resident Mt. Sinai Svcs. Elmhurst (N.Y.) Hosp. Ctr., 1983-85, clin. fellow, 1985-87; research fellow N.Y. State Office of Mental Retardation & Devel. Disabilities, 1987-89; instr. Mt. Sinai Sch. of Medicine, N.Y.C., 1987-88, NYU Sch. of Medicine, N.Y.C., 1988-89, Cornell U. Med. Coll., N.Y.C., White Plains, 1989—; clin. asst. Mt. Sinai Hosp., N.Y.C., 1987-88, NYU Med. Ctr., 1988-89; clin. affiliate The N.Y. Hosp., Westchester, N.Y., 1989—. Author: Sedatives Hypnotics, 1991; co-author: Research on School Refusal, 1989, Interviewing Children and Adolescents, 1989. Mem. Indo-Am. Cultural Assn. Westchester, 1987—. Recipient First Prize Photography Intermedical Arts Competition, 1979. Mem. AMA, Am. Acad. Child and Adolescent Psychiatry, Am. Psychiat. Assn., N.Y. Council on Child and Adolescent Psychiatry, World Fedn. for Mental Health. Home and Office: 21 Bloomingdale Rd White Plains NY 10605-1596

KISNER, JACOB, poet, editor, publisher; b. Chelsea, Mass., Apr. 30, 1926; s. Louis and Sarah (Kotel) K.; student Calvin Coolidge Coll., 1945-46, Burdett Coll., 1943-45, Harvard Extension, 1944-48; m. Gladys Selma Feinstein, May 29, 1947; 1 dau. Lesley Kisner Cafarelli. Sunday dept. writer Boston Globe, 1943-45; local news editor Jewish Advocate, Boston, 1945-46; founder, editor, pub. Dorchester (Mass.) Herald, 1946-47; trade reporter Fairchild News Service, Boston, 1948-49; sr. proof-reader Rec. and Statis. Corp., Boston, 1950-54; editor Crossroads, Toronto, Ont., Can., 1964-67; Am. editor View, 1967—; rsch. dir. N.Y. bur. Moneytree Publs., N.Y.C., 1972—; stamp and autograph dealer, 1973-82; owner/operator Penthouse F Stamps, 1982—; free-lance writer, 1943—; saxophonist, leader big band Jack Kenton, 1943-46; philatelic journalist; discussion moderator Great Books Found., Boston, 1948-51; judge of poetry contests, Rochester, N.Y., also N.Y. Poetry Forum, 1969—; N.Y. State dir. and N.Y.C. chmn. World Poetry Day Com., 1971—; v.p., incorporator N.Y. Poetry Forum, 1973-75; founder postmaster Park Ave Local Post, 1978—; author plays: First Came Paula, 1954, Speak of the Devil, 1955, The Monkey's Tail, 1956; author TV plays: The Late Mr. Honeywell, 1957, A World Apart, 1957; author: (poetry) I Am Hephaestus, 1966, numerous pub. articles, revs., research on stamps and postal hist.; contbr. poetry to various lit. jours. and anthologies. Recipient World Peace award Ky. State Poetry Soc., 1970, Gold Medal award Internat. Poets' Shrine, 1971, Radio award sta. WEFG, 1970, Spl. Citation award Poetry Pageant, 1970. Mem. Acad. Am. Poets, Wilson MacDonald Poetry Soc. Can. (exec. com. 1967-77, v.p. 1977—), Am. Philatelic Soc., Trans-Miss. Philatelic Soc., Soc. Philatelic Ams., Soc. Israel Philatelists, Am. Revenue Assn., Confederate Stamp Alliance, United Postal Stationery Soc., Scandinavian Collectors Club, Perfins Club, Am. Philatelic Rsch. Libr. Address: 254 Park Ave S Penthouse F New York NY 10010

KISSANE, JEAN CHARLOTTE, lawyer; b. Phila., Feb. 6, 1946; d. William C. and Grace A. (McGlade) K. AB, Lycoming Coll., 1968; JD, Widener U., 1986. Bar: Del. 1986, U.S. Dist. Ct. Dela. 1987. Tchr. history Colonial Sch. Dist., New Castle, Del., 1968-86; assoc. Skadden, Arps, Slate, Meagher & Flom, Wilmington, Del., 1986—. Recipient Am. Jurisprudence awards, 1986. Mem. ABA, Del. Bar Assn., Mensa, Phi Delta Phi, Phi Kappa Phi. Democrat. Office: Skadden Arps Slate Meagher & Flom PO Box 636 Wilmington DE 19899-0636

KISSANE, MARY ELIZABETH, communications executive; b. Westchester, N.Y.; d. Thomas Patrick and Marion (O'Shea) K. BA cum laude, Iona Coll., 1982, MS in Corp. Communications with honors, 1990. Asst. to chief fin. officer Aspen Systems Corp., 1984; account supr. Charles Barker, Inc., 1984-86; communications mgr. BET Fin., Inc., 1987; assoc. Bliss, Barefoot & Assocs., 1988; asst. v.p. Georgeson & Co., 1989-92, v.p., 1992—. Home: 91 Summit Ave Bronxville NY 10708-1814 Office: Georgeson & Co Wall St Plz New York NY 10016

KISSANE, THOMAS, criminologist, educator; b. Bronx, N.Y.; s. James M. and Elizabeth (Sheridan) K.; B.S., John Jay Coll.; M.S. Ed., Iona Coll.; Phd Fordham U.; m. Marion O'Shea, Nov. 18, 1950; 4 children. With N.Y.C. Police Dept., 1949-74, capt., 1965-74; dir. cargo theft program U. Louisville, 1975-76; assoc. prof. Iona Coll., New Rochelle, N.Y., 1976—; dir. staff services dept. public Safety City of White Plains (N.Y.), 1983-85; cons. on criminal receiving U.S. Senate Com. Mem. Bd. Police Commrs., Town of Eastchester, N.Y. Named Man of Yr., N.Y. State Motor Truck Assn., 1974, Nat. Assn. Former State Troopers, 1972. Mem. Capts. Endowment Assn., Nat. Assn. Former State Troopers, Ret. Detectives Assn., Am. Soc. Indsl. Security, N.Y. Police Dept. Honor Legion. Office: Iona Coll Dept Criminal Justice 715 North Ave New Rochelle NY 10801-1890

KISSEL, MICHAEL CASE, musician, composer, producer; b. N.Y.C.; s. William Thorn Kissel and Barbara (Eldred) Case; m. Elena Thornton, June 29, 1985; children: Siena Case, Lucy Elena. Student, Yale U. Pres. KMA, N.Y.C., 1987—. Producer, musician, vocalist, composer, lyricist, producer (album) Surrender by Robin Clark and the David Bowie Band, 1985; producer (albums) Healing Session by Babatunde Olatunji, 1991, Arnold Schwarzenegger's Total Body Workout, 1984, Peace Is The World Smiling with Babatunde Olatunji, Pete Seeger, Taj Mahal, 1989; producer, music dir. (film and soundtrack album) Pumping Iron II: The Women, 1985; producer (requiem) The Hocus Pocus Laundromat with Kurt Vonnegut and Edgar Grana, 1988; composer, music dir., performer, producer (film, soundtrack) In the Blood, 1990; composer , music dir. (film) Best Shots, 1990; musician, composer, lyricist, vocalist, producer for artists including The Pointer Sisters, The Drifters, Charles Moffet and the West Coast Jazz Allstars, Elvin Bishop, Freeze Peach, Jocelyn Brown, The Four Tops, Toots and the Maytals, Babatunde Olatunji and Drums of Passion, Ernie Isley, Otis Rush, Gloria Gaynor, Freeze Peach, mem Harlem All-Star Gospel Choir and others. Past group leader Los Amigos de las Americas, Lepaterique, Honduras. Recipient Gold medal Info. Film Producers of Am., 1984, Bronze medal Internat. Film and TV Festival of N.Y., 1983. Mem. ASCAP, NARAS, Songwriters Guild, Am. Fedn. Musicians, Spouting Rock Beach Assns. (R.I.), Racquet and Tennis Club, Newport (R.I.) Reading Rm. Club. Episcopalian. Office: KMA 1650 Broadway Ste 900 New York NY 10019-6833

KISSEL, WILLIAM THORN, JR., sculptor; b. N.Y.C., Feb. 6, 1920; s. William Thorn and Frances A. (Dallett) K.; grad. Choate Sch., 1939; B.A., Harvard U., 1944; postgrad. (Fellow), Pa. Acad. Fine Arts, 1951-53; grad. Barnes Found., 1953. Rinehart Grad. Sch. Sculpture, Balt., 1958; m. Barbara Eldred Case, June 17, 1943 (dec. June 8, 1978); children—William Thorn III (dec.), Michael C. Exhibited sculpture Lever House, N.Y.C., N.A.D., N.Y.C., Balt. Sculptor's Exhibit, York, Pa., Beverly, Mass., Gloucester, Woodmere Gallery, Germantown, Pa.; represented in pvt. collections, U.S.; executed large granite meml., Montclair, N.J., also many animal sculpture studies and commns. Served as pilot, lt. (j.g.) USNR, 1942-45. Recipient Mass. Sculptor's award Regional Exhibit, Beverly, Mass., 1958; Speyer award, NAD, 1966, 68, Am. Artists Profl. League award, 1966. Fellow Am. Artists Profl. League, Nat. Sculpture Soc.; mem. Soc. of Cincinnati. Republican. Episcopalian. Home: 223 Valley Rd Owings Mills MD 21117-4118

KISSICK, WILLIAM LEE, physician, educator; b. Detroit, July 29, 1932; s. William Leslie and Florence (Rock) K.; m. Priscilla Harriet Dillingham, June 16, 1956; children: William, Robert-John, Jonathan, Elizabeth. B.A., Yale U., 1953, M.D., 1957, M.P.H., 1959, Dr.P.H., 1961. Intern Yale-New Haven Med. Center, 1957-58; resident Montefiore Hosp. and Med. Center, N.Y.C., 1961-62; Div. Community Health Service, 1962-63; spl. asst. to asst. sec. for health U.S. Dept. HEW, 1964-65; dir. Office Program Planning Evaluation, Office of Surgeon Gen., USPHS, 1966-68; exec. dir., nat. adv. commn. health facilities The White House, Washington, 1968; prof., chmn. dept. community medicine Sch. Medicine U. Pa., 1968-71, George S. Pepper prof. public health and preventive medicine, 1969—, prof. research medicine, 1976—, prof. health care systems Wharton Sch., 1971—, prof. health policy and mgmt. Sch. Nursing, 1978—, dir. Center for Health Policy, 1981—; fellow, mem. exec. com. Nat. Ctr. for Health Care Mgmt.; dir. Health policy, chmn. bd. of govs. Leonard Davis Inst. Health Econs., 1989—; vis. prof. community medicine Guy's Hosp. Med. Sch.; vis. prof. dept. social sci. and adminstrn. London Sch. Econs. and Polit. Scis.; vis. prof. Inst. European Health Svcs. Rsch., Leuven U., 1974-75; cons. Nat. Ctr. Health Svcs. Rsch., Health Resources Adminstrn., Benedum Found., WHO, Appalachian Regional Commn., Smith Kline-Beckman, Pew Meml. Trust, Colonial Penn Group, Ctr. Disease Control; mem. Accrediting Commn. on Edn. for Health Svcs. Adminstrn., 1980-86; chmn. com. on med. affairs coun. Yale U., 1980-86, fellow Yale Corp., 1987—; mem. Mayor's Commn., 1981-83, coun. Coll. Physicians of Phila., 1983-88, coun. med. socs. Am. Coll. Physicians, 1983-88. Editor: Dimensions and Determinants of Health Policy, 1968. Contbr. articles to profl. jours. Bd. dirs. Met. Collegiate Ctr. Germantown; chmn. Yale U. Alumni Assn. Fund, 1988-90; trustee Appalachian Regional Hosps., 1969-76. With USPHS, 1962-68. Mem. AAAS, Am. Coll. Preventive Medicine, Am. Pub. Health Assn., Pa. Phila. Coll. Physicians, Assn. Health Svcs. Rsch. Assn. Tchrs. Preventive Medicine, Am. Coll. Physician Execs., Physicians for Social Responsibility, Nat. Assn. Pub. Health Policy. Home: Ellet Lane Philadelphia PA 19119

KISSICK, WILLIAM LEE, JR., academic director; b. New Haven, Jan. 25, 1958; s. William L. and Priscilla (Dillingham) K.; m. Catherine H. McGrath, Aug. 26, 1990. BA, Denison U., 1980; MBA, Wharton Sch., 1990. Asst. dir. alumni resources Denison U., Granville, Ohio, 1980-83; dir. ann. giving William Penn Charter Sch., Phila., 1983-84, asst. dir. devel., 1984-85; devel. officer St. Lawrence U., Canton, N.Y., 1985-86, devel. officer major gifts, 1986-88; cons. Barnes & Roche, Phila., 1989; assoc. dir. major gifts Dartmouth Coll., Hanover, N.H., 1990—; class agt. William Penn Charter Sch., Phila., 1985—. Mem. Hanover Country Club, Living End. Home: RR 1 Box 170 Orford NH 03777

KISSINGER, JOHN CALVIN, retired microbiologist; b. Shamokin, Pa., June 8, 1925; s. Claude Calvin and Flora (Smith) K.; m. Nancy Louise Wagner, Sept. 30, 1950 (dec. Jan. 1985); children: John A., George B.; m. Nancy Reamer, June 23, 1987. BS, Bucknell U., 1949, MS, 1950. Chemist Campbell's Soup, Camden, N.J., 1950-51; microbiologist Merck Sharpe & Dohme, Glenolden, Pa., 1951-53, Merck Sharpe & Dobme, Danville, Pa., 1953-55; supr. Grain Processing Corp., Muscatine, Iowa, 1955-57; rsch. microbiologist USDA, Phila., 1957-83; tech. cons. N.Am. Maple Producers Coun., Bainbridge, N.J., 1964-73. Contbr. articles to profl. jours. Prin. cellist North Penn Symphony Orch., Lansdale, Pa., 1971-89. With U.S. Army, 1943-46. Assn. of Ofcl. Analytical Chemists fellow, 1976; recipient Cert. of Merit U.S. Dept. Agr., 1969, Indsl. Wastes medal Fedn. Sewage and Indsl. Wastes Assns., 1957. Republican. Methodist. Home: 1018 S 10th St Emmaus PA 18049-3619

KISTLER, JAMES DONALD, minister; b. Watsonville, Calif., July 4, 1949; s. John Leonard Jr. and Eva Faye (George) K.;m. Kimberly Anne Berner, July 28, 1984; 1 child, Michelle Anne. BA, Azusa Pacific U., 1971; MDiv, Luther Rice Sem., 1983. Ordained to ministry Presbyn. Ch. in Am., 1990. Pastor Pioneer Presbyn. Ch., Ligonier, Pa., 1989—. Home and Office: Soli Deo Gloria Publs 213 W Vincent St Ligonier PA 15658-1139

KISTNER, JERRY LEE, information systems specialist; b. Rock Island, Ill., Oct. 4, 1950; s. Lawrence E. and Jacqueline R. Kistner; m. Mary Jane R. McConnel, Jan. 7, 1973; children: James, Erin, Patrick. AA in Acctg., Blackhawk Coll., 1975; BBA, Western Ill. U., 1978. Tech. tester J.J. Case Co., Racine, Wis., 1974-77; systems specialist Sperry Remington Corp., Davenport, Iowa, 1977-80, Donnegan Systems div. Sperry Row, Providence, 1980-86; owner PACS Inc., Providence, 1984-89; mgr. filing and storage systems Officeworks Inc., Rockville, Md., 1989—; owner PACS Inc., Providence, 1984—; guest speaker Coll. Bus. U. R.I., Kingston, 1983—. Mem. polit action com. VFW, R.I., 1985. Served with USN, 1969-73, Vietnam. Decorated Vietnam Cross Gallantry. Mem. Adminstrv. Mgmt. Soc. (pres. 1985-86, chmn. and dir. bus. show 1984, Diamond Merit award 1986). Roman Catholic. Office: Officeworks Inc 40 W Gude Dr Ste 100 Rockville MD 20850-1166

KITCHEN, JOHN HOWARD, economist; b. New Castle, Pa., May 14, 1957; s. Robert Henry and Betty Lee (Petry) K.; m. Rose Gemma Dukauskas. BA in Econs. and History, Coll. of William and Mary, 1979; MA in Econs., U. Pitts., 1982, PhD in Econs., 1983. Teaching fellow U. Pitts., 1981-83; asst. prof. Washington and Jefferson Coll., Washington, Pa., 1983-84; economist econs. rsch. svc. Econs. Rsch. Svc. USDA, Washington, 1984-91; sr. economist Pres.'s Coun. Econ. Advisors, 1991—. Contbr. articles to profl. jours. Mem. Am. Econs. Assn. Republican. Office: Coun Econ Advisors OEOB Rm 321 Washington DC 20500

KITTRIE, NICHOLAS N(ORBERT NEHEMIAH), legal educator, international consultant, author; b. en route Bilgoraj, Poland, Mar. 26, 1930; came to U.S., 1944; s. S.K. Kronenbergh and Perla F. (Ver Standig) K. (parents Brit. citizens); m. Sara Yudovic de Burak, June 1, 1962; children: Orde Felicien, Norda Nicole, Zachary McNair. Student, U. Cairo, 1946, U. London, 1947; LLB, U. Kans., 1950, MA, 1951; postgrad., U. Chgo., 1954-55; LLM, Georgetown U., 1963, SJD, 1968. Bar: Kans. 1953, D.C. 1958, U.S. Supreme Ct. Rsch. asst. U. London, 1947; instr. Western civilization dept. U. Kans., 1948-50; legal analyst Kans. Govt. Rsch. Ctr., 1951-54; asst. to dir. legis. svc. ABA, 1955-56, project dir., 1956-58; rsch. assoc. Yale Law Sch., 1958; legal asst. to U.S. Senator Wiley, 1959; counsel to U.S. Senator Estes Kefauver, antitrust and monopoly subcom. U.S. Senate, 1959-62; ptnr. DeGrazia & Kittrie, Washington, 1962-67; prof. criminal and comparative law Washington Coll. Law, Am. U., 1963—, dir. Inst. for Advanced Studies in Justice, 1970-78, dean, 1977-79, Mooers scholar and prof. law, 1983—; dean Sch. Justice Am. U., 1969-71; dir. Inst. Law and Policy, 1980—; lectr. U. Ottawa, summer 1966; rsch. scholar Univs. Warsaw and Berlin, summers 1967, 68; rsch. assoc. Ctr. Studies Criminal Justice U. Chgo., 1967-68; dir. Law and Policy Inst., Jerusalem, summers 1970-76, Inst. Law and Mass Media, 1978—; pres. Eleanor Roosevelt Inst. for Justice and Peace, 1989—; vis. fellow Inst. Advanced Legal Rsch. U. London, 1973-74, Nat. Inst. Justice U.S. Dept. Justice, 1979-80; vis. prof. London Sch. Econs., 1974; cons. Pres.'s Commn. Marijuana and Drug Abuse, 1972, v.p.'s commn. to combat terrorism, 1985; permanent rep. of AIDP to UN Social and Econs. Coun., 1975—; mem. task force on role of psychology in criminal justice Am. Psychol. Assn., 1975-76; dir. 1st Washington Devel. Corp., Bank of Chios, Athens, Greece; dir., gen. counsel Liberty House Investments; v.p. Nickal Corp.; chmn. KVK Communications Ltd. Author: International Legal Responsibility for Colonial People, 1951, Survey of Adminstration of Criminal Justice, 1956, (with others) The Mentally Disabled and the Law, 1959, The Right to be Different: Deviance and Enforced Law, 1971, The Comparative Law of Israel and the Middle East, 1971, The Real Estate Settlement Process and Its Cost, 1972, Crescent and Star: Arab-Israeli Perspectives on the Middle East Conflict, 1972, The Juvenile Drug Offender, 1972, Medicine, Law and Public Policy, 1975, Sanctions, Sentencing and Corrections, 1981, The Tree of Liberty: Rebellion and Political Crime in America, 1986, The Uncertain Future: Gorbachev's Eastern Bloc, 1988; chmn. editorial bd. Jour. Criminology, 1973-75, Justice mag., 1973-75; mem. editorial bd. Law and Human Behavior, 1976-80; mem. editorial adv. bd. The Washington Times; mem. exec. bd. Paragon House Pubs.; sr. cons. U.S. News and World Report Books; contbr. articles to profl. jours. Vice chmn. UN Alliance for Crime Prevention and Criminal Justice, 1976—, sci. com. U. Messina, Italy; mem. senate Am. U., 1964-72. Served with Brit. Middle East Command, 1944-45. Raymond fellow U. Chgo., 1954-55; sr. fellow NEH, 1973-74. Mem. ABA, Am. Soc. Criminology (pres. 1975), AAAS (coun. 1972—), Internat. Assn. Penal Law (Am. sect. v.p., sec.-gen. 1975-80), Internat. Assn. Comparative Pub. Law (dir. 1976—), Am. Soc. Pub. Adminstrn., Am. Judicature Soc., Am. Soc. Internat. Law, Internat. Inst. Space Law, Inter-Am. Bar Assn., Kans. Bar Assn., D.C. Bar Assn., Phi Delta Phi, Pi Sigma Alpha. Clubs: Rose Haven Yacht (dir.), Cosmos. Home: 6908 Ayr Ln Bethesda MD 20817-4902 also: Ramsbridge Farm Leesburg VA 22075 Office: Am U Sch Law 4400 Massachusetts Ave NW Washington DC 20016-8001

KITTS, JAMES JOSEPH, pharmacist; b. Cooperstown, N.Y., Feb. 18, 1943; s. Edward A. and Mildred (Filkins) K.; m. Janet Marx, June 17, 1967; children: Lisa Renee, Wendy Lee. BS in Pharmacy, Union U., Albany, N.Y., 1966. Pharmacy supr. C.U.S. Pharmacy, Albany, 1977—. Mem. Pharm. Soc. of N.Y. State, Chain Pharmacy Assn. of N.Y. State (v.p. 1977-89), N.Y. State Chain Pharmacy Assoc. (pres. 1989-92). Office: CUS Pharmacy PO Box 2011 Clifton Park NY 12065

KIVENKO, KENNETH, aerospace industry executive; s. Louis K.; m. Marilyn K., June 21, 1964; children: Leigh, Bram. B. in Engring., McGill U., 1964. With Dept. Nat. Def., Ottawa, Can., 1964-66; With Can. Marconi Co., 1966-84, v.p., 1979-84; with Bendix Avelex Inc. div. Allied-Signal Inc. (now Allied-Signal Aerospace Can.), 1984—; pres., chief exec. officer Bendix Avelex Inc., from 1984; now pres., chief exec. officer Allied-Signal Aerospace Can., Toronto; dir. Allied Can. Author: Managing Work-in-Process Inventory, 1981, Quality Control for Management, 1984; contbr. articles to profl. jours. Mem. Assn. Profl. Engrs. Ont., Am. Soc. Quality Control, Am Prodn. and Inventory Control Soc., Robotics Internat., Aerospace Industries Assn. Can. (chmn.), Assn. U.S. Army. Office: Allied-Signal Canada Inc, 240 Attwell Dr, Rexdale, ON Canada 9W6 L73

KIVIAT, STEPHEN HOWARD, architect; s. Louis and Lydia (Springer) K.; m. Susan E. Kimber, May 18, 1973; 1 child, Katherine Elizabeth. BA in Architecture, Cornell U., 1964; MA in Architecture, Harvard U., 1965. Archtl. designer William Lescaze, N.Y.C., 1966, Horowitz Chun, N.Y.C., 1967-70, Smith Munter, N.Y.C., 1970-71; archtl. design critic Cooper Union, N.Y.C., 1967-68; exec. v.p., founder Atelier Internat. Ltd., N.Y.C., 1967-78, pres., 1989-91. Chmn. Tenants Adv. Coun., N.Y.; pres. Designers Saturday, 1985-86; alumni adv. coun. Cornell U. Coll. of Architecture, 1989-91. Mem. Harvard Club of N.Y.C. Home: 114A E 36 St New York NY 10016

KIWIOR, CARLA MARIE, graphic artist, songwriter; b. Scranton, Pa., Jan. 8, 1964; d. Carl and Emily (Yablonsky) Snead; m. John Michael Kiwior Jr., Sept. 21, 1985; 1 child, Kirsten. BA in Advt./Art, Marywood Coll., 1985, postgrad. Buyer The Globe, Scranton, Pa., 1984-86, prodn. mgr. advt., 1986-88; editorial graphic artist The Scranton Times, 1988-92; owner Kiwi Graphics/Kiwi Music, Dickson City, Pa., 1992—; editorial graphic artist Knight-Ridder Tribune News Graphics, Washington, 1991. Author (children's cassette) Rudi & Friends, 1987, (cassette) Chemical, 1989; vocalist/musician Polka Jaks Orch., 1986. Named Flaming Foliage Queen, 1983-84; featured artist ITC Desktop Mag., 1990. Mem. NARAS, Nat. Acad. Songwriters, Songwriters Guild Am. Home and Office: Kiwi Graphics/Kiwi Music 404 Jackson St Dickson City PA 18519-1557

KJELLMARK, ERIC WILLIAM, JR., management consultant, opera company director; b. New Rochelle, N.Y., May 14, 1928; s. Eric William and Anna Sophia (Fogelstrom) K. BCE, Cornell U., 1950. Mgr. mktg. planning E. I. DuPont de Nemours, Wilmington, Del., 1980-87; dir. Far East task force E. I. DuPont de Nemours, Wilmington, 1987-89; gen. dir. Opera Del., Inc., Wilmington, 1985—; cons. Condux, Inc., Wilmington, 1985—; cons. Monkman-Rumsey, Inc., Wilmington, 1986—. Treas., v.p. Grand Opera House, Inc., Wilmington, 1971-91; panelist Del. State Arts Coun., Wilmington, 1987-89; bd. dirs. Opera Del., 1956—, Wilmington Waterways, Inc., 1985-89; chmn. level IV cos. Opera Am., 1989—, bd. dirs., 1992—; panelist Mid-Atlantic States arts Consortium, 1990—, NEA, 1991. Mem. Am. Chem. Soc., Am. Inst. Chem. Engrs., Alpha Chi Sigma. Republican. Episcopalian. Club: Rodney Square. Office: Opera Del 8th & Shipley St Wilmington DE 19801

KLAETKE, FRITZ, graphic designer; b. Detroit, June 3, 1966; s. Frank William and Valerie (Angers) K. BFA, U. Mich., 1988. Asst. art dir. Genesis Internat., Detroit, 1985-87; graphic designer Eclipse Jazz, Ann Arbor, Mich., 1987-88, Truzzi Design, Ann Arbor, 1988-89; prin. Visual Dialogue, Boston, 1989—. Recipient Cert. of Typographic Excellence, Type Dirs. Club, 1988, Am. Corp. Identity award Am. Corp. Identity, 1988. Mem. Am. Inst. Graphic Arts. Office: Visual Dialogue 429 Columbus Ave # 1 Boston MA 02116-5959

KLAHR, ARYEH LESLIE, psychiatrist; b. Bklyn., July 25, 1952; s. Robert and Eva (Richtman) K. BA, Yeshiva U., 1973; MD, U. Guadalajara, Mexico, 1977. Diplomate Am. Bd. Neurology and Psychiatry. Intern SUNY Sch. Medicine, Buffalo, N.Y., 1978; staff physician Bklyn., 1979-80; employee health physician Union Carbide Corp., N.Y.C., 1981; dir. employee health Gracie Sq. Hosp., N.Y.C., 1982-83; resident in psychiatry Hillside Hosp. Div. Jewish Med. Ctr., Glen Oaks, N.Y., 1984-87; fellow in Addictionology Fair Oaks Hosp., Summit, N.J., 1987-88; dir. alchoholism treatment svcs. Fair Oaks Hosp., Summit, 1988-90; med. dir. Indsl. Medicine Assocs., White Plains, N.Y., 1990—; clin. asst. prof. N.Y. Med. Coll. Dept. Psychiatry, 1991—. Contbr. articles to profl. jours. and chpts. to med. books. Recipient Regents scholarship State of N.Y. Bd. Regents, Albany, 1969-73. Fellow Am. Psychiat. Assn.; mem. AMA, Med. Soc. State of N.Y., Am. Soc. Addiction Medicine, Am. Acad. Clin. Psychiatrists. Jewish. Home: 50 W 75th St New York NY 10023

KLARFELD, JONATHAN MICHAEL, journalism educator; b. Springfield, Mass., Dec. 11, 1937; m. Patricia Holland, Sept. 7, 1974; children: Victoria, Alexander. AB, Colgate U., 1960. Reporter, editor Holyoke (Mass.) Transcript-Telegram, 1962-65, UPI, Springfield, Boston, 1965-66, Boston Globe, 1966-68; press sec. Boston Parks/Redevel. Auth., 1968-70; reporter, writer Boston Record-Am., 1970-72; mgr. pub. info. Mass. Blue Cross, 1972-74; assoc. professor journalism Boston U., 1975—, dir. print journalism, 1979—; editorial cons. Lawyers Weekly Pubs., Boston, Lansing, Mich., Richmond, Va., Providence, 1983-92; press analyst Oxbow Corp., West Palm Beach, Fla., Weston, Mass., 1984—; editorial cons. New Eng. Bus. mag., Boston. Contbr. articles to numerous newspapers, periodicals. Mem. Sorcerers Rugby Club (pres. 1974-80), The Squash Club (Allston,

Mass.), Delta Kappa Epsilon. Unitarian. Office: Boston U Sch Journalism Boston MA 02215

KLASS, ROSANNE TRAXLER, writer, editor, consultant; b. Cedar Rapids, Iowa; d. Raymond Nataliel and Ann (Traxler) K.; m. William K. Archer (div.). BA in Lit., U. Wis.; MA in Lit., CUNY. Instr. English Ministry of Edn., Kabul, Afghanistan, 1950s; freelance writer, editor, journalist, N.Y.C., 1961—; contbg. editor Internat. Ency. Art, 1968-72; mem. editorial staff Woman's Day mag., N.Y.C., 1972-77; arts editor The Trib, N.Y.C., 1977-78; mem. editorial staff Week in Rev., The N.Y. Times, 1978-79; writer, editor, cons., N.Y.C., 1980—; dir. Afghanistan and S.W. Asia program Freedom House, N.Y.C., 1980-91; specialist in Afghanistan and Southwest Asia, 1980—; sec. Afghanistan coun. Asia Soc., N.Y.C., 1959-65; co-founder, sr. v.p. Afghanistan Relief Com., N.Y.C., 1979—; script cons., MGM, 1968; lectr. in field. Author: Land of High Flags, 1964; co-author, editor: Afghanistan--The Great Game Revisited, 1988; editor Opera Spotlight mag., 1980-82; contbr. articles to books, newspapers and mags. Founding mem. N.Y.C. Opera Guild, 1959-83; co-founder Soc. Asian Music, N.Y.C., 1960; mem. exec. com. Norman Treigle Meml. Fund, N.Y.C. and Cin., 1975-85; mem., donor Met. Mus. Art., N.Y.C., 1976-78. Mem. Authors Guild Am., U.S. English. Office: Afghanistan/South Asia Resource Ctr PO Box 478 New York NY 10024-0478

KLATSKY, BRUCE J., apparel company executive; b. N.Y.C., July 14, 1948; s. Herbert W. and Pearl (Starkman) K.; m. Iris Ann Gussow, Aug. 15, 1970; 1 child, Peter. B.S., Western Res. U., 1970; postgrad., Georgetown U., 1970-71. Chmn. bd., chief exec. officer Van Heusen Group, Phillips-Van Heusen Corp., N.Y.C., 1971—; pres., chief operating officer Phillips-Van Heusen Corp. (parent), N.Y.C., 1987—. Office: Phillips-Van Heusen Corp 1290 Ave Of The Americas New York NY 10104-0095*

KLAUS, GEORGE LEONARD, corporate executive; b. Chgo., Aug. 17, 1924; s. George Michael and Marie Sophia (Schaaf) K.; m. Joan Ruthy, June 6, 1949; children: Cynthia, Susan, Jill Anna. BS in Acctg. with honors, U. Ill., 1949. CPA; cert. internal auditor. With auditing dept. W.H. Stout, CPAs, Chgo., 1949-50; acct. Darling and Co., Chgo., 1950-52; sr. auditor Arthur Andersen & Co., Chgo., 1952-58; corp. budget mgr., internal audit mgr. Brunswick Corp., Chgo., 1958-68; dir. spl. projects ITT, N.Y.C., 1968-72, dir. mfg. cost controls, 1972-85; exec. v.p. Mgmt. Controls Corp., Southport, Conn., 1985—; pres. Leisure Group Ltd., Milford, Conn., 1987—; v.p. Royal Cleaners, Milford, 1988—. Treas. Village of Glen Ellyn, Ill., 1959-62; mem. Police Pension Bd., Glen Ellyn, 1959-62. 1st lt. U.S. Army Air Force, 1942-45, ETO. Decorated Air medal, POW medal. Mem. Am. Prodn. Control Soc., 4th Fighters Group Assn. Republican. Home: 33 Glenwood Rd Weston CT 06883-2310 Office: Leisure Group Ltd 58 River St Milford CT 06460-3381

KLAUSNER, BENNETT, construction company executive; b. Jersey City, N.J., Mar. 23, 1939; s. Samuel and Eva (Favius) K.; m. Susan Irene Susser, June 25, 1961; children—Cynthia, Shari, Stacey. AB, Rutgers U., 1960; MBA, Pace U., 1970. CPA, N.Y. Claims supr. USF & G, N.Y.C., 1963-67; sr. auditor Ernst & Whinney, N.Y.C., 1967-72; v.p. fin. Titan Group Inc., Park Ridge, N.J., 1972-86; v.p. fin. E.E. Cruz & Co., Holmdel, N.J., 1986—. Served with U.S. Army, 1960-63. Mem. Am. Inst. CPAs, N.Y. State Soc. CPAs, Constrn. Fin. Mgmt. Assn. (bd. dirs., treas.). Office: EE Cruz & Co Inc Cruz Plz Holmdel NJ 07733

KLAVINS, JANIS VILIBERTS, oncologist, vocalist; b. Rugaji, Abrene, Latvia, May 6, 1921; came to U.S., 1951; s. Janis and Ida Aline K.; m. Ilga Minjona Krumins, July 4, 1950; children: Ilze Mara, Lize Kristine, Janis Peteris, Filips Klavs. MD, U. Kiel, Fed. Republic of Germany, 1948, PhD, 1959; D in Biology (hon.), U. Latvia, 1991. Prof. pathology Duke U., Durham, N.C., 1963-65, Columbia U. Coll. Physicians & Surgeons, N.Y.C., 1967-70, Downstate Med. Ctr., Bklyn., N.Y., 1965-85, SUNY, Stony Brook, 1970-85; dir. dept. labs. Queens Hosp. Ctr. Long Island Jewish Ctr. Affiliate, Queens, N.Y., 1970-77; prof. pathology Cornell U. Med. Coll., N.Y.C., 1985—; chmn. dept. pathology Cath. Med. Ctr. Bklyn & Queens, Jamaica, N.Y., 1977—. Author: (with others) Human Tumor Markers, Biological Basis and Nieburgs, 1983, Tumor Markers, Clinical and Laboratory Studies, 1985, Human Tumor Markers. Biology and Clinical Application, 1987; contbr. 160 articles to profl. jours.; editor-in-chief Jour. Tumor Marker Oncology, 1987—; singer Latvian songs in numerous recs., 1965—. V.p. Latvian Cultural Inst., N.Y.C., 1974-78; chmn. music sect. Latvian Cultural Found., Washington, 1988—; chmn., bd. dirs. Flushing Meadow Community Devel. Corp., Jamaica, N.Y., 1986-88; bd. dirs. N.C. State Ballet Co., 1963-65. Recipient Gt. Gold medal in music, Schubertbund, Vienna, Austria, 1984; named Laureate Musician Beaux Arts Internat., Inc., N.Y.C., 1980. Mem. Soc. Urban Physicians (sec.-treas. 1970-75), Assn. Clin. Scientists (pres. 1980-81, chmn. sci. sect. 1982-88, Scientist of Yr. 1983), Egyptian Soc. Tumor Mark Oncologists (hon.), Latvian Acad. Sci. (fgn. mem.), Interant. Acad. Tumor Mark Oncology (pres. 1984—), Latvian-Am. Assn. Univ. Profs. and Scientists (pres. 1985—). Home: 5 Broadmoor Rd Scarsdale NY 10583-7649

KLAY, ANDOR C., editor, author; b. Hungary, June 27, 1912; s. Alexander C. and Eva (Varga) K; m. Gerda Herz, Apr. 7, 1947; 1 child, Laurence Dennis. Editorial writer fgn. lang. dailies Cleve., 1935-42; polit. sect. chief U.S. Office Censorship, 1942-43; intelligence specialist U.S. State Dept., 1946-51; chief Hungary sect., intelligence rsch. for USSR and Ea. Europe, 1951-56; apptd. U.S. Fgn. Svc., 1956; consul, 2d sec. U.S. Embassy, Belgrade, 1958-59, 1st sec., 1959-61; chief polit. officer Frankfurt am Main, 1962-67, chief Ea. affairs div. U.S. Mission Berlin, 1967-70; spl. asst. legal div. U.S. State Dept., 1970-72; Washington corr. Am.-Hungarian AP, 1970-91; Washington editor Liberty Media, Inc., Cleve., 1991—; adj. prof. U.S. Fgn. Svc. Inst., Ctr. for Area Studies, 1970-79; dir. diplomacy seminars Mt. Vernon Coll., Washington, 1973. Author: The Visitor Speaks, 1950, Daring Diplomacy, 1957, other books in English and Hungarian; contbr. articles to profl. publs. Served with OSS, AUS, 1943-45, USAF, 1943-46. Recipient Lincoln award Am. Hungarian Found., Rutgers Univ., 1985, Golden Pen award Nat. Fedn. Hungarian Journalists, Budapest, 1990. Mem. Diplomatic and Consular Officers Assn., Nat. Press Club, Army & Navy Club. Home and Office: 3402 Garfield St NW Washington DC 20007-1439

KLECKNER, WILLARD RICHARDS, consultant, educator; b. Plainfield, N.J., Sept. 29, 1937; s. Willard Ralph and Gladys Alta (Richards) K.; 1 child, Tamara Lee. BSEE, Pa. State U., 1959, BBA, 1959, MBA, 1976; LLB, La Salle U., 1965; PhD in Bus. Adminstrn. and Engring., Calif. Western U., 1980. Cons. engr. Kleckner Enterprises, Whitehall, Pa., 1961-65, Whitehall, 1975-78, Hibernia, N.J., 1983—; labor rels. mgr. Eaton Corp., Phila., 1965-73; dir. labor rels. Beverage Mgmt. Corp., Columbus, Ohio, 1973-75; dir. adminstrn. Penn-Dixie Industries, Inc., Nazareth, Pa., 1978-81; v.p. adminstrn. Merrick Corp., Roseland, N.J., 1981-83; dir. engring., rsch. devel. AquaScis. Internat., Inc., Lincoln Park, N.J., 1988-90; cons. elec., environ. and R&D engr. Kleckner Assocs., Hibernia, 1990—; lectr. on indsl. rels., 1975—. Contbr. articles on pers. adminstrn. practices and policies and water tech. to profl. publs. Instr., lectr. on emergency rescue techniques, 1977—, on internal and external electronic security equipment, 1975—, on water tech., 1988. With USN, 1955-61. Mem. IEEE (sr.), AMA, Am. Soc. Safety Engrs., Am. Mgmt. Assn., Am. Paramedic Assn., Nat. Soc. Emergency Med. Technicians and Paramedics, Assn. Locksmiths Am., Internat. Soc. Profl. Cons., Pa. State U. Alumni Recruiting Coun., Assn. Energy Engrs., Assn. Ground Water Scientists and Engrs., Nat. Water Well Assn., Nat. Ground Water Assn., Am. Water Well Assn., Nat. Registry of Environmental Profls., NASA, Lions. Republican. Presbyterian. Home: 15 Colonial Rd Rockaway NJ 07866-4226 Office: Kleckner Assocs PO Box 357 Hibernia NJ 07842-0357

KLEIMAN, GARY HOWARD, radio station executive, consultant; b. Phila., Jan. 24, 1952; s. Leon and Martha (Rubin) K.; m. Annette Suzanne Vranich, Sept. 23, 1978; children: Aaron Jay, Jared Adam. Diploma, Am. Acad. Broadcasting, Phila., 1969, Pa. State Fire Sch., Media, 1969; BS, Temple U., 1972. Cert. radio mktg. cons. Gen. mgr. Sta. WFEC, Harrisburg, Pa., 1974-75; local sales mgr. Sta. WYSP-FM, Phila., 1976-79; pres. A.S.K. Advt., King of Prussia, Pa., 1976-80; v.p., gen. mgr. Sta. WGLU-FM, Johnstown, 1980-82, Sta. WAJE, Edensburg, Pa., 1982-84, Sta. WSBY-WQHQ-AM-FM, Salisbury, Md., 1984-86; mgr. Sta. WJDY, Salisbury, 1986-87; pres. Ideas Unltd. Mktg. and Advt. Co., Salisbury, 1986—; gen. mgr. Sta. WACS-FM, Schenectady, N.Y., 1988-89; v.p., gen. mgr. WDLE-FM, Federalsburg, Md., 1989-91; media cons., Sta. WMDT TV, Salisbury, Md., 1988; dir., tchr. Am. Acad. Broadcasting, Phila., 1976-79. Contbr. articles to profl. publs. Active campaigner Cambria County Dem. Com., 1982-84, Wicomico County Dem. Com., 1991—; com. chmn. Salisbury Revitalization, 1984—; bd. dirs. Salisbury Regional Urban Design Action Team, 1984—, Deers Head Hosp. Found., 1987—; co-sponsor projects Lower Shore Easter Seals, Salisbury, 1985, Am. Cancer Soc., 1984-85, Kidney Found., 1985, Epilepsy Assn., 1985; promotion coord. Salisbury Festival com., 1985, 87, 88, 89, 90, 91, vice-chmn., 1985-90; mem. exec. com. Lower Shore chpt. March of Dimes, 1984-89; bd. dirs. Am. Heart Assn., 1987—, Johnstown Area Regional Industries, 1981-84; scout leader Boy Scouts Am., 1988—. Recipient numerous awards from local civic orgns., 1981—. Mem. Downtown Salisbury Assn., Salisbury Area C. of C. (bd. dirs. 1990—), Caroline County C. of C. (bd. dirs. 1989), Salisbury Jaycees (Springboard award 1985), Johnstown Jaycees, Salisbury State U. Athletic Club (pres. 1985), Tall Timber Park Assn. (pres. 1992—). Democrat. Jewish. Home: 115 Tall Timbers Ln Fruitland MD 21826-1318 Office: Ideas Unltd Tall Timbers Ln Fruitland MD 21826-1319

KLEIMAN, GARY NEIL, international economic consultant; b. Harrisburg, Pa., Jan. 26, 1960; s. Raymond and Leah (Fishman) K.; m. Elizabeth Rennet Morrissey, Sept. 28, 1991. Cert., Inst. d'Etudes Politiques, Paris, 1980; BS in Fgn. Svc., Georgetown U., 1981; MS, London Sch. Econs., 1982. Chief exec. officer advisor European Community Bus. Cooperation, Tunis, Tunisia, 1982; refugee officer UN Devel. Program, Thailand and The Philippines, 1983; prin. Kleiman & Assocs., Harrisburg, Pa., 1983-84; sr. assoc. van Kloberg & Assocs. Ltd., Washington, 1984-85; sr. account exec. Curtis J. Hoxter, Inc., N.Y.C., 1985-87; pres. Kleiman Internat. Cons., Inc., N.Y.C., 1987—. Contbr. articles to profl. jours. Mem. U.S.-Yugoslav Econ. Coun., Internat. Bus. Group, Am. Friends of London Sch. Econs. Office: Kleiman Internat Cons Inc 80 Wall St New York NY 10005

KLEIMAN, HOWARD, mathematician, educator; b. N.Y.C., Apr. 15, 1929; s. Louis and Mollie (Blefeld) K.; m. Edna Madje Benjamin, July 26, 1956; children: Michele, Jeffery, Daniel. BA, NYU, 1950, MS, 1961; MA, Columbia, 1954; PhD, Kings Coll., U. London, 1969. Tchr. pub. schs. N.Y.C., 1955-65; asst. prof. Queensborough Community Coll., CUNY, 1967-70; asso. prof. math., 1970-78, prof., 1978-91, prof. emeritus, 1991—. Part-time lectr. math. S.I. Community Coll., 1960-63, Hunter Coll., 1963-69; adj. assoc. prof. Queens Coll City U. N.Y., 1970-74. David Diamond scholar music, 1951; Ernst Toch scholar, 1954; Berkshire Music Center scholar, Tanglewood, summer 1954. Mem. Am. Math. Soc. Author: (with E. Just) A Sourcebook of Fundamental Mathematics, part II, 1971. Contbr. articles to profl. jours. Home: 18883 85th Rd Jamaica NY 11423-1123 Office: Queensborough Community Coll Math Dept Bayside NY 11423

KLEIMAN, MARK ALBERT ROBERT, public policy educator; b. Phoenix, May 18, 1951; s. Allen and Jeanette (Albert) K. BA, Haverford Coll., 1972; M in Pub. Policy, Harvard U., 1977, PhD in Pub. Policy, 1985. Legis. asst. U.S. Rep. Les Aspin, Washington, 1974-75; spl. asst. to chmn. bd. dirs., chief exec. officer Polaroid Corp., Cambridge, Mass., 1975-76; dir. program analysis, Office Mgmt. and Budget City of Boston, 1977-78, dep. dir. for mgmt., Office of Mgmt. and Budget, 1978-79; assoc. dir. for drug enforcement programs Office of Policy and Mgmt. Analysis, U.S. Dept. Justice, Washington, 1979-82; dir. Office of Policy and Mgmt., Washington, 1982-83; lectr. in pub. policy Harvard U., 1987-91, assoc. prof. John F. Kennedy Sch. Govt., 1992—; pres. BOTEC Analysis Corp., Cambridge, 1985—; cons. Office of Nat. Drug Control Policy, Washington, 1991—. Author: Against Excess: Drug Policy for Results, 1992, Marijuana, Costs of Abuse, Costs of Control, 1989. Fellow Program in Criminal Justice Policy and Mgmt., John F. Kennedy Sch. Govt.; Assn. for Policy Analysis and Mgmt., Am. Soc. for Criminology. Office: Harvard U JFK Sch Govt 79 John F Kennedy St Cambridge MA 02138

KLEIN, AARON, small business owner; b. Bklyn., Oct. 6, 1948; s. Bernard and Paula (Pessah) K.; m. Katrina Carroll, Nov. 23, 1986; children: Francine, James. BFA, Adelphi U., 1970. Photo editor AP, N.Y.C., 1970-73; mgr. Wometco Photography, N.Y.C., 1973-78; owner Ultimate Photographics, Inc., N.Y.C., 1978—. Mem. N.Y. Woodturners Club. Jewish. Home: 14 John Cava Ln Cortlandt Manor NY 10566

KLEIN, ANNE SCEIA, public relations executive; b. Phila., Apr. 25, 1942; d. Charles B. and Kathryn L. (Lucas) Sceia; m. Gerhart L. Klein, June 19, 1976. BS in Econs., U. Pa., 1964, MA in Communications, 1965. Promotion asst. S.E. Pa. Transit Authority, Phila., 1965; pub. rels. dir. Pa. Lung Assn., Phila., 1965-68; info. dir. H2L2 Architects, Phila., 1968; pub. rels. officer Girard Bank, Phila., 1969-76; acct. exec. Aitkin-Kynett Co., Inc., Phila., 1977; mgr. media rels. Sun Co., Radnor, Pa., 1978-80; mgr. exec. communications Sun Co., Radnor, 1980-82; pres. Anne Klein & Assocs., Inc., Mt. Laurel, N.J., 1982—. Mem. Ethics Com., Mt. Laurel, 1988-92; Citizens Adv. Com., Mt. Laurel, 1988-92. Recipient Super Communicator of 80's award Women in Communications, 1987, Tribute to Women in Industry award YMCA, 1990; named Small Bus. Person of Yr. So. N.J. C. of C., 1991. Fellow Pub. Rels. Soc. Am.(accredited, pres. Phila. chpt. 1979, mid-Atlantic chmn. 1984, assembly del. 1980-82, 88—, exec. com. Counselors Acad. 1990—, Pepperpot awards, Coll. of Fellows 1991), Pub. Rels. Profls. So. N.J. (chmn. 1987—, pres. 1985-87), Forum Exec. Women (sec. bd. dirs. 1981-83), Phila. Pub. Rels. Assn., Harbor League Club, U. Pa. Faculty Club, Kappa Delta. Office: 533 Fellowship Rd Ste 250 Mount Laurel NJ 08054-3447

KLEIN, ARTHUR, foundation executive; b. Phila., June 27, 1934; s. Philip and Esther (Moyerman) K.; m. Marilyn A. Burnett, Mar. 12, 1961 (dec. Dec. 1990); children: Joshua, Rebecca Rose Clark, Alexander, Judith Amy. AB, Haverford Coll., 1955; MS, U. Pa., 1958; DHL, Combs Coll. Music, Bryn Mawr, Pa., 1983. Editor Phila. Jewish Times, 1958-71; pres. Rittenhouse Found., Phila., 1963—, Phila. Meml. Park, 1965-85, Gt. Valley Pet Cemetery, Frazer, Pa., 1968-85, Bristol Gardens, Inc. (Pa.), 1981—; trustee Mikveh Israel Cemetery Trust, Phila., 1977—. Pres. Phila. Jaycees, 1961, Ctr. City Residents Assn., Phila., 1963; chmn. Phila. Art Alliance, 1968-71; trustee The Provincial Found., Phila., 1965—, Friends of Independence Nat. Hist. Park, 1989—; exec. bd. Com. of Seventy, 1989—; hon. v.p. Temble Beth Zion-Beth Israel; trustee Combs Coll. Music, Bryn Mawr, Pa., 1983-85, Pa. Coll. Podiatric Medicine, Phila., 1983—, Independence Hall Preservation Fund, 1990ú, Big Bros./Big Sisters of Am., 1976—, chmn. bd. trustees Harcum Jr. Coll., Bryn Mawr, 1982—; committeeman 8th Ward Republican Exec. Com., Phila., 1979; bd. dirs. Mann Music Ctr., 1989—, Pan Am. Assn., 1991—. Recipient Eyerman award Pa. Jr. C. of C., 1962. Mem. Soc. Profl. Journalists (pres. Phila. chpt.), Jewish Cemetery Assn. Phila. (pres.), Locust Club, Plays and Players Club, Barnegat Light Yacht Club, Franklin Inn Club. Republican. Home: 2023 Pine St Philadelphia PA 19103-6522 Office: The Rittenhouse Found 225 S 15th St Ste 2034 Philadelphia PA 19102-3979

KLEIN, BARBARA WARD, communication arts educator, consultant; b. Newark; d. William Everett and Agnes Patricia (O'Toole) Ward; m. David G. Kennedy, May 2, 1970 (div. Aug. 1983); m. Bernard M. Klein, July 19, 1987. BA, Rutgers U., Newark, 1969; MA, Montclair State Coll., 1974; EdD, Rutgers U., New Brunswick, N.J., 1979. Tchr. 7th grade Queen of Peace Jr. High Sch., North Arlington, N.J., 1970-76; tchr. English Queen of Peace High Sch., North Arlington, 1976-80, chair dept. English, 1979-80; from asst. prof. to assoc. prof. communication arts St. Thomas Aquinas Coll., Sparkill, N.Y., 1980—, chair div. humanities, 1990—; founder, cons. Success Unltd., Mahwah, N.J., 1988—; lectr. in field. Producer, actress Actors Cafe Theatre, 1970-81; producer, editor video mktg. and tng., 1988; book reviewer. Sec. Overpeck Harriers, Ridgefield, N.J., 1983; advisor Girl Scouts U.S., Ridgewood, N.J., 1986; vol. Multiple Sclerosis, 1983—. Named Best Actress of Yr. in N.J. Regional Theatre, N.Y. Daily News, 1978, Outstanding Vocalist, N.Y. Voice Tchrs. Assn., 1968. Mem. Broadcast Edn. Assn., Assn. Communications Adminstrs., N.J. Bicycle Touring Club. Home: 8 Sandburg Ct Mahwah NJ 07430-3167 Office: St Thomas Aquinas Coll Rte 340 Sparkill NY 10976-9722

KLEIN, BERNARD ROBERT, ophthalmologist, surgeon; b. N.Y.C., Aug. 21, 1941; s. Leonard and Evelyn (Rotkowitz) K.; m. Jean Ann Hunt, Oct. 17, 1981; children: Ian David and Leah Renée (twins). BA, NYU, Bronx, 1962; MD, Dalhousie U., Halifax, N.S., Can., 1968. Diplomate Am. Bd. Ophthalmology, Am. Bd. Med. Examiners. Rotating intern Dalhousie U., 1967-68; resident in ophthalmology SUNY, Bklyn., 1968-71, chief resident in ophthalmology, 1971-72, clin. instr. in ophthalmology, 1972-73; clin. instr., ophthalmologist Albert Einstein Coll. Medicine, Bronx, 1972-85; chief of ophthalmology, dir. La Guardia Hosp., Forest Hills, N.Y., 1974—; assoc. ophthalmologist Beth-Israel Hosp., N.Y.C., 1986—. Lt. comdr. USNR, 1963-77. Fellow ACS, Am. Acad. Ophthalmology; mem. Am. Soc. Contemporary Ophthalmology (internat. glaucoma congress 1978—). Office: 66-07 102d St Forest Hills NY 11375

KLEIN, DENNIS BURTON, foundation administrator, educator, magazine editor; b. Cleve., May 28, 1948; s. Harold F. and Jean S. (Schwartz) K.; m. Libby A. Stein, Aug. 5, 1979; children: Aaron D., Leah T., Rachel E. BA cum laude, Hobart Coll., 1970; MA, U. Rochester, 1972, PhD, 1978. Vis. asst. prof. Ohio State U., Columbus, 1977-78; vis. prof. Mich. State U., East Lansing, 1978-79; post-doctoral fellow Harvard U., Cambridge, Mass., 1979-81; Dorot teaching fellow NYU, N.Y.C., 1981-84; exec. dir. Braun Ctr. Holocaust Studies, N.Y.C., 1984—, Jewish Found. Christian Rescuers, N.Y.C., 1991—, Hidden Child Found., N.Y.C., 1991—, mem. exec. com. Assn. Holocaust Orgns., N.Y.C., 1988—; cons. U.S. Dept. Edn., Washington, 1978; judge Nat. Jewish Book awards, N.Y.C., 1989-90; bd. dirs. U.S. Holocaust Meml. Coun., Washington. Author: Jewish Origins of the Psychoanalytic Movement, 1981, 85 (Choice Acad. Book of Yr. 1981); gen. editor book series Holocaust Studies Libr., 1984—; founding editor Dimensions: A Jour. of Holocaust Studies, 1984—; contbr. articles and revs. to profl. jours. Mem. Citizens Adv. Coun. on Schs., Teaneck, N.J., 1990—, Polit. Campaign Com., Teaneck, 1991—; den leader Cub Scouts Am., Teaneck, 1991—. Fulbright fellow U. Vienna, 1974-75, Spencer fellow Nat. Acad. Edn., 1982-84; recipient award NEH, 1984, award Meml. Found. Jewish Culture, 1984-85, Yavner award Disting. Contbns. to Human Rights Edn., N.Y. State Dept. Edn., 1987. Mem. Phi Beta Kappa. Office: Anti-Defamation League 823 United Nations Pl New York NY 10017

KLEIN, ELAINE, magazine publishing executive; b. Bklyn., Mar. 12, 1929; d. Sidney and Bertha (Smith) Laks; m. Melvin Klein, Dec. 23, 1951; children: Cyd Robin Klein Tomack, Amy Susan Klein Len. Exec. sec. to pres. Muzak Corp., N.Y.C., 1949-55; expeditor The Van Ard Co., Forest Mills, N.Y., 1968-70; dir. spl. sales, Calif. rep. Playbill Mag., N.Y.C., 1970—. Mem. The New Dramatists, Friars Club. Democrat. Jewish. Office: Playbill Mag 52 Vanderbilt Ave New York NY 10017

KLEIN, FREDERIC WILLIAM, manufacturing executive; b. Boston, Sept. 4, 1922; s. August C. and Maree (Keeling) K.; m. Isobel Marie Pinto, Nov. 4, 1950; children: Kathryn Sanders, Karen Anderson. BS in Marine Engring., U.S. Marchant Marine Acad., Kings Point, N.Y., 1944; BS in Gen. Engring., U. Maine, 1948; diploma, Columbia U., 1979. Registered profl. engr., N.Y. Engr. Ingersoll Rand, N.Y.C., 1948-55; from asst. sales mgr. to v.p., adminstrn. Thomson Industries, Inc., Port Washington, N.Y., 1955—; dir. Nuclear Equipment Corp., San Carlos, Calif. Contbr. articles to profl. jours. Committeeman Rep. Party, Glen Cove, N.Y., 1989—; pres. Elsinore Civic Assn., Glen Cover., 1978. Lt. USMC, 1942-44, ETO, PTO. Mem. ASME (Award of Merit 1973, treas. 1970-73, exec. com. 1970-73), Soc. Profl. Engrs., Sales Execs. Club, Am. Mgmt. Assn., Sea Cliff Yacht Club, U.S. Merchant Marine Acad. Officers Club, Navy League. Republican. Episcopalian. Home: 7 Woodland Rd Glen Cove NY 11542-1726 Office: Thomson Industries Inc Shore Rd at Channel Dr Port Washington NY 11050

KLEIN, HANS EMIL, accounting educator; b. Decin, Bohemia, Czechoslovakia, Dec. 4, 1939; came to U.S., 1966; s. Emil Franz and Irmgard (Hautmann) K.; m. Amelia Sokalski. Student, Munich Banking Acad., 1963; diploma in langs., Alliance Francaise, Paris, 1966; MS magna cum laude, U. Ky., 1973, DBA, 1977. Cert. mgmt. acct. Asst. prof. Boston U., 1976-79, Boston Coll., 1979-81; assoc. prof. acctg. and fin. U. Mass., Boston, 1981-83, vis. prof. acctg., 1990-91; assoc. prof. acctg. and fin. Am. Coll. of Switzerland, Leysin, 1983-85; vis. prof. Lubin Sch. of Bus. Pace U., N.Y.C., 1985-86; assoc. prof. Bentley Coll., Waltham, Mass., 1986-90, 91—; internal auditor, apptd. br. mgr. Sparkasse Dillingen a.d. Donau, Fed. Republic of Germany, 1961-63; internal auditor for fin., mgr. acctg., Paris, 1963-66; contr. U.S. ops., Chgo. and N.Y.C., 1966-70; internat. mfr. and distbr. Anker Werke AG, Bielefeld, Fed. Republic of Germany, 1963-70; contr. mus. instrument div. Pickwick Internat., N.Y.C., 1971; exec. ptnr. KM Assocs., Boston, 1981—, ASIDA, Boston, 1991—; exec. dir. World Assn. for Case Method Rsch. and Application, 1988—. Fellow Bank Adminstrn. Inst. Rsch. award 1976); mem. Inst. Mgmt. Acctg., Am. Acctg. Assn. (v.p. adminstrn. and financing Boston chpt. 1989), World Affairs Coun. of Boston, Internat. Acctg. Assn. (regional chair 1990—), Beta Alpha Psi, Beta Gamma Sigma. Office: WACRA 23 Mackintosh Ave Needham MA 02192-1218

KLEIN, HERBERT ALAN, nuclear physician; b. Milw., Mar. 28, 1936; s. David Xavier and Sophie (Posner) K.; m. Inara Berzins, Jan. 5, 1973; children: Benjamin C., Alexandra E. AB, Columbia U., 1956, MD, 1960; MA in Biochemistry, Harvard U., 1968, PhD in Biochemistry, 1975. Diplomate Am. Bd. Nuclear Medicine; lic. physician. Staff physician Wilford Hall USAF Hosp., Lackland AFB, Tex., 1962-64; teaching fellow Harvard Med. Sch., Boston, 1966-67; instr. NYU, 1970-72; summer faculty Manhattanville Coll., Purchase, N.Y., 1973; faculty SUNY Coll. Medicine, Bklyn., 1975-80; co-dir. nuclear medicine L.I. Coll. Hosp., Bklyn., 1975-76, dir. nuclear medicine, 1976-80; faculty U. Pitts. Sch. Medicine, 1980—; chief nuclear medicine VA Med. Ctr., Pitts., 1991—; med. staff Presbyn.-Univ. Hosp., Pitts., 1980—, Montefiore U. Hosp., Pitts., 1990—; assoc. dir. nuclear medicine dept. radiology U. Pitts., 1980—. Contbr. articles to profl. jours. Capt. USAF, 1960-62. Am. Cancer Soc. postdoctoral scholar, 1964; NIH spl. rsch. fellow, 1968; Wechsler Rsch. Found. grantee, 1984, Health Rsch. and Svc. Found. grantee, 1986. Mem. Soc. Nuclear Medicine (mem. brain imaging coun., computer coun., acad. coun.), Harvey Soc., Assn. Univ. Radiologists, Phi Beta Kappa. Home: 102 Pheasant Dr Pittsburgh PA 15238-2208 Office: VA Med Ctr University Dr C Pittsburgh PA 15240-1002

KLEIN, HILTON JAMES, veterinarian; b. Rochester, Pa., Dec. 6, 1950; s. Hilton George Klein and Jennie Inman; m. Charlotte Barchet, June 30, 1973; children: Alyssa, Meghann, Jacob. BS, Rutgers U., 1972; MS, Pa. State U., 1976; VMD, U. Pa., 1980. Diplomate Am. Coll. Lab. Animal Medicine. Dir. quality control Microbiol. Assocs., Walkersville, Md., 1974-76; mgr., vet. sci. Whittaker M.A. Bioproducts, Walkersville, 1980-83, dir., vet. medicine, 1983-85; staff vet. Merck, Sharp & Dohme Rsch. Labs, West Point, Pa., 1985-88, assoc. dir., 1988-91, dir. lab. animal resources, 1991—; cons. Am. Assoc. Accred. Lab. Animal Care, Rockville, Md., 1987—; adj. assoc. prof. U. Pa., Phila., 1988—, Hahneman U., Phila., 1987—. Patentee in field. Mem. Pa. Soc. Biomed. Rsch. (bd. dirs. 1990—), Am. Vet. Med. Assn., Am. Coll. Lab. Animal Medicine (chmn. sci. program com. 1991-92), Am. Assn. Lab. Animal Sci., Phi Sigma, Phi Zeta. Home: 107 Meadowood Dr Lansdale PA 19446-1610 Office: Merch Rsch Labs W44-201 West Point PA 19486

KLEIN, HOWARD BRUCE, lawyer, educator; b. Pitts., Pa, Feb. 28, 1950; s. Elmer and Natalie (Rosenzweig) K.; m. Lonnie Jean Wilets, Dec. 12, 1977; children: Zachary B., Eli H. Student, Northwestern U., 1968-69; BA, U. Wis., 1972; JD, Georgetown U., 1976. Bar: Wis. 1976, Pa. 1981, U.S. Ct. Appeals D.C., 1978, U.S. Dist. Ct. Pa. 1981, U.S. Ct. Appeals (3rd cir.) 1982, U.S. Supreme Ct. 1983. Law clk. to justice Robert Hansen Wis. Supreme Ct., Madison, 1976-77; asst. atty. gen. dept. justice State of Wis., 1977-80; chief criminal div. U.S. Atty.'s Office, Phila., 1980-87; ptnr., chmn. litigation dept. Blank, Rome, Comisky & McCauley, Phila., 1987—, chmn. litigation dept., 1991—; regional, nat. instr. Nat. Inst. Trial Advocacy, Phila. and Boulder, Colo., 1987—; lectr. introduction to trial advocacy, evidence Temple U., Phila., 1984—; instr. Atty. Gen. Advocacy Inst., Washington, 1983-87; lectr. pub. corruption and trial advocacy various law enforcement and community groups, 1983—; cons. Pa. Valley Neighborhood Assn., 1984—. Contbr. to profl. jours. Advisor Phila. Police Dept. Reform Commn., 1986—; campaign issues dir. Pa. Atty. Gen. campaign, Phila., 1988. Mem. ABA, Fed. Bar Assn. (chmn. criminal law com.), Phila. Bar

Assn., Wis. Bar Assn., D.C. Bar Assn., U.S. Attys. Alumni Assn. (co-founder, mem. exec. bd.). Democrat. Jewish. Club: Vesper (Phila.). Office: Blank Rome Comisky McCauley 1200 Four Penn Ctr Philadelphia PA 19103

KLEIN, ILONA, Italian educator; b. Geneva, Switzerland, Mar. 16, 1956. Laurea max. cum laude, Università di Rome, 1981; MA in Italian, U. Wis., 1982, PhD in Italian, 1986. Teaching asst. Italian U. Wis., Madison, 1981-86; asst. prof. Italian Loyola Coll. Md., Balt., 1986—. Conbtbr. articles to profl. jours., chpts. to books. Loyola Coll. in Md. faculty devel. summer grantee, 1988, 89, NEH travel to collections grantee, 1989; Albert Markham Traveling fellow, U. Wis., 1988-89, exchange fellow, 1984-85; L'Aquila scholar, U. Pa., summer 1983. Mem. MLA, Am. Assn. Tchrs. Italian, Rocky Mt. Modern Lang. Assn., Am. Assn. for Italian Studies. Office: Loyola Coll Modern Lang Dept 4501 N Charles St Baltimore MD 21210-2601

KLEIN, LAWRENCE ROBERT, economist, educator; b. Omaha, Sept. 14, 1920; s. Leo Byron and Blanche (Monheit) K.; m. Sonia Adelson, Feb. 15, 1947; children: Hannah, Rebecca, Rachel, Jonathan. B.A., U. Calif.-Berkeley, 1942; Ph.D., MIT, 1944; M.A., Lincoln Coll., Oxford U., 1957; LL.D. (hon.), U. Mich., 1977, Dickinson Coll., 1981; Sc.D. (hon.), Widener Coll., 1977, Elizabethtown Coll., 1981, Ball State U., 1982, Technion, 1982, U. Nebr., 1983; Dr. honoris causa, U. Vienna, 1977; Dr.Ed., Villanova U., 1978; Dr. (h.c.), Bonn U., 1974, Free U. Brussels, 1979, U. Paris, 1979, U. Madrid, 1980. Faculty U. Chgo., 1944-47; research assoc. Nat. Bur. Econ. Research, 1948-50; faculty U. Mich., 1949-54; research assoc. Survey Research Center, 1949-54, Oxford Inst. Stats., 1954-58; faculty U. Pa., Phila., 1958—, prof., 1958—, Univ. prof., 1964—, Benjamin Franklin prof., 1968—; vis. prof. Osaka U., Japan, 1960, U. Colo., 1962, CUNY, 1962-63, 82, Hebrew U., 1964, Princeton U., 1966, Stanford U., summer 1968, U. Copenhagen, 1974; Ford vis. prof. U. Calif. at Berkeley, 1968, Inst. for Advanced Studies, Vienna, 1970, 74; cons. Canadian Govt., 1947, UNCTAD, 1966, 67, 75, 77, 80, McMillan Co., 1965-74, E.I. du Pont de Nemours, 1966-68, State of N.Y., 1969, AT&T, 1969, Fed. Res. Bd., 1973, UNIDO, 1973-75, Congl. Budget Office, 1977—, Council Econ. Advisers, 1977-80; chmn. bd. trustees Wharton Econometric Forecasting Assocs., Inc., 1969-80, chmn. profl. bd., 1980—; trustee Maurice Falk Inst. for Econ. Research, Israel, 1969-75; adv. council Inst. Advanced Studies, Vienna, 1977—; chmn. econ. adv. com. Gov. of Pa., 1976-78; mem. com. on prices Fed. Res. Bd., 1968-70; prin. investigator econometric model project Brookings Instn., 1963-72, Project LINK, 1968—; sr. adviser Brookings Panel on Econ. Activity, 1970—; mem. adv. com. Inst. Internat. Econs., 1983; coordinator Jimmy Carter's Econ. Task Force, 1976; mem. adv. bd. Strategic Studies Center, Stanford Research Inst., 1974-76. Author: The Keynesian Revolution, 1947, Textbook of Econometrics, 1953, An Econometric Model of the United States, 1929-1952, 1955, Wharton Econometric Forecasting Model, 1967, Essay on the Theory of Economic Prediction, 1968, An Introduction to Econometric Forecasting and Forecasting Models, 1980; Author-editor: Brookings Quar. Econometric Model of U.S.; Ecometric Model Performance, 1976, Lectures in Econometrics, 1983; Editor: Internat. Econ. Rev, 1959-65; asso. editor, 1965—; Editorial bd.: Empirical Econs, 1976—. Recipient William F. Butler award N.Y. Assn. Bus. Economists, 1975; Golden Slipper Club award, 1977; Pres.'s medal U. Pa., 1980; Alfred Nobel Meml. prize in econs., 1980. Fellow Econometric Soc. (past pres.), Am. Acad. Arts and Scis., Nat. Assn. Bus. Economists; mem. Am. Philos. Soc., Nat. Acad. Scis., Social Sci. Research Council (fellow 1945-46, 47-48, com. econ. stability, dir. 1971-76), Am. Econ. Assn. (John Bates Clark medalist 1959, exec. com. 1966-68, pres. 1977), Eastern Econ. Assn. (pres. 1974-76). Office: U Pa Sch of Arts & Scis Dept Econs 3718 Locust Walk Philadelphia PA 19104-6209

KLEIN, MICHAEL ELIHU, physician; b. N.Y.C., Apr. 6, 1946; s. Leo and Edith (Rigrod) K.; m. Elizabeth Angela McGehee, Oct. 8, 1988; children: Michael, Debbie, Daniel. BA, Wesleyan U., Middletown, Conn., 1967; MD, Yale U., 1972, MPH, 1972. Diplomate Am. Bd. Internal Medicine. Asst. dir. hematology U. Md., Balt., 1979-83; sr. investigator U. Md. Cancer Ctr., Balt., 1979-83; pvt. practice specializing in hematology/oncology Cowley Assocs., Camp Hill, Pa., 1983—; cons. in hematology and oncology Polyclinic Hosp., Harrisburg, Pa., 1983—, Holy Spirit Hosp., Camp Hill, 1983—. Author: Political Dynamics National Health Insurance in New York, 1972; contbr. articles to profl. jours., chpts. to books. Founder, bd. dirs. Number Nine, New Haven, 1971. Comdr. lt. USPHS, 1974-77. Mem. AMA, Am. Soc. Clin. Research, Am. Soc. Clin. Oncology, Am. Soc. Hematology, Am. Legion, Masons, Balt. Blood Club (pres. 1979-83). Office: Cowley Associates 425 N 21st St Camp Hill PA 17011-2223

KLEIN, MICHAEL JAY, accountant, consultant; b. Balt., Oct. 31, 1947; s. Jack T. and Sarah B. (Flitt) K.; m. Arlene Hess, Sept. 4, 1969; children: Evan, Joey. BS, U. Md., 1969. CPA, Md. Staff acct. Alexander Grant & Co., Balt., 1970-75, rev. dept. head, 1975-79; dir. small bus. dept. Grant Thornton (formerly Alexander Grant), Balt., 1979-86, sr. ptnr., 1986—. Bd. dirs. Fellowship of Lights, Balt., 1975-80, Md. Food Com., Balt., 1988-90, The Chimes, Balt., 1990—. Mem. Nat. Retail Fedn. (bd. dirs. N.Y.C. chpt. 1988—). Office: Grant Thornton Two Hopkins Pla Baltimore MD 21201

KLEIN, MORTON, industrial engineer, educator; b. N.Y.C., Aug. 9, 1925; s. Norbert and Lottie (Wigdor) K.; m. Gloria Ritterband, July 31, 1949; children: Lisa, Melanie. B.S.M.E., Duke U., 1946; M.S., Columbia U., 1952, D.Engring. Sci., 1957. Engr. Picatinny Arsenal, Dover, N.J., 1950-54; instr. Sch. Engring and Applied Sci., Columbia U., N.Y.C., 1956; asst. prof. Sch. Engring and Applied Sci., Columbia U., 1957-61, asso. prof., 1961-69, prof. ops. research, 1969—, chmn. dept. indsl. engring. and ops. research, 1982-85; cons. to industry, govt. Author: (with Cyrus Derman) Probability and Statistical Inference for Engineers, 1959; editor: Management Science, 1960-77; research and pubs. on prodn. planning, scheduling early cancer detection examinations, network flows and ops. research. Served with USN, 1943-46. Mem. Ops. Research Soc. Am. Inst. Mgmt. Scis., Am. Inst. Indsl. Engrs., Pi Tau Sigma, Alpha Pi Mu, Omega Rho. Office: Columbia U 301 A SW Mudd New York NY 10027

KLEIN, PAUL E., insurance company executive, lawyer; b. N.Y.C., Apr. 26, 1934. AB, Cornell U., 1956; JD, Harvard U., 1960. Bar: Mich. 1960, Ill. 1965, N.Y. 1967, U.S. Supreme Ct. 1977, U.S. Ct. Appeals (2d cir.) 1980. Atty. Dow Chem. Co., Midland, Mich., 1960-65; assoc. Gunther & Choka, Chgo., 1965-66; atty. Esso Rsch. & Engring. Co., Linden, N.J., 1966-67; sr. mng. editor Matthew Bender & Co., N.Y.C., 1967-72; assoc. gen. counsel N.Y. Life Ins. Co., N.Y.C., 1972-80, v.p., assoc. gen. counsel, 1980-84; v.p., counsel Huggins Fin. Svcs., Inc., N.Y.C., 1984-86; exec. fin. svcs. office Ernst & Young, N.Y.C., 1986—; adj. asst. prof. L.I. U., 1972-79, adj. assoc. prof., 1979-80. Columnist Jour. Real Estate Taxation; writer; editor. Mem. ABA (past chmn. subcom. on life ins. cos./ins. cos. com., sect. taxation), Assn. Bar City N.Y. (com. on ins. law), Assn. Life Ins. Counsel (sec.-treas. 1979-83, bd. govs. 1983-87), N.Y. State Bar Assn. Office: Ernst & Young 277 Park Ave New York NY 10172-0003

KLEIN, PHILIP ALEXANDER, economist; b. Austin, Tex., Oct. 8, 1927; s. David Ballin and Rose (Schaffer) K.; m. Margaret A. McCormack, May 20, 1961; children—Kathleen Monico, Alan Schaffer. B.A., U. Tex., 1948, M.A., 1949; Ph.D., U. Calif., Berkeley, 1958. Instr. Carleton Coll., Northfield, Minn., spring 1955; mem. faculty Pa. State U., State College, 1955—, prof. econs., 1965—; rsch. assoc. Nat. Bur. Econ. Rsch., 1955-70, 73-79, Ctr. Internat. Bus. Cycle Rsch., Columbia U., 1979—; vis. prof. San Francisco State U., summer, 1963, U. Hawaii, summer, 1967, Inst. Europeen D'Adminstrn. des Affairs, Fontainbleau, France, 1963-64, 65, 66, 67, Mills Coll., spring, 1982; acad. visitor London Sch. Econs., 1973-74, 81; disting. Fulbright fellow U. Siena, Italy, 1989; adj. scholar Am. Enterprises Inst., Washington, 1976—; cons. UN, Ctr. Devel. Planning Projections Policies 1973, OECD, Paris, 1978-81, EEC, Brussels, 1979-82, World Bank, Washington, 1986, 87, 88. Mem. editorial bd. Internat. Jour. Forecasting, 1986—, Jour. Econ. Issues, 1976-81, 85-87; contbr. articles to profl. jours., chpts. to books. Served with M.C., AUS, 1944-47. Recipient Distinction in Social Scis. award Pa. State U., 1981; Fulbright fellow, 1963, 70, 89. Mem. Econs. Assn., Assn. Evolutionary Econs. (pres. 1977, Veblen-Commons award 1990), Assn. Comparative Econs., Phi Beta Kappa (pres. chpt. 1981). Home: 719 S Sparks St State College PA 16801-4114 Office: Pa State U 516 Kern Grad Bldg University Park PA 16802

KLEIN, RICHARD, botany educator; b. Chgo., Mar. 17, 1923; s. Harry and Grace (Flora) K.; m. Deana Tarson, Sept. 13, 1947. BS, U. Chgo., 1947, MS, 1949, PhD, 1951. Curator N.Y. Bot. Garden, Bronx, 1953-67; prof. U. Vt., Burlington, 1967—; cons. Time-Life Corp., N.Y.C., 1960-64, Union Carbide Corp., Westchester, N.Y., 1962-66. Author: Research Methods in Plant Science, The Green World, 1st and 2d edit., Discovering Plants, Principles of Plant Science. With U.S. Army, 1942-46. Recipient Bausch & Lomb Sci. medal Bausch & Lomb Corp., 1950; U. scholar U. Vt., 1989. Office: U Vt Marsh Life Sch Bldg Burlington VT 05405

KLEIN, STEPHEN THOMAS, symphony orchestra executive; b. Cleve., Mar. 9, 1947; s. Howard B. and Lilly (Gatchell) K.; m. Mary Ussery, Nov. 19, 1972; children—William Howard, Sarah Katherine. B.F.A., Boston U., 1970. Orch. Mgr. Cleve. Orch., 1978-82; exec. dir. Denver Symphony Orch., Colo., 1982-85, Nat. Symphony Orch., Washington, 1985—. Office: Nat Symphony Orch John F Kennedy Ctr Washington DC 20566

KLEIN, STEVEN GARY, personnel recruiting executive, personnel consultant; b. East Orange, N.J., Feb. 27, 1948; s. Lee and Lillian (Schneiderman) K.; m. Robin Beth Lehrer, Dec. 24, 1973; children: Jeffrey Michael, Jason Matthew. Cert. pers. cons. Mgr. Avco Pers. Svcs., East Orange, 1971-72; v.p. ops. Bus. Career, Ltd., Fairfield, N.J., 1972-73; pres. Century Pers. Svcs., Inc., Fairfield, 1974—. With USN, 1966-70. Recipient Presidents award N.J. Assn of Pers. Cons., 1983, 84, 85, Robert Allison award, 1986. Mem. Nat. Assn. Pers. Cons., N.J. Assn. Pers., Cons. (bd. dirs.), West Essex C. of C., Greater Wayne Area C. of C. Office: Century Pers Svc Inc 710 Rte 46 Fairfield NJ 07004-1540

KLEIN, SUSAN LYNN, financial analyst; b. Ft. Dix, N.J., June 5, 1967; d. Maurice and Judith Lee (Granoff) K. BS with honors in Fin. magna cum laude, Syracuse U., 1989. Fin. analyst Merrill Lynch & Co., N.Y.C., 1989—. Mem. Beta Gamma Sigma, Phi Kappa Phi.

KLEIN, SUSAN MARSHA, nursing service director, facility administrator, marketing consultant; b. Washington, May 23, 1953; d. Neil Bernard and Frances (Bass) Kabatchnick; m. Leigh Forrest Klein, June 16, 1974; children: Allison Michele, Scott Joseph. Diploma in nursing, Sinai Hosp. Sch. of Nursing, 1974; cert. legal asst. program, George Washington U., 1984. RN, Md. Educator childbirth, cardiopulmonary resuscitation Parent & Child, Inc., Bethesda, Md., 1978-85; instr. arthritic aquatic Jewish Community Ctr., Rockville, Md., 1983-84; legal asst. Kabatchnick & Kabatchnick, Washington, 1984; dir. accesible seating and svcs. ctr. mgmt. Capital Ctr. (Md.), Patriot Ctr. (Va.), Balt. Arena, Springfield (Mass.) Civ. Ctr., Springfield Symphony Hall, Balt. Arena, 1987—; mem. accesibility adv. coun. Box Office Mgmt. Inst., 1987—; pres., chmn. bd. Disabled Mktg. Cons., 1989—; v.p. Success Network, Inc., 1989—. Bd. dirs. Montgomery County Heart Assn., 1977-80; vol. chmn. com. for tchr. svcs. Parent & Child, Inc., 1978-91; v.p. Hadassah, 1980-81; rec. sec. Glenallan Elem. Sch. PTA, 1986-87, pres. 1987-89, E. Brooke Lee Mid. Sch., 1989-90; mem. Montgomery County Sch. Bd. Task Force on Arts, 1990-91; v.p. B'nai Shalom of Olney Sisterhood, 1990-91. Recipient Mid-Atlantic Regional award B'nai Brith, 1977, Hon. Mention for CPR, Montgomery County Heart Assn., 1977, Ann. award for Community Svc. Met. Washington Pub. Health Assn., 1978; named one of Outstanding Young Women in Am., 1980, Five Outstanding Young Marylanders, 1980. Mem. NAFE, Internat. Platform Assn., Nat. Assn. Profl. Cons., POWERS (bd. dirs. 1989—), Greater Gaithersburg Jaycee Women (external v.p. 1980-81), Md. Jayceetees (arthritis prog. mgr. 1980-83). Home and Office: Disabled Mktg Cons 1944 Autumn Ridge Cir Silver Spring MD 20906-5826

KLEIN, TOM CHAIM, accountant; b. Oslo, Norway, Sept. 21, 1951; came to U.S., 1954; s. Mendel Moses and Anna (Kohn) K.; m. Charna R. Kesler, July 23, 1975; children: Rochel, Mordechai, Rivka, David. BS in Acctg., Wayne State U., 1973; MBA in Taxation, Baruch Coll., 1980. CPA, N.Y. Staff acct. various CPA firms, 1974-77; mgr. tax Ernst & Young, N.Y.C., 1977-85; pvt. practice N.Y.C., 1985—. Contbr. articles to mags. Pres. Cong Crown of Israel, Bklyn., 1988—. Mem. AICPA, N.Y. State Soc. of CPAs, Bikur Cholim of Boro Park. Jewish. Office: 450 7th Ave New York NY 10123-0101

KLEIN, WILLIAM, II, lawyer; b. N.Y.C, June 18, 1919; s. Jacob and Gertrude (Bok) K.; m. Faith Z. Klein, Oct. 12, 1947 (div. Oct. 1980); children: William L., Nancy J., Margaret A.m. Sara Klein, Dec. 31, 1981 (div. Apr. 1991). BA, NYU, 1941; LLB, Yale U., 1943. Bar: N.Y. (2d cir.) 1943, U.S. Supreme Ct. 1968. Assoc. Hays, St. John, Abramson & Heilbron, N.Y.C., 1943-48, ptnr., 1949-58; gen. counsel ABC Internat. TV Co., Inc., N.Y.C., 1959-63; pvt. practice, N.Y.C., 1964-68; ptnr. Austrian, Lance & Stewart, P.C., N.Y.C., 1968-78; profl. corp. ptnr. Tenzer, Greenblatt, Fallon & Kaplan, N.Y.C., 1978-89, counsel, 1989—; assoc. gen. counsel Am. Soc. Travel Agts., Assn. Precious Stone dealers, Composers and Authors Guild, Authors League Am., N.Y.C., 1943-58; lectr. to internat. bankers and corp. execs., Geneva, 1989. Contbr. articles to legal jours. Mem. ABA, N.Y. State Bar Assn., Assn. Bar City N.Y., Washington Square U. Alumni Assn. (bd. dirs.), N.Y. U. Alumni Coun. Home: 120 E 34th St New York NY 10016-4609

KLEINELP, WILLIAM CHARLES, III, biology educator, editor; b. Yonkers, N.Y., Apr. 4, 1948; s. William Charles II and Lillian (Chytraus) K.; m. Mary Collins. BA, Fairleigh Dickinson U., 1970, MS, 1972; postgrad., William Paterson Coll., 1984-88. Tchr. sci. Dwight Morrow High Sch., Englewood, N.J., 1969-70; grad. fellow Fairleigh Dickinson U., Teaneck, N.J., 1970-72; assoc. prof. biology Middlesex County Coll., Edison, N.J., 1972&; critical editor W.C. Brown Publs., Dubuque, Iowa, 1981-87, Harper & Row, N.Y.C., 1985-88, Benjamin Cummings, Boston, 1986; editor Wood River Publs., North Brunswick, N.J., 1988—. Author: Investigations in Science, 1986, Experiments in Vertebrate Physiology, 1986, Experiments in Physiology, 1988; author computer module Anatomy and Physiology, 1987. Advisor Dept. Health, Piscataway, N.J., 1982; mem. Speakers Bur. Middlesex, Edison, 1986—. Recipient award N.J. Leukemia Soc., 1983. Mem. Am. Inst. Biol. Sci., AAAS, News in Physiologic Sci. Office: Middlesex County Coll 155 Mll Rd PO Box 3050 Edison NJ 08818-3050

KLEINER, ARNOLD JOEL, television station executive; b. N.Y.C., Apr. 7, 1943; s. Leo and Hannah K.; m. Carol Dunn, Aug. 15, 1965; children: Kim, Kerri, Keith. BBA, Pace Coll. 1967. Account exec. KDKA Radio, Pitts., 1968-69, WJZ-TV, Balt., 1969-71, TVAR, Chgo., 1971-72; sales mgr. WBZ-TV, Boston, 1972-74, TVAR (Group W), N.Y.C., 1974-75; gen. sales mgr. WJZ-TV, Balt., 1975-78; dir. sales WPVI-TV, Phila., 1978-81; v.p., gen. mgr. WMAR-TV, Balt., 1981—; chmn. media rels. com. United Way of Cen. Md., Balt., 1982-84; co-chmn. Md. reg. NCCJ, 1986-90, sr. co-chair, 1990-91; bd. dirs. Levindale, Balt., 1983-84; mem. adv. bd. Md. Fedn. Parents for Drug Free Use, Balt., 1986—, William Donald Schaefer Ctr. for Pub. Policy, Balt., 1986—; chmn. edn. com. Greater Balt. Com., 1986—, bd. dirs., 1989—, pres. chamber div., 1991—, Coll. of Notre Dame, Md., 1989—; mem. Mayor's Coordinating Com. on Criminal Justice, Balt., 1983-88, Variety Club of Md., 1984, Johns Hopkins Children Ctr.'s Devel. Com., 1984—; bd. dirs. Balt. Reads, Inc., Greater Balt. Com.; chmn. adv. com. Mayor's Office Internat. Programs; bd. dirs. Alvin Ailey Dance Theater Found. of Maryland, Inc., 1990—. Recipient Victorine Q. Adams Humanitarian award, Am. Men's ORT Community Achievement award, 1986. Mem. Md./D.C. Broadcasters Assn. (dir. 1984), TV Bur. Advt. (sales adv. com. 1975-78), Advt. Assn. of Balt., Advt. Club of Balt., Balt. Jewish Coun. (bd. dirs., mem. exec. com. 1985—), Nat. Assn. Broadcasters. Office: Sta WMAR-TV 6400 York Rd Baltimore MD 21212-2198

KLEINER, HENRY THOMAS, physician; b. Havana, Cuba, Jan. 21, 1922; came to U.S., 1923; s. Abraham Kleiner and Ida Nishnikoff; m. Eleanora Tubis; children: Suzanne Purdy, Pamela Gibbs. BA, U. Pa., 1941-44; DMS, Hahnemann Med. Coll., Phila., 1945-49. Diplomate Am. Bd. Psychiatry and Neurology. Intern Mt. Sinai Hosp., Phila., 1949-50; resident in psychiat. Phila. Psychiat. Ctr., 1950-51; resident U. Pa. Hosp., Phila., 1951-53; cons. student health svc. U. Pa., Phila., 1951-55; cons. Family Svc., Media, Pa., 1957-70. With USPHS, 1955-57. Mem. Phila. Assn. for Psychoanalysis (pres. 1974-76, cert. tng. and supr. analyst, 1968, chmn. ednl. com. 1980—), Am. Psychoanalytic Assn., Internat. Psychoanalytic Assn.

KLEINMAN, ARTHUR MICHAEL, medical anthropologist, psychiatrist, educator; b. N.Y.C., Mar. 11, 1941; s. Marcia F. (Kaplan) K.; m. Joan Andrea Ryman, Mar. 20, 1965; children: Peter John, Anna Simone. A.B., Stanford U., 1962, M.D., 1967; M.A., Harvard U., 1974. Diplomate: Nat. Bd. Med. Examiners, Am. Bd. Neurology and Psychiatry. Med. intern Yale-New Haven Hosp., 1967-68; surgeon USPHS, Bethesda, Md., Taiwan, 1968-70; resident in psychiatry Mass. Gen. Hosp., Boston, 1972-75; assoc. prof. U. Wash., Seattle, 1976-79, prof. psychiatry and anthropology, 1979-82; prof. med. anthropology and psychiatry Harvard U., Cambridge, Mass., 1982—, chmn. dept. social medicine, dir. Ctr. for Study Culture and Medicine, 1991—. Author: Patients and Healers in the Context of Culture, 1980 (Wellcome medal Royal Anthrop. Inst.), Social Origins of Distress and Disease, 1986, The Illness Narratives, 1988, Rethinking Psychiatry, 1988; co-editor: Relevance of Social Science for Medicine, 1981, Culture and Depression, 1985, Pain as Human Experience, 1992; editor-in-chief: Culture, Medicine and Psychiatry: A Jour. of Internat. Cross-Cultural Rsch., 1976-86. Recipient Rsch. award NIMH, 1977-79, Rockefeller Found., 1983-86, 88-89, NSF,1983-86, R.W. Johnson Found., 1988-89; grantee NIMH, 1984—, Carnegie Corp., 1990-92, MacArthur Found., 1992-94, Rockefeller Found., 1992-94; Guggenheim fellow, 1992. Fellow AAAS, Am. Psychiat. Assn., Am. Anthrop. Assn., Inst. Medicine of Nat. Acad. Scis. (chmn. com. on chronic pain, illness behavior and disability), Royal Anthrop. Inst., Am. Acad. Arts and Scis. Office: Harvard U 330 William James Hall Kirkland St Cambridge MA 02138

KLEINMAN, HYNDA KAREN, cell biologist; b. Boston, May 20, 1947; d. Ernest and Doris (Riman) Fisher; m. Joel C. Kleinman, Dec. 28, 1968; children: Dana, Ruth. BS, Simmons Coll., 1969; MS, MIT, 1971, PhD, 1974. Postdoctoral fellow Tufts U., Boston, 1974-75; staff fellow Nat. Inst. Dental Rsch. Nat. Inst. Dental Rsch., NIH, Bethesda, Md., 1975-79, rsch. chemist, 1980-89, chief cell biology, 1985—; vice chmn. Gordon Conf., N.H., 1990; mem. adv. com. Geisinger Inst., Danville, Pa., 1989; mem. program com. East Coast Connective Tissue Conf., Bethesda, 1990; Howard Hughes med. scholar adviser, 1990-93. Patentee in field. Recipient Helen Hay Whitney Found. award, 1975, Doerenkamp-Zbinden award Johns Hopkins U., 1987. Mem. AAAS, Am. Assn. Cell Biology (program com. 1989-90, sr. women in sci. award 1991), Soc. Complex Carbohydrates, Tissue Culture Assn. Office: Nat Inst Dental Rsch NIH 30/407 Bethesda MD 20892

KLEINMAN, LEONARD ISRAEL, pediatrician, pediatrics educator; b. Bklyn., June 29, 1935; s. Abraham Morris and Lillian (Rabinowitz) K.; m. Yorkette Rita Solomon, Oct. 8, 1961; children: Jonathan, David, Miriam. AB, Columbia U., 1956; MD, SUNY, Bklyn., 1960. Resident in pediatrics Mass. Gen. Hosp., Boston, 1960-62; rsch. fellow Harvard U., Boston, 1962-65; Fullbright fellow U. Milan (Italy), 1965-66; asst. prof. pediatrics and physiology U. Cin., 1966-70, assoc. prof. pediatrics and physiology, 1970-75, prof. pediatrics and physiology, 1975-83; prof. pediatrics SUNY, Stony Brook, 1983—; dir. neonatology SUNY, Stony Brook, 1983—. Contbr. articles to profl. jours. Pres. North Avondale Synagogue, Cin., 1974-83; v.p. Yavneh Day Sch., Cin., 1972-75. Fogarty Internat. fellow NIH, 1975-76. Mem. Am. Physiol. Soc., Am. Pediatric Soc., Am. Acad. Pediatrics, Com. on Fetus and Newborn, Internat. Soc. Nephrology, N.Y. Acad. Sci., AAAS, Soc. Pediaric Rsch. Jewish. Office: Coll of Medicine SUNY Dept of Pediatrics Health Science Ctr Stony Brook NY 11794-8111

KLEINMAN, MARTIN, health care executive; b. Bklyn., Aug. 16, 1952; s. Abraham and Ethel (Fischman) K.; m. Beth Indig, Mar. 12, 1974; children: Deena, Joseph S., Aliza. BA, Bklyn. Coll., 1974. Exec. dir. Brighton Sr. Citizens Cen., Bklyn., 1974-78; v.p. sales Sanidown Feather Corp., Bklyn., 1978-80; branch mgr. Quality Care, Inc., 1980-82; pres. and chief exec. officer Americare, Inc., Bklyn., 1982—. Contbr. articles to popular mags. Democrat. Jewish. Office: Americare Inc 929 Kings Hwy Brooklyn NY 11223-2336

KLEINROCK, VIRGINIA BARRY, public relations executive; b. Boston, Nov. 5, 1947; d. Robert Edmund and Anne Marie (Crowley) Barry; m. Lewis James Kleinrock, Dec. 15, 1984. AS, Garland Jr. Coll., Boston, 1967; BS, East Carolina U., 1969; MS, Simmons Coll., 1973; postgrad. Sch. Bus. Communications, Boston U., 1973, 86, 88. Tchr. Somerville (Mass.) Pub. Schs., 1969-70; tchr. Newton (Mass.) Pub. Schs., 1970-84, career edn. program coord., 1978-83; pres. Infinite Energy, Belmont, Mass., 1982—; cons. McKnight Pub. Co., Bloomington, Ill., 1976-82; publicity coord./intern Impact Communications, Boston, 1982. Contbr. articles to profl. jours. Recipient Commendation for Excellence for Pilot Occupational Training Program, New Eng. Assn. of Schs. and Colls., 1969. Mem. Pub. Rels. Soc. Am., Counselors Acad., Am. Home Econs. Assn., Home Economists in Bus. (exec. bd. 1985-87, chmn. program com. 1985-87), The Fashion Group, The Publicity Club of New Eng. (Disting. Svc. award 1984). Office: Infinite Energy 11 Hough Rd Belmont MA 02178-1104

KLEIN-SZANTO, ANDRES J. P., pathologist; b. Buenos Aires, Apr. 25, 1943; s. Geza and Madeleine K.-Z.; m. Maria U. Weyrauch, Dec. 30, 1972; children: Walter, Matias, Julian. MD, U. Buenos Aires, 1965, D.Med.Sci., 1970. Chief instr. dept. pathology U. Buenos Aires, 1967-73; staff scientist Argentine AEC, Buenos Aires, 1970-77; sr. med. scientist Oak Ridge (Tenn.) Nat. Lab., 1978-82; prof. U. Tex., Smithville, Houston, 1982-86; sr. pathologist and head exptl. histopathology service Fox Chase Cancer Ctr., Phila., 1986—; chief asst. dept. oral structural biology U. Zurich, 1974-76; mem. com. on role of tumor promoters, hormones, and other confactors in human cancer causation, Nat. Cancer Inst., Bethesda, Md., 1980, workshop on external radiation carcinogenesis, Oak Ridge, 1980, study sect. mechanisms of biol. and chem. prevention of carcinogenesis, NIH, Bethesda, 1981, chem. pathology study sect., 1986, 87-91, Am. Cancer Soc. reviewer for the rsch. devel. program, 1983. Assoc. editor: Acta Odontologica Latonoamericana, 1984—, Jour. of Cutaneous Pathology, 1981, editor-in-chief, 1981-83; editor 3 books; contbr. numerous articles to profl. jours., chpts. to books. Am. Assn. Cancer Rsch., AAAS, Radiation Rsch. Soc., Internat. Soc. Stereology, Internat. Acad. Pathology (sec. arg. div. 1978), European Soc. Pathology, Am. Assn. Pathologists. Office: Fox Chase Cancer Ctr 7701 Burholme Ave Philadelphia PA 19111-2497

KLEIS, JOHN DIEFFENBACH, physics consultant; b. Hamburg, N.Y., Feb. 1, 1912; s. Herbert and May Genevieve (Dieffenbach) K.; m. Marie Elizabeth Dahl, May 30, 1939; children: Lynne Marie, Cheryl Ann, John Dieffenbach. BA in Physics, U. Buffalo, 1932, MA in Physics, 1933; PhD in Physics, Yale U., 1936; Cert., Harvard U., 1957. Physicist Fan Steel Met. Corp., North Chgo., 1936-42, asst. dir. rsch., 1942-46, dir. rsch., 1946-52, v.p. rsch., 1952-58, v.p. mfg., 1958-69, dir., 1964-69; pres., v.p. Stern Metals, Mt. Vernon, N.Y., 1969-79, dir. rsch., 1979-82; cons. J.D. Kleis Assoc., Inc., Greenwich, Conn., 1982—; pres. John D. Kleis & Assocs., Inc., 1983—. Patentee in field. Recipient Ralph Armington Achievement award IEEE, 1991. Mem. IEEE (life, steering com. 1982-91). Republican. Home and Office: 161 Clapboard Ridge Rd Greenwich CT 02831

KLEMENTS, JOSEPH MICHAEL, lawyer; b. Cleve., May 17, 1953; s. Bernard J. and Marita A. (Best) K.; m. Elizabeth M. Melville, Sept. 6, 1978; children: William, Marita, David, Thomas. AB, Boston Coll., 1974; JD, Boston U., 1978. Assoc. Richardson and Tyler, Boston, 1978-83, ptnr., 1984—; mem. Cath. Lawyers Guild, Boston, 1988—. Chair, mem. Stoughton (Mass.) Planning Bd., 1981-91; mem. Stoughton (Mass.) Sch. Com., 1991—, Immaculate Conception Parish Fin. Com., Stoughton, Mass., 1988—; pres. Old Stoughton (Mass.) Mus. Soc., 1988—. Named Outstanding Family of Yr. Stoughton (Mass.) Jaycees, 1983. Mem. Mass. Bar Assn., Am. Bar Assn., Am. Transp. Assn. Office: Richardson & Tyler 15 Broad St Boston MA 02109-3803

KLEMM, RICHARD HENRY, investment company executive; b. N.Y.C., Aug. 10, 1931; s. Richard F. and Sophie (Leymann) K.; m. June Christ, Feb. 21, 1954; children: Janet, Lynda, Richard. BSCE, Bucknell U., 1953; MBA in Econs., NYU, 1964. Fin. planner N.Y. Tel., N.Y.C., 1956-65; div. mgr. AT&T Corp., N.Y.C., 1965-81; v.p. GTE Investment Mgmt. Corp., Stamford, Conn., 1981-85; sr. v.p. Warburg, Pincus Counsellors, N.Y.C., 1985-91; prin. Boxwood Inns, Akron, Pa., 1991—; prin. ExecuServ, Bernardsville, N.J., 1985—; bd. dirs. Ridge Oak, Inc., Basking Ridge, N.J., treas.-sec., 1990, v.p., 1991. Bd. dirs. Family Counselling Somerset County, Bound Brook, N.J., 1976-81, 85-87. Fellow Fin. Analysts Fedn.; mem. N.Y.

Soc. Security Analysts. Republican. Episcopalian. Office: Warburg Pincus Counsellors Inc 466 Lexington Ave New York NY 10017-3140

KLEMPERER, WILLIAM, chemistry educator; b. N.Y.C., Oct. 6, 1927; s. Paul and Margit (Freund) K.; m. Elizabeth Cole, Jan. 12, 1949; children—Joyce Hillary, Paul, Wendy Judith. A.B., Harvard U., 1950; Ph.D., U. Calif.-Berkeley, 1954. Instr. chemistry Harvard U., Cambridge, Mass., 1954-57, asst. prof., 1957-61, assoc. prof., 1961-65, prof., 1965—; asst. dir. NSF, Washington, 1979-81; vis. scientist Bell Telephone Lab., 1963-83; Evans lectr. Ohio State U., 1981, Pratt lectr. U. Va., 1984, Rollefson lectr. U. Calif., 1985, Oesper lectr. U. Cin., 1987, Kolthoff lectr. U. Minn., 1987, Mary E. Kapp lectr. Va. Commonwealth U., 1987, Linus Pauling Disting. lectr. Oreg. State U., 1988, Harry Emmett Gunning lectr. U. Alta., Can., 1988, Fritz London Meml. lectr. Duke U., 1989, Hinshelwood lectr. Oxford U., Eng., 1989, Neckers lectr. So. Ill. U., 1990. Served with A.C., USN, 1944-46. Recipient Wetherill medal Franklin Inst., 1978, Disting. Svc. medal NSF, 1981, Bomem Michelson award The Coblentz Soc., 1990. Fellow Am. Phys. Soc. (Earle Plyler prize 1983); mem. NAS, Am. Acad. Arts and Scis., Am. Chem. Soc. (Irving Langmuir award 1980). Home: 53 Shattuck Rd Watertown MA 02172-1310 Office: Harvard U 12 Oxford St Cambridge MA 02138-2900

KLEMPNER, MARK STEVEN JOEL, physician, research scientist, educator; b. Utica, N.Y., Jan. 18, 1949; s. Ben and Goldie (Rockoff) K.; m. Frances Borger, Sept. 9, 1979; children: Samuel Jacob, Jesse Maxwell, Hannah Rachel. Student, Tulane U., 1966-69; MD, Cornell U. Med. Coll., 1973. Diplomate Nat. Bd. Med. Examiners, Am. Bd. Internal Medicine, Am. Bd. Internal Medicine Subspecialty Infectious Disease. From intern to resident Mass. Gen. Hosp., Boston, 1973-75; clinical assoc. Nat. Inst. Health, Bethesda, Md., 1975-78; infectious disease cons. U.S.N. Med. Ctr., Bethesda, Md., 1976-78; asst prof. med. Tufts U. Sch. Med., Boston, Mass., 1978-83; asst. physician New England Med. Ctr., Boston, Mass., 1978-83; assoc. prof. med., assoc. prof., prof. medicine Tufts U. Sch. of Medicine, Boston, Mass., 1983—; assoc. editor Yearbook Infectious Diseases; editorial bd. Antimicrobial Agents & Chemotherapy; reviewer Jour. Infectious Diseases, Jour. Clinical Investigatio n, New England Jour. Medicine, Jour. Leukocyte Biology, Inflammation, Jour. I. Contbr. articles to numerous profl. jours. With USPHS, 1978—. Tulane U. scholar, Teagle scholar Cornell U. Med. Coll.; recipient Dean William Mecklenburg Polk Prize in Medicine, Cornell U. Med. Coll., Excellence in Teaching award Tufts U. Sch. of Medicine. Mem. AAAS, ACP, Am. Soc. Microbiology, Infectious Diseases Soc. Am., Am. Fed. Clinical Rsch., Am. Soc. Clinical Investigation, Phi Eta Sigma, Alpha Omega Alpha. Office: Dept Med Div Infectious Diseases New England Med Ctr Boston MA 02111-1526

KLENE, ROGER RALPH, financial investment company executive; b. Greensburg, Ind., May 4, 1949; s. Ralph J. and Doris (Lomax) K.; m. Deborah Louise Vehr, June 23, 1973; children: Megan Elizabeth, Sarah Jenifer. BS in Criminal Justice, Ind. U., 1974; MS in Indsl. Psychology-Orgnl. Behavior, U. New Haven, West Haven, Conn., 1978; MBA, U. Hartford, West Hartford, Conn., 1990. Sr. investigator United Techs. Corp., Hartford, Conn., 1974-82, exec. asst. to chmn., 1982-86, dep. dir. corp. aircraft dept., 1986-87; assoc. Harry Gray Assocs., Farmington, Conn., 1987-90, prin., 1991—. Sgt. U.S. Army, 1967-70, Vietnam. Republican. Congregationalist. Home: 32 Hope Valley Rd Amston CT 06231-1310 Office: Harry Gray Assocs 30 Stanford Dr Farmington CT 06032-2453

KLENOFF, BRUCE HOWARD, otolaryngologist; b. N.Y.C., May 6, 1944; s. Harry and Anne (Sager) K.; m. Joyce Ellen Potash, Nov. 30, 1968; children: Heather, Jason, Mindy. BS, Rensselaer Poly. Inst., 1965; MD, Tufts U., 1969. Diplomate Am. Bd. Otolaryngology. Resident in gen. surgery Albert Einstein Hosp., Bronx, N.Y., 1969-70, St. Elizabeth's Hosp., Boston, 1972-73; resident in otolaryngology, head and neck surgery Harvard U., Boston, 1973-76; dir. dept. eye, ear, nose and throat St. Joseph Hosp., Stamford, Conn., 1990—; attending physician Stamford Hosp. Inventor swim radio, 1987. Lt. comdr. USCG, USPHS, 1970-72. Fellow ACS, Am. Acad. Otolaryngology; mem. AMA, Conn. Med. Assn., Fairfield County Med. Soc. Office: 188 North St Stamford CT 06901

KLEPONIS, JEROME ALBERT, dentist; b. Ashland, Pa., July 26, 1955; s. Albert Francis and Anna Mae Catherine (Burns) K. BS in Biology summa cum laude, Allentown Coll. St. Francis de Sales, 1977; DMD, U. Pa., 1981. Resident in gen. dentistry Geisinger Med. Ctr., Danville, Pa., 1981-82; assoc. Office of Dr. Stephen D. Eingorn, Bethlehem, Pa., 1982-83; dir. dental svcs. Lock Haven (Pa.) Hosp., 1983-86; sr. staff dentist Tri-Town Med. Ctr., Williamstown, Pa., 1986-87; dir. dental svcs. Embreeville Ctr., Coatesville, Pa., 1987-92, Danville (Pa.) State Hosp., 1992—. Volunteer Chester County Buddies, West Chester, Pa., 1990—. Fellow Am. Assn. Hosp. Dentists, Acad. Gen. Dentistry; mem. ADA, Acad. Dentistry for Handicapped, Am. Soc. Geriatric Dentistry, Pa. Dental Assn., Tri-County Dental Soc., Am. Soc. Dentistry for Children, Am. Soc. Forensic Odontology, Am. Assn. Mental Retardation, Elks, Am. Hose Co., Am. Legion Sons of Vets., Allentown Coll. Alumni Assn. (bd. dirs. 1983—, sec. bd. 1985-87, pres. bd. 1991—), Psi Omega (editor Zeta chpt. 1979-81). Roman Catholic. Home: 1201 Arch St Ashland PA 17921-1213 Office: Danville State Hosp PO Box 700 Danville PA 17821-0700

KLEPPER, ANNE, journalist, speechwriter; b. Denver, Sept. 19, 1920; d. Max and Ethel (Perlstein) Lopatin; m. Sidney Lester Klepper, Feb. 3, 1951; 1 child, Leslie Klepper Arkin. BA magna cum laude, U. Colo., 1942. Intern Nat. Inst. Pub. Affairs, Washington, 1942; panel asst. disputes Nat. War Labor Bd., Washington, 1942-45; dep., chief of agy. Nat. Railway Labor Panel, Washington, 1946-47; researcher, reporter Time, N.Y.C., 1948-54; speechwriter, spl. asst. to pres., dir. corp. contbns. Time, Inc., 1955-73; sr. rsch. assoc., dir. contributions mgmt. inst. Conf. Bd., N.Y.C., 1974—; bd. dirs. WNYC Found., N.Y.C., 1984—. Bd. dir. Nat. Charities Info. Bur., N.Y.C., 1969-81,. Home: 520 E 90th St New York NY 10128-7850 Office: The Conference Bd 845 3rd Ave New York NY 10022-6601

KLEPPER, WILLIAM M., II, academic dean; b. Ft. Wayne, Ind., Aug. 31, 1944; s. William M. and Patricia F. (Teeple) K.; m. Susan A. Epstein, June 6, 1966; children: William III, Caroline, Michael. BS, St. Louis U., St. Louis, Mo., 1966; MEd, St. Louis U., 1967, PhD, 1975; postgrad, U. Pa., 1979. Asst. dean of men U.S.C., 1967-69; assoc. dean of students St. Louis U., 1969-71; dir., housing Trenton State Coll., Trenton, NJ, 1971-74; dir. group student devel. svcs. Trenton State Coll., 1974-85, dean of student life, 1985—; adj. prof. grad. sch. bus. Columbia U.; co-dir. Nat. Assn. Student Pers. Adminstrs., Intentional Student Devel. and Retention Consortium, 1984-86; chair edn. bd. Nat. Assn. of Coll. Aux. Svcs., 1980-84; pres. Mid-Atlantic Assn. of Coll. and Univ. Housing Officers Internat., 1975. Editor/author New Directions for Higher Education, 1987; editor Journal of College and University Student Housing, 1971-77. Pres. Mercer County Bd. of Chosen Freeholders, N.J., 1981-84; mayor Ewing Township, N.J., 1978-80; pres. Ewing Township Bd. Edn., 1975-77. Recipient: Humanitarian Award, Friends of the Handicapped, Mercer County, N.J., 1984. Mem. Am. Assn. Higher Edn., Nat. Assn. Student Pers. Adminstrs., Phi Delta Kappa. Democrat. Home: 70 Jacobs Creek Rd Trenton NJ 08628-1704 Office: Trenton State Coll Hillwood Lakes PO Box 4700 Trenton NJ 08650-4700

KLERER, MELVIN, computer science educator, researcher; b. N.Y.C., Feb. 17, 1926; s. Benjamin and Sadie (Horowitz) K.; m. Leona Wilt, June 1, 1951 (div. Jan. 1975); children: Burton, Robert. BA, NYU, 1948, MS, 1950, PhD, 1954. Instr. CUNY, N.Y.C., 1952-53, 54-57; sr. rsch. assoc. Columbia U., N.Y.C., 1957-67; prof. NYU, N.Y.C., 1967-73, N.Y. Poly. U., N.Y.C., 1973—; vis. scientist Weizman Inst. Sci., Israel, 1973-74. Category editor Assn. Computing Machinery Computing Revs., 1987—; author: User-Oriented Computer Languages, 1987, Design of Very High Level Computer Language, 1991; co-author: A New Table of Indefinite Integrals, 1971; co-editor: Digital Computer User's Handbook, 1967, Interactive Systems for Experimental Mathematics, 1968; contbr. more than 100 articles to profl. jours. Mem. AAAS, Computer Soc. of IEEE (chmn. social implications com. 1970-71), Assn. Computing Machinery (various offices 1957—), Am. Assn. for Artificial Intelligence. Office: NY Polytech U 333 Jay St Brooklyn NY 11201-2990

KLESSIG, DANIEL FREDERICK, molecular biologist, educator; b. Fond du Lac, Wis., Feb. 24, 1949; s. Edgard and Verona (Stecker) K. BS, U. Wis., 1971; BS (hons.), U. Edinburgh, Scotland, 1973; PhD, Harvard U., 1978. Staff scientist Cold Spring Harbor (N.Y.) Lab., 1979-80; asst. prof. U. Utah Med. Sch., Salt Lake City, 1980-83, assoc. prof., 1983-85; prof., assoc. dir. Waksman Inst. Rutgers U., Piscataway, N.J., 1985—; cons. NPI, Salt Lake City, 1981-85; acad. adv. bd. Am. Cyanamid, Princeton, N.J., 1985-89. Contbr. articles to profl. jours. Marshall scholar Govt. Great Britain, 1971, Searle Found. scholar, 1982, McKnight Found. scholar, 1983; recipient Faculty Rsch. award Am. Cancer Soc., 1984; grantee NIH, NSF, USDA, Am. Cancer Soc., 1980—. Mem. Am. Soc. Microbiology, Am. Phytopathology Soc., Internat. Soc. for Plant Molecular Biology, Am. Plant Physiology Soc. Office: Wakeman Inst Rutgers U PO Box 759 Piscataway NJ 08855-0759

KLETSKY, EARL JUSTIN, college dean, electrical engineer; b. Springfield, Mass., July 22, 1930; s. Julius and Lillian D. (Penn) K.; m. Trudy J. Wolkenberg, Aug. 31, 1958; 1 child, Jeffrey. BSEE, MIT, 1951, MSEE, 1953; PhD in Elec. Engring., Syracuse U., 1961. 1st lt. USAF, Bedford, Mass., 1953-55; asst. prof. elec. engring. Syracuse (N.Y.) U., 1961-67, assoc. prof. elec. engring., 1967-82, prof. bioengring., 1982—, asst. dean coll. engring., 1982—. Contbr. over 20 articles to profl. jours. Named Torchiana fellow Netherlands Govt., 1955. Mem. IEEE, Am. Soc. Engring. Edn., Soc. Sigma Xi, N.Y. Acad. Sci. Home: 113 Humbert Ave Syracuse NY 13224-2251 Office: Syracuse U 223 Link Hall Syracuse NY 13244

KLETT, EDWIN LEE, lawyer; b. Clearfield, Pa., Dec. 8, 1935; s. John L. and Gertrude Elizabeth (Larson) K.; m. Janis Lynn Gibson; children: David, Lauren, Krista, Kirklin, Keenan. BS in Commerce and Finance, Bucknell U., 1957; JD, Dickinson Sch. Law, Carlisle, Pa., 1962. Bar: Pa. 1963, U.S. Dist. Ct. (we. dist.) Pa. 1963, U.S. Ct. Appeals (3d cir.) 1967, U.S. Ct. Appeals (6th cir.) 1985, U.S. Supreme Ct. 1983. Assoc. Eckert, Seamans, Cherin & Mellott, Pitts., 1962, ptnr., 1969; sr. ptnr., co-chmn. Klett Lieber Rooney & Schorling, Pitts., 1989—; trustee Dickinson Sch. Law, 1982—. Mem. Pa. State Transp. Adv. Bd., Harrisburg, Pa., 1985-88, Rep. State Fin. Com., Harrisburg, 1986—, Allegheny County Rep. Fin. Com., Pitts., 1987—. Fellow Internat. Acad. Trial Lawyers, Am. Coll. Trial Lawyers, Am. Bar Found., Am. Bar Inst.; mem. Am. Judicature Soc., Acad. Trial Lawyers Allegheny County (bd. govs. 1986-88, pres. 1988-89). Home: 151 Ordale Blvd Pittsburgh PA 15228-1525 Office: Klett Lieber Rooney & Schorling 1 Oxford Ctr 40th Fl Pittsburgh PA 15219

KLEVANA, LEIGHTON QUENTIN JOSEPH, lawyer; b. Czechoslovakia, Oct. 7, 1934 (born Am. citizen); s. Joseph V. and Bellina N. (Karlovsky) K.; B.A., Cornell U., 1957; postgrad. U. Paris, The Sorbonne, 1958; J.D., U. Va., 1961. Admitted to N.Y. bar, 1963, Vt. bar, 1971; assoc. atty. Meyer, Kissell, Matz & Seward, N.Y.C., 1961-63, Olwine, Connelly, Chase, O'Donnell & Weyher, 1963-67; sec. Helme Products, Inc., N.Y.C., 1967, sec., gen. counsel, 1967-70; v.p., sec., dir. Transit Air Freight, Inc., 1966-75; ptnr. law firm Mahady & Klevana, 1973-76, Klevana & Rounds, P.C., 1977-79; pres., dir. Windsor County Properties, Inc., 1974-76, Practicing Real Estate Inst., Inc., 1974—, Klevana Inst. Inc., 1984—, Klevana Group, Inc., 1987—, Leighton Klevana Profl. Seminars, Inc., 1991—, Connecticut River Valley Properties, Inc., 1976-79; assoc. Norwood Group Realty, Inc., 1981-87; asst. atty. gen., Vt., 1970-73. Home: 115 N Adams St Manchester NH 03104-2321 Office: PO Box 1447 Manchester NH 03105-1447

KLEYMAN, GRETA, accountant; b. Odessa, U.S.S.R., Feb. 7, 1967; came to U.S., 1975; d. Ilya and Sofia (Shapiro) Blekher; m. Alexander Kleyman, Aug. 30, 1986; children: Robert Gabriel, Henry Richard. BBA, Temple U., 1988. Acct., mgr. Andrew Paul Goldner & Co., Phila., 1986-88; acct. Fishbein & Co., Elkins Park, Pa., 1988-90; acctg. coord. Lindy Property Mgmt., Elkins Park, Pa., 1990-91; acct., bus. cons. Profl. Svcs., Inc., Phila., 1991—. Republican. Home: 378 Tomlinson Pl Philadelphia PA 19116-3238

KLIDE, ROBERT, marketing executive; b. N.Y.C., Aug. 29, 1949; s. Everett and Yetta (Hilsenrod) K.; m. Silvia Irene Margulies, May 26, 1973; children: Rebecca Lynn, Jessica Sue. BA in Math., Hunter Coll., N.Y.C., 1972; MBA, St. John's U., 1982. Sr. clk. Ametalco Inc., N.Y.C., 1973-75, supr. raw matls. dept., 1975-78; raw mineral adminstr. and analyst Amax Copper Inc., N.Y.C., 1978-80, contract and phys. position coord. cooper, 1980-81, asst. mgr. primary copper raw matls., 1981-84; mgr. primary raw matls. Amax Metal Products, N.Y.C. and Greenwich, 1984-88; mgr. metals mktg. Commodity Exchange, Inc., N.Y.C., 1988—; lectr. in field. Mem. Empire Metal Merchants Assn. (sec. 1991), Wire Assn. Internat., AIME (N.Y. Sect.), The Copper Club. Office: Commodity Exchange Inc Four World Trade Ctr New York NY 10048

KLIGER, JACK, magazine publisher. Pub. Glamour mag., N.Y.C. Office: Glamour 350 Madison Ave New York NY 10017-3704*

KLIMCZAK, JANICE BEVERLY, educator; b. New Britain, Conn., Jan. 25, 1944; d. Edward John and Mary Sophie (Knapp) Folcik; m. Joseph Clement Klimczak, Sept. 5, 1965. BS, Cen. Conn. State Coll., 1965. Cert. elem. and secondary sci. tchr., Mass. Tchr. grades 7-8 Dracut, Mass., 1966—; cons. U. Lowell, Mass. Supt., tchr. Sunday Sch. St. Casimir's Ch., Lowell, 1965—, sec., 1968—, organist and dir. choir, 1981—. Horace Mann grantee State of Mass., 1986-88. Mem. NEA, Mass. Tchrs. Assn., Dracut Tchrs. Assn. Polish National Catholic. Home: 268 Lakeview Ave Lowell MA 01850-2313 Office: Englesby Jr High Sch 1580 Lakeview Ave Dracut MA 01826-3392

KLIMENT, CHARLES KAREL, chemical company executive; b. Prague, Aug. 2, 1932; s. Charles and Marie (Zizkova) K.; m. Daniela Tuckova, June 29, 1957; children: Zuzana, Charles III. PhD in Chemistry, Tech. U. Prague, 1956. Head press rooms Czechoslovakian Gramophone Industry, 1956-60; dept. head Inst. Macromolecular Chemistry Czechoslovakia Acad. Scis., Prague, 1960-69; dir. process devel. Hydron Labs., New Brunswick, N.J., 1969-78; dir. polymer rsch. NPD Optical Corp., New Brunswick, 1978-83; v.p. rsch. and devel. S.K.Y. Polymers, Princeton, N.J., 1983-84, Tyndale Plains-Hunter Ltd., Ringoers, N.J., 1984-90, Kingston Techs. Inc., Dayton, N.J., 1990—. Contbr. articles to profl. jours.

KLINDT, STEVEN, art museum director; b. Davenport, Iowa, Dec. 18, 1947. BA in Art, U. Iowa, 1971, MA in Photography, 1974. Dir. Evanston (Ill.) Art Ctr., 1976-79, Mus. Contemporary Photography and Columbia Coll. Art Gallery, Chgo., 1979-84, Tweed Mus. Art, Duluth, Minn., 1984-89; exec. dir. The Queens Mus. of Art, Queens, N.Y., 1989—; pres., bd. dirs. Upper Midwest Conservation Assn., Mpls., 1986-87; commr. Duluth Pub. Arts Commn., 1986-87; panel mem. Minn. State Arts Bd., St. Pau., 1985-87. Editor: (exhibition catalogues) Nathan Lerner: Fifty Years of Photographic Inquiry, 1984, Minnesota Sculpture Collections, 1988, The Tweed Museum of Art: 30 Years, 1988. Mem. Assn. of Art Mus. Dirs. Club: Cliff Dwellers (Chgo.). Office: The Queens Mus of Art Flushing Meadow Corona Pk Flushing NY 11368

KLINE, EMANUEL, textile engineer; b. N.Y.C., Aug. 17, 1921; s. Bernard Julius and Sarah (Spatt) K.; m. Roslyn Zuckerman, Sept. 11, 1954; children: Brett M., Mark S., Ivan O., Eric A. Student, CCNY, 1937-39, Cooper Union Coll., 1939-41; BS, New Bedford Textile Inst., 1949. Treas. PTA, Great Neck (N.Y.) High Sch., 1974-76; trustee Great Neck Libr., 1979—, Great Neck Community Fund, 1980—, Great Neck Reform Dem. Assn., 1984—. Staff sgt. USAF, 1942-45. Home: 1 Moreland Ct Great Neck NY 11024-1704

KLINE, H. CHARLES, theater educator; b. Macomb, Ill., Feb. 24, 1929; s. Carl G. and Mabel (Davis) K.; . Ruth M. Fifield, Feb. 14, 1954; children: Natalie R., Kline Signor, Amy E. BS in Ed., Cen. Mo. State U., 1951; MFA, Yale U., 1954; PhD, U. Denver, 1963. Dean men, dir. forensics Cen. Mo. State U., Warrensburg, 1956-57; asst. prof., dirs. theater Wheaton Coll., Norton, Mass., 1957-58; dir. ednl. TV Colo. State U., Greeley, 1960-62; head drama-speech dept., dir. theater Drake U., Des Moines, 1963-64; prof. theater SUNY, Plattsburgh, 1964—, chmn. dept., 1970-75, 78-83, 89-90;, 1989-90; cons. in theater Diagnostic Ctr., 1990-91, Dannemora (N.Y.) State Prison, 1968-76; mem., bd. dirs. Pattsburgh Summer Theatre, 1964-66, 68-83, 88-91, Ctr. Rsch. Frontier Theatre, U. Denver, 1966—. Contbr. articles to profl. jours. Chmn. bd. Clinton Essex Counties Coun. on Arts, 1968-72. With U.S. Army, 1954-56. AID fellow, Egypt, 1966, Nat. Endowment Humanities fellow U. N.C., 1977; Donnor Found. grantee, 1975-76. Mem. SUNY Theater Assn. (pres. 1971-72), Am. Theater Assn., N.Y. State Speech Assn., United Univ. Professions, N.Y. State United Tchrs., Assn. Coll., Univ. and Community Arts Adminstrs., Assn. Can. Theater History, Theatre Assn. N.Y. State . Home: 90 Brinkerhoff St Plattsburgh NY 12901-2704

KLINE, KATHERINE, film producer, distributor; b. N.Y.C., Nov. 8, 1945; d. Daniel Louis and Vivian (Bass) K.; m. Terence G. Benson, Jan. 3, 1981; children: Ross, Kara. BA, Am. U., 1963. Cultural affairs officer USIA, New Delhi, 1968-70, Mexico City, 1972-74; media program specialist Nat. Endowment for Arts, Washington, 1974-76, artist-in-schs., 1976-77; project coord. WNET-TV, N.Y.C., 1977-84; producer, distbr. Long Bow Group, Inc., N.Y.C., 1985-91, K. Kline and Co., N.Y.C., 1991—; founding bd. dirs. Alternative Media Info. Ctr., N.Y.C., 1981-87; chair steering com. New Day Films, N.Y.C., 1987-90; edn. coord., program specialist Dir.'s Creativity award USIA, 1971; panelist NEH, Washington, 1989, 90; screener N.Y. Emmy awards, 1980; judge Sinking Creek Film Celebration, Nashville, 1981. Co-producer films. Recipient George Peabody Award, 1986. Mem. Assn. Ind. Video and Film (sec. bd. dirs. 1978-83), Media Network (bd. dirs. 1981-87), Image Film Video Ctr. Democrat. Home: 617 W End Ave New York NY 10024-1607

KLINE, MILTON VANCE, psychologist; b. Bklyn., Mar. 25, 1923; s. Joseph and Elizabeth (Zimmerman) K.; B.A., Pa. State U., 1944; M.A., Columbia U., 1945; Ph.D., Western U., 1952; m. Dorothy Weller, Feb. 25, 1952; 1 dau., Jill. Chief psychologist Westchester Health Dept., White Plains, N.Y., 1948; dir. research dept. psychology L.I.U., 1948, research project dir. grad. sch., 1953; research cons. VA, N.Y.C., 1950; pvt. practice hypnoanalysis N.Y.C., 1950—, professorial lectr. Seton Hall Med. Sch., 1960-62; pres. Inst. for Research in Hypnosis, N.Y.C., 1954—; lectr. Fairleigh Dickinson U., Rutherford, N.J., 1964—; dir. Morton Prince Clinic for Hynotherapy; pres. Morton Prince Services, N.Y.C. and Balt., dir. substance abuse research lab., N.Y.C. and Mt. Kisco, 1987—, dir. employee asstance program consultation service, Mt. Kisco, 1987—; prof. med. psychology and hypnosis U. Milan New Sch. Medicine, Italy, 1988—; dir. Forensic Hypnosis Research and Consultation Center, Inst. for Research in Hypnosis, N.Y.C. and Mt. Kisco, N.Y.; co-dir. Internat. Soc. for Med. and Psychological Hypnosis; cons. NBC, Nat. Assn. Broadcasters; pres. Internat. Grad. U., Switzerland. Chmn. council sci. and profl. advs. Internat. Grad. Sch. Behavioral Scis., Switzerland; bd. advs. Am. Bd. Psychotherapy, 1982. Served with AUS, 1942-44. Recipient award for best book in hypnosis Soc. Clin. and Exptl. Hypnosis, 1958, 67, award for Best Paper on clin. hypnosis, 1973, Roy M. Dorcus award, 1971. Fellow Am. Med. Writers Assn., Acad. Psychosomatic Medicine; mem. Soc. Clin. and Exptl. Hypnosis (pres. 1961-63), Am. Psychol. Assn. (council reps.), Internat. Soc. Med. and Psychol. Hypnosis (bd. advisers), Authors Guild. Author: Hypnodynamic Psychology, 1955, A Scientific Report on The Search for Bridey Murphy, 1953; Freud and Hypnosis, 1958; The Nature of Hypnosis, 1962; Clinical Correlations of Experimental Hypnosis, 1965; Psychodynamics and Hypnosis, 1967; Forensic Hypnosis, 1983, Short Term Hypnotherapy and Hypnoanalysis, 1992; editor: Obesity: Etiology, Treatment and Research (C.C. Thomas), 1975. Editor emeritus Internat. Jour. Clin. and Exptl. Hypnosis. Home: 15 Kerry Ln Chappaqua NY 10514-1606 Office: 1991 Broadway New York NY 10023

KLINE, RICHARD DETHOFF, company executive; b. Harrisburg, Pa., Mar. 31, 1941; s. Thornton C. and Jermyle (Dethoff) K.; m. Ann M. Martinello, June 3, 1967; children: Susan, Michelle. BA, Dartmouth Coll., 1963; MBA, Columbia U., 1967. Product mgr. Gen. Foods Corp., White Plains, N.Y., 1967-74; group v.p. Carter Wallace, Inc., N.Y.C., 1974—. Lt. (j.g.) USN, 1963-65.

KLINEMAN, RONALD BRUCE, financial planner, lawyer; b. Rochester, N.Y., July 8, 1933; s. Albert Israel and Mildred (Kroll) K.; m. Linda Gilinsky, Aug. 19, 1962; children: Laurie, Janet, Karen. BA, Cornell U., 1955, JD, 1957. Bar: N.Y., 1959. Sole practice Ronald B. Klineman, P.C., Rochester, 1959-72, 73-80, 83-85; dir. tax planning Gradinger and Assocs., Rochester, 1980-82; fin. planner Personal Fin. Planners, Rochester, 1985—, v.p., 1987-88; chief exec. officer Capital Designs of Rochester, Inc., 1988—; sec. Genesee Funding, Inc., Genesee Capital, Inc., Rochester, 1983—. Councilman Town of Brighton, N.Y., 1969-73. Served to capt. U.S. Army, 1957. Fellow Estate Planning Council; mem. Nat. Acad. Elder Law Attys. Republican. Jewish. Lodge: Rotary (program chmn. 1978). Home: 93 Creek Rdg Pittsford NY 14534-4408

KLING, PHRADIE (PHRADIE KLING GOLD), small business owner; b. N.Y.C., July 2, 1933; d. Samuel A. and Mary Leah (Cohen) K.; m. Lee M. Gold, Sept. 5, 1955 (div. 1976); children: Judith Eileen, Laura Susan, Stephen Samuel, James David. BA, Cornell U., 1955; MA in Human Genetics, Sarah Lawrence Coll., 1971. Genetic counselor assoc. Coll. Medicine and Dentistry N.J., Newark, 1970-73; assoc. genetic counselor Sarah Lawrence Coll., Bronxville, N.Y., 1970-73; genetic counselor N.Y. Fertility Rsch. Found., N.Y.C., 1971-73; staff assoc., genetic counselor depts. pediatrics, ob-gyn and neurology Columbia U. Coll. Physicians and Surgeons, N.Y.C., 1973-78; asst. in genetics St. Luke's Hosp. Ctr., N.Y.C., 1977-79; health program assoc. Conn. Dept. Health Svcs., Hartford, 1978-84; edn. cons. Conn. Traumatic Brain Injury Assn., Rocky Hill, 1984-85; office mgr. Anderson Turf Irrigation Inc., Plainville, Conn., 1986-92; owner, mgr. KlingWorks, contract adminstrn., Avon, Conn., 1992—; speaker, instr. on health and health ethics issues, Conn., N.Y., N.J., 1971-85; dir. confs. on genetics and traumatic brain injury, 1980-85; project dir. ednl. field testing Biol. Scis. Curriculum Study, 1981-83; scientist AAAS Sci.-by-Mail, 1991—. Mem. Farmington River Watershed Assn., Simsbury, Conn., 1988—; docent Sci. Mus. Conn., West Hartford, 1989-90. Recipient citation for dedicated svc. Conn. Safety Belt Coalition, 1985. Mem. AAAS, Am. Human Genetics, Bus. and Profl. Microcomputer Users Group, Conn. Assn. for Jungian Psychology, Conn. Computer Soc., Hastings Ctr., Am. Mensa (chpt. coord. gifted children 1985—). Home and Office: 33 Hunter Rd Avon CT 06001-3618

KLINGEBIEL, ALBERT ARNOLD, soil scientist, consultant; b. Hinton, Iowa, Oct. 1, 1910; s. Herman August and Lena (Lotz) K.; m. Edith Mary Holmes, June 2, 1937; children: Keith and Kenneth (twins), John, Janice. BS in Agronomy, Iowa State U., 1936, MS in Soil Microbiology, 1937; postgrad., U. Ill., 1950-54. Field soil scientist Forest Svc., USDA, Ogden, Utah, 1937-38, Soil Conservation Svc., USDA, Midwest U.S. locations, 1938-40; dir. tng. sch. Soil Conservation Svc., USDA, LaCrosse, Wis., 1940-46; state soil scientist Soil Conservation Svc., USDA, Urbana, Ill., 1946-52; dir. soil conservation rsch. Agrl. Rsch. Svc., USDA, Urbana, 1952-54; dir. soil survey interpretations Soil Conservation Svc., USDA, Washington, 1954-73; ind. cons. soil sci. Silver Spring, Md., 1973—; guest lectr. U. Ill., Urbana, 1960; mem. sci. team FAO, UN, Rome, 1972, Nat. Rsch. Coun., Washington, 1975. Contbr. articles to Jour. Am. Soc. Agronomy, Agrl. Banking and Fin., Soil Conservation. Chmn. stewardship area Luth. Ch., Burtonsville, Md., 1975-90, pres. ch. coun., 1984. Recipient Superior Svc. award USDA, 1950, Merit awards USDA, 1965-73. Fellow Am. Soc. Agronomy (active various coms.), Soil Sci. Soc. Am. (com. mem.); mem. Soil Conservations Soc. Am., Ill. Soil Classifiers Assn. (hon.), Lambda Alpha. Home: 2413 Countryside Dr Silver Spring MD 20905-4524

KLINGMAN, JACK DENNIS, biochemistry educator, researcher; b. Johnson City, N.Y., Apr. 21, 1927; s. Lewis R. and Pearle A. (Dennis) K.; m. Gerda I. Schultz; 1 child, Karin L. BA, Syracuse (N.Y.) U., 1951; MS, Med. Coll. of Va., 1953; PhD, Duke U., 1958. Teaching asst. dept. biochemistry Med. Coll. Va., Richmond, 1951-53, rsch. assoc. dept. pharm., 1953; rsch. asst. dept. biochemistry Duke U., Durham, N.C., 1954-58; rsch. assoc. dept. biophysics The Johns Hopkins U., Balt., 1958-59; instr. dept. biophysics Johns Hopkin's U., Balt., 1959-61; from instr. to prof. SUNY, Buffalo, 1961—. Author: (chpt.) Automatic Ganglia and Their Biochemistry, 1984, Pharmacology of Ganglionic Transmission Ganglionic Metabolism, 1980; contbr. articles to Jour. Neurochem. Rsch. Synaptical Junctional Glycoconjugates. Staff sgt. U.S. Army, 1945-47, ETO. NIH fellow Duke U., 1954-57, Johns Hopkins U., 1957-58, Fulbright fellow

Monash U., Australia, 1971-72. Mem. AAAS, Am. Chem. Soc., Am. Neurochem. Soc., Am. Soc. Biochemistry and Molecular Biology, Am. Oil Chem. Soc., Am. Inst. Chemistry, Internat. Neurochem. Soc., Chem. Soc., Sigma Xi (pres. local chpt. 1972-74). Office: SUNY Sch of Medicine Dept of Biochemistry Buffalo NY 14214

KLINKENBERG, HILKA ELISABETH, management consultant; b. Bremen, Fed. Republic Germany, July 20, 1946; came to U.S., 1976; d. Lorenz and Agatha Margarete (Bohlen) K. BA, U. Toronto, Ont., Can., 1968. Mng. dir. Etiquette Internat., N.Y.C., 1989—. Author: At Ease...Professionally, 1992; contbr. articles to profl. jours. Vol. Vol. Svcs. for Children, N.Y.C., 1979-83, Helpline Telephone Crisis Counseling, N.Y.C., 1984-86; fund raising com. mem. Westchester Assn. for Retarded Citizens, White Plains, N.Y., 1991; fashion show coord. Guild for the Blind, N.Y.C., 1990. Mem. ASTD, NAFE, SIETAR, Am. Mgmt. Assn., Americas Soc., The Fashion Group, The Global Bus. Assn., Nat. Speakers Assn., Women in Communications. Office: Etiquette Internat 254 E 68th St New York NY 10021-6012

KLINKOWSKI, PETE R., business development consultant; b. Stamford, Conn., Dec. 16, 1947. BSCE, U. Mich., 1970; MBA, U. N.H., 1985. With Dorr-Oliver Inc., Stamford, 1970-80; mgr. Dorr-Oliver Div. Sohio, Stamford, 1980-86, tech. dir. strategic planning and implementation, 1986-88; v.p. Innotech Corp., Trumbull, Conn., 1988—; freelance cons. in field. Inventor 12 patents in field of ultrafiltration, membranes and electrokinetics; contbr. to book chpts. and articles to profl. jours. Mem. Am. Inst. Chem. Engrs., Electrochem. Soc., Internat. Assn. Colloid and Interface Scientists, Packaging Inst. Am. (assoc.).

KLINSKY, ARNOLD, communications executive; b. Chgo., Jan. 12, 1944; s. Nathan and Ruth (Fensin) K.; m. Hisako Tomisato, Dec. 8, 1970; children: Kevin, Ami. BS, U. Ill., 1966. News dir. and anchor Sta. WICD-TV, Champaign, Ill., 1968; dir. pub. affairs, reporter Sta. WOC AM-FM/TV, Davenport, Iowa, 1968-73; mng. editor news Sta. KTVI-TV, St. Louis, 1973-78; dir. news Sta. WVIT-TV, West Hartford, Conn., 1978-82; v.p. ops. Sta. WVIT-TV, 1982-83; v.p., gen. mgr. Sta. WHEC-TV 10, Rochester, N.Y., 1983—. Mem. com. Martin Luther King Festival, Rochester, 1987-88; chmn. Urban League, Rochester, 1987—; treas. Arts for Greater Rochester, 1988—; bd. dirs. Community Ptnrs. for Youth, 1988—. Mem. N.Y. State Broadcasting Assn. Jewish. Home: 18 Barrington Hls Pittsford NY 14534-4709 Office: Sta WHEC-TV 191 East Ave Rochester NY 14604-2695

KLINZING, GEORGE ENGELBERT, chemical engineering educator, consultant; b. Freeport, Pa., Mar. 22, 1938; s. Engelbert and Pearl (Zandona) K.; m. Sandra Moore, June 21, 1969; children: Matthew, Karey. BS, U. Pitts., 1959; MS, Carnegie Inst. Tech., 1961, PhD, 1963; hon. degree, Cen. U., Quito, Ecuador, 1966. From asst. prof. to prof. chem. engring. U. Pitts., 1963—. Author: Gas-Solid Transport, 1981; co-author: Pneumatic Conveying of Solids, 1989. Recipient Teaching award Western Electric, 1978. Fellow Am. Inst. Chem. Engrs.; mem. Am. Soc. Engring. Assn., Filtration Soc., Freight Pipeline Soc. (award 1984), Sigma Xi (local v.p.). Roman Catholic. Home: 5121 Beeler St Pittsburgh PA 15217-1001 Office: U Pitts 323 Benedum Hall Pittsburgh PA 15261-2232

KLIPP, TODD LAMONT CAUSEY, lawyer; b. Syracuse, N.Y., June 27, 1950; s. David Lawrence and Joyce (Axtell) K.; m. Anne MacRae Causey, Aug. 21, 1982; children: Austin, Hillary, Nathan. AB, Hamilton Coll., 1972; JD, Fordham U., 1976. Bar: N.Y. 1977, U.S. Dist. Ct. (so. and ea. dists.) N.Y. 1977, U.S. Tax Ct. 1978, Mass. 1980. Assoc. Mudge Rose Guthrie & Alexander, N.Y.C., 1976-79, Goodwin, Procter & Hoar, Boston, 1979-83; asst. gen. counsel Boston U., 1984-85, dep. gen. counsel, 1985-87, gen. counsel, 1987—; counsel Vol. Lawyers Project, Boston, 1982—. Notes editor Fordham U. Law Jour., 1975-76. Mem. Nat. Assn. Coll. and Univ. Attys. (publs. com. 1987-88, ann. conf. program com. 1988-89, continuing legal edn. com. 1990—), Mass. Bar Assn., Boston Bar Assn. Home: 19 Holmes Rd Lexington MA 02173-1916 Office: Boston U Office Gen Counsel 125 Bay State Rd Boston MA 02215-1785

KLITZMAN, ROBERT LLOYD, physician, author; b. N.Y.C., July 1, 1958; s. Joseph Arthur and Joan Marilyn (Kahn) K. AB, Princeton U., 1980; MD, Yale U., 1985. Diplomate Am. Bd. Psychiatry and Neurology. Rsch. asst. Nat. Inst. Health, Bethesda, Md., 1980-81; researcher Papua New Guinea Inst. Med. Rsch., 1980-81; intern The N.Y. Hosp. Cornell U. Med. Ctr., N.Y.C., 1985-86, resident, 1986-89; fellow Columbia Presbyn. Med. Ctr., N.Y.C., 1989—. Author: A Year-long Night 1989, book chpt. and articles in profl. jours. Recipient Keese prize Yale U., 1985; Robert Wood Johnson Found. clin. scholar, 1991—; MacDowell Colony fellow, 1991, DuPont fellow, 1982, Burroughs-Wellcome fellow Am. Psychiat. Assn., 1987. Mem. Am. Psychiatric Assn. (mem. N.Y. County dist. br. com. on AIDS 1989—, commn. on AIDS, 1988-89, steering com. of AIDS edn. project 1987-88). Home: 410 Central Park W Apt 16F New York NY 10025-4850

KLOCK, MARK STEVEN, finance educator; b. Plattsburg, N.Y., Sept. 2, 1958; s. Benny LeeRoy and Margaret Ann (Sherman) K.; m. Pamela Anne Megna, July 10, 1982; children: Nathan Vincent Klock. BA, Pa. State U., 1978; JD, U. Md., 1988; PhD, Boston Coll., 1983. Bar: Md. 1988, D.C. 1989. Rsch. assoc. Nat. Bur. Econ. Rsch., Cambridge, Mass., 1980-81, John Hancock, Boston, 1982-83, MCR, Inc., Falls Church, Va., 1983-84; asst. prof. Univ. of Balt., 1984-87; assoc. prof. George Washington U., Washington, 1987—; mng. editor Md. Jour. of Internat. Law and Trade, Balt., 1987-88; editorial rev. bd. Midwest Jour. of Econs. and Bus., Mankato, Minn., 1991; cons. in field. Contbr. articles to profl. jours. Recipient Am. Jurisprudence prize U. Md. Law Sch., Balt., 1986, 87, Bernstein prize, 1988. Mem. Am. Econ. Assn., Am. Fin. Assn., Fin. Mgmt. Assn., Md. State Bar Assn. (free legal advisor, Silver Spring, Md., 1989), D.C. Bar Assn., Ea. Fin. Assn. Democrat. Office: George Washington U 2023 G St NW # 101 Washington DC 20052-0001

KLOEPPER, DAVID ALAN, management consultant; b. Colby, Kans., Dec. 8, 1945; s. Robert Mayer and Justine (Peterson) K.; m. Evelyn Maria Gritzbach, June 27, 1969. BS in Metallurgy, MIT. Process devel. engr. Grumman Aerospace, Bethpage, N.Y., 1968-72; mgr. svc. engring. Hilti, Inc., Stamford, Conn., 1972-79; nat. sales mgr. F & S Cen. Mfg., Bklyn., 1979-82; v.p. ops. and adminstrn. Imperial Bolt & Mfg. Co., South Plainfield, N.J., 1982-85; nat. sales mgr. Indsl. Bolt & Nut, Irvington, N.J., 1985-86, T.A. & D.A. Troy, Fairfield, N.J., 1986-87; prin., project mgr. Don Aux Assocs., Hasbrouck Heights, N.J., 1987—, ptnr., 1992—. Pres. Van Vorst Park Neighborhood Assn., Jersey City, 1981-82. Republican. Home: 308 Varick St Jersey City NJ 07302-3404 Office: Don Aux Assocs 777 Terrace Ave Hasbrouck Heights NJ 07604-3110

KLOESMEYER, ILIANA MARISA, communications company executive; b. Harrisburg, Pa., Sept. 28, 1958; d. Jan and Sonia (Plynaer) K. Student, W.Va. U., Morgantown, 1976-78; cert., Katharine Gibbs, Boston, 1978-79; student, Temple U., Phila., 1981-83. Sr. media buyer Sonder Sevitt Advt., Phila., 1983-85; mktg. dir. Cable AdNet, Malvern, Pa., 1985-86; media dir. Phila. Coca-Cola, 1986-91; dir. corp. communications O'Brien Environ. Energy, Phila., 1991-92; pres. Blue Sky Media, 1992—; mem. advt. com. Red Cross, Phila., 1986. Counselor Women Organized Against Rape, Phila., 1981; com. mem. Am. Cancer Soc. Phila.; communications chairperson, corp. fundraiser United Negro Coll. Fund. Mem. Cable Advt. Bur., TV Radio Advt. Club (TV com.), UNCF Sports (chmn. 1990-91), Alpha Xi Delta Alumni. Democrat. Presbyterian.

KLOETZEL, JOHN ARTHUR, biology educator, cell biology researcher; b. Cambridge, Mass., Mar. 21, 1941; s. Milton Carl and Elizabeth (Gorder) K.; m. Judith Ann Nattress, Aug. 17, 1962; children: Jeffrey, Steven, Jennifer, Melanie. AB, U. So. Calif., 1962; PhD, Johns Hopkins U., 1967. NIH postdoctoral rsch. fellow U. Colo., Boulder, 1967-70; asst. prof. U. Md., Catonsville, 1970-76, assoc. prof., 1976—; vis. assoc. prof. Johns Hopkins Sch. Medicine, Balt., 1987-88. Contbr. rsch. articles to profl. jours. Host family Am. Field Svc., Catonsville, Md., 1987. Alexander von Humboldt Found. rsch. fellow, U. Tübingen, Fed. Republic Germany, 1978; Rsch. grantee NIH, NSF, Am. Cancer Soc. Mem. Am. Soc. for Cell Biology, Soc. Protozoologists, Electron Microscope Soc. Am., Chesapeake Soc. for Electron Microscopy (pres. 1981-82). Office: Univ of Maryland Balt Co Dept Biological Sci Catonsville MD 21228

KLOSE, JULES ZEISER, physicist; b. St. Louis, Aug. 7, 1927; s. Julius Harry and Florence (Zeiser) K.; m. Evelyn Yvonne Brady, Jan. 22, 1958; children: Linda Marie, Jules Stephen, Charles David, James Michael. AB in Physics, Washington U., 1949; MS, U. Rochester, 1953; PhD, Cath. U. of Am., 1958. Physics aid U.S. Naval Gun Factory, Washington, 1948; instr. Dunford Sch., St. Louis, 1949; asst. prof. physics U.S. Naval Acad., Annapolis, Md., 1953-58, assoc. prof. physics, 1959-61; physicist Nat. Inst. Standards and Tech., Gathersburg, Md., 1961-88, contractor, 1989-90; guest scientist Nat. Inst. Standards and Tech., Gaithersburg, 1991—; rsch. assoc. and lectr. U. Mich., Ann Arbor, 1960-61. Author: (book) Radiometric Standards in Vacuum Ultraviolet, 1987; contbr. articles to profl. jours. Basketball coach St. Mary's Elem. Sch., Annapolis, 1969-86; pres. Anne Arundel County Tennis Assn., Annapolis, 1970-71; soccer coach St. Mary's High Sch., Annapolis, 1978-79. With AUS, 1946-47, PTO. Mem. Am. Phys. Soc., Optical Soc. Am., Coun. for Optical Radiation Measurements, Severn Valley Racquet Club, Sigma Xi. Office: Nat Inst Standards and Tech Gaithersburg MD 20899

KLOSKOWSKI, VINCENT JOHN, JR., educator, school administrator, author; b. Sept. 30, 1934; s. Vincent and Mary Kloskowski; m. Gerri K.; 1 child, Vincent John III. B.S. with honors, Seton Hall U., N.J., 1960, M.A., 1971; postgrad. Newark State Coll., 1960-62, Trenton (N.J.) State Coll., 1961-64; M.Ed. (Asian Found. scholar), Rutgers U., 1964; Ph.D., U. Western Ont., 1971; postdoctorate Harvard U., 1975, Appalachian State U., 1979; Ed.D. in Ednl. Adminstrn., Nova U., Fla., 1976. Substitute tchr. South River (N.J.) High Sch., 1958-60; tchr. Madison Twp. (N.J.) Pub. Schs., 1960-64; co-adj. mem. staff Rutgers U., 1961-64; remedial specialist North Brunswick (N.J.) Public Schs., 1964-65; vice prin. Jamesburg (N.J.) High Sch., 1965-66; asst. supt., child study coord., curriculum coord., fed. coord. urban funding Pub. Schs. Jamesburg, 1966-77, prin. elem., jr. high sch. and spl. edn. bldg., 1966-77; ednl. specialist N.J. Dept. Edn., 1977—; cons. to paraprofls. Mercer County Community Coll., Trenton, 1972; pvt. practice ednl. counseling, 1973—; speaker ann. conf. on incoming students Seton Hall U., Jamesburg Pub. Schs. In-Service Program, Middlesex County Child Study Team, PTA Jamesburg Pub. Schs., 1970, 72, Middlesex County Curriculum Council, East Brunswick Vocat. Sch., Holy Innocence Soc., Avenel, N.J., St. Catherines PTA, Clayton, N.J.; panelist child study devel. Madison Twp. Pub. Schs.; participant Internat. Reading Assn., Somerville, N.J., 42d Summer Sch. Conf. Sch. Adminstrn., Harvard U., Scott Foresman New Programs in Reading, Freehold, N.J., Ann. Reading Inst., Rutgers U., McGraw-Hill-Sullivan Reading Program, Hightstown, N.J., use of paraprofls. in pub. schs. N.J. State Dept.-Middlesex County Community Coll., Edison; cons. Setting Up Pvt. Spl. Edn. Facility, South Brunswick, Ednl. Cons. Service N.J., 1971—, reading techniques for para-profl. Mercer County Community Coll., Trenton, 1971; merit badge counselor Boy Scouts Am.; mem. alumni resource bank counsel, mem. staff and adv. bd. transition program Rutgers U. Coll. Kettering Found. fellow. Mem. Acad. Fellows (speaker nat. confs.), Am. Assn. Sch. Adminstrs., N.J. Assn. Sch. Prins., NEA (life), N.J., Middlesex County, Jamesburg edn. assns., Nat. Ednl. Assn. Sch. Prins., N.J. Classroom Tchrs. Assn., N.J. Assn. Retarded Children, Internat., N.J. reading assns., Middlesex County Audio-Visual Assn., Am. Soc. Notaries, Phi Delta Kappa, Alpha Epsilon Mu, Kappa Delta Pi. Author: Didacticism-Montessori and the Special Child, 1969; Amish School System and Special Education; asst. editor Seton Hall U. Newspaper and Coll. Yearbook, 1959-60; book reviewer Narod Polski, nat. Polish-Am. newspaper, 1976—. Home: 41 Daily St South River NJ 08882-1421 also: Hart Brook Farm Eaton Rd West Brownfield ME 04010

KLOSNER, JEROME MARTIN, applied mechanics educator; b. N.Y.C., Mar. 23, 1928; s. Morris and Minnie (Gotchkofsky) K.; m. Naomi Beth Certner, May 31, 1965; children—Michael Robert, Lise Helaine, Marc Alexander. B.C.E., Coll. City N.Y., 1948; M.S., Columbia, 1950; Ph.D., Poly. Inst. Bklyn., 1959. Sr. structures engr. Republic Aviation Corp., Farmingdale, N.Y., 1952-56; sr. scientist Avco Research & Advanced Devel. Div., Wilmington, Mass., 1956; cons. Avco Research & Advanced Devel. Div., 1956-67; research assoc. Poly. Inst. Bklyn., 1956-59, asst. prof., 1959-62, assoc. prof., 1962-67, prof. applied mechanics, 1967—; cons. Gen. Applied Sci. Labs., Inc., L.I., N.Y., 1959, FTC, Washington, 1963, Ingersoll-Rand Corp. Research Center, Princeton, N.J., 1966, Technautics Corp., N.Y.C., 1968-69, Weidlinger Assocs., N.Y.C., 1976—, Hazeltine, L.I., 1985—, Beltran, Inc., N.Y.C., 1986—, Multiline Tech., 1987; vis. mem. Courant Inst. Math. Scis., N.Y.U., 1966-67; Mem. Nat. Research council com. on Recommendations for U.S. Army Basic Sci. Research, 1976-79, 85-88. Reviewer, contbr. articles profl. jours. Fellow Am. Inst. Aeros. and Astronautics (asso.), ASCE; mem. ASME, Acoustical Soc. Am., Sigma Xi, Sigma Gamma Tau. Office: Polytech U Dept Mech & Aerospace Engring RR 10 Farmingdale NY 11735

KLOSS, WILLIAM, art historian; b. Cleve., Dec. 23, 1937; s. Frank R. and Mary (Masters) K. BA, Oberlin Coll., 1962, MA, 1968; postgrad., U. Mich., 1972. Asst. prof. U. Va., Charlottesville, 1969-72; instr. U. Md., College Park, 1973-74; exhbn. coord. Smithsonian Instn. Traveling Exhbn. Svc., Washington, 1974-78; co-founder, dir. tours Washington Art Assocs., Inc., 1978—; ind. writer, curator, lectr., cons. Washington, 1985—; cons. Nat. Geographic Soc., Washington, 1988, Spanierman Gallery, N.Y.C., Theodore Robinson Catalogue Raisonne, 1990—; appointee Com. for Preservation of White House, Washington, 1990—. Author: Treasures from the National Museum of American Art, 1985, Samuel F.B. Morse, 1988, Art in the White House, 1992; co-author: Treasures of State, 1991. Fulbright scholar, Rome, 1967-69. Mem. Coll. Art Assn. Home: 1824 Wyoming Ave NW Washington DC 20009-1802

KLOTZBACH, WILLIS O'BRIEN, civil engineer; b. Milltown, N.J., June 7, 1915; s. John Henri and Josie Marie (O'Brien) K.; m. Mildred Myhalik, Apr. 27, 1949; 1 child, John. BSCE, Lafayette Coll., 1936. Registered profl. engr., N.J., Pa. Draftsman, surveyor Lehigh Valley RR Office of Bridge Engr., Bethlehem, Pa., 1936-38, 40; detailer N.J. State Hwy. Dept., Office of Bridge Engr., Trenton, 1938-40; structural designer Bessemer & Lake Erie RR Office of Chief Engr., Greenville, Pa., 1941-43; ensign, lt. USNR Active Duty, 1943-46; civil engr. Lehigh Valley RR Office of Chief Engr., N.Y.C., 1946-48; hwy. bridge engr. U.S. Bur. Pub. Roads Regional Office, Albany, N.Y., 1950-51; county bridge engr. County of Mercer, Trenton, 1951-56; engr. D.B. Steinman, Cons. Engr., N.Y.C., 1948-50, 57-65; cons. engr. self employed Trenton, Princeton, 1966—; speaker in field. Dep. coord. Mercer County Civil Def., Trenton, 1950-70; borough engr., Hightstown, N.J., 1974-75. Recipient Engr. Merit award Am. Concrete Inst., 1976. Mem. VFW, Am. Legion, Raritan Lodge 61, Constrn. Bd. Appeals Trenton, Phi Kappa Tau. Office: PO Box 7185 Princeton NJ 08543-7185

KLUEWER, JEFFERY DANE, educator of English; b. San Diego, May 3, 1947; s. Francis Xavier and Dorothy Ann (Sleva) K.; m. Susan Ellen Taylor, May 31, 1969; children: Jessica Lyn, Joshua Taylor, Benjamin Dane. BA in Lang. and Lit., U. Calif., Santa Cruz, 1969; MA in English, SUNY, Stony Brook, 1970, PhD in English, 1975. Inst. English to prof. English Suffolk Community Coll., Brentwood, N.Y., 1974—; editor Rockville Centre (N.Y.) Herald, 1991—. Author: In Print, 1983; contbr. articles to profl. jours. Bd. dirs. Rosa Lee Young Childhood Ctr., Rockville Centre, 1989—; exec. com. Shoreham Opponents Coalition, Smithtown, N.Y., 1979-85. Fellowship Woodrow Wilson Found., 1973, Andrew Mellon Found., 1987. Mem. MLA, Nat. Coun. Tchrs. of English, N.Y. Press Assn., Nat. Newspaper Assn. Home: 59 Woodland Ave Rockville Centre NY 11570-6015 Office: 143 E Park Ave Long Beach NY 11561-3522 also: 143 E Park Ave Long Beach NY 11561

KLUG, THOMAS LOREN, investment banker; b. Terre Haute, Ind., Aug. 1, 1949; s. Raymond Henry and Dorothy (Pihlstrom) K.; m. Doris Marie Rossiter, Aug. 30, 1986; 1 child, Michael Raymond. BS, Ohio State U., 1971; MBA, Columbia U., 1973, JD, 1976. Bar: Ohio 1977, D.C. 1978; CPA, Ohio. Staff acct. Price Waterhouse & Co., Columbus, Ohio, 1971-72; assoc. Vorys, Sater, Seymour & Pease, Columbus, 1976-78; sr. atty. U.S. SEC, Washington, 1978-80; cons. Booz Allen & Hamilton, N.Y.C., 1980-82; v.p. Lehman Bros. Kuhn Loeb, N.Y.C., 1982-84; dir. corp. devel. Thomson, McKinnon Securities, N.Y.C., 1984-87; v.p. Drexel Burnham Lambert, N.Y.C., 1987-90; mng. dir. Geneva Capital Markets, Teaneck, N.J., 1990-91; pres. Pvt. Bus. Exch., Inc., White Plains, N.Y., 1991—; mem. Columbia Legis. Drafting Rsch. Fund, N.Y.C., 1974-76, Columbia Jour. Law and Social Problems, N.Y.C., 1974-75; teaching asst. Columbia Law Sch., N.Y.C., 1975-76; lectr. Franklin U., Columbus, Ohio, 1977; speaker Tech. Transfer Inst. M&A Seminar, N.Y.C., 1987, Drexel Burnham Ctrs. of Influence Program, 1988-89, Inc., Conf. on Growing the Co., Chgo., 1989, Orlando, Fla., 1990. Researcher: CPA Law Review, 1978. Armistead fellow Columbia Bus. Sch., N.Y.C., 1973, internat. fellow Columbia U., N.Y.C., 1975-76. Mem. ABA, AICPA, Palnning Forum, The Nature Conservancy (trustee, sec. Ohio chpt. 1977-78), Chappaqua Swim and Tennis Club, Safari Club Internat. (pres. N.Y. Met. chpt. 1992—). Roman Catholic. Home: 8 Deborah Ln Chappaqua NY 10514 Office: Pvt Bus Exch Inc Westchester Fin Ctr 50 Main St Ste 1000 White Plains NY 10606

KLUGE, J. HANS, company executive; b. Kladno, Czechoslovakia, May 14, 1928; s. Johann and Elisabeth (Czeike) K.; m. Maria de Gyoeroessy-Czepreghy, Apr. 4, 1956; children: Florian, Clara. BA, U. Vienna, Austria, 1948; Cert. Elec. Tech., Ryerson Inst. Tech., Toronto, Ont., 1956; postgrad., U. Toronto, 1962-71. With W.M. Neilson Ltd., Toronto, Ont., 1952, DM Fraser Ltd., Toronto, 1952-57; estimator, sr. designer Ward Leonard of Can., Ltd., 1957-59, chief engr., mgr. engring. dept., 1959-61; v.p., gen. mgr. Ward Leonard of Can., Ltd., Toronto, Scarborough, 1961-67; pres. Ward Leonard of Can., Ltd., 1967-71, Ascolectric Ltd., Brantford, 1971-87; pres. internat. ops. Automatic Switch Co., Florham Park, N.J., 1987-90, pres., chief exec. officer, 1990—. Mem. N.J. Dist. Export Council, Princeton, 1989—; v.p. Can. Opera Co., Toronto, 1968-82. Mem. Can. Standards Assn. (bd. dirs., chmn. 1972), Quality Mgmt. Inst. (bd. dirs., chmn. 1982), Am. Nat. Standards Inst. (bd. dirs. 1990—), N.J. C. of C. (bd. dirs. 1989—), Brantford Club, Ontario Club. Office: Automatic Switch Co 50-60 Hanover Rd Florham Park NJ 07932

KLUGER, JOSEPH HARRIS, orchestra executive; b. Paterson, N.J., Feb. 9, 1955; s. Lawrence Alan and Eleanor (Glicksman) K.; m. Susan Elaine Lewis, Apr. 19, 1980; children: Daniel Adam, Julia Elizabeth, Andrew Lewis, Brian Thomas. BAin Music, Trinity Coll., 1977; MA in Arts Adminstrn., NYU, 1979. Prodn. asst. N.Y. Philharmonic, N.Y.C., 1978-79, asst. to mng. dir., 1979-81, asst. mgr., 1981-82, orch. mgr., 1982-85; gen. mgr. Phila. Orch., 1985-89, exec. dir., 1989-91, pres., chief operating officer, 1991—. Office: Phila Orch 1420 Locust St Ste 400 Philadelphia PA 19102-4297

KLUGMAN, PETER JAY, psychologist, consultant; b. Bklyn., May 19, 1942; s. Joseph and Shirley (Rich) K.; m. Marthanne Hamlin, Oct. 29, 1964 (dec. Dec. 1979). BA, U. Miami, 1964, MEd, 1965; MA, U. Fla., 1974, PhD, 1978. Diplomate Am. Acad. Pain Mgmt.; lic. psychologist, N.J., Pa. Commd. 2d lt. U.S. Army, 1966, advanced through grades to lt. col., 1983, ret., 1986; chief Community Mental Health Svc., Ft. Dix, N.J., 1976-86; clin. dir. Biofeedback Ctr. of South Jersey, Mount Holly, 1986—; pres. Orgnl. Potential, Medford, N.J., 1986—; cons. Pub. Svc. Electric and Gas, N.J., 1984—, Office Surgeon Gen. U.S. Army, 1986—. Contbr. articles to profl. jours. Bd. dirs. Burlington County (N.J.) Coun. Girl Scouts U.S., 1989—, Lenape Regional High Sch. Bd. Edn., N.J.; v.p. Medford Bd. Edn., N.J. Decorated Bronze Star, Legion of Merit, Army Commendation medal, Vietnam Svc. medal. Mem Am. Psychol. Assn., N.J. Psychol. Assn. (South Jersey rep. 1990—), South Jersey Psychol Assn. (bd. dirs. 1989—). Jewish. Office: Orgnl Potential PO Box 1551 Medford NJ 08055-6551

KLYBERG, ALBERT THOMAS, historian; b. Hackensack, N.J., Aug. 8, 1940. AB, Coll. Wooster, 1962; postgrad., U. Mich. Asst. curator manuscripts William L. Clements Libr., Ann Arbor, Mich., 1963-68; libr. R.I. Hist. Soc., Providence, 1968-69, exec. dir., 1969—; adj. prof. history U. R.I., 1974—, Providence Coll., 1986—. Compiler, bibliographer March of America series Univ. Microfilms, Inc., 1966; editor R.I. History; project dir. Papers of Gen. Nathanael Greene. Mem. R.I. Hist. Soc. Office: RI Hist Soc 110 Benevolent St Providence RI 02906-3103

KMIECIAK, D. LEE, publishing company executive; b. Albany, N.Y., June 29, 1950; d. Roland Joseph and Doris Louise (Rawlings) Rose; m. Alan Michael Kmieciak, Oct. 9, 1970 (div. 1983); 1 child, Michele Lynn; m. Gerald Owen Stoner, Aug. 3, 1983 (div. 1989). Student, U. Mich., 1968-71. With Office of the Counsel, State Health Dept., Albany, N.Y., 1971-73; editorial adminstr. Delmar Pubrs., Albany, N.Y., 1977-81; editorial dir. Coll. and Univ. Press Svcs., New Haven, Conn., 1981-85; pres., owner, chief exec. officer NCUP, Inc., Albany, 1985—. Contbr. articles to profl. jours. Mem. Citizen Ambassador Program to Soviet Union and Ea. Europe, 1991; rep. U.S.A. Publ. Mem. Guilderland C. of C., Nat. Assn. Self-Employed, Nat. Assn. Coll. Stores. Republican. writing, sketching, tennis, skiing. Office: NCUP Inc 292 Washington Avenue Ext Albany NY 12203-5346

KNACK, ARNOLD O., controller; b. Bklyn., Aug. 31, 1935; s. Harold Raymond and Jane (Fleischman) K.; m. 1960 (div. 1970); 1 child, Warren; m. Marjorie Ann Hirt, Apr. 11, 1973; 1 child, Benjamin. BBA, Pace U., 1963. Acct. Chem. Bank, N.Y.C., 1952-65; dir. fin. analysis Columbia Direct Mktg., N.Y.C., 1966-70; dir. budgets Bronx (N.Y.) Lebanon Hosp. Ctr., 1970; acctg. mgr. Kraft Inc. Dairy Group, Cherry Hill, L.I., N.J., N.Y., 1970-83; contr., sec. Apple & Eve, Inc., Roslyn, N.Y., 1984—. C.p., trustee Reli REACT Inc., L.I., 1984—; mem. Nassau County REACT, 1976-80; instr. 55 Alive/Mature Driving, Am. Assn. Ret. Persons, Suffolk, N.Y., 1989—. Office: Apple & Eve Inc 49 Bryant Ave Roslyn NY 11576-1123

KNACKSTEDT, MARY V., interior designer; b. Harrisburg, Pa., Oct. 26, 1940; d. Harry and Veronica Knackstedt. Student Pratt Inst., 1957-59, Cooper Union, Phila. Coll. Art. Pres. Knackstedt Inc., Harrisburg and N.Y., 1958—; mem. adv. com. CCNB Bank, N.A., New Cumberland, Pa., 1981—; pvt. practice cons.; speaker in field. Author: Interior Design for Profit, 1980, Profitable Career Options for Designers, 1985, The Interior Design Bus. Handbook, 1988, 92; columnist designer publs.; speaker on discipleship for Paulists of St. Paul's Ch., N.Y.C., 1991, bus. practices Harvard U., 1988—. V.p. Riverfront Peoples Park, Harrisburg, 1980—; bd. dirs. Harrisburg Symphony Assn., 1983—; mem. adv. bd. interior design U. Del., 1991. Mem. Am. Soc. Interior Designers, Internat. Furnishings and Design Assn., Illuminated Engring. Soc., Pres.'s Assn. Am. Mgmt. Assn., Human Factors Assn. Home and Office: 2901 N Front St Harrisburg PA 17110-1283 Address: 161 W 61st New York NY 10021

KNAPP, CHARLES HARRIS, electrical engineering educator; b. N.Y.C., June 8, 1931; s. Charles J. and Harriet M. (Harris) K.; m. Charleen A. Gaudet, Sept. 24, 1955; children: Linda Del Gizzi, Barry, Jennifer Knapp Johnson, Robert. BSEE, U. Conn., 1953, PhD, 1962; MS in Engring., Yale U., 1956. Engr. RCA, Camden, N.J., 1953, IBM, Poughkeepsie, N.Y., 1956-57; asst. prof. elec. engring. U. Conn., Storrs, 1961-74, prof. elec. engring., 1974—; cons. in field; vis. scientist IBM T.J. Watson Rsch. Ctr., Yorktown Hts., N.Y., 1969; vis. prof. Yale U., 1979; vis. scientist USN Underwater Systems Ctr., 1986. Contbr. articles to profl. jours. chmn. Ch. Coun., Storrs Congl. Ch., 1991—. Lt. USAF, 1953-55. Sperry Rand fellow, 1955. Mem. IEEE (sr. mem., pubs. chmn. 1975). Home: 113 Highland Rd Mansfield Center CT 06250-1504 Office: U Conn U-157 26 Glenbrook Rd Storrs Mansfield CT 06268

KNAPP, DAVID ALLAN, pharmaceutical educator, researcher; b. Cleve., Feb. 25, 1938; s. Frederick Allan and Ethel R. (Ogden) Kn.; m. Deanne Erma Evander, June 2, 1962; 1 child, Wendy Kay. BS, Purdue U., 1960, MS, 1962, PhD, 1965. Lic. pharmacist. Asst. prof. Coll. Pharmacy Ohio State U., Columbus, 1964-67, assoc. prof., 1967-71; prof. Sch. Pharmacy U. Md., Balt., 1972—, assoc. dean grad. edn. and rsch., 1981-83, chmn. dept. pharm. practice, 1987-91, dir. Ctr. on Drugs and Pub. Policy, 1987—, acting dean Sch. Pharmacy, 1989-91, dean, 1991—; vis. scholar U. Mich. Sch. Pub. Health, 1970-71; intramural researcher Nat. Ctr. for Health Svc. Rsch., Dept. HHS, Hyattsville, Md., 1978; scholar in residence Am. Assn. Colls. Pharmacy, Alexandria, Va., 1986-87. Author: Pharmacy Drugs and Medical Care, 5 edits., 1972-92; contbr. articles to profl. jours. Recipient numerous grants and contracts. Fellow AAAS, APHA, Am. Assn. Pharm. Scientists; mem. Am. Assn. Colls. Pharmacy (bd. dirs. 1986-89, Volwiler Rsch. Gold medal 1986), Am. Pharm. Assn. (rsch. achievement award 1984), Am. Soc.

Hosp. Pharmacists. Democrat. Unitarian. Office: Sch Pharmacy U Md at Balt 20 N Pine St Baltimore MD 21201-1180

KNAPP, DAVID WAYNE, electrical manufacturing company executive; b. Dixon, Ill., July 4, 1936; s. Burnelle W. and Margaret (Banker) K.; m. Wilma M. Miller, Dec. 19, 1960; children: Kristine, Valerie. BS, Northwestern U., 1961; postgrad., Harvard U., 1975. V.p. Westinghouse Credit Corp., Pitts., 1973-76; dir. corp. devel. Westinghouse Electric Corp., Pitts., 1976-79, dir. investor relations, 1979—; bd. dirs. Wesley Inst. Mem. bd. commrs. Upper St. Clair Twp., Pa., 1984-88. Served with U.S. Army, 1956-59. Mem. Investor Rels. Assn. (exec. com. 1988), Nat. Investor Rels. Inst. (exec. com., bd. dirs.), Internat. Investor Rels. Fed. (bd. dirs.). Office: Westinghouse Electric Corp 11 Stanwix St Pittsburgh PA 15222-1312

KNAPP, NANCY HAY, mental health administrator; b. Cleve., June 2, 1922; d. Henry Homer and Aurore Louise (LaCroix) Hay; m. Richard Dominick Knapp, Sept. 11, 1955; 1 child, Pamela Hay. BA, Hunter Coll., 1957; MSEd in Counseling Psychology, U. Pa., 1971, EdD in Counseling Psychology, 1987. Nat. cert. counselor; clin. assoc. Am. Bd. Med. Psychotherapists; cert. prevention specialist. Career and edn. counselor Johnson O'Connor Rsch. Found., N.Y.C., 1950-53; counselor, report writer The Pers. Lab., N.Y.C., 1953-63; cons. Chapel Hill, N.C., 1963-65; cons., Phila., 1965-69; counseling dir., resources for women U. Pa., Phila., 1972-78; dir. profl. svcs. Crossroads Career Planning Corp., Phila., 1978-80; dir. consultation and edn. Crozer-Chester Med. Ctr., Upland, Pa., 1980-90, chmn. tng. com., 1985-90; pvt. practice counseling, marital and family therapy, 1971—; mem. faculty Main Line Sch. Night, Ardmore, Pa., 1978-80; trainer Pa. Dept. Health, Harrisburg, 1982-85. Author: (tng. manuals) Prevention: Drug Misuse, 1983, Growing, Together, 1985. Bd. dirs. Resources for Women, U. Pa., Phila., 1976-80; mem. steering com. Coalition for Edn./Placement of Women, Phila., 1976-78, coord., 1978-80; mem. Chester (Pa.) Vocat./Ednl. Outreach, 1980-82, dir., 1982-84. Recipient Community Devel. award Pa. Cons. Edn. Coun., 1981; grantee Pa. Dept. Health, 1981, 83. Mem. AACD, APA (assoc.), Cons. Assn. Greater Phila., Phi Delta Kappa. Home: 326 Sprague Rd Narberth PA 19072-1124

KNAPP, PATRICIA ANN, psychologist, educator; b. Sandusky, Ohio, June 22, 1943; d. Charles Allan and Therma Eleanor (Kincade) Moore; m. Gary Robert Knapp, Dec. 15, 1963 (div. Dec. 1983); children: Chelsea Allison, Kirby Robert. BS, Colo. State U., 1968; MEd, Loyola U., 1976; MA, U. Md., 1986, PhD, 1988. Lic. psychologist, Md. Speech therapist Prince George's County Pub. Sch., Bladensburg, Md., 1968-70; dir. Womanscope, Inc., Columbia, Md., 1978-82; instr. Howard (Md.) Community Coll., 1982-86; intern in psychology Mt. Vernon Ctr. for Community Mental Health, Alexandria, Va., 1986-87; pvt. practice psychologist Towson, Md., 1987-89, Columbia, 1990—; adj. faculty U. Md. Baltimore County, 1988—. Contbr. articles to profl. jours. Mem. APA, Md. Psychol. Assn., Balt. Psychol. Assn., Nat. Register Health Svc. Providers in Psychology (registered), Phi Kappa Phi. Home: 9830 Pushcart Way Columbia MD 21045-3842 Office: 10715 Charter Dr Ste 270 Columbia MD 21044-2880

KNAPP, PHILIP BERNARD, business executive, inventor, lecturer, consultant; b. N.Y.C., Aug. 6, 1923; s. Litman Victor and Sophie (Klien) K.; m. Harriet D. Kramer, Mar. 11, 1952; children: John A., Joshua E., Josiah A. Student, Manhattan Sch. Music, 1946-51; BS, Clayton U., 1985, MBA, 1985, PhD in Bus., 1986. Mgmt. cons. Bruce Payne and Assoc., N.Y.C., 1957-60; nat. mgr. mktg. cons. Lybrand, Ross Bros and Montgomery, N.Y.C., 1962-65; v.p. Stewart Dougall and Assocs., N.Y.C., 1965-67; pres. Aptek Industries, Inc., Carle Place, N.Y., 1967-73, Hortigro, Inc., Lynbrook, N.Y., 1976-82, Apredel, Inc., Amityville, N.Y., 1974—; prof. SUNY, Farmingdale, 1985-87, lectr. in concept devel., process of invention, 1983-84; prof. engring. mgmt. Cooper Union, 1986-87; lectr., panelist N.Y. Soc. Profl. Inventors, Farmingdale, 1984; bd. dir. indsl. design lab. Pratt Inst., Bklyn., 1966-67, instr., cons., 1964-67. Author: The Process of Invention; Consultants Guide To Acquisitions, (tab books) Inventing-Creating and Selling Your Ideas, 1989; patentee in field; created over 50 inventions; designer, craftsman contemporary furniture. Active Le Bourget Soc., Amityville. With U.S. Army, 1943-45, ETO. Mem. AAAS, DAV, N.Y. Soc. Profl. Inventors (charter mem., chmn. legal com. 1983-86, chmn. fin. com. 1983-86, pres. 1987-88, editor newsletter 1989—), Fedn. Am. scientists, N.Y. Acad. Scis. Home: 116 Stuart Ave Amityville NY 11701-4226 Office: Apredel Inc 116 Stuart Ave Amityville NY 11701-4226

KNAPP, SHERRY LYNN, psychologist, mental health services administrator; b. Sellersville, Pa., Oct. 5, 1958; d. Kenneth Garvin Knapp and Ruth Elliott (Conard) Jefferis. BA in Psychology with honors, Indiana U. Pa., 1980; MA in Psychology, So. Ill. U., 1982, PhD in Psychology, 1985. Lic. psychologist, Mass., R.I., Pa. Psychology assoc. VA, Boston, 1984-85; staff psychologist Butler Hosp., Providence, 1985-86; dir. addiction svcs. Marlborough (Mass.) Hosp., 1986-89; dir. community support svcs. Community Counseling Ctr., Pawtucket, R.I., 1989-90; asst. dir. adolescent svcs. Southwood Community Hosp., Norfolk, Mass., 1990-91; v.p. clin. ops. The Stevens Ctr., Carlisle, Pa., 1992—. Mem. allocations bd. United Way of S.E. New England, Providence, 1985-87; co-chairperson com. on alcoholism Mass. Hosp. Assn., 1988-89; mem. substance abuse adv. com. City of Marlborough, 1988-89. Mem. APA, Am. Acad. Health Svcs. Providers in Addictions, Assn. Mental Health Adminstrs. (pres. local chpt. 1990), Mass. Psychol. Assn., Pa. Psychol. Assn., Soc. Psychologists in Addictive Behaviors, Nat. Register Health Svc. Providers in Psychology, Kiwanis, Phi Kappa Phi, Pi Gamma Mu, Psi Chi. Lutheran. Office: The Stevens Ctr 33 State Ave Carlisle PA 17013

KNAPP-STEEN, SUE, fund raising consultant. BS, The Juilliard Sch., 1967; postgrad. lang. studies, Alliance Française, 1979, '88; postgrad. mgmt. studies, NYU, 1989. Auditor N.Y. State Coun. on Arts, N.Y.C., 1975-78; asst. to presentations mgr. Met. Opera, N.Y.C., 1980-82; assoc. dir. Feldstone, Inc., Washington, N.J., 1983-91; exec. dir. Hunterdon Art Ctr., Clinton, N.J., 1992—. Recipient fellowship Nat. Endowment for Arts, 1979. Mem. Nat. Soc. Fund Raising Execs. (cert.). Office: Hunterdon Art Ctr 7 Center St Clinton NJ 08809

KNEAVEL, THOMAS CHARLES, JR., psychologist; b. Balt., Oct. 30, 1941; s. Thomas Charles and Caroline Frances (Noha) K.; BS, Loyola Coll., Balt., 1963, MEd, 1968; PhD, U. Ottawa, 1979; m. Ann Callanan, Dec. 18, 1970; children: Meredith, Thomas, Rebecca. Lic. psychologist, Del. Tchr. Ridge Sch., Towsen, Md., 1961-65; psychologist Balt. City Schs., 1965-69; clin. psychologist D.C. Children's Center, Laurel, Md., 1969-70; cons. to Joseph House, Balt., 1969-70; psychology intern Child Study Ctr., U. Ottawa, 1970-71, Child Diagnostic and Devel. Clinic, Children's Hosp. of Eastern Ont., Ottawa, 1971-72; sch. psychologist Cape Henlopen Sch. Dist., Nassau, Del., 1972-79; psychologist Community Mental Health Clinic, Beebe Hosp., Lewes, Del., 1973-79; program dir. child crisis unit Terry Children's Psychiat. Ctr., New Castle, Del., 1979-86, chief psychologist, 1982-86; mem. adj. faculty dept. psychiatry and human behavior Thomas Jefferson U. Med. Sch., 1980-86; pvt. practice, 1983—; psychologist Christina Sch. Dist., 1986—; clin. cons. Turnabout Counseling Ctr., Seaford, Del., 1987-91; cons. on compulsive gambling to dir. div. mental health, 1980-82; apptd. by Gov. DuPont and Gov. Castle to Del. Devel. Disabilities Planning Coun., 1982—, vice chmn., 1983-85, chmn., 1985-87; mem citizens adv. bd. Community Mental Health Clinic, Beebe Hosp., 1974-79; state rep. Nat. Assn. Devel. Disabilities, Washington, 1984-87, mem. child devel. com.; mem. state genetics adv. coun. A.I. Du Pont Inst. and State of Del., 1986-90; apptd. by Gov. Castle to State Bd. Psychol. Examiners, 1989, v.p., 1991—. Mem. Am., Del. psychol. assns., Nat. Assn. Sch. Psychologists (charter), Del. Sch. Psychologists Assn. (pres. 1976-77), Del. Psychol. Inc. (bd. dirs. 1987-89). Roman Catholic. Home: 7 Arthur Dr Hockessin DE 19707-1012 Office: The Pla 1303 Delaware Ave Ste 113 Wilmington DE 19806-3421

KNEEDLER, ALVIN RICHARD, university administrator; b. Ruffsdale, Pa., Apr. 8, 1943; s. Alvin Raymond and Louise (Mac Innes) K.; m. Suzette Gallagher, June 17, 1967; children: Eric, Rebecca. AB, Franklin and Marshall Coll., 1965; MA in French Language and Lit., U. Pa., 1967, PhD in French Language and Lit., 1970; cert. in Ednl. Mgmt., Harvard U., 1975. Instr. French Franklin and Marshall Coll., Lancaster, Pa., 1968-70, asst. prof. French, 1970-72, asst. to. dean, 1971-74, asst. to pres., 1974-77, sec. coll., 1977-79, v.p. adminstrn., 1979-84, v.p. devel., 1984-88, sec. bd. trustees, 1974-88, pres., 1988—; mem. exec. com. Pa. Commn. on Ind. Colls. and Univs., 1989—. Mem. Lancaster City Planning Commn., 1980-85, chmn. 1983-85, adv. bd. PRIME, Inc., 1991—; v.p., bd. dirs. Hist. Preservation Trust, Lancaster, 1984-87, sec., bd. dirs. Pa. Sch. Arts, Lancaster, 1985-89; bd. dirs. Lancaster Area Arts Coun., 1987-91, The Louise Von Hess Found. for Med. Edn., 1990—, Urban League of Lancaster County, Hamilton Bank, 1989—; chair Community Cultural Planning Com., 1989—; mem. Downtown Task Force, 1989-90; trustee Kiski Sch., 1988—; chair rsch. com. Pa. Ind. Coll. and Univ., 1991—. Mem. Am. Assn. Tchrs. French, Am. Soc. for 18th Century Studies, Lancaster C. of C. and Industry (bd. dirs. 1990—), Phi Beta Kappa, Phi Alpha Theta. Republican. Presbyterian. Home: 1416 Newton Rd Lancaster PA 17603-2461 Office: Franklin & Marshall Coll PO Box 3003 Lancaster PA 17604-3003

KNELL, GARY EVAN, television executive, lawyer; b. Sacramento, Feb. 27, 1954; s. David J. and Gertrude A. (Milkes) K.; m. Kim Larson, Oct. 18, 1981; children: Dwight M., Savannah B., Lucia L. BA, UCLA, 1975; JD, Loyola U., L.A., 1978. Bar: Calif. 1978. Asst. counsel sub-com. on intergovtl. relations U.S. Senate Govt. Affairs Com., Washington, 1978-79; counsel sub-com. on adminstrv. practice and procedure U.S. Senate Judiciary Com., Washington, 1979-81; spl. asst. to v.p., gen. counsel Sta. WNET-TV, N.Y.C., 1981-82, dir. telecommunications, 1982-84, sr. v.p., gen. counsel, 1984-89; v.p., dir. legal affairs Children's TV Workshop, N.Y.C., 1989—; mem. N.Y. Non-profit Coordinating Com., N.Y.C., 1984—. Contbr. articles to profl. jours. Mem. ABA (communications law sect. 1987—), Internat. Radio and TV Soc., Assn. Pub. Broadcasting Stas. (rep. 1982-89). Pub. TV Lawyers Assn. (chmn. 1985-89). Office: Children TV Workshop 1 Lincoln Pla New York NY 10023

KNEPLER, GAIL ORIT, graphic artist; b. Tel Aviv, Mar. 13, 1959; d. Abraham Israel and Eta (Kuchinsky) K. Student, Md. Inst., 1977-80, 88, 89. Graphic designer Gregory Assocs., Wilmington, Del., 1981, The Powerline, Inc., Newark, Del., 1982; layout artist, graphic designer Krell Corp., Wayne, Pa., 1986-88; freelance graphic artist Melton Communications, Wilmington, 1982, Franklin Lake Studios, Wilmington, 1982, Trimark Pub. Co., 1983-84, Phillips & Assocs., Wilmington, 1985, The News Jour. Co., 1985, Multigraphics, Wilmington, 1989—. Mem. Simon Wiesenthal Ctr., La., 1970-91. Grantee Md. Inst., 1980, Del. Postsecondary Scholarship Fund, 1980, 86, 90. Mem. Sierra Club. Republican. Jewish. Office: Multigraphics 1303 Stanford Rd Wilmington DE 19803-5135

KNER, ANDREW PETER, art director; b. Budapest, Hungary, Apr. 11, 1935; s. Albert and Susan (Gellert) K.; m. Carol Stevens, Sept. 16, 1961; children: Anne, Peter. BA, Yale U., 1957, MFA, 1959. Asst. art dir. Time, Inc., N.Y.C., 1961-63; asst. promotion dir. Look mag., N.Y.C., 1963-65; promotion art dir. Esquire mag., N.Y.C., 1965-69; exec. promotion dir. N.Y. Times, N.Y.C., 1969-84; creative dir. for promotion Backer Spielvogel Bates, N.Y.C., 1984-90; creative dir. R.C. Publs., N.Y.C., 1990—; art dir. Print Mag., N.Y.C., 1963—; advisor Nat. Endowment for the Arts, Washington, 1975-81. 1st lt. U.S. Army, 1958-60. Mem. Art Dirs. Club (pres. 1983-85, 7 Gold medals 1975-86, Cert. of Merit, 1965-88), Am. Inst. Graphic Arts (bd. dirs. 1981-83, Distinctive Merit award 1965-88), N.Y. Art Dirs. Club (pres. N.Y.C. chpt. 1983-85), Yale Club. Democrat. Home: 147 E 18th St New York NY 10003-2477 Office: Print Mag 104 5th Ave New York NY 10011-6901

KNERR, GEORGE FRANCIS, college vice-president; b. N.Y.C., Dec. 27, 1921; s. George Frank and Irene (Collins) K; m. Agnes Marie Doyle, Feb. 2, 1944; children: Kathleen, Maureen, Eileen, Joan, Paul, Rita, Francis, Bernadette, Marybeth. BA, St. John's U., Bklyn., 1948, MA, 1949; PhD, NYU, 1957. Tchr. Xavier High Sch., N.Y.C., 1948-49; asst. prof. St. John's U., Bklyn., 1949-56; assoc. prof. Pace U., N.Y.C., 1952—, dir., acting dean grad. div., 1958-63, dean admissions, 1959-61, dean student pers., 1961-65, asst. to pres., 1965-67, v.p., 1967—; cons. Peirce Jr. Coll., Phila., World U., N.Y. Inst. Credit, N.Y.C., San Juan (P.R.) Bautista Med. Sch.; pres., permanent sect. Mid Atlantic Assn. Colls. Bus. Adminstrn., 1979, 72-90. Trustee Maryknoll (N.Y.) Sch. Theology, 1983—. With U.S. Army, 1942-45, ETO. Home: 28 Holland Ln Monsey NY 10952-1322 Office: Pace U 1 Pace Pla New York NY 10038

KNESS, RICHARD MAYNARD, tenor; b. Rockford, Ill., July 23, 1937; s. Harry William and Helen Loretta (Curran) Kniess; m. Joann Danielle Grillo, July 23, 1967; 1 son, John Richard; children by previous marriage: Paul Richard, Kristin Elaine. B.A., San Diego State U., 1958. pres. Danielle Maynard Assocs., Inc.; five tours of China at invitation of Ministry of Culture; joint collaborator with Govt. Egypt, U.S.I.S., The Ambassadors of Opera and Am. Bus. Community. Performed in 36 countries, appeared with more than 60 opera cos., Europe, U.S., Middle East and Mexico, 1967-78; resident dramatic tenor, Met. Opera, N.Y.C. Opera, San Francisco, San Diego, San Antonio, Seattle, Cin., Hartford, Hawaii, Houston, Boston, Milw., 1967—, appeared with numerous symphony orchs., N.Y.C., Phila., Pitts., Cin., Washington, Atlanta, 1967—, leading dramatic tenor, Met. Opera Assn., N.Y.C., 1978—, co-dir. with wife Joann Grillo internat. opera co., The Ambassadores of Opera and Concert World Wide, 1979—, charitable and cultural performances in 36 countries include Beijing, Shanghai, Hong Kong, Taipei, Tokyo, Bangkok, Seoul, Jakarta, Singapore and others, 1989, Australia and New Zealand, 1990—, throughout Persian Gulf, 1990; performances for U.S. mil. in Middle East, 1990-91; Royal Command Performance for King and Queen of Thailand; last western singer to perform for Indira Gandhi; recs. include Beethoven's Ninth Symphony (Command Classics), Orff's Catulie Carmina (Columbia, Grammy award); performed for U.S. Forces in Persian Gulf. Served with U.S. Army, 1958-63. Recipient Grammy award for best classical rec., 1967. Republican. Clubs: Lions, N.Y. Athletic. Office: 240 Central Park Ste 16M New York NY 10019

KNEUER, PAUL JOSEPH, insurance company executive; b. Norfolk, Va., Dec. 6, 1960; s. Joseph George and Teresa Mary (Egan) K.; m. Melissa Leen Brown, July 3, 1988; 1 child, Elizabeth Devery. BS in Math., U. Notre Dame, 1982; MBA, Columbia U., 1991. Various positions Ins. Svcs. Office, Inc., N.Y.C., 1982-87; asst. v.p., assoc. actuary spl. ops. group Continental Ins. Cos., N.Y.C., 1987-91; officer property casualty ops. Continental Ins. Cos., Cranbury, N.J., 1992—; author and speaker at actuarial and ins. fourms, 1987—. Trustee parish endowment fund All Saints' Episcopal Ch., Hoboken, N.J., 1988-90. Fellow Casualty Acturarial Soc. (mem. exam. com. 1987-89, con. on fin. analysis 1989—); mem. Am. Acad. Actuaries, Beta Gamma Sigma. Home: 121 Haddon Pl Upper Montclair NJ 07043 Office: Continental Ins Cos 180 Maiden Ln New York NY 10038

KNICKERBOCKER, CHRISTINA MARY, student aid director; b. Medina, NY, May 7, 1959; d. Roy Arthur and Marie Edna (Van Why) K. B in Social Work, Lock Haven U., 1981; MEd, Cambridge Coll., 1988. Dir. social svc. Charles House Nursing Home, Boston, 1981; social worker geriatrics West Suburban Elder Svcs., West Newton, Mass., 1981-83; asst. dir. fin. aid Chamberlayne Jr. Coll., Boston, 1983-84, dir. fin. aid, 1984-88; dir. fin. aid Mount Ida Coll., West Newton, 1988; dir. student fin. aid and employment SUNY, Binghamton, 1988—. Mem. Nat. Assn. Fin. Aid Adminstrs., SUNY Fin. Aid Profls. (exec. coun. 1991—), N.Y. State Fin. Aid Assn. (workshop chmn. 1989—), Sigma Kappa. Democrat. Office: SUNY PO Box 6011 Binghamton NY 13902-6011

KNIERIM, THOMAS PATRICK, association executive; b. N.Y.C., May 12, 1963; s. Julius John and Patricia Marie (Connell) K. BA in History, Oberlin Coll., 1985; MS in Urban Affairs, CUNY, 1989. Legal asst. Friedman, Wang and Bleiberg, N.Y.C., 1986-87; Kramer, Levin, Nessen, Kamin and Frankel Kramer, Levin, Nessen, Kamin and Frankel, 1988-89; team leader City Vol. Corps, N.Y.C., 1987; project coord. Mayor's Office Ops., N.Y.C., 1988-89; assoc. dir. 14th St.-Union Sq. Local Devel. Corp., N.Y.C., 1989—; adv. bd. Washington Irving High Sch., N.Y.C., 1989—; mem. Coalition Neighborhood Econ. Devel., N.Y.C., 1989—. Project coord. N.Y. Cares, N.Y.C., 1988—; mem. N.Y.C. steering com. Mega Cities Project; founding mem. That Theater Thing, N.Y.C., 1990—; bd. dirs. St. George's Choral Soc., N.Y.C., 1991—. Urban fellow N.Y.C. Dept. Pers., 1988; featured in Manhattan Profile, N.Y. Newsday, 1989; recipient Top 10 Citizen award Manhattan Spirit, 1991. Mem. Hunter Coll. Alumni Coun., Oberlin Alumni Assn., N.Y.C. Urban Fellows Alumni Assn. (pres. 1989—). Home: 442 E 20th St Apt Mb New York NY 10009-8141 Office: 14th Street Union Sq LDC New York NY 10003-3558

KNIESLER, FREDERICK CORNELIUS, JR., real estate developer, city planner; b. Trenton, N.J., Feb. 12, 1954; s. Frederick Cornelius and Bernice Mary (Rottkamp) K.; m. Rebecca Lee Dorn, Aug. 8, 1981; children: Sarah Margaret, Martha Elizabeth. BS in Landscape Architecture, U. Va., 1976; M in City Planning, U. Pa., 1981. Dir. devel. Blackpoint Constrn. Co., Red Bank, N.J., 1983-85; sr. planner Fellows, Read & Assocs., Toms River, N.J., 1985; supr. transit project N.J. Transit/Rail Ops., Newark, 1985-88; dir. planning Birdsall Engring., Belmar, N.J., 1989—; assoc. N.J. State Bd. Architects and Landscape Architects, Newark, 1983-91. Contbr. articles to profl. jours. Mem. Little Silver (N.J.) Planning Bd., 1982, 83. Mem. Am. Inst. Cert. Planners, Am. Planning Assn. (N.J. chpt.), Am. Soc. Landscape Architects, Assn. Landscape Architects (N.J. chpt.), Monmouth County Hist. Assn. (trustee). Republican. Roman Catholic. Home: Halcyon Navesink Ave # 16 Rumson NJ 07760

KNIGHT, CHARLES ANTHONY, English educator; b. San Francisco, Sept. 3, 1937; s. Harry C. and Antoinette D. (Burr) K.; m. Katherine J. Kohlhas, Dec. 30, 1958; children: Christopher, Nathaniel, Jennifer, Lucy. BA, Haverford Coll., 1958; MA, U. Pa., 1960, PhD, 1964. Instr. Cath. U. Am., Washington, 1961-62, U. Mass., Amherst, 1962-65; asst. prof. English U. Mass., Boston, 1965-71, assoc. prof., 1971-80, prof., 1980—, assoc. dean, 1972-75, acting dean, 1975-76. Contbr. articles to profl. jours. Grantee Am. Coun. Learned Socs., 1987. Mem. Am. Soc. 18th Century Studies (chair ann. meeting 1984). Home: 177 Cypress St Newton MA 02159-2226 Office: U Mass Harbor Campus Boston MA 02125

KNIGHT, EDWARD R., lawyer, judge, educator, psychologist; b. Milw., Oct. 5, 1917; s. Harry and Lillian (Bachman) K.; m. Judith A. Weidberg, July 6, 1941; 1 dau., Barbara Jane. A.B., U. Wis., 1940, J.D., 1941; A.M., NYU, 1942, Ph.D., 1943. Bar: Wis. 1941, N.J. 1976; diplomate Am. Bd. Profl. Psychology. Master Oxford Sch., Pleasantville, N.J., 1941, psychologist, 1942, head psychologist, 1943, asst. headmaster, 1945-47, headmaster, 1947-73, emeritus, 1973—; U.S. magistrate judge, 1976—; judge Mcpl. Ct., Margate City, N.J., 1976-81; ptnr. Horn, Kaplan, Goldberg, Gorny & Daniels, Atlantic City, N.J.; dir. First Fidelity Bank, 1950-90. Pres., bd. govs. Atlantic City Med. Ctr., 1973-87, chmn. emeritus, 1987—; chmn. Master Planning Bd., Egg Harbor Twp., N.J., 1961-73; chmn. Atlantic County (N.J.) Charter Study Commn., 1973-74. Author: Self-Discipline and Academic Failure. Author articles edn., psychology; editorial. Parental Delinquency. Served to capt., USAAF, 1943-45; personnel com., personnel div. Air Tech. Service Command, Wright Field. Fellow Am. Psychol. Assn. (sch. psychologists div.); mem. Eastern, N.J. psychol. assns., Nat. Assn. Ind. Schs., N.J. Assn. Sch. Psychologists, Interam. Soc. Psychology, Boarding School Headmasters Assn. Middle States (pres. 1966-67), Wis. Alumni Assn., U. Wis. Mem. Union (life), Phi Delta Kappa, Kappa Delta Pi. Home: 7 N Thurlow Ave Margate City NJ 08402-1213

KNIGHT, GRACE PARKER, accountant; b. Phila., July 30, 1951; m. Tommie L. Knight, Oct. 17, 1981; children: Rahne, Tommie, Tomieka. BS, LaSalle U., Phila., 1980. CPA, Pa. Bookkeeper Greater Germantown Housing Devel. Corp., Phila., 1978-80; auditor Coopers and Lybrand, Phila., 1980-83; contr. Booth Maternity Ctr., Phila., 1983-88; owner Knights Acctg. Svc., Phila., 1988-90, Grace P. Knight, CPA,, Phila., 1990—; vol. Community Accts., Phila., 1990—; treas. Hola Kumba Ya, Phila., 1990—. Mem. Pa. Inst. CPAs (membership com.), Bus. and Profl. Womens Club (treas. 1990-92, 1st v.p. 1992—). Home and Office: 5555 Wissahkkon Ave Ste T-2 Philadelphia PA 19144

KNIGHT, HOWARD ATWOOD, oil company executive; b. Providence, Feb. 20, 1942; s. Richard B. and Helen (Atwood) K.; m. Bonnie Shields, June 9, 1961; children: Heather A., Heidi M., Howard A., Elizabeth R., Robert M. BA, Williams Coll., 1963; JD, Yale U., 1966. Assoc. Sullivan & Cromwell, N.Y.C., 1966-69; assoc. Cummings & Lockwood, Stamford, Conn., 1969-73, ptnr., 1973-82; mng. dir., pres., chief exec. officer Weeks Petroleum Ltd., Hamilton, Bermuda, 1982-84; chmn. bd., pres., chief exec. officer Avalon Corp., N.Y.C., 1984—; bd. dirs. Saugatuck Capital Co., Stamford, Avalon Corp., N.Y.C., Paringa Mining and Exploration Co. PLC, Melbourne, Australia. Mem. ABA, Am. Assn. Petroleum Geologists, Soc. Petroleum Engrs., Petroleum Soc. N.Y. Republican. Congregationalist. Clubs: Links, Racquet & Tennis (N.Y.C.), Wee Burn Country (Darien, Conn.). Office: Avalon Corp 101 E 52d St New York NY 10022-6018

KNIGHT, KENNETH GEORGE, non-profit healthcare association executive; b. Boston, Aug. 7, 1949; s. Harry V. and Anne M. (Ryan) K.; m. Joan M. Renouf, Dec. 27, 1982; children: Jane, Jeff. BS, Suffolk U., 1972; BSN, Boston U., 1974; postgrad., Oswego State U., 1990—. RN, N.Y. Physician's asst. Montreal Children's Hosp., 1975-79; instr. nursing Dawson Coll., Montreal, 1979-82; nurse mgr. Auburn (N.Y.) Meml. Hosp., 1982-86; exec. dir. Cayuga Health Assn., Auburn, 1986—. Mem. Leadership of Cayuga, Am. Cancer Soc. (bd. dirs. 1988-89). Home: 2581 Center Rd Scipio Center NY 13147-9702 Office: Cayuga Health Assn Inc 2 Easterly Ave # 3 Auburn NY 13021-3741

KNIGHT, MICHAEL J., accounting company executive; b. Bridgeport, Conn., Oct. 14, 1951; s. Ronald H. and R. Eleanor (Palumbo) K.; m. Darlene M. Hyland, Oct. 18, 1975; children: Marie, Matthew. BS in Mktg., Fairfield (Conn.) U., 1973. CPA, Conn. Staff acct. J. William Hope & Co., Bridgeport, 1975-76, Beers Hamerman, New Haven, 1976-78; from staff acct. to sr. mgr. Price Waterhouse, Bridgeport, 1978-84; prin. Michael J. Knight, CPA, Fairfield, 1984-89; co-owner Michael J. Knight & Co., CPAs, Fairfield, 1990—; past instr. Housatonic Community Coll.; del. White House Conf. on Small Bus., 1986; acct. advocate SBA Region I, 1992. Bd. dirs. Bridge House, Bridgeport, 1988—, pres., 1988-91; chmn. adv. bd. Sta. WSHU, Sacred Heart U.; mem. planned giving adv. com. Fairfield U. Mem. AICPAs (small bus. taxation subcom.), Nat. Small Bus. United (assoc. trustee), SBA of New Eng. (bd. dirs.), Conn. Soc. CPAs, Conn. Bus. Network (past pres.), Bridgeport Area CPAs Group (past pres.), Southern Conn. Bus. Assn. (past treas.). Home: 7 Crescent Ln Trumbull CT 06611

KNIGHT, NORMAN, broadcast executive; b. July 24, 1924; m. Susannah Howard Andre, Aug. 26, 1944; children: Norman Scott, Randolph Howard, Jeffrey Bryant, Robert Andre. LLD (hon.), Northeastern U.; DBA (hon.), Nathaniel Hawthorne Coll.; DCS (hon.), Merrimack Coll.; DHL (hon.), Suffolk U.; DCC (hon.), Anna Maria Coll. News reporter, scriptwriter Sta. WEW, WIL, WTMV, 1938-41; Announcer, host-producer Sta. WTMV, 1942; announcer, promotion mgr., news reporting continuity dir. Sta. KTHS, 1943; announcer Sta. WMC, 1943; announcer, news writer, reporter, salesman Sta. WMMN, 1944; gen. mgr. Sta. WAJR, 1944-46; Eastern dir. sta. relations MBS, 1946-49; v.p. sales, advt. and promotion Sponsor Publs., Inc., 1950-53; gen. mgr. Sta. WABD (now WNYW-TV), 1953-54; exec. v.p., gen. mgr. Yankee Network div. RKO Teleradio Pictures, Inc. (operating Yankee Network WNAC, WRKO, WNAC-TV); also dir. Yankee Network; v.p. RKO Teleradio Pictures, 1954-60; pres. Yankee div. RKO Teleradio Pictures, Inc., 1957-60, Yankee div. RKO Gen., Inc., 1958-60; treas., chmn. Knight Sales, Inc.; chmn., treas. Knight Radio, Inc. (WEZF, WGIR and WGIR-FM), Knight Broadcasting N.H., Inc. (WHEB and WHEB-FM); pres., treas. Knight Communications Corp. (WTAG and WSRS); chmn., treas. Quality Radio Corp. (WSAR), 1960—; chmn. Caribbean Communications Corp. Established first complete TV sta.: pub. affairs film unit which produced Brotherhood Series: River of Life, Wershmeitz (only film 1956 Hungarian revolt), Suffer the Little Children, Breast Cancer, over 100 programs Dangers of Apathy; TV documentaries, 1953-60; Author: (sales techniques radio/TV) The Cause of All Mankind, (film and TV) A Storm is Always a Challenge, Awake America, others. Radio-TV chmn. United Fund Greater Boston, Mass. Cancer Soc., ARC chpt. Met. Boston, Met. Boston chpt. ARC; bus. chmn. Easter Seal Soc.; radio chmn. Salvation Army; dir. Strawberry Banke; bd. dirs. New Eng. Nephrosis Found.; pres., founder New Eng. Kidney Disease Found.; pres. Norman Knight Charitable Found.; trustee Mass. Bd. Regional Community Colls., Agassiz Village Camps, Crippled Children's Non-Sectarian Fund, Boys and Girls Camps, Inc.; mem. nat. council, exec. com. New Eng. council Boy Scouts Am.; exec. com., dir. Rescue, Inc.; exec. com. The Jimmy Fund; exec. com., trustee Children's Cancer Research Found., Dana Farber Cancer Inst.; mem. fin. com. Com.

Econ. Devel.; mem. devel. council Boston U.; mem. pres.'s council Boston Coll.; bd. dirs. Freedoms Found.; also nat. co-chmn. Am. Freedom Center. Recipient Americanism award Am. Heritage Com., 1959, awards from VFW, Am. Legion, Amvets, Am. Legion Aux., 1959-60, award for contbn. to radio and TV industry Alpha Epsilon Rho; named one of ten Outstanding Young Men Boston Jr. C. of C., 1956, Man of Yr. Italian-Am. Police Assn.. Mem. Radio-TV Execs. Sec., Young Pres.'s Orgn., Broadcast Pioneers, AIM, Alpha Epsilon Rho. Clubs: Variety (Boston); Broadcasting Execs. New Eng, 100 of Mass. (co-founder, pres., dir.), 100 of N.H. (life), Univ. Office: 63 Bay State Rd Boston MA 02215-1892

KNIGHT, RICHARD, electrical engineer; b. Raunds, Northamptonshire, Eng., Dec. 22, 1955; came to U.S., 1985; s. Arthur Stephen and Edith (Robinson) K.; m. Pamela Jane Cross, June 21, 1985. BSc, Loughborough (Eng.) U. Tech., 1977, MSc, 1978, PhD, 1985; postdoctoral fellow, U. Minn., 1985-89. Chartered engr., Eng. Rsch. assoc. Loughborough U. Tech., 1980-85, Drexel U., Phila., 1989—. Contbr. 15 articles to prof. jours. Vol. United Way, Mpls., 1985-88. Mem. ASM Internat., IEEE, MIEE (UK). Office: Drexel U Materials Engring 32nd Chestnut Philadelphia PA 19104

KNIGHT, RICHARD G.H., III, restaurant owner; b. Fall River, Mass., July 18, 1949; s. Richard G.H. and Gladys-Elaine (McCrossan) K.; m. Laura C. Pitts, Apr. 11, 1981; children: Christopher Greene, Benjamin Fenner. BA, McGill U., 1971; JD, Western N.E. Law Sch., Springfield, Mass., 1979. Mgr. The Center Inn, Glenmont, N.Y., 1971-74, The Lark Tavern, Albany, N.Y., 1974-75; owner Holmes & Watson, Ltd., Troy, N.Y., 1978—. Charter pres. Bethlehem Jaycees, Delmar, N.Y., 1973-74; dist. pres. N.Y. State Jaycees, 1975-76, regional dir., 1979-81; pres. Downtown Troy Bus. Assn., 1983. Recipient Gold Shield, Troy Police Benevolent Assn., 1986. Mem. King Solomon's F&AM Lodge, Rensselaer County C. of C., N.Y. State Restaurant Assn., N.Y.State JCI Senate. Office: Holmes & Watson Ltd 450 Broadway Troy NY 12180

KNIGHT, SAMUEL NICHOLAS, electrical engineer; b. Jamestown, N.Y., Apr. 1, 1948; s. Frederick Richard and Margret Frances (Canning) K.; m. Nancy Mecke, Jan. 18, 1975 (div. Sept. 1979); 1 child, James David. BSEE, Clarkson U., 1970; MEE, Cornell U., 1982. Systems test engr. Link Flight Simulation Co., Binghamton, N.Y., 1970-72, systems engr., 1972-73; prin. engr. I Link Flight Simulation div. Singer, Binghamton, 1973-76, prin. engr. II, 1976-78, sr. systems engr., 1978-79, staff systems engr., 1979-84, sr. staff systems engr., 1984-88; staff scientist Link Flight Simulation div. CAE-Link, Binghamton, 1988-91; sr. staff scientist Link Flight Simulation div. CAE-Link, Binghamton, 1991—; mem. steering com., chmn. emissions subgroup Working Group for Interoperability of Def. Simulations, Orlando, Fla., 1990&. Contbr. papers to profl. publs. Mem. AIAA, Army Aviation Assocs. Am. (treas. 1990—), Assn. U.S. Army, Sons of Am. Legion. Roman Catholic. Home: Box 1548-5 Windsor NY 13865-9998

KNIGHT, WARREN VAN HORN, aerospace company executive; b. Pensacola, Fla., Jan. 23, 1945; s. Robert Clark and Patricia Gould (Roos) K.; m. Kimberly Elizabeth Stoutamyer, June 18, 1983; children: Brittany Elizabeth, Christopher Scott. BS in Engring., Va. Poly. Inst., 1967; MBA, Okla. City U., 1971; postgrad., Def. Systems Mgmt. Coll., Ft. Belvoir, Va., 1982. Commd. 2d lt. USAF, 1967, advanced through grades to lt. col., ret., 1988; sr. mission engr. Sci. Applications Internat., Washington, 1988-89; project mgr. Planetary Exploration Project, Washington, 1989-90; div. mgr. Solar System Exploration Support, Washington, 1990—. Active Civilian Mil. Coun., Cape Canaveral, Fla., 1987. Mem. AIAA (sr.), Planetary Soc., Air Force Assn. (life), Soc. Air Safety Investigators (founding), U.S. Parachute Assn. Home: 1212 Rowland Dr Herndon VA 22070 Office: Sci Applications Internat 400 Virginia Ave SW Washington DC 20024

KNIGHTS, PETER ROGER, history educator; b. Melrose, Mass., May 8, 1938; s. George Brownbill and Ruth Mary-Doris (Rother) K. Student, MIT, 1955-57; BA in Liberal Arts, Johns Hopkins U., 1959; postgrad., Cornell U., 1960-62; MA in Journalism & PhD in U.S. History, U. Wis., 1965, 69. Asst. prof. journalism U. Ill., Urbana, 1969-71; assoc. prof. history York U., Downsview, Ont., Can., 1971—. Author: The Plain People of Boston, 1830-1860: A Study in City Growth, 1971, Yankee Destinies: The Lives of Ordinary 19th Century Bostonians, 1991, (pamphlet) The Press Association War of 1866-67, 1965; contbr. articles to profl. jours. Rsch. grantee NEH, 1972-73, Social Scis. and Humanities Rsch. Coun. Can., 1981-83, 83-84, 87-88, York U., 1980-81, 90-91, 91-92; NDEA fellow, 1960-62, Andrew Mellon Postdoctoral fellow, 1968-69, Can. Coun. leave fellow, 1976-77, Fulbright scholar, West Germany, 1959-60. Mem. Orgn. Am. Historians, New England Historic Genealogical Soc., Urban History Assn., Social Sci. History Assn., Econ. History Assn., Soc. for History of Tech. Office: York U Dept Hist, Downsview, ON Canada M3J 1P3

KNISELY, CHARLES WILLIAM, JR., engineering educator, researcher, consultant; b. Johnson City, N.Y., Dec. 29, 1952; s. Charles William and Hattie Elnora (Miller) K.; m. Karin Ingrid Wegener, May 21, 1983; children: Katrina Marie, Carleton Perry. BSME, Bucknell U., 1975, MSME, 1978; PhD in Mech. Engring., Lehigh U., 1980. Rsch. engr. Sulzer Bros., Inc., Winterthur, Switzerland, 1980-83, U. Karlsruhe, Fed. Republic of Germany, 1983-85, David Taylor Naval Ship R & D Ctr., Bethesda, Md., 1985-87; lectr. Kyoto (Japan) U., 1987-90; asst. prof. Bucknell U., Lewisburg, Pa., 1990—. Inventee in field. Western Electric Co. scholar, 1972-75. Mem. ASME, AIAA, Am. Soc. Engring. Edn., Internat. Assn. Hydraulic Rsch., Internat. Conf. Bluff Body Aerodynamics and its Applications (sec. Kyoto meeting 1988). Office: Bucknell U Mech Engring Dept Lewisburg PA 17837

KNOLL, DAVID E., petroleum refining company executive; b. 1944. BS, Drexel U., 1966; MBA, U. Mich., 1967. Econ. analyst Sun Refining & Mktg. Co., 1967—, mgr., 1974—, v.p. unbranded fuels, 1981-83, v.p. Sunoco Mktg., 1983—, pres., until 1992; v.p. fin. Sun Petroleum Products Co., 1979; sr. v.p. Sun Co., 1992—. Office: Sun Refining & Mktg Co 1801 Market St Philadelphia PA 19103-2924*

KNOPF, PAUL MARK, immunoparasitologist; b. Trenton, N.J., Apr. 4, 1936; s. Chiam David and Beatrice (Safir) K.; m. Carol Lois Harrison, June 29, 1958; children: Jeffrey William, Steven Harrison, Rachel Analiese. BSc, MIT, 1958, PhD, 1962. Postdoctoral fellow MRC Lab. Molecular Biology, Cambridge, Eng., 1962-64; spl. research assoc. Salk Inst., La Jolla, Calif., 1964-72; prof. med. sci. Brown U., Providence, 1972—, Charles A. and Helen B. Stuart prof. med. sci., 1992—, chmn. sect. molecular, cellular and devel. biology, 1990—; mem. study sect. on parasitic disease NIH, 1985-87. Recipient Career Devel. award NIH, 1966-72; grantee NIH, 1966-76, 84-88, 91—, Rockefeller Found., 1972-8o, Edna McConnell Clark Found., 1976-85, WHO, 1979—, MS Soc., 1989-90; Fulbright-Hays sr. fellow, 1978-79, Fogarty sr. internat. fellow, 1986-87. Mem. AAAS, Am. Assn. Immunologists, Am. Soc. Tropical Medicine and Hygiene, Soc. Neuroscience. Home: 2 Dana Rd Barrington RI 02806-4614 Office: Brown U Div Biology and Medicine Providence RI 02912

KNOPP, MARVIN ISADORE, mathematics educator; b. Chgo., Jan. 4, 1933; s. Mitshel and Minnie (Israel) K.; m. Josephine Zadovsky, June 9, 1957; children: Seth David, Yudah Benjamin, Abby Alissa, Elana Melissa. B.S., U. Ill., 1954, A.M., 1955, Ph.D., 1958. Rsch. mathematician Space Tech. Labs., L.A., 1958-59; NSF postdoctoral fellow Inst. Advanced Study, Princeton, N.J., 1959-60; asst. prof. U. Wis., 1960-62, assoc. prof., 1962-67, prof., 1967-72; mathematician Nat. Bur. Standards, Washington, 1963-64; vis. prof. U. Basel, Switzerland, 1968-69; prof. U. Ill., Chgo., 1970-76, Temple U., Phila., 1976—, Bryn Mawr (Pa.) Coll., 1988-89; Mem. Inst. Advanced Study, Princeton, N.J., 1975, 78, 88; vis. prof. Ohio State U., spring 1979. Author: Theory of Area, 1969, Modular Functions in Analytic Number Theory, 1970, Number Theory and Related Analysis, 1992; contbr. articles to profl. jours.; editor: Ill. Jour. Math., 1971-78, Procs. of Conf. in Analytic Number Theory, 1981, Papers in Number Theory and Related Analysis, 1992. NSF grantee, 1960-90, Fulbright-Hays grantee NRC, 1975-76, Nat. Security Agy. grantee, 1990—. Mem. Am. Math. Soc., London Math. Soc. Democrat. Jewish. Home: 410 Lancaster Ave Apt 221 Haverford PA 19041-1333 Office: Temple U Dept Math Philadelphia PA 19122

KNOUR, ARTHUR, clinical psychologist; b. Bklyn.; s. Abe and Betty (Rosenberg) K. BBA, CCNY, 1957; MS, Yeshiva U., 1961, PhD, 1973. Jr. psychologist Psychopharmacology Unit Downstate Med. Ctr., Bklyn., 1961-64; clin. intern Bklyn. Psychiatric Ctrs., Inc., 1973-74; staff psychologist North Cen. Mental Health Ctr., Minot, N.D., 1977-79; staff psychologist Psychol. Svcs. Unit N.Y.C. Police Dept., 1979-85; sr. psychologist, clin. coord. N.Y.C. Police Dept., Corona, 1985—; pvt. practice Bklyn., 1983—. Mem. Am. Psychol. Assn. Home: 945 E 26th St Brooklyn NY 11210-3748 Office: NY Police Dept Psychol Svcs/Health Svcs Div 1 Lefrak Pla 59-17 Junction Blvd Corona NY 11368

KNOWLES, BRIAN J., finance and administration executive; b. Rockville, N.Y., July 21, 1956; s. Daniel Edmund and Kathleen (Armour) K.; m. Marion Josephine Armenio, Sept. 26, 1981; children: Adam, Eric, Allison. BS in Acctg., Manhattan U., 1978. Cost acct. Fairchild Republic, Farmingdale, N.Y., 1978-79; fin. analyst ITT World Hdqrs., N.Y.C., 1979-81; sr. acct. Sandvik Conveyor, Inc., Allendale, N.J., 1981-82; supr. gen. acctg. Sandvik Process Systems, Inc., York, Pa., 1982-85, contr., 1985-88; v.p. Sandvik Process Systems, Inc., Totowa, Pa., 1988—; corp. sec. Sandvik Process Systems, Totowa, Inc., 1985—; cons. Sandvik Can., Ltd., Guelph, Ont., 1985—; adminstrn. mgr. Sandvik Seamco, Inc., Louisville, 1991—. Mem. Am. Irish Polit. Edn. Com., Stonypoint, N.Y., 1990—; mem. N.J. Citizen Action, New Brunswick, N.J., 1991; coach West Milford (N.J.) Little League, 1991, West Milford Pal Soccer, 1991; mem. fin. com., ann. carnival com. Our Lady Queen of Peace Roman Cath. Ch., 1991. Mem. Swedish-Am. C. of C. Republican. Home: 162 Mountain Cir S West Milford NJ 07480-3214 Office: Sandvik Process Systems Inc 21 Campus Rd Totowa NJ 07512-1211

KNOWLES, CHRISTOPHER ALLAN, healthcare executive; b. Washington, Oct. 24, 1949; s. Charles Edward and Eleanor Patricia (Murphy) K.; m. Mary Margaret O'Loughlin, Feb. 14, 1988; children: Sean Christopher, James Charles, Thomas Patrick. BA, U. Nebr., 1975; MPA, Drake U., Des Moines, 1982. Adminstrv. asst. to dir. Nebr. Dept. Water Resources, Lincoln, 1976-78; environ. planner Iowa Natural Resources Council, Des Moines, 1978-81, Md. Environ. Trust, Balt., 1982; fin. analyst Norwest Corp., Des Moines, 1982-83; asst. dir., dir. fin. Hospice of Cen. Iowa, Des Moines, 1983-85; assoc. dir. home health svcs. dept. Hackensack Med. Ctr., N.J., 1985-86; fiscal mgr. Family Health Ctr, Montefiore Med. Ctr., N.Y.C., 1986-87; assoc. dir. and adminstr. Comprehensive Family Care Ctr., Albert Einstein Coll., N.Y.C., 1987-88; exec. dir. Hospice Care of L.I., 1988; assoc. dir. Bronx-Lebanon Hosp., N.Y.C., 1989; chmn., chief exec. officer Knowles Econometrics, Inc., Pelham Manor, N.Y., 1990-91; dir. Vis. Nurse Svc., Martha's Vineyard Community Svcs., Oak Bluffs, Mass., 1991—. U.S. Dept. Edn. grantee, 1981-82. Mem. Pi Sigma Alpha, Pi Alpha Alpha. Democrat. Episcopalian. Office: PO Box 369 Vineyard Haven MA 02568-0369

KNOWLES, GREGORY ADAMS, city manager; b. West Point, N.Y., Jan. 9, 1947; s. Harold Ferguson and Mercedes (Murphy) K.; m. Deberah Ann Hochwalt, Aug. 29, 1949; children: Jennifer Lynn, Emily Katherine, Sarah Beth. BA, Va. Poly. Inst. and State U., 1975, M Urban Affairs, 1977. Asst. county adminstr. Montgomery County, Christiansburg, Va., 1976; asst. to village mgr. Village of Winnetka, Ill., 1976-78; city adminstr. City of Monona, Wis., 1978-83; village mgr. Village of University Park, Ill., 1983-84; city mgr. City of Inkster, Mich., 1984-87, City of Greenville, N.C., 1987-89, City of Meadville, Pa., 1990—. Author, producer, dir. ednl. videos. Bd. dirs. Evergreen, Greenville, 1987-90; mem. adv. bd. Mar. of Dimes, Greenville, 1989; mem. allocation com. United Way, 1990—. Staff Sgt. USAF, 1966-73, Vietnam. Mem. Internat. City Mgmt. Assn., Rotary (pres. Inkster chpt. 1986-87), Kiwanis. Roman Catholic. Home: 766 Azalea St Meadville PA 16335-1003 Office: City of Meadville 984 Water St Meadville PA 16335-3443

KNOWLES, JEREMY RANDALL, chemist, educator; b. Rugby, Eng., Apr. 28, 1935; came to U.S., 1974; s. Kenneth Guy Jack Charles and Dorothy Helen (Swingler) K.; m. Jane Sheldon Davis, July 30, 1960; children: Sebastian David Guy, Julius John Sheldon, Timothy Fenton Charles. B.A., Balliol Coll., Oxford (Eng.) U., 1958; M.A., D.Phil., Christ Ch., 1961. Research fellow Calif. Inst. Tech., 1961-62; fellow Wadham Coll., Oxford U., 1962-74, univ. lectr., 1966-74; vis. prof. Yale U., 1969, 71; Sloan vis. prof. Harvard U., 1973; prof. chemistry Harvard U., 1974—, Amory Houghton prof. chemistry and biochemistry, 1979—, dean faculty of arts and scis., 1991—; Newton-Abraham vis. prof. Oxford U., 1983-84; hon. fellow Balliol Coll., Oxford U., Wadham Coll., Oxford U. Author papers, revs. bioorganic chemistry. Served as pilot officer RAF, 1953-55. Recipient Prelog medal ETH, Switzerland. Fellow Am. Acad. Arts and Scis., Royal Soc. (Davy medal 1991), Royal Chem. Soc. London (Charmian medal); mem. NAS (fgn. assoc.), Biochem. Soc. London, Am. Chem. Soc. (Bader award, Cope Scholar award), Am. Soc. Biol. Chemists, Am. Philos. Soc. Home: 7 Bryant St Cambridge MA 02138 Office: Harvard U Faculty Arts & Scis University Hall 5 Cambridge MA 02138

KNOWLES, JOCELYN WAGNER, health writer, women's health specialist; b. N.Y.C., Feb. 22, 1918; d. Frederick and Violet Alice (Swain) W.; m. Clive Dorman Knowles, 1950 (div. 1959); 1 child, Katherine Miranda. Student, London Sch. Econs., 1938; BS, Columbia U., 1939, MA, 1940; MPH, UCLA, 1970. Exec. dir. Nat. Physicians Forum, Inc., N.Y.C., 1945-49; West Coast editor Nat. Foremen's Inst. Prentice-Hall Co., L.A., 1959-68; writer, editor The Female Patient mag., N.Y.C., 1980-81; dir. Planned Parenthood of S.W., Silver City, N.Mex., 1981-83; freelance writer N.Y.C., 1977—; asst. to pres., lit. agt. Writers House, Inc., N.Y.C., 1989-92; book critic Kirkus Revs., 1989-90, 1PB, 1990—, Book of the Month Club, 1991—, Pubrs. Weekly, 1991—. Contbr. articles to med. mags.; staff book-reviewer L.A. Times. First woman organizer Brotherhood of Railway Trainmen, 1945-47; publicist Farmers Union of Iowa, Des Moines, 1951, Golden Gate Arboretum, San Francisco, 1976; bd. dirs. Nat. Womens Health Network, 1981-85. NIH grantee U. Calif., L.A., 1968-70; Va. Ctr. for the Arts fellow, Charlottesville, 1976, Woolrich fellow Columbia U., N.Y.C., 1977, Wurlitzer Found. fellow, Taos, N.Mex., 1981. Jewish.

KNOWLES, RICHARD JAMES ROBERT, medical physicist, educator, consultant; b. McPherson, Kans., Aug. 2, 1943; s. Richard E. and Pauline H. (Worland) K.; m. Stephanie R. Closter, May 14, 1970; 1 child, Guenevere Regina. BS, St. Louis U., 1965; MS, Cornell U., 1969; PhD, Poly. U., N.Y., 1979. Diplomate Am. Bd. Sci. in Nuclear Medicine, Am. Bd. Radiology. Chief med. physicist L.I. Coll. Hosp., Bklyn., 1977-81; dir. radiation physics lab. Downstate Med. Ctr., Bklyn., 1981-82; sr. med. physicist N.Y. Hosp. Cornell U. Med. Ctr., N.Y.C., 1982—; assoc. prof. physics in radiology Cornell U. Med. Coll., N.Y.C., 1989—. Author: Quality Assurance and Image Artifacts in Magnetic Resonance Imaging, 1988; contbr. articles to profl. jours. Mem. Am. Phys. Soc., Soc. Nuclear Medicine, Health Physics Soc., Am. Assn. Physicists in Medicine, N.Y. Acad. Scis., Soc. for Computer Applications in Radiology, Soc. Magnetic Resonance in Medicine, Sigma Xi. Office: NY Hosp-Cornell Med Ctr 525 E 68th St New York NY 10021-4873

KNUDSEN, RAYMOND BARNETT, clergyman, association executive, author; b. Denver, Nov. 11, 1919; s. Franklin Ole and Julia (Nielsen) K.; m. Edna Mae Nielsen, Jan. 26, 1940; children: Raymond Barnett, Silas John, Mark Allen, Ann DeLight (Mrs. Arthur James Semotan III). Student, Coll. Emporia, 1937-38, Wheaton Coll., 1938-39; B.A., U. Denver, 1941; Th.M., McCormick Theol. Sem., 1948; postgrad., U. Chgo., 1948; D.D., Burton Coll., 1955, LL.D., 1964; ThD, Miami Bible Inst., 1987. Pastor 1st Presbyn. Ch., Akron, Colo., 1937-39; Pastor 8th Ave. Presbyn. Ch., Denver, 1939-40; dir. Martin M. Post Larger Parish, Logansport, Ind., 1941-44; asst. Faith Presbyn. Ch., Chgo., 1945; pastor 1st Presbyn. Ch., Warsaw, Ill., 1946-52, 5th Presbyn. Ch., Springfield, Ill., 1952-63; sr. pastor Webb Horton Meml. Presbyn. Ch., Middletown, N.Y., 1963-70; exec. dir. for donor support Nat. Council Chs. of Christ in U.S.A., 1970-71, asst. gen. sec., 1971-77; pres. Nat. Consultation on Fin. Devel., 1977-85, chmn., 1985-88, chmn. emeritus, 1988—; lectr. philosophy Orange County (N.Y.) Community Coll., 1964-70; instr. Drew U. Sch. Theology, 1978-86, Perkins Sch. Theology So. Meth. U., 1986—; chmn. broadcasting press Synod of Ill., Presbyn. Ch., 1954-60, mem. gen. council, 1954-62; chmn. founding com. Ill. Presbyn. Home, Springfield, 1954; pres. Middletown Council Chs., 1967-69; chmn. Fifty Million Dollar Fund, Hudson River Presbytery, 1964-70; pres. Webb Horton Presbyn. Assocs.; v.p. Inst. Activation Research.; cons. Episc. Diocese of Pitts., 1977-85, Orthodox Ch. in Am., 1978-88, Christian Meth. Episc. Ch., 1983-88, Hawaii conf. United Ch. of Christ, 1983-86, Asbury Hills Camp, 1983-86; cons. Fla. Council of Chs., 1986—, Pitts. Experiment, 1987-88, Jesus Fellowship, Inc., 1987—, 1st Bapt. Ch., Washington, 1987-90, Cornstone Consultation, 1990—, Higher Dimensions, Tulsa, 1990, David M. Wright M.D. Found., Richmond, Va., 1991, Alfalit, Inc., Miami, Fla., 1991, Abundant Life, Richmond, 1991. Author: The Trinity, 1936, New Models for Financing the Local Church, 1974, 2d edit., 1985, New Models for Creative Giving, 1976, 2d edit., 1985, Models for Ministry, 1976, Developing Dynamic Stewardship, 1977, The Workbook, 1977, New Models for Church Administration, 1979, Christian Stewardship in a Period of Fiscal Change, 1984, Stewardship Enlistment and Commitment, 1986, Let Your Money Do the Talking, 1987, From "Commitment?" to "Commitment!", 1987, Wiltshire Village Cookbook, 1991; mem. rev. bd. Antenna, 1963-90; contbr. religious columns to publs.; syndicated newspaper column The Counselor. Mem. Middletown Narcotics Guidance Council, 1969-70; pres. bd. dirs. Occupations, Inc., 1964-69, treas., 1969-71, pres. emeritus, 1976—; bd. dirs. Aid to Retarded Children N.Y., 1963-66, United Presbyn. Student Found., 1962-70, Presbyn. Sr. Services, N.Y.C., 1981-85, Presbyn. Panel, 1981-87, Christian Collegiate Schs., Richmond, 1991; exec. bd. Orange County chpt. Aid Retarded Children; trustee Orange County Workshop for Disabled, 1963, Homemaker Service Orange County; pres. bd. trustees Camp Townsend, 1964-70. Recipient Author citation N.J. Inst. Tech., 1980, Cert. for Outstanding Ministry, Wheaton Coll., 1991; Dr. Raymond B. and Edna M. Knudsen Ann. Lectureship established in his honor, 1992; Edna Mae Knudsen Meml. Fund established to finance Knudsen Libr. and Needy Students at McCormick Theol. Sem., 1992. Mem. Nat. Temperance League (hon. v.p., chmn. nominating com. 1961-62), Alcohol Edn. Found. (dir.), Counselor Assn. Inc. (pres. 1954-82, chmn. bd. Ill. soc. 1955-88, chmn. emeritus 1988—), Greenview Shores Civic Assn. (founder, pres. 1989-90), Counselor Assn., Inc. (founder, pres. Fla. soc. 1990—). Clubs: Masons, Rotary (chmn. internat. contacts). Home and Office: 1457 Brampton Cove Wellington West Palm Beach FL 33414

KNUDSON, JERRY WAYNE, journalism educator, freelance writer; b. Rexford, Kans., Sept. 2, 1932; s. Jay Curtis Byron and Maybelle Edith (Cousins) K. BS, U. Kans., 1956; MA, U. Minn., 1958; PhD, U. Va., 1962. Instr. U. Kans., Lawrence, 1958-59; reporter Suffolk (Va.) News-Herald, 1957; asst. prof. SUNY, Oneonta, 1962-67, U. Ky., Lexington, 1967-71; assoc. prof. S.D. State U., Brookings, 1971-72; prof. journalism Temple U., Phila., 1972—; freelance writer; bd. dirs. Times of Ams. Edn. Found.; mem. press com. Latin Am. Studies Assn., Washington, 1974-80. Author: Bolivia: Press and Revolution, 1932-64, 1986; author 4 monographs, 35 articles on role of press in social change in Latin Am.; contbr. articles to various publs. With U.S. Army, 1954-56. Summerfield scholar U. Kans., 1950-54; Jefferson fellow U. Va., 1959-62; grantee Gannett Found., Ford Found., Tinker Found., Pa. Coun. Humanities, Doherty Found., Temple U., Ky. U. Mem. ACLU, Com. to Protect Journalists, Am. Hist. Assn., Latin Am. Studies Assn., Amnesty Internat. Home: 2101 Chestnut St Apt 1116 Philadelphia PA 19103-3121 Office: Temple Univ Dept Journalism Philadelphia PA 19122

KNUPP, MICHAEL DONALD, consulting company executive; b. Glenwood Springs, Colo., Sept. 10, 1947; s. Donald Eugene and Laurene W. (Grant) K.; m. Linda Ann Stevens, Jan. 20, 1973; children: Travis Grant, Emily Laurene. BS, Colo. State U., 1970; student, Golden Gate U., 1988. Warehouseman Koonce Co., Inc., Eagle, Colo., 1970-73; tech. editor ERT, Inc., Concord, Mass., 1973-74, cost analyst, 1974-76, contract adminstr., 1976-80, div. bus. mgr., 1980-85; mgr. adminstrn. ENSR Corp., Acton, Mass., 1985-88; v.p., gen. mgr. ENSR Health Scis., Alameda, Calif., 1988-89; v.p. fin. and adminstrn. Remediation Techs., Inc., Concord, Mass., 1989—. Chmn. Littleton (Mass.) Town Fin. Com., 1979-88; officer Littleton Rep. Com., 1985—; mem. Growth Study Com., Littleton, 1985-88, Bd. of Zoning Appeals, Littleton, 1990—. Recipient Cert. of Appreciation Mass. House Reps., Boston, 1988. Roman Catholic. Home: 27 Robinson Rd Littleton MA 01460-1907

KNUTH, CYNTHIA STROUT, educational consultant; b. Walpole, Mass.; d. Harold A. and Doris A. (Kendall) Strout; m. Count Adam Knuth. BA in French and Spanish, Middlebury Coll.; MA in Internat. Law and Govt., NYU. FAO Mission to Iraq, Baghdad, 1950-53; conf. precis-writer UN, Copenhagen, 1954-56; exec. sec. to UN legal counsel, N.Y.C., 1956-62, to pres. Gen. Assembly, 1962-63, UN Devel. Program, 1964-69; adminstrv. asst. Boston U., 1971-75; sec. to dir. Ctr. for Internat. Affairs, Harvard U., Cambridge, Mass., 1976-82; cons. to Bd. Regents of Higher Edn. in Mass., 1983-86. Founder Friends of the Wampanoag, Boston, 1986, Friends of Native Ams., 1989, Menotomy Indian Day, Arlington, Mass., 1991, Aberjona Indian Day, Winchester, Mass., 1992. Mem. Common Cause (exec. bd. Mass. 1986—), UN Assn. (exec. bd. 1970—), World Affairs Coun. Boston, Boston Jazz Soc. (exec. bd. 1975—), Mystic River Watershed Assn. (exec. bd. 1991—), Phi Delta Kappa (2s v.p. Harvard U. chpt. 1990). Home: 206 Massachusetts Ave Arlington MA 02174-8435

KO, EDMOND INQ-MING, chemical engineering educator; b. Hong Kong, July 8, 1952; came to U.S., 1970; BS, U. Wis., 1974; MS, Stanford U., Palo Alto, Calif., 1975, PhD, 1980. Rsch. fellow Exxon Rsch. & Engring. Co., Linden, N.J., 1975-76; asst. prof. Carnegie Mellon U., Pitts., 1980-84, assoc. prof., 1984-88, prof., 1988—; vis. assoc. prof. U. Calif., Berkeley, 1987-88. Editor: Catalytic Conversion with Niobium Materials, 1990 (Chem. Mfrs. Assn. catalyst award 1992); contbr. over 60 articles to profl. jours. Mem. AAAS, Am. Chem. Soc., Am. Inst. Chem. Engrs., Am. Soc. Engring. Edn., Materials Rsch. Soc., N.Am. Catalysis Soc., Phi Kappa Phi, Sigma Xi. Home: 363 S Highland Ave Apt 302 Pittsburgh PA 15206-4258 Office: Carnegie Mellon U Dept Chem Engring 5000 Forbes Ave Pittsburgh PA 15213-3816

KO, HON-SUM, immunologist, molecular biologist; b. Canton, Kwangdong, China, Oct. 3, 1946; s. Ching and Ching-Yee (Fong) K. MBBS, U. Hong Kong, 1971. Diplomate Am. Bd. Internal Medicine, Am. Bd. Allergy and Immunology. House officer Queen Elizabeth and Queen Mary Hosps., Hong Kong, 1971-72; intern medicine St. Louis City Hosp., 1972-73; resident medicine U. Toronto (Ont., Can.), 1973-74, resident clin. immunology, 1974-76; postdoctoral fellow Rockefeller U., N.Y.C., 1976-79; asst. prof. medicine U. Western Ont., London, 1979-86; Fogarty assoc. NIH, Bethesda, Md., 1987—; cons. in clin. immunology Univ. Hosp., London, 1979-86; vis. assoc. Fogarty Internat. Ctr., Bethesda, 1987—. Mem. Greenpeace, Washington, 1989—, Environ. Def. Fund, Washington, 1989—. Med. Rsch. Coun. Can. fellow, Ottawa, 1976-79; recipient Career Scientist award Ministry of Health, Toronto, 1983-86. Fellow Royal Coll. Physicians Edinburgh, Royal Coll. Physicians and Surgeons Can.; mem. Am. Assn. Immunologists.

KO, LI-WEN, pathologist, researcher; b. Taipei, Taiwan, Jan. 31, 1949; came to U.S., 1973; s. Wei-Dong and Tsang-Urr (Tsai) Ko.; m. Hwai-Hwa Chen, Dec. 17, 1976; children: Eric Chi-Ching, Michelle Chi-Hsun. BVM, Nat. Taiwan U., Taipei, 1972; MSc, U. Wash., 1975; PhD, Ohio State U., 1979. Postgrad. trainee U.S. Naval Med. Res. Unit 2, Taipei, 1972-73; postdoctoral fellow Sch. Medicine U. Washington, Seattle, 1973-75; grad. rsch. assoc. Ohio State U., Columbus, 1975-79, rsch. assoc., 1979-80; assoc. prof. Nat. Yang-Ming Med. Coll., Taipei, 1980-85; vis. rsch. scientist U. Mo., Kansas City, 1985-87; rsch. scientist Burke Rehab. Ctr., White Plains, N.Y., 1987—; dir. Brain Cell Culture Lab. Ohio State U., 1975-80, Ctr. Exptl. Animal Resources Nat. Yang-Ming Med. Coll., 1980-82; com. tissue culture core Dementia Rsch. Svc., Burke Rehab. Ctr., 1980—; instr. Cornell U. Med. Coll., N.Y.C., 1987-90, asst. prof., 1990—; reviewer Am. Jour. Pathology, 1990-91. Contbr. articles profl. jours. NIH fellow, 1975-80; recipient Ching-Ling Basic Med. Rsch. Chair award Ching-Ling Med. Found., 1981, Govt. Scholar award Min. Edn. Taiwan, 1973-76. Mem. Am. Soc. Cell Biology, Tissue Culture Assn., Soc. Exptl. Biology and Medicine, N.Y. Acad. Sci., N.Y. Soc. Electron Microscopy, Phi Zeta. Office: Burke Med Rsch Inst 785 Mamaroneck Ave White Plains NY 10605

KOBAK, JAMES BENEDICT, JR., lawyer, educator; b. Alexandria, La., May 2, 1944; s. James Benedict and Hope (McEldowney) K.; m. Carol Johnson, June 11, 1966; children: James Benedict III, Katherine Jean, Marcie Ann. BA magna cum laude, Harvard U., 1966; LLB, U. Va., 1969. Bar: U.S. Dist. Ct. (so. and ea. dists.) N.Y. 1972, U.S. Supreme Ct. 1977, U.S.

Ct. Appeals (2nd cir.) 1973, (5th cir.) 1982, U.S. Dist. Ct. (no. dist.) Calif. 1983. Asst. prof. U. Ala., 1969-70; assoc. Hughes Hubbard & Reed, N.Y.C., 1970-77, ptnr., 1977—; lectr. in law U. Va., 1986—; adj. assoc. prof. Fordham U., 1986—. Bd. editors Va. Law Review 1967-69 (assoc. editor 1968-69); contbr. articles to profl. jours., mags., and newspapers. Pres. bd. trustees N.J. Chamber Music Soc., Montclair, 1988-90. Mem. ABA (anti-trust sect.), Assn. Bar City N.Y., New York County Lawyers Assn. (dir. 1988—, chmn. trade rebulation com. 1987-88, chmn. com. on changing trends in profession 1990—), Order of Coif, Am. Law Inst., Adirondack 46ers Club, Keene Valley Country Club, Downtown Athletic Club. Home: Edge Hill Rd Llewellyn Park West Orange NJ 07052 Office: Hughes Hubbard & Reed One Battery Park Pla New York NY 10004

KOBAYASHI, SUKEYUKI, automotive industry administrator; b. Chiba-Ken, Japan, Dec. 21, 1946; came to U.S., 1976; s. Sukemi and Chizu (Inoue) K.; m. Eiko Ando, Nov. 4, 1972; children: Naho, Sow, Ken. BS, U. Tokyo, 1971, MS, 1973; MS, MIT, 1978, PhD, 1981. Engr. Ishikawajima-Harima Heavy Industries, Tokyo, 1973-76; sr. project staff ORI, Inc., Rockville, Md., 1981-85; prin. rsch. scientist Tracor Hydronautics Inc., Laurel, Md., 1985-88; mgr., Japanese auto bus. Airflow Rsch. & Mfg. Corp., Watertown, Mass., 1989—; cons., translator USN, Washington, 1982-89. Author: Laser Anemonetry in Fluid Mechanics, 1984. Mem. AIAA, Soc. Naval Architects & Marine Engrs. Home: 15 Emerson Rd Wayland MA 01778-4041 Office: Airflow Rsch & Mfg Corp 304 Pleasant St Watertown MA 02172-2401

KOBILINSKY, LAWRENCE, forensic science educator; b. N.Y.C., Nov. 7, 1946; s. Abraham and Sophie (Selkow) K.; m. Estelle Kartagener, June 10, 1971; 1 child, Hayley. BS, CUNY, 1969, MA, 1971, PhD, 1977. Adj. lectr. Bklyn. Coll., N.Y.C., 1972-74, Hunter Coll., N.Y.C., 1974-75; fellow, rsch. assoc. Sloan Kettering Inst. for Cancer Rsch., N.Y.C., 1977-80; mem. doctoral faculty grad. ctr. CUNY, N.Y.C., 1981—; prof. John Jay Coll. Criminal Justice, N.Y.C., 1975—; cons. forensic sci., 1978—. Contbr. numerous articles to sci. jours. 1st lt. U.S. Army, 1971-72. Recipient Civilian award Fed. Law Enforcement Officers Assn., 1988; fellow Am. Acad. Forensic Scis., 1991. Fellow N.Y. Microscopical Soc. (pres. 1986-89, Ashby award 1990); mem. Am. Assn. Immunologists, Am. Acad. Forensic Scis., Northeastern Assn. Forensic Scientists (chair edn. com. 1989—), N.Y. Acad. Scis., Masons, Sigma Xi. Home: 504 Rebecca Ln Oceanside NY 11572-2631 Office: John Jay Coll 445 W 59th St New York NY 10019-1104

KOBRIN, JAY ARTHUR, interior designer, fiber artist; b. N.Y.C., Nov. 30, 1936; s. Irving and Hortense (Freezer) K. BA, Brandeis U., 1958; MFA, Yale U., 1961. Theatre designer N.Y.C., 1961-64; prin. Jay Arthur Inc., N.Y.C., 1964-66; designer Bellciano Couture, N.Y.C., 1966-68, Masionette, N.Y.C., 1968-72, Malcolm Starr Boutique, N.Y.C., 1972, Damon Internat., N.Y.C., 1972-75, Goldworm Knits, N.Y.C., 1975-76; v.p. Gordon Micunis Designs, Inc., Stamford, Conn., 1976—. Artist, exhibitor Art of the N.E., 1990, Soc. of Conn. Craftsmen, 1991. Mem. bd. advisers Stamford Theatre Works, 1988-92; bd. dirs. Loft Artist Assn., Stamford, 1989—, Stamford Hist. Soc., 1985-87. Mem. Yale Club of Stamford (bd. dirs. 1983-85). Democrat. Jewish. Office: Gordon Micunis Designs Inc One Rogers Rd Stamford CT 06902

KOBRIN, ROBERT JAY, chemist, consultant; b. N.Y.C., Nov. 4, 1937; s. Alex and Helen (Tarnopol) K.; m. Eileen Debra Raden, Sept. 1, 1969; children: Michael, David, Daniel. BS in Chemistry, City Coll. N.Y., 1960; PhD in Phys. Chemistry, U. Del., 1969. Jr. chemist Sonneborn Chem. & Refining, Belleville, N.J., 1960-61; rsch. cons. Mobil R&D Corp., Paulsboro, N.J., 1961—; mem. editorial bd. Sci. Computing and Automation Jour., 1989-90. Contbr. articles to profl. jours. Recipient I-R 100 award Indsl. Rsch. mag., 1976. Mem. Assn. Computing Machinery, Am. Chem. Soc., Sigma Xi. Home: 16 Tracey Terr Cherry Hill NJ Office: Mobil R&D 600 Billingsport Rd Paulsboro NJ 08066-1034

KOBUS, LEE HENRY, university official, broadcasting educator; b. Phila., Apr. 11, 1955; s. Henry and Stella Catherine (Szozda) K.; m. Allison Elizabeth Fink, Oct. 24, 1986. BA, King's Coll., Wilkes-Barre, Pa., 1980. Staff announcer Sta. WILK, Wilkes-Barre, 1976-78, Sta. WBAX, Wilkes-Barre, 1978, Stas. WEJL and WEZX-FM, Scranton, Pa., 1978-80; news anchor Sta. WOBM, Toms River, N.J., 1980-82; dir. news and programming Clear TV Cable Corp., Toms River, 1982-83; news dir. Colony/U.S. Cablevision, Beacon, N.Y., 1984-87, Sta. WJRZ-FM, Toms River, 1987-89; dir. radio and TV, instr., prodn. technician SUNY, New Paltz, 1989—. Editor, dir. instrnl. video College 101, 1991. Recipient Voice of Democracy citation VFW, Tuckerton, N.J., 1987, hon. mention for best documentary N.J. AP, 1987. Mem. Broadcast Edn. Assn., Coll. Media Advisors, Radio and TV News Dirs. Assn., Soc. Profl. Journalists, Optimists (v.p. Toms River 1987-88). Office: SUNY Campus Media Ctr SUB 309 New Paltz NY 12561

KOBYLARZ, JOSEPH DOUGLAS, secondary education educator; b. Garfield, N.J., Dec. 18, 1948; s. Joseph H. and Josephine (Rys) K.; m. Joyce Ann Metzger, July 15, 1978; children: Lauren Ann, Kristen Ann. BS, Northwestern State Coll., 1970; MA, Montclair State Coll., 1976. Cert. tchr. indsl. arts, coord. C.I.E., supr., prin., N.J. Tchr. Garfield Bd. Edn., 1970—, master tchr., 1974-76, dept. chmn., 1976—, adminstrv. asst. to the supt., 1991—; mem. Am. Indsl. Arts Safety Com., 1978-81, adv. Am. Indsl. Arts Student Assn., Garfield, 1980-85; adj. instr. Montclair State Coll., Upper Montclair, N.J., 1982-86; transcript reviewer Bennett Pub. Co., Peoria, Ill., 1985-87. Co-author: (safety guide) New Jersey Industrial Arts Safety Manual, 1982; author (safety guide) Garfield District Safety Manual, 1981. County Committeeman Garfield Dem. Orgn., 1972-75; bd. govs. Ocean Beach and Yacht Club, Lavallette, N.J., 1972-78; mem. Garfield Housing Authority, 1979-84, chmn. 1984. Mem. Vocat. Edn. Assn. of N.J. (recording sec. 1982-86, pres. elect 1986-87, pres. 1987-88, past pres. 1988-91), Am. Vocat. Assn. (N.J. rep. region I 1990-91), Vocat. Edn. Assn. of N.J. (editor newsletter 1991), Phi Delta Kappa. Roman Catholic. Home: 97 Miller Rd Kinnelon NJ 07405-1544 Office: Garfield High Sch 500 Palisade Ave Garfield NJ 07026-2546

KOCH, EDWARD I., former mayor, lawyer; b. N.Y.C., Dec. 12, 1924; s. Louis and Joyce K. Student, Coll. City N.Y.; LLB, NYU, 1948. Bar: N.Y. State 1949. Sole practice law N.Y.C., 1949-64; sr. partner firm Koch Lankenau Schwartz & Kovner, N.Y.C., 1965-69; mem. N.Y.C. Council, 1967-68, 91st-92nd Congresses from 17th Dist. N.Y., 1969-72; mem. 93d-95th congresses from 18th Dist. N.Y., 1973-77, mem. appropriations com., sec. N.Y. Congl. del.; mayor N.Y.C., 1978-89; ptnr. Robinson Silverman Pearce Aronsohn and Berman, N.Y.C., 1990—; Democratic dist. leader Greenwich Village, 1963-65. Author: Mayor, 1984, Politics, 1985, His Eminence and Hizzoner, 1989, All the Best, Letters From a Feisty Mayor, 1990. Served with AUS, World War II. Office: Robinson Silverman Pearce Aronsohn & Berman 1290 Ave Of The Americas New York NY 10104-0095

KOCH, EDWARD RICHARD, lawyer, accountant; b. Teaneck, N.J., Mar. 25, 1953; s. Edward J. and Adelaide M. (Wunner) K. BS in Econs. magna cum laude, U. Pa., 1975; JD, U. Va., 1980; LLM in Taxation, NYU, 1986. Bar: N.J. 1980, U.S. Dist. Ct. N.J. 1980, U.S. Tax Ct. 1981, U.S. Ct. Claims 1981. Staff acct. Touche Ross & Co. (now Deloitte & Touche), Newark, 1975-77; assoc. Winne, Banta & Rizzi, Hackensack, N.J., 1980-82; tax atty. Allied Corp. (name now Allied-Signal, Inc.), Morristown, 1982-87; asst. v.p. Chem. Bank, N.Y.C., 1987-90; tax mgr. Paul Scherer & Co., N.Y.C., 1990—. Vice chmn. law and legis. com. Athletics Congress, Indpls., 1985—, chmn., 1989—, chmn. ins. com., 1984-88, bd. dirs., 1989—; pres. N.J. Athletics Congress, Red Bank, 1986-90; mem. Jury of Appeals, 1988, U.S. Olympic Men's Marathon Trials. Mem. ABA, AICPA, N.J. State Bar Assn., N.J. Soc. CPAs, Am. Assn. Attys.-CPAs, N.J. Striders Track Club (chmn. 1981—). Republican. Roman Catholic. Home: 47 Brandywine Dr Florham Park NJ 07932-2852 Office: Paul Scherer & Co 330 Madison Ave 15th Fl New York NY 10017

KOCH, MICHAEL IGNAZ, music business executive; b. Innsbruck, Austria, June 1, 1962; came to U.S., 1987; s. Otmar Koepfle and Margot (Dreier) K.; m. Laura Giadorou, June 15, 1991. D in Law, Leopold Franzens U., Innsbruck, Austria, 1984; diploma in bus. adminstrn., Leopold Franzeus U., Innsbruck, 1985. V.p., cons. Koch Internat. Europe, Austria, 1980—; asst. to judge Appellate Ct. Innsbruck, 1984-85; atty. Ladurner Leuprecht, Innsbruck, 1985-86; pres. Koch Internat. U.S.A., Westbury, N.Y., 1987—; bd. dirs. Shanachic Entertainment Corp., Newton, N.J. Civil servant Red Cross, Austria, 1985-86. Mem. Verein der Pauliner (bd. dirs. 1982-87). Home: 111 Hicks St # 25C Brooklyn NY 11201-1685 Office: Koch Internat Corp 177 Cantiague Rd Westbury NY 11590

KOCH, PHILIP, language educator; b. N.Y.C., Dec. 31, 1927; s. Samuel and Esther Florence (Goldstein) K.; m. Frances Ann Bonanno, June 15, 1952; children—Philip Samuel, Erec Russell. A.B. magna cum laude, Harvard U., 1949, A.M., 1951, Ph.D., 1955. Substitute instr. Phillips Exeter Acad., N.H., 1949; teaching fellow Harvard U., Cambridge, Mass., 1950-53, 54-55; instr. Northwestern U., Evanston, Ill., 1955-56; instr., then asst. prof. Bryn Mawr Coll., Pa., 1956-58, 58-61; asst. prof. U. Pitts., 1961-62, assoc. prof., 1962-66, prof., 1966-92, chmn. dept., 1965-72; cons. and lectr. in field; corrector Ednl. Testing Services, Princeton, 1960-65. Editor: Galiani Dialogues, 1968, Racine Andromaque, 1970. Contbr. articles to profl. jours., also revs. Vol. St. Margaret Meml. Hosp., 1980-88. Sr. research fellow Am. Council Learned Socs., Paris, 1969; grantee Fulbright Commn., 1953, 65. Mem. MLA, Am. Assn. Tchrs. French, N. Am. Soc. 17th Century French Studies, Am. Soc. 18th Century Studies, Soc. Francaise d'Etude du 18e Siecle, Phi Beta Kappa. Clubs: Harvard (Pitts.). Avocations: equitation; reading. Office: Dept French and Italian U Pitts Pittsburgh PA 15260

KOCH, ROBERT, art educator; b. N.Y.C., Apr. 7, 1918; s. Millard Fillmore and Ella (Heidelberg) K.; m. Gladys Leah Rooff, Aug. 5, 1942; children: B'rak Elana, Mitchell David. AB, Harvard U., 1939; MA, NYU, 1953; PhD, Yale U., 1957. Asst. instr. Queen's Coll., N.Y.C., 1951-53; grad. asst. Yale U., New Haven, 1953-56; asst. prof. So. Conn. State U., New Haven, 1956-59; lectr. U. Calif., Berkeley, 1960-61; assoc. prof. So. Conn. State U., New Haven, 1959-66, prof., 1966-79, prof. emeritus, 1979—. Author: Louis C. Tiffany, Rebel in Glass, 1964, Louis C. Tiffany's Glass, Bronzes, Lamps, 1971, Louis C. Tiffany's Art Class, 1977; contbr. articles to profl. jours. Pres. Temple Shalom of Norwalk, Conn., 1966-69. 1st Lt. U.S. Army, 1942-45. Recipient Faculty Scholar award So. Conn. State U., 1973-74. Mem. Coll. Art Assn., AAUP. Democrat. Jewish. Home: 143 Hyt St Apt 7G Stamford CT 06905

KOCH, STEPHEN BAYARD, author, educator; b. St. Paul, May 8, 1941; s. Robert Fulton and Edith (Bayard) K.; m. Frances Bernard Cohen, Apr. 25, 1987. BA, CCNY, 1962; MA, Columbia U., 1963, postgrad., 1963-66. Instr. English dept. SUNY, Stony Brook, 1965-70; adj. prof. Columbia U., N.Y.C., 1978-89, acting chmn., then chmn. writing div. Sch. Arts, 1989—; lectr. creative writing program Princeton (N.J.) U., 1979-86. Author: Night Watch, 1970, Stargazer: Andy Warhol's World and His Films, 1973, 3d edit., 1991, The Bachelors' Bride, 1986; contbr. articles to numerous publs. Democrat. Episcopalian. Home: 115 E 86th St New York NY 10028-1057

KOCHANSKI, GERALD JOHN, controller, educator, director of finance; b. Phila., May 2, 1953; s. Thaddeus Martin and Mary Catherine (Gonciarz) K.; m. Charlotte Diane Downing, June 22, 1973; children: Gerald John Jr., Brian, Michael, Lauren. BS in Acctg. magna cum laude, LaSalle U., 1975, MBA in Fin., 1984; postgrad., Villanova (Pa.) U. CPA, Pa. Sr. acct. Price Waterhouse, Phila., 1975-78; acctg. mgr. Air Shields Inc., Hatboro, Pa., 1978-86; controller Keystone Franklin, Inc., Ft. Washington, Pa., 1986-88, Gist-Brocades Food Ingredients, Inc., King of Prussia, Pa., 1988—; evening instr. LaSalle U., 1986—; dir. fin. coun. Nativity Parish, Warminster, Pa., 1989—. Administrator Boy Scouts Am., Warminster, 1984-87; coach Warminster Soccer Club, 1987—, treas., 1989. Republican. Roman Catholic. Home: 874 Aster Rd Warminster PA 18974-2115

KOCHER, BRYAN STANLEY, management consultant; b. Easton, Pa., July 3, 1948; s. Stanley C. and Virginia May (Paulson) K.; A.B. cum laude, Moravian Coll., 1970; M.S., U. Mass., 1975; m. Sandra Lee Wagner, Jan. 3, 1971; children—Ellen, Dana, Whitney. Data base project leader Comml. Union Assurance Co., Boston, 1976-77; mgr. bus. systems design Raytheon Data Systems Co., Norwood, Mass., 1977-80; software engr. Cullinane Corp., Westwood, Mass., 1980-82; project mgr. IDC, Waltham, Mass., 1982-85; cons., CMD, Cambridge, Mass., 1986-91; pres. G&E Systems, 1991—; adj. prof. computer sci. Boston U., 1979-81. Served with U.S. Army, 1970-73. Mem. Inst. Cert. Computer Profls. (cert. data processor), Assn. Computing Machinery (chmn. Boston chpt. 1978-80, mem. nat. bd. dirs., 1981-92, nat. pres. 1988-90), IEEE, Data Processing Mgmt. Assn., Ops. Research Soc. Am., Alpha Pi Mu, Phi Alpha Theta. Home: 250 Edge Hill Rd Sharon MA 02067-1017 Office: 250 Edge Hill Rd Sharon MA 02067-1017

KOCHERTHALER, MINA, painter; b. Munich. Student, Columbia U., 1942-45, Art Students League, 1955-62, Nat. Acad. Design, 1962-79. Del. U.S. Com. Internat. Assn. Arts., N.Y., 1960-62; vol. print collection N.Y. Hist. Soc., 1987—. Represented in permanent collection Norfolk Mus. Arts and Sci.; exhibited in group shows in Royal Soc. Painters Watercolours, London, 1962, 200 Yrs. Watercolor Painting Am., Met. Mus. Art, N.Y.C., 1966-67, Mus. Acuarela, Mexico City, 1968, Butler Inst. Am. Art, 1970, Can. Soc. Painters Watercolour, 1971-72. Vol. N.Y. Hist. Soc. Recipient John J. Karpick Meml. medal Audubon Artist, seven prizes Nat. Soc. Painters Casein & Acrylic, 1958-77, Grumbacher Polymer award Catharine Lorillard Wolfe Art Club, 1971. Mem. Am. Watercolor Soc. (recording sec., coord. chmn., 1962-82, bd. dirs. 1982, elected hon. mem. 1988), Aubdubon Artists, Nat. Soc. Painters Casein & Acrylic (v.p. 1962-84, bd. dirs. 1984-89), Allied Artists Am. (recording sec. 1974-78, mem. coord. 1978-86), Catharine Lorillard Wolfe Art Club.

KOCHHAR, DEVENDRA M., biomedical scientist, educator; b. Sialkot, Panjab, India, Mar. 10, 1938; came to U.S., 1960; s. Trilok Nath and Savitri D. (Abbi) K.; m. Omila Sagar, Sept. 14, 1962; children: Vineet Sagar, Romeen. BS with honors, Panjab U., Chandigarh, India, 1958, MS, 1959; PhD, U. Fla., 1964. Rsch. scholar Panjab U., Chandigarh, 1959-60; postdoctoral trainee Karolinska Inst., Stockholm, 1965-66; visiting scientist Strangeway Rsch. Lab., Cambridge, U.K., 1966-67; guest investigator Rockefeller U., N.Y.C., 1967-68; assoc. prof. U. Iowa, Iowa City, 1968-71; prof. U. Va., Charlottesville, 1971-76, Thomas Jefferson U., Phila., 1976—; editorial bd. Life Scis., 1979-89, Reproductive Toxicology, 1987—, Pergamon Press, N.Y.; study sect. mem. NIH, Bethesda, Md., 1986-90. Co-editor: Handbook of Exp. Pharmacology, 1983, In Vitro Techniques in Developmental Toxicology, 1990. Recipient medal Panjab U., 1958, Helen Hay Whitney fellowship, 1965-68, NIH merit award, 1988. Mem. Teratology Soc. (Warkany lectr. 1990, pres. 1982-83). Home: 75 Harrowgate Dr Cherry Hill NJ 08003-1939 Office: Thomas Jefferson U Dept Anatomy 1020 Locust St Philadelphia PA 19107

KOCISKO, STEPHEN JOHN, clergyman; b. Mpls., June 11, 1915; s. John Z. and Anna (Somosz) K. Ph.B., Propaganda Fide U., 1937, S.T.L., 1941. Ordained priest Roman Catholic Ch., 1941, consecrated bishop, 1956; chancellor Byzantine Cath. Diocese of Pitts., 1956; rector Byzantine Cath. Sem., Pitts., 1958-63; 1st bishop Byzantine Eparchy (diocese) of Passaic, 1963-69; met. archbishop of Pitts., 1969—. Address: 50 Riverview Ave Pittsburgh PA 15214

KODAKA, KUNIO, plastics company executive; b. Toyko, Apr. 4, 1932; s. Shintaro and Hana (Tonegawa) K.; m. Masako Kodaka, Oct. 10, 1959; children: Akiko, Ichiro. BS, Waseda U., Tokyo, 1955. V.p. gen. mgr. Achilles KCI Corp., N.Y.C., 1963-71; gen. mgr. internat. ops. Kohokoku Chem. Ind. Corp., Tokyo, 1971-73, dir., 1973-76; pres., chief exec. officer HOP Industries Corp., Carlstadt, N.J., 1977—; treas., dir. Have our Plastics Corp., Mississauga, Ont., Can., 1985—; dir. Tashin Shoji Co., Ltd., Osaka, Japan, 1981—. Mem. Haworth Country Club. Home: 190 Durie Ave Closter NJ 07624-1708 Office: HOP Industries Corp 130 Commerce Rd Carlstadt NJ 07072-2598

KODET, ALBERT CHARLES, systems engineer; b. N.Y.C., Feb. 28, 1958; s. Albert Charles and Laura (Cieplinski) K.; m. Lauren Buchinsky, June 11, 1983; children: Katherine Lee, Leslie Emily. AAS, SUNY, Farmingdale, 1978; BSME, U. Hartford, Conn., 1982; MSEE, Syracuse U., 1987. Assoc. staff engr. Gen. Elec. Co., Aerospace Controls Sys. Dept., Binghamton, N.Y., 1983-86; sr. sys. engr. Hercules Aerospace Co., Norwich, N.Y., 1986-89; group leader United Techs. Hamilton Standard, Windsor Locks, Conn., 1989-91. Author, presenter: Electroimpulse Deicing, 1988. Fund raiser Multiple Sclerosis, Broome County chpt., Binghamton, 1987, 88, Fidelco Guide Dog Found., Hartford, Conn., 1990. Recipient Outstanding Achievement award Gen. Elec. Co., 1986.

KODITSCHEK, DANIEL ELIEZAR, systems science educator, researcher; b. Montclair, N.J., July 26, 1954; s. Paul and Leah (Kusselewitz) K.; m. Anne Marie Teitelman, Aug. 23, 1984; 1 child, Benjamin Martin. BS, Yale U., 1977, PhD, 1983. Asst. prof. Yale U., New Haven, Conn., 1983-87, assoc. prof., 1987—. Recipient Henry Prentiss Becton prize Yale U., 1983, Presdl. Young Investigator award NSF, Washington, 1986; grad. rsch. fellow NSF, Washington, 1980, Lilly Endowment fellow Lilly Found., Evansville, Ill., 1986, Vis. rsch. fellow, Japan Soc. Promotion of Sci., Tokyo, 1990. Office: Yale U Ctr for Systems Sci 10 Hillhouse Ave New Haven CT 06520-1968

KODIYALAM, SRINIVAS, mechanical engineer, researcher; b. Madras, India, Apr. 21, 1960; came to U.S., 1983; BE, Annamalai U., India, 1983; MS, U. Iowa, 1985; PhD, U. Calif., Santa Barbara, 1988. Visiting faculty dept. mech. engring. U. Calif., Santa Barbara, 1989; rsch. engr. Vanderplaats, Muira & Assocs., Santa Barbara, 1988-90; mech. engr. GE Corp. R&D Ctr., Schenectady, N.Y., 1990—. Contbr. articles to profl. jours. and tech. books. Mem. ASME, AIAA (vice-chmn., treas. 1990—). Office: GE R&D Ctr Bldg K1 Rm 2A25 PO Box 8 Schenectady NY 12301

KOEDEL, JOHN GILBERT, JR., forge company executive; b. Pitts., June 25, 1937; s. John Gilbert and Elizabeth Marie (Kramer) K.; m. Fay Birren, Dec. 21, 1963; 1 son, John III. B.S. in Commerce, Washington and Lee U., 1959. V.p. Pitts. Nat. Bank, 1960-68; bd. dirs. Nat. Forge Co., Nat. Forge Europe N.V., Integra Fin. Corp., Pitts., Mitchell Shackleton & Co., Ltd., Manchester, Eng. Served to sgt., U.S. Army, 1960-65. Mem. Fin. Execs. Inst. Republican. Presbyterian. Clubs: Erie Yacht, Conenango. Lodge: Masons. Home: 337 Hickory St Apt C Warren PA 16365 Office: Nat Forge Co Irvine PA 16329

KOEHLER, GEORGE RICHARD, environmental engineer; b. Bklyn., Oct. 2, 1932; s. George Francis and Sarah Marie (Meehan) K.; m. Anna W. Brown, Sept. 21, 1958; children: Karen A., Sheryl L. B in Chem. Engring., N.Y. Poly. Inst., 1963; MSChemE, NYU, 1966; PhD, Western State U., 1985. Asst. engr. Hydrocarbon Rsch. Inc., N.Y.C., 1956-60; devel. engr. Macrosonics Corp., Cartaret, N.J., 1961-65; asst. prof. NYU, N.Y.C., 1965-70; engring. mgr. Chem. Constrn. Corp., N.Y.C., 1970-77; mgr. environ. compliance Am. Cyanamid Co., Wayne, N.J., 1977—; mem. U.S.-USSR Air Pollution Control Commn., Washington, 1973-75; mem. bd. examiners Inst. Hazardous Material Mgmt., Rockville, Md., 1991—. Author: S02 Control Process, 1976; patent in decoxing process; contbr. articles on environ. engring. to profl. jours. Mem. Middlesex County (N.J.) Planning Bd., 1992—; mem. fin. com. N.J. Sch. Bds., Trenton, 1972-74; pres. Old Bridge (N.J.) Bd. of Edn., 1970-76; vice chmn. Old Bridge Planning Bd., 1986-92; chmn. alumni vis. com. NYU, 1967-68, Dry Color Mfr.'s Assn., Arlington, Va., 1978-81. Sgt. USAF, 1952-56, Korea. Recipient Alumni award NYU, 1964. Mem. AICE (Profl. Devel. award 1985), N.Y. Acad. Sci., N.J. Assn. Planning Ofcls., Chem. Mfrs. Assn. (com. Washington chpt. 1986-92), Tau Beta Pi, Phi Lambda Upsilon, Sigma Xi. Home: 168-B Amboy Rd Matawah NJ 07747 Office: Am Cyanamid Co One Cyanamid Pla Wayne NJ 07470

KOEHNKE, JANET DEL, audiology educator, researcher; b. Newark, Aug. 26, 1954; d. George and Lotte (Heuman) Blustein. BS in Communication Disorders, U. Mass., 1976; MA in Audiology, SUNY, Geneseo, 1977; PhD in Communication Scis., U. Conn., 1983. Audiologist Waltham (Mass.) Pub. Schs., 1978-79, VA Med. Ctr., Newington, Conn., 1979-80; postdoctoral fellow MIT Rsch. Lab. Electronics, Cambridge, 1983-86; rsch. asst. prof. dept. communication disorders Boston U., 1985-90, sr. rsch. assoc. dept. biomed. engring., 1990—; asst. prof. dept. communication scis. U. Conn., Storrs, 1990-92; asst. prof. dept. communication disorders La. State U., Baton Rouge, 1992—; vis. scientist MIT Rsch. Lab. Electronics, Cambridge, 1986—. Contbr. articles to profl. jours. Recipient First Ind. Rsch. and Transition award NIH, 1987-92, Deafness Rsch. Found. award, 1989-90, 1990-91, 1991-92. Mem. Am. Speech-Lang.-Hearing Assn. (cert. clin. competence), Acoustical Soc. Am. Office: La State U Dept Communication Scis & Disorders 163 Music & Drama Arts Bldg Baton Rouge LA 70803

KOENEN, AUSTIN VOORHEES, investment banker; b. Morristown, N.J., Oct. 15, 1941; s. William and Elsie (Voorhees) K.; m. Kathleen Chase, June 19, 1966; children: Karestan C., Erin K., Austin V. Jr. BS, U.S. Naval Acad., 1964; MBA, Harvard U., 1972. Commd. ensign USN, 1964, advanced through grades to chief engr., 1969; staff nuclear engr. Nuclear Energy Liability Ins. Co., N.Y.C., 1969-71; v.p. Salomon Bros., N.Y.C., 1976-77; assoc. investment banker Kuhn Loeb & Co. (name changed to Shearson Lehman Bros. Inc.), N.Y.C., 1972-76; mng. dir. Kuhn Loeb Inc. (div. Shearson Lehman Bros. Inc.), N.Y.C., 1977-84, Shearson Lehman Hutton Bros. Inc., N.Y.C., 1984-89, Morgan Stanley & Co., Inc., N.Y.C., 1989—. Bd. dirs. Hurricane Island Outward Bound Sch., Rockland, Maine, 1987—; pres. Montclair Kimberly Acad. Mem. Securities Industry Assn. (bd. dirs., chmn. investment banking com.), Harvard Club, North Jersey Country Club, Windbeam Club. Office: Morgan Stanley & Co Inc 1251 Ave Of The Americas Fl 39 New York NY 10020-1104

KOENIG, ERL AUGUST, electrical engineer; b. Troy, N.Y., Nov. 7, 1935; s. Wilhelm Adolf Koenig and Elizabeth (Sofie) Ruedemann; m. Gail Barbara Cranston, July 24, 1964; children: Charles H., Barbara J., Hydee J. Elec. AES, HVCC, 1957; Physics, electricity, RIT, 1963. Researcher GE, Schenectady, N.Y., 1957-59, Utica, N.Y., 1959-60; owner Koenig Tool and Mfg. Co., Troy, N.Y., 1963-75; owner, cons. Mirror Image Magnetics, Averill Park, N.Y., 1975—; writer inventor The Family, Averill Park, N.Y. Patentee in field. Home: PO Box 81 Averill Park NY 12018

KOENIG, MARYJANE, secondary school educator; b. Erie, Pa., Sept. 15, 1947; d. William Frederick and Alma Florence (Hall) Phillips; m. Timothy Vincent Koenig, Aug. 18, 1984; children: Randolph Scott Golab, Brian Paul Golab. BA in French, Gannon U., Erie, Pa., 1969; MEd in English, Edinboro (Pa.) U., 1976. Cert. secondary school tchr. Tchr. French Sch. Dist. of City of Erie (Pa.), 1972-75, tchr. ESL, 1975-76; co-owner TK's Charter Fishing, Erie, 1985—; tchr. English Erie Sch. Dist., 1976—; workshop cons. Times Pub. Co. Newspaper in Edn., Erie, 1985—. Vol. U.S. Brig Niagara League, Erie, 1987—, Erie Art Mus., 1988—; acad. excellence coun. Erie Excellence Coun., 1989—. Named High Sch. Educator of the Yr. Erie Edn. Assn., 1980-81, High Sch. Tchr. of the Yr. City of Erie Sch. Dist., 1990. Mem. Nat. Coun. Tchrs. English, Erie Area C. of C. (liaison to Pa. Lake Erie Charter Capts. Assn.), N.W. Pa. Coun. Tchrs. English (dir. 1987—), Delta Kappa Gamma. Home: 1645 Skyline Dr Erie PA 16509-1169 Office: Erie East High sch 1151 Atkins St Erie PA 16503-1652

KOENIG-MACKO, JOANNE FRANCES, artist, small business owner; b. Cleve., Mar. 16, 1949; d. Frank Michael and Rose Marie (Peffer) Koenig; m. John Mark Macko, Aug. 29, 1980; children: Christopher, Robert. Student, Cuyahoga Coll., 1967-69. Artist Fed. Res. Bank, Cleve., 1967-73, Ortiz Art Studio, Cleve., 1973-74; artist prodn. Color-Mail, Inc., Cleve., 1974-80; v.p., owner Gourmet Graphics Inc., South Euclid, Ohio, 1980-84; owner, artist The Country Scene, Monroe, Conn., 1985—; ofcl. artist Dogwood Nat. Festival, Greenfield Hill, Conn., 1991, Orange (Conn.) County Fair, 1992. Author: Ohio, You Have Something to Crow About!, 1980. Dir. Town of Monroe Projects Fundraiser, 1984—; state and nat. coach Odyssey of the Mind. Recipient Best Artwork depicting community, Trumbull (Conn.) C. of C., 1990. Mem. Jr. Women's Club (life mem., dir. art shows 1984—), Fairfield County Arts Assn. Home and Office: The Country Scene 94 Lynn Dr Monroe CT 06468

KOEPP, LEILA HADDAD, biology educator; b. Haifa, Palestine, July 7, 1945; came to U.S., 1964; d. Khalil Salim and Martha (Kifawi) Haddad; m. Stephen John Koepp, June 2, 1969; children: Melanie, David. BA, Messiah Coll., 1968; MS, North Tex. State U., 1970; PhD, U. of Medicine & Dentistry, 1982. Bacteriologist Overlook Hosp., Summit, N.J., 1976-81; instr. Montclair State Coll., Upper Montclair, N.J., 1978-81; grad. teaching asst. U. Medicine & Dentistry, Newark, 1979-81; assoc. prof. Bloomfield (N.J.)

Coll., 1982—; cons. Met. Mus. of Art, N.Y.C., 1987-89. Author: Lab Exercises in Microbiology, 1990. Mem. Am. Soc. for Microbiologists, N.J. Acad. Sci. Home: 84 Edgemont Rd Montclair NJ 07043-1306 Office: Bloomfield Coll Bloomfield NJ 07003

KOERBER, JOAN C., educator; b. Newark, Mar. 23, 1929; d. George Vincent and Catherine Rose (Donahue) Callanan; m. John Calvin Koerber, June 27, 1953; children: John C., Joanne C. BS in Elem. Edn., Newark State Coll., 1952; MA in Adminstrn., Kean Coll., Union, N.J., 1984. Tchr. 15th Ave Sch., Newark, 1952-71; tchr. Lincoln Sch., Newark, 1971-78, tchr. chpt. I, 1978-79; chapter I coord. Lincoln Sch., 1979-84, basic skills tchr., 1984—; summer sch. coord. Lincoln Sch., 1979-84; pres. Kean Coll. Grad. Sch. Coun. Sec. Essex County PTA; hon. life mem. PTA, N.J. Named 25 yr. mem. PTA, hon. life mem., 1992. Mem. ASCD, AAUW, PTA (hon. life), NEA, N.J. Edn. Assn., Essex County Edn. Assn., Newark Edn. Assn., Newark Tchrs. Union, N.J. State Columbiettes (supreme bd. dirs., past state pres.), Kappa Delta Phi (past pres.), Phi Delta Kappa (past pres.). Home: 95 Midland Pl Newark NJ 07106-2805

KOETHER, PHILIP, architect; b. Denver, Apr. 7, 1956; s. Herbert Franklin and Sarah Louise (Jones) K. BA, Middlebury (Vt.) Coll., 1978; cert., Pushkin Russian Lang. Inst., 1978; MArch, Yale U., 1983. Registered architect, Conn. Intern Inst. for Architecture and Urban Studies, 1979-80; designer Cesar Pelli & Assocs. Inc., New Haven, 1983—; assoc. Cesar Pelli & Assocs., New Haven, 1989—. Mem. AIA, Conn. Soc. Architects, Yale Club (N.Y.C.), Phi Beta Kappa. Home: 327 Audubon Ct New Haven CT 06510-1204 Office: Cesar Pelli & Assocs Inc 1056 Chapel St New Haven CT 06510-2496

KOFF, ROBERT HESS, university dean; b. Chgo., June 5, 1938; s. Arthur Karl and Dorothy (Hess) K. BA, U. Mich., 1961; MA, U. Chgo., 1962, PhD, 1966. Lic. psychologist, Ill., Calif. Instr., counselor S. Shankman Orthogenic Sch. U. Chgo., 1961-64; tchr. U. Chgo. Lab. Sch., 1963-64; instr. U. Ill., Champaign, 1964, U. Chgo., 1964-66; vis. scientist, Lab. for Hypnosis Rsch., asst. prof. Stanford (Calif.) U., 1966-72; prof., dean Roosevelt U., Chgo., 1972-79, SUNY, Albany, 1979—; vis. scholar Oxford U., Eng., 1965; chmn. N.Y. State Ednl. Conf. Bd., Albany, 1981—. Mem. Nat. Adv. Coun. on Edn. of Disadvantaged Children, Washington, 1979-82, Gov.'s Adv. Commn. on Children and Youth, Albany, 1981—. Mem. Am. Ednl. Rsch. Assn., Am. Psychol. Assn. (com. chmn.), Nat. Register Health Svc. Providers in Psychology. Office: SUNY Sch of Edn 1400 Washington Ave Albany NY 12222-0001

KOFFLER, RUSSELL, federal agency executive; b. N.Y.C., Aug. 20, 1937; s. Nathan Koffler and Cecile (Reich) Shurgin; m. Ogechee L. Jenkins, July 26, 1967; 1 child, Aloyse Rene Cunningham. BS, CUNY, 1960; postgrad., Columbia U., 1961, Am. U., 1968. Rsch. meteorologist NOAA, Washington, 1962-72, project coord., 1972-74, chief environ. products br., 1974-79, dep. chief satellite svcs. div., 1979-81, chief land satellite ops. div., 1981-82, dir. Office of Satellite Data Processing and Distbn., 1982-88, dep. asst. adminstr. satellite and info. svcs., 1988—. Contbr. articles to profl. jours. Treasurer Sousa Jr. High Sch. PTA, Washington, 1969-70. Recipient Silver medal U.S. Dept. of Commerce, 1986. Mem. Am. Meteorol. Soc., Assn. for Computing Machinery, Am. Soc. Photogrammetry and Remote Sensing. Office: NOAA/Nat Environ Satellite Data and Info Svc FB 4 Rm # 2069 Ex 1 Washington DC 20233

KOFFSKY, ROBERT MICHAEL, biomedical engineering company executive; b. Albany, N.Y., Apr. 27, 1937; s. Samuel Koffsky and Nancy (Bittman) Raphael; m. Barbara Schwartz, Apr. 2, 1961. BS in Indsl. Engring., Calif. State Poly. Coll., 1965; MS in Indsl. Engring., Columbia U., 1966. Design engr. Achievement House, San Luis Obispo, Calif., 1963-64; systems analyst Gen. Foods Corp., White Plains, N.Y., 1965-66; sr. research assoc. Columbia U., N.Y.C., 1966-73; project leader ALZA Research Inc., Palo Alto, Calif., 1973-76; sr. bioengr. Mt. Sinai Med. Ctr., N.Y.C., 1976—; mng. ptnr. Alchemy Ptnrs., Hopewell Junction, N.Y., 1985—; cons. Miller Hill Ltd., Hopewell Junction, 1977—. Contbr. articles to profl. jours. Served with U.S. Army, 1956-59. Recipient Cert. Achievement Soc. Mfg. Engrs., 1965. Fellow Am. Inst. Chem. Engring., Am. Inst. Indsl. Engring., N.Y. Acad. Medicine; mem. Am. Heart Assn., Am. Soc. Artificial Internal Organs, Phi Kappa Phi, Tau Sigma. Office: Mt Sinai Med Ctr Box 1028 Fifth Ave at 100th St New York NY 10029

KOFKE, WILLIAM ANDREW, anesthesiologist, intensivist; b. Drexel Hill, Pa., Feb. 4, 1952; s. William Albert Jr. and Joan (Healey) K.; m. Marianne Lydia Maniet, July 24, 1976; children: Lauren Marie, Matthew Joseph, Marisa Anne, Elise Christine. BS in Chemistry, Bucknell U., 1974; MD, U. Pitts., 1978. Diplomate Am. Bd. Anesthesiology, Am. Bd. Critical Care Medicine. Intern Mercy Hosp., Pitts., 1978-79; resident Mass. Gen. Hosp., Boston, 1979-81; instr. in anesthesiology Harvard Med. Sch., Boston, 1981-82, resident, 1982-83; asst. prof. anesthesiology Pa. State U., Hershey, 1983-88; assoc. prof. anesthesiology U. Pitts., 1988—; bd. dirs. neurologic anesthesia and supportive care program U. Pitts. Med. Ctr., neurointensive care unit Montifiore U. Hosp., U. Pitts. Med. Ctr. Editor: Postoperative Critical Care Procedures of the Massachusetts General Hospital, 1986; contbr. articles to profl. jours. Named Parker B. Francis Investigator in Anesthesiology, Am. Soc. Anesthesiologists, 1984-86. Fellow Am. Coll. Critical Care Medicine; mem. Assn. Univ. Anesthesiologists, Pa. Soc. Critical Care Medicine (pres. 1990-92). Office: Univ Pitts Dept Anesthesia 1385 Scaife Hall Pittsburgh PA 15261

KOFMEHL, WILLIAM EARL, JR., religious organization administrator; b. Pitts., Dec. 5, 1943; s. William Earl and Ruth Elsie (DeLowry) K.; m. Linda Lou Meyer, May 27, 1972; children: Jennie Lynn, Amy Lou, Rebecca Lee, William Earl III. BA in History, U. Pitts., 1964, MEd, 1965, PhD in Foundations of Edn., 1973. 8th grade tchr. Baldwin-Whitehall Sch. Dist., Pitts., 1964; edn. officer transition program U.S. Army Edn. Ctr., Fort Dix, N.J., 1968-70; teaching fellow U. Pitts., 1970-73; rsch. cons. Literacy and Evangelism, Tulsa, Okla., 1973-77; exec. dir. Allegheny County Literacy Coun. Inc.; Christian Literacy, Pitts., 1975—; bd. dirs. Luth. Svc. Soc. Western Pa., 1978-91, Luth. Svc. Soc. Found., Pitts., 1978-91. Author: The Christian Literacy Series, 1976, (with others) Organization and Operation of the U.S. Army Reserve Schools, 1985; editor: Managing Methods and Materials, 1988, Game Plans and Guidelines, 1991. Active sch. bd. North Hills Sch. Dist., Pitts., 1978-85; v.p., pres. Northern Area Spl. Purpose Sch. Bd., Pitts. 1983-85; scoutmaster Boy Scouts Am. Capt. U.S. Army, 1965-68. Decorated Commendation medal. Mem. Internat. Reading Assn., Am. Assn. for Counseling and Devel., Pub. Offenders Counseling Assn., Coalition for Advancement of Literacy. Republican. Lutheran. Home: 541 Perry Hwy Pittsburgh PA 15229-1851 Office: Christian Literacy Assocs 311 Cumberland Rd Pittsburgh PA 15237-5484

KOGAN, RICHARD JAY, pharmaceutical company executive; b. N.Y.C., June 6, 1941; s. Benjamin and Ida K.; m. Susan Linda Scher, Aug. 29, 1965. BA, CCNY, 1963; MBA, NYU, 1968. Dir. planning and adminstrn. Ciba Corp., Summit, N.J., 1968-69; v.p. planning, pharm. div. Ciba-Geigy Corp., Summit, 1970-76; pres. Can. pharm. div. Ciba-Geigy Corp., Can., 1976-79; pres. U.S. pharm. div. Ciba-Geigy Corp., Summit, 1979-82; exec. v.p. pharm. ops. Schering-Plough Corp., Madison, N.J., 1982-86; pres., chief oper. officer Schering-Plough Corp., Kenilworth, N.J., 1986—; bd. dir. Schering-Plough Corp., Kenilworth; bd. dirs. Nat. Westminster Bancorp, Rite Aid Corp., Gen. Signal Corp. Trustee St. Barnabas Med. Ctr.; bd. overseers Sch. Bus. NYU. Office: Schering-Plough Corp 1 Giralda Farms Madison NJ 07940-1010

KOHAN, MARK ANTHONY, editor in chief, publishing executive; b. Lackawanna, N.Y., Mar. 24, 1960; s. Jon Francis and Mary Natalie (Winkowski) K.; m. Kyle Janice Stamer, June 20, 1987. BS in Mgmt., Canisius Coll., 1982. Advt. mgr. Polona Reporter Newspaper, Buffalo, 1982-83; spl. sect. editor Polish Am. Voice, Buffalo, 1983-85, assoc. editor, 1985-89; pres. Panagraphics, Inc., Buffalo, 1985—; editor in chief Polish Am. Jour., Buffalo, 1989—. Bd. dirs. Polish Community Ctr. Buffalo, 1984-86. Recipient Outstanding Achievement award Polish Community Ctr. Buffalo, 1991. Mem. Polish Am. Congress (del. 1989—), Polish Arts Club, Nat. Ralway Hist. Soc., Polish Union Am., U.S. Polka Assn., Internat. Polka Assn. (elector Chgo. chpt. 1987—). Democrat. Office: Polish Am Jour 1275 Harlem Rd Buffalo NY 14206-1980

KOHAN, MELVIN IRA, engineering thermoplastic consultant; b. Boston, Mar. 11, 1921; s. Max Charles and Sophie Pauline (Rashap) K.; m. Beatrice Nesson, Feb. 6, 1943; children: Stanford P., Allen M., Donald E., James M. AB, Harvard U., 1942; PhD, U. Ill., 1950. Chemist E. I. DuPont de Nemours, Niagara Falls, N.Y., 1942-44, 46-47; rsch. chemist E. I. DuPont de Nemours, Wilmington, Del., 1950-62, sr. rsch. chemist, 1962-74, rsch. assoc., 1974-82; cons. MIK Assocs., Wilmington, 1983—; adj. prof. Drexel U., Phila., 1983-86. Editor, prin. contbr. textbook: Nylon Plastics, 1973; contbr. articles to profl. jours. and encys.; patentee in field. With U.S. Army, 1944-46, Japan. Mem. Am. Chem. Soc. (emeritus), Soc. Plastics Engrs. (sr. emeritus, chmn. edn. com. Phila. sect. 1984-92). Jewish. Office: MIK Assocs 1913 Longcome Dr Wilmington DE 19810-3864

KOHIN, ROGER P., physics educator; b. Chgo., Mar. 2, 1931; s. Raymond Francis and Ruth Irene (Olmsted) K.; m. Barbara Jean Castle, July 17, 1959; children: Margaret E. Kohin-Nitschelm, Judith Ann, Suzanne. BSEE, U. Notre Dame, 1953; PhD, U. Md., 1961. Assoc. prof. physics Clark Univ., Worcester, Mass., 1962—; scientist Inst. Battelle, Geneva, 1961-62; fellow J. Stefan Inst., Ljubljana, Yugoslavia, 1968-69; Indo-Am. fellow Indian Inst. of Tech.-Kanpur, India, 1976-77; vis. prof. U. Nairobi, Kenya, 1987-88. Office: Dept Physics/Clark Univ Worcester MA 01610

KOHL, MARVIN, philosopher; b. N.Y.C., May 19, 1932; s. Jesse and Mollie (Wenzel) K.; m. Phylia Joyce Wurman, Sept. 2, 1955; children: Richard, Rhiana, Matthew, Maura. BA, CCNY, 1954; MA, NYU, 1958, PhD, 1966. Prof. philosophy SUNY, Fredonia, 1968, chair philosophy dept., 1983-88; assoc. dean faculty for arts and humanities SUNY, 1989-92; faculty exch. scholar SUNY, 1979—; vis. scholar Harvard U., 1987; v.p. Bertrand Russell Soc., 1985-87, pres., 1987-89, chair bd. dirs.; exec. dir. Assn. for Study and Advancement of Supportive Values. Author: The Morality of Killing, 1974; editor: Beneficent Euthanasia, 1975, Infanticide and the Value of Life, 1978; contbg. editor Free Inquiry, 1973—. Bd. dirs. Hospice, Chautauqua County, N.Y., 1989. With U.S. Army, 1954-56. Mem. Am. Philos. Assn., Internat. Assn. for Philosophy of Law and Social Philosophy, Concerned Philosophers for Peace. Jewish. Home: 168 Temple St Fredonia NY 14063-1757 Office: SUNY Philosophy Dept Fredonia NY 14063-9678

KOHL, SHELLEY JO, accounting administrator; b. Jeannette, Pa., Jan. 17, 1967; d. Dennis William and Catherine Lee (Sticca) Duez; m. Edward Paul Kohl, May 16, 1986; 1 child, Andrew Edward. BA, St. Vincent Coll., Latrobe, Pa., 1988. CPA, Pa. Retail acctg. intern Charley Brothers Co., Greensburg, Pa., 1987; staff acct. Boschini-Miller & Assocs., Greensburg, 1988; staff acct. and auditor Horner, Wible & Assocs., Greenburg, 1988-90; assoc. acctg. adminstr. Westinghouse, Bettis Atomic Power Lab, West Mifflin, Pa., 1990—. Mem. Am. Women's Soc. CPAs (dir.-at-large, newspaper com. 1990—). Democrat. Roman Catholic. Home: 1944 St Clair Ave Greensburg PA 15601-5242 Office: Westinghouse Bettis Atomic Power Lab PO Box 79 West Mifflin PA 15122-0079

KOHLENBERG, STANLEY, marketing executive; b. Bklyn., Aug. 19, 1932; s. Max and Minnie (Roth) K.; BS, Columbia U., 1953; postgrad. N.Y.U., 1956-58; m. Ruth Barbara Itkin, Dec. 11, 1955; children: Robin Sue, Mark Stuart, Howard Scott. Account supr. L.W. Frohlich, N.Y.C., 1959-62; advt. mgr. Pfizer Lab., N.Y.C., 1962-63; mktg. dir. Tussy Cosmetics, N.Y.C., 1964; sr. v.p., dir. client service Sudler & Hennessey, N.Y.C., 1964-66; pub. Cosmetics Fair mag., N.Y.C., 1966-68; exec. v.p. Spectrum Cosmetics, 1968-70; pres. Coty Inc., 1970-72; exec. v.p. Revlon Inc., N.Y.C., 1972-76; pres. Calvin Klein Cosmetics, Inc., N.Y.C., 1977-79; pres. CFT Mktg., Inc., N.Y.C., 1980-84; pres. Sanofi Beauty Products, Inc., N.Y.C., 1984-88; pres, chief exec. officer Alfin, Inc., N.Y.C., 1989—; cons., advt. and sales promotion. Served with M.D., AUS, 1953-55. Home: Shad Rd W Pound Ridge NY 10576 Office: Alfin Inc 720 5th Ave New York NY 10019-4107

KOHLER, JOHN CHARLES, packaging engineer; b. Rochester, N.Y., Mar. 30, 1944; s. Edward G. and Della (Wiles) K.; m. Jean Marie Morrison, June 24, 1967. BS, Mich. State U., 1966; MBA, Rochester Inst. Tech., 1971. Sect. supr., packaging engr. Eastman Kodak Co., Rochester, 1966—. Mem. Inst. Packaging Profl. (pres. 1988-92, cert. packaging profl.), Rochester Area Packaging Assn. (pres. 1980-81). Home: 6045 Slocum Road Ext Ontario NY 14519-9130

KOHLER, SAUL, public relations executive; b. N.Y.C., Oct. 4, 1928; s. Abraham and Nettie (Diamond) Kujavsky; m. Mary Virginia Baum, Jan. 10, 1956; children: Alan Craig, Barbara Ann. BA, Bklyn. Coll., 1948. Chief Harrisburg Bur. Phila. Inquirer, 1960-68, chief Washington Bur., 1969-70; legis. asst. to minority leader U.S. Senate, Washington, 1970-71; White Ho. corr. Newhouse Newspapers, 1972-78; editor Harrisburg Evening News, 1978-79; exec. editor Harrisburg Patriot and Evening News, 1979-84; dir. media rels. Bell Telephone Co. of Pa., Harrisburg, 1984—. Bd. dirs. Holy Spirit Hosp., Camp Hill, Pa., The Salvation Army, Harrisburg, Beth El Temple, Harrisburg, 1980-83, Tri-County United Way, 1979-83. Mem. Soc. Profl. Journalists, Pa. Soc. Newspaper Editors, Pa. Pub. RELs. Soc., White House Corrs. Assn. (bd. govs. 1976-79), Pa. Legis. Corrs. Assn. (pres. 1970-73). Jewish. Home: 443 Arlington Rd Camp Hill PA 17011-2108 Office: Bell of Pa Strawberry Sq Harrisburg PA 17101-1819

KOHLMANN, PHYLLIS BETH, alcohol and drug program administrator, counselor; b. N.Y.C., June 16, 1948. BA, U. Rochester, 1970; MEd, U. Md., 1973. Lic. prof. counselor, cert. clin. mental health counselor. Drug abuse counselor Arlington County Alcohol and Drug Program, Arlington, Va., 1972-75, clin. coord., 1975-77, dir., 1977—; pvt. practice Arlington, 1979—. Chmn. drug treatment com. Met. Washington Coun. Govts., 1988—; mem. met. surveys adv. group Nat. Inst. Drug Abuse, Washington, 1990—. Mem. AACD, Va. Assn Clin. Counselors. Office: Arlington County Alcohol & Drug Program 1725 N George Mason Dr Arlington VA 22205-3697

KOHN, HAROLD ELIAS, lawyer; b. Phila., Apr. 5, 1914; s. Joseph C. and Mayme (Rumm) K.; m. Edith Anderson, Dec. 30, 1946; children: Amy, Ellen, Joseph Carl. AB, U. Pa., 1934, LLB, 1937; LLD (hon.), Temple U., 1990. Bar: Pa. 1938, D.C. 1972. Pres. Kohn, Nast & Graf, P.C., Phila.; spl. counsel transit matters City of Phila., 1952-53, 56-62; counsel to gov. State of Pa., 1972; Mem. bd. Southeastern Pa. Transp. Authority, 1972-77; mem. Pa. Jud. Inquiry and Rev. Bd., 1973-77, Pa. Supreme Ct. Continuing Legal Edn. Bd., 1992—; bd. consultors Villanova U. Law Sch. Sec., treas., bd. dirs. Kohn Found.; pres., bd. dirs. Arronson Found., Lavine Found.; bd. dirs. Moss Rehab. Hosp., Phila. Geriatric Ctr.; trustee, mem. exec. com. Phila. Fedn. Jewish Agys.; trustee Temple U., U. of the Arts; past mem. exec. com. United Jewish Appeal; past mem. bd. dirs. Phila. Psychiat. Ctr.; past v.p., bd. dirs. Phila. chpt. ACLU, Wilma Theatre. Mem. ABA, Pa., Phila., D.C. Bar Assns., Internat. Acad. Trial Lawyers, Jud. Conf. 3d Circuit, Am. Law Inst., Order of Coif, Phi Beta Kappa. Office: 1101 Market St 24th Fl Philadelphia PA 19107

KOHN, JOACHIM BENJAMIN, chemistry educator; b. Munich, June 16, 1952; came to U.S., 1983; s. Jakob Kohn and Irmtraud (Orth) Walbeck; m. Naama Mizrahi, June 16, 1976; children: Anat, Tal. BS in Chemistry and Physics, Hebrew U., Jerusalem, 1976; PhD in Chemistry, Weizmann Inst., 1983. Postdoctoral fellow MIT, Boston, 1983-86; fellow in surgery Children's Hosp., Boston, 1985-86; asst. prof. Rutgers U., New Brunswick, N.J., 1986-92; assoc. prof. Rutgers U., New Brunswick, 1992—. Contbr. numerous articles to profl. jours.; patentee in field. Chaim Weizmann postdoctoral fellow; Henry Rutgers rsch. fellow, 1986; recipient Rsch. Career Devel. award NIH, 1990, Young Investigator award Controlled Release Soc., 1992. Mem. Am. Peptide Soc. (chmn. student affairs com. 1990-92). Office: Rutgers U Dept of Chemistry Piscataway NJ 08855-0939

KOHR, ROBERT LEON, risk management consultant; b. Carlisle, Pa., Aug. 19, 1952; s. Leonard Jacob and Marilyn Louise (Lau) K.; m. Shelley Beth Yondorf, Oct. 28, 1984; children: Robert, Jacob. BS, Va. Tech. U., 1976. Cert. safety profl., protection profl. Loss control rep. Aetna Life & Casualty, Richmond, Va., 1976-79; supr. safety Blake Constrn. Co., Washington, 1979-80; regional dir. loss prevention Marriott Corp., Washington, 1980-84, dir. tech. svcs., 1984-90, dir. design, 1990-91; prin. Kohr & Assoc., Mt. Airy, Md., 1991; sr. cons. Arthur D. Little, Inc., Cambridge, Mass., 1991—. Author: Accident Prevention for Hotels, Motels and Restaurants, 1991; contbr. articles to profl. jours. Mem.. ASTM (F13, C21.06, D21, F15 coms.), Am. Soc. for Indsl. Security (lodging com. 1989-91), Bldg. Ofcls. and Code Adminstrs. Internat., Am. Soc. Safety Engrs., Am. Hotel and Motel Assn., Nat. Safety Coun., Nat. Fire Protection Assn.

KOHRING, DAGMAR LUZIA, fundraiser, consultant; b. Lage, Fed. Republic Germany, Mar. 8, 1951; came to U.S., 1966; d. Wilfried and Luzia W. (Knichel) K.; m. Arthur Gingrande Jr., Dec. 29, 1976 (div. June 1982). BA, Am. U., 1972, MA, 1974. Cert. fundraising exec. Asst. dir. devel. Harvard Art Mus., Cambridge, 1981-83; campaign officer Harvard U., Cambridge, 1983-85; sr. cons., campaign dir. C.H. Benz Assocs., Westfield, N.J., 1985-88; v.p. Brakeley, John Price Jones, Inc., Stamford, Conn., 1988—. Nat. Endowment for the Arts fellow, 1983. Mem. Nat. Soc. Fundraising Execs., Women in Devel. Club: Harvard (N.Y.C.). Home: 36 Hancock St Apt 7A Boston MA 02114-4110 Office: Brakeley John Price Jones Inc 2777 Summer St Stamford CT 06905-4310

KOHUT, JOHN WALTER, corporate executive; b. N.Y.C., Nov. 13, 1946; s. Walter and Stelle (Dudar) K.; m. Linda Susan Ram, Jan. 3, 1987; 1 child, Katherine Grace. BBA in Fin. and Econs., U. Miami, Coral Gables, Fla., 1969. Mgmt. trainee Bankers Trust Co., N.Y.C., 1969-73, asst. treas. in comml. banking, 1973-76, asst. v.p. spl. loans, 1976-79; v.p. European Energy Bankers Trust Co., London, 1979-82, v.p. Global Aerospace, 1982-85; mng. dir. Pvt. Equity B.T. Securities Corp., N.Y., 1985-90; pres., chief exec. officer W. Atlee Burpee Co., Warminster, Pa., 1990-91, Ramko Venture Mgmt., Inc., N.Y.C., 1991—; bd. dirs. Quality Automotive Co., Washington; v.p. Pyramid Investors, N.Y.C., 1988-90. Bd. dirs. 309 E. 49th St. C.A., N.Y.C., 1985-91; elected committeeman Rep. County, Somerset, N.J., 1976-79; mem. adv. com. on comml. aspects of space NASA, 1984-87. Mem. AIAA (bd. dirs. 1987-91), Tau Kappa Epsilon. Roman Catholic. Home: 309 E 49th St New York NY 10017-1608 Office: Ramko Venture Mgmt Inc 200 Madison Ave New York NY 10016-3903

KOINIS, STEVEN W., environmental industry executive; b. Detroit, Nov. 12, 1956; s. John Alice (Retsinas) K.; m. Reem Jawharieh, Feb. 27, 1959; children: Zeina S., Christopher. BSMME, BSME, U. Mich., 1978; MBA, Harvard U., 1983. Mgr. new bus. devel. Owens-Corning Fiberglas Co., Athens, Greece, 1983-86; project mgr., mgr. prodn. planning, warehousing and distbn. N.V. Owens-Corning S.A., Owens-Corning G.B. Ltd., Wrexham, Eng., 1986-87; dir. bus. devel. and acquisitions BTR Paper Group, Wellesley Hills, Mass., 1988; v.p. rsch. Stowe Woodward Co., Southborough, Mass., 1988, v.p. spl. projects, 1988; v.p. mfg. Stowe Woodward Co., Middletown, Va., 1988-90; pres., chief oper. officer Cellin Mfg. Inc. and Am. Environ. Products, Inc., Elkwood, Va., 1990—; bd. dirs. Am. Environ. Products, Inc.; cons. in field. Mem. Am. Mgmt. Assn. (bd. dirs.), Cellulose Insulation Industry Assn. (bd. dirs.). Home: 10275 Cedar Ridge Dr Manassas VA 22110-6630 Office: 685 Hackney Dr # 38 Elkwood VA 22718

KOK, FRANS JOHAN, investment banker; b. Zaandam, Netherlands, May 14, 1943; came to U.S., 1963; s. Cornelis and Aaf K.; m. Mary M. Shirley, Dec. 23, 1971. BA in Econ., Occidental Coll., L.A., 1967; MA in Econs., Calif. State U., L.A., 1969; MBA, Insead, Fontainebleau, France, 1971, Harvard U., 1972. Assoc. Booz, Allen & Hamilton, Washington, 1974-78; chief economist Environ. Protection Agy., Washington, 1978-80; chief fin. officer, co-founder Long Lake Energy Corp., N.Y.C., 1980-83; mng. dir. Ferris, Baker-Watts, Inc., Balt., 1983-89, First Nat. Bank of Md., Balt., 1989—; bd. dirs. Envirosafe Svcs., Inc., Valley Forge, Pa., 1987-92, Automated Scis. Group, Inc., Silver Spring, Md., 1984—. Home: PO Box 1256 Purcellville VA 22132-1256

KOLB, FREDERICK JOHN, JR., technical specialist, retired; b. Rochester, N.Y., May 7, 1917; s. Frederick John Sr. and Emilie Ann (Haefele) K.; m. Priscilla Packard Pollock, Oct. 10, 1942 (dec. Oct. 1987); children: Carolyn, Katharine, Frederick John III, Merribeth. SB, MIT, 1938, SM, 1939, ScD, 1947. From project group leader to coord. project devel. mfg. Eastman Kodak, Rochester, 1942-83, tech. assoc. rsch. labs., 1983-86; ret., 1986; cons. imaging sci. Magnetic Records, 1986—; tech. specialist Internat. Standards Orgn./TC 36, 1970—. Patentee magnetic heads; contbr. articles to profl. jours. Chmn. ednl. coun. MIT, Rochester, 1950—; elder Summerville Presbyn. Ch., Rochester, 1959—. Fellow Tau Beta Pi 1938-39, Fedn. Paint and Varnish Prodn. Clubs 1940-42. Fellow SMPTE (Warner medal sound on film); mem. IEEE, AAAS, BKSTS, AIChE, Am. Chem. Soc., Soc. Imaging Sci. and Tech., Sigma Xi. Republican. Home and Office: 211 Oakridge Dr Rochester NY 14617-2511

KOLB, NANCY DWYER, museum director; b. Albany, N.Y., Nov. 23, 1940; d. Edward James and Elizabeth (McLachlan) Dwyer; m. W. Roy Kolb, June 16, 1962; children: Amy Elizabeth, William Roy, E. Anders. BA, Bucknell U., 1962. Social studies tchr. Abington (Pa.) Sch. Dist., 1962-65; editor Bucks County Chronicles, Doylestown, Pa., 1974-76; cons. in history, 1976-77; dir. Pennsbury Manor Historic Site, Morrisville, Pa., 1977-82; asst. exec. dir. Pa. Hist. and Mus. Commn., Harrisburg, 1982-87; dir. Bur. Historic Sites and Mus., Harrisburg, 1987-89; pres. Please Touch Mus., Phila., 1989—. Contbr. articles to profl. jours. Bd. dirs. Phila. Soc. for Preservation of Landmarks, 1990—, Friends of Fort Mifflin, Phila., 1990—; exec. com. Fairmound Park House Adv. Commn., Phila., 1987—; bd. dirs. Big Sisters Phila., 1989—. Mem. Mus. Trustee Assn., Pa. Hort. Soc., Assn. Youth Mus. (regional rep. 1990), Bucks County Hist. Soc. (bd. dirs. 1970-80), Am. Assn. Mus. (bd. dirs. 1991—), Am. Assn. for State and Local History (coun. 1988—), Mid Atlantic Assn. Mus. (bd. govs.). Office: Please Touch Mus 210 N 21st St Philadelphia PA 19103-1088

KOLBE, SHERRY LYNN, educational association executive; b. Marshalltown, Iowa, Mar. 29, 1957; d. Stanley Ernest and Wanda Lee (George) K. BA, Marshalltown Community Coll., 1977; BS, George Washington U., 1980. Architect of the capitol U.S. Capitol/U.S. Senate, Washington, 1978-82; constituent svcs. asst. to exec. asst. to legis. dir. Senator Lloyd Bentsen, Washington, 1982-86; adminstr. asst. to sr. v.p. CACI, Inc.-Fed., Washington, 1986; asst. dir. for fed. rels. Office of Govt. Rels., Am. Assn. State Colls. and Univs., Washington, 1987-90; exec. dir. Nat. Assn. Pvt. Schs. for Exceptional Children, Washington, 1990—; vol. chairperson Charity Retinitis Pigmentosa Found., Washington, 1986, Charity Fundraising Cyptic Fibrosis, Washington, 1988. Campaign vol. Clark for Senate, Iowa, 1978, Culver for Senate, Iowa, 1980, Kennedy for Pres., Iowa, 1980, Harkin for Senate, Washington (D.C.) and Iowa, 1984, 90. Democrat. Methodist. Office: NAPSEC 1522 K St NW Ste 1032 Washington DC 20005-1202

KOLE, JEFFREY HOLITSER, editor, reporter; b. Savannah, Ga., Apr. 17, 1960; s. Don and Kaye (Robinson) K. BA in Am. Studies, Brandeis U., 1982. Reporter Savannah Morning News, 1982, Portsmouth (Va.) Times, 1982-83; reporter, editor No. Va. Sun, Arlington, 1983-85; reporter Warren Pub., Washington, 1985—; mng. editor Pub. Broadcasting Report, Washington, 1986—. Mem. Brandeis U. Alumni Assn. (pres. Washington chpt. 1989-90).

KOLKER, BONNIE LYNNE, telecommunications professional; b. Phila., Mar. 26, 1953; d. Les and Sandee (Cantor) K. BS, Fairleigh Dickinson U., 1976, MBA, 1980. Asst. to v.p. Babcock & Wilcox, N.Y.C., 1974-79; account exec. AT&T, N.Y.C., 1979-82, sales mgr., 1982; nat. account exec. AT&T, Parsippany, N.J., 1983-85; product mgr. AT&T, Bridgewater, N.J., 1985-88, dist. mgr., 1988—. Mem. Am. Mktg. Assn., Assn. MBA Execs., Amnesty Internat. Nat. Wildlife Fedn., Ellis Island Found., Phi Omega Epsilon. Office: AT&T 55 Corporate Dr Bridgewater NJ 08807-1206

KOLLEN, MELISSA SUSAN, real estate licensing school owner; b. Queens, N.Y., Mar. 24, 1954; d. Loran and Joan (Wachman) Willing; divorced; 1 child, James Christopher. Lic. real estate broker. Property mgr. L.I. Real Estate Co., Plainview, N.Y., 1980-87; mortgage broker Dupont Funding Corp., Plainview, 1980-87; owner L.I. Property Mgmt. Corp., Hauppauge, N.Y., 1987-88; lectr., owner L.I. Real Estate Tng., Commack, N.Y., 1988—; owner MSK Prodns., 1990—; faculty Stony Brook (N.Y.) U.,

1987—, N.Y. Inst. Tech., Old Westbury, 1987—. Author: Buying Real Estate Foreclosures, 1991; contbr. articles to profl. jours. Mem. Nat. Assn. Realtors, L.I. Bd. Realtors, Ea. Suffolk Bd. Realtors, NAFE. Office: LI Real Estate Tng PO Box 803 Commack NY 11725-0803

KOLLER, ALAN MANUEL, mathematics educator; b. London, Feb. 12, 1945; came to U.S., 1949; s. Joseph and Theresa (Zernik) K.; m. Barbara Rose McHale, Nov. 23, 1968; children: David, Stephen. BS, CCNY, N.Y.C., 1965; MDiv, New Brunswick Theol. Sem., N.J., 1973; PhD, Fordham U., N.Y.C., 1977; MS in Edn., L.I. U., N.Y.C., 1984; MS, Columbia U., 1986, MPh, 1989, EdD, 1990. Adj. instr. history Western Conn. State U., Danbury, 1977-78; adj. instr. religion Coll. Mt. St. Vincent, N.Y.C., 1979, Manhattan Coll., N.Y.C., 1979; adj. instr. religion Mercy Coll., Dobbs Ferry, N.Y., 1977-80, adj. instr. math., 1979-84; adj. instr. math. Elizabeth Seton Coll., Yonkers, N.Y., 1981; tchr. math. Monsignor Scanlan High Sch., N.Y.C., 1984-85; adj. assoc. prof. math. Pace U., Pleasantville, N.Y., 1985-87; adj. asst. prof. math. Orange County Community Coll., Middletown, N.Y., 1988—; asst. prof. math. Dominican Coll., Orangeburg, N.Y., 1987—; pastor Walker Valley (N.Y.) United Meth. Ch., 1989—. Maj. U.S. Army Res., 1981—. Mem. Math. Assn. Am., Nat. Coun. Tchrs. Math. Mem. Reformed Ch. Am. Home: 5 Hayes Pl Washingtonville NY 10992-1231 Office: Dominican Coll 10 N Western Hwy Orangeburg NY 10962-1299

KOLLER, ALEXANDER JOSEPH, computer scientist; b. Subotica, Yugoslavia, July 23, 1957; came to U.S., 1957; s. Sandor and Anna (Kulisits) K.; m. Margaret Christine Ferlito, Oct. 6, 1979; children: Amanda Elizabeth, Jessica Alexis, Jennifer Lynn. BS in Computer Sci., Iona Coll., 1979; MS in Computer Sci., Poly. U., Bklyn., 1985. Systems analyst NCR Corp., Dayton, Ohio, 1979-81; sr. software engr. Perkin-Elmer Corp., Norwalk, Conn., 1981-86, Transitions Rsch. Corp., Bethel, Conn., 1986; pres. Koller Computer Techs., Woodbury, Conn., 1986—; mem. del. to visit China for technol. info. exchange, Beijing, 1985, 88. Contbr. articles to profl. jours. Recipient award Indsl. Rsch. and Devel. Inst., 1982, 85. Mem. AAAS, IEEE Computer Soc., Am. Chem. Soc., Assn. for Computer Machinery, N.Y. Acad. Scis. Republican. Roman Catholic. Office: 51 Sherman Hill Rd Ste 201A Woodbury CT 06798-3648

KOLLER, JOHN DRYDEN, educator; b. Newton, Mass., Apr. 14, 1942; s. George Frank K. and Charlotte Evelyn (Traylor) Clapper; m. Karen Elizabeth Anderson, Jan. 15, 1984; 1 child, Douglas Dryden. BA, Emerson Coll., 1964; MA, Suffolk U., 1966, Emerson Coll., 1971. Instr. speech & theatre, dir. theatre Suffolk U., Boston, 1966-68; asst. prof. speech & theatre Salem (Mass.) State Coll., 1970-73; founder, artistic dir. Am. Restoration Theatre Co., Inc., 1973-77; asst. prof. mass communications, dept. chmn. Ricker Coll., Houlton, Maine, 1977-78, Medaille Coll., Buffalo, 1979-82; asst. prof. journalism & broadcasting U. Maine at Orono, 1982-83; prof. broadcasting & TV Mt. Wachusett Community Coll., Gardner, Mass., 1983—; adj. prof. Franklin Pierce Coll., Rindge, N.H., 1984-91. Recipient Excellence award Nat. Inst. for Staff and Orgnl. Devel., 1991. Mem. Nat. Broadcasting Soc. (chpt. advisor 1982-92, Nat. Advisor of Yr. award 1987-88), Nat. Assn. Collegiate Broadcasters, Nat. Assn. Educators in Broadcastings, Women in Communications, Speech Communication Assn., Soc. Profl. Journalists. Office: Mt Wachusett Community Coll 444 Green St Gardner MA 01440

KOLLER, MARTIN FRANK, computer company executive; b. Phila., Sept. 23, 1948; s. Martin John and Sue (Barnet) K.; m. Sherri Lynn Pollock, June 15, 1982; children: Erica, Amanda, Daniel. BS, Temple U., 1974. Pres. MAM Products Inc., Huntingdon Valley, Pa., 1983-88, Datatron Inc., Warminster, Pa., 1986-90; sec., treas. Combined Automated Industrys, Doylestown, Pa., 1987-91; pres. Autobid Inc., Chalfont, Pa., 1988—; chmn. Stanley Systems, Chalfont, 1990—; VAR, Microrim, Redmond, Wash., 1987—; cons., VAR, Hayes, Washington, 1988-91. Author (software) Autobid, 1988, 89, 90. Member Vietnam Vets. of Am. With USMC, 1966-69, Vietnam. Mem. Bass Anglers Sportsmens Soc., N.Am. Fishing Club. Republican. Roman Catholic. Office: Stanley Systems 223 Diana Dr Chalfont PA 18914-2111

KOLLEVOLL, KRISTAN GEORGE, sales executive; b. Canton, N.Y., July 16, 1954; s. Olav Bernt Kollevoll and Barbara Ralph Deschaine; m. Gitte Nielsen, May 30, 1981; children: Steffan Kristan, Kennett Dane. BA, Princeton U., 1977. Hockey player Aalborg Boldspil Klub, Aalborg, Denmark, 1977-81; v.p. sales BRD Noise & Vibration Control Inc., Wind Gap, Pa., 1981—; cons. OSHA, Chgo., 1990—. Contbr. articles to profl. jours.; creator slide show seminar: Common Sense Approach to Noise and Vibration Control, 1989. Mem. Acoustical Soc. Am., Young Reps. Club. Office: BRD Noise & Vibration Contr 112 Fairview Ave Wind Gap PA 18091-1226

KOLLOCK, DAVID HALL, manufacturing executive; b. Phila., June 22, 1916; s. David Hall and Harriet (Crouse) K.; m. Marjorie Ann Tams, Mar. 30, 1940; children—David Peter, Helna Valentine Babcock, George Tams. Pres. Argosy Corp., Phila., 1984—. Republican. Methodist Episcopal. Clubs: Union League, Racquet, Merion Cricket, Phila. Cricket. Avocations: tennis, gardening. Home: 455 Australian Ave Palm Beach FL 33480-4532

KOLODNY, ABRAHAM LEWIS, physician; b. Norfolk, Va., July 2, 1917; s. William and Jennie (Eisenberg) K.; m. Mildred Fiske, Aug. 10, 1942; children: William (dec.), David Greene, Suki, Douglas, Merrill, Peggy Lee. Grad., U. Va., 1941. Intern South Balt. Gen. Hosp., 1941-42; residency Ashburn Army Arthritis Ctr., McKinney, Tex., 1944-46; with Arthritis Clinic/Sinai Hosp., Balt., 1948-70; chief, rheumatology N. Charles Hosp., Balt., 1951-90; co-chief, rheumatology Franklin Square Hosp., Balt., 1970-91; commr. Md. Commn. Rheumatic Diseases, 1987-91; pres. North Charles Gen. Hosp., 1963-67; staff mem. Franklin Sq. Hosp., 1984-85; state commr. Arthritis and Related Diseases, 1986-91; ret. chief rheumatology Homewood Hosp. Ctr.; active Johns Hopkins Med. Health Systems. Contbg. author textbooks in field, articles to profl. jours. Maj. U.S. Army, 1942-47, CBI. Decorated Bronze Star, Combat Med. badge, Victory medal, Chinese Victory medal, others. Fellow Am. Coll. Rheumatology, N.Y. Acad. Scis.; mem. AMA, Am. Soc. Clin. Pharmacology, Md. Arthritis Found. (bd. dirs. 1975-91), Md. Soc. for Rheumatic Diseases (co-founder), So. Med. Assn. Office: 9105 Franklin Square Dr Ste 214 Baltimore MD 21237-3995

KOLOMBATOVIC, VADJA VADIM, management consulting company executive; b. Belgrade, Serbia, Yugoslavia, Jan. 20, 1924; came to U.S., 1944; s. George Steven and Antigona (Kefala) K.; m. Virginia Doris Carter, 1946; children: Vadja Vadim Jr., Mimi Carter. BS, U. Ill., 1948; cert. in personnel mgmt., U. Richmond, Va., 1949. Office mgr. State Farm Ins. Co., Richmond, 1948-49; spl. agt. FBI, N.Y.C. and San Francisco, 1949-66; asst. legal attache FBI, Paris, 1966-69; legal attache FBI, Madrid, Spain, Paris, 1969-75; chief liaison sect. FBI, Washington, 1975-76; v.p. for internat. affairs Intertel, Washington, 1976-83, sr. v.p., 1983-85; exec. v.p. Intertel, Rockville, Md., 1985-89, pres., 1989—, also bd. dirs.; v.p. Chalk's Internat., Miami, Fla., 1976-91. Served to lt. U.S. Army, M.I., 1946-47. Mem. Am. Legion, Soc. Former Spl. Agts., Assn. Former Intelligence Officers, Assn. Former Legats, REs. Officers Assn., Masons (32 deg.), Shriners (Fairfax, Va.). Republican. Home: 1171 Dolley Madison Blvd Mc Lean VA 22101-3019 Office: Intertel 6110 Executive Blvd Rockville MD 20852-3903

KOLOR, MICHAEL GARRETT, research chemist; b. Bklyn., May 1, 1934; s. Michael Austin and Frances (Nugent) K.; B.S. in Chemistry, Queens Coll. CUNY, 1956; postgrad. Adelphi U., 1958-60; m. Agnes Theresa Fitzpatrick, June 29, 1957; children: Mary Catherine, Michael Francis, Agnes Theresa, Johanna Margaret. Chemist, Nat. Dairy Corp., Oakdale, N.Y., 1956-59; assoc. chemist Gen. Foods Corp., Tarrytown, N.Y., 1959-62, rsch. chemist, 1962-65, sr. rsch. chemist, 1965-70, rsch. specialist, 1970-72, sr. rsch. specialist, 1972-79, rsch. scientist, head mass spectrometry lab., 1972-87; sr. chemist Champion Internat. Corp., West Nyack, N.Y., 1989—. Mem. Am. Soc. for Mass Spectrometry, N.J. Am. Chem. Soc. Mass Spectrometry Group (program chmn. 1968-69). Co-author: Biochemical Applications of Mass Spectrometry, 1972; Supplementary Volume of Biochemical Application of Mass Spectrometry, 1980; Mass. Spectrometry (practical spectroscopy/series, 1979); patentee in field; contbr. articles on chemistry to profl. jours. Roman Catholic. Home: 71 Margaret Keahon Dr Pearl River NY 10965-1040

KOLOSKI, DIANE CAROL, special education educator; b. Bryn Mawr, Pa., Aug. 6, 1965; d. Joseph Kenneth and Margaret Mary (Moran) DiPhillips; m. John William Koloski, Aug. 26, 1989; 1 child, Julia Lauren. BS, Syracuse U., 1988. Cert. spl. edn. tchr. Sec. Angelo Ventresca Assocs., Montrose, Pa., 1989; tchr. Elk Lake Sch. Dist., Dimock, Pa., 1989—; tchr. and tutor, Montrose, 1989—; track coach Elk Lake Sch. Dist., Dimock, 1989-92. Active Libr. Assn., Montrose, 1992. Mem. Syracuse U. Orange Pack (Hall of Fame 1989). Democrat. Roman Catholic.

KOLTER, JOSEPH PAUL, congressman; b. McDonald, Ohio, Sept. 3, 1926; m. Dorothy Gray, 1949; children: Joseph Paul, James, David, Julie. B.S., Geneva Coll., Beaver Falls, Pa., 1950. Former acct., tchr.; city councilman New Brighton, Pa., 1961-65; mem. Pa. Ho. Reps., 1969-82; mem. 98th-102nd Congresses from 4th Pa. dist., 1983—. Mem. Beaver County Democratic Com., New Brighton Civil Service Commn. Served with U.S. Army, 1944-47. Mem. Nat. Assn. Accts., Am. Legion, VFW. Club: Marconi. Lodges: Eagles, Elks, Sons of Italy. Office: US Ho of Reps 212 Cannon House Office Bldg Washington DC 20515*

KOLTUN, FRANCES LANG, editor, publisher; b. N.Y.C.; d. Samuel and Rebecca (Lang) K. BA, Bklyn. Coll., 1942; MA, Columbia U., 1945. Editor Am. Girl Mag., N.Y.C., 1945-48, Charm Mag., N.Y.C., 1948-58, Mademoiselle Mag., N.Y.C., 1958-72; owner, pres. Frances Koltun Enterprises Ltd., N.Y.C., 1972—; radio and TV broadcaster NBC, N.Y.C., 1970-75; bd. dirs. Travel Industry Assn., Washington. Author: Frances Koltun's Complete Book for the Intelligent Woman Traveler, 1967; editor, pub. of ann. supplement A Fifth Avenue Christmas. Named as A Woman of Accomplishment Wings Club, N.Y.C., 1981. Mem. Trends, Women's Forum.

KOMISAR, ARNOLD, otolaryngologist, educator; b. N.Y.C., Nov. 27, 1947; s. Samuel and Sonia (Schwartz) K.; m. Lenora I. Felderman, Dec. 23, 1984; children: Alexandra Danielle, Jonathan Reed. BS, Bradley U., 1968; DDS, NYU, 1972; MD, Hahnemann Med. Coll., 1975. Diplomate Am. Bd. Otolaryngology. Resident in surgery Beth Israel Med. Ctr., N.Y.C., 1975-76; resident in Otolaryngology Mt. Sinai Med. Sch., N.Y.C., 1976-79; asst. prof. otolaryngology Albert Einstein Coll. Medicine, N.Y.C., 1979-85, assoc. prof., 1985-86, assoc. clin. prof., 1986-90; assoc. dir. head and neck surgery Albert Einstein Affiliated Hosps., N.Y.C., 1982-86; attending otolaryngologist Montefiore Hosp. and Med. Ctr., N.Y.C., 1979-90, Bronx Mcpl. Hosp. Ctr., N.Y.C., 1979-90, N. Cen. Bronx Hosp., N.Y.C., 1979-90; clin. assoc. prof. otolaryngology Cornell U. Med. Coll., N.Y.C., 1990—; otolaryngologist Lenox Hill Hosp., N.Y.C., 1986—, asst. to dir. resident edn. dept. otolaryngology, 1986—, adj. otolaryngologist, 1987—, attending otolaryngologist, 1989—, assoc. dir. otolaryngologist, 1990—; cons. otolaryngology N.Y. Eye and Ear Infirmary, N.Y.C., 1986-89; couresty staff surgery-otolaryngology Doctors Hosp., N.Y.C., 1986-90; presenter in field. Contbr. articles to profl. jours. Fellow Am. Coll. Surgeons, Am. Soc. Head and Neck Surgery, Am. Acad. Facial Plastic and Reconstructive Surgery, Am. Acad. Otolaryngology/Head and Neck Surgery (Honor award), Triological Soc. (Mosher award), Am. Bronchoesophalogical Soc., N.Y. Acad. Medicine; mem. AMA, Pan-Am. Soc. Broncho-esophagology, Soc. Univ. Otolaryngologists, N.Y. Head and Neck Soc., Med. Soc. N.Y., N.Y. County Med. Soc. Office: 1317 3d Ave New York NY 10021-2995

KOMP, RICHARD JOSEPH, solar scientist; b. Chgo., Aug. 7, 1938; s. Joseph C. and Rose Ann (Schatzman) K.; m. Vicky Patton, June 23, 1969 (div.); m. Mirdza Leskov, Oct. 24, 1983. BS, Loras Coll., Dubuque, Iowa, 1960; PhD, Wayne State U., 1964. Sr. physicist Xerox Corp., Webster, N.Y., 1964-68; assoc. prof. dept. physics and astronomy West Ky. U., Bowling Green, 1968-73; v.p. Zip Svcs. div. Ednl. Act., Columbus, Ohio, 1973-75; rsch. assoc. dept. chemistry Wayne State U., Detroit, 1975-81; exec. dir. Skyheat Assocs., English, Ind., 1979—; v.p. R&D Sunwatt Corp., Addison, Maine, 1981-88, pres., 1988—. Author: Practical Photovoltaics, 1981, rev. edit., 1984, (with Joel Davidson) The Solar Electric Home, 1983; contbr. articles to profl. jours.; patentee photovoltaics and copying machines. Bd. dirs. Urban Alternative Homestead, Louisville, 1981-87, Ind. Solar Industries Assn., Indpls., 1982-85. Mem. AAAS, Internat. Solar Energy Soc., Am. Phys. Soc., Maine Solar Energy Assn. (prs. 1989—), N.E. Sustainable Energy Assn. (bd. dirs. 1990—), Sigma Xi. Home: RFD Box 751 Addison ME 04606 Office: Sunwatt Corp RFD Box 751 Addison ME 04606

KON, MITCHELL ALLEN, marketing professional; b. Vineland, N.J., Dec. 26, 1957; s. Beno Robert and Rebecca (Rubin) K.; m. Jacqueline Saltzman, Oct. 17, 1982; children: Sarah Carla, Joseph Aaron. Franklin & Marshall Coll., 1980. Brand asst. Proctor & Gamble Co., Cin., 1980-81; asst. product dir. Johnson & Johnson Baby Products Co., Skillman, N.J., 1981-83, product dir., 1983-86, group product dir., 1986-88; dir. mktg. Johnson & Johnson, Athens, Greece, 1988-89; mktg. dir. Johnson & Johnson Consumer Products Inc., Skillman, 1989—. Home: 26 Marten Rd Princeton NJ 08558 Office: Grandview Rd Skillman NJ 08558

KONDZIELA, JOSEPH RICHARD, psychiatrist; b. Stamford, Conn., Oct. 27, 1954; s. Frank Joseph and Rose Dianne (Calitri) K. BS magna cum laude, Fairfield Coll., 1976; MD, St. Louis U., 1980. Diplomate Am. Bd. Psychiatry and Neurology. Resident in psychiatry Fairfield Hills Hosp., Newtown, Conn., 1980-83; chief resident in psychiatry N.Y. Med. Coll., Valhalla, N.Y., 1983-84; staff psychiatrist Dept. of Psychiatry Danbury (Conn.) Hosp., 1984-87; pvt. practice Fairfield, Conn., 1984—; cons. Danbury Hosp. Mental Health Clin., 1984-87; sec. Dept. of Psychiatry Danbury Hosp., 1984-85. Contbr. articles profl. jours. Vol. Spl. Olympics Found. for the Mentally Retarded, Fairfield, 1979-80; vol. med. faculty N.Y. Med. Coll., 1984--. Mem. Am. Psychiat. Assn., Conn. Psychiat. Soc., St. Louis U. Med. Alumni Club. Republican. Roman Catholic. Home: 953 Old Post Rd Fairfield CT 06430 Office: 1583 Post Rd Fairfield CT 06430-5910

KONECKY, GARY, accountant; b. Hollis, N.Y., Apr. 4, 1957; s. Jerome and Claire (Abramowitz) K. A.S. cum laude, Nassau Community Coll., Garden City, N.Y., 1977; BBA cum laude, Hofstra U., Hempstead, N.Y., 1979. CPA, N.Y. Jr. acct. Biller & Snyder CPAs, N.Y.C., 1979-80; staff acct. Larson, Ross & Co. CPAs, N.Y.C., 1980-81; sr. acct. Joel E. Sammet & Co. CPAs, N.Y.C., 1981-82; CPA exam grader AICPA, N.Y.C., 1982-85; pvt. practice acctg. New Hyde Park, N.Y., 1982-88; sr. acct. William A. Edid & Co. CPAs, N.Y.C., 1983; pres. Gary Konecky, CPA, P.C., New Hyde Park, 1989—; adj. prof. L.I. Univ., Greenvale, N.Y., 1985-87. Contbr. articles to community-based publs. and profl. jours. Treas. Hofstra U. Sch. Bus. Alumni, Hempstead, N.Y., 1988-89, pres., 1989-90; active L.I. AIDS Coalition to Unleash Power. Recipient Disting. Svc. award Hofstra U. Sch. Bus. Alumni, 1988. Mem. AICPA, Nat. Conf. CPAs, N.Y. State Soc. CPAs, Rotary (treas. Floral Park (N.Y.)-Bellerose chpt., 1985-88, v.p. 1988-89). Office: 16 Moore St New Hyde Park NY 11040-1304

KONECSNI, JOHN-EMERY, philosophy educator, university official; b. Bklyn., Sept. 1, 1946; s. Benjamin Francis and mary Elizabeth (Konecsni) Hannigan; m. Gail Maria DeLeonardo, Apr. 2, 1977; children: Margaret Eileen, John-Emery III. BSc, St. Johns U., Jamaica, N.Y., 1967, MA, 1968; PhD, NYU, 1972; hon. diploma pathologists asst. program, Cath. Med. Ctr., 1987. Clk. Bankers Trust Co., N.Y.C., 1963-67; microbiologist Kings County Hosp., Bklyn., 1967; prof. philosophy, chmn. dept. Caldwell (N.J.) Coll., 1968-78; chief exec. officer Declan Finn Career Mktg. Assocs., N.Y.C., 1978—; adj. assoc. prof. philosophy St. John's U., 1977—; asst. dean Grad. Sch. Pharmacy and Allied Health St. Johns U., 1980—; pastoral asst. St. Lucy-St. Patrick Roman Cath. Ch., Bklyn., 1976-77; mem. educators caucus Am. Assn. Pathologist Assts., 1982—; chmn. N.Y. State Coun. Physician Asst. Programs, 1986—. Author: Metabiology and Metascience, 1973, Biology and the Philosophy of Science, 1978, Scotus to Kant, 1978, A Post Kantian Anthropology, 1978, A Philosophy for Living, 2d edit., 1986; also articles and revs. Mem. Am. Soc. for Med. Tech. (treas. polit. action com. 1990-92), Empire State Assn. for Med. Tech. (pres. 1988, Mem. of Yr. award 1989), Am. Cath. Philos. Assn. (life), Amici Thomae Mori (life), Rho Chi, Lambda Tau. Home: 9320 222d St Queens Village NY 11428-1940 Office: St John's U Coll Pharmacy and Allied Health Jamaica NY 11439

KONES, RICHARD, cardiologist, medical service company executive; b. N.Y.C., Apr. 8, 1948; s. Joseph Irwin and Ruth (Winkler) K. BSChemE, NYU, 1960, MD, 1964; DSc in Physiology, Somerset U., Eng., 1988, PhD in Exercise Physiology and Nutrition, 1990. Diplomate Am. Bd. Internal Medicine. Intern Kings County Hosp., Bklyn., 1964-65; resident in surgery Bronx Mcpl. Hosp., N.Y.C., 1965-66; resident in medicine Lenox Hill Hosp., N.Y.C., 1966-68; fellow in cardiology, physician in charge ICU Arthur Logan Hosp., N.Y.C., 1968-69; USPHS-NIH fellow in cardiology, chief resident Sch. Medicine, Tulane U., New Orleans, 1969-71; asst. prof. cardiology N.Y. Med. Coll., N.Y.C., 1971, chief CCU, 1971-75; cons. and chief CCU Community Hosp., Flatbush Gen. Hosp. and others, N.Y.C., 1971-79; asst. physician, dir., ECG conf. coord. No. Westchester Hosp., Cornell Med. Ctr., Mount Kisco, N.Y., 1972-75; chief exec. officer Community Med. Offices, Inc., Houston and N.Y.C., 1974—; asst. physician, dir., ECG conf. coord. Cornell Med. Ctr. Park City Hosp., Bridgeport, Conn., 1975-78; physician and cons. in cardiology Westchester County Med. Ctr., Cornell Med. Ctr., Valhalla, N.Y., 1978-80, SW Meml. Hosp., 1979-81, Alief Gen. Hosp., Houston, 1979-81; lectr. medicine U. Tex., Houston, 1979—; asst. prof. then assoc. prof. medicine N.Y. Med.Coll., 1971—, pres. Nutrition, Sportsfitness and Preventive Wellness Med. Ctr. and Found., Houston; lectr. medicine and cardiology U. Tex. Health Sci. Ctr., Houston Med. Ctr., Baylor Coll. Medicine, 1979—; cons. Social Security Adminstrn., Tex. Dept. Health and Human Svcs., 1989—; med. dir., chief Nutrition-Medsport Health Clinic, Houston and Phila., 1989—; med. dir. Med. and Diagnostic Ctr., Phila., 1990—. Author, editor books on biochemistry, physiology, cardiology, nutrition, metabolism, nutrition and sports medicine; contbr. rsch. papers to profl. pubs. Fellow Am. Coll. Chest Physicians, Am. Thoracic Soc., Am. Coll. Cardiology, Royal Soc. Medicine, Royal Soc. Health, Am. Coll. Sports Medicine, Inst. Advancement of Health, Soc. Gen. Internal Medicine, Am. Coll. Angiology, Am. Geriatric Soc., Internat. Coll. Angiology, Am. Med. Athletic Assn.; mem. Am. Running and Fitness Assn., Nutritional Rsch. Coun., Nat. Strength and Conditioning Assn., Am. Coll. Nutrition, Am. Fedn. Clin. Rsch., Am. Dietetic Assn., Am. Soc. Internal Medicine, Am. Diabetes Assn., Am. Heart Assn., Am. Pub. Health Assn., So. Med. Assn., Am. Physiol. Soc., Am. Soc. for Cardiovascular and Pulmonary Rehab., Brit. Soc. of Nutritional Medicine, Ctr. Sci. in Pub. Interest, Soc. Nutrition Edn. Office: 1525 Locust St Fl 2D Philadelphia PA 19102-3732

KONIETZKO, KURT O., psychologist; b. Free City of Danzig, Germany, Sept. 25, 1924; came to U.S., 1939; s. Hermann and Anna (Baenfer) K.; m. Ruth Rittenhouse, 1949 (div. 1976); 1 child, Debra; m. Myrna DeVoren, 1982. BA, U. Chgo., 1951; MA, Temple U., 1953, PhD, 1959. Lic. clin. psychologist, Pa. Dist. supr. Commonwealth of Pa. Bd. of Parole, Phila., 1963-66; dir. Inst. for Rational Living, Phila., 1966-69, Inst. for Living, Inc., Phila., 1969-76; cons. Dept. of Edn., V.I., 1976-79; coord. Community Mental Health Svcs., V.I., 1976-77; dir. children's svcs. Mental Health Div., V.I., 1977-79; acting adminstr. Community Mental Health Ctr., V.I., 1976-77; pres. Self Mgmt. for Successful Living, Inc., Phila., 1979-91. Contbr. articles to profl. jours. Pres. World Federalists Assn. (Phila. chpt.), Brynford Civic Assn., Haverford, Pa., Delaware County Dem. Orgn., Phila.; candidate Haverford Twp. Commr., Phila. area, 1991. With USN, 1942-48. Mem. APA, Pa. Psychol. Assn., Phila. Soc. Clin. Psychologists, Delaware Valley Group Psychotherapy Soc.

KONIGSBERG, RICHARD LEE, accountant; b. Balt., July 3, 1953; s. Robert Lee and Helen Mae (Aronson) K. BA, Johns Hopkins U., 1975; cert., U. Balt., 1977; postgrad., Towson State U., 1979-86, U. Md., Balt., 1989—. CPA, Md. Jr. acct. Walpert, Smullian & Blumenthal, Towson, Md., 1977-78; jr. acct. Newman, Berfeld & Wolpert, Balt., 1978-80; sr. acct. Levy, Bronfein & Berliner, Pikesville, Md., 1980-82; pvt. practice acctg. Reisterstown, Md., 1982—; instr. tax seminars Md. Nat. Bank, Belair, 1986, Cable & Wireless Communications, Inc., Balt., 1987-89, Community Coll. Balt., 1989. Author: (with others) Tax Ideas; moderator radio call-in show Year Round Tax Planning Am. Radio Network, 1991. Big brother Jewish Big Brother League of Balt., 1990; bd. dirs. Cystic Fibrosis Found., Towson, 1980-83, Reisterstown-Owings Mills (Md.) C. of C., 1986-88; vol. Am. Heart Assn., Towson, 1980-88; mem. Jewish Community Ctr., Owings Mills, 1986—, Sinai Fitness Ctr., Owings Mills, 1988—; mem. Balt Mus. Art. Recipient 2nd prize Md. Psychol. Assn., Balt., 1970. Mem. AICPA, Md. Assn. CPA's, Md. Soc. Accts., Balt. Coun. Fgn. Affairs, Balt. Mus. of Art. Democrat. Jewish. Home: 221 Cedarmere Cir Owings Mills MD 21117-2447 Office: 100 Owings Ct Ste 3 Reisterstown MD 21136-3048

KONING, ROSS EDWARD, biology educator; b. Adrian, Mich., Oct. 5, 1953; s. David Ross and Evelyn Myrtle (De Meritt) K.; m. Christine Elizabeth Steeb, May 23, 1981; children: Hans Friederich, Kurt Nicolaas, Katje Anna. BS, U. Mich., 1975, MS, 1977, PhD, 1981. Asst. prof. biology Rutgers U., Piscataway, N.J., 1981-87; assoc. prof. Ea. Conn. State U., Willimantic, Conn., 1987—. Special papers editor Am. Jour. Botany, 1981-86; contbr. over 20 articles to profl. jours. Den leader Cub Scouts, Willimantic, 1989—. Mem. Am. Soc. Plant Physiologists (student rsch. awards), Bot. Soc. Am. (program dir. 1986—, chmn. physiol. sect. 1991—, student rsch. awards), Plant Growth Regulator Soc. Am. Home: 141 Oak St Willimantic CT 06226-2832 Office: Eastern Conn State U Biology Dept Willimantic CT 06226

KONKEL, R(ICHARD) STEVEN, environmental and social science consultant; b. Denver, June 27, 1950; s. E. Vernon and Jane (Templeman) K.; m. James Frances Ohlert, July 14, 1984; children: Kaitlin Brooke, Britt, Edward. BS in Archtl. Engring., U. Colo., 1972; M in City Planning, Harvard U., 1975; PhD in Urban and Environ. Planning, MIT, 1991. Economist, planner Edward C. Jordan Co., Portland, Maine, 1975-77; cost-benefit analyst Oak Ridge (Tenn.) Nat. Labs., 1977-79; prin. economist Konkel Environ. Cons., San Francisco, 1980-82; policy analyst State of Alaska Office of Gov. and Dept. Commerce and Econ. Devel., Juneau, 1982-84; pres. Konkel & Co., Cambridge, Mass., 1984—; Co-editor MIT faculty seminar on risk mgmt., 1989—. Author: Environmental Impact Assessment Rev., 1987; co-editor: MIT Faculty Seminar on Risk Management, 1989. Co-chairperson Juneau Energy Adv. Com., 1984. Research grantee Nat. Inst. Dispute Resolution, Washington, 1986-87. Mem. Am. Inst. Cert. Planners (charter), Am. Planning Assn., Am. Econ. Assn., Internat. Assn. Energy Econs., Assn. Environ. and Resource Economists. Home: 38 Maple Ave #2 Cambridge MA 02139 Office: MIT 77 Massachusetts Ave Rm 7338 Cambridge MA 02139-4307

KONKOL, ROBERT ANTHONY, psychiatrist; b. Perth Amboy, N.J., May 19, 1951; s. Robert Samuel and Irma (Martinak) K.; m. Nancy Isabel Ulanowicz, June 18, 1977. BA, Franklin and Marshall Coll., Lancaster, Pa., 1973; MD, U. Md., 1977. Diplomate Am. Bd. Psychiatry and Neurology. Dir. adolescent svcs. Springfield Hosp. Ctr., Sykesville, Md., 1979-82; chief exec. officer Regional Inst. for Children and Adolescents, Cheltenham, Md., 1982-83; dir. psychiatry Calvert Meml. Hosp., Prince Frederick, Md., 1983--; med. dir. Calvert County Mental Health Clinic, Prince Frederick, 1983-86; dir. psychiatry St. Mary's Hosp., Leonardtown, Md., 1988—; pres. Calvert Psychiat. Assocs., P.C., Prince Frederick, 1983—; v.p. med. staff Calvert Meml. Hosp., 1987-88; profl. advisor Nat. Mental Health Assn., 1984—. Mem. Am. Psychiat. Assn., Washington Psychiat. Soc. Republican. Roman Catholic. Home: 1911 Watson Rd Owings MD 20736-9720 Office: Calvert Psychiat Assocs PC 110 Hospital Rd Prince Frederick MD 20678

KONOVER, VICKI, clinical supervisor, family services administrator; b. Hartford, Conn., Oct. 7, 1951. BFA, U. Denver, 1973; MS, U. Hartford, 1981. Older adult caseworker Jewish Family Svc., Hartford, 1981-82; suburban outreach worker Jewish Family Svc., 1982-85, coord. suburban svcs., 1985-89, coord. older adult svcs., 1989—. Co-author: Surviving the Big Squeeze, 1991. Co-chmn. bd. dir. Our Children's Ctr., Hartford, 1986-87, bd. dirs., 1985-86; bd. dirs. United Cerebral Palsy, 1988. Mem. Gerontol. Soc. Am., Conn. Coalition on Aging, Am. Soc. Aging, Am. Assn. Counseling and Devel. Office: Jewish Family Svc 740 N Main St West Hartford CT 06117-2403

KONRAD, VICTOR ALEXANDER, educator; b. Schorndorf, Fed. Republic of Germany, Apr. 12, 1947; arrived in Can., 1948; s. Alexander Henry and Justine (Wiens) K.; m. Lee-Ann Partridge, July 20, 1974 (div. Jan. 1989); children: Laurianne Elizabeth, Joel Alexander; m. Lucie Marie

Bohac, Oct. 21, 1989. BA in Geography with honors, York U., Toronto, Can., 1971, MA in Geography, 1973; PhD in Geography, McMaster U., 1978. Asst. prof. anthropolgy and Can. Studies U. Maine, Orono, 1976-82, assoc. prof. anthropology and Can. Studies, 1982—; dir. Can. Am. Ctr. U. Maine, Orono, Can., 1982-90; vis. prof. dept. geography U. Ariz., 1984; Can. Studies Exch. fellow Western Wash. U., 1983; Pickerd Bell fellow; lectr.; cons. Can. Liaison Offices of Gov. and Legis., Maine, 1981—, Munsungun Archeol. Projet Exhibit, 1982-84, Maine State Planning Office, 1985—, Maine Coast Heritage Trust, 1986, Maine Devel. Found., 1987, Penobscot Hist. Project, 1987—, Maines Western Mountain Allaince, 1988, Columbia Ency., 1990-92; dir. Borderlands Project, 1988—; mem. adv. bd. Atlas of Maine Resources Project, 1983—; lectr. numerous orgns. including Mount Allsion U. Author 11 books and monographs; contbr. numerous articles to profl. jours. Can. Embassy fellow, 1983-84, Can. Embassy Faculty Enrichment award, 1983-84, Cen. Mortgage and Housing Corp. fellow, 1973-76, Can. Coun. Doctoral fellow, 1971-72; recipient Can. Assn. Geographers prize, 1971, York U. scholarship, 1971, Atkinson Found. Bursary, 1976; recipient numerous grants. Mem. Assn. Am. Geographers (hist. geography specialty group 1982-85, rsch. com. 1983-86, regional councilor 1983-86, com. on sci. responsibility 1983-87, liaison to CAG 1986-89, 91—, mem. editorial bd. IGC 1990-92), Assn. for Can. Studies in the U.S. (book rev. editor 1979-88, v.p. 1987-88, pres. 1989-91, various coms.), Assn. Living Hist. Farms and Agrl. Mus., Atlantic Assn. Historians, Can. Archeol. Assn., Can. Assn. Geographers (editorial com. 1986-88, 88-90, various coms.), Champlain Soc., Ea. Hist. Geography Assn. (conf. co-organizer and chmn. session on Heritage Rsch., Planning and Preservation 1979, conf. organizer 1985), Maine Coun. for Can. Studies (exec. dir. 1980-81, 82-83, 84—), New Eng.-St. Lawrence Valley Geog. Soc. (Maine rep. to exec. com. 1978-81, program chmn. ann. meeting 1982, regional councilor 1983-86), Ont. Archeol. Soc. (v.p. 1972, chmn. salvage com. 1972-74), Ont. Hist. Geographers Group (chmn. interdisciplinary session on Prehist. Geography 1976), Soc. for the N.Am. Cultural Survey, others. Office: Found Ednl Exch Can-US, Fulbright Program, 29 Beechwood at MacKay, Ottawa, ON Canada K1M 1M2

KONTOSTATHIS, KYRIAKOS, mathematician; b. Athens, Attiki, Greece, Dec. 7, 1959; came to U.S., 1978; s. Achilleus and Foto (Vagia) K.; m. April Edwards, May 18, 1990. BA, Coll. of Wooster, 1982; MA, Duke U., 1984, PhD, 1988. Asst. prof. Villanova (Pa.) U., 1988—. Mem. Am. Math. Soc., Assn. Symbolic Logic, Sigma Xi. Office: Villanova U Dept Math Villanova PA 19085

KONYHA, STEPHEN MICHAEL, management and data processing consultant; b. N.Y.C., Nov. 6, 1940; s. Stephen Joseph and Helen (Katcher) K.; m. Doris May Knappenberger, Dec. 12, 1970. BS, Fordham U., 1964, MBA, 1973. Cert. data processor. Internal cons. Bankers Trust Corp., N.Y.C., 1967-79, AFIA Ins. Co., Wayne, N.J., 1980-82; client cons. Morristown, N.J., 1982-88; owner, mgr., mgmt. cons. Steve Konyha and Assocs., Morristown, 1989-91; distbr. success motivation Inst. Personal & Profl. Devel., Waco, Tex., 1991—. Author, editor: The Ecology of Business Enterprise, 1971. Vol. ARC, Madison, N.J., 1984, cons., bd. dirs. S.E. Morris chpt., 1984-85. With U.S. Army, 1965-67. Mem. Data Processing Mgmt. Assn., Ind. Computer Cons. Assn. Republican. Methodist. Home: Two Lower State Rd North Wales PA 19454 Office: One Sentry Pkwy Blue Bell PA 19422

KOOL, LAWRENCE BERNARD, chemistry educator; b. Traverse City, Mich., Feb. 27, 1952; s. Bernard Paul and Cornelia Marjorie (Bergers) K.; m. Nancy Lois Globokar; m. Eva Anna Mehmetaj, Mar. 9, 1986; children: Olivia Isabella, Julia Lauren. BS in Chemistry, U. Mich., 1974; PhD in Chemistry, U. Mass., 1987. Chemist Transidyne Gen. Corp., Ann Arbor, Mich., 1974-75; scientist KMS Fusion, Inc., Ann Arbor, 1975-82; research fellow Harvard U., Cambridge, 1986-88; chemistry prof. Boston Coll., Chestnut Hill, 1988—. Mem. ACS, Matl. Research Soc., Internat. Union of Pure and Applied Chemistry. Home: 1811 Beacon St Brookline MA 02146-4206 Office: Boston Coll Dept Chem Boston MA 02135

KOOMEN, MARTIN JOHN, physicist; b. Bristol, N.Y., Dec. 30, 1917; s. Willem and Grietje (Veenis) K.; m. Nellie Faye Smith, Dec. 6, 1946 (dec. 1985); 1 child, William N. BS, U. Rochester, 1940, MS, 1943. Instrument inspector Bausch & Lomb Optical Co., Rochester, N.Y., 1940-42; physicist inst. of optics U. Rochester, 1942-46, Naval Rsch. Lab., Washington, 1946-82, SFA Inc., Landover, Md., 1982—. Fellow Optical Soc. Am.; mem. Am. Astron. Soc., Am. Inst. Physics, Am. Geophys. Union, AAAS. Home: 5194 Dungannon Rd Fairfax VA 22030 Office: Naval Rsch Lab Washington DC 20375

KOONCE, KENNETH TERRY, oil company executive; b. Corpus Christi, Tex., June 1, 1938; s. Hubert Allen and Nell Gustine (Lacy) K.; m. Beverly Anne Montgomery, Aug. 6, 1960; children—Diana K. Koonce Walla, Kenneth T., Jr., Kelly M. B.S. in Chem. Engring., Rice U., 1960, Ph.D. in Chem. Engring., 1964. Registered profl. engr., Tex. Research and mgmt. positions Exxon Co. U.S.A. and Exxon Prodn. Research, Houston, 1963-76; prodn. dept. planning coordinator Exxon Co. U.S.A., Houston, 1976-77; western div. ops. mgr. Exxon Co. U.S.A., Los Angeles, 1977-80, western div. mgr., 1980-83; prodn. dept. hdqrs. ops. mgr. Exxon Co. U.S.A., Houston, 1983-85; pres., chief exec. officer Esso Resources Can. Ltd., Calgary, Alta., Can., 1985-88; sr. v.p. Upstream Bus. Exxon Co. U.S.A., 1988-90; pres., chief exec. officer Exxon Rsch. and Engring. Co., 1990—, also bd. dirs.; bd. dirs. Exxon Rsch. and Engring. Co. Contbr. articles to profl. jours.; patentee in field. Pres. Rice U. Engring. Alumni, Houston, 1977; mem. adv. council George Brown Sch. Engring., Rice U., Houston; panel vice chmn. Gulf Coast United Way, Houston, 1984-85; dep. chmn. Calgary United Way, 1986, chmn. 1987; trustee Stevens Inst. Tech., Hoboken, N.J., 1990—; bd. dirs. YMCA of Houston, 1989-90, United Ways Tri-State, N.Y.C., 1991—, Liberty Sci. Ctr., Jersey City, 1992—; elder Ch. of Christ; mem. bd. regents Pepperdine U. Mem. Soc. Petroleum Engrs. (bd. dirs. 1981-84, Sect. Service award 1972, Disting. Svc. award), Am. Petroleum Inst., Can. Petroleum Assn. (gov., exec. com.), Tex. State Bd. Profl. Engrs., Tex. Mid-Continent Oil & Gas Assn. (budget & exec. coms. 1988-90), Mid-Continent Oil & Gas Assn. (exec. com. 1988-90), Nat. Ocean Industries Assn. (bd. dirs., fin., govt. & pub. Affairs coms. 1988—), Inst. for Christian Studies (adminstrv. and devel. bd.). Republican. Clubs: Calgary Petroleum, Calgary Golf and Country, Ranchmen's, Glencoe (Calgary); Petroleum (Houston), Houstonian. Office: Exxon Rsch and Engring Co PO Box 101 Florham Park NJ 07932-0101

KOONS, BETSY JEANNE, public relations executive; b. Lewisburg, Pa., Dec. 29, 1953; d. Arthur William and Betty Jane (Shively) K. BA, Shippensburg (Pa.) U., 1975. Exec. asst. The White House, Washington, 1981-84, dep. press sec. Office of First Lady Nancy Reagan, 1985-89; dir. pub. and consumer affairs Nat. Hwy. Traffic Safety Adminstrn., Washington, 1989; dir. pub. rels. and publs. Susquehanna U., Selinsgrove, Pa., 1990—. Mem. Coun. for Advancement and Support of Edn., Susquehanna Valley Visitors Bur., Selinsgrove C. of C. Republican. Office: Susquehanna U Dir Pub Rels Selinsgrove PA 17870-1001

KOONS, ROBERT HENRY, aerospace engineer; b. Morristown, N.J., Apr. 26, 1956; s. Henry Bailer and Susan Demarest (Roy) K.; m. Emily Alice Kelley, July 11, 1981; children: Douglas Robert, Elizabeth Kelley. BS in Aerospace Engring., U. Va., 1978, M Engring. in Aerospace Engring., 1980. Sr. engr. Boeing Aerospace Co., Kent, Wash., 1980-83; control systems engr. GE Astrospace Co., King of Prussia, Pa., 1983-90; sr. control systems engr. GE Astrospace Co., East Windsor, Pa., 1990—. Mem. Downingtown Area Sewer Task Force, Uwchlan, Pa., 1987-90; supr. Upper Uwchlan Twp., 1988—; chmn. Upper Uwchlan Bd. Suprs., 1990—. Mem. AIAA (sr.), U.S. Naval Inst. (assoc.), Sigma Gamma Tau. Republican. Presbyterian. Home: 17 Stephen Dr Downingtown PA 19335-1859 Office: GE Astrospace Co PO Box 800 Princeton NJ 08543

KOONTZ, ELDON RAY, financial consultant; b. Randolph County, Ind., Oct. 20, 1913; s. Irvin Delbert and Martha Caroline (Farmer) K.; m. Florence Gloria Gustus, Jan. 20, 1944; children: Rebecca Anne Koontz Stumm, Stephen Wickey Koontz. AB in Econs., Earlham Coll., 1938; Diploma in Bus. Adminstrn., Alexander Hamilton Inst., N.Y.C., 1956. Chief cost acct. and spl. assignments, Crosley Div. Avco Mfg. Corp., Richmond, Ind.; asst. to pres. F.C. Russell Co., Cleve.; controller, asst. sec. Pacific Mercury Electronics, Joplin, Mo.; sr. mgmt. engr. Bell Aerosystems Co., Wheatfield, N.Y.; controller, asst. sec. Fleet of America, Inc., Buffalo, N.Y.; asst. to pres., acting gen. mgr. Tycodyne Industries, Inc./Lakeside Mfg. Co., Lackawanna and Honeoye, N.Y.; chmn., pres. E.R. Koontz & Assocs., Inc., Williamsville, N.Y., 1970—; mng. dir. Koontzco (Div. E.R. Koontz & Assocs., Inc.), 1990—. Contbg. author: Mergers and Acquisitions Procedures, 1987. Treas. First English Luth. Ch., Richmond, Ind., 1950-55; v.p. Cen. Presbyn. Ch., Buffalo, N.Y., 1979-85; mem. The Chapel, Amherst, N.Y., 1986. Capt. U.S. Army, 1943-45. Mem. Richmond Accts. Assn. (pres. 1951-52), Nat. Assn. Cost Accts. (assoc. dir. for publs. Dayton, Ohio, 1951-55), Nat. Assn. Mergers and Acquistions Cons. (bd. dirs., sec. 1973-83), Internat. Assn. Mergers and Acquisitions Cons. (bd. dirs., sec. 1974-83), Am. Legion, Amherst C. of C., Rotary (Rotarian of Yr. North Amherst chpt. 1990). Republican. Home: 52B Williamsburg Sq Williamsville NY 14221 Office: ER Koontz and Assocs Inc PO Box 182 Buffalo NY 14221-0182

KOOPER, LAURENCE STANLEY, marketing administrator; b. N.Y.C., Apr. 6, 1957; s. Al Adam and Jean Eunice (Halwer) K. BA, NYU, 1986; MS, MIT, 1988. Cons. Walden Tech. Group, N.Y.C., 1978-83; project mgr. Reuters, Hauppauge, N.Y., 1988-90; tech. mgr. Reuters, N.Y.C., 1990, mktg. mgr., 1990—. Jewish.

KOPELMAN, RICHARD ERIC, management educator; b. N.Y.C., May 31, 1943; s. Seymour H. and Leona L. (Quint) K.; m. Carol Fialkov, June 7, 1970; children: Joshua Marc, Michael Adam. B.S., U. Pa., 1965, M.B.A., 1967; D.B.A., Harvard U., 1974. Instr. bus. Community Coll. of Phila., 1967-69; instr. mgmt. Baruch Coll., CUNY, N.Y.C., 1973-74, asst. prof., 1974-77, assoc. prof., 1978-80, prof., 1981—; cons. various corps. and pub. agys.; corp. dir. Aleph Null Corp., 1979-88, Applied Photonics, Inc., 1986-91, Infodex Systems, Inc., 1986-88, EMS Devel. Corp., 1992—; acad. dir. master of sci. in indsl. rels. program Baruch/Cornell U. Author: The Management of Productivity, A Practical People-Oriented Perspective, 1986; mem. editorial rev. bd. Jour. Social Behavior and Personality, 1985-89, Nat. Productivity Rev., Jour. Orgnl. Behavior Mgmt., Perceptions; contbr. numerous articles to profl. and acad. jours. Bd. dirs. Day Care Council, Nassau County, 1979-82; Nassau Symphony Orch., 1984-85. Recipient Teaching award Baruch Coll., 1987, Teaching Excellence award, 1989, 91; William B. Harding fellow Harvard U. Mem. Acad. Mgmt., Am. Psychol. Assn., Decision Scis. Inst., Soc. for Human Resource Mgmt. (accredited personnel diplomate), Am. Compensation Assn., Met. N.Y. Assn. for Applied Psychology (sec. 1986-87, treas. 1987-88, v.p. 1988-89, pres. 1989-90), Sigma Iota Epsilon. Home: 65 Colgate Rd Great Neck NY 11023-1501 Office: Baruch Coll Dept Mgmt 17 Lexington Ave New York NY 10010-5526

KOPEN, DAN FRANCIS, surgeon, consultant; b. Kingston, Pa., Aug. 14, 1948; s. Francis and Maryann (Kumiega) K.; m. Kathleen Elizabeth Roberts; children: Krystin, Derek, Kaytlin. BS in Chemistry, Wilkes Coll., 1970; MD, Milton S. Hershey Med. Ctr., 1974. Diplomate Am. Coll. of Surgeons. Surgical residency Washington U., St. Louis, 1975-80, surgical fellowship, 1976-77; clinical asst. in surgery Washington U. Sch. of Med., St. Louis, 1980-82; staff surgeon Nesbitt Meml. Hosp., Kingston, Pa., 1984—; pres. Northeastern Surg. Group, Kingston, 1986—, AIDS Awareness Com. of Luzerne County, 1990—. Editor Wilkes Physician's Report, 1988-89; contbr. articles to profl. jours. Bd. mem. Am. Cancer Soc., Wyoming Valley, Pa., 1985—, Wilkes Coll., Wilkes-Barre, 1987—; physicians com. United Way of Wyoming Valley, 1988; assoc. dir. Med. Explores Group, Nesbitt Hosp., 1987—; pub. issues chmn. Am. Cancer Soc., Wyoming Valley, 1985-88. Fellow ACS, Am. Soc. Abdominal Surgeons; me. AMA, Pa. Med. Soc., Am. Burn Assn., Am. Chem. Soc., Pa. Coun. for Humanities, Luzerne County Med. Soc. (bd. dirs. 1989—), Harrel Soc. of Milton S. Hershey Med. Ctr. of Pa. State U., Milton S. Hershey Med. Ctr. of Pa. State U. Alumni Assn. (bd. dirs. 1991—), Am. Chemistry Soc. (div. medicinal chemistry). Roman Catholic. Office: 480 Pierce St Ste 318 Wilkes Barre PA 18704-5521

KOPENHAVER, PATRICIA ELLSWORTH, podiatrist. Student, Columbia U., 1950-53; BA, George Washington U., 1954; MA, Columbia U., 1956; Dr. Podiatric Medicine, N.Y. Coll. of Podiatric Medicine, 1963; postgrad., N.Y. Coll. Podiatric Medicine, 1980. Diplomate Nat. Bd. Podiatry Examiners. Pvt. practice podiatry Greenwich, Conn., 1964—; mem. staff Laurelton Convalescent Hosp., Greenwich. Friends of Greenwich Libr.; publicity dir. Neighbors Club, YWCA, 1968—; bd. dirs. Monmouth Opera Guild, 1965; trustee Monmouth Opera Festival, 1966, v.p., 1964; mem. Greenwich Arts Council; program chmn. Greenwich Women's Republican Club, 1983-84, 4th dist. rep., 1984-85, 1987—; mem. Greenwich Exchange for Women's Work, 1984; chmn. bd. Greenwich Woman's Club Gardeners, 1986—. Recipient Hosp. Fund award for med. research translations ARC. Mem. AAUW (v.p. 1991, pres. Greenwich br. 1992—), NOW, Am. Podiatry Assn. (career guidance com.), Conn. Podiatry Assn., Fairfield Podiatry Assn., Am. Women's Podiatry Assn. (sec.), Am. Assn. Women Podiatrists (charter pres. 1969-78), Acad. Podiatry, Am. Podiatry Coun., UN Assn. U.S.A., Acad. Podiatric Medicine (chmn. nominating com. 1981, 1st v.p. 1983-84, chmn. fundraising 1984-85, chmn. women's issues 1985, chmn. community edn. 1989), Am. Podiatric Circulatory Soc., Am. Acad. Sports Medicine, Am. Acad. of Podiatric Sports Medicine (assoc. 1989), George Washington U. Alumni Assn., Columbia Alumni Assn., Fairfield County Alumni Assn. Columbia U., Nat. Fedn. Rep. Women, Bruce Mus., Nature Conservancy, Federated Garden Clubs Conn., Croquet Found. Am., St. Mary Ladies Guild, Greenwich Gardeners, Womans' Club (ways and means com. 1989), English Speaking Union, Soroptimists Internat. Am. (pres. Greenwich br. 1990—), Inc. (vice-chmn. program com. 1985—, regional med. scholarship chmn. 1987, med. scholarship chmn. N.E. region 1988, program dir. 1988—, pres. Greenwich br. 1990-92), Toastmasters, Travel Club (program com. 1984—, Indian com.), Greenwich Women's Club (chmn. civic & pub. affairs com. 1970, program com. 1983—, pres. 1985-88, scholarship chmn. 1985—, ways and means com. 1989), Pi Epsilon Chi. Home: 2 Sutton Pl S New York NY 10022-3070 Office: 8 Dearfield Dr Greenwich CT 06831-5348

KOPF, BENJAMIN, technical support manager; b. Warren, Pa., July 26, 1956; s. Harry Daniel Jr. and Ann (Newmaker) K. BA, Allegheny Coll. Ops. mgr. Aved Electronics, Andover, Mass., 1984-86; MIS Tregismans Catalog Showroom, Manchester, N.H., 1986-89; tech. support mgr. Aimtech Corp., Nashua, N.H., 1989—; pres. Choice Software, Bedford, N.H., 1989—; designer in field. Episcopalian. Home: 48 Birkdale Rd Bedford NH 03110-4300 Office: Aimtech Corp 20 Trafalgar Square Nashua NH

KOPF, PETER WILLIAM, physical chemist, consultant; b. Phila., Apr. 23, 1944; s. Christian August and Melba Theresa (Moennig) K.; m. Lynn Dobbin, Jan. 17, 1970; children: Robert Christian, Jennifer Lynn. AB, Rutgers U., 1966; PhD, U. Rochester, 1970. Chemist Union Carbide Corp., Bound Brook, N.J., 1970-80, group leader, 1980-85; cons. Arthur D. Little, Inc., Cambridge, Mass., 1985-89, dir., 1989—. Author: Environmental Packaging, 1991; contbr. articles to profl. pubs. Mem. Am. Chem. Soc., Soc. Advancement Materials and Process Engring., Soc. Mfg. Engrs., Phi Beta Kappa. Home: 29 Firecut Ln Sudbury MA 01776-1906 Office: Arthur D Little Inc Acorn Park Cambridge MA 02140-2303

KOPIT, ARTHUR, playwright; b. N.Y.C., May 10, 1937; s. George and Maxine (Dubin) K.; m. Leslie Ann Garis; 2 sons, 1 dau. A.B. cum laude, Harvard U., 1959. fellow Center for Humanities, Wesleyan U., 1974-75, playwright-in-residence, 1975-76; CBS fellow Yale U., 1976-77. Author: (plays produced at Harvard) Questioning of Nick, 1957, Gemini, 1957, On the Runway of Life You Never Know What's Coming Off Next, 1958, Across the River and into the Jungle, 1958, Sing to Me Through Open Windows, 1959, Aubade, 1959; Oh Dad, Poor Dad, Mamma's Hung You in the Closet and I'm Feelin' So Sad, 1960 (produced in London, 1961, on Broadway, 1963, released as motion picture, 1967), An Incident in the Park, 1968, What's Happened to the Thorne's House, 1972, Louisiana Territory, 1975, (6 one-act plays) The Day the Whores Came Out to Play Tennis, and Other Plays, 1965, Indians, 1969, Wings, 1977, Secrets of the Rich, 1978, (book of musical) Nine, 1982, Road to Nirvana, 1991; (adaptation) Ghosts (Ibsen), 1982, End of the World, 1984. Recipient Vernon Rice award, 1962, Outer Circle award, 1962; Shaw Travelling fellow Harvard U., 1959; Guggenheim fellow, 1967; Rockefeller grantee, 1968; NEH grantee, 1974. Mem. Writers Guild Am., Dramatists Guild (council), Hasty Pudding Soc., Signet Soc., PEN, Phi Beta Kappa. Club: Harvard (N.Y.C.). Address: care Audrey Wood Internat Creative Mgmt 40 W 57th St New York NY 10019

KOPLEWICZ, HAROLD SAMUEL, child and adolescent psychiatrist; b. Bklyn., Jan. 12, 1953; s. Joseph and Romana (Magid) K.; m. Linda Jane Sirow, June 22, 1980; children: Joshua, Adam, Sam. BS, U. Md., 1973; MD, Albert Einstein Coll. of Medicine, 1978. Diplomate Am. Bd. Psychiatry and Neurology, Am. Bd. Child Psychiatry. Med. dir. preschool hyperactivity program N.Y. State Psychiat. Inst., N.Y.C., 1982-85, med. dir. children's anxiety clinic, 1983-86; dir. gen. residency tng. child psychiatry Columbia Coll. Physicians and Surgeons, N.Y.C., 1985-86; chief div. child and adolescent psychiatry Schneider Children's Hosp. and Hillside Hosp. of L.I. Jewish Med. Ctr., N.Y.C., 1986—; cons. Riverdale Community Ctr., 1981-86, The Dalton Sch., The N.Y. Infirmary, 1991. Bd. dirs. Raoul Wallenberg New Leadership Soc., 1983-87, Community Mainstreaming Assocs., 1990; chmn. Simon Wisenthal Ctr., 1984-86; mem. adv. bd. The Hetrick-Martin Inst., 1989; cons. Jewish Child Care Assn. Recipient Lowenstein Found., 1986. Fellow Am. Acad. Child and Adolescent Psychiatry; mem. Am. Psychiat. Assn., Soc. Profs. Child and Adolescent Psychiatry, Am. Bd. Psychiatry and Neurology (examiner 1988—), Nat. Found. Depressive Illness (nat. bd. dirs. 1992—). Office: LI Jewish Med Ctr 27005 76th Ave New Hyde Park NY 11040-1433

KOPP, CHARLES GILBERT, lawyer; b. Hartford, Conn., Jan. 10, 1933; s. Henry and Grace (Goldberg) K.; m. Ann Weiss, June 10, 1962 (div. 1963). BA, Amherst Coll., 1955; LLB, U. Pa., 1960. Bar: Pa. 1961. Ptnr. Wolf, Block, Schorr and Solis-Cohen, Phila., 1960—; bd. dirs. Provident Nat. Bank, Thomas Jefferson U. Hosp. Contbr. articles to profl. jours. Commr. Delaware River Port Authority, 1986-87; co-chmn. select com. of U.S. Embassy, Bern, Switzerland, 1985; mem. Pa. Gov.'s Spl. Tax Commn., 1980; bd. dirs. Pennsylvanians for Effective Govt., Harrisburg, 1987; mem. Pa. Electoral Coll., 1988; mem. adv. bd. region I, Resolution Trust Corp.; mem. coun. The Pa. Soc. 1st lt. USAF, 1955-57. Recipient Pop Warner Gold Football award, 1988. Mem. ABA, Pa. Bar Assn., Phila. Bar Assn., The Union League of Phila., Philmont Country Club (Huntingdon Valley, Pa.)(pres. 1976-78), Locust Club. Republican. Jewish. Home: 210 W Rittenhouse Sq Ste 3306 Philadelphia PA 19103-5709 Office: Wolf Block Schorr & Solis-Cohen 1200 Packard Bldg Philadelphia PA 19102

KOPPEL, ANDREA ROTH, marketing company executive; b. Bklyn., Mar. 19, 1942; d. Jacob Harold and Iris Anita (Hausman) Roth; m. Alan Richard Koppel, June 30, 1963. BA, SUNY, Oswego, 1962; MS, Bklyn. Coll., 1965. Tchr. spl. edn. N.Y. Bd. Edn., N.Y.C., 1962-68; office mgr. Cert. Reports, Inc., Kinderhook, N.Y., 1978-82; v.p. Kinderhook Rsch., Inc., 1984-88, pres., 1988—. Mem. Canaan (N.Y.) Dem. Club, 1968-78, Canaan Fire Aux., 1969-78. Mem. Mktg. Rsch. Assn., Nat. Early Am. Glass Club, Order of Ea. Star (matron 1982-83). Jewish. Home: Rte 295 PO Box 399 Canaan NY 12029 Office: Kinderhook Rsch Inc Rte 9 Kinderhook NY 12106

KOPPEL, BARBARA SUE, neurologist; b. Cooperstown, N.Y., Sept. 9, 1952; d. Leopold and Lore (Baer) K.; m. Timothy A. Pedley, Mar. 17, 1984; children: Lauren, Nathaniel. BA, U. Rochester, 1974; MD, Columbia U., 1978. Intern Montefiore Hosp., Pitts., 1978-79; resident in neurology Neurol. Inst., Columbia U., N.Y.C., 1979-82; attending neurologist Met. Hosp., N.Y.C., 1982—, assoc. dir. neurology svc.; asst. prof. neurology N.Y. Med. Coll., Valhalla, N.Y., 1983-87, assoc. prof. neurology, 1987—; dir. Huntington's unit Terence Cardinal Cooke Health Ctr., N.Y.C., 1988—; chmn. pharmacy and therapeutics com. of med. bd. Met. Hosp., 1988—; cons. to AIDS patients in hosps., clinics and nursing homes. Contbr. chpts. to: Emergency Medicine, 1991, AIDS and Other Manifestations of HIV, 1986, rev. edit., 1992; contbr. articles to profl. jours. Sec. profession adv. bd. Epilepsy Soc. So. N.Y., Westchester, 1991—; co-dir. Neurofibromatosis Ctr., Valhalla, N.Y., 1987—. Fellow Am. Acad. Neruology, Am. Epilepsy Soc. Jewish. Home: 55 Grace Church St Rye NY 10580-3926 Office: Met Hosp 1901 1st Ave Rm 1315 New York NY 10029-7418

KOPROSKI, ALEXANDER ROBERT, real estate executive; b. Stamford, Conn., Apr. 6, 1934; s. Alexander J. and Gladys J. (Kryger) K.; m. Patricia A. Velliquette; children: Lisa, Susan, Gregory, Beth. Student, U. Conn., 1952-54; BS in Mktg. and Fin., Tri-State U., Angola, Ind., 1959. Lic. real estate broker, Conn., N.Y. Comml. and indsl. broker S.H. Silberman, Inc., Stamford, 1960-73; owner, comml. and indsl. broker, chief exec. officer Al Koproski Realty, Stamford, 1973—; mem. Coastal Mgmt. Adv. Com. Past pres. Holy Name Home and Sch. Assn.; past chmn. Poles for Ford Com., Kosciuszko Park Meml. Com., Southeastern Conn. Pulaski Meml. Com., Hartford; past mem. Stamford Bicentennial Commn., Resource Recovery Task Force, Polish Am. Affairs Council, Mayor's South End Adv. Com., Stamford C.E.T.A. Manpower Program; mem. Stamford Hist. Soc.; past chmn. lay adv. bd., past chmn. 75th ann. yr. book Holy Name of Jesus Cath. Ch.; past bd. dirs. Polish Am. Congress Conn., Polish Am. Cen. Com. Stamford; bd. dirs. Polish Slavic Info. Ctr., Stamford, 1975—, Am. Ctr. Polish Culture, Washington, 1990—. With U.S. Army, 1955-57. Named Citizen of Yr., Polish Am. World, N.Y.C., 1978, Layman of Yr., Stamford Kiwanis Club, 1979. Mem. Stamford Bd. Realtors, Am. Coun. Polish Cultural Clubs (nat. fundraising chmn. Washington project), Kosciuszko Found. (co-chmn. nat. coun.), Polish Am. Cultural Soc. (historian, Citizen of Yr. 1975), Am. Assn. Mil. Order of Malta. Republican. Roman Catholic. Clubs: Exch., Holy Name Athletic (Stamford) (pres., chief exec. officer, Citizen of Yr. 1982), Polish Am. Bus. and Profl. (past pres.), Oceanview Beach and Tennis (past treas.). Home: 222 Ocean Dr E Stamford CT 06902-8134 Office: Polish Slavic Info Ctr 36 Pulaski St PO Box 131 Stamford CT 06904

KOPROWSKA, IRENA, cytopathologist, cancer researcher; b. Warsaw, Poland, May 12, 1917; came to U.S., 1944; d. Henryk and Eugenia (Cwi) Grasberg; m. Hilary Koprowski, July 14, 1938; children: Claude, Christopher. BA, Popielewska/Roszkowska, Warsaw, 1934; MD, Warsaw U., 1939. Cert. Am. Bd. Pathology, Internat. Bd. Cytology. Intern in medicine Villejulf Lunatic Asylum, Seine, France, 1940; asst. pathologist Rio De Janeiro City Hosp., Miguel Couto, Brazil, 1942-44; rsch. fellow dept. pathology Cornell U. Med. Coll., N.Y.C., 1945-46, rsch. asst. dept. pharmacology, 1949-50, rsch. fellow dept. of anatomy, 1950-54; rsch. fellow applied immunology Pub. Health Rsch. Inst. of The City of N.Y., 1946-47; asst. pathologist N.Y. Infirmary for Women and Children, N.Y.C., 1947-49;, 1949-54; asst. prof. dept. pathology SUNY Downstate Med. Ctr., N.Y.C., 1954-57; assoc. prof. dept. pathology, dir. cytology lab. and sch. Hahnemann Med. Coll., Phila., 1957-64, prof. pathology dir. cytology lab., sch. cytotechnology, 1964-70; prof. pathology, dir. cytology lab. Temple U. Med. Sch., Phila., 1970-87, prof. emerita, 1987—; rsch. fellow dept. pharmacology Med. Coll. Cornell U., 1949-50; cons. WHO, Southeast Asia, India, 1960-85, Armed Forces Inst. Pathology, Air Force Cytology Rescreen Project, 1979-80. Contbr. articles on cancer rsch. to profl. and sci. jours. Named Woman Physician of Yr., Polish Am. Med. Assn., 1977; grantee USPHS-Nat. Cancer Insts., 1954-75, rsch. grantee Bender Co., Vienna, Austria, 1983-89. Fellow Am. Soc. Clin. Pathologists (emeritus), Coll. Am. Pathologists (emeritus), Coll. Physicians of Phila., Internat. Acad. Cytology (hon.), Internat. Acad. Pathology (emeritus); mem. Am. Assn. for Cancer Rsch. Inc. (emeritus), Am. Assn. Pathologists Inc. (emeritus), Am. Med. Women's Assn., Am. Soc. Cytology (life, Papanicolaou award 1985), Am. Soc. Exptl. Pathology, Argentinian Soc. Cytology (hon.), Path. Soc. Phila. Home: 334 Fairhill Rd Wynnewood PA 19096-1804

KOPROWSKI, HILARY, medical scientist; b. Warsaw, Poland; s. Pawel and Sarah (Berland) K.; m. Irena Grasberg; children: Claude Eugene, Christopher Dorian. BA, Nikolaj Rej Gymnasium of Luth. Congregation, Warsaw; MD, U. Warsaw; grad., Warsaw Conservatory Music and Santa Cecilia Acad., Rome; DSc (hon.), Ludwig-Maximilian U., Munich, Widener Coll.; D of Medicine & Surgery (hon.), U. Helsinki, Finland; D of Medicine (hon.), U. Uppsala, Sweden; LittD (hon.), Thomas Jefferson U.; D of Med. Sci. (hon.), U. Lublin, Poland. Rsch. asst. dept. exptl. and gen. pathology U. Warsaw, 1936-39; staff Yellow Fever Rsch. Svc., Rio de Janeiro, 1940-44; staff rsch. divsn. Am. Cyanamid Co., 1944-46; asst. dir. viral and rickettsial rsch. Lederle Lab., Pearl River, N.Y., 1946-57; dir. Wistar Inst., Phila., 1957-91, prof., 1957—; prof. microbiology Faculty Arts and Scis. U. Pa., Phila., 1957—, prof. microbiology and immunology, 1992—; prof. microbiology and

immunology Thomas Jefferson U., Phila., 1992—; prof. Ctr. Neurovirology; cons. WHO, 1950—; mem. microbiology study sect. NIH, 1956-60; mem. PAHO; mem. adv. com. Nat. Multiple Sclerosis Soc., 1970-78; mem. immunobiology adv. com. NIH, USPHS, 1975-76; mem. bd. sci. counselors div. cancer etiology Nat. Cancer Inst., 1982-86, chmn., 1987-90; mem. biol. response modifiers program decision network com. NIH, 1985-87. Co-editor: Methods in Virology, Viruses and Immunity, Current Topics in Microbiology and Immunology, 1965—, Cancer Research, Viral Immunology, Hybridoma. Decorated commandeur Ordre du Mérite pour la Recherche et l'Invention; chevalier Order Royal De Lion Belgium; recipient Alvarenga prize. Coll. Physicians Phila., 1959, Alfred Jurzykowski Found Polish Millenium prize, 1966, Felix Wankel Tierschutz prize, 1979, Alexander Von Humboldt Sr. U.S. Scientist award, Phila. Cancer Rsch. award Phila. Cancer Club, 1989, San Marino award, 1989, John Scott award, Nicolaus Copernicus medal Polish Acad. Scis., 1989, The Phila. award, 1990, John Scott award, 1990; Fulbright scholar Max Planck Inst. für Verhaltensphysiologie, Seewiesen, Fed. Republic Germany, 1971. Fellow N.Y. Acad. Medicine, Phila. Coll. Physicians; mem. Am. Acad. Arts and Scis., Nat. Acad. Scis., N.Y. Acad. Scis. (pres. 1959, trustee 1960-72), Yogoslavian Acad. Scis., Polish Acad. Scis. Office: The Wistar Inst 3601 Spruce St Philadelphia PA 19104-4265 also: Thomas Jefferson U 462 Jefferson Alumni Hall 1020 Locust St Philadelphia PA 19107

KORB, KENNETH ALLAN, lawyer; b. Boston, Oct. 11, 1932; s. Allan and Mynue (Herbert) K.; m. Jaclyn C. Patricof, June 30, 1962; 1 child, Jason B. BA magna cum laude, Harvard U., 1953, JD cum laude, 1956. Bar: Mass. 1956. Law clk. Supreme Jud. Ct., Mass., 1956-57; assoc. Hutchins & Wheeler, Boston, 1957-60, Kargman & Kargman, Boston, 1960-63; sr. ptnr. Brown, Rudnick, Freed & Gesmer, Boston, 1963-89, Posternak, Blankstein & Lund, Boston, 1990—; lectr. Mass. Continuing Legal Edn., Nat. Coun. Savs. Instns.; sec., bd. dirs., gen. counsel Safety Ins. Co., 1980—; sec., bd. dirs. Neb-Cell Inc., 1989—; underwriting mem. Lloyd's of London, 1984—. Legal columnist The Brookline Citizen, 1990-91; contbr. articles to profl. jours. Internat. pres. Soc. Israel Philatelists, 1974-76, bd. dirs. 1976-80; bd. dirs., treas. Watergate East Condominium U.S.V.I., 1989—. With USAR, 1956-62. Mem. Mass. Bar Assn. Democrat. Home: 24 Helene Rd Newton MA 02168-1025 Office: 100 Charles St Boston MA 02114-4609

KORBEN, DONALD LEE, counseling psychologist; b. Bklyn., Apr. 4, 1948; s. Abraham and Betty K.; BA, Butler U., 1972; MS, Ind. U., 1973, EdD, 1976; postdoctorate Duke U., 1982-84. Intern counseling and psychol. services Ind. U., 1974-76; counseling psychologist Counseling Ctr., St. Bonaventure U., 1976—, chmn. univ. scholastic evaluation com., 1976—, instl. rev. bd., 1980—, mem. adj. faculty Grad. Sch., 1977-80, chairperson pres.'s council alcohol and drug awareness program, 1982-89, dir., counselor, adminstr., dir. Drinking Driver Rehab. Program, 1976—; psychologist St. Bonaventure U. Men's Basketball Team, 1989—; cons. Proprietory Home Assn. Western N.Y., 1976-80, Alpha Phi Omega; cons., mem. Cattaraugus County Council Alcohol and Substance Abuse, 1980; cons. select com. alcohol and alcohol abuse N.Y. State Senate, 1980; advisor Alpha Phi Omega Nat. Service Orgn., 1984—, Students Against Drunk Driving, 1986—; bd. dirs. Pres.'s Council on Alcohol and Drug Abuse St. Bonaventure Univ., 1981—, Cattaraugus County Mental Health Assn. Adv. Com., 1988—; instr. Wyo. Sem. Inst. for drug and alcohol abuse, 1984—. Vol. Salvation Army, 1966-76, 1984—, Boy Scouts Am., 1966-72, Mental Health Assn. Ind., 1967-70, Nat. Epilepsy Found., 1973-76, 1985—; mem. host com. N.Y. State Spl. Olympics, 1979. Named Outstanding Young Man of Am., Jaycees, 1978; NSF grantee, 1970-71; Ind. U. grantee, 1976. Mem. Am. Psychol. Assn. (mem. div. psychotherapy), Am. Assn. Counseling and Devel., Am. Coll Pers. Assn., Am. Mental Health Counselors Assn., Phi Delta Kappa. Democrat. Jewish. Avocations: achievements include: research on the biophysics of neurological effects of hibernation monitoring regional cerebal circulation, factors in assertive tng. with females, construct validity of the strong-vocat. interest inventory, psychophysical effects on physiological optics, others. Home: 757 Main St Olean NY 14760-1550

KORD, VICTOR GEORGE, artist, educator; b. Satu Mare, Romania, Sept. 16, 1935; came to the U.S., 1943; s. Joseph and Clara (Steuer) K.; m. Elizabeth Mary Boyd, Aug. 11, 1971; children; Emily, Tyler. Student, Cleve. Inst. Art, 1953-57; BFA, Yale U., 1958, MFA, 1960. Instr. U. Ill., Champaign, 1960-65; asst. prof. U. Wis., Madison, 1965-67, assoc. prof., 1967-75, prof., 1975-81, prof., dept. chair, 1979-81; prof., dept. chair Va. Commonwealth U., Richmond, 1981-86, prof., 1986-87; prof., dept. chair Cornell U., Ithaca, N.Y., 1987—; mem. adminstrv. bd. Cornell U. Coun., Ithaca, 1991—. Bd. dirs. Federated Arts Coun., Richmond, 1983-85. With U.S. Army, 1960. Guggenheim fellow, 1962-63. Mem. Coll. Art Assn. Democrat. Jewish. Home: 710 Triphammer Rd Ithaca NY 14850-2505

KORENMAN, VICTOR, physics educator, dean; b. N.Y.C., Feb. 5, 1937; s. Morris and Theresa (Viess) K.; m. Joan Roberta Smolin, June 16, 1968; 1 child, Edward. AB, Princeton U., 1958; AM, Harvard U., 1959, PhD, 1966. Rsch. assoc. U. Md., College Park, 1965-67, asst. prof. physics, 1967-73, assoc. prof. physics, 1973-79, prof. physics, 1979—, assoc. dean, 1991—. Contbr. articles to profl. jours. Sloan Found. fellow, 1971-73; NSF grantee, 1973-87. Fellow Am. Phys. Soc.; mem. AAAS, Phi Beta Kappa. Office: U Md Physics Dept College Park MD 20742-4111

KORET, SYDNEY, psychologist, educator. BS, U. R.I., 1937; MSW, MA in Psychology, Boston U., 1949, PhD in Psychology, 1956. Cert. social worker, N.Y., psychologist, N.Y. Psychiatric social worker R.I. State Hosp. Mental Diseases, 1949-50; chief psychiatric social worker Emma Pendleton Bradley Hosp., 1950-58; pvt. practice Providence, and New Bedford, Mass., 1952-57, Rochester, N.Y., 1958—; sr. assoc. psychologist Strong Meml. Hosp., 1958—; instr. Sch. Social Work Boston U., 1951-57, Simmons Coll., 1954-57; instr. Colgate Rochester Bexley Hall Div. Sch., 1963-68; clin. assoc. prof. psychiatry (psychology) Sch. Medicine & Dentistry U. Rochester, 1958—, clin. assoc. prof. psychiatry (psychology) Grad. Sch. Psychology, 1961—; cons., group therapist Crippled Children and Adults R.I., 1952-55; rsch. cons. R.I. Coun. Social Agys., 1956-57; mem. gov.'s com. juvenile deliquency State of R.I., 1957-58; pres., chief exec. officer Convalescent Hosp. Children, 1958-88; mem. case com. Rochester Children's Nursery, 1960-64, cons., 1962-67, Newark State Sch., 1964-70, Batavia Sch. Blind, 1968-70, NIMH, 1974-77, 91—, application reviewer, 1991—; adivsor Nat. Orgn. Mentally Ill Children, 1961-62; prof. advisor League Emotionally Disturbed Children, 1961-63; lectr. SUNY, Geneseo, 1964-68; mem. adv. com. Monroe Devel. Ctr., 1970-72; clin. assoc. prof. Smith Coll., 1974-75. Author: (with others) Successful Innovations in Child Guidance, 1981; contbr. numerous articles to profl. jours. Treas. Concord Villa Home for Boys, 1968-72; mem. Gov. Rockefeller's Com. for Children, 1971-72; bd. dirs. Trinity Emmanuel Presbyn. Ch. Day Care Ctr., 1973-74; mem. steering com. Group Care Project Child Welfare League, 1974-76; mem. profl. adv. com. Monroe County Assn. Children with Learning Disabilities, 1965-70; mem. adv. bd. Parents without Ptnrs., 1969-80; bd. dirs. Ordway Sch., 1970-79, mem. long range planning com., 1975-79; chmn. fgn. bd. trustees Coun. Human Rels., Monrovia, Liberia, 1974-76; mem. pub. policy com. N.Y. State Coun. Voluntary Child Care Agys., Inc., 1972-74; bd. dirs. Mental Health Assn. Rochester & Monroe Counties, 1959-68, mem. profl. adv. com., 1960-68; bd. dirs. Community Child Care Ctr., Inc., 1968-80, pres., 1970-73; mem. task force region II Nat. Coun. Community Mental Health Ctrs., Inc., 1975, treas. N.Y. State br., 1975-77; com. mem. Nat. Consortium Child Mental Health Svcs., 1973-77, chmn., 1977-79; mem. task force standards psychiat. facilities for children Joint Commn. Accreditation Hosps., 1973-74, councilor, 1975-79; mem. Select Com. Psychiat. Care and Evaluation, 1976-78; chmn. adv. com. children and youth N.Y. State Office Mental Health, 1979-83; chmn. Svc. Providers Planning and Adv. Group Monroe and Livingston Counties, 1981-82; mem. Integrated Health Steering Com., 1979-85; bd. dirs. Planned Parenthood, 1975-79. With USAAF, 1942-46. Fellow Am. Orthopsychiat. Assn.; mem. Am. Assn. Children's Residential Ctrs. (treas. 1969-71, chmn. 1973-75), Am. Assn. Psychiat. Svcs. Children (bd. dirs. 1975-78, pres. 1982-84, chmn. div. accreditation 1985—, pres. regional affiliate 1969-71, exec. dir. 1988—), Am. Psychol. Assn., Am. Soc. Clin. Hypnosis, Nat. Mental Health Assn., Nat. Assn. Social Workers, Nat. Conf. Social Welfare, Internat. Assn. Applied Hypnosis, World Fedn. Mental Health, N.Y. State Psychol. Assn., Assn. N.Y. State Educators of Emotionally Disturbed, Genessee Valley Psychol. Assn. (pres.-elect 1967-68, pres. 1968-70), Coun. for Exceptional Children, Psychologists Interested in Advancement Psychotherapy, Rochester Coun. Sci. Socs., Inc., Acad. Cert. Social Workers, Rochester Assn. Edn. Young Children, Assn. Mental Health Adminstrs. Office: Am Assn Psychiat Svcs Children 1200-C Scottsville Rd Ste 225 Rochester NY 14624

KORETZKI, PAUL RICHARD, secondary educator, coach; b. Bklyn., Mar. 10, 1940; s. Paul Arthur and Dorothy Helen (Edwards) K.; m. Mary Joan Stampf, July 10, 1965; children: Krista, Kevin. BA, Hofstra U., 1963, MS in Edn., 1965. Cert. tchr., N.Y. Tchr. Brentwood High Sch., N.Y., 1963—, soccer coach, 1965-80; track coach Shoreham Wading River High Sch., N.Y., 1980—; v.p. Brentwood Soccer Club, 1972-76, North Shore Police Athletic League, Rocky Point, N.Y., 1979—. Dir. Calvary Luth. Basketball Program, Hauppauge, N.Y., 1967-82, Trinity Luth. Basketball Program, Rocky Point, 1982-87; coach L.I. Soccer Team, Empire State Games, 1979-82; committeeman Rocky Point Liberal Party, 1968-70. Named Coach of Yr., Suffolk Luth. Basketball League, 1968, 69, 72, Runner of Yr., Bohemia Track Club, 1979, Man of Yr. in Athletics Beacon Newspapers, 1990; recipient Outstanding Coach award Brentwood Schs., 1981, Shoareham-Wading River High Sch. Varsity Club, 1991; elected to Brentwood Sch. Soccer Hall of Fame, 1989. Mem. N.Y. State Tchrs. Assn., Suffolk County Soccer Coaches Assn. (pres. 1970-73; Coach of Yr. award 1978, 79), Suffolk County Winter Track Coaches Assn. (Coach of Yr. award 1983-91), Suffolk County Spring Track Coaches Assn. (Coach of Yr. award 1980-91), Suffolk County Cross Country Coaches Assn. (Coach of Yr. award 1985, 86, 87, 88, 90, 91), N.Y. State Coaches Assn. (honor award 1988), Nat. Track and Field Officials Assn. (National Coaching award 1989), Rocky Point Joggers (pres.—), Suffolk County Police Athletic League (County Vol. of Yr. 1986), Suffolk County Cross Country Coaches Assn. (Coach of Yr.). Democrat. Lutheran. Home: 81 Mahogany Rd Rocky Point NY 11778-9309 Office: Brentwood High Sch 1st St Brentwood NY 11717-6602

KORF, RICHARD PAUL, mycology educator; b. Bronxville, N.Y., May 28, 1925; s. Frederick and Evelyn F. (Krug) K.; m. Kumiko Tachibana, June 27, 1959; children: Noni, Mia, Ian, Mario. BSc, Cornell U., 1946, PhD, 1950. Lectr. botany U. Glasgow, Scotland, 1950-51; asst. prof. Cornell U., Ithaca, N.Y., 1951-55, assoc. prof., 1955-61, prof. mycology, 1961—, chmn. theatre arts, 1985-86; Fulbright rsch. prof. Yokohama (Japan) Nat. U., 1957-58; cons. prof. U. Ryukyus, Ryukyu Islands, 1969; adjunktvikar U. Copenhagen, 1973; Fulbright rsch. scholar U. Louvain, Belgium, 1972-73; dir. Exe Island Biol. Sta., Portland, Ont., 1973—; mem. sci. coun. Academia Sinica, Beijing, China, 1985—. Editor Mycotaxon, 1974-91; book rev. editor Mycologia, 1972-80; editorial bd. Persoonia, 1987—. State vice chair Liberal Party, N.Y.C., 1968. Sr. postdoctoral fellow NSF, Yokohama, 1957; recipient SUNY Chancellor's award for excellence in teaching, 1992. Mem. Internat. Mycol. Assn. (nomenclature chmn. 1971-84), Internat. Assn. Plant Taxonomy (mem. gen. com. 1975-91); Mycol. Soc. Am. (pres. 1971, disting. mycologist 1991). Home: 316 Richard Pl Ithaca NY 14850-3129 Office: Cornell U Plant Pathology Plant Sci Bldg Ithaca NY 14853

KORKEGI, ROBERT HANI, aerospace engineer; b. Milan, Italy, Dec. 3, 1925; came to U.S. 1941; s. Hani Jacob and Ethel Maud Essery (Pound) K.; m. Michele C. Caratini, Apr. 9, 1946; children: Paulette, Danielle. BSME, Lehigh U., 1949; MS in Aerospace Engring., Calif. Inst. Tech., 1950, PhD, 1954. Rsch. assoc. U. So. Calif., L.A., 1954-57; tech. dir. von Karman Inst., Brussels, 1957-64; dir. Hypersonic Rsch. Lab., ARL, Dayton, Ohio, 1964-75, NATO Adv. Group for Aero R&D, Paris, 1976-79; vis. prof. George Washington U., Washington, 1979-81; dir. Aero & Space Bd., NRC, Washington, 1981-90; cons. in aerospace engring. Washington, 1990—; bd. dirs. von Karman Inst., Brussels, 1976-79; active various coms. NRC, NATO, NASA, others. Editor: Viscous Interaction Phenomena at High Speed, 1969; contbr. numerous articles to profl. jours. With U.S. Army, 1944-46; ETO. Recipient Pub. Svc. award NASA, 1988, Group Recognition award, NRC, 1985, Sci. Achievement award, USAF, 1972. Fellow AIAA; mem. Kenwood Golf and Country Club. Home and Office: 4418 Springdale St NW Washington DC 20016-2716

KORMAN, BARBARA, artist, educator; b. N.Y.C., Apr. 8, 1938; d. David and Rose K. B.F.A. cum laude, N.Y. State Coll. Ceramics, 1959, M.F.A., 1960. Free-lance sculptor, 1961—; tchr. sculpture, design N.Y.C. Bd. Edn., 1961-91; photographer, producer audio-visual ednl. packages, 1973—. Group shows include, Albright-Knox Gallery, Buffalo, Rochester (N.Y.) Meml. Art Gallery, Bronx (N.Y.) Mus. Art, Met. Mus. Art, N.Y.C., Hudson River Mus., Yonkers, N.Y., Tiffany & Co., N.Y.C.; exhbns. include Tiffany Windows, N.Y. Recipient awards and prizes for sculpture and art edn. Mem. Nat. Assn. Women Artists, N.Y. Artists Equity Assn., Internat. Sculpture Ctr., Katonah Mus. Artists Assn. Address: 357 E 201st St New York NY 10458

KORMAN, EDWARD R., federal judge; b. N.Y.C., Oct. 25, 1942; s. Julius and Miriam K.; m. Diane R. Eisner, Feb. 3, 1979; children: Miriam M., Benjamin E. B.A., Bklyn. Coll., 1963; LL.B., Bklyn. Law Sch., 1966; LL.M., NYU, 1971. Bar: N.Y. 1966, U.S. Supreme Ct. 1972. Law clk. to judge N.Y. Ct. Appeals, 1966-68; assoc. Paul, Weiss, Rifkind, Wharton and Garrison, 1968-70; asst. U.S. atty. Eastern Dist. N.Y., N.Y.C., 1970-72; asst. to solicitor gen. of U.S., 1972-74; chief asst. U.S. atty. Eastern Dist. N.Y., 1974-78, U.S. atty., 1978-82; ptnr. Stroock & Stroock & Lavan, N.Y.C., 1982-84; prof. Bklyn. Law Sch., 1984-85; U.S. dist. judge Eastern Dist. N.Y., 1985—. Chmn. Mayor's Com. on N.Y.C. Marshals, 1983-85; mem. Temporary Commn. of Investigation of State of N.Y., 1983-85. Jewish. Office: US Dist Ct 225 Cadman Pla E Brooklyn NY 11201

KORMAN, LOUIS YVES, physician, educator; b. Paris, Apr. 2, 1947; came to U.S., 1951; s. Israel and Ester (Englard) K.; m. Iris Bernice Stein; children: Jessica, Zachary. BA, CUNY, 1967; B in Med. Sci., Free U., Brussels, 1973; MD, SUNY, Syracuse, 1975. Intern SUNY, Syracuse, 1975-76, resident, 1976-77, fellowship in gastrointestinology, 1977-78; clin. assoc. NIH, Bethesda, Md., 1978-81; chief gastrointestinal rsch. VA Med. Ctr., Washington, 1981—; prof. med. sch. George Washington U., Washington, 1981—; cons. Glaxo Rsch., Research Triangle Park, N.C., 1986-88, Parke Davis, Ann Arbor, Mich., 1990—, Fujinon Inc., Wayne, N.J., 1985—, NCRIC Ins., Washington, 1990—. Contbr. articles to profl. jours. Bd. dirs. Generation After, Washington, 1988—. Lt. Comdr. USPHS, 1978-81. Rsch. grantee VA, 1981—. Fellow Am. Coll. Gastroenterology; mem. AMA, AAAS, Am. Gastroent. Assn., Am. Soc. Gastrointestinal Endoscopy. Office: VA Med Ctr 50 Irving St NW Washington DC 20422

KORMES, JOHN WINSTON, lawyer; b. N.Y.C., May 4, 1935; s. Mark and Joanna P. Kormes; m. Frances W. Kormes, Aug. 19, 1978; 1 child, Mark Vincent. BA in Econs., U. Mich., 1955, JD, 1959. Bar: Pa. 1961, D.C. 1961, U.S. Sup. Ct. 1968. With License and Inspection Rev. Bd. Phila., 1972-73; asst. dist. atty. City of Phila., 1973-74, asst. city solicitor, 1974-80; pvt. practice, Phila., 1961—; moot ct. advisor. Mem. staff Re-Elect the Pres. Com., 1972, Rizzo for Mayor Com., 1971, 75, Phila. Flag Day Assn., 1965—. Served with USAF, 1956-57. Recipient N.Y. Intercoll. Legis. Assembly award, 1954; R.I. Model Congress award, 1954, Queens Coll. Speech Guild award. Fellow Lawyers in Mensa (charter), Triple Nine Soc. (elections officer 1991—, legal officer, new mem. welcome program officer), Internat. Soc. Philos. Enquiry (sr. fellow, pub. Best Telicom. 1986, 87, legal officer 1986-91, mgr. new mem. welcome program 1988-91, v.p. 1990-91); mem. Phila. Bar Assn., Phila. Trial Lawyers Assn., N.Y. State Trial Lawyers Assn., Am. Arbitration Assn., Fed. Bar Assn., Pitts. Inst. Legal Medicine, Assn. Trial Lawyers Am., Intertel, Internat. Platform Assn., Cincinnatus Soc., Masons, Shriners, KP, Lions, Delta Sigma Rho. Republican. Home: 1070 Edison Ave Philadelphia PA 19116-1342 Office: 2840 PSFS Bldg 12 S 12th St Philadelphia PA 19107-3620

KORN, BARRY PAUL, equipment leasing company executive; b. N.Y.C., May 27, 1944; s. Nat and Judith (Safro) K.; m. Judith Ann Kron, Aug. 2, 1969; children: Lisa Michele, Suzanne Leslie, Amy Beth. BBA in Acctg., CCNY, 1966; MBA in Fin., CUNY, 1969. Assoc. E.M. Warburg, Pincus & Co., Inc., N.Y.C., 1964-70; treas., sec. Interstate Brands (formerly DPF Inc.), Hartsdale, N.Y., 1970-75; pres. Barrett Capital & Leasing Corp., Mamaroneck, N.Y., 1975—; bd. dirs. Mid-Hudson Better Bus. Bur., 1983-88. Trustee Coun. for Arts in Westchester, 1990—, Emelin Theatre, 1991—. Mem. Am. Assn. Equipment Lessors (bd. dirs. 1974-77), Fin. Execs. Instr. (pres. Westchester chpt. 1976-77, bd. dirs. Conn./West chpt. 1989—), Computer Dealers and Lessors Assn. (treas. 1971-72, bd. dirs. 1979-84, chmn. industry practices com. 1979-82, v.p. 1982-84), Mamaroneck C. of C. (bd. dirs., chmn. indsl. div. 1988—). Office: 930 Mamaroneck Ave Mamaroneck NY 10543-1629

KORN, JOSEPH HOWARD, physician, educator; b. Augsburg, Fed. Republic of Germany, Jan. 31, 1947; came to U.S., 1947; s. Leo and Rose (Mann) K.; m. Paulette Jeremias, June 26, 1971; children: Naomi, Jerald, Joshua, Jonathan. BS, CCNY, 1968; MD, Columbia U., 1972. Cert. rheumatology: internal medicine. Intern N.C. Meml. Hosp., Chapel Hill, 1972-73, resident, 1973-75; fellow Med. U. S.C., Charleston, 1975-77, asst. prof. medicine, 1977-78; asst. prof. medicine U. Conn. Sch. Medicine, Farmington, 1978-84, assoc. prof., 1984-90, prof., 1990—; assoc. chief of staff R&D VA Med. Ctr., Newington, Conn., 1982—; mem. biomedical grant adv. panel Arthritis Found., Atlanta, 1986-91. Mem. editorial bd. Arthritis & Rheumatism, 1985-90, Clin. Immunology & Immunopathology, 1992—; contbr. over 60 articles to profl. jours. V.p. Congregation Agendas Action, West Hartford, Conn., 1991—, Hebrew Acad. Greater Hartford, Bloomfield, Conn., 1990—. Named to NIH Review Group, 1984-85. Fellow Am. Coll. Rheumatology; mem. AAAS. Office: VA Med Ctr 555 Willard Newington CT 06111

KORN, STEVEN ERIC, medical publisher; b. N.Y.C., Apr. 1, 1944; s. Otto and Melanie (Ungar) K.; m. Deborah Dee, Aug. 24, 1975; children: Adam, Emily, Justin. BA with honors, NYU, 1965. V.p. Intercontinental Med. Book Corp. (subs. Grune & Stratton), N.Y.C., 1965-70; chmn. bd. Futura Pub. Co., Mt. Kisco, N.Y., 1970—. Mem. N.Y. Acad. Scis. Office: Futura Pub Co 2 Bedford Ridge Rd PO Box 330 Mount Kisco NY 10549

KORNBERG, FRED, electronics executive; b. Lemberg, Poland, Jan. 28, 1936; s. Karl Kalman and Edith (Keller) K.; m. Rowena Birnbach, June 15, 1958; children: Michelle Caren, Matthew Eric, Tara Kim. BSEE, NYU, 1958, MSEE, 1959. Staff rsch. scientist Coll. Engring. NYU, Bronx, N.Y., 1958-59; sr. staff engr. Radio Engring. Labs., L.I., N.Y., 1956-62, dir. rsch., 1962-69; gen. mgr., v.p. Nardcom Group, Melville, N.Y., 1969-71; exec. v.p. Comtech Telecommunications Corp., Hauppauge, N.Y., 1971-76, pres., 1976—; also bd. dirs.; pres. Technotronic Data Systems, Inc., Dunloring, Va., 1985—; also bd. dirs.; bd. dirs. Octagon Communications Group, Tenafly, N.J. Mem. IEEE (sr. mem.), Armed Forces Communication and Electronics Assn. (sr. mem.). Republican. Jewish. Home: 17 Palatine Ct Syosset NY 11791-1105 Office: Comtech Inc 105 Baylis Rd 63 Oser Ave Melville NY 11747

KORNBLITH, HILARY STUART, academic administrator, philosophy educator; b. N.Y.C., Nov. 3, 1954; s. Borris Alexander and Gertrude (Chizik) K.; m. Robin D. Harris, Oct. 12, 1980; children: Benjamin Glen, Andrea Marie. BA, SUNY, Buffalo, 1975; MA, Cornell U., 1978, PhD, 1980. Asst. prof. U. Vt., Burlington, 1979-85, assoc. prof., 1985-91, prof., chair, 1991—; Editor: Naturalizing Epistemology, 1985; contbr. articles to profl. jours. NEH fellow, 1984-85, grantee, 1982. Mem. Am. Philos. Assn., Soc. for Philosophy and Psychology, Philosophy Sci. Assn. Office: U Vt Dept Philosophy 70 S Williams St Burlington VT 05401-3404

KORNBLUTH, RALPH ROSS, physician; b. Montreal, Que., Can., Apr. 18, 1938; came to U.S., 1965.; s. Max and Sarah (Tieger) K.; m. Anita DuBow, Apr. 2, 1966; children: Deborah Rochelle, Ira David, Michael Ari. BS, McGill U., 1962, MD, 1964. Diplomate Nat. Bd. Med. Examiners. Rotating intern Jewish Gen. Hosp., Montreal, 1964-65; cons. Douglas Hosp., Verdun, Can., 1965; resident psychiatrist Michael Reese Hosp., Chgo., 1965-68; cons. Ill. State Hosp. System, Chgo., 1968; staff psychiatrist Portsmouth (Va.) Psychiat. Ctr., 1970-71; attending psychiatrist Fairfax (Va.) Hosp., 1971-74; pvt. practice Fairfax, 1971—; supr. of psychologists, Fairfax, 1971—. Mem. com. B'nai Israel Congregation, Rockville, Md., 1978—; vice chmn. med. div. United Jewish Appeal, Washington, 1980. Lt. comdr. USN, 1968-71. Recipient Physician's Recognition award AMA, 1979—, Resident's award Ill. Psychiatry Soc., 1968, Rsch. award 1st place Psychosomatic and Psychiat. Inst., 1968. Mem. Am. Physicians Fellowship, Fairfax County Med. Soc. (credentials com. 1987—, mental health com. 1992), Am. Psychiat. Assn. (internat. affairs com. 1991—, pvt. practice com. 1991—), Washington Psychiat. Soc. Jewish. Home: 9812 Woodford Rd Rockville MD 20854-5034 Office: 8303 Arlington Blvd Ste 207 Fairfax VA 22031-2966

KORNHAUSER, KENNETH RICHARD, funeral director, executive; b. N.Y.C., Oct. 6, 1947; s. Martin and Gladys (Tuchman) K.; m. Ann Rona Morris, July 4, 1976; children: Evan Jason, Craig Morris. BS, Jacksonville U., 1969; MS, L.I. U., 1973; postgrad. in edn., N.Y.U., 1973-76; diploma, Am. Acad. McAllister Inst., 1977. Cert. corrective therapist, 1973. Phys. edn. tchr. Andrew Jackson High Sch., St Albans, N.Y., 1969-73; dean of boys Andrew Jackson High Sch., St Albans, 1973-76; assoc. prof., dir. spl. phys. edn. Queens Coll., Flushing, N.Y., 1973-75; athletic trainer U.S. Merchant Marine Acad., Kings Point, N.Y., 1975-76; exec. v.p. I. J. Morris Inc., Bklyn., 1976—; pres. IJM Computer Systems Inc., Hempstead, N.Y., 1985—; treas. Monuments by I.J. Morris, Inc., Bklyn., 1989—; bd. dirs. YM-YWHA of Suffolk, Commack, N.Y., 1986. Pres. Temple Beth Torah, Westbury, N.Y., 1992; bd. dirs. Gurwin Jewish Geriatric Ctr., Commack, N.Y., 1989, Nassau County Coun. Boys Scouts Am. Named Man of Yr., Suffolk County Region of Women's Am. Orgn. Rehab. Tng., 1987. Mem. Jewish Funeral Dirs. of Am., Masons, Knights of Pythias, Nat. Eagle Scout Assn.(mem. exec. bd. Nassau chpt. 1990). Democrat. Home: 3 Livingston Ave Jericho NY 11753-1510 Office: IJ Morris Inc 1895 Flatbush Ave Brooklyn NY 11210-4999

KORNHAUSER, STANLEY HENRY, medical administrator, educator, consultant; b. N.Y.C., Nov. 8, 1934; s. Max and Anna (Farrier) K.; m. Janet G. Divak, June 24, 1961; children: Stephanie, David. AB in Zoology/Physiology, Hunter Coll., 1956, AM in Biol. Scis., 1958; MA in Adminstrn. and Supervision, NYU, 1965; PhD, City U. Los Angeles, N.Y., 1985. Biology tchr. N.Y.C. (N.Y.) Bd. Edn., 1956-63, program adminstr., 1964-69, asst. adminstrv. dir., 1974-79; dir. rsch. and evaluation, dir. desegregation & integration Stamford (Conn.) Bd. Edn., 1971-73, dir. equal ednl. opportunity program Title IV, 1971-72; nat. dir. edn. Biomedical Instrumentation Svcs. Corp., N.Y.C., 1980-84; founder, exec. dir. Nat. Inst. Electromed. Info., N.Y.C., 1984—; adminstrv. cons. N.Y. State Office Commr., Albany, 1968-69; cons. Electromed. Products Internat., L.A., 1984—, N.Y. Inst. for Rsch. into Contemporary Medicine, Tarrytown, N.Y., 1988-89; adj. prof. LIU Grad. Sch. Edn., Bklyn., 1973-86; v.p. Brain Dysfunction Monitoring and Treatment Ctr., Mediscreen Inc., N.Y.C., 1987-89; exec. dir. Manhattan Westchester Med. Svcs., N.Y.C., 1988—; dir. counseling & guidance, ind. study programs N.Y. Coll. Podiatric Medicine, 1991—; assoc. dean grad. sch. electromed. scis. City U., L.A., 1986—. Contbr. articles to profl. jours. V.p. R & D Greater Safety Coun. of N.Y., N.Y.C., 1990—, N.Y. Consumer Assembly, N.Y.C., 1990—. Grantee NSF, Tucson, 1965, Kent, Ohio, 1966; recipient Alfred M. Sloan Found. scholarship in contemporary physics, Columbia Univ., 1961. Mem. Internat. Soc. for Meeting Planners, AAAS, N.Y. Acad. Scis., Cold Spring Harbor Bus. Devel. Assn. (electromed. tech. 1989, adv. bd.), N.Y. Soc. Assn. Execs. (membership com. 1990—), N.Y. Coll. Learning Skills Assn. Democrat. Jewish. Home: 21165 23rd Ave Flushing NY 11360-1947 Office: Nat Inst Electromed Info PO Box 4633 Flushing NY 11360-4633

KORNSTEIN, EDWARD, manufacturing executive; b. N.Y.C., Sept. 7, 1929; s. Max and Margit (Stahl) K.; m. Marion Beatrice Stein, Dec. 20, 1958; children: Sandra P., Martin R. BA, NYU, 1951; MA, Drexel U., 1954; postgrad., Boston U., 1957-59. Optics engr. RCA, Camden, N.J., 1951-57; group leader optical physics RCA, Burlington, Mass., 1966-70; mgr. optical physics group RCA, Burlington, 1970-72; cons. physical research lab. Boston U., 1958-60; v.p. Optel Corp., Princeton, N.J., 1970-72; pres. Kortron Cons., Princeton, 1972-78; v.p. Object Recognition Systems, Inc., Princeton, 1978-87; pres. ORS Automation, Inc., Princeton, 1987—; cons. Holographix, Inc., Burlington, 1986—, Waltham/Elgin Watch Co., Chgo., 1973-80, Ricoh Watch Co., Nagoya, Japan, 1974-78, Cosmo, Tokyo, 1978-80; bd. dirs. Affiliated Mfrs., Inc.; dir. ORS Automation, Princeton, Affiliated Mfrs., Inc., No. Branch, N.J. 3 patents in field; contbr. articles to profl. jours. Com. mem. Boy Scouts Am., West Windsor, N.J., 1973-85; mem. West Windsor Econ. Devel. com., 1972-78. Grantee Nat. Sci. Found., 1959. Mem. IEEE, Optical Soc. Am. (travel grantee 1959), Soc. Info. Display, Soc. Motion Picture and TV Engrs. (chmn. Boston area 1966-67),

Princeton C. of C., Rotary Club Princeton Corridor. Home: 10 Channing Way Cranbury NJ 08512-9721 Office: ORS Automation Inc 402 Wall St Princeton NJ 08540-1552

KORSON, ROY, pathology educator, cytopathologist; b. Phila., Oct. 24, 1922; s. David and Sarah (Gross) K.; m. Lorraine Bagdon, Sept. 8, 1946. AB, U. Pa., 1943; MD, Jefferson Med. Coll., Phila., 1947. Diplomate Am. Bd. Pathology. Intern Einstein Med. Ctr., Phila., 1947-48; postdoctoral fellow Columbia U., N.Y.C., 1948-49; postdoctoral fellow U. Vt., Burlington, 1949-50, resident pathology, 1949-52, asst. prof., 1951-57, assoc. prof., 1957-67, prof., 1967—; vis. scientist Middlesex Hosp. Med. Sch., London, 1961-62; dir. surg. pathology and cytology Med. Ctr. Hosp. of Vt., Burlington, 1974-89. Contbr. articles to profl. publs. Dir. Am. Cancer Soc., Atlanta, 1982—, pres. Vt. div., Burlington, 1976-78, 84-86. Capt. U.S. Army, 1952-54. Recipient practice prize in medicine Jefferson Med. Coll., Phila., 1947, Career Devel. award, USPHS, 1958-63; named Buttles prof. of pathology, U. Vt., 1984-89. Fellow Coll. Am. Pathologists; mem. AAAS, AMA, Internat. Acad. Pathology, Am. Soc. Cytology, N.Y. Acad. Scis., Alpha Omega Alpha, Sigma Xi.

KOSAKOW, JAMES MATTHEW, lawyer; b. New London, Conn., Apr. 12, 1954; s. Leonard Louis and Lois Ann (Rosen) K.; m. Yvonne Manijeh Bokhour, June 5, 1978; 1 child, Jonathan Daniel. BA, Conn. Coll., 1976; JD, Yeshiva U., 1984. Bar: N.Y. 1985, Conn. 1985, D.C. 1985, Fla. 1991, U.S. Dist. Ct. (so. and ea. dists.) 1985. Assoc. Vittoria & Forsythe, N.Y.C., 1986—; guardian ad litem N.Y. County Surrogate's Ct., N.Y.C., 1987—; lectr. trusts and estates, various instns., N.Y.; arbitrator Better Bus. Bur., N.Y.C., 1988-89. Trustee, bd. dirs. Internat. Nursery Sch., Queens, N.Y., 1987-89; mem. estates & trusts specialty group lawyers div. United Jewish Appeal-Fedn. Jewish Philanthropies of N.Y., Inc., 1990—. Mem. N.Y. State Bar Assn. (legis. com. on adminstrn. and distbn. of decedents estates, trusts and estates sect. 1987—), Assn. of Bar of City of N.Y. Office: Vittoria & Forsythe 630 5th Ave New York NY 10111-0002

KOSASKY, HAROLD JACK, gynecologist; b. Winnipeg, Man., Can., Oct. 19, 1927; s. Jack and Lillian (Resnick) K.; m. Shirley Anne Johnston, Sept. 3, 1955; children: Julia, Leah, Robert. BA, U. Manitoba, Can., 1948; MD, Licentiate, U. Manitoba, 1953. Diplomate Am. Bd. of Ob-gyn; lic. Coll. of Physicians and Surgeons of Ont. (8521), Ky. State Bd. of Health, Idaho State Bd. of Health (M2704), Mass. Bd. of Registration in Med. (29042), Med. Council of Can. Intern Deer Lodge VA and Grace Hosps., Winnipeg, Man., Can., 1952-53; resident in gen. surgery Col. Belcher Hosp., Calgary, Alta., Can., 1953-54; resident in psychiatry Warren (Pa.) State Hosp., 1955-56; jr. asst. resident, asst. resident, sr. resident in ob-gyn. Chgo. Lying-In Hosp., 1956-59; asst. and assoc. prof. U. Louisville Sch. Med., 1961-65; asst. and assoc. in Ob-gyn. various hosps., Boston, 1966-81; gynecologist and obstetrician Boston Hosp. for Women, 1965-81; gynecologist Brigham & Women's Hosp., Boston, 1981—; instr. ob-gyn. Harvard U., 1965—; cons. Ovutime, Inc., Boston, 1972—, Jordan Hosp., Plymouth, Mass., 1969—; asst. visiting surgeon, Boston City Hosp., 1967-69; mem. Ky. Govs. Task Force on Mental Retardation, 1964-65, Com. on Malignancy (chmn.), 1963-65. Contbr. numerous articles to profl. jours.; co-inventor Ovutime Ovulation group of instruments. Fellow Royal Coll. of Surgeons of Can. (cert. FRCS), Royal Soc. of Health, Boston Obstet. Soc. (emeritus), Am. Coll. Obstetricians and Gynecologists (cert. FACOG); mem. W.Va. Obstet. and Gynecol. Soc. (hon.), Am. Fertility Soc., AAAS, FRCS (Can.), ACS (lic. FACS), Gen. Med. Council of Great Britain (lic. C5086), Royal Coll. of Obstetricians and Gynecologists of Eng. (cert. MRCOG), Assn. of Profs. of Ob-gyn, Louisville Obstet. and Gynecol. Soc. (sec., treas. 1962-65), Louisville Med. Forum (v.p.). Episcopalian. Club: Harvard. Office: 25 Boylston St Chestnut Hill MA 02167-1710

KOSC, JEAN ROCHELLE, marketing professional; b. Northampton, Pa., Jan. 4, 1936; d. James and Anna (Gontar) Trobetsky; children: Deborah, Gregory, Robert Kosc Jr. Grad., Bethlehem Bus. Sch., 1963. Owner Eddies Market, Northampton, Pa., 1957-62; buyer Hess's Dept. Store, Allentown, Pa., 1964-73; owner Kemo-Sabays Restaurant, Northampton, 1980-85; asst. to dept. supr. Genesco-Phoenex Clothes, Allentown, 1973-80; market coordinator Leadership Inst., Allentown, 1985—. Sec. Lehigh Twp. PTA, Northampton, 1960, Pres., 1961; com. woman Leigh Twp., Northampton, 1961; pres. Northampton Bus. Profl. Women, 1986-87; pres. Northampton Exchangettes, 1986-87, 1990-91, bd. dirs., 1987-89, sec., 1991-92. Recipient Tiffany award Manpower, 1984. Mem. Bethlehem Area C. of C. (profl. women's com. 1987—). Democrat. Roman Catholic. Office: Leadership Inst 5000 W Tilghman St Ste 210 Allentown PA 18104-9101

KOSCIANSKI, LEONARD JOSEPH, artist; b. Cleve., Apr. 20, 1952; s. Ray Anthony and Ruth Ann (Malinowski) K.; m. Emily Anne Shrift; children: Nicholas, Daniel, Elizabeth. BFA, Cleve. Inst. Art, 1977; postgrad., Skowhegan (Maine) Sch., 1976; MFA, U. Calif., Davis, 1979. Prof. art U. Tenn., Knoxville, 1980-84, U. Md., College Park, 1984-87; represented by Karl Bornstein Gallery, L.A., 1980-90, Phyllis Kind Gallery, N.Y.C. and Chgo., 1982—, Barbara Fenderick Gallery, Washington, 1989—. Represented in permanent collections at Met. Mus. Art, N.Y.C., Newport Harbor Mus., Newport Beach, Calif. Fellow Rockefeller Found., 1989, NEA, 1985, 90; recipient Visual Arts award South Eastern Ctr. for Contemporary Art, 1984. Mem. Coll. Art Assn. Republican. Roman Catholic. Home and Studio: 1712 S Harbor Ln Annapolis MD 21401

KOSCIELNIAK, AUDREY A., placement office director; b. Buffalo, Dec. 14, 1944; d. Edward Vincent and Ann (Chmiel) K. AA, SUNY, Buffalo, 1969, BA, 1981, EdM, 1987. Dir., coord. career devel. office SUNY Sch. Law, Buffalo, 1978—. Office: SUNY Sch of Law 309 O'Brian Hall N Campus Buffalo NY 14260

KOSICH, GEORGE J., retail executive; b. Vancouver, B.C., Can., Aug. 3, 1934; s. John and Mary (Tomasevich) K.; m. Joan Alexandria Gray (dec. 1957); children: William, Georgina, John, Barbara, Robert. B in Commerce, U. B.C., 1959. With Hudson's Bay Co., Toronto, Ont., Can., 1960—, pres., COO, 1987-90, CEO, 1990—; dir. Hudson's Bay Co., Markborough Properties, Inc. Office: Hudson's Bay Co, 401 Bay St, Toronto, ON Canada M5H 2Y4

KOSIK, EDWIN MICHAEL, federal judge; b. 1925. BA, Wilkes Coll., Wilkes-Barre, Pa., 1949; LLB, Dickinson Sch. Law, Carlisle, Pa. Asst. U.S. atty. Pa. State Workmen's Compensation Bd., 1953-58, chmn., 1964-69; pvt. practice law Needle, Needle & Needle, 1958-64; judge 45th Jud. Dist. Ct. Common Pleas, 1969-86, U.S. Dist. Ct. (mid. dist.) Pa., Scranton, 1986—. Office: US Dist Ct US Courthouse Box 856 Scranton PA 18501

KOSKO, JOHN JOSEPH, vocational school administrator; b. Derby, Conn., Mar. 24, 1951; s. John and Helen (Sledziona) K.; m. Karen Nearhos, July 20, 1975; 1 child, Andrew. BA in English and Secondary Edn., Boston Coll., 1973; MS in Counselling, So. Conn. State U., 1980. Cert. tchr., counselor, adminstr. Instr. English, counselor, athletic coach Platt Regional Vocat. Tech. Sch., Milford, Conn., 1974-85; counselor South Shore Regional Sch. Dist., Hanover, Mass., 1985-88, prin., dir. campus, 1988—; pvt. practice Counseling Assocs., Stratford, Conn., 1983-85. Active Temp. Care Svcs., Cambridge, Mass., 1985—, City-Wide Neighborhood Adv. Coun., Cambridge, 1989—; bd. dirs., sec. YMCA, Milford, 1983-85. Mem. ASCD, Am. Vocat. Assn., Mass. Assn. Vocat. Adminstrs., Fresh Pond Golf Assn. (champion 1987, 90). Democrat. Roman Catholic. Home: 16 Griswold St Cambridge MA 02138-1012 Office: S Shore Regional Sch Dist 476 Webster St Hanover MA 02339-1215

KOSLOW, DIANE RUTH, psychologist; b. N.Y.C., June 14, 1942; d. Arthur O. and Sophia (Sobren) Heisler; m. Stephen H. Koslow, Aug. 18, 1962; children: Karin I., James D. BA, Hunter Coll., 1962; PhD, U. Md., 1983. Lic. psychologist, Md. Ind. cons. Washington, 1978-81; dir. counseling svcs. Naval Rsch. Lab., Washington, 1981-85; tng. dir. Internat. Counseling Ctr., Washington, 1985-87; ind. psychologist Rockville, Md., 1985—; cons. psychologist USPHS, Rockville, Md., 1987—; bd. dirs. The Multicultural Inst., Washington, 1989—; cons. in field. Co-editor: Crossing Cultures in Mental Health, 1989; co-author: (chpt.) Issues in Adult Career Counseling, 1991. Mem. APA, Md. Psychol. Assn. Office: 6201 Executive Blvd Rockville MD 20852

KOSLOW, MYRON ALAN, marketing executive; b. Bklyn., Dec. 29, 1936; s. Abraham and Helen (Gutman) K.; m. Hannah Luss, Aug. 19, 1962; children: Gregory J., Paul M. BEE, CCNY, 1958, MEE, 1963; MBA, L.I. U., 1979. Sr. engr. Republic Aviation Corp., Farmingdale, N.Y., 1959-62, Loral Electronics, Bronx, 1962-66; prin. engr. Instrument Systems Corp., Huntington, N.Y., 1966-74; dir. spl. applications Lambda Electronics Inc., Melville, N.Y., 1974-79, mktg. mgr., 1979-84, nat. sales mgr., 1984-86, dir. mktg., 1986-89, dir. field mktg., 1989-91; v.p. engring. Power Solutions Inc., Pompano Beach, Fla., 1991—. Contbr. articles to profl. jours. With U.S. Army, 1958-59. Mem. Power Sources Mfrs. Assn. (chmn. bd. 1986-88, bd. dirs. 1988-91). Home: 17 Hunters Ln Roslyn NY 11576-1305 Office: Power Solutions Inc 17 Hunters Ln Roslyn NY 11576-1305

KOSLOW, STEPHEN HUGH, science administrator, pharmacologist; b. N.Y.C., Oct. 14, 1940; s. Julius and Lillian (Kaye) K.; m. Diane Heisler, Aug. 18, 1962; children: Karin, James. BS, Columbia U., 1962; PhD, U. Chgo., 1967. Internat. postdoctoral fellow Swedish Med. Rsch. Coun., Karolinski Inst., 1968-69; pharmacologist, chief neurobiology unit St. Elizabeth's Hosp., Washington, 1970-77; chief biol. rsch. sect. Clin. Rsch. Br., Rockville, Md., 1975-81; chief div. Extramural Rsch. Neurosci. Rsch. Br. NIMH, Rockville, 1981-85, chief div. Basic Scis. Neurosci. Rsch. Br., 1985-88, acting dir. div. Basic Brain and Behavioral Scis., 1988-89, dir. div. Basic Brain and Behavioral Scis., 1990—; project dir. NIMH-CRB Collaborative Program on Psychobiology of Depression-Biol. Study, 1975-85; adv. bd. mem. Tourette Syndrome Assn., Bayside, N.Y., 1984. Named Swedish Med. Rsch. Coun. Internat. Postdoctoral fellow, 1968-69, Spl. NATO fellow, 1969; recipient NIMH Quality Increase award, 1977-78, Health Adminstr.'s award for Meritorious Achievement, 1979. Fellow am. Coll. Neuropsychopharmacology; mem. AAAS, Am. Soc. for Neurochemistry, Am. Soc. Pharmacology & Exptl. Therapeutics, Soc. for Neuroscience, Soc. Biol. Psychiatry. Office: NIMH 5600 Fishers Ln Rm 11103 Rockville MD 20857-0001

KOSMAN, JOHN GEORGE, executive; b. Johnstown, Pa. Dec. 22, 1930; s. Frank Joseph and Edith (Myeski) K.; m. Marian, June 9, 1962; children: John, Richard, Edward. BS, Pace Coll. Adminstrv. asst. N.Y. Credit and Fin. Mgmt. Assn., N.Y.C., 1962-76, sec., 1976-78, exec. v.p., 1978-79, pres., 1979—. Mem. Bredaglick Lodge. Office: NY Credit & Fin Mgmt Assn 520 8th Ace Ste 2201 New York NY 11018

KOSNER, EDWARD A(LAN), magazine editor and publisher; b. N.Y.C., July 26, 1937; s. Sidney and Annalee (Fisher) K.; m. Alice Nadel, Feb. 1, 1959; children: John Robbins, Anthony William; m. Julie Baumgold, Nov. 19, 1978; 1 dau., Lily. B.A., CCNY, 1958. Rewriteman, asst. city editor N.Y. Post, 1958-63; assoc. editor Newsweek Mag., N.Y.C., 1963-67; gen. editor Newsweek Mag., 1967-69, nat. affairs editor, 1969-72, asst. mng. editor, 1972, mng. editor, 1973-75, editor, 1975-79; editor N.Y. mag., N.Y.C., 1980—; pub. N.Y. mag., 1986-91; pres. N.Y. Mag., N.Y.C., 1991—. Recipient various journalism awards. Mem. Am. Soc. Mag. Editors (pres. 1984-86, exec. com.). Club: Century. Home: 180 E 79th St New York NY 10021-0437 Office: New York Mag 755 2d Ave New York NY 10017-5906

KOSOF, ANNA CLARA, radio station executive; came to U.S., 1957; d. Andras and Clara (Biro) Forgach; 1 child, Stefan. BA, CUNY; MA, Hunter Coll. Cons. Sydney Reynolds'; gen. mgr. Sta. WBAI, N.Y.C.; dep. dir. met. div. Sta. WNET-TV, N.Y.C.; cons. Marshall Cons., N.Y.C.; gen. mgr. Sta. WBGO, Newark, 1987—. Office: Sta WBGO 54 Park Pl Newark NJ 07102-4387

KOSTABI, MARK, artist; b. L.A., Nov. 27, 1960; s. Kaljo and Rita (Nirk) K. Artist, pres. Kostabi World, N.Y.C., 1988—. Author: Sadness Because the Video Store Was Closed, 1988, Kostabi, 1980, Kostabi, 1981, Upheaval, 1985; one-man shows at the Ronald Feldman Gallery, Martin Lawrence, Hanson, and Hokin Galleries; represented in permanent collections Met. Mus. of Art, N.Y., Mus. of Modern Art, N.Y., Guggenheim Mus., N.Y., Groninger Mus., Holland. Recipient Proliferation prize East Village Eye, 1984. Office: Kostabi World 544 W 38th St New York NY 10018-1104

KOSTECKY, JAMES FRANK, steel company executive; b. Ephrata, Pa., Apr. 4, 1943; s. John Michael and Sophia Frances (Basiago) K.; m. Joanne Christine Reddig, Aug. 28, 1965; children: Suzanne Elizabeth, Jennifer Michelle. BCE, Villanova (Pa.) U., 1965; MSCE, Carnegie Mellon U., 1967; MS in Mgmt. Sci., Lehigh U., 1971. Registered profl. engr., Pa. Rsch. engr. Bethlehem (Pa.) Steel Co., 1967-72, project engr., 1973-77, environ. and tech. coord., 1978-84, dir. corp. support programs, 1985—; bd. dirs. Burnside Plantation, Inc.; mem. corp. com. Allentown Art Mus., 1991—; assoc. dir. Northampton County Conservation Dist., Nazareth, Pa., 1986—. Inventor pedestal head for floor support, metal wall framing system, base bracket for shelving, pipe insulation system. Advisor United Way of Northampton and Warren County, Bethlehem, 1984—; mem. adv. coun. Minsi Trail coun. Boy Scouts Am., Lehigh Valley, Pa., 1989—; bd. dirs. Family Counseling Svcs., Bethlehem, 1979-81, ARC, Bethlehem, 1982-85. Mem. ASCE, Nat. Eagle Scout Assn. (chmn. Lehigh Valley chpt. 1990—), Assn. Iron and Steel Engrs., Am. Iron and Steel Inst., Saucon Valley Country Club. Republican. Roman Catholic. Office: Bethlehem Steel Corp 1170 8th Ave # 1711 Bethlehem PA 18016-7601

KOSTELANETZ, RICHARD, writer, artist; b. N.Y., May 14, 1940; s. Boris and Ethel (Cory) K. AB with honors, Brown U., 1962; postgrad. (Fulbright scholar), King's Coll., U. London, 1964-65; MA, Columbia U., 1966. Program assoc. thematic studies John Jay Coll. CUNY, 1972-73; sr. staff Ind. U. Writers' Conf., 1976; vis. prof. English and Am. studies U. Tex. at Austin, 1977; guest Mishkenot Sha'ananim, Jerusalem, 1979, 86, DAAD Berliner Kunstlerprogramm, 1981-83. Co-propr. Assembling Press, 1970-82; lit. dir. The Future Press, 1976—; propr. Words and Music (ASCAP), 1982—; guest artist WXXI-FM, Rochester, 1975, 76, Synapse, Syracuse U., 1975, Cabin Creek Ctr. for Work and Environ. Studies, 1978, Electronic Music Studio of Stockholm, 1981, 83, 84, 86, 88, Bklyn. Coll. Ctr. for Computer Music, 1984, Dennis Gabor Lab. Mus. of Holography, 1985, 89, Exptl. TV Lab., Owego, N.Y., 1985, 86, 87, 89, 90, 91, Real Art Ways, 1988, Film/Video Arts, 1989. Author: Music of Today, 1967, The Theatre of Mixed Means, 1968, 81, Master Minds: Portraits of Contemporary American Artists & Intellectuals, 1969, Visual Language, 1970, In the Beginning, 1971, The End of Intelligent Writing, 1974; 2d edit. as Literary Politics in Am, 1977; I Articulations/Short Fictions, 1974, Recyclings, vol. 1, 1974, complete text, 1984, Openings & Closings, 1975, Extrapolate, 1975, Come Here, 1975, Modulations, 1975, Portraits from Memory, 1975, Constructs, 1976, Rain Rains Rain, 1976, Numbers: Poems and Stories, 1976, Numbers Two, 1977, Illuminations, 1977, One Night Stood, 1977, Grants & the Future of Literature, 1978, Constructs Two, 1978, Tabula Rasa, 1978, Inexistences, 1978, Wordsand, 1978, Twenties in the Sixties, 1979, "The End" Appendix, 1979, "The End" Essentials, 1979, And So Forth, 1979, Exhaustive Parallel Intervals, 1979, More Short Fiction, 1980, Metamorphosis in Arts, 1980, The Old Poetries and the New, 1981, Autobiographies, 1981, Reincarnations, 1982, Turfs/Arenas/Fields/Pitches, 1983, American Imaginations, 1983, Epiphanies, 1983, Autobiographien New York Berlin, 1986, Prose Pieces/After Texts, 1987, The Old Fictions and the New, 1987, The Grants-Fix, 1987, Conversing with Cage, 1988, On Innovative Musici(an)s, 1989, Unfinished Business, 1990, The New Poetries and Some Olds, 1991, Politics in the African-American Novel, 1991, On Innovative Art(ists), 1992, Constructs Three, 1991, Constructs Four, 1991, Constructs Five, 1991, Constructs Six, 1991, Fifty Untitled Constructivist Fictions, 1991, Intermix, 1991, Flipping, 1991, Published Encomia, 1991, Solos, Duets, Trios & Choruses, 1991, A Dictionary of the Avant-Gardr, 1993; numerous others, works included various anthologies.; editor, contbr.: On Contemporary Literature, 1964, 69, The New American Arts, 1965, Twelve from the Sixties, 1967, The Young American Writers, 1967, Beyond Left & Right: Radical Thought for Our Times, 1968, Imaged Words & Worded Images, 1970, Moholy-Nagy, 1970, John Cage, 1970, 91, Possibilities of Poetry, 1970, Social Speculations, 1971, Human Alternatives: Visions for Us Now, 1971, Future's Fictions, 1971, Seeing Through Shuck, 1972, Breakthrough Fictioneers, 1973, The Edge of Adaptation, 1973, Essaying Essays, 1975, Language & Structure, 1975, Younger Critics in North America, 1976, Esthetics Contemporary, 1977, Assembling Assembling, 1978, Visual Literature Criticism, 1979, Text-Sound Texts, 1980, Scenarios, 1980, The Yale Gertrude Stein, 1980, A Critical Assembling, 1980, Aural Literature Criticism, 1981, American Writing Today, 1981, The Avant-Garde Tradition in Literature, 1982, Gertrude Stein Advanced, 1990, Writing About Merce Cunningham, 1992, John Cage: Writer, 1993, Writing About John Cage, 1993; others; composer: Praying to the Lord, 1977, 81, Invocations, 1981, 84, The Gospels/Die Evangelien, 1982, The Eight Nights of Hanukah, 1983, New York City, internat. version, 1984, Am. version, 1987, A Special Time, 1985, Baseball: Americas' Game, 1988, Onomatopoeia, 1988, Kaddish, 1990, I Was Borin New York City, 1992; producer numerous audiotapes, films, videotapes, extended radio features for stas. in Australia, Fed. Republic Germany, Sweden, U.S.; filmmaker: (with others) Openings & Closings, 1978, Constructivist Fictions, 1978, Epiphanies, 1981—, Ein Verlorenes Berlin/A Berlin Lost/Berlin Perdu/Ett Forlorat Berlin/El Berlin Perdido/Berlin Sche-Einena Jother, 1984-88 (prizewinner Ann Arbor, Mich., Film Festival); video art: Kinetic Writings, 1989, Video Strings, 1989, Stringsieben, 1989, Turfs/Grounds/Lawns, 1989, Invocations, 1988, Seductions, 1988, The Gospels Abridged, 1988, Relationships, 1988, Two Erotic Videotapes, 1988, Two Sacred Texts, 1988, Partitions, 1986, Three Prose Pieces, 1975, Onomatopoeia, 1989, Kaddish, 1991, Video Poems, 1992, Video Stories, 1992; contbg. editor: Pushcart Prize; writer, narrator: Camera Three, WCBS-TV, 1974; co-founder, compiler Assembling, 1970-82; co-pub., editor: Precisely, A Critical Jour., 1977—; contbr. articles, poems, revs., photographs and essays to mags.; numerous group exhbns. visual poetry, visual fiction, audiotapes, videotapes, films, holograms and numerical art; comprehensive exhbn.: Wordsand, at Simon Fraser U., U. Alta., Cornell Coll., Vassar Coll., U. N.D., Calif. State U., Bakersfield, Dade County Community Coll., Miami, Fla., 1978-81. Woodrow Wilson fellow, 1962-63; Pulitzer fellow in critical writing, 1965-66; Guggenheim Meml. Found. fellow, 1967-68; Nat. Endowment for Arts grantee, 1976, 78, 79, 81, 82, 84, 85, 86, 90, 91; N.Y. State Regents scholar, 1963-64; Internat. fellow Columbia U., 1963-64; Fund for Investigative Journalism fellow, 1980; Vogelstein Found. fellow, 1980, Editors Fellow CCLM, 1983, Am. Pub. Radio Program Fund, 1984, ASCAP Standard award, 1983-92 (annually). Mem. Artists Equity, Nat. Writers Union, Nat. Coalition Ind. Scholars, Internat. Assn. Art Critics, Soc. for Origination of Horspiel in Am., Phi Beta Kappa. Address: PO Box 444 Prince St New York NY 10012-0008

KOSTELEBA, NANCY ANN, dean, consultant; b. Wilkes-Barre, Pa., Mar. 20, 1947; d. Michael and Annastacia (Morika) K. BA, Syracuse U., 1969, MS, 1972; postgrad., Temple U., 1977-80. Cert. secondary education tchr. social studies, N.Y. Tchr. social studies Westhill Sch. Dist., Syracuse, 1970-73; edn. specialist Treatment and Rehab. Ctr. Northeastern Pa., Scranton, 1974-76; cons., edn. specialist Hazleton-Nanticoke Mental Health/Mental Retardation Ctr., 1976-80; edn. devel. officer Luzerne County Community Coll., Nanticoke, 1980-87, dir. Ctr. for Instructional Devel., 1982-89, dir. resource devel. and planning, 1987-89, assoc. dean instl. Devel., 1989—; crisis intervention team mem. Hazleton-Nanticoke Mental Health/Mental Retardation Ctr., 1977-80; adj. faculty Pa. State U., 1974-80. Dir. over 50 ednl. software programs, 1982-90; grant writer fed., state and pvt. found. grants, 1980—. Mem. Luzerne County Cultural Coun., 1990—. Named Outstanding Young Woman Am., 1979. Mem. Nat. Coun. Resource Devel., Quota Club. Office: Luzerne County CC 1333 S Prospect St Nanticoke PA 18634-3899

KOSTER, JAMES, trust company executive; b. Alkmaar, Netherlands, July 18, 1948; came to U.S., 1951; s. Simon and Tina M. (Timmerman) K.; m. Heather Wilson, Sept. 8, 1954; children: Erin, Asheley. BA, Hope Coll., 1970; MBA, Northwestern U., 1974; PMD, Harvard U., 1986. Mgr. product planning Midwest Securities Trust Co., Chgo., 1975-78; v.p. ops. Depository Trust Co., N.Y.C., 1978—. With U.S. Army, 1970-72. Republican. Mem. Dutch Reformed Ch. Office: Depository Trust Co 7 Hanover Sq New York NY 10004-2616

KOSTIS, JOHN BASIL, cardiologist; b. Yannina, Greece, June 14, 1936; came to U.S., 1964; s. Basil John and Vasiliki Ilia (Masouras) K.; m. Barbara Charleston, June, 1969; children: William Jason, Steven Lawrence. MD, U. Salonica, Greece, 1960; student, USAF Sch. Aerospace Medicine, 1963, U. Pa., 1967-68. Diplomate Am. Bd. Internal Medicine, subspecialty cardiovascular disease. Resident internal medicine Evangelosmos Hosp., 404 Gen. Hosp., Athens and Larissa, Greece, 1963-64; intern Bklyn.-Cumberland Med. Ctr., 1964-65, med. resident, 1965-67; fellow cardiology Phila. Gen. Hosp., 1967-69; instr. physiology and aviation medicine Sch. Aviation Medicine, Athens, 1969-70; assoc. clin. medicine, asst. prof. medicine U. Pa., Phila., 1971-72; assoc. prof. Coll. Medicine and Dentistry N.J.-Rutgers Med. Sch., New Brunswick, 1972-76; chief cardiology Robert Wood Johnson U. Hosp., New Brunswick, 1980—; adj. prof. biomed. engring. Rutgers U. Coll. Engring., Piscataway, N.J., 1975—, Grad. Sch. Biomed. Engring., 1976—; prof. medicine U. Medicine and Dentistry N.J.-Robert Wood Johnson Med. Sch., New Brunswick, 1976—, chief div. cardiovascular disease, 1982-84, chief div. cardiovascular disease and hypertension, 1984—, prof. pharmacology, 1986—, John G. Detwiler prof. cardiology, 1987—, chmn. dept. medicine, 1990—; cons. pharm. industry. Co-editor: Essentials of Cardiovascular Diagnosis, 1984, Beta Blockers in the Treatment of Cardiovascular Disease, 1984, The Prevention of Sudden Cardiac Death, 1990; mem. editorial bds. Am. Jour. Cardiology, Am. Heart Jour., Jour. Am. Coll. Cardiology, Circulation, Am. Jour. Hypertension, Jour. Human Hypertension, others; co-inventor device noninvasive diagnostic system for coronary artery disease. Grantee pharm. industry, NHLBI, NIH, NIA. Fellow ACP, Am. Coll. Cardiology; mem. Am. Heart Assn. (disting. leadership in rsch. award 1986), Assn. U. Cardiologists, Am. Coll. Angiology, Am. Coll. Chest Physicians, Am. Soc. Hypertension, Internat. Soc. Hypertension. Office: U Medicine and Dentistry NJ Robert Wood Johnson Med Sch 1 Robert Wood Johnson Pl CN19 New Brunswick NJ 08903-0019

KOSTKA, HEATHER SHARKEY, counselor; b. Orange, N.J.; d. Thomas Dunne and Doris (Halliwell) Sharkey; m. David G. Kostka, June 16, 1973; children: Brian David, Kevin Thomas. BA, Caldwell Coll., 1968; MA, Seton Hall U., 1974. Lic. elem. educator, student pers. svcs. Tchr. grades 1, 2, 6, 8, 1965-70; assoc. dir. publs. Seton Hall U., South Orange, N.J., 1970-74; acad. counselor Thomas A. Edison Coll., Trenton, N.J., 1974-77; dir. Statewide Edn. Hotline, Trenton, 1978-79; spl. edn. asst. Monmouth County Ednl. Svcs. Commn., Marlboro, N.J., 1990; guidance counselor Holmdel (N.J.) Sch. Dist., 1990—. Bd. trustees South Orange-Maplewood (N.J.) Adults Sch., 1977-83; bd. dirs. Colts Neck (N.J.) Sports Found., 1987—; mem. Colts Neck Community Alliance, 1988—; mem. exec. com. Colts Neck Vols. Fair, 1989—. Recipient Exemplary Contbn. Plaque, Freehold Regional High Sch. Dist., 1990. Mem. Am. Sch. Counselor Assn., N.J. Assn. Counseling and Devel., Monmouth County Guidance Counselor Assn. Home: 75 Blackbriar Dr Colts Neck NJ 07722 Office: Holmdel Sch Dist Crawfords Corner Rd Holmdel NJ 07733

KOSTMAYER, PETER HOUSTON, congressman; b. N.Y.C., Sept. 27, 1946; s. John Houston and Julia Claiborne (Carson) K.; divorced. B.A., Columbia U., 1971. Press sec. to atty. gen. State of Pa., 1972-73; dep. press sec. to gov. State of Pa., Harrisburg, 1973-76; mem. 95th-96th, 98th-101st Congresses from 8th Pa. dist., 1977-81, 1983—. Regional coordinator McGovern-Shriver campaign S.E. Pa., 1972. Democrat. Episcopalian. Office: US House of Reps Rayburn House Office Bldg Rm 2436 Washington DC 20515*

KOSTUCH, MITCHELL JOHN, venture capital company executive, publisher; b. Toronto, Ont., Can., Feb. 11, 1931; s. Antoni and Karolina (Novak) K.; m. June Regina Lulchak, June 8, 1958; children—James, Lynn. Student, Ryerson Inst. Tech., 1951, U. Western Ont., 1951; MBA, York U., 1962. With Southam Bus. Publs., Dons Mills, Ont., 1951-70, v.p., pub., 1973—; exec. v.p., dir. SB Capital Corp. Ltd., Toronto, Ont., 1973—; pres. Kostuch Communications Inc., Toronto, Ont., 1974; v.p. bd. dirs. N.Am. Ventures Mgmt. Ltd., Toronto; dir. Hemosol Inc., Toronto; v.p., bd. dirs. Assn. Can. Venture Capital Cos., Kostuch Engring. Ltd., Brockville, Ont., Kostuch Engring. Ltd., Brockville, Ont., Kostuch Communications, Inc., Toronto. Chmn. bd. Three Schs. for Edn. Through the Arts Ltd., Toronto and Hockley Valley, Ont., 1976-82; bd. dirs. Centre for Resource Machinery Tech., Sudbury, Ont. Mem. Am. Mktg. Assn. (bd. dirs.), Assn. Indsl. Advertisers (bd. dirs.), Am. Bus. Press, Can. Bus. Press, Donalda

Club. Home: 3 Alvarado Pl, Don Mills, ON Canada M3A 3E8 Office: SB Capital Corp Ltd, 2 Bloor St E Ste 3304, Toronto, ON Canada M4W 1A7

KOSTYNIAK, PAUL JOHN, pharmacology educator; b. Schenectady, N.Y., Apr. 8, 1947; s. Theodore John and Veronica Anne (Wojnarowski) K.; m. Carol Ann Kusak; children: Douglas, Gregory, Laura. BS, St. John Fisher Coll., 1970; PhD, U. Rochester, 1975. Diplomate Am. Bd. Toxicology. Asst. prof. pharmacology SUNY, Buffalo, 1977-84, assoc. prof., 1984—, dir. Toxicology Rsch. Ctr., 1985—; mem. sci. adv. bd. Immunozone Therapeutics, Inc., Port Jervis, N.Y.; mem. adv. b.d. N.Y. State Poison Prevention Control, Albany, 1990-91, Occupational Health Clinic Network N.Y. State. Contbr. articles to Jour. Applied Toxicology, Jour. Pharmacology and Exptl. Therapy, Toxicology Letters, Drugs of Future, In Vitro. Predoctoral fellow NIH; Young Environ. Scientist grantee Nat. Inst. Environ. Health Scis., 1979-82. Mem. AAAS, Am. Chem. Soc., N.Y. Acad. Scis., Soc. Toxicology (pres. metals specialty sect.). Office: SUNY Dept Pharmacology 102 Farber Hall Buffalo NY 14214

KOSTYRA, RICHARD JOSEPH, advertising executive; b. Winnipeg, Man., Can., Nov. 4, 1940; came to U.S., 1980; s. Joseph and Ann (Walashek) K.; m. Juleinne E. Lynden, Aug. 4, 1961 (div.); 1 son, Corwin Gregory; m. 2d Lorraine T. Antoniello, Sept. 19, 1981. With J. Walter Thompson, Toronto, Ont., Can., 1959-63, media dir., 1966-73, sr. v.p., dir. diversification, 1973-76; sr. v.p., gen. mgr. J. Walter Thompson, Montreal, Que., Can., 1976-80; sr. v.p., media dir. J. Walter Thompson, N.Y.C., 1980—; exec. v.p. U.S. dir. Media Services, 1987, bd. dirs.; dir. J. Walter Thompson Can., 1965-76. Home: 12H 245 E 35th St New York NY 10016 Office: J Walter Thompson USA Inc 466 Lexington Ave New York NY 10017-3140

KOTARU, SATYANARAYANA, computer scientist; b. Pulugurtha, Godavary, India, Apr. 15, 1944; s. Ganiraju and Bapadu (Adapa) K.; m. Venkata R. K. Seelamsetti, May 11, 1966; children: Chandra Shekar, Rajashekar, Chakradhar. BSME, Jawarlal Nehru Technol. U., Kakinada, India, 1966; MS, Indian Inst. Tech., 1982; PhD, Howard U., 1989. Sr. sci. asst. Def. Rsch. Devel. Orgn., Hyderabad, India, 1967-70; scientist, sr. engr. Indian Space Rsch. Orgn., Trivandrum, Kerala, India, 1970-72, Sriharikota, Nellore Dt, India, 1972-84; sr. analyst Informatics Inc., Greenbelt, Md., 1988-90; computer scientist Computer Scis. Corp., Lanham-Seabrook, Md., 1990—; head vehicles and flight test div. Indian Space Rsch. Orgn., 1972-84; computer scientist, leader task force flight dynamics of NASA Spacecraft Missions, Lanham-Seabrook, 1990—. Mem. AIAA, Sigma Xi. Home: 8100 Rycroft Ave Hyattsville MD 20784-3650 Office: Computer Scis Corp 10110 Aerospace Rd Lanham Seabrook MD 20706-2276

KOTCHER, RAYMOND LOWELL, public relations executive; b. N.Y.C., Nov. 19, 1951; s. Richmond and Elaine (Germaine) K.; m. Betsy Kasper, Sept. 10, 1978; children: Maris, Gregory. BS, SUNY, Geneseo, 1973; MS in Comm., Boston U., 1983. Account exec. Burson Marsteller, N.Y.C., 1978-79, 83; v.p., mgmt. supr. J. Walter Thompson Co., N.Y.C., 1979-84; v.p. Ketchum Pub. Rels., N.Y.C., 1983-85; exec. v.p. G.S. Schwartz & Co., N.Y.C., 1985-86; exec. v.p., chief U.S. ops. pub. rels. divsn. Ketchum Comm., N.Y.C., 1986—, also bd. dirs. Mem. exec. com. Boston U. Coll. Comm., 1988—. Mem. Pub. Rels. Soc. Am., Princeton Club. Office: Ketchum Pub Rels 1133 Ave Of The Americas New York NY 10036-6710

KOTHARI, AJAY PRASANNAJIT, engineering executive; b. Dhanera, Gujarat, India, Nov. 22, 1954; came to U.S., 1974; s. Prasannajit S. and Pushpa (P.) K. BS, U. Bombay, India, 1974; MS, U. Md., 1975, PhD, 1979. Sr. devel. engr. Bell Aerospace Textron, Buffalo, N.Y., 1979-81; rsch. engr. U. Md., College Park, 1982-89; pres., chief exec. officer Astrox Corp., Greenbelt, Md., 1985—. Profl. actor films and TV. Faculty adv. Indian Students Assn., U. Md., 1986-88, pres., 1976. Nat. Merit scholar Govt. India, 1966. Mem. AIAA (com. mem. nuclear propulsion tech. com.). Home: 3500 Marlbrough Way College Park MD 20740-3916 Office: Astrox Corp 7500 Greenway Center Dr Greenbelt MD 20770-3502

KOTHERA, LYNNE M., clinical neuropsychologist; b. Cleve., Dec. 18, 1938; d. Leonard Frank and Lillian (Shackleton) Kothera; m. Richard Litwin, Oct. 24, 1965. BA with hons., Denison U., Granville, Ohio, 1960; MA, NYU, 1983; PhD, L.I. U., Bklyn., 1989. Dancer Martha Graham Dance Co., N.Y.C., 1961-62, Carmen DeLavallade Dance Co., N.Y.C., 1965-68, Glen Tetley Dance Co., N.Y.C., 1965-69; prin. dancer John Butler's, N.Y.C., 1971; artist-in-residence Boston High Schs. - Title III, 1969-71, Hobart-Smith Coll./Denison U., 1973; auditor N.Y. State Council of the Arts, N.Y.C., 1974-78; predoctoral fellow clin. psychology Yale-New Haven Hosp., 1987-88; postdoctoral fellow neuropsychology Inst. of Living, Hartford, Conn., 1989-91; with dept. rehab. Mt. Sinai Med. Ctr., N.Y.C., 1991—. Mem. APA, Internat. Neuropsychological Soc. Democrat. Home: 23 E 11th St New York NY 10003-4450 Office: Mount Sinai Med Ctr Dept Rehab Medicine One Gustave Levy Pl Box 1241 New North Pavilion New York NY 10029

KOTIDIS, PETROS ANESTIS, aerospace scientist; b. Kozani, Greece, Aug. 9, 1960; came to U.S., 1983; s. Anestis and Penelope (Papistas) K. BS in Mech. Engring., Nat. Tech. U. Athens, 1983; MS in Aero. Engring., MIT, 1985, PhD in Aero. Engring., 1988. Rsch. asst. MIT, Cambridge, Mass., 1983-88; sr. scientist III Textron Def. Systems, Everett, Mass., 1989—. Contbr. articles to profl. jours.; patentee in field. Mem. AIAA, Combustion Inst., Sigma Xi (assoc.). Home: 12 Orchard Ave Newton MA 02168-2002 Office: Textron Def Systems 2385 Revere Beach Pky Everett MA 02149-5900

KOTIK, PETR, composer, performer, director; b. Prague, Czechoslovakia, Jan. 27, 1942; came to U.S., 1969; s. Jan Kotik and Paula Epstein Jerusalem; m. Charlotta Kotik, Sept. 30, 1966; children: Thomas, Jan. Grad. with distinction, Prague Conservatory, 1962, Music Acad., Vienna, Austria, 1966, Akademie Múzickych Ument, Prague, 1969. Creative assoc. Ctr. Creative and Performing Arts, Buffalo, 1969-73; dir. S.E.M. Ensemble, N.Y.C., 1970—; instr. York U., Toronto, Ont., Can., 1965-66, SUNY, Buffalo, 1972-77. Composer: Integrated Solos, 1988, Wilsie Bridge, 1989, Letters to Olga, 1991. Composition grantee Nat. Endowment Arts. Mem. ASCAP. Office: SEM Ensemble 25 Columbia Pl Brooklyn NY 11201

KOTITE, RICH, professional football coach; b. Oct. 13, 1942; m. Elizabeth Kotite; 1 child, Alexandra. Student, Wagner Coll. Football player N.Y. Giants, 1967, 69-72, Pitts. Steelers, 1969; asst. coach New Orleans Saints, 1977; receivers coach Cleve. Browns, 1978-82; receivers coach N.Y. Jets, 1983-89, offensive coord., 1985-89; offensive coord., quarterbacks coach Phila. Eagles, 1990-91, head coach, 1991—. Office: Phila Eagles Broad St and Pattison Ave Philadelphia PA 19148*

KOTOVSKY, KENNETH, psychology educator; b. Pitts., July 5, 1939; s. Jacob and Dorothy (Friedland) K.; m. Avis Brenda Lovit, June 10, 1962; children: Laura Lovit, Jack. BS in Econs./Polit. Sci., MIT, 1961; MS in Psychology, Carnegie Mellon U., 1970, PhD In Psychology, 1983. Systems analyst Stanford Rsch. Inst.-Control Systems Lab., Menlo Park, Calif., 1962-64 summers; USPHS trainee Biophys. Lab. Eye & Ear Hosp. of Pitts., Pitts., 1963-64; instr. biology Community Coll. of Allegheny County, Pitts., 1966-70, asst. prof. biology and psychology, 1970-75, assoc. prof., chmn. psychology, 1976-81, prof. psychology, 1981-89; assoc. prof., dir. undergrad. studies Carnegie Mellon U., Pitts., 1989—; rsch. assoc. psychology Carnegie Mellon U., Pitts., 1983-88, adj. prof. psychology, 1988-89. Editor: (with David Klahr) Complex Information Processing: The Impact of Herbert A. Simon, 1989; contbr. articles to profl. jours. Bd. dirs. Mid. East Forum, Pitts., 1987—; chmn. Troop com. Boy Scouts Am., Pitts., 1984-86; mem. Reizenstein Consortium Community Orgns., Pitts., 1979-82; com. on planning and allocation Pvt. Industry Coun. Allegheny County, 1988-91. Fellow NSF, 1964-66, grantee, 1981, 85-87. Mem. APA, Am. Psychol. Soc., Cognitive Sci. Soc. Democrat. Jewish. Home: 1310 Murray Ave Pittsburgh PA 15217-1223 Office: Carnegie Mellon U Psychology Dept Pittsburgh PA 15213

KOTTAMASU, MOHAN RAO, physician; b. Gudivada, India, Jan. 13, 1947; came to U.S., 1973; s. Janardana Rao and Kantharatnamma (Maddi) K. MBBS, Gulbarga Med. Coll., 1972. House surgeon Govt. Gen. Hosp., Gulbarga, India, 1971-72; intern St. Vincent's Med. Ctr. of Richmond, S.I., N.Y., 1973-74, resident, 1974-76, chief resident, 1976-77; assoc. Valley Pulmonary and Med. Assocs., Springfield, Mass., 1979-81, ptnr., v.p., 1981—; adj. asst. prof. clin. pharmacy Mass. Coll. Pharmacy and Allied Health Scis., 1984—. Pres. house staff St. Vincent's Med. Ctr., 1976; founding pres. Indian Assn. Greater Springfield, 1985-86; pres. med. staff Mercy Hosp., Springfield, 1989-91. Pulmonary Diseases fellow Deaconess Hosp., Boston, 1977-79, Clin. fellow Harvard Med. Sch., Boston, 1978-79. Fellow Am. Coll. Physicians, Am. Coll. Chest Physicians; mem. Am. Thoracic Soc., Mass. Med. Soc. Hindu. Home: 112 Twin Hills Dr Longmeadow MA 01106 Office: Valley Pulmonary Med Assocs 222 Carew St Springfield MA 01104

KOTUK, ANDREA MIKOTAJUK, public relations executive, writer; b. New Brunswick, N.J., Oct. 19, 1948; d. Michael and Julia Dorothy (Muka) Mikotajuk. BA, Douglass Coll., Rutgers U., 1970. Pub. relations asst. Wall St. Jour. Newspaper Fund, Princeton, N.J., 1970; editorial asst. Redbook mag., N.Y.C., 1970-71; asst. pub. relations dir. Children's Aid Soc., N.Y.C., 1971-75; assoc. pub. relations dir. Planned Parenthood, N.Y.C., 1975-80; pres. Andrea & Assocs., N.Y.C., 1980—. Writer publicist for healthcare corps., for non-profit agys.; contbg. editor Arts Mag., 1970-75. Mem. NAFE, Exec. Women Human Svcs. (bd. dirs.). Office: Andrea & Assocs 112 E 23d St New York NY 10010

KOTZ, JOHN CARL, chemistry educator; b. Massillon, Ohio, June 27, 1937; s. Fredrick M. and Shirley Marie (Longworth) K.; m. Kathrine Louise Ringland, July 15, 1961; children: David Frederick, Peter Joseph. BS, Washington and Lee U., 1959; PhD, Cornell U., 1963. Postdoctoral fellow Univ. Manchester, Eng., 1964, Ind. Univ., Bloomington, 1964-65; asst. prof. Kans. State Univ., Manhattan, 1965-70; assoc. prof. SUNY, Oneonta, 1970-78, prof., 1978-86, disting. teaching prof., 1986—; bd. dirs. Oneonta (N.Y.) Found., Project Seraphim and Jour. Chem. Edn. Software, Madison, Wis. Author: Inorganic Chemistry, 1977, Chemistry, 1987, 2d edit., 1991; editor: Chem Matters Mag., 1988—. Named Fulbright lectr., rsch. scholar, Lisbon, 1979; recipient Catalyst award Chem. Mfrs. Assn., 1992. Mem. Am. Chem. Soc. Home: RR 1 Box 567A Oneonta NY 13820-9777 Office: State Univ of New York Chemistry Dept Oneonta NY 13820

KOTZEN, MARSHALL JASON, educator; b. Malden, Mass., Dec. 29, 1942; s. Bernard and Regina (Katz) K.; m. Elizabeth Claudia Blondin, Aug. 24, 1980. BS in Math., Tufts U., 1964; MS in Math., U. N.H., 1967. Prof. math. Worcester (Mass.) State Coll., 1969—. Mem. Am. Math. Soc., Math. Assn. Am.

KOUBEK, EDWARD, chemist, educator; b. Bayshore, N.Y., July 25, 1937; s. Rudolph and Edna (Svec) K.p m. Elizabeth A. Smith, Oct. 6, 1963; children: Mary Anne, Edward. BS, SUNY, Albany, 1959; PhD, Brown U., 1963. Postdoctoral fellow Bell Labs., Murry Hill, N.J., 1963-64; prof. chemistry U.S. Naval Acad., Annapolis, Md., 1964—; vis. prof. Stanford U., Palo Alto, Calif., 1972, Dartmouth Coll., Hanover, N.H., 1981, Canterbury U., Christchurch, New Zealand, 1991. Contbr. articles to profl. jours. Mem. Am. Chem. Soc. Home: 1915 Old Annapolis Blvd Annapolis MD 21401-6204 Office: US Naval Acad Chemistry Dept Annapolis MD 21402

KOURY, THOMAS LEO, plastic and reconstructive surgeon, educator; b. Upland, Pa., Nov. 15, 1923; m. Elizabeth Koury; children: Carol Anne, Thomas Edwin, Virginia Lee, Jennifer Elaine. Student, Swarthmore Coll.; DDS, Temple U., 1948, MD, 1952. Intern Temple U. Hosp., Phila., 1952-53; gen. surg. resident Vets. Hosp., Phila., 1953-54; gen. surg. resident Kansas U. Med. Ctr., Kansas City, 1956-57, plastic surg. resident, 1957-59; pvt. practice plastic and reconstructive surgery Silver Spring, Md., 1959—; chief attending plastic surgeon D.C. Maternal Health-Children With Special Needs, Washington, 1963—; asst. prof. plastic surgery Georgetown U., Washington, 1963—; pres. I Care - Children of Peru Found., Silver Spring, 1990—; chief plastic surgery Holy Cross Hosp., Silver Spring, 1990—; lectr. cleft lip and palate and orthognathic surgery Howard U. Orthodontic Sch., Washington, 1982—; lectr. surg. procedures dept. plastic surgery Georgetown U. Med. Sch., Washington, 1963—; surgery tchr., contbr. Naval Hosp., Lima, Peru, 1989—. Mem. Woodside Pk. Civic Assn., Silver Spring, 1991. Lt., M.C., USN, 1954-56. Mem. Am. Med. Soc., Am. Soc. Plastic and Reconstructive Surgeons, Am. Craniofacial Soc., Md. State Med. Soc., Montgomery County Med. Soc. (Physician of Yr. 1992), Bladensburg Rotary Club. Office: 9801 Georgia Ave Ste 2-29 Silver Spring MD 20902

KOUSSA, HAROLD ALAN, marketing executive; b. Central Falls, R.I., June 20, 1947; s. Harold Albert and June Joann (John) K.; m. Marsha Lynn Heidenis, Dec. 1, 1973. B.S., U. R.I., 1969; M.B.A., U. Hartford, 1975; M.S. in Engring. Sci., Rensselaer Poly. Inst., 1977. Reactor engring. asst. Conn. Yankee Atomic Power Co., Haddam Neck, 1969-75, reactor engr., 1975-77; staff nuclear engr. Am. Nuclear Insurers, Farmington, Conn., 1977-79, sr. staff nuclear engr., 1979-81, prin. engr., 1981-82, mgr. ops., 1982-89, account exec., 1989—. Mem East Hampton Rep. Town Com., 1982-88; del. Conn. Rep. Conv., 1982, 84, 86; mem. East Hampton Water Pollution Control Authority, 1982-88, vice chmn., 1984-85, chmn., 1985-88. Engring. duty officer USNR, 1982—. Decorated Navy Commendation medal. Mem. Am. Nuclear Soc., ASME, Am. Soc. Naval Engrs., U.S. Naval Inst., Navy League U.S., Naval Res. Assn., Res. Officers Assn., Masons, U. R.I. Fast Break Club. Congregationalist. Home: 26 Meadowlark Dr Windsor CT 06095-1533 Office: Am Nuclear Insurers Town Ctr Ste 300 S 29 South Main St West Hartford CT 06107-2445

KOUTROULIS, ARIS GEORGE, artist, educator; b. Athens, Greece, May 14, 1938; came to U.S., 1953; s. George Aris and Julia (Eftimiades) K.; m. Mary Ann Schmid, 1964 (div. 1973); m. Jill Warren, July 4, 1982; 1 child, Georgina. BFA, La. State U., 1961; Master Printer, Tamarind Lithography Workshop, L.A., 1964; MFA, Cranbrook Acad. Art, Bloomfield Hills, Mich., 1966. Chmn. bd. Willis Gallery, Detroit, 1970-71; pres. Common Ground of the Arts, Detroit, 1969-72; guest artist Ox-Bow Summer Sch. Art, Saugatuck, Mich., 1973; co-dir. Ox-Bow Summer Sch. Art, Saugatuck, 1975; assoc. prof. art Wayne State U., 1966-75; head painting dept. Ctr. Creative Studies, Detroit, 1975-81; prof., chmn. Fine Arts Dept. Ctr. Creative Studies, 1981—. exhibited one-man shows Hanamura Gallery, Detroit, 1966, Montgomery Mus. Fine Arts, Ala., 1966, Va. Poly. Inst., 1968, Baton Rouge Gallery, 1968, Wayne State U., 1969, Mich. Council for Arts, 1969, Gertrude Kasle Gallery, Detroit, 1970, Detroit Artists Market, 1973, Klein-Vogel Gallery, Detroit, 1974, Detroit Inst. Arts, 1976, Gloria Cortella Gallery, N.Y.C., 1977, Gallery Renaissance, Detroit, 1980, Haber-Theodore Gallery, N.Y.C., 1980, OK Harris Gallery, N.Y.C., 1980, 81, 82, 83, 85, 87, Mich. Traveling Exhbn., 1981, Cantor/Cemberg Gallery, Birmingham, Mich., 1982, 88, Dubins Gallery, L.A., 1984, Nimbus Gallery, Dallas, 1986, Argo Gallery, Athens, Greece, 1988, Argo Gallery, Cypres, 1991, OK Harris Works of Art, Birmingham, Mich., 1991; exhibited group shows Decorative Arts Ctr., N.Y.C., 1973, Detroit Inst. Arts, 1974, Bykert Gallery, N.Y.C., 1974, Bklyn. Mus., 1977, Brooks Meml. Art Gallery, Memphis, 1977, La. State U. Gallery, 1978, Tyler Sch. Art, Temple U., 1978, Mus. Fine Arts, Springfield, Mass., 1978, Van Doren Gallery, San Francisco, 1978, Consulate Gen. Greece, N.Y.C., 1978, Landmark Gallery, N.Y.C., 1978, Cranbrook Mus. Art, Bloomfield Hills, Mich., 1979, Detroit Inst. Arts, 1980, Mus. Fine Arts Tampa, 1987, 51st nat. mid-yr. exhbn. Butler Inst. Am. Art, Youngstown, Ohio, 1987, Flint Mus. of Art. Mich., 1989, Japan Expo, Tokyo, 1989, Ctr. Gallery CCS, Detroit, MI.,1989; represented in pub. collections including Mus. Modern Art, Nat. Gallery Art, Detroit Inst. Arts, L.A. County Mus. Art, Cranbrook Mus. Art, Detroit Engring. Soc., Detroit Pub. Libr., U. Mich. Art Mus., Anglo-Am. Mus., Amon Carter Mus. Western Art, Ft. Worth, UCLA Grunwald Graphic Arts Found., Ball State U. Art Mus., Vores Mus., Athens, The Goulandis Mus. Modern Art, Andros, Greece; represented in corp. collections; commd. Standard Oil Corp., San Ramon, Calif., Arbor Drugs, Inc., Bracewell/Patterson, Washington, Mich. Found. for Arts, Detroit Engring. Soc., Art for Detroit, City of Detroit, WDIV-TV4, Detroit, Tampa Mus. Collection, Criterion Ctr., N.Y.C. Address: 51 Greene St New York NY 10013

KOUYOUMJIAN, CHARLES H., diversified financial services company executive; b. Cambridge, Mass., Nov. 20, 1940; s. Housep J. and Victoria M. (Madenjian) K.; BS in Bus. Adminstrn., Boston U., 1963; postgrad. Boston Coll., 1969-71; children: Joseph, Charles. Dir. purchasing Allis Chalmers Mfg. Co., Boston, 1968; investment broker Hornblower & Weeks Hemphill Noyes Inc., Boston, 1969-71, v.p., resident mgr., Springfield, Mass., 1971-76, regional hdqrs., Boston, 1976-77; v.p., resident mgr. Paine Webber, Inc., Boston, 1977-79, regional sales mgr. Fla. div., 1980-81, dir. Asset Mgmt. Group, nat. hdqrs., N.Y.C., 1982-83, v.p. spl. accounts dept. Boston, 1983-85; pres., chief exec. officer, Empire Nat. Securities, Buffalo, 1985-88, Charles Assocs., 1988—. Mem. camp com. Springfield YMCA, 1973-76; bd. dirs. Health Care Found. Western Mass., 1973-74. Served to capt. USAF, 1963-67. Mem. Boston Options Soc. (chmn.), Springfield C. of C. (dir. 1973-75), Nat. Assn. Securities Dealers (mem. quotation com. 1975-76), Boston Fin. Rsch. Assocs., Boston Univ. Alumni Assn. (bd. dirs.), Boston Investment Club, Boston Stockbrokers Club, Securities Industry Assn., Newcomen Soc. U.S. and Gt. Britain, Internat. Assn. Fin. Planning. Clubs: Bond of Boston, Bond of Buffalo. Home: 16 Greenridge Rd Weston MA 02193-1814 Office: Charles Assocs 205 Burlington Rd Bedford MA 01730-1406

KOVACH, ANDREW LOUIS, marketing executive; b. Greensboro, Pa., Feb. 4, 1948; s. Andrew and Pauline (Nassar) K.; m. Cindy Juliani, Nov. 28, 1970; 1 child: Courtney. BS in Indsl. Engineering, W.Va. U., 1969. Engr. DuPont, Marinsville, Va., 1970-73; supt. engr. Allied Corp., Syracuse, N.Y., 1973-75; mgr. employee relations Allied Corp., Morristown, N.J., 1976-80, mgr. orgnl. devel., 1980; dir. human resources Allied Corp., N.Y.C., 1981-82, dir. comml. devel., 1983-87; ptnr. Thomas Andrew Assoc., Morristown, N.J., 1987—; v.p. human resources Morristown Meml. Hosp., 1988—. Mem. pres. com. Morris County Hospice; bd. dirs. Fairleigh Dickinson Fed. Credit Union; mem. adv. group Fairleigh Dickinson U.; bd. dirs., vice-chmn. Morris County Rides; bd. dirs. Morristown Meml. Physician Hosp. Orgn. Mem. Indsl. Engring. Adv. Orgn., Morristown Club. Presbyterian. Office: Morristown Meml Hosp 100 Madison Ave Ste C Morristown NJ 07962-1956

KOVACH, BARBARA ELLEN, management and psychology educator; b. Ann Arbor, Mich., Dec. 28, 1941; d. Harry Arnold and Margaret Mayne (Buell) Lusk; m. Craig Randall Duncan, Dec. 28, 1963 (div. 1973); children: Deborah Louise, Mark Randall; m. Randall Louis Kovach, May 2, 1981; 1 child, Jennifer Elizabeth. BA magna cum laude, Stanford U., 1963, MA, 1964; PhD, U. Md., 1973. Asst. prof. psychology U. Mich., Dearborn, 1973-77, assoc. prof., 1977-82, prof., 1982-84, chair Dept. Behavioral Scis., 1980-83; dean Univ. Coll. Rutgers U., New Brunswick, N.J., 1984-88, prof. mgmt. and psychology, 1984—, dir. leadership devel. program, 1988—; pres. Leadership Devel. Inst., Princeton, N.J., 1990—; cons. Rochester (N.Y.) Products-Gen. Motors, Grand Rapids, Mich., 1982-87, Ford Motor Co., Dearborn, 1981-82, Mich. Bell Telephone, 1980-81. Author: Sex Roles and Personal Awareness, 1978, 90, Power and Love, 1982, Organizational Synch, 1983, Adolescent Experience, 1983, The Flexible Organization, 1984, Survival on the Fast Track, 1988, Organization Gameboard, 1989; producer videotape series Keys to Leadership, 1991; contbr. articles to profl. jours. Daniel E. Prescott fellow U. Md., 1972; recipient Susan B. Anthony and Faculty Recognition awards U. Mich., 1980. Mem. Am. Psychol. Assn., Acad. Mgmt., Organizational Devel. Network, Phi Beta Kappa. Republican. Episcopalian. Home: 95 Cuyler Rd Princeton NJ 08540-3460 Office: Rutgers U Sch of Bus New Brunswick NJ 08903

KOVAL, JENNIFER AMY, bank officer; b. Vineland, N.J., Oct. 19, 1965; d. Bernard C. and Elinorlou E. (Corso) K. BA in Econs., Dickinson Coll., 1987. Supr. customer svc. CoreStates-N.J. Nat., Trenton, N.J., 1987-90; mgr. Beneficial Savs. Bank, Phila., 1990—. Mem. Lower Bucks C. of C., Bensalem C. of C. Republican. Presbyterian.

KOVALCIK, KENNETH JOHN, accountant; b. Passaic, N.J., Nov. 9, 1946; s. Joseph Michael and Helen (Pavlinik) K.; m. Helene Mary Kurilko, Sept. 27, 1969; children: Kenneth Jason, Lucas Alan. BS in Acctg., Seton Hall U., 1968. Staff acct. Arthur Andersen & Co., Newark, 1968-71, sr. acct., 1972-73; mgr. Arthur Andersen & Co., N.Y.C., 1974-83, prin., 1984, asst. dir., internat. merger and acquisition prog., 1985-90, dir. corp. fin. cons. svcs., mergers and acquisitions. Co-author: Guide to Mergers and Acquisitions, 1988, Organizing & Implementing an Acquisition Program in the U.S. From Abroad, 1986, Guide to Performing a Businessman's Review, 1986. Treas. United Rep. Campaign Com., Rochelle Park, N.J., 1978—; mem. Zoning Bd. Adjustment, Rochelle Park, 1982-87, vice chmn., 1988-90. Named Father of the Yr., Twp. of Rochelle Park, 1987. Mem. AICPA, N.J. Soc. CPA's, N.Y. Soc. CPA's, Assn. for Corp. Growth (v.p. 1986, pres. 1990-91), Nat. Acctg. Assn., Am. Acctg. Assn., Am. Soc. Notaries. Republican. Roman Catholic. Office: Arthur Andersen & Co 1345 Ave Of The Americas New York NY 10105-0099

KOVALSKY, GEORGE BRIAN, telecommunications company executive, consultant; b. Johnstown, Pa., May 29, 1950; s. George and Florence Jean (Swegle) K.; m. Debra Lee Edge, June 1, 1974; children: Kristen Breeze, Shana Joy. BS summa cum laude, Loyola Coll., Balt., 1978. Site leader Unisys, Balt., 1973-79; sr. analyst Gen. Instrument Co., Lutherville, Md., 1978-80; sect. mgr. Digital Communications Corp., Germantown, Md., 1980-83; dept. mgr. M/A-Com Telecommunications, Germantown, 1983-85; dir. engring. and mktg. Hughes Network Systems, Germantown, 1985-90; founder, pres. Mobile Solutions, Inc., Mt. Airy, Md., 1990—. Mem. parish coun. St. Michael's Ch., Poplar Springs, Md., 1985, tchr., 1988, mem. Men's Club, 1989. Mem. IEEE, The Mastermind Group. Republican. Roman Catholic.

KOVARIK, DANIEL CHARLES, environmental and petroleum geologist, consultant; b. Patchogue, N.Y., Jan. 15, 1958; s. Vincent Joseph and Mary Josephine (Kriklava) K.; m. Colleen Ann Smith, July 11, 1981. B.S., SUNY-Stony Brook, 1980. Wellsite geologist Exploration Services, Inc., Midland, Tex., 1981-83, 84; geologist, ops. mgr., pres., 1983-84; petroleum geologists Midland, 1984—; cons. geologist, Midland, 1984-86; internat. cons. geologist, N.Y., 1986—; environ. cons. gealogist, N.Y., 1986—. Mem. Geol. Soc. Am., Am. Assn. Petroleum Geologists, Nat. Water Well Assn., Am. Inst. Profl. Geologists, Internat. Platform Assn. Republican. Roman Catholic.

KOVNER, RICHARD STEPHEN, neuropsychologist; b. N.Y.C., June 8, 1936; s. Milton and Evelyn (Schachner) K.; m. Fereshteh Yazdpour, May 19, 1965; 1 child, Linda. BA cum laude, Queens Coll., 1960; PhD, SUNY, Stony Brook, 1971. Diplomate Am. Bd. Profl. Psychology, Am. Bd. Clin. Neuropsychology. Vis. rsch. fellow dept. psychology Princeton (N.J.) U., 1971-73; postdoctoral fellow dept. neurology Montefiore Med. Ctr., Bronx, N.Y., 1973, staff psychologist div. neuropsychology, dept. neurology, 1974-76, dir. Ctr. Neuropsychol. Svcs., dept. neurology, 1982-85; instr. neurology Albert Einstein Coll. Medicine, Bronx, 1976-79, asst. prof neurology, 1979-86; sr. neuropsychologist depts. neurology Montefiore Med. Ctr. and Albert Einstein Coll. Medicine, 1976-82; asst. prof. neurosci. Cornell U. Med. Coll., N.Y.C., 1986—; chief adult neuropsychology dept. neurology North Shore U. Hosp., Manhasset, N.Y., 1985—; NSF trainee, 1967-71. Cons. reviewer Jour. Clin. and Exptl. Neuropsychology, 1970—; contbr. articles on memory and amnesia to profl. jours. Mem. APA, Internat. Psychol. Soc., Westchester Psychol. Assn., Phi BEta Kappa. Home: 6 Birch Grove Dr Armonk NY 10504-2521 Office: North Shore Univ Hosp 300 Community Dr Manhasset NY 11030-3800

KOWALSKI, CHRISTINE MARIE, human resources specialist; b. Phila., Feb. 9, 1949; d. Matthew Charles and Julia Regina (Tomaszewski) K.; m. Walter Patrick Brickley Jr., June 30, 1984; children: Nora Christine, Jacob Martin, Lucas Nathan. BA, U. Pa., 1971; MBA, Temple U., 1987. Tchr. St. Hugh of Cluny Sch., Phila., 1971-78; advisor Phila. Newspapers Inc., 1970-78, advt. supr., 1978-80, benefits mgr., 1980-88, compensation and benefits mgr., 1988-91, dir. compensation, benefits and HR systems, 1991—; bd. mem. Penjerdel Employee Benefit Assn., Phila., 1990—. Bd. mem., treas. U. Pa. Class 1971, 1986—. Mem. Human Resource Systems Profls., 1986—. Democrat. Roman Catholic. Office: Phila Newspapers Inc 400 N Broad St Philadelphia PA 19130-4099

KOWALSKI, KATHLEEN MADLAND, psychologist; b. Milw., Jan. 26, 1944; d. Lawrence F. and Dorothy H. (Grebe) Madland; children: Matthew J., Nicholas L. BS, U. Wis., 1966, MS, 1967; PhD, U. Pitts., 1989. Nat. cert. counselor. Tchr. Wayland (Mass.) Pub. Schs., 1967-69, Newton (Mass.) Pub. Schs., 1969-73; spl. edn. tchr. Nashville Pub Schs., 1973-74; grad. asst. U. Pitts., 1985-89; assoc. prof. psychology Community Coll. of Allegheny County, Pitts., 1990-91; rsch. psychologist Bur. of Mines, Dept. of Interior, Pitts., 1991—; adv. bd. SEARCH Displaced Homemakers Program, West

Mifflin, Pa., 1991—; guest lectr. U. Pitts. Leadership Conf., 1989, 90. U. Pitts. scholar, 1985-89; U. Wis. fellow, 1967. Mem. APA, ACA, Gamma Phi Beta (Pitts. chpt. pres. 1980-82). Home: 1276 Plantation Dr Bethel Park PA 15102-3595 Office: US Dept Interior Bur Mines Pitts Rsch Ctr PO Box 8070 Pittsburgh PA 15236-0070

KOWALSKI, LYNN MARY, podiatrist; b. Passaic, N.J., Aug. 15, 1955; d. George J. and Gladys L. (Kucera) K.; m. Donald Storbeck, Feb. 9, 1975 (div. Mar. 1982); children: Jason, Jessica. BSN, William Paterson Coll., 1984; DPM, N.Y. Coll. Podiatric Medicine, 1988. RN, N.J.; diplomate Am. Bd. Podiatric Med. Examiners; lic. physician N.Y, N.J. Resident in podiatric surgery N.Y. Coll. Podiatric Medicine & Affiliated Hosps., 1988-89; pvt. duty nurse Bergen County, N.J., 1989; pvt. practice podiatrist Brick, N.J., 1990—; guest speaker Eldermed, Brick, 1991, Diabetes Support Group, Point Pleasant, N.J., 1991, 92, Arthritis Support Group, 1991, Garden State Rehab. Hosp., Toms River, N.J., Community Svcs., Toms River and Brick, 1992, Laurelton Village Community Edn., Brick, 1992, Lions Head North, 1992, Family Wellness Fair, Toms River, 1992, Green briar 2, 1992, Post Polio Support Group-Garden State Rehab. Hosp., Toms River, 1992, Treat Your Feet-Med. Ctr. Ocean County Health Edn. Network, 1992, Parkinsons Support Group-Med. Ctr. Ocean County, 1992. Contbr. articles to profl. jours. Mem. Toms River-Ocean (N.J.) County C. of C., 1990, Brick C. of C., 1991, Community Svcs., Toms River, 1992, Laurelton Village and Community Edn., Brick, N.J., 1992, adult community Lions Head North, 1992, Family Wellness Fair, Toms River, 1992, Greenbriar 2, 1992, Post Polio Support Group-Garden State Rehab. Hosp., Toms River, 1992, Treat Your Feet, Med. Ctr. Olean County Health Edn. Network, 1992, point pleasant div. Diabetes Support Group, 1992, Parkinsons Support Group, 1992, Am. Diabetes Assn.-Tour de Cure, 1992. Mem. Am Diabetes Assn. (Tour de Cure 1992), Am. Coll. Foot Surgeons (assoc.), Am. Running and Fitness Assn., Am. Podiatric Med. Assn., N.J. Podiatric Med. Soc., Sigma Theta Tau (charter), Psi Chi. Office: 1608 Rte # 88 W Ste # 118 Brick NJ 08724

KOWALSKI, MICHAEL FRANCIS, podiatrist, surgeon; b. S.I., N.Y., Mar. 28, 1961; s. Theodore and Irene (Blois) K.; m. Traciann Rizzo, Nov. 8, 1986. BS in Biology, Marist Coll., 1983; D of Podiatric Medicine, N.Y. Coll. Podiatric Medicine, 1987. Chief podiatry resident Washington D.C. VA Med. Ctr., 1987-88; owner, sole practitioner Berdan Sq. Podiatry, Wayne, N.J., 1988—; speaker Roerig/Pfizer Pharm., 1991, Am. Diabetes Assn., 1991. Chmn. Shoes for the Shoeless, Passaic County, 1991. Mem. N.J. Podiatric Med. Assn. No. Div. (v.p. 1990-92), Am. Podiatric Med. assn., Am. Running and Fitness Assn., Am. Podiatric Sports Med. Assn., Am. Diabetes Assn. Roman Catholic. Home: 39 Harmon Pl Haledon NJ 07508-2320 Office: Berdan Sq Podiatry 87 Berdan Ave # 4A Wayne NJ 07470-3218

KOWALYSHYN, THEODORE JACOB, physician; b. Northampton, Pa., Dec. 12, 1935; s. Stephen and Anna (Kuzyk) K.; m. Mary Ann West, Aug. 19, 1967; children: Alexander West, Andrew Jacob. BS, Lehigh U., 1957; MD, Hahnemann U., 1966. Diplomate Am. Bd. Internal Medicine in Internal Medicine and Hematology. Intern St. Lukes Hosp., Bethlehem, Pa., 1966-67, resident, 1967-70; fellow in hematology U. Cin. Med. Ctr., 1970-72; pvt. practice East Stroudsburg, Pa., 1972—; staff physician Pocono Hosp., East Stroudsburg, Pa., 1972-84, cons. physician, 1985—; designated sr. med. examiner FAA, 1975—; clin. asst. prof. medicine Med. Coll. Pa., Phila., 1980-84; adj. clin. preceptor Sch. Nursing U. Pa., Phila., 1984-85. Contbr. articles to profl. jours. Bd. dirs. Am. Cancer Soc. of Monroe County, Pa., 1975-83, Pocono Hosp., 1978-81, Ea. Pa. Health Care Found., Allentown, Pa., 1977-82. With U.S. Army, 1958-60. Mem. ACP, Am. Soc. Internal Medicine, Pa. Soc. Hematology and Oncology, Alpha Omega Alpha. Ukrainian Orthodox. Home: 714 Sarah St Stroudsburg PA 18360-2122 Office: 214 Washington St East Stroudsburg PA 18301-2821

KOZAK, MICHAEL JOSEPH, clinical psychologist; b. Phila., May 17, 1952; s. Michael Longin and Hannah Elizabeth (Creely) K. AB in Psychology, U. Pa., 1974; MS in Psychology, U. Wis., 1978, PhD in Clin. Psychology, 1982. Instr., psychology intern Rush Presbyn. St. Luke's Hosp., Chgo., 1980-81; asst. prof. psychology U. Brit. Columbia, Vancouver, B.C., Can., 1981-82; rsch. assoc. psychiatry Temple U. Sch. Medicine, Phila., 1982-84, asst. prof. psychiatry, 1984-86; asst. prof. psychiatry Med. Coll. Pa., Phila., 1986-89, assoc. prof. psychiatry, 1989—; editorial cons. Clin. Psychology Review, Cognitive Therapy and Rsch., Jour. Abnormal Psychology, Jour. Behavior Therapy and Exptl. Psychiatry, Jour. Clin. and Exptl. Hypnosis, NSF, Psychosomatic Medicine, VA. Contbr. numerous articles to profl. jours; presenter at numerous sci. meetings. Vol. U. Wis. Crisis Line, Madison, 1978-79; mem. Women Organized Against Rape, Phila., 1990—, OCD Found., 1991—. Grantee NIMH, 1986-88, 1986-89, 89-94, Ciba-Geigy Corp., 1986-88, Kali-Duphar Labs., 1987-89, Smith, Kline, Beecham, 1991-92, others. Mem. Soc. for Psychophysiol. Rsch. (program com. 1985), APA, Assn. for Advancement of Behavior Therapy (program com. 1990), Phila. Behavior Therapy Assn. (bd. dirs. 1986-87, 89-90), Behavior Therapy and Rsch. Soc. Office: Med Coll of Pa Psychiatry 3200 Henry Ave Philadelphia PA 19129-1187

KOZARSKY, BRUCE LYLE, public relations executive, writer; b. Phila., May 11, 1957; s. Karl and Nancy (Rudel) K.; m. Megan Scribner, June 13, 1987; 1 child, Anya Lee. BA, U. Mich., 1979. Legis. corr. to Congresswoman Barbara Mikulski from Md., U.S. Ho. of Reps., Washington, 1979-80, office mgr., legis. coord., 1980-81; assoc. dir. Ohio Pub. Interest Campaign, Dayton, 1982-84, polit. dir., 1984-85; field dir. Coalition Against Double Taxation, Washington, 1985-86; pub. affairs dir. Citizen Action, Washington, 1987-89; account exec. The Kamber Group, Washington, 1989-90, sr. assoc., 1990-91, dir. media rels., 1990—, v.p., 1991—; cons. various polit. campaigns, Dayton, 1983-85, Project 500, Washington, 1986. Regional coord. Howard Metzenbaum for U.S. Senate, Dayton, 1982; campaign mgr. Mark Henry for City Commn., Dayton, 1983; Dayton GOTV coord. Dem. Nat. Com., 1984. Jewish. Office: The Kamber Group 1920 L St NW Ste 700 Washington DC 20036-5004

KOZBERG, DONNA WALTERS, rehabilitation administration executive; b. Milford, Del., Jan. 1, 1952; d. Robert Glyndwr and Gailey Ruth (Bedorf) Walters; m. Ronald Paul Kozberg, June 8, 1974. BA, U. Fla., 1973, M in Rehab. Counseling, 1974; MFA, CUNY, 1979; MBA, Rutgers U., 1986. Cert. rehab. counselor. Rehab. counselor Office Vocat. Rehab., N.Y.C., 1975-81; area dir. Lift, Inc., Staten Island, N.Y., 1981-83; ea. region dir. pub. relations, advt. Lift, Inc., Mountainside, N.J., 1983-85, v.p., 1985—, v.p., chief fin. officer, 1988, exec. v.p., 1991—; co-founder, mng. dir. Expert Strategies, Inc., Mountainside, N.J., 1992—; self-employed writer, editor, 1975—. Contbr. articles to profl. jours.; assoc. editor Parachute mag., 1978; editor-in-chief (newsletter) Counselor Adv, 1980. Pres. Com. on Employment of People with Disabilities; trustee Ctr. for Creative Living; bd. dirs. N.J. Adv. Coun. for Independent Living, adv. panel NYU. Mem. Nat. Rehab. Assn. (Spl. citation 1974, grantee 1973), Nat. Rehab. Adminstrs. Assn., Nat. Rehab. Counselors Assn., Poets and Writers. Home: 714 Woodland Ave Westfield NJ 07090-2339 Office: Lift Inc PO Box 1072 Mountainside NJ 07092-0072

KOZIKOWSKI, STANLEY JOHN, English and literature educator; b. Fall River, Mass.; s. Stanley S. and Mary (Barek) K.; m. Eunice Karin Rider, Aug. 14, 1965; children: Daria Lynn, Todd Michael. BS, U. Mass., Dartmouth, 1965; MA, U. Mass., 1968, PhD, 1971. Asst. prof. Elms Coll., Chicopee, Mass., 1965-75; asst. prof.. Bryant Coll., Smithfield, R.I., 1975-78, faculty dean, 1978-85, assoc. prof., 1981-86, prof., 1985—; program evaluator NEH, Washington, 1991. Contbr. articles to profl. jours. NEH grantee, 1973, 77, 83. Mem. Valley Forge Freedom Found. (Freedoms Found. award 1986). Democrat. Roman Catholic. Home: 21 Doner Cir Franklin MA 02038 Office: Bryant Coll Smithfield RI 02917

KOZLOWSKI, L. DENNIS, manufacturing company executive; b. Irvington, N.J., Nov. 16, 1946; s. Leo Kelly and Agnes (Kozell) K.; BS, Seton Hall U., 1968; MBA, Rivier Coll., 1976. V.p. fin. Grinnell Fire Protection Systems div., Providence, 1976-81; v.p., chief fin. officer Ludlow Corp., subs. Tyco Labs., Needham, Mass., 1981-82, pres., chief exec. officer, Grinnell Corp., 1982—; pres., chief oper. officer Tyco Labs., Inc., 1989—, also bd. dirs.; bd. dirs. Whitman and Howard Cons. Engrs., Atlantic Bank and Trust Co.; chmn., bd. dirs. Better Bus. Bur. of R.I.; bd. regents Seton Hall U. Office: 3 Tyco Park Exeter NH 03833

KRA, ETHAN EMANUEL, actuary; b. Port Chester, N.Y., Mar. 26, 1948; s. Michael Aaron and Bessie (Shragowitz) K.; m. Madeline Rollhaus, Jan. 4, 1976; children: Joseph, Rachel, Joshua. BA summa cum laude, MA, Yale U., 1969, M of Philosophy in Math., 1973, PhD, 1974. Enrolled actuary. Prize teaching fellow Yale U., New Haven, 1972-73; with Prudential Ins. Co., Newark, 1973-77; asst. actuary Prudential Ins. Co. Am., Newark, 1977; with William M. Mercer, Inc. (formerly Mercer-Meidinger-Hansen), N.Y.C., 1977—, prin., 1984-89, mng. dir., 1989—; bd. dirs. Cong Ahawas Achim, West Orange, N.J.; lectr. in field. Author: Infinitary Forcing for Languages with the Q-Quantifier, 1974; contbr. articles to profl. jours. Trustee Young Israel West Orange, N.J., 1987-89. Fellow Woodrow Wilson Found., 1969, NSF, 1969-72. Fellow Soc. Actuaries (pension sect. coun. 1991—), Conf. Cons. Actuaries; mem. Am. Acad. Actuaries, Phi Beta Kappa. Jewish. Office: William M Mercer Inc 1166 Ave Of The Americas New York NY 10036-2708

KRA, PAULINE SKORNICKI, French educator; b. Lodz, Poland, July 30, 1934; came to U.S., 1950, naturalized, 1955; d. Edward and Nathalie Skornicki; m. Leo Dietrich Kra, Mar. 10, 1955; children: David Theodore, Andrew Jason. Student Radcliff Coll., 1951-53; BA, Barnard Coll., 1955; MA, Columbia U., 1963, PhD, 1968; MA, Queens Coll., 1990. Lectr., Queens Coll., City U. N.Y., 1964-65; asst. prof. French, Yeshiva U., N.Y.C., 1968-74, assoc. prof. French, 1974-82, prof., 1982—. Mem. MLA, Am. Assn. Tchrs. French, Am. Soc. 18th Century Studies, Société française d'étude du XIII siècle, Soc. Montesquieu, Assn. for Computers and Humanities, Assn. for Literary and Linguistic Computing, Phi Beta Kappa. Author: Religion in Montesquieu's Lettres persanes, 1970; contbr. articles to profl. jours. Home: 109-14 Ascan Ave Forest Hills NY 11375 Office: 500 W 185 St New York NY 10033

KRAAR, LOUIS, journalist; b. Charlotte, N.C., July 26, 1934; s. Herbert and Ruth (Miller) K. BA, U. N.C., 1956. Staff reporter Wall St. Jour., N.Y.C., 1956-58; Pentagon reporter Wall St. Jour., Washington, 1958-62; Pentagon corr. Time mag., Washington, 1962-63; bur. chief Time mag., New Delhi, India, 1963-65, Bangkok, Thailand, 1965-68; Asia corr. Time mag., Singapore, 1969-74; bd. editors Fortune mag., N.Y.C., 1975—; Asian editor Fortune mag., Hong Kong, 1983-88. Fellow Coun. Fgn. Relations; mem. Overseas Press Club N.Y. Office: Fortune Mag 1271 Ave Of The Americas New York NY 10020-1300

KRAATZ, DAVID CHARLES, podiatrist, consultant; b. Newark, Apr. 25, 1954; s. Charles Joseph and Eva Minerva (Pilla) K.; m. Carolyn Jane Carpenter, June 28, 1986; children: Alessandra, Kara. AAS, Middlesex County Coll., 1976; BS, Monmouth Coll., 1979; D of Podiatric Medicine, Ohio Coll. Podiatric Medicine, 1983. Diplomate Am. Bd. Podiatric Surgery. Resident in podiatric surgery Met. Hosp., Phila., 1983-84; podiatrist Collingswood, N.J., 1984—; staff cons. Cooper River Convalalescent Ctr., Pennsauren, N.J., 1988—; sec. podiatry dept. JFK Hosp., Cherry Hill, N.J., 1986—, residency edn. dir., 1986—; lectr. Gerimed Nursing Staff, Pennsauren, 1988-91, Eldermed Sr. Citizen. Orgn., Stratford, N.J., 1986-91, N.J. Diabetic Assn., Am. Diabetic Assn., Cherry Hill, 1991. Fellow Am. Coll. Foot Surgeons; mem. Am. Podiatric Med. Assn., N.J. Podiatric Med. Assn. (del. N.J. State Assn. 1991). Home: 10 Burgundy Dr Marlton NJ 08053-3809 Office: 570 Haddon Ave Collingswood NJ 08108

KRACH, MITCHELL PETER, financial services executive; b. Westfield, Mass., Nov. 2, 1924; s. John Joseph and Sophie Mary (Swiatlowski) K.; cert. Mass. Extension U., 1944, Harvard U. Grad. Sch. Bus. Admnstrn., 1966; m. Theresa Florence Sanczuk, May 29, 1957; children—Susan, Gregory, Mitchell, Jonathan, Matthew. Auditor, H.F. Lynch Lumber Co., West Springfield, Mass., 1946-51, dir., 1951-79, sec. bd. dirs., 1951-79, mgr. purchasing, 1951-61, central mgr. purchasing, 1961-71, v.p. purchasing, 1971-76, v.p. purchasing and fin., 1976-79, treas. bd. dirs. 1976-79; treas., chmn. bd. dirs. Nat. Res. Corp., Longmeadow, Mass., 1957—; legal arbitrator bldg. materials. Exec. mem., vice-chmn. bd. govs. Shriners Hosp. for Crippled Children, Springfield, 1980. Cert. purchasing mgr.; notary public; registered and bonded real estate broker, Mass. Mem. Nat. Fedn. Ind. Bus. (nat. adv. council 1978), Nat. Assn. Purchasing Mgmt. (dir. nat. affairs 1965, nat. lumber chmn. 1970-80), Am. Soc. Notaries, Purchasing Mgmt. Assn. W. New Eng. (pres. 1963-64), Purchasing Mgmt. Assn. Worcester, Mfrs. Agts. Nat. Assn. Democrat. Roman Catholic. Clubs: Valley Press, 100 of Mass., Am. Turners, Elks (chmn. bd. trustees), Melha Temple, Masons, Shriners, K.T. Contbr. numerous articles to profl. jours. Home: Wood Hill Rd Monson MA 01057 Office: 1105 Main St West Springfield MA 01089-4245

KRACKOW, KENNETH ALAN, orthopaedic surgeon, educator, inventor; b. Balt., Sept. 6, 1944; s. Eugene Howard and Audrey Ruth (Goldstein) K.; m. Susan K. Lynch, June 11, 1966 (div. 1978); children: Sidney E., Andrea G.; m. Annamarie Abato, Apr. 16, 1983. AB in Math. with honors, Johns Hopkins U., 1966; postgrad., Duke U., 1968-69, MD, 1971. Diplomate Am. Bd. Med. Examiners, Am. Bd. Orthopaedic Surgeries. Intern in gen. surgery Johns Hopkins Hosp., Balt., 1971-72, asst. resident in gen. surgery, 1972-73, successively asst. resident, sr. asst. resident, chief resident in orthopaedic surgery, 1973-76, mem. staff in orthopaedic surgery; mem. staff in orthopaedic surgery Good Samaritan Hosp., Balt., 1976—, Children's Hosp., Balt., 1976—; mem. staff Union Meml. Hosp., Balt., 1986—; pvt. practice Drs. Filtzer, Reichmister & Becker, P.A., Balt., 1976-78; instr. orthopaedic surgery Johns Hopkins U., Balt., 1976-78, asst. prof., 1978-84, assoc. prof., 1984-90, prof., 1990—, acting chief div. arthritis surgery dept. orthopaedic surgery, 1986; pres. med. staff Good Samaritan Hosp., Balt., 1985-88, v.p. med. staff, 1984-85, sec. med. staff, 1980-83, med. exec. com., 1980-87, utilization rev. com. orthopaedic sect., 1976-81, ethics com., 1978-79; chmn. tissue com. Balt. County Gen. Hosp., 1977-78, by-laws com., 1977-78; chief divsn. orthopaedic surgery VA Hosp., Balt., 1980-87, cons., 1977—; vis. prof. U. Buffalo, 1983; bd. examiner Am. Bd. Orthopaedic Surgery, Chgo., 1989, 90-91; cons. Johns Hopkins Hosp., 1976-78, Balt. City Hosp., 1976—, Sinai Hosp. Balt., 1985—; lectr., presenter in field. Author: Technique of Total Knee Arthroplasty, 1990, (with others) Total Knee Arthroplasty: A Comprehensive Approach, 1983, Non-Cemented Total Hip Arthroplasty, 1988, Total Joint Replacement, 1991; editor Advances in Orthopaedic Surgery, 1982—; asst. chief editor Jour. Arthroplasty, 1988—; mem. editorial bd. Am. Jour. Knee Surgery, 1988—, Sports Medicine News, 1991—; contbr. articles and abstracts to profl. jours. Active Md. br. Arthritis Found., 1977—, Md. Soc. Rheumatic Diseases, 1977—. Recipient Peer Rev. award Genucom, 1986-88; Instl. grantee Johns Hopkins U., 1980-81; grantee O'Neil Found., 1979-80, Orthopaedic Rsch. and Edn. Found., 1980-81, Howmedica, Inc., 1988-90. Mem. AMA, Am. Orthopaedic Assn., Am. Acad. Orthopaedic Surgery, Am. Knee Soc., Md. Orthopaedic Soc., Md. Soc. Med. Rsch.,, Johns Hopkins Med. Surg. Soc., Acad. Orthopaedic Soc., Orthopaedic Rsch. Soc., Assn. Arthritic Hip and KNee Surgeons, Phi Beta Kappa. Home: 2331 Old Court Rd Apt 503 Baltimore MD 21208 Office: Johns Hopkins U Div Arthritis Surgery 5601 Loch Raven Blvd Ste G-1 Baltimore MD 21239

KRAEMER, JAMES PAUL, pharmacist; b. Putnam, Conn., Aug. 18, 1964; s. Kent Harold and Pauline Mary (Misorski) K.; m. Kathleen Sara Carroll, Jan. 5, 1991. BS in Pharmacy, Northeastern U., 1987; cert. spl. studies in mgmt.-adminstrn., Harvard U., 1990; MBA in Mktg., Bentley Coll., Waltham, Mass., 1992. Registered pharmacist, Mass. Computer installation specialist OSCO Drug div. Am. Stores Co., New England region, 1987-88; pharmacist OSCO Drug div. Am. Stores Co., Lynn, Mass., 1988-92; pharmacy mgr. F & M Distbrs., Chelmsford, Mass., 1992—; case writer Alanticare Med. Ctr., 1991. Mem. Mass. State Pharm. Assn., Boston Computer Soc. Home: 49 Poplar St Danvers MA 01923 Office: F & M Distributors 281 Chelmsford St Chelmsford MA 01824

KRAEMER, PHILIPP, manufacturing company executive, inventor; b. Hahn, Ger., Jan. 17, 1931; s. George Heinrich and Anna Erna K.; student vocat. sch., Darmstadt, Ger.; m. Rosemarie Sandner, June 2, 1956; children: Lynda, Irene, Sandra. Tool and die maker, 1956-61; tool maker Quality Tool & Massey Ferguson, 1961-64; founder Kraemer Tool & Mfg. Co., Ltd., Brampton, Ont., Can., 1964, since pres., gen. mgr. Mem. Pollution Control Assn., Can. Mfg. Assn. Lutheran. Patentee oil-sand separator, others (8); co-inventor of Sound Perfection, Spadafora violine bow-guide. Home: 34 Kendleton Dr, Rexdale, ON Canada M9V 1V4 Office: Devon Rd, Brampton, ON Canada L6T 5A4

KRAFT, WILLIAM FREDERICK, clinical psychologist, educator; b. Pitts., July 8, 1938; s. William F. and Margaret A. (Seman) K.; m. Patricia A. O'Brien, June 17, 1967; children: William P., Jennifer A. BA, Duquesne U., 1960, MA, 1962, PhD, 1965. Trainee Woodville Psychiat. Hosp., Pitts., 1961-63; dir. psychol. svcs. Somerset (Pa.) Psychiat. Hosp., 1965-68, Dixmont Psychiat. Hosp., Glenfield, Pa., 1968-70; pvt. practice, Pitts., 1965—; assoc. prof. Carlow Coll., Pitts., 1965-68, prof., 1969—; instr. Duquesne U., Pitts., 1965-69, adj. prof., 1985—; lectr. to various groups in U.S. and Italy, 1965—; psychologist to religious communities, Pitts., 1967—. Author: The Search for the Holy, 1971, A Psychology of Nothingness, 1974, Normal Modes of Madness, 1978, Sexual Dimensions of the Celibate Life, 1979, Achieving Promises: A Spiritual Guide for the Transitions of Life, 1981, Whole and Holy Sexuality, 1989; also numerous articles. Mem. APA, Pa. Psychol. Assn., Psychologists in Ind. Practice, Psychologists Interested in Religion. Democrat. Roman Catholic. Home: 8072 Brittany Pl Pittsburgh PA 15237-6357 Office: Carlow Coll 3333 5th Ave Pittsburgh PA 15213-3165

KRAFTSON, RAYMOND H., corporate executive; b. Delaware County, Pa., June 20, 1940; s. Harry A. and Elisabeth (Hallstrom) k.; m. Marguerite Knewstub; children: Donald W., Marguerite O., Audrey E., Michele S. BA, U. Pa., 1962; JD, Coll. of William and Mary, 1967. Trial atty. SEC, Washington, 1967-68; counsel Ringe, Peet & Mason, Phila., 1968-70, Monsanto Co., St. Louis, 1970-71; sr. v.p., gen. counsel Life of Pa. Fin. Corp., Phila., 1972-78; sr. staff counsel INA Corp., Phila., 1978-80; v.p., gen. counsel, dir. Safeguard Scientifics, Inc., Wayne, Pa., 1980-90; pres. Ailes Communications Inc., N.Y.C., 1990-91, The J.D. Group Ltd., Villanova, Pa., 1991—; bd. dirs. Hoffman Surgical Equipment Co., Conshohocken, Pa. Mng. editor William and Mary Law Rev., 1966-67. Pres. Gladwyne Montessori Sch., 1986-88; v.p., trustee The Baldwin Sch., Bryn Mawr, 1987—; vestry mem. St. David's Ch., 1988—. Mem. Nat. Assn. Corp. Dirs., Merion Cricket Club (Haverford), The Racquet Club (Phila.). Republican. Episcopalian. Office: The J D Group Ltd 804 The Safeguard Bldg 435 Devon Park Dr Wayne PA 19087

KRAH, JOHN GUEST NEALE, medical association executive; b. Pittsburgh, Dec. 10, 1953; s. Elwood Walter and Luella Carol (Neale) K.; m. Nancy Elizabeth Kerr, Jan. 2, 1981; children: Susan Alexandra, Elizabeth Ann. BA in Econs., Lafayette Coll., 1975; MBA, U. of Pitts., 1981. Exec. asst. Allegheny County Med. Soc., Pitts., 1975-79, asst. exec. dir., 1979-88, exec. dir., 1989—; exec. v.p. Allegheny Physicians Svc. Corp., Pitts., 1979-89, Allegheny MedCare, Pitts., 1984-89; exec. dir. Allegheny County Med. Soc. Found., Pitts., 1989—. Contbr. articles to med. bull. Dir. North Side Civic Devel. Coun., Pitts., 1991—, Consumer Credit Counseling Svc., Pitts., 1991—; sec., treas. Pitts. Soc. Assn. Execs., 1988-89, v.p., 1989-90, pres., 1990-91, dir., 1991-92; bd. dirs. Allegheny County Alliance on Aging. Mem. Am. Soc. Assn. Execs., Am. Assn. Med. Soc. Execs., Pitts Soc. Assn. Execs., Allegheny Club, Univ. Club. Republican. Presbyterian. Office: Allegheny County Med Soc 713 Ridge Ave Pittsburgh PA 15212-6098

KRAJEWSKI, JOEL ALAN, engineering executive; b. Detroit, Jan. 15, 1965; s. Robert Charles and Nancy Lee (Lackland) K. BS, U. Calif., Berkeley, 1987. Mem. tech. staff MITRE Corp., Bedford, Mass., 1987-90, group leader, 1990—. Buddy AIDS Action Com., Boston, 1988—; telephone counselor Fenway Community Health Ctr., Boston, 1991—. Mem. AIAA, Nat. Space Soc., Space Studies Inst., Planetary Soc. Home: 80 Wendell St # 3 Cambridge MA 02138 Office: MITRE Corp 8 Burlington Rd Bedford MA 01730

KRAJEWSKI, RYSZARD NORBERT, publisher; b. Jersey City, June 6, 1955; s. Feliks and Natalie (Bogdanova) K.; m. Liane Kobilak, Feb. 6, 1981; 1 child, Douglas. BE, Stevens Inst. Tech., 1977; MBA, Wharton Sch., 1991. With Sperry Rand, 1977-78, Bell Labs., 1978-81; prin. Tech. Assocs., Lawrenceville, N.J., 1981—. Contbr. articles to jours. Candidate for state senate Dem. Party, 15th Legis. Dist., N.J., 1991. Mem. IEEE, K.C. Democrat. Roman Catholic.

KRAKAUER, BARBARA, musician, educator; b. Bklyn., June 14, 1931; d. Hyman and Jean (Herships) Lieberman; m. William Krakauer, June 26, 1955; children: David, Elisabeth Krakauer Schultz. BA, Sarah Lawrence Coll., 1952; BS in Violin, Juilliard Sch. Music, 1954, MS in Violin, 1955. Tchr. violin and chamber music Turtle Bay Music Sch., N.Y.C., 1975-81, Mannes Coll. Music, N.Y.C., 1981—; pvt. practice N.Y.C., 1970—; tchr. Institut Internat. D'Etudes Musicales, Aix-En-Provence, France, 1977—, Alaria Chamber Ensemble, N.Y.C., 1983—. Recipient Heifetz award Tanglewood Music Ctr., 1953. Mem. AAUP, Am. String Tchrs. Assn. Home and Office: 40 E 83d St New York NY 10028-0843

KRAKOFF, ROBERT LEONARD, publishing executive; b. Pitts., May 4, 1935; s. Frank and Della (Zionts) K.; m. Sandra Gusky, June 22, 1958; children: Roger, Hope, Reed. BS with honors, Pa. State U., 1957; MBA, Harvard U., 1959. Staff v.p. mktg. planning TransWorld Airlines, N.Y.C., 1963-70; v.p., contr. consumer product div. Singer, N.Y.C., 1970-71; staff v.p. strategic planning RCA, N.Y.C., 1971-72; pres. Am. Internat. Travel Svc., Boston, 1972-73, Cahners Travel Group, N.Y.C., 1973-74, Cahners Expn. Group, N.Y.C., 1974-86; exec. v.p., CEO Reed Pub. (U.S.A.) Inc., Newton, Mass., 1986-89, pres., CEO, 1989-91, chmn., CEO, 1991—; mem. bd. dirs. Reed Internat. plc., 1990—; trustee Centennial Cash Mgmt. Trust. With USAR, 1957-63. Office: Reed Pub (U.S.A.) Inc 275 Washington St Newton MA 02158

KRAKOW, AMY GINZIG, advertising executive and consultant; b. Bklyn., Feb. 25, 1950; d. Nathan and Iris (Minkowitz) Ginzig; m. Gary Scott Krakow, Nov. 7, 1976. BA, Bklyn. Coll., 1971, postgrad. in TV prodn., 1974. Copy mgr. U.S. News & World Report, N.Y.C., 1977-80; promotion mgr. Sta. WINS-Radio, N.Y.C., 1980-82; promotion dir. CBS Mags., N.Y.C., 1982-84, The Village Voice, N.Y.C., 1984-85, N.Y. Woman (Am. Express Pub.), N.Y.C., 1987-89; cons. Silverman Collection, Santa Fe, 1985—; sem. leader Radcliffe Pub. workshop, 1986—, Mag. Pubs. Congress, 1989. Producer Festival of Street Entertainers, N.Y.C., 1984—, Albuquerque, 1986, Obies-Off-Broadway Theater Awards, 1984, 85; contbr. articles to consumer and trade mags. including New York, Family Circle, Working Woman, others; creater, producer, artistic dir. Ann. Coney Island Tattoo Festival, 1986—, The Psychedelic Festival, 1988; exec. dir. Radio Creative Mercury Awards, 1991—. Bd. dirs. Sideshows by the Seashore, Coney Island, U.S.A., Bklyn., 1985—, Bond Street Theater Coalition, 1985—, City Lore, N.Y.C., 1987—, Princeton Bio Ctr., 1991—. Recipient Addy award, 1985, BPA award, 1981. Mem. Advt. Women N.Y., Delta Phi Epsilon. Office: 57 Warren St New York NY 10007

KRALL, JOHN MORTON, biostatistician; b. Bellefonte, Pa., July 28, 1938; s. Harry LeVern and Nellie Chase (Morton) K.; m. Karen Dunham Prins, Aug. 19, 1967 (div. 1988); children: Philip, Andrew. BA, Pa. State U., 1960; MS, U. Iowa, 1962, PhD, 1969. Mathematician NIH, Bethesda, Md., 1962-65; NIH fellow U. Iowa, Iowa City, 1966-69; asst. prof. biometrics M.D. Anderson Hosp., U. Tex., Houston, 1969-70; asst. prof., assoc. prof., prof. biostats. W.Va. U. Med. Ctr., Morgantown, 1970-82; sr. biostatistician Am. Coll. Radiology, Phila., 1982—. Contbr. more than 50 articles to med. and stats. jours. Mem. Charter Bd., Morgantown, 1980-82. With USPHS, 1962-64. Mem. Am. Statis. Soc., Soc. for Clin. Trials, Biometric Soc., Phi Beta Kappa, Sigma Xi, Phi Eta Sigma, Phi Kappa Phi. Democrat. Lutheran. Office: Am Coll Radiology 1101 Market St Fl 14 Philadelphia PA 19107-2934

KRAM, SHIRLEY WOHL, federal judge; b. N.Y.C., 1922. Student, Hunter Coll., 1940-41, CUNY, 1940-47; LLB, Bklyn. Law Sch., 1950. Atty. Legal Aid Soc. N.Y., 1951-53, 1962-71; assoc. Simons & Hardy, 1954-55; pvt. practice law, 1955-60; judge Family Ct., N.Y.C., 1971-83, U.S. Dist. Ct. (so. dist.) N.Y., N.Y.C., 1983—. Author: (with Neil A. Frank) The Law of Child Custody, Development of the Substantive Law. Office: US Dist Ct US Courthouse 40 Foley Sq New York NY 10007-1502*

KRAMER, ALLAN FRANKLIN, II, botanical garden official, researcher; b. N.Y.C., Dec. 10, 1950; s. Walter Frederick and Dorothea (Russell-Hurley) K. AB, Coll. of Holy Cross, 1972; MS, Pratt Inst., 1979. Sr. document analyst Aspen Systems Corp., N.Y.C., 1979-81, team leader analyst, 1981-83, mgr. rsch. staff, 1983-86; sr. editor Bus. Guides, Inc. div., sr. rsch. mgr. Lebhar-Friedman, Inc., N.Y.C., 1987-91; conservator Bklyn. Botanic Garden, 1991—. Mem. exec. com. Bklyn. Botanic Garden Aux.; mem. pres.'s coun. Coll. of Holy Cross. Fellow Beta Phi Mu (life); mem. Soc. for Scholarly Pub., Am. Soc. for Info. Sci., Spl. Librs. Assn., New Eng. Soc. in City of Bklyn. (bd. dirs.), Royal Oak Found., Bklyn. Mus., Bklyn. Hist. Soc., Assn. St. George the Martyr (knight), Greek Order of St. Dennis of Zante, Montauk Club, Surf Club ofQueogue, English Speaking Union. Home: 35 Prospect Park W Brooklyn NY 11215-2369 Office: Bklyn Botanic Garden 1000 Washington Ave Brooklyn NY 11225-1099

KRAMER, BARNETT SHELDON, oncologist; b. Balt., July 29, 1948; s. Mervin and Muriel Hannah (Woolf) K.; m. Ruth Solomon, June 25, 1972; 1 child, Jeremy. Student, Johns Hopkins U., 1966-69, MPH, 1991; MD, U. Md., 1973. Intern Washington U., St. Louis, 1973-74, med. resident, 1974-75; fellow Nat. Cancer Inst., Bethesda, Md., 1975-78, sr. investigator, 1986-90, assoc. dir., 1990—; assoc. prof. U. Fla., Gainesville, 1978-83, 1983-86; mem. editorial bd. Physicians Data Query, Bethesda, 1988—, chairperson cancer prevention com., 1992—. Contbr. articles to profl. publs., chpts. to books; assoc. editor Jour. Nat. Cancer Inst., 1988—. With USPHS, 1975-78. Fellow ACP; mem. Am. Soc. Clin. Oncologists, Am. Assn. Cancer Rsch., Alpha Omega Alpha, Delta Omega. Office: Nat Cancer Inst EDCOP 9000 Rockville Pike EPN 300 Gaithersburg MD 20892

KRAMER, DIANA R., human resources executive; b. N.Y.C., Mar. 10, 1949; d. Joseph and Gloria S.; m. Steven Kramer, May 7, 1975. BA, Glassboro (N.J.) State Coll., 1972; MA, New Sch. Social Research, N.Y.C., 1975; PhD, Fordham U., 1979. Tchr. N.Y.C. Bd. Edn., 1972-80; mgr. human resources and tng. AT&T, Basking Ridge, N.J., 1980-87; mgr. human resources, planning and devel. BASF Corp., Parsippany, N.J., 1987-90; dir. human resources and tng. Miles Inc., Ridgefield Park, N.J., 1990—. Mem. APA, ASTD, Am. Psychol. Soc., Exec. Women N.J., N.J. Human Resource Planning Soc., N.Y. Human Resource Planning Soc., N.Y. Assn. Applied Psychology, Met. N.Y. Assn. for Applied Psychology, Orgn. Devel. Network of Greater N.Y., Soc. for Human Resource Mgmt., Soc. for Indsl. and Organizational Psychology. Home: 1 Colonial Way Chatham NJ 07928-2757

KRAMER, FRANKLIN, chemical engineering consultant, educator; b. N.Y.C., Mar. 6, 1923; s. Abraham H. and Anna (Schwartz) K.; m. Barbara Richter, Jan. 28, 1951; children: Nancy K. Goldman, Harold J. BChemE, CCNY, 1944; MChemE, Poly. Inst. of Bklyn., 1947. Registered profl. engr., Mass. Rsch. mgr. Gen. Foods, Hoboken, N.J., 1944-62; res. mgr. Bordens/Cracker Jack Div., Chgo., 1962-65; product/equipment devel. mgr. Kitchens Sara Lee, Deerfield, Ill., 1965-68; v.p. mgmt. La Touraine Foods, Newton, Mass., 1968-73; v.p. Sea Pak div. W.R. Grace & Co., St. Simons Island, Ga., 1973-75; prin. scientist, sr. lab. mgr. Gen. Foods Corp. Rsch., Tarrytown, N.Y., 1975-88; pres. Zuckerman, Kramer Assocs., Great Neck, N.Y., 1989—; adj. prof. Rutgers Univ., New Brunswick, N.J., 1990—. Patentee in field. Fellow Am. Inst. Chem. Engrs., mem. Am. Chem. Soc., Inst. Food Tech., Tau Beta Pi, Sigma Xi. Home: 132 Holbrook Rd Briarcliff Manor NY 10510-1126 Office: Zuckerman Kramer Assocs 111 Great Neck Rd Great Neck NY 11021-5402

KRAMER, HARRY, artist; b. Phila., Mar. 20, 1939; s. Samuel and Clayre (Sumerson) K.; m. Gertrude Murry Cader, Apr. 26, 1969. BFA in Painting, Phila. Coll. Art, 1962; MFA in Painting, Yale U., 1965. prof. Queens Coll., Flushing, N.Y., 1970—; instr. N.Y. Studio Sch., 1968-73, NYU, 1968-69. Artist Brata Gallery, N.Y.C., 1972, 55 Mercer Gallery, N.Y.C., 1973-81, Ted Greenwald Gallery, N.Y.C., 1983, Gruenebaum Gallery, N.Y.C., 1987, Charles Cowles Gallery, N.Y.C., 1991—; exhibitor Met. Mus., N.Y.C., Corcoran Gallery of Art, Washington, Bklyn. Mus., Detroit Inst. of Art, Hudson River Mus., Yonkers, N.Y. Fellow N.Y. State Coun. on Arts, 1973, 77, NEA, 1982.

KRAMER, HARVEY MERRILL, cardiologist; b. Atlantic City, N.J., May 18, 1952; s. Daniel David and Vivian Clarice (Bershaw) K.; m. Suzanne Carter, June 5, 1983. BA, Amherst Coll., 1974; MD, U. Va., 1978. Med. resident N.Y. Hosp.-Cornell Med. Ctr., N.Y.C., 1978-81, cardiovascular fellow, 1981-84; chief med. resident Meml. Sloan Kettering Cancer Ctr., N.Y.C., 1983-84; cardiologist Associated Internists of Danbury (Conn.), 1984—; mem. exec. com. med. staff Danbury Hosp., 1990-91; pres. Med. Ctr. Home Health Care, Danbury, 1986—; med. cons. Ris, Cassi, Darri, PC law firm, Hartford, Conn., 1987—; asst. clin. prof. medicine Yale Sch. of Medicine, New Haven, 1987—. Contbr. articles to profl. jours. Vol. attending physician West Haven (Conn.) VA Med. Ctr., 1989—. Fellow Am. Coll. Cardiology, ACP; mem. Am. Heart Assn. (pres. 1986-88, Spl. Recognition award 1988, Outstanding Community Svc. 1989, v.p. state of Conn. 1992-92, Outstanding state communications vol. award, 1991-92), AMA, Fairfield County Med. Assn., Am. Soc. Internal Medicine. Office: Associated Internists of Danbury 1 Medical Center Dr Danbury CT 06810

KRAMER, JOSEPH, accountant; b. N.Y.C., June 21, 1924; s. Marcus and Henrietta (Marks) K.; m. Sylvia Levine, Nov. 27, 1948 (div. 1992); children: Jeanne K. Simon, Marcia K. Snyder. BBA, CCNY, 1948. CPA, N.Y., Pa., Ohio. Staff acct. Kaiser & Fagin, CPAs, N.Y.C., 1948-51; sr. acct. Kabot Grouthuis & Co. CPAs, N.Y.C., 1951-52; controller Nat. Container Corp., N.Y.C., 1952-57, Owens-Ill. Forest Prodn. Div., Toledo, 1957-63; v.p. fin. Caron Spinning Co., Rochelle, Ill., 1963-66, St. Clair Metal Products Co., Detroit, 1966-67; v.p., treas. Brodart, Inc., Williamsport, Pa., 1967-74; owner Kramer & Hoffmann Assocs. CPAs, Williamsport, 1974—; bd. dirs. Indsl. Properties Corp., Williamsport, 1986—. Apptd. mem. Lycoming County Indsl. Devel. Auth., 1988—; dir. Nat. Conf. of Christians & Jews (Lycoming County chpt.), 1984—; v.p. Wililamsport Symphony Orch., 1988—. Mem. AICPAs, Pa. Inst. CPAs (edn. com. 1980—, exec. com. 1983-84, coun. 1982-84, v.p. 1989-90, pres. North Cen. cbpt.), Williamsport-Lycoming C. of C. (bd. dirs1982-88, exec. com. 1983-88, treas. 1984-86, chmn. 1986, 87). Jewish. Home: 142 Valley Heights Dr Williamsport PA 17701-1925 Office: Kramer & Hoffmand Assocs 1 Exec Plz 330 Pine St Ste 204 Williamsport PA 17701-6244

KRAMER, LAWRENCE ELIOT, musicologist, composer; b. Phila., Aug. 21, 1946; s. Arthur Kramer and Charlotte (Epstein) Ernst; m. Nancy Scott Leonard, Mar. 3, 1973; 1 child, Claire Kramer Leonard. BA, U. Pa., 1968; MPh, Yale U., 1970, PhD, 1972. Prof. U. Pa., Phila., 1972-78, Fordham U., N.Y.C., 1978—. Author: Music and Poetry: The Nineteenth Century and After, 1984, Music as Cultural Practice: 1800-1900, 1990; composer (mus. composition) Break of Day, 1987, Jornada del Muerto, 1988, Thresholds, 1989, Ursound, 1991. Mem. Am. Mus. Soc., Am. Music Ctr., Soc. for Music Theory, Modern Lang. Assn. Am. Office: Fordham U Lincoln Ctr New York NY 12572

KRAMER, MARC B., forensic audiologist; b. N.Y.C., Mar. 25, 1944; s. William C. and Rose G. (Bernstein) K. m. Diane Leslie Haas, Sept. 13, 1970; 1 child, Penny Colette. B.A., Temple U., 1965, M.A., 1967; Ph.D., City U. N.Y., 1972. Pvt. practice audiology; chief dept. audiology Lutheran Med. Ctr., 1969-73; asst. prof. speech scis. Hofstra U., 1972-77; dir. div. audiology, dir. auditory rsch. lab. L.I. (N.Y.) Coll. Hosp., 1973-81; prin. cons. Noise & Hearing Cons., N.Y.C., 1969—; assoc. Forensic Audiology Assocs., N.Y.C., 1978—; cons. in audiology Med. Div. Fire Dept., N.Y.C., 1972—, also hon. dep. chief; cons. in audiology Police dept., City of N.Y., hon. police surgeon; cons. med. dept. Port Authority N.Y./N.J., 1984—, Meml. Sloan Kettering Cancer Ctr., 1985—; adj. asst. prof., dir. hearing & speech svc. N.Y. Hosp. and Cornell U. Med. Coll., N.Y.C., 1982—; adj. assoc. prof. audiology Pace U., N.Y.C., 1981-83; med. cons. and expert witness in forensic audiology, occupational noise exposure and effects of noise on man; noise specialist and citizen mem. of N.Y.C. Environ. Control Board (appointed by Mayor Edward I. Koch), 1988—. Contbr. articles to profl. jours. and books; co-editor: Forensic Audiology, 1982; editor: Hearing Conservation, A Guide to Preventing Hearing Loss, 1983. Trustee The Floating Hosp. Fellow Am. Speech and Hearing Assn. (chmn. com. on hearing conservation and indsl. audiology, spl. course faculty 1982—, chmn. com. on profl. liability and risk mgmt.); mem. Am. Acad. Otolaryngology (instructional course faculty 1979—, Cert. of honor 1989), Internat. Soc. Audiology, Am. Acad. Audiology, Am. Auditory Soc., Acoustical Soc. Am. Jewish. Office: 159 E 69th St New York NY 10021

KRAMER, MARC D., city official; b. Coatesville, Pa., Feb. 1, 1961; s. Robert and Shelly (Stein) K.; m. Jacqueline Kadoch, Aug. 5, 1984; 1 child, Ariel. BS in Journalism, W. Va. U.; MA in Mgmt., Pa. State U., 1991. Feature writer Community Svc. Pub., Coatesville, 1983-84; field rep. Berkheimer Assocs., Exton, Pa., 1984-85; mgr. Schaefer Mgmt. Corp., Downingtown, Pa., 1985-87, Pa. State Tech. Devel. Ctr., Great Valley, 1987-90; exec. dir. and chief operating officer Tech. Coun. of Greater Phila., Wayne, 1990—. Vice chmn. United Way Sml. Bus., Phila., 1990—; bd. dirs. Drexel U. Engrng. Sch., 1991—. Mem. Pa. Pvt. Investors Group (bd. dirs., exec. dir. 1991), Pa. Innovation Network (bd. dirs. 1988-90), Entrepreneurs Forum (bd. dirs. 1988-90). Office: Tech Coun of Greater Phila 435 Devon Park Dr Wayne PA 19087-1935

KRAMER, PAUL R., lawyer; b. Balt., June 6, 1936; s. Phillip and Lee (Labovitz) K.; m. Janet Amitin, Sept. 1, 1957; children: Jayne, Susan, Nancy. BA, Am. U., 1959, JD, 1961. Bar: Md. 1961, D.C. 1962, U.S. Supreme Ct. 1965. Staff atty., dep. dir. Legal Aid Agy., D.C. Fed. Pub. Defender's Office, Washington, 1962-63; asst. U.S. Atty. Dist. Md., 1963-69; dep. U.S. atty. Md., Balt., 1969-83; exec. bd. Balt. Area coun. Boy Scouts Am., 1970-83, adv. counsel to exec. bd., 1983—; instr. U. Md. Sch. Law, 1975-80; assoc. prof. law Villa Julie Coll., 1976-80; assoc. professorial lectr. George Washington U., 1979; instr. Nat. Coll. Dist. Attys., 1979; permanent mem. 4th cir. fed. jud. conf. Mem. ABA, Fed. Bar Assn. (pres. Balt. chpt. 1973-74, nat. dep. sec. 1981-82, nat. sec. 1982-83, nat. cir. v.p. 1973-81, 85-86, chmn. nat. cir. v.p. 1978-80, mem. nat. coun. Fed. Bar Assn. 1973—, faculty Fed. Practice Inst. 1981-86), Md. Bar Assn., Balt. Bar Assn., Nat. Assn. Criminal Trial Attys., Md. Trial Lawyers Assn., Md. Criminal Def. Atty.'s. Assn., U.S. Atty. Alumni Assn., Masons (past master). Republican. Jewish. Home: 6804 Hunt Ct Baltimore MD 21209-1530 Office: 231 St Paul Pl Baltimore MD 21202-2003

KRAMER, RICHARD MARIO, telecommunications executive; b. Venice, Italy, May 19, 1950; came to U.S., 1951; s. Rodolfo and Adelina (Battistuzzi) K.; m. Judy Ann Allis, Dec. 17, 1972; children: Richard Michael, Michael Francis, Stacy Lynn. BS, Marist Coll., 1990. Field svc. technician Control Data Corp., N.Y.C., 1972-74; field svc. engr. IV Digital Equip. Corp., Melville and Tarrytown, N.Y., 1974-80, acting field svc. mgr., 1980-83; sr. support engr. Western Union Telegraph, Mahwah, N.J., 1983-84; mgr. MCI Corp., Ft. Lee, N.J., 1985-86; cons. Ft. Lee, N.J., 1986-88; sr. network control specialist Prudential Relocation Mgmt., White Plains, N.Y., 1989-90, acting network ops. mgr., 1990; prin. RK Assocs., Wappingers Falls, N.Y., 1990—. With USAF, 1968-72. Home and Office: 16 Elizabeth Ter Wappingers Falls NY 12590-3504

KRAMER, WILLIAM EDWARD, healthcare executive; b. N.Y.C., Apr. 27, 1952; s. Kenneth Lee and Blossom (Mover) K.; m. Melissa Cadwallader, Aug. 20, 1977; 1 child, Daniel Cadwallader. AB, Harvard U., 1974; MBA, Stanford U., 1982. Rsch. asst. Kennedy Sch. Govt., Harvard U., Cambridge, Mass., 1974-75; sr. budget analyst Wash. Dept. Social and Health Svcs., Olympia, 1975-79, chief Office Budget and Program Analysis, 1979-80; sr. med. economist Kaiser Permanente Med. Ctr., Oakland, Calif., 1982-85, dir. med. econs., 1985-91; mgr. health plan Kaiser Permanente, Farmington, Conn., 1991—; bd. dirs. Kaiser Found. Health Plan-Health Plan Inst., Oakland, 1991—. Mem. Woodridge Lake Assn., West Hartford, 1991—. Mem. Group Health Assn. Am. Office: Kaiser Permanente 76 Batterson Park Rd Farmington CT 06034

KRAMER-GANZ, KIM ALLISON, safety engineer; b. Manhasset, N.Y., June 18, 1965; d. Kenneth S. and Bonita Sheila (Walton) Kramer; m. David Harvey Ganz, May 27, 1991; 1 child, Alexis Sarah Ganz. BA in Biology, Colgate U., 1987; MS summa cum laude, Hunter Coll., 1991. Assoc. safety profl. Sr. loss control rep. Chubb & Son Inc., Uniondale, N.Y., 1989-90, unit supr., 1990—. Sec. 94-1169th Ave. Corp., Forest Hills, 1990-91. Nat. Inst. Occupational Safety Health fellowship grantee, Washington, 1990-91. Mem. APHA, Soc. Occupational and Environ. Health, Air and Waste Mgmt. Assn., Am. Indsl. Hygiene Assn., Am. Conf. Govtl. and Indsl. Hygientists, Am. Soc. Safety Engrs. Home: 94-11 69th Ave Apt 105 Forest Hills NY 11375 Office: Chubb & Son Inc 333 Earle Ovington Blvd Uniondale NY 11553

KRAMM, DEBORAH LUCILLE, lawyer; b. Milw.; d. Hartzell McDonald and Alice Lucille (Johnson) K.; m. Gary Baiz, June 19, 1988. Student, Trinity Coll., Deerfield, Ill., 1971-73; BS, Bradley U., 1974; JD, New Eng. Sch. of Law, 1977; postgrad., Georgetown U., 1978. Bar: N.Y. 1982, Ill. 1980, Mass. 1978. Trademark atty. U.S. Trademark Office, Washington, 1977-78; assoc. Hume, Clement, Willian, Brinks & Olds, Chgo., 1978-81; atty. Avon Products, Inc., N.Y.C., 1981-84; atty. Tiffany & Co., N.Y.C., 1981-84, v.p., sec., 1984-85; counsel Am. Brands, Inc., Old Greenwich, Conn., 1986—. Bd. dirs. Nat. Found. for Advancement for Arts, 1987-91; chmn. Martha Graham Guild, 1988—; trustee Martha Graham Ctr. for Contemporary Dance, Inc., N.Y.C., 1989—. Curt Tiege scholar, 1973. Mem. U.S. Trademark Assn. (bd. dirs. 1984-87), Cosmetic, Toiletry and Fragrance Assn. (chmn. trademark com. 1984). Office: Am Brands Inc 1700 E Putnam Ave Old Greenwich CT 06870-1300

KRAMVIS, ANDREAS CONSTANTINOS, electronics company executive; b. Nicosia, Cyprus, June 14, 1952; came to U.S. 1984; s. Constantinos Andreas and Electra (Nicolaou) K.; m. Shirley Anne Newcombe, July 16, 1977; children: Christopher, Nicholas, Catherine. BA, MA, Cambridge U., Eng., 1974; MBA, Manchester Bus. Sch., Eng., 1976. Subsidiary dir., gen. mgr., internat. fin. acct. Cadbury-Schweppes PLC, London, 1976-82; subsidiary pres. Combined Technologies Corp., London and Princeton, 1982-87; v.p. mktg. Ademco USA div. of Pittway Corp., Syosset, N.Y., 1987—; mng. dir. Ademco Internat. div. of Pittway Corp., Syosset, N.Y., 1989—; dir. numerous Ademco Subsidiaries. Home: 45 Cornflower Ln East Northport NY 11731-4720 Office: Ademco Mfg 180 Michael Dr Syosset NY 11791-5318

KRANEPOOL, HARRY ANTHONY, science educator; b. Bklyn., July 26, 1941; s. Harry M. and Marie R. (Sorrentino) K. BS, St. Francis Coll., Bklyn., 1962; MSED, Bklyn. Coll., 1972; MA in Edn., CCNY, 1977. Cert. sci., math., biology and chemistry tchr., N.Y., N.J., Pa. Sci. chmn. Bishop Loughlin Meml. High Sch., Bklyn., 1968—. Author: Chemistry, A Modern Approach, 1977-87. Fellow Sci. Assn. Tchrs. N.Y.; mem. AFT-AFL-CIO, N.Y. State Coun. of Ednl. Assns., Nat. Sci. Tchrs. Assn. (dir. Region II 1990—), Stanys (Svc. award 1985). Democrat. Roman Catholic. Home: 31-31 138 St 4D Flushing NY 11354-2625 Office: Lay Faculty Assn Local 1261 13825A 31st Dr Flushing NY 11354-2664

KRANKING, MARGARET GRAHAM, artist; b. Florence, S.C., Dec. 21, 1930; d. Stephen Wayne and Madge Williams (Dawes) Graham; BA summa cum laude (Clendenin fellow), Am. U., 1952; m. James David Kranking, Aug. 23, 1952; children: James Andrew, Ann Marie Kranking Eggleton, David Wayne. Asst. to head publs. Nat. Gallery Art, Washington, 1952-53; profl. artist, 1966—; tchr. art Woman's Club Chevy Chase (Md.), 1976-88; guest instr. Amherst Coll.; 1985; one-woman shows: Spectrum Gallery, Washington, 1974, 76, 78, 79, 83, 85, 87, 90, 92, Philip Morris U.S.A., Richmond, Va., 1982, 83, 86, Florence (S.C.) Mus., 1991; group shows include: Balt. Mus., 1974, 76, Corcoran Gallery Art, Washington, 1952, 72, USIA Traveling Exhibit, C. Am., 1978-79, AARP Traveling Exhibition, 1986; represented in permanent collection U. Va., 1979, Philip Morris U.S.A., 1982, 83, USCG, 1986-92, AT&T, 1986, 88, Freddie Mac, 1987, 88; traveling exhbn. Nat. Watercolor Soc., 1985-86, Watercolor U.S.A., 1987, Am. Watercolor Soc., 1988, Am. Artist mag., 1988, 91, 92, North Light Mag., 1990, Adirondacks Nat. Exhbn. of Am. Watercolor, 1988, 89, Artitude 7th Internat. Art Competition, N.Y., 1989, Shada Gallery, Riyadh, Saudi Arabia, 1991; ofcl. artist USCG. Mem. Spectrum Gallery Washington, So. Watercolor Soc., Artists Equity, Washington Watercolor Assn., M.W. Watercolor Soc., Potomac Valley Watercolorists (pres. 1981-83), Nat. Watercolor Soc, Southwestern Watercolor Soc. Roman Catholic. Home: 3504 Taylor St Bethesda MD 20815-4022

KRANTZ, DAVID S., medical psychology educator, researcher; b. N.Y.C., Feb. 9, 1949; s. Robert B. and Beatrice K.; m. Marsha L. Douma, June 27, 1982; children: Michael Douma, Della. BS, CCNY, 1971; PhD, U. Tex., 1975. Asst. prof. psychology U. So. Calif., L.A., 1975-78; asst. then assoc. prof. Uniformed Svcs. U. of The Health Svcs., Bethesda, Md., 1978-87, prof. med. psychology, 1987—; clin. prof. psychiatry Georgetown U. Sch. Medicine, 1991—. Co-author: Behavior, Health and Environmental Stress, 1982, Introduction to Health Psychology, 1989; assoc. editor: Health Psychology, 1988—; editorial bd.: Psychosomatic Medicine, 1990—; contbr. over 100 articles and chpts to profl. publs. Named one of Outstanding Young Scientists in Am., Sci. Digest, 1984. Fellow APA (Outstanding Contribution to Health Psychology award 1981, Disting. Sci. Early Career award 1982), Acad. Behavioral Medicine Rsch., Am. Psychol. Soc. Office: Uniformed Svcs Univ of the Health Scis/Med Psychology 4301 Jones Bridge Rd Bethesda MD 20814-4799

KRANTZ, JEROME, insurance agent; b. Bklyn., Feb. 18, 1955; s. Jacob and Gertrude (Poretsky) K.; m. Laurie Rae Silverstein, Apr. 9, 1978; children: Michelle, Brian, Michael. BA, Bklyn. Coll., 1976; chartered life underwriter, Am. Coll., Bryn Mawr, Pa., 1984, chartered fin. cons., 1986. Life ins. sales Phoenix Mutual Life, Hartford, Conn., 1978—. Jour. com. Ronald McDonald House, New Hyde Park, N.Y., 1991. Office: Phoenix Mutual Life Ste 600 50 Charles Lindbergh Blvd Uniondale NY 11553-3600

KRANYIK, ELIZABETH ANN, educator; b. Bridgeport, Conn., Nov. 15, 1957; d. Andrew Ladislaus and Marion Irene (Slater) K. BS summa cum laude, Western Conn. State U., 1979; MA, Fairfield U., 1989. Cert. elem. tchr., Conn. Tchr., program coordinator Fairfield (Conn.) Elem. Summer Sch., 1973-85; tchr. St. Maurice Sch., Stamford, Conn., 1980-82, Our Lady of Lourdes Sch., Melbourne, Fla., 1982-85, St. Pius X Sch., Fairfield, 1985-87, Bridgeport Pub. Schs., 1988—; freelance tutor; cons., tchr. Mill River Wetlands Prog., Fairfield, 1985-87, honors tchr., 1991; cons. Ocean Classroom, Bridgeport, Conn., 1989-90, NASA Newest Scholar, 1991, Sound Educators Assn., 1992—. Vol., tour guide H.M.S. Rose Found., Bridgeport, 1985—. Mem. Alliance Francais (Merit award 1979), Nat. Cath. Educators Assn., Sound Educators Assn., Phi Delta Kappa. Roman Catholic. Home: 1155 Huntington Tpke Bridgeport CT 06610-1034 Office: Capt's Cove Seaport PO Box 8517 Bridgeport CT 06605-0998

KRANZ, HARRY, education educator; b. N.Y.C., Dec. 25, 1923; s. Abraham Louis and Anna B. (Zimmerman) K.; m. Shirley L. Lipnick, Dec. 26, 1943; children: Sharlene Joy, Roger Gary. BLitt, Rutgers U., 1944; JD, Am. U., 1962, PhD, 1974. Reporter, editor N.J. Daily Newspapers, Plainfield, Asbury Park, Lakewood, 1944-47; legis. and pub. rels. dir. N.J. State Congress of Indsl. Orgns., Newark, 1947-57; asst. to pres. UAW Internat., Detroit, 1957-59; dep. dir. fgn. trade union tng. program Am. U., Washington, 1959-61; asst. to assoc. dir. Peace Corps., Washington, 1961-62; dir., recruit, selection, tng. pres. study group Nat. Svc. Corps., Washington, 1962-63; program mgr. U.S. Dept. Labor, Washington, 1963-81; adj. prof. Am. U., Washington, 1975—, U. Md., College Park, 1988—; arbitrator, panel chmn. Md. Health Claims Arbitration Office, Balt., 1981—. Author: The Participatory Bureaucracy, 1976 (APSA award 1975), CIO Guidebook on Unemployment Insurance, 1950; contbr. articles to profl. jours. Dem. candidate City Councilman, East Orange, N.J., 1954; candidate Del. to Dem. Nat. Conv., Bethesda, Md., 1988, 92. Mem. ASPA (nat. policy issues com. 1972—), Nat. Assn. Ret. Fed. Employees (pres. Bethesda-Chevy Chase chpt. 258 1987-89), Indsl. Rels. Rsch. Assn. (bd. dirs. D.C. chpt. 1986-88), Am. Arbitration Assn. (arbitrator 1989—), Montgomery County Commn. on Health, Trade Union Retirees Club (nat. cap area co-chmn., legis. com. 1990-92, pres. 1992—), Rutgers Club (pres. 1975). Home: 6527 Elgin Ln Bethesda MD 20817

KRARAS, GUST C., hotel executive; b. Terpsithea, Greece, Mar. 4, 1921; came to U.S., 1938; s. Christ I. and Ypapanti (Contos) K.; m. Stella Dialectos, Apr. 28, 1946; children: Christ, Angel, Ypapanti. Owner-operator Lorraine Hotel & Restaurant, Wildwood, N.J., 1955-73, White Star Motel, Wildwood, 1972—; owner-operator Nantucket Motel, Wildwood, 1973—, White Star Tours, Reading, Pa., 1975—; owner Two Mile Landing, Wildwood, 1982—; owner-operator Beach Terrace Motor Inn, Wildwood, 1985—, Rusty Rudder Restaurant, Wildwood, 1985—, Mansion Heights Assocs., Birdsboro, Pa., 1986—; owner-operator G.C.M., Reading, 1980—, Hopewell Heights, Birdsboro, 1988—. Editor hist. jours., 1954, 70, 75, 89. Pres. St. Constantine Ch., St. Helen Ch., Reading, 1958-59, 77, chpt. 61 Am. Hellenic Ednl. Progressive Assn., Reading, 1957; dist. gov. 5th dist. AHEPA, N.J., Del., 1981-82. With OSS, 1943-45, ETO. Mem. Nat. Tour Assn., Archon Depoutatos of Ecumenical Patriarchate of Constantinople, Masons, Shriners. Democrat. Greek Orthodox. Office: White Star Tours Inc 26 E Lancaster Ave Reading PA 19607-2693

KRASHNA, ROBERT WILLIAM, construction company executive; b. Pitts., Dec. 27, 1956; s. Joseph V. and Charlotte (Morgan) K.; m. Debra Bruss, Apr. 20, 1978 (div. 1990); children: Dustin, Christopher. Cert. Constrn. Mgmt., Orange Coast Coll., Costa Mesa, Calif., 1982. Carpenter Bruss Constrn., Lake Forest, Calif., 1979-81; project mgr. Turelk Inc., Long Beach, Calif., 1981-86, Blair Constrn., Pitts., 1986-87, Giffin Interior and Fixture, Bridgeville, 1987-89; owner, pres. Innertech Constrn., Bridgeville, 1990—. With USMC, 1975-79. Home: 1038 Ryeland Ct Bridgeville PA 15017-1143

KRASNO, RICHARD MICHAEL, academic administrator; b. Chgo., Jan. 20, 1942; s. Louis Richard Krasno and Adeline (Glassman) Kaplan; children: Jeffrey Patrick, Eric Peter. BS, U. Ill., 1965; PhD, Stanford U., 1970; LittD, Coll. St. Rose, 1983; LLD, Sacred Heart U., 1984. Asst. prof. U. Chgo., 1970-73; program advisor Latin Am. and Caribbean, Ford Found., Rio de Janeiro, Brazil, 1974-77, program officer Middle East and Africa, N.Y.C., 1978-80; dep. asst. sec. edn. U.S. Govt., Washington, 1980-81; exec. v.p. Inst. Internat. Edn., N.Y.C., 1981-83, pres., chief exec. officer, 1983—; commr. U.S.-Brazil Fulbright Commn., Rio de Janeiro, 1975-77; mem. U.S. del. U.S.-Mex. Bilateral Commn. on Cultural Cooperation, 1980, 84; commr. U.S. Nat. Commn. for UNESCO, Washington, 1983-85. Contbr. numerous articles on internat. edn. to profl. jours. Chmn. internat. transition team Dept. Edn., Washington, 1979-80; trustee Ralph Bunche Inst. on UN, 1986—; trustee Latin Am. scholarship program Am. Univs., Cambridge, Mass., 1980-82, Ctr. for Applied Linguistics, Washington, 1982-89. Named Nat. Def. Edn. fellow U.S. Govt., 1967-68; Sr. Fulbright lectr., 1973-74. Mem. Coun. on Fgn. Rels. Office: Inst Internat Edn 809 UN Plaza New York NY 10017

KRASNOFF, ABRAHAM, business executive; b. Newark. Grad. magna cum laude, NYU, post grad.; LHD (hon.), Long Island U., 1985. CPA, N.Y. From controller to treas. to v.p. to exec. v.p. Pall Corp., Glen Cove, N.Y., 1951-69, pres., vice chmn., chief exec. officer, 1969-89, chmn., 1989—. Past chmn. exec. council conf. bd.; past chmn. Glen Cove Planning Bd.; trustee, past chmn. bd. dirs. Long Island U.; bd. dirs. North Shore Community Hosp., Neighborhood Assn.; bd. overseers Stern Sch. of Boseners NYU. Recipient Madden award NYU, 1982. Mem. Am. Bus. Conf. (founding). Office: Pall Corp 30 Sea Cliff Ave Glen Cove NY 11542-3634

KRASS, PETER J., journalist, writer; b. Neptune, N.J., Nov. 22, 1956; s. Alvin and Suzanne (Freiwirth) K. BA, NYU, 1978. Editor Tech. News Am. Co., N.Y.C., 1979-84; freelance writer Bklyn., 1985-87; assoc. editor McGraw-Hill Inc., N.Y.C., 1988, mng. editor, 1989; sr. writer Info. Week Mag. CMP Publs. Inc., N.Y.C., 1990—; judge Ouellete & Assocs., Bedford, N.H., 1990-91. Author: Sojourner Truth, 1985; scriptwriter (video) Anti-Beta-Lactamase Inhibitors, 1986 (Cine Golden Eagle 1986). Winner Computer Press award, 1992. Mem. Computer Press Assn. Office: Info Week 360 Park Ave S New York NY 10010

KRATHWOHL, DAVID READING, educator; b. Chgo., May 14, 1921; adopted by Marie (Reimold) K.; m. Helen Jean Abney, Dec. 20, 1943; children: James D. (dec. Nov. 1967), David A., Ruth Anne Krathwohl Cleghorn, Kristin Jeanne. B.S., U. Chgo., 1943, M.S., 1947, Ph.D., 1953. Asst. dir. unit on evaluation Bur. Ednl. Research, Coll. Edn., U. Ill., 1949-55, instr., 1949-53; asst. prof., 1953-55; asso. prof. Mich. State U., 1955-58, prof., 1958-65, research coordinator, 1955-63; chmn. Psychol. Found. Edn., 1960-63; dir. Bur. Ednl. Research, 1963-65; dean Sch. Edn. Syracuse (N.Y.) U., 1965-76; prof. Sch. Edn., Syracuse (N.Y.) U., 1965-91, Hannah Ham-

mond prof. edn., 1982-91, prof. emeritus, 1991—; chmn. bd. trustees Eastern Regional Inst. for Edn., 1966-71; Hannah Hammond prof. emeritus, 1991—. Author: (with others) Taxonomy of Educational Objectives: Cognitive Domain, 1956, Affective Domain, 1964, Social and Behavioral Science Research: A New Framework for Conceptualizing, Implementing and Evaluating Research Studies, 1985, How to Prepare a Research Proposal, 3d edit., 1988, Methods of Educational and Social Science Research: An Integrated Approach, 1992. Served with USAAF, 1943-46. Fellow Center for Advanced Study in Behavioral Scis., 1980-81. Fellow Am. Psychol. Assn. (v.p. ednl. psychology div.); mem. Am. Ednl. Rsch. Assn. (pres.). Home: 9 Thornwood Ln Fayetteville NY 13066-2529 Office: Syracuse U Sch of Education Syracuse NY 13244-2340

KRATZER, GUY LIVINGSTON, surgeon; b. Gratz, Pa., Apr. 24, 1911; s. Clarence U. and Carrie E. (Schwalm) K.; m. Kathryn H. Miller, Jan. 27, 1940; 1 son, Guy Miller. Student, Muhlenberg Coll., 1928-31; M.D., Temple U., 1935; M.S., U. Minn., 1945. Diplomate: Am. Bd. Proctology. Intern Harrisburg Hosp., 1935-36; fellow proctology, surgery Mayo Clinic, 1942-46, fellow surgery, 1949-50; asso. surgeon Pottsville Hosp., 1936-41; asso. proctologist Allentown (Pa.) Hosp., 1946—, mem. tumor clinic, 1955—, chief, dept. proctology, 1958—; mem. cons. staff Sacred Heart Hosp., 1946—, chief dept. colon and rectal surgery, 1974—; clin. asso. prof. surgery Milton S. Hershey Med. Center, Pa. State U., 1972-75, clin. prof., 1975—, cons., 1975—; mem. Pa. Bd. Med. Edn. and Licensure, 1984—. Author: Disease of the Colon and Rectum, 1985; contbr. numerous articles to med. jours. Pres. Lehigh Valley chpt., bd. dirs. Am. Cancer Soc. Recipient Award for Exceptional Svc. and Significant Contbns. Am. Soc. of Colon and Rectal Surgeons, 1982. Mem. Fellow ACS (pres. S.E. Pa. 1965-66), Am. Proctologic Soc., Internat. Coll. Surgeons; mem. Shelter House Soc., Am. Med. Writers Assn., Pa. Proctologic Soc. (past pres.), Pa. Med. Soc., Am. Med. Authors, Lehigh Valley Med. Soc. (past pres.), Allentown C. of C. (gov.), Lions, Union League. Republican. Evangelical. Address: 1447 Hamilton St Allentown PA 18102

KRAUK, ELSIE ALEXANDRIA, educator; b. N.Y.C., Oct. 28, 1919; d. Harry and Katherine Huczko Harasym; B.A., Hunter Coll., 1941; M.A., Tchrs. Coll., Columbia U., 1942; postgrad. Johns Hopkins U., 1949-56, Towson State U., 1949-50, U. Md., 1956-59; m. Pembroke Mitchell Krauk, July 18, 1943; 1 son, James Mitchell. Tchr. phys. edn. Thomas Johnson Elem. Sch., Balt., 1942-43; social caseworker Dept. Public Welfare, Balt., 1948-49; tchr. grade 4 and 5 Guilford Ave. Elem. Sch., Balt., 1949-52, Glenmount Elem. Sch., 1952-77, ret., 1977; tutor, vol. work, 1977—. Tchr. rep. exec. bd. PTA, 1956-58, 63-65, area tchr. representing Balt., 1961-63. Mem. Ret. Public Sch. Tchrs. Assn., Md. Ret. Tchrs. Assn., NEA. Home: 6216 Walther Ave Baltimore MD 21206-2326

KRAUS, NORMA JEAN, industrial relations executive; b. Pitts., Feb. 11, 1931; d. Edward Karl and Alli Alexandra (Hermanson) K. BA, U. Pitts., 1954; postgrad. NYU , 1959-61, Cornell U., 1969-70. Pers. mgr. for several cos., 1957-70; corp. dir. personnel TelePrompter Corp., N.Y.C., 1970-73; exec. asst., speech writer to lt. gov. N.Y. State, Office Lt. Gov., Albany, 1974-79; v.p. human resources, labor relations and stockholder relations Volt Info. Scis., Inc., N.Y.C., 1979—. Co-founder, Manhattan Women's Polit. Caucus, 1971, N.Y. State Women's Polit. Caucus, 1972, vice chair N.Y. State Women's Polit. Caucus, 1978; bd. dirs. Ctr. for Women in Govt., 1977-79. Lt. (s.g.) USNR, 1954-57. Pa. State Senatorial scholar, 1950-54. Mem. Women's Econ. Roundtable, Indsl. Relations Research Assn., Employment Mgmt. Assn., Am. Compensation Assn. Democrat. Avocations: politics, women's rights, breeding Persian cats. Office: Volt Info Scis Inc 101 Park Ave New York NY 10178-0002

KRAUSE, HELEN FOX, physician, otolaryngologist; b. Boston, Mar. 20, 1932; d. Nathan and Frances Lena (Rich) Fox; m. Marvin Krause, Aug. 26, 1956; children: Merrick Eli, Beth Riva Krause-Harper, Kim Debra. BS, U. Maine, 1954; MD, Tuft U., 1958. Diplomate Am. Bd. Otolaryngology. Intern Health Ctr. Hosps. Pitts., 1958-59; resident Children's Hosp., 1959-62; pvt. practice Pitts., 1962—; pres. Am. Acad. of Otolaryngic Allergy, 1984-85, Pa. Acad. of Otolaryngology, 1989-90; Pres. Pitts. Otological Soc., 1983-85; cons. U.S. Pharmacopea, 1991—. Author, editor: Otolaryngic Allergy and Immunology, 1989; lectr., vis. prof. Singapore, Bangkok, Hong Kong (multiple tng. programs 1990); contbr. chpts. to books and articles to profl. jours. Pres. North Hills Jewish Community Ctr., Pitts., 1973-74; cons. North Allegheny Sch. Bd., Pitts., 1977; lectr. North Allegheny Sr. High Sch., Wexford, 1979-84; chmn. Desert Storm Project, North Hills Bus. and Profl. Women, 1991. Rsch. scholar Jackson Meml. Labs., Bar Harbor, Maine, 1954. Fellow Am. Coll. Surgeons, Am. Acad. Otolaryngologic Allergy, Am. Acad. Facial Plastic and Rsch. Surgery; mem. Phi Beta Kappa, Phi Kappa Phi. Office: 9104 Babcock Blvd Ste 4110 Pittsburgh PA 15237-5884

KRAUSE, LAURENCE ALAN, economics educator; b. N.Y.C., June 15, 1956; s. Cyrus and Florence (Langer) K. BA, Queens Coll., 1977; MA, U. Mass., 1985, PhD, 1988. Instr. to teaching asst. U. Mass., Amherst, 1980-85; instr. Coll. of William and Mary, Williamsburg, Va., 1985-86, Franklin and Marshall Coll., Lancaster, Pa., 1986-87; asst. prof. Fordham Coll. at Lincoln Center, N.Y.C., 1987-90; asst. prof. econs. SUNY, Old Westbury, 1990—. Author: Speculation and the Dollar, 1991; contbr. articles to profl. jours., book revs. Recipient Matthew Simon Meml. award, Queens Coll., 1978. Mem. Am. Econ. Assn., Eastern Econ. Assn., Union for Radical Polit. Econs. Office: SUNY Dept Politics Econs & Soc Old Westbury NY 11568

KRAUSE, MARTINE ANNE MARIE, manager production and distribution; b. Port-au-Prince, Haiti, Sept. 25, 1962; d. Yves and Anne Marie (Elie) Riveria; m. Charles Henry Krause, Apr. 28, 1984; 1 child, Charles Henry Jr. BA, St. John's U., 1986, MA, 1992. Communications asst. Mutual of Am., N.Y.C., 1986, asst. communications mgr., 1986-87, mgr. prodn. and distbr., 1987—. Office: Mutual of America 666 5th Ave New York NY 10103-0001

KRAUSS, JANET HENTOFF, English educator, poet; b. Cambridge, Mass., July 17, 1935; d. Simon Irving and Lena (Katzenburg) Hentoff; m. Bert Franklin K., June 16, 1957; children: David, Simon. BA in English and Am. Lit. cum laude, Brandeis U., 1957; MA in Am. Studies, Fairfield U., 1973. Asst. prof. St. Basil Coll., Stamford, Conn., 1973-88; adj. prof. Fairfield (Conn.) U., 1978—. Poetry editor Westport (Conn.) News, 1976-80, Norwalk (Conn.) News, 1981-85, Weston (Conn.) News, 1987-88; co-editor Conn. River Rev., Westport, 1985-86; contbr. essays and poems to mags. and newspapers. Winner poetry contest Yale Art Gallery, 1980, Triton Coll., 1979, 80, 88; nominee Puschcart prize, 1982. Mem. Poets and Writers, Poetry Soc. Am., Nat. Writers Union. Home: 17 Loren Ln Westport CT 06880-1220 Office: Fairfield U English Dept North Benson Rd Fairfield CT 06430

KRAUSS, LAWRENCE MAXWELL, physics, astronomy educator, researcher, author; b. N.Y.C., May 27, 1954; s. Alfred and Geraldine (Title) K.; m. Katherine Anne Kelley, Jan. 19, 1980; 1 child, Lillian Kelley. BSc in Math. and Physics with honours, Carleton U., Ottawa, Ont., Can., 1977; PhD in Physics, MIT, 1982. Jr. fellow Harvard Soc. Fellows, Cambridge, Mass., 1982-85; asst. prof. depts. physics and astronomy Yale U., New Haven, 1985-88, assoc. prof., 1988—; vis. scientist Harvard-Smithsonian Ctr. for Astrophysics, Cambridge, 1986-89; assoc. dept. physics Harvard U., 1987—; mem. panel astronomy and astrophysics survey com. NRC, Washington, 1989-90; Nesbitt lectr. Carleton U., 1988. Author: The Fifth Essence, 1989; editor: Cosmic Strings, 1988; also over 100 articles. Recipient 1st prize Gravity Rsch. Found., 1984, Young Investigator award Pres. U.S.-NSF, 1986. Mem. Am. Phys. Soc., Sigma Xi (com. on lectureships 1988-92, nat. lectr. 1990-92). Office: Yale U Ctr for Theoretical Physics Sloane Lab 217 Prospect St New Haven CT 06512

KRAUSS, MICHAEL IAN, educator, lawyer; b. N.Y.C., Apr. 21, 1951; s. Alfred Emmanuel Krauss and Geraldine (Teitelbaum) Appleton; m. Cynthia Mary Conner, Sept. 18, 1971; children: Rebecca Liane, Joshua Charles. BA cum laude, Carleton U., 1973; LLL, Universite de Sherbrooke, Quebec, Can., 1976; LLM, Yale U., 1978; postgrad., Columbia U., 1982-83. Bar: Que. 1978, Can. 1978, Va. 1990. With Le'Tourneau, Stein & Assocs., Quebec City, 1976-77; asst. prof. U. de Sherbrooke, Quebec, 1978-82; vis. prof. law U. Toronto (Ont.), 1983-84; assoc. prof. U. Sherbrooke, 1984-87; prof. law George Mason U., Arlington, Va., 1987—; commr. Quebec Human Rights Comm., Montreal, 1982-87; dir. Inst. Economique de Montreal, 1985-89. Editor: Affirmative Action: Theory and Consequences, 1989; mem. editorial bd. L'Analyste Mag., 1986-89, Foundations Mag., 1988—; contbr. articles to profl. jours. Named Commonwealth scholar, Brit. Commonwealth Office, Ottawa, 1978; fellow Law and Econs. Inst., Columbia Law Sch., N.Y.C., 1982, fellow Yale U., New Haven, Conn., 1977, Mackenzie-King scholar, Govt. Can., 1977. Mem. ABA, Quebec Bar Assn., Can. Bar Assn., Va. State Bar, Coun. on Competitiveness, Heritage Found. Republican. Jewish. Office: George Mason U Sch Law 3401 Fairfax Dr Arlington VA 22201-4498

KRAUSS, STEVEN JAMES, clothing executive; b. N.Y.C., Mar. 26, 1942; s. William Henry and Frieda (Greenblatt) K. BBA in Acctg., Hofstra U., 1964. Buyer Bloomingdale's, N.Y.C., 1965-69; mng. dir. Polo Fashions, N.Y.C., 1969-71; sales and mdse. exec. Rooster N.W., N.Y.C., 1971-76; v.p. Yves St. Laurant N.W., N.Y.C., 1976-79; pres. Saddle Club, N.Y.C., 1979-82; v.p. Damon Creations, N.Y.C., 1982-85; pres., prin. Prelude Neckwear, N.Y.C., 1985-86; owner The Chef's Connection, New Hope, Pa., 1986; v.p. mdse. and design Manhatten Menswear Group, N.Y.C., 1987—; pres. Steven J. Krauss & Assocs., Point Pleasant, 1990—. Chmn. local bd. Selective Svc. System, N.Y.C., 1972-76. Served with N.Y. Army N.G., 1964-65. Recipient United Cerebral Palsy citation, 1964, Am. Heart Fund citation, 1964, Selective Svc. Bd. medal and citation, 1973. Mem. Men's Neckwear Assn. (mem. com.). Jewish. Avocations: video, politics, building renovation. Home: PO Box 598 Point Pleasant PA 18950-0598

KRAUT, JEFFREY ALAN, health science center administrator; b. N.Y.C., Sept. 10, 1956; m. Ellen Pearl, Nov. 6, 1982; children: Dara, Brandon. BA, SUNY, Stony Brook, 1977; MBA, Baruch Coll., 1980. Adminstr. Montefiore Med. Ct., Bronx, N.Y., 1977-79; v.p. RMR Health Mgmt. Cons., Roslyn, N.Y., 1979-86, SUNY Health Sci. Ctr., Bklyn., 1988—; mgr. KPMG Peat Marwick, Bklyn., 1986-89; adj. lectr. Baruch Coll., N.Y.C., 1984—; bd. dirs. Morningside House Nursing Home Co., Bronx, N.Y., 1989—, N.Y. Regional Transplant Program, N.Y.C., 1989—, N.Y. Ctr. for Liver Transplantation, N.Y.C., 1988—, N.Y. Soc. Health Planning, N.Y.C., 1991—. Mem. Am. Hosp. Assn., Am. Assn. Med. Colls. Office: SUNY Health Sci Ctr 450 Clarkson Ave Brooklyn NY 11203-2098

KRAUT, JOEL ARTHUR, ophthalmologist; b. Jersey City, July 21, 1937; s. Alan and Lillian Betty (Kravitz) K.; m. Cathy Jane Kleven, June 30, 1963; children: David Terence, Amy Melissa. AB cum laude, Princeton U., 1958; MD, Columbia U., 1962. Diplomate Am. Bd. Ophthalmology. Intern Boston U. Med. Ctr., 1962-63; resident in ophthalmology NYU-Bellevue Med. Ctr., 1963-66; chief ophthalmology USAF Hosp., Tachikawa, Japan, 1966-68; pvt. practice specializing in ophthalmology Brookline, Mass., 1968—; clin. assoc., clin. instro. ophthalmology Harvard U. Med. Sch.; clin. instr. ophthalmology Tufts U. Sch. Medicine, 1968-91, clin. assoc. prof. ophthalmology 1977-81, assoc. surgeon ophthalmology 1981-91, surgeon in ophthalmology 1991—; dir. Low Vision Ctr., Mass. Eye & Ear Infirmary, 1968—, med. dir. Rehab. Ctr.; bd. dirs. physiol. optics dept. ophthalmology Tufts-New Eng. Med. Ctr., 1968-73; cons. U.S. 5th Air Force, Japan, 1966-68. Contbr. articles to med. and profl. jours. Chmn. United Way campaign, 1973; bd. dirs. Boston Aid to Blind, 1987; mem. adv. bd. Mass. Commn. for Blind, 1988; mem. adv. bd. Nat. Assn. of Visually Handicapped, 1991—. Cane scholar, 1958, St. John-Princeton scholar, 1962; U. Calif. research fellow, 1960. Fellow ACS; mem. Am. Acad. Ophthalmology (Honor award 1991), New Eng. Ophthal. Soc., Mass. Ophthal. Soc., Soc. Geriatric Ophthalmology, Intraocular Lens Soc., New Eng. Implant Soc. (sec. 1979-81, pres. 1981-83), Mass. Med. Soc., Greater Boston Med. Soc., Mass. Soc. Eye Physicians and Surgeons (exec. bd. 1988—, recorder 1991—), Hazel Hotchkiss Wightman Tennis Club, du Bailliage de la Chaine des Rotissurs, Phi Beta Kappa, Sigma Xi. Office: 16 Webster St Brookline MA 02146-4938

KRAUTHAMMER, CHARLES, columnist, editor; b. N.Y.C., Mar. 13, 1950; s. Shulim and Thea K.; m. Robyn Trethewey; 1 child, Daniel. BA, McGill U., 1970; postgrad., Balliol Coll. Oxford U., 1970-71; MD, Harvard U., 1975. Diplomate Am. Bd. Psychiatry and Neurology. Resident in pyschiatry Mass. Gen. Hosp., Boston, 1975-78; sci. advisor Dept. HHS, Washington, 1978-80; speech writer V.p. Walter Mondale, Washington, 1980-81; sr. editor The New Republic, Washington, 1981-88; essayist Time Mag., 1983—; syndicated columnist The Washington Post, 1984—. Author: Cutting Edges, 1985; contbr. sci. articles to psychiat. jours. Recipient Nat. Mag. award Am. Soc. Mag. Editors, 1984, Pulitzer prize for commentary, 1987, Commonwealth scholarship British Coun., Oxford, 1970-71.

KRAVITZ, JOHN JAY, gastroenterologist; b. Phila., Dec. 23, 1946; s. Alexander and Bertha (Rubin) K.; m. Nancy Freedman, Aug. 14, 1971; children: Fran, Marcy, Adam. BS, Ursinus Coll., 1968; MD, Temple U., 1972. Diplomate Am. Bd. Gastroenterology. Intern Med. Coll. Pa., 1972-73, resident, 1973-75, chief resident, 1974-75; gastroenterologist Larchmont Med. Ctr. II, Mt. Laurel, N.J., 1977—. Bd. dirs. Jewish Nat. Fund. Fellow Am. Coll. Gastroenterology; mem. AMA, Burlington County and Bucks County Med. Soc., Pa. and N.J. Med. Soc., Crohn's and Colitus Found. (med. bd. dirs.). Office: Larchmont Med Ctr II 210 Ark Rd Mount Laurel NJ 08054

KRAVITZ, MARJORIE RUTH, advertising copywriter; b. Chgo., Mar. 26, 1937; d. Nathan W. and Ester (Weiss) Helman; m. Lawrence C. Kravitz, June 9, 1957; children: Alan, Saul, Steven. AB, U. Chgo., 1957; postgrad., SUNY, Albany, Am. U., Washington. Mng. editor Nat. Criminal Justice Reference Svc., 1979-83; pres. Marjorie Kravitz Direct Mail Copy Specialist, Rockville, Md., 1983—. Mem. Direct Mktg. Assn. Washington (steering com. bus.-to-bus. coun. 1987—), Newsletter Assn.

KRAWITZ, RHODA NAYOR, clinical psychologist, psychoanalyst; b. Bayonne, N.J., Feb. 11, 1925; d. George and Lenette Bettina (Feldman) Nayor; m. Herman Everett, Feb. 17, 1952; children: David, Joshua. BA, Cornell U., 1944; MA, The New Sch., 1954; PhD, Adelphi U., 1960; cert. psychoanalysis, N.Y. Freudian Soc., 1984. Cert. clin. psychologist, N.Y. Remedial therapist Lawrence (N.Y.) Pub. Schs., 1954-58; faculty asst. Adelphi U., Garden City, N.Y., 1955-57; psychologist Little Red Sch. House, N.Y.C., 1957-58; pvt. practice psychodiagnostics, 1958-75; asst. clin. psychologist Child Psychiatry Dept. Mt. Sinai Hosp., N.Y.C., 1961-62; rsch. psychologist Child Devel. Ctr., N.Y.C., 1963-64; staff psychologist Lincoln Inst. for Psychotherapy, N.Y.C., 1975-78; pvt. practice N.Y.C., 1975—; instr. clin. psychology dept. psychiatry St. Luke's Hosp. Columbia U., N.Y.C., 1981-86. Mem. Am. Psychol. Assn. (div. of psychoanalysis), N.Y. State Psychol. Assn., N.Y. Soc. Clin. Psychologists. Jewish. Home: 333 E 57th St New York NY 10022 Office: 420 E 64th St New York NY 10021

KRAY, EUGENE JOHN, university dean, consultant; b. Jersey City, June 16, 1935; s. Anthony Walter and Jean (Lykowski) K.; m. Maureen Ellen Newsham, June 18, 1960; children: Kevin Patrick, Lisa Kathleeen Kray Mita. BS, St. Peter's Coll., 1957; MBA, Seton Hall U., 1965; EdD in Higher Edn. Adminstrn., Nova U., 1977. Bookkeeper, corr. Guaranty Trust Co. N.Y., N.Y.C., 1952-57; systems salesman Diebold, Inc., N.Y.C., 1957-58; tchr. Hudson County Youth House, Bayonne, N.J., 1959-60, Dickinson High Sch., Jersey City, 1960-61; chmn. bus. dept. West Milford (N.J.) High Sch., 1961-66; asst. prof. Montclair State Coll., Upper Montclair, N.J., 1966; dir. adult edn. High Point Regional High Sch., Sussex, N.J., 1967-69; dean community edn. Delaware County Community Coll., Media, Pa., 1969-85; dean Univ. Coll., West Chester (Pa.) U., 1985—; cons. to numerous colls., univs. and state systems on experiential learning and mktg., 1974—; mem. adv. bd. on community edn. Pa. Dept. Edn., 1975-80, mem. postsecondary task force on ednl. tech., 1979-81; mem. Title I Consortia Phila. Suburban Colls., 1969-75; chmn. Pa. Community Coll. Coun. Continuing Edn., 1972; ; mem. regional adv. bd. Del. External Degree Program, 1975. Contbr. numerous articles to ednl. and bus. jours. and newspapers. Pres. Apshawa Sch. PTA, 1965; mem. adv. com., vice chmn. cultural com. Delaware County Bicentennial, 1974-76; mem. lifelong learning adv. com. Free Libr. Phila., 1978; mem. edn. task force Chester County Partnership for Econ. Devel.; mem. Chester County Devel. Coun.; bd. dirs. Chester County Partnership for Econ. Devel., 1991, Chester County Internat. Initiative, 1991. Named Person of Yr., Nat. Coun. on Community Svcs. and Continuing Edn., 1983, to Practitioner's Hall of Fame, Nova U., 1991; recipient cert. of merit Chester County Adult Literacy Coalition, 1990. Mem. Assn. for Continuing Higher Edn. (chmn. region IV), Pa. Assn. for Adult and Continuing Edn. (chmn. membership com., Outstanding Adult Educator award 1989), Chester County C. of C. (pres. 1991), Exton Area C. of C. (pres.-elect 1991), Greater West Chester Area C. of C. (econ. devel. com.). Republican. Roman Catholic. Home: 325 Staghorn Way West Chester PA 19383-0001 Office: West Chester U Univ Coll Elsie O Bull Ctr Rm 143 West Chester PA 19383

KRAYBILL, HENRY LAWRENCE, retired physics educator; b. Washington, Apr. 13, 1918; s. Henry Reist and Mary Ruth (Grove) K.; m. Helen Earle Hardy, Sept. 15, 1944; children: April Ruth, Robert Hardy Gorham. SB in Physics, U. Chgo., 1938, PhD in Physics, 1949; MA (hon.), Yale U., 1982. Instr. physics Yale U., New Haven, 1948-51, asst. prof., 1951-57, assoc. prof., 1957-82, prof., 1983-84. Contbr. articles to profl. jours. Treas. West Rock Park Assn., Hamden, Conn., 1977-85. Capt. USAAF, 1940-45, ETO. Office: Yale U Physics Dept New Haven CT 06520

KREADEN, GERALD, real estate company executive; b. Kitchener, Ont., Can., May 30, 1935; s. Sydney and Norma (Gerofsky) K.; m. Pauline Drimer, June 30, 1957 (div. Jan. 1967); children: Lynn, Michael; m. Sheila Lubin, Mar. 17, 1967; children: Lynn, Cheryl, Michael, Andrew, Mitchell, Bryant. Grad. high sch., Montreal, Que., Can. With ops. Reliable Transport Ltd., Montreal, 1952-60, sales rep., 1954-55, sales mgr., 1955-56, terminal mgr., 1956-58; gen. mgr. maintenance Reliable Transport Ltd., Toronto, 1958-60, v.p., 1960-79; v.p. Kreadar Enterprises Inc., Montreal, 1960—; pres., chief exec. officer Geekay Internat., Montreal, 1980—; pres. Kreader Investments, Montreal, 1959—; v.p. Kreadar Enterprises Ltd., Montreal, 1957—; pres., chief exec. officer Gerald Kreaden Investments Ltd., Montreal, 1980—; v.p. Motor Transport Indsl. Rels. Bur., Toronto, 1962-79. Mem. Soc. Automotive Engrs., Maintenance Coun. Am. Trucking Assn. (chmn. S-7 study group 1978-80, chmn. S-4 study group 1981-85, dir. 1985-88, Silver Spark Plug 1989). Office: Geekay Internat, 5500 Fullum St Ste 204, Montreal, PQ Canada H2G 2H3

KREBS, FREDERICK JOHN, executive; b. Youngstown, Ohio, Dec. 18, 1949; s. Norman Frederick and Ruth Caroline (Demmel) K.; m. Cathryn Jane Stanley, Feb. 18, 1978; children: Stephen Frederick, Sarah Elizabeth. BA, Allegheny Coll., 1972; JD, Case Western Reserve U., 1975; postgrad., U. Manchester, England, 1970-71. Bar: Ohio 1975, D.C. 1976, Va. 1979. Asst. gen. counsel U.S. C. of C., Washington, 1975-79; ptnr. Stephens & Krebs, McLean, Va., 1979-84; mgr. dept. labor and human resources policy U.S. C. of C., Washington, 1984-91; exec. dir. Am. Corp. Counsel Assn., Washington, 1991—; mem. steering com. Health Policy Agenda for Am. People, Chgo., 1986-87; resource asst. White House Conf. Small Bus., Washington, 1986. Co-author: Associations and Lobbying Regulations, 1979. Mem. ABA, Am. Soc. Assn. execs., U. Club Washington. Presbyterian. Office: Am Corp Counsel Assn 1225 Connecticut Ave NW # 302 Washington DC 20036

KREBS, JAMES ARTHUR, JR., internist; b. Pitts., Aug. 23, 1948; s. James Arthur and Helen M. (McGrogan) K.; m. Cathy Ann Morrow, Aug. 5, 1988. BS, Pa. State U., 1970; MD, U. Pitts., 1974. Diplomate Am. Bd. Internal Med.; cert. geriatrics ACP, Am. Acad. Family Practice. Intern Mercy Hosp., Pitts., 1974-75; resident St. Francis Gen. Hosp., Pitts., 1975-77; assoc. mem. staff Washington (Pa.) Hosp., 1977-80, active mem. staff, 1981—; co-med. dir. Presbyn. Med. Ctr., Washington, Pa., 1992—. Mem. AMA, Pa. Med. Soc., Allegheny County Med. Soc. Democrat. Roman Catholic. Home: RR 2 Box 275 Washington PA 15301-8914 Office: Internal Med & Geriatrics Southminster Pl 825 S Main St Washington PA 15301-4757

KREBS, LOIS PONNOCK, chief development officer; b. Phila., July 3, 1938; d. Leon and Esther (Rader) Ponnock; divorced; children: Hope, Abbey K. Greenblatt, Wendy. BA, U. Pa., 1959. Pres. Surfside Motel, Inc., Lake George, N.Y., 1960-78; asst. to dir. Jewish Nat. Fund, Phila., 1979; exec. dir. Boys Town Jerusalem Found. Am., Phila., 1979-87; dir. devel. Albert Einstein Health-Care Found., Phila., 1987-89; assoc. v.p. Albert Einstein Health-Care Found., 1989-91, v.p. devel., 1991—. Pres. Har Zion Temple Sisterhood, Penn Valley, Pa., 1974-76; bd. dirs. State Israel Bonds, Women's Div., Phila., 1976—; bd. dirs. Har Zion Temple, 1974-86, trustee, 1986-88; mem. women's leadership bd. Fedn. Jewish Agys. of Greater Phila., 1990—. Named one of Outstanding Young Women of Am., 1970. Mem. Nat. Soc. for Fundraising Execs., Assn. Hosp. Devel., Phi Sigma Sigma (pres. 1958-59). Office: Albert Einstein Healthcare Found Braemer Bldg 5501 Old York Rd Philadelphia PA 19141-3098

KREBS, MARGARET ELOISE, publishing company executive; b. Clearfield, Pa., Apr. 20, 1927; d. Henry Louis and Delia Louise (Beahan) K.; grad. high sch. With Progressive Pub. Co., Inc., Clearfield, 1945—, bus. office mgr., 1956-60, bus. mgr., 1960-63, asst. to pub., 1963-69, asso. pub., 1981—, dir., exec. v.p., 1969-77, pres., 1977—; v.p./sec. Clearfield Broadcasters, Inc., Stas. WCPA-AM and WQYX-FM, 1965—, dir., 1971—. Mem. Pa. Newspaper Women's Assn., Clearfield Bus. and Profl. Women's Club (pres. 1952-53, dist. membership chmn. 1952-53), Sigma Delta Chi. Democrat. Roman Catholic. Club: Lake Glendale Sailing (sec. 1966—). Home: 526 Ogden Ave Clearfield PA 16830-2146 Office: 206 E Locust St Clearfield PA 16830

KREFT, ANTHONY FRANK, III, chemist, researcher; b. Detroit, May 28, 1948; s. Anthony Frank Jr. and Jane Teresa (Miedlar) K.; m. Margaret Mary Doyle, Aug. 25, 1979. BS, U. Mich., 1970; PhM, Columbia U., N.Y.C., 1973, PhD, 1976. Sr. scientist Wyeth Labs., Phila., 1978-83, supr., 1983-88; prin. scientist Wyeth Ayerst Rsch., Princeton, N.J., 1988-91, rsch. fellow, 1991—. Contbr. 50 articles to chemistry jours.; 38 patents in field. Mem. Am. Chem. Soc., Inflammation Rsch. Assn., N.Y. Acad. Scis. Democrat. Roman Catholic. Home: 43 Barley Ct Langhorne PA 19047-8102 Office: Wyeth Ayerst Rsch CN 8000 Princeton NJ 08543

KREFTING, ROBERT J(OHN), publishing company executive; b. Peoria, Ill., Apr. 29, 1944; s. Walter and Rebecca Juliana K.; m. Sally Ann Kingsmill, Aug. 27, 1978; children: Matthew, Nicholas; children by previous marriage: Gordon, Melissa, Sarah. BA magna cum laude with honors in History, Williams Coll., 1966. Subscription sales mgr. Time, Inc., N.Y.C., 1966-71; assoc. pub. Psychology Today, Del Mar, Calif., 1971-74; with CBS Publs., N.Y.C., 1974-83; v.p., group pub. spl. interest mags. CBS Publs., 1977-79, pres., 1979-83; pres. City Home Pub., Houston, 1984-85; exec. v.p. McCall Pub. Co., 1985-87; pres. Park Ave. Pub., N.Y.C., 1987-90, Holly Hill Pub., Katanah, N.Y., 1991—. Mem. Mag. Pubs. Assn., Young Presidents Orgn., Waccabuc Country Club, Sky Club, Phi Beta Kappa. Home: Mt Holly Rd Katonah NY 10536 Office: Holly Hill Pub 227 Mt Holly Rd Katonah NY 10536

KREIFELDT, JOHN GENE, engineering design educator; b. Manistee, Mich., Oct. 7, 1934; s. Chester Edward and Bernadine (Janicki) K.; children: Max, Alexander. BS, UCLA, 1961; MS, MIT, 1964, EE, 1964; PhD, Case Western Res. U., 1969. Prof. Tufts U., Medford, Mass., 1969—. Contbr. articles to profl. jours; inventor/patentee "Reach" toothbrush. Grantee NIH, NASA. Office: Dept Engring Design Tufts Univ Medford MA 02155

KREIGER, BARBARA SUE, writer, educator; b. Derby, Conn., Oct. 25, 1948; d. Samuel and Elaine Natalie (Chausky) Kreiger; m. Alan Lelchuk, Oct. 7, 1979; children: Saul, Daniel. BA, Russell Sage Coll., 1970; MA, Boston Coll., 1973; PhD, Brandeis U., 1978. Sr. lectr. and adj. asst. prof. Dartmouth Coll., Hanover, N.H., 1983—. Author: Living Waters: Myth, History and Politics of the Dead Sea, 1988. Office: Darmouth Coll Hanover NH 03755-1477

KREIGHBAUM, WILLIAM EUGENE, pharmaceutical company information analyst; b. Elkhart, Ind., June 17, 1934; s. Thaddeus William and Lillian Marjorie (Glace) K.; m. M. Carolyn Walsh, June 17, 1961; children: David William, Carol Kreighbaum Hoffman. AB, Wabash Coll., 1956; PhD, Ind. U., 1960. Postdoctoral fellow Ind. U., Bloomington, 1960-61; sr. rsch. scientist Mead Johnson & Co., Evansville, Ind., 1961-68, group leader, 1968-73; prin. rsch. assoc. Bristol-Myers Co., Evansville, 1973-81, sect. mgr., 1981-85; sci. info. analyst Bristol-Myers/Bristol Myers Squibb, Wallingford,

Conn., 1985—; research in field. Contbr. articles to profl. publs. Mem. Am. Chem. Soc., Phi Beta Kappa. Home: 210 Dogwood Ln Meriden CT 06450-2523 Office: Bristol-Myers Squibb Co Dept 809 PO Box 5100 Wallingford CT 06492

KREINBROOK, DENNIS WEHRLE, psychologist, educator; b. Greensburg, Pa., June 20, 1951; s. Theodore and Mildred (Wehrle) K.; children: Aaron, Dustin. BA, W.Va. U., 1974; MEd, Calif. Univ. of Pa., 1977; PhD, U. Pitts., 1981. Lic. psychologist, Pa. Faculty Westmoreland County Community Coll., Youngwood, Pa., 1980—; psychol. trainee Psychol. Assocs., Greensburg, 1980-85; psychologist Ramm Psychol. Svcs., Greensburg, 1985—. Author: The General Psychology Notebook, 1990. Mem. Pa. Psychol. Assn. Home: 1919 Keystone Ave Greensburg PA 15601-5520 Office: Ramm Psychol Svcs 1 Pineview Pl Ste 5 205 Humphrey Rd Greensburg PA 15601-4518

KREITZBERG, CHARLES BARRY, computer company executive; b. N.Y.C., Oct. 14, 1947; s. Irving and Sylvia Clair (Schwartz) K.; m. Valerie Jane Sasserath, June, 1972 (div. Oct. 1980). BA, CCNY, 1969; MS, Rutgers U., 1972; PhD, CUNY, 1978. Lic. psychologist, N.Y., N.J. Sr. systems programmer, corp. planner-assoc. rsch. scientist Ednl. Testing Svc., Princeton, N.J., 1969-78, dir. tech. devel., 1978-82; pres. Cognetics Corp., Princeton, 1982—; adv. bd. Human-Computer Interactive Lab., U. Md., College Park; cons. Citibank/Libr. of Congress, N.Y.C., Washington; postdoctoral fellow Multimodel Therapy Inst., Princeton; presenter various workshops and seminars, 1989—; advisor Hunterdon Regional Sch. Bd., Hunterdon County, N.J. Co-author: The Elements of Fortran Style, 1972, Fortran Programming: A Spiral Approach, 1975; (with N. Carpenter) Computer Fortran, 1984, Computer Basic, 1984; contbr. articles to profl. jours.; author software: Computer SAT, Amnesia, Hyperties. Mem. APA, ASTD (organizational tech. award 1991), Am. Ednl. Rsch. Assn., Software Pubs. Assn. Home: 80 Cranbury Rd Princeton Junction NJ 08550-1235 Office: Cognetics Corp 55 Princeton-Hightstown Rd Princeton Junction NJ 08550

KREITZER, LOIS HELEN, personal investor; b. Pitts., Feb. 2, 1933; d. Franklin and Helen Katherine (Leyda) Maroney; m. William Emil Kreitzer, Nov. 14, 1962. BS, Pa. State U., 1955. Stockbroker Parker Hunter (formerly McKelvy & Co.), Pitts., 1955-62; cons. Pitts., 1962-68, executrix of estates, 1968-82, personal investor, 1975—, shareholder activist, 1970—. Mem. AAUW (life, jrs. sec., v.p., pres. 1960-62), Pa. State U. Alumni Assn. (life), DAR (jrs. treas.-sec., v.p., pres. 1957-60), Colonial Dames 17th Century (charter treas.), Pa. State U. Club Allegheny County (pres. 1963), Coll. Club Pitts. (life, jr. v.p., pres. 1959-60), Soroptomists (life, v.p. Pitts. 1961). Republican. Presbyterian.

KREMPL, ERHARD, mechanics educator, consultant; b. Regensburg, Germany, Mar. 5, 1934; came to U.S., 1964, naturalized, 1983; m. Johanna A. Wunderlich, Dec. 19, 1961 (dec.); children: Christiane C., Ralph D. Dipl. Ing., Technische Hochschule Muenchen, W. Germany, 1956, Dr.Ing., 1962. Instr., research engr. Technische Hochschule Muenchen, 1956-59, wissenschaftl asst., 1959-64; mechanics of materials engr. Gen Electric Co., Schenectady, 1964-68; assoc. prof. Rensselaer Poly Inst., Troy, N.Y., 1968-75, prof. mechanics, dir. Mechanics of Materials Lab., 1975—, head dept. mech. engring., aero. engring. and mechanics, 1987—; vis. scientist Argonne Nat. Lab., Ill., 1974; Richard Merton guest prof. Institut für Statik und Dynamic der Luft und Raumfahrtkonstruktionen, Stuttgart, W.Ger., 1975-76. Author: (with Lai and Rubin) Introduction to Continuum Mechanics, 1974; contbr. numerous articles to profl. jours.; editor: Jour. Engring. Materials and Tech., 1981-84. Rsch. grantee NSF, Office Naval Rsch., NASA, Pressure Vessel Rsch. Com., Dept. Energy; Japanese Soc. Promotion Sci. fellow, 1984; Fulbright-Hayes grantee U. Innsbruck, Austria, 1985. Fellow ASME (chmn. materials div. 1977-78), Am. Acad. Mechanics; mem. ASTM, AAUP, Am. Soc. Engring. Edn., Soc. Engring. Sci. Office: Rensselaer Poly Inst Depts Mech & Aero Engring & Mechanics Troy NY 12180-3590

KRENS, THOMAS, museum administrator; b. N.Y.C., Dec. 26, 1946. BA in Polit. Economy with honors, Williams Coll., 1969; M in Art, SUNY, Albany, 1971, HHD (hon.), 1989; M in Pub. and Pvt. Mgmt., Yale U., 1984. Asst. prof. art Williams Coll., Williamstown, Mass., 1972-80, asst. prof. history art grad. program, 1977-80, adj. prof.; dir. Mus. Art Williams Coll. Mus. Art, Williamstown, Mass., 1980-88; cons. Solomon R. Guggenheim Mus., N.Y.C., 1986—, dir., 1988—; dir. The Peggy Guggenheim Collection, Venice, Italy, 1988—; dir., trustee Solomon R. Guggenheim Found. N.Y.C., 1988—; adv. com. mus. project NEA and Am. Fedn. Arts, Washington; adj. prof. art history Williams Coll., 1988—, dir. artist in residence program, 1976-80; lectr. in field. Author: Jim Dine Prints: 1970-1977, 1977, The Prints of Helen Frankenthaler, 1980, The Drawing of Robert Morris, 1982; exhibitions include Jim Dine Prints, 1970-77, 1976, The Prints of Helen Frankenthaler, 1980, The Drawing of Robert Morris: 1956-82, 1982, Refigured Painting: The German Image, 1960-1988. Honorary Award: Doctor of Humane Letters, SUNY. Mem. Assn. Art Mus. Dirs. (assoc.), Advisory Com. AFA., Yale Univ. Council Com. on the Art Gallery and Brit. Art Center. Office: Solomon R Guggenheim Mus 1071 5th Ave New York NY 10128-0173

KRESH, MICHAEL D., financial planner; b. Queens, N.Y., June 7, 1954; s. Leonard and Lona (Leibowitz) K.; m. Glenda Elaine Coren, May 30, 1977; children: Joshua Aaron, Daniel Scott. BS, SUNY, Cortland, 1977. CLU, Pa., cert. fin. planner, Colo., qualified pension adminstr., Washington. V.p. Intac Actuarial Svcs., Ramsey, N.J., 1980-84; pres. Tectum Fin. Svcs., Hicksville, N.Y., 1984-89; pres., exec. v.p. Snyder Kresh Fin. Svcs., Inc., Medford, N.Y., 1989—; adj. faculty L.I. Univ. and Coll. Fin. Planning, Denver, 1989—; host Money Wise WLIM Radio, Patchogue, N.Y., 1991. Mem. Am. Soc. Pension Actuaries, Inst. Cert. Fin. Planners (v.p. L.I. chpt. 1991—), Internat. Assn. Fin. Planners, Assn. Profl. Fin. Cons. (v.p. 1991—), L.I. Assn. Pension Actuaries (pres. 1991—). Office: Snyder Kresh Fin Svcs Inc 1721 N Ocean Ave Medford NY 11763-2649

KRESLOFF, RICHARD STEPHEN, ophthalmologist; b. Englewood, N.J., May 9, 1944; s. Morris and Sadie (Silver) K.; m. Judith Ina Rosenkranz, Dec. 17, 1966; children: Michael, Lisa, Lauren. BS, Muhlenberg Coll., 1966; MD, U. Pa., Phila., 1970. Diplomate Am. Bd. Ophthalmology. Rotating intern II Abington (Pa.) Meml. Hosp., 1970-71; resident Scheie Eye Inst., Phila., 1975-78; pvt. practice Collingswood, N.J., 1978—. Lt. comdr. USPHS, 1971-73. Fellow Am. Acad. Ophthalmology, Am. Coll. Surgeons. Office: Richard S Kresloff MD 900 Haddon Ave Collingswood NJ 08108

KRESS, ROY ALFRED, psychology educator; b. Elmira, N.Y., Oct. 4, 1916; s. Roy Alfred and Alice Elmira (Whitaker) K.; m. Doris Ethel Parker, Mar. 29, 1940 (dec. July 1969); children: Keith Denton, Lance Whitaker, Gene Gordon; m. Eleanor Murphy Ladd, Dec. 4, 1969. B.S. in Edn., Lock Haven State Coll., 1938; Ed.M., Temple U., 1949, Ph.D., 1956. Tchr. Woods Schs., Langhorne, Pa., 1938-43; tng. supr. VA, Phila., 1946-49; lectr. Temple U., Phila., 1949-55; prof. psychology Temple U., 1963-68, chmn. psychology of reading dept., 1968-70; assoc. dean Temple U. (Grad. Sch.), 1970-73, prof. psychology of reading, 1973-79, prof. emeritus, 1979—; acting dean Temple U. (Coll. Edn.), 1974-75; ednl. dir. Shady Brook Schs., Richardson, Tex., 1955-58; asso. prof. Syracuse (N.Y.) U., 1958-63; vis. lectr. Tex. Women's U., 1956, So. State Coll. Ark., 1957, U. Ark., 1958, State U. N.Y., 1960, U. Colo., 1961, Appalachian State U., 1970-79, U. S.C., 1980, Furman U., 1980; cons. edn. and psychology, U.S., Can., Australia. Author: A Place to Start, 1963, (with Marjorie S. Johnson) Informal Reading Inventories, 1965, (with J. Pikulskie), rev. edit., 1987, (with M.S. Johnson and J. McNeil) The Read System, rev. edit, 1971, American Book Company Reading Program, 1977. Editor: That All May Learn to Read, 1959, (with M.S. Johnson) Corrective Reading in the Elementary Classroom, 1967 (Outstanding Education Book of 1967, Pi Lambda Theta), Proc. Ann. Reading Insts. Temple U., 1963-70; proc. The Reading Teacher, 1967-71; editorial adv. bd.: Reading Research Quar, 1965-70, Jour. Learning Disability, 1968—, The Reading Tchr, 1971-72; adv. bd.: ERIC/CRIER, 1968-71, 73-75. Instl. rep., scoutmaster Circle Ten council, Onondaga Valley council Boy Scouts Am., 1955-63; faculty sponsor Alpha Phi Omega, Syracuse U., 1958-63. Served with USMCR, 1943-46. Recipient Disting. Service award Lock Haven State Coll. Alumni Assn., 1973; Disting. Service award Internat. Reading Assn., 1976; named to Reading Hall of Fame, 1986; Research grantee Phila. Bd. Edn., 1965-68. Mem. Am. Psychol. Assn., Internat. Reading Assn. (mem. bd. 1964-67), Nat. Council Research in English (bd. 1966-69, sec.-treas. 1972-75), Coll. Reading Assn. (bd. dirs. 1971-74, A.B. Herr award for disting. service in reading 1983), Nat. Soc. Study Edn., Am. Edn. Research Assn., Nat. Council Grad. Sch. Deans, Sigma Pi, Phi Delta Kappa, Alpha Phi Omega. Club: Masons. Home: 230 Pennsylvania Ave Kutztown PA 19530-1807

KREUTER, ERIC ANTON, accountant, human resources professional; b. Yonkers, N.Y., Aug. 16, 1959; s. Karl Anton and Bernice (Arby) K.; m. Maria Burke, Nov. 14, 1981 (div.); children: Christopher, Cathleen, Matthew. BSBA, Manhattan Coll., 1981; MA in Psychology, L.I. U., 1990. CPA, N.Y., N.J.; cert. fraud examiner, N.Y.; sr. prof. in human resources. Staff acct. Silver & Navon, CPA's, N.Y.C., 1980-83; staff acct. Borek, Stockel & Marden, CPA's, P.C., Port Chester, N.Y., 1983-86, pers. mgr., 1986-88, dir., shareholder, 1988—; chmn. bd. Levien-Rich Assocs., Inc., Port Chester, 1991—; chmn. acctg. curriculum com. Westchester Community Coll., Valhalla, N.Y., 1991, founder, leader CPA-student mentor program, 1989—. Author: A Bloodless Substitute for War, 1989, The Expression of Aggresion in the Game of War Using Chess, 1991; also articles. Mem. AICPA, N.Y. State Soc. CPA's, N.J. Soc. CPA's, Am. Arbitration Assn. (arbitrator 1991—), Nat. Assn. Accts., Am. Mgmt. Assn., Soc. for Human Resource Mgmt., Am. Compensation Assn., Assn. Cert. Fraud Examiners, U.S. Chess Fedn. Roman Catholic. Office: Borek Stockel & Marden One Gateway Pla Port Chester NY 10573

KREUTZ, AUSTIN THOMAS, clergyman; b. Queensvillage, N.Y., July 11, 1952; s. Austin Edward and Elaine Ann (Macksood) K.; m. Monica Kay Phillips, May 18, 1975; children: Andrew Michel, John Austin. BA, Heidelberg Coll., 1976; MA, Ashland Theol. Sem., 1983; postgrad., Trinity Sem., 1992—. Ordained to ministry Assemblies of God, 1982. Asst. pastor Calvary Temple, Royal Oak, Mich., 1982-83; sr. pastor New Life Assembly of God, Holland, Mich., 1983-88, Peekskill (N.Y.) Assembly of God, 1988-90, Light of the World, Yorktown, 1990—; exec. dir. Caring for the Homeless of Peekskill, 1990—, projects Jan Peek House/Noontime Meal Program. Pres., founder Holland (Mich.) Ministers Fellowship, 1986-88; bd. dirs. Prison Chaplins Saugatuck Dunes Correction, 1985-88. Mem. Peekskill Area Pastors Assn. (v.p. 1989-90). Home: PO Box 322 Buchanan NY 10511

KRIEG, ADRIAN HENRY, international trade, real estate and manufacturing executive; b. St. Gallen, Switzerland, Oct. 23, 1938; came to U.S., 1952, naturalized, 1957; s. Victor J. and Gertrude (Altheer) K. Student U. Mexico at San Miguel de Allende, 1957-58, Elmhurst Coll., 1959-60, CMfgE Soc. Mfg. Engrs. 1977, 82, 87; D Mfg. Sci. Word U., 1990; m. Audrey Ann Jones, Oct. 23, 1968; children: Ivan Victor, Alistair William. Cert. mfg. engr. Sec. Victor J. Kreig Inc., N.Y.C., 1960-62, exec. v.p., 1963; founder Widder Corp. (merged with Victor J. Krieg Inc.), Mamaroneck, N.Y., 1964, pres., chief exec. officer, 1965, chmn., 1977—; pres., chief cons. A. Krieg Cons. and Trading, Inc.; sec., treas., mgr. Mamaroneck Depot Pla. Corp., 1966-76; sec. Rovic Mfg. Co., 1976-78; sec., gen. mgr. Nugget Realty Co. of Conn., Inc., 1977-80; founder Widder Internat., London, 1983—, dir.; apptd. to fin. adv. group Soc. Standards. With USAF, 1960-62, Fed. Republic Germany. Recipient Polit. Adv. grant, Advt. Efficiency award Thomas Pub. Co., 1975, Sci. in Engring. award Soc. Mfg. Engrs., 1976, Nat. Welding and cutting award, 1983, Eli Whitney Entrepreneur of the Yr. Mem. Soc. Mfg. Engrs. (founder chpt. 216, vice-chmn. 1976), Am. Nuclear Soc., Am. Soc. for Metals, Soc. Mfg. Engrs., N.Y. Acad. Sci., Soc. Piping Engrs. and Designers, Am. Welding Soc., Nat. Jewelers and Silversmiths Assn., N.Y. Acad. Scis. Am. Supply and Machine Mfg. Assn., Am. Machine Tool Importers Group, NRA. Lodges: Masons (32 deg.), K.T., Shriners. Contbg. author: American Machinist Reference Book, The Problems with Welding Fumes and How to Solve Them, 1979; contbr. over 100 articles to tech. jours. and books; patentee in field; featured in The Wall St. Jour., The Hartford Courant, The Waterbury Rep., The Swiss Am. Rev. Achievements include designed welding fume elimantors, oxy-fuel pipe cutting and beveling equipment, remote controlled actuator for toxic gases, portable power hacksaws, railroad rail drill, 3 axis hydraulic lay shaft drill, 3 axis hydraulic turbine bore plug drill, BWR reactor control rod crusher, BWR velocity limiter shear, BWR stellite ball punch. Home: 119 Maplevale Dr Woodbridge CT 06525-1146 Office: Krieg Cons & Trading 119 Wayne Vale Dr Woodbridge CT 06125

KRIEG, ARTHUR FREDERICK, pathologist; b. East Orange, N.J., Oct. 23, 1930; s. Edwin Holmes and Helen Burnet (Mertz) K.; m. Monsita Alcaide, June 9, 1956; children—Arthur Mertz, Eric Andrew, Sandra Lee. A.B., Yale U., 1952; M.D., Tufts U., 1956. Diplomate Am. Bd. Pathology. Intern, resident Univ. Hosps., Cleve., 1956-60; instr. pathology Western Res. U. Sch. Medicine, Cleve., 1958-60; resident New Eng. Deaconess Hosp., Boston, 1963-64; asst. prof. pathology SUNY Sch. Medicine, Syracuse, 1964-68; assoc. prof. pathology Pa. State U. Sch. Medicine, Hershey, 1968-71; prof. pathology Pa. State U. Sch. Medicine, 1971—, dir. clin. labs., 1968—; cons. Beckman Instruments, Gen. Diagnostics div. Warner Chilcote, Baker Chem. Corp., DuPont Chem. Corp., Electronucleonics Corp. Author: Clinical Laboratory Computerization, 1970, Clinical Laboratory Communication, 1979, Computer Programming in ANS MUMPS, 1981, How to Make a Computer Work for You, 1985, Computer Programming in Standard MUMPS, 1985; contbr. chpts. to Clinical Diagnosis by Laboratory Methods, 1969, 74, 79, 82, 85, 90; contbr. numerous articles to profl. jours. Served to capt. USAF, 1960-62. Fellow Coll. Am. Pathologists (com. lab computers), Am. Soc. Clin. Pathologists (coun. on clin. chemistry, coun. on med. informatics), Assn. Clin. Scientists, Acad. Clin. Lab. Physicians and Scientists; mem. AMA, Pa. Assn. Clin. Pathologists (sec. com. on regional quality control 1972-73, chmn. 1974-75), Alpha Omega Alpha. Home: 237 Lamp Post Ln Hershey PA 17033-1881 Office: Pa State U Sch Medicine 500 University Dr Hershey PA 17033-2360

KRIEGER, JOSEPH BERNARD, physicist, physics educator; b. Bklyn., July 10, 1937; s. Samuel and Leah (Sussman) K.; m. Rose Meyerson, May 31, 1964; 1 child, Stephen. AB, Columbia Coll., 1959; PhD in Physics, Columbia U., 1965. Asst. prof. physics Poly. Inst. Bklyn., 1965-68, assoc. prof. physics, 1968-72; vis. assoc. prof. physics CUNY, Bklyn., 1971-72, assoc. prof. physics, 1972-73, prof. physics, 1973—, chmn., 1976-80, exec. officer PhD program, 1990—; cons. for govt. industry, Bklyn., 1980—. Contbr. articles to profl. jours. Fellow Am. Phys. Soc.; mem. Sigma Xi. Home: 243 McDonald Ave Brooklyn NY 11218-1449 Office: Bklyn Coll Bedford Ave H Brooklyn NY 11210-3102

KRIEGER, NORA JANE, nursery school director; b. N.Y.C., Apr. 13, 1946; d. Samuel and Lucy Clara (Bogage) Olchak; m. Mark Steven Krieger, Apr. 5, 1970; children: Nicole, Robert. BA, Queens Coll., 1967, MS, 1970. Lic. tchr., N.Y., N.J. Tchr. Community Sch. 6, Bronx, N.Y., 1967-74, UN Sch., Geneva, 1972-73; pers. adminstr. Whitesmiths Ltd., Woodbridge, N.J., 1980-81; tchr. Highland Park (N.J.) Pub. Schs., 1982-87; dir. Pine Grove Coop. Nursery Sch., Piscataway, N.J., 1987—. V.p. Highland Park Bd. Edn., 1979-82; mem., sec. bd. trustees Highland Park Pub. Libr., 1990—; mem. Childcare Task Force of Middlesex County, N.J.; pres. Friends of Highland Park Pub. Libr., 1982-87. Mem. ASCD, LWV (past bd. mem.), Nat. Assn. Edn. Young Children, Assn. Childhood Edn. Internat. Office: Pine Grove Coop Nursery Sch 40 Davidson Rd Piscataway NJ 08854-5604

KRIEGER-OLSEN, JOYCE, nurse; b. Jersey City, Sept. 2, 1950; d. Kenneth John and Sandy (Lipari) Krieger; m. Sept. 19, 1981 (div.); 1 child, Eric. RN, Christ Hosp. Sch. Nursing, 1971; BSN, Jersey City State Coll., 1982, MA in Counseling, 1992. Lic. RN; lic. sch. nurse. Staff nurse, charge nurse christ Hosp., Jersey City, 1971-75, Riverside Gen. Hosp., Secaucus, N.J., 1977-81; staff nurse Palisade Gen. Hosp., North Bergen, N.J., 1981—; sch. nurse, health educator Cliffside Park (N.J.) Sch. Bd. Edn., 1987-92; sch. nurse Ft. Lee Bd. Edn., 1992—. Mem. Bergen CitySch. Nurses Assn., N.J. State Sch. Nurses Assn., Nat. Sch. Nurses Assn., Am. Assn. Counseling and Devel., Sigma Theta Tau, Kappa Eta. Roman Catholic. Office: Ft Lee Bd Edn #2 School Cliffside Park NJ 07010

KRIEGSMAN, EDWARD MICHAEL, lawyer; b. Bridgeport, Conn., Oct. 29, 1965; s. Irving Martin and Marlene Sonya (Kates) K.; m. Meryl Gail Dennis, June 11, 1989; 1 child, Barry Alan. BS in Biology, MIT, 1986; JD, U. Pa., 1989. Bar: Pa. 1989, U.S. Patent and Trademark Office 1989, Mass. 1990, U.S. Ct. Appeals (Fed. cir.) 1990. Assoc. Finnegan, Henderson, Farabow, et al, Washington, 1989-90; ptnr. Kriegsman & Kriegsman, Framingham, Mass., 1990—. Mem. ABA, Am. Intellectual Property Law Assn., Mass. Bar Assn., Fed. Cir. Bar Assn., Boston Patent Law Assn., South Middlesex Bar Assn. Jewish. Home: 507 Windsor Dr Framingham MA 01701-3065 Office: Kriegsman & Kriegsman 883 Edgell Rd Framingham MA 01701-3973

KRIENKE, KENDRA CLIVER, art dealer, artist; b. Plainfield, N.J.; d. Edwin Kendall Cliver and Estelle (Blaine) Hufnagel; m. Douglas Elliot Krienke (div. 1991); m. Allan Daniel, 1992. BA, Drew U., 1969. Owner, portrait painter, frame designer, art dealer Whistler's Daughter Art Gallery, Basking Ridge, N.J., 1974-84; owner, frame designer, art dealer Whistler Gallery, Basking Ridge, 1985-90; dealer in original vintage art by illustrators for children Illustrators for Children and Fantasy, N.Y.C., 1989—. Contbg. author: American Illustrator Art, 1991; prepared 10 exhbns. and catalogues, 1978-84; curator Childhood Enchantments—British and American Illustration for Children, Mus. Cartoon Art, 1989. Mem. Soc. Illustrators. Address: 230 Central Park W New York NY 10024

KRIER, JEANNE DWYER, public relations executive; b. Chgo., Mar. 23, 1944; d. Edmund James and Marjorie (Muluihill) Dwyer; m. William John Krier, June 13, 1965; children: Sarah Caitlin, Michael. BA in Communication, Ind. U., 1967, MA in Theater, 1972. Promotion dir. U. Notre Dame (Ind.) Press, 1981-84; mng. dir. Barbara Hendra Assoc., N.Y.C., 1984-85; pub. rels. dir. Scholastic Inc., N.Y.C., 1985-91; bd. trustees M. R. Robinson Fund, N.Y.C., 1988-91. Mem. Nat. Adv. Com., Commn. Bicentennial U.S. Constitution, Washington, 1988-91. Home: 30 Christopher St Apt 3H New York NY 10014-3509

KRIESBERG, IRVING, painter; b. Chgo., Mar. 13, 1919; s. Max and Bessie (Turner) K.; m. Ruth Miller, Apr. 5, 1921 (div. 1973); children: Hadea, Matthias; m. Barbara Nimri Aziz, Dec. 2, 1974. BFA, Sch. of Art Inst. Chgo., 1941; MA, NYU, 1972. Tchr. Yale U. Grad. Sch., 1962-71; dir. state-wide honors studio program SUNY, 1972-77; tchr. painting Columbia U. Grad. Sch., 1977-79; tchr. painting and ceramics La. State U. Grad. Sch., 1980; Beaumont prof. painting Washington U., St. Louis, 1982; instr. terracotta, vis. artist Skidmore Coll., 1989; vis. artist painting Vt. Studio Sch., 1989; conductor lectrs. and workshops throughout the U.S. and India. Author: Looking at Pictures, 1955, Art, The Visual Experience, 1965, Working with Color, 1987; one-man shows at Guggenheim Mus., 1972, Fairweather-Hardin, Chgo., 1979, Dintenfass Gallery, N.Y.C., 1980-82, Everson Mus., Syracuse, N.Y., 1980, Rose Mus., Brandeis, 1980, Washington U. Art Mus., St. Louis, 1982, Graham Modern Gallery, N.Y.C., 1985, Montclair (N.J.) Art Mus., 1986; represented in permanent collections at Balt. Mus. Art, Cin. Mus. Art, Mus. Modern Art, N.Y.C., Whitney Mus., N.Y.C., Corcoran Gallery, Washington, Rose Mus., Brandeis, Nat. Gallery Am. Art, Washington. Recipient awards Ford Found., 1965, Fulbright, 1965-66, N.Y. State, 1974, 78, 91, Nat. Endowment Arts, 1984. Home: 160 6th Ave New York NY 10013-1502

KRIESBERG, LOUIS, sociologist, educator; b. Chgo., July 30, 1926; s. Max and Bessie (Turner) K.; m. Lois Ablin, Aug. 23, 1959; children: Daniel A., Joseph A. PhB, U. Chgo., 1947, MA, 1950, PhD, 1953. Instr. sociology sch. gen. studies Columbia U., N.Y.C., 1953-56; Fulbright rsch. scholar U. Cologne, Germany, 1956-57; sr. fellow in law and behavior scis. U. Chgo., 1957-58, rsch. assoc. dept. sociology, 1958-62; prof. dept. sociology Syracuse (N.Y.) U., 1967—, dir. program on analysis and resolution conflicts, 1985—. Author: Mothers in Poverty, 1970, Social Inequality, 1979, Social Conflicts, 1982, Internat. Conflict Resolution, 1992; editor: Research in Social Movements, Conflicts and Change, Vols. 1-14, 1978-92, Intractable Conflicts and Their Transformation, 1989, Timing the De-Escalation of International Conflicts, 1991. Active Syracuse Area Middle East Dialogue Group; commr. Human Rights Commn. Syracuse and Onondaga County. Grantee U.S. Inst. Peace, MacArthur Found., Hewlett Found. Fellow Am. Sociol. Assn. (chair peace and war sect. 1990-91), Internat. Peace Rsch. Assn. (co-chair internat. conflict 1989—), Internat. Sociol. Assn. (exec. com. 1982-86), Soc. for Study Social Problems (pres. 1983-84, Lee Founders award 1990), Eastern Sociol. Soc. (exec. com. 1977-81). Jewish. Home: 247 Kensington Pl Syracuse NY 13210-3307 Office: Analysis Resolution Conflict Syracuse U 712 Ostrom Ave Syracuse NY 13244-0001

KRIGSMAN, NAOMI, psychologist, consultant, photographer; b. Haifa, Israel; came to U.S., 1953, naturalized, 1961; d. Bezalel and Regina (Yacobi) Goussinsky; m. Ruben Krigsman; children—Michael W., Richard G., Jonathan H. MS, CCNY; PhD, Hofstra U.. Lic. psychologist, N.Y. State. Psychologist Mental Retardation Clinic, Flower-Fifth Avenue Hosp., N.Y.C., Children's Ctr., N.Y.C. Dept. Welfare, Rehab. Clinic, St. Barnabas Hosp., Newark, United Cerebral Palsy Ctr., Roosevelt, N.Y., Burke Rehab. Ctr., White Plains, N.Y., New Rochelle City Sch. Dist., N.Y.; v.p. Devel. Research Assocs. Inc.; cons. on employment selection, career devel., employee relocation, quality circles, U.S. and Israel; feature writer N.Y. Womensweek, 1978-79. Co-author tng. materials for quality circles; also author articles; exhibited in 2-person photography shows, 1990—. Fellow N.Y. State Mental Health Dept., 1958-59. Mem. Am. Psychol. Assn., Westchester County Psychol. Assn. (chmn. profl. edn. com. sch. psychology div. 1976-78, founder, pres. div. indsl./orgnl. psychology 1988-90, bd. dirs 1990), Westchester Photographic Soc. Home: 13 Dupont Ave White Plains NY 10605-3537

KRIKORIAN, ABRAHAM DER, biochemistry and cell biology educator; b. Worcester, Mass., May 5, 1937. PhD, Cornell U., 1965. Rsch. assoc. Lab. for Cell Physiology, Growth and Devel. Cornell U., Ithaca, N.Y., 1965, asst. prof. div. biol. scis., 1965-66, assoc. prof., 1972-73; asst. prof. dept. biol. scis. SUNY, Stony Brook, 1966-71, assoc. prof. dept. biology, 1971-81, assoc. prof. dept. biochemistry, 1981-88, prof. dept. biochemistry and cell biology, 1988—; mem. editorial bd. Indian Acad. Scis., 1985-91; vis. scientist div. internat. programs U. Philippines, Los Banos, 1979; guest biologist dept. biology Brookhaven nat. Lab., Upton, N.Y., 1968—; past mem. sci. adv. bd. United AgriSeeds, Inc., Champaign, Ill.; mem. Biotech Coun. Sci. Advisors, Brazil; mem. Internat. Adv. Bd. for Agricultural Biotech. and Chemistry, Kathmandu, Nepal. Contbr. numerous articles to profl. publs., including AIAA Bull., Annals of Botany, In Vitro, Am. Jour. Botany, others; mem. editorial bd., contbr. articles to Am. Soc. Gravitational and Space Biology Bull., 1987—; mem. editorial bd. Jour. Ethnopharmacology, 1979—, Phytomorphology, 1991—. Fellow AAAS; mem. Internat. Plant Growth Substances Assn., Am. Soc. Plant Physiolists, Bot. Soc. Am., Am. Soc. Pharmacognosy, Scandinavian Soc. Plant Physiology, Internat. Soc. Plant Morphologists, Soc. Econ. Botany, Internat. Palm Soc., History of Sci. Soc., Internat. Assn. Rsch. of Plantains and Bananas, Soc. for Devel. Biology, Internat. Assn. Plant Tissue Culture, Plant Growth Regulator Soc. Am., Tissue Culture Assn., Sigma Xi. Office: SUNY Dept Biochem & Cell Biology Stony Brook NY 11794-5215

KRIM, ARTHUR B., motion picture company executive, lawyer; b. N.Y.C., Apr. 4, 1910; s. Morris and Rose (Ocko) K.; m. Mathilde Galland, Dec. 7, 1958; 1 child, Daphna. B.A., Columbia U., N.Y.C., 1930, J.D., 1932, LL.D. (hon.), 1982. Bar: N.Y. 1933. With Phillips, Nizer, Benjamin, Krim & Ballon, N.Y.C., 1932—, sr. ptnr., 1935-78, of counsel, 1978—; pres. Eagle Lion Films, N.Y.C., 1946-49; chmn. United Artists Corp., N.Y.C., 1951-78; chmn. Orion Pictures Corp., N.Y.C., from 1978, named founder chmn., chmn. exec. com., 1991; dir. Occidental Petroleum Corp., Los Angeles, Cities Service Corp., Tulsa, Iowa Beef Corp., Iowa City. Editor in chief Columbia Law Rev., 1931-32. Spl. cons. to Pres. U.S., 1968-69; mem. Pres.'s Gen. Adv. Com. Arms Control, 1977-80; chmn. Democratic Nat. Fin. Com., 1966-68, Dem. Adv. Council Elected Ofcls., 1973-76; bd. dirs. Weizmann Inst. Sci., 1948—, UN Assn., 1961—, Lyndon Baines Johnson Found., 1969—, John F. Kennedy Library Found., 1964—, Arms Control Assn., 1985—; chmn. bd. trustee Columbia U., 1977-82, chmn. emeritus, 1982—. Served to lt. col. U.S. Army, 1942-45. Decorated Cavaliere Ufficiale Della award Republic of Italy, Chevalier dans l'Ordre Nat. de la legion d'Honneur (France); recipient Jean Hersholt Humanitarian award Acad. Motion Picture Arts and Scis., 1975. Office: Orion Pictures Corp 1325 Ave Of The Americas New York NY 10019-6011 also: Orion Pictures Corp 1888 Century Park E Los Angeles CA 90067*

KRIMS, LESLIE ROBERT, photographer, art educator; b. N.Y.C., Aug. 16, 1942; s. Leo and Sally (Leibowitz) K.; m. Patricia Louise O'Brien, Dec. 28, 1985; 1 child, Lauren. BFA, Cooper Union, 1964; MFA, Pratt Inst., 1967. Instr. Rochester (N.Y.) Inst. Tech., 1967-69; asst. prof. Buffalo State Coll., 1969-75, assoc. prof., 1975-79, prof., 1980—. Author: (books of photographics) Fictcryptokrimsographs, 1975, The Incredible Case of the Stack O'Wheats Murders, 1972; (original print portfolio) Idiosyncratic Pictures, 1980; (32 offset prints) Les Krims: Kodalith Images, 1968-75. NEA grantee, 1971, 72, 76. Mem. Nat. Pumpkin Fedn. Office: Buffalo State Coll 1300 Elmwood Ave Buffalo NY 14222-1095

KRIMS, MARVIN BENNETT, psychiatrist; b. Jan. 23, 1928. BS in Biochemistry, Tufts Coll., 1947; MD cum laude, Boston U., 1951. Diplomate Am. Bd. Psychiatry and Neurology, Am. Bd. of Psychiatry and Neurology in Child Psychiatry. Intern Boston City Hosp., 1951-52; resident Boston State Hosp., 1952-53, 55; staff psychiatrist R.I. div. of Alcoholism, 1955-58, Children's Hosp. Med. Ctr., 1957-67; supr. psychotheraphy study unit Mass. Mental Health Ctr., 1968-69; assoc. clin. prof. psychiatry Tufts Med. Sch., 1975—; psychiat. cons. Boston Com. on Alcoholism, 1956-58, Youth Svc. Bd., 1957-58, Jewish Family and Children's Svc., 1957-89, Walker Home for Children, 1965-66, Children's Mission to Children, 1965-66; asst. in psychiatry Harvard Med. Sch., 1957-67; assoc. vis. physician child psychiatry dept. Boston City Hosp., 1967-72; asst. clin. prof. Boston U. Sch. of Medicine, 1967-75, chief investigator rsch. project, 1980—, mem. faculty psychoanalytic lit. criticism Boston Psychoanalytic Soc., 1970—; cons. Mass. Dept. Pub. Health, 1974-75. Contbr. articles to profl. publs. With USN, 1953-55. Fellow Am. Psychiat. Assn.; mem. Boston Psychoanalytic Soc., New Eng. Psychiat. Assn. (chmn. childhood and adolescence com. 1966-71), Mass. Med. Soc., New Eng. Coun. Child Psychiatry (pres. 1973-75, chmn. program com. 1973-74, chmn. continuing edn. program 1974-83, chair psychoanalytic lit. criticism colloquium 1988—). Home: 184 Ward St Newton MA 02159-1328

KRIPPENDORFF, KLAUS HERBERT, communication educator, cybernetician, industrial designer; b. Frankfurt, Mar. 21, 1932; came to U.S., 1961; s. Herbert R. A. and Charlotte (Barthel) K.; children: Kaihan, Heike. Grad. in engring., Hanover Engring. Sch., 1952-54; diploma in design, ULM Sch. Design, 1956-60; PhD, U. Ill., 1962-67; MA hon. , U. Pa., 1974. Indsl. cons. Jarosch Engring., Düsseldorf, Germany, 1954-56; rsch. assoc. Inst. for Visual Perception, Germany, 1960-61; rsch. asst. Inst. for Communication Rsch., Urbana, Ill., 1963-64; prof. communication U. Pa., Phila., 1964—; cons. PBS, Washington, 1974, AT&T, N.Y., 1976-80, Philips, Eindhoven, Holland, 1987-89, Fitch-Richardson Smith, Worthington, Ohio, 1986-90. Author: Content Analysis, 1980, Information Theory, 1986; author, editor: Product Semantics, 1989, Theory and Analysis of Message Content, 1969, Control and Communication in Society, 1979. Intellectural contbr. Indsl. Design Soc. Am., Washington, 1984. Recipient Travel award, Fulbright, 1961. Fellow Netherlands Inst. Advanced Studies, AAAS, Internat. Communication Assn. former pres. ; mem. Am. Soc. for Cybernetics, Internat. Fed. Communication Assns. founding pres. . Office: University of Pa 3620 Walnut St Philadelphia PA 19104-6220

KRIS, EDWARD JOSEPH, chemist; b. Buffalo, Nov. 2, 1923; s. Walter and Frances K.; m. Irene B. Hoyczyk, June 1, 1946; children: Michael, Mark, Margaret. BA in Chemistry, Geology, Biology, U. Buffalo, 1945. Chemist Lucidol div. Wallace and Tiernan, Buffalo, 1945-52, Olin Mathieson, 1952-56, Roswell Park Meml. Inst., Buffalo, 1956-62, U.S. FDA, Buffalo, 1962-67; tech. dir. Buffalo Testing Labs., Buffalo, 1967—. Mem. ASTM, Am. Chem. Soc., Soc. Plastics Engrs., Profl. Businessmen's Assn. Republican. Roman Catholic. Office: BTL 902 Kenmore Ave Buffalo NY 14216-1495

KRISER, ANKA ANGELOWA, manufacturing and distributing company executive; b. Sofia, Bulgaria, Aug. 19, 1931; came to U.S., 1951; d. Angel Georgieff and Rayna (Tomoff) Georgiewa; m. David B. Kriser (div. 1978); m. Clarence Y. Palitz Jr., 1989. BA, Art Acad., Munich, 1950. Cert. interior design. V.p. Revlon, N.Y.C., 1955-61; pres. Decart Design, N.Y.C., Lancaster, Pa., 1978-83, also chmn., 1983-89; pres. The Baroness Collection, N.Y.C., Lancaster, Pa., 1983—; art dealer N.Y.C., 1989—. Contbr. articles to profl. jours. Bd. dirs. N.Y.C. Opera Guild, 1965-78, Beth Israel Hosp. Guild, N.Y.C., N.Y. Hosp. Nursing Com., 1975-78, 910 Fifth Ave bldg., N.Y.C., 1984—. Home and Office: 880 5th Ave New York NY 10021-4951

KRISHER, LAWRENCE CHARLES, investment company executive; b. Rochester, N.Y., Aug. 21, 1933; s. Lawrence Charles and Martha Elizabeth (Gilmore) K. AB, Syracuse U., 1955; AM, Harvard U., 1957, PhD, 1959. Asst. prof. Columbia U., N.Y.C., 1961-63; asst. prof. U. Md., College Park, 1963-66, part-time prof. phys. chemistry, 1975—; owner, investment mgr. The Stockworks, Riverdale, Md., 1977—; bd. dirs. Info. Security, Silver Spring, Md. Contbr. articles to profl. jours., also to Ency. of Physics. Mem. grad. coun. Harvard U., 1985-88. Republican. Office: The Stockworks PO Box 621 Riverdale MD 20738-0621

KRISHNAN, PALANIAPPA, agricultural engineering educator; b. Kanadukathan, Tamil Nadu, India, Apr. 25, 1953; came to U.S., 1974; s. Lakshmanan and Umayal (Thenappan) K.; m. Chitra Palaniappa Palaniappan, June 18, 1980; 1 child, Prashanth. BTech with honors, Indian Inst. Tech., Kharagpur, 1975; MS, U. Hawaii, 1976; PhD, U. Ill., 1979. Rsch. assoc. U. Ill., Urbana, 1979-80; rsch. assoc. Oreg. State U., Corvallis, 1980-83, asst. prof., 1983-85; asst. prof. agrl. engring. U. Del., Newark, 1985-91, assoc. prof., 1991—; cons. Am. Agrotech Lab., Sacaton, Ariz., 1983-86, Rodale Rsch. Ctr., Kutztown, Pa., 1986—; faculty advisor Indian Students Assn., Newark, 1988—. Contbr. articles to nat. and internat. jours.; patentee in field. Hunter fellow U. Ill., Urbana, 1977-78; rsch. grantee Oreg. State U., Corvallis, 1981; teaching grantee U. Del., Newark, 1987. Mem. ASTM, Am. Soc. Agrl. Engrs. (sec., vice-chmn., chmn. agrl. pest control and fertilizer application com. 1988—), Newark Lions (lion tamer 1989, bd. dirs. 1990—, pres. 1991—). Home: 21 N Fawn Dr Newark DE 19711-2565

KRISPIN, JACOB, research scientist; b. Tiberias, Israel, Dec. 29, 1952; came to U.S., 1984; s. Moshe and Bertha (Assa) K.; m. Tanya Rotgerber, May 26, 1980; children: Amit, Maya. BS cum laude, Israel Inst. Tech., Haifa, 1977, MS, 1984; PhD, U. Md., 1987. Aerospace engr., group leader Rafael (Israeli Armament Devel. Authority), Haifa, 1977-84, 87-89; grad. rsch. asst. U. Md., Dept. Aerospace Engring., College Park, 1984-87; program mgr. Enig. Assocs. Inc., Silver Springs, Md., 1990—; vis. asst. prof., math. U. Md., 1989-90. Contbr. tech. papers in field; patentee in field. NSF rsch. grantee, Washington, 1989, 90. Mem. AIAA. Office: Enig Assocs Inc 11120 New Hampshire Ave Silver Spring MD 20904-2633

KRISS, DOROTHY JEAN, medical company executive; b. Pitts., Sept. 17, 1947; d. Joseph Frank and Dorothy Ann (Crowley) K. Diploma in nursing, St. Joseph's Hosp., Pitts., 1968; BS in Biology, Mercy Coll., 1976; MBA, N.H. Coll., 1990. RN, N.Y., N.J. Asst. head nurse, dialysis and transplant unit Montefiore Hosp., Bronx, N.Y., 1968-71; head nurse, dialysis and transplant unit Mt. Sinai Hosp., N.Y.C., 1971-72; charge nurse Queen's Artificial Kidney Ctr., Queens, N.Y., 1972-73; nurse adminstr. Bronx Dialysis Ctr., Inc., Bronx, 1973-76; profl. svcs. coord., med. products div. Nat. Med. Care, Inc., Rockleigh, N.J., 1976-80; dialysis, sales specialist Nat. Med. Care, Inc., Rockleigh, 1980-82, sr. dialysis specialist, 1982-83, dir. customer service, 1983-87; v.p. clin. and tech. svcs., dialysis svcs. div. Nat. Med. Care, Inc., Waltham, Mass., 1988—. Office: Nat Med Care Inc PO Box 1653 Lowell MA 01853-1653

KRIST, BETTY JANE, mathematics educator, researcher; b. Buffalo, Dec. 4, 1946; d. Thomas James and Agnes (Ruchaczewska) K. BS, SUNY, 1968, MS, 1971; EdD, SUNY, Buffalo, 1980. Cert. permanent secondary math. tchr., N.Y. Rsch. assoc. Nat. Inst. Edn., SUNY, Buffalo, 1976-80, co-dir. Gifted Math. Program, 1980—, adj. assoc. prof. edn., 1985—; tchr. math. West Seneca (N.Y.) Schs., 1968-76, 78-80; assoc. prof. math. and computer sci. D'Youville Coll., Buffalo, 1980-87; prof. math. State U. Coll., Buffalo, 1987—, chmn. math. dept., 1991—; mem. adv. coun. Sci. Svc., Washington, 1987-90; dir. math. N.Y. State Summer Inst. for Sci. and Math., Albany, 1989-90. Co-author: Using Calculators in Mathematics ll, l2, 1980, Providing Opportunities for Gifted Students in Mathematics K-12, 1987; editor Math. Tchr., 1986-88; contbr. articles to math. jours. Speaker to schs.in western N.Y., 1980—. Named Tchr. of Yr., West Seneca Schs., 1976. Mem. ASCD, AAAS, Nat. Coun. Tchrs. Math. (editorial chmn. 1986-88, contbr. to yearbooks 1982, 85, 88), Math. Assn. Am. (founding mem. Strengthening Underrepresented Minorities Math. Achievement 1991—), Nat. Coun. Suprs. Math., Computing Educators League, Assn. Math. Tchrs. N.Y. State, AAUW (bd. dirs. Buffalo chpt. 1986-87). Democrat. Mem. United Ch. of Christ. Home: ll6 Iris Ave West Seneca NY 14224

KRISTAL, MARK BENNETT, psychologist, educator; b. N.Y.C., Apr. 19, 1944; s. Emanuel and Helen (Goldin) K.; m. Tova Iskovits, Oct. 8, 1967; 1 child, Morgan H. BA, Rutgers U., 1965; MS, Kans. State U., 1970, PhD, 1971. Postdoctoral trainee Jackson Lab., Bar Harbor, Maine, 1971-73; asst. prof. psychology SUNY, Buffalo, 1973-78, assoc. prof., 1978-90, interim assoc. dean sch. health related professions, 1986-88, assoc. dean faculty social scis., 1989—, prof. psychology, 1991—; editorial bd. Physiology and Behavior, 1989—. Contbr. 45 articles to profl. jours. NSF grantee, 1986-88, 89-91, Nat. Inst. on Drug Abuse grantee, 1989—. Mem. Soc. for Neurosci., Animal Behavior Soc., Internat. Soc. for Devel. Psychobiology, AAAS, Sigma Xi. Office: SUNY Dept Psychology Park Hall Buffalo NY 14260

KRITCHEVSKY, DAVID, biochemist, educator; b. Kharkov, Russia, Jan. 25, 1920; came to U.S., 1923, naturalized, 1929; s. Jacob and Leah (Kritchevsky) K.; m. Evelyn Sholtes, Dec. 21, 1947; children—Barbara Ann, Janice Eileen, Stephen Bennett. B.S., U. Chgo., 1939, M.S., 1942; Ph.D., Northwestern U., 1948. Chemist Ninol Labs., Chgo., 1939-46; postdoctoral fellow Fed. Inst. Tech., Zurich, Switzerland, 1948-49; biochemist Radiation Lab., U. Calif. at Berkeley, 1950-52, Lederle Lab., Pearl River, N.Y., 1952-57, Wistar Inst., Phila., 1957—; prof. biochemistry Sch. Vet. Medicine U. Pa., Phila., 1965—; prof. biochemistry Sch. Medicine U. Pa., 1970—, chmn. grad. group molecular biology, 1972-84; Mem. USPHS study sect. Nat. Heart Inst., 1964-68, 72-76; chmn. research com. Spl. Dairy Industry Bd., 1963-70; mem. food and nutrition bd. Nat. Acad. Sci., 1976-82. Author: Cholesterol, 1958, also numerous articles.; editor: (with G. Litwack) Actions of Hormones on Molecular Processes, 1964; co-editor: (with R. Paoletti) Advances in Lipid Research, 1963-89, (with P. Nair) 1973, Bile Acids, 1971; Western Hemisphere editor Atherosclerosis, 1978-90, cons. editor, 1990—. Recipient Research Career award Nat. Heart Inst., 1962, award Am. Coll. Nutrition, 1978, Herman award Am. Soc. Clin. Nutrition, 1992; research on role vehicle when cholesterol and fat produces atherosclerosis in rabbits, effects of saturated and unsaturated fat, deposition of orally administered cholesterol in aorta of man and rabbit, caloric restriction and cancer. Fellow Am. Inst. Nutrition (Borden award 1974, pres. 1979); mem. AAAS, Am. Soc. Biol. Chemists, Am. Chem. Soc. (award Phila. sect. 1977), Soc. Exptl. Biology and Medicine (pres. 1985-87), Arteriosclerosis Coun., Am. Heart Assn., Am. Soc. Oil Chemists (chmn. methods com. 1963-64), Internat. Soc. Fat Rsch. Home: 136 Lee Cir Bryn Mawr PA 19010-3724 Office: Wistar Inst 36th and Spruce Sts Philadelphia PA 19104

KROCKMAN, ARNOLD FRANCIS, publisher, advertising executive; b. N.Y.C., Sept. 4, 1945; s. Arnold W. and Alice Frances (Nowack) K.; m. Lorraine Edith Strunck, Jan. 19, 1980. BA, Fordham U., 1970; MFA, Pratt Inst., 1973. Editor Studio Photography Mag., Melville, N.Y., 1977-78; assoc. editor Billboard Publs., N.Y.C., 1978-79; photographer Wagner Internat. Photos, N.Y.C., 1979-81; editor PR Newswire, N.Y.C., 1988-89; pub. AK Publs., East Rutherford, N.J., 1990—; v.p. Meadowlands Advt. Agy., East Rutherford, 1991—. Mem. N.Am. Book Dealers Exch., Mensa. Office: AK Publs PO Box 7747 East Rutherford NJ 07073-0897

KROEGER, SUSAN JEAN, accountant; b. Glenridge, N.J., July 3, 1961; d. John Alfred and Patricia Ann (Ferrante) Kroeger; m. George Clarence Merrill, June 18, 1983; children: C.J., B.J., G.J. BA, William Paterson Coll., 1986. CPA, N.J., notary pub., ins. broker. Clk. Crum & Foster, Parsippany, N.J., 1980-86; internal auditor Crum & Foster, Parsippany, 1986-87; sr. acct. Ernst & Young & Co., Iselin, N.J., 1987-89; pvt. practice Susan J. Kroeger, CPA, Parsippany, 1989—; mortgage cons., ins. broker Kastle Fin. Group/America's First Mortgage, 1991—. Mem. Lake Parsippany Property Owners, 1989—. Mem. AICPA, N.J. Soc. CPAs. Republican. Roman Catholic.

KROEZ, HAROLD, paper and chemical company executive; b. N.Y.C., Apr. 19, 1937; s. Harold J. and Grace (Hoppe) K.; m. Barbara A. Fromwiller, Dec. 27, 1958; children: Thomas, Lorraine, John, Robert, Lawrence, Carolyn. BS in Chemistry, St. John's U., N.Y.C., 1958. Lab. asst. Andrews Paper & Chem. Co. Inc., Port Washington, N.Y., 1957-58, chemist, 1958—, v.p., 1975-87, pres., 1987—, also bd. dirs., trustee. Home: 392 Roxbury Rd S Garden City NY 11530 Office: Andrews Paper & Chem Co Inc 1 Channel Dr Port Washington NY 11050

KROGULSKI, JOHN LEO, sales executive; b. Fairview, Pa., Sept. 16, 1927; s. Anthony Stanley and Mary (Gunten) K.; m. Jennie Theresa Innocenti, Nov. 12, 1949; children: Judith Ann, Kenneth John. Student, Kings Coll., Wilkes-Barre, Pa. With Sordoni Enterprises, Forty Fort, Pa., 1944-78; lineman Sordoni Construction Co., Forty Fort, Pa., 1947-48; cable splicer helper Commonwealth Telephone Co., Dallas, Pa., 1948-50; mechanic Krogulski's Blvd. Garage, Ashley, Pa., 1951-54; several mgmt. positions Commonwealth Telephone Co., Dallas, 1954-70; v.p., gen. mgr. Sterling Products Co., Kingston, Pa., 1970-78; owner Northeastern Communications, Wilkes-Barre, 1978-86, Acrim Maintenance Co., Wilkes-Barre, 1987-91; with Kay Assocs., Wilkes-Barre, 1991—; dir. Ind. Telephone Pioneers, Dallas, Pa., 1980—, pres., 1986; bir. coun. commr., Penn Mt. coun. Boy Scouts Am., Wilkes-Barre, 1965—. Sgt. USMC, 1945-47, 1950-51. Mem. Wilkes-Barre C. of C. (dir., 1st v.p. 1985—), Kiwanis (bd. dirs. Dallas chpt.), George M. Dallas Club, Irem Temple Chanters, Masons, Scottish Rite. Republican. Roman Catholic. Office: Kay Assocs 421 N Pennsylvania Ave Wilkes Barre PA 18702-4414

KROL, JOHN CASIMIR, city manager, municipal planner; b. Chelmsford, Essex, Eng., June 1, 1949; came to U.S., 1951; s. Fortunat and Stanislawa (Kosowicz) K.; m. Linda Sue Wright, Jan. 2, 1971; children: Pamela, Suzanne, Michael. BS, Clarkson Coll. Technol., 1971; MS, SUNY, Buffalo, 1977. Planner St. Lawrence County, Canton, N.Y., 1971-74, county adminstrv. asst., 1984-85; sr. planner Town of Amherst, Williamsville, N.Y., 1974-77; planning dir. Clinton County, Plattsburg, N.Y., 1977-79, City of Ogdensburg(N.Y.), 1979-83; city mgr. City of Ogdensburg (N.Y.), 1987—; planning commr. Broome County, Binghamton, N.Y., 1986-87. Bd. dirs. Soc. United Helpers, Ogdensburg, 1983-84, Ogdensburg Boys and Girls Club, 1990—; co-chair annual city fund dr. Am. Cancer Soc., Ogdensburg, 1982. Mem. Am. Inst. Cert. Planners, Mcpl. Mgmt. Assn. N.Y. State (dir. 1987—), Internat. City Mgrs. Assn., St. Lawrence County C. of C. (bd. dirs. 1988—), Greater Ogdensburg C. of C. (bd. dirs. 1992—). Presbyterian. Lodge: Kiwanis. Home: 515 John St Ogdensburg NY 13669-2007 Office: City of Ogdensburg 330 Ford St Ogdensburg NY 13669-1626

KROLL, ALEXANDER S., advertising agency executive; b. 1937. BA, Rutgers U., 1962. Mem. profl. football team N.Y. Titans, Am. Football League, 1962; With Young & Rubicam, Inc., N.Y.C., 1962—, copywriter, 1962-68, v.p., 1968-69, sr. v.p., 1969-70, exec. v.p., worldwide creative dir., 1970-75, pres., chief operating officer, 1982, chief exec. officer, 1985—, chmn., chief exec. officer, 1986—, also dir.; mng. dir. Young & Rubicam U.S.A., N.Y.C., 1975-77, pres., 1977; Chmn. bd., Am. Assn. Adot. Agys., 1991-92. Recipient Kodak Life Achievement award, 1985, Nat. Collegiate Athletic Assn. Silver Anniversary award, 1987; named consensus All-Am. in football, 1961. Office: Young & Rubicam Inc 285 Madison Ave New York NY 10017-6401*

KROLL, LEONARD JOSEPH, secondary education educator; b. Jersey City, Oct. 13, 1935; s. Felix and Eleanor (Wrzesinski) K.; children: Andrew, Alison, Audrey. BS in Vocat. Edn., Rutgers U., 1972, ME in Vocat. Edn., 1975. Apprentice machinist Radio Corp. of Am., Harrison, N.J., 1953-57; 1st class machinist Radio Corp. of Am., Harrison, 1959-63, tool and die maker, 1963-68; secondary edn. educator Old Bridge (N.J.) Bd. of Edn., 1968—; com. mem. Cen. Jersey Student Crafts Fair, Inc., Perth Amboy, N.J., 1986—. With U.S. Army, 1957-59. Mem. Barnegat Bay Sail Club (founder, dir. 1970-72, life mem.), Barnegat Bay Power Squad (commdr. 1969-70, chair boating course 1986—), U.S. Power Squad (life mem.). Democrat. Roman Catholic. Home: 209 Cedar Island Dr Brick NJ 08723-7503 Office: Madison Cen High Sch Rt 516 Old Bridge NJ 08857

KROLL, MARTIN HARRIS, pathologist; b. Washington, June 19, 1952; s. Bernard Hilton and Doris (Weinblum) K.; m. Ellen Linda Coonin, June 22, 1975; children: Allison, Jonathan, Lauren. BS, U. Md., 1974, MD, 1978. Resident in pathology U. Md. Hosp., Balt., 1978-82, chief resident in pathology, 1981; fellow in clin. chemistry NIH, Bethesda, Md., 1982-84, med. staff, 1984—; cons. Baxter Travenol, Irving, Calif., 1988. Contbr. articles to profl. jours. Chmn. libr. com. North Potomac (Md.) Citizens Assn., 1988—, edn. com., 1991, Quince Orchard/Rt. 28 ad hoc Libr. Adv. Com., Montgomery County, Md., 1991. NSF fellow, 1973. Mem. Am. Chem. Soc., Assn. for Psychol. Type, Acad. Clin. Lab. Physicians and Scientists (Young Investigator award 1983), Am. Assn. for Clin. Chemistry (sec. Capital sect. 1988, chmn. 1990, Chmn. award 1990), NIH Interinstitute Chaos Coun. (steering com. 1990-91), Phi Kappa Phi. Democrat. Jewish. Home: 14070 Saddle River Dr Gaithersburg MD 20878-4249 Office: NIH Bldg 10 Rm 2C-407 Bethesda MD 20892

KROLL, RICHARD, corporate communications executive; b. L.A., July 3, 1952; s. Herbert David and Selma (Heimlich) Klynn; m. Elise Kroll (div. 1986); 1 child, Alexander; m. Tina Martin, June 19, 1988; 1 child, Amelia Kroll Martin. BA, UCLA, 1975, MA, 1979. Researcher, writer Office of Charles and Ray Eames, L.A., 1978-79, Richard Wurman & Assocs., L.A., 1979; researcher George Nelson Assocs., N.Y.C., 1980; rsch. dir. Carlos Ramirez & Albert H. Woods, Inc., N.Y.C., 1980-85, Siegel & Gale, N.Y.C., 1985-89; v.p. info. svcs. Siegel & Gale, 1989—; design rsch. cons., N.Y.C., 1980—; bd. advisers, Ctr. for Design Mgmt. Resources, 1989—. Researcher: Wall Street Jour. Guide to Understanding Money and Markets, 1989, Corporate Voice, 1989, American Dreams, 1990. Recipient Award of Excellence, Nat. Audio-Visual Assn., 1982. Mem. Design Rsch. Soc., Spl. Librs. Assn., Am. Soc. Picture Profls., Am. Assn. Mus. Democrat. Jewish. Office: Siegel & Gale 1185 Ave Of The Americas New York NY 10036-2601

KROMER, MICHAEL CHARLES, association executive; b. Rochester, N.Y., July 18, 1945; s. Charles J. and Mary (Dimon) K.; m. Patricia M. Foley, Aug. 2, 1969; children: Kelly Jasena, Kristy Michelle. BS, SUNY, Cortland, 1967; MS, Ind. State U., 1968. Asst. dir. nat. hdqrs. Am. Camping Assn., Martinsville, Ind., 1968-81; exec. dir. nat. hdqrs. Profl. Picture Framers Assn., Richmond, Va., 1981-89, U.S. Pony Clubs, West Chester, Pa., 1989—. Mem. Am. Soc. Assn. Execs. (cert. 1976—). Office: US Pony Clubs 893 S Matlack St S/110 West Chester PA 19382-4507

KRONE, IRENE, product consultant; b. N.Y.C., Oct. 12, 1940; d. Frederick Wilhelm and Gertrude (Gottschlich) Beckmann; m. Helmut Krone, Nov. 14, 1970; 1 child, Kathryn Maria. BS, Chestnut Hill Coll., 1962; postgrad., Sch. Visual Arts and Interior Design, 1962-64, NYU, 1967-68. Market rsch. analyst, then licensing mgr. Celanese Corp., N.Y.C. and Brussels, 1962-67; v.p. product devel. Doyle Dane Bernbach, N.Y.C., 1967-79; pres. I. Krone Assocs. Inc., N.Y.C., 1979—. Pres., founder Stop Traffic Offenses Program, N.Y.C., 1982—. Mem. Fashion's Inner Circle. Home: 1 E 62d St New York NY 10021 Office: 777 3d Ave New York NY 10017

KRONEGGER, MARIA ELISABETH, French and comparative literature educator; b. Graz, Austria, Sept. 23, 1932; came to U.S., 1962, naturalized, 1968; d. Karl and Josefine (Sparovitz) K. Grad., Karl-Franzens U., Austria, 1960; postgrad., Sorbonne, Paris, 1953-55; M.A. in English and Am. Lit., Kans. U., 1958; Ph.D. in French and Humanities, Fla. State U., 1960. Instr. French, German and humanities Fla. State U., 1958-60; mem. faculty Internat. Coll., St. Gallen, Switzerland, 1961-62; asst. prof. Hollins Coll., Va., 1962-64; asst. prof. French and comparative lit. Mich. State U., East Lansing, 1964-67, assoc. prof., 1967-70, prof., 1970—. Author: James Joyce and Associate Image Makers, 1968, Impressionist Literature, 1973, The Life Significance of French Baroque Poetry, 1988; editor: Phénoménologie et Littérature: L'origine de l'oeuvre d'art, Hommages à A.-T. Tymieniecka, 1986, Phenomenology and Aesthetics: Approaches to Comparative Literature and the Other Arts, 1990, Dordrecht (Kluver), vol. XXXIII of book series Analecta Husserliana, 1990; co-editor: Esthétique Baroque et Imagination Créatrice, 1992; contbr. numerous articles on 17th and 20th century French and English lit., lit. and the other arts, lit. and phenomenology to scholarly publs. Bd. dirs. World Inst. of Phenomenology, 1980—; pres. Internat. Soc. Phenomenology and Lit. Fulbright scholar, 1957-60; Ford Found. grantee, 1965-66. Mem. MLA, AAUP, Am. Soc. Aesthetics, Am. Comparative Lit. Assn., Semiotic Soc. Am., Chinese Comparative Lit. Assn., Internat. Soc. for Phenomenology and Lit. (pres. 1985—), Internat. Comparative Lit. Assn., Internat. Soc. Civilization, Internat. Semiotic Soc., South Atlantic MLA, Société Paul Claudel, Am. Assn. Tchrs. French, Fédération internationale de Langues et Littétures modernes, Gold Key Soc. (hon.; Rsch. award). Roman Catholic. Home: 1324 Chartwell Carriage N Stonelake East Lansing MI 48823 Office: Mich State U Old Horticulture East Lansing MI 48824

KRONENBERG, MARVIN LEE, electrochemist; b. Chgo., July 3, 1929; s. Max and Celia (Kissilove) K.; m. Marianne Lukacs, June 1, 1958; children: Alan, Judy, Jerry. MS, U. Chgo., 1951; PhD, Case Western U., 1960. Electrochemist Union Carbide, Cleve., 1960-77; project leader GE, Gainesville, Fla., 1977-80; rsch. electrochemist Argonne (Ill.) Nat. Lab., 1980-82; sr. staff electrochemist Duracell, Needham, Mass., 1982-87; tech. cons. and devel. mgr. Catalyst Rsch., Sparks, Md., 1988—. Author: (with others) Treatise on Electrochemistry, 1980, Encyclopedia of Electrochemistry; contbr. articles to profl. jours.; patentee in field. canvasser Am. Heart Assn., Boston, 1985-90. With U.S. Army, 1953-55. Harshaw fellow Case Western U., 1957-60. Mem. Am. Chem. Soc. (chmn. creative chemistry contest 1974, 75), Electrochem. Soc. (past session chmn. and treas. for nat. meetings, chmn. Cleve. sect. 1972, George Heise award 1977). Home: 85 Mary Chilton Rd Needham MA 02192-1148 Office: Catalyst Rsch 38 Loveton Circle Sparks MD 21152

KRONENTHAL, RICHARD LEONARD, chemist, consultant; b. N.Y.C., Oct. 6, 1928; s. Robert and Florence (Sichel) K.; m. Beverly R. Greenberg, Dec. 18, 1949; children: David, Susan. BSc, Bklyn. Coll., 1951; PhD, Poly. Inst. N.Y., 1955. Sr. project chemist Colgate Palmolive Co., Jersey City, 1954-57; chemist Ethicon, Inc., Somerville, N.J., 1957-60; sect. head Ethicon, Inc., Somerville, 1960-63, mgr., 1963-68, assoc. dir., 1968-85, dir. R & D, 1985-89; pres. Kronenthal Assocs., Inc., Rutherford, N.J., 1989—; cons. Viro-Tex Corp., Houston, 1989—, Neomorphics Rutherford, 1989—; sci. adv. bd. Ventures Med. Inc., Houston, 1990—; bd. dirs. Corvita Corp., Miami, Fla., 1991—. Author: Surgical Supplies Ency., 1990; author (with others): Biodegradable Polymers in Medicine and Surgery, 1975, Suture Material in Cataract Surgery, 1984. Recipient R & D medal Johnson & Johnson, 1984. Mem. AAAS, Am. Chem. Soc., Am. Inst. Chemists, N.Y. Acad. Scis., The Chem. Soc. Office: Kronenthal Assocs Inc 301 State Route 17 Ste 800 Rutherford NJ 07070-2575

KRONENWETT, FREDERICK RUDOLPH, microbiologist; b. Newark, July 29, 1923; s. Frederick Christian and Florence Margaret (Maelis/Kane) K.; m. Claire Elizabeth, June 18, 1950; children: Debora Claire, Pamela Fredericka, Gail Linda, Joyce Heidi, Erich Frederick. BS, Upsala Coll., 1948; MS, Rutgers U., 1950, PhD, 1953. Cert. specialist in microbiology. Pres. Am. Biol. Control Lab., Tenafly, N.J., 1957—; lectr. in chemistry Upsala Coll., East Orange, N.J., 1958-59; postdoctoral fellow Rutgers U., New Brunswick, N.J., 1958-59; asst. prof. Fairleigh Dickinson U., Teaneck, N.J., 1958-61, assoc. prof., 1961-70, prof., 1970-89; specialist in radioisotopic methods Oak Ridge (Tenn.) Assoc. Univs., 1969; mem. sterility com. U.S. Pharmacopeia XVIII, Rockville, Md., 1966-70, chmn. biol. indicator com., 1970-73; cons., microbiologist IAEA, Vienna, Austria, 1972. Co-author lab. manuals, 1959-61. Mem. Community Chest, Tenafly, 1960; bd. fellows Upsala Coll., 1972-76. With AC, USN, 1943-46. Fellow APHA; mem. Am. Soc. Microbiology, Am. Soc. Clin. Pathologists, Soc. Am. Parasitologists. Lutheran. Home: 45 Magnolia Ave Tenafly NJ 07670-2119 Office: Am Biol Control Labs 65 Hudson Ave Tenafly NJ 07670-1026

KRONENWETTER, JEFFREY ALAN, systems engineer; b. Chinon, France, Dec. 12, 1962; s. Joseph F. and Betty Sue (Saffrit) K.; m. Tamera Anita Mills, June 9, 1984; 1 child, Zachary. BS in Aerospace Engring., N.C. State U., 1984; postgrad., George Washington U., 1990—. Attitude determination and control specialist Computer Scis. Corp., Greenbelt, Md.,

1984-86; task leader, spacecraft attitude determination/control sect. Computer Scis. Corp., 1986-88, spacecraft systems engr., 1988—. Mem. AIAA, Soc. Computer Simulation. Home: 6425 Jodie St Hyattsville MD 20784-3633 Office: Computer Scis Corp 7404 Executive Pl Ste 200 Lanham Seabrook MD 20706-2268

KRONER, WALTER MANFRED, architect, educator; b. Neu-Ulm, Germany, June 28, 1934; came to U.S., 1954; s. Hans and Dora (Sellmer) K.; m. Francis Wilson Kroner (div.); m. Trudi Wybourn, Aug. 28, 1960; children: Robert, M. Renee, Kevin. BArch, U. Colo., 1966; MArch, Rensselaer Poly. Inst., 1967. Lic. architect. Head critic Boston (Mass.) Archtl. Ctr., 1967-69; assoc. Geometrics, Inc., Cambridge, Mass., 1968-69; rsch. assoc. Ctr. For Archtl. Rsch., Rensselaer Poly. Inst., Troy, N.Y., 1969-71; assoc. dir. to dir. Ctr. For Archtl. Rsch., Rensselaer Poly. Inst., Troy, 1972-77, 77—; asst. prof. Sch. of Architecture, Rensselaer Poly. Inst., Troy, 1971-75, assoc. prof., 1975-85, prof., 1985—, disting. prof., 1988; archtl. cons. Roman Cath. Diocese of Albany, N.Y., 1970—; prin. Walter Kroner Architects, Troy, 1971—; trustee Intelligent Bldg. Inst. Found., Washington, 1989—. Author: Energy Efficient Buildings, 1986; editor: A New Frontier, 1988; designer (bldg. design) Passive Solar Residences, 1978, Comml. Bldg. Concrete Design, 1984. With USAF, 1954-58. Fellow Am. Coun. for an Energy Efficient Economy; mem. ASHRAE, World Future Studies Fedn., Sierra Club. Office: Ctr for Archt Rsch Rensselaer Poly Inst Troy NY 12180

KRONFELD, LEOPOLD JAMES, manufacturing company executive, lawyer; b. Hartford, Conn., Sept. 5, 1941; s. Alexander James and Mae (Blumenthal) K.; m. Barbara Tillette, May 15, 1975; children: Alexander, Nicholas. BA, Syracuse U., 1963; MEd, U. Hartford, 1967; LLB, Cornell U., 1968. Bar: Conn., D.C. Legal asst. U.S. Ho. Reps., Washington, 1968-71, chief counsel, 1972-75; asst. gen. counsel CIA, Washington, 1975-78; pres. Mirror Pipe Co., Hartford, Conn., 1978-91; atty.-investor Hartford, Conn., 1991—; bd. dirs. Small Bus. Council, Hartford. Bd. dirs. Hartford Chamber Orch., 1978-84. Republican. Jewish. Home: 4 Hunter Dr West Hartford CT 06107-1014

KRONISH, RICHARD MARK, sports association executive; b. Bronx, N.Y., Oct. 1, 1961; s. William C. and Lillian B. (Hollinger) K. Student, CUNY, 1979-83. Chief exec. officer Kronish Sports Enterprises, N.Y.C., 1981—. Author: Draft Guide, 1985-91, 8th rev. edit., 1992. Democrat. Jewish. Home: 521 E 14th St New York NY 10009

KROPP, REGINA C., guidance counselor; b. Bethlehem, Pa.; d. Charles C. and Eileen (Hoffert) K. BA, Chestnut Hill Coll., Phila., 1972; MEd, Lehigh U., 1980. Guidance counselor, chairperson St. Mark's High Sch., Wilmington, Del. Mem. ACA, ASCA, DACD (bd. dirs., sec. 1991-92), DSCA. Office: St Marks High Sch Pike Creek Rd Wilmington DE 19808-3663

KROSER, ALBERT S., physician; b. Phila., July 15, 1930; s. Harry Z. and Florence (Budin) K.; m. Lila Stein, June 17, 1956; children: Marla Jill, Joyann Allison, Jonathan Mark. AB, Temple U., 1952; postgrad., Phila. Coll. Pharmacy & Sci., 1952-54; DO, Phila. Coll. Osteo. Medicine, 1958. Intern Met. Hosp., Phila., 1958-59; family practitioner Phila., 1959—; preceptor gen. practice Phila. Coll. Osteopathic Medicine, 1967—; clin. instr. dept. community and preventive medicine Med. Coll. Pa., 1985—; attending clinician child health conf. Phila. Dept. Health, 1960-63; bd. dirs. Del. Valley Geriatric Soc.; physician to consultate gen. of Israel, Phila., 1970—; med. dir. Ashton Hall Nursing Home, Phila., 1977-90; speaker in field. Coll. of Phys. of Phila. fellow, 1984. Fellow Internat. Coll. Gen. Practice; mem. Am. Osteo. Assn., Am. Coll. Gen. Practice in Osteo. Medicine and Surgery, Am. Geriatrics Soc., Am. Acad. Family Physicians, Pa. Osteo. Med. Assn. (elected mem. house of del. 1974—), Pa. Med. Soc., Pa. Osteo. Gen. Practitioners Soc., Pa. Acad. Family Physicians, Phila. County Osteo. Soc., Phila. County Med. Soc., Friends of Am. Med. Womens Assn. (pres. 1981-89, Camille Mermod award 1983), Cardozo Lodge Brith Shalom, Phi Alpha, Lambda Omicron Gamma. Republican. Jewish. Home and Office: 2855 Welsh Rd Philadelphia PA 19152-1697

KROTIUK, WILLIAM JOHN, mechanical engineer; b. Bklyn., July 7, 1948; s. William John and Regina Helen (Chrzanowski) K.; m. Claire Elise Guglielmelli, Oct. 20, 1973; 1 child, Elise Marie. BSME cum laude, Poly. U., Bklyn., 1970; MME, Poly. U., 1978; postgrad., Rensselaer Poly. Inst., 1970-71; MS in Nuclear Engring., Columbia U., 1972. Registered profl. engr., N.Y. R&D project engr. Combustion Engring., Windsor, Conn., 1970-71; supr. applied physics Ebasco Svcs., Inc., N.Y.C., 1972-85; prin. rsch. engr. Battelle Pacific Northwest Labs., Richland, Wash., 1985-87; prin. mem. tech. staff GE Astro Space, Princeton, N.J., 1988—; instr., organizer profl. symposia. Author, editor: Thermal-Hydraulics for Space Power, Propulsion and Thermal Management, 1990; contbr. articles, reports to profl. publs. Mem. ASME (reviewer fluids div. 1978—), AIAA, Amn. Nuclear Soc., Pi Tau Sigma, Tau Beta Pi. Office: GE Astro Space PO Box 800 Princeton NJ 08543-0800

KRUCENSKI, LEONARD JOSEPH, secondary education educator; b. Buffalo, June 15, 1931; s. Stanislous and Anna Victoria (Pyzanowska) K.; m. Estelle Ann Gaik, Oct. 19, 1957; children: Leonard S., Brian M., William G. BS cum laude, SUNY, Buffalo, 1976, MS in Edn., 1980. Electronics technician Bell Aero Space Inc., Niagara Falls, N.Y., 1953-62, Moog Valve Inc, East Aurora, N.Y., 1962-69; engring. aid Cornell Aero. Labs. Inc., Buffalo, 1969-75; jr. engr. Kistler Instruments Inc., Clarence, N.Y., 1975-79; tchr. electronics Buffalo Pub. Sch. System, 1979—. Recipient 85th Anniversary Alumni Disting. Svc. awrd Hutchinson Cen. Tech. High Sch., 1989. Mem. ASCD, NEA, Am. Vocat. Assn., Nat. Assn. Indsl. and Tech. Tchr. Educators, N.Y. State Occupational Edn. Assn., Vocat. Tech. Guild Buffalo, Buffalo Tchrs. Fedn. Home: 176 Lorelee Dr Tonawanda NY 14150-4325 Office: Hutchinson Cen Tech High Sch 256 S Elmwood Ave Buffalo NY 14201-2393

KRUEGER, ERIC EUGENE, construction company executive; b. Holyoke, Colo., Feb. 25, 1958; s. Chester Charles and Sibyl Noreen (Jackson) K.; m. Stephanie Wilke, May 20, 1986; children: Colton Matthew, Erica Elizabeth. BS, Colo. State U., 1980. Asst. dist. mgr. Armco Bldg. Systems, Cin., 1981; dist. mgr. Armco Bldg. Systems, Denver, 1981-83; bus. devel. mgr. Brae Constrn., Inc., San Antonio, 1983-85; v.p. Contemporary Constructors, Inc., San Antonio, 1985-87; dir. bus. devel. Centennial Contractors, Inc., Vienna, Va., 1987-90, OMNI Constrn., Inc., Bethesda, Md., 1990-91, The George Hyman Constrn. Co., Bethesda, 1991—. Mem. Soc. for Mktg. Profl. Svcs. (bd. dirs. 1985-87, 89-91), Nat. Assn. Indsl. & Office Parks, Internat. Facility Mgrs. Assn., D.C. Bd. Trade, Leadership Fairfax Alumni Assn. (bd. dirs. 1991—), Sigma Chi (hon.). Republican. Lutheran. Office: The George Hyman Constrn Co 7500 Old Georgetown Rd Bethesda MD 20814

KRUEGER, FRANCIS LEE, III, insurance company executive; b. Bklyn., Nov. 19, 1955; s. Francis Lee and Charlotte Nellie (Blind) K.; m. Cheryl Ann Camenzuli, June 30, 1979; 1 child, Alexandra Lee. BA in Econs., L.I. U., 1977. Acctg. mgr. Pan Atlantic Ins. Co., White Plains, N.Y., 1983-84; chief acct. Great Atlantic Ins. Co., N.Y.C., 1984-85, Moac Reins. Mgmt. Co., Cranbury, N.J., 1985—; pres., owner Krueger Fin. Mgmt., Inc., Glen Cove, N.Y., 1990—. Mem. Soc. Ins. Accts., Glen Cove C. of C. Republican. Methodist. Home and Office: Krueger Fin Mgmt 19 Alex Ln Glen Cove NY 11542-4105

KRUEGER, JAMES ELWOOD, pharmaceutical executive; b. Marinette, Wis., Apr. 2, 1926; s. Jesse and Beulah (Elwood) K.; m. Claire Pickener, June 20, 1953 (dec. 1966); children: David, Jonathan, Thomas; m. Virginia Cochrane Webb, Aug. 16, 1969; children: Virginia, Cynthia, Gregory. BS, U. Wis., 1949; PhD, MIT, 1954. Cert. quality auditor. Rsch. fellow Harvard Med. Sch., Brookline, Mass., 1953-55; rsch. chemist Dow Chem. Co., Midland, Mich., 1955-61; group leader Am. Cyanamid Co., Pearl River, N.Y., 1961-69, sr. rsch. chemist, 1969-79, sr. quality auditor, 1979-90; v.p. quality assurance I.N.D. Mgmt., Upper Saddle River, N.J., 1990—. Author: NMR Spectra Vol. I, 1965, Vol. II, 1966, ISO 9000: Guidelines For Use by the Chemical and Process Industries; patentee in field. Bd. dirs. Hudson River Counseling Svc., Mt. Kisco, N.Y., 1973-79. With U.S. Army, 1945-46. Mem. Am. Soc. Quality Control (sr., chair Tappan Zee sect. 1991—). Home: 6 Lucille Blvd New City NY 10956-4421 Office: IND Mgmt Inc 345 Rte 17 S Upper Saddle River NJ 07548

KRUEGER, RALPH ARTHUR, motel and food executive; b. Cleve., Apr. 14, 1952; s. Daniel and Florence (Myer) K.; m. Pamela Lynn Fredette, Aug. 6, 1978. AA, Adirondack Community Coll., Glen Falls, N.Y., 1983. Dept. mgr./inventory Telescope Furniture Co., Granville, N.Y., 1970-82; owner, mgr. Pine Grove Motel and Diner, Granville, 1979-89, Park Enterprises, Granville, 1987—, Valley Food Ct., Granville, 1988-89; owner Eagles Nest Homes of Granville, N.Y., 1990—; Notary Pub. State of N.Y., 1982—. Editor, pub.: (newsletter) Border Rider News, 1987—. Treas. Heritage Days Village of Granville, 1986; trustee Congl. Ch., 1985, cons. food svc., 1986; active Boy Scouts Am. Recipient Scouters Key award Boy Scouts Am., 1984, dist. award of merit, 1985, Leaders Woodbadge-Honor Campers award, 1985. Mem. Internat. Media and Info. Coun. (co-chmn. 1988), Internat. Snowmobile Coun. (Va.), Border Riders Snowmobile Club (pres. 1974-76, 87-90), Washington County Assn. Snowmobile Clubs (pres. 1983, Washington County coord. 1990—), Granville C. of C., Wakpominee Order of Arrow. Republican.

KRUEGER, ROBERT ALLEN, general manager; b. Oak Park, Ill., Dec. 29, 1935; s. Clarence A. and Edna A. (Polke) K.; m. Carol I. West, June 21, 1959; children: Jeffrey, Jerald, Thomas. AB, Knox Coll., 1957; PhD, Kans. State U., 1965. Dir. R & D B.F. Goodrich Chem., Independence, Ohio, 1975-78, v.p., 1978-80, sr. v.p., 1980-85; gen. mgr. ICI Resins U.S., Wilmington, Mass., 1985—; pres. ICI Resins Can., Brandtford, Ont., 1988—; bd. dirs. Image Polymers Co., Wilmington, Associated Industries of Mass., Boston. Editor: Research Management, 1976-79; patentee in field; contbr. articles to profl. jours. Mem. Am. Chem. Soc., Nat. Paint and Coatings Assn., Nat. Petroleum Refiners Assn. (bd. dirs. 1981-85), Indsl. Rsch. Assn. Office: ICI Resins US 730 Main St Wilmington MA 01887-3386

KRUGER, TRISTRAM COFFIN, dentist; b. Washington, Feb. 5, 1951; s. Gustav Otto and Helyn (Hollingsworth) K. BS, U. Md., 1973; DDS, Georgetown U., 1977; MS, U. Md., 1985. Lic. dentist, nutritionist, D.C., Md. Clin. instr. Georgetown U. Sch. Dentistry, Washington, 1978-88; rsch. assoc. nutrition dept. U. Md., College Park, 1980-85; pvt. practice Bladensburg, Potomac, Md., 1977—, nutritional counselor, 1984—. Contbr. articles to profl. jours. Pres. West Montgomery County Citizens Assn., Potomac, Md., 1987-88; vice chmn. Citizens Adv. Com. Md. Nat. Cap. Park and Planning Commn., 1991-92; v.p. Friends of the Libr., Potomac, mem. libr. adv. com.; chmn. Enriching the Lives of Aging Com., Kiwanis Club D.C., 1984-85. Fellow Acad. Gen. Dentistry; mem. ADA, So. Md. Dental Soc., Am. Med. Athletic Assn., Am. Nutrition Assn. (bd. dirs. 1986—, Am. Coll. Nutrition, Am. Cancer Soc., D.C. Dental Soc., Am. Dental Soc. Anesthesiology, Washington Study Club, Washington Running Club (pres. 1992), Kiwanis (bd. dirs. Washington, 1983-85, Disting. Svc. award 1984), Omicron Kappa Upsilon Nat. Honor Dental Frat., Delta Sigma Delta (grand master 1989, Anthony Gablione award 1977). Republican. Home and Office: 9641 Accord Dr Rockville MD 20854-4305 Office: 5102 Annapolis Rd Ste 101 Bladensburg MD 20710-1457

KRUH, DANIEL, chemist; b. Bklyn., May 22, 1934; s. Irving and Regina (Herbst) K.; m. Sheila Ruth Reinhard, Aug. 6, 1961; children: Andrew Scott, Ira Marc (dec.). BS in Chemistry, W.Va. Wesleyan Coll., Buckhannon, 1955; PhD in Organic Chemistry, Rensselaer Poly. Inst., Troy, N.Y., 1963. Rsch. chemist imperial color/chem. dept. Hercules, Inc., Glens Falls, N.Y., 1963-66; mgr. wire enamel devel. insulating materials Gen. Electric Co., Schenectady, 1966-72; supr. polymer tech. svc. Johnson & Johnson Dental Products Co., East Windsor, N.J., 1972-83; sr. chemist Electro-Sci. Labs., Pennsauken, N.J., 1983-84; project mgr. Internat. Hydron Rsch. Ctr., New Brunswick, N.J., 1984-87; sr. rsch. assoc., mgr. new tech., mgr. licensing/acquisitions Block Drug Co. Inc., Jersey City, 1987—. Contbr. articles to profl. jours. U.S. Army Devel. Command grantee, Troy, N.Y., 1959-63; recipient award Gen. Electric Inventors, Schenectady, 1970. Fellow Am. Inst. Chemists; mem. Soc. Plastics Engrs. (bd. dirs. med. plastics div. 1987-90), Am. Chem. Soc. (chmn. local sect. pub. rels. 1968-70), Internat. Assn. Dental Rsch., Soc. Cosmetic Chemists, Licensing Exec. Soc., Controlled Release Soc. Home: 8 Braddock St East Brunswick NJ 08816-2702 Office: Block Drug Co Inc 257 Cornelison Ave Jersey City NJ 07302-3113

KRULEWICH, HELEN D., lawyer; b. Paterson, N.J., Apr. 6, 1948; d. George and Kathrine P. (Vanderheide) Dworetzky; m. Leonard M. Krulewich, Sept. 2, 1972; children: Sara Heide, David Samuel. BS, Syracuse U., 1970; JD, Suffolk U., 1974. Bar: Mass. 1974, N.J. 1977, U.S. Supreme Ct. 1979. Clk. Nutter, McClennen & Fish, 1970-74, Rackemann, Sawyer & Brewster, Boston, 1974-75; pvt. practice, Boston, 1975-78, assoc. regional counsel real estate ops. Prudential Ins. Co. Am., Boston, 1978-85; counsel Karger & Arnowitz, Boston, 1985-86; pvt. practice, cons. 1987—; mem. L.M. Krulewich & Assocs.. Mem. LWV, Esplanad Citizens Adv. Met. Div., Mayor's Adv. Task Force on Elec. Outages, Newton, Parents Assn. Brimmert May; bd. dirs., chmn. edn. and enrollment coms. Govt. Ctr. Childcare Corp.; trustee Hist. Neighborhood Found.; mem. auction com. Big Sisters. Named Tufts U. Spl. Student 1988-89, Northeastern U. Ins. Inst. Mem. ABA, PIN, Am. Arbitrators Assn., Mus. Fine Arts, Condominium Assn., Beacon Hill and Chestnut Hill Civic Assn., The Children's Mus., Opera Assn., Inst. Contemporary Art, Mus. Modern Art, New Eng. Women in Real Estate, Urban Land Inst., Mass. Bar Assn., Boston Bar Assn. (daycare com., condo com. corp. lawyers com.), Mass. Conveyancers Assn. (legis. subcom. on interval ownership), Mass. Assn. Women Lawyers (scholarship found.), Women's Bar Assn., Friends Pub. Garden.

KRULL, IRA STANLEY, chemistry educator; b. N.Y.C., Oct. 21, 1940; s. Arthur and Anne (Nadelman) K.; m. Erica Meghid, Mar. 18, 1973; 1 child, Marc Arthur. BS in Chemistry cum laude, CUNY, 1962; MS in Organic Chemistry, NYU, 1966, PhD in Organic Chemistry, 1968; NIH postdoctoral fellow, U. Wis. Sch. Pharmacy, 1967-68. Postdoctoral fellow Union Carbide Corp., Tarrytown, N.Y., 1969-70; sr. postdoctoral fellow Weizmann Inst. Sci., Rehovot, Israel, 1970-73; asst. scientist Boyce Thompson Inst. for Plant Rsch., Yonkers, N.Y., 1973-76; sr. scientist New Eng. Inst. for Life Scis. Thermo Electron Corp., Waltham, Mass., 1977-79; sr. scientist and faculty fellow The Barnett Inst. Northeastern U., Boston, 1979—, assoc. prof. chem., 1984—; adv. bd. NIH, U.S. Food and Drug Adminstrn.; co-dir. and lectr. for the Ctr. for Prof. Advancement, East Brunswick, N.J., U.S. Food and Drug Adminstrn., Ctr. for Drug Analysis, St. Louis, Mo., 1985; vis. prof. and lectr. Project Specialist, Yunnan Provincial U., Yunnan Province, Kunming City, People's Republic of China, 1987; mem. organizing com. 3rd Internat. Symposium on Pharm. and Biomed. Analysis, Boston, 1988—, Column Liquid Chromatography 1990 Symposium, 1989—; bd. dirs. New Eng. Chromatography Coun., Northeastern U. Coun. on Rsch. and Scholarship, 1989—; cons. Waters Chromatography div. Millipore Corp., Milford, Mass., EM Sci., Inc., Cherry Hill, N.J., Lab. Data Control Milton Roy Corp., Riviera Beach, Fla., Ciba-Corning Diagnostics, Inc., Medfield, Mass., Med. Products Group Agrl. Chems. div. E.I. du Pont de Nemours & Co., Glasboro, Del., others; sci. advisor FDA, Boston, Bioanalytical Systems, Inc., West Lafayette, Ind.; vis. prof. analytical rsch. CIBAüGeigy AG, Basel, Switzerland, 1990; active numerous other career related activities. Mem. editorial adv. bd. Trends in Analytical Chemistry, 1985—, Jour. Pharm. Biomed. Analysis, 1987—; mem. editorial rev. bd. Jour. Liquid Chromatography, 1985—, Jour. Chromatography, 1987—, Analytical Letters, 1989—, BioChromatography, 1989—, assoc. editor; contbr. articles to Analytical Chemistry, Jour. Chromatography, Jour. Chromatographic Sci.; contbr. chpts. to various books in field. Mem. Am. Chem. Soc., Assn. Official Analytical Chemists, Soc. Electroanalytical Chemistry, New Eng. Sect. Analytical Chemistry Div., N.Y. Acad. Scis., Mensa, Sigma Xi, Phi Lambda Upsilon. Democrat. Jewish. Home: 86 Allen Rd North Easton MA 02356-2506 Office: Northeastern U 360 Huntington Ave # 341mu Boston MA 02115-5000

KRULL, JAMES SARGENT, marketing professional; b. Rockville Centre, N.Y., June 28, 1948; s. John Sargent and Jane (Davidson) K.; m. Mary Katherine Murtagh, Aug. 23, 1969; children: James, Jeffrey, Megan. BS in Econ., Cath. U., Washington, 1970; MBA, Villanova U., Pa., 1987. Mgmt. cons. R.L. Banks & Assocs., Inc., Washington, 1969-78; dir. passenger transp. Conrail, Phila., 1979-83; ptnr. Kenny Krull & O'Connor, Wayne, Pa., 1983-84; prin. J.S. Krull & Assocs., Wayne, Pa., 1984-88; v.p. mktg. & bus. devel. Internat. Computaprint Corp., Fort Washington, Pa., 1989—. Author: Logistics and Costing; contbr. articles to profl. jours. Cubmaster Boy Scouts Am., Strafford, Pa., 1982-85; treas. Devon (Pa.) Prep Parents Assn., 1989-91. Mem. Nat. Assn. Desktop Pub., Washington Directory Pub. Assn., MBA Execs., N.Y. Directory Pub. Assn., Beta Gamma Sigma. Republican. Home: 695 Vassar Rd Wayne PA 19087-5341 Office: Internat Computaprint Corp 475 Virginia Dr Fort Washington PA 19034-2792

KRUMHOLZ, WILHELM VILEM, psychiatrist; b. Vienna, Austria, Aug. 20, 1915; came to U.S., 1953; s. Josef and Fani (Engler) K.; m. Miriam Ryszelewska, Oct. 6, 1948 (dec. 1977); children: Ariane Denise Krumholz Lynn, Diana Noemi Krumholz McDonald. PhD, Universitaet Med. Sch., Vienna, 1938, postgrad., 1944; MD, Med. Sch. Basel (Switzerland), 1944, SUNY, Stony Brook, 1957. Clin. and surg. trainee Polyclinic Switzerland, Basel, 1948; rotating intern Hackensack (N.J.) Hosp., 1954-55; resident in psychiatry Cen. Islip (N.Y.) Psychiat. Ctr., 1955-58, staff psychiatrist, supr. psychiatry rsch. div., 1958-71; pvt. practice Islip Terr, 1959-80; sex therapist Human Sexuality Ctr., L.I. and Hillside, N.Y., 1974; asst. prof. Sch. Medicine SUNY, Stony Brook, 1976—; cons. Southside Hosp., Bayshore, N.Y., 1971-80; tchr. Cen. Islip Sch. Nursing, 1956-59, lectr. Contbr. articles to profl. jours. Fellow Am. Psychiat. Assn. (life), Am. Med. Soc. Vienna (life). Home: 15 Cleveland St Islip Terrace NY 11752-2602

KRUPP, IAMES ARTHUR GUSTAVE, manufacturing materials executive, consultant; b. Naples, Italy, Oct. 27, 1944; came to U.S., 1945; s. Ralph Gustave and Lydia (Guerroni) K.; m. Joyce Ann Draffan, Nov. 5, 1966; children: James Michael Douglas, Matthew Ralph Alexander. Student, U.S. Naval Acad., 1963-66; BSME magna cum laude, U. New Haven, 1971, EMBA, 1981. Cert. Fellow in Prodn. and Inventory Mgmt. Prodn. control mgr. Sargent & Co., New Haven, Conn., 1966-72; prodn. scheduling mgr. Stanley Tools, New Britain, Conn., 1972-75; materials mgr. Whitney Blake, Hamden, Conn., 1975-76; materials control mgr. Burndy Corp., Norwalk, Conn., 1976-79; prodn. and inventory mgr. Picker Corp., Northford, Conn., 1979-81; materials mgr. Carlyle Johnson Machine Co., Manchester, Conn., 1981-84; dir. advanced planning systems ITT Sealectro, New Britain, 1984-89; dir. corp. materials Echlin Inc., Branford, Conn., 1989—. Editorial review bd. mem. Production and Inventory Management Journal, 1988—; contbr. 31 articles to profl. jours. Chmn. Bd. Ethics, Wallingford, Conn., 1980-84; councilman Town Coun., Wallingford, 1984-85; mem. Charter Revision Comm., Wallingford, 1988-89. With USN, 1963-67. Mem. Am. Prodn. and Inventory Control Soc., Assn. for Mfg. Excellence. Democrat. Roman Catholic. Office: Echlin Inc 100 Double Beach Rd Branford CT 06405

KRUPP, JUDY-ARIN, national and international consultant; b. New London, Conn., Feb. 4, 1937; d. Harold and Minnie (Watchinsky) Peck; m. Alan Frederick Krupp, June 15, 1958; children: Peter, Larry, Susan, Karen. BA, Conn. Coll., 1958; MS in Edn., Queens Coll., 1960; 6th yr. cert., U. Conn., 1979, PhD, 1980. Tchr. gen. sci. Westbury (N.Y.) Pub. Schs., 1958-60; tchr. biology Roslyn (N.Y.) Pub. Schs., 1960-61; cons. edn. Europe, Near East and U.S., 1980—. Author: Adult Development: Implications for Staff Development, 1980, The Adult Learner, A Unique Entity, 1982, When Parents Face the Schools, 1984; contbr. over 40 articles to profl. jours. and chpts. to books. Trustee Home Care/Lutz Jr. Ms., Manchester, Conn., 1970-76; pres. Hosp. Aux., Manchester, 1976; vol. Conn. Arthritis Assn., Newington, 1980—, Ohio Arthritis Assn., Columbus, 1980. Recipient appreciation award Conn. Arthritis Assn., 1985; NSF grantee, 1959. Mem. Am. Assn. for Counseling and Devel., Am. Assn. for Adult and Continuing Edn., Am. Psychol. Assn., Assn. for Supervision and Curriculum Devel., N.Am. Assn. for Counsel and Supervision (rep. adult devel. and aging com. 1985-87), Nat. Staff Devel. Council (trustee 1987-88), Conn. Orgn. for Profl. Devel. (pres. 1984-85, Outstanding Leadership award 1984, Outstanding Ct. Staff Developer award 1989), Phi Delta Kappa, Phi Kappa Phi, Pi Lambda Theta. Home and Office: 40 Mcdivitt Dr Manchester CT 06040-2240

KRUPSKA, DANYA (MRS. TED THURSTON), director, choreographer; b. Fall River, Mass., Aug. 13, 1921; d. Bronislaw and Anna (Niementowska) Krupski; m. James M. Hanrihan (div. 1953); 1 child, Brion; m. Ted Thurston, May 27, 1954; 1 child, Tina Lyn. Student, Lankenau Sch. for Girls, Phila.; studied with, Ethel Phillips Dance Studio, Catherine Littlefield Ballet Studio, L. Egorova, Paris, Mikhail Mordkin, N.Y.C. and Phila.; studied, Aubrey Hitchens Studio, N.Y.C., Bobby Lewis Dir.'s Studio, N.Y.C. Performed concerts and toured in Poland, Roumania, Balkan Countries, Hungary, Vienna, Palestine, 1929-36; joined Phila. Ballet (Littlefield) for European tour, 1937, Chgo. Opera Season, 1938, Am. Ballet (Ballanchine), N.Y.C., 1938; soloist Broadway prodn.: Frank Fay Show, Radio City Music Hall Ballet; leading role on nat. tour: Johnny Belinda 1941; soloist in: Chouve Souris, 1943; dancer in role of Dream Laurie, 1st nat. co. of Okla., later Broadway co., 1945; asst. to choreographer Agnes de Mille on Rodgers and Hammerstein prodn.: Allegro; then in ballet prodn.: Fall River Legend; in opera prodn.: Rape of Lucrece; Broadway prodns.: Girl in Pink Tights, Gentlemen Prefer Blonds, Paint Your Wagon; assisted Michael Kidd in Broadway prodn.: Can Can; choreographer Broadway prodn.: Most Happy Fella (Tony award nomination), Seventeen, 1st Shoestring Revue, Carefree Heart, Happiest Girl in the World (Tony award nomination), Her First Roman, 1968, Apollo and Miss Agnes; choreographer Met. Opera prodn.: The Gypsy Baron; choreographer Italian mus.: Rugantino, 1962; choreographer: TV Salute to the Peace Corps, 1965; guest choreographer: Zorba, Nat. Theatre, Reykjavik, Iceland, 1971, Company for Stora Teatern, Gothenburg, Sweden, 1971, Fantastiks, Little Theatre, Gothenburg, 1971, No No Nanette, Malmö Stadsteater, Sweden, 1973, Porgy and Bess, Malmö Stadsteater, Sweden, 1974, Richard Rodger's Prodn. of Rex, Broadway, N.Y.C., 1976, Showboat, Malmö Stadsteater, 1976; dir., choreographer: Bernstein's The Mass, Malmö Stadsteater, 1975, Chicago, Det Danske Teater, Denmark, 1977, Our Man in Havana, Poland, 1977, Cabaret, Helsingborg Stadsteater, Sweden, 1978, Guys and Dolls, Aarhus Teater, Denmark, 1978, Once Upon a Mattress, Nat. Theater Reykjavik, Iceland, 1981, Animalen, Malmö Stadsteater, Sweden, 1985, Papushko, Colonade Theatre, N.Y.C., 1985; producer, dir.; choreographer: The King and I, Malmö Stadsteater, Sweden, 1984, Empress of China, Cin. Playhouse, 1984; produced, directed, choreographed Sound of Music, Malmo Stadsteater, Sweden, 1990; directed, choreographed Lerner and Loewe lost musical Day before Spring, N.Y.C., 1990; dance and mus. staging How it Was Done in Odessa, Walnut St. Theatre, Phila., 1991; dir. mus. prodns., N.Y. City Center; Most Happy Fella, 1959, Showboat, 1961, Fiorello, 1962 (also White House prodn. for gov.'s conf. 1968), Oklahoma, Nat. Theatre, Reykjavik, 1972; choreographer for Buick Hour, 1952, Colgate Comedy Hour, 1953, Omnibus; dir. U.S. Steel Theatre Guild Prodns; Ballets Outlook for Three (Ellington), Pointes on Jazz (Brubeck), Am. Ballet Theatre. Mem. Actors Equity Assn., Soc. Stage Dirs and Choreographers (exec. bd. mem.), Actors Studio (playwrights and dirs. unit). Office: 564 W 52d St New York NY 10019

KRUSE, REGINA BETH, elementary school counselor; b. Boston, Nov. 20, 1948; d. Irving and Evelyn Sarah (Egermann) Imber; m. Daniel Ray Kruse, Nov. 29, 1974; children: Charlotte Ann, Lillian Maia. BA, Conn. Coll., 1970; MEd, U. Mo., 1971, postgrad., 1973-74. Cert. sch. counselor. Elem. sch. tchr. Walpole (Mass.) Pub. Schs., 1971-72; elem. sch. counselor North Andover (Mass.) Pub. Schs., 1972-73; teaching asst. U. Mo., Columbia, 1973-74; elem. sch. counselor Columbia Pub. Schs., 1974-75, Los Alamos (N.Mex.) Pub. Schs., 1975-76, Daniel Boone Schs., Birdsboro, Pa., 1981, Muhlenberg Schs., Temple, Pa., 1981-82, Tulpehocken Schs., Bernville, Pa., 1982-84, Twin Valley Schs., Elverson, Pa., 1984—; house parent Dana Hall Sch., Wellesley, Mass., 1976-79; chmn. guidance task force Twin Valley Schs., 1988—, early childhood task force, 1990—. Chmn. religious edn. com. Unitarian-Universalist Ch. of Berks, Reading, Pa., 1981-83. Mem. NEA, Assn. Counseling and Devel., Pa. Sch. Counselor Assn., Pa. Sch. Edn. Assn., Twin Valley Edn. Assn., Berks Area Counselor Assn. (pres. 1992—). Democrat. Office: Twin Valley Schs Robeson Elem RD 3 Box 2042 Birdsboro PA 19607

KRUSHENICK, JOHN, artist, art consultant; b. N.Y.C., Mar. 18, 1927; s. John and Anna (Wilhowy) K.; m. Frances Harriet Greenberg, June 1, 1957; children: Andra Melissa, Joshua John, Jevon Jedidiah. Student, Art Students League, N.Y.C., 1948-51, Hans Hoffman Sch., N.Y.C., 1948-51; BFA, U. Wis., Milw., 1975. Owner, dir. Brata Gallery, N.Y.C., 1957-64;

dir., curator Dorsky Gallery, N.Y.C., 1970-71, Ft. Wayne (Ind.) Mus. Art, 1975-78; assoc. prof., dir. fine art galleries U. Wis., 1972-75; cons. C.S. Schulte Galleries, N.Y.C. and South Orange, N.J., 1981-90, Dupont Graphic Arts, Pinebrook, N.J., 1990—; mem. mus. adv. panel Ind. Arts Commn., Indpls., 1975-76; art critic News-Sentinel, Ft. Wayne, 1978-79; adj. instr. art Cooper Union, N.Y.C., 1968-69; tchr. art adult edn., Pequannock and Montclair, N.J., 1982-91. One-man shows include Bank State Coll., N.Y.C., 1970, Leo Castelli Downtown NYCLU Group NYC, 1971, Weatherspoon Gallery, U. N.C., 1973, Ft. Wayne Mus. of Art, 1976, 10th St. N.Y.C. 20th Anniversary Exhbn., 1977, Ten Park Gall One Man, Montclair, N.J., 1990, others; represented in permanent collections Mus. Modern Art, N.Y.C., Weatherspoon Gallery, U. N.C., Chapel Hill, Ft. Wayne Mus. Art, also pvt. collections. Leader Explorers troop Boy Scouts Am., Ft. Wayne, 1977. Mem. Fin and Feather Club (Pequannock) (pres. 1984-86). Home: 7 Windsor Pl Montclair NJ 07043-1109

KRUSOS, DENIS ANGELO, communications company executive; b. N.Y.C., Oct. 27, 1927; s. Angelo and Mary (Razzi) K.; B.S., CCNY, 1949; M.S., Newark Coll. Engring., 1951; J.D., St. Johns U., 1968; m. Catherine Bezas, July 30, 1955; children—Peri Denise, Denis Zachary. Devel. engr. missile div. Republic Aviation & Fairchild Engring. Corp., 1952-56; sr. engr. Arma div. Am. Bosch Arma Corp., 1956-60; founder dir. Automation Labs., Inc., Mineola, N.Y., 1955-65; founder, chmn. bd., dir. Integrated Electronics Corp., Huntington Station, N.Y., 1966-83; chmn. bd. Color Q Inc., Dayton, Ohio, 1969—; founder, pres., dir. Panafax Corp., Woodbury, N.Y., 1977-82; founder, chmn. bd., dir. Visual Scis., Inc., 1969-83; founder, chmn. bd., chief exec. officer, dir. CopyTele, Inc., Huntington Station, 1982—. Served with U.S. Army, 1946-47. Mem. Am., New York, Suffolk County bar assns., IEEE. Home: 1 Lloyd Harbor Rd Huntington NY 11743-9701 Office: CopyTele Inc 900 Walt Whitman Rd Melville NY 11747-2215

KRUT, STEPHEN FRANK, trade association administrator; b. Mt. Union, Pa., Sept. 26, 1943; s. John Joseph and Sophia (George) K.; m. Minerva Elizabeth Smith, Feb. 27, 1965 (div. Dec. 1977); children: Suzanne Marie, Stephen Vincent; m. Carol Lynn McCord, Feb. 11, 1978; 1 child, Shawn Lawrence. BA in Journalism, Pa. State U., 1964. Reporter Scranton (Pa.) Tribune, 1965, The Grit, Williamsport, Pa., 1966, Patriot-Evening News, Harrisburg, Pa., 1966-69; dir. pub. rels. Mfg. Housing Assn., New Cumberland, Pa., 1970-73; dir. pub. rels. Am. Assn. Meat Processors, Elizabethtown, Pa., 1974-76, asst. exec. dir., 1976-80, exec. dir., 1981—; mem. adv. com. on meat and poultry insp. USDA, Washington, 1985—; presenter Orgn. of Am. States, Montevideo, Uraguay, 1988. President Mechanicsburg (Pa.) Lions, 1976; lobbyist Am. Assn. Meat Processors, Elizabethtown, 1974—. Recipient Master Butcher award Belgium Meat Processors Fedn., 1990. Mem. Am. Soc. Assn. Execs., Pa. Soc. Assn. Execs. (pres. 1992), Livestock Industry Inst. (trustee). Office: Am Assn Meat Processors One Meating Pl Elizabethtown PA 17022

KRUZA, J. A., editor; b. Skrunda, Latvia, Jan. 23, 1940; came to U.S., 1947; married; 2 children. Editor Info-Quest Inc., Cambridge, Mass., 1960-72, Kaleidoscopix, Inc., Franklin, Mass., 1972-82; lobbyist State of Mass., Boston, 1976-82, State of R.I., Providence, 1976-82; mem. Successful Mag. Pub. Group, Maine and Ala., 1980-89. Author: Lighthouses of Massachusetts Handbook, 1989. With A.C., USN, 1964-70. Mem. Nat. Soc. Preservation of Covered Bridges, U.S. Lighthouse Soc., Photo Historic Soc. New Eng., Soc. Profl. Journalists in New Eng., Overseas Press Club, Masons (officer). Office: Kaleidoscopix Inc PO Box 389 Franklin MA 02038-0389

KRYGIER, STANLEY JAMES, former orthodontist; b. Phila., Nov. 18, 1903; s. Joseph and Felixa K.; m. Felicia A. Krygier, June 28, 1932; children: Kathleen P. Krygier Lewis, Patricia Ann Krygier Scott. DDS, Temple U., 1927; MS, U. Pa., 1950. Diplomate Am. Bd. Orthodontics. Pres. Orthodontic Internat. Svcs., 1970-85, Orthodontic Internat. Service, Inc., Wilmington, Del., 1977-87; v.p. OI Supply, Inc., Wilmington, 1987—; pres. Orthodonic Excellence Lab., Inc.; lectr. in field USA, Poland, Hong Kong, Thailand, Australia. Patentee 5 orthodontic devices. Fellow Am. Coll. Dentistry, Internat. Coll. Dentists; mem. Am. Orthodontic Assn. (del. 1971-73), Middle Atlantic Soc. Orthodontists (pres. 1970-71), Am. Dental Assn., Del. State Dental Assn. (pres. 1950-51), Kent-Sussex County Dental Soc. (pres. 1946-47), Tweed Orthodontic Research Soc., Ricketts Orthodontic Research Soc., Begg Soc. for Research, Ampol (Most Valued Person Polish Descent award 1980), Omicron Kappa Upsilon. Roman Catholic. Clubs: Greenville Country, Wilmington Univ. (Wilmington).

KRYSZTOFORSKI, JOSEPH THEODORE, company executive; b. Bklyn., Sept. 30, 1953; s. Theodore and Theresa Constance K.; m. Stavreoula Psihogous, Aug. 24, 1974 (div. Oct., 1982)m. Frances W. Berni, Dec. 31, 1986, 1 child, Byron Joseph. Student, Bklyn. Coll., 1972-73; BA, MA, SUNY, Stony Brook, 1977. Cert. secondary educator, N.Y. Programmer Carulli & Sons Produce, Bklyn., 1973-76; cons., owner SCDPI, Smithtown, N.Y., 1976-77; cons., pres. Stavjo Data Processing, Smithtown, 1977-78; sr. systems analyst Citicorp Credit Svcs., Inc., Melville, N.Y., 1978-79, project leader, 1979-80, ops. head, 1982-84; mgr. systems software Citicorp Sales Mgmt., Melville, 1980-82; dir. info. svc. Citicorp Card Acceptance Svcs., Melville, 1984-88; v.p. planning Citicorp Establishment Svcs., Huntington, N.Y., 1988—; cons. Smithtown Cen. Schs., 1977-78; rsch. analyst Cen. Islip (N.Y.) State Hosp., 1973-74. Photographer: American History, 1976; designer, developer: (computer software) Dental Office Management, 1980, Batch Authorization/POS, 1982, Abode, 1992 (Best in Category award 1992). Organizer Lake Grove (N.Y.) Civic Soc., 1987; organizer, tchr. First Steps, Stony Brook, 1988; mem., organizer Green Party, Lake Grove, 1988. Recipient Best in Show award Inst. Cert. PHotographers, 1977-80. Mem. Data Processing Mgmt. Assn., Am. Mgmt. Assn. Home: 12 Stonewood Ct Phoenix MD 21131 Office: Citicorp Establishment Svcs 2 Huntington Quad Huntington NY 11746

KRZYNOWEK, S. THEODORE, chemicals executive; b. Hartford, Conn., Apr. 9, 1943; s. Stanley Theodore and Agnes Francis (Brzezinski) K.; m. Judith Laming Krzynowek, Nov. 19, 1966; 1 child, Darcy. BS, Bates Coll., 1965. Chemist Polyvinyl Chemicals, Wilmington, Mass., 1966-69, sales rep., 1969-74, product mgr., 1974-77, sales rep., 1977-87; tech. svc. mgr. ICI Resins, Wilmington, Mass., 1987-89; v.p. Image Polymers, Wilmington, Mass., 1989—. Mem. Soc. Imaging Sci. and Tech. Office: Image Polymers 730 Main St Wilmington MA 01887

KRZYZANOWSKI, EVE, media executive; b. N.Y.C., July 19, 1951; d. Ludwik and Janine (Malinowska) K.; m. Charles Richard Novitz, Feb. 11, 1988. BA with honors, Vassar Coll., 1972. Mgr. ABC News, N.Y.C., 1972-80, producer, 1978-80; producer NBC News, N.Y.C., 1980-82; sr. producer CBS News, N.Y.C., 1982; mng. producer Santa Fe Communications, L.A., 1984; sr. producer Fin. News Network, N.Y.C., 1985-87, v.p., news dir., 1987-90; exec. producer This Morning Bus., N.Y.C., 1988-90; producer Viacom, N.Y.C., 1990; v.p. devel. BBC-Lionheart, N.Y.C., 1991—. Mem. Soc. Profl. Journalists. Office: BBC-Lionheart 630 5th Ave Rm 2220 New York NY 10111-0217

KSZEPKA, JOSEPH ANTHONY, insurance and real estate broker; b. Three Rivers, Mass., Oct. 6, 1931; s. Joseph and Helena (Sakowski) K.; student Alliance Coll., 1951, U. Mass., 1952; m. Frances H. Dragon, May 11, 1957; children: Louise, Paul, Jane, Joan, Irene. Lic. pub. acct. Owner ins. and real estate agy., broker, Three Rivers, 1956—; trustee Country Bank for Savs.; clk., Three Rivers Fire Dist., 1965-82; notary pub., 1960—; justice of peace, 1973—; mem. Palmer Bd. Health, 1957-62; chmn. bd. dirs. Wing Meml. Hosp., 1987-91, v.p. hosp. assn., 1982; chmn. bd. govs. Wing Health Systems, Inc., 1992; mem. Kosciuszko Found. Served with U.S. Army, 1953-55. Mem. Ind. Ins. Agts. Mass., Profl. Ins. Agts. New Eng., Ind. Ins. Agts. Hampden County (treas. 1983—), Three Rivers C. of C. (treas. 1960—, sec.-treas. 1966—, Man of Yr. 1972), Amvets, Polish Nat. Alliance, Polish Roman Cath. Union, St. Stanislaus Polish Lyceum (past pres.). Lodge: Rotary (pres. 1980). Address: 398 Main St Three Rivers MA 01080

KU, JENTUNG, mechanical and aerospace engineer; b. Hsinchu, Republic of China; came to U.S., 1974; BS, Tsing Hua U., Hsinchu, 1972; MS, Purdue U., 1976, PhD, 1980. Rsch. asst. Purdue U., West Lafayette, Ind., 1976-80; mem. tech. staff Advanced Tech. Ctr., Bendix Corp., Columbia, Md., 1980-83; section head/program mgr. OAO Corp., Greenbelt, Md., 1983-91; sr. engr. NASA Goddard Space Flight Ctr., Greenbelt, Md., 1991—. Contbr. articles on heat transfer and thermal control systems to profl. jours.; pioneer in developing capillary pumped loop heat transport systems (2 Tech. Innovation awards NASA). Bd. dirs. Columbia Chinese Bapt. Ch., 1991—. Mem. ASME, AIAA, Am. Nuclear Soc., Tau Beta Pi, Phi Tau Phi. Baptist. Home: 14208 Bradshaw Dr Silver Spring MD 20905 Office: NASA Goddard Space Flight Ctr Greenbelt MD 20771

KU, R. FASHUN, architect, urban development consultant; b. Meihsien, Kwontung, China, Feb. 16, 1949; s. Enfu and Gifung (Yae) K. MS, U. Wis., 1972; MBA, U. Rochester, 1989. Registered architect, N.Y. Sr. city planner, Planning Bur. City of Rochester, N.Y., 1975-78, chief tech. services, Devel. Services Bur., 1979-81, dir. downtown devel. Econ. Devel. Dept., 1982—; prin. Ku and Assocs., Rochester, 1981—. Mem. Rochester Internat. Friendship Coun., 1985-86; bd. dirs. Rochester Health Assn. Recipient Good Neighbor award Corn Hill Neighbor Assn., 1982. Mem. AIA, N.Y. State Assn. Architects, Am. Planning Assn. Democrat. Home: 877 Harvard St Rochester NY 14610-1528 Office: The City of Rochester 30 Church St Rochester NY 14614-1205

KU, Y. H., engineering educator; b. Wusih, Kiangsu, China, Dec. 24, 1902; came to U.S., 1950; s. Ken Ming Ku and Ching-Su Wang; m. Wei-zing Wang, Apr. 1, 1929; children: Wei-Lien, Wei-Ching, Wei-Wen (Mrs. Chi-Liang Hsieh), Walter, John, Victor, Anna (Mrs. Yuk-Kai Lau). S.B., MIT, 1925, S.M., 1926, Sc.D., 1928; M.A., LL.D., U. Pa., 1972. Prof. elec. engring., head dept. Chekiang U., China, 1929-30; dean engring. Cen. U., China, 1931-32; pres. Central U., 1944-45; dean engring. Tsing Hua U., China, 1932-37; vice minister Ministry Edn., Republic of China, 1938-44; edn. commr. Shanghai, 1945-47; pres. Nat. Chengchi U., Nanking, 1947-49; vis. prof. MIT, 1950-52; prof. U. Pa., 1952-71, prof. emeritus, 1972—; hon. prof. Jiao-Tong U., Shanghai, 1979—, Xi'an, Southwestern and Northern, 1985—, Northeastern U. Tech. and NW Inst. Telecommunications, 1986—, S.E. U. Nanjing, 1988—; cons. Gen. Electric Co., Univac, RCA. Author: Analysis and Control of Nonlinear Systems, 1958, Electric Energy Conversion, 1959, Transient Circuit Analysis, 1961, Analysis and Control of Linear Systems, 1962, Collected Scientific Papers, 1971; poems, plays, novels, essays in Chinese Collected Works, 1961; Woodcutter's Song, 1963, Pine Wind, 1964, Lotus Song, 1966, Lofty Mountains, 1968, The Liang River, 1970, The Hui Spring, 1971, The Si Mountain, 1972, 500 Irregular Poems, 1972, The Great Lake, 1973, 1000 Regular Poems, 1973, 360 Recent Poems, 1976, The Tide Sound, 1980, History of Chan (Zen) Masters, 1976, History of Japanese Zen Masters, 1977, History of Zen (in English), 1979, The Long Life, 1981, One Family-Two Worlds (in English), 1982, Poems after Chin Kuan, 1983, Poems after Tao Chien, 1984, 303 Poems after Tang Poets, 1986, Flying Clouds and Flowing Water, 1987, Poems After Wu Wen-Ying, 1988, Selected Plays, 1990, Eyebrows, 1991, Scientific Papers, 1992. Recipient Gold medal Ministry Edn., Republic of China; Pro Mundi Beneficio Gold medal Brazilian Acad. Humanities, 1975; Gold medal Chinese Inst. Elec. Engrs., 1972. Fellow Academia Sinica, IEEE (Lamme medal 1972), Instn. Elec. Engrs. (London); mem. Am. Soc. Engring. Edn., Internat. Union Theoretical and Applied Mechanics (mem. gen. assembly), U.S. Nat. Com. on Theoretical and Applied Mechanics, Sigma Xi, Eta Kappa Nu, Phi Tau Phi. Home: 1420 Locust St 22G Philadelphia PA 19102 Office: 200 S 33d St Philadelphia PA 19104

KUBASEK, ANTHONY JOSEPH, music educator; b. Kingston, Pa., Jan. 27, 1963; s. Anthony G. and Flora (Kadtke) K. MusB, Wilkes U., 1984. Music educator Northwest Area Sch. Dist., Shickshinny, Pa., 1985-86; studio music tchr. Mocanaqua, Pa., 1986—; music educator Wyo. Seminary, Kingston, Pa., 1988—; organist, choir dir. Holy Child Ch., Sheatown, Pa., 1985—. Choir mem. Wyoming Valley Oratorio Soc., Wilkes-Barre, Pa., 1987-89. Mem. Music Educators Nat. Conf., Am. Fedn. Musicians. Republican. Roman Catholic. Office: Wyoming Seminary 201 N Sprague Ave Wilkes Barre PA 18704-3593

KUBEJA, JUDITH WALLACE, higher education administrator; b. Pitts., Oct. 27, 1948; d. Kenneth Dale and Elizabeth Stoner (Wurtz) Wallace; m. J. Mark Kubeja, July 4, 1974. Student, Inst. for Am. Universities, Aix-en-Provence, France, 1969; BA, Wittenberg U., Springfield, OH., 1970; MS, Gannon U., Erie, Pa., 1991. Reporter Springfield Daily News-Sun, Springfield, Ohio, 1970-72; tchr. Ridgewood Sch., 1972-73; counselor Brown Ledge Camp, Mallett's Bay, Vt., 1973; sec. U. Vt., Burlington, 1973-74, Gannon U., Erie, Pa., 1975-85; asst. registrar Gannon U., 1985-88, asst. to pres., 1988-91; exec. asst. to the provost and v.p. for acad. affairs Edinboro U. of Pa., 1991—. Chair Girard Borough Zoning Hearing Bd., Pa., 1981—; v.p., exec. dir. Erie Summer Festival of the Arts, 1989—; mem. Pub. Art Com. of Erie Excellence Coun., 1990—. Recipient: various dog show awards. Mem. Phi Sigma Iota Romance Language honorary, 1970—, Psi Chi Psychology Honorary, 1991—. Home: 337 Main St E Girard PA 16417-1708

KUBIAK, JOHN MICHAEL, academic administrator; b. Pulaski, Wis., Jan. 15, 1935; s. Anton Joseph and Genevieve (McGuire) K.; m. Mary Dee Neville, Aug. 5, 1966; children: Michelle Jo, Leslie A. Welsh, Robert N. Welsh. BS in Mil. Engring., U.S. Mil. Acad., 1958; MBA, Washington U., St. Louis, 1976, M Data Processing, 1977; PhD, St. Louis U., 1981. Commd. 2d lt. USAF, 1958, advanced through grades to col., 1979; prof. aerospace studies Cornell U., Ithaca, N.Y., 1983-86; retired USAF, 1986; exec. dir. Ctr. Internat. Studies, Cornell U., 1986—. Decorated Legion of Merit (2), Air Force Commendation Medals (2), Air Medals (2). Mem. Air Force Assn., Am. Assn. Higher Edn., Rotary, Beta Gamma Sigma. Republican. Office: Cornell U Ctr Internat Studies 170 Uris Hall Ithaca NY 14853

KUCHARAVY, ROBERT M., public relations executive; b. Syracuse, N.Y., Nov. 25, 1946; s. Milton and M. Margaret (Lutz) K. BA, LeMoyne Coll., 1969; MA, Clark U., 1992. Account exec., dir. client service Rath Orgn., Syracuse, N.Y.C., 1969-76; pres. R.M.K. Assocs., Syracuse, 1976-81; mgr. pub. relations abrasives group Norton Co., Worcester, Mass., 1981-84; communications cons. Worcester, 1984-85; mgr. spl. programs Digital Equipment Corp., Maynard, Mass., 1985—; adj. prof. Syracuse U., 1978-81. Chmn. vol. resources div. United Way Cen. Mass., Worcester, 1985-90; bd. dirs. Big Bros., Big Sisters Worcester, 1990—; corporator Sta. WICN Pub. Radio, Worcester, 1982-84, Higgins Armory Mus., 1991, Worcester Area Mental Health Ctr., 1990—, Greater Worcester Community Found., 1990—, mktg. commr., 1990—. Mem. Pub. Rels. Soc. Am. (honors and awards com. 1988-90, Body of Knowledge bd. 1990—), Univ. Club Syracuse. Roman Catholic. Home: 11 Einhorn Rd Worcester MA 01609-2207 Office: Digital Equipment Corp 146 Main St Maynard MA 01754-2504

KUCHNER, EUGENE FREDERICK, neurosurgeon, educator; b. N.Y.C., Nov. 19, 1945; s. Morton H. and Edna Estelle (Marks) K. m. Joan Ruth Freedman, Sept. 2, 1968; children: Marc Jason, Eric Benjamin. AB, Johns Hopkins U., 1967; MD, U. Chgo., 1971. Resident in surgery Yale U. Sch. Medicine, New Haven, 1971-72; resident in neurosurgery Montreal (Que., Can.) Neurol. Inst., McGill U., 1972-76, spine fellow, 1976; neurosurgeon Sch. Medicine, SUNY, Downstate, 1976-79, Stony Brook, 1979—; mem. staff North Shore U. Hosp.-Cornell U. Med. Ctr., Univ. Hosp., Stony Brook, Nassau County Med. Ctr., St. John's Hosp.; cons. in field. Contbr. articles to profl. publs.; specialist in microsurgery, magnetic resonance imaging, spinal trauma, pituitary surgery. Recipient K.G. McKenzie Meml. award Royal Coll. Physicians and Surgeons Can., 1976, Open Scholarship award Johns Hopkins U., yearly, 1963-66, Scholarship award U. Chgo., yearly, 1967-70; NSF fellow, 1968, Blackman-Hoffman Found. fellow, 1969-70, USPHS fellow, 1969. Mem. ACS, AMA, Am. Assn. Neurol. Surgeons, Congress Neurol. Surgeons, N.Y. Acad. Scis., L.I. Neurosci. Acad., Suffolk Acad. Medicine, Montreal Neurol. Inst. Fellows Soc., N.Y. State Neurosurg. Soc., N.Y. State Med. Soc., N.Y. State Soc. Surgeons, Am. Epilepsy Soc., Am. Soc. Neuroimaging, Internat. Platform Assn., Nat. Alumni Schs. (chmn. com. Johns Hopkins U.), Assn. Yale Alumni in Medicine, Princeton Club N.Y., John Hopkins Club, Sigma Xi. Office: Stony Brook Med Ctr PO Box 721 Stony Brook NY 11790-0721

KUCHTA, JOHN ANDREW, management consultant; b. Bristol, Conn., June 24, 1943; s. John Stephen and Mildred (Reich) K.; m. Irene Barbara Levins, Sept. 16, 1965; children: Michelle Rachel, Tamara-Jean. AB, Brown U., 1965; MS, Fairleigh Dickinson U., 1983. Auditor Westinghouse Electric Co., Bloomfield, N.J., 1965-67; plant acct. Westinghouse Electric Co., Randolph, N.J., 1967-69; mgr. cost control Westinghouse Electric Co., Short Hills, N.J., 1969-71; account mgr. USV Pharm., Tuckahoe, 1971-74; mgr. inventory control Revlon Health Care, Tuckahoe, 1974-79; dir. material mgmt. Hudson Pharm., West Caldwell, N.J., 1979-84; cons. Gross & Assocs., Woodbridge, N.Y., 1984-86, 87—; dir. material mgmt. Superpharm Inc., Central Islip, N.Y., 1986-87. Author: How To Save Warehouse Space: 144 Tested Techniques, 1992. Mem. Am. Prodn. and Inventory Control Soc. (cert.), Warehouse Edn. and Rsch. Coun., Coun. Logistics Mgmt. Home: 15 Pawnee Ave Oakland NJ 07436 Office: Gross & Assocs 367 Berry St Woodbridge NJ 07095-3344

KUCHTA, RONALD ANDREW, art museum director, educator; b. Lackawanna, N.Y., June 23, 1935; s. Andrew and Clara May (Barnes) K.; m. Sique Stoll, Oct. 1, 1970 (div. 1974). B.A., Kenyon Coll., 1957; M.A., Western Res. U., 1961; postgrad. in mgmt., Cornell U., 1979. Curator Chrysler Mus., Provincetown, Mass., 1961-67, Santa Barbara Mus. Art, (Calif.), 1967-74; dir. Everson Mus. Art, Syracuse, N.Y., 1974—; adj. prof. Syracuse U., 1974—; trustee Fondo del Sol, Washington, 1974—, Nat. Conf. Educators Ceramic Arts, 1986, Quarry Rd. Sculpture Pk., Cazenovia, N.Y.; founding dir. Syracuse China Ctr. for Study Am. Ceramics; chmn. Urban Arts Commn., Syracuse; juror Mino '89 Internat. Competition for Ceramics, Gifu, Japan, 1989; juror Concorso Internazionale della Ceramica d'Arte, Faenza, Italy, 1990, Biennale Nationale de Ceramique, Trois Rivieres, Que., Can., 1992. Author: Provincetown Painters, 1975, Interior Vision, 1971, Batuz: Works in Paper, 1981, Robert Beauchamp: An American Expressionist, 1984; editor: A Century of Ceramics in the U.S., 1979, American Ceramics: Collection of Everson Museum of Art, 1989. Served with U.S. Army, 1958-60. Mem. Am. Assn. Mus., Am. Assn. Art Mus. Dirs. Democrat. Episcopalian. Clubs: Century, Nat. Arts. Home: 109 Euclid Ter Syracuse NY 13210-2611 Office: Everson Mus Art 401 Harrison St Syracuse NY 13202-3091

KUCIC, JOSEPH, computer component company executive, industrial engineer; b. Croatia, Yugoslavia, Dec. 21, 1964; came to U.S., 1967, naturalized, 1974; s. Roman Kucic and Esterina (Karcic) Milevoj. AAS, Coll. of Aeronautics, 1984; BS, Thomas A. Edison State Coll., 1986; B in Tech., N.Y. Inst. Tech., 1986; MBA, St. John's U., Jamaica, N.Y., 1989. Workload planner Butler Aviation-Newark, Inc., 1984-85; tech. planner N.Y. Airlines, Flushing, N.Y., 1985-86; product support engr. United Techs.-Pratt & Whitney, East Hartford, Conn., 1986; indsl. engr. Montefiore Med. Ctr., Bronx, 1986-88; sr. work mgmt. analyst Bank Leumi Trust Co., N.Y.C., 1988-89; sr. methods analyst Salomon Bros., Inc., N.Y.C., 1989-92; dep. gen. mgr., v.p. Romart Computer Products Corp., Manhasset, N.Y., 1992—. Contbr. articles to profl. jours. Mem. AIAA, IEEE (assoc.), SAE (affiliate), Inst. Indsl. Engrs. (chpt. pres. 1988-89, chmn. bd. N.Y.C. chpt. 1989-90, Cert. of Recognition 1988, bd. govs. 1988—), MBA Execs., Coll. of Aeronautics Alumni Assn. (pres. 1990—), St. John's U. Coll. of Bus. Adminstrn. Alumni Assn. (bd. dirs. 1991—), The Wings Club (N.Y.C.), Tau Alpha Pi. Democrat. Roman Catholic. Home: 13-14 125th St Flushing NY 11356 Office: Romart Computer Products Corp 1180 Northern Blvd Manhasset NY 11030

KUCZYNSKI, PEDRO PABLO, economist; b. Lima, Peru, Oct. 1938; m. Jane Casey; children: Carolina, Alexandra, John-Michael. BA, MA in Philosophy, Politics & Econs., Oxford (Eng.) U., 1959; MPA, Princeton U., 1961. Sr. economist Western Hemisphere dept. IMF, 1969-71; v.p., ptnr. Kuhn Loeb Internat., 1973-75; chief economist Internat. Fin. Corp. World Bank, 1975-77, chief of the policy planning divsn., 1972-73, chief economist Mex., Cen. Am., Caribbean, 1971-72, loan officer and economist, 1961-67; pres., CEO Halco (Mining) Inc., 1977-80; min. of energy and mines Govt. of Peru, 1980-82; mng. dir., chmn. First Boston Corp., 1982-92; pres., CEO Nueva Mgmt. Inc., Coconut Grove, Fla., 1992—; lectr. econs. U. Pitts., 1977-80; bd. dirs. Coun. of the Ams., ROC Taiwan Fund, 1988—; mem. adv. coun. Rockefeller U., 1984—, Overseas Devel. Coun., 1987—, Internat. Ctr. for Econ. Growth, 1987. Author: Peruvian Democracy under Economic Stress: An Account of the Belaunde Administration 1963-68, 1977, (with others), The Impact of the Higher Oil Prices on the LDCs, 1975, Contemporary Venezuela, 1977, Toward Renewed Economic Growth in Latin America, 1986, Latin American Debt, 1988; contbr. articles to profl. jours. Home: 11 E 87th St Apt 3E 2 Grove Isle Coconut Grove FL 33133 Office: Nueva Mgmt Inc Grand Bay Plz Ste 1101 2665 S Bayshore Dr Cocunut Grove FL 33131

KUDRICK, LLOYD JOSEPH, quality assurance professional; b. Streator, Ill., Jan. 29, 1936; s. Lloyd Louis and Lucille Isabelle (Foltin) K.; m. Imogene Odle, Sept. 23, 1962; children: Benjamin, Jonathon, Rachel. Cert. tech., Comml. Trades Inst., 1966; student, Fisher Jr. Coll., 1978. Cert. indsl. electronics tech. Shift supr. Owens-Ill. Glass Co., Streator, 1972-78; dept. supr. Owens-Ill. Glass Co., Mansfield, Mass., 1978-81; shift supr. Owens-Ill. Glass Co., Clarion, Pa., 1981-87; quality assurance mgr. Owens-Ill. Glass Co., Clarion, 1987—. With U.S. Army, 1958-60. Lutheran. Home: RD 2 Knox PA 16232 Office: Owens Ill Glass Co 150 Grand Ave Clarion PA 16214

KUEBELER, GLENN CHARLES, engineering executive; b. Sandusky, Ohio, Aug. 1, 1935; s. William Louis and Helen Amelia (Johnson) K.; m. Iris Elaine Parker, Sept. 7, 1957; children: Mark Kenton, Gregory Glen. B-SChemE, Case Inst. Tech., 1957. Project engr. Hercules Inc., Cumberland, Md., 1957-61, program mgr., 1962-69; field resident rep. Hercules Inc., Sunnyvale, Calif., 1961-62; sr. tech. specialist Hercules Inc., Wilmington, Del., 1969-77, aero mktg. mgr., 1977-80, sr. sales rep., 1980-87, quality mgr. purchasing, 1987-88, div. mgr. purchasing, 1988-91, dir. safety, 1991—. Co-author: Composite Materials: Testing and Design, 1974, Beer Advertising Openers, 1978, Commercial Opportunities for Advanced Composites, 1980. Bd. dirs. Suppliers Advanced Composite Materials Assn., Arlington, Va., 1985-87; bd. dirs. Sci. Alliance Del., Wilmington, 1991—, vice-chair, 1992—; adv. bd. dirs. Ctr. for Composite Materials, Newark, Del., 1982-87, Del. Aerospace Edn. Found., Wilmington, 1991—. Mem. NRA, Soc. Advancement Material and Process Engring. (chpt. chmn. 1983-84), Del. County Field and Stream Assn., Palatines to Am., Nat. Assn. Breweriana Collecting, Ea. Coast Breweriana Assn., Hercules Country Club, Johnny Appleseed Postcard Club, Ohio Bottle Club, Firelands Hist. Soc., Zeta Psi, Alpha Chi Sigma. Republican. Home: 2410 Dacia Dr Wilmington DE 19810 Office: Hercules Inc 1313 N Market St Wilmington DE 19894

KUECHENMEISTER, KARL THOMAS, broadcast advertising executive; b. Detroit, Nov. 30, 1946; s. Karl Mooers and Frances Evelyn (Hubbell) K.; m. Elizabeth Ann Lynch, May 6, 1983; children: Karl Mooers II, Britt Elizabeth. BA, Dickinson Coll., 1968. Sales devel. analyst CBS, N.Y.C., 1973-75; mgr. sales devel. CBS, Chgo., 1975-77; sales account exec. NBC, Chgo., 1977-79; v.p. western sales NBC, Burbank, Calif., 1979-80; v.p. daytime sales NBC, N.Y.C., 1980-83; sr. v.p. media sales Warner Bros., Inc., N.Y.C., 1983—. Lt. USN, 1968-72. Roman Catholic. Office: Warner Bros 1325 Ave of Americas New York NY 10019

KUEHLER, JACK DWYER, computer company executive; b. Grand Island, Nebr., Aug. 29, 1932; s. August C. and Theresa (Dwyer) K.; m. Carmen Ann Kubas, July 16, 1955; children—Cynthia Marie, Daniel Scott, Christina L., David D., Michael P. BSME, U. Santa Clara. Design engr. jet engines dept. Gen. Electric Co., Evandale, Ohio, 1954-55; with IBM, 1958—; dir. IBM Raleigh Comunications Lab., 1967-70, IBM San Jose and Menlo Park Labs., 1970-72; v.p. devel. gen. products div. IBM, 1972-77, asst. group exec. data processing product group, 1977-78, pres. system products div., 1978-80, corp. v.p., from 1980; pres. gen. tech. div. IBM, White Plains, N.Y., 1980-81, info. systems and tech. group exec., 1981-82, sr. v.p., 1982-88, vice chmn., 1982-88, pres., 1988—; bd. dirs. Olin Corp. Patentee in field. Trustee U. Santa Clara (Calif.). Served as 1st lt. U.S. Army, 1955-57. Mem. IEEE (sr.), Nat. Acad. Engring., Am. Electronics Assn. Office: IBM Old Orchard Rd Armonk NY 10504-1709 also: IBM Info Systems & Tech Group 1000 Westchester Ave White Plains NY 10604*

KUEHNEMAN, GENE GEORGE, JR., economist; b. St. Paul, Sept. 1, 1953; s. Gene George and Jacquelyn Ann (Harris) K.; m. Adrienne Marla Weissman, June 5, 1989. BA in Econs., U. Chgo., 1976, MA in Econs., 1978, PhD in Econs., 1986. Lectr. Ind. U. N.W., Gary, 1979-84; cons. ICF,

Inc., Washington, 1986-87; sr. economist Syllogistics Inc., Springfield, Va., 1987, GAO, Washington, 1988—. Bd. dirs. 2501 M Street Condominium, Washington, 1989—, pres., 1990—; fundraiser U. Chgo. Alumni Fund, Washington, 1988—. Mem. Am. Econ. Assn., Am. Contract Bridge League. Home: 2501 M St NW Washington DC 20037-1303 Office: GAO 441 G St NW Washington DC 20548-0002

KUEHNLE, NORMAN BRUCE, minister; b. Balt., Feb. 20, 1940; s. Norman Ellsworth and Rae (Bruce) K.; m. Doris Stepp, June 23, 1962; children: Karen Joy, Matthew Bruce, Christina Lyn. BA, Am. U., 1960, EdD, 1972; STB, Wesley Theol. Seminary, 1963. With Balt. conf. United Meth. Ch., 1961-87; comml. real estate broker O'Conor, Piper & Flynn, Annapolis, Md., 1987-91. Methodist. Home: 538 Kenora Dr Millersville MD 21108-1317

KUENNE, ROBERT EUGENE, economics educator; b. St. Louis, Jan. 29, 1924; s. Edward Sebastian and Margaret (Yochum) K.; m. Janet Lawrence Brown, Sept. 7, 1957; children: Christopher Brian, Carolyn Leigh. Student, Harris Jr. Coll., St. Louis, 1941-42; B.J., U. Mo., 1947; A.B., Washington U., St. Louis, 1948, A.M., 1949; A.M., Harvard, 1951, Ph.D., 1953; Ph.D. (hon.), Umea U., 1985. Asst. prof. econs. U. Va., 1955; mem. faculty Princeton, 1956—, asso prof., 1960-69, prof. econs., 1969—; cons. U.S. Naval War Coll., 1954, 55, Inst. Def. Analyses, Arlington, Va., 1968—, Inst. for Energy Analysis, Washington, 1978-82; vis. prof. mil. systems analysis U.S. Army War Coll., 1967-85; mem. sci. and mgmt. adv. com. U.S. Army Computer Systems Command. Author: The Theory of General Economic Equilibrium, 1963, The Attack Submarine: A Study in Strategy, 1965, The Polaris Missile Strike: A General Economic Systems Analysis, 1966, Monopolistic Competition Theory: Studies in Impact, 1967, Microeconomic Theory of the Market Mechanism, 1968, Eugen von Böhm-Bawerk, 1971, Rivalrous Consonance, 1986, Economics of Oligopolistic Competition, 1992, General Equilibrium Economics, 1991, Economic Justice in American Society, 1992. Served with AUS, 1943-46. Named Oliver Ellsworth Bicentennial preceptor, 1957-60. Clubs: Princeton (N.Y.C.); Harvard (Phila.). Home: 63 Bainbridge St Princeton NJ 08540-3901

KUES, MARY CAROLYN, career counselor, educational administrator; b. Balt., Oct. 24, 1936; d. James Andrew and Jennie Frances (Robertson) Gaff-Becker; m. Irvin William Kues, Oct. 24, 1959; children: Pamela A., Janet M., Lynne P., Leslie F. BA, Mt. St. Agnes Coll., 1958; MS, Loyola Coll., Balt., 1979; cert. advanced study, Johns Hopkins U., 1988. Nat. cert. counselor, nat. cert. career counselor. Intelligence researcher Nat. Security Agy., Fort Meade, Md., 1958-60; career advisor asst. Loyola Coll., Balt., 1975-77, career cons., 1978, career advisor, 1979-83, asst. dir. career planning, 1983-87, assoc. dir career planning, 1987—; career counselor Balt. New Directions, 1978-79; part-time faculty Johns Hopkins U., Balt., 1988-89. Contbr. articles, reviews to profl. jours. Mem. AACD, Mid. Atlantic Placement Assn. (mem. com.), Md. Career Devel. Assn. (sec. 1989-91). Democrat. Roman Catholic. Office: Loyola Coll 4501 N Charles St Baltimore MD 21210-2699

KUGLER, DANIEL EDWARD, agricultural economist, government official; b. Rochester, N.Y., Jan. 26, 1947; s. Robert Edward and Marilyn Lucile (Betz) K.; m. Ann Elizabeth Haman, Aug. 12, 1977; children: Nicholas C.L., Elizabeth H., Katherine H., Sara H. BS in Physics, Mich. State U., 1969, MS in Resource Devel., 1977, PhD in Agrl. Econs., 1984. Vol., supr. math. and sci. Peace Corps, Afghanistan, 1971-73; economist Econ. Rsch. Svc., USDA, East Lansing, Mich., 1976-85; mgr. fibers program Coop. State Rsch. Svc., USDA, Washington, 1986-89, dir. Office Agrl. Materials, 1989—. Recipient R & D 100 award R & D mag., 1988; cert. of merit, 1988, 90, Tech. Transfer award 1990, Disting. Svc. award, 1991. Mem. Am. Econ. Assn., Assn. for Advancement Indsl. Crops, Internat. Kenaf Assn. Office: USDA Coop State Rsch Svc-SP 14th and Independence Ave SW Washington DC 20250-2200

KUHLTHAU, JOHN SUYDAM, judge; b. New Brunswick, N.J., May 16, 1937; s. Kearney Y. and Eleanor (Suydam) K.; m. Carol Collier, June 21, 1958; children: Ellie Molloy, Ann Caspari, Leslie. AB, Princeton U., 1958; JD, Rutgers U., 1962. Bar: N.J. 1963. Asst. dep. pub. defender Office N.J. Pub. Defender, New Brunswick, 1967-68; prosecutor Middlesex County, New Brunswick, 1971-74, dist. ct. judge, 1976-83; judge N.J. Superior Ct., New Brunswick, 1983—. Mem. ABA, N.J. Bar Assn., World Peace Through Law. Home: 402 Franklin Rd N Brunswick NJ 08902-2718 Office: NJ Superior Ct Middlesex County Courthouse New Brunswick NJ 08903

KUHN, FRANK RUDOLF, environmental consultant; b. Montreal, Quebec, Can., May 1, 1962; s. Joseph and Erika (Oberbeck) K. BS in Aerospace Engring, magna cum laude, Boston U., 1984, MS in Mech. Engring., 1986. Teaching fellow Boston U., 1984-86; wind tunnel cons. Tech. Integration & Devel. Group, Billerica, Mass., 1984-86; air quality/noise cons. Bolt, Beranek & Newman, Cambridge, Mass., 1986-91; sr. engr. K. M. Chng Environ., Cambridge, Mass., 1991; sr. environ. scientist Louis Berger Group, Waltham, Mass., 1991—. Honor scholar Boston U., 1984-86. Mem. AIAA, ASME, Tau Beta Pi. Home: 126 Lexington Rd Lincoln MA 01773 Office: Louis Berger Internat 303 Bear Hill Rd Waltham MA 02154-1016

KUHN, HANSJOERG KARL (GEORGE KUHN), transportation executive; b. Zuerich, Switzerland, Feb. 23, 1939; arrived in Can., 1978; s. Karl and Josephine (Tschallener) K.; m. Kathleen Margaret Roddy, Apr. 18, 1970; 1 child: Joergen Lucas. Cert., Zuerich Sch. Commerce, 1959; degree (hon.), Canadian Inst. Traffic and Transp., Toronto, 1991. Various pos. LEP Group Cos., N.Y.C., London, and Marseilles, France, 1960-70; acct. exec. Lintas Advt. Co., Zuerich, 1970-72; N.Am. area mgr. Internat. Transport Jour., Basel, Switzerland, 1972-73; Japan area mgr. Danzas Ltd. Switzerland, Tokyo, 1974-75; gen. mgr. Far East area for Japan, Korea, Hong Kong, and Taiwan Danzas Ltd., Tokyo, 1975-78; pres. Danzas Can. Ltd., Toronto, 1978—; dir. Canadian Internat. Freight Forwarders Assn., Toronto, 1980-90, pres., 1981-82, author edn. course, 1982, 86. Active Pub. Policy Forum, Ottawa, Can., 1989—. Home: 275 Glen Manor Dr E, Toronto, ON Canada M4E 2Y4 Office: Danzas Can Ltd, 5580 Explorer Dr 6th Fl, Mississauga, ON Canada L4W 4Y1

KUHN, RICHARD JOHN ALOIS, pharmacist; b. Johnson City, N.Y., Feb. 9, 1936; s. Frank Alois and Maria Antonia (Fuhr) K.; m. Margarete Hildegarde Nitschke, July 14, 1962; children: Martin Richard, Michele Luise. BS in Pharmacy, Albany Coll. Pharmacy, 1958. Lic. pharmacist, N.Y., Calif., Vt. Intern pharmacist E-J Med. Dept., Johnson City, 1956-58, pharmacist, 1960-63; pharmacist L-F Hamlin Inc., Binghamton, N.Y., 1958-60, Geroulds Pharmacy, Elmira, N.Y., 1964—. Mem. Am. Pharm. Assn., Nat. Assn. Retail Druggists, N.Y. State Pharm. Soc., Am. Soc. History of Pharmacy, Nat. Rifle Assn., N.Y. State Rifle and Pistol Assn. (life), Assn. Rsch. and Enlightenment, Elks. Republican. Lutheran. Home: 933 Palisades Blvd RD 1 Elmira NY 14903 Office: Geroulds Pharmacy 130 S Main St Elmira NY 14904-1392

KUHNLY, BARRY SCOTT, insurance company executive, consultant; b. Simsbury, Conn., Feb. 3, 1966; s. Barry David and Elizabeth Ann (Gallagher) K.; m. Joan Marie Esper, Apr. 20, 1991. AS in Safety Studies/BS in Mgmt., Keene (N.H.) State Coll., 1988. Cert. fire protection specialist. Sr. loss control rep. Crum and Forster Comml. Ins., Glastonbury, Conn., 1988—. Mem. Am. Soc. Safety Engrs., Nat. Fire Protection Assn. (cert.). Republican. Roman Catholic. Home: 70 Plank Hill Rd Simsbury CT 06070-2105 Office: Crum and Forster Comml Ins 95 Glastonbury Blvd Glastonbury CT 06033

KUHNS, (ALICE) POLLY, education educator, administrator; b. Pitts., July 2, 1947; d. Howard Dale and Alice (King) K. BA, U. Md., 1969; M in Ednl. Adminstrn., George Mason U., 1976; EdD, Va. Poly. Inst. and State U., 1986. Tchr. Loudoun County Sch. System, Leesburg, Va., 1971-76, asst. prin., 1976-87; assoc. prof. Shippensburg U. of Pa., 1988—; ctr. dir. student teaching Adams and York Counties. Mem. ASCD, Nat. Mid. Sch. Assn., Phi Delta Kappa. Home: 191 Longstreet Dr Gettysburg PA 17325-8929 Office: Shippensburg U Horton Hall Shippensburg PA 17257

KUJAWA, HENRY RICHARD, drafting detailer; b. Camden, N.J., Aug. 11, 1959; s. Felix and Agnes (Kurtas) K. AAS, Art Inst. Am., 1988. Drafting detailer Electronic Enclosures, Inc., Pennsauken, N.J., 1976-79, Kulicke & Soffa, Horsham, Pa., 1979-80, RF Products, Inc., Camden, 1980-88; drafting detailer Ad-Tek/VL Technical, Cherry Hill, N.J., 1989, tech. illustrator, 1990; drafting detailer Star Design, Inc., Moorestown, N.J., 1990, John Eppler Machine Works, Inc., Phila., 1991-92. Writer, artist, editor, publisher: (comic book) 2230, 1984. Home: 1202 Everett St Camden NJ 08104-3510

KUKLIN, BAILEY HOWARD, law educator; b. Lincoln, Nebr., Mar. 28, 1941; s. Harry H. and Reba (Magid) K.; m. Susan Gussman Greenbaum, July 7, 1974. BS, U. Nebr., 1963; JD, U. Mich., 1966. Bar: Calif. 1967, N.Y. 1970. Teaching fellow Stanford Law Sch., Palo Alto, Calif., 1966-67; Reginald Heber Smith fellow Legal Aid Soc. of Westchester County, White Plains, N.Y., 1969-70; asst. dean U. Mich. Law Sch., Ann Arbor, 1970-74; asst. prof. U. Tenn. Law Sch., Knoxville, 1974-76; from assoc. prof. to prof. Bklyn. Law Sch., 1976—; vol. Peace Corps, Nepal, 1967-69. Office: Bklyn Law Sch 250 Joralemon St Brooklyn NY 11201

KULESZA, FRANK WILLIAM, chemical engineer; b. Cambridge, Mass., Apr. 6, 1920. BSChemE, Northeastern U., 1950. Prodn. chemist Synthon Inc., Cambridge, Mass., 1950-51; R & D chemist Borden Chem., Bainbridge, N.Y., 1951-53; assoc. engr. IBM, Poughkeepsie, N.Y., 1953-66; pres. Epoxy Tech. Inc., Billerica, Mass., 1966—; chmn. Poly-Organics Inc., Newburyport, Mass., 1981—, Optical Fiber Tech. Inc., Westford, Mass., 1981—; bd. dirs. Epotecny, Velizy, France. Sgt. USAF, 1941-45, CBI. Mem. Am. Chem. Soc., Internat. Soc. Hybrid Mfrs., Semi-Conductor Equipment and Materials Inst. Home: 3 Grant Rd Winchester MA 01890-1016 Office: Epoxy Tech Inc 14 Fortune Dr Billerica MA 01821-3922

KULHAWY, FRED HOWARD, engineering educator; b. Topeka, Kans., Sept. 8, 1943; s. Fred and Gloria Katherine (Hahn) K.; m. Gloria Ianna, Sept. 4, 1966. BSCE, N.J. Inst. Tech., 1964; MS, Newark Coll., 1966; PhD, U. Calif., Berkeley, 1969. Registered profl. engr., N.Y., N.J., Pa., Calif., geotech. engr., Calif. Asst. instr. N.J. Inst. Tech., 1964-66; soil engr. Storch Engrs., East Orange, N.J., 1966; research asst. U. Calif., Berkeley, 1966-67, jr. research specialist, 1967-69; assoc. Raamot Assocs., Syracuse, N.Y., 1969-71; asst. prof. civil engring. Syracuse U., 1969-73, assoc. prof., 1973-76; assoc. prof. Cornell U., Ithaca, N.Y., 1976-81, prof. civil and environ. engring.and geology, 1981—; cross-Can. lectr, Can. Geotech. Soc., 1988; vis. prof. Cambridge (Eng.) U., U. Sydney, Australia, U. Hawaii, Honolulu, 1985-86; cons. in field.. Author: (with C. S. Desai, J.T. Christian, et al) Numerical Methods in Geotechnical Engineering, 1977; editor: Recent Developments in Geotechnical Engineering for Hydro Projects, 1981, Foundation Engineering: Current Principles and Practices, 1989; contbr. over 190 articles to profl. jours. Fulbright scholar, 1985. Fellow ASCE (pres. Syracuse sect. 1974-75, Edmund Friedman young engr. award 1974, Walter L. Huber rsch. prize 1982), Geol. Soc. Am.; mem. IEEE (sr.), ASTM, Am. Soc. Engring. Edn., Assn. Engring. Geologists, Internat. Assn. Engring. Geology, Internatl. Soc. Rock Mechanics, Internat. Soc. Soil Mechanics and Found. Engring., Transp. Rsch. Bd., U.S. Com. on Large Dams, Assn. Drilled Shaft Contrs. (hon. tech. affiliate), Deep Founds. Inst. Home: 113 Orchard St Ithaca NY 14850-2733 Office: Cornell U Hollister Hall Ithaca NY 14853-3501

KULICK, RICHARD JOHN, computer scientist; b. New Kensington, Pa., Mar. 27, 1949; s. John Anthony and Anna Teresa (Tuzik) K. BS, Pa. State U., 1971; MBA, U. Md., 1973. Project acct. PPG Indusries, Inc., Ford City, Pa., 1973-75; programmer analyst Allegheny Ludlum Steel Corp., Brackenridge, Pa., 1975-77, systems analyst, 1977-82, sr. systems analyst, 1982, sr. MIS planner, 1982-86; system design specialist Allegheny Ludlum Corp., Brackenridge, 1986-91; mgmt. info. systems assoc. Allegheny Ludlum Corp., Vandergrift, Pa., 1991—. Author: (manual) Data Modeling Standards, 1988. Mem. Computer Soc. of IEEE, Nat. Systems Programmers Assn., Assn. for Computing Machinery (voting), Datamation High Tech. Panel, Smithsonian Assocs., Pa. State U. Club Alle-Kiski Valley. Home: 483 Lillian Rd Leechburg PA 15656 Office: Allegheny Ludlum Corp 130 Lincoln Ave Vandergrift PA 15690-1232

KULIN, KEITH DAVID, cinematographer; b. Bogota, N.J., Jan. 24, 1948; s. Joseph Julius and Ava L. (Finestone) K. BA, Ramapo Coll. N.J., 1973. News photographer Ridgewood Newspapers, Paramus, N.J., 1967; desk asst. TV news CBS Inc., N.Y.C., 1975-77, newsreel photographer, 1977-84, documentary photographer, 1984—; staff documentary cinematographer for 60 Minutes, West 57th, CBS Reports, 48 Hours, Saturday Night with Connie Chung, other CBS news programs. Contbr. photography to Ridgewood newspapers, N.Y. Times, Womens World, 1966-75. Served with U.S. Army, 1968-70, Vietnam. Recipient Outstanding Photog. Achievement award Eastman Kodak Co., 1985, Spot News and Feature News awards, 1967; nominee Emmy award, 1985. Mem. Internat. Brotherhood Elec. Workers, TV and Radio Working Press Assn. Home: 217 Pond Ter Westwood NJ 07675-5121 Office: CBS News 555 W 57th St New York NY 10019-2925

KULL, FRANCIS RAYMOND, manufacturing company executive, consultant; b. Phila., Sept. 26, 1921; s. John Hans and Hattie (Nickles) K.; m. Pauline Elizabeth Brown; children: Francis Jr., Richard, Patricia, James. BSME, Drexel U., 1953, MS in Engring Mgmt., 1973. Registered profl. engr., Pa. Sr. machine designer STD Pressed Steel Co., Jenkintown, Pa., 1940-50, project engr., 1950-60; mgr. product devel. SPS Techs., Jenkintown, 1960-70, mgr. rsch. svcs. and contract rsch., 1970-87; pres. FRK Cons., Warminster, Pa., 1987—; mgr. contract referrals Govt. Contracts Prin. Investigator; lectr. in field. Contbr. articles to profl. jours.; inventor of fasteners, fastener tools, mfg. equipment and tools. Mem. ASME. Republican. Home: 800 Bluebell Rd Warminster PA 18974-5508 Office: FRK Cons 800 Bluebell Rd Warminster PA 18974

KULLA, MICHAEL, psychologist; b. N.Y.C., Feb. 20, 1929; s. Maxwell and Jean (Michaels) K.; m. Ofrah Ben-Joseph, 1962 (div. Aug. 1989); children: Jamie, David, Mia. BA, Syracuse U., 1950; MA, New Sch. for Social Rsch., N.Y., 1956; PhD, U. Okla., 1966. Psychologist State of Okla., 1966—; sch. psychologist State of N.Y., 1962—, psychologist, 1968—; psychologist Coun. Nat. Register of Health Svcs. Providers Psychology, Washington, 1976—; dir., profl. in charge of tng. Mid-Hudson Cons. Ctr. Mental Health, Wappingers Falls, N.Y., 1969—; working with Am. Indians, hypnosis, tng. in psychotherapy. Contbr. articles to newspapers, mags. and profl. jours. Dir. community mental health ctr., 1969—; mem. adv. com. Dutchess Community Coll., 1973-75, mem. adv. bd. Dutchess County div. Youth Citizens, N.Y., 1983-84. With U.S. Army, 1951. Mem. Am. Psychol. Assn., Psychologists in Pvt. Practice, Soc. Psychol. Study Social Issues, Peace Psychology and Study Introgenic Practice and Rsch., Group Psychology and Group Psychotherapy, Hudson Valley Psychol. Assn. Home and Office: Drake Rd Pleasant Valley NY 12569

KULLBERG, GARY WALTER, advertising agency executive; b. White Plains, N.Y., Dec. 15, 1941; s. Walter George and Neva Virginia (Franz) K. B.S., U. R.I., 1963; m. Audrey Ellen Greenwald, June 20, 1976; 1 child, Eric Alan. Contr. WCD, Inc., N.Y.C., 1963-66; v.p., mgmt. supr. Ogilvy & Mather, N.Y.C., 1966-77; sr. v.p., account group head Wells, Rich, Greene, N.Y.C., 1977-83; chief executive officer, chief fin. officer, co-founder Fredericks Kullberg Amato Pisacane, Inc., 1983-88; pres. Kullberg Amato Pisacane/ABP, Inc., 1987-89; pres., chief oper. officer Pan Com Internat. Corp., 1989—; guest speaker univs. Mem. bd. advisors and communications com. Manhattan Salvation Army. Mem. West Point Soc. N.Y. (career adv. com.), Am. Numismatic Assn., N.Y. Athletic Club, Phi Gamma Delta. Home: 50 E 89th St New York NY 10128-1225 Office: PanCom Internat Corp 2015 W Main St Stamford CT 06902-4536

KULOK, WILLIAM ALLAN, entrepreneur, venture capitalist; b. Mt. Vernon, N.Y., July 24, 1940; s. Sidney Alexander and Bertha (Lembeck) K.; m. Susan B. Glick, June 26, 1965; children: Jonathan, Brian, Stephanie. BS in Econs., U. Pa., 1962. CPA, N.Y. Acct. David Kulok Co., N.Y.C., 1962-67; asst. to pres. Syndicate Mags., N.Y.C., 1967-70; founder Kulok Capital Inc., N.Y.C., 1970, pres., 1970—; bd. dir. Listcomp Corp., Mail Mgmt. Corp., Mag. Devel. Fund, Lazard Spl. Equities Fund, N.Y. Import/Export Ctr., Inc., Ctr. for Exec. Edn., Arts & Events, Inc., Sax and Co., Art Horizons Internat.; lectr. Wharton Sch., U. Chgo., NYU. Pres. N.Y. Soc. Ethical Culture, 1978-80; vice chmn. bd. Ethical Culture Schs., 1979, chmn., 1982-86. Mem. Am. Inst. CPAs, Rockaway River Country Club, Sleepy Hollow Country Club, Tryall Golf and Beach Club (Jamaica, W.I.). Home: 40 E 84th St New York NY 10028-1115 Office: Waldorf Astoria 301 Park Ave Ste 1855 New York NY 10022-6806

KULP, J. ROBERT, metal company executive; b. Buffalo, June 23, 1935; s. Joseph Francis Kulp and Mary Gertrude (O'Brian) Kulp O'Hearn; m. Suzanne Frances Schultz, Jan. 26, 1957; children: J. Robert Jr., Kaaren S., Kevin E., Kenneth C. BS in Bus., U. Buffalo, 1967; MBA, Canisius Coll., 1972. Sales Reynolds Metals Supply Co., Miami, Fla., 1957-58, Ryerson Steel Co., Buffalo, 1958-72; ptnr., v.p. Oehler Industries Inc., Buffalo, 1972—; ptnr., pres. Machines for Industry, Buffalo, 1983—, Denler Metal Products, Buffalo, 1984—; bd. dirs. Erie County Industry Devel. Agy., Buffalo, 1980-86. Pres. Episcopal Charities Bd., Buffalo, 1979-83; mem. bd. regents Canisius Coll., Buffalo, 1980-84, 89—, v.p. bd. regents, 1991—; mem. pres.'s Adv. Coun. D'Youville Coll., Buffalo, 1987—. Recipient Bernard J. Martin Outstanding M.B.A. award Canisius Coll., 1979, LaSalle medal. Mem. Internat. Assn. Fabricators and Mfrs. (bd. dirs. 1991—), Am. Soc. Metals, Engring. Soc. Buffalo (bd. dirs. 1982-85), Frontier Metal Trades Assn. (pres. 1984-86), Canisius Coll. Alumni Assn. (pres. 1985, v.p. 1984), MBA Alumni Assn. (pres. 1979), Buffalo C. of C. (chmn. existing industries com. 1978-79), Beta Gamma Sigma. Republican. Roman Catholic. Clubs: Orchard Park Country (N.Y.) (bd. dirs., sec. 1988-89, v.p. 1989-90); Saturn (Buffalo). Lodge: Shrine. Home: 12 Briar Hill Rd Orchard Park NY 14127-3527 also: 15 Hedding Chautauqua Instn Chautauqua NY 14722 also: 303 Brackenwood Circle PGA Nat Palm Beach Gardens FL 33418 Office: Oehler Industries Inc Elk and Smith Sts Buffalo NY 14210

KULP, JONATHAN B., educator; b. Norristown, Pa., July 18, 1937; s. Abraham Moyer and Frances Mann (Connelly) K.; m. Priscilla Lory June 20, 1959 (div. 1968); m. Carol Janice (Nabinger) Apr. 5, 1968; children: Julie E., Penny S. BA, Dickinson Coll., Carlisle, Pa., 1959; MA, Am. U., 1963. Cert. tchr., Pa. Tchr., coach The Mercersburg (Pa.) Acad., 1959-60; tchr., coach The Episcopal Acad., Merion, Pa., 1963—, head history dept., 1983-89; dir. curriculum and faculty devel., 1989—; Adv. com. Project Cares, Exton, Pa., 1979-82; mem. Dodge Found. seminar on Women in History, Bryn Mawr, Pa., 1985-86; reader for Am. History Advanced Placement Program of Coll. Bds., Princeton, 1987; cons. in field. Active ARC, Montrose, Pa., 1974—; mem. Downingtown Area Sch. Bd., Downingtown, Pa., 1975-79, pres. 1978-79; The Exton Chorale, Exton, Pa., 1976—, v.p., 1977-79, pres. 1981. Served with USAR, 1960-66. Cert. of Achievement Teaching fellow Commonwealth Partnership, 1986; Fellowship award, 1986; ind. study in humanities fellow Coun. for Basic Edn. and Nat. Endowment, 1987, Woodrow Wilson fellow in Am. History, 1989. Mem. Ind. Sch. Tchrs. Assn. Phila. (chmn. history program 1985-88, profl. devel. chair 1991—), Nat. Interscholastic Swim Coaches Assn. Am., Coun. Basic Edn., Orgn. Am. Historians, Phila. Area Coun. for Women in Ind. Schs. (co-chmn. 1987-88, mem. exec. com. 1986-90). Republican. Home: 1230 Street Rd Chester Springs PA 19425-1606 Office: The Episc Acad 376 N Lathces Ln Merion Station PA 19066

KULSTAD, GEORGE ARTHUR, international economic developer; b. Shanghai, China, Sept. 30, 1935; came to U.S., 1949; s. Peter A. and Helen (Thomas) K.; m. Ruth Mary Kingerlee, July 31, 1965; children: Erik B., Helen C. BA, U. Calif., Berkeley, 1960; MBA, U. Geneva, 1962. Dep. exec. dir. N.Am. Assn. Venezuela, Caracas, 1965-67; 2d sec. U.S. Dept. State, Port au Prince, Haiti, 1967-70; dep. chief Fla. Dept. Commerce, Tallahassee, 1974-75; owner, operator Mather & Assocs., Rockville, Md., 1975—. Mem. Am. Econ. Devel. Coun., Northeastern Indsl. Devel. Assn., Md. Indsl. Developers Assn. Office: Mather & Assocs 90 W Montgomery Ave Rockville MD 20850-4211

KUMAR, AKHIL, business educator; b. Ambala, India, Oct. 8, 1956; came to U.S., 1984; s. Mukut Behari and Saroj (Agarwal) Lal; m. Nilima Gupta, Nov. 23, 1980; children: Anshul, Anurag. BSEE, Indian Inst. Tech., New Delhi, 1978; MBA, Indian Inst. Mgmt., Ahmedabad, India, 1980; MS in Computer Sci., U. Calif., Berkeley, 1986, PhD in Bus. Adminstrn., 1988. Asst. prof. Cornell U. Grad Sch. Mgmt., Ithaca, N.Y., 1988—. Rsch. grantee NSF, Washington, 1991; Rsch. fellow Arthur Andersen Found., 1987. Mem. Assn. for Computing Machinery. Office: Cornell Univ 551 Malott Hall Ithaca NY 14853

KUMAR, HARINATH V., urologist, surgeon; b. Hyderabad, Andhra Pradesh, India, Sept. 2, 1938; came to U.S., 1964; s. Ramchander and Seetha Rao; m. Leela Murthy, Mar. 13, 1967; children: Vivek, Naveen, Veena. MB BS, Gandhi Med. Coll., Hyderabad, 1963. Diplomate Am. Bd. Urology. Intern Lawrence and Meml. Hosp., New London, Conn., 1965; resident in surgery Norwalk (Conn.) Hosp., 1966-67; resident in urology Bellevue Hosp., N.Y.C.; resident in urology Montefiore Hosp. and Med. Ctr., Bronx, N.Y., fellow in urology, 1970-72; attending urologist Morrisania City Hosp., Bronx, 1972-74; attending urologist Northwestern Med Ctr., Oil City, Pa., 1975—, Franklin, Pa., 1980—; attending urologist Titusville (Pa.) Area Hosp., 1976—. Fellow ACS, Internat. Coll. Surgeons; mem. AMA, Am. Assn. Clin. Urologists, Pa. Med. Assn., Urol. Assn. Pa. Inc. Home: 3 Crestview Dr Oil City PA 16301 Office: 32 Seneca St Oil City PA 16301

KUMAR, TOBI JEANNE, photographer, poet; b. Long Beach, Calif.; d. John Stewart O'Denny and Helen Ruth (Thompson) Denny; m. Prem Kumar Mago, July 1, 1973. BA, Kent State U., 1963; cert. in photography, N.Y. Inst. of Photography, 1973. Photo colorist Am. Photograph Corp., N.Y.C., 1973-75; air brush artist Leichtner's Photog. Studios, Rochester, N.Y., 1976; freelance India, 1976-77; freelance oil painter Let There Be Dragons, Fairport, 1991—. Photos exhibited at 41 Union Sq., West Sixth Ann. Open Studios, N.Y.C., 1990—; author poems. Freedom rider Martin Luther King's Congress of Racial Equality, N.Y.C. to Balt., 1963; tutor, news mgr. Harlem Edn. Project, N.Y.C., 1963; active The Peace and Freedom Party, San Francisco, 1968. Recipient Golden Poet award World of Poetry, 1989, 90, 91. Mem. The Statue of Liberty-Ellis Island Found., Inc. Democrat.

KUMAR, VIJAY, immunologist, microbiologist, educator, researcher; b. Rampura Phul, Punjab, India, Apr. 15, 1945; came to U.S., 1969; s. Megh Raj and Puran (Devi) Goel; m. Asha Jain, July 1, 1973; children: Sasha, Sabina. BSc with honors, Punjab U., Chandigarh, India, 1965, MSc with honors, 1968; PhD, SUNY, Buffalo, 1973. Diplomate Am. Bd. Med. Lab. Immunology, Am. Bd. Med. Microbiology; cert. Am. Registry in Clin. Chemistry. Asst. prof. microbiology SUNY, Buffalo, 1980-87, rsch. assoc. prof. microbiology, 1987—; pres. Immco Diagnostics Inc., Buffalo, 1988—; asst. dir. Ernest Witebsky Ctr. for Immunology, Buffalo, 1991—. Author: Immunopathology of the Skin, 1987, Serological Diagnosis of Celiac Disease, 1990; contbr. articles to profl. jours. Fogarty Internat. fellow NIH, 1985. Mem. Am. Soc. for Microbiology, Am. Soc. for Investigative Dermatology, Am. Fedn. for Clin. Rsch., Am. Assn. for Clin. Chemistry. Home: 47 Stonybrook Ln Williamsville NY 14221 Office: Immco Diagnostics Inc 963 Kenmore Ave Buffalo NY 14223

KUMP, PETER CLARK, school system administrator; b. L.A., Oct. 22, 1937; s. Ernest Joseph and Josephine Clark (Miller) K.; m. Carolyn Curme Davis, May 7, 1960 (div. 1967); 1 child, Christopher. BA in Speech and Drama, Stanford U., 1961; MFA, Carnegie-Mellon U., 1969. Cert. culinary profl. Exec. producer Comedia Repertory Co., Palo Alto, Calif., 1957-66; dir. Evelyn Wood Reading Dynamics, Pitts., 1967-69; nat. dir. edn. Diversified Edn. and Rsch. Corp., N.Y.C., 1970-74; pres. Breakthrough Rapid Reading, N.Y.C., 1974-81, Peter Kump's N.Y. Cooking Sch., N.Y.C., 1974—; cons. Stanley H. Kaplan, Ltd., N.Y.C., 1982—. Author: Quiche and Pate, 1982 (Tastemaker award 1983); syndicated columnist The Practical Cook, 1985—. Mem. Internat. Assn. Culinary Profls. (pres. 1987-88), N.Y. Assn. Cooking Tchrs. (pres. 1980-81), Am. Inst. Wine and Food, The James Beard Found. (pres. 1985—). Independent. Office: Peter Kump's NY Cooking Sch 307 E 92d St New York NY 10128

KUNDRAT, STEPHANIE L., psychologist; b. Danville, Pa., Oct. 5, 1962; d. Stephen and Gloria (Woolever) K. BA in Psychology, Pa. State U., 1984; MA in Clin. Psychology, Loyola Coll., Balt., 1990. Crisis intervention counselor Oasis Help Ctr., State Coll., Pa., 1982-84; asst. human resources cons. Berkshire Assocs. Inc., Balt., 1985-86; intern in clin. psychology VA

Outpatient Clinic, Balt., 1986; counselor Dundalk Youth Svc. Ctr., Balt., 1986-90; psychology assoc. Franklin Sq. Hosp. Ctr., Balt., 1990—. Mem. Orthodox Christian Assn. Medicine Psychology and Religion, Am. Psychol. Assn. Democrat. Eastern Orthodox. Home: 1304 Deanwood Rd Baltimore MD 21234 Office: Franklin Sq Hosp Ctr White Sq Profl Bldg 9105 Franklin Square Dr Baltimore MD 21237-3930

KUNDSIN, RUTH BLUMFELD, microbiology educator, epidemiologist; b. N.Y.C., July 30, 1916; d. John David and Emily (Krumin) Blumfeld; m. Edwin Stanley, June 17, 1935; children: Andrea Dupree, Dennis. BA, Hunter Coll., 1936; MA, Boston U., 1949; ScD in Pub. Health, Harvard U., 1958; ScD (hon.), Lowell (Mass.) U., 1975. Diplomate Am. Med. Microbiology. Microbiologist Peter Bent Brigham Hosp., Boston, 1951-58; asst. to surgery Brigham and Women's Hosp., Boston, 1958-64, assoc. staff mem., 1964-70, hosp. epidemiologist, 1970—, lab. dir., 1976—; assoc. prof. microbiology and molecular genetics Harvard Med. Sch., Boston, 1976—; founder, mgr. Kundsin Lab., Inc., Boston, 1981—; mem. adv. panel U.S. Pharmacopeia, Rockville, Md., 1981-86. Editor: Women and Success, 1974; contbr. numerous articles to profl. jours. Named to Hall of Fame Hunter Coll.; neonatology grantee NIH, 1978-85. Fellow N.Y. Acad. Scis., Am. Acad. Microbiology, Phi Beta Kappa; mem. Latvian Acad. Scis. (fgn. mem.). Home: 71 Pratt Rd Quincy MA 02171-1141 Office: Kundsin Lab 75 Francis St Boston MA 02115-6195

KUNES, JOHN CHARLES, chemical company executive; b. Canandaigua, N.Y., Apr. 13, 1949; s. Vernon James and Ruby Harriet (Jones) K.; m. Pamela Elizabeth Vanderwall, May 1, 1971; children: John Charles Jr., Summer Margaret. BS in Acctg., Rochester Inst. Tech., 1976, MBA in Fin., 1978. Rin. trainee Mobil Chem. Co., Macedon, N.Y., 1976-78, internal auditor, 1978-79, fin. analyst, 1979-80; sr. fin. analyst Mobil Chem. Co., Temple, Tex., 1980-82; fin. mgr. Mobil Chem. Co., Pittsford, N.Y., 1982-85; regional congr. Mobil Chem. Co., Frankfort, Ill., 1985-88; bus. mgr. Mobil Chem. Co., Pittsford, 1988-90, mfg. mgr., 1990, recycle mgr., 1990—; mem. operating com. Nat. Polystyrene Recycling Co., Lincolnshire, Ill., 1990—. With U.S. Army, 1967-70. Mem. Mensa. Republican. Methodist. Office: Mobil Chem Co 1159 Pittsford Victor Rd Pittsford NY 14534-3876

KUNG, PATRICK CHUNG-SHU, biotechnology executive; b. Nanjing, Republic of China, July 10, 1947; came to U.S., 1969; s. Tao and Yuing (Li) K.; m. Rita Wu, Feb. 11, 1980; children: Julia, Calvin. BS, FuJen U., Republic China, 1968; PhD, U. Calif., Berkeley, 1974. Rsch. fellow MIT, Cambridge, 1974-77; sr. rsch. fellow Ortho Pharm. Co., Raritan, N.J., 1978-81; v.p. rsch. Centocor Inc., Malvern, Pa., 1982-83; co-founder, exec. v.p. T Cell Scis., Inc., Cambridge, 1984-88; vice chmn. bd. T-Cell Scis., Inc., Cambridge, 1989-91; exec. bd. Coll. Letters and Scis., U. Calif., Berkeley, 1989-91. Contbr. articles to profl. jours. Recipient Philip Hoffman award Johnson & Johnson Co., 1979, Achievement award Chinese Inst. Engrs., 1988, Discoverers award Pharm. Mfrs. Assn., 1991, Thomas Alva Edison award N.J. Rsch. Coun., 1991. Mem. Am. Assn. Immunologists, N.Y. Acad. Scis., Sigma Xi. Roman Catholic. Office: T Cell Scis Inc 38 Sidney St Cambridge MA 02139-4160

KUNIN, MADELEINE MAY, educator, former governor of Vermont; b. Zurich, Switzerland, Sept. 28, 1933; came to U.S., 1940, naturalized, 1947; d. Ferdinand and Renee (Bloch) May; m. Arthur S. Kunin, June 21, 1959; children—Julia, Peter, Adam, Daniel. B.A., U. Mass., 1956; M.S., Columbia U., 1957; M.A., U. Vt., 1967; numerous hon. degrees. Newspaper reporter Burlington Free Press, Vt., 1957-58; guide Brussels World's Fair, Belgium, 1958; TV asst. producer Sta. WCAX-TV, Burlington, 1960-61; freelance writer, instr. English Trinity Coll., Burlington, 1969-70; mem. Vt. Ho. of Reps., 1973-78; lt. gov. State of Vt., Montpelier, 1979-82, gov., 1985-91; disting. vis. in Pub. Policy Bunting Inst., Cambridge, Mass., 1991-92; fellow Inst. Politics, Kennedy Sch. Govt., Harvard U., 1983; lectr. Middlebury Coll., St. Michael's Coll., 1984; Disting. Pub. Policy Visitor, Rockefeller Ctr., Dartmouth Coll.; Vt. Joint Fiscal Com., 1977-78; mem. exec. com. Nat. Conf. Lt. Govs., 1979-80. Author: (with Marilyn Stout) The Big Green Book, 1976; contbr. articles to profl. jours., mags. and newspapers. Mem. exec. com. Dem. Policy Council. Named Outstanding State Legislator, Eagleton Inst. Politics, Rutgers U., 1975. Mem. Nat. Gov.'s Assn. (mem. exec com.), Nat. Govs.' Conf. (chair com. on energy and the environ.), New Eng. Gov.'s Conf. (chairperson). Democrat. Office: Rockefellow Center Dartmouth College Hanover NH 03755

KUNISCH, ROBERT DIETRICH, business services company executive; b. Norwalk, Conn., July 7, 1941; s. Irving William and Margaret (Diedrich) K.; m. Alicia Stephenson, Aug. 22, 1964; children: Alicia Mary, Robert D. BS, NYU, 1964. Regional mgr. residential sales Homequity, Wilton, Conn., 1966-68, dir., 1968-69, dir. corp. mktg., 1969-71, sr. v.p. mktg. and svcs., 1971-76, pres., 1976-84; exec. v.p. PHH Corp., Inc., Hunt Valley, Md., 1981-84, pres., chief oper. officer, 1984-88, pres. chief exec. officer, dir., 1988—; chmn. bd. dirs. 1989—; bd. dir. Corp., Merc. Bankshares Corp., Balt., Alex Brown & Sons Inc., Preston Corp.; Disting. exec. lectr. NYU. Trustee Johns Hopkins U., Johns Hopkins Hosp., Johns Hopkins Health Systems; bd. dirs. Greater Balt. Co.; mem. United Way Cen. Md.; past trustee Am. Shakespearean Theatre; past mem. devel. com. John F. Kennedy Inst., Balt., 1984. Democrat. Roman Catholic. Office: PHH Corp 11333 Mccormick Rd Cockeysville Hunt Valley MD 21031-1001

KUNJUKUNJU, PAPPY, insurance company financial executive; b. Punalur, Kerala, India, Aug. 26, 1939; came to U.S., 1974.; s. Varghese and Thankamma (Yohannan) Chacko; m. Kunjamma Zachariah, Dec. 31, 1971; children: Grace, Nancy, Samuel. B of Commerce, U. Ranchi, India, 1965; MBA, N.Y. Inst. Tech., 1976. CPA, N.Y.; cert. mgmt. acct. Cost. acct. Nat. Tobacco Co. India, Calcutta, 1964-68; exec. asst. Gen. Electric Co. of India (sub. of GEC/Eng.), Calcutta, 1968-69; mgr. mfg. div. GEC India, Coimbatore, 1969-74; examiner ins. dept. N.Y. State, N.Y.C., 1977-83, sr. examiner ins. dept., 1983-87; contr. Golden Eagle Mut. Life Ins. Corp., Bklyn., 1987-88, treas., 1988-89; v.p., treas. Golden Eagle Mutual Life Ins. Corp., Bklyn., 1989—. Mem. AICPA, Nat. Assn. Accts., Inst. Cost and Works Accts. India (assoc. mem.). Mem. Assembly of God Ch. Home: 156 Bellevue Pl Yonkers NY 10703-1625 Office: Golden Eagle Mut Life Ins Corp 105 Court St Brooklyn NY 11201-5645

KUNSCH, LOUIS, artist; b. Bronx, N.Y., Dec. 1937. Student, Art Students League N.Y., 1961-65, Sch. Visual Arts, N.Y., 1972. Artist Metropolitan Museum of Art Islamic Art Dept., 1970-75, Metropolitan Museum of Art Egyptian Art Dept., 1978-88. One-man shows include Main St. Gallery, Brewster, N.Y., 1975, Long Beach Libr., N.Y., 1977, The Exhibitionists, Jamaica, N.Y., 1977, P.S. 1, L.I., N.Y., 1979, Queens Pub. Libr., N.Y., 1991; exhibited in group shows at Audubon Artists, Staten Island Mus., Ball State U., Purdue U., Berkshire Mus.; curator for six, Citicorp, 1991, Medium Matters, 1991, Contrasts, 1991, Citicorp Bldg., L.I., Different Angles, La Guardia Community Coll., L.I., others. Recipient Ford Found. scholarship, 1964-65. Founding mem. Hunters Point Community of Artists, The Exhibitionists, Inc. Office: Art Space Inc 10 20 45th Rd 4th Fl Long Island City NY 11101

KUNSTADTER, GERALDINE S., foundation executive; b. Boston, Jan. 6, 1928; d. Harry Herman and Nettie Sapolsky; m. John W. Kunstadter, Apr. 23, 1949; children: John W., Lisa, Christopher, Elizabeth. Student, MIT, 1945-48. Draftsman U. Chgo. Cyclotron Project, 1948; engring. asst. Gen. Electric Corp., Lynn, Mass., 1948-49; pres. Capricorn Investments Corp., 1971—; chmn., dir. A. Kunstadter Family Found., N.Y.C., 1966—; host family program dir. N.Y.C. Commn. for UN, 1971-86; pres. Nat. Inst. Social Scis., 1979-81. Bd. dirs. Ptnrs. of Ams. Found., Washington, Menninger Clin., Topeka, Nat. Com. on U.S.-China Rels., Inst. Current World Affairs, Feld Ballet, N.Y.C., Ctr. U.S.-China Arts Exch., N.Y. Regional Assn. Grantmakers, Inst. World Affairs, Am. Forum; mem. resource coun. Ptnrs. of Ams., Washington; mem. adv. coun. Bridges to Asia Found., East Asian studies program MIT Sch. Architecture; mem. Peace Links Leadership Network, Nat. Coun. of Women (internat. hospitality com.), Overseas Devel. Coun., Atlantic Coun., Vol. Devel. Coun. for UN Delegations, Inc., N.Y.-Beijing Friendship City Com., MIT Corp. Devel. Com., Vol. Devel. Coun. for UN Delegations, Inc.; hon. bd. dirs. Govs. of Nat. Women's Employment and Edn., Inc. Recipient Windham award, 1970, silver medal Nat. Inst. Social Sci., 1981. Mem. Am. Women's Club, Hurlingham Club, Lansdowne Club (London).

KUNTZ, WILLIAM FRANCIS, II, lawyer, educator; b. N.Y.C., June 24, 1950; s. William Francis I and Margaret Evelyn (Brown) K.; m. Alice Beal, May 20, 1978; children: William Thaddeus, Katharine Lowell, Elizabeth Anne. AB, Harvard U., 1972, AM, 1974, JD, 1977, PhD, 1979. Bar: N.Y. 1978. Assoc. Shearman & Sterling, N.Y.C., 1978-86; mem. Varet Marcus & Fink, N.Y.C., 1986—; assoc. prof. Bklyn. Law Sch., 1987—. Author: Criminal Sentencing, 1988. Bd. dirs. MFY Legal Svcs., Inc., N.Y.C., 1984-90, Boys Brotherhood Republic, N.Y.C., 1986-90, Habitat for Humanity, N.Y.C., 1987—; chmn. Resources for Children with Spl. Needs, N.Y.C., 1986-89; mem. N.Y. Civilian Complaint Rev. Bd., 1987—. Mem. ABA, N.Y. State Bar Assn., New York County Lawyers Assn. (bd. dirs. 1991—), Assn. Bar City N.Y. (chmn. mcpl. affairs com. 1992—, judiciary com.), Bklyn. Bar Assn., Met. Black Bar Assn. Democrat. Roman Catholic. Office: Varet Marcus & Fink 53 Wall St New York NY 10005-2834 also: Milgrim Thomajan 53 Wall St New York NY 10005

KUNZ, HAROLD RUSSELL, electrochemistry researcher, educator; b. Troy, N.Y., Oct. 3, 1931; s. William Gottlob and Amelia (Miller) K.; m. Nancy Metcalf, July 28, 1956; children: Daryl Lynne Kunz Gottier, Roderick Russell. B in Mech. Engring., Rensselaer Polytech Inst., 1953, MSME, 1958, PhD, 1966. Analytical engr. Pratt & Whitney Aircraft, East Hartford, Conn., 1954-57; sr. analytical engr. Pratt & Whitney Aircraft, East Hartford, 1957-60; asst. project engr. Advanced Power Systems United Techs. Inc., East Hartford, 1960-63, chief, rsch. engr., 1963-65, project engr., 1965-67; project engr. Advanced Power Systems United Techs. Inc., South Windsor, Conn., 1967-68; devel. engr. advanced tech. Internat. Fuel Cells, South Windsor, 1968-92; lectr. Hartford Grad. Ctr., Rensselaer Poly. Inst., 1962-66, adj. asst. prof., 1966-70, adj. assoc. prof., 1970—; adj. prof. U. Conn., 1992—. Contbr. articles to The Electrochem. Soc., Jour. of Electrochem. Soc. Mem. ASME, The Electrochem. Soc., Sigma Xi, Tau Beta Pi, Pi Tau Sigma. Mem. United Ch. of Christ. Home: 26 Valley View Ln Vernon Rockville CT 06066-4153 Office: U Conn Dept Chem Engring Box U-139 Rm 204 191 Auditorium Rd Storrs CT 06269-3139

KUNZ, JOHN EDWARD, JR., financial operations, accounting analyst; b. Pitts., Aug. 17, 1964; s. John Edward and Constance (Wagner) K. BBA in Acctg., U. Notre Dame, 1986; MBA in Fin., J. L. Kellogg Grad. Sch., Evanston, Ill., 1991. CPA, Pa. Supervising sr. acct. KPMG Peat Marwick, Pitts., 1986-90; with PNC Fin., Pitts., 1991-92; fin. analyst Weirton (W.Va.) Steel Corp., Pitts., 1992—. Mem. Notre Dame Club Pitts. Republican. Roman Catholic. Home: 415 Glen Arden Dr Pittsburgh PA 15208

KUNZE, RICHARD SPENCER, veterinarian; b. Newark, Feb. 8, 1948; s. Eldon Clark and Doris (Davis) K.; div. 1984; children: Joanna, Matthew; m. Penny Platoff, Feb. 10, 1990. BS, Tex. A&M U., 1969, BS in Vet. Sci. cum laude, 1973, DVM magna cum laude, 1974; cert. internal medicine, Colo. State U., 1980. Intern Animal Med. Ctr., N.Y.C., 1974-75; assoc. surgeon, clin. cardiologist Telephone Rd. Park Pl. Vet. Hosp., Houston, 1975-77; clin. cardiologist Colo. State U. Vet. Hosp., Ft. Collins, 1977-80; assoc. in medicine and cardiology Ramsey (N.J.) Vet. Hosp., 1980-88; pres., cons. in medicine and cardiology Vet. Consulting and Relief Svc., Mahwah, N.J., 1988—; ptnr. vet. Ramsey (N.J.) Vet. Hosp. Contbr. articles to profl. publs. Delegate Rep. Nat. Com., mem. 1992 Presdl. Trust. Mem. Am. Vet. Med. Assn., N.J. Vet. Med. Assn. (v.p. sci. edn. No. N.J. chpt. 1987-88, chpt. v.p. 1988-89), Met. N.J. Vet. Med. Assn., Sports Car Club Am. Republican. Home: Stag Hill Rd # 495 Mahwah NJ 07430-1019 Office: Vet Cons and Relief Svc Aranwood-Staghill Rd Mahwah NJ 07430

KUNZENDORF, ROBERT GODFREY, psychologist, educator, researcher; b. Lincoln, Nebr., Feb. 18, 1951; s. Godfrey and Mabel Roberta (Valentiner) K.; m. Elizabeth Ann Ritvo, June 5, 1971; children: Jennifer Ritvo, Rebecca Ritvo. BA, Yale U., 1973; PhD, U. Va., 1979. Asst. prof. U. Lowell, Mass., 1979-85, assoc. prof., 1985-90; prof. U. Mass.-Lowell, 1990—; mem. editorial bd. Internat. Review of Mental Imagery, 1983—. Editor: (book) Mental Imagery, 1991; co-editor (book) Psychophysiology of Mental Imagery, 1990; contbr. over 3 dozen articles to profl. jours. Grantee NIMH, 1982-83. Mem. Am. Psychol. Assn., Am Assn. for Study of Mental Imagery (pres. 1990-91), Soc. for Clin. and Exptl. Hypnosis, Internat. Soc. for Clin. and Exptl. Hypnosis, Am. Psychol. Soc. Office: U Mass-Lowell Dept Psychology Lowell MA 01854

KUO, CHIH-CHENG, electrical engineer; b. Pingtung, Taiwan, July 14, 1956; s. Ching-Yang and Yoeh-Wo (Yeh) K.; m. Minwen Lo, June 4, 1990; 1 child, Jennifer. BSEE, Nat Cheng-Kung U., Tainan, Taiwan, 1978; MSEE, Nat. Taiwan U., 1980; MSCS, U. Md., 1987. Design engr. AOC Internat., Chung-Ho, Taiwan, 1982-84; systems engr. ABSS, Riverdale, Md., 1987-88; software engr. Telecommunications Tech. Corp., Germantown, Md., 1988-89; sr. systems engr. Applied Systems Inst., Washington, 1989-91; communication engr. RDC/INTELSAT, Washington, 1991—. Home: 1400 Arbor View Rd Silver Spring MD 20902 Office: RDC/INTELSAT 3400 International Dr Washington DC 20008

KUO, JOHN TSUNGFEN, geophysicist, educator, researcher; b. Hangchow, Chejiang, China, Apr. 1, 1922; came to U.S., 1949; s. Lee Chen and Che Chen (Ping) K.; m. Marilyn Dunlap, Apr. 14, 1957; children: Ping Andrea, Sonya Sue, J. David. BS in Physics, Math and Geology, U. Redlands, 1952, ScD (hon.), 1978; MS, Cal. Inst. Tech., 1954; PhD, Stanford U., 1958. Registered geophysicist, Calif. Asst. prof. San Jose (Calif.) St. Coll., 1957-60; rsch. assoc. Stanford U., 1958-60; rsch. scientist Columbia U., N.Y.C., 1960-64, assoc. prof., 1964-67, prof., 1967-83, Vinton prof., 1983-85, Ewing and Worzel prof., 1985—; participant DEEPSCAN, 1963; dir. Lamont-Doherty's Geophys. Obs., Ogdensburg, N.J., 1967-77, project MIDAS (Migration, Inversion, Diffraction, and Scattering), 1979-89; asst. Mobil Anvil Point Expt. Mine, Colo., 1969; disting. vis. scholar, U. Cambridge, Eng., 1970-71; vis. prof., U. Tex., Austin, 1977-78, Cornell U., N.Y., 1978; Columbia U. del. People's Republic of China, 1979; tech. adv. 23rd Dist. Congressman, 1983—; cons. dept. Theoretical and Applied Mechanics, Cornell U., 1984-87; prof. (hon.) and co-dir. Integrated Basin Studies, Chengdu Coll., People's Republic of China, 1986; prin. investigator, grantee numerous orgns. including NSF, NASA, U.S. Geol. Survey. Editorial bd. Bollettino di Geofisica, Italy, 1985-89; contbr. over 120 articles to profl. jours. Danforth teaching fellow, 1957, NSF postdoctoral fellow, 1970; recipient Alexander von Humboldt award for Disting. U.S. Sr. Scientist, Fed. Republic Germany, 1986. Fellow Geol. Soc. Am., Royal Astron. Soc. U.K.; mem. Internat. Union Geodesy and Geophysics (fellow Assn. Geodesy), Am. Geophys. Union (life, assoc. editor Geophysics Rev.), Soc. Exploration Geophysicists (rep.-at-large, mem. numerous coms.), Seismol. Soc. Am., Petroleum Exploration Soc. N.Y., Redlands Round Table (hon.), Sigma Xi. Home: 11 Hoffmann Ln Blauvelt NY 10913 Office: Columbia U New York NY 10027

KUPFER, CARL, ophthalmologist, science administrator; b. N.Y.C., Feb. 9, 1928; s. James and Hannah Kupfer; m. Muriel I. Kaiser, Dec. 9, 1969; children: Charles, Sarah. AB, Yale U., 1948; MD, Johns Hopkins U., 1952; DSc (hon.), U. Pa., 1982, SUNY, 1992. Diplomate Am. Bd. Ophthalmology. Intern, resident Johns Hopkins U., 1952-55, 57-58; asst. prof. Harvard U. Med. Sch., Boston, 1960-66; prof., chmn. dept. ophthalmology U. Wash. Sch. Med., Seattle, 1966-69; dir. Nat. Eye Inst. NIH, Bethesda, Md, 1979—. Capt. USAF, 1954-56. Recipient Migel award Am. Found. for the Blind, 1976, Pisart award Lighthouse for the Blind, N.Y.C., 1984, Presdl. Rank award, 1991. Mem. Johns Hopkins Soc. Scholars, Insts. Medicine, NAS. Office: HHS 9000 Rockville Pike Bethesda MD 20892-0001

KUPFERMANN, IRVING, neurobiology educator, researcher; b. Jan. 26, 1938; s. Paul and Anna Kupfermann; m. Aug. 19, 1965; children: David, Celina. BS, U. Fla., 1959; PhD, U. Chgo., 1964. Asst. prof. NYU, N.Y.C., 1969-73, assoc. prof., 1973-74; assoc. rsch. scientist N.Y. State Psychiat. Inst., N.Y.C., 1973—; Columbia U., N.Y.C., 1979—, prof., 1979—; assoc. rsch. scientist N.Y. State Psychiat. Inst., N.Y.C., 1974—. Contbr. over 100 articles to profl. jours. Grantee NIMH; recipient Merit award NIMH, Career Devel. award. Office: Columbia U Sch of Medicine 722 W 168th St New York NY 10032-2603

KUPIEC-WEGLINSKI, JERZY WOJCIECH, transplantation immunologist; b. Warsaw, Poland, July 11, 1951; came to U.S., 1979; s. Antoni and Aleksandra (Kolbusz) K.; m. Grazyna Szafarkiewicz, Oct. 27, 1979 (dec. Mar. 1980); m. Kasia Krystyna Czerpak, July 14, 1992. MD, Med. Acad., Warsaw, 1975; PhD, Polish Acad. Scis., Warsaw, 1979. Cons. surgery 2d Dept. Surgery, Warsaw, 1976-78; asst. surg. rsch. Polish Acad. Scis., Warsaw, 1978; rsch. fellow Harvard Med. Sch., Boston, 1979-82, instr. surgery, 1982-84, asst. prof., 1985-87; reader in surgery Oxford (England) U., 1986-87; assoc. prof. Harvard Med. Sch., 1987-91; prof. transplantation immunology German Heart Ctr., Berlin, 1990—; prof. surgery Harvard Med. Sch., 1992—; cons. BAYER Pharms., Wuppertal, Germany, 1987—, SmithKline Beecham Pharms., King of Prussia, Pa., 1990—; speaker in field. Contbr. to 12 books and over 150 papers to profl. jours. NIH grantee, 1988—, NATO grantee, 1990—; Grant-In-Aid award Am. Heart Assn., 1987-90, Horatio Symmonds award U. Oxford, 1986-87. Mem. Fedn. Am. Socs. Exptl. Biology, Am. Soc. Transplant Physicians, Am. Fedn. Clin. Rsch., European Soc. Surg. Rsch., Internat. Soc. Lymphology, The Transplantation Soc. Office: Harvard Med Sch 260 Longwood Ave Boston MA 02115

KUPPENHEIMER, JOHN DANIEL, physicist, educator; b. Orange, N.J., Sept. 15, 1941; s. John Daniel and Selma (Hauser) K. BS in Physics, Lafayette Coll., 1963; MA in Physics, Boston U., 1965; PhD in Physics, Worcester Poly. Inst., 1969. Asst. prof. Worcester Poly. Inst., Mass., 1969-71; optical physicist Diffraction Ltd., Bedford, Mass., 1971-73; dir. optical metrology lab Sanders Assocs., Nashua, N.H., 1973-79, sr. prin. physicist, 1979-84, physics fellow, 1984—; adj. prof. U. Lowell, Mass., 1975-87; prof. physics Tufts U., Medford, Mass., 1984—. Contbr. articles to tech. jours. Patentee in field. Active Greater Lowell Fly Fishers, Drucut, Mass., 1975—. Recipient Robert E. Gross award Lockheed Corp., 1987. Mem. Optical Soc. Am., Sigma Xi. Avocations: fly fishing, sound reproduction, photography. Home: 100 Brookfield Rd Tewksbury MA 01876-2123 Office: Sanders Assocs MS MER15-1813 Nashua NH 03061-2035

KURALT, CHARLES BISHOP, television news correspondent; b. Wilmington, N.C., Sept. 10, 1934; s. Wallace Hamilton and Ina (Bishop) K.; m. Suzanna Folsom Baird, June 1, 1962; children by previous marriage: Lisa Bowers White, Susan Guthery Bowers. B.A., U. N.C., 1955. Reporter, columnist Charlotte (N.C.) News, 1955-57; writer CBS News, 1957-59, corr., 1959—; corr., host. CBS News Sunday Morning. Author: To The Top of the World, 1968, Dateline America, 1979, On the Road with Charles Kuralt, 1985, Southerners, 1986, North Carolina Is My Home, 1986, A Life on the Road, 1990. Recipient Ernie Pyle Meml. award, 1956, George Foster Peabody Broadcasting award, 1969, 76, 80, Emmy award, 1969, 78, 81, 86, 87, 88, 89; named Broadcaster of Yr., Internat. Radio-TV Soc., 1985. Club: Players (N.Y.C.). Address: care CBS News 524 W 57th St New York NY 10019*

KURAS, THOMAS FRANCIS, total quality management professional; b. Phila., Mar. 6, 1947; s. Charles Joseph and Jean Anna Kuras; m. Margaret Clare Manser, Feb. 15, 1969; children: Kimberly Clare, Alison Jean. BS in Mgmt. and Mktg., Phila. Coll. Textiles & Sci., 1973; postgrad., Drexel U., 1977-78. Mgmt. and total quality coord. Kingston-Warren Corp., Newfields, N.H., 1984-88; mgr. total quality systems New Eng. Bus. Svc., Inc., Groton, Mass., 1988—; mfg. mgmt., quality assurance, new product devel. in textile and food processing inds., 1974-84. With USAF, 1966-70. Home: 240 Middle Rd Brentwood NH 03833

KURIANSKY, JUDY, television and radio talk show host, reporter, psychologist, writer, lecturer; b. N.Y.C., Jan. 31, 1947; d. Abraham and Sylvia (Feld) Brodsky; m. Edward Kuriansky, Aug. 24, 1969. BA, Smith Coll., 1968; MEd, Boston U., 1970; PhD, NYU, 1980. Reporter Sta. WABC-TV, N.Y.C., 1980-82, Sta. WBZ-TV, Boston, 1981-82, Sta. WCBS-TV, 1982-86, CBS-TV, N.Y.C., 1986-88, Sta. WPIX-TV, N.Y.C., 1987-89, Sta. CNBC-TV, Ft. Lee, N.J., 1989—; host Total Wellness for Women program Sta. WDBB-TV, Birmingham, Ala., 1988-89; program host Sta. WABC-AM, N.Y.C., 1980-87, Sta. WOR-AM, 1987-88; temp. program host ABC Talk Radio, N.Y.C., 1988-90; host Modern Satellite Network, 1981; TV host J.C. Penney Golden Rule Network, Dallas, 1988-90; feature contbr. Attitudes Show LifeTime, 1992—; cons. Lily of France, Val Mode Lingerie, Charles of the Ritz, The Rolland Co., Taylor-Gordon Arons Advt., Clairol; tchr. Columbia U. Med. Sch., 1974-79, Inst. for Health and Religion, 1980-82; adj. prof. psychology NYU, 1989-90; judge Most Unforgettable Women contest Revlon, 1990; therapy coord. Nat. Inst. for Psychotherapists, 1977-79; therapist Ctr. for Marital and Family Therapy, 1986—; v.p. Quezon Corp., 1978-79; sr. rsch. scientist N.Y. State Psychiat. Inst., 1970-78; lectr. Blanton Peale Inst., 1979-81. Author: Sex, Now That I've Got Your Attention, Let Me Answer Your Questions, 1984, How to Love a Nice Guy, 1990, Italian and Japanese translations; columnist Family Circle mag., 1984-89, Whole Life Times, 1986-87, King Features Newspaper, 1984-86; writer New Woman, Ad Age, Boardroom Reports, Am. Advt. Fedn. mag., Chgo. Tribune Woman News; contbg. editor Beauty Mag., 1989-90. Bd. dirs. Scientists Com. for Pub. Info., 1977-79; mem. adv. bd. N.Y. City Self Help Orgn., 1983-85; mem. benefits com. Mental Health Svcs. for Deaf, 1980-82. Recipient Civilian Commendation, N.Y.C. Police Dept., 1984, Cert. for Unique Pub. Svc., AWRT, 1984, Maggie award Planned Parenthood, 1985, Freedoms Found. award Children for a Better Soc., 1986, Olive award Coun. of Chs., 1986, Mercury award Larimi Communications, 1987. Fellow Am. Psychol. Assn.; mem. Am. Women in Radio and TV (pres. N.Y. chpt. 1988-89, nat. found. vice chair 1988-90—), Soc. Sex Therapy and Rsch. (charter) TV Acad. of N.Y. (gov. 1987—), Friars Club. Office: CNBC 244 W 72nd St Apt 14D New York NY 10023-2815

KURIEN, SANTHA T., psychiatrist; b. Perumpavoor, Kerala, India, June 15, 1945; came to U.S., 1973; d. Varghese and Mary (Thomas) Koshy; m. Thomas K. Kurien; children: Susan, Miriam. MD, Calicut Med. Coll., Kerala, India, 1970. Diplomate Am. Bd. Psychiatry and Neurology; cert. geriatric psychiatry. Sr. house surgeoncy Vellore (Madras) Med. Coll., 1970-71; gen. med. practice St. Thomas Memorial Hosp., Vadasserikara, Kerala, India, 1971-72; psychiat. residency Fairfield Hills Hosp., Newtown, Conn., 1973-76; staff psychiatrist Fairfield Hills Hosp., Newtown, 1976-77, Danbury (Conn.) Hosp., 1977-82; psychiatrist pvt. practice, Danbury, 1982—. Mem. Am. Psychiat. Assn., Am. Assn. Geriatric Psychiatry, New Haven County Med. Assn., Danbury Med. Soc., Assn. Kerala Med. Grads. Office: Santha T Kurien MD PC 27 Hospital Ave Ste 304 Danbury CT 06810-5970

KURK, MITCHELL, physician; b. N.Y.C., Aug. 25, 1931; s. Benjamin and Frieda (Steinbaum) K.; m. Marcia Carol Leon (dec. 1981); children: Hope, Nancy, Cindy. BS, MS, Columbia U., 1954; OD, Mass. Coll. Optometry, 1955; DO, Phila. Coll. Osteopathic, 1960; MD, U. Calif., 1962. Diplomate Am. Bd. Gen. Practice. Clin. asst. Queens (N.Y.) Gen. Hosp.; pvt. practice N.Y.C., 1962—; dir. Biomed. Revitalization Ctr., Lawrence, N.Y., 1980-85; attending physician Peninsula Hosp. Ctr.; mem. alcohol adv. bd. Southshore Hosp., Queens, 1978-80. Author: Kurkian Way To Hold Back the Aging Process, 1989. Fellow Internat. Coll. Applied Nutrition; mem. Internat. Acad. Preventive Medicine, Am. Holistic Med. Assn., AMA, N.Y. State Med. Soc., Nassau County Med. Soc., Nassau Acad. Medicine. Republican.

KURKE, LANCE BROWNSON, business educator; b. Fargo, N.D., May 19, 1952; s. John Mathew and Eleanor Francis (Bergen) K.; m. Florence Emily Mendelson, Sept. 17, 1988. BS, Stetson U., 1974; MBA, Cornell U., 1979, MA, 1980, PhD, 1981. Assoc. prof. Carnegie Mellon U., Pitts., 1980-86; asst. prof. Wake Forest U., Winston-Salem, N.C., 1986-89, Duquesne U., Pitts., 1989—. Contbr. chpts. to books and articles to profls. Recipient Rsch. Support award Ford Found., 1981, Innovations in Teaching award Exxon/Am. Assn. Collegiate Schs. of Bus., 1987. Mem. APA, Am. Sociol. Assn., Acad. Mgmt., Strategic Mgmt. Soc. Home: 1542 Asbury Pl Pittsburgh PA 15217 Office: AJ Palumbo Sch Bus Adminstr Rockwell Hall Duquesne Univ Pittsburgh PA 15282

KURLAN, MARVIN ZEFT, surgeon; b. Wilkes-Barre, Pa., Feb. 20, 1934; s. Ephraigm Joseph and Fannye Lillian (Rosenbluth) Kurlancheek; m. Eleanor Frank, June 21, 1964; 1 child, Todd. BA, Wilkes Coll., 1957; MS, U. Ill., 1958; MD, SUNY, Buffalo, 1964. Diplomate Nat. Bd. Med. Examiners, Am. Bd. Surgery. Intern then resident in surgery Millard Fillmore Hosp., Buffalo, 1964-69, dir. trauma svcs., 1974-82, sr. attending surgeon, 1984—;

plant surgeon Bethlehem (Pa.) Steel Corp., 1969-74; med. dir. Bros. of Mercy Health Facilities, Clarence, N.Y., 1976-80; assoc. examiner Am. Bd. Surgery, Phila., 1987—. Contbr. articles to profl. jours. Vol. Empire State Games, Buffalo, 1986; mem. Jack Kemp Forum, Buffalo, 1985—; bd. dirs. Jewish Fedn. Allentown, Pa., 1972-74. Served to lt. col. M.C., USAR, 1965-91. Fellow Am. Coll. Gastroenterology, Am. Trauma Soc. (founder); mem. Assn. Mil. Surgeons, Buffalo Surg. Soc. (v.p. 1988-89, pres. 1989-90, sec. 1986-88), ACS (life fellow leadership soc.), Am. Biog. Inst. (dep. gov.), Internat. Biog. Assn. (dep. dir. for the Americas), Grand Coun. World Parliament, Confederation of Chivalry, Knight of Humanity, Order White Cross Internat. (dist. comdr. N.Y., U.S.A.), Chevalier Grand Cross, Ordre Souverain et Militaire de la Milice du Saint Sepulcre. Republican. Club: Sci. Progress Research (Buffalo) (v.p. 1983-84). Lodges: Masons, Shriners. Home and Office: 413 Dan Troy Dr Buffalo NY 14221-3558

KURLAND, SHERYL PAULA, freelance writer, marketing consultant; b. Live Oak, Fla., June 20, 1957; d. Irwin and Bette Ann (Fleet) Leider; m. Steven David Kurland, Sept. 3, 1989. BA cum laude, U. Ga., 1978. Pub. rels. mgr. Sun Bank, N.A., Orlando, Fla., 1981-88; investor rels. mgr. Ryland Acceptance Corp., Columbia, Md., 1987-91; freelance writer, mktg. cons. Ellicott City, Md., 1991—. Contbr. articles to mags. Recipient State award Best Newsletter Fla. Pub. Rels. Assn., 1985, cert. Merit, 1987, Golden Image award, 1988. Mem. Am. Mktg. Assn., Nat. Investor Rels. Inst./Roundtable (bd. dirs. Washington chpt. 1991-92, chmn. 1991—), Advt. and Graphic Arts Soc., 1991—. Office: PO Box 644 Ellicott City MD 21041

KURLANDER, HONEY WACHTEL, artist, educator; b. Bklyn.; d. Charles Bernard and Sara F. (Alexander) Wachtel; m. Neale Kurlander, June 25, 1949; children: Harold Michael, Susan Laurie. Student, Parsons Sch. Design; cert. in illustration, Pratt Inst., 1948. Freelance textile designer N.Y.C., 1948-58, freelance children's book illustrator, 1950-60; art instr. East Meadow (N.Y.) High Sch., 1958-60, Kurlander Studio, East Meadow, 1958-79, Kurlander Art Studio, Old Westbury, N.Y., 1979—. Exhibited in one-man shows at Garden City (N.Y.) Galleries Ltd., 1960-90, Robley Gallery, Roslyn, N.Y., 1971, Madison Ave. Gallery, N.Y.C., 1975, Salmagundi Club, N.Y.C., 1978; executed mural Astoria Queens, 1985, poster Centennial Celebration of Statue of Liberty; represented in permanent collections at Dietz Mus., Wasserberg, Germany, C.W. Post Coll. Art Ctr., Brookville, N.Y., DeServersky Conf. Ctr., Greenvale, N.Y. Recipient 1st prize Heckscher Mus., 1966; 1st prize Eastern Regional Exhibit, 1968. Mem. Nat. League Am. Penwomen (Best in Show award 1978, 81, 84, 1st prize 1962-91), Art League Nassau County, Salmalgundi Club (Williams award 1979). Home and Studio: Kurlander Studio 6 Kings Dr Old Westbury NY 11568

KURLANDER, NEALE, accounting and law educator, lawyer; b. Bklyn., Jan. 1, 1924; s. Sol and Eleanor Kurlander; m. Honey Wachtel, June 25, 1949; children: Harold M., Susan L. BS, Long Island U., 1948; JD, N.Y. Law Sch., N.Y.C., 1951; MBA, Adelphi U., 1967. Bar: N.Y. 1952; CPA, N.Y. V.p., chief fin. officer Profit Motivation Svcs., Inc., Garden City, N.Y., 1967-71; cons.-reviewer Ernst & Ernst, Garden City, 1967-72; lectr. Practicing Law Inst., N.Y.C., 1974; chmn. dept. acctng and law Adlphi U., Garden City, 1964-82; cons. Regent's External Degree, Albany, N.Y., 1974-87; pvt. practice law Old Westbury, N.Y., 1952—; pvt. practice acct., CPA Old Westbury, 1960—; prof. acctg. and law Adelphi U., Garden City, 1962—; profl. developer Harris, Kerr, Forster & Co., N.Y.C., 1969-71; treas. Fin. Execs. Inst., Long Island, N.Y., 1974-76, chmn. acad. rels., 1975—, bd. dirs. 1975—; faculty Found. for Acctg. Edn., 1975—, bd. trustees, 1976-79. Author: Basic Accounting, 1962, Auditing, Vol. I and II, 1978; contbr. articles to profl. jours. Comdr. post 6081 VFW, Bklyn., 1953-54; mem. Bd. Elections, Nassau County, N.Y., 1964-70, Citizens Adv. Com. N.Y. State Dept. Taxation, Albany, 1975-87, Bd. Appeals, Old Westbury, 1988—; legis. adv. coun. mem. N.Y. State Assembly 15th Dist., 1991—. Recipient cert. Delta Mu Delta, 1982; named Outstanding Acctg. Educator, Found. for Acctg. Edn., N.Y., 1982, Acct. of Yr. Acctg. Soc., 1992. Mem. N.Y. State Soc. CPA's, AICPA, Am. Acctg. Assn., Nassau County Bar Assn., N.Y. State Assembly 15th Dist. (legis. adv. coun.). Home: 6 Kings Dr Old Westbury NY 11568-1108 Office: Adelphi U South Ave Garden City NY 11530

KURTH, WALTER RICHARD, association executive; b. Normal, Ill., Jan. 21, 1932; s. Walter H. and Irene (Freitag) K.; m. Mary Elisabeth Taylor, Aug. 23, 1958; children: Mary Helen, Sarah Jane, Elisabeth Irene. B.S., U. Ill., 1954. Cert. assn. exec. Publ. dir. Assoc. Credit Burs. of Am., Inc., St. Louis, 1954-57; mktg. dir. Assoc. Credit Burs. of Am., Inc., 1957-62, asst. gen. mgr., 1962-66; asst. gen. mgr., treas. Assoc. Credit Burs. of Am., Inc., Houston, 1966-68; adminstrv. v.p., treas. Assoc. Credit Burs. of Am., Inc., 1968-69; exec. v.p., treas. Assoc. Credit Burs., Inc., 1969-75; sec.-treas. Credit Bur. Automation, Inc., Houston, 1966-75; vice chmn. bd. Credit Services Internat., 1970-75; pres., sec.-treas., vice chmn. bd. ACB Services, Inc., 1970-75; sr. v.p. Nat. Consumer Finance Assn., Washington, 1976-77; exec. v.p. Nat. Consumer Finance Assn., 1977-80, pres., 1980-82; pres. Am. Fin. Services Assn., 1983, Assoc. Credit Burs. Inc., 1983—; chmn. bd. ACB Svcs. Inc., 1983-90. Mem. Houston dist. council SBA, 1971-75; mem. adv. council Purdue Credit Research Ctr., 1977—, chmn. 1986-87, mem. gov. bd.; chmn. Republican Dist. Fund Drive; Rep. precinct chmn., 1969-75; bd. mgrs. Thompson Retreat Center, St. Louis, 1963-64; bd. dirs. Econ. Edn. Found. for Clergy, 1976-82. Mem. Am. Soc. Assn. Execs. (dir. 1982—, vice chmn. bd. 1985-86), Tex. Soc. Assn. Execs., Houston Soc. Assn. Execs. (pres. 1974), St. Louis Soc. Assn. Execs. (pres. 1962), Star and Scroll (pres. 1953), U.S. C. of C. (bd. dirs. 1986-88, assn. com. 1978—, chmn. 1986—), Am. Mgmt. Assn., Univ. Club, Washington Golf and Country Club, Masons (32d degree), Shriners, Alpha Kappa Lambda (pres. 1953). Republican. Presbyterian (elder). Home: 7302 Aynsley Ln Mc Lean VA 22102-2931 Office: Assoc Credit Burs Inc 1090 Vermont Ave NW Ste 200 Washington DC 20005-4905

KURTZ, ELAINE, artist; b. Phila., June 10, 1928; d. George and Tillie (Goldberg) Kahn; m. Jerome Kurtz, July 28, 1956; children: Madeleine, Nettie Kurtz Greenstein. Cert. with honors, U. Arts, Phila., 1950; student, Barnes Found., Merion, Pa., 1963-65. One-woman shows include Martha Jackson Gallery, N.Y.C., 1978, Osuna Gallery, Washington, 1980, 82, 84, 88, Gross McCleaf Gallery, Phila., 1986, 89, Anita Shapolsky Gallery, N.Y.C., 1987, 90, 91; exhibited in group shows, including Indpls. Mus. Art, 1978, Internat. Festival Painting, France, 1981, Nat. Mus. Am. Art, Washington, 1985, XXIV Internat. Prix Contemporary Art, Monte Carlo, 1991; represented in permanent collections Hirschhorn Mus. and Sculpture Garden, Nat. Mus. Am. Art, Phila. Mus. Art, Portland (Maine) Mus. Art, also others. Recipient alumni award in painting U. Arts, 1977. Home and Studio: 17 E 16th St New York NY 10003

KURTZ, JOEL BARRY, finance executive; b. Bklyn., Aug. 2, 1944; s. Milton and Claire (Diamond) K.; BBA, Pace U., 1970; MBA, C.W. Post Coll., 1981; m. Judith M. Austin, Aug. 11, 1968; children: Brian, Steven, Stacey. CPA, N.Y. Staff acct. Arthur Andersen & Co., Melville, N.Y., 1970-73; div. controller Elec. Comp. div., Gould Inc., Farmingdale, N.Y., 1973-78; controller CBS-Holt, Rinehart & Winston, N.Y.C., 1979-80; controller Siemans Data Switching Systems, formely Databit Inc., Hauppauge, N.Y., 1981-87; v.p. fin. Linotype-Hell Co., Hauppauge, N.Y., 1987—. Active L.I. Assn., 1981—. With U.S. Army, 1966-68. Mem. AICPA, Nat. Assn. Accts. (chpt. pres. 1976-77), N.Y. Soc. CPAs, Am. Mgmt. Assn. Home: 84 Vera Ln Commack NY 11725-1922 Office: 425 Oser Ave Hauppauge NY 11788-3607

KURTZ, MAX, civil engineer, consultant; b. Bklyn., Mar. 25, 1920; s. Samuel and Ida (Malkin) K.; B.B.A., CCNY, 1940; postgrad. Rutgers U., 1943-44; m. Ruth Ingraham, Sept. 9, 1967. Structural engr. Kurtz Steel Constrn. Corp., Mineola, N.Y., 1946-56; pvt. practice cons. engring., Flushing, N.Y., 1956—; condr. seminars on ops. research. Served with U.S. Army, 1943-45. Registered profl. engr., N.Y. Mem. N.Y. State Soc. Profl. Engrs. (Honor award Kings County chpt. 1970), Nat. Soc. Profl. Engrs. Author: Structural Engineering for P.E. Examinations, 3d edit., 1978; Engineering Economics for P.E. Examinations, 3d edit., 1985; Comprehensive Structural Design Guide, 1968; Handbook of Engineering Economics, 1984; Handbook of Applied Mathematics for Engineers and Scientists, 1991; editor Kings County Profl. Engr., 1967-71; project editor Civil Engineering Reference Guide, 1986. Home and Office: 33-47 91st St Flushing NY 11372

KURTZ, PAUL, philosopher, educator; b. Newark, Dec. 21, 1925; s. Martin and Sara (Lasser) K.; m. Claudine C. Vial, Oct. 6, 1960; children—Valerie L., Patricia A., Jonathan. B.A., NYU, 1948; M.A., Columbia U., 1949, Ph.D., 1952. Instr. Queens Coll., 1950-52; instr. philosophy Trinity Coll., Hartford, Conn., 1952-55; asst. prof. Trinity Coll., 1955-58, assoc. prof. 1958-59; assoc. prof. Vassar Coll., Poughkeepsie, N.Y., 1960-61; vis. prof. New Sch. Social Rsch., N.Y.C., 1960-65; assoc. prof. Union Coll., Schenectady, 1961-64; prof. Union Coll., 1964-65; vis. prof. U. Besancon, France, 1965; prof. philosophy SUNY, Buffalo, 1965—; moderator TV series. Author: (with Rollo Handy) A Current Appraisal of the Behavioral Sciences, 1964, Decision and the Condition of Man, 1965, The Fullness of Life, 1974, Exuberance, 1977, In Defense of Secular Humanism, 1983, A Skeptics Handbook of Parapsychology, 1985, The Transcendental Temptation, 1986, Forbidden Fruit, 1988, Eupraxophy, 1989, Philosophical Essays in Pragmatic Naturalism, 1990, The New Skepticism, 1992; editor: American Thought Before 1900, 1966, American Philosophy in the Twentieth Century, 1966, Sidney Hook and the Contemporary World, 1968, Moral Problems in Contemporary Society, 1969; co-editor: International Directory of Philosophy and Philosophers, 4th edit, 1978-81, Tolerance and Revolution, 1970, Language and Human Nature, 1971, A Catholic/Humanist Dialogue, 1972, The Humanist Alternative, 1973, Idea of a Modern University, 1974, The Philosophy of The Curriculum, 1975, The Ethics of Teaching and Scientific Research, 1977, University and State, 1978, Sidney Hook: Philosopher of Democracy and Humanism, 1983, Building A World Community, 1989; mem. editorial bd.: The Humanist, 1964-78, editor, 1967-78; mem. editorial bd. Philosophers Index, 1969-85, Question, 1969-81; editor-in-chief: Prometheus Books, 1970—; mem. editorial bd.: The Skeptical Inquirer, 1976—; editor: Free Inquiry Mag., 1980—. chmn. Council for Dem. and Secular Humanism, 1980—, Council on Internat. Studies and World Affairs, 1966-69; trustee Behavioral Research Council, Great Barrington, Mass.; bd. dirs. U.S. Bibliography of Philosophy, 1958-70, Univ. Ctrs. for Rational Alternatives, 1969—; bd. dirs. Internat. Humanist and Ethical Union, 1968—, co-chmn., 1986—; chmn. Com. for Sci. Investigation Claims of Paranormal, 1976—. Served with AUS, 1944-46. Behavioral Research Council fellow, 1962-63; French Govt. fellow, 1965; John Dewey fellow, 1986-87; recipient Bertrand Russell Soc. award, 1988. Fellow AAAS; mem. Acad. Humanism. Home: 660 Lebrun Rd Buffalo NY 14226-4234 Office: 59 John Glenn Dr Buffalo NY 14228-2197

KURTZ, ROBERT GARY, publishing company accounting executive; b. Newark, Nov. 1, 1952; s. Franklin and Estella (Wright) K.; m. Bonnie Scheer, Jan. 23, 1977; children: Lauren, Daniel. BS, NYU, 1974, MBA, 1978, Advanced Profl. Cert., 1983. CPA, N.Y.; cert. info. systems auditor, date processor, systems profl., internal auditor. Programmer Bache & Co., N.Y.C., 1974; analyst N.Y. Bank for Savs., N.Y.C., 1975-76; EDP auditor Gen. Foods, N.Y.C., 1976-78; sr. EDP auditor N.Y. Times, N.Y.C., 1979, EDP audit supr., 1980, EDP audit mgr., 1981, mgr. info systems unit, 1983-87, asst. dir. corp. internal audit, 1987-89, asst. corp. contr., 1989—. Contbr. articles to profl. jours. Mem. AICPA, EDP Auditors Assn., Inst. for Cert. of Computers Profls., Internat. Benefits Assn., Fin. Exec. Inst. Office: NY Times Co 1120 Ave of Americas 8th Fl New York NY 10036

KURTZ, SHELDON IAN, executive recruiter; b. N.Y.C., Mar. 12, 1938; s. Herman and Rebecca (Garbo) K.; m. Diana Lawrence; children: Jack, Adam. BS in Bus., NYU, 1959, MBA, 1961. Nat. account mgr. Burroughs Corp., N.Y.C., 1960-63; regional sales mgr. Addo Machine Co., Malmo, Sweden, 1963-69; regional v.p. Pitney Bowes-Alpex, Inc., Danbury, Conn., 1969-74; v.p. EDP World, Inc., N.Y.C., 1974-86; pres., chief exec. officer Kurtz Pro-Search, Inc., Warren, N.J., 1986—; cons., exec. recruiter AT&T, N.Y.C., 1976—. Contbr. articles to profl. jours. Dir. PANN, N.J., 1987-90. Office: Kurtz Pro-Search Inc PO Box 4263 Warren NJ 07059-0263

KURTZ, THEODORE STEPHEN, psychoanalyst, educator; b. N.Y.C., Apr. 25, 1944; s. Maxwell Arthur and Evelyn R. (Rosenberg) K.; A.B., Boston U., 1964; M.A., N.Y. U., 1965; postgrad. N.Y. Soc. Freudian Psychologists, 1968-74; m. Maritza J. Zurita, Sept. 12, 1975. Caseworker, N.Y.C. Dept. Social Services, 1965-66; tchr., coordinator classes for emotionally disturbed Northport (N.Y.) Pub. Schs., 1966-70; pvt. practice psychoanalytic psychotherapy, 1968—; prin. Luther E. Woodward Sch. for Emotionally Disturbed Children, Freeport, N.Y., 1970-74; asst. prof. edn. C.W. Post Coll., L.I. U., Greenvale, N.Y., 1974-81; psychol. cons. to pvt. industry, 1971—. Diplomate Am. Inst. Counseling and Psychotherapy; cert. Soc. for Psychoanalytic Psychotherapy. Fellow Am. Orthopsychiat. Assn.; mem. Am. Assn. Marriage and Family Counselors (clin. mem.), Am. Acad. Psychotherapists, Am. Group Psychotherapy Assn., Am. (asso.), Nassau County (exec. bd. 1977-78, chmn. com. on acad. psychology 1977-78) psychol. assns., N.Y. Soc. Clin. Psychologists (asso.), Am. Inst. Profl. Con.'s (sr.), Am. Soc. Tng. and Devel., Acad. Psychologists in Marital, Sex and Family Therapy, Council Advancement of Psychol. Professions and Scis. Jewish. Contbr. articles to profl. jours. Home: Willow Brook Rd PO Box 529 Cold Spring Harbor NY 11724-0529

KURTZBERG, EVELYN CLAIRE, school psychologist; b. N.Y.C., Mar. 23, 1942; d. Leon and Henrietta (Reinfield) Bach; m. Richard L. Kurtzberg, Dec. 24, 1964; children: Kimberly, Terri. BS, Queens Coll., 1962, MA, 1964; PhD, NYU, 1972. Lic. psychologist, N.Y., Conn. Sch. psychologist Boces of Westchester, Elmsford, N.Y., 1965-72; assoc. prof. U. Bridgeport, Conn., 1972-74; adj. prof. Fairfield (Conn.) U., 1982-84; psychotherapist in pvt. practice South Salem, N.Y., 1973—; sch. psychologist New Canaan (Conn.) High Sch., 1974—; participant in tng. films on group process Assn. of Specialists in Group Work, Fairfield, 1985. Mem. APA, Am. Assn. Marriage and Family Therapists, Nat. Register of Mental Health Providers. Home and Office: Route 4 Hastings Ct South Salem NY 10590 Office: New Canaan High Sch Farm Rd New Canaan CT 06840-6608

KURUC, ALVIN RONALD, mathematician; b. Passaic, N.J., Apr. 3, 1957; s. Andrew William and Elizabeth (Handago) K.; m. Donna Joy Winn, June 30, 1990. SB, MIT, 1979, postgrad., 1990—; MD, Yale U., 1984; postgrad., U. Calif., San Diego, 1989-90. Rsch. assoc. Children"s Hosp., Boston, 1984-85; signal processing analyst MIT Lincoln Lab., Lexington, 1985-89, cons., 1989—. Nat. Def. Sci. and Engring. fellow Dept. of Def., 1991—. Mem. Am. Math. Soc. Home: 113 Columbia St Cambridge MA 02139-2729

KURZMAN, STEPHEN ALAN, accountant; b. Boston, Feb. 24, 1945; s. H. Edward and Gertrude (Blake) K.; B.S., Northeastern U., 1968; M.S., Bentley Coll., 1977; m. Marilyn Verna Baker, June 30, 1968; children—David Eric, Jessica Susan. Asst. to treas. Home Owners Fed. Savs. & Loan Assn., Boston, 1968-70; sr. acct. Martin D. Braver & Co., Chestnut Hill, Mass., 1970-73; tax supr. Laventhol & Horwath, Boston, 1973-76; ptnr. Kurzman & Scibetta, Dedham, Mass., 1976—; adj. asst. prof. taxation Bentley Coll., 1978—, chmn. tax adv. bd., grad. tax program adv. com.; bd. dirs Congregation Mishkan Tefila. Chmn. IRS Dist. Dirs. Liaison Commn. for Mass.; program chmn. Bentley Coll. Nat. Tax Conf. Contbr. articles to profl. jours. Mem. AICPA (instr. 1982—), Mass. Soc. CPAs (past chmn. fed. tax com., bd. dirs., chmn. tax forum com., co-chmn. tax conf.), Bentley Coll. Alumni Assn. (dir. edn. found.), Beta Alpha Psi. Lodge: B'nai B'rith. Home: 8 David Rd Newton MA 02159-2712 Office: Kurzman & Scibetta 1017 Turnpike St Canton MA 02021-2828

KUSH, CHARLES ANDREW, III, mechanical, aerospace, software engineer; b. Somerville, N.J., Dec. 30, 1964; s. Charles A. Jr. and Barbara A. (Zuris) K. BS in Mech. and Aerospace Engring., Rutgers U., 1987. Registered profl. engr. in tng., N.J. Prodn. engr. ITT Avionics, Clifton, N.J., 1987-88, project engr., 1988, program transition engr., 1988-89; pres. Creative Products, Middlesex, N.J., 1989—; info. mgr. AT&T, Piscataway, N.J., 1990—. Recipient George R. Bolmer Meml. scholarship Bound Brook Rotary, 1983, Fisk Assocs. Engring. scholarship Fisk Assocs., 1983, Carl Rabke award for Citizenship and Scholarship, 1983. Mem. ASME, AIAA, Nat. Soc. Profl. Engrs., Soc. Mfg. Engrs. (sr.), Internat. Platform Assn., Soc. Automotive Engrs. Republican. Roman Catholic. Home: 114 Jay Pl Middlesex NJ 08846-1613

KUSHEL, GERALD, management consultant, educator; b. Melville, N.Y., July 18, 1930; s. Benjamin and Bella (Gordon) K.; m. Selma Pearl Plaxsun, Apr. 14, 1957; children: Joan Elan Kushel Davis, Lynne Ora. BS, Rider Coll., 1952; MA, Columbia U., 1959, EdD, 1966. Lic. counselor, N.Y. Tchr. Teaneck (N.J.) and Great Neck Schs., 1957-67; rep., salesman William Jennings, Co., Englewood, N.J., 1960; sch. adminstr. Teaneck Pub. Schs., 1966-67; prof. counseling L.I. U., Brookville, 1967—; pres. Inst. for Effective Thinking, Melville, N.Y., 1986—. Author: Discord in Teacher Counselor Relations, 1967, Fact and Folklore, 1975, Centering, 1979, Fully Effective Executive, 1983, Effective Thinking, 1991. Mem. AACD, Am. Assn. Marriage and Family Therapist (cert.), N.Y. State Assn., L.I. Counseling Assn. (pres. 1970). Democrat. Home and Office: 10 Earl Rd Melville NY 11747-1314

KUSHEN, BETTY SANDRA, writer, educator; b. N.Y.C., Nov. 8, 1933; d. Moses and Betty (Cohen) Cohen; m. Allan Stanford Kushen; children: Annette Joyce, Robert Allan. BEd, U. Miami, 1954; MA, NYU, 1959, PhD, 1969. Author: (biography) Virginia Woolf and The Nature of Communion; assoc. editor Jour. Evolutionary Psychology; contbr. articles to Early Am. Lit., Lit. and Psychology, Am. Imago, Am. Writers Before 1800, Jour. Evolutionary Psychology. Mem. MLA, Virginia Woolf Soc. Jewish. Home: One Raynor Rd West Orange NJ 07052

KUSHNER, HARVEY WOLF, criminal justice educator; b. Manhattan, N.Y., Dec. 9, 1941; s. Albert and Iryne (Fieman) K.; m. Sara Yerich, May 23, 1970; 1 child, Meredith Hope. BA, Queens Coll., Flushing, N.Y., 1969; MA, NYU, 1970, PhD, 1974. Dir. grad. studies Coll. Arts & Scis., C.W. Post/L.I. U., Brookville, N.Y., 1976; prof. dept. Criminal Justice, C.W. Post/L.I. U., Brookville, N.Y., 1974-88, chmn., 1988—; cons. U.S. Dept. Justice, Trenton, N.J., 1991, Suffolk County Police Dept., Suffolk, 1991; evaluator Edn. assistance Corp., Mineola, N.Y., 1986-87; program dir. Correctional Ednl. Consortium, 1986-90. Author: Understanding Basic Statistics, 1980; editor Justice Profl. Jour., 1990, Criminal Organizations/IASOC newsletter, 1991; editorial bd. Jour. Correctional Edn., 1989. Mem. Mayor's Adv. Blue Ribbon Panel on Criminal Justice, Village of Freeport, 1990—; bd. dirs. Correctional Ednl. Consortium, N.Y.C., 1988—. Recipient Founders Day award, NYU, 1974, Commrs. award, Nassau County Police Dept., 1991; fellow, NYU, 1970, 71. Mem. Narcotic Enforcement Officers Assn., Internat. Assn. Chiefs of Police, Nassau County Mcpl. Police Chiefs Assn. Office: CW Post/LI Univ Brookville NY 11548

KUSKA, JOHN JOSEPH, JR., accountant; b. Balt., Feb. 27, 1953; s. John Joseph and T. Virginia (Branham) K.; 1 child, Jennifer L. BA magna cum laude, Lycoming Coll., 1975. CPA, Md. Staff acct. Deloitte & Touche (H & S), Balt., 1975-76; sr. acct. Henry E. Pear & Co., Laurel, Md., 1977-78; corp. sec. Nu-Homes, Inc., Columbia, Md., 1979-80; mgr. Barry S. Fishman & Assocs., Bethesda, Md., 1981-87; prin. John J. Kuska, Jr. & Co., Columbia, 1987—. Winner Durant Furey Meml. award (first in class) Lycoming Coll., 1975. Mem. AICPA, Md. Assn. CPAs, Laurel, Columbia C. of C. Republican. Office: John J Kuska Jr & Co 9891 Broken Land Pkwy Columbia MD 21046-1165

KUSNETZOV, HOWARD, marketing executive; b. Bklyn., July 3, 1942; s. Joseph Kusnetzov and Lillian Gaslowitz; m. Susan Berman; children: Cheryl, Ira. Grad., Dale Carnegie Inst., N.Y.C., 1985. V.p. sales Kusnetzov Bros., Bklyn., 1963-72; asst. sales mgr. Dannon Yogurt div. Beatrice Foods, N.Y.C., 1972-87; sales mgr. hotel-bar-foods div. Secaucus, N.J., 1972-87; sales mgr. Gel Spice Co., Bayonne, N.J., 1987—; sales mgr. U.S. ops. food svc. div. Info Food Corp., Plainview, N.Y., 1988—; sales mgr. food svc. div., 1988-90; sales mgr., dir. U.S. ops. Internat. Cheese Co., Hinesberg, Vt., 1990—; chmn. bd. Piwacket Prodns. Designer yogurt vending machine, 1975 (award 1981). Served with U.S. Army, 1960-61. Mem. Purveyors Club of N.Y. (cons. 1985-87), Ea. Dairy Deli Assn, One-to-One (bd. dirs.). Lodges: Masons, Knights of Pythians.

KUSTIN, KENNETH, chemist; b. Bronx, N.Y., Jan. 6, 1934; s. Alex and Mae (Marvisch) K.; m. Myrna May Jacobson, June 24, 1956; children—Brenda Jayne, Franklin Daniel, Michael Thorpe. B.Sc., Queens Coll., 1955; Ph.D., U. Minn., 1959. Postdoctoral fellow Max Planck Inst. for Phys. Chemistry, Gottingen, W. Ger., 1959-61; asst. prof. chemistry Brandeis U., 1961-66, asso. prof., 1966-72, prof., 1972—, chmn. dept. chemistry, 1974-77; vis. prof. pharmacology Harvard U. Med. Sch., 1977-78; Fulbright-Hays lectr., 1978; program dir. NSF, 1985-86. Research, publs. in field; editor: Fast Reactions, vol. 16 of Methods in Enzymology, 1969; bd. editors Internat. Jour. Chem. Kinetics. Mem. Am. Chem. Soc. (councilor 1983-85), Phi Beta Kappa. Office: Brandeis U Dept Chemistry PO Box 9110 Waltham MA 02254

KUTASI, KATALIN ERZSEBET, investment executive; b. Ann Arbor, Mich., Sept. 7, 1956; d. Karoly and Margaret (Vidonyi) K. BA in Acctg., Mich. State U., 1978; MBA in Fin., DePaul U., 1983. Cost acct. Continental Ill. Nat. Bank and Trust Co. Chgo., 1978-80, banking officer trade fin., 1980-85, 2d v.p., 1985-88, v.p., 1988; workout specialist FDIC, Chgo., 1989; v.p. Equitable Capital Mgmt. Corp., N.Y.C., 1989—; bd. dirs. White Wave Rising Dance Co., Webcraft Tech. Inc. Hotel Property Holdings, Inc. Active Am. Coun. for Arts, Chgo. Coun. for Arts, Bus. Vol. for Arts. Mem. Am. Coun. for the Arts, Gamma Phi Beta.

KUTHY, ARNOLD ROBERT, laundry company executive; b. Detroit, Mar. 23, 1932; s. Wendell Basil and Elizabeth Rosalie (Silagyi) K.; m. Helen Louise Smith, Sept. 5, 1953; children: Michael E., Virginia M., William A. BS, Wayne State U., 1954. Various positions Mobil Oil Corp., N.Y.C., 1956-68; gen. mgr. Phillips Fuel Co., Inc., Hackensack, N.J., 1968-69; nat. sales mgr. Walker Mfg. Co., Inc., Racine, Wis., 1969-70; pres. and chief operating officer Chateau Estates, Rochester, Mich., 1970-75; pres. and owner Kuthy-Beveridge & Assocs., Orchard Lake, Mich., 1975-76; v.p. mktg. Mary MacIntosh Svcs., Inc., Allentown, Pa., 1976-78; exec. v.p. and chief operating officer Geo. W. Kistler, Inc., Allentown, Pa., 1978-82; exec. v.p. and chief operating officer Mary MacIntosh Svcs., Inc., Allentown, 1982-85, pres. and chief exec. officer, 1985-90, also bd. dirs.; pres., chief exec. officer Managed Benefit Systems, Inc., 1990-91; pres., chief oper. officer ACME Cryogenics, Inc., 1992—; also bd. dirs.; bd. dirs. Retail Assocs., Inc., Turnersville, N.J., Liberty Mut. Ins. Co., Phila. Author (with others) two tng. syllabi, 1964, 66. Chair bd. dirs. Better Bus. Bur., Allentown, 1976, Allentown Literacy Coun., 1985; bd. dirs. Indsl. Devel. Corp. of LeHigh County, 1989. Mem. Allentown C. of C. (legis. com. 1988), Rotary. Republican. Roman Catholic. Home: 4380 Knollwood Dr Emmaus PA 18049

KUTLINA, MARY LOUISE, elementary school educator; b. Niagara Falls, N.Y., Dec. 1, 1963; d. Joseph William and Frida Marlene (Reumel) K. BA in Communications, Niagara U., 1985, MS in Edn., 1988. Cert. elem. tchr., English tchr. Elem. tchr., jr. high English tchr. St. Joseph Elem. Sch., Niagara Falls, 1988-90; sub. tchr. Niagara Falls Bd. of Edn., 1990—; vol. Blind Info. Svc., Niagara Falls, 1978-87; asst. Jolly Jokebook. Author: (poems) Friends of Mary, 1991, (play) Friends of Blondin, 1985. Fund-raiser March of Dimes Birth Defects Found., 1981-85. Named 1st runner-up Polish Princess Contest, Echo Club, Niagara Falls, 1982. Mem. Substitute Tchrs. United (bd. dirs. sec. 1991—), Pi Lambda Theta. Home: 2634 Welch Ave Niagara Falls NY 14303 Office: Niagara Falls Bd of Edn 607 Walnut Ave Niagara Falls NY 14302

KUTSCHER, EUGENE BERNARD, educational administrator; b. N.Y.C., Aug. 19, 1947; s. Irving and Babette (Dreyfuss) K.; m. Robin Gerri Rochstein, June 23, 1974; children: Lauren Allison, Scott Jason. BA, Queens Coll., 1968, MA, 1972; postgrad., St. John's U., Jamaica, N.Y., 1976-82. Tchr. Brentwood (N.Y.) Pub. Schs., 1968-78; acting sch. adminstr. Brentwood East Jr. High Sch., 1975-78; lectr. in physics Queens (N.Y.) Coll., 1969-70; dist. chmn. sci. and health edn. Malverne (N.Y.) Pub. Schs., 1978-83, dist. coordinator computer services, 1981-83; dist. chmn. sci. Roslyn (N.Y.) Pub. Schs., 1983—, coordinator sci. research, 1983—; cons., frequent lectr. in field. Author: Physics Research Activities, 1988, Creative Science Activities, Grades 5-9, 1990, Environmental Science Activities, 1991; contbr. articles to profl. jours. Bd. dirs. Zero Population Growth, Washington, 1987—. Grantee N.Y. State Energy R&D, 1983-92. Mem. Nat. Sci. Suprs. Assn. (exec. com., del. Alliance for Environ. Edn. 1988—, chair environ. edn. com. 1991—), Nat. Sci. Tchrs. Assn., N.Y. Sci. Suprs. Assn. (bd. govs. N.Y.State Sci. Honor Sci. Soc. 1991—), Nassau County Sci. Suprs. Assn., Sci. Tchrs. Assn. of N.Y., Guitar Club N.Y.C. Jewish. Home: 80-26 189th

St Jamaica NY 11423 Office: Roslyn Pub Schs Adminstrn Bldg Roslyn NY 11576

KUTTEN, L(AWARENCE) J(OSEPH), lawyer, writer, publisher; b. St. Louis, May 10, 1953; s. Joseph and Carolyn Jane (Yalem) K.; m. Linda Gail Ishibashi, Oct. 20, 1979; 1 child, Carolyn. BA, Claremont McKenna Coll., 1974; JD, Washington U., St. Louis, 1977. Bar: Mo. 1977, Ill. 1978, Hawaii 1987, Pa. 1988. Assoc. Mann & Poger, St. Louis, 1977-78; ptnr. Chartrand Harvey & Kutten, St. Louis, 1978-81; writer St. Louis, 1981—; pub. Software Law Bull., 1988—, Software Taxation Letter, 1990—. Author: Computer Buyer's Protection Guide, 1984, Computer Software, 1987, Executive and Professional Employment Contracts, 1988, An Overview of United States Export Controls, 1989, Electronic Contracting Law: EDI and Business Transactions, 1991. Mem. ABA (patent and copyright sect.). Office: PO Box 113 Wayne PA 19087-0113

KUYPER, JOAN CAROLYN, foundation administrator; b. Balt., Oct. 22, 1941; d. Irving Charles and Ethel Mae (Pritchett) O'Connor; m. L. William Kuyper, Dec. 20, 1964; children: Susan Carol, Edward Philip. BA in Edn., Salisbury State U., 1963; postgrad. Columbia U., 1978; MA in Arts Mgmt. and Bus., NYU, 1988. Elem. sch. tchr. Prince Georges County Schs., Md., 1963-68; free lance singer, opera, oratorio, chamber music Amato Opera, N.Y.C., 1967-80; owner, mgr. Privette Artists' Registry, Placement Service for Singers, Teaneck, N.J., 1969-78; exec. dir. Teaneck Artists Perform-Chamber Music Series, 1975-80; program dir. Vols. in Arts & Humanities, Vol. Bur. Bergen County, N.J., 1978-81; dir. Bergen Mus. Art and Sci., 1981-83; cons. Am. Soc. Prevention Cruelty to Animals, 1984, Am. Council for the Arts, 1987; dir. ops. Isabel O'Neil Found. and Studio, 1984-85. Dir. vol. services March of Dimes Birth Defects Found. of Greater N.Y., 1985-88; dir. chpt. devel. Huntington's Disease Soc. Am., 1988-91; bd. dirs Pro Arte Chorale and adv. bd. on the arts, Teaneck, 1976-81; mgmt. cons. metro svc. cluster Girl Scouts U.S., 1992—. Mem. N.Y. Soc. Assn. Execs. (membership com. 1991-92), Am. Soc. Assn. Execs., Am. Assn. Mus., Mus. Coun. N.J., Am. Mktg. Assn., Assn. for Vol. Adminstrn. (author handbook). Democrat. Presbyterian. Clubs: Altrusa (bd. dirs. 1984-86, 90—, pres. 1986-88), P.E.O., Phi Alpha Theta. Home: 345 W 58th St 14X New York NY 10019

KUZMA, GREGORY PAUL, treasurer, accountant; b. Pitts., Dec. 5, 1950; s. Paul Kenneth and Florence (Moran) K.; m. Maureen Elizabeth McGrath, May 4, 1951; children: Sarah Elizabeth, Amanda Clare, Katherine Alexandra. BS in Acctg., Georgetown U., 1972; MBA in Fin., Columbia U., 1979. Staff auditor Price Waterhouse & Co., Washington, 1972-73; comml. banker, 2d. v.p. Chase Manhattan Bank, N.Y.C., 1973-78; asst. treas. Chesebrough-Pond's Inc., Greenwich, Conn., 1979-88, Pittston Co., Greenwich, 1988, Duracell Inc., Bethel, Conn., 1988-89; treas. Catalyst Energy Corp., N.Y.C., 1989—. Roman Catholic. Home: 104 Highland Rd Stamford CT 06902-2845 Office: Catalyst Energy Corp 535 Madison Ave New York NY 10022-4212

KVEDERIS, PAUL MARK, coal company executive. BA in Journalism, Duquesne U., Pitts., 1959. Various editorial positions Pitts. Sun-Telegraph, 1953-60; copy editor Pitts. Post-Gazette, 1960; with publs. dept. PPG Industries, 1960-63; press rels. rep. Bethlehem Steel Corp., 1963-72, news media rels. rep., 1972-74, asst. editor news media div., 1974-77; pub. rels. spokesman Nat. Steel Corp., 1977-82; mgr. pub. rels. Consol Inc., 1982—; bd. dirs. St. Clair Hosp., chmn. pub. rels. com. Bd. dirs., mem. pers. practices com. Canonsburg Gen. Hosp.; former dir. Wesley Inst.; mem. Village Acad. Com.; pub. rels. coord. Diamond Jubilee Skill-O-Rama, Boy Scouts Am., also mem. planning com. for Scouting for Food project, 1989. Mem. NRA, Ky. Coal Assn. (pub. rels. com.), W.Va. Press Assn., Libr. Sportmen's Assn., Rotary (past pres., chmn. pub. rels. com.). Home: 851 Fredericka Dr Bethel Park PA 15102-3766

KVENVOLD, TONY MARK, electronics executive, consultant; b. Madison, S.D., Oct. 28, 1956; s. Alden Theodor Kvenvold and Dorothy Clara (Verhay) Johnson; m. Wynne Whiting Treanor, June 23, 1979; children: Kristopher, Allyssa, Laura, Colleen. AA, Rochester Community Coll., 1980; BS, Winona State U., 1986. Electronic design engr. Watlow Co., Winona, Minn., 1980-86; pres. Finch Systems, Winona, 1983—; sr. design engr. Quantem Corp., Trenton, N.J., 1986-89; chief engr. PSG Industries, Inc., Perkasie, Pa., 1989—; Inventor electronic computer chip, 1985. Inventor single chip micro temperature control, 1990. Office: PSG Industries Inc 1225 Tunnel Rd Perkasie PA 18944

KWA, RAYMOND PAIN-BOON, cardiologist; b. Rangoon, Burma, Dec. 25, 1944; s. Wun Hoke and Sue Ain (Tay) K.; m. Stella Jih-Ming Juh, May 19, 1975; children: Rosemary, Maryann. BS, BM, Inst. Medicine I, Rangoon, 1970. Diplomate Am. Bd. Internal Medicine, Am. Bd. Cardiovascular Disease. Med. resident Cabrini Med. Ctr., N.Y.C., 1973-76, chief med. resident, 1976-77, cardiology fellow, 1977-79, attending med. asst. div. cardiology, 1979-82, attending med. assoc. div. cardiology, 1982—, chief non-invasive cardiology lab., 1985—; clin. instr. medicine N.Y. Med. Coll., N.Y.C., 1981—; med. cons. Greater Chinatown Community Assn., N.Y.C., 1979—. Contbr. numerous articles to profl. jours. Fellow ACP, Am. Coll. of Cardiology; mem. AMA (Physician's Recognition award 1981—), ACP, Am. Soc. Echo-Cardiography. Republican. Office: 105 Mosco St New York NY 10013-4380

KWITEROVICH, PETER OSCAR, JR., medical science educator, researcher, physician; b. Danville, Pa., June 24, 1940; s. Peter O. Sr. and Mary E. (Marks) K.; m. Kathleen Ann Justin, Aug. 14, 1965; children: Kris Ann, Peter III, Karen Ann. AB, Holy Cross Coll., Worcester, Mass., 1962; B in Med. Sci., Dartmouth Coll., 1964; MD, Johns Hopkins U., 1966. Intern Boston Children's Meml. Hosp., 1966-67; staff assoc. NIH, Bethesda, Md., 1967-70; resident Johns Hopkins Hosp., Balt., 1970-72; from asst. prof. to assoc. prof. in med. sci. Johns Hopkins U., Balt., 1972-84, prof. in med. sci., 1984—; bd. dirs. various clinics Johns Hopkins Hosp., 1971—. Author: Beyond Cholesterol, 1989 (Blakeslee award 1991); contbr. articles to profl. jours. Platt rep., Roland Park Civic League, Balt., 1986-88, v.p., 1988-89, pres., 1989-91. Surgeon USPHS, 1967-70. Fellow Coun. Arteriosclerosis; mem. Soc. Pediatrics Rsch., Am. Soc. Clin. Investigation. Republican. Roman Catholic. Office: Johns Hopkins Hosp 600 N Walye St Baltimore MD 21205

KYBAL, DALIMIL, government/industrial consulting executive; b. Prague, Czechoslovakia, June 21, 1916; came to U.S., 1935; s. Vlastimil and Ana (Saenz) K.; m. Elisa Alvarado, June 8, 1952. BL, Montpellier (France) U., 1934; BS, Calif. Inst. Tech., 1938, BS in Aero., 1939, MS, 1940. Asst. prof. Oreg. State Coll., Corvallis, 1940-42; asst. chief engr. Yates/Naco Aircraft, Troy, Ohio, 1942-43; aero. project engr. Chance Vought Aircraft, Stratford, Conn., 1943-47; asst. to chmn. GM project MIT, Cambridge, 1947-51; dep. asst. weapon systems evaluation USAF Hdqrs., Washington, 1951-57; spl. asst. to group pres. Lockheed Missiles & Space Co., Palo Alto and Sunnyvale, Calif., 1957-75; cons., asst. dir., acting dir. Fed. Prep. Agy., GSA, Washington, 1975-79; chief sci. advisor to dir. Fed. Emergency Mgmt. Agy., Washington, 1979-86; pres. DEAK Corp., Washington, 1986—; cons. Office Emergency Preparedness, Washington, 1957, 59-72, Dept. State, 1959-74, ACDA, 1959-67, Dept. Def., 1959-72, 86—, SRI, Palo Alto, 1963-73, Hudson Inst., 1960-76. Contbg. author: Issues and Arms Control, 1960, others; also articles. Scholar Govt. of Czechoslovak, 1937-38. Fellow AIAA (assoc.); mem. AAAS, Internat. Inst. Strategic Studies, Internat. Inst. Geopolitics, Cosmos Club. Republican. Roman Catholic. Home: 3900 Watson Pl NW Washington DC 20016-5701

KYBURG, HENRY GUY ELY, JR., philosophy and computer science educator; b. N.Y.C., Oct. 9, 1928; s. Henry Guy Ely and Margherita (Abbey) K.; m. Sarah Randlev, Feb. 4, 1967; children: Henry Guy Ely III, Sarah Abbey; by previous marriage: Robin Margherita, Christopher Ely, Alice Independence, Peter David. BChemE, Yale, 1948; MA in Philosophy, Columbia, 1953; PhD, Columbia U., 1955. Asst. prof. math. Wesleyan U., Middletown, Conn., 1958-61; rsch. assoc. Rockefeller Inst., 1961-62; assoc. prof. math. and philosophy Denver U., 1962-63; assoc. prof. philosophy Wayne State U., 1963-65; prof. philosophy U. Rochester, N.Y., 1965—, Luther W. Burbank prof. moral and intellectual philosophy, 1981—, prof. computer sci., 1986—, chmn. dept., 1969-81; mem.-at-large U.S. nat. com. Internat. Union History and Philosophy of Sci., 1978-83; v.p. engrng. Montana Wind Turbine, Inc., also bd. dirs. Author: Probability and the Logic of Rational Belief, 1961, Philosophy os Science, 1968, Probability and Induction, 1970, Probability Theory, 1969, The Logical Foundations of Statistical Inference, 1974, Induction, Some Current Issues, 1962, Studies in Subjective Probability, 2 edit., 1979, Epistemology and Inference, 1982, Theory and Measurement, 1984, Knowledge Representation and Defeasible Reasoning, 1990, Science and Reason, 1990. With USCG, 1951. Am. Coun. Learned Socs. grantee, 1962; NSF grantee, 1964-75, 78-80, 81-82, 90—; Guggenheim fellow, 1980-81; recipient Butler Medal for Philosophy in Silver, 1986. Fellow AAAS; mem. Assn. for Computing Machines, Am. Philos. Assn. (exec. com. Eastern div. 1978-81), Philosophy Sci. Assn. (governing bd. 1978-80), Assn. Symbolic Logic, Am. Math. Soc., Am. Assn. Artificial Intelligence, Sigma Xi. Home: 1018 Eyer Rd Lyons NY 14489-9754 Office: U Rochester Dept Philosophy and Computer Sci Rochester NY 14627

KYNE, SISTER MARY THERESA, English educator; b. Pitts., July 23, 1953; d. Edward and Mary (Lydon) K. BA in English summa cum laude, Seton Hill Coll., 1975; MA in English, Carnegie Mellon U., 1987; PhD in English, Duquesne U., 1991. Cert. secondary edn., English and French tchr., Pa.; joined Sisters of Charity of Greensburg, Pa., 1975. Tchr. English, French Elizabeth Seton High Sch., Pitts., 1977-79, Seton-LaSalle High Sch., Pitts., 1979-82, 84-87; asst. dean of students Seton Hill Coll., Greensburg, Pa., 1982-84, asst. prof. English, 1992—; disting. juror of poetry Westmoreland Arts and Heritage Festival, 1992. Author: George Herbert and Gerard Manley Hopkins: A Comparative Study in Spiritual Autobiography, 1992. Board dirs., mem. adv. coun. Project Forward, Greensburg, 1983-84; mem. admissions coun. Carnegie Mellon U.; mem. adv. bd. Western Pa. Symposium World Lits., 1990—. Mem. MLA, Nat. Coun. Tchrs. English, Pa. Coun. Tchrs. English, We. Pa. Symposium on World Lits. (sec. to dir. 1990—, co-chair 1990-91). Roman Catholic. Home and Office: Seton Hill Coll PO Box 373 Greensburg PA 15601-0373

KYNOCH, JAMES BRENT, environmental engineering executive; b. Columbia, S.C., Jan. 2, 1959; s. R. Kirkland and Peggy Joan (Berry) K. BEME, Vanderbilt U., 1981. Sales engr. Trane Co., Washington, 1982-84, Combustioneer, Washington, 1984; pres. Asbestos Abatement Services, Inc., Washington, 1984—; panelist asbestos policy dialogue roundtable EPA; testified U.S. Senate inspections for asbestos in schs. and comml. bldgs., 1986; lectr. Ga. Tech. Rsch. Inst., Atlanta, 1984—, Tufts U., Boston, 1985-91, NYU, 1985-91, Inst. for Environ. Edn., 1987-91. Author (contbg.): Hazardous Substances in Buildings-Liability, Litigation and Abatement, 1992; contbr. articles to profl. jours. Mem. council on young ministries Grace United Meth. Ch., 1983-87; chmn. bd. trustees Chevy Chase United Meth. Ch., 1992—; chmn. young adult Grace United Meth. Ch., 1984-85. Named one of Outstanding Young Men of Am., 1987. Mem. ASME, ASHRAE, Nat. Asbestos Coun. (sec. 1986-87, pres.-elect 1987-88, pres. 1988-89), Rotary, Univ. Club. Home: 4004 E West Hwy Bethesda MD 20815-5915 Office: Asbestos Abatement Svcs Inc 4801 Massachusetts Ave NW Washington DC 20016-2069

KYRIAZIS, ARTHUR JOHN (ATHANASIOS IOANNIS KYRIAZIS), lawyer; b. Thessaloniki, Greece, Nov. 2, 1958; came to U.S., 1960; s. George A. and Elpis (Halkedis) K.; m. Maria M. Zissimos, Aug. 31, 1986. AB, Harvard U., 1981; JD cum laude, Temple U., 1985. Bar: Pa. 1985, U.S. Dist. Ct. (ea. dist.) Pa. 1985, N.J. 1986, U.S. Dist. Ct. N.H. 1986, Calif. 1987, U.S. Dist. Ct. (ea. dist.) Calif. 1988, U.S. Ct. Appeals (3d cir.) 1991. Spl. aide to pres. and former dean law sch. Temple U., 1983-84; intern to presiding justice U.S. Dist. Ct. (ea. dist.) Pa., 1984; law clk. to presiding justice Commonwealth Ct. Pa., Phila., Harrisburg, 1985-86; assoc. Cohen, Shapiro, Polisher, Shiekman & Cohen, Phila. and Princeton, N.J., 1986-87, Rawle & Henderson, Phila. and Marlton, N.J., 1987-88, Lesser & Kaplin and predecessor firm, Phila., Blue Bell, Pa. and Marlton, N.J., 1988-89; prin. Kyriazis & Assocs., Phila., Cherry Hill, N.J. and Delaware County, Pa., 1989—; arbitrator Phila. Ct. Common Pleas, 1988—; corr. coounsel Miller & Fleisher, Phila., 1989-90. Pa. co-coord. Dukakis for Pres., 1987-88; del. Nat. Fin. Com., Dem. Conv., Atlanta, 1988, 1982 Dem. Mid-Term Conv., Phila.; mem. Young Lawyers for Dukakis, Hellenic Am. for Dukakis, Pa., 1987-88; founder Am. Assn. Univ. Students, Cambridge, Mass. and Phila., 1978-79, pres., 1990—; v.p. Hercules-Spartan Phila. chpt. 26 Am. Hellenic Progressive Edn. Assn., 1989-90, pres., 1990-91, bd. govs., 1987—; fundraiser Edgar for Senate, Pa., 1986; co-coord. Mondale for Pres., 1984; fieldworker Cranston for Pres. 1983. Mem. ABA (young lawyers div., litigation and bus. law sect., bus., real estate sects.), Phila. Bar Assn. (exec. com. young lawyers sect. 1988-90, fin. sec. exec. com. 1990, sec. exec. com. 1989, co-chmn. law related edn. com. 1988—, mem. bar edn. found. com. 1988—, mem. Bill Rights 200 coms., mem. fed. cts. 200 com., chmn. debate com. and mock trial 1987—, debate dir. fed. cts. 200 nat. high sch. debate tournament 1990—), Camden County Bar Assn. (young lawyers, pub. benefits, debtor-creditor relations), Pa. Bar Assn. (litigation, young lawyers jud. administrn.), N.J. State Bar Assn. (young lawyer banking law sect., consumer fin. com.), L.A. County Bar Assn., Am. Arbitration Assn. (comml. arbitrator 1988—), State Bar Calif. (litigation, real estate, entertainment), Am. Assn. Univ. Students (legal counsel 1989—). Greek Orthodox. Home: 408 Drew Ave Swarthmore PA 19081-2406

KYSOR, DANIEL FRANCIS, school psychologist; b. Corry, Pa., Aug. 3, 1956; s. Darrell Francis and Louise Mary (Caglio) K.; m. Kate Galbraith Morrison Kysor, Sept. 7, 1991. BS, Edinboro U., 1980; MS in Edn., Edinboro U., Pa., 1988. Cert. elem. edn., guidance, elem. and secondary adminstr., sch. psychologist. House parent Assn. for Retarded Citizens, Meadville, Pa., 1980-81; tchr. Calhoun County Schs., Grantsville, W.Va., 1982; counselor, tchr. Bradford Children's Home, Bradford, Pa., 1983; residential program counselor Assn. for Retarded Citizens, Meadville, Pa., 1984-86; resident hall dir. Edinboro U., Edinboro, Pa., 1984-86; guidance counselor Cranberry Sch. Dist., Seneca, Pa., 1986; student Edinboro U., Edinboro, Pa., 1987; dropout prevention counselor Erie Sch. Dist., Erie, Pa., 1988; sch. psychologist Seneca Highlands IU #9, Coudersport, Pa., 1989—. Mem. Potter County Democratic Party, Pa., 1990. Recipient Rural Leadership Program scholarship, Penn State, Pa, 1989. Mem. Nat. Assn. of Sch. Psychologists, Am. Assn. Counseling and Devel., Am. Sch. Counselor Assn., Nat. Fed. Interscholastic Officials Assn., Pa. Interscholastic Athletic Assn., Am. Coll. Personnel Assn., Assn. Supr. and Curriculum Devel. Democrat. Methodist. Home: RR 3 Union City PA 16438-9803 Office: Seneca Highlands IU #9 306 N Main St Coudersport PA 16915-1626

LAANO, ARCHIE BIENVENIDO MAAÑO, cardiologist; b. Tayabas, Quezon, Philippines, Aug. 10, 1939; naturalized U.S. citizen; s. Francisco M. and Iluminada (Maaño) L.; m. Maria Eleazar, May 2, 1964; 1 child, Sylvia Marie. A.A., U. Philippines, 1958, B.S., 1959, M.D., 1963. Diplomate Am. Bd. Internal Medicine. Rotating intern Hosp. St. Raphael, New Haven, 1963-64; resident internal medicine, 1964-65; rotating resident pulmonary diseases Laurel Heights Hosp., Shelton, Conn., 1965; affiliated rotating resident Yale-New Haven Med. Ctr., 1965; resident internal medicine Westchester County Med. Ctr., Valhalla, N.Y., 1965-66, resident cardiology, 1966-67; resident fellow cardiology Maimonides Med. Ctr., Bklyn., 1967-68; rotating sr. resident cardiology Coney Island Hosp., Bklyn., 1967-68; fellow internal medicine Mercy Hosp., Rockville Centre, N.Y., 1968-70; med. dir. 54 Main St. Med. Ctr., Hempstead, N.Y., 1971-76, Bloomingdale's, Garden City, N.Y., 1972—, Esselte Pendaflex Corp., Garden City, 1976—; attending staff Nassau County (N.Y.) Med. Ctr., Hempstead Gen. Hosp.; practice medicine specializing in cardiology, internal medicine, Nassau County, 1971—; chief med. svcs., chief profl. svcs. U.S. Army 808th Sta. Hosp., Hempstead, N.Y., 1979—; brig. gen. 1st U.S. Army AMEDD Augmentation Detachment, Ft. Meade, Md., 1989—, M.C., chief of staff, chief profl. svcs. U.S. Army Meddac Hosp., Ft. Dix., N.J., 1990—; med. dir. Cities Svc. Oil Co. (CITGO), L.I. div., 1972— ; mem. adv. bd. Guardian Bank, Hempstead, chmn. adv. coun., 1973-89; clin. prof. medicine SUNY at Stony Brook, 1979—; professorial lectr. medicine (cardiology) U.S. Mil. Acad.-Keller Army Med. Ctr., West Point, N.Y., 1979; affiliated teaching hosp. Harvard Med. Sch, 1979; vis. prof. Harvard U., 1979—; cons. physician ICC, Citgo, Liberty Mut. Ins. Co. Boston, 1972—, U.S. Dept. Transp.; counsel White House Commn. on Mil. Medicine, 1988—. Decorated Silver Star, Bronze Star, Legion of Merit, Soldiers medal, Joint Svc. Command medal, Army Meritorious Svc. medal, Dept. Def. Joint Svc. Achievement award, Southwest Asia Svc. award-Desert Storm, others. Fellow Internat. Coll. Angiology, Am. Coll. Angiology, Am. Coll. Internat. Physicians, Internat. Coll. Applied Nutrition, Am. Soc. Contemporary Medicine and Surgery, Acad. Preventive Medicine, Internat. Acad. Med. Preventives, Philippine Coll. Physicians, Am. Coll. Acupuncture, N.Y. Acad. of Sci.; mem. AMA, Am. Coll. Cardiology, N.Y. Med. Soc., Nassau County Med. Soc., Am. Heart Assn., N.Y. Cardiol. Soc., World Med. Assn., Royal Soc. Medicine (overseas, London), Nassau Acad. Medicine, Am., N.Y. State, Nassau Soc. Internal Medicine, N.Y. Soc. Acupuncture for Physicians, Am. Geriatrics Soc., Nassau Physicians Guild, Res. Officers Assn. U.S., Assn. Mil. Surgeons, Assn. Philippine Physicians Am. (bd. govs. rep. N.Y. State 1984-86, v.p. 1988-89, chmn. com. nominations and election 1987-88. spl. counsel to pres. 1986-87), Philippine Med. Assn. Am. (spl. counsel 1988-89, bd. dirs. 1989-90, spl. counsel to pres. 1989-90, dir. continuing med. edn. 1990—, chmn. scholarship com. 1989—), Assn. Philippine Physicians of N.Y. (founding v.p., pres. 1985-87, pres. emeritus 1988—, chmn. com. on constitution and by-laws, nominations and election, med. coord. Internat. Games for Disabled Olympics 1984), Soc. Philippine Surgeons Am. (Medallion of Honor 1991), U.S. Knights of Rizal, U. Philippines Med. Alumni Soc. (pres. class of 1963, 1981—), U. Philippines Med. Alumni Soc. Am. (chmn. bd. 1985—), Royal Soc. Medicine Club, The Oxford Club, Rolls Royce Club L.I., N.Y. Club (chmn. 1987—), West Point OfficersClub, Garden City Country Club, Phi Kappa Mu (overseas coord. U. Philippines 1985—), Beta Sigma (coun. adivsers Ea. U.S. 1990—)program chmn. 1975—, chmn. bd. 1978—, pres. 1978-79), Lions (Garden City program chmn. 1975—, chmn. bd. 1978—, pres. 1978-79). Home: 80 Stratford Ave Garden City NY 11530-2531 Office: 230 Hilton Ave Ste 106 Plaza 230 Profl Condo Hempstead NY 11

LABAKI, GEORGES T., French civilization educator; b. Baabdat, Lebanon, Apr. 23, 1955; came to U.S. 1985; s. Tanous P. and Ezabel (Melki) L. PhD in French Civilization, Paris XII, 1981; PhD in Law, Sorbonne, Paris, 1984. Prof. Pascal Coll., Paris, 1978-84; prof. cons. Ctr. Internat. Devel. and Conflict Mgmt. U. Md., 1985-88; prof. Georgetown U., Washington, 1989—, Johns Hopkins U., 1991—; contbr. Le Quotidien Juridique, Paris, 1984—, Encyclopaedia Universalis, Paris, 1985—; cons. Assoc. des Universite Partiellement ou Entierement de Langue Francaise, 1988—. Author: Housing in Lebanon & France, 1987, The Lebanon Crisis, 1986. Recipient Excellency award Ctr. for Univ. & Scholarly Activities, Paris, 1986; grantee French Ministry Cultural Affairs, Paris, 1983, Sorbonne U., 1978-84. Mem. Internat. Assn. Francophonic Studies. Maronite Catholic. Home: 1414 17th SH NW 308 Washington DC 20036

LABAREE, BENJAMIN WOODS, history educator; b. New Haven, Conn., July 21, 1927; s. Leonard Woods and Elizabeth Mary (Calkins) L.; m. Linda Carol Prichard, June 27, 1959; children: Benjamin Woods Jr., Jonathan Martin, Sarah Calkins. BA, Yale U., 1950; AM, Harvard U., 1953, PhD, 1957. Instr. history Conn. Coll., New London, 1957-58; from asst. prof. history to Allston Burr Sr. Tutor Harvard U., Cambridge, Mass., 1958-63; dean Williams Coll., Williamstown, Mass., 1963-67, assoc. to prof. history, 1963-77, Ephraim Williams Prof. Am. History, 1972-77; dir. Williams Coll.-Mystic Seaport Program/Mystic Seaport Mus., Mystic, Conn., 1977-89; dir. Ctr. for Environ. Studies Williams Coll., 1989-91; prof. history and environ. studies Williams Coll., Williamstown, 1989—; adj. prof. Williams Coll., 1977-89; dir. Munson Inst. Am. Maritime Studies, Mystic, 1974—; managing editor Essex Inst. Hist. Collections, Salem, Mass., 1956-60. Author: Patriots and Partisans, 1962, The Boston Tea Party, 1964, America's Nation-Time, 1972, Colonial Massachusetts, 1979; co-author: New England and The Sea, 1972, Empire or Independence, 1976. Mem. Mt. Greylock Regional High Sch. Com., Williamstown, 1971-74. With USNR, 1945-46, ATO. Recipient Wilbur Cross award Conn. Humanities Coun., 1990. Mem. Am. Hist. Assn. (com. 1971-73), Am. Antiquarian Soc., Colonial Soc. Mass., Mass. Hist. Soc., Inst. for Early Am. History and Culture (coun. mem. 1983-86), others. Democrat. Congregationalist. Home and Office: 2 Andrews Ln Amesbury MA 01913

LABARGE, KARIN PETERSON, financial economics educator, researcher; b. Cadillac, Mich., Oct. 14, 1953; d. Carl Edwin Lindell and Frances Agda (Hodges) Peterson; m. Richard Allen LaBarge, June 28, 1980; 1 child; Robert Edwin Justin. BS in Edn. magna cum laude, Cen. Mich. U., 1975; MA, U. New Orleans, 1979; PhD in Bus. Adminstrn., U. Calif., Berkeley, 1986. Teaching asst. U. New Orleans, 1978-79; teaching asst. U. Calif., 1980-81, rsch. asst., 1981-83; rsch. assoc. Ctr. for Study of Futures Markets Columbia U., N.Y.C., 1983-84; asst. prof. fin. U. New Orleans, 1984-89, Rutgers U., Camden, N.J., 1989—. Chairperson fin. com. St. Andrew's Luth. Ch., New Orleans, 1985. Mem. Am. Fin. Assn., Western Fin. Assn., Eastern Fin. Assn., So. Fin. Assn., Fin. Mgmt. Assn., Midwest Fin. Assn., Southwestern Fin. Assn., Phi Kappa Phi, Omicron Delta Epsilon. Republican. Lutheran. Office: Rutgers U Sch Bus Camden NJ 08102

LABARGE, RICHARD ALLEN, financial analyst, educator; b. Salt Lake City, May 6, 1934; s. Oza Joseph and Mae (Erdman) LaB.; m. Catherine Eulalie Laurent, June 10, 1953 (div. 1979); children: R. Allen Jr., Catherine, Joseph Laurent, Nedra Anne, Eve Marie, Mary Evangeline, Louis E.R.; m. Karin Louise Peterson, June 28, 1980; 1 child, Robert E.J. AB, U. Mich., 1954, MA, Tulane U., 1955; PhD, Duke U., 1960. Chartered fin. analyst, 1982. Asst. prof. So. Methodist U., Dallas, 1957-60; treas., fin. analyst, spl. legis. analyst world hdqrs. Ford Motor Co., Dearborn, 1960-65; assoc. prof. Fla. State U., Tallahassee, 1965-67; prof. econs. and fin. U. New Orleans, 1967-89, chair dept., 1967-73; prof. Rutgers U., Camden, N.J., 1990-92; prin. Capital Choices, Inc., 1992—; fin. economist U.S. SEC, Washington, summer, 1977; cons. bd. regents State U. System Fla., Tallahassee, Miami, 1989; lectr. Fin. Analysts' Rev., Raleigh, N.C., 1989-92, Zurich, Switzerland, 1990. Author: (monograph) Impact of United Front on Economic Development of Guatemala, 1960; contbr. articles to profl. jours. Rsch. tng. fellow Social Sci. Rsch. Coun., Washington, 1956-57, Sr. Fulbright-Hays prof., Mexico, 1973-74. Mem. Assn. for Investment Mgmt. Rsch. N.Y. Soc. Security Analyst, Nat. Assn. Bus. Economists (New Orleans chpt., pres. 1972-73, 75-76), Mich. Alumni Assn. (New Orleans chpt., pres. 1985-89). Republican. Home: 160 Ardmore Ave Haddonfield NJ 08033-1428 Office: Sch Bus Rutgers U Camden NJ 08102

LABATON, STEPHEN, journalist, lawyer; b. Queens, N.Y., May 3, 1961; s. Edward and Laura (Wasserman) L. BA, Tufts U., 1983; MA, JD, Duke U., 1986. Legal affairs corr. N.Y. Times, N.Y.C., 1987-90; Washington corr. N.Y. Times, 1990—. Home: 2501 Porter St NW Apt 720 Washington DC 20008-1258 Office: NY Times 1627 I St NW Washington DC 20006-4007

LABBAUF, FARSAD REZA, product designer; b. Tehran, Iran, Oct. 28, 1965; came to U.S., 1979; s. Habib and Media Labbauf. BFA, B Indsl. Design with honors, R.I. Sch. Design, 1987. Product designer Origo Corp., Boston, 1990—. Designer Oasis Mannequin, 1987; artwork in tourikng exhbns. in Tex. Mem. Indsl. Designers Soc. of Am. (hon.). Office: Origo Corp 1050 Commonwealth Ave Boston MA 02116

LABELLE, EDWARD FRANCIS, physiologist; b. Worcester, Mass., Aug. 11, 1948; s. Edward F. and Viola Louise (Trudel) L.; m. Constance Miriam Reichmann, Aug. 19, 1972; children: Devon, Ross. AB, Holy Cross Coll., 1970, MS, 1970; PhD, U. Mich., 1974. Postdoctoral fellow Cornell U., Ithaca, N.Y., 1974-76; asst. prof. Western Ill. U., Macomb, 1976-78; asst. prof. U. Tex. Med. Br., Galveston, 1978-86, assoc. prof., 1986-87; rsch. scientist Grad. Hosp., Phila., 1987—; adj. assoc. prof. U. Pa., Phila., 1988—. Contbr. articles to profl. jours. Grantee NIH, 1978-84, 87—, Am. Heart Assn., 1986, 88. Mem. Am. SOc. Biochemistry and Molecular Biology, Soc. Gen. Physiologists.

LABELLE, MICHAEL MAURICE, science educator; b. Biddeford, Maine, June 11, 1951; s. Maurice Donat and Lorraine (Lachance) LaB.; m. Sue Ellen Mooney, Aug. 4, 1979; children: Evan Michael, Janet Nicole. BS, U. Maine, 1973; MS, U. N.H., 1978. Cert. sci. supr., N.J., sci. tchr., N.H., Maine. Sci. tchr. Stevens High Sch., Claremont, N.H., 1973-79, Mt. Pleasant Mid. Sch., Livingston, N.J., 1979—; basketball coach Mt. Pleasant Mid. Sch., 1982-85, 87—; adj. instr. Fairleigh Dickenson U., Teaneck, N.J., 1985; sci. instr. weekend workshops, Short Hills, N.J., 1987. Author: (video series) Silver Burdett Video Labs, 1984-85. Recipient Honorable Mention award Profl. Best Learning Mag., 1991. Mem. NEA, N.J. Edn. Assn., Livingston Edn. Assn., YMCA. Home: 10 Longview Ave Madison NJ 07940-1712 Office: Mt Pleasant Mid Sch 11 Broadlawn Dr Livingston NJ 07039-3117

LABER, JERI LIDSKY, association executive; b. N.Y.C., May 19, 1931; d. Louis and Mae (Zias) Lidsky; m. Austin Laber, Oct. 3, 1954 (div. 1982); children: Abigail, Pamela, Emily. BA, NYU, 1952; MA, Columbia U., 1954; Cert., Russian Inst. Coll. U., N.Y.C., 1952-54. Sr. editor Current Digest of Soviet Press, N.Y.C., 1954-56; pubs. dir. Inst. for Study of USSR, N.Y.C., 1956-70; staff dir. Internat. Freedom to Pub. Com., Assn. Am. Pubrs., N.Y.C., 1975—; exec. dir. Fund for Free Expression, N.Y.C., 1976-78, U.S. Helsinki Watch Com., N.Y.C., 1978—; mem. exec. com. Human Rights Watch, N.Y.C., 1988—; bd. dirs. fund for Free Expression, N.Y.C., 1977—, Asia Watch, N.Y.C., 1983—; vis. com. New Sch. for Social Rsch., N.Y.C., 1990—. Co-author: A Nation is Dying: Afghanistan Under the Soviets, 1988; contbr. articles to profl. jours. Office: US Helsinki Watch Com 485 Fifth Ave New York NY 10017

LABOMBARDE, PETER MICHAEL, bank officer; b. Manchester, N.H., Aug. 25, 1954; s. Philip deGaspé and Frances Ann (Merritt) L.; m. Irene Mary Albano, Aug. 22, 1981. BA, Colby Coll., 1976; MA, Cornell U., 1983; MMus, Fla. State U., 1983; grad. with honors, Northwestern U., 1989. Trust mgmt. trainee Bank of N.H., Nashua, 1983-85, personal trust mgr., 1985-88, asst. v.p., 1988-90; v.p., regional trust officer Bank of N.H., Manchester, 1990—; Mem. N.H. Estate Planning Coun., Manchester, 1987—; chmn. N.H. div. Am. Cancer Soc., Manchester, 1988-90, treas., 1991—; mem. adv. bd. Rivier Coll., Nashua, 1989—, chair, 1991—; trustee Nashua Symphony Assn., 1988—. Recipient Nat. Leadership medal Am. Cancer Soc., 1990. Mem. Rotary. Mem. United Ch. of Christ. Office: Bank of NH 300 Franklin St Manchester NH 03101-2318

LABOON, LAWRENCE JOSEPH, personnel consultant; b. St. Louis, Aug. 4, 1938; s. Joseph Warren and Ruth (Aab) LaB.; children: Lindsey Beth, Allison Ruth; m. Glynys M. Brown, Sept. 16, 1989; children: Lawrence Bradley, Meredith Ashley. BS magna cum laude, Tex. Wesleyan U., 1962. Cert. pers. cons. Operating mgr. Firestone Tire & Rubber Co., Akron, Ohio, 1962-66; pres. Met. Pers., Inc., Phila., 1966—, Metro Tech, Valley Forge, Pa., 1977—, Metro Temps, Valley Forge, 1978—; dir. Alpha-Indian Rock Savs. and Loan Assn., chmn. compensation com., 1986-90; chmn. pvt. employment agy. adv. coun. Pa. Dept. Labor and Industry, 1973—; guest lectr. Drexel U., 1976-91; human resources del. to USSR, Citizen Amb. Program, 1991. With USAF, 1954-60. Mem. Nat. Employment Assn. (state certification bd. chmn. 1969-71, bd. dir. 1972-74, chmn. bd. regents 1973), Pa. Assn. Pers. Svcs. (pres. 1971-72, Blanchet Meml. award 1973), Nat. Assn. Pers. Cons., Am. Soc. Pers. Adminstrn., Mid-Atlantic Assn. Temporary Svcs. (pres. 1983-84), TEMPNET (bd. dir. 1986-88), Exec. Riders Ltd. (pres. 1986-88), Glenhardic Condominium Assn. (non-resident exec. bd. mem. 1989), Alpha Chi. Republican. Methodist. Home: 255 Country Ln Valley Forge PA 19481 Office: 565 Swedesford Rd Ste 220 Valley Forge PA 19481

LABORDE, TERRENCE LEE, small business owner, research subcontract administrator, negotiator; b. DuBois, Pa., June 20, 1947; s. Donald Leo and Anna Lee (Wise) LaB.; m. Brenda Sue Roberts, May 16, 1970 (div. 1975); 1 child, Terrence Lee II; m. Elisa Jean Meenan, Sept. 12, 1975; children: Marc Elliott, Dawn Ann. BS, Nat. Coll., 1973. Sr. auditor Def. Contract Audit Agy., State Coll., Pa., 1973-84; contract negotiator Pa. State U., State Coll., 1984-88, subcontract adminstr., 1988-91, mgr. grant & subcontract adminstrn., 1991-92; owner LaBorde Enterprises and Higher Edn. Fin. Aid Opportunities, Pennsylvania Furnace, Pa., 1991—. Sgt. USAF, 1966-70. Democrat. Lutheran. Home: Ramblewood 1 110 Elm Rd Pennsylvania Furnace PA 16865

LA BRACK, KENNETH ALAN, service manager; b. Winchendon, Mass., Oct. 9, 1947; s. Kenneth Leon and Doris Louise (Nadeau) La B.; m. Vicki Lynn Raymond, June 14, 1975; children: Kyle Raymond, Jay Alan. Assoc. in Engring., Mt. Wachusett Community Coll., 1971; BS, Fitchburg State Tchrs. Coll., 1973. High sch. tchr. Narragansett Regional High, Baldwinville, Mass., 1973-75; tech. rep. field svc. Simplex Time Recorder, Gardner, Mass., 1975-82; field svc. mgr. Worcester br. Simplex Time Recorder, Auburn, Mass., 1982-84; field svc. mgr.-Auburndale br. Simplex Time Recorder, Boston, 1984-87; regional svc. mgr. Simplex Corp. Hdqrs., Gardner, 1987—. Coach Little League, 1987-91. With USN, 1965-68. Mem. Am. Legion (commdr. 1973-74). Democrat. Roman Catholic. Office: Simplex Time Recorder Simplex Plz Gardner MA 01441-0001

LABRECQUE, PAUL GERARD, electrical engineer; b. Holyoke, Mass., Sept. 14, 1946; s. Gerard D. and Emid M. (Cross) L. BSEE, Western New Eng. Coll., Springfield, Mass., 1968; MBA, U. Balt., 1982. With Raytheon, Wayland, Mass., 1968-74, Frequency Sources, North Chelmsford, Mass., 1974-75; sr. engr. Westinghouse Co., Balt., 1976—. Telephone counselor Contact Balt. Crisis Intervention Hot Line, 1977-81; pres. Elvaton Towne Condominium, Glen Burnie, Md., 1988-90. Mem. Am. Mgmt. Assn., Delta Mu Delta. Home: 7682 Bush Ave Pasadena MD 21122-3534

LABRECQUE, THEODORE JOSEPH, lawyer; b. Portland, Oreg., Mar. 8, 1903; s. Herman F. and Clara (Thibault) L.; m. Marjorie Uprichard, Jan. 31, 1931; children: Theodore J., Katherine Labrecque Skiba, Thomas G., Jeanne M. Labrecque Gagliano, Robert S., David F., Susan Labrecque Woolley, Barbara Anne Labrecque Danowitz. Ed., Manhattan Coll., 1920-21; LLB, Fordham U., 1924; LLD (hon.), Georgian Ct. Coll., 1986. Bar: N.J. 1925, ICC 1936, U.S. Tax Ct. 1943, U.S. Supreme Ct. 1957. Gen. practice law Red Bank, N.J., 1925-60; mem. Quinn, Parsons & Doremus, 1929-37, Parsons, Labrecque, Canzona & Blair, and predecessor firms, 1937-60; mem. N.J. Div. of Tax appeals, 1946-60, pres., 1956-60; judge N.J. Superior Ct., 1960-73; judge appellate div. Superior Ct., 1964-73, presiding judge part D, 1972-73; of counsel Parsons & Cappiello (and predecessor firms), Red Bank, N.J., 1973—. Chmn., Monmouth County Transp. Coordinating Com., 1973—; chmn. North Jersey Transit Adv. Com., 1980-87; mem. Monmouth County Hist. Commn., 1988-90. Fellow Am. Coll. Trial Lawyers, Am. Bar Found.; mem. ABA, N.J. State Bar Assn. (pres. 1960), Essex County Bar Assn., Monmouth Bar Assn., Am. Judicature Soc., Elks, Red Bank Lions Club (pres. 1939), Phi Delta Phi (hon.). Democrat. Roman Catholic. Home: 410 Rumson Rd Little Silver NJ 07739-1610 Office: 612 River Rd Fair Haven NJ 07704-3221

LABRIE, J. ROLAND, principal; b. Eagle Lake, Maine, Mar. 30, 1948; s. Claude Charles and Rella (Marquis) LaB.; m. Claire C. Roy, Dec. 28, 1970; children: Shelly Ann, Shantelle Marie. BS, U. Maine, 1971, MEd, 1980, postgrad., 1988—. Tchr. Cunningham Middle Sch., Presque Isle, Maine, 1971-72; tchr. Ft. Kent (Maine) Elem. Sch., 1972-77, prin., 1986—; prin., tchr. Market St. Sch., Ft. Kent, 1977-80; tchr. Community High Sch., Ft. Kent, 1980-86; mem. Cert. Adv. Com., Augusta, Maine, 1988—; bd. dirs. Maine Prin. Acad., Augusta. Recipient Disting. Teaching award Nat. Coun. for Geographic Edn., 1985. Mem. Maine Elem. Prins. Assn., Nat. Assn. Elem. Prins., Aroostook County Prin.'s Assn., Assn. Supervision and Curriculum Devel., Maine Assn. Supervision and Curriculum Devel., Rotary (bd. dirs. Ft. Kent chpt. 1988—). Office: Ft Kent Elem Sch 15 Pleasant St Fort Kent ME 04743-1213

LABRUNA, VINCENT FRANCIS, podiatrist; b. Queen, N.Y., Apr. 29, 1958; s. Joseph S. and Lynn R. (Altomare) LaB.; m. Donna Marie Valerio, Dec. 10, 1989. BS, Rutgers U., 1980; D in Podiatric Medicine, N.Y. Coll. Podiatric Medicine, 1984. Resident surgery, pediatric surgery Fairlawn, Mass.; pvt. practice Oakland, N.J., 1986—. Mem. N.J. Podiatric Med. Soc. Office: 388 State Route 202 Oakland NJ 07436-2793 Office: 707 S Orange Ave South Orange NJ 07079-2698

LABUZ, RONALD MATTHEW, design educator; b. Utica, N.Y., Nov. 17, 1953; s. Emil John and Elsie (Pritchard) L.; m. Carol Ann Altimonte, Sept. 5, 1975. BA, SUNY, Oswego, 1975; MA, Ohio State U., 1977. Acquisition dir. Collegiate Pub., Columbus, Ohio, 1977-78; pres. Advt., Pub. and Avatar Media Advt. Agy., Columbus, 1978-80; prodn. specialist Am. Ceramic Soc., Columbus, 1980-81; assoc. prof. advt. Mohawk Valley Community Coll., Utica, 1981-85, prof., dept. head advt. design, 1985—. Author: Contemporary Graphic Design, Typography and Typesetting, The Computer in Graphic Design, 5 other books; contbr. articles and revs. to profl. jours. Recipient Chancellor's award for excellence, SUNY, 1989, faculty exch. scholar, 1990. Mme. Printing History Soc., Am. Printing History Assn., Graphic Design Educators Assn. (bd. dirs. 1989—), Am. Ctr. for Design, Internat. Graphic Arts Educators Assn., Am. Inst. Graphic Arts, N.Y. State Assn. Two-Yr. Colls. (bd. dirs. 1990-91). Office: Mohawk Valley CC 1101 Sherman Dr Utica NY 13501-5308

LACATTIVA, CLAIRE ANTOINETTE, educator; b. L.I., N.Y., Feb. 14, 1931; d. Joseph and Lucy (Bennett) L.; 1 child, Paul. BA, St. John's U., N.Y.C., 1952; MS, Fordham U., 1954, PhD, 1964. Elem. tchr. N.Y.C. Bd. Edn., 1952-61; assoc. prof. St. John's U., Jamaica, N.Y., 1961—; Cert. prin., N.Y. Mem. Nat. Coun. Tchrs. English, Ea. Ednl. Rsch. Assn., Am. Ednl. Rsch. Assn., St. John's Coun. of Tchrs. of English (dir.). Roman Catholic. Office: St John U Grand Central & Utopia Pkwy Jamaica NY 11439

LACEY, PAMELA ANNE, lawyer; b. Annapolis, Md., Apr. 5, 1955; d. Douglas Raymond Lacey and Mary (Millington) Nohrden; m. Richard Eugene Bradshaw, June 3, 1989. AB cum laude, Bryn Mawr Coll., 1977; JD, George Washington U., 1984. Bar: Pa. 1984, D.C. 1985. Assoc. Bishop, Liberman, Cook, Purcell and Raynolds, Washington, 1984-86, Newman and Holtzinger, P.C., Washington, 1986—. Spl. events chmn. St. Mark's Episc. Ch., Washington, 1986-88, seminarian's lay com., 1982-84; co-author spl. report League Women Voters, Washington, 1979. Mem. Fed. Energy Bar Assn. (vice chmn. tax devels. com. 1988, chmn. 1989, environ. com. 1991), ABA (natural resources sect. 1984—). Democrat. Office: Newman & Holtzinger PC 1615 L St NW Washington DC 20036-5610

LACHANCE, PAUL ALBERT, food science educator, clergyman; b. St. Johnsbury, Vt., June 5, 1933; s. Raymond John and Lucienne (Landry) L.; m. Therese Cecile Cote; children: Michael P., Peter A., M.-Andre, Susan A. BS, St. Michael's Coll., 1955; postgrad., U. Vt., 1955-57; PhD, U. Ottawa, 1960; cert. in pastoral counseling, N.Y. Theol. Sem., 1981; DSc (hon.), St. Michael's Coll., 1982. Ordained deacon Roman Cath. Ch., 1977. Aerospace biologist Aeromed. Research Labs., Wright-Patterson AFB, Ohio, 1960-63; lectr. dept. biology U. Dayton, Ohio, 1963; flight food and nutrition coordinator NASA Manned Spacecraft Center, Houston, 1963-67; assoc. prof. dept. food sci. Rutgers U., New Brunswick, N.J., 1967-72, dir. Sch. Feeding effectiveness research project, 1969-72, prof., 1972—, faculty rep. to bd. trustees, 1988-90, dir. grad. program food sci., 1988-91, chmn. food sci. dept., 1991—, chmn. univ. senate, faculty rep. to bd. govs., 1990—; assigned to St. Paul's Ch., Princeton, N.J.; cons. Nutritional aspects of food processing; mem. sci. adv. bd. Roche Chem. div. Hoffmann LaRoche Co., 1976-88; mem. nutrition policy com. Beatrice Foods Co., 1979-86; mem. religious ministries com. Princeton Med. Ctr.; bd. dirs. J.R. Short Milling Co., 1990—. Mem. editorial adv. bd., Sch. Food Service Research Rev., 1977-82, Jour. Am. Coll. Nutrition, 1986—, Jour. Med. Consultation, 1985—, Nutrition Reports Internat., 1963-83, Profl. Nutritionist, 1977-80; contbr. articles to profl. jours. Served to capt. USAF, 1960-63. Recipient Endel Karmas award for excellecne in teaching food sci., 1988, William Cruess award for excellence in teaching Inst. Food Technologists, 1991. Fellow Inst. Food Technologists, Am. Coll. Nutrition; mem. Am. Assn. Cereal Chemists, AAAS, Am. Inst. Nutrition, N.Y. Inst. Food Technologists (chmn. 1977-78), Am. Soc. Clin. Nutrition, N.Y. Acad. Sci., Am. Dietetic Assn., Soc. Nutrition Edn., Am. Public Health Assn., Nat. Assn. Cath. Chaplains, Sociedad Latino Americano de Nutricion, Sigma Xi, Delta Epsilon Sigma. Home: 34 Taylor Rd Princeton NJ 08540 Office: Rutgers U PO Box 231 New Brunswick NJ 08903-0231

LACHANCE, ROGER WILLIAM, electronics manufacturing executive; b. Rochester, N.H., Feb. 14, 1944; s. Armand Raymond and Rose Marie (Levesque) L.; m. Jean Ann Adams, June 28, 1969; children: Jennifer, Jason, Justin. BSEE, U. N.H., 1968; MBA, Northeastern U., 1974. Mfg. foreman GE, Somersworth, N.H., 1968-72, human resource specialist, 1972-74, mfg. engr., 1974-77, shop ops. mgr., 1977-82, mgr. quality control, 1982-88, mgr. quality and customer svc., 1988-90, mgr. quality and materials, 1990—. Bd. trustees Frisbie Meml. Hosp., Rochester, N.H., 1988—; treas. Rochester Westside Little League, 1983-91. Office: GE 130 Main St Somersworth NH 03878-3194

LACHAPELLE, CLEO EDWARD, real estate broker; b. West Warwick, R.I., Aug. 16, 1925; s. Wilfrid Maxim and Alice (Michaud) L.; m. Ann Wilcox, July 17, 1954; children: Linda, Susan. BA in Sociology, St. Bonaventure U., 1950. Cert. social worker, R.I.; lic. real estate broker, R.I. Probation officer R.I. Dept. Social Welfare, Cranston, 1951-53; prevention coord. juvenile dept. R.I. Family Ct., Providence, 1953-63; asst. dir. Providence Youth Progress Bd., Inc., 1963-64, exec. dir., 1965-67; exec. dir. Progress for Providence, Inc., 1967-70; adminstr. Marathon House, Inc., Providence, 1970-77; dir. Washington Hosp. and Ctr. for Addictions, Boston, 1977-80; state refugee coord. R.I. Office Refugee Resettlement, Cranston, 1980-85; broker, owner C.E. Lachapelle Real Estate Agy., Warwick, 1986—; social svcs. cons. VA Hosp., 1971-72, City of Providence, 1976-77, HHS, 1985, NIMH, 1985, and others; part-time detached youth worker Providence Recreation Dept., 1953-63; mem. mayor's adv. bd. City of Providence Model Cities Program, 1968-70; mem. adv. panel Nat. Inst. Drug Abuse, Rockville, Md., 1978; chair gov.'s study com. spl. needs population State of R.I., 1982-85; chair refugee policy Northeastern Regional Consultations, Boston, 1983, and others. Sgt. USAF, 1943-46, PTO. Mem. Nat. Bd. Realtors, R.I. Bd. Realtors, Kent County Bd. Realtors, Inc. Roman Catholic. Home: 39 Winslow Ave Warwick RI 02886-4724 Office: CE Lachapelle Real Estate 2905 Post Rd Warwick RI 02886

LACHOWICZ, FRANCISZEK, foreign language educator; b. Poland, July 12, 1908; came to U.S., 1951; s. Ignacy and Anastazja (Szarejko) L.; m. Helena M. Pogonowska, Dec. 8, 1944; children: Barbara, Lech. MA, U. Warsaw, 1935; MS in Edn., U. Bridgeport, 1962, profl. diploma, 1966, MS in Math., 1970. Asst. U. Warsaw, Poland, 1936-39; tchr. Polish Tchrs.' Coll., Univ. Edinburgh, Scotland, 1943-45; prin. Polish Bus. Coll., England, 1946-48; math. tchr. Masuk High Sch., Monroe, Conn., 1961-77, Housatonic Community Coll., Stratford, Conn., 1966-67; adj. assoc. prof. Sacred Heart Univ., Fairfield, Conn., 1978—. Contbr. articles to profl. jours. 2d lt. Polish Army, 1939-43. Mem. Polish Am. Hist. Soc., Polish Nat. Alliance, Kosciuszko Found., Polish Inst. Arts and Scis. Am., Polish Am. Edn. Soc. (first pres. 1973, pres. 1989), Jozef Pilsudski Inst., Polish Heritage Soc. (Man of the Yr. 1986), Polish Army Vet. Assn. Democrat. Roman Catholic. Home: 95 Houston Ave Bridgeport CT 06606-3041 Office: Sacred Heart Univ 5151 Park Ave Fairfield CT 06432-1000

LACHTER, GERALD DAVID, psychologist, educator; b. N.Y.C., May 3, 1941; s. Lazar and Leah (Weisberg) L.; m. Abbie J. Lowenstein, May 19, 1973; children—Katie Mae, Eloise Rebecca. B.A., C.W. Post Coll., 1964; M.A., Columbia U., 1966; Ph.D., CUNY, 1970. Cert. psychologist, N.Y. Asst. prof. psychology L.I. U., C.W. Post Coll., Greenvale, N.Y., 1970-74, assoc. prof., 1974-82, prof., 1982—; cons. psychologist Suffolk Child Devel. Ctr., Smithtown, N.Y., 1981-87, Suffolk AHRC, Commack, N.Y., 1976-81; dir. grad. programs in psychology C.W. Post Coll., 1973-80. Author: Behavior Objectives Unit Handbook, 1974, (with others) Stimulus Schedules: The T-Tau Systems, 1972. Contbr. articles to profl. jours. Mem. Am. Psychol. Soc., Psychonomic Soc., Assn. for Behavior Analysis, Eastern Psychol. Assn., Sigma Xi (v.p. C.W. post coll. club 1990-91, pres. 1991-92). Democrat. Jewish. Office: LIU-CW Post Campus Psychology Dept Greenvale NY 11548

LACK, JAMES J., state senator, lawyer; b. N.Y.C., Oct. 18, 1944; s. Harry A. and Eve (Kaufman) L.; m. Therese M. Gutleber, Jan. 19, 1969; children—Kara Shana, Jeremy David. B.A., U. Pa., 1966; J.D., Fordham U., 1969. Bar: N.Y. 1970. Counsel to Betty Furness, N.Y. State Consumer Protection Bd., 1970-72; prin. asst. frauds bur. dist. attys. office County of Suffolk, N.Y., 1972-73; commr. Suffolk County Dept. Consumer Affairs, Hauppauge, N.Y., 1974-77; pres. Better Bus. Bur. Met. N.Y., 1977-78; ptnr. Smyth & Lack, Huntington, N.Y., 1983—; mem. N.Y. Senate, 1979—; chmn. Senate Labor com., 1985—, Majority Steering com., 1989—, Nat. Commn. Employment Policy. Republican. Office: NY State Senate State Capitol Albany NY 12224

LACKEY, JAMES EDWARD, retail executive; b. Niskyuna, N.Y., Sept. 4, 1953; s. Dale Franklin and Helen Joan (Goodell) L.; m. Linda Marie Luoma, May 20, 1984; children: James Edward Jr., Jennifer Elizabeth. Student, Worcester Polytechnic Inst., 1971-75. Asst. mgr. Tech HiFi, Cambridge, Mass., 1974-75; pres. Natural Sound Inc., Framingham, Mass., 1975—; treas. Profl. Audio Retailers Assn., Kansas City, Mo., 1982-84. Republican. Roman Catholic. Home: 730 Edgell Rd Framingham MA 01701-3906 Office: Natural Sound Inc 401 Worcester Rd Framingham MA 01701-5382

LACKS, SANFORD ABRAHAM, geneticist; b. N.Y.C., Jan. 28, 1934; s. Charles Jonas and Goldie Rose (Dranoff) L.; m. Elaine Rose Norris, Nov. 22, 1959; children: Jennifer, Daniel, Julia. BS, Union Coll., 1955; PhD, Rockefeller U., 1960. Vis. investigator Pasteur Inst., Paris, 1957-58; instr. Harvard U., Cambridge, Mass., 1960-61; from asst. geneticist to sr. geneticist Brookhaven Nat. Lab., Upton, N.Y., 1961—; vis. investigator Hebrew U., Jerusalem, 1970-71; mem. genetics program faculty SUNY, Stony Brook, 1986—. Contbr. over 90 articles to profl. jours. and books. Grantee USPHS, 1978— 81—. Mem. Am. Soc. for Microbiology, Am. Soc. for Biochemistry and Molecular Biology, Genetics Soc. Am. Office: Brookhaven Nat Lab Biology Dept Upton NY 11973

LACLAIR, RICHARD JAY, English educator; b. Silver Creek, N.Y., May 26, 1942; s. Joseph F. and Marjorie LaClair; m. Mary Jo Uebbing, Aug. 6, 1966; children: James J., Jeanne M., Jennifer A. BA in English, Canisius Coll., 1965; MA in English, Niagara U., 1972. Cert. English tchr., N.Y. Prof. Erie Community Coll North, Williamsville, N.Y., 1972—; advisor Element Campus Newspaper, Erie Community Coll. North, Williamsville, 1975-81, Insight Lit. Mag., 1989—. Author: Methods of Environmental Impact Assessment, 1976. Chmn. Town of Amherst (N.Y.) Conservation Coun., 1975-80; con. County of Erie (N.Y.) Conservation Coun., 1976. Mem. N.Y. Coun. on Writing. Office: Erie CC North Main St at Youngs Rd Buffalo NY 14221

LACZ, STANLEY JOHN, architect; b. Paterson, N.J., Mar. 8, 1938; s. John Stanley and Harriet (Strezeski) L.; m. Diane Ormsby, Feb. 12, 1961 (div. Oct. 1973); children: Darria, Kimberly, Scott, Kristin; m. Peggy Dujets, June 23, 1974; children: Sarah, Katie. B in Architecture, U. Notre Dame, Ind., 1960. Registered architect Bd. of Architects, N.J., 1964; profl. engr. Bd. Profl. Engrs., N.J., 1965; profl. planner Bd. Profl. Planners, N.J., 1967; registered architect NYU, 1973, Registration Bd., Conn., 1973, Bd. Examiners, Pa., 1973; certification architect Nat. Coun. Archtl. Registration Bds., Washington, 1973; prin. AEP Assoc., Little Falls, N.J., 1965—; cons. Planning Bd./Bd. Adjustment, Litle Falls, N.J., Planning Bd., Wanaque, N.J.; mcpl. engr. Governing Body, Stafford Township, N.J. Mem. Passaic COunty Transp. Com., Paterson, N.J., 1978; pres. Passaic County Hist. Soc., Paterson, N.J., 1980; trustee Great Falls Preservation and Devel. Corp., Paterson, N.J., 1991. Recipient Honor award Passaic County Hist. Soc., 1991. Mem. AIA, Nat. Soc. Profl. Engrs., North Cen. Jersey Soc. Profl. Engrs., Passaic County Internat. Profl. Coun., Notre Dame Club of No. N.J. Republican. Roman Catholic. Office: AEP Assocs 485 Notch Rd Little Falls NJ 07424-1955

LADAS, ALICE KAHN, psychologist; b. N.Y.C., May 30; d. Myron O. Kahn and Rosalie (heil) Blum; m. Harold S. Ladas (dec. Mar. 7, 1989); children: Robin Janis, Pamela. BA, Smith Coll., 1943, M in Social Scis., 1947; EdD, Columbia U. Tchrs. Coll., 1970; postgrad., Inst. Bioenergetic Analysis, 1971-75. Diplomate Am. Bd. Sexology, Am. Bd. Clin. Social Work. Various positions as assts. to psychologists, Washington, N.Y.C., 1943-51; dir. Child Guidance Dept. Pub. Schs., Caldwell, N.J., 1952-58; asst. to dir. Maternal Care Adoption Svc., Lakeville, Conn., 1958-60; staff Ballard Sch. of YWCA, 1967-73; analyst, marriage counselor pvt. practice, 1967—; staff Hamilton Sch. for Marriage and Family Life, 1970—; cons. Found. for Religion and Mental Health, 1979—; staff Family Life Inst.-Westchester County, 1979—; pvt. practice, 1979—. Author: The G Spot, 1982. Recipient fellowship to Nat. Inst. Pub. Affairs, 1944; named William Alan Nielson fellow, 1941. Democrat. Home: 42 Whippoorwill Rd Armonk NY 10504-1333 Office: 241 Central Park W New York NY 10024-4530

LADAY, JEROME MICHAEL, employment and compensation manager; b. New Brunswick, N.J., May 2, 1953; s. Joseph Martin and Theresa Susan (Grebely) L.; m. Elaine Marilyn Powers, May 8, 1982; children: Jason Michael, Kathleen Lillian. BA in History, St. Francis U., Loretto, Pa., 1975; cert. in human resource mgmt., Middlesex County Coll., 1985. Human resources adminstrv. asst. Amalgamated Credit Bur., East Brunswick, N.J., 1980-81; pers. supr. Amalgamated Credit Bur., East Brunswick, 1981-82; pers. mgr. Amalgamated Credit Bur., Old Bridge, N.J., 1982-88; mgr. employee rel. Noble Lowndes, East Orange, N.J., 1989-90; mgr. employment and compensation Noble Lowndes, Roseland, N.J., 1990—; seminar instr. Middlesex County Coll., Edison, N.J., 1988—, Raritan Valley Community Coll., Somerville, N.J., 1991—, Holy Family Coll., Phila., 1992—. Treas. Milltown (N.J.) Jaycees, 1977-78. Named Jaycee of the mth. Milltown (N.J.) Jaycees, 1977. Mem. Soc. Human Resource Mgmt. (cen. N.H. chpt. sec. 1988-89, 91-92, pres. 1992-93). Office: Noble Lowndes 3 Becker Farm Rd Roseland NJ 07068-1726

LADD, EVERETT CARLL, political science educator, author; b. Saco, Maine, Sept. 24, 1937; s. Everett Carll and Agnes Mary (MacMillan) L.; m. Cynthia Louise Northway, June 13, 1959; children: Everett Carll, III, Corina Ruth, Melissa Ann, Benjamin Elliot. A.B. magna cum laude, Bates Coll., 1959; Ph.D. (Woodrow Wilson fellow, Social Sci. Research Council fellow), Cornell U., 1964. Asst. dean students for pub. affairs Cornell U., Ithaca, N.Y., 1963-64; asst. prof. U. Conn., Storrs, 1964-67, assoc. prof., 1967-69, prof. polit. sci., 1969—, dir. Inst. for Social Inquiry, 1968—, co-exec. dir. Roper Ctr. for Pub. Opinion Research, 1977-79, exec. dir., pres. Roper Ctr. for Pub. Opinion Research, 1979—; research fellow Ctr. for Internat. Studies, Harvard U., Cambridge, Mass., 1969-75; mem. exec. council Inter-Univ. Consortium for Polit. and Social Research, 1975-77; adj. scholar Am. Enterprise Inst. Pub. Policy Research, 1978—; adv. editor in social scis. W.W. Norton & Co., 1977—; rsch. assoc. Ctr. for Study Social and Polit. Change, 1986—, Inst. for Study Econ. Culture, 1986—; trustee Nat. Coun. Pub. Polls, 1987-90. Author: Negro Political Leadership in the South, 1966, Ideology in America: Charge and Response in a City, a Suburb and a Small Town, 1969, rev. edit., 1986, American Political Response, 1970 (with S.M. Lipset) Professors, Unions and American Education, 1973, Academics, Politics and the 1972 Election, 1943, The Divided Academy: Professors and Politics, 1975, (with C.D. Hadley) Political Parties and Political Issues: Patterns in Differentiation Since the New Deal, 1973, Transformations of the American Party System: Political Coalitions from the New Deal to the 1970s, 2d edit., 1978, Where Have All the Voters Gone?, 1978, 2d edit., 1982, The American Polity, 1985, 4th edit., 1991; sr. editor Pub. Opinion mag., 1979-89, Am. Enterprise mag., 1990—; editor: Pub. Perspective mag., 1989—. Ford Found. fellow, 1969-70; Guggenheim fellow, 1971-72; Rockefeller Found. fellow, 1976-77; Hoover Instn. fellow, 1976-77, 79-80; Center Advanced Study in Behavioral Scis., 1979. Mem. Am. Polit. Sci. Assn., Am. Sociol. Assn., Am. Assn. Pub. Opinion Rsch., New Eng. Polit. Sci. Assn. (pres. 1982-83), Acad. Polit. Sci., Cosmos Club (Washington), Phi Beta Kappa, Delta Sigma Rho. Home: 86 Ball Hill Rd Storrs Mansfield CT 06268-2007 Office: Roper Center PO Box 440 Storrs Mansfield CT 06268-0440

LADD, LAWRENCE R., educator; b. Worcester, MA, July 30, 1949; s. Lawrence Firmin and June (Fisk) L.; m. Susan E. Cartmell, Jan. 4, 1975; children: Jonathan, Elizabeth, Sarah. AB, U. Mass., Amherst, 1973; EdM, 1974. Ast. budget dir. U. Mass., Amherst, Mass., 1973-74; asst. to pres. Duke U., Durham, NC, 1974-76; asst. provost Boston U., Boston, 1976-78; assoc. dean Tufts U., Medford, Mass., 1978-84; dean of adminstrn. Tufts U., 1984-92; assoc. dir. Woods Hole (Mass.) Oceanographic Inst., 1992—; mem. exec. com., bd. Mass. Assn. Schools and Colleges, Boston 1989—. Mem. finance com. Town of Winchester, Mass. 1984-88. Home: 12 Lawrence St Winchester MA 01890-2402 Office: Woods Hole Oceanographic Woods Hole MA 02543

LADENHEIM, HARRY, chemical engineer; b. Vienna, Austria, Oct. 17, 1932; s. Emanuel and Anna (Harnik) L.; m. Rosel Srill, Aug. 21, 1955; children: Lawrence, Leonard. BS, CCNY, 1954; PhD, Poly. Inst. Bklyn., 1958; postgrad., Ill. Inst. Tech., 1958-59. Rsch. chemist Esso Rsch. and Engring. Co., Linden, N.J., 1959-63; rsch. chemist Air Products and Chem., Inc., Linwood, Pa., 1964-70, sr. rsch. chemist, 1970-76, sr. devel. engr., 1976-79; prin. rsch. engr. Air Products and Chem., Inc., Linwood, 5, 1979-81; process engr. Air Products and Chem., Inc., Paulsboro, N.J., 1981-87, sr. process engr., 1987—. Contbr. articles to profl. publs.; patentee in field.

Mem. Am. Chem. Soc. Office: Air Products & Chem Inc Billingsport Rd Paulsboro NJ 08066-1003

LADEROUTE, CHARLES DAVID, engineer, economist, consultant; b. Helena, Mo., Aug. 2, 1948; s. Estel and Anna Maude (Stuart) L.; m. Linda Dodd, June 8, 1985; 1 child, Lindsay; 1 stepchild, Erik. BS in Engring. Mgmt., U. Mo., Rolla, 1971, BS in Econs., 1972; MA in Econs., Ea. Mich. U., 1980; postgrad., Harvard U., 1979-81. Sr. rate analyst Consumers Power Co., Jackson, Mich., 1972-79; prin. cons. Chas. T. Main, Inc., Boston, 1979-81; pres., chief exec. officer Charles D. Laderoute, Ltd., Topsfield, Mass., 1981—, also chmn. bd. dirs.; mem. supplemental faculty Jackson Community Coll., 1974-78; course dir. Ctr. for Profl. Advancement, East Brunswick, N.J., 1981—; ptnr. Knowledge Applications Software, LP, Acton, Mass., 1986—; lectr. in field. Contbr. articles to profl. jours. Mem. Nat. Rep. Senatorial Com., 1990-91, Rep. Nat. Com., 1990—; charter mem. Rep. Campaign Coun., 1991. Mem. Am. Econs. Assn., Am. Meteorol. Soc., Nat. Assn. Bus. Economists, Nat. Soc. Rate of Return Analysts, Internat. Assn. Energy Economists (charter, pres. N.E. chpt. 1984-86), Am. Soc. Engring. Mgmt. (charter, life), Planning Engrs. Desktop Computer Users Group (charter, pres. 1987-88), ABA (assoc.), Am. Gas. Assn. (assoc.), Can. Gas. Assn. (assoc.), Assn. Energy Engrs., Demand-Side Mgmt. Soc. (charter), Assn. Demand-Site Mgmt. Profls. (charter), Omicron Delta Epsilon. Republican. Office: Charles D Laderoute Ltd PO Box 376 Topsfield MA 01983-0576

LADIN, LEONARD IRWIN, management consultant; b. N.Y.C., Mar. 29, 1933; s. Samuel Ladin and Ann Dora Geist;m. Myrna Lee Greenberg, Oct. 25, 1964 (dec. Feb. 1979); children: Miles Geist, Brett Ian; m. Kathleen Ann O'Connor, June 25, 1983. AB in Chemistry, Cornell U., 1955; postgrad., NYU, 1960-61. Cert. mgmt. cons. Inst. Mgmt. Cons. From mktg. analyst to sr. mktg. analyst Roger Williams Tech. and Econ. Svcs., Princeton, N.J., 1960-65; mgr. internat. mktg. rsch. Celanese Plastics Co., Newark, 1965-67, mgr. new venture analysis, 1967-70; mng. dir. Technomic Rsch. Assocs. Ltd., London, 1970-76; prin. assoc. Technomic Rsch. Assocs. Ltd., N.Y.C., 1976-80; v.p. internat. Technomic Consultants, N.Y.C., 1960-87; v.p. Technomic Consultants Internat. Inc., N.Y.C., 1987—. Bd. dirs. Landmark Found., Prides Crossing, Mass., 1990—. Lt. USNR, 1956-60. Mem. Cornell Club of N.Y.

LADJEVARDI, HAMID, investment company officer; b. Tehran, Iran, June 11, 1948; came to U.S., 1948; s. Ahmad and Banoo (Barzin) L.; m. Manijeh Mirdamad, July 19, 1978; children: Adella, Lilly. BA in Econs., BA in Polit. Sci., U. Calif., Berkeley, 1971; MBA, Harvard U., 1973. Dep. mng. dir. Behshahr Indsl. Group, Tehran, 1974-79; vice chmn., fin. dir. Akam Group of Cos., Tehran, 1975-79; investment mgr., v.p. Morgan Stanley & Co., N.Y.C., 1980—; instr. Fairleigh Dickinson U., Rutherford, N.J., 1984; chmn. Iran Am. Trade Coun., Inc. Mem. Coun. Internat. Bus. Risk Mgmt., Fgn. Policy Assn., Carnegie Coun. on Ethics and Internat. Affairs, U.S. Senatorial Club, Harvard Club. Home: 66 Brite Ave Scarsdale NY 10583-1637 Office: Morgan Stanley & Co 1251 Ave Of The Americas New York NY 10020-1104

LADUE, EDDY LORAIN, agricultural economics educator, consultant; b. Middlesex, N.Y., June 23, 1939; s. George Jay and Ester (Eddy) LaD.; m. Lorraine Judith Frankish, June 27, 1964; children: Steven George, Scott Philip, Shelley Ester. Cert. Cornell U., 1959, BS, 1964, MS, 1966; PhD, Mich. State U., 1972. Farm owner, operator George LaDue & Sons, Canadaigua, N.Y., 1959-62; extension assoc. Cornell U., Ithaca, N.Y., 1965-67, asst. prof., 1971, assoc. prof., 1976, prof. agrl. econs., 1984—; grad. asst. Mich. State U., 1967-71; agrl. economist U.S. Dept. Agr., 1977-78; cons. Congl. Budget Office, Washington, 1979; cons. in field. Assoc. editor Jour. Agrl. Fin. Rev., 1983-90, editor, 1991, co-editor, 1992—. Mem. Am. Agr. Econs. Assn., Am. Dairy Sci. Assn., Am. Econs. Assn., Northeastern Agr. and Resource Econs. Assn., Phi Kappa Phi. Republican. Avocations: golf, fishing, gardening. Home: 1132 Snyder Hill Rd Ithaca NY 14850-8701 Office: Cornell U 155 Warren Hall Ithaca NY 14853

LADUE, WILLIAM STUART, security company executive; b. St. Albans, Vt., June 5, 1955; s. Robert Allen and Edna (McKillop) L. Student, Vt. Tech. Coll., 1973-74, Pa. State U., 1989-90. Floor supr., tech. specialist Vt. Precision Resistor Co., 1977-79; dir. tech. svcs. Codeco Corp. Vt., Stowe, 1979-87; engring. mgr. Catalpa, Inc., Brattleboro, Vt., 1987-89, Cressona Aluminum Co., 1989—. Inventor demand control system.

LADZINSKI, G(ERARD) ROBERT, sales representative; b. Perth Amboy, N.J., Mar. 9, 1962; s. Robert J. and Evelyn C. (Meszaros) L.; m. Michele Carroccia, Nov. 22, 1986. BGS in Biochemistry, Villanova (Pa.) U., 1984. Sales intern MSA, Malvern, Pa., 1985-87; sales rep. MSA, Mountainside, N.J., 1987—; lectr. Mid-Atlantic Asbestos Tng. Ctr., Piscataway, N.J., 1988, N.J. Inst. Tech., 1988—. Bd. dirs. Reynard Run Townhouse Assn., Marlton, N.J., 1989—. Mem. Am. Indsl. Hygienists Assn., Am. Soc. Safety Engrs. (lectr. 1989). Roman Catholic. Home: 114 Crown Prince Dr Marlton NJ 08053-1415 Office: MSA 1100 Globe Ave Mountainside NJ 07092-2904

LA FALCE, JOHN JOSEPH, congressman, lawyer; b. Buffalo, Oct. 6, 1939; s. Dominic E. and Catherine M. (Stasio) La F.; m. Patricia Fisher, 1979. BS, Canisius Coll., 1961; JD, Villanova U., 1964; LLD (hon.), Niagara U., 1979, St. Johns U., 1989; LHD (hon.), Canisius Coll., 1990; LLD (hon.), Villanova U., 1991. Bar: N.Y. 1964. Mem. N.Y. State Legislature, 1971-74, 94th-102nd Congresses from 32d Dist. N.Y., 1975—; chmn. Small Bus. Com.; mem. Banking Com. Served as capt., Adj. Gen. Corps AUS, 1965-67. Democrat. Home: 35 Danbury Ln Buffalo NY 14217-2101 Office: US Ho of Reps Rm 2367 Rayburn House Office Bldg Washington DC 20515

LAFERRIERE, MARY ELIZABETH, nursing educator; b. Orange, N.J., Dec. 21, 1938; d. Leonard Robert and Mary Frances (Shea) Gardner; m. Leo CHarles Laferriere, Dec. 30, 1967; children: Meg Ann, Lynn Beth. Diploma in Nursing, St. Michael's Hosp. Sch., of Nursing, Newark, N.J., 1959; BSN, Boston Coll., Newton, Mass., 1963; MS in Nursing, U. Colo., 1965. RN. Staff nurse Mountainside Hosp., Montclair, N.J., 1959-60, Mass. Gen. Hosp., Boston, 1960-61; pvt. duty nurse various hosps., Boston, 1961-63; staff nurse Loeb Ctr., Montefiore Med. Ctr., Bronx, N.Y., 1966; pub. health nurse East Orange (N.J.) Health Dept., 1963; instr. St. Mary's Hosp., Orange, N.J., 1963-64, Seton Hall U., Newark, 1966; per diem nurse Med. Ctr. Hosp. Vt., Burlington, 1981-90; instr. nursing U. Vt., Burlington, 1966-68, lectr., 1983—. Chmn. Waitsfield (Vt.) Health Coun.; co-chmn. Waitsfield Blood Drive/ARC, 1987-91; bd. dirs. Mad River Valley Health Ctr., 1982-83, pres. 1983; bd. dirs. Cen. Vt. Home Health Agy., 1992—; leader Girl Scouts U.S. Mem. NAACOG, Vt. Nurses Assn., Sigma Theta Tau (chmn. nominating com. 1991). Home: RFD Box 360 Waitsfield VT 05673 Office: U Vt Burlington VT 05405

LAFF, JAY E., health facility acquisition executive, entrepreneur; b. Yonkers, N.Y., Dec. 9, 1942; s. Jesse M. and Charlotte (Greenstein) L.; m. Linda F. Glass, Dec. 26, 1965; children: Joshua F., Hillary J. BSBA, Bryant Coll., 1964; MBA in Hosp. Adminstrn., Wagner Coll., 1969. Cert. nursing home adminstr. Asst. adminstr. Albert Einstein Hosp., Bronx, N.Y., 1966-69; adminstr. French Hosp., N.Y.C., 1969-74; exec. dir. Freeport (N.Y.) Hosp., 1974-75; dir. bur. of long term care Pa. Dept. Health, Harrisburg, 1975-79; pres. Med. Ctr. for Aging, Inc., Doylestown, Pa., 1979-82, Med. Mgmt. Group, Inc., Doylestown, 1982-90; ptnr. Sencit Health Facility Acquisition Group, Harrisburg, 1986—; mem. nursing home Pa. State Bd. Examiners, Harrisburg, 1975-79. Mem. citizen adv. panel Doylestown Intelligencer, 1991. Fellow Am. Coll. Health Care Adminstrs. (bd. dirs. Pa. chpt. 1990—, cert. com. 1989—, advancement and cert. com. 1989—). Office: Sencit Health Facility Acquisitions Group PO Box 1110 Doylestown PA 18901-0037

LAFFERTY, JAMES MARTIN, physicist; b. Battle Creek, Mich., Apr. 27, 1916; s. James V. and Ida M. (Martin) L.; m. Eleanor J. Currie, June 27, 1942; children: Martin C., Ronald J., Douglas J., Lawrence E. Student, Western Mich. U., 1934-37; B.S. in Engring. Physics, U. Mich., 1939, M.S. in Physics, 1940, Ph.D. in Elec. Engring, 1946. Physicist Eastman Kodak Research Lab., Rochester, N.Y., 1939; physicist Gen. Electric Research Lab., Schenectady, 1940, 42-81; mgr. power electronics lab. Gen. Electric Research Lab., 1972-81; with Carnegie Instn., Washington, 1941-42; past pres. Internat. Union Vacuum Sci. Technique and Applications, 1980-83; People to People citizen ambassador program group leader for Vacuum Sci. and Tech. delegation to Europe, 1984, China, 1986, Australia, 1988, Soviet Union, 1990. Editor, contbg. author: Scientific Foundations of Vacuum Technique (Dushman), 1962; editor: Vacuum Arcs, Theory and Applications, 1980; asso. editor: Jour. Vacuum Sci. and Tech, 1966-69; Editorial bd.: Internat. Jour. Electronics, 1968-89; contbr. articles to profl. jours. Mem. greater consistory Ref. Ch.; trustee Schenectady Museum, 1967-73, sec., 1971-72, pres., 1972-73. Recipient Devel. award Bur. Naval Ordnance, 1946; Distinguished Alumnus citation U. Mich., 1953; IR-100 award, 1968. Fellow Am. Phys. Soc., IEEE (Lamme medal 1979), AAAS; mem. Nat. Acad. Engring., Am. Vacuum Soc. (hon. life mem.; dir. 1962-70, sec. 1965-67, pres. 1968-69), U.S. Power Squadrons (comdr. Lake George squadron 1975-76, comdr. Dist. 2 1981-82, nat. rear comdr. 1987-90), Sigma Xi, Phi Kappa Phi, Iota Sigma, Tau Beta Pi. Home: 1202 Hedgewood Ln Niskayuna NY 12309-4605

LAFFERTY, MARTIN CURRIE, broadcast executive; b. Schenectady, N.Y., Dec. 24, 1947; s. James Martin and Eleanor Jean (Currie) L.; m. Sari Stevens, June 1, 1979; children: Alana Hope, David Aaron. BA, Williams Coll., Williamstown, Mass., 1969; MFA, Yale U., 1972; postgrad., GE Devel. Inst., Crotonville, N.Y., 1989. Chmn. dept. Milton (Mass.) Acad., 1972-74; asst. prof., resident producer Rutgers U., Camden, N.J., 1974-78; mgr. communications svcs. GE Advt. and Sales Promotion Ops., Stamford, Conn., 1978-80; dir. programming Cox Cable Communications, Atlanta, 1980-83; v.p. programming and mktg. Group W Broadcasting and Cable, N.Y.C., 1983-84; v.p. Turner Direct Broadcast Svcs. Turner Broadcasting System, Atlanta, 1984-87; pres. Tempo Devel. Corp., Atlanta, 1987-88; v.p. cable svcs. GE Americom, Princeton, N.J., 1988-90; v.p. pay-per-view Olympics NBC, N.Y.C., 1990—. Author: (plays) Machination, 1968, Bald, 1974. Recipient Pres.'s award Nat. Cable TV Assn., 1983, Founders award Satellite Broadcasting and Communications Assn., 1987. Mem. Nat. Acad. Cable Programming (founder), Cable TV Adminstrn. and Mktg. Soc. (TAMI award 1985), Am. Mktg. Assn. (exec. mem.), William Coll. Alumni Assn. (pres. Atlanta chpt. 1982), Mercedez-Benz Club Am. Republican.

LAFFOLEY, PAUL GEORGE, JR., artist, architect; b. Cambridge, Mass., Aug. 14, 1935; s. Paul George and Mary Ellen (Lyons) L. BA, Brown U., Providence, R.I., 1958; postgrad., Harvard U., 1958-62, MIT, 1964-65, Boston Archtl. Ctr., 1967-69. Registered architect, Mass. Apprentice in sculpture The Studio of Mirko Baseldella, Cambridge, 1961-62, The Studio of Frederick J. Kiesler, N.Y.C., 1962-63; archtl. designer Emery Roth and Sons, Architects, N.Y.C., 1963-64, Techbuilt Inc., North Dartmouth, Mass., 1964-66, James Lawrence Jr., Architect, Brookline, Mass., 1966-67; concept designer The Tufts New England Med. Ctr. Planning Office, Boston, 1967-70; pres. The Boston Visionary Cell, Inc., 1971—. Exhibiting mem. The Ward-Nasse Gallery, Boston and N.Y.C., 1970-84, Stux Gallery, Boston and N.Y.C., 1985-88, Kent Fine Art, Inc., 1989 and numerous one-person and group nat. and internat. exhibits, 1966—; author: The Phenomenology of Revelation, 1989; contbr. author and artworks various books, featured writer and artist: Sulfur 17: A Literary Tri-Quarterly of the Whole Art, 1986, The Pnenomenology of Revelation, 1989. Named finalist Fellowships of the Creative Artists' Svcs., U. Mass., 1976, Mass. Arts and Humanities Found., Boston U. Gallery, 1978; printing fellow Mass. Artists Found., 1989; grantee The Marie Walsh Sharpe Art Found., 1991-92. Mem. Inst. of Contempory Art (Englehard award 1985), Theosophical Soc., U.S. Psychotronics Assn., World Future Soc. (Boston-Cambridge chpt.), New England Soc. Psychic Sci. Researchers (earned recognition 1982), Faculty Club Harvard U. Office: Boston Visionary Cell Inc 36 Bromfield St Unit 200 Boston MA 02108-5210

LA FLAMME, PAUL H., marketing and sales professional; b. Springfield, Mass., Jan. 12, 1943. BS in Chemistry, Holy Cross Coll., 1965; MAT, U. Mass., 1967. Program mgr. Springborn Labs., Enfield, Conn., 1980-85; mktg./sales dir. Spectrum Internat., Palmer, Mass., 1987—; pres. Soquela, Monson, Mass., 1991—; pres. ACTFANE, Manchester, N.H., 1987—. Author: The Cross and the Chameleon, 1975; contbr. articles to profl. jours. Mem. Am. Chem. Soc. Office: Spectrum Internat Palmer Indsl Park Palmer MA 01069

LAFRANCE, NORMAN DAVID, pharmaceutical company executive; b. Waterbury, Conn., Aug. 6, 1947; s. Roger A. and Clara S. (Pagano) LaF.; m. M.C. Muran, Dec. 21, 1975; children: Katherine, Adrienne. BS in Nuclear Engring. and Sci., Rensselaer Polytech. Inst., 1969, M of Engring. in Nuclear Engring. & Sci., 1970; MD, U. Ariz., 1977. Clin. dir. Nuclear Medicine Johns Hopkins Hosp., Balt., 1982-88; exec. dir. Med. Rsch. DuPong Merck, Wilmington, Del., 1988-92; v.p. rsch. divsn. Sterling Winthrop Pharms., Malvern, PA, 1992—; mem. med. ethics bd. Johns Hopkins Hosp., Balt., 1982-88; cons. med. imaging FDA, Rockville, Md., 1984-86, mem. adv. com., 1987-88. Contbr. articles to profl. jours. Lt. USPHS, 1970-73. Fellow ACP, Am. Coll. Nuclear Physicians; mem. Radiol. Soc. on N.Am., Am. Coll. Radiology, Soc. of Nuclear Medicine (trustee 1987-90). Home: 5610 Enderly Rd Baltimore MD 21212-2939

LAFRENIERE, RAYMOND LEE, school administrator; b. Haverhill, Mass., Apr. 15, 1949; s. Raymond Walter and Honorine Suzanne (Berard) L.; m. D. Anne Skinner, June 18, 1977; children: Justin Paul, Nicole Lee. BA, Merrimack Coll., 1971; MEd, U. Maine, Orono, 1972, C.A.S., 1976. Tchr. Jordan Jr. High Sch., Lewiston, Maine, 1972-73; guidance counselor Windham (Maine) High Sch., 1973-74; edn. liaison Dept. of the Navy, Boston, 1974-91; owner Career Concepts, Poland, Maine, 1988-91; asst. prin. Poland Community Sch., 1991—. Bd. dirs. Gov.'s Adv. Coun. on Career Edn., Augusta, Maine, 1975-78, Gov.'s Adv. Coun. on Vocat. Edn., Augusta, 1978-81, Poland Sch. Com., 1987-90; mem. exec. bd. Maine Sch. Bds., Augusta, 1987-90, Mainelead, Augusta, 1988-90. Named Edn. Liaison of Yr., Navy Recruiting Command, 1981. Mem. Cen. Maine Guidance (pres. 1981), Maine Vocat. Guidance (founder), Maine Guidance Assn., Nat. Career Devel. Assn., AACD, Lewiston-Auburn C. of C. Home: RR 1 Box 667 Poland ME 04273-9618 Office: Poland Community Sch Poland ME 04273

LAGAKOS, WILLIAM GEORGE, food and restaurant operation educator, musician, author; b. Camden, N.J., May 2, 1911; s. George B. and Stavroula (Alikakos) L.; m. Lola Carapanos, June 17, 1945; children: George, Matina, Stacy, Phillip. BA, Rutgers U., Camden, N.J., 1934; postgrad. law, Temple U., 1935-38, BS, 1970. Chef various restaurants, N.Y.C., 1938-39; propr., chef, mgr. various restaurants, N.J. and Pa., 1939-70; instr. food theory Bucks County Community Coll., Phila., 1961; tchr. Manpower Devel. Tng. Act Program, Phila., 1961-62, Phila. Bd. Edn., 1962-75; food preparation cons. Delaware Valley, Pa., 1976-88; substitute instr. Phila. Sch. System, 1975—; instr. in rehabilitation for ex-offenders Urban Coalition League Inst., Phila., 1972-86. Author: Profile of a Family: The Story of George B. and Stavroula Lagakos, 1981. Greek Orthodox. Home and Office: 252 Buckner Ave Haddonfield NJ 08033-2914

LAGASSE, THOMAS JOSEPH, English educator; b. Bristol, Conn., Jan. 28, 1964; s. Joseph A.W. and Yolanda (Beardsley) L. BA in Mass Communication, Bonaventure U., 1986; MA in English, Trinity Coll., Hartford, Conn., 1992. Claim rep. Cigna Corp., Kansas City, Mo., 1986-87; sr. claim rep. Cigna Corp., Sherman, Tex., 1987-88; admissions counselor St. Bonaventure (N.Y.) U., 1988-89; researcher ESPN, Bristol, Conn., 1991-92; instr. Tunxis Community Coll., 1992—. Home: 24 Briarwood Rd Bristol CT 06010

LAGATOL, NANCY LYNN, educator; b. N.Y.C., Dec. 20, 1948; d. Method Joseph and Ernestine (Wagner) Kocak; 1 child, Jennifer Kim. BA in Elem. Edn., William Paterson Coll. N.J., Wayne, 1971, MEd, 1982, Supr.'s cert., 1986; postgrad., 1990. Title I tchr. Westwood (N.J.) Regional Schs., 1973-76, tchr., 1977, compensatory educator, 1978-84, supplemental tchr., 1984-89; basic skills/ESL/testing coord. Hawthorne, N.J., 1989—; tchr. Reading Improvement Ctr., North Haledon, N.J., 1986-87; speaker in field. Mem. NEA, N.J. Edn. Assn., Internat. Reading Assn., N.J. Reading Assn., N.J. Assn. Fed. Program Adminstrs. Home: 154 Sibbald Dr Park Ridge NJ 07656-2334 Office: Lincoln Mid Sch Hawthorne Ave Hawthorne NJ 07506-1309

LAGERFELD, STEVEN DAVID, editor, writer; b. N.Y.C., Jan. 31, 1955; s. Theodore David Lagerfeld and Irene (Hayman) Jordan; m. Frances Conklin, June 21, 1985; children: Nathalie, Elizabeth. BA, Cornell U., 1977. Asst. editor The Public Interest, N.Y.C., 1977-78, asst. mng. editor, 1978-79; program officer Inst. for Ednl. Affairs, N.Y.C., 1979-80; assoc. editor The Wilson Quar., Washington D.C., 1981-85, sr. editor, 1985-89, acting editor, 1990-91, deputy editor, 1989—. Contbr. articles to popular mags. Home: 2012 Virginia Ave Mc Lean VA 22101-4939 Office: Wilson Quarterly 740 L'Enfant Promenade SW Washington DC 20024

LAGOUDAS, DIMITRIS CHRISTOS, civil engineering educator; b. Serres, Greece, Dec. 1, 1959; came to U.S., 1983; s. Christos and Anastasia (Karapepera) L.; m. Magdalini Zabuki, July 25, 1983; children: Anastasia D., Georgia Kerasia. Diploma in mech. engring., Aristoteles U. Thessaloniki, Greece, 1982; PhD in Applied Math., Lehigh U., 1986. Registered profl. engr., Greece. Asst. mech. engr. Bor (Yugoslavia) Copper Mines, 1979, Adra Sugar Factory, Damascus, Syria, 1981; teaching asst. Aristoteles U. Thessaloniki, 1979-80, Lehigh U., Bethlehem, Pa., 1983-86; postdoctoral assoc. Cornell U., Ithaca, N.Y., 1986-88; asst. prof. civil engring. Rensselaer Poly. Inst., Troy, N.Y., 1988—; vis. scientist Max Planck Inst., Stuttgart, Fed. Republic Germany, 1987. Co-author: Gauge Theory and Defects in Solids, 1988; co-editor: Microcracking Induced Damage in Composites, 1990; also articles. Recipient rsch. initiation award Engring. Found., 1991. Mem. ASME, ASCE (assoc.), Am. Acad. Mechanics, Soc. Engring. Sci., Materials Rsch. Soc., Internat. Soc. for Interaction Mechanics and Mathematics. Office: Rensselaer Poly Inst Dept Civil Engring Troy NY 12180-3590

LAHEY, MARGARET MARY, speech-language pathology educator, researcher; b. Hartford, Conn., Apr. 1, 1932; d. George Joseph and Jeannette A. (Wall) Malloy; m. Henry C. Lahey, Aug. 17, 1957; children: Diane Marie, Denise Louise. BS, SUNY, Geneseo, 1952; MA, Ohio State U., 1953; EdD, Tchrs. Coll., Columbia U., 1972. CCC in speech-language and audiology; lic. speech pathologist, Mass. Speech and hearing clinician Youngstown (Ohio) Speech and Hearing Soc., 1953-54; instr. U. Conn., Storrs, 1955-59; speech pathologist Bd. Edn., Ellington, Conn., 1965-68; assoc. prof. Montclair State Coll., Upper Montclair, N.J., 1971-76; prof. Hunter Coll., Grad. Ctr. CUNY, N.Y.C., 1976-87; prof. div. comm. disorders Div. Comm. Disorders Emerson Coll., Boston, 1987—; chmn. div. Emerson Coll., Boston, 1989-91. Author: Language Disorders and Language Development, 1988; co-author: (with L. Bloom) Language Development and Language Disorders, 1978; editor: Childhood Language Disorders, 1978; contbr. numerous articles to profl. jours. Recipient Profl. Achievement award N.Y.C. Speech-Language-Hearing Assn., 1987, Disting. Achievement award N.Y. State Speech-Language-Hearing Assn., 1983. Fellow Am. Speech-Language-Hearing Assn. Office: Emerson Coll 168 Beacon St Boston MA 02116-1401

LAHEY, REGIS HENRY, bank executive; b. Pitts., July 15, 1948; s. Michael Patrick and Henrietta (Szczesny) L. Diploma in Indsl. Mgmt., Ednl. Inst. Pitts., 1968; BS, Robert Morris Coll., Pitts., 1981; grad., Bucknell U., 1991. Corp. trustee Union Nat. Bank, Pitts., 1968-70; asst. supr. Mellon Bank, N.A., Pitts., 1978-80, supr., 1980-83, unit mgr., 1983-84, asst. ops. officer, 1984-86, ops. officer, 1986-87, trust and investment officer, 1987—; instr. cash mgmt. Master Trust U., Pitts., 1987—. Mem. Am. Mgmt. Assn. Republican. Roman Catholic. Office: Mellon Bank One Mellon Ctr Pittsburgh PA 15258-0001

LAHMAN, H. S., software design engineer; b. Flushing, N.Y., Mar. 20, 1938; s. Howard S. and Catherine (Wainwright) L. BS, MIT, 1961, MS, 1971. Ops. mgr. Geosci., Inc., Cambridge, Mass., 1964-72; rsch. assoc. MIT, Cambridge, 1972-74; programmer, analyst Gillette, Boston, 1974-75; v.p. Martindale, Inc., Cambridge, 1975-77; systems analyst Stop & Shop, Boston, 1977-79; sr. mktg. engr. Teradyne, Inc., Boston, 1979-82, software engr., 1982—. Author: The Evolution and Utilization of Marine Resources, 1972. With U.S. Army, 1962-64. Mem. IEEE, Assn. Computing Machinery. Home: 12 Middlesex St Framingham MA 01701 Office: Teradyne Inc 621 Harrison Ave Roxbury MA 02118-2303

LAHNEMAN, WILLIAM JAMES, naval officer, political science educator; b. Darby, Pa., July 18, 1952; s. William Herman and Catherine Bernadette (Robinson) L.; m. Leslie Jean de Moustes, Nov. 8, 1975; children: William, Brooke, Grace, David. BS in Mgmt., U.S. Naval Acad., 1974; MBA in Mgmt., Golden Gate U., 1990; MA in Nat. Security, Naval Postgrad. Sch., 1990. Commd. ensign USN, 1974, advanced through grades to comdr., 1988; div. officer U.S.S. Truxtun, San Diego, 1976-78; ops. officer U.S.S. Samuel Eliot Morison, Mayport, Fla., 1981-83; damage control asst. U.S.S. Theodore Roosevelt, Norfolk, Va., 1984-86; exec. officer U.S.S. Tex., Alameda, Calif., 1987-88; dept. sr. mem. Nuclear Propulsion Mobile Tng. Team, San Diego, 1990-92; assoc. chmn. polit. sci. dept. U.S. Naval Acad., Annapolis, Md., 1992—. Mem. U.S. Naval Inst., Mensa, U.S. Naval Acad. Alumni Assn. Roman Catholic. Office: Polit Sci Dept US Naval Acad 589 McNair Rd Annapolis MD 21402

LAI, MARY MANERI, financial executive; b. Bklyn., June 20, 1921; d. Joseph and Concettina (DiPeri) Maneri; m. William T. Lai, July 25, 1943; children: William Thomas, Richard Joseph. BS, L.I. U., 1942, LHD (hon.), 1986; MS, Fordham U., 1951. Jr. acct. Klein Hinds Finke, CPA (now Alexander Grant), N.Y.C., 1942-43; bookkeeper USN, 1943-45; acct. Arthur Young and Co., N.Y.C., 1946; bursar L.I. U., Brookville, N.Y., 1946-54, dir. fin., 1954-63, treas., 1963—, v.p. fin., 1983—; mem. Coll. Entrance Exam. Bd., trustee com. on fin., 1978-80; mem. fin. com. Coun. Higher Ednl. Instns., 1965-67; mem. N.Y. State adv. com. ednl. policy analysis, 1975—; cons. various colls. and univs. including Gannon U., Fordham U., Union Theol. Sem.; cons. N.Y. State Dept. Edn., Dormitory Authority State of N.Y.; bd. dirs. East N.Y. Savs. Bank, Mfrs. and traders Trust Co., First Empire State Corp.; adv. bd. Chem. Bank, 1977—; mem. budget rev. com. L.I. Assn. Commerce and Industry, 1977. Bd. dirs. Bklyn. Tuberculosis and Lung Assn., 1965-75, budget./;fin. com., 1965-75; bd. dirs. Family Svc. Assn. Nassau County, 1982-87, also mem. fin. com.; bd. dirs. Breezy Point Coop, Inc., 1965-68, asst. treas., 1965, treas., 1966-68, employee rels. com., 1965—, fin. com., 1965—, pension fund trustee, 1965-85, nominating com.; bd. trustees Barton Coll., 1972-80, chmn. fin. com., 1973-75; bd. trustees LeMoyne Coll., 1972-79, fin. com., vice chmn. bd., 1977-79; fin. com. St. Joseph Coll., 1981—. Mem. AAUW, Nat. Assn. Coll. and Univ. Bus. Officers (pres. 1979-80), Ea. Assn. Coll. and Univ. Bus. Officers (pres. 1974-75), Nat. Assn. Ednl. Buyers Met. Group (sec. 1960-65), Ednl. and Instl. Coop. Svcs. (bd. dirs. 1978-85), Higher Ednl. Adminstrv. Referral Svc. (mgmt. com. 1971-73), Nassau Consortium Bus. Officers. Home: 19 Norgate Rd Glen Head NY 11545-2607

LAI, RALPH WEI-MEEN, physical scientist; b. Tou-Lu, Taiwan, Dec. 17, 1936; s. Chungetn and Chen Chu Lai; m. Cindy S. Chen, aug. 6, 1967; children: Naline, Melisa. BS, Cheng Kong U., Tainan, Taiwan, 1959; MS, S.D. Sch. M & Tech., 1964; PhD, U. Calif., Berkeley, 1970. Engr. Cyprus Minerals Co., Trenton, N.J., 1969-73; metulligic engr. Kennecott Copper Co., Lexington, Mass., 1974-80; scientist Kennecott Copper Co., Salt Lake City, 1980-85; pres. Toshi Co., Pitts., 1986—; phys. scientist U.S. Dept. Energy, Pitts., 1985—. Author: The Overlooked Law of Nature, 1991; contbr. articles to profl. jours.; patentee in field. Republican. Home: PO Box 12722 Pittsburgh PA 15241-0722 Office: Pitts Energy Tech Ctr PO Box 10940 Pittsburgh PA 15236-0940

LAING, JOANN MILLS, manufacturing executive; b. Mpls., Nov. 16, 1957; d. Joseph Mills and Jane (Anthony) Garneau. BS, Syracuse U., 1980; MBA, Harvard U., 1986. Cons. Citibank N.A., Citicorp., N.Y.C., 1980-82; asst. treas. The Chase Manhattan Bank, N.A., N.Y.C., 1982-84; intern Ing. C. Olivetti & Co., S.p.A., Ivrea and Cambridge, Italy and Eng., summer 1985; dir. strategy and corp. devel. Olivetti Advanced Tech. Ctr., N.Y.C. and Ivrea, 1986-87; contr. internat. investment Olivetti Advanced Tech. Ctr., Ivrea, 1987-88; dir. joint venture fin. and adminstrn. Ing. C. Olivetti & Co., S.p.A., Paris and Ivrea, 1988-89; comml. contr. Ing. C. Olivetti & Co., S.p.A., Ivrea, 1989-90; gen. mgr., chief fin. officer Olivetti Supplies, Inc., Middletown, Pa., 1990—. Office: Olivetti Supplies Inc 137 4th St-HIA Middletown PA 17057

LAING, JOHN WAILON, neurosurgeon; b. Cannelton, W.Va., Apr. 14, 1937; s. Clarence Robert and Irene Elizabeth (Hudnall) L.; m. Judith

Marcum (div.); children: JOhn Wailon Laing Jr., Mark Robert Laing; m. Patricia Ann Laing, Nov. 11, 1967; children: Matthew Robert Laing, Daniel Patrick Laing. BA, Marshall U., 1959; MD, Vanderbilt U., 1963. Intern Vanderbilt U. Hosp., Nashville, 1959-60, resident in surgery, 1960-61; resident in neurosurgery U. Miss. Med. Ctr., Jackson, 1971-76; gen. practitioner Permanente Med. Group, San Raphael, Calif., 1969-71; neurosurgeon U.S. Naval Hosp., San Diego, 1977-83, Al Hada Hosp., Taif, Saudi Arabia, 1983-85, Cumberland Valley Neurosurg. Cons., Chambersburg, Pa., 1985—; cons. in neurosurgery Nat. Naval Med. Ctr., Bethesda, 1990; asst. clin. prof. neurosurgery Uniformed Svcs., U. Health Svcs., Bethesda, 1990. Contbr. articles to profl. jours. Mem. AMA, Assn. of Mil. Surgeons, N.Y. Acad. Scis., Pa. State Med. Soc., Congress of Neurol. Surgeons. Office: Cumberland Valley Neurosurg 764 Lincoln Way E Chambersburg PA 17201-2768

LAIOU, ANGELIKI E., history educator; b. Athens, Greece, Apr. 6, 1941; came to U.S., 1959; d. Evangelos K. and Virginia I. (Apostolides) Laios; m. Stavros B. Thomadakis, July 14, 1973; 1 son, Vassili N. B.A., Brandeis U., 1961; M.A., Harvard U., 1962, Ph.D., 1966. Asst. prof. history Harvard U., Cambridge, Mas, 1969-72; Dumbarton Oaks prof. Byzantine history Harvard U., 1981—; assoc. prof. Brandeis U., Waltham, 1972-75; prof. Rutgers U., New Brunswick, N.J.., 1975-79, disting. prof., 1979-81; chmn. Gennadeion com. (Am. Sch. Classical Studies), Athens, Greece, 1981-84; dir. Dumbarton Oaks, 1989—. Author: Constantinople and The Latins, 1972, Peasant Society in the Late Byzantine Empire, 1977; editor: Charanis Studies, 1980. Guggenheim Found. fellow, 1971-72, 79-80, Dumbarton Oaks sr. fellow, 1983-88, Am. Coun. Learned Socs. fellow, 1988-89. Mem. Am. Hist. Assn., Medieval Acad. Am., Societa Ligure di Storia Patria, Greek Com. Study of South Eastern Europe. Office: Dumbarton Oaks 1703 32nd St NW Washington DC 20007-2961

LAIR, JUDITH ANNE TREVVETT, social services administrator, counselor; b. Richmond, Va., Mar. 26, 1942; d. William Thomas and Thelma A. (Dyson) Trevvett; m. Robert E. Lair, Jr., Sept. 15, 1962; children: Marlene, Karen, Gregory. Student, Mary Washington Coll., 1960-62, U. N.C., 1974-75; BA in Psychology, U. N.C., Asheville, 1977; MA in Edn., Western Carolina U., 1979; DSc in Counseling, George Washington U., 1992. Probation/parole officer N.C. Dept. Correction, Asheville, 1981-82; vocat. evaluator Sheltered Workshop, Columbus, N.C., 1982; mgr. N.C. Welcome Ctr., Columbus, 1982-85; asst. mgr. Eckerd's Drugs, Monroe, N.C., 1985-86; mgr. J.E's Dress Shop, Monroe, 1986; child support enforcement agent div. social services N.C. Dept. Human Resources, Charlotte, N.C., 1986—; counselor, office mgr. Nat. Ctr. Treatment of Phobias, Anxiety and Depression, Washington, 1989-91, Ft. Balvoir Counseling Ctr., 1991-92; grad. asst. in counseling George Washington U., 1992; bereavement cons.Hospice of Union County, Monroe, N.C., 1986-87. Mem. Thermal Belt Bus. and Profl. Women (Woman of the Yr. 1981, 84, Employee of the Yr. 1985), Psi Chi. Republican. Methodist. Home: 1009 Brantham Ct Charlotte NC 28211-2400

LAIRD, RICHARD H., securities dealer; b. Gulfport, Miss., Jan. 17, 1951; s. Travis H. and Carole Ann (Bladon) L.; m. M. Kathleen Miller, Apr. 24, 1976 (div. Nov. 1987); 1 child, Travis J. BS in Aero. Sci., Embry Riddle U., 1973; MBA in Fin., Xavier U., 1976. Cons. Booz Allen & Hamilton, Cin., 1972-74; pres. Am. Group Cos., Cin., 1974-77; v.p. corp. devel. Offshore Logistics, Inc., Houston, 1977-81; v.p. pvt. investment Legg Mason Wood Walker, Balt., 1981-82; pres. Equity Group, Washington, 1983—; chmn. bd. dirs. Mountain Rain Inc.; mng. ptnr. Tartan Farms, Potomac, Md., 1987—. With Med. Svc. Corps, U.S. Army, 1969-71, Vietnam. Office: The Equity Group 1100 Connecticut Ave #1200 Washington DC 20036

LAJOIE, ROLAND, army officer; b. Nashua, N.H., Aug. 11, 1936; s. Ernest Joseph and Alice (Bechard) L.; m. Joann Theresa Sinibaldi, Feb. 11, 1961; children: Michelle, Christopher, Renee. BA in Govt., U. N.H., 1958; MA in History, U. Colo., 1971; diploma, Army Command & Staff Coll., 1973, U.S. Army War Coll., 1981. Commd. 2d lt. U.S. Army, 1958, advanced through grades to maj. gen., 1991; served as asst. army attache Am. Embassy, Moscow, 1973-76; commandant U.S. Army Russian Inst., Garmisch, Fed. Republic Germany, 1976-79; bn. comdr. 1st Psychol. Ops. Bn., Ft. Bragg, N.C., 1979-80; rsch. fellow U.S. Army War Coll., Carlisle, Pa., 1980-81, Harvard U., Cambridge, Mass., 1980-81; army attache Am. Embassy, Moscow, 1981-83; chief of mission U.S. Mil. Liaison Mission, Berlin, Potsdam, German Dem. Republic, 1983-86; def. and army attache Am. Embassy, Paris, 1986-88; dir. U.S. On-Site Inspection Agy., 1988-91; dep. dir. internat. negotiations JS, The Joint Staff, Washington, 1991-92; assoc. dep. dir. for ops. and mil. affairs CIA, Washington, 1992—. Decorated Bronze Star, Legion of Merit, Def. Meritorious Svc., Def. Superior Svc., Nat. Order Merit (France). Mem. VFW. Home: 5 Fairfax Dr Fort Belvoir VA 22060-2105

LAKE, CHRISTOPHER ROBERT, transportation executive; b. Bklyn., June 27, 1952; s. Edward Theron and Mildred Katherine (Rhodes) L.; m. Gia C. Garel. BA in Engl., SUNY, Stony Brook, 1973. Tech. asst. SUNY, Stony Brook, 1974-75; mgmt. trainee, then asst. mgr. Friendly Ice Cream, Inc., Long Island, N.Y., 1975-77; food and beverage supr. Host Svcs. N.Y., Queens, 1977-78; staff analyst, then assoc. staff analyst N.Y.C. Transit Authority, Bklyn., 1978-85; dir. personnel, surface transit N.Y.C. Transit Authority, 1985-88, sr. dir. human resources, surface transit, 1988-90; asst. chief officer human resources Surface Transit, Bklyn., 1990—. Mem. Conf. Minority Transp. Ofcls. (v.p. N.Y.C. chpt. 1988-90). Episcopalian. Office: NYC Transit Authority 25 Jamaica Ave Brooklyn NY 11207-1894

LAKEMAN, PAUL ERIC, foundation executive; b. Roslyn, N.Y., Feb. 16, 1950; s. James Parson and Helen Katherine (Johnson) L.; m. Nancy Jane Schaeffer, May 4, 1974 (div. 1989); m. Brenda Lynn Lokushek, July 8, 1990; 1 child, Kirsten Nicole. BA, Rider Coll., Trenton, N.J., 1972; MHA, Duke U., 1986. Pub. rels. asst. Monmouth Med. Ctr., Long Branch, N.J., 1974-76; pub. rels. rep. Newport News Shipbuilding, 1976-79; employee communications rep. Ethyl Corp., Richmond, Va., 1979-84; pres. Kent Gen. Hosp. Found., Dover, Del., 1986—. Recipient First Place in Typography Design award, N.J. Press Assn., 1974, First Place Corp. Mag., Internat. Assn. Bus. Communicators, 1977. Mem. Assn. Hosp. Philanthropy, Nat. Soc. Fund Raising Execs., Am. Coll. Healthcare Execs., Rotary. Lutheran. Office: Kent Gen Found 640 S State St Dover DE 19901-3503

LAKSHMINARAYANA, BUDUGUR, aerospace engineering educator, consultant; b. Shimoga, India, Feb. 15, 1935; came to U.S., 1963; s. Budugur and Seethamma Srinivasachar; m. Saroja Lakshminarayana, Feb. 27, 1965; children: Anita, Arvind. B Mech. Engring., Mysore (India) U., 1958; D in Mech. Engring., U. Liverpool, Eng., 1963, U. Liverpool, Eng., 1981. Vis. asst. prof. aerospace engring. Pa. State U., University Park, 1963-69, assoc. prof., 1969-74, prof., 1974-85, disting. alumni prof., 1985-86, Evan Pugh prof., 1986—, dir. computational fluid dynamic studies, 1980-87; vis. assoc. prof. MIT, Cambridge, 1972; Fulbright sr. vis. prof. Tech. U. Aachen, Germany, 1988, Nat. Ctr. for Sci. Rsch. vis. prof. Ecole Cen. Lyon, France, 1987-88; cons. Pratt & Whitney, GE, GM, Warren, Mich., 1989—, European Space Agy., Vernon, France, 1988. Editor 2 books; contbr. over 200 articles to profl. jours. Fellow AIAA (chmn. Cen. Pa. chpt., Pendray Aero. Lit. award 1989), ASME (Freeman scholar 1990); mem. Am. Soc. for Engring. Edn. Home: 843 Wheatfield Dr State College PA 16801-4229 Office: Pa State U 153H Hammond Bldg University Park PA 16802

LAKY, ANTHONY JOSEPH, pharmaceutical executive; b. Phila., Feb. 22, 1941; s. Joseph John and Rosalie (Deutsch) L.; m. Wanda Marie Jones, Sept. 21, 1975; children: Michael, Joette, Joseph, Karen. BS, Rutgers U., 1967, B Pharmacy, 1967. Registered pharmacist, N.J., Va. Pharmacist/mgr. Marr Drug Inc, Clifton, N.J., 1968-75; staff pharmacist Automated Pharm. Svcs., Fairfield, N.J., 1975-77; dir. pharmacy ops. Automated Pharm. Svcs., Fairfield, 1977-90; asst. v.p. ops. Automated Pharm. Svcs., Whippany, N.J., 1990-91; v.p. ops. Automated Pharm. Svcs., Whippany, 1991—. Auxiliary police sgt., Clifton, 1960-70; fireman West Milford Vol. Fire Co. #1, 1973-74. Mem. N.J. Pharm. Assn., Am. Soc. Cons. Pharmacists, Passaic County Pharm. Assn., Elks. Home: 18 George St West Milford NJ 07480-3416 Office: Automated Pham Svcs 121 Algonquin Pky Whippany NJ 07981-1601

LA LIMA, SALVATORE JOHN, college dean; b. Bklyn., Apr. 26, 1931; s. Salvatore and Anna (La Cova) La L.; m. Nora Margaret Ruxton, June 27, 1964; children: Kathleen, Theresa, Jeanne, Paul, Christopher, Nancy. AAS, Hofstra U., 1957, BBA, 1959, MS, 1963. Statis. quality contorl mgr. Fairchild-Stratos Corp., Brightwaters, N.Y., 1958-63; bus. tchr. Wm. Floyd High Sch., Shirley, N.Y., 1963-65; instr. acctg. and data processing Suffolk Community Coll., Selden, N.Y., 1965-68, head dept. acctg. and data processing, 1968-71, chmn. bus. div., 1971-80; dean of instrn. Suffolk Community Coll., Brentwood, N.Y., 1980-84, exec. dean, 1984—; lectr. SUNY, Stony Brook, 1979-80, Dowling Coll., Oakdale, N.Y., 1970-80. Author quality control reference manual. Treas. Soundview Civic Assn., Inc., Shoreham, N.Y., 1975-80, 90, pres., 1987-88, 91. Sgt. USAF, 1951-53. Recipient Long Island U. Edn. award, 1986, Spl. Appreciation award Nat. Assn. Negro Bus. and Profl. Women, 1987. Mem. Long Island Forum for Tech., Loyal Order Sons of Italy in Am., Phi Theta Kappa, Alpha Beta Gamma. Roman Catholic. Home: 11 Southgate Shoreham NY 11786-1626 Office: Suffolk CC Crooked Hill Rd Brentwood NY 11717-1006

L'ALLIER, JAMES JOSEPH, educational software company executive, instruction designer; b. St. Paul, June 24, 1945; s. Charlemagne Joseph and Mildred Marie (LeVasseur) L'A.; m. Susan Kay Margulies, Apr. 28, 1973. BS magna cum laude, U. Wis., River Falls, 1969, MS, 1973; PhD, U. Minn., 1980. Isntr. English River Falls Sr. High Sch., 1969-71; instr. English Stillwater (Minn.) Sr. High Sch., 1971-80; mgr. computer assisted instrn. Wilson Learning Corp., Mpls., 1980-83, dir. R&D, 1983-86; v.p. R&D Wilson Learning Interactive Tech. Group, Santa Fe, 1986-89; v.p. product devel. Nippon Wilson Learning, Tokyo, 1989-90; v.p., gen. mgr. Whole Systems Software, Inc., Cambridge, Mass., 1990—; expert witness Universal Tng., Chgo., 1989-91. Author: (video prodns.) Who Shot the Terminal?, 1984, The Tenth Woman, 1987, Working Toward the Future, 1991, America's Workforce: A Vision for the Future, 1992; mem. editorial bd. Learning Age, Mpls., 1987-89; product reviewer Ednl. Tech., N.Y.C., 1981-83; assoc. editor Performance and Instrn., Washington, 1983-85. Curriculum chair Total Info. Ednl. Systems, St. Paul, 1971-76; fund raiser U. Minn. Alliance, Mpls., 1983-89; contbr. Am. Cancer Soc., Washington, 1987—; mem. pub. svc. com. Instructional Systems Assn., Sunset Beach, Calif., 1988—. U. Minn. Grad. Sch. Edn. sr. fellow, 1984; U.S. Dept. Labor grantee, 1991. Mem. U. Wis. Alumni Assn., Instructional Systems Assn. (conf. chair 1980, 84), U. Minn. Alumni Assn., Boston Computer Soc., Pres.'s Club U. Minn., Heritage Soc. U. Wis. Home: 14 Kings Way Waltham MA 02154 Office: Whole Systems Software Inc 26 Lansdowne St Cambridge MA 02139

L'ALLIER, JEAN-PAUL, mayor. BA, U. Montreal, 1959; LLM, U. Ottawa, 1962, diploma of superior studies, 1963. Mem. law firms Ville de Quebec, Ottawa and Hull, Ont., Can.; mem. law faculty U. Ottawa; rsch. officer Centre africain de formation et de recherches adminstratives pour le développment, Morocco, 1964-66; dir. coop. Ministry of Cultural Affairs Que., 1966-68; sec. gen. l'Office franco-que. pour la jeunesse, 1968, chmn. bd. dirs., 1970-76; mem. Deux-Montagnes Nat. Assembly Que., 1970-76; pres. Jean-Paul L'Allier & Assocs., 1976-89; mayor City of Que., 1989—; ministe youth recreation and sports Nat. Assembly Que., 1970, minister pub. svc., 1970-72, minister communications, 1970-75, minister cultural affairs, 1975-76, mem. treasury bd. and legislative com., 1970-76; pres. ministerial com. Quality of Life,, 1970-76; gen. del. Que. in Belgium, 1981-84, hon. consul, 1985-88; legal advisor Langlois, Trudeau, Tourigny, Montreal; counselor GAMMA Inst. Montreal, Inst. Entrepreneurial Devel. Que. Chmn. provisional exec. com. World Heritage Cities, 1991—. Office: Hotel de Ville, CP 700, Quebec, PQ Canada G1R 4S9

LALLY, DOUGLAS ROBERT, credit rating officer, lawyer; b. Ridgewood, N.J., Dec. 21, 1962. BA, U. Chgo., 1986; JD, U. Tulsa, 1989. Bar: Pa. 1990. Gold prospector Lally's Recources, Fairbanks, Alaska, 1983-85; jud. intern U.S. Dist. Ct. for No. Okla., Tulsa, 1989; prof. Taylor Inst., East Orange, N.J., 1989; securities analyst Value Line Securities Inc., N.Y.C., 1989-91; rating officer Standard & Poor's Rating Group, N.Y.C., 1991—. Mem. ABA, Assn. Investment Mgmt. and Rsch. Republican. Lutheran. Home: 240 Montana Dr Brick NJ 08723-5962 Office: Standard & Poor's Rating Group 26 Broadway New York NY 10004

LALLY, WILLIAM JOSEPH, financial planner; b. N.Y.C., Sept. 28, 1937; s. William Joseph and Madeline (Bradley) L.; m. Janet Lou Miars, July 30, 1960; children: Catherine Mary, Elizabeth Ann, Maureen Susan, Monica Eileen, Patricia Jude. AB in Econs., Coll. Holy Cross, 1959; MBA, Rutgers U., 1961. CPA, Conn., N.Y., N.J. Mgr. Peat, Marwick, Mitchell & Co., Newark, 1960-70; ptnr. Peat, Marwick, Mitchell & Co., White Plains, N.Y., 1970-76; sr. v.p. Gregg Group, Inc., Falls Village, Conn., 1977-83; pres. Hamilton Gregg Fin. Services, Falls Village, 1983-84, Lally & Assocs., Inc., Stamford, Conn., 1984—; bd. dirs., lectr. Inst. Fin. Planning, Quinnipiac Coll., Hamden, Conn., 1986-91. Adv. bd. Cath. Family Svcs., Stamford, Conn., 1988—. Mem. AICPA, Conn. Soc. CPA's, Internat. Fin. Planning Assn. (bd. dirs. Fairfield chpt. 1989—), Registry Fin. Planning Practitioners, Chemists Club (N.Y.C.). Republican. Roman Catholic. Office: Lally & Assocs Inc 979 Summer St Stamford CT 06905-5512

LAM, CHUN-MING GORDON, aerodynamicist; b. Hong Kong, Nov. 6, 1964; came to U.S., 1987; s. Kam-Chien and Yuet-Mei (Shum) L. B in Engring., Imperial Coll. Sci. & Tech., London, 1987; MS, MIT, 1989. Staff assoc. Continuum Dynamics Inc., Princeton, N.J., 1989—. Mem. AIAA, Am. Helicopter Soc. Office: Continuum Dynamics Inc PO Box 3073 Princeton NJ 08543-3073

LAMARRE, BERNARD, engineering, contracting and manufacturing advisor; b. Chicoutimi, Que., Can., Aug. 6, 1931; s. Emile J. and Blanche M. (Gagnon) L.; m. Louise Lalonde, Aug. 30, 1952; children: Jean, Christine, Lucie, Monique, Michèle, Philippe, Mireille. BSc, Ecole Poly., Montreal, Que., Can., 1952; MSc, Imperial Coll., U. London, 1955; LLD, St. Francis Xavier U., N.S., Can., 1980; D in Engring. (hon.), U. Waterloo, Ont., 1984; LLD (hon.), U. Concordia, Montreal, 1985; D in Engring. (hon.), U. Montreal, 1985; D in Applied Sci. (hon.), U. Sherbrooke, Que., 1986; D in Bus. Adminstrn. (hon.), U. Chicoutimi, Que., 1987; D in Sci. (hon.), Queen's U., Kingston, Ont., 1987; D in Engring. (hon.), U. Ottawa, Ont., 1988, Tech. U. N.S., 1989, Royal Mil. Coll., Kingston, 1990. Structural and founds. engr. Lalonde-Valois, Montreal, 1955-60, chief engr., 1960-62; ptnr., gen. mgr., pres. Valois, Lalonde, Valois, Lamarre, Montreal, 1962-72; chmn., chief exec. officer Lavalin Group, 1972-91; sr. advisor SNC-Lavalin Inc., 1991—; adv. Publicité Martin Inc., Télésystème Inc., Bellechasse Santé Inc. Contbr. articles to profl. jours. Bd. dirs. l'Ecole Polytechnique, Mus. Fine Arts, Coll. Stanislas; chmn. Can. cultural property export rev. bd. Decorated officer Ordre nat. du Quèbec, Order of Can.; Athlone fellow, 1952. Fellow Engring. Inst. Can., Can. Soc. Civil Engring.; mem. ASCE, Order Engrs. of Que., Mont-Royal Club, Laval-sur-le Lac Club. Roman Catholic. Home: 4850 Cedar Crescent, Montreal, PQ Canada H3W 2H9

LAMARRE, PAUL RONALD, artist; b. Monroe, Mich., Sept. 3, 1950; s. Theophile Conrad and Geraldine Ann (Goodnagh) L.; m. Melissa Wolf, Jan. 1, 1986. BFA, U. Mich., 1978. lectr. in field. Exhbns. include Dooley Le Cappellaine Gallery, N.Y.C., 1991, 92, Richard/Bennett Gallery, L.A., 1991, Richard Green Gallery, L.A., 1990, Montecarotto Mail Art Mus., Italy, 1990, Gracie Mansion Gallery, 1987, 86, Shuttle Theatre, Westbeth Gallery, 1984, Barbara Braathen Gallery, N.Y.C., 1984, 22 Wooster Gallery, N.Y.C., 1980, 80 Washington Sq. Gallery, N.Y.C., 1980, Chgo. Art Expo, 1979, others; one man show at Barbara Braathen Gallery, 1989; works in permanent collections at Inst. Contemporary Art, London, Toledo Mus. Art, pvt. collectors; co-editor, pub. Food Sex Art: Starving Artists' Cookbook, 1991. Recipient award for best non-narrative video San Francisco Internat. Film Festival, 1986; N.Y. Found. for the Arts Video fellow, 1987, Kitchen, Media Bur. grantee, 1984, 85, CAPS fellow, 1982, Robert Rauschenberg "Change" Found. grantee, 1983. Home and Office: Eidia Arts PO Box 11 New York NY 10012-0001

LAMB, EDGAR ANDREW, musician, composer; b. Clinton, N.C., Aug. 26, 1958; s. Edgar Thomas Herring and Ercelle Lamb; m. B. Madaha Kinsey, May 6, 1990. AA, LaGuardia Coll., 1979; postgrad., Old Westbury Coll., 1979-84. Musician, sideman, soloist Chelsea Performing Arts, N.Y.C., 1981—; composer, musician, band leader KiLa Music/Andrew Lamb Quartet, Bklyn., 1982—; musician, sideman, soloist various orchestras, N.Y.C., 1981—; cons. Chelsea Performing Arts, N.Y.C., 1985—; lectr., tchr. KiLa Music Co., Bklyn., 1989—. Author multiple compostions, 1979—. Speaker, performer Magnolia Tree Earth Ctr., Bklyn., 1992. Mem. Concerned African-Am. Artists Bklyn. (cons. 1991). Home: 22 Herkimer St Brooklyn NY 11216 Office: KiLa Music Co 22 Herkimer St Brooklyn NY 11216

LAMB, HENRY GRODON, safety engineer; b. Saco, Maine, Feb. 9, 1906; s. Charles Barnard and Fannie Mabel (Prentiss) L.; 1 child, Patricia Miller Lamb Steen. BS, Dartmouth Coll., 1926; BS in CE, MIT, 1928. Cert. profl. safety engr.; registered profl. engr., Calif. Civil engr. Stone & Webster Engring., Boston, 1928-31; safety engr. Liberty Mutual Ins., Boston, 1931-38, Scott Paper Co., Chester, Pa., 1938-42, Am. Nat. Stds. Inst., N.Y.C., 1942-71; ret. Mem. Sch. Bd., Freedom, N.H., 1983-89. Mem. Am. Soc. Safety Engrs. (pres. 1968-69), Am. Indsl. Hygiene Assn., ASME, Masons (worshipful master 1986-88). Republican. Congregationalist. Address: Scarboro Rd PO Box 211 Freedom NH 03836

LAMB, KARL A(LLEN), political scientist, educator, dean; b. Worland, Wyo., Jan. 24, 1933; s. Lawrence and Floribel (Krueger) L.; m. Sally Ann Walker, July 12, 1959; children: Steven Bayard, Amy Kristine, Martin Andrew, Cynthia Marlene. BA, Yale U., 1954; PhD, Oxford (Eng.) U., 1958. Asst. prof. U. Mich., Ann Arbor, 1958-63; from asst. prof. to prof. U. Calif., Santa Cruz, 1963-85; prof. U.S. Naval Acad., Annapolis, Md., 1986—; acad. dean U.S. Naval Acad., Annapolis, 1985-89; provost Cowell Coll. U. Calif., Santa Cruz, 1978-79. Author: The People, Maybe, 1971, As Orange Goes, 1974, The Guardians, 1982; co-author: Apportionment and Representative Institutions, 1963, Congress: Politics and Practice, 1964, Campaign Decision-Making, 1968; contbr. over 20 articles to profl. jours. Bd. dirs. Mich. Citizenship Clearing House, Ann Arbor, 1959-62; faculty intern Rep. Nat. Com., Washington, 1964; from mem. to pres. bd. dirs. Santa Cruz County Fair, 1965-75. Capt. USAR, 1957-58. Rhodes scholar Oxford U., 1954-57; recipient rsch. fellowship Social Sci. Rsch. Coun., 1970, humanities fellowship Rockefeller Found., 1977, faculty rsch. grant Earhart Found., 1983, 91. Mem. Am. Polit. Sci. Assn., U.S. Naval Acad., Officers and Faculty Club. Office: US Naval Acad Polit Sci Dept Annapolis MD 21402

LAMBDIN, CRAIG HASKELL, investment counselor; b. Summit, N.J., July 25, 1958; s. Jack Haskell and Jane Marie (Starko) L.; m. Karen Hansen, May 3, 1986; children: Derek Hansen, Gavin Haskell. AB, Dartmouth Coll., 1980; MBA, NYU, 1985. Chartered fin. analyst. Portfolio mgr. First Fidelity Bancorp., Newark, 1980-83; investment assoc. Brundage, Story and Rose, N.Y.C., 1983-86; v.p. The Bank of N.Y., N.Y.C., 1986—. Fellow Assn. for Investment Mgmt. and Rsch.; mem. N.Y. Soc. Security Analysts. Republican. Roman Catholic. Home: 517 Wolfs Ln Pelham NY 10803-2429 Office: The Bank of NY 706 Madison Ave New York NY 10021-7293

LAMBERGS, GUNTIS J., investment banker; b. Boston, May 16, 1956; s. Aristids and Dzidra (Alsins) L.; m. Anne T. Tilley, Dec. 31, 1978; children: Kathryn, Victoria. BS in Bus., Boston U., 1980. V.p. L.F. Rothschild, Boston, 1985-87; chmn., chief exec. officer Mark Computer Systems, Milford, Mass., 1988-90; v.p. Josephthal, Lyon & Ross, Boston, 1990—; lectr. in investing Westwood High Adult Edn., 1985-86. Contbr. articles to profl. jours.; appeared on FNN and other local cable TV bus. stas. Republican. Office: Josephthal Lyon & Ross 30 Rowes Wharf Boston MA 02110

LAMBERT, ABBOTT LAWRENCE, retired accountant; b. N.Y.C., Mar. 19, 1919; s. Woolf W. and Estelle (Wittcover) L.; m. Lois H. Ribman, Oct. 9, 1958 (dec.); children: Nancy Lambert Rodgers, Jane Lambert Peck. BA Columbia U., 1940, MS in Acctg., 1946. Acct., N.Y.C., 1940-42, 46-48, 71—; v.p. Chopak Mills, Inc., N.Y.C., 1948-71; pres. Carthage Fabrics Corp. (N.C.), 1964-71; pres., dir. 1025 Fifth Ave. Corp., N.Y.C., 1965-71, dir., 1975-78, 81-82. Trustee Associated Camps, 1972—, v.p., 1985—, Fedn. Jewish Philanthropies N.Y., 1958-75, life 1975-86; founding mem. council Overseers UJA Fedn., N.Y., 1986—; life rep. assembly Domestic Affairs Div. UJA Fedn. 1986—; trustee Assn. Jewish Sponsored Camps, 1964—, pres., 1964-67, 76-79, hon. pres., 1990—. Served to capt. AUS, 1942-46. Decorated Bronze Star. C.P.A., N.Y. State. Mem. N.Y. State Soc. C.P.A.s, Fairview Country Club, Golf and Racquet at Eastpointe Club, Zeta Beta Tau. Home: 1025 5th Ave New York NY 10028-0134 Office: 535 Fifth Ave New York NY 10017

LAMBERT, DEBORAH KETCHUM, public relations executive; b. Greenwich, Conn., Jan. 22, 1942; d. Alton Harrington and Robyna (Neilson) Ketchum; m. Harvey R. Lambert, Nov. 23, 1963 (div. 1985); children: Harvey Richard Jr., Eric Harrington. BS, Columbia U., 1965. Researcher, writer The Nowland Orgn., Greenwich, Conn., 1964-67; model Country Fashions, Greenwich, Conn., 1964-67; owner, mgr. Paper Collectables, McLean, Va., 1973—; freelance writer to various newspapers and mags., 1977-82; press sec. Va. Del. Gwen Cody, Annandale, Va., 1981-82; assoc. editor Campus Report, Washington, 1985—; adminstrv. asst. Accuracy in Media, Inc., Washington, 1983-84, dir. pub. affairs, 1985—; bd. dirs. Accuracy in Academia, Washington; film script cons. The Seductive Illusion, 1988-89. Columnist: The Eye, The Washington Inquirer, 1984—, Squeaky Chalk, Campus Report, 1985—; contbr. articles to various mags. Co-founder, mem. Va. Rep. Forum, McLean, 1983—. Mem. Pub. Rels. Soc. Am., DAR., World Media Assn., Am. Platform Assn. Republican. Presbyterian. Home: 1945 Lorraine Ave Mc Lean VA 22101-5331 Office: Accuracy in Media Inc 1275 K St NW Washington DC 20005-4006

LAMBERT, EUGENE LOUIS, engineer, manufacturing executive; b. Providence, R.I., Jan. 26, 1948; s. Louis Eugene and Concetta (Russo) L.; m. Maureen McHugh, Feb. 1, 1969 (div. June 1979); children: Kenneth Patrick, Margaret Mary; m. Julia Coy Hadeka, Dec. 21, 1988. BS in Elec. Engring., U. R.I., 1969; MBA, N.H. Coll., 1981. Registered profl. engr., N.Y., N.H., Mass., Maine. Elec. engr. Kaiser Aluminum, Bristol, R.I., 1969-70; plant engr. Milliken & Co., Exeter, N.H., 1971-81; consulting engr. Jones & Beach, Engrs., Stratham, N.H., 1981-82; salesman Simplex Wire & Cable Co., Newington, N.H., 1982; sales engr. The Valve Co., Portsmouth, N.H., 1982-83; engring. mgr. TVC Systems, Portsmouth, 1983-90; mgr. instrument engring. Herzog-Hart Corp., Boston, 1990—; cons. Automation & Power Elec. Engrs., Exeter, N.H., 1982—; guest lectr., U. N.H., Durham, 1987, 88; faculty mem. work curriculum com. Boston Archtl. Ctr., 1991—. Capt. U.S. Army, 1970-71. Mem. IEEE, Am. Inst. Plant Engrs., Instrument Soc. Am. (sr. mem.), Internat. Dist. Heating & Cooling Assn. (chmn. Controls Com. 1988-89), Boston Computer Soc., Kiwanis, (bd. dirs. Exeter, N.H. 1981). Office: Herzog-Hart Corp 200 Berkeley St Boston MA 02116-5022

LAMBERT, JOHN BERNARD, mechanical construction contractor, restauranteur; b. Massena, N.Y., June 16, 1948; s. Bernard Francis and Mary Agnes (Conway) L.; m. Frances Anne Meisinger, Apr. 8, 1972; children: Matthew Rene, Jeffrey Paul, Sara Elizebeth. AS in Acctg., SUNY, Canton, 1972; BA Acctg. Fin. and Law, Clarkson U., 1975. Acct. Whalen, Davey & Looney, CPA's, Ogdensburg, N.Y., 1976-77; supr. Reynolds Metals Co., Massena, N.Y., 1979-90; ptnr. F&L Assocs., Massena, 1983—; pres., chief exec. officer Lambert Corp., Massena, 1985—; v.p., treas. MJS Properties, Inc., Massena, 1985—; mng. ptnr. East Massena Water Agy., Massena, 1987—; gen. mgr. U.S. ops. LaFramboise Group, Ltd., 1990—; chmn. supervisory com. Twin Rivers Fed. Credit Union, Massena, 1982-85. Trustee Massena Ctrl. Sch. Bd. Edn., 1982-85, 92—. Sgt. U.S. Army, 1968-71, Vietnam. Mem. Alpha Theta Gamma (bd. dirs. 1983—). Republican. Roman Catholic. Office: Lambert Corp RR 2 Massena NY 13662-9802

LAMBERTH, ROYCE C., district judge; b. 1943. BA, U. Tex., 1965, LLB, 1967. With civil dir. U.S. Atty's. Office, Washington, 1974-77, asst. chief, 1977-78; chief U.S. Atty's. Office, 1978-87; judge U.S. Dist. Ct. (D.C. dist.), Washington, 1987—. Capt. (j.a.g.) U.S. Army, 1967-74. Mem. ABA (chmn. armed svcs. and vets. affairs com. sect. adminstrv. law 1983-83), Fed. Bar Assn. (chmn. fed. litigation sect. 1986—), Jud. Conf. D.C. Cir. (arangements com. 1985, D.C. Bar, D.C. Bar Assn. (Cert. Appreciatio 1977), State Bar Tex. Office: US Dist Ct US Courthouse 3rd & Constitution Ave NW Washington DC 20001*

LAMENDOLA, MICHAEL JOHN, manufacturing executive; b. Corry, Pa., Apr. 25, 1953; s. Tom Joseph and Autumn Marie (McCaslin) L.; m. Karol Elizabeth Kelsey, Aug. 18, 1973; children: Valerie Lynn, Gretchen Michelle, Amy Elizabeth. BS, Penn State U., 1975. Mktg. specialist Barnes Group,

Inc., Corry, 1976-80; product mgr., corp. mgr. mkt. R&D, gen. mgr. Snaptite, Inc., Erie, Pa., 1980-88; mktg. mgr., v.p. Alliance Plastics div. Bunzl Plastics, Inc., Erie, 1988—; officer Multiquip, Ltd., Oakdale, Ont., Can., 1990—; speaker Penn State U., Internat. Trade Conf., Erie, 1990, Nat. Assn. Accts., Erie, 1990. Recipient Distinctive Merit award Erie Ad Club, 1989, award of excellence Internat. Assn. Bus. Communicators, Erie, 1990. Recipient Distinctive Merit award Erie Ad Club, 1989, Project award of excellence Internat. Assn. Bus. Communicators, Erie, 1990. Mem. Am. Mktg. Assn., Penn State Alumni Assn., Mikes of Am. Republican. Roman Catholic. Home: 3925 Lewis Ave Apt 7 Erie PA 16504-2270 Office: Alliance Plastics div Bunzl Plastics Inc 3123 Station Rd Erie PA 16510-6599

LAMI, CHARLES NICHOLAS, forester; b. Paterson, N.J., May 28, 1954; s. Charles Benjamin and Katherien Louise (Vander Voort) L. BS in Forest Mgmt., Utah State U., 1976. Dist. forester, firewarden Utah Forestry and Fire Control, Salt Lake City, 1976-77; Peace Corps vol., asst. regional forester Jamaica Ministry of Agr. Forest Dept., 1978-80; project dir. Bent Nail Labs., Inc., Trenton, N.J., 1980; forester N.J. Bur. Forest Mgmt., New Lisbon, 1981-82; forest firewarden N.J. Bur. Forest Fire Mgmt., Franklin, 1982-91; vol., natrual lands forester Peace Corps, West Africa, 1991—. Treas. Swartswood (N.J.) Vol. Fire Dept., 1984-91; fire policeman Sussex County Fire Police Assn., N.J., 1984-89. Recipient Beyond War award, Beyond War Assn., Princeton, N.J., 1987. Home: 295 N 12th Pl Haledon NJ 07508-2216

LAMKIN, SELMA HOFFMAN, accounting executive, consultant; b. Boston, Mar. 29, 1925; d. Irving and Julia (Levine) Hoffman; children: Barry D., Deborah Rund, Leonard. Diploma; PhD in Econs., Pacific Western U., 1987. Pres. Acctg. Microsystems, Canton, Mass., 1978-90, Nikmal Fin. Svcs., Hyde Park, Mass., 1980—. Author various bus. manuals. Bd. dirs. NSC, 1981—, U.S. Congl. Adv. Com., 1982—, Mass. Human Svcs., 1986, Health for All; treas. Jo-Col Scholarship, 1987-89; founder Roslindale (Mass.) Health Ctr., 1980. Mem. Bus. and Profl. Women (treas. Boston 1987-89). Office: 23 Victoria Heights Rd Hyde Park MA 02136-3257

LAMM, CAROLYN BETH, lawyer; b. Buffalo, Aug. 22, 1948; d. Daniel John and Helen Barbara (Tatakis) L.; m. Peter Edward Halle, Aug. 12, 1972; children: Alexander P., Daniel E. BS, SUNY Coll. at Buffalo, 1970; JD, U. Miami (Fla.), 1973. Bar: Fla., 1973, D.C., 1976, N.Y. 1983. Trial atty. frauds sect. civil div. U.S. Dept. Justice, Washington, 1973-78, asst. chief comml. litigation sect. civil div., 1978, asst. dir., 1978-80; assoc. White & Case, Washington, 1980-84, ptnr., 1984—; mem. Sec. State's Adv. Com. Pvt. Internat. law, 1988-91. Mem. bd. editors Can./U.S. Rev. Bus. Law; mem. editorial adv. bd. Inside Litigation; contbr. articles to legal publs. Fellow Am. Bar Found.; mem. ABA (chmn. young lawyers div., rules and calendar com., chmn. assembly resolution com., sec. 1984-86, chmn. internat. litigation com. coun. 1991—, sect. litigation, ho. dels. nominating com. 1982—, del. Union Internat. Des Avocats), Am. Arbitration Assn. (arbitrator, com. on fed. arbitration act), Fed. Bar Assn. (chmn. sect. on antitrust and trade regulation), Bar Assn. D.C. (bd. dirs., sec.), D.C. Bar (bd. govs., steering com. litigation sect.), Am. Law Inst., Women's Bar Assn. D.C., Am. Soc. Internat. Law, Internat. Bar Assn. (bus. law sect., internat. litigation com.), Am. Turkish Friendship Coun. (bd. dirs., chair comml. com.), Washington Fgn. Law Soc., Am. Indonesian C. of C. (bd. dirs.), Nat. Women's Forum, City Tavern Club, Columbia Country Club. Democrat. Home: 2801 Chesterfield Pl NW Washington DC 20008-1015 Office: White & Case 1747 Pennsylvania Ave NW Washington DC 20006-4692

LAMMERS, LENNIS LARRY, nuclear utility executive; b. Hardin, Mont., July 16, 1937; s. George Joseph and Mayma Rose (Bolten) L.; m. Bea Marilyn Jones, Nov. 25, 1961; children: Laura Bea, Lennis Steven. BSEE, U.S. Naval Acad., 1960; MS in Ocean Engring., U.S. Naval Postgrad. Sch., 1971; postgrad., Duke U., 1982. Commd. ensign USN, 1960, advanced through grades to capt., 1981, various submarine assignments, 1960-68; ship supt. and docking office Mare Island Naval Shipyard, Vallejo, Calif., 1971-76; repair officer USS L.Y. Spear (AS 36), 1976-78; plan and estimate supt. Charleston Naval Shipyard, Charleston, S.C., 1978-81; Trident ILS officer integrated logistics systems Naval Sea Systems Command, Washington, 1981-82; planning officer Mare Island Naval Shipyard, Vallejo, 1983-84; commanding officer Portsmouth Naval Shipyard, Portsmouth, N.H., 1984-87; dir. plant material and maintenance Oyster Creek NGS, GPU-Nuclear, Forked River, N.J., 1987—; guest lectr., sr. mgr. tng. course Naval Sea Systems Command, Washington, 1984-87, Engring. Duty Officer Sch., Vallejo, 1983-87; host and sponsor Navy League, Portsmouth, 1984-87; founder, lifetime mem. Ports Navy Shipyard Hist. Found., 1985—; founder Shipyard Employees Assn., Portsmouth, 1986. Pres., Navy Relief Soc., Portsmouth, 1984-87; chmn. YMCA Bldg. Fund-Greater Portsmouth area, 1985-87; hon. mem. Police Soc., Portsmouth Naval Shipyard, 1987, Rotary Club, Portsmouth, 1984-87; scoutmaster Boy Scouts Am., Charleston, 1980-81. Decorated Vietnam Svc. medal, Meritorious Svc. medal. Mem. Soc. Indsl. Engring., Am. Soc. Naval Engrs., Am. Nuclear Soc., Naval Inst., U.S. Naval Submarine League, U.S. Naval Acad. Alumni Assn. Republican.

LAMONICA, THOMAS EDWARD, banker; b. Urbana, Ill., Mar. 18, 1945; s. Tom P. and Barbara (Fritz) LaM.; m. Karen Troutman, Aug. 24, 1968; 1 child, Mark Fritz. BS in Econs., Lehigh U., 1967, MS in Econs., 1969. Asst. gen. mgr. Chase Manhattan Bank, Bangkok, 1972-76; country mgr. Chase Manhattan Bank, Taipei, Taiwan, 1976-79; regional credit mgr. Chase Manhattan Bank, Hong Kong, 1979-82; mgr. trade fin. Bankers Trust Co., Hong Kong, 1982-85; sr. v.p. corp. banking Hibernia Bank, San Francisco, 1985-88; dir. Arab Australia Ltd., Sydney, 1988-90; mgr. bus. banking Chase Manhattan Bank, N.Y.C., 1990—; instr. Berkeley (Calif.) U., 1985-89, U. Calif., San Francisco, 1985-89; dir. Reflect Inc., San Rafeal, Calif. Editor: Fundamental of Trade Finance, 1986. Mem. The Banking Law Inst., Am. Mgmt. Assn., Am. C. of C. Home: 34 Benenson Dr Cos Cob CT 06807-1407 Office: Chase Manhattan Bank 30 Rockefeller Pla New York NY 10112

LAMONT, BARBARA, television executive; b. Paget, Bermuda, Nov. 9, 1939; came to U.S., 1949; d. Theophilus and Muriel (Aird) Alcántara; m. Ludwig Gelobter, Dec. 20, 1959; children: Michel, David, Elisabeth. BA in Internat. Law, Sarah Lawrence Coll., 1960; MPA, Harvard U., 1985. Reporter Sta. WINS, N.Y.C., 1971-73; reporter, anchor Sta. WNEW-TV, N.Y.C., 1973-76; writer, reporter CBS News, N.Y.C., 1976-82; dir. ops. Nigerian TV Authority, Lagos, Nigeria, 1982-84; writer ABC News, N.Y.C., 1985-86; pres., CEO New Orleans Teleport, 1987—; adj. assoc. prof. journalism Columbia U., N.Y.C., 1980-82, 82-86. Author: City People, 1976; mem. editorial bd. Amsterdam News, N.Y.C., 1986—; contbr. articles to the N.Y. Times. Dist. leader N.Y. County Dem. Com., N.Y.C., 1969-72; mem. Coun. Elected Black Dems., N.Y.C., 1969-72; bd. dirs. Planned Parenthood N.Y.C., 1971; mem. Nat. Women's Polit. Caucus, Washington, 1972; mem. exec. coun. Kennedy Sch. Alumnae Assn., Cambridge, Mass., 1985—; mem. parents com. Williams Coll., Williamstown, Mass., 1986—, fiscal reform com. Urban League; mem. adv. bd. New Orleans Mus. of Art. Recipient AP award, 1973, Ret. Detectives award N.Y.C. Detectives Assn., 1975. Mem. Nat. Assn. Broadcasters, New Orleans Ctr. for the Creative Arts, Greater New Orleans Exec. Assn. (bd. dirs.), Friends of New Orleans Ctr. for Creative Arts. Republican. Club: Harvard. Office: WCCL-TV 620 Desire St New Orleans LA 70117-6266

LAMONT, BILLY, television executive; b. West Islip, N.Y., July 19, 1962; s. William Porter and Carmel Anne (Amoreno) L. AD, SUNY, Farmingdale, 1982; BFA, N.Y. Tech., 1984. Reporter Beacon Newspaper, Babylon, N.Y., 1981-83; transmission operator Telicare, Uniondale, N.Y., 1984; tech. dir. MTV Networks Inc., Smithtown, N.Y., 1984—. Author: (poems) Eulogy: Flowers for the Living, 1990, Gallery of Light, 1992; performer Joe Franklin Show, 1991; singer, writer (music video) A Game of Chess With Love, 1988; performer (nat. radio show) Religion and Rock, 1988. Home: 119 Dickinson Ave East Northport NY 11731-1018

LA MONTE, ANGELA MAE, painter; b. New Britain, Conn., May 19, 1944; d. James Michael and Angeline (D'Agata) La M. MFA, CCNY, 1977; MS, Bank St. Coll., 1982. Instr. of painting and drawing Malcolm-King Coll., N.Y.C., 1979-89, chair dept. of arts, 1984-89; lectr. in field. Exhibited in group shows at Multi-Media Arts Gallery, N.Y.C., 1991, 92, Boniface Gallery of Cathedral of St. John the Divine, N.Y.C., 1986, Atlantic Gallery, N.Y.C., 1990, Castillo Gallery, N.Y.C., 1987, Gallery M, N.Y.C., 1988, Gallery Art 54, N.Y.C., 1988, Adelphi U., Garden City, N.Y., 1977, Harlem State Office Bldg. Gallery, 1981, Malcolm-King Coll., N.Y.C., Art '84 Tobago, 1984; represented in pvt. collections. Louis Comfort Tiffany Found. scholar, 1968-69; recipient Louis La Beaume prize Nat. Acad. Fine Arts, 1969.

LAMORIELLO, FRANCINE CYNTHIA, international business consultant; b. Providence, Dec. 27, 1957; d. Frank Schiano Lamoriello and Carmela DeLuise. Cert. Soviet Studies, U. Fribourg, Switzerland, 1977-78; BA, Georgetown U., 1979; postgrad., John Hopkins Bologna Ctr.., Italy, 1980-81; MA, John Hopkins SAIS, Washington, 1982. Internat. economist U.S. Dept of Commerce, Washington, 1982-89; internat. practice mgr., than sr. mgr. KPMG Peat Marwick, Washington, 1989-91, 91—. Office: KPMG Peat Marwick 2001 M St NW Washington DC 20036

LAMPE, DAVID ALAN, business owner; b. Grand Haven, Mich., Sept. 10, 1960; s. Jerome K. and Rosemarie S. (Goetz) L. BM, Berklee Coll., 1982. V.p. Marsh Labs., Pitts., 1982-88, pres., 1988—; bd. dirs. Caress Inc., Grand Haven, Mich., 1989—. Mem. Am. Chem. Soc. Republican. Office: Marsh Labs 2437 Waverly St Pittsburgh PA 15218-2626

LAMPE, DAVID ELWOOD, educator; b. Storm Lake, Iowa, Jan. 18, 1941; s. Elwood Carl and Verna Marcella (Peterson) L.; m. Ruth Elaine Eickstaedt, Feb. 1, 1963; children: Jeffrey, Paul. BA cum laude, Buena Vista Coll., 1962; MA, U. Nebr., 1964, PhD, 1969. Instr. Bemidji (Minn.) State Coll., 1964-65, Buena Vista Coll., Storm Lake, Iowa, 1965-66, U. Nebr., Lincoln, 1966-69; asst. prof. State Univ. Coll., Buffalo, N.Y., 1969-73, assoc. prof., 1973-76, prof., 1976—; founder, dir. Western N.Y. Medievalists, Buffalo, 1974—, Poets and Writers State U. Coll. at Buffalo, 1978—, bd. dirs. faculty-student assn., 1984—; bd. dirs. White Pine Press, Fredonia, N.Y., 1985—. Editor: The Legend of Being Irish, 1989, The 15th Century, 1989, Five Irish Poets, 1990, Born in Brooklyn, 1991. Mem. Parkside Community Assn. Summer rsch. grant SUNY, 1970, NEH, Duke U., 1978. Mem. Medieval Acad. Am., Am. Conf. on Irish Studies. Democrat. Lutheran. Home: 73 Crescent Ave Buffalo NY 14214 Office: English Dept/SUCB 1300 Elmwood Ave Buffalo NY 14222

LAMPHIER, BLAISE MICHAEL, city manager assistant, consultant; b. Meriden, Conn., Jan. 29, 1963; s. Frank Alfred Jr. and Anne Mary (DeMaria) L. BA, Wesleyan U., 1986; MBA, Coll. of William and Mary, 1987. Legis. intern Gen. Assembly, Office Speaker of the House, Hartford, Conn., 1983-84; state pub. rels. officer Ams. for Hart, Storrs, Conn., 1984; opers. mgr. Sta. WMMW-AM, Meriden, 1987-88; asst. to city mgr./ombudsman City of Meriden, 1988-92, asst. to city mgr./devel. asst., 1992—; mcpl. rep. Nat. League of Cities Conf., Boston, 1988, Atlanta, 1989, Houston, 1990; liaison to Meriden Redevel. Agy., Office of City Mgr., 1988; mem. Checknote rock band. Author: (screenplay) Yearning to Breathe Free, 1991; released album Daze & Knights, 1992 with Checkmate. Mem. Dem. Town Com., Meriden, 1982-84, Downtown Revitalization Adv. Com., Meriden, 1989-91. Harry S. Truman scholar U.S. Senate/Truman Found., 1983; Blaise Lamphier Day proclaimed By City of Meriden, 1983. Mem. Internat. City Mgrs. Assn. (affiliate mem.), Holy Family Retreat League (pres. Meriden chpt. 1988—), Masons, Kiwanis (bd. mem. 1990—). Roman Catholic. Home: 243 Hamilton St Meriden CT 06450 Office: City Hall 142 E Main St Rm 218 Meriden CT 06450

LAMPMAN, GEORGE JAMES, insurance executive; b. Kingston, Pa., Mar. 16, 1945; s. George James and Alberta (Fey) L.; m. Andrea Loretta Aceituno, Oct. 1, 1966; children: George, Paul, Aileen. BS in acctg., King's Coll., 1966. Ins. adjuster Royal Ins. Co., Wilkes Barre, Pa., 1967-71; claim mgr. Royal Ins. Co., Erie, Pa., 1971-74; br. mgr. Nickerson & Co., Meadville, Pa., 1974-77, Gay & Taylor, Co., Meadville, Pa., 1977-78; regional mgr. Gay & Taylor, Co., Erie, Pa., 1979-80; pres. Lampman Claim Svc., Edinboro, Pa., 1980—. Pres. Newman Apostolate Parish Coun., Edinboro, 1983. With U.S. Army, 1966-70. Mem. Pa. Assn. Ind. Ins. Adjusters, Pa. Claim Assn. (editor svc. directory, pres. 1989-90), Lake Erie Claim Assn. Office: Lampman Claim Svc Inc PO Box 828 Edinboro PA 16412-0828

LAMPOS, JAMES, musician; b. Norwich, Conn., July 10, 1962; s. Theofanis and Christina (Karambovitous) L. BA, Brandeis U., 1984; MA, New Sch. Social Rsch., 1986. Dir. devel. Community Access, Inc., N.Y.C., 1984-87; freelance musician, alternative rock guitarist N.Y.C., 1987—; exec. producer Bklyn. Beat Records, 1991—. Composer musical recording One World Now, 1991. Mem. Phi Beta Kappa, Pi Alpha Alpha. Home: 276 19th St Brooklyn NY 11215

LAMSTER, IRA BARRY, academic administrator; b. N.Y.C., Mar. 6, 1950; s. Nathan and Mollie (Garber) L.; m. Gail Maxine Marcovitz, Aug. 28, 1971; children: Rachel Amy, Stephanie Anne. BA, CUNY, 1971; SM, U. Chgo., 1972; DDS, SUNY, Stony Brook, 1977; M in Med Sci., cert. in periodontology, Harvard U., 1980. Assoc. prof., dir. rsch. ctr. Coll. Dental Medicine Fairleigh Dickinson U., Hackensack, N.J., 1980-88; dir. div. periodontics Sch. Dental and Oral Surgery Columbia U., N.Y.C., 1988—; cons. VA, various oral health care companies. Inventor in field; contbr. chpts. to books and articles to profl. jours. Bd. trustees Temple Beth Rishon, Wyckoff, N.J., 1991. Recipient Young Investigator Rsch. award PHS 1982-85, Individual Rsch. award 1985-89, prin. Investigator Program Project 1991—; fellow Am. Coll. Dentists 1990. Mem. AAAS, ADA, Am. Acad. Periodontology (editorial bd.), Am. Assn. Dental Rsch., Am. Acad. Oral Medicine, N.Y. Acad. Scis., Northeastern Soc. Periodontists (contbg. editor). Office: Columbia U Sch Dental and Oral Surgery 630 W 168th St New York NY 10032-3702

LA NATRA, JODI ANN, music educator; b. Bklyn., Aug. 30, 1943; d. Claude and Rose (Cipolla) Pellegrino; m. George Salvatore La Natra, Dec. 10, 1966; children: Danielle, Nicole. BA, Bklyn. Coll., 1966; postgrad., Kean Coll., 1991—. Primary tchr. N.Y.C. Bd. Edn., Bklyn., 1966-72; pvt. practice music instr. Millburn, N.J., 1973—; early childhood, music literacy tchr. Music Preludes, Inc., Millburn, 1981-89; early childhood, music literacy dir. Musically Yours, Inc., Millburn, 1989—. Co-author: (music/early childhood literacy curriculum) Music Preludes, 1981. Recipient Comprehensive Musicianship cert. Internat. Piano Teaching Found. Mem. Music Educators Assn., Piano Tchrs. Soc. N.J. (exec. bd. mem. 1983—, judge of music evaluations 1984-86, high honor tchr. award 1982, 83, 84, 86). Roman Catholic. Office: Musically Yours Inc 875 Ridgewood Rd Millburn NJ 07041-1412

LANCASTER, ALDEN, educational consultant; b. Balt., Feb. 25, 1956; d. Henry Carrington and Martha (Roe) L. BA magna cum laude, Duke U., 1977; MA, George Washington U., 1979. Program designer, coord. Duke U., Durham, N.C., 1977-79; mgr. profl. devel. programs Nat. Assn. Coll. and Univ. Bus. Officers, Washington, 1979-80; assoc. dir. refugee relief program Ch. of the Saviour, Bangkok, Thailand, 1980-81; nat. project dir. Bread for World, Washington, 1982-83; edn. dir., exec. dir. Ptnrs. for Global Justice, Washington, 1983-85; dir. adult edn. programs, tchr. Spanish Ednl. Devel. Ctr., Washington, 1983-86; exec. dir., cons. Samaritan Ministry Greater Washington, 1985-87; career counselor, tng. cons. Rockport Inst., Washington, 1985—; dir. nat. literacy tng., ednl. cons. Assn. for Community Based Edn., Washington, 1987—; ednl. cons. George Washington U., Washington, 1989—; ednl. cons. Pub./Pvt. Ventures, Phila., Savannah, Ga., Ft. Lauderdale, Fla., 1990—; ednl. cons., dir. nat. literacy projects Wider Opportunities for Women, Washington, 1991—. Author: An Introduction to Intergenerational Literacy, 1992; co-author: (with Thomas g, Sticht) Functional Context Education: A Primer for Program Providers, 1992; editor, primary author: Literacy for Empowerment: A Resource Handbook for Community Based Educators, 1989. Home and Office: 1537 Monroe St NW Washington DC 20010-3140

LANCASTER, KELVIN JOHN, economics educator; b. Sydney, Australia, Dec. 10, 1924; s. John Kelvin and Margaret Louise (Gray) L.; m. Deborah Grunfeld, June 10, 1963; children—Clifton John, Gilead. B.Sc., Sydney U., 1948, B.A., 1949, M.A., 1953; B.Sc. in Economics, London U., 1953, Ph.D. (Leon fellow), 1958. Asst. lectr., lectr. London Sch. Economics, 1954-59; reader economics U. London, 1959-62; prof. polit. economy Johns Hopkins U., 1962-66; prof. econs., 1966-78, John Bates Clark prof. econs., 1978—; John Bates Clark prof. econs. Columbia U., N.Y.C.; Ford faculty fellow, 1968-69, chmn. dept. econs., 1970-73, 89-90, Wesley Clair Mitchell research prof., 1973-74; vis. prof. U. Birmingham, Brown U., 1961-62, CUNY, 1965-66, NYU, Australian Nat. U., 1969-77, Ottawa U., 1972; fellow Inst. Advanced Studies Hebrew U., Jerusalem, 1976-77; dir. Nat. Bur. Econ. Rsch., 1971-73; trustee BT Investment Funds, 1986—. Author: Mathematical Economics, 1968, Introduction to Modern Microeconomics, 1969, Consumer Demand: A New Approach, 1971, Modern Economics: Principles and Policy, 1973, Variety, Equity and Efficiency, 1979, Modern Consumer Theory, 1991; contbr. articles in economics to profl. jours. Served with Royal Australian Air Force, 1943-45. Fellow Econometric Soc., Am. Acad. Arts and Scis.; mem. Am. Economic Assn., N.Y. State Economic Assn. (pres. 1974-75), AAAS, AAUP. Home: 35 Claremont Ave New York NY 10027-6823 also: 8 Island View Dr Sherman CT 06784 Office: Columbia U Dept Econs New York NY 10027

LANCASTER, OTIS EWING, engineering educator, consultant; b. Pleasant Hill, Mo., Jan. 28, 1909; s. Hayden Guard and Ida May (Seaton) L.; m. Hildreth Adele Herald, Dec. 5, 1942; children: Elaine Adele, Hayden Ewing, Dale Burkham. BS, Central Mo. U., Warrenburg, 1929; MA, Mo. U., Columbia, 1934; PhD, Harvard U., Cambridge, 1937; aeronautical engr., Calif. Inst. of Tech., Pasadena, 1945. Engr. Tchr. High Schs., Oak Grove, Independence, Mo., 1929-33; instr. Harvard U., Cambridge, Mass., 1936-37; asst. prof. U. Md., College Park, Md., 1939-42; rsch. div. Bur. Aeronautics, Washington, 1945-54; statistician planning staff IRS, Washington, 1954-55; dir. econs. and stats. U.S. Post Office Dept., Washington, 1955-57; westinghouse prof. for engring. edn. Pa. State U., University Park, 1957-75; assoc. dean Coll. Engring. Pa. State U., University Park, Pa., 1967-74; chief math. and stats. Interstate Commerce Commn., Washington, 1976-80; cons. NASA, Washington, 1965-69, FAA, ICC. Co-author: Gas Turbine for Aircraft, 1955; author: Effective Teachng and Learning, 1974; editor: Jet Propulsion Engines, 1959. Served to capt. USN, from 1942. Recipient Meritorious Civil Svc. award U.S. Navy, 1952. Mem. AIAA, ASME, Am. Soc. for Engring. Edn. (pres. 1977-78, Disting. Svc. citation 1982). Home: 268 Ellen Ave State College PA 16801-6305

LANCASTER, RICHARD ANDREW, electrical engineer; b. Buffalo, Sept. 20, 1943; s. Richard Leon and Mary Clara (Farkas) L.; m. Susan Mary Mickel, Nov. 25, 1967 (div. 1980); children: Talley, Susanna. BEE, Cath. U., Washington, 1965. Project mgr. IIT Rsch. Inst., Annapolis, Md., 1973-82, ARINC Rsch. Corp., Annapolis, Md., 1982-85; sr. EMC engr. MILCOM Systems Corp., Annapolis, Md., 1985-90; sr. EMC engr., project mgr. CTO, Inc., Annapolis, Md., 1990—; dir. Arundel Trunked Partnership, Annapolis, Md., 1991—; mem. U.S. del. to Internat. Telecommunications Union, CCIR, Geneva, 1989. Contbr. articles to internat. profl. jours. Asst. scoutmaster Boy Scouts Am., Weisbaden, 1970, Arnold, Md., 1986. Capt. USAF, 1965-73. Decorated Purple Heart, Air Force Commendation medal, Bronze Star. Mem. Nat. Assn. Radio and TV Engrs., U.S. Naval Inst., Armed Forces Communications and Electronic Assn. Home: 420 Holly Dr Annapolis MD 21403-4011 Office: CTO Inc 170 Jennifer Rd Annapolis MD 21401-3064

LANCE, STEVEN, author. BA in English, Upsala Coll., 1976. Dir. mktg. Monmouth County Arts Coun.-Count Basie Theatre, Red Bank, N.J., 1990, The Two River Times, 1991; founder, exec. dir. Silent Running Soc., 1985—. Actor Star Trek: The Motion Picture, 1980, Stardust Memories, 1981. Home: PO Box 529 Howell NJ 07731-0529

LAND, ROLAND JOHN, insurance broker, executive; b. Jersey City, Apr. 11, 1936; s. August and Isabella (Antolovich) L.; m. Mary Woerner, Nov. 23, 1963; children: Elizabeth M., Ann M., John W. MA, NYU, 1963; BS, U.S. Merchant Marine Acad., 1957. Registered profl. engr., assoc. risk mgmt. 3d asst. engr. United Fruit Co., N.Y.C., 1960-61; engring. rep. The Employers Liability Assurance Corp. Ltd., N.Y.C., 1961-63; safety and fire protection engr. E.I. duPont de Nemours & Co., Inc., Wilmington, Del., 1963-66; safety engr. Monsanto Co., Springfield, Mass., 1966-68; sr. safety engr. Hoffmann-LaRoche, Inc., Nutley, N.J., 1968-76; safety mgr. Mobil Chem. Co., Short Hills, N.J., 1976-84; v.p. Jardine Ins. Brokers NY Inc., N.Y.C., 1985—; curriculum devel. cons. Jersey City State Coll., 1975-76; adv. com. indsl. tech. program Middlesex County Coll., Edison, N.J., 1975-77; adj. asst. prof. County Coll. Morris, Dover, N.J., 1975-76; adj. instr. Passaic County Community Coll., Paterson, N.J., 1976. Lt. USNR, 1957-60. Mem. Am. Soc. Safety Engrs. (v.p. N.J. chpt. 1974-75), Am. Indsl. Hygiene Assn., Safety Execs. N.Y. Inc., Nat. Fire Protection Assn., Nat. Safety Coun., Soc. Fire Protection Engrs. (affiliate), The Boiler & Machinery Assn., Inc. (assoc.). Republican. Presbyterian. Home: 4 Crestwood Dr Chatham NJ 07928-1721 Office: Jardine Ins Brokers NY Inc 1155 Ave Of The Americas New York NY 10036-2711

LANDAU, ARTHUR NORMAN, ophthalmologist; b. Bklyn., Mar. 11, 1948; s. Saul and Esther (Wlodinger) L.; m. Carron L. Klein, Feb. 24, 1980; children: Ross, Seth. BS, Rensselaer Polytech., 1968, MS, 1970; MD, Albert Einstein Coll., 1975. Diplomate Am. Bd. Ophthalmology. Pvt. practice N.Y.C., 1979—; attending surgeon Manhattan Eye Ear Throat Hosp., N.Y.C., 1979—. Mem. Internat. Soc. Refractive Keratoplasm, Am. Soc. Cataract and Refractive Surgeons, Am. Acad. Ophthalmology, Eta Kappa Nu, Tau Beta Pi. Office: 44 W 62d St New York NY 10023

LANDAU, IRWIN, magazine publishing company executive. BA, Bklyn. Coll., 1954; MS in Journalism, Columbia U., 1955. Reporter N.Y. Daily Mirror, 1951-55; asst. mng. editor Engring. News-Record, 1957-60; sr. editor Med. Econs., 1960-66; mng. editorr Consumer Reports, 1966-71, now editorial dir. Office: Consumer Reports 101 Truman Ave Yonkers NY 10703-1057*

LANDE, LAWRENCE MONTAGUE, writer, bibliophile; b. Ottawa, Ont., Can., Nov. 11, 1906; s. Nathan and Rachel (Freiman) L. m. Helen Vera Prentis, June 14, 1939 (dec.); children: Denise Lande Brown, Nelson Prentis; m. Helen Ackerman. BA, McGill U., 1928, LittD, 1967; diploma, U. Grenoble, France, 1928; LLB, U. Montreal, 1931. Bibliog. research in Canadiana; founder Lawrence Lande Found. for Canadian Hist. Research, McGill U. Composer works for piano; author poems Author: Psalms Intimate and Familiar, 1945; Towards the Quiet Mind, 1954; The Third Duke of Richmond, 1956; Old Lamps Aglow, 1957; Experience, 1963; Lande Bibliography of Canadiana, 1965, Supplement, 1971; Adventures in Collecting Books, 1975; Canadian Historical Documents and Manuscripts, 7 vols., 1977-83; The Rise and Fall of John Law 1716-1720, 1982, The Political Economy of New France, 1983; The Founder of Our Monetary System; John Law, 1984; The Beginning of Exploration, Trade and Paper Money, 1985; John Law-The Influence of his System on the American and French Revolutions and its Lasting Effect on World Economics, 1986, John Law-The Creditability of Land and the Development of Paper Money and Trade in North America, 1987, John Law-Early Trade Rivalries Among Nations and the Beginnings of Banking in North America, 1988, John Law The Evolution of His System, 1989, The Development of The Voyageur Contract, 1989, A Second Short Title Catalogue of The Lawrence M Lande Collection, 1989, John Law-His System and Its Influence on Trade and Industry in North America-An Eighth Bibliography, 1990, Bound Together with the French Navy, Events During the Naval Wars Since 1740-An Unpublished Manuscript by Louis-Antoine Bougainville Translated into English from the Original French, 1990, A Third Short Title Catalogue of the Lawrence M. Lande Collection of Manuscripts, Numismatics, Arrets, Books, Maps and Other Printed Material Reflecting the Influence of John Law and Paper Money on the Early Economic Development of N. Am., 1991, others, also recs. Past pres. Montreal Friends of Hebrew U. Gov. Montreal Children's Hosp. Decorated officer Order of Can., knight Order of Malta. Recipient Centennial medal, 1968, Sir Thomas More medal Gleeson Library Assocs., 1988. Fellow Intercontinental Biog. Assn. (life); mem. Canadian Writer's Found. (dir.), P.E.N. (past pres. Can.), Royal Soc. Arts (London) (hon. corr. Que.), Montefiore Club, Palm Beach Country Club, Beaver Club, Grolier Club, NYU Club. Jewish. Home: 4870 Cedar Crescent, Montreal, PQ Canada H3W 2H9 Office: McGill U, McLennan Libr Lande Rm, Montreal, PQ Canada H3A 2T5 also: 147 Dunbar Rd Palm Beach FL 33480

LANDE, RUTH HARRIET, photographer, language educator; b. N.Y.C., May 17, 1929; d. Julius Dewey and Josie (Rosenberger) Schlesenger; m. Bernard Lande, Dec. 21, 1951 (div. 1983); 1 child, Stephen. BS, Adelphi U., 1964; MS, Hofstra U., 1988. Cert. tchr., N.Y. Tchr. E. N.Y. Vocat. High Sch., Bklyn., 1968-70; freelance photographer Muttontown and Great Neck, N.Y., 1979—; adj. prof. English as 2d lang. C.W. Post Coll., Brookville, N.Y., 1989—; tchr. photography Bethpage Adult Edn., 1991—. Recipient Pell grant, Hofstra U., 1986. Mem. Nassau Assn. Continuing Community Edn., Syosset Camera Club (sec. 1987-89), Nassau Counselors Assn., Rockport Art Assn., Great Neck Camera Club. Home: Apt 209 1 Ipswich Ave Great Neck NY 11021

LANDEO, LUIS AMADOR, surgeon; b. Lima, Peru, Apr. 30, 1933; came to U.S., 1960; s. Sergio Landeo and Atanilda Hinojosa; m. Eva Luz Perez, July 17, 1962; children: Luis, Eva. MD, U. Buenos Aires, 1959. Diplomate Am. Bd. Surgery. Intern Aguadila Dist. Hosp., P.R., 1960-61; resident in gen. surgery Fasardo Dist. Hosp., P.R., 1962-65; preceptoship in gen. surgery Alexandria La. VA Hosp., 1965-67; pvt. practice N.Y.C., 1967—; pres. Hispanish Am. Med. Soc. N.Y., 1989. Democrat. Home: 40 Lake Shore Dr Eastchester NY 10709 Office: 685 West End Ave New York NY 10025

LANDESBERG, JOSEPH M., chemistry educator; b. N.Y.C., Apr. 21, 1939; s. Leon and Ethel (Chazin) L.; m. Lucy Gold, June 7, 1964; children—Leonard John, Jeffrey Eric. B.S., Rutgers U., 1960; M.A., Harvard U., 1962, Ph.D., 1965. Research assoc. Columbia U., N.Y.C., 1964-66; prof. chemistry Adelphi U., Garden City, N.Y., 1966—. Contbr. articles to profl. jours. Scoutmaster Boy Scouts Am., 1979—; coach, v.p. Rockville Ctr. Soccer Club, 1980—. Mem. Am. Chem. Soc., Sigma Xi., Nat. Assn. Watch and Clock Collectors. Avocations: Antiques; camping; hiking. Office: Dept Chemistry Adelphi U Garden City NY 11530

LANDESMAN, LINDA YOUNG, health services researcher, educator; b. Flint, Mich., Mar. 20, 1949; d. Samuel Morrie and Bertha (Sills) Young; m. Paul Landesman, May 29, 1983; 1 child, Andrew David. BA, U. Mich., 1971, MSW, 1974; DPH, Columbia U., 1990. Lic. clin. social worker, Calif.; cert. social worker. Clin. social worker L.A. County Health Svcs., Long Beach, Calif., 1974-76, Children's Hosp., L.A., 1976-79; mem. faculty Perinatal Outreach, Orange, Calif., 1980-83; clin. social worker U. Calif.-Irvine, Orange, Calif., 1979-84; cons. Newhall & Landesman, Palos Verde, Calif., 1982—; asst. prof. Albert Einstein Coll. Medicine, Bronx, N.Y., 1991—; mem. adj. faculty Fed. Emergency Mgmt. Agy., Emmitsburg, Md., 1982-83; advisor in health Assemblywoman Cecile Singer, 84th Assembly Dist., White Plains, N.Y., 1991—; mem. environ. subcom. N.Y. Acad. Medicine, N.Y.C., 1990—; reviewer Mosby Books, 1988-90, AMA Commn. on EMS, Chgo., 1988-90, NSF, Washington, 1988-90. Contbr. articles to profl. jours., chpts. to books. Pres. dist. 6 B'nai B'rith Youth Orgn., Flint, Mich., 1966-67. Recipient Doctoral Dissertation award The Health Svcs. Improvement Fund, Inc. Empire Blue Cross and Blue Shield, N.Y.C., 1990. Mem. APHA, ASTM, LWV (dir. 1990-92), NASW (cert.). Office: Albert Einstein Coll Medicine Dept Pediatrics Pelham Pkwy & Eastchester Rd Bronx NY 10461

LANDIN, THOMAS MILTON, lawyer, pharmaceutical company executive; b. Bradford, Pa., July 21, 1937; s. Charles Milton and Agnes Eleanor (Fredrickson) L.; m. Johanna Sue Johnson, July 2, 1966; children: Jane, Ahna, Amanda, Joya. BS in Biology, Grove City Coll., 1959; JD, U. Denver, 1967. Bar: Colo. 1967, D.C. 1976. Mktg. rep. Atlantic Refining Co., Pitts. and Phila., 1963-64; asst. to v.p. McNeil Labs., Johnson & Johnson, Ft. Washington, Pa., 1967-72; dir. pub. affairs SmithKline Corp., Phila., 1972-76, dir. govt. affairs, 1977-80; Presdl. interchange exec. Dept. Def., Washington, 1976-77; v.p. corp. communications SmithKline Beckman Corp., Phila., 1980-86, v.p. govt. rels., 1986-90; v.p. govt. and pub. affairs SmithKline Beechman Corp., 1990—; bd. dirs. Mfrs. Assn. Del. Valley; trustee Caribbean/Latin Am. Action. Bd. dirs. YMCA Greater Phila., Citizens Crime Commn., Am. Music Theatre Festival. Comdr. USNR ret. Mem. ABA, D.C. Bar Assn., Pub. Affairs Coun. (bd. dirs. 1986—), Georgetown Club (Washington), Capitol Hill Club (Washington), Army and Navy Club (Washington), Union League of Phila., Vesper Club. Republican. Home: 510 Heather Circle Villanova PA 19085 Office: SmithKline Beecham One Franklin Pla Philadelphia PA 19101

LANDINO, RITA ANN, psychologist; b. New Haven, May 1, 1942; d. Michael and Rose (Di Meola) L.; 1 child, Michael Joseph. BS in English Edn., So. Conn. State U., 1964; MA in Liberal Studies, Wesleyan U., 1966; postgrad., Fairfield U., 1971; PhD in Ednl. Psychology, U. Conn., 1985. Cert. nat. counselor. English tchr. Hamden (Conn.) Pub. Schs., 1964-65; English instr. So. Conn. State U., New Haven, 1966-69, counselor, 1969-73, counselor, asst. prof., 1973-85, counselor, assoc. prof., 1985-90, counselor, prof., 1990—, adj. prof., 1982—; dir. Greater new Haven YWCA Bd., 1987-90; trainer, cons. in field. Contbr. articles to profl. jours.; patentee in field. Mem. Bd. of Fin., North Haven, 1989-93; trustee Meml. Libr. Bd., North Haven, 1987-89; mem. Dem. Town Com., North Haven, 1986—. Recipient Rsch. fellowship U. Conn. Rsch. Found., 1983. Mem. AAUP, APA, Am. Assn. for Counseling and Devel., Am. Coll. Personnel Assn., Conn. Coll. Personnel Assn. (pres. 1988-91), Nat. Assn. for Women in Edn., Conn. Assn. for Women in Edn. Office: So Conn State U 501 Crescent St New Haven CT 06515-1355

LANDIS, KEITH ALLEN, mortgage company executive; b. Chambersburg, Pa., Mar. 26, 1964; s. Richard Lee and Lois Jean (Kuhns) L.; m. Caroline Faith Bendshaw, Apr. 30, 1983; children: Jacqueline Elise, Mariah Carri. BS, Messiah Coll., Grantham, Pa., 1986. Account exec. Supreme Title Agy. Encore Mortgage, Voorhees, N.J., 1986-87; br. mgr. Am. Title Co. Inc., Lancaster, Pa., 1987-88; pres., owner Willow Abstract Inc., Willow Street, Pa., 1988—, Lancorp Mortgage Svcs., Lancaster, 1987—. Bd. dirs. Morning Star Ministries, Manila, 1990—; chmn. Lancorp Found., Lancaster, Pa., 1990—; fin. cons. Christ the King Community Ch., Silver Springs, Pa., 1989—, trustee, 1989—; bd. dirs. Spl. Olympics, Lancaster, 1989. Mem. Am. Mgmt. Assn., Mortgage Bankers Assn., Mortgage Brokers Assn., Lancaster County Bd. Realtors, Rotary, Jaycees (bd. dirs. Lancaster chpt. 1989). Home: 240 E Clay St Lancaster PA 17602-2082 Office: Lancorp Mortgage Svcs 255 Butler Ave Lancaster PA 17601-6308

LANDIS, PAMELA ANN YOUNGMAN, tribologist; b. Lancaster, Pa., Nov. 14, 1941; d. George Baldwin and Hazel Elizabeth (Ray) Youngman; m. Carrol Paul Landis, Aug. 21, 1971. BA in Chemistry, Millersville (Pa.) State U., 1973. Chief chemist Howmet Aluminum Corp., Lancaster, 1974-87; corp. inter plant tribologist, supr. chem. lab. Alumax Mill Products, Inc., Lancaster, 1987-89; sr. lubrication engr. Alumax, Inc., Hinsdale, Ill., 1989—; presenter papers in field. Patentee in field. Advisor Jr. Achievement of Lancaster County, 1979, exec. advisor, 1980-83; judge Lancaster Sci. and Engring Fair, Quarryville, Pa., 1983; vol. Easter Seal Soc., Lancaster County, 1983-85. Recipient Company of Yr. award Jr. Achievement of Lancaster County, 1983. Mem. Soc. Tribologists and Lubrication Engrs. (program com. 1985-91, sec. 1988, vice chmn. 1989, chmn. program com. 1990), Non Ferrous Metals Coun. (session chmn. 1980—, sec.-treas. exec. com. 1983-84, vice chmn. 1984-85, chmn. 1985-86, asst. indsl. coord. 1991—). Republican. Presbyterian. Home and Office: RR 4 Box 171 Salem Rd Pound Ridge NY 10576 Office: Alumax Inc 901 N Elm St Hinsdale IL 60521-3632

LANDIS, ROBERT KUMLER, III, investment banker, lawyer; b. Dayton, Ohio, June 20, 1953; s. Robert Kumler Landis Jr. and Rebecca (McCall) Baird; m. Robin Lee Taylor, June 2, 1979; children: Robert Kumler IV, Taylor McCall, Samuel Tufts. AB, Princeton (N.J.) U., 1975; JD, Harvard U., 1978. Bar: N.Y. 1978. Assoc. Simpson Thacher & Bartlett, N.Y.C., 1978-83; dir. Merrill Lynch & Co., N.Y.C., 1984—. Mem. Short Hills Club, Harvard Club. Republican. Episcopalian. Home: 43 Park Pl Short Hills NJ 07078-2840

LANDON, FRED BARRY, hospital official, lawyer; b. Bklyn., June 9, 1951; s. Edward Gordon and Anne (Goldsmith) Lipschitz; m. Susan Dorothy Villanella, Aug. 2, 1975; 1 child, Jonathan. BA magna cum laude, Bklyn. Coll., 1972; JD, U. S.C., 1975; MPA, NYU, 1976. Asst. adminstr. Bklyn. Jewish Hosp., 1977-78; dir. risk mgmt. Good Samaritan Hosp., West Islip, N.Y., 1978—. Maj. USAR, 1972—. Mem. Am. Hosp. Assn., Assn. for Hosp. Risk Mgmt. N.Y., Res. Officers Assn., Southward Ho Country Club. Republican. Jewish. Home: 325 Lakeview Ave W Brightwaters NY 11718-1904 Office: Good Samaritan Hosp 1000 Montauk Hwy West Islip NY 11795

LANDOWNE, ROBERT A., computer consultant; b. Bklyn., Feb. 24, 1931; s. Morris and Frances (Miller) L. BS in Chemistry, U. Mich., 1952; MA, Johns Hopkins U., 1953; PhD, Yale U., 1958. Asst. prof. medicine Yale U., New Haven, 1958-66; group leader Am. Cyanamid Co. Rsch. Labs., 1966-72; chief clin. chemist, dir. computer ops. St. Joseph Hosp., Stamford, Conn., 1972-82; cons. computer applications using databases (R-base) Westport, Conn., 1982—. Contbg. author books in field; contbr. articles to profl. jours. Mem. Bd. Tax Rev., Town of Westport, Conn., 1979-87. With U.S. Army, 1953-55, Korea. Recipient NIH Career Devel. award, 1965-66.

LANDRON, MICHEL JOHN, lawyer; b. Santurce, P.R., June 15, 1946; s. Francis Xavier and Francisca (Carretero) Healy; m. Carol McQuade, Apr. 22, 1989; children, Michael Francis, Ryan McQuade. BA, Lehman Coll., 1968, postgrad., 1969-73; JD, Fordham U., 1977. Bar: N.Y. 1978, U.S. Dist. Ct. (so. dist.) N.Y. 1978, U.S. Dist. Ct. (ea. dist.) N.Y. 1978. asst. atty. gen. Office of Atty. Gen., N.Y. State Dept. Law, N.Y.C., 1978-80; enforcement atty. N.Y. Stock Exch., N.Y.C., 1980-81; pvt. practice, Bklyn., 1981-82, 84—; mem. Leaf, Duell, Drogin P.C., N.Y.C., 1982-84; gen. counsel Rockcom, Inc., 1985-87, adminstr. law judge City of N.Y., 1987; of counsel Berger and Paul, N.Y.C., 1984-85; assoc. area counsel Digital Equipment Corp., 1988-89; adj. instr. N.Y. Law Sch., Ramapo Coll.; arbitrator U.S. Dist. Ct. (ea. dist.) N.Y.; guest lectr. Lehman Coll.; cons. in field; arbitrator Civil Ct. N.Y.C., No Fault Ins. Panel State of N.Y. Author: Armed Services, Personal Injury: Actions, Defenses and Damages, Conflicts of Law, Products Liability Guide. Mem. med. malpractice panel appellate div., 2d dept. Author: rev. Prologue to Nuremburg; arbitrator Am. Arbitration Assn. Mem. ABA (forum com. on entertainment and sports law), Bklyn. Bar Assn. (past chmn. patents trademark and copyrights com., past chmn. arbitration com.), N.Y. State Bar Assn. (com. to cooperate with law revision comm.), Assn. Arbitrators City of N.Y., Am. Judges Assn., Phi Alpha Delta (Disting. Svc. award 1977). Republican. Roman Catholic. Avocations: music, reading, sports. Office: 323 46th St Brooklyn NY 11220-1109

LANDRY, (JOSEPH) ALFRED RONALD, judge; b. Robichaud, N.B., Can., Apr. 21, 1936; s. Joseph Albert P. and Agnes (Thibodeau) L.; m. Alfreda Hazel Leger, July 4, 1964; children—Christian, Chantal. BA, St. Joseph U., 1957; B in Commerce, U. Ottawa, 1958; MA in Jurisprudence, Oxford U., 1963; DCL (hon.), St. Thomas U., Fredericton, N.B., 1973, U. Moncton, 1977. Created Queen's Counsel, 1978. Sr. ptnr. Landry & McIntyre, Moncton, N.B., 1964-85; chmn. bd. U. Moncton, 1971-76; chmn. N.B. Liquor Corp., Fredericton, 1976-79; dir., mem. exec. com. N.B. Telephone Co., St. John, 1973-85; pres. N.B. Bicentennial Commn., Fredericton, 1983-85. Pres. N.B. Progressive Conservative Assn., Fredericton, 1981-83. Rhodes scholar, 1960. Mem. Can. Barristers' Assn., N.B. Barristers' Soc., Moncton Barristers' Soc. (treas. 1966-68). Roman Catholic. Lodge: Rotary. Home: 85 Sackville St, Shediac, NB Canada

LANDRY, ESTHER FRANCES, health services executive; b. Swampscott, Mass., Aug. 13, 1935; d. George Murdock Landry and Esther Louise (Gott) Hopkins; m. James Joseph Fernald (div. 1981); children: Scott Edward, Esther Louise; m. David Elmer Howes (div. 1963); 1 child, David Ralph. BS, Fitchburg State U., 1957; student, U. Mass., 1990-91. Cert. RN. Pvt. practice Cape Cod, Mass., 1959-63; operating room nurse Cape Cod Hosp., Hyannis, Mass., 1963-64; dir. health svcs. Cape Cod Community Coll., W. Barnstable, Mass., 1967—, acting chair div. life fitness/wellness edn., 1988—; active Health Promotion Resource Ctr., Barnstable, 1986—; cons. health svc. devel. Mass. Bd. Regional Community Colls., 1969-76; pres. bd. dirs. Cape Cod Coun. Alcoholism and Drug Dependence, Hyannis, Mass., 1989—. Author: Jour. Am. Coll. Health Assn., 1975. Sec. Cape & Islands Area Bd. mental Health, 1978; active Substance Abuse Prevention Com., CC Baseball League, Cape Cod, 1988; chair com. svc. March of Dimes, S.E. Mass., 1988; smoking cessation instr. Am. Lung Assn., 1987—; safety svcs. com. sec. ARC, 1985. Recipient Governors Pride in Performance award Commonwealth of Mass., 1987. Mem. Am. Coll. Health Assn. (chair nurse directed health svcs. 1986-88), New England Coll. Health Assn., Am. Pub. Health Assn., Am. Nurses Assn. Home: 17 Hampshire Ave Hyannis MA 02601-2627 Office: Cape Cod Community Coll Rte 132 West Barnstable MA 02668

LANDRY, JEAN EDA, art educator, consultant; b. Worcester, Mass., Jan. 16, 1950; d. Herbert Richard and Eda Justine (Riopel) L.; m. Gerald Lee Bourassa, June 6, 1973 (div. Oct. 1987); children: Corey, Amy Lynn, Kimberly. BA, Plymouth (N.H.) State Coll., 1972; postgrad., Sch. of Worcester Art Mus., 1972; MAT in Fine Arts, Assumption Coll., 1983; postgrad., Phoebe Flory Watercolor Sch., 1984-85. Cert. art specialist grades kindergarten-12, N.H. Tchr. Worcester Alternative Sch., 1972-73, Craftsworkers Guild, Bedford, N.H., 1979-80; substitute tchr. Goffstown (N.H.) High Sch., 1980-82, Villa Augustina Acad., Goffstown, 1982-83; instr. Notre Dame Coll., Manchester, N.H., 1983—; art tchr., cons. Enrichment Program, Derry, N.H., 1985; cons. Guided Advanced Instruction in Exceptional Students, 1985; cons. N.H. Pub. Schs., 1984—; organizer, chairperson N.H. Youth Art Month, 1985-88; regional and state site coord. scholastic art awards Boston Globe, 1987-89. Organizer youth art exhibit Notre Dame Coll., 1983-88, NDC student and faculty art exhibit, 1983—; instr. Summer Art Program for Teens, 1985-86; mem. Villa Augustina Home Sch. Assn., Goffstown, 1987-91, Parents Club of Trinity High Sch., Manchester, 1991—; mem. adv. bd. Scholastic Art Awards, 1987-89, bd. dirs., 1990-91. Mem. Nat. Art Edn. Assn. (N.H. Art Educator of the Yr. 1989), N.H. Art Educators Assn. (bd. dirs., chairperson youth art month 1985-88), N.H. Art Assn. (juried), Phi Delta Kappa. Office: Notre Dame Coll 2321 Elm St Manchester NH 03104-2213

LANDY, MARCIA, English educator; b. Cleve., June 24, 1931; d. Isidore and Goldie (Baratz) Kanevsky; m. Alvin Landy, June 24, 1953 (div. 1971); children: Hilary Joyce, Anne Rebecca. BA, Ohio U., 1953; MA, U. Rochester, 1961, PhD, 1962. Asst. prof. English U. Rochester, N.Y., 1962-67; prof. U. Pitts., 1967—. Author: Fascism in Film, 1986, British Genres, 1991; editor: Imitations of Life, 1991; contbr. articles to profl. jours. Grantee Am. Coun. Learned Socs., 1987, Am. Philos. Soc., 1987. Mem. MLA, Am. Assn. Italian Studies, Soc. for Cinema Studies. Office: U Pitts 526 CL Dept English Pittsburgh PA 15217

LANDZBERG, JOEL SERGE, cardiologist; b. N.Y.C., Dec. 20, 1958; s. Sol and Marilyn Joy (Aboff) L.; m. Barbare Eugene Ross, May 1, 1983; children: Rebecca, Elizabeth. BA summa cum laude, Columbia Coll., 1979; MD, Columbia U., 1983. Resident medicine Vanderbilt U., Nashville, 1983-86, chief resident medicine, 1987-88; rsch. fellow cardiology U. Calif. San Francisco, Cardiovascular Rsch. Inst., 1986-87; cardiology fellow Brigham & Woman's Hosp., Boston, 1988-90; instr. medicine Harvard U., Boston, 1990-91; pvt. practice cardiology Westwood, N.J., 1991—. Fellow Am. Coll. Cardiology; mem. AMA, Am. Med. Athletic Assn., Phi Beta Kappa. Office: Westwood Cardiology 336 Westwood Ave Westwood NJ 07423

LANE, ADELAIDE IRENE, graphics application programmer, researcher; b. Bronx, N.Y., Sept. 27, 1939; d. Anton John and Constance Mary (Fogle) Pospisil; m. Robert Walton Lane, Sept. 26, 1964; children: Frank Anton, Miriam Helen, Robin Ann. BS in Edn. cum laude, SUNY, Oneonta, 1961; MS in Edn., Hofstra U., 1963; MS in Computer Sci., Rensselaer Poly. Inst., 1983. Cert. tchr., N.Y., Vt. Tchr. Island Trees Jr. High Sch., Levittown, N.Y., 1961-64; copy editor, typesetter Pennysaver & Press, Bennington, Vt., 1976-77; tchr. Mt. Anthony Jr./Sr. High Sch., Bennington, Vt., 1977-80; computer operator Rensselaer Poly. Inst., Troy, N.Y., 1981-82, graphics application programmer, 1982-87, sr. graphics application programmer, 1987-92, mgr. instrnl. computing support, 1992—; tchr. computer sci. Russell Sage Coll., Troy, N.Y., 1984-85; cons. Union Coll., Schenectady, N.Y., 1990. Editor: The Rock Ribs of Bennington Town, 1977; contbr. articles to profl. jours. Asst. coach Bennington (Vt.) Swim Team, 1972-75; troop leader Girl Scouts Am., Hoosick Falls, N.Y., 1973-79; tchr. Hoosick Falls Ice Skating Club, 1975-80. Interuniv. Consortium for Ednl. Computing fellow, 1984. Mem. Nat. Computer Graphics Assn., Ednl. Uses of Info. Tech./EDUCOM (Joe Wyatt Challenge selection com. 1990-91), NAFE. Republican. Roman Catholic. Office: Rensselaer Polytech Inst ECS-CII 3111 Troy NY 12180

LANE, BERNARD PAUL, medical educator; b. Bklyn., June 27, 1938; s. Jack Robert and Rose L. (Weiss) L.; m. Dorothy Ellen Spiegel, Aug. 2, 1962; children: Erika, Andrew, Matthew. AB, Brown U., 1959; MD, NYU, 1963. Asst. prof. Sch. of Medicine, NYU, N.Y.C., 1965-69, assoc. prof., 1969-71; assoc. prof. Sch. of Medicine, SUNY, Stony Brook, 1971-75, prof., 1975—. Author chpts. in books; contbr. articles to profl. jours. Active L.I. div. Am. Cancer Soc., 1977—. Maj. USAF, 1969-71. Decorated Air Force medal; NIH fellow NYU, 1964-65; NIH grantee SUNY, 1972-78. Fellow Am. Soc. Clin. Pathologists, Coll. of Am. Pathologists; mem. Am. Assn. Pathologists, Am. Soc. Cell Biology, Internat. Acad. Pathology, Suffolk Pathologists Soc. Office: SUNY-HSC Dept of Pathology Stony Brook NY 11794

LANE, ELIZABETH ANN, small business owner; b. N.Y.C., Oct. 29, 1959; d. Paul Gerard and Judith (Gray) Lane. Grad. high sch. Salesperson Waterbed City, Ft. Lauderdale, Fla., 1980, Winer Motors/WinSports, Stratford, Conn., 1981, Matress Discounters, Arlington, Va., 1982-83, Artisans in Mirror, Phoenix, 1983-84; mgr. Del. Discount Bedding, Wilmington, 1984-88; owner Mattress Queen, New Castle, Del., 1988—; real estate investor. Chmn. Ron Paul for Pres. Com., Wilmington, 1988. Mem. Am. Mensa. Libertarian. Home: 3600 16th St NW Washington DC 20010-1102 Office: Mattress Queen 132 Sunset Blvd Rte 13 and 273 New Castle DE 19720

LANE, ERNEST EDWARD, III, military officer; b. Albuquerque, Nov. 27, 1948; s. Ernest Edward and Eloise Kathryn (Basham) L.; m. Catherine Sue Garrison, Sept. 6, 1967; children: Susan Marie, Garrison Andrew. BS, Purdue Univ., 1970; postgrad., Aarhus (Denmark) Univ., 1975-77; MS, Fla. State U., Tallahassee, 1982. Platoon leader 82nd Airborne Div., Fort Bragg, N.C., 1971, 101st Airborne, Vietnam, 1971-72; aide-de-camp 82nd Airborne Div., Fort Bragg, N.C., 1972-74; co. commdr. 25th Inf. Div., Schofield Barracks, Hawaii, 1978-81; intelligence analyst Defense Intelligence Agy., Washington, 1983-84; politico-mil. planner Orgn. of Joint Chiefs of Staff, Washington, 1984-87; mil. observer UN Truce Supervision Orgn., Cairo, Egypt, 1987-88; country dir. Defense Security Assistance Agy., Washington, 1988-91; program mgr. Hercules Defense Electronics Systems, Clearwater, Fla., 1991—. Recipient: Bronze Star, Air Medal, Defense Meritorious Svc. Medal, Meritorious Svc. Medal. Episcopalian. Home: 2305 Oxford Ct Safety Harbor FL 34695-5622 Office: Hercules Def Electronics Systems Clearwater FL 34618

LANE, GARY STEPHEN, parks and recreation director; b. St. Louis, Oct. 4, 1941; s. William Thomas and Willa Freda (Beals) L.; m. Judith Ann Aepler, June 19, 1965; children: Gregory Jon, Lisa Lynn. BS in Health and Physical Edn., SUNY, 1965; MEd, U. Buffalo, 1972. Cert. tchr. N.Y.; cert. leisure profl. N.Y. Recreation leader Town of Tonawanda (N.Y.), 1965-67, recreation supr., 1967-78, asst. dir. recreation, 1978-91, dir. parks and recreation, 1991—. Mem., com. chmn. Chmns. Club. Tonawanda, 1986-92; com. mem., chmn. Bicentennial Com., Tonawanda, 1975-76; coach Tonawanda Baseball League, 1981-90. Capt. USAF, 1966-70. Mem. Nat. Recreation and Parks Assn., N.Y. State Recreation and Parks Soc. (com. mem. 1992, 93), Niagara Frontier Parks and Recreation Soc., VFW. Republican.

LANE, GILBERT MANUEL, educator; b. N.Y.C., Jan. 27, 1938; s. Herbert Daniel and Margaret Ann (Massenberg) L.; m. Norma Beane Lalor, Aug. 22, 1970; 1 child, Gilbert Manuel Jr. BA in Liberal Arts, CCNY, 1962; MA in Edn., CUNY, 1974. Tchr. Jr. High Sch. 117 Bd. Edn., N.Y.C., 1963-88; asst. dir. Key Sch. - Bd. Edn., N.Y.C., 1988—; pres. Lane & Lane Enterprise, N.Y.C., 1991—. Inventor utility cart, 1978, family game Family Ladder, 1987, geog. game Flagships, 1990. Pres. 880 Colgate Tenant Assn., Bronx, N.Y., 1973-75. Roman Catholic. Home and Office: 4017 Secor Ave Bronx NY 10466

LANE, JAMES WELDON, musician; b. Oakfield, Ga., Oct. 16, 1926; s. Charles and Rebecca (Allen) L.; m. Virginia, 1956 (div. Feb. 28, 1987); children: Toni Rebecca, Curtis, Andre, Andrea, Warner, Sherrie, Donna; m. Christine Royster, May 5, 1987. Cert. of Music, Acad. Theatre Arts, 1947-50. Sr. sales mgr. Merit Metalcraft Corp., Phila., 1950-56; pres. Spiro's News and Advt. Svc., Phila., 1958-62; A&R dir., arranger Master Sound and Dee Records, Phila., 1962-64; pres. Spiro's Music Svc., Inc., Phila., 1964—; pres. October Love Prodns., Inc., J. Weldon Lane Music Co., Inc.; music dir. Jazz at Home Club, Phila., 1962-70; piano and voice tchr. Granoff Sch. Music, Phila., 1965-70; piano tchr. Acad. Theatre Arts, Phila., 1950-52. Playwright, dir. (music drama play) King: A Man With So Much Love, 1990; composer music for King's speech I Have a Dream, 1990. Pres. 60th St. Businessman's Assn., Phila. 1972; census taker U.S. Dept. Commerce, Phila., 1970. Recipient Best Sch. Song Acad. Theatre Arts, 1949, Best Philly Song Phila. daily News, 1971, No. 1 Bicentennial Song "Happy, Happy Birthday America", 1976, 1st Pl. Winner Jazz Combo, 1980, Jazz Appreciation award L.G.'s Blue Note, 1985. Mem. ASCAP (composer mem., pub. mem. 1973—), Masons (sr. deacon 1980-81, sr. warden 1981-83, worshipful master 1983-84, meritorious cert. 1st masonic dist. 1984), Shriners (cert. appreciation 1979). Democrat. Baptist. Home: 6157 W Columbia Ave Philadelphia PA 19151-4504 Office: Spiro's Music Svc Inc 6056 Market St Philadelphia PA 19139-3023

LANE, KELLY FLEMMING, human resources executive; b. Endicott, N.Y., Dec. 16, 1964; d. Gregory Francis and Barbara Elizabeth (Schwanzer) Flemming; m. Kevin Michael Lane, Sept. 15, 1990. Student, Franklin Coll., Lugano, Switzerland, 1985; BS in Mgmt. with honors, Babson Coll., 1986; postgrad., Boston U., 1990—. Asst. personnel mgr. Lechmere, Inc., Cambridge, Mass., 1986-87; personnel mgr. Lechmere, Inc., Rochester, N.Y., 1987-88, Danvers, Mass., 1988; exec. recruiter Lechmere, Inc., Woburn, Mass., 1988-89; exec. devel. specialist Lechmere, Inc., Woburn, 1989-90, supr. exec. devel., 1990, mgr. stores personnel div., 1990—. Alumni rep. Babson Coll., Wellesley, Mass., 1988—; advisor N.H. Coll. Coun. of Bus. Advisors, 1990. Mem. Internat. Assn. of Personnel Women, Eastern Coll. Personnel Officers. Home: 26 Wedgewood Rd Lawrence MA 01843-3671 Office: Lechmere Inc 275 Wildwood St Woburn MA 01801-6809

LANE, KENNETH ROBERT, producer, distributor; b. N.Y.C., Dec. 3, 1942; s. Carl Lane and Freda Rosalind; m. Marjory Horowitz, Dec. 1965 (div. 1967); m. Nicole Sloan Helguero (div.); m. Yolanda Natalia Bianco, Mar. 1990. BA, CUNY, 1965. Cert. engring. Prodn. mgr. Saul Bass & Assocs., Los Angeles, 1968-70; cameraman, prodn. mgr. Nat. Film Bd. Can., Vancouver, 1970-71; producer, distbr. Troma Inc., N.Y.C., 1976-77; prin. Ken Lane Films, N.Y.C., 1976—; producer, prodn. mgr. Platinum Prodns./Platinum Pictures, N.Y.C., 1977-78, Ganymede Prodns., N.Y.C., 1978-80; cameraman, audio mixer Madison Sq. Garden Network, N.Y.C., 1981-82; tech. dir. Sta. WNET Channel 13 (PBS), N.Y.C., 1983; cameraman Fox Broadcasting Co., Sta. WNYW, N.Y.C., 1981—; audio mixer, engr. ABC, N.Y.C., 1982—, CBS, N.Y.C., 1988—, NBC, N.Y.C., 1991—. producer/distbr.: (motion pictures) Delora, 1977, Legacy of Horror, 1981, The Navy vs. the Night Monsters, 1981, Women of the Prehistoric Planet, 1981. Treas. Washington Market Community Park, N.Y.C., 1985-86. Mem. Internat. Alliance Theatrical and Stage Employees, Nat. Assn. Broadcast Engrs. Technicians, Internat. Brotherhood Elec. Workers, Dirs. Guild. Am. Jewish. Home: 69-51 Cloverdale Blvd Bayside NY 11364 Office: 80 N Moore St Apt 18K New York NY 10013-2732

LANE, NATHAN, insurance agency executive; b. Poland, Oct. 1, 1921; came to U.S., 1929; s. Max and Anna (Cypris) Leizerowitz; m. Helen Andercheck, June 12, 1948; children: Linda, Robert. Student, Fairleigh Dickinson Coll., 1946-47. Ins. salesman Automobile Assn. N.J., Dover, 1948-51; pres. Nathan Lane Agy. Inc., Wyckoff, N.J., 1951—. Advisor Republican Party, Passaic County, N.J., 1951—. Sgt. USAF, 1942-45, PTO. Recipient Air Force Assn. citation, 1962, Air Force Assn. medal of merit, 1962, Air Power award Curtiss Wright Corp., 1964. Mem. Ind. Ins. Agts. N.J. (pres. 1975-77, Plaque 1977), Profl. Ins. Agts., Am. Legion, VFW, DAV, Air Force Assn. (comdr. Bergen Squadron 1961-66). Jewish. Office: Nathan Lane Agy 545 Goffle Rd Wyckoff NJ 07481-2937

LANE, ROBERT EDWARDS, political scientist; b. Phila., Aug. 19, 1917; s. Robert Porter and Bess (Edwards) L.; m. Helen Sobol, Nov. 15, 1944; children: Robert Lawrence, Thomas Edwards. BS, Harvard Coll., 1939;

PhD, Harvard U., 1950. Instr. to prof. polit. sci. Yale U., New Haven, 1948-85, prof. emeritus, 1985—. Author: Political Ideology, 1962, The Market Experience, 1991; contbr. articles to profl. jours. Capt. USAAF, 1942-46. Fellow Ctr. for Advanced Study in Behavioral Scis., 1956-57, Woodrow Wilson Internat. Ctr., 1970-71, Fulbright-Hays scholar, 1972-73; Netherlands Inst. for Adv. Study fellow, 1982-83; Australian Nat. U. fe-lalow, 1985. Mem. Am. Polit. Sci. Assn. (pres. 1970-71), Policy Studies Orgn. (pres. 1973), Internat. Soc. Polit. Psychology (pres. 1978-79). Democrat. Office: Yale Univ 3532 Yale Sta New Haven CT 06520

LANE, SHERRY See UNGER, SHARON LOUISE

LANE-ARRONS, MARION JEAN, artist; b. Bklyn., July 8, 1928; d. Herman and Anita (Gordon) Arrons; children: Spencer, George. BA, William Paterson Coll., 1975; MFA, Rutgers State U. N.J., 1978. Free-lance designer N.Y.C., 1953-60; art instr. N.J. colls., 1979-1985; art therapist Manhattan Psychiat. Ctr., N.Y.C., 1986—. Works represented in pvt. collections. Art Students League scholar, Woodstock, N.Y., 1953; recipient Grumbacher award Bklyn. Mus. Alumni Juried, N.Y.C. 1958; fellow Edward Albee Found., 1983, grantee N.J. State Coun. of the Arts, 1983, 88.

LANESE, JILL RENEE, computer and management consultant; b. Neptune, N.J., June 3, 1952; d. William Herman and Blossom Roslyn (Feldman) Epstein; m. Louis Lanese, June 10, 1984. BA, C.W. Post Coll., 1974. Word processing specialist Nat. Produce Co., Inc., Neptune, 1974-78; systems mgr. AT&T, Basking Ridge, N.J., 1978-81; sr. systems mgr. ITT, N.Y.C., 1981-84; info. systems mgr. Breed, Abbott & Morgan, N.Y.C., 1984-86; word processing/data processing dir., advisor Compu-group, N.Y.C., 1985-88; automation cons, Jill Lanese Computer Cons., N.Y.C., 1986-88, pres. ComputerForce Inc., N.Y.C., 1988—, Jill Lanese, Inc., N.Y.C., 1989—. adv., bd. dirs. ComputerPro,N.Y.C., 1987—. Contbr. articles to newspapers, jours., mags. Bd. dirs., pres. Am. Found. for Animals, West End, N.J., 1982—, dir. fundraiser, 1985-88. Mem. Internat. Platform Assn., Doris Day Animal League, Ind. Computer Cons. Assn., Assn. Info. Systems Profls., Assn. for Women in Computing, Nat. Assn. Female Execs, World Wildlife Fund, Greenpeace, Jacques Cousteau Soc., Humane Soc. U.S., Fund for Ethical Treatment to Animals, Internat. Platform Assn. Republican. Avocations: writing, floral and interior design, nutrition, dogs, photography, travel. Home: 8874 24th Ave Brooklyn NY 11214-6502 Office: 314 W 53rd St New York NY 10019-5702

LANFORD, WILLIAM ARMISTEAD, physics educator; b. Albany, N.Y., Nov. 15, 1944; s. Oscar Erasmus and Caroline (Sherman) L.; m. Cynthia Smith, Aug. 26, 1966; children—Catherine, William, Anne. B.S. in Physics, U. Rochester, 1966, Ph.D., 1972. Asst. prof. Yale U., New Haven, 1973-78, assoc. prof., 1978-79; assoc. prof. physics SUNY-Albany, 1979-83, prof. physics, 1983—, chair, 1989—. IBM, Yorktown Hts., N.Y., 1978—, Exxon, Annandale, N.J., 1979—; editor Radiation Effects, N.Y.C., 1983-90. Contbr. articles to profl. jours. Alfred P. Sloan Found. fellow, 1979-81. Mem. Am. Phys. Soc. (exec. com. 1981-85, vice chmn. N.Y. State sect. 1985-87, chmn. N.Y. State sect. 1987-89), Am. Ceramic Soc., Metall. Soc. of AIME, Hist. Metallurgy Soc. Avocations: history of technology, Am. decoration arts. Home: PO Box 53 Malden Bridge NY 12115-0053 Office: SUNY 1400 Washington Ave Albany NY 12222-0001

LANFRANCHI, RONALD GREGORY, nutritional biochemist, chiropractor; b. Bklyn., Apr. 14, 1953; s. Alfred Charles and Helen (Graniti) L.; m. Joan M. Weich, Dec. 3, 1983; 1 child, Alyssia. MS, NYU, 1976, M of Med. Sci., 1978; Dr. of Chiropractic, N.Y. Chiropractic Coll., 1987; PhD, Cornell U., 1989. Dir. Parkside Chiropractic, N.Y.C., 1987—; prin. scientist Metro Diagnostics, N.Y.C., 1988—; asst. prof. N.Y. Chiropractic Coll., Glen Head, N.Y., 1989—, chmn. dept. nutritional sci., 1991—. Mem. N.Y. Chiropractic Assn. (chmn. state com. on nutrition 1991—), Am. Coll. Nutrition. Office: 4 E 89th St New York NY 10128-0636

LANG, C. MAX, veterinarian, educator; b. Paris, Ill., Dec. 29, 1937; s. Acel G. and O. Nadine (Beaver) L.; m. Sylvia Smith, Jan. 10, 1965; children: Karen E., John A., Susan C. BS, U. Ill., 1959, DVM, 1961. Diplomate Am. Coll. Lab. Animal Medicine. Capt., vet. corp. Walter Reed Army Inst. Research, Washington, 1961-63; asst. prof. Pa. State U. Coll. Medicine, Hershey, 1966-69, assoc. prof., 1969-72, prof., 1972-84, George T. Harrell Jr. prof., 1984—, asst. dean continuing edn., 1984—. Contbr. over 120 articles to profl. publs. Served to capt. U.S. Army, 1961-63. Recipient Research award Am. Assn. Lab. Animal Sci., 1980-81, Charles River award Am. Vet. Med. Assn., 1987; Bowman Gray Sch. Med. postdoctoral fellow, 1963-66. Mem. Am. Vet. Med. Assn., Am. Assn. Lab. Animal Sci., Am. Coll. Lab. Animal Medicine (pres.). Home: 472 Hilltop Rd Hummelstown PA 17036-8512 Office: Pa State U Milton S Hershey Med Ctr PO Box 350 Hershey PA 17033-0351

LANG, CHARLES WILLIAM, personnel director; b. Chgo., Dec. 1, 1943; s. Charles and Marguerite (Meyer) L. AA, Wright Jr. Coll., 1966; BBA, Loyola U., Chgo., 1968; postgrad., De Paul U., 1970. Program analyst Dept. of Navy, Chgo., 1968-70; pers. rep. Def. Supply Agy., Chgo., 1970-72; team leader U.S. Dept. HEW, Chgo., 1972-74; regional rep. U.S. Dept. Health and Human Svcs., Washington, 1974-79; chief, Western field office U.S. Dept. Health and Human Svcs., San Francisco, 1979-82; program mgr. U.S. Dept. Health and Human Svcs., Washington, 1982-88; dep. dir. pers. Commodity Futures Trading Commn., Washington, 1988—; instr. Fed. Regional Coll., Chgo., 1973; communications com. Pub. Employees Roundtable, Washington, 1985. Tng. chmn., asst commr., coun. membership chmn., Boy Scouts Am., Chgo., San Francisco, and Washington, 1966-90. Mem. Internat. Pers. Mgmt. Assn. (treas. Chgo. chpt. 1973-74), Pers. Mgmt. Assn. (mem. fed. sect. internat. awards com. 1989, chmn. workgroup on classification 1988), Pers. Testing Coun. of Met. Washington. Home: 4906 28th St S Arlington VA 22206-1409 Office: Commodity Futures Trading Commn 2033 S St NW Washington DC 20581-0001

LANG, DAVID WAYNE, law librarian; b. Kewanee, Ill., Aug. 13, 1954; s. Wayne Victor and Joan Audrey (Fairchild) L.; m. Susan Rochelle White, July 25, 1975; children: Barret Wesley, Audrey Rochelle. BS, U. Md., 1980; MSLS, Cath. U. Am., 1985. Law librarian Wilkes, Artis, Hedrick & Lane, Washington, 1976-90; law libr. Venable, Baetjer, Howard & Civiletti, Washington, 1990—. Author: D.C. Code Updater, Subject Index to Bills D.C. Council; contbr. articles to law library jours. Mem. ALA, Am. Assn. Law Librs., Law Librs. Soc. Washington (pres., v.p. legis. spl. interest sect. 1990-92, rec. sec. 1992—). Republican. Methodist. Home: 2008 Howard Chapel Turn Crofton MD 21114-1832 Office: Venable Baetjer Howard & Civiletti 1201 New York Ave NW # 1000 Washington DC 20005-3917

LANG, GERHARD, psychology educator; b. Germany, Mar. 19, 1925; came to U.S., 1940; s. Bertold and Else Lang; m. Adell Lang, Dec. 27, 1951; children: Kenneth, Judith Lang Knutsen. BS in Psychology, CCNY, 1952, MA in Sch. Psychology, 1954; PhD in Devel. and Ednl. Psychology, Columbia U., 1958. Cert. psychologist, N.Y.; lic. psychology, N.J. Teaching fellow, rsch. asst., cons., lectr. CCNY, 1954-60; instr., asst. prof. psychology Fairleigh Dickinson U., Rutherford, N.J., 1958-63, assoc. prof., 1963-64; assoc. prof. psychology and edn. Montclair State Coll., Upper Montclair, N.J., 1966-70, prof., 1970—, chmn. dept. ednl. rsch. and evaluation, 1970-73, team leader, 1973—; cons. N.Y.C. Bd. Edn., 1966-90, rsch. assoc. bd. examiners, 1964-66; cons. Jewish Edn. Svc. N.Am., N.Y.C., 1960-84, Title I reading project Dist. 29, Queens, N.Y., 1973-77, Twp. of Montclair, 1991; pvt. practice, 1971—. Author: A Practical Guide to Statistics for Research and Measurements, 4th edit., 1991, A Practical Guide to Research Methods, 4th edit., 1991; contbr. articles to profl. jours., also chpts., pamphlets and monographs. Grantee James McKeen Cattel Fund, 1957, U.S. Dept. Edn., 1962-64, 65-67. Mem. APA, Am. Ednl. Rsch. Assn., Nat. Coun. on Measurements in Edn., Northeastern Ednl. Rsch. Assn. Jewish. Home: 4-39 Lyncrest Ave Fair Lawn NJ 07410 Office: Montclair State Coll Dept Psychology Upper Montclair NJ 07043

LANG, JOHN FRANCIS, lawyer; b. Bayonne, N.J., June 8, 1915; s. Lewis F. and Pauline M. (Norwich) L.; m. Eleanor Bradford Cook, Jan. 26, 1952; children: Elaine L., Anita L. Knowlton. BA, Georgetown U., 1937; JD, Harvard U., 1940. Bar: N.Y. 1941, U.S. Dist. Ct. (so. dist.) N.Y., U.S. Ct. Appeals (2d cir.), U.S. Supreme Ct., 1947. Assoc. Buckley & Buckley, N.Y.C., 1940-41, Law Office of D. J. Mooney, N.Y.C., 1946-51, Nash, Ten Eyck, N.Y.C., 1951-53; ptnr. McNutt & Nash, N.Y.C., 1953-56; ptnr. Hill, Betts & Nash, N.Y.C., 1956-86, of counsel, 1986—; bd. dirs. numerous corps.; chmn. biennial seminar in Paris on ship and aircraft fin. Lt. comdr. USN, 1941-45. Decorated Knight Comdr. (Republic of Liberia). Mem. ABA, Internat. Bar Assn., Maritime Law Assn., Harvard Club of N.Y. Office: Hill Betts & Nash One World Trade Ctr New York NY 10048

LANG, MARY ELIZABETH, freelance writer, educator; b. New London, Conn., Feb. 21, 1947; d. Hubert Gregory and Frances Morgan (Alling) L.; m. Ward J. McFarland Jr., May 30, 1969 (div. 1981); 1 child, Rebecca Jean; m. Bruce Everett Neild, June 25, 1982; stepchildren: Kimberly Ann, Joel Edward. BA cum laude, Barnard Coll., 1969; MAT with honors, Yale U., 1970; postgrad., So. Conn. State U., 1978-80. Tchr. Branford (Conn.) Pub. Schs., 1970-71; editor Dushkin Pub. Group, Guilford, Conn., 1971-72; freelance writer, editorial cons. New Haven, 1974—; writing coach talented and gifted program Jackie Robinson Middle Sch., New Haven, 1980; rsch. asst., tech. writer, publicist Yale Bush Ctr. in Child Devel. and Social Policy, New Haven, 1981-87; composition instr. So. Conn. State U., New Haven, 1987—. Co-author: Childcare Choices, 1991; author curriculum materials; contbr. articles to various publs. Diocesan rep. St. James the Apostle Ch., New Haven, 1975-81, lay reader, chalicist, 1976-82; newsletter editor St. Peter's Episc. Ch., Cheshire, Conn., 1986—; cons. Episc. Social Svc., Bridgeport, Conn., 1987. Mem. AAUP, Nat. Coun. Tchrs. English (assembly on sci. and humanities). Democrat. Home: 51 Currier Way Cheshire CT 06410-1431 Office: Dept English So Conn State Univ 501 Crescent St New Haven CT 06515-1355

LANG, PAUL JOSEPH, financial services executive; b. Amityville, N.Y., Jan. 13, 1947; s. Jerome and Hannah (Hauft) L.; Lucia Molteni, July 13, 1969 (div. June 1975); 1 child, Heather C.; m. Stephanie Laudenbach, July 1, 1977. BS in Commerce, Rider Coll., 1968; MS in Mgmt., Am. Coll., Bryn Mawr, Pa., 1986; postgrad., Yale U., 1986. Cert. internal auditor, life underwriter; chartered fin. cons. Various internal audit positions Prudential Ins., Newark, 1973-78; treas. Prudential Reinsurance Co., Newark, 1978-80; mgr. acctg. ea. home office Prudential Ins., Woodbridge, N.J., 1980-82, dir. individual ins. ea. home office, 1982-85; v.p. individual ins. ea. home office Prudential Ins., Ft. Washington, Pa., 1985-87; v.p. auditing Prudential Securities, Inc., N.Y.C., 1987-88; v.p. exec. edn. human resources Prudential Ins., Newark, 1988-89; v.p. adminstrn. Prudential Power Funding, Newark, 1989-90; v.p., comptr. pvt. placement svcs. Prudential Ins., Newark, 1990—. Chmn. sch. bus. adminstrn. adv. bd. Rider Coll., Trenton, N.J., 1990—. Capt. USAF, 1968-73. Fellow Life Mgmt. Inst. Home: 224 Lorraine Dr Berkeley Heights NJ 07922 Office: The Prudential 100 Mulberry St 7GC4 Newark NJ 07102

LANG, SCOTT WILLIAM, management consultant, accountant; b. Buffalo, Dec. 5, 1959; s. David John and Edith (Wurster) L. BS, SUNY, Oswego, 1981; MBA, Columbia U., 1987. CPA, N.Y. Sr. acct. Price Waterhouse, Buffalo, 1981-85; asst. treas. Irving Trust Co., N.Y.C., 1987-89; sr. cons. Deloitte and Touche, N.Y.C., 1989-90; mng. ptnr. Wolverine Ptnrs., L.P., Snyder, N.Y., 1990—. Mem. AICPA. Roman Catholic. Office: Wolverine Ptnrs LP 140 Parkwood Dr Snyder NY 14226

LANG, STANLEY ALBERT, chemist, consultant; b. Cleve., Mar. 30, 1944; s. Stanley Albert and Patricia Jean (Cummings) L.; m. Irene Marion Slattery, May 8, 1975; children: Amy Elizabeth, Steven Joseph. BS, John Carroll U., 1966; PhD in Chemistry, Brown U., 1970. Rsch. fellow Ohio State U., Columbus, 1970-71; rsch. chemist Am. Cyanamid Co., Pearl River, N.Y., 1971-75, group leader, 1975-80, dept. head, 1980-90, project dir., 1990—. Author: Progress in Heterocyclic Chemistry, 1991; also numerous articles; patentee in field. Cons. South Orangetown (N.Y.) Cen. Sch. Dist., 1989—. Fellow Petroleum Rsch. Found., 1964-66, Nat. Cancer Inst., 1971. Mem. Am. Chem. Soc., Internat. Soc. Heterocyclic Chemistry (adv. com. 1988—), N.Y. Acad. Scis. Office: Am Cyanamid Co MRD Lederle Labs Pearl River NY 10965

LANGACKER, PAUL GEORGE, physics educator; b. Evanston, Ill., July 14, 1946; s. George Rollo and Florence (Hinesley) L.; m. Irmgard Sieker, June 25, 1983. BS, MIT, 1968; PhD, U. Calif., Berkeley, 1972; MA, U. Pa., 1981. Postdoctoral assoc. Rockefeller U., N.Y.C., 1972-74; postdoctoral assoc. U. Pa., Phila., 1974-75, asst. prof. physics, 1975-81, assoc. prof. physics, 1981-85, prof. physics, 1985—; exec. com. Div. Particles & Fields of Am. Phys. Soc., Washington, 1989—; mem. editorial bd. Phys. Rev., 1987-88, 91—; sci. dir. Theoretical Advanced Study Inst., Boulder, Colo., 1990. Editor: Testing the Standard Model, 1991. Recipient Humboldt award A.V. Humboldt Soc., 1987-88. Fellow Am. Phys. Soc.; mem. AAAS. Office: U of Pa Dept of Physics Philadelphia PA 19104

LANGAN, ROGER FLEMMING, lyricist; b. Mar. 29, 1961; s. William and Maureen (Hurley) L. BA in History, SUNY, Stony Brook, 1984. Shipping clk. Cowin Enterprises, Smithtown, N.Y., 1979-84; projectionist New Community Cinema, Huntington, N.Y., 1985-87; therapy aide Kings Park (N.Y.) State Hosp., 1988-89; usher Commack (N.Y.) Multiplex, 1989—. Author over 300 copyrighted lyrics including: Soul of the City, Go Mad my Revoler.

LANGBEIN, JOHN HARRISS, lawyer, educator; b. Washington, Nov. 17, 1941; s. I. L. and M. V. (Harriss) L.; m. Kirsti M. Hiekka, June 24, 1973; children: Christopher, Julia, Anne. AB, Columbia U., 1964; LLB, Harvard U., 1968, Cambridge U., 1969; PhD, Cambridge U., 1971; MA (hon.), Yale U., 1991. Bar: D.C. 1969, Fla. 1970; barrister-at-law Inner Temple, Eng., 1970. Asst. prof. law U. Chgo., 1971-73, assoc. prof. law, 1973-74, prof. law, 1974-80, Max Pam prof. Am. and fgn. law, 1980-90; Chancellor Kent prof. law and legal history Yale U., New Haven, 1990—; commr. Nat. Conf. Commrs. on Uniform State Laws, 1984—. Author: Prosecuting Crime in the Renaissance, 1974, Torture and the Law of Proof: Europe and England in the Ancient Regime, 1977, Comparative Criminal Procedure: Germany, 1977, (with L. Waggoner) Selected Statutes on Trusts and Estates, 1987, rev. edits. 1991, 92, (with B. Wolk) Pension and Employee Benefit Law, 1990; contbr. numerous articles on law and legal history and profl. jours. Mem. ABA, Am. Coll. Trust and Estate Counsel, Am. Law Inst., Am. Soc. Legal History, Am. Hist. Assn., Selden Soc., Gesellschaft fuer Rechtsvergleichung, Am. Acad. of Arts and Scis., Internat. Acad. Estate and Trust Law, Internat. Acad. Comparative Law. Republican. Episcopalian. Office: Yale U Sch Law 127 Wall St New Haven CT 06511-6636

LANGDANA, FARROKH KEKI, economics and finance educator; b. Bombay, Feb. 15, 1958; s. Keki Darabshaw and Zarrin (Daruvala) L.; m. Mary E. Wills, May 3, 1987; children: Christopher, Jenelle. B. Tech. in Civil Engring., IIT Kanpur, Kanpur, India, 1979; MBA in Fin., Va. Poly. Inst. and State U., 1981, PhD in Econs., 1987. Asst. prof. grad. sch. mgmt. Rutgers U., 1987—; exam-setter Ednl. Testing Svc., Princeton, N.J., 1988; referee Routledge, Chapman & Hall, London. Author: Sustaining Budget Deficits in Open Economies, 1989, (with Richard Burdekin) Budget Deficits and Economic Performance, 1992; editor Macrocast, econ. forecasting newsletter. Recipient teaching excellence awards and rsch. award. Mem. Am. Econ. Assn., So. Econ. Assn. Zoroastrian. Home: 986 Robin Rd Somerville NJ 08876-4437 Office: Rutgers Grad Sch Mgmt 92 New St Newark NJ 07102-1818

LANGDON, GEORGE DORLAND, JR., museum administrator; b. Putnam Conn., May 20, 1933; s. George Dorland and Anne Claggett (Zell) L.; m. Agnes Domandi; children—George Dorland, III, Campbell Brewster. A.B. cum laude (Coolidge scholar), Harvard Coll., 1954; M.A., Amherst Coll., 1957; Ph.D. (Coe fellow), Yale U., 1961; LHD (hon.), Colgate U. Instr. in history and Am. studies Yale U., 1959-62, asst. provost, lectr. in history, 1969-70, asso. provost, lectr. in history, 1970-72, dep. provost, lectr. in history, 1972-78; asst. prof. history Calif. Inst. Tech., 1962-64; asst. prof. Vassar Coll., 1964-67, asso. prof., 1967-68, spl. asst. to pres., 1968; pres., trustee Colgate U., 1978-88, pres. emeritus, 1988—; pres. Am. Mus. Natural History, N.Y.C., 1988—; bd. dirs. Quest for Value Dual Purpose Fund, Inc. Author: A History of New Plymouth 1620-1691, 1966 (State and Local Assn. of History award of Merit). Trustee The Kresge Found., St. Lukes/Roosevelt Hosp. Ctr., Wenner-Gron Found. for Anthrop. Rsch. Lt. U.S. Army, 1954-56. Fellow Pilgrim Soc. Office: Am Mus Natural History Cen Pk W 79th St New York NY 10024-5192

LANGE, NANCY POST, program director; b. Trenton, N.J., May 5, 1950; d. James Magnus and Nancy McCullough (Post) L. AB, U. Cin., 1972, BS, 1972. Owner The Gallery Florist, Oneida, N.Y., 1976-83; gen. mgr. The Kenan Ctr., Inc., Lockport, N.Y., 1983-90; annual fund dir. Niagara U., Niagara Falls, N.Y., 1990—. Planning commr. City of Oneida, 1980-83; vice chmn. Oneida Arts Coun., 1982; bd. dirs. Kenan Ctr., Inc., Lockport, N.Y., 1983-90, Niagara Edn. Found., Sanborn, N.Y., 1991—, sec., 1992—; sec. Leadership Niagara, 1986-89, 1st vice chmn., 1989—, chmn.-elect, 1982-84; vice chmn. Niagara Coun. of the Arts, Niagara Falls, N.Y. Mem. Lockport Jr. League, Lockport Zonta, Lockport Town and Country Club. Republican. Episcopalian. Office: Niagara U Barrows Hall Niagara Falls NY 14109

LANGE, STEPHAN CHARLES, neurosurgeon; b. Ogden, Wash., June 4, 1950; s. Charles J. and Christiane R. Lange; m. Elizabeth Ann Lange; children: Christine, Katherine, Jennifer. BS, Loyola U., L.A., 1972; MS, U. Calif., Irvine, 1976, MD, 1976. Asst. clin. prof. surgery U. Conn.; chmn. dept. neurosurgery St. Francis Hosp., Hartford, Conn.; with Neurolsurg. Assocs., Hartford. Maj. U.S. Army Med. Corps, 1980-84. Fellow ACS; mem. Am. Assn. Neurol. Surgeons, Congress of Neurol. Surgeons, Conn. State Med. Soc., Hartford Conn. Med. Soc. Office: Neurosurg Assocs PC 1000 Asylum Ave Hartford CT 06107

LANGENBERG, DONALD NEWTON, physicist, educational administrator; b. Devils Lake, N.D., Mar. 17, 1932; s. Ernest George and Fern (Newton) L.; m. Patricia Ann Warrington, June 20, 1953; children: Karen Kaye, Julia Ann, John Newton, Amy Paris. B.S., Iowa State U., 1953; M.S., UCLA, 1955; Ph.D. (NSF fellow), U. Calif. at Berkeley, 1959; D.Sc. (hon.), U. Pa., 1985, MA (hon.), 1971. Electronics engr. Hughes Research Labs., Culver City, Calif., 1953-55; acting instr. U. Calif. at Berkeley, 1958-59; mem. faculty U. Pa., Phila., 1960-83; prof. U. Pa., 1967-83; dir. Lab. for Research on Structure of Matter, 1972-74; vice provost for grad. studies and research, 1974-79; chancellor U. Ill.-Chgo., 1983-90, U. Md. System, Adelphi, 1990—; maître de conference associe Ecole Normale Superieure, Paris, France, 1966-67; vis. prof. Calif. Inst. Tech., Pasadena, 1971; guest researcher Zentralinstitut für Tieftemperaturforschung der Bayerische Akademie der Wissenschaften and Technische Universität München, 1974; dep. dir. Nat. Sci. Found., 1980-82. Researcher, contbr. to publs. on solid state and low temperature physics including electronic band structure in metals and semiconductors, quantum phase coherence and nonequilibrium effects in superconductors and science policy and research adminstrn. Recipient John Price Wetherill medal Franklin Inst., 1975, Disting. Contribution to Research Adminstrn. award Soc. Research Adminstrs., 1983, Disting. Achievement Citation, Iowa State Alumni Assn., 1984, Significant Sig award Sigma Chi, 1985; fellow NSF, 1959-60, Alfred P. Sloan Found., 1962-64; Guggenheim Found., 1966-67. Fellow AAAS (pres. 1990), Am. Phys. Soc., Sigma Xi. Office: U Md System 3300 Metzerott Rd Hyattsville MD 20783-1600

LANGER, AMY SCHIFFMAN, educational association administrator; b. N.Y.C., July 22, 1954; d. Jacob Henry Schiffman and Frances Sylvia (Hammer) Goldenberg; m. Michael Hoffman, Sept. 9, 1979 (div. 1984); m. Charles Andrew Langer, Feb. 3, 1990. BA cum laude, Yale Coll., 1975; MBA, Harvard U., 1977. Various positions ending with sr. v.p. corp. fin. Shearson Lehman Bros., N.Y.C., 1977-85; cons. N.Y.C., 1985-88; adminstrv. dir. Nat. Alliance Breast Cancer Orgns., N.Y.C., 1988-90, exec. dir., 1990—; mem. various adv. panels on breast cancer, 1989—. Office: Nat Alliance Breast Cancer Orgns 2d Fl 1180 Ave of Americans New York NY 10036

LANGER, ARTHUR MARK, mineralogist; b. N.Y.C., Feb. 18, 1936; s. Morton Livingston and Ruth Regina (Lewitz) L.; m. Catherine Chilcott Josi, apr. 11, 1977; children: Erica Margaret, Andrew Michael, Elliott Mark, Christopher Morton. BA, Hunter Coll., 1956; MA, Columbia U., 1962, PhD, 1965. Exploration geologist Rosario Exploration Chibougamau Mining and Smelting, 1956; field asst. in geology Bear Tooth Mountain, Mont. Columbia U., N.Y.C., 1957-58, teaching asst. dept. geology, 1958-59, cons. mineralogist, 1960-65, rsch. asst. dept. geology, 1961-64; lectr. CUNY, 1964-65, mem. grad. faculty, 1982—; rsch. assoc. environ. medicine, dept. medicine Mt. Sinai Hosp., N.Y.C., 1965-67, asst. prof. dept. community medicine, 1967-68; assoc. prof. mineralogy, dept. community medicine Mt. Sinai Sch. Medicine, N.Y.C., 1968-86, 87-88, head phys. scis. sect., assoc. dir. Environ. Scis. Lab., 1969-86, sci. adminstr. Environ. Scis. Lab., 1983-84, assoc. prof. Ctr. for Polypeptide and Membrane Rsch., 1986-88; rsch. assoc. dept. mineral scis. Am. Mus. Natural History, N.Y.C., 1979—; dir. Environ. Scis. Lab. Inst. of Applied Scis. CUNY, 1988—; adj. assoc. prof. mineralogy grad. div. CUNY, 1969-69; expert cons. NIH, 1974—, WHO, 1975—, Nat. Heart, Lung and Blood Inst., 1975—, EPA, 1975—, Nat. Inst. for Environ. Health Scis., 1975—, Nat. Inst. for Occupational Safety and Health, 1975—, EPA Superfund cases, 1985—, other regional consultations; cons. Inst. Pub. Health, Norway, 1977, Ministry of Mines, South Africa, 1977, Internat. Agy. Rsch. Cancer, 1976, 86, Internat. Program Chem. Safety (WHO), 1985, Internat. Fedn. Bldg. Wood Workers, 1989; mem. internat. coms. on pollution and health. Assoc. editor Environ. Rsch., 1978-85, adv. editor, 1985-87; asst. editor Am. Jour. Indsl. Medicine, 1980-85, assoc. editor, 1985-86; mem. editorial rev. bd. Journ. Environ. Pathology and Toxicology, 1978-82, Jour. Environmental Pathology, Toxicology and Oncology, 1983—; mem. editorial adv. bd. Advances in Modern Eenviron. Toxicology, 1981-82; manuscript reviewer many jours.; reviewer, author fed. and industry documents, 1978—; contbr. chpts. to books, articles and abstracts to profl. jours. and symposia proc. Recipient award Dept. Geology, Hunter Coll., 1956, Dust Rsch. award Polachek Found., 1965-67, Career Scientist award Nat. Inst. Environ. Health Scis., 1969-74; named to Hall of Fame, Hunter College-CUNY, 1978; grantee Health Rsch. Coun., 1966-67, 75-77, Polacheck Found., 1966-68, NIH, 1967-78, Johns-Manville Corp., 1968-73, Am. Cancer Soc., 1971-74, 80-81, EPA, 1973, Ford Motor Co., 1973-75, Nat. Inst. Occupational Safety and Health, 1976-79, 82-84, Nat. Inst. Environ. Health Scis, 1978-86, Nat. Cancer Inst., 1979-81, Mobil Found., 1979—, Vanderbilt Talc Co., 1988, Battelle, Columbus, 1988—, Consumer Products Safety Commn., 1987-90, Ga. Pacific, 1989-91, others. Fellow Collegium Ramazzini, Geol. Soc. Am., Mineral. Soc. Am., N.Y. Acad. Scis.; mem. Phi Beta Kappa, Sigma Xi. Home: 6 Rochambeau Dr Hartsdale NY 10530 Office: Bklyn Coll of CUNY Brooklyn NY 11210

LANGER, SANDRA LOIS (CASSANDRA LANGER), writer; b. Montecello, N.Y., Dec. 18, 1941; d. Moe Morris and Doris Lillian (Tractenburg) L. BA, U. Miami, 1967, MA, 1969; PhD, NYU, 1974. Asst. prof. Fla. Internat. U., Miami, 1973-78; asst. prof. U. S.C., Columbia, 1978-81, assoc. prof., 1982-86; pres. Langer Fine Arts Svcs., N.Y.C., 1986—; vis. assoc. prof. art dept. Hunter Coll., CUNY, 1989-90; cons. Robert R. Preato Collection, N.Y.C., 1991-92. Co-author: Impressionism/Post Impressionism, 1988, Feminist Art Criticism: An Anthology, 1989; author: Mother and Child in Art, 1992; also various catalogues and articles. Postdoctoral fellow Smithsonian Instn./Nat. Mus. Am. Art, 1984. Mem. Nat. Writer's Union, Coll. Art Assn., Women's Caucus for Art, Assn. Authors and Journalists, Nat. Women's Studies Assn., Assn. Art Critics USA. Home: 32-22 89th St Apt 605 Jackson Heights NY 11369 Office: care Javors 215 E 23d St 3d Fl New York NY 10010

LANGHAM, NORMA, playwright, poet, composer; b. California, Pa.; d. Alfred Scrivener and Mary Edith (Carter) L. BS, Ohio State U., 1942; B in Theatre Arts, Pasadena Playhouse Coll. Theatre Arts, 1944; MA, Stanford U., 1956; postgrad., Summer Radio-TV Inst., 1960, Pasadena Inst. Radio, 1944-45. Tchr. sci. California High Sch., 1942-43; asst. office pub. info. Denison U., Granville, Ohio, 1955; instr. speech dept. Westminster Coll., New Wilmington, Pa., 1957-58; instr. theatre. California U. of Pa., 1959, asst. prof., 1960-62, assoc. prof., 1962-79, prof. emeritus, 1979—, co-founder, sponsor, dir. Children's Theatre, 1962-79; founder, producer, dir. Food Bank Players, 1985, Patriot Players, 1986. Writer: (plays) Magic in the Sky, 1963, Founding Daughters (DAR award 1991), Women Whisky Rebels (Pa. DAR award 1992), John Dough (Freedoms Found. award 1968), Who Am I?, Hippocrates Oath, Gandhi, Clementine of '49, Soul Force, Dutch Painting, Esther, Music in Freedom, The Day the Moon Fell; composer-lyricist (plays) Why Me, Lord?, (text) Public Speaking; inventor CBMT champion driver game. Recipient award exceptional acad. svc. Pa. Dept. Edn., 1975, Ap-

preciation award Bicentennial Commn. Pa., 1976, Gregg award Calif. chpt. U. Pa. Assn., 1992; Henry C. Frick Ednl. Commn. grantee. Mem. Theatre Assn. Pa., Internat. Platform Assn., Calif. U. of Pa. Assn. Women Faculty (founder, pres. 1972-73), AAUW (co-founder Calif. br., 1st v.p. 1971-72, pres. 1972-73, Outstanding Woman of Yr. 1986), Dramatists Guild, DAR, California (Pa.) Community Choir, Brownsville (Pa.) Hist. Soc., Whiskey Rebellion Task Force, Internat. Platform Assn., Theatre Assn. Pa., Mensa, Alpha Psi Omega, Omicron Nu. Presbyterian (elder). Home: Box 459 California PA 15419

LANGHANS, LESTER FRANK, III, construction company executive; b. Corning, N.Y., Apr. 7, 1948; s. Lester Frank and Lois Jane (Keller) L.; B.S. in bldg. constrn., Va. Poly. Inst. and State U., 1970; m. Patricia Jane Wood, May 6, 1972 (div. Aug. 1991); children—Kristen, Daniel, David, Ellen. Vice pres. Cape Assocs., Inc., North Eastham, Mass., 1971-75; treas. Langhall Builders, Inc., East Dennis, Mass., 1976-77; project mgr. The Green Co., Inc., East Falmouth, Mass., 1977-83; project mgr. CMJ Builders, Inc., Quincy, Mass., 1983-84; project coordinator Corcoran Mullins, Jennison, Inc., 1984-85; prin. TEL Assocs., Barnstable, Mass., 1985; dir. devel. LBC, Inc., Rockland, Mass., 1985-86, v.p. planning and devel., 1986-88; constrn. and devel. mgr. Olde Forge Realty, Boston, 1988-89; pres., treas. Job Busters, Eastham, Mass., 1990—. Mem. choir East Dennis Community Ch., 1970-79, elder, 1972-75, clk., 1973-74, deacon, 1981—, treas. 1985-90. Served with U.S. Army, 1970-71, with Res., 1971-76, 92—, with U.S. Navy Res., 1982-85. Home: 5 Ben's Way North Eastham MA 02651 Office: c/o Job Busters PO Box 4 Eastham MA 02642-0004

LANGLEY, KENNETH H., physics educator; b. Ft. Collins, Colo., Sept. 1, 1935; s. Glenn and Dorothy (Douglass) L.; m. Joan Eleanor Pannier, June 27, 1959; children: Christine Ruth, Mark Douglass. SB, MIT, 1958; PhD, U. Calif., Berkeley, 1958. Asst. prof. U. Mass., Amherst, 1966-72, assoc. prof., 1972-80, prof. physics, 1980—; founder, prin. Langley-Ford Instruments, Amherst, 1977-83. Contbr. articles to profl. publs. Grantee NSF, 1969—, U.S. Army. Mem. AAAS, Am. Phys. Soc. Office: U Mass Dept Physics Amherst MA 01003

LANGLEY, PATRICIA COFFROTH, psychiatric social worker; b. Pitts., Mar. 1, 1924; d. John Kimmel and Anna (McDonald) Coffroth; m. George J. Langley, May 1, 1946; children: George Julius III, Mary Patricia, Kelly Joan; stepchildren: Robin Spencer, Veronica Bell. BA, Empire State Coll., 1976; MSW, Hunter Coll., 1980. Diplomate Clin. Social Worker; cert. ind. social worker, Conn. Psychiat. rehab. worker, alcoholism treatment unit Bronx Mcpl. Hosp. Center, Albert Einstein Med. Coll., 1970-74, case worker, comprehensive alcoholism treatment center, dept. psychiatry, 1974-80; asst. coordinator outpatient psychiat. alcoholism Meridian Ctr., Stamford, Conn., 1980-83; dir. family treatment Meridian Ctr.; pvt. practice and consultation. Vol., DuBois Day Clinic, Stamford, 1966-67, Greenwich Hosp., 1966-67. Mem. NASW, Conn. Soc. for Clin. Social Workers, Nat. Assn. Mental Health Counselors. Republican. Home and Office: 25 W Elm St Greenwich CT 06830-6465

LANGLEY, ROGER RICHARD, editor; b. Amsterdam, N.Y., Aug. 22, 1930; s. Walter B. and Anna Mae (McCaffrey) L.; m. Norma A. Sekinger, Feb. 5, 1960; children: David, Jennifer, Michael. AB, Syracuse U., 1958, AM, 1965. Cert. tchr. N.Y. Salesman Underwood-Olevitti Corp., Syracuse, 1960-61; editor Ind. Newspaper Chain, Marathon, N.Y., 1961-64; reporter Syracuse Herald-Jour., 1964-66; asst. city editor Ithaca (N.Y.) Jour., 1966-68; gen. editor Best Medium Pub., Englewood Cliffs, N.J., 1968-74; chief bur. World News Corp., Washington, 1974-76; syndicated columnist Washington (D.C.) Writers' Syndicate, 1978-82, sr. editor, 1977—, chief exec. officer, 1982—; instr. U. Md., College Park, Am. U., Washington, George Washington U., Washington, Montgomery Coll., Md.; dean workshops on humor in the workplace, humor and health Comedy Coll.; speaker and tng. cons. NIH, Washington, 1982—; mem. White House Press Corp, 1974-84. Author: Wife Beating: The Silent Crisis, 1977, You Can Chart Your Career Path, 1992; author audio tape presentation Speak With Humor; contbr. articles to mags. and newspapers. Pres. Woodly Gardens Home Owners Assn., Rockville, Md., 1975; mem. Keep Montgomery County (Md.) Beautiful, 1985-89, Fuel Oil Task Force, Montgomery County, 1985-89, Emergency Mgmt. Com., Montgomery County, 1985-89, Bethesda (Md.) Action Group, 1989—. Served with USN; 1950-54, Korea. Recipient Enterprise Writing award N.Y. A.P., 1967, Nat. Assn. Counties awards, Excellence in Writing award Chevy Chase C. of C.; named Toastmaster of Yr., 1986, 91. Mem. Nat. Press Club, Am. Legion Post of Nat. Press Club, Soc. Profl. Journalists, Beta Theta Pi. Club: Toastmasters (various offices Silver Spring, Md. chpt.). Home: 625 Smallwood Rd Rockville MD 20850-1918 Office: Washington Writers' Syndicate 1377 K St NW Ste 131 Washington DC 20005-3303

LANGMUIR, CHARLES HERBERT, geology educator; b. Chalk River, Ont., Can., Nov. 24, 1950; came to U.S., 1954; s. David Bulkeley and Marianna (Lawrence) L.; m. Diane Marie Langmuir, Sept. 22, 1973; 1 child, Molly Kathryn. BA, Harvard U., 1973; MS, SUNY, Stony Brook, 1978, PhD, 1980. From asst. to assoc. prof. Lamont-Doherty Geol. Observatory Columbia U., Palisades, N.Y., 1981-88, prof. Lamont-Doherty Geol. Observatory, 1988—, Arthur D. Storke Meml. prof., 1989—; vis. scientist Inst. de Physique du Globe, Paris, 1989-90; mem. adv. com. on ocean scis., NSF, 1990—; mem. lithosphere panel Joint Oceanographic Instns. for Deep Earth Sampling, 1984-87; chmn. Conf. on Sci. Ocean Drilling II, Working Group on Mantle-Crust Interactions, 1986-87; mem. steering com. Ridge Interdisciplinary Global Experiments; chmn. coord. com. Project French-Am.-Ridge Atlantic, 1989—. Editor: Earth and Planetary Sci. Letters, 1989—; mem. editorial bd. Chem. Geology, 1985—; contbr. over 30 articles to profl. jours. Alfred Sloan Rsch. fellow, 1983-85, Henry Shaw fellow Harvard U., 1974. Mem. Am. Geophys. Union, Geol. Soc. Am. Office: 37 Iroquois Ave RFD 1 Box 86 Palisades NY 10964

LANGO, PAUL JAMES, graphic designer; b. Springville, N.Y., Nov. 20, 1956; s. James Albert and Marjorie (Flick) L.; m. Myra Sue Nisenfeld, June 5, 1977; children: Jonathan David, Sean Michael. AAS, Fashion Inst. Tech., N.Y.C., 1980. Stock clk. Super Duper, Springville, N.Y., 1971-74; fork lift driver to plant mgr. William J. Elwood, Copiague, N.Y., 1976-78; salesman Macy's, N.Y.C., 1978-80; engraving trainee, mgr. M. Lowenstein, Inc., Lyman, S.C., 1981-84; staff artist Guilford Mills, N.Y.C., 1984-85; laser graphics mgr. Pan Graphics, Inc., Garfield, N.J., 1985—. Tribal chief Indian Guides-YMCA, Verona-Montclair, N.J., 1989—.

LANGSAM, GERTRUDE FEINSTEIN, education educator; b. Bklyn., June 27, 1918; d. Max and Lena (Kroman) Feinstein; m. Henry Langsam, Nov. 8, 1942; 1 child, Barbara Langsam Blosveren. BA magna cum laude, Adelphi Coll., 1938; MA, Adelphi U., 1965. Adj. instr. L.I. U., Greenvale, N.Y., 1967; adj. asst. prof. Dowling Coll., Oakdale, N.Y., 1968-84; adj. prof. Adelphi U., Garden City, N.Y., 1968-84; adj. prof. emerita Adelphi U., Garden City, 1984. Co-editor: Global Images of Peace: Transforming The War System, 1985, reprint, 1987. Recipient Cert. of Recognition NCCJ, 1975, UN Assn. award, 1988, Leadership award New Haven YWCA, 1990, Mustard Seed award, 1991. Mem. Soc. for Ednl. Reconstrn. (founder, adv. com. 1969-90, sec. 1990, Gertrude Langsam award 1981), Phi Delta Kappa, Delta Kappa Gamma. Democrat. Jewish. Home: 123 York St New Haven CT 06511-5614

LANGSTON, CHARLES ADAM, geophysics educator; b. Athens, Ohio, Nov. 23, 1949. BS, Case Western Res. U., 1972; MS, Calif. Inst. Tech., 1974, PhD, 1976. Rsch. asst. Calif. Inst. Tech., Pasadena, 1972-74, 75-76, Louis D. Beaumont fellow, 1974-75, rsch. fellow, 1976-77; asst. prof. Pa. State U., University Park, 1977-82, assoc. prof., 1982-86, prof. geophysics, 1986—; cons. Arms Control and Disarmament Agy., Washington, 1986-90. Contbr. articles to profl. jours. Recipient Outstanding Jr. Faculty award ARCO, 1981. Mem. AAAS, Am. Geophys. Union, Seismol. Soc. Am. (pres. 1990-91), Geol. Soc. Am. Office: Pa State U Dept Geophysics 440 Deike Bldg University Park PA 16802

LANGTON, RAYMOND BENEDICT, III, manufacturing company executive; b. N.Y.C., Oct. 26, 1944; s. Raymond B. II and Viola M. (Swanson) L.; m. Regina M. Rose, July 20, 1968; children: Raymond B. IV, Tyler J. BA in History, U. Va., 1966; MBA, U. Pa., 1971. Dir. sales and mktg. Continental Forest Industries (Continental Group), Greenwich, Conn., 1974-78, dir. planning and devel., 1978-79; v.p. mktg, bus. devel. Fram (Allied Signal), Providence, 1979-81, v.p., gen. mgr. div. indsl. filtration, 1981-83, v.p. ops., 1983-86; pres. SKF Automotive Products, King of Prussia, Pa., 1986-87, SKF Bearing Industries Co., King of Prussia, 1987-91; pres., chief exec. officer SKF USA Inc., King of Prussia, 1991—, also bd. dirs. Mem. Antifriction Bearing Mfrs. Assn. (treas. 1990, vice chmn., pres. 1991). Office: SKF USA Inc 1100 1st Ave King Of Prussia PA 19406

LANGWEILER, MARK JAY, chiropractic physician, life science educator; b. Atlantic City, N.J., June 8, 1952; s. Burton Langweiler and Barbara E. (Feingold) Carp; m. Judith Hyman, June 6, 1976; children: Abigail, Norah. BA, Rutgers U., 1975; postgrad., U. Ark., 1976-78; DC, Cleve. Chiropractic Coll., 1988. Diplomate Am. Acad. Pain Mgmt. Product mgr. Springer-Verlag N.Y., Inc., N.Y.C., 1978-84; pvt. practice Northfield, N.J., 1988—; life sci. faculty Atlantic Community Coll., Mays Landing, N.J., 1990—; rsch. fellow Cleve. Chiropractic Coll., Kansas City, Mo., 1985-87. Editorial bd.: Am. Jour. Pain Mgmt., 1991—; host: (weekly radio broadcast) Innovations in Wellness. Mem. Internat. Arts-Medicine Assn., Inst. Noetic Scis., Atlantic County Chiropractic Soc. (founding), Somatic Soc., Rotary Internat. (substance abuse chmn. 1990-91). Jewish. Home: 219 N Douglas Ave Margate NJ 08402 Office: 600 New Rd Northfield NJ 08225

LANGWORTHY, JAMES BRIAN, research physicist; b. Billings, Mont., Feb. 18, 1934; s. Alan Wadleigh and Rhea Ellen (Kline) L.; m. Alva Edith Lawhorne, Jan. 16, 1965; children: Alan, Shelby. BS in Physics, U. Colo., 1956; MS in Physics, U. Md., 1966. Rsch. physicist Naval Rsch. Lab., Washington, 1959—. Pres. bd. dirs. Youth Resources Ctr., Inc., Hyattsville, Md., 1971-89. Lt. USN, 1956-59. Mem. Am. Phys. Soc., AAAS, Sigma Xi. Office: Naval Rsch Lab Code 4613 Washington DC 20375-5000

LANGWORTHY, KEITH CHARLES, chemical company executive; b. Phila., Oct. 2, 1956; s. David Collie and Norma Jane (Shea) L.; m. Diane Julie Joseph, Oct. 1, 1983; children: Kyle, Nicole. BS, NYU, 1978, MBA, 1981. V.p. Amivest Corp., N.Y.C., 1981-86; dir. acquisitions HMK Group Cos., Inc., Waltham, Mass., 1986-88; chief fin. officer S.A.Y. Industries, Inc., Leominster, Mass., 1988-89; mgr. acquisitions Uniroyal Chem. Co., Inc., Middlebury, Conn., 1989—. Mem. Soc. Chem. Mfrs. Republican. Home: 9 Limekiln Rd Ridgefield CT 06877 Office: Uniroyal Chem Co Inc Benson Rd Middlebury CT 06749

LANIER, RICHARD BLACKBURN, architect; b. Boston, May 7, 1958; s. Robert Blake Sims and Erma LaBelle (Lanier) L. BA, U. Va., 1980; BArch, Pratt Inst., 1983; M of Environ. Design, Yale U., 1986. Registered Architect, N.Y. Designer Stephen Lepp Assocs., N.Y.C., 1981-82, Tonetti Assocs. Architects, N.Y.C., 1983-86; assoc. Ted Reeds Assocs., N.Y.C., 1987-88, architect, 1988-90; prin. Automated Design Systems, N.Y.C., 1989—; systems cons., project architect Gwathmey Siegel & Assocs., N.Y.C., 1990—; mem. admissions com. Yale Sch. Architecture, 1984-85, mem. rules com., dean search com., 1984-86; instr. computer-aided design SUNY, 1991—; cons. in field. Author: Landmarks of the Vertical City, 1986; contbr. articles to Newsday, N.Y. Times, N.Y. Tribune. Mem. Computer Graphics Assn. Libertarian. Episcopalian. Home: 300 W 49th St New York NY 10019 also: 4334 Crawford Ave San Diego CA 92105 Office: Automated Design Systems 730 Wall St Sta New York NY 10268

LANIER, THOMAS, chemical and export company executive; b. Cienfuegos, Cuba, Sept. 18, 1923; came to U.S., 1938; s. Joseph and Irene (Medina) L.; divorced; children: Margie, Robert, George, Thomas Emil; m. Julie Gonzalez, May 1, 1980. Student, Bowens Bus. Coll., 1939-40, Latin Am. Inst., 1940-41; BBA, Havana U., 1948; postgrad., St. Mary's U., San Antonio, 1955. Mgr. sales Joskes of Tex., San Antonio, 1949-51; mgr. office investment corp. San Antonio, 1951-55; v.p. internat. sales Sun-X Internat. Export Corp., San Antonio, 1955-59; pres. Sun-X Internat. Ltd., Houston, 1963-66; pres., mgr. Tri-X Internat. Co., North Bergen, 1963—; pres., chief exec. officer Lanier Shipping Co., Inc., North Bergen, N.J., 1966-87; internat. trade cons. Falor Assocs. Inc., North Bergen, 1987—, Factory Assocs. & Exporters, East Hanover, N.J., 1987—. Served with USAF, 1943-45. Recipient E award U.S. Govt., 1963. Mem. Am. Soc. Internat. Execs., C. of C. of Shipping (pres. North Bergen 1982-88), Bogota (N.J.) Tenants Assn., Am. Radio Relay League. Democrat. Roman Catholic. Office: Tri-X Internat Co 7500 Bergenline Ave North Bergen NJ 07047-9995

LANIGAN, JAMES JOSEPH, public relations professional; b. N.Y.C., Sept. 4, 1924; s. Irving Terrence and Audrey (Shapiro) L.; m. Christine Johnstone, Feb. 11, 1952; children: John, Cataline, Brendan, Lotus Blossom, Angela, Manny. BA, Fordham U., 1943; FEA, Harvard U., 1946; MA, Columbia U., 1947. Commd. 2d lt. U.S. Army, 1943, advanced through grades to lt. col., served with Mil. Intelligence, 1943-63; desk chief Voice of Am., N.Y.C., 1952-54; Chinese affairs officer USIA, Bangkok, 1954-56; project mgr. Sylvania Electric Products, Inc., N.Y.C., 1956-62; advanced to lt. col., 1966; ret. U.S. Army, 1968; dir. pub. affairs GTE Govt. Systems Corp., Waltham, Mass., 1962—. Columnist Ag-Pilot and Conair mags.; contbr. articles to mil. publs. Pres. Waltham Boys and Girls Club, 1970-71; bd. dirs. Chinese Golden Age Ctr., 1987—. Fellow in Chinese studies Chinese Ministry Culture, Columbia U., 1947. Mem. Aviation Space Writers Assn. Home: 19 Abbott Rd Wellesley Hills MA 02254 Office: GTE Govt Systems Corp 100 1st Ave Charlestown MA 02129-2024

LANKFORD, JOHN LLEWELLYN, energy technology consultant; b. Hampton, Va., Sept. 13, 1920; s. Stephen Foster and Frances (Llewelling) L.; B.S., Va. Poly. Inst., 1942; postgrad. U. Va., 1947-48; m. Mary Louise Charlton, June 29, 1945; children—John Foster, Susan Charlton. With Nat. Adv. Com. for Aeros., Hampton, Va., 1945-52, Westinghouse-Melpar, Alexandria, Va., 1952-53; head gas dynamics lab. Experiment, Inc., Richmond, Va., 1954-58; project mgr. Naval Surface Weapons Center, Washington, 1958-61, cons. Dept. Navy, 1964-76; chief advanced studies NASA, Washington, 1961-64; acting dept. head, lectr. Montgomery Coll., Rockville, Md., 1977-78; cons. energy program U. Md., College Park, 1979-80; cons. energy tech., Silver Spring, Md., 1980—; mentor, advisor, lectr. sci. fair competitions and magnet programs Montgomery County Schs., 1985—. Served with U.S. Army, 1942-45. Decorated Purple Heart. Fellow AIAA (assoc.). Methodist. Contbr. articles in field to profl. jours. Home and Office: 1717 Marymont Rd Silver Spring MD 20906-1240

LANKS, KARL WILLIAM, pathologist, educator; b. Phila., Nov. 1, 1942; s. Gustav Wilhelm and Elizabeth Emma (Rentschler) L.; m. Jane Simon, June 3, 1967 (div. June 1976); children: Claire, Belinda; m. Nena Chin, Apr. 16, 1979; children: Paul, Charles, Cristina. BA, Cen. U., Phila., 1960; BS, Pa. State U., 1963; MD, Temple U., 1967; PhD, Columbia U., 1971. Diplomate Am. Bd. Pathology. Intern Columbia P & S, N.Y.C., 1967-68; instr. Columbia U., N.Y.C., 1970-72; rsch. fellow Francis Delafield Hosp., N.Y.C., 1968-70, Harvard U., Boston, 1970-72; asst. prof. SUNY, Bklyn., 1974-78, assoc. prof., 1978-88, prof., 1988—; cons. Staten Island (N.Y.) Hosp., 1988—, StressGen Biotechnologies, Victoria, Can., 1991—. Author: Academic Environment, 1990; contbr. numerous articles and papers to profl. jours. Maj. USA, 1972-74. Grantee NIH, Am. Cancer Soc. Mem. Am. Soc. Cell Biology, Am. Soc. Exptl. Pathology, Am. Soc. Biochemistry and Molecular Biology, Am. Assn. Univ. Pathologists. Office: SUNY HSC at Brooklyn PO Box 25 Brooklyn NY 11203-0001

LANNAMANN, RICHARD STUART, executive recruiting consultant; b. Cin., Sept. 4, 1947; s. Frank E. and Grace I. (Tomlinson) L. AB in Econs., Yale U., 1969; MBA, Harvard U., 1973; m. Margaret Appleton Payne, June 21, 1969; children: Thomas Cleveland, Edward Payne, John Stewart. Investment analyst U.S. Trust Co. N.Y., N.Y.C., 1969-71; rsch. analyst Smith, Barney & Co., N.Y.C., 1973-75, 2d v.p., 1975-77, v.p. successor firm rsch. div. Smith Barney Harris Upham & Co., 1977-78; v.p. Russell Reynolds Assocs., Inc., N.Y.C., 1978-83, mng. dir. 1983-86, 87—; sr. v.p. Mgmt. Asset Corp., Westport, Conn., 1986-87. Mem. N.Y. Soc. Security Analysts, Assn. for Investment Mgmt. and Rsch., Inst. Chartered Fin. Analysts, Riverside Yacht Club, Yale Club of N.Y., Links Club. Home: 25 Cathlow Dr Riverside CT 06878-2602 Office: 200 Park Ave New York NY 10166-0005

LANNON, KATHLEEN MARIA, information consultant; b. Cumberland, Md., Jan. 21, 1949; d. Clifton Miller and Agnes Josephine (Walsh) Marsh; m. Peter Francis Lannon, Apr. 29, 1983. AA cum laude, Mt. Aloysius Jr. Coll., 1969; BA, George Mason U., 1979; postgrad., George Washington U., 1987-88. Mgmt. analyst Nat. Archives and Records Adminstrn., Washington, 1970-80, Gen. Svcs. Adminstrn., Washington, 1980-85, Dept. of State, Washington, 1985-90; prin. Lannon Info. Cons., Vienna, Va., 1990—. Editor college literary magazine, 1969; contbr. articles to profl. jours. Home and Office: 2781 Grovemore Ln Vienna VA 22180-7069

LANSKY, AARON JONATHAN, non-profit organization executive; b. New Bedford, Mass., June 17, 1955; s. Sidney and Edith (Bieler) L.; m. Gail Judith Sharpe, Apr. 1, 1990. BA, Hampshire Coll., 1977; cert., Columbia U., 1977; MA, McGill U., Montreal, Que., Can., 1980. Founder and exec. dir. Nat. Yiddish Book Ctr., Amherst, Mass., 1980-90, pres., 1990—. Contbr. articles to profl. jours. Named Tzedakah Hero Coalition for Alternatives in Jewish Edn., 1986; recipient Yiddish Citation award Jewish Book Coun., 1986, Myrtle Wreath award Hadassah, 1987, Community Svc. award Moment mag., 1989, Disting. Humanitarian award Ohio State U.; MacArthur fellow John D. and Catherine T. MacArthur Found., 1989. Mem. ACLU, Amnesty Internat., Jewish Peace Fellowship, Assn. for Jewish Studies. Home: 55 Yale St Holyoke MA 01040 Office: Nat Yiddish Book Ctr 48 Woodbridge St South Hadley MA 01075

LANTOS, GEOFFREY PAUL, marketing educator; b. West Chester, Pa., June 20, 1952; s. Peter Richard and Janice Hope (Kirchner) L.; m. Lori Lynn Heath, Aug. 24, 1984; children: Joshua Paul, Kristina Lynn. BA, Gettysburg Coll., 1974; MBA, U. Rochester, 1976; PhD, Lehigh U., 1980. Asst. prof. mktg. Ea. Mich. U., Ypsilanti, 1980-81, Bentley Coll., Waltham, Mass., 1981-86, Stonehill Coll., North Eaton, Mass., 1986-89; assoc. prof. mktg. Stonehill Coll., North Eaton, 1989—; adj. prof. mktg. Muhlenberg Coll., Allentown, Pa., 1977, Allentown Coll., 1977, N.H. Coll., Manchester, 1986; adj. prof. econs. Moravian Coll., Bethlehem, Pa., 1978, 80; lectr. mktg. River Coll., Nashua, N.J., 1985; cons. to media, edn. workshops; mem. editorial Jour. Ministry Mktg. and Mgmt.; bd. contbrs. Jour. Consumer Mktg., Jour. Svcs. Mktg. Author: Fundamentals of Direct Mail Marketing, 1985, Pricing Strategies and Practices, 1988, Successful Product Management: How to Make Your Product a Winner, 1989; contbr. articles to profl. jours.; various radio talk show appearances and acad. conf. presentations. Sunday sch. tchr. Trinity Bapt. Ch., Nashua, 1985-86, Attleboro (Mass.) Advent Christian Ch., 1988-91, Foxboro Bapt. Ch., 1992—; mem. Christian Bus. Faculty Assn. Scholar U. Rochester, 1974-76, Carnegie fellow Lehigh U., 1976-80; faculty rsch. grantee Bentley Coll., 1984, faculty rsch. grantee Stonehill Coll., 1987, 90. Mem. Am. Acad. Advt., Am. Mktg. Assn., N.E. Decision Sci. Inst., Product Devel. and Mgmt. Assn. (jour. abstract reviewer), Phi Beta Kappa, Beta Gamma Sigma, Pi Lambda Sigma. Republican. Baptist. Home: 3 Crane St Norton MA 02766-2908 Office: Stonehill Coll Bus Adminstrn Dept North Easton MA 02357

LANTZ, DAVID CARSON, mathematics educator; b. Topton, Pa., Nov. 15, 1946; s. Carson Oliver and Harriet Mary (Smith) L. BS in Secondary Edn., Kutztown U., 1968; MA, U. Kans., 1972, PhD, 1975. Tchr. Palmyra (Pa.) Area High Sch., 1968; vis. asst. prof. U. Nebr., Omaha, 1975-76; vis. instr. U. Ga., Athens, 1976-77; prof. Colgate U., Hamilton, N.Y., 1977—; vis. prof. Purdue U., West Lafayette, Ind., 1984-75, 90-91. Mem. Am. Math. Soc., Math. Assn. Am. Home: RR 2 Box 324 Hamilton NY 13346-9574 Office: Colgate U Math Dept Hamilton NY 13346

LANZA, KENNETH ANTHONY, foreign service officer; b. Bklyn., Dec. 29, 1953; s. Anthony Robert and Carmela (Alfano) L.; m. Sheri Ross, May 22, 1981; children: Kelsey Anastasia, Jessica Kimberly. AB, Colgate U., 1977; MBA, U. Miami, 1979. Gen. mgr. O.H.S. Ltd., London, 1977-78; adminstrv. and fin. mgr. Burroughs Corp., Miami, Fla., 1979-80; mktg. coord. C.B.S. Internat., Miami, 1980-84; chief, pvt. sector U.S. Fgn. Svc., A.I.D., Washington, 1984—; fgn svc. officer, consular officer, sec. Diplomatic Svc. U.S.A., 1989—. Author: The Art of Market Planning, 1982, Spanish edit., 1982. Recipient Meritorious awards U.S. Govt., 1988, 90, 91. Home and Office: Agy for Internat Devel Dept of State APO AA 34020

LANZAFAME, RAYMOND JOSEPH, surgeon, researcher; b. Rochester, N.Y., Sept. 30, 1952; s. Ray J. and Mary Vera (DeMeis) L.; m. Patricia Marie Volkmar, Apr. 26, 1980; children: Mark Raymond, Karen Elizabeth. BS with honors and distinction, Cornell U., 1974; MD, George Washington U., 1978. Diplomate Nat. Bd. Med. Examiners, Am. Bd. Surgery. Clin. asst. prof. U. Rochester, N.Y., 1983-87, asst. prof., 1987—; mem. laser task force N.Y. State Dept. of Health, 1990; dir. laser tng., chmn. laser usage com., Rochester Gen. Hosp. 1983—, dir. surg. laser rsch. lab., 1988—, dir. Laser Ctr., 1984—; bd. dirs. Rochester Gen. Hosp. Found., 1990—. Sr. editor Jour. Clin. Laser Surgery and Medicine; mem. editorial bd. Laser Surgery and Medicine, 1987—, referee, 1987—; mem. editorial bd. Laser Medicine and Surgery News and Advances, 1988-90, Jour. of Laparoendoscopic Surgery, 1991—, Surgery Alert, 1991—. Grantee Am. Cancer Soc. Fellow ACS (young surgeon rep. 1992); mem. AMA, Southern Med. Assn., Med. Soc. State of N.Y., Monroe County Med. Soc., Rochester Surg. Soc., Rochester Acad. Medicine, Am. Soc. for Laser Medicine and Surgery, Assn. for Acad. Surgery, Collegium Internationale Chirugie Digestive, N.Y. Acad. Sci., Acad. Surg. Rsch., Internat. Soc. for Lasers in Surgery and Medicine, Internat. Soc. Surgery, Soc. for Surgery of Alimentary Tract, Cen. Surg. Assn., Cen. N.Y. Surg. Soc., Soc. Photo-Optical Instrumentation Engrs. Office: 1445 Portland Ave # 202 Rochester NY 14621-3008

LANZANO, RALPH EUGENE, civil engineer; b. N.Y.C., Dec. 26, 1926; s. Ralph and Frances (Giuliano) L.; B.C.E., NYU, 1959. Engring. aide Seelye, Stevenson, Value, Knecht, N.Y.C., 1957-58; jr. civil engr. N.Y.C. Dept. Public Works (name changed to N.Y.C. Dept. Water Resources), 1960-63, asst. civil engr., 1963-68; civil engr., 1968-71; sr. san. engr. Parsons, Brinckerhoff, Quade & Douglas, N.Y.C., 1971-72; civil engr. N.Y.C. Dept. Water Resources, 1972-77, N.Y.C. Dept. Environ. Protection, 1978-90; ret., 1990. Registered profl. engr., N.Y. Mem. NRA (life), ASCE (life), ASTM, Nat., N.Y. socs. profl. engrs., Water Pollution Control Fedn., Am. Water Works Assn., Am. Public Health Assn., Am. Fedn. Arts (contbg.), U.S. Inst. Theatre Tech., NYU Alumni Assn., Am. Nat. Theatre and Acad., Lincoln Center Performing Arts, Film Soc. Lincoln Ctr., U.S. Lawn Tennis Assn. (life), Nat., Internat. wildlife fedns., Nat. Parks and Conservation Assn., Nat. Geog. Soc., Nat. Audubon Soc., Am. Automobile Assn., Bklyn. Bot. Garden, Am. Mus. Natural History, Chi Epsilon. Home: 17 Cottage Ct Huntington Station NY 11746-1104

LANZILOTTI, THOMAS ANTHONY, cardiologist; b. Washington, Dec. 7, 1953; s. Anthony Edward and Maureen Ann (Haney) L.; m. Jean Marie Donohue, Oct. 10, 1981; children: Joseph, John, Mary Jean, Ann Marie. BS in Physics, Premed., Fairfield U., 1976; MD, SUNY, 1980. Diplomate Am. Bd. Internal Medicine. Intern internal medicine SUNY Downstate, King County Hosp., Bklyn. VA, 1980-81, resident internal medicine, 1981-83, fellow cardiology, 1983-85; attending cardiologist Wallhill Valley Hosp. Ctr., Sussex, N.J., 1985—, chief ICU, critical care unit, 1992—, co-chmn. dept. medicine, 1991—; instr. ACLS, Am. Heart Assn., 1990. Active Right to Life, 1992. Fellow Am. Coll. Cardiology; mem. ACP, Am. Heart Assn. (pres. Sussex County unit 1987-88), Sussex County Med. Soc., N.J. Med. Soc. Roman Catholic. Office: Viking Village Ste 5F RR 4 Vernon NJ 07462

LANZKRON, ROLF WOLFGANG, manufacturing company executive; b. Hamburg, Fed. Republic of Germany, Dec. 9, 1929; came to U.S., 1951, naturalized, 1961; s. Aron Artur and Hanna (Farbstein) L. m. Amy Virginia Yarri, Mar. 5, 1961; children: Paul Joshua, Sophie Miriam, Lisa Rachel. BS, Milw. Sch. Engring., 1953; MS, U. Wis., 1955, PhD, 1956. Registered profl. engr. Calif. Computer designer Univac Sperry Rand, St. Paul, 1956-58; guidance and control systems integrations staff Martin Marietta, Orlando, Fla., 1958-61; systems engr. Martin Marietta, Balt., 1961-68; became chief command and svc. module flight project div. NASA Manned Spacecraft Ctr., Apollo Program, Houston, 1963; graphic ops. mgr. Raytheon Co., Marlborough, Mass., 1968-82, dep. dir. air traffic control, 1982-92, dir. air traffic control, 1992—; Registered profl. engr., Calif. With Israeli Army, 1948-51. Recipient NASA Outstanding Achievement award, 1964, Spl. Svc. award, 1966. Mem. AIAA, Am. Math. Soc., IEEE, Am. Mgmt. Assn.,

Sigma Xi. Home: 8 Hickory Dr Medfield MA 02052-1131 Office: Raytheon Co Equipment Div Boston Post Rd Marlborough MA 01752-3503

LAPADULA, ROBERT MAURO, social worker; b. Lowell, Mass., Jan. 8, 1938; s. Mauro and Emily Evelyn (McElroy) L. Student, Dartmouth Coll., 1955-58; AB, Boston U., 1967. Lic. social worker, Conn. Supr. social svcs. Mass. Dept. Social Svc., Boston, 1969-78; retail buyer Batus Corp.-Frederick-Nelson, Seattle, 1978-82; sales rep. Universal Foods Corp., San Francisco, 1982-86; social worker Conn. Dept. Child & Youth Svc., Rockville, 1986—. Home: 123 Hall Hill Rd Somers CT 06071-1415 Office: Conn Dept Child & Youth Svc 1 Court St Vernon Rockville CT 06066-3611

LAPCHICK, RICHARD EDWARD, educator, civil rights specialist; b. Yonkers, N.Y., July 16, 1945; s. Jopseph Bohumiel and Elizabeth (Sarubbi) L.; m. Sandra Miller (div. Oct. 1988); children: Joseph Michael, Elisa Chamy; m. Ann Lavaughn Pasnak, Feb. 18, 1992; 1 child, Emily. BA in Polit. Sci., St. John's U., 1967; MA in Internat. Studies, U. Denver, 1970, PhD in African Studies, 1973. Assoc. prof. polit. sci. Va. Wesleyan Coll., 1970-78; sr. liaison officer UN Ctr. Against Apartheid, N.Y.C., 1978-80, World Conf. for UN Decade for Women, N.Y.C., 1980-81, Internat. Conf. on the Mid. East, N.Y.C., 1982-83; dir. Ctr. for the Study of Sport in Soc. Northeastern U., Boston, 1984—. Author: The Politics of Race and International Sport: The Case of South Africa, 1975, Resisting Oppression: The Saga of Women in Southern Africa, 1982, Broken Promises: Racism in American Sport, 1984, On the Mark: Putting the Student Back in the Student-Athlete, 1986, The Rules of the Game: Ethics in College Sports 1989, Five Minutes to Midnight: Race and Sport in the 1990s, 1991; editor Jour. Sport & Social Issues, 1975-78, World Conf. of UN Decade for Women, 1981; mem. editorial bd. various refereed jours.; contbr. over 150 articles to profl. jours. Dir. Phelps Stokes Fund, N.Y., 1981; nat. chairperson ACCESS, Boston, 1976—; exec. dir. ARENA, The Inst. for Sport and Social Analysis, Boston, 1974—, exec. bd. dirs. Am. Com. on Africa, N.Y., 1978-86; exec. dir. PRIDE, Denver, 1968-70. Recipient Humanitarian of Yr. award United Meth. Ch. Fedn., N.Y., 1978, Tenn. Coalition Against Racism and Apartheid, 1978, Kenneth Kuanda Humanism award Kenneth Kuanda Assn., N.Y., 1987, World of Difference award Anti-Defamation League, Boston, 1991, Dryslongo award for Combatting Racism Community Exch., 1991, Man of Yr. award Nat. Invitation Tournament, 1992; Martin Luther King fellow Ford Foun., 1969. Mem. Am. Polit. Sci. Assn., African Studies Assn., N.Am. Soc. for Sport Sociology. Office: Northeastern U/Ctr for the Study of Sport in Soc 360 Huntington Ave 161 CP Boston MA 02115

LAPHAM, LOWELL WINSHIP, physician educator, researcher; b. New Hampton, Iowa, Mar. 20, 1922; s. Percy Charles and Altha Theresa (Dygert) L.; m. Miriam Amanda Sellers, June 22, 1945 (div. 1982); children: Joan, Steven, Judith, Jennifer. BA, Oberlin Coll., 1943; MD cum laude, Harvard U., 1948. Diplomate Am. Bd. Pathology in neuropathology, Am. Bd. Psychiatry and Neurology in neurology. Instr. Case Western Res. U. Sch. Medicine, Cleve., 1955-57, asst. prof., 1957-64, assoc. prof., 1964; assoc. prof. U. Rochester (N.Y.) Sch. Medicine, 1964-69, prof., 1969—; cons. in neuropathology Cleve. Met. Gen. Hosp., 1957-64, Cleve. VA Hosp., 1957-64, Genesee Hosp., Rochester, 1966—, Rochester Gen. Hosp., 1966—. Contbr. numerous articles to profl. jours. 1st lt. USAR, 1951-53. Fellow Nat. Multiple Sclerosis Soc., 1957-59; rsch. grantee NIH, USPHS. Mem. Am. Assn. Neuropathologists. Unitarian. Home: 1380 Elmwood Ave Apt 4 Rochester NY 14620-3150 Office: U Rochester Med Ctr 601 Elmwood Ave Rochester NY 14642-9999

LAPIDES, JULIAN LEE, state senator, lawyer; b. Balt., Sept. 17, 1931; s. Solomon M. and Doris (Racusin) L.; m. Linda Zeva Fishman, 1964. BS, Towson State U., 1954; LLB, U. Md., 1961. Tchr. sci. pub. schs., 1956-60; admitted to Md. bar, 1965; practice law, Balt., 1965—; mem. Md. Ho. of Dels., 1963-67, Md. State Senate, 1967—; mem. senate budget and taxation com., 1967—, co-chmn. joint com. legis. ethics, joint budget and audit com. Mem. Md. State Arts Council, 1967—, Md. Hall Records Commn., Md. State Planning Commn., Md. State Housing Policy Commn.; pres. Mt. Royal Democratic Club. Served with AUS, 1954-56. Recipient Md. Pub. Health Assn. Ann. Achievement award, 1971, Nat. Kidney Found. Disting. Service award, 1971, Young Democrat of Md. Outstanding State Ofcl. award, 1973, Cert. of Merit Common Cause Md., 1982. Mem. Am. Antiquarian Soc. (council 1983—). Address: 1528 Bolton St Baltimore MD 21217 Office: Md State Senate Office Bldg Annapolis MD 21401

LAPIDUS, ARNOLD, mathematician; b. Bklyn., Nov. 6, 1933; s. Morris and Mollie L. m. Nancy Beatrice Latner, Aug. 9, 1952. BS, Bklyn. Coll., 1956; MS, PhD, N.Y. U., 1967. Research scientist Courant Inst., N.Y.C., 1956-68; computer application math. analyst Goddard Inst. for Space Studies, N.Y.C., 1968-70, math. analyst programming methods, 1970-71, sr. mem. tech. staff computer scis., 1971-73; assoc. prof. quantitative analysis Fairleigh Dickinson U., Teaneck, N.J., 1973-83, prof., chair dept. computer and decision systems, 1983-85; sr. engr. Singer Electronic Systems Corp., Little Falls, N.J., 1986-87; owner Advanced Math. Co., Englewood, N.J., 1987—; pvt. practice Englewood, 1987—. Contbr. articles to profl. publs. Mem. AAAS, Math. Assn. Am., Am. Math. Soc., Soc. Indsl. and Applied Math. Home and Office: 160 Rockwood Pl Englewood NJ 07631-5028 Office: 160 Rockwood Pl Englewood NJ 07631-5028

LAPIDUS, LEAH BLUMBERG, clinical psychologist, educator; b. Chgo., Apr. 6, 1938; d. Louis and Kay (Kahan) Blumberg; m. I. Richard Lapidus, Feb. 28, 1959 (dec. 1988); children: Louise Jesse Wind, Lenora Michelle, Kyle A. Blumberg. Early entrant, U. Chgo., 1954; cert. (12th grade), 1955; BA in Biology, Psychology, Sociology, NYU, 1960, PhD in Clin. Psychology, 1968; MA in Devel. Psychology, Columbia U., 1961. Lic. psychologist, N.Y., N.J., Calif., Israel; diplomate Am. Bd. Profl. Psychology, Nat. Register of Health Svc. Providers in Psychology. Clin. psychology trainee Bronx (N.Y.) VA Hosp., 1962-63; psychotherapy trainee NYU Psychology Clinic, 1966-67; researcher NYU Rsch. Ctr. for Mental Health, 1966-67; clin. psychology intern VA, N.Y.C., 1967-68; instr. in clin. psychology, psychologist in charge NYU Med. Ctr., Bellevue Hosp., 1968-72; from asst. prof. to prof. dept. clin. psychology Columbia U. Tchrs. Coll., N.Y.C., 1972—; vis. prof. UCLA, Hebrew U., 1980, 86-87; vis. scientist Weizmann Inst. Sci., Rehovot, Israel, 1986-87, 88; vis. lectr. Oxford U., U. London Med. Sch., 1982; psychotherapist Group Health Ins., N.Y.C., 1969—; com. mem. Chancellor's Adv. Commn. on Child Abuse, N.Y.C. Bd. Edn., 1988; cons. psychology ACLU, 1969—, VA Hosps. and Clinics, 1969—, Amnesty Internat., 1969—. Contbr. articles on rsch. and intervention on social experience and neurophysiology to profl. jours. USPHS/NIMH and Indian Health Svc. grantee, 1966-67, 90-91. Fellow APA, Am. Psychol. Soc., Am. Ortho-Psychiat. Assn., N.Y.C. Soc. Clin. Psychologists (exec. bd. 1974-75, clin. assoc. psychol. svc. ctr. 1969—), Psychologists for Social Action (nat. exec. bd. 1969-75); mem. AAAS, AAUP, N.Y. Acad. Scis., Internat. Soc. Psychosomatic Obstetrics and Gynecology. Office: Columbia U Tchrs Coll 525 W 120th St New York NY 10027-6625

LAPIDUS, LEONARD, insurance company executive; b. N.Y.C., June 10, 1929; s. Abram and Mary (Leichter) L.; m. Jacqueline Gale Smith, Feb. 6, 1981. BS, City Coll. of N.Y., 1951; MA, NYU, 1960, PhD, 1975. Mid. mgmt. N.Y. Telephone Co., N.Y.C., 1953-62; v.p. Fed. Res. Bank of N.Y., N.Y.C., 1962-75; supt. of banks N.Y. State Banking Dept., N.Y.C., 1975-77; spl. asst. to chmn. FDIC, Washington, 1977-79; pres. Cen. Liquid Facility Nat. Credit Union Adminstrn., Washington, 1979-81; pres. Mut. Savs. Cen. Fund, Boston, 1981—. Author, editor: Public Policy Toward Mutual Savings Banks in New York State, 1974, State and Federal Regulation of Commercial Banks, 1980. Sgt. U.S. Army, 1951-52, Korea. Mem. Am. Econ. Assn., Nat. Assn. of Bus. Economists, Phi Beta Kappa. Republican. Jewish. Home: 34 Ledyard Rd Winchester MA 01890-4039 Office: Mut Savs Cen Fund Inc One Linscott Rd Woburn MA 01801

LAPIDUS, NORMAN ISRAEL, food broker; b. N.Y.C., July 20, 1930; s. Rueben and Laurette (Goldsmith) L.;m. Myrna Sue Cohen, Nov. 20, 1960; children: Robin Anne, Jody Beth. BBA, CCNY, 1952; postgrad. internat. Relations, CCNY, NYU, 1957-60. Salesman Rueben Lapidus Co., N.Y.C., 1954-56, pres., 1960—; sales trainee Cohn-Hall-Marx, N.Y.C., 1955; salesman to v.p. Julius Levy Co., Millburn, N.J., 1964-66, pres., 1966—; salesman Harry W. Freedman Co., Millburn, N.J., 1975-76, v.p., treas., 1976-84, pres., 1984—; pres. Julius Levy/Rueben Lapidus and Harry W. Freedman Cos. div. Pezrow Corp., Millburn, N.J., 1985-86, L&H Food Brokers, Millburn, N.J., 1986-87. Mem. Maplewood (N.J.) Bd. Adjustment, 1975-82; gen. chmn. Maplewood Citizens Budget Adv. Com., 1977-79, chmn. Maplewood United Jewish Appeal Drive, 1975-76, 83-84; vice-chmn. Maplewood First Aid Squad Bldg. Fund Dr., 1978-79; co-founder Citizens for Charter Change in Essex County (N.J.), 1974, mem. exec. bd., 1974—, treas., 1983-84; founder, chmn. Music Theatre of Maplewood; pres. Maplewood Civic Assn., 1983-85; bd. mgrs. Essex County unit Am. Cancer Soc., v.p., 1984-87, chmn. 1991—; mem. adv. bd. Essex County Coll., West Essex, N.J., chairperson bd., 1991—. Served with U.S. Army, 1952-54, Korea Active local theatricals. Recipient Leadership Medallion United Jewish Appeal, 1970, 84. Mem. Nat. Food Brokers Assn. (regional dir., Cert. Exceptionally Meritorious Svc.), Nat. Food Svc. Sales Com., Met. Food Brokers Assn. (chmn. 1982-90), Assn. Food Industries (bd. dirs.), Nat. Food Processors Assn., Young Guard Soc., Old Guard Soc., CCNY Alumni Assn., U.S. Navy Inst., Acad. Polit. Sci., Archaeol. Inst. Am., Nat. Trust for Historic Preservation, Assn. Food Distbrs., LWV, Am. Legion, Lions (bd. dirs.), B'nai Brith. Republican. Jewish. Club: Maplewood Glee. Home: 21 Lewis Dr Maplewood NJ 07040-1005 Office: 2204 Morris Ave Ste 310 Union NJ 07083-5914

LAPIN, ABRAHAM, chemical engineer; b. Cairo, Sept. 30, 1923; s. Leib and Frida (Shlank) L.; m. Barbara Lapin, May 4, 1950 (dec.); children: Jonathan, Josh. BSChemE, U. Mich., 1949; MS, Poly. Inst. Bklyn., 1955; PhD, Lehigh U., 1963. Asst. engr. Am Israeli Shipping Co., Inc., N.Y.C., 1949-51; sales mgr. Dapor Trading Co., Inc., Englewood, N.J., 1951-52; materials engr. U.S. Corps Engrs., N.Y.C., 1953; chem. engr. mineral beneficiation lab. Columbia U., N.Y.C., 1954; chem. engr. Air Products and Chems., Inc., Allentown, Pa., 1955-57, project engr., 1957-59, group leader, 1959-63, sect. mgr. cryogenic engring. R&D, 1963-75; lectr. Pa. State U., Allentown, 1961, Lehigh U., Bethlehem, Pa., 1964-75. Cpl. USAF, 1945-46. Mem. Am. Chem. Soc., Am. Inst. Chem. Engring. Jewish. Home: 845 Palmer Ave Mamaroneck NY 10543-2406

LAPINSKI, FRANCES CONSTANCE, data processing systems executive; b. Flushing, N.Y., Sept. 19, 1950; d. Frank Stanley and Frances A. (Giziano) L. BS in Edn., SUNY, Oswego, 1972, MS in Edn., 1974; postgrad. in program edn., adminstrn., Syracuse U., 1976; MBA, NYU, 1990. Tchr. Mexico (N.Y.) Boces, 1971-72; chancellor's intern SUNY, Oswego, 1972-74; coordinator housing Lemoyne Coll., Syracuse, 1974-76; project coordinator Am. Assn. State Colls. and Univs., Washington, 1976-79; project mgr. Robt Bell & Co., Balt., 1979-81; asst. treas. Chase Manhattan Bank, N.Y., 1981-84; mgr. systems and computing Depository Trust Co., N.Y., 1984—. Vol. Spl. Olympics, N.J., N.Y., 1984—; chmn. Outreach Program, St. Andrew and Holy Communion Ch., South Orange, N.J., 1991—. Mem. Microcomputer Mgrs. Assn. (vendor liaison 1986—, bd. dirs., 1991). Home: 11 S Kingman Rd South Orange NJ 07079-2611

LAPORTE, WILLIAM FRANCIS, education educator; b. Hartford, Conn., May 27, 1933; s. William Francis Sr. and Alice (Rhoades) LaP.; m. Justine Mac Carthy, May 4, 1957; children: Lee Ann, David. BA, Trinity Coll., 1955, MA in Econs., 1967. V.p. investments CIGNA Corp., Hartford, 1955-88; adj. prof. U. Hartford, 1990—, Greater Hartford Community Coll., 1990—; chmn. Capital Region Edn. Coun., Hartford, 1975-77, Gov.'s Task Force on Health Care Fin., Conn., 1978-80, Conn. Housing Investment Fund, Hartford, 1987-89, bd. dirs. Elected mem. Newington (Conn.) Bd. of Edn., 1971-75; chmn. Rep. Party, Newington, 1975-78, mem. town com., 1973-78; mem. West Hartford Rep. Town Com., 1980—; chmn. Human Rights Commn., West Hartford, Conn., 1980-85. Fellow Assn. Investment Mgmt. and Rsch.; mem. Co. of Fifes and Drummers, Hartford Soc. Fin. Analysts, Hartford Club. Roman Catholic. Home: 26 Tumblebrook Ln West Hartford CT 06117-1457

LAPRADE, JAMES NICHOLAS, electrical and design engineer; b. Teaneck, N.J., Jan. 21, 1956; s. James Wallace and Elizabeth Henshall (Keeton) LaP.; m. Melissa Mary Tysenn; children: Matthew, Jeffery. BSEE, Va. Poly. Inst., 1978; MSEE, Drexel U., 1982, postgrad., 1982-84. Cert. engr.-in-tng., Va. Assoc. mem. tech. staff Astro Electronics Div. RCA, East Windsor, N.J., 1978-80; mem. tech. staff RCA, East Windsor, 1980-84, sr. mem. tech. staff, 1984-85, mgr. microwave cir. tech. devel., 1985-86, mgr. antenna systems tech., 1986-87; mgr. microwave power systems design Astro Space Div. GE, Princeton, N.J., 1987-91; dir. communications payload engring. Fairchild Space, Germantown, Md., 1991—. Contbr. articles to profl. jours.; patentee microwave cir. interconnect system, overdrive control of FET power amplifier. Elder Presbyn. Ch., 1987. Mem. IEEE, AIAA (chmn. publs. subcom. tech. com. communication systems 1988—), IEEE Microwave Theory and Techniques Soc. (chmn. Princeton, N.J. chpt. 1989-91). Home: 8704 Snow Valley Ct Gaithersburg MD 20879-4628 Office: Fairchild Space 20301 Century Blvd Germantown MD 20874-1181

LA PRE, LISA MARIE, treasury analyst; b. N.Y.C., May 4, 1968; d. Cordell Herbert and Lynette Marina La Pre. BSBA cum laude, Boston U., 1990. Fin. mgmt. profl. Am. Express Co., N.Y.C., 1990-91; asst. v.p. Shearson Lehman Bros., Inc., N.Y.C., 1991—; fin. analyst Am. Express Travel Related Svcs., N.Y.C., 1990. Vol. Street Project, N.Y.C., 1991. Mem. Boston U. Young Alumni Club, Golden Key. Roman Catholic. Office: Shearson Lehman Bros/Am Express Co World Fin Ctr 200 Vesey St 12th Fl New York NY 10285-0001

LAPRIME, JEAN-HENRI ANTONIN, insurance investigator; b. Boston, Sept. 7, 1952; s. Henri Jean A. and Maria (Moshides) L.; m. Ruth A. Payne Laprime, Feb. 4, 1978; children: Martine M. Laprime, Jean-Robert H. Laprime. AA, Newton Jr. Coll., 1972; BA cum laude, Boston U., 1974; MA, Eastern Nazarene, 1979. Sales trainee Shell Oil Co., Boston, 1977-78; mgr. Tile Fashions, Norwood, Mass., 1978-81; dept. mgr. Stowell's, Newton, Mass., 1981-85; claims dept. Allstate Ins., Wellesley, Mass., 1985-89; investigations Commonwealth Auto. Reinsurance, Boston, 1989—; mem. Internat. Assn. of Arson Investigators, Saugus, Mass., 1989—; coord. Car 005 Task Force or Ins. Fraud, Boston, 1989—; com. mem. N.E. chpt. Internat. Assn. of Autotheft Investigators, Boston, 1991; v.p. Merrimack Valley Auto Theft Investigators, Manchester, N.H., 1991—. Com. mem. Boy Scouts Am., Norwood, Mass., 1989—; cert. instr. Nat. Rifle Assn., 1989—. Recipient Honors award, Newton (Mass.) Jr. Coll., 1971-72. Mem. Beth-horon Lodge AF&AM, Ancient and Accepted Scottish Rite Valley of Boston, Q.C. Corr. Cir., Philalethes Soc., Norfolk County Deputy Sheriff's Assn. Republican. Office: Commonwealth Auto Reinsurers 100 Summer St 21st Fl Boston MA 02110

LAPSLEY, JAMES NORVELL, JR., minister, pastoral theology educator; b. Clarksville, Tenn., Mar. 16, 1930; s. James Norvell and Evangeline (Winn) L.; m. Brenda Ann Weakley, June 4, 1953 (dec. May 1989); children: Joseph William, Jacqueline Evangeline; m. Helen Joan Winter, Feb. 24, 1990. BA, Rhodes Coll., 1952; BD, Union Theol. Sem., 1955; PhD (Div. Sch. fellow, Rockefeller fellow), U. Chgo., 1961. Ordained to ministry Presbyn. Ch., 1955; asst. min. Gentilly Presbyn. Ch., New Orleans, 1955-57; instr. Princeton (N.J.) Theol. Sem., 1961-63, asst. prof., 1963-67, assoc. prof., 1967-76, prof. pastoral theology, 1976-80, Carl and Helen Egner prof. pastoral theology, 1980—, acad. dean, 1984-89. Editor: The Concept of Willing, 1967, Salvation and Health, 1972; chmn. editorial bd.: Pastoral Psychology Jour., 1975-84. Bd. dirs. Westminster Found., Princeton U., 1970-76. Danforth fellow Menninger Found., 1960-61. Mem. Am. Acad. Religion. Presbyterian. Home: 95 Mercer St Princeton NJ 08540-6826 Office: Princeton Theol Sem CN 821 Princeton NJ 08540

LARD, EDWIN WEBSTER, retired chemist; b. Waterloo, Ala., July 17, 1921; s. John Robert and Mamie Alice (Webb) L.; m. Virginia Faye Howard, June 11, 1945; children: Ronald, William, Sheryl, Kenneth. BS in Chemistry, Ark. State U., 1949; MS in Chemistry, Memphis State U., 1961. Chemist, physicist Ethyl Corp., Baton Rouge, 1949-52; chemist Chemstrand Corp., Decatur, Ala., 1952-54, W. R. Grace & Co., Columbia, Md., 1954-74, Naval Ship Rsch. and Devel. Ctr., Annapolis, Md., 1974-79; chemist, chem. engr. Naval Sea Systems Command, Crystal City, Va., 1979-84; ret., 1984. Contbr. articles to sci. publs.; patentee in field. Lt. (j.g.) USNR, 1949-57. Home: 12703 Beaverdale Ln Bowie MD 20715-3913

LARDE-ARTHES, ENRIQUE RAFAEL, writer; b. San Salvador, El Salvador, June 30, 1899; s. Jorge Larde and Amelie Arthes; BS summa cum laude Instituto Nacional, El Salvador, 1917; DDS, U. El Salvador, 1927; m. Marina Bellegarrigue, Nov. 22, 1930; children: Marina (Mrs. Jean Pierre Abbat), Enrique Roberto, Odette (Mrs. John M. Danskin), Roger. Came to U.S., 1943. Dir., pub. Espiral mag., San Salvador, 1920-23; prof. natural scis. and philosophy Escuela Normal de Varones' El Salvador, 1917-23, Colegio Garcia Flamenco, El Salvador, 1924-30, Instituto de Larde, El Salvador, 1931-38; prof. radiology and physics U. El Salvador, 1932-40; pvt. practice dentistry, San Salvador, 1927-43, Atlanta, 1944-45. Author: Historia de Centro-America, 1922; El Centenario de la Fundacion de San Salvador Cuscatlan, 1925; La Cabala de los Atlantes, 1960; Occult Christianity, 1972; The Crown Prince Rudolf, His Mysterious Life After Mayerling, 1981; The Real Democracy-What the Ruling Classes Ought to Know. Club: Masons.

LAREAU, MARYBETH BASS, marketing professional; b. N.Y.C., July 12, 1941; d. James Gordon and Marjorie (Mestell) B.; m. Gerard Arthur Lareau, June 6, 1970 (div. Nov. 1984). AB in Biology, Bucknell U., 1963. V.p., creative group head Dancer Fitzgerald Sample, Inc., N.Y.C., 1966-78; sr. v.p., creative dir. Norman Craig & Kummel, N.Y.C., 1978-79; creative dir., pres. Lareau & Assocs., N.Y.C., 1980—; guest lectr. St. John's U., N.Y.C., 1980-83; adj. instr. Fashion Inst. Tech. SUNY, N.Y.C., 1982-84, 87—. Contbr. articles to mags., jours.; prin. works include L'eggs Pantyhose, 1974-78, corp. advt. campaign Gen. Electric Corp., 1981. Recipient ANDY award Advtg. Club N.Y., 1975, EFFIE award Am. Mktg. Assn., 1976. Mem. Internat. Wine and Food Soc., Advt. Women N.Y. (chair pub. svc. com. 1986-88), Women's Direct Response Group. Episcopalian. Home and Office: 140 W End Ave New York NY 10023-6131

LAREW, KARL GARRET, history educator; b. Ithaca, N.Y., Dec. 9, 1936; s. Walter Byron and Catherine Willard (Phisterer) L.; m. Sonya Carol Louise Jensen, Mar. 4, 1959 (div. Feb. 1969); m. MariLynn Elizabeth Melton Terry, Feb. 19, 1972. BA, U. Conn., 1959; MA, Yale U., 1960, PhD, 1964. Asst. historian U.S. Army Signal Corps, Washington, summers 1956-57, summers 1959-61; teaching asst./asst. instr. So. Conn. State Coll., New Haven, 1960-64; reader Yale U., New Haven, 1961-64; lectr. U. Conn., Waterbury, summer 1962; instr. U. Md., Balt. and College Park, 1964-66, 72; asst. prof. history Towson (Md.) State U., 1966-69, assoc. prof., 1969-73, prof., 1973—. Author: Garret Larew, Civil War Soldier, 1975; author poetry; contbr. articles to prof. jours. 1st lt. U.S. Army, 1964-66. Recipient Merit award Towson State U., 1987, summer rsch. grant, 1987. Mem. AAUP, Am. Hist. Assn., Assn. U.S. Army, Phi Beta Kappa, Phi Alpha Theta (internat. councillor 1989-91, adv. bd. 1991-93). Democrat. Office: Towson State U History Dept Towson MD 21204

LARGEY, JOSEPH CHARLES, electronics design engineer; b. St. Marys, Pa., Dec. 6, 1952; s. Charles Michael and Anne Marie (Lombardi) L.; m. Lou Ann Maris Nissel, Aug. 6, 1977; children: Krystal Marie, Tiffany Anne. Degree in Biol. Engring., U. Pitts., 1981. Retail mgr., pres. Largey Electronics & Rsch., St. Marys, 1976-86; design engr. N.S.C., Kersey, Pa., 1986—. Author: I'm the Alien, 1988; patentee in field. Recipient Humanitarian award A.R.P. (Elk County Spl. Olympics Com.). Recipient Humanitarian award A.R.P., 1984. Fellow Pure and Power Health and Spiritual Club, Life on Other Side Club, Unusual Aircraft Club, Robots and Use Club; mem. Toby Valley Grange, Toby Leisure Club. Home and Office: 257 Coal Hollow Rd Kersey PA 15846-9672

LARIC, MICHAEL VICTOR, marketing educator, consultant, author; b. Split, Yugoslavia, Feb. 8, 1945; came to U.S., 1971; s. Joseph and Ljubica (Abraham) L.; m. Roberta Kine; children: Shai Samuel, Pnina Leora, Ari Nathaniel. BA in Econs. and Polit. Sci., Hebrew U. of Jerusalem, 1968, MA in Bus., 1971; PhD, CUNY, 1976. Economist Israel Hotel & Motel Owners, Tel Aviv, 1968-69; gen. mgr. Galia Laundries, Jerusalem, 1969-71; economist Risk Analysis Corp., Alpine, N.J., 1971-72; lectr. CUNY, N.Y.C., 1972-73; asst. prof. Rutgers U., State U. N.J., Newark, 1974-75, U. Conn., Storrs, 1975-81; prof. mktg. U. Balt., 1981—, assoc. dean; course dir. Data Tech. Inst., Clifton, N.Y., 1986—, Frost & Sullivan, N.Y. and U.K., 1990—; cons. Ecomares Internat., Ellicott City, Md., 1981—. Author: Marketing Management: Analysis Using Spreadsheets, 1988, Lotus Exercises for Principles of Marketing, 1986, 14 others; contbr. numerous articles, monographs and case to profl. jours. Named Outstanding Young Man of The Yr. Jaycees, 1979, 80. Mem. Am. Mktg. Assn. (bd. mem. Balt. chpt. 1976-82, Outstanding Contbr. of Conn. 1978), Product Devel. and Mgmt. (bd. mem. 1981, 82), Am. Econs. Assn., Beta Gamma Sigma. Home: 4609 Morning Ride Ct Ellicott City MD 21042-5927 Office: U Balt 1420 N Charles St Baltimore MD 21201-5720

LARIMER, DAVID GEORGE, district judge; b. Rochester, N.Y., Mar. 3, 1944; s. John and Mary (Sullivan) L.; m. Karen Moore, July 29, 1967; children: Amy, Beth, John. BA, St. John Fisher Coll., 1966; JD, Notre Dame U., 1969. Bar: N.Y. 1970, D.C. 1971. Law clk. to Hon. Joseph C. McGarraghy U.S. Dist. Ct. (D.C. dist.), 1969-70; asst. U.S. atty. U.S. Dept. Justice, Washington, 1970-73, Rochester, 1973-75; chief appellate law asst. Supreme Ct. (4th Dept.), Rochester, 1979-81; mem. firm Greisberger, Zicari, etal, Rochester, 1982-87; U.S. magistrate U.S. Dist. Ct., Rochester, 1983-87, judge, 1987—; law instr. St. John Fisher Coll., Rochester, 1979-81. Office: US Dist Ct 100 State St 250 US Courthouse Rochester NY 14615

LARISH, JOHN JOSEPH, image consultant, journalist; b. Cleve., Dec. 15, 1928; s. John and Francis (Per) L.; m. Rose Ellen Quinn, June 10, 1961; children: John F., Mary M., James P., Susan C. BS, Empire State Coll., 1980. Media rep. Westinghouse Broadcasting, Cleve., 1956-59; plant mgr. Cleve. Color Svc., 1958-59; dist. sales mgr. GAF Corp., San Francisco, 1959-69; sr. market analyst Eastman Kodak Co., Rochester, N.Y., 1969-84; prin. Jonrel Imaging Cons., Rochester, N.Y., 1984—. Author: Understanding Electronic Photography, 1990, Digital Photography, 1992; editor: Electronic Photography News, 1988—; contbg. editor: Focal Encyc. of Phytography, 1992; columnist Advanced Imaging mag., 1990—. Bd. dirs. Empire State Coll. Student/Alumni Found., Saratoga Springs, N.Y., 1980; asst. dist. comr. Boy Scouts Am., Rochester, 1983. Lt. U.S. Army, 1952-56. Mem. Computer Press Assn. (charter). Office: Jonrel Imaging Cons Inc 70 Southwick Ct Rochester NY 14623

LARIVIERE, LAWRENCE JOSEPH, interior designer; b. Portsmouth, N.H., Sept. 9, 1938; s. Robert Amadee and Irene Mary (Morin) L.; m. Pamela Ann St. Lawrence, May 30, 1962; children: Leanne Lariviere Knight, Paul Lawrence, Philip Steven, Lauren. AA in Interior Design, R.I. Sch. Design, 1975; cert., U. N.H., 1982. Apprentice Model Upholstery Shop, Portsmouth, 1962-70; owner, pres. Larry's Custom Interiors, Inc., North Hampton, N.H., 1970—; tchr. U. N.H., Durham, 1986-87. Contbr. articles to profl. publs. Devel. com. The Music Hall, Portsmouth, 1990-91. With USAF, 1958-59. Mem. Boston Curtain and Drapery Club (edn. chair 1991—). Office: Larrys Custom Interiors 225 Atlantic Ave North Hampton NH 03862-2313

LARIVIERE, SUSAN MARIE, mathematics educator; b. Webster, Mass., Jan. 29, 1967; d. Adelard Maurice and Genevieve Alice (Lazarowski) L. BA in Math. cum laude, Clark U., 1989; postgrad., WPI. Cert. secondary tchr. math., Mass., Conn. Tchr. math. Edwin O. Smith High Sch., Storrs, Conn., 1989—. Mem. Nat. Coun. Tchrs. Math., Assn. Tchrs. Math. Conn., Am. Math. Soc., Assn. for Women in Math. Roman Catholic. Home: 30 Whitcomb St Webster MA 01570-2431

LARKIN, ANYA, designer; b. Washington, July 30, 1945; d. Brooks S. and Elizabeth (Pratt) L. Student, Silvermine Coll. Fine Arts, 1964-65. Fabric designer Mary McFadden, Inc., N.Y.C., 1974-84, Anya Larkin Ltd., N.Y.C., 1984—. Mem. Decorative Fabric Assn. Office: Anya Larkin Ltd 39 W 28th St New York NY 10001-4203

LARKIN, JAMES THOMAS, financial services company executive; b. Quincy, Mass., Sept. 6, 1931; s. Richard James and Alice Wedd (Murphy) L.; m. Susan Gardiner, Dec. 28, 1968; children: James Thomas Jr., Kathleen Tracey. BS, Coll. of Holy Cross, Worcester, Mass., 1953; postgrad., U. Pa., 1958. Dir. internat. bus. ABC, N.Y.C., 1958-70; v.p. internat. travelers cheque div. Am. Express Co., N.Y.C., 1970-74, sr. v.p. travelers cheque and

money order divs., 1975-77, exec. v.p. Travelers cheque and money order divs., 1977-80; exec. v.p. Am. Express Internat., Inc., N.Y.C., 1980-81; pres. travel related services, Europe and Mid-East Africa div. Am. Express Europe, Ltd., London, 1982-86; exec. v.p. Am. Express Co., N.Y.C., 1986-90; vice chmn. Am. Express Internat., N.Y.C., 1991—; bd. dirs. Am. Express Internat., Inc., San Francisco Ins. Co., Ltd., London, Travelers Cheque Assocs., Ltd., London, Soc. Francaise du Cheque de Voyage S.A., Paris. Board dirs. Rock Ridge Assn., Greenwich, Conn., 1976—, pres., 1987-91; founding mem., exec. com. Cooperation Ireland, London, 1984—. Capt. USMC, 1953-56. Fellow Inst. Dirs.; Royal Inst. Internat. Affairs, Coll. Holy Cross Regents Council. Republican. Roman Catholic. Clubs: Met. N.Y.C., Indian Harbor Yacht Club. Home: 5 Hillside Dr Greenwich CT 06831-4502 Office: Am Express Co 200 Vesey St New York NY 10285-0001

LARKIN, MAYO, architect; b. Boston, July 25, 1916; s. Julius Kenicott and Frances (Szathmary) Larkin; m. Martha Goorno, June 14, 1942; children: Geoffrey, Sandra. BS, Mass. Coll. Art, 1938; MA, Boston U., 1940; MArch, MIT, 1942. Prin. Mayo Larkin Arch., Boston, 1947-49; pres. Larkin & Glassman Assoc., Inc., Boston, 1950-58; pres., chief exec. officer Larkin, Glassman & Prager Assoc., Inc., Boston, 1959-86; pres. Mayo Larkin Assoc., Inc., Newton and Needham, Mass., 1987—; pvt. pilot, 1947—. Prin. works include HUD Housing Units, numerous indsl., hosp. and med. facilities, schs., mcpl. and state projects. Trustee dir. Mass. Coll. Art. 1st lt. USAF, 1941-45, ETO. Fellow Soc. Am. Registered Architects; mem. AIA, Boston Soc. Architects, Am. Ex-Prisoners of War Assn. (jr. vice comdr.), Temple Emanuel Brotherhood (past pres.), MIT Stein Club (past pres.), New Century Club, VFW, DAV, Jewish War Vets., Masons, B'nai B'rith (past pres.). Home: 47 Alderwood Rd Newton MA 02159-1226 Office: 145 Rosemary St Needham MA 02194-3259

LARKIN, MICHAEL HOWARD, choral conductor, composer, educator; b. Cumberland, Md., Apr. 10, 1951; s. William James and Carolyn Maxine (Crouse) L.; m. Kathleen Winchell, May 11, 1979 (div. Oct., 1986); children: Amy Leigh, Jonathan Michael; m. Linda Jean Taylor, Nov. 29, 1986. BMus, U. Del., 1973; MusM, Catholic U., 1975; D of Musical Arts, Temple U., 1985. Instr. in Music Wesley Coll., Dover, Del., 1975-79; chmn. music dept. Sanford Sch., Hockessin, Del., 1979-81; minister of music White Clay Creek Presbyn. Ch., Newark, Del., 1981-85; programmer, cons. U. Del. Plato Project, Newark, 1981-85; asst. prof. in music Misericordia Coll., Dallas, Pa., 1985-86; founder, music dir. New Ark Chorale, Newark, 1977—; chmn. vocal music dept. Wilmington (Del.) Music Sch., 1986—; dir. music St. Mary Annes Episcopal Ch., North East Md., 1989—; mem. faculty senate Misericordia Coll., Dallas, Pa., 1985-86, commn. on liturgy and music, Episcopal Diocese of Easton, Md., 1990—; guest conductor Cecil County (Md.) Honors Chorus, 1989. Composer over 40 published works, hymns and carols including My Lord, What a Morning, Brightest and Best of the Stars of the Morning, Glory to God, Alleluia, Sing to Jesus, Somebody's Knockin at Your Door, 1990, Now Thank We All Our God, Coventry Carol, Come Thou Long Expected Jesus, 1991. Recipient 4th place award Internat. Elsledlel Solo Competition, Lilangallon, Wales, 1972, fellowship, Temple U., Phila., 1982-85. Mem. Music Educators Nat. Conf., Am. Choral Directors Assn. (chmn. Del. com. for worship 1991—), Del. State Music Educators Assn., Am. Guild of Organists, Assn. Lutheran Musicians. Lutheran. Home and Office: 605 W 22nd St Wilmington DE 19802-3926

LARKIN, ROBERT HAYDEN, chemicals executive; b. N.Y.C., Mar. 26, 1946; s. James Michael and Rita Evelyn (Hayden) L.; m. Eileen Dunkak, Dec. 16, 1967; children: Brian, Tracy, Colleen, Kelly. BS in Chemistry, Providence Coll., 1968; PhD in Phys. Chemistry, U. Mass., 1972. Rsch. assoc. MIT, Cambridge, 1972-73; rsch. scientist Rohm and Haas Co., Spring House, Pa., 1973-78, rsch. sect. mgr., 1978-86; mgr. regulatory affairs Rohm and Haas Co., Phila., 1986-90, dir. regulatory affairs, 1990—. Mem. Am. Chem. Soc., Nat. Agrl. Chem. Assn. (registration com. 1991—). Roman Catholic. Home: 207 Hemlock Cir North Wales PA 19454-2663 Office: Rohm and Haas Co Independence Mall W Philadelphia PA 19105

LARMIE, WALTER ESMOND, floriculturist, retired; b. Smithfield, R.I., Sept. 6, 1920; s. Charles A. and Clara (Wilding) L.; m. Una Mullen, May 1, 1943; children: Walter, Wayne, Wendy. BS, U. R.I., 1949, MS, 1954. Apprentice coremaker Brown & Sharp Mfg. Co., Providence, 1939-41, coremaker, 1941-42; flight instr. Jenning Bros. Air Svc., Fitchburg and Grafton, Mass., 1942-44; chief pilot Woonsocket (R.I.) Airways, 1945-47, Howard Aviation, Westerly, R.I., 1947-50; instr. to prof. U. R.I., Kingston, 1949-83, prof. emeritus, 1983—; owner Welco Floral Crafts, West Kingston, R.I., 1983—. Author: Flower Arranging: Basics to Advanced Design, 1980. Lt. USNR, 1944-68. Recipient Presdl. citation R.I. Fedn. Garden Clubs. Mem. R.I. Dahlia Soc., Rotary. Home: 65 Blackbird Rd West Kingston RI 02892-1414

LAROE, EDWARD TERHUNE, III, marine biologist, government official, educator; b. Suffern, N.Y., June 15, 1943; s. Edward Terhune II and Mary Louise (Ritter) LaR.; m. Margaret Ann Engel, Mar. 24, 1964 (div. July 1979); children: Dale Ritter, Tracy Ann; m. S. Elisabeth Sheiry, Aug. 22, 1981. AB in Biology, Stanford U., 1964; MS in Marine Sci., U. Miami, Fla., 1967, PhD Biol. Oceanography, 1970. Rsch. scientist U. Miami, 1970-71; exec. dir. Collier County Conservancy, Naples, Fla., 1971-73; sr. scientist NOAA, Washington, 1973-77; coastal specialist Oreg. Dept. Land Conservation and Devel., Salem, 1975-77; chief Bur. Coastal Zone Mgmt. Fla. Dept. Environ. Regulation, Tallahassee, 1977-79; spl. asst. to asst. sec. Fish, Wildlife and Parks U.S. Dept. Interior, Washington, 1980; dep. chief div. biol. svc. Fish and Wildlife Svc., Washington, 1981-82, chief, 1982-87; dir. coop. rsch. units U.S. Fish and Wildlife Svc., Washington, 1987—; tech. advisor South Fla. Regional Planning Com., Miami, 1972-73; mem. tech. adv. bd. Fla. Dept. Pollution Control, Tallahassee, 1973; mem. faculty USDA Grad. Sch., Washington, 1982—; del. leader Indo-U.S. Conf. on River Conservation, New Delhi, 1987; U.S. del. Intergovtl. Panel on Climate Change, Moscow, 1989; lectr. Moscow State U., 1991; exec. sec. White House Wetlands Rsch. subcom. FCCSET, 1991—. Co-author: Classification of Wetlands, 1979. Expert witness Environ. Def. Fund, N.Y.C., 1971-75; bd. dirs. Big Cypress Nature Ctr., Naples, Fla., 1972-73; v.p. Fla. Audubon Soc., 1972-73. Recipient Disting. Svc. award Naples Jaycees, 1972, Conservationist of Yr. award Fla. Audubon Soc., 1973, Silver medal Meritorious Svc. Dept. Interior, 1991. Mem. AAAS, Soc. Conservation Biologists, Wildlife Soc., Coastal Soc. (bd. dirs. 1974-79, pres. 1977-78), Natural Areas Assn. (bd. dirs. 1991—), Iron Arrow. Democrat. Home: 2001 N Monroe St Arlington VA 22207 Office: Fish and Wildlife Svc Coop Rsch Units Ctr MS 725 Washington DC 20240

LAROSA, DANIEL CARMEL, hypnotist; b. Meriden, Conn., July 15, 1949; s. Domenick and Antoinette (Martorelli) LaR.; m. Sharon Swabski, Aug. 22, 1970 (div. Sept. 1975). BS in Social Scis. Edn., Cen. Conn. State U., 1971; M Hypnotherapy, Am. Inst. Hypnotherapy, Danbury, Conn., 1981. Master hypnotist. Owner Dan LaRosa and Assocs., Meriden, 1976—; motivational speaker and entertainer throughout U.S. and P.R. for major corps. and colls. Author: Q & A on Hypnosis, 1987. Named Entertainer of Yr., Nat. Guild Hypnotists, 1990; named to Internat. Hypnosis Hall of Fame, 1991. Mem. Internat. Platform Speakers, Nat. Speakers Assn., Internat. Councilors and Therapists Assn. Home: 146 N Pearl St Meriden CT 06450-4419

LAROSA, JULIUS, engineering company official; b. Jacksonville, Fla., Aug. 11, 1956; s. John Wesley and Mandy (McKinnon) LaR.; m. Elnora Elizabeth Bradford, July 26, 1980; children: Jason Christopher, Steven Andrew, Kristie Renee. Student, Lincoln (Pa.) U., 1976-79. Salesman Kaufmann's Dept. Store, Monroeville, Pa., 1980-81, 83-87; commn. salesman Montgomery Ward Dept. Store, Monroeville, 1981-82; mgr. reprodn. dept. Salvucci Engrs., Inc., Pitts., 1981-87; supr. adminstrv. svcs., mgr. reprodn. dept., supr. document control Eichleay Engrs. Inc., Pitts., 1987—; printing cons. NAACP, Monroeville, 1986-88. Mem. In-Plant Mgrs. Assn. Democrat. Baptist. Office: Eichleay Engrs Inc 6585 Penn Ave Pittsburgh PA 15206-4483

LAROSA, ROBERT A., trade association executive; b. Boston, May 29, 1938; s. Alphonso LaRosa and Lillian D. (Cacciotta) Pierce; m. Naida L. Janes, July 30, 1961; children: Robert A. Jr., Terry Ann, Jon A., Deana Marie. Student, Bentley Coll., 1963. Pres. Associated Industries of Mass. Svc. Corp., Boston, 1959—; chmn. Mass. Employers Ins. Exch., Boston, 1989—; governing bd. Workers Compensation Rating Bur., Boston, 1990—. With U.S. Army, 1955-58. Mem. Am. Soc. Assn. Execs. (bd. dirs. 1985-88, mgmt. edn. award 1983, 84). Home: 2 Harwood Dr PO Box 533 Monument Beach MA 02553 Office: Associated Industries Mass 222 Bekeley St Boston MA 02116

LAROSE, LAWRENCE ALFRED, lawyer; b. Lowell, Mass., Oct. 26, 1958; s. Alfred M. and Rita B. (Plunkett) L.; m. Janet G. Yedwab, Aug. 12, 1984. BA summa cum laude, Tufts U., 1980; JD magna cum laude, Georgetown U., 1983. Bar: N.Y. 1984. Assoc. Sullivan & Cromwell, N.Y.C., 1983-85, 87-90, Melbourne, Australia, 1985-87; assoc. Cadwalader, Wickersham & Taft, N.Y.C., 1990—; vis. fellow Faculty of Law, U. Melbourne, 1986-87. Contbr. articles to profl. publs. Bd. dirs. Soho 20 Art Gallery. Mem. ABA, N.Y. State Bar Assn., N.Y. County Lawyers Assn., Assn. Bar City N.Y., Am. Soc. Internat. Law, Georgetown U. Nat. Law Alumni Bd. (exec. com., sec.), Down Town Assn. in City of N.Y., Phi Beta Kappa. Office: Cadwalader Wickersham & Taft 100 Maiden Ln New York NY 10038-4818

LARRABEE, RICHARD M., Coast Guard officer; b. New Rochelle, N.Y.; m. Pamela L.; 1 child, Jennifer. Grad., USCG Acad.; MS in Ocean Engring., U. R.I. Formerly skipper cutter Cape Hatteras; commdg. officer USCG Marine Safety Office, Detroit; now Capt. Port of N.Y. N.Y.C. Office: Capt Port of New York Bldg 109 Governor's Island New York NY 10004

LARRICK, MICHAEL PAUL, insurance company executive; b. Balt., June 5, 1943; s. Anthony Albert and Mary Ann (Corusy) L.; m. Nancy Toby Mandels, Oct. 9, 1976; 1 child, Jillian Paige. BS, Ohio U., 1966. CPCU. Prodn. mgr. Am. Internat., Boston, 1980-86, regional mgr., 1990—; exec. v.p. Ins. Diagnostics, Newton, Mass., 1986-87; v.p.mgr. Sullivan Risk Mgmt. Group, Waltham, Mass., 1987-88; br. mgr. New Hampshire Ins., Cambridge, Mass., 1988-90. Mem. Soc. CPCU. Republican. Unitarian. Home: 12 Westlake Rd Natick MA 01760-1753 Office: Am Internat 101 Federal St Boston MA 02110-1823

LARSEN, ANITA MARGARET, public relations executive; b. Poughkeepsie, N.Y., Jan. 8, 1960; d. Arne H. and Margaret E. (Sanderson) L. BA, SUNY, Plattsburgh, 1982. Journalist Southern Dutchess News, Wappingers Falls, N.Y., 1982; broadcast journalist Cable News 10, Beacon, N.Y., 1983; media rels. specialist Texaco Inc., White Plains, N.Y., 1984-87, asst. mgr. media rels., 1987-89, mgr. media rels., 1989—; disting. alumni vis. prof. SUNY, Plattsburgh, 1991. Office: Texaco Inc 2000 Westchester Ave White Plains NY 10650-0001

LARSEN, ANNETTE, economic services executive; b. Provo, Utah, Oct. 7, 1951; d. Richard Lewis and Lois Elaine (Fowlke) L.; BS, Brigham Young U., 1974, MBA, 1978. Data contr. D.H.I. Computing Svc., Provo, 1968-72; testing clk. Testing Ctr., Brigham Young U., Provo, 1973, sr. analyst Ctr. for Bus. and Econ. Rsch., 1974-76; analyst Tex. A&M U., College Station, summer 1977; grad. rsch. asst. Grad. Sch. Mgmt., Brigham Young U.; 1977-78, mem. faculty, 1978, rsch. assoc., 1978-79; bus. cons. Larsen & Assocs., Provo, 1974-80; cons. to Utah Energy Consortium, U.S. SBA, Weidner Communications, 1979—; mgr. Strategic Info., Burlington, Mass., 1980-83; pres. Decision Scis., cons. firm to fin. instns., 1982; dir. Dun & Bradstreet Tech. Econ. Svcs., 1983-85; regional mgr. Tenenbaum Hill Assocs., Inc., Boston, 1985-89; pres. Beacon Fin. Assocs., 1989—, Met. Ins., 1991—. Pres. Woman's Svc. Orgn., 1975-76, 79-80. Mem. Assn. for MBA Execs., Am. Fin. Assn. Republican. Mormon. Contbr. articles on bus. mgmt. to profl. publs. Home: 1 Devonshire Pl Apt 2204 Boston MA 02109-3514 Office: Met Ins 822 Boylston St Brookline MA 02167

LARSEN, EDGAR ROBERT, JR., electrical engineer; b. Plainfield, N.J., Oct. 8, 1950; s. Edgar Robert Sr. and Margaret Hedwig (Schmidt) L.; m. Virginia Grace Lienhart, Sept. 14, 1974; children: Scott, Bethany. AAS in Elec. Tech., Middlesex County Coll., 1970; BS in Elec. Engring. Tech., Milw. Sch. Engring., 1972, MS in Engring. Mgmt., 1984. Application engr. Square D Co., Milw., 1972-77, project engr., 1977-79, sr. project engr., 1979-80, mktg. sect. mgr., 1980-82; product planning mgr. Square D Co., Cedar Rapids, Iowa, 1982-87, mng. engr., 1987-90, product mgr., 1990-91; dir. engring. Heinemann Electric Co., Salisbury, Md., 1991—; mem. industry adv. com. Underwriters Labs., 1991—. Inventor illuminated two color selector switch, 1977. Mem. curriculum adv. com. Cedar Rapids Pub. Schs., 1984-87; chmn. publicity com. Trinity Luth. Sch. Midwinter Basketball Tournament, Cedar Rapids, 1989-91. Mem. IEEE (mem. low voltage protection subcom., low voltage circuit breaker application guide working group 1983-91). Home: 146 Westbrooke Dr Salisbury MD 21801-8344 Office: Heinemann Electric Co 2300 Northwood Dr Salisbury MD 21801-7807

LARSEN, ERIC, writer, English educator; b. Northfield, Minn., Nov. 29, 1941; s. Erling Lauritz and Eileen (Dilley) L.; m. Anne Schnare, June 5, 1965; children: Flynn, Gavin. BA, Carleton Coll., 1963; MA, U. Iowa, 1964, PhD, 1971. Prof. English John Jay Coll. of Criminal Justice CUNY, 1971—. Author: (novels) An American Memory, 1988, I Am Zoe Handke, 1992. Recipient Heartland prize Chgo. Tribune, 1988. Office: CUNY John Jay Coll of Criminal Justice 445 W 59th St New York NY 10019-1104

LARSEN, ERIK ALLAN, astrospace engineer; b. Mar. 6, 1968; s. Allan Warren and Lois Ann (Sommer) L.; m. Elizabeth Ann Williams, Aug. 10, 1991. BS in Aerospace Engr., U. Va., 1990. Sales rep. Omni Co. Computers, Charlottesville, Va., 1988-90; astrospace engr. GE Astrospace, Princeton, N.J., 1990-91, BDM Internat., Washington, 1992—. Leader Holy Cows Youth Group, West Windsor, N.J., 1990-92. Mem. AIAA. Democrat. Roman Catholic.

LARSEN, JOHN CHRISTIAN, librarian, consultant; b. Menominee, Mich., Aug. 1, 1929; s. Julius Christian and Bozena Mary (Blahnik) L. BDes, U. Mich., 1950, MA, 1951, MLS, 1955, PhD, 1967. Adminstrv. asst. styling sect. GM, Detroit, 1951-54; reference libr. Detroit Pub. Libr., 1954-57; head art and music sect. Mich. State Libr., Lansing, 1958-61; assoc. dir. pub. svcs. Towson State U. Libr., Balt., 1961-64; instr. U. Mich., Ann Arbor, 1965-68; asst. prof. U. Ky., Lexington, 1968-71; assoc. prof. Columbia U., N.Y.C., 1971-77; prof. No. Ill. U., DeKalb, 1977-88; cons., Balt., 1989—. Editor: Museum Librarianship, 1985, Researcher's Guide to Archives and Local History Collections, 1988; editorial bd. Reference Books Bull., ALA, 1976-79, 83-85, 89—; contbr. articles on art librarianship to profl. publs. Grantee Danforth Found., 1963. Mem. ALA (coun. 1970-72, chair libr. edn. div. 1974-76, chair art sect. 1980-82), Art Libr. Soc. N.Am., Am. Friends Attingham Trust, Victorian Soc. Am. (bd. dirs. 1984-87), Friends of Johns Hopkins U. Librs., Phi Kappa Phi, Beta Phi Mu. Presbyterian. Home and Office: 4000 N Charles St Unit 1407 Baltimore MD 21218-1737

LARSEN, LARRY LEE, psychologist; b. Amarillo, Tex., Jan. 9, 1937; s. Ross H. and Eloise (Stubbs) L.; m. Nancy Louise Farrell, June 21, 1958; children: Peter, Ann. BA, Baylor U., 1958, MA, 1959; MS, Wesleyan U., 1964; PhD, Boston U., 1970. Lic. clin. psychologist, Mass. Intern Beford (Mass.) VA, 1964-65, Brockton (Mass.) VA, 1965-66, Cambridge (Mass.) Mental Health Ctr., 1966-71; staff psychologist Douglas A. Thom Clinic, Boston, 1967-68; dir., chief psychologist St. Ann's Home, Methuen, Mass., 1968-74; clin. psychologist Larry L. Larsen and Assocs., Andover, Mass., 1972—; instr. U. Mass., Boston, 1967-69, Met. Coll., Boston U. Author: (weekly columns) Family Matters, 1976—, Dr. Nettles, 1980-86, (book) Parents and Families, 1977. Selectman Andover, Mass., 1991-93; campaign chmn. United Fund, Greater Lawrence, Mass., 1980; chmn. Elder Opportunities Panel, Andover; 1st pres. Fidelity House, Methuen, Mass., Greater Lawrnece Mental Health and Retardation Area Bd. Mem. Kiwanis (bd. dirs.), Creative Living (pres. 1986), Mass. Psychol. Assn., Am. psychol. Assn., Childrens Lobby for the Commonwealth of Mass., Masons. Mem. Ch. of Christ. Home: 53 Birch Rd Andover MA 01810-3348 Office: 63 Park St Andover MA 01810-3662

LARSEN, MARK ARVID, lawyer; b. San Francisco, Sept. 12, 1948; s. Frank and Klara M. (Ashman) L.; m. Joan Holcombe, Aug. 29, 1970; children: Hannah Holcombe, Faith Froelicher. BA in Religious Studies, Beloit Coll., 1970; JD, U. Calif., San Francisco, 1973. Bar: Calif. 1973, N.H. 1974. Atty. N.H. Legal Assistance, Lebanon, 1974-79; ptnr. McNamara & Larsen, Lebanon, 1979-88; assoc. Nighswander Martin & Mitchell, P.A., Lebanon, 1988-90, ptnr., 1990—. Editor, contbr. N.H. Bar Jour., 1981-86. Chmn. Canaan Dem. Com., 1988—; mem. Mascoma Valley Regional Sch. Bd., Grafton County Dem. Com. Recipient vol. award N.H. Mental Health Assn., 1986. Mem. ABA, N.H. Bar Assn. (Disting. Svc. citation 1986), Calif. Bar Assn., Assn. Trial Lawyers Am., N.H. Trial Lawyers Assn. Home: Granite Ledge Farm RR 2 Box 940 Canaan NH 03741-9316 Office: Nighswander Martin & Mitchell 23 Bank St Lebanon NH 03766-9003

LARSEN, NEIL ALLYN, literature, language educator; b. N.Y.C., Jan. 3, 1952; s. Leonard Hills and Beatrice (Rosenblum) L.; m. Emma Luna, Aug. 31, 1979; 1 child, Emil Luna-Larsen. BA, Reed Coll., Portland, Oreg., 1974; MA, U. Minn., 1979, PhD, 1983. Asst. prof. lit. and lang. Northeastern U., Boston, 1983-89, assoc. prof. lit. and lang., 1989—. Contbg. editor: Postmodem Culture Jour., 1990—; editor: The Discourse of Power, 1983, Modernism and Hegemony, 1990; contbr. numerous articles to profl. jours. Mem. MLA, Latin Am. Studies Assn. Office: Northeastern U Modern Lang 360 Holmes Boston MA 02115

LARSEN, RALPH STANLEY, health care company executive; b. Bklyn., Nov. 19, 1938; s. Andrew and Gurine (Henningsen) L.; m. Dorothy M. Zeitfuss, Aug. 19, 1961; children: Karen, Kristen, Garret. BBA, Hofstra U., 1962. Mfg. trainee, then supr. prodn. and dir. mfg. Johnson & Johnson, New Brunswick, N.J., 1962-77; v.p. ops., v.p. mktg. McNeil Consumer Products Co. div. Johnson & Johnson, Ft. Washington, Pa., 1977-81; pres. Becton Dickenson Consumer Products, Paramus, N.J., 1981-83; pres. Chicopee div. Johnson & Johnson, New Brunswick, 1983-85; co. group chmn. Johnson & Johnson, New Brunswick, N.J., 1985-86, vice chmn., exec. com., bd. dirs., 1986—, chmn. bd., chief exec. officer, 1989—, also bd. dirs., mem. exec. com.; bd. dirs. N.Y. Stock Exch., Xerox Corp. Bd. dirs. United Negro Coll. Fund; bd. govs. United Way Am.; mem. bd. visitors Grad. Sch. Bus., U. N.C.; trustee Ednl. Broadcasting Corp.; mem. Found. Malcolm Baldridge Nat. Quality Award, U.S. Coun. Internat. Bus. Mem. Bus. Coun., Bus. Roundtable (policy com.). Republican. Office: Johnson & Johnson 1 Johnson & Johnson Pla New Brunswick NJ 08933

LARSEN, RONALD JOHN, potter; b. Chgo., Jan. 1, 1937; s. John Adolph and Emily (Maas) L.; m. Joan Audrey Bricker, June 14, 1962; 1 child, Nils Erik. BS in Math., Mich. State U., 1957, MS in Math., 1959; PhD in Math., Stanford U., 1963. Instr. in math. Yale U., New Haven, 1963-65; asst. prof. U. Calif., Santa Cruz, 1965-70; assoc. prof. Wesleyan U., Middletown, Conn., 1970-75; vis. assoc. prof. SUNY, Binghamton, 1975-76, Albany, 1976-77; vis. assoc. prof. Clarkson U., Potsdam, N.Y., 1977-78; owner, operator Crary Mills (N.Y.) Pottery, 1978—. Author: Theory of Multipliers, 1970, Functional Analysis, 1973, Banach Algebras, 1973, A Potter's Companion, 1992; contbr. articles to profl. publs. Fulbright rsch. grantee U. Oslo, 1968-69, Fulbright travel grantee U. Oslo, 1973-74. Mem. Am. Craft Coun., Empire State Craft Alliance, Dinosaur Club (corr. sec. 1986—, co-founder). Home and Office: RR 4 Box 252 Canton NY 13617

LARSON, ALLAN BENNETT, pharmacist; b. Chgo., Feb. 9, 1943; s. Nils Ragnar and Mary Frances (Quigley) L.; m. Virginia Louise, Apr. 16, 1971; children: Michael Allan, Jacie Lynn. BS in Pharmacy, Drake U., Des Moines, 1966; MS in Phys. Pharmacy, U. Wis., 1969; PhD in Indsl. and Phys. Pharmacy, Purdue U., 1972. Sr. rsch. pharmacist Dorsey Labs., Lincoln, Nebr., 1972-76; sr. pharm. scientist Vicks Rsch. & Devel., Mt. Vernon, N.Y., 1976-77, group leader skin care/toiletries, 1977-80; mgr. tech. svcs. Vicks Rsch. & Devel., Shelton, Conn., 1980-84; dir. process rsch. & devel. Wyeth-Ayerst Rsch., Rouses Point, N.Y., 1984—. Contbr. articles to profl. jours. Chmn. summer festival Rowayton (Conn.) Civic Assn., 1983; chmn. Peru (N.Y.) Activity and Recreation Ctr., 1985-86; chmn. Peru Bicentennial Com., 1990-92; lay leader Peru Community Ch., 1991—. Mem. Am. Pharm. Assn., Am. Assn. Pharm. Scis., Acad. Pharm. Scis., Soc. Cosmetic Chemists, Internat. Soc. Pharm. Engrs., Drug Info. Assn., Phi Lambda Upsilon. Republican. United Ch. of Christ. Home: RR 2 Box 112C Peru NY 12972-9409 Office: Wyeth-Ayerst Rsch 64 Maple St Rouses Point NY 12979-1424

LARSON, DONALD CLAYTON, physics educator, consultant; b. Wadena, Minn., Jan. 29, 1934; s. Clyde Melvin and Selma (Wilson) L.; m. Susan Dunnet, July 17, 1960; children: Tor Frederick, Jun Dunnet, Erika Rose. BS, U. Wash., 1956; SM, Harvard U., 1957, PhD, 1962. Asst. prof. U. Va., Charlottesville, 1962-67; assoc. prof. Drexel U., Phila., 1967-83, full prof., 1983—; vis. prof. Universidad De Chile, Santiago, 1969, 73, Tel-Aviv (Israel) U., 1984; vis. scientist Naval Air Devel. Ctr., Warminster, Pa., summers 1981-91; cons. NIST, Gaithersburg, Md., 1984-91. Author: Physics of Thin Films, vol. VI, 1971, Experimental Methods in Preparation and Measurement of Thin Films, vol. II, 1974. Mem. Optical Soc. Am., Phi Beta Kappa, Tau Beta Pi, Sigma Xi. Home: 409 Drew Ave Swarthmore PA 19081-2407 Office: Drexel U Physics Atmospheric Sci Dept Philadelphia PA 19104

LARSON, ERIC MARTIN, demographer; b. Detroit, Feb. 22, 1950; s. Lee Martin and Mary Elizabeth (Klaila) L. B of Journalism (with honors), U. Tex., 1974, MA, MS in Community & Regional Planning, 1976, 79, MA, 1984, PhD, 1987. Instr. journalism Tarleton State U., Stephenville, Tex., 1975-77; newspaper reporter The San Jose (Costa Rica) News, 1977-78; rsch. specialist Tex. A&M U., College Sta., 1980-83; cons. self-employed Austin, Tex., 1984-86; social sci. analyst U.S. Gen. Acctg. Office, Washington, 1987-88, sr. evaluator, 1989—. Contbr. articles to profl. jours. Recipient Fulbright Group Project grant U.S. Dept. Edn., 1983, Dissertation Rsch. grant William and Flora Y. Hewlett Found., 1986; recipient Spl. Commendation award U.S. Gen. Acctg. Office, 1988, 90, Outstanding Performance award, 1989. Mem. Soc. Study Narrative Lit., NRA (life). Office: US Gen Acctg Office 441 G St NW Rm 5729 Washington DC 20548-0002

LARSON, JANE WARREN, ceramist; b. San Francisco, June 2, 1922; d. Stafford Leak and Viola (Lockhart) Warren; m. Clarence Ernest Larson, Apr. 21, 1957; children: Lawrence Ernest, Lance Stafford. Student, Swarthmore Coll., 1939-41; BA with honors, U. Rochester, 1943; MFA in Ceramics, Antioch Coll., 1982. Tech. editor Tenn. Eastman Corp., Oak Ridge, 1943-46; chief Tech. Info. Ctr. Carbide & Carbon Chem. Corp., Oak Ridge, 1946-51; tech. editor physics div. Rand Corp., Santa Monica, Calif., 1954-55; tech. editor libr. Rand Corp., Washington, 1955-57; ceramist Janeware, Santa Monica, 1953-55; pres., bldg. founder Oak Ridge Community Art Ctr., 1963-66, ceramic tchr., 1965-69; ceramic tchr. Inst. Learning in Retirement Am. U., Washington, 1985-88; juror in ceramics Montgomery Potters, Md. Fedn. Art, Md./Va., 1980—. One-person shows at AAAS, Washington, 1990, Studio Gallery, Washington, 1992, others 1973—; group shows at Bader Gallery and others, 1971—, Internat. Sculpture Conf., Washington, 1990; mural artist Guest Quarters Hotel gardens, Bethesda, Md., 1987, Oak Ridge Com. Ctr. garden, 1992, Fed. City Shelter, Washington, 1988; sculptor Johns Hopkins Ctr. Internat. Studies, Washington, 1990, Nat. Acad. Engring., Beckman Ctr., Irvine, Calif., 1990; contbr. articles and reviews to profl. jours. including Ceramics, 1989; commns. include 4 murals 20 vases Germaines Restaurant, Washington, 1978, lobby mural Nat. Milk Producers Assn., Rosslyn, Va., 1983, others. Commr. Cable TV Commn., Montgomery County, Rockville, Md., 1989-90. Mem. Ind. Agy. Women (pres. 1964-65), Kiln Club Washington, Achievement Rewards Coll. Sci., Inc. (v.p. 1980-81), Artists Equity, Internat. Sculpture Ctr., Bethsda Ceramic Guild, Studio Gallery. Republican. Home and Office: 6514 Bradley Blvd Bethesda MD 20817-3248

LARSON, LINDA K., university administrator; b. Henry County, Iowa, Aug. 14, 1942; d. Elwood LeRoy and Helen Inez (Garmoe) Holaday; m. Brian John Larson, June 8, 1963; 1 child, April Kay. BA, Point Loma (Calif.) Coll., 1965; MA, Calif. State U., Sacramento, 1972; postgrad., U. Pa., 1988-89. Cert. elem. and reading tchr., Calif. Tchr. Sunnymead (Calif.) Sch. Dist., 1964-65; tchr. San Juan Sch. Dist., Carmichael, Calif., 1965-70, specialist tchr. of reading, 1970-72; freelance cons. Columbus, Ohio, 1972-75; prof. Mt. Vernon (Ohio) Coll., 1975-76; lang. arts coord. West Grove (Pa.) Middle Sch., 1978-84; mem. staff reading study skills U. Pa., Phila., 1984-88, supr. student tchrs., 1988—; freelance tchr. and reading specialist, Carmichael, 1965-72; coord. lang. arts program Avon Grove Middle Sch.,

West Grove, 1978-84. Bd. dirs. Fairview Christian Acad., Fairview Village, Pa., 1986—. Mem. Internat. Reading Assn., Nat. Coun. Tchrs. of English, Assn. Supervision and Curriculum, Phi Delta Kappa, Pi Lambda Theta. Home: PO Box 29 Worcester PA 19490-0029

LARSON, LLOYD WARREN, economist; b. Barrett, Minn., Sept. 2, 1920; s. John Arthur and Jennie Constance (Nygren) L.; B.A., U. Minn., 1946, M.A., 1947; postgrad. U. Minn., George Washington U. Assoc. prof. history and polit. sci. Carthage (Ill.) Coll., 1948-49; with Dept. Labor, Washington, 1950-78; chief div. state workers' compensation standards, 1974-78; mem. research faculty Cornell U. Sch. Indsl. and Labor Relations, 1979-81; writer, cons. U.S. Task Force on Safety, 1968, Interdeptl. Workers Compensation Task Force, 1974-77, Nat. Commn. on State Workmen's Compensation Laws, 1971-72; officer, mem. exec. bd. local Am. Fedn. Govt. Employees, 1962-73. Served with U.S. Army, 1942-46. Mem. Am. Polit. Sci. Assn., Center for Study of Presidency, Internat. Soc. Polit. Psychology, Nat. Peace Found., Internat. Platform Assn., Am. Legion (past post comdr.), Order Ky. Cols. Lutheran. Clubs: Statler, Cornell (N.Y.C.). Author books, reports, bulls., papers in field. Home: 641 Erie St SE Minneapolis MN 55414-3110

LARUSSA, LUANN, small business owner; b. Scranton, Pa., Apr. 3, 1954; d. Dominick Anthony and Anita Marie (Piraino) LaR.; m. Charles S. Lehnert, June 21, 1975; children: Charles L., Keith L. BFA, Kutztown U., 1972-75. Camera supr. Pinwheel, N.Y.C., 1975-80; owner, pres. Parsippany (N.J.) Pinwheel, 1987—; grad. asst. Dale Carnegie, N.Y.C., 1978. Mem. Assn. Graphic Arts. Republican. Roman Catholic. Home: 25 Cottage Ln Sparta NJ 07871-4001 Office: Parsippany Pinwheel 1279 Route 46 Parsippany NJ 07054-4904

LASAK, JOHN JOSEPH, lawyer; b. Moosic, Pa., Jan. 18, 1944; s. Frank J. and Ann (Grudzinski) L.; m. Julilee Werteen, Mar. 17, 1973; children: Jennifer Ann, James Michael, Jessica Lee, Jill Emily. AB cum laude, U. Pa., 1965; JD, Harvard U., 1968. Bar: Pa. 1968. Assoc. Crumlish & Kania, Phila., 1968, Kania & Garbarino, Rosemont, Pa., 1971-76; ptnr. Kania & Garbarino, Bala Cynwyd, Pa., 1977-82, Kania, Lindner, Lasak & Feeney, Bala Cynwyd, 1982—. Vice chmn. Haverford Twp. (Pa.) Planning Commn., 1983; mem. Radnor Twp. (Pa.) Zoning Bd., 1985-91, vice chmn., 1987-91, chmn. 1992—. Mem. ABA, Pa. Bar Assn., Phila. Bar Assn., Harvard-Radcliffe Club (Phila.), St. Albans Club (Newtown Square, Pa.), Phi Beta Kappa. Republican. Roman Catholic. Office: Two Bala Pla 2 Bala Pla Ste 525 Bala Cynwyd PA 19004

LASCHENSKI, JOHN PATRICK, accountant; b. Darby, Pa., Nov. 20, 1937; s. Sigmund Joseph and Mary (Oldham) L. BS in Physics, Holy Cross Coll., 1959; MS in Physics, U. Wis., 1965; MBA, Rochester Inst. Tech., 1978. CPA, N.Y. Engr., mgr. IBM, N.Y., 1964-72; system engr. mgr. Xerox Corp., Rochester, N.Y., 1972-78, div. controller, 1978-82; pvt. practice acctg. Rochester, 1982-85; ptnr. Heveron, Laschenski & Walpole, Rochester, 1985—; adj. prof. Rochester Inst. Tech., 1983—, St. John Fisher Coll., Rochester, 1986—. Lt. USN, 1959-63. Mem. N.Y. State Soc. CPAs (bd. dirs. Rochester 1986—), Am. Inst. CPAs. Republican. Home: 6 Portsmouth Ter Rochester NY 14607-1513 Office: Heveron Laschenski & Walpole 144 Exchange Blvd Rochester NY 14614-2110

LASH, JAMES WILLIAM (JAY LASH), embryology educator; b. Chgo., Oct. 24, 1929; s. Joseph and Alice (Smith) L.; m. Natalie Novak, Sept. 10, 1954; 1 child, Rebecca. Phd, U. Chgo., 1954; MS (hon.), U. Pa., 1981. Postdoctoral fellow NIH, Phila., 1955-57; sr. rsch. fellow NIH, London, 1986; from asst. prof. to prof. U. Pa., Phila., 1957—; Helen Hay Whitney fellow Helen Hay Whitney Found., Phila., 1958-61, Helen Hay Whitney Established Investigator, 1961-66; cons. NSF, Washington, 1967-70; mem. adv. bd., cons. NIH, 1970-83. Co-editor 6 books in field. Fellow Lalor Found., 1957, Paulo Found., 1969, NIH, 1986; recipient rsch. award Wellcome Found., 1960. Office: Dept Cell & Dev Biol U Pa Sch Medicine Philadelphia PA 19104-6058

LASH, NATHANIEL ROBERT, corporate executive; b. Burlington, Vt., Apr. 19, 1922; s. Myron Simon and Martha (Katz) L.; m. Millicent C. Mandel, June 22, 1947; children: Michael, David, Roger. BS in Bus. Adminstrn., Boston U. Pres. Lash Furniture Co., Burlington, 1950-74, Plattsburgh, N.Y., 1957-69; pres. Town and Country Furniture Shop, South Burlington, 1965—, Burlington House, South Burlington, 1962—, Modern Design, Inc., Shelburne, Vt., 1970—. Chmn. City of Burlington Parking and Traffic Com., 1965-71. Cpl. USAF, 1942-46. Mem. Exch. Club (gov.), Nat. Home Furnishing Assn. (gov. 1982-86), Tau Epsilon Phi (consul). Home: 68 Crescent Rd Burlington VT 05401 Office: Town and Country Furniture 1515 Shelburne Rd South Burlington VT 05403-7714

LASHLEY, BARBARA THERESA, psychologist, educator, mental health counselor; b. Cambridge, Mass., Feb. 26, 1944; d. Frederick Karl and Theresa Sarah (Greelish) Petersen; m. Leonard A.G.O. Lashley Jr., Oct. 1, 1964 (div. 1972); children; Leonard A.G.O. III, Matthew Adrian. AS in Psychology, Massasoit Community Coll., Brockton, Mass., 1977; BSEE in Phys. Geog., Bridgewater State Coll., 1979, MEd in Counseling Psychology, 1989. Therapist Mass. Treatment Ctr., Bridgewater, 1982-83; pers. dir. Dept. of Mental Health, Plymouth, Mass., 1983-84; maximum tier priviledge coord. Mass. Treatment Ctr., Bridgewater, 1985-88; guidance intern Martha Burwell Lab. Sch., Bridgewater, 1988; guidance counselor Epping (N.H.) Elem. Sch., 1989-90; cons. to nursing homes Somerville, Mass., 1991—; counselor, tchr. Nutri System, Kingston, Mass., 1991-92; owner, therapist Children's and Family Guidance, 1989—; cons. Easton (Mass.) Children's Mus., 1991. Sec. Rocky Nook Point Improvement Assn., Kingston, 1984, treas., 1985; mem. adv. bd. Red Cloud Indian Sch. Mem. AACD, Am. Sch. Guidance Assn., Mass. Assn. Counseling and Devel., Mass. Mental Health Counselors Assn. Mem. Christian Ch. Home and Office: 57 Robins St East Bridgewater MA 02333-2557

LASHLEY, MARK ALAN, physician assistant; b. Balt., Sept. 17, 1959; s. William George and Verna Joan (Buterbaugh) L.; m. Mary Ellen Cadogan, June 21, 1986. BA in Biology, U. Md., Balt., 1981; AA in Physician Asst., Essex (Md.) Community Coll., 1984; MBA, Loyola Coll., Balt., 1987. Cert. physician asst., Md. Emergency room registrar Church Hosp., Balt., 1980-84; surg. physician asst. Baltimore County Gen. Hosp., Balt., 1984, South Balt. Gen. Hosp., 1984-85; physician asst. supr. Union Meml. Hosp., 1985—; guest speaker dept. nursing Towson State U., Balt., 1987—; part time faculty Essex Community Coll., 1990—. U.S. Senate scholar, 1977. Fellow Am. Acad. Physician Assts., Md. Acad. Physician Assts. Republican. Baptist. Home: 2513 Tally-Ho Dr Fallston MD 21047 Office: Union Meml Hosp Emergency Dept 201 E University Pkwy Baltimore MD 21218

LASHNER, MARILYN AUERBACH, communication content analyst, forensic expert; b. Phila., Dec. 11, 1929; d. Jacob and Mildred (Goodrich) Auerbach; m. Melvin Lashner, Aug. 19, 1951; children: Bret Auerbach, Jane Leslie, William Mark, Suzanne. BS in English and Edn., U. Pa., 1950, MS in English and Edn., 1954; PhD in Communications., Temple U., 1979. Cert. secondary English tchr., Pa. Tchr. English, dir. dramatics Cheltenham High Sch., Elkins Park, Pa., 1951-54; instr. English, Pa. State U., Abington, 1967-75; tchr. effective English communication Tng. div. U.S. Civil Svc., Phila., 1974; pres., dir. rsch. Inst. for News Media Analysis, Meadowbrook, Pa., 1979-84; asst. prof. communications Temple U., Phila., 1980-81; prin. researcher Media Analysis & Communicaitons Rsch., Meadowbrook, 1984—; forensic expert on meaning and interpretation of communication content in cases of libel, slander, invasion of privacy, prejudicial publicity, product liability, change of venue, fraudulent advertising, copyright infringement, contract interpretation. Author: The Chilling Effect in TV News: Intimidation by the Nixon White House, 1984; also articles. Recipient 1st place nat. award for First Amendment essay Nat. Assn. Broadcasters, 1977; fellow Temple U., 1976-79. Mem. Nat. Forensic Ctr. for Disting. Experts, Pi Delta Theta. Office: Media Analysis & Comm Rsch PO Box 3165W Meadowbrook PA 19046

LASKIN, CAROL RUBIN, non-profit organization director, consultant; b. Phila., July 20, 1948; d. Henry M. and Ruth (Mosheim) Rubin; children: Benjamin L., Michael R. BA, Case Western Res. U., 1970; M of City and Regional Planning, U. N.C., 1972. Health care cons. Macro Systems, Inc., Silver Spring, Md., 1972-75; staff officer Nat. Acad. Scis., Washington, 1975-76; health care cons. Washington, 1976—; exec. dir. Formula, Inc., Washington, 1979—. Contbr. articles to profl. jours. Recipient Loula D. Lasker award City Planning, 1970, Nat. Vol. award Washington Vol. Community, 1984. Mem. APHA. Home: 7111 Ridgewood Ave Chevy Chase MD 20815 Office: Formula Inc PO Box 39051 Washington DC 20016

LASKIN, LEE B., lawyer, state senator; b. Atlantic City, June 30, 1936; student Am. U., Temple U.; Rutgers U., 1960; m. Andrea Solomon; 1 dau., Shari. Bar: N.J.; asst. atty. City of Camden (N.J.), from 1962; asst. U.S. atty. N.J., 1964-68; mem. N.J. Gen. Assembly, 1968-70; mem. Camden County Bd. Chosen Freeholders, 1970-73; mem. N.J. Senate, 1977—; mcpl. atty. Audubon, Berlin Borough, Berlin Twp., Clementon, Laurel Springs, Mt. Ephraim and Waterford, N.J., and Winslow Twp.; counsel Bellmawr Bd. Edn., Berlin Zoning Bd., Camden County Welfare Bd., Non-Resident Taxpayers Assn., Animal Welfare Assn., Brith Sholom Fed. Credit Union, Camden Hebrew Fed. Credit Union, Union Fed. Savs. and Loan Assn., Div. 880 Amalgamated Transit Union, Local 18 of Am. Fed. Tech. Engrs., Camden Fire Officers Assn., Am. Postal Workers Union, Fuel Mchts. Assn., Glendale Nat. Bank; field counsel Fed. Nat. Mortgage Assn.; founder, 1st chmn. Glendale Nat. Bank; del. Rep. Nat. Conv., 1984. Served with USMCR. Office: NJ State Senate 1878 Route 70 E Cherry Hill NJ 08003-2090

LASKY, ELIZABETH MARCHELEWICZ, professional organization administrator; b. Springfield, Mass., Nov. 25, 1945; d. Joseph Louis and Josephine (Purda) Marchelewicz; m. Roy Edward Lasky, Apr. 19, 1969; children: David Roy, Gregory Joseph. BA, Smith Coll., 1967. Cert. tchr., Mass. Editorial asst. Houghton Mifflin Co., Boston, 1967-68; tchr. Palmer (Mass.) Pub. Schs., 1968-72, Agawam (Mass.) Pub. Schs., 1973-76; exec. dir. N.Y. State Assn. City Couns., Albany, 1983-86; freelance writer, editorial cons. Albany, 1983-86; exec. dir. Pharm. Soc. N.Y. State, Albany, 1986—; vol. editorial adviser N.Y. State Assn. Learning Disabled, Northeast Assn. of Blind, Wildwood Sch.; tchr. Temple Beth Emeth Nursery Sch., Albany, 1981-82. Editor: N.Y. State Pharmacist Century II, 1983-86. Program chmn. Loudonville (N.Y.) Sch. PTA, 1981-84; newsletter editor Capital Dist. PTA, Albany, 1982-84. Mem. State Assn. Execs. N.Y. State, Am. Soc. Assn. Execs. Office: Capital Pub Affairs Inc 111 Washington Ave Albany NY 12210-2207

LASNER, MARK SAMUELS, book collector, bibliographer; b. New Haven, July 1, 1952; s. Morton Henry and Bryna Jane (Samuels) Spero. BA, Conn. Coll., 1974. Hon. cons. Boston U. Librs., 1976-82; hon. cons. Victorian lit. Georgetown U. Libr., Washington, 1989—; dir. The Browning Inst., N.Y., 1987—. Co-editor: Poems and Drawings of Elizabeth Siddal, 1978; co-author: England in the 1880s, 1989, England in the 1890s, 1990; contbr. articles to profl. jours.; curator of exhbns. Dante Gabriel Rossetti, Fogg Art Mus., Harvard U., 1982. Bd. dirs. Friends of Conn. Coll. Libr., 1974—; vol. Fogg Art Mus., Harvard U., Cambridge, 1975-76; vol. bibliographer U. Va. Libr., Charlottesville, 1982-86. Winthrop scholar, 1973. Mem. William Morris Soc. in the U.S. (pres. 1988—), Bibliog. Soc. U.S., Tennyson Soc. (Am. rep. 1986—), Bibliog. Soc., William Nuthead Soc., Eighteen-Nineties Soc., Williams Club, Grolier Club, Phi Beta Kappa. Home: 1870 Wyoming Ave NW Washington DC 20009

LASNER, RUSSELL PAUL, insurance company executive; b. Fort Meade, Md., Aug. 15, 1956; s. William Paul and Carmela Mary (Candela) L.; m. Theresa Thomas, Oct. 22, 1977 (div. Mar. 1981). Grad. high sch., Croom, Md. CLU. Mgr. Duron Paint and Wallcovering, Marlow Heights, Md., 1976-78; field agt. KC, Davidsonville, Md., 1978-82, N.Y. Life, Landover, Md., 1982-87; agt. supr. Prudential Inst. of Am., Bethesda, Md., 1987-89; v.p. agy. Am. Citizens Life Ins., Washington, 1989-90; pres. Lasner & Assocs., Inc., Upper Marlboro, Md., 1989—. Bd. dirs. Washington Area Wheelchair Assn., 1989—, Arthritis Found., 1991-92, telethon chmn. 1992; bd. dirs. Prince George's County Fair Bd., 1990-93; adv. bd. Xmas in April, Prince George County, 1991-92; fundraising dir. Prince George's County Drug Awarness, 1992. Mem. Upper Marlboro Jaycees (pres. 1990-91, Jaycee of the Yr. 1990, other awards), Md. Jaycees (bd. dirs. dist. 6, 1991-92, bd. dirs. region III 1992—, numerous Dir. of the Month awards, Dist. Dir. of Yr. 1991-92, M. Keith Upson Meml. award 1991-92, Top Ten Jaycees of the Quarter 1991, others), KC, Moose, Fraternal Order of Police. Democrat. Mem. Christian Ch. Office: Lasner & Assocs Inc Ins Brokers 14806 Pratt St 2nd Flr Upper Marlboro MD 20772

LASPAGNOLETTA, BENJAMIN JOSEPH, infosystems specialist; b. Rochester, N.Y., Apr. 9, 1946; s. Joseph and Madeline (Sciora) LaS.; m. Susan Ann Appelt, Sept. 6, 1975. AS cum laude, Rochester Bus. Inst., 1967; BS cum laude, U. Rochester, 1972. Computer programmer U. Rochester, 1969-72; systems analyst Blue Cross and Blue Shield, Rochester, 1972-73; project leader Xerox Corp., Rochester, 1973—. Mem. Data Processing Mgmt. Assn., Xerox Mgmt. Assn. Republican. Roman Catholic. Home: 14 Brookshire Ln Penfield NY 14526-1614 Office: Xerox Corp PO Box 1540 Rochester NY 14644-0001

LASPINA, PETER JOSEPH, educator; b. Bay Shore, N.Y., June 28, 1951; s. Peter Celestine and Barbara Elizabeth (Rodee) L.; m. Julia Mary Gunther, July 10, 1982; 1 child; Joseph Peter. BMus, N.Y. State Coll., Potsdam, 1973; MS in Music Edn., L.I. U., 1978; MS in Tech. Sys. Mgmt., SUNY, Stony Brook, 1987. Tchr. music E. Meadow (N.Y.) pub. schs., 1974-75; tchr. music Northport-East Northport pub. schs., 1975-86, computer resource tchr., 1986—; part-time faculty SUNY, Stony Brook, 1991—; writer master trainer N.Y. State Edn. Dept., Albany, 1987—; cons. edni. tech., Smithtown, N.Y., 1987—; conf. presenter. Contbr. articles to profl. jours. Mem. Am. Fedn. Tchrs., N.Y. State United Tchrs., Suffolk County Music Educators Assn., Nat. Assn. Sci., Tech. and Soc., N.Y. State Assn. Computers and Techs. Presbyterian. Home: 749 Meadow Rd Smithtown NY 11787-1621

LASRY, CLAUDE, retail distribution executive; b. Tangiers, Morocco, Jan. 26, 1956; came to U.S., 1980; MS in Engring., Ecole Des Mines, Nancy, France, 1980; MBA, Columbia U., 1982. Registered profl. engr., France. Account officer Citibank, N.A., N.Y.C. and Madrid, 1982-85; assoc. dir. Continental Ill. Bank, N.Y.C., 1986-88; v.p. fin. Def. Software & Systems, Mahwah, N.J., 1988-89; v.p. GEC Alsthom Internat., Inc., N.Y.C., 1990-91; v.p. fin. and adminstrn. Carrefour (USA), Inc., Phila., 1991—. Home: 53 Chatham Pl Newtown PA 18940 Office: Carrefour (USA) Inc 1 Franklin Blvd Philadelphia PA 19154

LASSEN, JOHN KAI, lawyer; b. Youngstown, Ohio, Mar. 28, 1942; s. Kai Kierulff and Helen Susanne (Elsaesser) L.; m. Marion duPont McConnell, Sept. 26, 1987; children: Christian K., Laura Wick, William duPont, James Tyler. BA, Yale, 1964; LLB, U. Pa., 1967. Bar: Del. 1971, U.S. Dist. Ct. Del. 1972. Assoc. Lord, Day & Lord, N.Y.C., 1967; assoc. Morris, Nichols, Arsht & Tunnell, 1971-77, ptnr., 1977-83; ptnr. Lassen, Smith, Katzenstein & Furlow, 1984-91; pres. Chesapeake Industries, Inc., 1992—. Lt. USNR, 1967-70. Fellow Am. Coll. of Trusts & Estates Counsel; mem. ABA, Am. Judicature Soc., Del. Bar Assn. (chmn. decedents, estate and trusts, 1979-81), Del. World Affairs Coun., Nat. Assn. Bond Counsel, Del. Com. of 100, Soc. Mayflower Descendants (dep. gov. 1990—), Del. C. of C., Friends of Winterthur, Wilmington Club, Wilmington Country Club, Vicmead Hunt Club, Lincoln Club, Rotary. Republican. Episcopalian. Home: Crooked Billet PO Box 3712 3510 Kennett Pike Wilmington DE 19807-3019 Office: 29 Hill Rd Wilmington DE 19806

LASSERRE, JEAN PAUL, reinsurance company president; b. Mirande, France, Feb. 2, 1942; s. Henry and Renée (Bertin) L. Degree in engring., Ecole Centrale, Paris, 1965; MBA, Insead, Fontainebleau, France, 1977. Design engr. S.O.M., Chgo., 1965; project engr. Eurochemic, Mol, Belgium, 1966; area mgr. mid. east OTH Internat., Paris, 1972; internat. contracts mgr. CMP-EI, Paris, 1977; with SCOR Group, Paris, 1981; pres. SCOR Reins. Co. of Can., Toronto, Ont., 1987. Mem. Reins. Rsch. Coun. (bd. dirs., v.p.), Cercle Can. (bd. dirs.), French Can. C. of C. (bd. dirs.). Office: Scor Reinsurance of Canada, 123 Front St W, Toronto, ON Canada M5J 2M2

LASTER, LEONARD, physician, academic administrator; b. N.Y.C., Aug. 24, 1928; s. Isaac and Mary (Ehrenreich) L.; m. Ruth Ann Leventhal, Dec. 16, 1956; children: Judith Eve, Susan Beth, Stephen Jay. A.B., Harvard U., 1949, M.D., 1950. Diplomate Nat. Bd. Med. Examiners, Am. Bd. Internal Medicine (gastroenterology). From intern to resident in medicine Mass. Gen. Hosp., Boston, 1950-53; fellow gastroenterology Mass. Meml. Hosp., 1958-59; vis. investigator Pub. Health Rsch. Inst., N.Y.C., 1953-54; lt. commd. USPHS, 1954, advanced through grades to asst. surgeon gen. (rear adm.), 1971; mem. staff Nat. Inst. Arthritis, Metabolic and Digestive Diseases, NIH, Bethesda, Md., 1954-73, chief digestive and hereditary diseases br., 1969-73; spl. asst., then asst. dir. human resources President's Office Sci. and Tech., 1969-73; exec. dir. Assembly Life Scis.; also div. med. scis. NAS-NRC, 1973-74; ret. USPHS, 1973; v.p. acad. affairs and clin. affairs Med. Ctr., also dean Coll. Medicine, prof. medicine Downstate Med. Ctr., SUNY, Bklyn., 1974-78; pres. Oreg. Health Scis. U., Portland, 1978-87, prof. medicine, 1978-87; chancellor U. Mass. Med. Ctr., Worcester, 1987-90; prof. medicine, 1988-90; disting. univ., prof. medicine, health policy Oreg. Health Scis. U., Portland, 1990—, chancellor emeritus, 1990—; bd. dirs. Thermo Cardiosystems, Inc., Protein Engring. Corp., Inc., Cambridge, Mass.; cons. mgmt. and productivity of R & D programs for numerous pharm. corps., R & D strategic planning, orgn. corp. health care programs for multinat. paper corp.; lab investigator Marine Biol. Lab., Woods Hole, Mass., summers 1962-69, chmn., organizer symposia on nat. policy and biomed. scis., summers 1971-72, libr. reader, summers 1973-76. Author articles on gastrointestinal disease, inborn errors metabolism, devel. biology. Bd. dirs. Found. Advanced Edn. Scis., Bethesda, 1965-69, Bedford Stuyvesant Family Health Ctr., Bklyn., 1975-78, Med. Rsch. Found., Oreg., 1979-87, Oreg. Symphony, 1979-85, Oreg. Contemporary Theatre, 1981-83; pres. Burning Tree Elem. Sch. PTA, Bethesda, 1972-73; bd. dirs. Internat. Artists Series, Worcester, 1988-91, Mass. Biotech. Ctrs. for Excellence, Boston, 1988—, Mass. Biotech. Rsch. Inst., Worcester, 1988-90, Worcester Bus. Devel. Corp., 1988-91; co-chmn. United Way Cen. Mass., COMEC Campaign, 1989; exec. com. Worcester Econ. Club, 1988-91; mem. citizen gov. bd. Worcester Fights Back, 1990—. With USPHS, 1952-73. Fellow ACP; mem. Am. Fedn. Clin. Rsch., Am. Gastroenterol. Assn., Am. Soc. Biol. Chemists, Am. Soc. Clin. Investigation (emeritus), Marine Biol. Lab. Corp., Harvey Soc. N.Y., Portland C. of C. (dir. 1980-84), Mass. Med. Soc., Worcester Dist. Med. Soc., Worcester Club, Cosmos Club (Washington), Harvard Club (N.Y.C.), Univ. Club (Portland, Oreg.), Phi Beta Kappa, Sigma Xi. Home: 47 Pine Arden Dr West Boylston MA 01583-1024 Office: U Mass Med Ctr S1 866 55 Lake Ave N Worcester MA 01655

LASTER, PAUL ALAN, artist; b. Flint, Mich., Oct. 14, 1951; s. George Winston Laster and Virginia Joyce (Ingram) Lehman; m. Renee Ann Riccardo, May 21, 1983. One-person shows at Pence Gallery, Santa Monica, Calif., 1989, 90, Hirschl & Adler Modern, N.Y.C., 1990, Runkel-Hue-Williams, London, 1991, Barbara Krakow Gallery, Boston, 1991, Greenberg Gallery, St. Louis, 1992, Baudoin Lebon, Paris, 1992, Hirschl & Adler Modern, N.Y.C., 1992; exhibited in group shows at Pace Gallery, N.Y.C., 1991, Barbara Krakow Gallery, Boston, 1991, Pence Gallery, Santa Monica, 1991, Cantor Art Gallery, Worcester, Mass., 1991, Betsy Rosenfield Gallery, Chgo., others; represented in permanent collections at Met. Mus. Art, N.Y.C., Bklyn. Mus., others; contbr. articles to profl. jours. Grantee N.Y. Dept. Cultural Affairs, 1983, Nat. Endowment for Arts, 1985, 89, Art Matters, Inc., 1988, 89. Office: Hirschl & Adler Modern 851 Madison Ave New York NY 10021-4908

LASUCHIN, MICHAEL, artist, educator; b. Kramatorsk, Russia, July 24, 1923; came to U.S. 1951; s. Sergei F. and Agafia I. (Okolelova) L.; m. Dorothy L. Roschen, Aug. 26, 1988. BFA, Phila. Coll. Art, 1970; MFA, Temple U., 1972. Prof. art The Univ. of the Arts, Phila., 1972-90. Author/pubr.: Interpolated Voids, 1970; One man shows include Capital Air Ctr. Gallery, Taichung, Taiwan, 1989, Univ. of the Arts, Phila., 1991; permanent collections include Phila. Mus. Art, Brooklyn Art Mus., Mus. Modern Art, N.Y., Mus. Modern Art, Barcelona, Spain, Libr. Nat., Paris, Berlin Mus. of Art, Russian State Mus., Tretjakow Gallery, Moscow, Victoria Albert Mus., London. Mem. Watercolor USA, Nat. Watercolor Soc., Color Print Soc., Soc. Am. Graphic Artists, Phila. Print Club, Boston Printmakers. Home: 120 E Cliveden St Philadelphia PA 19119-2309

LATANISION, RONALD MICHAEL, materials science and engineering educator, consultant; b. Richmondale, Pa., July 2, 1942; s. Stephen and Mary (Kopach) L.; m. Carolyn Marie Domenig, June 27, 1964; children—Ivan, Sara. B.S., Pa. State U., 1964; Ph.D. in Metall. Engring., Ohio State U., 1968. Postdoctoral fellow Nat. Bur. Standards, Washington, 1968-69; research scientist Martin Marietta, Balt., 1969-73, acting head materials sci., 1973-74; dir. H.H. Uhlig Corrosion Lab. MIT, Cambridge, 1975—, Shell Disting. prof. materials sci. and engring., 1983-88, dir. Materials Processing Ctr., 1984-91; chmn. MIT Coun. on Primary and Secondary Edn., 1991—; tech. adv. bd. MODAR, Inc., Natick, Mass., 1981—; sci. advisor U.S. Ho. of Reps. Com. on Sci. and Tech., Washington, 1982-83; chmn. ad hoc com. Mass. Advanced Materials Ctr., Boston, 1985—; mem. adv. bd. Mass. Office Sci. and Tech.; co-chair steering com. for systemic change in teaching and learning math. and sci. Commonwealth of Mass. Editor: Surface Effects in Crystal Plasticity, 1977, Atomistics of Fracture, 1983, Chemistry and Physics of Fracture, 1987, Advances in Mechanics and Physics of Fracture, 1981, 83, 86; contbr. articles to profl. jours. Coach Winchester Soccer Club, Mass. Recipient A.B. Campbell award NACE, 1971, Sr. Scientist award Humboldt Found., 1974-75, David Ford McFarland award Pa. State U., 1986; named Henry Krumb lectr. AIME, 1984, Disting. Alumnus, Ohio State U. Coll. Engring., 1991, hon. alumnus MIT, 1992. Fellow Am. Soc. Metals Internat.; mem. NAE, Am. Soc. Metals (mem. govt. and pub. affairs com. 1984), Nat. Assn. Corrosion Engrs., New Eng. Sci. Tchrs. (founder, co-chmn.), Nat. Materials Adv. Bd. Roman Catholic. Office: MIT Materials Sci & Engring 77 Massachusetts Ave Rm 8202 Cambridge MA 02139-4307

LATCHIS, KENNETH SPERO, emergency physician; b. Brattleboro, Vt., July 5, 1935; s. Spero Demetrius and Angelika (Katsimanis) L.; m. Erika Mechthild Daucher, June 25, 1966; children: Mark T., Christine A., Ingrid K. AB, Brown U., 1957; MD, U. Vt., 1961. Diplomate Am. Bd. Surgery, Am. Bd. Emergency Medicine. Intern George Washington U. Hosp. Med. Ctr., Washington, 1961-62, resident in gen. surgery, 1964-69; fellow in gen. surgery Lahey Clinic, Boston, 1969-70; pvt. practice Fairfax, Va., 1970-77; attending emergency physician Newport (R.I.) Hosp., 1977-83, dir. emergency dept., 1979-83; attending emergency physician R.I. Hosp., Providence, 1983-85; attending emergency physician Washington (D.C.) Hosp. Ctr., 1985—, assoc. dir. emergency dept., 1989—; tumor bd. dirs. Fairfax Hosp., Falls Church, Va., 1970-77; clin. instr. surgery Georgetown U., Washington, 1971-77; clin. instr. surgery Brown U., Providence, 1983-85; instr. mil. medicine Uniformed Svcs. U. for Health Scis., Bethesda, MD., 1989—. Contbr. articles to profl. jours. Capt. USAF, 1962-64. Fellow Am. Coll. Surgeons, Am. Coll. Emergency Physicians, Southeastern Surg. Congress. Lutheran. Office: Washington Hosp Ctr 110 Irving St NW Washington DC 20010

LATCHUM, JAMES LEVIN, federal judge; b. Milford, Del., Dec. 23, 1918; s. James H. and Ida Mae (Robbins) L.; m. Elizabeth Murray McArthur, June 16, 1943; children: Su-Allan, Elizabeth M. A.B. cum laude, Princeton U., 1940; J.D., U. Va., 1946. Bar: Va. 1942, Del. 1947. Assoc. Berl, Potter & Anderson, Wilmington, 1946-53; partner Berl, Potter & Anderson, 1953-68; judge U.S. Dist. Ct. Del., Wilmington, 1968-73; chief judge U.S. Dist. Ct. Del., 1973-83, sr. judge, 1983—; New Castle County atty. Del. Hwy. Dept., 1948-50; asst. U.S. atty., 1950-53; atty. Del. Interstate Hwy. Div., 1955-62, Delaware River and Bay Authority, 1962-68. Chmn. New Castle County Democratic Com., 1953-56, Wilmington City Com., 1959-63. Served to maj. Insp. Gen. Corps AUS, 1942-46, PTO. Mem. Am., Del., Va. bar assns., Order of Coif, Sigma Nu Phi. Presbyn. Clubs: Wilmington, Univ. Office: US Dist Ct 844 N King St # 34 Wilmington DE 19801-3519

LATELLA, SALVATORE PHILIP, songwriter; b. Bronx, N.Y., Oct. 27, 1919; s. Joseph and Caroline (DeFiore) L.; m. Carmela Marie Yerace, May 22, 1954; 1 child, Joseph. Student in voice culture, N.Y. Sch. Music, 1950-52. Clk. U.S. Post Office, N.Y.C., 1949-55; park ranger U.S. Dept. of Interior, N.Y.C., 1955-63; freelance writer N.Y.C., 1963—; stock transfer clk., speaker The Bank of N.Y., N.Y.C., 1965-77; clk. U.S. Post Office, Pitts.,

1977-80. Author 2 nationally recognized poems. Served with U.S. Army, 1943-45. Recipient award N.Y.C. Lighthouse for Blind, 1963. Mem. Am. Hist. Soc., Internat. Platform Assn. Republican. Roman Catholic. Lodge: KC. Home: 5918 Nell Ln Ellenwood GA 30049-4076

LATHAM, ALLEN, JR., manufacturing company consultant; b. Norwich, Conn., May 23, 1908; s. Allen and Caroline (Walker) L.; m. Ruth Nichols, Nov. 11, 1933; children: W. Nichols, Harriet (Mrs. William S. Robinson), David W., Thomas W. B.S. in Mech. Engring, MIT, 1930, Sloan fellow, 1936. Devel. engr. E.I. duPont, Belle, W.Va., 1930-35; engr., treas. Polaroid Corp., Cambridge, Mass., 1936-41; engr., v.p. Arthur D. Little, Cambridge, 1941-66; pres. Cryogenic Tech., Waltham, Mass., 1966-71; founder Haemonetics, Braintree, Mass., 1971—. Recipient New Eng. Inventor award, 1987, Morton Grove-Rasmussen award Am. Assn. Blood Banks, 1989; named Engr. of Yr. Socs. New Eng. Engring., 1970. Mem. ASME, AAAS, Am. Inst. Chem. Engrs., Instrument Soc. Am., Nat. Acad. Engring. Club: Country (Brookline, Mass.). Home: 143 Whitcomb Ave Jamaica Plain MA 02130-3436 Office: Haemonetics 400 Wood Rd Braintree MA 02184-2486

LATHAM, CHRISTOPHER DANIEL, lawyer; b. Bklyn., Oct. 16, 1951; s. Ernest R. and Rosemary (McVarish) L.; m. Catherine Gleason Ruggiero, Oct. 6, 1979; children: Rita, Elizabeth, Christopher. BA in Music, U. Ariz., 1975; JD, N.Y. Law Sch., 1979. Bar: N.Y. 1980. Ptnr. Johnson, Tannen et al., N.Y.C., 1980—. Mem. N.Y. County Lawyers Assn., N.Y. State Trial Lawyers Assn., Assn. Trial Lawyers Am. Roman Catholic. Office: Johnson Tannen et al 225 Broadway New York NY 10007-3001

LATHAM, EUNICE STUNKARD (MRS. JOHN R. LATHAM), educational administrator; b. N.Y.C., Sept. 4, 1923; d. Horace Wesley and Frances Grace (Klank) Stunkard; BA, Wellesley Coll., 1945; m. John Ralph Latham, June 9, 1962. Reports officer UNRRA, Washington, Germany and France, 1945-47, acting dir. div. reports and analysis, Europe and Middle East, 1947; editor Unitarian Svc. Com., N.Y.C., 1947-49; copywriter J. Walter Thompson Co., N.Y.C., 1949-56, Lambert & Feasley, Inc., N.Y.C., 1956-62, Fuller & Smith & Ross, N.Y.C., 1962-65; v.p., creative supr. Lennen & Newell, Inc., 1965-70; headmistress Barnard Sch., N.Y.C., 1970-85, 87-88, dir. devel., 1985-88. Election dist. capt. Bronx County, 1948-54; committeewoman Bronx County, 1950-62; trustee Barnard Sch., Antoinette Fischer Williams Fund, Barnard Sch. Money Purchase Pension Plan, Baldwin Sch., Bryn Mawr, Pa., Profl. Children's Sch. Mem. Nat. Assn. Prins. Schs. for Girls (councilor), Head Mistresses Assn. of East (pres.), Guild Ind. Schs. N.Y.C. (v.p.), Shakespeare Soc., Soc. Mayflower Descs., Riverdale-on-Hudson Garden Club (pres.). Home: PO Box 171 Eagle Bridge NY 12057-9998 Office: 554 Ft Washington Ave New York NY 10033-2003

LATIF, MARY KOON, association-development director; b. Columbia, S.C.; d. Edwin Riser and Ruth Enoise (Wheeler) K.; m. Salam Karim Latif, Dec. 11, 1987. BA in Interdiciplinary Studies, U. S.C., 1983; MA in Edn. and Human Devel., George Washington U., 1986. Adminstrv. asst. Lancaster County Bd. Edn., Lancaster, S.C., 1974-76; instr. Williamsburg Tech. Coll., Kingstree, S.C., 1976-78, coord. rsch. and devel., 1978-84; spl. asst. Senator Ernest F. Hollings, Washington, 1984-90; dir. devel. Am. Assn. Community and Jr. Colls., Washington, 1990—; mem. Nat. Orgn. on Disability, Washington, 1990—; mem. employment preparation com. Pres. Com. on Employment of People with Disabilities, Washington, 1990—; mem. Coalition of Adult Edn. Orgns., 1992—. Co-author: Case Study of the Role of Title III Staff at the Department of Education, 1986. Mem. Nat. Coun. Fundraising Execs., Golden Key, Phi Delta Kappa. Office: Am Assn Community and Jr Colls 1 Dupont Cir NW Ste 410 Washington DC 20036-1176

LATIMER, JAMES HEARN, systems engineer; b. Texarkana, Ark., Oct. 27, 1941; s. James Hearn and Helen (Harris) L.; m. Michele Renee Halbeisen, July 5, 1969; children: Eric James, Veronique Claire. BS, MIT, 1963. Engr. Smithsonian Astrophys. Obs., Cambridge, Mass., 1963-71; applied mathematician Smithsonian Astrophys. Obs., 1971-77, mgr. satellite data, 1977-83; tech. staff The MITRE Corp., Bedford, Mass., 1983-90, lead engr., 1990—. Contbg. author: 1973 Smithsonian Standard Earth (III), 1973. Mem. ACM, AIAA (tech. com. on astrodynamics 1988-91). Republican. Methodist. Office: The Mitre Corp Burlington Rd Bedford MA 01730-1306

LATIMER, JONATHAN PEABODY, publisher, editor, writer; b. San Diego, June 19, 1942; s. Jonathan Wyatt and Ellen Baxter (Peabody) L.; m. Mari Alice Ryan, June 26, 1966; children: Jonathan Peter, Ryan Elizabeth. BA, Occidental Coll., 1964. Coll. traveller Harcourt Brace Jovanovich, Cin., 1965-68, editor, 1969-71; exec. editor St. Martin's Press, N.Y.C., 1971-73; freelance writer San Diego, 1973-77; pub. HP Books, Tucson, 1977-81; pub. Golen Press divsn. Western Pub., N.Y.C., 1981-87; reference pub. Houghton Mifflin, Boston, 1987-91; pub., owner Lightbeam Comm., Boston, 1991—; cons. Howard Graham Assn., N.Y.C., 1991—, Ligature, Boston, Simon & Schuster, San Rafael, Calif. Contr. revs. to L.A. Times. Judge Nat. Christina Found., Boston, 1991; mem. pres.'s bd. Scripp's Hosp., La Jolla, Calif., 1988—; active Blue Ribbon Ednl. Curriculum Panel, Tucson, 1979-80. With M.C., U.S. Army, 1968-69. Mem. Am. Book Producers Assn.

LATIMER, STEPHEN PAUL, real estate investment executive; b. Providence, June 1, 1957; s. George Thomas and Frances (Szwed) L.; m. Carol Gardner, Aug. 24, 1985; 1 child, Sally Gardner. BS, Providence Coll., 1979; MBA, Columbia U., 1986. CPA, R.I. Auditor Arthur Young & Co., Providence, 1979-83; sr. auditor Arthur Young & Co., N.Y.C., 1984; assoc. Jones Lang Wootton Realty Advisors, N.Y.C., 1986-88, v.p., 1989-90, dir., 1991—. Mem. Real Estate Bd. N.Y. Roman Catholic. Office: Jones Lang Wootton Realty Advisors 101 E 52d St New York NY 10022

LATORTUE, RÉEGINE ALTA GRÂCE, Africana studies educator; b. Port-au-Prince, Haiti, May 24, 1952; came to U.S., 1964; d. Charles Francçois and Yva (Richard) L.; m. Charles A. Dougall, May 26, 1973 (div. 1977); m. Jean Jacques Senechal, Aug. 27, 1985. BA, Trinity Coll., 1970; MA, U. Ill., 1972; MPhil, Yale U., 1975, PhD, 1982. Tchrs. asst. U. Ill., Urbana-Champaign, 1970-72; tchrs. asst. Yale U., New Haven, Conn., 1974-75, lectr. African-Am. studies, 1975-77; lectr. Hartford (Conn.) U., 1978; instr. Bklyn. Coll., 1978-83, asst. prof., 1983-87, assoc. prof., 1987-88, chmn., assoc. prof. African studies dept., 1988—. Co-author, editor: Les Cenelles: A Collection of Poems by Creole Writers, 1979; co-author: Femmes Haitiennes En Diaspora, 1986; contbr. articles to profl. jours. Recipient 11 awards for untiring efforts on behalf of Haitians, HASA-Bklyn. Coll., 1990, award for outstanding svc. to Vietnam era vets. Bklyn. Coll., 1981; Ford Found. postdoctoral fellow, 1987-88; grantee ACLS, 1988, So. Fellowships Fund, 1976-78. Mem. MLA, Coll. Lang. Assn. (life), Caribbean Studies Assn., African Lit. Assn., Mid. Atlantid Writers Assn., N.Y. State Women's Assn. Democrat. Roman Catholic. Office: Bklyn Coll Africana Studies Dept Bedford Ave and Ave H Brooklyn NY 11222-3102

LATSHAW, DAVID RODNEY, chemist; b. Allentown, Pa., Nov. 4, 1939; s. Willis Drehs and Augusta Mary (Minnich) L.; m. Patricia Mary Fix, Oct. 2, 1971; children: Jonathan David, Rebekah Ruth. BS, Muhlenberg Coll., Allentown, Pa., 1961; MS, Lehigh U., 1963, PhD, 1966. Lab. tech. Bethlehem (Pa.) Steel Co., 1961; rsch. asst. Lehigh U., Bethlehem, 1963-66; from chemist to mgr. Air Products & Chems., Inc., Allentown, 1966—. Contbr. articles to profl. jours. Trustee, pres. Bethany Evang. Ch., Allentown, 1967-74, 75-83, 89—, pres. official bd., 1972-75, 83-89, Sunday sch. tchr., 1966—; treas. Macungie (Pa.) Band, 1973—; active Lehigh County Hist. Soc., Anthracite Ry. Hist. Soc., Reading Co. Tech. and Hist. Soc., Nat. Ry. Hist. Soc., Ry. Locomotive and Hist. Soc. Mem. Am. Chem. Soc., Sigma Xi. Home: 944 Belford Rd Allentown PA 18103-3646 Office: Air Products and Chems Inc 7201 Hanilton Blvd Allentown PA 18195-1501

LATTIN, ALBERT FLOYD, banker; b. Everett, Wash., May 23, 1950; s. Albert S. and Erma Victoria (Hunt) L. Student, U. Nairobi, Kenya, 1970-71, Am. U. Cairo, Egypt, 1972; BA, Antioch U., 1973; MA, NYU, 1979; MBA, Columbia U., 1984. Asst. curator The Bklyn. Mus., 1973-76, assoc., 1976-79; sec. of the mus. Solomon R. Guggenheim Mus., N.Y.C., 1979-80, cons. in arts, 1980-83; assoc. Bankers Trust Co., N.Y.C., 1984-86, v.p., 1988—; v.p., trustee Mus. Holography, N.Y.C., 1980-87; bd. adv. Gallery Assn. N.Y. State, 1988—; treas. The Theban Found., 1991—. Editor, researcher book and catalogue Africa in Antiquity: The Arts of Ancient Nubia and the Sudan, 1978; organizer exhibition/movie The Heritage of Islam, 1982. Mem. Bklyn. Hist. Soc., Bklyn. Heights Assn., 1986—. Mem. Am. Banking Assn., Urban Land Inst., Internat. Council of Mus., Am. Assn. Mus., Internat. Assn. Egyptologists, Roundout Valley Country Club, Columbia Club. Home: 242 Henry St Brooklyn NY 11201-4662 Office: Bankers Trust Co 280 Park Ave New York NY 10017-1216

LAU, HARRY HUNG-KWAN, acoustical and interior designer, consultant; b. Hong Kong, May 8, 1939; s. Kang Hoi and Yuk Jing (Chan) L. B.Arch., Ohio State U., 1965, M.Arch., 1966. Acoustical designer Bolt, Beranek & Newman, N.Y.C., 1967-69; archl. designer Marcel Breuer & Asscos., N.Y.C., 1969-70; archl. designer Edward L. Barnes & Assocs., N.Y.C., 1970-74; pres. MKC Design, N.Y.C., 1975-76; pres. Lau & Assocs., N.Y.C., 1977—; instr. of design N.Y. Inst. Tech., 1974. Summer grantee Harvard U., 1966. Mem. Acoustical Soc. Am., Nat. Council Interior Design, Am. Soc. Interior Design. Address: 30 E 95th St New York NY 10028

LAU, HENRY YAN-CHUNG, cardiologist; b. Chekiang, China, Nov. 21, 1943; came to U.S., 1974; s. Tsee-Pang and Fong-Ting (Lin) L.; m. Siew-Yin Foo, May 7, 1973; children: Jolie Roh-Ying, Evan Yee-Fan. B. Medicine, Nat. Taiwan U. Med. Coll., Taipei, Republic of China, 1973. Cert. State Bd. Med. Examiners of N.J., Am. Bd. Internal Medicine, Am. Bd. Internal Medicine-Cardiovascular Disease. Intern Nat. Taiwan U. Hosp., Taipei, 1971-73; resident in medicine Hackensack (N.J.) Med. Ctr., 1974-77, chief resident internal medicine dept., 1977-78, cardiology fellow, 1978-80; assoc. Michael D. Yablonski, M.D., P.A., Hackensack, 1980-82; pres. Henry Lau M.D., P.A., Hackensack, 1982—. Fellow Am. Coll. Cardiology, N.Y. Cardiology Soc.; mem. AMA, ACP, Bergne County Med. Sco., Med. Soc. N.J., Nat. Taiwan U. Med. Coll. Alumni Assn. Office: 155 Polifly Rd Ste 106 Hackensack NJ 07601

LAU, ROBERT KEITH, videotape director and editor, musician, actor; b. Hackensack, N.J., Oct. 20, 1958; s. Grant Franklin and Mary Teresa (Lee) L. BA, U. Md., 1981; profl. cert., Convergence Corp., N.Y.C., 1984; quality improvement cert., Phil Crosby and Assocs., 1986; postgrad., U. Md., 1989-. Intern, prodn. asst. PM Mag., camera operator asst. Eyewitness News Sta. WDVM-TV (now WUSA), Washington, 1981; sr. engr., staff announcer The Washington Ear, Inc.-Radio Reading Service for Blind & Handicapped, Silver Spring, Md., 1981-84; tech. dir. NUS Tng. Corp., Gaithersburg, Md., 1984-86, assoc. dir., sr. video editor, 1986-90, dir., editor, 1990—; audio cons. Fine Arts div. U. Md., College Pk., 1981, communications dept. Montgomery Coll., Rockville, Md., 1983, Arena Stage Theater, Washington, 1984; video editor pub. service announcement Am. Lung Assn., 1985, tng. video Digital Circuits 5, 1985 (Merit award), sales video NUS Tng. Corp., 1986 (Merit award), computer graphics animation Sta. WETA, 1987 (Merit award), Atlas Video, Inc., Hyattsville, Md., 1986, Hyattstown Vol. Fire Dept., Germantown, Md., 1987, Montgomery County Police Dept., 1987; video tech. PM/Evening Mag., San Francisco, 1987; music cons. The Source Theater, Washington, 1986. Keyboardist, vocalist, Rockville, Md., 1973-85; extra actor feature films, 1986, 87, feature films, 1986-92; composer music Chlorep Theme, 1987 (Merit award); composer music series opening Microprocessor Series, 1985, photographer textbook and catalogue, 1987 (Merit award); video photographer Washington Grove Heritage Com., Gaithersburg, 1987. Elections judge Montgomery County, Rockville, 1977-79; mem. Nat. Rep. Congl. Com., Washington, 1979-85. Dist. winner nat. auditions Nat. Guild Piano Tchrs., 1970-76, state winner 1977-79; recipient Nebr. Interactive Videodisc award, 1987. Mem. AFTRA, SAG, Internat. TV Assn. (award of Excellence 1986, 2 Merit awards 1986, Golden Reel of Excellence award 1987), Hawaii State Soc. Washington, Am. Film Inst., Friends of Kennedy Ctr., Interactive Multimedia Assn., Internat. Interactive Communications Soc. (bd. dirs. Washington chpt. 1991—), U. Md. Alumni Assn. (life), Internat. Platform Assn., Alpha Epsilon Rho. Lutheran. Home: 12034 Winding Creek Way Germantown MD 20874-1954 Office: NUS Tng Corp 910 Clopper Rd PO Box 6032 Gaithersburg MD 20877-0962

LAUB, STEPHEN W., artist; b. Oakland, Calif., July 10, 1945. BA, U. Calif., Berkeley, 1968, MA, 1970. Acting instr. U. Calif., Berkeley, 1972-73, lectr., 1974-75, 77; asst. prof. Temple U., Tyler Sch. of Art, Phila., 1979-84, SUNY, Old Westbury, 1987, Rutgers U., Newark, N.J., 1987—; internat. co-editor Leonardo, Jour. of the Internat. Soc. Arts, Scis. and Tech., San Francisco, 1983-87. One-man shows include Ealan Wingate Gallery, N.Y.C., 1991, Koury Wingate Gallery, N.Y.C., 1989, 88. Recipient Chancellor's fellowship U. Calif., 1969-70, Fulbright fellowship Coun. for Internat. Exch., 1971-72, Artist's fellowship NEA, 1978-79, Henry Rutgers Rsch. fellowship, 1987-89, Artist's fellowship N.Y. Found. for the Arts, 1989-90. Office: Rutgers U 110 Warren St Newark NJ 07102-1809

LAUBACH, DAVID CLAIR, English educator; b. Danville, Pa.; s. Joseph Bedford and Melva Kathryn (Kile) L.; m. Glenda Cheryl Laubach, June 16, 1969; children: Kristi Ann, Karina Jo. BS, Bloomsburg (Pa.) U., 1960, MEd, 1966; EdD, U. Mass., 1985. Head English dept. Loyal Sock Twp. High Sch., Williamsport, Pa., 1960-69; English tchr. St. Nicholas Sch., Northwood, England, 1969-70; dir. English dept. Westfield (Mass.) Pub. Schs., 1970-85; coord. lang. arts and reading Colonial Sch. Dist., Plymouth Meeting, Pa., 1985-88; assoc. prof. English Kutztown (Pa.) U., 1988—; cons. Pa. Dept. Edn., 1989—. Author: Introduction to Folklore, 1986; film columnist Valley Advocate, 1975—; contbr. articles to profl. jours. Deacon United Ch. of Christ. Fulbright scholar, 1969-70; NEH fellow, 1985, Pa. Acad. for Teaching fellow, 1989. Mem. Nat. Coun. Tchrs. English (rural com., conf. on English edn. 1985—). Democrat. Home: PO Box 85 Stony Run PA 19557-0085 Office: Kutztown U Kutztown PA 19530

LAUBER, JOHN K., research psychologist; b. Archbold, Ohio, Dec. 13, 1942; s. Kenneth Floyd and Fern Elizabeth (Rupp) L.; m. Susan Elizabeth Myers, Sept. 16, 1967; 1 stepchild, Sarah H. BS, Ohio State U., 1965, MS, 1967, PhD, 1969. Rsch. psychologist U.S. Naval Tng. Equipment Ctr., Orlando, Fla., 1969-73; chief aero. human factors office NASA Ames Rsch. Ctr., Moffett Field, Calif., 1973-85; mem. Nat. Transp. Safety Bd., Washington, 1985—; mem. aeros. adv. com. NASA, 1987—, U.S. Air Force Studies Bd., NAS, Washington, 1987-89. Contbr. articles to profl. jours. Recipient Industry Svc. award Air Transport World, N.Y.C., Disting. Svc. award Flight Safety Found., Tokyo, 1987, Joseph T. Nall Meml. award Nat. Air Traffic Controllers Assn., 1992. Fellow Aerospace Med. Assn. (chmn. aviation safety com. 1978-82, R. F. Longacre award 1990).; mem. Human Factors Soc. Democrat. Office: Nat Transp Safety Bd 490 L'Enfant Pla E SW Washington DC 20594

LAUDANO, WILLIAM BONAVENTURA, JR., banker, accountant; b. New Haven, Conn., Oct. 26, 1953; s. William Bonaventura and Margaret Marie (DeRosa) L.; m. Anne Neidlinger, Oct. 29, 1982; 1 child, Alexander August. BS with high honors, Quinnipiac Coll., 1975. CPA, Conn. Sr. mgr. Ernst & Young, Hartford, Conn., 1975-90; chief fin. officer Amity Bancorp., Inc., Woodbridge, Conn., 1990—. Bd. dirs. Quinnipiac Coun. Boy Scouts Am. Mem. Conn. Soc. CPAs (Acad Achievement award 1975), AICPA, Quinnipiack Club, Delta Mu Delta. Roman Catholic. Home: 191 Saddle Hill Dr Guilford CT 06437-1433 Office: Amity Bancorp Inc 128 Amity Rd Woodbridge CT 06525-2229

LAUDER, ESTEE, cosmetics company executive; b. N.Y.C.; m. Joseph Lauder; children: Leonard, Ronald. LLD (hon.), U. Pa., 1986. Chmn. bd. Estee Lauder Inc., 1946—. Author: Estee: A Success Story, 1985. Named One of 100 Women of Achievement Harpers Bazaar, 1967, Top Ten Outstanding Women in Business, 1970; recipient Neiman-Marcus Fashion award, 1962; Spirit of Achievement award Albert Einstein Coll. Medicine, 1968; Kaufmann's Fashion Fortnight award, 1969; Bamberger's Designer's award, 1969; Gimbel's Fashion Forum award, 1969; Internat. Achievement award Frost Bros., 1971; Pogue's Ann. Fashion award, 1975, Golda Meir 90th Anniversary Tribute award, 1988; decorated chevalier Legion of Honor France, 1978; medaille de Vermeil de la Ville de Paris, 9, 1979; 4th Ann. award for Humanitarian Service Girls' Club N.Y., 1979; 25th Anniversary award Greater N.Y. council Boy Scouts Am., 1979; L.S. Ayres award, 1981; Achievement award Girl Scouts U.S.A., 1983; Outstanding Mother award, 1984; Athena award, 1985; honored Lincoln Ctr., World of Style, 1986; 1988 Laureate Nat. Bus. Hall of Fame. Office: Estee Lauder Inc 767 5th Ave New York NY 10153-0002*

LAUDER, RONALD STEPHEN, investor; b. N.Y.C., Feb. 26, 1944; s. Joseph H. and Estee (Josephine) (Mentzer) L.; m. Jo Carole Knopf, July 8, 1967; children: Aerin Rebecca, Jane Alexandra. Degree in French lit., U. Paris, 1964; B.S. in Internat. Bus., U. Pa., 1965. With Estee Lauder, Inc., Brussels, Paris, N.Y.C., 1965-83, also bd. dirs.; chmn. Estee Lauder Internat., Inc., 1980-83; dep. asst. Sec. of Def., Washington, 1983-85; ambassador to Austria Vienna, 1986-87; chmn., pres. Lauder Investments, Inc.; pvt. investor Ea. and Cen. Europe; founder, chmn. Cen. European Devel. Corp. Author: Fighting Violent Crime in America, 1985. Mem. N.Y. State Econ. Devel. Bd., 1972-78; fin. chmn. N.Y. State Republican Com., 1979-82; chmn. 500 Club of N.Y. Rep. Com., 1979-83; trustee Mus. Modern Art, 1975—, Mt. Sinai Med. Ctr., 1981—; Rep. candidate, Conservative nominee for Mayor of N.Y.C., 1989. Recipient Ordre De Merit, France, 1985, Disting. Pub. Svc. medal award Dept. Def., 1986; decorated Great Cross of the Order of Aeronautical Merit with White Ribbon, Spain, 1985; Ronald S. Lauder Drawing Gallery at Mus. Modern Art named in his honor, 1984. Office: 660 Madison Ave Ste 850 New York NY 10021-8405*

LAUFER, ALLAN HENRY, chemist; b. N.Y.C., Mar. 27, 1936; s. William and Helen G. (Lipsey) L.; m. Sondra Pallant, June 20, 1959; children: Terri M., Andrea J. BA, NYU, 1956; MS, Lehigh U., 1958, PhD, 1962. Staff chemist Gulf R&D Co., Pitts., 1962-64, Nat. Bur. Standards, Washington, 1964-83; staff chemist Basic Energy Scis.-Dept. Energy, Washington, 1983-86, supervisory chemist, br. chief fundamental interactions, 1986—. Contbr. over 50 articles to scholarly and profl. jours. Past pres. local elem. and jr. high sch. PTAs; area v.p. county PTA; active county sch. bd. panels. Recipient Silver Medal award Dept. Commerce, 1983. Office: Basic Energy Scis Dept Energy ER 141 GTN Washington DC 20585

LAUFER, HILDA, physician, neuropathologist; b. Vienna; came to U.S., 1939; d. Richard and Franziska; 2 children. BS in Edn., CCNY, 1946; MD, Syracuse U., 1950. Neuropathologist Queens Hosp. Ctr., N.Y.C., 1965—, Long Island Jewish Med. Ctr., New Hyde Park, N.H., 1971—. Office: Queens Div Long Island Jewish Med Ctr 82-68 164th St Jamaica NY 11432

LAUFER, IRA JEROME, physician; b. N.Y.C., Mar. 29, 1928; s. Irving and Evelyn (Weisman) L.; m. Barbara Alfandari, July 10, 1955; children: Tina, David. BA, NYU, 1948; MD, NYU Sch. Medicine, 1953. Diplomate Am. Bd. Internal Medicine. Instr. clin. medicine NYU Sch. Medicine, N.Y.C., 1959-69, asst. prof. clin. medicine, 1969-83, clin. assoc. prof. medicine, 1983—; dir. diabetes svc. Cabrini Med. Ctr., N.Y.C., 1966-89; dir. medicine N.Y. Eye and Ear Infirmary, N.Y.C., 1978-91; med. dir. Diabetes Treatment Ctr., N.Y.C., 1985—; attending physician Cabrini Med. Ctr., N.Y.C., 1989—; lectr. and cons. in field. Co-author: Diabetes Explained, 1976. Capt. USAF, 1955-57, Korea. Recipient Svc. award Am. Diabetes Assn., 1990. Fellow Am. Coll. Clin. Pharmacology; mem. Am. Coll. Physicians. Office: 247 Third Ave New York NY 10010

LAUFFER, MAX AUGUSTUS, JR., biophysicist, educator; b. Middletown, Pa., Sept. 2, 1914; s. Max Augustus and Elsie (Keiper) L.; m. Dorothy Easton, Dec. 20, 1936 (dec. 1963); 1 child, Edward William; m. Erika Erskine, Mar. 21, 1964; children—Susan, Max, John. B.S., Pa. State Coll., 1933, M.S., 1934; Ph.D., U. Minn., 1937. Asst., instr. biochemistry U. Minn., 1935-37; fellow, asst., asso. Rockefeller Inst. Med. Research, Princeton, 1937-44; asso. prof. U. Pitts., 1944-47, prof. biophysics, 1947—, head dept., 1949-56, dean div. natural scis., 1956-63, dean emeritus, 1984—, Andrew Mellon prof. biophysics, 1963-84, prof. emeritus, 1984—, chmn. dept., 1963-67, 71-75, cons. to provost, 1984-86; Vis. prof. U. Bern, Switzerland, 1952, Max Planck Inst. Virus Research, Tubingen, Germany, 1965-66, U. Philippines, 1967; sci. adv. bd. Delta Regional Primate Research Center, Tulane U., 1964-67; nat. advisory gen. med. scis. council NIH, 1963-67; mem. teaching staff Marine Biol. Lab., Woods Hole, Mass., 1953-56; sci. adv. com. Boyce Thompson Inst. Plant Research, 1953-83; cons. Research and Devel. Bd., 1947-53, surgeon gen., 1961-63. Author: Entropy-Driven Processes in Biology, 1975, Motion in Biological Systems, 1989; bd. editors: Archives Biochemistry and Biophysics, 1944-54, Biophys. Jour., 1960-64, editor, 1969-73; co-editor: Advances in Virus Research, 1953-85; contbr. articles to profl. jours. Mem. bd. Christian edn. U.P. Ch. U.S.A., 1963-72, mem. coun. ch. and soc., 1963-71, chmn., 1968-71; trustee Pitts. Theol. Sem., 1964-79, 80-89, trustee emeritus, 1990—, chmn., 1971-74; bd. dirs. Health Rsch. and Svcs. Found., Pitts., 1961-67, 75-81; trustee Coll. Wooster, 1967-87, trustee emeritus, 1987—. Recipient Eli Lilly Research award in biochemistry Am. Chem. Soc., 1945; Outstanding Achievement award U. Minn., 1964. Fellow N.Y. Acad. Sci.; mem. Am. Chem. Soc. (chmn. div. biol. chemistry 1949-50, Pitts. award 1958), Fedn. Am. Scientists (chmn. Pitts. br. 1958-59), Biophys. Soc. (exec. bd. 1958-62, pres. 1961, archivist 1981-91), Am. Soc. Biol. Chemists, Soc. Exptl. Biology and Medicine, World Federalist Assn. (vice chmn. Pitts. chpt.), Phi Beta Kappa, Sigma Xi, Alpha Zeta, Alpha Chi Sigma, Gamma Alpha, Phi Kappa Phi, Phi Eta Sigma, Gamma Sigma Delta, Phi Lambda Upsilon, Sigma Pi Sigma, Phi Sigma. Presbyterian. Home: 190 Lauffer Rd Middletown PA 17057-3863

LAUFMAN, HAROLD, surgeon; b. Milw., Jan. 6, 1912; s. Jacob and Sophia (Peters) L.; m. Marilyn Joselit, 1940 (dec. 1963); children: Dionne Laufman Weigert, Laurien Laufman Kogut; m. June Friend Moses, 1980. BS, U. Chgo., 1932; MD, Rush Med. Coll., 1937; MS in Surgery, Northwestern U., Chgo., 1946, PhD, 1948. Diplomate: Am. Bd. Surgery. Intern Michael Reese Hosp., Chgo., 1936-39; resident in gen. surgery St. Marks Hosp., London, Northwestern U. Med. Sch., Cook County Hosp., Hines VA Hosp., 1939-46; mem. faculty Northwestern U., 1941-65; from clin. asst. to prof., attending surgeon Passavant Meml. Hosp., Chgo., 1953-65; prof. surgery, history of medicine Albert Einstein Coll. Medicine, N.Y.C., 1965-82, prof. emeritus, 1982—; dir. Inst. Surg. Studies, Montefiore Hosp. and Med. Center, Bronx, N.Y., 1965-81; pvt. practice gen. and vascular surgery Chgo., 1941-65, N.Y.C., 1965-81; ret. professorial lectr. surgery Mt. Sinai Sch. Medicine, N.Y.C., 1979—; attending surgeon Mt. Sinai Hosp., N.Y.C., 1979-83; cons., lectr. in field; chmn. FDA Classification Panel Gen. and Plastic Surgery Devices, 1975-78; chmn. Medinvent, Inc., 1977-92; pres. Harold Laufman Assocs., Inc., 1977—, sr. ptnr., 1988—. Author: (with S.W. Banks) Surgical Exposures of the Extremities, 1953, 2d edit. 1986, (with R.B. Erichson) Hematologic Problems in Surgery, 1970, Hospital Special Care Facilities, 1981, The Veins, 1986; chmn. editorial bd.: Diagnostica, 1974-79; mem. editorial bd.: Surgery, Gynecology and Obstetrics, 1974—, Infection Control, 1980-88, Med. Instrumentation, 1972-83, Med. Research Engring, 1972-79; contbr. articles to sci. pubis. Chmn. bd. dirs. N.Y. Chamber Soloists, 1974-80, Chamber Music Conf. and Composers Forus of the East, 1975-91. Maj. AUS, 1942-46. Fellow ACS; mem. Assn. Advancement Med. Instrumentation (pres. 1974-75, chmn. bd. 1976-77), Am. Assn. Hosp. Cons., Am. Med. Writers Assn. (pres. 1968-69), Am. Surg. Assn., Société Internationale de Chirurgie, Western Surg. Assn., Cen. Surg. Assn., N.Y. Surg. Soc., Soc. Vascular Surgery, Internat. Cardiovascular Soc., Soc. Surgery Alimentary Tract, Surg. Infection Soc. (councillor 1980-84), Sigma Xi, Alpha Omega Alpha, Phi Sigma Delta, Zeta Beta Tau. Jewish. Clubs: Standard (Chgo.); Harmonie (N.Y.C.); Willow Ridge Country (Harrison, N.Y.). Home and Office: 31 E 72d St New York NY 10021

LAUGHLIN, ROBERT ARTHUR, accountant; b. Towanda, Pa., Mar. 2, 1939; s. Robert Donald and Mary Ann (Lewis) L.; m. Judith Ann Jerico, Sept. 4, 1960 (div. 1973); children: Maryann, Susan, Robert J. BS, Bklyn. Coll., 1961. CPA, N.Y., Ill. Investment analyst Dupont & Co., N.Y.C., 1958-60; acct. S.P. Cooper & Co., CPAs, N.Y.C., 1960-69, sr. ptnr., 1969—; gen. ptnr. Cal III. Ltd., Fort Lee, N.J., 1981—; fin. cons. Old Boston Sq. Assocs., L.A., 1981—; bd. dirs., treas. CYNWYD Corp., Del., 1988, Gilpin Pl., Inc., Wilmington, Del., 1986—, 1506 Delaware Ave. Corp.; bd. dirs., treas. MMA Financo, Hong Kong; bd. dirs. Myanmar Am. Fisheries Corp., Yangon, Myanmar, 1990—. Mem. U. Wyo. Pres.'s Coun. With U.S. Army N.G., 1956-62. Mem. AICPA, N.Y. State Soc. CPAs, Internat. Fiscal Assn. (bd. dirs. 1991—), Le Club, Non-Club (Paris), Players Club, N.Y. Athletic Club, Le Club De La Tour. Republican. Roman Catholic. Office: SP Cooper & Co CPAs 733 3d Ave New York NY 10017

LAUGHLIN, STANLEY IRA, patent lawyer; b. N.Y.C., Oct. 2, 1924; s. Michael Francis and florence (Kennedy) L.; m. Edith Brown, Sept. 3, 1949; children: David Alvin, Sheryl Laughlin Mihopulos. BEE, Pratt Inst., 1949; MSEE, Poly. Inst., Bklyn., 1963; JD, N.Y. Law, 1970. Lic. profl. engr., N.Y. Load dispatcher L.I.L.C.O., Hicksville, N.Y., 1949-57; engr. Sperry Gyroscope, Lake Success, N.Y., 1957-64; patent engr. A.I.L., Div. Cutler-Hammer, Deer Park, N.Y., 1964-70; patent agt. U.S. Philips Corp., Briarcliffe Manor, N.Y., 1970-73; sole proprietor North Babylon, N.Y., 1971—. Mem. Suffolk County Bar Assn. Christian Scientist.

LAUGHTON, JOHN CHARLES, music educator, musician; b. Sioux City, Iowa, Oct. 9, 1946; s. Richard Laughton and Carolyn Mae (Bogenrief) Wood; m. Katherine Elaine Kendall, Oct. 25, 1969; children: Benjamin Kendall, Nicholas Dehner. BMus, U. Iowa, 1968, D Musical Arts, 1980; MMus, Cath. U., 1972. Instr. music Cornell Coll., Mt. Vernon, Iowa, 1972-74; assoc. prof. music St. Mary's Coll. of Md., St. Mary's City, 1974—, head div. arts and letters, 1984-90; performer/coach Ctr. for Chamber Music, Keene, N.H., 1974-84; dir. Tidewater Music Festival, St. Mary's City, 1982-85; exec. dir., founder Chesapeake Summer Arts, St. Mary's City, 1985-90; Fulbright prof. Fed. U. Bahia, Salvador, Bahia-Brazil, 1983-84; mem. panel Arts Internat., N.Y.C., 1989; cons. Southwestern U., Georgetown, Tex., 1990. Performer in solo recital, China, Soviet Union, 1990, Brazil, 1989. Advisor Md. State Arts Coun., Balt., 1984-88; bd. dirs. St. Mary's Arts Coun., St. Mary's County, Md., 1984-90. With USN, 1968-72. Fulbright grantee, Brazil, 1983-84, China, 1990; NEH grantee, Austin, Tex., 1991; acad. specialist USIA, 1986, 89. Mem. Fulbright Assn. (v.p. 1989-90). Democrat. Home: PO Box 83 Saint Marys City MD 20686-0083 Office: St Mary's Coll of Md Saint Mary's City MD 20686

LAULICHT, MURRAY JACK, lawyer; b. Bklyn., May 12, 1940; s. Philip and Ernestine (Greenfield) L.; m. Linda Kushner, Apr. 4, 1965; children: Laurie Hasten, Pamela Hirt, Shellie Davis, Abigail. BA, Yeshiva U., 1961; LLB summa cum laude, Columbia U., 1964. Bar: N.Y. 1965, N.J. 1968, U.S. Supreme Ct. 1976. Mem. legal staff Warren Commn., Washington, 1964; assoc. Kaye, Scholer, Fierman, Hays & Handler, N.Y.C., 1965-68; ptnr. Lowenstein, Sandler, Brochin, Kohl & Fisher, Newark, N.J., 1968-79, Pitney, Hardin, Kipp & Szuch, Florham Park, N.J., 1979—. Mem. N.J. Consumer Affairs Adv. Com., 1991—; vice chmn. N.J. Commn. on Holocaust Edn., 1992—. Recipient Julius Cohn Young Leadership award Jewish Fedn. Metrowest, 1976. Mem. ABA, N.J. State Bar Assn. (dist. X ethics com. 1986-89, bd. editors N.J. Law Jour. 1986—, N.J. Lawyer, vice chmn. 1991—). Democrat. Home: 18 Crestwood Dr West Orange NJ 07052-2004 Office: Pitney Hardin Kipp & Szuch PO Box 1945 200 Campus Dr Florham Park NJ 07962-1945

LAUMAN, RICHARD H., JR., nuclear energy executive; b. Rockville Center, N.Y., Aug. 12, 1956; s. Richard H. and Joane M. (Albright) L.; m. Laura H. Cady, Aug. 28, 1982; 1 child, Richard H., III. B in Mech. Engring., Villanova U., 1978; postgrad., Pace U. Field engr. Gen. Electric Co., Phila., 1979-81; mech. engr. Ebasco Svcs., Inc., N.Y.C., 1981-82; engr. nuclear ops. and maintenance N.Y. Power Authority, White Plains, 1982-86, sr. engr., 1986-88, dir. nuclear ops. and maintenance, 1988—. Mem. ASME, Am. Mgmt. Assn., Planning Forum. Home: 9 Serendipity Ln Wilton CT 06897 Office: NY Power Authority 123 Main St White Plains NY 10601

LAUMONT, PHILIPPE EMILE, communications executive; b. Liege, Belgium, June 17, 1944; came to U.S., 1957; s. Gustave J. and Germaine (Cattet-Thellier de Poncheville) L.; m. Anne Colton Adams, July 19, 1978; children: Anne Sophie, Julia Adams, Laura Philippa. BA, U. Louvain, Belgium, 1964, MA, 1965; MBA, Columbia U., 1978. Film producer CBS Inc., N.Y.C., 1969-78; pres. Laumont Labs Inc., N.Y.C., 1979—. Mem. Coffee House Club, Ausable Club, Tuxedo Club. Office: Laumont Labs 333 W 52nd St New York NY 10019

LAURANS, PATRICIA WEBSTER, counselor; b. Fall River, Mass., Aug. 12, 1939; d. Raymond Theodore and Anne Vondele (Rudnick) L. BS, Boston U., 1961; MEd, U. Bridgeport, 1969. Instr. phys. edn., coach The Walnut Hill Sch., Natick, Mass., 1961-68; coach Kent (Conn.) Sch. for Girls, 1968-69; guidance counselor Brookfield (Conn.) High Sch., 1970—. Del. Am. Kennel Club, N.Y.C., 1980—; state dir. Morris Animal Found., Denver, 1985—.

LAURENCE, DAVID ERNST, language association administrator; b. Boston, Apr. 16, 1947; s. Maurice Kamm and Elizabeth Erica (Zimmermann) L.; m. Laura Griffith Mathews, May 31, 1986. AB, Amherst Coll., 1969; PhD, Yale U., 1976. Researcher Yale Media Design Studio, New Haven, Conn., 1976-78; asst. prof. English SUNY, Stony Brook, 1978-86; asst. dir. English program MLA, N.Y.C., 1986-88, dir. English program, 1988—. Editor: Association of Department of English Bull., N.Y.C., 1988—. Office: MLA 10 Astor Pl New York NY 10003-6981

LAURENDI, NAT, criminal investigator; b. Sant'Eufemia d'Aspromonte, Reggio Calabria, Italy, Aug. 7, 1923; s. Domenick and Grace (Crea) L.; grad. RCA Insts., 1951; A.A.S., Coll. City N.Y., 1969; m. Laura Autelitano, Mar. 28, 1946; children: Domenick, Susan (dec.), Adrienne, Loretta, Diana, Robert. With N.Y. Police Dept., 1951-75, N.Y. Dist. Atty's Office, 1952-75, criminal investigator, 1951-75, polygraph expert, 1962-75; pres. Certified Lie Detection, N.Y.C., 1975—, Nat. Laurendi, 1975—; mem. Frank S. Hogan Assocs., Hogan-Morgenthat Assocs.; author, lectr. on polygraph. Served with CIC, AUS, 1943-46. Decorated Bronze Star medal; recipient Excellent Police Duty award N.Y. Police Dept., 1954, 62, also Meritorious Police Duty awards. Fellow Acad. Certified Polygraphists; mem. ABA (criminal justice assoc.), AAAS, N.Y.C. CIC Assn. (pres. 1956), N.Y. State Polygraphists (chmn. membership com., 1964—), Am. Polygraph Assn., N.Y. State Assn. Criminal Def. Lawyers, N.Y. Acad. Scis., N.Y. State Defenders Assn., Am. Assn. Police Polygraphists, Detectives Endowment Assn., N.Y. Police Dept. Patrolmens Benevolent Assn., N.Y. Police Dept. Ret. Detectives, Ret. Patrolmen N.Y. Police Dept., Am. Soc. for Indsl. Security, Nat. Law Enforcement Assos., N.Y. Vet. Police Assn., N.Y.C. Ret. Employees Assn., Soc. Profl. Investigators. Roman Catholic. Home: 108 Village Rd S Brooklyn NY 11223-5237 Office: Certified Lie Detection 299 Broadway New York NY 10007

LAURENT, PIERRE-HENRI, history educator; b. Fall River, Mass., May 15, 1933; married; 4 children. A.B., Colgate U., 1956; A.M., Boston U., 1960, Ph.D., 1964. Instr. polit. economy Boston U., 1961-64; asst. prof. history Sweet Briar Coll., 1964-66; vis. asst. prof. history U. Wis., Madison, 1966-67; asst. prof. history Tulane U., New Orleans, 1967-68, assoc. prof., 1968-70; assoc. prof. history Tufts U., Medford, Mass., 1970-75, prof., 1975—, chmn. dept., 1987-89, adj. prof. diplomatic history/Fletcher Sch. Law and Diplomacy, 1977, 84, chmn. Exptl. Coll., 1973-75, acting dir. internat. relations program, 1979, dir. internat. relations program, 1984-88; co-dir. Internat. Relations Inst. Tufts U., France, 1979-80; mem. history devel. bd. Ednl. Testing Svc. of Princeton, 1979-82; instr. JFK Inst. Polit., Harvard U., Cambridge, 1989; mem. nat. screening com. Fulbright-Hays program Inst. Internat. Edn., 1988-91; rsch. assoc. Ctr. for Internat. Affairs, Harvard U. Mem. editorial bd. Jour. Social History, 1966-74; sect. editor Am. Hist. Rev., 1967-77; contbr. chpts. to books, articles to profl. jours., mags., encys. Served with USAF, 1956-59. NATO fellow, 1967, NEH fellow, 1969, Paul-Henri Spaak Found. fellow, 1976-77; Sweet Briar Faculty rsch. grantee, 1965, Tufts Faculty rsch. grantee, 1972, Inst. European Studies-Exxon Ednl. Fund grantee, 1983; Fulbright Rsch. scholar, 1992-93. Fellow Inst. des Rels. Internationales, Acad. Assoc. Atlantic Coun.; mem. AAUP (exec. com. Mass. State Conf. 1974-76, pres. Tufts U. chpt. 1982-84), European Community Studies Assn. (exec. com. 1988, chmn. 1991-92), Belgian-Am. Edn. Found. (bd. govs. 1986-90). Office: Tufts Univ Dept History Medford MA 02155

LAURICELLA, LEONARD JOHN, lawyer; b. N.Y.C., June 28, 1948; s. Bart T. and Annette (Crescimanno) L.; m. Victoria Facchini, July 28, 1985; children: Annette Rose, Rose Victoria. BSBA, Georgetown u., 1970, JD, 1973; LLM in Taxation, NYU, 1986. Bar: D.C. 1973, U.S. Tax Ct. 1975, U.S. Ct. Claims 1975; CPA, Md. Acct. Hurdman and Cranstoun, Washington, 1973-75, tax mgr., 1975-76; tax mgr. Hurdman and Cranstoun, London, 1977-80, Main Hurdman, N.Y.C., 1981-83; v.p. Shearson Lehman Bros., N.Y.C., 1984-89, sr. v.p., 1990—; adj. prof. taxation Stern Sch. Bus. grad. divsn. NYU, N.Y.C., 1982—. Vice chmn., treas. Weehawken (N.J.) Housing Authority, 1985—; mem. grad. adv. bd. Georgetown U., 1987-90. Mem. ABA (tax. sect.), Am. Inst. CPAs (tax sect.), N.Y. Bar Assn., Internat. Tax Assn. (pres. 1987-88), Internat. Tax Inst., Internat. Fiscal Assn., NYU Tax Soc. (pres. 1991—), Wall St. Tax Assn. Republican. Roman Catholic. Office: Shearson Lehman Bros Inc 388 Greenwich St 31st Fl New York NY 10013

LAURILA, NORMAN THOMAS EDWARD, executive, owner; b. Nipigon, Ontario, Canada, Jan. 16, 1955; s. Toivo Elias and Bernice Ethel (MacDonald) L. BS, SUNY, 1984. Pres. Androgyny Books Inc., L.A., West Hollywood,, San Francisco and N.Y., 1979—; owner Norman Laurila Literary Mgmt., N.Y.C., 1987—; founder's circle mem. Lesbian & Gay Community Svc. Ctr., N.Y.C., 1989—. Recipient Bus. of the Yr. award Christopher St. West Com., 1989. Mem. Am. Booksellers Assn. (com. mem. 1989—, panel mem. 1987—), Human Rights Campaign Fund, Nat. Gay Lesbian Task Force, Gay Men's Health Crisis. Office: A Different Light 548 Hudson St New York NY 10014-3233

LAURINO, JOHN ALAN, marketing professional; b. Bklyn., Dec. 5, 1949; s. Andrew James Sr. and Helen Lenore (Schneider) L.; m. Deborah Denneen, Aug. 29, 1969; children: Elizabeth Higby, Jennifer Thurston. BA, Franklin and Marshall Coll., 1971; MBA, U. Conn., 1975. Mktg. mgr. Equitable Life, N.Y.C., 1970-75; v.p. Citibank N.A., N.Y.C., 1975-82; sr. v.p. Hosp. Trust Nat. Bank, Providence, 1982-84, RIHT Fin. Corp., Providence, 1982-84; pres., chief exec. officer Bay Loan & Investment Bank, Providence, 1985-87; sr. v.p. Colonial Pen Group, Phila., 1984-87; sr. v.p., chief mktg. officer Bowery Savs. Bank, N.Y.C., 1987-88; prin. Mktg. Corp. of Am., Westport, Conn., 1988; mng. dir. Westport Cons. Group, 1988—. Chmn. Hist. Dist. Commn., Westport, 1989; pres. Greens Farms Assn., Wesport, 1981-82. Mem. Hope Club. Republican. Episcopalian. Office: Westport Cons Group PO Box 223 8 River Ln Westport CT 06881

LAURO, MARY VIOLA, chemical consultant; b. N.Y.C., May 4, 1926; d. Joseph Mario and Rita (Carcaterra) L. BA, CUNY, 1947. Chemist Adhesive Products Corp., N.Y.C., 1947-60, chief chemist, 1960-91; ind. chem. cons. N.Y.C., 1991—; cons. Boise Adhesive, N.Y.C., 1992—, Adhesive Techs., N.Y.C., 1992—, Adhesive Products, N.Y.C., 1992—. Apptd. mem. Community Bd., Bronx, 1986—; pres. Wakefield (N.Y.) Taxpayers & Civic League, Inc., 1984—; chairperson community action com. St. Frances of Rome, N.Y., 1990—. Republican. Roman Catholic. Home: 4330 Matilda Ave Bronx NY 10466-1315

LAUTENBERG, FRANK R., senator; b. Paterson, N.J., Jan. 23, 1924; s. Samuel and Mollie L.; children: Ellen, Nan, Lisa, Joshua. BS, Columbia U., 1949; DHL, Hebrew Union Coll., Cin. and N.Y.C., 1977; PhD (hon.), Hebrew U., Jerusalem, 1978; postgrad., Rutgers U., UPsala Coll. Founder Automatic Data Processing, Inc., Clifton, N.J., 1955; exec. v.p. adminstrn. Automatic Data Processing, Inc., 1961-69, pres., 1969-75, chief exec. officer, 1975-82, former chmn. bd.; mem. U.S. Senate from N.J., 1982—. Commr. Port Authority N.Y. and N.J., 1978-82, N.J. econ. devel. coun.; trustee Sch. Bus., Columbia U.; nat. pres. Am. Friends Hebrew U., 1973-74; former gen. chmn., pres. Nat. United Jewish Appeal, 1975-77; mem. bd. overseers N.J. Symphony Orch.; mem. Pres.'s Commn. on the Holocaust; founder Lautenberg Center for Gen. and Tumor Immunology, Med. Sch., Hebrew U., Jerusalem, 1971; mem. fin. council Nat. Democratic Com. Served with Armed Forces, 1943-46, ETO; bd. mem. Montclair Art Mus., mem. adv. bd. Interfaith Hunger Appeal; trustees Tri-County Scholarship fund. Recipient Torch of Learning award Am. Friends Hebrew U., 1971, Scopus award, 1975. Mem. Nat. Assn. Data Processing Service Orgns. (pres. 1968-69, dir. from 1974), Patrons Soc. Met. Opera. Office: US Senate Hart Senate Office Bldg Washington DC 20510

LAUTIN, EVERETT MARC, radiologist, educator; b. N.Y.C., Oct. 5, 1946; s. Arthur and Fredda B. Lautkin; m. Dona Andrea Cass, Jan. 21, 1978; children: Douglas Edward, Dana Valerie. AB, Columbia Coll., 1967; MD, SUNY, Bklyn., 1971. Diplomate Am. Bd. Radiology. Med. intern SUNY Downstate Med. Ctr., Bklyn., 1971-72; radiology resident Mount Sinai Hosp., N.Y.C., 1972-75; instr. radiology Albert Einstein Coll. Medicine, Bronx, 1975-78, asst. prof. radiology, 1978-83, assoc. prof. radiology, 1983—, dir. uroradiology, 1991—; staff radiologist Montefiore Med. Ctr., Bronx, 1975—, dir. uroradiology, 1977—; cons. Office of Chief Med. Examiner, N.Y.C., 1986-89. Reviewer Radiographics, Easton, Pa., 1989—; author: Genitourinary Radiology, 1989; contbr. chpt. to book and articles to profl. jours. Mem. work group on low osmolar contrast Greater N.Y. Hosp. Assn., 1988-89. With USAR, 1972-78. Mem. AMA, Am. Roentgen Ray Soc., Am. Coll. Radiology, Radiol. Soc. N.Am., Soc. Uroradiology, N.Y. Roentgen Soc., N.Y. County Med. Soc. (radiology com. 1982—, nominating com. 1983, alt. del. 1983-88). Home: 245 E 93rd St Apt 27G New York NY 10128-3699 Office: Montefiore Med Coll Dept Radiology 111 E 210th St Bronx NY 10467

LAUVER, DAVID ALAN, photographer, educator; b. Harrisburg, Pa., Aug. 14, 1947; s. Joseph Roy and Pauline Mildred (Leister) L. BA, Am. U., 1970; student in bus. adminstrn., Strayer Coll., Washington, 1967-68; student in photography, U. Ariz., 1970-72; student in fine arts, Susquehanna U., 1973-74. Freelance photographer Selinsgrove, Pa., 1975—; owner, operator Images Selinsgrove, 1976—; lectr. fine arts, photography and photojournalism Susquehanna U., Selinsgrove, 1985—. One-man shows include Temple U., Phila., 1980, U. Del., Newark, 1985, U. Nebr., Lincoln, 1985, Susquehanna U., 1986, Anita Shapolsky Gallery, N.Y.C., 1991, Pa. State U., 1991, Arthur Griffin Ctr. of Photography, 1992, Pa. State Mus., 1992, ; group show include Doshi Gallery, Harrisburg, 1985, 86, Art Assn. Harrisburg, 1988, 89, Pa. State Mus., 1980-89, Ledel Gallery, N.Y.C., 1990, Susquehanna U., 1990, Shapolsky Gallery, N.Y.C.; represented in permanent collections at Phila. Mus. Art, Bucknell U., Amish Hist. Soc. of Ont., Mennonite Hist. Soc., Richfield, Pa., Mellon Bank, Pitts., NBC-TV, N.Y.C., Gulf Oil Corp., Pitts., collection of former pres. Ronald Reagan, others; prin. works document Amish and Old Order Mennonite communities; publications include CelebraAtion '76, Plain Buggies, 1986, Amish Crib Quilts, 1986, The World of Amish Quilts, 1986, Who Are the Amish?, 1986, A Treasury of Amish Quilts, 1990. Recipient spl. achievement award Pa. Senate, 1989, Best of Show award 9th Ann. N.E. U.S.A. Exhbn., 1992; grantee Pa. Humanities Coun., 1987. Mem. Art Assn. Harrisburg, Susquehanna Art Soc., Am. Photog. Hist. Soc., Friends of Photography (Carmel, Calif.), Print Club Phila. Democrat. Lutheran. Home: 705 University Ave Selinsgrove PA 17870-9412 Office: Images Photog Svcs 29 S Market St Selinsgrove PA 17870-1836

LAUX, RUSSELL FREDERICK See DULAUX, RUSSELL FREDERICK

LAUZON, RODRIGUE VINCENT, colloid scientist; b. Ottawa, Ont., Can., Oct. 24, 1937; s. Rodrigue Alphonse and Alice (Lacombe) L.; children: Alicia, Rod Jr. BA, U. Toronto, 1960; MS, U. Conn., 1962; PhD, Clarkson U., 1971. Rsch. chemist Dow Chem., Midland, Mich., 1970-74; dir. latex R&D Dart Industries, Paramus, N.J., 1974-77; mgr. rsch. NL Baroid, Houston, 1977-83; rsch. scientist Hercules Inc., Wilmington, Del., 1983—. Contbr. articles to profl. jours. Mem. Am. Chem. Soc., Materials Rsch. Soc., Tappi. Home: 63 Quail Hollow Dr Hockessin DE 19707-1403 Office: Hercules Rsch Ctr Wilmington DE 19894

LAVALLE, SHARLENE HARTLE, retail executive; b. New Haven, Aug. 16, 1949; d. Paul L. and Helen (Mikenis) Hartle; m. Joseph M. LaValle, Feb. 14, 1970. Grad. high sch., North Branford, Conn. Sec. Prudential Ins. Co., New Haven, 1967-70; owner Little Bit Tack Shop, Guilford, Conn., 1971-72, Little "B" Barn, North Franklin, Conn., 1972-89; pres. Bar B Corp. dba Little "B" Barn, North Franklin, 1990—; designing cons. western wear and leather wear, 1991. Designer Equestrian gift items. Mem. Am. Qtr. Horse Assn., New Eng. Pinto Horse Assn., Western/English Retailers Assn., C. of C., Better Bus. Bur. Office: Little B Barn 43 Manning Rd North Franklin CT 06254

LA VANISH, GEORGE RONALD, artist, illustrator, publisher; b. Ft. Belvoir, Va., Mar. 24, 1953; s. Richard Lysle and Nancy Jane (Anderson) LaV.; m. Jannette Arlene Ober, Apr. 6, 1974; children: Timothy, Kristin, Beth. AS, Art Inst. of Phila., 1974. Graphic artist Pa. State U., University Park, 1974-85; freelance artist University Park, 1976—; sr. illustrator HRB Systems, State College, Pa., 1985—; mem. hon. art bd. Nat. Hunting and Fishing Mus. Am., Meyersdale, Pa., 1991—. Author: Shooters Bible, 1979, Joe Humphrey's Trout Tactics, 1984, 50 Years of Game News, 1986, Rabbit Hunting, 1987, On the Trout Stream, 1989, Birds of Pennsylvania, Fishes of Pennsylvania, 1990, Reptiles of Pennsylvania, 1991. Mem. Pa. Game Commn., Pa. Fish Commn. Named Artist of Yr., Whitetails Unltd., Sturgeon Bay, Wis., 1992. Mem. Pa. Outdoors Writers Assn., Nat. Wildlife Fedn., Trout Unltd., Am. Wild Turkey Soc., Rocky Mountain Elk Found., Audubon Soc. Lutheran. Home: RD# 1 Box 73 Warriors Mark PA 16877 Office: HRB Systems PO Box 60 State College PA 16804-0060

LAVELL, THOMAS EUGENE, surgeon; b. N.Y.C., June 2, 1928; s. Thomas Eugene and Kathleen (MacDonald) L.; m. Anne M. Prosser, July 10, 1954 (div. 1985); children: Thomas III, Christopher, Patrick, Melissa; m. Jeanne P. Taber, Apr. 23, 1988. BA, Cornell U., 1949; MD, NYU, 1953; MS, Russell Sage Coll., 1980. Diplomate Am. Bd. Surgery. Intern St. Vincent's Hosp., N.Y.C., 1953-54; resident in gen. practice U. Colo. Med. Ctr., Denver, 1957-58; resident in surgery U. Vt. Med. Ctr., Burlington, 1958-60, 63-65; practice gen. medicine Hancock, N.Y., 1960-63; practice medicine specializing in surgery, mem. attending staff Delaware Valley Hosp., Walton, N.Y., 1965—, chief of surgery, 1974—; adj. instr. health adminstrn. Russell Sage Coll., Albany, 1981—; clin. asst. prof. surgery SUNY Upstate Med. Ctr., Binghamton, 1986—. Pres. Community Svcs. Bd., Walton, 1966-73; bd. dirs., past pres. William B. Ogden Libr., Walton, 1973-91; pres. Health Systems Agy., N.E. N.Y., Albany, 1981-83; mem. N.Y. State Hosp. Rev. and Planning Coun., 1992—. Served as lt. USNR, 1954-57. Richard P. Ettinger fellow N.Y. State div. Am. Cancer Soc., 1976. Fellow ACS; mem. AMA, Med. Soc. State N.Y. (pres. 6th dist. 1984-86), Delaware County Med. Soc. (pres. 1972-75), Am. Health Planning Assn., Am. Pub. Health Assn., Am. Evaluation Assn. Republican. Office: Delaware Valley Hosp 1 Titus Pl Walton NY 13856-1457

LAVELLE, PATRICK BRIAN, JR., accountant; b. Holyoke, Mass., Nov. 8, 1961; s. Patrick B. and Arlene (Ramsey) L. AS in Acctg., Holyoke Community Coll., 1981; BSBA in Fin., Western New Eng. Coll., 1983; MPA, Am. Internat. Coll., 1990. Asst. to treas. HFP Sprinkler, Holyoke, 1983-85; fiscal officer Holyoke Chicopee Headstart, 1985-87; acctg. mgr. Brightside, West Springfield, Mass., 1988—; dir. Credit Union Providence Systems, Springfield, 1989—. Mem. Citizens Adv. Coun., City of Holyoke, 1984—; Whiting St. Fund com., 1987—; treas. Western Mass. Track & Field Ofcls. Assn., West Springfield, 1988—; auditor Grace United Ch. of Christ. Mem. Inst. Mgmt. Accts. Home: PO Box 6382 Holyoke MA 01041-6382

LAVENAS, SUZANNE, editor; b. Buenos Aires, Dec. 17, 1942; came to U.S., 1955; d. Carlos Fernando and Mary (Sharp) Lavenas; m. Wesley First, Jan. 9, 1982. Student, Antioch Coll., 1960-64, 65-66. Computer programmer N.Y. Telephone, N.Y.C., 1966-68; prodn. editor, then copy editor Travel Weekly, N.Y.C., 1968-76, chief copy editor, 1976-79; mng. editor Indsl. Chem. News, N.Y.C., 1981-82; editor, writer cons. N.Y.C., 1986—. Author numerous articles. Mem. Overseas Press Club, Soc. Silurians. Republican. Episcopalian. Home: Montauk Manor Apt 413 236 Edgemere St Montauk NY 11954

LAVENSON, SUSAN BARKER, consultant; b. L.A., July 26, 1936; d. Percy Morton and Rosalie Laura (Donner) Barker; m. James H. Lavenson, Apr. 22, 1973; 1 child, Ellen Ruth Stanclift. BA, Stanford U., 1958, MA, 1959. Cert. secondary tchr., Calif. Tchr. Benjamin Franklin Jr. High Sch., San Francisco, 1960; french dept. head Lowell High Sch., San Francisco, 1961-61; v.p. Monogram Co., San Francisco, 1961-62; creative dir. Monogram Co., N.Y.C., 1973-76; pres. SYR Corp., Santa Barbara, Calif., 1976-89; ptnr. Lavenson Ptnrs., Camden, Maine, 1989—; mem. commn. on co-edn. Wheaton Coll., Norton, Mass., 1985-87; mem. Relais et Chateaux, Paris, 1978-89. Author: Greening of San Ysidro, 1977 (Conf. award 1977). Trustee Camden Pub. Libr., 1989—, v.p., 1991-92. Mem. Camden Yacht Club, Stanford Alumni Assn., Com. of 200 (treas. 1985-86), Phi Delta Kappa. Home and Office: 158 Chestnut St Camden ME 04843-2224

LAVER, STEVEN GEORGE, lawyer; b. Phila., May 2, 1941; s. Louis A. and Hester (Horenstein) L.; m. Anita Targan, Dec. 16, 1962; children: Miriam, David. BS, Temple U., 1962; JD, Cleve. State U., 1968. Bar: Ohio 1968, Pa. 1969. Instr. Cuyahoga Community Coll., Cleve., 1966-68; asst. prof. Community Coll. of Phila., 1968-70; assoc. Nix & Randolph, Phila., 1971; sr. trial atty. Defender Assn. of Phila., 1969-70, 72-91; instr. Phila. Inst., 1975—; dir. of tng. Dist. Atty. of Phila., 1991—. Nat. pres. Nat. Tay-Sachs and Allied Diseases, Boston, 1982-87; commr. B'nai B'rith Internat. Youth Comm., Washington, 1984—; exec. com. ACLU, Pa., 1975-80; trustee Upper Moreland Free Libr., Willow Grove, Pa., 1976-81. Mem. Phila. Bar Assn. (chmn. criminal justice sect. 1992). Office: Dist Atty of Pa 1421 Arch St Philadelphia PA 19102

LAVERY, BARRY, photography educator, photo journalist; b. Gary, Ind., Nov. 2, 1944; s. Bernard L. and Florence G. (Foley) L.; m. Beth Ann Womer, Nov. 24, 1965 (div. June 1989); children: Sarah, Kerri, Maggie; m. Katyna Manis, June 17, 1990. BA, Westminster Coll., New Wilmington, Pa., 1966; BD, Temple U., 1969. Wholesale rep. Fortress Press, Phila., 1969-70; photographer WPHL-TV, Phila., 1970; freelance photographer Phila., Pitts., 1970; mgr. Pitts. Power & Light Co., 1970-71; tchr. Art Inst. Pitts., 1971—, dept. head, 1980-84; tchr. Photo Forum Gallery, Pitts., 1987—; photojournalist, Impact Images, N.Y.C., 1989—, Photo Researchers, N.Y.C., 1989—; freelance documentarian, Haiti, 1986—. Photo editor and writer for mags., 1985; photographer, N.Y. Times, 1991, Macmillan Pub. Co., 1991. Recipient Community Svc. award Pitts. Jaycees, 1980, 81, Vectors, Pitts., 1982-83. Mem. Nat. Press Photographers Assn., Blatant Image. Zen Buddhist. Office: Art Inst of Pitts 526 Penn Ave Pittsburgh PA 15222-3269

LAVERY, ROBERT CREIGHTON, commercial artist; b. Glen Ridge, N.J., Apr. 21, 1954; s. Hugh Thomson and Marie Antonette (Fasanella) L. Staff artist Creative Prodns., Orange, N.J., Landmark Assocs., East Orange, N.J.; asst. art dir. Ron Ton Agy. (Maxon Pontiac), Union, N.J.; art dir. Silk Screen Photo Svc., East Orange; v.p. Pro Arts Screen Graphics Inc., Montclair, N.J.; creative/art dir. Peter Pan Industries, Newark; art dir. E.J. Barrie Advt. Inc., Bloomfield, N.J.; pres. Lavery Graphics and Advt., Glen Ridge, N.J., 1975—. Composer, arranger and performer all instruments (guitars, keyboards, bass and drum programming) for title song (MGM film) "Crooked Hearts", 1991, (songs) "Sparks", 1986 (regional winner Electra Records Undiscovered Artist of Yr. award 1986); lead guitarist The Burns Sisters Band, "Listen to the Beat of a Heart" (charted #11 nationwide adult contemporary radio), "I Wonder Who's Out Tonight" (top ten hit radio stas.), 1980-86, others; opening act various groups. Office: Lavery Graphics & Advt 17 Sommer Ave Glen Ridge NJ 07028-2014

LAVIENA, LUIS R., psychologist, educator; b. Humacao, P.R., Mar. 29, 1955; s. Angel and Julia (deLeon) L. BA in Psychology, U. Puerto Rico, Rio Piedras, 1977; MS in Clin. Psychology, Caribbean Ctr. for Advanced Studies, San Juan, P.R., 1981; PhD in Devel. Psychology, Yeshiva U., 1991. Lic. psychologist, sch. psychologist, N.Y.; cert. hypnotherapist, Puerto Rico, neuropsychologist, N.Y. Bilingual psychologist Bd. Edn. City of N.Y., N.Y.C., 1981-85, 90—, supr. project devel. of norms of Spanish WISC-R, 1986-88; clin. psychotherapist Manhattan Children Psychiat. Ctr., Wards Island, N.Y., 1987-88; neuropsychol. trainee Columbia Presbyn. Hosp., N.Y.C., 1987-88; dir. psychol. svcs. for people with AIDS Luth. Med. Ctr., Bklyn., 1988-90; coord. children's bilingual svcs., specialist psychologist Hearing Handicapped and Visually Impaired Unit, N.Y.C., 1991—; adj. prof. Seton Hall U., South Orange, N.J., 1991—; cons. Caribbean Biofeedback Assn. P.R., 1979—, Latino Issues in Inst. Human Identity, P.R., 1985—, AIDS films, N.Y.C., 1989—, Hispanic Issues in Gay Men's Health Crisis, N.Y.C., 1989—; presented articles to profl. confs., 1989—. Fellow Nat. Coun. LaRaza, Office of Bilingual Edn. and Minority Lang. Affairs, Neuropsychology Dept. Columbia Presbyn. Hosp. Mem. AAAS, NASP, Am. Orthopsychiat. Assn., Assn. Devel. Behavioral Scis., Assn. Hispanic Mental Health Profls., N.Y. State Assn. Sch. Psychologists, Asociación de Psicologos de Puerto RIco. Home: 401 E 64th St # 4E New York NY

10021-7589 Office: Seton Hall U - Hearing Hand icapped and Vision Impaired 400 1st Ave New York NY 10010-4004

LAVIETES, MARC HARRY, medical educator; b. New Haven, July 7, 1941; s. Paul H. and Ruth (Swedler) L.; m. Aug. 13, 1966 (div.); children: Bryan, Jonathan. BA, Yale U., 1963; MD, Case Res. U., 1969. Med. intern & resident Harlem Hosp. Ctr., N.Y.C., 1969-71; pulmonary clinical fellowship Bellevue Hosp., N.Y.C., 1971-73; pulmonary rsch. fellowship Columbia-Presbyn. Med. Ctr., N.Y.C., 1973-75; assoc. prof. medicine U. Medicine and Dentistry N.J., Newark, 1975—. Contbr. articles to Am. Rev. Respiratory Diseases, Chest. Fellow Am. Coll. Chest Physicians; mem. Am. Thoracic Soc., N.J. Thoracic Soc (pres. 1984-86), Physicians for Social Responsibility (pres. No. N.J. chpt. 1986—). Jewish. Office: Univ Hosp 100 Bergen St Rm 1354 Newark NJ 07103-2406

LAVIN, PHILIP TODD, biostatistician, consultant; b. Rochester, N.Y., Nov. 21, 1946; s. Albert A. and Mary (Rapkin) L.; m. Mary Ellen Saunders, Aug. 23, 1970; children: Andrew, Abby. AB, U. Rochester, 1968; PhD, Brown U., 1972. Rsch. asst. prof. Brown U., Providence, 1972-74, SUNY at Buffalo, Amerst, 1974-77; asst. prof. sch. pub. health Harvard U., Boston, 1977-83, assoc. prof. surgery Med. Sch., 1983—; pres. Boston Biostatistics, Inc., Framingham, Mass., 1983—, Boston Biostat Rsch. Found., Newton Upper Falls, Mass., 1988—; mem. editorial bd. Drug Info. Assn., Phila., 1986-88, Anti-microbial Agents and Chemotherapy, Boston, 1987—; cons. FDA, 1983-86. Contbr. articles to on medicine and stats. to scholarly jours. Bd. dirs. William Graves Fund, Boston, 1989—. NSF trainee, 1968-72; grantee Nat. Cancer Inst., 1976-80, 87—, Nat. Heart, Lung, Blood Inst., 1985-89. Mem. Biometric Soc., Am. Statis. Assn., Soc. Clin. Trials, Regulatory Affairs Profl. Soc., Phi Beta Kappa. Home: 3 Cahill Park Dr Framingham MA 01701-6105 Office: Boston Biostat Rsch Fedn 1007 Chestnut St Newton MA 02164-1101

LAVINE, ADAM, entrepreneur; b. N.Y.C., Jan. 4, 1967; s. David and Gladys Holmes (Bozyan) L. MA in English, U. Mass., 1990, MS in Ednl. Computer Animation, 1990. Sr. instr. New Eng. Computer Camp, Avon, Conn., 1985-87; vis. juggler Tama Tech Amusement Parks, Tokyo, 1987-88; arts editor Mass. Daily Collegian, Amherst, 1987-88; pres., chief exec. officer Specular Internat., Amherst, 1989-90; rsch. scientist Ctr. for Knowledge Communication, U. Mass., Amherst, 1988-89, dir. animation, 1989—. Dir. animated production Robomation. Democrat. Jewish.

LAVINE, CHARLES IRA, company executive; b. Trenton, N.J., Nov. 23, 1947; s. Ivan and Geraldine (Shapolsky) L.; m. Jane Elizabeth Heald, Sept. 18, 1976. BS, MIT, 1970. Pres. Chasz Realty Corp, N.Y.C., 1972-80, Great Am. Resources, Cambridge, Mass., 1980-85, Boston Tech. Svcs., 1985—; cons. Computer Literacy Inc., Boston, 1985-88, U. Computer Stores, Boston, 1985-88. Recipient Young Entrepeneur award Chivas Regal, 1987. Mem. Am. Inst. of Wine and Food, MIT Alumni Assn. Jewish. Office: Boston Tech Svcs 3 Center Plz Boston MA 02108-2003

LAVINE, EILEEN MARTINSON, communications executive; b. N.Y.C., Dec. 28, 1924; d. Herman and Sylvia (Eichler) Martinson; m. Richard Bennett, Jan. 13, 1957; children: Michael, Amy. BA, U. Wis., 1945; MS, Columbia U., 1946. Reporter Standard-Times, New Bedford, Mass., 1946-47; asst. to moderator youth forums N.Y. Times, N.Y.C., 1948-50; writer Joint Def. Appeal, N.Y.C., 1952-55; editor Better Times Community Coun. Greater N.Y., N.Y.C., 1955-59; writer, editor PR Assocs., Washington, 1962-68; writer, editor Info. Svcs., Bethesda, Md., 1968—, pres., 1979—; info. counsel Intesoc. Com. on Pathology Info., Bethesda, 1984—. Author: Manual of Administration for Occupational Therapists, 1978. Mem. Nat. Assn. Women Bus. Owners, Washington Ind. Writers. Democrat. Jewish. Home: 4978 Sentinel Dr Bethesda MD 20816-3516 Office: Info Svcs Inc 4733 Bethesda Ave Bethesda MD 20814-5228

LAVINE, JERROLD LEWIS, automotive executive, consultant; b. Providence, Dec. 10; s. Edward H. and Doris (Millen) L.; m. Barbara Ellen Showstack, Aug. 26, 1961; children: Jeffrey, Jonathan, Marc, Elisa. Student, Boston U. Pres., CEO Stencil Ease, Lincoln, R.I.; mng. gen. ptnr. Powder Hill Assocs., Lincoln, R.I. & Ga.; chmn. Allied Accessories, Detroit; chmn., CEO Globe Distbn., Lincoln; chmn., chief exec. officer Southporte Group, Ltd., Providence, 1992—; chmn., chief exec. officer R.I. Solid Waste Mgmt. Corp., Providence, 1992—; cons., stratetic planner pub. and pvt. cos.; prin. speaker econ. trends and industry forecasting Automotive Parts & Accessories Assn. Mem. transition bd., chmn. inauguration com. State of R.I.; amb. Israel Bonds, R.I.; R.I. Philharm., RI Commodores; fin. chmn. Gov. Sundlun; trustee Home for Aged; bd. dirs. Temple Emanu-El, FOP, 100 Club. Named Automotive Man of the Yr., Automotive News, 1987. Mem. Internat. Mass Retail Assn., Ledgemont Country Club, Jonathan's Landing, C. of C., Atrium Club, Turks Head Club, Masons (32 degree), Shriners. Office: Southporte Group Ltd 4 Richmond Sq Providence RI 02906-5741

LAVINE, JUDITH BAZARSKY, psychotherapist; b. Newport, R.I., Jan. 7, 1945; d. Samuel Z. and Beatrice (Berman) Bazarsky; divorced; children: Jill, James, Meredith, Elizabeth, Samantha, Gregory. BA, U. R.I., 1966; MA, R.I. Coll., 1986; postgrad., Boston U., 1989—. Cert. tchr. for Systematic Tng. for Effective Parenting. Tchr. Hugh B. Bain Jr. High Sch., Cranston, R.I., 1966-67; tutor/writer-author Seekonk, Mass., 1967-87; consumer coord. Mental Health Assn., Providence, 1985-86; psychotherapist Counseling and Psychiat. Rehab. Svc., Rumford, R.I., 1986—; consumer affairs assoc. R.I. Div. Mental Health, Cranston, 1986—. Recipient Boston U. scholarship, 1989. Mem. ASCD, Assn. for Counselor Edn. and Supervision; R.I. Assn. Tng. and Devel.; Am. Rehab. Counseling Assn., R.I. Protection and Advocacy Systems (adv. bd.), Nat. Assn. for Rights Protection and Advocacy, Nat. Assn. for Rehab. Counseling. Home: PO Box 16311 Rumford RI 02916-0694 Office: 9 Newman Ave Rumford RI 02916-1944

LAVINE, MARLAINE, information services executive,training consultant; b. N.Y.C., June 4, 1946; d. Abraham and Marion Irene (Moscowitz) Levine; m. Alfred Edward Lavine, June 13, 1976. BS in Sociology cum laude, NYU, 1967; MA in Indsl./Organizational Psychology, Columbia U., 1975, postgrad., 1975-80. Testing cons. N.Y. State Dept. Labor, N.Y.C., 1970-76, employment mgr., 1974-76; mgr. human resource selection systems Port Authority of N.Y. & N.J., N.Y.C., 1976-83, mgr. mgmt. assessment and devel., 1979-83, tng. and orgn. devel. cons., 1983-86, dir. info. svcs. staff devel. and planning, 1985-90, dir. info. svcs. orgn. and staff devel., 1988-91; dir. info. svc. effectiveness and quality, 1991—; adj. prof. bus. studies Baruch Coll., N.Y.C., 1982-84, pers. mgmt. Queens (N.Y.) Coll., 1984-85. Contbg. author: Job Analysis Content Validity Manual, 1978; editor: Human Resources Forum, 1978-82. Mem. Am. Psychol. Assn., Am. Soc. Tng. and Devel., Soc. for Indo. Mgmt., Orgn. Devel. Network. Home: 111-20 73rd Ave Forest Hills NY 11375-5532 Office: Port Authority NY & NJ 1 World Trade Ctr # 71N New York NY 10048-0202

LA VITA, ROBERTO, art director; b. Lecce, Apulia, Italy, July 23, 1950; came to U.S., 1979; s. Ugo and Jolanda (Romano) LaV.; m. Barbara Jameson, Dec. 19, 1988; children: Ananda, Giacomo. Student, U. Florence, Italy, 1978, Cappiello Acad., Florence, Italy, Ctr. for Media Arts, N.Y.C. Prin. La Vita Products, Florence, Italy, 1975-79; ptnr. Secrest and La Vita, Inc., Bethesda, Md., 1975-79; prin. La Vita Fine Arts, Inc., Bethesda, Md., 1983-87, Unica Design, Bethesda, Md., 1984-87; dir. Washington Gallery of Fine Arts, 1986-88; freelance art dir. and graphic designer, 1987—; art dir., mktg.-advt. cons., Italy and U.S.A., 1988—. Mem. Am. Inst. Graphic Arts, Am. Assn. Advt. Agys., Art Dirs. Club N.Y., The One Club.

LAVOIE, DENNIS JAMES, secondary education educator; b. Syracuse, N.Y., Aug. 31, 1955; s. James Jay and Mary (Gadwood) L.; m. Allegra Ann Beahan, Oct. 11, 1980. BA in Spanish, St. John Fisher Coll., 1977; MA in Spanish Lang. and Lit., Middlebury Coll., 1982. Cert. tchr. Spanish, French, N-12, N.Y. Fgn. lang. educator Fairport (N.Y.) Cen. Sch., 1977—, mentor tchr., 1990-91. Recipient N.Y. Coun. for the Humanities scholarship, Colgate U., 1991, MCES scholarship N.Y. State Edn. Dept. of Spanish Govt., Universidad de Salamanca, 1989, NEH grant, U. Va., 1989. Mem. Fgn. Lang. Assn. of Tchrs. of the Rochester Area (pres. 1980-81, v.p. 1979-80), Am. Assn. Tchrs. of Spanish and Portuguese (pres. Rochester chpt. 1990-92, v.p. 1988-90, treas. 1984-86). Democrat. Roman Catholic. Office: Fairport High Sch 1358 Agrault Rd Fairport NY 14450

LAW, BERNARD FRANCIS CARDINAL, archbishop; b. Torreon, Mex., Nov. 4, 1931; s. Bernard A. and Helen A. (Stubblefield) L. B.A., Harvard U., 1953; postgrad., St. Joseph Sem., St. Benedict, La., 1953, Pontifical Coll. Josephinum, Worthington, Ohio, 1955. Ordained priest Roman Catholic Ch., 1961, consecrated bishop, 1973; editor Natchez-Jackson diocesan paper, Jackson, 1963-68; exec. dir. U.S. Bishops Com. for Ecumenical and Interreligious Affairs, 1968-71, chmn., from 1975; vicar gen. Diocese of Natchez-Jackson, 1971-73; bishop Diocese of Springfield-Cape Girardeau, Mo., 1973-84; archbishop Archdiocese of Boston Brighton, Mass., 1984—; created cardinal, 1985; mem. adminstrv. com. Nat. Conf. Cath. Bishops, from 1975; mem. communication com. U.S. Cath. Conf., 1974, mem. adminstrv. bd., from 1975; mem. Vatican Secretariat for Promoting Christian Unity, from 1976; consultor Vatican Commn. Religious Relations with the Jews, from 1976; chmn. bd. Pope John XXIII Med.-Moral Research and Edn. Ctr., St. Louis, 1980-82; ecclesiastical del. of Pope John Paul II for matters pertaining to former Episcopal priests, 1981. Trustee Pontifical Coll. Josephinum, 1974-85, Nat. Shrine of Immaculate Conception, from 1975; bd. regents Conception (Mo.) Sem. Coll., from 1975. Office: Cardinal's Residence 2121 Commonwealth Ave Brighton MA 02135-3193

LAW, BRIAN JOHN, conductor; b. London, Apr. 14, 1943; Immigrated to Can., 1965.; s. John William and Ethel (Taylor) L. Ed., Royal Sch. Ch. Music, Croydon, Eng. Organist, choirmaster St. Matthew's Ch., Ottawa, Can., 1965-80; mus. dir. Cantata Singers of Ottawa, 1965-87; condr., chorus master Festival Ottawa, 1970-83, 88—; founding condr. Ont. Youth Choir, 1971, condr., 1987; mus. dir. Ottawa Symphony Orch., 1974—, Ottawa Choral Soc., 1967—; asst. condr., chorus master L'Opera de Montreal, 1986-89, 90-91. conducting debut Nat. Arts Ctr. Orch., 1970, Victoria Symphony, 1976, Calgary Philharm., 1978; numerous other conducting appearances. Office: Ottawa Symphony Orch, PO Box 3644, Sta C, Oshawa, ON Canada K1Y 4J7*

LAW, TERENCE R., bank officer; b. N.Y.C., Nov. 10, 1960; s. Thomas and Kathleen (O'Hanlon) L. Student, Syracuse U., 1979; BA, U. San Francisco, 1982. With credit mgmt. tng. program Bank of N.Y., N.Y.C., 1984-85; mgr. fin. instns. group Credit Lyonnais, USA, N.Y.C., 1989—. Vol. Save the Theatres, N.Y.C., 1985-87, N.Y.C. Mission Soc., 1990—. Mem. Securities Industry Assn., Capital Markets Credit Analysts Soc. Home: 322 W 57th St Apt 40E New York NY 10019-3713

LAWARE, JOHN PATRICK, banker, federal official; b. Columbus, Wis., Feb. 20, 1928; s. John Henry and Ruth (Powles) L.; m. Margery Ann Ninabuck, Dec. 22, 1952; children: John Kevin, Margaret Ann. BA in Biology, Harvard, 1950; grad., Advanced Mgmt. Program, 1975; MA in Polit. Sci., U. Pa., 1951; LHD (hon.), Suffolk U., D in Polit. Sci. (hon), Northeastern U. Trainee Chem. Bank & Trust Co., N.Y.C., 1953-54, with credit dept., 1954-56, asst. sec., 1957-60, asst. v.p., 1960-62, v.p., 1962-65, v.p. in charge mktg. div., 1965-68, sr. v.p., 1968-72; sr. v.p. in charge holding co. ops. Chem. N.Y. Corp., from 1972; pres., dir. Shawmut Corp., 1978-88, Shawmut Bank of Boston N.A., 1978-80, chmn., dir., 1980-88; pres., dir. Shawmut Assn., Inc., 1978-80; chmn., chief exec. officer Shawmut Corp., 1980-88; mem. bd. govs. Fed. Res. System, Washington, 1988—; pres., dir. Devonshire Fin. Svc. Corp., 1978-88; chmn., treas. Boston Clearing House Assn., Inc.; Shawmut Corp. subs.; mem. Internat. Fin. Conf.; chmn. Mass. Bankers Assn., 1982-83, Assn. Bank Holding Cos., 1986-87. Trustee, vice chmn., chmn. fin. com. Northeastern U., 1981-88; trustee, mem. fin. com. Mt. Holyoke Coll., 1984-88; chmn. Children's Hosp. Med. Ctr., 1989-91; past chmn., bd. dirs. Mass. Bus. Roundtable; chmn. coordinating com. Boston Bus. Leaders Orgn.; trustee Holyoke Coll., 1983-88, Northeastern U., 1982-83, vice chmn. 1985-88, chmn. fin. com., 1985-88. 2d lt. USAF, 1951-53. Recipient Disting. Citizen award Minuteman Coun. Boy Scouts Am., Chief Exec. Officer of Yr. award Northeastern U. Coll. Bus., Outstanding Citizen award B'nai Brith-Antidefamation League. Mem. Assn. Bank Holding Cos. (past chmn. and dir.). Home: 11505 Skipwith Ln Rockville MD 20854-1642 Office: FRS 20th & C Sts NW Washington DC 20551

LAWBER, HAROLD ERNEST, JR., economist, educator; b. Tampa, Fla., Mar. 8, 1950; s. Harold Ernest and Virginia (Gustafson) L.; m. Katherine Margaret Leary, June 9, 1990; 1 child, Matthew Christopher. BA, N.C. State U., 1972, M in Econs., 1974; PhD, U. Conn., 1990. Asst. mgr. trainer Liberty Loans, Belmont, N.C., 1974-75; instr. econs. Belmont Abbey Coll., 1975-77, U. Conn., Storrs, 1985-86, Trinity Coll., Hartford, Conn., 1986-87; instr. econs. Salve Regina Coll., Newport, R.I., 1988-90, asst. prof. econs., 1990—, dir. MBA in global bus. and fin. program, 1990—. Mem. Am. Econs. Assn., Econ. History Assn., History Econs. Soc., Omicron Delta Epsilon. Methodist. Home: 150 Atlantic Dr Middletown RI 02840 Office: Salve Regina Coll Ochre Point Ave Newport RI 02840-6906

LAWES, JAMES SIDNEY, education educator; b. Fordingbridge, Hants., Eng., Dec. 2, 1926; s. Wilfred Sidney and Fanny Elizabeth (Spratt) L.; m. Dorothy Elizabeth Bennison, Aug. 14, 1952. BSc, U. Durham, Eng., 1951; MEd, U. Durham, 1961; PhD, U. Southampton, Eng., 1985. Tchr. sci. various high schs., Eng., 1952-59; lectr. (prof.) edn. Westminster Coll., Oxford, Eng., 1959-86; prof. edn. Westminster Coll., New Wilmington, Pa., 1987—. Author: Understanding Children, 1966; contbr. articles to profl. jours. Chmn. governing body Penhurst Sch. for Physically handicapped, Chipping Norton, Eng., 1975—. With RAF, 1945-48. Mem. Brit. Psychol. Soc. Methodist. Office: Westminster Coll Dept Edn New Wilmington PA 16172-0001

LAWLER, JOHN KEVIN, real estate consultant; b. Norwalk, Conn., May 10, 1948; s. W.J. and Agnes Clare (Eastley) L.; m. Laurie Mc. Baker, Apr. 26, 1980 (div. Sept. 1988). BS, Mich. State U., E. Lansing, 1971; MCP, Harvard U., Cambridge, 1973. Assoc. v.p. Gladstone Assocs., Washington, 1973-81; sr. v.p. GA Partners, Washington, 1981-88; prin. Arthur Andersen & Co., Washington, 1988—; adv. Nat. Trust Hist. Preservation, Washington, 1977-80; asst. prof. George Washington U., 1976-79; sr. lectr., U. Md., College Park, 1990. Mem. The Corinthians, Md. Capital Yacht Club, Annapolis Yatch Club, Urban Land Inst. Home: 42 Chesapeake Lndg Annapolis MD 21403-2616 Office: Arthur Andersen & Co Arthur Andersen & Co. 1 Thomas Cir NW Washington DC 20005-5802

LAWLEY, SUSAN MARC, management consultant; b. N.Y.C., July 5, 1951; d. Romolo and Catherine (Giacalone) Marcucci; m. Robert Lawley, Feb. 11, 1978; 1 child, Gregory. BA with honors, Herbert H. Lehman Coll., N.Y.C., 1972; MBA, Fairleigh Dickinson U., 1982; postgrad., Fielding Inst., 1990—. With AT&T, N.Y.C. and Bedminster, N.J., 1972-80; v.p., head adminstrn. investment banking dept. Bankers Trust Co., N.Y.C., 1980-87; v.p. head planning and adminstrn. mortgage securities dept. Goldman, Sachs & Co., N.Y.C., 1987-89; pres., mgmt. cons. Camelot Con, N.Y.C. and Parsippany, N.J., 1989—; strategic planning dir. GAIN Communications, Inc., 1989-92; co-founder New View Prodns., 1989—; founder Lasting Corrections Found., 1992—. Bd. dirs. Katherine Gibb Scholarship Found., N.Y.C., 1986—; v.p. Edith Imre Found., N.Y.C., 1985—. Mem. NAFE, Am. Soc. Pers. Adminstrn., AWED, Am. Mgmt. Soc., Women's Club Fairfield.

LAWN, GREGORY T., financial executive; b. Englewood, N.J., Nov. 22, 1950; s. Andrew and Helen (Kapus) L.; m. Mary Beth Drew, Sept. 7, 1974; children: Michael Drew, Elizabeth Marie, Medridith Ann. BS, U. Dayton, 1972; MBA, Fairleigh Dickenson U., 1977. CPA, N.Y., Conn., N.J. Div. controller Ingredient Tech. Corp., Woodbridge, N.J., 1980-81; asst. corp. treas. Ingredient Tech. Corp., Dariane, Conn., 1981-83; dir. internal audit Iroqwis Brands, Ltd., Greenwich, Conn., 1983-86; v.p. fin. Jenderan Assoc., Inc., North Caldwell, N.J., 1986-92; contr. Imperial Schrade, Inc., N.Y.C., 1992—. Bd. trustees, treas. Kosciuszko Found., Inc., N.Y.C., 1987—; mem. Citizens Adv. Com. Mt. Laurel, Haworth, N.J., 1988-89; bd. dirs. Haworth Rep. Com., 1989; councilman Haworth, N.J., 1990—. Mem. AICPA, N.Y. Soc. CPA's. Republican. Roman Catholic. Office: Imperial Schrade Corp 99 Madison Ave New York NY 10016

LAWRENCE, ALBERT WEAVER, insurance company executive; b. Newburgh, N.Y., Aug. 4, 1928; s. Claude D. and Janet (Weaver) L.; m. Barbara Corell, June 28, 1950; children: David, Janet, Elizabeth. BSAE in Engring., Cornell U., 1950; grad. advanced mgmt. program, Rensselaer Poly. Inst., 1975. Ins. agt., exec., 1953—; founder, chmn. A.W. Lawrence and Co. Inc., Schenectady and Albany, N.Y., 1954-82; chmn. bd. dirs. United Community Ins. Com., N.Y.C., 1982—, Lawrence Agy. Corp., Albany, 1982—, Lawrence Ins. Group Inc., Albany, 1986—, Lawrence Group Inc., Schenetady, 1986—, ADAPT, Inc., Schenectady, 1989; mem. bus. adv. bd. Health Svcs. Agy. N.Y., Albany, 1985—; underwriting mem. Lloyds of London; bd. dirs. Ctr. for Econ. Growth, Inc., Capital Dist. Ctr. for Econ. Devel.; dir. Fleet Bank Capital Region Adv. Bd., Fleet Upstate Governing Bd., the Hudson and Mohawk Adv. Coun. Bd. overseers Grad Sch. Bus. Rensselaer Poly. Inst., Troy, N.Y.; past pres. Schenectady Girls Club, Family and Child Svc. Schenectady; bd. dirs. Ind. Living for Physically Disabled, Proctor's Theatre; co-founder (with Barbara Lawrence) The Lawrence Inst. for physically disabled rsch.; past chmn. Schenectady United Fund Drive, Jr. Achievement Capital Dist.; trustee Russell Sage Coll., Troy, Sunnyview Hosp. & Rehab. Ctr., Poly. Tech. Inst.; bd. dirs. N.Y. State Olympic Regional Devel. Authority, 1989. Served with U.S. Army, 1946-47. Recipient Sca-Nec-Ta-De Civic award, 1967. Mem. Schenectady C. of C. (past pres.), Mohawk Golf Club, Mohawk Club, Cornell Club (N.Y.C.), N.Y. Athletic Club, N.Y Yacht Club, No. Lake George Yacht Club (past commodore), Univ. Club Albany. Republican. Mem. Dutch Reformed Ch. Home: 708 Riverview Rd Rexford NY 12148-1433 Office: Lawrence Group Inc 108 Union St Schenectady NY 12305-1788

LAWRENCE, AUDREY BETH, dental hygienist; b. Bklyn., Dec. 27, 1954; d. Martin R. and Ruth (Katz) L.; m. Glenn Rosenberg, Apr. 11, 1992. Degree in Dental Hygiene, Northwestern U., 1976; BS, NYU, 1981; Dr. (hon.), Am. Dental Assn., 1976. Registered dental hygienist. Dental hygienist Drs. Shelby, Maitland, N.Y.C., 1976-79, Dr. Lawrence Rubin, N.Y.C., 1980-85, Drs. Eitches & Lorinsky, N.Y.C., 1981-84, Smile Ctr., N.Y.C., 1981-83, Dr. Malvin F. Braverman, N.Y.C., 1981-85, Drs. Stahl, Buonocore, N.Y.C., 1988-92; del. to state First Dist. Dental Hygienists Assn., Albany, N.Y., 1980-81. Author, illustrator: Tooth Survival Book, 1976; rschr., developer circular method of toothbrushing, 1986. Mem. Am. Acad. TV Arts & Scis. Home: 229 E 51st St New York NY 10022

LAWRENCE, BRIAN DAVID, wedding professional; b. Bklyn., Feb. 21, 1958; s. Matthew Martin Lawrence and Gloria Blacker Peyser; m. Stacy Fran Lipner, Nov. 23, 1985; 1 child, Eric Harlan. BA, Bklyn. Coll. Pres. Do Me A Favor, Rutherford, N.J., 1981-82, Bridal Fashions, Inc., Rutherford, N.J., 1983—; v.p. Elite Limosine, West N.Y., N.J., 1987—; pres. Able Mind Cons., Teaneck, N.J., 1990—. Author: Wedding Expert's Guide to Sales and Marketing, 1991; author casette: Stop Smoking for Life, 1990; contbr. articles to mags. Educator Community Edn. Programs of Paramus, Teaneck, Waldwick, Garfield; partisan Nat. Assn. for Remembrance of the Holocaust, 1990—. Mem. Assn. Bridal Cons. Jewish. Home: 268 Griggs Ave Teaneck NJ 07666-3305 Office: Bridal Fashions Inc 200 Park Ave Rutherford NJ 07070-2347

LAWRENCE, DAVID STEPHEN, financial planner, forecaster; b. Seattle, June 21, 1959; s. Samuel Crocker and Julia Belle (Franklin) L. AB in Econs., Harvard U., 1981, postgrad., 1981-88. Founder, pres. Fractals and Fin., Cambridge, Mass., 1987—; researcher Harvard U., Cambridge, 1980-82, lectr., 1981-88; cons. The Admission Ctr., Phila., 1984—; lectr. Boston Soc. Security Analysts, 1989—. Econs. editor The Harvard Internat. Review, 1981; founding editor The Harvard Salient, 1982. Speaker Christ Ch. Episcopal, Cambridge, 1991, mem. choir, soloist, 1988-91; organizer 10th reunion Class of 1981, Harvard U.-Radcliffe Coll. Mem. Harvard Wine and Food Tasting Soc. (pres. 1983-84). Home and Office: Fractals & Fin 18 Leonard Ave Cambridge MA 02139-1020

LAWRENCE, EDGAR, association executive; b. Freeport, N.Y., Sept. 27, 1944; s. Edgar Boyd Lawrence and Mary Margaret (Giddings) Lawrence-Harper; m. Carmen Barrett, Mar. 6, 1964; children: Lexi B. Nelson, Lane H. Lawrence. BS, Grove City (Pa.) Coll., 1966; postgrad., U. Md., 1966-69, Am. U., 1970; M in Hosp. Adminstrn., George Washington U., 1972. Field rep. Calgon Corp., Silver Spring, Md., 1966-70; adminstrv. resident Md. Hosp. Assn., Lutherville, Md., 1971-72, dir. planning, assoc. dir., sr. v.p., 1972-90; exec. v.p. Md. Hosp. Assn., Lutherville, 1990—; bd. dirs. State Sales and Svc. Corp., Balt.; v.p. Carmen Lawrence Interiors, Lutherville, 1981—; instr. Essex Community Coll., Baltimore County, Md., 1973-74. Author: (booklet) Duplication and Regulation, 1979; editor: (booklet) Access Achievement Accountability, 1988, (manual) Guide to Rate Review, 1989. Mem. Baltimore County Leadership, Towson, Md.; bd. dirs. Calvert Hall Parents Club, 1983; registrar Ch. of the Holy Comforter, 1988-91, head usher, 1987—. NSF grantee, 1965. Mem. Am. Assn. Hosp. Accts., Balt. Econ. Soc., Mid-Atlantic Planning Assn., Forum for Health Care Planning (pres. 1987-88, dir. emeritus 1988—). Democrat. Episcopalian. Office: Md Hosp Assn 1301 York Rd Lutherville MD 21093

LAWRENCE, ERNEST RICHARD, entrepreneur, management executive; b. Muskogee, Okla., Mar. 18, 1944; s. Ernest Curlee and Dorothy Clare (Schaefer) L.; m. Janice Mary Ann Herzog, Nov. 25, 1967; children: Stacy Lynette, Shannon Elise, Susan Shari. BA in English, St. John's U., 1966; MBA, U. Denver, 1974. Media buyer, account mgr. Campbell-Mithun, Inc., Mpls. and Denver, 1969-74; dir. advt., product mktg. and devel. Samsonite Corp., Denver, 1974-79; v.p. mktg. The Stiffel Co., Chgo., 1979-81; exec. v.p., chief operating officer N.Y. Graphic Soc., Greenwich, Conn., 1982-84; pres., chief operating officer, dir. Chartwell Group Ltd., Carlstadt, N.J., 1981-87; prin. EJS Enterprises, Randolph, N.J., 1987-89; pres., chief exec. officer, dir. New Century Edn. Corp., Piscataway, N.J., 1989—; bd. dirs. Ctr. for the Media Arts, N.Y.C. 1st lt. U.S. Army, 1966-69, ETO.

LAWRENCE, FRANCIS LEO, language educator, educational administrator; b. Woonsocket, R.I., Aug. 25, 1937. B.S., St. Louis U., 1959; Ph.D. in French and Italian, Tulane U., 1962. Mem. faculty Tulane U., New Orleans, 1962—, chmn. dept. French and Italian, 1969-76, acting dean Newcomb Coll., 1976-78, dep. provost, 1978-81, acting provost, grad. dean, 1981-82, prof. French, from 1971, acad. v.p., provost, 1982-90; pres. Rutgers, New Brunswick, N.J., 1990—. Author numerous publs. on French 17th century lit. Contbr. articles, revs. and essays to profl. publs. Decorated chevalier, Palmes Academiques, 1977. Mem. Am. Assn. Tchrs. French, N.Am. Soc. 17th Century French Lit., MLA. Office: Rutgers U Office of President New Brunswick NJ 08903*

LAWRENCE, HENRY SHERWOOD, physician, educator; b. N.Y.C., Sept. 22, 1916; s. Victor John and Agnes (Whalen) L.; m. Dorothea Wetherbee, Nov. 13, 1943; children: Dorothea, Victor, Geoffrey. AB, NYU, 1938, MD, 1943. Diplomate Am. Bd. Internal Medicine. Mem. faculty NYU, N.Y.C., 1947—; John Wyckoff fellow in medicine NYU, 1948-49, dir. student health, 1950-57, head infectious disease and immunology div., 1959—, prof. medicine, 1961-79, Jeffrey Bergstein prof. medicine, 1979—, co-dir. med. svcs., 1964—, dir. Cancer Ctr., 1974-79; dir. Ctr. for AIDS Rsch., 1989—; vis. physician Tisch Hosp., Bellevue Hosp., 1964—; cons. medicine Manhattan VA Hosp., 1964—; infectious disease program com. VA Rsch. Svc., 1960-63; cons. allergy and immunology study sect. USPHS, 1960-63, chmn., 1963-65; assoc. mem. commn. on streptococcal and staphylococcal diseases Armed Forces Epidemiol. Bd., Dept. Def., 1956-74; mem. coms. Nat. Acad. Scis.-NRC, 1957-65, chmn. com. transplantation, 1963-65; mem. NRC, 1970-72; mem. allergy and infectious disease panel Health Rsch. Coun., N.Y.C., 1962-75, co-chmn., 1968-75; mem. sci. adv. council Am. Cancer Soc., 1973-75. Editor: Medical Clinics of North America, 1957, Cellular and Humoral Aspects of Hypersensitive States, 1959, (with M. Landy) Mediators of Cellular Immunity, 1969, (with Kirkpatrick and Burger) Immunobiology of Transfer Factor, 1983; mem. editorial bd. Transplantation, Ann. of Internal Medicine; founder, editor in chief: Cellular Immunology. Served to lt. M.C. USNR, World War II. Commonwealth Found. fellow Univ. Coll., London, 1959; recipient Research Career Devel. award USPHS, 1960-65, prize Alpha Omega Alpha, 1943; Meritorious Sci. Achievement award NYU Alumni Assn., 1970, von Pirquet Gold medal Ann. Forum on Allergy, 1972, Award for Disting. Achievement in Sci. of Medicine ACP, 1973, Sci. Achievement award Am. Coll. Allergists, 1974, Sci. medal N.Y. Acad. Medicine, 1974, Bristol Sci. award Infectious Diseases

Soc. Am., 1974, Charles V. Chapin medal, 1975, Lila Gruber honor award Am. Acad. Dermatology, 1975, Alumni Achievement award NYU Washington Sq. Coll., 1979. Fellow ACP (Bronze medal 1973), Am. Acad. Allergy (hon.), Royal Coll. Physicians and Surgeons Glasgow (hon.); mem. Nat. Acad. Scis., Assn. Am. Physicians, Am. Soc. for Clin. Investigation, Am. Assn. Immunologists, Soc. for Exptl. Biology and Medicine (editorial bd. procs.), Interurban Clin. Club, Harvey Soc. (sec. 1957-60, lectr. 1973—, councillor 1974-77), Peripatetic Clin. Soc., Infectious Diseases Soc. (charter, councillor 1970-72, Bristol Sci. award 1974), Royal Soc. Medicine (affiliate) (Eng.), Internat. Transplantation Soc. (chmn. constn. com., councillor), Société Française d'Allergie (corr.), Alpha Omega Alpha. Home: 343 E 30th St New York NY 10016-6417

LAWRENCE, HOWARD RAY, architecture educator; b. San Francisco, Mar. 21, 1936; s. Ray Palmer and Ina Mabel (Sharp) L.; divorced; children: Thomas Fairchild, Anna Marie, Katharine Marie. BArch, U. Calif., Berkeley, 1962, MA in Art, 1964. Apprentice various cos., 1964-70; asst. prof. City Coll. San Francisco, 1970-71, Hampton (Va.) Inst., 1971-72, U. Kans., Lawrence, 1972-73; asst. prof. architecture Pa. State U., University Park, 1973—. Office: Pa State U Dept Architecture University Park PA 16802

LAWRENCE, JUDIANA, English educator; b. Pretoria, Transvaal, South Africa, Jan. 3, 1936; came to U.S., 1969; d. Jan and Christina J. P. (Du Preez) Vorster; m. Christopher William Lawrence, Aug. 5, 1961; children: Nicholas R., Andrew G., Peter J. BA, U. of the Witwatersrand, Johannesburg, South Africa, 1956; MA, U. Rochester, 1976, PhD, 1983. Tchr. Pietersburg (South Africa) Sch., 1957-58, Goedehoop High Sch., Germiston, South Africa, 1958-59, Peckham Manor Sch., London, 1960-61, Icknield Sch., Wantage, Oxon, Eng., 1962-64; instr. U. Rochester (N.Y.), 1978-82; vis. asst. prof. St. John Fisher Coll., Rochester, N.Y., 1982-86, asst. prof., 1986-91, assoc. prof., 1991—. Author of book chpt.; contbr. articles to profl. jours. U. Rochester dissertation fellow, 1978-79, St. John Fisher Coll. summer rsch. fellow, 1986, NEH summer rsch. seminar fellow, 1989; recipient Dissertation Prize, U. Rochester, 1982, Grad. Teaching Prize, U. Rochester, 1983. Mem. Modern Lang. Assn., N.Y. Coll. English Assn. (sec.-treas. 1989-91), Shakespeare Assn. Am., Delta Kappa Gamma.

LAWRENCE, LARRY JAMES, computer systems executive, consultant; b. Petersburg, Va., Mar. 22, 1944; s. Charles Barnes Jr. and Catherine (Saponar) L.; m. Paula Elizabeth Andersen, Oct. 12, 1968; children: David James, Erich Paul. Student, Pa. State U., 1962-65; AB, U. New Haven, 1974. Supr. ops. Western Electric Corp., Orange, Conn., 1968-74; cons. Computer Techs., West Haven, Conn., 1974-75; supr. mfg. and warehousing systems Sikorsky Aircraft div. United Techs. Corp., Stratford, Conn., 1975-85; supr. office systems Norden Systems Inc. div. United Techs. Corp., Norwalk, Conn., 1985-88, supr. application devel. and implementation, 1988—; cons., Guilford, Conn., 1985—. Contbr. articles to profl. jours. Active Boy Scouts Am., North Haven, Conn., 1983-84; mgr. Little League Baseball, North Haven, 1983-84, Guilford, 1985-86. 1st lt. U.S. Army, 1965-68. Mem. Data Processing Mgrs. Assn. (cert. APICS CIPM 1973). Republican. Episcopalian. Home: 3ll White Birch Dr Guilford CT 06437 Office: Norden Systems Inc Norden Pl Norwalk CT 06855-1441

LAWRENCE, LESLIE GAIL, graphic designer; b. Albany, N.Y., Sept. 20, 1961; d. Sanford Edward Slawsky and Anne Ruth (Andresen) Little; m. David Andrew Lawrence, Aug. 1, 1987 (div.). BS in Graphic Design, SUNY, Buffalo, 1983, MA in Advt. Design, 1992. Freelance designer Syracuse, N.Y., 1983—; graphic artist Carrols Corp., Syracuse, 1984-86; creative designer Automated Graphics, Syracuse, 1986-87; graphics mgr. Carrols Corp., Syracuse, 1987-89; mktg. and promotions designer The Syracuse Newspapers, 1989—; guest lectr. Baldwinsville (N.Y.) Schs., 1988, Onondaga County Community Coll., 1990; substitute instr. Univ. Coll., Syracuse, 1987—; adj. prof. Sch. Visual and Performing Arts, Syracuse U., 1990—. Recipient 2 merit awards Syracuse Ad Club, 1990, 2 merit and 1 excellence awards, 1991, 2 gold and 1 silver awards, 1992.k. Mem. World Wildlife Fedn., Nat. Humane Soc., People for Ethical Treatment Animals. Democrat. Home: 133 Paul Ave Syracuse NY 13206-3218 Office: The Syracuse Newspapers Clinton Sq PO Box 4915 Syracuse NY 13221-4915

LAWRENCE, RANDOLPH THOMAS, sales executive; b. N.Y.C., July 19, 1949; s. Everard Edward and Shirley (Hoffman) L.; m. Barbara Ann La Greca, Mar. 30, 1980; children: Jacqueline Rae, Daniel Steven. Grad., Phillips Acad., 1967; BA in Dramatic Lit. and Criticism, U. Denver, 1971. Rep. sales various firms, 1972-82; v.p. sales, mgr. Universal Printing Co., N.Y.C., 1982—. Mem. Mensa. Republican. Episcopalian. Office: Universal Printing Co 420 Lexington Ave Ste 2735 New York NY 01710

LAWRENCE, RICHARD SELLERS, actor, director; b. Morgantown, W.Va., June 2, 1934; s. Richard Rudolph and Virginia (Sellers) L.; m. Mary Courtney, June 25, 1969; 1 child, Jenna Mara. BA, W.Va. U., 1956. Actor, summer stock Pricilla Beach Theatre, Plymouth, Mass., 1954, Maxincuccki Playhouse, Culver, Ind., 1956; actor Broadway Actor's Guild, N.Y.C., 1959-60, The Cafe Cino, N.Y.C., 1960-61; dir., actor Residential Community Theatre, Boston and Winchester, Mass., 1970-83; dir. Theatre in Process, Boston, 1983-85; founder Acting Co. for the Pirandello Lyceum, Boston, 1986; dir. Theatre in Process, Boston, 1986; actor Boston, 1988—; pres. Theatre in Process, Inc., Boston, 1986—; bd. dirs. The Footlight Club, Boston, 1977-80, The Amateurs, Inc., Brookline, Mass., 1972-76; rehab. specialist U.S. Dept. Edn., 1974—. Composer, lyricist numerous songs. Mem. StageSource, Inc. Democrat. Home: 200 Church St Newton MA 02158-1906

LAWRENCE, ROBERT ASHTON, investment company executive; b. Boston, Aug. 11, 1926; s. Edward and Frances Wilcox (Gaither) L.; m. Patricia Perrin, Mar. 20, 1948; children: Robert Ashton Jr., John P., George W., Frances G. AB, Yale U., 1947. Salesman Estabrook & Co., Boston, 1947-53; v.p. Loomis Sayles, Boston, Phila., 1967-85; ptnr. State Street Rsch. & Mgmt. Co., Boston, 1960—, Saltonstall & Co., Boston, 1980—; bd. dirs. Affiliated Publs., Boston, McCaw Cellular Communications, Kirkland, Wash., Fifty Assocs., Boston, various mut. funds, Boston. Trustee Wellesley (Mass.) Coll., 1979-80, Noble and Grenborough Sch., Dedham, Mass., 1970-78, pres. bd. trustees. Capt. USMCR, 1951, Korea. Home: 423 Sandy Valley Rd Westwood MA 02090-1129 Office: Saltonstall & Co 50 Congress St Rm 800 Boston MA 02109-4007

LAWRENCE, SIGMUND JOSEPH, chemical engineer; b. Chgo., May 20, 1918; m. Helen Agnes Shields (dec. 1964); children: Clifford, Keith, Claudia, Karen; m. Helen Asquith, July, 14, 1973 (div.); children: Joan, Mary. BS, Ill. Inst. Tech., 1939; MS, U. Iowa, 1942, PhD, 1943. Registered profl. engr., N.Y. With Shell Devel., 1943-46; chem. engr. GE Hanford Works, 1946-48, Knolls Atomic Power Lab., 1948-51; rsch. assoc. GE Rsch. Lab., 1951-52; with Gen. Electric, 1946-73; chem. engr., Silicone Prodn. dept. Gen. Electric, Waterford, N.Y., 1953-57; chem. engr., Gen. Engring. lab. Gen. Electric, Schenectady, N.Y., 1957-59; systems engr., Systems Sales and Engring. Gen. Electric, Schenectady, 1959-67; mgr. sensor programs, Instrument dept. Gen. Electric, West Lynn, Mass., 1967-69; cons. instrumentation, Re-entry div. Gen. Electric, Phila., 1969-73; process engr. Catalytic, Inc. United Engrs. and Constructors, Phila., 1974-91; pvt. cons. engr., 1991—; lectr. in field. Citizens sch. bd., Schenectady, 1958; ops. chief Civil Def., Schenectady, 1955-67. Mem. Am. Inst. Chem. Engrs. (treas. nat. meeting Lake Placid, N.Y., 1956, chmn. automation seminar Troy, N.Y., 1962, sect. chmn. 1965, emeritus), Am. Chem. Soc. (emeritus). Republican. Unitarian.

LAWRENCE, STEPHEN REID, public relations professional; b. Bklyn., Feb. 12, 1921; s. Frederick William Lawrence, Sr. and Elvira (Scherpich) Lawrence John; m. Elizabeth Harriet Smith, Aug. 23, 1947. AB, Duke U., 1941; MA, Middlebury Coll., 1951; postgrad., U. Pa., 1954-57. English instr., coach Peddie Sch., Hightstown, N.J., 1947-51, Girard Coll., Phila., 1951-54; instr. English U. Pa., Phila., 1954-57; mgr. publs. Ins. Co. N.Am., Phila., 1957-65, dir. pub. rels., 1965-76; assoc. dir. pub. rels. INA Corp., Phila., 1976-82; communications cons. Cigna, Phila., 1982-91; pres. Steve Lawrence Assocs., Inc., Phila., 1991—; bd. dirs. Better Bus. Bur. East Pa. Chmn. Phila. chpt. Nat. Safety Coun., 1976-78; bd. dirs. Phila. C. of C., 1976-78. Lt. USN, 1942-46, ETO, PTO. Named Communicator of Yr. Delaware Valley Indsl. Editors, Phila., 1960. Mem. Pub. Rels. Soc. Am. (bd. dirs., soc. of fellows), Phila. Pub. Rels. Assn. (bd. dirs.), Insurers Pub. Rels. Coun. Democrat. Presbyterian. Home: 637 W Ellet St Philadelphia PA 19119-3428

LAWRENCE, WILLIAM WALTER, editor, publisher; b. Roeblins, N.J., May 3, 1929; s. Jacob and Anna (Lockett) L.; m. Margaret Jane Lozinak Lawrence; children: William Walter II, Robert James, Christopher Anthony. Student, Temple U., 1955-58. Police reporter Phila. Daily News, 1955-60; writer, reporter, editor Phila. Bull., 1960-82; editor, pub. County Press, Haverford Press, Drexel Hill Press, Del. County, Pa., 1982—. V.p. Nat. Kidney Found., Phila., 1968; chmn., founder Del. Valley Kidney Funds, Phila., 1969. Sgt. U.S. Army, 1947-54. Named Man of Yr. Am. Legion, 1973, one of Brotherhood Phila. Post Office, 1973. Mem. Phila. Press Assn. Republican. Mem. Christian Ch. Home: 18 Windsor Cir Media PA 19064-1422 Office: County Press 3732 W Chester Pike Newtown Square PA 19073-3285

LAWRENCE, WINIFRED GILLEN, special education educator; b. Beardstown, Ill., Nov. 14, 1935; d. Francis Henry and Helen (Skiles) Gillen; m. John Robert Lawrence, Sept. 24, 1954; children: Robert Francis, Jane Winifred, William Clyde. BS, Pace Coll., 1975; MA, Manhattan Coll., 1979, postgrad., 1981-82. Cert. reading and spl. edn. tchr., N.Y. Tchr. aide Bd. Coop. Ednl. Svcs., Yorktown Heights, N.Y., 1969-72, acad. instr., 1972-79, tchr., coms. on spl. edn. liaison, 1979—; mem. policy bd. Bd. Coop. Ednl. Svcs. Tchr. Ctr., Yorktown Heights, 1988—. Mem. PTA bd., Yorktown Heights, 1963-69; neighborhood chair Girl Scouts U.S., Yorktown Heights, 1966-71. Mem. No. Westchester-Putnam Reading Coun. (treas. 1981—), N.Y. State Reading Assn. (award 1990), Alpha Upsilon Alpha, Kappa Delta Pi. Republican. Presbyterian. Office: Bd Coop Ednl Svcs Pinesbridge Rd Yorktown Heights NY 10598

LAWS-MOSELEY, BARBARA LEE, communications company executive; b. Media, Pa., Jan. 3, 1946; d. Philip and Dorothy (Adams) Laws; m. Charles R. Moseley (dec.; children: Brenda L., Charles R. Student, Ben Franklin Bus. Sch., Phila., 1962, Pa. State U., 1976, Temple U., 1986, Ophelia Devore Sch. Modeling, N.Y.C., 1978. With Bell Telephone Co./ AT&T, 1957; gospel singer various locations, 1958-69; with N.B.N.A. & Black Caucus, Washington, 1964; freelance writer Relevant Mag., N.Y.C., 1972; fashion coordinator Relevant & Karl Owen, N.Y.C., 1972; sr. clk. AT&T, Bala Cynwyd, Pa., 1984-86, adminstrv. clk., 1986-89, supr., 1989—. Author poetry. Active various charitable orgns. in past. Mem. NAACP, Nat. Council Negro Women. Home: 609 Vernon St Media PA 19063-3908 Office: AT&T 3 Bala Plz # 700 Bala Cynwyd PA 19004-3481

LAWSON, JANET ANN, improvisational singer, composer, lyricist; b. Balt., Nov. 13, 1940; d. Oscar Jack and Helene Elizabeth (Kocur) Polun. Student, Balt. Jr. Coll., 1958-59; pvt. study, N.Y.C., 1960—. Educator, performer Jamey Aebersold Clinics, Denver and San Jose, Calif., 1980-81; co-founder, performer Improvised Music Collective, N.Y.C., 1981—; performer Women's Work, Stroudsburg, Pa., 1989-90; performer, co-producer Audio-Holograms, East Stroudsburg, Pa., 1990; head vocal jazz adj. prof. William Paterson Coll., Wayne, N.J., 1981-88; mem. faculty Janice Boria Local Jazz Camp, Lisle, Ill., 1989—; performer, facilitator Family of Artists, Delaware Water Gap, Pa., 1990—; co-producer, performer Jazz for Children, Millburn, N.J., 1991—; singer univs., clubs., hotels throughout U.S., Can., Italy, S.Am., Cen. Am.; workshop facilitator Living Potentials Holistic Health Orgn., Effort, Pa., 1990—; artist in resident Pa. State Coun. Arts, 1990-91. Performer, lyricist: (album) Dreams Can Be, 1984, 91; performer: (albums) The Janet Lawson Quintet, 1981, Real Jazz for Folks Who Feel Jazz, 1982, The Main Man, 1981; composer, co-producer: (musical) Jass Is a Lady, 1983; contbg. writer Women's Resources, 1991. Organizer ACLU, 1977-80, Women Against Pornography, 1977-80. Recipient Grammy Nomination, NARAS, 1981; co-fellow Pa. State Coun. Arts, 1991; grantee Nat. Endowment Arts, N.Y.C., 1978, 80. Mem. Nat. Jazz Educators Assn. Home: 101 Fawn Rd East Stroudsburg PA 18301

LAWSON, JENNIFER, broadcast executive; b. Birmingham, Ala., June 8, 1946; d. Willie DeLeon and Velma Theresa (Foster) L.; m. Elbert Sampson, June 1, 1979 (div. Sept. 1980); m. Anthony Gittens, May 29, 1982: children: Kai, Zachary. Student, Tuskegee U., 1963-65; MFA, Columbia U., 1974; LHD (hon.), Teikyo Post U., Hartford, Conn., 1991. Assoc. producer William Greaves Prodns., N.Y.C., 1974-75; asst. prof. film studies Bklyn. Coll., 1975-77; exec. dir. The Film Fund, N.Y.C., 1977-80; TV coord. Program Fund Corp. for Pub. Broadcasting, Washington, 1980-83, assoc. dir. TV Program Fund, 1983-89, dir. TV Program Fund, 1989; exec. v.p. programming PBS, Alexandria, Va., 1989—; v.p. Internat. Pub. TV, Washington, 1984-88; panelist Fulbright Fellowships, Washington, 1988-90. Author, illustrator: Children of Africa, 1970; illustrator: Our Folktales, 1968, African Folktales: A Calabash of Wisdom, 1973. Coord. Nat. Coun. Negro Women, Washington, 1969. Office: PBS 1320 Braddock Pl Alexandria VA 22314-1649

LAWSON, JOEL SMITH, III, financial services executive; b. N.Y.C., June 18, 1947; s. Joel Smith and Grace (Rumbough) L.; m. Mary Ann Benone, Apr. 26, 1975; children: Elizabeth, Joel, Victoria. BA in Econs. cum laude, Yale U., 1969; MBA with distinction, U. Pa., 1980. Pres. Cork & Keg, Inc., Rockville, Md., 1973-76; bus. mgr. Parks and History Assn., Washington, 1975-78; proprietor Lawson Ent., Phila., 1978-80; mng. ptnr. Howard, Lawson & Co., Phila., 1980—; bd. dirs. Sechan Electronics, Inc., Lancaster, Pa., Datacap System, Inc., Horsham, Pa., Urban Outfitters, Inc., Phila. Pub. newsletter Going Public: The IPO Reporter, 1980-85, Private Placements, 1982-85, Growth Capital, 1981-85; contbr. articles to profl. jours. Bd. dirs., pres. Phila. Art Alliance, 1985-91; bd. dirs. Buten Mus., Lower Merion, Pa., 1982-84; bd. dirs., chmn. Germantown Citizens Assn., 1976-78; vice chmn. United Way Phila. Lt. (j.g.) USN, 1969-73. Mayer fellow, 1978-79. Mem. Coll. Fin. Planning, Alexis de Tocqueville Soc. (vice chmn.), Wharton Club of Pa. U., Yale Club, Beta Gamma Sigma. Home: 888 Parkes Run Lane 216 Pheasant Run Dr Villanova PA 19085 Office: Howard Lawson & Co 2 Penn Center Plz Philadelphia PA 19102-1701

LAWSON, JONATHAN NEVIN, academic administrator; b. Latrobe, Pa., Mar. 27, 1941; s. Lawrence Winters and Mary Eleanor (Rhea) L.; m. Leigh Farley (div.); children: Paul, Joshua, Jacob; m. Leesa G. Olson (div.). AA, York Coll. Pa., 1962; BFA, Tex. Christian U., 1964, MA, 1966, PhD, 1970. Dir. composition St. Cloud (Minn.) State U., 1971-77, assoc. dean, 1977-81; asst. vice chancellor Minn. State U. System, St. Paul, 1980-81; dean liberal arts Winona (Minn.) State U., 1981-84; dean arts and scis. U. Hartford, West Hartford, Conn., 1984-86; sr. v.p., dean of faculty U. Hartford, 1986—; pres. Bus. Sch. U. Hartford, Paris, 1990—. Author: Robert Bloomfield, 1980; editor: Collected Works: Robert Bloomfield, 1971; contbr. articles and papers to scholarly publs; assoc. editor Rhetoric Soc. Quar., St. Cloud, 1974-79. Mem. regional adv. bd. Greater Hartford Community Coll., 1992—; mem. bd. trustees Hartford Coll. for Women, 1992—. Mem. Am. Coun. Edn., Coun. Fellows Alumni, Coun. Liberal Learning, Assn. Gen. and Liberal Studies, Assn. Am. Colls., N.E. Assn. Schs. and Colls. (mem. instnl. appeals com. commn. on instns. of higher edn. 1992—), Lambda Iota Tau. Democrat. Episcopalian. Home: 207 Bloomfield Ave West Hartford CT 06117-1503 Office: U Hartford 200 Bloomfield Ave West Hartford CT 06117-1500

LAWSON, NEWAVERY GLOVER, cosmetologist, educator; b. St. Augustine, Fla., Dec. 21, 1922; m. Paul M. Lawson, June 21, 1943; children: Byron M., Pauletta B. Grad., Myers Poro Beauty Sch., Balt., 1940. Cert. cosmetologist, Md., Fla. Owner/mgr. Avery's Beauty Salon, Balt., 1944-88, Avery's Sch. of Advanced Cosmetology, Balt., 1955-87; ret., 1975. Recipient numerous awards in field. Democrat. Methodist. Home: 4323 Kennison Ave Baltimore MD 21215-4208

LAWSON, WILLIAM BURTON, clergyman; b. Mpls., Oct. 14, 1930; s. Lawrence Burton and Mabel Lucille (Lund) L.; m. Grace Elizabeth Dickson, July 30, 1955; children: William Lawrence, Thomas Baxter. BA, U. Minn., 1952; MDiv cum laude, Berkeley Div. Sch., New Haven, 1955, DD (hon.), 1979. Ordained priest Episcopal Ch., 1955. Vicar St. Edward's Episcopal Ch., Duluth, Minn., 1955-59; rector St. Stephen's Episcopal Ch., Bloomfield, Conn., 1959-65, St. Paul's Episcopal Ch., Natick, Mass., 1965-75, St. Stephen's Meml. Ch., Lynn, Mass., 1975—; presiding minister United Parish Natick, 1971-75; ecumenical officer Episcopal Diocese Mass., 1972—, mem. coun., 1972-76, 79-83; mem. exec. com. Episcopal Diocesan Ecumenical Officers, 1973-83, pres., 1978-82; mem. planning com. Nat. Workshop on Christian Unity, 1978-83, chmn., 1982-83; mem. Standing Commn. on Ecumenical Rels., 1978—; mem. governing bd. Nat. Coun. Chs. U.S.A., 1981—; mem. Anglican-Roman Cath. Dialogue, U.S.A., 1984-87; also numerous other career related offices. Author: A New Concept of Ordained Ministry, 1970; contbr. articles to religious publs. Trustee John Walcott Fund, Natick, 1970-75, Lynn Pub. Library, 1975-86, Union Hosp. Mental Health Ctr., 1977-81; mem. Natick Urban Redevel. Authority, 1973-75, Lynn Shelter Assn., 1984-87; pres. St. Stephen's Housing Corp., Lynn, 1975—. Diocese of Mass. Norman Nash fellow, 1984. Mem. N.Am. Acad. Ecuminists, Anglican Ctr. Com. in Rome, Rotary, Delta Tau Delta. Home: 35 Grant Rd Lynn MA 01904-1212 Office: 74 S Common St Lynn MA 01902-4594

LAWSON-JOHNSTON, PETER ORMAN, foundation executive; b. N.Y.C., Feb. 8, 1927; s. John R. and Barbara (Guggenheim) L.; m. Dorothy Stevenson Hammond, Sept. 30, 1950; children: Wendy, Tania, Peter, Mary. Reporter, yachting editor Balt. Sun Papers, 1951-53; exec. dir. Md. Classified Employees Assn., Balt., 1953-54; pub. info. dir. Md. Civil Def. Agy., Pikesville, 1954-56; sales mgr. Feldspar Corp. subs. Zemex Corp. (formerly Pacific Tin Consol.), N.Y.C., 1956-60, v.p. sales, 1961-66, v.p., 1966-72, chmn., 1972-81, bd. dirs., 1959—; v.p. Zemex Corp., 1966-72, vice chmn. 1972-75, pres., 1975-76, chmn., 1975—, also bd. dirs.; chmn. Anglo Energy, Inc., 1973-86; trustee Solomon R. Guggenheim Found. (operating Guggenheim Mus., N.Y.C. and Peggy Guggenheim Collection, Venice, Italy), 1964—, v.p. bus. adminstrn., 1965-69, pres., 1969—; dir. Harry Frank Guggenheim Found., 1968—, chmn., 1971—; ptnr. Guggenheim Bros., 1962-70, sr. ptnr., 1971—; ltd. ptnr. emeritus Alex. Brown & Sons, Inc.; pres., bd. dirs. Elgerbar Corp.; bd. dirs. McGraw Hill Inc., Nat. Rev. Inc., William H. Donner Found. Mem. adv. bd. Jeffersonian Restoration, U. Va.; trustee The Lawrenceville Sch., pres. 1990—; bd. dirs. Coun. for U.S. and Italy. Served with AUS, 1945-47. Mem. Pilgrims of U.S., Carolina Plantation Soc., U.S. Srs. Golf Assn., Edgartown Yacht Club, Edgartown Reading Room Club, Green Spring Valley Hunt Club, River Club, Century Assn., Links, Nassau Gun Club, Bedens Brook Club, Pretty Brook Tennis Club, Md. Club, Seminole Golf Club, Island Club, Brook Club (N.Y.C.), Yeamans Hall Club. Republican. Episcopalian. Home: 215 Carter Rd Princeton NJ 08540-2104 Office: Solomon R Guggenheim Found 527 Madison Ave New York NY 10022-4304

LAWTON, HENRY WILLIAM, social worker; b. Trenton, N.J., July 1, 1941; s. William Joseph and Bettina Lawton (Bowers) L.; m. Helen Claire Sieswerda, June 22, 1968; children: Jennifer, Jason. BA, Trenton State Coll., 1968; MA, Fairleigh Dickinson U., 1971; MLS, Rutgers U., 1977. Social caseworker N.Y.C. Dept. Social Svcs., 1968-71, Passaic (N.J.) County Welfare Bd., 1971; family svc. specialist N.J. Div. Youth and Family Svcs., Hackensack, 1971—; presenter workshops at profl. confs. Author: The Psychohistorian's Handbook, 1988; contbg. editor Jour. Psychohistory, N.Y.C., 1977—, book rev. editor, 1981—; contbr. articles, revs. to profl. publs. With USAF, 1959-63. mem. Internat. Psychohistorical Assn. (charter, sec. 1984—), Psychohistory Forum (co-foounder), Group for Psychohistorical Study of Film (founder and dir. 1989—), Inst. Psychohistory (rsch. assoc. 1976—). Democrat. Home: 266 Monroe Ave Wyckoff NJ 07481-1915 Office: NJ Div Youth/Family Svcs Bergen Dist Office 60 State St Hackensack NJ 07601-5451

LAWTON, LORILEE ANN, pipeline supply company owner, accountant; b. Morrisville, Vt., July 17, 1947; d. Philip Wyman Sr. and Margaret Elaine (Ather) Noyes; m. Lee Henry Lawton, Dec. 6, 1969; children: Deborah Ann, Jeffrey Lee. BBA, U. Vt., 1969. Sr. acct., staff asst. IBM, Essex Junction, Vt., 1969-72; owner, treas. Red-Hed Supply Inc, Colchester, Vt., 1972—; bd. dirs. Greater Burlington Indsl. Corp. Mem. Bus. Edn. Adv. Com., Colchester High Sch. Mem. Assoc. Gen. Contractors Am., Assoc. Gen. Contractors Vt., Am. Water Works Assn., Vt. Water Works Assn., New Eng. Water Works Assn., No. Vt. Homebuilders Assn., Water and Sewer Distbrs. Am. (bd. dirs., treas.). Republican. Home: 53 Middle Rd Colchester VT 05446-1118

LAWTON, WILLIAM JOHN PENSON, investment company official; b. San Francisco, Dec. 19, 1950; s. William J.P. and Harriett Jean (Frazer) L.; m. Heidi Mary Stauch, Jan. 15, 1977. BA in Econs., U. Calif., Berkeley, 1972; MA in Internat. Econs., Monterey (Calif.) Inst., 1976; MBA in Fin., Columbia U., 1981; Cert., Japanese/Am. Inst., Tokyo, 1974. Internat. banking officer Sumitomo Bank, San Francisco, 1976-80; investment officer Fireman's Fund Ins., San Francisco, 1982-84; trading mgr. First Interstate Bank, L.A., 1984-87; chief investment officer Nikko Capital Mgmt., N.Y.C., 1987—. Author: Interest Rate Comparisons, 1989; contbr. articles to profl. jours. Named one of 1000 Most Influential, Am. Banker, 1990. Republican. Episcopalian. Office: Nikko Capital Mgmt 350 Park Ave 27th Fl New York NY 10022

LAWYER, VIVIAN MOORE, college administrator; b. Cleve., Jan. 6, 1946; d. Walter Frank and Everine (Stanton) Moore; m. Cyrus Jefferson Lawyer III, June 8, 1968; children: Lenaye Lynne, Sonya Alyse, Cyrus Jefferson IV, Stanton Moore Bosley. BS in Edn., Bowling Green U., 1967, MEd, 1969; JD, Cath. U. Am., 1981. Bar: Md. 1989. Asst. dean students Bowling Green (Ohio) U., 1967-72, dir. EEO, 1972-75; dir. Affirmative Action Montgomery Coll., Rockville, Md., 1975-89, dir. employment and devel., 1989—. Pres. Columbia chpt. Jack & Jill of Am., Inc., 1989-91; treas. Longfellow Elem. PTA, Columbia, 1989-91; participant Howard County Leaders Program, 1991—. Recipient Outstanding Woman award First Bapt. Ch. of Guilford, Columbia, 1986. Mem. ABA, Md. Assn. Affirmative Action Officers (pres. 1989-91), Waring Mitchell Law Soc., Nat. Forum for Black Pub. Adminstrs., Delta Sigma Theta. Office: Montgomery Coll 900 Hungerford Dr Ste 130 Rockville MD 20850-1740

LAX, JAMES DAVID, internist, gastroenterologist, educator; b. N.Y.C., Jan. 28, 1954; s. Peter and Anneli (Kahn) L.; m. Jocelyn Brown, Sept. 11, 1982; children: Thomas, Jean, Timothy, Emile, Pierre Henri. BA, Columbia U., 1976; MD, NYU, 1981. Diplomate Am. Bd. Internal Medicine, Am. Bd. Gastroenterology. Intern Roosevelt-St. Luke's Hosp., 1981-82, resident, 1982-84, fellow in gastroenterology, 1984-86; pvt. practice N.Y.C., 1986—; clin. instr. medicine Columbia U. Med. Ctr., N.Y.C., 1986—. Contbr. articles to med. jours. Mem. ACP. Democrat. Office: 160 E 72d St New York NY 10024

LAX, MELVIN, theoretical physicist; b. Bklyn., Mar. 8, 1922; s. Morris and Rose H. L.; m. Judith Heckelman, June 26, 1949; children: R. Laurie, David A, Jonathan R., Naomi A. B.A. in Physics (Charles Hayden scholar 1938-42), NYU, 1942; M.S. in Physics; M.S. (fellow in applied math. 1942-43), MIT, 1943, Ph.D. (fellow in physics 1943-46, research asso. 1946-47), 1947. Mem. faculty Syracuse (N.Y.) U., 1947-55, Princeton U., 1961, Oxford (Eng.) U., 1961-62; mem. tech. staff Bell Labs., Murray Hill, N.J., 1955-72; head theoretical physics research dept. Bell Labs., 1962-64, cons., 1972—; mem. faculty CCNY, 1971—, Disting. prof. physics, 1971—; cons. to govt. and industry. Author books and numerous papers in field; bd. editors Phys. Rev., 1958-60, 84-86; editor: Advanced Series in Applied Physics, 1988—; mem. adv. bd. Modern Physics Letters, Internat. Jour. Modern Physics. Fellow Am. Phys. Soc. (publs. com. 1980-83); mem. NAS (sec. applied scis., math. and engring. class), Optical Soc. Am. (publs. tech. com. 1992—). Jewish. Home: 12 High St Summit NJ 07901-2413 Office: CCNY 138th St and Convent Ave New York NY 10031

LAY, CHRISTOPHER DAVID, defense and national security analyst; b. Houston, Nov. 9, 1946; s. Carl Franklin and Maurine L. BS in Physics and Math., Tex. Christian U., 1969; MA in Nat. Security Studies, Georgetown U., 1985. Rsch. engr. Martin Marietta Corp., Denver, 1970-72; legis. and adminstrv. asst. U.S. Congress, Washington, 1973-81; staff asst. undersec. def. rsch. and engring. U.S. Dept. Def., Washington, 1982-84; dep. dir. congl. affairs U.S. Arms Control & Disarmament Agy., Washington, 1984-86; spl. asst. to undersec. def. for policy U.S. Dept. Def., Washington, 1986-88; mgr. policy-requirements analysis Lockheed Missiles & Space Co., Washington, 1989—. Vol. Citizens for Reagan, 1976, Reagan for Pres., 1980; exec. com. Young Rep. Nat. Fedn., 1973-75. Mem. AIAA, U.S. Strategic Inst.

Methodist. Office: Lockheed Missiles & Space 1725 Jefferson Davis Hwy Ste 300 Arlington VA 22202

LAY-DOPYERA, MARGARET ZOE, early childhood and elementary education educator; b. Warren County, Pa., Apr. 18, 1931; d. Darell Hillard and Berdena (Smith) Lay; m. John Edward Dopyera, Oct. 26, 1978. BS, Edinboro State U., 1952; MEd, Pa. State U., 1958; EdD, U. Fla., 1967. Elem. tchr. Jamestown (N.Y.) Pub. Schs., 1952-57; instr. Pa. State Univ., University Park, Pa., 1957-58; asst./assoc. prof. Antioch Coll., Yellow Springs, Ohio, 1958-65; asst. prof. to prof. early childhood and elem. edn. Syracuse (N.Y.) Univ., 1967—, assoc. dean for acad. programs, 1985-88. Author: (textbook) Becoming a Teacher of Young Children, 1977, 2d edit., 1981, 3d edit., 1987, 4th edit., 1990, 5th edit., 1993. Mem. Nat. Assn. for Edn. Young Children (tchr. edn. panel 1989—), Nat. Assn. for Early Childhood Tchr. Educators (bd. mem. 1984-87), Am. Edn. Rsch. Assn. Democrat. Unitarian Universalist. Home: RR 1 Box 148E Grand Valley PA 16420-9732 Office: Syracuse Univ Sch of Edn Syracuse NY 13244

LAYMAN, CLIFFORD PAUL, data processing executive; b. Schenectady, N.Y., Aug. 7, 1946; s. Clarence W. and Genevieve C. (Green) L.; m. Holly Jane D'Addurno, Oct. 18, 1986; 1 child, Emily H. BA, Ithaca (N.Y.) Coll., 1972. Sr. systems analyst N.Y. State Dept. of Audit and Control, Albany, 1973-80; dir. fiscal policy and analysis N.Y. State Office of Mental Health, Albany, 1980-85; dep. dir. E.D.P. N.Y. State Unified Ct. System, Albany, 1985-91; dir. admnisntrn. N.Y. State Div. Probation and Correctional Alternatives, Albany, 1991—. With U.S. Army, 1967-71. Home: 4 Lea Ct Niskayuna NY 12309-1953 Office: NY State Unified Ct System 125 Jordan Rd Troy NY 12180-8343

LAYTON, MARJORIE REBECCA, publishing manager; b. Genesee, Pa., Feb. 26, 1928; d. Max and Faith Matilda (Withey) Linza; m. Lloyd Spencer Layton, Nov. 15, 1946; children: William, Brian, Janet. AA, Auburn (N.Y.) Community Coll., 1975. Pvt. sec. G.L.F., Ithaca, N.Y., 1945-48; rsch. assoc. Chronicle Guidance Publs., Moravia, N.Y., 1966-74, asst. editor, 1974-76, assoc. editor, 1976-83, adminstrv. mktg. mgr., 1983-88, print product mgr., 1988—. Secretary, bd. dirs. Southern Cayuga Non-Profit Housing Corp., Moravia, 1979-91. Republican. Baptist. Home: 11 School St Moravia NY 13118 Office: Chronicle Guidance Publs Inc 66 Aurora St Moravia NY 13118

LAZAR, GEORGE THEODORE, orthopaedic surgeon; b. Bulgaria, Apr. 24, 1931; came to U.S., 1973; s. Theodore Raitcho and Maria George (Ianakieva) Lazarov; m. Christina Pavlova Christova, Dec. 4, 1959; 1 child, Theodore G. MD, I.P. Pavolov Inst., Plovdiv, Bulgaria, 1956. Resident orthopaedic surgery Trauma Ctr. Inst. Specialization Physicians, Children's Hosp., Kotel, Madan and Sofia, Bulgaria, 1956-60; asst. prof. othopaedics I.P. Pavlov Inst., Plovdiv, 1960-71; specialization hand Inst. Specialization Physicians, Sofia, 1963-68; surgeon Bengiasi, Libya, 1972-73, Prof. R. Judet, Paris, 1973; intern Westchester County Med. Ctr., Balt., 1974-75; resident, fellow Union Meml./Children's/Hopkins, Balt., 1975-78; pvt. practice Drs. Elias, Lazar & Assocs., Balt., 1978—. Bd. mem. Bulgarian St. George Ch., Washington, 1983. Mem. ACS, Am. Assn. Surgery Hand, Am. Soc. Surgery Hand, Am. Assn. Orthopaedic Surgeons, Balt. City Med. Soc., Johns Hopkins Club. Republican. Greek Orthodox. Office: Drs Elias Lazar & Assocs 1050 Old North Point Rd Baltimore MD 21224

LAZAR, MARK HOWARD, neurologist; b. N.Y.C., Oct. 25, 1952; s. Irving and Blanche (Goldhirsch) L. BA, Lehman Coll., 1973; MD, NYU, 1977. Intern in internal medicine SUNY Affiliated Hosps., Stonybrook, 1977-78; resident in neurology NYU Med. Ctr., 1978-81; fellow in neurology Cornell Med. Ctr., N.Y.C., 1981-82, Columbia U. Coll. Physicians & Surgeons, Neurol. Inst., 1982-83; dir. electroencephalographic and evoked potential lab. John F. Kennedy Med. Ctr., Edison, N.J., 1983-85, med. dir. muscular dystrophy clinic, 1985-86, med. dir. clin. neurophysiology labs., 1985-91; clin. instr. neurology NYU Med. Ctr., N.Y.C., 1983-91; clin. asst. prof. neurology Robert Wood Johnson Med. Sch., New Brunswick, N.J., 1985—; cons. in neurology Robert Wood Johnson Univ. Hosp., 1986—, St. Peters Med. Ctr., New Brunswick, 1986-91, John F. Kennedy Med. Ctr., 1983—. Mem. Am. Acad. Neurology, Am. Assn. for Study Headache, Am. Electroencephalographic Soc., AMA, Middlesex County Med. Soc. Republican. Jewish. Office: 573 Cranbury Rd Ste 5A East Brunswick NJ 08816-4026

LAZAR, NORMAN DONALD, pharmacist; b. Bklyn., Oct. 14, 1942; s. Louis and Frieda (Leventer) Lazarowitz; m. Sharon Lowitt Lazar, Aug. 15, 1965; children: Howard, Jason. BS, Long Island U., Bklyn., 1965. Lic. pharmacist, N.Y., N.J., Fla., Calif., Mass. Pharmacist Lowitt Labs, Inc., Arverne, N.Y., 1966-71, pres., 1971—; pres. Central Surg. Svc., Inc., Arverne, N.Y., 1981—. Pres. C. of C. of the Rockaways, Rockaway, N.Y., 1991-92; pres., dir. Kiwanis Club of the Rockaways, Rockaway, N.Y., 1987-88; v.p. Temple Beth El, Cedarhurst, N.Y., 1987-88. Recipient Rockaway Means Bus. award Rockaway Revitilization and Devel. Corp., 1990. Mem. Am. Pharm. Assn., Empire State Pharm. Assn., Nat. Assn. Retail Druggists, Knights of Pythias, Masons, Eastern Assn. Intercollegiate Football Officials, Pub. Schs. Athletic League Football Officials Assn. Republican. Jewish. Home: 324 Buckingham Rd Cedarhurst NY 11516-1109 Office: Lowitt Labs Inc 69-19 Rockaway Beach Blvd Arverne NY 11692

LAZARCHICK, MICHAEL COX, career counseling administrator; b. Chicopee, Mass., Mar. 29, 1947; s. Michael and Elsie (Cox) L.; m. Susan Jean Lacy, Jan. 2, 1981; 1 child, Aron Michael. BA, U. Miami, Coral Gables, Fla., 1968; MA, Glassboro (N.J.) State U., 1975. Cert. counselor, career counselor; registered profl. counselor, N.J. Counselor N.J. Div. Employment Svcs., Atlantic City, 1975-77; employment officer supr. N.J. Div. Employment Svcs., Pleasantville, 1978-79; counselor N.J. Dept. Labor, Atlantic City, 1980—; project coord. N.J. Career Counseling Ctrs., 1989—. Editor: N.J. Jour. Profl. Counseling, 1991. Chairperson South Jersey Employment Svcs. Cooperative for Disabled, 1986—. With USAF, 1969-71. Mem. Am. Assn. for Counseling and Devel., Assn. for Religious and Values Issues in Counseling (exec. bd. 1989—), Nat. Employment Counselors Assn. (pub. rels. com. 1984-88), N.J. Assn. for Counseling and Devel. (pres. 1983-84, exec. bd., Disting. Profl. Svc. award 1990), N.J. Assn. for Religious and Values Issues in Counseling (exec. bd., pres. 1989-91, Leadership award 1991, editor newsletter 1989—), N.J. Employment Counselors Assn. (editor newsletter 1981—, exec. bd., pres. 1981-82).

LAZAREV, GREGORY LEIVIK, software company executive, consultant; b. Moscow, U.S.S.R., Dec. 3, 1946; came to U.S., 1976; s. Leivik G. and Hanna M. (Liberman) L.; m. Inna E. Bren, June 25, 1969; children: Mark G., Katya F. MS, Inst. Steel and Alloys, Moscow, 1969; postgrad., Inst. Energy Sources, Moscow, 1969-76. Group leader Datacomp Corp., Phila., 1978-80; mgr. devel. group IDBS Inc., Phila., 1980-82; mgr. product devel. 202 Data Systems, Wayne, Pa., 1982-85; pres. Applied Logic Programming, Wynnewood, Pa., 1986—; sr. course instr. Integrated Computer Systems, L.A., 1985-89. Author: Why Prolog?, 1989; contbr. papers to profl. jours. Mem. Assn. Object-Oriented Programming, Assn. for Logic Programming, Am. Assn. for Artificial Intelligence. Office: Applied Logic Programming 262 Tomkenn Rd Wynnewood PA 19096-3328

LAZARIS, NICHOLAS G., corporate executive; b. Dixon, Ill., Sept. 26, 1950; s. George and Olga (Ktenas) L.; m. Stephanie J. Racin, June 14, 1975; children: Alexander, Katherine, Madeline. BS, MIT, 1972; MBA, Harvard U., 1975. CPA, Va. CPA Ernst & Young, Charleston, W.Va., 1975-77; asst. state treas. Charleston, 1977-78; commr. dept. employment security State of W.Va., Charleston, 1978-80; chief of staff Gov.'s Office, Charleston, 1980-85; dir. bus. devel. Barry Wright Corp., Newton, Mass., 1985-86; v.p. mktg. Wright Line Inc., Worcester, Mass., 1986-88, v.p. fin. and adminstrn., 1988-89; v.p. sales and mktg. M.W. Carr and Co., West Somerville, Mass., 1989-90, pres., chief exec. officer, 1990—. Office: MW Carr & Co 63 Gorham St Somerville MA 02144-2700

LAZARUS, ARTHUR LOUIS, psychiatrist; b. Phila., Jan. 19, 1954; s. Aaron and Lenore (Rubin) L.; m. Cheryl Ruth Barrist, June 8, 1980; children: Joshua, Karen, Heather. BA, Boston U., 1975; MD, Temple U., 1980. Diplomate Am. Bd. Psychiatry and Neurology, Am. Bd. Med. Examiners. Instr. in psychiatry Temple U. Sch. Medicine, Phila., 1984-86, asst. prof., 1986-88, clin. asst. prof., 1988-91; clin. assoc. prof. TAO, Inc., Phila., Pa., 1992—; med. dir. network svcs. TAO Inc., Phila., 1992—. Author: Neuroleptic Malignant Syndrome, 1989; editor Transactions, 1988-91. Recipient Grant in Aid Rsch., Sigma Xi, 1974, Upjohn Achievement award Temple U., 1980, AMA Physicians Recognition award AMA, 1988, 91. Mem. AMA, Alpha Omega Alpha. Democrat. Jewish. Home: 2317 Holly Ln Lafayette Hill PA 19444-2237 Office: TAO Inc 1901 Market St PO Box 15988 Philadelphia PA 19103

LAZARUS, BARRY A., urologist; b. Balt., Dec. 2, 1942; s. Louis and Gladys (Cohen) L.; m. Frances Solomon, June 26, 1965; children: Jeffrey Victor, Kate Michelle. BA, Western Md. Coll., 1964; MD, U. Md., 1968; MA, Trinity Coll., 1984. Diplomate Am. Bd. Urology. Urologist Urology Assocs. Inc., Bloomfield, Conn., 1976—; chief dep. urology Mt. Sinai Hosp., Hartford, Conn., 1986—. Scoutmaster Boy Scouts Am., West Hartford, Conn., 1983—. Maj. U.S. Army, 1970-72, Vietnam. Fellow ACS; mem. Am. Fertility Soc., Hartford County Med. Assn., Conn. State Med. Soc., Am. Urol. Assn., Orgn. Am. Historians. Office: Urology Assocs Inc 580 Cottage Grove Rd Bloomfield CT 06002

LAZARUS, GERALD SYLVAN, physician; b. N.Y.C., Feb. 16, 1939; s. Joseph W. and Marion (Goldstein) L.; m. Sandra Jacob, Sept. 3, 1961 (dec. 1985); children: Mark, Elyse, Lynne, Laura; m. Audrey Jakubowski, Apr. 7, 1990. B.A., Colby Coll., 1959; M.D., George Washington U., 1963. Intern, then resident U. Mich., Ann Arbor, 1963-64; resident in medicine U. Mich., 1964-65; NIH research asso. NIH, Bethesda, Md., 1965-68; resident in dermatology Harvard U., Cambridge, Mass., 1968-70; research fellow Strangeways Labs., Cambridge, Eng., 1970-72; assoc. prof. medicine, co-dir. dermatology tng. program Albert Einstein Med. Coll., N.Y.C., 1972-75; J. Lamar Callaway prof. Duke U., Durham, N.C., 1977-82; chief dermatology Duke U., 1975-82; Milton B. Hartzell prof. U. Pa. Sch. Medicine, Phila., 1982—, chmn. dept. dermatology, 1982—; mem. study sect. NIH, 1976-80. Author: (with L. Goldsmith) Diagnosis of Skin Disease, 1980, (with Herman Beerman) Tradition of Excellance: History of Dermatology at Univ. Pa. Sch. of Medicine; asso. editor: Jour. Investigative Dermatology, 1977-82; contbr. numerous articles to profl. jours. Served with USPHS, 1965-68. Carl Herzog fellow Am. Dermatology Assn., 1970-72; John Simon Guggenheim fellow U. Geneva, 1986; sr. investigator Arthritis Found., 1972-77; grantee NIH. Fellow ACP, Assn. Am. Physicians, Am. Soc. Clin. Investigation; mem.Am. Dermatol. Assn., Soc. Investigative Dermatology (dir.), Biochem. Soc., Am. Acad. Dermatology (Sultzberger award 1986). Republican. Jewish. Office: U Pa Sch Medicine 221 Clin Rsch Bldg Dermatology 422 Curie Blvd Philadelphia PA 19104-6140

LAZARUS, JOAN A., business executive; b. Newark, Sept. 22, 1929; d. Louis Henry and Jeanette (Flitman) Alter; m. Barry Lazarus, Sept. 22, 1951; children: Linda, Amy, Leslie. BS, Stern Sch., 1951. Acct. Monument Industries, Bennington, Vt., 1971-74; office mgr. DGM, Inc., Saxtons River, Vt., 1975-79; v.p. Fall Mountain Furniture, Inc., Templeton, Mass., 1979—.

LAZARUS, ROCHELLE BRAFF, advertising executive; b. N.Y.C., Sept. 1, 1947; d. Lewis L. and Sylvia Ruth (Eisenberg) Braff; m. George M. Lazarus, Mar. 22, 1970; children: Theodore, Samantha, Benjamin. AB, Smith Coll., 1968; MBA, Columbia U., 1970. Product mgr. Clairol, N.Y.C., 1970-71; account exec. Ogilvy & Mather, N.Y.C., 1971-73, account supr., 1973-77, mgmt. supr., 1977-84, sr. v.p., 1981—, account group dir., 1984-87; gen. mgr. Ogilvy & Mather Direct, N.Y.C., 1987-88, mng. dir., 1988-89, pres., 1989-91; pres. Ogilvy & Mather, N.Y.C., 1991—. Mem. Smith Coll. Career Counseling Bd., Northampton, Mass., 1978—. Recipient YWCA Women Achievers award 1985. Mem. Am. Assn. Adv. Agys. (ea. div., adv. ednl. found., Ann Taylor bd. dirs.), Advt. Women N.Y., Women's Direct Mktg. Group, Direct Mktg. Assn. Home: 530 E 86th St New York NY 10028-7535 Office: Ogilvy & Mather Direct Worldwide Pla 309 W 49th St New York NY 10019-7316

LAZINSKY, JO ANNE MARIE, advertising executive; b. Bklyn.; d. Guy A. and Lillian (Chiarello) Cimino. Student, Duquesne U., 1960-62; BA cum laude, St. John's U., Jamaica, N.Y., 1964. Cert. in secondary edn. English tchr. Wantagh (N.Y.) High Sch., 1964-65; advt. media analyst Advt. Info. Services, N.Y.C., 1965-66; editor, copywriter J.C. Penney Co., Inc., N.Y.C., 1973-76; editor Avon Products, Inc., N.Y.C., 1976-79; advt. copywriter Conklin, Labs & Bebee, Syracuse, N.Y., 1980-83; advt. mgr. Will & Baumer Candle Co., Syracuse, 1983-84; sales promotion supr. Carrier Corp. div. United Techs., Syracuse, 1984-85; advt. cons. Liverpool, N.Y., 1985-87; copy chief New England Bus. Svc., Inc., Groton, Mass., 1987-91, assoc. advt. mgr. div. mktg. products, 1991—. Contbg. editor style guide for Avon Products Co., Inc., 1977-78; contbr. articles to newspapers and various trade jours. Mem. bd. mgrs. North Area Syracuse YMCA, 1981-86, mem. mktg. com., 1984-85. Recipient Advt. award Assn. of Advt. Agys. Internat., 1982. Mem. New England Direct Mktg. Assn. Home: 13L Bonnie Ln Derry NH 03038-4009 Office: New England Bus Svc Inc Div Mktg Products 500 Main St Groton MA 01471

LAZORCHAK, JOSEPH MICHAEL, economist; b. Paterson, N.J., June 7, 1957; s. Michael and Lena Madeline (Nejmeh) L. BS, Montclair State Coll., 1979; MA, Fordham U., 1980. Asst. staff mgr. AT&T, Basking Ridge, N.J., 1980-83; mem. tech. staff bus. rsch. Bellcore, Livingston, N.J., 1984-86; mem. tech. staff ops. technology Bellcore, Morristown, N.J., 1987—. Mem. Am. Econ. Assn. Republican. Roman Catholic. Office: Bellcore 435 South St Morristown NJ 07960-6422

LEAB, DANIEL JOSEF, history educator; b. Berlin, Aug. 29, 1936; s. Leo and Herta (Marcus) L.; B.A., Columbia U., 1957, M.A., 1961, Ph.D., 1969; m. Katharine Kyes, Aug. 16, 1964; children—Abigail Elizabeth, Constance Martha, Marcus Rogers. With Columbia U., 1966-73, Seton Hall, 1974—; pub., co-editor Am. Book Prices Current; mng. editor Labor History; dir. Bancroft-Parkman; cons. AEC, 1972-73; sr. Fulbright lectr., 1977, 86-87. Fellow Met. Mus. Art. NEH fellow, 1981. Mem. Am. Hist. Assn., AAUP, Orgn. Am. Historians. Clubs: Century, Grolier. Author: A Union of Individuals, 1970; From Sambo to Superspade: the Black and Film, 1975; The Auction Companion, 1981; The Labor History Reader, 1985. Home: PO Box 1216 Washington Depot CT 06793-0216

LEACH, HARRISON LANGFORD, retail executive; b. Fayette County, Ga., May 7, 1923; s. Roy Hugh and M. Jewell (Moody) L.; m. Sylvia Wynn, May 27, 1967 (div. 1987); children: Jalah, Brooke, Kim, Dawn, Joy; m. Fay Wykhuis, July 11, 1987. Grad., West Ga. Coll., 1942; postgrad., Ga. Tech. U., 1947-50. Lic. comml. pilot. Sales rep. Rexall Drug Co., 1951-53; dist. mgr. Rexall Drug Co., N.Y., 1956-63; owner, mgr. S.E.A. Distbrs., Atlanta, 1964-67; v.p. Gilpin Drug Co., Washington, 1967-79; exec. dir. Circle Drug Inc., Washington, 1979—. Lt. USN, 1942-46, 53-55. Republican. Episcopalian. Home: 15518 Royal Crescent Ct Dumfries VA 22026-1071 Office: Circle Drug Inc 8401 Corporate Dr Ste 660 Landover MD 20785

LEACH, JOAN GENEVIEVE, information service executive; b. New Brunswick, N.J., Jan. 15, 1941; d. Andrew J. and Irma (Chato) Stasik; m. Thomas E. Leach, July 23, 1960; children: Thomas, Merrill, Craig. BA with high honors, Douglass Coll., 1962; MBA, Rutgers U., Newark, N.J., 1987. Prodn. coordinator and paste-up artist Angel Advt. Assocs., Manville, N.J., 1972-75; freelance copy editor Behavioral Publs., Inc., N.Y.C., 1970-76; paste-up artist Hermitage Press, Trenton, N.J., 1976-77; freelance copy editor Haworth Press, N.Y.C., 1974-79; co-owner, pres. Capitol Information Svc., Inc., Trenton, N.J., 1978—. Mem. Somerset County (N.J.) Commn. on Women, 1988-91. Mem. NAFE, N.J. Assn. Womenn Bus. Owners (bd. dirs. hosp. chmn. Somerset chpt. 1989—), N.J. Assn. Pub. Records Search Cos., Phi Beta Kappa, Sigma Delta Pi. Roman Catholic.

LEACH, LYNNE E., nursing educator; b. Ridley Park, Pa., July 24, 1949; d. David J. and Mildred Elizabeth (Wynn) Fleming; m. Joseph P. Leach. RN, Bryn Mawr Hosp. Sch. Nursing, Pa., 1970; BS in Edn., Millersville (Pa.) U., 1975; MS, U. Del., Newark, 1983; postgrad., Widener U., Chester, Pa., 1990—. Staff nurse Queen's Med. Ctr., Honolulu, 1972, Crozer-Chester Med. Ctr., Upland, Pa., 1970-71, 72-76; instr. nursing Bryn Mawr Hosp. Sch. Nursing, 1976-80; asst. prof. nursing Widener U., Chester, 1983—. Mem. NAACOG (edn. coord. Pa. sect. 1985-87, coord. Delco chpt. 1987-88, sec.-treas. Pa. sect. 1988-90, chair Pa. sect. 1991—, dist. III adv. coun. 1988—), Sigma Theta Tau.

LEACH, MARY MOYNIHAN, academic administrator; b. Lawrence, Mass., Nov. 8, 1943; d. Joseph Daniel and Margaret Lawn (Byrne) M.; m. Ronald Jacob Leach, Aug. 29, 1965; children: John Stephen, Anne Teresa, David Louis. AB, Merrimack Coll., 1964; PhD, U. Md., 1973. Asst. prof. math., dir. learning resources ctr. U. Md. Baltimore County, Balt., 1978-84; ACE fellow U. Md. System, Adelphi, 1982-83, spl. asst. to exec. v.p., 1983-84; asst. to pres. U. Md. Baltimore County, Balt., 1984-88; asst. to chancellor U. Md. System, Adelphi, 1988—; cons. Nat. Fire Acad., Hagerstown, Md., 1978-82, Balt. City Pub. Schs., 1975-80. Author: Statistics, 1978, Logic with Computer Applications, 1976. Bd. dirs. Women's Ordination Conf. Fellow Am. Coun. on Edn., 1982-83; NSF grantee, 1979-80, 80-81, grantee U.S. Office Edn., 1979-82. Democrat. Roman Catholic. Home: 10 E Lee St Unit 2101 Baltimore MD 21202-6008 Office: U Md System 3300 Metzerott Rd Hyattsville MD 20783-1600

LEACH, ROBERT ELLIS, physician, educator; b. Sanford, Maine, Nov. 25, 1931; s. Ellis and Estella (Tucker) L.; m. Laurine Seber, Aug. 20, 1955; children: Cathy, Brian, Michael, Craig, Karen, Diane. A.B., Princeton U., 1953; M.D., Columbia U., 1957. Resident orthopedic surgery U. Minn., 1957-62; orthopedic surgeon Lahey Clinic, Boston, 1964-68; chmn. dept. Lahey Clinic, 1968-70; prof., chmn. dept. Boston U. Med. Sch., 1970—; lectr. Tufts U. Med. Sch., Medford, Mass., 1971—; head physician U.S. Olympic Team, 1984; chmn. sports medicine council U.S. Olympic Com., 1984—. Editor-in-chief Am. J. Sports Med.; contbr. articles to profl. jours. Served to lt. comdr. USNR, 1962-64. Am., Brit., Canadian Orthopedic Travelling fellow, 1971. Mem. Am. Acad. Orthopedic Surgeons, Continental Orthopedic Soc. (sec. 1966—), Am. Orthopedic Assn. (pres. elect 1993), Am. Orthopedic Soc. Sports Medicine (pres. 1983). Club: Longwood Cricket (Brookline). Home: 40 Rockport Rd Weston MA 02193-1428 Office: 75 E Newton St Roxbury MA 02118-2347

LEADER, ALAN H., thread company executive; b. N.Y.C., Feb. 6, 1938; s. Julius A. and Edna Rhoda (Silverman) L.; m. Bernice Jean Kramer, July 31, 1966; children: Anne Beth, Audrey Dale. BA, Brown U., 1958; MBA, Columbia U., 1960. V.p. Leader Thread Corp., N.Y.C., 1960-81, pres., 1981—. Commr. Wayne Township Zoning Bd., 1977-78, vice chmn., 1979, chmn., 1980; mem. Blue Ribbon Master Plan Com., 1976-89. Democrat. Jewish. Office: Leader Thread Corp 555 8th Ave New York NY 10018-4308

LEADER, BERNICE KRAMER, art consulting company executive; b. N.Y.C., Nov. 18, 1938; d. Stanley Julius and Anne Helen (Benedick) Kramer; m. Alan Harvey Leader, July 31, 1966; children: Anne Beth, Audrey Dale. BA magna cum laude, Barnard Coll., 1959; MA, Columbia U., 1962, MPhil, 1977, PhD, 1980; cert. in bus. adminstrn. Careers in Bus. Program, NYU, 1981. Teaching asst. Barnard Coll., Columbia U., N.Y.C., 1961; instr. art history Fashion Inst. Tech., N.Y.C., 1969-71, Wayne (N.J.) Adult Sch., 1973-79, Fairleigh Dickinson U., Rutherford, N.J., 1980-81, Ramapo Coll., Mahwah, N.J., 1980-81, Cooper Union, N.Y.C., 1980-81; assoc. prof. art history SUNY, Stony Brook, 1981; dir. ops. Kennedy Sinclaire Inc., Wayne, 1982-83; supr. graphics prodn. Timeplex Inc., Woodcliff Lakes, N.J., 1984-86; pres. Leader Assocs., Wayne, 1987—. Author exhbn. catalogue entries; contbr. articles to profl. jours. Mem. Friends Wayne Pub. Libr., 1984-86. Grantee Columbia U., 1962, Smithsonian Instn., 1978, Woodrow Wilson Found., 1978. Mem. Nat. Assn. Corp. Art Mgrs., N.J. Bus. Network, N.J. Network Bus. and Profl. Women (newsletter columnist 1988-91, trustee 1989-90), Mensa, Phi Beta Kappa. Office: 7 Nottingham Rd Wayne NJ 07470-3246

LEAF, ALEXANDER, physician, educator; b. Yokohama, Japan, Apr. 10, 1920; came to U.S., 1922, naturalized, 1936; s. Aaron L. and Dora (Hural) L.; m. Barbara Louise Kincaid, Oct. 1943; children—Caroline Joan, Rebecca Louise, Tamara Jean. B.S., U. Wash., 1940; M.D., U. Mich., 1943; M.A., Harvard, 1961. Intern Mass. Gen. Hosp., Boston, 1943-44; mem. staff Mass. Gen. Hosp., 1949—, physician-in-chief, 1966-81; resident Mayo Found., Rochester, Minn., 1944-45; research fellow U. Mich., 1947-49; practice internal medicine Boston, 1949-90; faculty Med. Sch., Harvard, 1949—, Jackson prof. clin. medicine, 1966-81, Ridley Watts prof. preventive medicine, 1980-90, chmn. dept. preventive medicine and clin. epidemiology, 1980-90, Jackson prof. emeritus clin. medicine, 1990—; Disting. physician VA Medical Ctr. Brockton/W. Roxbury Hosps., Boston, 1992—. Served to capt. M.C. AUS, 1945-46. Recipient Outstanding Achievement award U. Minn., 1964; vis. fellow Balliol Coll., Oxford, 1971-72; Guggenheim fellow, 1971-72; named Disting. Physician, VA, 1991—. Fellow Am. Acad. Arts and Scis.; mem. NAS, Inst. Medicine, ACP (master), Am. Soc. Clin. Investigation (past pres.), Am. Physiol. Soc., Biophys. Soc., Assn. Am. Physicians. Home: 1 Curtis Cir Winchester MA 01890-1703 Office: Mass Gen Hosp Boston MA 02114

LEAHY, CHARLES FARRINGTON, lawyer; b. Claremont, N.H., Feb. 27, 1935; s. Albert D. and Helen (Farrington) L.; m. Barbara Shimanski, June 18, 1960 (div. June 1975); children: Mary Siobhan Leahy Ulrich, Charles Farrington Jr., Matthew Edward, Susan B. Leahy Gummere, Jonathan Norton; m. Mary Susan Stein, Oct. 22, 1977. Bar: N.H. 1963, U.S. Dist. Ct. N.H. 1963, U.S. Supreme Ct. 1967, U.S. Tax Ct. 1970, U.S. Ct. Appeals (1st cir.) 1971. Mem. Orr and Reno, P.A., Concord, N.H., 1963—; of counsel to gov. State of N.H., 1971-72; chmn. Long Range Planning Task Force N.H. Supreme Ct., 1988-90; bd. dirs. Fidelity Bank & Trust Co., Salem, N.H., Chubb Securities Corp., Concord, Hampshire Funding Inc., Concord; adj. faculty U Maine Law Sch., Portland. Mem. bd. editors Harvard U. Law Rev., 1962-63. Trustee St. Mary's in-the-Mountains, Bethlehem, N.H., 1966-71; mem. bd. edn., Concord, 1977-82; mem. bd. visitors Antioch/New England Grad. Sch., Keene, N.H., 1981-90; mem. bd. govs. N.H. Pub. TV, Durham, 1986—. Spl. agt. U.S. Army Mil. Intelligence, 1957-60. Fellow Am. Coll. of Probate and Estate Counsel; mem. ABA, Am. Law Inst., N.H. Bar Assn. Republican. Episcopalian. Office: Orr and Reno PA 1 Eagle Sq # 709 Concord NH 03301-4903

LEAHY, KEITH W., insurance professional, singer, songwriter; b. Southington, Conn., June 13, 1961; s. Thomas Howard and Ann Marie (Venditto) L.; m. Marissa Ann Leahy, Aug. 16. Student, Cen. Conn. U., 1981-83, U. Bridgeport, 1983. Ins. adjustor Toensmeier Adjustment Svc., Prospect, Conn., 1985-87, Frank B. Hull Co., Hartford, Conn., 1987-89; sr. adjustor Orion Capital Co., West Hartford, Conn., 1989-90; ins. mgr. Alexsis Inc., Hartford, 1991—; owner, mgr. Messenger Prodns./Recording Studio, New Britain, Conn., 1990—; songwriter, performer RSPN Prodn. Co., Nashville, 1990-91; assoc. prof. corr. course in songwriting UCLA. Vocalist album Kindom/Serious, 1991. Home: 92 Rockyhill Ave New Britain CT 06051 Office: Alexsis Inc PO Box 5048 Hartford CT 06102-5048

LEAHY, PATRICK JOSEPH, senator; b. Montpelier, Vt., Mar. 31, 1940; s. Howard and Alba (Zambon) L.; m. Marcelle Pomerleau, Aug. 25, 1962; children: Kevin, Alicia, Mark. B.A., St. Michael's Coll., Vt., 1961; J.D., Georgetown U., 1964. Bar: Vt. 1964, U.S. Supreme Ct. 1964, D.C. 1979, U.S. Ct. Appeals (2d cir.). State's atty. Chittenden County, Vt., 1966-75; U.S. senator from Vt., 1975—, chmn. com. on agrl., nutrition and forestry, mem. com. on apporiations, chmn. jud. subcom. tech. and law, chmn. jud. subcom. tech. and law; mem. judiciary com., chmn. fgn. ops. subcom., mem. appropriations com., mem. appropriations com., vice chmn. senate intelligence com., 1985-86. Mem. Nat. Dist. Attys. Assn. (v.p. 1971-74). Office: US Senate 433 Russell Senate Office Bldg Washington DC 20510

LEAHY, ROBERT DAVID, communications executive; b. Arlington, Va., Feb. 17, 1952; s. Robert David Joseph and Margaret Ellen (Kennedy) L.; m. Eliabeth Ann McCahey, Jan. 15, 1959. BA in Polit. Sci. cum laude, Loyola U., New Orleans, 1974; MA in Internat. Rels., Johns Hopkins U., 1976; postgrad., MIT, 1976-77, NYU, 1984; PhD, Brandeis U., 1976-78. Mem. overseas liaison com. Am. Coun. on Edn., Washington, 1974-76; staff mem. U.S. Dept. Labor, Washington, 1978-79; staff writer Congl. Quar. Inc., Washington, 1979-80; rsch. dir. Ernest Wittenberg Assocs. Inc., Washington, 1980-81; v.p. The Hannaford Co., Inc. (formerly Deaver & Hannaford, Inc.), Washington, 1981-84, Padilla and Speer, Inc., N.Y.C., 1984-85; dir. pub. and media rels. Internat. Telecommunications Satellite Orgn., Washington, 1985-87; v.p. corp. communications Andal Corp., N.Y.C., 1987-89; dir. media

communications Internat. Paper, Purchase, N.Y., 1989—. Mem. Nat. Investor Rels. Inst., Internat. Assn. Bus. Communicators, Pub. Rels. Soc. Am., Nat. Press Club., World Affairs Coun., Am. Polit. Sci. Assn., Am. Soc. Internat. Law, Ctr. for the Study of the Presidency, Univ. Club. (Washington), Georgetown Club (Washington). Republican. Episcopalian. Home: 320 Strawberry Hill Ave # 9 Stamford CT 06902-2580 Office: Internat Paper Two Manhattanville Rd New York NY 10577

LEAHY, ROBERT LOUIS, psychologist; b. Alexandria, Va., Mar. 8, 1946; s. James J. and Lillian (DeVita) L.; m. Helen Butleroff, Aug. 8, 1987. BA, Yale U., 1967, MS, 1972, MPhil, 1972, PhD, 1974. Lic. psychologist, N.Y., Pa. Postdoctoral fellow dept. psychiatry U. Pa. Med. Sch., Phila., 1982-83; assoc. prof. New Sch. for Social Rsch., N.Y.C., 1976-81; vis. assoc. prof. U. B.C., Vancouver, 1981-82; assoc. prof. Hofstra U., Hempstead, N.Y., 1984-86; assoc. clin. prof. dept. psychiatry N.Y. Hosp.-Cornell Med., N.Y.C., 1991—; dir. Am. Inst. for Cognitive Therapy, N.Y.C., 1985—. Editor: Development of the Self, 1985, Child's Construction of Social Inequality, 1983; contbr. articles to profl. jours. NIMH grantee, 1976-79. Mem. Am. Psychol. Assn., Assn. for Advancement of Behavior Therapy. Republican. Office: Am Inst for Cognitive Therapy 30 E 60th St Ste 1007 New York NY 10022-1008

LEAHY, THOMAS FRANCIS, broadcasting executive; b. N.Y.C., June 30, 1937; m. Patricia B. Flanagan, May 5, 1962; children: Patricia Ann, Allison Marie, Thomas Francis, Kirsten Elizabeth, Caitlin Coxe. B of Elec. Engring., Manhattan Coll., 1959; D. Comml. Sci. (hon.), St. John's U., Jamaica, N.Y., 1983. With CBS-TV, N.Y.C., 1962—; exec. v.p. CBS/Broadcast Group, N.Y.C., 1981-86; pres. CBS-TV Network, N.Y.C., 1987-88, Mktg. div. CBS, N.Y.C., 1988-90; sr. v.p. CBS Broadcast Group, N.Y.C., 1990—. Past mem. exec. com. N.Y.'s Better Bus. Bur.; past trustee Fordham Prep. Sch., Stonehill Coll.; mem. Mayor's Mid-Town Com., Assn. for a Better N.Y.; foundind dir. Youth Suicide Nat. Ctr., Washington; bd. dirs., exec. com. Just Say No Internat., Oakland, Calif.; past bd. dirs. Found. Ind. Higher Edn. Inc., Am. Edn. Fedn., Big Bros. N.Y., Red Cross of Greater N.Y.; grad. dir., past mem. exec. com., mem. campaign revs. com., Advt. Coun., Inc.; bd. dirs. Advt. Ednl. Found., Inc. Am. Advt. Fedn. Recipient Nat. Disting. Achievement in Communications award Am. Jewish Com., 1985, Joseph E. Connor Meml. award Phi Alpha Tau, Emerson Coll., Boston, 1986. Mem. NATAS (past pres. internat. coun.), Network TV Assn. (chmn. 1990—), Am. Irish Hist. Soc. (exec. coun.), Siwanoy Country Club, Met. Club. Office: CBS Broadcast Group 51 W 52nd St New York NY 10019-6101

LEAK, LEE VIRN, cell biologist; b. Chesterfield, S.C., July 22, 1932; s. Robert Lincoln and Lucille Elizabeth (Moore) L.; m. Eleanor Carrol Merrick, July 11, 1964; children: Alice Elizabeth, Lee Virn Jr. BS, S.C. State Coll., 1954; PhD, Mich. State U., 1962. Asst. prof. Mich. State U., Lansing, 1962; rsch. fellow Harvard Med. Sch., Boston, 1962-64, instr. dept. anatomy, 1965-67, asst. prof. dept. anatomy, 1967-71; prof., chmn. dept. anatomy Howard U., Washington, 1971-81, rsch. prof., 1983—; mem. anat. sci. tng. com. NIH, Bethesda, Md., 1972-73; mem. anatomy test com. Nat. Bd. Med. Examiners, Phila., 1973-76; adv. coun. Nat. Heart Lung Inst., NIH, Bethesda, 1982-86. Contbr. chpt.: Handbuch der Allgemeine Pathologie, 1972, Inflammatory Process, 1974, Respiratory Defense Mechanisms, 1977, Blood Vessel and Lymphatics in Organ Systems, 1984, The Lungs, Scientific Foundations, 1991. Pres. Md. Grape Growers Assn., 1983, Md. Angus Assn., 1991; regional v.p. Md.-D.C. Am. Wine Soc., 1980-83. 1st lt. U.S. Army, 1954-56. Grantee Nat. Inst. Allergy and Infectious Diseases/NIH, 1966-85, Nat. Heart Lung and Blood Inst./NIH, 1971-86, Nat. Inst. Gen. Med. Scis./NIH, 1974-84, NSF, 1990-93; recipient Ardelle Melbourne rsch. award Am. Heart Assn., 1989-91. Mem. Am. Assn. Anatomists (bd. dirs. 1965—), Am. Physiol. Soc., Am. Soc. Cell Biology, Internat. Soc. Lymphology, N.Am. Soc. Lymphology, Microcirculatory Soc. Office: Coll Medicine Howard Univ 520 W St NW Washington DC 20059-0001

LEAMAN, J. RICHARD, JR., paper company executive; b. Lancaster, Pa., Sept. 22, 1934; s. J. Richard and Margaret B. (Leaman); m. Helen Brown, June 15, 1957; children: Lynda B., J. Richard, III. BA, Dartmouth Coll., 1956, MBA, 1957; PhD (hon.), Widener U., 1988. With Scott Paper Co., Phila., 1960—, v.p. comml. products, 1975-78; exec. v.p. mktg. and sales Scott Paper Co., 1978—, pres. Packaged Products div., 1983—, dir., 1986; pres. Scott Worldwide, 1986; vice chmn. Scott Paper Co., 1991—; pres. S.D. Warren Co. div. Scott Paper, 1991—; bd. dirs. Church & Dwight Co., Inc., Pep Boys. Vice chmn. exec. com., trustee Widener U., 1987; mem. conf. bd.'s coun. Global Bus. Mgmt.; trustee Tyler Arboretum. Capt. USAF, 1957-61. Recipient Disting. Performance in Mgmt. award Widener U. Mem. Am. Paper Inst. (internat. bus. com.), Conf. Bd.'s Coun. on Global Bus. Mgmt. Republican. Episcopalian. Clubs: Dartmouth (Phila.); Rose Tree Media Optimists. Home: 317 Boot Rd Malvern PA 19355-3317 Office: Scott Paper Co Scott Pla Philadelphia PA 19113

LEAN, JEROME HOWARD, sales executive; b. Phila., Mar. 1, 1945; s. Samuel H. and Lucille (Roseman) L.; m. Sheryl Rosenman, Nov. 28, 1971; children: David, Michael, Brett. BS, Pa. State U., 1966. Staff acct. Coopers & Lybrand, Phila., 1967-69; stockbroker DuPont & Co., Phila., 1970-72; leasing exec., v.p. HBE Leasing, Phila., 1973-81; v.p. leasing Copelco Leasing Co., Pennsauken, N.J., 1982—. With USAF, 1967-73. Home: 12 Banner Rd Cherry Hill NJ 08003-1515 Office: Copelco Leasing Co 1 Mediq Plz Pennsauken NJ 08110-1439

LEAR, GAIL HOLLENBECK, college administrator; b. Long Beach, Calif., Mar. 12, 1951; d. Floyd Lee Hollenbecak and Barbara Breck (Neathery) Margolis; m. John Louis Lear, July 6, 1991; 1 child, Dorian LoBato. BS in Human Resources, U. Del., 1987. Adminstrv. aide Del. Tech. and Community Coll., Dover, 1977-81; statewide housing coord. State Div. Mental Health, Wilmington, 1986-88; allocations assoc. United Way of Del., Wilmington, 1981-86, 88-89; dir. admissions Goldey-Beacom Coll., Wilmington, 1989—; speaker in field. Instr. Del. Safety Coun., Wilmington, 1989-91; v.p. Del. Health Coun., Wilmington, 1979-82; bd. dirs. Del. Guidance Svcs., Wilmington, 1987. Mem. Kiwanis Club of Wilmington West (pres. 1991—). Office: Goldey-Beacom Coll 4701 Limestone Rd Wilmington DE 19808-1927

LEAR, PHILLIP EPHRIAN, surgeon, educator; b. New Haven, Dec. 7, 1905. B.S., Yale U., 1926; M.D., State U. N.Y, 1934. Diplomate Am. Bd. Surgery, 1940. Intern. 1934-35; then resident in surgery; then practice medicine specializing in surgery, Bklyn.; asst. in surgery Health Sci. Ctr. Bklyn., 1934-35, instr. surgery, 1935-39, asst. prof., 1939-42, assoc. prof., 1942-48, prof. clin. surgery, 1948—; mem. staff including chmn. emeritus surgery, L.I. Jewish Med. Ctr. and Queens Gen. Hosp., N.Y., 1970—; cons. Bklyn.-Caledonian, Bklyn. Vets., L.I. Coll., St. Johns Episc. hosps. Recipient Dudley Meml. medal for best surgical thesis; Master Tchrs. award; Frank L. Babbott award. Phillip E. Lear Lectureship in Surgery established in his honor, 1982. Fellow ACS (bd. govs. 1961-70); mem. Alpha Omega Alpha. Home: 50 Nassau Dr Great Neck NY 11021-1441 Office: LI Jewish Med Ctr Manhasset Div 1554 Northern Blvd Manhasset NY 11030-3006

LEARN, RICHARD LELAND, corrections school principal; b. New Kensington, Pa., Nov. 29, 1955; s. Leland Leroy Learn and Gendolyn Leora (Furman) George; m. Rosamond Amelia Kautz, July 31, 1982. BS in Music Edn., Indiana U. of Pa., 1977, MA in Adult/Community Edn., 1984; PhD in Edn., U. Pitts., 1991. Adult edn. instr. PIC of Westmoreland County, Greensburg, Pa., 1980-82; corrections edn. specialist Pa. State Correctional Instn., Greensburg, 1984-87; sch. prin. Pa. State Correctional Instn., Mercer, 1989—; acad. support coord. Indiana U. of Pa., 1987-89. Chmn. bd. dirs. Young Adult Handicapped, Inc., Apollo, Pa., 1980-82. Mem. ASCD, Am. Vocat. Assn., Pa. Assn. for Adult and Continuing Edn., Corrections Edn. Assn. Democrat. Presbyterian. Office: State Correctional Inst 801 Butler Pike Mercer PA 16137-9651

LEARN, RICHARD LISLE, school administrator; b. Indiana, Pa., June 1, 1935; s. Lisle W. and M. Helen (Ross) L.; div.; 1 child, Nancy Learn Storck. BS, Indiana U. of Pa., 1956, MEd, 1962; postgrad., U. Pitts., 1970. Cert. tchr., sch. bus. adminstr., Pa. Tchr. North Cambria Sch. Dist., Spangler, Pa., 1956-61; tchr. Ford City (Pa.) Union Sch. Dist., 1961-65, curriculum coord., 1965-66; acctg. supr. Armstrong Sch. Dist., Ford City, 1966-70; dir. bus. affairs Armstrong Sch. Dist., 1970-77, Sch. Dist. Lancaster, Pa., 1977-87; dir. mgmt. svcs. Chester County Intermediate Unit, Exton, Pa., 1987-91; dir. bus. affairs, sch. bd. sec. Bethlehem (Pa.) Area Sch. Dist., 1991—; pres., then v.p. Lancaster County Tax Collection Bur., 1979-87; pres. bd. govs., Pa. Ins. Consortium for Schs., Lancaster, 1981—. Contbr. articles to profl. publs. Pres., v.p. Lancaster Recreation Commn., 1980-87; football and basketball ofcl., Pa. Interscholastic Athletic Assn., Harrisburg, 1954-79. With U.S. Army, 1958-64. Mem. Assn. Sch. Bus. Ofcls. (registered adminstr., chmn. negotiations 1987—), Pa. Assn. Sch. Bus. Ofcls. (bd. dirs. 1981-88, pres. 1986-87; Gary Reeser Meml. award 1989), Pa. Sch. Bds. Assn., Rotary, Masons. Presbyterian. Home: 863 Jefferson Way West Chester PA 19380-6908 Office: Bethlehem Area Sch Dist 1516 Sycamore St Bethlehem PA 18017-6099

LEARY, CAROL ANN, academic administrator; b. Niagara Falls, N.Y., Mar. 29, 1947; d. Angelo Andrew and Mary Josephine (Pullano) Gigliotti; m. Noel Robert Leary, Dec. 30, 1972. BA, Boston U., 1969; MS, SUNY, Albany, 1970; PhD, Am. Univ., 1988. Asst. to v.p. for student affairs, dir. women's programs Siena Coll., Loudonville, N.Y., 1970-72; asst. dir. housing Boston U., 1972-78; dir. residence Simmons Coll., Boston, 1978-84, assoc. dean, 1984-85; assoc. dir. The Washington Campus, Washington, 1985-86; adminstrv. v.p., asst. to pres. Simmons Coll., Boston, 1988—. Chair, coll. and univ. devel. com. St. Francis Homeless Shelter, Boston, 1990—. Fellow SUNY, Albany, 1969-70, Am. U., 1986-88; Ednl. Policy Fellowship Program fellow, 1990-91. Mem. Coun. for the Advancement and Support of Edn., Am. Assn. Higher Edn., Am. Coun. Edn. (rep. Mass. div. 1991—), Phi Beta Kappa. Office: Simmons Coll 300 The Fenway Boston MA 02115

LEARY, GENEVIEVE LOESCH, transportation executive; b. N.Y.C., Dec. 15, 1927; d. George and Jane (Black) Loesch; m. William P. Leary, Jr., 1955 (dec. 1966); children: Brian Michael, Kevin Douglas. AB, Coll. New Rochelle, 1948; MBA, Adelphi U., 1976. Statistician A&P, N.Y.C., 1948-51; bus. editor Dun & Bradstreet, N.Y.C., 1951-55; economist Am. Petroleum Inst., N.Y.C., 1956, 59-64; rsch. dir. N.Y. Dept. Transp., Albany, 1964-71; transit commnr. Westchester County, White Plains, N.Y., 1971-76; econ. cons. Tri State Regional Planning, N.Y.C., 1975-76; transp. mgmt. staff mem. Montgomery County, Rockville, Md., 1976-87; exec. dir. Silver Spring (Md.) Transp. Mgmt. Dist., 1988—. Rep. candidate N.Y. Assembly, 1958, N.Y.C. precinct capt., 1958-66; treas. Grosvenor Park Condo II, Rockville, Md., 1982-86, 92; dir. Silver Spring C. of C. Mem. Assn. for Commuter Transp. Roman Catholic. Home: 10500 Rockville Pike Rockville MD 20852 Office: Silver Spring Transp System 8601 Georgia Ave Silver Spring MD 20910

LEARY, JAMES FRANCIS, pathology and pediatrics educator; b. Portsmouth, N.H., Apr. 12, 1948; s. Frank Joseph and Etta Myrtle (Ford) L.; m. Rosemary Conrad, May 27, 1978; children: Charles, Elaine, Selena, Michael. SB in Aeros. and Astronautics, MIT, 1970, SB in Philosophy, 1970; MS in Physics, U. N.H., 1974; PhD in Biophysics, Pa. State U., 1977. Postdoctoral fellow Los Alamos (N.Mex.) Nat. Lab., 1977-78; asst. prof. pathology U. Rochester, N.Y., 1978-83, assoc. prof. pathology and pediatrics, 1983—; dir. cell analysis and sorting facility dept. pathology, U. Rochester, 1983—. Contbr. articles to profl. jours.; patentee in field. Sch. bd. Our Sch., Rochester, 1990—; coach/asst. Penfield (N.Y.) mini league football/Penfield Little League baseball, 1990—. Mem. Internat. Soc. for Analytical Cytology, N.Y. Acad. Scis. Democrat. Unitarian. Office: U Rochester Dept Pathology PO Box 626 Rochester NY 14642-0001

LEARY, JAMES HENRY, real estate broker and executive; b. Chester, Pa., Feb. 20, 1950; s. James Henry Sr. and Mildred Mae (Barlow) L.; m. Denise Benedict, July 16, 1976; children: Summer, Lauren. Student, Temple U., 1967-69, 75-76; grad., Realtors Inst. Cert. residential specialist Residential Sales Coun., Chgo. Asst. terminal mgr. McLean Trucking Co., Aston, Pa., 1976-81; owner Rainbow Creative Graphics, Brookhaven, Pa., 1980-84; profl. firefighter City of Chester Fire Dept., Pa., 1983-87; real estate salesperson Carr Real Estate Co., Aston, 1985-87; real estate office mgr. Carr Real Estate Co., 1987-88, real estate broker, v.p., 1988—; v.p. Am. Mortgage Corp., Lansdowne, Pa., 1988—; designated spokesperson Penna Assoc. Realtors, Harrisburg, Pa., 1989—. Contbr. articles on real estate and pub. info. to area newspapers. Pres. Aston Bus. & Profl. Assn., 1988—; life mem. Realtors Polit. Action Com., Springfield, Pa., 1988—. With USN, 1969-73. Mem. Del. County Bd. Realtors, Residential Sales Coun., Residential Brokerage Coun., Pa. Assn. Realtors, Del City Bd. Realtors (edn. com. 1988—, chmn. edn. com. 1991—, standard forms com. 1991—), KC. Republican. Roman Catholic. Office: Carr Real Estate Co 892 Concord Rd Chester PA 19014-1218

LEARY, KEVIN MICHAEL, stockbroker; b. Springfield, Mass., May 21, 1955; s. Thomas D. and Marie T. (Hussey) L. BA, Holy Cross Coll., 1977; MBA, U. Notre Dame, South Bend, Ind., 1979. Fin. analyst IBM, White Plains, N.Y., 1979-82; v.p. Kidder, Peabody & Co., Inc., Boston, 1982—; trustee Harbor Towers, Boston, 1988. Mem. N.Y. Athletic Club. Office: Kidder Peabody 100 Federal St Boston MA 02110-1904

LEARY, THOMAS PATRICK, dean; b. Kingston, Pa., Aug. 22, 1951; s. John Joseph and Mary (Graham) L.; m. Margaret, Feb. 17, 1979; 1 child, Patrick. BA, King's Coll., 1973; MA, U. Scranton, 1976; postgrad., Temple U., 1980-82. Asst. dir. admissions Luzerne County Community Coll., Nanticoke, Pa., 1974-76, assoc. dir. admissions, registrar, 1977-80, dir. admissions, registrar, 1981-83, dean admissions, student affairs, 1983—. Chmn. Wyoming Valley Heart Assn., Kingston, 1983. Mem. Am. Assn. Collegiate Registrars, Pa. Assn. Student Svcs., Pa. Assn. Community Coll. Admissions Officers (pres. 1987-88), Luzerne County Counselors Assn., Luzerne County Deans Assn. (pres. 1988-89). Home: 240 E Dorrance St Wilkes Barre PA 18704-5230 Office: Luzerne County Community Coll Propect St Nanticoke PA 18634

LEARY, VIRGINIA ANNE, law educator; b. Salt Lake City, Aug. 15, 1926; d. William H. and Catherine (Flanagan) L. BA, U. Utah, 1947; JD, U. Chgo., 1950; PhD, U. Geneva, Switzerland, 1980. Bar: Ill. 1951. Assoc. lawyer Sidley and Austin, Chgo., 1950-53; staff mem., U.S. dir., internat. v.p. Internat. Coop. Assn., Chgo., Brussels, Geneva, 1953-70; ofcl. Internat. Labor Orgn., Geneva, 1972-75; assoc. prof., prof. SUNY, Buffalo, 1976—; bd. dirs. Asia Watch, N.Y., 1987—, Human Rights Ctr. SUNY, Buffalo, 1985—, Internat. Labor Rights and Edn. Fund, Washington, 1985—. Author: International Labor Conventions and National Law, 1982; co-editor: Asian Perspectives on Human Rights, 1990. Pres. Buffalo Coun. on World Affairs, 1980. Grantee Ford Found., 1989-94. Mem. Am. Soc. Internat. Law (v.p. 1990-92), Internat. Law Assn., Order of Coif, Phi Beta Kappa. Roman Catholic. Home: 24 Norwood Ave Buffalo NY 14222-2104 Office: SUNY Faculty of Law Buffalo NY 14260

LEAS, DOROTHY RANDALL, financial services company executive; b. Nuremburg, Germany, Feb. 24, 1950; d. John Bruce and Marjory (Moore) L. BS, Pa. State U., 1972; MBA, U. Pa., 1977. CPA, N.Y., 1974. Staff acct. Ernst and Young, N.Y.C., 1972-74; asst. to officer J.P. Morgan and Co., Inc., N.Y.C., 1974-78; v.p. and asst. treas. Paine Webber Group, Inc., N.Y.C., 1978-89; v.p., group mgr. Merrill Lynch and Co., Inc., N.Y.C., 1989-91. Mem. Fin. Women's Assn. Home: 55 E End Ave New York NY 10028-7928

LEASON, ROBERT W., utility advertising executive; b. Boston, July 24, 1930; s. Edwin Everett and Charlotte (Pickard) L.; m. Barbara M.A. Walker, Dec. 31, 1955; children: Cynthia C.A. Leason Crowe, Steven Walker. BBA, U. Mass., 1959; postgrad., U. Mich., 1969, Northwestern U., 1990. Sales rep. Am. Airlines, Buffalo and N.Y.C., 1960-61; with sales and mktg. depts. Corning Glass Works, Detroit, Grand Rapids, Mich., and Cleve., 1961-66; asst. to mgr. mktg., asst. mgr. mktg. Cen. Maine Power Co., Augusta, 1966-68, mgr. mktg., 1968-73, mgr. customer, mktg. and rate svcs., 1973-78, staff asst. to sr. v.p., 1978-80, mgr. customer communications, 1980-84, dir. advt., 1984-91, advt. mgr., 1991—. Bd. dirs. Salvation Army, Augusta, 1969; del. Maine Rep. Conv., 1968, 71; chmn. Kennebec Valley YMCA, Augusta, 1978. Capt. USAF, 1950-56. Mem. Mil. Order World Wars (comdr. 1972), Advt. Club. Portland, Kennebec Valley C. of C., Maine Heart Assn., Utility Communicators Internat. (regional chair), Augusta Country Club, Masons, Kiwanis (pres. Augusta 1972). Episcopalian. Office: Cen Maine Power Co Edison Dr Augusta ME 04336-0002

LEASURE, FREDERICK H., foundation executive, consultant; b. Pitts., Aug. 2, 1948; s. Raymond C. and Pauline N. L.; m. Cathy Ann Loughner, Apr. 7, 1984; children: Joshua G., Zachary C. BA, W. Va. Weslyan Coll., 1970; MDiv, Drew U., 1974. Pastor Valley United Meth. Ch., Conneautville, Pa., 1974-78, Asbury United Meth. Ch., Waterford, Pa., 1978-83; exec. dir. United Meth. Found. of Western Pa., Mars, 1983—. Author: Federal Tax Reporting and Filing, 1989; contbr. article to profl. jour. chmn. Conneautville Borough Planning Com., 1977-78; bd. dir. Magee Women's Health Found. Pitts., 1989—, Wesbury Community, Meadville, Pa., 1980-83. Mem. Nat. Soc. Fund Raising Execs. (pres. local chpt. 1991, Outstanding Fund Raising Exec. 1991), Nat. Assn. United Meth. Founds. (exec. com. local chpt. 1986—), Pitts. Planned Giving Coun. (charter mem. 1988). Republican. Methodist. Office: United Meth Found 1204 Freedom Rd Mars PA 16046-8801

LEATH, KENNETH THOMAS, research plant pathologist; b. Providence, Apr. 29, 1931; s. Thomas and Elizabeth (Wootten) L.; m. Marie Andreozzi, Aug. 1955; children: Kenneth, Steven, Kevin, Maria Beth. BS, U. R.I., 1959; MS, PhD, U. Minn., 1966. Rsch. plant pathologist U.S. Regional Pasture Rsch. Lab. USDA-ARS, University Park, Pa., 1966—; prof. Pa. State U., University Park, 1966—; advisor numerous state and nat. orgns. Contbr. numerous articles to profl. jours. With USN, 1951-55. Mem. Elks. Office: US Regional Pasture Rsch La Curtin Rd University Park PA 16802

LEATH, PAUL LARRY, university official, physicist, educator; b. Moberly, Mo., Jan. 9, 1941; s. James Lewis and Naomia (Burton) L.; m. Rosemary Rippel, June 2, 1962; children: Steven, Kimberly. Grad., Moberly Jr. Coll., 1960; BS, U. Mo., 1961, MS, 1963, PhD, 1966. Rsch. officer Oxford U., Eng., 1966-67; asst. prof. physics Rutgers U., New Brunswick, 1967-71, assoc. prof., 1971-78, prof., 1978—, assoc. provost for acad. affairs, 1978-87, provost, 1987—; sr. vis. fellow Oxford U., 1972-73; researcher in theoretical physics, especially properties of alloys and disordered materials, percolation processes, breakdown phenomena, and vibrational and electronic properties. Co-author: The Theory and Properties of Randomly Disordered Crystals and Related Physical Systems, 1974. Mem. Millstone (N.J.) Borough Coun., 1979-84, pres., 1984; bd. dirs. New Brunswick Tomorrow, 1989—, R&D Coun. N.J., 1980-83. Mem. Am. Phys. Soc., Inst. Physics, AAAS, N.Y. Acad. Sci., Sigma Xi. Office: Rutgers U 18 Bishop Pl New Brunswick NJ 08901-1103

LEATHERDALE, MARCUS ANDREW, art photographer; b. Montreal, Que., Can., Sept. 18, 1952; came to U.S., 1979; s. John Bruce and Grace (Andersen) L.; m. Claudia Ann Summers. BFA, San Francisco Art Inst., 1977. Curator Sam Wagstaff Pvt. Photo Collection, N.Y.C., 1979-81; pvt. practice art photographer N.Y.C., 1981—. One-man shows include Brent Sikkema Fine Art, N.Y.C., 1990, Wessel-O-Connor Gallery, N.Y.C., 1989, Claus Runkel Fine Arts Ltd., London, 1988, Greathouse, N.Y.C., 1984, 85, 86, 87, Form & Function Gallery, Atlanta, 1983, Inst. for Art & Urban Resources, N.Y.C., 1982, Stilwende, N.Y.C., 1981, Club 57, N.Y.C., 1980; exhibited in many group exhbns. Home: 281 Grand St # 3 New York NY 10002-4416

LEATHERMAN, CHARLES JUNIOR, small business owner; b. Keyser, W.Va., May 7, 1928; s. Charles Maslin and Louise Dorothy (Kelley) L.; m. Anna Marie Cook, June 19, 1948; children: Anna Louise, Jeffrey Charles, David John, James Ralph. Enlisted USAF, 1947, ret., 1969; with CSC, 1970-89; owner, 1989—. Mem. Masons, Scottish Rite, Shriners (sec. Capitol Hill chpt.). Democrat. Presbyterian. Home: 12010 Ft Washington Rd Fort Washington MD 20744-6003

LEAVITT, CHARLES LOYAL, English language educator, administrator; b. Randolph, Maine, Apr. 30, 1921; s. Charles Warren Franklin and Alice Mabel (Sparrow) L.; m. Emily Raymond Stewart, June 12, 1951 (dec. 1966); m. Virginia Louise Kracke, Sept. 6, 1969. Diploma in Edn., U. Maine, Farmington, 1941; BS in Edn., U. So. Maine, 1946; MA in English, Boston U., 1947; PhD in English, U. Wis., 1961; MLS, Columbia U., 1969. Cert. tchr. English and history, elem., secondary, coll. Tchr. pub. schs., Vanceboro, Maine, 1941-42; tchr., prin. pub. schs., York Village, Maine, 1945-47; Instr. English and history Endicott Jr. Coll., Beverly, Mass., 1947-48; assoc. prof. English Lyndon State Coll., Lyndon Center, Vt., 1948-53, 54-55; teaching asst. in English U. Wis., Madison, 1953-54, 55-59; instr. Wayne State U., Detroit, 1959-61; assoc. prof. Montclair (N.J.) State Coll, 1961-68; v.p., sec., dir. edn. Universal Learning Corp., N.Y.C., 1968-69; assoc. dir. admissions Sarah Lawrence Coll., Bronxville, N.Y., 1970-71; dir. continuing edn., asst. dean, prof. Bloomfield (N.J.) Coll., 1971-74; chmn. liberal arts, prof. Coll. of Ins., N.Y.C., 1975-86, prof. emeritus, 1987—. Cons. editor Monarch Lit. Guides, N.Y.C., 1963-68; author Ten Lit. Study Guides, 1964-66. Treas. Youth Community Funds, York Village, Maine, 1946-47; asst. scoutmaster Boy Scouts Am., York Village, 1946-47; v.p. Overseas Neighbors, Montclair, 1974-75; tchr. Adult Sch. of Montclair, 1963-68. With USAAF, 1942-45. Named Most Popular Prof., Montclair State Coll., 1967, Prof. of Yr., Coll. of Ins., 1978; yearbook dedications Lyndon State Coll., 1950, Bloomfield Coll., 1974, Coll. of Ins., 1987; Nat. Audubon scholar, Garden Clubs York Village, 1947. Mem. AAUP, MLA, Coll. English Assn., Internat. Platform Assn., Princeton Club (N.Y.C.), Faculty Columbia U. Club, New Eng. Soc. N.Y.C. Club, Kiwanis (trustee Manhattan found. 1989—). Republican. Baptist. Home: 93 Stonebridge Rd Montclair NJ 07042-1632 Office: One Insurance Pla 101 Murray St New York NY 10007-2165

LEAVITT, JULIAN JACOB, chemist; b. Boston, Sept. 4, 1918; s. Joshua William and Isabel (Wolper) L.; m. Frances Victoria Albert, Dec. 25, 1943; children: Robert Matthew, Phyllis Ellen, Anne Irene. AB, Harvard U., 1939, AM, 1940, PhD, 1942. Rsch. chemist Nat. Def. Rsch. Com., Cambridge, Mass., 1942, Phila., 1942-44; rsch. chemist, group leader Am. Cyanamid, Bound Brook, N.J., 1944-60, mgr. dyes R&D, exploratory rsch., 1960-69, tech. dir. decision making systems, 1969-70; mgr., dir. tech. acquisition and licensing, chems. group Am. Cyanamid, Bound Brook and Wayne, N.J., 1970-85, Stamford, Conn., 1970-85; v.p. The Chemists Group, Inc., Stamford, Conn., 1986—; mem. adv. bd. Mil. Pers. Supplies, Natick, Mass., 1967-68, Com. on Textile Dyeing and Finishing, Nat. Acad. Scis./NRC, Natick, 1967-68; mem. adv. bd. Chem. Abstracts Svc., Columbus, Ohio, 1966-78. Sect. editor Chem. Abstracts Svc., Columbus, 1961—. Mem. AAAS, Am. Chem. Soc. (coun. com. on publs. 1968-72), Licensing Execs. Soc. Jewish. Home: 227 Silver Hill Ln Stamford CT 06905-3122 Office: The Chemists Group Inc PO Box 3365 Stamford CT 06905-0365

LEAVITT, MICHELE JOLIE, lawyer, writing educator; b. Jacksonville, Fla., May 10, 1957; d. Victor and Teresa Rae (Genzale) L.; m. Donald R. Bumiller, June 11, 1983. BA cum laude, Suffolk U., 1979, JD, 1981; MA in English, Salem State Coll., 1989. Bar: Mass. 1981, U.S. Dist. Ct. Mass. 1981. Pvt. practice Lynn, Mass., 1981-85; ptnr. Leavitt and Bumiller, Attys., Lynn, 1985—; vis. instr. English composition Salem (Mass.) State Coll., 1990—. Bd. dirs. Help for Abused Women and Their Children, Salem, 1988-90, pres., 1991. Mem. MLA, Mass. Bar Assn., Northshore Women Lawyers (bd. dirs. 1986-90), Essex Inst. Office: Leavitt and Bumiller 447 Broadway Lynn MA 01904-2650

LEAVITT, THOMAS WHITTLESEY, museum director, educator; b. Boston, Jan. 8, 1930; s. Richard C. and Helen M. (Pratt) L.; m. Jane O. Ayer, June 23, 1951 (div. 1969); children: Katherine, Nancy, Hugh; m. Lloyd B. Carter, Sept. 14, 1978 (div. 1985). A.B., Middlebury (Vt.) Coll., 1951; M.A., Boston U., 1952; Ph.D., Harvard, 1958. Asst. to dir. Fogg Mus., Harvard, 1954-56; exec. dir. fine arts com. People to People Program, 1957; dir. Pasadena (Calif.) Art Mus., 1957-63, Santa Barbara (Calif.) Mus. Art, 1963-68; dir. Andrew Dickson White Mus. Art, Cornell U., Ithaca, N.Y., 1968-73, Herbert F. Johnson Mus. Art, 1973-91; univ. prof. history art Cornell U., 1968-91, prof. emeritus, 1991—; Dir. mus. program Nat. Endowment for Arts, 1971-72, mem. museum panel, 1972-75; vice chmn. Council on Museums and Edn. in Visual Arts, 1972-76; trustee Gallery Assn. N.Y. State, 1972-78; mem. mus. panel N.Y. State Council Arts, 1975-78, 1980-82; chmn. art adv. com. Nat. Air and Space Mus., 1988-89. Author exhbn. catalogs, articles. Trustee Am. Fedn. Arts, 1972-91; bd. dirs. Am. Arts Alliance, 1976-82, Ind. Sector, 1980-84; bd. govs. N.E. Mus. Conf., 1973-76; bd. trustees Williamstown Regional Art Conservation Lab., 1979-91, pres., 1984-87. Mem. Assn. Art Mus. Dirs. (pres. 1977-78, trustee 1978-

80), Am. Assn. Museums (council 1976-79, v.p. 1980-82, pres. 1982-85). Home: 17 South St Trumansburg NY 14886-9530 Office: Cornell U Herbert F Johnson Mus Art Ithaca NY 14853

LEBEAU, PAUL ANDREW, paper industry executive; b. Troy, N.Y., Nov. 3, 1950; s. Charles Paul and Doris Mary (Nicoll) LeB. BS, Boston Coll., 1972. Sales mgr. Thmas River Tube Co., Inc., Ashaway, R.I., 1972-78, v.p., 1978-88, sr. v.p., 1988—. Bd. dirs. Hopkinton (R.I.) Econ. Devel. Com., 1980-81; vice chair Help Our People Endure Found., New London, Conn., 1991—. Mem. Eastern Conn. Yacht Racing Assn. (exec. bd. 1974-76), Thames Yacht Club (rear commodore 1977-78, 84, vice commodore 1979-80), Watch Hill Yacht Club. Republican. Roman Catholic. Home: 7 Carnot Ct Pawcatuck CT 06379-2424 Office: Thames River Tube Co Inc 64 High St # 206 Ashaway RI 02804-1502

LEBEL, GREGORY GALEN, college dean, researcher; b. Portsmouth, N.H., Apr. 12, 1950; s. Emile Henry Jr. and Willetta Jane (Vigue) L. BA, U. N.H., 1972, MPA, 1981; MA, U. Md., 1991, postgrad., 1991—. Chief program ops. to program planner N.H. Dept. of Health and Welfare, Concord, 1974-83; nat. staff Americans with Hart, N.H., 1983-84; campaign mgr. Asbury for Congress, Albuquerque, 1984-85; chief ops. officer Ctr. for a New Democracy, Washington, 1985; spl. asst. U.S. Sen. Gary Hart, Washington, 1985; exec. dir. The Vol. Com., Washington, 1986-87; dir. nat. scheduling Friends of Gary Hart, Denver, 1987; nat. polit. dir. League of Conservation Voters, Washington, 1987; nat. campaign mgr., dep. nat. campaign mgr. Hart for Pres., N.H., 1987-88; rsch. assoc. and lectr. The Grad. Sch. of Polit. Mgmt., N.Y.C., 1988—; asst. dean The Grad. Sch. Polit. Mgmt., N.Y.C.; tech. advisor White House Conf. on Aging, Concord, 1981; cons. Global Tomorrow Coalition, Washington, Voter Edn. Project Atlanta, Dem. Congl. Campaign Com., Americans with Hart, N.H. Dept. Health and Human Svcs.; guest lectr. Williams Coll., U. N.Mex., U. Md., Am. U.; guest scholar John Hopkins U. Ctr. for Study Am. Govt. Co-Author: Sustainable Development: A Guide to Our Common Future, 1989; author: The Advance Manual, 1986. Del. Democratic Nat. Convention, San Francisco, 1984. Mem. Am. Polit. Sci. Assn., Am. Assn. on Polit. Cons. (ethics com.), Am. Soc. Pub. Adminstrn. Democrat. Roman Catholic. Office: George Washington U Phillips Hall T 409 Washington DC 20052

LEBENSBAUM, HENRY, lawyer; b. Bergen-Belsen, Germany, May 31, 1948; came to U.S. 1959; s. Samuel and Frieda L. BA, CUNY, 1971; MA, Alfred (N.Y.) U., 1973; JD cum laude, Calif. Western Sch. Law, San Diego, 1990. Bar: Mass. 1991, U.S. Dist. Ct. (Mass.) 1991; cert. sch. psychologist, Mass., N.Y. Dir. testing Mass. Dept. Corrections, Norfolk, 1973-74; sch. psychologist Tewksbury (Mass.) Pub. Schs., 1974-86; psychologist in pvt. practice Andover, Mass., 1975-86; mgmt. cons. Princess House, North Deighton, Mass., 1986-88; cons. assoc. Klieman, Lyons, Schindler, Gross & Pabian, Boston, 1990—. Chmn. bd. dirs. Office for Children, Lawrence, Mass., 1985; bd. dirs. Big Bro./Big Sisters of Greater Lawrence, 1983. Recipient Am. Jurisprudence award, Miller Tax award, Calif. Western Sch. Law. Mem. Assn. Trial Lawyers Am., Boston Bar Assn., Mass. Bar Assn., Mass. Acad. Trial Attys., Am. Psychol. Assn., Essex County Bar Assn., Lawrence Bar Assn., Phi Alpha Delta.

LEBER, R(ALPH) ERIC, chemist; b. Seattle, Nov. 30, 1949; s. Ralph Theodore and Ann Elisa (Ellsworth) L.; m. Lori Ramonas, Apr. 27, 1978; 1 child, Christopher T. BA in Chemistry, Reed Coll., 1972; MS in Chemistry, Yale U., 1973, M Ph in Chemistry, 1974, PhD in Chemistry, 1975. Postdoctoral rsch. fellow Lawrence Berkeley Lab., Berkeley, Calif., 1975-77; Congl. fellow Capitol Hill, Washington, 1977-78; dir. of energy rsch. Am. Pub. Power Assn., Washington, 1978-84; dir. Dept. of Pub. Affairs. Am. Chem. Soc., Washington, 1984, dir. Pub. Policy and Communication, 1984-87, Smithsonian fellow, 1987-90, dir. Spl. Programs, 1990-91; mgr. U. Programs Battelle Pacific NW Labs., Richland, Wash., 1992—; exec. dir. Coun. of Sci. Soc. Pres., Washington, 1984-91. Contbr. articles to profl. jours. Mem. AAAS, Am. Chem. Soc., Assn. Sci.-Tech. Ctrs., Internat. Union of Pure and Applied Chemistry, Women's Coun. on Energy and Environment, Aircraft Owners and Pilots Assn., U.S. Yacht Racing Union, Washington State Soc., Griffin Soc. of Reed Coll., Yale Club of Washington, Phi Beta Kappa, Sigma Xi. Home: 2455 George Washington Way A11 Richland WA 99352 Office: Battelle Pacific NW Labs Battelle Blvd Richland WA 99352

LEBLANC, PAUL JOSEPH, historian, educator; b. Huntingdon, Pa., Apr. 30, 1947; s. Gaston and Shirley Dorothy (Harris) LeB.; m. Sandra Joanne Hoffberger, Apr. 7, 1968 (div. 1973); 1 child, Gabriel Seth. BA, U. Pitts., 1971, MA in History, 1980, PhD in History, 1989. With history dept. Slippery Rock (Pa.) Univ., 1989-91. Mem. editorial bd.: (mag.) Bulletin in Def. of Marxism, 1985—; gen. editor: (book series) Revolutionary Studies, 1990—; editor : C.L.R. James: Revolutionary Marxism and Modern Politics, 1992; author: Lenin and the Revolutionary Party, 1990; contbr. articles to profl. jours.

LEBMAN, ROBERT RICHARD, social services administrator; b. Amsterdam, N.Y., Sept. 20, 1945; s. Harry and Catherine (Spitzkopf) L. BA cum laude, Harpur Coll., Binghamton, N.Y., 1967; MA, Pa. State U., 1968. With Peace Corps, 1968-72; project dir. AID mission, Afghanistan, 1972-73; cons. Rochester (N.Y.) Sch. Dist., 1973; rsch. assoc. Applied Behavioral Rsch. Assocs., Rochester, 1973-74; caseworker, then clin. dir. Delphi House, Rochester, 1974-78; dir. N.W. Youth Ctr. of Charles Settlement House, Rochester, 1978-80; exec. dir. Livingston County Youth Bur., Rochester, 1981-83, Monroe County Youth Advocacy, Rochester, 1983-86; dir. in-patient svcs. DayBreak Alcoholism Treatment Facility, Rochester, 1986-89; exec. dir. Huther-Doyle Meml. Inst., Webster, N.Y., 1989—. Author: English Language Teaching in Afghanistan, 1972. Pres. bd. dirs. Nat. Coun. on Alcoholism; bd. dirs. Helping People with AIDS, Jewish Family svcs., Mental Health Assn., Health Assn. Rochester, Extension Found., Coop. Extension Monroe County, Operation U-Turn, Inc., Roca Assocs., Inc.; mem. Monroe County Task Force on Youth and Alcohol, 1976-86, 4-H adv. com. Monroe County Coop. Extension, 1978-80, Black Seeds Scholarship Com., 1981-86, Jewish Chem. Dependency Task Force Com. on Youth and Alcohol; mem. budget adv. com. Rochester City Schs., 1983-85; chmn. Regional Youth Workers Tng. Network. NDEA fellow, 1967. Mem. Acad. Polit. Sci., Am. Polit. Sci. Assn., Acad. Polit. and Social Sci., Am. Judicature Soc., Nat. Coun. Crime & Delinquency, Arts & Scis. Acad. Rochester (bd. dirs.). Democrat. Jewish. Home: 6 Queensberry Ln Rochester NY 14624-4308 Office: Huther-Doyle Meml Inst 2112 Empire Blvd Webster NY 14580-1935

LEBOUITZ, MARTIN F., financial services industry executive, consultant; b. Phila., May 16, 1946; s. William and Sylvia (Magen) L.; m. Helene A. Pepe, Oct. 15, 1977; 1 child, Clarke S. BS, U.S. Air Force Acad., Colorado Springs, Colo., 1971; MA, The Fletcher Sch. of Law and Diplomacy, 1972. Asst. v.p. Bankers Trust Co., N.Y.C., 1976-82; v.p. mgr. of planning Barclays Bank of N. Am., N.Y.C, 1982-85; v.p. corp. devel. Chase Manhattan Bank, N.Y.C., 1985-88; v.p. planning and devel. Paine Webber Group Inc., N.Y.C., 1988-90; prin. DRI/McGraw-Hill, N.Y.C., 1990-91, mng. dir., 1991—. Bd. dirs., chmn. sch. rels. com. N.Y. chpt. Fletcher Sch. Capt. USAF, 1971-76. Mem. Planning Forum, Assn. for Corp. Growth, Am. Mgmt. Assn., USAF Acad. Alumnae (treas. N.Y. metro area chpt.), Harvard Club, Fletcher Sch. Club N.Y. (chmn. sch. rels. com.). Office: DRI/McGraw-Hill 11 Broadway New York NY 10004-1302

LEBOWITZ, MARSHALL, publishing company executive; b. Boston, Mar. 4, 1923; s. Max Nathan and Rissah (Zangwill) L.; m. Charlotte Lily Meyersohn, Aug. 7, 1949; children: Wendy Ann, Marian Kay, Mark Louis. AB, Harvard U., 1942. Statis. analyst U.S. WPB, Washington, 1942-43; periodicals mgr. J.S. Canner & Co. Inc., Needham Heights, Mass., 1946-68, gen. mgr., 1968-86, v.p., 1987—; v.p. Plenum Pub. Corp., 1977—. Mem. Natick (Mass.) Planning Bd., 1964-69, chmn., 1968-69; mem. Natick Town Meeting, 1954—, chmn. town by-laws revision com., 1965-67; pres. Greater Framingham Mental Health Assn., 1963-64, dir. 1954-63; mem. Greater Framingham Mental Health Area Bd., 1972-78, v.p., 1974-75, pres., 1975-77; mem. Regional Drug Rev. Bd., 1973; chmn. Natick Regional Vocat. Sch. Planning Com., 1974-77; mem. Natick Sch. Com., 1978-81, clk., 1979-81; chmn. legis. impact study comm. Town of Natick, 1980; chmn. town commn. to rev. by-laws and mcpl. charter, 1980-90; mem. trustees adv. coun. Leonard Morse Hosp., 1973-91, vice chmn., 1974-77, mem. mental health adv. com., 1972-91; chmn. Natick Land-Use Com., 1983—; mem. Mcpl. Charter Rev. Com., 1985-88, Framingham-Natick Golden Triangle Planning Com., 1988—; trustee Morse Inst. Libr., 1989—; bd. dir. Framington-Natick Cemetery Assn., 1991—. With AUS, 1943-46. Jewish (fin. sec. temple 1954-56, treas. 1952-54, vice-chmn. bd. 1958-59). Home: 2 Abbott Rd Natick MA 01760-1913 Office: 10 Charles St Needham MA 02194-2900

LEBOWITZ, STEVEN MARK, lobbyist; b. Queens, N.Y., July 17, 1965; s. Bernard Arnold and Jane Marie (Solomon) L. BA, Dickinson Coll., Carlisle, Pa., 1987. Legis. coord. N.Y. State Assembly Commerce Com., Albany, 1987-90; pres. Steven Lebowitz Strategies, Towson, Md., 1990—; dir. Md. Traditional Brewers Assn., Balt., 1990—, Agglomerate Stone Importers Consortium, Wilmington, Del., 1990—, Am. Stone Distbrs. Com. Zone leader Nassau Dem. County Com., Oyster Bay, N.Y., 1987-90; del. Dem. Nat. Conv., Atlanta, 1988; mem. Md. Dem. State Cen. Com., 1990—; dirs. Friends of Yevoli, Old Bethpage, N.Y., 1987-90. Mem. Nat. Dem. Club, Kiwanis, Toastmasters, 9-4-2 Dem. Club, Beta Theta Pi, Oyster Bay Dem. Club. Jewish. Home and Office: 82 Dunkirk Rd Baltimore MD 21212

LEBRECHT, THELMA JANE MOSSMAN, reporter; b. Indpls., Feb. 21, 1946; d. Elmore Somerville and Lois Thelma (Johnson) Mossman; m. Roger Dublon LeBrecht, May 4, 1968. BS in Journalism, U. Fla., 1968. Pub. affairs reporter WBT and WBTV, Charlotte, N.C., 1967-72; freelance reporter Toronto and N.Y.C., 1972-76; reporter KYW Newsradio, Phila., 1976-80; editor ABC Radio Network, N.Y.C., 1980-81; reporter AP Broadcast, Washington, 1981—. Mem. Radio and TV Corrs. Assn. in U.S. Capitol (chmn. 1991). Office: AP Broadcast 1825 K St NW Washington DC 20006-1202

LECASH, LEON PAUL, photographer; b. London, Oct. 20, 1951; came to U.S., 1980; s. Henry and Ann (Green) L.; 1 child, Chloe. Student, St. Pauls, London, 1963-67. Self-employed photographer, 1973—. Home: 284 5th Ave New York NY 10001-4507

LECCE, FRANK ANTHONY, investments executive; b. Calabria, Italy, Apr. 9, 1947; came to U.S., 1958; s. Felice Anthony and Rachael (Lombardo) L.; m. Kathleen Ann Gettemy, June 27, 1950; children: John Jacob, Nora Jane. BA, U. Conn., 1973. Stockbroker Advest, Inc., Hartford, Conn., 1973-77; mcpl. bond salesman Conn. Bank & Trust Co., Hartford, 1977-80; v.p. mcpl. bond Trading Advest, Inc., Hartford, 1980-83; pres., co-founder Conn. Securities Investment Corp., Hartford, 1983—. Com. mem. Dem. Town Com., Farmington, Conn., 1978-84. Mem. Nat. Securities Traders Assn. Club: Bond of Hartford (pres. 1987). Home: 56 Outlook Ave West Hartford CT 06119-1431 Office: Conn Securities Investment Corp 15 Lewis St Ste 212 Hartford CT 06103

LECHER, RICHARD CLINTON, social welfare association administrator; b. Morristown, N.J., Jan. 28, 1945; s. Francis Dean and Ruth (Firstbrook) L.; m. Susan Moran, June 21, 1969; children: Jennifer, Todd. BA, W.Va. Wesleyan Coll., 1967; MA, Seton Hall U., 1969. Cert. tchr. of handicapped, sch. prin., sch. adminstr. Tchr. spl. edn. Roxbury Pub. Schs., Succasunna, N.J., 1968-72; exec. dir. Sussex County Assn. for Retarded Citizens, Newton, N.J., 1972—, Sussex County Assn. for Retarded Citizens Found., Inc., Newton, 1985—, Sussex County Assn. for Retarded Citizens Guardianship Svcs., Newton, 1989—; pres. Dove Industries Sussex County, Inc., Newton, 1985—; chmn. N.J. Conf. Execs. of ARC, North Brunswick, 1991-93, Sussex County Human Svcs. Adv. Coun., Newton, 1991-93. Elder, Emmanuel Bible Ch., Schooley's Mt., N.J., 1985—. Mem. Am. Assn. on Mental Retardation, Coun. for Exceptional Children, Am. Soc. Assn. Execs., Assn. for Retarded Citizens of the U.S. Home: 76 Lawrence Dr Hackettstown NJ 07840-2526 Office: Sussex County Assn for Retarded Citizens 8 Hampton House Rd Newton NJ 07860-1409

LECHNER, BERNARD JOSEPH, consulting electrical engineer; b. N.Y.C., Jan. 25, 1932; s. Barnard Joseph and Lillian Veronica (Stevens) L.; m. Joan Camp Mathewson, Nov. 21, 1953. BSEE, Columbia U., 1957; postgrad., Princeton U., 1957-60. Mem. tech. staff RCA Labs., Princeton, N.J., 1957-62, project leader, 1966-67, group head, 1967-77, lab. dir., 1977-83, staff v.p., 1983-87; pvt. practice cons. Princeton, 1987—; bd. dirs. Palisades Inst., N.Y.C., 1981—; chmn. adv. commn. Mercer County Coll., Trenton, N.J.. 1968-85. Contbr. articles to profl. jours.; holder 10 patents. Reader Recording for the Blind, Princeton, 1967-72. Served to cpl. U.S. Army, 1953-55. Recipient David Sarnoff Gold medal RCA Corp., 1962. Fellow Soc. for Info. Display (pres. 1978-80, other offices, Frances Rice Darne award 1971, Beatrice Winner award 1983), IEEE (chpt. chmn. 1964-66, Best Paper award Solid State Cirs. Conf. 1966); mem. Soc. Motion Picture & TV Engrs., Am. Relay Radio League, Sigma Xi, Tau Beta Pi, Eta Kappa Nu. Episcopalian. Club: Princeton Sqs. (pres. 1981-87). Address: 98 Carson Rd Princeton NJ 08540

LECHTER, GEORGE STEVE, computer company executive; b. Brookline, Mass., Sept. 24, 1954; s. Abraham and Zita (Perczek) L.; m. Candy Keezer, July 31, 1982; children: Michael, James. BME, MIT, 1975, MBA, 1977. Pres. Rorrim, Inc., Cambridge, Mass., 1976-77; cons. Harbridge House, Boston, 1977-80, Braxton Assocs., Boston, 1980-81; mini-computer specialist Nixdorf Computer Co., Waltham, Mass., 1981-82; co-founder Alpha Software Co., Burlington, Mass., 1982-85; exec. v.p. Keezer Properties, Newton, Mass., 1985-88; pres. Technologies Corp., Needham, Mass., 1988—. Patentee, positive reflection mirror, side collision safety belt, radiation-free video display terminal, power line radiation detector and TV "PET" radiation detector. Office: Safe Technologies Corp 33 William St Needham MA 02194-3259

LE CLAIR, RICHARD ALFRED, JR., wholesale grocery executive; b. Johnson City, N.Y., Apr. 7, 1943; s. Richard Alfred and Anne Barbara (Barsosky) L.; m. Carolyn Jean Drislane, Oct. 19, 1960; children: Richard A III, David Alan, Renee Carol. Student, Orange County Community Coll., 1966. Crew chief John F. Purdy Land Surveyor, Vestal, N.Y., 1962-64; exec. v.p. John L. English Co., Inc., Cohoes, N.Y., 1965-88; owner, pres. Richlyn Marine, Inc (doing bus. as Gabry's Marine), Watervliet, N.Y., 1989—; pres. Martserve Inc., Cohoes, 1985-87. With USN, 1960-62. 6th and 7th Lake Assn. (Inlet, N.Y., pres. 1974-80). Democrat. Presbyterian. Home: 2137 Galway Rd Galway NY 12074-2404 Office: Richlyn Marine Inc 2137 Galway Rd Galway NY 12074

LECLERC, PAUL, college president; b. Lebanon, N.H., May 28, 1941; s. Louis and M. Juliette (Trottier) LeC; m. Judith Ginsberg, Oct. 26, 1980; 1 child, Adam Louis. BS, Coll. Holy Cross, 1963; student, U. Paris, 1963-64; MA, Columbia U., 1966, PhD with distinction, 1969. Assoc. prof. French Union Coll., Schenectady, 1969-79, chmn. dept. modern langs. and lit., 1972-77, chmn. humanities div., 1975-77; univ. dean for acad. affairs CUNY, 1979-84; provost and acad. v.p. Baruch Coll., CUNY, 1984-88; pres. Hunter Coll., CUNY, 1988—; bd. dirs. N.Y. Alliance for Pub. Schs., N.Y.C., 1981-84, El Museo del Barrio, The Feminist Press; pres. N.Y. Tchr. Edn. Conf. Bd., Albany, N.Y., 1983-84. Author: Voltaire and Crebillon Pere, 1972, Voltaire's Rome Sauvée, 1992; co-editor: Lettres d'André Morellet, 1991; contbr. articles to profl. jours. Decorated officier Palmes Académiques (France); grantee NEH, 1971, 79, Am. Coun. Learned Socs., 1973, Ford Found., 1979. Mem. MLA, Am. Soc. for 18th Century Studies. Office: CUNY Hunter Coll 695 Park Ave New York NY 10021-5085

LECOUNT, ROSCOE DALE, JR., dean; b. Cin., July 8, 1940; s. Roscoe Dale and Dorothy Margaret O'Brien LeC.; m. Margaret Blaine Nutt, June 18 1964; children: Melinda, Andrew, Scott. BA, Princeton U., 1962; MA, Columbia U., 1967, EDD, 1971; postgrad., Harvard U., 1982. Tchr. Casady Sch., Oklahoma City, 1962-63; asst. dir. admission Princeton (N.J.) U., 1963-67; asst. prof. edn. Franklin and Marshall Coll., Lancaster, Pa., 1970-72, asst. dean of students, 1972-73; dean of students Muhlenberg Coll., Allentown, Pa., 1973-80, dean ednl. svcs., 1980-86, dean continuing edn., 1986—. Bd. dirs. Lehigh County United Way, Allentown, 1988—, chair allocation and allocation com., 1988-91; elder Presbyn. Ch. U.S.A., 1980-86. NDSL fellow, 1967-70. Mem. Assn. Continuing Higher Edn., Am. Assn. Higher Edn. Democrat. Office: Muhlenberg Coll 2400 W Chew St Allentown PA 18104-5564

LEDBETTER, MARY LEE STEWART, cell biologist; b. Monterrey, Nuevo Leon, Mexico, Aug. 30, 1944; d. William Sheldon and Maria Rosalind (Markham) Stewart; m. Steven John Ledbetter, Sept. 10, 1966; children: William, Joanna. BA, Pomona Coll., 1966; PhD, The Rockefeller U., 1972. Rsch. trainee NYU Sch. Medicine, N.Y.C., 1971-72; rsch. assoc. Dartmouth Med. Sch., Hanover, N.H., 1972-75, 77-79; instr. Dartmouth Med. Sch., Hanover, 1975-78; vis. asst. prof. Dartmouth Coll., Hanover, 1977; rsch. asst. prof. Dartmouth Med. Sch., Hanover, 1979-80; asst. prof. Coll. of Holy Cross, Worcester, Mass., 1980-86; assoc. prof. Coll. of Holy Cross, Worcester, 1986—; cell biology adv. panel NSF, Washington, 1986-90; NSCORT peer rev. panel AIBS/NASA, Washington, 1990; NSF young investigator selection panel, Washington, 1992. Contbr. articles to profl. jours. Violinist Newton (Mass.) Symphony Orch., 1984—. Recipient postdoctoral fellowship Leukemia Soc. Am., 1973-75, 77-78, NIH, 1975-77; grantee Muscular Dystrophy Assn., 1980-84, NSF, 1984-88, NIH, 1988-91. Mem. Am. Soc. for Cell Biology, Coun. on Undergrad. Rsch. (councilor 1989-91), Assn. for Women in Sci., Sigma Xi, Phi Beta Kappa. Democrat. Office: Coll of the Holy Cross 1 College St # B Worcester MA 01610-2322

LEDDICOTTE, GEORGE COMER, business executive, consultant; b. Oak Ridge, Tenn., May 28, 1947; s. George W. Leddicotte and Virginia (Comer) Leddicotte Stratton; m. Connie Laverne Sterrett, Jan. 25, 1969; 1 child, Matthew Sterrett. BA in Polit. Sci., U. Mo., 1970. Cert. relocation profl. Customer service supr. Crown Zellerbach, San Francisco, 1973-74; exec. recruiter Christopher & Long, St. Louis, 1974; regional ops. mgr. Curtin Matheson Scientific, Inc., Houston, 1974-80; regional mgr., mng. cons. Merrill Lynch Relocation Mgmt., White Plains, N.Y., 1980-82, regional v.p., nat. accounts, 1982-83, regional v.p. govt. svcs., 1983-84; dir. govt. svcs. Coldwell Banker Relocation Mgmt., Washington, 1984-85; dir. sales., account mgmt. Homequity, Wilton, Conn., 1985-87; v.p. nat. sales Premier Relocation Svcs., Inc., Irvine, Calif., 1987-88; v.p., sr. mng. cons. Premier Decision Mgmt., Irvine, 1988—; pres., mng. dir. Feasibllity Inc., Brookfield, Conn., 1988—. First lt. U.S. Army, 1970-72, Korea. Mem. Am. Mktg. Assn., Am. Mgmt. Assn., Soc. for Human Resource Mgmt., Employee Relocation Coun. Home and Office: Feasibility Inc 9 Broadview Rd Brookfield CT 06804-1802

LEDEBUR, GARY WILLIAM, psychologist, government official; b. New Brighton, Pa., Mar. 22, 1949; s. Linas Vocroth Ledebur and Lois (Binzley) Calenback; m. Diane Snow, June 27, 1970; children: Lee Ann, Linas Edward. BA, W.Va Wesleyan Coll., 1971; MEd, Edinboro (Pa.) U., 1972; EdD, Lehigh U., 1981. Psychologist Carbon-Lehigh Intermedia Unit, Allentown, Pa., 1972-77; supr. Carbon-Lehigh Intermedia Unit, Harrisburg, Pa., 1977-86; advisor sch. psychology Pa. Dept. Edn., Harrisburg, 1986-89, bur. dir., 1989—; mem. Inter-state Migrant Edn. Coun., Denver, 1989—. Author: Adolescent Suicide, 1987, Pregnant and Parenting Students, 1990. Bd. dir. Lehigh Valley Child Care, Bethlehem, Pa., 1980-83. Mem. Am. Psychol. Assn., Pa. Psychol. Assn., Phi Delta Kappa, Psi Chi, OMicron Delta Kappa. Office: Pa Dept Edn 333 Market St Harrisburg PA 17101-2210

LEDERBERG, JOSHUA, geneticist, educator; b. Montclair, N.J., May 23, 1925; s. Zwi Hirsch and Esther (Goldenbaum) L.; m. Marguerite S. Kirsch, Apr. 5, 1968; children: David Kirsch, Anne. BA, Columbia U., 1944; PhD, Yale U., 1947. With U. Wis., 1947-58; prof. genetics Sch. Medicine, Stanford (Calif.) U., 1959-78; pres. Rockefeller U., N.Y.C., 1978-90, Univ. prof., 1990—; adj. prof. Columbia U., 1990—; mem. adv. com. med. rsch. WHO, 1971-76; mem. bd. sci. advisors Affymax N.V., Palo Alto, Calif., Hoechst-Celanese Corp., Summit, N.J.; mem. study sects. NSF, NIH; cons. U.S. Def. Sci. Bd.; mem. adv. bd. U.S. Dept. Energy; cons. NASA, ACDA; bd. dirs. Inst. Sci. Info. Inc., Phila., Proctor & Gamble Co., Cin., Ann Revs., Inc., Palo Alto. Trustee Revson Found., Carnegie Corp., Camille and Henry Dreyfus Found.; bd. dirs. Chem. Industry Inst. Toxicology, N.C., Am. Type Culture Coll., Wash., OTA Assessment Adv. Coun. With USN, 1943-45. Recipient Nobel prize in physiology and medicine for rsch. in genetics of bacteria, 1958, U.S. Nat. Medal of Sci., 1989. Fellow AAAS, Am. Philos. Soc., Am. Acad. Arts and Scis., N.Y. Acad. Medicine (hon.); mem. Nat. Acad. Scis. (Inst. of Medicine), Royal Soc. London (fgn.), N.Y. Acad. Scis., Sackler Found. Office: Rockefeller U 1230 York Ave Ste 400 New York NY 10021-6399

LEDERER, NORMAN, labor association administrator; b. Milw., Mar. 1, 1938; s. Maximilian George and Anna (Mueller) L.; m. Sally Ann Naquin, Aug. 20, 1966; children: Maximilian, Katrina Marie. BS, U. Wis., Milw., 1960; postgrad., Rice U., 1960-61; MA, La. State U., 1963, postgrad., 1963-65, 68-70. Asst. prof. social scis. Nicholls State Coll., Thibodaux, La., 1965-68; asst. prof. history U. Wis., Platteville, 1970-72; exec. dir. U. Wis. System Ethnic and Minority Studies Ctr., Platteville and Stevens Point, Wis., 1972-74; dir. Menard Jr. Coll., Merrill, Wis., 1973-74; dean scis. Camden County Coll., Blackwood, N.J., 1974-77; dean instrn. Washtenaw Community Coll., Ann Arbor, Mich., 1977-81, Lower Columbia Coll., Longview, Wash., 1981-85; sr. program advisor Edison State Coll., Trenton, N.J., 1986-87, adj. faculty, 1987—; dir. edn. and tng. United Auto Workers Dist. 65, Woodbridge, N.J., 1987-89; dean devel. edn. Stevens State Sch. Tech., 1989—; cons. N.J. Commn. for the Humanities, Middlesex County Coll. Inst. for Mgmt. and Tech. Devel.; mem. Middlesex County Coll. Commn. on Edn., Employment and Economy, Rutgers Labor Edn. Ctr. Trade Union Con.; mem. Lancaster County human rels. com. Lancaster County Hist. Soc. Contbr. numerous book and record revs. to mags. Mem. adv. bd. Washtenaw County Coop. Ednl. Tng. Assistance planning coun., Ann Arbor, 1978-81, Greater Raritan Pvt. Industry Coun., N.J. Plus Lit. Task Force; adv. coun. Coop. Ednl. Tng. Assistance planning coun., Ann Arbor, 1978-81; bd. dirs. Cowlitz County Community Action Program, Longview, 1981-83, Middlesex Literacy Vols. Am.; advisor Wash. Commn. for the Humanities, 1983-84; pres. S.W. Wash. Youth Symphony, Longview, 1983-84; mem. Middlesex County Lit. Adv. Task Force. Mem. Nat. Assn. for Industry-Edn. Cooperation, Am. Tech. Edn. Assn., Am. Soc. Tng. and Devel. Democrat. Roman Catholic. Home: 329 N Donerville Rd Mountville PA 17554-1312 Office: Thaddeus Stevens State Sch Tech 750 E King St Lancaster PA 17602-3198

LEDERER-ANTONUCCI, YVONNE, management information educator, consultant; b. Phila., May 5, 1958; d. Jay William and Elizabeth (Stratton) Lederer; m. Michael F. Antonucci, Aug. 23, 1986. BSBA in Mgmt. Sci., Shippensburg U., 1980; MS in Mgmt. Sci., Lehigh U., 1983; PhD, Drexel U., 1992. Programmer Shared Med. Systems, Malvern, Pa., 1980-81; prof. MIS, Widener U., Chester, Pa., 1983—; computer cons., co-owner Simplex Computing Svcs., Media, Pa., 1984—; ptnr. Totem Software, Media, 1988-90; lectr. presenter profl. conf. Mem. Data Processing Mgmt. Assn. (edn. coord. 1987-89, coord. student chpt. 1988-91), Assn. Computer Machinery. Lutheran. Home: 44 Stirling Way Chadds Ford PA 19317-9415 Office: Widener U Sch Mgmt Chester PA 19013

LEDLEY, CHRISTIAN SALVESEN, social worker, researcher; b. Edinburgh, Scotland, Aug. 4, 1925; d. John Stephen and Magda Virginie (Salvesen) Elliot; m. Brian Gunning Ledley, Aug. 9, 1958; 1 child, Jean Elliot Ledley. Cert. in Social Work, U. Edinburgh, 1948; Cert. in Child Welfare, U. Leeds, Eng., 1949; AM in Social Svc. Adminstrn., U. Chgo., 1958. Cert. social worker. Child care worker Northumberland County Coun., Newcastle, Eng., 1950-56, Chgo. Child Care Soc., 1958-59; vol. social worker U. Md. Extension Svc., Silver Spring, 1965-77, Extended Hand Inc., Silver Spring, 1966-77; researcher Montgomery County, Rockville, Md., 1977-79; tenant liaison, researcher Franklin Assocs./Montgomery Oaks Mgmt., Takoma Park, Md., 1979—. Developer, coord. Colesville (Md.) Parent Edn. Program, 1966-77; chmn. Community Credit Fund, Colesville, 1966-69; family aid and fin. counselor U. Md. Extension Svc., 1966-91; mem. Takoma Park-East Silver Spring Adv. Commn., 1981—, chmn., 1986-88, vice chmn., 1991—. Cpl. Brit. Army, 1943-46, ETO. Named Outstanding Vol., Channel 7, Washington, 1972; recipient svc. awards. Democrat. Presbyterian. Home: 13114 Venetian Rd Box 4026 Silver Spring MD 20914-4026 Office: Montgomery Oaks Mgmt 11900 Tech Rd Silver Spring MD 20904

LEDONNE, ROBERT J., television news producer, writer; b. Leominster, Mass., Dec. 1, 1929; s. Alfred and Ida (Santucci) LeDonne; m. Joyce LeDonne, June 21, 1962; children: Denise, Robert L., Christopher. BA in Journalism, Northeastern U., 1952. Bur. mgr. United Press Internat., Concord, N.H., 1954-56; publicist NBC, N.Y.C., 1956-58; producer Sta. WNBC,

N.Y.C., 1958-59; writer, producer Sta. WNEW Radio News, N.Y.C., 1959-61; producer, writer ABC News Spl. Events, N.Y.C., 1962-80, ABC News Nightline, N.Y.C., 1980—. Producer, reporter The Ken Meeks Story, The Courage of Priscilla Diaz, 1987 (Ohio State Achievement of Merit award, Gabriel award, NEA award, Monte Carlo TV Festival award, Columbus Internat. TV and Film Festival award, N.Y. Internat. TV and Film Festival award, gold medal 1992, Monitor award, Am. Med. Writers award). Served to sgt. U.S. Army, 1947-49. Recipient Emmy award, 1985, 86, 91, Gold medal N.Y. Internat. TV and Film Festival, 1987, 91. Mem. Writers Guild Am. Office: ABC News Nightline 47 W 66th St New York NY 10023-6290

LEDUC, EUGENE JOSEPH, designer; b. Newburyport, Mass., Mar. 9, 1953; s. Eugene Ovila and Anna Jacques (Eaton) L.; m. Marcia Ann Demers, Nov. 15, 1980; 1 child, Eric Joseph. Student, United Tech. Inst., Boston, 1971-73. Lobsterman Portland, Maine, 1967-72; draftsman Fairchild Semiconductor, South Portland, Maine, 1972-73; elec. draftsman Neil & Gunter Inc., Falmouth, Maine, 1976-79; tool designer Data Gen. Corp., Westbrook, Maine, 1979-81; designer ABB Environ. Svcs. Inc., Portland, 1981—. Sgt. USAF, 1973-76. Republican. Roman Catholic. Home: 86 Bailey Ave Portland ME 04102 Office: ABB Environ Svcs Inc 110 Free St Portland ME 04106

LEE, BETTY JANE, nursing educator; b. Chester, Pa., Oct. 6, 1928; d. Harvey and Elizabeth Mary (Edwards) Warner; children: Barton Warner, Barry Court, Byron Tucker. BS in Nursing, Keuka Coll., 1950; MS in Nursing, W.Va. U., 1979. Instr. Salem (W.Va.) Coll., 1973-78, Albright Coll., Reading, Pa., 1979-86, York (Pa.) Coll. Pa.; with Med. Personnel Pool Reading, 1987-89; instr. St. Joseph Hosp., Reading, 1987-88; dir. nursing Lehigh County Community Coll., Schnecksville, Pa., 1988—. Mem. Am. Nurses Assn., NLN, Sigma Theta Tau. Home: 3423 Kutztown Rd Reading PA 19605-2646

LEE, CHEN HSI, structural engineer; b. Shanghai, China, Oct. 26, 1923; came to U.S., 1948, naturalized, 1962; s. Kung and Teh-Ling (Yu) L.; B.S., Chiao-Tung U., Shanghai, 1947; M.S., U. Mich., 1950; m. Stella T., Nov. 19, 1955; 1 dau., Grace T. Registered profl. engr., N.Y. Prin. structural designer J.G. White Engring Corp., N.Y.C., 1950-63; aerospace stress analyst Grumman Aerospace Corp., Bethpage, N.Y., 1963-78, stress and fatigue structure engr., 1978-90; ret. Recipient Apollo Achievement award NASA, 1969, Lunar Module Structure Sci. award Grumman Aerospace Corp., 1969. Assoc. fellow: AIAA (L.I. sect. council man, pub., sec. L.I. sect., editor L.I. sect. Flier, chmn. L.I. sect. 1987-88), N.Y. Profl. Engrs. Soc., Alpha Lambda. Club: Toastmasters Internat. Home: 21 Joyce Rd Plainview NY 11803-3911 Office: Grumman Aerospace Corp Bethpage NY 11714

LEE, CHI-JEN, supervisory research chemist; b. Yi-Lan, Taiwan, Republic of China, Feb. 8, 1936; came to U.S., 1962; s. Chao-Huei and Sian-Sim (Chiong) L.; m. Sue-Yuan Lee, Oct. 10, 1960; children: Johns Y., Lucia H., Benjamin R. BS in Pharmacy, Nat. Taiwan U., Taipei, 1957; ScD in Biochemistry, Johns Hopkins U., 1966. Pharmacist China Chem. & Pharm. Co., Shu-Lin, Taiwan, 1959-62; rsch. assoc. Dept. Biochemistry Johns Hopkins U., Balt., 1966-67; rsch. assoc. Rockefeller U., N.Y.C., 1967-68, asst. prof. chemistry, 1968-73; sr. staff fellow NIH, Bethesda, Md., 1973-74; supervisory rsch. chemist FDA Ctr. Biologics Evaluation and Rsch., Bethesda, 1974—; vis. prof. Nat. Cheng Kung U., Coll. Medicine, Tainan, Taiwan, 1984; chmn. Third Pneumococcal Workshop, FDA, Bethesda, 1979; bd. dirs. Chinese Med. & Health Assn., Washington. Referee: (book) Handbook of New and Recent Drugs, 1991; contbr. articles to profl. publs. Pres., bd. dirs. Culture Sch., Wheaton, Md., 1990—; elder Taiwanese Presbyn. Ch., Wheaton, 1990—. Recipient Disting. Achievement award, Nat. Taiwan U. Alumni Assn. in N.Am., 1988. Mem. Am. Assn. Immunologists, Am. Soc. Biochemistry and Molecular Biology. Democrat. Home: 9807 Belhaven Rd Bethesda MD 20817-1731 Office: Ctr Biologics Evaluation 8800 Rockville Pike Bethesda MD 20892-0001

LEE, CLEMENT WILLIAM KHAN, association administrator; b. N.Y.C., Feb. 7, 1938; s. William P. and Helen M. BTh, Concordia Coll., 1958; MDiv, Concordia Theol. Sem., 1962; MA, New Sch. for Social Research, 1976. Asst. exec. dir. Greater Detroit Luth. Ctr., 1962; editor Detroit and Suburban Luth. Newspaper, 1963; assoc. communications dir. Met. Detroit Council of Chs., 1964; dir. media ops. Am. Bible Soc., N.Y.C., 1967; dir. media relations Luth. Council U.S.A., N.Y.C., 1971-82, asst. exec. dir. communications and interpretation, 1977-82; dir. dept. telecommunications Luth. Ch. in Am., N.Y.C., 1983-87; dir. electronic media Episcopal Ch., N.Y.C., 1987—, program dep. for communication, 1989—; media cons. Luth. Ch.-Mo. Synod, Spaulding for Children, Metro News of Metro N.Y., Synod of Luth. Ch. Am., archtl. newsletter Window, Luth. Deaconess Assn., Concordia Coll., Bronxville, Physicians for Social Responsibility, Wheatridge Found., Luth. Sch. Theology, Chgo.; chmn. broadcast ops. com. Nat. Council Chs. of Christ U.S.A., 1976-80; vice chmn. bd. mgrs. Communications Commn., 1977-80; chmn. inter-faith Media Data System, 1981; mem. TV awards com. N.Y. Council Chs.; mgr. Lutherans-in-Media Conf. I and II, 1980, Luth. Audio-Visual Conf., 1981; project dir. Lambeth Conf. Inter-Anglican Telecommunication Network, 1988; internat. computer network resource leader Religious Communications Congress 90, 1990; bd. dirs. FACTA TV News, Inc.; pres. N.Y. chpt. Religious Pub. Rels. Coun.; telecommunication cons. World Coun. of Chs., Canberra Assembly, 1990-91. Editor: Media Alert newsletter, 1980-86, Luth. Communication newsletter, 1983-87, Episcopal Media Adv. newsletter, 1989—; creator children's TV series Storyline; producer multi-image sequences, Augustana Jubilee, 1980, multi-image program Proclaim, 1984, multi-image effects, Milw. Conv., 1986, (films) Mission on Six Continents, 1975, Room for a Stranger, 1978, Winter Wheat, 1982; exec. producer, One in Mission, 1985, Gathering of the Family, 1988, Doers of the Word, 1988, The Tully-Freeman Report, 1988, Outpourings of Love, 1989, Faith on a Tightrope, 1989, Fresh Winds Blowing, 1989, Prophecy Fulfilled in Me, 1990, President Carter Center Health Video, 1990, To Walk in Beauty, 1990, Pathways for Peace, 1990, Word in the World, 1991, Executive Council Presents, 1991. Mem. Metro N.Y. Synod Evangelical Luth. Ch. in Am. Communication Commn., Religious Pub. Rels. Coun. Recipient award Detroit Press Club Found., 1963, silver medal Internat. Film and TV Festival, 1975, 79, Creative Excellence award U.S. Indsl. Film Festival, 1986, Brit. Telecommunications award, 1988, Polly Bond award, 1989, 90, 91, N.Y. TV Festival finalist, 1990. Mem. Assn. Edn. Communication Tech., Internat. Assn. Bus. Communicators, Internat. TV Assn., World Assn. Christian Communication (chmn. N.Am. broadcast sect. 1975), Nat. Interfaith Cable Coalition VISN (members' com.), Satellite TV Network (bd. dirs.). Office: Episcopal Ch Nat Office 815 2nd Ave New York NY 10017-4503

LEE, DANIEL YONG-GEUN, economics educator; b. Naju, Korea, May 21, 1954; m. Deborah C. Lee, July 16, 1977; children: Daniel J., Sarah H., Esther G. BS, Chonnam Nat. U., Korea, 1976; MA in Econs., U. Pitts., 1984, PhD in Econs., 1986. Adj. prof. econs. Pa. State U., McKeesport, 1984-85; assoc. prof. econs. Shippensburg (Pa.) U., 1986-91, prof. econs., 1991—. U. Pitts. fellow, 1980-85, 85-86. Mem. Am. Econ. Assn., Eastern Econ. Assn., So. Econ. Assn., Pa. Econ. Assn., Cen. Pa. Internat. Bus. Assn. Home: 627 Glenn St Shippensburg PA 17257-2129 Office: Shippensburg U Shippen Hall 215 Shippensburg PA 17257

LEE, DONALD JOHN, district judge; b. 1927. AB, U. Pitts., 1950; LLB, Duquesne U., 1954. Bar: Pa. Supreme Ct. 1955; U.S. Supreme Ct. 1984. Assoc. George Y. Meyer and Assocs., 1954-57, Wilner, Wilner and Kuhn, 1958-61; ptnr. Dougherty, Larrimer & Lee, Pitts., 1961-84, 86-88; judge Ct. Commnon Pleas of Allegheny County, Pa., 1984-86, 88-90, U.S. Dist. Ct. (we. dist.) Pa., Pitts., 1990—; councilman Borough Green Tree, Pitts., 1963-74, solicitor, 1963-84, 86-88; spl. asst. atty. gen. Office of Atty. Gen. Commonwealth of Pa., 1963-74; spl. legal counsel Home Rule Study Comm. Municipality of Bethel Park and Borough Green Tree, 1973-74, City of Pitts., 1978-80, various municipalities, 1970-86; chmn. Home Rule Charter Transition Com. Bethel Park, 1978. Mem. ad hoc com. Salvation Army. With USN, 1945-47. Mem. ABA, Assn. Trial Lawyers Am., Allegheny County Bar Assn., Pa. Trial Lawyers Assn., St. Thomas More Legal Soc., Adv. Com. on Appellate Ct. Rules of Supreme of Pa., Air Force Assn., Am. Legion, Western Pa. Conservancy, Am. Youth Hostel, Ancient Order of Hibernians, Knights of Equity, Woodland Hills Swim Club, Gaelic League, Smithsonian Assocs. Office: US Dist Ct 7th & Grant Sts Rm 916 Pittsburgh PA 15219

LEE, DRUN-SUN JOHN, environmental engineer; b. Nanjing, People's Republic China, July 14, 1944; came to U.S., 1969; s. Chung-yung and Cheh Lin Lee; m. Litzu Lin, Feb. 2, 1974; children: Vanessa N., Tiffany T. BSChemE, Nat. Taiwan U., Taipei, Republic of China, 1967; MSChemE, U. Tex., 1971, Rutgers U., 1973; PhD in Civil & Environ. Engring., Rutgers U., 1977. Registered profl. engr., Va., Mass. Environ. engr. Stone & Webster Engring. Corp., Boston, 1978-81; process environ. engr. Badger Am., Inc., Cambridge, Mass., 1981-82; chem. engr. Charles T. Main, Inc., Boston, 1982-83; pres. Aneptek Corp., Natick, Mass., 1983—. Contbr. rsch. papers to profl. jours. Recipient Waste Reduction for Nickel Plating award R.I. Dept. Environ. Mgmt., 1988. Mem. ASCE, Am. Inst. Chem. Engrs., Am. Acad. Environ. Engrs. (diplomate).

LEE, ELIZABETH BRIANT, sociological researcher; b. Pitts., Sept. 9, 1908; d. William Wolfer and Adah May (Riley) Briant; m. Alfred McClung Lee II, Sept. 15, 1927 (dec.); children: Alfred McClung III, Briant Hamor. BA, U. Pitts., 1930, MA, 1931; PhD, Yale U., 1937. Lectr. dept. sociology Bklyn. Coll., CUNY, 1949-50; lectr. Hartford Theol. Sem. Found., 1951-53; vis. prof., acting chair dept. sociology and anthropology Conn. Coll., New London, 1953-54; rsch. assoc. Ctr. for Sociol. Rsch., Cath. Univ. of the Sacred Heart, Milan, Italy, 1957-58; lectr. dept. sociology and anthropology Fairleigh Dickinson Univ., Teaneck, 1962-63; assoc. dir., Irish Culture and Personality Project Bklyn. Coll., CUNY, 1965-80; vis. scholar dept. anthropology Drew Univ., Madison, N.J., 1981—; student asst. dept. sociology U. Pitts., 1928-31; rsch. editor Hill Survey Com., urban League, Pitts., 1930; lectr. Sch. Nursing, Wayne State U., Detroit, 1944-46; field researcher Italy, Sicily, 1957-58, 60-61, 67, Ireland, 1955, 58, 61, 66, 70, 75; lectr. dept. sociology and anthropology Fairleigh Dickinson U., Madison, 1965-66; Am. specialist lectr. U.S. Dept. State, Far East, Middle East, Europe, Iceland, 1967. Editorial bd. mem. History of Sociology; author: Personnel Aspects of Social Work in Pittsburgh, 1931, Eminent Women" A Cultural Study, 1937; co-author: The Fine Art of Propaganda, 1939, Social Problems in Am., 1949, 2d edit., 1955, Marriage and the Family, 1961, 2d edit. 1967; co-editor: Mental Health and Mental Disorder: A Sociological Approach, 1955; contbr. articles to profl. jours. Bd. dirs. Am. Protestants for Truth about Ireland, dir. women's issues; mem. Ctr. for Constl. Rights, Common Cause, Fellowship of Reconciliation, Friends Com. on Nat. Legislation, Gray Panthers, Nat. Abortion Rights Action League, NAACP, Nat. Emergency Civil Liberties Com., Nat. Urban League, People for Am. Way, Planned Parenthood Fedn. Recipient Sarah P. Sloan scholarship Univ. Pitts., 1926-27, grad. scholarship in sociology Yale Univ., 1932-33. Mem. Am. Sociol. Assn. (Disting. Career award 1990), Ea. Sociol. Soc. (life, sec.-treas. 1956-57, 58-59, chair various coms., merit award 1979), Soc. for Study of Social Problems (founder, life mem., v.p. 1976-77), Assn. for Humanist sociology (founder, pres. 1977-78), Sociol. Practice Assn., Sociologists for Women in Soc., N.J. Sociol. Assn., Sociol. Assn. Ireland (hon.), Am. For Religious Liberty (nat. adv. coun. 1983—), AAUW, ACLU, Am. Friends Svc. Com. and many others. Quaker-Unitarian. Home: 17 Holden Ln Madison NJ 07940-2614

LEE, ELIZABETH SOSENHEIMER, insurance company executive; b. Paterson, N.J., Aug. 21, 1941; d. George Richard and Mary (Betterbed) Sosenheimer; children: John R. Lee Jr., Patricia A. Lee. AS, Union Coll., 1975. Caseworker Union City Welfare Bd., Plainfield, N.J., 1974-75; asst. dir. pub. relations Mt. Carmel Guild, Newark, 1975-76; dir. pub. relations Meml. Gen. Hosp., Union, N.J., 1977-78; project staff recruiter Meml. Gen. Hosp., 1978-79; personnel asst. Muhlenberg Hosp., Plainfield, N.J., 1979-80; adminstrv. mgr. St. Paul Fire & Marine Ins., Edison, N.J., 1980-85; personnel adminstr. Western World Ins. Group, Ramsey, N.J., 1985-87; asst. v.p. Western World Ins. Group, 1988, v.p., 1989—. Mem. N.J. Ins. Personnel Dirs. (chair 1985-87, 89), Nat. Assn. Ind. Insurers (vice chmn. personnel com. 1987-90, chair 1991—), Coll. Ins. (profl. adv. com. 1988-89), English as 2d Lang. (lit. vol. Am.). Republican. Episcopalian. Office: Western World Ins Group 48 S Franklin Tpke Ramsey NJ 07446-2558

LEE, ERIC KIN-LAM, chemical engineer; b. Hong Kong, June 25, 1948; came to U.S., 1969; m. M. Cecilia Wan, Aug. 14, 1972; 1 child, Claudia Y. BS in Textile Chemistry, N.C. State U., 1970, MS, 1972, PhDChemE, 1976. Postdoctoral fellow Max-Planck Inst. for Biophysics, Frankfurt, Germany, 1976-77; project mgr. Bend (Oreg.) Rsch. Inc., 1977-84; sr. rsch. engr. DuPont de Nemours & Co., Wilmington, Del., 1984-86; dir. membrane rsch. and tech. devel. Sepracor Inc., Marlborough, Mass., 1986—. Author: Synthetic Membrane Applications, Ency. of Phys. Sciences and Technology, 1985, 87, 92; contbr. articles to profl. jours.; patentee in field. Mem. N.Am. Membrane Soc. (dir., treas. 1990—), Am. Chem. Soc., Am. Inst. Chem. Engrs. Office: Sepracor Inc 33 Locke Dr Marlborough MA 01752-1183

LEE, GENE F., city manager, accountant; b. Bklyn., July 8, 1960; s. Gam and May Ngon (Tom) L. BBA, Pace U., 1982; MBA, Fordham U., 1988. CPA, N.Y. Bookkeeper part-time McCarthy, Ried, Crisanti & Maffei, Inc., N.Y.C., 1980; account reconcilier part-time Paine, Webber, Jackson & Curtis, Inc., N.Y.C., 1980-81; project analyst part-time Mfrs. Hanover Trust Co., N.Y.C., 1981-82; staff acct. Richard A. Eisner & Co., CPAs, N.Y.C., 1982-84; acct. Cometals, Inc., N.Y.C., 1984-85; fin. analyst The Hertz Corp., N.Y.C., 1985-86; housing analyst, mortgage officer, mgmt. auditor City of N.Y. Dept. Housing Preservation and Devel., N.Y.C., 1988—; part-time acct. Exam. Grader, N.Y.C., 1989-91. Vol., chaperone St. Bartholomew Ch. & Sch., Queens, N.Y., 1987—. Scholar N.Y. Regents, 1978-82, United Fedn. Tchrs., Pace U. Mem. Beta Gamma Sigma, Alpha Chi. Roman Catholic. Office: NYC Dept Housing 100 Gold St Rm 9H New York NY 10038-1605

LEE, GENEVIEVE BRUGGEMAN, publishing company executive; b. Mahnomen, Minn., May 23, 1928; d. Joseph William and Mary Martha (Bastain) Bruggeman; m. Joel Kenneth Lee, Aug. 23, 1946; children: Rebecca Marie, Joel Gregory. Clk. Family Service Assn., N.Y.C., 1946-47; counselor Cin. Employment Service, 1968-70; exec. sec. Ch. Bulls. of Buffalo, Inc., 1970-73, v.p., 1973—; bd. dirs. Woodgate Assn., East Amherst, N.Y.; mem. adv. bd. Schofield Residence,Buffalo, 1983-85, now bd. dirs., exec. bd., sec. 1985-90, vice chmn./sec., 1991—. Mem. Ken-Ton C. of C., Zonta (pres. Kenmore 1984-86, bd. dirs. area 3, 1986-88, sec. dist. IV 1988-90). Republican. Roman Catholic. Home: 258 Old Meadow Dr East Amherst NY 14051-2405 Office: Ch Bulls of Buffalo Inc 745 Englewood Ave Buffalo NY 14223-2493

LEE, JOHN CHONGHOON, SR., financial executive, international lawyer, consultant; b. Seoul, Korea, July 4, 1928; came to U.S., 1948; s. Sung Han and Song Soh (Chae) L.; m. Mary Aniela Cyrulik, May 6, 1967; children: Suzanne, Daniel, Judy, Jeannette, John Jr. BSFS, Georgetown U., 1954; univ. doctorate in laws, faculty of laws, U. Paris, 1957. Spl. asst. to Korean ambassador UN, Geneva, Switzerland, 1955; v.p. Stanford Corp., Washington, 1958-60; chmn., pres. Overseas Investment Corp., Washington, N.Y.C., 1961-70, 76—; chmn. Amfico Corp./Allnations Devel. Bank, 1971-76; co-chmn. Brit. Indsl. Bank, London, 1965-68; chmn. Agronomica Internat. BV, Inc.; speaker internat. law soc. Am. U., 1987-88; founder Global Econ. Action Inst., N.Y.C., Washington; participant World Conf. Econ. and Social Order, Geneva, 1983; bd. dirs., chmn. logistic com. Fulbright Assn.; dir. Inst. Behavioral Rsch., Washington; mem. adv. com. Behavioral Law Ctr., Washington; hon. chmn. World Bus. Rsch. Ctr./Mag., Ark. Fulbright scholar, 1950-54. Office: Overseas Investment Corp Ste 400 4801 Massachusetts Ave NW Washington DC 20016-2087

LEE, JOHN J., petroleum, fertilizer company executive; b. 1933. With Barber Oil Co., N.Y.C., 1970-80, Fibre Sullivan Resources Co., 1980-83; pres. Lee Devel. Corp., 1983—; chmn. d., CEO Seminole Fertilizer Corp., 1989—; pres. Tosco Corp. Office: Tosco Corp 72 Cummings Point Rd Stamford CT 06902-7912*

LEE, JOHN JONGJIN, librarian; b. Seoul, June 7, 1933; came to U.S., 1962; s. Donkyu and Sun Young (Woo) L.; m. Wolsue Chun; children: Carol, Christopher. MA in Internat. Rels., Kon-Kuk U., Seoul, 1962; MA in Polit. Sci., Tufts U., 1968; MLS, George Peabody Coll. for Tchrs., 1969. Tng. officer U.S. 8th Army Civilian Personnel Tng. Office, Seoul, 1960-62; regional rep. Ency. Brit., Boston, 1963-65; reference libr. N.Y. Pub. Libr., N.Y.C., 1968-70; libr. readers' svcs. SUNY Maritime Coll., Bronx, 1971—, editor Maritima, 1971—; mem. chancellor's adv. com. for excellence in librarianship SUNY, Albany, 1984-87. Author: An Annotated List of Currently Published Maritime Periodicals. Acad. del. Maritime chpt. N.Y. State-United Univ. Professions, Albany, 1975—, mem. affirmative action com., 1984—. Recipient Chancellor's award SUNY, Albany, 1983. Mem. N.Y. State Libr. Assn., SUNY Librs. Assn. (exec. bd. 1976-84), United Univ. Professions (rsch. grantee 1985-86, 87-88). Republican. Home: 5 Country Ridge Rd Scarsdale NY 10583-6621 Office: SUNY Maritime Coll Ft Schuyler Bronx NY 10465

LEE, JOSEPH WILLIAM, sales executive; b. Florence, S.C., Sept. 19, 1943; s. Warner Lou and Rosalee (Hyman) L.; m. Rita Martin, Sept. 8, 1962; children: Mark Stephen, Allison Lynette. Grad. high sch., Florence. Clk. Atlantic Coast Line R.R., Florence, 1962-69; sales rep. Durham (N.C.) & So. Rwy., 1969-74; dist. sales mgr. Westmoreland Coal Sales Co., Charlotte, N.C., 1974-82; v.p. purchasing Westmoreland Coal Sales Co., Phila., 1982-85, v.p. purchasing distbn., 1985-88, v.p. purchasing and northern sales, 1988-91; sr. v.p. Westmoreland Coal Sales Co., Phila., Pa., 1991; pres. Westmoreland Coal Sales Co., Charlotte, N.C., 1991—, also bd. dirs.; bd. dirs. Ea. Coal & Coke Corp., ECC Leasing Co., Ky. Criterion Coal Co. Mem. N.C. Coal Inst., So. Coals Conf., Inc. (trustee 1989-92). Republican. Office: Westmoreland Coal Sales Co 200 S Broad St Philadelphia PA 19102-3803

LEE, J(OSEPHINE) PATRICIA, nursing educator; b. Equinunk, Pa., Sept. 6, 1924; d. Blanche Elizabeth (Frisbie) Trout; m. Maurice J. Lee (dec. 1985); children: Valerie Marie Lee Zaba, Terry Granville. BSN, Keuka Coll., 1949; MS in Nursing Edn., Syracuse U., 1984. Tchr. health edn. Binghamton (N.Y.) North High Sch., 1965-68; assoc. prof. Broome Community Coll., Binghamton, 1968—. Deacon presbyn. ch., Binghamton, 1991. Home: 940 River Rd # 97 Binghamton NY 13901-1441

LEE, JUDITH ANNE, marketing professional, magazine editor; b. McAlester, Okla., July 8, 1950; d. Eddie W. and Irene Laverne (Hicks) L.; m. James Lavern Hodge, Jan. 30, 1970 (div. Dec. 1977); 1 child, Joshua Lee. AA in Bus., Crowder Coll., 1972. Pres. J.L.I., Neosho, Mo., 1981—; founder, editor In... Joplin (Mo.) Metro mag., 1984—; founder The Epicenter, Joplin, 1987—; dir. mktg. Techmark Ltd., Neosho, 1987—; bd. dirs. Ozark Ctr., Joplin, 1983, Am. Heart Assn., Joplin, 1987. inventor card games Josh, 1982, E.W. Lee, 1988. Pres. Neosho PTA, 1982-84; Cub Scout leader troop 34, 1982-84; host parent Internat. Ednl. Found., 1983-88; pres. Gifted Assn., Neosho, 1985-86. Named Woman of Yr., Beta Sigma Phi, Neosho, 1983-84; recipient Bringing Out Your Best award Budweiser Light, 1983. Mem. Am. Mktg. Assn. (exec.), Neosho C. of C. (retail dir. 1983-84), Kansas City Mktg. Assn., Joplin Advt. Club (Addy Award of Merit 1987, Addy Award of Excellence 1988), Mensa Internat. Club, Soroptimist Club (treas. 1984-85). Home: 23 Brimmer St TH 1 Boston MA 02108

LEE, KEUN SOK, business educator; b. Pusan, Korea, May 12, 1954; came to the U.S., 1981; s. Namho and Okki (Ryo) L.; m. Youn Lee, Apr. 15, 1980; children: Grace, Daniel. BA, Hankuk U. of Fgn. Studies, Seoul, 1979; MBA, U. No. Iowa, 1983; DBA, U. Ky., 1987; postgrad., Columbia U. Rsch. cons. U. No. Iowa, Cedar Falls, 1982-83; rsch. asst. U. Ky., Lexington, 1983-84, teaching asst., 1984-85; instr. Hofstra U., Hempstead, N.Y., 1986-87; asst. prof. Hofstra U., 1987—. Author numerous publs. in mktg. jours. and confs. Recipient best article award Mu Kappa Tau, 1989. Mem. Acad. Mktg. Svc., Acad. Internat. Bus., Assn. for Consumer Rsch., Am. Mktg. Assn. (assoc.). Home: 17 Stanwich Rd Smithtown NY 11787-2356 Office: Hofstra U 110 and 222 Weller Hall Hempstead NY 11550

LEE, KWAN IL, anesthesiologist; b. Kwangju, Chonnam, Korea, Dec. 13, 1943; came to U.S., 1970; s. Chongman Lee and Ockja Oh; m. Shang Ock, Jan. 27, 1972; children: Daewon, Sara. MD, Chonnam U. Med. Sch., Kwangju, 1967. Lic. physician, Pa.; lic. in acupuncture, Pa.; diplomate Am. Bd. Anesthesiologists, Am. Soc. of Pain Mgmt. Anesthesiologist, dept. dir. Ohio Valley Gen. Hosp., McKees Rocks, Pa., 1975—. Office: Ohio Valley Gen Hosp Heckel Rd McKees Rocks PA 15136

LEE, LILLIAN VANESSA, microbiologist; b. N.Y.C., June 1, 1951; d. Wenceslao and Ada (Otero) Cancel; B.S. in Biology, St. Johns U., 1972; M.S. in Microbiology, Wagner Coll., 1974; m. Thomas Christopher Lee, June 11, 1972; children—Tovan, John-Peter, Phillip-Michael. Grad. lab. asst. in microbiology Wagner Coll., S.I., N.Y., 1972-74; clin. microbiology technologist Queens Hosp. Center, Jamaica, N.Y., 1974-81, clin. microbiology supr., 1981-84; sect. head microbiology Nyack Hosp. (N.Y.), 1984—. Cert. registered microbiologist and specialist in microbiology, clin. lab. specialist. Mem. Am. Soc. Clin. Pathologists, Am. Soc. Microbiology, Am. Acad. Microbiology, Med. Mycology Soc., N.Y., N.Y. Acad. Scis., Nat. Cert. Agy. Med. Lab. Personnel, Synergists Soc. Home: 14 Continental Dr West Nyack NY 10994-2803 Office: Nyack Hosp N Midland Ave Nyack NY 10960

LEE, MARILYN (IRMA) MODARELLI, law librarian; b. Jersey City, Dec. 8, 1934; d. Alfred E. and Florence Olga (Koment) Modarelli; m. Alfred McC. Lee III, June 8, 1957 (div. July 1985); children: Leslie K., Alfred McClung IV, Andrew Modarelli Lee. BA, Swarthmore (Pa.) Coll., 1956; JD, Western New Eng. Sch. of Law, 1985. Bar: Mass. 1986. Claims rep., supr. region II Social Security Adminstrn., Jersey City, 1956-59; law libr. County of Franklin, Greenfield, Mass., 1972-78; libr. I Franklin Law Libr. Mass. Trial Ct., Greenfield, 1978—. Chmn. Franklin County (Mass.) Regional Tech., Turners Falls, Mass., 1974-76, Sch. Bldg Com., 1974-76; clk. Franklin County Tech. Sch., 1976-81; vice chmn. Greenfield Planning Bd., 1987—, Franklin County Planning Bd., 1989—. Mem. Mass. Bar Assn., Franklin County Bar Assn. (vice chmn. lawyer referral com. 1991—), Law Librs. of New Eng., Am. Assn. Law Librs. Office: Mass Trial Ct Franklin Law Libr 425 Main St Greenfield MA 01301-3313

LEE, PATRICK CHRISTOPHER, general surgeon, surgical intensivist; b. Grand Haven, Mich., Mar. 11, 1955; s. Raymond Thomas and Beatrice (Chao) L.; m. Barbra Ann Masel, Mar. 14, 1986; children: Benjamin, Megan, Andrew. AB cum laude, Harvard Coll., 1976; MD, U. Mass., Worcester, 1982. Diplomate Am. Bd. Surgery. Dir. SICU Worcester City Hosp., 1988-91; internship U. Mass. Med. Ctr., Worcester, 1982-83; residency U. Mass. Med. Ctr., 1983-87; asst. prof. surgery U. Mass. Med. Sch., Worcester, 1988—; assoc. dir. SICU St. Vincent Hosp., Worcester, 1991—. Contbr. articles to med. jours. Maj. U.S. Army, 1991. Recipient Cecile Lehman Mayer Rsch. award Am. Coll. Chest Physicians. Fellow Am. Coll. Surgeons (assoc.); mem. Soc. Critical Care Medicine, Assn. Mil. Surgeons of U.S. Home: 4 Coachman Ridge Shrewsbury MA 01545 Office: St Vincent Hosp Dept Critical Care Medicine 25 Winthrop St Worcester MA 01604

LEE, PATRICK PAUL, manufacturing executive; b. Portsmouth, Va., Oct. 16, 1938; s. Gordon R. Lee and Helen (Ragenard) Frerichs; m. Nancy Clarke Jackson, Jan. 2, 1958 (dec. Sept. 1983); children: Barbara Lee Rhee, Patrick W., Elizabeth J., Christopher; m. Mary Sidney Sander, Aug. 2, 1984. BSAE, St. Louis U., 1959. Pres. Enidine Inc., Orchard Park, N.Y., 1966—; chmn. bd. dirs. Enine Inc., Orchard Park, Enidine GmbH., Weil am Rhein, Fed. Republic Germany, Enidine AG, Sarnen, Switzerland, Enidine Co Ltd., Tokyo. Inventor, patentee in field. Mem. governing bd. Buffalo (N.Y.) Gen. Hosp. Mental Health Ctr., 1988, steering com. Greater Buffalo C. of C., 1988. Mem. Country Club Buffalo (Williamsville, N.Y.), Saturn Club (Buffalo), Orchard Park Country Club. Republican. Roman Catholic. Home: 16 Hillsboro Dr Orchard Park NY 14127-3411 Office: Enidine Inc 7 Centre Dr Orchard Park NY 14127-2293

LEE, PETER BERNARD, marketing executive; b. Salem, Mass., July 18, 1959; s. Raymond Thomas and Beatrice (Chao) L.; m. Jiliana Helen, June 14, 1986; children: Brendan Christopher, Garrett William. BBA in Mktg. cum laude, U. Mass., Amherst, 1981. Salesman Keebler Co., Manchester, Conn., 1981-82; tchr. English English Lang. Schs., Inc. (ELSI), Taipei, Republic of China, 1982-86; account supr. Cambridge Advtg., Taipei, 1983-85; account mgr. Gaynor Assocs. Internat., Taipei, 1985-86; asst. account exec. Giardini/Russell, Inc., Watertown, Mass., 1986-87; placement specialist Fidelity Investments, Inc., Boston, 1987-88; dir. mktg. svcs. Mass. Office of

Travel & Tourism, Boston, 1988—; founder Scholarship Rsch. Svc., 1991. Contbr. articles to profl. jours.; inventor "10 PACE" method for learning and teaching lang., 1983. Bd. dirs. Boston Ctr. for Internat. Visitors, 1989-90, South Cove Community Health Ctr., 1991—. Mem. U. Mass. Greater Boston Alumni Club (bd. dirs. 1988—, v.p. devel. 1990—). Roman Catholic.

LEE, REBECCA, college administrator; b. N.Y.C.. BA in Psychology, U. Pa., 1978, MS in Edn., 1979. Resident dir. U. Calif., Davis, 1980-82; area coord. Oberlin (Ohio) Coll., 1982-84, asst. dean of residential life, 1984-86; asst. dean of students Amherst (Mass.) Coll., 1986-89, assoc. dean of students, 1989—. Mem. Asian and Asian Am. Women's Network, 1988—. Mem. Nat. Assn. for Women in Edn. (chair 1993 Conf. program, Dorothy Truex award 1991), Nat. Women's Student Leadership Project (adv. bd.), Asian Pacific Ams. in Higher Edn. Office: Amherst Coll Assoc Dean Students Amherst MA 01002

LEE, RICHARD STEWARD, vocational educator, school system administrator; b. Woodbury, N.J., Dec. 14, 1941; s. George Walton and Ethel (Steward) L.; m. Loretta Green, June 20, 1964; children: Darryl Keith, Tamela Nicole. BS in Indsl. Arts Edn., Cen. State Coll., Wilberforce, Ohio, 1964; MS in Human Growth and Devel., Fairleigh Dickinson U., 1978; degree in Bibl. Counseling, Christian Rsch. & Devel. Sch., Phila., 1981. Cert. tchr. of indsl. and tech. edn., supr. of vocat. and tech. edn. from K thru 12th grade. Auto mechanic George Lee's Auto, Deptford, N.J., 1955-70; tchr. Deptford High Sch., 1964-67, Woodrow Wilson High Sch., Camden, N.J., 1967-70; tchr. coord. Hatch Mid. Sch., Camden, N.J., 1970-72, Camden High Vocat., 1972-88; supr. Adminstrn. Bldg. Camden City Bd. Edn., 1988—; instr. Fairleigh Dickinson U., Rutherford, N.J., 1979, Christian Rsch. Child Devel., 1982, facilitator bibl. counseling, 1982. Named Deacon of the Yr. NAACP, Deptford, 1985, Dir. of Yr. Woodbury Jaycees, 1971. Mem. Four Chaplains (hon.). Baptist. Home: 1732 Dayton Ave Paulsboro NJ 08066-1507 Office: Camden City Bd Edn 1656 Kaighns Ave Camden NJ 08103-3607

LEE, ROBERT B., educator; b. Columbus, Miss., May 20, 1944; s. Johnnie and Martha E. (Armstrong) L.; m. Peggy Perkins, Dec. 30, 1972; children: Robert II, Candace. BA, Howard U., 1966, MA, 1970; PhD, Ga. State U., 1986. Asst. dir. career planning Fisk U., Nashville, 1968-69; guidance counselor Montclair (N.J.) High Sch., 1969-71; mgmt. trainee Ford Motor Co., Atlanta, 1971-72; asst. dean of students Clark Coll., Atlanta, 1972-78; asst. dir. fin. aide Lamar U., Beaumont, Tex., 1978-80, dir. spl. svcs., 1980-88; asst. dean student devel. York Coll., CUNY, Jamaica, 1988-90; dean student affairs Medgar Evers Coll., CUNY, Bklyn., 1990-91, assoc. prof., dir. pub. policy, 1991—; founder, prin. Creative Writing Cons., Beaumont, 1986-88; presenter in field. Contbr. articles to profl. jours. Campaign coord. Jesse Jackson for Pres., Beaumont, 1984, 88; elected Leadership Beaumont, 1987; chmn. bd. Steinhagen YMCA, Beaumont, 1984-85. Regents scholarship Ga. State U., 1983-84. Mem. Nat. Assn. Student Personnel, Assn. of Black Psychologists, Phi Delta Kappa, Kappa Alpha Psi. Home: 111 Mulberry St Apt 2T Newark NJ 07102-4010 Office: Medgar Evers Coll 1150 Carroll St Brooklyn NY 11225-2298

LEE, ROBERT DORWIN, public affairs educator, academic administrator; b. Detroit, Jan. 14, 1939; s. Robert Dorwin Sr. and Virginia (Stanow) L.; m. Barbara Marvin, June 4, 1968; children: Robert, Craig, Cameron. BA, Wayne State U., 1960; MA, Syracuse (N.Y.) U., 1963, PhD, 1967. From asst. to prof. Pa. State U., University Park, 1966—, head pub. adminstrn. dept., 1988—. Author: Public Personnel Systems, 2d edit., 1987; lead author: Public Budgeting Systems, 4th edit., 1989. Home: 672 Devonshire Dr State College PA 16803-3231 Office: Pa State U Dept Pub Adminstrn 205 S Burrowes St State College PA 16801-4009

LEE, ROBERT EDWARD, JR., lawyer; b. Bklyn., Feb. 6, 1941; s. Robert E. and Edna C. (Koerber) L.; m. Janet A., July 12, 1975; children: Kristen A., Robyn E. B.A. summa cum laude, Niagara U., 1962; LL.B., St. John's U., 1967. Bar: N.Y. 1967, N.J. 1975. Asso. Cunningham & Lee, and predecessor firms, N.Y.C., 1967-72, jr. ptnr., 1972-78, sr. ptnr., 1978—; assoc. Snevily, Ely & Williams, Westfield, N.J.; instr. St. Francis Coll., 1975-76. Served to 1st lt. U.S. Army, 1963-65. Mem. ABA, N.J. State Bar Assn., Bklyn. Bar Assn., Cath. Lawyers Guild (past pres.). Republican. Roman Catholic. Clubs: Lawyers of Bklyn. (past pres.); KC (Westfield, N.J.). Home: 957 Woodmere Dr Westfield NJ 07090-4235 Office: Cunningham & Lee 111 Fulton St New York NY 10038-2711

LEE, ROBERT SANFORD, psychologist; b. Bklyn., Nov. 16, 1924; s. Mark and Celia (Edelstein) L.; m. Barbara Kaplan, June 9, 1963 (div. 1980); children: David, Daniel. Student, U. Chgo., 1943-46; B.A., NYU, 1947, Ph.D., 1956. Psychologist, N.Y. Program dir. U.S. Bur. Census, N.Y.C., 1947-50; research assoc. NYU, 1952-58; asst. dir. The Psychol. Corp., N.Y.C., 1959-61; research advisor for communications IBM, Armonk, N.Y., 1961-81; sr. v.p. McCann-Erickson, Inc., N.Y.C., 1981-84; assoc. prof. mktg. Lubin Grad. Sch. Bus. Pace U., N.Y.C., 1984—. Author: (with Chein, Gerard and Rosenfeld) The Road to H, 1964. Served with U.S. Army, 1943-45. Mem. AAAS, Am. Assn. for Pub. Opinion research (exec. council 1967-68, 71-72), Am. Psychol. Assn., N.Y. Assn. for Pub. Opinion Research, Am. Mktg. Assn. Home: 277 W 10th St #ph-j New York NY 10014-2517 Office: Pace U LGSB 1 Pace Plz New York NY 10038-1598

LEE, SAMUEL DENNIS, agency examiner; b. Dayton, Ohio, Sept. 23, 1958; s. Samuel Jr. and Joyce Eileen (Mitchell) L.; m. Cinda Haven Lansaw, Aug. 6, 1988; 1 child, Monika Eileen. Cert., USN, 1979, USN, 1982, USN, 1983. Enlisted USN, 1975, 1st class petty officer, resigned, 1985; sr. insp. Aeronca Aerospace, Middletown, Ohio, 1986-87; NAVSEA examiner Trans Eastern Ins., Inc., Washington, Pa., 1987—; tchr. Community Coll. of Allegheny County, Pitts., 1987; cons. Jefferson Tech. Coll., Jefferson County, Ohio, 1987, Aeronca Aerospace, Middletown, 1988. Mem. Am. Soc. for Non-Destructive Testing, Am. Welding Soc., Am. Mgmt. Assn. Republican. Presbyterian. Home: 495 Mckinley Ave Washington PA 15301-3936 Office: TEI Analytical Svcs Inc 35 W Point Rd Washington PA 15301-5453

LEE, SHENG YEN, publisher; b. Xinyang, Henan, China, Dec. 28, 1924; s. Yi-San and Qin-Yuan (Gan) L.; m. Winnie Cho, Aug. 25, 1949; 1 child, Yin May. BS in Chemistry, Nat. Northeastern U., 1946; PhD in Chemistry, U. Colo., 1964. Chemist inspector Agrl. Inspection Bur., Taiwan, 1948-51; lang. interpreter Chinese Army, Taiwan, 1951-53; chem. engr. Agrl. Chem. Works, Kaohsiung, Taiwan, 1953-59; chemist Polymer Corp., Ltd., Sarnia, Ontario, Can., 1965-68; chemist, supr. Harry Diamond Labs., U.S. Army, Adelphi, Md., 1969-79; chemist Goddard Space Flight Ctr., NASA, Greenbelt, Md., 1979-91; pres., editor Chinese Am. Forum, Inc., Silver Spring, Md., 1982—; prof. hon. Xinyang Tchrs. Coll., 1991. Founder Chinese Am. Forum, 1984—; patentee in field; contbr. sci. papers to profl. publs. Dir. Assn. for Promoting Democracy in China, Washington, 1989—. Named Inventor-of-the-yr. finalist NASA, 1990. Home: 606 Brantford Ave Silver Spring MD 20904 Office: Chinese Am Forum Inc 606 Brantford Ave Silver Spring MD 20904

LEE, SUN-OCK, dancer, choreographer, educator; b. Seoul, Jan. 14, 1943; came to U.S., 1969; d. Chong Ha and Kisoon (Kim) L.; div. 1985; 1 child, Honey Lee. MA, NYU, PhD, 1984. Founder Sun Ock Lee Studio Theater, N.Y.C., 1976—; founding mem. Asian New Dance Coalition, 1978—; teaching fellow Zen dance NYU, N.Y.C., 1978-80; artist in residence N.Y. State Arts Coun., 1981-82; instr. U. Hawaii, 1987; asst. dir.performing arts dept. Asia Soc., N.Y.C., 1992—; choreographer, performer Festival 2000, Hong Kong; coord. Mini Asian Music and Dance Festival, at LaMama; pioneer, founder Zen Dance, 1972—, N.Y. premiere Lotus I, II, II, IV, Asia Soc., 1991; tchr. Zen dance N.Y. Open Ctr., Beijing Dance Acad., 1988, organizer Zen Performing Arts Festival, 1979; participant with Zen dance at Internat. Jazz Festival at Seoul Olympic, 1988; adj. prof. NYU Dept. Arts Communication, 1984—; lectr., demonstrator colls. and schs. throughout Asia, Europe, U.S. Author: Zen Dance: Mediation in Movement, 1985, Zen Dance: Meditation in Movement II, 1990, Zen Quest: Enlightenment in Daily Life, 1990; N.Y. debut Carnegie Hall, 1972; appeared at Alice Tully Hall, Town Hall, Avery Fisher Hall, All Nation's Co.; collaborator video art prodn. Global Groove, 1973; resident artist Asian Soc. Performing Arts, 1974—; toured Europe and Asia with own co., 1975, 1984, France, 1981; performer Zen dance Internat. Theater Inst. Conf., Stockholm, 1977, Festival Traditional Arts, Rennes, France, 1978, Asian Dance Conf., Hawaii, 1978, numerous other events. Nat. Endowment Choreographer's award, 1980. Home and Office: Zen Temple of Cresskill 185 6th St Cresskill NJ 07626-2046

LEE, TED CHOONG KIL, biochemist; b. Seoul, Korea, Dec. 3, 1940; came to U.S. 1965; s. Jong Hyun and Soon Yea (Kim) L.; m. Sue Jane Moon, Sept. 10, 1966; children: Shirley Moon, Charles Young, Michelle Sara. BS, Korea U., Seoul, 1965; PhD, Okla. State U., 1971. Rsch. assoc. Rockefeller U., N.Y.C., 1971-73; asst. prof. Med. Coll. Howard U., Washington, 1973-78; vis. asst. prof. Cornell U., Ithaca, N.Y., 1978-81; sr. rsch. scientist Revlon Health Care Group, Tuckahoe, N.Y., 1981-85; prin. scientist Meloy Labs., Springfield, Va., 1985-88; sect. mgr. process devel. Rhone-Poulenc Rorer Biotech., Inc., King of Prussia, Pa., 1988—. Contbr. articles to profl. jours. Cpl. Korean army, 1961-63. Mem. Am. Chem. Soc., Am. Soc. Biochemistry and Molecular Biology. Office: Rhone-Poulenc Rorer Biotech 640 Allendale Rd King Of Prussia PA 19406

LEE, TSUNG-DAO, physicist, educator; b. Shanghai, China, Nov. 25, 1926; s. Tsing-Kong L. and Ming-Chang (Chang); m. Jeannette Chin, June 3, 1950; children: James, Stephen. Student, Nat. Chekiang U., Kweichow, China, 1943-44, Nat. S.W. Assoc. U., Kunming, China, 1945-46; PhD, U. Chgo., 1950; DSc (hon.), Princeton U., 1958; LLD (hon.), Chinese U., Hong Kong, 1969; DSc (hon.), CCNY, 1978. Research assoc. in astronomy U. Chgo., 1950; research assoc., lectr. physics U. Calif., Berkeley, 1950-51; mem. Inst. for Advanced Study, Princeton (N.J.) U., 1951-53, prof. physics, 1960-63; asst. prof. Columbia U., N.Y.C., 1953-55, assoc. prof., 1955-56, prof., 1956-60, 63—, adj. prof., 1960-62, Enrico Fermi prof. physics, 1964—, also Univ. prof.; Loeb lectr. Harvard U., Cambridge, Mass., 1957, 64. Editor: Weak Interactions and High Energy Nutrino Physics, 1966, Particle Physics and Introduction to Field Theory, 1981. Recipient Albert Einstein Sci. award Yeshiva U., 1957, (with Chen Ning Yang) Nobel prize in physics, 1957. Mem. NAS, Acad. Sinica, Am. Acad. Arts and Scis., Am. Philos. Soc., Acad. Nazionale dei Lincei. Office: Columbia U Dept Physics Morningside Heights New York NY 10027*

LEE, WANDA DARLENE, small business owner; b. Easton, Pa., Feb. 26, 1951; d. Ernest Henry and Dorothy Mae (DeReamer) Hoffner; m. Clarence Omar Dietterich, Oct. 3, 1970 (div. 1972); 1 child, Derek John; m. Larry Warren Lee, Apr. 4, 1981; 1 child, Ryan Carmen. Grad. high sch., Pen Argyl, Pa. Dental asst. College Hill Dental Group, Easton, 1969-79; owner K&L Masonry, Wind Gap, Pa., 1982—. Author poems. Home: 111 S Fairview Ave Wind Gap PA 18091-1416

LEE, WILLIAM LAMBORN, literature educator; b. Amarillo, Tex., Oct. 17, 1947; s. William Lamborn and Louise Monning (Elliott) L.; m. Carla Jo Shatz, May 20, 1973 (div. June 1978); m. Barbara de Cerchio, Sept. 5, 1981. BA, Dartmouth Coll., 1969; BA, MA, Oxford (Eng.) U., 1971, 86; MPhil, Yale U., 1973, PhD, 1980. Instr. Yale U., New Haven, Conn., 1973-74, Colby Coll., Waterville, Maine, 1974-75, 76-77, Tufts U., Medford, Mass., 1978-79; instr. history and lit. Harvard U., Cambridge, Mass., 1978-80, lectr., 1980-83; asst. prof. Yeshiva U., N.Y.C., 1983—, acting chair dept. English, 1986-87, chair Yeshiva Coll. Senate, 1987-88, 91-92. Contbr. articles to profl. publs. Chair, founder West Side Neighborhood Assn., Englewood, N.J., 1988—, newsletter editor, 1990—. Recipient Sr. Prof. award for disting. teaching Yeshiva U., 1985, 87, 89; Marshall scholar, 1969-71; Kent fellow, 1971-74, prize teaching fellow, 1974; grantee Mellon Found., 1984. Mem. MLA, AAUP, Nat. Coun. Tchrs. English (program com. 1986-87, 88—), Soc. for Values in Higher Edn., Danforth Found. (exec. com. 1971-72), N.E. Victorian Studies Assn., William Morris Soc., Phi Beta Kappa. Democrat. Home: 163 W Demarest Ave Englewood NJ 07631-2240 Office: Yeshiva U 500 W 185th St New York NY 10033-3201

LEE, WILLIAM SWAIN, judge; b. Phila., Dec. 18, 1935; s. Walter Hutchison and Virginia (Swain) L.; m. Mary McGrew, June 12, 1965 (div. Jan. 1985); children: Mary Caroline, William Swain Jr., Virginia Hutchison, John Edwin Berry. BA, Duke U., 1957; JD, U. Pa., 1960. Bar: D.C. 1961, U.S. Ct. Mil. Appeals 1962, Del. 1964, U.S. Dist. Ct. Del. 1965. Dep. atty. den. Del. Dept. Justice, Georgetown, 1966-69; ptnr. Betts and Lee, Attys., Georgetown, 1969-77; assoc. judge Family Ct., State of Del., Georgetown, 1977-86; assoc. judge Superior Ct., State of Del., Georgetown, 1986-89, resident judge Sussex County, 1989—; county atty. Sussex County Coun., Georgetown, 1971-73; chmn. Sussex County Bd. Adjustment, Georgetown, 1960-71; master Family Ct., Georgetown, 1972-77. Chmn. Sussex County Rep. Exec. Com., Georgetown, 1973-77; del. Rep. Nat. Convention, Kansas City, Mo., 1976; mem. State Tax Appeals Bd., Wilmington, Del., 1970-72; chmn. adminstrv. bd. Epworth United Meth. Ch., Rehoboth Beach, Del., 1975-91; pres. Old Union Ch. Soc., Townsend, Del., 1976—. 1st lt. USMC, 1961-64. Republican. Home: 27 Bay Harbor Dr Rehoboth Beach DE 19971-1550 Office: Superior Ct State of Del Sussex County Courthouse PO Box 152 Georgetown DE 19947-0152

LEE, WOONG MAN, pathologist; b. Seoul, Korea, Dec. 3, 1938; came to U.S., 1967; s. Jay Hyuck and Sung Yong Lee; m. Young Sook Kim, 1968; children: Danny Eugene, Francis Eusun, Peggy Eurie. BS, Seoul Nat. U., 1960, MD, 1964. Asst. resident Albany (N.Y.) Med. Ctr. Hosp., 1967-70, resident, 1970-72, asst. attending pathologist, 1974-79; instr. Albany Med. Coll., 1970-74, asst. prof., 1974-79; attending pathologist Albany VA Hosp., 1974-79; pathologist Glens Falls (N.Y.) Hosp., 1979—. Roman Catholic. Office: Glens Falls Hosp 100 Park St Glens Falls NY 12801-4447

LEEB, BRUCE HARVEY, advertising executive; b. Milw., Aug. 16, 1941; s. Harry and Claire (Mugier) L.; m. Kay Carol Lachman, Aug. 15, 1964 (div. Oct. 1979); children: Ellen Claire, Aimee Estelle; m. Rona Michele Eagle, June 8, 1980; 1 child, Aaron Nathan. BA, San Jose (Calif.) State U., 1964. Various positions Roerig Div. Pfizer/Pfizer Pharms., San Francisco and N.Y.C., 1967-78; group mktg. mgr. Pfizer, Inc., N.Y.C., 1978-80; dir. mktg. Becton Dickinson, Orangeburg, N.Y., 1980-82; account supr. Gross, Townsend, Frank, Inc., N.Y.C., 1982-83; various positions Rolf Werner Rosenthal, Inc., N.Y.C., 1983-87; v.p., account group supr. Rolf Werner Rosenthal Div. Ogilvy & Mather, N.Y.C., 1987-89; sr. v.p., dir. client svcs. RWR Advt., Nelson Communications, N.Y.C., 1989-91; pres. Bruce Leeb & Co., Wyckoff, N.J., 1991—. Pres. Marin County-San Rafael (Calif.) Homeowners Assn., 1973. With U.S. Army, 1959-60. Office: 666 Godwin Ave Ste 300 Midland Park NJ 07432

LEECE, WILLIAM ALFRED, lawyer; b. Plainfield, N.J., Sept. 18, 1912; s. William Rowland and Ethel Emily (Goodson) L.; m. H. Patricia Murphy, June 25, 1947; children: Mary Patricia, Elizabeth Anne, William A. Jr. AB, George Washington U., 1940; LLB, Georgetown U., 1950. Bar: Conn. 1950, D.C. 1950, U.S. Dist. Ct. D.C. 1950, U.S. Supreme Ct. 1958. Spl. agt. FBI, Washington, 1941-51; asst. counsel com. on govt. ops. U.S. Senate, Washington, 1951-53; spl. asst. to the atty. gen. U.S. Dept. Justice, Washington, 1953-54; gen. counsel, staff dir. com. on labor and pub. welfare U.S. Senate, Washington, 1954-55; v.p. Prudential Ins. Co., Newark, 1955-77; security dir. com. on intelligence U.S. Ho. of Reps., Washington, 1977-80. Board dirs. ARC, Litchfield, Conn., Vis. Nurse Assn., Litchfield Vol. Soc. for the Blind and Handicapped, Litchfield Hist. Soc. Mem. Soc. Former Senate Aides, Soc. Former Spl. Agts. FBI, Bar Assn. of D.C., Litchfield County Bar Assn. Republican. Episcopalian. Home: 7 Emerson Ct Litchfield CT 06759-3313

LEE-CURRY, JANETTE MARIE, physical therapist; b. Phila., Mar. 9, 1957; d. Wheeler Edward and Sadie (Young) Lee; m. Wallace Edward Curry, Sept. 26, 1981; children: Nicole, Wallace Jr. (dec.), Karey. BS in Phys. Therapy, Temple U., 1980. Lic. physical therapist, Pa., N.J. Phys. therapy aide Phila. State Hosp., 1977-78; phys. therapist Suburban Gen. Hosp., Norristown, Pa., 1980-83, St. Joseph's Hosp., Phila., 1983-85, Pa. Home Health Svcs., Phila., 1984-85; dir. phys. therapy Haverford (Pa.) State Hosp., 1985-86; cons. phys. therapist Mid-Atlantic Rehab. Svcs., Phila., 1986-87; phys. therapist, owner Old York Rd. Phys. Therapy and Cons. Svcs., Phila., 1987—. Co-chmn. West Oak Ln. Concerned Citizens, Phila., 1983; co-block capt. 500 E. Washington Ln. Neighbors, 1989-90. Mem. Am. Phys. Therapy Assn. (legis. ambassador 1989-91), 5900 Block Old Yk. Rd. Bus. Assn. (pres. 1990-91). Office: Old York Rd Phys Therapy 5910 Old York Rd Philadelphia PA 19141-1806

LEED, CAROL ANN, language professional, educator; b. Lancaster, Pa., Feb. 9, 1949; d. Paul Myers Groff and Evelyn Louise (Yost) Getz; m. Allen Wilmer Leed, Sept. 24, 1971 (div. 1988); children: Heather Michelle, Adam Jason. AB in Spanish, Wilson Coll., Chambersburg, Pa., 1971; MEd, Marywood Coll., Scranton, Pa., 1982. Spanish tchr. Octorara Area Sch. Dist., Atglen, Pa., 1971-72; ESL tchr. Sch. Dist. of Lancaster (Pa.), 1972—; career cons., mentor Wilson Coll., Chambersburg, 1981—; mentor for grad. students Immaculata (Pa.) Coll., 1987-88; core team facilitator Edward Hand Jr. High Sch., Lancaster, 1988—. Bd. dirs. YWCA, Lancaster, 1972-73. Mem. Tchrs. of English to Speakers of Other Languages, Wilson Coll. Alumni Club (pres. 1988—). Office: Sch Dist of Lancaster Hand Jr High Sch S Ann & Juniata Sts Lancaster PA 17602

LEEDS, BARRY HOWARD, English educator; b. N.Y.C., Dec. 6, 1940; s. Andrew Samuel and Paula (Stark) L.; m. Robin Leigh Flowers, Apr. 20, 1968; children: Brett Ashley, Leslie Robin. BA, Columbia U., 1962, MA, 1963; Phd, Ohio U., 1967. Lectr. CUNY, 1963-64; instr. U. Tex., El Paso, 1964-65; asst. prof. Cen. Conn. State U., New Britain, 1968-71, assoc. prof., 1971-76, prof., 1976-91; disting. prof., 1991—; cons. Am. lit. Choice mag., Middletown, Conn., 1968—; vis. mem. faculty Yale U., 1984-85. Author: The Structured Vision of Norman Mailer, 1969, Ken Kesey, 1981; editor: Conn. Rev., 1989—, mem. editorial bd., 1986—; contbg. editor D.C. Heath Anthology Am. Lit., 1986—; contbr. numerous articles to profl. jours. including Saturday Rev., Modern Fiction Studies. Alumni interviewer Columbia Coll., N.Y.C., 1982—. Conn. State U. grantee, 1986—; recipient Disting. Svc. award Cen. Conn. State U., 1982. Home: 133 Jerome Ave Burlington CT 06013-2433 Office: Cen Conn State U Dept of English 1615 Stanley St New Britain CT 06053-2439

LEEDS, DOROTHY, author, lecturer, consultant; b. N.Y.C., Jan. 7, 1934; d. Hyman and Tonia (Perkins) Adelsberg; m. Arnold D. Weinstock, Dec. 19, 1955; children: Laura, Ian. BA, Adelphi U., 1955; MA, Columbia U., 1956. Tchr. Great Neck (N.Y.) High Sch., 1956-57, Martin Van Buren High Sch., N.Y.C., 1957-58; actress Broadway tour Stop the World I Want to Get Off, 1960-66; pres. Dorothy Leeds Knits, N.Y.C., also Ireland, 1970-77; sr. account exec. Chislovsky Design div. Grey Advt., N.Y.C., 1977-78; cons. Am. Mgmt. Assn., N.Y.C., 1978—; bd. dirs. The Fashion Group, N.Y.C., 1980-82, The Lighthouse, N.Y.C., 1986—; cons. Mobil Oil, Citibank, Equitable, Digital Equipment, Conde Nast. Author: Smart Questions, 1987, Power Speak, 1988, Marketing Yourself, 1991, Smart Questions to Ask Your Doctor, Lawyer, Broker and Insurance Agent, 1992. Mem. River Park Assn., N.Y.C., 1990—, Save the Children, 1985—, Concerned Citizens Montauk, N.Y., 1969—. Mem. NATAS, ASTD, AFTRA, Nat. Speakers Assn. Home: 800 W End Ave # 10A New York NY 10025-5467 Office: Organizational Techs 800 W End Ave # 10A New York NY 10025-5467

LEEDS, MORTON WILLIAM, chemical company executive; b. N.Y.C., Dec. 18, 1916; s. William and Ida (Witkin) L.; m. Norma Sterne, Feb. 4, 1945; 1 child, Valerie. BS in Chemistry, Poly. U., Bklyn., 1937, MS in Chemistry, 1939, PhD in Chemistry, 1944. Assoc. dir. rsch. Ohio Med. Products div. Airco Corp., Murray Hill, N.J., 1952-71; asst. dir. med. products mgmt. Pharm. div. Ciba-Geigy Co., Summit, N.J., 1971-82; pres. Med-Chem Assocs., Murray Hill, 1982—. Mem. Am. Chem. Soc., Am. Soc. for Pharmacology and Therapeutics, Sigma Xi, Phi Lambda Upsilon. Home and Office: Med Chem Assocs 100 Chestnut Hill Dr Murray Hill NJ 07974

LEEDS, ROBIN LEIGH, executive; b. Athens, Ohio, Jan. 4, 1942; d. Clarence Thomas and Jean B. (Foster) Flowers; m. John A Cornwell, Oct. 28, 1957 (div. Jan. 1968); children: Michael John, Brian Arthur; m. Barry H. Leeds, Apr. 20, 1968; children: Brett Ashley, Leslie Robin. BS in Edn., Ohio U., 1967. Cultural arts dir. Regional Sch. Dist. # 10, Burlington, Conn., 1978-81; exec. dir. Conn. Sch. Transp. Assn., West Hartford, Conn., 1982—; exec. sec. Northeast Sch. Transp. Safety Inst., West Hartford, 1987—; chmn. Conn. Sch. Transp. Safety Commn., 1990—; state del. Nat. Standards Congress, Warrensburg, 1990; mem. Gov.'s Motor Carrier Adv. Com., Conn., 1989—, Dept. Motor Vehicles Safety Task Force, Conn., 1991—. Chmn. gifted edn. task force, Regional Sch. Dist., 1976-78; pres. Parent-Tchr. Orgn., Burlington, 1977-79; bd. dirs. Burlington Libr. Assn., 1987-80. Named Contractor of Yr., Sch. Bus Fleet Mag., 1990. Mem. Nat. Sch. Transp. Assn., Nat. Assn. Pupil Transp., Nat. Safety Coun. Home: 133 Jerome Ave Burlington CT 06013-2433 Office: Conn Sch Transp Assn 630 Oakwood Ave Ste 406 West Hartford CT 06110-1505

LEEMING, DAVID ADAMS, English and comparative literature educator; b. Peekskill, N.Y., Feb. 26, 1937; s. Frank Clifford and Margaret Adams (Reeder) L.; m. Pamela Elaine Fraser, July 1, 1967; children: Margaret, Juliet, Paul. BA, Princeton (N.J.) U., 1958; MA, NYU, 1964, PhD, 1970. Instr. Robert Acad., Istanbul, Turkey, 1958-61; English dept. head Robert Coll. Lycee, Istanbul, Turkey, 1961-63, 66-69; lectr. U. Conn., Storrs, 1969-70, asst. prof., 1970-76, assoc. prof., 1976-91, prof., 1991—; sec., asst. to James Baldwin, N.Y.C., Istanbul, 1963-67. Author: Mythology: the Voyage of the Hero, 1972, rev. 1981, Mythology, 1979, The World of Myth, 1990, Introduction to James Baldwin, Notes of a Native Son, 1990; editorial bd. Parabola Mag., N.Y.C., 1978—, Henry James Rev., Baton Rouge, 1988—. Fellowship Am. Coun. of Learned Socs., 1975-76, Camargo Found., 1983, Nat. Endowment for the Humanities, 1989, Schomburg Ctr. for Rsch. in Black Culture, 1990. Mem. AAUP, MLA, C.G. Jung Found., Schomburg Soc. for the Preservation of Black Culture, Henry James Soc. Democrat. Episcopalian. Home: 22 Pearl St Stonington CT 06378-1327 Office: English Dept U Conn U-25 Storrs CT 06269

LEERBURGER, BENEDICT ALLEN, writer; b. N.Y.C., Jan. 2, 1932; s. Benedict Aron and Kathleen (Goodman) L.; m. Julie Loeb, June 22, 1958; children: Marian, Ellen. BA, Colby Coll., 1954. Science editor Look Mag., N.Y.C., 1968-72; v.p. Nat. Micropublishing Corp., Wilton, Conn., 1972-73; dir. publs. Microfilming Corp. Am. divsn. N.Y. Times, N.Y.C., 1973-75; dir. publs. Kraus Thompson Orgn. Press, Millwood, N.Y., 1975-77; editor-in-chief McGraw-Hill Book Co., N.Y.C., 1977-82; freelance writer, 1982—. Author: Josiah Willard Gibbs, 1968, Marketing the Library, 1986, 2d edit., 1989, Insiders Guide to Foreign Study, 1989, Insider's Guide to Overseas Employment, 1992, Getting a Job in the Middle East, 1992. Pres. Westchester Libr. System, White Plains, N.Y., 1989-91, Scardsale (N.Y.) Pub. Libr., 1986-89; trustee Scarsdale Adult Sch., 1974-90. Recipient Antarctic award NSF, 1967. Mem. Nat. Assn. Sci. Writers, Am. Soc. Journalists and Authors.

LEES, A. BRYAN, chemistry educator; b. Providence, June 19, 1943; s. Alfred and Bertha (Bryan) L.; m. Paula A. Whitlock, Dec. 26, 1972; children: Alyssa W., Brandon W. BSc, Brown U., 1964; PhD, SUNY, Stony Brook, 1973. Postdoctoral rsch. assoc. Wayne State U., Detroit, 1973-76; asst. prof. Bloomfield (N.J.) Coll., 1976-79; asst. prof. Kean Coll. of N.J., Union, 1979-85, assoc. prof., 1986-88, prof. chemistry, 1989—; mem. adj. faculty Wayne State U., 1975-76; coord. gen. chemistry labs. Kean Coll of N.J., 1982—, co-coord. gen. edn. and pilot program, 1984-86. Author coll. textbook; contbr. articles to profl. jours. Mem. AAAS, Am. Chem. Soc., N.J. Acad. Sci. (pres.-elect 1988-89, pres. 1990-91, Outstanding Svc. award 1991), Sigma Xi. Office: Kean Coll of NJ Chemistry-Physics Dept Morris Ave Union NJ 07083-7117

LEES, ALFRED WILLIAM, writer, former magazine editor; b. Kansas City, Kans., June 12, 1926; s. Alfred Whitaker and Blanche (Pontius) L. BA, Stanford U., 1950. Editor, writer Home Craftsman, N.Y.C., 1953-59, Family Handyman, 1960; editor, writer Popular Sci., N.Y.C., 1960-62, sr. editor, writer, 1967-71, group editor, reader activities, 1972-88; editor, writer Popular Mchanics, 1962-66; home care columnist Cosmopolitan, 1965-67; dir., judge nat. ann. design competition Am. Plywood Assn., Tacoma, 1976-86; pres. Nat. Assn. Home and Workshop Writers. Author: Leisure Homes, 1980; 67 Prizewinning Plywood Projects, 1984; co-author: Wood Finishing and Painting, 1955; DIY Projects for Your Own Backyard, 1978, 84, What's Wrong With My Car?, 1990, Decks & Sunspaces, 1991. Served with USAAF, 1944-45. Republican. Presbyterian. Club: Dutch Treat (N.Y.C.). Avocations: world travel; film making. Home: 140 Nassau St Apt 9B New York NY 10038-1501

LEES, MARJORIE BERMAN, biochemist, neuroscientist; b. N.Y.C., Mar. 17, 1923; d. Isadore I. and Ruth (Rogalsky) Berman; m. Sidney Lees, Sept. 17, 1946; children: David E., Andrew, Eliot. BA, Hunter Coll., 1943; MS, U. Chgo., 1945; PhD, Harvard U., Radcliffe Coll., 1951. Assoc. biochemist, asst. biochemist McLean Hosp., Belmont, Mass., 1953-58; rsch. assoc. Darmouth Med. Sch., Hanover, N.H., 1962-66; assoc. biochemist McLean Hosp., Belmont, 1966-76; prin. and sr. rsch. assoc. Harvard Med. Sch., Boston, 1966-85; biochemist E.K. Shriver Ctr., Waltham, Mass., 1976—; prof. biochemistry neurology Harvard Med. Sch., Boston, 1985—; biochemist Mass. Gen. Hosp., Boston, 1976—; assoc. dir. biochemistry E.K. Shriver Ctr., Waltham, 1982-90, dir. biochemistry, 1990—. Chief editor Jour. of Neurochemistry, 1986-90; author (with others) books; contbr. articles to profl. jours. Mem. adv. coun. Nat. Inst. Neurological Disorders, Bethesda, Md., 1979-82; chmn. Radcliffe Grad. Soc., Cambridge, Mass., 1978-80. Predoctoral fellow USPHS, 1947-50, postdoctoral fellow Am. Cancer Soc., 1951-53; Javitz Neurosci. grantee NIH, 1983—, prin. grantee NIH, 1962—; named to Hunter Coll. Hall of Fame, 1982. Mem. Am. Soc. Biol. Chemistry, Internat. Soc. Neurochemistry, Am. Soc. Neurochemistry (treas. 1975-81, pres. 1981-85), Soc. for Neurosci., Am. Assn. Neuropathology (assoc.), Internat. Soc. Neuroimmunology, N.Y. Acad. Scis., Phi Beta Kappa. Office: E K Shriver Ctr 200 Trapelo Rd Waltham MA 02254-6319

LEES, THOMAS MASSON, retired analytical and microbiological chemist; b. N.Y.C., June 16, 1917; s. Andrew and Helen (Davidson) L.; m. Nola C. Winters, 1943; children: David, Christine. BS, L.I. U., 1939; MS, Iowa State U., 1942, PhD, 1944. Rsch. chemist Am. Distilling Co., Pekin, Ill., 1944-46; penicillin supr. Pfizer, Inc., Bklyn., 1946-49, rsch. chemist fermentation, 1949-53; rsch. chemist analytical Pfizer, Inc., Groton, Conn., 1953-77; sr. rsch. chemist analytical Pfizer, Inc., Groton, 1977-80; ret., 1980. Contbr. articles to profl. jours.; patentee in field. Mem. Zoning Bd. Appeals, Ledyard, Conn., 1962-88. Mem. Am. Chem. Soc., Sigma Xi, Phi Kappa Phi, Phi Lambda Upsilon. Home: 35 Woodridge Cir Gales Ferry CT 06335-1137

LEESON, LEWIS JOSEPH, research pharmacist, scientist; b. Paterson, N.J., Apr. 26, 1927; s. Alfred Elias and Rose (Sandow) L.; m. Barbara Rothstein, Dec. 20, 1953; children: Suzanne, Erica, Alex. BS in Pharmacy, Rutgers U., Newark, 1950, MS in Pharm. Chemistry, 1954; PhD in Pharm. Chemistry, U. Mich., 1957. Registered pharmacist, N.J., N.Y., Mich. Pharmacist Mack Drug Co., Paterson, N.J., 1950-52, Fried's Drugs, Paterson, 1952-54; lab. asst. Rutgers U. Coll. Pharmacy, Newark, 1952-54, U. Mich., Ann Arbor, 1954-57; rsch. pharmacist, project leader Lederle Labs., Pearl River, N.Y., 1957-66; dir. product R & D, Union Carbide Co., Greenburgh, N.Y., 1966-68; asst. dir. product R & D, Geigy Pharm., Suffern, N.Y., 1969-71; dir., sr. dir., sr. rsch. fellow Ciba-Geigy Pharm., Summit, N.J., 1971-84; disting. rsch. fellow Ciba-Geigy Corp., Summit, 1984—. Editor: Dissolution Technology, 1971; contbr. over 40 articles to profl. jours; patentee in field. Recipient Disting. Alumnus award U. Mich., 1990. Fellow Acad. Pharm. Sci., Am. Assn. Pharm. Scientists; mem. Am. Pharm. Assn., Sigma Xi, Rho Chi, Phi Lambda Upsilon. Jewish. Home: 48 Pitcairn Dr Roseland NJ 07068-1022 Office: CIBA-GEIGY Corp 556 Morris Ave Summit NJ 07901-1398

LEFER, ALLAN MARK, physiologist; b. N.Y.C., Feb. 1, 1936; s. I. Judah and Lillian G. (Gastwirth) L.; m. Mary E. Indoe, Aug. 23, 1959; children—Debra Lynn, David Joseph, Barry Lee and Leslie Ann (twins). B.A., Adelphi Coll., 1957, Western Res. U., 1959; Ph.D. (NSF fellow), U. Ill., Urbana, 1962. Instr. physiology, USPHS-NIH fellow Western Res. U., 1962-64; asst. prof. physiology U. Va., 1964-69, assoc. prof., 1969-71, prof., 1972-74; vis. prof. Hadassah Med. Sch., Jerusalem, 1971-72; prof., chmn. dept. physiology Jefferson Med. Coll., Thomas Jefferson U., Phila., 1974—; dir. Ischemia-Shock Research Inst., 1980—; cons. Merck & Co., Upjohn Co., Genentech Inc., Syntex, Inc., Ciba-Geigy, NIH, Smith, Kline and Beecham Labs., Bristol-Myers Squibb; Wellcome Found. vis. prof., 1985-86. Author: Pathophysiology and Therapeutics of Myocardial Ischemia, 1977, Prostaglandins in Cardiovascular and Renal Function, 1979, Cellular and Molecular Aspects of Shock and Trauma, 1983; Leukotrienes in Cardiovascular and Pulmonary Function, 1985; mng. editor: Eicosanoids, 1988-92; cons. editor Circulatory Shock, 1973-80; mem. editorial bd. Critical Care Medicine, Am. Jour. Physiology, Drug News and Perspectives; contbr. to World Book Ency. Sci. Yearbook, 1979; contbr. over 500 sci. articles to profl. jours. Active Acad. Com. on Soviet Jewry, 1970—; chmn. United Jewish Appeal, 1973-74; established investigator Am. Heart Assn., 1968-73; coach basketball and baseball Huntingdon Valley Athletic Assn., 1975-78. Recipient Pres. and Visitor's prize in research U. Va., 1970. Fellow Am. Coll. Cardiology; mem. Am. Physiol. Soc., Am. Soc. Pharmacology and Exptl. Therapeutics, Internat. Heart Research Soc., Am. Heart Assn. (established investigator 1968-73, fellow circulation coun.), Pa. Heart Assn. (research com.), Shock Soc. (chmn. membership com., pres. 1983-84, chmn. devel. com. 1985-89), AAAS, Soc. Exptl. Biology and Medicine, Israel Soc. Physiology and Pharmacology, Phila. Physiol. Soc. (pres. 1978-79), Sierra Club, B'nai B'rith (Charlottesville chpt., v.p. 1967-68, chmn. Va. Hillel 1970-71), Sigma Xi. Democrat. Home: 3590 Walsh Ln Huntingdon Valley PA 19006-3226 Office: 1020 Locust St Philadelphia PA 19107-6799

LEFEVER, MARK BARRETT, accounting firm manager; b. Allentown, Pa., Oct. 2, 1964; s. Paul Carlton and Constance (Angelo) L. BS in Acctg., Villanova U., 1986. CPA, N.J. Staff acct. Arthur Andersen & Co., Roseland, N.J., 1986-88, sr. acct., 1988-92, mgr., 1991—. Mem. AICPA, N.J. Soc. CPAs. Roman Catholic. Home: 417 Morris Ave Apt 25 Summit NJ 07901-1501 Office: Arthur Andersen & Co 101 Eisenhower Pky Roseland NJ 07068-1028

LEFEVER, RICHARD R., lawyer; b. Carlisle, Pa., Mar. 19, 1936; s. LeVerne B. and Etta (Roop) L.; m. Linda Pearson, Feb. 29, 1964; children: Elizabeth Harris Lefevr, Richard Pearson. AB, Princeton (N.J.) U., 1958; LLB, Harvard U., 1961. Assoc. McNees, Wallace & Nurick, Harrisburg, Pa., 1961-66, ptnr., 1967—. Chmn. campaign Capitol area United Way, Harrisburg, 1973, pres., 1976; bd. dirs. Harrisburg Area YMCA, 1987-91; campaign chair, bd. dirs. Allied Arts Fund, 1990—. Fellow Am. Coll. Trust and Estate Counsel; mem. ABA (tax sect.), Pa. Bar Assn. (tax sect.), Dauphin County Bar Assn. (bd. dirs. Harrisburg chpt. 1980-87, pres. 1986), West Shore Country Club, Princeton Club N.Y.C., Rotary (pres. Harrisburg chpt. 1984-85). Republican. Presbyterian. Home: 1029 Mccormick Rd Mechanicsburg PA 17055-5970 Office: McNees Wallace & Nurick 100 Pine St Harrisburg PA 17101-1228

LEFEVRE, ANN HAMILTON, writer, sales representative; b. East Orange, N.J., May 28, 1956; d. Raymond Sherwood Jr. and Nancy Anna (Jones) Hamilton; m. Jeffrey Scott LeFevre, June 17, 1978; children: Erick Richard, Christopher Scott. BA in Fine Arts, Bethany Coll., 1978. Sr. asst. clk. West Caldwell (N.J.) Pub. Libr., 1979-81; sales assoc. Star of Hope Bookstore, Paterson, N.J., 1988-89; libr. Star of Hope Ministries, Paterson, N.J., 1988-89; children's libr. Dawn Treader Christian Sch., Paterson, N.J., 1989-91, art tchr., 1989-90; ind. sales rep. Avon, Stockholm, N.J., 1987—, rep. tng. program instr., 1991—. Author, co-dir. (drama) Scripture Dog, 1990; author (puppet drama) Love Calling, 1989. Co-dir. Fellowship of Christian Photographers, Montclair, N.J., 1986—; asst. disc jockey David and Goliath Show W.F.M.U., East Orange, N.J., 1982-92; mem. planning bd. Wordseekers, Jacksonville Chapel, Lincoln Park, N.J., 1991-92; co-leader Boydlife, Lincoln Park, N.J., 1989-92; tchr. women's ministries Jacksonville Chapel, Lincoln Park, 1989-92; mem. Hardyston (N.J.) PTA, 1992, Sterling Mine Hist. Soc., Densburg, N.J., 1992. Recipient scholarship N.J. Libr. Assn., 1980. Mem. Nature Conservancy, Consumer Buyline Inc., Messengers of the New Covenant. Republican. Evangelical. Home: 207 Rte 23 RD 1 Stockholm NJ 07460

LEFFAND, MICHAEL, psychologist; b. N.Y.C., June 12, 1937; s. Isaiah and Margaret (Steinberger) L.; m. Sava A. Kenner, Apr. 17, 1966; children: Zachary, Amy. AB, Columbia U., 1960; PhD, Princeton U., 1965. Lic. psychologist, N.J., N.Y. Prin. psychologist Essex County, East Orange, N.J., 1966-68; asst. prof. CUNY, 1968-71; clinic coord. Mt. Carmel Guild, Cranford, N.J., 1971-76; dir. Family Guidance Ctr., Belvidere, N.J., 1976-77; asst. adminstr. South Amboy (N.J.) Meml. Hosp., 1977-85; dir. mental health program J.F.K. Med. Ctr., Edison, N.J., 1985—. With USN, 1955-57. Office: JFK Med Ctr 65 James St PO Box 3059 Edison NJ 08840-3059

LEFFEL, ROBERT CECIL, research agronomist; b. Woodbine, Md., Apr. 26, 1925; s. Claude Spencer and Katherine Lee (Childress) L.; m. Ruth Ann Green, Oct. 10, 1959; children: Margaret Ann, Robert James. BS, U. Md., 1948; MS, Iowa State U., 1950, PhD, 1952. Rsch. agronomist USDA, Beltsville, Md., 1952-57; forage breeder U. Md., College Park, 1957-62; clover investigations leader USDA, Beltsville, 1962-72, lab. chief, 1972-76, staff scientist, 1976-83, rsch. agronomist, 1983—. Contbr. over 80 articles to profl. jours. Pres. Calvert Hills Citizen Assn., College Park, 1963-65, College Park PTA, 1972-73; cubscout master, 1972-73; bd. dirs. City of College Park, 1972-75. Sgt. USMC, 1943-46. Recipient Spl. Honor award Nat. Agrl. Rsch., 1983. Mem. Crop Sci. Soc. Am., Am. Soc. Agronomy, Am. Soybean Assn. Lutheran. Home: 4509 Amherst Rd College Park MD 20740-3633 Office: Agrl Rsch Svc USDA Bldg 011 HH19 BARC-West Beltsville MD 20705

LEFFELL, DAVID JOEL, surgeon, dermatologist, educator, researcher; b. Montreal, Que., Can., Feb. 28, 1956; came to U.S., 1973; s. Allen Bernard and Freda (Deckelbaum) L. BS, Yale U., 1977; MD, McGill U., Montreal, 1981. Diplomate Am. Bd. Dermatology, Am. Bd. Internal Medicine. Resident in internal medicine Meml. Sloan-Kettering Cancer Ctr., N.Y.C., 1981-84; instr. medicine Cornell U. Sch. Medicine, N.Y.C., 1983-84; lectr. dermatology U. Mich., Ann Arbor, 1987-88; resident in dermatology Yale U. Sch. Medicine, New Haven, 1984-86, asst. prof. dermataology, chief Mohs micrographic surgery, 1988—; dir. Yale skin cancer detection program Yale U. Sch. Medicine, 1988—; sci. advisor Nat. Hereditary Hemorrhagic Telangiectasia Found., New Haven, 1991—. Inventor laser flourescence device to measure photoaging. Recipient Frederic Mohs award Skin Cancer Found., 1988, 91. Home: 69 Mumford Rd New Haven CT 06515-2431 Office: Yale Sch Medicine 333 Cedar St New Haven CT 06510-3289

LEFKOWITZ, JEREMY SAMSON, investment manager; b. Paris, Tex., June 1, 1945; s. Samuel Charles and Ruth Rebecca (Samson) L.; m. Judith Ann Cohen, Aug. 17, 1975; children: Lisa Sharon, Joshua David. BS in Engring., Columbia U., 1967, MBA, 1969. Mfg. control analyst The Singer Co., Little Falls, N.J., 1968-74; v.p. Citibank NA, N.Y.C., 1974-82; v.p., contr. Citicorp Investment Mgmt., N.Y.C., 1982-84; sr. portfolio mgr., mng. dir. Chancellor Capital Mgmt., N.Y.C., 1984—. Mem. Nat. Options and Futures Soc. (bd. dirs. 1989-90). Office: Chancellor Capital Mgmt 153 E 53rd St Fl 23 New York NY 10022-4696

LEFTIN, BARTON BENNETT, rabbi; b. Providence, Feb. 9, 1949; s. Eli and Pearl (Gordon) L.; m. Cathy Genkin, Sept. 1, 1974; children: Avigdor, Benjamin. BA, Boston U., 1970; MA, Brown U., 1972, Jewish Theol. Sem., 1975; DMin, Andover Newton Theol. Sch., 1991. Rabbi, 1977. Rabbi Temple Bnai Abraham, Beverly, Mass., 1977-81, Bethel Temple, Norfolk, Va., 1981-85, Beth El Synagogue, Waterbury, Conn., 1985—; mem. pastoral care com. Waterbury (Conn.) Hosp., 1991. Recipient Rabbinic Leadership award Combined Jewish Philanthropies, 1986. Mem. AACD, The Rabbinical Assembly, Conn. Valley Rabbinical Assembly. Jewish.

LEFTON, HARVEY BENNETT, gastroenterologist; b. Cleve., May 17, 1944; s. Nat L. and Edith (Waintrup) L.; m. Paulette Lipkowitz, Aug. 24, 1968; children: Allison rachel, Daniel Adam. BS, U. Pitts., 1966; MD, Jefferson Med. Coll., Phila., 1970. Cert. Nat. Bd. Med. Examiners, Am. Bd. Internal Medicine, Am. Bd. Gastroenterology. Intern medicine Cleve. Clinic, 1970-71, resident internal medicine, 1971-72, fellow fastroenterology, 1972-74; chief gastroenterology Scott AFB, Belleville, Ill., 1974-76; asst. clin. prof. medicine Med. Coll. Pa., Phila., 1976-78, assoc. clin. prof. medicine, 1978-81, clin. prof. medicine, 1981—; cons. gastroenterology, Friends Hosp., Phila. Psychiat. Hosp., Pa., 1980—. Contbr. articles to profl. jours. Maj. USAF, 1974-76. Fellow ACP, Am. Coll. Gastroenterology; mem. Am. Sic. Gastroenterology Endoscopy, Pa. Soc. Gastroenterology, Coll. Physicians Phila. Home: 559 Long Ln Huntingdon Valley PA 19006 Office: 2 Bala Plz Ste IL 22 Bala Cynwyd PA 19004

LEGASPI, RUFINO ENCARNACION, accountant, statistician; b. Cavite, Rosario, Philippines, July 10, 1921; came to U.S., 1967; s. Maximino A. and Biatrice A. (Encarnacion) L.; m. Brigida Vivas Fajutag, July 3, 1967. BSBA, U. of the East, Manila, 1955; cert. spl. mgmt., Tech. Inst. Philippines, Manila, 1967; cert. programmer, analyst, CPU, Inst. Data Processing, N.Y.C., 1969. Audit examiner Bur. Treasury, Dept. Fin., Manila, 1957-65; chief tariff bur. Philippine Nat. Rwy., Manila, 1965-69; chmn. bd. admissions F.A.C.T. Essex County Coll., Newark, 1980-84; dep. sheriff Hudson County, Jersey City, 1981-89. Recipient Leadership award Asian-Pacific Am. Heritage, 1983. Mem. Congress Filipino Am. Citizens (v.p. adminstrn., treas. Fed. Credit Union 1979-85, county chmn. Jersey City chpt. 1979-89, merit award 1979, medal of leadership award 1980), United Filipino Am. Assn. (founder, adviser Jersey City 1975-87, meritorious svc. award 1982), Philippine Am. Guild Educators (bd. dirs. 1982-89, Man of Achievement award 1988), Filipino Am. Cath. Action (adviser Jersey City 1980-85). Home: 485 Manila Ave Jersey City NJ 07302-1721 Office: Congress Filipino Ams PO Box 3215 Jersey City NJ 07303-3215

LEGASSE, DAVID STEPHEN, advertising agency executive; b. Derry, N.H., Nov. 18, 1949; s. Alfred and Dorothy Kimbal (Lockhart) L.; grad. High sch., Nashua; m. Lynn Marie Fritts, Dec. 16, 1978; children: Melissa Shawn, Steffan Philip, Amanda Elizabeth. Advt. account exec. Keene Sentinel Pub. Co., Keene, N.H., 1968-71, The Day Pub. Co., New London, Conn., 1971-72; pres., creative dir. Legasse Assocs. Advt. Inc., Walpole, N.H., 1972—; pres., mktg. dir. Utility Products, Inc., Savannah, Ga. and Walpole, N.H.; exec. dir. Groton (Conn.) Shopping Plaza, 1972; incorporator Savs. Bank of Walpole; instr. in field. Inventor, patentee locking device for utility industry, 1988. Dir. exec. com. Monadnock United Way, Keene, 1975-83, chmn. communications com., 1974-77, allocations/program rev. com., 1981, agy. relations com., 1982. Recipient numerous awards including Gold Community Award, Nat. Gold Award; dir. Keene Day Care Center, 1977-79; chmn. Concerned Citizens for Improved Schs., Monadnock Sch. Dist., 1977; mem. Gov.-Apptd. Sponsors Child and Youth Conf., Manchester, N.H., 1981; town chmn. Rep. Party, Walpole, 1980-89; mem. Walpole Fin. Com., 1991, town mgr., 1991; com. mem., treas. St. John's Ch., Walpole, 1991—; co-chmn. Walpole Recreational Park Fund Dr., 1981, 82; ex-officio dir./adv. Keene State Coll. Campus Ministry, 1977-86; incorporator Cheshire Hosp., Keene, N.H., 1983—, Walpole Players Theater Group; trustee Fort No. 4, Charlestown, N.H., 1984-88; drive chmn. fund drive N.H. Assn. for Blind, Walpole, 1983, 84; elected to Rep. State Convention, 1988; chmn. fund drive Walpole Volunteer Ambulance Corp., 1989. Recipient 2 1st place awards Best of Broadcasting in New Eng., 1983, 2 2d awards, 1983, 84; 1st place Hatch award Boston Advt. Club, 1983, 2 2d place awards, 1983, 84, 1st place Marketing Achievement awards Info. Industry Assn., 1986, 87, Achievement award Printing Industry Am., 1986, 1st place TV comml. award N.E. Bank Marketing Assn., 1989, Mktg. award Bus./Profl. Advt. Assn., 1990. Mem. Grand Monadnock Arts Council (dir. 1978, 79), Walpole Trade Assn. (chmn. 1978), Monadnock Advt. Club (pres. Keene 1975), Boston Ad Club (Hatch Awards com.), N.H. Advt. Club (Graniteer awards: 7 1st pl., 7 2d place, 9 3d place). Home: PO Box 348 Walpole NH 03608-0348 Office: Westminster St Walpole NH 03608

LEGATES, JOHN CREWS, information scientist; b. Boston, Nov. 19, 1940; s. Eber Thomson and Sybil Rowe (Crews) LeG. BA in Math., Harvard U., 1962. Edn. svcs. mgr. Telcomp Dept. Bolt Beranek & Newman, Cambridge, Mass., 1966-67; v.p. Washington Engring. Svcs., Cambridge, 1967-69; v.p., co-founder Cambridge Info. Systems, 1968-69; v.p., founder Computer Adv. Svc. to Edn., Wayland, Mass., 1966-72; exec. dir. Educom Interuniversity Communications Coun., Boston, 1969-72; founder, mng. dir. Program on Info. Resources Policy Harvard U., 1973—, founder, pres. Ctr. Info. Policy Rsch., 1978—; cons. in field. Contbr. articles to profl. jours. Bd. dirs. Nat. Telecommunications Conf., Washington, 1979. Kent fellow, 1964. Mem. NAS/NRC (telecommunications privacy, reliability and integrity panel), IEEE, Nat. Sci. Found., Soc. for Values in Higher Edn. Episcopalian. Club: Nashuba Valley Hunt (Pepperell, Mass.) (pres. 1974-80). Home: PO Box 331 Lincoln MA 01773-0012

LEGGAT, JANET COCHRANE, nutritionist; b. Lowell, Mass., Nov. 18, 1954; d. William Douglas and Doris (Russell) L. BS in Human Nutrition, U. Mass., 1976; MBA in Human Resources, Rivier Coll., Nashua, N.H., 1986. Asst. dir. Chelmsford (Mass.) Sch. Food Svcs., 1977-79; sales rep. Princess House Products, Nashua, N.H., 1981-82; program mgr. St. Joseph Community Svcs., Inc., Merrimack, N.H., 1979-87; enterprise mgr. St. Joseph Community Svcs., Inc., Merimack, N.H., 1987—; state rep. Nat. Assn. Meals Programs, Washington, 1985—. Vol. Hands Across Am. Mass., Boston, 1986, gen. Greater Lowell (Mass.) Regatta Festival Com., 1975—, Nat. Park Svc., Lowell, 1986—, Headstart Nutrition Edn., 1989. Mem. NAFE, Am. Dietetic Assn., N.H. Dietetic Assn. (sec. bd. dirs.), Kiwanis (2d v.p. Lowell chpt.). Republican. Episcopalian. Office: St Joseph Community Svcs PO Box 910 Merrimack NH 03054-0910

LEGGE, ROBERT SCOTT, manufacturing company executive; b. Rochester, N.Y., Nov. 10, 1951; s. Richard Claude and Patricia (Roney) L.; m. Julie Anne Seaver, July 11, 1982; children: Robert Jr., Katherine. BA, Coll. of Wooster, 1973; MA in Communication Arts, U. Wis., 1978, MBA, 1979. Sr. assoc. cons. Hay Mgmt. Cons., Chgo., 1980-82; prin. Legge Assocs., Rochester, N.Y., 1982-85; v.p. human resources Sentry Group (John D. Brush & Co., Inc.), Rochester, 1985—; chmn. human resources group Indsl. Mgmt. Coun., Rochester, 1991; adjunct faculty mem., Rochester Inst. Tech., 1991. Agy. evaluator United Way of Greater Rochester, 1989—; dir. Rochester Jobs Inc., 1990—; coun. mem. Finger Lakes Health Systems Planning Agy., Rochester, 1982-87. Mem. Am. Mgmt. Assn., Soc. for Human Resource Mgmt., Am. Compensation Assn. Home: 42 Nelson St Fairport NY 14450-1333 Office: Sentry Group 900 Linden Ave Rochester NY 14625-2710

LEGGETT, JOHN CARL, sociology educator; b. Detroit, Sept. 18, 1930; s. Norval John and Eileen Elizabeth (McVeigh) L.; m. Iris Leja Leggett (div. Feb. 1989); children: Britt Erika, Shannon Kelley. BA, U. Mich., 1954, MA in Polit. Sci., 1956, MA in Sociology, 1958, PhD in Sociology, 1962. Various positions U. Mich., Ann Arbor, 1954-62, lectr. dept. sociology, rsch. assoc. Sch. Social Work, 1961-62; instr. sociology U. Calif., Berkeley, 1962-63, asst. prof., 1963-66, rsch. assoc., 1964-65; asst. prof. Simon Fraser U., Berkeley, 1966-67; assoc. prof. Simon Fraser U., 1967-70; lectr. sociology U. Calif., Davis, 1968, lectr. black studies, 1971; assoc. prof. sociology Rutgers U., New Brunswick, N.J., 1971—; vis. assoc. prof. Sacramento State Coll., 1967-68; prof. U. Conn., 1968-69; vis. lectr. U. B.C. (Can.), Vancouver, 1970; cons. to labor union, including United Farm Union, AFL-CIO. Author: Class, Race and Labor: Working Class Consciousness in Detroit, 1968, paperback edit., 1971, Race, Class and Political Consciousness, 1973, Taking State Power, 1973, (with others) Allende, His Exit and Our Times, 1978, Whither Black Studies, 1971, The American Working Class, 1979, Mining the Field, A Photo History of American Farm Worker Struggles, 1991, Newspaper Analysis: The Natural History of a Counter-Revolutionary News Story, 1992; contbr. numerous articles and book revs. prof. publ. Active Free Speech Movement, Berkeley, 1964, Farm Labor Support Com., Berkeley and Delano, Calif., 1965, Vietnam Day Com., Berkeley, 1965-66, Rainbow Coalition Cen. N.J., 1984—; candidate for local polit. offices; union ofcl.; chmn. Raritan Inst. With USN, 1949-50. Recipient Disting. Faculty Person award Livingston Coll. Assn. Grads., 1987; Ford Found. fellow, 1954-55; Social Sci. Rsch. Coun. grantee, 1960-61, 64, Can. Coun. grantee, 1968-70, Trans-Action rsch. grantee, 1984-85. Mem. AAUP (officer Rutgers U.), Am. Sociol. Soc., So. Sociol. Soc., Midwestern Sociol. Soc., North Cen. Sociol. Soc., Assn. for Humanist Sociology, Soc. for Study Social Problems, Students for Dem. Soc. (charter Ann Arbor chpt. 1960). Home: 320 Lawrence Ave Highland Park NJ 08904-1840 Office: Rutgers U Dept Sociology New Brunswick NJ 08904

LEGGIERE, PHILIP SAMUEL, trucking executive, consultant; b. Bergenfield, N.J., July 1, 1926; s. Frank S. and Philomena (Chiaradio) L.; m. Maureen C. Ives, Oct. 31, 1953; children: Philip G., Brian K. Student, Fairleigh Dickinson U., 1946-48. Freight agt. N.Y. Cen. R.R., Weehawken, N.J., 1948-57; regional mgr. No. Haulers Corp., Watertown, N.Y., 1957-63, Carolina Freight Corp., Winston-Salem, 1963-68; v.p. Fla. Tex. Freight, Miami, 1968-84; founder, pres., and ceo Traileroad Distbn. Specialists, Inc., North Arlington, N.J., 1982—. Trustee Englewood (N.J.) Hosp., 1986—; mgr. Bergenfield Little League, 1950-62; mem. citizens com. P.A.L., pres., 1962-68. With USN, 1944-46; PTO. Mem. VFW (charter), Meadowlands C. of C., Knickerbocker Country Club. Republican. Roman Catholic. Home: Cove Ln N # 5D North Bergen NJ 07047-6236 Office: Trailerload Distbn Special 500 Belleville Tpke North Arlington NJ 07031-6719

LEGLER, JENNIFER ONAITIS, mental health nurse, administrator; b. Pitts., Sept. 8, 1952; d. Norbert and Albina (Storolis) Onaitis; m. John A. Legler, Nov. 25, 1978; children: Julia Marie. BS in Nursing, U. Pitts., 1974; MS in Nursing, Marymount U., 1987. Cert. ANA mental health nursing and nursing adminstrn. Head nurse inpatient mental health South Hills Health System, Pitts., 1977-78; head nurse psychiat. unit Suburban Hosp., Bethesda, Md., 1980-81; nursing unit administr. Psychiat. Inst. of Montgomery County, Rockville, Md., 1981-85; program dir., 1985-90; asst. adminstr. Psychiat. Inst. of Montgomery County, Rockville, Md., 1990-92; assoc. adminstr., dir. nursing Psychiat. Inst. Montgomery County, Rockville, Md., 1992—. Mem. Bus. and Profl. Women's Assn. of Great Falls (sec., past treas.), Sigma Theta Tau. Home: 9105 Weant Dr Great Falls VA 22066-4133

LEGLER, JOHN ANTHONY, trade association executive; b. Pitts., Mar. 8, 1952; s. Cyril A. and Josephine D. (Demma) L.; m. Jennifer Onaitis, Nov. 25, 1978; 1 child, Julia M. BS/BA, U. Pitts., 1973. Regional supr. GAB Bus. Svcs., Washington, 1974-82; v.p. Corroon & Black Mgmt., Inc., Nashville, 1982-87; dir. transp. and safety Nat. Solid Wastes Mgmt. Assn., Washington, 1987—; reporting sec. com. on refuse industry Am. Nat. Standards Inst., N.Y.C., 1987—; dir. Nat. Truck Weight Adv. Coun., Washington, 1988—; bd. mem. Am. Nat. Standards OSHA coord. coms., N.Y.C., 1989—; bd. mem. Am. Nat. Standards Inst. Safety and Health Standards Bd., N.Y.C., 1989—. Contbr. articles to profl. jours. Mem. Am. Soc. Safety Engrs., Soc. Automotive Engrs., Nat. Safety Coun. Roman Catholic. Home: 9105 Weant Dr Great Falls VA 22066-4133 Office: Nat Solid Wastes Mgmt Assn 1730 Rhode Island Ave NW Washington DC 20036-3101

LEGO, PAUL EDWARD, corporation executive; b. Centre County, Pa., May 16, 1930; s. Paul Irwin and Sarah Elizabeth (Montgomery) L.; m. Ann Sepety, July 7, 1956; children: Paul Gregory, Debra Ann, Douglas Edward, Michael John. B.S. in Elec. Engring, U. Pitts., 1956, M.S., 1958. With Westinghouse Electric Corp., 1956—; gen. mgr. Westinghouse semiconductor div. Westinghouse Electric Corp., Pitts., 1970-74; gen. mgr. electronic tube div. Westinghouse Electric Corp., Elmira, N.Y., 1974-75; bus. unit gen. mgr. electronic components divs. Westinghouse Electric Corp., Pitts., 1975-77; v.p., gen. mgr. lamp divs. Westinghouse Electric Corp., Bloomfield, N.J., 1977-80; exec. v.p. electronics and control group Westinghouse Electric Corp., Pitts., 1980-83, exec. v.p. control equipment, 1983-85, sr. exec. v.p. corp. resources, 1985-87, pres., chief oper. officer, 1988-90, chmn., chief exec. officer, 1990—, also bd. dirs.; bd. dirs. Pitts. Nat. Bank, PNC Fin. Corp., USX Corp., Consol. Natural Gas Co. Trustee U. Pitts., exec. com., Penn's S.W. Assn., 1992—; chmn. bd. visitors U. Pitts. Sch. Engring.; v.p., exec. com. Allegheny Conf. on Community Devel., Pitts.; gen. campaign chair United Way Allegheny County, Pitts., 1992; mem. Bus. Coun., Conf. Bd., Bus. Roundtable; bd. overseers N.J. Inst. of Tech., Newark, 1979—. With AUS, 1948-52. Recipient Westinghouse Order of Merit 1975, Disting. Alumni award U. Pitts. Sch. Engring., 1986, Bicentennial Medallion of Distinction award U. Pitts., 1987. Mem. Am. Soc. Corp. Execs., Valley Brook Country Club, Duquesne Club, Club at Pelican Bay (Naples, Fla.), Laurel Valley Golf Club, Rolling Rock Club (Ligonier, Pa.), Sigma Xi. Republican. Roman Catholic.

LEGUM, JEFFREY ALFRED, automobile company executive; b. Balt., Dec. 16, 1941; s. Leslie and Naomi (Hendler) L.; m. Harriet Cohn, Nov. 10, 1968; children: Laurie Hope, Michael Neil. BS in Econs., U. Pa., 1963; grad. Chevrolet Sch. Merchandising and Mgmt., 1966. With Park Circle Motor Co., Balt., 1963—, exec. v.p., 1966-77, pres., 1977—, also dir.; ptnr. Pkwy. Indsl. Ctr., Dorsey, Md., 1965-91; ltd. ptnr. Circle Ltd. Partnership, Glen Burnie, Md., 1991; v.p., dir. P.C. Parts Co., 1967—; v.p. Westminster Motor Co. (Md.), 1967-72, pres., dir., 1972—; pres. One Forty Corp., Westminster, 1972—; dir., exec. com. United Consol. Industries, 1970-73; dist. chmn. Chevrolet Dealers Council, 1975-77, chmn. Washington zone, 1982-83. Chmn. transp. div. Associated Jewish Charities, Balt., 1966-69; mem. Md. Svc. Acad. Review Bd., 1975-77, Bus. Adv. Bd. to Atty. Gen., 1985-87; trustee The Legum Found., Balt., 1967—, Balt. Mus. Art, 1992—;

trustee, treas., mem. exec. com., chmn. fin. com., The Park Sch., Balt., 1979—; mem. pres.'s com. U. Toronto, 1983—; bd. dirs. Assoc. Placement Bur. (Jewish Vocat. Svc.), Balt., 1964-76, v.p., 1972-76; adv. bd. The Competitive Edge, Albuquerque, 1977-81; mem. investment com. Balt. Hebrew Congregation, 1980—, bd. electors, 1990—; bd. dirs. Preakness Celebration, Inc., 1988-89, Associated Jewish Community Fedn. Balt., 1992—; mem. adv. coun. Wilmer Eye Inst., The Johns Hopkins Hosp., 1991, mem. instl. rev. bd. Francis Scott Key Med. Ctr. Bayview Rsch. Campus Johns Hopkins U., 1992—. Recipient award of honor Assoc. Jewish Charities of Balt., 1967, 68; Cadillac Master Dealer award, 1980-88, 91; Cadillac Pinnacle of Excellence award, 1986; Young Pres.'s Orgn. Cert. Appreciation, 1984; Nissan Nat. Merit Master award, 1982-88; Chevrolet Nat. Svc. Supremacy award, annually 1979-89, Sales Giant award Automotive News, 1987. Mem. Md. New Car and Truck Assn., Young Pres. Orgn. (pres.'s forum 1977-92), World Pres.' Orgn., Greater Balt. Com., Benjamin Franklin Assocs., Johns Hopkins Assocs., Carroll County C. of C., Md. Hist. Soc. (exec. com. Library of Md. History 1981-90), Suburban Club (Baltimore County), U. of Pa., Center Club, U. Toronto Faculty Club (hon.). Home: 10 Stone Hollow Ct Baltimore MD 21208-1860 Office: 1829 Reisterstown Rd Baltimore MD 21208-6301

LEHAN, PATRICIA ELLEN, marketing director; b. Melrose, Mass., May 16, 1960; d. Charles M. and Ellen F. (Finnegan) L.; m. Randall Keeping, Oct., 1991. BA in Polit. Sci. & Eng., Westfield State Coll., 1983. Acct. exec. QPA Cons., Boston, 1984; mktg. rep. Nutritional Mgmt. Inc., Boston, 1985, Software Internat., Andover, Mass., 1986; mgr. mktg. svcs. Cullinet Software Inc., Westwood, Mass., 1986-89; mgr. field mktg. programs Coenos Inc., Burlington, Mass., 1989—. Author of poem. Mem. Mass. Choice, Boston, 1988—, So. Poverty Law Ctr., 1990—, Alzheimer's Assn., 1989—, NARAL, Washington, 1990—. Mem. Am. Mktg. Assn., New Eng. Direct Mktg. Assn., Nat. Abortion Rights Action League. Home: 29 Hancock St Newburyport MA 01950 Office: Cognos Inc 67 S Bedford St Burlington MA 01803-5152

LEHMAN, ARNOLD LESTER, museum official, art historian; b. N.Y.C., July 18, 1944; s. Sidney and Henrietta F. L.; m. Pamela Gimbel, June 21, 1969; children—Nicholas Richard, Zachary Gimbel. B.A., Johns Hopkins, 1965, M.A., 1966; M.A., Yale U., 1968, Ph.D., 1973. Chester Dale fellow Met. Mus. Art, N.Y.C., 1969-70; lectr. art history Cooper Union and Hunter Coll., 1969-72; dir. Urban Improvements Program, N.Y.C., 1970-72, Parks Council of N.Y.C., 1972-74, Met. Mus. and Art Centers, Miami, Fla., 1974-79, Balt. Mus. Art, 1979—; adj. prof. dept. art history Johns Hopkins U., 1986—; dir. or trustee several corps. Author: The Architecture of Worlds Fairs 1900-1939, 1972, The New York Skyscraper: A History of its Development 1870-1939, 1974; editor: Oskar Schlemmer, 1986; also various mus. catalogs. Trustee several non-profit orgns. Mem. Assn. Art Mus. Dirs. (trustee 1987—, pres. 1990-91), Harmonie Club (N.Y.C.). Office: Balt Mus Art Art Museum Dr Baltimore MD 21218-3898

LEHMAN, DONALD RICHARD, physicist, educator; b. York, Pa., Dec. 13, 1940; s. Frederick Hinkle and Wilhelmina Emma (Ruesskamp) L.; m. Elyse Joan Brauch, Aug. 24, 1962. BA in Physics, Rutgers U., 1962; PhD in Theoretical Physics, George Washington U., 1970. NAS NRC postdoctoral rsch. assoc. Nat. Bureau Standards, Gaithersburg, Md., 1970-72; from asst. to assoc. prof. physics George Washington U., Washington, 1972-82, prof. physics, 1982—, dep. chair physics, 1986-87, chair physics, 1987—, dir. ctr. nuclear studies, 1990—; guest worker Nat. Bureau Standards, Gaithersburg, 1972-89, program analyst, 1974; vis. staff mem. and collaborator Los Alamos (N.Mex.) Nat. Lab., 1973—; speaker at internat. confs. Contbr. over 75 articles to profl. jours. Grantee Rsch. Corp., N.Y., 1974-76, Dept. Energy, Germantown, Md., 1979—, NATO, Belgium, 1987-91. Fellow Am. Phys. Soc. Office: George Washington U Dept Physics Washington DC 20052

LEHMAN, LAWRENCE BRAD, neurosurgeon; b. N.Y.C., July 7, 1953; s. Elmore Gerald and Martha (Solomon) L. BA, Hofstra U., 1975; MD, Columbia U., 1979. Diplomate Am. Bd. Neurol. Surgery. From asst. to dir. of surgery Maimonides Med. Ctr., Bklyn., 1985—; chief, div. neurosurgery Coney Island Hosp., Bklyn., 1987—; asst. clin. prof., neurosurgery SUNY, Bklyn., 1987-88, asst. prof. neurosurgery, 1989—; attending neurosurgeon Kings County Hosp., Bklyn., 1989—; dir. Blood Utilization Com., Bklyn., 1990—; cons. Physicians for Quality, 1990—, Nat. Med. Audit, Calif., 1992—; mem. bioethics com., 1991—, quality of care exec. com., 1992—. Editor: Postgraduate Medicine jour., 1987—; inventor in field; contbr. articles to profl. jours. Mem. Alumni Assn. of Columbia U., Sigma Xi, Phi Beta Kappa. Office: Chief Neurosurgery Coney Island Hosp 2601 Ocean Pkwy Brooklyn NY 11235

LEHMAN, WAYNE ERIC, industrial company executive; b. N.Y.C., Oct. 30, 1949. BBA, U. Mich., 1971; MBA, CUNY, 1975. Product mgr. Pirelli Cable, Union, N.J., 1971-78; product mktg. mgr. Amax, Orangeburg, S.C., 1978-81; asst. to pres. Matec Corp., Hopkinton, Mass., 1981-86; pres. Cobebi, Inc., Dover, N.H., 1986—. Office: Cogebi Inc 14 Faraday Dr Dover NH 03820-4384

LEHMANN, DORIS ELIZABETH, elementary educator; b. Ramsey, N.J., Aug. 17, 1933; d. Alfred Harrison and Anna Elizabeth (Gerhold) Rockefeller; m. Victor S. Lehmann, June 25, 1955; children: Joanne E. Cathy Lynn, Victor A., Kristie Sue. BS in Edn. magna cum laude, Wagner Coll., 1955; student in edn., Columbia U., summers 1988-91, Jersey City State, 1990—, William Paterson, 1971. Elem. tchr. Sch. St. Sch., Ramsey, 1955-56; bedside instr. N. Bergen County schs., N.J., 1966-71; elem. tchr. Edith A. Bogert Sch., Upper Saddle River, N.J., 1971—. Author numerous poems; author: (with others) Curriculum for Values Education in New Jersey, 1991. Indian cons. Bergen County Mus. of Art and Sci., Paramus, N.J., 1983—. Recipient Fellowship of Life award Luth. Layman's Movement, 1955. Mem. Upper Saddle River Edn. Assn. (fellow, social sec. 1972-73, v.p. 1974-75, 84-85, liaison to USR hist. soc. 1986—) N.J. Edn. Assn. (fellow), N.J. North Edn. Assn. (fellow). Republican. Lutheran. Office: Edith A Bogert Sch 395 W Saddle River Rd Saddle River NJ 07458-1622

LEHMANN, FREDERICK GLIESSMANN, university administrator; b. Hinsdale, Ill., Nov. 1, 1930; s. Frederick William and Hermine Barbara (Gliessmann) L.; m. Betty Ann Ferguson, Sept 13, 1952 (div. 1984); children: Karl F., Pamela J., Karen L., Andrew W. SB, MIT, 1951. Cert. Inst. for Ednl. Mgmt., Harvard Bus. Sch., 1973. Adminstrv. staff member MIT, 1953-54; prodn. dept. mgr. Procter & Gamble Co., Kansas City, Kans., 1954-59; asst. sec. MIT Alumni Assn., Cambridge, Mass., 1959-62; advanced to fin. v.p. MIT Alumni Assn., 1973-77; dir. devel. Boston U., 1977-79; exec. dir. devel. & pub. affairs The Rockefeller Univ., 1979-84; v.p. for instl. advancement N.Y. Med. Coll., Valhalla, 1984-89; dep. v.p. for devel. Columbia U., N.Y.C., 1989—; cons. Nat. Acad. Scis., Washington, 1982-84, devel. div. visiting com., Carnegie-Mellon Univ., Pittsburgh, 1965-68. Trustee, Boxford (Mass.) Town Lib., 1969-78; mem. gov.'s adv. coun. on comprehensive health planning, Boston, 1971-77. 1st lt. USAF, 1951-53. Recipient, U.S. Steel Award 1978, Time/Life Award, 1977. Mem. AAAS, N.Y. Acad. Scis., Am. Assn. Med. Colls./GPA, MIT Alumni Ctr. of N.Y. (exec. com./govs. 1978-79), Harvard Club of N.Y.C. Home: 541 W 113th St #6E New York NY 10025-8039 Office: Columbia U Health Scis 100 Haven Ave New York NY 10032-2601

LEHR, BARBARA AUGUSTA, sales executive; b. New Haven, July 1, 1924; d. Frederick Lincoln and Julia Elizabeth (Mattson) L. Student, Vassar Coll., 1941-43; BS in Religious Edn., NYU, 1964. Comml. mgr. Sta. WBIB-FM, New Haven, 1943-45; record librarian OWI, N.Y.C., 1945-47; with CBS, N.Y.C., 1947-49, R.H. Donnelley, N.Y.C., 1949-86; sales rep. Sta. WMCA, N.Y.C., 1987; freelance writer N.Y.C., 1987-90. Lay mem. to ann. conf. N.Y.C. Meth. Ch., 1978-86; mem. Marble Collegiate Ch. Mem. Telephone Pioneers Am., Order Eastern Star. Republican. Home: 7 Stuyvesant Oval Apt 1H New York NY 10009-1902

LEHR, DAVID, physician, educator, scientist; b. Sadagura, Austria, Mar. 22, 1910; came to U.S., 1939, naturalized citizen, 1945; s. Salomon and Esther (Buck) L.; m. Lisa Fellner; children: Karin Elizabeth, Jonathan Mathias. MD, U. Vienna, Austria, 1935. Intern Krankenhaus Wieden, Vienna, 1935-36; instr. in pharmacology Royal U., Lund, Sweden, 1938-39; pharmacologist, rsch. assoc. dept. pathology Newark Beth Israel Hosp., 1939-42; instr. in pharmacology and medicine N.Y. Med. Coll., 1941-44, asst. prof. pharmacology and medicine, 1944-49, assoc. prof., 1949-54, prof., dir. dept. pharmacology, 1954-56, prof., chmn. dept. physiology and pharmacology, 1956-64, prof., chmn. dept. pharmacology, 1964-79, prof. emeritus, 1979; asst. vis. physician Met. Hosp., Welfare Island, N.Y., 1942-54; assoc. attending physician Flower and Fifth Ave Hosps., 1949-78, poison control officer, 1955-78; vis. physician Met. and Bird S. Coler Hosps., 1954—; Claude Bernard prof. Inst. Exptl. Medicine and Surgery, U. Montreal, 1961; cons. in field. Mem. editorial bd. Jour. Clin. Pharmacology, 1969—, Jour. Cardiovascular Pharmacology, 1977-91, Magnesium Bull., 1979—; contbr. numerous articles to profl. jours. Recipient Disting. Alumni Svc. medal N.Y. Med. Coll., 1965, 76, cert. merit for exhibit Med. Soc. N.J., 1941, cert. proficiency Chem. Warfare Sch., 1942, cert. merit original investigation AMA, 1948, 1st award clin. rsch. Med. Soc. N.Y., 1949, cert. merit excellence sci. exhibit Assn. Am. Mil. Surgeons, 1949, Edward Henderson gold medal award Am. Geriatric Soc., 1972. Fellow ACP, AAAS, N.Y. Acad. Medicine, N.Y. Acad. Scis., Am. Coll. Cardiology, Am. Heart Assn., Am. Coll. Clin. Pharmacology and Chemotherapy, Am. Coll. Nutrition (hon., cons. editor jour. 1981—); mem. AAUP, Am. Soc. Pharmacology and Exptl. Therapeutics, Soc. Exptl. Biology and Medicine, Sci. Rsch. Soc. Am., Harvey Soc., Internat. Soc. Internal Medicine, Am. Soc. Arteriosclerosis, Virchow Med. Soc. (pres. 1970-72), Pirquet Soc. (pres. 1958-60), Contin Soc. (hon.), Med. Soc. N.Y., Med. Soc. County N.Y., Alumni Assn. N.Y. Med. Coll., Assn. Am. Med. Colls., Am. Soc. Exptl. Pathology, N.Y. Soc. Med. Rsch. (v.p. 1961-63), N.Y. Heart Assn., Coun. Arteriosclerosis, Virchow-Pirquet Med. Soc. (v.p. 1977-78, pres. 1979-81), Sigma Xi, Alpha Omega Alpha, Phi Delta Epsilon. Home and Office: 125 W 96th St New York NY 10025-6419

LEHRER, JOEL FREDRIC, otolaryngologist; b. Bklyn., May 2, 1941; s. Isidore and Helen (Barach) L.; m. Nancy-Dean Murray, June 15, 1962; children: Brian, Hilary. AB, Cornell U., 1952; MD, SUNY, Bklyn.; 1956. Diplomate Am. Bd. Otolaryngology. Intern Kings Co. Hosp., Bklyn., 1956-57, resident in otolaryngology, 1959-61; resident in otolaryngology Mt. Sinai Hosp., N.Y.C., 1961-63, fellow, 1963-64; pvt. practice N.Y.C., 1964-73, Teaneck, N.J., 1968—; chief dept. otolaryngology Bergen Pines Hosp., Paramus, N.J., 1977-83, Holy Name Hosp., Teaneck, 1979-85. Contbr. articles to med. jours. Patroller Nat. Ski Patrol, Haystacks Mountain, Vt., 1973-88. Capt. M.C. USAF, 1957-59. Fellow ACS, Am. Neurootology Soc.; mem. AMA, Med. Soc. N.J., Bergen County Soc. Otlaryngologists (pres. 1979-81), Lotos Club (N.Y.C., pres. 1987-91). Office: 315 Cedar Ln Teaneck NJ 07666

LEHRER, PAUL MICHAEL, clinical psychologist; b. N.Y.C., Aug. 30, 1941; s. Samuel and Ethel (Lubin) L.; m. Phyllis Claire Alpert, June 13, 1965; children: Jeffrey, Suzanne. AB, Columbia U., 1963; PhD, Harvard U., 1969. Lic. clin. psychologist, N.J. Psychology instr. Sch. Medicine Tufts U., Boston, 1969-70; asst. prof. psychology Rutgers U., New Brunswick, N.J., 1970-72; from asst. prof. to prof. psychology Robert W. Johnson Med. Sch. (formerly Rutgers U. Med. Sch.), Piscataway, N.J., 1972—; pres. SERV, Inc., Trenton, N.J, 1988-91. Editor: Principles and Practice of Stress Management, 1984; contbr. articles to profl. jours. Grantee NIH, 1988—. Fellow APA (sec.-treas. clin. psychology rsch. sect. 1986-90). Democrat. Jewish. Office: UMDNJ RW Johnson Med Sch Dept Psychiatry 671 Hoes Ln Piscataway NJ 08854-5633

LEIBLUM, SANDRA RISA, psychology educator; b. Bklyn., Aug. 18, 1943; divorced; 1 child, Jonathan Kassen. AB, Bklyn. Coll. CUNY, 1965; MA, U. Ill., 1968, PhD, 1971. Staff mem. U. Ill. Psychol. Clinic, Urbana, 1967-68; adult clin. pschology intern Worcester (Mass.) Youth Guidance Ctr., 1968-69, child clin. psychology intern, 1969-70; counseling psychologist Worcester Poly. Inst., 1970-71; postdoctoral fellow U. Colo. Med. Ctr., Denver, 1971-72; asst. coord. North Community Focus Team, Dunellen, N.J., 1972-76; grad. psychology faculty Rutgers U., New Brunswick, N.J., 1972—; assoc. prof. clin. ob-gyn. U. Medicine and Dentistry N.J. Robert Wood Johnson Med. Sch., New Brunswick, 1984—; prof. clin. psychiatry U. Medicine and Dentistry N.J. Robert Wood Johnson Med. Sch., Piscataway, N.J., 1988—; con. Neighborhood Youth Corps, Worcester, 1968-69; co-dir. sexual counseling svc., UMDNJ Robert Wood Johnson Med. Sch., 1972—, dir. internship in clin./community psychology, 1988—. Co-editor Sexual Desire Disorders, 1988, Principles and Practices of Sex Therapy --update 90s, 1989; author: How to Do Psychotherapy and How to Evaluate It. Mem. APA, Soc. for Sex Therapy and Rsch. (pres. 1991), Am. Assn. for Sex Educators, Counselors and Therapists, N.J. Psychol. Assn., Am. Soc. Psychosomatic Ob-Gyn., Internat. Acad. Sex Rsch. Home: 6 Kathleen Pl Bridgewater NJ 08807-1816 Office: UMDNJ R W Johnson Med Sch Dept Psychiatry 401 Central Ave # Erbld Stratford NJ 08084-1156

LEIBOWITZ, BERNICE, artist, educator; b. Bklyn., Nov. 2, 1929; d. Nathan and Shirley (Gilman) Ottenstein; m. Herbert J. Leibowitz, Jan. 28, 1950; children: Kenneth, Lori, Paul. BA, Hunter Coll., 1950, MA, 1953. Cert. art tchr., N.Y. Instr. art Hunter Coll. High Sch., N.Y.C., 1950-53, Bergenfield (N.J.) Adult Sch., 1967-74, Ft. Lee (N.J.) Adult Sch., 1969-73; community svcs. lectr. Bergen Community Coll., Paramus, N.J., 1981-83, lectr. fine arts, 1983-85, instr. art, 1974-83, 85—; mem. edn. com. Arts Ctr. No. N.J., New Milford, 1981—, chmn. edn. com., 1987-91, bd. dirs., 1987-91. One-woman shows include Pleiades Gallery, N.Y.C., 1983, 85, 87, 90, 92; exhibited in group shows Silvermine Guild, Conn., 1990, gallery in Barcelona, Spain, 1990, Ambiente Gallery, Gelhausen, Germany, 1992. Mem. Nat. Assn. Women Artists (Molly M. Canaday award for painting 1991), Artists Equity.

LEIBOWITZ, NORMAN, contractor, real estate developer; b. Albany, N.Y., Sept. 21, 1947; s. Morris and Fay (Spiegel) L.; children: Jesse Morris, Alex Kirsch. Student, Plattsburgh State U., 1985-89. Real estate cons. First Albany Corp., 1986-87; pres. Utility Source, Inc., Albany. Chmn. Israel Anniversary Com., Albany; mem. Tri-County Vietnam Vets. Mem. Com.

LEIBOWITZ, PAUL JASON, pharmaceutical and life sciences company executive; b. N.Y.C., July 14, 1941; s. Edward and Sylvia Leibowitz. BA, NYU, 1963; MA, SUNY, Buffalo, 1970, PhD, 1972. Various positions Schering-Plough Corp., Bloomfield, N.J., 1977-85, dir. molecular and analytical biology, 1986-87; prin. Redding BioPharm. Assocs., Hackensack, N.J., 1988-89; v.p. corp. planning and devel. Immunomedics, Inc., Warren, N.J., 1989-90; sr. v.p. R & D, TSI Corp., Worcester, Mass., 1990—; postdoctoral fellow Tufts U. Med. Sch., Boston, 1972-74; rsch. assoc. MIT, Cambridge, 1975-76. Contbr. articles to sci. jours. Office: TSI Corp Innovation Dr Worcester MA 01605-4305

LEIBSOHN, LUDWIG, dentist; b. Paris, France, Apr. 1, 1939; came to U.S., 1939; s. Simon and Clare (Wallenstein) L.; Irene Leibo, Aug. 6, 1961; children: Laura, Jacqueline Trinkler, David. BS, CCNY, 1959; DDS, NYU, 1963. Pvt. practice dentist N.Y.C. Capt. U.S. Army, 1963-65. Fellow Acad. Gen. Dentistry (dir. 1983-89, v.p. 1989-90, pres. elect 1990-91, pres. 1991-92.), Am. Coll. Dentists, Internat. Coll. Dentists, Acad. Dentistry Internat., Royal Coll. Medicine. Office: 145 W 86th St New York NY 10024-3406

LEIBTAG, BERNARD, accountant; b. Balt., Oct. 24, 1950; s. Aaron H. and Rose Sarah (Miller) L.; m. Susan Ann Weintraub, Aug. 4, 1974; children: Gila M., Aaron D., Aliza C. BA in History, Yeshiva U., 1973; MA in History, Columbia U., 1975, M Phil in History, 1976, MBA in Acctg., 1979. CPA, Md. Staff acct. Arthur Young & Co., N.Y.C., 1979; mgr. Grant Thornton, Balt., 1979-86; sr. mgr. KPMG Peat Marwick, Balt., 1987-90; tax mgr. Kamanitz, Uhlfelder & Permison, Balt., 1990—; cons. Nat. Bus. Inst., Eau Claire, Wis., 1989—, Balt. Assn. Tax Counsel, 1990—, Comptroller of Treasury, Annapolis, Md., 1985-86. Contbr. articles to profl. jours. Mem. Assn. Jewish Charities Young Leadership Coun., Balt., 1982-84; mem. Associated Way Balt., 1982—. Fellow Nat. Found. Jewish Culture, 1976, Yivo Inst., N.Y.C., 1973-76. Mem. AICPAs, Md. Assn. CPAs (chmn. state tax com. 1989-91, cert. appreciation 1989-91), Balt. Assn. Tax Counsel, Balt. Estate Planning Coun., Beta Gamma Sigma, Eta Sigma Phi, Pi Gamma Mu. Democrat. Jewish. Office: Kamanitz Uhlfelder Permison 4 Reservoir Cir Baltimore MD 21208

LEIBU, HENRY JOACHIM, consulting chemist; b. Germany, Apr. 22, 1921; came to U.S., 1949; s. Wolfgang and Paula (Probst) L.; m. Coralie T. Timmermann, 1959; children: Jacques D., Katherine A. ChemE, Swiss Fed. Inst. Tech., Zurich, 1942, DSc in Chemistry, 1946. Rsch. assoc. Swiss Fed. Inst. Tech., 1946-49; researcher polymers E.I. Du Pont de Nemours & Co., Wilmington, Del., 1949-52, rsch. assoc. plant ops., 1952-59, rsch. assoc. internat. tech. svc. isocyanates, 1959-65, elastomers tech. sales assoc., 1965-85; cons., chemist Wilmington, 1985—. Patentee fields intermediates, high polymers, elastomers and composites, plastics, liquid chromatography. Mem. Am. Chem. Soc. Home and Office: 4905 Threadneedle Rd Wilmington DE 19807-2527

LEIBY, BRUCE RICHARD, educator; b. Media, Pa., Aug. 30, 1947; s. Edward Charles and Margaret Ellen (Strawbridge) L.; m. Linda Pauline Flounders, June 26, 1971. BSBA, Tusculum Coll., Greeneville, 1969; postgrad. West Chester U., 1970, 72. Tchr. Interboro Sch. Dist., Prospect Park, Pa., 1969-70, Delaware County Community Coll., Media, 1974, Upper Darby Adult Sch., Pa., 1970-88, Upper Darby Sch. Dist., 1970—; staff asst. Upper Darby High Sch., 1987—, former mem. bus. edn. adv. bd., co-sponsor Bus. Club, 1987-88. Author for Greenwood Press, Westport, Conn., 1988—; author: Gordon Macrae - A Bio-Bibliography, 1988, 91, Howard Keel - A Bio-Bibliography, 1992. Mem. Am. Film Inst., NEA, Pa. Edn. Assn., Upper Darby Edn. Assn. (past membership chmn.), Suburban Bus. Edn. Assn. Republican. Methodist. Home: 13 E 6th St Media PA 19063-5913 Office: Upper Darby High Sch Lansdowne Ln Upper Darby PA 19082-5410

LEIBY, RICHARD ARTHUR, historian, educator; b. Allentown, Pa., Apr. 11, 1954; s. Robert William Leiby and Grace June (Grim) Christman; m. Cathy Jo Benchoff, June 17, 1989; children: Michael Paul Scott, Andrew Thomas Scott. AB, Albright Coll., 1976; MA, U. Del., 1978, PhD, 1984. Vis. instr. Franklin and Marshall Coll., Lancaster, Pa., 1981-82; vis. asst. prof. Kutztown (Pa.) U., 1985-87; mem. continuing edn. faculty Ea. Mich. U., Ypsilanti, 1987; asst. prof. history Rosemont (Pa.) Coll., 1988—; cons. Ednl. Testing. Svc., Lawrenceville, N.J., 1991. Contbr. articles, book revs. to profl. publs. Grantee Pew Meml. Trust Fund, 1990, German Acad. Exch. Svc., 1990. Mem. Am. Hist. Assn., German Studies Assn., Arbeitskreis Nachkriegsgechichte, Greater Phila. Area Modern European Historians (coun. mem. 1990—). Office: Rosemont Coll Montgomery Ave Bryn Mawr PA 19010-3403

LEICH, JOHN FOSTER, political scientist, European languages educator; b. Evansville, Ind., June 27, 1920; s. Clarence and Josephine (Foster) L.; m. Jean Elizabeth Ferriss, June 24, 1950; children: Ellen Leich Moon, Christopher Martin. BA, Swarthmore Coll., 1942; MA, Yale U., 1947; PhD, U. Mass., 1976. Fgn. svc. officer U.S. Dept. State, Gdansk, Warsaw, Munich, Bremen, 1947-50; dep. divisional dir. Free Europe, Inc., N.Y.C. and London, 1950-65; rsch. scientist, cons. George Washington U., Washington, 1965-67; prof. polit. sci. and fgn. langs. La. Tech. U., Ruston, 1967-90; mem. faculty Taconic Learning Ctr. and Inst. World Affairs, Salisbury, Conn., 1990—. Author: The Communist Parties in the European Parliament, 1976; contbr. articles to profl. jours. Pres. Greenwich Village Brotherhood Com., N.Y.C., 1959-60; dist. capt. Rep. party, N.Y.C., 1956; founder Ruston (La.) Community Theatre, 1977. Mem. Coun. on Fgn. Rels., Conf. Group on Italian Politics, Southeastern Assn. Latin Americanists, Phi Beta Kappa. Republican. Episcopalian. Home: 34 Dudley Town Rd Cornwall Bridge CT 06754-1313 also: PO Box 1402 Sharon CT 06069

LEICHT, R. T., fire protection specialist; b. Phila., Feb. 28, 1951; s. Joseph Earl and Betty (Lewis) L. AS, Del. County Ct. Coll., 1976; BS in Fire Protection, Madonna U., Livonia, Mich., 1982; MS in Safety, St. Joseph U., Phila., 1988. Cert. fire protection specialist, fire inspector. Firefighter Lower Merion Fire Dept., Phila., 1973-77; field engr. IRM Svcs., Charlotte, N.C., 1977-83; fire protection specialist CUGNA Corp., Phila., 1984—; adjunct prof. Del. Tech. Coll., Stanton, 1986—, Del. County Community Coll., Media, 1990—. Vol. firefighter Springfield Fire Co., Pa., 1990—; fire marshal Springfield Township, 1982—. With USAF, 1970-76. Mem. Soc. Fire Protection Engrs. (scholarship com. 1988), Cert. Protection Specialist Bd. (sec. 1987—), Fire Marshal Assn. Del. Valley (dir. 1990—), Am. Soc. Safety Engrs., Nat. Fire Protection Assn. Home: PO Box 569 Bear DE 19701-0569 Office: CIGNA Loss Control 09 TLP 1601 Chestnut St Philadelphia PA 19192-0003

LEICHTMAN, HARRY MACGREGOR, psychologist; b. Washington, Nov. 3, 1949; s. Edwin Sylvester and Dorothy Esther (Moore) L.; m. Susan Turriff, Aug. 26, 1978; children: Andrew, Jeffrey. B.A., Coll. William and Mary, 1972; M.A., Northwestern U., 1973, Ph.D., 1978. Lic. psychologist, Mass. Predoctoral clin. intern Judge Baker Guidance Ctr., Boston, 1975-76; assoc. dir. Wediko Children's Svcs., Boston, 1976-82; cons. delinquency sect. Judge Baker Children's Ctr. and Childrens Hosp., Boston, 1979-80; corp. cons., 1981—; dir. HaML Clin. Assocs., Needham, Mass., 1982—. Fellow Mass. Psychol. Assn., Am. Orthopsychiat. Assn.; mem. Mass. Coun. of Human Svc. Providers. Home: 26 Whitney Rd Newton MA 02160-2429 Office: HaML Clin Assocs 388 Hillside Ave Needham MA 02194-1262

LEIFER, MARVIN WILLIAM, physician; b. Albany, N.Y., Feb. 8, 1945; Seymour and Anne (Swidler) L.; m. Lynn Joy Burkes, Nov. 14, 1976. BA, Univ. Chgo., 1966; MD, SUNY, Bklyn., 1970. Diplomate: Am. Bd. Psychiatry and Neurology. Intern L.I. Jewish Med. Ctr., New Hyde Park, N.Y., 1970-71; resident in psychiatry Albert Einstein Coll. Medicine, Bronx, N.Y., 1971-74, rsch. fellow in psychopharmacology, 1974-76; dir. univ. psychiat. svcs. SUNY, Stony Brook, N.Y., 1976-77; dir. outpatient psychopharmacology svcs. Bellevue Hosp. Ctr., N.Y.C., 1977-81; dir. clerkship program in psychiatry NYU Sch. of Medicine, 1981-83; dir. cen. evaluation svc. Bellevue Psychiatric Hosp. Outpatient Clinics, N.Y.C., 1981-83; dir. outpatient dept. St. Vincent's Hosp. Westchester, Harrison, N.Y., 1983-90; dir., chmn. dept. psychiatry Helene Fuld Med. Ctr., Trenton, N.J., 1990—; asst. prof. SUNY, Stony Brook, 1976-77; asst. prof. NYU Sch. of Medicine, 1977-82; clin. assoc. prof. NYU, 1982-83; clin. assoc. prof. N.Y. Med. Coll., Valhalla, 1983—. Author and co-author articles in profl. jours. Recipient: individual rsch. fellowship, NIMH, 1974-76. Mem. Am. Psychiat. Assn. Office: Helene Fuld Med Ctr 750 Brunswick Ave Trenton NJ 08638

LEIFER, RICHARD, management educator, management consultant; b. N.Y.C., Oct. 9, 1942; s. Meyer and Bella (Axelrod) L.; m. Jane Dermon; children: Gabriel, Jeffrey. AB, U. Calif., Berkeley, 1964, MS, 1966; PhD, U. Wis., 1975. Asst. prof. U. Mass., Amherst, 1975-80; vis. assoc. prof. U. Santa Clara, Calif., 1980-82; assoc. prof. mgmt. Rensselaer Poly. Inst., Troy, N.Y., 1983—; cons. Community Health Plan, Albany, N.Y., 1988-91, GM, Warren, Mich., 1989—, GE, Huntsville, Ala., 1989—; numerous presentations in field. Capt. USAF, 1966-70. Mem. Acad. Mgmt., Inst. Mgmt. Sci., Decision Scis. Inst. Office: Rensselaer Poly Inst Sch Mgmt Troy NY 12180

LEIFMAN, HOWARD DAVID, psychotherapist; b. Miami, Fla., Aug. 24, 1956; s. Harvey and Renee (Ellis) L. BA, Syracuse U., 1977, MA, 1978; MSW, NYU, 1987, postgrad., 1992—. Cert. social worker. Acct. exec. Bozell & Jacob, N.Y.C., 1978-79; acct. supr. PR AIDS, N.Y.C., 1979-81; dir. mktg. Hearst Corp.-King Features, N.Y.C., 1982-84; acct. dir. West Glen Com., N.Y.C., 1984-86; dir. social svcs. Stuyvesant Polytech, N.Y.C., 1987-88; dir. counseling NYU, N.Y.C., 1988—; workshop leader Stern Sch. Bus., N.Y.C., 1989—; bd. dirs. Appleby Found., 1985—. Mem. NASW, Coll. Placement Coun. Democrat. Jewish. Office: NYU Stern Sch 44 W 4th St New York NY 10010

LEIGH, PENNY RUTH, executive speech consultant; b. Springfield, Ill.; d. Lloyd Edwards and Ruth (Stinson) Leka; married, Dec. 18, 1965. MusB, U. Ala., 1957; MS, Columbia U., 1960. Cons. Scholastic Mag., N.Y.C., 1972-75, Frederick Knapp Assocs., N.Y.C., 1976—. Author 3 record-book companions, 1974; co-author 4 record-book companions, 1975;; co-author: (music) Fruitcake, 1965 (Novelty of the Decade award). Bd. mem. Interlocken Ctr. for the Arts, 1975-77. Mem. ASCAP, Women in Communications, Nat. Speaker's Assn., U. Ala. Alumni Assn. (exec. bd., past pres. Greater N.Y. chpt.). Office: Frederick Knapp Assocs 280 Madison Ave New York NY 10016-0801

LEIGH, STEPHEN, industrial designer; b. N.Y.C., May 21, 1931; s. Herman Lerner and Rhea (Drinkhouse) L.; m. Barbara Lynn Haim, Feb. 14, 1984; children: Harvey Alan, Madeleine Beth. BFA, Cooper Union, 1951. Interior designer Robert Gruen Assocs., N.Y.C., 1951-55; designer, project

dir. Michael Saphier Assocs., N.Y.C., 1955-59; pres. Stephen Leigh & Assocs. Inc., N.Y.C., 1959—; interior designers, cons. specializing in comml. usage, United Jewish Appeal, 1963, U.S. Pavilion, Venezuelan Pavilion, N.Y. World's Fair, 1964-65, Random House, 1969, Mitsubishi Internat. Corp., 1980, Rapid Am. Corp., 1982, Bowery Savs. Bank, 1986; lectr. NYU. Columnist Real Estate Weekly, 1963-65, The Office Mag., 1985—; one-man shows of sculpture at Cartier and East River Savings Bank; recent prin. works include Union Chelsea Nat. Bank, Faberge, Fino Restaurant, Il Menestrello Restaurant, Schenley, redesign of landmark facade at 111 8th Ave., 1989; sculpted permanent team trophy for Eisenhower Golf Tournament. Recipient AIA design award for Venezuelan Pavilion N.Y. World's Fair, 1964-65, Excellence award The Archtl. Woodwork Inst., 1988. Mem. Am. Soc. of Interior Designers (N.Y. chpt.), Charge des Missions of the Confrerie de la Chaine des Rotisseurs (Bronze Star of Excellence), Brotherhood of the Knights of the Vine. Office: 201 E 57th St New York NY 10022-2800

LEIGHTEN, PATRICIA, art history educator; b. Providence, Nov. 11, 1946; d. George David and Barbara Edith (Greeno) L.; m. Steven Helmling, Sept. 17, 1982. BA, U. Mass., Boston, 1973; MA, Rutgers U., 1975, PhD, 1983. Lectr. U. Del., Newark, 1982-83, asst. prof., 1983-88, assoc. prof., 1988—. Author: Re-Ordering the Universe: Picasso and Anarchism, 1897-1914, 1989; editor spl. edition Art Jour., 1988. Rsch. grantee Am. Philos. Soc.; postdoctoral fellow J. Paul Getty Found., 1985-86, Kress Sr. fellow Ctr. for Advanced Study in the Visual Arts, Nat. Gallery of Art, 1989-90, fellow Guggenheim Found., 1990-91. Mem. Coll. Art Assn. Office: U Del 318 Old College Newark DE 19716

LEIGHTON, LAWRENCE WARD, investment banker; b. N.Y.C., July 1, 1934; s. Sidney and Florence (Ward) L.; m. Mariana Stroock, June 21, 1959; children: Sandra Florence, Michelle Stroock. BSE, Princeton U., 1956; MBA, Harvard U., 1962. Vice pres. Kuhn Loeb & Co., N.Y.C., 1962-69, Clark, Dodge & Co., Inc., N.Y.C., 1970-74, Norton-Simon, Inc., N.Y.C., 1974-78, ltd. ptnr. Bear, Stearns & Co., N.Y.C., 1978-82; mng. dir. Chase Investment Bank, 1983-88; pres., chief exec. officer Union d'Etudes et Investissements Mcht. Bank of Credit Agricole, 1989—. Mem. exec. com. Princeton U. Alumni Council, 1975-80; vice chmn. nat. schs. com. Princeton U., 1980—; chmn. Harvard Bus. Sch. Fund of N.Y., 1964-65; mem. nat. fin. com. Pete DuPont for Pres., 1986-88. Served to lt. (j.g.) USN, 1957-60. Clubs: Stanwich (Greenwich, Conn.); Princeton Club of N.Y. (scholarship com. 1970—, bd. govs. 1989—); Coral Beach and Tennis (Bermuda). Avocations: flying; golf. Home: 1088 Park Ave New York NY 10128-1132 Office: UI-USA 610 5th Ave New York NY 10020-2403

LEIMAN, JOAN MAISEL, university administrator; b. Rochester, Minn., Apr. 26, 1934; d. John Josiah and Ida (Rubenstein)Maisel; m. Leonard M. Leiman June 26, 1955; children: Elizabeth, Alan. BA, Wellesley (Mass.) Coll., 1955; MA, Columbia U., 1958, MPhil, 1976, PhD, 1977. Prog. analyst N.Y.C. Bur. Budget, 1966-68, sr. budget examiner, 1968-69, asst. budget dir., 1969-71; dep. commr. N.Y.C. Addiction Svcs. Agy., 1971-72; spl. advisor to Mayor N.Y.C. Govt., Office of Mayor, 1972-74; v.p. prog. devel. and budget Manpower Demonstration Research Corp., N.Y.C., 1977-81; v.p. planning Interfaith Med. Ctr., N.Y.C., 1982-84; dep. v.p. Columbia U. Health Scis., N.Y.C., 1984—; pres., past pres. Grad. Faculties, Alumni of Columbia U., 1988—; dir., vice-chair N.Y. Found., 1985—; adj. lectr. pub. health Col. Sch. Pub. Health, 1991—; cons. in field. Fellow N.Y. Acad. Medicine; mem. Acad. of Polit. Sci., Health Care Exec. Forum (v.p. 1986-87), Women's City Club, Women and Founds., Am. Assn. Med. Colls., N.Y. Health Planning Soc. Office: Columbia U 630 W 168th St Rm 2-463 New York NY 10032

LEIMER, PHYLLIS HANCOCK, personnel consultant; b. Kansas City, Mo., June 27, 1936; d. Kenton L. and Lois (Post) Hancock. BA, Coll. of Wooster, Ohio, 1958; postgrad., NYU. Pers. cons. Girl Scouts U.S.A., N.Y.C.; pers. adminstr. Rsch. Hosp. and Med. Ctr., Kansas City; speaker in field. Tutor Lenox Hill Neighborhood; vol., shelter for homeless; elder, deacon Fifth Ave. Presbyn. Ch. Mem. Soc. for Human Resource Mgmt., N.Y. Personnel Mgmt. Assn. Home: 405 E 54th St Apt 7G New York NY 10022-5125

LEINER, MURRAY J., advertising and marketing executive, consultant; b. N.Y.C., Dec. 2, 1929; s. Samuel Wolf and Jean (nee Baron) L.; m. Joan Lois Rubenstein; children: Mindy Leiner-Jacobson, Barbara Leiner-Greenstein, Amy Jo Leiner-Epstein. BS in Advt. and Mktg., N.Y. U., 1953, postgrad., 1953. Asst. editor Town & Country Mag., N.Y.C., 1953-54; creative dir. Erland Advt. Agy., N.Y.C., 1954-55; v.p. mktg. Leeds Travelwear Inc., N.Y.C., 1955-67; pres. Murray Leiner Assocs. Inc., N.Y.C., 1967-70, Doak Mktg., Inc., N.Y.C., 1970—; speaker's roster AFA, N.Y.C., 1953-55; speaker Video World Conf., N.Y.C., 1975. Trustee Community Synagogue, Sands Point, N.Y., 1965-78, Brotherhood pres., 1972-74; pres. Harbor Hills Owners Assn., Port Washington, N.Y., 1972. Served with U.S. Army, 1948-49. Republican. Jewish. Club: Ensign Fleet 9. Lodge: Mason. Home: 36 Lewis Ln Port Washington NY 11050-2513 Office: Doak Mktg Inc PO Box 47 Port Washington NY 11050-0100

LEINWEBER, BRUCE KORNBLATT, obstetrician/gynecologist; b. Phila., Sept. 11, 1935; s. Arthur Richter and Florence (Kornblatt) L.;m. Nancy Schwartz, 1960 (dec. 1971); children: Cynthia Beth, Melanie Joy; m. Joan Halperin Glick, 1976; stepchildren: Suzanne Lynn Glick, Jennifer Beth Glick, Adam Brett Glick; 1 child, Dara Hope. BA in Biology, Lafayette Coll., 1955; DDS, Temple U., 1959; MD, Jefferson Med. Coll., 1963. Lic. dentist, N.Y., Pa.; lic. MD, Pa.; diplomate Nat. Bd. Dental Examiners, Nat. Bd. Med. Examiners, Am. Bd. Ob-gyn. Rotating intern, then resident in ob-gyn. Albert Einstein Med. Ctr., Phila., 1963-67, mem. active staff, 1967—; mem. active staff Rolling Hill Hosp. divsn. United Hosps. of Phila., Elkins Park, Pa., 1967-91, Frankford Hosp., Phila., 1967-91; pvt. practice ob-gyn. Phila., 1967-78, 86—, Bensalem, Pa., 1978-91; founder Bensalem Premenstrual Syndrome Ctr., 1984; clin. asst. prof. ob-gyn. Med. Coll. Pa., Phila., 1976-91; clin. asst. prof. ob-gyn. Sch. Medicine Temple U., Phila., 1991—; cons. numerous orgns. including Prudential Ins. Co., Blue Shield of Pa., Med. Assistance Program of Pa., Amalgamated Clothing and Textiles Workers Union, Pvt. Health Care Systems; mem. med. adv. bd. Jon D. Fox State Rep., Pa.; panelist Med. Malpractice of southeastern Pa. Contbr. articles to profl. jours. Capt. USAR, 1957-65. Ford scholar, 1953-55. Mem. AAAS, AARP, AMA, Acad. Natural Scis. Phila., Am. Assn. Gynecol. Laparascopists, Am. Assn. Sex Educators, Counselors and Therapists, Am. Coll. Ob-Gyn., Am. Fertility Soc., Fedn. State Med. Bds., Obstet. Soc. Phila., Pa. Med. Soc., Philadelphia County Med. Soc., World Med. Assn., World Affairs Coun. Phila., Zool. Soc. Phila., Assn. Vol. Sterilization, Phi Lambda Kappa. Republican. Jewish. Office: Dept Ob/Gyn Levy 2 5501 Old York Rd Philadelphia PA 19141-3098 also: 9880 Bustleton Ave Center One Ste # 306 Philadelphia PA 19115

LEIS, HENRY PATRICK, JR., surgeon, educator; b. Saranac Lake, N.Y., Aug. 12, 1914; s. Henry P. and Mary A. (Disco) L.; m. Winogene Barnette, Jan. 8, 1944; children—Henry Patrick III, Thomas Frederick. B.S. cum laude, Fordham U., 1936; M.D., N.Y. Med. Coll., 1941. Diplomate Am. Bd. Surgery. Intern Flower and Fifth Ave Hosps., N.Y.C., 1941-42, resident, 1943-44, 46-49, attending surgeon, chief breast service, 1960-81; resident in surgery Kanawa Valley Hosp., Charleston, W.Va., 1942-43; attending surgeon, chief breast service Met. Hosp., N.Y.C., 1960-81, emeritus chief breast service, 1982—; attending surgeon Coler Meml. Hosp., N.Y.C., 1960-76; chief breast surgery Cabrini Hosp. Med. Ctr., 1978-85, cons. breast surgery, 1985—; emeritus surgeon Lenox Hill Hosp., N.Y.C., 1980-83, hon. surg. staff, 1984—; hon. surg. staff Drs. Hosp., N.Y.C., Grand Strand Gen. Hosp., Myrtle Beach, S.C., 1985—; attending surgeon Westchester County Med. Ctr., 1977-81, emeritus surgeon, 1982—; clin. prof. surgery U. S.C. Sch. Medicine, Breast Surg. Oncology, Columbia, 1985—; hon. dir. breast cancer ctr., cons. in breast surgery Winthrop Univ. Hosp., Mineola, 1971—; cons. in breast surgery VA Hosp., Columbia, S.C., 1985—; cons. in breast surgery St. Claires Hosp., N.Y.C., 1979; attending surg. staff Richland Meml. Hosp., Columbia, 1986-90; clin. prof. surgery, 1960-81, prof. emeritus, 1982—, co-dir. Inst. Breast Diseases, 1978-82, emeritus, 1982—, chief breast svc. N.Y. Med. Coll., 1960-81, emeritus, 1982—; cons. in breast surgery SUNY Div. Rehab., 1965—, Med. and Surg. Specialists Plan N.Y.; mem. Am. Joint Com. on Breast Cancer Staging and End Results; v.p. N.Y. Met. Breast Cancer Group, 1975-76, pres., 1977-79; cons. Med. Advs. Selective Svc. System, N.Y.C. Alumni trustee N.Y. Med. Coll., 1971-76; adv. coun. Fordham Coll. Pharmacy, 1968—; bd. dirs. Hall Fame and Mus. Surg. History and Related Scis. Author: Diagnosis and Treatment of Breast Lesions: The Breast, 1970, Management of Breast Lesions, 1978, Breast Cancer: Conservative and Reconstructive Surgery, 1989, Breast Lesions: Diagnosis and Treatment, 1988; co-editor: Breast; hon. editor Internat. Surgery Jour.; mem. editorial bd. jour. Senolgia, 1982—, Breast: An Internat. Jour.; contbr. articles to profl. jours. Mem. Women's Cancer Task Force of S.C. Capt. M.C., AUS, 1944-46, PTO. Decorated knight comdr. with star Equestrian Order Holy Sepulchre Jerusalem, knight Mil., Order of Malta, Knight Noble Co. of the Rose; recipient award of Merit Am. Cancer Soc., 1969, 87, cert. and award for outstanding and devoted services to indigent sick City N.Y., 1965, Dr. George Hohman Meml. medal, 1936, N.Y. Apothecaries medal, 1936, Internat. cert. merit for disting. service to surgery, 1970, award of merit N.Y. Met. Breast Cancer Group, 1976, medal of Ambrogino (Italy), 1977, Service award of Honor N.Y. Med. Coll., 1969, medaille d'Honneur (France), medal of City of Paris, 1979. Fellow ACS (cancer liaison physician Surgeons commn. on Cancer 1987—, Peruvian Acad. Surgery (hon.), Am. Acad. Compensation Medicine, Am. Soc. Clin. Oncology, Am. Assn. Cancer Rsch., Am. Geriatrics Soc., Indsl. Med. Assn., Internat. Coll. Surgeons (1st v.p. 1973-74, pres. 1977-78, v.p., chmn. coun. examiners U.S. sect. 1962-68, pres. 1971, Svc. award of honor 1971), Internat. Paleopathology Assn. (founder), N.Y. Acad. Medicine, N.Y. Coun. Surgeons, Royal Soc. Health (Eng.); mem. AMA, AAAS, AAUP, Am. Cancer Soc. (com. breast cancer), Am. Med. Writers Assn., Am. Profl. Practice Assn., Assn. Am. Med. Colls., Am. Coll. Radiology (com. mammography and breast cancer), Assn. Mil. Surgeons U.S., Cath. Physicians Guild (pres. N.Y. 1970-78), Gerontol. Soc., Internat. Platform Assn., N.Y. Cancer Soc., N.Y. County Med. Soc., N.Y. Surg. Soc., Pan Am Med. Assn. (v.p. N.Am. sect. on cancer 1967—), Pan Pacific Surg. Assn. (v.p. 1980, Res. Officers Assn. U.S., Soc. Acad. Achievement (editorial bd. 1969—), Soc. Med. Jurisprudence, Soc. Nuclear Medicine SurSoc. N.Y. Med. Coll., WHO, World Med. Assn., Alumni Assn. N.Y. Med. Coll. (gov. 1960—, pres. 1971), Assn. Mil. Surgeons U.S., Catholic War Vets Assn., VFW, Hollywood Acad. Medicine (hon.), Alpha Omega Alpha, Phi Chi; hon. mem. Argentine Soc. Mammary Pathology, Argentina Cardiac and Thoracic Surg. Soc., Ecuador Med. Assn., Mo. Surg. Soc., Venezuela Surg. Soc., Italian Surg. Soc., S.C. Oncology Soc., So. Med. Assn. Club: Ocean Dunes, Surf. Lodge: K.C. (4th deg.).

LEISHMAN, J(OHN) GORDON, aeronautics/astronautics educator; b. Scotland, Aug. 11, 1958; came to U.S., 1986; s. John and Alice B. (Millar) L. BSc, U. Glasgow, 1980, PhD, 1984. Aerodynamicist Westland Helicopters, Yeovil, Eng., 1983-86; rsch. assoc. Ctr. for Rotocraft Edn. and Rsch., College Park, Md., 1986-87; asst. prof. U. Md., College Park, 1988—. Contbr. articles to profl. jours. Mem. AIAA, Am. Helicopter Soc. Home: 11351 Broken Bow Ct Beltsville MD 20705-1452

LEISMAN, GERALD, neuroscientist; b. London, Oct. 18, 1947; s. Bernard Louis and Olga (Bjelinki) L.; m. Naomi Esther Leisman, Sept. 5, 1968 (div. Jan. 1987); children: Yael M., Akiba J., Daniel E.; m. Debra Ellen Blaine, Sept. 22, 1987. MSc, U. Manchester, U.K., 1970, MB, ChB, 1972; PhD, Union Grad. Sch., 1979; MD, U. Compl. Medicine, Colombo, Sri Lanka, 1990. Assoc. prof. physiology/psychology CUNY, Flushing, Bklyn., 1972-79; dir. clin. neurosci. labs. VA Hosp., East Orange, N.J., 1973-79; v.p. R&D Sercenco Scientific Systems Corp., Mamanoneck, N.Y., 1979-82, Am. Electromedics Corp., Hudson, N.H., 1982-84, Hai Surg. Corp., Nashua, N.H., 1984-86; rsch. prof. neurosci., dir. conservative health Rsch. Inst. N.Y. Chiropractic Coll., Old Brookville, N.Y., 1987-90; pres., chief scientific officer Nat. Inst. Complementary Medicine, Manhasset, N.Y., 1990-92; prof. neurosci., psychology and biomed. engring. Touro Coll., Dix Hills, N.Y., 1992—; dir. and assoc. dean Inst. Biomed. Engring. and Rehab. Svcs., Dix Hills, N.Y., 1992—; vis. scholar Palmer Coll. Chiropractic, 1990; adj. assoc. prof. neurology N.J. Med. Sch., Newark, 1973-79, adj. prof. neurology and biomed. engring. Harvard U. Med. Sch. Children's Hosp., Boston, 1982-86; adj. prof. life sci. and elec. engring. N.Y. Inst. Tech., Old Westbury, 1986-91; cons. in field. Author textbooks; contbr. articles to profl. jours.; patentee in field. Recipient Human Factors Citation Israel Ministry Health, 1979, Contbn. to Psychiatry award Am. Acad. Gen. Practice, 1974, Outstanding Contbn. Vision Sci. Am. Optimetric Assn., 1982. Fellow Am. Psychol. Soc., N.Y. Acad. Sci., Acad. Medicine N.J.; mem. IEEE (sr.), AAAS, Internat. Neuropsychol. Soc., Assn. for the Advancement of Med. Instrumentation. Jewish. Home: 215 Sycamore St West Hempstead NY 11552-2409

LEIST, JOSEPH ANTHONY, appeals officer, lawyer; b. Bklyn., Jan. 3, 1945; s. Louis August and Antoinette Mary (Barone) L.; m. Bonnie Lorraine Tillery, Feb. 14, 1986. BBA, CCNY, 1966; JD, N.Y. Law Sch., 1978. Field agt. IRS, N.Y.C., 1966-67, 69-78, team coord., 1978-82, appeals officer, 1982—; adj. prof. Borough of Manhattan Community Coll., N.Y.C., 1979-82. 1st lt. U.S. Army, 1967-69. Regents scholarship N.Y. State Bd. Regents, 1962. Mem. Nat. Treasury Employees Union. Democrat. Roman Catholic.

LEISTER, LORI ANN, guidance counselor; b. Pottsville, Pa., Mar. 22, 1962; d. Chester Mark and Nancy Arlene (Straw); m. William Harvey Leister, Mar. 16, 1985; children: Kristin Pamela, Shane William. BA, Bloomsburg U., Pa., 1980-84; MEd, Kutztown U., Pa., 1991. Secondary Sch. Counseling. Fieldworker Campus Child Ctr., Bloomsburg, Pa., 1983; intern Columbia County Children & Youth, Bloomsburg, Pa., 1984; in-house coord. Regional Devel. Corp., Pottsville, Pa., summers 1982-84; caseworker Pinebrook Svcs., Whitehall, Pa., 1984-86; grad. asst. Kutztown U., Kutztown, Pa., 1987, study skills instr., 1987; guidance counselor intern N.E. Mid. Sch., Bethlehem, Pa., 1990-91. Mem. Am. Assn. for Univ. Women, Am. Assn. of Counseling and Devel., Pa. Sch. Counselors Assn., Alpha Kappa Delta. Home: 522 Raub St Easton PA 18042-1569

LEITER, DONALD EUGENE, religious organization executive; b. Ashland, Ohio, Feb. 5, 1932; s. Harold Lewis and Sadie Helena (Watson) L.; m. Crystal Dianne Berkey, June 15, 1957; children: David Alan, Donald Eugene Jr., Dianne Elizabeth, Daniel Scott. BA, Manchester Coll., 1954; MDiv, Bethany Theol. Seminary, 1958; postgrad., Garret Theol. Seminary and Northwestern U., 1972. Ordained to ministry Ch. of the Brethren, 1956. Min. West Side Christian Parish, Chgo., 1955-58; pastor Ch. of the Brethren, Everett, Pa., 1958-59, Germantown Ch. of the Brethren, Phila., 1959-61; pastor, organizer Immanuel Ch. of the Brethren, Paoli, Pa., 1959-66; assoc. pastor Washington City Ch. of the Brethren, 1966-72; coord. Capitol Hill Group Ministry, Washington, 1968-72; exec. dir. Delmarva Ecumenical Agy., Wilmington, Del., 1972-81; pastor, organizer Christ Ch. of the Brethren, Carol Stream, Ill., 1981-84; exec. dir. Ga. Christian Coun., Macon, 1984-90, Christian Assocs. Southwest Pa., Pitts., 1991—. Scoutmaster, agy. rep. Boy Scouts Am., 1963-72; co-chmn. Upper Main Line Com. Conscience, 1965-66; mem. Neighborhood Planning Coun., Washington, 1967-72, Leadership Pitts., Citizens League S.W. Pa., Interfaith/Impact for Justice and Peace, Pitts. Points of Light Leadership Coun., Nat. Conf. Christians and Jews, 1973-81, Habitat for Humanity, Ctr. Dem. Renewal. Mem. Nat. Assn. Ecumenical Staff, Nat. Coun. Chs., Ecumenical Networks. Office: Christian Assocs SW Pa 239 Fourth Ave Ste 1817 Pittsburgh PA 15222-1769

LEITERSTEIN, STEVEN JAY, technical company executive; b. N.Y.C., Nov. 24, 1947; s. Edward Samuel and Pauline (Solomon) L.; m. Susan F. Shapiro; children; Matthew, Rachel. B.S., CCNY, 1968; M.S., Yeshiva U., 1972. Math. tchr. N.Y.C. Bd. Edn., NYU, York Coll., 1968-77; dean students Elizabeth B. Browning Intermediate Sch., N.Y.C., 1977-81; area tech. mgr. TYMSHARE, Stamford, Conn., 1981-83; sr. cons. McDonnell Douglas, Stamford, 1983-85; dir. client support Decision Support Svcs., Stamford, 1985-89; sr. v.p. systems devel. Arbeit & Co., N.Y.C., 1989-90; sr. v.p. info. tech. DecisionBase Resources, N.Y.C., 1990-92; dir. fin. info. systems Young and Rubicam, Inc., N.Y.C., 1992—. Home: 71 Fox Hill Rd Stamford CT 06903-2221 Office: Young and Rubicam Inc 285 Madison Ave New York NY 10017

LEITNER, MELINDA JO, vocational rehabilitation counselor; b. Springfield, Mo., Apr. 21, 1958; d. Charles E. and Mary A. (Flanagan) Gottas; m. Peter L. Leitner, May 13, 1988. BS, S.W. Mo. State U., 1980; MA, U. Mo., 1983. Nat. cert. counselor. Counselor Mich. Tech. U., Houghton, 1983-84; family adv. specialist Dept. Def., Bindlach, Germany, 1984-89; counselor youth svcs. Children's Home and Aid Soc. of Ill., Belleville, 1990; rehab. specialist Comprehensive Rehab. Assocs., White Plains, N.Y., 1991—. Bd. dirs. Dial Help Crisis Line, Houghton, 1983-84. Mem. AACD, Am. Coll. Pers. Assn. Methodist. Home: 8 Hilltop Cir Fishkill NY 12524

LEKSE, WILLIAM JOHN, water transportation executive; b. Pitts., July 18, 1947; s. William Charles and Mary Ann (Iacomini) L.; m. Babette S. Brody, June 22, 1972; 1 child, Jaclyn Mary. BS, U.S. Merchant Marine Acad., 1969; MBA, Duquesne U., 1972; postgrad., U. Pitts., 1990. Lic. marine engr. Marine engr. U.S. Merchant Marine, 1969; nuclear test engr. electric boat div. Gen. Dynamics, Groton, Conn., 1972-73; from asst. to pres. to pres. Campbell Barge Line, Pitts., 1973—; from v.p. to pres. Haney Barge Line, Charleroi, Pa., 1978—; pres. Blue Danube Inc., Charleroi, 1984—, Campbell Transp. Co., Charleroi, 1985—, Kanowha River Twoing, Port Pleasant, W.Va.; dir. Nat. Waterways Conf., Washington, 1986. Bd. dirs. DINAMO, Ohio Valley, 1984. Lt. USN, 1971-72. Recipient Cert. of Merit U.S. Dept. Transp., 1985; named Admiral of Port Port Authority and County Commrs., Pitts., Allegheny County, Pa., 1983. Mem. Waterways Assn. Pitts. (pres. 1982-83, bd. dirs. 1978—), Am. Waterways Operators (chmn. Ohio Valley region 1986-87, bd. dirs. 1982—), Duquesne Club, St. Clair Country Club. Democrat. Roman Catholic. Home: 1320 Bower Hill Rd Pittsburgh PA 15243-1308 Office: Campbell Transp Co PO Box 124 Charleroi PA 15022-0124

LELLINGER, DAVID BRUCE, botanist; b. Chgo., Jan. 24, 1937; s. Nicholas Francis and Rose (Kreicker) L.; m. Linda Mae Kuhles, June 15, 1963; children: Richard Eric, Anne Marie. AB, U. Ill., 1958; MS, U. Mich., 1960, PhD, 1965. Curator ferns Smithsonian Instn., Washington, 1963—. Author: A Field Manual of the Ferns and Fern-allies of the United States and Canada, 1985, The Ferns and Fern-allies of Costa Rica, Panama and the Chocó. Named Hon. Assoc. Curator of Pteridophyta, Museo Nacional de Costa Rica, 1978. Mem. Am. Fern Soc. (editor, coun. mem., pres. 1990-91), Internat. Assn. Plant Taxonomy (sec. of com. for pteridophyta 1988—). Office: Smithsonian Instn US Nat Herbarium MRC-166 Washington DC 20560

LELYVELD, GAIL ANNICK, actress; b. Boston, May 22, 1948; d. Edward I. and Beatrice Elizabeth (Hewitt) L. BA in Polit. Sci., Boston U., 1970; MA in Polit. Sci., Goddard Coll., 1974; studies with Paul Barry, Peter Donat, Ray Reinhardt, Darrell Lauer, others. Actress, 1970—; tech. staff USA Prodns. and Midseason, Hempstead, N.Y., 1986-87, prodn. stage mgr., 1987—; tech. staff Gray Wig, Hempstead, 1986, 87; cons. Talking With prodn. M.A., C.W. Post. Appeared in numerous films including Frances, Halloween III, Children on Their Birthdays, Project 1917, Rocky II, Happy Endings, Seeds of Innocence, Bonfire of the Vanities, The Tale of 109th, (TV shows) Archie Bunker's Place, Mister Clown Says, White Noise, The Gentle Creature, (ABC Afterschool Spl.) Summer Stories: The Mall, The Tale of 109th; actor (theatre) Alice in Wonderland, Not so Grimm Fairytale Players; actress (Littletop Theatre Co.) Toby Tyler, Marmalade Gumdrops, (theatre) Bohemian Lights; singer Musicum Collegium Hofstra U., Pala Opera Assn., St. Patrick's Cathedral Choir; theatre tech. involvement includes stage mgr., sound asst. Wings; sound asst. Danton's Death; asst. stage mgr. Endgame, Breaker Morant; lighting, stage mgr. The Foreigner. Mem. AFTRA, Freeport Arts Coun. Jewish. Home: 291 Saville Rd Mineola NY 11501 Office: USA Prodns care Hofstra Cultural Ctr Hofstra U Hall Hempstead NY 11550

LELYVELD, JOSEPH SALEM, newspaper editor, correspondent; b. Cin., Apr. 5, 1937; s. Arthur Joseph and Toby (Bookholz) L.; m. Carolyn Fox, June 16, 1958; children: Amy, Nita. BA summa cum laude, Harvard U., 1958, MA, 1959; MS in Journalism, Columbia U., 1960. Reporter, editor N.Y. Times, 1963—, fgn. corr., Johannesburg, New Delhi, Hong Kong, London, 1965-86, columnist mag., staff writer, 1977, 84-85, fgn. editor, 1987-89, mng. editor, 1990—. Author: Move Your Shadow, 1985 (Pulitzer prize, L.A. Times Book prize, Sidney Hillman award, Cornelius P. Ryan award, all 1986). Recipient George Polk Meml. award, 1972, 84. Mem. The Century Assn. Office: The NY Times 229 W 43d St New York NY 10036-3913

LEMA, JO-ANNE S., academic administrator; b. Worcester, Mass., Nov. 5, 1947; d. James Patrick and Florence Marie (Howard) Sullivan; m. Luis E. Lema, Sept. 25, 1971; children: Maria, James. BA, Merrimack Coll., 1969; EdM, Boston U., 1975; EdD, Harvard U., 1981. Researcher MIT, Cambridge, Mass., 1969-71, 79-81; tchr. Colegio Bolivar, Cali, Columbia, 1971-73; contracts adminstr. Educators Cons. Svc., Shrewsbury, Mass., 1973-75; tchr., rsch. asst. Harvard Univ., Cambridge, 1977-79; dir. inst. rsch. Bryant Coll., Smithfield, R.I., 1982-89; asst. v.p. Bryant Coll., Smithfield, 1989—. Rep. town meeting mem. Town Govt., North Attleboro, Mass., 1990—; scholarship com. Harvard Radcliffe Club of R.I., Providence, 1991—. Mem. Soc. for Coll. & Univ. Planning (regional rep. 1991—, bd. dirs. 1991—). Home: 106 Blackberry Rd North Attleboro MA 02760-3504 Office: Bryant Coll 1150 Douglas Pike Smithfield RI 02917-1220

LEMA, MARK JOSEPH, anesthesiologist; b. Buffalo, June 18, 1949; s. Joseph Patrick and Grace Lucille (Sante) L.; m. Suzanne Czamara, Jan. 7, 1972; children: Gareth, Jordan, Bethany. BA in Polit. Sci., Canisius Coll., 1972; MS in Natural Scis., SUNY, Buffalo, 1976, PhD in Physiology, 1978; MD, SUNY, Bklyn., 1982. MD, N.Y., Mass.; diplomate Am Bd. Anesthesiology, Nat. Bd. Med. Examiners. Intern S.I. Hosp., 1982; clin. fellow in anesthesiology Brigham and Women's Hosp., Boston, 1983-84; instr. anesthesiology Med. Sch. Harvard U., Boston, 1985-87; asst. prof. anesthesiology Sch. Medicine SUNY, Buffalo, 1987-91, assoc. prof., 1992—, dir. rsch. dept. anesthesia, 1987—; head anesthesiology, critical care medicine Roswell Park Cancer Inst., 1987—, dir. chronic pain svcs., 1988—; vis. prof. SUNY-Buffalo, Naval Med. Command, Bethesda, Md., Cornell U., Dartmouth-Hitchcock Med. Ctr., Lebanon, N.H., SUNY-Syracuse; lectr. hosps., univs., 1983—; prin. investigator Parker B. Francis Investigatorship in Anesthesiology, Purdue Frederick Inc., Internat. Technidyne Inc., Roxanol Inc., Electronetics Inc., Pharmaco Inc., E.I. duPont de Nemours and Co. Inc., others. Mem. AMA, Am. Soc. Anesthesiologists, Internat. Anesthesia Rsch. Soc., Am. Soc. Regional Anesthesia, Soc. Critical Care Medicine, Anesthesia History Assn., Cardiovascular-Pulmonary Group Western N.Y., Med. Soc. State N.Y., Anesthesia Patient Safety Found., Med. Soc. County Erie, N.Y. State Soc. Anesthesiologists. Roman Catholic. Office: Roswell Park Cancer Inst Buffalo NY 14263

LEMAHIEU, JAMES JOSEPH, business consultant; b. Milw., Feb. 23, 1936; s. Harold William and Genieveve Azalea (Christman) LeM.; m. Barbara M. Pratt, July 3, 1989; children: Paul George, Ann Genieveve, Charles William. BS, Yale U., 1958; MBA cum laude, Boston U., 1969. Cert. prodn. and inventory mgmt. mgr. System analyst USM Co., Beverly, Mass., 1961-68; system cons. IMF, Inc., Waltham, Mass., 1968-70; mgr. inventory, prodn. control Gorton Group div. Gen. Mills, Gloucester, Mass., 1970-77, dir. forecasting, 1977-91; cons. in field, Derry, N.H., 1965—. Chmn. Derry (N.H.) Sch. Survey Com., 1963-66; active Derry Sch. Bd., 1964-79; coach, organizer Derry Recreation Prog., 1974-80; trustee, pres. Pinkerton Acad., Derry, 1980-91. Mem. Internat. Inst. Forecasters, Am. Prodn. and Inventory Control Soc., Beta Gamma Sigma. Lodge: Kiwanis. Home: 431 Sprucewood Ln San Antonio TX 78216-6417

LEMARBE, EDWARD STANLEY, engineering manager, engineer; b. Chicago Heights, Ill., June 30, 1952; s. Gerald Joseph and Irene Helen (Jelen) LeM.; m. Patricia Ann Czyz, May 28, 1977; children: Kyle Bradford, Randall Jered. BS in Mech. Tech., Purdue U., 1976; MBA, Lewis U., 1984. Field engr. Morrison Constrn. & Engring., Hammond, Ind., 1976-78; sr. engr. Miner Enterprises, Inc., Geneva, Ill., 1978-85; mgr. product devel. Alco Dispensing Systems div. Alco Standard, Torrington, Conn., 1985-88; v.p. engring. Jet Spray Corp., Norwood, Mass., 1988—; mem. pres.'s staff Alco Dispensing/Selmix-Alco, Torrington, 1986-88; mem. exec. com. Jet Spray Corp., Norwood, 1988—. Mem. Am. Soc. Testing and Materials (subcom. 1988—), Am. Mgmt. Assn. (assoc.), Internat. Food Svc. Mfrs. Assn. (corp. mem.), Hickory Bend Condo Assn. (bd. dirs. 1984-85). Republican. Roman Catholic. Office: Jet Spray Corp 825 University Ave Norwood MA 02062-2662

LEMASTER, ARTHUR JAMES, educator; b. San Angelo, Tex., Sept. 2, 1933; s. Arthur Brookshire and Ruth (Denham) L. BBA, U. North Tex., 1955; MA, Sul Ross State U., 1957; EdD, U. North Tex., 1962. Tchr. Odessa (Tex.) Schs., 1955-60; instr. Cooke County Community Coll., Gainesville, Tex., 1961-62; assoc. prof. Univ. Houston, Tex., 1962-69; editor in chief McGraw Hill Inc., N.Y.C., 1969-74, 76-81; assoc. prof. CUNY, Baruch Coll., N.Y.C., 1974-76; prof. Rider Coll., Lawrenceville, N.J., 1981—. Author: Gregg Shorthand for Colleges, Transcription, 1981, College Dictation for Transcription, Diamond Jubilee Series, 1981, Gregg Shorthand, Individual Progress Methods, 1982, Gregg Dictation and Transcription, Individual Progress Method, 1983, SuperWrite Brief Course, 1990, Notemaking, 1990, SuperWrite Dictionary, 1990, SuperWrite, Vols. One and Two, 1991, and others; contbr. over 100 articles to profl. jours. Mem. Nat. Bus. Edn. Assn., Delta Pi Epsilon. Democrat. Home: 231 Youngs Rd Trenton NJ 08619-1023 Office: Rider Coll Lawrenceville Rd Trenton NJ 08648-4308

LE MAY, MOIRA KATHLEEN, psychology educator; b. N.Y.C., Apr. 12, 1934; d. Bernard Howard and Kathleen (Sullivan) Fitzpatrick; m. Joseph Albert Le May, June 14, 1958; children: Valerie H. (Le May) Teal, Joseph B. BS, Queens Coll., 1956; MS, Pa. State U., 1960, PhD, 1970. Engring. psychologist USN Rsch. Lab., Washington, 1960-62, ITT Fed Labs., Nutley, N.J., 1962-64; instr. psychology Manhattanville Coll., Purchase, N.Y., 1964-68; asst. prof. Skidmore Coll., Saratoga Springs, N.Y., 1968-70; prof. Psychology Montclair State Coll., Upper Montclair, N.J., 1970—; cons. in engring. psychol. USAF-WPAFB, Human Resources Lab., Dayton, Ohio, 1978-79, NASA Calif. Tech. Jet Propulsion Lab., Pasadena, 1982-83, USN Air Devel. Ctr. Warminser, Pa., 1986-87, NASA Langley Rsch. Ctr., Hampton, Va., 1989-90. Contbr. numerous artticles to profl. jours and papers to sci. meetings. Campaign worker, Ridgewood (N.J.) Dem. Orgn., 1974-89, com. rep. corresponding sec. 1978-86. Fellow Am. Psychol. Soc.; mem. IEEE, AAAS, APA, Human Factors Soc. (liaison to AAAS 1984—). Roman Catholic. Home: 1023 Hillcrest Rd Ridgewood NJ 07450-1030 Office: Montclair State Coll Upper Montclair NJ 07043

LEMBERGER, NORMA, financial executive; b. Monticello, N.Y., July 21, 1944; d. Joe J. and Ellen Anna (Rosman) L. BS summa cum laude, Bklyn. Coll., 1965. With IBM, Armonk, N.Y., 1965—; dir. spl. fin. IBM Credit Corp., Stamford, Conn., 1985—; gen. mgr. Rolm Credit Corp. IBM, Santa Clara, Calif., 1985-87; pres. Rolm. Credit Corp. and dir. financing programs IBM Credit Corp., Stamford, Conn., 1987-88; treas. IBM Americas Group, Mt. Pleasant, N.Y., 1988-89; program dir. investor rels. IBM Corp., Armonk, 1989-91, dir. investor rels., 1991—. Mem. Women's Econ. Round Table.

LEMBO, GLORIA ANN, bank executive; b. Bronx, N.Y., Oct. 22, 1949; d. Salvatore and Antoinette (Grande) Fulia; m. Richard Andrew Lembo, May 21, 1972; 1 child, Kimberly. BA, Queens Coll., 1971; MBA, Fordham U., 1976. Systems analyst Bankers Trust Co., N.Y.C., 1971-73, asst. treas., 1973-77, asst. v.p., 1977-83, v.p., 1983-84; cons. U.S. Dept. of Treasury, Washington, 1984-85; v.p. Riggs Nat. Bank, Washington, 1985-87, sr. v.p., 1987—. Mem. Am. Bankers Assn. (NOAC planning com. Washington chpt. 1988-89, wholesale ops. com. 1990), Mid Atlantic Clearing House Assn. (chmn. edn. com. Linthicum, Md. chpt. 1988-90). Roman Catholic. Home: 2 Pennforest Way Rockville MD 20853 Office: Riggs Nat Bank 808 Seventeenth St NW Washington DC 20074-0143

LEMCO, JONATHAN MARTIN, research director, political science educator; b. Montreal, Que., Can., Apr. 2, 1956; came to U.S., 1985; s. Frank and Ruth (Fischer) L.; m. Judy Yellen, May 17, 1987; children: Alexandra Pauline, David Benjamin. BA, Clark U., 1977; MA, U. Rochester, 1980, PhD in Polit. Sci., 1982. Prof. U. Victoria, B.C., Can., 1982-83, McGill U., Montreal, 1983-84, Wilfrid Laurier U., Waterloo, Ont., Can., 1984-85, The Johns Hopkins U., Washington, 1985—; rsch. dir. Nat. Planning Assn., Washington, 1989—; prof. Fgn. Svc. Inst. of the U.S., Arlington, Va., 1985—; scholarship referee Govt. Can., Washington, 1986—, Internat. Assn. of Machinists, Washington, 1985—. Author: Canada and the Crisis in Central America, 1991, Political Stability in Federal Govts. 1991, Turmoil in the Peaceable Kingdom, 1992; editor: State and Development, 1988, Energy and Environmental Concerns in Canada and the United States, 1992. Campaign worker Udall for Pres. Com., Worcester, Mass., 1976; polit. commentator CKO Radio Network, Can., 1986-89. Recipient Rsch. support Inco Fellowship, 1977, Donner Found., 1990, Ford Found., 1990. Mem. Am. Polit. Sci. Assn., Can. Polit. Sci. Assn. Home: 2004 Rampart Dr Alexandria VA 22308 Office: Nat Planning Assn 1424 16th St NW #700 Washington DC 20036

LEMENTOWSKI, MICHAL, surgeon; b. Warsaw, Poland, Sept. 20, 1943; came to U.S., 1972; s. Wlodzimierz and Tamara (Bakurewicz) L.; m. Celeste Gallo, Mar. 29, 1983; children: Maria, Michal Jr., Jennifer, Lisa, Jason, Sean. MD, Acad. Medicine, Warsaw, 1968. Diplomate Am. Bd. Surgery. Surg. intern Kings County Hosp., Bklyn., 1974-75; surg. resident St. Francis Hosp. Med. Ctr., U. Conn., Hartford, 1975-79; asst. dept. urology Grochowski Hosp., Warsaw, 1970-72; clin. instr. surgery SUNY Downstate Med. Ctr., Bklyn., 1974-75, U. Conn., Hartford, 1978-79; pvt. practice Monessen, Pa.; chmn. dept. surgery Brownville (Pa.) Gen. Hosp., 1988, Monongahela (Pa.) Valley Hosp., 1989—. Fellow ACS, Internat. Coll. Surgeons; mem. AMA (physician recognition award 1989), Pa. Med. Soc., Fayette County Med. Soc., Monessen C. of C. Republican. Roman Catholic. Home: 30 Heritage Hills Rd Uniontown PA 15401-5620 Office: 331 Schoonmaker Ave Monessen PA 15062-1210

LEMKE, JAY LAWRENCE, education educator; b. Chgo., June 1, 1946; s. David Louis and Xenia Dora (Shapiro) L. BS, U. Chgo., 1966, MS, 1968, PhD, 1973. Rsch. fellow Enrico Fermi Inst., Chgo., 1968-72; prof. edn. CUNY, Bklyn., 1972—; vis. scholar U. London, 1980-81, U. Sydney, Australia, 1981-85; cons. Deakin U., Victoria, Australia, 1983; mem. editorial bd. Linguistics and Edn., 1988—. Author: Using Language in Classrooms, 1985, Talking Science, 1990; contbr. articles to profl. publs. NSF fellow, 1967; recipient rsch. award NSF, 1980. Mem. Am. Ednl. Rsch. Assn., Am. Anthrop. Assn., Internat. Systemic Linguistics Assn., Phi Beta Kappa. Office: CUNY Bklyn Coll Sch Edn Brooklyn NY 11210

LEMLE, ROBERT SPENCER, lawyer; b. N.Y.C., Mar. 6, 1953; s. Leo Karl and Gertrude (Bander) L.; m. Roni Sue Kohen, Sept. 5, 1976; children: Zachary, Joanna. AB, Oberlin Coll., 1975; JD, NYU, 1978. Bar: N.Y. 1979. Assoc. Cravath, Swaine & Moore, N.Y.C., 1978-82; assoc. gen. counsel Cablevision Systems Corp., Woodbury, N.Y., 1982-84, v.p., gen. counsel, 1984-86, sr. v.p., gen. counsel, sec., 1986—; bd. editors Cable TV and New Media Law and Fin., N.Y.C., 1983—, bd. dirs. Cablevision Systems Corp., 1988—. Mem. ABA, N.Y. State Bar Assn. Home: 7 Grace Dr Old Westbury NY 11568-1228 Office: Cablevision Systems Corp 1 Media Crossway Dr Woodbury NY 11797-2062

LEMLEY, BARBARA WINK, business educator; b. Gettysburg, Pa., Mar. 26, 1930; d. Howard Lamar and Anna Beamer (Tawney) Wink; m. Leo Wayne Lemley, Mar. 2, 1963; children: Susan Lee, Mark Christopher. BA, Pa. State U., 1951, MS, 1955; EdS, George Washington U., 1978, EdD, 1981. Tchr. high sch. N.J., Pa., and Md., 1951-63; asst. prof. bus. U. D.C., Washington, 1971-82, assoc. prof., 1982-86, prof., 1986—, dept. chmn., 1985-88, assoc. dean, 1988-91. Contbr. articles to profl. jours. Co-chmn. fundraiser Columbia Lighthouse for Blind, Washington, 1985, mem. adv. bd. 1986—; co-chmn. antiques show Our Lady of Mercy Ch., Potomac, Md., 1983, 84. Rsch. grantee Cheasapeake and Potomac Tel. Co., Washington, 1984, U. D.C., 1984. Mem. D.C. Bus. Edn. Assn. (pres.), Nat. Bus. Edn. Assn., Ea. Bus. Edn. Assn., Assn. Bus. Communication, Kiwanis, Phi Delta Kappa, Delta Pi Epsilon. Republican. Roman Catholic. Home: 8326 Turnberry Ct Potomac MD 20854 Office: U DC 900 F St NW Washington DC 20004-1404

LEMMON, WILLIAM THOMAS, JR., surgeon; b. Phila., June 11, 1934; s. William T. and Madeleine (Pierce) L.; m. Jean Moyer, Sept. 30, 1961; children: Kelly, Tracy. AB, Princeton U., 1956; MD, Jefferson U., 1960. Diplomate Am. Bd. Gen. Surgery. Intern Jefferson Med. Coll. Hosp., Phila., 1960-61, resident in surgery, 1961-63, 65-67; pres. Lemmon Surg. Assocs., Ltd., Lansdale, Pa., 1973—. Lt. comdr. USPHS, 1963-65. Mem. Alpha Omega Alpha. Home: 102 Tanglewood Dr Lansdale PA 19446 Office: Lemmon Surg Assocs Ltd Cowpath at Line St Lansdale PA 19446

LEMMOND, CHARLES D., JR., lawyer, state senator; m. Barbara Northrup; children: Charles N., Judy, John P., David H. AB, Harvard Coll., 1952; LLB, U. Pa., 1955. Assoc. Silverblatt and Townend; judge Ct. Common Pleas, Luzerne County; first asst. dist. atty., asst. dist. atty. Luzerne County; solicitor various boroughs, twps., sch. dists. Northeastern Pa.; mem. Pa. Senate, Harrisburg, 1985—; chmn. state govt. com., vice chmn. inter-govtl. affairs com., mem. fin. com.,, judiciary com., local govt. com., mil. and vet. affairs com.; bd. dirs. 1st Ea. Bank, N.A. Trustee Wyoming Conf., United Meth. Ch.; bd. dirs. Nesbitt Meml. Hosp., Wyoming Sem.; mem. adv. bd. dirs. Pa. State U., N.E. Tier of Ben Franklin Partnership Program, Salvation Army. With U.S. Army, 1946. Mem. ABA, Pa. Bar Assn., Wilkes-Barre Law Libr. Assn., Masons. Office: Pa Senate State Capitol Harrisburg PA 17120

LEMMONDS, DOUGLAS HARPER, banker; b. Richmond, Va., Feb. 18, 1947; s. Elmo Van Buren and Francis (Penn) L.; m. Pamela Ceresi, May 22, 1971; children: Kimberly Diane, Christine Michelle. BA, Va. Poly. Inst. and State U., 1969; postgrad., U. Amsterdam, 1969; B.Internat. Mgmt., Am. Grad. Sch. Internat. Mgmt., Phoenix, 1970. Examiner Fed. Res. Bank, Richmond, Va., 1970-73; asst. v.p. Bank of Am., London, 1974-79; v.p. Bank of Am., Amsterdam, Holland, 1979-81, Washington, 1981-83, London, 1983-87; v.p., mgr. Bank of Am., N.Y.C., 1987—. Treas. bd. trustees Somers Libr., N.Y., 1988—; pres. Somers Dem. Club, 1991—; trustee Westchester (N.Y.) Libr. System. Mem. Robert Morris Assocs. Democrat. Episcopalian. Office: Bank of Am 335 Madison Ave New York NY 10017-4605

LEMNIOS, WILLIAM ZACHARY, research laboratory administrator; b. Athens, Greece, Sept. 13, 1925; came to U.S., 1929; s. Zachary Vasilios and Evangelia (Malamoglou) L.; m. Angelina Pazar, Jan. 24, 1954; children: Zachary John Lemnios, Starla Catherine Colosimo, Philip Evan Lemnios, Lucian Nicholas Lemnios. BSEE, MIT, 1949; MS in Physics, U. Ill., 1951. Contbr. articles to profl. jours. M.I.T./Lincoln Lab. M.I.T./Lincoln, Nebr., 1952-63, 1963-70, 1970—. Sgt. U.S. Army, 1943-46. Mem. IEEE (sr.), AIAA, AAAS, Am. Phys. Soc., Sigma Xi. Greek Orthodox. Home: 36 Independence Ave Lexington MA 02173-5945 Office: MIT/Lincoln Lab 244 Wood St Lexington MA 02173-6499

LEMONCELLI, JOHN JOSEPH, psychology educator; b. Archbald, Pa., May 4, 1948; s. Samuel L. and Mary Jean (McAndrew) L.; m. Margaret A. Kolmansberger, June 12, 1971; children: Mark James, Mauri Theresa. BA, U. Scranton, 1971, MS, 1972; EdD, Temple U., 1983. Lic. psychologist, Pa. Dir. community svcs. Luzerne-Wyoming County Mental Health, Wilkes-Barre, Pa., 1973-83; lectr. U. Scranton, Pa., 1984-87; psychologist intern G.D. Boroios, M.D. & Assocs., Scranton, 1983-87; psychologist Forum Psychol. Assn., Scranton, 1987—; asst. pro. Marywood Coll., Scranton, 1987—; instr. Pa. State Police Commn., Harrisburg, 1980—; cons. Sister Servants IHM, 1989—, clergy Diocese of Scranton, 1989—. Contbr. articles to profl. jours., 1978—. CCD tchr. St. Thomas Aquinas Ch., Archbald, 1981—; bd. dir. Commn. on Cath. Edn., Scranton, Pa., 1989—. Recipient Prevention Progress award, Pa. Consultation Coun., 1981, Exemplary Svc. award, 1982; named Disting. Svc. Profl., Counseling and Devel. Assn., 1990. Mem. Pa. Consultation and Edn. Assn. (pres. 1981), No. Psychology Assn., Pa. Counseling Assn., Am. Psychology Assn., Pa. Psychol. Assn., Chi Sigma Iota. Democrat. Office: Marywood Coll CHS Dept Counseling & Psych Scranton PA 18503-1936

LEMOR, PIERRE CHARLES, industrial company executive; b. Paris, Sept. 9, 1933; came to U.S., 1982; s. Jean René Louis and Andree Jeanne (Besse) L.; m. Diane Gabrielle Sibelle, Aug. 23, 1968; 1 child, Emmanuel Xavier. Diploma in engring., Ecole Centrale, Paris, 1957; diploma in bus. adminstrn., Institut de Controle Gestion, Lyon, France, 1976. Field engr. Electro-Entreprise, Paris, 1957-59; sales engr. Forges de Vulcain, Paris, 1959-64; export mgr. S.E. Languepin, St. Denis, France, 1964-67; export sales mgr. Transrol SKF, Chambery, France, 1967-72, mktg. and sales mgr., 1972-82; product mgr. SKF Component Systems Co., Allentown, Pa., 1982-88; gen. mgr. SKF Component Systems Co., Bethlehem, Pa., 1988—; counsellor for fgn. trade to the French govt., N.Y.C., 1982—. Contbr. articles to profl. jours.; inventor screw driven rack, high helix ball screw. V.p. Assn. des Centraliens aux U.S.A., N.Y.C., 1986—, Alliance Francaise LeHigh Valley, Allentown, 1989—; dir. Union des Francais àl'Etranger-U.S.A., Phila., 1990—. Lt. French Air Force, 1957-59. Home: 1811 Elmhurst Dr Whitehall PA 18052-3714 Office: SKF Component Systems Co 1530 Valley Center Pky Bethlehem PA 18017-2266

LEMP, MICHAEL ALBERT, ophthalmology educator; b. Washington, May 19, 1937; s. Albert William and Gladys (O'Neal) L.; m. Joan Bernadette Ahern, May 6, 1961; children: Patrick, Regina, Deirdre. BS, Georgetown U., 1958, MD, 1962, MSc, 1968. Asst. clin. prof. ophthalmology Georgetown U., Washington, 1970-78, assoc. clin. prof. ophthalmology, 1978-83, chmn. dept. ophthalmology, prof. ophthalmology, 1983-92; pres. Univ. Ophthalmic Cons., Washington, 1992; cons. Walter Reed Army Med. Ctr., Washington, 1975—, Nat. Eye Inst., Bethesda, Md., 1978—. Author (book) Clinical Anatomy of Eye, 1990; author, editor (book) The Dry Eye, 1992; contbr. articles to profl. jours. Capt. USAF, 1963-65. Recipient Lacrima award Soc. of Dacriology, 1986, Achievement award Japan Contact Lens Soc., 1980. Mem. Am. Acad. Ophthalmology (Honor award 1988), Met. Club, Cosmos Club, Am. Ophthal. Soc. Roman Catholic. Office: Univ Ophthalmic Cons 4910 Massachusetts Ave NW Washington DC 20016

LEMPICKI, ALEXANDER, physicist, educator; b. Warsaw, Poland, Jan. 26, 1922; came to U.S., 1955; s. Dominik and Janina (Czaplicki) L.; m. Antonina Hirschberg, Sept. 27, 1952; children: Maria, Veronica. PhD, Imperial Coll., London, 1960. Rsch. physicist EMI, Eng., 1949-55, Sylvania, N.Y., 1955-72, GTE Labs., Waltham, Mass., 1972-82; prof. physics and chemistry Boston U., 1983—; cons. NASA, Washington, 1979, Baxter Troverwl, 1985, Corning Glassworks, 1983-87. 2nd lt. Inf. Fellow Am. Phys. Soc., Optical Soc. Am. Home and Office: 303 Commonwealth Ave # A Boston MA 02115-2009

LENA, ADOLPH JOHN, specialty steel company executive; b. Latrobe, Pa., Oct. 10, 1925; s. Attilio and Leona (Robb) L.; m. Dolores Ruth Cunningham, June 9, 1948 (div. 1978); m. Beverly Ann Prue, Sept. 15, 1979; children: Mario, Carol, Kathleen, Lisa, Lauren, Lydia. BS in Metallurgy, Pa. State U., 1948; M MetE, Carnegie Mellon U., 1950, D MetE, 1952. Assoc. dir. research Allegheny Ludlum Steel Corp., Pitts., 1953-56, mgr. basic research dept., 1956-63, dir. product devel., 1963-68, dir. research, 1968-69, v.p., tech. dir., 1969-71, v.p., gen. mgr. bar prodn., 1971-76; chmn., chief exec. officer A1 Tech Splty. Steel Corp., Dunkirk, N.Y., 1976-84; exec. v.p., chief operating officer Carpenter Tech. Corp., Reading, Pa., 1986-87, pres., chief operating officer, 1987—, also bd. dirs., 1987-91; ret., 1991; cons. Carpenter Tech. Corp., Reading, 1985-86. Contbr. articles to 20 tech. jours; patentee in field. Trustee Reading (Pa.) Hosp., 1987—. Served to lt. (j.g.) USN, 1944-46, World War II. Recipient McFarland award Pa. State U.; named Disting. Citizen N.Y. State, SUNY Bd. Regents; Pa. State U. alumni fellow. Fellow Am. Soc. Metals (past chmn. Pitts. chpt., past nat. trustee, past nat. sec., Disting. Life Mem. award). Republican. Roman Catholic. Club: Berkshire Country (Reading). Home: 1743 Reading Blvd Reading PA 19610-2605 Office: Carpenter Tech Corp 101 W Bern St PO Box 14662 Reading PA 19612-4662

LENARD, JOHN, physiology and biophysics educator; b. Vienna, Austria, May 17, 1937; s. George and Frances (Perten) Lenard; m. Nancy Stevenson, Oct. 5, 1973; children: Eric, Keith, Karen, Steven. BA, Cornell U., 1958, PhD, 1964. Postdoctoral fellow U. Calif. at San Diego, La Jolla, 1964-67; asst. prof. Albert Einstein Coll. of Medicine Yeshiva U., Bronx, N.Y., 1967-68; assoc. Sloan-Kettering Inst., N.Y.C., 1968-72; assoc. prof. U. Medicine & Dentistry N.J. Robert Wood Johnson Med. Sch., Piscataway, 1973-76, prof., 1976—. Contbr. numerous articles to profl. jours. Mem. Am. Soc. Biochemistry and Molecular Energy, Biophys. Soc., Am. Soc. for Cell Biology, Am. Soc. Microbiology, Am. Soc. for Virology. Office: U Medicine & Dentistry NJ Robert Wood Johnson Med Sch 675 Hoes Ln Piscataway NJ 08854-5635

LENDERKING, WILLIAM RAYMOND, foreign service officer; b. Great Neck, N.Y., Mar. 26, 1934; s. William Raymond and Marion (Groser) L.; m. Lois Allen Haskell Stratton (div.); children: William R. III, Timothy A., Eben P.; m. Susan Joan Halbert, Oct. 6, 1972; children: Justin A.H., Alexandra Q. BA, Dartmouth Coll., 1955; postgrad., Johns Hopkins U., Bologna, Italy, 1973-74. Chief officer plans and operational policy USIA, Washington, 1971-73; press attache U.S. Embassy USIA, Rome, 1974-76, Bangkok, 1976-80; pub. affairs officer U.S. Embassy USIA, Lima, Peru, 1980-83; dir. Cen. Am. Task Force USIA, Washington, 1983, dep. dir. office East Asian and Pacific Affairs, 1985-88; pub. affairs officer U.S. Embassy USIA, Islamabad, Pakistan, 1989—; spokesman, Bur. East Asian and Pacific Affairs U.S. Dept. State, Washington, 1984-85; adviser polit. and security affairs U.S. Mission to UN 43d gen assembly, N.Y.C., 1988; exec. com., bd. dirs. Roosevelt Sch., Lima, 1980-83. Contbr. articles, book revs. to various mags. Lt. (j.g.) USN, 1955-57. Mem. Am. Fgn. Svc. Assn. (exec. com. 1971-73; Rifkin award 1977). Democrat. Episcopalian. Office: USIA Am Embassy PSC Box 13 APO AE 09614

LENEY, GEORGE WILLARD, air pollution administrator, consulting geologist; b. Wausau, Wis., Nov. 13, 1927; s. Bert and Iva Irene (Skoog) L.; m. Arax G. Tefankjian, June 25, 1955 (dec. Aug. 1983); children: Sara Ann, Janet Ellen, John Alan, Ruth Alison. BS, U. Mich., 1950, MS, 1952, MA, 1955. Teaching fellow U. Mich., 1951-53, 53-55; geophysicist Gulf Oil Co., Harmarville, Pa., 1955-56; chief geophysicist Hanna Mining Co., Cleve., 1956-64; staff geophysicist Shell Oil Co., Houston, 1964-66; chief geologist H.K. Porter Co., Inc., Pitts., 1966-76, cons., 1976-77, 81-86, regional geologist U.S. Dept. Energy, 1977-81; air pollution adminstr. Allegheny County Health Dept., Pa., 1986—; v.p., bd. dirs. Pacific Asbestos Corp., 1970-75. Trustee, Hamilton Presbyn. Ch., 1974-77. With USN, 1946-48. Mem. Soc. Econ. Geologists, Am. Inst. Mining Engrs., Soc. Exploration Geophysicists, Geologic Soc. Am., Pitts. Geol. Soc., Pa. Acad. Sci., Air and Waste Mgmt. Assn. Address: 5335 Tomfran Dr Pittsburgh PA 15236

LENGEL, DIANE, elementary education student; b. Belle Vernon, Pa., June 26, 1962; d. Joseph David and Erminia Rose (Manzini) Pastorkovich; m. Elliott Gordon Lengel, May 6, 1989. BA, Calif. Univ. of Pa., 1984, MEd, 1986; postgrad., Slippery Rock U. of Pa., 1991—. Cert. ednl. specialist, sch. guidance. Teen parenting program coord. Midwestern Intermediate Unit IV, Grove City, Pa., 1986-89; cons. and edn. coord. Community Mental Health and Counseling Ctr., Hermitage, Pa., 1989-90. Vol. Grove City Area Sch. Dist., 1991—. Mem. AAUW, AADC, Pa. Counseling Assn. Democrat. Roman Catholic. Home: RR 5 Box 5253 Mercer PA 16137-9630

LENGEL, JEROME KENNETH, financial consultant; b. Reading, Pa., May 18, 1933; s. George Frank and Emma (Smith) L.; m. Kathryn Grim, Dec. 29, 1956; children: Lori Kay, Amy Marie. BS in Econs., Albright Coll., 1955. Mgr. CNA Fin. Co., Reading, 1960-67; fin. cons. Jerome K. Lengel Assocs., Reading, 1967—. Chmn. Heart Fund Reading, 1968. Lt. comdr. USN, 1956-60. Mem. Masons. Republican. Lutheran. Home and Office: 16 Victory Cir RD #9 Reading PA 19605-9664

LENHARTH, WILLIAM HOWARD, program director; b. St. Louis, Dec. 16, 1946; s. Howard Henry and Ellen Ida (Young) L.; m. Jane Levett, Apr. 25, 1969; children: William Allen, Ross David. AA, Meramec Community Coll., 1967; BS in Indsl. Engring., St. Louis U., 1969; MS in Mech. Engring., U. N.H., 1974, PhD, 1978. Machinest Vandeventer Machine, St. Louis, 1963-67; indsl. engring. asst. Combustion Engrs., St. Louis, 1967-68; indsl. engr. Naval Air Systems Command, Washington, 1969-70; ops. rsch. analyst Naval Weapon Systems Analysts, Quantico, Va., 1970-72; indsl. arts instr. Fall Mountain High Sch., Charlestown, N.H., 1972-73; teaching/rsch. assoc. U. N.H., Charlestown, 1973-78; dir. rsch. com. U. N.H., Durham, 1979—; ptnr. G.W. Assocs., Charlestown, 1978-79; v.p. ops. Prime Computing Svcs., Charlestown, 1977-78; cons. in field, Durham, 1979—. Co-author: Arctic Flying, 1977. Active League of Conservation, Concord, N.H., 1991; vol. Owls Head Transp. Mus., 1989-91. Mem. Am. Inst. Indsl. Engrs. (sr.), Prime Computer Users Group (pres. 1984, pres.-elect 1982-83, sec.-treas. 1985, dir. 1987). Home: 55 New Mkt Rd Durham NH 03824 Office: U NH Rsch Computing Engring Sci Rsch Bldg Durham NH 03824

LENNON, MARILYN ELLEN, environmentalist; b. Paterson, N.J., Feb. 7, 1954; d. George Henry and Florence (Buczek) L. BA, Ramapo Coll., 1976; M in City Regional Planning, Rutgers U., 1978. Environ. and land use planner Bergen County Planning Bd., Hackensack, N.J., 1975-78; project planner Pandullo Quirk Assoc., Wayne, N.J., 1978-80; environ. planning cons. Enviro Resource, Inc., Allendale and Atlantic City, N.J., 1980-81, Lennon Assoc., Inc., Atlantic City, 1981-83; sr. v.p., prin.-in-charge Paulus Sokolowski & Sartor, Inc., Warren, N.J., 1983—; assoc. bd. dirs. United Jersey Bank. Author: (chpt. in book) Advances in Environmental Science and Engineering, 1986. Bd. dirs. Liberty Sci. Mus., 1991—; mem. adv. bd. Paramus Cath. Girls High Sch., 1992—. Named one of Outstanding Young Women in Am., 1982, Pioneer Woman of the 90's Bergen County, 1990. Mem. Am. Planning Assn. (legis. com. N.J. chpt. 1986), Atlantic City C. of C. (v.p. 1982, bd. dirs. 1984). Democrat. Roman Catholic. Home: 484 Lanza Ave Garfield NJ 07026-2035 also: 126 9th Ave Seaside Park NJ 08752 Office: Paulus Sokolowski & Sartor Inc 67A Mountain Boulevard Ext Warren NJ 07059-5626

LENSBOWER, JEFFREY LYNN, school psychologist, consultant; b. Chambersburg, Pa., Jan. 15, 1957; s. Frank Lawrence and Ruth Louise (Griffith) L.; m. Melodie Dawn Criswell, May 27, 1978; children: Justin, Chad. BA in Psychology, Shippensburg (Pa.) State Coll., 1979, MS in Psychology, 1982; postgrad., Johns Hopkin's U., 1986—; cert. in sch. psychology, Millersville (Pa.) U., 1991. Community drug and alcohol cons. Franklin/Fulton Drug & Alcohol Program, Chambersburg, 1982-83; program dir. spl. project Potomac Comprehensive Diagnostic Ctr., Romney, W.Va., 1983; lead tchr. Potomac Comprehensive Diagnostic Ctr., Ramsey, W.Va., 1983-84; dir. profl. svcs. Washington County Assn. for Retarded Citizens, Hagerstown, Md., 1984-88; psychology asst. Psychol. Assessment & Therapy, Owings Mills, Md., 1985-88; v.p., co-owner Lycher, Inc., Hagerstown, 1988-90; sch. psychologist Chambersburg Area Sch. Dist., 1988—. Mem. human rights com. Washington County ARC, Hagerstown, 1985-88. State of Md. grantee, 1989, 90. Mem. APA, Assn. Retarded Citizens, Eastern Psychol. Assn., Elks. Home: 304 Norland Ave Chambersburg PA 17201-1224 Office: Chambersburg Area Sch Dist 611 S 6th St Chambersburg PA 17201-3607

LENT, NORMAN FREDERICK, JR., congressman; b. Oceanside, N.Y., Mar. 23, 1931; s. Norman Frederick and Ellen (Bain) L.; m. Barbara Ann Morris, Aug. 4, 1979; children from previous marriage: Norman Frederick 3d, Barbara Anne, Thomas Benjamin. BA, Hofstra U., 1952; LLB, Cornell U., 1957; LLD (hon.), Kyung Hee U., Seoul, Republic of Korea, 1975, Molloy Coll., 1985, Hofstra Coll., 1988. Bar: N.Y. 1957, Fla. 1976. Assoc. police judge East Rockaway, N.Y., 1958-60; confidential law sec. to N.Y. State Supreme Ct., 1960-62; mem. N.Y. State Senate, 1963-70, chmn. joint legislative com. public health, 1966-70; mem. 92nd Congress 5th Dist. N.Y., 1971-73; mem. 93rd-102d Congresses 4th Dist. N.Y., 1973—; vice chmn. Energy and Commerce com. 100th-102nd Congresses U.S. Ho. Reps., 1986—, vice chmn. Mcht. Marine subcom., 1987—; Rep. exec. leader, East Rockaway, N.Y., 1968-70. Trustee Franklin Hosp. Med. Ctr., Oceanside; mem. bd. visitors U.S. Mcht. Marine Acad., Kings Point, N.Y. With USNR, 1952-54. Recipient George Estabrook Disting. Service award Hofstra U., 1967, Israeli Prime Minister's medal, 1977, Disting. Achievement medal N.Y.C. Holland Soc., 1987, Tree of Life award Jewish Nat. Fund., 1987, Anatoly Sharansky Freedom award L.I. Com. for Soviet Jewry, 1983. Mem. ABA, Nassau County Bar Assn., Fla. Bar Assn. Office: US Ho of Reps 2408 Rayburn Office Bldg Washington DC 20515

LENZ, WILLIAM HARDING, podiatrist; b. Canton, Ohio, Sept. 23, 1953; s. George Francis and Christine (Harding) L.; m. Barbara Carter, Aug. 7, 1982; children: Brian, Hilary, Kahle. BA, Thiel Coll., 1975; D Podiatric Medicine, Ohio Coll. Podiatric Medicine, 1980. Diplomate, Am. Bd. Podiatric Surgery. Ptnr. Allegheny Podiatry Foot and Ankle Med. Ctrs., Pitts., 1982—; pres. Allegheny Podiatry Investors Group, Pitts., 1987—; mem. residency com., Podiatry Hosp. Pitts., 1982-86; adj. clinician, Ohio Coll. Podiatric Medicine, Cleve., Pa. Coll. Podiatric Medicine, Phila., 1982—. Bd. dirs., Contact Pitts., Inc., 1988-89. Fellow Am. Coll. Foot Surgeons; mem.

Am. Podiatric Med. Assn., Pa. Podiatric Med. Assn. Republican. Presbyterian. Home: 3 Fieldvue Ln Pittsburgh PA 15215-1510

LEO, DOUGLAS WILLIAM, camera manufacturing company official; b. Rochester, N.Y., Apr. 27, 1951; s. Eugene William and Beverly Ruth (Powley) L.; m. Paula Barbara Romano, Mar. 20, 1970 (div. Feb. 1979); 1 child, Douglas Michael; m. Susan Danette Bailey, July 30, 1983. AS in Gen. Studies, Monroe Community Coll., Rochester, 1991; BS in Mgmt., Roberts Wesleyan, 1992; postgrad., Rochester Inst. Tech. Loan adjuster Security Trust Co., Rochester, 1971-73; metal fabricator Eastman Kodak Co., Rochester, 1973-88, constrn. estimator, 1988—. Bd. dirs. Long Pong Home Owners Assn., Rochester. Mem. Harro East Athletic Club, Phi Theta Kappa (treas. 1990-91). Democrat. Roman Catholic.

LEODORA, ANTHONY E., sports editor, journalist; b. Phila., Jan. 28, 1951; s. Anthony J. and Lena A. (D'Orsi) L.; m. Laura Cecilia Martin, Apr. 14, 1973 (div. 1986); m. Candida M. Chichearo, Sept. 8, 1990. BS in Secondary Edn., Villanova U., 1972, M in Secondary Edn., 1976. Freelance writer, 1973—; asst. sports editor The Times Herald, Norristown, Pa., 1977-80, sports editor, 1980—; cons. Phila. PGA, 1990—. Contbr. articles to profl. jours. Recipient Keystone Press award Pa. Newspaper and Pubs. Assn., 1990. Mem. Nat. Golf Reporters Assn., Baseball Writers Assn. Am., Golf Writers Assn., Am. Phila. Sports Writers Assn. (bd. govs. 1982—, pres. 1988-89, Good Guy award 1992). Home: 1943 Yorktown N Jeffersonville PA 19403 Office: The Times Herald 410 Markley St Norristown PA 19404

LEONARD, DANIEL GERARD, counselor; b. Auburn, N.Y., Sept. 28, 1962; s. William Paul and Marjorie Anne (Hickey) L. BS in Spl. and Elem. Edn., SUNY, Buffalo, 1988, MS in Rehab. Counseling, 1991. Cert. rehab. counselor, N.Y. Evening program instr. People Inc., Buffalo, 1986-91; vocat. rehab. specialist U.S. Dept. Vet. Affairs, Buffalo, 1991—; counselor Crisis Svcs., Buffalo, 1987-90. Sgt. U.S. Army, 1980-83, with USANG, 1984-86. Mem. AACD, Nat. Rehab. Assn., Coun. for Exceptional Children. Democrat. Roman Catholic. Home: 473 Colvin Ave Buffalo NY 14216

LEONARD, EDWIN DEANE, lawyer; b. Oakland, Calif., Apr. 22, 1929; s. Edwin Stanley and Gladys Eugenia (Lee) L.; m. Judith Swatland, July 10, 1954; children: Garrick Hillman, Susanna Leonard Hill, Rebecca, Ethan York. BA, The Principia, 1950; LLB, Harvard U., 1953; LLM, George Washington U., 1956. Bar: D.C. 1953, Ill. 1953, N.Y. 1957. Assoc. Davis Polk Wardwell Sunderland & Kiendl, N.Y.C., 1956-61; ptnr. Davis Polk & Wardwell, N.Y.C., 1961—. Trustee the Brearley Sch., N.Y.C., 1980-90. Served to 1st lt. JAGC, 1953-56. Mem. ABA, N.Y. Bar Assn., N.Y. County Bar Assn., Assn. of Bar of City of N.Y. (chmn. various coms.), Millbrook Equestrian Ctr. (pres.). Home: 1148 5th Ave New York NY 10128-0807 Office: Davis Polk & Wardwell 450 Lexington Ave New York NY 10017

LEONARD, EMILY, public relations executive; b. N.Y.C., Oct. 18, 1928; d. Thomas J. and Emily V. (Gibney) Heffernan; m. Robert D. Leonard, Sept. 23, 1950 (wid. 1963); 1 child, John D. BA, Hunter Coll., 1950; MS, Rensselaer Polytechnic Inst., 1966. Special events coordinator Hartford Nat. Bank & Trust, 1966-68; youth cons. Nat. Assn. Retarded Children, N.Y.C., 1968-70; v.p. communications and program devel. Keep Am. Beautiful, Inc., N.Y.C., 1970-78; copr. affairs Philip Morris Cos., N.Y.C., 1978—. Recipient Clarion Women in Communications award, 1974. Mem. Council Protocol Execs. (founder, bd. dirs. 1988—), Women Execs. in Pub. Rels. (bd. dirs., sec. 1978-80), Pub. Rels. Soc. Am. Office: Philip Morris Cos 120 Park Ave New York NY 10017-5523

LEONARD, JOHN, television critic. With N.Y. Mag., 1983—. Office: New York Mag 755 2nd Ave New York NY 10017-5906*

LEONARD, JOHN CLAY, III, physical education educator, gymnastics coach; b. Washington, May 2, 1950; s. John Clay Jr. and Liliane Justine (Schumacher) L.; m. Christine Marellan Flowers, Dec. 23, 1973 (div. Sept. 1983); m. Kaye Anne DeFranceaux, Dec. 24, 1983; stepchildren: Mary Kay, Carolyn, Timmy, Lynn. BS in Edn., Ohio State U., 1973. Counselor, instr. Ctrl. Atlantic Gymnastics Camp, Edgewater, Md., 1967-71; physical edn. instr. Montgomery County Pub. Schs., Rockville, Md., 1973—, boys' high sch. gymnastics coach, 1973-83, girls' high sch. gymnastics coach, 1983—; gymnastics coach Rockville Marvateens, 1974-76, Hill's Gymnastics Tng. Ctr., Gaithersburg, Md., 1988—; owner, dir. Jack Leonard Gymnastics, Woodbine, Md., 1983—; expert gymnastics litigation Andrew Greenwald Atty., Greenbelt, Md., 1977—; instr., dir. Mid. Eas. Gymnastics Camp, Highview, W.Va., 1972-81; athlete rep. U.S. Tumbling and Trampline Rules Com., Cedar Rapids, Iowa, 1972. Designer, performer children's fitness video Toe-Belly-Up-Belly, 1992. Recipient Contbn. Medal award World Tumbling Championships Com., 1973; named Nat. Gymnastics Champion, YMCA, 1970, '71, '72, '73. Nat. Tumbling Champion, U.S. Tumbling and Trampoline Assn. and AAU, 1972-73, Coach of Yr., Montgomery County Coaches Assn., 1975-80, '87, Nat. High Sch. Gymnastic Coaches Assn., 1981. Mem. NEA, U.S. Gymnastics Fedn., Montgomery County Edn. Assn., Delta Upsilon. Home: 705 Morgan Station Rd Woodbine MD 21797-8733 Office: Jackson Rd Elem Sch 900 Jackson Rd Silver Spring MD 20904

LEONARD, JOSEPH HOWARD, association organization executive; b. Cambridge, Md., Oct. 20, 1952; s. Joseph Francis and Catherine (Hill) L.; m. Jacquelyn Lee McCall, June 7, 1975 (div. Dec. 1981); m. Margaret Ann Shenton, June 26, 1982; children: Stephanie Kristina, Jacquelyn Margaret. BA in Psychology, Salisbury State U., 1976; MA in Rehab. Counseling, Gallaudet U., 1979; postgrad., Washington Coll., Chestertown, Md., 1984, 88, U. Md., 1986-87. Cert. profl. counselor, Md. Staff electrician John W. Tieder, Inc., Cambridge, Md., summers 1973-74; prodn. supr. W.H. Leonard & Sons, Inc., Seward, Md., summers 1968-70, 75; instr., program coord. Dorchester Devel. Unit, Inc., Cambridge, 1976-77; rehab. counselor Tex. Rehab. Commn., Austin, 1979; instr. Am. Sign Lang., developmental disabilities Chesapeake Coll., Wye Mills, Md., 1979—; case mgr., coord. spl. programs Dorchester County Health Dept., Cambridge, 1979-80; ind. interpreter Am. Sign Lang. Md., 1979—; exec. dir. Deaf Ind. Living Assn., Inc., Salisbury, Md., 1990—; bd. dirs. Md. Assn. of the Deaf, 1982-86; v.p. bd. dirs. Deaf Ind. Living Assn., Inc., Md., 1984-90; dir. bd. vis. Md. State Sch. for the Deaf, 1985—; mem. adv. bd. Devel. Disabilities program Chesapeake Coll., 1986-90; mem. Gov.'s Commn. on the Hearing Impaired, Md., 1984-90; surveyor Applied Rsch. and Evaluation U., U. Md., 1988-89; bd. dirs. Md. Assn. Community Svcs.; mem. mental health adv. com. for deaf and hearing impaired, Md., 1990—. Asst. scoutmaster Boy Scouts Am., Cambridge, 1973-78; v.p. bd. dirs. Dorchester County Family YWCA, 1985; pres. bd. dirs. Dorchester Assn. for Devel. Disabled, 1979-88. With USN, 1970-73, with USCGR, 1975-86. Mem. Am. Deafness and Rehab. Assn., Am. Assn. Mental Retardation, The Assn. for Severely Handicapped, Nat. Assn. Deaf, Md. Assn. Deaf, Md. Assn. for Retarded Citizens, Chi Sigma Iota, Psi Chi, Rho Sigma Chi. Roman Catholic. Home: 29972 Holly Acres Rd Trappe MD 21673 Office: Deaf Ind Living Assn Inc 106 W Main St Ste 402 Salisbury MD 21801-4943

LEONARD, LAURENCE, metallurgist, consultant; b. N.Y.C., Jan. 9, 1932; s. Newman and Rose (Lipkin) L.; m. Marjorie Aronoff, June 15, 1958; children: Michael, Stephen, Rachel, Eric. SB, MIT, 1954, SM, 1956, ScD, 1962. Asst. prof. Case Western Reserve U., Cleve., 1962-69; group leader SKF Industries, King of Prussia, Pa., 1969-71; sr. staff metallurgist Franklin Rsch. Ctr., Phila., 1971-88, Valley Forge, Pa., 1988—; adj. assoc. prof. Drexel U., Phila., 1978—, Pa. State Grad. Ctr., Malvern, 1990—. Contbr. articles and reports to profl. jours. Home: 505 Princeton Dr Kng Of Prussa PA 19406-1913 Office: Franklin Rsch Ctr 2600 Monroe Blvd Norristown PA 19403-2417

LEONARD, LEO DONALD, educational sociologist; b. Salt Lake City, Nov. 23, 1938; s. Leo Bradford and Florence (Robbins) L.; m. Marilynn Rae Hoyt, Jan. 2, 1962; 1 son, Richard Corey. BS, U. Utah, 1961, student U. Wash., 1961-62, 64-65; MS, Utah State U., 1967, EdD, 1969, postdoctoral U. Mich., 1975-76; MA, George Washington U., 1992. Acting head King County Dept. Mental Health and Adoptions, Seattle, 1962; dir. programs and youth Snoline YMCA, Seattle, 1962-64; instr. Shorecrest High Sch., Wash., 1967-68, Roy (Utah) High Sch., 1966-67; instr. ednl. methods Utah State U., 1968-69; prof. edn. U. Toledo, 1969-80; dean Sch. Edn., U. Portland, Oreg., 1979-88, Sch. Edn. and Human Devel., The George Washington U., Washington, 1988-91; univ. coord. Catholic Diocese of Toledo Curriculum Devel. Project, 1970-75; coll. dir. Canadian Dissemination Project, 1971-74; bd. dirs. Internat. Tchrs. Edn. Council, 1970—; mem. Nat. Task Force on Tchr. Edn., 1984-86. Dir cons. D.C. Pub. Schs., curriculum project, 1988—, Nat. Model Schs. Project, 1988-91. Bd. dirs. Toledo Symphony Orch., 1970-79; trustee, v.p. Choral Arts Soc. Portland, 1983-85; trustee Tucker Maxon Sch., Open Meadows Learning Ctr.; cons. Marine Corps U.; coord. edn. programs USMC Recruiting Svc., 1989—. Fellow Internat. Tchr. Edn. Council, 1971—; Fulbright scholar, Africa, 1967; grantee U.S. Office Edn-Tchr. Corps, 1970, many others. Mem. Am. Assn. Individual Guided Edn., Am. Edn. Research Soc., Comparative Edn. Soc. U.S., Comparative Edn. Soc. Can., Am. Assn. Colls. of Tchr. Edn. (pres. state coun. deans of edn. 1983-85), Marine Corps League (commandant Toledo Detachment 1977-78, Portland detachment 1983-84), VFW, Phi Kappa Phi, Phi Alpha Theta, Phi Delta Kappa. Author: (with Robert T. Utz) Building Skills for Competency Based Teaching, 1974, The Foundations of Competency Based Education, 1975, A Competency Based Curriculum, 1971, La Enseñanza como Desarrollo de Competencias, 1979; (with others) 7 instructors guides for individually guided edn.; contbr. chpts. to books and articles to profl. jours. Office: Sch Edn & Human Devel Dept Ednl Leadership George Washington U Washington DC 20052

LEONARD, THOMAS ALOYSIUS, lawyer; b. Phila., Sept. 5, 1946; s. Thomas Aloysius and Mary Teresa (Kelly) L.; m. Kathleen Mary Duffy; children: Sarah, Mary Kate, Tom. BS, Drexel U., 1968; JD, Temple U., 1971. Bar: Pa., U.S. Supreme Ct., U.S. Ct. Appeals (3d cir.), U.S. Dist. Ct. (ea., mid., we. dists.) Pa., U.S. Dist. Ct. (so. dist.) N.J., U.S. Dist. Ct. Utah, U.S. Dist. Ct. (so. dist.) N.Y. Assoc. Dilworth, Paxson, Kalish & Kauffman, Phila., 1972-76, ptnr., 1976-79, 83-87, sr. ptnr., mem. exec. com., 1987—; controller City of Phila., 1987-91; chmn. litigation dept., sr. ptnr., permanent mem. mgmt. com. Obermayer, Rebmann, Maxwell and Hippel, Phila., 1991—; vice chmn. Phila. Gas Commn., 1979-83; register of wills City of Phila., 1976-79; mem. disciplinary bd. Supreme Ct., Pa., 1991—. Mem. editorial bd. Amran's Pa. Practice, 1972; contbr. articles to profl. publs. Mem. Dem. Nat. Com., Washington, 1976-83, mem. fin. com., 1988; del. Dem. Nat. Convention, 1976, 80, 92; chmn. Pa. fin. com. Clinton for Pres.; mem. coun. Phila. Orch., 1981-86; bd. dirs. Acad. Scis., Phila., 1981-85; pres. Pa. chpt. Irish Am. Partnership. Capt. U.S. Army, 1971-77. Recipient Man of Yr. award Emerald Soc., 1979, Korean-Am. Friendship Soc., 1982, Carmel Humanitarian award Haifa U., 1981, Merit award Chapel of Four Chaplains, 1983. Mem. ABA, Pa. Bar Assn., Phila. Bar Assn. (bd. govs. 1979-82), Union League, Phila. Racquet Club, Serra Club (past pres.). Roman Catholic. Office: Obermayer Rebmann Maxwell and Hippel 14th Fl Packard Bldg Philadelphia PA 19102

LEONARDOS, GREGORY, chemist, odor consultant; b. Cambridge, Mass., Dec. 30, 1935; s. Nicholas C. and Evangeline (Niarchos) L.; m. Virginia Shinopoulos, May 23, 1965; children: Nicholas, Charles. AB in Biochem. Sci., Harvard U., 1957; MS in Chemistry, Northeastern U., 1964, MBA, 1969. Rsch. assoc. Protein Found., Boston, 1960-63; sr. project leader Arthur D. Little Inc., Cambridge, Mass., 1963-80; prin. G. Leonardos Cons., Arlington, Mass., 1980—. Contbr. articles to profl. jours. Mem. Am. Chem. Soc., Air and Waste Mgmt. Assn. (chmn. TT-4 com. 1975-78). Greek Orthodox. Home and Office: 43 Ronald Rd Arlington MA 02174-1421

LEONDAR, BARBARA, academic administrator; b. N.Y.C., Jan. 19, 1928; d. Marcy and Pauline (Spiwack) L.; m. Aaron Reuben Cohn, Dec. 21, 1947 (div. 1962); children: D'Vera, Daniel Charles, Joel Jacob. BA, NYU, 1947; MA, Calif. State U., Northridge, 1964; EdD, Harvard U., 1968. English tchr. Taft High Sch., Woodland Hills, Calif., 1960-64; asst. prof. Harvard U., Cambridge, 1967-68, 1969-72, U. Mass., Boston, 1968-69; asst. dean, assoc. prof. Rutgers U., New Brunswick, N.J., 1972-74; assoc. dean Boston U., 1974-80; v.p. acad. affairs Worcester (Mass.) State Coll., 1980-86; pres. U. Maine, Ft. Kent, Maine, 1986-89; sr. assoc. presdl. search consultation svc. Assn. of Governing Bds. of Univs. and Colls., Washington, 1989-91; cons. Northwind Assocs., Londonderry, N.H., 1991—. Editor: The Arts and Cognition, 1977; contbr. articles to prof. jours. Kent fellow Danforth Found., 1966-68, Fulbright fellow, 1984. Mem. Modern Lang. Assn., Am. Soc. for Aesthetics, Nat. Council Tchrs. of English, New England Assn. Schs. and Colls. (mem. various accreditation teams 1978-84).

LEONE, DANIEL CESIDIO, pharmaceutical executive; b. Norwich, Conn., Apr. 23, 1932; s. Daniel C. Sr. and Mary Catherine (Luzzi) L.; m. Maryanne V. Ozga; children: Maryanne Loretta, Stephanie Carol, Susan Elizabeth. BS in Pharmacy, U. Conn., 1953. With Leone's Pharmacy, 1955-61, ptnr., mgr., 1961-75; exec. v.p. Conn. Pharm. Assn., Rocky Hill, 1975—; cons. pharmacist Norwichtown Conv. Home, Elmachri Conv. Home, 1973-75; clin. assoc. U. Conn. Sch. Pharmacy, 1986—. cons. pharmacist Norwichtown Conv. Home, Elmachri Conv. Home, 1973-75; clin. assic. U. Conn. Sch. Pharmacy, 1986—. Mem. Norwich Jaycees, 1956-68, v.p. 1958, pres. 1959; co-chmn. United Fund, Small Bus. Div. Fund Drive, 1960-62; mem. Citizens Adv. Con. on Urban Renewal, 1967-71, Norwich Charter Revision Commn., 1967; chmn. Am. Cancer Crusade, Norwich, 1967; mem. Am. Cancer Soc., bd. trustees, 1967-69, 73-79, Norwich CDAP Agy., 1970-71, Norwich Health Dist. Study Com., 1970-71; bd. dirs. Conn. Pub. Health Assn., 1981-85; bd. trustees U. Conn., 1987—, co-chmn. budget and fin. com., 1991. Mem. Am. Soc. Assn. Execs., Am. Pharm. Assn., Nat. Assn. Retail Druggists, Nat. Coun. State Pharm. Assn. Execs. (3d party com. 1983-88, bd. dirs. 1984-90, pres. 1989), Ea. Conn. Pharm. Assn. (v.p. 1964, pres. 1965), Conn. Pharm. Assn. (various exec. positions 1965-74), Norwich Area C. of C. (bd. dirs. 1972-74), Kappa Psi, U. Conn. Alumni Assn. (bd. dirs. Southeastern chpt. 1971—, treas. 1978-83), U. Conn. Century Club, KC, Order of Alhambra. Home: 11 Meadow Ln Norwich CT 06360-5240 Office: Conn Pharm Assn 35 Cold Spring Rd Ste 125 Rocky Hill CT 06067-3167

LEONE, LOUIS J., marketing and communications executive; b. Union City, N.J., Mar. 17, 1936; s. Louis J. and Catherine (DeVercelly) L.; m. Susan I. Sawtelle, Aug. 3, 1957; children: Louis C., Marian K., Mark O. BA, U. Tampa, 1972; MA, Cen. Mich. U., 1979. Enlisted U.S. Army, 1959, advanced through grades to lt. col.; pub. affairs officer US Forces in Iran U.S. Army, Tehran, 1974-76; brigade advisor 56th Infantry, 28th Infantry U.S. Army, 1976-78; chief tng. br. U.S. Army Readiness Region II U.S. Army, Ft. Dix, N.J., 1978-79; chief civil liaison br. hdqrs. Dept. of Army U.S. Army, Washington, 1979-82; dir. pub. affairs U.S. Mil. Acad. U.S. Army, Westpoint, N.Y., 1982-84; ret. U.S. Army, 1984; dir. devel. Northeastern Assn. of Blind, Albany, N.Y., 1984-87; mil. liaison Regents Coll. SUNY, Albany, 1989-90, dir. mktg. & communications, 1990—. Mayor Greenwich Village, 1986—, trustee, 1985-86; dir. Tri-County Am. Heart Assn., Glens Falls, N.Y., 1987-89. Mem. VFW, Am. Legion, Greenwich C. of C. (bd. dirs. 1989—), Greenwich Village Bus. Assn. (bd. dirs. 1986-89), Am. Assn. Counseling and Devel., Mil. Edn. Counselors Assn., Assn. of U.S. Army, Ret. Officers Assn., Elks, Lions, Alpha Chi. Republican. Roman Catholic. Home: 181 Main St Greenwich NY 12834-1009

LEONI, MARK ANTHONY, diplomat; b. Anaheim, Calif., June 21, 1961; s. Joe Gabriel and Sarah Alice (Combs) L. AA, Cypress (Calif.) Coll., 1982; BA, Calif. State U., Fullerton, 1984; cert., Def. Intelligence Coll., Washington, 1990. Intelligence analyst Dept. Def., Camp Smith, Hawaii, 1986-90; vice consul U.S. Fgn. Svc., Kingston, Jamaica, 1990—. Ensign USN, 1984-85, Lt. USNR, 1986—. Mem. Delta Sigma Phi (pledgemaster).

LEONTIEF, WASSILY, economist, educator; b. Leningrad, Russia, Aug. 5, 1906; s. Wassily and Eugenia (Bekker) L.; m. Estelle Helena Marks, Dec. 25, 1932; 1 child, Svetlana Eugenia Alpers. Student, U. Leningrad, 1921-25; grad. Learned Economist; PhD, U. Berlin, 1928; PhD honoris causa, U. Bruxelles, Belgium, 1962, U. York, Eng., 1967, U. Louvain, 1971, U. Paris, 1972, U. Pa., 1976, U. Lancaster, Eng., 1976; D honoris causa, Adelphi Coll., 1988; LHD (hon.), Rensselaer Poly. Inst., 1988; D honoris causa, U. Cordoba, 1990. Rsch. economist Inst. Weltwirtschaft U. Kiel, Germany, 1927-28, 30; econ. adviser to Chinese govt. Nanking, 1929; with Nat. Bur. Econ. Rsch., N.Y.C., 1931; instr. econs. Harvard U., Cambridge, Mass., 1932-33; asst. prof. Harvard U., Cambridge, 1933-39, assoc. prof., 1939-46, prof., 1946-75, dir. econ. project, 1948-72, Henry Lee prof. econs., 1953-75; prof. econs. NYU, 1975—, univ. prof., 1983—, founder Inst. Econ. Analysis, 1978-85, mem. rsch. staff, 1986; cons. Dept. Labor, 1941-47, OSS, 1943-45, UN, 1961-62, Dept. Commerce, 1966-82, EPA, 1975-80 , UN, 1980—. Author: The Structure of the American Economy, 1919-29, 2d edit., 1976, Studies in the Structure of the American Economy, 1953, 2d edit., 1977, Input-Output Economics, 1966, 2d edit., 1986, Collected Essays, 1966, Theories, Facts and Policies, 1977, The Future of the World Economy, 1977, (with Faye Duchin) The Future Impact of Automation on Workers, 1986; Contbr. articles to sci. jours. and periodicals U.S. and abroad. Mem. Commn. to Study Orgn. of Peace, 1978; trustee N.C. Sch. Sci. and Math., 1978; mem. issues com. Progressive Alliance, 1979; mem. com. for Nat. Security, 1980. Decorated officer Order Cherubim Univ. Pisa, 1953, Legion of Honor (France), 1967, Order of Rising Sun (Japan), 1984, French Order of Arts and Letters, Commdr., 1985; recipient Bernhard-Harms prize econs. Fed. Republic Germany, 1970, Nobel prize in econs., 1973; Guggenheim fellow, 1940, 50; recipient Takemi Meml. award Inst. of Seizon Life Scis., Japan, 1991. Fellow Soc. Fellows Harvard (sr. fellow, chmn. 1964-75), Econometric Soc., Royal Statis. Assn. (hon.), Inst. de France (corr.); mem. NAS, AAAS, Am. Philos. Soc., Internat. Statis. Inst., Am. Econ. Assn., Am. Statis. Assn., USSR Acad. Scis. (fgn.), 1988, Royal Econ. Soc., Japan Econ. Rsch. Ctr. (hon.), Brit. Acad. (corr.), French Acad. Scis. (corr.), Royal Irish Acad. (hon.), Brit. Assn. Advancement Sci. (pres. Sect. F 1976), USSR Acad. Scis. (fgn.), Soc. of the Optimate Italian Cultural Isnt., Century Club. Mem. Greek Orthodox Church. Office: NYU 269 Mercer St New York NY 10003-6633

LEOPOLD, SUSAN ELIZABETH, photographer, artist; b. Chgo., July 13, 1960; d. Robert Louis and Ann (Cunnyngham) L. Student, Boston U., 1978-80; BFA, Sch. Visual Arts, 1982. Dir. Young Artist Painting Workshop, Bklyn., 1985-92; stock photographer Allford/Trotman Assoc., Jacksonville, Fla., 1989—; represented by John Weber Gallery, N.Y.C., 1986—. Indo-Am. Program fellow, 1989-90.

LEOUS, STEPHEN FRANCIS, restaurant executive; b. Buffalo, Aug. 7, 1958; s. Thomas Matthew and Beatrice Cecilia (Batt) L.; m. Susan Marie Cody, June 13, 1987; 1 child, Courtney Suzanne. BA, Williams Coll., Williamstown, Mass., 1980; M Mgmt., Northwestern U., 1985. Salesman Rich Products Corp., Buffalo, Calif., Chgo., 1980-83; assoc. Aetna Realty Investors, Hartford, Conn., 1985-87; asst. v.p. Marine Midland Bank NA, Buffalo, 1987-88; dir. U.S. francising O'Toole's Restaurants Inc., Buffalo, 1989—. Mem. Crag Burn Golf Club, Univ. Club Buffalo (long range planning com. 1989), Williams Coll. Alumni Assn. Western N.Y. (pres.). Roman Catholic. Home: 812 Auburn Ave Buffalo NY 14222-1419

LEPAGE, WILBUR REED, electrical engineering educator; b. Kearny, N.J., Nov. 16, 1911; s. Wilbur Nicholas and Gertrude Elizabeth (Reedt) LeP.; m. Eveline Marie Jacobsen, June 9, 1936; 1 dau., Margaret Ann. E.E., Cornell U., 1933, Ph.D., 1941; M.S. in Physics, U. Rochester, 1939. Instr. engrng. U. Rochester, 1933-38; grad. student, teaching asst. Cornell U., 1939-41; mem. staff advanced devel. lab. RCA, 1941; physicist radiation lab. Johns Hopkins, 1942-45; sr. research engr. Stromberg Carlson Co., 1946; prof. elec. engrng. Syracuse U., 1947—, chmn. dept., 1956-74; initiated ann. Sagamore Conf. Elec. Engrng. Edn., 1952; cons. to Signal Corps. U.S. Army, 1953; ednl. cons. UNESCO, 1967; guest lectr. Rumanian Assn. Scientists, 1977; mem. Nat. Com. on Elec. Engrng. Films, 1964-71. Author: Analysis Alternating Current Circuits, 1952, (with S. Seely) General Network Analysis, 1952, Complex Variables and The Laplace Transform for Engineers, 1961, (with N. Balabanian) Electrical Science, Book I, 1970, Book II, 1972, Applied APL Programming, 1978. Recipient Gen. Electric award for teaching excellence, 1985. Fellow IEEE (chmn. com. basic scis. 1955-56), AAUP, N.Y. Acad. Scis., Sigma Xi. Home: 217 Dewitt Rd Syracuse NY 13214-2006 Office: Syracuse U Link Hall Syracuse NY 13244

LEPORE, JOHN ANTHONY, engineering educator; b. Phila., Feb. 19, 1935; s. Anthony Donald and Louise E. (Di Sipio) L.; m. Patricia Ann Luning, June 25, 1959; children: William, Thomas, Jacqueline, John Jr. MSME, U. Pa., 1965, PhD, 1967. Registered profl. engr., Pa. Winterstan asst. prof. dept. civil engrng. U. Pa., Phila., 1970-73, undergrad. chair, assoc. prof. dept. civil and urban, 1973-78, prof., dept. chair civil engrng. dept., 1978-81, prof., undergrad. chair dept. of systems, 1986—; owner, proprietor Engrng. & Sci. Consultants, Springfield, Pa., 1975—. Co-author: Developments in Mechanics, Part III, Solid Mechanics, 1971, An Interactive Modelling System for Policy Disaster Analysis, 1978, Lecture Notes in Mathematics: Stability of Stochastic Dynamical Systems, 1972; contbr. 31 engrng. mechanics articles to profl. jours. NSF fellow, 1970. Mem. ASCE, EERI, AAUP, ASEE, Sigma Xi. Home: 731 Timber Trail Ln Media PA 19064-1138 Office: U Pa Towne Bldg Philadelphia PA 19109

LEPORE, MICHAEL JOSEPH, gastroenterologist, educator; b. N.Y.C., May 8, 1910; s. Joseph and Florence (Melucci) L.; m. Ardean Clough Everett, Sept. 18, 1937; 1 son, Frederick Everett. B.S., N.Y. U., 1929; M.S., U. Rochester, 1931, M.D. with honor, 1934. Diplomate: Am. Bd. Internal Medicine. Intern Duke Hosp., asst. resident in medicine, 1934-37; fellow in medicine Yale U., 1935-36; asst. in medicine Columbia U., 1937-46, instr., 1946-52, assoc. in medicine, 1952-56, asst. clin. prof. medicine, 1956-63; practice medicine specializing in internal medicine and gastroenterology, 1937—; cons. in field; dir. Upjohn Gastrointestinal service Roosevelt Hosp., 1962-66, St. Vincent's Hosp. and Med. Center, 1966-75; mem. staffs Englewood (N.J.) Hosp., St. John's Riverside Hosp., Yonkers, N.Y.; attending physician St. Vincent's Hosp. and Med. Center, N.Y.C., Univ. Hosp., Bellevue Hosp. Center; assoc. prof. clin. medicine Sch. Medicine, N.Y. U., 1968-70, prof., 1971—; profl. cons. Tripler Gen. Hosp., Oahu; chief of medicine 148th Gen. Hosp., Saipan, Marianas Islands. Author: Death of the Clinician— Requiem or Reveille?, 1981; Contbr. articles to med. jours. Pres. Upjohn Gastrointestinal Found., 1962-79; mem. pres.'s leadership council U. Rochester. Served as lt. col. M.C. AUS, 1942-46. Decorated Army Commendation medal; Michael J. Lepore Professorship in Gastroenterology endowed in his honor U. Rochester Sch. Medicine, 1986; recipient St. Vincent de Paul Disting. Physician award St. Vincent's Hosp./Med. Ctr. N.Y.C., 1990. Fellow A.C.P., N.Y. Acad. Scis., N.Y. Acad. Medicine; mem. AMA, Am. Gastroenterol. Assn., N.Y. Gastroenterol. Assn., Physiol. Soc. Phila., AAAS, Royal Soc. Medicine, Alpha Omega Alpha, Sigma Xi. Office: 36 7th Ave New York NY 10011

LEPOWSKY, JAMES, mathematician; b. N.Y.C., July 5, 1944; s. Edward and Frances (Rice) L. AB, Harvard U., 1965; PhD, Mass. Inst. Tech., 1970. Lectr., rsch assoc. Brandeis U., 1970-72; asst. prof. Yale U., 1972-77; assoc. prof. Rutgers U., 1977-80, prof., 1980—; mem. Inst. Advanced Study, 1975-76, fall 1980, spring 1985, 87-88, Mathematical Scis. Rsch. Inst., 1983-84. Co-author: (with I. Frenkel and A. Meurman) Vertex Operator Algebras and the Monster, 1988; contbr. articles to profl. jours. Sloan Fellow, 1976-78, Guggenheim Fellow, 1987-88. Mem. Am. Math. Soc., Math. Assn. Am., Am. Phys. Soc. Office: Rutgers U Dept Math New Brunswick NJ 08903

LEPPERT, PHYLLIS CAROLYN, obstetrician-gynecologist; b. Phila., July 7, 1938; d. Walter Jennings and Alice (Brubach) L. BS, Columbia U., 1961, MS, 1964; MD, Duke U., 1973; PhD, Columbia U., 1986. Diplomate Nat. Bd. Med. Examiners, Am. Bd. Obstetrics and Gynecology. Clin. scholar Duke U., Durham, N.C., 1973-74; resident in pediatrics Duke U. Med. Ctr., Durham, 1974-76; resident in obstetrics/gynecology Yale U. Med. Sch., New Haven, 1976-79; assoc. in ob-gyn. Columbia U., N.Y.C., 1979-81, asst. prof. ob-gyn., 1981-88; visiting prof. Tokyo (Japan) Coll. of Pharmacy, Hachioji, Tokyo, Japan, 1989; chmn. dept. ob-gyn., assoc. prof. Rochester (N.Y.) Gen. Hosp., U. Rochester, 1989—; bd. dirs. Maternity Ctr. Assn., N.Y.C., 1988—, Preferred Care, Rochester, 1990—, Riverdale Mental Health Assn., 1986-89, St. Luke/Roosevelt Hosp., N.Y.C., 1986-88. Co-editor: The Extracellular Matrix of the Reproductive Tract; contbr. numerous articles to profl. jours. Vestry Christ Ch. Riverdale, Bronx, N.Y., 1984-86; adv. com. Office of Technology U.S. Congress, 1984. Recipient Berlex Found. Internat. Research Fellowship, 1989, Irving Friedman Award in Ob-Gyn. Yale U., 1978. Fellow Am. Coll. Obstetrics/Gynecology; mem. N.Y. Obstetrical Soc., Soc. for Exptl. Medicine, AAAS. Episcopalian. Office: Rochester Gen Hosp 1425 Portland Ave Rochester NY 14621-3001

LEQUERICA, MARTHA, psychologist, educator; b. Iquitos, Peru; came to U.S., 1969; d. Cesar and Maria Del Pilar (Durand) L.; m. David Sternberg, Dec. 12, 1982; 1 child, Paula Marissa L. BA, Pontifical U., Lima, Peru,

1963; MA in Spl. Edn., NYU, 1972, PhD in Ednl. Psychology, 1982. Lic. psychologist, N.Y. Staff learning disability therapist Maimonides Mental Health Ctr., Bklyn., 1969-82, staff psychologist, 1982-83; mental health cons. East Harlem Headstart, Manhattan, N.Y., 1983—; supervising psychologist, asst. prof. pediatrics Lincoln Hosp. & Mental Health Ctr., Bronx, 1985-89; asst. prof. psychology Montclair (N.J.) State Coll., 1989—; cons. in field; workshop leader, lectr. on child devel. & parenting skills; researcher of behavior problems in minority populations. Mem. APA, Assn. Hispanic Mental Health Profls., N.Y. World Fedn. Mental Health. Office: Montclair State Coll Russ Hall Upper Montclair NJ 07043

LERAY, MARGARET MAY, social services administrator, consultant; b. Bridgeport, Conn., July 22, 1954; d. Francis V. and Elanor (Galvin) Feroleto; m. Alan C. LeRay (div. 1991); children: Elizabeth, Kathryn. BA in Psychology, Trinity Coll., Burlington, Vt., 1976. Devel. disabilities worker United Counseling Svcs., Bennington, Vt., 1978-80; dist. field dir. Vt. coun. Girl Scouts U.S.A., Essex Junction, 1986-89; dir. edn. and devel. No. Berkshire Mental Health, North Adams, Mass., 1989—; mem. task force on substance abuse and violence No. Berkshire Health and Human Svcs. Coalition, 1989—, mem. steering com., 1989—; mem. exec. com. Western Mass. Svc. Providers, Springfield, 1991—. Bd. dirs. Southwestern Vt. Supervisory Union, Bennington, 1984-89; bd. dirs. Bennington Sch. Dist., 1984-89, chmn., 1986-89; trainer Beyond War, Bennington, 1983-87; bd. dirs. Burr & Burton, Manchester, Vt., 1979-80. Recipient President's Circle award Bennington C. of C., 1986, Outstanding Alumna award Trinity Coll., 1986, Vermonter of Yr. award Times Argus-Rutland Herald, 1986, Person of Yr. for South Vt., Beyond War, 1989. Home: 207 Crescent Blvd Bennington VT 05201-2418

LERCH, BETH ANN, editor; b. Reading, Pa., Aug. 20, 1965; d. Richard Dennis and Janet (Nagle) L. BA, Temple U., 1989. Edit. asst. Philly Sport Mag., Phila., 1988-89; mng. editor BFIA/Hosiery Mag., N.Y.C., 1989—; cons. Phila. Fitness, 1988-89; publisher Phila. People Student Mag., 1988-89. Author of poems. Mem. NAFE, NOW (publicity and media 1988—). Home: 101 Gerald Ave Reading PA 19607

LERCH, IRVING ABRAM, medical physicist, radiology educator; b. Chgo., June 29, 1938; s. Abraham and Rissel (Lutwak) L.; m. Sharon Primack, Feb. 24, 1963. BS, U.S. Mil. Acad., 1960; MS, U. Chgo., 1966, PhD, 1969. Rsch. assoc. Univ. Chgo. (Ill.) Hosps., 1969-73; first officer Internat. Atomic Energy Agy., Vienna, Austria, 1973-76; prof. NYU Sch. of Medicine, N.Y.C., 1976—; dir. internat. sci. affairs Am. Phys. Soc., N.Y.C., 1991—; cons., mission expert Internat. Atomic Energy Agy., Vienna, 1976-87; cons. physicist Nat. Cancer Inst., Bethesda, Md., 1978-82; cons. expert World Health Orgn., Geneva, Switzerland, 1980-81; telecommunications cons. PW Communications, Secaucus, N.J., 1985. Editor: Biomedical Dosimetry, 1976; contbr. articles to profl. jours. 1st lt. U S. Army, 1960-63. Recipient Investigator grant USPHS, Univ. Chgo., 1969-73, Rsch. grant, 1973, Clin. Programs grant Nat. Cancer Inst., N.Y.U. Med. Ctr., 1978, Equipment grant ENI, Inc., N.Y.U. Med. Ctr., 1985, monetary grants L.G. Bodkin, Johnson & Johnson, N.Y.U. Med. ctr., 1987. Mem. AAAS, Am. Assn. Physicists in Medicine and Biology (editorial bd. 1980-82), Am. Phys. Soc. (pub. info. and edn. com. 1980-82), Radiation Rsch. Soc., Radiol. and Med. Physics Soc. N.Y. Office: New York Univ Med Ctr 566 1st Ave New York NY 10016-6402 also: Am Phys Soc 335 E 45th St New York NY 10017

LERESCU, NICK, tour operator executive; b. Bucharest, Romania, Mar. 22, 1948; came to U.S., 1976; s. Romulus and Pauline (Ionescu) L.; children: Nicole, Jacqueline. Student Internat. Trade, Acad. Econs., Bucharest, Romania, 1976. Group cons. Englewood (N.J.) Travel Agy., 1986-88; dir. Leslie Travel Agy., Closter, N.J., 1988-90; pres. Advantage Tours, Fort Lee, N.J., 1990—. Republican. Roman Catholic. Office: Advantage Tours 2017 Center Ave Fort Lee NJ 07024-4707

LERMAN, ROBERT ALLAN, investment banker; b. N.Y.C., Jan. 23, 1935; s. Nathan and Eva (Nichomoff) L.; m. Ellen Finkelstein, Nov. 28, 1957. B of Mech. Engring., CCNY, 1957; MS in Math., Adelphi Coll., 1961; MSEE, U. Conn., 1964. Various engring. and math. positions Kollsman Instrument Corp., Adler Electronics, United Aircraft Corp. (not United Technologies), 1957-68; instr. dept. elec. engring. U. Conn. Grad Sch., 1961-62; founder, dir., pres. Predictor Mgmt. Corp., 1966-78; founder, dir., v.p., treas. Spectrum Inc., 1966—; dir. Internat. HRS Industries Inc., 1978-85; dir., pres., treas. Thermodynetics Inc., 1978—, Advanced Energy Concepts Inc., 1980—; pres., treas., dir. Applied Tech. Systems Inc., 1983-89; founder, dir., sec., treas. Pioneer Capital Corp., 1988—; pres., treas., dir. World Wide Art Inc., 1989—; mem. Gov. task force study methods encouraging the fin. of recycling facilities, Conn., 1989-90; lectr. Hartford Grad. Sch., Electrical Engring. Dept., 1989—. Co-author: Nonlinear System Dynamics, 1992; contbr. articles to profl. jours. Office: 651 Day Hill Rd Windsor CT 06095-1719

LERMAN, STEVEN IRA, consulting chemist, industrial hygienist; b. N.Y.C., Nov. 14, 1944; s. Cyprus and Pauline (Ranchwarger) L.; m. Ruth Judy Mandle, Sept. 6, 1965; children: Craig, Tracy, Erica. BA, Queens Coll., N.Y.C., 1965; MS, Adelphi U., 1971. Chemist Con Edison, Queens, 1965-86; sr. chemist N.Y. Power Authority, White Plains, 1986-88; cons. SIL Cons., N.Y.C., 1988—; tech. expert U.S. Dept. Commerce, Gaithersburg, Md., 1988—; instr. Tall Oaks Pubs., Denver, 1989—, FED Tng. Ctr., Nassau, N.Y., 1990—; sr. cons. CBDA Cons. Group, Suffolk, N.Y., 1990—. Contbr. articles to profl. jours. Member Bethpage (N.Y.) Jewish Community Ctr., 1970—, Mid-Island YM-WHA, Plainview, N.Y., 1983—. Fellow Am. Inst. Chemists; mem. ASTM (chmn., Outstanding Svc. award 1988), Am. Chem. Soc. (congl. sci. rep. 3d congl. dist. 1980-85), Nat. Asbestos Coun., Mensa. Office: SIL Cons 3 Allan Gate Plainview NY 11803-6112

LERNER, ABRAM, retired museum director, artist; b. N.Y.C., Apr. 11, 1913; s. Hyman and Sarah (Becker) L.; m. Pauline Hanenberg, Oct. 7, 1940; 1 child, Aline. B.A., NYU, 1935; student, Ednl. Alliance, Art Students League, Bklyn. Mus. Asso. dir. A.C.A. Gallery and Artist's Gallery, N.Y.C., 1945-57; curator Joseph H. Hirshhorn Collection, N.Y.C., 1957-66; dir. Joseph H. Hirshhorn Mus. and Sculpture Garden, Smithsonian Instn., Washington, 1967-85, founding dir. emeritus, ret., 1985; Adv. bd. Archives Am. Art, 1970—. Author: Hirshhorn Museum and Sculpture Garden - Inaugural Book, 1974, Gregory Gillespie, 1977; contbr. to mags., mus. catalogues.; one man show, Davis Gallery, N.Y.C., 1958, group shows include, A.C.A. Gallery, Peridot Gallery, Bklyn.-Mus., Pa. Acad., Davis Gallery, represented in pvt. collections. Decorated commandeur in de Orde Van Oranje-Nassau (The Netherlands); chevalier dans L'Ordre des Arts et des Lettres (France). Home: 98 Lewis St Southampton NY 11968-5006

LERNER, BARBARA, public policy consultant, researcher, writer; b. Chgo., Mar. 31, 1935; d. Jacob Israel and Mary (Turen) L. BA with honors, U. Ill., 1956; MA, U. Chgo., 1961, PhD, 1965, JD, 1977. Bar: Ill. 1977; registered psychologist, Ill. Intern U. Chgo. Hosp. and Clinic, 1962-63; instr. Coll. Medicine U. Ill., 1963-64; clin. psychologist Ill. Mental Health Ctr., Chgo., 1965-68; assoc. prof. Ohio U., Athens, 1968-70; pvt. practice clin. psychologist Chgo., 1970-78; assoc. prof. Roosevelt U., Chgo., 1972-74; study dir. Nat. Acad. Scis., Washington, 1977-78; pres. Lerner Assocs., Princeton, N.J., 1981—; vis. scholar Ednl. Testing Svc., Princeton, 1978-79, sr. rsch. scientist, 1980-81; expert witness fed. cts. Debra P. vs. Turlington, Tampa, Fla., Marshall vs. Ga., 1983; vis. prof. U. Tex., Austin, 1989. Author: Therapy in the Ghetto, 1972, Minimum Competence, Maximum Choice, 1980; assoc. editor U. Chgo. Law Rev., 1975-77; contbr. articles to profl. jours., newspapers, and mags. Pres. nominee U.S. Dept. Edn., Washington, 1986; mem. adv. com. U.S. Commn. Civil Rights, N.J., 1985-87. Recipient Cert. of Appreciation award for outstanding service U.S. Dept. Edn., 1985. Mem. Am. Psychol. Assn., ABA, Nat. Council Measurement in Edn., Am. Ednl. Research Assn., Phi Beta Kappa, Sigma Xi. Jewish. Office: Lerner Assocs 111 Carter Rd Princeton NJ 08540-2112

LERNER, FREDERICK ANDREW, librarian, information scientist; b. Mt. Vernon, N.Y., Dec. 27, 1945; s. Ira Gerald and Shirley (Nagorsky) L.; m. Sheryl Dianne Rubin, June 29, 1980; 1 child, Elizabeth. AB, Columbia U., 1966, MS, 1969, DLS, 1981. Reference libr. Hamilton Coll., Clinton, N.Y., 1969-70; info. specialist Rsch. Found., CUNY, 1970-72; head reference svcs. unit Vt. Dept. Librs., Montpelier, 1974-78; head tech. info. svcs. Spectra, Inc., Hanover, N.H., 1979-89; info. scientist Nat. Ctr. for Post-Traumatic Stress Disorder, White River Junction, Vt., 1989—. Author: Modern Science Fiction and the American Literary Community, 1985, A Silverlock Companion, 1988. Bd. dirs. Vt. Pub. Radio, Winooski, 1975—; pres. Congregation Beth Jacob, Montpelier, 1977. With U.S. Army, 1966-68. Mem. Spl. Librs. Assn., Am. Soc. for Info. Sci., Med. Libr. Assn., Kipling Soc., Sci. Fiction Rsch. Assn. (sec.-treas. 1970-72), Sci. Fiction Writers Am. (affiliate), Internat. Soc. for Traumatic Stress Studies. Home: 5 Worcester Ave White River Junction VT 05001-1609

LERNER, GERALD MICHAEL, aerospace systems engineer; b. Balt., Feb. 13, 1943; s. Philbert Fred and Sylvia (Finkelstein) L.; m. Barbara Lehman, July 2, 1968; children: David, Andrew, Jamie. BA, Johns Hopkins U., 1964; PhD, U. Md., 1972. Rsch. assoc. Tex. A&M U., College Station, 1971-72; dept. mgr. Computer Scis. Corp., Silver Spring, Md., 1971-79; analyst CIA, Washington, 1979-85; program mgr. ESL, Reston, Va., 1985-89; sect. mgr. GE Aerospace, Blue Bell, Pa., 1989—. Author: Spacecraft Attitude Determination and Control, 1978; contbr. articles to profl. jours. Recipient cert. special achievement CIA, 1981. Home: 1422 Cambridge Dr North Wales PA 19454-3686 Office: GE PO Box 1000 Blue Bell PA 19422-0240

LERNER, LEONARD JOSEPH, endocrinology and pharmacology educator; b. Roselle, N.J.; s. Hyman and Esther (Honig) L. BS in Pharmacy, Rutgers U., 1943, BA, 1951, MS, 1953, PhD, 1954. Head endocrine rsch. sect. William S. Merrell Co. (now Marion Merrell Dow), Cin., 1954-58; head endocrinology sect. Squibb Inst. for Med. Rsch., New Brunswick, N.J., 1958-65, dir. dept. endocrinology, 1965-70; dir. dept. endocrinology Lepetit Rsch. Labs. div. Dow Lepetit, Milan, Italy, 1971-77; rsch. prof. dept. ob-gyn and pharmacology Jefferson Med. Coll., Thomas Jefferson U., Phila., 1977—, prof. pharmacology, 1988—; adj. prof. Sch. Nursing, U. Pa., Phila., 1990—; cons. NIH, WHO, FDA, various other govt and non-profit orgns., 1958—, pharm. cos., 1977—; mem. numerous sci. adv. bds., coms. and rev. bds. Mem. editorial bd. Steroids, Transactions of N.Y. Acad. Scis., others; contbr. articles to profl. jours.; patentee in field. Bd. dirs. N.J. affiliate Am. Diabetes Assn., 1990—. With U.S. Army, 1944-46. Grantee in field. Fellow AAAS, N.Y. Acad. Scis. (vice chair, then chair sect. biomedicine 1968-72); mem. Endocrine Soc., Am. Assn. Cancer Rsch. (mem. program com., Cain Meml. award 1989), Soc. Study of Reproduction (animals in rsch. com.), Am. Physiology Soc., Am. Fertility Soc., Soc. for Exptl. Biology and Medicine, Sigma Xi. Home: C-5 Windsor Castle Apts Cranbury NJ 08512 Office: Thomas Jefferson U Dept Pharmacology 1020 Locust St Philadelphia PA 19107-6799

LERNER, LINDA JOYCE, human resources executive; b. N.Y.C., Aug. 19, 1944; d. Morris and Victoria (Mizrahi) L. BS in Bus., U. Bridgeport, 1966. Asst. dir. pers. Bridgeport (Conn.) Hosp., 1969-73; dir. pers. Tufts U., Boston, 1973-80; sr. v.p. human resources Provident Instn. Savs., Boston, 1981-88; sr. v.p. UST Corp. Bank Holding Co., Boston, 1988—. Past bd. mem. Living is For the Elderly, Boston, 1984-90, Boy Scouts Am., Boston, 1985-90; bd. dirs. Jewish Vocat. Svc., Boston, 1989—, Horizons for Youth, Boston, 1991—. Fellow Internat. Mktg. Inst., Boston, 1978. Mem. ASTD, Internat. Assn. Pers. Women (past dir., com. chair), N.E. Human Resources Assn., Am. Bankers Assn. (human resources exec. com. 1991—), Mass. Bankers Assn. (human resources com. 1989—), Fin. Women Internat., The Boston Club. Office: UST Corp 40 Court St Boston MA 02108-2202

LERNER, RITA GUGGENHEIM, association executive, information scientist, physicist; b. N.Y.C., May 7, 1929; d. Karl and Fannie (Gottesman) Guggenheim; m. Arnold Lerner, Feb. 14, 1954; children—James, Richard. A.B. cum laude, Radcliffe Coll., 1949; M.A., Columbia U., 1951, Ph.D., 1956. Research assoc. Columbia U., N.Y.C., 1956-64, dir. biol. sci. labs., 1968; mgr. info. analysis Am. Inst. Physics, N.Y.C., 1964-67, mgr. planning and devel., 1969-74, mgr. spl. projects, 1974-79, mgr. mktg. div., 1979-84, mgr. books div., 1985-90; consulting editor VCH Pubs., Inc., 1990—; mem. adv. com. on 108(i) U.S. Copyright Office, 1974-79; cons. editor Hutchinson & Ross, 1975-85. Editor: Encyclopedia of Physics, 1980, 2d edit., 1990, Concise Encyclopedia of Solid State Physics, 1984; contbr. articles to profl. jours. Pres. Ardsley PTA, N.Y., 1955-56. NSF grantee, 1975-80. Fellow AAAS (council, com. on council affairs 1981-84); mem. Assn. Info. Dissemination Ctrs. (pres. 1981-83), Am. Phys. Soc., Am. Chem. Soc., Am. Soc. for Info. Sci., Sigma Xi. Home: Winding Rd S Chauncey Ardsley NY 10502 Office: VCH Pubs Inc 220 E 23d St New York NY 10010

LEROUX, SYLVAIN GUY, musician; b. Montreal, Quebec, Can., May 4, 1956; s. Maurice and Marthe (Lavallée) L.; m. Kathi Alyn Spadanuta, Apr. 12, 1983 (div. Jan. 1992). Grad., Paul-Gerin Lajoie High Sch., Quebec, 1972; student, Creative Music Studio, 1978-80. Sideman Yaya Diallo Band, Montreal, 1978-81; leader Mysterioso, Montreal, 1981-83, Sylvain Leroux Quartet, L.I., N.Y., 1987-90, Sylvain Leroux and The Maintenance Crew, N.Y., 1990—; sideman Nego Gato Band, Woodstock, N.Y., 1991—; flutist Viva Brasil Dance Co., 1991—. Composer (songs) Windsong, 1987, No More Trouble, 1987, Northern Blues, 1986, Keep on Trucking, 1990.

LESAK, DAVID MICHAEL, emergency response and planning educator, consultant; b. Phila., July 5, 1952; s. Joseph Michael and Charlotte (Rockel) L.; m. Lora Jean Schmoyer, June 12, 1976; children: Jana Bryn, Scott David. BS, Kutztown U., 1976. Lab technician Air Products and Chems. Inc., Trexlertown, Pa., 1976-78; sci. tchr. Parkland Sch. Dist., Orefield, Pa., 1978-79, Quakertown (Pa.) Sch. Dist., 1980; owner, pres. Hazard Mgmt. Assocs., Allentown, Pa., 1981—; adj. prof. Nat. Fire Acad., Emmitsburg, Md., 1981—, devel. team mgr. Hazmat courses; adj. prof. Emergency Mgmt. Inst., Emmitsburg, 1985—. Author: Chemistry of Hazardous Materials, 1983, (study guide) Fire Chemistry I and II, 1991; author, producer, narrator video tape Fire Fighter Safety, 1984; author, presenter video tape Oxidizers, 1991. Chmn. Lehigh County Hazardous Materials Adv. Commn., Allentown, 1990, 91; chief Lehigh County Hazmat Team, Allentown, 1990, 91; fire chief Lower Macangie Twp., Pa., 1984-86. Mem. Nat. Fire Protection Assn., Am. Soc. of Safety Engrs. Home and Office: Hazard Mgmt Assocs PO Box 3004 Allentown PA 18106-0004

LESER, BERNARD H., publishing executive. Formerly pub. Vogue Australia; pres. Condé Nast Publs., N.Y.C., 1987—. Office: Condé Publs 350 Madison Ave New York NY 10017-3704*

LESHER, RICHARD LEE, association executive; b. Doylesburg, Pa., Oct. 28, 1933; s. Richard E. Lesher and Rosalie Orabelle (Meredith) Lesher Ehrhart; m. Agnes Marie Plocki, June 13, 1981; children by previous marriage: Douglas Allen, Laurie Lynn, Betsy Lee, Craig Collin. BBA, U. Pitts., 1958; MS, Pa. State U., 1960; DBA, Ind. U., 1963, LLD (hon.), 1979; D of Pub. Service (hon.), Ferris State Coll., 1981; DBA (hon.), Lawrence Inst. Tech., 1985. Asst. prof. Coll. Commerce and Adminstrn., Ohio State U., Columbus, 1963-64; cons. NASA, Washington, 1964-65; dep. asst. adminstr. NASA, 1965-66, asst. adminstr., 1966-69; bus. and mgmt. cons. Washington, 1969-71; pres. Nat. Ctr. for Resource Recovery, Washington, 1971-75, U.S. C. of C., Washington, 1975—; bd. dirs. SHL Systemhouse, Inc.; mem. bd. advs. CORDECOM. Author: (book) Economic Progress...It's Everybody's Business, 1980, syndicated newspaper column; participant (weekly syndicated debate show) It's Your Business. Board dirs. Wolf Trap Found.; mem. bd. visitors Coll. Bus. Adminstrn., Pa. State U.; mem. Sch. Bus. Dean's Adv. Coun., Ind. U. With U.S. Army, 1954-56. Recipient Superior Achievement award NASA, 1968, Exceptional Svc. award, 1968, Alumni Achievement award Pa. State U., 1976, Acad. of Alumni Fellows award Ind. U., 1977, Religious Heritage award 1978, Horatio Alger award 1980, Bicentennial Medallian of Distinction U. Pitts., 1987, Golden Exec. medal Gen. C. of C. of Taiwan, 1988, Disting. Alumni fellow Pa. State U. 1990, Am. Soc. of Assn. Execs. Spl. Key award, 1992. Mem. Am. Soc. Assn. Execx. (Spl. Key award 1992), Washington Soc. Assn. Execs., Internat. Platform Assn., Am. C. of C. Execs. (bd. dirs.), Phi Alpha Kappa, Beta Gamma Sigma (Dir.'s Table, Nat. award 1977). Club: Congressional Country, Met. Office: US C of C 1615 H St NW Washington DC 20062-0002

LESIEUTRE, GEORGE ANDRÉ, aerospace engineering educator, consultant; b. Detroit, Nov. 29, 1958; s. George Pierre and Josephine Anne (O'Rorke) L.; m. Anne Johnston, Aug. 1, 1981; children: John Daniel, William Andrew. BS in Aero. and Astron. Engring., MIT, 1981; PhD in Aerospace Engring., UCLA, 1989. Staff engr. Rockwell Internat., Seal Beach, Calif., 1981-83; dynamic systems scientist HR Textron, Inc., Irvine, Calif., 1983-85; dir. space structures SPARTA, Inc., Laguna Hills, Calif., 1985-89; asst. prof. aero. engring. Pa. State U., University Park, 1989—; cons. SPARTA, Inc., La Jolla, Calif., 1989—. Contbr. articles to profl. jours.; inventor high damping graphite fiber. Treas. Hawk Valley Homeowners Assn., 1991—. GM scholar, Indpls., 1980-81; Material and Structural Damping rsch. grantee NSF, 1990. Mem. AIAA (sr., structural dynamics tech. com. 1990—), Am. Soc. for Engring. Edn., Sigma Xi, Tau Beta Pi. Unitarian. Office: Pa State U Dept Aerospace Engring University Park PA 16802

LESIKAR, JAMES DANIEL, II, physicist; b. Houston, Feb. 24, 1954; s. James Daniel and Ludine Luella (Kosel) L. BSME cum laude, Rice U., 1976, MME, 1978, MA, 1981, PhD in Physics, 1982. Registered prof. engr., Va., Md. Rsch. asst. T.W. Bonner Nuclear Labs. Rice U., Houston, 1976-81; asst. prof. physics U.S. Naval Acad., Annapolis, Md., 1984-85; sr. analyst system scis. div. Computer Scis. Corp., Lanham, Md., 1986—. Author (with others) NASA reports, 1990; contbr. articles to Physics Letters, Phys. Rev., Phys. Rev. Letters. Co-moderator Math Counts Program, Annapolis, Md., 1991. Capt. U.S. Army, 1981-85; maj. USAR, 1988—. Recipient Bronze Cross for Achievement Legion of Valor, Inc.; Grad. fellow Rice U., Houston, 1976-77, Nettie S. Autrey Meml. fellow in sci., 1978-79. Mem. AIAA, ASME, AAAS, IEEE, Nat. Soc. Profl. Engrs., Am. Phys. Soc., Optimist Club (bd. dirs. 1983-84), Am. Def. Preparedness Assn., Sigma Xi, Sigma Pi Sigma. Home: 1037 Oak Tree Ln Annapolis MD 21401-5011 Office: Computer Scis Corp 10110 Aerospace Rd Lanham Seabrook MD 20706-2262

LESKO, JAMES JOSEPH, designer, educator, sculptor; b. Windber, Pa., Mar. 20, 1939; s. John George and Mildred (Shimko) L.; m. Marcia Ann Papak, June 9, 1979. BFA, Carnegie Inst. Tech., 1965; MFA, Carnegie-Mellon U., 1971. Asst. prof. indsl. design Purdue U., West Lafayette, Ind., 1972-77; assoc. prof. U. Cin., 1977-79; spl. lectr. N.J. Inst. Tech., Newark, 1980-81; owner, operator Lesko Design, N.Y.C., 1983; assoc. prof. Carnegie Mellon U., Pitts., 1986-89; vis. prof. Ohio State U., 1975, N.Y. Inst. Tech., 1989—; adj. assoc. prof. Pratt Inst., Bklyn., 1983-86, 89—; cons. Westinghouse Electric Corp., Pitts., 1985-89. Sculptor, 1963—. Bd. dirs. Kew Gardens (N.J.) Civic Assn., 1985, 91—. Recipient Agusta Fisher Porter prize Carnegie Inst. Tech., 1963, Westinghouse Electric Corp. award Three Rivers Arts Festival, 1966, Mrs. H.J. Heinz II award Soc. Sculptors, 1968. Mem. Indsl. Designers Soc. Am. (chmn. Western Pa. chpt. 1988-89). Republican. Home and Office: 12318 Metropolitan Ave Jamaica NY 11415-2710

LESLIE, JANIS ETHLYN, employee assistance counselor; b. Buffalo, July 9, 1960; s. Edeston Vincent and Viola Agatha (Brown) L. BA, Buffalo State Coll., 1982; MEd, Howard U., 1985. Tchr. aide NBC Lab Sch. for Gifted Children, Washington, 1982-83; counselor Spl. Approaches to Juvenile Assistance, Washington, 1985-86; mental health specialist D.C. Govt. Mental Health Svcs., Washington, 1987-90; employee assistance counselor Bev Anderson & Assocs./Met. Police Dept., Washington, 1990—. Vol. telephone counselor/trainer Families and Children in Trouble Hotline, Washington, 1984-90. Mem. AACD, Psi Chi. Democrat. Episcopalian. Office: Met Police Employee Assistance Program 1220 L St NW Ste 515 Washington DC 20005-4018

LESLIE, JOHN, artist, printmaker, photographer, sculptor; b. Phila., July 11, 1923; s. John Joseph and Mary Kathryn (Bauermees) L.; m. Kathryn Elizabeth Frame, Feb. 4, 1946 (div. 1948); m. Mary Frances Huggins, Apr. 2, 1950; children: Karol Ann, John Joseph III, Mary Lee. Grad. comml. art, Murrell Dobbins Tech., Phila., 1941; postgrad., Fleisher Art Meml., Phila., 1939-42, Phila. Mus. Sch. Indsl. Art, 1944, Pa. State U., 1982—. Staff artist Phila. Daily News, 1942; founder, creative dir. Graphic Ad Displays, Inc., Phila., 1944; parade designer Gimbel Bros. Dept. Stores, Phila., 1945; pres., art dir. Duplex Display and Mfg. Co., Inc., Phila., 1947-54; pres., designer Leslie Creations, Inc., Lafayette Hill, Pa., 1954-65; pres., founder Mail Order Methods, Inc., Lafayette Hill, 1954-67; pres. World Treasures, Seven Seas House, Inc., Lafayette Hill, 1960-65; founder, creative dir. Kopy Kat Inc., Fort Washington, Pa., 1968-77; catalog design cons. Jesse Jones Industries, Inc., Phila., 1978-79; co-founder, art dir. Galerie Marjole, Inc., Sanatoga, Pa., 1987-89, lectr. ltd. edition prints, 1987—; fine art spokesman radio, TV, 1989—; advt. mktg. cons. Ottawa Group, Inc., Futura Mktg., Inc., Pottstown, Pa., 1985—; guest speaker Hundred Million Club, N.Y.C., 1963; stage set designer Bessie V. Hicks Sch. Dramatic Arts, Phila., 1944-46. Patentee U.S. Kopy Kat, Inc. trademark; prin. works include site selection Jeanes Meml. Libr., Lafayette Hill, Pa.; executed murals and dioramas Phila. Savings Fund Soc., Commonwealth Land Title Co., Penn Fruit Co., E.F. Houghton Co., Victor Tarello, 1945-53; created wrought iron and chromed steel functional metal sculptures, 1954-79; designer the Crystal Mall concept, 1990; artworks in many U.S. Museums. Pres., founder Cen. Citizens Com., Inc., Whitemarsh Twp., Pa., 1960-75; active Big Bros. Am., Phila., 1957-65, YMCA Indian Guides, Montgomery County, Pa., 1965-68; conservationist, animal rights activist Am. Anti-Vivisection Soc., 1959—. With U.S. Army, 1943-44. Named Citizen of Week Ambler (Pa.) Gazette, 1978; recipient Direct Mail Leaders award Direct Mail Advt. Assn., 1957, 60, Artistic Merit award Playboy Mag., 1958, Japanese Graphic Arts Indstry award, 1975, King of Prussia Fine Arts award Upper Merion Cultural Ctr., 1966, Disting. Svc. award Citizens Com. on Pub. Edn., Phila., 1981; inducted into Artist's Hall of Fame Murrell Dobbins Tech., 1988. Mem. N.Y. Oil Pastel Assn., Woodmere Art Mus., Boca Grande Fla. Art Alliance, Les Amis de Veterans Francais. Roman Catholic. Studio: Blueberry Hill 6318 Zeno Cir Port Charlotte FL 33981

LESMAN, MICHAEL STEVEN, lawyer; b. N.Y.C., May 26, 1953; s. Herman and Estelle (Levy) L.; m. Gail R. Grossman, May 26, 1980; children: Adam, Laura. BA magna cum laude, CUNY, 1975; JD, Bklyn. Law Sch., 1982. Bar: N.Y. 1983. Assoc. Jacobowitz & Lysaght, N.Y.C., 1983-85; supervising atty. Jacobwitz & Lysaght, N.Y.C., 1985-88; atty. of record, mng. atty. Jacobowitz, Spessard, Garfinkel & Lesman, N.Y.C., 1989—; staff counsel Am. Internat. Group, N.Y.C., 1989—. Mem. ABA, N.Y. State Bar Assn., N.Y. State Trial Lawyers Assn., N.Y. County Lawyers Assn. Office: Jacobowitz Spessard et al 7 Hanover Sq New York NY 10004-2594

LESNIAK, ROBERT JOHN, education educator; b. Herkimer, N.Y., Sept. 10, 1936; s. John and Mary (Hinotsky) L.; m. Mary Anne Quinn, Sept. 4, 1965; children: John Francis, Kristin Anne, Nicole Marie. BA, Hope Coll., 1958; MA, Syracuse U., 1964, PhD, 1969. Head tchr. Herkimer Cen. Schs., 1962-63; assoc. dir. instructing urban tchr. program Syracuse (N.Y.) U., 1965-69; asst. prof. edn. Pa. State U. Harrisburg, Middletown, 1969-72, assoc. prof. edn., coord. grad. teaching and curriculum, 1972-86, coord. grad. edn. program, 1983-86, acting assoc. dean rsch. and grad. studies, 1986-87, coord. tng. and devel. and adult edn., 1987-90, acting div. head behavioral sci. and edn., 1988-90, coord. grad. program tng. and devel., 1990—; cons. L.A. Pub. Schs., 1970, Harrisburg Police Dept., 1984. Author: (video script) Sensitivity for Teaching, 1985; developer classroom behavior task for urban tchrs., 1972. Pres., v.p. Lower Dauphin Sch. Bd., Hummelstown, Pa., 1976-82; chmn. adult edn. task force com. State Adults Edn. Plan, Harrisburg, 1982-85; rep. Nat. Sch. Bds. Assn., Washington, 1983. Lt. USNR, 1959-62. Recipient Disting. Merit award Am. Assn. Colls., 1966, Continuing Edn. Excellence for Home Child Care Providers award Nat. U. Continuing Edn. Assn., 1987, Community Svc. award Lower Dauphin Sch. Dist., 1982. Mem. ASTD (cen. Pa. chpt., bd. dirs. 1984-87, Svc. award 1988), Am. Edn. Rsch. Assn., Pa. Assn. of Colls. and Educators; Phi Delta Kappa. Home: 4336 Snavely Rd Elizabethtown PA 17022-9068 Office: Pa State Harrisburg Rte 230 Middletown PA 17057

LESSE, ETTA GORDON (MRS. S. MICHAEL LESSE), psychiatric social worker; b. Trenton, N.J.; d. H. Charles and Rose (Miers) Gordon; B.A., Beaver Coll.; M.Social Sci., Smith Coll.; postgrad. Bryn Mawr Coll. Sch. Social Economy; U. Pa. Sch. Social Work; m. S. Michael Lesse; children—Toni Gordon and Cathy Ross (twins). Exec. sec. Clinic for Child Psychiatry, Temple U. Med. Sch., Phila.; psychiat. social worker Bur. Family Service, Orange, N.J., Family Welfare Soc., Newport, R.I.; intake worker Bur. Family Service, Orange, N.J.; case supr., asst. to chief social worker VA, Phila.; consultant for social agys. and ct. Social and health counsellor to

Draft Bd., Orange, N.J.; organizer steering com. for establishment case work sect. Council Social Agys., Newport, R.I.; chmn. Workshop for Profl. Social Workers Lehigh Valley; group chmn. regional conf. pub. edn. Gov.'s Commn. Pub. Edn., Pa. Gov.'s Commn. on Aging; cons. foster home devel. Northampton County Children's Aid Soc.; profl. participant in religion and psychiatry seminars, Easton, Pa.; interviewer Easton-Phillipsburg (Pa.) Commn. Human Relations; mem. adv. bd. Northeastern region Pa. Dept. Pub. Welfare. Lectr. to child study group PTA, Easton, Pa. Bd. dirs. Lehigh Valley Center Performing Arts Assn., v.p.; bd. dirs. Lehigh Valley Community Council, 1975—, Planned Parenthood of Northampton County; exec. bd. Am. Heart Assn., 1978—; mem. adv. bd. Jr. League of Lehigh Valley. Mem. Nat. Assn. Social Workers, Acad. Certified Social Workers, AAUW (past br. pres., dir. Eastern br., chmn. career advancement loan fund, named Outstanding Woman of Yr. 1981-82, founder, chair meml. fund 1987—), Lehigh Valley Mental Health Assn. (dir., chmn. com. on personnel and nominating), Allentown Art Mus., Women's Com. Phila. Assn. Psychoanalysis, Northampton County Med. Soc. Aux., (dir. 1980—, v.p., pres., chmn. scholarships, chmn. med. and profl. nursing students loan fund), Phila. Orch. Assn., Met. Opera Assn., Smith Coll. Alumni Assn. Contbg. author Two Hundred Years of Life in Northampton County, Pa. Home: 2768 Stephens St Easton PA 18042-2633

LESSELL, SIMMONS, neuro-ophthalmologist; b. Bklyn., May 25, 1933; s. Bernard Benjamin and Augusta (Coleman) L.; m. Irma Frances Miller, June 12. 1955; children: Miller, Jason (dec.), Newell, Ephraim. BA, Amherst Coll., 1954; MD, Cornell U., 1958; MA (hon.), Harvard U., 1984. Prof. ophthalmology Boston U., 1967-83, Harvard U., Boston, 1984—; dir. neuro-ophthalmology Mass. Eye and Ear, Boston, 1984—. Editor: Current Neuro-ophthamology. Home: 20 Saddle Club Rd Lexington MA 02173

LESSER, ALLEN, retired government official, editor; b. Bklyn., Sept. 21, 1907; s. Louis and Betty (Schlesinger) L.; m. Frances Hauser, Apr. 4, 1939; children: Lawrence M., Howard M. BA, NYU, 1929, MA, 1932. Editor Contemporary Jewish Record Am. Jewish Com., N.Y.C., 1940-43; chief European intelligence Office War Info., N.Y.C., 1943-45; editor Jewish News Essex County Community Coun., Newark, 1946-47; mng. editor Menorah Jour., N.Y.C., 1947-50; editor, pub. Cross-Section, U.S.A., N.Y.C., 1950-53; dir. pub. rels. B'nai B'rith, Washington, 1953-56; editor Near East Report Am. Zionist Pub. Affairs Com., Washington, 1956-59; exec. asst. to Senator Javits U.S. Senate, Washington, 1959-65; dir. civil rights U.S. Office Edn., Washington, 1965-66; dir. Vets. Edn. USOE, 1966-74; ret., 1974. Author: Weave a Wreath of Laurel, 1938, Enchanting Rebel, 1947, Israel's Impact, 1950-51, 1984; contbr. articles to mags. Mem. Zionist Orgn. Am., Am. Jewish Hist. Soc., Am. Jewish Archives. Republican. Home and Office: 3527 Runnymede Pl NW Washington DC 20015-2419

LESSER, LAURENCE, music conservatory president, cellist, educator; b. Los Angeles, Oct. 28, 1938; s. Moses Aaron and Rosalyne Anne (Asner) L.; m. Masuko Ushioda, Dec. 23, 1971; children—Erika, Adam. AB, Harvard U., 1961; student of Gaspar Cassádo, Germany, 1961-62; student of Gregor Piatigorsky, 1963-66. Mem. faculty U. So. Calif., Los Angeles, 1963-70; mem. faculty Peabody Inst., Balt., 1970-74; mem. faculty New Eng. Conservatory Music, Boston, 1974—, pres., 1983—; former vis. prof. Eastman Sch. Music, Rochester, N.Y.; vis. prof. Toho Gakuen Sch. Music, Tokyo, 1973—; performed with New Japan Philharm., Boston Symphony, London Philharm., Los Angeles Philharm. and Marlboro, Spoleto, Casals, Santa Fe and Banff fesitvals; rec. artist; overseer Boston Symphony Orch. trustee WGBH Ednl. Found.; mem. adv. council Chamber Music Am. Recipient prize Tchaikovsky Competition, Moscow, 1966; Fulbright scholar, 1961-62; Ford Found. grantee, 1972. Mem. Harvard Musical Assn., Phi Beta Kappa, Pi Kappa Lambda, Sigma Alpha Iota. Jewish. Club: Tavern (Boston). Home: 65 Bellevue St Newton MA 02158-1918 Office: New Eng Conservatory Music 290 Huntington Ave Boston MA 02115-5000

LESSER, LAWRENCE J., advertising agency executive; b. Bklyn., June 1, 1939; m. Joanna Savarese, Aug. 26, 1962; children: Eileen, Kristin. AAS, N.Y.C. Community Coll., 1959. Asst. acct. exec. Friend Reiss Advt., 1959-63; v.p., acct. supr. sr. v.p. L.W. Frohlich, 1963-72; sr. v.p Medicus Communications Inc., N.Y.C., 1972-76, pres., chief exec. officer, from 1976; chmn., chief exec. officer Medicus Intecon Internat. Office: Medicus Intercon Internat Inc 1675 Broadway New York NY 10019-5820 also: Scripps Howard 1100 Central Trust Tower Cincinnati OH 45202*

LESTER, BIJOU YANG, educator; b. Sinchu Hsian, Taiwan, Republic of China, Apr. 2, 1950; d. Gwei-Far and Yuei-Mey (Chou) Y.; m. Shi-Tao Yeh, (div. Oct. 1986); children: Andrew C. Yeh, Cynthia Yeh; m. David Lester, Oct. 22, 1987. BA in Econs., Nat. Taiwan U., Taipei, 1971, MA in Econs., 1974; AM in Econs., U. Pa., 1975, PhD in Econs., 1981. Economist Wharton Econometric Forecasting Assn., Phila., 1981-83; asst. prof. Villanova (Pa.) U., 1983-85, Stockton State Coll., Pomona, N.J., 1985-86, Trenton (N.J.) State Coll., 1986-87, Drexel U., Phila., 1987—. Author: Economic Perspectives in Suicide, 1992. Pres. Chinese Student Club at U. Pa., Phila., 1978-79. Mem. Am. Econ. Assn. (mem. com. on status of women in econ. profession), Eastern Econ. Assn., Pa. Econ. Assn., Soc. Advancement Behavioral Econ. Assn. (treas. 1992). Home: 5 Stonegate Ct RR 41 Blackwood NJ 08012-5356 Office: Drexel U Dept Econs 32nd Market St 11-504D Philadelphia PA 19104-2875

LESTER, MALCOLM COLTRANE, secondary school educator; b. N.Y.C., July 12, 1967; s. Julius Bernard and Joan B. (Steinau) L. BA, Springfield (Mass.) Coll., 1989; MA, Coll. William and Mary, 1991. English tchr. St. Albans Sch., Washington, 1991—, head varsity lacrosse coach, 1991—. Class coord. Springfield Coll. Alumni Fund, 1989—. Mem. Nat. Coun. Tchrs. English, Nat. Assn. Black Journalists, Nat. Assn. Black Coaches, Emily Dickinson Internat. Soc., Sports Lit. Assn., Am. Lit. Assembly, Washington D.C. Road Runners Club. Office: Saint Albans Sch Mount Saint Alban Washington DC 20016

LESTER, MARK CHARLES, neurosurgeon; b. Pitts., Sept. 23, 1952. AB, Cornell U., 1973; MD, U. Pitts., 1977. Diplomate Am. Bd. Neurol. Surgery. Intern gen. surgery U. Health Ctr. Hosps., Pitts., 1977-78, resident in neurological surgery, 1978-83; neurosurgeon Allentown, Pa., 1983—; assoc. chief div. neurosurgery Lehigh Valley Hosp. Ctr., Allentown, 1990—; clin. asst. prof. Hahnemann U., Phila., 1988—; med. dir. cen. nervous system unit Lehigh Valley Hosp. Ctr., Allentown, 1987-91, head sect. neurotrauma, 1991—. Fellow Am. Coll. Surgeons; mem. Am. Assn. Neurolog. Systems, AAAS. Office: Allen Neurosurg Assn Inc 1210 S Cedar Crest Blvd Allentown PA 18103-6208

LESTER, STEVEN BURT, military non-commissioned officer, musician; b. Port Jervis, N.Y., Dec. 19, 1954; s. Caryle Wilmarth Lester and Margery Ann (Becker) Wilson; 1 child, Jason Gabriel Galambos. BA in Journalism, Pa. State U., 1978; studies with Christopher Parkening, Messiah Coll., 1984-85; BA in Music performance, Salisbury State Coll., 1985. Musician, writer pvt. practice Frederic, Md., 1978-80; educator, journalist, musician pvt. practice Salisbury, Md., 1980-85; enlisted U.S. Army, 1985, advanced through grades to staff sgt., 1992; musician 392d Army Band U.S. Army, Ft. Lee, Va., 1986-89; sgt., musician 8th Army Band U.S. Army, Seoul, Korea, 1989-90; musician 26th Army Band U.S. Army, Bklyn., 1990-92; with 8th Army Band, Seoul, Republic of Korea, 1992—; vocalist St. Peter's Episcopal Ch., Salisbury, 1985; vol. vocalist St John's Episcopal Ch., Hopewell, Va., 1986-89, St. John's Episcopal Ch., Bklyn., 1990—. Section leader, pub. rels. writer Salisbury Choral Arts Soc., 1984-85. Recipient Herbert D. Brent Meml. scholarship, Salisbury-Wicomico Arts Coun., 1984. Home and Office: HQ East EUSA Band APO San Francisco CA 11252

LESTINGI, JOSEPH FRANCIS, engineering educator, dean, consultant; b. Long Island City, N.Y., Apr. 24, 1935; s. Michael and Virginia Lestingi; m. Jean Lucille Boggia, July 4, 1957; children: Michael, Gene, Daniel, John. BCE, Manhattan Coll., 1957; MS, Va. Poly. Inst., 1959; DEng, Yale U., 1966. Registered profl. engr., N.J., Ohio. Structural rsch. engr. Gen. Dynamics/Electric Boat, Groton, Conn., 1960-64; sr. mech. engr. Battelle Meml. Inst., Columbus, Ohio, 1965-67; prof. civil engring. U. Akron, Ohio, 1967-78; head of mech. engring. GMI Engring. and Mgmt. Inst., Flint, Mich., 1978-83; dean of engring. Manhattan Coll., Riverdale, N.Y., 1983-92; dean sch. engring. U. Dayton, Ohio, 1992—; cons. Gen. Tire & Rubber Co., Akron, 1972-78, Union Metal Mfg. Co., Canton, Ohio, 1973-78, Macomber Inc., Canton, 1972-74, Babcock and Wilcox Co., Barberton, Ohio, 1968-71. Bd. dirs. KIDS of North Jersey, Secaucus, N.J., 1988-92. Jour. Am. scholar, 1952; named Danforth assoc., 1972; NASA-ASEE fellow, 1977. Fellow ASCE, ASME; mem. Am. Soc. for Engring. Edn., Soc. Automotive Engrs., Sigma Xi, Chi Epsilon, Omicron Delta Kappa, Phi Eta Sigma, Tau Beta Pi, Sigma Tau. Roman Catholic. Home: 181 Crossridge Dr Kettering OH 45429 Office: Univ Dayton Sch Engring 300 College Park Dayton OH 45469

LESTOURGEON, DIANA ELIZABETH, English educator; b. Covington, Ky., Apr. 6, 1927; d. Percy Earle and Mollie Monday (Chapman) LeS. AB, U. Pa., 1949, AM, 1950, PhD, 1960. Asst. instr. U. Mo., Columbia, 1954-55, Pa. State U., University Park, 1955-56; asst. instr. U. Pa., Phila., 1956-59, instr., 1960-63; asst. prof. Widener U., Chester, Pa., 1965-68, assoc. prof., 1968-77, prof., 1977—. Author: Rosamond Lehmann, 1968. Mem. AAUP, Nat. Coun. Tchrs. of English, Modern Lang. Assn. Home: 30 E Jefferson St Apt 103 Media PA 19063-3746 Office: Widener U Chester PA 19013

LETSOU, GEORGE VASILIOS, cardiothoracic surgeon; b. Boston, 1958; s. Vasilios George and Helen (Valacellis) L.; m. Jane Elizabeth Carter, June 1, 1985; 1 child, Christopher George. AB magna cum laude, Harvard U., 1979; MD, Columbia U., 1983. Diplomate Am. Bd. Surgery. Resident in gen. surgery Yale-New Haven Hosp., 1983-88, chief resident, 1987-88, clin. fellow in cardiothoracic surgery, 1988-89, resident in cardiothoracic surgery, 1990—, chief resident in cardiothoracic surgery, 1991-92; instr. surgery Yale U., New Haven, 1987-88, 91-92, asst. prof., 1992—. Mem. AMA, ACS, Am. Coll. Cardiology, Am. Coll. Chest Physicians, Soc. Thoracic Surgeons. Office: Yale U Sch Medicine Divsn Cardiothoracic Surgery 333 Cedar St New Haven CT 06510

LETTERMAN, DAVID, television personality, comedian, writer; b. Indpls., Apr. 12, 1947. Grad., Ball State U., 1969. Radio and TV announcer, Indpls.; performer The Comedy Store, Los Angeles, 1975—; appearances on TV include (variety series) Mary, CBS; frequent guest host The Tonight Show; host (morning comedy/variety program) David Letterman Show, NBC, 1980, Late Night with David Letterman, 1982— (also writer); writer for TV including Bob Hope Special, Good Times, Paul Lynde Comedy Hour, John Denver Special. Recipient 6 Emmy awards, 1981-88. Office: NBC 30 Rockefeller Pla New York NY 10112

LETTIERI, RONALD JOHN, college administrator, educator; b. Chelsea, Mass., May 13, 1950; s. Roy R. and Genevieve Helen (Sokolowski) L.; m. Janet May O'Brien, Aug. 17, 1974; 1 child, Colleen Janet. BA in History, U. Mass., 1972; MA in History, Ind. State U., 1974; postgrad., U. N.H., 1974-79. Teaching asst. Ind. State U., Terre Haute, 1973-74; teaching asst. U. N.H., Durham, 1975-79, lectr. humanities, history, 1976-81; instr. history Mt. Ida Jr. Coll., Newton Ctr., Mass., 1981-88, also dir. devel., 1981-88, assoc. prof., 1988—, dir. instl. advancement, 1988—; assoc. dir. Naples (Fla.) Inst., Newton Centre, Mass., 1989—; lectr. New Eng. Found. for Humanities, Middletown, 1986—; researcher Deer St. Project Strawberry Banke Mus., Portsmouth, N.H., 1978; cons. grants reviewer N.H. Council for Humanities, Concord, 1977-82. Author: Connecticut's Young Man of the Revolution: Oliver Ellsworth, 1978; editor: Coll. Bd. Aptitude Test in Am. History, 1990—; co-editor: Kirby's Connecticut Law Reports: 1785-1789, 1986, Publius in New England, 1987; contbr. articles to profl. jours.; contbg. editor: Education in Massachusetts: A Statistical Inventory, 1991. Mem. speakers bur. Nat. Commn. on Bicentennial of U.S. Constitution, Washington, 1986—, N.H. Council for Humanities, Concord, 1987—; mem. master plan com. City of Somersworth, N.H., 1977-78; state del. for Mass. Jefferson Found. Debates, Lexington, 1987; project dir. "Rights and Duties" Coll. community forum program Nat. Commn. of U.S. Constn., 1989-91. Curf grantee U. N.H., 1978; summer inst. fellow NEH, 1989. Mem. Orgn. Am. Historians. Roman Catholic. Office: Mt Ida Coll 777 Dedham St Newton MA 02159-3310

LETTOW, CHARLES FREDERICK, lawyer; b. Iowa Falls, Iowa, Feb. 10, 1941; s. Carl Frederick and Catherine (Reisinger) L.; m. Sue Lettow, Apr. 20, 1963; children: Renee, Carl II, John, Paul. BS in Chem. Engring., Iowa State U., 1962; LLB, Stanford U., 1968. Bar: Calif. 1969, Iowa 1969, D.C. 1972, Md. 1991. Law clk. to Hon. Ben C. Duniway U.S. Ct. Appeals (9th cir.), San Francisco, 1968-69; law clk. to Hon. Warren E. Burger U.S. Supreme Ct., Washington, 1969-70; counsel Council on Environ. Quality, Washington, 1970-73; assoc. Cleary, Gottlieb, Steen & Hamilton, Washington, 1973-76, ptnr., 1976—; pres. Busy Way Farms, Inc., 1989—. Contbr. articles to profl. jours. Trustee Potomac Sch., McLean, Va., 1983-90, chmn. bd. trustees, 1985-88. 1st lt. U.S. Army, 1963-65. Mem. ABA, D.C. Bar Assn., Iowa Bar Assn., Order of Coif. Club: University. Office: Cleary Gottlieb 1752 N St NW Washington DC 20036-2806

LETTS, LINDSAY GORDON, pharmacologist, educator; b. Warragul, Victoria, Australia, Jan. 9, 1948; came to U.S., 1987; m. Barbara Dawn Hawkey, Sept. 13, 1969; children: Michelle Maree, Kathryn Jane, David Gordon. BS, Monash U., Australia, 1971; PhD, Sydney U., 1980. Tutor Sydney (Australia) U., 1976-80; rsch. scientist Royal Coll. Surgeons Eng., London, 1980-82; sr. rsch. fellow Merck Frosst Can. Inc., 1982-87; dir. pharmacology Boehringer Ingelheim Pharms., Inc., Ridgefield, Conn., 1987—; adj. assoc. prof. Yale U. Sch. Medicine, New Haven, 1991—. Editor Mediators of Inflammation, 1992—; sect. editor Prostaglandins, 1986—. Bd. dirs. Nat. Inst. for Community Health Edn., Quinnipiac Coll., Hamden, Conn., 1990—, Conn. United Rsch. Excellence, Wallingford, 1991—; dir. Inflammation Rsch. Assn., 1992—, Conn. Biomed. Rsch. Assn., 1992—. Office: Boehringer Ingelheim Pharms 90 E Ridge Rd PO Box 368 Ridgefield CT 06877

LETTS, NANCY BARLOW, counselor, educator; b. Taunton, Mass., Apr. 27, 1942; d. Kenneth John and Julia Marsh (Dunham) Barlow; m. Jeffrey Starlin Letts, Sept. 14, 1963; children: Douglas Barlow, Laurie Anne, Allison Lynne. BA in Psychology, Bucknell U., 1963; MS in Counseling, So. Conn. State Coll., 1980; postgrad., R.I. Coll., 1984; cert., Inst. for Healing & Wholeness, 1990. Caseworker Am. Red Cross, Alton, Ill., 1963-65; employment interviewer State Ill., Alton, 1965-66; social worker Hallworth House Nursing Home, Providence, 1981-89; counselor, group facilitator Feeling & Healing Groups, Inc., Warwick, R.I., 1991-92; bd. dirs., officer support group Social Workers in Long-Term Care Facilities, Warwick, 1982-88; tchr. personal growth workshops Learning Connection, Providence, 1988—. Named Outstanding Young Woman of the Yr. for community svc., 1978. Mem. AACD, Assn. for Specialists in Group Work, Assn. for the Study of Dreams, New Eng. Holistic Counselors Assn. Home: 5570 Post Rd Unit 8 East Greenwich RI 02818 Office: 2123 Warwick Ave Warwick RI 02889

LETTVIN, THEODORE, concert pianist; b. Chgo., Oct. 29, 1926; s. Solomon and Fannie (Naktin) L.; m. Joan Rorimer; children: Rory, Ellen, David. Mus. B., Curtis Inst. Music, 1949; postgrad., U. Pa. vis. lectr., U. Colo., 1956-57; head piano dept. Cleve. Music Sch. Settlement, 1957-68; prof. piano New Eng. Conservatory Music, Boston, 1968-77; prof., dir., doctoral program in piano performance U. Mich. Sch. Music, Ann Arbor, 1977-87; disting. prof. dept. music, dir. doctor of musical arts/artist's diploma program Rutgers U., New Brunswick, N.J., 1987—; concerts, tchr. master classes U. S.E. Mass., summer 1973; mem. faculty Chamber Music Sch., U. Maine, Orono. First appeared as concert pianist, 1931, solo debut with, Chgo. Symphony Orch., 1939, solo, orchestral appearances include, Boston Symphony Orch., N.Y. Philharmonic, Phila. Orch., Cleve. Orch., Chgo. Orch., Washington Nat. Symphony, Pitts. Symphony, Seattle Symphony, Mpls. Symphony, Atlanta Symphony, other Am. orchs., also European orchs.; radio appearance, Bell Telephone Hour, 1948, debut, Ravinia Festival, 1951, apprentice condr., William Steinberg, Buffalo Symphony Orch., 1950-51, concertized, throughout U.S., Can., Europe, Africa, 1952—, recent concert appearances, Pitts., Cin., Atlanta, Boston, N.Y.C., Phila., Chgo., Cleve., Mpls. and Chautauqua, Ravinia, Interlochen and New Coll., Town Hall, Alice Tully Hall concerts, in N.Y.C., Boston Symphony Orch; performances in concert with Bernard Greenhouse, cellist; concert tours, Europe, 1952, 55, 58, 60, 62—, Israel, 1973, Africa and Japan, 1974; also numerous performances with European orchs., summer festivals, TV; asst. artist: Africa and Japan, Marlboro Music Festival, 1963. Recipient award Soc. Am. Musicians, 1933, Naumberg award, 1948, Michaels Meml. award, 1949, Belgian Internat. Music Competition prize. Mem. Am. Fedn. Musicians, Am. Guild Mus. Artists, AAUP (exec. com.), Music Tchrs. Nat. Assn., Am. Liszt Soc., Curtis Inst. Music Alumnae Assn. (bd. dirs.). Home: Bradford NH 03221 also: 12 Bernard Rd East Brunswick NJ 08816 Office: Rutgers U Old Music Bldg Douglass Campus New Brunswick NJ 08903

LEUBERT, ALFRED OTTO PAUL, international business executive; b. N.Y.C., Dec. 7, 1922; s. Paul T. and Josephine (Haaga) L.; m. Celestine Capka, July 22, 1944 (div. 1977); children: Eloise Ann (Mrs. Kevin B. Cronin), Susan Beth (Mrs. Stephen E. Melvin); m. Hope Sherman Drapkin, June 4, 1978 (div. 1982). Student, Dartmouth Coll., 1943; BS, Fordham U., 1946; MBA, NYU, 1950. Account mgr. J.K. Lasser & Co., N.Y.C., 1948-52; controller Vision, Inc., N.Y.C., 1952-53; with Old Town Corp., 1953-58, controller, 1953-54, sec., controller, 1954-56, sec.-treas., 1956-57, v.p., treas., 1957-58; dir. subsidiaries Old Town Corp. (Old Town Internat. Corp., Old Town Ribbon & Carbon Co., Inc.), Mass. and Calif., 1955-58; v.p., controller Willcox & Gibbs, Inc., N.Y.C., 1958-59; v.p., treas. Willcox & Gibbs, Inc., 1959-65, pres., dir., chief exec. officer, 1966-76; founder, pub., pres. Leubert's Compendium of Bus. (Fin. and Econ. Barometers), 1978-82; pres. Alfred O.P. Leubert Ltd., 1981-82; chmn., chief exec. officer Solidyne, Inc., 1982; chmn. bd., pres., chief exec. officer, dir. Chyron Corp., 1983-91, pres., chief oper. officer, 1992—; chmn. bd., chief exec. officer, bd. dirs. Chyron Group (U.K.) Ltd., 1985-89, CMX Corp.; bd. dirs. Aurora Systems, 1988-91; chief exec. officer, dir. CGS Units, Inc., 1988-90, chmn. of the bd., 1989-90; bd. dirs. Digital Svcs. Corp.; vice chmn. bd. dirs. CMX Laser Systems, Inc., 1988—; instr. accountancy Pace Coll., 1955-57. Bd. dirs. United Fund of Manhasset, 1963-69, pres., 1964-65; bd. dirs. Actor's Studio, 1972-76; adv. bd. St. Anthony's Guidance Clinic, 1967-69. Served to 1st lt., inf. USMCR, 1943-46. Decorated Bronze Star; recipient Humanitarian award Hebrew Acad., N.Y.C., 1971. Mem. AICPA, N.Y. State Soc. CPAs, Fordham U. Alumni Assn. Roman Catholic. Club: N.Y. Athletic (N.Y.C.). Home: 1 Lincoln Pla New York NY 10023 Office: 265 Spagnoli St Melville NY 11747

LEUNG, CHRISTOPHER CHUNG KIT, anatomy educator; b. Hong Kong, Jan. 3, 1939; came to U.S., 1960; s. Nai Kuen and Sau Wah (Chan) L.; m. Stella M. Tang, May 11, 1970; children: Jacquelyn, Therese. PhD, Jefferson Med. Coll., 1969. Instr. Jefferson Med. Coll., Phila., 1969-71; asst. prof. Jefferson Med. Coll., 1971-74, assoc. prof., 1974-75; asst. prof. U. Kans. Med. Sch., Kansas City, 1975-79; assoc. prof. La. State U. Med. Sch., Shreveport, 1979-85, N.J. Med. Sch., Newark, 1985—; cons. study section NIH, 1985. Contbr. 21 articles to Am. Jour. Anatomy, Devel. Biology, Jour. Immunology, Jour. Exptl. Medicine, Am. Jour. Zoology, Anatomical Record. Rsch. grantee NIH, 1978-89. Mem. Am. Assn. Immunologists, Am. Assn. Anatomists, Am. Soc. Cell Biology, Teratology Soc. Office: NJ Med Sch Dept Anatomy 185 S Orange Ave Newark NJ 07103-2714

LEUNISSEN, DOROTHY ANN PIATNEK, internist; b. Lawrence, Pa., Feb. 8, 1928; d. Andrew Paul and Mary Theresa (Batrla) Piatnek; m. R.L.A. Leunissen, May 12, 1962. BA, Seton Hill Coll., 1949; MA, Mt. Holyoke Coll., 1951; PhD, U. Pitts., 1956; MD, Med. Coll. Pa., 1974. Rsch. asst. Jefferson Med. Coll., Phila., 1951-53; rsch. fellow U. Pitts. Grad. Sch. Pub. Health, 1956-58, rsch. assoc., 1958-62; asst. prof. physiology Hahnemann Med. Coll., Phila., 1962-69; pvt. practice internal medicine Med. Cardiology Assocs., Media, Pa., 1976—. Contbr. articles to profl. jours. Mem. Humane Soc. USA, World Wildlife, Natural Conservancy, Greenpeace, Brandywine Conservancy, Phil. Art Mus., Pro Life. Recipient postdoctoral fellowship USPHS, 1956-57. Mem. Del. County Med. Soc., Pa. Med. Soc., Am. Med. Soc., Am. Physiology Soc., N.Y. Acad. Scis., Sigma Xi, Kappa Gamma Pi. Republican. Roman Catholic. Office: Med Cardiology Assocs Ste 209 RHCCI 1978 W Baltimore Pike Media PA 19063

LEV, ALEXANDER SHULIM, mechanical engineer; b. Tselinograd, USSR, May 4, 1945; came to U.S., 1979; s. Borukh and Golda (Kopitman) L.; m. Polina Zhdanovskaja, Aug. 31, 1968; 1 child, Victoria. MSME, Lvov Polytech Inst., 1968. Project mgr. Glavspetsavtotrans, Lvov, USSR, 1968-78; sr. engr. Machine Plant, Lvov, USSR, 1978-79; metalurgist Ronson Metals Corp., Newark, N.J., 1980-82, foundry quality control mgr., 1982-83, reduction dept. mgr., 1986-86; project mgr. FMB Systems Inc., Harrison, N.J., 1986—. Patentee in field. Mem. Am. Metals Soc., Metallurgical Soc. Home: 16 Princeton St Maplewood NJ 07040

LEVA, NEIL IRWIN, psychotherapist; b. N.Y.C., Sept. 18, 1929; s. Charles and Alice Lee (Peirce) L.; m. Jean Kathryn Walters, Dec. 4, 1952 (div. May, 1988); children: Steven L., Michael N., Scott A.; m. Susan Mary Callagy, Aug. 12, 1988. BA in Govt., U. Tex., 1963; MA in Systems Mgmt., U. So. Calif., 1973; MA in Psychology, Cath. U. Am., 1976; MSW, U. Md., 1990. Commd. 2d. lt. U.S. Army, 1953, advanced through grades to col., 1976, retired, 1976; with psych. factors div. Quadraennial Bd. for Rev. of Mil. Compensation, Washington, 1974-76; psychotherapist Village Counselling Ctr., Potomac, Md., 1978-86, Met. Psychotherapist Group, Bethesda, 1986-90, Village Counseling Ctr., Potomac, Md., 1990—; human factors cons. The Artery Orgn., Washington, 1978-83, Mont County Schs., Rockville, Md., 1979-81. Decorated D.F.C., Bronze Star with V device and 4 oak leaf clusters, Air Medal with V device and 10 oak leaf clusters, Purple Heart, Legion of Merit. Mem. NASW, DAV, Am. Assn. Family Counselors, Internat. Transactional Analysis Assn., Mil. Order of Purple Heart, Am. Legion. Democrat. Home: 10011 Counselman Rd Rockville MD 20854-5019 Office: Village Counseling Ctr 10011 Counselman Rd Potomac MD 20854-5019

LEVAL, PIERRE NELSON, federal judge; b. N.Y.C., Sept. 4, 1936; s. Fernand and Beatrice (Reiter) L. B.A. cum laude, Harvard U., 1959, J.D. magna cum laude, 1963. Bar: N.Y. 1964, U.S. Ct. Appeals 2d Circuit 1964, U.S. Dist. Ct. So. Dist. N.Y 1966. Law clk. to Hon. Henry J. Friendly, U.S. Ct. Appeals, 1963-64; asst. U.S. atty. So. Dist. N.Y., 1964-68, chief appellate atty., 1967-68; assoc. firm Cleary, Gottlieb, Steen & Hamilton, N.Y.C., 1969-74; ptnr. firm, 1973-75; 1st asst. dist. atty. Office of Dist. Atty., N.Y. County, 1975-76; chief asst. dist. atty. Office of Dist. Atty., 1976-77; U.S. dist. judge So. Dist. N.Y., N.Y.C., 1977—. Served with U.S. Army, 1959. Mem. Am. Law Inst. (council), Assn. Bar City N.Y., N.Y. County Lawyers Assn. Office: US Dist Ct US Courthouse Foley Sq New York NY 10007-1501*

LEVALLEY, GUY GLENN, speech communication educator; b. Phila., Oct. 21, 1942; s. Glenn Henry and Mary Jane (Henderson) LeV.; BA, Glassboro State Coll., 1964; MA, U. Iowa, 1967; m. E. Raye Gerlack, June 17, 1967 (div. 1981); 1 son, Ian G. Designer, tech. dir. Glassboro (N.J.) Summer Theatre, 1963-67, Monticello Coll., Godfrey, Ill., 1967-68; asst. tech. dir. N.Y. Shakespeare Festival Mobile Theatre Unit, N.Y.C., 1967; asst. prof. theatre Prince George's Coll., Largo, Md., 1968-73, assoc. prof. speech communication, designer, tech. dir. theatre, 1974—; lighting designer Murray Spalding Movement Arts Inc., 1975—, City Dance '77; bldg. cons. Church St. Theatre, Capitol Hill Arts Workshop; co-dir. 94th Combat Bomb Wing Research Group. Mem. Am. Theatre Assn., U.S. Inst. Theatre Tech., 8th USAF Hist. Soc., Eastern Communication Assn. Democrat. Quaker. Reviewer, cons. Choice mag., 1974—. Author: Annotated Bibliography of Stage Lighting for the Dance, 1974, 77; Technical Elements of Stage Lighting; Technical Theatre: A Critical Bibliography, 1985; contbg. author: A Handbook of Stage Lighting; contbr. articles to profl. jours. Home: 7305 Hopkins Ave College Park MD 20740-3411 Office: 301 Largo Rd Largo MD 20870

LE VAN, DANIEL HAYDEN, business executive; b. Savannah, Ga., Mar. 29, 1924; s. Daniel Hayden and Ruth (Harner) LeV. Grad., Middlesex Sch., 1943; BA, Harvard U., 1950; postgrad., Babson Inst., 1950-51. Underwriter Zurich Ins. Co., N.Y.C., 1951-52; co-owner, dir. Overseas Properties, Ltd., N.Y.C., 1970—; dir. Colonial Gas Co., N.Y.C., 1973—. With AUS, 1943-46. Mem. Harvard Club (N.Y.C. and Boston).

LEVANDOWSKY, MICHAEL, marine biologist; b. Knoxville, Tenn., Aug. 15, 1935; s. Daniel and Evelyn (Mooney) L.; m. Jane Adams, 1959 (div. 1962). BA in Math., Antioch Coll., 1961; MA in Zoology, Columbia U., 1965, PhD in Biol. Scis., 1970; MS in Math., NYU, 1975. Instr. biology Bard Coll., Annandale-on-Hudson, N.Y., 1967-69; asst. prof. biology York Coll., CUNY, Jamaica, N.Y., 1973-74; rsch. sci. Haskins Lab., Pace U., N.Y.C., 1970—; visiting sci. math. dept. U. British Columbia, Vancouver,

BC, Can., 1980, 81, U. Heidelberg, West Germany, 1983, 85, 86; trustee The River Project, N.Y.C., 1986—. Editorial adv. bd.: The Jour. of Protozoology, 1981-84, Marine Ecology Progress Series, 1979—; editorial bd.: (jour.) Art & Academe, 1988—; editor: (with S.H. Hutner) (4 vols.) Biochemistry and Physiology of Protozoa, 1978, 81. Mem. steering com. Citizens Adv. Com. Resource Recovery, Bklyn.; sec. Environ. Scis. for Global Survival, N.Y.C., 1982-91. Named Disting. Lectr. N.E. Algal Symposium, Woods Hole, Mass., 1986, co-convenor, 1992; recipient Sci. Faculty Fellowship NSF, Washington, 1971-72; grantee Hudson River Found., N.Y.C., 1989-91, Sea Grant Inst. N.Y., Stony Brook, 1989-91. Mem. Am. Soc. Microbiology, AAAS, Assn. for Chemoreception Soc., Soc. of Protozoologists, N.Y. Acad. Scis. Office: Pace U Haskins Labs 41 Park Row New York NY 10038-1508

LEVEE, HARRIS HAROLD, construction executive; b. N.Y.C., Aug. 9, 1919; s. Joseph George and Stella (Segal) L.; m. Pearl Rosner, July 26, 1942; children: Stephen Van, Leslie Lynn. BS in Mech. Engring., Ill. Inst. Tech., Chgo., 1949; MBA, Pace U., 1967. Registered profl. engr. Ill., N.Y., N.J., Pa., Md., Va., D.C. Cons. engr., mech. engr. Pioneer Svc. & Engring., Chgo., 1946-50; chief engr. U.S. Refrigeration, Bklyn., 1950-51; mgr. Far East, project engr. Gibbs & Hill Inc., N.Y.C., 1951-67; v.p., gen. mgr. Norair Engring. Corp., Washington, 1967-74; chmn. bd. Halco Engring. Inc., Gaithersburg, Md., 1974-90; tchr. constrn. and estimating constrn. Montgomery Coll., 1975-87; arbitrator constrn. Am. Arbitration Assn., Washington, 1981-91. Author, editor: Intermediate Construction, 1984. With C.E., U.S. Army, 1943-46. Mem. Mech. Constrn. Assn. Am. (pres., spl. svc. award 1975). Home: 10504 Great Arbor Dr Rockville MD 20854-4217 Office: Halco Engring Inc 13-15 E Deer Park Dr Gaithersburg MD 20877

LEVEEN, PAULINE, history government educator; b. N.Y.C., Mar. 5, 1925; d. Aaron and Sophie (Karp) Ugelow; m. Seymour Leveen, Nov. 5, 1944; children: David Ian, Amy Frances, Adriane Beth. Student, Coll. City N.Y., 1941-44; BA, Elmira Coll., 1963, MS, 1965; postgrad., Cornell U., 1967, 71-72, Syracuse U., 1981-82. Cert. tchr. permanent secondary social studies. Substitute tchr. Elmira (N.Y.) Sch. Dist., 1960-65; prof. history govt. Corning Community Coll., 1965—, dir. paralegal program, 1975—, chairperson div. social scis., 1984-91; lectr. Elderhostel, Painted Post, N.Y., 1982—. Mem. Phi Alpha Theta, Beta Chi/Delta Kappa Gamma Corning (profl. affairs 1968, 75, legis. 1989—). Home: 60 Ohio Ave Elmira NY 14905-1822 Office: Corning CC Spencer Hill Rd Corning NY 14830-9417

LEVEN, ANN RUTH, arts administrator; b. Canton, Ohio, Nov. 1, 1940; d. Joseph J. and Bessie (Scharff) L. AB, Brown U., 1962; cert. with distinction in program in bus. adminstrn., Harvard-Radcliffe Univs., 1963; MBA, Harvard U., 1964. Product mgr. household products div. Colgate-Palmolive, N.Y.C., 1964-66; account exec. Grey Advt., N.Y.C., 1966-67; fin. asst. Met. Mus. Art, N.Y.C., 1967-69; asst. treas. Met. Mus. Art, 1970-72, treas., 1972-79; v.p., sr. corp. planning officer Chase Manhattan Bank, N.Y.C., 1979-83; pres. ARL Assocs., N.Y.C., 1983—; treas. Smithsonian Instn., 1984-90; dep. treas. Nat. Gallery Art, Washington, 1990—; adj. asst. prof. Grad. Sch. Bus., Columbia U., 1975-77, adj. assoc. prof., 1977-79, adj. prof., 1980—; exec.-in-residence Amos Tuck Sch., Dartmouth Coll., winter 1976, spring 1984; dir. Alliance Capital Res., Inc., 1978-79; Short Term Asset Res., 1985—, Oreg. Tax Free Trust, 1986—, Churchill Tax-Free Fund of Ky., 1987—, Cascades Cash Fund, 1989—, Del. Group, 1989—; trustee Carnegie Corp. of N.Y., 1981-90. Artist (awarded prizes for painting and graphic arts); author articles on grad. bus. edn., mgmt. studies on the arts. Mem. exec. bd. new leadership div. Fedn. Jewish Philanthropies, 1968-70; mem. council N.Y. Public Library, mem. exec. com., 1976-79; mem. mus. adv. panel N.Y. State Council on Arts, 1977-79; bd. dirs. Camp Rainbow, 1970-84, v.p., 1976-78, treas., 1982-84; bd. overseers Amos Tuck Sch., 1978-84, chmn. ednl. affairs com., 1979-84; trustee Brown U., 1976—, also mem. fin. and budget com., student life com., devel. com., adv. and exec. coms.; bd. mem. Ctr. for Fgn. Policy Devel., 1989—; trustee Artists' Choice Mus., 1979-87; bd. dirs. Reading is Fundamental, 1987-91; mem. vis. com. Harvard U. Bus. Sch., 1979-84; trustee ARC Endowment Fund, 1985-90; bd. dirs. Am. Arts Alliance, 1990—; bd. dirs. Twyla Tharp Dance Found., 1982-87; bd. overseers Hood Mus.-Hopkins Ctr. Dartmouth Coll., 1984-91, chmn., 1988-91; mem. staff Presdl. Task Force on Arts and Humanities, 1981. Recipient Young Leadership award Council Jewish Fedns. and Welfare Funds, 1968; named N.Y. State's Outstanding Young Woman, 1976. Mem. Harvard Bus. Sch. Alumni Assn. (exec. coun. 1976-79, v.p. 1978-79), Women's Fin. Assn., Women's Forum, Econ. Club of Washington, Cosmopolitan Club, Harvard Bus. Sch. Club, Radcliffe Club, Brown Club. Home: 1160 3d Ave New York NY 10021 Office: Nat Gallery Art Washington DC 20565

LEVENSALER, WALTER LOUIS, human resources consultant; b. Somerville, Mass., Jan. 18, 1934; s. Leon Walter and Elizabeth Mary (Adreani) L.; m. Mary Frances Cronin, Sept. 26, 1964; children: Karen, Linda, Renee. BBA, Northeastern U., Boston, 1961; MA in Sociology, Northeastern U., 1977. Wage and salary analyst ITEK Corp., Lexington, Mass., 1960-62, personnel adminstr., 1962-65; personnel adminstr. MITRE Corp., Bedford, Mass., 1965-68; wage and salary adminstr. Univ. Hosp., Boston, 1968-70, personnel dir., 1970-73, adminstr. labor relations, 1973-76, adminstr. personnel, 1976-82, adminstr. human resources, 1982-88; ind. cons., 1988—; ind. cons., 1988—; wage and salary cons. New Eng. Rehab. Hosp., Woburn, Mass., 1982-83; labor rels. cons. Resthaven Nursing Home, Roxbury, Mass., 1980—, Armenian Nursing Home, Jamaica Plain, Mass., 1984-86; pers. cons. Martha's Vineyard (Mass.) Hosp., 1978-82, Nevins Home, Methuen, Mass., 1990—, Orthopedic Assn. of Portland, Maine, 1991—, Litle & Co., Salem, N.H., 1991—. Com. mem. Town of Acton (Mass.) Personnel Bd., 1977-83. Served with USAF, 1952-56. Mem. Am. Soc. Personnel Adminstrs., Am. Acad. Polit. and Social Scis., Am. Mgmt. Assn., Mass. Health Care Human Resources Assn. (pres. 1976-77), Indsl. Relations Research Assn., N.E. Geneol. & Hist. Soc., Boston Mus. Sci., N.E. O.D. Network. Democrat. Roman Catholic.

LEVENSON, ALAN BRADLEY, lawyer; b. Long Beach, N.Y., Dec. 13, 1935; s. Cyrus O. and Jean (Kotler) L.; m. Joan Marlene Levenson, Aug. 19, 1956; children—Scott Keith, Julie Jo. A.B., Dartmouth Coll., 1956; B.A., Oxford U., Eng., 1958, M.A., 1962; LL.B., Yale U., 1961. Bar: N.Y. 1962, U.S. Dist. Ct. D.C. 1964, U.S. Ct. Appeals (D.C. cir.) 1965, U.S. Supreme Ct. 1965. Law clk., trainee div. corp. fin. SEC, Washington, 1961-62, gen. atty., 1962, trial atty., 1963, br. chief, 1963-65, asst. dir., 1965-68, exec. asst. dir., 1968, dir., 1970-76; v.p. Shareholders Mgmt. Co., L.A., 1969, sr. v.p., 1969-70, exec. v.p., 1970; ptnr. Fulbright & Jaworski, Washington, 1976—; lectr. Cath. U. Am., 1964-68, Columbia U., 1973; adj. prof. Georgetown U., 1964, 77, 79-81, U.S. rep. working party OECD, Paris, 1974-75; adv. com. SEC, 1976-77; mem. adv. bd. Securities Regulation Inst., U. Calif., San Diego, 1973—, vice chmn. exec. com., 1979-83, chmn., 1983-87, emeritus chmn., 1988—; mem. adv. coun. SEC Inst., U. So. Calif., L.A., Sch. Acctg., 1981-85; mem. adv. com. Nat. Ctr. Fin. Svcs., U. Calif.-Berkeley, 1985—; mem. planning com. Ray Garrett Ann. Securities Regulation Inst. Northwestern U. Law Sch.; mem. adv. panel to U.S. compt.-gen. on stock market decline, 1987, panel of cons., 1989—; mem. audit com. GAO, 1992—. Mem. bd. editorial advisors U. Iowa Jour. Corp. Law, 1978—; Bur. Nat. Affairs adv. bd. Securities Regulation and Law Report, 1976—; bd. editors N.Y. Law Jour., 1976—; bd. advisors, corp. and securities law advisor Prentice Hall Law & Bus.; contbr. articles to profl. jours.; mem. adv. bd. Banking Expansion Reporter. Recipient Disting. Service award SEC, 1972; James B. Richardson fellow Oxford U., 1956. Mem. ABA (exec. com., fed. regulation securities com., former chair subcom. on securities activities banks), Fed. Bar Assn. (emeritus mem. exec. com. securities law com.), Am. Law Inst., Practicing Law Inst. (nat. adv. com. 1974), AICPA (pub. dir., bd. dirs. 1983-90, fin. com. 1984-90, chmn. adv. coun. auditing standards bd. 1979-80, future issues com. 1982-85), Nat. Assn. Securities Dealers (corp. fin. com. 1981-87, nat. arbitration com. 1983-87, gov.-at-large, bd. govs. 1984-87, exec. com. 1986-87, long range planning com. 1987-90, chmn. legal adv. com. 1988—, spl. com. governance and structure 1989-90, numerous adv. coms.). Home: 12512 Exchange Ct S Potomac MD 20854-2431 Office: Fulbright & Jaworski 801 Pennsylvania Ave NW Washington DC 20004-2615

LEVENSON, HARVEY STUART, manufacturing company executive; b. N.Y.C., May 1, 1940; s. Abraham and Lucile (Lichtenstein) L.; m. Merrilee Borenstein, Aug. 28, 1960; children: Lee Alan, Gary Scott. BA, Drake U., 1962, JD, 1963; LLM, Georgetown U., 1966. Bar: Iowa 1963, N.Y. 1964, Conn. 1968. Atty. IRS, Washington, 1964-68; assoc. Murtha, Cullina, Richter & Pinney, Hartford, Conn., 1968-69; ptnr. Murtha, Cullina, Richter & Pinney, Hartford, 1970-82; sr. v.p., chief fin. officer Kaman Corp., Bloomfield, Conn., 1982-90; pres., chief oper. officer Kaman Corp., Bloomfield, 1990—, bd. dirs.; lectr. U. Conn. Law Sch., Hartford, 1972-76; bd. dirs. Conn. Natural Gas Corp.; adv. bd. dirs. Conn. Nat. Bank; corporator St. Francis Hosp., Hartford Hosp., Inst. of Living. Co-author: Depreciation & The Investment Tax Credit, 1983; contbr. various articles on taxation to profl. jours. Mem. Conn. Bus. and Industry Assn. (bd. dirs.).

LEVENSON, NATHAN S., architect; b. Pitts., Apr. 22, 1916; s. Max and Anne (Ashinsky) L.; BArch, Carnegie Inst. Tech., 1941; m. Bernice K. Klein, Aug. 31, 1947; children: David, Laura. Sr. draftsman various cos., Pitts., 1939-43; pvt. practice architecture, Pitts., 1948-89; tchr. Coll. of Phillipines, 1945-46; substitute prof. archtl. practice Carnegie Tech., 1959; instr. U. Pitts., 1978; pres. Bldg. Inspection Cons. Inc., 1973-92. Bd. dirs. AIA Pitts. Charitable Assn., 1982-85, Allegheny County Plumbing Bd., 1981-89; pres. bd. dirs. Bower Hill, 1979. Served to 1st lt. C.E., AUS, 1943-46; ETO, PTO. Registered architect, Pa., Ohio, N.J., Ark., Mich., Md., W.Va. Certified fallout shelter analyst, 1970; recipient 1st pl. award Illuminating Engring. Soc., Pitts., 1965. Mem. AIA (emeritus, regional rep., housing commn. 1972-77, treas. Pitts. chpt. 1980), Pa. Soc. Architects, Nat. Council Archtl. Registration Bds., Electric League Western Pa. (dir. 1984-86), Pitts. Architecture Club (dir. 1979), Clan-Carnegie-Mellon U. (v.p. 1970-72). Democrat. Jewish. Patentee Terrace Town House, multi-housing (U.S. and Israel). Home: Apt 307 220 N Dithridge St Pittsburgh PA 15213-1420 Office: Two Gate Ctr 14 S Pittsburgh PA 15222

LEVENSTEIN, HAROLD, electronics engineer, consultant; b. Phila., June 28, 1923; s. Solomon and Fannie (Liebman) L.; m. Gloria Elaine Potasnick, Nov. 16, 1947; children: Paula Butler, Marcia Weisman, Alissa Onigman. BEE, Cooper Union, N.Y.C., 1943; MEE, Bklyn. Poly. Inst., 1949; MS, Columbia U., 1979. Mem. tech. staff Draper Lab., MIT, Cambridge, Mass., 1955-56; dir. rsch. W.L. Maxson Corp., N.Y.C., 1956-60; lab. mgr. Servo Corp. Am., Hicksville, N.Y., 1960-62; sect. head. ARMA, Mineola, N.Y., 1962-64; dept. head ops. rsch. AIL, Deer Park, N.Y., 1964-71; program mgr. RCA Missile & Surface Radar, Moorestown, N.J., 1971-73; tech. dir. Perkin Elmer Mil. Systems, Danbury, Conn., 1973-88; electro optics systems cons. Danbury, Conn., 1988—; mem. DARPA/MIT Studies of Optical Discrimination of ICBM, Lexington, Mass., 1983, 84, 85, 86; lectr. in field; mem. adv. bd. Fed. Agy., Washington, 1988—. Editor: Adaptive Control Systems, 1962; contbr. over 50 articles to profl. jours.; patentee in field of control systems - optics. Mem. IEEE (sr.), Am. Statis. Assn., Ops. Rsch. Soc. Am., Soc. for Indsl. and Applied Math. Home and Office: 7 Golden Heights Rd Danbury CT 06811-3626

LEVENTHAL, MARVIN, physicist; b. N.Y.C., Dec. 4, 1937; s. Jerome and Helen (Treppel) L.; m. Alice Judith Smilowitz, Apr. 16, 1961; children: Liza, Tama. BS in Physics, CCNY, 1958; PhD in Physics, Brown U., 1964. Postdoctoral fellow Yale U., New Haven, Conn., 1964-66, asst. prof., 1966-68; mem. tech. staff AT&T Bell Labs., Murray Hill, N.J., 1968-91; NRC sr. rsch. assoc. NASA/Goddard Space Flight Ctr., Greenbelt, Md., 1992—. Contbr. numerous articles to profl. jours. Owens-Ill. fellow, 1962-64. Fellow Am. Phys. Soc.; mem. Am. Astron. Soc. (exec. com. high energy astrophysics div. 1984-86), Sigma Xi. Home: 28 Sunset Dr Summit NJ 07901 Office: NASA/Goddard Space Flight Ctr Greenbelt MD 20770

LEVENTHAL, NATHAN, performing arts executive, lawyer; b. N.Y.C., Feb. 19, 1943; s. Harry and Fay (Bronstein) L. B.A. in Pub. Affairs, Queens Coll., 1963; J.D. cum laude, Columbia U., 1966. Bar: N.Y. 1967. Commr. Rent and Housing Maintenance, N.Y.C., 1972-73; chief counsel U.S. Senate Subcom. Adminstrv. Practice and Procedure, Washington, 1973-74; assoc. and ptnr. Poletti, Freidin, Prashker, Feldman & Gartner, N.Y.C., 1974-78; commr. Housing Preservation and Devel., N.Y.C., 1978-79; dep. mayor ops. City of N.Y., 1979-84; pres. Lincoln Ctr. for Performing Arts, N.Y.C., 1984—; lectr. govt. housing policy New Sch. Social Research, N.Y.C., 1979; lectr. health care and pub. policy Columbia Law Sch., N.Y.C., 1971. Editor-in-chief: Columbia Law Rev., 1965-66. Adv. com. City Univ. Law Sch., N.Y.C., 1983—; active Council on Jud. Adminstrn., Bar Assn. N.Y. City, 1983—; dir. Nat. Youth Service Corp. for N.Y.C., 1983—; commnr. N.Y.C. Charter Revision Commn., 1986—. Harlan Fiske Stone scholar Columbia Law Sch., 1963-65, Jerome Michael scholar, 1965-66; Disting. Service award Citizens Housing and Planning Council, N.Y.C., 1984, Am. Soc. Pub. Adminstrn. outstanding pub. adminstr. award 1982, Columbia Univ. Medal for Excellence, 1985.*

LEVENTHAL, RUTH, university provost and dean, educator; b. Phila., May 23, 1940; d. Harry Louis Mongin and Bertha (Rosenberg) Mongin Blai; children—Sheryl Anne, David Alan. B.S., U. Pa., 1961, Ph.D., 1973, M.B.A., 1981. Cert. med. technologist, clin. lab. scientist. Trainee NSF, 1971; trainee USPHS, 1969-70, 73; asst. prof. med. tech. U. Pa., Phila., 1974-77; acting dean U. Pa., 1977-81; dean Hunter Coll., N.Y.C., 1981-84; provost, dean, prof. biology Capitol Coll. Pa. State U., Middletown, 1984—; site visitor Middle State Assn. Colls. and Secondary Schs., Phila., 1983—. Author: (with Cheadle) Medical Parasitology: A Self Instructional Text, 1979, 2d edit., 1985; contbr. chpt. to book and articles to profl. jours. Chmn. pub. service div. Tri-County United Way, South Central Pa., 1985—; mem. health found. bd. Harrisburg Hosp., Pa., 1984—; bd. dirs. Tri-County Planned Parenthood, 1984—, Harrisburg Acad., Wormleysburg, Pa., 1984—, Metro Arts of Harrisburg, 1984—. Recipient Alice Paul award Women's Faculty Club, U. Pa., 1981; Recognition award NE Deans of Schs. of Allied Health, 1984; fellow U. Pa., 1972. Mem. Am. Soc. Parasitologists, Am. Assn. Higher Edn., N.Y. Soc. Tropical Medicine, N.J. Soc. Parasitology, AAUW (bd. dirs. Pa. br. 1985—), Sigma Xi. Office: Pa State U-Harrisburg Capital Coll Rte 230 Middletown PA 17057*

LEVENTHAL, STUART GARY, sales and marketing executive; b. N.Y.C., Oct. 23, 1947; s. David A. and Ruth L. (Tesser) L.; m. Lisa Hirsh, Sept. 7, 1980; children: Shawn Jared, Justin Reed. BA, Queens Coll., N.Y.C., 1970. Prodn. asst. Sta. ABC-TV, N.Y.C., 1968-70; art dir. Sta. WPIX-TV, N.Y.C., 1970-73; design dir. Merrill Lynch, N.Y.C., 1973-78; sales and mktg. exec. A. Colish Color Lithographers, Mt. Vernon, N.Y., 1978—; print cons., N.Y.C. With USAR, 1970-76. Mem. Am. Inst. Graphic Artists (awards 1978, 83, 88), Thomas Paine Assn., New Rochelle Hist. Assn. Home: 45 Disbrow Ln New Rochelle NY 10804-3210 Office: Sandy/Alexander Inc Clifton NJ 10503

LEVERSEE, GORDON JEPSON, academic administrator; b. Cohoes, N.Y., Apr. 18, 1944; s. Gordon Jepson and Florence (Pagel) L.; m. Marcia Mahaffey, Sept. 6, 1969; children: Katherine, Anna. AB, Dartmouth Coll., 1966; PhD, Duke U., 1972. Assoc. biology Nasson Coll., Springvale, Maine, 1970-78; asst. ecologist, acting assoc. dir. Savannah River Ecology Lab. U. Ga., Aiken, S.C., 1978-81; dean scis. Keene (N.H.) State Coll., 1981-91, interim v.p. acad. affairs, 1991—; vis. scientist marine inst. U. Ga., Sapelo Island, 1987. Contbr. articles to profl. jours. Bd. dirs. Childrens Performing Arts Ctr., Keene, 1982-85; founder Monadnock Childrens Mus., 1988. Rsch. grantee U.S. EPA, 1980-81. Mem. AAAS, Am. Soc. Limnology and Oceanography, Am. Soc. Zoologists. Home: 71 Terrace St Keene NH 03431-3210 Office: Keene State Coll Main St Keene NH 03431-3732

LEVESQUE, ALLEN H(ENRY), electronics engineering manager; b. Jewett City, Conn., Nov. 1, 1936; s. Henry A. and Bertha C. (Slonski) L.; m. Barbara Ann Lyons, Aug. 27, 1960; children: Karen A., Amy E., Steven L. BSEE, Worcester Poly. Inst., 1959; M Engring., Yale U., 1960, D Engring., 1965. Registered profl. engr., Mass. Mem. tech. staff Sylvania Applied Research Lab., Waltham, Mass., 1965-69; sr. mem. tech. staff GTE Labs. Inc., Waltham, 1969-74, GTE Govt. Systems Corp., Needham, Mass., 1974-83; sr. scientist Natick, Mass., 1983-88; staff scientist Waltham, Mass., 1988—. Author: Error Control Techniques for Digital Communication, 1985; contbr. articles to profl. jours. and confs. Chmn. Ednl. Adv. Com. for Pub. Schs., Chelmsford, Mass, 1970-74; chmn. alumni fund Worcester Poly. Inst., 1984-87. Mem. IEEE (sr., chpt. chmn. 1973-76, assoc. editor Transactions on Communications 1986—). Republican. Roman Catholic. Home: 49 Brentwood Rd Chelmsford MA 01824-1348 Office: GTE Govt Systems Corp Waltham MA 02254

LEVEY, HAROLD ABRAM, physiologist, educator; b. Boston, Aug. 14, 1924; s. Maurice J. and Dora G. (Seckman) L.; widowed, Sept. 1989; children: Karen L., Christopher B. AB, Harvard U., 1947; PhD, UCLA, 1956. Instr. to assoc. prof. SUNY Health Sci. Ctr., Bklyn., 1956—. Contbr. articles to profl. jours. Pres. Bd. Health, Mountain Lakes, N.J., 1973-74. With Army Air Corps, 1943-45. Grantee NIH. Mem. AAAS, Am. Physiol. Soc., N.Y. Acad. Scis., Endocrine Soc., Harvey Soc., Harvard Club (N.Y.C.). Democrat. Home: 160 Columbia Heights # 9B Brooklyn NY 11201 Office: SUNY Health Sci Ctr Dept Physiology 450 Clarkson Ave Brooklyn NY 11203

LEVI, ENRICO, engineering educator; b. Milan, Italy, May 20, 1918; s. Mario and Virginia Marcella (Levi) L.; m. Nechama Bitia Froimberg, Sept. 11, 1941. BSc in Mech. and Elec. Engring., Technion, Haifa, Israel, 1940, diploma in engring., 1941; MEE, Poly., Bklyn., 1956, PhD, 1958. Registered profl. engr., N.Y. Lectr. Technion, IIT, Haifa, 1945-55; prof. Poly. U., Bklyn., 1958—; pres., treas. Enrico Levi, Inc., Forest Hills, N.Y., 1976—. Author: Electromechanical Power Conversion, 1965, Russian translation, 1969, Polyphase Motors, 1984, Chinese translation, 1989; contbr. articles to profl. jours.; patentee in field. Recipient IEEE Charles J. Hirsch award, 1980, Disting. Faculty Rsch., Sigma Xi, 1983. Office: Poly U 333 Stuart St Brooklyn NY 11229-6604

LEVI, MARK, mathematician; b. Riga, Latvia, USSR, Nov. 25, 1951; s. Ber and Dvora (Lurie) L.; m. Olga Gelfand, Aug. 3, 1984; children: Vivian, Nicole, Max, Eric. MS, Latvian State U., 1973; PhD, NYU, 1978. Asst. prof. Northwestern U., Evanston, Ill., 1978-80, Duke U., Durham, N.C., 1980-82; asst. prof. Boston U., 1982-85, assoc. prof. math., 1986—; assoc. prof. math. Rensselaer Poly. Inst., Troy, N.Y., 1991—; cons. Sci. Applications Inc., McLean, Va., 1984. Author: Qualitative Analysis, 1981; coeditor: New Approaches..., 1988 (Jay Krakauer award 1979); editorial bd. 2 jours.; contbr. articles to profl. jours. Mem. Am. Math. Soc., Soc. for Indsl. and Applied Math. Office: Rensselaer Poly Inst Math Sci Troy NY 12180

LEVI, ROY ELLIOTT, information services executive; b. N.Y.C., May 9, 1945; s. Henry and Else (Plaut) L.; m. Linda R. Theilheimer, Feb. 2, 1969; children: Daniel H., Karen C. BS, CCNY, 1966; MBA, Pace U., 1970. Systems analyst Western Electric Co., N.Y.C., 1966-72; programming mgr. McGraw Hill, Inc., Hightstown, N.J., 1972-76; cons., sr. mgr. Price Waterhouse, Morristown, N.J., 1976-84; dir. of sytems devel. Cabletek, Inc., Sewaren, N.J., 1984-89; v.p. info. svcs. Primetime 24, N.Y.C., 1989—; subchmn. task force Pres.'s Pvt. Sector Survey on Cost Control, Washington, 1982-83. Treasurer East Brunswick (N.J.) Jaycees, 1974-76. Mem. Inst. Mgmt. Cons., EDP Auditors Found. Home: 29 Buffalo Run East Brunswick NJ 08816-4078 Office: Primetime 24 342 Madison Ave New York NY 10173-0002

LEVI, VICKI GOLD, picture editor, historical consultant, actress; b. Atlantic City, N.J., Sept. 16, 1941; d. Albert and Beverly Valentine Gold; m. Alexander Hecht Levi, May 31, 1970; 1 child, Adam Hecht Levi. Student, Montclair State Coll., 1959-60, New Sch. Social Rsch., N.Y.C., 1970-73, Sch. Visual Arts, N.Y.C., 1972, Lee Strass Berg Sch. Acting, N.Y.C., 1961. Actress Atlantic City, N.Y.C and L.A., 1945—; asst. to pres. Family Fare, Inc., N.Y.C., 1966; advt. rep. Cosmopolitan Mag., N.Y.C., 1967; publicity dir. Misty Harbor, Ltd., N.Y.C., 1968; freelance picture researcher, 1972—; contbg. picture editor Esquire Mag., N.Y.C., 1980—, Mirabella Mag., N.Y.C., 1991—, Atlantic City Mag., 1988—; story cons. Alvin Cooperman Prodns., N.Y.C., 1985—; hist. cons. various, Atlantic City; lectr. on Atlantic City, 1979—; guest exhibitor Internat. Ctr. Photography, N.Y.C., 1979; guest exhibitor and lectr. Cooper Hewitt, N.Y.C., 1980; guest curator Songwriters Hall of Fame, N.Y.C., 1979; guest lectr. Mcpl. Arts Soc., N.Y.C., 1979; co-founder Atlantic City Hist. Mus., 1985—, bd. dirs.; hist. cons. Toast to Times Square Com., N.Y.C., 1988—; picture cons. Am. Mus. of the Moving Image, Astoria, N.Y., 1988—. Co-author: Atlantic City: 125 Years of Ocean Madness, 1979, Live and Be Well: A Celebration of Yiddish Culture in American, 1982, You Must Have Been a Beatiful Baby, 1992; columnist: Phila. Bull., The Way It Was, 1980; prodr./dir. (hist. video) Boardwalk Ballyhoo, 1992. Reviewer of grants, Nat. Endowment for Humanities, Washington. Recipient Author's Citation, N.J. Inst. Tech., Div. Continuing Edn., 1980, Senate Resolution, N.J. State Senate, 1979, Outstanding Achievement award, Atlantic City Women's C. of C., 1981, Proclamation from mayor of Atlantic City, 1981; named An Atlantic City Treasure, Atlantic City Women's C. of C., 1989. Mem. Nat. Acad. TV Arts and Scis. (Emmy judge 1987—, spl. events com. 1989-90), Screen Actors Guild, Am. Fedn. TV and Radio Artists, Am. Soc. Picture Profls. (bd. dirs. 1984), Ziegfeld Club. Democrat. Jewish. Home and Office: 211 Central Park W New York NY 10024-6020

LEVIN, EDWARD M., lawyer, government administrator; b. Chgo., Oct. 16, 1934; s. Edward M. (dec.) and Anne Meriam (Fantl) L. (dec.); children from previous marriage: Daniel Andrew, John Davis. BS, U. Ill., 1955; LLB, Harvard U., 1958. Bar: Ill. 1958, U.S. Supreme Ct. 1968. Mem. firm Ancel, Stonesifer, Glink & Levin and predecessors, Chgo., 1958, 61-68; draftsman Ill. Legis. Reference Bur., Springfield, 1961; spl. asst. to regional adminstr. HUD, Chgo., 1968-71, asst. regional adminstr. community planning and mgmt., 1971-73; asst. dir. Ill. Dept. Local Govt. Affairs, Chgo., 1973-77; of counsel Holleb, Gerstein & Glass, Ltd., Chgo., 1977-79; chief counsel Econ. Devel. Adminstrn., U.S. Dept. Commerce, Washington, 1979-85; sr. fellow Nat. Gov's. Assn., 1985-86; sr. counsel U.S. Dept. Commerce, Washington, 1987—; lectr. U. Ill., 1972-73, adj. assoc. prof. urban scis., 1973-79; lectr. Loyola U., 1976-79, No. Va. law Sch., 1988. Assoc. editor Assistance Mgmt. Jour., 1990—; contbr. articles to profl. jours. Mem. Ill. Nature Preserves Com., 1963-68, Northeastern Ill. Planning Commn., 1974-77, Ill.-Ind. Bi-State Commn., 1974-77; bd. dirs. Cook County Legal Assistance Found., 1978-79; mem. Ill. div. ACLU, 1965-68, 77-79, v.p., 1977-78. With AUS, 1958-60. Mem. Fed. Bar Assn. (chmn. Fed. grants com. 1991—), Ill. Bar Assn. (Lincoln award 1977), Washington Coun. Lawyers, Nat. Grants Mgmt. Assn. (bd. dirs. 1988-92). Home: 5343 43rd St NW Washington DC 20015-2007 Office: US Dept Commerce Rm 7001-H 14th St & Constitution Ave NW Washington DC 20230

LEVIN, FREDRICK, financial services company executive; b. Phila., July 31, 1944; s. Milton Joseph and Mae Lillian (Glickman) L.; m. Marlene Finkelstein, June 25, 1966 (div. April 1977); children: Scott Howard, Pamela Hope; m. Janice Ann Egnatz, Aug. 22, 1987. BS, U. Pa., 1967. Ins. and investment exec. Corp. Fin. Service, Phila., 1967—; dir. Life Underwriters Assn., Phila., 1970—; co-chmn. Equities Assn., Del., Pa., N.J., 1984—; v.p. legislation com. lobby, Pa., 1985-87. Contbr. articles to mags. Treas. Pa. Kidney Found., 1979-81; com. leader Phila. polit. caucus, 1980-81; v.p. Phila. Boosters, 1981-82, 86-87; chancellor pres.'s council, Phila., 1984-86; fund raiser Fed. Jewish Agys., 1983; co-chairperson Temple Emmanuel Gala 40th Avnniversity, 1990. Served with U.S. Army, 1964-70. Named Man of Yr. Rising Stars, 1984, Phoenix Mutual Life Ins. Co. Hall of Fame, 1960's Man of Decade N.E. High Sch. Centennial. Mem. Phila. C. of C. (recipient Young Leaders award 1985, v.p. 1986-87), Variety Club (exec. v.p. 1988-89, pres. 1989-90, internat. amb. 1988—, internat. v.p. 1989—, membership com. chair 1990, co-chair audit and ethics com.1991—, co-chmn. internat. telethon com. 1991, lifeline com. 1990, mem. internat. lifeline com. honoring former Prime Minister Margaret Thatcher 1991), Phila. Roast Com., Million Dollar Round Table (life, Hall of Fame 1991). Office: The Bellevue 4th Fl Broad at Walnut St Philadelphia PA 19102

LEVIN, GERALD MANUEL, publishing company executive; b. Phila., May 6, 1939; s. David and Pauline (Schantzer) L.; m. Carol S. Needleman, Aug. 30, 1959 (div. Aug. 1970); children: Laura, Leon, Jonathan; m. Barbara J. Riley, Oct. 11, 1970; children: Michael, Anna. BA, Haverford Coll., 1960; LLB, U. Pa., 1963; LLD (hon.), Tex. Coll., 1985. Assoc. Simpson, Thacher & Bartlett, N.Y.C., 1963-67; gen. mgr., chief operating officer Devel. and Resources Corp., N.Y.C., 1967-71; rep. Internat. Basic Economy Corp., Tehran, Iran, 1971-72; v.p. programming Home Box Office, N.Y.C., 1972-73, pres., chief exec. officer, 1973-76, chmn., chief exec. officer, 1976-79; group v.p. video Time, Inc., N.Y.C., 1979-84, exec. v.p., 1984-88, vice chmn., dir., 1988-90; vice chmn., dir. Time Warner Inc., N.Y.C., 1990—, chief oper. officer, 1991-92, pres., co-chief exec. officer, 1992—; bd. dirs. Whittle Communications Partnership, N.Y.C. Trustee Hampshire Coll., 1983—, Haverford Coll., 1983—, chmn. bd. dirs., 1990—; bd. dirs., treas. N.Y.

Philharm., 1989. Recipient Nat. Disting. Achievement award Am. Jewish Com., 1984. Mem. Nat. Coun. for Families and TV (sec.-treas. 1985), Internat. Radio and TV Soc. (1st v.p. 1991), Phi Beta Kappa. Office: Time Warner Inc 75 Rockefeller Pla New York NY 10019

LEVIN, JOAN ELLEN, social worker; b. Newark, N.J., July 20, 1947; d. Belle (Brody) Yeselson; m. William F. Adler, June 22, 1969 (div.); children: Joshua, Deborah; m. Stanley Levin, Robb, David. BS, Emerson Coll., 1969; MA, Hunter Coll., 1972; MEd, Am. U.; MSW, Cath. U. Lic. clin. social worker. Speech pathologist Yonkers (N.Y.) Pub. Schs., 1969-72, Christ Ch. Child Ctr., Bethesda, Md., 1972-74, 78-79; guidance counselor Mont. County Pub. Schs., Rockville, Md., 1979—; part-time instr. grad. counseling dept. Trinity Coll., Washington. Talk show hostWomens Issues Cable TV Show, Montgomery Community TV, 1987-91, MCPS Cable-Tips for Raising Kids, 1991—. Mem. AACD, NASW, AASW. Office: 4610 W Frankfort Dr Rockville MD 20853

LEVIN, LOIS ANN, psychologist; b. Boston, Dec. 1, 1941; d. Sidney and Pearl (Koufman) L. BA, Brandeis U., Waltham, Mass., 1964; EdM, Harvard U., 1965; MA, Boston U., 1966, PhD, 1973. Lic. psychologist, Mass.; diplomate Am. Bd. Profl. Psychology. Dir. psychoedn. Boston U. Med. Ctr., Dept. Child psychiatry, 1972-73, staff psychologist, 1973-76; rsch. psychologist Boston U. Sch. Medicine, 1974-76; chief psychologist Westborough State Hosp./Cambridge-Somerville unit, 1976-80; dir. inpatient psychology The Cambridge Hosp., 1976-81, rsch. psychologist, 1977-82; cons. in psychology Newton-Wellesley Hosp., Newton Lower Falls, Mass., 1983—; asst. attending psychologist McLean Hosp., Belmont, Mass., 1984—; pvt. practice psychology Waban, Mass., 1977—. Editor: Facilitating Psychotherapy: Selected Papers of Sidney Levin, M.D., 1987. Corporator, All Newton Music Sch., 1987—. Mem. Am. Psychol. Assn., Mass. Psychol. Assn., Mass. Soc. Clin. Psychologists (pres. 1991-92). Home and Office: 497 Chestnut St Newton MA 02168-1220

LEVIN, M. PENNY, clinical psychologist, consultant; b. Phila., June 7, 1956; d. Bernard Rice and Goldie (Kauffman) Levin; m. Philip David Rosenberg, July 3, 1978; children: Sarina Claire, Brenna Michelle. BA, Northwestern U., 1977; MA, Temple U., 1983, PhD, 1987. Lic. psychologist. Counselor Jewish Employment and Vocat. Svcs., Phila., 1977-78; resettlement counselor Jewish Family Svc., Phila., 1978-80; psychology intern Friends Hosp., Phila., 1983-84; staff psychologist St. Gabriel's Hall, Audobon, Pa., 1984-85, Achievement and Guidance Ctrs. in Am., Bensalem, Pa., 1985-87; clin. dir. Phila. Inst. for Rational-Emotive Therapy, Phila., 1988-90; pvt. practice Phila., 1986—; counselor Childbirth Edn. Assn., Phila., 1987-89; psychologist Human Svcs. Ctr., Phila., 1990. Temple U. fellow, 1980-81, 82-83. Mem. Am. Psychol. Assn., Pa. Psychol. Assn. (chmn. internal communications 1989-90), Phila. Soc. Clin. Psychologists, Delaware Valley Group Psychotherapy Soc. Jewish. Home: 14 Pear Tree Ln Lafayette Hill PA 19444-2302 Office: Benjamin Franklin Bldg 9th and Chestnut Sts Ste 311 Philadelphia PA 19107

LEVIN, MARCIA ALISON, graphic designer; b. Boston. BA, Brandeis U., 1988. Publs. asst., now editor Mass. Assn. Sch. Coms., Boston, 1989—. Editor-in-chief The Lighter Side of Brandeis University, 1988. Mem. Burlington Players Inc. Home: 31 Dix Road Ext Woburn MA 01801-6104

LEVIN, MICHAEL JOSEPH, lawyer; b. Detroit, Feb. 1, 1943; s. Bayre and Lydia Ruth (Kahn) L.; m. Adah Hanson, Aug. 3, 1974; children: Andrew, Stephen. BA, Johns Hopkins U., 1964; JD, U. Mich., 1967. Bar: Mich. 1968, N.Y. 1973. Assoc. Milbank, Tweed, Hadley & McCloy, N.Y.C., 1971-86; ptnr. Boyle, Vogeler & Haimes, N.Y.C., 1986—. Served to lt. col. USMCR, 1963-90. Mem. Mich. Bar Assn., Assn. of Bar of City of N.Y. Office: Boyle Vogeler & Haimes 1270 Ave Of The Americas New York NY 10020-1700

LEVIN, NORMAN CYRIL, real estate developer; b. Cape Town, Republic of South Africa, Oct. 30, 1949; came to U.S., 1977; s. Morris and Rosette (Khodara) L. B. Bus. Sci. with honors, U. Cape Town, Rep. of South Africa, 1972, M Urban Regional Planning, 1977. Pres. A.I.E.S.E.C. SA, Johannesburg, 1973; mgr. real estate Foschini Ltd., Cape Town, 1974-75; project mgr. Robert P. Gersin Assocs., N.Y.C., 1978-80; project dir. The Gruzen Partnership, N.Y.C., 1980-82; v.p. Sideco of N. Am., Macri Group, N.Y.C., 1982-84; exec. v.p. The Trump Orgn., N.Y.C., 1985—. Mem. N.Y.C. Parks Coun., 1985—. Mem. West Side C. of C. (bd. dirs. 1985—), City Club N.Y., Humanitas. Jewish. Office: The Trump Orgn 725 5th Ave New York NY 10022-2519

LEVIN, ROBERT EDMOND, electrical engineer, educator; b. Orange, Calif., Oct. 11, 1931; s. Morris and Lydia Ruth (Simpson) L.; m. Karen Noel Andree, July 19, 1958; children: Kristen Roberta, Erik Noel. BS, Stanford U., 1953, MS, 1954, Engr., 1957, PhD, 1960. Registered profl. engr., Calif., Mass. Asst. prof. San Jose (Calif.) State U., 1958-62, assoc. prof., 1962-63; sr. scientist GTE Products Corp., Salem, Mass., 1963—; cons., san Jose, 1959-63; instr. continuing edn. Northeastern U., Boston, 1969-82; adj. prof. elec. engring. U. N.H., Durham, 1982—; adj. assoc. prof. architecture Rensselaer Poly. Inst., Troy, N.Y., 1990—. Co-author, co-editor books, handbooks and articles in field; patentee in field. Fellow NSF, 1954-56, GE Co., 1956-58. Mem. Internat. Brotherhood Magicians, Soc. Am. Magicians, Phi Beta Kappa, Sigma Xi, Tau Beta Pi. Office: GTE Products Corp 60 Boston St Salem MA 01970-2194

LEVIN, RONA F., nursing administrator and educator; b. Bronx, N.Y., Mar. 5, 1945; d. Martin and Ruth Eva (Grossman) Kaufman; m. LeRoy Levin, June 8, 1969; children: Sherry, Robert. AAS, Queens Coll., 1965; BS, Adelphi U., 1968, MS, 1973; PhD, NYU, 1981. Asst. dir. nursing rsch. L.I. Jewish Med. Ctr., New Hyde Park, N.Y.; dir. Master's Program Adelphi U., Garden City, N.Y.; dir. div. health scis. Felician Coll., Lodi, N.J.; cons. in field. Contbr. articles to profl. jours. USPHS trainee, 1967-68, 69-71; grantee Sigma Theta Tau, 1982, 84, Midwest Nursing Diagnosis Assn., 1987. Mem. ANA, Nat. League for Nursing, N.J. Nurses Assn., N.Y. State Nurses Assn. (coun. nurse rschrs.), Mid-Atlantic Regional Nursing Diagnosis Assn. (v.p.), N.Am. Nursing Diagnosis Assn., Internat. Pain Soc., Sigma Theta Tau (treas. chpt. 1983-84, chmn. rsch. com. 1984-86).

LEVINE, ALAN HILLEL, investment company executive, petroleum economist; b. Jersey City, Mar. 3, 1937; s. Robert Harry and Bertha (Allen) L.; m. Priscilla Reinhart, Sept. 24, 1961; children: Victoria Anne, Jason Harris. BS, Rutgers U., 1958; MS, Columbia U., 1959. Mgr. of econs. Johnson & Johnson, New Brunswick, N.J., 1964-69; sr. analyst W.J. Levy Cons. Corp., N.Y.C., 1969-76, Petroleum Industry Rsch. Found., N.Y.C., 1976; v.p. Energy Decisions, Inc., Washington, 1976-79; sr. analyst Resource Planning Assoc., Washington, 1979-81; exec. v.p. Energy Futures Group, Bethesda, Md., 1981-83; fin. cons. Merrill Lynch, Washington, 1983-86; 2d v.p. Shearson Lehman Bros., Bethesda, 1986—. Contbr. articles to profl. jours. Chmn. Traffic & Transp. Commn., Rockville, Md., 1991-92. Lt. USNR, 1959-64. Mem. Internat. Assn. Energy Econs. (founder 1978, chpt. pres. 1980). Home: 9 Echo Ct Rockville MD 20854 Office: Shearson Lehman Bros 7315 Wisconsin Ave Bethesda MD 20814

LEVINE, BENJAMIN, lawyer; b. New Haven, May 22, 1931; s. George and Frances (Levovsky) L.; m. Arleen Ella Rosenblatt, Jan. 14, 1962; children: Joshua, Sarah. BA, U. Conn., 1953; JD, Rutgers U., 1963. Bar: N.Mex. 1964, N.Y. 1965, N.J. 1967, U.S. Sup. Ct. 1980; cert. civil trial atty., 1986. Law clk. N.Mex. Sup. Ct., 1963-64; spl. asst. N.J. Commr. Conservation and Econ. Devel., 1965-67; dep. atty. gen. State of N.J., 1967-70; pvt. practice, Newark and N.Y.C., 1970—; adj. prof. law Ramapo Coll., Mahwah, N.J., 1978-80; arbitrator U.S. Dist. Ct. N.J., 1989. Author Medical Malpractice, (with D. Moore) Zoning Guide for Local Officials; contbr. articles to profl. jours. Pres. Environ. Action Inst. N.J., 1977-80; chmn. North Plainfield (N.J.) Environ. Commn., 1974-76; trustee South Branch Watershed Assn., 1976-80. Served to lt. (j.g.) U.S. Navy, 1956-60. Mem. Am. Arbitration Assn. (arbitrator 1973—, mem. policy com. ins.), Assn. Trial Lawyers Am., Trial Attys. N.J., N.J. Bar Assn., N.Y. State Trial Lawyers Assn., N.Y. County Lawyers Assn. (com. on civil cts. 1982—), B'nai B'rith, Anti-Defamation League, Jewish Club.

LEVINE, DAVID M., newspaper editor; b. Newark, Oct. 2, 1949; s. Seymour I. and Fay D. Levine; m. Arleen Weintraub, Apr. 5, 1987. BA, Montclair State Coll., 1971; MS, Columbia U., 1973. Reporter, state house corr. Herald-News, Passaic, N.J., 1971-74; editorial writer Phila. Bull., 1974-79; night mng. editor Trenton (N.J.) Times, 1979-83; exec. fin. editor Washington Times, 1983-85; exec. editor Lebhar-Friedman Co., N.Y.C., 1985-86; editor Daily Jour., Elizabeth, N.J., 1986-87, Hudson Dispatch, Union City, N.J., 1987-91, The Daily Jour., Elizabeth, N.J., 1990-92; editor, v.p. The Herald-News, Passaic, N.J., 1992—; adj. instr. English dept. Rutgers U., Newark, 1987—; prin. Jour. Publs., Trenton, 1971—. Author: Editorial Style, 1974. Office: The Herald-News 988 Main Ave Passaic NJ 07055

LEVINE, EUGENE, health services researcher; b. N.Y.C., Jan. 11, 1925; s. Maurice and Rebecca (Spector) L.; m. Barbara Jean Stevenson, July 23, 1971; m. Julia Raisner, June 26, 1948 (div. July 1971); children: Gary Mitchell, Jeffrey Howard, Douglas Edward. BBA, CCNY, 1948; MPA, NYU, 1950; PhD, Am. U., 1960. Statistician N.Y.C. Health Dept., 1948-50; chief rsch. and statistics div. nursing USPHS, Washington, 1950-77, dep. dir. div. health profl. svc. analysis, 1977-80; cons. Levine Assocs., Kensington, Md., 1982—; cons. Nat. League Nursing, N.Y.C., 1984-88, Indian Health Svc., Washington, 1986—, NAS, Washington, 1981-84; adj. prof. Georgetown U., Washington, 1982-91. Author: Better Patient Care through Nursing Research, 1984 (award ANA 1988), Needs for Environmental Health Personnel, 1988, Nursing in North America and United Kingdom, 1992; editor Proc. Nursing Productivity Conf., 1987; also articles. With USAAF, 1942-45, ETO. Recipient Outstanding Svc. award D.C. League Nursing, 1971. Mem. APHA, Am. Statis. Assn., Nat. League Nursing. Democrat. Jewish. Home: 8135 Inverness Ridge Rd Potomac MD 20854-4014 Office: 5020 Nicholson Ct Kensington MD 20895-1007

LEVINE, FAITH LAUREL, educational administrator; b. Richmond Hill, N.Y., May 10, 1939; d. Henry and Pearl (Freedman) Brofman; children: Debra Sue Goldberg, Heidi Beth Levine. BA, Queens Coll., 1960; MS in Early Childhood Edn., Bklyn. Coll., 1965; postgrad., St. John's U., NYU, Pace U. Lic. elem. sch. tchr., prin., dir. early childhood edn., N.Y. Head tchr. Headstart, Bklyn., 1965; tchr. English as second lang. Hato Rey, P.R., 1966-67; tchr. early childhood N.Y.C. Bd. Edn., Bklyn., 1960-79, coord. early childhood, 1979—, coord. dist. 23 mentor tchr. internship program, 1989-91, asst. to the dir. spl. projects, 1991—; dir. nursery unit Jewish Community House, Bkyn., 1985-86; tchr. ESL Sta. WIPR-TV, P.R., 1966-67. Contbr. to manuals. Recording sec. Flatlands Civic Assn. N.Y. State grantee, 1978; recipient N.Y.C. Sch.-Community Human Rels. prize, 1978. Mem. N.Y. Pub. Sch. Early Childhood Assn. (v.p. 1984—), United Fedn. Tchrs. (chpt. leader 1967-69), Nat. Assn. Adminstrv. Women Edn., Brownsville Boys Alumni Assn. (chpt. pres. 1975-79), Hadassah Club (program chmn. 1968-70), Kings Square Dance Club (recording sec. 1987-88), Queens Square Dance Club (corresp. sec. 1991—). Democrat. Jewish. Home: 2775 E 16th St Apt 2F Brooklyn NY 11235-4017 Office: Dist Office 23 2240 Dean St DO 23 Brooklyn NY 11233

LEVINE, GEOFFREY, pharmacist; b. Sept. 2, 1942. BS in Pharmacy, Temple U., 1965, MS in Radiol. Health, 1967; PhD, Northwestern U., 1978. Bd. cert. in nuclear pharmacy; cert. pharmacist, Pa. Pharmacist Profl. Practice-Community Peoples Drug Stores, 1965-67; radioisotope chemist Abbott Labs., Chgo., 1966-68; dir. radiopharmaceutical svcs. U. Pitts. Health Ctr., 1972—; asst. prof. radiology U. Pitts. Sch. Medicine, 1972-83, assoc. prof., 1983—; nuclear pharmacist Presbyn.-Univ. Hosp., 1972—; dir. nuclear pharmacy Cen. Imaging Svcs., Inc., 1985—; assoc. mem. Pitts. Cancer Inst., 1987—; clin. prof. Allegheny County Community Coll., 1984—; adj. faculty U. Pitts. Sch. Pharmacy, Dept. Pharm., 1981. Contbr. numerous articles to profl. jours. and publs. Recipient AEC-AUA-ANL fellowship, USPHS traineeship, Teaching assistantship, W.P. Murphy fellowship; recipient Plaque, Am. Pharm. Assn., 1978. Mem. Am. Pharm. Assn., Health Physics Soc., Soc. Nuclear Medicine, AAAS, Am. Soc. Hosp. Pharmacists, Pa. Coll. Nuclear Medicine and Nuclear Physicians, Sigma Xi, Rho Chi Pharm. Honor Soc. Home: 6360 Monitor St Pittsburgh PA 15217-2720 Office: Presbyn U Hosp Dept Radiology Div Nuclear Medicine Pittsburgh PA 15213

LEVINE, GERALD RICHARD, investment banker, estate planning specialist, philanthropy specialist; b. N.Y.C., Nov. 7, 1936; s. Irving Arthur and Lillian (Kronstadt) L.; m. Linda L. Paige, May 17, 1991.; children from previous marriage: Jodi Levine Avergun, Debby Levine Rifkin, James H. AB, Brown U., 1958; MBA, GM Inst. Tech., Flint, Mich., 1960; postgrad., Pohs Inst. Ins., N.Y.C., 1978, Securities Tng. Inst., N.Y.C., 1981. Pres. Town and Country Motors (Div. KLZ Corp.), Woodmere, N.Y., 1959-78, TAR Brokerage Corp., 1977—; nat. mktg. dir. Performance Dynamics Inc., N.Y.C., 1978-81; v.p. Oppenheimer & Co., N.Y.C., 1981-84; sr. v.p. Twenty-First Securities Corp., N.Y.C., 1984-89; assoc. nat. dir. corp. and instl. investment programs Devel. Corp. for Israel, N.Y.C., 1989-91; assoc. dir. estate planning div. Prudential Securities/Ins., N.Y.C., 1991-92; dir. corp. philanthropy Anti-Defamation League, N.Y.C., 1992—. Pres. 5 Towns div. Salvation Army, Woodmere, 1968-85; mem. exec. com., adv. bd. commerce and industry div. State of Israel Bonds, N.Y.C., 1988-89; mem. exec. com. Brown Ann. Fund, Providence, 1987-89, 92—, Brown Corp. Com. on Devel., 1987-89, 92—, major gifts chmn. 30th Reunion, 1988, N.Y.C. Brown Reg. Devel. Com., 1988—; advisor Brown U. Sports Found., 1987—; bd. dirs. Brown U. Football Assn., Providence, 1988—; dir. Assoc. Alumni Brown U. (Disting. Alumni Svc. award 1988, Head Marshall Alumni 1983-84, 88-89, head class agt. 1978-88, treas. class of 1958, 1988—). Mem. Brown U. Club N.Y. (pres. 1990-92, v.p., exec. dir. 1989-90), K.P. (mem. at large), Princeton Club, Nat. Arts Club. Republican. Jewish. Office: Anti-Defamation League 823 United Nations Plz New York NY 10017

LEVINE, HARVEY ROBERT, biology educator, parasitologist, entomologist; b. N.Y.C., Sept. 15, 1931; s. William and Molly (Heinberg) L.; m. Rosalyn Freides, Oct. 7, 1956; children: Nancy Levine Fichman, David. BS, CCNY, 1953; MS, U. Mass., 1955, PhD, 1958; postgrad. Ind. U., 1955-56. Cert. in med. entomology Am. Registry Profl. Entomologists. Faculty Bemidji State U., Minn., 1958—, prof., 1965-68; prof. biology Quinnipiac Coll., Hamden, Conn., 1968—, chmn. dept. biol. sci., 1968-76, dir. Title II Math. Sci. Computer Inst., 1991—. Contbr. articles to profl. jours. Trustee Quinnipiac Coll., Hamden, 1984—. Grantee NSF, HEW. Mem. NRTA, Soc. Vector Ecologists, Conn. Sci. Tchrs. Assn., Conn. Sci. Suprs. Assn., Entomol. Soc. Am., Am. Fedn. Tchrs., Am. Assn. for Lab. Animal Sci., Am. Mus. Natural History, Sigma Xi, Phi Kappa Phi, Beta Beta Beta, Alpha Phi Sigma. Jewish. Avocations: philately; gardening. Home: 1141 King Rd Cheshire CT 06410-3410 Office: Dept Biol Sci Quinnipiac Coll Mount Carmel Ave Hamden CT 06518

LEVINE, IRA NOEL, chemistry educator; b. Bklyn., Sept. 8, 1937; s. Louis and Fannie (Davidoff) L. BS in Chemistry, Carnegie Inst. Tech., 1958; AM in Chemistry, Harvard U., 1959, PhD in Chemistry, 1963. Instr. Bklyn. (N.Y.) Coll., 1964-66, asst. prof., 1967-70, assoc. prof., 1971-77, prof. of chemistry, 1978—. Author: Molecular Spectroscopy, 1975, Physical Chemistry, 3d edit., 1988, Quantum Chemistry, 4th edit., 1991. Mem. Am. Chem. Soc. (Petroleum Rsch. Fund grant 1965-67), Am. Phys. Soc. Office: Brooklyn Coll Chemistry Dept Brooklyn NY 11210

LEVINE, JANICE R., clinical psychologist; b. Cleve., Mar. 4, 1954; d. Bennett and Lenore (Tracht) L.; m. Brian Richard Igoe, Aug. 31, 1980; children: Brennan Joseph, Sarah Ann. BA cum laude, Yale U., 1976; MA, Harvard U., 1979, PhD, 1983. Lic. psychologist, Mass. Sr. ptnr., cons. Cambridge (Mass.) Consortium; staff psychologist Ayer (Mass.) Clinic; lectr. psychology Harvard U., Chambridge; pvt. practice clin. psychologist Lexington, Mass.; lectr., pub. speaker, workshop leader, cons. in field. Founder, dir. Third Thursday Parent Edn. Series, Lexington. Margaret Yardley fellow, 1980, Devel. Trainee fellow NIH, 1978-79. Mem. APA, MPA, Soc. for Family Therapy and Rsch. Office: 76 Bedford St Ste 19 Lexington MA 02173

LEVINE, JEROME FREDRIC, internist; b. N.Y.C., Apr. 10, 1949; s. Bernard and Anna (Bluman) L.; m. Helaine C. Damask, July 18, 1951; children: Jason, Lauren. BSEE summa cum laude, Union Coll., 1971; MD, NYU, 1976. Diplomate Am. Bd. Internal Medicine, Nat. Bd. Med. Examiners (subspeciality of infectious diseases). Intern, then residen in medicine Manhattan VA Hosp.-NYU Med. Ctr., 1976-79; chief med. resident Manhattan VA Hosp., 1979-80, fellow in infectious diseases, 1980-82; clin. asst. infectious disease sect. Hackensack (N.J.) Med. Ctr., 1982-83, asst. attending, then attending physician infectious disease, 1983—, dir. fellowship program infectious disease sect., 1984—, asst. prog. dir. internal medicine, 1986—; clin. asst. prof. medicine, U. Medicine & Dentistry of N.J./N.J. Med. Sch., 1983—; cons. infectious diseases, Valley Hosp., Ridgewood, N.J., 1982—, Good Samaritan Hosp., Suffern, N.Y., 1983-84. Contbr. articles to profl. jours. Fellow ACP; mem. ASIM, AMA, Infectious Diseases Soc. Am., Am. Soc. Microbiology, Assn. for Practitioners in Infection Control. Office: Hackensack Med Ctr 123 Johnson Ave Hackensack NJ 07601-4827

LEVINE, JILL, psychological associate; b. Shamokin, Pa., Aug. 20, 1958; d. Marshall Edwin and Elizabeth Mae (Carter) Hornberger; m. Michael Mark Levine, May 24, 1981; children: Alexandra Bette, Mara Suzanne. BA, Bloomsburg State Coll., 1980; MA, Towson State U., 1982. Domestic violence counseling coord. Women's Ctr., Bloomsburg, Pa., 1983-85, sexual assault counselor, 1983; counselor Ednl. Opportunity Ctr., Bloomsburg, 1986-88; psychol. assoc. Shamokin (Pa.) State Gen. Hosp., 1991—, Nittany Rehab. Ctr., Middleburg, Pa., 1991—; auditor Willowbrook Spl. Master's Office, Queens, N.Y., 1990. Mem. AACD, Psi Chi. Jewish. Home: RR 3 Box 374 Catawissa PA 17820-9582 Office: Shamokin State Gen Hosp Shamokin St Shamokin PA 17872-5455

LEVINE, JULIE GORCHOW, career planning administrator, consultant; b. Mpls., June 24, 1956; d. Neil N. and Roslyn Diane (Wein) Gorchow; m. Robert G. Levine, Nov. 28, 1981; 1 child, Stephanie Ann. BA in Anthropology, Northwestern U., 1978; MEd, U. Pa., 1986. Group sales mgr., asst. buyer Hecht's Dept. Store, Washington, 1978-81; exec. recruiter Sweeney Cons., Denver, 1982; asst. store mgr. Casual Corner, Denver, 1983-84; assoc. dir. career devel. and placement U. Pa. Wharton Grad. Sch., Phila., 1984-90; pvt. practice Phila., 1991—; presenter in field. Leadership trainer Fedn. Jewish Agys., Phila., 1988-90; bd. observer Hillel Greater Phila., 1990. Mem. Pa. Counseling Assn., Nat. Career Devel. Assn., Nat. Assn. Women Educators , Counselors, Am. Coll. Personnel Assn., Am. Assn. for Counseling and Devel. Home and Office: 758 Cornerstone Ln Bryn Mawr PA 19010

LEVINE, LAURENCE E., investment banker; b. N.Y.C., Dec. 17, 1941; s. Martin and Beulah (Brandt) L.; m. Laura Lynn Vitale; 1 child, Blair Brandt. BA (Francis Biddle prize 1961), Princeton U., 1964; LLB, Stanford U., 1967. V.p., voting shareholder Drexel Burnham Lambert, N.Y.C., 1968-71; corp. planning officer Office of Chmn., Ogden Corp., N.Y.C., 1971-73; pres. Investment Research Assos., West Chester, Pa., Fla., 1973-80; sr. v.p., dir. investment banking Kramer Capital Cons., Inc., N.Y.C., 1981; exec. v.p. Henry Ansbacher Inc., N.Y. and London, 1982-84; sr. v.p. Rothschild Inc., N.Y., 1984-86; exec. v.p. and dir. corp. fin. Smith New Ct. Inc., N.Y. and London, 1986-90; chmn. Blair Corp., N.Y. and London, 1990—, dir. First Internat. Fin. Group, Hamburg, London and Bermuda, Signature Fin. Group, Boston, Landmark Funds Broker-Dealer Svcs., Inc., N.Y.C.; mem. bd. visitors Stanford U. Law Sch., 1968-71, exec. com., 1970. Dir. Musica Sacra, N.Y., 1981-86, Concert Artists Guild, N.Y., 1989—, Fla. Reperatory Theatre, 1989—. With USMCR, 1961-65. Mem. N.Y. State Bar Assn., Pa. Bar Assn., City Athletic Club, Harmonie Club, St. James Club (London), Princeton Club (N.Y.), Govs. Club (Palm Beach), Old Oaks Country Club (Purchase, N.Y.), Kennett Sq. (Pa.) Golf and Country Club, Palm Beach (Fla.) Country Club. Office: Blair Corp 437 Madison Ave 39th Fl New York NY 10022

LEVINE, LES, artist; b. Dublin, Ireland, Oct. 6, 1935; came to U.S., 1964; s. Charles and Muriel (MacMahon) L.; m. Catherine Kazuko Kanai, Aug. 26, 1973; 1 son, Sean. Student, Central Sch. Arts and Crafts, London, 1953-56. Pres. Mus. of Mott Art, Inc., N.Y.C., 1971—; assoc. prof. art NYU, N.Y.C., 1971-73; assoc. editor Arts Mag., N.Y.C., 1973-74; video instr., prof. William Paterson Coll., Wayne, N.J., 1974-76; vis. artist U. Ill., Chgo., 1975-76, Columbia U., N.Y.C., 1978; assoc. prof. art William Paterson Coll., Wayne, N.J., 1974-76, U. Ill., Chgo., 1975-76, Columbia U., N.Y.C. Artist-in-residence, Aspen Inst. Humanistic Studies, 1967-69, asst. prof. art, N.Y. U., 1971-73, N.S. Coll. Art and Design, 1972-73; assoc. editor Arts Mag, N.Y.C., 1973-74; organizer Jimmy Carter Collection, Ga. Mus. Art, Athens, 1977. Author: Culture Hero, 1969, Using the Camera as a Club, 1976, Media the Bio-Tech Rehearsal for Leaving the Body, 1979; contbg. author: New Artists Video, A Critical Anthology, 1978, The Art of Performance, 1984; One-man shows include Lower Manhattan Cultural Coun. and Pub. Art Fund, Mass Media Subway Campaign, N.Y.C., 1981, 90, Feldman Fine Arts Gallery, N.Y.C., 1981, 83, Elizabeth G Fine Art, Ossining, N.Y., 1982, 84, Internat. Cultureel Centrum, Antwerp, Belgium, 1978, Inst. Contemporary Art, London, 1985, Carpenter and Hochman Gallery, N.Y.C., 1986, Art Frankfurt, Fed. Republic of Germany, 1989, Everson Mus. Art, Syracuse, N.Y., 1990, MAI 36 Galeries, Luzern, Switzerland, 1988, 90, Muhka, Antwerp, 1992, Albright-Knox Gallery, Buffalo, 1977, Wadsworth Atheneum, Hartford, Conn., 1976, Adler Castillo, Caracas, Venezuela, 1975, Galeria Schema, Florence, Italy, 1974, Isaacs Gallery, Toronto, Ont., 1973, 83, Finch Coll. Mus. Art, N.Y.C., 1972, group shows include, Canadian Sculpture Biennale, 1967 (1st prize sculpture), Tokyo Biennale, 1974, Sao Paulo Biennale, 1975, Sydney (Australia) Biennale, 1976, Internat. Video Festival, San Francisco, 1983, Mus. Modern Art, N.Y.C., 1983, Documenta 6 Kassel, Fed. Republic of Germany, 1977, Documenta 8, 1987. U.S. rep. Documenta, Kassel, W. Ger., 1977; pres. Mus. Mott Art, Inc., 1970—. Fellow Nat. Endowment for Arts 1974, 80. Address: 20 E 20 St New York NY 10003-1316

LEVINE, MARILYN MARKOVICH, lawyer, arbitrator; b. Bklyn., Aug. 9, 1930; d. Harry P. and Fannie L. (Hymowitz) Markovich; m. Louis L. Levine, June 24, 1950; children: Steven R., Ronald J., Linda J. Morgenstern. BS summa cum laude, Columbia U., 1950; MA, Adelphi U., 1967; JD, Hofstra U., 1977. Bar: N.Y. 1978, U.S. Dist. Ct. (so. and ea. dists.) N.Y. 1978, D.C. 1979, U.S. Supreme Ct. 1982. Sole practice Valley Stream, N.Y., 1978—; contract arbitrator bldg. svc. industry, N.Y.C., 1982—; panel arbitrator retail food industry, N.Y.C., 1980—; arbitrator N.Y. dist. cts., Nassau County, 1981—; mem. Nat. Acad. Arbitrators, 1992—. Panel arbitrator Suffolk County Pub. Employee Relations Bd., 1979—, Nassau County Pub. Employee Relations Bd., 1980—, Nat. Mediation Bd., 1986—, N.Y. State Pub. Employee Relations Bd., 1984—; mem. adv. council Ctr. Labor and Industrial Relations, N.Y. Inst. Tech., N.Y., 1985—; counsel Nassau Civic Club, 1978—. Mem. ABA, N.Y. State Bar Assn., D.C. Bar Assn., Nassau County Bar Assn., N.J. Bd. Mediation (panel arbitrator), Am. Arbitration Assn. (arbitrator 1979—), Fed. Mediation Bd. (arbitrator 1980—). Home and Office: 1057 Linden St Valley Stream NY 11580-2135

LEVINE, MARVIN, business educator; b. Bklyn., June 26, 1924; s. Sol and Sadie (Trager) L.; m. Eva Silver, Jan. 17, 1976; children: Burton Charles, Gail Susan. BS, NYU, 1945, MBA, 1946. Instr. NYU, N.Y.C., 1950-55, 58-67; adj. assoc. prof. NYU, 1967-82; instr. Bklyn. Coll., 1955-58; asst. prof. Orange County Community Coll., Middletown, N.Y., 1982-86, coord. weekend coll., 1985-88, assoc. prof., 1986—; cons. U.S. Agy. Internat. Develop., Washington, 1964, U.S. Dept. Labor, Washington, 1966-67, U.S. Joint Econ. Com., Washington, 1967, N.J. Bd. Pub. Utility Commn., Newark, 1975. Contbr. articles to profl. jours. Chmn. Coun. New Rochelle (N.Y.) Neighborhood Civic, 1965-67; mem. planning bd. New Rochelle, 1968-83. Recipient citation United Way of New Rochelle, 1965, commendation New Rochelle City Coun., 1966. Mem. AAUP, Am. Mktg. Assn., Am. Econ. Assn. Jewish. Home: 172 Taymil Rd New Rochelle NY 10804-2211

LEVINE, MELVIN CHARLES, lawyer; b. Bklyn., Nov. 12, 1930; s. Barnet and Jennie (Iser) L. BCS, NYU, 1952; LLB, Harvard U., 1955. Bar: N.Y. 1956, U.S. Supreme Ct. 1964. Assoc., Kriger & Haber, Bklyn., 1956-58, Black, Varian & Simons, N.Y.C., 1959; sole practice, N.Y.C., 1959—; devel. multiple dwelling housing. Mem. N.Y. County Lawyers Assn. (civil ct. com., housing ct. com., uniform housing ct. rules com., liaison to Assn. Bar City of N.Y. on selection of housing and civil ct. judges, task force on tort reform). Democrat. Jewish. Home: 146 Waverly Pl New York NY 10014-3848 Office: 271 Madison Ave Ste 1404 New York NY 10016-1001

LEVINE, OSCAR, lubricant coatings company executive; b. Bklyn., Feb. 6, 1923; s. Benjamin and Celia (Richman) L.; m. Betty Lee Palais, Sept. 12, 1948; children: Douglas Stewart, Jan Louise. BS, CCNY, 1943; AM, Columbia U., 1948; PhD, Georgetown U., 1958. Rsch. scientist Lewis Flight Propulsion Lab., Cleve., 1948-52, U.S. Naval Rsch. Lab., Washington, 1952-58, Gillette Co., Boston, 1958-85; owner RO-59, Inc., Pembroke, Mass., 1985—. Contbr. rsch. papers to profl. publs. With U.S. Army, 1944-46. Home: 1 Cabot Pl Stoughton MA 02359-1510

LEVINE, PAUL HOWARD, physician; b. N.Y.C., Sept. 11, 1937; s. Joseph L. and Esther (Katzman) L.; m. Miriam Gray, June 19, 1960; children: Jane, David, Daniel. BA, Cornell U., 1959; MD, U. Rochester, 1963. Intern Strong Meml. Hosp., Rochester, N.Y., 1963-64; resident U. Colo., Denver, 1966-68; cancer rsch. investigator Nat. Cancer Inst., NIH, Bethesda, Md., 1964—. Contbr. over 200 articles to profl. jours. Sr. surgeon USPHS, 1964—. Fellow Am. Coll. Physicians. Office: NCI/NIH EPN 434 Bethesda MD 20892

LEVINE, ROBERT JOHN, physician, educator; b. N.Y.C., Dec. 29, 1934; s. Benjamin Bernard and Ruth Florence (Schwartz) L.; m. Jeralea Fooshee Hesse, Nov. 28, 1987; children from previous marriage: John Graham, Elizabeth Hurt. Student, Duke U., 1951-54; M.D. with distinction, George Washington U., 1958. Med. house officer Peter Bent Brigham Hosp., Boston, 1958-59; asst. resident medicine Peter Bent Brigham Hosp., 1959-60; clin. assoc. Nat. Heart Inst., Bethesda, Md., 1960-62; investigator Nat. Heart Inst., 1963-64; chief med. resident VA Hosp., West Haven, Conn., 1962-63; attending physician VA Hosp., 1966—; mem. faculty Yale U. Depts. Medicine and Pharmacology, New Haven, Conn., 1964-73; chief sect. clin. pharmacology Yale U., 1966-74, prof. medicine, lectr. pharmacology, 1973—, dir. physician's assoc. program, 1973-75; mem. med. staff Yale-New Haven Med. Center, 1964-68, attending physician, 1968—; mem. Conn. Adv. Com. on Foods and Drugs, 1967-82, sec., 1969-71, chmn., 1971-73; mem. working group on mech. circulatory support Nat. Heart, Lung and Blood Inst., 1983-86; mem. adv. com. AIDS program U.S. Dept. Health Human Svcs., 1989—; cons. Nat. Commn. for Protection of Human Subjects of Biomed. and Behavioral Research, 1974-78; chmn. award com. Nellie Westerman prize for Research in Ethics, 1975-79; bd. dirs. Medicine in the Pub. Interest, Inc., 1976—, sec., 1983—; vice chmn. Commn. on Fed. Drug Approval Process, 1981-82. Author: Ethics and Regulation of Clinical Research, 1981, 2d edit., 1986; hon. adv. editorial bd. Biochem. Pharmacology, 1968-83; assoc. editor, 1969-74; editor: Clin. Research, 1971-76; editor: IRB: A Review of Human Subjects Research, 1978—; contbr. numerous articles to profl. jours. Mem. Conn. Humanities Council, 1983-89, chmn. 1988-89. Served with USPHS, 1960-64. Multiple Research grantee. Fellow ACP, Am. Coll. Cardiology, The Hastings Ctr.; mem. AAAS (coun. del. 1987-91), Am. Soc. Clin. Investigation, Am. Soc. Clin. Pharmacology and Therapeutics (dir. 1981-85), Am. Fedn. Clin. Rsch. (nat. coun. 1967-76, exec. com. 1971-76), Am. Soc. Pharmacology and Exptl. Therapeutics (exec. com. 1974-77), Am. Soc. Law and Medicine (bd. dirs. 1986—, pres.-elect 1988-89, pres. 1989-90), Soc. for Bioethics Consultation (bd. dirs. 1988—), Sigma Xi, Alpha Omega Alpha. Office: Yale U Sch Medicine 333 Cedar St New Haven CT 06510-3289

LEVINE, RONALD JAY, lawyer; b. Bklyn., June 23, 1953; s. Louis Leon and Marilyn Priscilla (Markovich) L.; m. Cindy Beth Israel, Nov. 18, 1979; children: Merisa, Alisha. BA summa cum laude, Princeton U., 1974; JD cum laude, Harvard U., 1977. Bar: N.Y. 1978, U.S. Dist. Ct. (so. and ea. dists.) N.Y. 1978, D.C. 1980, N.J. 1987, U.S. Supreme Ct. 1982, U.S. Ct. Appeals (2d cir.) 1983, N.J. 1987, U.S. Dist. Ct. N.J. 1987, U.S. Dist. Ct. (we. dist.) N.Y. 1991, U.S. Ct. Appeals (3d Cir.) 1991. Assoc. Phillips, Nizer, Benjamin, Krim & Ballon, N.Y.C., 1977-80, Debevoise & Plimpton, N.Y.C., 1980-84; assoc. Herrick, Feinstein, N.Y.C., 1984-85, ptnr., 1985—; gen. counsel Greater N.Y. Safety Council, N.Y.C., 1979-81; arbitrator Small Claims Ct. of Civil Ct. of City of N.Y., 1983-85. Mem. Site Plan Rev. Adv. Bd., West Windsor, N.J., 1986, planning bd., 1987. Mem. ABA (litigation sect.), N.Y. State Bar Assn. (chmn. com. on legal edn. and bar admission 1982—, com. on profl. discipline 1989-90), N.J. State Bar Assn. (product liability com. 1991—), Assn. of Bar of City of N.Y. (com. on profl. responsibility 1980-83, com. on legal assistance 1983-86, product liability com. 1987-91, trustee career devel. awards 1989-90), Phi Beta Kappa. Home: 6 Arnold Dr Princeton Junction NJ 08550-1521 Office: Herrick Feinstein 2 Park Ave New York NY 10016-5603

LEVINE, SAMUEL HAROLD, nuclear engineering educator; b. Hazlehurst, Ga., Nov. 30, 1925; s. Abraham and Rebecca (Starfsky) L.; married; children: Reneé, Lisa, Suzanne. BS, Va. Poly. Inst. and State U., 1947; MS, U. Ill., 1948; PhD, U. Pitts., 1954. Instr. Va. Poly. Inst. and State U., Blacksburg, 1949-50; mgr. A1W exptl. reactor physics Westinghouse Bettis, Pitts., 1954-59; reactor physicist Gen. Atomic, San Diego, 1959-61; group head Rocketdyne, Canoga Park, Calif., 1961-62; head nuclear sci. lab. Northrop Space Lab., Hawthorne, Calif., 1962-68; dir. Breazeale Rsch. Reactor Pa. State U., University Park, 1968-86, prof. nuclear engring., 1968—; cons. IAEA, 1977—, Pa. Power & Light Co., Allentown, 1986—. Contbr. articles to Nuclear Tech., Ann. Nuclear Energy, Health Physics, Nuclear Sci. and Engring. With USAF, 1943-44. Recipient Invention award NASA, 1973; fellow Westinghouse Electric Corp., 1953; Lady Davis fellow Technion, 1976, 89. Fellow Am. Nuclear Soc.; mem. ASTM, Am. Phys. Soc., Phi Kappa Phi, Sigma Xi. Jewish. Office: Pa State U 231 Sackett Bldg University Park PA 16802

LEVINE, SAMUEL J., biology educator; b. N.Y.C., May 19, 1934; s. Rose (Teich) L.; m. Rhoda L. Lucker, Mar. 4, 1967; children: Richard A., Caren D. BS cum laude, NYU, 1959, MA, 1960, PhD, 1964. Asst. biology prof. NYU, N.Y.C., 1959-67, adj. asst. prof., 1967-70; prof. Borough of Manhattan Community Coll., N.Y.C., 1967—; cons. N.Y. State Narcotic Addiction Control Commn., N.Y.C., 1967-68. Author: (manual) Lab. Manual for Microbiology, 1975, 78, Lab Manual for General Biology, 1977. Cpl. U.S. Army, 1953-55. Home: 10 Woodland Rd Valley Stream NY 11581-1733 Office: Borough of Manhattan Community Coll 199 Chambers St New York NY 10007-1006

LEVINE, STANLEY A., lawyer; b. Phila., Sept. 4, 1936; s. Henry and Hilda (Weisgrow) L.; m. Binney Safier, June 21, 1958; children—Glenn, John. B.A., Pa. State U., 1958; LL.B., Temple U., 1961. Bar: Pa., 1961, D.C., 1972. Assoc. Maurice Abrams, Phila., 1961-65; assoc. Tabas and Smith, Phila., 1965-67; asst. resident atty. Prudential Ins. Co., Phila., 1967-71; resident atty. Prudential Ins. Co., Washington, 1971-75; asst. gen. counsel Prudential Ins. Co., Newark, 1975-77; assoc. Danzansky and Dickey, Washington, 1977-80; ptnr. Finley, Kumble, Wagner, Heine, Underberg, Manley and Casey, Washington, 1981-87, Hazel & Thomas, Washington, 1987—. Bd. dirs. McLean Chamber Orch., Va., 1980-82. Mem. ABA, D.C. Bar Assn. Office: Hazel & Thomas 2001 Pennsylvania Ave NW Washington DC 20006-1813

LEVINE, SUZANNE MARIN (DR.), podiatrist; b. N.Y.C., June 28, 1951; d. Maurice and Miriam (Kraus) Marin; dovroced; children: Marisa Allison, Heather Danielle. BA, CUNY, 1971; MS, Columbia U., 1972; D of Podiatric Medicine, N.Y. Coll. Podiatric Medicine, 1977. Diplomate Am. Bd. Podiatric Surgery. Prin. Yorkville Foot Ctr., N.Y.C., 1977—; writer Am. Podiatric Med. Writers Assn.; adj. clin. prof. N.Y. Coll. Podiatric Medicine, 1982—; clin. instr. emeritus Mt. Sinai Hosp., N.Y.C. Author: My Feet are Killing Me!, 1987, Walk It OFF!, 1990; contbr. articles to mags. Contbg. author Am. Diabetes Assn., N.Y.C.; lectr., leader Multiple Sclerosis Walkathon, N.Y.C.; benefactor N.Y. Commn. on the Arts, N.Y.C., N.Y. Coll. Podiatric Medicine, N.Y.C. Mem. Brae Burn Country Club. Office: Yorkville Foot Ctr 885 Park Ave New York NY 10021-0325

LEVINE, THOMAS MARK, venture capitalist, lawyer; b. Pitts., May 5, 1949; s. Arnold I. and Adelyne Esther (Roth) L.; m. Susan Todd Floyd, Oct. 9, 1976; children—Elizabeth Floyd, Robert Scott. B.A., Colgate U., 1971; J.D., U. Chgo., 1974. Bar: Pa. Ptnr. Berkman, Ruslander, Pohl, Lieber, & Engel, Pitts., 1974-82; exec. v.p. Fostin Capital Corp., Pitts., 1982—. Mem. ABA, Pa. Bar Assn., Nat. Venture Capital Assn. Democrat. Jewish. Office: Fostin Capital Corp 681 Andersen Dr Pittsburgh PA 15220-2747

LEVINE, WALTER DANIEL, lawyer, accountant; b. Paterson, N.J., July 19, 1941; s. Samuel M. and May (Zaretzky) LeV.; m. Joy Herman, Dec. 24, 1964 (div. 1972); children: Lee Jason, Stephen Ian; m. Ellen R. Ignatoff, Feb. 12, 1976; children: Elissa Whitney, Evan Harris. BA, Rutgers U., 1962; JD, Temple U., 1965; BS, Fairleigh Dickinson U., 1967. Bar: N.J. 1965. Assoc. atty. Gutkin & Miller, Newark, 1965-72; ptnr. firm Gutkin Miller Shapiro Berson, Millburn, N.J., 1972-78; sole practice Fairfield, N.J., 1978-88; sr. ptnr. Friedman LeVine & Brooks, Florham Park, N.J., 1988-91; sole practice Florham Park, 1991—; sec., dir. Tekimage Inc., Florham Park, 1986—; pres., dir. Macet Corp., Florham Park, 1988—. Author: Prentice Hall Tax Reports, 1971. Bd. dirs. v.p. Men's Club Congregation B'nai Jeshurun, Short Hills, N.J., 1991; coach, mgr. Livingston (N.J.) Little League, 1988—. Mem. N.J. Bar Assn., Passaic County Bar Assn. (chmn. tax com. 1989), K.P. (chancellor-comdr. Passaic chpt. 1987). Democrat. Jewish. Home: 345 Walnut St Livingston NJ 07039-5011 Office: Walter D LeVine PA 23 Vreeland Rd Florham Park NJ 07932-1510

LEVINE-SHNEIDMAN, CONALEE, psychologist; b. N.Y.C., Feb. 22, 1930; d. Robert and Lillian (Kurlander) Levine; m. J. Lee Shneidman, Sept. 3, 1961; children—Philip, Jack. Student Black Mountain Coll. (N.C.); Ph.D., NYU, 1959. Cert. in psychoanalysis and psychotherapy. Pvt. practice psychoanalysis and psychotherapy, N.Y.C., 1961—; assoc. prof. psychology NYU, 1965-70; adj. assoc. prof. Yeshiva U., 1970-73. USPHS grantee, 1958. Author: Too Smart For Her Own Good?, 1985. Mem. Am. Psychol. Assn., Am. Orthopsychiat. Assn., N.Y. State Psychol. Assn., Psychoanalytic Soc. of Postdoctoral Program for Tng. and Research. Office: 27 W 86th St New York NY 10024-3615

LEVINGER, BERYL BETH, cultural organization administrator, consultant; b. N.Y.C., July 31, 1947; d. Adolph Seymour Schapira and Beatrice Glickman Lemeshnik; m. Samuel Levinger, June 17, 1967; children: Lisa, Andrea. BS, Cornell U., 1968; MA, U. Ala., 1974, PhD, 1977. Vol. U.S. Peace Corps, Colombia, 1967-69; assoc. dir U.S. Peace Corps, Bogota, Colombia, 1974-75; tchr., adminstr. Am. Schs. Abroad, Honduras and Colombia, 1970-74; edn. advisor AID, Bogota, 1975-77; spl. asst. to pres. Save the Children, Westport, Conn., 1977-79; dep. dir. tech. svcs. unit World Edn., N.Y.C., 1979-81; sr. rsch. assoc., adj. asst. prof. Columbia U., N.Y.C., 1981-84; dep. exec. dir. CARE, N.Y.C., 1984-89; pres. AFS Intercultural Programs, N.Y.C., 1989—; cons. in field. Mem. Cornell Club. Democrat. Jewish. Home: 17 Woods Grove Rd Westport CT 06880-2427 Office: AFS Intercultural Programs 313 E 43d St New York NY 10017

LEVINSON, ALFRED LINDEN, economist, management consultant; b. Newark, Nov. 28, 1933; s. Irving and Edith (Linden) L. AB, U. Pa., 1955; MA, U. Calif., Davis, 1968; PhD, U. Calif., Berkeley, 1978. Staff scientist Lawrence Berkeley Lab., Berkeley, Calif., 1975-79; rsch. assoc. Washington U., St. Louis, 1979-81; assoc. prof. N.J. Inst. Tech., Newark, 1981-90; prin. A. L. Levinson Assocs., Flanders, N.J., 1990—. Author: Energy and Materials in Three Sectors of the Economy; contbr. articles to profl. jours. Mem. Am. Econ. Assn., Soc. for Risk Analysis.

LEVINSON, BARRY LEWIS, biochemist; b. Camden, N.J., July 2, 1955; s. Morris Mordechai and Pauline Rose (Gitzes) L.; m. Marcia Ellen Wagner, June 14, 1981; children: Eliron Meir, Aviyam Chanan. AB magna cum laude, Princeton U., 1977; M.Phil. with honors, Yale U., 1980, PhD, 1983. Postdoctoral fellow U. Southampton, Hampshire, U.K., 1983-85; rsch. scientist Ecogen Inc., Langhorne, Pa., 1985-89, sr. rsch. scientist, 1989; scientist Berlex Labs., Inc., Cedar Knolls, N.J., 1989—. Editor Yale Jour. of Biology and Medicine, 1979-83; contbr. articles to profl. jours.; patentee in field. Postdoctoral fellow NATO, 1984-85, Muscular Dystrophy Assn., 1983-84; Rensselaer Poly. Inst. award, 1973, Nat. Merit scholar, 1973-77, Berlex Dirs. Rsch. award, 1991. Mem. AAAS, N.Y. Acad. Sci., Am. Soc. for Biochemistry and Molecular Biology, Am. Chem. Soc. Orthodox Jewish. Home: 419 Becker St Highland Park NJ 08904-2616 Office: Berlex Labs Inc 110 E Hanover Ave Cedar Knolls NJ 07927-2095

LEVINSON, DEBORAH JOY, accounting company executive; b. Orangeburg, N.Y., Aug. 1, 1957; d. Pearl Levinson. BBA, CCNY, 1978. CPA, N.Y. Staff acct. Anchin, Block & Anchin, N.Y.C., 1978-80; ptnr. Kenneth Leventhal & Co., N.Y.C., 1980—. Mem. N.Y. Soc. CPAs (sec. 1991—), Comml. Real Estate Women (bd. dirs. 1991—). Office: Kenneth Leventhal & Co 805 3d Ave New York NY 10022-7513

LEVINSON, DEBORAH SUE, family therapist; b. Balt., June 22, 1946; d. Alder I. and Pearl (Boxer) Simon; m. A. Joel Levinson, June 19, 1968 (dec. May 1991); children: P. Andrew, Jonathan B. BA, Goucher Coll., 1968; MEd, Johns Hopkins U., 1972, CASE, 1980. Cert. profl. counselor Nat. Acad. Cert. Clin. Mental Health Counselors. Dir. parent program Southeastern Community Mental Health Ctr., Balt., 1979-85; asst. prof. edn. Dundalk, Catonsville, Essex Community Coll., Balt., 1979—; pvt. practice family therapy, individual therapy, hypnosis C.M. Citvenbaum Assocs., Balt., 1987—; pvt. practice family therapy, 1980-87. Mem. Am. Orthopsychictric Assn., AACD, Am. Mental Health Counselors Assn., Md. Mental Health Counselors Assn., Phi Beta Kappa, Phi Lambda Theta. Office: CM Citrenbaum Assocs PA 416 E Quadrangle Village of Cross Keys Baltimore MD 21210

LEVINSTONE, BERTRAM, surgeon; b. N.Y.C., Nov. 11, 1921; s. Aaron and Etta Miriam (Goldstein) L.; m. Mildred Dolores Rothfeld, Nov. 16, 1946; children: Edward Ira, Daniel Everett. BS, Muhlenberg Coll., 1942; MD, U. Pa., 1945. Diplomate Am. Bd. Surgery. Intern Newark Beth Israel Med. Ctr., 1945-46, surg. resident, 1947-50; pvt. practice Newark and Maplewood, N.J., 1951—, West Orange, N.J., 1977—; attending surgeon St. Barnabas Med. Ctr., Livingston, N.J., 1951—, clin. chief surgery, 1980-83; sr. attending surgeon Newark Beth Israel Med. Ctr., 1951—; attending surgeon St. James Hosp., Newark, 1953—; surg. cons. U.S. VA Hosp., Lyons, N.J., 1953-88; clin. instr. surgery N.Y. Med. Coll., N.Y.C., 1963-66; clin. assoc. prof. surgery U. Medicine and Dentistry N.J., N.J. Med. Sch., Newark, 1970—; lectr. surgery Mt. Sinai Med. Sch., N.Y.C., 1983-86; med. dir. Harrison (N.J.) Alloys, 1953-89, Penick Corp., Newark, 1953—, Mannkraft Corp., Neawrk, 1953—; regional med. dir. Aetna Health Plans N.J., Parsippany, 1987—. Trustee Jewish Family Svc. Metrowest, Florham Park, N.J., 1963—, Jewish News of Metrowest, East Orange, N.J., 1955-60; mem. Community Rels. Com. Metrowest, East Orange, 1983—; exec. com. Met. Orch. West Orange, 1972—; med. com. Am. Cancer Soc., 1983—, vice-chmn., 1984. Capt. U.S. Army, 1946-48, capt. USAF, 1953. Fellow ACS, Internat. Coll. Surgeons, Acad. Medicine N.J. (pres. 1981-82); mem. AMA, Med. Soc. N.J. (ho. dels. 1980—), N.J. Gastroent. Soc., N.J. Soc. Surgeons, Oncology Soc. N.J. (pres. 1991-92), Essex County Med. Soc. (editor Bull. 1973-78), Orange Lawn Tennis Club. Home: 26 Korwel Cir West Orange NJ 07052 Office: 769 Northfield Ave Orange NJ 07052

LEVINTHAL, CHARLES FREDERICK, research psychologist; b. Cin., July 6, 1945; s. Sam and Mildred Carolyn (Greenburg) L.; m. Beth Ellen Kuby, Dec. 16, 1973; children: David Justin, Brian Ross. AB, U. Cin., 1967; MA, U. Mich., 1968, PhD, 1971. Lic. psychologist, N.Y. Asst. prof. Hofstra U., Hempstead, N.Y., 1971-78, assoc. prof., 1978-87, prof., 1987—. Author: Messengers of Paradise: Opiates and the Brain, 1988, Introduction to Physiological Psychology, 3d edit., 1990; contbr. articles to profl. jours. With USAR, 1968-74. Fellow Woodrow Wilson Found., 1967, NSF, 1967-71. Mem. Am. Psychol. Assn., Soc. Psychophysiol. Rsch., Soc. Neurosci. Jewish. Home: 9 Royal Oak Dr Huntington NY 11743-4427 Office: Hofstra U 1000 Hempstead Tpke Hempstead NY 11550-1090

LEVITAN, HERBERT, zoology educator; b. Bklyn., Apr. 25, 1939; s. Meyer and Lena (Kohl) L.; m. Karen Merle Brounstein, Aug. 23, 1964; children: James, Danielle. Student Bklyn. Coll., 1956-58; BEE, Cornell U., 1962, PhD, 1965. Postdoctoral fellow Brain Research Inst., UCLA, 1965-67, CNRS, Paris, 1968-69; spl. fellow NIMH, Bethesda, Md., 1970-71; assoc. prof. zoology U. Md., College Park, 1972-79, prof., 1982—; neurophysiologist Nat. Inst. Aging, Balt., 1979-82. U.S. Yugoslav health scientist exchange scholar NIH, Belgrad, Yugoslavia, 1979; program dir., sect. head undergrad. sci. edn. NSF, 1990—. Contbr. articles to profl. jours. Recipient Disting. Tchr. Scholar award U. Md., 1985; Fulbright-Hays scholar, 1987—. Mem. Soc. Neuroscience, Am. Soc. Cell Biologists, Soc. Gen. Physiologists, Am. Physiol. Soc., Sigma Xi. Home: 212 Dale Dr Silver Spring MD 20910-5502 Office: Dept Zoology U Md College Park MD 20742

LEVITAN, LAURENCE, state senator, lawyer; b. Washington, Oct. 22, 1933; s. Maurice Land Nathlie (Rosenthal) L.; BS, Washington and Lee U., 1955; JD, George Washington U., 1958; m. Barbara E. Levin, 1957; children: Jennifer, Michelle, Lisa. Admitted to Md. bar, 1964; prin. Frank Bernstein Co. and Goldman, 1988; mem. Md. Ho. of Dels., 1971-74; mem. Md. Senate, 1975—, chmn. budget and taxation com., policy com., spending affordability com., mem. joint com. on mgmt. pub. funds., legis. com. on budget and audit, gov.'s commn. to rev. state taxes & taxes structure, joint legis. com. on tax reform, govtl. commn. to revise annotated code of Md., joint subcom. on program open space, chmn. drunk and drugged driving task force, chmn. joint com. on ins. tax reform; mem. Montgomery County Exec.'s Commn. for Higher Edn. in High Tech.; past mem. Gov.'s Commn. To Study Unification of Circuit Ct., Gov.'s Commn. to Study Condominium Laws, Gov.'s Commn. Law Enforcement and Adminstrn. Justice, Gov.'s Subcom. on Revenue Structure of Task Force to Study State-Local Relationships; mem. Gov.'s Commn. To Study Feasibility of Biennial Budget, Gov.'s Task Force on Real Property Closing Costs, Task Force To Study Md. Tax Ct. Mem. ABA, D.C. Bar Assn., Md. Bar Assn., Nat. Conf. State Legislatures (mem. subcom. on fed. budget and taxation com., fiscal affairs govt. oversight com.), So. Legis. Conf. (chmn. fiscal affairs and govt. ops. steering com. 1991-92), Am. Legis. Exch. Coun. (tax task force). Democrat. Jewish. Office: 11426 Georgetowne Dr Rockville MD 20854-3722 also: James Senate Office Capitol Bldg Annapolis MD 21401

LEVITAS, ANDREW STEPHEN, child psychiatrist, educator; b. Bklyn., Feb. 17, 1948; s. Louis and Laura (Perlman) L.; m. Phyllis Malin, Apr. 19, 1970; children: Joshua, Matthew. BS, Union Coll., 1968; MD, Albert Einstein Coll. Medicine, 1972. Diplomate Am. Bd. Psychiatry and Neurology. Intern Montefiore Hosp. and Med. Ctr., Bronx, N.Y., 1972-73; resident in psychiatry Downstate-Kings County Hosp. Ctr., Bklyn., 1973-75; fellow in child psychiatry U. Colo. Health Scis. Ctr., Denver, 1975-77, asst. clin. prof., 1982-86; staff psychiatrist Denver Children's Hosp., 1977-79; pvt. practice Denver, 1979-86; asst. prof. U. Nebr. Med. Ctr., Omaha, 1986-88; asst. prof. U. Medicine and Dentistry N.J. Sch. Osteo. Medicine, Cherry Hill, 1988—, med. dir. devel. disabilities project, 1988—; cons. psychiatrist T.I.M. House, Devel. Pathways, Aurora, Colo., 1982-86; mem. sci. adv. bd. Fragile-X Soc., Denver. Contbr. numerous articles to profl. jours. Mem. MLA, Am. Psychiat. Assn., Am. Acad. Child and Adolescent Psychiatry. Office: U Medicine and Dentistry NJ Sch Oste Medicine Dept Psy 2250 Chapel Ave Cherry Hill NJ 08002-2051

LEVITE, LAURENCE ALLEN, communications executive; b. Buffalo, Apr. 26, 1940; s. Samuel and Estelle (Tishman) L.; student U. Pa., 1958-60; grad. Am. Acad. Dramatic Arts, 1962; student U. Buffalo Law Sch., 1965; m. Sharon Cohen, Aug. 15, 1965; children—Adam, Joshua. Gen mgr. McLendon Broadcasting, WYSL & WPHD Radio, Buffalo, 1970-74; exec. v.p., gen. mgr. Queen City Radio Corp., WEBR Radio, Buffalo, 1974-77; founder, pres., chief exec. officer Algonquin Broadcasting Corp., Buffalo, 1977—. Bd. govs. Jewish Fedn. Buffalo, 1982—; chmn. media div. United Way campaign, 1985; adv. bd. Jr. League, 1981, Medaille Coll., 1980, Jewish Center of Buffalo, 1979-82, Episcopal Charities, 1981-83. Mem. Profl. Communicators of Western N.Y. (pres.), Buffalo Radio Assocs. Group (pres. 1972), N.Y. Broadcasters, N.Y. State Broadcasters Assn. (bd. dirs. 1983—, chmn. 1987), ABC radio adv. bd. Nat. Assn. Broadcasters, Radio Advt. Bur., Buffalo Exec. Assn. Jewish. Clubs: Buffalo, Univ., Westwood Country. Office: Sta WBEN-AM 2077 Elmwood Ave Buffalo NY 14207-1903

LEVITSKY, WALTER SIMEON, JR., neurologist, researcher; b. Bklyn., Sept. 30, 1932; s. Walter Simeon and Mary (Zwoliak) L.; m. Katherine Lang, June 2, 1963 (div. Sept. 1965); m. Margaret Anne Cantwell, June 11, 1966; children: Walter Simeon III, Elizabeth Walsh Levitsky, Kristen Cantwell Levitsky. BS, Rutgers U., 1954; MD, Albany Med. Coll., 1958. Diplomate Am. Bd. Neurology, Am. Bd. Med. Examiners, Am. Soc. EEG. Medical intern Seton Hall Coll. of Medicine and Jersey City Med. Ctr., 1958-59; fellow in neuropsychiatry Cleve. Clinic, 1959-60; resident in neurology Jersey City Med. Ctr., 1960-61; fellow neuropathology Mallory Inst. and Boston City Hosp., 1962-64; instr. and rsch. assoc. VA Hosp. and Boston U. Sch. of Medicine, 1964-66; pres., cons. North Shore Neurol. Assocs., Peabody, Mass., 1966-90; pres. The Autism Rsch. Found., Boston, 1989—; dir. neurology Boston State Hosp., Mattapan, Mass., 1966-67, Danvers (Mass.) State Hosp., 1967-77. Bd. dirs. North Shore Mental Health Guidance Ctr., Salem, Mass., 1970-81, Am. Heart Assn., Mass., 1972-79, New Bldg. Capital Campaign, Boston, 1990-91, North Shore Homeles Shelter Com., Ipswich, Mass., 1990-91; founder, chmn. stroke com. N.E. chpt. Am. Heart Assn., 1972-79; chmn. State Task Force on Stroke, 1974-76. Mem. Boston Soc. Psychiatry and Neurology. Russian Orthodox. Office: The Autism Rsch Found 818 Harrison Ave Roxbury MA 02118-2999

LEVITT, ANNETTE SHANDLER, language educator; b. Phila.; d. Samuel Harry and Sarah (Gould) Shandler; m. Morton Paul Levitt. BA, Temple U., MA; PhD, Pa. State U. Instr. English Pa. State U., Ogontz, 1964-68; asst. prof. Temple U., Phila., 1973-79; asst. prof. Drexel U., Phila., 1985-89, asst. dean Coll. Humanities and Social Scis., 1989-90, assoc. prof. humanities, 1989—; vis. prof. Concordia U., Montreal, Ont., summer 1985; Pa. Humanities Coun. Commonwealth speaker, 1992-93. Editor: William Blake and the Moderns, 1988; contbr. numerous articles to profl. and acad. jours. Bd. dirs. Center City Residents Assn., Phila., 1981-83. Fellow The Camargo Found., 1990, Am. Coun. of Learned Socs., 1987. Mem. MLA, Northeastern MLA, Women's Caucus of MLA. Democrat. Jewish. Office: Drexel U Dept Humanities 32d and Chestnut Philadelphia PA 19104

LEVITT, BRIAN MICHAEL, consumer products and services company executive, lawyer; b. Montreal, Que., Can., July 26, 1947; s. Eric and Rya Levitt; children: Marie-Anne, Katherine; m. Claire Gonier, Jan. 25, 1992. BASc, U. Toronto, Ont., Can., 1969, LLB, 1973. Spl. asst. to provost U. Toronto, 1969-73; dir. interpretation Anti-Inflation Bd. Govt. Can., Ottawa, 1975-76; assoc. Osler, Hoskins & Harcourt, Toronto, 1976-79, ptnr., 1979-91; pres. Imasco Ltd., Montreal, 1991—; also, bd. dirs.; bd. dirs. First Fed. Savs. & Loan Assn., Rochester, N.Y., CT Fin. Svcs., Inc., Westbury Can. Life Ins. Co., Finsco Svcs. Ltd.; spl. lectr. facility of law U. Toronto; mem. adv. bd. faculty of mgmt. McGill U., Montreal. Contbr. articles to profl. jours. Bd. dirs. Montcrest Schs.; mem. adv. coun. Soc. Ednl. Visits and Exchanges in Can. Mem. ABA (bus. law subsect.), Can. Bar Assn., Law Soc. Upper Can., Caledonia Ski, Toronto Club. Office: Imasco Ltd, 600 de Maisonneuve Blvd W, Montreal, PQ Canada H3A 3K7

LEVITT, JESSE, retired foreign language educator; b. N.Y.C., June 15, 1919; s. Louis and Mollie (Goldstein) L.; m. Selma Kojan, May 9, 1958; children: Vera Louise, Lorraine Elizabeth Levitt Katz. BA magna cum laude, CCNY, 1938; MA in French, Columbia U., 1940, PhD in Romance Philology, 1963. Translator, news wire editor U.S. Fgn. Broadcast Info. Svc., Washington, 1941-54; tchr. high sch. Balt., 1955-56; tchr. jr. high sch. Greenlawn, N.Y., 1956-57; tchr. French, Spanish, Latin Rye Neck High Sch., Mamaroneck, N.Y., 1957-59; asst. prof. Wash. State U., Pullman, 1960-65; prof. fgn. langs. U. Bridgeport, Conn., 1965-89; ret., 1989. Author: The Grammaire des Grammaires of Girault-Duvivier, a Study of 19th Century French, 1968; co-editor Geolinguistic Perspectives, 1987, Justice: Interdisciplinary and Global Perspectives, 1988; contbr. articles on linguistics, onomastics and French lit. to scholarly publs. Mem. MLA, Am. Soc. Geolinguistics (editor 1974—), Am. Name Soc., U.S. English, Simon Wiesenthal Ctr., Amnesty Internat., Phi Beta Kappa. Democrat. Home: 485 Brooklawn Ave Fairfield CT 06432-1805

LEVITT, MARK HOWARD, government official; b. N.Y.C., Sept. 21, 1952; s. Sol H. and Beatrice (Belman) L.; m. Shelley Beth Robbins, Jan. 30, 1988; children: Zachary, Sarah. BS, Am. U., 1974, MPA, 1977. Compensation and personnel analyst govt. office personnel County of Prince Georges, Upper Marlboro, Md., 1977-79; supervisory labor relations officer D.C. Office Labor Relations and Collective Bargaining, 1979-85, dep. dir., 1985-87, dir., 1987-91; labor rels. and human resources officer D.C. Dept. Corrections, Washington, 1991—; pres. Zara Consulting, Inc., 1991—; bd. dirs. Com-Ex Corp.; commr. Commn. on Domestic Partnership Benefits, Washington, 1989—; chmn. health benefits com. Task Force Health, Life,

Retirement Benefits, Washington, 1986—; guest lectr. U. Md., Am. U., U. D.C., 1982—; pres. Zara Consulting, Inc., 1992—. Mem. Nat. Assn. Pub. Labor Relations. Democrat. Jewish. Home: 915 Crest Park Dr Silver Spring MD 20903 Office: DC Dept Corrections 1923 Vermont Ave NW Washington DC 20001-4103

LEVITT, MORTON, pharmacologist; b. N.Y.C., Jan. 4, 1929; married; 3 children. BSS, CCNY, 1951; BS in Pharmacy, Fordham U., 1957; MS, George Washington U., 1959; PhD, Howard U., 1966. Rsch. asst. George Washington U., Washington, 1957-58, teaching fellow, 1958-59; pharmacologist Nat. Heart Inst., Lab. Clin. Biochemistry, 1962-67; rsch. biologist Sterling-Windthrop Rsch. Inst., 1967-70; rsch. assoc. Columbia U., N.Y.C., 1971-82, rsch. scientist, 1982—; assoc. rsch. scientist, pharmacologist N.Y. State Psychiat. Inst., N.Y.C., 1971-76, rsch. scientist V, 1976—. Office: NY State Psychiatric Inst 722 W 168th St New York NY 10032-2603

LEVKOWITZ, HAIM, computer science educator and researcher; b. Haifa, Israel, Aug. 30, 1953; came to U.S., 1982; m. Ethel Schuster, 1984; children: Merav, Shir. BA in Math. and Computer Sci., U. Haifa, 1980; M in Computer and Info. Sci., U. Pa., 1983, PhD in Computer and Info. Sci., 1988. Rsch. fellow dept. radiology U. Pa., Phila., 1982-88; dir. computer R&D, dept. radiology and divsn. cardiology Children's Hosp. of Phila., 1988-89; asst. prof. computer sci. U. Mass., Lowell, 1989—; speaker in field. Contbr. articles to profl. jours., chpts. to books. Sgt. maj. Israeli Air Force, 1972-76. Mem. IEEE, IEEE Computer Soc., Assn. for Computing Machinery. Office: U Mass at Lowell 1 University Ave Lowell MA 01854

LEVNER, LOUIS JULES, contract administrator; b. N.Y.C., Feb. 10, 1951; s. Carl and Hildea (Moses) L.; m. Efrat Zohar. BS in Aero. Adminstrn., Parks Coll., 1973. Sales engr. Israel Aircraft Industries, Ltd., Tel Aviv, Israel, 1979-82; contract adminstr. Tadiran, Ltd., Holon, Israel, 1982-85; aircraft specification engr. Lockheed Ga. Co., Marietta, Ga., 1985-87; sr. subcontract adminstr. AAI Corp., Hunt Valley, Md., 1987-90; sr. contracts adminstr. Diversified Internat. Scis. Corp., Lanham, Md., 1990—. Mem. Nat. Contract Mgmt. Assn. (cert.), Alpha Eta Rho. Home: 14 Windy Meadow Ct Randallstown MD 21133-4346 Office: Diversified Internat Scis Corp 9901R Business Pky Lanham Seabrook MD 20706-1840

LEVY, ARTHUR JAMES, public relations executive, writer; b. Bklyn., Dec. 23, 1947; s. Bernard and Bernice (Lipner) L.; m. Andrea Susan Hall, May 11, 1980; children: Zoe Jess, Jake Benjamin. BA, Brandeis U., 1969. Account exec., disc jockey Sta. WBUS-FM, Miami Beach, Fla., 1971; pop music critic Magic Bus Newspaper, Miami Beach, 1971; sr. editor, writer Zoo World mag., Ft. Lauderdale, Fla., 1971-74; chief writer Atlantic Records, N.Y.C., 1975-78; assoc. dir. Press and Pub. Info. dept. Columbia Records, N.Y.C., 1978-88, nat. dir. media services, publicity dept., 1988—; so. regional v.p. Rock Writers of the World, 1973-74; seminar panelist United Jazz Coalition, N.Y.C., 1983—, CMJ Folk, 1987—, New Music Seminar Folk, 1989—. Writer, researcher album and video liner notes for Rolling Stones, Eric Andersen, Herbie Mann, Taj Mahal, Al Kooper, Robert Johnson, Jan Hammer, Julio Iglesias, Boomtown Rats, Jimmy Webb, Pete Seeger, Montreux Festival '77, Elvis Presley: Golden Celebration, 1985 (Grammy nomination), Songs of the Civil War; appeared on album session (Finnadar Records) Idil Biret's New Line Piano, 1978, (Columbia) Jaroslav Jakubovic's Checkin' In, 1978. Named Publicist of Yr. Columbia Records, 1982, 87, Media Man of Yr. Record World mag., N.Y.C., 1981. Mem. NARAS (gov. N.Y. chpt., Grammy voting com., crafts com.), Rock and Roll Hall of Fame (nominating com., mus. experts com.), Nat. Acad. Popular Music.

LEVY, ARTHUR THEODORE, real estate executive; b. N.Y.C., Nov. 25, 1926; s. Louis Levy and Minnie Goldbart; m. Barbara Gay Witmondt, Sept. 15, 1957; children: Lauren Michelle, Scott Jeffrey, Jennifer Ellen. BS, NYU, 1949. Ptnr. Assoc. Sales, Inc., Whippany, N.J., 1963-70; pres. Art Levy Assocs., Inc., Roxbury, N.J., 1970-86; dir. land div. Weichert Realtors, Morris Plains, N.J., 1986-90; sr. property analyst The Heller Group, Madison, N.J., 1990-91; dir. spl. projects U.S. Land Resources, Morristown, N.J., 1991—. Home: 11 Fieldstone Dr Morristown NJ 07960-2629

LEVY, BENJAMIN, artist; b. Tel-Aviv, Feb. 28, 1940; s. Ovadia and Bat-Sheva (Mizrachi) Nahum-Levy; student Meirovitch and Yaskil Art Sch., Haifa, Israel, 1957-58, Ecole DeMont Parnass, Paris, 1959, Pratt Graphic Art Center, 1966-67; m. Hanna Vroman, Oct. 10, 1962; children: Ofer, Bat-Sheva, Amnon, Jhonathan; came to U.S., 1965, naturalized, 1970. Exhibited one-man shows Dugit Gallery, Tel-Aviv, 1961, Tchermerinsky Gallery, Tel-Aviv, 1964, Israeli Art Gallery, N.Y.C., 1966, Morris Gallery, Woodstock, N.Y., 1966, Everyman Gallery, N.Y.C., 1968, 71, Morris Gallery, N.Y.C., 1969, New Haven Jewish Center, 1970, Aleph Gallery, Mexico City, 1971, Miami Mus. Modern Art, 1971, Graphic Art Gallery, Tel-Aviv, 1971, Galerias Del Centro Deportivo, Mexico City, 1972, Nat. Mus. Panama, 1973, Carol Halsband Gallery, N.Y.C., 1973, Israel Art Gallery, N.Y.C., 1973, Gallery T, Amsterdam, 1975, 76, Tel-Aviv Mus., 1976, Delson Richter Galleries, Jaffa and Jerusalem, 1976, La Cadre Gallery, Toronto, Ont., Can., 1976, Mus. Modern Art, Utrecht, Holland, 1978, Galerij 565, Aalst, Belgium, 1978, 79, 80, Wetering Gallery, Amsterdam, Holland, 1978, 79, Palm Springs (Calif.) Mus., 1978, Ordan Gallery, Israel, 1979, L'Affiche Galerie, N.Y.C., 1979, Mus. of S.C., Columbia, 1979, U. S.C., Columbia, 1979, JAS Gallery, Utrecht, 1980, Nat. Print Center for Graphics, Kasterlee, Belgium, 1980, Kaneda Gallery, Tokyo, 1980, Marquis Gallery, Flisingen, Netherlands, 1980, D Cercle, Oostende, Belgium, 1981, Montjoi Gallery, Brussels, 1981, McKissik Mus., Columbia, S.C., 1982, Holdsworth Galleries, Australia, 1983, Galerie Fabien Boulakia, Paris, 1985, Sander Fine Arts Gallery, Daytona Beach, Fla., Goldman Fine Arts Mus., Washington, 1985, Roslyn Fine Art Mus., N.J., 1990, Sailor Gallery, Phila., 1991, Union League, N.Y.C., 1991, Yeshiva U. Mus., N.Y.C., 1991, Geneva Art Fair, 1992, Gallery Guy Marain, Geneva; group shows: Georgetown Gallery, Washington, 1969, Mus. Modern Art, Utrecht, Holland, 1972, Mus. Tel-Aviv, 1973, Cabinet, São Paulo, Brazil, 1977, Mus. Israel, 1978, Malmo (Sweden) Mus., 1978, UN, N.Y.C., 1979, Museo Vial, Venezuela, 1982, Museo Sefardi, Toledo, Spain, Am. Acad. and Inst. Arts and Letters, 1983-84, musee suquemart Andre Paris, 1992, numerous others; represented in permanent collections: Haifa Mus. Modern Art, Pub. Library N.Y.C., Mus. Detroit, Miami Mus. Modern Art, Utrecht Mus. Modern Art, Nat. Mus. Panama, Joseph Hirshhorn Mus., Stedelejke Mus., Amsterdam, Skirball Mus., Calif., McKissic Mus., Columbia, S.C., Jewish Mus., N.Y.C., Mus. Contemporary Art, Caracas, Venezuela, Transito Mus., Toledo, Spain, other pvt. and public collections. Illustrator children's books Bobbs Merrill Co.; illustrator yearly UN envelope, also lithographs, 1976; artist jacket for jazz record Garry Burton and Pat Mathini-Reunion, 1990. Recipient prizes Young Israeli Artists, 1965; Helena Rubenstein Norman Fund, 1966; Audubon Artists, 1969. Address: 317 W 89th St New York NY 10024

LEVY, BENJAMIN, medical research executive; b. N.Y.C., June 12, 1937; s. Martin Luther and Alice (Marks) L.; m. Ellen Lois Goldberg, Sept. 1, 1963; children: Michael, Daniel, Mark. BS, Union Coll., Schenectady, N.Y., 1956; MD, N.J. Coll. Medicine, 1960. Diplomate Am. Bd. Internal Medicine. Intern Jersey City Med. Ctr., 1960-61; resident Boston City Hosp., 1961-63; fellow NIH, N.Y.C., 1963-65; practice internal medicine Hartford (Conn.) Hosp., 1965-83; research dir., pres. Nat. Med. Research Corp., Hartford, 1983—, also bd. dirs.; dir. courses, lectr. Ctr. for Profl. Advancement, New Brunswick, N.J., 1985—. Contbr. articles to profl. jours. Bd. dirs. Conn. Opera Co., Hartford, 1978-82; trustee Westwood Hill Assn., West Hartford, Conn., 1980—. Recipient numerous grants for med. research. Mem. AMA, Am. Soc. Clin. Pharmacology and Therapeutics, Conn. Med. Soc., Drug Info. Assn., Soc. for Clin. Trials, Am. Coll. Clin. Pharmacology, Am. Heart Assn., Hartford C. of C. (com. mem. 1984—), Hartford Club, Tumblebrook Country Club (Bloomfield, Conn.). Home: 47 Westwood Rd West Hartford CT 06117-2253 Office: Nat Med Rsch Corp 25 Main St Hartford CT 06106-1806

LEVY, BENJAMIN, insurance consultant; b. N.Y.C., Feb. 22, 1903; s. Joseph and Yetta L.; married; children: Joel, Emily. Grad., Bklyn. Law Sch., 1927. Ins. broker and agt. various, N.Y.C., 1927-37; underwriter and loss adjuster, pvt. practice N.Y.C., 1937-40; pvt. ins. cons. Ins. Surveys Co., Liberty, N.Y., 1940—; ins. cons. to sch. and municipalities, various, N.Y., Conn., 1940—. Author publs. in field. Mem. sch. bd. Liberty Cen. Sch., 1946-71; pres. local synagogue, Liberty, 1960-62, trustee, 1974—. Mem. Masons. Home: PO Box 1058 44 Highview Ave Liberty NY 12754 Office: Ins Surveys Co 52 East Liberty NY 12754

LEVY, BRUCE FARRELL, cardiologist; b. N.Y.C., May 14, 1951; s. Theodore Steinburg and Enid Sue (Gerstner) L.; m. Lynne Robin, Sept. 24, 1978; children: Joshua, Rebecca, Meghan. BS in Biology, Rensselaer Poly. Inst., 1973; MD, Albany Med. Coll., 1975. Cert. critical care medicine, internal medicine, cardiovascular disease. Intern internal medicine St. Elizabeth Hosp., 1975-76, resident in internal medicine, 1975-78; cardiology fellow St. Elizabeth Hosp., Brighton, Mass., 1980-82; staff cardiologist Falmouth (Mass.) Hosp., 1982—, chief cardiac svc., 1986—. Fellow Am. Coll. Cardiology; mem. AMA, Mass. Med. Soc. Office: Falmouth Cardiology Assocs 21 Bramblebush Pk Falmouth MA 02540

LEVY, DAVID CORCOS, art gallery director; b. N.Y.C., Apr. 10, 1938; s. Edgar Wolf and Lucille (Corcos) L.; m. Janet Meyer, June 7, 1959 (separated 1983); children: Jessica Anne, Thomas William. BA, Columbia U., 1960; MA, NYU, 1969, PhD, 1979; DFA (hon.), New Sch. for Social Rsch., 1989. Asst. dir. admissions Parson Sch. Design, N.Y.C., 1961-62, dir. admissions, 1962-67, v.p., 1967-70, dean, chief adminstrv. officer, 1970-79, exec. dean, chief adminstrv. officer, 1979-89; chancellor New Sch. for Social Rsch., N.Y.C., 1989-90; pres., dir. The Corcoran Gallery of Art, Washington, D.C., 1991—. Photographer of works exhibited in Guggenheim Mus., Mus. Modern Art; art dir. jours., books, posters; contbr. articles to jours. and newspapers. Decorated Chevalier des Arts et des Lettres (France). Home: 16 E 23d St New York NY 10010 Office: Corcoran Gallery of Art 17th St & New York Ave NW Washington DC 20006 also: Corcoran Gallery of Art 17th St & NY Ave NW Washington DC 20006*

LEVY, HAROLD DAVID, psycholinguist; b. Rochester, N.Y., Aug. 25, 1938; s. Barnet Lewis and Ada Sylvia (Zimmerman) L.; m. Jan Patricia Schwartz, Mar. 3, 1959 (div. 1961); children: Marvin Lee; m. Natalie Miller, Nov. 27, 1969 (div. 1982); children: Benjamin Eli. BS in Psychology, U. Rochester, 1969, MA in Edn., 1971. Permanent cert. to teach langs. (7-12). Sociotherapist Convalescent Hosp. for Children, Rochester, 1971-76; tutor City Sch. Dist., Rochester, 1973-83; editor, ednl. dir. Operaton Friendship, Rochester, 1983-88; pvt. tutor home and social agencies Rochester, 1982—; activity therapist Genesee Hosp., Rochester, 1983—. Author: (textbooks) Forced Categories: A Taxonomy for Languages, 1971, Languages: Their Common Elements, 1990, Linguistics: Theory of Names, 1990, Language Learning by Slices, 1990, Linguistics: The Binary System, 1990. Home: 111 East Ave Apt 719 Rochester NY 14604-2542

LEVY, HAROLD JAMES, physician, psychiatrist; b. Buffalo, Feb. 15, 1925; s. Sidney Harold and Evelyn (Sperling) L.; m. Arlyne Adelstein, July 3, 1958; children: Sanford Harvey, Richard Alan, Kenneth Lee. MD, U. Buffalo, 1946. Diplomate in psychiatry Am. Bd. Neurology and Psychiatry. Intern Meyer Meml. Hosp., Buffalo, 1946-47, asst. resident in psychiatry, 1947-48; fellow in psychosomatic medicine Med. Sch. U. Buffalo, Meyer Meml. Hosp., 1950-53; psychiatrist Buffalo, 1950—; mem. courtesy staff Millard Fillmore Hosp., 1957, clin. asst., 1958, asst. attending physician, 1959-63, assoc. attending physician, 1963-64, attending physician, 1964-90, chmn. dept. psychiatry, 1968-90, cons., 1990—; attending psychiatrist BryLin Psychiat. Hosp. (formerly Linwood Bryant Hosp.), Buffalo, 1955—, clin. dir. psychiatry, 1966—; attending psychiatrist Meyer Meml. Hosp., 1953—, asst. chief psychiatry, 1953-59; staff psychiatrist Psychiat. Clinic, Family Ct. Erie County, N.Y., 1959-63, psychiat. dir. clinic, 1963-80; mem. courtesy staff in psychiatry St. Joseph's Intercommunity Hosp., Buffalo, 1969-71, cons. in psychiatry, 1971—; cons. in psychiatry St. Francis Hosp., 1972—, Sisters of Charity Hosp.; asst. in psychiatry Med. Sch. SUNY, Buffalo, 1950-52, asst. 1952-55, instr. 1955-61, assoc. 1955-70, clin. asst. prof. 1970-86, clin. assoc. prof., 1986—; mem. psychiat. staff Rosa Coplon Jewish Home and Infirmary, 1957-72, chmn. dept. psychiatry, 1969-72; staff psychiatrist Chronic Disease Rsch. Inst., sect. on alcoholism Med. Sch. SUNY, Buffalo, 1950-53; psychiat. cons. Dent Clinic Found. Millard Fillmore Hosp., 1967—, Sisters of Charity Hosp., Buffalo, 1987—, Lafayette Gen. Hosp., Buffalo, 1973-88. Pres. Lemezo Enterprises Inc., Buffalo, 1970, Sanricken Enterprises Inc., Buffalo, 1970—; mem. exec. com. Blue Shield Western Ky. Served to capt. M.C., AUS, 1948-50. Fellow Am. Psychiat. Assn. (life, pres. Western N.Y. dist. br. 1969-70), Am. Soc. Psychoanalytic Physicians, Am. Soc. Advancement Electrotherapy; mem. AMA, Israel Med. Assn., N.Y. State Med. Soc., Erie County Med. Soc. (chmn. com. on mental health, econs. com., publ. com. for bull. 1969-70), Buffalo Acad. Medicine, Jerusalem Acad. Medicine, Maimonides Med. Soc. (pres. 1968-69), N.Y. State Soc. Med. Rsch., Western N.Y. Neuropsychiat. Soc. (pres.-elect 1965-66), Western N.Y. Psychiat. Assn. (past pres. 1974-75), U.S. Trotting Assn., Gen. Alumni Assn. SUNY, Buffalo (treas. exec. bd. 1967-69, numerous offices), SUNY-Buffalo Sch. Medicine Alumni Assn. (past pres., numerous offices), Med. Students' Aid Soc. (past. nat. pres., now -chmn. bd. dirs.), B'nai B'rith (exec. com. Anti Defamation League), Cherry Hill Golf and Country Culb, Alpha Omega Alpha, Phi Lambda Kappa (nat. dir., past nat. v.p., past nat. pres., now chmn. bd. dirs.), Beta Sigma Rho. Home: 47 Longleat Dr Buffalo NY 14226-4199 Office: Psychiat Assocs of Western NY 2740 Main St Buffalo NY 14214-1702

LEVY, HARRY ALAN, entrepreneur, physician, film maker; b. N.Y.C., Nov. 4, 1944; s. Sidney and Ethel (Chafetz) L.; m. Carol Ross Woodward, Dec. 27, 1972 (div. Dec. 1987); children: Zachary, James, Samuel. AB, Columbia U., 1965; MD, NYU, 1969; MPH, Yale U., 1982. Diplomate Am. Bd. Preventive Medicine. Dir. office spl. projects Mt. Sinai Med. Sch., N.Y.C., 1970-73; pres., founder Physicans Examining Svc., N.Y.C., 1977—, Health Opinion Rsch., Inc., N.Y.C., 1982—, M/O/R/E, Inc., N.Y.C., 1982—, Employee Info. Network, Inc., N.Y.C., 1989. Author: (film) Take a Deep Death, 1970, Interned, 1972 (Helsinki Film Archives 1973), (screenplay) The Househusband, 1978; inventor. Coach Yorkville Community Coun., N.Y.C., 1987-90. Office: Health Opinion Rsch 970 Lexington Ave New York NY 10021-5049

LEVY, HERBERT MONTE, lawyer; b. N.Y.C., Jan. 14, 1923; s. Samuel M. and Hetty D. L.; m. Marilyn Wohl, Aug. 30, 1953; children: Harlan A., Matthew D., Alison Jill. A.B., Columbia U., 1943, LL.B., 1946. Bar: N.Y. 1946, U.S. Dist. Ct. (so. dist.) N.Y. 1946, U.S. Ct. Appeals (2d cir.) 1949, U.S. Dist. Ct. (ea. dist.) N.Y. 1949, U.S. Supreme Ct. 1951, U.S. Ct. Appeals (10th cir.) 1956, U.S. Tax Ct. 1973, U.S. Ct. Appeals (4th cir.) 1988. Assoc. Rosenman, Goldmark, Colin & Kaye, 1946-47, Javits & Javits, 1947-48; staff counsel ACLU, 1949-56; sole practice, 1956-64; ptnr. Hoffman, Gartlir, Hoffheimer, Gottleib & Gross, 1965-69; sole practice, N.Y.C., 1969—; faculty N.Y. County Lawyers Assn.; former lectr. Practising Law Inst. Exec. com. on law and social action Am. Jewish Congress, 1961-66; bd. dirs., chmn. bd. trustees Congregation B'nai Jeshurun, 1988-91, gen. counsel, 1991—. Mem. Fed. Bar Coun. (past trustee), Bar Assn. City N.Y., N.Y. County Lawyers Assn., 1st Amendment Lawyers Assn. Democrat. Author: How to Handle an Appeal (Practising Law Inst.), 1968, rev. edit. 1982, 2d rev. edit., 1990; also legal articles. Home: 285 Central Park W Apt 12W New York NY 10024-3006 Office: 60 E 42d St Ste 4210 New York NY 10165

LEVY, IVAN MARSHALL, engineering executive; b. Newport News, Va., Jan. 23, 1937; s. Maxwell and Goldie Ruth (Peltz) L.; m. Sandra Mirmelstein, June 19, 1960; children: Eric Sheldon, Stuart Jay, Gordon Ross. B in Aero. Engring., U. Va., 1960; MSME, Drexel U., 1967; M in Engring. Adminstrn., George Washington U., 1981. Engr. Martin-Marietta Corp., Balt., 1962-65; sr. engr. Hittman Assocs., Columbia, Md., 1965-69, Westinghouse Space and Defense, Balt., 1969-71; mgr. engring. Chesapeake Instrument Corp., Shady Side, Md., 1971-74; project engr. TRACOR, Rockville, Md., 1974-84; mgr. engring. Defense Systems Inc., McLean, Va., 1984-87; program mgr. Fairchild Space and Defense Corp., Germantown, Md., 1987—. Author: (with others) Energy Sources, 1968. With USN, 1960-62. Mem. AIAA. Home: 11812 Seven Locks Rd Rockville MD 20854-3395 Office: Fairchild Space 20301 Century Blvd Germantown MD 20874-1181

LEVY, JEROME E., dean, consultant, engineering educator; b. N.Y.C., June 2, 1918; s. Harry and Mollie (Raab) L.; m. Freda Levy, Aug. 1, 1947; children: Ellen, Richard. BS, CCNY, 1938; MA, NYU, 1940. Cert. gen. sci. tchr., N.Y. Instr. in math. and physics N.Y.C. Bd. Higher Edn., 1937-39, tchr. math. secondary sch., 1939-41; tng. specialist USN Bur. of Ordnance, Washington, 1946-51; founder, pres. Washington Engring. Svcs. Co., Kensington, Md., 1951-69; cons. Systems Cons., Magnolia, Mass., 1970-86; dean Gordon Inst., Wakefield, Mass., 1987—; cons. Instrumentation Lab., MIT, Cambridge, 1957-65; cons. Analugie Corp., Peabody, Mass., 1969-85, Mass. Gen. Hosp., Siemens Corp. Mem., chair com. Peabody Edn. Coun., 1985-91. Lt. comdr. USNR, 1941-46, PTO. Decorated Legion of Merit; Charles Hayden Found. scholar, 1938. Mem. IEEE, Am. Soc. Engring. Edn., Assn. Computing Machinery, Phi Beta Kappa. Office: Gordon Inst 9 Audubon Rd Wakefield MA 01880-1273

LEVY, JOEL N., financial executive; b. N.Y.C., Aug. 17, 1941; s. Louis N. and Rena Levy; m. Rona Levy, July 8, 1973; children: Marcy, Jeremy. BA, Am. U., 1963. Formerly mgr. Leveraged Acquisition Fund Resource Holdings Capital Group, N.Y.C.; now mng. dir. LBO Group, N.Y.C. Home: 14 Saint George Rd Great Neck NY 11021

LEVY, JOHN FELDBERG, retail executive; b. Newton, Mass., Jan. 20, 1947; s. Milton and Shirley (Feldberg) L.; m. Gail Rothenberg, June 9, 1974; children—Sara, Scott. BA, Trinity Coll., Hartford, Conn., 1969; MBA, Harvard U., 1973. With Zayre Corp., Natick, Mass., 1973—; div. mdse. mgr. Zayre Corp., Framingham, Mass., 1973-78, sr. v.p., gen. mdse. mgr., 1982-85, exec. v.p., gen. mdse. mgr., 1985-86, sr. exec. v.p., 1986, corp. exec. v.p., group exec. wholesale divs., 1986-89; pres. Waban, Inc. (spin-off wholesale div. Zayre Corp.), 1989—; dir. sales ops. Hit or Miss div. Zayre Stores, Stoughton, Mass., 1978-80, gen. mdse. mgr. Hit or Miss, 1980-82. Home: 200 Kent Rd Newton MA 02168-1108 Office: Waban Inc 1 Mercer Rd Natick MA 01760-2479*

LEVY, JORDAN, mayor; b. Worcester, Mass., Nov. 4, 1943; m. Maxine Levine; children: Tammi, Sherri. Assocs. in Acctg. and Bus. Adminstrn., Worcester Jr. Coll. Asst. store mgr. C.T. Sherer Co.; buyer William Filene's; gen. merchandise mgr. Marcus Co.; exec. v.p. Parker Affiliated Co.; mem. Worcester City Coun., 1974-80; mayor City of Worcester, 1988—. Chmn. Worcester Sch. Com; past chmn. bd. trustees, bd. dirs. Worcester State Coll.; past bd. dirs. Alcoholism Coun. Greater Worcester; bd. dirs. Downtown Worcester Devel. Corp., local YWCA. Recipient numerous awards Ancient Order of Hibernians, Disting. USMC and N.G., Lions Club, Am. Business-women's Assn., Credit Women's Internat., Entertainment Club. Mem. Knights of Pythias (past pres., Outstanding Pythian award). Office: 455 Main St Worcester MA 01608-1805*

LEVY, LEON SHOLOM, computer scientist; b. Perth Amboy, N.J.; s. Simcha and Minnie (Drazin) L.; m. Millie Lea Barish, Aug. 15, 1954; children: Gary, Jordan, Sharon Gail. BA, Yeshiva Coll., 1952; SM, Harvard U., 1955, ME, 1958; PhD, U. Pa., 1970; MBA, Fairleigh Dickinson U., 1986. Engr. RCA, Camden, N.J., 1955-58; sr. staff engr. Hughes Aircraft, Culver City, Calif., 1958-63; mgr. Aerospace Corp., El Segundo, Calif., 1963-66; sr. engr. IBM, Owego, N.Y., 1966-67; assoc. prof. U. Del., Newark, 1970-79; disting. mem. tech. staff AT&T Bell Labs., Middletown, N.J., 1979—; vis. prof. Ben Gurion U. of the Negev, Beer Sheba, Israel, 1983-84; fellow U. Pa., 1970. Author: Discrete Structures, 1979, Taming the Tiger, 1987. RCA David Sarnoff fellow, 1956. Mem. IEEE (disting. lectr. 1988-91), Am. Assn. for Artificial Intelligence, Assn. Computing Machinery. Jewish.

LEVY, LEWIS LAWRENCE, neurologist; b. N.Y.C., Feb. 18, 1922; s. Jack Ellis and Ida (Schwartz) L.; m. Dorothy, June 16, 1946; children: Robert, Susan, Joan, David. AB, Temple U., 1943, MD, 1946. Diplomate Am. Bd. Psychiatry and Neurology; lic. MD, Pa., N.Y., Ky., Conn. Intern Temple U. Hosp., Phila., 1946-47; capt. U.S. Army Med. Corps, 1947-49; resident in neurology VA Hosp., Louisville, 1949-50; resident in psychiatry VA Hosp., Bronx, N.Y., 1950-51; fellow in neurology U. Louisville Med. Sch., 1951-52, instr. in medicine, asst. prof. medicine, 1952-53, 53-54; asst. clin. prof. neurology Yale U. Sch. Medicine, 1954-64, assoc. clin. prof. neurology, 1964-71, clin. prof. neurology, 1971—; chief neurology svc. VA Hosp. Med. Ctr., 1955-83; attending physician Yale New Haven Hosp., 1956—; dir. stroke acute care unit VA Med. Ctr., 1971-76, chief cerebrovascular sect., 1979-83. Contbr. numerous articles to profl. jours. Fellow Am. Acad. Neurology; mem. Am. Neurol. Assn., Am. Epilepsy Soc., Am. EEG Soc., Assn. for Rsch. of Nervous and Mental Disease. Home: 230 Pleasant Point Rd Branford CT 06405

LEVY, MARGUERITE ELIZABETH, psychology educator, researcher; b. Buffalo, Dec. 20, 1925; d. Matthias and Mary Elizabeth (deStasio) Fine; m. Louis Harold Levy, May 23, 1925; B.A., U. Buffalo, 1952; M.A., NYU, 1964, Ph.D., 1968. Licensed psychologist. Research scientist NYU, N.Y.C., 1968-69; research assoc. CUNY, 1969-70; asst. prof. Queens Coll., CUNY, Flushing, 1970-76; dir. research and evaluation Community Mental Health Ctr., Paterson, N.J., 1976-77; dir. research Med. and Health Research Assn., N.Y.C., 1978-82; adj. Baruch Coll.; adj. CUNY, 1982-85, assoc. prof., 1985—; cons. Bd. Edn., Bklyn., 1975-76, Bd. Higher Edn., N.Y.C., 1972-73, Columbia U., N.Y.C., 1978, Fashion Inst. Tech., SUNY, N.Y.C., 1983-85. Editor: Research and Theory in Developmental Psychology, 1983; assoc. editor The Corporation and Its Publics, 1963. Contbr. articles to profl. jours. Fellow NIMH-USPHS, NYU, 1966-67; recipient Creative Talent award Am. Inst. Research, 1967-68. Fellow APA; mem. N.Y. State Psychol. Assn. (pres. social div. 1977-78, 83-84), Sigma Xi. Club: Women's City (N.Y.C.) (sec. 1983-85). Home: 241 Sackett St Brooklyn NY 11231-3604 Office: Queens Coll CUNY Flushing NY 11367

LEVY, MARILYN, photographic scientist; b. N.Y.C., Apr. 3, 1922; d. Morris and Rachel (Meisel) L. AB, Hunter Coll., 1942; postgrad., Poly. Inst. Bklyn., 1942-45. Chemist N.Y. Quinine, Bklyn., 1942-43, Roxalin Flexible Finishes, Elizabeth, N.J., 1943-46, Valspar Corp., South Kearny, N.J., 1946-48; inspector N.Y. Quartermaster Agy., N.Y.C., 1951-52; rsch. chemist U.S. Army, Ft. Monmouth, N.J., 1953-75, chief photo div., 1975-79; pvt. practice Little Silver, N.J., 1979—. Patentee in field; contbr. 21 articles to profl. jours. Fellow Soc. Photo Scientists and Engrs. (v.p. membership, chair processing sect., editorial rev. bd. 1955-89, pres. Monmouth chpt.). Home: 56 Cheshire Sq Little Silver NJ 07739-1433

LEVY, MARK, lawyer; b. N.Y.C., Oct. 25, 1948; s. Leon and Elsi (Kovacs) L.; m. Lillian Haimann, Jan. 24, 1971; children: Lora, Lisa. BS in Physics, Poly. U. Bklyn., 1970; JD, N.Y. Law Sch., 1979. Registered patent atty. Mng. editor Key Pubs., Denver, 1971-72; tech. writer Hewlett Packard Co., Loveland, Colo., 1972-74, Digital Equip. Corp., Maynard, Mass., 1974-76, Foxboro Co., Foxboro, Mass., 1976-77; patent atty. Pitney Bowes, Inc., Stamford, Conn., 1977-82, GE Corp., N.Y.C., 1982; corp. patent counsel U.S. Surg. Corp., Norwalk, Conn., 1982-83; patent atty. IBM Corp., Endicott, N.Y., 1983-88; ptnr. Salzman & Levy, Binghamton, N.Y., 1988—. Contbr. articles to profl. jours.; author videotape: The Patentable Idea, 1991. Pres. Broome County Coalition for Free Choice, Binghamton, 1983—, bd. dirs., 1983—. With Air N.G., 1970-76. Mem. Cen. N.Y. Patent Law Assn. (pres. 1988-90), Computer Law Assn., Soc. of Am. Ind. Inventors (bd. dirs. 1989—), Tier Area Elec. Vehicle Assn. (bd. dirs. 1990—). Office: Salzman & Levy 19 Chenango St Binghamton NY 13901

LEVY, MATTHEW DEGEN, management consultant; b. N.Y.C., Dec. 5, 1958; s. Herbert Monte and Marilyn (Wohl) L.; m. Laura Ann Goldin, Aug. 20, 1989. BA magna cum laude and spl. honors, Tufts U., 1980; M in Pub. and Pvt. Mgmt., Yale U., 1983. Rsch. assoc. State St. Cons., Boston, 1980-81; cons. to vice chmn. Yankelovich, Skelly & White, Inc., Stamford, Conn., 1982; staff fin. analyst IBM Corp., White Plains, N.Y., 1983-86; co-founder, prin. WSY Cons. Group, Inc., Greenwich, Conn., 1986—; cons. Yale Sch. Mgmt. Alumni Assn., 1989; bus. mgr., anchorman WMFO Radio, Medford, Mass., 1977-80; co-instr. course on decision-making Tufts U., 1977. Bd. dirs. DOROT, N.Y.C., 1986—, pres. bd., 1991—; mem. allocations com. United Way of Greenwich, 1984-86. Mem. Yale Club of N.Y. Home: 415 E 85th St New York NY 10028-6355 Office: WSY Cons Group Inc 15 Valley Dr # 300 Greenwich CT 06831-5205

LEVY, MICHAEL SCOTT, psychologist; b. Newburgh, N.Y., Oct. 23, 1953; s. Beverly (Kalish) Mark; m. Laurie Paige Bristow, Aug. 19, 1978; 1 child, Brianna Nicole. BA, Boston U., 1975; PhD, Calif. Sch. Profl. Psychology, Berkeley, 1981. Lic. psychologist, Mass. Staff psychologist

Chenango County Mental Health Clinic, Norwich, N.Y., 1981-83; consulting psychologist Delphi Ctr., Reading, Mass., 1983-86; clin. dir. dual diagnosis unit Met. State Hosp., Waltham, Mass., 1984-91; dir. of psychology Dr. Solomon Carter Fuller Mental Health Ctr., Boston, 1991-92; dir. program devel. Norcap, Southwood Community Hosp., Norfolk, Mass., 1992—; clin. instr. in psychology, med. sch. Harvard U., Cambridge, Mass., 1987—; pvt. practice Andover, Mass., 1986—; consulting psychologist Project COPE, Lynn, Mass., 1984-85; mem. faculty Colgate U., Hamilton, N.Y., 1983, Ctr. Addiction Studies, Cambridge, 1987—. Contbr. articles to profl jours. Mem. adv. com. ARC Boston, Lexington, Mass., 1988—; bd. dirs. Ea. Middlesex Coun. Children, Wakefield, Mass., 1984-87. Mem. APA, Mass. Psychol. Assn. Jewish. Home: 52 Charles St Reading MA 01867-1753 Office: 2 Elm Sq Andover MA 01810-3668

LEVY, ROCHELLE FELDMAN, artist; b. N.Y.C., Aug. 4, 1937; d. S. Harry and Eva (Krause) Feldman; m. Robert Paley Levy, June 4, 1955; children: Kathryn Tracey, Wendy Paige, Robert Paley, Angela Brooke, Michael Tyler. Student Barnard Coll., 1954-55, U. Pa., 1955-56; BFA, Moore Coll. Art, 1979. Mgmt. cons. Woodlyne Sch., Rosemont, Pa., 1983-84; sr. ptnr. DRT Interiors, Phila., 1983—; ptnr. Phila. Phillies, 1981—. One-woman shows: Watson Gallery, Wheaton Coll., Norton, Mass., 1977, U. Pa., 1977, Med. Coll. Pa., Phila., 1982, Aqueduct Race Track, Long Island, N.Y., 1982, 68, Phila. Art Alliance, 1983, Moore Coll. Art, Phila., 1984. Pres., League of Children's Hosp., Phila., 1969-70; chmn. bd. trustees Moore Coll. Art, 1988—. Recipient G. Allen Smith Prize, Woodmere Art Gallery, Chestnut Hill, Pa., 1979; Woman honoree Samuel Paley Day Care Ctr., Phila., 1990, Jefferson Bank Declaration award, 1991. Trustee Moore Coll. Art, 1988—, chmn. bd. trustee, 1990—; mem. selections and acquisitions com. Pa. Acad. Fine Arts, 1979—; bd. mgrs., 1975—, chmn. exec. com., 1982—, bd. trustee, 1990—. Mem. Allied Artists Am., Artist's Equity, Phila. Art Alliance, Phila. Print Club.

LEVY, ROSS STUART, medical educator; b. Bklyn., Jan. 26, 1951; s. Zachary Franklin and Rhoda (Fuerth) L.; m. Janet Sisman, Aug. 8, 1982; children: Adam, Andrew, Alana. BS, CUNY, 1973; MD, Albert Einstein Coll. Medicine, 1976. Diplomate Am. Bd. Dermatology. Med. intern Montefiore Hosp., Bronx, N.Y., 1976-77, resident in internal medicine, 1977-78; resident, then chief resident in dermatology Albert Einstein Coll. Medicine, Bronx, 1978-81, instr., 1981-82, asst. prof., 1982-88, assoc. clin. prof., 1988—; dir. div. dermatology North Cen. Bronx Hosp., 1983—; dir. dermatologic laser Montefiore Hosp., 1983—; dir. dermatologic surgery Albert Einstein Coll. Medicine, 1985—. Contbr. articles to profl. jours. Fellow Am. Acad. Dermatology, Am. Soc. Dermatologic Surgery, Am. Soc. Laser Medicine and Surgery; mem. Am. Soc. Acad. Dermatologic Surgeons, N.Y. State Dermatologic Soc., Greater N.Y. Dermatologic Soc., Bronx County Med. Soc. Office: 2600 Netherland Ave Bronx NY 10463

LEVY, SIDNEY, psychologist; b. Bklyn., June 5, 1909; s. Benjamin and Minnie (Zwickel) L.; BS, CCNY, 1932, MS, 1936; PhD, NYU, 1948; m. Estelle Turteltaub, Jan. 22, 1931; 1 son, Richard. Supr. social work N.Y.C. Dept. Welfare, 1941-45; chief psychologist Westover Air Force Hosp., 1944-45; rsch. assoc. Bur. Naval Rsch., NYU, 1947; pvt. practice psychology, N.Y.C., 1947—; faculty NYU, 1947-67; staff psychologist Northport (N.Y.) Psychiatric Hosp., 1947-52; dir. profl. tng. VA Mental Hygiene Svc., 1950-52; exec. dir. Rsch. Inst. Personality, Psychotherapy and Edn., N.Y.C., 1956-75, Atlantic Inst. Internat. Conflict and Behavioral Analysis, N.Y.C., 1969-75; dir. Profl. Seminars in Diagnosis and Therapy, 1962—. Served in USAAF, 1944-45. Mem. Am. Psychol. Assn., N.Y. State Psychol. Assn., AAAS, AAUP, N.Y. Acad. Sci., Phi Delta Kappa. Originator: Levy Animal Symbol Test, 1944; Little Momsa Technique in Psychotherapy, 1952. Office: 9511 Shore Rd Brooklyn NY 11209-7506

LEVY, (ALEXANDRA) SUSAN, construction company executive; b. Rockville Centre, N.Y., Apr. 26, 1949; d. Alexander Stanley and Anna Charlotte (Galasieski) Jankoski; m. William Mack Levy, Aug. 12, 1977. Student, Suffolk Community Coll., Brentwood, N.Y., 1976. Cert. constrn. assoc. Supr. N.Y. Telephone Co., Babylon, 1970-74; v.p. Aabbacco Equipment Leasing Corp., Lindenhurst, N.Y., 1974-81; pres., owner Femi-9 Contracting Corp., Lindenhurst, 1981—. Mem. affirmative action adv. coun. N.Y. State Dept. Transp., Albany, 1984-88, human resources adv. panel Long Island Project 2000; mem. Presdl. Task Force, Washington, 1982—. With U.S. Army, 1967-69. Recipient Henri Dunant Corp. award ARC Suffolk County, 1986; named honoree Women on the Job, 1989. Mem. Nat. Assn. Women in Constrn. (founder L.I. chpt., pres. 1983—, regional chmn. woman-owned bus. enterprise com., nat. chmn. pub. rels. and mktg. com., nat. dir. Region 1 1988—, Mem. of Yr. L.I. chpt. 1987, Exec. of Yr. L.I. chpt., nat. dir., 1988-89, nat. treas. 1991—), Nassau Suffolk Contractors Assn. (sec. 1984-87, sec.-treas. 1987—, bd. dirs.), Nat. Assn. Women Bus. Owners (charter), Am. Plat form Assn. Republican. Roman Catholic. Avocations: reading, writing, golf. Home: 133 Hollins Ln East Islip NY 11730-3006 Office: Femi-9 Contracting Corp 305 E Sunrise Hwy Lindenhurst NY 11757-2589

LEW, FRAN, artist. BA in Art with honors, Bklyn. Coll., 1966; MFA, Boston U., 1968; postgrad., Internat. Ctr. Painting and Costume Design, Venice, Italy, 1978, Art Student's League, N.Y.C., 1978-79, Reilly League of Artists, White Plains, N.Y., 1979-84. One-man shows include Grand Ctrl. Art Galleries, N.Y.C., 1990, Manhattan Borough Pres.'s Art Gallery, N.Y.C., 1989, Pen and Brush Club, N.Y.C., 1989, Columbus Club, N.Y.C., 1982; group shows include John Pence Gallery, San Francisco, 1987, Salmagundi Club, Nat. Arts Club, Am. Artists Profl. League; represented in public collections Gov.'s Mansion, N.Y.C., Consulate of Israel, N.Y.C.; portraits include Gov. Mario M. Cuomo, First Lady Matilda Cuomo, Nobel Laureate Dr. Vincent duVigneaud, Philip H. Geier Jr., Daniel Damiano, trilogy Golda Meir, David Ben Gurion, and Moshe Dayan. Artist Westchester 2000, White Plains, 1989. Recipient Crescent Cardboard Corp. prize Am. Artist Mag., 1987. Mem. Art Students' League (life), Reilly League Artists, Knickerbocker Artists (Gold medal 1984), Hudson Valley Art Assn. (Mrs John Newington award 1989), Catherine Lorillard Wolfe Art Club (Margaret Dole award 1988), Pen and Brush Club (Solo award 1987). Home: 150 Lake St 3F White Plains NY 10604

LEWACK, LARRY, college official, fund raising consultant; b. Queens, N.Y., Mar. 30, 1958; s. Harold Irving and Maxine Jane (Gersten) L.; m. Margaret Jean MacDonald, Sept. 18, 1982; 1 child, Forrest L. MacDonald. BA, New Coll., Sarasota, 1980. Mktg. dir. Good Money Newsletters, Montpelier, Vt., 1984-86; dir. devel. and pub. rels. Champlain Assn. for Retarded Citizens, Winooski, 1986-87; dir. devel. Vt. Symphony Orch., Burlington, 1987-88; nat. sales mgr. Pointer Systems, Burlington, 1988-90; dir. admissions Burlington Coll., 1990—; cons. Peace and Justice Coalition, Burlington, 1986-90, Bernie Sanders for Congress, Burlington, 1990. Del. Vt. Dem. Conv., 1984; mem. Winooski Zoning Bd. Adjustment, 1986-88, Winooski Planning Commn., 1988—. Mem. Vt. CoHousing (bd. dirs. 1990—). Office: Burlington Coll 95 North Ave Burlington VT 05401-2998

LEWAN, DOUGLAS, communications engineer; b. Somerville, N.J., Oct. 5, 1957; s. William Douglas and Phebe (Badgley) L. BS, U. N.H., 1979; MSc, Brown U., 1982. Mem. tech. staff Bell Labs., Holmdel, N.J., 1982-90; communications engr. CSF Corp., Somerset, N.J., 1990—. Mem. Am. Math. Soc., Math. Assn. Am., Internat. Jugglers Assn. Home: 100 Hudson Ave West Keansburg NJ 07734-3264

LEWANDOWSKI, ANDREW ANTHONY, utilities executive, consultant; b. Kiel, Fed. Republic of Germany, Nov. 29, 1946; came to U.S., 1949; s. Kazimierz and Emily (Lewandowski) L.; m. Mary Ann Zuza; 1 child, Adam Christopher. Student, Rutgers U., 1964-66; BS in Mech. Engring., N.J. Inst. Tech., 1969; postgrad., Pa. State U., 1969-70; MS in Mech. Engring., N.J. Inst. Tech., 1973. Registered profl. engr., N.J.; cert. profl. planner, N.J. NSF trainee N.J. Inst. Tech., 1970-72; Engr. I DeLeuw, Cather & Co., Newark, 1970; gas utilities engr. DeLeuw, Cather & Co. of N.Y., Inc., N.Y.C., 1972, specifications writer, 1972-74, chief specifications, 1974-75; supv. engr. Elizabethtown Gas Co., Iselin, N.J., 1976-79; mgr. planning, system improvement Elizabethtown Gas Co., Iselin, 1979-81, mgr. planning, budgets, 1981-86; internal cons., computer mgmt. Elizabethtown Gas Co., Elizabeth, N.J., 1986-87; internal cons. ops., engring. Elizabethtown Gas Co., Iselin, N.J., 1987-89; internal cons. engring., budgets Elizabethtown Gas Co., Union, N.J., 1989—. Editor Jaycee newsletter, 1979-80, local Rep. newsletter, 1986. Den leader, asst. cubmaster Cub Scouts Boy Scouts Am.; active various local govt., religious, polit. and charitable orgns. Recipient Dir. of Yr. award South Plainfield Jaycees, 1972, Disting. Svc. award, 1975, Outstanding Young Man of Yr. award N.J. Jaycees. 1975, South Plainfield Jaycees, 1976; named one of Outstanding Young Men of Am., 1977. Mem. NSPE, ASME, KC, Internat. Platform Assn., South Plainfield Polish Nat. Home. Republican. Roman Catholic. Home: 1910 Murray Ave South Plainfield NJ 07080-4713 Office: Elizabethtown Gas Co 1 Elizabethtown Plz Union NJ 07083-7138

LEWIN, WALTER H. G., physics educator; b. The Hague, The Netherlands, 1936; came to U.S., 1966; s. Walter S. and Pieternella J. (v.d. Tang) L.; children: Pauline, Emanuel, Yakob, Emma. Doctorate, Tech U. Delft, The Netherlands. Tchr. Libanon Lyceum, Rotterdam, The Netherlands, 1960-66; rsch. fellow U. Delft, 1960-66; asst. prof. physics MIT, Cambridge, 1966-68, assoc. prof., 1968-74, prof., 1974—. Editor 5 books; contbr. over 250 articles on astrophysics to sci. jours. Recipient award for exceptional sci. work NASA, 1978, Alexander von Humboldt award, 1984, 91, prize for excellence in teaching MIT Sci. Coun., 1984, Buechner teaching prize, 1988; Guggenheim fellow, 1984. Mem. Am. Astron. Soc., Am. Phys. Soc., Internat. Astron. Union. Office: MIT 37-627 Cambridge MA 02139

LEWIS, ALEXANDER INGERSOLL, III, lawyer; b. Detroit, Apr. 10, 1946; s. Alexander Ingersoll Jr. and Marie T. (Fuger) L.; m. Gretchen Elsa Lundgren, Aug. 8, 1970; children: Jennifer L., Katherine F., Elisabeth M., Alexander Ingersoll IV. BA with honors, Johns Hopkins U., 1968; JD cum laude, U. Pa., 1971. Bar: Md. 1972, U.S. Dist. Ct. Md. 1972, U.S. Ct. Appeals (4th cir.) 1975, U.S. Supreme Ct. 1976, D.C. 1982. Assoc. Venable, Baetjer and Howard, Balt., 1972-75, 78-80, ptnr., 1981—; asst. atty. gen. State of Md., Balt., 1975-77; cons. subcom. on probate rules, standing com. on rules and procedures Md. Ct. Appeals, 1976—; mem. Md. Gov.'s Task Force to Study Revision Inheritance and Estate Tax Laws, 1987-88; lectr. Md. Inst. Continuing Profl. Edn. Lawyers, 1978—, Nat. Bus. Inst., 1986-87, 92—, Cambridge Inst., 1986-90, Nat. Law Found., 1988—. Contbr. articles to legal jours. Vice chmn. Md. Gov.'s Task Force on Long-Term Fin. Planning for Disabled Individuals, 1990—. 1st lt. U.S. Army, 1972. Fellow Am. Coll. Trust and Estate Counsel; mem. ABA, Md. Bar Assn. (chmn. probate reform and simplification com. estates and trusts coun. 1984-86, sec. 1987-88, chmn. 1989-90), Bar Assn. City Balt., D.C. Bar Assn., Am. Immigration Lawyers Asns., Balt. Estate Planning Coun., Johns Hopkins Club. Republican. Roman Catholic. Home: 922 Army Rd Baltimore MD 21204-6703 Office: Venable Baetjer & Howard 1800 Two Hopkins Pla Baltimore MD 21201

LEWIS, ALVIN BOWER, JR., lawyer; b. Pitts., Apr. 24, 1932; s. Alvin Bower Sr. and Ethel Weidman (Light) L.; m. Marilyn Snyder Ware; children: Alvin B. III, Judith W., Robert B. II. BA, Lehigh U., 1954; LLB, Dickinson Sch. Law, 1957. Bar: Pa. 1957, U.S. Dist. Ct. (mid. and ea. dists.) Pa. 1958, U.S. Ct. Appeals (3d cir.) 1958, D.C. 1979. Ptnr. Lewis & Lewis, Lebanon, Pa., 1957-66, Lewis, Brubaker, Whitman & Christianson, Lebanon, 1967-76; spl. counsel, acting chief counsel, dir. select com. on assassinations of M.L. King, and J.F. Kennedy U.S. Ho. of Reps., Washington, 1976-77; ptnr. Lewis & Kramer, Phila., 1977-78, Hartman, Underhill & Brubaker, Lancaster, Pa., 1979—; dist. atty. County of Lebanon, Pa., 1962-70; chmn. Gov.'s Justice Commn., Pa., 1969-74; mem., chmn. Pa. Crime Commn., Pa., 1979-85. Fin. chmn., exec. com. Rep. County Com., Lebanon, 1959-76; bd. dirs., chmn. adv. com., nominating com. Urban League Lancaster County, 1986-91. Recipient Furtherance of Justice award Mercyhurst Coll., 1979, Dist. Service award Ho. of Reps. Pa., 1982, Award of Distinction Pa. Senate, 1982, Outstanding Service award Gov. and Atty. Gen. Pa., 1974. Mem. ABA, Pa. Bar Assn. Lancaster County Bar Assn., Preservation Fund Pa., Inc., Lebanon County Bar Assn. (pres. 1974-76, bd. dirs. 1982-90), Nat. Dist. Attys. Assn. (bd. dirs. 1966-68), Pa. Dist. Attys. Assn. (officer, pres. 1964-68). Lutheran. Lodge: Masons. Home: 550 Bunker Hill Rd Strasburg PA 17579-9770 Office: Hartman Underhill & Brubaker 221 E Chestnut St Lancaster PA 17602-2782

LEWIS, CHARLES JOSEPH, journalist; b. Bozeman, Mont., July 10, 1940; s. Vern Edward James and Mary (Brooke) L.; m. Sarah Withers; children: Peter, Patrick, Barbara. BS in Humanities with Honors, Loyola U., Chgo., 1962; JD, Columbia U., 1965. Bar: Ill. 1965. Atty. McDermott, Will & Emery, Chgo., 1965-67; reporter City News Bur., Chgo., 1967-68; reporter, editor Chgo. Sun-Times, 1968-73; with AP, 1974-89, reporter, editor, Washington, 1974-78, reporter, editor, L.A., 1978-80, personnel mgr., N.Y.C., 1981-83, bur. chief, Hartford, Conn., 1980-81, bur. chief, Washington, 1984-89; bur. chief Hearst Newspapers, Washington, 1989—. Bd. dirs. Nat. Press Found., Washington, 1985—, treas., 1987—, vice chmn., 1988-90, chmn. 1990-92. Cpl. USMCR, 1963-67. Mem. Gridiron Club, Sigma Delta Chi (v.p. Washington chpt. 1988-89). Office: Hearst Newspapers 1701 Pennsylvania Ave NW Washington DC 20006-5805

LEWIS, CHARLES THOMAS, arts administrator, lawyer; b. Denver, July 7, 1956; s. Robert Edward Lewis and Alma Louise (Bell) Holcomb. BA, Howard U., 1978, JD, 1985; MBA, SUNY, Binghamton, 1982. Exec. intern Office Cultural Diversity Affairs John F. Kennedy Ctr. for Performing Arts, Washington, 1986-87; supr. instant-charge/info. John F. Kennedy Ctr. for Performing Arts; gen. mgr. Creative Ascent Theatre Co., Washington, 1986-87; arts adminstrn. intern Feig & Taubman, N.Y.C., 1982, Kolmar-Luth Entertainment, N.Y.C., 1982. NEA fellow, 1980. Mem. N.W. Kiwanis Club (treas. 1990-91, v.p. 1991-92), Phi Beta Sigma (asst. exec. dir. 1978-79, assoc. regional dir. 1981-82). Home: 103 G St SW # 718B Washington DC 20024-4341 Office: John F Kennedy Ctr Performing Arts 2700 F St NW Washington DC 20566-0002

LEWIS, CHRISTINE LYNNE, human resources administrator; b. Phila., July 22, 1950; d. Alexander Elias and Regina Ann (Czarkowski) Matkowski; m. Edwin William Lewis, Dec. 19, 1970; 1 child, Jennifer Anne. BS, Temple U., 1972, PhD, 1982; MA, Villanova U., 1975. CPCU, CLU, ChFC, ARP, RHU. Tchr., cons. for gifted Montgomery County Intermediate Unit, Norristown, Pa., 1975-80; supr. gifted programs Owen J. Roberts Sch. Dist., Coventry, Pa., 1980-81; dir. student svcs. The Am. Inst., Malvern, Pa., dir. edn. svcs., dir. examinations, asst. v.p. Co-author: Gemini, 1978, Pegasus, 1979; contbr. articles to profl. jours. Mem. Soc. Ins. Rsch. (v.p. rsch., bd. dirs. 1990-91), Soc. CPCU, Soc. CLU, ASTD. Home: 217 Knapp Rd Lansdale PA 19446-1700 Office: The American Inst 720 Providence Rd Malvern PA 19355-3443

LEWIS, CHRISTOPHER ALAN, lawyer; b. Phila., Sept. 16, 1955; s. Charles Edward and Florence (Scott) L.; m. Sheilah Diane Vance, Oct. 18, 1986. BA magna cum laude, Harvard U., 1975; JD magna cum laude, U. Mich., 1978. Bar: Pa. 1979, U.S. Dist. Ct. (ea. dist.) Pa. 1979, U.S. Ct. Appeals (3d cir.) 1979. Law clk. to judge U.S. Dist. Ct. (ea. dist) Pa., Phila., 1978-80; assoc. Dilworth, Paxson, Kalish & Kauffman, Phila., 1980-85, ptnr., 1986-87; exec. dep. gen. counsel Commonwealth of Pa., Harrisburg, 1987-89, sec., 1989-91; ptnr. firm Blank, Rome, Comisky & McCauley, Phila., 1991—. Mem. steering com. 21st Century Inst. for Polit. Action, 1985—, Com. on Seventy; bd. dirs. Pub. Interest Law Ctr. of Phila., 1984-87, Crime Prevention Assn., 1982-85. Mem. ABA, Fed. Bar Assn., Phila. Bar Assn., Barristers' Assn. Phila., Kappa Alpha Psi (treas. alumni chapt. 1981-83), Sigma Pi Phi. Democrat. Episcopalian. Home: 6425 Wayne Ave Philadelphia PA 19119-3630 Office: Blank Rome Comisky McCauley 1200 Four Penn Ctr Pla Philadelphia PA 19103

LEWIS, CLAYTON WILSON, foundation program administrator; b. Washington, Aug. 4, 1936; s. Albert Clayton and Elizabeth Jane (Kenerly) L.; m. Beverly Hardcastle, Dec. 29, 1958 (div. Oct. 1977); m. Huston Diehl, July 20, 1979 (div. Jan. 1985); children: Jennifer Hopkins Lewis, Daniel Clayton, Susannah Simons, Elizabeth Bauer; m. Joan Marie Biskupic, May 19, 1990. BA, Duke U., 1958; MFA, U. Iowa, 1969, MA, 1970. Advt. writer Brown Shoe Co., St. Louis, 1961-62; advt. copy writer Gardner Advt. Agy., St. Louis, 1962-64; asst. to dir. alumni affairs Duke U., Durham, N.C., 1964-65, asst. to dir. admissions, 1965-67; teaching asst. English U. Iowa, Iowa City, 1967-70; from instr. to asst. prof. SUNY, Geneseo, 1970-80; asst. prof. to assoc. prof. U. Okla., Norman, 1980-89; grants officer NEH, Washington, 1989—. Contbr. fiction, essays, autobiography and revs. to various jours. 1st lt. USMC, 1958-61. Recipient Roll of Honor award Best Am. Short Stories, 1974, 75, Chancellor's award for Excellence in Teaching, SUNY Geneseo, 1975, Amoco award for Disting. Teaching, U. of Okla., Norman, 1989; fellow SUNY Rsch. Found., Geneseo, 1972, 73, 78, Summer fellow NEH Johns Hopkins U., 1976, U. Okla., Norman, 1988. Mem. MLA, Am. Studies Assn., Soc. for the Study of So. Lit. Democrat. Episcopalian. Home: 4436 Faraday Pl NW Washington DC 20016 Office: NEH Div Fellowships and Seminars 1100 Pennsylvania Ave NW Washington DC 20506-0005

LEWIS, CLIFFORD, III, financial analyst; b. Utica, N.Y., Sept. 8, 1904; s. Clifford and Isabel Marriner (Kernan) L., Jr.; m. Mary Butler, Jan. 21, 1942 (dec.); children: Eleanor Reed Lewis Koppe, Clifford Butler; m. Virginia Gray Gibson Bullitt, Aug. 27, 1970 (dec.); m. Mary W. Pitz, June 18, 1988. BA, U. Pa., 1928. Chartered fin. analyst. Researcher, asst. surveyor Mut. Assurance Co., Phila., 1930-49; stock broker Battles & Co. (now Janney Montgomery Scott), Phila., 1949-88; fin. analyst, 1963—. Author: Nicholas Devereux, 1791-1855, 1974; contbr. articles to hist. jours. Sec. bd. Atwater Kent Mus., 1938-86, sec. emeritus, 1986—; mem. Brandywine Battlefield State Park Commn., Chadds Ford, Pa., 1981—, vice chmn., 1982-83, chmn., 1983-87. Recipient Del. County Hist. Achievement award, 1988; Am. Philos. Soc. grantee, 1972, 73. Mem. Phila. Fin. Analysts, SR, Soc. War of 1812, Colonial Soc. Pa. (gov. 1973-74), Pa. Soc. of Cincinnati (chmn. Am. hist. com. 1972—, pres. 1978-81), Gen. Soc. Cincinnati (chmn. Bicentennial Exhbn. Project 1980-83, history com. 1983—, chmn. subcom. Revolutionary Period Book prize, 1985-89), Upper Providence Twp. Citizens Assn. (pres. 1965-66), Numis and Antiquarian Soc. Phila. (pres. 1981-84), Rittenhouse Club, Franklin Inn Club (Phila.). Republican. Home: 2008 Hilltop Rd Flourtown PA 19031-1615

LEWIS, COURTLAND STANLEY, science policy consultant, writer; b. Coral Gables, Fla., June 4, 1949; s. Weldon Bell and Eleanor Jane (Tarilton) L.; m. Margaret Wild Lewis. Student U. Rochester, 1967-68; BS/BA, U. Fla., 1973. Scriptwriter, Vetter Prodns., Montreal, Que., Can., 1974-76; tchr. English, chemistry and math. pvt. high sch., Washington, 1976-77; sci. writer, editor Carnegie Inst. of Washington, 1977-78; research analyst Biotechnology, Inc., Falls Church, Va., 1978-83; pvt. practice cons., govt., ednl., ind. clients, Washington, 1983—; prin. clients Nat. Rsch. Coun., 1983—, Nat. Sci. Found., 1990—. Mng. editor quar. jour. USSR Space Life Sci. Digest, 1980-82; contbg. author: Space Physiology and Medicine, 1982, The Space Station, 1984, Soviet Space Programs, 1981-87, 88, Adapting to the Future, 1991; dir. publs. Space Commerce Corp., 1989—; author numerous reports and articles on space sci./tech. and engring. rsch., edn. and practice. Mem. Am. Inst. Aero. and Astronautics, Am. Soc. for Engring. Edn., N.Y. Acad. of Sci. Avocations: sailing, fishing, bicycling. Office: 4851-B S 28th St Arlington VA 22206

LEWIS, DONALD EMERSON, banker; b. Orange, N.J., Apr. 3, 1950; s. Donald Emerson Lewis and Marie (Gannon) Slaght; m. Suzanne Kimm, Oct. 12, 1974; children: Andrew Gannon, Meredith Marie, Carolyn Ann. AB, Villanova U., 1972; MBA, Boston Coll., 1974. V.p. Citibank N.A., N.Y.C., 1974-85, Boston Safe Deposit & Trust Co., N.Y.C., 1985-87; sr. v.p. United Jersey Banks, Princeton, N.J., 1987-91; v.p. Nat. Westminster Bank, Jersey City, 1991—. Republican. Roman Catholic. Club: Canoe Brook Country. Office: Nat Westminster Bank 1125 Rte 22 W Bridgewater NJ 08807

LEWIS, DONNA CUNNINGHAM, banker, communications consultant; b. Salt Lake City, Aug. 23, 1945; d. Aloysius Cabre Cunningham and Margaret Louise (Jacobs) Brown; m. Gary K. Lewis, Dec. 10, 1976; children: Gary Alexander, Zoe Kit. Student, Ea. Mont. Coll., 1963-65, U. Mont., 1965, NYU, 1990. Mgr. telephone communications Bank of Calif., San Francisco, 1966-70; with Mfrs. Hanover Trust Co. (name now Chem. Banking Corp.), N.Y.C., 1970—, asst. sec., mgr. video prodns., 1972-75, asst. v.p., dir. mgmt. communications, then v.p. and dir., 1975-88; v.p., mgr. internal communications, editor MHC Newspaper, 1988—. Mem. Audio-Visual Mgmt. Assn. (chair membership com. 1986-89, assoc. Cert. of Accreditation 1988, Outstanding com. Chmn. 1988-89), Assn. Nat. Advertisers (chair audio visual communications com. 1980-85), Women in Communications, Inc., Jr. Achievement. Democrat. Home: 411 W End Ave New York NY 10024-5719 Office: Chem Banking Corp 270 Park Ave New York NY 10017-2014

LEWIS, DOUGLAS, art historian; b. Centreville, Miss., Apr. 30, 1938; s. Charles Douglas and Beatrice Fenwick (Stewart) L. B.A. in History; B.A. in History of Art, Yale U., 1960, M.A., 1963, Ph.D., 1967; B.A. in Fine Arts, Clare Coll., Cambridge (Eng.) U., 1962, M.A., 1966. Asst. in instrn. Yale U., 1962-64; asst. prof. art Bryn Mawr Coll., 1967-68; vis. lectr. U. Calif., Berkeley, spring 1970, fall 1979; adj. prof. Johns Hopkins U., 1973-77; curator sculpture and decorative arts Nat. Gallery Art, Washington, 1968—; professorial lectr. Georgetown U., 1980—; adj. prof. U. Md., 1988—; mem. art adv. com. Mt. Holyoke Coll. Art Mus.; vis. com. Smith Coll. Mus. Art; vice-chmn. nat. citizens stamp adv. com. U.S. Postal Service; adv. bd. Centro Palladiano, Vicenza, Italy, Friends of Benaki Mus. in Am. Author: The Late Baroque Churches of Venice, 1979, The Drawings of Andrea Palladio, 1981, intro. to Renaissance Master Bronzes, 1986. Mem. Am. fellowship com., Belgian-Am. Ednl. Found.; bd. dirs. Bauman Found. Recipient Copley medal Nat. Portrait Gallery, 1981; Chester Dale fellow; David E. Finley fellow Nat. Gallery Art, 1964-67; Rome Prize fellow Am. Acad. Rome, 1964-66. Mem. Coll. Art Assn. Am., Soc. Archtl. Historians, Nat. Trust Historic Preservation, Washington Collegium for the Humanities (adv. bd.), Manuscript Soc. Episcopalian. Clubs: Yale (N.Y.C.); Falcons (Cambridge U.). Office: Nat Gallery Art Washington DC 20565

LEWIS, DOUGLAS GRINSLADE, Canadian minister, parliament member; b. Toronto, Ont., Can., Apr. 17, 1938; s. Horace Grinslade and Brenda Hazeldine Reynolds; m. Linda Diane Haggans, July 14, 1962; children: Justin, Matthew, Penny, Gillian, Susan. Grad. Chartered Acct., 1962; JD, Osgoode Hall Law Sch., 1967. Bar: Ont. 1969. Assoc. Crawford Lewis Worling Ewart & MacKenzie, Orillia, Ont., 1969-79; mem. Ho. of Commons, 1979—, mem. parliament from Simcoe North, Ont., parliamentary sec. to minister supply and services, 1979-80, spokesman for housing, 1980, dep. opposition house leader, interim opposition house leader, 1983, chmn. pub. accounts com., chmn. fed. Ont. Prog. Conservative Caucus, 1983-84, parliamentary sec. to pres. treasury bd., 1984-85, parliamentary sec. to pres. Queen's privy council for Can., 1985-86, parliamentary sec. to dep. prime minister and govt. house leader, 1986-87, minister of state dep. house leader, minister of state treasury bd., 1987-88, minister of justice and atty. gen. Can., govt. house leader, 1989-90, minister of transport, 1990-91; solicitor gen. of Can., 1991—. Past pres. Toronto Jr. Bd. Trade, Ont. Jaycees, Can. Jaycees; active various polit. campaigns, 1971-79. Named Queen's counsel, 1984; sworn to Privy Coun., 1987. Fellow Inst. Chartered Accts. Conservative. Mem. United Ch. Office: Ho of Commons, Confedn Bldg Rm 356, Ottawa, ON Canada K1A 0A6 also: 41 Peter St N, Orillia, ON Canada L3V 4Y9 also: 517 Dominion Ave, Midland, ON Canada L4R 1P7

LEWIS, EDWARD, publisher; b. Bronx, N.Y., May 15, 1940; s. George and Jewell (Spencer) Clark. B.A., U. N.Mex., 1964, M.A., 1966; postgrad., NYU, 1966-69. Lectr. for Peace Corps at U. N.Mex., 1963; adminstrv. analyst City Mgr.'s Office, Albuquerque, 1964-65; financial analyst First Nat. City Bank, N.Y.C., 1966-69; pub. Essence mag., N.Y.C., 1969—; chief exec. officer Essence Communications, Inc.; dir. Freedom Nat. Bank, N.Y.C. Bd. dirs. Rheeland Found., Negro Ensemble N.Y.C. Recipient Minority Buisnessman of Yr. award Internat. Coun. for Bus. Opportunityfor, 1970; named Businessman of Year Blackfrica Promotions, Inc., 1974. Mem. 100 Black Men, Inc., Uptown C. of C., N.Y.C. Chamber Commerce and Industry. Office: Essence Mag 1500 Broadway New York NY 10036-4015*

LEWIS, FELICE FLANERY, lawyer, educator; b. Plaquemine, La., Oct. 5, 1920; d. Lowell Baird and E. Elizabeth (Lee) Flanery; m. Francis Russell Lewis, Dec. 21, 1944. BA, U. Wash., 1947; PhD, NYU, 1974; JD, Georgetown U., 1981. Bar: N.Y. 1982. Dean L.I. Univ., Liberal Arts & Scis., Bklyn., 1974-78; assoc. Harry G. English, Bklyn., 1983-85, 91—; adj. prof., polit. sci. L.I. Univ., Bklyn., 1983—. Author: Literature, Obscenity and Law, 1976; co-editor: Henry Miller, Years of Trial & Triumph, 1962-64, 1978. Home: 28 Whitney Cir Glen Cove NY 11542-1316 Office: Harry G English 7219 3rd Ave Brooklyn NY 11209-2131

LEWIS, HENRY DONALD, fund raising executive; b. N.Y.C., Sept. 28, 1941; s. David and Ruth (Beck) L. BA, C.W. Post Coll., Greenvale, N.Y., 1966; MA, Adelphi U., Garden City, N.Y., 1972. Cert. fund raising exec. Prog. dir. Health Care Fin. Cons., Corona del Mar, Calif., 1977-79, Instl. Devel. Counsel, Bloomfield, N.J., 1979-81; v.p. Instl. Devel. Counsel, 1981-82, sr. v.p., 1982-83; pres. Devel. Cons. Assocs., 1983—; sr. ptnr. Single Source Internat., 1985—; cons. U.S. Merchant Marine Acad. Found., Kings Point, N.Y., 1985—, Va. Mil. Inst., Lexington, 1980—, N.J. Symphony Orch., Newark, 1988-90. Trustee Alumni Assn. of Bronx High Sch. of Sci., 1986-91. With U.S. Army, 1961-64. Mem. Nat. Soc. Fund Raising Execs. Office: Devel Cons Assocs 38 Park Ave Bloomfield NJ 07003-2610

LEWIS, JAMES EARL, investment banker; b. Chgo., Aug. 1, 1939; s. J. Earl and Elsie L. (Danneberg) L.; m. Patricia Ann Martin, Jan. 19, 1980. BA, DePauw U., 1961; MBA, U. Chgo., 1966. Analyst Harris Trust & Savs. Bank, Chgo., 1966-68; v.p. Paine, Webber, Jackson & Curtis, Boston, 1968-70; mgr. corp. loan component Gen. Electric Credit Corp., Stamford, Conn., 1971-77; v.p. Rauscher Pierce Refsnes Inc., Dallas, 1978-82; sr. v.p., mgr. corp. fin. dept. First Oklahoma Bancorp. Inc., Dallas and Oklahoma City, 1982-84; v.p., mgr. corp. fin. group PNC Mcht. Banking Co., Phila., 1984-87; v.p., dir. corp. fin. Ferris & Co., Inc., Washington, 1987-88; v.p. Washington Sq. Capital Markets Inc., Bala Cynwyd, Pa., 1988-90; pres., founder Mid. Atlantic Capital, Inc., Wayne, Pa., 1990—. With U.S. Army, 1962-64. Mem. Internat. Assn. Fin. Planning, Phila. Fin. Assn. Home: 852 Briarwood Rd Newtown Square PA 19073-2620 Office: Mid Atlantic Capital Inc 175 Strafford Ave Ste 1 Wayne PA 19087

LEWIS, JEROME XAVIER, II, lawyer, retired army officer; b. Chgo., June 12, 1938; s. Michael John and Eva (Lisewski) Brown; m. Mary Caroline Kickham, Sept. 17, 1960; children: Michael John, Thaddeus Thomas, John William, Mary Caroline. BS, U.S. Mil. Acad., 1960; JD, Georgetown U., 1965. Bar: D.C. 1966, U.S. Supreme Ct. 1980. Commd. 2d lt. U.S. Army, 1960, advanced through grades to col., 1981; sr. advisor to judge adv. gen. Republic of Vietnam, 1970-71; assoc. prof., dep. judge adv. law dept. U.S. Mil. Acad., West Point, N.Y., 1970-71, assoc. prof., acting prof., head dept. law, 1983-87; staff judge adv. 2d Armored Div., Ft. Hood, Tex., 1975-78, U.S. Army Cen. Command/3d Army, Ft. McPherson, Ga., 1987-90; appellate judge U.S. Army Ct. Mil. Rev., Washington, 1978-83; ret., 1990; dir. adminstrn., mng. atty. law dept. Digital Equipment Corp., Maynard, Mass., 1990—; mem. various governing bds. U.S. Mil. Acad., 1983-87. Contbr. book revs. to legal jour. Decorated Bronze Star, Legion of Merit with oak leaf cluster. Mem. Assn. Legal Adminstrs., D.C. Bar Assn. Republican. Roman Catholic. Home: 15 S Meadow Rdg Concord MA 01742-3051 Office: Digital Equipment Corp Law Dept 111 Powder Mill Rd Maynard MA 01754

LEWIS, JOCELYA (GRO MAMBO ANGELA NOVANYON IDIZOL), ethnologist, religious leader, choreographer, dancer; b. Phila., June 9, 1953; d. Joseph and Bertha (Hack) Smith; m. Ahmed Lewis, Dec. 2, 1977; 1 child, Ahmed Jr. Bus. student, C.C. Phila., 1971-72; dance student, Arthur Hall Dance Ensemble, Phila., 1971; studied under Nana Parabia, 1977-78; studied under Papa Hilaire Michel, Mariane, Haiti, 1978-83; studied under Mambo Josephine, Delmas, Haiti, 1978-83; studied under Hungan Rejje', Kenscoff, Haiti, 1978-83; studied under Hungan Daniel, St. Louis, Haiti, 1978-83; studied under Hungan Marcell, Mais Jace, Haiti, 1978-83; studied under Hungan Lieonells, Haiti, 1978-83. Cert. master dancer. Instr. Arthur Hall Dance Ensemble, Phila., 1973-77; founder, dir. Spirit Cultural Dance Ensemble, Phila., 1975—; founder, high priestess LePeristyle Haitian Sanctuary, Phila., 1982—; Dir. African Dance Dept. Lacher Latari, 1976; bd. dirs. Le Peristyle Sanctuary, Mariane, 1990—, Ctr. African Culture, Phila., 1991—; dance instr. various colls. and univs. Author: Divine Messages of the Loas, 1990, Vol. II, 1991, The African Way, 1992; presented dance recitals Walnut St. Theatre, 1976; appeared in Ayida, Acad. of Music, Phila., 1974, Aqua Suite, Robin Hood, Dell Theatre, 1982. Tour condr., lectr. Ile Ife Mus., 1974. Recipient J.J. Desslaine award J.J. Desslaine Soc., 1990, Spl. Achievement award Level Movement, 1990; Choreographer grantee Pa. Coun. Arts, 1991.

LEWIS, JOHN RAYMOND, retired chemical company executive; b. Phila., July 25, 1918; s. Charles C. and Barbara Elizabeth (Reeser) L.; m. Rachel Elizabeth Brinard, Sept., 1942; 1 child, Sondra Elaine Sperati. BS, Franklin & Marshall U., 1942; postgrad., U. Del., 1946-50. Rsch. chemist Hercules Inc., Wilmington, Del., 1942-44, rsch. supr., 1945-56, rsch. mgr., 1956-59, rsch. assoc., 1959, rsch. devel. mgr., 1959-63, projects mgr. new enterprise, 1964-74, mgr. corp. acquisitions and planning, 1974-83, cons. exec. dept., 1983-84; shift supr. Sunflower Ordnance Works, Lawrence, Kans., 1944-45. Patentee in field. Bd. dirs. YMCA Del., 1953—, Sojourners' Place Homeless; lay leader, elder Elsmere Presbyn. Ch., New Castle Presbytery. Mem. Am. Chem. Soc. Republican. Home: 118 Dickinson Ln Wilmington DE 19807-3138

LEWIS, LIONEL STANLEY, sociology educator; b. Ottawa, Ont., Can., July 29, 1933; m. Ann Winifred Herman, Nov. 9, 1962; children: Peter, Andrew. AB in Sociology with honors, Washington U., 1957; MA in Sociology, Cornell U., 1958; PhD in Sociology, Yale U., 1961. Asst. prof. sociology U. Nevada, Reno, 1961-63; asst. prof. SUNY, Buffalo, 1963-67, assoc. prof., 1967-73, dir. grad. studies, 1971-72, prof., 1973—, chmn., 1988-91. Author: Scaling the Ivory Tower: Merit and Its Limits in Academic Careers, 1975, Cold War on Campus: A Study of the Politics of Organizational Control, 1988. With U.S. Army, 1951-53. Woodrow Wilson fellow, 1957-58; Social Sci. Rsch. Coun. faculty rsch. grantee, 1969-70. Fellow Am. Sociol. Assn.; mem. AAUP, Phi Beta Kappa. Democrat. Home: 17 Morningside Ln Buffalo NY 14221-5030 Office: SUNY Buffalo Dept Sociology 438 Park Hall Amherst NY 14260

LEWIS, MICHAEL, pediatrics educator; b. Bklyn., Jan. 10, 1937; s. Bernard Lewis and Leah Cohen; m. Rhoda Rosenzweig, Aug. 18, 1962; children: Benjamin, Felicia. BA, U. Pa., 1958, PhD, 1962. Cert. N.J. State Bd. Psychol. Examiners. Dir. infant lab. Ednl. Testing Svc., Princeton, N.J., 1961-68, sr. rsch. psychologist, 1968-72; vis. prof. grad. ctr. CUNY, N.Y.C., 1973-78; sr. rsch. scientist Roosevelt Hosp.-St. Lukes, N.Y.C., 1977-82; dir. inst. study exceptional children Ednl. Testing Svc., Princeton, 1977-82; prof. psychology Rutgers U., New Brunswick, N.J., 1979—; vis. prof. dept. psychology Princeton U., 1981; prof. pediatrics and psychiatry Univ. Medicine and Dentistry N.J.-Robert Wood Johnson Med. Sch., New Brunswick, N.J., 1982—; chief Inst. for Study of Child Devel. Univ. Medicine and Dentistry N.J.-Robert Wood Johnson Med. Sch., New Brunswick, 1983—; adj. prof. psychology Temple U., Phila., 1979-80, dept. pediatrics UMDNJ-RWJ Med. Sch., New Brunswick, 1980-82. Author: Shame The Exposed Self, 1991, Social Cognition & Acquisition of Self, 1979, Children's Emotions and Moods, 1983; editor: Handbook of Development Psychopathology, 1990. Fellow N.Y. Acad. Scis., AAAS, Am. Psychol. Assn., Japan Soc. for Promotion of Sci.; mem. Family Resource Coalition, N.J. Assn. for Infant Mental Health, Internat. Assn. for Infant Mental Health (bd. dirs.), Ea. Psychol. Assn., Soc. for Psychol. Study of Social Issues (chmn. com. on children and social issues 1987—). Home: 95 Linwood Cir Princeton NJ 08540-3623 Office: U Medicine & Dentistry NJ Robert Wood Johnson Med Sch 97 Paterson St CN 19 New Brunswick NJ 08903-2160

LEWIS, MICHAEL, office products retailing executive; b. St. Thomas, Ont., Can., Dec. 18, 1950; m. Krystyna Katherine Ballantyne; 1 child, Shannon. BS, Queen's U., Kingston, Ont., Can., 1973, MBA, 1978. Sr. cons. CLC Can. Mktg. Assn. Ltd, Toronto, Ont., Can., 1981-85; v.p. No Frills Divsn. Loblaws Supermarkets Ltd., 1985-89; pres. Willson Stationers, Mississauga, Ont., Can., 1989—; bd. dirs. Kennedy Marchant Shields Inc., Toronto, 1991—. Mem. Young Pres.'s Orgn., Toronto Criket and Skating Club (capt. squash team). Home: 115 Melrose Ave, Toronto, ON Canada M5M 1Y8 Office: Willson Stationers, 6625 Millcreek Dr, Mississauga, ON Canada L5N 4G4

LEWIS, MICHAEL SETH, health facility administrator; b. Bklyn., Dec. 11, 1953; s. Irving Abraham and Beatrice Rachel (Fishman) L.; m. Arlene Feigenbaum, June 27, 1976; children: Adam, Sara. BA, Bklyn. Coll., 1974; MS, Fordham U., 1975; MBA, Temple U., 1977. Grad. asst. Temple U., Phila., 1975-77; adminstrv. asst. Cherry Hill (N.J.) Med. Ctr., 1976-77; adminstr. Brachfeld Med. Assocs., Willingboro, N.J., 1977—. Candidate Voorhees Twp. Bd. Edn. Mem. Med. Group Mgmt. Assn., Am. Coll. Hosp. Adminstrs., Am. Pub. Health Assn., Nat. Found. for Ileitis and Colitis, Beta Gamma Sigma. Home: 24 Abington Rd Mount Laurel NJ 08054-4720 Office: Brachfeld Med Assocs Rancocas Hosp Willingboro NJ 08046

LEWIS, PAUL LE ROY, pathology educator; b. Tamaqua, Pa., Aug. 30, 1925; s. Harry Earl and Rose Estella (Brobst) L.; m. Betty Jane Bixby, June 2, 1953; 1 child, Robert Harry. AB magna cum laude, Syracuse U., 1950; MD, SUNY, Syracuse, 1953. Diplomate Am. Bd. Pathology. Intern Temple U. Hosp., Phila., 1953-54; resident in pathology Hosp. of U. Pa., Phila., 1954-58, asst. instr., 1957-58; instr. pathology Thomas Jefferson U. Coll. Medicine, Phila., 1958-62, asst. prof., 1962-65, assoc. prof., 1965-75, prof., 1975—; pathologist Thomas Jefferson U. Hosp., 1958—; attending pathologist Meth. Hosp., Phila., 1975—, dir. clin. labs., chmn. dept. pathology, 1975—; pres. Penndel Labs. Inc., Ardmore, Pa., 1974-85; cons. VA Hosp., Coatesvillle, Pa., 1976-85; mem. med. adv. com. ARC Blood Bank, Phila., 1978—. Contbg. author: Atlas of Gastrointestinal Cytology, 1983; contbr. articles to med. jours. 2d lt. USAAF, 1943-46. Fellow Am. Soc. Clin. Pathologists, Coll. Am. Pathologists; mem. AMA, Pa. Med. Soc., Philadelphia County Med. Soc., Internat. Acad. Pathology, Am. Soc. Cytology, Masons, Phi Beta Kappa, Alpha Omega Alpha, Nu Sigma Nu. Republican. Methodist. Home: 521 Baird Rd Merion Station PA 19066 Office: Methodist Hosp Dept Path 2301 S Broad St Philadelphia PA 19148-3594

LEWIS, RHODA HABER, art educator; b. Yonkers, N.Y., Sept. 13, 1932; d. Sol and Rita (Friedman) Haber; children: Jeff, Shanna. BS, CUNY, 1970. Tchr. Riverdale (N.Y) Country Sch., 1966-67, White Plain (N.Y.) Sch. Dist., 1968-70, Carmel (N.Y.) Union Free Sch., 1971-72; tchr., treas. Hudson Glass Co., Peekskill, N.Y., 1972—; treas. Tchrs. Union, Carmel, 1971. Exhibited works in group shows including R. Hunter Gallery, N.Y.C., 1970. Vol. East Fishkill Libr., 1986-90. Recipient various awards for art. Democrat. Home: 41 Dogwood Hills Rd Newburgh NY 12550-2029

LEWIS, RICHARD ALLAN, financial planner; b. Pitts., Feb. 25, 1952; s. Harry C. and Vera E. (Williams) L. BS in Econs., Allegheny Coll., 1974; MBA in Fin., U. Pitts., 1978. Trainee Mellon Bank, Pitts., 1974-75, various positions with, 1975-84, v.p. N.Am. ops., 1984-86; pres., chief operating officer WorkWell, Pitts., 1987-89; sr. fin. planner The Acacia Group, Pitts., 1989—. Mem. Nat. Automated Clearing House Assn. (bd. dirs. 1981-86), Tri-State Automated Clearing House Assn. (pres. 1984-86, treas. 1980-83, v.p. 1984-85), Phi Beta Kappa, Delta Tau Delta (pres. house corp. 1976—). Republican. Methodist. Lodges: Masons, Blue. Home: 1 Trimont Ln Pittsburgh PA 15211-1252 Office: Acacia Group Acacia Bldg Pittsburgh PA 15220

LEWIS, SIMON, transportation executive; b. Cardiff, Wales, Nov. 21, 1953; came to U.S., 1983; s. John Frederick and Patricia Jeane (Davies) L. BSc, U. East Anglia, England, 1977; MSc, Imperial Coll., England, 1977-78, MIT, 1985; student, MIT, 1986. Cons. London, 1978-83, World Bank, Washington, 1985-86; instr. MIT, Cambridge, Mass., 1983-90; pres. GIS/Trans., LTD., Cambridge, 1990—. Rep. London Borough of Southwark, 1981-82. Mem. Am. Soc. Civil Engrs. (assoc.), Inst. Transp. Engrs., Urban and Regional Info. Systems Assn., Chartered Inst. Transport (Eng.), Inst. Transport and Hwys. (Eng.). Home: 77 Bay State Ave Somerville MA 02144-2133 Office: GIS/Trans LTD 675 Massachusetts Ave Cambridge MA 02139-3309

LEWIS, STUART WESLIE, surgeon; b. Bellefield, Mandeville, Jamaica, Oct. 23, 1938; came to U.S., 1959; s. Phillip Augustus and Ivy Hyacinth (Glegg) L.; m. Cordia L. Beverley; children: Camille, Hope Louise, Denise, Hara. BA, NYU, 1965; MD, Harvard U., 1974. Dir. Youth in Action, Neighborhood Youth Corps, Bklyn., 1966-69; resident in surgery NYU Med. Ctr.-Bellevue Hosp., N.Y.C., 1974-76; resident in surgery SUNY Downstate Med. Sch.-Kings County Hosp., Bklyn., 1976-79, chief surg. resident, 1979-80; pres. Monad Med. Svcs., Bklyn., 1981—; med. dir. N.Y.C. Transit Authority, Bklyn., 1989—. Chair David Dodge Bedford Stuyvesant Neighborhood House, Bklyn., 1990—. Recipient Marcus Garvey award Com. to Honor Marcus Garvey, Bklyn., 1991, Recognition award Cen. Bklyn. Coord. Coun., 1992. Mem. Med. Execs., 100 Black Men. Home: 45 E 89th St New York NY 10128

LEWIS, TIMOTHY EDWARD, environmental scientist; b. Chester, Pa., May 6, 1956; s. Henry Dasso and Elizabeth Carol (Kasarsky) L.; m. Betty Anne Deason. BA in Biology, West Chester (Pa.) U., 1977; MS in Platn Pathology, Rutgers U., 1980, PhD in Environ. Sci., 1984. Lab. asst. Dept. Biology, West Chester U., 1976-77; rsch. asst. Dept. Plant Pathology, Rutgers U., 1978-80, Dept. Environ. Sci., Rutgers U., 1980-84; lab. supr. Lockheed Engring. & Sci. Co., Las Vegas, Nev., 1984; postdoctoral fellow Rutgers U., 1985; prin. scientist Lockheed Engring. & Sci. Co., Las Vegas, 1985—; cons. N.J. Dept. Environ. Protection, Trenton, 1985. Editor: Environmental Chemistry & Toxicology of Aluminum, 1989; contbr. numerous articles to profl. jours.; author: 17th Edit. of Standard Methods, 1989. Asst. scoutmaster Boy Scouts Am., Aston, Pa., 1976-81; citizen amb. to USSR, 1989. Recipient Excellence award U.S. EPA, 1988, Silver Performance award and Robert Gross award nominee Lockheed-ESC, 1989, 90. Mem. Am. Chem. Soc., AAAS, Soc. Applied Spectroscopy, Soc. Environ. Toxicology and Chemistry. Home: 1048 Yucca Ave Las Vegas NV 89104-1507 Office: Lockheed Engring & Sci Co 1050 E Flamingo Rd Las Vegas NV 89119-7427

LEWIS, WILLIAM MARK, construction company executive, civil engineer; b. Pitts., June 26, 1952; s. Sidney G. and Geraldine (Shuklansky) L.; children: Zachary, Sarah. BS in Civil Engring., U. Pitts., 1974; MBA in Fin., U. Conn., 1986. Project engr. and mgr. Proctor & Gamble, Cin. and Greenville, N.C., 1974-79; project mgr. Pepsi-Cola, Purchase, N.Y., 1979-81; mgr. constrn. div. ITT, Rye, N.Y., 1981-83, Pitney Bowes, Stamford, Conn., 1983-86; v.p. Al Shankle Constrn. Co., Anaheim, Calif., 1986-89; pres. Shankle East, Inc., Trumbull, Conn., 1989—, also bd. dirs.; bd. dirs. Greenhouse Assocs., Newtown, Conn. Mem. ASCE. Republican. Office: Shankle East Inc 126 Monroe Tpke Trumbull CT 06611-1300

LEWIS, WILLIAM SCHEER, electrical engineer; b. Mt. Vernon, N.Y., Feb. 7, 1927; s. Perley Linwood and Nellie Cora (Scheer) L.; m. Jane Alexander, Feb. 4, 1950 (div. 1972); children: Christopher A., Pamela Scheer Shaw, David Robert; m. Barbara Johnson, June 24, 1972. SB, MIT, 1950, SM, 1950. Registered profl. engr. Mass, N.Y. Sales engr. Gen. Electric Co., Erie, Pa., 1950-53, Morrissey Tractor Co., Burlington, Mass., 1953-56, Hubbs Engine Co., Cambridge, Mass., 1956-57; mgr. contract div. Payne Elevator Co., Cambridge, 1957-69; sales mgr. diversified systems Otis Elevator Co., N.Y.C., 1969-72, mktg. analyst/gen. sales, 1972-73; mgr. vertical transp. Jaros, Baum & Bolles, N.Y.C., 1973-91, ptnr., 1978-91, ret., 1991—. Author: (handbooks) Materials Handling, Freight Elevators, 1985, Building Structural Design-Vertical Transportation, 1987; editor: (monograph) Tall Buildings—Vertical and Horizontal Transportation, 1978. Mem. Wayland (Mass.) Bd. Assessors, 1954-69, chmn., 1963-69. Recipient 1st prize award N.Y. Assn. Consulting Engrs., 1987, Honor award Am. Consulting Engrs. Council, 1987. Mem. ASME. Republican. Unitarian. Home: The Chase House RR2 Box 909 Cornish NH 03745-9743 Office: Jaros Baum & Bolles Cons Engrs 345 Park Ave New York NY 10154-0004

LEWIS, WILLIAM V., JR., investment consultant; b. Wilkes-Barre, Pa., May 27, 1959; s. William V. and June McGuire; m. Mary Ellen Judge, Sept. 2, 1989. BA, Wilkes U., 1980, MBA, 1986; MPA, Lehigh U., 1982, doctorate, 1992. Staff asst. U.S. Senator Arlen Spector, Allentown, Pa., 1983-85; rsch. coord. Wilkes Coll., Wilkes-Barre, 1982-83; staff asst. U.S. Congressman James Nelligan, Washington, 1981-82; sr. fin. cons. Merrill Lynch, Wilkes-Barre, 1986—; adj. prof. polit. sci. Wilkes U., 1991—. Elected mem. Rep. State Com. Pa., 1984—; state treas. Young Reps. Pa., 1984-88; sec. Luzerne County Rep. Party, 1989-90; chmn. 6th Dist. Rep. Com., 1992—; chmn. Wyo. Valley chpt. ARC, Wilkes-Barre, 1991— (Player award 1990). Parkhurst fellow, 1983. Mem. Wyo. Hist. Soc., St. David's Soc. Wyo. Valley, Family Svc. Assn. (vice chmn. 1990—), Ctr. for Study of Presidency (nat. adv. bd. 1987—), United Way (PARD com. 1985—), SAR (pres. N.E. chpt. 1982-88), Westmoreland Club, The Pa. Soc., Masons, Order of Chevalier. Republican. Presbyterian. Home: 183 W River St Wilkes Barre PA 18702 Office: Merrill Lynch 39 Public Sq Wilkes Barre PA 18701

LEWIS, WINFIELD ELLSWORTH, piano technician, composer, retired; b. Bath, Maine, July 14, 1924; s. Ralph Clenwood Lewis and Elizabeth Augusta (Cressey) Glidden; m. Mary Elizabeth Bedrosian, Oct. 24, 1970. Degree in Piano Tuning Tech., Perkins Sch. for Blind, Watertown, Mass., 1946. Piano tuner technician Bath Schs., 1946-55, Lewiston, Maine, 1955-70, Worcester (Mass.) Schs., 1970-75; piano tuner technician Worcester, 1975-81, ch. and nursing home musician, 1981-92. Author: Marshmallow World, 1985; composer, Hallelujah, Old Fashioned Christmas Mass, 1991. Recipient Ky. Fried Chicken Song Contest Cert. Achievement, 1990. Mem. Nat. Fed. for Blind. Democrat. Baptist.

LEWITT, MICHAEL HERMAN, physician, educator; b. Hartford, Conn., Nov. 27, 1948; s. Bernard and Celeste (Garfunkel) LeW.; m. Lynne Rubin, Apr. 1, 1979; children: Mattea, Jeremy, Rachel. BA, Lafayette Coll., 1970; MD, Jefferson Med. Coll., 1974. Diplomate Am. Bd. Preventive Medicine, Am. Bd. Emergency Medicine, Am. Bd. Family Practice. FMC Corp., 1975-80, U.S. Steel Corp., 1978-81, Jeans Hosp., 1981-84, Chester County Hosp., 1984-90; Instr. Jefferson Med. Coll., Phila., 1983—; pvt. practice, 1990—; cons., 1990—. Fellow Phila. Coll. Physicians, Am. Coll. Emergency Physicians, Am. Coll. Occupational and Environ. Medicine, Am. Acad. Family Practice; mem. Am. Coll. Physicians.

LEWNES, PETER A., sales account executive; b. Queens, N.Y., Mar. 15, 1929; s. Andrew P. and Stamateke (Anagnostakos) L.; m. Barbara D. Pappas, Sept. 13, 1953; children: Andrew P., Christina G. Michaels. MS in Fin. Svcs., Am. Coll., 1983. CLU, chartered fin. cons. Structural draftsman Voorhies, Walker, Foley & Smith, N.Y.C., 1950-55, Parco, Inc., N.Y.C., 1956-57; sr. structural draftsman Ford, Bacon & Davis, Inc., N.Y.C., 1958-65; sales rep. Met. Life Ins. Co., Bklyn., 1965—; fin. planner Metlife Securities, Inc., Bklyn., 1986—; moderator Life Underwriter Tng. Council, Bklyn., 1976-79; lectr. SBA Wksp., N.Y.C., 1975-76. Trustee Three Hierarchs Greek Orthodox Ch., Bklyn., 1955-59; youth advisor Three Hierarchs Youth, Bklyn., 1955-65; treas. Holy Order of Three Hierarchs Ch., Bklyn., 1979—. Mem. Nat. Assn. Life Underwriters, Am. Soc. CLU and ChFC, Internat. Assn. Fin. Planners. Republican. Home: 2019 E 15th St Brooklyn NY 11229-3309 Office: Met Life 9920 4th Ave Ste 201 Brooklyn NY 11209

LÊ XUÂN HY, social science analyst, educator; b. Saigon, Vietnam, Feb. 25, 1957; came to U.S., 1975; s. Joseph Ty Dinh Lê and Anna Liêu Thi Nguyên. AA, Alice Lloyd Coll., Pippa Passes, Ky., 1977; BS and BA, St. Louis U., 1982; MA, Washington U., St. Louis, 1984, PhD, 1986. Asst. prof. Rockhurst Coll., Kansas City, Mo., 1986-88, Washington U., St. Louis, 1988-90; analyst U.S. GAO, Washington, 1990—. Recipient Beck award Soc. Personality Assessment, 1989. Mem. Am. Psychol. Assn. Roman Catholic. Office: US GAO Program Evaluation & Methodology Div 441 G St NW Ste 5729 Washington DC 20548-0002

LEY, RONALD, psychologist, educator; b. Buffalo, Oct. 19, 1929; s. August Andreas and Marie (Jerge) L.; m. Carmen De Brito, Jan. 16, 1965; 1 child, Jessica Elizabeth. BA, U. Buffalo, 1951; PhD, Syracuse U., 1963. Rsch. dir. Madison Area Project, Syracuse, 1962-63; asst. prof. psychology No. Ill. U., DeKalb, 1963-64, Grad. Faculty, New Sch. for Social Rsch., N.Y.C., 1964-66; prof. psychology and stats. SUNY, Albany, 1966—; cons. Nat. Inst. for Occupational Safety and Health; vis. prof. psychology U. P.R., 1969, cardiac dept., Charing Cross Hosp., London, 1988. Author: A Whisper of Espionage, 1990; editor: Behavioral and Psychological Approaches to Breathing Disorders, 1992; editorial bd. Jour. Behavior Therapy and Exptl. Psychiatry, 1983—; contbr. numerous articles to profl. jours. Bd. dirs. Father's Assn. of the Albany Acad. for Girls, 1981-84. Overseas fellow Royal Soc. Medicine, London, 1988; SUNY rsch. fellow, 1967,68, 70, 74, 76, 78, 91, grantee, 1967-68, 69-70, 71-72, 74-75, 76, 78, 87-88, 91-92; Nat. Inst. Occupational Safety and Health grantee, 1982-83, 87, 88, others; recipient Jour. award Pergamon Press, 1988. Mem. APA, Assn. for Advancement Behavior Therapy, Authors Guild, Authors League Am., Behavior Therapy and Rsch. Soc., Ea. Psychol. Assn., New Eng. Soc. Behavior Analysis and Therapy, Psychol. Assn. Northeastern N.Y. (sec. 1967-68, pres. 1983-84), Soc. for Psychophysiol. Rsch., Psychonomic Soc., Sigma Xi. Home: 22 Marion Ave Albany NY 12203-1823 Office: SUNY 1400 Washington Ave Albany NY 12222-0001

LEZDEY, JOHN, lawyer; b. Bklyn., Oct. 9, 1931; m. Noreen Viola Bishop, June 24, 1961; children: Darren B., Jarett R. BS in Chemistry, Rutgers U., 1953; JD, Bklyn. Law Sch., 1962; LLM, Georgetown U., 1970. Rsch. chemist E.R. Squibb & Sons, New Brunswick, N.J., 1953-60; from patent agt. to patent atty. Olin Mathieson Corp., N.Y.C., 1960-64; patent atty. Am. Home Products, N.Y.C., 1964-68; mng. atty. Marks & Clerk, Washington, 1968-73; patent atty. John Lezdey Assocs., Phila., 1973—; pres. Protease Scis. Inc., Phila., 1992—; trademark counsel Teleflex Corp., Limerick, Pa., 1985—; cons. Dow Chem. Corp., Freeport, Tex., 1987—. Patentee in chem. field; co-author: Dermatology Perspectives and l-PI in AT & Psoriasis, 1991. 1st lt. U.S. Army, 1954-56. Mem. Phila. Patent Law Assn. (chmn. chem. practice 1976-83). Office: 400 Market St Philadelphia PA 19106

L'HEUREUX, DENNIS PAUL, hospital information officer; b. Woonsocket, R.I., Dec. 1, 1950; s. Bertrand Joseph and Alice (Giguere) L'H.; m. Pauline Emelia Lefrançois, July 1, 1972; children: Christopher, Matthew, Sarah. BSIE, Northeastern U., 1974, MS in Engring. Mgmt., 1977. Engring. technician Owens-Corning Fiberglas, Ashton, R.I., 1970-71; indsl. engring. asst. Johnson & Johnson, New Brunswick, N.J., 1971-72; dir. mgmt. systems engr. Haricomp Inc., Providence, 1972-80; assoc. vice chancellor info. resources U. Mass. Med. Ctr., Worcester, 1980-86; v.p. clin. and mgmt. support svcs. Leonard Morse Hosp., Natick, Mass., 1986-91; v.p. info. systems, chief info. officer MetroWest Med. Ctr., Framingham, Mass., 1992—; bd. dirs. West Suburban Joint Diagnostics MRI Ctr., S.W. Suburban Emergency Svcs. Fellow Healthcare Info. and Mgmt. Systems Soc. (bd. dirs. 1981-83, 90-91, pres. 1992); mem. Inst. Indsl. Engring. (sr. mem.), Healthcare Fin. Mgmt. Assn. (sr. mem.), Alpha Pi Mu, Tau Beta Pi. Roman Catholic.

LI, CHOU HSIUNG, electrical engineer, materials scientist; b. Haining, Chekiang, China, June 8, 1923; came to U.S., 1948; s. Chou T. Li and Sze T. Chang; m. Shao M. Yuan, Mar. 29, 1953; children: Lawrence, Suzanne. BS, Chiao Tung U., China, 1944; MS, Purdue U., 1949, PhD, 1951. Metallurgist RCA, Harrison, N.J., 1951-59; sr. scientist Shockley Transistor Corp., Palo Alto, Calif., 1959-60; mgr. rsch. and devel. Gen. Instrument, Hicksville, N.Y., 1960-62; sr. scientist Grumman Aerospace, Bethpage, N.Y., 1962-77; staff technologist Singer, Fairfield, N.J., 1978-79; dir. rsch. and devel. Semi-Alloys, Mt. Vernon, N.Y., 1979-80; pres. Lintel Tech., Roslyn, N.Y., 1981—. Recipient David Gessner award Am. Soc. Engring. Edn., 1956, New Tech. Innovation award NASA, 1977. Sr. mem. IEEE, Am. Soc. Quality Control; mem. AIME, Am. Phys. Soc. Buddhist. Office: Lintel Tech Inc 379 Elm Dr Roslyn NY 11576-3045

LI, PEARL NEI-CHIEN, library director, consultant; b. Jiangsu, China, June 17, 1946; came to U.S., 1968; d. Ping-Yung and Yao-Hwa (Li) Chu; m. Terry Teng-Fang Li, Sept. 20, 1969; children: Ina Ying, Ping Li. BA, Nat. Taiwan U., Taipei, 1968; MA, W.Va. U., 1971; cert. advanced study in info. studies, Drexel U., 1983. Cert. sr. libr., N.J. Instr. Nat. Tchr.'s Coll., Chang-Hua, Taiwan, 1977-78; reference libr. Camden County Libr., Voorhees, N.J., 1981-82; libr. Kulzer and Dipadova, P.A., Haddonfield, N.J., 1982-87; libr. dir. Am. Law Inst., Phila., 1987—; cons. Kulzer & Dipadova, P.A., Haddonfield, N.J., 1988—; tchr. South Jersey Chinese Sch., Cherry Hill, N.J., 1978-82. Editor: (book) CLE Around the Country (annually), 1988—, (directory) ALI and ALI-ABA Directory (semi-annual), 1987—, (newsletter) Calendar of Courses and Meetings, 1987— (monthly); contbr. articles to profl. pubs. Bus. mgr. Chinese Community Ctr., Voorhees, 1981. Mem. Am. Assn. Law Librs., Chinese-Am. Librs. Assn., Greater Phila. Law Libr. Assn., Phila. Area Reference Librs. Info. Exch., Spl. Librs. Assn. Home: 1132 Sea Gull Ln Cherry Hill NJ 08003-3113 Office: The Am Law Inst 4025 Chestnut St Philadelphia PA 19104-3019

LIANG, CHANG-SENG, cardiologist, educator; b. Chang Chow, Fukien, China, Jan. 6, 1941; came to U.S. 1966; s. You Rang and Mu Lan (Cheng) L.; m. Betty Pei Pei Wang, July 29, 1967; children: Marilyn G., Marybeth L., Michelle C. MD, Nat. Taiwan U., 1965; PhD, Boston U., 1971. Diplomate Am. Bd. Internal Medicine. Intern Brookdale Hosp. Med. Ctr., N.Y., 1967-

68; resident Univ. Hosp., Boston, 1971-72; fellow Boston City Hosp., 1972-73; instr. medicine Boston U., 1973-74, asst. prof., 1973-78, assoc. prof., 1978-82; assoc. prof. U. Rochester, N.Y., 1982-86, prof. medicine, 1986—; study sect. reviewer NIH, Bethesda, Md., 1981-85. Contbr. articles to profl. jours. Mem. Am. Physiol. Soc., Am. Soc. for Pharmacology and Exptl. Therapeutics, Am. Soc. for Clin. Investigation, Am. Coll. Cardiology. Office: Univ of Rochester Med Ctr 601 Elmwood Ave Rochester NY 14642-9999

LIANG, CHARLES CHI, management and technology consultant; b. Nanking, Peoples Republic of China, June 9, 1934; came to the U.S., 1958; s. Tsai-Yung and Jean-Yu (Lee) L.; m. Anna Rosabella Juan, Jan. 28, 1961; children: Anita, Bertrand, Bryan. BS, Taiwan U., 1956; PhD, Baylor U., 1962. Rsch. chemist Houdry Process & Chem. Co., Marcus Hook, Pa., 1962-63; asst. prof. W.Va. Inst. Tech., Montgomery, 1963-64, assoc. prof., 1964-65; from group leader to assoc. tech. dir. P.R. Mallory & Co. Lab. for Phys. Sci., Burlington, Mass., 1965-77; v.p. Wilson Greatbatch Ltd., Clarence, N.Y., 1977-79; pres. Electrochem Industries, Clarence, 1979-82, Omnion Enterprises Inc., Clarence, 1982—. Contbr. numerous articles to profl. jours.; patentee in field. Recipient IR 100 award Indsl. Rsch. Mag., 1971. Mem. Am. Chem. Soc., Electrochem. Soc. Office: Omnion Enterprises Inc 9460 Greiner Rd Clarence NY 14031-1213

LIANG, ISABELLA YEE-SHAN, health scientist administrator; b. Kweilin, China; came to U.S., 1979; d. Chi-Chin and Kin-Sam (Wong) L. BS, Chinese U. Hong Kong, 1966; grad. summa cum laude, Pontificia Facultas Theologic, Rome, 1972; M, U. Hong Kong, 1976, PhD, 1979. Rsch. assoc. U. Okla. Health Scis. Ctr., Oklahoma City, 1979-83; instr., sci. assoc. Tex. Coll. Osteopathic Medicine, Ft. Worth, 1983-87; sr. fellow NIH, Bethesda, Md., 1988-90, health scientist adminstr., 1990—. Mem. Am. Heart Assn. (basic sci. coun.), Am. Sect. Internat. Soc. Heart Rsch., Am. Physiol. Soc., Microcirculatory Soc., Soc. Exptl. Biology and Medicine, Sigma Xi. Office: 9000 Rockville Pike Bethesda MD 20892-0001

LIANG, MICHAEL THEAN-CHONG, physiologist, health and wellness researcher; b. Klang, Selangor, Malaysia, July 25, 1942; came to U.S., 1968; s. Fong-Wong and Yee-Bei (Tan) L. BEd, Nat. Taiwan Normal U., Republic of China, 1966; MS, Springfield (Mass.) Coll., 1970; PhD, U. Minn., 1974. Dir. cardiac rehab. Divine Redeemer Meml. Hosp., South St. Paul, Minn., 1975-80; pres., cons. Prevention & Rehab. Inc., Bethesda, Md., 1980-84; assoc. prof. George Williams Coll., Downers Grove, Ill., 1983-85, Chgo. Coll. Osteo. Medicine, 1985-89; prof. Sch. Osteo Medicine, dir. human performance lab. U. Medicine and Dentistry N.J., Stratford, 1989—; vis. prof. Nat. Coll. Phys. Edn. and Sports, Taoyuan, Republic of China, 1990—; v.p. Ill. Soc. Cardiac Health and Rehab. Contbr. rsch. articles to profl. jours. Nat. YMCA scholar, 1971, 72. Fellow Am. Coll. Sports Medicine (cert. exercise specialist, cert. program dir. preventive and rehab. exercise); mem. AAHPER, Am. Physiol. Soc., Am. Heart Assn. (coun. on artherosclerosis), Assn. Tchrs. Preventive Medicine. Office: U Medicine and Dentistry NJ 301 S Central Plz Rm 1200 Stratford NJ 08084-1503

LIAO, KAREN ANNE, real estate executive; b. N.Y.C., Nov. 13, 1945; d. Joseph Henry and Virginia Rita (Martin) Pravetz; m. Paul F. Liao, Aug. 31, 1968; children: Teresa, Joanna. BA, Hunter Coll., CUNY, 1967; AAS, Brookdale Community Coll., Lincroft, N.J., 1984. Rsch. assoc. N.Y. Hosp./Cornell Med. Sch., N.Y.C., 1967-68, Mt. Sinai Med. Sch., N.Y.C., 1968-71; learning asst. Brookdale Community Coll., Lincroft, 1982-84; computer programmer AT&T Bell Labs., Holmdel, N.J., 1984-90; real estate salesperson Hartshorne Realty, Atlantic Highlands, N.J., 1989-90, Weichert Realtors, Rumson, N.J., 1990—. Office: Weichert Realtors 30 Ridge Rd Rumson NJ 07760-1830

LIAU, MARY CHONG-CHIN, engineer; b. Bangkok, Thailand; came to U.S., 1977; d. You-ming and Lily Liau. BSEE, Tufts U., 1985; MSEE, Boston U., 1988. Registered profl. engr., Mass. Assoc. engr. Raytheon, Marlboro, Mass., 1985-87; engr. Digital Equipment Corp., Littleton, Mass., 1987—. Mem. IEEE, Soc. Women Engrs., Eta Kappa Nu. Home: 1 Agawam Rd Acton MA 01720-2501 Office: Digital Equipment Corp 305 Forest St Marlborough MA 01752

LIBBY, JOHN KELWAY, financial services company executive; b. Washington, June 13, 1926; s. John H.and Violet K. (Bamber) L.; m. Mary Seymour Kindel, Dec. 30, 1960; children: Carolyn K., Anne K., Virginia K. BA, Haverford Coll., 1945; postgrad., Harvard U., 1946. With U.S. Dept. State, Washington, 1947-48, Capital Airlines Inc., 1949-51, S.G. Warburg & Co., London, 1954; assoc. and v.p. Kuhn Loeb & Co., N.Y.C., 1955-66, gen. ptnr., 1967-77; mng. dir. Lehman Bros. Kuhn Loeb, Inc., N.Y.C., 1977-80; chmn., chief exec. officer Parkstar, Inc., N.Y.C., 1980—, chmn. Parkstar Ltd. Bahamas, 1987—; gen. ptnr. K.L. Assocs., N.Y.C., 1985—; adviser Cen. Bank Venezuela, 1974-75; bd. dirs. various corps. Trustee Brearley Sch., N.Y.C., 1977-85. Served to lt. USN, 1944-46, PTO, 1951-53. Office: K L Assocs 450 Park Ave New York NY 10022-2605

LIBBY, JULIANNA, naval architect; b. Westbrook, Maine, Mar. 10, 1956; d. Clifford Emery and Elizabeth Phipps (Bennett) L. BCE, U. N.H., 1978; MS in Ocean & Marine Engring., George Washington U., Washington, 1982. Naval architect David Taylor Rsch. Ctr., Bethesda, Md., 1978-88; with Bath (Maine) Iron Works Corp., 1988—. Assoc. mem. Am Soc. Naval Engrs., Am. Soc. Civil Engrs. Republican. Mem. United Ch. of Christ. Office: Bath Iron Works Corp Bath ME 04530

LIBBY, PAUL MARC, sales executive, consultant; b. Newark, May 27, 1947; s. Dexter Kalman and Jean J. (Zessin) L.; m. Marlene Ellen Hirschel, May 1, 1973; 1 child, Sarah Lindsay. BS, E. Tex. State U., 1969. Salesman Met. Life Ins. Co., Maplewood, N.J., 1970-75; tchr. Newark Bd. Edn., 1969-75; salesman Amerada Hess Corp., Woodbridge, N.J., 1975-81; cons. PML Sales Assn., West Orange, N.J., 1977—; nat. sales mgr. Gladstone Electric, West Orange, 1982-84, Cabletenna Corp., East Brunswick, N.J., 1985—; cons. ABM Guarantee Group, Clifton, N.J., 1984-85, Tec Sales, Short Hills, N.J., 1983-84; Thoughtware/IMI, Coconut Grove, Fla., 1983-85, cons., mktg. dir. TCI Industries, Buffalo, 1983-85. Mem. Am. Mgmt. Assn. Home: 376 St Cloud Ave West Orange NJ 07052-2520 Office: Cabletenna Corp 440 Forsgate Dr Cranbury NJ 08512

LIBERTY, LEONA HELEN, rehabilitation services professional; b. Troy, N.Y., Nov. 2, 1940. BS cum laude, Syracuse U., 1976, MS, 1979; EdD, La. State U., 1985. Asst. prof. St. John's U., Jamaica, N.Y., 1984-91; rehab. coord. Capabilities Evaluation Ctr., Albany, N.Y., 1991—; adj. prof. SUNY, Albany, 1991—. Home: PO Box 442 East Greenbush NY 12061-0442

LICHSTEIN, EDGAR, cardiologist; b. N.Y.C., Nov. 27, 1936; s. Joseph and Ruth (Weisner) L.; m. Marilyn Dorf, June 19, 1966; children: Adam Robert, Amy Ruth. AB, Columbia Coll., 1957; MD, SUNY, Bklyn., 1961. Diplomate Am. Bd. Internal Medicine, Am. Bd. Cardiovascular Disease. Intern Lenox Hill Hosp., N.Y.C., 1961-62, resident in medicine, 1962-63; resident in medicine NYU, N.Y.C., 1963-64; fellow in cardiology NYU-Nat. Heart Inst., 1964-66; chief cardiology Mt. Sinai Med. Services Elmhurst, N.Y.C., 1971-77; dir. cardiology Maimonides Med. Ctr., Bklyn., 1977-89, dir. dept. medicine, 1989—; bd. dirs. Maimonides Rsch. and Devel. Found., Bklyn., N.Y. Heart Assn. Author: Hemodynamict's Reference File, 1971; contbr. articles to profl. jours. Mem. New Rochelle (N.Y.) Sch. Bd., 1977-81; bd. dirs. New Rochelle Youth Soccer LEague, 1976. Served to capt. USAF, 1966-68. Fellow Am. Coll. Cardiology, Am. Coll. Physicians, Am. Coll. Chest Physicians, Council Clin. Cardiology; mem. N.Y. Heart Assn. (chmn. council community programs, bd. dirs. 1983—). Jewish. Office: Maimonides Med Ctr 4802 10th Ave Brooklyn NY 11219-2999

LICHT, STUART LAWRENCE, chemistry educator; b. Boston, July 24, 1954; s. Truman and Reeva (Snyder) L.; children: Dov, Ariel, Yacov. BA, Wesleyan U., 1976, MA, 1981; PhD, Weizmann Inst. Sci., Rehovot, Israel, 1986. Astrophysics cons. Princeton (N.J.) U., 1977-78; vis. asst. prof. Northeastern U., Boston, 1985-86; vis. scientist MIT, Cambridge, 1986-88; prof. chemistry Clark U., Worcester, Mass., 1988—; faculty fellow Office of Naval Rsch., Newport, R.I., 1991. Contbr. articles to profl. jours.; patentee in field. Mem. Am. Chem. Soc., Electrochem. Soc., Soc. Electroanalytical Chemistry, Boston Computer Soc., Sigma Xi. Office: Clark Univ Chemistry Dept 950 Main St Worcester MA 01610-1473

LICHTBLAU, MYRON IVOR, language educator; b. N.Y.C., Oct. 10, 1925; s. Samuel and Sadonia (Weinberg) L.; m. Bernice Glanz, June 23, 1956; children—Mark (dec.), Anita, Eric. BA, CCNY, 1947; MA, U. Nacional Mex., 1948; PhD, Columbia U., 1957; diploma (hon.), U. de Nuevo Leon, Mex., 1964. Tchr. spanish secondary schs., N.Y.C., 1948-57; instr. Ind. U., Bloomington, 1957-59; prof. Syracuse U., N.Y., 1959—, chmn. dept. fgn. langs., 1967-74, 86-88; vis. prof. Colgate U., Hamilton, N.Y., 1970, SUNY-Binghamton, 1975; coordinator language program Peace Corps, 1966. Author: The Argentine Novel in the Nineteenth Century, 1959, El Arte estilistico de Eduardo Mallea, 1967, Manuel Galvez, 1972, A Practical Reference Guide to Reading Spanish, 1977, Rayuela y la creatividad artistica, 1989; editor: Manuel Galvez: Las dos Vidas del Pobre Napoleon, 1963, E. Caballero Calderon: Manuel Pacho, 1980, Eduardo Mallea Ante La Critica, 1985, Emigration and Exile in Twentieth-Century Hispanic Literature, 1988, Mario Vargas Llosa: A Writer's Reality, 1990, Manuel Galvez: La maestra normal, 1991; translator: Eduardo Mallea: History of an Argentine Passion, 1983; book rev. editor Symposium, 1966—, Hispania, 1974-83; mem. editorial bd. Critica Hispánica, 1985—. Bd. dirs. Syracuse Jewish Community Ctr., 1973; pres. Rabbi Jacob Epstein Sch. Jewish Studies, 1981-83; trustee Temple Beth Sholom, 1987-88. With U.S. Army, 1944-46. Mem. AAUP, MLA, Am. Assn. Tchrs. of Spanish and Portuguese (assoc. editor 1974-83), Inst. Internat. de Lit. Iberoamericana (exec. sec. 1959-63), Internat. Assn. Hispanistas, Latin Am. Jewish Studies Assn., Drumlins Tennis Club. Jewish. Office: Syracuse U Dept Fgn Langs Syracuse NY 13210

LICHTENBAUM, STEPHEN, mathematics educator; b. Bklyn., Aug. 24, 1939; s. Reuben and Rose (Garbus) L.; m. Marilyn Harris, June 25, 1961; children: Karen, Peter, Erica, Roger, Amy. AB, Harvard U., 1960, AM, 1961, PhD, 1964. Prof. math. Brown U., Providence, R.I. Contbr. numerous articles to profl. jours. Recipient Guggenheim fellowship Guggenheim Found., 1973. Mem. Am. Math. Soc. Home: 201 Freeman Pky Providence RI 02906-4649 Office: Brown U Dept Math Providence RI 02912

LICHTENBERG, PHILIP, social work educator; b. Schenectady, N.Y., Oct. 1, 1926; s. Chester and Bertha (Stein) L.; m. Elsa Russell, June 15, 1949; children: Erik Russell, Andrew Adam, Thomas Philip, Peter Alexander. BS, Case Western Res. U., 1948, MA, 1950, PhD, 1952. Lic. psychologist, Pa. Rsch. fellow in clin. psychology Harvard U., 1951-52; rsch. asst. prof. of Psychology NYU, N.Y.C., 1952-54; rsch. psychologist Michael Reese Hosp., Chgo., 1954-57; assoc. social psychologist N.Y. State Dept. of Mental Hygiene, Syracuse, N.Y., 1957-61; from assoc. prof. to prof. social work and social rsch. Bryn Mawr (Pa.) Coll., 1961—; bd. dirs. The Gestalt Therapy Inst. of Phila., Bala Cynwyd, Pa. Author (book) Psychoanalysis: Radical and Conservative, 1969, Getting Even, 1988, Undoing the Clinch of Oppression, 1990; co-author (book) Motivation for Child Psychiatry Treatment, 1960; contbr. articles to profl. jours. Sgt. USAF, 1944-46, ETO. Mem. Am. Psychological Assn., Coun. on Social Work Edn., AAAS, AAUP, Am. Orthopsychiatric Assn., Pa. Psychological Assn., Bertha Capen Reynolds Soc. Home: 25 S Lowrys Ln Bryn Mawr PA 19010-1402 Office: Bryn Mawr Coll 300 Airdale Rd Bryn Mawr PA 19010-1697

LICHTENBERGER, HORST WILLIAM, chemical company executive; b. Yugoslavia, Nov. 5, 1935; came to U.S., 1950, naturalized, 1955; s. Andrew W. and Hella L.; m. Patricia Ann Thomas, June 15, 1957; children: Erich, Lisa. B.A., U. Iowa, 1957, B.S. in Chem. Engring., 1959; M.B.A., SUNY, Buffalo, 1962. With Union Carbide Corp., 1959—; bus. mgr. Union Carbide Corp., N.Y.C., 1972-75; v.p., gen. mgr. Linde div. Union Carbide Corp., Geneva, 1975-80; v.p. mktg. Union Carbide Corp., N.Y.C., 1980-82; v.p., gen. mgr. gas products Union Carbide Corp., 1982-85, pres. Solvents and Coatings div., from 1985, pres. Chemicals and Plastics group, 1986-92; pres., CEO Praxair Inc., 1992—. Mem. Iowa N.G., 1954-62. Mem. Am. Iron and Steel Inst., Chem. Mfg. Assn., Soc. of Chem. Industry. Republican. Office: Praxair Inc 38C Grove St Ridgefield CT 06877-4657*

LICHTER, ROBERT LOUIS, science foundation administrator, chemist; b. Cambridge, Mass., Oct. 26, 1941. AB, Harvard U., 1962; PhD, U. Wis., 1967. NIH postdoctoral fellow Technische U. Braunschweig, Fed. Republic of Germany, 1967-68; rsch. fellow Calif. Inst. Tech., Pasadena, 1968-70; from asst. prof. to prof. Hunter Coll. CUNY, N.Y.C., 1970-83; chair dept. chemistry Hunter Coll. CUNY, N.Y.C., 1977-81; regional dir. grants Rsch. Corp., Port Washington, N.Y., 1983-86; v.p. for rsch. and grad. studies SUNY, Stony Brook, 1986-89; exec. dir. Camille & Henry Dreyfus Found., N.Y.C., 1989—; vis. scientist Sandoz Rsch. Labs., 1981-82, Exxon Rsch. and Engring. Co., 1981-82; treas. Exptl. NMR Confs., Inc., 1981-85. Co-author: N-15 Nuclear Magnetic Resonance Spectroscopy, 1979, C-13 Nuclear Magnetic Resonance Spectroscopy, 1980, NMR Spectroscopy Techniques, 1987; editor Concepts in Magnetic Resonance Jour., 1989—; mem. editorial bd. Magnetic Resonance in Chemistry Jour., 1983-87; mem. edn. adv. bd. N.Y. Acad. Scis., 1991—; contbr. over 36 articles to profl. jours. Mem. Am. Chem. Soc. (chair NMR topical group Northern Jersey chpt. 1982-83), N.Y. Acad. Scis. (chair sect. on chem. scis. 1987). Office: Camille & Henry Dreyfus Found 555 Madison Ave Ste 1305 New York NY 10022-3301

LICHTIG, LEO KENNETH, health economist; b. Bklyn., Oct. 20, 1953; s. Samuel and Alyne Norma (Strauss) L.; m. Susan Mary Walsh, May 15, 1977; children: Brielle Joy, Danica Jill. BS, MS, Rensselaer Poly. Inst., 1974, PhD, 1976. Asst. prof. SUNY, Albany, 1976-77; project specialist, econometrician N.J. State Dept. Health, Trenton, 1977-82; dir. utilization econs. and rsch. Empire Blue Cross/Blue Shield, Albany, 1982-90; v.p. rsch. and demonstration Health Care Rsch. Found., Albany, 1982-90; v.p. Network, Inc., Latham, N.Y., 1990—, Randolph, N.J., 1990—; pvt. practice cons., Latham, 1982-90; mem. nat. diagnosis related group, steering com. health care fin. adminstrn. Yale U., Washington, 1979-81; mem. adj. faculty Russell Sage Grad. Sch. Health Adminstrn., Albany, 1986—, Union Coll. Grad. Mgmt. Inst., Schenectady, N.Y., 1991—; expert reviewer Health Care Financing Adminstrn., Washington, 1987, 89. Author: Hospital Information Systems for Case Mix Management, 1986; contbg. editor (newsletter) Nat. Report on Computers & Health, 1982-85; contbr. articles to profl. jours. Mem. tech. adv. com. Statewide Planning and Rsch. Coop. System. Mem. Am. Mgmt. Assn., Assn. for Health Svcs. Rsch., Am. Statis. Assn. (com. on privacy and confidentiality 1981-84, subcom. on quality and productivity measures 1988-90), N.Y. State Dept. Health.

LICK, DALE WESLEY, mathematician, university president; b. Marlette, Mich., Jan. 7, 1938; s. John R. and Florence M. (Baxter) L.; m. Marilyn Kay Foster, Sept. 15, 1956; children: Lynette (dec.), Kitty, Diana, Ronald. BS with honors, Mich. State U., 1958, MS in Math, 1959; PhD in Math, U. Calif., Riverside, 1965. Research asst. physics Mich. State U., East Lansing, 1958; teaching asst. math. Mich. State U., 1959; instr., chmn. dept. math. Port Huron (Mich.) Jr. Coll., 1959-60; asst. to comptroller Mich. Bell Telephone Co., Detroit, 1961; instr. U. Redlands, 1961-63; teaching asst. math. U. Calif., Riverside, 1964-65; asst. prof. math. U. Tenn., Knoxville, 1965-67; postdoctoral fellow Brookhaven Nat. Lab., Upton, N.Y., 1967-68; assoc. prof. U. Tenn., 1968-69; assoc. prof., head dept. math. Drexel U., Phila., 1969-72; adj. assoc. prof. dept. pharmacology Med. Sch., Temple U., Phila., 1969-72; v.p. acad. affairs Russell Sage Coll., Troy, N.Y., 1972-74; prof. math. and computing scis. Old Dominion U., Norfolk, Va., 1974-78; also dean Old Dominion U. (Sch. Scis. and Health Professions); pres., prof. math. and computer sci. Ga. So. Coll., Statesboro, 1978-86; pres., prof. math. U. Maine, Orono, 1986-91, Fla. State U., Tallahassee, 1991—; textbook and manuscript reviewer for Appleton-Century Crofts, Bogden and Quigley, Macmillan and Prentice-Hall, 1966—; cons. Va. Health Planning and Resources Devel. Agy., 1976-78, Norfolk State U., Va., 1977, U. Central Fla., 1977; proposal reviewer divs. higher edn. in sci. and public understanding of sci. NSF, 1972-76; appeared in interviews, discussions and spl. topic presentations various radio and TV programs, 1974—, mem. faculty 7 day tng. programs series in health adminstrn., 1977-79, guest lectr. various conf. and symposia on health care and interinstnl. cooperation, 1975—; bd. dirs. Blue Cross/Blue Shield, 1987-88. Author: Fundamentals of Algebra, 1970; contbr. articles to profl. jours. Bd. dirs. Statesboro/Coll. Symphony, 1978-86, Statewide Health Coordinating Coun. Va., 1976-78; chmn. higher edn. adv. bd. Reorganized Ch. of Jesus Christ of Latter Day Sts., 1986—; mem. planning com. Bulloch Meml. Hosp., 1979-86; active Costal Empire coun. Boy Scouts Am., 1982-86, Katalidin coun., 1986-91; bd. dirs. Health Care Ctrs. Am., Virginia Beach, Va., 1978, Ea. Va. Health Systems Agy., 1976-78; chmn., bd. dirs. Assembly Against Hunger and Malnutrition, 1977-78, pres., 1977-78. Mem. AAUP, AAAS, Am. Math. Soc., Math. Assn. Am., Am. Assn. Univ. Adminstrs., Am. Soc. Allied Health Professions, Am. Assn. State Colls. and Univs. (chmn. com. agr. resources and rural devel. 1981-86), Am. Assn. Higher Edn., Sigma Xi, Phi Kappa Phi, Pi Mu Epsilon (governing coun. 1972-77), Beta Gamma Sigma, Pi Sigma Epsilon. Mem., high priest Reorganized Ch. of Jesus Christ of Latter-day Saints. Lodge: Rotary. Office: Fla State U Office of Pres Tallahassee FL 32306

LICKEM, CONNI LEEBIDOW, literary consultant; b. Ferndale, Wash., Jan. 29, 1960; d. Phil A. and Elma (Finsk) Thatchet; m. Martin E. Lickem, Jan. 29, 1981. BA, U. Zaire, Africa, 1982, PhD, 1987. Community devel. Lubasho et Dimba, Lubvmbashi, Zaire, 1979-85; prof. U. Zaire, 1985-91; literary cons. Lickem & Assocs., Washington, 1992—. Editor and writer daily paper Dimbu Ata, 1981-90. Development Peace Corps, Zaire, 1989-91. Mem. Zaire and Am. Reading Club (pres. 1992—). Civil Libertarian. Roman Catholic. Office: Lickem & Assocs 114 S Pitt St Alexandria VA 22314

LICKLIDER, ROY EILERS, political science educator; b. Seattle, Jan. 27, 1941; s. Woodburn Jennings and Agnes (Eilers) L.; m. Patricia Minichino, July 10, 1971; 1 child, Virginia Anne. BA, Boston U., 1963; MA, Yale U., 1964, PhD, 1968. Asst. prof. polit. sci. Tougaloo (Miss.) Coll., 1967-68; asst. prof. polit. sci. Rutgers Univ., New Brunswick, 1968-72, assoc. prof. polit. sci., 1972-89, prof. polit. sci., 1989—; program officer Exxon Edn. Found., N.Y.C., 1977-78; vis. prof. polit. sci. Princeton (N.J.) Univ., 1989; vis. researcher Ctr. for the Study of Social Change, New Sch. for Social Rsch., N.Y.C., 1990-91. Author: Private Nuclear Strategists, 1971, Political Power and the Arab Oil Weapon, 1988; editor: When the Killing Stops: How Civil Wars End, 1992, mem. editorial bd. Nat. Collegiate Software, 1990-91. Recipient Conf. grant U.S. Inst. of Peace, Washington, 1990. Mem. Internat. Studies Assn. (pres. comparative fgn. policy 1979-80, v.p. 1978-79, exec. com. internat. polit. econ., bd. editors internat. polit. econ. yearbook 1982-87). Home: 39 S Adelaide Ave Highland Park NJ 08904-1601 Office: Rutgers Univ Polit Sci Dept PO Box 270 New Brunswick NJ 08903-0270

LICOPANTIS, DEAN PETER, podiatrist; b. Queens, N.Y., July 5, 1961; s. Peter Gus and Yolanda (Diamantis) L.; m. Katherine J. Kozakis, June 18, 1988. BS, U. Albany, 1983; D of Podiatric Medicine, Pa. Coll. Podiatric Medicine, 1988. Podiatric surg. resident Osteo. Med. Ctr., Phila., 1988-89; podiatric surgeon Ctr. for Advanced Foot Surgery, Paramus, N.J., 1989—; staff podiatrist Ridgewood (N.J.) Manor, 1990—, Kennedy Meml. Hosp., Saddle Brook, N.J., 1991—, Wayne (N.J.) Gen. Hosp., 1991—, Bergen Pines County Hosp., Paramus, 1991—. Mem. Am. Bd. Podiatric Surgery, Am. Podiatric Med. Assn., N.Y. State Podiatric Med. Assn., Am. Podiatric Circulatory Soc. Greek Orthodox.

LIDDELL, JANE HAWLEY HAWKES, civic worker; b. Newark, Dec. 8, 1907; d. Edward Zeh and Mary Everett (Hawley) Hawkes; A.B., Smith Coll., 1931; postgrad. in art history, Harvard U., 1933-35; M.A., Columbia U., 1940; Carnegie fellow Sorbonne, Paris, 1937; m. Donald M. Liddell, Jr., Mar. 30, 1940; children: Jane Boyer, D. Roger Brooke. Pres., Planned Parenthood Essex County (N.J.), 1947-50; trustee Prospect Hill Sch. Girls, Newark, 1946-50; mem. adv. bd., publicity and public relations chmn. N.J. State Mus., Trenton, 1952-60; sec., then v.p. women's br. N.J. Hist. Soc.; women's aux. prodn. chmn. Englewood (N.J.) Hosp., 1959-61; pres. Dwight Sch. Girls Parents Assn., 1955-57; v.p. Englewood Sch. Boys Parents Assn., 1958-60; mem. Altar Guild, women's aux. bd., rector's adv. council St. Paul's Episcopal Ch., Englewood, 1954-59; bd. dir. N.Y. State Soc. of Nat. Soc. Colonial Dames, 1961-67, rep. conf. Patriotic and Hist. Socs., 1964—; bd. dirs. Huguenot Soc. Am., 1979-86, regional v.p., 1979-82, historian, 1983-84, co-chmn. Tercentennial Book, 1983-85; bd. dirs. Soc. Daus. Holland Dames, 1965-82; nat. jr. v.p. Dames of Loyal Legion, USA; bd. dirs., mem. publs. com. Daus. Cin., 1966-72; bd. dirs. Ch. Women's League Patriotic Service, 1962—, pres., 1968-70, 72-74; bd. dirs., chmn. grants com. Youth Found., N.Y.C., 1974—; chmn. for Newark, Smith Coll. 75th Ann. Fund, 1948-50; pres. North N.J. Smith Club, 1956-58; pres. Smith Coll. Class 1931, 1946-51, 76-81, editor 50th anniversary book, 1980-81. Author: (with others) Huguenot Refugees in the Settling of Colonial America, 1982-85. Recipient various commendation awards. Republican. Mem. Colonial Dames Am. (N.Y.C. chpt.). Clubs: Colony, City Gardens, Church (N.Y.C.); Jr. League Bergen County; Needle and Bobbin, Nat. Farm and Garden . Editor: Maine Echoes, 1961; research and editor asst., Wartime Writings of American Revolution Officers, 1972-75.

LIDDICOAT, BRIAN, producer; b. Butte, Mont., Sept. 27, 1944; s. Albert Earl and Marie Elizabeth (McNaughton) L.; m. Allison Davis Casey, Dec. 4, 1984 (div.); m. Charmaine Henninger, Dec. 7, 1985; children: Julie Millicent, Gillian Devon, Gabrielle Corinne. AA, Am. River Community Coll., Sacramento, Calif., 1964; postgrad., U. Utah, 1966. Co. mgr. Columbia Artists Mgmt., 1968-80, Dancin', A Chorus Line, 1980-84; exec. dir. Shubert Performing Arts Ctr., New Haven, 1984-85; co. mgr. Dream Girls, Gigi, 1985-86, Cats, 1986-87; gen. mgr. Big Apple Circus, N.Y.C., 1982-92, Archdos, N.Y.C., 1992; producer Winterschau-Holiday Circus, N.Y.C., 1992—; co-producer opening gala Shubert Pac, New Haven, 1984. Home: 50 Barn Rd Deep River CT 06417

LIDE, DAVID REYNOLDS, scientific editor; b. Gainesville, Ga., May 25, 1928; s. David Reynolds and Laura Kate (Simmons) L.; m. Mary Ruth Lomer, Nov. 5, 1955 (div. Dec. 1988); children: David Alston, Vanessa Grace, James Hugh, Quentin Robert; m. Bettijoyce Breen, 1988. BS, Carnegie Inst. Tech., 1949; PhD, Harvard U., 1952, AM, 1951. Physicist Nat. Bur. Standards, Washington, 1954-63, chief molecular spectroscopy sect., 1963-69; dir. standard reference data Nat. Bur. Standards, Gaithersburg, Md., 1969-88; editor-in-chief Handbook of Chemistry and Physics, CRC Press, 1988—; pres. Com. on Data for Sci. and Tech., Paris, 1986-90. Editor Jour. Phys. and Chem. Reference Data, 1972—; contbr. over 100 articles to profl. publs. Recipient Skolnik award for Chem. Info., Am. Chem. Soc., 1988, Patterson-Crane award, 1991, Presdl. Rank award in sr. exec. svc., 1986. Mem. Internat. Union Pure and Applied Chemistry (pres. phys. chemistry div. 1983-87). Home and Office: 13901 Riding Loop Dr Gaithersburg MD 20878-3879

LIDSTROM, ESTHER MARIE, art educator; b. Rockville Centre, N.Y., Aug. 18, 1947; d. Carl John and Helen Marie (Benzie) L. BA, Adelphi U., 1969, MA, 1971. Lic. art educator, N.Y. Tchr. Sayville (N.Y.) Pub. Schs., 1972-84; police officer Nassau County Police Dept., Mineola, N.Y., 1984-86; high sch. art tchr. Sayville High Sch., 1986—; guest speaker Nat. Audubon Soc., East Islip, N.Y., 1989, Nassau County Visual Arts Ctr., East Norwich, N.Y., 1990, Bryant Libr., Roslyn, N.Y., 1991, KC, Amityville, N.Y., 1991. Group shows include Rochester (N.Y.) Mus. and Sci. Ctr., 1989, Boston Mus. Sci., 1989, Cleve. Mus. Natural History, 1991, Va. Mus. of Natural History, 1992, The Witte Mus., San Antonio, 1992, San Bernardino County Mus., Redlands, Calif., 1992, Anniston (Ala.) Mus. Natural History, 1992; contbr. articles to profl. jours. Recipient Showcase award Visual Art Alliance of L.I. and Nassau County Office Cultural Devel., 1989, Sax award Nat. League Am. Pen Women, Suffolk County, N.Y., 1990. Mem. Soc. Animal Artists (award of excellence 1988), Salmagundi Club, N.Y. Zool. Soc., East African Wildlife Soc., Friends of Conservation. Office: Wildlife Impressions PO Box 781 Sayville NY 11782-0781

LIEB, ANDREW MARC, wholesale distributor executive; b. Pottstown, Pa., June 12, 1955; s. Alan Morton and Barbara Lois (Goald) L.; m. Deborah Richardson, Apr. 29, 1979 (div. Oct. 1987); 1 child, Brian; m. Pamela Susan Cluck, June 25, 1989; stepchildren: Adam Zummo, Rachael Zummo, Daniel Zummo. Student, Bucknell U., 1973-75. Pres. Pottstown (Pa.) News Co., 1975—, Nala Corp., Pottstown, 1984-85. Chief, pres. Phoenixville YMCA Indian Guides, 1989-91; coach Phoenixville Area Soccer Club; treas. Temple Brith Achim, 1992—. Named Vol. of the Yr., Phoenixville YMCA, 1991. Mem. Atlantic Coast Ind. Distbr. Assn. Jewish. Office: Pottstown News Co 557 W High PO Box 274 Pottstown PA 19464

LIEBENSON, GLORIA KRASNOW, interior design executive; b. Chgo., Apr. 6, 1922; d. Henry Randolph and Margaret (Rivkin) Krasnow; m.

Herbert Liebenson, March 11, 1944; children: Lauren Ward, Lynn Liebenson. Student, Int. Inst. Interior Design, Washington, 1961; B Am. Studies, Dunbarton Coll., Washington, 1974. Lic. Interior Designer, D.C. Numerous positions Journalism, Advt., editing, 1942-62; interior design exec. Creative Interiors, 1962—; tchr. interior design YMCA, Washington, 1980-82. Mem. editorial staff Champlin Encyclopedia, 1945-47; journalist Shreveport Jour., 1944. Bd. Dirs. Jewish Social Svc. Agy., Washington, 1983-85, Nat. Coun. Jewish Women. 1982-84; pres. Friends Nat. Museum African Art, 1983-85, D.C. Mental Health Assn., 1986-88. Mem. Womens Nat. Dem. Club. Democrat. Jewish. Home and office: 2703 Unicorn Ln NW Washington DC 20015-2233

LIEBERGALL, GORDON S., ophthalmologist; b. N.Y.C., July 16, 1934; s. Harry and Rose (Rotner) L.; m. Florence H. Worton, June 13, 1959; children: Caryn, David, Jonathan. BS, Syracuse U., 1955; MD, Chgo. Med. Sch., 1959. Ophthalmologist pvt. practice, Suffern, N.Y. Fellow Am. Acad. Ophthalmology, Am. Coll. Surgeons. Home: 8 Longbow Rd Suffern NY 10901

LIEBERMAN, EDWIN JAMES, psychiatrist; b. Milw., Nov. 21, 1934. AB, U. Calif., 1955, MD, 1958. Intern USPHS Hosp., Staten Island, 1958-59; resident in psychiatry Mass. Mental Health Ctr., 1959-61, Putnam Children's Ctr., Boston, 1962-63, Hillcrest Children's Ctr., 1965-66; asst. clin. prof. Howard U. Sch. Medicine, Washington, 1967-76; assoc. clin. prof. George Washington U. Sch. Medicine, Washington, 1976-87; adj. prof. dept. family and community devel. U. Md., 1987-90; clin. prof. George Washington U. Sch. Medicine, 1990—; pvt. practice Family Inst., Chtd.; psychiatrist extramural program NIMH, 1963-67, chief ctr. for child and family mental health, 1969-73; cons. Peace Corps, 1963-64, UNICEF, 1965-66, WHO, 1974; coord. family therapy Hillcrest Children's Ctr., 1971-74; lectr. Internacia Esperanto Kongresa U., Beijing, 1986; bd. chmn. Ctr. for Population Options, 1981-83; population rsch. adv. com. NIH, 1967-70. Author: Acts of Will: The Life and Work of Otto Rank, 1955. Capt., med. dir. USPHSR. Fellow Am. Psychiat. Assn., Am. Pub. Health Assn. (project dir. mental health/family planning 1972-77), Am. Assn. for Marriage and Family Therapy (bd. dirs.); Esperantic Studies Found. (bd. dirs.), Universala Esperanto Asocio (del. in medicine). Office: 3900 Northampton St NW Washington DC 20015-2951

LIEBERMAN, HARVEY JOEL, mental health administrator, psychologist; b. Bklyn., Dec. 7, 1943; s. Leonard and Sylvia Lieberman; m. Carol M. Schneider, Apr. 12, 1970; 1 child, Jay. BE, Cooper Union, 1966; MS in Psychology, Pa. State U., 1970, PhD in Clin. Psychology, 1974. Lic. psychologist, N.Y. Dir. Bayview Manor/South Beach Psychiat. Ctr., Bklyn., 1974-79; chief community residential treatment svc. South Beach Psychiat. Ctr., S.I., 1979-87; exec. dir. Inst. for Community Living, Bklyn., 1986-87; dir. treatment svcs. South Beach Psychiat. Ctr., Staten Island, 1987—; internat. cons. in field; adj. prof. L.I. U., Bklyn., 1985—; faculty mem. NYU, 1991—. Contbr. articles to profl. jours. Mem. APA, AAAS, Eastern Evaluation and Rsch. Soc., Am. Coll. Mental Health Adminstrs. Home: 31 Oxford Pl Rockville Centre NY 11570-1829

LIEBERMAN, HARVEY MICHAEL, hepatologist, gastroenterologist, educator; b. N.Y.C., Feb. 24, 1949; s. Louis and Ellie (Miller) L.; m. Lewette Alexandra Fielding, Nov. 24, 1985. BA magna cum laude, NYU, 1972, MD, 1976. Intern Bronx (N.Y.) Mcpl. Hosp./Albert Einstein Coll. Medicine, N.Y.C., 1976-77, jr. and sr. resident, 1977-79; fellow in gastroenterology and liver disease Albert Einstein Coll. Medicine, 1979-81, rsch. assoc. Liver Rsch. Ctr., 1983; asst. prof. Albert Einstein Coll. Medicine, Bronx, N.Y., 1984-86; dir. gastroenterology Gouverneur Hosp., N.Y.C., 1986-90; asst. chief gastroenterology Lenox Hill Hosp., N.Y.C., 1992—; clin. asst. prof. Sch. Medicine NYU, 1986—; prin. investigator Liver Rsch. Ctr. Albert Einstein Coll. Medicine, 1984-87; med. adv. bd. Crohn's and Colitis Found. of Am., Am. Liver Found., N.Y. chpts., 1987—; researcher in molecular biology of hepatitis B virus and relationship to viral infection and liver cancer. Author: Relationship of Hepatitis B Viral Infection in Serum to Viral Replication, 1983. Recipient Clin. Investigator award NIH, 1984-87. Fellow ACP, Am. Coll. Gastroenterology, N.Y. Acad. Gastroenterology (pres. 1990-91). Office: 345 E 37th St New York NY 10016-3217

LIEBERMAN, HENRY RICHARD, retired editor, consultant; b. St. Louis; s. Joseph Morris and Saragolda (Spector) L.; m. Kathryn Gwenith Martin, June 11, 1949; children: Peter Martin, Linda Susan Lieberman Teurlinckx. AB, Columbia U., 1937, MA, 1950. Reporter N.Y. Times, N.Y.C., 1937-40; reporter, Washington corr. Newspaper PM, N.Y.C., 1940-41; editor U.S. Office War Info., Washington, 1941-44; chief news editor U.S. Office War Info., Chungking, China, 1944-45; Far East corr. N.Y. Times, various locations, 1946-57; editor N.Y. Times, N.Y.C., 1957-60, dir. sci. dept., 1960-70, asst. to exec. editor computer ops., 1970-81, cons., 1981-84; pres. H.R. Lieberman Assocs., Ltd., Scarsdale, N.Y., 1981-86. Author: China Versus Russia in Sinkiang, 1950; author spl. series for N.Y. Times on computer operation in USSR, Alaska Pipeline. Fellow Coun. Fgn. Rels.; mem. IEEE, N.Y. Acad. Scis., Phi Beta Kappa. Home: 3 Medford Ln Scarsdale NY 10583-3315

LIEBERMAN, JAMES, city health official; b. N.Y.C., June 2, 1921; s. Elias and Rose (Kiesler) L.; m. Lucille Nan Goldstein, Nov. 7, 1943; 1 child, Margaret Ann. Student Cornell U., 1938-40; D.V.M., Middlesex (now Brandeis) U., 1944; M.P.H., U. Minn., 1947. Sr. cons. UNRRA, 1946; commd. USPHS, 1948; assigned as cons. food borne diseases Bur. State Services, Kansas City, Mo. and Washington, 1948-50, 52-54, chief spl. projects program (emergency health), 1951-52; liaison officer U.S. Navy Bur. Medicine and Surgery, 1952; epidemiologist on detail to N.Y. State Health Dept., Albany, 1954-55; developer of first field training program in epidemiology Communicable Disease Ctr., Atlanta, 1955-59, chief Med. Audiovisual Br., 1958-67; founding dir. Nat. Med. Audiovisual Ctr. Atlanta, 1967-70; assoc. dir. for Audiovisual and Telecommunications, Nat. Library of Medicine, NIH, Washington, 1967-70; v.p. med. div. Videorecord Corp. Am., Westport, Conn., 1970-73; cons. in health scis. edn. Westport, 1973-76; dir. Dept. Health, Greenwich, Conn., 1976—; vis. prof. Sch. Medicine Hahnemann U., Phila., 1973—. Contbr. articles to med. jours. Author: (with others) Instructor's Guide to Sanitary Food Service, 1952. Editor: Animal Disease and Human Health, 1958; (with others) Comparative Medicine in Transition, 1960; Biomedical Communication: Problems and Resources, 1967. Served to asst. surg. gen., rear adm. USPHS, 1948-70; served with USNR, 1944-46. Recipient Meritorious Service medal USPHS, 1965; Brenda award Theta Sigma Phi, 1968; Hadassah Myrtle Wreath award, 1969; Exceptional Service award Ga. Easter Seal Soc., 1970. Fellow Am. Pub. Health Assn. (elective councilor 1959-62, 66), Nat. Easter Seal Soc. (councilor, prof. adv. council 1969-75); mem. Assn. Mil. Surgeons (life), N.Y. Acad. Scis., AVMA, Greenwich Med. Soc. (hon.), U.S. Conf. Local Health Officers (trustee 1979-87), Sigma Xi. Home: 12 Silver Brook Rd Westport CT 06880-1521 Office: Dept Health 101 Field Point Rd Greenwich CT 06836

LIEBERMAN, JETHRO KOLLER, law educator, writer; b. Washington, Oct. 23, 1943; s. J. Ben and Elizabeth (Koller) L.; m. Susan E. Viuker, Aug. 14, 1966 (div. Oct. 1985); children: Jessica D., Seth K.; m. Jo Shifrin, Apr. 8, 1990. BA, Yale U., 1964; JD, Harvard U., 1967. Bar: N.Y. 1967, D.C. 1968. Staff writer Bus. Week, N.Y.C., 1967-68, legal affairs editor, 1973-82l; assoc. Arent, Fox, Kintner, Plotkin & Kahn, Washington, 1971-72; v.p., gen. counsel Stein and Day Pubs., N.Y.C., 1972-73; v.p. Ctr. for Pub. Resources, N.Y.C., 1982-85; prof. Law Sch. N.Y. Law Sch., 1985—; vis. assoc. prof. Fordham U. Law Sch., N.Y.C., 1983-85; proprietor Goldstein & Lieberman Writing Workshop for Lawyers, Hastings-on-Hudson, N.Y., 1985—, Dialogue Press, Berkeley, Calif. and Hastings-on-Hudson, 1988—. Author: The Litigious Society, 1981 (Silver Gavel award 1982), The Enduring Constitution, 1987 (Silver Gavel award 1988), Lawyer's Guide to Writing Well, 1990, and others. Lt. USNR, 1968-71. Mem. ABA, OCD Found. Office: N Y Law Sch 57 Worth St New York NY 10013-2959

LIEBERMAN, JOSEPH I., senator; b. Stamford, Conn., Feb. 24, 1942; s. Henry and Marcia (Manger) L.; m. Hadassah Freilich, Mar. 20, 1983; children: Matthew, Rebecca, Ethan, Hana. B.A., Yale U., 1964, J.D., 1967. Bar: Conn. 1967. Mem. Conn. Senate, 1971-81, Senate majority leader, 1975-81; ptnr. Lieberman, Segaloff & Wolfson, New Haven, 1972-83; atty. gen. State of Conn., Hartford, 1983-89; U.S. Senator from Conn., 1989—. Author: The Power Broker, 1966, The Scorpion and the Tarantula, 1970, The Legacy, 1981, Child Support in America, 1986. Democrat. Jewish. Office: 502 Hart Senate Office Bldg Washington DC 20510

LIEBES, RAQUEL, import and export company executive, university lecturer; b. San Salvador, El Salvador, Aug. 28, 1938; came to the U.S., 1952, naturalized, 1964; d. Ernesto Martin and Alice Bella Juliane (Philip) L.; m. Richard Paisley Kinkade, June 2, 1962 (div. 1977); children: Kathleen Paisley, Richard Paisley Jr., Scott Philip. BA, Sarah Lawrence Coll., 1960; MEd, Harvard U., 1961; MA, Yale U., 1962, postgrad., 1961-65; PhD in English, Oxford (Eng.) U., 1992. Instr. Spanish Sarah Lawrence Coll., Bronxville, N.Y., 1958-60; econ. teaching fellow Yale U., New Haven, 1964-65, instr. Spanish, 1964-66; exec. stockholder, bd. dirs. Import Export Co., San Salvador, 1968—; exec. stockholder, bd. dirs., ptnr., owner St. Ann's Coll. Oxford (Eng.) U., 1989; lectr. Am. U., Washington, 1989—; lectr. Am. U., Wash., 1989, dept. fgn. lang. and linguistics, dept. fgn. studies Georgetown U., Washington, 1990—. Contbr. glossary of Spanish med. terms. Hon. consul Govt. of El Salvador, 1977-80; docent High Mus. of Art, Atlanta, 1972-77; vol. Grady Hosp., Atlanta, 1966-71; instr. Spanish for med. drs. Tucson Med. Ctr., 1966-71; chmn. Atlanta Coun. for Internat. Visitors, 1966-71; mem. Outreach Group on Latin Am., Washington, 1982-86; founding mem. John Kennedy Ctr. for Performing Arts, 1980—; mem. Folger/Shakespeare Libr., Smithsonian Inst., Agape, El Salvador. Fellow Yale U., 1963, econ. fellow Yale U., 1964-65; fellow Corcoran Mus. of Art, 1984-85. Mem. Modern Lang. Assn., Am. Biog. Inst. (dep. gov. 1992-93), Jr. League of Washington, Harvard Club (Washington, Boston, N.Y.C.), Yale Club (Washington). Republican. Home: 700 New Hampshire Ave NW Washington DC 20037-2406

LIEBICH, MARCIA TRATHEN, community volunteer; b. Troy, N.Y., Mar. 10, 1942; d. Roland Henry and Ida Mae (Horsfall) Trathen; m. Donald Herbert Liebich, May 13, 1941; children: Kurt Roland, Mark Christian. BA, Elmira Coll., 1964. With Sunnyview Hosp. and Rehab. Ctr., Schenectady, 1982—, dir. devel., 1992—. Co-founder Parent Anonymous Lay Therapy, Schenectady, 1974-80; trustee Elmira (N.Y.) Coll., 1978—; bd. dirs. United Way, Schenctady, 1980-81, pres. 1985, bd. dirs. United Way, N.Y., 1991—, Sunnyview Rehab. Hosp., Schenectady, 1982, pres. 1988-91; social svcs. Women's Legis. Forum, Albany, 1984-91; bd. dirs. Leadership Schenectady, 1987—, Schenectady C. of C., 1987-90, YMCA Capital Dist., 1991—, WMHT Pub. Radio and TV, 1991—; pres. Samaritan Counseling Ctr., Schenectady, 1988-91; bd. dirs., treas. Bridge Ctr. Drug Treatment, Schenectady, 1988-91. Recipient YWCA Community Vol. award, 1986, K.S. Rozendaal award Community Svc. Schenectady, 1987, Liberty Bell award Schenectady Bar Assn., 1990, Women of Vision Betty Bean award YWCA, 1990. Mem. AAUW (pres. 1978), Jr. league Schenectady (Vol. of Yr. award 1981), Phi Beta Kappa. Republican. Lutheran. Home: 6 Brian Dr Rexford NY 12148-1415

LIEBMAN, JOEL FREDRIC, chemistry educator; b. Bklyn., May 6, 1947; s. Murray and Lucille Henrietta (Spitz) L.; m. Deborah Van Vechten, June 12, 1970. BS, Bklyn. Coll., 1967; MA, Princeton U., 1968, PhD, 1970. Postdoctoral fellow NATO, Cambridge (U.K.) Eng., 1970-71, NRC-Nat. Bur. Standards, Gaithersburg, Md., 1971-72; asst. prof. chemistry U. Md., Balt., 1972-77, assoc. prof., 1977-82, prof., 1982—; cons. Nat. Inst. Standards and Tech., Nat. Bur. Standards, Gaithersburg, 1980—; cons. editor Structural Chemistry, N.Y.C., 1990—. Contbr. book chpts. and articles to profl. jours. NSF fellow Princeton U., 1968-70, U.S. hon. Ramsey fellow, 1970, faculty fellow German Acad. Exch. Svc., 1976; Norwegian Marshal Fund travel/study grantee, 1992. Mem. Am. Chem. Soc. (exec. com. fluorine div. 1990—). Office: U Md Balt County 5401 Wilkens Ave Baltimore MD 21228-5329

LIEBMAN, LAWRENCE HOWARD, finance company consultant; b. Phila., Feb. 10, 1957; s. Emmanuel and Anita (Forman) L.; m. Marica Cohen, Feb. 10, 1988. BA, Syracuse (N.Y.) U., 1980. V.p. investments Dean Witter, Cherry Hill, N.J., 1984-86; 2d v.p., fin. consultant Shearson Lehman Bros., Cherry Hill, 1986—. Guest host (cable show) Finance Week, 1990-91. Member B'nai B'rith. Mem. Greater Cherry Hill C. of C. Office: Shearson Lehman Bros 325 Rte #70E Cherry Hill NJ 08034

LIEBMAN, RONALD STANLEY, lawyer; b. Balt., Oct. 11, 1943; s. Harry Martin and Martha (Altgenug) L.; m. Simma Liebman, Jan. 8, 1972; children: Shana, Margot. BA, Western Md. Coll., Westminster, 1966; JD, U. Md., 1969. Bar: Md. 1969, D.C. 1977, U.S. Dist. Ct. (ea. dist.) Va. 1970, U.S. Dist. Ct. Md. 1970, U.S. Dist. Ct. D.C. 1982, U.S. Ct. Appeals (4th cir.) 1972, U.S. Ct. Appeals (D.C. cir.) 1982, U.S. Ct. Appeals (5th cir.) 1985. Law clk. to chief judge U.S. Dist. Ct. Md., 1969-70; assoc. Melnicove, Kaufman & Weiner, Balt., 1970-72; asst. U.S. atty. Office of U.S. Atty., Dept. Justice, Balt., 1972-78; ptnr. Sachs, Greenebaum & Tayler, Washington, 1978-82, Patton, Boggs & Blow, Washington, 1982—. Author: Grand Jury, 1983; co-editor: Testimonial Privileges, 1983. Recipient spl. commendation award U.S. Dept. Justice, 1978. Mem. ABA, D.C. Bar Assn., Md. Bar Assn. Club: Sergeants Inn (Balt.). Office: Patton Boggs & Blow 2550 M St NW Washington DC 20037-1301

LIEBOVICH, SIDNEY, engineering educator; b. Memphis, Apr. 2, 1939; s. Harry and Rebecca (Phlant) L.; m. Gail Barbara Colin, Nov. 24, 1962; children: Bradley Colin, Adam Keith. BS, Calif. Inst. Tech., Pasadena, 1961; PhD, Cornell U., 1965. NATO postdoctoral fellow U. Coll., London, 1965-66; asst. prof. thermal engring. Cornell U., Ithaca, N.Y., 1966-70, assoc. prof. thermal engring., 1970-78, prof. mech. and aerospace engring., 1978-89, Samuel B. Eckert prof. mech. and aerospace engring., 1989—. Editor: Nonlinear Waves, 1974; assoc. editor Jour. Fluid Mechanics, 1982—; co-editor: Acta Mechanca, 1986—; mem. editorial bd. Ann. Revs. of Fluid Mechanics, 1989—. Disting. lectr. Naval Ocean Rsch. Devel. Activity, 1983. Recipient MacPherson prize Calif. Inst. Tech., 1961. Fellow ASME (chmn. applied mechanics div. 1987-88), Am. Phys. Soc. (chmn. div. fluid dynamics 1987-88), Am. Acad. Arts and Scis., U.S. Nat. Com. for Theoretical and Applied Mechanics (chair 1990—). Office: Cornell U Upson Hall Ithaca NY 14853

LIEBOVITCH, LARRY S., scientist. BS, CCNY, 1972; PhD, Harvard U., 1978. Postdoctoral fellow Mt. Sinai Sch. Medicine, N.Y.C., 1978-79; postdoctoral fellow Coll. Physicians and Surgeons Columbia U., N.Y.C., 1979-82, assoc. rsch. scientist, 1982-85, asst. prof., 1985—. Contbr. articles to Biophys. Jour., Math. Biosci., Jour. Theoretical Biology, others. Office: Coll Physicians and Surgeon Columbia U 630 W 168th St New York NY 10032-3702

LIEBOW, CHARLES, dentist, educator, researcher; b. Bklyn., June 17, 1944; s. Raymond and Ruth (Slavitsky) L.; m. Roslyn Lee Raskin, July 4, 1968; children: Bradley, Adam, Lisa. BA, NYU, 1966; DMD, Harvard U., 1970; PhD in Physiology, U. Calif., San Francisco, 1973. Asst. prof. of physiology Cornell U. Med. Coll., N.Y.C., 1973-80; assoc. prof. of surgery La. State U. Med. Sch., New Orleans, 1980-84; prof. of oral surgery SUNY, Buffalo, 1984—; sci. dir. Nat. Pancreatic Cancer Program, New Orleans, 1980-84, Nat. Pancreatic Cancer Project, Buffalo, 1984-86; mem. user insertion device team Lawrence Berkeley Lab., 1988—. Contbr. articles to Proceedings of NAS, 1991. Nat. Inst. Dental Rsch. grantee, 1987—; oncogenes and oral cancer grantee Smokeless Tobacco Rsch. Coun., 1988-91. Home: 123 Blue Heron Ct East Amherst NY 14051-1639 Office: SUNY Dept Oral & Maxillo Surgery 112 Squire Hall Buffalo NY 14214

LIEBSON, MILT, sculptor, educator, author; b. N.Y.C., Dec. 12, 1923; s. Ely and Gertrude (Kern) L.; m. Lila Jacobs, Mar. 5, 1944; children: Richard, Ellen Liebson Porges, Donald. BS, St. John's U., 1948; MS, L.I. U., 1960. Tchr. Mercer Community Coll., West Windsor, N.J., 1987—, Artworks, Princeton, N.J., 1989—. One-man shows include Gallery 100, Princeton, N.J., George B. Markle Gallery, Hazelton, Pa., Bergen Mus., Paramus, N.J., Rutgers U., New Brunswick, N.J., Baron Art Ctr., Woodbridge, N.J., Monmouth Mus., Lincroft, N.J., AT&T Corp. Gallery, Hopewell, N.J., Ellarslie Mus., Trenton, N.J., Strand Gallery, Summit, N.J., Trenton City Mus., Mus. of Artists, Moscow, Delann Gallery, Plainsboro, N.J., others; represented in various permanent collections; author: Direct Stone Sculpture, 1991. With U.S. Army, 1942-44. Mem. Internat. Sculpture Ctr., Trenton Artists Workshop Assn., Allied Artists of Am. (assoc. mem.), Clearbrook Tennis Club (pres. 1991—), Rho Chi. Home and Office: 69B Picea Plz Cranbury NJ 08512

LIEBSON, SIDNEY HAROLD, research and development consultant; b. N.Y.C., July 9, 1920; s. George and Rose (Gelasno) L.; m. Jeanette Burman, Jan. 18, 1947; children: Alice Ruth, Gail Audrey. BS, CCNY, 1939; MS, U. Mich., 1940; PhD, U. Md., 1947. Head electromagnetics U.S. Naval Rsch. Lab., Washington, 1940-55; mgr. R & D, Nuclear Devel. Corp. Am., White Plains, N.Y., 1955-60; mgr. phys. rsch. NCR, Dayton, Ohio, 1960-66; mgr. xerographic tech. Xerox, Stamford, Conn., 1966-82; R & D cons., Stamford, Conn., 1982—. Contbr. articles on radiation detectors, fluorescence to profl. jours.; inventor halogen geiger counters. Recipient Civilian Meritorious Svc. award USN, 1945. Fellow Am. Phys. Soc.; mem. IEEE (sr.), Sigma Xi, Sigma Pi Sigma. Home and Office: 15 Forestwood Dr Stamford CT 06903-3618

LIEN, ERIC L., pharmaceutical executive; b. Hammond, Ind., Apr. 9, 1946; s. Arthur P. and Rowena (Woltz) L.; m. Winifred A. Latham, July 23, 1987; children: Caroline, Steven, Janet, Elizabeth, Jeffrey, Alison. BA, Coll. of Wooster, 1968; MSc, U. Ill., 1971, PhD, 1972. Postdoctoral fellow Sch. Medicine U. Pa., Phila., 1972-75; rsch. biochemist Wyeth Labs., Phila., 1975-82, mgr. metabolic disorders, 1982-87, assoc. dir. nutritional rsch., 1987-90; dir. nutritional rsch. Wyeth-Ayerst Labs., Phila., 1990—; mem. U.S. delegation CODEX Alimentarius, Washington and Rome, 1988—; mem. tech. adv. group com. on nutrition Am. Acad. Pediatrics, Oak Park, Ill., 1988—; mem. Com. on Nutritional Scis. Infant Formula Coun., Atlanta, 1988—. Contbr. articles to profl. publs., chpts. to books. Recipient award Am. Heart Assn., 1974. Mem. AAAS, Am. Soc. Parenteral and Enteral Nutrition, Am. Inst. Nutrition, Phi Beta Kappa. Presbyterian. Home: 1 Anthony Dr Malvern PA 19355-1973 Office: Wyeth-Ayerst Labs PO Box 8299 Philadelphia PA 19101-8299

LIEUWMA, ALEX S., company executive; b. Hilversum, Netherlands, June 1; came to U.S. 1962; s. Harmen Sybrandus and Katy (Matteman) L.; m. Lien Sarah Waas, Aug. 25, 1959; children: Simone Yvonne, Ronald Herman. Patroon Dipl., Bovag, The Hague, 1960. Parts dir. Sanato Volkswagen B.V., Zeist, Netherlands, 1958-62; svc. mgr. Allingham Volkswagen Inc., Manhattan, Kans., 1962-66; ops. mgr. Volkswagen Mid-Am., Inc., St. Louis, 1966-69; gen. svc. mgr. Northgate Volkswagen, Inc., St. Louis, 1969-74; reg. mgr. Fiat Mtrs. of N. Am., Chgo., 1974-78; nat. svc. mgr. Saab Scania of Am., Inc., Orange, Conn., 1978-87, dir. cons. affairs, 1987-89; pres. Lieuwma Ent., Inc., North Haven, Conn., 1989—. Mem. Over the Hill Gang Internat. (sec. 1985—), Lions. Home: 65 Bartlett Dr Madison CT 06443-1727 Office: Lieuwma Ent Inc 110 Washington Ave North Haven CT 06473-1707

LIEW, FAH POW, mechanical engineer; b. Kuala Lumpur, Selangor, Malaysia, Sept. 30, 1960; s. Yeam Shoon and Park Yuen (Yong) L. BA in Computer Sci., SUNY, Buffalo, 1983; BS in Aerospace Engring., SUNY, 1983, MS in Mech. Engring., 1987. Teaching asst. SUNY, Buffalo, 1983-85; research asst. SUNY, 1985-87; engr. E.I. DuPont de Nemours & Co., Buffalo, 1988—. Mem. AIAA, ASME, N.Y. Soc. Profl. Engrs., S.E. Asian Student Assn. (pres. 1980-81). Office: EI DuPont de Nemours Sheridan Dr at River Rd Buffalo NY 14207

LIFLAND, JOHN C., district judge; b. 1933. BA, Yale U., 1954; LLB, Harvard U., 1957. Pvt. practice law, 1957-59; law sec. to Hon. Thomas F. Meaney U.S. Dist. Ct. N.J., 1959-61; mem. firm Stryker, Tams & Dill, 1961-88; dist. judge U.S. Dist. Ct. N.J., Newark, 1988—; mem. N.J. State Bd. Bar Examiners, 1968-77. 1st lt. U.S. Army, 1958. Fellow Am. Bar Found., Assn. Fed. Bar (v.p. 1986—), N.J. State Bar Assn., Essex County Bar Assn.; mem. ABA (antitrust sect. publs. com., books editor/co-editor Antitrust Law Jour. 1981-87), Clearwater Seim Club, Essex Club, Harvard Law Sch. Assn. Office: US Dist Ct 235 US Courthouse 402 E State St Trenton NJ 08608-1507*

LIGGETT, BONNIE JOHNSTONE, product executive; b. Buffalo, N.Y., Dec. 31, 1960; d. Angus Jr. and Diane Martha (Carpenter) Johnstone; m. Charles Franklin Liggett Jr., Nov. 22, 1986. BA, Mt. Holyoke Coll., 1983; MBA, U. Rochester, 1985. Fin. analyst, intern Xerox Corp., Rochester, N.Y., 1984-85; mktg. analyst Autex Systems, Wellesley, Mass., 1985-86; product specialist Autex Systems, N.Y.C., 1986-87; mktg. mgr. DRI/McGraw-Hill, N.Y.C., 1987-89, product mgr., 1989—; product dir. DRI/McGraw-Hill, Lexington, Mass. Home: 199 Weston Rd Wellesley MA 02181-5719 Office: DRI/McGraw-Hill 24 Hartwell Ave Lexington MA 02173-3144

LIGGETT, MALCOLM HUGH, labor economist, educator; b. Balt., Sept. 3, 1929; s. Francis Marion and Neva Ruth (Crandall) L.; m. Suzanne LaPaugh, June 6, 1962. BA in Govt. with honors, U. Tex., 1957; PhD in Econs., Cornell U., 1967. Instr. Cornell U., Ithaca, N.Y., 1962-63; asst. prof. U. Calif., Santa Barbara, 1963-66, San Francisco State U., 1967-70; labor economist EEOC, Washington, 1970-73, U. Tex., Austin, 1973-75, Coun. on Wage and Price Stability, Washington, 1975-81; cons. Washington, 1981-83; assoc. prof. Pa. State U. Harrisburg, Middletown, Pa., 1983-91; with Holland Point Enterprises, North Beach, Md., 1991—; faculty senate Pa. State U., 1986-88. Author: Employment Discrimination, 1978, Aluminum Prices, 1976; contrbr. articles to profl. jours. With USAF, 1950-53. Mem. Am. Arbitration Assn., Am. Econ. Assn., Assn. for Evolutionary Econs., Indsl. Rels. Rsch. Assn., Soc. Profls. in Dispute Resolution, Pi Sigma Alpha. Home: 901 Walnut Ave North Beach MD 20714-9646 Office: Holland Point Enterprises PO Box 40 North Beach MD 20714-0040

LIGGETT, TWILA MARIE CHRISTENSEN, public television company executive; b. Pipestone, Minn., Mar. 25, 1944; d. Donald L. Christensen and Irene E. (Zweigle) Christensen Flesher. BS, Union Coll., Lincoln, Nebr., 1966; MA, U. Nebr., 1971, PhD, 1977. Dir. vocal and instrumental music Sprague (Nebr.)-Martell Public Sch., 1966-67; tchr. vocal music, pub. schs., Syracuse, Nebr., 1967-69; tchr. Norris Pub. Sch., Firth, Nebr., 1969-71; cons. fed. reading project, pub. schs., Lincoln, 1971-72; curriculum coord. Westside Community Schs., Omaha, 1972-74; dir. State program Right-to-Read, Nebr. Dept. Edn., 1974-76; asst. dir. Nebr. Commn. on Status of Women, 1976-80; asst. dir. project adminstrn./devel. Great Plains Nat. Instructional TV Libr., U. Nebr., Lincoln, 1980—; exec. producer Reading Rainbow, Pub. Broadcasting Svc. nat. children's series, 1980— (3 Emmy awards 1990, 91, 92); cons. U.S. Dept. Edn., 1981; Far West Regional Lab., San Francisco, 1978-79; panelist, presenter AAAS, NEA, NEH, Corp. Pub. Broadcasting, Internat. Reading Assn., Blue Ribbon panelist, Acad. TV Arts & Scis., 1991-92. Bd. dirs. Planned Parenthood, Lincoln, 1979-81. Mem. Assn. Supervision and Curriculum Devel., Phi Delta Kappa. Presbyterian. Home: 665 W Lakeshore Dr Lincoln NE 68528-1012 also: 301 E 79th St 23P New York NY 10021 Office: PO Box 80669 Lincoln NE 68501-0669 also: Reading Rainbow 601 W 50th St New York NY 10023

LIGGIO, JEAN VINCENZA, artist, educator; b. N.Y.C., Nov. 5, 1927; d. Vincenzo and Bernada (Terrusa) Verro; m. John Liggio, June 6, 1948; children: Jean Constance, Joan Bernadette. Student, N.Y. Inst. Photography, 1965, Elizabeth Seton Coll., 1984, Pasons Sch. of Design, 1985. Hairdresser Beatuy Shoppe, N.Y.C., 1947-65; freelance oil colors and portraits N.Y.C., 1958-75; instr. watercolor N.Y. Dept. Pks., Recreation and Conservation, Yonkers, 1985-89, Bronxville (N.Y.) Adult Sch., 1989—; substitute tchr. cosmetology Yonkers Bd. Edn., 1988-89. Paintings pub. by Donald Art Co., C.R. Gibson Greeting Card Co. Recipient numerous awards. Mem. Mt. Vernon Art Assn. (bd. dirs. membership com. 1983—), Mamaroneck Artist's Guild, Hudson River Contemporary Artist's, Scarsdale Art Assn. (publicity chmn. 1984-89), New Rochelle (N.Y.) Art Assn., Katonah Mus. Artists Assn., Italian Club. Home and Office: 166 Helena Ave Yonkers NY 10710-2524

LIGHT, ERNEST ISAAC, dental educator; b. Watkins, Iowa, Oct. 5, 1931; s. Robert Isaac and Anna (Becker) L.; m. Dorothy Kaplan, Dec. 28, 1960; children: Christina, William, Samuel, David. DDS, U. Iowa, 1961, MS, 1966. Pvt. practice Marshalltown, Iowa, 1961-64; from asst. prof. to prof. coll. dentistry U. Iowa, Iowa City, 1966-71; from assoc. prof. to prof., chmn. operative dentistry U. Medicine and Dentistry N.J., Newark, 1971-82, prof.

gen. and hosp. dentistry, 1982—; cons., nat. rev. com. Project Accorde NIH, Washington, 1975; mem. Internat. Symposium on Composits U. N.C., 1982. Editor: Operative Dentistry Handbook and Lab Manual, 1975; contbr. articles to profl. jours.; author, producer numerous audio-visual tng. programs; contbr. chpt.: Comprehensive Review of Dentistry, 1977. Active Pres. Club Rep. Nat. Com., Washington, 1990-91. Sgt. U.S. Army, 1952-54, Korea. Named one of Outstanding Educators Am., 1972. Fellow Internat. Coll. Dentists; mem. ADA, Am. Assn. Dental Schs., Acad. Operative Dentistry, Am. Assn. Endodontists, Internat. Assn. Dental Rsch., Fedn. Dentarie Internat., Omicron Kappa Epsilon. Roman Catholic. Home: 81 Dwight Rd Middletown NJ 07748-3118 Office: U Medicine Dentistry NJ 100 Bergen St Newark NJ 07103-2407

LIGHT, (MARVIN) LAWRENCE, advertising agency executive; b. Montreal, Que., Can., June 12, 1941; s. Louis and Celia L.; m. Joyce Wax, June 18, 1966; children: Laura, Michelle. B.S., McGill U., Montreal, 1962; M.A., Ohio State U., 1965, Ph.D., 1967. Exec. v.p. Batten Barton Durstine & Osborn Inc., N.Y.C., 1966-81; chmn., chief exec. officer Backer Spielvogel Bates Internat., N.Y.C., 1981-89, bd. dirs. Calif. and Washington Cos.; pres., chief operating officer Arcature Corp., Stamford, Conn., 1989—; lectr. exec. program Northwestern U. Grad. Sch. of Mgmt.; bd. dirs. Calif. & Wash., Inc. Office: Three Stamford Landing Three Stamford Landing Ste 300 Southfield Ave Stamford CT 06902

LIGHT, MURRAY BENJAMIN, newspaper editor; b. Bklyn., Oct. 14, 1926; s. Paul and Rose (Liatsk) L.; m. Joan M. Cottrell; children: Lee Light Monier, Laura Light Arbogast, Jeffrey Eugene. B.S., Bklyn. Coll., 1948; M.S. in Journalism, Northwestern U., 1949. Copy editor New York World-Telegram, 1949; with Buffalo Evening News, 1949—, news editor, 1962-69, mng. editor for news, 1969-79, editor, v.p., 1979—, sr. v.p., 1983—; mem. arts adv. coun. SUNY, Buffalo, 1987—, N.Y. State Jud. Screening Com. for 4th Dept., 1983—; mem. nominating jury for journalism Pulitzer Prize, 1990, 91. Mem. adv. coun. to pres. on journalism St. Bonaventure U., 1980—; mem. community adv. coun. SUNY, Buffalo, 1979—; mem. community adv. bd. Assn. for Rsch. Childhood Cancer, 1989—; steering com. State Citizen Bee, 1990—. With AUS, World War II, PTO. Mem. N.Y. State Soc. Newspaper Editors (pres. 1977), Am. Soc. Newspaper Editors, A.P. Mng. Editors Assn., N.Y. Fair Trial Free Press Conf. (past chmn.). Office: Buffalo News 1 News Plz Buffalo NY 14203-2994

LIGHT, RICHARD JAY, statistician, education educator; b. N.Y.C., Sept. 10, 1942; s. Solomon Julius and Muriel (Szwarcman) L.; m. Patricia Kahn, June 27, 1965; children: Jennifer Susan, Sarah Elizabeth. BS, U. Pa., 1962, AM, 1964; PhD, Harvard U., 1969; LLD (hon.), U. Winnipeg, Can., 1991. Mem. faculty Harvard U., Cambridge, Mass., 1969—, prof. stats., 1975—; dir. faculty studies John F. Kennedy Inst. Politics, 1971-76; mem. panel children's and family policy Nat. Acad. Scis., 1977—, chmn. panel on evaluation, 1982; panel program evaluation Social Sci. Research Council, 1977—; bd. dirs Huron Inst., Cambridge, Mass., 1971—; cons. World Bank, 1975—; dir. Harvard Assessment Seminar, Cambridge, 1986—. Co-author: Data for Decisions, 1982, Summing Up, 1984, By Design, 1990; editor: Learning from Experience, 1982, Evaluation Studies Rev., 1983. Trustee Buckingham, Browne and Nichols Sch., Cambridge, 1977—; policy adv. group Mass. Office of Children, 1977—. N.Y. State Advanced Coll. Teaching fellow, 1965; vis. fellow Ctr. Analysis Health Practices, Harvard U. Sch. Pub. Health, 1977-78; Sr. Research award Spencer Found., Chgo., 1978-84; research fellow Ford Found., N.Y.C., 1981; recipient Paul Lazarsfeld award for contbns. to sci., 1992. Mem. Am. Assn. Higher Edn., Am. Ednl. Research Ass., Am. Sociol. Assn., Am. Evaluation Assn. (pres. 1986), Council Applied Social Research, Evaluation Research Soc. (Paul lazarsfeld award 1991). Home: 31 Dunbarton Rd Belmont MA 02178-2458 Office: Harvard U John F Kennedy Sch Govt Cambridge MA 02138

LIGHT, RICHARD TODD, corporate medical director, internist; b. Rochester, N.Y., May 1, 1948; s. Glenn Wallace and Gloria C. (Capparelli) L.; m. Susan Kathryn Nelson, Nov. 2, 1974. BS, Yale U., 1970; MD, U. Rochester, 1975. Diplomate Am. Bd. Internal Medicine, Am. Bd. Pathology. Intern Johns Hopkins Hosp., 1975-76, resident, 1976-78; resident clin. pathology U. Minn., Mpls., 1978-79, fellow chem. pathology, med. hematology, 1979-82; asst. prof. Vanderbilt U. Med. Sch., Nashville, 1983-88; dir., asst. chief Nashville VA Med. Ctr. Lab. Svc., 1987-88; assoc. dir. Bristol-Myers Squibb Human Pharmacology, Princeton, N.J., 1988-90; corp. med. dir. Becton Dickinson Co., Franklin Lakes, N.J., 1990-92; med. dir. CIBA-GEIGY Corp., Summit, N.J., 1992—. Contbr. articles to profl. jours. Mem. Am. Soc. for Clin. Pharmacology and Therapeutics, Am. Heart Assn., Am. Assn. Clin. Chemistry, Am. Fedn. for Clin. Rsch., Assn. Clin. Lab. Physicians and Scientists, Sigma Xi. Home: C-17 Carver Pl Lawrenceville NJ 08648 Office: CIBA-GEIGY Corp Pharmaceuticals Div 556 Morris Ave Summit NJ 07901

LIGHT, TRUMAN S., chemist; b. Hartford, Conn., Dec. 16, 1922; s. Joseph and Lillian (Ginsburg) L.; m. Reeva Snyder, Dec. 29, 1946 (dec. 1977); children: Edward N., Stuart Licht, Joel M.; m. Arlene C. Wick, June 29, 1980. SB, Harvard U., 1943; MS, U. Minn., 1949; DrChem, U. Rome, 1961. Asst. prof. Boston Coll., Newton, Mass., 1949-59; staff scientist rsch. div. Avco Corp., Wilmington, Mass., 1959-64; prin. rsch. scientist Foxboro (Mass.) Co., 1964-88; cons. chemistry Lexington, Mass., 1988—; adj. prof. Boston Coll., Newton, 1987, Suffolk U., Boston, 1991. Contbr. articles to profl. jours. Lt. comdr. USN, 1943-46, PTO; with USNR retired, 1982—. NSF fellow, 1960-61. mem. Am. Chem. Soc. (councilor 1976-91, chmn. Northeastern sect. 1977-79), Instrument Soc. Am., Electrochem. Soc., Sigma Xi. Home and Office: 4 Webster Rd Lexington MA 02173-8222

LIGHTBODY, GEORGE PHILLIPS, fundraiser; b. Cleve., Feb. 19, 1962; s. James Davies and Patricia (Calkins) L. BA, Harvard Coll., 1984; M in Internat. Affairs, Colubmia U., 1992. Tchr. Am. Internat. Sch., Vienna, Austria, 1984-85; major gift officer Columbia U., N.Y.C., 1985-88; assoc. dir. major gifts Harvard U., Cambridge, Mass., 1988—. Steering com. City Tear, Boston, 1988—; bd. dirs. Double Discovery Ctr., N.Y.C., 1985-88; founder Urban Soccer Program, N.Y.C., 1986-88. Mem. Nat. Soc. Fundraising Execs., Planned Giving Group New Eng., Harvard Alumni Assn. (com. chair 1987-91), Class Leadership Assn. (pres. 1986-91), Owl Club (libr. 1983-84), Griffin Club. Home: 2 Ware St Apt 203 Cambridge MA 02138-4029 Office: Harvard Devel Office 124 Mt Auburn St 3d Fl Cambridge MA 02138-5758

LIGHTBOURNE, ROBERT EDWARD ARTHUR, population researcher; b. Birmingham, Eng., Jan. 22, 1944; came to U.S., 1961; s. Robert Charles and Dorothy Helen (Hinman) L.; m. Susheela Devi Singh, May 22, 1985; 1 child, Robert Vickram. AB, Harvard U., 1967; MSc, U. W.I., 1970; PhD, U. Calif., Berkeley, 1977. Asst. prof. Howard U., Washington, 1977-79; rsch. officer World Fertility Survey, London, 1979-84; cons. Westinghouse Health Systems, Columbia, Md., 1984-85, UN, N.Y.C., 1985-91, Population Coun., N.Y.C., 1988-89; dir. rsch. Edison Population Inst., N.Y.C., 1989—. Contbr. articles on human reproductive motives, fertility and mating in developing countries to profl. jours. Mem. Internat. Union for Sci. Study Population, Population Assn. Am., Am. Sociol. Assn. Home: 41 Essex Ave Metuchen NJ 08840-2335

LIGHTDALE, CHARLES J., physician, educator; b. Jersey City, Apr. 25, 1940; s. Harold B. and Dorothy R. (Raynes) L.; m. Reina S. Silverman, Sept. 8, 1968; children: Jenifer, Hallie, Nina, Sarah. AB, Princeton U., 1962; MD, Columbia U., 1966. Itnern Yale-New Haven Hosp., 1966-67, med. resident, 1967-68; resident Cornell Med. Coll., N.Y.C., 1968-69; fellow gastroenterology Meml. Hosp., N.Y.C., 1971-73; asst., assoc. attending physician Meml. Sloan-Kettering Cancer Ctr., N.Y.C., 1973-91, attending physician, 1991—, dir. endoscopic rsch. gastroenterology svc., 1991—; asst., assoc. prof. clin. medicine Cornell U. Med. Coll., N.Y.C., 1973-92, prof. medicine, 1992—. Editor Gastrointestinal Endoscopy, 1989—. Fellow ACP, Am. Coll. Gastroenterology (trustee 1982-84); mem. Am. Gastroent. Assn., Am. Soc. Gastointestinal Endoscopy, N.Y. Gastroent. Assn. (pres. 1988-89), N.Y. Soc. Gastointestinal Endoscopy (master endoscopist 1987, pres. 1981-82), N.Y. Acad. Gastroenterology (pres. 1980-81). Office: Meml Sloan Kettering Cancer Ctr 1275 York Ave New York NY 10021

LIGHTMAN, HAROLD ALLEN, marketing executive; b. Gloucester, Mass., Oct. 23, 1925; s. Abraham and Gertrude (Chait) L.; m. Irma Shorell, Feb. 19, 1954; children: Timothy, Harold, Jr., Stacey. Student, Norwich U., 1943; student, Cambridge U., Eng., 1946; BBA, U. Miami, 1949. Acct. exec. Grant Advt., Miami, Fla., 1948-50; advt. dir. Sears Roebuck & Co., Tampa, Fla., 1950-51; account exec. Robert Otto Internat., N.Y.C., 1952-53; account exec., field supr. Amos Parish & Co., N.Y.C., 1954-56; acct. exec. Dowd, Redfield & Johnstone, N.Y.C., 1957-59; chmn. bd. dirs. H. Allen Lightman Inc., N.Y.C., 1959—; bd. dirs. Irma Shorell Inc., N.Y.C.; pres., bd. dirs. Ind. Cosmetic Mfg. and Distbrs. U.S.A., v.p. nat. legis. affairs, 1974—; exec. v.p. Alfin Fragrances, Inc., 1985-87; pres. I.S. Labs. Inc., 1987—. Author newspaper column: Seen & Heard, 1965-83; producer: Cable TV program Seen & Heard, 1978—. Sgt. U.S. Army, 1943-46, ETO. Decorated Purple Heart, Bronze Star (2), Combat Infantry Badge; recipient Pub. Rels. Gold Key award, 1987. Fellow Winston Churchill Meml. Libr., Harry S. Truman Meml. Libr.; mem. Nat. Fedn. Ind. Bus. (del. 1979), Alpha Delta Sigma (founder, 1st pres. 1947-48), DAV, Am. Legion (vice comdr. 1948-49), Vets. of the Battle of the Bulge, The Jockey Club. Office: 75 E End Ave Ste 11E New York NY 10028

LIGHTNER, ARDYCE LEAH STEVENS, business educator; b. Leigh, Nebr., July 21, 1932; d. John Wesley and Anna Louise (Leuschen) Stevens; m. Jerry P. Lightner, Sept. 13, 1953 (div. 1967). BA, Wayne State Coll., 1952; MA, U. No. Colo., 1954, EdD, 1966; JD, U. Dayton, 1982. Bar: Ohio, 1982. Instr. East Jr. High Sch., Great Falls, Mont., 1961-63; with Coll. Great Falls, 1963-67, Morehead (Ky.) State U., 1967-69; dean, sch. of bus. Radford (Va.) U., 1969-79; prof. bus. D'Youville Coll., Buffalo, 1983—. Treas. Rep. Women's Club, Radford, 1974-78. Presbyterian. Office: DYouville Coll 320 Porter Ave Buffalo NY 14201-1084

LIGHTNER, JAMES EDWARD, mathematics educator; b. Frederick, Md., Aug. 29, 1937; s. Norman Edward and Lydia Irene (Biddle) L. BA, Western Md. Coll., 1958; AM, Northwestern U., 1962; PhD, Ohio State U., 1968. Math. and English tchr. Frederick County Pub. Schs., 1958-62; math. instr. Western Md. Coll., Westminster, 1962-65, asst. math. prof., 1965-68, assoc. math. prof., 1968-77, prof. math. and edn., 1977—, dir. math. proficiency, 1982—; cons. Md. State Dept. Edn., Balt., 1975—; reader-advanced placement Calculus Testing Svc., Princeton, N.J., 1980-88; speaker in field. Author: (with others) Geometry, 1980, 84; contbr. articles to profl. jours. Mem.Nat. Coun. Tchrs. Math., Md. Coun. Tchrs. Math. (pres. 1982-83, exec. sec. 1988—, Outstanding Md. Math. Educator 1986), Rotary, Westminster Club (pres. 1980-81, Paul Harris fellow 1990), Phi Beta Kappa (sec.-treas. local chpt. 1980—), Phi Delta Kappa, Kappa Mu Epsilon (nat. pres. 1977-81), Sigma Xi, Phi Delta Theta. Home: 3 Marbeth Hl Westminster MD 21157-4320 Office: Western Md Coll 2 College Hl Westminster MD 21157-4303

LIGI, BARBARA JEAN, architectural and interior designer; b. Binghamton, N.Y., June 13, 1959; d. Robert Richard and Helen Margaret (Wagner) Taylor; m. Alan Joseph Ligi, July 24, 1982; children: Curtis John, Ryan Robert. AA, Mt. Ida Coll., 1979; BFA, Syracuse U., 1982. Designer Norman Davies, Architect, Binghamton, 1982—; adj. faculty design Community Coll., Binghamton, 1987—. Mem. Am. Soc. Interior Designers, Nat. Trust for Historic Preservation, Gold Key. Democrat. Roman Catholic. Home: 2703 Robins St Endwell NY 13760 Office: Norman J Davies Architect 783 Chenango St Binghamton NY 13901

LIGOTTI, EUGENE FERDINAND, retired dentist; b. N.Y.C., June 10, 1936; s. Eugene A. and Lee (D'Agata) L.; m. Corbina Theresa Loscalzo, Nov. 21, 1959; children: Gina Maria Ligotti Aliperti, Lisa Anne. BA, Adelphi U., 1958; DDS, NYU, 1962. Pvt. practice Huntington, N.Y., 1962-90; instr. operative dentistry NYU, N.Y.C., 1962-65. Author historic fiction. Patentee dental apparatus to prevent loss of precious metal. Founder, pres. Upper Bay Civic Assn., Inc., Huntington, 1979—. Mem. ADA, N.Y. State Dental Soc., Suffolk County Dental Soc., German Shepherd Dog Club (pres. 1971-75), Xi Psi Phi (founder, pres. alumni chpt. 1981-82), Chi Sigma. Republican. Roman Catholic.

LIJOI, CHRISTINE CONFROY, educator; b. Newark, Jan. 20, 1954; d. James Richard and Ida Patricia (Sunder) Confroy; m. Peter Bruno Lijoi, Aug. 19, 1978; children: Jonathan, Christopher. BA in Biology, Montclair State Coll., 1976; MS in Spl. Edn., Long Island U., 1983. Sci. tchr. Edison Jr. High Sch., West Orange, N.J., 1976-77, Summit (N.J.) Middle Sch., 1977—. Teacher, trustee Summit Ednl. Found. Grantee Starlab, 1989. Roman Catholic. Home: 124 Canoe Brook Pky Summit NJ 07901-1436 Office: Summit Middle Sch 272 Morris Ave Summit NJ 07901-2579

LIJOI, PETER BRUNO, lawyer; b. Suffern, N.Y., Sept. 2, 1953; s. Salvatore and Josephine (Gentile) L.; m. Christine Louise Confroy, Aug. 19, 1978; children: Jonathan Peter, Christopher Andrew. BA in History and Econs., Montclair State Coll., 1975; postgrad. in urban planning, Rutgers U., 1975-76; JD, Pace U., 1979; postgrad., Harvard U., 1992. Bar: N.J. 1981, N.Y. 1988. Rsch. intern N.J. Dept. Edn., Trenton, 1976; intern Office U.S. Atty., N.Y.C., 1977-78; energy coord. Rockland County, 1979-80; dep. dir., of counsel Pvt. Industry Coun., Pearl River, N.Y., 1980-91; pvt. practice law Mahwah, N.J., 1981—; dir., counsel County of Rockland Indsl. Devel. Agy., 1981—; v.p., gen. counsel Rockland Econ. Devel. Corp., Pearl River, 1990-91; cons. U.S. Dept. Energy, Washington, 1980; mem. program of instrn. for lawyers Law Sch. Harvard U., 1992. Bd. dirs. Rockland County coun. Girl Scouts U.S., 1982—, Washington Elem. Sch. PTA, Summit, N.J., 1986—. Mem. ABA, N.J. Bar Assn., N.Y. Bar Assn., Bergen County Bar Assn., Assn. Trial Lawyers Am., Nat. Assn. Bond Lawyers. Republican. Roman Catholic. Home: 124 Canoe Brook Pky Summit NJ 07901-1436 Office: County of Rockland Indsl Devel Agy 1 Blue Hill Plz Ste 1024 Pearl River NY 10965-8576

LILIENFIELD, LAWRENCE SPENCER, physiology and biophysics educator; b. Bklyn., May 5, 1927; s. Henry Jacob and Lee (Markman) L.; m. Eleanor Marion Russ, Oct. 22, 1950; children: Jan, Adele, Lisa. BS, Villanova (Pa.) U., 1945; MD, Georgetown U., 1949, MS, 1954, PhD, 1956. Diplomate Am. Bd. Med. Examiners, Am. Bd. Intenal Medicine. Intern Georgetown U. Hosp., Washington, 1949-59, 1949-50, resident in internal medicine, 1950, 52-54, rsch. fellow, 1954-55; instr. medicine Sch. Medicine Georgetown U., Washington, 1955-56, asst. chief cardiovascular rsch. lab., dept. mediine, 1956-63, asst. chief cardiovascular rsch. lab. dept. medicine, 1956-63, assoc. prof. physiology, biophysics and medicine Sch. Medicine, 1961-64, prof. physiology and biophysics Sch. Medicine, 1964—61, prof., chmn. dept. physiology and biophysics Sch. Medicine, 1963—; attending pysician VA Hosp., Washington, 1956-70; cons. USPHS, 1964-69, NASA, 1964-70, U.S. Dept. of State, 1967-74; established investigator Am. Heart Assn., 1958; vis. prof. Faculty of Mediicne, U. Saigon, Republic of Korea, 1965-74. Contbr. numerous articles to profl. jours. Bd. dirs. Washington Heart Assn., 1962-67, chmn., 1966. With USN, 1945; capt. USAF, 1950-52. Recipient Established Investigator award Am. Heart Assn., 1958; Rsch. Career Devel. award USPHS, 1963, Rsch. Career award, 1963, Kaiser-Permanente Teaching award, 1987; USPHS rsch. and rsch. tng. grantee, 1987. Fellow ACP; mem. Am. Soc. for Clin. Investigation, Am. Physiol. Soc., Soc. for Exptl. Biology and Medicine, Am. Fedn. for Clin. Rsch. (chair ea. sect. 1965-66). Office: Georgetown U Sch Medicine 3900 Reservoir Rd NW Washington DC 20007-2187

LILLIE, MASHALL SHERWOOD, safety and security director, instructor; b. Corry, Pa., May 23, 1953; s. Lloyd G. and Jalean R. (Sherwood) L.; m. Anita M., Aug 16, 1975; children: Amanda M., Sarah N., Rebekah L., Reuben L. ASB, Erie Bus. Ctr., Pa., 1974; BA, Olivet Nazarene U., Kankakee, Ill., 1980; MS, Mercyhurst Coll., Erie, Pa., 1984. Municipal Police Officer Training. Dir., security Olivet Nazarene U., Kankakee, Ill., 1977-81; administr. asst. Mercyhurst Coll., Erie, Pa., 1981-86; dir., security Thiel Coll., Greenville, Pa., 1986—; chmn. ASIS, Lake Erie Chpt., Erie, Pa., 1990-91, Western Pa. Security Dirs., 1989-90; instr. Thiel Coll., Greenville, Pa., 1990—. Master Sunday Sch. Supr. Ch. of Nazarene, 1991; Mayor's Adv. com., Greenville, Pa., 1990. Mem. N.E. Coll. & Univs. Security Assn., Western Pa. Coll., Security Dirs. Assn., Internat. Assn. Campus Law Enforcement Adminstrs., NRA, Am. Soc. Indsl. Security. Republican. Mem. Ch. of Nazarene. Office: Thiel Coll 75 College Ave Greenville PA 16125-2186

LILLY, FRANK, biomedical researcher; b. Charleston, W.Va., Aug. 28, 1930; s. Frank Otho and E. Verna (Zimmerman) L.; 1 child, Matthew T. PhD, U. Paris, 1959, Cornell U., 1965. Asst. prof. dept. genetics Albert Einstein Coll. Medicine, Bronx, N.Y., 1967-70, assoc. prof., 1970-74, prof., 1974—, chmn. dept., 1976-89; Am. Cancer Soc. rsch. prof. oncogenetics Albert Einstein Coll. Medicine, Bronx, 1989—; mem. bd. scientific overseers Jackson Lab., Bar Harbor, Maine, 1989—; mem. scientific adv. coun. Cancer Rsch. Inst., N.Y.C., 1975—; mem. scientific adv. com. Wistar Inst., Phila., 1979—. Author or co-author 140 scientific articles. Mem. Presdl. Commn. on the HIV Epidemic, Washington, 1987-88. With U.S. Army, 1952-53. Fellow N.Y. Acad. Scis.; mem. NAS (mem. Com. on a Nat. Strategy 1986-87), Am. Assn. for Cancer Rsch. Office: Albert Einstein Coll of Med Genetics Dept 1300 Morris Park Ave Bronx NY 10461-1924

LILLY, THOMAS MORE, insurance executive; b. Pitts., May 14, 1942; s. Joseph H. and Mary Jo (Lippert) L.; m. Roberta M. Maloney, Dec. 31, 1966. BA, U. Pitts., 1966, JD, 1973. Bar: Pa. 1973, U.S. Dist. Ct. (we. dist.) Pa., 1973; CLU, 1983. Asst. to dir. Assoc. Indsl. Advertisers, N.Y.C., 1966-67; media planner Ketchum, MacLeod & Grove Advt., Pitts., 1967-70; mktg. mgr. Cahners Pub. Co., Chgo., 1970-71; media cons. Thomas M. Lilly, Pitts., 1971-73; asst. dist. atty. Allegheny County, Pitts., 1973-75; law clk. Common Pleas Ct., Pitts., 1975-76; atty. Hickton, Dean, Tighe & Lilly, Pitts., 1976-77; agt. State Mut. Life, Pitts., 1977-86; owner Thomas M. Lilly, JD CLU, Pitts., 1986-90, Strategic Benefits Group, Pitts., 1990—. Contbr. articles to profl. jours. Mem. Am. Soc. CLU's and Chartered Fin. Cons., Internat. Assn. Fin. Planners, Allegheny County Bar Assn. Democrat. Roman Catholic. Home: 5 Colonial Pl Pittsburgh PA 15232-1418 Office: 5401 Walnut St The Hartwell Bldg Pittsburgh PA 15232

LIM, RALPH WEI HSIONG, finance educator; b. N.Y.C., Oct. 3, 1953; s. Yuen and Huan Lim. BSE, Princeton (N.J.) U., 1975; MBA, U. Pa., 1977. Fin exec. Internat. Paper Co., N.Y.C., 1977-82; cons. Darien, Conn., 1982—; prof. Sacred Heart U., Fairfield, Conn., 1984—; vis. fellow Yale U., New Haven, 1988-89. Mem. CAP, Ark., 1978-80, Conn., 1980—; rep. Darien Town Legis., Darien, 1988-89; commr. Darien Housing Authority, 1991—. Republican. Home: PO Box 938 Darien CT 06820-0938

LIME, JAMES CRAIG, energy industry executive; b. Paterson, N.J., Jan. 29, 1951; s. Daniel Abraham and Barbara Ruth (McDougall) L.; m. Kimberly Elaine Kelly; children: Brian James, Kathryn Kimberly. BA in Bus., Rutgers Coll., 1973; MS in Forest Mgmt., Syracuse U., 1975. Sales trainee Westvaco Corp., N.Y.C., 1976, fin. analyst, 1976-77, asst. purchasing agt., 1977-79, mgr. raw materials and fuels, 1979-81, mgr. group purchasing, 1981-84; mgr. raw material purchases Colgate-Palmolive Co., N.Y.C., 1984-87; v.p. corp. purchasing J.M. Huber Corp., Edison, N.J., 1987-88, v.p. purchasing and transp., 1988-90; dir. corp. purchasing, v.p. environ. affairs Warner Lambert Co., 1990-91. Asst. scout master Boy Scouts Am., Pluckemin, N.J.; deacon Pluckemin Presbyn. Ch., 1992—. Named Eagle Scout, Boy Scouts Am., 1965. Office: Warner Lambert Co 201 Tabor Rd Morris Plains NJ 07950

LIMPERT, JOHN ARTHUR, editor; b. Appleton, Wis., Mar. 15, 1934; s. John Adam and Olga Charlotte (Lindstrom) L.; m. Jocelyn Roberta Minarik, 1957 (div. 1971); 1 child, John; m. Jean Ann Vincent, July 3, 1975; children—Ann, Jean. B.S., U. Wis., Madison, 1959; student, Stanford U. Law Sch., 1959-60. Reporter UPI, Minn., 1960-61; regional exec. UPI, St. Louis, 1961-63, Detroit, 1963-64; editor Warren Progress, Mich., 1964-65; mng. editor San Jose Sunpapers, Calif., 1965-67; editor DC Examiner, 1967-68, The Washingtonian, Washington, 1969—. Recipient Distimg. Reporting of Pub. Affairs award Am. Political Sci. Assn., 1970; Congl. fellow Am. Political Sci. Assn., 1968. Mem. Am. Soc. Mag. Editors, Soc. Profl. Journalists. Office: Washingtonian 1828 L St NW Ste 200 Washington DC 20036-5169

LIN, ALICE LEE LAN, physicist, researcher, educator; b. Shanghai, China, Oct. 28, 1937; came to U.S., 1960, naturalized, 1974; m. A. Marcus, Dec. 19, 1962 (div. Feb. 1972); 1 child, Peter A. AB in Physics, U. Calif., Berkeley, 1963; MA in Physics, George Washington U., 1974. Statis. asst. dept. math. U. Calif., Berkeley, 1962-63; rsch. asst. in radiation damage Cavendish Lab. Cambridge (Eng.) U., 1965-66; info. analysis specialist Nat. Acad. Scis., Washington, 1970-71; teaching fellow, rsch. asst. George Washington U., Catholic U. Am., Washington, 1971-75; physicist NASA/Goddard Space Flight Ctr., Greenbelt, Md., 1975-80, Army Materials Tech. Lab., Watertown, Mass., 1980—. Contbr. articles to profl. jours. Mencius Ednl. Found. grantee, 1959-60. Mem. AAAS, N.Y. Acad. Scis., Am. Phys. Soc., Am. Ceramics Soc., Am. Acoustical Soc., Am. Men and Women of Sci., Optical Soc. Am. Democrat. Home: 28 Hallett Hill Rd Weston MA 02193-1753 Office: Army Materials Tech Lab Mail Stop MRS Bldg 39 Watertown MA 02172

LIN, KUANG FARN, chemist; b. Taipei, Republic of China, Feb. 25, 1936; came to U.S., 1961; s. May-Po and Bao-Yi (Lu) L.; m. Grace C. Yang, Feb. 22, 1958; children: Robert, Alexander. BScChemE, Cheng Kung U., Tainan, Republic of China, 1957; PhD in Chemistry, N.D. State U., 1970. Supt. ALKYD Yung Koo Paint & Varnish Co., Taipei, 1959-61; chemist coatings Hercules Inc., Wilmington, Del., 1963-67, rsch. chemist material sci., 1969-73, rsch. scientist meaterial sci., 1973-78, tech. mgr. mineral processing, 1978-81, project leader coatings, elastomers, adv. materials, 1981-89; venture mgr. Hercules Inc., Wilmington, 1989—. Fellow Am. Inst. Chemists; mem. Am. Chem. Soc., The Tire Soc. Office: Hercules Inc Hercules Plz Wilmington DE 19894-0001

LIN, MIN-CHUNG, obstetrician-gynecologist; b. Nan-Tou, Republic of China, Aug. 24, 1944; s. Chi-Hsien and Yue (Chen) L.; m. Miaw-Chyung, June 26, 1971; children: Susie, Judy, Nancy, Frances. MD, Tapei Med. Coll., Republic of China, 1970. Diplomate Am. Bd. Ob-Gyn. Chmn. obgyn dept. Cuba (N.Y.) Meml. Hosp., 1976-80, Ira Davenport Meml. Hosp., Bath, N.Y., 1980—. Fellow Am. Coll. Ob-Gyn; mem. AMA. Republican. Presbyterian. Office: Valley Med Bldg Rte 54 PO Box 751 Bath NY 14810

LIN, SUNG PIAU, mechanical engineering educator; b. Taipei, Taiwan, China, Apr. 18, 1937; came to U.S., 1959; s. Zu Yang and Hsueh-Zhau (Hsieh) L.; m. Charlotte A. Bordin, Apr. 9, 1966; children: Anna L., Martin T. MS, U. Utah, 1961; PhD, U. Mich., 1965. Lectr. U. Mich., Ann Arbor, 1965-66; asst. prof. Clarkson U., Potsdam, N.Y., 1966-68, assoc. prof., 1968-72, prof., 1972—; vis. prof. U. Rochester (N.Y.), 1980-81, Stanford (Calif.) U., 1981; sr. visitor Cambridge (U.K.) U., 1972-73; cons. Eastman Kodak, Rochester, 1974-82; mem. adv. bd. NASA Univ. Consortium, Potsdam, 1990—. Mem. editorial bd. Internat. Jour. Engring. Fluid Mechanics, 1988—; contbr. articles to Jour. Fluid Mechanics, Physics of Fluids, Encyclopedia Fluid Mechanics. NASA fellow, 1983, Rackham grad. fellow U. Mich., 1963. Mem. AIAA, ASME, Am. Physical Soc. Home: 9 Wellings Dr Potsdam NY 13676 Office: Clarkson U Old Main Potsdam NY 13676

LIN, SUSAN TU, retired librarian; b. Taipei, Taiwan, Republic of China, June 10, 1923; arrived in U.S., 1961, naturalized, 1976; d. Tsungming Tu and Sonsui Lin; 4 children. BA, Utah State U., 1965; MA, U. Utah, 1971; MSLS, La. State U., 1973, cert. of med. librarianship, 1975, MEd, 1977, postgrad., 1976-77. Chief libr. Saints Coll., Lexington, Miss., 1974-76; hosp. libr. U.S. Army, Ft. Polk, La., 1977-79; dist. libr. Rock Island (Ill.) dist. U.S. Army Corps Engrs., 1979-83; div. libr. North Atlantic div. U.S. Army Corps Engrs., N.Y.C., 1984-88; dist. libr. N.Y. Dist., N.Y.C., 1988-90. Coproducer various videos, slide prodns., TV program. Mem. Spl. Librs. Assn., Chinese-Am. Librs. Assn., Photographic Soc. Am.

LIN, THOMAS FU YUAN, defense engineer, nuclear engineering educator; b. Taipei, Taiwan, Mar. 15, 1954; came to U.S., 1976; s. Chun Ju and Ho (Wang) L.; m. Fen-Fen Hung, Aug. 8, 1981; children: Steven, Cynthia. BS, Nat. Tsing Hua U., Hsin-chu, Taiwan, 1976; MS, U. Wis., 1978; PhD, Rensselaer Poly. Inst., 1984. Accelerator physicist Stanford (Calif.) Linear Accelerator Ctr., 1984-85; sr. rsch. assoc. and assoc. prof. nuclear engring. Pa. State U., State College, 1985—; project dir. magnetohydrodynamics Applied Rsch. Lab. Pa. State U., 1989—. Author: Measuring Techniques in Gas-Liquid Two-Phase Flows, 1984 (Karen and Lester Gearhart prize 1984). Mem. AIAA, Am. Nuclear Soc. Home: 642 Berkshire Dr State College PA

16803 Office: Applied Rsch Lab Pa State u PO Box 30 State College PA 16804

LINAWEAVER, F. PIERCE, environmental services consultant; b. Woodstock, Va., Aug. 22, 1934; s. Dorothy (Dade) L.; m. Karen Crain, Jan. 20, 1968; children: Kelly C., Stephen P. BES, Johns Hopkin's U., 1955, PhD, 1965. Civil engr. Balt. Bur. of Water Supply, 1955, 58-61; mem. rsch. faculty environ. engrng. sci. dept. Johns Hopkin's U., Balt., 1961-66; White House fellow Sec. of Interior, Washington, 1966-67, assoc. prof. environ. engrng. sci. dept., 1967-68; dir. pub. works City of Balt., 1969-74; pvt. practice cons. environ. and civil engr. Balt., 1974-78; ptnr. Rummell, Klepper & Kahl Cons. Engrs., Balt., 1978-87; pres. EA Engrng., Inc., Hunt Valley, Md., 1987-90; exec. v.p. EA Engrng., Sci. and Tech., Inc., Hunt Valley, 1987-91; prin. F. Pierce Linaweaver and Assoc., Inc., Balt., 1991—; ind. dir. T. Rowe Price Mut. Funds, Balt., 1979—; trustee Johns Hopkin's U., 1980-86, 87—. Contbr. articles to profl. jours. Mem. bus. svcs. coun. Greater Balt. Com., 1978-82; nat. chmn. ann. fund Johns Hopkin's U., 1981-83; trustee Johns Hopkin's Hosp. Endowment Fund, Inc., Balt., 1982-86. 1st lt. USAF, 1955-58. Fellow ASCE (pres. Md. chpt. 1969-70), AAAS; mem. Am. Acad. Environ. Engrs. (diplomate), Am. Water Works Assn. (life, trustee Chesapeake chpt. 1973-74), Water Pollution Control Assn., Am. Cons. Engrs. Coun., Engrng. Soc. of Balt. (pres. 1973-74), Nat. Soc. Profl. Engrs. Democrat. Episcopalian. Home: 224 Wendover Rd Baltimore MD 21218-1837 Office: The Legg Mason Tower 111 S Calvert St Ste 2700 Baltimore MD 21202-6198

LINCOLN, CARL CLIFFORD, JR., auditor; b. Connellsville, Pa., Sept. 23, 1928; s. Carl Clifford and Mary Elizabeth (Pierce) L.; m. Clara May Collins, May 1, 1950; children: Patricia J., William E., Carl Clifford III, Ralph C., Charles D., James B., John D., Richard D. Student, LaSalle Extension U., 1962. Flight agt. All Am. Airways, Pitts., 1951-52; prodn. control expeditor Bryant Heaters, Inc., Cleve., 1952-53; asst. to plant engr. Osborne Mfg. Co., Cleve., 1953-54; driver salesman Nat. Biscuit Co., Cleve., 1954-55; prodn. control expeditor Rockwell Mfg. Co., Uniontown, Pa., 1955-56; clk., salesman various cos., Connellsville, Pa., 1956-65; investigator tax Dept. Revenue Pa., Harrisburg, 1965-68; revenue adminstr. Indstl. Collections, Harrisburg, 1968-70; field office mgr., field inspector engrng. dept., auditor Pa. Turnpike Commn., Harrisburg, 1970—; ret., 1991. County chmn. Young Reps., Uniontown, 1965-69; chmn. western Pa. chpt. Heart Assn., Connellsville, 1968; mem. Rep. Coun. Community Leaders, St. Ho. of Reps., Harrisburg, 1987-88, 89, 90, 91, 92. With USN, 1944, 46-48, ETO. Mem. SAR (pres., v.p., publicity chmn. deputy dist. #5 Pa. Somerset Cambria chpt. 1991), Toastmasters Internat., Masons, VFW (life), Am. Legion, Berlin Hist. Soc., Ancient Accepted Scottish Rite (32 degree, v.p.), Last Mans Club (Berlin). Mem. Ch. of Christ. Home: 713 Stewart St Berlin PA 15530-1507 Office: Pa Turnpike Commn Harrisburg PA 17120

LIND, ROBERT CLARENCE, economist, educator; b. Seattle, June 23, 1937; s. Clarence Samuel and Harriet (Schreur) L.; m. Gretchen Gayle (div. 1967); m. Joan Squires-Lind, Feb. 21, 1968; children: Jason Mark-Alexander, Vanessa Antonia-Alexandra. BA, Yale U., 1960; PhD, Stanford U., 1966. Asst. prof. econs. U. Wash., Seattle, 1966-67; asst. prof. engrng., econs. systems Stanford (Calif.) U., 1967-70, assoc. prof., 1970-71, assoc. prof. grad. sch. bus., 1971-74; prof. econ. mgmt., pub. policy Cornell U., Ithaca, 1974—; pres. The Washington Campus, Inc., 1979-85. Co-author: Discounting for Time and Risk in Energy Policy, 1982. Dir. Inst. for Pub. Policy Analysis, 1969-71. Recipient Leavey award Freedoms Found., 1983. Mem. Am. Soc. Pub. Adminstrn., Acad. Mgmt., Am. Econ. Assn., Internat. Assn. Energy Econs., Yale Club N.Y., Cornell Club, Capital Hill Club. Home: PO Box 188 Lansing NY 14882-0188 Office: Cornell U Grad Sch Mgmt 562 Malott Hall Ithaca NY 14853

LINDAMOOD, GEORGE EDWARD, computer consultant; b. Marietta, Ohio, Sept. 15, 1938; s. Lee Marcus and Mildred Katherine (Young) L.; m. Diane Kay Haugen, Feb. 2, 1962 (div. July 1980); children: Brian Avery, Elden Kirk; m. Annette Irene Powell, July 18, 1980; 1 stepchild, Nina Powell. BS, Wittenberg U., 1960; MA, U. Md., 1964, postgrad., 1964-69; postgrad., Johns Hopkins U., 1972-73. Assoc. engr. Westinghouse Electric Corp., Balt., 1962-63; instr. in computer sci. U. Md., College Park, 1963-70; sr. computer scientist Nat. Bur. Standards, Gaithersburg, Md., 1970-81; visiting fellow MIT, Cambridge, 1981-82; sr. scientist U.S. Office Naval Rsch., Tokyo, 1982-84; dir. industry analysis Burroughs Corp., Tokyo, 1984-85; assoc. prof. computer sci. Hood Coll., Frederick, Md., 1986-87; prog. dir. industry svc. Gartner Group, Inc., Stamford, Conn., 1987-90, dir. high performance computing, 1991, v.p., high performance computing, 1991—; cons. to numerous pvt. cos. and fed. agencies, 1963-87; mem. numerous adv. coms. and study teams of U.S. govt., 1971-87; U.S. rep. at internat. meetings, Manila, Paris, Bangkok, India, Jamaica, 1976-84. Author pub. poems, humorous articles; contbr. articles to profl. jours. Mem., sec. Planning & Zoning Commn., Woodsboro, Md., 1975-78; pres. Woodsboro Elem. PTA, 1976-77, v.p. 1975-76; pres. Frederick (Md.) County Coun. PTAs, 1978, v.p., 1977. Recipient Silver medal U.S. Dept. Commerce, 1973, fellowship Woodrow Wilson Found., 1960-61, scholarship Nat. Merit Scholarship Found., 1956-60. Mem. IEEE. Lutheran. Home: 51 Schuyler Ave Stamford CT 06902-3728 Office: Gartner Group Inc 56 Top Gallant Rd Stamford CT 06902-7700

LINDEMANN, KATE, philosophy and meditation educator; b. N.Y.C., July 28, 1935; d. William and Elizabeth (Kane) L. BA, Seton Hall U., 1963; MA, Fordham U., 1966; PhD, Mich. State U., 1975. Lectr. Mount St. Mary's Coll., Newburgh, N.Y., 1966, instr., 1967-71, asst. prof., 1972-76, assoc. prof., 1977-81, prof. philosophy, dept. chmn., 1981—; non-profit health and ednl. cons., N.Y., N.J., Conn. 1974—; meditation educator,N.Y. Contbr. articles to profl. jours. Bd. mem. Marisndale Ctr., Ossining, N.Y., 1989—; mem. Dem. Club, Newburgh, N.Y., 1991—. Mem. APA, Assn. Philosophy of Liberation, Soc. for Women in Philosophy. Democrat. Roman Catholic. Office: Mt St Mary's Coll Powell Ave Newburgh NY 12550-3412

LINDEN, BARNARD JAY, electrical engineer; b. Bklyn., May 18, 1943; s. Abraham and Beatrice (Westler) L.; m. Janet Sigrid Jaffe, Sept. 12, 1965; 1 child, Michelle. BS, Monmouth Coll., 1965; postgrad., Adelphi U., 1966, N.Y. Inst. Tech., 1970-71. Registered profl. engr., N.Y., N.J. Electronics engr. Grumman Aerospace, Bethpage, N.Y., 1965-72; sr. electronics engr. Litton Industries, Melville, N.Y., 1972-73; elec. engr. N.Y.C. Bd. Edn., 1973-75, N.Y. State Div. Housing, N.Y.C., 1975—; cons. in field, N.Y. Vol. Spl. Olympics, Patchogue, N.Y., 1991. Mem. N.Y. State Soc. Profl. Engrs. (legis. chmn. 1986-88, chair membership 1988-90, treas. 1990-91), Nat. Soc. Profl. Engrs., Sigma Pi Sigma. Jewish. Office: NY State Div Housing One Fordham Pla Bronx NY 10458

LINDEN, HAROLD ARTHUR, interior designer, consultant; b. N.Y.C., May 25, 1941; s. Moses Lindenman and Rose Barmack. BA in Art, CCNY, 1964, MA in Design, 1967. design cons. Forecast Furniture, Inc., Winchester, Va., 1969-87; Charlton Co., Leominster, Mass., 1968-71; Archt. CBT Corp., N.Y.C., 1971-86. Mem. Nat. Soc. Interior Designers, Kappa Phi Omega. Jewish. Home: 62-05 Alderton St Rego Park NY 11374

LINDEN, KURT JOSEPH, electronics engineer; b. Berlin, Germany, Dec. 27, 1936; came to U.S., 1947; s. Fred I. and Ruth B. (Salomon) L.; m. Susan M. Alpert, July 8, 1962; children: Judith A., Philip A., Benjamin N. BS, U. Utah, 1959; MS, MIT, 1962; PhD, Purdue U., 1966. Group leader Raytheon, Waltham, Mass., 1966-76; mgr. Laser Analytics, Bedford, Mass., 1976-84; dir. electronic materials div. Spire Corp., Bedford, Mass., 1984—; sr. lectr. Northeastern U., Boston, 1976—; lectr. MIT, Cambridge, Mass., summers 1980—. Contbr. over 35 articles to scholarly and profl. jours. Mem. IEEE, SPIE, Am. Phys. Soc. Home: 17 Keith Rd Wayland MA 01778-4560 Office: Spire Corp 1 Patriots Park Bedford MA 01730-2396

LINDENBERG, STEVEN PHILLIP, counselor, consultant; b. Lancaster, Pa., Dec. 6, 1945; s. Sidney David and Ruth Lillian (Levine) L.; m. Linda Kathleen Young, Aug. 26, 1967; children: Sara Michelle, Karen Rebecca, Elisabeth Claudine. BS, Millersville U., 1968; MEd, Shippensburg State U., 1974; PhD, U. Ga., 1977. Cert. clin. mental health counselor, Nat. Acad. Cert. Clin. Health Counseling, cert. counselor Nat. Bd. Cert. Counselors, cert. sch. psychologist, Pa. Jr. high sci. tchr. Chambersburg (Pa.) Area Sch. Dist., 1972-74; grad. asst. dept. counseling edn. Univ. Ga., Athens, 1974-77; ptnr., cert. clin. mental health counselor Hershey (Pa.) Psychiat. Assocs., 1977—; co-founder, 1st vice-chair Nat. Acad. Cert. Clin. Mental Health Counselors, Falls Church, Va., 1978-80; founder Lindenberg & David, Assocs., Hershey, 1990—. Mem. editorial bd.: Jour. Mental Health Counseling, 1991—; author: Group Psychotherapy with People Who Are Dying, 1983; contbr. articles to profl. jours. Founding bd. mem. Hospice of Cen. Pa., Enola, 1978-87, past. pres., mem. bereavement com. 1978—; mem. profl. devel. com. Am. Cancer Soc., Harrisburg, Pa., 1986-87; past pres., mem. bd. sch. dirs. No. Lebanon Sch. Dist., Fredericksburg, Pa., 1988—. Sgt. USAF, 1968-72. Decorated Am. Spirit of Honor medal Citizens Com. for Army, Navy and Air Force, Inc., Lackland AFB, Tex., 1968. Mem. AACD (bd. mem. 1979-80), Am. Mental Health Counselors Assn. (pres. 1979-80, profl. recognition awards 1981, 89, charter mem.), Am. Sch. Bd. Assn., Pa. Counselors Assn. (eminent practitioner 1988), Pa. Sch. Bd. Assn., Phi Kappa Phi, Kappa Delta Pi. Office: Hershey Psychiat Assocs 20 Briarcrest Sq Ste 205 Hershey PA 17033-2331

LINDENBERGER, GEORGE FERDINAND, former insurance executive; b. N.Y.C., Sept. 6, 1924; s. Richard George and Anna (Aulbach) L.; m. Hazel Maude Gueldenapfel, July 25, 1947; 1 child, Linda Marlene Curle. Student public schs. Pearl River, N.Y. With Equitable Life Ins. Co., N.Y.C., 1941-84, asst. v.p., 1980-81, v.p., 1981-84. Mem. Am. Pension Conf., Washington, 1980-81. Developed and installed 1st pvt. national system for direct deposit of pension benefits by electronic fund transfer. Mem. council Good Shepherd Ch., Pearl River, 1967-74, sec., 1971-73. Served with USAAF, 1943-45. Recipient Oustanding Performance award Equitable Ins. Co., 1975. Mem. Life Office Mgmt. Assn. (chmn. program com. 1980-81), Spray Beach (N.J.) Yacht Club, Ocean Acres Country Club (Stafford Township, N.J.), All Am. Photo (Park Ridge, N.J.) (pres. 1983-84). Republican. Lutheran. Avocations: boating, tennis, golfing, traveling, horticulture. Address: 1 Cleveland Ave Holgate NJ 08008 also: River Club 1600 NE Dixie Hwy Jensen Beach FL 34957

LINDENMUTH, ELISE BELL, counselor, educator; b. Hagerstown, Md., Jan. 22, 1945; d. W. Leigh and Gladys Marilee (Henkel) Bell; m. G. Frank Lindenmuth, Nov. 23, 1968; children: Joshua, Jacob. Student, NYU, 1966; BS, Gettysburg Coll., 1967; MA, MillersvilleU., 1971; postgrad., Am. U., 1989—. Cert. instrnl. III, Pa. Master tchr. West York (Pa.) Area Schs., 1967-75; dept. chmn. West York (Pa.) Schs., 1970-71; dir. Temple Child Program, York, 1979-80; counselor, speaker Psychol. Cons., York, 1981—; adj. faculty York (Pa.) Coll. of Pa., 1984—; researcher The Am. Univ., Washington, 1989-91; cons. York (Pa.) City Schs., 1985—. Author: Economic Education For Elementary School, 1972; co-author: Teachers, Schools and Society: Student Guide, 1991, Instructor's Manual to Accompany Teachers, Schools and Society, 1991. Recipient fellowship The Am. Univ., Washington, 1989. Mem. AAUP, AACD, Assn. Mental Health Counselors, Assn. for Adult Devel. and Aging. Home: 405 Hillcrest Rd York PA 17403-4711 Office: York Coll of Pa Country Club Rd York PA 17403-3644

LINDENTHAL, JACOB JAY, public health educator; b. Roanoke, Va., July 21, 1941; s. Haskel and Naomi Bracha (Weinberg) L.; m. Lorelle Naomi Michelson, Sept. 16, 1984. BA, Yeshiva U., 1963; PhD, Yale U., 1967, Yeshiva U., 1973; DrPH, Columbia U., 1978. Rsch. assoc. Yale U., New Haven, 1967-71; asst. prof. Rutgers U., Newark, 1971-73, assoc. prof., 1973-77; assoc. prof. U. Medicine & Dentistry of N.J., Newark, 1978-82, prof., 1982—; lectr. Columbia U., N.Y.C., 1982—; adj. univ. prof. Yeshiva U., N.Y.C., 1985—. Author: Health Concerns of Hispanics in New York City, 1991; co-editor: Psychiatry and Mental Health Handbook, 1988. Fellow N.Y. Acad. Medicine (assoc.), N.Y. Acad. Sci., Acad. Medicine of N.J., Am. Assn. for Social Psychiatry; mem. Am. Sociol. Assn. Office: NJ Med Sch 185 S Orange Ave Newark NJ 07103-2714

LINDHOLM, CHARLES THOMAS, anthropologist, educator; b. Mankato, Minn., Dec. 18, 1946; s. Wilbur Theodore and Viola Maimie (Schmidt-Lauffler) L.; m. Cherry Denise Korklin, Nov. 18, 1972; 1 child, Michelle. BA, Columbia U., 1968, PhD, 1979. Asst. prof. Barnard Coll., N.Y.C., 1979-82, Columbia U., N.Y.C., 1982-83; assoc. prof. Harvard U., Cambridge, Mass., 1983-90; assoc. prof. anthropology and social theory Univ. Profs. Program of Boston U., 1990—. Author: Charisma, 1990, Generosity and Jealousy, 1982; contbr. articles to profl. jours. Clark and Milton Funds rsch. grantee, 1985-89, NEH grantee, 1982, Fulbright-Hayes/NSF grantee, 1977; Henry Evans Travelling fellow of Columbia U., 1968. Mem. Am. Anthropol. Assn., Am. Ethnological Assn., Assn. for Psychol. Anthropology. Office: Boston U Univ Profs Program 745 Commonwealth Ave Boston MA 02215

LINDHOLM, CLIFFORD FALSTROM, II, engineering executive, mayor; b. Passaic, N.J., Dec. 8, 1930; s. Albert William and Edith (Neandross) L.; m. Margery Nye (div.); children: Clifford, Elizabeth, John; m. Karen Cooper, Oct. 7, 1989. BS in Engrng., Princeton U., 1953; M in Engrng., Stevens Inst. Tech., 1957. Supr. prodn. GM, Linden, N.J., 1953-56; pres. Falstrom Co., Passaic, N.J., 1956—; Bd. dirs. N.J. Mfg. Ins. Co., Trenton. Mayor Twp. Montclair, N.J., 1988—; pres. Montclair Bd. Edn., 1968-72; bd. dirs. Albert Payson Terhune Found., N.J., 1976—. Mem. N.J. Bus. and Industry Assn. (bd. dirs. 1977—), Princeton Club N.Y., Upper Montclair Golf Club, Mantoloking Yacht Club. Republican. Mem. Ch. of Christ. Home: 10 Mountainside Park Ter Montclair NJ 07043-1209 Office: Falstrom Co 3 Falstrom Ct Passaic NJ 07055-4443

LINDMAYER, JOSEPH, physicist; b. Budapest, Hungary, May 8, 1929; s. Stephen Joseph and Aranka (Borza) L.; m. Clara Boldvai (dec. 1982); 1 child, Monika Clara Lindmayer Lavine. B in Elec. Engrng., Tech. U. of Budapest, 1956; MS, Williams Coll., 1963; PhD, Rhein-Westphalian U., Aachen, Fed. Republic Germany, 1968. Mgr. physics lab. Sprague Electric Co., North Adams, Mass., 1957-68; dir. physics lab. Comsat, Clarksburg, Md., 1968-73; pres. Solarex Corp., Rockville, Md., 1973-82, Semix Inc., Rockville, 1979-83; pres., chmn. Quantex Corp., Rockville, 1984—; chmn. Photonex Corp., 1990—; bd. dirs. Optex Corp., Rockville. Co-author: Fundamentals of Semiconductor Devices, 1965; contbr. more than 100 articles to profl. jours.; more than 70 patents in field. Recipient Research and Devel. award Nat. Energy Resources Orgn., Washington, 1980, Recognition award NASA, Washington, 1979, 81. Office: Quantex Corp 2 Research Ct Rockville MD 20850-3211

LINDNER, CHARLOTTE K., librarian; b. N.Y.C., Feb. 28, 1922; d. Louis B. and Ada (Kreitman) Fisch; children: Carol, Gregory, Amy. BA, NYU, 1942; MLS, Columbia U., 1958. From asst. cataloger to dir. Albert Einstein Coll. Medicine Libr., Bronx, N.Y., 1958-89; ret. Office: Albert Einstein Coll 1300 Morris Park Ave Bronx NY 10461-1924

LINDNER, ISAAC NEWTON, physician; b. N.Y.C., Sept. 24, 1921; s. Jacob B. and Bertha Lindner; m. Rheba Ginsberg, Sept. 18, 1949; children: Mark, Richard, Judith. BA, Columbia Coll., 1942; MD, SUNY, Bklyn., 1945. Diplomate Am. Bd. Internal Medicine. Intern Kings County Hosp., Bklyn., 1945-46, 48-49; resident VA Hosp., Bronx, N.Y., 1948-50; pvt. practice Franklin Square, N.Y., 1952—; mem. staff internal medicine L.I. Jewish Hosp., New Hyde Park, N.Y., 1954-83; attending physician Franklin Hosp. and Med. Ctr., Franklin Square, 1964—; pres. med. staff Franklin Hosp. Med. Ctr., Franklin Square, N.Y., pres. med. bd., 1992—. Capt. U.S. Army, 1945-53. Mem. AMA, ACP, Am. Soc. Internal Medicine. Office: 397 Franklin Ave Franklin Square NY 11010-1227

LINDNER, MARIA CHRISTINA, professional society official; b. Harrisburg, Pa., Feb. 20, 1960; d. Kenneth Dale and Lena Annette (Detoma) S. BSBA, Shippensburg State, 1982; MBA, Loyola Coll., Balt., 1989. Tax staff Arthur Andersen & Co., Balt., 1982-84; acct. Enterprise Found., Columbia, Md., 1984-86; exec. recruiter Don Richard Assocs., Balt., 1986-91; mem. svcs. mgr. Md. Assn. CPAs, Lutherville, 1991—; bd. dirs. Pet-Coke, Inc., Houston; part-time instr. U. Md. Baltimore County, 1989—. Bd. dirs. Santa Claus Anonymous, Balt., 1986-87. Mem. Nat. Assn. Accts. (bd. dirs. 1986-88), Balt. Jr. Assn. Commerce (bd. dirs. 1988-89, v.p. 1987-88, treas. 1986-87, Key Mem. award 1988, President's citation, 1986, 89, Outstanding New Mem. award 1986). Republican. Roman Catholic. Office: Md Assn CPAs 1300 York Rd Ste 10 PO Box 4417 Lutherville Timonium MD 21094

LINDROTH, LINDA HAMMER, artist; b. Miami, Sept. 4, 1946; d. Mark Roger and Mae Lang Hammer; m. David George Lindroth, May 26, 1968 (div. Mar. 1985); m. Craig David Newick, June 6, 1987; 1 child, Zachary Eran Newick. BA in Art, Douglass Coll., 1964; MFA in Art, Rutgers U., 1979. Represented in permanent collections The Mus. of Modern Art, N.Y.C., The Met. Mus. of Art, N.Y.C., The Mus. of City of N.Y., Polaroid Collection/Artist Program, N.J. State Mus., Trenton, The Bibliotheque Nationale, Paris, Ctr. for Creative Photography, Tucson, The Newark Mus., The Jane Voorhees Zimmerli Art Mus., New Brunswick, N.J., Price Waterhouse & Co., N.Y.C., First Bank of Boston, Bear, Stearns Co.; exhibited at Aetna Gallery, 1991, 89, 87. Dir. Artspace, Inc., New Haven; mem. Mayor's Task Force on Pub. Art, New Haven. Recipient Ann. Design Rev. award ID Mag., 1990, 91, Honorable Mention, Nat. Peace Garden Design Competition, 1989, Archtl. Design Competition, 1988, Individual Artist fellow N.J. State Coun. on Arts, 1974-75, 83-84; grantee Found. for Contemporary Performance Arts, Inc., 1989, 90, Fission Fusion NEA InterARts, 1989, grantee New Eng. Found. for Arts, 1992. Office: 219 Livingston St New Haven CT 06511

LINDSAY, DONALD J., banker; b. Utica, N.Y., Oct. 13, 1941; s. Robert Nelson and Gertrude Esther (Vaeth) L.; m. Andrea Takacs Sohonyai, July 30, 1977. BA, Harvard Coll., 1963; LLB, Columbia U., 1966; MBA, 1968. Bar: N.Y. 1966. Various lending and mgmt. pos. Chase Manhattan Bank, N.A., N.Y.C., 1968-85; pres. Chase Manhattan Bank So. Tier, Binghamton, N.Y., 1974-75, Chase Manhattan Bank Greater Rochester, N.Y., 1975-76, Chase Manhattan Bank Cen. N.Y., Syracuse, 1976-77; v.p., dep. credit policy area head State St. Bank and Trust Co., Boston, 1985—. Trustee, exec. com. Cantata Singers, Inc., Boston, 1987; trustee Everson Mus. Art, Syracuse, 1975-76. Mem. Harvard Club, Century Club. Republican. Episcopalian. Home: 68A Monmouth St Brookline MA 02146-5607 Office: State St Bank and Trust Co 225 Franklin St Boston MA 02110-2804

LINDSAY, FRANKLIN ANTHONY, business executive, author; b. Kenton, Ohio, Mar. 12, 1916; s. Harry Wyatt and Ruth (Andrews) L.; m. Margot Coffin, Dec. 17, 1948; children: Catherine, Alison, John Franklin. A.B., Stanford U., 1938; postgrad., Harvard U., 1946. With Columbia div. U.S. Steel Corp., 1938-39; exec. asst. to Bernard Baruch, U.S. del. UN Atomic Energy Commn., 1946; cons. Ho. of Reps. Select (Herter) Com. on Fgn. Aid, 1947-48, ECA, Paris; rep. to exec. com. OEEC, 1948-49; with CIA, 1949-53; with pub. affairs program Ford Found., 1953-56; prin. McKinsey & Co., Inc., N.Y.C., 1956-61; exec. v.p., dir. Itek Corp., Lexington, Mass., 1961-62, pres., dir., 1962-75, chmn. bd., 1975-81, chmn. exec. com., 1981-83; chmn. Engenics, Inc., Menlo Park, Calif., 1983-85, Vectravision, Inc., Nashua, N.H., 1985-87; rsch. assoc. Inst. Politics, Harvard U., 1967-71; cons. 2d Hoover Commn., 1954, The White House, 1955; mem. Rockefeller Spl. Studies Panel Econ. Policy, 1956, Gaither Com. Nat. Security Policy, 1957; asst. staff dir. President's Com. World Econ. Policy, 1958; mem. President Elect's Task Force on Disarmament, 1960; dir. Com. for Nat. Trade Policy, 1956-71; adv. coun. dept. econs. Princeton U., 1961-64; mem. Wilson Ctr. adv. coun. Smithsonian Instn., 1980—; trustee Bennington Coll., 1963-73; chmn. bd. trustees Edn. Devel. Ctr., 1967-73; mem. vis. com. dept. econs. Harvard U., 1976-80; mem. President's Adv. Com. on Trade Negotiations, 1976-79; bd. dirs. Nat. Bur. Econ. Rsch., 1976—, mem. exec. com., 1980—, chmn., 1983-86; mem. adv. coun. Gas Rsch. Inst., 1977-83; vice chmn. energy and raw materials, bus. and industry advisory com. OECD, 1977-82; bd. dirs. Corp. Pub./Pvt. Ventures, 1978-82, chmn., 1980; mem. advisory bd. Pub. Agenda Found., 1978-84; mem. NRC Commn. Engrng. Systems, 1978-84, panel on balancing nat. interest NAS, 1985-87; bd. dirs. Resources for the Future, 1978-86; assoc. Ctr. for Internat. Affairs, Harvard U., 1988—. Author: New Techniques of Mgmt. Decision Making, 1958, War and Revolution in Yugoslavia 1941-45, 1992; contbg. author: Preparing Tomorrow's Business Leaders Today, The Conscience of the City, Removing Obstacles to Economic Growth, Wars within a War: Yugoslavia, 1992; contbr. articles on nat. and fgn. policy to profl. jours. Fellow Woodrow Wilson Ctr. for Scholars, Washington, 1987-88, 90. Served to lt. col. AUS, 1940-45; with guerrilla forces 1944-45, Europe (OSS); chief U.S. Mil. Mission to Yugoslavia, 1945. Decorated Legion of Merit. Mem. Nat. Planning Assn. (vice chmn. com. arms control 1959-62), Coun. Fgn. Relations, Inst. Strategic Studies (London), Com. for Econ. Devel. (trustee 1967—, vice chmn. 1974-88, mem. rsch. and policy com. 1976—, chmn. 1976-83), UN Assn. U.S. (gov. 1968-75), Can.-Am. Com., Hudson Inst. (pub. mem.), Saturday Club, Century Club, Phi Beta Kappa, Tau Beta Pi.

LINDSAY, GEORGE NELSON, lawyer; b. N.Y.C., Oct. 20, 1919; m. Mary Sloan Dickey, Apr. 13, 1946; children: George Nelson Jr., Louise Dickey, Stephen Whitney, Peter Vliet. BA, Yale U., 1941, LLB, 1947. Bar: N.Y. 1947. Assoc. Debevoise & Plimpton and predecessor firms, N.Y.C., 1947-54, ptnr., 1955-90, presiding ptnr., 1980-87; resident ptnr. Debevoise & Plimpton and predecessor firms, London, 1989-90; of counsel Debevoise & Plimpton, N.Y.C., 1991—; mem. adv. coun. of Africa, Dept. State, 1964-68; mem. exec. com. Lawyers Com. for Civil Rights Under Law, 1969—, co-chmn. 1969-71. Mem. urban design coun. City of N.Y., 1969-75; bd. dirs. African-Am. Inst., 1969—, chmn. bd. dirs., 1981-84; trustee, mem. coun. Yale U., 1973-78, 81-86, v.p., 1976-78, 81-86; bd. dirs. Planned Parenthood-World Population, 1965-68, chmn. bd. dirs., 1965-66; trustee Carnegie Endowment for Internat. Peace, 1981-91, vice chmn., 1986-89, hon. trustee, 1991—; bd. dirs. The Ogilvy Group, Inc., 1962-89, Am. Ditchley Found., 1985—. Recipient Whitney North Seymour award for civil right, 1988. Fellow Am. Bar Found., N.Y. Bar Found.; mem. ABA, N.Y. State Bar Assn., Assn. of Bar of City of N.Y. (mem. exec. com. 1973-77, chmn. exec. com. 1976-77, v.p. 1977), Am. Judicature Soc., Am. Assn. Internat. Commn. Jurists (bd. dirs. 1969—, chmn. bd. dirs. 1983-88), Coun. Fgn. Rels., Overseas Devel. Coun. Home: 16 Sutton Pl New York NY 10022-3057

LINDSAY, JOHN VLIET, former mayor, former congressman, author, lawyer; b. N.Y.C., Nov. 24, 1921; s. George Nelson and Eleanor (Vliet) L.; m. Mary Harrison, June 18, 1949; children—Katharine, Margaret, Anne, John Vliet. Grad., St. Paul's Sch., Concord, N.H., 1940; B.A., Yale U., 1944, LL.B., 1948; LL.D. (hon.), Harvard U., 1969, Williams Coll., 1968. Bar: N.Y. State 1949, N.Y. Dist. Ct. (so. dist.) N.Y 1950, U.S. Supreme Ct. 1955, D.C. 1958. Mem. firm Webster & Sheffield, N.Y.C., 1953-60, 74-91, presiding ptnr., 1989-91; of counsel Mudge Rose Guthrie Alexander & Ferdon, N.Y.C., 1991—; exec. asst. to U.S. atty. gen., 1955-56; mem. 86th-89th Congresses from 17th Dist. N.Y.; mayor N.Y.C., 1965-73; Commentator on TV. Author: Journey Into Politics, 1966, The City, 1970, The Edge, 1976. Bd. mem. emeritus Lincoln Ctr. for Performing Arts; chmn. emeritus Lincoln Ctr. Theatre Co. Lt. USNR, 1943-46. Mem. Assn. of Bar of City of N.Y. (exec. com. 1956-60), ABA, N.Y. State Bar Assn., Assn. Former Mems. Congress (pres. 1987-88). Episcopalian. Democrat.

LINDSEY, JOANNE MEREDITH, dean, law educator; b. West Palm Beach, Fla.; d. James Jacob and Mildred (Hooper) Meredith; m. Raymond Edwin Lindsey, Dec. 1, 1957; children: Meredith, Lorraine, Jennifer. Student, U. Fla., 1954-57; BA magna cum laude, Neumann Coll., 1975; JD, Temple U., 1978. Bar: Pa. 1978. Counsel J.E. Brenneman Co., Phila., 1978-81; pres., co-founder Waterfront Corp., Phila., 1980-84; dir. placement Sch. of Law Widener U., Wilmington, Del., 1984-86, asst. dean Sch. of Law, 1986—. Mem. Marple Twp. Planning Commn., Broomall, Pa., 1979; leader Girl Scouts U.S., Broomall, 1970-75; pres. Phila. chpt. Planning Execs. Inst., 1981. Mem. ABA, Del. Bar Assn. (assoc.), Nat. Assn. Law Placement, Law Sch. Admission Coun. Republican. Episcopalian. Home: 67 Lindbergh Ave Broomall PA 19008-2604 Office: Widener U Sch Law PO Box 7474 Wilmington DE 19803-0409

LINDSEY, LAWRENCE BENJAMIN, economist; b. Peekskill, N.Y., July 18, 1954; s. Merritt Hunt and Helen Ruth (Hissam) L.; m. Susan Ann McGrath, Aug. 28, 1982. AB magna cum laude, Bowdoin Coll., Brunswick, Maine, 1976; MA, Harvard U., 1981, PhD, 1985. Economist Coun. Econ. Advisers, Washington, 1981-84; from asst. prof. to assoc. prof. Harvard U., Cambridge, Mass., 1985-89; faculty rsch. fellow Nat. Bur. Econ. Rsch., Cambridge, 1985-89; assoc. dir. The White House Office Policy Devel., Washington, 1989-90; spl. asst. to pres. for policy devel. White House Office Policy Devel., Washington, 1991—; Gov. of Fed. Res. System, 1991—.

Author: The Growth Experiment, 1990; contbr. articles to profl. jours. Recipient Walter Wriston award Manhattan Inst., 1988. Mem. Phi Beta Kappa. Office: Fed Res Bd Washington DC 20551

LINDSTROM, JANET ELENA, non-profit executive; b. Erie, Pa., Jan. 27, 1934; d. Charles and Emma Marie (Brummer) Ramandanes; m. Gary Edward Lindstrom, June 19, 1958 (wid. Jan. 1980); children: Maren, Jennifer. BS, Pa. State U., 1956; MA, Columbia U., 1960. Tchr. Erie Sch. Dist., 1956-58, New Canaan (Conn.) Schs., 1958-62, Foxglove Sch., New Canaan, 1982-83; exec. dir. New Canaan Hist. Soc., 1983—. Sec. Dirs. of Vols., Stamford, Conn., 1990—. Commr. Hist. Dist. Commn., New Canaan, 1989—; sec. Day Care Ctr. of New Canaan, 1984—, vice-chmn., 1992—; pres. New Canaan High Sch. Parent Facility, 1980-81, New Canaan Hist. Soc., 1983-85; co-chmn. NCHS Scholarship Found., New Canaan, 1982-84. Mem. AAUW (pres. 1971-73, grantee 1973), Rep. Woman's Cl;ub, New Canaan Field Club. Republican. Presbyterian. Office: The New Canaan Hist Soc 13 Oenoke Rdg New Canaan CT 06840-4195

LINDSTROM, JON MARTIN, medical research scientist; b. Moline, Ill., Oct. 9, 1945; s. Herbert Martin and Melnotte Elanore (Anderson) L.; m. Dona Meiko Chikaraishi, June 29, 1969 (div. 1972); m. Suzanne Stevenson, Nov. 23, 1977; children—Laurel Anne, Kara Martine, Jon Kenneth. BA, U. Ill., 1967; PhD, U. Calif.-San Diego, 1971. Asst. prof. Salk Inst., La Jolla, Calif., 1973-78, assoc. prof., 1978-83, assoc. prof. and mem., 1983-90, trustee prof. U. Pa. Med. Sch. Dept. Neurosci., 1990—. Author over 250 articles; discovered cause of myasthenia gravis; patentee radioimmunoassay for myasthenia gravis; mem. editorial bd. Jour. Neuroimmunology. Mem. Sci. adv. com. Muscular Dystrophy Assn. Grants and awards include NIH, Jacob Javits award, Muscular Dystrophy Assn., Sloan Found., McKnight Found., Onassis Found., Office Naval Research, U.S. Army. Home: 110 Rock Rose Ln Radnor PA 19087 Office: U Pa Med Sch 217 Stemmler Hall Philadelphia PA 19104-6074

LINDVALL, MICHAEL LLOYD, clergyman, writer; b. Mpls., June 24, 1947; s. Lloyd Calvin and Jean Elizabeth (Painter) L.; m. Terri V. Smith, Sept. 8, 1973; children: Madeline, Benjamin, Grace. BA, U. Wis., Oshkosh, 1970; MDiv, Princeton U., 1974. Ordained to ministry United Presbyn. Ch., 1974. Assoc. pastor Drayton Avenue Presbyn. Ch., Ferndale, Mich., 1974-79; pastor 1st Presbyn. Ch., Northport, N.Y., 1979—; bd. dirs. United Presbyn. Residence, Woodbury, N.Y., 1987—. Author: (novel) The Goal News from North Haven, 1991; contbr. short stories and articles to popular mags. Chaplain Northport Vol. Fire Dept., 1988—. Mem. Enigma Club (N.Y.), Bass Lake Sailing Club (Mich.). Home: 5 Woodhull Pl Northport NY 11768-2864 Office: 1st Presbyn Ch Church and Main Sts Northport NY 11768

LINDZEN, RICHARD SIEGMUND, meteorologist, educator; b. Webster, Mass., Feb. 8, 1940; s. Abe and Sara (Blachman) L.; m. Nadine Lucie Kalougine, Apr. 7, 1965; children: Eric, Nathaniel. A.B., Harvard U., 1960, S.M., 1961, Ph.D., 1964. Research assoc. U. Wash., Seattle, 1964-65; Research asso. U. Oslo, 1965-66; with Nat. Center Atmospheric Research, Boulder, Colo., 1966-68; mem. faculty U. Chgo., 1968-72; prof. meteorology Harvard U., 1972-83, dir. Center for Earth and Planetary Physics, 1980-83; Alfred P. Sloan prof. meteorology MIT, 1983—; Lady Davis vis. prof. Hebrew U., 1979; Sackler prof. Tel Aviv U., 1992; Vikram Sarabhai prof. Phys. Research Lab., Ahmedabad, India, 1985; cons. NASA, Jet Propulsion Lab., others; mem. space studies bd. and bd. on atmospheric scis. and climate NRC. Author: Dynamics in Atmospheric Physics; co-author: Atmospheric Tides; contbr. to profl. jours. Recipient Macelwane award Am. Geophys. Union, 1968. Fellow NAS, Am. Geophys. Union, Am. Meteorol. Soc. (Meisinger award 1969, councillor 1972-75, Charney award 1985), Am. Acad. Arts and Scis., Internat. Commn. Dynamic Meteorology, Woods Hole Oceanographic Instn. (corp.), Institut Mondial des Sciences. Jewish. Office: MIt 54-1720 Cambridge MA 02139

LINEBACK, HARVEY LEE, media specialist; b. Key West, Fla., Jan. 2, 1946; s. Paskel Lee Lineback and Mabel Ida (Collins) Griffitts. BS, Appalachian State U., 1968; postgrad., Western Md. Coll., 1970, Cath. U., 1974-75. Media specialist St. Mary's County Pub. Schs., Leonardtown, Md., 1968—; lab. tech. U. Md., Solomons, 1986. Co-author: The Beroth Roots, 1987; author: Our Collins Family, 1988, Our Frye Family, 1989. Mem. Pub. Libr. Planning Com., Leonardtown, 1984, parish coun. St. Aloysius Ch., Leonardtown, 1987-89, liturgy com., 1987-89, So. Md. Reading Coun. Mem. NEA, Md. Tchrs. Assn., Md. Ednl. Media Orgn., Edn. Assn. St. Mary's County, St. Mary's County Hist. Soc., U.S. Capital Hist. Soc. (Outstanding Tchr. award 1983), Md. Soc. SAR (sec. chpt. 1990). Republican. Roman Catholic. Home: RR 1 Box 772 Hollywood MD 20636-9736 Office: Esperanza Mid Sch 201 Maple Rd Lexington Park MD 20653-9449

LINEK, HENRY, podiatrist; b. Somerville, N.J., Oct. 28, 1947; s. Matthew and Hedwig (Rusinski) L.; m. Patricia Korbeil, Nov. 17, 1985. BS in Biology, Alliance Coll., 1970; D of Podiatric Medicine, Ohio Coll. Podiatric Medicine, 1974. Diplomate Nat. Bd. Podiatry Examiners. Resident St. Luke's Childrens and Med. Ctr., Phila., 1974-75; assoc. practice Morristown, N.J., 1975-77; podiatrist pvt. practice Morristown, 1977—; podiatrist, ptnr. Rockaway, N.J., 1989—; mem. cons. staff Morristown Meml. Hosp., St. Clare's-Riverside Hosp., Denville, N.J., VA Med. Ctr., Lyons, N.J., 1977-83; instr. podiatry residents Podiatry Clinic, 1983—; staff podiatrist Preakness Hosp., Totowa, N.J., 1978, Little Brook Nursing Home, Califon, N.H., Hunterdon Med. Ctr., Flemington, N.J., 1989, Somerset Valley Nursing Home, 1991, Hunterdon Hills Residential Care, 1991. Fellow Acad. Ambulatory Foot Surgeons; mem. Am. Podiatric Assn., N.J. Podiatric Med. Soc. Office: Henry Linek DPM 88 Maple Ave Morristown NJ 07960-5221

LINEWEAVER, PAUL KELTON, educator; b. Berkelcy Spring, W.Va., May 30, 1925; s. Allen Lee and Bessie May (Fredman) L.; m. Hilda Eloise Crane, Nov. 16, 1947; 1 child, Amanda Storm. BS in Econs., Ind. U., 1955; MEd, Shippensburg (Pa.) State Coll., 1962. With Fairchild Aircraft, Hagerstown, Md., 1942-43; hosp. tech. VA, Martinsburg, W.Va., 1947-51; project coordinator Fairchild Aircraft, 1955-59; tchr. social studies Chambersburg (Pa.) High Sch., 1961-86; ret. With U.S. Army, 1943-47. Mem. Ind. U. Alumni Assn., Chambersburg Club, NEA, Pa. Edn. Assn., Masons, Delta Sigma, Alpha Kappa Delta. Address: 1619 Clinton Ave Chambersburg PA 17201

LING, DOUGLAS CHIH-YEN, entrepreneur, consultant; b. Hong Kong, Mar. 23, 1960; came to U.S., 1981; s. Francis Cho-Feng and Vivian Hsiao-Wen (Shen) L. Student, U. B.C., 1978-81; BSc in Aeros., Rensselaer Poly. Inst., 1983; SM in Aeros., MIT, 1987. Rsch. assoc. Dept. Nat. Def., Quebec City, Toronto, 1982; rsch. asst. MIT, Cambrige, Mass., 1983-90; co-founder Fire Sta. Earth, Inc., Portsmouth, N.H., 1991—; dir. MIT Entrepreneurs Club, Cambridge, 1988—; founder, dir. MIT $10k Entrepreneurial Competition, Cambridge, 1989—; prin. cons. FTL Group, Cambridge, 1990—. Recipient Norman McKenzie scholarship Univ. B.C., Vancouver, 1978. Mem. AIAA, Tau Beta Pi, Sigma Gamma Tau, Sigma Xi.

LING, SUILIN, management consultant; b. Shanghai, China, Oct. 13, 1930; s. Chunchen and Maisan (Dunn) L.; came to U.S., 1949, naturalized, 1963; B.S., U. Mich., 1952; Ph.D., Columbia U., 1961; m. Avril Marjorie Kathleen Button, Apr. 4, 1964; children—Christopher Charles, Charmian Avril. Mech. engr. Ebasco Services, Inc., 1953-54; with research div. Foster Wheeler Corp., 1954-64; mgmt. cons. The Emerson Cons., Inc., 1964-65; sr. economist Communications Satellite Corp., 1965-67; chief economist Northrop-Page Communication Engrs., Inc., 1967-70; founder-dir., chief economist Teleconsult, Inc., Washington, 1970-82; founder, pres. Communications Devel. Corp., 1982-87, chmn. bd. dirs., 1987—; lectr. econs. Bernard M. Baruch Sch. Bus. and Pub. Adminstrn., CCNY. Mem. Am. Mgmt. Assn., Am. Econ. Assn., Am. Soc. M.E., Am. Acad. Polit. and Social Sci. Author: Economies of Scale in the Steam-Electric Power Generating Industry, 1964. Home: 2735 Unicorn Ln NW Washington DC 20015-2233 Office: 2828 Pennsylvania Ave NW Washington DC 20007

LINGAPPA, YAMUNA, microbiologist, researcher; b. Nanjangud, Mysore, India, Dec. 6, 1929; came to U.S., 1953; d. Anantha L. and Kamla Achar; m. Banadakoppa T. Lingappa, Mar. 21, 1953; children: Vishwanath, Jaisri, Jairam. BS, Mysore U., 1950; BT, Madras U., India, 1952; MS, Purdue U., 1955, PhD, 1958. Rsch. assoc. U. Mich., Ann Arbor, 1958-60; pool officer U. Madras, India, 1960-61; rsch. assoc. Mich. State U., East Lansing, 1961-62, Holy Cross Coll., Worcester, Mass., 1963-70; pres. Annapurna Inc., Worcester, 1976—. Office: Holy Cross Coll Worcester MA 01610

LINGELBACH, DAVID CHARLES, financial company executive; b. Oct. 25, 1961; s. Clayton Thomas and Fern Marion (Sanders) L.; m. Jeannette Alison Wentz, June 2, 1990. Student, London Sch. Econs., 1981-82; BS in Polit. Sci., MIT, 1984, BS in Econs., 1984, MS in Polit. Sci., 1984. Comml. officer nat. div. First Wisc. Nat. Bank, Milw., 1984-87; intelligence analyst intern Dept. State, Washington, 1981, policy planning staff intern, 1982; internat. econs. analyst The Heritage Found., Washington, 1983; asst. v.p. northeast corp. dept. Phila. Nat. Bank, 1987-90, v.p. fgn. corp. dept., 1989-91; v.p. credit rev. Core States Fin. Corp., Phila., 1991—. Mem. World Affairs Coun., Phila., 1989—. Home: 1638 Naudain St Philadelphia PA 19146-1521 Office: 30 S 15th St 6th Fl Philadelphia PA 19101

LINK, ANTHONY EDWARD, educational administrator, educator; b. N.Y.C., July 31, 1932; s. Edward Anthony and Beatrice Johanna (Moxter) L.; m. Marilyn Ann Gaylord, Aug. 3, 1957; children: Gretchen Ann, Elizabeth Ann. BA, SUNY, Brockport, 1955; MS in Adminstrn., SUNY, Buffalo, 1961. Cert. sch. dist. adminstr., N.Y. Prin. North Tonawanda (N.Y.) Sch. Dist., 1964-66; tchr. Williamsville (N.Y.) Cen. Sch. Dist., 1957-61, asst. prin., 1961-64, dir. differentiating staffing, 1970-71, prin., 1964-70, 71—, acting asst. supt. for instrn., 1979; adj. prof. SUNY, Buffalo, 1986—; SED visitor U.S. Dept. Edn., Washington, 1989-90; co-dir. Adminstrv. Assessment Ctr. Western N.Y., 1990—; chmn. Western N.Y. Prin.'s Ctr., Buffalo, 1987—. With U.S. Army, 1955-57. Recipient Nat. Disting. Prin. award U.S. Dept. Edn., 1989, Dean's Svc. award SUNY, Buffalo, 1990. Mem. NAESP, ASCD, Nat. Staff Devel. Coun., Internat. Reading Assn., Sch. Adminstrs. Assn., Sch. Adminstrs. Assn. N.Y. State (Disting. Prin. award), Phi Delta Kappa (Outstanding Contbn. to Edn. award 1990). Presbyterian. Home: 224 Brantwood Rd Buffalo NY 14226-4306 Office: Maple West Elem Sch 851 Maple Rd Buffalo NY 14221-3297

LINKE, HARALD A.B., microbiology educator, consultant; b. Bautzen, Fed. Republic Germany, Aug. 18, 1936; came to U.S., 1967; s. Helmuth and Kathe Linke; m. Christa Bolte, Dec. 21, 1971; 1 child, Arthur. BSc, Humboldt U., Berlin, 1961; MSc, U. Gottingen, Fed. Rep. Germany, 1963, PhD, 1967; prof. oral microbiology. Postdoctoral fellow Rutgers U., New Brunswick, N.J., 1967-69; rsch. microbiologist Allied Chem. Corp., Morristown, N.J., 1969-72; rsch. assoc. Waksman Inst. Rutgers U., 1972-73; prof. NYU, 1973—. Co-author: Developments in Sweeteners-3, 1987; co-patentee method of reducing dental caries. Mem. Am. Soc. Microbiology, German Chem. Soc., European Orgn. Caries Rsch., Internat. Assn. Dental Rsch., U.S. Fedn. Culture Collections, N.Y. Acad. Scis., Sigma Xi. Home: 138 Barnard St Highland Park NJ 08904-3510

LINKSZ, JAMES JOSEPH, administrator; b. Hanover, N.H., Dec. 19, 1941; s. Arthur and Magdalena (Orban) L.; m. Donna Elaine Hill, June 14, 1986; children: Timothy, Justin, Elizabeth. AB, Dartmouth Coll., 1963; MA, Columbia U., 1964, EdD, 1971. Asst. to pres. Catonsville Community Coll., Catonsville, Md., 1966-68; ednl. cons. Eaton-Burnett Jr. Coll., Balt., 1968-69; faculty art, head libr. Catonsville Community Coll., 1970-71; dean instrn. Rappahannock Community Coll., Glenns, Va., 1971-75; chmn. humanities, prof. art Catonsville Community Coll., 1975-80, dean instrn., 1980—; adv. bd. Project ACCLAIM, N.C. State U./Kellogg Found.; bd. dirs. Nat. Coun. Instn. Adminstrs., Washington, 1986-89. Pres. Middlesex Lions Club, Va., 1975; EMT tng. officer Middlesex Rescue Squad, 1973-75; bd. dirs. We. Family YMCA, Catonsville, 1968-69. W.K. Kellogg fellow, 1965, 66. Mem. Dartmouth Club Md.

LINN, ANN MARIE, nurse; b. Ashland, Pa., June 23, 1937; d. Raymond Joseph and Hilda Minnie (Burgund) Maher; m. Clayton Henry Linn, Sept. 13, 1958. Lic. practical nurse, Danville Area Sch., Washingtonville, Pa., 1985. Lic. practical nurse. Optometric asst./reccptionistl, receptionist office of pvt. practice optometrist, Shamokin, Pa., 1978-82; charge nurse, supr. Maria Hall Nursing Home for Elderly Nuns, Danville, Pa., 1985; charge nurse Gold Star Nursing Home, Danville, 1985—, plan of care nurse, 1985-89; charge nurse Mt. Carmel (Pa.) Nursing Ctr., 1990-91. Democrat. Roman Catholic. Home: 22 S Walnut St Mount Carmel PA 17851-2312 Office: Mt Carmel Nursing Ctr 3D W St Mount Carmel PA 17851

LINN, ANTHONY BLANE, engineering firm executive; b. Houston, Mar. 27, 1951; s. Edward Roy and Lorraine Gloria (Robsham) L.; m. Kathleen Conley, Jan. 15, 1975 (div. Feb. 1988); children: Shannon, Eric. BSME, U. Mass., 1973. Registered profl. engr., N.H. Project engr. Kingsbury Machine Tool Co., Keene, N.H., 1976-77; project engr. MFE, Salem, N.H., 1978-80; pres. Linn Tool & Electronics, Jaffrey, N.H., 1981-87; dir. engring. RWT Rsch. & Engring., North Kingstown, R.I., 1987—. Mem. Jaffrey C. of C., 1988-89, Jaffrey Recycling Com., 1989. Mem. ASME, AIAA, Exptl. Aircraft Assn., Internat. Aerobatics Club. Republican. Office: Aerotek Engring Corp 22 Fitzgerald Dr Jaffrey NH 03452-1918

LINN, RICHARD THOMAS, neuropsychology educator; b. Lexington, Ky., Oct. 20, 1953; s. Richard Thomas and Harriet Semple (Field) L.; m. Susan Benz, Sept. 15, 1990. BA, U. R.I., 1975; MA, U. N.Mex., 1980, PhD, 1986. Lic. psychologist, Mass. Neuropsychologist McLean Hosp., Belmont, Mass., 1983-90, Framingham (Mass.) Heart Study, 1984-90; rsch. asst. prof. SUNY, Buffalo, 1990—; rsch. dir. Rsch. Rehab. and Tng. Ctr., Buffalo, 1990-91. Contbr. articles to profl. jours. Mem. Am. Psychol. Assn., Am. Heart Assn., Internat. Neuropsychol. Soc. Office: SUNY 197 Farber Hall 3435 Main St Buffalo NY 14214-3000

LINN, ROBERT ALLEN, chemical company executive, lawyer; b. Akron, Ohio, June 9, 1932; s. Robert Albertus and Rita Marie (Hogl) L.; m. Eileen Marie Ryan, Nov. 22, 1956 (div. 1986); children—Nancy Ann, Thomas Patrick, Michael Joseph, Mary Lisa; m. Patricia Moreland Gwinner, Aug. 16, 1986; stepchildren: Kelli Ann Gwinner, Susan Lynne Gwinner. B.S. in Chemistry, Xavier U., Cin., 1954, M.S., 1956; postgrad. Wayne State U., 1956-58; LL.B., U. Detroit, 1961; M.B.A., Mich. State U., 1980. Bar: Mich. 1961, U.S. Dist. Ct. (ea. dist.) Mich. 1962, U.S. Patent & Trademark Office, 1963. Toxicologist, Wayne County, Detroit, 1957-61; patent atty. Ethyl Corp., Ferndale, Mich., 1961-64, mgr. patent sect., 1964-80, economist, Baton Rouge, 1980-81, dir. corp. bus. devel., Richmond, Va., 1981-86, patent atty., Baton Rouge, 1986-88; patent atty. Eastman Kodak Co., Rochester, N.Y., 1988-92, dir. licensing and bus. devel. photographic materials, 1992—. Contbr. articles to profl. jours. Mem. Product Devel. and Mgmt. Assn. (pres. 1984-85, Cresheim award for best conf. paper 1982), Am. Intellectual Property Assn., Rochester Intellectual Property Law Assn. (pres. elect 1991). Episcopalian. Office: Eastman Kodak Co 343 State St Rochester NY 14650-0001

LINNANE, JAMES JOSEPH, state official, consultant; b. Boston, Oct. 24, 1941; s. James Joseph and Mary Elizabeth (Devine) L.; m. Eileen Veronica Walsh, Apr. 12, 1968. BA, Columbia U., 1974; MPA, NYU, 1982. Researcher Ctr. for Community Health, N.Y.C., 1974-76; planner Woodhull Hosp., Bklyn., 1976-78; facilities cons. R.I. Dept. Health, Providence, 1978-83, supervising planner, 1983-84; planning dir. Health Systems Agy., Hartford, Conn., 1984-88; lead planner Conn. Medicaid, Conn. Dept. Income Maintenance, Hartford, 1988—; cons. R.I. Dept. Health, Providence, 1984—; cons. Bus. Coalition on Health, Hartford, 1988—. Contbr. articles to profl. publs. Pres. Abbey Lane Condominium, Foster, R.I., 1983-84. With U.S. Army, 1960-62. Mem. APHA, Am. Soc. Pub. Adminstrn., Farmington River Watershed Assn., Appalachian Mountain Club, Mensa, Phi Beta Kappa. Democrat. Home: 122 Ratlum Rd 6 Greenwoods Rd Barkhamsted CT 06022 Office: Dept Income Maintenance 110 Bartholomew Ave Hartford CT 06106-2201

LINNEN, THOMAS FRANCIS, international strategic management consulting firm executive; b. Carbondale, Pa., Sept. 29, 1925; s. John Joseph and Marie Dolores (Fitzpatrick) L.; m. Mary Joanne, Dec. 28, 1951 ; children: Nancy, Paula, Michele, Thomas F. Jr., Mary J. Jr. BS in Fgn. Svc., Georgetown U., 1949; MA, Am. Univ., Washington, 1951; postgrad., U. Rochester, 1987-88. Writer Congl. News Reports, Washington, late 40's; congl. press asst. Washington, 1949; asst. for pub. relations office of pres. Georgetown U., 1950; officer psychol. and spl. ops., counter-intelligence U.S. Army, Ft. Bragg, N.C., 1951-53; mgr. Retail Credit Company, Atlanta, 1953-56, 59-72; various mgr. assignments including gen. mgr. Equifax Inc., Chgo., 1972-80; regional mgr. ops. and sales Equifax Inc., Upstate, N.Y., 1980-89; vice chmn. bd. dirs., pres. The NORAM Group Ltd., Buffalo, 1990—; bd. dirs. Gaflin Communication Group Inc., Chgo.; on spl. assignment CIA, 1956-59. Author: articles various jours. and mags. Active in Fgn. Policy Assn. of U.S., United Nations Assn. of U.S.; adv. bd. Barat Coll., Buffalo Coun. on World Affairs, Internat. Inst. Buffalo, Chgo. Coun. Fgn. Rels., United Way, Crusade of Mercy, Heart Fund Campaigns, and other civic orgns. Maj. USAR, Ret., also maj. USAF. Mem. Res. Officers Assn. of U.S. (former officer), Mortgage Bankers Assn., Nat. Coun. Life Underwriters. Republican. Roman Catholic. Home: 20 Fir Top Dr Orchard Park NY 14127-3517 Office: The NORAM Group Ltd 650 Statler Towers Buffalo NY 14202

LINNENBERG, CLEM CHARLES, JR., economist; b. Houston, May 20, 1912; s. Clem Charles and Maggie (White) L.; student So. Meth. U., 1930; B.A., M.A., U. Tex., 1933; Ph.D., Yale U., 1941; postgrad. Am. U., 1954; m. Marianne Sakmann, Aug. 15, 1942. Economist, Dept. Labor, 1934-35, Social Security Bd., 1936, antitrust div. Dept. Justice, 1938-39, Bur. Budget, 1939-51; program planning officer Office Sec. Commerce, 1951-53; chief econ. analysis sect. Office Internat. Trade, Dept. Commerce, 1953; transp. economist Gen. Services Adminstrn., 1953-54, Dept. Agr., 1954-59; chief div. statistics and studies Office Vocational Rehab., Dept. Health Edn. and Welfare, 1959-62; economist USPHS, 1962-69; ind. cons. in econs. and statistics, 1969—. Lectr. in transp. Georgetown U., 1956-57. Mem. Am. Pub. Health Assn., Phi Beta Kappa, Pi Sigma Alpha, Sigma Delta Pi. Democrat. Methodist. Author: Twixt Chaos and Conformism, 1950; The Agricultural Exemptions in Interstate Trucking: Mend Them or End Them?, 1960; Economics in Program Planning for Health, 1966; Organizing and Staffing for the Program Planning Function, 1967; other monographs. Home and Office: 4000 Cathedral Ave NW Apt 806B Washington DC 20016-5249

LINNER, DONALD, business educator; b. N.Y.C., Oct. 25, 1939; s. Carl and Johanna (Hanzlik) L. BS, Cen. Conn. State U., 1961; MA, Columbia U., 1964, MEd, 1968; MBA, Seton Hall U., 1974. Tchr. bus. edn. Brien McMahon High Sch., Norwalk, Conn., 1961-68; instr. bus. div. Essex County Coll., Newark, 1968-71, asst. prof., 1971-75, assoc. prof., 1976-91, prof., 1991—, chair bus. div., 1987-92. Author: Investment and Stock Market Practice Set, 1986. Grantee State of N.J., 1987. Mem. NEA, Nat. Bus. Edn. Assn., Ea. Bus. Edn. Assn. (registration chair 1987, session chair 1982, 84, 86, 90, session speaker 1986), N.J. Bus. Edn. Assn., Delta Pi Epsilon. Home: 555 Mt Prospect Ave Newark NJ 07104-1545 Office: Essex County Coll 303 University Ave Newark NJ 07102-1798

LINZER, ELLIOT, indexer; b. Bklyn., July 11, 1946; s. Sam and Charlotte (Hanin) L.; m. Maxene Sternberg, Sept. 13, 1987. BA, New Sch. for Social Rsch., N.Y.C., 1969; MA, CUNY, Flushing, 1980. Freelance indexer Flushing, 1971—. Mem. editorial bd. WIN mag., N.Y.C., 1966-82. Mem. Sci. for the People, N.Y., Boston, 1973-90, Computer Profls. for Social Responsibility, N.Y., 1988—. Mem. AAAS, Editorial Freelancers Assn. (bd. dirs. 1977-79, bd. govs. 1990, co-exec. 1990-92), Am. Soc. Indexers (bd. dirs. 1980's). Home and Office: 43-05 Crommelin St Flushing NY 11355

LINZNER, CHARLES, lawyer; b. Phila., Aug. 30, 1948; s. Lewis and Freda (Bealsky) L.; m. Nancy J. Meyer, Nov. 14, 1970. AB, Columbia U., 1970; JD, NYU, 1974. Bar: N.Y. 1975. Assoc. Dewey, Ballantine, Bushby, Palmer & Wood, N.Y.C., 1974-77, 80-83, Paris, 1977-80; v.p., gen. counsel Squibb Med. Systems, Bellevue, Wash., 1983-85; assoc. gen. counsel Squibb Corp., Princeton, N.J., 1985-90; gen. counsel U.S. ops. Squibb Pharm. Group, Princeton, 1988-91; v.p., sr. counsel strategic mgmt. Bristol-Myers Squibb Pharm. Group, Princeton, 1991—. Mem. ABA, N.Y. State Bar Assn., Internat. Bar Assn. Republican. Office: Bristol-Myers Squibb Corp PO Box 4000 Princeton NJ 08543-4000

LIONARONS, JOYCE TALLY, English educator; b. Chgo., Nov. 19, 1952; d. James Foy and Colette (Valiquet) Tally; m. John Stewart Lionarons, July 25, 1983. BA in English, U. Colo., 1975; MA in English, U. Denver, 1978, PhD in English, 1983. Lectr. U. Denver, 1981-83; vis. asst. prof. Ill. Coll, Jacksonville, Ill., 1983-84; asst. prof. Ursinus Coll., Collegeville, Pa., 1984-90, assoc. prof. English, 1990—. Mem. MLA, Del. Valley Medieval Assn., Medieval Acad. Office: Ursinus Coll English Dept Collegeville PA 19426

LIPARI, JOSEPH L., accounting and taxation educator; b. Passaic, N.J., July 11, 1955; s. Angelo G. and Irvina A. (Bolcar) L.; m. Deborah Ann Ingoldsby, Sept. 3, 1977; children: Joseph, Michael, Amanda. BS, Montclair State Coll., 1977; MBA, Fairleigh Dikinson U., 1981. CPA, N.J. Divisional contr. R.C. Diocese of Paterson, Clifton, N.J., 1978-84, contr., 1984-88; asst. prof. acctg. and taxation Montclair State Coll., Upper Montclair, N.J., 1988—. Contbr. articles to Jour. of Taxation of Exempt Orgns., 1990, Bus. and Tax Planning Quarterly, 1990, Jour. of Personal Fin. Planning, 1991, Exempt Orgn. Tax. Review, 1991. Mem. parish fin. coun. St. Paul's R.C. Church, Prospect Park, N.J., 1990. Mem. U.S. Cath. Conf. (acctg. practices com. 1990—), N.J. Soc. CPAs Edn. Found. (community svc. com., acctg. educators and students com.), Montclair Faculty Senate. Roman Catholic. Home: 236 Dorothy Dr Haledon NJ 07508-2843 Office: Montclair State Coll Upper Montclair NJ 07043

LIPICKY, RAYMOND JOHN, physician, researcher; b. Cleve., May 3, 1933; s. John and Margaret Karolina (Szanto) L.; m. Janet Lee Eisenhut, Mar. 8, 1958 (div. 1983); children: Laura Lee, Josh Wesley; m. Freda Sanders Jacobsen, Apr. 25, 1983; stepchildren: Ronald Lowell Jr., Robert Bordwell, Elizabeth Dorinda. BA, Ohio U., 1955; MD, U. Cin., 1960. Diplomate Nat. Bd. Med. Examiners. Asst. prof. pharmacology and medicine U. Cin., 1966-71, assoc. prof. pharmacology and medicine, 1971-72, prof. pharmacology assoc. prof. medicine, 1972-73, prof. pharmacology and medicine, dir. div. pharmacology, 1973-79; med. officer FDA, Rockville, Md., 1979-82, acting dir. div. cardio-renal drug products, 1982-86, dir. div. cardio-renal drug products, 1986—. Contbr. over 50 articles to profl. jours. NIH grantee, 1966-79. Mem. Am. Physiol. Soc., Am. Soc. Pharmacology and Exptl. Therapeutics, Biophys. Soc., Soc. Neurosci., Corp. of Marine Biol. Lab. Home: 15201 Apricot Ln Gaithersburg MD 20878-2321 Office: FDA Div Cardio-Renal Drug Products 5600 Fishers Ln Rockville MD 20857-0001

LIPINSKI, EDWARD R., illustrator, consultant, designer, educator; b. Jersey City, Nov. 2, 1943; s. Joseph Anthony and Margaret (Logan) L.; m. Clarice Jones, Aug. 29, 1969 (div. Dec. 1989). BA, Wilkes U., 1965; postgrad., Sch. of Visual Arts, 1975. Cert. tchr., N.Y. Asst. art dir. Greystone Pub., N.Y.C., 1970-71; with MacMillan Pub., N.Y.C., 1971-74; book designer Harcourt-Brace-Jovanovich, N.Y.C., 197-76; designer Reader's Digest, N.Y.C., 1976-82; freelance illustrator, designer N.Y.C., 1982—; instr. Ctr. for the Media Arts, N.Y.C., 1989—. Illustrator (column) N.Y. Time Home Improvement, Popular Mechanics; author, illustrator (children's book) The Cat Who Wanted To Be An Artist, 1974. Capt. USAF, 1965-70. Recipient S.I. award Artists Fedn., 1982. Home and Office: 5908 5th Ave # 1R Brooklyn NY 11220-4031

LIPINSKI, JAMIE LYNNE, computer systems programmer, analyst; b. Balt., Aug. 13, 1962; d. Edward Eugene Jr. and Sylvia Lynne (Esslinger) L. BS, Towson State U., 1990. Bus. systems programmer, analyst Tex. Instruments, Hunt Valley, Md., 1984—. Mem. Digital Equipment Users Soc. Democrat. Roman Catholic. Home: 198 E Jackson St York PA 17403 Office: Tex Instruments 10909 McCormick Rd Cockeysville Hunt Valley MD 21031-1406

LIPINSKY DE ORLOV, LUCIAN CHRISTOPHER, account marketing representative; b. N.Y.C., Feb. 21, 1962; s. Lino Sigismondo and Leah Safier (Penner) L.; m. Ann Marie Coffey, Aug. 23, 1986. BS in Computer Sci., SUNY, Binghamton, 1984, MS in Advanced Tech., 1985. Ptnr., cons. Computer Solutions Unltd., Johnson City, N.Y., 1983-85; programmer IBM Corp., Tarrytown, N.Y., 1985; assoc. info. ctr. analyst IBM Corp., Tarrytown, 1986-87; mktg. rep. IBM Media Br., N.Y.C., 1987-90, account mktg.

rep. U.S. mktg. and svcs., 1990—. Editor: IBM Corp. Hdqtrs. Info. Systems Jour., 1985—, IBM Corp. Hdqtrs. Info. Products and Software Services Product Catalogue, 1985—; contbr. to profl. newsletter. Mem. bus. adv. coun. Norman Thomas High Sch., N.Y.C., 1988—; mem. Katonah-Bedford Hills (N.Y.) Vol. Ambulance Corps, 1979-85, North Salem (N.Y.) Vol. Ambulance Corps, 1985—, line officer 1988-89; vol. Caramoor Ctr. for Music and the Arts, Katonah, 1976—, head usher, 1978; bd. mem., bus. adv. coun. Norman Thomas High Sch., N.Y.C. Bd. Edn., 1988—; adminstrv. advisor AIS Hudson Valley Support Group, Pomona, N.Y., 1988—; judge Distributed Edn. Clubs Am. Northeast Regional Mktg. Competition Finals, N.Y.C., 1989-90; Eagle scout Boy Scouts Am., 1977. Recipient Bernard V. Deutchman Bus. Person of Yr. award Norman Thomas High Sch., 1991. Mem. IEEE, Assn. Computing Machinery, Soc. Am. Magicians, Internat. Brotherhood Magicians, Nat. Eagle Scout Assn. (life), Mensa, N.Y. State Emergency Med. Technicians, Aircraft Owners and Pilots Assn. Home: PO Box 524 Rte 22 Goldens Bridge NY 10526 Office: IBM Corp 590 Madison Ave New York NY 10022-2505

LIPKIN, CAREN RUBINSON, graphic designer; b. Phila., Sept. 10, 1958; d. Ernest and Elaine Iris (Segal) Rubinson; m. Drew Alan Lipkin, Nov. 25, 1989. BFA in Graphic Design, Tyler Sch. Art, Elkins Park, Pa., 1980; MS in Publ. Mgmt., Drexel U., 1990. Freelance graphic artist/designer Phila., 1980-83; graphics coord. Drexel U., Phila., 1983-87; graphic design specialist Consol. Rail Corp., Phila., 1987-91; art dir. Mueller and Wister, Inc., Norristown, Pa., 1991—; freelance design cons., Phila., 1980—. Mem. Am. Inst. Graphic Arts (treas. bd. dirs. 1989—). Jewish. Office: Mueller & Wister Inc 801 E Germantown Pike Ste J-4 Norristown PA 19401

LIPMAN, EUGENE JAY, rabbi; b. Pitts., Oct. 13, 1919; s. Joshua and Bessie (Neaman) L.; m. Esther Marcuson, July 4, 1943; children: Michael H. (dec.), Jonathan N., David E. AB, U. Cin., 1941; MHL, Hebrew Union Coll., 1943, DD (hon.), 1968. Ordained rabbi, 1943. Rabbi Temple Beth El, Ft. Worth, 1943-44; dir. B'nai B'rith Hillel Found. U. Wash., Seattle, 1949-50; dept. dir. Union of Am. Hebrew Congregations, N.Y., 1951-61; rabbi Temple Sinai, Washington, 1961-85, rabbi emeritus, 1985—; lectr. in religion Am. U., Washington, 1961-68; lectr. in theology Cath. U. Am., Washington, 1967-79. Author: Yamim Nora'im, 1988; (with A. Vorspan) A Tale of Ten Cities, 1962, Justice and Judaism, 1956; editor: (textbook) The Mishnah, 1970; contbr. numerous articles to profl. jours. and chpts. to books. Pres. Cen. Conf. Am. Rabbis, 1987-89, Interfaith Conf. Met. Washington, 1982-84, Washington Bd. Rabbis, 1971-2; mem. bd. dirs., past pres. Nat. Capitol Area ACLU, 1965-77. Chaplain with armed forces 1944-46, 50-51. Teaching fellow Hebrew Union Coll., 1948-49. Mem. Commn. on Social Action. Democrat. Home and Office: 3512 Woodbine St Bethesda MD 20815-4039

LIPMAN, IRA ACKERMAN, security service company executive; b. Little Rock, Nov. 15, 1940; s. Mark and Belle (Ackerman) L.; m. Barbara Ellen Kelly Couch, July 5, 1970; children: Gustave K., Joshua S., M. Benjamin. Student, Ohio Wesleyan U., 1958-60; LLD (hon.), John Marshall U., Atlanta, 1970. Salesman, exec. Mark Lipman Svcs. Inc., Memphis, 1960-63; v.p. Guardsmark, Inc., Memphis, 1963-66; pres. Guardsmark, Inc., 1966—, chief exec. officer, 1968—, chmn. bd., 1968—; bd. dirs. Nat. Coun. Crime and Delinquency, 1976, chmn. exec. com., 1986, chmn. fin. com., treas., 1978-79, vice chmn. bd., 1982-86—, exec. com. 1976—; bd. dirs. Greater Memphis Coun. Crime and Delinquency, 1976-78, entrepreneurial fellow Memphis State U., 1976; mem. environ. security com., pvt. security adv. council Law Enforcement Assistance Adminstrn., 1975-76; mem. conf. planning com. 2d Nat. Law Enforcement Explorer Conf., 1980. Author: How to Protect Yourself From Crime, 1975, 3d edit., 1990; contbr. numerous articles to profl. jours., mags. and newspapers. Bd. dirs. Memphis Jewish Community Center, 1974, Memphis Shelby County unit Am. Cancer Soc., 1980-81, Memphis Orchestral Soc., 1980-81, Memphis Jewish Fedn., 1974-83; chmn. Shelby County com. U.S. Savs. Bonds, 1976; mem. president's coun.l Memphis State U., 1975—, mem. visual arts coun., 1980-82; Memphis met. chmn. Nat. Alliance Businessmen, 1970-71; mem. task force Reform Jewish Outreach, Union Am. Hebrew Congregations, 1979-83; mem. young leadership cabinet United Jewish Appeal, 1973-78, mem. S.E. regional campaign cabinet, 1980; exec. bd. Chickasaw council Boy Scouts Am., 1978-81; bd. dirs., exec. com. Tenn. Ind. Coll. Fund, 1979; trustee Memphis Acad. Arts, 1977-81; mem. president's club Christian Bros. Coll., 1979; bd. dirs. Future Memphis, 1980-83, 83-86; nat. trustee NCCJ, 1980—, exec. com., 1981—, nat. Jewish co-chmn., 1985-88, nat. chmn., 1988—; bd. dirs. Memphis chpt., 1980-85, life bd. dirs. Memphis chpt. 1985—; group II chmn. for 1982 campaign United Way Greater Memphis, 1981; vp., exec. com. Internat. Coun. Christians and Jews, 1992—; bd. govs. United Way of Am., 1992—, bd. gov.'s liaison, 1991-92; trustee Memphis Brooks Mus. Art, 1980-83, Yeshiva U., Simon Wiesenthal Ctr., 1982—, chmn. campaign com., 1983—; bd. dirs. Nat. Alliance against Violence, 1983-85, Nat. Ctr. Learning Disabilities, 1989—, United Way of Greater Memphis, 1984-85, gen. campaign chmn., 1985-86; founder, bd. overseers B'nai Brith, 1980; bd. dirs. Tenn. Gov.'s Jobs for High Sch. Grads. Program, 1980-83; vol. United Way Am. Second Century Initiative Vol. Involvement com. and chmn. task force on critical mkts., 1987, exec. cabinet, 1990—, bd. govs. liaison, 1991—; trustee Ohio Wesleyan U., 1988—; vice chmn. spl. task force on endowment growth Ohio Wesleyan U., 1990—; mem. bd. overseers Wharton Sch., U. Pa., 1991—; assoc. trustee U. Pa., 1991—; hon. chmn. and past nation chmn. NCCJ, 1992—, nat. bd. trustees, 1980-92, exec. com., 1981-92; Nat. Jewish Co-Chmn., 1985-88, nat. chmn., 1988-92; mem. exec. com. Am. Israel Pub. Affairs Com., 1991—. Recipient Humanitarian of Yr. award NCCJ, 1985, Outstanding Community Sales award Sales and Mktg. Execs. Memphis, 1987, Jr. Achievement Master Free Enterprise award, 1987; one of 10 cited as Best Corp. Chief Exec. of Achievement, Gallagher Pres.'s Report, 1974. Mem. Internat. Assn. Chiefs Police, Am. Soc. Criminology, Internat. Soc. Criminology, Am. Soc. Indsl. Security (cert. protection profl.). Republican. Clubs: 100, B'nai B'rith, Ridgeway Country, Racquet, Summit, Economic bd. dirs. 1980-85, v.p. 1983-84, pres. 1984-85, chmn. exec. com. 1984-85), Petroleum (Memphis); Internat. (Washington).

LIPMAN, JACK, manufacturing engineer; b. N.Y.C., May 30, 1920; s. Joseph and Blanche (Marshak) L.; m. Norma Dawn Rubin, Dec. 27, 1942; children: Gwynne Amy Safier, Joseph Laurence. BSME, Pa. State U., 1942; postgrad., SUNY, 1977. Registered profl. engr., Pa. Salvage engr. Solar Aircraft/U.S. Rubber, Des Moines, 1943-44; mfg. engr. Murray Corp., Scranton, Pa., 1946-47; prin. Internat. Corr. Schs., Scranton, 1947-50; group leader Daystrom Inc., Archbald, Pa., 1950-58; project mgr. W.L. Maxson Inc., Old Forge, Pa., 1958-60; chief mfg. engr. Ronson Inc., Delaware Water Gap, Pa., 1960-61; sr. staff engr. IBM, Endicott, N.Y., 1961-90; mfg. cons. Scranton, 1990—; lectr. U. Scranton, 1958-60, Pa. State U., Wilkes-Barre, 1990—, Scranton, 1990—. Editor: Machine Tool Operation, 1948. 2d v.p. Concerned Citizens About Taxes, Scranton, 1989-91. With USN, 1944-46. Mem. Nat. Soc. Profl. Engrs., Soc. Mfg. Engrs., Pa. Soc. Profl. Engrs. (treas. N.E. 1961-63). Home: 602 Taylor Ave Scranton PA 18510-1817

LIPMAN, RICHARD PAUL, pediatrician; b. Cambridge, Mass., Aug. 1, 1935; s. Hyman Zelig and Betty (Likovsky) L.; m. Mary Alice Wilcox, Aug. 25, 1963; children: Gregory, Susan. AB magna cum laude, Harvard U., 1957; MD cum laude, Tufts U., 1961. Diplomate Am. Bd. Pediatrics. Intern Boston Floating Hosp., 1961-62, jr. resident, 1962-63, sr. resident, 1963-64, chief resident, 1964; rsch. fellow infectious disease Med. Sch. U. N.C., Chapel Hill, 1967-69; practice pediatrics Peabody and Lynn, Mass., 1969—; mem. staff North Shore Children's Hosp., Salem, Mass., assoc. chief of staff, 1974-76, pres., chief of staff, 1976-79, chief of medicine, 1979-83, trustee, 1980-84, corporator, 1985-86, mem. staff Tufts-New Eng. Med. Ctr., Boston, Boston Children's Hosp. Med. Ctr., AtlantiCare Med. Ctr., Salem Hosp.; clin. instr. pediatrics Tufts U. Sch. Medicine, Boston, 1969-74, asst. clin. prof., 1974-78, assoc. clin. prof., 1978—; bd. dirs. Tufts Assoc. Health Maintanance Orgn., 1988—. Contbr. articles to profl. jours. Capt. M.C., AUS, 1964-66. Fellow Am. Acad. Pediatrics; mem. AMA, Am. Soc. Microbiology, New Eng. Pediatric Soc., Mass. Med. Soc., Tufts Alumni Assn., Nat. Assn. Watch and Clock Collectors. Office: 1 Roosevelt Ave Peabody MA 01960-2227 also: 225 Boston St Salem MA 01970

LIPMAN, WYNONA M., state legislator; b. Ga.; children—Karen Anne, William (dec.). BA, Talladega Coll.; MA, Atlanta U.; Ph.D., Columbia U.; LL.D. (hon.), Kean Coll., Bloomfield Coll. Former high sch. tchr., lectr. Seton Hall U., Assoc. prof. Essex Community Coll.; mem. N.J. State Senate, 1971—, state govt. com., joint appropriations com., revenue, fin. and appropriations com. chmn., Commn. on Sex Discrimination in the Statutes. Mem. NAACP, Nat. Coun. Negro Women, Women's Polit. Caucus, Essex County Urban League. Recipient Outstanding Woman award Assn. Women Bus Owners, 1983. Democrat. Home: Ste 1035 50 Park Pl Newark NJ 07102-4301 Office: NJ State Senate Capitol Trenton NJ 08625

LIPNACK, JESSICA PAULI, research and consulting company executive; b. Pottstown, Pa., June 4, 1947; d. Marvin and Ethel A. Lipnack; m. Jeffrey Spaulding Stamps, Jan. 18, 1972; children: Miranda, Eliza. BA in Philosophy, Antioch Coll., 1970; student, Oxford U., Eng. Reporter The Pottstown (Pa.) Mercury, 1963-67; co-owner Whitewood Stamps, Inc., Newton, Mass., 1970-80; pres. The Networking Inst., Inc., West Newton, Mass., 1982—; lectr. in field of human networking; online faculty Internat. Exec. Forum, 1984; co-designer PresbyNet, The Presbyn. Ch. Computer Conferencing Network, 1986. Co-author, pub.: Cable in Boston, 1974; co-author: The Networking Book: People Connecting with People, 1986, Networking: The First Report and Directory, 1982; contbr. articles to profl. jours. and publs. including The Boston Globe, The Christian Sci. Monitor, Esquire, The Futurist, Mothering, New Age Jour. Office: The Networking Inst Inc 505 Waltham St West Newton MA 02165

LIPNER, ARTHUR CHARLES, music educator, musician; b. Miami Beach, Fla., Sept. 29, 1958; s. Daniel Sherman and Judith Gertrude (Levine) L.; m. Kathryn S. Caprino. BS, U. Del., 1981. Adj. faculty mem. U. Bridgeport (Conn.), 1985-91; guest faculty mem. Brabants Conservatory, Tilburg, the Netherlands, 1990—; invited performer Percussive Arts Soc. Internat. Conf., Phila., 1990; guest lectr. and performer 50 univs., U.S., Europe, Japan, 1987—. Author: Solo Jazz Vibraphone Etudes, 1990; participant five recordings for U.S. and fgn. record cos.; contbr. articles to profl. jours.. Mem. Am. Fedn. Musicians, Percussive Arts Soc., Broadcast Music Inc. Home: PO Box 7106 New York NY 10163-7106

LIPP, SUSAN KLOTZ, sales executive; b. Syracuse, N.Y., Sept. 15, 1947; d. Fred Guth Jr. and Mary Jane (Cairns) Klotz; children: Alexandra Cairns Santiago, Molly Mable Molloy; m. G. Irwin Lipp, Dec. 28, 1991. BFA, Syracuse U., 1969; diploma, Am. Edn. Inst., 1988. Acct. exec. WILM News Radio, Wilmington, Del., 1980-83; mktg. staff specialist Dorothea B. Lane Schs., Wilmington, Del., 1983-84, dir., 1985; pub. rels. dir., ins. coord. USA Tng. Acad., Newark, Del., 1985-89; sales rep. Interactive Design, Wilmington, Del., 1990—; dir. sales Arden Films and Video, Wilmington, Del., 1989—; adv. bd. Girls Inc., Newark, Del., 1989-92. Mem. Pub. Rels. Soc. Am. (program dir. 1990-92, exec. bd. 1991-92), Wilmington Women in Bus. (newsletter photographer 1989-92, exec. com. 1991). Democrat. Presbyterian. Office: Arden Films and Video 1501 N Walnut St Wilmington DE 19801-3133

LIPPA, ERIK ALEXANDER, ophthalmologist; b. Mpls., Nov. 7, 1945; s. Walter and Cecilie (Buchman) L.; m. Linda Susan Mottow, Mar. 6, 1980; children: David Abram, Andrew Moss. BS, Calif. Inst. Tech., 1967; MS, U. Mich., 1968, PhD in Math., 1971; MD, Albert Einstein Coll. Medicine, 1980. NATO postdoctoral fellow Oxford (Eng.) U., 1971-72; asst. prof. Purdue U., West Lafayette, Ind., 1972-78; med. intern NYU Med. Ctr./Manhattan (N.Y.) VA Hosp., 1980-81; resident ophthalmology Ill. Eye and Ear Infirmary, Chgo., 1981-84; ophthalmologist St. Paul, 1984-85; asst. dir. clin. rsch. Merck & Co. Inc., West Point, Pa., 1985-89, dir. clin. rsch., 1989—; adj. clin. asst. prof. Jefferson Med. Coll., Phila., 1986-91, adj. clin. assoc. prof., 1991—; clin. assoc. U. Pa., Phila., 1987—; asst. surgeon Wills Eye Hosp., Phila., 1991—, instr., 1986-91. Author: Mathematics for Freshmen in the Life Sciences, 1976; contbr. articles to profl. jours. Treas. Cub Scout Pack #665, Ft. Washington, Pa., 1988—. Fellow Am. Acad. Ophthalmology; mem. AMA, Assn. Rsch. in Vision and Ophthalmology, Internat. Soc. Eye Rsch., Am. Glaucoma Soc., European Glaucoma Soc., Pa. Med. Soc., Phila. County Med. Soc., Sigma Xi, Tau Beta Pi. Home: 1045 Stevens Dr Fort Washington PA 19034-1633 Office: Merck Rsch Labs Clin Rsch West Point PA 19486

LIPPERT, ALBERT, health service executive; b. Bklyn., Apr. 23, 1925; s. Hyman and Becky (Shapiro) L.; m. Felice Sally Mark, June 21, 1953; children: Keith Lawrence, Randy Seth. B.B.A., Coll. City N.Y., 1949. Asst. buyer Goldrings, 1949-51; buyer, mdse. mgr. Mangel Stores Corp., 1951-67; v.p. Weight Watchers Internat., Inc., Manhasset, N.Y., 1967-68; chmn. bd.. pres. Weight Watchers Internat., Inc., 1968-79, chmn. bd., from 1979, chief exec. officer, 1979-81; treas., past dir. W.W. Twenty First Corp. Active City of Hope; active Mr. and Mrs. League, Grand St. Boys Club. Served with AUS, 1943-46, ETO. Named Man of Yr., N.Y. Council Civic Affairs, 1968. Club: Sands Point Golf. Office: Weight Watchers Internat Jericho Atrium 500 N Broadway Jericho NY 11753-2111

LIPPINCOTT, HELEN ZABRISKIE, volunteer; b. N.Y.C., Apr. 20, 1921; d. Charles Lemaire and Frances M. (Hyde) Zabriskie; m. William J. Lippincott, Dec. 2, 1942; children: Helene M. Lippincott Peterson, Suzanne H. Lippincott Crase, William III, John L. Student, Smith Coll., 1941; BA, Empire State Coll., 1976. Chmn. New Eyes for the Needy, Short Hills, N.J., 1957-58; dir. religious edn. Christ's Ch., Rye, N.Y., 1959-73, 1st vestrywoman, 1967-70; co-chair Rye Youth Coun.; founder Rye Youth Employment Svc.; founder, chair SUNY-Purchase Affiliates, 1979-82; vol. United Hosp., Port Chester, N.Y., 1978—. Bd. dirs. Westchester Community Found., White Plains, N.Y., 1982-91, chmn., 1984-89; bd. dirs. Port Chester Carver Ctr., 1982—, Rye Human Rights Commn., 1984-90, FIRST, White Plains, 1988—; bd. dirs. Sound Shore Area Mental Hygiene Coun., White Plains, 1967—, vice chmn., 1991—. Episcopalian. Home: 265 Grace Church St Rye NY 10580-4201

LIPPMAN, ADAM BART, mechanical and aerospace engineering executive; b. Newark, June 4, 1965; m. Patricia Anne Landry, Mar. 23, 1991. AA, U. South Fla., 1985; BSME, U. Southern Fla., 1988. Sr. quality assurance engr. Curtiss Wright Flight Systems, Inc., Fairfield, N.J., 1988-89, assoc. program adminstr., 1989-90, program mgr., 1990—; mem. total quality mgmt. com., 1989—. Mem. spl. olympics com., Tampa, Fla., 1986-88; active N.J. Pub. Interest Group, Trenton, 1988—, World Wildlife Fund. Mem. ASME (Promotion and Devel. award 1988), AIAA. Home: 58 Tremont Ter Livingston NJ 07039-3340

LIPPMAN, BARRY, publishing executive; b. N.Y.C., Sept. 9, 1949; s. Mark and Edythe (Beck) L.; m. Chris Conover, Oct. 17, 1980. BA in English, SUNY, Buffalo, 1971; MFA, U. Montana, 1973. Editorial asst. New Am. Libr., N.Y.C., 1973-74, editor, 1974-78; sr. editor Doubleday & Co., N.Y.C., 1978-81; gen. mgr. paperbacks Little, Brown & Co., Boston, 1981-83; v.p., pub. Collier Books, Macmillan Pub. Co., N.Y.C., 1983-85, Macmillan & Collier Books, N.Y.C., 1985-87; pres., pub. adult trade div. Macmillan Pub. Co., N.Y.C., 1988—; chmn. Keter Pub. Co., Maxwell-MacMillan. Mem. Am. Assn. Pubs. (exec. com.), Internat. Freedom to Publish Com.

LIPPMAN, CRAIG HARRIS, marketing and sales executive; b. L.A., Mar. 31, 1949; s. Burt Bernard and Jeanne (Linnick) L.; m. Leslee Joan Duda, June 3, 1973; children: Ahren Royal, Devan Joshua, Kaelan Sears. BSEE, U. Calif., Santa Barbara, 1970. Engr. Burrough Corp., Santa Barbara, Calif., 1970-73, Northeast Utilities, Berlin, Conn., 1973-75; mgr. Data General, Westborough, Mass., 1975-81, dir., 1984-88; dir. Avatar Tech., Hopkinton, Mass., 1981-83, Nixdorf Computer, Waltham, Mass., 1983-84, Data Gen., Westborough, Mass., 1984-88, Wang Info. Svcs., Lowell, Mass., 1988-90; exec. v.p. First Phone of New Eng., Boston, 1990—; grad. Greater Worcester Exec. Program, Mass., 1986. Chmn. Inland Wetlands Commn., Woodbury, Conn., 1976-77. Home: 28 Old Nourse Rd Westborough MA 01581 Office: First Phone of New Eng 300 Ocean Ave Revere MA 02151

LIPPMAN, DAVID HENRY, Navy journalist, writer; b. N.Y.C., Nov. 7, 1962; s. Paul and Barbara Patricia (Sheridan) L. BA in History and Journalism, NYU, 1983. Field reporter Stan Fischler, syndicated sports columnist Toronto Star, 1980-84; editor Mets Inside Pitch, N.Y.C., 1984-85; reporter Sports Press Svc., N.Y.C., 1986; assoc. editor Hudson Dispatch, Union City, N.J., 1987-89; editorial writer Boca Raton (Fla.) News, 1990; commd. USN, 1990—; broadcast journalist USN, Susebo, Japan, 1990—; lectr. in field. Contbr. articles to profl. jours. Mem. campaign team Thomas Vezzetti for Mayor, Hoboken, N.J., 1985; press dir. Aaron Miranda-Forman for Hoboken City Coun., 1st Ward, 1987; U.S. Census enumerator Hoboken, 1990; mem. Hoboken Hist. Mus., 1990—. Recipient Navy Commendation, Nat. Def. medal, 1st place awards N.J. Press Assn. Better Newspapers Contest, 1989, North Jersey Pica Club contest, 1989, N.J. Soc. Profl. Journalists ann. contest, 1989, others. Mem. Def. Info. Sch. Alumni Assn., Stuyvesant High Sch. Alumni Assn., Elec. Railroaders Assn., Jewish War Vets, U.S Naval Inst. Democrat. Home: 1216 Garden St Hoboken NJ 07030-4406

LIPPMAN, NEAL, cardiologist; b. Bklyn., Feb. 25, 1962; s. Edward and Helen (Weisbard) L.; m. Cathi Lynn Cohen, Oct. 9, 1988. BS, MIT, 1982; MD, Cornell U., 1986. Diplomate Am. Bd. Internal Medicine. Intern in medicine N.Y. Hosp., Cornell Med. Ctr., 1986-87, resident in medicine, 1987-89, fellow in cardiology, 1989-91, fellow in electrophysiology, 1991—. Joseph Collins scholarship Joseph Collins Found., 1982-86, David Scherf scholarship N.Y. Acad. of Medicine, 1985. Mem. AMA, ACP, Am. Coll. Chest Physicians (affiliate in-tng.), Am. Coll. Cardiology (affiliate in-tng.), N.Y. Acad. Scis., Sigma Xi, Sigma Pi Sigma. Office: New York Hosp 525 E 68th St New York NY 10021-4873

LIPPMANN, HEINZ ISRAEL, physician, educator, researcher; b. Breslau, Fed. Republic of Germany, May 21, 1908; came to U.S., 1940; s. Felix and Sophie (Moskiewicz) L.; m. Alisa Moscato, Mar. 15, 1936; children: Ruth Lippmann Gordon, Robert, Lawrence. MD, U. Berlin, 1931, U. Geonoa, Italy, 1933. Diplomate Italian Med. Bd., diplomate Am. Bd. Phys. Medicine and Rehab. Asst. prof. Albert Einstein Coll. Medicine, N.Y.C., 1955-59, assoc. prof., 1959-69, prof. rehab. medicine, 1969-, prof. emeritus, 1976—; chief peripheral vascular diseases clinic Bronx Med. Ctr. Medicine, N.Y.C., 1957—; chief OPD clinic Bronx Mcpl. Hosp. Ctr., Albert Einstein Coll. of Medicine, 1957—; cons. rehab. medicine St. Joseph Hosp., Paterson, N.J., Engelwood (N.J.) Hosp., E-O VA Med. Ctr., East Orange, N.J., 1960—. Fellow Am. Coll. Physicians; mem. AMA (sr.), N.Y. Acad. Medicine (life), N.Y. Acad. Scis. (life), Am. Acad. PMR (sr., Disting. Clinician 1986), Am. Congress Rehab. Medicine (sr., Gold Medal 1959), N.J. State Med. Soc. (sr.). Home: 597 Sunderland Rd Teaneck NJ 07666 Office: Albert Einstein Coll of Medicine 1600 Tenbroeck Ave Bronx NY 10461

LIPPMANN, JANET GURIAN, artist, art gallery owner; b. Bklyn., May 10, 1936; d. William and Gertrude (Shukousky) Gurian; m. Morton Lippmann, Nov. 24, 1956; children: Amy, Stanley, David. BA in Art and Edn., CUNY, 1956, MA in Art and Edn., 1960. Permanent cert. art tchr., N.Y. Tchr. art pub. schs., N.Y.C., Cin., Westchester, N.Y., 1956-74; founder, tchr. Children's Art Workshop, Mt. Vernon, N.Y., 1964-76; pres., dir. The River Gallery, Irvington-on-Hudson, N.Y., 1974-89, Janet Lippmann Fine Arts, Irvington-on-Hudson, 1989—. Contbr. articles to profl. jours.; one-woman shows include River Gallery, 1986, 88, Nat. Arts Club, 1991; represented in many pvt. collections including The Reader's Digest Collection. Mem. Nat. Arts Club (exhibiting artist, hon. mention 1990). Studio: 15 Grammercy Park S New York NY 10003 Office: 8 N Dutcher St Irvington NY 10533-1518

LIPPMANN, MICHAEL, physician; b. N.Y.C., June 30, 1944; s. Ernest and Margot (Rosenow) L.; m. Julie Ann Cohn, June 8, 1969; children: Elisa, Sara. BS, CCNY, 1966; MD, SUNY, Buffalo, 1970. Intern medicine Bronx Mcpl. Hosp. Ctr., N.Y.C., 1970-71; sr. asst. surgeon USPHS-NIOSH, Morgantown, W.Va., 1971-73; resident medicine Yale New Haven Hosp., New Haven, 1973-75; fellow Bronx Mcpl. Hosp., N.Y.C., 1975-76; attending pulmonary Albert Einstein Med. Ctr., Phila., 1977—; chief pulmonary disease Albert Einstein Med. Ctr., 1980—. Contbr. articles on pulmonary diseases to profl. jours. Pres. Camp Ramah Poconos, Lake Como, Pa., 1988-91. Fellow Am. Coll. Chest Physicians, ACP; mem. Am. Toracic Soc., Soc. Critical Care Medicine. Fellow ACCP, ACP; mem. ATS, SCCM. Democrat. Jewish. Office: Albert Einstein Med Ctr York & Tabor Philadelphia PA 19141

LIPPNER, LEWIS ALAN, health facility administrator; b. Bklyn., Mar. 10, 1948; s. Sidney and Ruth (Wolitz) L.; m. Cosette Burke, Apr. 27, 1991. Fellow in Comparative Econs., U. Oslo, 1968; BA in Econs., U. Pitts., 1969; MA in Health Care Adminstrn., George Washington U., 1972. Resident King's County Hosp. Ctr., Bklyn., 1971-72; facilities planning and fin. cons. Block, McGiboney & Assocs./Health and Hosp. Cons., Silver Springs, Md., 1972-73; asst. dir., planner The Bklyn. Hosp./Bklyn.-Cumberland Med. Ctr., 1973-75; asst. hosp. adminstr. John E. Runnells Hosp. of Union County, Berkley Heights, N.J., 1975-78; adminstr. Rush Presbyn. St. Luke's Med. Ctr., Chgo., 1978-88; chief operating officer N.Y.C. Health and Hosps. Corp., 1988-90; chief exec. officer Fairfield Hills Hosp., Newtown, Conn., 1990—; adminstr. fin. cons. Pritzker Med. Sch., Chgo., 1988; planning cons. Internat. Sci. and Tech. Inst., Washington, 1988. Univ. scholar U. Pitts., 1967-69; recipient Frederick Schaeffer Meml. fellowship U. Oslo, Norway, 1968, U.S. Pub. Health traineeship George Washington U., 1970-71. Mem. Am. Coll. Hosp. Adminstrs., Am. Hosp. Assn., Chgo. Health Execs. Forum, George Washington U. Alumni Assn. for Health Svcs. Adminstrn., Omicron Delta Epsilon.

LIPPSON, ROBERT LLOYD, marine biologist, educator; b. Detroit, Apr. 18, 1931; s. Jack C. and Shirley Ann (Milstein) L.; m. Alice Jane O'Brien, Apr. 5, 1972; children—Steven, Lisa, Kevin, Marisa, Christopher, James, John. B.S., Mich. State U., 1963, M.S., 1964, Ph.D., 1975. Research scientist U. Md., Solomons, 1968-71; fisheries biologist Nat. Marine Fisheries Service, Oxford, Md., 1971-73, research coordinator, 1975-81, mid-Atlantic liaison officer, 1981-82, asst. regional dir., 1982—; adj. prof. zoology Mich. State U., East Lansing, 1977-89; dir. NOAA Chesapeake Bay program; Author: (with others) Life in the Chesapeake Bay, 1984. Recipient Bronze medal U.S. Dept. Commerce, 1980. Mem. Estuarine Research Fedn., Atlantic Estuarine Research Soc., Am. Fisheries Soc., Sigma Xi. Avocations: fishing; boating; writing; travel. Home: North Winds Bozman MD 21612 Office: Nat Marine Fisheries Svc 904 Morris St Oxford MD 21654

LIPSCHULTZ, FREDERICK PHILLIP, physics educator; b. L.A., Aug. 27, 1937; s. Julius C. and Esther (Robinson) L. BS, Stanford U., 1959; PhD, Cornell U., 1966. Postdoctoral fellow Brookhaven Nat. Lab., Upton, N.Y., 1965-67; asst. prof. physics U. Conn., Storrs, 1967-72; assoc. prof. physics U. Conn., 1972—; sabbatical, U. Nottingham, Eng., 1976-77. Trustee Joshua's Trust, Storrs, 1985-90; v.p. Friends Bd. Conn. Pub. TV, Hartford, 1986-89, pres. 1989—. Mem. IEEE, Am. Phys. Soc., Sigma Xi (chpt. pres. 1988-89). Democrat. Jewish. Office: U Conn Dept Physics 2152 Hillside Rd Storrs Mansfield CT 06268

LIPSCOMB, SYLVESTER HIRRAM, educator; b. Cumberland, Va., Oct. 9, 1958; s. Claude H. and Maude (Agee) L.; m. Chandra Rachelle Norman, June 20, 1987; 1 child, Myah. BS in Plant and Soil Sci., Va. State U., 1980; MS in Turf Mgmt., U. Md., 1986. Rsch. asst. Va. State U., Petersburg, 1977-78; soil conservationist USDA-Soil Conservation Svc., Harrisburg, Pa., 1978-79; teaching asst. Va. State U., Petersburg, 1979-80; asst. mgr. Grand Union Co., Landover, Md., 1980-82; grad. teaching asst. U. Md., College Park, 1982-85; extension agt. U. D.C., Washington, 1985-87; horticulture tchr. D.C. Pub. Schs., Washington, 1987—; cons. D.C. Dept. of Housing and Urban Devel., Washington, 1986, U. D.C. Extension Svc., Washington, 1986, freelance, Washington, 1987—. Author: Greenleaf Newsletter, 1986-87. Cafritz Found. fellow, 1990. Mem. Am. Vocat. Assn., Nat. FFA Orgn. (state exec. sec. 1988-91), Va. State U. Alumni Assn., Alpha Phi Alpha. Democrat. Baptist. Home: 2521 Hughes Rd Adelphi MD 20783 Office: DC Pub Schs 26th St and Benning Rd NE Washington DC 20002

LIPSCOMB, WILLIAM NUNN, JR., retired physical chemistry educator; b. Cleve., Dec. 9, 1919; s. William Nunn and Edna Patterson (Porter) L.; m. Mary Adele Sargent, May 20, 1944; children: Dorothy Jean, James Sargent; m. Jean Craig Evans, 1983. BS, U. Ky., 1941, DSc (hon.), 1963; PhD, Calif. Inst. Tech., 1946; DSc (hon.), U. Munich, 1976, L.I. U., 1977, Rutgers U., 1979, Gustavus Adolphus Coll., 1980, Marietta Coll., 1981, Miami U., 1983, U. Denver, 1985, Ohio State U., 1991; Transylvania U., 1992, DSc (hon.). Phys. chemist Office of Sci. R&D, 1942-46; faculty U. Minn., Mpls., 1946-59, asst. prof., 1946-50, assoc. prof., 1950-54, acting chief phys. chemistry div., 1952-54, prof. and chief phys. chemistry div., 1954-59; prof. chemistry

Harvard U., Cambridge, Mass., 1959-71, Abbott and James Lawrence prof., 1971-90, prof. emeritus, 1990—; mem. U.S. Nat. Commn. for Crystallography, 1954-59, 60-63, 65-67; chmn. program com. 4th Internat. Congress of crystallography, Montreal, 1957; mem. sci. adv. bd. Robert A. Welch Found.; mem. rsch. adv. bd. Mich. Molecular Biology Inst.; mem. adv. com. Inst. Amorphus Studies; mem. sci. adv. com. Nova Pharms., Daltex Med. Svc., Gensia Pharms., Binary Therapeutics. Author: The Boron Hydrides, 1963, (with G.R. Eaton) NMR Studies of Boron Hydrides and Related Compounds, 1969; assoc. editor: (with G.R. Eaton) Jour. Chemical Physics, 1955-57; contbr. articles to profl. jours.; clarinetist, mem.: Amateur Chamber Music Players. Guggenheim fellow Oxford U., Eng., 1954-55; Guggenheim fellow Cambridge U., Eng., 1972-73; NSF sr. postdoctoral fellow, 1965-66; Overseas fellow Churchill Coll., Cambridge, Eng., 1966, 73; Robert Welch Found. lectr., 1966, 71; Howard U. distinguished lecture series, 1966; George Fisher Baker lectr. Cornell U., 1969; centenary lectr. Chem. Soc., London, 1972; lectr. Weizmann Inst., Rehovoth, Israel, 1974; Evans award lectr. Ohio State U., 1974; Gilbert Newton Lewis Meml. lectr. U. Calif., Berkeley, 1974; also lectureships Mich. State U., 1975, U. Iowa, 1975, Ill. Inst. Tech., 1976, numerous others; also speaker confs.; Recipient Harrison Howe award in Chemistry, 1958; Distinguished Alumni Centennial award U. Ky., 1965; Distinguished Service in advancement inorganic chemistry Am. Chem. Soc., 1968; George Ledlie prize Harvard, 1971; Nobel prize in chemistry, 1976; Disting. Alumni award Calif. Inst. Tech., 1977; sr. U.S. scientist award Alexander von Humboldt-Stiftung, 1979; award lecture Internat. Acad. Quantum Molecular Sci., 1980. Fellow Am. Acad. Arts and Scis., Am. Phys. Soc.; mem. NAS, Am. Chem. Soc. (Peter Debye award phys. chemistry 1973, chmn. Minn. sect. 1949-50), Am. Crystallographic Assn. (pres. 1955), The Netherlands Acad. Arts and Scis. (fgn.), Math. Assn. Bioinorganic Scientists (hon.), Academie Europeenne des Sciences, des Arts et des Lettres, Royal Soc. Chemistry (hon.), Phi Beta Kappa, Sigma Xi, Alpha Chi Sigma, Phi Lambda Upsilon, Sigma Pi Sigma, Phi Mu Epsilon. Office: Harvard U Dept Chemistry Cambridge MA 02138

LIPSEY, ROBERT EDWARD, economist, educator; b. N.Y.C., Aug. 14, 1926; s. Meyer Aaron and Anna (Weinstein) L.; m. Sally Irene Rothstein, Nov. 24, 1948; children—Marion, Carol, Eleanor. B.A., Columbia, 1944, M.A., 1946, Ph.D., 1961. Research asst. Nat. Bur. Econ. Research, N.Y.C., 1945-53; research assoc. Nat. Bur. Econ. Research, 1953-60, sr. research staff, 1960—, v.p. research, 1970-75, dir. internat. studies, 1975-78, dir. N.Y. Office,, 1978—; lectr. econs. Columbia, 1961-64; prof. econs. Queens Coll. and Grad. Ctr., CUNY, 1967—; cons. Dept. Commerce, Fed. Res. Bd., UN, World Bank; mem. Pres.'s Adv. Bd. Internat. Investment, 1977-78. Author: Price and Quantity Trends in the Foreign Trade of the U.S, 1963, (with Raymond W. Goldsmith) Studies in the National Balance Sheet of the U.S, 1963, (with Doris Preston) Source Book of Statistics Relating to Construction, 1966, (with Irving B. Kravis) Price Competitiveness in World Trade, 1971, (with Phillip Cagan) Financial Effects of Inflation, 1978, (with Irving B. Kravis) Saving and Economic Growth: Is the U.S. Really Falling Behind, 1987; editor: (with Helen Stone Tice) The Measurement of Saving, Investment and Wealth, 1989, (with Magnus Blomström and Lennart Ohlsson) Economic Relations Between the U.S. and Sweden, 1989; assoc. editor Rev. of Econs. and Stats., 1989—; mem. editorial bd. Rev. of Income and Wealth, 1992—; contbr. articles to profl. jours. Fellow Am. Statis. Assn.; mem. Acad. Internat. Bus., Nat. Assn. Bus. Economists, Am. Econ. Assn., Econometric Soc., Internat. Assn. for Rsch. in Income and Wealth, Conf. on Rsch. in Income and Wealth. Home: 70 E 10th St New York NY 10003-5102 Office: 269 Mercer St New York NY 10003-6633

LIPSEY, STANFORD, newspaper publisher; b. Omaha, Oct. 8, 1927; s. Jacob and Molly (Brick) L.; m. Jeanne Blacker, June 15, 1949 (div. 1981); children—Janet Gail, Daniel Jacob. AB in Econs., U. Mich., 1948. Sales rep., pub. relations rep. Libby, McNeil & Libby, Los Angeles, 1948-50; reporter, advt. mgr., editor, pub. owner Sun Newspapers Omaha, 1952-80; vice-chmn. The Buffalo News, 1980-83, pres., pub., 1983—. Pres., founder Nebr. chpt. Multiple Sclerosis Soc., Omaha, 1951; bd. dirs., founder Strategic Aerospace Mus., Nebr., 1972; bd. dirs. Canisius Coll., Greater Buffalo Devel. Found., The Buffalo News Inc., U. at Buffalo Found., Inc., Bus. Coun. of N.Y. State, Roswell Park Inst.; mem. Newspaper Advt. Bur. Jr. League. With USAF, 1950-52. Pub. 1st weekly group to receive Pulitzer prize for investigative reporting Sun. Newspapers, Omaha. Office: Buffalo News 1 News Plz Buffalo NY 14203-2994

LIPSHER, MOLLY BARBARA, real estate executive; b. New Haven, Dec. 29, 1952; d. Charles M. and Beatrice (Shapiro) L. BA, U. Conn., 1975; MLA, Harvard U., 1983. Planner Cambridge (Mass.) Community Devel. Dept., 1977-78; planner, urban designer Met. Area Planning Coun., Boston, 1978-80; devel. mgr. The Rouse Co., Columbia, Md., 1982, 83, Am. Landmark Devels., N.Y.C., 1983-84; assoc. Landauer Assocs., N.Y.C., 1984-87; pres. The Property Rsch. Group, N.Y.C., 1987—. Prin. work includes Beverly (Mass.) Square, 1978. Mem. Harvard Bus. Sch. Club of Greater N.Y. (chairperson real estate com. 1989—). Office: The Property Rsch Group 35 W 71st St New York NY 10023-4134

LIPSITT, MARTIN FREDERIC, advertising agency executive; b. Detroit, May 9, 1934; s. Murray Jack and Betty L.; m. Judith Melnikoff, Sept. 8, 1957; children: Nancy, Katherine. BFA, Pratt Inst., 1956. With William Douglas McAdams, N.Y.C., 1957-59, DKG, Inc. (now Calet, Hirsch & Ferrell, Inc.), N.Y.C., 1962-65, 69—; exec. v.p., creative dir. DKG, Inc. (name now Calet, Hirsch & Spector, Inc.),, N.Y.C., 1974-90; with McCann-Erickson Advt., N.Y.C., 1965-67, Carl Ally, Inc., N.Y.C., 1967-68; pres., dir. of design The Lipsitt Design Unit, 1991—; guest lectr. Photo Club, Sch. Visual Arts, Pratt Inst., 1970-78; instr. design essentials Parsons Sch. Design, 1980-81. Bd. dirs. Montessori Sch., Brooklyn Heights, N.Y., 1967-69; mem. fund raising com. St. Ann's Episcopal Sch., Bklyn., 1975, Internat. TV Festival of N.Y. Finalist, 1987. Recipient Gold medal One Show Club, 1980, Silver medal, 1966, 83, 89, Distinctive merit, 1984, Andy award, 1967, 1984, 85, 87, Clio award, 1971, cert. of merit Art Dirs. Club, 1965, 68, 69, 78, 79, 80, 81, 82, 83, 85, 86, 90, award of distinctive merit, 1981, 85, Creativity award Art Direction mag., 1990, Print Casebook award, 1976, 79, cert. of design excellence, 1981, Best in Advt. award, 1982, C.A. award, 1965, 70, 76, 79, 80, 81, Illustrators Club award, 1970, 71, Progressive Architecture Annl. Advt. award, 1987; Kelly award finalist, 1990. Mem. Art Dirs. Club.

LIPSITZ, LAWRENCE IRWIN, publishing executive; b. Paterson, N.J., July 24, 1937; s. Samuel and Rachel (Hammerman) L.; m. Janice Shapiro, July 3, 1966; children: David, Jill, Julie. BS, NYU, 1959, AM, 1960. Tchr. Saddle Brook (N.J.) High Sch., 1961-63; pub. rels. NYU, N.Y.C., 1963-69; pub. Ednl. Tech. mag. and Ednl. Tech. Publs. Edn. Technology Publs., Englewood Cliffs, N.J., 1969—. Editor: Technology and Education, 1972, Test Score Decline, 1978, Instructional TV, 1979, Telecommunications in Learning, 1991. Pres. Temple Emeth, Teaneck, N.J., 1984-87; chmn. alumni communications NYU, 1989—; com. mem. United Jewish Community, River Edge, N.J., 1986—. With USAF, 1960-61. Fellow Jewish Acad. Arts and Scis.; mem. NYU Alumni Fedn. (com. chmn.). Jewish. Home: 1147 Trafalgar St Teaneck NJ 07666-1931 Also: 154 Old Farms Rd Torrington CT 06790 Office: Ednl Technology 700 E Palisade Ave Englewood Cliffs NJ 07632-3040

LIPSITZ, ROBERT JOEL, lawyer, corporate executive; b. Pitts., June 30, 1949; s. Herman and Helen Virginia (Nobel) L.; m. Susan Dale Schechter, July 5, 1970; 1 child, Samantha Beth. BBA, U. Miami, 1971; JD, U. Balt., 1975. Bar: Pa. 1975, U.S. Dist. Ct. (we. dist.) Pa., U.S. Ct. Appeals (3rd cir.), U.S. Supreme Ct. 1985. Ptnr. Lipsitz, Nassau, Schwartz & Leckman, Pitts., 1975—; corp. counsel B. Lipsitz Co., Pitts., 1976—; counsel various other corps.; trustee several pension plans. Mem. Upper St. Clair Cable Commn., Pa., 1983, chmn., 1984-86; mem. Upper St. Clair Planning Commn., 1985—, sec., 1986, vice chmn., 1987; bd. dirs. Avent Garde Found., 1991—. Recipient Merit award U. Balt. Sch. Law, 1975. Mem. ABA, Allegheny County Bar Assn., Am. Trial Lawyers Assn., Am. Biog. Inst. Rsch. Assn. (bd. gov's.), Masons, Shriners. Office: Lipsitz Nassau Schwartz & Leckman 1100 5th Ave Pittsburgh PA 15219-6204

LIPSKI, SHARYN ANN, nurse; b. Springfield, Mass., Apr. 14, 1945; d. James Joseph and June Lorraine (Cordes) Kennedy; m. Peter Allan Lipski, July 28, 1962; children: Michael, Michelle, Mark. AS with honors, Greenfield Community Coll., Mass., 1987. RN, Mass. Nurse Monson Devel. Ctr., Mass., 1977; nurse Narraguagus Health Care Facility, Milbridge, Maine. Vol. Healthcare for Homeless, Springfield, 1988. Mem. Mass. Nurses Assn. Roman Catholic. Home: RR 1 Steuben ME 04680-9801

LIPSKY, LEONARD, merger, management and acquisition specialist, financial and marketing consultant; b. Boston, May 12, 1936; s. Samuel M. and Marian E. (Quint) L.; m. Arline M. Cohen, Sept. 8, 1957 (div. Aug. 1982); children: Sheryl L. Reback, Alan S.; m. Judith Russell, July 8, 1984. BBA, Boston U., 1957. Lic. real estate broker. Owner, operator L & L Assocs. Restaurant Corp., Brookline, Mass., 1957-59; mgr. sales Beacon Builders Supply, Brookline, 1959-61; pres. Teletracer Internat., Inc., N.Y.C., 1961-74; dir. internat. mktg. Nira Internat., Emmen, Netherlands, 1975-79; pres. The Nimark Group, Mamaronek, N.Y., 1979—; regional v.p. Corp. Fin. Assocs., Ft. Lee, N.J., 1984-86; v.p. spl. projects Duro-Test Corp., Fairfield, N.J., 1989-91; exec. v.p. Advt. Display Co., Englewood Cliffs, N.J., 1991—; dir. Corp. Acquisition and Merger Affiliates; cons. internat. mktg. and distbn. problems. Mem. Am. Mgmt. Assn., Sales and Mktg. Execs. Internat., Assn. Corp. Growth. Jewish. Home: 238 Osborn Rd Harrison NY 10528-1304 Office: Advt Display Co 570 Sylvan Ave Englewood Cliffs NJ 07632

LIPSMAN, RICHARD MARC, lawyer, educator; b. Bklyn., Aug. 17, 1946; s. Abraham W. and Ruth (Weinstein) L.; m. Geri A. Russo, 1979; children: Eric, Dana Briana. BBA, CCNY, 1968; JD, St. John's U., Jamaica, N.Y., 1972; LLM in Taxation, Boston U., 1976. Bar: N.Y. 1973, Mass. 1975, U.S. Dist. Ct. (ea. and so. dists.) N.Y. 1977, U.S. Supreme Ct. 1978, U.S. Tax Ct. 1979; CPA, N.Y., Mass. Tax atty. Arthur Young & Co., N.Y.C., 1972-74; assoc. Gilman, McLaughlin & Hanrahan, Boston, 1974-76, Lefrak, Fischer & Meyerson, N.Y.C., 1976-77; ptnr. Tarnow, Landsman & Lipsman, N.Y.C., 1978; sole practice N.Y.C., 1979—; adj. faculty Baruch Coll. CUNY, 1984-86, curriculum specialist Research Found. CUNY, 1977-78; faculty Pratt Inst., Bklyn., 1974, Queensboro Coll., Bayside, N.Y., 1978-80. Author, producer book/cassette program Learning Income Taxes, 1978—. Mem. ABA, AICPA, Am. Assn. Atty.-CPA's, N.Y. State Bar Assn., Assn. of the Bar of the City of N.Y., N.Y. State Soc. CPA's. Jewish. Office: 605 3d Ave New York NY 10158

LIPSON, ABIGAIL, psychologist; b. Washington, Mar. 6, 1956; d. Leon Samuel and Dorothy Ann (Rapoport) L. BA, Hampshire Coll., 1977; PhD, Duke U., 1981. Lic. clin. psychologist. Instr., teaching asst. Duke U., Durham, N.C., 1977-79; staff psychotherapist Duke Psychol. Svcs., Durham, N.C., 1977-81; clin. psychology intern Harvard U., Cambridge, Mass., 1981-82; sr. counselor Bur. Study Counsel Harvard U. Bur. Study Counsel, Cambridge, Mass., 1982—; pvt. practice Cambridge, Mass., 1983—; vis. faculty Cambridge Coll., 1984, Kennedy Sch. Govt., Cambridge, 1985, 91; rsch. assoc. U. Mass., Amherst, 1989-91. Co-author: BLOCK, 1990; contbr. articles to psychology and edn. jours. Mem. APA, Am. Ednl. Rsch. Assn., Mass. Psychol. Assn. Office: Harvard U Bur Study Counsel 5 Linden St Cambridge MA 02138-5004

LIPSON, HERBERT GEORGE, retired physicist; b. Boston, July 4, 1925; s. Louis Emanuel and Sara Lillian (Bashaway) L.; m. Gloria Freedman, July 1, 1951; children: Neil, Jerold, Elayne. BS in Physics, MIT, 1948; MS in Physics, Northeastern U., 1964. Jr. physicist Sylvania Electric Products Inc., Bayside, N.Y., 1948-50; physicist Brookhaven Nat. Lab., Upton, N.Y., 1951, Naval Rsch. Lab., Washington, 1951-55; staff physicist MIT, Lexington, 1955-58; physicist Rome Air Devel. Ctr., Hanscom AFB, Bedford, Mass., 1958-90; ret., 1990. Contbr. articles to sci. jours.; patentee in field. Pres. Brotherhood, Temple Emmanuel, Wakefield, Mass., 1969, 79. Mem. ASTM (chmn. subcom. infrared lasers and materials 1974-79), Am. Phys. Soc., Materials Rsch. Soc. Home: 68 Aldrich Rd Wakefield MA 01880-4941

LIPSON, MARJORIE YOUMANS, education educator; b. Fond du Lac, Wis., Mar. 15, 1947; d. Vernon John and Kathleen (Kearns) Youmans; m. Michael Herber Lipson, Sept. 7, 1974; children: Nora Rose, Theodore Lawrence. BS in Elem. Edn. with distinction, U. Wis., 1969; MEd in Tchr. Edn., U. Vt., 1976; PhD in Curriculum and Instrn., U. Mich., 1981. Bilingual tchr. grades 4-5 Milw. Pub. Schs., 1969-70; tchr., team leader grades 4, 5, 6 Washington Pub. Schs., 1970-74; substitute tchr. grade 4 Burlington (Vt.) Pub. Schs., 1975; lectr., grad. asst. Coll. Edn. and Social Svcs. U. Vt., 1976-78, vis. asst. prof. edn., 1982-83, assoc. prof. profl. edn. and curriculum devel., 1985—80; grad. asst. U. Mich., Ann Arbor, 1978-80; asst. prof. edn. Coll. Edn. Ea. Mich. U., Ypsilanti, 1981-85; rsch. coord. Metacognition and Reading Comprehension, U. Mich., Ann Arbor, 1980-81. Author: Instructor's Manual: Reading Instruction for Today, 1986; (with others) Experiences in Literature (K-8 Reading Series), 1991, Assessment and Instruction of Reading Disability: An Interactive Approach, 1991; editor (with others) Improving Basal Reading Instruction, 1989; contbr. articles to profl. jours., chpts. to books; editorial adv. bd. Reading Rsch. Quar., 1988-90, Jour. Reading Behavior, 1985-89, Nat. Reading Conf. Ann. Yearbook, 1984—. Recipient Disting. Faculty, Jr. Teaching award Ea. Mich. U., 1984, Kroepsch-Maurice award for teaching excellence, 1991.; grantee Ea. Mich. U. Grad. Sch., 1984-85, 85-86, 86-89, Dean's Fund Spl. Allocation for Scholarly Activity, 1983, U. Vt., 1983, 88-89. Mem. Internat. Reading Assn. (mem. task force on issues in lit. assessment 1988—), Vt. Coun. on Reading (mem.-at-large exec. com. 1986-91), Nat. Reading Conf. (mem. student rsch. award com. 1987, field coun. rep. 1985—), Coll. Reading Assn. (Vt. state chairperson 1987-88), Mich. Reading Assn. (co-chair com. on microcomputers and reading 1984-85), Am. Ednl. Rsch. Assn., New Eng. Reading Assn. Office: U Vt 538 Waterman Bldg Burlington VT 05405

LIPTON, CHARLES, public relations executive; b. N.Y.C., May 11, 1928; s. Jack B. and Bertha (Lesser) L.; m. Audrey Williams, Nov. 11, 1951; children—Susan, Jack. AB, Harvard U., 1948. Market researcher Cecil & Presbury, Inc., N.Y.C., 1948-49; spl. events dir. 20th Century Fox Film Corp., N.Y.C., 1949-52; account exec. Ruder & Finn, Inc., N.Y.C., 1953-58; v.p. Ruder & Finn, Inc., 1958-63, sr. v.p., 1963-69, chmn. bd., 1969—; buest lectr. Boston U., 1967-68. Mem. coun. Ctr. for Vocat. Arts, Norwalk, Conn., 1966-74; trustee Norwalk Jewish Ctr., 1966-70; treas., mem. exec. com. Norwalk Symphony Soc., 1972-85; chmn. parent's counsel Washington U., St. Louis, 1976-77, trustee, 1977—. Mem. Am. Soc. Colon and Rectal Surgeons (trustee), Internat. Pub. Rels. Assn., Am. Mgmt. Assn., USIA (pub. rels. pvt. sector com. 1988—), Nat. Emphysema Soc., Nat. Investor Rels. Inst., Harvard Club, Midday Club, Harvard Varsity Club. Home: 18 Douglas Dr Norwalk CT 06850-1730 Office: Ruder Finn Inc 165 W End Ave Apt 14F New York NY 10023-5520

LISA, CLAIRE JEANNETTE, philanthropic organization administrator; d. Max Werner and Clara Elise (Weder) Gigandet; children: James J., Robert J., David J. BSBA, Ramapo Coll., 1985. Dir. adminstrn. Community Action Coun., Pompton Lakes, N.J., 1973-79; computer specialist Ingersoll Rand, Woodcliff Lake, N.J., 1979-82; analyst, consultant Computer Visions, Hawthorne, N.J., 1982-85; dir. adminstrn. Jewish Fedn. North Jersey, Wayne, N.J., 1985—; computer cons. Jewish Community Housing Corp., Paterson, 1985—, Jewish Fedn. Clifton Passaic, 1985—, Endowment Corp., Wayne, 1985—; software tng. cons. Quality Software, Dallas, 1991—; tech. asst. various orgns., N.J., 1991—. Video producer Fair Lawn Creative Cable and Skyline Prodns., Ringwood. Den mother, publicity dir. Boy Scouts Am., Ringwood, 1970-73; com. woman Passaic County Dems., Ringwood, 1981-83; vol. Am. Heart Assn., 1986, March of Dimes, 1992. Mem. NAFE, Am. Mgmt. Assn., N.J. Personal Computer Users Group, Pick Profls., Smithsonian Instn., Greenpeace, Amnesty Internat. Home: 191 Lakeview Ave Ringwood NJ 07456-2108

LISANTE, STEPHEN JAMES, government official; b. Bklyn., Jan. 30, 1950; s. Theodore Richard and Frances Josephine (Fiorenza) L. BA, CCNY, 1971; postgrad., Baruch U., 1973-75. Tax auditor IRS, Bklyn., 1972-74, mgmt. analyst, 1974-77; budget analyst IRS, Washington, 1977-80, chief, compliance progs. analysis sect./fin. div., 1980-85, chief, service-wide budget execution sect., 1985-87, chief internat. budget, rsch. and oversight staff, 1988—. Mem. Am. Soc. Pub. Adminstrs. Home: 5312 Weymouth Dr Springfield VA 22151-1502 Office: IRS 950 L Enfant Plz Washington DC 20024

LISCH, HOWARD, accountant, tax lawyer; b. N.Y.C., Dec. 30, 1950; s. Simon and Edith (Sachs) L.; m. Audrey Robin Ginsberg, 1973; children—Sari Victoria, Melissa Dawn, Jeremy Harold, Simon Alexander. B.S., NYU, 1972; J.D., Bklyn. Law Sch., 1975. CPA, Conn., N.J., N.Y. Tax acct. Arthur Andersen & Co., N.Y.C., 1975-77; tax supr. Coopers & Lybrand, Stamford, Conn., 1977-79; internat. tax mgr. Pitney Bowes, Stamford, 1979-80; tax mgr. Deloitte, Haskins & Sells, N.Y.C., 1980-82; chief fin. officer Campus Entertainment Network, N.Y.C., 1982-83, Black Tie Network, N.Y.C., 1982-83; tax mgr. Schachter & Co., White Plains, N.Y., dir. tax services Sobel & Co., Roseland, N.J., 1983-85; tax mgr. Rosenberg, Leffler & Zach, N.Y.C., 1985-86; prin. Howard Lisch Acctg. Offices, N.Y.C., N.J., L.A., 1986—. Active Freehold Twp. Transp. Bd. Mem. Am. Arbitration Assn. (arbitrator), ABA, Am. Inst. CPA's, N.J. Soc. CPA's, N.Y. Soc. CPA's. Republican. Jewish. Home: 11 Nathan Hale Pl Freehold NJ 07728-1386 Office: 305 Broadway Ste 601 New York NY 10007

LISCHEWSKI, HANS-CHRISTIAN, architect, educator; b. Sensburg, Germany, Aug. 23, 1944; came to U.S., 1976; s. Hans and Gerda (Lerch) L.; m. Sabine Faust, May 15, 1970 (div. July 1975); m. Martha Leinroth, Feb. 3, 1982 (div. Mar. 1986); m. Jane Elizabeth Pike, May 28, 1989; 1 child, Marc. Dipl Ing Arch, U. Karlsruhe, 1975; MArch in Advanced Studies, MIT, 1979. Asst. prof. dept. architecture U. Karlsruhe (Fed. Republic Germany), 1975-76; rsch. affiliate dept. architecture U. Stuttgart (Fed. Republic Germany), 1975-76; rsch. affiliate architecture machine group MIT, Cambridge, 1978-81; pres. Most Media, Inc., Somerville, Mass., 1981-83; dir. systems devel. Sota Assos., Inc., Stamford, Conn., 1983-84; dir. computer svcs. Russo & Sonder, N.Y.C., 1984-90, Perkins & Will, N.Y.C., 1990—; assoc. prof. sch. architecture Pratt Inst., Bklyn., 1984—, assoc. prof., 1989—; mem. adv. bd. AEC Expo Conf., Pratt Ctr. for Resource Mgmt. Co-author: Design Simulation, 1984. Lt. German Army, 1964-66. MIT Graham travelling scholar, 1977; Govt. Fed. Republic Germany grantee, 1978-80. Mem. AIA (assoc., unbuilt products group award 1985), Assn. for CAD in Architecture, Assn. for Computing Machinery, IEEE Computer Soc. Home: 222 Park Ave S Apt 9C New York NY 10003-1509 Office: Perkins & Will One Park Ave New York NY 10016 also: Pratt Inst Sch Architecture 200 Willoughby Ave Brooklyn NY 11205

LISH, JENNIFER DAWN, clinical psychology educator; b. Tucson, Oct. 5, 1957; d. Gordon Jay and Frances (Fokes) L. AB, Brown U., 1980; PhD, NYU, 1986. Lic. psychologist, N.Y. Postdoctoral fellow Columbia U., N.Y.C., 1986-88, asst. prof., 1988-91; asst. prof. U. Pa., Phila., 1992—. Contbr. articles to profl. jours. Mem. APA, Am. Psychol. Soc., Assn. for Psychosocial Clin. Rsch. Democrat. Jewish. Home: 880 N 22d St Philadelphia PA 19130 Office: U Pa 3600 Market St Philadelphia PA 19104

LISK, PENELOPE TSALTAS, artist; b. N.Y.C., June 16, 1959; d. Theodore-Theodosios and Margaret (Owen) Tsaltas; m. Douglas Crumback Lisk, July 7, 1990; 1 child, Christina Margaret. AB in Fine Arts, Bryn Mawr (Pa.) Coll., 1981; MFA, Cranbrook Acad. of Art, 1985. Tchr., intern Phila. Mus. of Art, 1983; gallery asst. Noël Butcher Gallery, Phila., 1985-87; account mgr. Archibald Allan Assocs., West Conshohocken, Pa., 1987-91; artist Media, Pa., 1985—; asst. organizer alumnae exhbn. Baldwin Sch., Bryn Mawr, 1989. One-woman shows include The Chilton Co., Radnor, Pa., 1990, Cabrini Coll., Radnor, 1988, Quisset, Haverford, Pa., 1987, Wayne (Pa.) Hotel, 1986, others; group shows include ARTREACH/AURA Soc., Villanova U., Phila., 1991, Villanova U., 1990, The Baldwin Sch., Bryn Mawr, Pa., 1989, Sishuan Inst. of Fine Art, Tin Sin U., China, 1986, Cranbrook Acad. of Art, Bloomfield Hills, Mich., 1985, others; work represented in collections at Detroit Inst. of Art, Nelson Atkins Mus., Newport Harbor Mus., others. Recipient 2nd prize painting, Villanova U., purchase price/Nat. Drawing 1987, Trenton (N.J.) State Coll. Mem. Artists Uniting Religion and Art, Print Club, Pa. Arts Coalition. Republican. Episcopalian.

LISKIN, BARBARA ANN, psychiatrist; b. Englewood, NJ, Nov. 24, 1952; d. Louis and Anita (Merker) L.; m. Vincent Robert Bonagura, June 3, 1982; children: Elizabeth, Rebecca. AB, Smith Coll., Northampton, 1974; MS, Columbia U., N.Y.C., 1974, MD, 1979. Boarded in Pediatrics and Psychiatry. Research asst. Columbia U., N.Y.C., 1974-75; asst. psychiat. instr. Columbia U., 1985-87, asst. clin. prof. pediatrics and psychiatry, 1987—, dir. young adult psychiatry, 1987—; clin. dir. Barnard Coll. Mental Health Svcs., 1988—; pvt. practice psychiatry, 1985—. Recipient NIMH Jr. Faculty award 1985; Resident Research award 1985. Mem. Am. Psychiatry Assn. Office: Barnard Coll Health Svcs 3009 Broadway New York NY 10027-6598

LISMAN, GERARD WILLIAM, sales executive; b. Wilkes Barre, Pa., Mar. 5, 1955; s. Robert J. and Anne M. (Piatt) L.; m. Connie E. Bisulca, July 12, 1980; children: Jennifer, Michael. Grad. high sch., Wilkes Barre, 1973. Owner, operator Drafco Inc., Parkway Blueprinting, Wilkes Barre, 1974-79; ops. mgr. Joseph's Fund Raising, Pittston, Pa., 1979; sales rep. Marshall Electronics, Skokie, Ill., 1980-83; Eastern sales mgr. Marshall Electronics, Marshall Products, Omron Healthcare, Lincolnshire, Ill., 1983-91; nat. sales mgr. Omron Healthcare, Vernon Hills, Ill., 1991—; movie projectionist Gen. Cinema Corp., Wilkes Barre, 1976-80. Treas. Big Bros./Big Sisters, Wilkes, 1989—; active Newtown Fire Dept., Hanover Twp., Pa., 1973—; vice chmn. Eastside Landfill Authority, Wilkes Barre, 1978-90. Mem. Am. Mktg. Assn., Masons. Democrat. Roman Catholic. Home and Office: 84 W Liberty St Wilkes-Barre PA 18706-1797

LIST, DOUGLASS WILLIAM, management consultant, civil engineeer; b. Phila., Nov. 27, 1955; s. Harold Adams and Marie Laura (Fisher) L.; m. Sherri Elisabeth Anderson, June ll, 1982; children: Brittany Anderson, Peyton Elizabeth. BSCE, MSCE, U. Va., 1977; MBA, Harvard U., 1982. Ops. analyst So. Ry., Atlanta, 1977-78; svc. analyst Union Pacific R.R., Omaha, 1979-80; cons. Merrimac Transport Assocs., Newburyport, Mass., 1980-81, McKinsey & Co., Atlanta and Boston, 1982-85; v.p. mktg. and strategic planning CSX Equipment Co., Balt., 1986-87; pres. List & Co., Inc., Balt., 1988—; gen. mgr. Ry. Engring. Assocs., Balt., 1988—; bd. dirs. Harmon Industries. Contbr. articles on mgmt. of r.r. equipment to profl. jours. Mus. dir. Redeemer Theatre Co., Balt., 1987—; mem. planning com. United Way, 1989—; trustee Center Stage, 1992—; bd. dirs. Alliance, Inc., Friends of Paquin Found. Baker scholar Harvard U., 1982. Mem. Transp. Rsch. Forum (nat. bd. 1989—, pres. Md. chpt. 1990), Am. Mktg. Assn., Am. Rwy. Engring. Assn., Harvard Bus. Sch. Club Md., Ctr. Club. Episcopalian. Office: List & Co Inc World Trade Ctr Ste # 2233 Baltimore MD 21202

LISTON, ALAN A., lawyer; b. Hamilton, Ont., Oct. 11, 1946; s. Ambrose James and Kathleen Frances (Burns) L. BA, U. Western Ont., 1968, B. Laws, 1972. Solicitor Domgroup Ltd., Toronto, 1976-81, dir. legal svcs., 1981-82, gen. counsel, sec., 1982-84, v.p., gen. counsel, sec., 1984-85, sr. v.p., gen. counsel, sec., 1986-88, pres., 1988—, also bd. dirs. Home: 29 Notley Pl, Toronto, ON Canada M4B 2M7 Office: Domgroup Ltd, 10 Toronto St, Toronto, ON Canada M5C 2B7

LISTON, RONALD ARGYLE, mechanical engineer; b. Buffalo, Apr. 11, 1926; s. William Combe and Ruby Blanche (Morrison) L.; m. Mary Jean Cook, Dec. 16, 1926 (div. July 1980); children: William Argyle, Deborah Jane, Thomas Ian, John Alexander, Susan Eloise, Sally Jo; m. Nancy Harriet Cummings, Aug. 9, 1981; children; SCott Ian, Robin Argyle, Alexis Siobhan. BSc in ME, U. Vt., 1949; MSc in ME, U. Mich., 1958, MSc in Engring. Mechanics, 1961; PhD in EM and ME, Mich. Tech. U., 1973. Registered profl. engr., N.H. Rsch. engr. Tank Automotive Command, Warren, Mich., 1961-70; rsch. engr. Colo Region Rsch. and Engring. Lab., Hanover, N.H., 1970-74, rsch. mech. engr., 1976—; dir. Kaneenaw Rsch. Ctr., Houghton, Mich., 1974-75; treas. Am. Precision Mus., Windsor, Vt., 1985—. Contbr. articles to profl. jours. Mem. sch. bd., Windsor, 1987-91. With Ordnance Corps, U.S. Army, 1950-61. Mem. ASME, Internat. Soc. Terrain/Vehicle Systems (gen. sec. 1975—), Sigma Xi. Home: 8 Lowell St RR 3 Box 263 Cornish NH 03745 Office: US CRREL 72 Lyme Rd Hanover NH 03755

LITKE, JOHN DAVID, technology executive, researcher; b. Winchester, Mass., May 30, 1944; s. E. David and Clara Edna (Killenberg) L.; m. Louise M. Lockier, June 11, 1966. BS in Physics, MIT, 1965; PhD in Physics, Johns Hopkins U., 1976. Instr. Johns Hopkins U., Balt., 1966-76; mem. tech. staff Bell Labs., Holmdel, N.J., 1976-80; prin. scientist Photocircuits, Glen Cove, N.J., 1980-84; dep. dir. software technology Grumman Data Systems,

Woodbury, N.Y., 1984-88, dir. computing and controls rsch. Copr. Rsch. Ctr., 1988—; mfg. technology cons., Huntington, N.Y., 1984—. Contbr. articles to computer sci. jours. Inventor in field of circuit technology. Mem. IEEE, AIAA, Assn. for Computing Machinery, Am. Phys. Soc., N.Y. Acad. Scis., Inst. for Interconnecting and Packaging Electronic Circuits (mem. computer standards com. 1982-84). Home: 645 Park Ave Huntington NY 11743-3756 Office: Grumman Corp Rsch Ctr MS AOS-35 Bethpage NY 11714-3580

LITMAN, ROBERT BARRY, physician, author, television and radio commentator; b. Phila., Nov. 17, 1947; s. Benjamin Norman and Bette Etta (Saunders) L.; m. Niki Thomas, Apr. 21, 1985; children: Riva Belle, Nadya Beth, Caila Tess, Benjamin David. BS, Yale U., 1967, MD, 1970, MS in Chemistry, 1972, MPhil in Anatomy, 1972, postgrad. (Life Ins. Med. Rsch. Fund fellow) Yale U., Univ. Coll. Hosp., U. London, 1969-70; Am. Cancer Soc. postdoctoral rsch. fellow Yale U., 1970-73. Diplomate Am. Bd. Family Practice. Resident in gen. surgery Bryn Mawr (Pa.) Hosp., 1973-74; USPHS fellow Yale U. Sch. Medicine, 1974-75; pvt. practice medicine and surgery, Ogdensburg, N.Y., 1977—; mem. med. staff A. Barton Hepburn Hosp.; commentator Family Medicine Stas. WWNY-TV and WTNY-Radio; clin. preceptor dept. family medicine State Univ. Health Ctr., Syracuse. Author: Wynnefield and Limer, 1983, The Treblinka Virus, 1991, Allergy Shots, 1992; contbr. articles to numerous sci. publs. Pres. Am. Heart Assn. No. N.Y. chpt., 1980-84. Fellow Am. Coll. Allergy and Immunology, Am. Acad. Family Physicians; mem. AMA (Physicians Recognition award 1970—), N.Y. State, St. Lawrence County med. assns., Joint Coun. Allergy and Immunology, Nat. Assn. Physician Broadcasters (charter), Acad. Radion and TV Health Communicators, Book and Snake Soc., Gibbs Soc. of Yale U. (founder), Sigma Xi, Nu Sigma Nu, Alpha Chi Sigma. Home: 604 Crescent PO Box 29 Ogdensburg NY 13669-0029 Office: PO Box 29 124 King St Ogdensburg NY 13669-0029

LITOFF, JUDY BARRETT, history educator; b. Atlanta, Dec. 23, 1944; d. John and Dorothy (Woodall) Barrett; m. Harold Lawrence Litoff, Sept. 30, 1966; children: Nadja Barrett, Alyssa Barrett. BA, Emory U., Atlanta, 1967; MA, Emory U., 1968; PhD, U. Maine, 1975. Asst. prof. history Bryant Coll., Smithfield, R.I., 1975-81; assoc. prof. history Bryant Coll., 1981-87, prof. history, 1987—; scholarly reader U. Ga. Press, Greenwood Press, U. Ill. Press. Author: American Midwives, 1978, American Midwife Debate, 1986; co-author: Miss You, 1990, Since You Went Away, 1991, Dear Boys, 1991; contbr. articles to profl. jours.; book reviewer many profl. jours. Bd. dirs. R.I. Com. for Humanities, 1982-86; bd. overseers The Lincoln Sch., Providence 1982-88, The Moses Brown Sch., Providence, 1984—; leader Girl Scouts R.I., 1978-87. Recipient Disting. Faculty award, Bryant Faculty Fedn., 1988, Bryant Alumni Assn., 1989; Ford Career scholar Emory U., 1965-67. Mem. Orgn. Am. Historians, Am. Hist. Assn., So. Hist. Assn., R.I. Hist. Soc., R.I. Black Heritage Soc., Coordinating Com. on Women in the Hist. Profession, So. Assn. Women Historians, Phi Kappa Phi, Phi Alpha Theta. Soc. of Friends. Home: 248 Morris Ave Providence RI 02906-2424 Office: Bryant Coll 450 Douglas Pike Smithfield RI 02917-2346

LITTERER, JOSEPH AUGUST, management educator; b. N.Y.C., Oct. 16, 1929; s. Charles Frank and Gladys (Bader) L.; m. Marie E. Wilson, Oct. 15, 1953 (div.); children: Karin, Susan, David; m. Mariann Jelinek, Aug. 1987. BSEE, Drexel U., 1950, MBA, 1955; PhD, U. Ill., 1959. Supr., RCA, Camden, N.J., 1952-55; instr. to prof. mgmt. U. Ill., Urbana, 1955-69; prof. mgmt. U. Mass., Amherst, 1969—; cons. to mgmt. firms. Author: Analysis of Organizations, 1973, Managing for Organizational Effectiveness, 1976, Management: Concepts and Controversies, 1978, Organizations: Structure and Behavior, 1980, Organization by Design, 1981, An Introduction to Management, 1984, Negotiating, 1985, Systematic Management, 1987. With U.S. Army, 1950-52. Mem. Acad. Mgmt. (pres. 1969-70), Am. Sociol. Assn. Democrat. Home: 313 Burns Ln Williamsburg VA 23185 Office: U Mass Dept Mgmt Amherst MA 01003

LITTLE, CHRISTOPHER MARK, publishing company executive, lawyer; b. Tazewell, Va., Mar. 11, 1941; s. Haskin Vincent and Janet Koe (Kessinger) L.; m. Virginia Elizabeth Silver, Dec. 27, 1963 (div. Oct. 1988); children: Timothy Mark, Margaret Elizabeth; m. Elizabeth Foster Anderson, Oct. 15, 1988. BA, Yale U., 1963; LLB, U. Tex., 1966. Bar: D.C. 1966. Assoc. Covington & Burling, Washington, 1966-68, 70-75; adminstrv. asst. to Congressman Bob Eckhardt, U.S. Ho. of Reps., Washington, 1968-70; asst. gen. counsel EPA, Washington, 1975-76; v.p., counsel The Washington Post, 1976-80; pres., pub. The Herald, Everett, Wash., 1980-84; sr. v.p. adminstrn. Newsweek, Inc., N.Y.C., 1984-86, pres., 1986-89; pres. Cowles Mags., Inc., Harrisburg, Pa., 1989—. Vice chmn., chmn. exec. com., internat. bd. trustees Am. Field Svc., N.Y.C., 1989—. Mem. Mag. Pubs. Am. (bd. dirs., chmn. govt. affairs coun. 1990—). Episcopalian. Office: Cowles Mags Inc 6405 Flank Dr Harrisburg PA 17112

LITTLE, JAMES MORRIS, artist; b. Memphis, Tenn., July 21, 1952; s. Roger and Annie (Simmons) L.; m. Fatima Shaik, June 23, 1986; children: Dialene, Celeste. BFA, Memphis Acad. Art, 1974; MFA, Syracuse U., 1976. Represented in permanent collections Ark. Art Ctr., N.J. State Mus. Democrat. Baptist/Pentecostal. Home: 315 7th Ave Apt 9A New York NY 10001-6014 Office: Little 210 Kent Ave Brooklyn NY 11211-3908

LITTLE, JILL ANN, education educator; b. Syracuse, N.Y., Sept. 4, 1940; d. Wilfred Samuel and Frances Elgy (Webb) Lowe; m. Edward Serens Little, July 7, 1962; children: William Richard, Deanna Kristen, Kelly Anne. BS, Syracuse U., 1961; MEd, Temple U., 1966; PhD, Syracuse U., 1979. Elem. tchr. Jamesville Dewitt Schs., Dewitt, N.Y., 1961-62, Springfield Twp., Ambler, Pa., 1962-64; spl. tchr. Liverpool (N.Y.) Sch. Dist., 1964-66, B.O.C.E.S., East Syracuse, N.Y., 1966-67; adj. prof. LeMoyne Coll., Syracuse, N.Y., 1979-88, asst. prof., 1988-91, adj. asst. prof., 1991—. Mem. N.Y. State Assn. Tchr. Educators (bd. dirs. 1984-86, 90—), N.Y. State Reading Coun. (bd. dirs. 1990—), Beta Kappa (rsch. com., 1989—). Republican. Roman Catholic. Home: 4200 Taylor Rd Jamesville NY 13078-9618

LITTLE, NED ALLEN, aviation training analyst; b. Fredrick, Md., July 15, 1940; s. David S. and Marion (Hawk) L.; m. Sarah Rang, Nov. 7, 1959; children: Ned A. Jr., David J., Scott A., Mark E., Kristin M. AS, State Tech. Inst. at Memphis, 1975. Enlisted man USMC, 1957, advanced through grades to master sgt., 1974; ret., 1979; aviation tng. analyst ECC Internat. Corp., Wayne, Pa., 1979—. Decorated Air medal with gold stars. Mem. AIAA (assoc.), NRA, VFW, Marine Corps League. Republican. Mem. United Ch. of Christ. Home: 362 Heritage Ln King Of Prussia PA 19406 Office: ECC Internat Corp 175 Strafford Ave Wayne PA 19087

LITTLE, R. DONALD, architect; b. Gastonia, N.C., Mar. 18, 1937; s. Coy Marshall and Stella May (Pruett) L.; B.A., U. Md., 1972; B.Arch., Catholic U. Am., 1980, M.Arch., 1981; m. Jacqueline Beatrice Mandel, June 10, 1967; children by previous marriage—Tina June Whitman, Diana Dawn Little, Laura Marie Van Meel. Blood bank and med. technologist Dr. Oscar B. Hunter Meml. Lab., Washington, 1961-66; biol. lab. technologist Navl. Med. Research Inst., Bethesda, Md., 1966-68; blood bank and med. technologist, supr. Central Lab., Doctor's Hosp., Washington, 1959-79; jr. architect VVKR Inc., University Park, Md.; supr. architect; br. head design div. Naval Surface Weapons Center, Silver Spring, Md., 1981-87; supr. architect, chief facility engring.br. Agrl. Research Service, USDA, 1987—. Served with USN, 1956-61. Mem. Am. Assn. Blood Banks, Am. Soc. Med. Technologists. Home: 13417 Rich Lynn Ct Highland MD 20777-9790 Office: USDA-Agrl Rsch Svc Facility Engring Br Bldg 426 BARC-E Beltsville MD 20705

LITTLE, THOMAS EDWARD, adult educator; b. Altoona, Pa., Oct. 5, 1948; s. Fred O. and Mary M. (Finnegan) L.; m. Patricia Jordan, Sept. 20, 1980; children: Matthew, Sarah, Rebecca. BA, St. Mary's Coll., 1970; MA, St. Mary's U., 1974; MS, Johns Hopkins U., 1976; EdD, N.C. State U., 1979. Cert. adult edn. tchr. Assoc. prof. edn. St. Mary's U., Balt., 1979-85; instr. Johns Hopkins U., Balt., 1979—, La Salle U., Phila., 1979-82, Coll. Notre Dame, Balt., 1991—, Nat. Louis U., McLean, Va., 1991—; ednl. cons. small businesses, svc., health care and ednl. instns., 1979—. Author Sales Manager's Manual, 1986; contbr. articles on adult edn. to profl. publs. Home and Office: 722 Dryden Dr Baltimore MD 21229-1419

LITTLEFIELD, ROY EVERETT, III, association executive, legal educator; b. Nashua, N.H., Dec. 6, 1952; s. Roy Everett and Mary Ann (Prestipino) L.; m. Amy Root; children: Leah Marie, Roy Everett IV. BA, Dickinson Coll., 1975; MA, Catholic U. Am., 1976, PhD, 1979. Aide U.S. Senator Thomas McIntyre, Democrat, N.H., 1975-78, Nordy Hoffman, U.S. Senate Sergeant-at-arms, N.H., 1979; dir. govt. rels. Nat. Tire Dealers and Retreaders Assn., Washington, N.H., 1979-84; exec. dir. Svc. Sta. and Automotive Repair Assn., Washington, N.H., 1984—; cons. Am. Retreaders Assn., 1984—; mem. faculty Catholic U. Am., Washington, 1979—. Author: William Randolph Hearst: His Role in American Progressivism, 1980, The Economic Recovery Act, 1982, The Surface: Transportation Assistance Act, 1984; editor Nozzle mag.; contbr. numerous articles to legal jours. Mem. Nat. Dem. Club, 1978—. Mem. Am. Soc. Legal History, Md. Hwy. User's Fedn. (pres.), Nat. Hwy. User's Fedn. (bd. dirs.), Nat. Capitol Area Transp. Fedn. (v.p.), N.H. Hist. Soc., Kansas City C. of C., Capitol Hill Club, Phi Alpha Theta. Roman Catholic. Home: 1707 Pepper Tree Ct Bowie MD 20721-3021 Office: 9420 Annapolis Rd Ste 307 Lanham Seabrook MD 20706-3028

LITTLETON, CHARLES THOMAS, association administrator; b. Atlanta, July 23, 1938; s. Charles Thomas and Lucile (Cooper) L.; m. Madeleine Hollier, Aug. 10, 1957 (div. 1979); m. Diane Crouch, June 30, 1979. BS in Food Distbn., U. So. Calif., L.A., 1967. Dir. S.E. sales Philip Morris USA, Atlanta, 1961-83; pres. Met. Distbrs., N.Y.C., 1983-86; exec. dir. New Eng. Assn. Tobacco and Candy Distbrs., Walpole, Mass., 1987—; bd. dirs. Mass. Candy Tobacco Distbrs., Conn. Assn. Tobacco Candy Distbrs. With U.S. Army, 1957-60. Mem. Nat. Candy Wholesalers Assn., Am. Soc. Assn. Execs. Democrat. Roman Catholic. Office: New Eng Assn Tobacco and Candy Distbrs PO Box 659 Walpole MA 02081-0659

LITTLETON, JOSEPH COOK, glass company executive, consultant; b. Corning, N.Y., Oct. 30, 1920; s. Jesse Talbot and Bessie (Cook) L.; m. Barbara Ann Gunnell, June 2, 1945; children: Nancy Jo, Margaret Ann, William John. BEE, Cornell U., 1942. Registered profl. engr., N.Y. Engr., bus. exec. Corning (N.Y.) Glass Works, 1945-69, v.p., 1970-85, cons., 1985-89; chmn. bd. Diagnostic Research Inc., Roslyn, N.Y., 1972-75; pres. Hodes Lang Corp., North Bergen, N.J., 1969-75, Cormedics Inc., Somerville, N.J., 1971-74; chmn. bd. Kansas City Biol. Co., Lenexa, Kans., 1982-83; bd. dirs. Hardinge Bros., Inc., Elmira, N.Y., J.H. Ullman & Assocs., Corning, N.Y. Patentee in field. Mem. Corning Bd. Pub. Works, 1954-60, Corning Zoning Bd., 1951-53; chmn. Urbana (N.Y.) Zoning Bd. Appeals, 1988—. Capt. U.S. Army, 1942-45, PTO. Named to Corning Painted Post Sports Hall of Fame, 1979. Republican. Methodist. Clubs: Bath County (N.Y.), Castle Creeek Fishing (Corning). Home: 190 E Lake Rd Hammondsport NY 14840-9526 Office: Corning Glass Works HP CB 09 Corning NY 14830

LITTMAN, BRUCE HENRY, physician, researcher; b. N.Y.C., Nov. 18, 1944; s. William and Francis (Brody) L.; m. Estelle Young, June 2, 1975 (div. Nov. 1982); m. Catherine Irving, May 11, 1986; 1 child, Sarah W. BS, U. Wis., 1966; MD, SUNY, 1970. Intern, resident Tufts New Eng. Med. Ctr., Boston, 1970-71, 73-74; staff fellow Nat. Cancer Inst. USPHS, NIH, Bethesda, Md., 1971-73; rsch. fellow, asst. in medicine Robert B. Brigham/Harvard Med. Sch., Boston, 1974-76; asst. prof. Med. Coll. of Va., Richmond, 1976-81, assoc. prof., 1981-89; sr. assoc. dir. Pfizer Cen. Rsch., Groton, Conn., 1989—; mem. adv. bd. Lipus Found. Am., Richmond, 1986-89. Contbr. chpts. to books and articles to profl. jours. Sr. surgeon USPHS, 1971-73. Recipient Fellowship award Am. Cancer Soc., Boston, 1974-76, Rsch. Career Devel. award NIH, 1977-82. Fellow Am. Rheumatism Assn. (founding mem., councilor 1984-89), Am. Coll. Rheumatology (v.p. S.E. region 1989-90), Am. Coll. Physicians; mem. Am. Fedn. Clin. Rsch., Am. Assn. Immunologists, Va. Soc. Rheumatologists (pres. 1988-89). Office: Pfizer Cen Rsch Eastern Point Rd Groton CT 06340-4947

LITTMAN, JULES SANFORD, lawyer; b. Detroit, Nov. 8, 1946; s. Henny and Mary Blanche (Kaftan) L.; m. Mary Andrea Max, Aug. 18, 1968; children: Justin, M. Jared, Kyle. Student, Wayne State U., 1964-67; BA, Mich. State U., 1968; JD, Rutgers, 1973. Tchr. N.Y.C. Bd. Edn., Bronx, 1968-69; social worker N.J. Div. of Youth and Family Svcs., Paterson, 1969-71; staff atty. Middlesex County Legal Svcs. Corp., New Brunswick, N.J., 1973-77; assoc. Arthur H. Miller, P.A., New Brunswick, 1977-79, 80; ptnr. Miller & Littman, P.A., New Brunswick, 1980—; bd. trustees Women Aware, Inc., New Brunswick, 1979—; bd. dirs. Middlesex County Legal Svcs. Corp., New Brunswick. Bd. dirs. Freehold (N.J.) Soccer League, Inc., 1987—. Recipient Community Svc. award United Way of Cen. Jersey, 1983, Cert. of Merit, 1979, Cert. of Appreciation for Vol. Svc., Rutgers Med. Sch. Community Adv. Bd., 1982, Equal Justice award Legal Svcs. N.J., 1990. Mem. Assn. Trial Lawyers Am., N.J. State Bar Assn., Middlesex County Bar Assn. (mem. judge's family law com.. Spl. Merit Recognition Vol. Atty. Program 1987-89), New Brunswick Bar Assn. Democrat. Jewish. Office: Miller & Littman PA 96 Paterson St New Brunswick NJ 08901-2175

LITWACK, GERALD, biochemistry educator, academic administrator; b. Boston, Jan. 11, 1929; s. David and Edith Jean (Berkman) Lytell; m. Patricia Lynn Gorog, Feb., 1956 (div. 1973); 1 child, Claudia; m. Ellen Judith Schatz, Aug. 31, 1973; children: Geoffrey Sandor, Katherine Victoria. BA, Hobart Coll., 1949; MS, U. Wis., 1950, PhD, 1953. Postdoctoral fellow Biochem. Labs. U. Paris, 1953-54; asst. prof. Rutgers U., New Brunswick, N.J., 1954-60; assoc. prof. U. Pa., Phila., 1960-64; Carnell prof., dep. dir. Fels Inst., Sch. of Medicine Temple U., Phila., 1964-91; prof., chair dept. pharmacology Thomas Jefferson U., Phila., 1991—, also dep. dir. Jefferson Cancer Inst., 1991—; chmn. adv. com. Am. Cancer Soc., N.Y.C., 1977-80; mem. adv. panel NSF, Washington, 1980-84; mem. ad hoc panels NIH, Bethesda, 1985, 89; councilor Soc. for Exptl. Biology and Medicine, N.Y.C., 1984-88. Author, co-author: Experimental Biochemistry, 1960, Hormones, 1987; editor: Biochemical Actions of Hormones, Vol. XIV, 1970-87, Receptor Purification, 1990; co-editor: Actions of Hormones on Molecular Processes, 1964; mem. editorial bd. Chemtracts, Cancer Communications, Cancer Rsch., Endocrinology, Anticancer Rsch.; editor-in-chief Jour. Receptor, 1990—. Recipient Pub. Svc. award Chapel of Four Chaplains, 1977. Home: 517 S Roberts Rd Bryn Mawr PA 19010-2034 Office: Thomas Jefferson U 10th & Locust Sts Philadelphia PA 19107

LITWAK, MANUEL, therapist, computer scientist; b. N.Y.C., May 10, 1938; s. Harry and Gertrude (Bergman) L.; m. Suzanne Tarazi, Aug. 9, 1987; 1 child, Jason Paul. BEE, CCNY, 1961; MEE, NYU, 1964; MS in Counseling, U. Bridgeport, 1981; PhD in Psychology, Union Inst., Cin., 1985. Planner IBM, Poughkeepsie, N.Y., 1964—; psychotherapist Fishkill (N.Y.) Cons. Group for Psychiatry and Psychology, 1986—; cons. Counseling Ctr. for Cancer and Meaninful Living, Poughkeepsie, N.Y., 1987-91. Cons. Parents Without Ptnrs., Poughkeepsie, 1982-87. Recipient Black Belt, World Tae Kwon Do Assn., N.Y.C., 1976. Mem. AACD, APA, Am. Guild of Hypnotherapists. Home: Grand Ave Poughkeepsie NY 12603-2304 Office: Fishkill Cons Group Fishkill NY 12524

LITZSINGER, ORVILLE JACK, aerospace executive; b. Richmond Heights, Mo., Sept. 11, 1936; s. Orville Frank and Irma Helen (Krisay) L.; m. Frances Elaine Shepard, June 14, 1958; children: Karen Elaine, Cheryl Denise. BS, U. Mo., 1958; MBA, Auburn U., 1972. Commd. USAF, 1958-82, advanced through grades to col., ret. 1982; ICBM program dir. USAF, Ogden, Utah, 1979-82; pres., cons. OJL Inc., Alexandria, Va., 1982-85, 92—; dir. Aerojet, Washington, 1985-92; cons. Textron, Titan Systems, Aerojet, Washington, 1982-85, NASA HQ, 1992. Pres. Clermont Woods Community Assn., Fairfax County, Va., 1980-81. Recipient Key to City of Omaha, 1967, City of San Bernardino, Calif., 1970. Mem. AIAA, Am. Space Transp. Assn. (bd. dirs. 1991—), Washington Space Bus. Roundtable, Air Force Assn. Home and Office: 5824 Wessex Ln Alexandria VA 22310-1437

LIU, CHARLES CHUNG-CHA, transportation engineer, consultant; b. Ping-Tung, Taiwan, Oct. 6, 1953; came to U.S., 1977; s. Lian-Chyan and Sheue-Er (Chen) L.; m. Ing-Ing Tsai, Aug. 19, 1979; children: Alexander Charles, Andrew Huey. BSCE, Nat. Taiwan U., 1975; MSCE, Purdue U., 1979, PhD, 1982. Registered profl. engr., Tenn. Instr. Chinese Army Engr. Sch., Taipei, Taiwan, 1975-77; grad. instr. Sch. Civil Engring. Purdue U., West Lafayette, Ind., 1977-82; asst. prof. civil engring. Tenn. State U., Nashville, 1982-84; chief engr. Allstar Engring. Internat., Inc., Annandale, Va., 1984—; prin. engr. SRA Techs., Inc., Alexandria, Va., 1984-89; on-site contract mgr. Turner-Fairbank Hwy. Research Ctr., Fed. Hwy. Adminstrn., McLean, Va., 1988—; dir. transp. engring. AEPCO, Inc., Rockville, Md., 1989—; cons. Cumberland Tectonics, Inc., Nashville, 1984, Engring. Directions Internat., Leesburg, Va., 1986—, UN Devel. Program People's Republic of China, 1991. Contbr. articles to profl. jours. Mem. ASCE (referee Jour. of Transp. Engring. 1989—), Inst. Transp. Engrs. (Past Pres.'s award 1988), Ops. Soc. Am., Sigma Xi, Omega Rho. Office: AEPCO Inc 15800 Crabbs Branch Way Ste 300 Rockville MD 20855-2604

LIU, PAMELA PEI-LING, graphic designer; b. Taipei, Taiwan, Republic of China, Jan. 31, 1951; came to U.S., 1968; d. Hoh-Tu and Julia C.Y. (Sheng) L. BS, Marywood Coll., 1972. Calligrapher Geyer Studio, N.Y.C., 1972-74; artist James Bell Graphic Design, N.Y.C., 1974-75; freelance artist, designer, art dir. N.Y.C., 1975-82; ptnr. Triptic Graphics Inc., N.Y.C., 1982-92; pres. LIU Communications & Design, Inc., N.Y.C., 1992—. Bd. dirs. N.Y. New Music Ensemble. Mem. NOW, Women in The Arts (charter), Smithsonian Inst., Nat. Geographic Soc., Cousteau Soc., Common Cause, China Inst. Am., Sierra Club. Office: LIU Communications & Design Inc 149 Wooster St New York NY 10012

LIU, RALPH YIEH-MIN, investment management and banking executive; b. Ping Tung, Republic of China, Aug. 24, 1958; came to U.S., 1983; s. Tseng-Pao and Man-Feng (Chang) L.; m. Laura Teresa Razzano, Dec. 23, 1988. BSE, Nat. Taiwan U., 1981; M ChemE, Rice U., 1984; postgrad., U. Mich., 1985; MBA, MSE, U. Pa., 1987; postgrad., NYU, 1989. Assoc. 1st Boston Corp., N.Y.C., 1986; investment rep. Morgan Stanley & Co., N.Y.C., 1987-89; pres. RYL Corp., N.Y.C., 1989—; currency options dealer Global Securities and Fgn. Exch., Chem. Banking Corp., N.Y.C., 1989-90; pres., chief exec. officer RYL Corp., N.Y.C., 1990—; treas. AT&T Capital Corp., Morristown, N.J., 1990-91; derivative products mgr., head trader Equitable Capital Mgmt. Corp., N.Y.C., 1991-92; v.p. trading, sales and risk mgmt. Union Bank of Switzerland, Singapore, 1992—. Author software Portfolio Analysis. Mem. coun. Fresh Air Fund, N.Y.C., 1988—, Fedn. Protestant Welfare Agys., N.Y.C., 1988—, Morris-Jumel Mansion, Inc., N.Y.C., 1992—. Rice U. fellow, 1983, Rackham grad. fellow U. Mich., 1984, IBM Mgmt. Info. fellow U. Pa., 1986. Mem. IEEE, Am. Inst. Chem. Engrs., Ops. Rsch. Soc. Am., Am. Mgmt. Soc., Asian Fin. Soc., Princeton Club, Wharton Bus. Sch. Club N.Y., Am. Stock Exch. Club. Home: 40 Cinnamon Tree Ln Berkeley Heights NJ 07922 Office: Union Bank of Switzerland 299 Park Ave New York NY 10171

LIVI, IVAN DAVID, educational administrator; b. Belle Vernon, Pa., June 17, 1920; s. Attilio Ausilio and Maria (Lazzari) L.; m. Annabelle Rigotti, Apr. 14, 1945; 1 child, Darla. Student, U. Pitts., 1958-64. Technician Mid-States Aviation, Northbrook, Ill., 1945-51; instr. Pitts. Inst. of Aero., 1951-54, dir. tng., 1954-64, v.p., 1964-72, exec. dir., 1972-78, pres., 1978—; pres. Aviation Tech. Edn. Coun., Harrisburg, Pa., 1975-77. Contbr. articles to profl. jours. Recipient Award of Excellence FAA, 1989, Clifford Ball award Aero Club of Pitts., 1990, Award of Excellence Profl. Aviation Maint. Assn., 1991. Mem. Pa. Assn. Pvt. Sch. Adminstrs. (pres. 1977-79). Home: 210 Melvin Dr Pittsburgh PA 15236-1432 Office: Pitts Inst Aero PO Box 10897 Pittsburgh PA 15236-0897

LIVINGSTON, COLLEEN M., psychiatrist; b. Ogdensburg, N.Y., May 2, 1946; d. Roy and Gloria (Morgan) L.; m. Clarence Henry Gratto, June 6, 1968; children: Christopher, Andre. AB, Cornell U., 1967; MD, SUNY, Buffalo, 1971. Diplomate Am. Bd. Psychiatry and Neurology. Resident in psychiatry Johns Hopkins U. Med. Sch., Balt., 1971-73; resident in psychiatry Yale U. Sch. Med., New Haven, 1973-74, fellow in community psychiatry, 1974-75; dir. edn. and tng. St. Lawrence Psychiat. Ctr., Ogdensburg, 1975-79; pvt. practice Ogdensburg, 1975-86, Canton, N.Y., 1986—; cons., staff psychiatrist Hepburn Hosp., Ogdensburg, 1976—; cons. in psychiatry St. Lawrence County Community Mental Health Ctr., Potsdam, N.Y., 1978-80, St. Lawrence U., Canton, 1982—, Vietnam Vets. Pathfinders Program, Canton, 1988—. Bd. dirs. Helping Hand, Canton, 1975-76, Curtis Hall-Jack and Jill Day Care Ctr., Ogdensburg, 1983-86; mem. adv. bd. SUNY Nursing Sch., Canton, 1978-83; elder 1st Presbyn. Ch., Ogdensburg, 1985-86. Fellow Am. Psychiat. Assn. (legis. rep. 1977); mem. AMA, Med. Soc. State N.Y., St. Lawrence County Med. Soc. (v.p. 1985-86, pres. 1986-87). Home: 2 Crary Dr Canton NY 13617-1003 Office: 80 E Main St Canton NY 13617-1450

LIVINGSTON, GIDEON ELEAZAR, food scientist, consultant; b. Rotterdam, The Netherlands, Feb. 1, 1927; came to U.S., 1940, naturalized, 1945; s. Morris S. and Rachel (Grunfeld) L.; m. Cilla Mahr, Sept. 18, 1948 (div. Apr. 1987); children: David J., Gary M., Nina J. Livingston Phillis; m. Joan Bendel Adams, July 13, 1991. B.A., NYU, 1948; M.S., U. Mass., 1951, Ph.D., 1952. Asst. prof. U. Mass. Amherst, 1951-53, assoc. prof., 1953-59; pres. Food Sci. Assocs., Dobbs Ferry, N.Y., 1956—; adj. prof. Columbia U., N.Y.C., 1966-72, Pratt Inst., Bklyn., 1972-78, NYU, N.Y.C., 1978—; chmn. food and nutrition council Am. Health Found., N.Y.C., 1970-91; bd. dirs. Sierra Sunset, Ins., 1988—, DeLuca Pasta co., 1987—, Mitchell Lane Kitchens, Inc., 1991—. Co-author: Food Service Systems: Analysis, Design and Implementation, 1979; editor: Nutritional Status Assessment of the Individual, 1989; co-editor: Role of Product Development in Implementing Dietary Guidelines, 1982; Environmental Aspects of Cancer, 1984. Served with U.S. Army, 1945-47, ETO. Recipient Research award U. Mass. chpt. Sigma Xi, 1957. Fellow Inst. Food Technologists (pres. N.Y. sect. 1969-70); mem. Am. Chem. Soc., Research Devel. Assocs. Avocation: running. Office: Food Sci Assocs Inc 110 Draper Ln Burlington VT 05401-4140

LIVINGSTON, GORDON STUART, psychiatrist; b. Memphis, June 30, 1938; s. Stanton Knowlton and Barbara (Keegan) L.; m. Katharine Stuart Lowry, Feb. 4, 1961 (div. June 1975); children: Kirsten, Nina, Michael; m. Clare Vickers King, Mar. 19, 1977; 1 child, Emily. BS, U.S. Mil. Acad., 1960; MD, Johns Hopkins U., 1967. Commd. 2nd lt. U.S. Army, 1960; intern Walter Reed Gen. Hosp. U.S. Army, Washington, 1967-68; regimental surgeon 11th Armored Cavalry Regiment U.S. Army, Vietnam, 1968-69; resigned U.S. Army, 1969; resident psychiatry Johns Hopkins Sch. Medicine, Balt., 1969-72; fellow in child psychiatry Johns Hopkins Sch. Medicine, 1972-74; psychiatrist Columbia Med. Plan, Columbia, Md., 1974-77; chief psychiatry Columbia Med. Plan, 1977—; asst. prof. psychiatry Johns Hopkins U. Sch. Medicine, Balt., 1972—. Contbr. articles to profl. jours. and newspapers. Mem. Am. Psychiat. Assn., Md. Regional Coun. on Child Psychiatry, AMA. Democrat. Home: 5993 The Bowl Columbia MD 21045-3830 Office: Columbia Med Plan Knoll North 2 Columbia MD 21045

LIVINGSTON, LEE FRANKLIN, recreation industry executive, real estate and finance consultant; b. Boston, Feb. 20, 1942; s. William and Frances (Turner) L.; m. Elaine Wiesenfeld, June 9, 1968; children: Eli, Jed. Student, Sch. Visual Arts, 1959-62, Georgetown U., 1964. With pub. rels. and promotion dept. Cowles Communications Co., N.Y.C., 1961-62, Newsweek, N.Y.C., 1965-70; exec. mng. dir., sec., treas. Carolier Lanes Inc., North Brunswick, N.J., 1970-79; mng. dir., sec., treas. Anasarca Corp., North Brunswick, 1971—; pres. Imperial Cons., Inc., 1971—; ptnr. Bess & Co., Phila. Stock Exch.; cons. on charitable fund raising to various charities, 1971—. Active charities for autistic children and retarded citizens, Spl. Olympics; bd. trustees, treas. Anshe Emeth Meml Temple. With C.E., U.S. Army, 1962-64. Recipient Am. Svc. award Girl Scouts U.S., Bronze Svc. award Spl. Olympics, Svc. award Spl. Edn., 1989, 91. Mem. N.J. Soc. for Retarded Citizens, Mu Sigma, Greenacres Country Club, Phila. Stock Exch. Club. Democrat. Home: 12 Derby Ln # 4 North Brunswick NJ 08902-4729 also: 3300 S Ocean Blvd Palm Beach FL 33480 Office: Carolier 790 US Hwy One North Brunswick NJ 08902

LIVINGSTON, ROBERT GERALD, university official, political scientist; b. N.Y.C., Nov. 17, 1927; s. Robert Teviot and Geraldine (Gray) L.; m. Jeanne Andrée Nettel, May 12, 1955; children: Catherine Schuyler Livingston Fernandez, Robert Eric. AB, Harvard U., 1953, AM, 1953, PhD, 1959. Fgn. svc. officer U.S. Dept. State, Washington, 1956-74; v.p. German Marshall Fund U.S., Washington, 1974-77, pres., 1977-81; writer Washington, 1981-83; acting dir. Am. Inst. for Contemporary German Studies, Johns Hopkins U., Washington, 1983-87, dir., 1987—; commentator Radio Saarbruecken (Fed.

Republic Germany), 1984—, BBC German Svc., London, 1986—, Deutschlandfunk, Cologne, 1991—. Co-author, editor: The Federal Republic in the 1980s, 1983, West German Political Parties, 1986; contbr. over 200 articles to polit. jours. and newspapers. Sgt. U.S. Army, 1946-49. Mem. Internat. Inst. for Strategic Studies, German Studies Assn. U.S., Coun. on Fgn. Rels., N.Y. Soc. Sons of Cincinnati, Cosmos Club, Chevy Chase Club, Barnstable Yacht Club (Mass.), Phi Beta Kappa. Democrat. Episcopalian. Office: Am Inst Contemporary German Studies 11 Dupont Cir NW Ste 350 Washington DC 20036

LIVINGSTON, WILLIAM LAFAYETTE, mechanical engineer; b. Bklyn., Nov. 4, 1932; s. William Lafayette and Gladys Irene (Hopkins) L.; m. Hattie June Harwood, Dec. 23, 1955 (dec. 1981); children: Carole, William, Sarah; m. Carolyn Bonnie Crosby, May 19, 1984. BSME, Rutgers U., 1954. Registered profl. engr., Mass. Engr. Combustion Engring., Windsor, Conn., 1954-64; design supr. Honeywell, Mpls., 1964-66; projects mgr. FM Rsch. Corp., Norwood, Mass., 1966-73; cons. engr. EBASCO, N.Y.C., 1973—; editor F.E.S. Pub., N.Y.C., 1981—; cons. R.A. Whitney & Co., West Orange, N.J., 1989—. Author: The New Plague, 1986, Have Fun at Work, 1988, Friends in High Places, 1990; patentee in field. Mem. ASME, N.Y. Acad. Sci., Internat. Soc. of Systems, Profl. Reactor Operator Soc., Soc. of Profl. Engrs. Lutheran. Home: 35-24 211 St Bayside NY 11361 Office: EBASCO 2 World Trade Ctr New York NY 10048

LIVINGSTONE, HARRISON EDWARD, author; b. Urbana, Ill., May 23, 1937; s. Harry E. and Elsie (Harrison) L. BA, Harvard U., 1970; JD, U. Balt., 1963. Pres., owner The Conservatory Press, Balt., 1976—. Author: High Treason 2, 1992 (N.Y. Times Bestseller), High Treason, 1989 (N.Y. Times Bestseller), Harvard John, 1987, The Wild Rose, 1985, David Johnson Passed Through Here, 1971; author numerous poems. Cert. of Honor Balt. City Police, 1964. Office: The Conservatory Press PO Box 7149 Baltimore MD 21218

LIVOLSI, VIRGINIA ANNE, pathologist; b. N.Y.C., July 29, 1943; d. Epifanio and Mary Ann (LaPorta) LiV. BS cum laude, Coll. Mt. St. Vincent, N.Y.C., 1965; MD, Columbia U., 1969; MA honoris cause, U. Pa., 1983. Instr. pathology Columbia U., N.Y.C., 1973-74; attending pathologist Yale-New Haven Hosp., 1974-83; asst. prof. Yale U. Sch. Medicine, 1974-79, assoc. prof., 1979-83; dir. cytology Yale U., 1975-77; dir. surg. pathology Hosp. U. Pa., Phila., 1983—, prof. pathology, 1983—; cons. in pathology Chester County Hosp., 1985—, VA Med. Ctr., 1988-90. Mem. U.S. and Can. Acad. Pathology, Am. Soc. Clin. Pathologists (abstract rev. com. 1991—), Arthur Purdy Stout Soc. Surg. Pathologists (sec. 1987—), Am. Thyroid Assn., Coll. Am. Pathologists, Assn. Dirs. Anatomic and Surg. Pathology. Office: Hosp U Pa 3400 Spruce St # F6042 Philadelphia PA 19104-4220

LIZANICH-ARO, SUZANNE, health care consultant; b. Newark, Sept. 17, 1953; d. Frank and Natalie Ann (Kotch) L.; m. Karl Stephen Aro, July 1, 1978; 1 child, Stephen Christopher. AAS in Nursing, County Coll. Morris, 1973; BA in English, Fairleigh Dickinson U., 1975; MA in Am. Studies, Seton Hall U., 1976; MPH in Health Svcs. Adminstrn., Johns Hopkins U., 1982. RN, Md., D.C., N.J. Relief charge nurse, staff nurse Dover (N.J.) Gen. Hosp., 1973-76; student health nurse Student Health Ctr. Fairleigh Dickinson U., Madison, N.J., 1973-75; chief occupational health nurse Nat. Health Svcs., Inc., Washington, 1976-77; community health nurse Vis. Nurse Assn., Washington, 1977-78; program asst., ambulatory care mgr. Nat. Capital Med. Found., Inc., Washington, 1978-81; program mgr., project mgr., rev. specialist United Mineworkers Health & Retirement Funds, Washington, 1982-85; dir. utilization rev. Am. PsychMgmt. Inc., Washington, 1985-86; health systems cons. SLA Cons., Inc., Silver Spring, Md., 1986—; program devel. cons. Green Spring Mental Health Svcs., Columbia, Md., 1989—; system design cons. Medecision Inc., Paoli, Pa., 1987—. Mem. APHA. Office: SLA Cons Inc 1008 Balmoral Dr Silver Spring MD 20903-1303

LLEWELLYN, IRENE BEATRICE, educator; b. Hartford, Conn., May 5, 1940; d. Alvin Bernard and Margaret Beatrice (Morris) Wood; m. Basil A. Llewellyn, Aug. 14, 1965 (div. 1978); 1 child, Sheryl Anne. BS, Boston U., 1962; MS, U. Hartford, 1969; postgrad., Cen. Conn. State U., 1988. Tchr. Metacomet Sch., Bloomfield, Conn., 1962-71; tchr. computers Bloomfield Adult Edn., 1983-85; tchr. Laurel Sch., Bloomfield, 1971—. Author computer curriculum: Introduction to Computers, 1984; co-author Laurel Sch. Parent Handbook, 1991. Panelist, Oak Park Exchange Congress, Bloomfield, 1983; mem. Cicusa Club Scholarship Com., Hartford, 1983—, Union Bapt. Ch. Scholarship Com., 1981—; bd. dirs. Bloomfield Early Learning Ctr., 1973-76; chmn. Laurel Sch. Multicultural Interdisciplinary Com., 1990—. Named Bloomfield Tchr. of Yr., 1985, Conn. Educator, Nat. Educator award award Milken Family Found., 1991. Mem. NEA, Bloomfield Edn. Assn. (rep.-at-large), Conn. Edn. Assn., N.E. Coalition Ednl. Ldrs., Inc., Links Inc., Cicuso Club, Alpha Kappa Alpha (edn. com.), Iota Phi Lambda (Apple for Tchr. award 1989). Democrat. Baptist. Home: 7 Alexander Rd Bloomfield CT 06002-2857 Office: Bloomfield Bd of Edn 1 Filley St Bloomfield CT 06002-1855

LLEWELLYN, JOHN SCHOFIELD, JR., food company executive; b. Amsterdam, N.Y., Jan. 10, 1935; s. John S. and Dorothea (Breedon) L.; m. Mary Martha Pallotta, June 9, 1962; children: Mary M., John S. III, Robert J., James P., Timothy J. AB, Holy Cross Coll., 1956; MBA, Harvard U., 1961. With mktg. Gen. Foods Corp., White Plains, N.Y., 1961-69, Sunshine Biscuit div. Am. Brands, N.Y.C., 1973-77; exec. v.p. Morton Frozen Foods div. ITT Continental Baking Co., Charlottesville, Va., 1977-79; gen. mgr. Continental Kitchens ITT Continental Baking Co., Rye, 1980-81; sr. v.p. Ocean Spray Cranberries Inc., Plymouth, Mass., 1982-86; exec. v.p., chief operating officer Ocean Spray Cranberries Inc., Plymouth, 1986-87, pres., chief exec. officer, 1988—. Trustee Derby Acad., Hingham, Mass., 1984—, St. Sebastian's Country Day Sch., Needham, Mass., 1991—; bd. dirs. Mass. Environ. Trust, 1991—. Capt. USMC, 1957-63. Mem. Nat. Food Processors Assn. (bd. dirs., exec. com., vice chmn.). Roman Catholic. Home: Steamboat Ln Hingham MA 02043-1928 Office: Ocean Spray Cranberries Inc 1 Ocean Spray Dr Middleboro MA 02349-1000

LLOYD, JOHN EUGENE, manufacturing executive; b. Tucson, Ariz., Jan. 11, 1940; s. Burton Lewis and Beuluh Grace (Gibson) L.; m. Patsy Jo Weaver, June, 1959 (div. Feb., 1992); children: Sandra Lee Quigley, Jeffrey Burton, John Jr., Omer L. Grad. high sch., Flint, Mich., 1958. Night mgr. Midway Enterprises, Dandalk, Md., 1959-62; machine operator Bremner Biscuit Co., Balt., 1962-63; packaging mechanic E.H. Koester Bakery, Balt., 1963-67; plant & corp. engr. H&S Bakery Inc., Balt., 1967-73; bakery equipment cons. Adam Equipment Corp., Belmar, N.J., 1973-74; dir. sales ops. Adam Equipment Corp., Eatontown, N.J., 1981-85; v.p. ops. Sur Flo Silo Mfg. Corp., Eatontown, N.J., 1974-81; dir. tech. ops. Gemini Bakery Equipment, Phila., 1985—; design cons. MTV, Bantln, Fed. Republic Germany, 1974-80; cons. Oshikiri Machinery Ltd., Tokyo, 1985-88, Oshikiri Corp. Am., Phila., 1988—. Home: 10300 Clark St Philadelphia PA 19116-3816 Office: Gemini Bakery Equipment 9990 Gantry Rd Philadelphia PA 19115-1097

LLOYD, JUNE DICKSON, vocational educator; b. Monaca, Pa., June 17, 1936; d. Harry Ross and Mabel Pearl (Yoho) Dickson; m. William Howard Lloyd, Sr., Jan. 24, 1957; children: Kathleen Gay, William Howard Jr., Richard Lewellyn. BS in Home Econs., Carnegie Mellon U., 1971; MEd in Vocat. Edn., U. Pitts., 1976. Cert. home econ. tchr., vocat. tchr. Instr. Pitts. Sch. Dist., 1973—; sec. Future Directions Task Force, Home Econ. in Pa., 1990-91; trainer Pa. Home Econs. Leadership Training, 1991. Mem. league of Women Voters, Churchill, Pa., 1965-70; chmn. PTA, Churchill, 1968-80, Beulah Women's Orgn., Churchill, 1968-80. Recipient grant Pa. Dept. Edn., 1987-88. Mem. Am. Vocat. Assn., Am. Home Econs. Assn., Pa. Vocat. Assn. (bd. dirs. 1990-91), Pa. Home Econs. Assn. (pres. 1989-91), Phi Delta Kappa, Kappa Omicron Phi. Home: 914 Treasure Lk Du Bois PA 15801-9023 Office: Schenley High Tchrs Ctr 4410 Bigelow Blvd Pittsburgh PA 15213-2661

LLOYD, MARKLAND GALE, health facility administrator; b. Troy, Ohio, Sept. 1, 1948; s. Solomon Garfield and Melba D. (Fisher) L.; m. Therese L. Heretick, Sept. 4, 1971; children: Brian, Maegan. BA, Wittenberg U., 1970; MA, Ohio U., 1971, PhD, 1975. Asst. prof. Augusta (Ga.) Coll., 1975-79; dir. community rels. St. Joseph's Hosp., Parkersburg, W.Va., 1979-82; mgr. pub. affairs Geisinger Med. Ctr., Danville, Pa., 1982-85; v.p. corp. communication Geisinger System Svcs., Danville, 1985—. Editor Geisinger Mag., 1982 (award 1983). Dir. Diocesan Pastoral Coun., Diocese of Harrisburg, Pa., 1988—; mem. parish coun. St. Columba Parish, Bloomsburg, Pa., 1986, 87; pres. sch. bd. St. Columba Sch., Bloomsburg, 1988, 89; bd. dirs. YMCA, Bloomsburg, 1987, Danville Revitalization Authority, 1991—. Recipient Silver Touchstone, Am. Soc. Hosp. Mktg. and Pub. Rels., 1989, MacEachern award Pub. Rels. Soc. Am., 1987; named Best in East, Va. Soc. Healthcare Mktg., 1984, 85. Mem. Am. Mktg. Assn., Am. Soc. Hosp. Mktg. and Pub. Rels. (Gold Touchstone 1984, Silver Touchstone 1989, regional coun. 1989), Pub. Rels. & Mktg. Soc. (pres. 1989). Roman Catholic. Office: Corp Communication GSS Geisinger Office Bldg Danville PA 17822-3013

LLOYD, ROBERT ALBERT, foundation administrator; b. Pitts., Apr. 21, 1930; s. Robert Morgan and Martha Elizabeth (Sauter) L.; student Carnegie Mellon U., 1948, 50, 51. Adminstrv. supr. Pitts. Inf. Sch., USAR, 1951-71; ret., 1971; asst. mgr. meml. dept. Sears Roebuck & Co., Pitts., 1960-71, mem. staff 1971-91, ret. Chmn. Boro of Dormont (Pa.) Rep. Com., 1974-76, committeeman 7th Dist., Allegheny County, 1970-76; bd. dirs., v.p. Concerned Citizens of Dormont Boro Inc., 1982—. With USAR, 1951-90. Recipient Good Citizenship medal SAR, 1943; Legion of Honor, Order of DeMolay; named Warrior Apache Nation, 1984. Mem. NAACP, VFW, Hist. Soc. We. Pa., Assn. U.S. Army, Am. Soc. Notaries, Pa. Assn. Notaries, Nat. Rifle Assn., Vietnam Vets., Inc., Nat. Assn. Uniformed Services, Am. Legion, Sons. of Union Vets. of Civil War, Pitts. History and Landmarks Found., Fraternal Order Police (assoc.), Allegheny Club, Masons, K.T. (life sponsor Eye Found.), Knights of Malta, Elks, Moose, Shriners (Legion of Honor). Presbyterian. Home: 3089 Pinehurst Ave Pittsburgh PA 15216-2434

LLOYD-DAVIES, PETER R., economist; b. Ashridge, Herts., U.K., Nov. 18, 1943; s. John Robert and Margery (McClelland) Lloyd-D.; m. Karen Sagstetter, 1969 (div.); m. Louise M. Lynch, Aug. 28, 1982. BA, Oxford U., Eng., 1965; MA, McMaster U., Hamilton, Ont., 1966; PhD, Rice U., Houston, 1970. Asst. prof. Baruch Coll., CUNY, 1970-72, U. Rochester, 1972-76; sr. economist Fed. Res. Bd., Washington, 1976-86; dir., v.p. fin. research Freddie Mac, Reston, Va., 1986-91; dir. rsch. Trepp & Bergman, Inc., N.Y.C., 1991—. Contbr. articles to profl. jours. Home: 25 Glen Eagles Dr 2012 Virginia Ave Larchmont NY 10538 Office: Trepp & Bergman Inc 477 Madison Ave 18th Fl New York NY 10022

LO, CHU SHEK, medical physiology educator; b. Hong Kong, Nov. 8, 1936; came to U.S., 1962; s. Hong Yuen and Miu Ling (Wong) L.; m. Theresa L. Nong, Dec. 27, 1969; 1 child, Francesca C. BS, Nat. Taiwan U., Taipei, 1962; MS, U. Notre Dame, 1965; PhD, Ind. U., Indpls., 1972. NIH postdoctoral trainee U. Calif., San Francisco, 1972-75; asst. prof. med. physiology Sch. Med., U. Md., Balt., 1975-77; asst. prof. Uniformed Svcs. U. Health Scis., Bethesda, Md., 1977-81, assoc. prof., 1981—; guest worker NIDDK/NIH, Bethesda, 1976-78; Sidney C. Werner lectr. Columbia U., N.Y.C., 1980; participant sci. exch. with Switzerland, Roche Rsch. Found., 1976. Co-contbr. articles to Jour. Biol. Chemistry, Am. Jour. Physiology. Mem. peer rev. subcom., mem. rsch. com., mem. coun. on circulation Md. affiliate Am. Heart Assn., Balt., 1990—; active Orgn. Chinese Ams., Md., 1984—. Grantee Md. affiliate Am. Heart Assn., 1976, 89, NIH, 1981. Mem. Am. Physiol. Soc., Biophys. Soc., Am. Soc. for Cell Biology, Soc. Chinese Bioscientists in Am. Office: Uniformed Svcs U Health Scis Dept Physiology 4301 Jones Bridge Rd Bethesda MD 20814-4799

LO, RON, system engineer; b. Taipei, Taiwan, Republic of China, July 8, 1956; came to U.S., 1980; s. Chi-Sun and Hsiu-Fun (Hu) Lo; m. Cher Yee-Gu Liu, June 29, 1980; children: Daniel, Mary, David. BS, Tamkang U., 1978; MS, SUNY, Buffalo, 1982; PhD, Ariz. State U., 1988. Grad. asst. SUNY, 1980-81, rsch. asst., 1981-82; rsch. assoc. Ariz. State U., Tempe, 1982-85, teaching assoc., 1985-87; mem. tech. staff AT&T Bell Labs., Holmdel, N.J., 1988—. Contbr. articles to profl. jours. Mem. Monmouth Chinese Christian Fellowship, Upsilon Pi Epsilon. Home: 10 Knollwood Rd Holmdel NJ 07733 Office: AT&T Bell Labs Crawfords Corner Rd RM 2M613 Holmdel NJ 07733

LOACH, KENNETH WILLIAM, chemistry educator; b. Portsmouth, Eng., Sept. 5, 1934; s. William Alfred Francis and Josephine Kathleen (Wilkes) L.; m. Sandra Kendis Miller, June 11, 1966; children: Matthew William, Catherine Genna. BS, Auckland Univ., New Zealand, 1956, MS, 1958; PhD, U. Wash., 1969. Analytical chemist Ruakura Animal Rsch. Sta., Hamilton, New Zealand, 1958-60, C.S.I.R.O. Div. Plant Industry, Canberra, Australia, 1960-63; teaching asst. U. Wash., Seattle, 1963-69; asst. prof. SUNY, Plattsburgh, 1969-75, assoc. prof., 1975—. Office: SUNY Dept Chemistry Plattsburgh NY 12901

LOBBAN, RICHARD ANDREW, JR., anthropologist, educator; b. Balt., Nov. 3, 1943; s. Richard Andrew and Dorothy (Dietz) L.; m. Carolyn Fluehr, Aug. 31, 1968; children: Josina, Nichola. BS in Biology, Bucknell U., 1966; MA in Anthropology, Temple U., 1968; PhD in Anthropology, Northwestern U., 1973. Prof. anthropology R.I. Coll., Providence, 1972—; tchr. Dartmouth U., Am. U. in Cairo, U. Pitts., U. Khartoum, U. Ill., Bucknell U.; head urban devel. unit Am. U. Cairo, 1982-84; dir. program African and Afro-Am. studies R.I. Coll., 1985-90. Author: Historical Dictionary of Cape Verde, 1979, of Guinea-Bissau, 1988, of Sudan, 1991; Urban Research in Egypt, 1983. Fellow Am. Anthrop. Assn., Soc. Applied Anthropology; mem. Sudan Studies Assn. (pres. 1980-81), Middle East Studies Assn. (chair Kerr award com.), African Studies Assn. (chair Herskovits award com.). Office: R I Coll 600 Mt Pleasant Ave Providence RI 02908-1924

LOBO, ANGELO PETER, synthetic chemist, researcher; b. Masindi, Uganda, May 19, 1939; came to U.S., 1960; s. Thomas Joseph and Mary Malagrina (Siqueira) L.; m. Victoria Kam Hau Leong, Sept. 9, 1967; children: Stephen, Michael. BSc, U. Bombay, 1958; PhD, Ind. U., 1966. Spl. lectr. in organic chemistry Makerere U. Coll., Kampala, Uganda, 1966-68; Rockefeller Found. postdoctoral fellow Rensselaer Poly. Inst., Troy, N.Y., 1968-70; rsch. scientist Wadsworth Ctr. for Labs. & Rsch., Albany, N.Y., 1970—. Mem. Am. Chem. Soc. Home: 25 Milner Ave Albany NY 12203-2021 Office: NY State Dept Health Wadsworth Ctr of Labs/Rsch Empire State Plz Albany NY 12201

LOBRON, BARBARA L., writer, editor, photographer; b. Phila., Mar. 19, 1944; d. Martin Aaron and Elizabeth (Gots) L.; student Pa. State U., 1962-63; B.A. cum laude, Temple U., Phila., 1966; student photography Harold Feinstein, N.Y.C., 1970, 79-80. Reporter, writer Camden (N.J.) Courier-Post, 1966-68; editorial asst. Med. Insight mag., N.Y.C., 1970-71; mng. editor Camera 35 mag., N.Y.C., 1971-75, also asso. editor photog. anns. for U.S. Camera/Camera 35, 1972, 73; freelance editor as Word Woman, N.Y.C., 1975-77, 79—; acct. exec. Bozell & Jacobs, N.Y.C., 1977-79; copy editor Camera Arts mag., N.Y.C., 1981-83; editorial coord. Center mag., Nat. Ctr. Health Edn., 1985; editorial coord. Popular Photography mag., 1986—; contbg. editor Photograph; photographer, group exhbns. include: Photograph Gallery, N.Y.C., 1981, Rockefeller Center, N.Y.C., 1976, Internat. Women's Art Festival, N.Y.C., 1975; represented in collection Library of Calif. Inst. Arts, Valencia. Recipient 1st pl. honors Dist. 1, Internat. Assn. Bus. Communicators, 1977. Copy editor: Camera Arts, 1981-83, The Complete Guide to Cibachrome Printing, 1980, The Popular Photography Question and Answer Book, 1979, The Photography Catalog, 1976, Strand: Sixty Years of Photography, 1976, You and Your Lens, 1975; contbr. articles to comml. publs., chpts. to books. Mem. NAFE. Buddhist. Avocations: acting, ballroom dancing, reading. Home: 85 Hicks St Apt 7 Brooklyn NY 11201-6825

LOBSENZ, AMELIA, public relations executive; b. Greensboro, N.C.; d. Leo and Florence (Scheer) Freitag; m. Harry Abrahams, Aug. 17, 1957; children: Michael, Kay. BA, Agnes Scott Coll., 1944. Dir. mag. dept. Edward Gottlieb & Assocs., N.Y.C., 1952-56; pres. Lobsenz Pub. Rels. Co., N.Y.C., 1956-75; chmn. bd., chief exec. officer Lobsenz-Stevens Inc., N.Y.C., 1975—; pres. Pinnacle Group Cos., 1983-84, chmn., 1985-86, chmn. internat. affairs, 1986—; mem. bd. advisors, bd. dirs. Mercomm Inc.; lectr. in field. Author: Kay Everett Calls CQ, 1951 (Jr. Lit. Guild Selection), Kay Everett Works DX, 1952; contbr. 300 articles to profl. mags. Bd. govs. Nat. Women's Econ. Alliance. Recipient award for best article on ins. Mag. Writers, 1974; named to Acad. Women Achievers YWCA, 1978. Fellow Pub. Rels. Soc. Am. (accredited, bd. dirs. N.Y. chpt. 1971-79, chmn. nat. com. pub. rels. 1977-79, nat. bd. dirs. 1980-81, pres.' adv. com. 1988, Pres.' awards for outstanding svc. 1975-79); mem. Am. Soc. Journalists and Authors, Am. Med. Writers Assn., Am. Women in Radio and TV, Nat. Assn. Sci. Writers, Internat. Pub. Rels. Assn. (bd. mgmt. 1984-85, pres. 1986), Nat. Women's Econ. Alliance (bd. dirs.), Overseas Press Club, Racquet Club Old Westbury, Cornell Club (spl. events com. 1991). Office: 460 Park Ave S New York NY 10016-7315

LOBUR, JULIA MARIE, computer systems analyst, state official; b. New Kensington, Pa., Feb. 25, 1955; d. John and Anna Julianna (Surowski) L. AA, Harrisburg (Pa.) Area Community Coll., 1992; student, Pa. State Univ., 1991—. Computer systems analyst Pa. Dept. Transp., Harrisburg, 1986—. Recipient Sec.'s quar. award for excellence Pa. Dept. Transp., 1989. Mem. Math. Assn. Am., Am. Statis. Assn., Phi Theta Kappa. Home: 210 Harris St Harrisburg PA 17102-2430 Office: Pa Dept Transp Bur Constrn and Materials 1118 State St Harrisburg PA 17101-2417

LOCHER, MARIANNE, business development professional; b. Washington, Oct. 27, 1959; d. Paul R. and Anne (Farrelly) L. BA cum laude, Rosemont Coll., 1981; Cert., N.Y. Sch. Interior Design, 1986; MFA, Columbia U., 1989. Asst. to dir. of mktg. Sotheby's, N.Y.C., 1983-85; spl. asst. to pres. Asprey, N.Y.C., 1985-88; asst. to exec. dir. Assoc. Art Mus. Dirs., N.Y.C., 1988-89; dir. communications Paul Segal Assocs., Architects, N.Y.C., 1989; bus. devel. profl. Archtl. Interiors, Washington, 1991-92; bus. devel. cons. Kentfield, Calif., 1992—. Mem. Delta Epsilon Sigma.

LOCHHEAD, JACK VAN SLYKE, educator, director; b. Burlington, Vt., June 7, 1944; s. John Hutchison and Margit (Szabo) L.; m. Danielle Naomi Garrick, June 10, 1967. BA in Physics, Johns Hopkins U., 1966; MS in Physics, U. Mass., 1969, EdD, 1973. Dir. cognitive devel. project U. Mass., Amherst, 1976-88, dir. sci. reasoning rsch. inst., 1988—; dir. programs Ventures in Edn., N.Y., 1991—; adj. assoc. prof. dept. psychology U. Mass., 1987—. Author: (with others) Cognitive Process Instruction, 1979, Developing Mathematical Skills, 1980, Beyond Problem Solving and Comprehension, 1982, Problem Solving & Comprehension, 4th edit., 1986. Schumann fellow Harvard U., 1988-89. Office: U Mass 314 Hasbrouck Lab Amherst MA 01003

LOCHMAN, WILLIAM HERSHEY, JR., banking executive; b. Reading, Pa., July 31, 1947; s. William Hershey and June Lorainne (Segler) L.; m. Loretta Bianco, Sept. 13, 1980; children: Matthew Hershey, Dana Marie. BS in Psychology, Kutztown (Pa.) U., 1969; MS in Indsl. Rels., Saint Frances Coll., Loretto, Pa., 1979. Sales rep. Syntex Labs., Palo Alto, Calif., 1970-72; employment counselor S.H.S. Internat., Hamsburg, Pa., 1972-73; asst. personnel mgr. CCNB Bank, N.A., New Cumberland, Pa., 1973-76, personnel dept. head, 1976-82, v.p. human resources, 1982-87; sr. v.p. corp. svcs. CCNB Bank, N.A., Camphill, Pa., 1987—. With U.S. Army, 1969-75. Mem. Capital Area C. of C., Am. Inst. Banking (bd. dirs., chair, pres., v.p.), Adminstrv. Mgmt. Soc., Opportunities Industrialization Ctr. (treas., bd. dirs.), Soc. for Human Resources Mgmt., Harrisburg Area Personnel Assn., Bank Mktg. Assn., Pa. Employer Adv. Coun. (chair). Office: CCNB Bank NA 4242 Carlisle Pike Camp Hill PA 17011-4158

LOCHTENBERG, BERNARD HENDRIK, chemical company executive; b. Singapore, Mar. 10, 1931; came to U.S., 1979; s. Jan Bernard and Anna Lochtenberg; m. Margaret Lynch, June 16, 1956; children: Jan, Anna, Mark, Michael, Benedict, Margaret, Lucy. B.Engring., U. Western Australia, 1953; D. Phil., Oxford U., 1956. Planning and devel. mgr. ICI Australia, Melbourne, 1971-73; dir. plastics div. ICI PLC Welwyn Garden City, Eng., 1973-79; sr. v.p. ICI Americas, Inc., Wilmington, Del., 1979-88; prin. exec. officer ICI Splty. Chems., Wilmington, 1984-88; pres., chief exec. officer C-I-L, Inc., North York, Ont., Can., 1988—; chmn. ICI Ams. Inc., ICI Can., 1989—; also bd. dirs. Trustee Wilmington Med. Ctr., 1980-88, Sanford Sch., Hockessin, Del., 1982-88. Australian Rhodes scholar, 1954-56. Fellow Plastics and Rubber Inst.; mem. Soc. Chem. Industry, CMA (bd. dirs.), Leander Rowing Club, Greenville Country Club. Office: ICI Ams Inc PO Box 751 Wilmington DE 19897-0001

LOCKE, HAROLD OGDEN, chemist; b. Camden, N.J., Sept. 14, 1931; s. Harold Glenwood and Grace Reynolds (Ogden) L.; m. Elizabeth Janet Bellmer, Aug. 22, 1959; children: Bruce Charles, David Edward. BA, Wesleyan U., Middletown, Conn., 1953, MA, 1955; PhD, Rutgers U., 1962. Chemist Armstrong Cork Co., Lancaster, Pa., 1961-65; analytical chemist GAF Corp., Wayne, N.J., 1965—. Patentee on insoluble vinyl lactam clarifiers. With U.S. Army, 1958. Mem. ASTM (vice chmn. com. D12.12, 1976—), Am. Chem. Soc. Republican. Episcopalian. Home: 816 Prince St Easton PA 18042-2435 Office: GAF Corp 1361 Alps Rd Wayne NJ 07470-3700

LOCKE, JOHN WILLIAM, association executive; b. La Salle, Ill., Jan. 27, 1933; s. George Ferguson and Blanche Elizabeth (Shilling) L.; m. Margaret Mary Kincius, July 9, 1955; children: William, Barbara, Louise, Jean, Mary, Jim. BS in Aero. Engring., U. Ill., 1955. Cert. safety profl., quality auditor. Aerodynamicist McDonnell Aircraft, St. Louis, Mo., 1955-62; rsch. dir. Booz Allen, Bethesda, Md., 1962-66; v.p. NUS, Washington, 1966-68; project mgr. Nat. Bur. Standards, Gaithersburg, Md., 1968-72, dir. lab. accreditation, 1978-85; assoc. dir. Bur. Product Safety, FDA, Washington, 1972-73; exec. dir. Consumer Product Safety Commn., Washington, 1973; tech. dir. Can Mfrs. Inst., Washington, 1973-78; pres. Am. Assn. Lab. Accreditation, Gaithersburg, 1986—. Deacon local Roman Cath. Ch. Recipient Bronze medal Nat. Bur. Standards, Gaithersburg, 1984. Mem. ASTM (chmn. com. F-15 on product safety 1979-85, Margaret Dana award 1985, chmn. com. E 36 on lab. accreditation 1985-91). Republican. Office: Am Assn Lab Accreditation 656 Quince Orchard Rd # 304 Gaithersburg MD 20878-1409

LOCKE, RALPH P., music educator; b. Boston, Mar. 9, 1949; s. Merle Irving Locke and Doris Helen (Tobis) Schwartz; m. Lona Miriam Farhi, May 27, 1979; children: Martha, Susannah. BA cum laude, Harvard U., 1970; MA, U. Chgo., 1974, PhD, 1980. From instr. to prof. Eastman Sch. Music, Rochester, N.Y., 1975—. Author: Music, Musicians and the Saint-Simonians; contbg. author: Mendelssohn and Schumann Essays (Todd and Finson), 1984, Music in Paris in the 1830s (Bloom), 1987, Music and Society: The Early Romantic Era (Alexander Ringer), 1991, Royal Opera House Covent Garden Program Book, 1991—; contbr. articles to New Grove Dictionary, New Harvard Dictionary, scholarly jours.; composer, condr. Mother Courage, Loeb Drama Ctr., Cambridge, Mass., 1969; guest condr. Esterhazy Chamber Ensemble, 1985-88. Recipient award Govt. of France, 1975, Marc Perry Galley prize U. Chgo., 1981, Best Article award, 1982; fellow Am. Coun. Learned Socs., 1984. Mem. Am. Musicological Soc. (program com. 1983-84, council mem. 1985-88). Office: Eastman Sch Music 26 Gibbs St Rochester NY 14604-2599

LOCKE, STANLEY, mathematician; b. N.Y.C., June 18, 1934; s. Emmanuel and Ida (Pollack) L.; m. Jane Laura Hershkowitz, Dec. 20, 1958; children: Cathy-Lynn, Peter Stuart, Ilene Jill. B of Mech. Engring., NYU, 1955, MS in Math., 1957, PhD in Math., 1960. Prin. engr. Schlumberger Doll Rsch., Ridgefield, Conn., 1960-88; consulting engr. Teleco Oilfield Svcs., Inc., Meriden, Conn., 1988—. Patentee in field; contbr. articles to profl. jours. Mem. IEEE (sr.), Sigma Xi. Home: 17 Deerwood Ct Norwalk CT 06851-2605

LOCKE BERGER, KATHLEEN CAROL, micrographics service bureau executive; b. Wakefield, Mass., Feb. 6, 1963; d. Birtley Quentin and Virginia Faye (Russell) Locke; m. Timothy Berger, June 22, 1990. BS, Plymouth (N.H.) State Coll., 1985. In sales Am. Computer Group, Boston, 1985-87; pres. Info. Svcs. Inc., Derry, N.H., 1987—; cons. NEC Techs. Inc., Boxborough, N.H., 1989-91. Mem. NAFE, Assn. for Info. and Image Mgmt., Assn. for Record Mgrs. Office: Info Svcs Inc 2 Treasure Ln Derry NH 03038

LOCKMAN, NORMAN ALTON, newspaper editor, journalist; b. West Chester, Pa., July 11, 1938; s. Norman James Lockman and Olive (Whyte) Lockman; m. Virginia Trainer; children: Holly Beth, Carey Paige, Sarah Elizabeth. Student, Pa. State U, 1957; Grad., U.S. Army Info. Sch., Ft. Slocum, N.Y., 1964. Govt. editor The News Journal Papers, Wilmington, Del., 1970-73, Washington corr., 1973-75, mng. editor, 1984-90, assoc. ed., 1990—; state house reporter The Boston Globe, 1975-79, editorial bd., 1979-81, state house bur. chief, 1981-84. Served with USAF, 1961-65. Recipient Pulitzer prize in Journalism, 1984. Mem. Nat. Press Club, Nat. Assn. Black Journalists. Office: News Jour PO Box 15505 Wilmington DE 19850-5505

LOCKWOOD, HELSHI, advertising executive; b. East Orange, N.J., May 18, 1941; d. Warren Sewell and Ann Frances (Gleason) L.; m. Bertram A. Tunnell Jr., Dec. 13, 1969 (div. Oct. 1976); children: Bertram A. III, Tory Lockwood; m. William B. Hewson Jr., May 30, 1981; 1 child, Charles W.; stepchildren: William B. III, Andrew L., Elizabeth S. BA, Pa. State U., 1963. Promotion asst. Vogue Mag., London, 1963-64; advt. sales rep. Brides Mag., London, 1964-65; west coast mgr. Status Mag., L.A., 1965-67; asst. advt. mgr. Status Mag., N.Y.C., 1968-69; advt. sales rep. Eye Mag., N.Y.C., 1967-68; N.Y. mgr. Phil. and Boston Mags., N.Y.C., 1969-76; v.p. Metro Mag., N.Y.C., 1976-78; exec. v.p., ptnr. Catalyst Communications, N.Y.C., 1978-80; account mgr. Dun's Rev., N.Y.C., 1980-82; ea. advt. dir. Dun's Bus. Month, N.Y.C., 1982-84, advt. dir., 1984-85; dir. nat. accounts Chgo. Mag., N.Y.C., 1986; ea. advt. mgr. Mediatex, N.Y.C., 1987-88, v.p., nat. sales dir., 1989—. Deacon Brick Ch., N.Y.C., 1983. Mem. Advt. Women N.Y. Republican. Episcopalian. Home: 8 Hanson Rd Darien CT 06820-2502 Office: Mediatex 420 Lexington Ave Ste 1908 New York NY 10170-0156

LOCKWOOD, MOLLY ANN, communications company executive; b. London, Sept. 19, 1936; d. Warren Sewell and Ann Frances (Gleason) L.; BS, Pa. State U., 1958. With exec. tng. program Lord & Taylor, N.Y.C., 1958-60; assoc. merchandising editor House & Garden Mag., N.Y.C., 1960-65; advt. dir. Status Mag., N.Y.C., 1965-70; merchandising dir. Holiday Mag., N.Y.C., 1970; account mgr. Ladies' Home Journal Mag., N.Y.C., 1970-72; adv. dir. Girl Talk Mag., N.Y.C., 1972-74; mktg. dir./assos. pub. East/West Network Mag., N.Y.C., 1974-77; pres., chief exec. officer, ptnr. Catalyst Communications, Inc., N.Y.C., 1977—; pres. Catalyst Pub. Inc., 1987—; sec. bd. 244 Madison Realty Corp., 1984—; mktg. and sales dir. Mus. Mag., 1979-83. Mem. Advt. Women N.Y., Am. Soc. Travel Agts., Rear Guard, Kappa Kappa Gamma Alumnae Assn. Home: 1133 Park Ave New York NY 10128-1246 Office: Catalyst Communications Inc 244 Madison Ave New York NY 10016

LODER, MICHAEL WESCOTT, librarian; b. Easton, Pa., July 11, 1945; s. Theodore Charles Loder Jr. and Mary Sue (Wescott) Ubben; m. Linda Ellen Zuryk, Dec. 21, 1968; Michael Wescott Jr., Laura Ellen, Lisa Sue. BA, Union Coll., 1967; MS in Journalism, U. Oreg., 1974, MLS, 1978. Media technician Olympic Coll., Bremerton, Wash., 1975-77; asst. libr. Coll. Ganado, Ariz., 1978-80; reference libr. Bethany Coll., W.Va., 1980-83; libr. Pa. State U., Schuylkill Haven, 1983—. Scoutmaster Boy Scouts Am.; leader pipe band. Capt. USAF, 1967-71. Mem. ALA, Ea. U.S. Pipe Band Assn., Pa. Libr. Assn. Office: Pa State U Schuylkill Campus 200 University Dr Schuylkill Haven PA 17972-2202

LODEWICK, PHILIP HUGHES, equipment leasing company executive; b. Bklyn., Dec. 31, 1944; s. Robert John and Louise Mary (Bockhold) L.; m. Christine Helen Lobeck, July 5, 1969; children: Alyssa Erin, Kendra Blythe. BS, U. Conn., 1966, MBA, 1967. With sales dept. IBM Corp., N.Y.C., 1969-71; officer Boothe Fin. Corp., San Francisco, 1971-80; pres. The Tradewell Corp., equipment leasing co., Ridgefield, Conn., 1980—; gen. ptnr. Sierra Assoc. IV, San Francisco, 1981-88; chief fin. officer Wicklo's Maple Hill Farm, Ridgefield, 1983—. Bd. dirs. St. Andrew's Luth. Ch., Ridgefield, 1979—; mem. Conn. Refugee Resettlement Commn., 1985-88; bd. dirs., treas. Family Y in Ridgefield, 1985-89; founder, dir. Discovery Ctr., 1986—; founder, pres. A Better Chance in Ridgefield, 1987—. With AUS, 1967-69, Korea. Mem. Computer Lessors and Dealers Assn., Golden Bridge Hounds, L.I. Golden Retriever Club (pres. 1979-80). Republican. Lutheran. Home: 201 Spring Valley Rd Ridgefield CT 06877-1229 Office: Tradewell Corp Ridgefield CT 06877

LODGE, THOMAS RUSSELL, SR., manufacturing executive; b. Bryn Mawr, Pa., May 17, 1943; s. Howard Thomas and Lois (Rinehart) L.; m. Susan Marie Fridlington, May 3, 1944; children: Thomas R., Jr., Andrew N., Susan Sarah. BA, Ursinus, 1965. Mgmt. trainee Sears and Roebuck, St Davids, Pa., 1965-66; sales trainee Delaware Ribbon Mfrs., Inc., N.Y.C., 1967-68; Eastern sales mgr. Delaware Ribbon Mfrs., Inc., Menlo Park, N.J., 1969-72; v.p. sales Delaware Ribbon Mfrs., Inc., Princeton Junction, N.J., 1972-90; sr. v.p. Delaware Ribbon Mfrs., Inc., Phila., 1990; pres. Delaware Ribbon Mfrs., Inc., 1991—. Deacon First Presbyterian Ch., Dutch Neck, N.J., 1971-74, elder, 1977-80; asst. to scoutmaster Troop #40, Dutch Neck, 1977-80. Recipient Eagle Scout award Boy Scouts Am., Bryn Mawr, Pa., 1958. Mem. Hist. Soc. West Windsor (bd. dirs. 1984-87). Republican. Home: 240 Spruce St Philadelphia PA 19106-4322 Office: Delaware Ribbon Mfrs Inc PO Box 15271 Philadelphia PA 19125-0271

LODMELL, DEAN WALTER, investment banker; b. N.Y.C., July 19, 1959; s. Dean Struthers and Marilyn (Maki) L. AB, Dartmouth Coll., 1981; MBA, Harvard U., 1985. Field engr. Ebasco Services, Inc., N.Y.C., 1979-80; assoc. Capital Devel. Co., Olympia, Wash., 1980-83; prin. Kideral Internat., N.Y.C., 1983—; ptnr. Enright & Co., 1987—; bd. dir. Harmouth Holdings, Inc., 1989—, The Kimberly Found., 1991—. Mem. N.Y. Soc. Security Analysts, Harvard Club.

LOEB, FRANCES LEHMAN, civic leader; b. N.Y.C., Sept. 25, 1906; d. Arthur and Adele (Lewisohn) Lehman; student Vassar Coll., 1924-26; L.H.D. (hon.), NYU, 1977; m. John L. Loeb, Nov. 18, 1926; children: Judith Loeb Chiara, John L., Ann Loeb Bronfman, Arthur Lehman, Deborah Loeb Brice. N.Y.C. commr. for UN and Consular Corps, 1966-78. Exec. com. Population Crisis Com., Washington; life mem. bd. Children of Bellevue, Inc., 1974—; bd. dirs. Internat. Presch., Inc., N.Y. Landmarks Conservancy; chmn. bd. East Side Internat. Community Ctr., Inc.; mem. UN Devel. Corp., 1972—; life trustee Collegiate Sch. for Boys, N.Y.C.; trustee Cornell U., 1979-88, trustee emeritus, 1988—; trustee Vassar Coll., 1988—; bd. overseers Cornell U. Med. Coll., 1983-88 (life mem. 1988—), Inst. Internat. Edn. (life). Mem. UN Assn. (dir.). Clubs: Cosmopolitan, Vassar, Women's City (N.Y.C.). Home: 730 Park Ave New York NY 10021-4945 also: Anderson Hill Rd Purchase NY 10577 also: Lyford Cay, Nassau The Bahamas

LOEB, JOHN LANGELOTH, JR., investment counselor; b. N.Y.C., May 2, 1930; s. John Langeloth and Frances (Lehman) L.; children: Nicholas, Alexandra. Grad., Hotchkiss Sch., 1948; A.B. cum laude, Harvard, 1952, M.B.A., 1954; LL.D. (hon.), Georgetown U. With Loeb, Rhoades & Co., N.Y.C., from 1956; gen. ptnr., mem. mgmt. com. Loeb, Rhoades & Co., 1959-73, mng. ptnr., pres., 1971-73, ltd. ptnr., 1973-84; chmn. bd. Holly Sugar Co., Colo., 1969-71; amb. to Denmark Copenhagen, 1981-83; chmn. John L. Loeb, Jr. Assocs., N.Y.C., 1984—; U.S. del. to 38th Session Gen. Assembly of UN; spl. advisor environ. matters to Gov. Nelson A. Rockefeller, 1967-73; chmn. Gov. N.Y. Coun. Environ. Advisors, 1970-75; pres. Winston Churchill Found., 1981—; trustee Ednl. Testing Svc., Princeton, N.J. Trustee Montefiore Hosp. and Med. Ctr., Mus. City N.Y., NCCJ, John and Frances L. Loeb Found.; Am. U., Washington; mem. vis. com. Loeb Drama Ctr.; mem. vis. com. Sch. Pub. Health. Served as 1st lt. USAF, 1954-56. Decorated Grand Cross of the Order of Dannebrog (Denmark); recipient Lee Max Friedman award Am. Jewish Hist. Soc. Mem. Downtown Assn. (N.Y.C.), City Midday Club, Harvard Club, Century Country Club, Sleepy Hollow Club (Westchester, N.Y.), Buck's Club, Brooks's Club, Hurlingham Club (London), Royal Swedish Yacht Club (Stockholm), Royal Danish Yacht Club (Copenhagen), Lyford Cay Club (Nassau, Bahamas). Office: Loeb Family Office 375 Park Ave Ste 801 New York NY 10152-0047

LOEB, NACKEY SCRIPPS, publisher; b. Los Angeles, Feb. 24, 1924; d. Robert Paine and Margaret (Culbertson) Scripps; m. William Loeb, July 15, 1952 (dec. 1981); children—Nackey Loeb Scagliotti, Edith Loeb DuBuc. Student, Scripps Coll. Pub. Union-Leader Corp., Manchester, N.H., 1981—. Republican. Baptist. Home: Paige Hill Rd Goffstown NH 03045-2237 Office: Union Leader Corp 100 William Loeb Dr Manchester NH 03103

LOEBENSTEIN, WILLIAM VAILLE, research chemist, consultant; b. Providence, R.I., Aug. 9, 1914; s. Lester and Lillian R. (Marcus) L.; m. Sara Ann Clements, Nov. 12, 1949; children: Linda C., J. Roger, Frances L., Cynthia L. BS, Brown U., 1935, MS, 1936, PhD, 1940. Rsch. chemist Corning Glass Works, Central Falls, R.I., 1940-41, Bone Char Rsch. Project, Inc., Washington, 1946-52; physical chemist Nat. Bureau Standards, Washington, 1952-82; cons. and instr. Silver Spring, Md., 1982—. Patentee in field; contbr. 35 articles in profl. jours. Maj. U.S. Army, 1941-46, South Pacific. Recipient Meritorious Svc. medal U.S. Dept. Commerce, Washington, 1958. Fellow Washington Acad. Scis. (liaison rep. 1981-82); mem. Am. Chem. Soc. (50 year mem. 1989), Sigma Xi. Jewish. Home and Office: 8501 Sundale Dr Silver Spring MD 20910-5033

LOEDDING, PETER ALFRED, trade association executive; b. Sewickly, Pa., July 29, 1934; s. Peter Herbert and Alice Regina (Bourne) L.; m. Mary Ellen Cahalan, June 28, 1958; children—Peter, Joseph, Jeffrey. BSBA, Youngstown U., 1967; Grad. Inst. for Orgn. Mgmt., 1988. Credit mgr. Gen. Foods Corp., Newark, Del., 1962-64; v.p. John Blackson Assn., New Castle, Pa., 1964-70, Modulage Homes Co., Niles, Ohio, 1970-72; exec. dir. Redevel. Auth. Authority, Sharon, Pa., 1972-77, Shenango Valley C. of C., Pa., 1982-85; free-lance cons., Sharon, 1977-82; adminstr. Mercer County Devel. Corp., Sharon, 1982-85; exec. dir. Shenango Valley Indsl. Devel. Corp., 1982-85, Mercer County Indsl. Devel. Authority, 1982-85, Mercer County PTA, 1982-85. Bd. dirs. Shenango Valley Campus, Pa. State U., 1984—, Shenango Valley Urban League, 1984—. Mem. Am. Inst. Cert. Planners, Am. Planning Assn. (pres. Pitts. region 1972-73), Pa. Assn. Redevel. Ofcls. (v.p. 1976), Williamsport-Lycoming C. of C. (pres. 1985—). Home: 1160 Canterbury Rd Williamsport PA 17701-4016 Office: Williamsport-Lycoming C of C 454 Pine St Williamsport PA 17701-6200

LOEFFEL, BRUCE, software company executive, consultant; b. Bklyn., Aug. 13, 1943; s. Samuel and Loretta (Bleiweiss) L.; children: Alisa, Joshua. BBA, Pace U., 1966; MBA, St. John's U., 1971. Certified data processor. Mgr. fin. systems Gibbs & Hill Inc., N.Y.C., 1973-76; mgr. sales, tech. support Mgmt. Sci. Am. Inc., Fort Lee, N.J., 1976-81; dir. mktg. Info. Scis., Inc., Montvale, N.J., 1981-82; dir. bus. devel. Cullinet Software, Inc., Westwood, Mass., 1982-85; exec. v.p. strategic planning Online Data Base Software Inc., Pearl River, N.Y., 1985-88; pres. Corp. Application Software, Inc., Nyack, N.Y., 1988—. With U.S. Army, 1966-71. Mem. Inst. Cert. Computer Profls. Democrat. Jewish. Home and Office: 107 High Ave Apt 308 Nyack NY 10960-2500

LOEPER, F. JOSEPH, state senator; b. Dec. 23, 1944; m. Joann M. Loeper; children: F. Joseph III, James H., Joanne M. BS in Edn., West Chester U., 1966; MEd, Temple U., 1970. Tchr. social studies, asst. basketball coach, advisor sch. paper Aldan Sch. Dist., 1966-67; tchr. social studies, football coach Drexel Hill Jr. High Sch. Upper Darby Sch. Dist., 1967-68; dir. leisure svcs. Upper Darby Sch. Dist. Upper Darby Twp., 1968-78; instr. Pub. Svc. Inst. Millersville, Kutztown and West Chester U., 1972; mem. Rep. State Com. 26th Senatorial Dist., 1972-74; co-adj. instr. Delaware County Community Coll., 1973-74; mem. Uppser Darby Gov. Study Commn., 1973-74; treas. Upper Darby Sch. Dist., 1973-78; senator Pa. Senate, 1978—, senate majority caucus sec., 1980-83, senate majority whip, 1984; chmn. Rules and Exec. Nominations com.; mem. Appropriations Com., Banking and Ins. Com., Intergovernmental Affairs com.; bd. govs. State Systems of Higher Edn. com.; mem. exec. com. Joint State Gov. Commn. Past chmn. Eastern Delaware County Br. ARC, past bd. dirs. southeastern Pa. chpt.; past bd. dirs. Delaware County Assn. for Retarded Citizens; past pres. Garrettford-Drexel Hill Fire Co., Upper Darby Twp. Fireman's Relief Assn. Recipient Delaware County Citizen of Yr. award, 1990, West Chester Univ. Disting. Alumni award, 1989, Presdl. award Delaware County Fed. Sr. Svcs., 1988, Legis. award Fraternal Order Police, 1985, Legion Honor award Chapel Four Chaplains, 1982, St. Charles Cath. Youth Assn. award, Delaware County Saving League award, YMCA Youth in Gov. award. Mem. Pa. Recreation and Park Soc. (Governmental svc. award, 1982), Nat. Edn. Assn. (life), Upper Darby Assn. Suprs. and Adminstrators, Nat. Rep. Legislators Assn. (Legislator of Yr. 1988), Senate Rep. Campaign Com. (treas.). Office: Pa State Senate State Capitol Rm 362 Harrisburg PA 17120 also: 403 Burmont Rd Drexel Hill PA 19026

LOESSNER, G. ARNO, III, university executive, consultant; b. Washington, Nov. 23, 1942; s. G. Arno and Pauline E. (Guessford) L.; m. Mary Kremer, June 13, 1964; children: Michael Douglas, Laura Lynn. BA in Econ., U. Del., 1964, MA in Econ., 1970; PhD, U. Pa., 1993. Armor officer USA, Germany, 1965-67; planner Del. Planning Office, Dover, Del.; asst. dir., asst. prof. U. Del. Coll. Urban Affairs and Pub. Policy, 1969-78; from exec. asst to pres. to v.p. and univ. sec. U. Del., 1978—; permanent UN rep. Internat. Union Local Authorities, 1978—; bd. dirs. WHYY Pub. TV/Radio, Phila., 1985—; active Govs. Adv. Commn. Devel. Impact, 1989—; cons. UN Div. of Devel., 1991. Vice chair Bd. Del. Acad. Youth, Wilmington, 1989; active Centreville Sch. Bd., 1990; chmn. Reapportionment Commn., 1991; bd. dirs. New Castle County Del. Libr. Found. Mem. Wilmington Club, Omicron Delta Epsilon (excellence in econ. 1970), Kappa Alpha Order (James Ward Wood court of honor 1979). Democrat. Methodist. Address: Blackbird Lake Farm 124 Mill Lane Townsend DE 19734 Office: Univ of Delaware 132 Hullihen Hall Newark DE 19716-0001

LOEVINGER, LEE, lawyer; b. St. Paul, Apr. 24, 1913; s. Gustavus and Millie (Strouse) L.; m. Ruth Howe, Mar. 4, 1950; children: Barbara L., Eric H., Peter H. BA summa cum laude, U. Minn., 1933, JD, 1936. Bar: Minn. 1936, Mo. 1937, D.C. 1966, U.S. Supreme Ct., 1941. Assoc. Watson, Ess, Groner, Barnett & Whittaker, Kansas City, Mo., 1936-37; atty., regional atty. NLRB, 1937-41; with antitrust div. Dept. Justice, 1941-46; ptnr. Larson, Loevinger, Lindquist & Fraser, Mpls., 1946-60; assoc. justice Minn. Supreme Ct., 1960-61; asst. U.S. atty. gen. charge antitrust div. Dept. Justice, 1961-63; commr. FCC, 1963-68; ptnr. Hogan & Hartson, Washington, 1968-85; of counsel Hogan & Hartson, 1986—; v.p., dir. Craig-Hallum Corp., Mpls., 1968-73; dir. Petrolite Corp., St. Louis., 1978-83; U.S. rep. com. on restrictive bus. practices Orgn. for Econ. Cooperation and Devel., 1961-64; spl. asst. to U.S. atty. gen., 1963-64; spl. counsel com. small bus. U.S. Senate, 1951-52; lectr. U. Minn., 1953-60; vis. prof. jurisprudence U. Minn. (Law Sch.), 1961; professorial lectr. Am. U., 1968-70; chmn. Minn. Atomic Devel. Problems Com., 1957-59; mem. Adminstrv. Conf. U.S., 1972-74; del. White House Conf. on Inflation, 1974; U.S. del. UNESCO Conf. on Mass Media, 1975, Internat. Telecommunications Conf. on Radio Frequencies, 1964, 66; mem. legal adv. coun. Atlantic Legal Found. Author: The Law of Free Enterprise, 1949, An Introduction to Legal Logic, 1952, Defending Antitrust Lawsuits, 1977; author first article to use term-Jurimetrics, 1949; contbr. articles to profl. jours.; editor, contbr.: Basic Data on Atomic Devel. Problems in Minnesota, 1958; adv. bd. Antitrust Bulletin, Jurimetrics Jour. Served to lt. comdr. USNR, 1942-45. Recipient Outstanding Achievement award U. Minn., 1968; Freedoms Found. award, 1977, 84. Fellow Am. Acad. Appellate Lawyers; mem. ABA (del. of sci. and tech. sect. to Ho. of Dels. 1974-80, del. to joint conf. with AAAS 1974-76, 90—, liaison 1984-90, chmn. sci. and tech. sect. 1982-83, coun. 1986-89, standing com. on nat. conf. groups 1984-90), Minn. Bar Assn., Hennepin County Bar Assn., N.Y. Acad. Sci., D.C. Bar Assn., FCC Bar Assn., AAAS, Broadcast Pioneers, U.S. C. of C. (antitrust coun.), Am. Arbitration Assn. (comml. panel), Atlantic Legal Found. (legal adv. coun.), Cosmos Club (pres. 1990), City Club (Washington), Phi Beta Kappa, Sigma Xi, Delta Sigma Rho, Sigma Delta Chi, Phi Delta Gamma, Tau Kappa Alpha, Alpha Epsilon Rho. Home: Apt 17D 5600 Wisconsin Ave Bethesda MD 20815-4414 Office: Hogan & Hartson 555 13th St NW Washington DC 20004-1109

LOEWENHEIM, HAROLD ARTHUR, insurance sales executive, retired; b. N.Y.C., Mar. 8, 1911; s. Arthur and Irene (Simonsfeld) L.; m. Virginia Speyer, June 12, 1934 (dec. Aug. 1969); children: Barbara Jacobs, Patricia Franke, Roger; m. Susan Weingarten, Feb. 12, 1971. BA, Princeton U., 1932. Sales agt. Continental Am. Life Ins. Co., N.Y.C., 1932-35; asst. mgr. Mutual Benefit Life Ins. Co., N.Y.C., 1935-44; regional field asst. Home Life Ins. Co. N.Y., N.Y.C., 1944-47, mgr., 1947-77, mgr. emeritus, 1977—. Pres. Larchmont (N.Y.) Community Chest, 1946; chmn. Larchmont Campaign Fedn., 1948, N.Y. City Campaign Jewish Philanthropies, N.Y.C., 1944. Mem. N.Y. City Life Underwriters Assn. (pres. 1949-50, 55-56, 63-64), N.Y. City Life Mgrs. Assn. (pres. 1949-50), N.Y. State Life Underwriters Assn. (pres. 1963-64). Jewish. Office: Loewenheim Assocs 575 Lexington Ave New York NY 10022-6102

LOEWENTHAL, STANLEY, controller; b. Newark, Feb. 12, 1947; s. Leo and Mildred Gertrude (Greenberg) L.; m. Marilyn Sue Rand, July 5, 1971; children: Elana Joy, Carrie Beth. BA in History, Rutgers U., 1968, MA in History, 1970, MBA in Acctg., 1973. CPA, N.J. Tchr. history South Plainfield (N.J.) High Sch., 1970-71; auditor Arthur Anderson, Newark, 1973-75; staff acct. Liesure Tech. Corp., Lakewood, N.J., 1975-76; contr. Morse/Diesel Inc., N.Y.C., 1976-83, Herbert Constrn. Co., N.Y.C., 1983-84; cost contr. Tishman Constrn. Corp., N.Y.C., 1984-91; v.p., contr. Linpro Co., N.Y.C., 1991—. Sgt. USAR, 1970-79. Mem. AICPA, N. Soc. CPA's, Constrn. Fin. Mgmt. Assn. Democrat. Jewish. Home: 22 Dale Dr Edison NJ 08820 Office: Linpro Co 245 Park Ave New York NY 10167

LO FASO, FRED JOSEPH, sales and marketing professional; b. N.Y.C., Sept. 9, 1932; s. Antonio and Angelina Tina (Cirrincione) L.; m. Emily Luz Rodriguez, Sept. 12, 1953; children: Diana, Janice, Phillip, Thomas. BS in Internat. Trade, NYU, 1954. With Pfizer Internat., N.Y.C., 1955-59; asst. mgr. Price Dept. The Mearl Corp., N.Y.C., 1959-69, internat. sales mgr., asst. v.p. sales and mktg., 1969-79, v.p. sales and mktg., 1979-90, sr. v.p. global sales and mktg., 1990—; sec., dir. Mearl Hong Kong Ltd., 1991—. Pres. Holy Name Soc., Merrick, N.Y., 1969-70. Mem. Fgn. Trade Club (pres. 1953-54), Soc. Cosmetic Chemists, Cosmetic Industry Buyers and Sellers, Nat. Assn. Printing Ink Mfrs., Delta Phi Epsilon (pres. 1952-53). Republican. Roman Catholic. Office: The Mearl Corp 41 E 42d St New York NY 10017

LOFLIN, WILLIAM EUGENE, JR., college official; b. Salisbury, N.C., Mar. 13, 1959; s. William Eugene and Shirley Yvonne (Trexler) L. Student, U. N.C., 1977-78; BA in Religion, Mars Hill (N.C.) Coll., 1980; MA in Reading Edn., Appalachian State U., Boone, N.C., 1981; PhD in Reading and Lang. Arts, Fla. State U., 1985. Cert. tchr., Fla., N.C., S.C. Grad. teaching asst. dept. reading edn. Appalachian State U., 1980-81; tchr. reading Tift County Jr. High Sch., Tifton, Ga., 1982; dir. instrnl. support Sampson Community Coll., Clinton, N.C., 1983-87; chmn. devel. edn. div. Spartanburg (S.C.) Meth. Coll., 1987-89; dir. devel. edn. and support svcs. Catonsville (Md.) Community Coll., 1989—; ednl. cons. Loflin Ednl. Svcs., 1981—; presenter in field, 1981—; condrs. workshops. Editor (booklet) Year of the Reader, 1987, The Bookend newsletter, 1989. Chmn. Yr. of Reader Com., Clinton, 1987; mem. Baltimore County Literacy Works, Balt., 1989—; mem. adv. coun. Balt. Assn. for Retarded Citizens, 1990—. Mem. Nat. Coun. Instrnl. Adminstrs., Internat. Reading Assn. (pres. Sampson County chpt. 1984-87, resolutions and program com. N.C. coun. 1986-87, chmn. studies and rsch. com. 1985-87, pub. rels. com. 1987, mem. bylaws com. Spartanburg County chpt. 1988, editor newsletter 1988-89, chmn. publs. com. 1988-89, del nat. conv. 1985), Md. Assn. for Adult, Community and Continuing Edn., Phi Kappa Phi, Phi Delta Kappa (award com. Fayetteville Area chpt. 1986-87). Office: Catonsville C C 800 S Rolling Rd Baltimore MD 21228-5317

LOFQUIST, WILLIAM SPENCER, industry specialist; b. Orange, N.J., Mar. 31, 1936; s. Spencer Oscar and Esther (Olson) L.; m. Toshiko Sugiyama, Dec. 11, 1965; children: Lisa Esther, James Spencer. Cert., The Holderness Sch., 1954; AB, Middlebury Coll., 1958; MBA, NYU, 1970. Researcher G.M. Basford Co., N.Y.C., 1960-63, Young & Rubicam, Inc., N.Y.C., 1963-64; industry analyst U.S. Dept. Commerce, Washington, 1966-72, industry specialist, 1974—; industry econ. U.S. Postal Rate Commn., Washington, 1972-74; assoc. editor Research Quar., Rutgers U., New Brunswick, N.J., 1982—. With U.S. Army, 1958-60. Recipient Bronze medal, Silver medal U.S. Dept. Commerce, 1976, 87. Mem. Washington Book Pub. (bd. dirs. 1984-85), Soc. for Scholary Pub. Episcopalian. Office: US Dept Commerce ITA Room 4312 Washington DC 20230

LOFTIS, JOSEPH MICHAEL, water treatment chemical executive; b. Pitts., Mar. 12, 1941; s. Joseph Herbert and Reba Marie (Townsend) L.; m. Barbara Durkin, July 31, 1965; children: Megan, Joseph, Kevin, Wendy. BSc, Duquesne U., 1963; MSc, U. Pitts., 1974. Criminalist Pitts./Allegheny Crime Lab., 1964-68; bus. devel. engr. Calgon Corp., Pitts., 1968-75; sales mgr. Ionics, Inc., Bridgeville, Pa., 1975-85, v.p. fabricated products, 1985-91, v.p., gen. mgr., 1991—; bd. dirs. Applied Health Physics, Decon Internat., Costa Builders, Inc. Coach "C" lic. Western Pa. State Youth Soccer Assn., Pitts., 1980-90. Mem. Engrs. Soc. Western Pa. (dir. 1982-89, exec. com. Internat. Water conf., Cert. of Merit 1992), Shannopin Country Club. Republican. Home: 8697 Breezewood Dr Pittsburgh PA 15237 Office: Ionics Inc 3039 Washington Pike Bridgeville PA 15017

LOFTUS, ANDREW JOHN, foundation administrator, researcher; b. Hastings, Mich., Dec. 20, 1961. BS in Fisheries Biology, Mich. State U., 1984, MS in Fisheries Population Dynamics, 1986. Rsch. asst. Mich. State U., East Lansing, 1984-87; estuarine biologist Md. Dept. Natural Resources, Annapolis, 1987-90; rsch. specialist Sport Fishing Inst., Washington, 1990—; mng. dir. FishAm. Found., Washington, 1990—; mem.-at-large Citizens Adv. Com. to the Chesapeake Exec. Coun., Balt., 1990—; mem. adv. bd. Pacific Salmon Sportfishing Coun., Olympia, Wash., 1990—. Mem. Am. Fisheries Soc. Office: Sport Fishing Inst 1010 Massachusetts Ave NW Washington DC 20001

LOFTUS, WILLIAM PETER, computer company executive; b. Phila., Nov. 23, 1963; s. John A. and Dolores A. (Dwyer) L.; m. Veena Shyamalan, Dec. 6, 1986; 1 child, Isaac Shyamalan. BS in Computer Sci., Villanova U., 1985, postgrad.; postgrad., Villanova U. Programmer Unisys, Paoli, Pa., 1984-85, sr. programmer, 1985-87, project leader, 1987-89, tech. mgr., 1989-90; pres. WPL Labs., Inc., Penn Valley, Pa., 1990—. Contbr. articles to profl. jours. Mem. Assn. for Computing Machinery, IEEE, Phila. Arts, Amnesty Internat., Del. Valley SIGAda (chmn. 1991—). Office: WPL Labs 216 Wynne Ln Narberth PA 19072

LOGAN, BRUCE DAVID, physician; b. Salem, Mass., Nov. 17, 1945; s. Jack Merill and Mariam Jane (Buckley) L.; m. Ann Marie Viola, Mar. 24, 1983; children: Anna Leah, Jennifer Mary. AB, Colby Coll., 1967; MD, Columbia U., 1972. Dir. ambulatory care Beekman Hosp., N.Y.C., 1981-87; pvt. practice N.Y.C., 1987—; chief of medicine N.Y. Downtown Hosp., N.Y.C., 1991—. Mem. AAAS, AMA, Assn. Program Dirs. in Internal Medicine, Phi Beta Kappa.

LOGAN, DAN, investment professional; b. Chgo., Dec. 10, 1946; s. David S. and Reva (Frumkin) L.; m. Gloria Jean Blasz, July 8, 1973; children: Elizabeth, Andrew. BA, Knox Coll., 1969. Sr. speechwriter, asst. Ill. Gov. Daniel Walker, Springfield, Ill., 1975-76; spl. asst. U.S. Sen. Joseph Biden, Jr., Washington, 1977; speechwriter, cons. U.S. Rep. Max Baucus Senate campaign, Washington, 1978; speechwriter U.S. Sen. Edmund S. Muskie, Washington, 1979, Charles Ferris, chmn. FCC, Washington, 1980; exec. dir. Free Men, Inc., Washington, 1980-90; co-founder Nat. Congress for Men, Washington, 1981; ptnr. Mercury Investments, Chgo., 1988—. Contbr. articles to newspapers. Unitarian.

LOGAN, FRANCIS DONALD, historian, educator; b. Boston, Mar. 9, 1930; s. Joseph and Laura (MacDonald) L. AB, St. John's Sem., 1951, AM, 1954; MA, U. Toronto, 1959; Lic. in Mediaeval Studies, Pontifical Inst. Medieval Studies, Toronto, Ont., 1959, D in Mediaeval Studies, 1966. From asst. prof. to assoc. prof. Emmanuel Coll., Boston, 1964-73, prof., 1973—. Author: Excommunication and the Secular Arm in Medieval England, 1969, Vikings in History, 1983; contbr. articles to profl. jours. Recipient Fulbright scholar, London U., 1960-62, Guggenheim fellow, 1969-70. Fellow Royal Hist. Soc., Soc. Antiquaries. Home: 321 Tappan St Brookline MA 02146-4335 Office: Emmanuel Coll 400 The Fenway Boston MA 02115

LOGAN, GRACE ELEANOR MILLER (MRS. HENRY WHITTINGTON LOGAN), English educator; b. Valencia, Pa., June 22, 1908; d. Alvah John and Lillian (Gibson) Miller; B.S., Temple U., 1930, M.S., 1931; postgrad., 1955-56; m. Henry Whittington Logan, Mar. 16, 1940; 1 son, Henry Whittington III. English instr. Temple U., 1930-33; asst. prof. to dept.

head Moravian Coll., Bethlehem, Pa., 1933-42; assoc. prof. edn. and philosophy Widener U., Chester, Pa., 1956-67, prof. English, 1967-85, prof. emeritus, adj. prof. 1985—; dir. Coll. Reading Services, 1958-85; dir. Fed. Office of Edn. Equal Opportunities Tng. Br. Insts., 1965—; bd. dirs. 1683 Caleb Pusey House, Upland, Pa., dir. Bd. of Friends, 1986—, Emergency Aid Found.; cons., lectr. in biblical studies, 1985—; only woman on faculty any mil. coll. U.S. for 8 yrs. Elder, Presbyn. Ch.; mem. adv. bd. Pa. Inst. Tech. Mem. AAUP, Delaware County Hist. Soc. (dir.), Nat. Council Tchrs. English, Coll. English Assn., Coll. Reading Assn., Internat. Reading Assn., Pa. Council of Tchrs., Am. Acad. Religion, Questers Potpourri, Kappa Delta Epsilon, Pi Delta Epsilon. Home: 201 Sykes Ln Wallingford PA 19086 Office: Widener U 1 University Pl Chester PA 19013

LOGAN, TERENCE, insurance company executive; b. Cleve., Feb. 4, 1949; s. Walter Olin and Eileen Colleta (Sammon) L.; m. Starlyn DeLony, Oct. 17, 1970; children: Delony, Alexandra. BS, Ohio State U., 1973; MBA, U. Conn., 1979. Asst. dir. rates and rsch. Travelers Ins. Cos., Hartford, Conn., 1979-83, assoc. dir. managed care and employee benefits, 1983-88, dir., 1988—. Mem. Winsted (Conn.) Sch. Bd., 1986-90, chmn. sch. bldg. com., 1988-89. Mem. Internat. Soc. Cert. Employee Benefit Specialists. Republican. Methodist. Home: 208 Old New Hartford Rd Winsted CT 06098 Office: Travelers Ins Cos One Tower Sq Hartford CT 06183

LOGGINS, DONALD ANTHONY, analyst; b. Bklyn., June 13, 1951; s. Sal and Patricia (Smith) Amari. BA in Psychology, Richmond Coll., 1975, BA in Econs., 1975; MPA in Pub. Adminstrn., L.I. U., 1976, MPA in Environ. Sci., 1976. Analyst City of N.Y., 1976—. Author: Natural History-NYC, 1976, Managing Non Profits, 1977, Urban Tree Inventories, 1978, Careers in the Environment, 1979. Recipient Cert. EPA, 1979, Bklyn. Borough Pres. 1990, N.Y.C. Dept. Parks, 1985. Mem. N.Y. Audobon Soc., Richmond Coll. Alumni Assn., Mcpl. Arts Soc., Sierra Club, Nat. Inst. of Urban Wildlife. Office: Mgmt Info Systems 111 8th Ave New York NY 10011-5201

LOGIO, THOMAS, colon and rectal surgeon; b. Jersey City, Sept. 17, 1941; m. Eloise DeDonato; children: Jill, Lia, Kim, Thomas, Michael. BS, St. Peters Coll., 1963; MD, St. Louis U., 1967. Diplomate Am. Bd. Surgery, Am. Bd. Colon and Rectal Surgery. Surgeon Summit (N.J.) Colon & Rectal Surg. Assn. Mem. AMA, ACS, N.J. Med. Soc., N.J. Soc. Colon & Rectal Surgeons, N.Y. Soc. of Colon and Rectal Surgeons. Office: Summit Colon & Rectal Surg Assn 137 Summit Ave Summit NJ 07901

LOGUE, EDWARD JOSEPH, development company executive; b. Phila., Feb. 7, 1921; s. Edward J. and Resina (Fay) L.; m. Margaret DeVane, June 7, 1947; children: Katherine, William DeVane. B.A., Yale U., 1942, LL.B., 1947. Bar: Pa. 1948, Conn. 1950. Practiced in Phila., 1948; legal sec. Gov. Chester Bowles, Hartford, Conn., 1949-51; spl. asst. to ambassador Chester Bowles, New Delhi, 1952-53; devel. adminstr. City of New Haven, 1954-60, City of Boston, 1961-67; vis. Maxwell prof. govt. Boston U., 1967-68; pres., chief exec. officer N.Y. State Urban Devel. Corp., 1968-75; pres. Roosevelt Island Devel. Corp., 1969-75, Logue Devel. Co., Inc., 1976—, South Bronx Devel. Orgn., Inc., 1978-85; chief exec. officer Logue Boston, 1987—; Thomas Jefferson prof. Sch. Architecture, U. Va., spring 1985; sr. lectr. Sch. Architecture and Planning, MIT, 1985-89; prin. devel. cons. to Ft. Lincoln New Town, Washington, 1968; vis. lectr. Yale Sch. Law, 1957-77; chmn. Task Force on Housing and Neighborhood Improvement, N.Y.C., 1966; mem. Critical Choices Commn., 1973-76; founder Vineyard Open Land Found., 1970; mem. vis. com. Harvard U. Sch. Design, 1969-75; mem. resource team Mayor's Inst. on City Design. Chmn. Dukes County Charter Commn., 1991-92. With USAAF, 1943-45. Decorated Air medal with clusters. Mem. AIA (hon. mem.), Am. Acad. Arts and Scis., Tavern Club (Boston), Century Club (N.Y.C.), Union Boat Club (Boston), Saturday (Boston), Yale Club (N.Y.C.), Phi Beta Kappa (hon.). Democrat. Home: Scotchman's Bridge Ln West Tisbury MA 02575 Office: Logue Devel Co 94 Charles St Boston MA 02114-4643

LOGUE, JOHN JOSEPH, psychologist; b. Phila., Nov. 16, 1929; s. Edwin J. and Ellen V. (Mallon) L.; m. Evelyn Bortnick, Apr. 24, 1954; 1 child, Eileen Logue Handel. BS, Temple U., 1954, MEd, 1958, EdD, 1966. Lic. psychologist Pa., Md., N.J., Del. Ptnr., sr. cons. RHR Internat., Phila., 1966-88; mgmt. psychologist pvt. practice Phila, 1988—. With U.S. Army, 1954-56. Fellow Royal Soc. Health; mem. APA (indsl., orgn., cons., counseling, edn. divs.), Vesper Club, Quaker City Yacht Club. Home: 710 Kenilworth Ave Philadelphia PA 19126-3715 Office: 205 Keith Valley Rd Horsham PA 19044-1499

LOGUE-KINDER, JOAN, public relations executive; b. Richmond, Va., Oct. 26, 1943; d. John T. and Helen (Harvey) Logue; m. Lowell A. Henry Jr., Oct. 6, 1963 (div. Sept. 1981); children: Lowell A. Henry III, Catherine D. Henry, Christopher Logue Henry; m. Randolph S. Kinder, Dec. 13, 1986. Student, Wheaton Coll., 1959-62; BA in Sociology, Adelphi U., 1964; cert. in edn., Mercy Coll., Dobbs Ferry, N.Y., 1971; postgrad., NYU, 1973; cert. in edn., St. John's U., 1974. Asst. to dist. mgr. U.S. Census Bur., N.Y.C., 1970; tchr. and adminstr. social studies Yonkers (N.Y.) Bd. Edn., 1971-75; dir. pub. relations Nat. Black Network, N.Y.C., 1976-83; corp. v.p. NBN Broadcasting, N.Y.C., 1984-90; sr. v.p. The Mingo Group/Plus, N.Y.C., 1990-91; v.p. Edelman Pub. Rels. Worldwide, N.Y.C., 1991—; cons. in field. Mem. alumnae recruitment council Wheaton Coll.; mem. Nigerian-Am. Friendship Soc., 1978-81; bd. dirs. Westchester Civil Liberties Union, 1974-77, Greater N.Y. Council, Girl Scouts U.S., 1985—, Operation PUSH, 1985—; del. White House Conf. on Small Bus.; active Morris Udall for Pres. Campaign, Howard Samuels for Gov. Campaign; sr. black media advisor Dukakis/Bentsen 1988; state del. nat. conv. N.Y. State Women's Polit. Caucus, 1975, pres. Black caucus, 1976-77. Recipient Excellence in Media award Inst. New Cinema Artists, 1984. Mem. World Inst. Black Communications (bd. dirs. 1983—), Women in Communications, Inc., Nat. Assn. Market Developers, Advt. Women of N.Y., 100 Black Women. Home: 1800 7th Ave New York NY 10026-3601 Office: Edelman Pub Rels Worldwide 1500 Broadway New York NY 10036

LOH, ARTHUR TSUNG YUAN, finance company executive; b. Shanghai, People's Republic of China, Dec. 2, 1923; came to U.S., 1948; s. Chengor and Kwei N. (Wang) L.; m. Monica K.L. Chen, Apr. 16, 1955; children: Stephanie T.L., Pamela T.K. BA, St. John's U., Shanghai, 1945; MS, U. Ill., 1949, PhD, 1952. V.p., co-owner R.W. Pressprich & Co., N.Y.C., 1952-69; exec. v.p. fin. GAC Corp., Allentown, Pa., 1970-71; v.p., co-owner N.Y. Securities Co., N.Y.C., 1972-74; sr. v.p., chief fin. officer Govt. Employees Ins. Co., Criterion Ins. Co., Washington, 1974-80; chief fin. officer Rotary Internat., Evanston, Ill., 1981-88; founder, chmn. Loh Assocs., Greenwich, Conn., 1988—; chmn. bd. GAC Securities Co., Ft. Lauderdale, Fla., 1973-74. Chmn. devel. com. Travelers Aid Soc., N.Y.C.; active Rep. Nat. Com., Washington, Heritage Found. Mem. Internat. Soc. Security Analysts, Am. Econ. Assn., Fin. Execs. Inst., Inst. Chartered Fin. Analysts (chartered), N.Y. Soc. Security Analysts, Wall Street Club, Bankers Club Am., Windmill Club, Rotary, Downtown Assn. (N.Y.C.), City Midday Club (N.Y.C.). Methodist. Home: 9 North Ln Armonk NY 10504-2238 Office: Loh Assocs 30 Milbank Ave Greenwich CT 06830-5730

LOHMANN, GEORGE YOUNG, JR., neurosugeon, hospital administrator; b. Scranton, Pa., Aug. 9, 1947; s. George Young Lohmann and Elizabeth (Nichols) Frantzen; m. Joette Calabrese, May 15, 1973 (div. 1981); m. Rosemary Ei-Ling Ma, Sept. 24, 1988; 1 child, Norelle Christa Victoria. AB, Hobart Coll., 1968; MD, SUNY, Buffalo, 1972. Resident gen. surgery Wesley Meml. Hosp., Chgo., 1972-73; from jr. resident to chief resident Georgetown U. Hosp., Washington, 1975-79; asst. med. dir. West Side Orgn., Chgo., 1973-74; emergency physician St. James Hosp., Chicago Heights, Ill., 1973-74; pvt. practice Baton Rouge, 1979-81, 81-84; dir. dept. neurosurgery Brookdale Hosp. Med. Ctr., Bklyn., 1984—; mem. Med. Dir. Com., Risk Mgmt. Com., Exec. Quality Assurance Com., 1987—; mem. Med. Bd. Com., 1985—, Exec. Bd. Com., 1984—, Pain Mgmt. Com., 1988—. Patentee in field; contbr. articles to profl. jours, poetry to lit. mags. Adv. bd. Ctr. Latin Affairs, Baton Rouge, 1982-84; mem. Senatorial Inner Cir., 1988. Fellow ACS; mem. AMA, Am. Assn. Neurologic Surgeons (spine sect.), N.Y. State Neurosurg. Soc., N.Y. Soc. Neurosurgery, Congress Neurologic Surgeons (spine sect.). Office: Brookdale Hosp Med Ctr 1 Brookdale Plz Brooklyn NY 11212

LOHMANN, KEITH HENRY, police department official, consultant; b. Brookhaven, N.Y., Dec. 26, 1955; s. Henry August and June Dorothy (Friberg) L.; m. Margaret Lynch, Mar. 31, 1984. A.S. in Law Enforcement, Guilford Coll., 1977, B.S. in Adminstrn. of Justice, 1981, M pub. affairs U. N.C., 1987. Ops. mgr. H. Lohmann and Son, Brookhaven, 1973-75, 81-82; ops. supr. Powers Detective and Patrol, Greensboro, N.C., 1975-81; pub. safety officer Chapel Hill Police Dept., N.C., 1982-84, police planner, 1984-87; security cons. Hotel Europa, Inc., Chapel Hill, 1982-83; law enforcement coordinator U.S. Dept. Justice dist. of N.H., Concord, 1987-89, spl. asst. to U.S. atty., 1989—. Justi. Mem. Nat. Assn. Police Planners, Am. Soc. Pub. Adminstrn. Lutheran. Avocations: golf, tennis, snow skiing, snowmobiling. Office: Cleve Fed Bldg PO Box 480 Concord NH 03302-0480

LOHMEYER, DOUGLAS EDWARD, engineering executive, civil engineer; b. Takoma Park, Md., Nov. 17, 1948; s. Harry Edward and Elva Juanita (Brann) L.; m. Jeannie Marie Ucci, June 5, 1971; children: Marcie Gail, Brandon Edward. AS, Montgomery Coll., 1978. Registered profl. engr., Md., Va., D.C. Draftsman Matz-Childs, Inc., Rockville, Md., 1970-71; engr. PRC-Toups, Rockville, 1971-75, 77-80, Rodgers & Assocs., Rockville, 1975-77; v.p., gen. mgr. Loiederman Assocs., Inc., Rockville, 1980—; co-owner, mem. exec. com. Loiederman Assocs., Inc., 1988—. Bd. dirs. Olney (Md.) Boys and Girls Club, 1985-91, Leadership Montgomery, Rockville, 1990—, Mont. Housing Partnership, 1992—. With USMC, 1969-74, with U.S. Army, 1974-75. Recipient Bus. Svc. award Montgomery County Coun., 1990. Mem. Nat. Soc. Profl. Engrs., Suburban Md. Engrs. Soc., Suburban Md. Bldg. Industry Assn. (assoc.), Real Estate Profl. Club, Montgomery County C. of C. Office: Loiederman Assocs Inc 15200 Shady Grove Rd Rockville MD 20850

LÖHNER, RAINALD, engineering research educator; b. Braunschweig, Fed. Republic Germany, Mar. 23, 1959; came to U.S., 1986; s. Roland and Elisabeth K. (Niebuhr) L.; m. Claudia S. Fleige, Sept. 8, 1982; children: Nils S., Maria A., Johannes L. Diploma in engring., Tech. U. Braunschweig, 1982; PhD, Univ. Coll. Wales, Swansea, 1984. Lectr. Univ. Coll. Wales, 1984-85; rsch. scientist Berkeley Rsch. Assocs., Springfield, Va., 1985-88; assoc. rsch. prof. dept. civil, mech. and environ. engring. George Washington U., Washington, 1988—; cons. Vigyan Rsch. Assocs., Hampton, Va., 1985—, Huntsville (Ala.) Scis. Corp., 1988—, McDonnell-Douglas Co., St. Louis, 1990—. Contbr. over 100 articles to profl. jours. Mem. AIAA, Sigma Xi. Episcopalian. Home: 1211 Pine Hill Rd Mc Lean VA 22101-2906 Office: George Washington U Sch Engring and Applied Sci Washington DC 20052

LOHSE, DAVID JOHN, physicist; b. N.Y.C., Sept. 14, 1952; s. Edward and Mildred Edna (Hofmeister) L.; m. Maria Isabel Magdalena Garcia, Sept. 2, 1978. BS, Mich. State U., 1974; PhD, U. Ill., 1978. Rsch. assoc. Nat. Bur. of Standards, Gaithersburg, Md., 1978-80; rsch. engr. Exxon Chem. Co., Linden, N.J., 1980-89; staff engr. Exxon Rsch. & Engring. Co., Annandale, N.J., 1989—. Inventor graft polymers; contbr. articles to profl. jours. NRC/NSF fellow, 1978-80. Mem. Am. Chem. Soc., Am. Phys. Soc., N.Y. Acad. Scis. (chmn. polymers div. N.Y.C. chpt. 1991—). Home: 556 Stony Brook Dr Bridgewater NJ 08807-1947 Office: Exxon Rsch & Engring Corp Rte # 22 E Annandale NJ 08801

LOIEDERMAN, A. MARIO, engineering company executive; b. Buenos Aires, Dec. 30, 1934; came to U.S., 1947; s. Lazaro and Kathlyn Catalina (Tucker) L.; m. Rona Wasserman, Aug. 22, 1956; children: Karen Fleming, Eric. B in Engring., Johns Hopkins U., 1955. Registered profl. engr., Md., D.C., N.Y., N.J., Del., Pa., Va., W.Va., N.C., S.C., Ga., Fla., Ill. Design engr. Whitman Requardt and Assocs., Balt., 1955-60; staff engr. Baltimore County Dept. Pub. Works, Towson, Md., 1960-64; assoc., then chief engr. Matz, Childs and Assocs., Rockville, Md., 1964-71; v.p., gen. mgr. Toups and Loiederman, Rockville, 1971-76; exec. v.p., regional mgr. PRC Toups, Rockville and Orange, Calif., 1976-80; pres., chief exec. officer Loiederman Assocs., Inc., Rockville, 1980—; bd. dirs. SMBIA Health Benefit Trust, Landover, Md., Bldg. Devel. Guaranty Group, Landover, Strathmore Hall Arts Ctr., North Bethesda; chmn. bd. trustees Md. Coll. Art and Design, Silver Spring, 1990—. Prin. editor Sediment Control in Residential Areas, 1976; contbr. articles to constrn. publs. Mem. Md. Non-Tidal Wetlands Policy Task Force, Annapolis, 1988; fin. com. chmn. U.S. Congresswoman Constance Morella, Montgomery County, Md., 1988—. Recipient Award of Excellence Nat. Assn. Indsl. and Office Parks, 1990, Vol. Pub. Svc. award Montgomery County Coun., 1990. Fellow ASCE; mem. NSPE, Am. Water Works Assn., Water Pollution Control Fedn., Washington Bldg. Congress, Suburban Md. Bldg. Industry Assn. (bd. dirs. 1983—, Milton Kettler award 1991). Office: Loiederman Assocs Inc 15200 Shady Grove Rd Rockville MD 20850-3218

LOIELLO, JOHN PETER, public affairs executive, consultant; b. Oceanside, N.Y., Aug. 16, 1943; s. Rosario Paul and Mary Agnes (Butler) L.; m. Elaine Margaret Robinson, June 14, 1944. BA in History, Fordham U., 1965; MA in History, SUNY, Buffalo, 1973; PhD in African History, U. London, 1980. Tchr. history The Gow Sch., South Wales, N.Y., 1967-71; instr. U. Md. (U.K.), London, 1976-78; exec. dir. Dem. Party Com. Abroad, Washington and London, 1978-80; sr. cons. Assn. Am. Chambers of Commerce in Latin Am., Washington, 1980; spl. asst. to chmn. NEH, Washington, 1978-82; assoc. dir. Democracy Prog., Washington, 1982-83; founding exec. dir. Nat. Dem. Inst. for Internat. Affairs, Washington, 1983-85; pres. Gowran Internat., Washington, 1985—; pres. Alcide de Gaspari Found. (USA), Washington, 1987-89. Contbr. articles to profl. jours. Commr. Commn. on Platform Accountability, Dem. Nat. Com., Washington, 1981-85, chmn. fgn. policy subcom., 1980, platform com., 1980; sec. Tax Equity for Ams. Abroad, London, 1977-79; sec. Dems. Abroad, London, 1976-79. African Studies scholar, U. London, 1974-78, grantee, 1975. Mem. Nat. Italian Am. Found., Royal African Soc. Democrat. Roman Catholic. Office: Gowran Internat 1215 17th St NW Washington DC 20036-3089

LOISELLE, GILLES, federal official, legislator; b. Ville Marie Teriscamingue, Que., Can., May 20, 1929; m. Lorraine Benoît; children: Anne, Frédéric. BA in Arts, Laval U., Que., 1951. Prof. Lycée Tafari Makonnen, Addis Ababa, Ethiopia, 1951-53; reporter Le Droit, Sta. CKCH, Ottawa, Can., 1953-56; prof., dir. Inst. Berhane Zarie Neo Lycée Haile Sélassié, Addis Ababa, 1956-62; reporter, dir. Telejournal/Radio Can., Montreal, 1962-65; corr. Radio Can., Paris, 1965-67; exec. dir. govt. affairs. Govt. of Can., Québec, 1972-76; fin. min. state Govt. Can., Ottawa, 1988—; pres. Inter-Ministry Com. for Olympic Yr., Montreal, 1976; dir. for pres. Interparliamentary Rels., Québec, 1977; del. gen. of Que. to U.K. Eng., 1977-82; asst. dep. min. Can. affairs Govt. of Québec, Can., 1982-83; asst. dep. min. cultural affairs Govt. of Québec, 1983-84, del. gen. to Rome, 1985-88; M.P. from Quebec City Progressive Conservative Party, 1988—; pres. Treasury Bd., Ottawa; min. of state for fin. Govt. of Can., 1991—. Office: Office of Pres Treasury Bd, 140 O'Connor St 9th Fl, Ottawa, ON Canada K1A 0R5

LOKIEC, LIORA, historian; b. Rio de Janeiro, June 28, 1946; came to U.S., 1988; s. Moises and Ester (Migdal) L.; children: Irad, Yanai. BA, Sorbonne U., Paris, 1972; MA, Hebrew U., Jerusalem, 1981; PhD, London Sch. Econs., 1988. Rsch. asst. Truman Inst. Hebrew U., Jerusalem, 1978-81; rsch. fellow Ctr. Mid. Ea. Studies, Harvard U., Cambridge, Mass., 1988—; head Arabic and Turkish Archives, Israeli State Archives, Jerusalem, 1976-80. Author: Iraq, In Search for National Identity, 1992. Office: Ctr Mid Ea Studies Harvard U 1737 Cambridge St Cambridge MA 02138

LOKIS, MARIANNA, advertising executive; b. Manchester, N.H., June 29, 1967; d. Demetrios and Sophie (Yanakis) L. BBA magna cum laude, Baruch Coll., 1989. Mktg. asst. Eigen Software, N.Y.C., 1988-89; advt. asst. Travers, Inc., Flushing, N.Y., 1989-90; advt. mgr. Lazar Stricker & Assocs., N.Y.C., 1990—; cons. various firms, N.Y.C., 1990—. 1st pl. regionally, 3rd pl. nationally Am. Advt. Fedn. competition, 1989. Mem. Beta Gamma Sigma. Office: Lazar Stricker & Assocs 15 W 39th St New York NY 10018-3806

LOLLAR, THOMAS WILLIAM, ceramics department head; b. Detroit, Mar. 19, 1951; s. Harold Robert and Marjorie Bernice (Rowe) L. BFA, W. Mich. U., Kalamazoo, 1973, MA, 1979. Ceramics faculty Kalamazoo Art Inst., Kalamazoo, Mich., 1973-79, Parsons Sch. of Design, N.Y.C., 1979-82; dir. Shippee Gallery, N.Y.C., 1984-87; ceramics faculty Crafts Students League, N.Y.C., 1982-89; head Tchrs. Coll. Columbia U., N.Y., 1989—; art cons., Upjohn Co., Kalamazoo. Mich., Revlon, Inc., N.Y.C.; juror, N.Y. State Art Competition, Albany, N.Y. Prin. works include Homage to Albany clay mural, 1988, Manhattan mural, 1990, Washington mural, 1990. Mem. Artist Equity of N.Y. Home: 50 W 106th St New York NY 10025-3819 Office: Columbia U Tchrs Coll Art in Edn Macy Hall New York NY

LOMAX, PEGGY JEAN, physician; b. Neptune, N.J., Nov. 22, 1960; d. John William and Margaret Anne (Gegan) L. BS cum laude, Trinity Coll., 1982; MD, Georgetown U., 1987. Chief resident in psychiatry Georgetown U. Hosp., Washington, 1990-91; staff psychiatrist Northern Va. Doctor's Hosp., Arlington, 1991—; clin. instr. dept. psychiatry sch. medicine Georgetown U., 1991—. Mem. AMA, Am. Psychiat. Assn., Phi Beta Kappa. Office: 611 S Carlin Springs Rd Ste 309 Arlington VA 22204-1079

LOMBARD, JAMES RAYMOND, real estate executive; b. Bridgeport, Conn., Aug. 27, 1942; s. John Joseph and Margaret Ann (Spencer) L. BA in Econs., Fairfield U., 1965, MA in Counseling, 1968; MBA in Bus. Adminstrn., Calif. State U., 1976. Lic. real estate broker, Conn., Fla., Calif.; lic. mortgage broker, Fla. Bank examiner N.Y. State Banking Dept., N.Y.C., 1965-66; asst. to v.p. People's Bank, Bridgeport, 1966; vol. Peace Corp, Dominican Republic, 1967; asst. to the dean Kenyon Coll., Gambier, Ohio, 1969-72; sr. acct. Deloitte and Touche, Stamford, Conn., 1976-79; pres. Lombard Assocs. of Conn., Inc., Branford, 1979—; pres. Homequarters, Inc., Hartford, 1984-91. Trustee Hartt Sch. of Music at the U. Hartford, 1987—, Hartford (Conn.) Ballet, 1982-89, Fairfield U. Alumni Assn., 1979-84. Roman Catholic. Office: Lombard Assocs of Conn Inc 1140 Chapel St Stratford CT 06497

LOMBARDO, MICHAEL JOHN, assistant attorney general, educator; b. Willimantic, Conn., Mar. 25, 1927; s. Frank Paul and Mary Margaret (Longo) L.; children: Nancy C., Claire M. BS, U. Conn., 1951, MS, 1961, JD, 1973. Bar: Conn. 1974, U.S. Dist. Ct. Conn. 1975, U.S. Supreme Ct. 1979, U.S. Ct. Appeals (2d cir.) 1980. Div. controller Jones & Laughlin Steel Corp., Willimantic, 1956-67; adminstrv. officer health ctr. U. Conn., Hartford, 1968-69; dir. adminstrv. svcs. South Central Community Coll., New Haven, 1969-70; asst. dir. adminstrn. Norwich (Conn.) Hosp., 1970-77; asst. atty. gen. State of Conn., Hartford, 1977—; adj. asst. prof. U. Hartford, 1961-70; adj. prof. bus. Old Dominion U., 1973-81; adj. lectr. in law and bus. Ea. Conn. State U., 1973—, disting. adj. faculty 1990. Vol. Windham Center (Conn.) Fire Dept. Sgt. U.S. Army, 1945-46; 1st lt. USAF, 1951-53, col. Res., 1953-87, ret., 1987. Mem. AAUP, Retired Officers Assn., Conn. Bar Assn., Windham County Bar Assn., Mensa Internat., Am. Legion, VFW, Lions (bd. dirs. Willimantic chpt. 1960-64). Home: 35 Oakwood Dr Windham CT 06280-1520 Office: 55 Elm St Hartford CT 06106-1773

LOMBARDO, ROBIN ANN, therapeutic recreation director, educator; b. Mineola, N.Y., July 28, 1956; d. John Donald and Irene (Pepe) Alexander; m. Ralph John Lombardo, Dec. 30, 1980; 1 child, Jason Alexander. BA, SUNY, Stony Brook, 1978; MS in Recreation Edn., CUNY, 1985. Cert. therapeutic recreation specialist; cert. leisure profl. Activities aide A. Holly Patterson Home, Uniondale, N.Y., 1975-76; activities asst. Franklin Park Nursing Home, Franklin Square, N.Y., 1977; recreation leader Brunswick Hosp. Nursing Home, Amityville, N.Y., 1978-80; dir. recreational therapy Brunswick Hosp. Ctr. Rehab., Amityville, N.Y., 1980-86; recreation therapist Kings Park (N.Y.) Psychiat. Ctr., 1986-87, VA Med. Ctr., Northport, N.Y., 1988-91; dir. therapeutic recreation L.I. State Vets. Home, Stony Brook, 1991—; adj. instr. Suffolk County Community Coll., Selden, N.Y., 1985—; cons. N.Y. State Civil Svc. Exam. Bd., N.Y.C., 1984; vol. med. staff N.Y. State Games for the Physically Challenged, East Meadow, N.Y., 1984-86. Pres. Masons, Westbury, N.Y., 1973-74. Named one of Outstanding Young Women of Am., 1985. Fellow Nat. Recreation & Park Assn., N.Y. State Recreation & Park Soc., Inc.; mem. L.I. Recreation, Parks & Leisure Svcs. Assn. (exec. bd. mem., pres. 1989-90, Citation 1989, 91). Unitarian. Office: LI State VA Home 100 Patriots Rd Stony Brook NY 11790-3300

LOMBARDO, STEPHEN JOHN, physician; b. Bklyn., N.Y., Jan. 5, 1952; s. Ludwig and Mary Virginia (Stewart) L.; m. Resa Ann Mazzuoccola, Jan. 20, 1980 (div. June, 1984); m. Elena Marie Pace, Oct. 23, 1986. BS in Biol. Sci., SUNY, Stony Brook, 1973; MD, SUNY, Bklyn., 1977. Diplomate Nat. Bd. Med. Examiners, Am. Bd. Quality Assurance and Utilization Rev. Physicians. Pres. Stephen J. Lombardo, MD, PC, Staten Island, N.Y., 1980—; attending physician Staten Island Mcpl. Hosp., 1980—, Bailey Seton Hosp., Staten Island, 1982—; clin. instr. medicine SUNY Health Scis. Ctr. of Bklyn., 1981—. Bd. dirs. Am. Cancer Soc., Staten Island, 1987-89, CTV, Staten Island, 1991—, Island Peer Rev. Orgn., Lake Success, N.Y., 1988-89. Mem. AMA (Physician Recognition award 1980, '82, '85, '88, '91), N.Y. Acad. Scis., N.Y. State Soc. Internal Medicine, Undersea and Hyperbaric Med. Soc., Staten Island Sport Divers (pres. 1990—, Disting. Svc. award 1991), Profl. Assn. Dive Instrs., Richmond County Yacht Club. Republican. Roman Catholic. Office: Stephen J Lombardo MD 1324 Victory Blvd Staten Island NY 10301

LONABOCKER, LOUISE MADORE, registrar; b. Pittsfield, Mass., Nov. 6, 1948; d. Alcide Alexis and Lillian Claire (Delisle) Madore; m. Thomas Michael Lonabocker, Aug. 29, 1970 (div. 1981). BS, Boston Coll., 1974, MEd, 1976, PhD, 1981. Dir. transfer admission Boston Coll., Chestnut Hill, Mass., 1973-76, asst. registrar, 1976-77, assoc. registrar, 1977-80, univ. registrar, 1980—. Contbr. articles to profl. jours. Vol. Boston Symphony Orch., 1989—. Mem. New Eng. Assn. of Collegiate Registrars and Admissions Officers (pres. 1991—), Cumrec Conf. (Best Paper 1990). Roman Catholic. Home: 86 Griggs Rd Brookline MA 02146-4719 Office: Boston Coll Chestnut Hill MA 02167

LONARDO, CARMEN GIUSEPPE, low income housing rehabilitation specialist; b. Toronto, Ont., Can., July 13, 1963; s. Arcangelo and Maria Giuseppina (Marcogliese) L. BA in Polit. Sci., St. John Fisher Coll., Rochester, N.Y., 1985; MPA, SUNY, Brockport, 1988. With The Housing Coun. in The Monroe County Area, Inc., Rochester, 1989-90; housing rehab. adminstr. Rural Opportunities Inc., Rochester, 1990—. Newspaper editor GOP Trunkline, 1991, 92; contbr. articles to profl. jours. Hispanic consumer roundtable mem. Rochester Telephone Corp., 1989; sch. bd. cand. Penfield (N.Y.) Bd. Edn., 1990; energy issues com. Rochester Gas & Elec. Corp., 1990—, Ctr. for Environ. Info., Inc., Rochester, 1991. Mem. Am. Soc. Pub. Adminstrn. (program com. chmn. 1989-91, bd. dirs. 1991, pres. 1992—), K.C. (coun. advocate 1985-87, community activities com. chmn. 1989-91). Republican. Roman Catholic. Home: 118 Highledge Dr Penfield NY 14526-2435 Office: Rural Opportunities Inc 339 East Ave Rochester NY 14604-2615

LONDON, CHARLES STUART, communications executive, sound designer, producer, director; b. N.Y.C., Feb. 5, 1946; s. Robert Lincoln and Frances (Abes) L. Student, U. Mich., 1962-66. Dir. prodn. 1492 Prodns., Inc., N.Y.C., 1968-72; v.p. prodn. Motiva, Ltd., N.Y.C., 1972-76; resident sound designer Circle Repertory Co., N.Y.C., 1972—; freelance producer N.Y.C., 1976-78; pres. London MultiMedia, Ltd., N.Y.C., 1978-88; cons. on-air advt. and promotion ABC News, 1988—; designs all sounds for Pulitzer Prize winning playwright Lanford Wilson. Bd. dirs. N.Y. CitiWorks, N.Y.C., 1982-84. Recipient Silver awards Internat. Film and TV Festival, 1980, 84, 87, 90, Gold award, 1987, 90, Finalist award, 1990. Mem. Theatrical Sound Designers Assn. (charter), Nat. Assn. TV Arts and Scis., Nat. Assn. Recording Arts & Scis., Dirs. Guild of Am. Office: CLU Inc 60 Madison 2d Fl New York NY 10010

LONDON, DAVID BRUCE, psychiatrist; b. Chgo., Sept. 25, 1948. AB, George Wash. U., 1970, MD, 1974. Diplomate Am. Bd. Psychiatry and Neurology. Intern in internal medicine George Wash. U., Washington, 1974-75; fellow in psychiatry Yale U., New Haven, 1975-78, forensic fellow in psychiatry, 1984-86; clin. and research fellow Yale Psychiat. Inst., New Haven, 1978-80; sr. staff psychiatrist Inst. of Living, Hartford, Conn., 1980-82; pvt. practice Madison, Conn., 1982—, Waterford, Conn., 1984—; cons. in psychiatry Waterford Country Sch., 1983—, Madison (Conn.) Youth Svcs., 1987-90, Norwich (Conn.) Ct. Diagnostic Clinic, 1988-92; med. dir. Chem. Addiction Recovery Enterprise, New London, Conn., 1987-91, asst.

clin. prof. psychiatry Yale U., New Haven, 1987. Contbr. articles to profl. jours. Mem. Am. Psychiat. Assn., Am. Acad. Psychiatry and the Law, Am. Soc. Adolescent Psychiatry, Am. Acad. Med. Acupuncture. Office: 567 Vauxhall St Ext Ste 320 Waterford CT 06385-4332 also: 147 Durham Rd PO Box 1158 Madison CT 06443

LONDON, ELEANOR, apparel designer, computer-aided design consultant; b. N.Y.C., Sept. 17, 1955; d. Cornelius and Ireta (Riddles) L. BFA in Fashion Design, Parson Sch. of Design, N.Y.C., 1976. Designer Lommtogs, Inc., N.Y.C., 1976-79; designer, merchandiser United Apparel Group, N.Y.C., 1980-82; merch. asst. Bloomingdales div. Federated, N.Y.C., 1982-87; sr. design cons. London Tech. Mgmt., N.Y.C., 1987—; mem. faculty New Sch. for Social Rsch., N.Y.C., 1985—, Parson Sch. Design, N.Y.C., 1987—, Sch. Visual Arts, N.Y.C., 1985—. Guest speaker Assn. Coll. Prof. Textiles, N.Y.C., 1988. Cooper Union rsch. grantee, 1985; recipient Most Innovative Design award Corduroy Coun. Am., 1976, Cert. of Appreciation, Bloodmingdales, 1984. Mem. Am. Guild Variety Artists. Baptist. Home: 235 E 95th St New York NY 10128-4012

LONDON, MICHAEL JEFFREY, public relations executive; b. Waterbury, Conn., Apr. 20, 1952; s. Sherman David and Arlene Dolores (Freedman) L.; m. Allison Brook Spitzer, June 27, 1976; 1 child, Jordan Maxwell. BA, U. Conn., 1974; MS, Rensselear Poly. Inst., 1987. Pub. rels. assoc. Combined Ins. Co. Am., Chgo., 1974; reporter The Hartford (Conn.) Courant, 1975-78, asst. bus. editor, 1978-80, bur. chief, 1980-82; news rep. Northeast Utilities, Hartford, 1982-83, sr. news rep., 1983-85; dir. corp. rels. Lone Star Industries, Inc., Stamford, Conn., 1985-90; prin. Michael J. London and Assocs., Trumbull, Conn., 1990—; instr. U. Conn., Storrs, 1981-82. Mem. Nat. Investor Rels. Inst., Pub. Rels. Soc. Am., Soc. Profl. Journalists, Newcomen Soc. N.Am., Internat. Assn. Bus. Communicators. Jewish. Office: Michael J London & Assocs 15 Lake Ave Trumbull CT 06611-2233

LONDYNSKY, SAMUEL, marine consultant; b. Poland, Jan. 17, 1921; came to U.S., 1927; s. Itzhak and Gittel (Tenenbaum) L.; m. Betty Hilda Olchin, Mar. 17, 1952 (dec. Mar. 1982); children: Jeffrey Morgan, Paul Ansell; m. Joan Welch Stevenson, Mar. 27, 1989. Diploma, U.S. Mcht. Marine Acad., 1944. Deck officer U.S. Mcht. Marine and Army Transport Svc., 1944-45; port ops. asst. U.S. War Shipping Adminstrn., 1945-47; various deck officer positions U.S. Mcht. Marine, 1947-50, deck officer, 1954-57; officer-in-charge mobile ship repair unit USN, N.Y.C., 1953-54; capt. Omnium Freighter Corp., N.Y.C., 1957-59; pilot Panama Canal Co., Balboa, Canal Zone, 1959-77, asst. port capt., 1977-79, canal port capt., 1979-82; marine cons. in ship handling, marine and boating safety, Ramsey, N.J., 1982—. Columnist on safe boating Hudson River Boating News, 1992—. Pres. Gatun (Canal Zone) Civic Coun., 1965-68; EEO counselor Panama Canal Co., 1972-80; poll watcher Ramsey Rep. Club, 1985—. Lt. USN, 1950-53. Recipient gov.'s svc. achievement award Govt. of Canal Zone, 1973, safety award, 1973, 75. Mem. U.S. Power Squadron (comdr. 1976-78), USCG Aux. (vice flotilla comdr. 1991-93), Combat Mcht. Mariners World War II, Soc. Marine Cons., Coun. Am. Master Mariners, Alumni Assn. U.S. Mcht. Marine Acad., Heroes of 76 (comdr. 1970-73), Nat. Sojourners (pres. 1969-71), Masons (32 degree), Shriners. Home: PO Box 4 Ramsey NJ 07446-0004 Office: PO Box 67 Blauvelt NY 10913-0067

LONE, MOHAMMED SALIM, editor-in-chief; b. Jhelum, Pakistan, Mar. 3, 1943; came to U.S., 1982; s. Mohammed Siddiq and Saffia Begum (Mir) L.; m. Patricia Stephanie Foley, Sept. 4, 1965; children: Samir, Saahir. BA cum laude, Kenyon Coll., 1965; MA, NYU, 1967. Spl. asst. N.Y. Times, N.Y.C., 1970-72; mng. editor Sunday Post, Nairobi, Kenya, 1972-74; editor-in-chief Viva Mag., Nairobi, 1974-82; info. officer UNICEF, N.Y.C., 1982-84; editor Africa Emergency UN Office for Emergency Ops. in Africa, N.Y.C., 1985-86; chief info., spokesman UN Africa Recovery Programme, N.Y.C., 1987—; 1st vice chmn. E. African Newspapers & Periodical Assn., Nairobi, 1980-82; chmn. bd. chief editors Journalism of Yr. awards, Nairobi, 1980-82; mem. steering com. Secretariat, UN Africa Recovery Programme, 1987-; keynote speaker internat. conf. on Africa. Editor-in-chief Africa Recovery, 1987—; contbr. articles to several newspapers. Recipient Rockefeller lectureship Rockefeller Found., MakerereU., Kampala, Uganda, 1968; Danforth Grad. fellow Danforth Found, 1965-68; ASPAU scholar African Am. Inst., N.Y.C., 1961-65. Mem. Inst. for African Alternatives. Muslim.

LONG, CARL DEAN, management consultant; b. Lutesville, Mo., Mar. 8, 1938; s. Curtis E. and Cleo A. (Crites) L.; m. Lee Ann Skinner, Nov. 11, 1961 (div. Nov. 1968); 1 child, Timothy Lee; m. Rose-Carol Washton, Mar. 28, 1970; 1 child, Daniel Keith. BS, St. Louis U., 1959; MPA, NYU, 1974. Cert. mgmt. cons.; registered orgn. devel. cons. Area supr. GM Inst., Flint, Mich., 1962-67; mgr. Touche, Ross & Co., N.Y.C., 1967-71; sr. cons. Mobil Corp., N.Y.C., 1971-86; pres. Mgmt. Cons. Internat., N.Y.C., 1986-91; mng. ptnr. Long & Vickers Inc., N.Y.C. and Charlotte, N.C., 1991—. Author Manual for Cons. Svcs. in Human Resources Mgmt., 1967; contbr. The Practice of Mgmt. Devel., 1988. Capt. USAF, 1959-62. Mem. Inst. Mgmt. Cons., Internat. Registry of Orgn. Devel. Profls., Profl. Ski Instrs. Am.

LONG, CEDRIC WILLIAM, health research facility executive; b. Mpls., Mar. 4, 1937; s. Tracy Steven and Clarice Cecilia (Robertson) L. BA, UCLA, 1960, MA, 1962; PhD, Princeton U., 1966. Postdoctoral fellow U. Calif., Berkeley, 1966-68; instr. NYU Med. Sch., N.Y.C., 1969-70; lab. chief Flow Labs., Rockville, Md., 1968-70, Litton Industries, Frederick, Md., 1976-80; preclin. chief NIH, Nat. Career Inst., DCT, Bethesda, Md., 1980-86; gen. mgr. Nat. Cancer Inst.- Frederick Cancer R&D Ctr., 1986—. Home: 2 Basildon Cir Rockville MD 20850-2724

LONG, CIEL M., counselor; b. Jersey City, N.J., Mar. 9, 1936; d. James Aloysius and Hilda Margaret (Vogel) L.; children: Jennifer, Kathleen, Elizabeth, Sarah, William. BS, Seton Hall U., 1971; MTS, Drew U., 1975. Cert. profl. counselor. Dir. religious edn. Dioceses of Paterson and Metuchen, N.J., 1980-84; counselor Headstart of Morris County, Dover, N.J., 1984-85; counselor, social worker Nat. Multiple Sclerosis Soc., Montclair, N.J., 1985-86; adj. faculty County Coll. of Morris, Randolph, N.J., 1986-87; dir. Community Soup Kitchen, Morristown, N.J., 1987-89, Multiple Sclerosis Svc. Orgn., Randolph, 1989-90; counselor Reach-Career Counseling Ctr., Convent, N.J., 1989-90; social worker Lutheran Children Family Svc., Phila., 1990—. Mem. AACD, NASW, Nat. Career Devel. Assn., Assn. for Multi-Cultural Counseling and Devel.

LONG, DAVID RUSSELL, academic program director; b. Worcester, Mass., Feb. 12, 1942; s. Wendell Russell and Eleanor May (Ohlund) L.; children: Daphne Ruth Evdokia, Payson David Cheslov. BA, Emerson Coll., 1965; MS in Ednl. Communication, U. Albany, 1970, MS in Ednl. Adminstrn., 1977. TV producer-dir. U. Albany, N.Y., 1968-69, dir. audio-visual svc., 1969—; pres., cons. Media Assocs., Scotia, N.Y., 1982—; asst. to dir. White Funeral Home, Scotia, 1982—. Creator slide programs for fire chiefs, police, children's mus.; author: (videotape) Children's Participation Play (selected for inclusion in Libr. of Congress). Fin. sec., mem. pub. rels com. Scotia Fire Dept., 1975-85, commr., 1985-88; bd. dir. Scotia-Glenville Children's Mus., 1980-84, Schenectady Acess Cable Coun., 1980-84. With U.S. Army, 1966-67, Vietnam. Recipient Chancellor's award for excellence in profl. svc. U. Albany, 1982. Mem. Capital Dist. Media Assn., Hudson-Mohawk Vol. Fireman's Assn., Glenville Fire Fighters Assn. (pub. rels. com. 1978-86). Republican. Methodist. Home: 144 Van Buren Rd Ballston Spa NY 12020-3800 Office: U Albany 1400 Washington Ave Albany NY 12222

LONG, JANET LOUISE, academic program director; b. Phila., July 10, 1954; d. Melvin Henry and Ruth Elizabeth (Chandley) L. BA, King's Coll., 1976; MPA, Pace U., 1991. Ins. rep. Social Security Adminstrn., Phila., 1977-87; dir. alumni affairs King's Coll., Briarcliff Manor, N.Y., 1987-91, dir. fin. aid, 1991—. Chmn. Holmesburg Bapt. Christian Sch., Phila., 1983-86. Republican. Home: 40 James St Apt 2 Ossining NY 10562-5412 Office: Kings Coll 150 Lodge Rd Briarcliff Manor NY 10510-1200

LONG, JOAN HAZEL, accountant; b. Colchester, Vt., Sept. 26, 1952; d. Ray Lawrence Sr. and Bernice Ethel (Reynolds) Wells; m. Joseph Andre Long; 1 stepchild, Tracy Kendrew Long Stevens. A in Acctg., Community Coll. Vt., St. Albans, 1990. Cert. motorcycle rider tng. instr. Vt. Dept. Motor Vehicles, 1992. Receptionist, sec. Vis. Nurse Assn., Burlington, Vt., 1971-72; accounts receivable bookkeeper Surg. Assocs., Inc., Burlington, 1972-73; sec., bookkeeper Munson Earth Moving, South Burlington, Vt., 1973-74; corp. sec., acct. Engelberth Constrn., Inc., Winooski, Vt., 1975-82; mgr., owner Long Properties, 1983—; acct. Joan Long Acctg. Svcs., 1983—; asst. upholsterer Essex Upholstery Shop, 1974—. Activist, pres. Vt. Motorcyclist Rights Orgn., Essex Junction, 1975-78; govtl. affairs dir. Freedom of the Rd.-Vt., Inc., 1991-92; active Greenpeace. Home and Office: PO Box 970 East Fairfield VT 05448-9998

LONG, JOSEPH FRANCIS, II, manufacturing company executive; b. Suffern, N.Y., Mar. 26, 1963; s. Joseph F. and Winifred (Lally) L. BS in Acctg., Bus. Adminstrn., Marist Coll., Poughkeepsie, N.Y., 1985. Staff acct. Helme Tobacco Corp., N.Y.C., 1985-86; fin. analyst J. Walter Thompson, N.Y.C., 1986-87; corp. acct. Am. Natural Beverage Corp., N.Y.C., 1987; asst. controller, systems mgr. Fisher Skylights, Inc., West Nyack, N.Y., 1987—. Basketball coach CYO, St. Anthony's Ch., Nanuet, N.Y., 1983-85. Mem. Am. Mgmt. Assn. Republican. Roman Catholic. Home: 59 Lenox Ave Congers NY 10920-2517 Office: Fisher Skylights Inc 50 Snake Hill Rd West Nyack NY 10994-1624

LONG, MICHAEL HOWARD, landscape architect; b. Rochester, N.Y., July 20, 1956; s. Howard M. and Barbara K. (Leonard) L.; m. Diane M. Olshefski, Mar. 11, 1979; children: Kristan M., Jessica A., Brendan M. AAS in Architecture, Dutchess Community Coll., 1976; BS in Environ. Design, SUNY, Syracuse, 1979, B Landscape Architecture, 1980; postgrad., Syracuse U., 1990. Registered landscape architect, N.Y. Constrn. foreman Landscape Concepts, Millbrook, N.Y., 1976-80; site designer, estimator F.W. Cunningham, Inc., Auburn, N.Y., 1980; landscape architect Environ. Design and Research, Skaneateles, N.Y., 1981-84; sr. planner Cayuga County Planning Bd., Auburn, N.Y., 1980—; cons. Brennan Lorenzini Architects, Auburn, 1984-88; sec.-treas. New Directions Therapeutics, Inc., Auburn, 1989—; mng. ptnr. E.A. Huntington House Partnership, Auburn, 1990—; prin., cons. Liberatore, Long Preservation Planners, Auburn, 1987; co-dir. Willard Meml. Chapel Project, 1988—. Chmn. Community Preservation Com., Inc., Cayuga County, N.Y., 1984-88, City of Auburn Hist. Resources Adv. Bd., 1987—; trustee Cayuga Mus. History and Art, 1985-92; bd. dirs. Auburn Bicentennial Com., 1991—. Grantee Fulbright scholarship, 1979; recipient award Preservation League N.Y. State, 1990. Mem. Am. Soc. Landscape Architects (juror nat. student awards design competition 1986, 88, 90), Am. Planning Assn. (speaker Upstate N.Y. conf.), Nat. Trust for Hist. Preservation. Office: Cayuga County Planning Bd 160 Genesee St 5th Fl Auburn NY 13021-3423

LONG, RONALD ALEX, real estate and financial consultant, educator; b. Scranton, Pa., Dec. 9, 1948; s. Anthony James and Dorothy Agnas (Posgay) L.; m. Geraldine Sinneway, July 17, 1976; 1 child, Elizabeth Dorothy. BA, Bethany Coll., Lindsburg, Kans., 1971; MAT, Trenton (N.J.) State Coll., 1973; BS, Spring Garden Coll., 1980; MBA, St. Joseph's U., Phila., 1985; cert., Grad. Realtor Inst., 1990. Cert. tchr., N.J., Pa., real estate instr., Pa.; lic. mortgage broker, Pa. Substitute tchr. Hackettstown and Roxbury (N.J.) Sch. Bds., 1971-72; prof., chmn. bus. adminstrn. dept. Spring Garden Coll., Phila., 1973—; sales assoc. Red Carpet Real Estate, Doylestown, Pa., 1980—; cons. real estate Doylestown, 1980—; cons. mgmt. Budd Wheel Corp., Phila., 1978-82; pres., prin. Aladdin Fin. Svcs., Inc.; prin. Loan Finders, Inc. Co-author: Explorations in Macroeconomics, 1988, Explorations in Microeconomics, 1989; contbr. articles to area newspapers. Site dir. ARC Blood Mobile, 1975—; bd. dirs. Buckingham (Pa.) PTA, 1984-88. Recipient Legion Honor award Chapel of the 4 Chaplains, Phila., 1984. Mem. Nat. Assn. Realtors, Pa. Assn. Realtors, Bucks County Assn. Realtors, Profl. Assn. Diving Instrs. (cert.), Bus. Club (treas. 1969-71, pres. 1970-71), Alpha Chi, Pi Sigma Chi, Eta Beta Phi. Republican. Home: 2698 Cranberry Rd Doylestown PA 18901-1770 Office: Spring Garden Coll 7500 Germantown Ave Philadelphia PA 19119-1651

LONG, WILLIAM PENUEL, JR., chemical company executive; b. Bainbridge, Md., Sept. 11, 1944; s. William Penuel and Bertha (Graham) L.; m. Cynthia C. Cary (div. 1984); children: Kelly, Michael; m. Susan Marie May (div. 1991); children: Andrew Melissa. BS in Chem. Engring., U. Del., 1966. Process engr. Atlas Chem. Co., New Castle, Del., 1966-68; product devel. chemist Atlas Chem. Co., Wilmington, Del., 1968-72; lab. supr. ICI Ams. Inc., Wilmington, 1972-76, devel. mgr., 1976-82, bus. mgr., 1982-87, gen. mgr., 1987—. Patentee in field. Pres. Crescendo Dance Club, Wilmington, 1976-77, Sharpley Civic Assn., Wilmington, 1987; advisor Jr. Achievement, Wilmington, 1969; coach Kirkwood Soccer Club, Wilmington, 1981-83. Home: 125 Fair Hill Dr 604 Halstead Rd Wilmington DE 19808 Office: ICI Ams Inc Concord Pike Wilmington DE 19897

LONGCOPE, CHRISTOPHER, physician, endocrinology educator; b. Lee, Mass., Aug. 5, 1928; s. Warfield Theobald and Janet Percy (Dana) L.; m. Julia C. Coffin, Oct. 6, 1961; children: Dana, Peter, David. AB, Harvard U., 1949; MD, Johns Hopkins U., 1953. Intern, then asst. resident Presbyn. Hosp., N.Y.C., 1953-55, fellow in endocrinology, 1959-60; asst. resident in medicine Johns Hopkins Hosp., Balt., 1955-56; staff scientist Worcester Found. for Exptl. Biology, Shrewsbury, Mass., 1966-70, sr. scientist, 1970-80; prof. ob/gyn and medicine U. Mass. Med. Sch., Worcester, 1980—. Contbr. articles to Jour. Clin. Investigation, Jour. Clin. Endocrinology and Metabolism. Mem. Am. Physiol. Soc., Endocrine Soc., Soc. for Exptl. Biol. Medicine. Office: U Mass Med Sch 55 Lake Ave N Worcester MA 01655-0001

LONGLEY, JAMES WILDON, mathematician, researcher; b. San Saba, Tex., Oct. 29, 1913; s. Leon and Emily Araminti (Patton) L.; m. Letitia J. Robinson, 1961 (dec. 1988); 1 child, Roger Wayne. BA, Tex. A&M U., 1936, MS, 1937; MA, Harvard U., 1946, PhD, 1947. Economist, numerical analyst Bur. Labor Stats. U.S. Dept. Labor, Washington, 1955-83, researcher in applied math. and stats., 1983—. Author: Least Squares Computations Using Orthogonalization Methods, 1984, 2d edit., 1989; contbr. articles on least squares and the Gram-Schmidt process for the computer to profl. jours. Mem. Assn. for Computing Machinery, Am. Statis. Assn., Am. Math. Soc., Soc. Indsl. and Applied Math. Republican. Methodist. Home: 8200 Cedar St Silver Spring MD 20910-5558

LONGO, DAN LOUIS, research physician; b. St. Louis, Apr. 25, 1949; s. Dominic L. and Alene V. (Bratcher) L.; m. Nancy Kay Schiffman, May 29, 1971; children: Jennifer Alene, Adam Daniel, Paul Anthony. AB, Washington U., St. Louis, 1970; MD cum laude, U. Mo., 1975. Diplomate Am. Bd. Internal Medicine, Am. Bd. Oncology., Am. Bd. Nat. Examiners. Resident in medicine Peter Bent Brigham Hosp., Boston, 1975-77; fellow in oncology Nat. Cancer Inst., Bethesda, Md., 1977-78; postdoctoral fellow in immunology Nat. Inst. Allergy and Infectious Diseases, Bethesda, 1978-80; sr. investigator Medicine Br. Nat. Cancer Inst., Bethesda, 1980-85; assoc. dir. Biolog. Response Modifiers Program Nat. Cancer Inst., Frederick, Md., 1985—; mem. editorial bd. Critical Reviews in Oncology/Hematology. Editor: Clin. Oncology Alert, 1985—, Cancer Chemotherapy and Biol. Response Modifiers Annual, 1987—; asst. editor: Am. Jour. Clin. Nutrition, 1981-91; assoc. editor: Cancer Rsch., Jour. Nat. Cancer Inst., Yr. Book of Oncology, Jour. Immunology, Jour. Immunotherapy; contbr. chpts. to text books and over 300 articles to profl. jours. Capt. USPHS, 1977—. Recipient Harvard Book award 1965, Young Physician award U. Mo. Alumni Assn. Fellow ACP (MKSAP IX Oncology Subspecialty Co. 1989-91); mem. AAAS, Am. Fedn. for Clin. Rsch., Am. Soc. for Microbiology, N.Y. Acad. Scis., Am. Inst. Nutrition, Am. Soc. Clin. Nutrition, Am. Soc. Clin. Oncology (program com. 1986, 90, award com. 1989—), Am. Assn. Immunologists, Am. Assn. Cancer Rsch. (program com. 1991), Am. Soc. Hematology (subcom. on Neoplasia 1989—, chmn. 1990), Am. Soc. Clin. Investigation, Clin. Immunology Soc. (councilor 1987-90), Sigma Xi, Phi Kappa Phi, Alpha Omega Alpha. Office: Nat Cancer Inst FCRDC Bldg 576 Rm 101 Frederick MD 21702-1201

LONGO, KATHRYN MILANI, pension consultant; b. Jersey City, N.J., July 22, 1946; d. Joseph John Baptiste and Kathryn (Sacco) Milani; BA, Adelphi U., 1969; postgrad. N.Y. U., 1968-69, Hunter Coll., 1969-70; m. John Carmine Longo, Mar. 15, 1970 (div. June 1984). Pension cons. Laiken, Siegel & Co., N.Y.C., 1967-84, ptnr., 1977-84; mng. ptnr. Laventhol & Horwath Retirement and Employee Benefit Cons. Div., 1984-88; pres. Pension Alternatives Inc., 1988, mgmt. cons. Creative Pension Systems, 1988—. cons., 1988—; pres., creative cons. Pinch-Hitters, Inc., North Bergen, N.J., 1978-82. Co-founder, co-chmn. Greater N.Y. Pension Cons. Workshop, 1974-88; jazz dance tchr. Kay Marie Sch. Dance Arts, Hammonton, N.J., 1976-83; guest choreographer Regis Drama Soc., Regis High Sch., N.Y.C., 1978-79. Bd. dirs. Phila. Chamber Orch., 1988. Adelphi U. scholar, 1964-68. Mem. Am. Soc. Pension Actuaries (assoc.), N.J. Assn. Women Bus. Owners, Nat. Assn. Female Execs., Am. Soc. Profl. and Exec. Women, Women Entrepreneurs of N.J., Women Bus. Ownership Ednl. Coalition, Inc. (bd. dirs. 1988). Roman Catholic. Office: 2200 Fletcher Ave 7th Fl Fort Lee NJ 07024

LONGO, PAUL, college dean; b. Albany, N.Y., Nov. 10, 1934; s. Paul B. and Angeline (Vigilante) L.; m. Virginia Brown; children: Sharon, Kim, Teresa, Lisa. BS in Edn., SUNY, Oneonta, 1956; MS in Edn., SUNY, New Paltz, 1963; EdD, NYU, N.Y.C., 1971. lic. tchr. elem. edn., social studies, elem. supr. and adminstr. Tchr. Colonie (N.Y.) Cen. Schs., 1956-58, Harborfields Sch. Dist., Greenlawn, N.Y., 1958-63, Commack (N.Y.) Sch. Dist., 1963-65; adminstr. Garden City (N.Y.) Sch. Dist., 1965-67; tchr., adminstr. Queens Coll., Flushing, N.Y., 1967—; dir. Ctr. for Improvement Edn., Flushing, 1986-90, 91; evaluator N.Y.C. Schs. Dist. 1, 5, 17, 27, 32, 1970-80; cons. N.Y.C. Bd. Edn., Dists. 8,2 5, 27, N.Y.C., 1975-90; dir. Project City Sci. Evaluation, N.Y.C., 1977-79. Author: A College Works With a School, 1984. Mem. ASCD, Am. Fedn. Tchrs. (coll. exec. com. 1969-71), Mid. Sch. Tchrs. Assn., Nat. Mid. Sch. Assn. Office: Queens Coll 65-30 Kissena Blvd Flushing NY 11367

LONGO, RICHARD ANTHONY, hospital administrator; b. Scranton, Pa., May 31, 1952; s. Angelo and Consetta (D'Angola) L.; m. Lillian Solomon, Oct. 12, 1985. BSN, Duquesne U., 1975; M in Nursing Adminstrn., U. Pitts., 1981. RN, Pa. Staff nurse VA Med. Ctr., Wilkes-Barre, Pa., 1975, Allegheny Gen. Hosp., Pitts., 1975-76; head nurse VA Med. Ctr., Pitts., 1976-78, supr., 1978-81; assoc. dir. profl. svcs. Hosp. Coun. of West Pa., Warransdale, Pa., 1981-85; dir. physician support svcs. Shadyside Hosp., Pitts., Pa., 1986—; pvt. practice cons., Pitts., 1991—. Mem. Allegheny County Young Reps., Pitts., 1992—. Mem. Am. Market Assn., Am. Coll. Health Care Execs. (affiliate), Health Care Exec. Forum, Brookline C. of C., K.C. Roman Catholic. Office: Shadyside Hosp 5230 Centre Ave Pittsburgh PA 15232

LONGO, ROBIN WEISBARTH, foundation executive; b. Berea, Ohio, Feb. 9, 1954; d. Jack Charles and Margie Clare (Funk) Weisbarth; m. Gregory Anthony Longo, Mar. 5, 1976 (div. 1982). BS in Journalism, W.Va. U., 1980, MS in Indsl. Rels., 1982. Asst. mgr. Season's Restaurant, Woburn, Mass., 1982-83, Nature Fund Ctr., Boston, 1984-86; tchr. Boston Pub. Schs., 1988-90; asst. of v.p./fundraiser Share Systems, Inc., Cambridge, Mass., 1988-90; mgr. mem. outreach WGBH Ednl. Found., Boston, 1990—; telemarketer Share Systems, Inc., 1986—. Fundraiser Dem. Nat. Com., Boston, 1988; mem. membership com. Cambridge Family Y., 1991-92; treas. bd. dirs. The Theatre Co. of Cambridge, 1991. Mem. NAFE, Women in Devel., Nat. Soc. Fundraising Execs. Democrat. Methodist. Home: 390 The Riverway #12 Boston MA 02115 Office: WGBH Ednl Found 125 Western Ave Boston MA 02134

LONGOBARDI, JOSEPH J., federal judge; m. Maud L.; 2 children: Joseph J. Longobardi III, Cynthia Jean Hermann. BA, Washington Coll., 1952; LLB, Temple U., 1957. Deputy atty. Gen. State Del., Wilmington, 1959-61, tax appeal bd., 1973-74; ptnr. Longobardi & Schwartz, Wilmington, 1964-72, Murdoch, Longobardi, Schwartz & Walsh, Wilmington, 1972-74; judge Superior Ct. State of Del., Wilmington, 1974-82; vice chancellor Ct. Chancery, State Del., Wilmington, 1982-84; federal judge U.S. Dist. Ct. Del., Wilmington, 1984—, chief judge, 1989—; assoc. editor Temple Law Rev. Recipient Paul C. Reardon award Nat. Ctr. for State Cts., 1981, S.S. Shull Meml. awrd for excellence in legal rsch. and writing. Office: US Dist Ct 844 N King St # 40 Wilmington DE 19801-3519*

LONGO-MUTH, LINDA LOUISE, artist; b. Nyack, N.Y., Mar. 25, 1948; d. Frank Peter and Amelia Theresa (Maiorano) Longo; m. Ernest Michael Muth, Mar. 14, 1971; 1 child, Jason Jon Muth. Student, Rome, 1969; BS, Southern Conn. State Coll., New Haven, 1970; postgrad., Paris, 1971; MA, Montclair State Coll., N.J., 1975. Studio art tchr. Ramapo Cen. Sch. Dist., Suffern, N.Y., 1970-88; artist, 1970—; bd. advisors Resources for Artists with Disabilities, N.Y.C., 1989-91; exhibits IBM Gallery Soc. & Art, N.Y.C., 1989. Lincoln Ctr., 1989-91, 92. One-woman shows including Thomsen Gallery, Tappan, N.Y., 1992, Stock Exch. Bldg., N.Y.C., 1992, Brickell Corporate Gallery, Miami, 1992, Galeria, Scottsdale, Ariz., 1992, Rittenhouse Hotel, Phila., 1992; exhibited at Metlife Gallery, N.Y.C., 1991, 333 Gallery, Chgo., 1991, Bay Front Gallery, San Franciscom 1991; interviews ABC News Mag. TV Program, N.Y.C., 1991, CBS affiliate WJW-TV, Ohio Life Choices TV Program, L.A., Atlanta, 1991, WBAI N.Y. Radio, 1991. Lectr. Mus. Modern Art., N.Y., 1990. Recipient Zuita and Joseph Akston Found. award, 1991, Sondra Gittis award, 1991, Wayne Becker award, 1991, Dorothy Seligson Meml. award, Guy Ford Money Penny award. Mem. Nat. Assn. Women Artists, N.Y. Soc. Women Artists, N.Y. Artists Equity. Home: 4 Reina Ln Valley Cottage NY 10989

LONKART, GEORGIA FAITH, banker; b. Trenton, N.J., Jan. 17, 1947; d. George W. and Laura L. (Tilghman) Balles; m. Robert S. Lonkart, Apr. 8, 1967; children: Kevin L., Scott C. Student, Rutgers U., Camden, 1972-75; BA in English, U. R.I., 1982. Fin. aid officer Brown U., Providence, 1980-84; ops. mgr. R.I. Hosp. Trust Nat. Bank, Providence, 1984-85, ops. officer, 1985-86, asst. v.p., 1986-87, v.p., 1987-89; mgr. sr. ops. Bank of Boston, 1989-90, dir. consumer fin. ops., 1991—; 1st v.p. R.I. Hosp. Trust (subs. Bank of Boston), Providence, 1990-91; dir. cons. fin. ops. Bank of Boston, 1991—. Mem. Am. Inst. Bankers, Consumer Bankers Assn. Home: 62 Carue Dr North Scituate RI 02857-1013

LONSFORD, FLORENCE ELIZABETH HUTCHINSON, artist, designer, writer; b. Lebanon, Ind., Jan. 7, 1914; d. Frank Edwin and Jennie Cecelia (Pugh) Hutchinson; m. Graydon Lee Lonsford, Dec. 18, 1938 (dec. Sept. 1958). BS in Sci., Purdue U., 1936; postgrad., Nat. Acad. Fine Arts, 1956-58; MA, Hunter Coll., 1963; postgrad., John Herron Art Inst., 1963, Barnard-NBC Inst. Radio-TV, 1963. Tchr. fine arts N.Y. Pub. Schs., 1960-80; owner, operator greeting card design bus., 1966-69. Freelance artist and designer; freelance artist, copywriter Harper's Pub. House; illustrator Morningstar Prodns.; greeting card artist Curzart, Rust Craft Pubs., Dedham, Mass., Nat. Arcrafts, Detroit; illustrator ch. publs.; editor The Key of Kappa Kappa Gamma, 1947—; paintings shown nat. and regional shows including Hoosier Salon (Indpls.), Cooperstown, N.Y., Brockton, Mass., Mystic, Conn., Ind. State Fair, Jackson, Miss., N.Y., Ky., Ohio and Mich.; graphics rev. in Revue Moderne, Paris, 1967; writer Artists Equity; contbr. to Woman's Home Companion, Christian Sci. Monitor, Saturday Rev., N.Y. Times, Woman's Day, small verse and lit. mags.; paintings sold in decorating dept. of Lord & Taylor. Recipient art prizes Ind. State Fair, Nat. Art League, Salmagundi, Hoosier Salon; named Outstanding Educator Met. Mus. and N.Y. Center Arts and Humanities, 1977; recipient Prix de Honneur, Monaco, 1966; finalist Deauville and Cannes Grand Prix, 1973; elected to Watercolor Soc. Ind. Mem. Nat. Coun. Tchrs. of English, Am. Artists Profl. League, Nat. Art League, Cooperstown Art Assn., Artists Equity, Met. Portrait Soc. (Am. Portrait Soc.), Nat. Opera Club Am. (bd. dir.), Oil Pastel Soc. Am., N.Y. Art Tchrs. Assn. (exec. bd.), Poetry Soc. Am. (cert. USCG artist), Greensward Found., Wilderness Soc., Kappa Kappa Gamma (nat. officer), Mortar Bd., Alpha Lambda Delta. Republican. Presbyterian. Home and Office: 311 E 72d St New York NY 10021

LOOMIS, LEE RODGER, data processing executive; b. Fulton, N.Y., June 28, 1951; s. Lee Earl and Eleanor Jean (Mansfield) L.; m. Sandra J. Forbes, June 14, 1970; children: Brick, Joshua, Trevor, Luke. N.Y. State Regent's Sci. degree, Mexico (N.Y.) Acad., 1969. Regional mgr. Gulf Oil Corp., Phila., 1975-79; exec. v.p. Cen. Computer Svcs. Corp., Syracuse, N.Y., 1979-83; pres. Digital Svc. Inc., Syracuse, 1983-87; pres., chief exec. officer Delta Computec Inc., Syracuse, 1987—; pres. R&M Assocs., S. Hackensack, N.J., 1990. V.p. Bd. Edn. Mexico Acad., 1982-86; dir. Upstate Dist. Men's Retreat, 1988—; mem. Dist. Adv. bd. Nazarene Ch., 1990-91. Home: RR 4 Box 248 Fulton NY 13069-9235 Office: DCI Cos 6647 Old Thompson Rd Syracuse NY 13211

LOOMIS, RONALD EARL, biophysicist; b. Elmira, N.Y., June 22, 1954; s. Donald Earl and Liselotta Hedwig (Hammer) L.; m. Pamela Marie Wingert, Dec. 28, 1974; children: Donald Arthur, Arthur Scott, Theodore Thom. BA in Chemistry and Biology, SUNY, Brockport, 1976; PhD in Biophysics, Roswell Park Cancer Inst., 1983. Postdoctoral rsch. fellow U. Oreg., Eugene, 1983-84; rsch. asst. prof. U. Buffalo, 1984-85, asst. prof. health scis., 1985-92, clin. assoc. prof. health scis., 1992—. Contbr. articles to Biopolymers, Biophys. Jour., Jour. Adhesive Sci. Tech., others. Grantee NIH, 1986—, Health Inst. Devices Inst., 1986-90. Mem. Am. Chem. Soc., Am. Phys. Soc., Soc. for Biomaterials, N.Y. Acad. Sci., Am. Assn. Dental Rsch., Internat. Soc. Magnetic Resonance, Biophys. Soc., Internat. Union Pure and Applied Chemistry (afffiliate), Trout Unltd., Fedn. of Fly Fishers, Sigma Xi. Presbyterian. Home: 53 Puritan Pl Orchard Park NY 14127-4615 Office: SUNY Buffalo 321-322 Foster Hall Buffalo NY 14214

LOONEY, WILLIAM FRANCIS, JR., lawyer; b. Boston, Sept. 20, 1931; s. William Francis Sr. and Ursula Mary (Ryan) L.; m. Constance Mary O'Callaghan, Dec. 28, 1957; children: Willam F. III, Thomas M., Karen D., Martha A. AB, Harvard U., JD. Bar: Mass. 1958, D.C. 1972, U.S. Supreme Ct. 1972, U.S. Dist. Ct. (ea. dist.) Mich. 1986. Law clk. to presiding justice Mass. Supreme Jud. Ct., 1958-59; assoc. Goodwin, Procter & Hoar, Boston, 1959-62; chief civil div. U.S. Attys. Office, 1964-65; ptnr. Looney & Grossman, Boston, 1965—; asst. U.S. atty. Dist. Ct. Mass., 1962-65; spl. hearing officer U.S. Dept. of Justice, 1965-68; mem. Mass. Bd. Bar Overseers, 1985-91, vice chmn., 1990-91. Mem. Zoning Bd. of Appeals, Dedham, Mass., 1971-74; bd. dirs. Boston Latin Sch. Found., 1981-85, pres., 1981-84, chmn. bd. dirs., 1984-86; trustee U.S. Coast Guard Found., 1987—. Fellow Am. Coll. Trial Lawyers; mem. Mass. Bar Assn. (co-chmn. standing com. lawyers responsibility for pub. svc. 1987-88), Boston Bar Assn. (pres. 1984-85, coun. mem. 1985-90), Nat. Assn. Bar Pres.'s, Boston Latin Sch. Assn. (pres. 1980-82, life trustee 1982—, Man of Yr. 1985), U.S. Coast Guard Found. (bd. dirs. 1987—), Norfolk Golf Club, Harvard Club. Democrat. Roman Catholic. Home: 43 Coronation Dr Dedham MA 02026-6230 Office: 101 Arch St 9th Fl Boston MA 02110-1112

LOPER, JOHN ROBERT, environmental services company, consultant; b. Houston, Oct. 1, 1951; s. Joe William and Mary (Lohmann) L.; m. Lorraine Elizabeth Dudley, Dec. 29, 1973; children: Jarrod Wesley, Thomas Benjamin. BA in Applied Sci., Lehigh U., 1973, BSChemE, 1973; MSChemE, W.Va. Coll. Grad. Studies, 1979. Profl. engr., Pa., N.J., N.Y.; lic. indsl. waste water treatment operator. Mgr. prodn., environ. and tech. speciality chem. plant FMC Corp., Charleston, W.Va., 1975-79; mgr. group safety and health indsl. chem. group FMC Corp., Phila., 1979-81, mgr. product sales speciality chems. div., 1981-83, mgr. industry mktg. specialty chems. div., 1983-84; bus. dir. aquifer remediation systems FMC Corp., Princeton, N.J., 1984-85; v.p. Roux Assocs., Inc., West Deptford, N.J., 1985—. Contbr. articles to profl. jours. Elder, bd. trustees, Sunday sch. tchr. Ashland Evang. Presbyn. Ch., Voornees, N.J., 1984—; speaker Nat. Youth Sci. Camp, Webster Springs, W.Va., 1979; mem. Environ. Adv. Bd., Voornees, 1985-86; chair Students for McGovern, 1972, Plant United Way Campaign, South Charleston, W.Va., 1982; scouting coord. pack troop 127 Boy Scouts Am., Voornees, 1984-85. Mem. NSPE, Am. Inst. Chem. Engrs., Nat. Water Well Assn., Environ. Law Inst., Am. Water Works Assn., Water Pollution Control Fedn. Republican. Home: 14 Katherine Ct Glassboro NJ 08028-2826 Office: Roux Assocs Inc 1222 Forest Pky Ste 190 Paulsboro NJ 08066-1728

LOPEZ, JOSEPH JACK, oil company executive, consultant; b. N.Y.C., July 26, 1932; s. Florentino Estrada and Leah (Bodner) L.; m. June Elliott, June 20, 1953; children: Karen Marie Lopez Lynch, Debra Jo Lopez Newton, Laura Jean Lopez Berrell. Student, CCNY, 1955-59. Project estimator Chem. Constrn.-Engrs., N.Y.C., 1960-64, Dorr Oliver-Engrs., Stamford, Conn., 1964-66; chief estimator R.M. Parsons-Engrs., Frankfurt, Germany, 1966-74; mgr. project svcs. A.G. McKee-Engrs., Berkley Heights, N.J., 1974-76; mgr. tech. svcs. Rsch. Cottrell Corp., Sommerville, N.J., 1976-78; cons. Booz Allen & Hamilton, Abu Dhabi, United Arab Emirates, 1978-84; v.p. XL Tech. Corp., N.Y.C., 1984-87; cons. Qatar Gen. Pete Corp., Doha, 1987-90; pres. J. Lopez Cons., Babylon, N.Y., 1990—; estimator Combustion Engring. Co., N.Y.C., 1955-60. With USAF, 1950-54. Mem. Am. Assn. Cost Engrs., Project Mgmt. Inst. Republican. Roman Catholic. Home and Office: 15 Hinton Ave. Babylon NY 11702

LOPEZ, RALPH IVAN, physician educator; b. San Juan, P.R., Jan. 3, 1942; s. Ralph and Aida (Miranda) L.; m. Paula, July 30, 1964; 1 child, Jennifer Abigail. AB cum laude, Fordham Coll., 1963; MD, NYU, 1967. Intern pediatrics NYU Bellevue Hosp., N.Y.C., 1967-68; resident pediatrics NYU Bellevue Hosp., 1968-69, Boston Children's Hosp., Harvard Med. Ctr., 1969-70; asst. prof. pediatrics N.Y. Hosp., N.Y.C., 1973-79; assoc. prof. pediatrics N.Y. Hosp., 1979-83, clin. assoc. prof. pediatrics, 1983—; cons. physician The Dalton Sch., N.Y.C., 1973-86, Nightingale Bamford, N.Y.C., 1986—. Editor: Adolescent Medicine Topics, 1976, 2d edit. 1980; contbr. articles to profl. jours. Bd. dirs. Louis August Jones Found., Rhinebeck, N.Y., 1973-91, chmn. bd., 1990—; bd. dirs. Covenant House, N.Y.C., 1990—; mem. nominating com. Girl Scouts U.S., N.Y.C., 1991. Lt. comdr. USNR, 1971-73. Mem. Phi Beta Kappa. Home: 239 Central Park W New York NY 10024-6038 Office: 418 E 71st St New York NY 10021-4802

LOPINTO, JOSEPH MICHAEL, visual artist; b. Bklyn., Apr. 21, 1958; s. John Salvatore and Athena Marie (Pabst) LoP. Assoc. Graphic Art Prodn. Mgmt., N.Y.C. Community Coll., Bkly., 1979. Illustrator Mark 5 Sales Inc., Manhattan, N.Y., 1977-79; advt. traffic mgr. Time Square Stores Inc., Bklyn., 1979-80; graphic artist Exhibit Group N.Y., Bklyn., 1980-81; asst. publs. dir. N.Y.C. Tech. Coll., Bklyn., 1981—; coll. lab. technician graphic arts dept. N.Y.C. Tech. Coll., Bklyn., 1983-85, art and advt. design dept., 1986-90; freelance graphic artist Gene Discala Assocs., Manhattan, N.Y., 1980-82; founder Dragoncrafts, Bklyn., 1990—. Exhibited in group shows at Bklyn. Arts and Cultural Assn., Promenade Art Show, 1987, Triumvirate Prodns./Make a Wish Found., Renaissance Fair, Sommerset, N.J., 1991, history dept. C.W. Post Coll., Renaissance Festival, L.I., N.Y., 1991; Washington Heights and Inwood Devel. Corp. Ann. Medieval Fair at Cloisters, 1991, 92; photographs represented in permanent collections at N.Y. City Tech. Coll., 1987; featured photographs Bklyn. Skills Exch., 1987. Mem. Gamma Epsilon Tau. Office: NYC Tech Coll 300 Jay St Brooklyn NY 11209

LOPKER, ANITA MAE, psychiatrist; b. San Diego, May 25, 1955; d. Louis Donald and Betty Jean (Sayman-Campbell) L. BA magna cum laude, U. Calif., San Diego, 1978; MD, U. Rochester, 1982. Diplomate Nat. Bd. Med. Examiners. Intern in internal medicine Yale U. Sch. Medicine-Greenwich Hosp., 1982-83; resident in psychiatry Yale U. Sch. of Medicine, 1983-86; postdoctoral fellow Yale U. Sch. Medicine, New Haven, Conn., 1982-86; clin. instr. Yale U. Sch. Medicine, New Haven, 1986-88; pvt. practice specializing in eating disorders Westport, Conn., 1987—; cons. psychiatrist Yale-New Haven Hosp Lyme Disease Study Clinic, 1987—, Yale U. Lyme Disease Rsch. Project, 1986—, Alcoholism and Drug Dependency Coun., Inc., 1989-90; internat. lectr. on Lyme psychiat. syndrome; nat. lectr. on eating disorders, substance abuse. Contbr. articles to profl. jours. Founding mem. Nat. Mus. for Women in the Arts, Washington, 1987; patron Menninger Found., Met. Opera. Mem. AAAS, N.Y. Acad. Scis., Am. Psychiat. Assn., Conn. Psychiat. Soc., World Fedn. Mental Health, Menninger Found., Alpha Omega Alpha, Phi Beta Kappa. Home: 27 Strathmore Ln Westport CT 06880-4700 Office: 7 Whitney St Ext Westport CT 06880-3761

LOQUASTO, SANTO, theatrical set designer; b. Wilkes-Barre, Pa.. Grad., King's Coll., Wilkes-Barre; student, Yale U. Drama Sch. Set designer for repertory cos. including Hartford Stage Co., Long Whart Theater, New Haven, Conn., 1967-68, Yale Sch. Drama Repertory Theater. N.Y.C. debut Astor Place, 1970; set designer Broadway and off-Broadway prodns. Sticks and Bones, 1971, That Championship Season; designer other prodns. including The Secret Affairs of Mildred Wild, 1972, Siamese Connections, The Orphan, As You Like It, King Lear, A Public Prosecutor is Sick of It All, Washington, 1973, The Tempest, The Dance of Death, Pericles, The Merry Wives of Windsor, Richard III, Mert and Phil, Cherry Orchard, Hartford Stage Co., That Championship Season, London, 1974, A Midsummer Night's Dream, A Doll's House, Hamlet, The Comedy of Errors, Awake and Sing, Kennedy's Children, 1975, Murder Among Friends, Heartbreak House, Legend, Measure for Measure, The Glass Menagerie, Hartford, 1976, The Lower Depths, The Cherry Orchard, Agamemnon, Cafe Crown (Antoinette Perry award, 1989); scenery and costume design, Jakes's Women, 1992; film prodn. designer, Shadows and Fog, 1992; costumes only Golda, 1977, Curse of the Starving Class, The Play's the Thing, The Mighty Gents, Stop the World - I Want to Get Off, King of Hearts, 1978, Sarava, The Goodbye People, Bent, 1979, Grand Hotel, 1990; prin. designer costumes only, Twyla Tharp Dance Found.; other ballet design includes Don Quixote for Am. Ballet Theater, 1978, Heart of the Matter for Joffrey Ballet, 1986, costumes for La Salle des Pas Perdus for Les Grand Ballets Canadiens, 1988, set and costumes for Pastorale, Nat. Ballet Can., 1990; designer sets and costumes for opera including La Dafne, Spoleto Festival, Italy, 1973; designer sets for opera including San Diego Opera, Opera Soc. Washington, San Francisco Spring Opera. Recipient Drama Desk award and Variety Poll of N.Y., Drama Critics award for Sticks and Bones and That Championship Season 1971, 72,; prodn. designer films Radio Days, 1987, Bright Lights, Big City, 1988, Big, 1988. Recipient Antoinette Perry award (Tony), 1990. *

LORANTAS, RAYMOND MARTIN, historian, educator; b. Elizabeth, Pa., Feb. 1, 1928; s. Justin and Agnes (Supanis) L.; m. Barbara Anne Bradshaw, Aug. 2, 1969; 1 child, Glenn Seng. PhD, U. Pa., 1963. Asst. to assoc. prof. Drexel U., Phila.; sr. lectr. The Chinese U. of Hong Kong; prof. Tianjin Fgn. Langs. Inst., China. Recipient fellowships NEH, 1976, 80, Mary and Christian Lindback Teaching award, 1968, Educator of Yr. award Interfraternity Coun., Drexel U., 1976. Mem. World History Assn. (pres. 1992—), Am. Hist. Assn. (Africa travel/study grant 1982), Modern European Historians of Phila. (pres. 1965-66, 75-76), Assn. Asian Studies, North Am. Assn. for Cameroonian Studies, ACLU, AAUP, Nat. History Teaching Alliance. Home: 518 Coffman Ave Malvern PA 19355-1512 Office: Drexel U Dept History & Polit Sci Philadelphia PA 19104

LORBER, DANIEL LOUIS, endocrinologist, educator; b. N.Y.C., Sept. 21, 1946; s. Jerome Zachary Lorber and Ruth (Frank) Cook. AB, Columbia U., 1968; MD, Albert Einstein, 1972. Diplomate Am. Bd. Internal Medicine, Endocrinology and Metabolism. Intern medicine Bronx (N.Y.) Municipal Ctr., 1972-73; resident medicine Albert Enstein, Bronx, 1973-75; fellow in endocrinology Vanderbilt U., Nashville, 1975-77; from asst. prof. to asst. dean NYU Sch. Medicine, N.Y.C., 1977-84; from asst. clin. prof. to assoc. clin. prof. Albert Einstein Coll. Medicine, Bronx, 1984—; med. dir. Diabetes Control Found., Flushing, N.Y., 1986—; bd. dirs. Am. Diabetes Assn., N.Y., 1982—. Editor in chief Practical Diabetology Magazine, 1987—. Fellow Am. Coll. Physicians; mem. Am. Diabetes Assn. (N.Y. Downstate Affiliate), Endocrine Soc. Democrat. Jewish. Office: Diabetes Control Found 138-26 58th Ave Flushing NY 11355-5232

LORBER, MORTIMER, physiology educator, researcher; b. N.Y.C., Aug. 30, 1926; s. Albert and Frieda (Levin) L.; m. Eileen Segal, May 20, 1956; children: Kenneth, Stephanie. BS, NYU, 1945; DMD cum laude, Harvard U., 1950, MD cum laude, 1952. Diplomate Nat. Bd. Med. Examiners. Rotating intern A.M. Billings Hosp., 1952-53; resident in hematology Mt. Sinai Hosp., N.Y.C., 1953-54, asst. resident, 1957; asst. resident medicine Georgetown U. Hosp., Washington, 1958; instr., asst. prof. dept. physiology and biophysics Georgetown U., Washington, 1959-68, assoc. prof., 1968; lectr. physiology U.S. Naval Dental Sch., Bethesda, Md., 1962-70, Walter Reed Army Inst. Dental Rsch., Washington, 1963-70; guest scientist Naval Med. Rsch. Inst., Bethesda, 1978-83. Contbr.: The Merck Manual, 14th and 15th edit., 1982, 87; contbr. articles to profl. jours. Lt. USNR, 1954-56. Recipient Lederle Med. Faculty award Lederle Co., Pearl River, N.Y., 1960-63, USPHS Rsch. Career Devel. award Nat. Inst. Dental Rsch., Bethesda, 1963-70; grantee Am. Cancer Soc., USPHS. Mem. Am. Physiol. Soc., Am. Soc. Hematology, Assn. Rsch. in Vision and Ophthalmology, Internat. Assn. Dental Rsch. Jewish. Home: 5823 Osceola Rd Bethesda MD 20816-2032 Office: Georgetown U Sch Medicine 3900 Reservoir Rd NW Washington DC 20007-2187

LORBER, RICHARD JAN, broadcasting and film company executive; b. Bklyn., Dec. 9, 1946; s. Hyman and Evelyn (Fladell) L.; m. Dovie Frances Wingard. BA, Columbia U., N.Y.C., 1967, MA, 1970, EdD, 1977. Freelance art critic Art Forum, Arts Mags., N.Y.C., 1973-79; dir. community edn. Mus. Modern Art, N.Y.C., 1976-77; asst. prof. art history, criticism, edn. NYU, 1977-79; dir. mktg. Nat. Video Clearing Ho., N.Y.C., 1979-81; pres., chief exec. officer, founder Fox/Lorber Assocs., Inc., N.Y.C., 1981—; editor Dance Scope mag., 1973-79. Author: The Gap, 1968. Home: 161 W 16th St Ph C New York NY 10011-6286 Office: Fox/Lorber Assocs Inc 419 Park Ave S New York NY 10016-8410

LORBER, STEPHEN NEIL, artist; b. Bklyn., Aug. 30, 1943; s. Henry and Sophie (Haber) L. Student, Yale U., 1964; BFA, Pratt Inst., 1966; MGA, Bklyn. Coll., 1969. Exhibited in one-person shows at A.M. Sachs Gallery, N.Y.C., 1974, 75, 76, 77, 78, Delahunty Gallery, Dallas, 1975, 77, Alexander Milliken Gallery, N.Y.C., 1981, 83, 84, 85, Dubins Gallery, L.A., 1983; group shows include Pa. Acad. Fine Arts, Phila., 1969, Rotunda Gallery, Bklyn., 1984, Hokin/Kaufman Gallery, Chgo., 1990; works in permanent collections at Chgo. Inst. Art, Bklyn. Mus., Roswell Mus. and Art Ctr., Harvard U. Libr., IBM Inc., 3M Corp., Tulsa Bank of Commerce, Xerox Corp., others. Stoeckel fellow Yale U., 1964, Yaddo fellow, 1971, 74, artist-in-residence grantee Roswell Mus., 1973, 74, Artists fellow Nat. Endowment for Arts, 1976. Home: RR 3 Box 198 Greenwich NY 12834-9124

LORCH, MARISTELLA DE PANIZZA (MRS. INAMA VON BRUNNENWALD), educator, writer; b. Bolzano, Italy, Dec. 8, 1919; came to U.S., 1947, naturalized, 1951; d. Gino and Giuseppina (Cristoforetti) de Panizza; m. Claude Bové, Feb. 10, 1944 (div. 1955); 1 dau., Claudia; m. Edgar R. Lorch, Mar. 25, 1956; children: Lavinia Edgarda, Donatella Livia. Ed., Liceo Classico, Merano, 1929-37; Dott. in Lettere e Filosofia, U. Rome, 1942. Prof. Latin and Greek Liceo Virgilio, Rome, 1941-44; assoc. prof. Italian and German Coll. St. Elizabeth, Convent Station, N.J., 1947-51; faculty Barnard Coll., 1951—, prof., 1967—, chmn. dept., 1951—, chmn. medieval and renaissance program, 1972—; founder, dir. Ctr. for Internat. Scholarly Exch., Barnard Coll., 1980—; dir. Casa Italiana, Columbia U., 1972-76, chmn. exec. com. Italian studies, 1990—, dir. Italian Acad. Advanced Studies in Am., 1991—. Author: Critical edit. L. Valla, De vero falsoque bono, Bari, 1970, (with W. Ludwig) critical edit. Michaelida, (with K. Hieatt) On Pleasure, 1981, A Defense of Life: L. Valla's Theory of Pleasure, 1985, (with E. Grassi) Folly and Insanity in Renaissance Literature, 1986, (with F. Colombo, M. Spaziani, Sinisca) All' America, 1990; editor: Il Teatro Italiano del Renascimento, 1981, Humanism in Rome, 1983, La Scuola, New York, 1987; mem. editorial bd. Italian jour. Romanic Review; dir. Italieu Acad. for Advanced Studies in Am. at Columbia U., 1991—, also articles on Renaissance lit. and theater. Chmn. Am. Ariosto Centennial Celebration, 1974; chmn. bd. trustees Scuola N.Y. G. Marconi, 1986—; trustee Lyceé Français de N.Y., 1986—; bd. dirs. Internat. Congress on Renaissance Theater of No. Italy, 1978. Decorated Cavaliere della Repubblica Italiana, 1973, Commendatore della Repubblica Italiana, 1988; recipient AMITA award for Woman of Yr. in Italian Lit., 1973, Columbus '92 Countdown prize of excellence in humanities, 1990, Elena Cornaro award Sons of Italy Woman of Yr., 1990. Mem. MLA (chmn. Italian Renaissance sect. 1973-74), Medieval Acad. Am., Renaissance Soc. Am., Am. Assn. Tchrs. Italian, Am. Assn. Italian Studies (hon. pres. 1990-91), Internat. Assn. for Study of Italian Lit. (assoc. pres. 8th Congress 1973), Pirandello Soc. (pres. 1972-78), Arcadia Acad. Home: 445 Riverside Dr New York NY 10027-6842

LORD, ANTHONY WILLIAM GRATTAN, executive search consultant; b. Plymouth, Devon, Eng., Aug. 12, 1942; s. William Francis Grattan and Kathleen Joan (Thomsen) L.; m. Victoria Jean Wallis, Nov. 18, 1967; children: Karen Victoria, Scott Anthony. AIB, Heriot Watt U., Edinburgh, Scotland, 1962. Trainee Brit. Linen Bank, Edinburgh, 1958-62, Chartered Bank, London, 1962-64; sub-acct. Chartered Bank, Hong Kong, 1964-68; trainee Chase Manhattan Bank N.A., N.Y.C., 1968-70; v.p. Chase Manhattan Bank N.A., Singapore, Manila, 1970-74; chief exec. Baring Sanwa Multinational, Hong Kong, 1974-75; pres. Crocker Bank Internat., N.Y.C., 1975-81; s.v.p., div. exec. Marine Midland Bank N.A., N.Y.C., 1981-86; ptnr. Johnson, Smith, Knisely, N.Y.C., 1986—. Office: Johnson Smith Knisely 475 5th Ave New York NY 10017-6220

LORD, GEORGE DEFOREST, English educator; b. N.Y.C., Dec. 2, 1919; s. George deForest and Hazen (Symington) L.; m. Ruth Ellen du Pont, Mar. 22, 1947 (div. 1978); children: Pauline, George deForest Jr., Edith (dec. 1954), Henry; m. Louise Robins Hendrix, 1978; stepchildren: Louisa, Leslie. BA, Yale U., 1942, PhD, 1951. Instr. English Yale U., New Haven, 1947-66, prof., 1966—; master Trumbull Coll., 1963-66, dir. directed studies, 1966-70, assoc. chmn. English dept., 1983-86; dir. Fiduciary Trust, N.Y., 1969-91; cons. PBS TV program Transformations of Myth Through Time, 1982-90; lectr. in field. Author: Homeric Renaissance: the "Odyssey" of George Chapman, 1956, Andrew Marvell: Poems on Affairs of State, 1963, Complete Poetry, 1968, rev. edit., 1985, Andrew Marvell: A Collection of Critical Essays, 1968, Anthology of Poems on Affairs of State, 1975, Heroic Mockery: Variations on Epic Themes from Homer to Joyce, 1977, Trials of the Self: Heroic Ordeals in the Epic Tradition, 1983, Classical Presences in Seventeenth-Century English Poetry, 1987 (outstanding acad. book 1987 Choice mag.); gen. editor Poems on Affairs of State: Augustan Satirical Verse: 1660-1714, 7 vols., 1963-75; contbr. articles, reviews to acad. jours. Trustee Winterthur Mus., 1952-80, Mary Holmes Coll., West Point, Miss., 1971-80, Fair Haven Housing, 1972-78; trustee, advisor Outward Bound USA, 1977—; vestryman Calvary Episcopal Ch., Stonington, Conn., 1986-89. Morse fellow 1954-55, NEH sr. fellow, 1982. Mem. MLA, English Inst., Renaissance Soc. Am., Am. Acad. in Rome, The Century Assn. Home: 9 Grand St Stonington CT 06378-1352 Office: Yale U Dept English New Haven CT 06520

LORD, JOHN GOVAN, writer, television producer; b. Rochdale, Lancashire, Eng., May 7, 1924; s. Edmund and Doris (Milnes) L.; m. Alison Annette Megroz, 1955 (div. 1963); children: Annette, Nicholas; m. Karolyn Louise Kennedy, 1972. Dipl. in adminstrn., Manchester (Eng.) U., 1943; BA in English, Oxford (Eng.) U., 1950. Tchr. Bancroft's Sch., London, 1950-57; writer, producer Associated Rediffusion, London, 1957-59; TV cons. Govt. Western Nigeria, 1959-60; researcher ABC, N.Y.C., 1960-61; producer NBC, N.Y.C., 1961-72; prof. TV and film arts Boston U., 1972-79; v.p. devel. and prodn. Air Time Internat., N.Y.C., 1979-82; freelance writer, producer various TV networks, N.Y., 1982-89; exec. v.p. Media Access Corp., N.Y.C., 1989—; cons. Nat. Humanities Faculty, Concord, Mass., 1973-76, Inst. Nat. Health Initiatives, Washington, 1985. Author: Duty, Honor, Empire, 1969, The Maharajahs, 1971; co-author: The Valiant Years, 1962; contbr. articles to Life, Atlantic Monthly, Am. Heritage. Capt. inf. British Army, 1943-47, ETO, Mideast. Home: 46 Highland Ave Montclair NJ 07042-1910 Office: Media Access Corp 150 E 58th St New York NY 10155

LORD, MARION MANNS, retired educator; b. Fort Huachuca, Ariz., Dec. 17, 1914; d. George Wiley and Annie May (Pellett) Manns; children: Caroline L. Gross, Polly Steadman, Jane Chapin Humphries. BS, Northwestern U.; MEd, Harvard U., 1962; MA, U. Wis., 1968, PhD, 1968. Columnist, exec. sec. Boston Am., 1936-38; dean women, dir. counseling Henniker, N.H., 1962-64; psychology tchr. Cen. Mich. U., Washington, 1975-79; higher edn. adminstr. U.S. Office Edn., Washington, 1968-75; dean faculty Borough of Manhattan Community Coll., CUNY, 1975-79, Cottey Coll., Nevada, Mo., 1979-80; English tchr. high sch., 1982-84, realtor, 1984-90; ednl. cons. N.H. Coll. and Univ. Coun., 1974-80, David W. Smith & Assocs., Washington, U.S. Office Edn., 1975-80. Editor, contbr.: A Survey of Women's Experiences and Perceptions Concerning Barriers to Their Continuing Education, Review of the Literature. State rep. Gen. Ct. N.H., 1957-62; active various polit. campaigns; active in past numerous civic orgns. E.B. Fred fellow, 1964-68; Breadloaf Coll. scholar, 1936, Northwestern U. scholar, 1933-36. Mem. Am. Psychol. Assn., Pi Lambda Theta. Republican. Home: RR 4 Box 402 Laconia NH 03246-8907

LORD, RICHARD J., advertising executive; b. 1925. Copywriter Cunningham & Walsh, 1954-56; with Young & Rubicam Advt. Agy., N.Y.C., 1956-61; with Benton & Bowles, N.Y.C., 1961-64; v.p., creative dir. Warwick & Legler, N.Y.C., 1964-67; with Lord Geller Federico Einstein, pres., then chmn. bd., chief exec. officer, 1967-88; chmn., chief exec. officer, ptnr. Lord Einstein O'Neill & Ptnrs., N.Y.C., from 1988; now chmn., c.e.o. Lord Dentsu & Ptnrs., N.Y.C. Office: Lord Dentsu & Ptnrs 810 Seventh Ave New York NY 10019*

LOREE, PAUL JAMES, ophthalmologist, consultant; b. Buffalo, Mar. 1, 1936; s. Howard Martin and Victoria Ann (Kirchmeyer) L.; m. Grace C. Langlois, June 29, 1959 (div. Sept. 1984); children: Ruth Langlois Houser, Howard M. Loree II, Paul Edward Loree. BA, Syracuse U., 1954-57; MD, U. Buffalo, 1957-62, Ophthalmologist residency, 1965-68. Am. Bd. Med. Examiners Diplomate, Am. Bd. Ophthalmology Diplomate. Dir. low Vision Svc. SUNY at Buffalo Sch. Medicine, 1970-89, assoc. prof. Ophthalmology, 1968—; pvt. practice Tonawanda, N.Y., 1968—; cons. Batavia (N.Y.) State Sch. for Blind, 1968—; lectr. Am. Acad. Ophthalmology, Treatment of Eye Trauma, 1971-72. Regent Canisius Coll. Bd. Regents, Buffao, N.Y., 1979—. Capt. U.S. Army, 1963-65. Mem. County State Nat. Med. Soc., N.Y. State Ophthalmology Soc., Christian Med. Soc., Christian Ophthalmology Soc., Buffalo Launch Club. Methodist. Home: 2057 Bush Rd Grand Island NY 14072 Office: 2211 Sheridan Dr Tonawanda NY 14150

LORELLI, MICHAEL KEVIN, division president; b. N.Y.C., Apr. 17, 1950; s. Domenic and Effie (Stankevich) L.; m. Judith Bryant; children: Karen, Elizabeth. BE, NYU, 1972, MBA in Mktg., 1973. Dir. mktg. Clairol Co., N.Y.C., 1973-81; v.p., gen mgr. Internat. Playtex, Stamford, Conn., 1981-84; v.p. mktg. Apple Computer, Cupertino, Calif., 1984-85; exec. v.p. Pepsi-Cola Co., Somers, N.Y., 1985-88; pres. Pepsi-Cola East, Somers, N.Y., 1989—; bd. dirs. Allied Beverage. Bd. dirs. Keep Am. Beautiful, United Way, Rosenthal Travel, Am. Health Found.; trustee Sarah Lawrence Coll. Republican. Roman Catholic. Home: 25 Winding Ln Darien CT 06820-5516 Office: Pepsi-Cola Co Rtes 35 & 100 Somers NY 10589

LORENTE, RODERICK DANA, optometrist; b. Lynn, Mass., Mar. 9, 1949; s. Roderick Mariano and Cassie V. (Petrykowski) L.; m. Carol Ann London, Jan. 1, 1972 (div. 1987). BA, Northeastern U., 1971; OD, New Eng. Coll., 1975. Optometrist G. Burtt Holmes & Assoc., Worcester, Mass., 1975-83, Med. East Community Health Plan, Peabody, Mass., 1986—; pvt. practice Belmont, Mass., 1979-84; mgr. clin. programs Soft Contact Lens div. Am. Optical (named changed to Ciba Vision Care), Framingham, Mass., 1984-86, Atlanta, 1984-86; asst. prof. New Eng. Coll. Optometry, Boston, 1983—. Contbr. articles to profl. jours. Mem. Am. Optometric Assn., New Eng. Coun. Optometrists, Mass. Soc. Optometrists (contact lens com. 1980-84), Belmont Lions, Beta Nu. Home: 62 Crescent Hill Ave Arlington MA 02174-2530 Office: Med East Community Health Northshore Peabody MA 01960

LORENZ, ALBERT, illustrator, educator; b. N.Y.C., Dec. 9, 1941; s. Albert Carl and Josephine (Thomas) L.; m. Maureen McCartney, Oct. 17, 1965; children: Margaret, Kirsten. BArch, Pratt Inst., 1965; MArch, Columbia U., 1969; postgrad., Princeton U., 1971. Prin. Albert Lorenz Studio, Floral Park, N.Y., 1969—; mem. faculty Pratt Inst., Bklyn., 1972—, mem. faculty continuing edn., 1978-80, coord. media, 1980—, disting. prof., 1989-90; lectr. Tuskegee Inst., 1972, U. of South, 1972, Auburn U., 1972, U. La., 1972, U. Ala., 1973, Tulane U., 1973, N.Y. Inst. Tech., 1985-86. Author, illustrator: Illustrating Architecture, 1985, Architectural Illustration Inside and Out, 1988, Drawing In Color, 1991; illustrator: AB to ZOGG, 1977, The Dictionary of American English, 1983, The Terra Beyond, 1984, The Bible for Students, 1988; exhbns. include Mus. Modern Art, 1974, Nat. Gallery Art, 1975, Pratt Inst., 1977, Soc. Typographic Arts 100, 1980, Art Dirs'. Show, 1985, 91, N.Y. Soc. Renderers, 1987, Soc. Illustrators, 1987, 90, 91, Illustrators Art Show, 1990; work included in numerous books, jours. and mags. Kinne Traveling fellow Columbia U., 1969; recipient Design award Progressive Architecture, 1973, Outstanding Illustration award Soc. Publ. Designers, 1976, award Chgo. Pub.'s Guild, 1976, ANDY award Merit Advt. Club N.Y., 1980, Exceptional Achievement award PRINT, 1981, award of Excellence Communication Arts Mag., 1983, Silver medal Art Dirs'. Show, 1985, DESI award Graphic Design USA, 1985, First Pl. award Nat. Newspaper of Admissions Mktg., 1991. Mem. AIGA (cert. excellence 1978, 83), Assn. Collegiate Schs. Architecture, Nat. Inst. Archtl. Edn., Soc. Illustrators (edn. com. 1990-91, cert. merit 1982, 90, 91, lectr. 1988). Roman Catholic. Home and Studio: 49 Pine Ave Floral Park NY 11001

LORENZ, DONALD HENRY, polymer chemist; b. Bklyn., Oct. 18, 1936; s. Henry and Florence (Schneider) L.; m. Patricia Ann Marshall, June 2, 1962; children: Peter M., Jeanne C. BS in Chemistry, Poly. Inst. N.Y., 1958, PhD in Organic Chemistry, 1963. Polymer chemist Tex. U.S. Chem. Co., Parsippany, N.J., 1963-65; sr. product chemist GAF Corp., Easton, Pa., 1965-70; group leader polymers GAF Corp., Wayne, N.J., 1970-75, mgr. polymers, 1975-80; dir. R&D Hydromer Inc., Whitehouse, N.J., 1980-88, exec. v.p., 1988-91; pres. Ridge Sci. Enterprises, Inc., Basking Ridge, N.J., 1991—. Author: (with others) Vinylether Monomers, 1968; patentee in field. Republican. Roman Catholic. Office: Ridge Sci Enterprises Inc 12 Radel Pl Basking Ridge NJ 07920

LORENZ, SUSAN JEAN, food service company executive; b. Allentown, Pa., Aug. 7, 1954; d. Norman Curtis and Bernice Isobel (Knauss) L. BS in Nutrition Edn., Indiana U. Pa., 1976; teaching cert., U. Scranton, 1980. Asst. dir. food svc. Servomation Corp., Stamford, Conn., 1976-77, dir. food svc., 1977-84; dist. mgr. Servomation/Svc. Am., Stamford, 1984-87, sales dir., 1987-88, dist. mgr., 1988-91; gen. mgr. food svc. Daka, Inc., Danvers, Mass., 1991—. Mem. Am. Sch. Food Svc. Assn., Pa. Assn. Sch. Bus. Ofcls. Republican. Home: 4190 Newport Dr Emmaus PA 18049-3300

LORENZEN, LOUIS OTTO, art educator; b. Akron, Ohio, Apr. 20, 1935; s. Lorenz Jack and Anne (Stramphér) L.; m. Veronica Ann Lorenzen, Dec. 10, 1978; children: Michelle Melody Raitt, Teresa Ann Turner, Lisette Marie Jackson, Anthony Frederick, Nicholas Joseph. BSEd in Art, Bowling Green (Ohio) State U., 1959; MEd in Adminstrv. Counseling, Bridgewater State Coll., 1964; MAT, Assumption Coll., 1970; MFA, Syracuse (N.Y.) U., 1982. Cert. art tchr., Mass.; cert. secondary English, counseling and guidance, secondary adminstrn., Mass. Art tchr. K-12 Bluffton (Ohio) City Schs., 1959; dir. pubs. Illustrator, graphic designer Greater Cleve. Regional Rsch. Coun., 1959; English tchr. DUEL Vocat. Inst. Calif. Dept. Corrections, Tracey, 1960-61; spl. needs tchr. Old Rochester Regional High Sch., Mattapoisett, Mass., 1961-62; English tchr. Roosevelt Jr. High Sch., New Bedford, Mass., 1962-63, New Bedford Vocat. High Sch., 1963-65; full prof. art Fitchburg (Mass.) State Coll., 1965—; chair program rev. com. Mass. Dept. Edn. Certification, Quincy, Mass., 1991, program rev. com., 1987-90; artist-in-residence Mt. Washington Hotel, 1981. One man shows include LaGardina Gallery, San Francisco, 1960, Fitchburg State Coll., 1968, 80, 82, Jaffrey Civic Ctr., 1972, The Elms Coll., 1985, Borgia Gallery; exhibited in group shows at Rockport Art Assn., 1980-82, 84, Fitchburg Art Mus., 1978, 79, 81-83, 90, Fitchburg State Coll. Faculty Shows, 1982-89, Brick House Gallery, Boothbay Harbor, Maine, 1984-90 (3 ann. shows), New Eng. Art Educators Conf. Show, 1983, also represented in permanent collections. Adv. bd. dirs. Boston Globe Art awards, 1980-85; judge ann. show Westfield (Mass.) State Coll. Dept. Art, 1985. Mem. NEA (life), Mass. Tchrs. Assn., State Coll. Edn. Assn. (local bd. dirs. 1989-90, promotion com. 1988-90, curricula com. 1991—), Mass. Art Edn. Assn. (recording sec. 1968-69, corr. sec. 1970-72, chmn. nominations com. 1972-74, v.p. 1981-83, pres. 1983-86), Mass. Art Edn. Assn., Nat. Art Edn. Assn. (chair authored coee of ethics 1985, ea. rep. to exec. com. for the com. of minority concerns 1986-90, Cert. of Appreciation), Internat. Soc. for Edn. Through Art (ea. alt. rep. nat. chpt. 1989-91), Amnesty Internat., Phi Delta Kappa. Office: Fitchburg State Coll 160 Pearl St Fitchburg MA 01420-2697

LORENZINI, ENRICO CARLO, astrophysical scientist; b. Rome, Sept. 22, 1954; came to U.S., 1983; s. Luciano and Maria Luisa (Lallo) L.; m. Catherine Mannick, Sept. 3, 1988. D in Aeronautics, U. Pisa, Italy, 1980. Registered profl. engr., Italy. System engr. Aermacchi, Varese, Italy, 1981, Aeritalia (Space Div.), Turin, Italy, 1981-84; staff scientist Smithsonian Astrophys. Obs., Cambridge, Mass., 1984—; assoc. Coll. Obs. Harvard U., Cambridge, 1986—; vis. scientist Smithsonian Astrophys. Obs., 1983; vis. prof. U. Naples, Italy, 1990. Patentor device for gravity gradient stabilization. Ordine dei Cavalieri S. Stefano fellow, 1981; Von Karman Inst. Fluid Dynamics scholar, 1978. Mem. AIAA (sr.), Am. Geophys. Union, Am. Astron. Soc., Italian Assn. Engrs. Office: Harvard-Smithsonian Ctr Astrophysics 60 Garden St Stop 80 Cambridge MA 02138-1596

LORGE, TIMOTHY SEAN, real estate developer, musical entrepreneur; b. Camden, N.J., Jan. 23, 1969; s. Eugene Philip and Elizabeth Jeanne (O'Brien) L. Salesman Prudential Preferred Properties, Cherry Hill, N.J.; recruiting and tng. dir. Century 21 Hearst Realty Inc., Turnersville, N.J., 1988-92, salesman, 1988-92, dir. automation, 1988-92, dir. pub. rels., 1990—; pres., founder, chief exec. officer Lorge Devel. Co., Turnersville, 1990—; pres., CEO Tim Lorge Music Ltd., 1992—. Contbr. articles to pubs.; author songs. Mem. Camden County Bd. Mem. Nat. Assn. Realtors, N.J. Assn. Realtors, Gloucester County Bd. Realtors. Republican. Roman Catholic. Office: Lorge Devel Co 6 Bancroft Ct Turnersville NJ 08012

LORI, JOHN MARTIN, financial officer, accountant; b. Harrisburg, Pa., July 31, 1951; s. Robert and Doris (Baugh) L.; m. Sandra Ann Millett, June 2, 1973 (div. Feb. 1980); m. Vicki Lee Shrawder, June 7, 1990. AA in Bus., Harrisburg Community Coll., 1971; BS in Acctg., Elizabethtown Coll., 1973. CPA, Pa. Sr. acct. Schmidt/Garrett Assocs., CPA's, Camp Hill, Pa., 1973-76; contr. Broadscope, Inc., Harrisburg, 1976-80; chief fin. officer Harold H. Hogg, Inc., York, Pa., 1980-85; v.p. Richard D. Poole, Inc., York, 1986-87; pres. Fin. Equity Investments, Inc., Mechanicsburg, Pa., 1988-90; exec. v.p. The McFarland Co., Inc., Harrisburg, 1990-91; chief fin. officer Skelly & Loy, Inc., Harrisburg, 1991—; bd. dirs. Venture Investment Forum of Cen. Pa., Harrisburg; co-founder Cen. Pa. Tech. Coun., Harrisburg, 1990. Contbr. articles to profl. jours. Mem., bd. dirs. Harrisburg (Pa.) Area Community Theatre, 1990—. Mem. AICPA, Pa. Inst. CPAs, Cen. Pa. Internat. Bus. Assn. (treas., bd. dirs.). Republican. Roman Catholic. Office: Skelly & Loy Inc 2601 N Front St Harrisburg PA 17110-1185

LORING, RICHARD WILLIAM, psychotherapist; b. Bronx, N.Y., May 26, 1928; s. William Maurice and Jeannette Edith (Bass) L.; B.A., DePauw U., 1952; M.A., Ind. U., 1954; Ph.D., Columbia Pacific U., 1982; m. Janet Teetor, Aug. 22, 1953; children—Steven, David, Lynne. Psychiat. social worker Richmond (Ind.) State Hosp., 1954-56; asst. dir. Tippecanoe County Mental Health Center, Lafayette, Ind., 1956-62; exec. dir. Venango County Mental Health Center, Oil City, Pa., 1962-71; adminstr. Mental Health/Mental Retardation Authorities, Oil City, 1970-71; dir. Venango Human Services Center, Franklin, Pa., 1971-75; clin. program dir., dir. consultation and edn. Erie County Mental Health Dept.; pvt. practice psychotherapy, Oil City, 1976—; mem. staff dept. psychiatry Oil City Hosp.; sr. psychotherapist Vets. Adminstrn. Vietnam Vets. Outreach Program, 1986—; part-time prof. sociology DePauw U., 1956-62; part-time prof. psychology Pa. State U., 1968-69; field prof. U. Pitts., 1969-74; prof. sociology Clarion State Coll., part-time, 1972-73; part-time prof. mental health counseling Gannon Coll., 1975; spl. cons. Corps Chaplains, U.S. Army, 1971-75; mem. profl. adv. com. Crippled Children and Adults Com., 1971-75; mem. profl. adv. com. Clarion State Coll. Sch. Nursing, 1981—. Bd. dirs. Pa. Mental Health Assn., 1969-77, mem. exec. com., 1973-77; del., mem. task force on aging White House Conf. on Aging, 1971; del. Nat. Conf. on Mental Health, 1975; bd. dirs. Franklin Light Opera Co., 1970-74; chmn. project rev. com. Venango Regional Comprehensive Health Planning, 1973-75; chmn. Gt. Lakes Forum on Primary Prevention in Mental Health, 1976; chmn. N.W. Pa. Family Planning Council, 1974; mem. N.W. region steering com. Pub. Com. for Humanities in Pa., 1971-74. Served with AUS, World War II. Named Boss of Yr., Ft. Venango chpt. Nat. Secs. Assn., 1972. Mem. Psychiat. Outpatient Centers Am. (exec. sec. 1966-74), Am. Pub. Health Assn., Am. Coll. Clinic Adminstrs. Editor: Selected Papers of Psychiatric Outpatient Centers, 1967; Psychiatric Outpatient Centers and Low Income Populations, 1968. Home: 406 W 7th St Oil City PA 16301-3040 Office: Glenview Profl Bldg 9 Glenview Ave Oil City PA 16301-2137

LORION, RAYMOND PAUL, psychologist, educator; b. Worcester, Mass., May 19, 1946; s. Edmond Gerard and Irene Agnes (Brodeur) L.; m. Shelia Catherine O'Connor, Nov. 24, 1967; children: Jennifer, Matthew. BS in Psychology and French summa cum laude, Tufts U., 1968; PhD in Clin. Psychology, U. Rochester, 1972. Lic. clin. psychologist, N.Y., Pa., Tenn., Md. Asst. prof., rsch. assoc., rsch. coord. Primary Mental Health Project and Ctr. for Community Study U. Rochester, N.Y., 1972-74; assoc. prof. Temple U., Phila., 1974-79; prof. psychology and ednl. counseling psychology, dir. community psychology program, dir. sch. psychology program U. Tenn., Knoxville, 1979-85; prof. psychology, dir. clin./community psychology U. Md., College Park, 1985—; clin. psychology trainee VA Outpatient Mental Health Clinic, Rochester, 1970-71; clin. psychology intern Strong Meml. Hosp., Rochester, 1972; clin. instr. psychiatry (psychology) med. sch. U. Rochester, 1973-74; clin. psychologist Park West Hosp., Knoxville, 1982-85; co-dir. stress mgmt. programs Wellnes Ctr. Park West Hosp., Wellnes Ctr., Knoxville, 1982-84; acting head M.A. community psychology program, Temple U., 1978; mem. exec. com. Coun. Community Psychology Program Dirs., 1982-84, chair, 1983-84; vis. scientist Ctr. for Prevention Rsch. div. Prevention and Spl. Mental Health Programs NIMH, Rockville, Md., 1982-84; acting assoc. adminstr. Prevention, Alcohol/DHHS, Drug Abuse, and Mental Health Adminstrn., Rockville, 1983-84; child and family interventions cons. YMCA Child Care Svcs. Washington, 1987-88; cons. clin. psychologist, Ctr. for Human Svcs. Episc. Community Svcs. of the Diocese of Pa., Phila., 1975-79; rsch. cons. WESTAT Corp., Rockville, 1989—, Nat. Rsch. Ctr. on Asian Am. Mental Health UCLA, 1989—; mem. rsch. adv. com. Prevention Intervention Rsch. Ctr. Albert Einstein Coll. Medicine, Bronx, N.Y., 1988—; mem. tng. adv. bd. Dept. Health and Mental Hygiene State Md., 1987-89; sr. cons. Office of Substance Abuse Prevention, Alcohol, Drug Abuse and Mental Health Adminstrn., Rockville, 1986-89; mem. prevention/edn. staff com. Gov.'s Drug and Alcohol Abuse Commn., Balt., 1990—; rsch. assoc. Prince George's County Pub. Schs., Upper Marlboro, Md., 1988—; mem. Gov.'s Task Force on Youth, Alcohol, and Drug Abuse, Nashville, 1984-85; rsch. cons. dept. child psychiatry Children's Meml. Hosp., Chgo., 1984-89; active numerous other mental health orgns. Co-author: New Ways in School Mental Health: Early Detection and Prevention of School Maladaptation, 1975, Effective Behavior and Human Development, 1977; editor: Ajuriaquerra's Handbook of Child Psychiatry and Psychology, 1980, Protecting the Children: Strategies for Optimizing Emotional and Behavioral Development, 1990; co-editor: Fourteen Ounces of Prevention: A Casebook for Practioners, 1988; editor Jour. Community Psychology, 1989—, 1986-88; assoc. editor Am. Jour. Community Psychology, 1983-87, mem. editorial bd., 1974-83, 89—, editorial cons.; mem. editorial bd. Internat. Jour. Applied Psychology, 1986—, Child and Adolescent Psychotherapy, 1984-90, Internat. Jour. Mental Health, 1978-85, Paraprofl. Jour., 1980-81; editorial cons. Jour. Consulting and Clin. Psychology, Am. Psychologist, Community Mental Health Jour., Developmental Psychology, Jour. Nervous and Mental Diseases, Psychol. Bull., Profl. Psychology Psychotherapy, Theory, Rsch. and Practice, Acad. Press, St. Martins Press, MacMillan Press, Wiley, Pergamon; book rev. editor Internat. Jour. Mental Health; contbr. numerous article to profl. jours. Recipient Adminstr.'s award for Meritorius Achievement Alcohol, Drug Abuse and Mental Health Adminstrn., 1983; grantee Office for Substance Abuse Prevention, NIMH., 1990. Fellow Am. Psychol. Soc.; mem. Am. Psychol. Assn. (fellow clin. div., fellow community div., fellow child, youth and family svc. div.), Soc. for Rsch. in Child Devel., Ea. Psychol. Assn., Coun. Community Programs Dirs., Coun. Univ. Dirs. Clin. Psychology (chair 1989-92), Phipa, Sigma Xi. Roman Catholic. Office: Univ Md Dept Psychology 1123K Zoology-Psychology Bldg College Park MD 20708

LOSAPIO, KATHLEEN (TONI LOSAPIO), technical editor; b. Rochester, N.Y., July 3, 1955; d. Anthony and Grace (Castiglione) L. AAS in Profl. Photography, Rochester Inst. Tech., 1975, BS with honors in Profl. Photography and Communications, 1979. Photographer Eastman Kodak Co., Rochester, 1975-78, specialist customer svc., 1978-84, tech. editor, 1984—; adj. faculty Rochester Inst. Tech., 1982-84. Vol. Wesley-on-East Home for Elderly; mem. Young Leadership div. Jewish Community Fedn.; trustee Internat. Sister Cities of Rochester, 1992; chair Rochester-Rehovot Sister City Com., 1992. Fellow Kodak Camera Club (pres. 1987-88, pres. elect 1986-87, trustee 1983-86); mem. Soc. Tech. Communicators (3 Achievement awards 1987, Merit award 1988, 90, Achievement award 1989, Disting. Tech. Communication award 1990, Merit and Achievement awards Internat. Competition 1990, 2 Disting. Tech. Comm. awards 1991), Soc. Photographic Scientists and Engrs., Photographic Soc. Am. (area rep., ranked 7th to Top Ten Nature Print Exhibitors in World 1984), Women in Communications, Writers and Books, Internat. Platform Assn. Home: 273 Barrington St Rochester NY 14607-3303 Office: 343 State St Rochester NY 14650

LOSCALZO, JOSEPH, biochemist, cardiologist; b. Camden, N.J., Oct. 26, 1951; s. Joseph and Dolores Rita (Ventura) L.; m. Anita Beth Sendrow, Mar. 10, 1974; children: Julia, Alexander. AB summa cum laude, U. Pa., 1972, MD and PhD, 1978. Diplomate Am. Bd Internal Medicine; cert. in cardiovascular disease. Postdoctoral fellow U. Pa., Phila., 1978; resident in internal medicine Brigham and Women's Hosp., Boston, 1978-81, clin. fellow cardiology, 1981-83, chief med. resident, 1983-84, instr. medicine, 1983-85; clin. fellow medicine Harvard Med. Sch., Boston, 1978-81, asst. prof. medicine, 1985-88, assoc. prof., 1989—; chief cardiol. sect. Brockton West Roxbury VA Med. Ctr., Boston, 1989—; mem. rsch. rev. com. Am. Heart Assn., 1988—; med. advisor W.W. Smith Charitable Trust, Phila., 1989—; rsch. rev. cons. Nat. Heart, Lung and Blood Inst., Bethesda, Md., 1990—. Author: (with others) books on vascular biology and medicine; contbr. articles to profl. jours. Recipient Med. Scientist Tng. award NIH, 1972-77, Rsch. Career Devel. award, 1989—; Clin. Scientist award Am. Heart Assn., 1983-88. Fellow ACP, Am. Coll. Cardiology; mem. Am. Fedn. Clin. Rsch., Am. Soc. Clin. Investigators, Am. Soc. Biol. Chemistry, Phi Beta Kappa. Office: Brigham and Womens Hosp 75 Francis St Boston MA 02115-6195

LOSCUTOFF, LYNN LEON, artist; b. San Francisco, Aug. 10, 1934; d. Edward Joseph and Mabel (Robins) Leon; m. James Loscutoff Jr., 1952; children: James III, Holly Lynn, Carol Alice. Student, U. So. Calif., 1952; B in Speech and English, Staley Coll., 1959; student, Boston U., 1960, Art Inst. Boston, 1984, Mus. Sch. Boston, 1985. Cert. camp dir., learning disabilities instr, art adminstr. Camp dir. Camp Evergreen, Andover, Mass., 1964-74; pres. and owner Ideas Inc., Andover, Mass., 1970-76; exec. dir. Copley Soc. of Boston, 1976-84; freelance artist Andover, 1950-87. Fund raiser March Dimes, Gov. Michael Dukakis re-election campaign, 1986, YWCA, Cambridge, Mass. Mem. LWV, North Shore Art Assn., Copley Soc. Boston (Copley medal 1986), Rockport Art Assn. Democrat. Home and Studio: 166 Jenkins Rd Andover MA 01810 Studio: 84 Langsford St Gloucester MA 01930

LOSI, MAXIM JOHN, medical communications executive; b. Jersey City, Dec. 27, 1939; s. Maxim Fortune and Carrie (Rivoli) L.; m. Mary Ann De Grandis, May 30, 1968; children: Christopher, Benjamin. AB, Princeton U., 1960; postgrad. N.Y. Med. Coll., 1960-61, Albert Einstein Coll. Medicine, 1961-62, PhD, NYU, 1972. Lectr. English C.W. Post Coll. L.I. U., Greenvale, N.Y., 1965-67; instr. English, Centenary Coll. for Women, Hackettstown, N.J., 1967-71, chmn. dept., 1970-71; med. abstractor/indexer Coun. for Tobacco Rsch., N.Y.C., 1972-73; freelance med. writer, 1973-74; sr. clin. info. scientist Squibb Inst. Med. Rsch., Princeton, N.J., 1974-77, project team leader, 1975-77; chief med. writer ICI Ams., Wilmington, Del., 1977-79; dir. biomed. communications Revlon Health Care Group, Tuckahoe, N.Y., 1979-86; pres. Max Losi Assocs. Biomed. Writers, Trenton, N.J., 1986-87; exec. dir. documentation mgmt. G.H. Besselaar Assocs., Princeton, N.J., 1987—; FDA cons. Microbiol. Assocs., Bethesda, Md., 1973; mgmt. cons. Robert S. First Assocs., N.Y.C., 1974; vis. lectr. med. writing techniques St. George U. Med. Sch., Grenada, W.I., 1977. Mem. Am. Med. Writers Assn. (N.Y. chpt. pres. 1984-85, nat. pres. 1987-88), Drug Info. Assn., Soc. Tech. Communication. Roman Catholic. Home: 1194 Parkside Ave Trenton NJ 08618-2626

LOSTEN, BASIL HARRY, bishop; b. Chesapeake City, Md., May 11, 1930; s. John and Julia (Petryshyn) L. BA, St. Basil's Coll., 1953; STL, Cath. U., Washington, 1957. Ordained priest Ukranian Cath. Ch., 1957. Personal sec. to archbishop, 1962-66; contr. Archdiocese, 1966-75; apptd. monsignor, 1968; apptd. titular bishop of Arcadiopolis and aux. bishop Ukrainian Cath. Archeparchy of Phila., 1971-77; vicar gen., 1971, apostolic adminstr., 1976-77; bishop of Stamford, Conn., 1977—. Pres. Ascension Manor. Club: Union League (Phila.). *

LOTEMPIO, JULIA MATILD, accountant; b. Budapest, Hungary, Oct. 14, 1934; came to U.S., 1958, naturalized 1962; d. Istvan and Irma (Sandor) Fejos; m. Anthony Joseph LoTempio, Mar. 11, 1958. AAS in Lab. Tech. summa cum laude, Niagara County C.C., Sanborn, N.Y., 1967; BS in Tech. and Vocat. Edn. summa cum laude, SUNY, Buffalo, 1970; MEd in Guidance and Counseling, Niagara U., 1973, BBA in Acctg. summa cum laude, 1983. Sr. analyst, rschr. Gt. Lakes Carbon Co., Niagara Falls, N.Y., 1967-71; tchr. sci. Niagara Falls Schs., 1973-75; tchr. sci. and English Starpoint Sch. System, Lockport, N.Y., 1975-77; instr. acctg. principles Niagara County Community Coll., Sanborn, N.Y., 1989—; club adminstr., acct. Twinlo Racquetball, Inc., Niagara Falls, 1979-81; bus. cons. Twinlo Beverage, Inc., Niagara Falls, 1981-85; staff acct. J.D. Elliott & Co. PC, CPAs, Buffalo, 1986-87; acct., Lewiston, N.Y., 1988—; instr. applied chemistry Niagara County C.C., 1979, instr. acctg. principles, 1989—; bd. dirs. Niagara Frontier Meth. Home Inc., Niagara Frontier Nursing Home Inc., The Blocher Homes Inc., Buffalo. Mem. faculty continuing edn., speaker, chairperson fin. and community rels. coms. United Meth. Ch., Dickersonville, N.Y., 1985-90; guest speaker, counselor, tchr. Beechwood Svc. Guild, Buffalo, 1987-91; bd. dirs. Niagara Frontier Meth. Home, Inc., Getzville, N.Y., 1988—; bd. dirs., mem. fin., investment, pension, ins., and community rels. coms. Niagara Frontier Nursing Home Co., Inc., Getzville, 1988—, Blocher Homes, Inc., Williamsville, N.Y., 1988—; asst. sec., bd. dirs., mem. exec., quality and assurance coms., chmn. community rels. com. Beechwood/Blocher Community, Buffalo, 1990—; mem. Coop. Parish Coun., Sanborn, N.Y., 1991—; mem. adminstrv. bd., chmn. outreach com. Pekin (N.Y.) United Meth. Ch., 1992—; sec. to bd. dirs. Beechwood/Blocher Found., Amherst, N.Y., 1992—. Mem. NAFE, Nat. Assn. Accts., Nat. Fedn. Bus. and Profl. Women's Club, Internat. Platform Assn., Niagara U. Alumni ASsn., SUNY Coll. Buffalo Alumni Assn., Niagara County C.C. Alumni Assn. Home and Office: 1026 Ridge Rd Lewiston NY 14092-9704

LOTHROP, KRISTIN CURTIS, sculptor; b. Tucson, Feb. 8, 1930; d. Thomas and Elizabeth (Longfellow) Curtis; m. Francis B. Lothrop, Jr., Dec. 27, 1951; children—Robin B., Thornton K. and Jonathan C. (twins). B.A., Bennington Coll., 1951. Exhbns. include: Nat. Sculpture Soc., 1967-71, NAD, 1968-71, Hudson Valley Art Assn., 1968, Allied Artists Am., 1969, Concord Art Assn., 1970; represented in permanent collection, Brookgreen Gardens, S.C. Recipient Mrs. Louis Bennett award Nat. Sculpture Soc., 1967; Thomas R. Procter award N.A.D., 1968; Dessie Greer award, 1969; Daniel Chester French medal, 1970; hon. mention Hudson Valley Art Assn., 1968; 1st prize Concord Art Assn., 1970, 83; 1st prize Manchester Arts Assn., 1975; 1st prize Hamilton-Wenham Art Show, 1980; Liskin purchase prize Nat. Sculpture Soc., 1986. Mem. Nat. Sculpture Soc., New Eng. Sculptor's Assn. (1st prize 1987). Address: 71 Bridge St Manchester MA 01944

LOTTA, (ANTHONY) TOM, artist; b. Rochester, N.Y., Mar. 28, 1924; s. Joseph and Julia (Roncone) L.; m. Rosemary Alionello, June 18, 1949; children: Tom, Karen. AS, Rochester Inst. Tech., 1950. Freelance artist Rochester, 1951—. Committeeman Rep. Cen. Com., Greece, N.Y., 1970—. Sgt. U.S. Army, 1943-45. Named to Boxing Hall of Fame, Can., 1977; recipient numerous awards for paintings. Mem. Am. Watercolor Soc., Soc. Illustrators, Rochester Art Club (pres. 1976-77). Roman Catholic. Home: 1337 Beach Ave Rochester NY 14612-1895 Office: 100 Rockwood St Rochester NY 14610-2693

LOTTI, VICTOR JOSEPH, pharmaceutical executive; b. Trenton, N.J., Jan. 6, 1938; s. Joseph and Elizabeth (Persiano) L.; m. Jo Ann Pitcock, July 7, 1961 (div. 1971); children: Lynn E., Victor J., Lisa A.; m. Barbara Ozoroski, Nov. 17, 1976. BS in Pharmacy, U. Conn., 1959; MS in Pharmacology, U. Mo., 1961; PhD in Pharmacology, UCLA, 1965. NIH postdoctoral fellow UCLA Brain Rsch. Inst., 1965-66, Nat. Inst. Med. Rsch., London, 1966-67; sr. rsch. pharmacologist Merck & Co., West Point, Pa., 1967-69, rsch. fellow, 1969-73, dir., 1973-75, sr. dir., 1975-77, sr. scientist, 1979—; sr. dir. Merck & Co.-Chibert, Clemont, France, 1977-79. Member editorial bd. Jour. Ocular Pharmacology, 1985—; U.S. and fng. patentee in field; contbr. numerous articles to profl. jours. NIH fellow UCLA, 1964-65; recipient Goldman award U. Conn., 1959. Mem. Am. Chem. Soc., Assn. Rsch. in Vision and Ophthalmology, Mid-Atlantic Pharm. Soc., Western Pharm. Soc., Fedn. Am. Soc. Exptl. Medicine. Roman Catholic. Home: 214 Brookside Cir Harleysville PA 19438-1810 Office: Merck & Co W26A-3025 West Point PA 19486

LOTZ, GEORGE MICHAEL, computer graphics executive; b. Balt., Aug. 28, 1928; s. Michael Henry and Mina Catherine (Fleck) L.; m. Anna Mae Carlson, July 21, 1951; 1 child, Georgeanna. Student Md. Inst. Art, 1956-58, Johns Hopkins U., 1957-58, Catonsville Community Coll., 1975, Essex Community Coll., 1976-78. Mech. draftsman, designer Sinclair Scott Canning House Machinery Co., Balt., 1943-50; illustrator, designer Communications div. Bendix Corp., Towson, Md., 1950-69, supr. graphic arts, photography, 1969-73, art dir., 1974-78, mgr. computer graphics dept., 1978—; art dir., pres. Glen Arm Graphic, 1963-74; advisor Md. State Dept. Art Edn., 1973-78, U. Md. Coll. Human Ecology, 1981—, Essex Community Coll. Computer Graphics, 1981—, Community Coll. Balt. Graphics, 1978—, Goucher Coll., 1991—; mem. panel Nat. Endowment Arts. 1977-78; conf. chmn. Indsl. Graphics Internat. U. Md., 1974, adv. Coll. of Human Ecology & Art Design, 1981—; advisor graphic arts Community Coll. Balt., 1978—, Essex Community Coll., 1981—; tchr. tech. writing Goucher Coll.; guest speaker various local colls., 1973, 77, profl. groups, 1967-78. Judge, Jr. Miss Pagent, Reisterstown, Md., 1971, 72. Served with USNR, 1947-48. Recipient 38 nat. awards for art direction, graphics design including 1st pl. newsletter design Nat. Assn. Indsl. Artists. 1970; 1st pl. award Assoc. Printing Industries Am., 1976, 1st place award Soc. Tech. Communications, 1977; award of excellence Printing Industries Md., 1978, 79; 1st place in photography 1982 World's Fair Design. Competition. Mem. Indsl. Graphics Internat. (pres. 1975-77, exec. dir., 1980—, Award of Merit 13th ann. design competition for promotional photography, Vancouver, B.C., 1986), Council Communication Soc. (dir. 1984-85), Advt. Assn. Balt. (dir. 1971-78), Profl. Photographers of Am. Inc. Clubs: Bendix Emblem, Bendix Mgmt. (pres. 1982-83), Balt. Camera. Contbr. articles on graphic art and edn. to profl. jours. Home: 11212 Old Carriage Rd Glen Arm MD 21057-9415 Office: Allied Signal Corp Bendix Communications Div 1300 E Joppa Rd Baltimore MD 21204-5917

LOU, PETER LOUIS, ophthalmologist; b. Shanghai, China, Dec. 9, 1945; s. J.T. and Huang (Chin) L.; m. Vibeke Emilie Pedersen, Sept. 20, 1980; children: Jared, Kristina, Elizabeth. BSc with honors, U. Ottawa, Ont., Can., 1967; MD, U. Ottawa, 1974; MSc, McMaster U., 1970; diplomate ophthalmic sci., U. Toronto, 1977. Diplomate, Am. Bd. Ophthalmology. Intern U. Toronto, 1974-75, resident, 1976-77; instr. biology McMaster U., Hamilton, Ont., Can., 1967-70; fellow in vitreo-retinal disorders Retina Assocs./Mass. Eye and Ear Infirmary, Boston, 1977-78; instr. ophthalmology Harvard U., Boston, 1979-82; clin. instr. ophthalmology Harvard U., 1982—; pvt. practice ophthalmology Boston, 1982—; dir. ultrasound unit, dir. diabetes clinic Mass. Eye and Ear Infirmary, 1979-82. Author: Retinal Vascular Disorders, 1987; contbr. articles to sci. jours. Fellow Am. Acad. Ophthalmology; mem. AMA, Mass. Med. Soc., New Eng. Ophthal. Soc., Harvard Travellers Club, Harvard Club. Episcopalian. Office: 75 Blossom Ct Boston MA 02114-2352

LOUALLEN, SHARON, film producer; b. Cleve., Aug. 19, 1960; d. James Trekur and Evelyn Hardy Louallen. AS, Va. Marti Coll., Lakewood, Ohio, 1987; Cert., Am. Acad. Dramatic Arts, N.Y.C., 1981-82, Charlee Kebbe on Camera, N.Y.C., 1981-82; cert., H/B Studios, William Hickey, 1987. Account exec. TV Facts Sales & Promotions, Cleve., 1983-84; tchr. Casablanca Modeling Sch., Cleve., 1984-85; pub. rels. staff Roland Co. & Norman Winters, N.Y.C., 1987-89; exec. film producer N.Y.C., 1989—; v.p. ops. Centron Internat., N.Y.C., 1989—; account exec. The Computer Tng. Co., Commack, N.Y., 1991—. Inventor in environ. field. Mem. NAFE, Nat. Assn. Women Bus. Owners. Home: PO Box 7299 New York NY 10150-7299 Office: Centron Internat 14407 Sanford Ave Flushing NY 11355-1672 Office: Tambourine Prodns 200 Rector Pl Ste 25G New York NY 10280

LOUCKS, A. PAUL, academic administrator; b. Jamestown, N.Y., Dec. 24, 1943; s. Arthur P. and Genevieve J. (Peterson) L.; m. Melinda Wallace, Aug. 27, 1966; children: Amy Lynne, Alison Wallace. BA, Allegheny Coll., 1965, MA, 1969. Tchr. high sch. English Cleveland Hts.-U. Hts. Schs., Cleve., 1966-68; counselor Cleveland Hts.-U. Hts. Schs., 1968-70, Valley Cen. Schs., Montgomery, N.Y., 1970-72, SUNY, Potsdam, N.Y., 1972-77; dir. acad. svcs. ctr. SUNY, 1978-86, dir. new student programs & parents rels., 1987—; project dir. AASCU Grant/Potsdam Coll., 1979-82, sec. faculty assembly,

1982-84; mem., SUNY contract negotiations United U. Profls., Albany, N.Y., 1976-80; exec. coun. Nat. Student Exchange Program, Ft. Wayne, Ind., 1982-84. Contbr. articles to profl. jours. Fin. chmn., ch. bd. Unitarian Universalist Ch. of Canton, N.Y., 1976-80; v.p. Potsdam Figure Skating Assn., 1991—. Mem. Nat. Orientation Dirs. Assn., Nat. Acad. Advising, Assn. Democrat. Home: RR 1 Box 242 Potsdam NY 13676-9735 Office: SUNY Potsdam Potsdam NY 13676

LOUDEN, WILLIAM HERBERT, telecommunications executive, consultant; b. Cleve., Nov. 22, 1946; s. William Hugh and Marie Rose (Barry) L.; m. Sherry Lee Soronen, June 27, 1970; children: Heather, Summer. BA in English and Japanese, Ohio State U., 1972; MA in Internat. Mgmt., U. Md., 1992. Asst. elec. engr. Union Carbide Corp., Cleve., 1966-68; retail sales mgr. Tandy Corp., Columbus, Ohio, 1972-80; dir. product mktg. CompuServe, Inc., Columbus, 1980-84; v.p. mktg. Internat. Software Database, Ft. Collins, Colo., 1984; gen. mgr. GE Network for Info. Exch., Rockville, Md., 1985-92; v.p. fin. and mktg. U.S. Videotel, Houston, 1992—; mem. editorial adv. bd. Online Access mag., Chgo., 1986—. Telecommunications editor Portable 100 mag., 1982-84. Mem. GE Polit. Action Com., Washington, 1991. With USN, 1963-66. Named One of Top 50 Contbrs. to Personal Computer Industry, Microtimes mag., 1986, One of Top 150 Contbrs. to Personal Computer Industry, 1987. Mem. Videotex Industry Assn. (bd. dirs. 1988-90), Info. Industry Assn. (Immy award 1990), Am. Mgmt. Assn., Elfun Soc. for GE Leaders. Democrat. Home: 12208 Triple Crown Rd Gaithersburg MD 20878-3785

LOUGEE, ROBERT WAYNE, JR., banker; b. Winchester, Mass., Mar. 14, 1945; s. Robert Wayne and Grace (Hayes) L.; m. Sandra Marie Modean, June 29, 1968; children: Loren Marie, Robert W. III, Jennifer Lynn. BA in English, U. Conn., 1968; MS in Journalism, Boston U., 1971. Reporter, editor Hartford Courant, Hartford, Conn., 1968-70; reporter, editor Worcester Telegram & Gazette, Worcester, Mass., 1970, Boston Herald Traveler, 1970-71, Boston Globe, 1971-72; bus. editor Gannett Co. Inc. Democrat & Chronicle, Rochester, N.Y., 1972-76; mgmt. editor McGraw-Hill, Bus. Week, N.Y.C., 1976-78; bur. chief McGraw-Hill, Bus. Week, Boston, 1978-81; sr. v.p. corp. communications Fleet/Norstar Fin. Group, Providence, 1981—. Mem. Greater Providence C. of C., 1983-88, communications com., 1984-86; mem. communications com. Meeting St. Sch., E. Providence, R.I., 1983-85. Recipient Gold Quill, Internat. Assn. Bus. Communicators, 1985. Mem. Bank Investor Rels. Assn. (bd. dirs. 1983-88, pres. 1986), Nat. Investor Rels. Inst. (bd. dirs. Boston chpt. 1987-88), Pub. Rels. Soc. Am. Office: Fleet Norstar Fin Group 50 Kennedy Plz Providence RI 02903-2393

LOUGHLIN, DONALD ALEXANDER, real estate broker, retired high school principal; b. Bklyn., Dec. 4, 1926; s. James and Isabel (Black) L.; m. Patricia Quinn, July, 1960 (div. 1986); chilren: Ted, Peter, Tim; m. Sue Anne Stark, Oct. 10, 1986. BS, Adelphi U., 1950; MA, Columbia U., 1954, profl. diploma, 1960. Tchr., Lacrosse coach Huntington (N.Y.) High Sch., 1952-58, asst. prin., 1958-68; prin. James E. Sperry High Sch., Henrietta, N.Y., 1968-87, prin. emeritus, 1987—; real estate broker ERA Lighthouse Properties, Fairport, N.Y., 1988—; dir. I/D/E/A Fellows Program, Kettering Found., Agnes Scott Coll., Decatur, Ga., 1975; co-dir. Nat. Leadership Workshop, Plattsburgh, N.Y., 1982-83. Lacrosse Official, Westet N.Y. Ofcls. Assn., 1983; bd. dirs., Jr. Achievement of Rochester, Inc., 1973-81. Served with USN, 1944-46, PTO. Fellow John Hay Found., 1964; named Lacrosse Man of Yr., U.S. Intercoll. Lacrosse Assn.-U.S. Lacrosse Coaches Assn., 1966. Mem. Sch. Adminstrs. Assn. of N.Y. (past pres.), Nat. State Adv. Com., Middle States Assn. of Colls. and Schs., Nat. Assn. of Secondary Sch. Prins., Alumni trustee, Adelphi U. Republican. Presbyterian. Lodge: Kiwanis (pres. 1964). Home: 58 Cambridge Ct Fairport NY 14450-9175 Office: ERA Lighthouse Properties 137 N Main St Fairport NY 14450-1463

LOUGHNEY, JOHN ANTHONY, philosopher educator; b. Scranton, Pa., Apr. 3, 1947; s. John Clifford and Elizabeth Katherine (Swift) L.; m. Amy A. Oliver, May 12, 1980. BS, St. Joseph's U., 1969; MA, Purdue U., 1971, PhD, 1977. Grad. asst. Purdue U., West Lafayette, Ind., 1969-77, vis. lectr., 1977-79; asst. prof. Westfield (Mass.) State Coll., 1979-83, assoc. prof., 1983-87, prof., 1987—; exec. dir., editor-in-chief Social Philosophy Rsch. Inst., Westfield, 1991—; exec. dir., trustee Soc. Philosophers in Am., Yale U., 1986—; pres., dir. Conf. Philos. Socs., 1988—. Dir. Archmere Acad. Alumni Bd., Claymont, Del., 1988. Recipient Disting. Svc. awards Westfield State Coll., 1985, 88; Sumemr Seminar participant Ford Found., 1984, NEH, 1983; David Ross fellow Purdue U., 1976. Mem. Am. Philos. assn., Methaphysical Soc. of Am., Soc. for Phenomenology and Existential Philosophy, Soc. for Iberian and Latin Am. Philosophy, North Am. Soc. for Social Philosophy (dir. 1987—), Soc. for Advancement Am. Philosophy, Am. Studies Assn. Office: Westfield State Coll Dept of Philosophy Westfield MA 01086

LOUGHRAN, MATTHEW GEORGE, sports operations manager; b. Teaneck, N.J., Sept. 11, 1962; s. George Leo and Catherine (Burns) L.; m. Katie Berry, June 22, 1991. Student, Fordham U., 1985—. Adminstrv. mgr. Nat. Hockey League Svcs., N.Y.C., 1982-86; mgr. team svcs. N.Y. Rangers, N.Y.C., 1986—; statistician Madison Sq. Garden Network, N.Y.C., 1987-90. asst. editor: 1986-87 N.Y. Rangers Yearbook, 1986, 1987-88 N.Y. Rangers Yearbook, 1987. Office: NY Rangers 4 Penn Plz New York NY 10001-2819

LOUIE, KWOK YING, space and naval electronics logistic specialist; b. Hagerstown, Md., Sept. 4, 1953; s. Foom You and Yip Chun (Hung) L. BS in Economics summa cum laude, Mt. St. Mary's Coll., Emmittsburg, Md., 1975; MBA, Pepperdine Univ., 1981. Officer USN, 1975-86; assoc. Booz-Allen & Hamilton, Arlington, Va., 1986-87; mgr. integrated logistic support Space and Naval Warfare Systems Command, Washington, 1987—; comdg. officer NR FOSSAC 106 USNR, Norfolk, Va., 1991—. Recipient Navy Commendation Medal, 1979, 81, Navy Achievement Medal, 1984, 89, DOD Civilian Desert Shield Support Medal, 1992. Mem. Delta Epsilon Sigma, Delta Mu Delta. Home: 12801 Valleyhill St Woodbridge VA 22192-6421 Office: Space & Naval Warfare Systems Command Washington DC 20363

LOUIS, BRIAN P., architect; b. Buffalo, Feb. 7, 1958; s. Paul Leo and June Marie (Marvin) L.; m. Sandra Lee Adelmann, Sept. 9, 1984; 1 child, Alison Marie. B of Profl. Studies in Architecture, SUNY, Buffalo, 1980; MArch, SUNY, 1982. Registered architect, N.Y., Fla. Intern architect Hodge Design Svcs., Buffalo, 1982-83, Fullerton, Carey & Johnston, Tampa, Fla., 1983-85; staff architect Johnston Dana Assocs., Tampa, Fla., 1985-88, Schneider Design Assoc., Buffalo, 1988-90; ptnr. Caley & Louis Architects, Buffalo, 1990—; sole proprietor Brian Paul Louis, Architect, Buffalo, 1988-90. Bd. dirs. St. Columbans Retreat Ctr., Derby, N.Y., 1990—. Mem. Buffalo Networking Assoc. (dir. 1991), Internat. Facilities Mgmt. Assn., Free Trade Bus. Assn. (exec. v.p. 1992—), West Seneca N.Y. C. of C., Buffalo C. of C. Home: 186 Main St W Seneca NY 14224 Office: Caley & Louis Architects 520 Franklin St Buffalo NY 14202

LOUISELLE, ROGER WILLIAM, roofing company executive; b. Keene, N.H., Mar. 16, 1951; s. William R. and Elaine Ann (Sharkey) L.; m. Donna Marie Cameron, July 22, 1977; children: Scott Cameron, Jeffrey William. AS, North Hampton (Mass.) Jr. Coll., 1971. Exec. v.p. Vt. Roofing Co. Inc., Rutland, 1973—; gen. mgr. Tri-State Acoustical Inc., Rutland, 1973—, Al Melamson Co. Inc., Rutland, 1973—. Mem. Rutland South Rotary (pres. 1982-83, Paul Harris fellow 1987, 92). Office: Vt Roofing Co Inc PO Box 237 Rutland VT 05702

LOUNSBURY, JAY WILLARD, small business owner; b. Lynbrook, N.Y., Jan. 16, 1944; m. Sariann Cayton; children: Vanessa, Gregory, Sarah. BA, George Washington U., 1970. Free lance cons., editor, 1975-83; pres. Challenger Services, Dunkirk, Md., 1983—. Author: Discontinued and Renamed Post Offices in the ZIP Era, 1963-92, 4th rev. edit., 1992. Dir. communications Calvert County Mental Health Assn., 1983-86; v.p. Dunkirk Area Concerned Citizens Assn., 1985—; county coordinator Md. Vietnam Vets. Meml., 1987—. Served with USAF, 1964-68. Mem. Postmark Collectors Club, Inc. (dir. 1976-85), MENSA (coordinator spl. interest group on impact of TV 1979-84).

LOURIE, ALAN DAVID, federal judge; b. Boston, Jan. 13, 1935. A.B., Harvard U., 1956; M.S., U. Wis., 1958; Ph.D., U. Pa., 1965; J.D., Temple U., 1970. Bar: Pa. 1970. Chemist Monsanto Co., St. Louis, 1957-59; lit. scientist, chemist, patent agt. Wyeth Labs., Radnor, Pa., 1959-64; with Smithkline Corp., Phila., 1964-90, successively as patent agt., atty., dir. corp. patents, asst. gen. counsel, v.p. corp. patents; cir. judge U.S. Ct. Appeals (fed. cir.), Washington, 1990—; mem. U.S. del. to Diplomatic Conf. on Revision of Paris Conv. for Protection of Indsl. Property, 1982, 84; vice chmn. industry functional adv. com. to U.S. Trade Rep. and Dept. Commerce, 1987-90; chmn. U.S. group of U.S.-Japan Bus. Coun. Task Force on Patents. Mem. ABA, Phila. Patent Law Assn. (pres. 1984-85), Am. Intellectual Property Law Assn. (bd. dirs. 1982-85), Assn. Corp. Patent Counsel (treas. 1987-89), Pharm. Mfrs. Assn. (chmn. patent com. 1981-86), Am. Chem. Soc., Harvard Club of Washington. Office: US Ct Appeals Fed Cir 717 Madison Pl NW Washington DC 20439-0002*

LOUZIOTIS, DEMETRIOS, SR., executive director; b. New London, Conn., May 23, 1927; m. Mary Melligon, Feb. 19, 1962; 1 child, Demetrios Jr. BS in Fin., Northeaster U., Boston, 1953. Cert. mcpl. assessor, Conn. Owner Louziotis Agy., New London, Conn., 1953—; br. mgr. Soc. for Savs., Old Saybrook, Conn., 1972-79; bail commr. Judicial dept. State of Conn., New London, 1983—. 1st vice-chmn. Housing Authority, 1958-64; negotiator City of New London, 1964; coord. Joseph Goldberg for Congress Com., 1966; chmn. Presdl. Electors Conn., 1972; dist. coord. Steele for Gov. Com., 1974; commr. Commn. on Spl. Revenue, Conn., 1971-79; chmn. New London Harbor Improvement Agy., 1984-91; mem. Weicker for Gov. Com., 1990. With U.S. Army, 1945-47. Mem. Am. Assn. Cert. Appraisers (sr.), Nat. Assn. State Racing Commrs. (mem. country wide greyhound com. 1971-79), F.L. Allen Hood and Ladder Co., Northeastern Alumni Club Conn., VFW, Order of Am. Hellenic Ednl. Progressive Assn. (Hellene of Yr. award). Home: 72 Parkway S New London CT 06320 Office: Div of Spl Revenue 555 Russell Rd Newington CT 06111

LOVAS, FRANCIS J., chemist; b. Cleve., July 29, 1941; s. Frank J. and Anne (Noonan) L. BS, U. Detroit, 1963; PhD, U. Calif., Berkeley, 1968. Postdoctoral fellow NATO Free U., Berlin, 1968-70; NRC postdoctoral fellow Nat. Bur. Standards, Gaithersburg, Md., 1970-72; rsch. chemist Nat. Inst. Standards and Tech., Gaithersburg, 1972—. Office: Nat Inst Standards and Tech Bldg 221 Rm B265 Gaithersburg MD 20899

LOVE, DERROLD JON, telecommunications industry executive; b. Washington, July 3, 1961; s. Charles James and Anne Lucinda (Vinson) L.; m. Jeanette Victoria Dorsey, July 6, 1985; children: Ryan Michael, Jonee Denise. Student, Knoxville (Tenn.) Coll., 1979-81; BS, Bowie (Md.) State U., 1983. Sales rep. Gap Stores Inc., Landover, Md., 1980; sales specialist AT&T, Hunt Valley, Md., 1983-84; supr. AT&T-Network Svcs., Oakton, Va., 1984-88; mgr. AT&T-Network Svcs., Bedminster, N.J., 1988-90, AT&T Fed. Systems Sales, Washington, 1990—; cons. Image Mktg. Group, Silver Spring, Md., 1990-92. Mem. Am. Soc. Quality Control, Alpha Phi Alpha. Baptist. Home: 13244 Whiteholm Dr Upper Marlboro MD 20772 Office: AT&T Fed Systems 8403 Colesville Rd Silver Spring MD 20910

LOVE, WILLIAM JEFFREY, actor, comedian, playwrite; b. Denver, Feb. 11, 1958; s. William Jr. and Marian Olivia (Andersen) L. Author, appeared in Nose Job, 1989, The Inner City Avon Lady, 1989, The Bunny and Doris Show, 1991, P.M.S. I Love You, 1992.

LOVEJOY, MARGOT R., artist, educator; b. Campbellton, N.B., Can., Oct. 21, 1930; came to U.S., 1965; d. John W. and Hazel (Mowab) MacDonald. Student, Mt. Allison U., 1947-49, St. Martin's Sch. Art, London, 1950, Pratt Graphics Ctr., 1966-71, NYU. Instr. Pratt Graphics Ctr., N.Y.C., 1972-79, Parsons Sch. Design, N.Y.C., 1975-78, SUNY, Purchase, 1978—. One-woman shows MacIntosh Gallery, Glasgow, Scotland, 1982, Inst. for Contemporary Art, Long Island City, N.Y., 1987, Alternative Mus., N.Y.C., 1990, Islip (N.Y.) Art Mus., 1992 also others; exhibited in group shows, 1971—, including Queens Mus., 1983, Mus. Modern Art, Paris, 1983, Bronx Mus., 1985, 87, Va. Mus., 1985, Mus. Contemporary Hispanic Art, 1987, Mus. Modern Art, N.Y.C., 1988, San Antonio Art Inst., 1991; represented in permanent collections N.B. Mus., St. John, Hudson River Mus., Bibliotheque Nat., Paris, Dresden Mus., Mus. Modern Art, others. Recipient purchase award Soc. Am. Graphic Artists, 1978, Nat. Copier Art Exhbn., 1984, faculty leave award SUNY, 1985; grantee Can. Coun., 1976, N.Y. State Coun. on Arts, 1987, Art Matters, Inc., 1989; Offset Inst. fellow, 1984, Guggenheim fellow, 1987. Home and Studio: 166-04 81st Ave Jamaica NY 11432 Office: SUNY Purchase Visual Arts Div Purchase NY 10577

LOVELL, CHRISTOPHER WARD, psychology educator; b. San Pedro, Calif., Sept. 7, 1943; s. James Reynolds and Laura Marcia (Gere) L.; m. Ellen McCulloch, Mar. 1, 1969; 1 child, Evan McCulloch. BA, Goddard Coll., 1974; MEd, U. Vt., 1980; PhD, Am. U., Washington, 1990. Nat. cert. counselor. Dir. admissions Goddard Coll., Plainfield, Vt., 1977-81; assoc. dean Norwich U., Montpelier, Vt., 1981-86; asst. prof. psychology and counseling The Am. U., Washington, 1986—. Home: 5020 Smallwood Dr Bethesda MD 20816-2830

LOVELL, FRANCIS JOSEPH, III, investment company executive; b. Boston, Mar. 21, 1949; s. Frank J. and Patricia Anna (Donnellan) L. BBA, Nichols Coll., 1971. With Brown Bros. Harriman & Co., Boston, 1971—, deputy mgr., 1990—. Mem. New Eng. Hist. Gen. Soc., United Way Loaned Exec. Assn., Union Club of Boston. Republican. Home: 25 Pomfret St West Roxbury MA 02132-1809 Summer Home: 48 Hidden Village Rd West Falmouth MA 02574 Office: 40 Water St Boston MA 02109-3661

LOVELL, ROBERT EUGENE, police administrator; b. N.Y.C., Oct. 17, 1939; s. William Joseph and Anna (Shannon) L.; m. Carol Werthmann, Sept. 23, 1961; children: Christopher, Karen, Susan. BS, U. New Haven, 1980; MPA, Western Conn. State U., Danbury, 1983. Cert. master police instr., Conn. Police officer Danbury Police, 1968-73, patrol supr., 1973-82, comdg. officer spl. ops., 1978—, tng. dir., 1982—; pres. Police Pension Bd., Danbury, 1979-86; sec. Police Benevolent Assn., Danbury, 1971-91; vice chmn. Fairfield Regional Tng. Coun., Greenwich, Conn., 1986-90. Chmn. Tarrywile Park Authority, Danbury, 1991. Recipient Meritorious Svc. medal City of Danbury, 1985. Mem. Nat. Tactical Officers Assn., Nat. Rifle Assn. (life), Internat. Assn. Chiefs of Police, Nat. Criminal Justice Assn., Internat. Assn. Law Enforcement Firearms Instrs. (charter), Am. Soc. Law Enforcement Trainers, Danbury Lions (2d v.p. 1991). Republican. Roman Catholic. Office: Danbury Police Dept 120 Main St Danbury CT 06810-7894

LOVELL, ROBERT MARLOW, JR., investment company executive; b. Orange, N.J., June 24, 1930; s. Robert Marlow and Agnes Whipple (Keen) L.; m. Barbara Jane Cronin, Jan. 16, 1960; children—Kimberley, Kerry, Anthony, Matthew. B.A. with honors in History, Princeton U., N.J., 1952. Trainee Halsey, Stuart & Co., N.Y.C., 1955-57; assoc. Lehman Bros., N.Y.C., 1957-64, assoc. dir., investment adv. service, 1965-67; v.p. New Court Securities Corp., N.Y.C., 1968-70; fin. v.p. Crum & Forster, Morristown, N.J., 1970-73, sr. v.p. fin., 1973-85; pres. First Quadrant Corp., 1985-88, chmn. bd., 1988—; trustee Coll. Retirement Equities Fund; chmn. fin. com. Morristown Meml. Hosp. Contbr. articles to profl. jours. Former chmn. fin. com. Morristown Meml. Hosp. Served to lt. (j.g.) USNR, 1952-55. Mem. Fin. Analysts Fedn., N.Y. Soc. Securities Analysts. Ins. Investment Officers, Am. Fin. Assn. Republican. Club: Princeton Quadrangle. Home: Featherbed Ln PO Box 561 New Vernon NJ 07976 Office: First Quadrant Corp 299 Madison Ave Morristown NJ 07960-6100

LOVELL, WALTER CARL, engineer, inventor; b. Springfield, Vt., May 7, 1934; s. John Vincent and Sophia Victoria (Klementovicz) L.; m. Patricia Ann Lawrence, May 6, 1951; children: Donna, Linda, Carol, Patricia, Diane, Walter Jr. B of Engring., Hillyer Coll., Hartford, Conn., 1959. Project engr. Hartford Machine Screw Co., Windsor, Conn., 1954-59; design engr. DeBell and Richardson Labs., Enfield, Conn., 1960-62; cons. engr. Longmeadow, Mass., 1962—; freelance inventor Wilbraham, Mass., 1965—. Numerous patents include Egg-Stir mixer, crown closure sealing gasket and circular unleakable bottle cap; composer over 50 country-and-Western songs. Office: 348 Mountain Rd Wilbraham MA 01095-1724

LOVETT, JOHN ROBERT, chemical company executive; b. Norristown, Pa., June 17, 1931; s. James and Margaret (Creighton) L.; m. Sandra Miller, May 26, 1956; children: Judy, Jackie, John Robert Jr. BS, Ursinus Coll., 1953; MS, U. Del., 1955, PhD, 1957. Rsch. chemist Exxon Rsch., Linden, N.J., 1957-64; lab. dir. Exxon Rsch./Exxon Chem., Linden, 1964-70; v.p. Paramins Exxon Chem., Houston, 1970-74; tech. mgr. Exxon Chem., Linden, 1974-76; v.p. rsch. Air Products and Chems., Inc., Allentown, Pa., 1976-81; pres. Europe Air Products and Chems., Inc., Hersham, Eng., 1981-88; group v.p. chems. Air Products and Chems., Inc., Allentown, 1988-92, exec. v.p. gases and equipment div., 1992—. Mem. Chem. Mfrs. Assn. (bd. dirs. 1990—), Am. Inst. Chem. Engring., Am. Chem. Soc., Soc. Chem. Industry. Office: Air Products & Chems Inc 7201 Hamilton Blvd Allentown PA 18195-9642

LOVETT, MILLER CURRIER, management educator, clergyman; b. Lynn, Mass., Mar. 18, 1923; s. Charles William and Phoebe Frances (Miller) L.; m. Dorothy Johnsen, Feb. 14, 1946 (div.); children: Anne E., Celeste M., Peter W., Rebecca J.; m. Virginia Lavelli, May 26, 1979. BSBA, Boston U., 1944, STB, 1946, PhD, 1964; postgrad., MIT, 1970-72. Pastor Wesley United Meth. Ch., Medford, Mass., 1946-52; sr. pastor United Meth. Ch., Ellensburg, Wash., 1952-62, Congl. Ch., Laconia, N.H., 1965-70; assoc. prof. bus. adminstrn. Belknap Coll., Center Harbor, N.H., 1970-73; prof. bus. adminstrn. Bunker Hill Community Coll., Charlestown, Mass., 1973-77; assoc. prof. mgmt. Boston State Coll., 1977-82, U. Mass., Boston, 1982—; founder and exec. dir. Social Ventures Trust, Lexington, Mass., 1985—. Contbr. articles to profl. jours. Lt. col. CAP USAF, 1955—. Recipient Disting. Svc. award Ellensburg Jr. C. of C., 1956. Mem. Am. Mgmt. Assn., Mass. Tchrs. Assn., Masons. Home: 25 Spindle Point Rd Meredith NH 03253-1669 Office: U Mass Coll Pub & Community Svc Boston MA 02125-3393

LOVICK, NORMAN, accountant; b. Wilson, N.C., July 10, 1942; s. Henry J. and Ella (Lovick) Webb; m. Delores P. Lovick, Dec. 23, 1967; children: Norman Lovick Jr., Michael D. BS, Durham (N.C.) Coll., 1963; AA, N.C. Cen. Coll., Durham, 1961; MS, Am. U., 1964; Adv. Deg., USDA Grad. Sch., Washington, 1971. Acctg. analyst U.S. Dept. Treasury, Washington, 1967-76; fin. analyst Midland Nat. Corp., Wheaton, Md., 1976-78; cpa, cert. fin. planner Lovick's Fin. Assocs., Hyattsville, Md., 1978-88, chief exec. officer, pres., 1985—; gen. agt. Bankers United, Cedar Rapids, Iowa, 1977-79; notary pub. With U.S. Army, 1965-67. Mem. Nat. Assn. Accts., D.C. Life Underwriters Assn., Nat. Assn. Life Underwriters, Nat. Soc. Pub. Accts., Am. Inst. Profl. Bookkeepers, D.C. Soc. Ind. Accts., Am. Mgmt. Assn., Masons (32 deg., chaplain). Democrat. Pentecostal Ch. Office: Lovick's Fin Assocs 3420 Hamilton St Ste 6 Hyattsville MD 20782-3954

LOVIG, LAWRENCE, III, management consultant; b. Norfolk, Va., Nov. 17, 1942; s. Lawrence Jr. and Edith McDowell (Burfoot) L.; m. Gail Helena Halsted, Aug. 27, 1966 (div. Dec. 1984); children: Justine Helene, Jessica; m. Annika Marie Olsson, Apr. 5, 1985; 1 child, Lydia Charlotte. BS, U.S. Naval Acad., 1964; MBA, Harvard U., 1970. Commd. ensign USN, 1964, advanced through grades to lt. comdr., 1971, resigned, 1974; asst. to N.Am. head 1st Nat. Bank Chgo., 1974-75; sr. engagement mgr. McKinsey & Co., Inc., Chgo., Copenhagen and Stockholm, 1976-82; pres. Larlo, Westport, Conn., 1983-84; v.p. mktg. Kontron, Inc., Everett, Mass., 1984; mgr. Bain & Co., Inc., Boston, 1985-89; prin. Putnam, Hayes & Bartlett, Cambridge, Mass., 1989-90; pres. Real Estate Cost Mgmt., Natick, Mass., 1990-92; prin. DRI/McGraw-Hill, Lexington, Mass., 1992—. Bd. dirs. Chgo. Lung Assn., 1976-79. Mem. ASTM (dir. rsch. and tech. planning com. 1986-90). Home: 11 Rice St Natick MA 01760-3528

LOVINGOOD, REBECCA BRITTEN, educator; b. Bethlehem, Pa., June 5, 1939; d. Clyde Robert and Helen Cauffiel (Britten) L. BS, Syracuse U., 1961; MA, Guildhall Sch. of Music, London, 1962; cert., Jagiellonian U., Krakow, Poland, 1985. Cert. tchr., N.Y., Pa. Newspaper reporter The Christian Sci. Monitor, Boston, 1963-65; music tchr. Devereux Found., Devon, Pa., 1965-66; elem. sch. tchr. The Episcopal Acad., Merion, Pa., 1966-90; tchr. Diocese Wilmington Schs., 1991—; edn. tchr. U. Ala., Tuscaloosa, 1988; dir. children's theater, Saratoga Performing Arts, Saratoga Springs, N.Y., 1969; dir. music events, Aldeburgh Music Festival, Suffolk, Eng., 1970. Author numerous children's plays. Vol. The Musical Fund Soc., Phila., The Coll. of Physicians. Recipient Legion of Honor, Chapel of Four Chaplains, Phila., 1981; travel grant, Kosciuszko Found., N.Y.C., 1985. Mem. Am. Assn. for the History of Medicine. Democrat. Roman Catholic. Home: Brandywine Hundred 400 Foulk Rd Apt 22B Wilmington DE 19803-3839

LOW, WYE MING, lawyer, law educator; b. Hong Kong, Sept. 5, 1960; came to U.S., 1986; d. Wing Kee and Siew Kheng (Ng) Low; 1 child, Nicholas ReMINGton Low Wolf. LLB with honors, U. Hong Kong, 1982; postgrad., London Sch. of Econs. and Polit. Sci., 1982-83, Inns of Ct. Sch. of Law, London, 1983-84. Bar: Eng. 1984, Wales 1984, Hong Kong 1986, N.Y. 1990, U.S. Dist. Ct. (so. and ea. dists.) 1990, U.S. Ct. Mil. Appeals 1990, U.S. Ct. Appeals (fed. cir.) 1991, U.S. Ct. Internat. Trade, 1991. Barrister-at-law Chambers of A.E. Diamond, Esq., Q.C., London, 1984-85, Chambers of T.A. Blanco-White, Esq., Q.C., London, 1985, Chambers of Wye Ming Low, Esq., Hong Kong, 1986—; assoc. Pennie & Edmonds, N.Y.C., 1986-87; lawyer, cons. on laws of England Weg & Myers, P.C., N.Y.C., 1988; regional dir., paralegal lectr. BOSSI, Inc., N.Y.C., 1989-90; prof. law Baruch Coll. CUNY, 1989—; examiner exams. div. AICPA, N.Y., 1989-91; tchr. Royal Acad. Dancing, London, Hong Kong, U.S., 1973—. Contbr. articles to profl. publs. Arbitrator Better Bus. Bur. of Met. N.Y., 1989—. Mem. ABA (vice-chair young lawyers div. com. on patents, trademarks and copyrights 1990—, sect. on patent, trademark and copyright law 1990—, sect. on entertainment and sports law 1990—, spl. com. on rels. with fgn. intellectual property attys. 1990—), N.Y. State Bar Assn. (com. amateur and Olympic sports 1990—, com. on law office econs. and mgmt. 1990—, com. on securities regulation 1991—, sect. on entertainment, arts and sports law 1990—, sect. on bus. law 1990—, sect. on internat. law and practice 1991—), Honourable Soc. Inner Temple, Hong Kong Bar Assn., N.Y. Patent, Trademark, and Copyright Law Assn., Gen. Coun. Bars of England and Wales, Fed. Cir. Bar Assn. Mailing Address: PO Box Gen Post Office, Hong Kong Hong Kong Office: CUNY Baruch Coll Law Dept 17 Lexington Ave New York NY 10010-5526 also: Chambers Wye Ming Low Esq, Barrister-at-Law, 1323A Prince's Bldg, Central Hong Kong

LOWE, ALFRED MIFFLIN, III, advertising agency executive, writer; b. Phila., Mar. 18, 1948; s. Alfred Mifflin Jr. and Marian (Higginson) L.; m. Patricia Ann Coppage; 1 child, Alden Mifflin. BA in Art History, Princeton U., 1970. Writer Lansdale & Carr Advt. Agy., Newport Beach, Calif., 1970-72, Asher Gould Advt. Agy., Los Angeles, 1972-73, Wilson, Haight & Welch Advt. Agy., Boston, 1973-74, Creamer, Inc., Providence, 1974-76; owner Loweco Music Co., Providence, 1976-80; v.p. Harold Cabot Advt. Agy., Boston, 1980-81; creative dir. Duffy & Shanley Advt. Agy., Providence, 1981-87, Pagano, Schenck & Kay, Providence, 1987—. Author: The Cheapskate's Handbook, 1986, Beasts by the Bunches, 1987, How to be a Celebrity, 1989, I Hate Fun, 1991. Recipient Clio awards, 1987, Silver Pencil award The One Show, 1988, 2 Bronze Pencil awards, 1991, 5 Boston Creative Club awards, 3 New Eng. Broadcasting Assn. awards, 33 HATCH awards Boston Advt. Club; winner of 2 radio best awards, 1989. Episcopalian. Club: Saunderstown Yacht (R.I.). Home: 51 Spencer Ave East Greenwich RI 02818 Office: Hill Holliday Connors Cosmopulous John Hancock Tower Boston MA 02113

LOWE, ETHEL BLACK, artist; b. Kiowa County, Olka., Jan. 30, 1904; d. Benjamin Alonzo and Harriet Ann (Heaton) Black; m. William Glenn Lowe, June 5, 1939 (dec. 1942). BA, Cen. State U., Okla., 1926; MA, U. Tulsa, 1937; postgrad., U. Okla., U. Colo., Columbia, U. Hawaii. Tchr. pub. schs. Okla., 1922-39, N.Y., 1942-49, 50-68; ret.; teaching prin. Dragon Sch., Sasebo, Kyushu, Japan, 1949-50. Exhibits include Nat. Assn. Women Artists, 1953, 55, 71, 75, 77, Terry Nat. Art Exhibit, 1952, Provincetown Art Assn., 1952-53, Nassau Community Coll., 1971; represented in schs. and pvt. collections; reproductions of works in newspapers, mags, paintings in schs. and pvt. homes. Mem. N.Y. State Ret. Tchrs. Assn., Nat. Assn. Women

Artists, Am. Watercolor Soc., Nat. Ret. Tchrs. Assn., Delta Kappa Gamma. Home: 48-50 44th St Woodside NY 11377

LOWE, FLORENCE SEGAL, public relations executive; b. N.Y.C.; d. Samuel I. and Rose (Cantor) Segal; BS in Edn., U. Pa., 1930; postgrad. Sch. Social Svc., 1935-36; m. Herman Albert Lowe, June 27, 1935; children: Lesley Ellen Lowe Israel, Roger Bernard. Guidance counsellor Phila. Pub. Schs., 1935-41; Washington corr. Variety and Daily Variety, Phila. Daily News, Manchester Union Leader, TV Guide, 1942-58; spl. pub. rels. Radio Sta. WIP, Phila. and Metromedia, 1958-60; coord. spl. projects Metromedia, 1960-70; spl. asst. to chmn. pub. affairs Nat. Endowment for Arts, Washington, 1970-86; sr. cons. arts and cultural communications Kamber Group, 1986—. Mem. pub. rels. and advt. com. Nat. Symphony, 1952-56; mem. Sec. State's Commn. on Travel, 1970-71; mem. Coordinating Com. for Ellis Island, 1982-87; mem. Com. for Nancy Hanks Endowment for Arts, Duke U. Recipient All-Army Entertainment Contest award, 1958; spl. achievement award Nat. Endowment for Arts Chmn., 1983; Spl. Merit award Fed. Govt., 1981, Spl. Achievement award, 1983, Disting. Svc. award, 1985. Mem. Am. Women in Radio and TV (founder, pres. 1954-55), Am. News Women's Club, Coun. Jewish Women, Women in Communications (citation for meritorious reporting 1962), Nat. Press Club, Women's Nat. Press Club (treas. 1954, v.p. 1956), Washington Press Club (bd. dirs. 1968-71, 83-84), Am. News Women's Club (v.p. 1969-70), Washington Press Club Found. Republican. Home: 2801 New Mexico Ave NW Washington DC 20007-3921 Office: Kamber Group 1920 L St NW Washington DC 20036-5004

LOWE, IDA BRANDWAYN, librarian; b. Bogota, Colombia, Oct. 5, 1946; came to U.S., 1964; d. Jacobo and Donna (Ghelman) Brandwayn; m. Fredric Robert Lowe, Aug. 16, 1970; children: Evin, Laurence. BA, Cornell U., 1968; MA, New Sch. Social Rsch., 1971; MSLS, Columbia U., 1972; MBA, Baruch Coll., 1988. Cataloger Baruch Coll. Libr., N.Y.C., 1973-80, mgr. info. svcs., 1981-86, asst. dean, 1987, coord. for systems, 1988—, dep. dir., 1990—; cons. UN Ctr. on Transnational Corp., Ethiopia, 1990-91, UN Devel. Prog., N.Y.C., 1989, various librs., 1987—, various corps., 1986—. Contbr. articles to profl. jours. Home: 81 Old Rd Westport CT 06880-4145 Office: Baruch Coll 17 Lexington Ave New York NY 10010-5526

LOWE, MARY JOHNSON, federal judge; b. N.Y.C., June 10, 1924; m. Ivan A. Michael, Nov. 4, 1961; children: Edward H. Lowe, Leslie H. Lowe, Bess J. Michael. BA, Hunter Coll., 1952; JD, Bklyn. Law Sch., 1954; LLM, Columbia U., 1955; LLD, CUNY, 1990. Bar: N.Y. 1955. Pvt. practice law N.Y.C., 1955-71; judge N.Y.C. Criminal Ct., 1971-73; acting justice N.Y. State Supreme Ct., 1973-74, justice, 1977-78; judge Bronx County Supreme Ct., 1975-76; justice 1st Jud. Dist., 1978; judge U.S. Dist. Ct. (so. dist.) N.Y., 1978—, now sr. judge. Recipient award for outstanding service to criminal justice system Bronx County Criminal Cts. Bar Assn., 1974, award for work on narcotics cases Asst. Dist. Attys., 1974. Mem. Women in Criminal Justice, Harlem Lawyers Assn., Bronx Criminal Lawyers Assn., N.Y. County Lawyers Assn., Bronx County Bar Assn., N.Y. State Bar Assn. (award for outstanding jud. contbn. to criminal justice Sect. Criminal Justice 1978), NAACP, Nat. Urban League, Nat. Council Negro Women, NOW. Office: US Dist Ct US Courthouse Foley Sq New York NY 10007-1501*

LOWELL, ALAN I., security company executive; b. New Haven, Sept. 8, 1939; s. Leonard and Violet L.; m. Phyllis, Dec. 25, 1960; children: Mitchell, Scott, Richard. BS, NYU, 1961. Exec. Dale System Inc., Garden City, N.Y., 1961—. Mem. Am. Polygraph Assn., N.Y. State Polygraphists. Office: Dale System 1101 Stewart Ave Garden City NY 11530-4808

LOWELL, FRANK, film producer; b. Richmond Hill, N.Y., June 25, 1960; s. James and June (Moser) L. BFA in Film, NYU, 1982. Producer, owner, mgr. Proof Prodns. Ltd., N.Y.C., 1983—. Republican. Office: Proof Prodns Ltd 104-51 109th St Richmond Hill NY 11419

LOWELL, HOWARD PARSONS, government records administrator; b. Rockland, Maine, May 10, 1945; s. Chauncey Vernon Lowell and Delia Coffin (Parsons) Morey; m. Marcia Barrell, Feb. 15, 1969 (div. 1980); m. Charlesa Ann Gatson, July 27, 1985, 1 stepson, Garrett Timmons. BA, U. Me., Orono, 1967, Simmons Coll., 1974. Adminstrn. svcs. officer Maine state archives, Augusta, 1968-72; ednl. specialist Mass. bur. libr. ext., Boston, 1974-75; dir. Revere (Mass.) Pub. Libr., 1975-76; freelance cons. Salem, Oreg., 1976-81, Denver, 1976-81; adminstr. Okla. resources br. Okla. Dept. Librs., Oklahoma City, 1981-89; archivist and records administrator State of Del., 1990—; acting dir. N.E. Document Conservation Ctr., Andover, Mass., 1978. Mem. Acad. Cert. Archivists, Nat. Assn. Govt. Archives and Records Adminstrs. (bd. dirs. 1985-87, pres. 1992—), Phi Beta Kappa, Phi Kappa Phi, Phi Alpha Theta, Beta Phi Mu. Democrat. Mem. Unitarian Ch. Office: Bur Archives and Record Mgmt Hall of Records Dover DE 19901

LOWELL, STANLEY EDGAR, accountant; b. N.Y.C., Oct. 12, 1923; s. benjamin and Valerie (Steinberg) L. Student Tchrs. Coll., Columbia U., 1945; B.B.A. cum laude, CCNY, 1948. C.P.A., N.Y. Staff acct. S. D. Leidesdorf & Co., Chgo., 1952-54; chief acct. Polyplastex United Inc., Union, N.J., 1955-57; chief auditor Hudson Pulp & Paper Inc., N.Y.C., 1957-62, chief acct., 1962-64; internal audit mgr. Screen Gems div. Columbia Picture Industries, N.Y.C., 1966-74; chief auditor Alpha Metals, Inc., Jersey City, 1974-77; asst. dir. internal audit CUNY, N.Y.C., 1977—. Served with USAAF, 1943-44. Mem. Am. Inst. C.P.A.s, N.Y. State Soc. C.P.A.s, Inst. Internal Auditors (cert. internal auditor), Internat. Platform Assn. Home: 302 W 12th St New York NY 10014-1945

LOWELL, STANLEY HERBERT, lawyer; b. N.Y.C., Apr. 13, 1919; s. Isidore and Mildred (Cohen) Lowenbraun; BS in Social Sci., CCNY, 1939; LLB, Harvard U., 1942; LLD (hon.), CUNY, 1981; m. Vivian Abrams, Mar. 29, 1947 (div. 1973); children: Jeffrey, Darcy, Lauri; m. 2d, Leona Schaevitz, June 20, 1974. Admitted to N.Y. bar, 1942; asst. U.S. atty., N.Y., 1943-47; partner law firm Lowenbraun & Lowell, N.Y.C., 1947-58, Lowell & Karassik and predecessors, N.Y.C., 1966-78, Fink, Weinberger, Fredman, Berman & Lowell, 1978—; former lectr. CCNY; vis. prof. grad. sch. CUNY; adj. prof. Fordham U. Sch. Social Services. Asst. to borough pres., Manhattan, 1950-53; exec. asst. to mayor, N.Y.C., 1954-58, dep. mayor, 1958; chmn. N.Y.C. Commn. Human Rights, 1960-65; U.S. pub. del. Madrid Conf. Helsinki Final Act, 1979. Chmn., N.Y.C. com. Am. Jewish Tercentenary; past chmn. lawyers com., trustee United Jewish Appeal-Fedn. Jewish Philanthropies; chmn. Nat. Conf. on Soviet Jewry, 1974-76; past chmn. Greater N.Y. Conf. on Soviet Jewry; mem. praesidium Brussels World Conf. on Soviet Jewry; past chmn. Com. for Pub. Higher Edn.; past pres., chmn. Citizens Com. for Children of N.Y.; past vice chmn. Nat. Jewish Community Relations Adv. Council. Del. Dem. Nat. Conv., 1960, 64, 68; exec. com. Dem. State Com., 1960-68; trustee Jewish Communal Fund N.Y., 1981—; trustee-at-large, v.p. Jewish Community Relations Coun., N.Y., 1982—, United Jewish Appeal, Fedn. Jewish Philanthropies, 1984—; spl. counsel pro bono Kings County Hosp., investigation mem. Mayor's Commn. on Health & Hosp. Corps., 1991. Recipient medal City N.Y., 1965; John F. Kennedy Peace award Jewish Nat. Fund, 1966; Judge Joseph Proskauer award Lawyers United Jewish Appeal and Fedn.; John H. Finley Medal CCNY Alumni Assn., 1980, Pres.'s medal, 1980; Establishment of Stanley H. Lowell Ann. Humanitarian award N.Y.C. Commn. on HUman Rights, 1988. Mem. N.Y. State Bar Assn., Assn. Bar City N.Y., Harvard Law Sch. Assn. N.Y. (past trustee), Coll. City N.Y. Alumni Assn. (past pres.). Home: 15 Paxford Ln Scarsdale NY 10583-3329 Office: 420 Lexington Ave New York NY 10170-0002

LOWEN, THEODORE WHITNEY, III, publishing executive; b. N.Y.C., May 12, 1955; s. Theodore Whitney and Eileen (Halpin) L. AB, Hamilton Coll., 1977; MBA, NYU, 1982. Reporter Forbes Mag., N.Y.C., 1982-85; v.p., dir. econ. devel. Hill and Knowlton, N.Y.C., 1985—. Contbr. articles to profl. jours. Mem. Overseas Press Club, Asia Soc., Japan Soc., Garden City Golf Club, Hong Kong Football Club, Phi Beta Kappa. Roman Catholic. Office: Hill and Knowlton 420 Lexington Ave New York NY 10170-0002

LOWENFELS, ALBERT BROWNOLD, surgeon, educator; b. New Rochelle, N.Y., May 10, 1927; s. Albert Lowenfels and Corrine (Brownold) L.; m. Doris Rosett Becker, June 20, 1948; children: Kate, Charles, Robert, Ann. BS, U. Vt., 1948; MD, NYU, 1952. Diplomate Am. Bd. Surgery. Intern Bellevue Hosp., N.Y.C., 1952-53; resident in surgery NYU, 1953-58; assoc. dir. dept. surgery Westchester County Med. Ctr., Valhalla, N.Y., 1966—; prof. surgery N.Y. Med. Coll., Valhalla, 1979—, prof. community and preventive medicine, 1981—; vis. scientist Internat. Agy. for Rsch. on Cancer, WHO, Lyon, France, 1977—. Author: Alcoholic Patient in Surgery, Companion Guide to Surgery; contbr. articles on surgery, epidemiology, alcoholism and pub. health to profl. jours. Recipient award Smithers Found., Mill Neck, N.Y., 1969—. Mem. ACS, Am. Gastroent. Assn., Phi Beta Kappa. Office: NY Med Coll Monger Bldg Valhalla NY 10595

LOWENSTEIN, ALFRED SAMUEL, cardiologist; b. Frankfurt, Germany, Oct. 19, 1931; came to U.S., 1938; s. Ernst and Babette (Stern) L.; m. Mirjam Stern, June, 1957 (div. Feb. 1981); children: Esther, David, Eve; m. Lucy Zilbersweig, Nov. 1, 1981; children: Elie, Daniel, Ariel. BA cum laude with honors in German, NYU, 1953; MD, SUNY, Bklyn., 1957. Diplomate Am. Bd. Internal Medicine, Am. Bd. Cardiology. Intern Montefiore Hosp., Bronx, N.Y., 1957-58, resident, 1959-60, fellow in cardiology, 1960-61; resident Bklyn. VA Hosp., 1958-59; fellow in cardiology St. Vincent's Hosp., N.Y.C., 1970-72; internist Far Rockaway, N.Y., 1963-70; attending cardiologist Beilenson Hosp., Petah Tikva, Israel, 1972-75; pvt. practice Cedarhurst, N.Y., 1975—. Capt. U.S. Army, 1961-63. Fellow Am. Coll. Cardiology, N.Y. Cardiol. Soc.; mem. AMA, N.Y. State Nassau County Med. Soc., Phi Beta Kappa. Jewish. Office: 123 Grove Ave Cedarhurst NY 11516

LOWENSTEIN, DEREK IRVING, physicist; b. Hampton Court, Eng., Apr. 26, 1943; came to U.S., 1946; s. Siegfried and Ilse (Mildenberg) L.; m. Elaine Hartmann, July 6, 1968; children: Jessica R., Peter D. BS, CCNY, 1964; MS, U. Pa., 1965, PhD, 1969. Postdoctoral fellow U. Pa., Phila., 1969-70; research assoc. U. Pitts., 1970-73; asst. physicist Brookhaven Nat. Lab., Upton, N.Y., 1973-75; assoc. physicist Brookhaven Nat. Lab., 1975-77, physicist, 1977-83, sr. physicist, 1983—, head Exptl. Planning and Support div., 1977-84, dep. chmn. accelerator dept., 1981-84, chmn. Alternating Gradient Synchrotron dept., 1984—; assoc. mem. U.S.-USSR Joint Coordinating Commn. on Fundamental Properties of Matter, 1983—, U.S.-Japan Commn. on High Energy Physics, 1984—. Contbr. articles on particle and accelerator physics to profl. jours. Fellow Am. Phys. Soc.; mem. AAAS, N.Y. Acad. Scis., Sigma Xi. Office: Brookhaven Nat Lab AGS Dept 35 Lawrence Dr Bldg 911 Upton NY 11973-9999

LOWEY, NITA M., congresswoman; b. July 5, 1937; m. Stephen Lowey, 1961; children: Dona, Jacqueline, Douglas. BS, Mt. Holyoke Coll., 1959. Community activist, prior to 1975; asst. sec. state State of N.Y., 1975-87; mem. 101st, 102nd Congresses from 20th N.Y. dist., 1989—. Democrat. Office: US Ho of Reps Office House Mems Washington DC 20515*

LOWI, THEODORE J(AY), political science educator; b. Gadsden, Ala., July 9, 1931; s. Alvin R. and Janice (Haas) L.; m. Angele M. Daniel, May 11, 1963; children: Anna Amelie, Jason Daniel. BA, Mich. State U., 1954; MA, Yale U., 1955, PhD, 1961; HLD (hon.), Oakland U., 1972; LittD (hon.), SUNY, Stony Brook, 1988; Docteur honoris causa, Fondation Nationale des, Sciences Politiques, Paris, 1992. Mem. faculty dept. govt. Cornell U., 1959-65, 72—, asst. prof., 1961-65, John L. Senior prof. Am. instns., 1972—; assoc. prof. U. Chgo., 1965-69, prof., 1969-72; Gannett disting. prof. Rochester Inst. Tech., 1986-87, 90-91; fellow Ctr. Advanced Study in Behavioral Scis., 1977-78; chair Am. civilization U. Paris, 1981-82. Author: At the Pleasure of the Mayor, 1964, (with Robert Kennedy) The Pursuit of Justice, 1964, The End of Liberalism, 2d edit, 1979, Japanese edit., 1981, French edit., 1987, The Politics of Disorder, 1971, Poliscide, 1976, (with others) Nationalizing Government: Public Policies in America, 1978, Incomplete Conquest: Governing America, 1981, The Personal President: Power Invested, Promise Unfulfilled, 1985, (with B. Ginsberg) American Government: Freedom and Power, 1990, 2d edit., 1992; Anthologies: Private Life and Public Order, 1968, Legislative Politics U.S.A., 3d edit, 1973. Recipient J. Kimbrough Owen award Am. Polit. Sci. Assn., 1962, French-Am. Found. award, 1981-82, Fulbright award, 1981-82, Harold Lasswell award Policy Studies Orgn., 1986, Richard Neustadt award for Best Book on Presidency, 1986; Social Sci. Rsch. Coun. fellow, 1963-64; Guggenheim Found. fellow, 1967-68; Nat. Endowment for Humanities fellow, 1977-78; Ford Found. fellow, 1977-78; Fulbright 40th Anniversary Disting. fellow, 1987. Mem. Internat. Polit. Sci. Assn. (v.p. 1991—), Am. Polit. Sci. Assn. (v.p., adminstrv. com. 1985-86, pres. 1991), Am. Acad. Arts and Scis. (nomination com., publs. com.), Policy Studies Orgn. (pres. 1977), Yale Grade Assn. (exec. com.). Home: 101 Delaware Ave Ithaca NY 14850-4707

LOWREY, JOYCE ANN, education educator, academic program administrator; b. Meadville, Pa., Feb. 18, 1939; d. John Adams and Virginia (Anderhalt) L. BS in Elem. Edn., Villa Maria Coll., Erie, Pa., 1973; MEd, Ind. U. of Pa., 1978. Sister of St. Joseph, Roman Cath. Ch. Various office positions Traveler's Ins. Co., Pitts., 1956-64; elem. edn. tchr. Diocese of Erie, Pa., 1965-77; elem. tchr. Notre Dame Sch., Hermitage, Pa., 1968-77; learning disabilities tchr. Perceptual Devel. Ctr., Erie, 1977-78, dir., 1978-81; adj. faculty Villa Maria Coll., Erie, 1981-86; learning disabilities tchr. Villa Maria Elem. Sch., Erie, 1981-85; dir. learning disabilities program, instr. Villa Maria Coll., Erie, 1986-89; dir. learning disabilities program, asst. prof. Gannon U., Erie, 1989—; cons. Erie Diocese Confraternity of Christian Doctrine, 1988; presenter, mem. Pa. Planning Team for Secondary Learning Disabilities Program, 1988-90; adv. bd. mem. Inst. for Students with Learning Disabilities at Coll. Misericordia, Dallas, Pa., 1990—; founding bd. dirs. Living Independent for Everyone House, Inc., 1985—. Author, reviewer State Newsletters, Nat. Notes, 1989—. Bd. dirs. L'Arche Erie, 1987—; adv. People with Learning Disabilities, Pa., 1982—, Erie Diocesan Marriage Tribunal, 1980-86. Recipient Letter of Acclamation, Barbara Bush, 1989, award Pa. Assn. for Children & Adults with Learning Disabilities, 1988, Erie County Assn. for Children & Adults with Learning Disabilities, 1984. Mem. Learning Disabilities Assn. of Pa. (pres. 1988-91), Learning Disabilities Assn. of Am., Coun. for Exceptional Children, Orton Dyslexia Soc., N.Y. Coll. Learning Skills Assn., Coun. for Learning Disabilities. Office: Gannon Univ Sch Edn 2551 W 8th St Erie PA 16505-4494

LOWREY, RICHARD WILLIAM, architect; b. Phila., June 11, 1938; s. Charles William and Ethel May (Straley) L.; m. Eileen Joanne Wallace, Jan. 28, 1989; children: Jodi, Erika, Melanie, Ian. BArch, Pa. State U., 1962. Registered architect, Mass., Pa.; registered real estate salesman, Mass. Project mgr. Nolen, Swinburne & Assocs., Phila., 1962-64, project architect, 1968-69; project architect Harold E. Wagoner FAIA, Phila., 1964-68; constrn. mgr. Cape Lands Realty & Bldg. Corp., Brewster, Mass., 1969-70; v.p. David M. Crawley Assocs., Inc., Plymouth, Mass., 1970-75; owner Lowrey Assocs., Architects, Plymouth, 1975-84; pres. Architects Lowrey & Blanchard, Inc., Plymouth, 1984-88; pvt. practice Plymouth, 1988—. South Shore editor Mugs Away, 1989-90. Mem. Plymouth Hist. Dist. Commn., 1979—; trustee Old Colony Natural History Soc., 1979—; corp. mem. Plymouth Pub. Libr., 1984—, Old Colony Club, 1986—; chmn. design com. Plymouth Downtown/Harbor Project. Recipient Plymouth County Renaissance award, 1980, 87, 88. Mem. Minute Man Dart League, (award 1989, area rep. 1989-90), Am. Darts Orgn. (area coord. 1989-90), Nat. Coun. Archtl. Registration Bds. (cert.), Masons, Kiwanis (disting. past pres. Plymouth chpt. 1980-81). Congregationalist. Home and Office: 39 Megansett Dr Unit 3A Plymouth MA 02360-4870

LOWRIGHT, RICHARD HENRY, geology educator, consultant; b. Bethlehem, Pa., Aug. 31, 1940; s. Raymond Charles and Marion Helen (Schaffer) L.; m. Margaret Mary Brockbank, June 26, 1966. AA, Hershey (Pa.) Jr. Coll., 1960; BA, Franklin and Marshall Coll., 1962; PhD, Pa. State U., 1971. Tchr. sci. Horace Greeley High Sch., Chappaqua, N.Y., 1964-66; asst. prof. geology Susquehanna U., Selinsgrove, Pa., 1972-78, assoc. prof., 1978—; hydrogeologist EnvironMetrics, Selinsgrove, 1973—. Mem. Soc. Econ. Paleontologists and Mineralogists, Computer Oriented Geol. Soc., Yellowstone-Big Horn Rsch. Assn. Office: Susquehanna U Selinsgrove PA 17870

LOWRY, WILLIAM KETCHIN, JR., insurance company executive; b. Columbia, S.C., Oct. 4, 1951; s. William Ketchin and Beverly Hubbard (Frazee) L.; m. Elaine Diana Kent, June 22, 1984; children: Jennifer Lyn, Julia Ann. BS in Bus. Adminstrn., U. S.C., 1972, M in Acctg., 1973. CPA, S.C. Supr. Ernst & Whinney, Columbia, 1973-81; sr. mgr. Price Waterhouse, Hartford, Conn., 1981-83, Phila., 1983-84; dir. corp. systems devel. and analysis Am. Can Co., Greenwich, Conn., 1984-86; v.p., treas., chief fin. officer Phoenix Re Corp. and Reinsurance Co., N.Y.C., 1986-90, sr. v.p., treas., chief fin. officer, 1990; v.p., treas. Transnational Ins. Co., N.Y.C., 1989-90; bd. dirs., v.p., treas. Nat. Bus. Brokers, Inc., Greenlawn, N.Y., 1989-90; sr. v.p./chief fin. officer SCOR U.S. Corp., SCOR Reins. Co. Gen. Security Assurance Corp., Unity Fire & Gen. Ins. Co., N.Y.C., 1990—; bd. dirs. Calif. Reinsurance Mgmt. Corp., S.W. Internat. Reinsurance Co., Morgard Inc. Pres., bd. dirs. Groves Homes Assn., Columbia, 1980-81; diaconate West Side Presbyn. Ch., Ridgewood, N.J., 1989-91. Fellow Life Office Mgmt. Soc.; mem. AICPA, S.C. Assn. CPAs, Fin. Execs. Inst., Am. Soc. CLUs, City Midday Drug & Chem. Club, Forest Lake Club, Beta Gamma Sigma, Omicrom Delta Kappa, Beta Alpha Psi, Omicron Delta Epsilon, Sigma Phi Epsilon. Presbyterian. Home: 314 Elizabeth Ave Ramsey NJ 07446-2422 Office: SCOR US Corp 110 William St New York NY 10038-3901

LOWY, HARVEY DAVID, computer science educator, consultant; b. N.Y.C., Dec. 17, 1947; s. Karl and Zilla (Daum) L.; m. Caryn Audrey Stern, July 31, 1977; children: Joshua, Rachel, Benjamin. BS in Math., CCNY, 1969; MS in Computer Sci., SUNY, Stony Brook, 1974, PhD in Computer Sci., 1976. Programmer Airborne Instruments, Deer Park, N.Y., 1969-70; mgr. Leslo Import Corp., N.Y.C., 1971-72; mem. tech. staff Bell Labs., Whippany, N.J., 1976-82; dir. Fin. Info. Svcs. Agy., N.Y.C., 1982-84; prof. computer sci. Fairleigh Dickinson U., Teaneck, N.J., 1984—; cons. Profl. Computer Svcs., Teaneck, 1984—. Contbr. articles to profl. jours. Mem. Assn. Computing Machinery, Phi Beta Kappa.

LOZANSKY, EDWARD DMITRY, physicist, consultant; b. Kiev, Ukraine, Feb. 10, 1941; s. Dmitry R. and Dina M. (Chizhik) L.; m. Tatiana I. Yershov, Feb. 27, 1971; 1 child, Tania. MS, Moscow Phys. Engring. Inst., 1966; PhD, Inst. Atomic Energy, Moscow, 1969. Asst. prof. Moscow State U., 1969-71; assoc. prof. Mil. Tank Acad., Moscow, 1971-75, U. Rochester, N.Y., 1977-80, Am. Univ., Washington, 1981-83; prof. L.I. U., Bklyn., 1983-87; pres. Independent U., Washington, 1987—; pres. Andrei Sakharov Inst., Washington, 1981-86, Russia House, Inc., Washington, 1991—. Author: Theory of the Spark, 1976, For Tatiana, 1984, Andrei Sakharov, 1986, Mathematical Competitions, 1988. Republican. Jewish. Office: Russia House 1800 Connecticut Ave NW Washington DC 20009

LOZIER, DANIEL WILLIAM, mathematician; b. Portland, Oreg., Apr. 10, 1941; s. Elmer William and Helen Cleo (Hilton) L.; m. Elaine Marie Tolnitch, June 6, 1966; 1 child, Daniel William Jr. BA, Oreg. State U., 1962; MA, Am. U., Washington, 1969; PhD, U. Md., 1979. Mathematician U.S. Army Mobility Equipment Rsch. and Devel. Ctr., Ft. Belvoir, Va., 1963-69, Nat. Inst. Standards and Tech., Gaithersburg, Md., 1969—; adj. prof. Inst. Phys. Sci. and Tech., U. Md., College Park, 1986—. Contbr. articles to profl. jours. Mem. Soc. Indsl. and Applied Math., Assn. Computing Machinery, Math. Assn. Am., Sigma Xi. Democrat. Methodist. Home: 5230 Sherrier Pl NW Washington DC 20016-3324 Office: Nat Inst Standards and Tech Math Div Gaithersburg MD 20899

LOZIER, GILMOUR GREGORY, academic administrator; b. Dumont, N.J., Feb. 13, 1945; s. George Henry Jr. Lozier and Dorothy Anne (Gilmour) Lozier Engler; m. S. Lee Partridge, Aug. 19, 1967; children: Andrew John, Jeannine Anne, Edward Theodore. BA, Rutgers U., 1966; MS in Edn., So. Ill. U., 1968; DEd, Pa. State U., 1973. Counselor So. Ill. U., Carbondale, 1966-68; dean of men Atlantic Christian Coll., Wilson, N.C., 1968-70; rsch. asst. Pa. State U., University Park, 1970-72, sr. planning analyst, 1972-75, univ. planning specialist, 1975-79, assoc. dir., 1979-83, exec. dir., 1983—; cons. Cornell U., SUNY Oswego, U. Montreal, U. Kans., N.C. State U., Miami U. Ohio, U. S.C., Western Wash. U., Oreg. State U., Fayetteville State U., Nicholls State U., Va. Poly. Inst. and State U., U. Calif. State System; presenter of workshops and panels. Contbr. chpts. to books and articles to profl. jours. Mem. State College (Pa.) Sch. Dist. Planning Team, 1985-88; chair Pers. and Adminstrn. Com., Ferguson Twp., Pa., 1985-90; bd. dirs. Cen. Pa. Festival of the Arts, State College, 1988-91, treas., 1989-91; planning facilitator State Coll. C. of C., 1990. Mem. Am. Soc. Quality Control, Assn. Instl. Rsch., Soc. Coll. and U. Planning (internat. conf. chair 1988), Assn. for Study Higher Edn., Acad. Academic Pers. Adminstrn. (sec.-treas. 1976-77), European Assn. Instl. Rsch., Phi Kappa Phi, Kappa Delta Pi. Democrat. Methodist. Home: 316 Mcbath St State College PA 16801-2743 Office: Pa State U 405 Old Main University Park PA 16802-1505

LOZNER, JERROLD STANLEY, surgeon; b. N.Y.C., May 20, 1947; s. Joseph and Etta (Bring) L.; m. Barbara Dicter, July 4, 1970; children: Amy, Joshua, Stacy. BA, Columbia U., 1967; MD, U. Louisville, 1971; MHA, U. Colo., 1991. Diplomate Am. Bd. Surgeons, Am. Bd. Thoracic Surgeons. Intern in Surgery, resident in gen./cardiothoracic surgery U. Cin. Med. Ctr., Cin., 1971-78; mem. staff in thoracic, vascular and gen. surgery Overlook Hosp., Summit, N.J., 1980—, asst. v.p. med. affairs, 1990—; asst. clin. prof. surgery Columbia Coll. of Physicians and Surgeons, N.Y.C., 1982—. Bd. dirs. Summit Med. Group, Summit, 1988—. Lt. Comdr. USN, 1978-80. Fellow ACS; mem. AMA, Am. Coll. Physician Execs., N.J. Vascular Soc., N.J. Soc. of Thoracic Surgeons. Home: 79 Old Hollow Rd Short Hills NJ 07078 Office: Summit Med Group 120 Summit Ave Summit NJ 07901

LOZOWSKI, THOMAS EDWARD, mechanical engineer, utilities industry manager; b. Pitts., May 26, 1963; s. Stanley Charles and Mary Ann (Kronenberger) L.; m. Cheryl Snyder, Mar. 4, 1989. BS in Mech. Engring., Villanova U., 1985; MBA, Rider Coll., 1991; cert. of modern mfg. system and mgmt., N.J. Inst. Tech., 1992. Field engr. Stonhard Corp., Maple Shade, N.J., 1985-86; mktg. engr. Pub. Svc. Electric & Gas, Princeton, N.J., 1986-89, applications engr., 1989-91, industry mgr., 1991—; task force mem. for alternative waste techs., N.J. Hosp. Assn., Princeton, 1991. Mem. ASHRAE (assoc.). Office: Pub Svc Electric & Gas PO Box 2021 Princeton NJ 08543

LU, I-LI, federal agency administrator, researcher; b. Taipei, Taiwan, China, Apr. 24, 1956; came to the U.S., 1980; s. Dou-Yen and Tan J. (Liang) L.; m. Katrina Huang, July 8, 1983; children: Darlene, De-chi. BS with highest honors, U. Wis., LaCrosse, 1983; MA, U. Va., 1987, PhD, 1991. Statis. analyst Commonwealth Clin. System, Charlottesville, Va., 1984-87; math. statistician U.S. Bur. Census, Washington, 1991—. Mem. Am. Math. Soc., Am. Statistical Assn., Inst. Math. Statistics. Home: 10150 Marshall Pond Rd Burke VA 22015 Office: US Dept Commerce Census Washington DC 20233

LU, KEH-MING, computer science professional; b. I-Lan, Taiwan, China, June 19, 1949; came to U.S. 1973, naturalized 1981.; s. Kung-Yun and Rye-Lian (Jiang) L.; m. Helen Sheau-Feng Chen Lu, Mar. 24, 1974; children: Julie I-Wei, Margaret I-Chia, Alan Yao-Jen. BS, Nat. Chiao Tung U., Hsin-Chu, Taiwan, 1971; MS, Mich. State U., 1974, Washington U., St. Louis, 1976; DS, Washington U., 1977. Sr. systems engr. Link div. Singer Co., Silver Spring, Md., 1977-79; staff engr. Link div. Singer Co., 1979-80; sr. mem. tech. staff Systems Sci. div. Computer Sci. Corp., 1980-81; sr. sect. head Link div. Singer Co., 1981-85; sr. engr. Control Command div. Westinghouse Elec. Corp., Balt., 1985-87; pres. ISC Systems, Inc., Chantilly, Va., 1987-91; sr. program mgr. Hughes Network Systems, Germantown, Md., 1991—; cons. Westinghouse Electric Corp., Balt., 1987-91. Contbr. articles to profl. jours. Mem. Rep. Senatorial Inner Cir., Washington, 1988; group ldr., bass Tung-Hsin Choral Soc., Potomac, Md., 1981. Mem. IEEE, Sigma Xi. Republican. Methodist. Home: 9408 Fox Hollow Dr Rockville MD 20854-2082 Office: Hughes Network Systems 11717 Exploration Ln Germantown MD 20876-2700 Office: Hughes Network Systems 11717 Exploration Ln Germantown MD 20876-2700

LU, LINYU LAURA, business educator; b. Taipei, Taiwan, Dec. 30, 1957; d. Bingie and Jingpo Lu; m. Hao Chun Chang, Sept. 10, 1983. BS, Fu-Jen Cath. U., Taipei, 1980; MS, Nat. Chung-Hsing U., Taipei, 1982; PhD, SUNY, Stony Brook, 1988. Rsch. assoc. Chung-Hua Inst. for Econ. Rsch., Taipei, 1982-84; asst. prof. L.I. U., Greenvale, N.Y., 1988-89; asst. prof. bus. dept. Plymouth State Coll.-U. System N.H., 1989—; coord. econs. discipline Plymouth State Coll., U. System N.H., 1990-91, faculty advisor Nat. Assn.

Bus. Economists, 1990-91. Mem. Am. Econ. Assn., Ea. Econ. Assn., Assn. Mgmt., Western Econ. Assn. Internat. Midwest Econs. Assn. Office: Plymouth State Coll Bus Dept Plymouth NH 03264

LU, PANG-CHIA, chemical company executive; b. Chia-yi, Taiwan, China, Aug. 28, 1949; came to U.S., 1973; BS, Tunghai U., 1971; PhD, Ga. Inst. Tech., 1977. Rsch. chemist Scott Paper Co., Westbrook, Maine, 1977-78; sr. rsch. scientist Am. Can Co., Neenah, Wis., 1979-81; rsch. assoc. Mobil Chem. Co., Macedon, N.Y., 1981—. Patentee in field. Pres. Rochester (N.Y.) Chinese Choral Soc., 1986-87. Mem. Am. Chem. Soc., AAAS. Office: Mobil Chem Co 729 Pittsford-palmy Rd Macedon NY 14502

LUBAN, NORMAN ALAN, neurologist; b. N.Y.C., Dec. 27, 1945; s. Morris and Lillian L.; m. Naomi Corman, May 23, 1971; children: Matthew, Benjamin. BA, SUNY, Buffalo, 1967; MD, Albert Einstein Coll. Medicine, 1971. Intern Bellevue Hosp., N.Y.C., 1971-72; rsch. assoc. NIH, Bethesda, Md., 1972-74; resident Presbyn. Hosp., N.Y.C., 1974-77; pvt. practice neurology Bethesda, 1977—. Physician Community for Creative Non-Violence, Washington, 1990—. Lt. comdr. USPHS, 1972-74. Recipient Bernton award Providence Hosp., D.C., 1979. Fellow Am. Acad. Neurology. Jewish. Home: 4101 Leland St Chevy Chase MD 20815 Office: 10215 Fernwood Rd Bethesda MD 20817-1106

LUBBOCK, FIONA CONSTANCE, anthropologist, nurse; b. Salem, Mass., Jan. 24, 1957; d. Homer E. and Eleanor Erica Mary (Watson) Harris; m. Geoffrey Orr, Oct. 24, 1981; children: Francesca, Caroline. Student, St. Michael's Sch., Limpsfield, Eng., 1975-76; BS in Nursing, Boston U., 1980; postgrad., Brown U., Providence, 1984-88. RN. Staff nurse ICU Tufts-New Eng. Med. Ctr., Boston, 1980-81; with paralegal Parker, Coulter, Daley & White, Boston, 1981-83; staff nurse obstetrics Raleigh Gen. Hosp., Beckley, W.Va., 1983-84; teaching asst. Brown U., Providence, 1986-87, researcher. cons., 1987—; staff nurse Lynn (Mass.) Vis. Nurse Assn., 1988—; clin. nurse dept. urology Brigham and Women's Hosp., Boston, 1988—; case contr. Hospice Raleigh County, Beckley, 1983-86; researcher investigation in pregnancy Cultural Barriers Prenatal Care, 1987-88. Researcher video prodn. on pregnancy and prenatal care in R.I., 1987-88. Mem. children's edn. Old North Congl. Ch., Marblehead, Mass., 1987—. Recipient Gold award, Duke of Edinburgh, 1985; grantee Brown U. Med. Sch., 1987-88; recipient Harvard Book Prize. Democrat. Congregationalist. Home: 33 Bubier Rd Marblehead MA 01945-3630 Office: Brown U Dept Anthropology PO Box 1921 Providence RI 02912-0001

LUBENSKY, AMY RUTH, psychologist; b. N.Y.C., May 4, 1943; d. Morris L. and Lenore (Koslan) Waldstreicher; m. Tom C. Lubensky, Sept. 21, 1968; children: David, Ellen. BA, Brown U., 1965; PhD, Harvard U., 1972. Lic. psychologist, Pa.; cert. sch. psychologist, Pa. Staff psychologist West Philadelphia Children's Svcs., 1971-81; pvt. practice Merion, Pa., 1981—. Pres. Merion Sch. Home and Sch., 1984-87; v.p. Lower Merion High Sch. Home and Sch., Ardmore, Pa., 1991-92. Mem. APA, Pa. Psychol. Assn. Home and Office: 121 Glenwood Rd Merion Station PA 19066-1305

LUBENSKY, TOM CARL, physics educator; b. Kansas City, Mo., May 7, 1943; s. Earl Henry and Anita Ruth (Price) L.; m. Amy Ruth Waldstreicher, Sept. 21, 1968; children: David K., Ellen P. BS, Calif. Inst. Tech., 1964; MA, Harvard U., 1965, PhD, 1969. NSF postdoctoral fellow U. Paris, Orsay, France, 1969-70; postdoctoral fellow Brown U., Providence, 1970-71; asst. prof. physics U. Pa., Phila., 1971-75, assoc. prof., 1975-80, prof., 1980—; vis. prof. Ecole Nomale Supérieur, Paris, 1981-82; cons. Exxon Rsch. and Engring., Annandale, N.J., 1990-91. Contbr. 120 articles to profl. jours. Fellow Alfred P. Sloan Found., 1975-77, Guggenheim Found., 1981. Fellow Am. Phys. Soc. Office: U Pa Dept Physics Philadelphia PA 19104

LUBIC, BENITA JOAN ALK, travel executive; b. Green Bay, Wis., May 18, 1936; s. Isadore George and Marion (Segal) Alk; m. Robert Bennett Lubic, May 31, 1959; children—Wendy Alison, Bret David, Robin Kimberly. B.B.A., U. Wis. 1958. Cert. travel cons. Inst. Cert. Travel Agts. Pres., owner Transeair Travel, Inc., Washington, 1959—; instr. Internat. Travel Tng. Sch., 1982-91. Mem. SKAL, Washington; mem. adv. bd. Braniff Airlines, Republic Airlines, Sonesta Hotel Corp. Mem. Am. Soc. Travel Agts. (pres. Washington sub chpt. 1985-88, bd. dirs. 1979—), Prost Exec. Women in Travel (v.p. 1982-83, treas. 1984-85). Contbr. articles on incentive travel to mags. Democrat. Jewish. Avocations: golf, tennis, swimming, bicycling, travel. Home: 2813 Mckinley Pl NW Washington DC 20015-1104 Office: Transeair Travel Inc 4710 41st St NW Washington DC 20016

LUBIT, ROY HOWARD, psychiatrist; b. N.Y.C., Dec. 3, 1953; s. Erwin Ciril and Esther (Levine) L. BA, Cornell U., 1975; MD, NYU, 1979; postgrad., Harvard U., 1987—. Diplomate Am. Bd. Psychiatry and Neurology. Intern Greenwich (Conn.) Hosp., 1979-80; Resident psychiatry Yale U., New Haven, 1979-83; resident child psychiatry Children's Hosp., Boston, 1983-85; clin. instr. psychiatry Harvard Med. Sch., Boston, 1985-87; research dir. Inst. Social and Behavioral Pathology, 1987; acting med. dir. Danvers State Hosp., Danvers, Mass., summer 1988, Family & Children's Clinic New Eng Home for Little Wanderers, Boston, summer 1988; acting med. dirs. Cape and the Islands Mental Health Ctr., summer 1990; assoc. Ctr. for Internat. Affairs Harvard U., 1990—; non-resident tutor Lowell House, Harvard U., 1989—; speaker in field. Contbr. articles to profl. jours. Harvard MacArthur scholar in internat. security, 1990-91. Home and Office: 213 Holden Grn # D Cambridge MA 02138-2054

LUBITZ, CECIL ROBERT, nuclear physicist; b. Bklyn., Mar. 18, 1925; s. Harry and Lilian (Burrows) L.; m. Betty Baum, Aug. 23, 1946 (div. Feb. 1982); chhildren: Faith, Martha, Benjamin; m. Lois New, Dec. 28, 1991. BS, U.S. Naval Acad., 1945; MEE, U. Mich., 1949, PhD in Physics, 1960. Rsch. assoc. elec. engring. Rsch. Inst. U. Mich., 1949-54; physicist Knolls Atomic Power Lab., Schenectady, 1960—. Fellow NSF, 1954. Office: Knolls Atomic Power Lab PO Box 1072 Schenectady NY 12301-1072

LUBKIN, HOWARD, education administrator, consultant; b. Bklyn., July 13, 1934; s. Louis and Beatrice (Murstein) L.; m. Arlene Frances Miller, June 28, 1959; children: Richard, Carolyn Lubkin Siegall. BA, Bklyn. Coll., 1955, MS, 1957; cert. teaching, Hebrew Union Coll., 1964. Cert. tchr., guidance counselor, edn. and vocat. counselor, sch. adminstr., ednl. adminstr., N.Y. Tchr. pub. sch. 83 Bd. Edn. N.Y.C., Bklyn., 1955-59, tchr. jr. high sch. 166, 1959-65, guidance counselor spl. edn. pub. sch. 63 and 159, 1965, guidance counselor pub. sch. 260, 1965-68, edn. and vocat. counselor jr. high sch. 64, 1968-75; edn. and vocat. counselor I.S. 218 Intermediate Sch. 218, Bklyn., 1975-79; dir. pupil pers. svcs. dist. 19 Bd. Edn. N.Y.C., Bklyn., 1979-87; dir. pupil pers. svcs. dist. 6 Bd. Edn. N.Y.C., N.Y.C., 1987-90, edn. cons. dist. 6, 1990—. Officer, mem. sch. bd. Temple Beth Am., Merrick, N.Y., 1975-80. Sgt. U.S. Army, 1957, USAR, 1963. Mem. N.Y. State Pers. and Guidance Assn., N.Y. State Pupil Pers. Adminstrs. Jewish. Home: 3000 Lonnie Ln Merrick NY 11566-5136 Office: Bd Edn Dist 6 NYC 665 W 182d St New York NY 10033

LUBKIN, SAUL, mathematician, educator; b. Bklyn., June 18, 1939; s. Meyer Yaakov and Fannie Rebecca (Frieden) L.; m. Maxine Werner, Oct. 18, 1983; children: Ashira Leah, Meira Jaffa. AB in Math., Columbia Coll., 1960; PhD in Math., Harvard U., 1963. Rsch. assoc. Brandies Univ., Waltham, Mass., 1962-63; NSF postdoctoral fellow Univ. Oxford, Eng., 1963-64, Stanford (Calif) Univ., 1964-65; mem. Inst. for Advanced Study, Princeton, N.J., 1965-66, 70-71; asst. prof. dept. math. Univ. Calif., Berkeley, 1966-70; hon. rsch. fellow dept. math. Harvard Univ., Cambridge, 1968-70; full prof. dept. math. Pa. State Univ., University Park, 1971-74, Univ. Rochester, N.Y., 1974—; project ALP, Inst. for Def. Analysis, Stanford and UCLA, summer 1960, 61; vis. prof. U. Witwatersrand, Johannesburg, South Africa, 1985; mem. Inst. for Advanced Study, Princeton, 1981-82. Author: Cohomology of Completions, 1982; contbg. editor: Computer Shopper Mag., 1989—; contbr. articles to profl. jours. Mem. Am. Math. Assn., Phi Beta Kappa. Republican. Jewish. Home: 134 Hemingway Dr Rochester NY 14620-3314 Office: U Rochester Dept Math Rochester NY 14627

LUBKIN, VIRGINIA LEILA, ophthalmologist; b. N.Y.C., Oct. 26, 1914; d. Joseph and Anna Fredericka (Stern) L.; m. Arnold Malkan, June 6, 1944 (div. 1949); m. Martin Bernstein, Aug. 28, 1949; children: James Ernst, Ellen Henrietta, Roger Joel, John Conrad. BS, NYU, 1933; MD, Columbia U., 1937. Diplomate Am. Bd. Ophthalmology. Intern Harlem Hosp., N.Y.C., 1938-40; asst. resident neurology Montefiore Hosp., N.Y.C., 1940, asst. resident pathology, 1940-41, fellow in ophthalmology, 1941-42; resident ophthalmology Kings County Hosp., Bklyn., 1942-43, Mt. Sinai Hosp., N.Y.C., 1943-44; attending opthalmologist, assoc. clin. prof. emeritus Mt. Sinai Sch. Medicine, 1944—; pvt. practice N.Y.C., 1945-90; rsch. prof. N.Y. Med. Coll., 1986—; creator, chief of rsch. bioengineering lab. N.Y. Eye and Ear Infirmary (name now The Aborn), N.Y.C., 1978—; creator first grad. course in oculoplastics and bi-yearly symposia in devel. dyslexia Mt. Sinai Sch. Medicine; educator courses in psychosomatic ophthalmology Am. Acad. Ophthalmology, 1950-60, educator course in complications of blepharoplasty, 1980-90; bd. dirs. Jewish Guild for the Blind; tchr. surg. ophthalmology in French Cameroon, Presbyn. Mission, 1951; lectr. in numerous countries.*. Author: (with others) Ophthalmic Plastic and Reconstructive Surgery, 1989; contbr. articles to profl. jours. Grantee Intraocular Lens Implant Mfrs., 1989. Fellow AMA, AAAS, Am. Soc. Ophthalmic Plastic and Reconstructive Surgery (founding), N.Y. Acad. Medicine, N.Y. Acad. Scis., Am. Acad. Ophthalmology, Am. Soc. Cataract and Refractive Surgery, PanAm. Soc. Ophthalmology. Democrat. Home and Office: One Blackstone Pl Bronx NY 10471

LUBOT, EUGENE STEPHEN, academic administrator; b. Boston, May 22, 1942; s. Martin and Molly (Zaslaw) L.; m. Donna Lou Young, Jan. 18, 1965; children: Karyn, Kevin. BA, U. Pa., 1963; MA, U. S.C., 1965; PhD, Ohio State U., 1970. Asst. prof. Wheaton Coll., Norton, Mass., 1969-77; head history dept. Univ. Tenn., Chattanooga, 1977-81, acting dean arts and scis., 1978-79; v.p. acad. affairs Albright Coll., Reading, Pa., 1981—. Author: Liberalism in an Illiberal Age: New Culture Liberals in Republican China, 1919-1937, 1982; contbr. articles to profl. jours. Sec. Friends of the Reading (Pa.) Mus., 1983-87. Recipient Nat. Def. Fgn. Lang. fellowships U.S. Dept. Edn., Columbia U., 1967-68. Office: Albright Coll PO Box 15234 Reading PA 19612-5234

LUBOW, NATHAN MYRON, accountant; b. N.Y.C., Aug. 4, 1929; s. Cornelius W. and Blanche (Igstaedter) L.; m. Joyce S. Litt, Dec. 17, 1955; children: Susan M. Russak, Andrew M. PhB, U. Chgo., 1948; BS in Econs., U. Pa., 1950. CPA, N.Y. Ptnr. Aronson & Oresman, CPAs, 1969-73, Clarence Rainess & Co., N.Y.C., 1973-78, Main Hurdman, N.Y.C., 1978-87, KPMG Peat Marwick, N.Y.C., 1987-90; v.p., mem. Mahoney Cohen & Co., P.C., N.Y.C., 1990—; trustee banking and fin. unit B'nai B'rith, N.Y.C., 1969; bd. dirs. 465 WEA Owners Corp., N.Y.C., Westmoor Corp., Ft. Worth. Contbg. editor: The Secured Lender mag., 1988—. Mem. AICPAs, N.Y. State Soc. CPAs, Nat. Assn. Credit Mgmt., Empire Credit Club, Decorum Credit Club, Friars Club. Home: 465 W End Ave New York NY 10024-4926 Office: Mahoney Cohen & Co PC 111 W 40th St New York NY 10018-2506

LUBOWSKY, JACK, academic director; b. Bklyn., July 11, 1940; m. Marcelle Kaplan, Jan. 1, 1986. BEE, CCNY, 1962; MSEE, Polytech. Inst. Bklyn., 1966, PhD in Elec. Engring., 1973. Registered profl. engr., N.Y. Project engr. Airborne Instruments Lab., Melville, N.Y., 1962-66; dir. sci./acad. computing ctr. SUNY-Health Sci. Ctr., Bklyn., 1966—. Contbr. 35 articles to profl. jours. Recipient Congrl. Sci. fellow AAAS, Washington, 1983. Mem. IEEE (chmn. U.S. govt. activities coun., chmn. fed. legis. agenda task force for 100th and 101st Congress, chmn. Washington internships for students of engring. program, mem. supercomputer com., congl. fellows com., computer soc., instrumentation soc., engring. in biology and medicine soc.), Eta Kappa Nu, Sigma Xi. Home: 2064 Beverly Way Merrick NY 11566-5416 Office: Sci/Acad Computing 450 Clarkson Ave # 7 Brooklyn NY 11203-2098

LUBOWSKY, SUSAN, curator, arts administrator; b. Bklyn., Jan. 16, 1949; children: MacKay, Maggie. BFA, Pratt Inst., 1970, MFA, 1975. Asst. coord. exhbns. Pratt Inst., Bklyn., 1972-75; gallery dir. SUNY, Brockport, 1975-77; asst. curator McCrory Corp., N.Y.C., 1977-80; asst. dir. Queens Mus., Flushing, N.Y., 1980-82; br. dir. Whitney Mus. Am. Art at Philip Morris, N.Y.C., 1982-87, Whitney Mus. Am. Art at Equitable Ctr., N.Y.C., 1987-89; dir. visual arts program Nat. Endowment for Arts, Washington, 1989-92; dir. Southeastern Ctr. for Contemporary Art, Winston-Salem, N.C., 1992—. Author: (exhbn. catalog) George Ault, 1988; co-author: (exhbn. catalogs) Spaces '88, 1988, Yasuo Kuniyoshi, 1990. Bd. dirs. 42d Street Edn., Theater and Culture, N.Y.C., 1982-87; mem. Art Table, Inc., N.Y.C., 1988-89. Office: SECCA 750 Marguerite Dr Winston Salem NC 27106

LUCAS, ALFRED WINSLOW, JR., management consulting company executive; b. Washington, Oct. 14, 1950; s. Alfred Winslow and Mildred Elizabeth (Lawson) L.; m. Debra Denise DeBerry, Aug. 20, 1977; children: Michael Maurice, Marlé. BA in Sociology and Social Welfare, St. Augustine's Coll., Raleigh, N.C., 1972; MSW, Syracuse U., 1974; MPA, Roosevelt U., Chgo., 1979, PhD, 1983. Planner United Way Cen. N.Y., 1973-74; adminstrv. asst. to dir. community devel. People's Equal Action Community Effort Inc., Syracuse, N.Y., 1972-73; rsch. cons. Urban Inst., Washington, 1974-75; exec. dir. New Birth Community Devel., Elgin, Ill., 1975-79; pres. Rasen Mgmt. Cons., Inc., Chgo. and Washington, 1979—; assoc. dir. Centers for New Horizons, Chgo., 1979-80; cons. in field. Author: Getting Funded, Grantsmanship and Proposal Development, 1982; author, editor: Classic and Contemporary African American Quotations, 1990. Chmn. bd. dirs. Kane County (Ill.) Community Action Agy., 1976-77; bd. dirs. Kane County Overall Econ. Devel. Com., 1977-78; trustee Mildred Lawson Lucas Meml. Found., 1981—. NIMH fellow, 1972-74. Mem. Am. Mgmt. Assn., Nat. Assn. Social Workers, Acad. Cert. Social Workers, Am. Soc. Pub. Adminstrs., Nat. Urban League, Am. Soc. Profl. Cons., Kappa Alpha Psi. Roman Catholic. Home: 3441 Easton Dr Bowie MD 20716-1360

LUCAS, BILLY JOE, philosophy educator; b. Houston, Jan. 7, 1942; s. Joseph Cuthel and Billie Louise (Smith) L.; m. Diana Stephens, July 13, 1965 (div. 1976); children: Lisa Ann, Deborah Lynn; m. Shelby Hearon, Apr. 19, 1981. BA, U. Houston, 1970; MA, McMaster U., 1972; PhD, U. Tex., 1981. Instr. Houston Community Coll., 1973-77; asst. instr. U. Tex., Austin, 1978-81; asst. prof. Manhattanville Coll., Purchase, N.Y., 1981-86, assoc. prof., 1986-89, prof., 1989—; edn. policy cons. to the pres. Manhattanville Coll., 1990-91. Assoc. editor Internat. Jour. for Philosophy of Religion, 1990—; contbr. articles to profl. jours. Mem. AAAS, Soc. for Philosophy of Religion (exec. coun. 1986—, v.p. 1989-90, pres. 1990-91), Assn. for Symbolic Logic, Computer Soc. of IEEE (tech. com. on multiple valued logic 1987—), Am. Acad. Religion, Am. Philos. Assn. (logic sect. adv. com. 1990—), N.Am. Soc. for Social Philosophy (exec. coun., co-chair Eastern div. 1986-90), Am. Math. Soc., N.Y. Acad. Scis., Phi Kappa Phi. Office: Manhattanville Coll 125 Purchase St Purchase NY 10577-2400

LUCAS, GEORGE RAMSDELL, JR., philosophy educator; b. San Angelo, Tex., Sept. 8, 1949; s. George Ramsdell and Clare Elizabeth (Baldwin) L.; m. Patricia Cook; children: Jessica, Kimberly, Theresa. BS summa cum laude, Coll. William and Mary, 1971; PhD, Northwestern U., 1978. Asst. prof., chmn. dept. philosophy Randolph-Macon Coll., Ashland, Va., 1978-82; assoc. prof., chmn. dept. philosophy Santa Clara (Calif.) U., 1982-86; assoc. prof. Emory U., Atlanta, 1986-87; prof. philosophy Clemson (S.C.) U., 1987-91; asst. dir. rsch. div. NEH, Washington, 1990—. Author: The Genesis of Modern Process Thought, 1983, The Rehabilitation of Whitehead, 1989; editor: Lifeboat Ethics: Moral Dilemmas of World Hunger, 1976, Poverty, Justice and the Law, 1986; philosophy editor SUNY Press, Albany, 1989—; also articles. Am. Coun. Learned Socs. fellow, 1982; Fulbright rsch. fellow, 1989. Mem. Am. Philos. Assn., Soc. for Philosophy in Am. (trustee 1989—), Metaphys. Soc. Am. (exec. coun. 1987-92), Hegel Soc. Am., Soc. for Process Philosophy (program chmn.), Phi Beta Kappa. Office: NEH 1100 Pennsylvania Ave NW Rm 318 Washington DC 20506-0005

LUCAS, ROBERT ALAN, mechanical engineering educator, researcher; b. Allentown, Pa., June 13, 1935; s. Robert Horace and Helen Marguerite (Koons) L.; m. Joanne Adele Wetherhold, June 15, 1957; children: Michael John, Elizabeth Adele, Leslie Anne, Marya Courtney. BS in Mech. Engring., Lehigh U., 1957, MS, 1959, PhD, 1964. Design engr. Air Products and Chems., Inc., Trexlertown, Pa., 1957-58; grad. asst. dept. mech. engring. Lehigh U., Bethlehem, Pa., 1958-59, instr., 1959-64, asst. prof., 1964-65, 66-69, assoc. prof. mech. engring. and mechanics dept., 1969—; postdoctoral rsch. asst. Naval Rsch. Labs., Washington, 1965-66; prin. Robert A. Lucas, Cons., Bethlehem, 1965—. DuPont Sci. and Engring. fellow, 1970, Nat. Rsch. Coun. fellow, 1965-66, Koppers Co. fellow, 1961. Mem. ASME, Sigma Xi. Lutheran. Home: 2604 W Walnut St Allentown PA 18104-6231 Office: Lehigh U Dept Mech Engring/Mechanics Bethlehem PA 18015

LUCCI, WILLIAM RALPH, JR., college dean, credit and collections consultant; b. Great Falls, Mont., Dec. 23, 1956; s. William Ralph and Priscilla (Blake) L.; m. Margaret Teresa Hoar, July 15, 1982; 1 child, Alexander William. BS, North Adams State Coll., 1980; MEd, Bridgewater State Coll., 1982. Dir. campus ctr. Xavier U., Cin., 1982-85; asst. dean U. Cin., 1985-87; dean students Coll. St. Joseph, Rutland, Vt., 1987—. Vol. Rutland Open Door Mission, March of Dimes; chair blood drive Hoxworth Blood Ctr. Dept. Edn. Title IV grantee, 1991; named Outstanding Young Man in Am., 1988. Mem. Am. Coll. Pers. Assn., Vt. Coll. Student Pers. Assn. (bd. dirs. 1988—), NASPA, Smithsonian Instn. Republican. Baptist. Home: 4 Allen Ave Fair Haven VT 05743-1102 Office: Coll St Joseph Clement Rd Rutland VT 05701-3825

LUCE, JAMES EDWARD, chemical engineer; b. Toronto, Ont., Can., Aug. 24, 1935; s. Ivor Stanley and Hazel Audrey (Fernley) L.; m. Lee Heinsohn, June 29, 1980; 1 child, James Allan. B of Applied Sci., U. Toronto, 1956; PhD, McGill U., 1960; MBA, N.Y. Inst. Tech., 1980. Rsch. assoc. CIP Rsch. Ltd., Hawkesbury, Ont., 1960-68, asst. mgr. basic rsch., 1968-71; sr. adminstrv. officer Atomic Energy of Can., Ltd., Chalk River, Ont., 1971; group dir. paper tech. Internat. Paper Co., Tuxedo, N.Y., 1972-78, assoc. dir. advanced devel., 1978-83, mgr. papermaking tech., 1983-87, mgr. paper sci., 1987—. Fellow TAPPI; mem. Can. Pulp and Paper Assn., Paper Industry Tech. Assn. Office: Internat Paper Co Long Meadow Rd Tuxedo Park NY 10987

LUCE, JAMES JAY DUDLEY, non-profit political agency executive; b. Hamilton, Ohio, July 24, 1959; s. Stanford Leonard Luce and Frances Dudley Alleman-L. Student, Ctr. Estudiar U. Colombino-Am., Bogota, Columbia, 1979, Waseda U., Tokyo, 1980-81; BA, Coll. Wooster, 1982. Co-founder, assoc. exec. dir. Fundamentalists Anonymous, N.Y.C., 1985-91, coord. legal task force, 1988-91; pres. Com. to Explore an Alternative Candidacy, N.Y.C., 1991. State campaign mgr. Dump D'Amato in '92!, N.Y.C., 1992; vol. Partnership for the Homeless, N.Y.C., 1983-91; trustee Madison Ave. Baptist Ch. N.Y.C., 1989-92. Named Alternate Internat. scholar, Rotary, 1982. Democrat. Episcopalian. Office: Dump D'Amato in '92! 298 Fifth Ave Ste 285 New York NY 10001

LUCERO, FRANK ANTHONY, utility company executive; b. Pasadena, Calif., May 19, 1935; s. Frank Lucero Sr.; m. Aug. 1971 (div. Mar. 1979); m. Karolyne J. Lucero, Aug. 26, 1980; children: Lyndsay J., Mari E. Student, U. Calif., Berkeley, 1963; BS, Calif. State U., 1970; MBA, Golden Gate U., 1972; postgrad., Harvard U., 1976. Pres. Nuclear Internat. Corp., Boston, 1971-79, Stafford Labs., Phoenix, 1979-84, Whitmoyer Labs., Myerstown, Pa., 1982—, Utility Products Co., Bernville, Pa., 1988—; bd. dirs. Tech. Chems. Inc.; chmn. Equitec Corp., Lexington, Ky., 1986—. Advisor Reading (Pa.) Symphony Orch. Lt. USN, 1959-63. Mem. Heidelburg Country Club. Republican. Office: Utility Products Co RR 4 Box 165A Bernville PA 19506-9522

LUCHETTI, ROBERT JAMES, architect, industrial designer; b. San Francisco, June 1, 1949; s. Lawrence Leo and Petranella Helen (Mortiga) L.; m. Leita Hagemann, May 9, 1987. AB in Environ. Design, U. Calif., Berkeley, 1971; MArch, Harvard Grad. Sch. Design, 1974. Registered architect, Mass., Tex., S.C., Minn., Fla. Asst. prof. dept. visual & environ. studies Harvard U., Cambridge, Mass., 1975-76, 78-84; asst. prof. sch. environ. design King Abdulaziz U., Jeddah, Saudi Arabia, 1976-78; assoc. Cambridge Seven Assocs., Inc., 1975-76, 78-87; prin., pres. Robert Luchetti Assocs., Inc., Cambridge, 1987—. Contbr. articles to profl. jours. Recipient Boston Exports award Boston Soc. Architects, 1986, Julia Amory Appleton Travelling fellowship Harvard U., 1974, Honor award Boston Soc. of Architect, 1991; winner Internat. Competition for a New Office Furniture System, 1983. Mem. AIA, Nat. Coun. Archtl. Registration. Office: Robert Luchetti Assocs Inc 14 Arrow St Cambridge MA 02138-5106

LUCIANO, ROBERT ANTHONY, packaging engineer; b. Orange, N.J., July 15, 1934; s. Anthony Alfred and Rose Lillian (Borello) L.; m. Lorraine B. Chennette, Nov. 27, 1955; children: Susan L., Robert A., Lawrence W. BSME, N.J. Inst. Tech., 1963, MS, 1966. Registered profl. engr., N.J., R.I., P.R. Mech. designer Bell Telephone Labs., Whippany, N.J., 1951-56, Rayonier, Inc., Whippany, 1956-60; automatic machinery engr. Colgate Palmolive, Jersey City, N.J., 1960-64; mgr. packaging engring. Ortho Pharms., Raritan, N.J., 1964-72; cons. engr. Robert A. Luciano Assocs., Lebanon, N.J., 1972—; pres. Luciano Packaging Techs., Inc., Lebanon, 1990—, also bd. dirs., chmn., 1990—; bd. dirs. Inst. Packaging Profls., Reston, Va.; lectr. NYU, N.Y.C., 1973-80, Rutgers U., 1984, Inst. of Packaging Profls., 1989—. Tech. editor: Modern Packaging Mag., 1975-82; contbg. editor: Packaging Mag., 1982—. Chmn. Bd. Health, Warren, N.J., 1968-72; mem. Planning Bd., Warren, 1972, Tewksbury Twp. Rep. Club, Lebanon, 1974. Named Packaging Man of Yr., Inst. Packaging Profls., Reston, 1990; recipient Young Engr. of Yr. award Soc. Profl. Engrs., Somerset County, N.J., 1968-69. Mem. Packaging Coms. Coun. (chmn. 1988-91), Met. N.Y. Chpt. Packaging Inst. (pres. 1975-77), Soc. Mfg. Engrs. (sr.), Robotics Internat. (sr.), Raritan Valley Soc. Profl. Engrs. Home: 95 Bissell Rd Lebanon NJ 08833 Office: Luciano Packaging Techs Inc 29 County Line Rd Somerville NJ 08876

LUCKOW, SHERRY LOUISE, career counselor; b. Crystal Falls, Mich., Mar. 2, 1963; d. Virgil Edward and Ann Louise (Bicigo) L. BSW, U. Wis., Milw., 1986, MS in Ednl. Psychology, 1990. Career devel. intern, then career course instr. Alverno Coll., Milw., 1989, 90, alternative plans counselor, 1990; career devel. intern Cardinal Stritch Coll., Milw., 1990; career counselor St. Mary's Coll. Md., St. Mary's City, 1990—. Literacy tutor St. Mary's County Literacy Program, 1991—. Mem. Mid-Atlantic Placement Assn. Presbyterian. Office: Career Ctr Lower Charles Saint Mary's Coll Maryland Saint Mary's City MD 20686

LUDDEN, JOHN FRANKLIN, financial economist; b. Michigan City, Ind., May 6, 1930. BS in Econs., U. Wis., 1952, MS in Econs., 1955; postgrad., U. Mich., 1955-59. Wage and hour investigator U.S. Dept. Labor, 1960, mgmt. intern, 1960-61, labor economist, 1963; economist, instr. U.S. Bur. of Labor Statis., 1961-63; economist Office of Internat. Ops. IRS, 1963-68, fin. economist Audit div., 1968-86, fin. economist Office of the Asst. Commr. Internat., 1986—. With U.S. Army, 1952-54. Recipient Spl. Svc. award U.S. Dept. of Treasury, 1967, 68, Spl. Achievement award U.S., 1984, Spl. Svc. award, 1987, Spl. Act award, 1990. Mem. Am. Econ. Assn.

LUDEKING, JUDSON SCOTT, safety insurance consulting company executive; b. Amesbury, Mass., Apr. 29, 1951; s. Charles W. and Ann May (Petherick) L.; m. Christine Barbaro, Dec. 23, 1988. Assoc., No. Essex Community Coll., Haverhill, Mass., 1971; BA, U. Mass., 1973; postgrad., Northeastern U., Burlington, Mass., 1978. Safety cons. Risk Control Svcs., Newton, Mass., 1973-84; pres. Contractors Risk Mgmt., Inc., Concord, N.H., 1984—. Inventor protective throwing balls. Sponsor Men's Softball Team, Suncook Div., Concord, 1986-87, Contractors Risk Mgmt. City Basketball Team, Concord, 1987. Mem. N.H. Assn. Ins. Profl. (bd. dirs. 1988—). Baptist. Office: Contractors Risk Mgmt Inc PO Box 211 Concord NH 03302-0211

LUDGIN, DONALD HUGH, editor; b. Chgo., Sept. 16, 1929; s. Earle and Mary King (MacDonald) L.; m. Sue Keating Conway, Oct. 26, 1957; children: Sarah, Katherine, Peter. AB, Oberlin Coll., 1951. Asst. editor World Book Ency., Chgo., 1953-56, sr. editor, 1956-62, editorial coord., London and Sydney, Australia, 1962-66, assoc. editor, Chgo., 1966-69, dir. spl. projects, 1969-83; pres. Electronic Scribe, Evanston, Ill., 1983-86, Georgetown, Maine, 1986—. Trustee Mus. Contemporary Art, Chgo., 1971-79, sec., 1974-78; mem. Joseph Jefferson Theatre Awards Com., Chgo., 1979-81. Served with U.S. Army, 1951-53. Mem. Graphic Communications Assn. (editorial bd. jour. 1978). Democrat. Roman Catholic. Home and Office: 446 Indian Rd Georgetown ME 04548

LUDLUM, DAVID BLODGETT, pharmacologist, educator; b. N.Y.C., Sept. 30, 1929; s. C. Daniel and Elsie B. (Blodgett) L.; B.A., Cornell U., 1951; Ph.D., U. Wis., 1954; M.D., N.Y.U., 1962; m. Carlene L. Dyke, Dec. 23, 1952; children—Valerie Jean Ludlum Wright, Kenneth David. Research scientist Dupont Co., Wilmington, Del., 1954-58; intern Bellevue Hosp., N.Y.C., 1962-63; asst. prof. pharmacology Yale U., 1963-68; assoc. prof. U. Md., 1968-70, prof., 1970-76; prof. pharmacology Albany (N.Y.) Med. Coll., 1976-86 , chmn. dept. pharmacology, 1976-80, prof. medicine, 1980-86, dir. oncology research, 1980-86; prof. pharmacology and medicine U. Mass. Med. Sch., 1986—; adj. prof. chemistry Rensselaer Poly. Inst., Troy, N.Y., 1977-80; vis. prof. oncology Johns Hopkins U., 1973-76; vis. prof. Courtauld Inst., London, 1970. WARF fellow, 1951-52; NSF fellow, 1952-54; Am. Heart Assn. fellow, 1960-62; grantee in field; recipient NIH Research Career Devel. award 1968; Markle scholar in acad. medicine, 1967-72; lic. physician, N.Y., Conn., Md. Mem. Am. Soc. Pharmacology and Exptl. Therapeutics, Am. Soc. Clin. Pharmacology and Therapeutics, Am. Assn. Cancer Research, Am. Soc. Biochem. and Molecular Biology, Am. Chem. Soc., Phi Beta Kappa, Sigma Xi, Phi Kappa Phi, Alpha Omega Alpha. Assoc. editor Cancer Rsch., 1980-87, 89—; contbr. articles to profl. jours.; patentee in field. Home: 24 Linda Ct Delmar NY 12054-3512 Office: U Mass Med Sch Worcester MA 01655

LUDMER, ALBA, psychologist, pharmacist; b. Pereira, Risaralda, Colombia, Aug. 2, 1940; came to U.S., 1967; d. Rafael and Josefina (Patiño) Orozco; m. Raul Isidro Ludmer, Oct. 26, 1968; children: Pamela, Andrea, Julian. Chem. Pharmacist, U. Nat., Bogota, Colombia, 1965; MA in Teaching in Sci., Fairleigh Dickinson U., Teaneck, N.J., 1980; EdM in Psychology, Columbia U., 1986, EdD in Psychology, 1988. Lic. psychologist, N.J. Asst. prof. U. Nat., Bogota, Colombia, 1965-67; instr., researcher Chgo. Med. Sch., 1967-69; tchr. molecular biology Dwight Englewood (N.J.) High Sch., 1978-80; program developer Newark Hispanic Community, 1983; psychotherapist Mid-Bergen Mental Health Ctr., Paramus, N.J., 1985-86; psychologist Elizabeth (N.J.) Gen. Hosp., 1987-89, Columbia Presbyn. Hosp., N.Y.C., 1989-91; pvt. practice Ridgewood, N.J., 1990—; adj. asst. prof. Columbia U., N.Y.C., 1988—; presenter several confs. in child abuse, psychotherapy with Hispanic patients, women's profl. and psychol. devel. Contbr. rsch. papers to profl. jours. Tchr. illiterate adults Priests of 3d World Movement, Bogota, 1964; leader parent tng. Bergen County Parent Workshop, Paramus, 1982; speaker at various local high schs.; vol. teaching course developer Willard Sch., Ridgewood, 1982. Mem. Colombian Basketball Team, 1962-64. Mem. Am. Psychol. Assn., Assn. Hispanic Mental Health Profls., N.Y. State Psychol. Assn., N.Y.C. Coalition for Women's Mental Health, N.J. Psychol. Assn., Bergen County Assn. Lic. Psychologists, Internat. Soc. for Prevention of Child Abuse. Republican. Roman Catholic. Office: 88 W Ridgewood Ave Ridgewood NJ 07450-3141

LUDTKE, JOHN LEROY, business management and computer consultant; b. Waterloo, Iowa, Nov. 23, 1950; s. Gene L. and Dorothy J. (Tebrake) L.; m. L. Joy Dixon (div. 1973); 1 child, Robin N.; m. Lesley M. Mills, May 9, 1987. Gen. edn. diploma, Thousand Oaks, Calif., 1974. Salesperson Harris & Frank, Covina, Calif., 1969-71; mgr. outlet Harris & Frank, Covina, 1971-73; mgr. store The World's Fair, Northridge, Calif., 1973-75; supr. dist. Mode 'O Day, Burbank, Calif., 1975-77; ptnr. Woodworks W., Sonoma, Calif., 1977-80; v.p., dir. Harbour Landing Devel. Corp., New Haven, Conn., 1980-90, Marina Landing Devel. Corp., New Haven, 1982-90; cons. Conn. Marine Studies Consortium, New Haven, Conn., 1982-90; ptnr. Vital Care Ptnrs., Milford, Conn., 1991-92; owner Regency Mgmt., Milford, 1989—; also bd. dirs. FDIC, N.Y.C., $D, $D; pres. Iota, Inc., Milford, 1992—; co-producer Aircastle Prodns., New Haven, 1986—. Pres. Blvd. Devel. Assn., New Haven, 1985, 868, bd. dirs., 1987; bd. dirs. Friends of Orch. of New Eng., New Haven, 1986-87; trustee Orch. New Eng., 1992—. Mem. The Waterfront Ctr. (speaker 1987), Am. Mgmt. Assn., Internat. Platform Soc., Cousteau Soc., Nature Conservancy. Office: 132 Beach Ave Milford CT 06460-8004

LUDWIG, EDMUND VINCENT, federal judge; b. Phila., May 20, 1928; s. Henry and Ruth (Viner) L.; children: Edmund Jr., John, Sarah, David. AB, Harvard U., 1949, LLB, 1952. Assoc. Duane, Morris & Heckscher, Phila., 1956-59; ptnr. Barnes, Biester & Ludwig, Doylestown, Pa., 1959-68; judge Common Pleas Ct., Bucks County, Pa., 1968-85, U.S. Dist. Ct. (ea. dist.), Phila., 1985—; mem. faculty Pa. Coll. of the Judiciary, 1974-85; presenter Villanova (Pa.) U. Law Sch., 1975-80, lectr., 1984—; vis. lectr. Temple Law Sch., 1977-80; clin. assoc. prof. Hahnemann U., Phila., 1977-85; mem. Pa. Juvenile Ct. Judge's Commn., 1978-85; chmn. Pa. Chief Justice's Ednl. Com., 1984-85; pres. Pa. Conf. State Trial Judges, 1981-82. Contbr. articles to profl. jours. Chmn. Children and Youth Adv. Com., Bucks County, 1978-83; mem. Pa. Adv. Com. on Mental Health and Mental Retardation, 1980-85; founder, bd. dirs. Today, Inc., Newtown, Pa., 1971-85, Probation Vols., Bucks County, 1971-81; bd. dirs. Program Women Offenders, Del. Valley, 1988; mem. Pa. Joint Coun. Criminal Justice, Inc., 1979-80; mem. Joint Family Law Council Pa., 1979-85; vice chmn. Human Services Council Bucks County, 1979-81; mem. Com. to Study Unified Jud. System Pa., 1980-82, Pa. Legislative Task Force on Mental Health Laws, 1986-87. Recipient Disting. Service award Bucks County Corrections Assn., 1978, Spl. Service award Big Bros., 1979, Humanitarian award United Way Bucks County, 1980, Founder's award Vol. Services, 1982, Spl. award Bucks County Juvenile Ct., 1985. Mem. ABA, Pa. Bar Assn. (chmn. com. legal svcs. to disabled 1990—), Fed. Bar Assn. (hon.). Club: Harvard (N.Y.C. and Phila.) (v.p. 1979-80), Phila. Office: 12614 US Courthouse Independence Mall W 601 Market St Philadelphia PA 19106-1510

LUDWIG, EDWARD LEE, director athletics, eduator, coach; b. Lebanon, Pa., Sept. 7, 1948; s. William Franklin and Kathleen Jane (Gerberich) L.; m. Elaine Faye Stine, Mar. 30, 1968; children: Terry Lee, Travis Lew. BS, East Stroudsburg (Pa.) U., 1970. Cert. edn. tchr., Pa. Tchr., coach No. Lebanon Sch. Dist., Fredericksburg, Pa., 1970—, intramural and athletics dir., 1986—. Vice pres. coun. Zion Luth. Ch., Jonestown, Pa., 1986-90. Republican. Lutheran. Office: No Lebanon High Sch PO Box 100 Fredericksburg PA 17026-0100

LUDWIG, JEANNETTE MARIE, French linguistics educator; b. Denver, Sept. 29, 1949; d. George Robert Ludwig and Jessie Ruth (Mann) Ludwig-Miller; m. Claude Emerson Welch Jr., June 13, 1981; stepchildren: Lisa, Sarah, Martha, Christopher. BA, Drake U., 1971; PhD, U. Mich., 1977. Asst. prof. French linguistics U. Buffalo, 1977-83, assoc. prof., 1983—. Presbyterian. Office: U Buffalo Dept Modern Langs 910 Clemens Buffalo NY 14260

LUDWIG, PATRICIA A., manufacturing executive, consultant; b. Rochester, N.Y., Apr. 30, 1949; d. James J. and F. Miriam (Price) L. BA in Polit. Sci., U. Wis., 1971; MBA in Mktg. and Econs., U. Hartford, 1980. Media buying asst. Batten, Barton, Durstine & Osborn, Boston, 1972-73; corp. rsch. asst. Needham, Harper & Steers, Chgo., 1974-75; account exec. Potyra Assocs., Hartford, 1976-77; sr. advt. svc. mgr. Torin Corp., Torrington, Conn., 1977-80; sr. mktg. rsch. analyst Emhart Corp., Farmington, Conn., 1981-85; sr. product mgr. The Darwarth Co., Avon, Conn., 1985-86; mgr. corp. product div. Rule Industries, Gloucester, Mass., 1986-88; pres. Stratman Group, Inc., Torrington, 1988—; Guest speaker econ. forecasting Cen. Conn. Coll., New Britain, 1981. Recipient Gold and Silver Drummer award Bldg. Supply and Home Ctrs. Assn., 1986. Mem. N.Am. Soc. Corp. Planning (sec. Hartford chpt. 1985-86). Home: 56 Union Ave Saratoga Springs NY 12866-4362 Office: Stratman Group Inc 265 E Elm St PO Box 1277 Torrington CT 06790

LUDWIG, ROBERT PAUL, musician, educator; b. St. Petersburg, Fla., Oct. 28, 1953; s. George Wilford Ludwig, Sr. and Phoebe Jane (Owenby) Allen; m. Nancy Greig Shearer, Aug. 20, 1977; children: James Fowler, Samuel Alexander. AB, Davidson Coll., 1975; MusM, Yale U., 1977. Organist, choirmaster Christ Ch. Episcopal, Lexington, Ky., 1978-87, Cathedral of the Incarnation, Garden City, N.Y., 1987—; organist, lectr. in music Mercer Sch. of Theology, Garden City, 1987—. Contbg. author: Harper's Ency of Religious Edn., 1990; composer: Saint John Passion, 1984, Preces and Responses, 1986, Fraction Anthem, 1986. Mem. Assn. Anglican Musicians, Am. Guild Organists. Office: Cathedral of Incarnation 50 Cathedral Ave Garden City NY 11530-4435

LUEBKE, BARBARA FRANCINE, journalism educator; b. Green Bay, Wis., Jan. 23, 1949; d. Glenn F. and Barbara E. (Walker) L. BA, U. Wis., Eau Claire, 1971; MS, U. Oreg., 1972; PhD, U. Mo., 1981. Reporter, society editor Antigo (Wis.) Daily Jour., 1972-73; news editor DeKalb (Ill.) Chronicle, 1973-74; instr. journalism U. Mo., Columbia, 1974-77, asst. prof., assoc. prof., 1980-84; instr. U. Wis., Eau Claire, 1977-80; assoc. prof. dept. communication U. Hartford, West Hartford, Conn., 1984-89; assoc. prof. journalism, chmn. dept. U. R.I., Kingston, 1989—; cons. La Crosse (Wis.) Tribune, 1978. Copy editor Hartford Courant, 1985-89; contbr. articles to profl. jours. Mem. R.I. Women's Health Collective, Providence. Mem. Assn. for Edn. in Journalism and Mass Communication, Nat. Fedn. Press Women, Nat. Women's Studies Assn., New England Women's Studies Assn., Kappa Tau Alpha. Office: U RI Dept Journalism 230 Chafee Hall Kingston RI 02881

LUECKEL, WILLIAM JOHN, JR., engineering executive; b. N.Y.C., Aug. 2, 1928. BS in Econs. and Engring., MIT, 1950, MSME, 1950; D of Engring. Sci., Rensselaer Poly. Inst., 1968. Engr. Pratt & Whitney Aircraft, East Hartford, Conn., 1950-57; sr. engr. Peslo Pump, Cleve., 1957-59; sr. scientist Thompson Ramb Wooldridge, Redondo Beach, Calif., 1959-60; mgr. programs and mktg. fuel cell ops. United Techs. Corp., South Windsor, Conn., 1960-84; gen. mgr. Internat. Fuel Cells Inc., South Windsor, 1984-90, v.p., 1990—. Pres. Congl. Ch. in South Glastonbury, Conn., 1975-76, Glastonbury Interfaith Housing Corp., 1980—. With USN, 1944-46. Home: 72 Crossroads Ln Glastonbury CT 06033 Office: Internat Fuel Cells 195 Governors Hwy South Windsor CT 06074

LUECKEN, PETER GRANT, chiropractor; b. N.Y.C., Jan. 18, 1950; s. Herbert Robert and Inge Gertrude (Spandau) L.; m. Roxanne Virginia Sammis, Sept. 20, 1975. BA, Hofstra U.; DC, N.Y. Chiropractic Coll. Lic. chiropractor Conn., N.J.; diplomate Nat. Bd. Chiropractic Examiners. Pvt. practice Fairfield, Conn.; dir. Fairfield Chiropractic Office; lectr. in field; cons. in field. Recipient Outstanding Svc. award Fairfield C. of C., Disting. Svc. Citation N.Y. Chiropractic Coll., Distinguished Leadership award Nat. Found. March of Dimes; knighted Sovereign Mil. Order of the Temple of Jerusalem. Fellow Am. Coll. Chiropractic; mem. Am. Chiropractic Assn., Internat. Chiropractic Assn., Conn. Chiropractic Assn., Parker Chiropractic Rsch. Found., Found. for Chiropractic Edn. and Rsch., Am. Health Assn., Internat. Assn. Chiropractic Indsl. Injury Cons., Am. Assn. Chiropractic Ins. Cons., N.Y. Chiropractic Alumni Assn. (bd. dirs.), Fairfield C. of C. (past v.p. profl. div., bd. dirs.), Fairfield Rotary (past v.p. internat. affairs), Masons, Pyramid Soc., Conn. Arabian Horse Assn. Office: Fairfield Chiropractic Off 527 Tunxis Hill Rd Fairfield CT 06430-4442

LUEDKE, FREDERICK LEE, manufacturing company executive; b. Milw., Jan. 19, 1938; s. Frederick William and Martha Marie (Widiger) L.; m. Wilma Jeanne Seacat, July 3, 1960; children; Tracy Jeanne, Frederick William II. BSIE, Wichita State U., 1960; MBA, Harvard U., 1966. Mfg. tng. program GE, 1960-64; prodn. gen. supr. Polaroid Corp., Waltham, Mass., 1966-70; mgr. mfg. Millipore Corp., Bedford, Mass., 1970-76; dir. mfg. Berol Corp., Danbury, Conn., 1976-87; exec. v.p. WPM Inc., Waterbury, Conn., 1987—. President bd. trustees East Hill Woods Retirement Ctr., Southbury, Conn., 1989—; pres. 1st Luth. Ch., Waterbury, 1988-89, Luth. Ch. of Newtons, Mass., 1974-75; active Danbury ARC, YMCA; mem. Waterbury Found., 1991—. Republican. Lutheran. Home: 98 Woodlawn Ter Waterbury CT 06710-1929 Office: WPM Inc 407 Brookside Rd Waterbury CT 06708-1418

LUEKE, DONNA MAE, national retail manager; b. Toledo, Sept. 18, 1946; d. Herbert Henry and Margery Alberta (Welsh) L. BA, Adrian Coll., 1968. Tchr. Anchor Bay Schs., Adrian, Mich., 1968-74; salesperson Jacobson's, Birmingham, Mich., 1974-76; sales rep. Stark & Co., Detroit, 1976-80; regional retail supr. Norwich-Eaton Consumer Pharms., Louisville, 1974-76; territory rep. Procter & Gamble, Louisville, 1983-84; dir. Progressive Retail, Raleigh, N.C., 1984-89; nat. retail mgr. CIBA Consumer Pharms. and CIBA Vision Corp., Wayne, Pa., 1989—. Student govt. v.p. Adrian Coll., 1966, 67. Mem. Nature Conservancy Acorn Club, Sierra Club, Amnesty Internat., NOW. Office: CIBA Retail 565 E Swedesford Rd Ste 309 Wayne PA 19087-1611

LUERS, WILLIAM HENRY, art museum administrator; b. Springfield, Ill., May 15, 1929; s. Carl U. and Ann L. (Lynd) L.; m. Wendy Woods Turnbull, Oct. 18, 1979; children by previous marriage: Mark B., David L., William F., Amy L. A.B., Hamilton Coll., 1951, LL.D. (hon.), 1984; M.A., Columbia U., 1957; postgrad., Northwestern U., 1951-52. Commd. fgn. service officer Dept. State, 1957; vice consul Naples, Italy, 1957-60; 2d sec. Am. Embassy, Moscow, 1963-65; polit. counselor Am. Embassy, Caracas, Venezuela, 1969-73; dep. exec. sec. Dept. State, 1973-75; dep. asst. sec. for inter Am. affairs, Washington, 1975-77; dep. asst. sec. European affairs (Soviet-Eastern Europe), 1977-78; ambassador to Venezuela, Caracas, 1978-82, Czechoslovakia, Prague, 1983-86; pres. Met. Mus. Art, N.Y.C., 1986—; bd. dirs. Transco Energy Co., Houston, IDEX Corp., Northbrook, Ill., Discount Corp. N.Y., Scudder New Europe Fund, N.Y., Scudder Global/Internat. Funds; dir.'s visitor Inst. Adv. Study, Princeton, N.J., 1982-83; vis. lectr. Woodrow Wilson Sch., Princeton U., 1983; bd. trustees Rockefeller Bros. Fund., N.Y.C. Mem. trustee adv. coun. Appeal of Conscience Found., N.Y.C. With USNR, 1952-55. Mem. Council on Fgn. Relations. Episcopalian. Office: Met Mus Art 1000 5th Ave New York NY 10028-0198

LUETH, FAITH M., music educator; b. Washington, Feb. 13, 1943; d. Francis and Ellen D. (Parsons) Musker; m. Richard A. Lueth, Dec. 26, 1968; 1 child, Rachel. BA, Boston U., 1964; MA, MM, Boston Conservatory, 1986. Cert. music tchr. K-12. Condr. Wheaton Coll. Chorale, Norton, Mass.; choral dir. Pollard Middle Sch., Needham, Mass.; asst. prof. music edn. Berklee Coll. Music, Boston, choral clinician adolescent voice; condr. Wheaton Coll. Chorale, Norton, Mass.; guest condr. Contbr. chpt. to book. Recipient Disting. Tchr. award Ednl. Coop. Supts.; Mann grantee. Mem. Am. Choral Dirs. Assn., Music Educators Nat. Conf., Mass. Music Edn. Assn., Mu Phi Epsilon. Address: 8 Irving Dr Walpole MA 02081

LUETZELSCHWAB, JOHN WILLIAM, physics educator; b. Hammond, Ind., Sept. 8, 1940; s. Edgar John and Willette Elizabeth (Feder) L.; m. Marcia Ann Bonnemort, Sept. 7, 1963; children: Dana, Mark. AB, Earlham Coll., 1962; MS, Washington U., St. Louis, 1968, PhD, 1968. Asst. prof. physics Dickinson Coll., Carlisle, Pa., 1968-73, assoc. prof., 1973-83, prof., 1983—. Author: Household Energy Use and Conservation, 1980; contbr. articles to profl. jours. Mem. troop com. Boy Scouts Am., Etters, Pa., 1982-86. Office: Dickinson Coll PO Box 1773 Carlisle PA 17013-2896

LUFF, GERALD MEREDITH, JR., sales and marketing executive; b. Vineland, N.J., Oct. 19, 1937; s. Gerald Meredith and Harriet Mary (Lippincott) L.; m. Kathryn Margaret Desmond, Dec. 12, 1964; children: Gerald M., Kelleen M., Jeffrey P., Jennifer D., Bradley S., Valerie A. B Chem. Engring., Rensselaer Poly. Inst., 1960. Various positions Linde Div. Praxair (formerly Union Carbide Indsl. Gases), various locations, 1961—; product mgr. Linde div. Union Carbide Corp., N.Y. hdqrs., 1973-74, area bus. mgr., 1974-76; mktg. mgr. Linde div. Union Carbide Corp., various locations, 1977-87; sales mgr. Linde div. Union Carbide Corp., Danbury, Conn., 1988-90; dir. sales and mktg. Union Carbide Corp., 1990—. Commr., Nottingham Civic Assn., Houston, 1972-73; dist. leader New Canaan (Conn.) Republicans, 1978—; commr. New Canaan Parks and Recreation, 1979-88, com. chmn., 1987. Mem. Am. Chem. Soc., Country Club of New Canaan. Roman Catholic. Home: 234 Main St New Canaan CT 06840-5607 Office: Carbide Ctr Old Ridgebury Rd Danbury CT 06817-0001

LUFTMAN, MICHAEL ERIC, public affairs executive; b. N.Y.C., Jan. 22, 1946; s. Walter and Leonore (Perlstein) L.; m. Susan Wolfe Swiger, Mar. 4, 1973 (div. Aug. 1989); children: Andrew David, Jonathan Louis. BA, Dickinson Coll., 1968. Staff writer Time-Life Books, N.Y.C., 1971-76; writer corp. pub. affairs Time Inc, N.Y.C., 1977-79, sr. assoc. corp. press, 1980-81, chief spokesman, 1982-88; v.p. corp. pub. affairs Am. TV and Comm. Corp., Stamford, Conn., 1988—. Mem. Cable TV Pub. Affairs Assn. Office: Am TV & Comm Corp 300 Leslie Pl Stamford CT 06902-4641

LUGENBEEL, EDWARD ELMER, publisher; b. Balt., June 6, 1932; s. Nimrod Augustus and Victoria Elizabeth (Shilling) L.; m. Alice Marie Smith, June 12, 1953; children: Craig Edward, Susan Elizabeth, Douglas Paul, Leslie Jean. B.S., U. Md., 1954. With Prentice-Hall, Inc., N.J., 1957-76; exec. editor, asst. v.p. Prentice-Hall, Inc., 1972-76; pres. D. Van Nostrand Co., div. Litton Ednl. Pub., Inc. (pubs. coll. textbooks), N.Y.C., 1976-81; v.p. Lynne Palmer Exec. Recruitment, Inc., N.Y.C., 1981-83; v.p., editorial dir. W.B. Saunders Med. Pubs., Phila., 1983-85; exec. editor Columbia U. Press, N.Y.C., 1985—. Served as 1st lt. USAF, 1954-57. Mem. AAAS, Am. Inst. Biol. Scis., Am. Geophys. Union, Soc. Vertebrate Paleontology, Internat. Assn. Landscape Ecology, Delta Sigma Pi. Office: 136 S Broadway Irvington NY 10533

LUGT, HANS JOSEF, physicist; b. Bonn, Germany, Sept. 12, 1930; came to U.S., 1960; s. Josef and Elisabeth (Pütz) L.; m. Anneliese W. Scheller, Nov. 22, 1957; children: Christian H., Brigitte M. Prae Diploma, Bonn U., Fed. Republic of Germany, 1953; diploma, Aachen U., Fed. Republic of Germany, 1954; PhD, Stuttgart U., Fed. Republic of Germany, 1960. Asst., physics lab. Ruhrgas Co., Essen, Fed. Republic of Germany, 1954-57, head, physics lab., 1957-60; rsch. physicist U.S. Naval Weapons Lab., Dahlgren, Va., 1960-66; sci. cons. David Taylor Rsch. Ctr., Bethesda, Md., 1967-74, div. head, 1974-78, sr. rsch. physicist, 1978—; Author: Vortex Flow in Nature and Technology, 1983; contbr. over 110 articles to profl. jours. Recipient Humboldt award Fed. Republic of Germany, 1981, Disting. Civilian Svc. award USN, 1982. Fellow Am. Physical Soc.; mem. Am. Hist. Soc., Am. Goethe Soc. (pres. 1985-87), German Soc. for Applied Math. and Mechanics, Sigma Xi. Office: David Taylor Rsch Ctr Bethesda MD 20084-5000

LUHRS, H. RIC, toy manufacturing company executive; b. Chambersburg, Pa., Mar. 22, 1931; s. Henry E. and Pearl (Beistle) L.; m. Grace Barnhart, June 12, 1973; children by previous marriage: Stephen Frederick, Christine Michelle, TerriAnn, Patricia Denise. BA, Gettysburg Coll., 1953. With The Beistle Co., Shippensburg, Pa., 1948-53, 1959—; pres., gen. mgr. Beistle Co., 1962-90, chmn. bd., 1978—; bd. dirs. Mellon Bank, Commonwealth Region, Capital Tech. Corp.; bd. dirs., vice chmn. CompuPix Tech. Inc., 1984—, pres., 1986—, gemologist, 1977—, owner. Pres. Shippensburg Public Library, 1964-66, 1970-72, 76-78, bd. dirs., 1963-82; pres. Community Chest, 1965, bd. dir., 1963-72; pres. Shippensburg Area Devel. Corp., 1966-72; bd. dirs., trustee Carlisle (Pa.) Hosp., 1967-71, Chambersburg Hosp., 1969-75; mem. consumer advisor council Capital Blue Cross, 1976-78; bd. dirs. Fla. Atlantic U. Found., 1988-91, Shippensburg U. Found., 1991—. Capt. USAF, 1953-59. Mem. Shippensburg Hist. Soc. (bd. dir. 1968), Nat. Sojourners, SAR (life), Shippensburg C. of C. (pres. 1965, bd. dir. 1964-65), Toy Mfrs. Assn. (bd. dir. 1969-71), Nat. Small Businessmen's Assn., NRA (life, benefactor), Shippensburg Fish and Game Assn. (pres. 1963), Am. Legion. Lutheran. Clubs: Cumberland Valley Indsl. Mgmt, York of Printing House Craftsmen. Lodges: Masons (32 deg.), Shriners, Elks, Tall Cedars of Lebanon. Office: 1 Beistle Plz Shippensburg PA 17257-9623

LUI, ERIC MUN, engineering educator; b. Hong Kong, Feb. 2, 1958; came to U.S., 1977; s. Kui Leung and Yin Fong (Leung) L. BS in Civil and Environ. Engring., U. Wis., 1980; MS in Civil Engring., Purdue U., 1982, PhD, 1985. Teaching asst. Purdue U., W. Lafayette, Ind., 1981-82; rsch. asst. Purdue U., W. Lafayette, 1983-85, post-doctoral rsch. asst., 1985-86, lectr., 1985-86; asst. prof. Syracuse (N.Y.) U., 1986-92, Assoc. prof., 1992; advisor Grad. Student Orgn., Syracuse, N.Y., 1988—. Co-author: Structural Stability-Theory and Implementation, 1987, Stability Design of Steel Frames, 1991; contbr. over 40 articles to profl. jours., papers to sci. proceedings and chpts. to books and monographs. Recipient Bleyer scholarship U. Wis., 1979, Bates & Rogers Found. scholarship, 1980, David Ross fellowship Purdue U., 1982, 82. Mem. ASCE, AAUP, Am. Concrete Inst., Am. Acad. Mechanics, Am. Inst. Steel Constrn., Am. Soc. Engring. Edn., Structural Stability Rsch. Coun., Tau Beta Pi, Phi Kappa Phi, Sigma Xi. Office: Syracuse U 220 Hinds Hall Syracuse NY 13244-1190

LUIZZO, ANTHONY JOHN, loss prevention executive, consultant; b. Bklyn., May 26, 1942; s. Philip and Bessie (Pellegrino) L.; (div. Mar. 1973); children: Philip, Anthony Jr. BS in Security Mgmt., Pacific Western U., 1983, MA in Criminology, 1985. Cert. security trainer; cert. fraud examiner; lic. master locksmith. Police officer N.Y.C. Police Dept., 1964-84; dir. security N.Y.C. Pub. Devel., 1984-86, N.Y.C. Office for Econ. Devel., 1986-87; corp. dir. loss prevention N.Y.C. Health & Hosps. Corp., 1987—; pres. L.C. Security Cons. Group, Inc., N.Y.C., 1990—. Contbr. articles to profl. jours. Bd. dirs. People Against Sexual Violence, N.Y.C., 1989—, Tri Pack, Inc. (civilian crime prevention program), 1989—. Recipient Legis. citation N.Y.C. Legis., 1984, citation Bklyn. Borough Pres.'s Office, 1989, Congl. citation 98th Congress, 1985. Mem. ASTM, Nat. Assn. Cert. Fraud Examiners (v.p. commerce chair 1990—), Am. Soc. Indsl. Security, Acad. Security Educators & Trainers (bd. dirs. 1990—), Crime Prevention Practitioners Assn. Home and Office: LC Security Cons Group 326 Bay Ridge Ave Brooklyn NY 11220-5316

LUJAN, MANUEL, JR., secretary of the interior of U.S., former congressman; b. San Idlefonso, N.Mex., May 12, 1928; s. Manuel and Lorenzita (Romero) L.; m. Jean Kay Couchman, Nov. 18, 1948; children: Terra Kay Everett, James Manuel, Barbara Frae, Robert Jeffrey. BA, Coll. Santa Fe, 1950; postgrad., St. Mary's (Calif.) Coll., 1946-47. Engaged in ins. bus. Santa Fe and Albuquerque, 1948; mem. 91st-100th Congresses 1st N.Mex. Dist., 1969-89; mem. interior and insular affairs com., energy and environ. subcom., sci. and tech. com. Dept. of Interior, 1969, sec., 1989—. Office: Dept Interior 1849 C St NW Washington DC 20240-9996*

LUKACH, TERESA ANN, media specialist, writer; b. Waterbury, Conn., Dec. 5, 1948; d. Daniel and Teresa Agnes (Rocco) Santovasi; m. John Edward Lukach (div.); children: John Edward, Dustin Thomas. Grad. high sch., Waterbury, Conn., 1966. Campaign news sec. GOP primary and gen. election campaigns, Conn., 1980-83; adminstrv. asst. to Dep. Under-Sec. for Policy Devel. U.S. Dept. Interior, Washington, 1982-83; staff asst. to Pres. for pub. liaison The White House, Washington, 1983; spl. asst. for pub affairs U.S. Dept. Edn., Washington, 1983-85; speechwriter to sec. HHS, Washington, 1985-86; dep. dir./dir. communications, editor Newswatch High Frontier Inc., Washington, 1986-88; dir. media rels. Nat. Telecommunications and Info. Adminstrn., Washington, 1988-89; dir. pub. affairs Office Human Devel. Svcs., HHS, Washington, 1989, dir. comm., 1990-91; with Romano & Assocs., Columbia, Md.; justice of the peace Hartford, Conn., 1980-84; mem. U.S. Dept. Commerce Consumer Coun., Washington, 1989, World Affairs Coun. of Washington, 1986-88. Contbr. articles to profl. jours. Past mem. Hartford Rep. Town Com., Farmington Rep. Town Com. Recipient Bronze Medal award for superior federal svc. U.S. Dept. Commerce, 1989. Roman Catholic. Home: 806 N Jordan St Alexandria VA 22304 Office: Romano & Assocs 10630 Little Pautaxet Hwy Columbia MD 21044

LUKACS, MICHAEL EDWARD, communications researcher; b. N.Y.C., Mar. 25, 1946; s. William and Hannah (LeWitter-Wolf) L.; m. Diane Harriet Katz, Oct. 29, 1967. Student, CUNY, Queens, 1965-68; T-3, Radio Corp. Am. Inst. now Tech Careers Inst., N.Y.C., 1968-69. Tech. aide Bell Telephone Labs., Holmdel, N.J., 1969-72, sr. tech. aide, 1972-77, assoc. mem. tech. staff, 1977-81, mem. tech. staff, 1981-83; mem. tech. staff Bell Communications Rsch., Red Bank, N.J., 1983—. Patentee cathode ray tube dynamic focus apparatus, cathode ray tube electro-optic linearization device; (co-inventor) pel recursive motion compensated video coder; (inventor) "Lukacs" coding, disparity corrected predictive coding for 3-D video. Recipient Notable Achievement award Bell Labs Research Lab. 113, 1983. Mem. IEEE, Assn. Computing Machinery, Soc. Motion Picture TV Engrs. Office: Bell Comm Rsch 331 Newman Springs Rd Red Bank NJ 07701-7040

LUKAS, JOAN DONALDSON, mathematics and computer science educator; b. New Haven, June 19, 1942; d. Walter George and Rose (Shor) Donaldson; m. George Lukas, Sept. 1, 1963 (div. 1980); children: David Imre, Jonathan; m. Seamus Edmond Kearney, July 14, 1990. AB, Barnard Coll., 1963; PhD, MIT, 1967. Asst. prof. U. Mass., Boston, 1967-74, assoc. prof. math. and computer sci., 1974—; cons. Bolt, Beranek & Newman, Cambridge, Mass., 1978, 87-90, Intermetrics, Inc., Cambridge, 1981-85, Compass, Inc., Wakefield, Mass., 1984-91, Advanced Computer Rsch. Inst.,

Lyon, France, 1992; vis. lectr. Brandeis U., Waltham, Mass., 1970, 79; mem. grad. rev. com. NSF, Washington, 1991, 92. Co-author: Learning Mathematics Through Programming, 1977, Logo: Principles, Programming, Projects, 1986; contbr. articles to profl. publs. Vol. My Sister's Place-Nameless Women's Advocacy, Boston, 1988-91; mem. Peace and Social Concerns, Friends Meeting, Cambridge, 1988—. Mem. IEEE Computer Soc., Assn. for Computing Machinery. Home: 9 Highland Park Malden MA 02148-2429 Office: U Mass Harbor Campus Boston MA 02125

LUKASIK, JOHN PETER, JR., therapist, counselor; b. Scranton, Pa., June 19, 1947; s. John Peter and Mary Ann (Minich) L.; 1 child, Thomas Volk. BA in Mgmt., Park Coll., 1980; MA in Counseling, Webster U., 1982; MS in Counselor Edn., U. Scranton, 1990. Enlisted U.S. Army, 1968, advanced through grades to chief warrant officer, ret., 1988; athletic dir. Cath. Youth Ctr., Scranton, 1989-91; psychotherapist Children's Svc. Ctr., Wilkes Barre, Pa., 1990-91; therapist, counselor Specialized Counseling Svcs., Scranton, 1989—; guidance counselor Bishop Hannan High Sch., Scranton, 1991—. Mem., student advisor sch. psychology adv. bd. Marywood Coll., Scranton. Mem. Am. Psychol. Assn., Am. Assn. Counseling and Devel., Assn. Curriculum Supervision and Devel., Am. Career Devel. Assn. Republican. Roman Catholic. Home: 101 Bengar Dr Scranton PA 18505-3421 Office: Bishop Hannan High Sch 330 Wyoming Ave Scranton PA 18503-1278

LUKASZEWSKI, JAMES EDMUND, communications executive; b. Kewaunee, Wis., Aug. 27, 1942; s. Edmund Ignatius and Virginia Francis (Sprague) L.; m. Barbara Ann Bray, Dec. 18, 1964; children: Charles Todd, James Moir. BA, Metropolitan State U., 1974. Asst., press sec. State of Minn., Office of Governor Wendell R. Anderson, St. Paul, 1974-76; deputy commr. Dept. of Econ. Devel., State of Minn., St. Paul, 1976-78; pres. Media Info. Systems Corp., New Brighton, Minn., 1978-83, Brum & Anderson Exec. Tng., Inc., Mpls., 1984-86; ptnr. Chester Burger Co., N.Y.C., 1986-87; sr. v.p., dir. exec. communication programs Georgeson & Co., Inc., 1987-89; pres., chmn. bd. The Lukaszewski Group Inc., White Plains, N.Y., 1989—; lectr. East Coast Comdr.'s Media Tng. Symposium, USMC, 1986—, Nat. Media Conf., N.Y.C., 1986-89; adj. asst. prof. communications NYU Mgmt. Inst., 1991—; civilian advisor to the Internat. Disaster Adv. Com., U.S. Dept. State, 1990—, to USMC, 1986—. Author: Executive Television Training Handbook, 1983, The Publicity Handbook, 1984, Having Effective Media Interviews, 1984, The Tactical Ingenuity Pyramid, 1989, Executive Action Crisis Management Anthology, 1992, Executive Action Crisis Management Workbook, 1992, Executive Action Emergency Media Relations Guide, 1992, Influencing Public Attitudes: Reducing Media Power, 1992; contbr. articles to profl. jours. Chmn. Bklyn. Park Tater Daze Celebration, Minn., 1972, Met. State U. Alumni Assn., St. Paul, 1974; chmn. venture fund drive Met. State U., 1990-91; trustee, v.p. Met. State U. Found., St. Paul, 1976-86. Recipient Silver Key award Bklyn. Park Jaycees, Minn., 1973, named Sound Citizen of Yr., 1972. Mem. Pub. Rels. Soc. Am. (accredited, Pres.'s Citation award 1991), Counselors Acad. Pub. Rels. Soc. Am. (chmn. monograph com., pub. affairs/govt. sect., newsletter editor), Ctr. for Study of Presidency, Internat. Churchill Soc., The Issues Exchange. Home: 10B Olde Willow Way Briarcliff Manor NY 10510-1452 Office: Ten Bank St Ste 530 White Plains NY 10606-1933

LUKER, JEFFREY PAUL, management information consultant; b. Baytown, Tex., June 11, 1954; s. Norman Elvoy and Shirley Jean (Rinear) L.; m. Joyce Mary Gilbertson, Aug. 6, 1977; children: Jeffrey Paul Jr., Christian Korthaus, Mary Kathryn. BS, Lehigh U., 1976. Staff analyst Arthur Andersen & Co., N.Y.C., 1976-78; sr. analyst Arthur Anderson & Co., N.Y.C., 1978-80, mgr., 1980-86, ptnr., 1986—; ptnr., nat. dir. quick response Arthur Andersen & Co., N.Y.C., 1988—. Contbr. articles to profl. jours. Bd. dirs. Holy Cross Luth. Ch., Springfield, N.J., 1988-89, 87-88. Mem. Vol. Interindustry Communications, Nat. Retail Merchants, Internat. Mass Retailers, Met. Retail Fin. Execs. Assn., Coral Beach & Tennis Club, Canoe Brook Country Club. Republican. Lutheran. Home: 521 Colonial Ave Westfield NJ 07090-3010 Office: Andersen Cons PO Box 765 100 Campus Dr Florham Park NJ 07932

LUKS, JONATHAN CERF, dancer, educator, composer; b. Bklyn., June 26, 1954; s. Alan Cerf Luks and Emily (McGee) Kidwell; m. JoAnna Schnoll, Aug. 26, 1990; 1 child, Noah Maxwell. Student, SUNY, New Paltz, 1973-74; studies in tap with Honi Coles, Gregory Hines, Copasetics, 1974—; student, Dee Erickson Acad., Yorktown, N.Y., 1977-78, Ballet Arts, N.Y.C., 1980-84, Ronnie DeMarco, N.Y.C., 1979-82. Performer Brenda Bufalino's Dancing Theatre Co., New Paltz, N.Y., 1974-76, Coca Cola High Sch. Assembly Tour, 1977, Pepsi Cola High Sch. Assembly Tour, 1980-81, Off Broadway/TV, N.Y.C., 1979-87; choreographer 50 musicals, N.Y., Can., Germany, 1979-92; instr. dance N.Y.C. Studios, 1981-87, Ray Lynch N.Y.C. Sch.-Dance, Stuttgart, Germany, 1986; instr., owner Delhi (N.Y.) Dance Ctr., 1987-92, Liberty Dance Ctr., Walton, N.Y., 1991—; acting tchr. Goshen (N.Y.) Ctr. Boys, 1975; jazz/rock guitarist bands, shows, recordings, N.Y. and tours, 1973—; mus. theatre instr. Delhi Dance Ctr., 1990—. Composer: (mus. plays) Androcles and the Lion, 1980, Romeo and Juliet, 1983; author, composer: (mus. plays) The Fool and the Flying Ship, 1990, The Falcon's Magic Feather, 1991, Z the Musical, 1992. Mem. AFTRA, Actor's Equity Assn. Home: State Rd Andes NY 13731 Office: Delhi Dance Ctr 56 Main St Delhi NY 13753

LULLA, JACK DAVID, polymer engineer; b. N.Y.C., Jan. 15, 1929; s. Joseph and Fannie L.; m. Rita Vernon, Apr. 2, 1955; children: Bruce, Joel, Stephen, Margot. BS, CCNY, 1950. Rsch. chemist Tech. Tape, N.Y.C., 1951-55, plant mgr., 1955-56; v.p. R & D Tech. Tape, New Rochelle, N.Y., 1956-88, Tesa Tuck Inc., New Rochelle, 1988—. Cpl. U.S. Army, 1952-54. Home: 40 E 88th St Apt 11D New York NY 10128-1176 Office: Tesa Tuck Inc Le Fevre Ln New Rochelle NY 10801

LUMADUE, DONALD DEAN, hobby and crafts executive; b. El Reno, Okla., Sept. 30, 1938; s. Harry Basil and Muriel Ellen (Craven) L.; m. Joyce Anne Hayes, June 28, 1958; children: Dawnia, Donald, Robert, Ronald. Student USCG Acad., 1956-57. Lab. technician Charles Pfizer & Co., Groton, Conn., 1957-60; indsl. engr. Sonoco Products, Mystic, Conn., 1960-67; partner Joydon's, New London, Conn., 1958—, House of Leisure, New London, 1965—; Hobby Crafts, New London, 1968—; pres. NEI, Inc., New London, 1968-83. Mem. New Eng. Hobby Industry Assn. (pres. 1973-74, 86-88, bd. dirs. 1983-90), Hobby Industry Assn. Am. (chmn. Wholesaler bd. 1976-78, 82—, exec. show bd. 1985—, Pres.'s award 1986), Nat. Assn. Wholesalers (trustee 1976—), Mgmt. Club S.E. Conn. (pres. 1961-62, 77-78). Office: 78-88 Captains Walk New London CT 06320

LUMBARD, ELIOT HOWLAND, lawyer, educator; b. Fairhaven, Mass., May 6, 1925; s. Ralph E. and Constance Y. L.; m. Jean Ashmore, June 21, 1947; m. Kirsten Dehner, June 28, 1981; children: Susan, John, Ann, Joshua Abel, Marah Abel. BS in Marine Transp., U.S. Mcht. Marine Acad., 1945; BS in Econs., U. Pa., 1949; JD, Columbia U., 1952. Bar: N.Y. 1953, U.S. Supreme Ct. 1959, Pa. 1983. Assoc. Breed, Abbott and Morgan, N.Y.C., 1952-53; asst. U.S. atty. So. Dist. N.Y., 1953-56; assoc. Chadbourne, Parke, Whiteside & Wolff, N.Y.C., 1956-58; ptnr. Townsend & Lewis, N.Y.C., 1961-70; ptnr. Spear and Hill, N.Y.C., 1970-75; ptnr. Lumbard and Phelan, P.C., N.Y.C., 1977-82, Saul, Ewing, Remick & Saul, N.Y.C., 1982-84; pvt. practice law, N.Y.C., 1984-86; ptnr. Haight, Gardner, Poor & Havens, N.Y.C., 1986-88; pvt. practice law, N.Y.C., 1988—; chief counsel N.Y. State Commn. Investigation, 1958-61; spl. asst. counsel for law enforcement to Gov. N.Y., 1961-67; criminal justice cons. to Gov. Fla., 1967; chief criminal justice cons. to N.J. Legis., 1968-69; chmn. com. on organized crime N.Y.C. Criminal Justice Coordinating Coun., 1971-74; mem. departmental disciplinary com. First Dept., N.Y. Supreme Ct., 1982-88; trustee bankruptcy Universal Money Order Co., Inc., 1977-82, Meritum Corp., 1983-89; spl. master in admiralty Hellenic Lines Ltd., 1984-86; chmn. Palisades Life Ins. Co. (former Equity Funding subs. 1974-75); bd. dir. RMC Industries Corp.; lectr. trial practice NYU Law Sch., 1963-65; mem. vis. com. Sch. Criminal Justice, SUNY-Albany, 1968—; adj. prof. law and criminal justice John Jay Coll. Criminal Justice, CUNY, 1975-86; arbitrator Am. Arbitration Assn. and N.Y. Civil Ct.-Small Claims Part, N.Y. County; mem. Vol. Master Program U.S. Dist. Ct. (so. dist.) N.Y. Contbr. articles to profl. jours. Bd. dirs. Citizens Crime Commn. N.Y.C., Inc.; Big Bros. Movement, Citizens Union; trustee Trinity Sch, 1964-78, N.Y.C. Police Found., Inc., 1971—, chmn., 1971-74. Lt. j.g. USNR, 1943-52. Recipient First Disting. Svc. award Sch. Criminal Justice, SUNY-Albany, 1976. Mem. Assn. Bar City N.Y., N.Y. County Lawyers Assn., ABA, N.Y. State Bar Assn., Maritime Law Assn., Down Town Assn. Club. Republican. Home: 300 Central Park W New York NY 10024-1513

LUMER, MARK JOSEPH, government executive; b. Bklyn., Sept. 6, 1951; s. Seymour and Bernice (Endlich) L.; m. Beatty Gail Elson, Sept. 7, 1972; children: Michael, Anne, Sarah. BA, SUNY, Buffalo, 1972; MBA, Am. U., 1984. Cert. assoc. contracts mgr. Contracting officer U.S. Army CECOM, Ft. Monmouth, N.J., 1986; chief compliance U.S. Army CECOM, Ft. Monmouth, 1986-88, ombudsman, 1988-90; dep. dir. procurement procedures U.S. Army SARDA, Pentagon, Washington, 1990-91, rep. DAR coun., 1991—; adj. prof. Brookdale Community Coll., Lincroft, N.J., 1989-90. Contbr. articles to profl. jours. Ky. col. Hon. Order of Ky. Cols., Louisville, 1990; guest lectr. Nat. Def. U.-Info. Resources Mgmt. Coll., Washington, 1990-91. Recipient Comdr.'s award for Civilian Svc., 1984, Superior Civilian Svc. medal, 1990, Order of Mercury Bronze medal Signal Corps Regimental Assn., 1990; named Top 100 Fed. Employee, 1989-90. Fellow Nat. Contract Mgmt. Assn. (dir. 1991—, functional co-dir. chartering 1991—), Armed Forces Communication Electronics Assn., Signal Corps Regimental Assn. Hebrew. Office: US Army SARDA Pentagon SARD-PP Washington DC 20310-0103

LUMPKIN, BRUCE KEYSER, television station executive; b. Balt., Aug. 11, 1944; s. William R. and Doris E. (Keyser) L.; m. Lynn A. Harmon, Feb. 17, 1973; children—Tad W., Elin M. B.A., U. Md., 1971. Local sales exec. Sta. WBFF-TV, Balt., 1971-72, nat. sales mgr., 1972-77, sales mgr., 1977-82; gen. sales mgr. Sta. KSTW-TV, Seattle-Tacoma, 1982-84, v.p. gen. mgr., 1984-86; gen. sales mgr. Sta. WDCA-TV, Bethesda, Md., 1986-87; gen. mgr. Sta. WBFF-TV, Balt., 1987—. Bd. dirs. Concerts Artists Balt. Sgt. E-5 U.S. Army, 1968-69, Vietnam. Decorated Purple Heart, Bronze Star, Air medal. Mem. Wash. State Assn. Broadcasters, Nat. Assn. Broadcasters, Nat. Assn. TV Program Execs., Assn. Ind. TV Stas., TV Bur. Advt., Advt. Assn. Balt. (bd. dirs.), Md., D.C. and Del. Assn. Broadcasters (bd. dirs.). Office: Sta WBFF-TV 2000 W 41st St Baltimore MD 21211-1420

LUMSDEN, IAN GORDON, art gallery director; b. Montreal, Que., Can., June 8, 1945; s. Andrew Mark and Isobel Dallas (Wilson) L.; m. Katherine Elizabeth Carson, July 28, 1979; 1 child, Craig Ian. B.A., McGill U., 1968; postgrad., Mus. Mgmt. Inst., U. Calif., Berkeley, 1991. Curator art dept. N.B. Mus., Saint John, 1969; curator Beaverbrook Art Gallery, Fredericton, N.B., 1969-83, dir., 1983—; bd. dirs. ArtsAtlantic; mem. Cultural Property Export Rev. Bd., 1982-85; mem. program com. 49th Parallel Ctr. for Contemporary Can. Art. Author exhbn. catalogues; contbr. numerous articles to Can. art periodicals. Mem. Can. Museums Assn. (sec.-treas. 1973-75), Can. Art Mus. Dirs. Orgn. (1st v.p. 1977-83, pres. 1983-85), Atlantic Provinces Art Gallery Assn. (chmn. 1970-72), Am. Assn. Museums, Union Club (St. John, N.B.). Mem. Anglican Ch. of Can. Home: Fernholme, 725 George St, Fredericton, NB Canada E3B 1K6

LUMSDEN, ROBERT DOUGLAS, plant pathologist; b. Washington, June 21, 1938; s. George Napier and Mary Louise (Shropshire) L.; m. Valerie Theresa Brook, June 11, 1960; children: Douglas Robert, Thomas Brook. BS, N.C. State U., 1961, MS, 1963; PhD, Cornell U., 1966. Rsch. leader, biocontrol plant diseases lab. USDA/ARS, Beltsville, Md., 1966—. Co-editor: Biotechnology of Fungi, 1989; patentee in field. NDEA fellow Cornell U., 1963, NIH fellow U.S. HHS, 1965. Mem. Am. Phytopathol. Soc., Brit. Mycological Soc., Phi Kappa Phi, Sigma Xi. Office: USDA Beltsville Agrl Rsch Ctr Beltsville MD 20705

LUNA, JOSEPH LUIS, III, architect; b. L.A., Mar. 27, 1960; s. Jose Luis II and Nancy Maureen (Gerber) L.; m. Robin Anne Goyette, Sept. 23, 1989; 1 child, Joseph Robert. AS, Don Bosco Tech. Inst., San Gabrial, Calif., 1979; BArch, Calif. Poly. U., Pomona, 1984. Registered architect, Mass. Archtl. designer Gin Wong Assocs., L.A., 1982-84; archtl. draftsman, designer Spl. Prodns. Inc., San Pedro, Calif., 1984; project architect, project mgr. ADD Inc., Cambridge, Mass., 1984-88; project architect, mgr. Cubellis & Assocs., Boston, 1988-90; prin. Luna Design Group, Beverly, Mass., 1990—. Big brother Boston Big Bros. Assn., 1985-91. Mem. AIA, Boston Soc. Architects, Small Bus. Assn. New Eng., Beverly Bus. Assn. , Cert. Minority Bus. Enterprise: Commonwealth of Mass. Democrat. Roman Catholic. Office: Luna Design Group 38 Ashton St Beverly MA 01915-4014

LUNA, WILSON, college program director; b. Cumuy, P.R., Dec. 15, 1951; came to U.S., 1962; s. Rufino and Elvira (Tosado) L.; m. Elie Maldonado, July 24, 1976; children: Erik and Jaime (twins). AA, Norwalk Community Coll., 1972; BA, So. Conn. State U., 1974; MS, U. Bridgeport, 1976; postgrad., Nova U., 1991—. Tutor, counselor project upward bound U. Bridgeport, Conn., 1973-76, grad. fellow higher edn. opportunities program, 1975-76; student counselor Sacred Heart U., Fairfield, Conn., 1976-78; assoc. dir. admissions Sacred Heart U., 1978-85; counselor, div. fin. aid Greater New Haven Tech. Coll., North Haven, Conn., 1985—, evening adminstr., 1986—. Mem. task force on strategic plan to ensure racial and ethnic diversity Conn. Pub. Higher Edn.; fin. aid div. exec. com. New Eng. Coll. Bd.; mem. Gov. O'Neill Student Fin. Aid Task Force; mem. task force on minority enrollment and retention New Eng. Bd. Higher Edn. Recipient Recognition award League United Latin Ams., Program of Yr. award Am. Coll. Pers. Assn.; named Outstanding Young Man Am. Mem. Conn. Assn. Latin Ams. in Higher Edn. (past pres.), Conn. Assn. Profl. Fin. Aid Adminstrs. (treas.), Conn. Coll. Pers. Assn. (pres., Outstanding Contbns. award), Ea. Assn. Student Fin. Aid Adminstrs., Phi Sigma Iota. Democrat. Roman Catholic. Home: 70 Harvest Ln Milford CT 06460-1705 Office: Greater New Haven State Tech Coll 88 Bassett Rd North Haven CT 06473-1999

LUND, EDWIN HARRISON, business accounting systems executive; b. Erie, Pa., Apr. 4, 1954; s. John Freeman and Shirley (Nick) L.; m. Michele C. Lund, July 9, 1988; children: Christian John Chaffee, Harrison Taylor VonNick. Student, U. Tex., Dallas, 1981. Pres., mgr. Flowerama of Am., Erie, Pa., 1973-79; acctg. mgr. Diversified Human Resources Group, Dallas, 1980-83; acctg. rep. Tex. Dept. Human Resources, Dallas, 1983-84; mgr. Progressive Bookkeeping Systems, Erie, 1984-85; pres. Presque Isle Group Cos. Inc., Erie, 1985—, Rising Star Recordings, Inc., Erie, 1989—; treas. North Coast Fin. Svcs., Erie, 1989—. Author: How to Value An Accounting Business, 1988. Mem. Leadership Erie Class of 1990. Mem. Nat. Exchange Club (pres. Erie chpt. 1989-91), Nat. Assn. of Accts., Nat. Soc. Pub. Accts., Pa. Notary Soc.; Nat. Red Cross (bd. dirs. Erie chpt.). Office: Lund Acctg Systems 1920 W 8th St Erie PA 16505-4935

LUND, GEORGE EDWARD, retired electrical engineer; b. Phila., Feb. 17, 1925; s. Harold White and Hannah (Lawford) L.; m. Shirley Bolton Stevens, Sept. 24, 1960; children: Marsha, Roger, Sharon Stevens, Gretchen. BEE, Drexel U., 1952; MEE, U. Pa., 1959; postgrad. in computer sci., Villanova U., 1981-83. Project engr. Burroughs Corp., Paoli, Pa., 1952-86; project engr. UNISYS Corp., Paoli, 1986-90, ret., 1990. Assoc. editor, contbr.: Digital Applications of Magnetic Devices, 1960; patentee in field. With USN, 1943-46, ETO. Mem. IEEE (sr.), Eta Kappa Nu. Republican. Methodist. Home: 923 Pinecroft Rd Berwyn PA 19312-2123

LUND, JON PAUL, university administrator; b. Faribault, Minn., Feb. 28, 1964; s. Lloyd Arthur and Donna Jean (Kopp) L. BA cum laude, St. Olaf Coll., 1986; MA, Mich. State U., 1990. Head resident St. Olaf Coll., Northfield, Minn., 1986-88; grad. advisor Mich. State U., East Lansing, 1988-90; asst. area coord. U. Del., Newark, 1990—. Mem. Capitol Area Drug Coalition, East Lansing, 1988-90; English lang. tutor lit. Vols. Am., Wilmington, Del., 1991—. Mem. AACD, Am. Coll. Pers. Assn. (commn. XVIII directorate, newsletter editor 1991—). Lutheran. Office: U Del 5 Courtney St Newark DE 19711-5325

LUNDAHL, STEVEN MARK, musician, consultant; b. Bloomington, Minn., Aug. 19, 1955; s. John Miles and Zita Marguerite (Otto) L.; m. Genevieve Catherine Munoz, May 24, 1980; children: Alexandra Maia, Anders Braeden. MusB in Edn., Coll. of St. Scholastica, 1979. Music dir. Utah Shakespearean Festival, Cedar City, Utah, 1979-81; pres. Boston Early Music Ctr., 1980-84; mem. New Eng. Baroque Ensemble, Boston, 1981-86, Waverly Consort, N.Y.C., 1985—; pres. Lundahl Assocs., 1990—; artist-in residence Duluth Pub. Schs., Minn., 1979-80; founding mem. Boston Shawm and Sackbut Ensemble, Boston, 1981—; computer cons., 1984—. Performer, interpreter of medieval, Renaissance and Baroque instruments; rec. artist Smithsonian Chamber Players, Musical Heritage Soc., Nat. Pub. Radio, Deutsche Harmonia Mundi, Erato; guest artist Boston Camerata, 1984—, Calliope: A Renaissance Band, 1985—, Boston Symphony Orch.: Early Instrument Collection, 1985—. Del. Minn. Dem. state conv., 1974. Recipient Rose Reese award, 1974. Mem. Am. Fedn. Musicians 1974—. Home and Office: 139 Tina Dr Suncook NH 03275-1337

LUNDBERG, ROBERT DEAN, consulting chemist and researcher; b. Valley City, N.D., May 30, 1928; s. Alvin Andrew and Ella Frances (Brechwald) L.; m. Patricia Elaine Goeschel, July 11, 1953; children: Michael Robert, Barbara Ann. BA, Harvard U., 1953, MA, PhD, 1957. Scientist Union Carbide Corp., Charleston, W.Va., 1957-67, polymer chemist, 1967-69; tech. leader Exxon Chem. Co., Linden, N.J., 1984-90; sect. head Exxon Rsch. & Engring. Co., Linden, 1969-84; cons., part-time researcher Exxon Rsch. & Engring. Co., Clinton, N.J., 1990—. Contbr. over 100 articles to tech. jours.; over 200 patents on polymer sci. Sgt. USMC, 1946-48. Fellow Am. Inst. Chemists (Chem. Pioneer award 1986); mem. Am. Chem. Soc. Home: 4 Brian Dr Bridgewater NJ 08807-2016 Office: Exxon Rsch & Engring Co Rte 22 E Annandale NJ 08801

LUNDEBERG, ROGER VICTOR, inventor; b. Hartford, Conn., Jan. 18, 1934; s. Edgar C. and Olga Maybel (Wadlund) L. Student, Charter Oak Coll., Farmington, Conn., 1988-90; AS, Manchester Community Coll., 1983; student, Hartford Tech. Coll., 1977-80, 84-86, U. Hartford, 1957, 87. Inventor, sec.-treas. Parts Feeders Corp., Hartford, 1958-61; inventor Lundeberg Engring. Co., Hartford, 1954-87; cons. AMSCO, East Hartford, Conn., 1985-87; editor AMSCOR, East Hartford, Conn., 1987-92, Jour. of Applied Sci., Manchester, Conn., 1992—; cons. AMSCOR, 1987-90. Inventor rotary engine prime movers; author: My World, 1985. Vol. Friendship Ctr., East Hartford, 1981. Mem. AAAS, N.Y. Acad. Sci. (assoc.), Am. Mensa. Home: PO Box 508 Norwich CT 06360

LUNDEEN, JOHN ANTON, finance company executive; b. Passaic, N.J., Jan. 7, 1952; s. Joel Waldemar and Doris Menurva (Nordling) L.; m. Gael Barbara Simonson, Apr. 20, 1985; children: Berent Anton Winslow, Anders Gordon Frederic. AB, Harvard U., 1974; MA in Am. Studies, U. Minn., 1976; MA in Pub. Policy, Harvard U., 1978. Presdl. mgmt. intern SBA, Boston, 1978-79; budget examiner Office Mgmt. and Budget, Washington, 1980-81; planner, urban and regional policy Dept. of Transp., Cambridge, Mass., 1981-82; mgr., pub. policy issues analysis Aetna Life & Casualty, Hartford, Conn., 1982-84; mgr., internat. fin. svcs. Aetna Life & Casualty, Hartford, 1984-85; assoc., pub. fin. dept. Piper, Jaffrey & Hopwood, Mpls., 1985-86; sr. assoc., pub. fin. group Merrill Lynch Capital Markets, N.Y.C., 1986-89; v.p. derivative products group Nat. Westminster Bank Capital Markets, N.Y.C., 1990—. Democrat. Lutheran. Home: 3 Hollister Ln Darien CT 06820-5404 Office: Nat Westminster Bank Capita Derivative Products Group 175 Water St 20th Fl New York NY 10038

LUNDINE, STANLEY NELSON, state government official, former congressman, lawyer; b. Jamestown, N.Y., Feb. 4, 1939; children: John Ludwig, Mark Andrew. Mayor of Jamestown, 1969-76; mem. 95th-97th Congresses from 39th N.Y. Dist., 98th-99th Congress from 34th N.Y. Dist., 1976-87; lt. gov. State of N.Y., Albany, 1987—; mem. banking, fin. and urban affairs coms., sci. and tech. com., select com. on aging. Office: State Capitol Office of Lt Gov Rm 326 Albany NY 12224

LUNDQUIST, DANA R., health systems company executive; b. Mpls., Sept. 12, 1941; s. R. Dana and Mary Jane (Norton) L.; children: Brenda A., Shiela R. BA, Valparaiso U., 1963; postgrad., U. Hawaii, 1963-64, U. Colo., 1963; MBA, U. Chgo., 1966. Adminstrv. asst. U. Chgo. Hosps. and Clinics, 1966-67, asst. supt., 1967-68, asst. dir., 1968-70; officer, bd. dirs. affiliates Hamot Health Systems, Inc., Erie, Pa., 1970—, pres. parent co., 1981—; lectr. grad. program in hosp. adminstrn. U. Chgo., 1967-70; mem. Erie County Hosp. Coun., 1978—, pres. 1982; mem. bd. dirs. Hosp. Coun. Western Pa., 1978—, vice chmn.; mem. exec. com. Pa. Coun. Teaching Hosps., 1986-90; mem. adv. coun. risk mgmt. Pa. Hosp. Ins. Co., 1982-90, bd. dirs. Vol. Hosps. Am. of Pa., 1985—, chmn. bd.; bd. dirs. Marine Bank, 1987—; bd. visitors The Behrend Coll., Pa. State u., 1990; bd. mem. Pa. Med. Coll., 1991; bd. dirs. Hardware Hawaii, 1989—. Mem. Erie Conf. on Community Devel., 1981—, bd. dirs., 1988—; bd. dirs. N.W. Pa. Buy Right Coun., 1986—, United Way Erie County, 1983—; mem. pres.'s coun. Villa Maria Coll., Erie, 1981-90; mem. bd. incorporators Gannon U., Erie, 1981—; mem. governing bd. St. Paul's Luth. Ch., Erie, 1973-78, v.p., 1974-78; mem. steering com. Erie Down Town Coalition, 1990, chmn., 1991; bd. dirs., mem. coms. The Achievement Ctr., 1974—; numerous other activities. Fellow Am. Coll. Healthcare Execs. (former regents adv. coun. Pa.); mem. Am. Hosp. Assn. (governing coun. sect. for met. hosps. 1987, alt. ho. of dels. 1988), Hosp. Assn. Pa. (polit. action com. 1981—), Pa. C. of C., Newcomen Soc. N.Am., U. Chgo. Hosp. Alumni Assn. (exec. com. 1967-70, 87-92, sec.-treas. 1988, pres. 1990-91), Erie Club, Kahkwa Club, Aviation Country Club of Erie, Rotary. Office: Hamot Health Systems Inc 100 State St Ste 500 Erie PA 16507-1457

LUNDQUIST, KATHLEEN KAPPY, psychologist, management consultant; b. Bronxville, N.Y., July 2, 1953; d. Thaddeus Roman and Eileen Marie (McEntee) Kappy; m. Wade Allyn Lundquist, Oct. 13, 1990. BA, Coll. Mt. St. Vincent, N.Y.C., 1974; MA, Fordham U., 1975, PhD, 1979. Rsch. assoc. NAS, Washington, 1977-78; sr. rsch. assoc. Ednl. Testing Svc., Evanston, Ill., 1978-79; indsl. psychologist So. Calif. Edison, Rosemead, Calif., 1979-82, mgr. human resources, 1982-89; cons. Hewitt Assocs., Rowayton, Conn., 1989-90; v.p., mng. prin. H.R. Strategies, Stamford, Conn., 1990—; nat. coord. Edison Elec. Inst., Washington, 1976-79. Mem. APA, Soc. for Indsl. and Orgnl. Psychology, Met. N.Y. Assn. Applied Psychology, Phi Beta Kappa. Office: HR Strategies 1281 Main St Stamford CT 06902

LUNDREGAN, WILLIAM JOSEPH, lawyer; b. Peabody, Mass., Nov. 8, 1940; s. William J. and Suzanne G. (Hichens) L.; m. Jane T. Lundregan, July 15, 1967; children: Catherine S., William J., Anne T. BS in BA, Boston Coll., 1962, LLB, 1967. With office of tax counsel United Shoe Machinery Corp., Boston, 1967; atty. tax dept. Arthur Young & Co., Boston, 1967-69; first asst. clk. magistrate First Dist. Ct. of Essex, Salem, Mass., 1969-74; ptnr. Welch & Lundregan, Salem, Mass., 1974-88, Lundregan Law Offices, Salem, Mass., 1988—; corporator, trustee, bd. investment Salem Five Cents Savs. Bank. Bd. dirs. North Shore Cath. Charities, Peabody; trustee, pres. Salem Atheneum; pres., dir. Boys and Girls Club, Salem. 1st lt. U.S. Army, 1962-64. Mem. Mass. Bar Assn., Salem Bar Assn., Essex County Bar Assn. (exec. com.), Rotary (bd. dirs., pres. 1985-86), Corinthian Yacht Club (membership com.). Roman Catholic. Home: 8 Faye Cir Marblehead MA 01945-3714

LUNDSTEDT, PETER SANFORD, stockbroker, investment consultant; b. Princeton, N.J., Apr. 10, 1958; s. Sven Birtle and Jean (Sanford) L. BS in Internat. Bus., Ohio State U., 1986. With Smith Barney, Harris Upham, 1986; account exec. Merrill Lynch, 1986-87; v.p. Kopstein, Van Alen & Co. Inc., Poughkeepsie, N.Y., 1987-91; with A.G. Edwards, White Plains, N.Y., 1991—. With U.S. Army, 1976-80. Mem. So. Dutchess C. of C., Nat. Exchange Club, Hudson Valley Ski Club. Republican. Home: 25 Tamarack Cir Fishkill NY 12524-2641 Office: AG Edwards 10 Bank St White Plains NY 10601

LUNETTA, VINCENT NORMAN, academic administrator; b. Boston, June 24, 1937; m. Lois Kathryn Waldeck, July 1, 1961; children: Mark, Kathryn. AB, Harvard Coll., 1959; MA, Tufts U., 1961; PhD, U. Conn., Storrs, 1972. Tchr., dept. chair various Conn. schs., 1962-72; prof. U. Iowa, Iowa City, 1972-87; program dir. NSF, Washington, 1986-87; assoc. dean for rsch. and grad. programs Coll. of Edn. Pa. State U., University Park, 1987—; active in profl. leadership and cons. Contbr. numerous articles to profl. jours. Recipient STAR awards, Gustav Ohaus award Nat. Sci. Tchrs. Assn.; named Outstanding Sci. Educator, Assn. for Edn. Tchrs. in Sci.

Fellow AAAS. Home: 763 Storch Rd State College PA 16801-4221 Office: Pa State U 241 Chambers Bldg University Park PA 16802

LUNNEY, JOAN KATHERINE, research immunologist; b. Phila., July 19, 1946; married, 1979. BS in Chemistry, Chestnut Hill Coll., 1968; PhD in Biochemistry, Johns Hopkins U., 1976. Rsch. chemist Corning Glass Works, Painted Post, N.Y., 1967; tchr. sci. Camden (N.J.) Cath. High Sch., 1968-71; chemist lab. biochem. pharmacology NIH, Nat. Inst. Arthritis, Metabolism & Digestive Diseases, Bethesda, Md., 1973-76; postdoctoral fellow immunology br. NIH, Nat. Cancer Inst., Bethesda, 1976-79; sr. staff fellow immunology br. NIH, NCI, 1979-83; rsch. immunologist Helminthic Diseases lab. USDA Agrl. Rsch. Svc., Beltsville, Md., 1983—; adv. coun. Portuguese NSF, 1987-90; com. rsch. in animal genome U.S. Exptl. Sta. Com. on Planning, 1990; nat. animal genetic resources com. USDA, 1991—. Assoc. editor Jour. Immunology, 1989-93; mem. editorial bd. Vet. Immunology Immunopathology, 1989—, Animal Biotech., 1989—. Recipient Women's Equality Day Supr. award USDA Women's Action Task Force, 1991. Mem. Am. Assn. Immunologists (vet. immunology com. 1990—), Am. Assn. Vet. Parasitologists, Am. Assn. Vet. Immunologists, Internat. Union Immunological Sci. (chair monoclonal antibody cluster differentiation workshop for swine 1990-92), Internat. Soc. Animal Genetics, Transplantation Soc., Assn. Women in Sci. Home: 8903 Grant St Bethesda MD 20817-3513 Office: USDA Agrl Rsch Svc Helminthic Diseases Lab Bldg 1040 Rm 2 Beltsville MD 20705

LUONGO, JANET DUFFY, speaker, educator, artist; b. N.Y.C., Mar. 2, 1949; d. Edmund John Duffy and Frances Barbara (Beyer) Savin; m. James Paul Luongo, 1976. BA, Adelphi U., 1972; MS, CUNY, 1977. Cert. art tchr., N.Y., Conn. Trainer, v.p. It Works, Inc., Bridgeport, Conn., 1986-88; tchr. art Acad. St. Joseph's, Brentwood, N.Y., 1975-78; tchr. art, chmn. Internat. Sch. Geneva, Chataigneraie, Switzerland, 1981-86; tchr. art Wilton (Conn.) Pub. Schs., 1988-92, tchr. adult edn., 1974—; art history tchr. Sacred Heart U., Fairfield, Conn., 1992—; workshop trainer Unitarian Universalist Ch., Ferry Beach, Maine, 1989; founder, pres. Conn. chpt. Women's Caucus for Art, 1990—, nat. bd. mem., 1991—. One-woman art show Galerie Motte, Geneva, 1986; cartoon illustrator P.C. mag., 1988; pub. works in The World, Sept., 1989. Mem. Unitarian Universalist Svc. Com., Boston, 1988—; mem. NOW, Nat. Mus.-Women in the Arts. Recipient human rels. award Dale Carnegie Sch., Conn., 1987. Mem. AAUW, Nat. Art Educators Assn., Entrepreneurial Women's Network, Amnesty Internat., Greenpeace, Mensa. Home and Office: 1145 Capitol Ave Bridgeport CT 06606

LUONGO, LUCILLE FRANCESCA, communications company executive; b. N.Y.C., May 29, 1948; d. Carmine and Jean (Gubitosi) Ariniello. BA in English and Speech, Hofstra U., 1970, MA in Communications, 1975. Tchr. Roosevelt (N.Y.) High Sch.; exec. sec. Katz Communications, Inc., N.Y.C., 1978-79, asst. dir. corp. communications, 1979-81, dir. communication svcs., 1981-82, dir. corp. rels., 1982-85, v.p. corp. rels., 1985-91, sr. v.p. corp. communications, 1991—. Mem. Internat. Radio and TV Soc., Am. Women in Radio and TV (pres. N.Y. chpt.), NAFE, Broadcast Promotion and Mktg. Execs. Office: Katz Comm Inc 125 W 55th St New York NY 10019

LUPERT, LESLIE ALLAN, lawyer; b. Syracuse, N.Y., May 24, 1946; s. Reuben and Miriam (Kaufman) L.; m. Roberta Gail Fellner, May 19, 1968; children: Jocelyn, Rachel, Susannah. BA, U. Buffalo, 1967; JD, Columbia U., 1971. Bar: N.Y. 1971. Ptnr. Orans Elsen & Lupert, N.Y.C., 1971—. Contbr. articles to profl. jours. Mem. ABA, N.Y. State Bar Assn. (trial lawyers sect.), Assn. of Bar of City of N.Y. (com. fed. legislation 1977-80, profl. and jud. ethics com. 1983-86, com. on fed. cts. 1986-89), Phi Beta Kappa. Office: Orans Elsen & Lupert 1 Rockefeller Pla New York NY 10020

LUPIANI, DONALD ANTHONY, psychologist; b. N.Y.C., June 7, 1946; s. Louis and Josephine (Boccia) L.; m. Linda Moyik, June 20, 1970; 1 child, Jennifer. BA, Iona Coll., 1968; MA, Columbia U., 1971, PhD, 1973; postdoctoral, Behavior Therapy Inst., White Plains, N.Y., 1976. Lic. psychologist, N.Y. Clin. assoc. Columbia U., N.Y.C., 1974-85, Fordham U., Bronx, N.Y., 1979-81; dir. psychology and spl. edn. svcs. Riverdale Country Sch., Bronx, 1973-87; chief psychologist Franciscan Order of Priests, N.Y.C., 1983—; pvt. practice Yonkers, N.Y., 1975—; dir. spl. svcs. Riverdale Country Sch., Bronx., 1973-87; bd. dirs. St. Ursula Learning Ctr., Mt. Vernon, N.Y. Contbr. articles to profl. jours. Bd. dirs., mem. The St. Ursula Learning Ctr. Fellow Am. Orthopsychiat. Assn., Am. Coll. Psychology; mem. APA, N.Y. State Psychol. Assn., Westchester County Psychol. Assn. (chmn. ethics com. 1980-87). Roman Catholic. Home and Office: 227 Mile Square Rd Yonkers NY 10701-5369

LURKIS, ALEXANDER, electrical engineer; b. N.Y.C., Oct. 1, 1908; s. Louis and Rebecca (Friedman) L.; m. Carin Tendler, Nov. 8, 1930; 1 child, Jeffry. BSEE, Cooper Union, N.Y.C., 1930, NYU, 1934; postgrad., SUNY, N.Y.C. Registered profl. engr., N.Y., Fla. Asst. engr. 8th & 9th Ave. Rwy. Co., N.Y.C., 1925-28; elec. draftsman N.Y.C. Bd. Edn., 1928-30; from jr. engr. to sr. elec. engr. N.Y.C. Transit Authority, 1930-58; acting commr. Dept. Water Supply, Gas and Electricity, City of N.Y., 1961; chief engr. N.Y.C. Bur. Gas and Electricity, 1959-64; prin. ptnr. Alexander Lurkis Assocs., N.Y.C., 1964-80; pres. Alexander Lurkis P.C., Cons. Engrs., N.Y.C., 1971-90; prin. Alexander Lurkis, P.E., N.Y.C., 1991—. Author: The Power Brink, 1983; contbr. articles to profl. jours. Formerly active various civic orgns. Fellow Illuminating Engring. Soc. (chmn. energy mgmt. com. 1974-77), N.Y. Acad. Sci.; mem. IEEE (sr.), Cooper Union Alumni Assn. (bd. govs. 1960-66), Queens Mus., Nat. Geog. Soc., Holliswood Civic Assn. (v.p. 1974-76). Jewish. Home and Office: 19312 Nero Ave Jamaica NY 11423-1154

LUSCH, CHARLES JACK, physician; b. Lehighton, Pa., Feb. 15, 1936; s. Charles Norman and Loretta (Gaumer) L.; m. Carole Faye Eckart, Aug. 17, 1957; children: Marjorie, Susan, Stephen, Robert. AB in Biology magna cum laude, Lafayette Coll., Easton, Pa., 1957; MD, Temple U., 1961. Bd. cert. in med. oncology, Hematology, and internal medicine. Pres. Berks Hematology-Oncology Assocs., Reading, Pa., 1968—; chief sect. of med. oncology & hematology Reading Hosp. & Med. Ctr., Reading, 1970—; dir. Pa. State Hemophilia Ctr., Reading Hosp. & Med. Ctr., 1973—; v.p. Lusch Motor Parts, Lehighton, Pa., 1975—; chief sect. med. oncology & hematology Community Gen. Hosp., Reading, 1980—; asst. chief medicine Reading Hosp. and Med. Ctr., 1986—; med. dir. Pocono Internat. Raceway, 1980-85; chmn. institutional rev. bd. Reading Hosp. and Med. Ctr., 1986—, dir. continuing med. edn., 1987—; med. dir. Berks County Hospice, Berks County Vis. Nurse Assn., Reading, 1987—; dir. oncology svcs. Reading Hosp. and Med. Ctr., 1990—; med. adv. com. Pa. Blue Shield, Camp Hill, Pa., 1987—; bd. dirs. Berks Home Health Car, Reading Cancer Ctr., Reading Hosp.; malpractice cons. Med. Protective Ins. Co., Ft. Wayne, Ind., 1985—; cons. in hematology and oncology Pottsville (Pa.) Hosp. and Good Samaritan Hosp., 1975—; clin. asst. prof. medicine Pa. Med. Sch., 1984—, Pa. State Med. Sch., 1981—, Temple U. Med. Sch., clin. assoc. prof. 1990; sr. clin. instr. Mahnemann U. Med. Sch., 1968—; prin. investigator Ea. Coop Oncology Group, 1975-90, Nat. Surg. Adj. & Breast Project, 1986—. Contbr. articles to profl. jours.; editor The Med. Record (regional med. jour.), 1970-71. Advisor Future Physicians Am., Reading, 1965; bd. dirs. Berks County unit Am. Cancer Soc., Reading, 1968-78, Keystone Community Blood Bank, Reading, 1970-80; adv. com. The Women's Ctr., Reading Hosp., 1987-88. Lt. comdr. USPHS, 1965-67. Fellow ACP; mem. Pa. Soc. Hematology-Oncology (sec.-treas. 1986-87), Am. Soc. Clin. Oncology, Am. Soc. Hematology, Am. Fedn. Clin. Rsch., Acad. Hospice Physicians (publs. com. 1989—), Lafayette Coll. "The Graduates" Choir, U.S. Amateur Ballroom Dance Assn. (pres. Reading chpt.), Sports Car Club Am., Phi Beta Kappa, Alpha Omega Alpha. Republican. Lutheran. Home: 1617 Meadowlark Rd Reading PA 19610-2820 Office: Berks County Oncology Assoc 301 S 7th Ave Reading PA 19611-1410

LUSH, SAMUEL ROBERT, furniture store owner, bed and breakfast owner; b. Wellsboro, Pa., Oct. 14, 1961; s. Henry William and Jean (Wolfe) L.; m. Fredrica Walbridge, Oct. 31, 1987; 1 child, Alyson Laney. BS cum laude, U. N.H., 1983. V.p. Lush Bros., Inc., State College, Pa., 1984—; bd. dirs. Commonwealth Bank. Deacon, State College Presbyn. Ch. Mem. Nat. Home Furnishing Assn. (pres. Pa. chpt. 1991), State College Kiwanis Club (v.p. 1990-91). Republican. Home: RR 1 Box 135 Spring Mills PA 16875-9624 Office: Lush Bros Inc 137 Elmwood St State College PA 16801-6890

LUSHINGTON, NOLAN, library science educator, educator; b. Kingston, Jamaica, Feb. 15, 1929; arrived in U.S., 1933; s. Neville and Margaret (Calder) Landor; m. Gertruda Brooks, Mar. 15, 1951 (div. 1983); children: Christopher, Nancy, Michael; m. Louise Blalock, Mar. 12, 1983. AB, Columbia U., 1950, MA in History, 1953, MS in Libr. Sci., 1958. Libr., master St. Andrews Sch., Middletown, Del., 1953-60; libr. Free Libr. Phila., 1960-61; libr. Greenwich (Conn.) Libr., 1962-64, asst. dir., 1964-66, dir., 1966-87; asst. prof. So. Conn. State U., New Haven, 1987—; cons. for numerous libr. bldgs. Author: Libraries Designed for Users, 1980; co-author: Design and Evaluation of Public Library Buildings, 1991; inventor Locator, 1990. With USMC, 1950-52, col. res., 1950-72. Fellow Coun. on Libr. Resources, 1972. Mem. ALA (chair bldgs. sect. 1981-82), Pub. Libr. Assn. (GGS com. 1991-93), Conn. Libr. Assn. (pres. 1970-71). Episcopalian. Home: 167 W Norwalk Rd Norwalk CT 06850-4410 Office: So Conn State U 231 Crescent St New Haven CT 06511-1624

LUSHT, KENNETH MICHAEL, business administration educator; b. N.Y.C., Dec. 22, 1942; m. Elizabeth Enloe Hall; children: Elizabeth, Alexander. BBA, Emory U., 1964; PhD, Ga. State U., 1973. Prof. bus. adminstrn. Pa. State U., University Park, 1973—, acad. program dir. continuing edn., 1983—, dir. inst. for real estate studies, 1986—, chmn. dept. ins. and real estate, 1989—; pres. Kenneth M. Lusht Cons., State College, 1983—. Author 2 textbooks; editorial bd. Jour. of the Am. Real Estate and Urban Econs. Assn., 1986—, Jour. of Property Rsch., 1990—, Appraisal Jour., 1991—; contbr. articles to profl. jours. Recipient Wagner award Am. Inst. of Real Estate Appraisers, 1986. Mem. Am. Real Estate and Urban Econs. Assn. (pres. 1987, bd. dirs. 1982-84, 88-90), Am. Real Estate Soc., VFW. Office: Coll Bus Pa State U 409 BAB University Park PA 16802

LUST, ELENORE (NORLIST), artist; b. Chgo.; d. Herbert and Dora (Koumas) Lust; m. Robert Eising, Jan. 7, 1932 (div.). Student, Smith Coll., 1929-30; BA, NYU, 1935, MA, 1957. Cert. tchr., N.Y., N.J. Dir., co-founder Norlyst Art Gallery, N.Y.C., 1940-49; art tchr. Cape of Good Hope Sem., Capetown, South Africa, 1952-55, St. Siprian's Sch., Capetown, 1952-55, N.J. High Schs., 1957-79; art lectr. Herald Tribune N.Y.C., 1944-49, art tchr. Little Red Sch. House, N.Y.C., 1944-49, Bklyn. Mus. Art Sch., 1947-49, Rancocas Valley Region High Sch., 1959-68; spl. edn. tchr. Lenape High Sch. System, 1970-79. Exhibited in one-woman shows at Norlyst Art Gallery, 1944, Stuttaford's Gallery , Capetown, 1952, Cafe Gallery, Burlington, N.J., 1988, Ft. Dix, Pemberton, N.J. , 1988, Nat. Mus. Women in Arts, Washington; represented in permanent collection at Fort Dix and 74 other private and corporate collections. Docent Burlington County Cultural and Heritage Commn., Smithville, N.J., 1984—; vol. Chatsworth (N.J.) Festival, 1988—. Mem. AAUW, Burlington County Art Guild (pres. 1983-85, v.p. 1989), Atlantic City Art Ctr., Trenton Artists' Workshop Assn., So. N. J. Advocates for Arts, Artworks/Princeton. Democrat. Episcopalian. Studio: PO Box D Mount Holly NJ 08060

LUST, HERBERT COHNFELDT, II, finance executive; b. Chgo., Oct. 31, 1926; s. Herbert Cohnfeldt and Jennie (Friedman) L.; m. Virginia Wertheimer; children: Herbert Cohnfeldt III, Conrad. MA, U. Chgo., 1948. Pres. Pvt. Water Supply, Inc. Greenwich Assocs., N.Y.C., 1961—, co-owner, dir. Gallery Bernard, 1969-87; dir. First Va. Real Estate Trust, Washington, 1981-83; chmn. bd. BRT, Great Neck, N.Y., 1983-85; chmn. bd. dirs. United Merchants & Mfg., Teaneck, N.J., 1991—; lectr. comparative lit. U. Chgo., 1956-59; chmn. bd. United Merchants and Mfg., 1991—; bd. dirs. Prime Motors Inv. 1992—. Author: 12 Principals of Art Investment, 1969, Alberto Giacometti, 1970, Enrico Baj, 1972, Violence and Defiance, 1983. Served in USN, 1944-46. Named Fulbright scholar, 1949-51. Jewish. Office: 1356 Madison Ave New York NY 10128-0728

LUSTE, JOSEPH FRANCIS, JR., land use, transportation, planning specialist; b. Troy, N.Y., Dec. 7, 1940; s. Joseph Francis and Catherine (Coler) L.; m. Migdalia Malissa Gallardo, Jan. 31, 1970; children: Kimberly, Jonathan. AAS in Engring., Hudson Valley Community Coll., 1960; BA in Planning, Rutgers U., 1979; M in Aviation Mgmt., Embry-Riddle Aero. U., 1985; PhD in Property Mgmt., Western States U., 1987. Jr. engr. Tallamy Assocs., Inc., Washington, 1965-71; staff engr., planner Barrett & Hale, Inc., Hato Rey, P.R., 1971-73; sr. engr., planner T&M Assocs., Inc., Middletown, N.J., 1973-80; dir. planning and devel. Twp. of Middletown, 1980-82; head planning, engring. and devel. County of Atlantic, Atlantic City, 1982-84; prin. planner, office mgr. Edwards and Kelcey, Inc., Atlantic City, 1984-86; dir. planning, assoc. Pennoni Assocs., Inc., Haddon Heights, N.J., 1986-90; exec. dir., chief exec. officer Cross County Connection Transp. Mgmt. Assn., Marlton, N.J., 1990—. Author planning, housing and transp. reports. Dir. aerospace edn. USAF, CAP, McGuire AFB, N.J., 1984; exec. com. Cross County Transp. Mgmt. Assn., Burlington County, N.J., 1989-90, trustee, 1989-90. With USN, 1961-65. Recipient Assistance award Sr. Citizens Council, 1981., Cert. Appreciation Atlantic County Pvt. Industry Council, 1983. Mem. Am. Planning Assn. (charter, exec. com. N.J. chpt. 1982), Urban Land Inst., Met. Assn. Urban Designers and Environ. Planners, Internat. Real Estate Inst., Greater Atlantic City C. of C. (chmn. transp. com. 1986-91), South Jersey C. of C. (transp. com. 1986—), Greater Mainland C. of C. (bd. dirs.), Burlington County (N.J.) Cross Country Transp. Mgmt. Assn. (exec. com., trustee 1989—), Nat. Coun. Urban Devel. (planning and devel. com. N.J. chpt. 1989—), Internat. Platform Assn., World Affairs Coun., Assn. Commuter Transp., U.S. Nature Conservancy. Republican. Seventh Day Adventist. Home: 28 Harding Ave Cherry Hill NJ 08002-3516 Office: Ste 107 One Greentree Ctr Marlton NJ 08053

LUSTGARTEN, STEWART J., marketing executive; b. N.Y.C., Jan. 4, 1943; s. Samuel H. and Kate (Motelson) L.; m. Susan Figa, Aug. 14, 1969; children: Jennifer, Shelby, Jillian. Student, U. Miami, Fla., 1960-63. Asst. v.p. Columbia Dentoform Corp., N.Y.C., 1964-77; dir. bio-materials div. Parkell Inc., Farmingdale, N.Y., 1977; v.p. Healthco Internat., Inc., Boston, 1977-86; chief exec. officer Lustgarten Multi-Tech Internat. Inc., Framingham, Mass., 1986—; chief exec. officer Pharmex, Inc., Framingham and New Eng., Mass., 1989—, Englewood, Colo., 1989—; chief exec. officer Vaifivre/Laser Ams., Inc., Framingham, 1989—, Pharmex Internat. Inc., Framingham, 1989—, Restorative Technics Div., Framingham, 1989—; v.p., bd. dirs. Roeko U.S.A., Inc., Framingham, 1987—, Algotec Ams. Inc., Framingham; cons. Roeko GmbH, Langenau, Fed. Republic Germany, 1987—, Accutek, Inc., Cranston, R.I., 1988; Adiesse Founitures Dental, Florence, Italy, 1986—, P.S.P. Dental Ltd, Belv. Kent, England, 1986, Macrochem Corp., Woburn, Mass., 1987, Biodmed. Devel. Corp., San Antonio, 1989—, Avitar Corp, Canton, Mass., 1989—, Algotec, Colombes, France, 1989, Symbalon, Inc., Ashland, Mass., 1989, Euronda, Vicenza, Italy, 1988, Warner Lambert Corp., Morristown, N.J., 1972-74, Primary Med. Communications, Inc., N.Y.C., 1971-74, Denar Corp., Anaheim, Calif., 1977-78, dept. dental materials Coll. Dentistry, NYU, 1974-77, dept. dental materials N.J. Coll. Dentistry, Newark, 1974-77 and numerous other cos.; bd. dirs. Dental Mfrs. Am., Phila., 1974-77, mem., 1988—; v.p. DuraGLove, Inc., Framingham, 1989—, Algotec Am., Framingham, 1989—. Developer worldwide dental product mktg.; patentee dental materials and methods. With USNR, 1964-70. Recipient cert. of appreciation Mass. Dental Assts. Assn., 1983, 84. Mem. Am. Assn. Dental Schs., Am. Assn. for Dental Rsch., Acad. Operative Dentistry. Home: 73 Dalton Rd Holliston MA 01746-2470 Office: 1661 Worcester Rd Framingham MA 01701-5401

LUSTIG, BARBARA ELLEN, publications manager; b. N.Y.C., Jan. 24, 1946; d. Fred and Sylvia (Lotringer) L. BA in English, Psychology, U. Rochester, 1967; MA in Communications, U. Pa., 1973; MEd in Orgn. Devel., Temple U., 1982; grad., 1st New Brunswick Leadership Inst., 1991. Tng. cons. Mfrs. Hanover Bank, Huntingdon Valley, Pa., 1983-85; tng. officer Conn. Nat. Bank, Hartford, 1986-87; cons. Unisys Corp., Blue Bell, Pa., 1987-88; assoc. mgr. Bell Communications Rsch., Piscataway, N.J., 1988—; tng. dir., tng. cons. various fin. svcs. corps, 1971-83. Author of self-instructional tng. programs, seminar leader's guides and computer software manuals, 1970—; editor: (newsletter) Internat. Assn. Pers. Women, 1978-79, Pa. Mfrs. Assn. Ins. Co., 1970-73. Dir. Energy for Employment, Phila., 1985-86. Recipient 4 scholar incentive awards N.Y. State Bd. Regents, 1963-67, Helen M. Loane Meml. award Ins. Soc. Phila., 1972; Nat. Merit scholarship finalist, 1963, Annenberg scholar U. Pa., 1967-69. Mem. ASTD (position referral com. 1988—), Holistic Health Assn. of Princeton Area (festival planning com. 1990—), Toastmaster's Internat. Club (pres. 1990), Sierra Club (N.J. exec. com. 1991—, congl. coord. 1991—, officer Raritan Valley sect. 1991—). Home: 85 Phelps Ave # D New Brunswick NJ 08901-3719

LUSTIG, DAVID VERNON, consumer products company executive; b. Balt., May 1, 1947; s. Frederick and Ethel Lustig; m. Constance Beth Tanner, Nov. 29, 1970; children: Gretchen, Randolph. BA in Polit. Sci., Northeastern U., 1969. Legis. asst. Mass. State Senate, Boston, 1971-73; dir. pub. rels. New England Mut. Life Ins. Co., Boston, 1973-78; mgr. pub. affairs Lever Bros. Co., N.Y.C., 1978-80; mgr. pub. affairs Unilever U.S., Inc., N.Y.C., 1980-88, dir. govt. affairs, 1988—. Author: (with others) The People vs. Presidential Wars, 1970. Pres. Roosevelt Island Residents Assn., N.Y.C., 1982-83; dir. Roosevelt Island Tennis League, N.Y.C., 1985—; mem. N.Y. County Dem. Com., N.Y.C., 1989—; advisor State Legis. Leaders Found. Recipient commendation award United Way of Boston, 1978, Silver Anvil award Pub. Rels. Soc. Am., 1978. Fellow Nat. Govs. Assn. (corp. fellow), Pub. Affairs Coun. Office: Unilever US Inc 390 Park Ave New York NY 10022-4613

LUSTIG, IRVIN JAY, operations research educator; b. Miami, Fla., Mar. 15, 1961; s. Edward V. and Hillelene Sherman (Bluming) L.; m. Susan Ellen Barksy, Oct. 30, 1988; 1 child, Joanna Rose. ScB and ScM, Brown U., 1983; MS, Stanford U., 1986, PhD, 1987. Asst. prof. Princeton (N.J.) U., 1987—; cons., mem. XMP Software, Inc., Tucson, 1990—. Contbr. numerous articles to profl. jours. Mem. Assn. Computing Machinery, Math. Programming Soc., Soc. Indsl. and Applied Maths., Ops. Rsch. Soc. Jewish. Home: 48 Harriet Dr Princeton NJ 08540-3935 Office: Princeton U Dept Civil Engring Ops Rsch Princeton NJ 08544

LUSTIG, JOANNE, librarian; b. Newark, July 22, 1952; d. Melvin and Grace Ann (Kertsmar) L.; m. Glenn Seggel, Mar. 26, 1988. BA summa cum laude, Montclair State Coll., 1975; MLS, Rutgers U., 1978. Asst. libr. Sterling Drug Inc., N.Y.C., 1979-80, sr. editor, 1980; info. specialist Knoll Pharms., Whippany, N.J., 1980-82, sr. info. specialist, 1982-84, mgr. med. and sci. info., 1984—; bd. dirs. N.W. Regional Libr. Coop., Chester, N.J., 1990-92, pres., 1991-92; mem. N.J. Libr. Network Strategic Planning Com., 1990-91. Mem. N.J. Chpt. Spl. Librs. Assn. (pres. 1987-88, v.p. 1986-87, editor bull. 1984-86), Pharm. Div. Spl. Librs. Assn. (archivist 1989-90, chair regional program planning com. 1985-86), Pharm. Mfrs. Assn. (communications support liaison 1989—), Drug Info. Assn. Jewish. Office: Knoll Pharms 30 N Jefferson Rd Whippany NJ 07981-1045

LUSTIG, NORA CLAUDIA, researcher; b. Buenos Aires, Argentina, Jan. 13, 1951; came to U.S., 1989; d. Xavier Friedrich and Anna (Tenenbaum) L.; m. Antonio Carlos Martin-Del-Campo, Mar. 22, 1975; children: Carlos Javier, Liliana. BA in Econs., U. Calif., Berkeley, 1972, MA in Econs., 1974, PhD in Econs., 1979. Prof. econ. studies ctr. El Colegio de Mex., Mex., 1975—, acad. coord., 1975-76, 86-88; vis. scholar econs. dept. MIT, Cambridge, 1982; vis. prof. dept. natural resources and agrl. econs. Inst. of Internat. Studies U. Calif., Berkeley, 1984; vis. fellow Fgn. Policy Studies Program The Brookings Inst., 1989—; cons. Office of Econ. and Social Planning, Ministry of Budget and Programming, Mexico City, Mexican Food Sstem, Office of Advisors to the Pres., Mexico City, Viceministry of Planning, Ministry of Agriculture, Nicaragua, 1981-82, econ. commn. for Latin Am., Mexico City, 1984-85. Contbr. numerous articles to profl. jours. Office: Brookings Institution 1775 Massachusetts Ave NW Washington DC 20036-2188

LUTER, MELVIN A., aerospace engineer; b. Tylertown, Miss., July 10, 1944; s. Marcus A. and Era (Grubbs) L.; m. Jannis Dianne McGehee, July 5, 1968; 1 child, Matthew. BS in Aero. Engring., Miss. State U., 1967. Engr. trainee NASA, Wallops Island, Va., 1963-67; performance engr. Naval Air Systems Command, Washington, 1967-81, supr. performance engr., 1981-87, head performance sect., 1987—. Mem. AIAA. Home: 8117 Gale St Annandale VA 22003 Office: Naval Air Systems Command Dept Navy Washington DC 20361

LUTES, JOSEPH WYCOFF, financial executive; b. Phila., May 30, 1950; s. William Edward and Margaret Rose (Corcoran) L.; m. Linda Rita Ricchetti, Oct. 1, 1977; children: Joseph Jr., Daniel, Timothy. BS in Acctg., Drexel U., 1979; postgrad., Drexel U. Grad. Sch. Bus., 1980. Asst. treas. Del. Group of Funds, Phila., 1980-84, treas., 1984-88, fin. v.p., 1988—; treas. Del. Service Co., Phila., 1982-88, fin. v.p., 1988—; treas. Del. Distbrs. Inc., Phila., 1982—, Del. Mgmt. Co., Phila., 1984-88; chief fin. officer, v.p. Del Mgmt. Co., Phila., 1988—; treas. Del. Group of Funds, Phila., 1988—; v.p., chief fin. officer Del. Mgmt. Holdings, Inc., Del. Mgmt. Co., Inc., Del. Distbrs., Inc., 1989—; sr. v.p., chief fin. officer, dir. Del. Mgmt. Trust Co., 1991—; dir. Del. Internat. Advisers Ltd., 1991—; bd. dirs. Pa. Economy League, Greater Phila. Citizens Crime Commn. Mem. Nat. Corp. Cash Mgmt. Assn. (charter), Investment Co. Inst. (acctg./treas. com.), Securities Industry Assn. (internat. ops. assn.), Fin. Execs. Inst. Republican. Roman Catholic. Home: 210 Forrest Dr Southampton PA 18966-2100 Office: Delaware Mgmt Co Inc 1 Commerce Sq Philadelphia PA 19103

LUTFI, SULTAN NAJIB, diplomat; b. Salt, Jordan, Oct. 1, 1941; arrived in U.S., 1986; s. Najib ayed and Mariam (Zawwad) L.; m. Norah M. Barger, July 15, 1980. BA in Math., Am. U. Beirut, Lebanon, 1962; Diploma Internat. Realtins, Oxford U., Eng., 1965; MA in Econs., Howard U., 1970; PhD in Econs., George Washington U., 1979. Asst. chief Ministry of Nat. Economy, Amman, Jordan, 1962-64; asst. dir. Ministry of Fgn. Affairs, Amman, 1964-67; counselor Ministry of Fgn. Affairs, 1980, dir., 1984-86; 1st sec. Jordanian Embassy, Washington, 1967-75, minister, 1982-84, amb., 1988-92; exec. dir. asst. The World Bank, Washington, 1992—; econ. adv. HRH Crown Prince Hassan, Arman, 1975-79. Decorated Silver Star, Rep. of Austria, 1976. Mem. Omieron Delta Epsilon. Office: 3273 A Sutton Pl NW Washington DC 20016

LUTHER, WILLIAM LEE, construction company executive; b. Philipsburg, Pa., Dec. 10, 1952; s. William Denis and Edna Patricia (Culp) L.; m. Carolyn Jane Shadburn, May 27, 1976 (div. June 1983). BS, Pa. State U., 1975. Tchr. Huntingdon (Pa.) Sch. Dist., 1977-79; carpenter Zimmerman Homes, Inc., State College, Pa., 1981-83, sales mgr., 1983-86, dir. sales, 1986—; bd. dirs. Zimmerman Homes, Inc., State College; owner, ptnr. Housewrights, Inc., State College, 1991—. Mem. Pa. Builders Assn., Nat. Assn. Home Builders, Nat. Inst. Residential Mtkg. Republican. Roman Catholic. Home: 1019 Tanney St Bellefonte PA 16823-2417 Office: Housewrights Inc 2790 W College Ave State College PA 16801-2605

LUTHER-LEMMON, CAROL LEN, educator; b. Waverly, N.Y., May 8, 1955; d. Carl Ross and Mary Edith (Auge) Luther; m. Mark Kevin Lemmon, June 21, 1986; children: Matthew C., Cathryn M. BS, Ithaca Coll., 1976; MS in Edn., Elmira Coll., 1982. Cert. elem. and secondary tchr., Pa. Reading aide Waverly (N.Y.) Central Schs., 1978-80; tchr. reading N.Y. State Div. for Youth, Lansing, 1981-82; tchr. chpt. I reading, mem. student assistance program and instructional support team Rowe Mid. Sch., Athens (Pa.) Area Sch. Dist., 1982—. Basketball coach Youth Activities Dept., Athens, 1982-85, asst. softball coach, 1990—; mem. ad hoc com. Waverly Sch. Dist., 1990-91; active Girls' Softball League, Waverly, 1978-80, commr., 1980; bd. dirs. Waverly Community Ch., 1976-78; choir mem. Meth. Ch., Waverly, 1976-90, adminstrv. bd., trustee; mem. Valley Chorus, Pa. and N.Y., 1983-86. With USAR, 1977-83. Mem. AAUW (v.p. 1982-83, pres. Waverly br. 1992—), Am. Legion Aux. (girl's state rep. 1972, girl's state chmn. 1976-80, counsleor 1977), Chemung Area Reading Coun., N.Y. State Reading Assn. Republican. Home: 490 Waverly St Waverly NY 14892-1102 Office: Athens Area Sch Dist Pennsylvania Ave Athens PA 18810-1438

LUTHY, RICHARD GODFREY, environmental engineering educator; b. June 11, 1945; s. Robert Godfrey Luthy and Marian Ruth (Ireland) Haines; m. Mary Frances Sullivan, Nov. 22, 1967; children: Matthew Robert, Mara Catherine, Jessica Bethlin. BSChemE, U. Calif., Berkeley, 1967; MS in Ocean Engring., U. Hawaii, 1969; MSCE, U. Calif., Berkeley, 1974, PhDCE, 1976. Registered profl. engr., Pa.; diplomate Am. Acad. Environ. Engrs. Rsch. asst. dept. civil engring. U. Hawaii, Honolulu, 1968-69; rsch. asst. div. san. and hydraulic engring. U. Calif., Berkeley, 1973-75; asst. prof. civil

engring. Carnegie Mellon U., Pitts., 1975-80, assoc. prof., 1980-83, prof., 1983—, assoc. dean Carnegie Inst. Tech., 1986-89, head dept. civil engring., 1989—; cons. sci. adv. bd. U.S. EPA, 1983—, Bioremediation Action Com., 1990-92; cons. U.S. Dept. Energy, 1978—, various pvt. industries; del. water sci. and tech. bd. NAE, Washington and Beijing, 1988; mem. tech. adv. bd. Remediation Techs. Inc., Concord, Mass., 1989—. Contbr. articles to tech. and sci. jours. Chmn. Conf. on Fundamental Rsch. Directions in Environ. Engring, Washington, 1988. Lt. C.E. Corps, USN, 1969-72. Recipient George Tallman Ladd award Carnegie Inst. Tech., 1977. Mem. ASCE (Pitts. sect. Prof. of Yr. award 1987), Assn. Environ. Engring. Profs. (pres. 1987-88, Nalco award 1978, 82, Engring. Sci. award 1988), Water Pollution Control Fedn. (rsch. com. 1982-86, awards com. 1981-84, 89-91, std. methods com. 1977—, groundwater com. 1989-90, editor jour. 1989-92, Eddy medal 1980), Internat. Assn. on Water Pollution Rsch. and Control (Founders award U.S. Nat. Com. 1986, orgnl. com. 16th Biennial Conv. Washington 1992), Am. Chem. Soc. (div. environ. chemistry, editorial adv. bd. Environ. Sci. Tech. 1992—). Presbyterian. Home: 620 S Linden Ave Pittsburgh PA 15208-2813 Office: Carnegie Mellon U Dept Civil Engring Pittsburgh PA 15213-3890

LUTTER, RUDOLPH VICTOR, JR., communications law educator, lawyer; b. Phila., Feb. 9, 1932; s. Rudolph Victor and Elizabeth (Matzko); m. Marilyn Warburton, Sept. 29, 1979. BA in Sociology with honors, Pa. State U., 1956; JD, Harvard U., 1960; postgrad., Oxford U., 1968, Northwestern U., 1989. Bar: Pa., U.S. Dist. Ct. (ea. dist.) Pa., U.S. Dist. Ct. D.C., U.S. Tax Ct., U.S. Ct. Mil. Appeals, U.S. Ct. Appeals (1st, 2d, 3d, D.C. cirs.), U.S. Supreme Ct. Assoc. Brown, Brown and Wieland, Phila, 1960-62; sr. atty. advisor Broadcast Bur., FCC (now Mass. Media Bur.), Washington, 1962-80; pvt. practice Lutter Washington Communications Cons., Washington, 1980-81; faculty mem. Howard U. Sch. Communications, Washington, 1981—; mem. faculty NYU, 1966-67; evaluator mass media in 56 fgn. countries, 1964—. Participant Vols. for the Visually Handicapped, Phila. Assn. for Retarded Citizens, Mental Health Assn. Southeastern Pa., Gov.'s Com. on Employment of the Handicapped Commonwealth of Pa., Pa.'s Gov.'s Conf. on Handicapped Individuals, Pres.'s Com. on Employment of People with Disabilities, Am. Coalition Citizens with Disabilities Del. Assembly, Del. Assembly of Affiliated Leadership League, White House Conf. on Handicapped Individuals, Coun. Citizens with Low Vision, Children's Aid Soc. Pa. Mem. AAUP, Harvard Law Sch. Assn., World Future Soc., Am. Blind Lawyers Assn., Fellowship Commn. Phila. (lawyers div.), Pa. State U. Alumni Assn., Harvard Club Washington, Harvard Club Phila. Home: 2122 Massachusetts Ave NW #2 Washington DC 20008 Office: Howard U Sch Communications Washington DC 20059

LUTTON, LEWIS MONTFORT, biology educator, researcher; b. Cin., July 14, 1945; s. Edwin Scott and Virginia (Melchior) L.; m. Marianne C. Hendow, Nov. 26, 1982; children: Wolf M., Bram V. BA, Swarthmore Coll., 1968; PhD, Cornell U., 1976. Instr. Allegheny Coll., Meadville, Pa., 1974-75, asst. prof., 1975-80; with Mercyhurst Coll., Erie, Pa., 1980-83, assoc. prof., 1983—; rsch. assoc. Brooks Air Force Base Armstrong Labs., San Antonio, Tex., 1990-91; chmn. sci. div. Mercyhurst Coll., 1986-90, chmn. honors program, 1982-90, premed. advisor, 1981—. Contbr. articles to profl. jours. Mem. AAAS, Nat. Assn. Biology Tchrs., Soc. for Neursci., Soc. for Biological Rhythms, Phi Kappa Phi, Sigma Xi. Unitarian. Home: 4706 Upland Dr Erie PA 16509-2248 Office: Mercyhurst Coll Glenwood Hills Erie PA 16546

LUTTRELL, GREGORY BRENT, financial executive; b. Decatur, Ill., Dec. 7, 1962; s. John Wesley and JoAnne Delores (Bourland) L.; m. Barbara Padula, Aug. 24, 1991. BS in Fin., Ind. U., 1985; MBA with distinction, NYU, 1992. Corp. lender Sovran Bank, Springfield, Va., 1985-87; fin. mgr., asst. v.p. Merrill Lynch, Plainsboro, N.J., 1987-90; security analyst TIAA-CREF, N.Y.C., 1992—; sr. ptnr. Whitestone Interfunding, Hamilton Square, N.J., 1990—; security analyst TIAA-CREF, N.Y.C., 1992—. Marcus Nadler scholar, 1991, Stern scholar, 1991; Lew Glucksman Inst. for Security Analysis fellow, 1991. Mem. Beta Gamma Sigma. Republican. Presbyterian. Home and Office: 1011 Hughes Dr Apt 15 Hamilton Square NJ 08690

LUTTS, JOHN ALBERT, math and computer science educator; b. Balt., Feb. 26, 1932; s. John A. and Hilda L. (Kostelak) L.; m. June 10, 1967; children: Judith, John, Eric, Irene, Claire, Paul, Laetitia. BS in Math., Spring Hill Coll., 1957; MA in Math., U. Pa., 1959, PhD in Math., 1961; STL in Theology, Woodstock Coll., 1965. Lectr. Loyola Coll., Balt., 1964, asst. prof., 1965-66; sr. engr. Westinghouse Aerospace Div., Balt., 1966; asst. prof. Univ. Mass., Boston, 1966-70, assoc. prof., 1970—; cons. in computer sci. Quincy (Mass.) Schs., 1982-83. Chairperson PTO of Furnace Brook Sch., Quincy, 1987-90; v.p. Quincy (Mass.) Citizens for Quality Edn., 1989—. Mem. Am. Math. Soc., Math. Assn. Am. Democrat. Roman Catholic. Office: U Mass Boston Dept Math & Computer Sci Harbor Campus Boston MA 02125

LUTZE, RUTH LOUISE, retired textbook editor, public relations executive; b. Boston, Apr. 19, 1917; d. Frederick Clemons and Louise (Rausch) L. BA with honors, Radcliffe Coll., 1938; postgrad., Boston U., 1938-39. Tchr. Winthrop (Mass.) Pub. Schs., 1938-39; with pub. relations dept. The Boston City Club, Boston, 1939-42; sr. projects editor D.C. Heath & Co., Lexington, Mass., 1942-82; book reviewer, lectr., 1939—; cons. pub. rels. 1991—. Bd. Winthrop Improvement and Hist. Assn., 1980—; vol. tchr. Boston Pub. Schs., 1967-77; mem. Winthrop Rep. Town Com., 1970—. Recipient cert. appreciation for vol. in edn., Kiwanis Club of East Boston, 1972. Mem. Radcliffe Club Boston, First Luth. Ch. Boston (v.p. 1986, deacon 1980--). Lutheran. Home: 110 Circuit Rd Winthrop MA 02152-2819

LUTZKY, FRANK JOSEPH, JR., science educator; b. Flagtown, N.J., Feb. 4, 1934; s. Frank J. and Esther (Buckshaw) L.; m. Donna Wyglendowski, June 17, 1943; children: Angela, Robert, Albert, David, Kristen, Scott. BS in Engring., Rutgers U., 1955. Lic. real estate broker. Engr. def. projects Western Electric Co., N.Y.C., 1955-61; supr. svc. ops. Bell Labs., Murray Hill, N.J., 1961-69; dep. head ops. svc. ops. Bell Labs., Holmdel, N.J., 1969-72; dept. head engring. svc. ops. Bell Labs., Murray Hill, N.J., 1972-75, dept. head space planning plant engring., 1975-79; dir. svc. ops. Bell Labs., Holmdel, 1979-84, dir. facilities mgmt. adminstrn. systems, 1984-86; v.p. Weichert Comml. Realtors, Princeton, N.J., 1986-89; pres. Weichert Comml. Realtors, Morris Plains, N.J., 1989—; sci. instr. Cen. Oreg. Community Coll., Bend, 1991; cons., 1988. Mgr. Little League, Hillsborough, 1980-83; sponsor dir. Jr. Achievement, Holmdel, 1976-86. 2d lt. U.S. Army, 1957-58. Mem. Nat. Assn. Corp. Real Estate Execs., Morris County Bd. Realtors, Princeton Area C. of C. Roman Catholic. Home: 60612 Brasada Way Bend OR 97702 Office: Weichert Comml Realtors 1625 State Route 10 Morris Plains NJ 07950-2934

LUX, JOHN H., corporate executive; b. Logansport, Ind., Feb. 3, 1918; s. Carl Harrison and Mary Emma (Dunn) L.; m. Betty F. Passow, Aug. 27, 1940; children—John Ernst, Courtney Rae; m. Bernice Weitzel Brown, 1965; m. Linda Merrill Brown, Mar. 2, 1978; children—Julia Elizabeth, Jenifyr Claire. B.S., Purdue U., 1939; Ph.D., 1942. Asst. dir. research and devel. The Neville Co., 1943-46; v.p., cons. Atomic Basic Chems., 1946-47; dir. research Witco Chem. Co., 1947-50; mgr. new product devel. Gen. Electric Co., 1950-52; v.p. Shea Chem. Co., 1952-55; pres., dir. Haveg Industries, Inc., Wilmington, Del., 1955-66, Haveg Corp., Tourlux Mgmt. Corp. (P.R.); chmn. bd. Hemisphere Products Corp. (P.R.), Reinhold Engring. & Plastics Co., Norwalk, Calif., Am. Super-Temperatures Wires Co.; pres. Ametek, Inc., 1966-69, chmn. bd., chief exec. officer, 1969-90, chmn. bd., 1990—. Mem. Am. Inst. Chem. Engrs., Am. Chem. Soc., Phi Lambda Upsilon. Club: Met. Office: Ametek Inc 430 N Cedar St Ste A Escondido CA 92025-4650 also: Ametek Inc Station Sq 2 Paoli PA 19301

LUX, SAMUEL EDWARD, IV, hematologist, oncologist, pediatrics educator; b. Topeka, Dec. 17, 1940; s. Samuel E. III and Mary (Guild) L. AB, U. Kans., Lawrence, 1962; MD, U. Kans., Kansas City, 1967; MA, Harvard U., 1982. Diplomate Am. Bd. Pediatrics. Staff assoc. Nat. Heart, Lung and Blood Inst., Bethesda, Md., 1969-72; intern, resident in pediatrics Children's Hosp., Boston, 1967-69, clin. fellow in medicine, 1972-73, asst. in medicine (hematology), 1973-76, assoc. in hematology and oncology, 1976-77, sr. assoc., 1977—, chief hematology and oncology div., 1985—; rsch. fellow in pediatrics Harvard Med. Sch., Boston, 1972-73, instr., asst. prof., 1973-77, assoc. prof., 1977-82, prof., 1982—, mem. program on cell and devel. biology, 1977—; asst. physician Dana-Farber Cancer Inst., Boston, 1977-80, assoc. physician, 1980-82, assoc. in pediatrics, 1983—. Lt. comdr. USPHS, 1969-72. Recipient prize for excellence in teaching Harvard Med. Sch., 1982, award for rsch. in pediatrics E. Mead Johnson, 1983, award for excellence in teaching Boylston Soc., 1984, merit award NIH, 1988, Dameshek prize for rsch. in hematology, 1989. Mem. Am. Soc. Clin. Investigation (councilor), Am. Assn. Physicians, Am. Soc. Hematology, Am. Soc. Biol. Chemists, Am. Soc. Cell Biology, Internat. Soc. Hematology. Office: Children's Hosp 320 Longwood Ave Boston MA 02115-5746

LUXEMBURG, JACK ALAN, rabbi; b. Feb. 16, 1949; s. Milton Irwin and Bernice Esther (Adler) L.; m. Barbara Elaine Etkind, June 15, 1975; children: Daniel, Michael. BA, Trinity Coll., 1970; MA in Hebrew Letters, Hebrew Union Coll., 1973; D of Ministry, Wesley Theol. Sem., 1987. Ordained rabbi, 1976. Rabbi intern B'nai B'rith Hillel at Ohio State U., Columbus, Ohio, 1973-74; regional dir. Hashachar/Young Judaea, Cin., 1972-75; student rabbi Temple Ahavat Shalom, Coriopolis, Pa., 1975-76; assoc. rabbi Main Line Reform Temple, Wynnewood, Pa., 1976-81; rabbi Temple Beth Ami, Rockville, Md., 1981—; bd. dirs. Jewish Social Svc. Agy., Rockville, United Jewish Appeal Fedn., Greater Washington Charles E. Smith Jewish Day Sch., Rockville; exec. com. mem. Jewish Community Coun. of Greater Washington, 1985-87, 92—. Mem. Montgomery County (Md.) Civil Rights Minority Group, 1988, Inter-Religious Com. on Drug Abuse, Montgomery County, 1989; bd. dirs. Washington Area Community Investment Fund, Washington, 1988-89; mem. Citizens Adv. Coun. Montgomery County (Md.) Sch. Bd., 1981-83; nat. coord. synagogue campaign U.S. Holocaust Meml. Mus. Recipient Leadership award Am. Jewish Congress, 1988, 92, Rabbinic award Coun. of Jewish Fedns., 1991. Mem. Nat. Rabbinical Cabinet of United Jewish Appeal (exec. com. 1986—), Am. Jewish Congress (regional pres. 1987-92, nat. governing coun. 1987—), Cen. Conf. Am. Rabbis (regional pres. 1990-92, nat. exec. com. 1990-92), Washington Bd. Rabbis (v.p. 1989—). Office: Temple Beth Ami 800 Hurley Ave Rockville MD 20850-3000

LUXTON, RICHARD N., South American literature educator, researcher; b. Lima, Peru, Jan. 21, 1950; came to U.S., 1984; s. Henry and Dorothy Eleanor (Inkster) L. BA with honors, Essex U., Colchester, Eng., 1972, PhD, 1978. Prof. Nat. U., Sacramento, 1985-89, Chapman Coll., Sacramento, 1985-89, Western New Eng. Coll., Springfield, Mass., 1989—; chair dept. human studies Western New Eng. Coll., 1992—. British Acad. fellow, 1979, Harvard U. fellow, 1981. Mem. Latin Am. Indian Lit. Assn. (symposium chmn. 1986—, v.p. 1986-89, pres. 1989-92). Anglican. Office: Western New Eng Coll 1215 Wilbraham Rd Springfield MA 01119-2693

LUYTEN, JAMES REINDERT, oceanographer; b. Mpls., Dec. 26, 1941; s. Willem Jacob and Willemina (Miedema) L.; m. Meredith Luyten, June 18, 1966; children: Dylan, Laura, Elijah. AB, Reed Coll., 1963; AM, Harvard U., 1965, PhD, 1969. Rsch. fellow Harvard U., Cambridge, Mass., 1968-70; asst. scientist Woods Hole (Mass.) Oceanographic Instn., 1971-74, assoc. scientist, 1971-86, sr. scientist, 1986—, chmn. phys. oceanography, 1991—; vis. scientist Nat. Ctr. for Atmospheric Rsch., Boulder, Colo., 1983. Office: Woods Hole Oceanographic Instn Woods Hole MA 02543

LYBARGER, ADRIENNE REYNOLDS (MRS. LEE FRANCIS), college administrator; b. Boston, Mar. 8, 1926; d. Joseph Anthony and Albertine (Mouton Drevet) Reynolds; BA, Mills Coll., Calif., 1947; cert. Katharine Gibbs Sch., 1948; m. Lee Francis Lybarger, Jr., Sept. 15, 1955 (dec); children: Linda, Lauretta, James (dec.), Lisa, Leslie (dec.), Jeffrey (dec.), Lucia, Lana. Asst. to dir. Mid-Century convocation M.I.T. Cambridge, 1949, asst. to dir. West Coast regional office Mid-Century devel. program, 1949-50, asst. dir. So. regional office, 1950-51; asst. to dir. convocation devel. program Ithaca (N.Y.) Coll., 1951; asst. to dir., devel. program U. Buffalo, 1951-52; asst. to dir. Diamond Jubilee program Case Inst. Tech., Cleve., 1952-54; asst. to dir., expansion and improvement program John D. Archbold Hosp., Thomasville, Ga., 1955-61; ptnr. Lybarger Prodns., comml. films, N.Y.C.; asst. dir., dir. regional campaigns, Ohio, Boston, Mass., N.Y.C., also supr. all other nat. regional campaigns Mount Holyoke Coll. Fund for Future, South Hadley, Mass., 1961-63; fund-raising cons. to capital programs, Vocation Svc. Ctr. and Bronx-Westchester YMCA, YMCA Greater N.Y., 1963-65; dir. devel. and pub. rels. Bank St. Coll. Edn., N.Y.C., 1965-79; cons. S. Bronx Overall Econ. Devel. Corp., 1978-79; v.p. devel. Wells Coll., 1979—, dir. Wells Capital campaign; cons. capital campaign Borough of Manhattan Community Coll., 1979-80; Realtor assoc./mktg. cons. Century 21, Clinton, N.J., 1978-81; Pres., Birch Island (Maine) Corp., 1979; mem. Nat. Women's Hall of Fame, 1987-90, bd. dirs., 1987—. Mem. Am. Prospect Rsch. Assn. Author: (with L. F. Lybarger) Proven Guides to Effective Soliciting (slide film), 1950, rev., 1960, 81; exec. producer, Scriptwriter Now More than Ever, Wells Coll. Home: Kings Manor Pittstown NJ 08867 Office: Wells Coll Aurora NY 13026

LYDON, MICHAEL CLERY, musician, writer; b. Boston, Sept. 14, 1942; s. Patrick Joseph and Alice Louise (Joyce) L.; m. Ellen Mandel, Oct. 11, 1981; 1 child, Shuna. BA cum laude, Yale U., 1965. Freelance reporter Boston Globe, 1964 summer; corr. Newsweek Mag., London and San Francisco, 1965-68; freelance writer Elk and Berkley, Calif., 1968—; musician Calif., 1970—, N.Y.C., 1976—. Author: Rock Folk, 1971, Boogie Lightning, 1974, How to Succeed in Show Business by Really Trying, 1985; composer (with Ellen Mandel) Passion in Pigskin, 1985. Democrat. Home: 311 E 9th St New York NY 10003-7742

LYLE, JOHN WILLIAM, JR., state senator, social sciences educator; b. Providence, May 19, 1950; s. John William and Lois (Smith) L.; m. Lori A. Lyle, Feb. 16, 1992. BA, Barrington Coll., 1973; MEd, Providence Coll., 1978; JD, Suffolk U. Tchr. Lincoln (R.I.) Sch. Dept., 1974—; senator State of R.I., Dist. 34, 1981-87, 91—, dep. leader R.I. Senate, 1983—; tchr. William Davies Vocat. Sch.-Summer Sch., Lincoln, 1975, 77; dir. student affairs Brown U. Summer Acad., Providence, 1987; mem. adj. faculty R.I. Coll., Providence, 1990—, Community Coll. R.I., Lincoln, 1991—. Contbr. articles to profl. jour. Bd. dirs. Blackstone Valley Tourism Council, also women's shelter, Providence, 1987; trustee Cumb-Line Boys and Girls Club, Cumberland, R.I., 1982; mem. R.I. Rep. Cen. Com., Providence, 1979—; Rep. candidate for Sec. of State of R.I.; lines person USTA, N.Y.C., 1985—; mem. Nat. Head Injury Found., No. R.I. Assn. Retarded Citizens, Common Cause. Robert A. Taft Inst. fellow, 1975, 79; recipient Outstanding Alumnus award Barrington Coll., 1982, Disting. Alumnus award, 1984; Appreciation award No. R.I. Sr. Services, 1983, Johns Hopkins U. Close Up fellow. Mem. R.I. Fedn. Tchrs., R.I. Assn. Social Studies Tchrs., Nat. Conf. State Legis., Nat. Rep. Legis. Assn., Lincoln Tchrs. Assn. (exec. bd. 1987—), NOW, Save the Bay, Blackstone Valley Hist. Soc., R.I. Women's Polit. Caucus, Kirkbrae Country Club. Avocations: travel, reading, running, tennis. Office: RI Senate State House Providence RI 02865

LYLE, QUENTIN ERNEST, banker; b. Phila., May 12, 1958; s. Quentin Ernest and Barbara (Touw) L. BS, Davidson Coll., 1980; MBA, Georgetown U., 1989. Tchr. Kingswood-Oxford Sch., West Hartford, Conn., 1981-87; portfolio control analyst Md. Nat. Bank, Columbia, 1988; comml. banker, asst. treas. The Bank of N.Y., N.Y.C., 1989—. Mem. bd. advisors Safe rides of West Hartford, 1983-87; dir. Joe Valonis 10K and 5K races Hartford Track Club. 1985-87. Mem. Fin. Mgmt. Assn., Beta Gamma Sigma. Episcopalian. Home: 355 S End Ave Apt 4K New York NY 10280-1055 Office: The Bank of NY 1 Wall St 16th Fl New York NY 10286-0001

LYLES, BARBARA DIGGS, human development educator; b. Sewickley, Pa., Aug. 12, 1930; d. Lucien M. Diggs and Ruselle (Turner) Bembry; children: Jocelyn J., Russell B. III, Lauri C. BS, Marietta Coll., 1951; MA, Howard U., 1954; PhD, U. Md., 1971. Assoc. prof. human devel. Howard U., Washington, 1964—. Editor: (with Charlene and A.M. Tibbetts) Strategies: Rhetoric and Reader, 1991; contbr. article to Newsweek, 1989. NSF grantee, 1961; Ford Minority grantee Ford Found., 1970-71. Democrat. Home: 6800 Liberty Rd Baltimore MD 21207-5860 Office: Howard U Sch Edn ASA 302 Dept Psychol Studies Washington DC 20059

LYMAN, MELVILLE HENRY, laboratory administrator, consultant; b. Glen Ridge, N.J., Apr. 4, 1942; s. Melville Henry Jr. and Frances Fridley (Needham) L.; m. Elizabeth Ann Farquharson, May 10, 1969; 1 child, Christopher Melville. BS, U.S. Naval Acad., 1964; MA, Webster U., 1979. Enlisted U.S. Navy, 1960, advanced through grades to capt., 1985, comdr. U.S.S. Casimir Pulaski, comdr. U.S.S. Daniel Boone, asst. to dir. strategic systems programs, 1985-90, ret., 1990; asst. for opers. strategic systems dept. Applied Physics Lab., The Johns Hopkins U., Laurel, Md., 1990—. Decorated Legion of Merit. Mem. Naval Submarine League, Nat. Space Club, U.S. Naval Inst., U.S. Naval Acad. Alumni Assn. Episcopalian. Office: The Johns Hopkins U Applied Physics Lab Johns Hopkins Rd Laurel MD 20723-6099

LYNCH, BARBARA DEUTSCH, sociologist, rural development consultant; b. Bklyn., Sept. 6, 1940; d. Jack Gordon and Rue (Bunzelman) Deutsch; children: Elizabeth, Jean, Julia. BA, Cornell U., 1961, PhD, 1988. Asst. dir. irrigation studies group Cornell U., Ithaca, N.Y., 1983-88, extension assoc., 1988—; vis. prof. Carleton Coll., Northfield, Minn., 1991; cons. Internat. Irrigation Mgmt. Inst., Colombo, Sri Lanka, 1991, USAID, Washington, 1988-90. Author: The Vicos Experiment, 1982; co-author: Indigenous Land Claims, 1982; editor: Right to Know: Opportunity to Learn, 1990; contbg. editor: Handbook of the Latin Am. Studies. Mediator Community Dispute Revolution Ctr., Ithaca, 1988—. Postdoctoral fellow Soc. for Humanities, Cornell U., 1992; Danforth Found fellow. Mem. Am. Sociol. Assn., Rural Sociol. Soc., Latin-Am. Studies Assn. Office: Cornell U 16 Fernow Hall Ithaca NY 14850

LYNCH, CHARLES ANDREW, chemical company executive; b. Bklyn., Jan. 6, 1935; s. Charles Andrew and Mary Martina (McEvoy) L.; m. Marilyn Anne Monaco, July 30, 1960; children: Nancy Callan, Cara Martina. BS, Manhattan Coll., 1956; PhD, U. Notre Dame, 1960. Rsch. chemist Esso Rsch. & Engring. Co., Linden, N.J., 1960-65; rsch. supr. FMC Corp., Organic Chem. Div., Balt., 1965-72; rsch. mgr. FMC Corp., Indsl. Chem. Div., Princeton, N.J., 1972-74; exec. v.p. Am. Oil & Supply Co., Newark, 1974-80; tech. dir., dir. sales & mktg., dir. rsch. & bus. devel. Hatco Corp., Fords, N.J., 1981-90; v.p. tech. Hatco Advanced Technologies CP, Fords, N.J., 1990—. Contbr. articles to profl. jours.; patentee in field (U.S. and foreign). Mem. Am. Chem. Soc., Am. Oil Chemists Soc., Soc. Automotive Engrs., Soc. Tribiologists and Lubrication Engrs. (N.Y. sect. chmn. 1980-81), Ind. Lubricant Mfrs. Assn. (bd. dirs. 1985-88), Commercial Devel. Assn., Chem. Mgmt. and Resources Assn. Office: Hatco Corp 1020 King George Post Rd Fords NJ 08863-0601

LYNCH, DANIEL, newspaper editor, writer; b. Elmira, N.Y., Feb. 27, 1946; s. Joseph Patrick and Betty (Reed) L.; m. Donna L. Rimmer, Aug. 16, 1969; children: Kathleen Ellen, Kevin Rimmer. BS, Temple U., 1969. Polit. reporter Phila. Inquirer, 1970-74; Queens editor Newsday, L.I., N.Y., 1974-79; mng. editor Times Union, Albany, N.Y., 1979—; bd. dirs. N.Y. State AP. Author: (novels) Deadly Ernest, 1986, A Killing Frost, 1987, Deathly Pale, 1988, Brennan's Point, 1988, Bad Fortune, 1989, Yellow, 1992. Sgt. N.J. Air N.G., 1969-75. Named Author of Yr. Albany Pub. Libr., 1989; recipient first prize award for columns N.Y. AP, 1988. Mem. N.Y. State Soc. Newspaper Editors (pres. 1990-91). Roman Catholic. Office: Times Union Box 15000 Albany NY 12212

LYNCH, DONALD FREDERICK, psychology educator; b. Augusta, Maine, Dec. 31, 1950; s. Donald and Phyllis (Willett) L. BA, U. Maine, 1973, MEd, 1974. Cert. social worker. Complex coord. U. Maine, Orono, 1974-77; outpatient therapist Community Health and Counseling Svcs., Bangor, Maine, 1977-84, dir. outpatient svcs., 1984-86; asst. prof. psychology Unity (Maine) Coll., 1986-92, assoc. prof. psychology, 1992—; cons. Maine State Dept. Corrections, Augusta, 1985—, St. Michael's Ctr., Bangor, Maine, 1987—; dir. peer counseling program Unity Coll., 1987—. Mem. New Eng. Assn. Ednl. Opportunity Program Pers. Home: RR 1 Box 972 Hampden ME 04444-9713 Office: Unity Coll Quaker Hill Rd Unity ME 04988

LYNCH, FRAN JACKIE, real estate development executive; b. Bklyn., Dec. 15, 1948; d. William R. and Ruth (Slaiman) Diamondstein; m. James P. Lynch, Jan. 8, 1969; children: Cheryl Ann, Christopher, Kevin. BA, Bklyn. Coll., 1969; student, Suffolk Community Coll., Brentwood, N.Y., 1980-82; postgrad, L.I. U., 1983. V.p. Castle Capital Corp., N.Y.C., 1971-74; agt. Jerome Castle Found., N.Y.C., 1970-74; dir. office services Penn-Dixie Industries, N.Y.C., 1970-74; exec. asst. Med. Fin. Advisor, N.Y.C., 1974; v.p. Sept. Capital Corp., Glen Cove, N.Y., 1977-80; controller Bobgar Inc., Wallweaves Inc. and N.Y. Twine, Syosset, N.Y., 1980-86, The Kapson Group, Commack, N.Y., 1987-91, Westbury Transport ETAL, Astoria, N.Y., 1991—; cons. Women's Times, Queens, N.Y., 1987. Sec. Elwood Booster Club, East Northport, N.Y., 1987; mem. Harley Ave. PTA, 1980-87; coach Northport Youth Soccer, 1982; tchr. Confraternity Christian Doctrine Project St. Elizabeth's Ch., 1972-80, bd. dirs. Parish council, S. Huntington, N.Y., 1978-80. Home: 25 Hooper Ct East Northport NY 11731-4945

LYNCH, SISTER FRANCIS XAVIER, nun, development director; b. Watertown, N.Y., Oct. 21, 1918; d. George Francis and Sarah Emma (Nicholson) L. BS in Nursing, Cath. U. Am., 1944, MS in Adminstrn., 1948, postgrad. in chemistry, 1949-51; Dr. Humane Letters (hon.), Long Island U., 1967. Tchr. St. Leo Sch., N.Y.C., 1939-40, Holy Angels Sch., Buffalo, N.Y., 1940-41; operating room supr. Champlain Valley Hosp., Plattsburgh, N.Y., 1941-42; instr. Biology & Biol. Scis. D'Youville Coll., Buffalo, N.Y., 1944-48; head dept. Biology D'Youville Coll., Buffalo, 1948-51, dean Sch. of Nursing, 1951-62, pres., 1962-68; initiator expansion program Grey Nuns Motherhouse, Yardley, Pa., 1969-71; dir. devel. Grey Nuns of the Sacred Heart, Yardley, Pa., 1971—; cons. to Hosps. operated by Grey Nuns and their schs. of Nursing, 1955-62; mem. N.Y. State Bd. Nurse Examiners (Regents), 1952-64. Bd. dirs. A. Barton Hepburn Hosp., Ogdensburg, N.Y., 1976—. Mem. AAUW, Nat. Cath. Dev. Conf. (charter, v.p., bd. dirs., Disting. Svc. award), Am. Biographical Inst. (bd. advisors), Ctr. for the Study of the Presidency, World Affairs Coun., Am. Acad. Polit. Sci., Nat. Soc. of Fund Raising Execs., Lower Bucks County C. of C., Phila. Mus. Art. Democrat. Home and Office: Grey Nuns of Sacred Heart 1750 Quarry Rd Morrisville PA 19067-3998

LYNCH, GERALD WELDON, college president, psychologist; b. N.Y.C., Mar. 24, 1937; s. Edward Dewey and Alice Margaret (Weldon) L.; m. Eleanor Gay Sherry, Dec. 5, 1970; children: Timothy, Elizabeth. B.S., Fordham Coll., 1958; Ph.D., N.Y. U., 1968. Tech. employment rep. Bell Telephone Labs., N.Y.C., 1958-63; psychologist VA Hosp., N.Y., Palo Alto, Calif., 1964-68; asst. prof. psychology John Jay Coll. Criminal Justice, N.Y.C., 1967-71; dir. student activities John Jay Coll. Criminal Justice, 1968-70, asso. prof., 1971-74, prof., 1974—, dean students, 1968-71, v.p., 1971-76, pres., 1976—; chmn. Use of Force in Jails, N.Y.C., 1987—. Contbr. articles to profl. jours. Chmn. N.Y.C. Police Found., 1979—; chmn. N.Y. State Casino Gambling Study Panel, 1979, N.Y. State Fire Fighting Personnel Edn. and Standards Com., 1980—, Westchester County Spl. Task Force on Dept. Public Safety Services; mem. N.Y. State Fire Safety Task Force, 1981, N.Y. State Crime Control Planning Bd., 1979—; chmn. bd. advs. Channel 13, 1984-87; chmn. N.Y.C. Fire Safety Found., 1984—; vice chmn. U.S. Marshals Found., 1987—; pres. Cath. Interracial Coun., 1990-91; chmn. Mayoral Search Com. for Police and Fire Commn. Recipient Criminal Justice award N.Y. State Bar Assn., 1977; Disting. Alumni award in edn. Fordham Coll. Alumni Assn., 1978; Brotherhood award NCCJ, 1985; named Person of Yr., N.Y.C. chpt. Indsl. Security Soc., 1987, N.Y.C. Police Dept. Patrolwomen's Endowment Assn., 1987, Man of Yr., Police Self Support Group, 1989. Mem. Acad. Criminal Justice Scis., Am. Soc. Criminology, Am. Assn. State Colls. and Univs., AAAS, Am. Psychol. Assn. Democrat. Roman Catholic. Office: CUNY John Jay Coll Criminal Justice 899 10th Ave New York NY 10019

LYNCH, HARRY JAMES, biologist; b. Glenfield, Pa., Jan. 18, 1929; s. Harry James and Rachel (McComb) L.; m. Pokum Lee Lynch. BS, Geneva Coll., Beaver Falls, Pa., 1957; PhD, U. Pitts., 1971; postgrad. Bio-Space Tech. Tng. Program, NASA and U. Va., 1970. Clin. chemist West Penn Hosp., Pitts., 1955-56; grad. teaching asst. U. Pitts., 1966-71, sr. teaching fellow, 1971; postdoctoral fellow MIT, Cambridge, 1973-75, rsch. assoc. dept. nutrition, lab. neuroendocrine regulation, 1973-75, lectr., 1976-81, rsch. scientist dept. brain and cognitive sci., 1982—. Contbr. over 50 articles to profl. jours., books; patentee on implantable programmed microinfusion apparatus, 1981. With USN, 1950-54. NIH postdoctoral fellow 1971-73.

Mem. Soc. Light Treatment and Biol. Rhythms. Democrat. Office: MIT E25-615 77 Massachusetts Ave Cambridge MA 02139-4307

LYNCH, J. MICHAEL, real estate executive; b. Balt., Oct. 9, 1952; s. James F. and Amelia M. (Rolek) L.; m. Elizabeth Daher, May 6, 1989. BS in Econs., Mt. St. Mary's Coll., 1978; MArch, Va. Poly. Inst., 1983. Statistician U.S. Commerce Dept. Bur. Econ. Analysis, Washington, 1978-80; real estate cons. James Canestaro, Blacksburg, Va., 1982-83; asst. v.p., sr. project mgr. real estate investment dept. First Wachovia Corp., Winston-Salem, N.C., 1983-88; mgr. devel. and cons. The Circle Cos., Balt., 1988—; steering com. Urban Land Inst., Balt., Winston-Salem, 1985-92; real estate broker N.C. Bd. of Realtors, Winston-Salem, 1985-88; appraisal com. mem. NCREIF, 1986-88; real estate cons. Engring. Technologies Assoc., Ellicott City, Md., 1991-92. Bd. dirs. Villages of Homeland H.O.A., Balt., 1991-92. With USN, 1972-76. Recipient Bldg. Design Excellence award, 1986, 87, 88, Brochure Design Excellence award, 1990, 87. Democrat. Home: 356 Homeland Southway Baltimore MD 21212

LYNCH, JANIS ELIZABETH, education director, consultant; b. Perth Amboy, N.J., Dec. 10, 1948; d. Joseph Andrew Lynch and Elizabeth Ann (Horvath) Hochfelder. BA, Montclair State Coll., 1971; MA, New Sch. for Social Rsch., 1979. Media specialist Parsippany (N.J.)-Troy Hills Bd. Edn., 1971-90, supr., 1990—; prof. Jersey City (N.J.) State Coll., 1984-91; cons. Apple Support Coords., Edison, N.J., 1990—, Apple's Community Educators, Edison, 1990—, N.J. Sch. Leaders in Tech., Trenton, N.J., 1990—, Newtwork for Action in Microcomputer Edn., Wayne, N.J., 1990—; workshop presenter in field. Co-author: (curriculums) Media Education: Grades 7 & 8, 1978, Computers: A Running Start, 1984, Mathematics and the Computer, 1985. Trustee, chair pers. com. Parsippany (N.J.)-Troy Hills Twp. Pub. Libr., 1990—. Scholarship N.J. Assn. for Ednl. Comm. and Tech., 1976, mini-grant Jersey Cen. Power and Light, Morris County Area, 1983, several mini-grants Parsippany (N.J.)-Troy Hills Bd. Edn. Mem. ASCD, Assn. for Ednl. Communications and Tech., Prins. and Suprs. Assn., Edn. Media Assn. N.J. (jour. editor), N.J. Libr. Trustees Assn., N.J. Prins. and Suprs. Assn., Ednl. Media Assn. N.J. Roman Catholic. Office: Ednl Tech Ctr 20 Rita Dr Morris Plains NJ 07950

LYNCH, JOAN DRISCOLL, theatre and film educator; b. Boston, Nov. 9, 1935; d. James S. and Bridget Agnes (Delaney) Driscoll; m. Thomas Alexander Lynch, Apr. 18, 1959; children: Maureen, Christopher, Julie. BS in Edn., Boston Coll., 1957; MA in Theatre, Villanova U., 1970; EdD in Film, Temple U., 1980. Prof. theatre and film Villanova (Pa.) U., 1972—. Author: Film Education in Secondary Schools, 1983; contbr. articles to profl. jours. Mem. U. Film and Video Assn. (exec. v.p. 1989-91, bd. dirs. 1987-89), Soc. for Cinema Studies. Home: 1115 Signal Hill Ln Berwyn PA 19312-2024 Office: Villanova Univ Communication Arts Dept Villanova PA 19085

LYNCH, JOHN A., lawyer, state senator; b. New Brunswick, N.J., Oct. 21, 1938; s. John A. Lynch; m. Deborah A. Lynch; children: Patricia, John P., Matthew J. L. Grad. Holy Cross Coll., 1960; LLB, Georgetown U., 1963. Bar: N.J. 1963; ptnr. Lynch, Martin, Philobosian, Chansky, Fitzgerald & Kane, North Brunswick, Brielle and Somerville; pres. N.J. Senate, 1990-92, minority leader, 1992—; mayor City of New Brunswick, 1979-91. Mem. Gov.'s Commn. on Sci. and Tech. Mem. Middlesex County Trial Lawyers Assn. (past pres.). Home: 11 Cotter Dr New Brunswick NJ 08901-1506 Office: 100 Bayard St New Brunswick NJ 08901-2102 also: NJ State Senate Trenton NJ 08625

LYNCH, JOSEPH JOHN, infosystems specialist; b. Manhattan, N.Y., Sept. 16, 1949; s. Walter Joseph and Irene Elizabeth (Moran) L.; m. Cathy Elaine Marshal, Nov. 15, 1986. BA in Math., Iona Coll., 1972. Computer systems specialist dept. finance City of N.Y., 1977-82; sr. systems programmer Gen. Foods Corp., White Plains, N.Y., 1982-85; virtual machine operating system analyst NYNEX, White Plains, 1986-88; systems programming cons. S/SE Systems/Software Engring., Wayne, Pa., 1988—. Mem. Nat. Systems Programmers Assn. Roman Catholic. Home: 129 Fenimore Rd Mamaroneck NY 10543-3502 Office: S/SE Systems Software Engring 940 W Valley Rd Ste 1603 Wayne PA 19087-1823

LYNCH, KATHRYN LEONA, English educator; b. L.A., Mar. 30, 1951; d. Frank William and Marilyn Leona (Hopwood) L.; m. Robert Edward McDonnell, July 27, 1974; children: Michael Kelly, Madeline Leona, Leo Aeneas. AB, Stanford U., 1973; MA, U. Va., 1978, PhD, 1982. Postdoctoral scholar Ctr. Medieval/Renaissance Studies, UCLA, 1982-83; lectr. UCLA Writing Programs, 1982-83; asst. prof. English, Wellesley (Mass.) Coll., 1983-89, assoc. prof., 1989—, co-dir. 1st yr. writing program, 1988-91. Author: The High Medieval Dream Vision, 1988; contbr. articles to scholarly publs. NEH fellow, 1987. Mem. MLA, N.E. MLA, Medieval Acad., Gower Soc., New Chaucer Soc. Office: Wellesley Coll Dept English Wellesley MA 02181

LYNCH, LUBA HOLOD, human service director; b. Regenburg, Bavaria, Germany, Feb. 28, 1947; came to Can., 1949; d. Stephen and Sophia (Kopcsiuk) Holod; m. James Edward Lynch, Sept. 23, 1972; 1 child, Andrew Michael Lynch. BA, U. Toronto, 1968; AA, Royal Conservatory of Music, Toronto, 1967; MEd, Bank St Coll. of Edn., N.Y.C., 1984. Rsch. asst. Children's Def. Fund Juvenile Justice Div., N.Y.C., 1974-77, Hon. Justine Wise Polier, N.Y.C., 1977-79; program officer Field Found., N.Y.C., 1979-83; exec. dir. A.L. Mailman Family Found., White Plains, N.Y., 1983—; chair, mem. Grantmakers for Children, Youth & Families, Washington, 1989-91; bd. mem. Family Redsource Coalition, Chgo., 1987—, N.Y. Regional Assn. of Grantmakers, N.Y.C., 1988—. Mem. Nat. Assn. for Edn. Young Children, Am. Orthopsychiatric Assn.; bd. mem. Viola W. Bernard Found. Office: A L Mailman Family Found 707 Westchester Ave White Plains NY 10604-3102

LYNCH, MARK JEFFREY, hospital manager; b. Youngstown, Ohio, July 5, 1954; s. Harry Joseph and Joyce Roseanne (Hanzel) L.; m. Kathleen Ann Hoffmaster; children: Andrew Patrick, Kevin Robert. BS, Alfred (N.Y.) U., 1976. Admissions counselor Alfred U., 1976-80, Allegheny Coll., Meadville, Pa., 1980-81; cons. Ketchum, Inc., Pitts., 1981-85; hosp. mgr. Sewickley (Pa.) Valley Hosp., 1985—. Mem. Quaker Valley Rotary. Office: Sewickley Valley Hosp 720 Blackburn Rd Sewickley PA 15143-1498

LYNCH, PAUL VINCENT, safety engineer; b. Bklyn., Apr. 11, 1932; s. John Andrew and Mary Catherine L.; m. Nancy Lynch; children: David, Marianne. BA, St. Anselm's Coll., Manchester, N.H., 1954; postgrad. Fordham U., 1958-59, U. N.H., 1969-71. Reg. profl. engr. in safety engring. Corp. ins. specialist Allied Chem. Corp., 1959-66; asst. to dir. risk mgmt. Am. Metal Climax, Inc., N.Y.C., 1966-68; lectr. risk mgmt., adminstr. safety U. N.H., Durham, 1969-71; assoc. prof. safety N.H. Vocat.-Tech. Coll., 1971-75; pres. Lynch Assocs., Inc., cons., Pittsfield, N.H., 1972-75; regional safety officer GSA, 1976-79; safety mgr. Calif., Bur. Land Mgmt., U.S. Dept. of the Interior, Sacramento, 1979-86, chief safety mgmt., Washington, 1986—; v.p. N.H. Safety Coun., 1972-74; instr. safety mgmt. Am. River Coll., Sacramento, 1975-76. Active Boy Scouts Am., 1962—, dist. vice chmn. Nat. Capitol Area coun., 1987—, membership chmn., mem. exec. bd. Golden Empire Coun., 1978-86, dist. chmn., 1984-85. With U.S. Army, 1955-57. Recipient Silver Beaver award Boy Scouts Am., 1977. Mem. Am. Soc. Safety Engrs. (pres. Sacramento chpt. 1981-82; regional v.p., nat. long range planning com., chmn. legis. affairs com., adminstr. pub. sector div., named div. Safety Profl. of Yr. 1986, Sacramento chpt. Safety Profl. Yr. 1986, chmn. sch. safety task force Nat. Safety Coun. 1988-91), Am. Indsl. Hygiene Assn., Vets of Safety (pres. Sacramento chpt. 1984-85), Rotary (sec. Pittsfield club 1970-73). Author, editor govt. publs.

LYNCH, PETER GEORGE, artist; b. Aug. 5, 1932. BFA, Pratt Inst., Bklyn., 1954; postgrad., CCNY. pub. Limited Editions Prints (11 eds.), News-n-viewsletter; cons. photolithography and mktg. for artists. Exhibitions include: (internat. and nat.) The Art Gallery of La Merced, Maracaibo, Venezuela, Nephente Mundi Internat. Competition, Allied Artist Am., Nat. Arts Club, Chautauqua Instn., Acad. Artist Assn. Nat. Exhibition, Internat. Festival of The Arts, Mexico-Douglas, Wiesner Gallery Intertnat., Global Visions, Fed. Pla., Gallery Cozumel, Yergeau Mus. Internat. d'Art, Montreal, Que. (Named One of Best Am. Painters, One of Best Am. Printmakers, 1991, Deuxieme prix Ann. Ctr. P.R.D. Montreal Exhbn., 1992), and numerous others; (regional and local) Arsenal Gallery, Coler Meml., Vega Fine Arts, Casino Gallery, Fulton Gallery, Artifax Galleries, Cabrini Gallery, Ten Talents Gallery, Inroads Multimedia Ctr. among others; author: (dossiers), Collaborative Photolithographic Prints: Publishing Your Own, 1990, Direct Marketing: Survival Factors and the Artist, 1990, Succeeding as a Fine Artist: Professionalism in a Difficult Environment, 1991, Artist's Eye vs. Photographers Eye: Shooting Your Art Right, 1991, Overused and Underexplored: The Paradox of Print Media: Effective Advertising for Creative People, 1991, Direct-Contact Marketing: Art Fairs and Festivals, 1991, The Video Portfolio: A New User-Friendly Marketing Tool, 1991. With U.S. Army, 1956-58. Recipient Citation for Superior Competence, U.S. Army Air Def. Command, 1958, Hon. Mention Nat. Exhibition at Bakersfield, 1985, Second Place Assn. Artist Nat. Exhibition, 1985, Cert. of Merit, Academic Artist Assn. Annual Nat. Exhibition, 1986, First Place Nephente Mundi Internat. Art Competition, 1987, Watson-Guptill award Lake Worth Silver Anniversary Exhbn., 1991.

LYNCH, ROSE PEABODY, art gallery executive; b. Dallas, June 6, 1949; d. Russell Vincent and Rose Peabody (Parsons) L.; m. Peter Stuart Milhaupt, Feb. 12, 1972 (div. 1977); m. James Alexander Torrey, Apr. 22, 1989. AAS, Bennett Coll., 1969; BA, Princeton U., 1971; MBA, Harvard U., 1982. Personal asst. Halston, Ltd., N.Y.C., 1975-76; assoc. dir. retail promotion Revlon, Inc., N.Y.C., 1976-80; dir. mktg. devel. Elizabeth Arden, N.Y.C., 1982-85; dir. mktg. Charles of the Ritz, N.Y.C., 1985-87; pres. Danskin, N.Y.C., 1987-89, Trowbridge Gallery, U.S., N.Y.C., 1989—; cons., acting chief operating officer LeRoi Princeton Inc., 1991—; bd. dirs. Harmony Group, Manhattan Theatre Club. Republican. Episcopalian. Office: 1155 Park Ave New York NY 10128-1209

LYNCH, SEAN DENNIS, health care executive; b. Bethlehem, Pa., Apr. 1, 1957; s. Bernard Joseph Jr. and Elizabeth (Murphy) L. BA, East Stroudsburg U., 1981; postgrad., Lehigh U., 1981-83, Dale Carnegie Leadership Inst., 1981, 86. Supr. Community Found. for Human Devel., Sellersville, Pa., 1983-85, asst. dir., 1985-87; program supr. partial hospitalization Wiley House, Allentown, Pa., 1987—. Mem. Fountain Hill (Pa.) Borough Coun., 1986—, v.p. 1989; mem. Fountain Hill Hist. Soc., 1991—; mem. drug task force Northampton County, Pa., 1990—, Lehigh Valley Child Care Coalition, 1990—, Northampton County Anti-Drug Initiative, 1990—. Mem. Am. Mgmt. Assn., Fountain Hill Jaycees (state rep. 1988-91), Holy Name Soc., Bethlehem Rugby Club, Rod and Gun Club, Mack Ski Club, Alpha Chi Rho. Democrat. Roman Catholic. Home: 615 Lechauweki Ave Bethlehem PA 18015 Office: Wiley House 1610 Emmaus Ave Allentown PA 18103

LYNCH, SONIA, data processing consultant; b. N.Y.C., Sept. 17, 1938; d. Espriela and Sadie Beatrice (Scales) Sarreals; m. Waldro Lynch, Sept. 18, 1981 (div. Oct. 1983). BA in Langs. summa cum laude, CCNY, 1960; cert. in French, Sorbonne, 1961. Systems engr. IBM, N.Y.C., 1963-69; cons. Babbage Systems, N.Y.C., 1969-70; project leader Touche Ross, N.Y.C., 1970-73; sr. programmer McGraw-Hill, Inc., Hightstown, N.J., 1973-78; staff data processing cons. Cin. Bell Info. Systems, 1978-89; sr. analyst AT&T, 1989-92; sr. analyst Automated Concepts Inc. Bell Atlantic, Arlington, Va., 1992—. Elder St. Andrew Luth. Ch., Silver Spring, 1992—. Downer scholar CUNY, 1960, Dickman Inst. fellow Columbia U., 1960-61. Mem. Assn. for Computing Machinery, Phi Beta Kappa. Democrat. Home: 13705 Beret Pl Silver Spring MD 20906-3030

LYNCH, THOMAS GREGORY, educational program administrator; b. Seaford, Del., Jan. 17, 1954; s. Thomas Parsons and Jane Frances (Kenney) L.; m. Patricia Anne Yearsley, Aug. 27, 1977. BA, U. Del., 1982, M in Ednl Leadership, 1989. Reporter/photographer Kent Pub. Co., Chestertown, Md., 1977-78; photojournalist Chesapeake Pub. Co., Easton, Md., 1978-81; copy editor, The Delaware State News Ind. Newspapers, Inc., Dover, Del., 1983-84; pub. info. officer Del. Pub. Svc. Commn., Dover, 1984-86; asst. program specialist U. Del., Lewes, 1986-89; assoc. program specialist U. Del., Wilmington, 1989, program mgr., 1989—. Contbr. to conf. procs.; contbr. photographs to numerous gen. interest publs. Dem. committeeman; alt. del. Del. State Dem. Conv., 1988. Mem. Nat. Univ. Continuing Edn. Assn. (region parliamentarian 1989—, chair region by-laws com. 1990-91), Nat. Press Photographers Assn., Lions, Ducks Unltd. (committeeman Naticoke chpt. 1987—), Nat. Hole-in-One Assn., Sigma Phi Epsilon. Methodist. Home: 233 Benjamin Blvd Caravel Farms Bear DE 19701 Office: Univ Del John M Clayton Hall Newark DE 19716

LYNE, DOROTHY-ARDEN, educator; b. Orangeburg, N.Y., Mar. 9, 1928; d. William Henry and Janet More (Freston) Dean; m. Thomas Delmar Lyne, Aug. 16, 1952 (div. June 1982); children: James Delmar, Peter Freston, Jennifer Dean. BA, Ursinus Coll., 1949; MA, Fletcher Sch. Law and Diplomacy, 1950. Assoc. editor World Peace Found., Boston, 1950-51; editorial assoc. Carnegie Endowment Internat. Peace, N.Y.C., 1951-52; dir. Assoc. of Internat. Rels. Clubs, N.Y.C., 1952-53; editor The Town Crier, Westport, Conn., 1966-68; editorial assoc. Machinery Allied Products Inst., Wash., 1959-63; tchr. Helen Keller Mid. Sch., Easton, Conn., 1967-89; vice chmn. Cooperative Ednl. Svcs., Fairfield, 1983-85. Editor: Documents in American Foreign Rels., 1950, Current Rsch. in Internat. Affairs, 1951. Chmn. Westport Zoning Bd. of Appeals, 1976-80, Westport Bd. of Edn., 1985-87; vice chmn. Westport Bd. of Edn., 1980-85; mem. Westport Charter Revision Commn., 1966-67. Mem. NEA, Assn. Supervision and Curriculum Devel., Coop. Ednl. Svcs., Westport Charter Commn. Republican. Episcopalian.

LYNN, DONNA MARIA, public relations and marketing executive, writer; b. Hollywood, Calif., Oct. 4, 1945; d. Kane Wallace Lynn and Rita (Piazza) Maxwell; m. Dennis D. Schreffler, 1965 (div. 1973); children: Scott G. Schreffler, Susan M. Schreffler. Student, UCLA, 1963-65, U. Utah, 1965-68; BA, U. Ark., 1970; postgrad. in law, U. Balt., 1973-74. Lobbyist, UniServ dir. NEA, Washington, 1970-77; pres., chief exec. officer Lynn Assocs., Inc., Westport, Conn., 1977—; mgr. media rels. Perrier/Great Waters of France, N.Y.C., 1978-79; sr. cons. The Nestle Co., Washington and White Plains, N.Y., 1979-83; dep. dir. sports div. Hill & Knowlton, N.Y.C., 1983-85; mgr. pub. relations Avon Products, Inc., N.Y.C., 1985-86; supr. account group Daniel J. Edelman, N.Y.C., 1979-81. Features editor: Flight Attendant mag., 1986-87; contbr. numerous articles to newspapers and mags. Founder, dir. Earth Day in Ark., 1970; del. White House Conf. on Children and Youth, Washington, 1970; nat. pres. Women's Aux. to Student AMA, 1971-73; liaision White House Press Office, Dem. Nat. Conf., N.Y.C., 1979; mem. Md. Commn. for Women, Annapolis, 1976-77; pres. Annapolis Summer Garden Theatre, 1976-78; mem. bus. adv. bd. Nat. Down Syndrome Soc., N.Y.C., 1985-89. Mem. Am. Mgmt. Assn., Boating Writers Internat., Pub. Rels. Soc. Am., NEA (life, legis. chair Ark. chpt. 1970-73), Phi Alpha Theta. Office: 7 Punch Bowl Dr Westport CT 06880-2126

LYNN, FREDERICK ANSON, investment counselor; b. Memphis, Aug. 7, 1946; s. Harvey Don and Marcia Helen (Diamond) L.; m. Ann M. Coleman, Nov. 24, 1973; 1 child, Jeffrey Anson. AB, Tulane U., 1968. Securities analyst Mfrs. Nat. Bank Detroit, 1969-71, Goldman, Sachs & Co., N.Y.C., 1971-72, Pershing & Co., N.Y.C., 1972-74; prin. Lynn Capital Mgmt., N.Y.C., 1974-75; pres. F.A.L. Capital Mgmt., Norwalk, Conn., 1976—. Bd. dirs. 92d St. YM & YWHA, N.Y.C., 1975-84. Mem. Amex Club N.Y., N.Y. Soc. Securities Analysts. Republican. Club: City Athletic (N.Y.C.). Home: 183 Lantern Ridge Rd New Canaan CT 06840-2416 Office: FAL Capital Mgmt 98 East Ave Norwalk CT 06851-5079

LYNN, MERISSA SHERRILL, educational organization executive, editor; b. Exeter, N.H., July 7, 1942; d. Raymond Wilson and Geneva Lake (Orvis) Southwick. BA in Philosophy, U. N.H., 1971. Founder, exec. sec. Tiffany Club, Wayland, Mass., 1978-88; founder, mng. dir. Tapestry Publs., Wayland, 1981—; founder, exec. dir. Internat. Found. for Gender Edn., Waltham, Mass., 1986—; founder, dir. Coming Together Conv., Waltham, 1987—; lectr. various colls. and univs. Author: TV/TS Terms and Definitions, 1990; author/editor TV/TS Tapestry Jour., 1981—; editor: Wives, Partners, & Others, 1987, rev. edit., 1991, Transsexualism, 1988, rev. edit., 1990, Religion, 1989, Legal Aspects of Transsexualism, 1990, Hormones, 1992. With U.S. Army, 1961-64. Recipient Dr. Virginia Prince Lifetime Svc. award, 1988, Community Svc. award Soc. for the Second Self, 1990, Outstanding Svc. award Metamorphosis Med. Rsch. Found., 1990. Mem. Am. Contract Bridge League (life master). Home: Box 367/36 Alpine Rd Wayland MA 01778 Office: Internat Found Gender Edn & Indentification 6 Cushing St 2nd Fl Waltham MA 02154

LYNN, RICHARD BRIAN, physician, internist, gastroenterologist; b. N.Y.C., June 20, 1956; s. Marvin S. and Nancy J. Lynn; m. Carolyn J. Cohen, June 2, 1991. BA, Columbia U., 1978, MD, 1982. Cert. internal medicine and gastroenterology. Intern, resident U. Mich., 1982-85; fellow in gastroenterology U. Pa.; asst. prof. medicine Thomas Jefferson U., Phila., 1990—. Office: Thomas Jefferson U 1025 Walnut St Rm 901 Philadelphia PA 19107

LYNN, STEPHEN, financial executive; b. Takoma Park, Md., Apr. 14, 1956; s. Bernard and Lila (Winokor) L.; m. Melodie Lee Lawrence, May 24, 1980; children: Krystle, Shannon. BS in Econ., U. Pa., 1978, MBA, 1981. Sr. fin. analyst Am. Can Co., Greenwich, Conn., 1978-80, LTV, Dallas, 1981-82, A.H. Belo, Dallas, 1983-84; v.p., controller A.H. Belo-DFW Sub Papers, Dallas, 1985-87; dir. fin. planning and reporting A.H. Belo, Dallas, 1988-89; chief fin. officer Pepsi Cola East, Balt., 1990—. Sponsor John Hopkins Children's Ctr., Balt., 1990—. Mem. Wharton Club of Balt. Home: 8460 Spring Showers Way Ellicott City MD 21043-6057 Office: Pepsi-Cola E 7 E Redwood St # 1100 Baltimore MD 21202-1115

LYNN, VERNE LAURISTON, electronics executive; b. Seattle, Sept. 5, 1930; s. Eldin Verne and Irma (Tuell) L.; m. Jean Badger, Oct. 4, 1952 (div. 1988); children: Stuart A., Allison B.; m. Shirley Marie Lynn, Sept. 27, 1988. BS, Tufts U., 1951. Assoc. div. head, mem. steering com. MIT Lincoln Lab., Lexington, Mass., 1953-79; dir. defensive systems Office Undersec. of Def., Washington, 1979-81; dep. dir. Def. Advanced Rsch. Projects Agy., Washington, 1981-85; v.p., chief operating officer Atlantic Aerospace Electronics Corp., Greenbelt, Md., 1985—; mem. Army Sci. Bd., Washington, 1989—; cons. Def. Sci. Bd., Washington, 1988—, mem. 1992—; bd. dirs. Atlantic Aerospace; chmn. numerous studies U.S. Dept. Def. Lt. (j.g.) USNR, 1951-53. Mem. AIAA (sr.), IEEE (sr.), Assn. Old Crows, SASA. Home: 6324 Manchester Way Alexandria VA 22304 Office: Atlantic Aerospace 6404 Ivy Lane # 300 Greenbelt MD 20770

LYNN, YEN-MOW, mathematics educator; b. Shanghai, China, Jan. 17, 1935; came to U.S., 1956; s. Thuinli and Pao-Chiung (Tcheng) L.; children: Edward, Kirk, Genevieve. BS, Nat. Taiwan U., 1955; MS, Calif. Inst. Tech., 1957, PhD, 1961. From asst. to assoc. rsch. scientist Courant Inst. Math. Sci NYU, N.Y.C., 1960-64; assoc. prof. Ill. Inst. Tech., Chgo., 1964-67; from assoc. prof. to prof. U. Md., Balt., 1967—, chmn. dept. math., 1976-82; cons. NASA Ames Rsch. Ctr., Moffett Field, Calif., 1966, U.S. Army Ballistics Rsch. Lab., Aberdeen, Md., 1969-75; sr. resident rsch. assoc. Nat. Acad. Sci.-NRC NASA Ames Rsch. Ctr., Moffett Field, 1966, 67. Contbr. articles to profl. jours. Mem. Am. Math. Soc., Soc. Indsl. and Applied Math., Am. Phys. Soc. Office: Univ of Md Baltimore County 5401 Wilkens Ave Baltimore MD 21228-5398

LYNT, RICHARD KING, microbiologist; b. Washington, Feb. 25, 1917; s. Richard King and Elsie Ackerman (King) L.; m. Elizabeth Mackenzie Cissel, Nov. 17, 1944; children: Richard, Margaret, David. BS in Bacteriology, U. Md., 1939, MS in Bacteriology and Food Technology, 1942. Grad. asst. bacteriology U. Md., College Pk., Md., 1939-40; food inspector, bacteriologist D.C. Health Dept., Washington, 1940-42; lab officer, hosp. corps, med. svc. corps USNR, Bethesda, Md., Oceanside, Calif., 1942-46; bacteriologist E.R. Squibb & Sons, New Brunswick, N.J., 1946-48; rsch. fellow Rutgers U., New Brunswick, 1948-49; bacteriologist NIH Nat. Inst. Allergy and Infectious Disease, Bethesda, 1951-63; microbiologist U.S. FDA Div. Microbiology, Washington, 1963-83; microbiologist cons., retired Silver Spring, Md., 1983—; mem. interagy. botulism rsch. coordinating com., Washington, 1968-83; faculty mem. Am. Soc. for Microbiology Continuing Edn. Com., Dallas, 1981; mem. People to People Enzymology Del. to People's Republic of China, 1985. Author: (with others) Clostridium Botulinum, 1970-84; contbr. chpts to books, articles to profl. jours. Mem. Pinecrest Citizens Assn., Silver Spring, 1960—; adminstrv. bd. Marvin Meml. United Meth. Ch., Silver Spring, 1985—; judge of elections Bd. Suprs. Elections, Montgomery County, Md., 1988-92. Served to lt. Med. Svc. Corps, USNR, 1942-46. Recipient Awards of Merit, U.S. FDA, 1974. Mem. N.Y. Acad. Sci., Inst. Food Technologists, Naval Res. Assn., Am. Soc. for Microbiology, AAAS. Republican. Methodist. Home: 316 Penwood Rd Silver Spring MD 20901-2716

LYON, ANDREW BENNET, economics educator; b. Elmhurst, Ill., June 6, 1958; s. Richard M. and Rhee Lyon; m. Jennifer A. Sour, May 31, 1987; 1 child, Sarah. AB, Stanford U., 1980; PhD, Princeton U., 1986. Economist Jt. Com. on Taxation, U.S. Congress, Washington D.C., 1985-87; asst. prof., dept. econ. U. Md., College Park, 1987—; cons. various firms, 1987-92; dir. Unisys Credit Corp., Detroit, 1991-92; sr. economist Coun. Econ. Advisers, 1992—. Contbr. numerous articles to profl. jours. Nat. Bur. Econs. fellow, 1987—; KPMG Peat Marwick Found. grantee, 1990; various fellowships and grants, 1981-89. Mem. Am. Econ. Assn., Nat. Tax Assn. (Outstanding Doctoral Dissertation award 1986, Fed. Tax Com. 1991), Phi Beta Kappa. Office: Univ of Maryland Dept of Economics College Park MD 20742

LYON, ANN PATTERSON DURR, social worker; b. Birmingham, Ala., Feb. 12, 1927; d. Clifford Judkins and Virginia Heard (Foster) Durr; m. Walton Lyon, May 19, 1951; children: Nancy, Clifford, Paul, James. BA, U. Wis., 1949; MSW, Howard U., 1954. Cert. Acad. Cert. Social Workers, NASW; lic. social worker, Pa. Group worker Hull House, Chgo., 1949-51; psychiat. social worker Child Study Ctr., Phila., 1954-56, Ea. Pa. Psychiat. Inst., Phila., 1956-57; therapist Treesler Luth. Svcs., Mechanicsburg, Pa., 1979-86, 88-89; prof. Harrisburg (Pa.) Area Community Coll., 1971—, coord. human svcs., 1973-83. Mem. Cumberland County Bd. of Assistance, Carlisle, Pa., 1980-90; elected commr. E. Pennsboro Twp., 1990—. Vocat. Edn. grantee Pa. Dept. Edn., 1973-75, 77, Human Svcs. grantee Pa. Dept. Welfare, 1972, 79; recipient Lifetime Achievement award Ctrl. Pa. div. NASW, 1992. Mem. NASW (past bd. mem. cen. Pa., clin. register), Mid Atlantic Consortium Human Svc. (conf. chair 1988). Democrat. Unitarian. Home: 20 Clifton Rd Camp Hill PA 17011-1607

LYON, GORDON EDWARD, computer scientist; b. New London, Wis., June 8, 1942; s. Gordon Martin and Dorothy Alice (Hooper) L.; m. Carla Susan Kaiser, Jan. 3, 1971; children: Merritt, Adrienne. BS, Mich. Technol. U., 1964; MS in Math., U. Mich., 1966, MS, 1967, PhD in Computer Science, 1972. Rsch. mathematician GM Rsch. Labs., Warren, Mich., 1967-68; rsch. assoc. U. Mich., Ann Arbor, 1970-72; supr. computer scientist Nat. Inst. Standards and Tech., Gaithersburg, Md., 1972—; assoc. prof., lectr. George Washington U., Washington, 1978-79; sr. lectr. George Mason U., Fairfax, Va., 1984; mem. bd. rev. Jour. Supercomputing, Lanham, Md., 1987—. Editor: Using ANS Fortran, 1980. Recipient Silver medal Dept. Commerce, Washington, 1978. Mem. IEEE Computer Soc., Assn. Computing Machinery, Soc. Indsl. and Applied Math., Potomac Pedalers Touring Club, Inc. Office: Nat Inst Standards & Tech Gaithersburg MD 20899

LYON, JAMES BURROUGHS, lawyer; b. N.Y.C., May 11, 1930; s. Francis Murray and Edith May (Strong) L. BA, Amherst Coll., 1952; LLB, Yale U., 1955. Bar: Conn. 1955, U.S. Tax Ct. 1970. Asst. football coach Yale U., 1953-55; assoc. Murtha, Cullina, Richter and Pinney (and predecessor), Hartford, Conn., 1956-61, ptnr., 1961—; mem. adv. com., lectr. and session leader NYU Inst. on Fed. Taxation, 1973-86. Chmn. 13th Conf. Charitable Orgns. NYU on Fed. Taxation, 1982; trustee Kingswood-Oxford Sch., West Hartford, Conn., 1961-91, hon. trustee, 1991—, chmn. bd. trustees, 1975-78; trustee Old Sturbridge Village, Mass., 1974—, chmn. bd. trustees, 1991—; trustee Ella Burr McManus Trust, Hartford, 1980—, Hartford YMCA, 1985—, St. Francis Found., 1991—; trustee Wadsworth Atheneum, Hartford, 1968—, pres., 1981-84; corporator Inst. Living, 1981—, Hartford Hosp., 1975—, St. Francis Hosp., Hartford, 1976, Hartford Art Sch., 1979—, Hartford Pub. Libr., 1979—, Hartford Sem., 1991; bd. dirs. Hartford Conv. and Visitors Bur., 1990—, Conn. Policy and Econ. Coun., Inc., 1991—; mem. Conn. adv. com. New Eng. Legal Found., 1991—. Recipient Eminent Service medal Amherst Coll., 1967, Nathan Hale award Yale Club Hartford, 1983, Disting. Am. award No. Conn. chpt. Nat. Football Found. Hall of Fame, 1983. Fellow Am. Coll. Tax Counsel; mem.

ABA (mem. exempt orgn. com., co-chair subcom. on mus. and other cultural orgns. sect. of taxation 1988—), Am. Law Inst., Hartford Golf Club, Univ. Club of Hartford, Yale Club, Union Club of N.Y.C., Dauntless Club (Essex, Conn.), Wianno Club (Osterville, Mass.), Phi Beta Kappa. Office: City Pl I 185 Asylum St City Hartford CT 06103

LYON, RICHARD KENNETH, chemist; b. Cleve., Dec. 22, 1933; s. Aaron Richard and Shirley (Peck) L.; m. Ina Helga Hoffmann, Mar. 30, 1968; children: John, David. BS, Coll. William and Mary, Williamsburg, Va., 1955; PhD, Harvard U., Boston, 1960. Sci. advisor Exxon Rsch. & Engring., Linden, N.J., 1960-81, Annandale, N.J., 1981-86; sr. scientist Energy &Environ. Rsch. Corp., Whitehouse, N.J., 1986—; cons. in field. Contbr. articles to profl. jours.; inventor Thermal DeNOx process, 1974; patentee in field; author 4 novels. Recipient IR 100award, Indsl. Rsch. Mag., 1976. Mem. Am. Chem. Soc. (award 1984), Combustion Inst., Sci. Fiction Writers of Am. Home: RR 3 Box 267 Pittstown NJ 08867-9445 Office: Energy & Environ Rsch Corp Rt 22 E PO Box 189 Whitehouse NJ 08888

LYON, RONALD EDWARD, management consultant; b. Kansas City, Kans., Apr. 13, 1936; s. William Edward and Lillian (Gee) L.; m. Josette Paula Larré, July 24, 1959; children: Michael Alan, Mark Alexander, Matthew Adam, Collette Allison. Owner Hansler Outboard & Austin Aqua Sports, Austin, Tex., 1959-63; gen. mgr. Wayne Green Ent.-73 Mag., Peterboro, N.H., 1963-65; with Computer Control Corp., Peterboro, N.H., 1965-71; sales person Radio Shack (Tandy) & Sterling Elec. Co., Maine, N.H., Vt. areas, 1971-82; sales engr. Pall Corp./Russell Assocs., Inc., Watertown, Mass., 1982-87; mgr. eastern region Fansteel/Wellman Dynamics, 1984-87; chief exec. officer, chief operating officer Laryon Assocs., Inc., Keene, N.H., 1987—. With USAF, 1955-59. Mem. U.S. Power Squadron (comdr.). Home: Mcintire Rd Munsonville NH 03457 Office: Laryon Assocs Inc 178D Main St Keene NH 03431

LYON-LOFTUS, GREGORY THOMAS, family physician, psychologist; b. Washington, July 16, 1944; s. Joseph Phillip and Margaret Mary (Boland) Loftus; m. Diana Joan Lyon, July 12, 1975; children: Michael Thomas, Anthony Eric. BA, Wheeling (W.Va.) Jesuit Coll., 1966; MA, Mich. State U., 1970, PhD, 1975, MD, 1977. Diplomate Am. Bd. Family Practice. Intern dePaul Hosp., Norfolk, Va., 1978-79; resident in family practice Ea. Va. Med. Sch., Norfolk, 1978-81; dir. emergency med. svcs., acting dir. mental health svcs. Indian Health Svc., USPHS, Keams Canyon, Ariz., 1982-84; pvt. practice, Mont Alto, Pa., 1984—. Officer USPHS, 1982-84. Mem. Am. Acad. Family Practice, Pa. Acad. Family Practice (del. 1990—), Am. Diabetes Assn. (bd. dirs. Waynesboro, Pa. chpt. 1987—), Rotary (bd. dirs. Waynesboro 1990—). Roman Catholic. Home: 916 E Main St Waynesboro PA 17268-2337 Office: Mont Alto Family Practice 6155 Anthony Hwy Mont Alto PA 17237

LYONS, CATHY, executive director; b. Conn, Apr. 28, 1943. BS in Edn., Cen. State U., 1965. Tchr., spl. edn., trade show prodn.; assn. svcs. mgmt. Daniels Prodns Inc, West Hartford, Conn. Mem. Plainville (Conn.) Choral Soc., United Meth. Ch. Trustees, Plainville. Mem. Am. Soc. Assn. Execs., Conn. Soc. Assn. Execs.

LYONS, CHARLES HENRY, academic director; b. Boston, July 20, 1941; s. John Laurence and Adelaide (English) L.; m. Anne Warner Nason, Nov. 30, 1968; children: Mary Littlefield, Paul Laurence, Charles Philip. BA, Harvard Coll., 1963; MAT, Harvard Grad. Sch. Edn., 1964; PhD, Columbia U., 1970. Lectr. Syracuse (N.Y.) Univ., 1969-70; asst. to assoc. prof. Tchrs. Coll., Columbia Univ., N.Y.C., 1970-76; dir., overseas liaison Am. Coun. on Edn., Washington, 1976-82; exec. dir. Fulbright Found., Monrovia, Liberia, 1982-85; dir. Internat. Rsch. Univ. of Ill., Chgo., 1985-87; dir. internat. affairs Conn. State Univ., New Britain, 1987—; cons. U.S. Agy. for Internat. Devel., Washington, 1980-82. Author: To Wash An Aethiop White, 1975. Vol. U.S. Peace Corps, Nigeria, 1964-66; dir. Nat. Coun. Returned Peace Corps Vols., Washington, 1980-82; chmn. edn. com. Conn. World Trade Assn., Hartford, 1988-90. Recipient fellowship Fulbright Program, Germany, 1989. Home: 35 School St Burlington CT 06013-2532

LYONS, IVAN, publisher, writer; b. N.Y.C., Oct. 5, 1934; s. Martin Pleskow and Ruth Lyons; m. Nan Bauer, May 18, 1958; 1 child, Samantha Kelly. BS in Social Sci., CCNY, 1956; postgrad., Boston U., 1956-57. Adv. and sales mgr. Plenum Pub., N.Y.C., 1958-64; cons. Unesco Publs., N.Y.C., 1965-67, Tech. Press, Ltd., London, 1966-67, The Faraday Press, N.Y.C., 1966-69. Publisher and editor: Information Hotline Jour. Office: Sci Assocs Internat Inc 465 W End Ave New York NY 10024-4926

LYONS, JOHN MATTHEW, telecommunications executive, broadcasting executive; b. N.Y.C., Nov. 5, 1948; s. Matthew Joseph and Anna (Coroneos) L.; Natalia Astakhova, Apr. 12, 1992. BSEE, Roosevelt U., Chgo., 1970, MSEE, 1976; BSE, Century U., L.A., 1981, MBA in Engring. Mgmt., 1982; PhD in Communications, Loyola U., Chgo., 1979; PhD in Broadcasting (hon.), Sicluna U. Found., 1987. Registered profl. engr. Engr., producer Sta. WRFM, N.Y.C., 1965-69; sr. facilities planning and project engr. Sta. WWRL-Radio, N.Y.C., 1969-76; sr. facilities planning, project engr. Sta. WWRL/WRVR, N.Y.C., 1976-78; asst. chief engr. Sta. WOR, Inc., N.Y.C., 1978-80; chief engr. Sta. WRKS-FM, N.Y.C., 1980-90; sr. project mgr. DSI Communications, Kenilworth, N.J., 1990—; pres. Lyon Records, N.Y., 1971—, Short Lines Co., N.Y., 1980—; chmn. master antenna com. Empire State Bldg., N.Y., 1980—; bd. dirs. The Document Ctr., N.Y.; cons. broadcasting and telecommunications; ofcl. photographer U.S. Imperial Soc. Tchrs. of Dance, 1991—, Blackpool Dance Festival, 1992—. Producer: (radio broadcast) The Cuban Missile Crisis, 1962 (Peabody award 1963); exec. producer: (broadcast series) Radio: The First 50 Years, 1970, Sta. WOR 60th Anniversary Program, 1982 (Armstrong award 1983, Internat. Radio Festival award 1983), Sta. WOR 65th Anniversary Program, 1987; photography editor Amateur Dancers mag., Ability Mag.; contbg. photographer to Dance Scene mag., Dance News, Eng.; photographer Dance Beat, U.S.A., Japan Dance News, U.S. Imperial Soc. Tchrs. of Dance, 1991—. Chmn. media curriculum com. Westchester Community Coll., N.Y., 1987—; v.p. U.S. Amateur Ballroom Dancers Assn., 1987—. With USAF, 1967-70. Fellow Soc. Broadcast Engrs. (sr., cert., bd. dirs. 1974-78), Internat. Biog. Assn.; mem. Nat. Assn. Radio and Telecommunications Engrs. (cert.), Broadcast Music, Inc., Audio Engring. Soc., IEEE, Internat. Radio and TV Soc., VA Hosp. Radio and TV Guild (v.p. 1976-82, 84—, pres. 1982-84, chmn. exec. com. 1984—, Bennie award 1981), Broadcast Pioneers, Am. Soc. Composers, Authors, and Pubs., Broadcast Music, Am. Inst. Plant Engrs., U.S. Amateur Ballroom Dancers Assn. (regional v.p. 1987-89, dir. for internat. liaison 1989—), Knights of Malta, 1986. Avocation: competitive ballroom dancing, photography. Home: 305 E 86th St New York NY 10028-4702 Office: DSI Communications 627 Boulevard Kenilworth NJ 07033-1639

LYONS, JOHN W(INSHIP), government agency administrator, chemist; b. Reading, Mass., Nov. 5, 1930. A.B. in Chemistry, Harvard U., 1952; A.M. in Phys. Chemistry, Washington U., St. Louis, 1963, Ph.D. in Phys. Chemistry, 1964. With Monsanto Co., 1955-73, group leader, sect. mgr. research dept., inorganic chems. div., 1962-69, mgr. comml. devel., head fire safety center, 1969-73; mem. ad hoc panel on fire research Nat. Bur. Standards, Washington, 1971-73; dir. Center for Fire Research, 1973-77, Inst. Applied Tech., 1977-78, Nat. Engring. Lab., 1978-89; acting dep. dir. Nat. Bur. Standards, 1983; dir. Nat. Inst. Standards and Tech., Gaithersburg, Md., 1990—; chmn. Products Research Com. (trust which adminstrs. fire research funds), 1974-79; vis. lectr. various univs.; co-chmn. U.S.-Japan Natural Resources Panel on Fire Research, 1975-78; mem. adv. com. on engring. NSF, 1981-90; mem. bd. visitors U. Md. Coll. Engring., 1980-90; mem. adv. com. Naval Research Lab., 1985—; mem. com. on fed. labs. Office Sci. and Tech. Policy. Author: Viscosity and Flow Measurement, 1963, The Chemistry and Uses of Fire Retardants, 1970; Fire, 1985; contbr. numerous articles to profl. publs. Served with U.S. Army, 1953-54. Recipient Gold medal Dept. Commerce, 1977, Pres.'s Mgmt. Improvement award White House, 1977, Pres.'s Disting. Exec. Rank award, 1981, E.U. Condon award, 1986. Fellow AAAS, Washington Acad. Sci.; mem. Am. Chem. Soc. (chmn. St. Louis sect. 1971-72), Nat. Fire Protection Assn. (bd. dirs. 1978-84), ASTM (bd. dirs. 1985-87), Nat. Acad. Engring., Sigma Xi. Office: Nat Inst Standards & Tech Gaithersburg MD 20899

LYONS, NICK, publishing executive; b. N.Y.C., June 5, 1932; s. Nathan and Rose (Bernstein) Ress; m. Mari Blumenau, Sept. 1, 1957; children: Paul, Charles, Jennifer, Anthony. BS in Econs., U. Pa., 1953; MA in Am. Lit., U. Mich., 1961, PhD in Am. Lit., 1963. Prof. English Hunter Coll., N.Y.C., 1961-88; exec. editor Crown Pubs., Inc., N.Y.C., 1963-78; pres. Nick Lyons Books, N.Y.C., 1979-84, Lyons & Burford, Pubs., N.Y.C., 1984—. Author: The Sony Vision, 1975, The Seasonable Angler, 1970, Bright Rivers, 1978, Confessions of a Fly Fishing Addict, 1988. With U.S. Army, 1954-55. Office: Lyons & Burford Pubs 31 W 21st St New York NY 10010-6806

LYONS, PATRICK JOSEPH, management educator; b. N.Y.C., Dec. 12, 1943; s. Joseph Raphael and Catherine (Albrecht) L.; m. Georgette Marie Tumasonis, June 27, 1970; children: Michael, Theresa, George. BEE, Manhattan Coll., 1965; MS in Applied Math., Case Western Res. U., 1967; PhD in Applied Math., Adelphi U., 1973. Systems analyst Grumman Aerospace, Bethpage, N.Y., 1967-75, asst. mgr., 1975-76; prof. mgmt. St. John's U., Jamaica, N.Y., 1976—; cons. mgmt. sci., 1978—. Contbr. articles to profl. jours. Adult edn. instr. Sacred Heart Ch., Bayside, N.Y., 1983—. Mem. Am. Assn. for Artificial Intelligence, Inst. Mgmt. Sci. Roman Catholic. Office: St John's U Coll Bus Jamaica NY 11439

LYONS, RICHARD GERALD, education educator, researcher; b. Cambridge, Mass., Oct. 13, 1934; s. Maurice and Abbie (Brennan) L.; m. Grace Marie Rotigliano, Aug. 16, 1958; 1 child, Richard Douglas. BS, Boston U., 1959, EdM, 1961, PhD, 1964. Instr. Boston U., 1963-64; prof. U. Mass., Lowell, 1964—; cons. Lexington (Mass.) Pub. Schs., 1962-64, Mass. Fedn. Tchrs., Lynn, 1972-74, Lawrence (Mass.) Pub. Schs., 1988-91. Editor: Working to Schooling, 1990, Controversies Over the Purposes of Schooling and the Meaning of Work, 1990; contbr. articles to profl. jours. Mem. Needham (Mass.) Hist. Soc. Nat. Def. Grad. fellow, 1959-63. Mem. New Eng. Philosophy Edn. Soc. (pres. 1972-73), Boston Mus. Fine Arts, John Dewey Soc., Soc. for Ednl. Reconstruction, Fin, Fur and Feather Club (pres. 1989-91). Democrat. Home: 25 Mallard Rd Needham MA 02192-1814 Office: Univ of Mass 1 University Ave Lowell MA 01854-2881

LYONS, RICHARD KENT, economics educator; b. Palo Alto, Calif., Feb. 10, 1961; s. J. Richard and Ida (Primavera) L.; m. Barrie Ann Fiske, 1992. BS in Bus. with highest honors, U. Calif., Berkeley, 1982; PhD, MIT, 1987. Rsch. analyst SRI Internat., Menlo Park, Calif., 1983-84; summer intern Orgn. for Econ. Cooperation & Devel., Paris, 1985, Bd. Govs., Fed. Res. System, Washington, 1986; asst. prof. Columbia U., N.Y.C., 1987-91; assoc. prof., 1991—; faculty rsch. fellow Nat. Bur. Econ. Rsch., Cambridge, Mass., 1989—. Assoc. editor Jour. Internat. Fin. Markets, Insts. & Money, Carbondale, Ill, 1989—; contbr. articles to profl. jours. NSF grad. fellow, 1984. Mem. Am. Econ. Assn. (coun. on fgn. rels.), Phi Beta Kappa, Beta Gamma Sigma, Sigma Alpha Epsilon. Democrat. Office: Columbia U 606 Uris Hall New York NY 10027

LYONS, THOMAS PATRICK, economics educator; b. Groton, Conn., Sept. 8, 1953. BA in Asian Studies, Cornell U., 1979, MA in Econs., 1982, PhD in Econs., 1983. Asst. prof. econs. Dartmouth Coll., Hanover, N.H., 1983-87; vis. asst. prof. Cornell U., Ithaca, N.Y., 1986-88, asst. prof., 1988-91; assoc. prof., 1991—; dir. East Asia program Cornell U., Ithaca, N.Y., 1991—. Author: Economic Integration and Planning in Maoist China, 1987; contbr. numerous articles to profl. jours. With USN, 1972-76. Rsch. grantee Ford Found., 1987. Mem. Am. Econ. Assn., Assn. for Asian Studies. Office: Cornell U Dept Econs Uris Hall Ithaca NY 14853

LYONS, WARREN, health care adminstrator; b. N.Y.C., Mar. 6, 1949; m. Pamela Adrien, Aug. 4, 1984; children: Noah, Estather. BA, Fordham U., 1970; MBA, Columbia U., 1975, MPH, 1976. Adminstr.P.A. program Bklyn. Hosp., 1971-73; adminstrv. asst. to exec. dir. JFK Med. Ctr., Edison, N.J., 1975-78; adminstrv. asst. Providence Hosp., Southfield, Mich., 1978-79; asst. adminstr. Heritage Hosp., Taylor, Mich., 1979-81; dir. planning MacNeal Hosp., Berwyn, Ill., 1981-84; v.p. Victory Meml. Hosp., Waukegan, Ill., 1984-87; exec. dir. Community Health Alliance, Warrington, Pa., 1987—. Fellow Am. Coll. Health Care Execs.; mem. Nat. Assn. Health Svc. Execs., Bucks County Physicians Hosp. Alliance (bd. dirs. 1990—). Roman Catholic. Home: 26 Belmont Sq Doylestown PA 18901-4432 Office: Community Health Alliance 949 Easton Rd Warrington PA 18976-1849

LYSKOWSKI, STAN ALBIN, personnel placement executive; b. Elizabeth, N.J., Sept. 3, 1947; s. Albin J. and Adele (Yourglivich) L.; m. Chris Rossi, Dec. 1973 (div. June 1985); children: Cynthia, Sharon, Donna; m. Rose D. Liccardi, June 7, 1987. Student, Union Coll. Pres. recruiter Career Ctr., Somerset, N.J., 1970-74; sales mgr. ITT Continental Baking Co., East Brunswick, N.J., 1974-85; pres. Delta Pers., Somerset, 1985—. Republican. Office: Delta Personnel 100 Franklin Square Dr Somerset NJ 08873-4109

LYSUN, GREGORY, artist, educator; b. Yonkers, N.Y., Oct. 24, 1924; s. John and Paraska (Petryszyn) L. Student Art Students League N.Y., 1947-53. Instr. painting and drawing Westchester Art Workshop of Westchester Community Coll., White Plains, N.Y., 1969—; art dir., instr. Fairview Greenburgh Community Ctr., White Plains, 1972—; artist-in-residence and instr. painting and drawing Pelham Art Ctr., 1978—; instr. painting and drawing Hudson River Mus., Yonkers, 1978-79, SUNY-Purchase, 1982—. One man shows: Berkshire Mus., Pittsfield, Mass., 1971; group exhbns. include: 74th Ann. Exhbn. Allied Artists Am., 1985-87, Nat. Arts Club, N.Y.C., Conn. Acad. Fine Arts, William Benton Mus., 1988, Berkshire Mus., 1980, Cooperstown (N.Y.) Art Assn., 1980, Knickerbocker Artists of Am., Nat. Arts Club, 1979; represented in permanent collections: Butler Inst. Am. Art, Youngstown, Ohio, New Britain (Conn.) Mus. Am. Art, Berkshire Mus., Pittsfield, Mass., De Cordova Mus., Lincoln, Mass. Contbr. articles on painting to mags. Served with USCG, 1942-45; ETO, NATOUSA. Recipient Gen. Telephone and Electronics Corp. award, 1972; Council Am. Art Socs. award, 1971; Best Landscape award Conn. Acad. Fine Arts, 1977, Best Portrait award, 1983. Fellow Am. Artists Profl. League; mem. Conn. Acad. Fine Arts (prize 1986), Allied Artists of Am., Art Students League N.Y.C. (life). Address: 481 Winding Rd N Ardsley NY 10502

LYTLE, RICHARD, artist, educator; b. Albany, N.Y., Feb. 14, 1935; s. Ralph Dudley and Mary (Putnam) L.; m. Berit Ore Lytle, June 16, 1959; children: Mara, Claudia, Dorian. Diploma, Cooper Union, N.Y.C., 1955; BFA, Yale U., 1957, MFA, 1960. Instr. Yale Sch. Art, New Haven, 1960-63, assoc. prof., 1966-80, acting dean, 1980-81, 90, prof. art, 1980—; dean Silvermine Coll. Art, New Canaan, Conn., 1963-66; cons. Rockefeller Fund, N.Y.C., 1970; dir. Yale Summer Sch., Norfolk, Conn., 1976, 77; vis. artist-in-residence Dartmouth Coll., Hanover, N.H., 1986. One-man shows in N.Y.C., New Haven and other locales; exhibited in group shows at Mus. Modern Art, N.Y.C., 1959, Whitney Mus. Art, 1963, Pa. Acad. Art, 1983, Bruce Mus., Greenwich, Conn., 1989. Chmn. Region 5 Bd. Edn., Woodbridge, Conn., 1988—. Fullbright fellow, 1958-59; recipient St. Gaudens award Cooper Union, N.Y.C., 1985. Home: 14 Sperry Rd Woodbridge CT 06525-1234 Office: Yale Sch of Art 180 York St West Haven CT 06516-3549

MA, YUAN YUAN, investment banking executive; b. Shanghai, China, Dec. 2, 1952; came to U.S., 1973; s. Chee-Tsin and Chi-Hwa (Wang) M.; m. Linda Teh-Ying Pan, Aug. 20, 1983. BA, U. Cambridge, Eng., 1973, MA, 1977; MA, Princeton U., 1975, PhD, 1982. Sr. analyst Sci. Applications, Inc., McLean, Va., 1978-82; analyst Salomon Bros., Inc., N.Y.C., 1982-83, v.p., 1983-90, dir., 1990—. Mem. Ops. Rsch. Soc. Am., Soc. Indsl. and Applied Maths. Home: 28 Summit Rd Riverside CT 06878-2107 Office: Salomon Bros Inc 7 World Trade Ctr New York NY 10048-1102

MAASS, ALFRED ROLAND, health science consultant; b. Plymouth, Wis., Apr. 14, 1918; s. George Edward and Mabel (Eichenberger) M.; m. Eleanor Anderson, Jan. 26, 1947; children: Andrew, David, Philip. BS, Antioch Coll., 1942; MS, U. Wis., 1948, PhD, 1950. Abbott lab. fellow Argonne Nat. Labs., North Chicago, Ill., 1950; sr. biochemist Smith Kline & French Labs., Phila., 1951-56, group leader biochemistry dept., 1956-57, asst. sect. head biochemistry dept., 1957-62, sect. head biochemistry dept., 1962-67, assoc. dir. biochemistry dept., 1967-75, assoc. dir. biol. rsch., 1975-78, dir. analytical biochemistry dept., 1978-79, dir. analytical biochemistry dept. preclin. devel., 1980-81, dir. sci. adminstrn., 1981-82; radiol. safety chair Smith Kline & French Labs., 1952-75, worldwide dir., 1974-78. Contbr. numerous articles to profl. jours. Lt. (j.g.) USNR, 1944-46, PTO. Home: RR 2 Box 50 New Milford PA 18834-9616

MAAZEL, LORIN, conductor, musician; b. Neuilly, France, Mar. 6, 1930; s. Lincoln and Marie (Varencove) M.; m. Dietlinde Turban, 1986; 2 children; 4 children from previous marriages. Studies with, Vladimir Bakaleinikoff; student, U. Pitts., Mus. D. (hon.), 1968; H.H.D., Beaver Coll., 1973. Debut as condr., 1938; condr. Am. symphony orchs., 1939—; violin recitalist; European debut, 1953; festivals include Bayreuth, Salzburg, Edinburgh; tours include S.Am., Australia, USSR, Japan, Korea, People's Republic China; artistic dir. Deutsche Opera Berlin, 1965-71; assoc. prin. condr. New Philharm. Orch., London, 1970-72; dir. Cleve. Orch., 1972-82, condr. emeritus, 1982-86; dir. Vienne State Opera, 1982-84; music dir. Pitts. Symphony Orch., 1988—, Orchestre Nat. de France, 1988-90. Decorated officer Legion d'Honneur 1981; Finnish Commdr. of the Lion; Portuguese Commdr.; Bundesverdienstkreuz, Germany. Office: Pitts Symphony Orch 600 Penn Ave Pittsburgh PA 15222-3209

MACALISTER, ROBERT LEE, real estate developer; b. Glens Falls, N.Y., June 21, 1956; s. Robert Lee and Louise (Didio) MacA.; m. Julia Spanos, Feb. 16, 1986; 1 child, Logan Kaythern. AAS in Mktg., Adirondack Coll., 1978. Dir. leasing Pyramid Cos., Syracuse, N.Y., 1981-85; leasing ptnr. Windsor Devel., Albany, N.Y., 1986—; leasing ptnr. Mountain Magic Leather, Keene, N.H., 1985—. Bd. dirs. Hope Prison Ministry. Mem. Internat. Coun. Shopping Ctrs. (roundtable leader 1989, 90, panelist, 1991). Office: Windsor Devel Group 5 Washington Sq Albany NY 12065

MACARIO, ALBERTO JUAN LORENZO, physician; b. Naschel, Argentina, Dec. 1, 1935; came to U.S., 1974, naturalized, 1980; s. Alberto Carlos and Maria Elena (Giraudi) M.; MD, Nat. U. Buenos Aires, 1961; m. Everly Conway, Mar. 16, 1963; children: Alex, Everly. Intern, Ramos Mejia Hosp., Buenos Aires, 1958-60, resident 1960; resident Rivadavia Hosp., Buenos Aires, 1961-62, physician-hematologist, 1962-64; fellow NRC Argentina, Buenos Aires, 1964-69; head dept. radioactive isotopes Inst. Hematological Investigations, Nat. Acad. Medicine Argentina, Buenos Aires, 1967-69; Eleanor Roosevelt fellow Internat. Union Against Cancer, Dept. Tumorbiology, Karolinska Inst., Stockholm, 1969-71; mem. sci. staff Lab. Cell Biology, NRC Italy, Rome, 1971-73; head Lab. Immunology, Internat. Agy. Rsch. on Cancer, WHO, Lyons, France, 1973-74; research scientist Brown U., Providence, 1974-76, Div. Labs. and Rsch., N.Y. State Dept. Health, Albany, 1976-79; chief hematology Clin. Lab. Center, N.Y. State Dept. Health, Albany, 1979-81, dir. clin. and exptl. immunology sect. Lab. Medicine Inst., 1981-83; rsch. physician, 1981—, Wadsworth Ctr. for Labs. and Rsch. N.Y. State Dept. of Health; prof. Dept. Biomed. Scis. Sch. Pub. Health U. at Albany, SUNY-N.Y. State Dept. Health, 1985—, mem. senate, 1989—; adj. prof. pathology and lab. medicine Albany Med Coll., 1991—; grant reviewer for nat. and internat. agys.; manuscript reviewer for sci. jours. Recipient Diploma de Honor prize Nat. U. Buenos Aires, 1961, Bernardino Rivadavia prize Nat. Acad. Medicine Argentina, 1967, Ciencia e Investigation prize Argentinian Soc. Advancement Sci., 1967; Ford Found.-NAS travel fellow, 1968, Eleanor Roosevelt fellow, 1969. Mem. Scandinavian Soc. Immunology, Italian Assn. Immunologists, French Soc. Immunology, Am. Assn. Immunologists, Am. Soc. Microbiology (sect. editor Manual of Clin. Lab. Immunology 4th edit. 1989—), Am. Assn. Pathologists. Achievements include two patents, 1981, 87; developed method for immunologic identification of bacteria that produce methane gas; discovered antigenic diversity of these bacteria in natural and manufactured ecosystems; described structural topography of methanogenic bacteria and population dynamics in granular microbial consortia; found novel multicellular forms of archaebacteria; isolated for the first time a dnaK gene from an archaebacterium. Sect. editor: Manual of Clinical Laboratory Immunology, 4th edit., 1989—; editor multivol. treatise Monoclonal Antibodies Against Bacteria and treatise Gene Probes for Bacteria; contbr. articles to profl. jours., chpts. to books. Office: Empire State Pla/Dept Health Wadsworth Ctr Labs Rsch PO Box 509 Albany NY 12201

MACARTHUR, BRIAN HENRY, hotel executive; b. Bronxville, N.Y., July 25, 1949; s. Chester Wallace and Arline (Simmen) MacA. BS in Hotel and Restaurant Adminstrn., Okla. State U., 1971. Cert. hotel adminstr. Mgr. food and beverage Quality Inn Cen., Arlington, Va., 1971; budget and cost analyst Quality Hotels & Resorts Inc., Silver Spring, Md., 1972-82, contr. hotel ops., 1982-86; contr. Quality Inns, Inc., 1986-89, Manor Care, Inc., Quality Inns div., 1989—. Mem. Internat. Assn. Hospitality Accts. Republican. Presbyterian. Home: 11411 Oak Leaf Dr Silver Spring MD 20901-5006 Office: Manor Care Inc Quality Inns Div 10750 Columbia Pike Silver Spring MD 20901-4427

MACARTHUR, JOHN RODERICK C. G. (RICK MACARTHUR), magazine publisher, journalist; b. N.Y.C., June 4, 1956; s. J. Roderick and Christiane (L'Etendart) MacA. AB, Columbia U., 1978. Reporter Wall Street Jour., Chgo., summer 1977, Washington Star, 1978, Bergen Record, Hackensack, N.J., 1978-79, Chgo. Sun Times, 1979-82; asst. fgn. editor UPI, N.Y.C., 1982; pres., pub. Harper's Mag., N.Y.C., 1983—. Author: Second Front: Censorship and Propaganda in the Gulf War, 1992. Bd. dirs. J. Roderick MacArthur Found., Com. to Protect Journalists, Death Penalty Info. Ctr. Mem. Overseas Press Club (bd. dirs.), Econ. Club of N.Y. Office: Harper's Mag 666 Broadway 11th Fl New York NY 10012

MACAULAY, COLIN ALEXANDER, mining engineer; b. Montreal, Que., Can., Dec. 26, 1931; s. Kenneth Douglas and Eunice S. (Guild) M.; m. Elizabeth Ann Rowsell, Aug. 27, 1955; children: Douglas C., James. R., Robert C. B.Engring. in Mining, McGill U., Montreal, 1954, M.Engring., 1955. Registered profl. engr., Ont. Gen. mgr., dir. Palabora Mining Co., Transvaal, Republic South Africa, 1972-82; dep. chmn., mng. dir., chief exec. Rössing Uranium Ltd., Namibia, 1982-88; pres., chief operating officer Rio Algom Ltd., Toronto, Ont., Can., 1988-91, pres., ceo, 1991—, also bd. dirs.; bd. dirs. Pan Orvana Resources, B.C., Can.; chmn. bd. dirs. Highland Valley Copper, B.C. Mem. Ont. Mining Assn. (bd. dirs. 1990-91), Mining Assn. Can. (dir.), Mining Industry Tech. Coun. Can., Can. Inst. Mining and Metallurgy, Assn. Profl. Engrs. Ont. Home: 70 Roxborough Dr, Toronto, ON Canada M4W 1X1 Office: Rio Algom Ltd, 120 Adelaide St W, Toronto, ON Canada M4W 1X1

MACAUSLAND, MARY ANN, accountant, educator; b. Sellersville, Pa., Dec. 23, 1959; d. Howard Grant and Ruth Shirley (Garges) Bardsley; m. D. Stuart MacAusland, Sept. 7, 1985; children: Sarah Elizabeth, Sean Andrew. BS in Bus., Temple U., 1990. CPA, Pa. Jr. acct. Roberson, Keown Co., CPAs, Souderton, Pa., 1982-85; payroll acct. Adult Communities Total Svcs., Springhouse, Pa., 1985; contr. Total Care Systems, Springhouse, 1985-90; instr. acctg. Reading (Pa.) Area Community Coll., 1991—; Instr. of taxation Alvernia Coll., Reading, 1991. Chmn. Dist. Twp. recreation com., 1990. Republican. Home: PO Box 313 Boyertown PA 19512-0313

MACBRAYNE, PAMELA SUE, university administrator; b. Savannah, Ga., Oct. 8, 1948; d. John Morrison and Mildred (Hubbs) MacB.; m. Denis Lyon Moonan, May 28, 1978; 1 child, Tavis Lyon MacBrayne Moonan. BA in Sociology, St. Lawrence U., 1970; MS in Ednl. Adminstrn., SUNY, Albany, 1975; postgrad., U. Maine, 1984—. Adminstrv. asst. corp. banking Chem. Bank, N.Y.C., 1970-72; trading analyst Am. Stock Exch., N.Y.C., 1972-73; rsch. assoc. Coun. for Fin. Aid to Edn., N.Y.C., 1973-74; devel. and info. counselor U. Maine, Augusta, 1976, dir. mid-coast community coll., 1976-86, spl. asst. to pres. for community coll. planning, 1986-87, exec. dir. of community coll. planning, 1987-88, exec. dir. distance edn., 1988-91, exec. dir. student svcs. and distance edn., 1991—; cons. Daytona (Fla.) Beach Community Coll., 1991—; instr. Hurrican Island Outward Bound Sch., Rockland, Maine, 1986—; bd. dirs. Rockport (Maine) Apprenticeship, Camden (Maine) Conf. Contbr. articles to profl. jours. Pres. Children's Ho. Montessori Sch. Bd., Camden, 1990—; vice chair Appleton (Maine) Village Sch. Com., 1985—; chair Mid Coast Tchrs. Ctr., Rockport, 1978-85; admission assoc. St. Lawrence U., Canton, 1977—. Mem. Coun. for Adult and Exptl. Edn. Office: U Maine Augusta ME 04330

MACCARIO, MAURICE MALCOLM, oral and maxillofacial surgeon, consultant; b. Newark, Jan. 17, 1942; s. Melchiorre Malcolm and Susan (Bocchino) M.; m. Rosemarie Agnes Nocera; children: Lenora, Marcus. BA,

Villanova U., 1964; DDMedicine, Fairleigh Dickinson U., 1968. Diplomate Am. Bd. Oral and Maxillo Facial Surgery. Intern Bklyn. Jewish Hosp., 1969; resident Bklyn. Vets. Hosp., 1970; chief resident Bklyn. Cumberland Med. Ctr., 1971; sr. registrar North Staffordshire Royal Infirmary, Eng., 1971-72; tchr. oral surgery Bklyn. Hosp., 1972-82; pvt. practice Oakland, N.J., 1972—; staff Valley Hosp., Ridgewood, N.J., 1971—, dir. dentistry, 1980-88; cons. St. Joseph Hosp., Paterson, N.J., 1971—. contbr. articles to profl. jours. V.p. Oakland (N.J.) Rep. Club., 1986-88. Fellow Am. Assn. Oral and Maxillofacial Surgeons, Oral Surgery Soc. N.J., Am. Mensa Soc. Roman Catholic. Home: 160 Long Hill Rd Oakland NJ 07436-3113 Office: 180 Ramapo Valley Rd Oakland NJ 07436-2524

MACCAUSLAND, JANET, apparel designer, educator, small business owner; b. Newton, Mass., Sept. 17, 1947; d. James Paul and Ethel (Sanderson) MacC.; m. Salvatore DeMaio, June 18, 1973 (div. 1976); 1 child, Pasquale; m. David Lawrence Smith, Feb. 13, 1981. Student, Mass. Coll. of Art, 1978-79, Mass. Coll. of Art, 1987-88; BFA in Fashion Design, Moore Coll. of Art, 1970. Designer, artist The Needlework Shop, Boston, 1971-72; freelance designer and photographer Vt. and Mass., 1972-77; designer Garland, Brockton, Mass., 1977-80; head designer Whittenton Garment Corp. Inc., Taunton, Mass., 1980-83; designer Cheenos by Donrich Industry Inc., Framingham, Mass., 1983-85; design mgr. Goodman Knitting Co. Inc., Brockton, 1985-88; designer Fall River (Mass.) Knitting Co. Inc., 1988-89; owner, designer N.E. Design, Raynham, Mass., 1989—; head design dept. Worcester (Mass.) Knitting Co. Inc., 1991—; design cons. men's div. David Brett Sales, Inc., Easton, Mass., 1988—; instr., lectr. R.I. Sch. Design, Providence, 1991—. Designer (ofcl. sweater) Boy Scouts Am., 1991. Mem. New Eng. Knitwear Sportswear Assn., New Eng. Aquarium Dive Club, Divers Environ. Survey. Home: 26 Lakeview Dr Raynham MA 02767-1611 Office: Worcester Knitting Co Inc 1 Brussels St Worcester MA 01610-2903

MACCECCHINI, MARIA-LUISA, biochemist, molecular biologist; b. Bern, Switzerland, Jan. 15, 1951; came to U.S., 1980; d. Paola and Alfreda Maccecchini. Ph.D. in Biochemistry, U. Basel, 1978; vis. student Rockefeller U., 1977-78. Postdoctoral fellow Basel (Switzerland) Inst. Immunology, 1978-79, Calif. Inst. Tech., Pasadena, 1980-82; group leader molecular biology IMC Corp., Northbrook, Ill., 1982-86; exec. v.p., chief operating officer Bachem Biosci. Inc., Phila., 1986-91; pres., chief exec. officer Symphony Pharms., Inc., 1991—; asst. prof. molecular biology Ind. State U. Chmn. Leadership Terre Haute, 1983. Mem. AAAS, Am. Soc. Microbiology, Genetics Soc. Am., Sigma Xi (exec. bd.), Greater Phila. Internat. Network (bd. dirs.), Pa. Biotech. Assn. (program chmn.). Contbr. articles in biochemistry and genetics to sci. jours.; patentee in field. Home: 2400 Chestnut St Philadelphia PA 19103-4316 Office: Symphony Pharms Inc 3624 Market St Philadelphia PA 19104-2611

MACCHI, I. ALDEN, retired biology educator, researcher; b. Bologna, Italy, Feb. 21, 1922; came to U.S., 1929; s. Elio and Ida Anna (Gamberini) M.; m. Joan Mary Shiminski, July 6, 1953; 1 child, Deborah Joan. BA, Clark U., 1947, MA, 1950; PhD, Boston U., 1954. Rsch. scientist Worcester (Mass.) Found. for Exptl. Biology, 1950-54; asst. prof. physiology Clark U., Worcester, 1954-56; asst. prof. biology Boston U., 1956-58, assoc. prof., 1958-64, prof., 1964-83, exec. asst. for rsch. dept., 1956-67, interim chmn. dept., 1974-76, assoc. chmn. dept., 1976-77, prof. emeritus, 1983—; vis. lectr. zoology U. Sheffield, Eng., 1962-63; cons. NIH, NSF, Washington. Editor: Comparative Aspects of the Endocrine Pancreas, 1973; mem. internat. editorial adv. bd. Gen. and Comparative Endocrinology, 1971-81, mem. bd. editors, 1975-78; also over 60 articles. With USAAF, 1942-45, ETO. Fellow Lalor Found., 1955, sr. rsch. fellow U.K. Div. Sci. Indsl. Rsch., 1962-63; rsch. grantee USPHS, NIH. Fellow AAAS; mem. Am. Physiology Soc., Am. Soc. Zoologists (nominating com. 1974), Endocrine Soc. (travel awards), Soc. Exptl. Biology and Medicine, Sigma Xi. Home: 52 Roundwood Rd Newton MA 02164-1217 Office: Boston U 5 Cummington St Boston MA 02215-2406

MACCLAREN, JOEL DANIEL, publisher; b. Rochester, N.Y., May 25, 1955; s. Robert H. Macclaren and Marcia (Rietmann) Macclaren Finley; m. Darcy J. Rieman, June 29, 1985; children: Whitney, David. BA, St. Lawrence U., 1977. Asst. controller Wentworth By The Sea, Portsmouth, N.H., 1978-80; employee computer systems Inter Continental Hotels Corp., N.Y.C., 1980-88; pres. 1st Coastal Corp., Branford, Conn., 1983-85; pub. Bus. Times, New Haven, Conn., 1985—. Office: Bus Times 315 Peck St New Haven CT 06513-2933

MACCLEERY, RUSSELL ELDRIDGE, SR., lobbyist; b. Boston, Jan. 10, 1913; s. Watson Aubrey and Ethel Eldridge (Smith) MacC.; m. Georgie Lee Dawson, Feb. 19, 1953 (div. Mar. 1990); children: Russell Jr., Stephen. BS, U. Mass., 1934. Vocat. agrl. instr. various high schs., Mass., Vt., 1934-36; New Eng. rep. Nat. Hwy. Users Conf., 1936-45; mgr. state svcs. Nat. Hwy. Users Conf., Washington, 1945-59; exec. dir. N.H. Petroleum Coun., Concord, 1959-66; mgr. field svcs. dept. Mfrs. Assn., Detroit, 1966-67; sr. v.p. Mfrs. Assn., Detroit and Washington, 1967-78; cons. in govt. affairs N.H., D.C., 1978—. Mem. Chichester (N.H.) Sch. Bd., 1960-66, Bd. of Selectmen, Chichester, 1982-85, N.H. Traffic Safety Comm., Concord, 1963—; pres. Merrimack County Farm Bur., Chichester, 1963-65; v.p. N.H. Farm Bur., Concord, 1965-66. Mem. Engrs. Soc. Detroit. Republican. Methodist. Home: RR 2 Pittsfield NH 03263-9802

MACCOULL, LESLIE SHAW BAILEY, papyrologist; b. New London, Conn., Aug. 7, 1945. AB summa cum laude, Vassar Coll., 1965; MA, Yale U., 1966; PhD with honors, Cath. U., 1973. Curator Inst. Christian Oriental Rsch. Cath. U., Washington, 1973-77; dir. of studies Soc. for Coptic Archaeology, Cairo, 1978-84; sr. rsch. scholar Soc. for Coptic Archaeology, Washington, 1984—; personal asst. to Mirrit Boutros Ghali, 1978—. Author: Dioscorus of Aphrodito, 1988; contbr. numerous articles to profl. jours. Mem. Am. Soc. Papyrologists, Internat. Assn. Coptic Studies. Office: Soc Coptic Archaeology 2800 Wisconsin Ave NW Washington DC 20007

MACCOY, CLINTON VILES, biologist; b. Brookline, Mass., Mar. 27, 1905; s. William E. MacCoy; m. Mildred Seymour, Sept. 3, 1936. AB, Harvard U., 1928, AM, 1929, PhD, 1934. Asst. prof. biology U. Mass., Amherst, 1938-41; prof. biology Wheaton Coll., Norton, Mass., 1942-70; biologist Norwell (Mass.) Labs., 1970—. Editor: Bull. New Eng. Mus. Natural History, 1928-38; contbr. articles to profl. publs. Mem. conservation com. Town of Norwell, 1940-51. Mem. Am. Soc. Limnology and Oceanography, Internat. Soc. Limnology. Republican. Uniterian-Universalist. Home and Office: Norwell Labs 77 Winter St Norwell MA 02061-1413

MACCULLOUGH, MARTHA ELIZABETH, education educator; b. Bristol, Va., Dec. 2, 1940; d. Robert George and Beryl Lyda (Phipps) Kilgore; m. Donald Lansing MacCullough, June 3, 1962; children: Sheryl Ann, Debbie Lynn. BS, Phila. Coll. of Bible, 1962; MA, Wheaton Coll., 1969; EdD, Temple U., 1983. Cert. tchr. K-8 elem., K-12 profl., Pa. Tchr. Smith Meml. Schs., Phila., 1958-62; tchr., adminstr. Faith Christian Sch., Roslyn, Pa., 1964-65, 69-74; faculty Lancaster (Pa.) Bible Coll., 1974-80; faculty Phila. Coll. of Bible, 1980-84, dept. chair tchr. edn., 1984—; ednl. workshop leader Assn. Christian Schs. Internat., 1984-91, Internat. Inst. for Tchrs., Grace Coll., Winona Lake, Ind., 1983-90; retreat/seminar leader, Pa., N.J., N.Y. Contbr. articles to profl. jours. Recipient Salute to Teaching award Pa. Acad. for the Profession of Teaching, 1990. Mem. ASCD, Nat. Sci. Tchr. Assn., Assn. Tchr. Educators, Assn. Christian Tchr. Educators (v.p. 1982-85, exec. com.), Phi Delta Kappa, Delta Epsilon Chi. Republican. Office: Philadelphia Coll of Bible 200 Manor Ave Langhorne PA 19047-2990

MACCUTCHEON, EDWARD MACKIE, naval architect, ocean engineer; b. Bridgeport, Conn., Nov. 12, 1915; s. Edward Mackie and Laura (Stout) MacC.; BS, Webb Inst. Naval Arch., N.Y.C., 1937; postgrad. U. Md., 1948-49; M in Engring. Adminstrn., George Washington U., 1958; m. Jean Loeffler, June 20, 1942; children: Barbara Jean MacCutcheon Smith, Maryann MacCutcheon Lucero. Registered profl. engr., Md., D.C. With N.Y. Shipbldg. Co., Camden, N.J., 1937-38, U.S. Coast Guard, Washington, 1938-48, David Taylor Model Basin, Dept. Navy, 1948-49, Bur. Ships, 1949-55, Office of Naval Rsch., Washington, 1955-57; tech. dir. Naval Civil Engring. Lab., Port Hueneme, Calif., 1957-62; chief rsch. and devel. Maritime Adminstrn., Dept. Commerce, Washington, 1962-66; dir. systems devel., Nat. Ocean Survey, NOAA, Rockville, Md., 1966-72; cons. engr., Bethesda, Md., 1973—. Lt. comdr. USCGR, 1943-46. Fellow Soc. Naval Architects and Marine Engrs., Marine Tech. Soc.; mem. Am. Soc. Naval Engrs. Address: 6405 Earlham Dr Bethesda MD 20817

MACDONALD, BRUCE RAYMOND, urologist; b. Salem, Mass., Aug. 12, 1942; s. Raymond Septimus and Barbara (Upton) MacD.; m. Estelle Goodell, July 5, 1976; 1 child, Allexis II. BA, Washington & Lee U., 1964; MD, Med. Coll. Va., 1968. Intern, resident in surgery Med. Coll. Va., Richmond, 1968-70, resident in gen. surgery, 1972-73, resident in urology, 1973-76; attending urologist dept. surgery Bassett Hosp., Cooperstown, N.Y., 1976—; v.p. Island Peer Review Orgn., Queens, N.Y., 1988—, chmn. upstate quality review com.; mem. urology steering com. Ea. Coop. Oncology Group. Lt. comdr. USN, 1970-72. Recipinet fellowship Am. Coll. Surgeons. Mem. Am. Urol. Assn., Capital Dist. Urol. Assn., N.Y. State Urol. Assn. Office: Bassett Hosp Atwell Rd Cooperstown NY 13326

MACDONALD, DONALD STONE, international resources executive, educator; b. Boston, Mar. 28, 1919; m. Jean Carroll Macdonald; 1 child, Thomson Stone. BSBA, MIT, 1938; MA in Polit. Sci., Harvard U., 1960; PhD in Polit. Sci., George Washington U., 1978. Fgn. svc. officer U.S. Dept. State, 1947-69; prin. staff Ops. Rsch., Inc., Carlisle Barracks, Pa., 1969-71; cons. U.S. Dept. State, 1969-75; prof. polit. sci. East Stroudsburg (Pa.) U., 1971-80; coord. adv. area studies, Korea, Foreign Svc. Inst. U.S. Dept. State, 1982—; rsch. prof. Korea studies Sch. Foreign Svc., Georgetown U., Washington, 1984-89; sr. assoc. Sr. Internat. Resources, Inc., Washington, 1989—; internat. rels. officer Hdqs. U.S. Forces Korea, 1975-77; dir. Office of Intelligence Coord., U.S. Dept. State, 1980-83. Author: The Koreans: Contemporary Politics and Society, 1990; editor Mid-Atlantic Bull. of Korean Studies, 1984—; contbr. articles to profl. jours. Bd. dirs. Harbour Sq. Owners, Inc., 1987-90, S.W. Neighborhood Assy., 1982-86. Recipient Citation Comdr.-in-Chief, UN Command, 1977, John Jacob Rogers medal U.S. Dept. of State, 1983; Fulbright scholar, 1990-91. Mem. AAUP, ACLU, Am. Fgn. Svc. Assn., Am. Polit. Sci. Assn., Asia Soc., Assn. for Asian Studies (pres. Mid-Atlantic region 1984-85), Common Cause, Diplomatic and Consular Officers Retired, Internat. Studies Assn., Kings Chapel, Korean-Am. Assn., Royal Asiatic Soc., Smithsonian Resident Assocs., VFW, Rotary, Pi Sigma Alpha. Republican. Home: 1311 4th St SW Washington DC 20024-2201

MACDONALD, DUNCAN, broadcaster, writer, communications consultant; b. Beaumont, Tex.; d. William Whyte MacDonald and Martha (Schalies) Hammond. Grad. high sch., Houston. Supr. women's and religious programming DuMont TV Network, N.Y.C., 1950-53; prodr. Home show NBC-TV, N.Y.C., 1954; broadcaster Yankee Network, Boston, 1955-59, Sta. WQXR, N.Y.C., 1962-67; monthly article writer House Beautiful, N.Y.C., 1966-67, exec. asst. to editor, 1967-70; pres. The Media Group, Edgartown, Mass., 1967—; exec. dir. Nat. Friends Pub. Broadcasting, N.Y.C., 1970-72; adminstrv. aide Dukes County Commrs., Edgartown, 1976-82; features editor Martha's Vineyard (Mass.) Forum, 1983-88; mem. White House Conf. Nutrition, Washington, 1969. Author: Rain, Hail & Baked Beans, 1958; home editor Yankee Mag., 1956-63; food editor Old Farmer's Almanac, 1957-65. Founder, pres. Com. for the Ams., N.Y.C., 1963-67; trustee Nat. Coun. Women, N.Y.C., 1962-72, Am. Youth Hostels, N.Y.C., 1968-73, Am. Friends Scottish Opera, N.Y.C., 1982-87, pres., 1986-87; trustee Caledonian Found., Inc., Laurinburg, N.C., 1987—, exec. v.p., treas. Recipient UN Children's Fund award UNICEF, 1957, citation Pres.'s Com. on Aid to Physically Handicapped, 1957, citation OAS, 1970. Mem. Am. Women in Radio and TV (pres. N.Y.C. chpt.), Overseas Press Club. Baptist. Address: PO Box 1242 Edgartown MA 02539

MACDONALD, GARY BRUCE, communications executive; b. Spokane, Wash., Apr. 17, 1950; s. William and Thelma (Wilhelm) MacD.; m. Joy Bea Fukumoto, June 1973 (div. Dec. 1980). BA, Fairhaven Coll., 1973. Fgn. svc. officer U.S. Info. Agy., Washington, 1976-84; asst. cultural attache U.S. Embassy, Rabat, Morocco, 1977-78; dir. Am. Cultural Ctr., Damascus, Syria, 1978-82; planning officer Office Acad. Programs, Washington, 1982-83; country affairs officer Office of N. African Near Eastern and South Asian Affairs, Washington, 1983-84; exec. dir. AIDS Action Coun., Washington, 1984-87; coord. Asia/Near East programs AIDSCOM Acad. Ednl. Devel., Washington, 1987-91; dep. dir. Acad. Ednl. Devel. AIDS Communication Support, Washington, 1991—; cons. U.S. Agy. for Internat. Devel., Washington, 1987-89, WHO, Geneva, 1987, Pan Am. Health Orgn., Mexico City, 1987, govts. of Philippines, Thailand, Indonesia, 1987-89. Editor: Five Experimental Colleges, 1973; contbr. articles to profl. jours. Clark county coord. Youth for McCarthy, Vancouver, Washington, 1968; v.p. Gay Activists Alliance, Washington, 1983-84; chmn. com. on human rels. Met. Police, Washington, 1985. Recipient Pub. Svc. award Franklin E. Kameny, 1985, Cert. of Honor City and County of San Francisco, 1986, Harvey Milk Pub. Svc. award Nat. Gay and Lesbian Health Found., 1987, Alumni Fellow award Fairhaven Coll., 1991. Office: Acad Ednl Devel 1255 23rd St NW Washington DC 20037

MACDONALD, JAMES KENNEDY, JR., executive search consultant; b. Providence, Mar. 6, 1956; s. James Kennedy and Virginia (Spargo) M.; m. Julie Ann Kuhn, Jan. 2, 1988. BA, Yale U., 1978; MBA, Cornell U., 1984; postgrad., N.Y. Law Sch., 1985. Tchr. Westminster Sch., Simsbury, Conn., 1978-79; systems support analyst The New Eng., Boston, 1979-82; pers./labor rels. adminstr. Nat. Broadcasting Co., Inc., N.Y.C., 1984-87; cons./assoc. Russell Reynolds Assocs., Inc., N.Y.C., 1987-89, chief of staff, 1990—. Mem. dean's alumni exec. coun. The Johnson Sch.-Cornell U., 1987-89, class officer, 1989—; devel. com. Stamford (Conn.) Ctr. for the Arts, 1989—; active United Way, 1982-90, mem. chmn.'s campaign cabinet, 1987; mem. alumni schs. com. Yale U., 1988—, hockey bd. dirs., 1984—. Francis Ouimette Caddie scholar, 1974-77; The Johnson Sch.-Cornell U. scholar, 1982-84. Mem. Southwestern Area Conf. of Ind. Assns. (pres. search com. 1990, pub. policy task force 1990), Yale Club of N.Y.C. (admissions com. 1985-87). Office: Russell Reynolds Assocs 200 Park Ave New York NY 10166-0005

MACDONALD, JEROME EDWARD, consultant, school psychologist; b. Newark, Aug. 16, 1925; s. Jerome A. and Olvinia Regina (McKenna) MacD.; m. Nan Elizabeth Kennington, June 2, 1951; children: Jerome C., Mary Jane, Charles, Blanche Kohler, Ruth, Gregory, Paul, Robert, Carol. BS, Niagara U., 1947, MA (grad. fellow), 1950; MA in Ednl. Psychology (experienced tchr. fellow), profl. diploma in sch. psychology, Jersey City State Coll., 1970; postgrad., Fordham U., 1950-55. Asst. prof. philosophy Seton Hall U., South Orange, N.J., 1948-55; lectr. in philosophy, edn. Seton Hall U., South Orange, 1955-61; tchr. English Newark Pub. Schs., 1955-60, guidance counselor, 1960-62, chmn. dept., 1963-69, psychologist, 1969-71; psychologist Metuchen (N.J.) Pub. Schs., 1971-86; vis. tchr. NDEA Reading Inst. Bowling Green (Ohio) U., 1966-67; extern psychologist N.J. Diagnostic Ctr., Menlo Park, 1969; consulting psychologist Dept. Health and Social Svcs., Province of Prince Edward Island, Can., 1987—. Editor: (with Eli Levinson) The English Curriculum in Secondary Schools: Ninth Grade, 1964. Troop treas. Boy Scouts Am., 1967-69. With inf., AUS, 1943-46. Decorated Bronze Star medal. Mem. Nat. Assn. Sch. Psychologists, Internat. Reading Assn., NEA, Am. Psychol. Assn., N.J. Psychol. Assn., N.J. Assn. Sch. Psychologists, Middlesex County Sch. Psychologists Assn. (pres. 1976-77, 81-82), Psychol. Assn. Prince Edward Island, N.J. Catholic Tchrs. Guild (pres. 1966), VFW, Am. Legion, DAV, Holy Name Soc., Can. Legion, Mensa, Phi Delta Kappa, Lions. Roman Catholic. Home: 1 MacDonald Rd Cavendish, PO Box 71, North Rustico, PE Canada C0A 1X0

MACDONALD, JOHN A., newspaper reporter, columnist; b. Columbus, Ohio, Aug. 12, 1943; s. Frank J. and Ruth K. MacD.; m. Georgia Paul, June 18, 1966; 1 child, Daniel. BA, Ohio State U., 1965, MA, 1967; cert. in Asian studies, U. Hawaii, 1979. Reporter, editor Akron (Ohio) Beacon Jour., 1969-73, Courier-Jour., Louisville, 1973-84; nat. editor Hartford (Conn.) Courant, 1984-86, sr. Washington corr., 1986—. 1st lt. U.S. Army, 1965-71, Vietnam. Office: Hartford Courant Ste 300 1730 Rhode Island Ave NW Washington DC 20036

MACDONALD, JOHN COURY, lawyer; b. Ft. Myers, Fla., May 14, 1966; s. John William and Darlene J. M. AA in Polit. Sci., U. S. Fla., Tampa, 1985; BA in Polit. Sci., U. S. Fla., 1986; JD, Nova U., Ft. Lauderdale, Fla., 1989; LLM in Internat. Trade & Banking, Am. U., Washington, 1990. Bar: Fla. 1990, D.C. 1991. Intern Congressman Connie Mack, Washington, summer 1988; atty. Legal Assets Corp., Washington, 1989; atty. legal counsel's office Exec. Office of U.S. Attys. U.S. Dept. of Justice, Washington, 1989-91; assoc. Sedam & Emerson, P.C., Washington, 1991—. Contbr. articles to profl. jours. Student liaison and rep. Youth for Understanding, Washington, 1983-89. Toyota Motor Sales scholar, 1983. Mem. Am. Soc. Internat. Law, Internat. Law Soc. (sec. 1986-89), Japan-Am. Soc. of Cen. Fla., Fed. Am. Inn of Ct., Zeta Chi (founder, chmn. 1984-86), Phi Alpha Delta. Republican. Baptist. Home: PO Box 18123 Washington DC 20036-8123

MACDONALD, KAREN CRANE, occupational therapist, geriatric counselor; b. Denville, N.J., Feb. 24, 1955; d. Robert William and Jeanette Wilcox (Crane) M. BS, Quinnipiac Coll., 1977; MS, U. Bridgeport, 1982; postgrad., NYU, 1983—. Cert. occupational therapist. Occupational therapist, coord. of spl. care unit Jewish Home for the Elderly, Conn., 1987—, N.Y. Inst., N.Y.C., 1984-86; pvt. practice Fairfield County, Conn., 1977-88; instr. NYU, 1985-89, Quinnipiac Coll., 1986—; lectr., cons. in field. Contbr. articles to profl. jours. Youth leader, deacon Union Meml. Ch., Stamford, Conn., 1980-88; deacon Southport Congl. Ch., 1992—. Teaching fellow NYU, 1983-86. Mem. World Fedn. Occupational Therapy, Am. Occupational Therapy Assn. (scholar 1985, coun. edn.), Conn. Occupational Therapy Assn. (gerontology liaison 1980-83). Home: 2600 Park Ave Apt 3Y Bridgeport CT 06604-1352 Office: Jewish Home for Elderly 175 Jefferson St Fairfield CT 06432-1098

MACDONALD, MARCELLA ANNE, podiatrist; b. Manchester, Conn., Nov. 24, 1963; d. John H. and Teresa M. (Lashenske) MacD. BA, Am. Internat. Coll., 1985; D Podiatric Medicine, N.Y. Coll. Podiatric Medicine, 1989. Pvt. practice N.Y.C., 1989—, Manchester, Conn., 1991. Mem. N.Y. State Podiatric Med. Assn. Roman Catholic. Home: 158 Mckee St Manchester CT 06040-4828

MACDONALD, MARK DOUGLAS, counselor, teacher; b. Erie, Pa., Dec. 30, 1955; s. Richard Allen, Sr. and Sarah Louise (Young) MacD.; M. Kim Elaine MacDonald, Feb. 22, 1975 (div. July 1984); children: Nicole Marie, Claire Allison. BS in Sec. Edn., Clarion U., Pa., 1973-77; Med. Off. Comp., Mercyhurst Coll., erie, Pa., 1984-85; New Testament Course, Schofield Bible Inst., Chgo., 1982-85; MA in Guidance Counseling, Edinboro U., 1991. Instrnl. I. Tchr. Millcreek Sch. Dist., Erie, Pa., 1977-79; yard clk. Union Railroad, Pitts., 1979-85; co-dir. of youth New Life Ctr., Erie, Pa., 1986-88; tchr. Vision Quest, Franklin, Pa., 1988-89; counselor Harborcreek Youth Svc., Erie, Pa., 1989—; lifeguard and water safety instr., Red Cross, Erie, Pa., 1985—. Recipient Eagle award, Boy Scouts of Am., Erie, Pa., 1972, PTA Acad. Scholarship, Millcreek PTA, Erie, Pa., 1973-77. Mem. AACD, ASCA. Democrat. Presbyterian. Home: 3358 W 42nd St Erie PA 16506-4226

MACDONALD, R. FULTON, venture developer, business educator; b. Monmouth County, N.J., Dec. 24, 1940; s. James Fleming Smith Macdonald and Jane Macfarlane Barnes Abbott; m. Carol Jean Archer (div.); 1 child, Paige Brubaker Smith; m. Laura Boswell; children: George Dewey Boswell, James Fleming Smith Macdonald II. AB, U. Pa., 1963, MBA, 1969; postgrad. sr. mktg. mgmt., Stanford U., 1979. Systems mgr., mcht. John Wanamaker, Inc., Phila., 1969-74; prin. Booz, Allen & Hamilton, N.Y.C., 1974-79; pres. Irwill Industries, N.Y.C., 1979-82, Internat. Bus. Devel. Corp., N.Y.C., 1982—; chmn. IBEX Mktg. Corp., N.Y.C., 1988—; pres. Simfer Operatinal Internat., Inc., N.Y.C., 1984; vice chmn. Neusteter Co., Denver, 1984-85; dir. Fragrances Selective, Inc., 1985-87; mng. dir. Stuyvesant Group Internat., Dutch Am. Bus. Advisors, N.Y.C. and Amsterdam, 1987-88; chmn. Am. Bus. Media, Inc., 1989-90; adj. prof. Grad. Bus. Sch., Columbia U., N.Y.C., 1984-85, Mgmt. Inst. NYU, 1992—. Designer Manpower Mgmt. Concepts computer system, 1972—; contbr. articles to bus. publs. Capt. inf. U.S. Army, 1963-67, Vietnam. Decorated Bronze Star. Mem. Ripon Soc., Inst. Mgmt. Consultants (cert. mgmt. cons. 1989), Global Econ. Action Inst., Soc. Mayflower Descendants, Soc. Coll. Alumni U. Pa. (pres. 1973-74, bd. mgrs. 1975—). Republican. Christian Scientist. Home: Trump Tower 721 Fifth Ave New York NY 10022-2523 Office: Internat Bus Devel Corp 237 Park 21st Ave New York NY 10017-3142

MACDONALD, ROBERT BRUCE, county official; b. Delhi, N.Y., Dec. 28, 1930; s. Ernest Jamison and Daisy (Beers) MacD.; m. Ferne Huffman, Aug. 17, 1965; 1 child, Robert Bruce II. BS Govt., Pub. Adminstrn., Am. Univ., 1961; postgrad., U. Okla., 1981-83. Enlisted USAF, 1950-59; adminstrv. officer U.S. Govt., Washington, 1961-68; asst. to assoc. adminstr. rsch. and devel. Nat. Hwy. Traffic Safety Adminstrn., Washington, 1968-78; exec. dir. Delaware County Indsl. Devel. Agy., Delhi, N.Y., 1978—. Mem. SUNY Bus. & Industry Counsel, So. Tier East Planning and Devel. Bd., Econ. Devel. Com., Kiwanis (pres. Delhi chpt. 1984-85). Home: 41 Delview Ter Delhi NY 13753-1055 Office: Delaware County Indsl Devel Agy PO Box 506 Delhi NY 13753-0506

MACDONALD, ROBERT RIGG, JR., museum director; b. Pitts., May 11, 1942; s. Robert Rigg and Ruth (Johnson) M.; m. Catherine Ronan, Nov. 27, 1965; children: Matthew, Robert, Catherine. B.A., U. Notre Dame, 1964, M.A., 1965; M.A., U. Pa., 1970. Asst. curator Smithsonian Instn., Washington, 1965; curator Mercer Mus., Doylestown, Pa., 1966-70; dir. New Haven Colony Hist. Soc., 1970-74, La. State Mus., New Orleans, 1974-85, Mus. of City of N.Y., 1985—; adj. prof. mus. studies NYU, 1989—; mem. Commn. on Mus. for a New Century. Editor: New Haven Colony Furniture, 1973, Louisiana Images 1880-1920, 1975, Louisiana Black Heritage, 1977, Louisiana Portraitures, 1979, Louisiana Legal Heritage, 1981, The Sun King: Louis XIV and the New World, On Being Homeless in New York, 1987, Broadway! 125 Years of Musical Theater. Active Nat. Endowment for Humanities. Decorated chevalier de l'Ordre des Arts et des Lettres (France), cruz de Caballero de la Order de Isabel La Catolica (Spain); assoc. fellow Berkeley Coll., Yale U., 1978; Hagley fellow U. Del., 1970-71; Univ. scholar U. Notre Dame, 1964-65. Mem. Am. Assn. State and Local History (coun.), Am. Assn. Mus. (pres. 1985-88, chmn. ethics task force 1988-91), Century Assn. Roman Catholic. Home: 35 Edgewood Ln Bronxville NY 10708-1946 Office: Mus NYC Fifth Ave at 103rd St New York NY 10029

MACDONALD, ROD, singer, songwriter; b. Southington, Conn., Aug. 17, 1948; s. Harold Owen and B. Joan (Walsh) MacD. BA with high honors, U. Va., 1970; JD, Columbia U., 1973. Reporter Hartford (Conn.) Courant, 1969-70; bur. corres. Newsweek, Atlanta, Washington, 1970-71; singer-songwriter Greenwich Village, N.Y.C., 1973—; music dir. N.Y. Musicians Coop., Greenwich Village, N.Y.C., 1982-85; recording artist Cinemagic Records, Greenwich Village, N.Y.C., 1983-87, Brambus Records, Chur, Switzerland, 1989—, Mountain R.R. Records, Venice, Calif., 1987-90, Shanachie Records, Newtown, N.J., 1991—; producer, pres. Greenwich Village Folk Festival, 1987—; lead singer The Hitchikers, Gradisca, Italy, 1989—; pres. Blue Flute Music, N.Y.C., 1980—. Contbg. editor: Fast Folk Music Mag., N.Y.C., 1983—; singer/composer record albums: No Commercial Traffic, 1983, White Buffalo, 1987, Bring on the Lions, 1989, Highway to Nowhere, 1992. Benefit artist Greennpeace, Greenwich Village Coalition Against Nuclear Arms, 1985—. Mem. Am. Soc. Composers and Pubrs. Home: 114 MacDougal St # 2 New York NY 10012 Office: PO Box 262 Harvard MA 01451

MACDONALD, RONALD FRANCIS, securities insurance company executive; b. Detroit, July 23, 1946; s. Alfred and Marianne Dorothy (Paddock) Mac.; m. Harriet Pratt Higgins, Dec. 18, 1982; children: John Higgins, Peter Brewer. BS, U. Detroit, 1968; MBA, Mich. State U., 1970. V.p. Northern Trust Co., Chgo., 1970-84, Bankers Trust Co., N.Y.C., 1984-89; sr. v.p. Capital Markets Assurance Corp., N.Y.C., 1989—. Treas./dir. 829 Park Ave Corp., N.Y., 1988—. Mem. N.Y. Athletic Club, Royal Oak Soc. Roman Catholic. Home: 829 Park Ave New York NY 10021-2846

MACDONALD, SHARON ETHEL, dancer; b. Pittsfield, Mass., Mar. 24, 1952; d. Harry and Angeline (Saracco) MacD. BA, Skidmore Coll., 1974; MA, Smith Coll., 1992. Faculty Smith Coll., Northampton, Mass., 1974-76; dancer, tchr. Berkshire Ballet, Pittsfield, 1976-77; dance dir. Becket (Mass.)

Arts Ctr., Mass., 1977-80; faculty mem. Williams Coll., Williamstown, Mass., 1979-80; co-artistic dir., owner N.E. Am. Ballet, Northampton, 1980-85; devel. dir., tchr. Berkshire Ballet, Pittsfield, 1984-85; adminstr., tchr. Hartford (Conn.) Ballet, Inc., 1985-90; asst. choreographer Easthampton Mass. Community Theatre Assn., 1981-83, Project Opera, 1982; bd. dirs. Jacob's Pillow Dance Festival, Becket, 1978-81; bd. trustees Becket Arts Ctr., 1979-80; tchr. Trinity Coll., Hartford, Conn., 1990—; guest artist numerous pub. schs., pvt. studios, colls., and univs. Pres. Friends of Jacob's Pillow, Becket, 1978-81, Friends of the Hartford Ballet, 1988—, Jacob's Pillow Alumnae/Archives Com., 1988—, Dance History Scholars, 1976-79, 91—. Mass. Arts Lottery Grantee Mass. Arts Coun., 1984, Arts Lottery Grantee Northampton Arts Coun., 1984; Smith Coll. Fellow. Mem. AAHPERD, Nat. Dance Assn., Congress for Rsch. in Dance. Democrat. Baptist. Home: PO Box 697 Stockbridge MA 01262-0697

MACDONALL, JAMES SINCLAIR, psychology educator; b. N.Y.C., July 14, 1946; s. Donald Angus and Maye Vance (Sinclair) MacD.; m. Marilyn Lois Fartely, July 31, 1982; 1 child, Scott. BA, Oglethorpe U., 1970; MA, Boston U., 1973, PhD, 1976. Research psychologist Washingtonian Ctr. for Addictions, Boston, 1975-78; asst. prof. Fordham U., Bronx, N.Y., 1978—; scientist, cons. Boston U., 1978-80; cons. Montefiore Hosp. Med. Ctr., Bronx, 1986-88, N.Y. State Psychiat. Inst., 1987—. Contbr. numerous articles to profl. jours. Research grantee Nat. Inst. Alcoholic Abuse and Alcoholism, 1982; equipment grantee Digital Equipment Corp., 1983. Mem. Am. Psychol. Soc., Ea. Psychol. Assn., Psychonomic Soc., Soc. for Neurosci., Trout Unltd., Fedn. Fly Fishers, Theodore Gordon Flyfishers (bd. dirs.), Sigma Xi. Home: 52 Washington Pl Hasbrouck Heights NJ 07604-1220 Office: Fordham U Psychology Dept Bronx NY 10458

MACDONELL, CAMERON, graphic artist, wood carver; b. Elmira, N.Y., May 29, 1938; s. Gerald Angus and Mary (Yedenek) MacD. BS in Art Edn., SUNY, Buffalo, 1961. Art tchr. Owego (N.Y.) Cen. Sch., 1961-63, Corning/Painted Post (N.Y.) Cen. Sch., 1963-71; graphic artist Signs-660, Galeta, Calif., 1971-76; mgr. Sign Shop, Elmira, 1984-91; owner, operator Studio 605, Elmira, 1991—; art dir. Art Made Famous, Galeta, 1976-79; vocat. instr. Assn. for Retarded Citizens, Elmira, 1979-84. Designer medalion for Santa Barbara (Calif.) County Bicentenial, 1976; executed mural Komer Ctr., Elmira, 1991, Midtown Pla., Elmira, 1991; designer Arctic League telethon backdrop Clemens Ctr., Elmira, 1991, scenery for Halina Sch. Dance Arts, 1991; paintings represented in numerous pvt. collections. Founder Elmira's Ann. Chmn. Arts in the Park, So. Tier Arts Assn., Elmira, 1975. Home and Office: Studio 605 Yale St Elmira NY 14904-2641

MACDOUGALL, HUGH COOKE, diplomat, historian; b. Boston, Aug. 30, 1932; s. C. Hugh and C. Ursula (Cooke) MacD.; m. Eleanore Taylor Ellsworth, Dec. 26, 1970. AB, Harvard U., 1954; MA, JD, Columbia U., 1958. Bar: N.Y. 1959. Fgn. svc. officer U.S. Dept. of State, 1958-81; counselor polit. and econ. affairs Am. Embassy, Rangoon, Burma, 1981-84; coord. polit. studies Fgn. Svc. Inst., Washington, 1984-86, ret., 1986. Author: Cooper's Otsego County, 1989; editor: (periodical) Burma Press Summary, 1987—. Mem. Cooperstown (N.Y.) Planning Bd., 1988-91; trustee Village of Cooperstown, 1988-91; bd. dirs. Friends of Cooperstown Libr., 1987—, Burma Studies Found., 1990—; bd. dirs. Cooperstown Art Assn., 1987—, vol. councilor, 1991—. Mem. James Fenimore Cooper Soc. (sec.-treas. 1989—), Otsego 2000 (bd. dirs. 1988—), Rotary (bd. dirs. Cooperstown 1988-89). Democrat. Episcopalian. Home: 32 Elm St Cooperstown NY 13326-1214

MAC DOWELL, SAMUEL WALLACE, physics educator; b. Camaragibe, Brazil, Mar. 24, 1929; came to U.S., 1963; s. Samuel Wallace and Maria Anita (Amazonas) Mac D.; m. Myriam Ramos Da Silva, Feb. 2, 1953; children: Ana Myriam, Samuel Wallace, Maria Dolores. BSc in Engring., U. Pernambuco, Brazil, 1951; PhD in Math. Physics, Birmingham (Eng.) U., 1958. Rsch. assoc. Princeton (N.J.) U., 1959-60; assoc. prof. Centro Brasileiro De Fisicas Pesquisas, Rio de Janeiro, 1960-63; fellow Inst. for Advanced Study, Princeton, 1963-65; assoc. prof. Yale U., New Haven, 1965-67, prof., 1968—. Fellow Am. Phys. Soc.; mem. Brazilian Acad. Scis. Roman Catholic. Office: Yale U Sloane Physics Lab PO Box 6666 New Haven CT 06511-8101

MACER-STORY, EUGENIA ANN, writer, artist; b. Mpls., Jan. 20, 1945; d. Dan Johnstone and Eugenia Loretta (Andrews) Macer; divorced; 1 child, Ezra Arthur Story. BS in Speech, Northwestern U., 1965; MFA, Columbia U., 1968. Writing instr. Polyarts, Boston, 1970-72; theater instr. Joy of Movement, Boston, 1972-75; artistic dir. Magik Mirror, Salem, Mass., 1975-76, Magick Mirror Communications, 1977—. Author: Congratulations: The UFO Reality, 1978, Angels of Time, 1982, Project Midas, 1986, Dr. Fu Man Chu Meets the Lonesome Cowboy: Sorcery and the UFO Experience, 1991, 2d edit., 1992, Gypsy Fair, 1991, The Strawberry Man, 1991; (plays) Fetching the Tree, Archeological Politics, Strange Inquiries, Divine Appliance, 1989, The Zig Zag Wall, 1990, The Only Qualified Huntress, 1990, Telephone Taps Written up for Tabloids, 1991, Wars with Pigeons, 1992, others; philosophy writer; contbr. articles to profl. jours.; author poetry in Woodstock Times, Lamia Ink!, Manhattan Poetry Rev., others; feature writer, editorial cons. Body, Mind, Spirit mag., Anomalous Encounters mag. Shubert fellow, 1968. Mem. AAAS, Dramatists Guild, N.Y. Acad. Sci., U.S. Psychotronics Assn., Ctr. for UFO Studies. Democrat. Office: Magick Mirror Communications PO Box 741 New York NY 10116-0741

MACEWAN, CRAIG EDWARD, small business owner; b. Glens Falls, N.Y., Aug. 4, 1954; s. Auger Adolf and Marion Elsie (Smith) MacE.; m. Honey Lynn Miller, Aug. 31, 1985; 1 child, Salvatore. Cert., Internat. Corrs. Sch., 1975, Computervision Sch., 1984, Adirondack Community Coll., Glens Falls, 1991. Engring. technician Kamyr, Inc., Glens Falls, 1973-78, from graphic artist to systems designer, 1978-81, from cadd designer to rsch. and devel. cadd designer, 1981-90; v.p., chief oper. officer Temploy, Inc., Queensbury, N.Y., 1987—. Active Ch. the Messiah, Glens Falls, 1984—. Mem. Nat. Assn. Temproary Svcs., Nat. Fedn. Ind. Bus., Tech. Assn. Pulp & Paper Industry, Adirondack Regional C. of C., Queensbury Businessmans Assn. Republican. Episcopalian. Office: Temploy Inc 76 Quaker Rd Quaker Vill Queensbury NY 12804

MACFADDEN, PATRICIA ANN LAURA, bookseller; b. Brantford, Ont., Can., Aug. 12, 1936; d. F.A. Ray and Victoria R. (Harvey) MacF; m. E.W. Trasewick, July 30, 1960 (div. 1984); children: Timothy Alexander, Stephanie Ann. BA, U. Toronto (Can.), 1960. Investment researcher Fin. Post Corp. Svc., Toronto, 1960-61; investment analyst Merrill Lynch, Toronto, 1961-62, Elliott & Page, Toronto, 1962-64; mgr., proprietor Old Niagara Bookshop, Niagara on the Lake, Ont., Can., 1969—. Mem. Univ. Women's Club of Toronto. Anglican. Home: 45 The Promenade, Niagara on the Lake, ON Canada L0S 1J0 Office: Old Niagara Bookshop, 44 Queen St, Niagara on the Lake, ON Canada L0S 1J0

MAC GILLIS, ROBERT DONALD, artist; b. Bayonne, N.J., June 30, 1936; s. Angus Roy and Catherine Ellen (Bull) Mac G.; m. Marie Eugenia Sharkey, Jan. 9, 1960; children: Linda Ann, Mary Therese, Robert Martin, Dawn Marie, Eugene Thomas, Doreen Ellen. Indsl. artist electric boat div. Gen. Dynamics, Groton, Conn., 1960-76; profl. artist Groton, 1976—. With U.S. Army, 1956-58. Recipient over 70 nat. and regional awards in various juried exhibits. Mem. Hudson Valley Art Assn., Acad. Art Assn., Conn. Watercolor Soc., Salmagundi Club, KC (grand knight 1964-65). Roman Catholic. Home: 96 School St Groton CT 06340-3941

MACGUIGAN, MARK R., Canadian federal judge; b. Charlottetown, P.E.I., Can., Feb. 17, 1931; s. Mark R. MacG.; m. Maryellen MacGuigan, June 17, 1961 (div.); children: Ellen, Mark, Thomas; m. Patricia D. Robinson, Dec. 26, 1987. BA, St. Dunstan's U., 1951; MA, U. Toronto, 1953, PhD, 1957; LLB, York U., Toronto, 1958; LLM, Columbia U., 1959, JSD, 1961; LLD, U. P.E.I., 1971, St. Thomas U., 1981, U. Windsor, 1983, Law Soc. Upper Can., 1983. Called to Ont. bar, 1958. Read law with Hon. Mr. Justice Arthur Kelly, 1956-58; asst. prof. law U. Toronto, 1960-63, assoc. prof., 1963-66; vis. assoc. prof. criminal law NYU, 1966; prof. law Osgoode Hall Law Sch., 1966-67; dean Faculty of Law U. Windsor, 1967-68; mem. Fed. Govt. Spl. Com. on Hate Propaganda, 1965-66; advisor to Fed. Govt. Spl. Counsel on Constn., 1967-68; constl. advisor to Gov. P.E.I., 1968; mem. Ho. of Commons for Windsor-Walkerville, 1968-84, chmn. spl. com. on statutory instruments, 1968-69, chmn. spl. joint com. on constn. Can., 1970-72; parliamentary sec. to Minister of Labour, 1974-75, chmn. standing com. on justice and legal affairs, 1975-79; chmn. subcom. on penitentiary system in Can., 1976-77, chmn. spl. joint com. on constn. Can., 1978, opposition critic for solicitor-gen., 1979, Sec. of State for External Affairs, 1980-82, minister of justice, 1982-84; judge Fed. Ct. Appeal, Ottawa, 1984—. Office: Fed Ct Can, Kent & Wellington Sts, Ottawa, ON Canada K1A 0H9

MACGUNNIGLE, BRUCE CAMPBELL, manufacturing company executive; b. Providence, Mar. 18, 1947; s. Douglas Campbell and Dorothy Stewart (Greene) McGunigle; m. Kathleen Marie Walsh, Aug. 4, 1973; children: Douglas Campbell II, Alison Campbell. BS, U. R.I., 1970. From export credit mgr. to export sales mgr. Brown & Sharpe Mfg. Co., North Kingstown, R.I., 1982-89; bus. mgr. W.R. Cobb Co., Cranston, R.I., 1989—; dir. Varnum House Mus., East Greenwich, R.I., 1990—. Author: Rhode Island Freemen 1747-1755; A Census of Registered Voters, 1976, Docents' Guide to the James Mitchell Varnum House Museum, 1989, Mayflower Families, Vol. 4, 1990, Edward Fuller and His Descendants for Five Generations, East Greenwich Rhode Island Historical Cemetery Inscriptions, 1991; editor: New England's Victory at Louisburg in 1745, 1986, Rhode Islanders Misbehave at Surinam in 1744: A Complaint Against the Captain and Crew of the Prince Charles of Loraine of Bristol, Rhode Island, 1987, Carnage at Cartagena: Captain William Hopkins and His Rhode Island Recruits in the Campaign Against Cartagena and Cuba 1741, 1988, John Brown of Providence and His Chariot, 1989, Delenda est Canada--Canada Must be Conquered, 1990, Red Coats and Yellow Fever: Rhode Island Troops at the Siege of Havana 1762, 1991. Bd. dirs. East Greenwich Preservation Soc., 1984—; vestry mem. St. Martin's Episcopal Ch., Providence, 1973-76, St. Luke's Episcopal Ch., East Greenwich, 1984-86; exec. com. mem. Varnum Continentals, East Greenwich, 1986—; mem. Troop 2 com., Boy Scouts Am., East Greenwich, 1988—; mem. Hist. Dist. Commn., East Greenwich, 1982—. Mem. Soc. Mayflower Descendants (gov. 1986-89, capt. gen. 1987-90), New Eng. Hist. and Geneal. Soc., R.I. Soc. Colonial Wars (historian 1984—), R.I. Geneal. Soc. (pres. 1980-83), R.I. Hist. Soc. Huguenot Soc. R.I. (pres. 1989—), East Greenwich Vet. Firemen's Assn., Providence Art Club, Univ. Club Providence. Home: 80 Rector St East Greenwich RI 02818-3313 Office: WR Cobb Co 850 Wellington Ave Cranston RI 02910-3729

MACH, LETA MARIE, communications specialist; b. Detroit, June 6, 1947; d. Theodore Louis and Martha Marie (Nordstrom) Cogut; m. Darrell Lee Mach, Aug. 17, 1968; children: Ryan Lee, Amy Marie. BA, Mich. State U., 1969. Tchr. Prince George's County Pub. Schs., Md., 1969-73; freelance writer Greenbelt, Md., 1973-82; info. specialist Greenbelt Homes, Inc., 1982-87; publs. mgr. Nat. Coop. Bus. Assn., Washington, 1987-88, communications dir., 1988—. Co-author: (book) Greenbelt: History of a New Town, 1988, Going Places in Washington with Children, 1988. Pres. Eleanor Roosevelt Parent Tchr. Student Assn., Greenbelt, Md., 1992—. Mem. Prince George's County Pub. Rels. Soc., Coop. Communicators Assn. (3rd pl. video award 1991). Office: Nat Coop Bus Assn 1401 New York Ave NW Ste 1100 Washington DC 20005-2115

MACHADO, JAIME ULISES, architect, designer, artist, photographer; b. Quito, Eduador, Nov. 30, 1962; m. Anne Elizabeth Scarano. BArch, Syracuse U., 1986. Project leader, designer Mario Campi Archtl. Exhibit, Syracuse, N.Y., 1985-86; archtl. designer Rose, Beaton & Rose, White Plains, N.Y., 1986-91; architect Ebasco Infrastructure, N.Y.C., 1991—. Author house designs, numerous art paintings. Mem. AIA, Nat. Hist. Soc., KC.

MACHANIC, HARMON JACK, radiologist; b. Burlington, Vt., Feb. 2, 1923; s. Morris Robert and Rose (Levin) M.; B.S., U. Vt., 1944, M.D., 1946; m. Betty Hetler, Sept. 13, 1965; children—Mindy R., Scott L. Intern, Jewish Hosp. Bklyn., 1946, resident in radiology, 1950-53; resident in pulmonary diseases Montefiore Hosp., Bronx, N.Y., 1950-53; chief radiologist Divine Providence Hosp., Williamsport, Pa., 1953-84; radiologist Troy (Pa.) Community Hosp., 1972-84, North Penn Health Services, Inc., Blossburg, Pa., 1979-84; cons. radiologist Eastern Fed. Penitentiary, Lewisburg, Pa., 1965-68; radiologist Muncy (Pa.) Valley Hosp., 1963-72; dir. radiologic tech. program Williamsport Area Community Coll., 1971-84. Pres., Lycoming County unit Am. Cancer Soc.; bd. mgrs. Divine Providence Hosp., 1974-80. Served with U.S. Army, 1942-46. Diplomate Am. Bd. Radiology. Fellow Am., Internat. colls. radiology, Am. Geriatrics Soc.; mem. AMA, N.Am., Pa. radiol. socs., Lycoming Radiology Assn. (pres. 1974-84), Pa. (ho. of dels. 1973-84), Lycoming County (bd. censors 1979, pres. 1982) med. socs. Republican. Home: 2001 SE Giffen Ave Port Saint Lucie FL 34952-5823 Office: 2002 SE Giffen Ave Port Saint Lucie FL 34952-5824

MACHIAVERNA, FRANK EDWARD, surgeon; b. Newark, Jan. 1, 1951; s. Frank Howard and Muriel Marie (Price) M.; m. Christene Lee DeWitt, June 27, 1981; children: Jennifer, Jeffrey. BS in Pharmacy, Temple U., 1976; AOA (hon.), Univ. Med./Dental N.J., 1979, MD, 1980. Diplomate Am. Bd. Surgery. Resident Univ. Med./Dental N.J., Newark, 1980-85; attending surgeon Med. Ctr. Ocean Co., Point Pleasant, N.J., 1985—. Bd. dirs. Brielle (N.J.) Bd. Edn., 1991. With USN, 1969-70. Mem. Med. Soc. N.J., Ocean County Med. Soc., Rho Chi. Republican. Methodist. Office: 2701 Hwy 70 Manasquan NJ 08736

MACHINSKI, MICHAEL FRANCIS, controller, finance company executive; b. Scranton, Pa., Aug. 11, 1950; s. Henry C. and Marie Rose (Sabatini) M. BS in Acctg. cum laude, U. Scranton, 1972. CPA, N.Y. Audit supr. Touche Ross & Co., N.Y.C., 1972-80; controller, N. Am. Sea Containers Group, N.Y.C., 1980-82; controller, v.p. fin. and acctg. Russell Reynolds Assocs., Inc., N.Y.C., 1982—. Bd. dirs., treas. Valley Ponds Homeowners' Assn., Inc., Wayne, N.J., 1987—, pres., 1985-86; mem. Assn. Condominiums and Townhomes, Wayne, 1988-89. Recipient Wall Street Jour. award, U. Scranton, 1972. Mem. AICPA, N.Y. State Soc. CPAs. Republican. Roman Catholic. Home: 45 Pond Cir Wayne NJ 07470-3560 Office: Russell Reynolds Assocs Inc 200 Park Ave New York NY 10166-0005

MACHLOWITZ, MARILYN MARCIA, business executive; b. Phila.; d. Roy A. and Eleanore (Levin) M.; m. Edward C. Katz, Jan. 5, 1986; 1 child, Karen N. AB, Princeton U., 1974; PhD, Yale U., 1978. Cons., mgr. N.Y. Life Ins. Co., N.Y.C., 1978-80; cons. N.Y.C., 1981-89; exec. dir., corporate bd. resource Catalyst, N.Y.C., 1989—. Author: Workaholics, 1980, Inside Moves, 1984, Whiz Kids, 1985. Office: Catalyst 250 Park Ave S New York NY 10003-1402

MACHOVER, CARL, computer graphics consultant; b. Bklyn., Mar. 26, 1927; s. John Herman and Rose (Alter) M.; m. Wilma Doris Simon, June 18, 1950; children: Tod, Julie, Linda. BEE, Rensselaer Poly. Inst., 1951; postgrad., NYU, 1953-56. Mgr. applied engring. Norden div. United A/C Corp., 1951-59; mgr. sales Skiatron Electronics & TV, N.Y.C., 1959-60; v.p. mktg., dir. Info. Displays, Inc. Info. Displays, Inc., Mount Kisco, N.Y., 1960-73; v.p., gen. mgr., Info. Displays, Inc., Mount Kisco, 1973-76; pres. Machover Assocs. Corp., White Plains, N.Y., 1976—; adj. prof. Rensselaer Poly. Inst. Author: Gyro Primer, 1957; Basics of Gyroscopes, 1958, mem. editorial bd. IEEE Computer Graphics and Applications, Computers and Graphics, Spectrum, S. Klein Newsletter on Computer Graphics; editor C4 Handbook, 1989; co-editor CAD/CAM Handbook, 1980, Computer Graphics Rev.; contbr. articles to profl. jours. Mem. adv. bd. Pratt Ctr. for Computer Graphics in Design. With USNR, 1945-46. Recipient Frank Oppenheimer award Am. Soc. for Engring. Edn., 1971, Orthagonal award N.C. State U., 1988; named to Computer Graphics Hall of Fame Fine Arts Mus. of L.I., Hempstead, N.Y., 1988. Fellow Soc. for Info. Display (pres. 1968-70); mem. IEEE, Assn. for Computing Machinery, Am. Inst. Design and Drafting, Nat. Soc. Profl. Engrs., Nat. Computer Graphics Assn. (bd. dir., pres. 1989-90), Computer Graphics Pioneer, Sigma Xi, Tau Beta Pi, Eta Kappa Nu. Home: 152 Longview Ave White Plains NY 10605-2314 Office: Machover Assocs Corp 199 Main St White Plains NY 10601-3200

MACHTLEY, RONALD KEITH, congressman, lawyer; b. Johnstown, Pa., July 13, 1948; s. Kenneth C. Machtley and Doris Larson; m. Kathryn A. Croft, Apr. 10, 1971; children: Erin C., Todd R. BS, U.S. Naval Acad., 1970; JD, Suffolk U., 1978. Bar: R.I. 1978, Mass. 1978, Fla. 1980. Ptnr. Hall, D'Addario & Machtley, Newport, R.I., 1978-82; prin. ptnr. Machtley & Assocs., Newport, 1982-89; mem. 101st-102nd Congresses from 1st R.I. dist., 1989—. Past bd. dirs. Save the Bay, Providence, R.I, Townsand Fund for Aged; chmn. Armed Svcs. YMCA; elder 1st Presbyn. Ch., Newport. Officer USN, 1970-75, capt. Res. Mem. R.I. Bar Assn., Mass. Bar Assn., Fla. Bar Assn., Army Navy Club, Rotary. Republican. Office: US Ho of Reps Longworth Bldg Rm 1123 Washington DC 20510 also: 200 Main St Pawtucket RI 02860

MACIELAG, MICHAEL, banker; b. Spokane, Wash., Dec. 27, 1949; s. Frank and Ann Elizabeth (Waterman) M. BA, Washington Coll., Chestertown, Md., 1973; student, Manhattan Coll., Bronx, 1968-70. Counselor Kent County Health Dept., Chestertown, 1973-74; dir. Publick House, Chestertown, 1974-76; with Chestertown Bank of Md., 1976-83, v.p., 1980-83; mgr. spl. projects Chestertown, 1983-85; acting dir. devel. Washington Coll., Chestertown, 1984; founder Chesapeake Bank & Trust Co., Chestertown, 1986; pres. Chesapeake Bank & Trust Co., 1986—; legis. com. IBAA, 1991-92. Trustee Washington Coll. Mem. Md. Bankers Assn., Bank Adminstrn. Inst. (pres. Ea. Shore chpt. 1980-81), Chester River Yacht Club (commodore 1978-81), Washington Coll. Alumni Assn. (pres. 1980-82). Democrat. Roman Catholic. Office: Chesapeake Bank & Trust 245 High St Chestertown MD 21620-1500

MACINTOSH, MONICA BERNADETTE, art director; b. Phila., Sept. 27, 1957; d. Lawrence John and Alice Elizabeth (Spering) Blake; m. William Leslie MacIntosh, Oct. 9, 1982. AS, Art Inst. Phila., 1980. Artist Quicksilver Printing Services, Inc., Bryn Mawr, Pa., 1980-84; art dir. BPM Enterprises, Inc., Merion, Pa., 1984-91, To Coin a Phrase, Bridgeport, Pa., 1991—; freelance artist, 1978—. Mem. Assn. Sci. Fiction and Fantasy Artists. Republican. Roman Catholic. Office: To Coin A Phrase Bridgeport PA 19408

MACINTOSH, ROBERT EDWARD, graphic designer; b. Boston, Aug. 25, 1945; s. James Lloyd and Dorothy (Moneritt) MacI.; m. Anna Rosalba Barbarino, Nov. 9, 1969; children: Scott, Jamison. BFA, Mass. Coll. Art, 1969. Dir. communications Greater Boston YMCA, 1969-72; pres., creative dir. Rob MacIntosh Communications, Inc., Boston, 1972—; mgr. graphic design Hale and Dorr, Boston, 1990—; cons. Nat. Coun. YMCAs Urban Action Commn., N.Y.C., 1970-72; vice-chair, bd. trustees Mass. Coll. Art, Boston, 1987—. Active Big Sister Assn. Boston Devel. Com., 1972-74, Am. Cancer Soc. Pub. Informat, Boston, 1974—; bd. dirs. Greater Boston YMCA, West Roxbury, Mass., 1983-84. Recipient Hatch award Boston Advt. Club, 1970, Clio award, N.Y., 1988. Mem. Nat. Assn. Desktop Pub., Boston Computer Soc., Mass Coll. Art Alumni Assn. (dir., pres. 1977—), Appalachian Mountain Club. Office: Hale and Dorr 60 State St Boston MA 02109

MACINTYRE, JOHN ALEXANDER, financial planner; b. Boston, June 6, 1937; s. John Alexander and Alice Thelma (Miers) MacI.; m. Karen Anderson, July 3, 1969; children: Gregory, Jeffrey. BA, Pa. Mil. Coll., 1961; MS, George Washington U., 1972; MHA, Trinity U., 1975. Cert. fin. planner. Commd. 2d lt. U.S. Army, 1961, advanced through grades to col., 1987; fin. advisor Alexanda Armstrong Advisors, Washington, 1987-91, Armstrong, Welch & MacIntyre, Washington, 1991—. Decorated Legion of Merit, U.S. Army, Germany, 1985. Mem. Internat. Assn. for Fin. Planning (pres. Washington chpt. 199-91). Office: Armstrong Welch & MacIntyre 1155 Connecticut Ave NW Washington DC 20036

MACIOCIA, GABRIEL JAMES, record producer, singer/songwriter; b. Providence, Oct. 8, 1948; s. Michael J. and Mary M. (Lolio) M. Student, Boston Conservatory, 1967-68, Berklee Coll. Music, Boston, 1968-69; Assocs., Roger Williams Coll., 1970; BS., R.I. Coll., 1972. Cert. tchr. Producer Slack Records, North Providence, R.I., 1973-87, 90-92, RJD Records, Las Vegas, Nev., 19887-90; New Eng. A&R dir. Caprice Internat. Records, Lititz, Pa., 1992—; pub. Broadcast Music Inc., N.Y.C., L.A., Nashville, 1978—, ASCAP, N.Y.C., L.A., Nashville, 1986—. Author: Whispering Pines, 1990; composer mus. score Never Feel Feeling, 1983, Elvis Is Smiling, 1989, Please, Don't Go, 1991; writer Satisfied, Wild Weekend and Sexy Lady for 4 Tops singing group. Organizer Jimmy Fund, Boston, 1988; entertainer Say No to Drugs, Las Vegas, 1989-90, M.S. Fund, Chgo., 1991. Democrat. Roman Catholic. Home and Office: Slack Record Co 108 Humbert St North Providence RI 02911

MACISCO, JOHN JOSEPH, sociology educator, consultant; b. Bronx, N.Y., May 23, 1936; s. John Joseph and Emma Rita (Ciuci) M.; m. Elizabeth Gelabert, Nov. 30, 1963; children: Elizabeth, Rosalina Emma. BS, Fordham Coll., 1958, MA, 1959; PhD, Brown U., 1966. Rsch. assoc. George Washington U., 1960-61; asst. prof. Georgetown U., Washington, 1963-69, assoc. prof., chair, assoc. dir. Ctr. for Population Rsch., 1971-72; project specialist Ford Found., Santiago, Chile, 1969-71; instr. sociology Fordham U., Bronx, 1959-60, prof. sociology, 1972—; adj. prof. Cornell U., 1971, U. Pa., 1973-74; cons. UN Fund for Population Activities, UN Tech. Assistance Div., 1990-91, The World Bank, Washington, 1980, The Population Coun., N.Y.C., 1973. Author: Migrants to Metropolitan Lima: A Case Study, 1975; (with others) El Exodo de Los Colombianos, 1980; co-author: (with J.C. Elizaga) Migraciones Internas: Teoria, Metodo y Factores Sociologicos, 1975; (with M. Powers) Labor Force Characteristics of Puerto Rican Migrants in New York, 1979, Los Puertorriqueños En Nueva York: Un Analisis de su Participacion Laboral y Experiencia Migratoria, 1982; contbr. articles to profl. jours. 1st lt. U.S. Army, 1960-61. Urban Tng. grantee NIMH, 1972; grantee Ford Found., 1956-70, USPHS, 1967-69, The Manpower Adminstrn., U.S. Dept. Labor, 1974-79, Interdisciplinary Population Program, The Smithsonian Instn., 1974-77, NIMH, 1972-77, 79-84, Nat. Inst. Child Health and Human Devel., 1984-87. Mem. Am. Sociol. Assn., Population Assn. Am., Population and Social Change (co-chair seminar Columbia U. 1980-90), Internat. Union for Sci. Study of Population, Itnernat. Sociol. Assn. (mem. rsch. com.). Democrat. Roman Catholic. Office: Fordham U Dept Sociology E Fordham Rd Bronx NY 10468-5445

MACK, DANIEL RICHARD, furniture designer; b. Rochester, N.Y., Dec. 23, 1947; s. Richard Cornelius and Virginia Anne (Brayer) M.; m. Theresa Marie Husted, May 31, 1969; children: Kendra, Jessica, Eliza. BA, U. Toronto, Ont., Can., 1969; MA, New Sch. for Social Rsch., 1975. Journalist Sta. WRVR-FM, N.Y.C., 1971-73; spl. journalist NBC Radio, N.Y.C., 1973-75; jouranlist NBC TV, N.Y.C., 1981-83; asst. prof. Fordham U., Bronx, N.Y., 1975-81; pres. Daniel Mack Rustic Furnishings, Inc., Warwick, N.Y., 1983—; treework cons. Centerbrook Architects, Essex, Conn., 1990-91. Author: Making Rustic Furniture, 1992. Fellow N.Y. Found. for Arts, 1985-86, 90-91, Mid-Atlantic Arts Found., 1989-90. Mem. Am. Crafts Coun. Home: 14 Welling Ave Warwick NY 10990-1514 Office: 3280 Broadway New York NY 10027-7921

MACK, DONALD ROY, electrical engineer; b. Seattle, Mar. 14, 1925; s. Roy Austin and Edna Bell (Moore) M.; m. Sally Sears, Feb. 20, 1954; children: Melissa, Meredith. BEE, U. Wash., 1948; MS in Systems Sci., Poly. Inst. Bklyn., 1967, PhD in Systems Sci., 1969. Registered profl. engr., N.Y. Engr. Gen. Electric Co., various cities, 1948-56; supr. project engring. Gen. Electric Co., Schenectady, N.Y., 1956-61, cons. engring. edn., 1961-70, mgr. advanced course in engring., 1970-78; mgr. tech. edn. Gen. Electric Co., Fairfield, Bridgeport, Conn., 1978-87; adj. prof. Rensselaer Poly. Inst., Troy, 1969-78. Author: Engineering Analysis, 1982; contbr. articles to profl. jours.; patentee temperature measuring device. Staff sgt. U.S. Army, 1943-46... Mem. IEEE (sr., editor jour. 1985—), Tau Beta Pi, Sigma Xi, Phi Beta Kappa. Democrat. Unitarian. Home: 404A Montauk Ln Stratford CT 06497-8127

MACK, EARLE IRVING, real estate company executive; b. N.Y.C., July 11, 1939; s. H. Bertram and Ruth (Kaufman) M.; m. Carol L. Dickey, July 26, 1990; 1 child, Andrew Mack. BBA, Drexel U., 1960; postgrad., Fordham Law Sch., 1961-62. Owner, breeder thoroughbred horses Fla., Ky., N.J., N.Y., Md., 1964—; with The Mack Co., Rochelle Park, N.J., since 1964; chmn. Mack/Taylor Prodns., N.Y.C., 1985-89. Producer-dir. film The Children of Theater Street, 1977 (Acad. Award nomination). Bd. dirs. Benjamin N. Cardozo Sch. of Law, N.Y.C., 1980—, chmn. exec. com., 1990, vice chmn. bd. dirs., 1991; bd. dirs. N.Y.C. Ballet, 1988—, The New 42nd St., Inc., 1990—; chmn. N.Y. State Racing Commn., 1983-90; mem. bldg.

devel. com. N.Y.C. Holocaust Commn., 1985—, N.Y. State Thoroughbred Racing Capital Investment Fund, 1987—; bd. dirs. Dance Thatre of Harlem, N.Y.C., 1987, elected ch-chmn. bd., 1988-89; trustee N.Y. Racing Assn., Inc. 1990—. 1st lt. USAR, 1960-68. Named outstanding alumnus and one of Drexel 100, Drexel Univ., 1992. Mem. Nat. Realty Com. (bd. dirs., exec. com. 1986-88), Urban Land Inst., Union League Club, Univ. Club, Reading Room Club, Turf & Field Club. Office: The Mack Co 370 W Passaic St Rochelle Park NJ 07662-3009

MACK, GEORGE FRANCIS, superintendent schools; b. Bklyn., July 12, 1944; s. George Francis Mack and Eileen (Drew) Murphy; m. Gail Audrey Zinke, July 10, 1971; children: Joseph, James, David. AB, U. Rochester, 1966; MS, SUNY, Brockport, 1970; PhD, Syracuse U., 1974. Cert. sch. dist. adminstr. Tchr. grades 4-6 Rochester (N.Y.) City Sch. Dist., 1967-69; adminstrv. asst. Syracuse (N.Y.) U., 1972-74, Geneva (N.Y.) City Sch. Dist., 1974-76; asst. supt. Phoenix (N.Y.) Cen. Sch. Dist., 1976-79; supt. Worcester (N.Y.) Cen. Sch. Dist., 1979-83, Walton (N.Y.) Cen. Sch. Dist., 1983—; ho. of dels. N.Y. State Coun. Sch. Supts., Albany, 1986-88; pres. Susquenango Athletic Assn., 1988-90. Contbr. articles to profl. jours. Mem. nominating com. Delaware Valley Hosp., Walton, 1987—; bd. mem. Pvt. Industry Coun., Walton, 1988—. With U.S. Army, 1967-69. Kettering fellow IDEA Found., Columbia, Mo., 1981, 83-85, Appleton, Wis., 1986-90; recipient Delaware County Youth Svc. award, Delhi, N.Y., 1989. Mem. Occupational Edn. Adv. Coun., BOCES Facilities Task Force, 1990-91, Am. Assn. Sch. Adminstrs., 1988-91, Kiwanis Club (bd. mem. 1983—), Phi Delta Kappa. Office: Walton Cen Sch Dist Stockton Ave Walton NY 13856-9701

MACK, GREGORY JOHN, financial consultant; b. Buffalo, Oct. 11, 1954; s. Henry and Dorothy Catherine (Boone) M.; m. Rosemary Lynn Testa, Aug. 17, 1979; children: Lindsey Marie, Stephanie Kaitlyn. BS in Polit. Sci., SUNY, Buffalo, 1978. Cert. tchr., N.Y. Police officer Town of Amherst, N.Y., 1978-81; fin. cons. Cigna Individual Fin. Svcs. Co., Amherst, 1981—; speaker in field. Mem. Buffalo Life Underwriters Assn., Buffalo C. of C., Gen. Agts. and Mgrs. Assn. (Agt. of Yr. 1987, 88, 89, 90, 91, 92), Cigna's Pres. Club (pres. 1990-91), Cigna's Honor Table (pres. 1987-89), Cigna's Gold Key (chmn. 1988), Cigna's Excalibur (life). Republican. Roman Catholic. Home: 241 Halston Pkwy East Amherst NY 14051 Office: Cigna Individual Fin Svcs Co 6255 Sheridan Dr Ste 300 Amherst NY 14221

MACK, JOHN EDWARD, III, utility company executive; b. Poughkeepsie, N.Y., Feb. 20, 1934; s. John Edward Jr. and Agnes D. (Albrecht) M.; m. Maureen Whitworth, Sept 1, 1970; children: John, Todd, Ellen, David. BS, Siena Coll., 1956, MBA, 1966. With Central Hudson Gas & Electric Corp., Poughkeepsie, 1958—, v.p. corp. services, 1974-76, v.p. customer services, 1976-79, exec. v.p., 1979-82, pres., 1982—, chief exec. officer, 1986—, chmn. bd., 1989—, also bd. dirs.; bd. dirs. Edison Electric Inst., Inst. Gas Tech.; mem. exec. com. N.Y. Power Pool. Mem. exec. com. Dutchess County (N.Y.) Boy Scouts Am.; bd. dirs. Astor Home for Children, Rhinebeck, N.Y., Marist Coll., N.Y. Bus. Devel. Corp.; chmn. bd. St. Francis Hosp. Capt. U.S., 1956-58. Recipient Alexis de Tocqueville Volunteerism award United Way, Poughkeepsie, 1988, Americanism award Anti Defamation League, 1988, Citizenship award Hudson-Del. Boy Scouts, 1987, Disting. Citizen award Dutchess County Boy Scouts Am. Mem. Am. Gas Assn., Edison Electric Inst. of Gas Technology (bd. dirs.), Energy Assn. N.Y. State (chmn.), N.Y. Power Pool. Roman Catholic. Office: Cen Hudson Gas & Electric Corp 284 South Ave Poughkeepsie NY 12601-4879

MACK, STAN, cartoonist; b. Bklyn., May 13, 1936; s. Frank and Pearl (Kamaiko) M.; m. Gail Kredensek, Dec. 7, 1965 (div. July 1987); children: Kenneth, Peter. BFA, R.I. Sch. Design, 1958. Art dir. Book Week N.Y. Herald Tribune, N.Y.C., 1964-66, Book and Edn. div. Book Rev. and Sunday Mag. N.Y. Times, N.Y.C., 1967-71; advt./editorial illustrator N.Y.C., 1965—, Stan Mack's Real Life Funnies The Village Voice, N.Y.C., 1975—, Stan Mack's Out-Takes Adweek Mag., N.Y.C., 1981-92; co-creator non-fiction graphic books for young adults, author, illustrator Real Life Funny History Books, N.Y.C., 1992—. Author, illustrator: The ABC of Bumptious Beasts, 1966, Potato Talk, 1969, One Dancing Drum, 1971, 10 Bears in My Bed, 1974, Where's My Cheese?, 1977; writer, artist two animated shorts for children's program Electric Co. Pub. TV, 1979. With U.S. Army, 1959-61. Recipient Soc. of Illustrators award, 1967, Jr. Literary Guild award, Aiga Children's Book Coun. Showcase award. Mem. The Graphic Artists Guild. Office: The Village Voice 36 Cooper Sq New Yori NY 10014

MAC KAY, DONALD MACGREGOR, manufacturing executive, consultant; b. Providence, May 13, 1935; s. Richmond Cameron and Barbara Louise (Woodward) M.; m. Deborah Fowler, June 28, 1958; children: Glenn, Allyn, Laura, Janet. BSME, Cornell U., 1958; postgrad., Ohio State U., 1958-59, U. So. Calif., 1959-60, Rensselaer Polytech. Inst., 1961-62. Cert. mfg. engr. Systems engr. Pratt & Whitney Aircraft, East Hartford, Conn., 1961-65; dir. engring. Union/Butterfield, Athol, Mass., 1965-73, mgr. mktg., 1978-84; dir. engring. Waukeshau (Wis.) Cutting Tools, 1973-77; engring. mgr. The Moore Co., Springfield, Mass., 1977-78; regional sales mgr. Multi-Arc Vacuum Systems, St. Paul, 1984-85, Litton/CITCO, Chardon, Ohio, 1985-88; pres. D.M. Mac Kay Co., Athol, Mass., 1988—; sr. mem. bd. investment, Athol Savs. Bank, 1980—. Bd. dirs. Athol Area YMCA, 1980—; bd. advisors Salvation Army; former chmn. Athol chpt. ARC, Athol sch. com. Lt. USAF, 1958-61. Mem. Soc. Mfg. Engrs. (chmn. local chpt. 1970), ASME, Masons. Republican. Congregationalist.

MACKAY, ELMER MACINTOSH, Canadian government official; b. Hopewell, N.S., Can., Aug. 5, 1936; s. Gordon Barclay and Laura Louise (MacIntosh) MacK.; m. Macha Bredin Delap, July 17, 1962 (div. July 1973); children: Cethlyn, Peter, Mary Louise, Andrew; m. Laura Agnes Macaulay, July 17, 1974; 1 child, Rebecca. B.A., Acadia U., 1959; LL.B., Dalhousie U., 1962. Bar: N.S. 1962. Ptnr. MacKay Parker & White, New Glasgow, N.S., Can., 1962-71; mem. parliament House of Commons, Ottawa, Ont., Can., 1971-79, minister regional econ. expansion, 1979-80, solicitor gen. Can., 1984-85; min. nat. rev. Can., from 1985, min. pub. works, min. Atlantic Can. Opportunities Agy. Act, until 1991, min. pub. works, min. responsible for Can. Mortgage and Housing Corp., 1991—. Progressive Conservative. Presbyterian. Home: RR 1, Hopewell, NS Canada B0K 1C0 Office: Ho of Commons, Confederation Bldg Rm 509, Ottawa, ON Canada K1A 0A6

MACKAY, NEIL DUNCAN, plastic company executive; b. Chelsea, Mass., Nov. 5, 1931; s. Allan Foster and Helen May (Smith) MacK.; m. Marcia Ann McCarthy, Aug. 22, 1953 (dec. 1979); children: Duncan, Jerry, Alan, Neil, Bonnie; m. Beverly J. Burke, May 31, 1991. BS, BA, Northeastern U., Boston, 1954. Gen. mgr. Plastic Molding Corp., Newtown, Conn., 1954-67; market specialist Chem. div. Uniroyal, N.Y.C., 1967-70; project mgr. Colt Ind. Korean Project, N.Y.C., 1970-76; pres. Automatic Injection Molding Corp., Berkeley Heights, N.J., 1976-87, Diamond Mgmt. Cons., Inc., Winchester, N.H., 1988—; bd. dirs. Frazier & Son, Inc., Clifton, N.J., 1987—, Lor-Tech Plastics, Inc., Berkeley Heights, N.J. Author: Korean Plastics, 1973. Mem. Rep. Nat. Com., Washington, 1986-92. Recipient Outstanding Performance award Ministry Nat. Def. Republic of Korea, 1974. Mem. Am. Profl. Capt.'s Assn., Soc. Plastics Engrs. (sec. 1963-70, treas. 1983-86), Scottish-Am. Cultural Soc., St. Andrews Soc. N.Y., Plastic Pioneers Assn., Stuyvesant Yacht Club, Am. Yacht Club. Republican. Presbyterian. Home: 19 Lovely Ln Winchester NH 03470 Office: Diamond Mgmt Cons Inc PO Box 40 Winchester NH 03470

MACKEN, DANIEL LOOS, internist, educator; b. Rochester, N.Y., May 7, 1933; s. Daniel Edward and Mary Frances (Loos) M.; m. Elaine Kathryn Audi (div. 1979); children: Elizabeth Redford, Diana Loos; m. Maria Luisa Medina de Palma, Nov. 16, 1979. AB, Holy Cross Coll., Worcester, Mass., 1955; postgrad., Yale U., 1956-57; MD, Boston U., 1960. Resident Roosevelt & Columbia-Presbyn. Hosps., N.Y.C., 1960-63; fellow Am. Heart Assn., asst. physician N.Y. Heart Assn., N.Y.C., 1964-65; dir. coronary care unit Walter Reed Gen. Hosp., Washington, 1968; staff rsch. physician Walter Reed Army Inst. of Rsch., Washington, 1970; instr. Columbia U., N.Y.C., 1966-78, asst. clin. prof., 1979—; pres. Medica Found., Inc., N.Y.C., 1971—; bd. dirs. Medica Endowment Fund, N.Y.C., 1975—. Contbr. chpts. in book and articles to profl. jours. Lt. Col. U.S. Army, Med. Corp, 1967-70, Vietnam. Recipient Bronze Star medal U.S.A. 1970; Vietnam Cross 1969. Fellow Am. Coll. Cardiology, Royal Soc. Medicine, N.Y. Acad. Medicine, Harvey Soc.; mem. AMA, Assn. Mil. Surgeons of U.S., Am. Heart Assn., Mil. Govs. Island Officers Club. Republican. Roman Catholic. Home: 570 Park Ave New York NY 10021-7370 Office: Columbia-Presbyn Med Ctr 161 Ft Washington Ave New York NY 10032-3713

MACKEN, MARIA LUISA MEDINA, management consultant; b. Merida, Yucatan, Mex.; came to U.S., 1947; d. Luis Felipe Medina and Maria Antonia Palma; m. Donald Ernest Hibbard (div. 1979); children: Gary, Mark, Marisa, Donald; m. Daniel Loos Macken, Nov. 17, 1979. Pres. Hibbard Internat. Interiors, Key Biscayne, Fla., 1972-80; exec. v.p. GHM Mgmt. Co., N.Y.C., 1981—. Asst. treas. Musicians Emergency Fund, N.Y.C., 1987—; bd. dirs. Berkshire Choral Inst., Sheffield, Mass., 1986—; vol. Vanderbilt Clinic, N.Y.C., 1988—; charter mem. Miami (Fla.) Ballet Soc., 1967—. Mem. Am. Cancer Soc., Allied Bd. Trade, Presbyn. Hosp. Aux., Met. Club. Roman Catholic. Home: 570 Park Ave New York NY 10021-7370 Office: GHM Mgmt Co 322 W 57th St New York NY 10019-3701

MACKENZIE, JAMES, fire protection and industrial safety executive; b. Camden, N.J., Sept. 1, 1933; s. Murdo James and Pearl (Mickle) M.; m. Sally Ann Park, July 22, 1960. BS in Sci., Muhlenberg Coll., 1957; MA in Chemistry, Trenton State Coll., 1969. Cert. safety profl., hazardous material supr. Project leader ESB, Inc., Yardley, Pa., 1959-70; supr. process engring. CBS Records, Pitman, N.J., 1970-71; quality assurance supr. C and D Batteries, Conshohoken, Pa., 1971-72; ptnr. MacWell Enterprises, Medford, N.J., 1972-73; fire protection engr. Merck and Co., Inc., Rahway, N.J., 1973-88; pres. Teaberry Assocs., Medford, 1988—; mem. Tng. & Edn. Adv. Coun., N.J. Fire Com., Trenton, 1986—, HazMat Tng. Adv. Com., N.J. State Police, Trenton, 1988—; chmn. Occupational Safety Conf., Cranford, N.J., 1984-88; fire official N.J. Bur. Fire Safety, Trenton, 1979—. Pub: HazMat Tech., 1986—, Haz Packs, 1989—; author: Firefighter Guide Sheets, 1978. Safety officer Taunton Vol. Fire Co., Medford, 1961— (Chief's award 1991); vol. instr. Burlington County Girl Scouts, Westhampton, N.J., 1989; instr. Burlington County Fire Acad., Mt. Holly, N.J., 1962—. Recipient Disting. Svc. award N.J. State Safety Coun., Cranford, 1988, Dedicated Svc. award Taunton Vol. Fire Co., 1989. Mem. Nat. Fire Protection Assn., Am. Soc. Safety Engrs. (editor 1973-89), Am. Soc. for Testing & materials (F23 com. 1976, 89), Internat. Soc. Fire Svc. Instrs., Internat. Assn. Fire Chiefs, Natural Sci. Club. Republican. Methodist. Office: Teaberry Assocs 21 Saw Mill Rd RR 21 Medford NJ 08055

MACKENZIE, JOHN ANDERSON ROSS, educator, minister; b. Edinburgh, Scotland, Aug. 26, 1927; came to U.S., 1959; s. Donald Ross and Edith Agnes (Anderson) M.; m. Flora Margaret Duncan, July 14, 1951; children: Sheena, Donald, Alasdair. MA with honors, Edinburgh U., 1949, BD with Distinction, 1952, PhD, 1962; Teol. Lic., U. Lund, Sweden, 1964. Ordained to ministry Ch. of Scotland, 1953. Min. St. Andrew's Clermiston, Edinburgh, 1954-59, Westminster Presbyn. Ch., Richmond, Va., 1959-64; prof. ch. history Union Theol. Sem., Va., 1964-81; sr. min. 1st Presbyn. Ch., Gainesville, Fla., 1981-89; dir. dept. religion Chautauqua (N.Y.) Instn., 1989—; adj. prof. Cath. U., Washington, 1965-71; vis. prof. Orthodox Theol. Sem., Kottayam, India, 1972-73. Author: Trying New Sandals, 3d edit., 1977, Christian Passages, 1986, (with Elaine Kaye) William Edwin Orchard: A Study in Christian Exploration, 1990. Mem. Downtown Redevel. Agy., Gainesville, 1983-89; bd. dirs. North Fla. Retirement Village, Gainesville, 1984-89, chmn. 1987-89; bd. dirs. Samaritan Ctr., Gainesville, 1987-89. Recipient Patronal medal Cath. U. Am., Washington, 1977. Democrat. Home: 65 W Summit St Lakewood NY 14750-1127 Office: Chautauqua Instn Dept Religion Chautauqua NY 14722

MACKENZIE, MARK SCOTT, manufacturing sales professional; b. Anchorage, May 31, 1959; s. Norman Lloyd and Lillian Theresa (Kelly) MacK.; m. Mary Patricia Healy, Oct. 18, 1986. AS in Gen. Bus., Thomas Coll., 1979, BS in Mktg., 1981. Sales rep. Lloyds, Oxford, Mass., 1981-82; sales and mktg. mgr. Paperworld div. the Ziff Group, Worcester, Mass., 1982-87; territory sales mgr. A.E. Staley Mfg. Co., Inc., Decatur, Ill., 1987-92; dir. sales and mktg. ingredient div. Schlotterbeck & Foss Co., Portland, Maine, 1992—. Campaign coordinator Cen. Mass. State Rep., 1981, 82. Mem. Am. Mktg. Assn., New Eng. Food Processors Assn., Emerald Club (bd. dirs. 1989—), Nat. Beverage Packaging Assn., New England Dairy Tech Soc., Inst. Food Techs. Republican. Home: 1 Old Village Rd Sturbridge MA 01566-1041 Office: Schlotterbeck & Foss Co 117 Preble St Portland ME 04104

MACKENZIE, WILLIAM FORBES, III, non-profit organization executive; b. Allentown, Pa., Nov. 22, 1959; s. William Forbes Jr. and Jane Loretta (McLaughlin) M. Grad. high sch., Allentown. Sec., dir. Pa. Assn. Songwriters, Composers and Lyricists, Allentown, 1983—. Author: (anthology) Marilyn's Readings, 1988, (chapbook) The Unreality of Truth, 1988; songwriter, composer: (cassette) Conceptis, 1988. Mem. Lehigh Valley Arts Coun., Allentown, 1991. Recipient hon. mention amateur song div. Music City Song Festival, Nashville, 1988. Home: 1826 Turner St Allentown PA 18104

MACKERTICH, SEROJ, engineering educator; b. Feb. 1, 1942; s. Galestan and Manooshak M.; m. Rebecca Baker, Apr. 9, 1983; children: Galestan, Hendrick. BS, Tex. A&M U., 1969; MS, U. Mo., 1971; PhD, Pa. State U., 1979. Structural engr. Brown & Root Inc., Houston, 1969-70; asst. prof. engring. Lafayette Coll., Easton, Pa., 1979-85, Pa. State Univ. Harrisburg, Middletown, Pa., 1985—. Mem. ASCE (chmn. structural tech. group 1987-90, dir. Cen. Pa. sect. 1990—), Acoustical Soc. Am., Am. Soc. Engring. Edn. Home: 6160 Pine Knolls Dr Harrisburg PA 17111-3852 Office: Pa State Univ Harrisburg W-261 Olmsted Bldg Middletown PA 17057

MACKEY, JEFFREY ALLEN, minister; b. Kingston, N.Y., July 12, 1952; s. Allen William and Vivian Mathilda (Hornbeck) M.; m. Martha LaVonne Webster, Dec. 18, 1971; children: Guy Linwood, Kenyon Paul, Geoffrey Joel. BS, Nyack Coll., 1974; D of Sacred Lit., Ridgedale Theol. Sem., 1975; M Ministry, Trinity Coll., Andover, N.Y., 1976; D Ministry, Mansfield Sch. Div., 1985, Grad. Theol. Found., 1990; diploma in Angelican Studies, Gen. Theol. Sem. Ordained to ministry Congl. Christian Ch., 1974. Min. music Neversink Valley Bapt. Ch., Huguenot, N.Y., 1969-70; pastor Ponckhockie Congl. Ch., Kingston, 1971-74, The Alliance Ch., Andover, 1974-76; acad. dean Macon (Ga.) Bible Inst., 1976-78; min. Oak Grove Gospel Tabernacle, Williamsport, Pa., 1977-80, 69th St. Alliance Ch., Phila., 1980-83; sr. min. Vestavia Alliance Ch., Birmingham, Ala., 1983-87, Hope Alliance Ch., New Hartford, N.Y., 1987-91; pastoral assoc. Grace Ch., Utica, N.Y, 1991—. Author: A Worship Manifesto, 1986, Indicatives and Imperatives, 1987, Christ's Centripetal Cross, 1990; contbr. numerous articles to profl. jours. Mem. Nat. Fedn. for Decency, Birmingham, Alcohol and Drug Abuse Prevention Treatment Program, Birmingham, 1987-88. Mem. Am. Assn. Christian Schs., Fellowship Christian Sch. Adminstrs., Evang. Theol. Soc., Am. Assn. Sch. Adminstrs., Am. Guild Organists, Kiwanis. Republican. Home: RR 1 Box 246B New Hartford NY 13413-9801 Office: Grace Ch Episcopal 6 Elizabeth St PO Box 389 Utica NY 13501

MACKEY, LYNN MARIE, film director, copywriter, editor; b. Washington, May 27, 1964; d. Richard Andrew and Eileen Francis (Rawa) M. BA, Boston Coll., 1986; MA, Emerson Coll., 1989. Asst. editor Jour. Film and Video, Boston, 1988-89; teaching asst. Emerson Coll., Boston, 1989; apprentice film editor Full Moon Prodns., Hollywood, Calif., 1991; prodn. sec. The Mambo Kings Warner Bros., Burbank, Calif., 1991; freelance writer, editor Sherman Oaks, Calif., 1991-92. Dir., producer: (video documentary) Mudisuila Volunteer, 1989, Body and Soul, 1990; cinematographer: (corp. video) A Place to Be, 1990. Vol. The Peace Corps, Micronesia, Pohnpei, 1992—. Mem. New England Producers Assn. (print editor 1990-91), Assn. Ind. Video and Film Makers. Home: 49 Webster St Westwood MA 02090

MACKINNON, GEORGE E., federal judge; b. St. Paul, Apr. 22, 1906; s. James Alexander Wiley and Cora Blanche (Asselstine) MacK.; m. Elizabeth Valentine Davis, August 20, 1938; children: Catharine Alice, James Davis, Leonard Davis. Student, U. Colo., 1923-24; LL.B., U. Minn., 1929. Bar: Minn. 1929, U.S. Supreme Ct. 1947. Asst. gen. counsel Investors Syndicate, Mpls., 1929-42; engaged pvt. practice law, 1949-53, 58-61; elected mem. Minn. Ho. of Reps. from 29th dist., 1934, 36, 38, 40; mem. 80th Congress, 1947-49, 3d Minn. Dist.; U.S. Atty. for Minn., 1953-58; spl. asst. to U.S. Atty. Gen., 1960; gen. counsel, v.p. Investors Mut. Funds, Mpls., 1961-69; judge U.S. Ct. Appeals for D.C. Cir., 1969—; pres. judge U.S. Fgn. Intelligence Surveillance Ct. of Rev., 1979-82; U.S. del. UN Congress Prevention of Crime and Treatment of Offenders, 1985; presiding judge div. U.S. Ct. Appeals for Appointment of Ind. Counsels, 1985—; mem. U.S. Sentencing Commn., 1985-91. Author: Minn. State Reorganization Act, 1939, State Civil Service Law, 1939, Old Age Assistance Act, 1936. Republican nominee for Gov. of Minn., 1958. Served to comdr. U.S. Navy Air Force, 1942-46. Cited for meritorious service by comdr. Air Force U.S. Atlantic Fleet. Mem. ABA, Minn. Bar Assn., Hennepin County Bar Assn., Delta Tau Delta, Phi Delta Phi. Republican. Episcopalian. Clubs: Minneapolis; Lawyers (Washington); Masons (32 deg.). Home: 11333 Willowbrook Dr Rockville MD 20854-2568 Office: US Ct Appeals 3rd & Constitution Aves NW Washington DC 20001

MACKINNON, JOYCE LESLIE, physical therapist; b. Buffalo, Nov. 21, 1950; d. J. Bruce and Evelyn J. (Lindberg) MacK.; m. Jonathan E. Morris, Nov. 6, 1983. BA, Ohio Wesleyan U., 1973; M in Phys. Therapy, Baylor U., 1974; EdD, N.C. State U., 1987. Staff phys. therapist Martin Army Hosp., Ft. Benning, Ga., 1974-76; dir. phys. medicine Miami (Fla.) Internat. Hosp., 1976-77; coord. phys. rehab. Dorothea Dix Hosp., Raleigh, N.C., 1977-85; instr. phys. therapy U. N.C., Chapel Hill, 1977-81, asst. prof. phys. therapy, 1981-87; assoc. prof., chmn. phys. therapy U. New Eng., Biddeford, Maine, 1987—. Author 2 book chpts.; contbr. articles to profl. jours. (Jack Walker award 1986); reviewer: (manuscript) Physical Therapy, 1984—; editorial bd. Jour. Phys. Therapy Edn., 1990—. Lt. U.S. Army, 1974-76. Tng. grantee Dept. Health Human Svcs., 1991—. Mem. Am. Phys. Therapy Assn. (state treas. 1981-83, state del. nat. conf. 1980, 83, 89). Home: 22 Orchard Hill Dr Old Orchard Beach ME 04064-1561 Office: U New Eng 11 Hills Beach Rd Biddeford ME 04005-9526

MACKINNON, ROGER ALAN, psychiatrist; b. Attleboro, Mass., Feb. 13, 1927; s. Irville Herbert and Helen (Junk) MacK.; m. Florence Lundgren, Apr. 8, 1949 (div. 1970); children: Carol Louise, Stuart Alan; m. Nadine Trassenster, May 28, 1971. Student, Princeton U., 1944-46; MD, Columbia U., 1950, Cert. Psychoanalytic Med., 1957. Diplomate Am. Bd. Psychiatry and Neurology. Intern E.W. Sparrow Hosp., Lansing, Mich., 1950-51; resident in psychiatry N.Y. State Psychiatric Inst., N.Y.C., 1951-52, 52-54; chief psychiatry Vanderbilt Clinic, Presbyn. Hosp., N.Y.C., 1959-77; prof. clin. psychiatry Coll. Physicians & Surgeons, Columbia U., N.Y.C., 1986—; tng., supervising analyst Columbia U. Psychoanalytic Ctr., 1970—, asst. dir. for selection, 1981-91, dir., 1991—; attending psychiatrist Presbyn. Hosp., N.Y.C., 1972—, N.Y. State Psychiatric Inst., N.Y.C., 1972—; asst. examiner Am. Bd. Psychiatry and Neurology, 1960-70; lectr. in field. Co-author testbook: The Psychiatric Interview, 1971, The Psychiatric Evaluation, 1986; contbr. articles to profl. jours., chpts. to books. Lt. USNR, 1952-54. Recipient George Goldman award, Columbia U. Psychoanalytic Ctr., 1989. Fellow Am. Psychiatric Assn. (life), N.Y. Acad. Medicine; mem. Am. Psychoanalytic Assn., N.Y. Psychiatric Soc. (pres. 1987-88). Home: 11 Edgewood St Tenafly NJ 07670-2909 Office: 11 E 87th St New York NY 10128-0527

MACKINNON, WALTER ALLAN, employee benefits administration company executive; b. Pitts., Dec. 16, 1929; s. Allan Douglas and Elizabeth (Bernkopf) MacK.; m. Carolyn Hanson, Sept. 12, 1953 (div. 1964); children: Kathryn Dale, Patricia Lee ; m. Constance Ann Sorber, Dec. 20, 1987. BSBA, Lehigh U., 1951; CLU, Rutgers U., 1958. Spl. agt. Prudential Ins. Co., Newark, 1951-55; pres. Aero Marine Corp., Chatham, N.J., 1955-60; ptnr. Robert Heller & Assoc., Cleve., 1960-65; sr. cons. Booz-Allen-Hamilton, Cleve., 1965-67; cons. MacKinnon Assoc., Cleve., 1967-69, also bd. dirs.; pres. The MacKinnon Co., Inc., Wayne and Fairfield, N.J., 1969—, also bd. dirs.; chmn., pres., bd. dirs. MacKinnon & Gomperz, Inc., Fairfield; chmn., bd. dirs. Matrix Rsch. Inc., Wayne and N.Y.C.; adj. prof. Centenary Coll., Hackettstown, N.J., 1978. Del. White House Conf. on Small Bus.; dir. Beta Delta Bldg. Bd., LeHigh U. Served with USAF, 1951-53. Mem. Am. Coll. CLUs, Soc. Profl. Benefit Adminstrs., Self Ins. Inst. Am., Newcomen Soc., U.S. C. of C., Beaver Brook Country Club, Chi Psi. Republican. Home: 179 Buffalo Hollow Rd Glen Gardner NJ 08826-3210 Office: The MacKinnon Co Inc 23 Kulick Rd Fairfield NJ 07004-3377

MACKO, JOHN, lawyer, farmer; b. Franklin, N.J., Apr. 2, 1947; s. John S. and Dorothy (Kruppa) M.; m. Anna Elin Kjartansson, July 12, 1975; 1 child, John H. BSEE, BS in Mgmt., MIT, 1965-70, MS in Mgmt., 1970; MS in Acctg., Syracuse U., 1978, JD summa cum laude, 1978. Bar: N.Y. 1979, Fla. 1979, D.C. 1980. Fin. analyst Xerox Corp., Rochester, N.Y., 1970-72; mkt. planning mgr. Xerox Corp., 1972-74, fin. mgr., 1974-76; assoc. Harris, Beach, Wilcox, Rubin & Levey, Rochester, 1978-82; ptnr. Githler, Samloff, Rochester, 1982-86, Githler, Samloff, Macko & Githler, Rochester, 1986-87; mng. ptnr. Githler, Macko, Reichert & Clawson, Rochester, 1987—; owner Barrister Farms, Geneseo, N.Y., 1983—, Macko Apartments, Rochester, 1972—. Vice-pres., treas bd. Southeast Area Coalition, Rochester, 1978-82; treas. bd. Rochester Housing Coun., 1978-82; chmn. Rochester Sch. Budget Com., 1981, 12th Ward Rep. Com. Mem. Jaycees (chmn. Xerox chpt.), Order of Coif, Law Rev., Justinian Soc., MIT Club, Beta Alpha Psi. Home: 42 Second St Geneseo NY 14454-1223 Office: Githler Macko Reichert & Clawson 600 Reynolds Arc Rochester NY 14614-1803

MACKOWIAK, ELAINE DECUSATIS, pharmacist, educator; b. Hazleton, Pa., Apr. 28, 1940; d. Stanley Joseph and Veronica Marie (Zabrosky) DeCusatis; m. Robert C. Mackowiak, Sept. 5, 1964 (wid. Sept. 1984); children: Jeffrey, Lisa. BS in Pharmacy, Temple U., 1962, MS in Radiation Health, 1965; PhD in Pharmacology, Thomas Jefferson U., 1974. Registered pharmacist. Asst. chief pharmacist Holy Redeemer Hosp., Huntingdon Valley, Pa., 1962-63; lectr. Sch. Dist. Phila., 1964-68; instr. Temple U., Phila., 1964-73, asst. prof., 1973-77, assoc. prof., 1977-86, prof., 1986—; vis. prof. Montgomery County Community Coll., Blue Bell, Pa., 1974—; radiation cons. AIRCO, Rare and Speciality Gases, Riverton, N.J., 1982-88, N.J. Bur. of Environ. Labs., Trenton, 1985. Author: (book chpt.) Sterile Dosage Forms, 1987; contbr. articles to profl. jours. Active parents' bd. Mt. St. Joseph Acad., Flourtown, Pa., 1987-91. Recipient several awards Temple U. Sch. Pharmacy, 1962. Mem. Am. Pharm. Assn., Pa. Pharm. Assn., Am. Assn. Colls. of Pharmacy, Health Physics Soc., Pharmacy Alumni Assn. of Phila. (bd. dirs. 1965—, cert. honor 1979),Temple U. Alumni Assn. (bd. dirs. 1977—), Thomas Jefferson U. Grad. Sch. Alumni Assn. (bd. dirs. 1980-86), Rho Chi, Sigma Xi, Magnet Honor Soc. Roman Catholic. Home: 189 Hillcrest Rd Philadelphia PA 19118-2621 Office: Sch of Pharmacy/Temple Univ 3307 N Broad St Philadelphia PA 19140-5193

MACLEAY, RONALD EDWARD, research chemist; b. Buffalo, Dec. 3, 1935; s. Roderick Lister and Mildred Christina (Veith) MacL; m. Janet Marie Shepardson, June 25, 1960; children: James, Ann, Jean, Thomas. BS in Chemistry, St. Bonaventure U., 1957, MS in Chemistry, 1959; PhD in Chemistry, SUNY, Buffalo, 1965. Chemist Lucidol Div. Wallace & Tiernen, Buffalo, 1959-61; rsch. chemist Licidol Div. Pennwalt, Buffalo, 1964-67, rsch. group leader, 1967-75, sr. group leader, 1975-79, mgr. process devel., 1980-81, rsch. fellow, 1981-89; rsch. fellow Atochem N.A. Div. Elf Acquitaine, Buffalo, 1989—. Patentee in field. Baseball coach Christy Mathewson Little League, Williamsville, N.Y., 1968-83; football coach Williamsville Jr. Football, 1971-91. 2d lt. U.S. Army, 1958-59. NIH grantee, 1963. Mem. Am. Chem. Soc. Roman Catholic. Home: 10 Mahogany Dr Buffalo NY 14221-2419

MACLEAY, WILLIAM BRANSON, III, consultant; b. Windsor, Vt., Oct. 10, 1947; s. William B. Jr. and Maryon (Behrends) M.; m. Margaret J. Stevenson, Mar. 10, 1972; children: Andrew S., Michael P. BA, Ohio Wesleyan U., 1969; MEd, U. Vt., 1970; PhD, U. No. Colo., 1974. Exec. dir. mgmt. info. systems Vt. Coun. Community Mental Health, Essex Junction, 1977-81; instr. Community Coll. Vt., St. Albans, 1981—; v.p. Burlington (Vt.) Coll., 1985-88; owner, operator Basic Employment Skills Tng., Colchester, Vt., 1988—. Contbr. articles to profl. jours. Chair selectboard Town of Colchester, 1979-82, 84-87, 89—; exec. bd. Green Mountain coun. Boy Scouts Am., Waterbury, Vt., 1990—. Capt. USAF, 1970-73. Home and Office: PO Box 396 Colchester VT 05446-0396

MACLEOD, EDWARD JAMES WARING, manufacturing executive, marketing professional; b. Plainfield, N.J., Jan. 4, 1950; s. Robert Frederic MacLeod and Carolyn (Waring) Verbeck; m. Susan M. Strate; children: Merrielle Skye, Kelly Marie, Edward James Jr. AA, Santa Monica Coll., 1970; BA, San Fernando Valley State, 1972. Mktg. mgr. Superior Industries Internat., Van Nuys, Calif., 1975-83; v.p., gen. mgr. Hollywood Accessories, Compton, Calif., 1983-85; nat. mktg. mgr. G&O Mfg. Co., New Haven, Conn., 1985-90; mng. ptnr. Advantage, Inc., Fenton, Mich., 1990—. Recipient Best New Automotive-Indsl. Chemist of Yr. award, Chem. Packagers N.Am., Ontario, Calif., 1983; runner-up World Bumper Pool Championships, 1991. Mem. Automotive Parts and Accessories Assn. (advocate 1987-92, chmn. membership com. 1989—), Automotive Mktg. Profls., N.Am. Cons. Alliance (v.p. bd. dirs. 1990—). Episcopalian. Home: 43 Madison Ave Madison CT 06443-3135 Office: Advantage Inc 43 Madison Ave Madison CT 06443-3135

MACMILLAN, CLAIRE ELIZABETH, travel agency executive; b. Phila., Sept. 20, 1953; d. William Harry and Claire Elizabeth (Bergman) Schoellhorn; 1 child, William Leedom MacMillan IV. BS, Beaver Coll., 1971; postgrad., Fla. Atlantic U., 1972-74; cert. in orgn. mgmt., U. Del., 1982. Cert. K-12 tchr., N.J. Treas. Abbey Color & Chem. Co., Phila., 1969-91; exec. v.p. Assn. Hdqrs., Marlton, N.J., 1976—; pres. A Better Way To Go, Inc., Ocean City, N.J., 1990—; lobbyist LWV/NOW, N.J., 1974-79; gen. mgr. Inst. Newspaper Controllers & Fin. Officers, 1978-81; trade show dir. Juvenile Products Mfrs. Assn., Marlton, 1979-89; seminar lectr. N.J. Assn. Women Bus. Owners, 1991. Mem. N.J. Assn. Women Bus. Owners, Atlantic City Conv. and Vis. Bur., N.J., LWV (various offices Trenton and Moorestown, N.J., Cape May County chpt.), ABWA (bd. dirs. Ocean chpt. 1989—), Meeting Planners Internat., Hotel Sales Mkgt. Execs., IAMC, ASAE, Ocean City C. of C., Women's Aux. Betty Bachrach Rehab. Hosp. Office: A Better Way To Go Inc 834 Asbury Ave Ocean City NJ 08226-3362

MACMURREN, HAROLD HENRY, JR., psychologist; b. Jersey City, Sept. 18, 1942; s. Harold Sr. and Evelyn (Almone) MacM.; m. Margaret Bartro, Nov. 21, 1970. BA, William Paterson Coll., Wayne, N.J., 1965; MA, Jersey City Coll., 1973; EdD, St. Johns U., N.Y.C., 1985; JD, Rutgers U., 1989. Cert. secondary tchr., N.J.; Bar: N.J. 1989. Instr. Wanaque (N.J.) Bd. Edn., 1965-66, cons. psychologist, 1983-84; instr. Elmwood Park (N.J.) Bd. Edn., 1967-70; coll. faculty mem., psychologist Assoc. Clinic, Jersey City, 1971-72; cons. psychologist Rockaway (N.J.) Bd. Edn., 1972-83; intern lawyer Environ. Law Clinic, Newark, N.J., 1988-89; cons. psychologist Pequannock (N.J.) Bd. Edn., 1984—; speaker and writer in field. Mem. N.J. Edn. Assn., NEA, N.J. Psychologist Assn., N.J. Bar Assn., ABA, Sierra Club. Home: 4 Sytsema Pl Sussex NJ 07461 Office: Pequanock Bd Edn Pequannock NJ

MACNEAL, EDWARD ARTHUR, economic consultant; b. Winona Lake, Ind., Apr. 19, 1925; s. Kenneth Forsyth and Marguerite Josephine (Giroud) MacN.; m. Priscilla Creed Perry, Dec. 27, 1952; children: Catherine Wright, Madeleine Creed. Student Harvard, 1943; B.A., U. Chgo., 1948, M.A., 1951. Exec. sec. Internat. Soc. Gen. Semantics, Chgo., 1947-51; staff cons. James C. Buckley, Inc., N.Y.C., 1951-55; market researcher Socony Mobil Oil Co., N.Y.C., 1955-58; research dir. O.E. McIntyre, Inc., N.Y.C., 1958-61; econ. cons., N.Y., 1956-66, Wayne, Pa., 1966—; adv. local govt. agys. Served with AUS, 1943-46; ETO. Mem. ABA, Am. Statis. Assn., Am. Econ. Assn., Internat. Soc. Gen. Semantics (dir.), Inst. Gen. Semantics (dir.), Am. Sociol. Assn., Am. Assn. Airport Execs., Travel Research Assn., Travel Research Forum. Clubs: Nat. Aviation; Harvard (Phila.); Wings. Author: The Semantics of Air Passenger Transportation, 1981, MacNeal's Master Atlas of Decision Making, 1988. Home: 348 Louella Ave Wayne PA 19087-4804 Office: PO Box 249 Wayne PA 19087

MACO, PAUL STEPHEN, JR., lawyer; b. Allentown, Pa., May 14, 1952; s. Paul Stephen and Rose Mary (McFadden) M. BA, Lehigh U., 1974; JD, NYU, 1977. Bar: N.Y. 1978, U.S. Dist. Ct. (so. dist.) N.Y. 1978, Mass. 1987. Staff atty. div. enforcement SEC, N.Y.C., 1977-79; assoc. Hawkins, Delafield & Wood, N.Y.C., 1979-81, Debevoise & Plimpton, N.Y.C., 1981-85; assoc. Mintz, Levin, Cohn, Ferris, Glovsky & Popeo, P.C., Boston, 1985-88, ptnr., 1988—; mem. M.S.I.L. adv. bd. Mcpl. Security Rulemaking Bd. Co-author: Fundamentals of Municipal Bonds Part 3: Federal Securities Law, 1991; editor: Disclosure Roles of Counsel in State and local Government Securities Offerings, 1987; editorial advisor Mcpl. Fin. Jour. Mem. ABA, Nat. Assn. Bond Lawyers (chmn. com. on fed. securities law and disclosure 1987-89, bd. dirs.), Assn. Bar City N.Y., Boston Bar Assn., Traditions for Tomorrow (bd. dirs.). Office: Mintz Levin Cohn Ferris Glovsky & Popeo 340 Commercial St Fl 3 Manchester NH 03101-1121

MACOMBER, RICHARD WILTZ, earth science educator; b. Chgo., June 6, 1932; s. William W. and Dorothy L. (Wiltz) M.; m. Lenore Baker, Nov. 30, 1957. BS, Northwestern U., 1954, MS, 1959; AM, Harvard U., 1963; PhD, U. Iowa, 1968. From instr. to prof. earth sci. Bklyn. campus L.I. U., 1966—. Contbr. articles to profl. jours. Mem. Sigma Xi, Phi Beta Kappa. Office: LI U Dept Physics University Plz Brooklyn NY 11201-5301

MACOSKO, PAUL JOHN, II, psychotherapist; b. Erie, Pa., May 15, 1952; s. Paul Sr. and Susan Ann (Miraldi) M.; m. Marsha Gail Blystone, July 1, 1978; children: Paul John III, Benjamin Jamison. BA in Psychology, Mercyhurst Coll., 1976; postgrad., Grand Rapids Bapt. Bible Sem., and Edinboro U., 1976-78; MA in Bibl. Counseling, Grace Theol. Sem., Winona Lake, Ind., 1983; DPhil, Oxford U., 1992. Protective svc. caseworker I Trumbull County Children's Svcs. Bd., Warren, Ohio, 1976-77; counselor Regular Bapt. Children's Agy., St. Louis, 1978-81; coord. devel. dual diagnosis program Dr. Gertrude A. Barber Ctr., Erie, 1987—; pvt. practice marriage, family and crisis counseling Erie, 1984—. Mem. AACD, Am. Assn. Christian Counselors, Assn. Religious and Value Issues in Counseling, Pa. Counseling Assn., Nat. Disting. Svc. Registry. Baptist. Office: 1561 W 38th St Ste 10 Erie PA 16508-2384

MACPHAIL, DANIEL DAVID, psychologist; b. Springfield, Mass., Mar. 15, 1948; s. Robert Daniel and Theresa Maria (D'Amore) M. BA, U. Mass., 1971; MEd, Springfield Coll., 1973; EdD, Boston U., 1986. Tchr. Enfield (Conn.) Pub. Schs., 1971-72; counselor Downey Side, Springfield, 1972-73; child welfare social worker Div. Family and Child Svcs., Springfield, 1973-75; alcohol counselor Dept. Pub. Welfare, Springfield, 1975-77; psychologist Mass. Correctional Inst., Concord, 1977-85, Human Resource Inst., Lowell, Mass., 1980-89; dir. court clinic Waltham (Mass.) Dist. Ct., 1985—; psychol. cons. Mass. Rehab. Commn., Woburn, 1986-88; psychologist Psychiatric Med. Assn., Inc., Billerica, Mass., 1988-90; pvt. practice Lexington, Mass., 1988—. Mem. Am. Psychol. Assn., Am. Assn. Correctional Psychologists, Mass. Psych. Assn. Office: Custance Pl 76 Bedford St Ste 21 Lexington MA 02173

MACPHERSON, RICHARD FREDERICK (DICK MACPHERSON), professional football coach; b. Old Town, Maine, Nov. 4, 1930; s. Hugh Allen and Marie Odella (Moreau) MacP.; m. Sandra Jean Moffitt, Dec. 28, 1958; children: Maureen, Janet. BS, Springfield Coll., 1958, HHD (hon.), 1987; MS, U. Ill., 1959. Asst. football coach U. Cin., 1961-65, U. Md., College Park, 1966-67, Denver Broncos, 1967-71; head football coach U. Mass., Amherst, 1971-78; asst. football coach Cleve. Browns, 1978-81; head football coach Syracuse (N.Y.) U., 1981-91, New Eng. Patriots, Foxboro, Mass., 1991—; asst. coach East West Shrine Football Classic, 1989-91; head coach Japan Bowl, Tokyo, 1989; con. NCAA Rules Com.; bd. dirs. Knight Found. Bd. dirs. Eye Rsch. Found., Syracuse, Salvation Army, Syracuse, Easter Seals, Syracuse, Am. & Juvenile Diabetes, Syracuse; spokesman Camp Good Days and Spl. Times, Syracuse. Recipient Bear Bryant award (Football Writers Coach of Yr.), 1987, Charles Richard Drew Trophy (NCAA Coach of Yr.), 1987, Joseph F. Sheehan Meml. award (Football Writers Assn. N.Y. Coach of Yr.), 1987; named Coach of Yr., UPI, 1987, Coach of Yr., Sporting News, 1987, Coach of Yr., Sports Illustrated, 1987, Coach of Yr., Bobby Dodd, 1987, Coach of Yr., Scripps Howard, 1987, Coach of Yr., Toyota Nat., 1987, Walter Camp Coach of Yr., 1987, Gold Helmet Coll. Coach of Yr., 1987, Coach of Yr., CBS/Chevrolet, 1987, MacGregor Coach of Yr., 1987, Bud Lite Coach of Yr., 1987. Mem. Am. Football Coaches Assn. (Kodak Coach of Yr. 1987), Coll. Football Assn., Century Club (Syracuse). Roman Catholic. Office: New England Patriots Sullivan Stadium Foxboro MA 02035

MACPHERSON, ROBERT DUNCAN, mathematician; b. Lakewood, Ohio, May 25, 1944; s. Herbert G. and Jeanette (Wolfenden) MacP. BA, Swarthmore Coll., 1966; MA, PhD, Harvard U., 1970. Instr. Brown U., Providence, 1970-72, asst. prof., 1972-74, assoc. prof., 1974-77, prof., 1977-85, Florence Pirce Grant prof., 1985-87; prof. MIT, Cambridge, Mass., 1987—; mem. Inst. des Hautes Etudes Sci., Paris, France, 1980-81, Steklov Math Inst., Moscow, USSR, 1980; visiting prof. U. Rome, 1985. Co-author: Stratified Morse Theory, 1988, Nilpotent Orbits, 1989; contbr. numerous articles to profl. jours. Recipient Research Grant NSF, 1970—, Math. award NAS, 1992; named Herman Weyl Lectr. Inst. for Advanced Study, 1982. Mem. NAS, AAAS, Am. Acad. Arts and Scis., Am. Math. Soc., Soc. for Applied & Indsl. Math., Phi Beta Kappa. Home: 77 Sea Ave Quincy MA 02169-3127 Office: MIT Dept Math Cambridge MA 02139

MACQUIDDY, JEAN ELIZABETH, health organization administrator; b. Watsonville, Calif., May 22, 1943; d. Thomas Malcolm and Elizabeth Geary (Wilson) MacQ.; m. Peter Mills Baptiste, Dec. 11, 1939 (div. Sept. 1977); children: Geary, Ruth. BA, Mills Coll., 1965; MBA, Northeastern U., 1982. Staff asst. Harvard Sch. of Edn., Cambridge, Mass., 1965-67; staff asst. Market Structure Studies, Cambridge, 1967-68; conv. coord. Interactive Learning Systems, Brighton, Mass., 1968-69; adminstrv. asst. Harvard Law Sch., Cambridge, 1969-70; exec. officer Harvard Med. Sch., Boston, 1971-84; bus. planning mgr. Allied Health & Scientific Products, Andover, Mass., 1984-85; adminstrv. officer Mass. Eye and Ear Infirmary, Boston, 1985—; bd. dirs. Weston Drama Workshop, Weston, Mass. Mem. Weston Traffic Commn., 1988-89, Weston Neighborhood Assn., 1989. Mem. Med. Group Mgmt. Assn., Cambridge Boat Club, Harvard Cooperative Soc. (bd. dirs. 1980-84). Episcopalian. Home: 107 North Ave Weston MA 02193-2033

MACRAE, DUNCAN ALEXANDER, bank officer; b. Aberdeen, N.S., Can., Sept. 29, 1943; came to U.S., 1964; s. Gordon and Mary Jane (MacKinnon) MacR.; m. Mary Faith Elson, Apr. 17, 1965 (div. July 1978); 1 child, Melanie Beth; m. Patricia Lynn Kazenko, July 25, 1987. BS, U. Balt., 1986, MBA, 1988. Asst. comml. credit mgr. Comml. Credit Bus. Loans, Balt., 1970-73, Mercantile Safe Deposit and Trust, Balt., 1973-74; v.p. MNC Fin., Balt., 1974-80; asst. v.p. comml. fin. Walter E. Heller and Co., Chgo., 1980-82; v.p. comml. fin. Security Pacific Bus. Credit, Chgo., 1982-85; sr. v.p. credit and loan policy Bank of Balt., 1985—. With U.S. Army, 1966-69. Mem. Robert Morris Assocs., Beta Gamma Sigma. Presbyterian. Home: 147 Hershey Cir Stewartstown PA 17363

MACRAKIS, A. LILY, history educator, researcher; b. Athens, Greece; came to U.S., 1953; d. Chryss and Irene (Carabini) Chryssanthacopoulos; m. Michael S. Macrakis, Oct. 1, 1953; children: Stavros M., Michele A., Kristie I. Professorat, Inst. Français, Athens, 1946; diploma, U. Athens, 1951; MA, Radcliffe Coll., 1955; PhD, Harvard U., 1983. Fellow Radcliffe Inst., Cambridge, Mass., 1961-63; assoc. prof. history, chmn. dept. Regis Coll., Weston, Mass., 1962-83, prof., dir. internat. rels., 1983—, dir. Greek programs, 1971; co-founder, moderator Greek group Ctr. for European Studies, Harvard U., Cambridge, 1975-77; vis. prof., George Seferis chair classics dept. Harvard U., 1982-83; vis. prof. U. Crete, Greece, 1987-88, U. Aegean, Mytiline and Rhodes, Greece, 1988, 89, Boston Coll., 1990, 91; bd. dirs. Aegean Inst., Poros, Greece, 1971—. Author: Cretan Rebel: E Venizelos in Crete, 1983, E. Venizelos: The Formation of a Leader (in Greek), 1992; editor books on Modern Greece Historiography and Women in Greece; contbr. numerous articles to profl. jours. Recipient Biography Prize, Acad. Athens, 1988; Fulbright sr. rsch. grantee Coun. for Internat. Exch. Scholars, Athens, 1987-88. Mem. AAUP (pres. Regis Coll. chpt. 1990—), Modern Greek Studies Assn. (pres. 1977-79, chmn. Endowment Fund 1980—), Bunting Inst. Fellows, Friends of Gennadeion, Pi Gamma Mu. Home: 24 Fieldmont Rd Belmont MA 02178-2607 also: 17 Loukianou St, Athens 10675, Greece Office: Regis Coll Dept History Weston MA 02193

MACRIS, RICHARD GEORGE, investment banking manager; b. N.Y.C, Sept. 7, 1957; s. Nicholas B. and Mary (Joanas) M.; m. Lisa Ann Meierdiercks, Sept. 28, 1985; children: Richard Nicholas, Elizabeth Caroline. BA, N.Y. U., 1980, MBA with distinction, 1982. Ops. strategist Smith Barney, N.Y.C., 1983-84; asst. v.p. First Boston Corp., N.Y.C., 1984-86; sr. v.p. Lehman Bros., N.Y.C., 1986—. Author: (with others) Market Makings/Changing Structure of Securities Industry, 1985. Beta Gamma Sigma. Republican. Office: Lehman Bros World Fin Ctr 6th Fl New York NY 10285

MACRURY, KING, management counselor; b. Manchester, N.H., Oct. 14, 1915; s. Colin H. and Lauretta C. (Shea) MacR.; 1 son, Colin C. A.B., Rollins Coll., 1938; postgrad., St. Anselms Coll., L.I. Coll. Medicine, Princeton. Asst. personnel dir. Lily-Tulip Cup Corp., 1939; asst. dir. market research Ward Baking Co., 1940-41; staff mem. Nat. Indsl. Conf. Bd., 1941-43; cons. indsl. relations and orgn. planning McKinsey & Co., 1946-48; internal cons. Oxford Paper Co., 1949-50; installer, dir. indsl. relations Champion Internat. Co., 1950-51; pvt. practice mgmt. counselor, 1951—; lectr. Indsl. Edn. Inst., 1962-68, Mgmt. Center, Cambridge, 1968-71, Dun & Bradstreet, 1979—; extension div. U. N.H., 1968—; extension program U. Maine, 1978—; also U. Bridgeport, extension program U. Conn.; coordinator mgmt. edn. extension div. U. Conn., 1964-68, Philippine Council Mgmt., 1969—, Econ. Devel. Found. Philippines, 1969—, Am. Metal Stamping Assn., 1969—; condr. mgmt. seminars for Asian Assn. Mgmt. Orgns. C.I.O.S., 1972; Mem. Indsl. Devel. Commn. Andover, 1957-58; manpower com. U.S. Dept. Labor Bus. Adv. Council, 1958-61. Author: Developing Your People Potential; Contbr. numerous articles in field to profl. jours. Served to lt. USNR, 1943-46. Mem. Nat. Dental Soc. (hon.), Smaller Bus. Assn. N.E., Res. Officers Assn. Office: PO Box 215 Rye NH 03870-0215

MACY, TERRENCE WILLIAM, social services administrator; b. Springfield, Mass., Apr. 13, 1946; s. Thomas William and Bertha (Johnson) M.; m. Linda Kautz, Aug. 28, 1971; children: Arianne, Tyler. BA, Assumption Coll., 1970; MA, Ohio State U., 1977, PhD, 1980. Instr. Hartford Regional Ctr., Newington, Conn., 1970-73, residential program supr., 1973-74; adminstrv. asst. to supt. Orient (Ohio) Developmental Ctr., 1974-77, dir. transition office, 1977-79; supt. SW Ohio Developmental Ctr., Fairfield, 1979-83; dir. residential services DATAHR, Inc., Brookfield, Conn., 1983-86, dir. residential and vocat. services, 1986-89, dir. vocat. svcs., 1989-90; exec. dir. SARAH TUXIS Residential Svcs., Guilford, Conn., 1990—; cons. Fla. Dept. Mental Retardation, 1982. Author: A Resource Manual on Transition Shock, 1985. Vice pres. Bethel (Conn.) Coop Ext. Svc. Coun., 1987-91; mem. Brookfield Dem. Town Com., Brookfield Planning commn., 1989-91; vice chmn. Dem. Town Com., Brookfield, 1990-91. Recipient commendation Ohio Legislature, 1983, Statesman award Conn. Jaycees, 1989. Fellow Am. Assn. Mental Retardation (sec. 1977-81, pres. Ohio chpt. 1983-84, chmn. adminstrv. div. 1982-83, chmn. Conn. chpt. residential div. 1991, 2d vice chair 1992); mem. U.S. Jaycees (Gov.'s Civic Leadership award 1985, 89, mem. town Brookfield planning com., Dem. town com.), Conn. Coun. Execs. (vice chair). Roman Catholic. Home: 93 Flintlock Rd Madison CT 06443-2425 Office: SARAH TUXIS Residential Svc 55 Park St Guilford CT 06437-2629

MADAMA, PATRICK STEPHEN, academic official; b. Rochester, N.Y., Jan. 4, 1951; s. Anthony L. and Mary S. (Silvio) M. AS, Monroe Community Coll., Rochester, 1971; BS, SUNY, Brockport, N.Y., 1977, MS Edn., 1987. Acct. Monroe Community Coll. Assn., Inc., Rochester, 1973-81; dir. alumni affairs & devel. SUNY, Brockport, 1981-87, exec. dir. for coll. devel., 1987—; bd. dirs. SUNY Coun. for Univ. Affairs & Devel., Albany, 1982-90; senator alt. SUNY faculty senate, Albany, 1985-89; senator SUNY, Brockport Coll. Faculty Senate, 1983-87. Contbr. articles to profl. jours. Exec. committeeman Monroe County Dem. Party, Rochester, 1988-92; bd. dirs. Edgerton Day Care Ctr. Bd., Rochester, 1988—, Monroe Community Coll. Alumni Assn., Rochester, 1971-86; chmn. Holy Family Parish Coun., Rochester, 1971-75. Recipient Monroe Community Coll. Disting. Alumnus award, 1983. Mem. Nat. Soc. Fund Raising Execs., Coun. for the Advancement and Support of Edn. Democrat. Roman Catholic. Home: 173 Augustine St Rochester NY 14613-1445 Office: SUNY 306 Allen Brockport NY 14420-2926

MADAN, STANLEY KRISHEN, retired chemistry educator, researcher; b. Lahore, Punjab, India, May 1, 1922; came to U.S., 1955; s. Madan Lal and Vimla (Galani) M.; m. Carol Schlaretzki, June 7, 1958; 1 child, John S. BSc, Forman Christian Coll., Lahore, Pakistan, 1945; MA in Psychology, Punjab U., 1950; MS in Teaching of Chemistry, U. Ill., 1957; MS in Chemistry, Punjab U., 1954; PhD in Inorganic Chemistry, U. Ill., 1960. Rsch. asst. Punjab Irrigation Rsch. Inst., Lahore, 1945-48; lectr. Forman Christian Coll., 1948-55; teaching asst. U. Ill., Urbana, 1957-60; asst. prof. chemistry SUNY, Binghamton, 1960-63, assoc. prof., 1963-67, prof., 1967-88, prof. emeritus, 1988—. Contbr. over 60 articles on coordination complexes and kinetics of coordination to profl. jours. Office: SUNY Dept Chemistry Vestal Pkwy E Binghamton NY 18902-6000

MADDEN, EDWARD GEORGE, JR., lawyer; b. Newark, Feb. 21, 1924; s. Edward and Catherine (Mahon) M.; m. Mary B. Haveron, June 20, 1959; children: Maurica, Margaret, Thomas, Mary, Jane. BS, St. Peter's Coll., 1950; JD, U. Mich., 1953. Bar: N.J. 1954, U.S. Dist. Ct. N.J. 1954, U.S. Ct. Appeals (3d cir.) 1981, U.S. Supreme Ct. 1959. Assoc. McCarter & English, Newark, 1954-56, Donohue & Donohue, Nutley, N.J., 1956-61; ptnr. Troast, Mattson & Madden, Newark, 1961-65, Mattson, Madden & Polito, Newark, 1965—; mem. N.J. State Legislature, 1960-62. With USN 1943-46. Fellow Am. Bar Found.; mem. ABA, N.J. Bar Assn. (trustee, treas. 1972-78), Essex County Bar Assn. (trustee 1971-75), Internat. Assn. Def. Counsel, Transp. Lawyers Assn. Democrat. Roman Catholic. Office: One Gateway Ctr Newark NJ 07102

MADDEN, GERALD PATRICK, finance educator; b. Phila., Dec. 17, 1942; s. Edward Ignatius and Helen Ruth (McCarthy) M. BSBA, St. Joseph's Coll., Phila., 1964; MBA, Temple U., 1971; PhD in Bus. Adminstrn., Pa. State U., 1976. Auditor Sun Oil Co., Phila., 1965-67; sr. asst. acct. Haskins and Sells, CPA's, Phila., 1967-69; instr. of fin. Pa. State U. Capitol campus, Harrisburg, 1975-76; asst. prof. fin. U. Conn., Storrs, 1976-80; assoc. prof. bus. adminstrn. Northeastern U., Boston, 1980-85; assoc. prof., coord. of fin. sch. bus. Fairfield (Conn.) U., 1985-91, assoc. prof. fin. Sch. Bus., 1985—. Author: Investment Analysis with Value/Screen Plus, 1991; co-author: Handbook of Business Strategy; contbr. articles to profl. jours. Served with USAR, 1964-70. J.W. Van Dyke scholar, 1961-63; faculty research grantee Fairfield U., Northeastern U., U. of Conn., 1977-88. Mem. Am. Fin. Assn., Ea. Fin. Assn., Fin. Mgmt. Assn., So. Fin. Assn., European Fin. Assn. Office: Fairfield U Sch Bus Fairfield CT 06430

MADDEN, KENNETH CROMWELL, JR., school administrator; b. Hot Springs, Va., Aug. 7, 1950; s. Kenneth Cromwell Sr. and Mabel Alice (Failes) M.; m. Alice Patrice Everhart, Jan. 18, 1980; children: Kenneth Cromwell III, Tyler Rice. BA, Shippensburg (Pa.) State U., 1972; MEd, U. Del., 1979. Cert. elem., secondary and spl. edn. tchr., N.J., Del. Sch. psychologist Christina Sch. Dist., Newark, Del., 1978-85, prin. Medill Sch., 1985-89; asst. prin. Delcastle Tech. High Sch., 1989; pres. EMS Assocs., Newark, 1989—; prin. Polytech High Sch., Woodside, Del., 1991—. With U.S. Army, 1974-77. Mem. ASCD, Assn. Quality and Participation, Internat. Platform Assn. Methodist. Home: 6 Cardiff Ct E Newark DE 19711-3443

MADDEN, PETER ROBERT, secondary education educator; b. N.Y.C., Oct. 16, 1939; s. James C. and Julia (Baronowicz) M.; m. Frances Hogan Madden, July 2, 1960; children: Ann Madden Bhatt, CArol, Julie. BS, U. Conn., 1960; MS, So. Conn. State U., 1971; postgrad., Wesleyan U., 1991—. Sales and office mgr. Asgrow Seed Co., Milford, Conn., 1960-63; tchr., coach Amity Regional High Sch., Woodbridge, Conn., 1963—. Mem. Dem. Town Com., Bethany, 1978-84, Inland Weltand Commn., Bethany, 1980-82. Named Outstanding Grand Masters Runner, Hartford Track Club, 1990; recipient many 1st pl. running awards. Mem. Conn. Edn. Assn. (chmn. negotiation com. 1975), Conn. High Sch. Coaches Assn., Amity Edn. Assn. (pres. tchrs. assn. 1971-76), Amity Coaches Assn. (Outstanding Coach award 1988). Democrat. Roman Catholic.

MADDIN, ROBERT, metallurgist educator; b. Hartford, Conn., Oct. 20, 1918; s. Isadore I. and Mae (Jacobs) Levine; married, July 8, 1945; children: Leslie, Jill. BS in Metall. Engring., Purdue U., 1942; DEng., Yale U., 1948. Registered profl. engr., Pa. Asst., assoc. prof. Johns Hopkins U., Balt., 1949-55; prof. U. Pa., phila., 1955-73, univ. prof., 1973-83; vis. prof. Harvard U., Cambridge, Mass., 1983-87; curator Harvard U., Cambridge, 1987—; vis. prof. Oxford U., Eng., 1970; fellow Wolfson Coll., Oxford, Eng., 1970; vis. prof. U. Birmingham, Eng., 1953-54; vis. scholar Hebrew U., Jerusalem, 1976; hon. prof. Beijing Iron and Steel U., 1986; hon. mem. Japan Metals. Contbr. more than 150 publs. to profl. jours. 1st Lt. USAF, 1942-45. Disting. Sr. Sci. fellow A. von Humboldt Found., Germany, 1989-90. Fellow Am. Soc. Metallurgists, TMS; mem. Mus. Fine Arts-Boston.

MADDOX, DONALD, French and Italian educator; b. Billings, Mont., Apr. 2, 1944; s. Howard William and Allene (Beckett) M.; m. Sara Sue Whitney, Oct. 9, 1976. BA, U. Kans., 1966; MA, Duke U., 1969, PhD, 1970; Diplome d'Etudes Francaises, Sorbonne, Paris. Teaching assoc. Duke U., Durham, N.C., 1968-70; asst. prof. U. Okla., Norman, 1970-71, U. Calif., Santa Barbara, 1971-76; Andrew W. Mellon fellow Brandeis U., Waltham, Mass., 1976-79; vis. prof. Boston Coll., Chestnut Hill, Mass., 1981-82; prof. French U. Conn., Storrs, 1980-89; prof. and chmn. dept. French and Italian U. Mass., Amherst, 1990—. Author: The Arthurian Romances of Chretien de Troyes, 1991, Semiotics of Deceit, 1984, Structure and Sacring, 1978; contbr. articles to profl. jours. NEH fellow, 1974-75, Mellon fellow, 1976-79, Camargo Found. fellow, France, 1978, Sachar Found. grantee, 1978, Am. Coun. Learned Socs. grantee, 1978. Mem. MLA, Medieval Acad. Am., Internat. Courtly Lit. Soc. (v.p. 1989—), Internat. Arthurian Soc., Societe des Anciens Textes Francais, Societe Internationale Rencesvals, Pi Delta Phi. Office: U Mass Dept French/Italian 316 Herter Hall Amherst MA 01003

MADER, THOMAS FRANCIS, communications educator; b. Bklyn., May 29, 1930; s. William and Margaret Mary (O'Hara) M.; m. Diane Helen Castellano, June 17, 1963; chilren: Janine Claire, Christopher Keith. BA cum laude, St. John's U., 1952; MA, NYU, 1955; PhD, Northwestern U., Evanston, Ill., 1963. Asst. prof. St. John's U., Jamaica, N.Y., 1955-61; asst. prof., chair Amherst (Mass.) Coll., 1963-66; faculty fellow Princeton U., 1966-67; assoc. prof. communications Hunter Coll., N.Y.C., 1967—; exch. prof. U. P.R., Rio Piedras, 1990-91; cons. Edn. Testing Svc., Princeton, N.J., 1987, Jr. Statesman Found., New Haven, Conn., 1991, Stanford, Calif., 1992; prof. CUNY Hiroshima Rsch. Ctr., 1992-93. Author: Understanding One Another, 1990; contbr. articles to profl. jours. Trustee Syosset (N.Y.) Bd. Edn., 1970-73. Sgt. U.S. Army, 1952-54. Faculty fellow Northwestern U., 1961-62. Mem. Speech Communication Assn., Internat. Hist. Soc., Princeton Club. Democrat. Roman Catholic. Home: 31 Camel Hollow Rd Huntington NY 11743 Office: Hunter Coll 695 Park Ave New York NY 10021

MADERAZO, EUFRONIO GALA, physician, educator; b. Camiguin, The Philippines, Aug. 3, 1942; came to U.S., 1967; s. Perfecto Gillamac and Natividad (Gala) M.; m. Norma V. Baer, Feb. 14, 1970; children: Alan, Alicia, Alex. BS, Xavier U., The Philippines, 1961; MD, U. Santo Tomas, The Philippines, 1966. Intern USAF Hosp. Clark, Pampanga, The Philippines, 1965-66, Bristol (Conn.) Hosp., 1967-68; med. resident Hartford (Conn.) Hosp., 1968-72, infectious desease fellow I, 1972-73, infectious disease fellow II, 1973-74, dir. med. rsch. lab., 1974—; chief med. resident U. Conn. Sch. Medicine, Farmington, 1972-73, assoc. prof. medicine and pathology, 1988—; assoc. dir. infectious diseases Hartford Hosp., 1988—, program dir. antibiotic mgmt., 1991—, chmn. antibiotic subcom., 1991—; co-founder Conn. Assn. Philippine Physicians, 1988. Contbr. articles to profl. jours. Founder Fedn. of Filipino Assn. in Conn., 1990. Recipient award for excellence in med. sci. Good Samaritan, 1987. Fellow Infectious Diseases Soc. Am. (Joseph Susman Meml. Award 1987), Am. Acad. Microbiology, Am. Coll. Physicians; mem. Am. Fedn. Clin. Rsch., Am. Soc. Microbiology, Sigma Xi (pres. Hartford chpt. 1985-86). Roman Catholic. Home: 78 Blue Ridge Dr Manchester CT 06040 Office: Hartford Hosp 80 Seymour St Hartford CT 06115

MADEY, RONALD ELIOT, pension fund investment manager; b. Patchogue, N.Y., Nov. 12, 1959; s. Richard and Mary L. (Kirch) M. Student, Miami U., Oxford, Ohio, 1977-79; BBA cum laude, Kent State U., 1982, MBA, 1983. Chartered fin. analyst. Planning coord. Cole-Layer-Trumble, Dayton, Ohio, 1983-84, sr. project supr., 1984-85, implementation cons., 1985; money market trader DuPont Pension Fund, Wilmington, Del., 1985-

86, internat. bond, fgn. exch. trader, 1986-87, head fixed income trading, 1988-90, portfolio mgr. fixed income, 1990-92, dir. fixed income, 1992—. Soc. Real Estate Appraisers scholar, 1982; recipient Culler award, 1978. Mem. Fin. Analysts Wilmington, Fin. Analysts Fedn., Beta Gamma Sigma. Episcopalian.

MADIGAN, EDWARD R., secretary of agriculture; b. Lincoln, Ill., Jan. 13, 1936; m. Evelyn M. George, 1955; children—Kimberly, Kellie, Mary Elizabeth. Grad., Lincoln Coll., 1955, LHD (hon.), 1975; LHD (hon.), Millikin U., Ill. Wesleyan U. Mem. Ill. Ho. of Reps., 1967-72, 93d-102nd Congresses from 15th Ill. dist., 1973-91; former mem. House Energy and Commerce Com.; former ranking Rep. House Agr. Com.; sec. agr. Dept. Agr., Washington, 1991—. Recipient Outstanding Legislator award Ill. Assn. Sch. Supts., 1968, Outstanding Pub. Service award Lincoln Coll. Alumni Assn. Mem. Ill. Jaycees (past v.p.), Lincoln C. of C. Lodges: Elks, Kiwanis. Office: Dept of Agriculture Office of Sec 14th & Independence Ave SW Washington DC 20250

MADIGAN, MICHEAL GERARD, artist, educator; b. Altoona, Pa., Nov. 13, 1957; s. Gerald Desales and Mary Theo (Beck) M.; m. Elaine Kay Taraba; 1 child, Ceilidh. BFA, Indiana U. of Pa., 1980, MA in Fine Arts, 1986. Instr. art Indiana U. of Pa., 1980-81, Antonelli Inst. Art, York, Pa., 1983-84, St. Francis Coll., Loretto, Pa., 1987, Artworks, Princeton, N.J., 1987—. Paintings in numerous pub. and pvt. collections, including Mus. Art, Carnegie Inst., Pitts. Hoyt Inst. Art, Squibb Internat., Am. Blue Cross & Blue Shield, SunChem., Univ. Mus. Ind. U. Pa. Home: 2019 Greenwood Ave Trenton NJ 08609-2311

MADISON, EDDIE LAWRENCE, JR., public affairs specialist, editor, writer; b. Tulsa, Sept. 8, 1930; s. Eddie Lawrence Sr. and Laverta (Pyle) M.; m. Davetta Jayn Cooksey, Nov. 17, 1956; children: Eddie Lawrence III, Karyn Devette, David Cooksey. BJournalism, Lincoln U., Jefferson City, Mo., 1952; MA, U. Tulsa, 1959. Editor-in-chief Okla. Eagle, Tulsa, 1954-59; assoc. editor Chgo. Daily Defender, 1959-61; dep. editor Assoc. Negro Press, Chgo., 1961-63; sect. editor Chgo. Tribune, 1963-65; dep. dir. Publs. Div. Domestic and Internat. Commerce U.S. Dept. Commerce, Washington, 1965-69; mgr. community svcs. Evening Star Broadcasting Co., Washington, 1969-78; asst. editor Bus. Am. Mag., Washington, 1978-81; press asst. Ho. of Reps., Washington, 1981-82; pub. affairs specialist U.S. Dept. HHS, Washington, 1982—, mgr. HHS radio, 1991—; founder Nat. Broadcast Assn. for Community Affairs, Washington, 1974, 1st pres., 1974-77. Pres. Brightwood Civic Assn., Washington, 1969-72; bd. dirs. Opportunities Industrialization Ctr., Washington, 1971-77, D.C. United Way, 1972-77, Boy Scouts Am., Washington, 1972-77. Cpl. U.S. Army, 1952-54. Mem. Alpha Phi Alpha (nat. dir. pub. rels. 1985—, v.p. Montgomery County chpt. 1987-89, assoc. editor Sphinx Mag.). Methodist. Home: 1120 Netherlands Ct Silver Spring MD 20905-6039 Office: US Dept HHS 200 Independence Ave SW Washington DC 20201

MADLE, ROBERT ALBERT, writer; b. Phila., June 2, 1920; s. Vincent Robert and Mary Virginia (Kidwell) M.; m. Billie Franklin Lindsay, Nov. 7, 1943; children: Robert, Richard, Jane, Mary Anne. BS, Drexel U., 1951, MBA, 1953. Asst. to sales mgr. Masland Duraleather, Phila., 1951-53; asst. to dir. indsl. rels. Chadbourne Hosiery, Charlotte, N.C., 1953-54; pers. and credit mgr. Shaw Mfg. Co., Charlotte, 1954-56; pers. rsch. specialist U.S. Army, Washington, 1956-59; rsch. psychologist, program mgr. USN, Washington, 1959-80; guest speaker sci. fiction confs. Contbr. articles to sci. fiction and sports mags.; specialist in field of sci. fiction and fantasy lit.; condr. search svcs. rare books in field of sci. fiction and fantasy lit. With U.S. Army, 1942-46. Nominated for Hugo, 1956; guest of honor World Sci. Fiction Conv., Miami, 1977, U. Md. Sci. Fiction Conv., 1982. Mem. Sci. Fiction Writers Am., Washington Sci. Fiction Assn., First Fandom (pres. 1959-82, 1st Fandom Hall of Fame award 1990). Home and Office: 921 N Queen St Martinsburg WV 25401-3544

MADONIA, TINA, artist; b. Bay Shore, N.Y., Aug. 17, 1955; d. Mario Vincent and Josephine (Budzilek) M.; m. William Robert Brown, July 26, 1980; children: Megan Madonia Brown, Melissa Madonia Brown. AA, Suffolk Community Coll., Selden, N.Y., 1977. Artist. One-person shows include Town Hall, Sommers, Conn., 1980, Colonie (N.Y.) Libr., 1983, The First Unitarian Soc., Schenectady, 1987, Gloversville (N.Y.) Art Ctr., 1988, Voorheesville (N.Y.) Libr., 1989, Connexions Gallery, Easton, Pa., 1992; exhibited in group shows at Clinton St. Gallery, Schenectady, 1990, The Island Gallery, Shelter Island, N.Y., 1990, 91, 92; juried exhibits include 23rd Show Allentown Art Mus., 1992, 53rd and 54th Nat. Art Exhibits, Cooperstown, N.Y., 1988, 89, Nat. 87 Small Works Exhibit, Cobleskill, N.Y., 1987, So. Vt. Art Ctr. Juried Selection, 1985-87, 88, 89. Recipient 3rd place award for oil painting Clinton St. Gallery Juried Exhibit, Schenectady, 1989, Colonie Art League Judged Exhibit, Albany, N.Y., 1985, 87, 89, 1st place awards and hon. mention, 1983, 84, Parkland Art League Fall Exhibit, Allentown, Pa., 1991. Mem. So. Vt. Artists, Colonie Art League, Parkland Art League (spring show chmn. 1992). Home and Office: Tina Madonia Studio 5533 Ridge Rd Slatington PA 18080

MAFFEI, STEPHEN ROGER, medical products executive, treasurer; b. N.Y.C, July 24, 1939; s. Roger S. and Catherine E. (Premo) M.; m. Barbara A. Tomek, Apr. 15, 1961; children: Stephen, Matthew, Joseph. BS, U. Bridgeport, 1960; MBA, Pace U., 1976. Analyst Dun & Bradstreet, N.Y.C., 1961-63; sr. analyst Burlington Industries, N.Y.C., 1963-66; asst. treas. U.S. Mineral, Stanhope, N.J., 1966-71; sec.-treas. Mueller Group, Alpha, N.J., 1971-73; chief fin. officer, v.p., sec.-treas. Landis & Gyr Inc., Elmsford, N.Y., 1973-84; chief fin. officer, v.p. fin., treas. Meadox Meds. Inc., Oakland, N.J., 1984—; treas. Meadox U.K., Ltd., Dunstable, Eng., 1985—; treas., dir. Meadox FSC, Inc., St. Thomas, V.I., 1985—; treas. Meadox France S.A., Rungis, 1986—, Meadox Germany Gmbtl., Dusseldorf, 1988—, Meadox Sverge S.A., Helsingborg, Sweden, 1989—; dir. P.A. Inc., Dayton, Ohio, 1982—, Ramco Inc., Dumont, N.J., 1989—. Home: 345 Webster Dr New Milford NJ 07646-1045 Office: Meadox Meds Inc 112 Bauer Dr Oakland NJ 07436-3105

MAFFEO, GILBERT JOSEPH, JR., communications educator; b. Pitts., Dec. 16, 1947; s. Gilbert J. Sr. and Mary V. (Duco) M.; m. Connie A. Dell'Accio, Aug. 17, 1969; children: Sharon Kaye, Gilbert J. III. BS, Duquesne U., 1969; MA, Bowling Green State U., 1970, PhD, 1972. Assoc. prof. Cen. Mich. State U., Mt. Pleasant, 1972-78; investment broker Merrill Lynch, Hartford, Conn., 1978-80; adminstr. U. Hartford, West Hartford, Conn., 1980-84; v.p. Johnson Meml. Hosp., Stafford Springs, Conn., 1985-87, Waterbury (Conn.) Hosp. Health Ctr., 1987-89; assoc. prof. dept. corp. communication So. Conn. State U., New Haven, 1990—; adj. lectr. Hartford Grad. Ctr., 1986—; cons., presenter in field. Contbr. articles to profl. publs. Pres. Conn. chpt. Unico Nat. Simsbury, 1983-84. Mem. Conn. Hosp. Assn. (chmn. dirs. mktg. and pub. rels. 1988-89). Home: 4 Windham Dr Simsbury CT 06070-1228 Office: So Conn State U Communication Dept New Haven CT 06515

MAGARGAL, LARRY ELLIOT, ophthalmologist; b. Bethel, Conn., June 14, 1941; m. Helga Olsen, Dec. 31, 1966; children: Lauren Elizabeth, Larry Elliot, Geoffrey Robb. AB in Biology with honors, Temple U., 1965, MD with honors, 1969. Am. Bd. Ophthalmology/Surgery. Dir. med. edn. dept. opthalmology Temple Med. Sch., Phila., 1975-78; co-dir. retina vascular unit Wills Eye Hosp., Phila., 1976—, assoc. fellow Retina Svc., 1980—; assoc. clin. prof. ophthalmology Thomas Jefferson U., 1980—; assoc. vice regent Internat. Coll. of Surgeons, 1983—; cons. in field. Contbr. articles to profl. jours., textbooks. Mem. Inner Circle, Rep. Party, Washington; charter mem. Book of Normandy Mus., Washington, Ronald Reagen Libr., Washington. Capt. U.S. Army, 1972-73. Recipient Eli Lily award, 1969, Robert Shoemacker award, Pa. Acad. Ophthalmology, 1979, others. Fellow Am. Coll. Surgeons, Am. Ophthalmology Acad., others. Home: 9601 Milnor St Philadelphia PA 19114-3198

MAGAZINER, ELLIOT ALBERT, musician, conductor, educator; b. Springfield, Mass., Dec. 25, 1921; m. Sari Fromkin; 2 children. Student, Nat. Orch. Assn., 1937-40, Princeton U., 1943, Juilliard School of Music, 1946-50. Music dir., prof. music Manhattanville Coll., Purchase, N.Y., 1970—; faculty Westchester Conservatory Music. Debut: Town Hall, N.Y.C., 1952; staff artist, concertmaster CBS-TV and Radio; Networks: condrs. Reiner, Ansermet, Beecham, Stokowski; condr. and sr. violin instr. Westchester Conservatory of Music; vis. condr. Dubuque Symphony; soloist N.Y. Philharm. Symphony, Symphony of the Air, Kol Visrael, symphonies in Chgo., Ft. Myers, Dubuque, York, St. Petersburg; recitals in N.Y.C., Washington, Detroit, Amsterdam, Paris, Jerusalem; star of CBS-TV, The Violin. Recs.: Charles Ives Sonata #2, Charles Ives Trio (with Frank Glazer and David Weber); Vivaldi Concerto in C and Concerto in B (with orchestre Symphonique de Paris); conductor Westchester All County Festival Orch. Mem. AAUP, N.Y. TV Musicians (pres.), CBS Musicians Fund (sec.). Home: 250 Garth Rd #2B3 Scarsdale NY 10583 Office: Westchester Conservatory Symphony Orch 20 Soundview Ave White Plains NY 10606

MAGEE, CHARLES THOMAS, international consultant, retired diplomat; b. Clifton Forge, Va., Mar. 6, 1932; s. Charles Thomas and Dorothy Elizabeth (McPherson) M.; m. Maideh Mazda, May 30, 1959; 1 child, Maya. BA, Harvard U., 1953. With Fgn. Svc. Dept. State, 1961-89; dep. dir. for ops. Exec. Secretariat Dept. State, Washington, 1971-72, officer-in-charge French desk, 1972-74; polit. officer, exec. asst. to amb. Am. Embassy, Paris, 1974-77; dep. chief mission Am. Embassy, Sofia, Bulgaria, 1977-80; chief jr. officer div. Bur. Pers. Dept. State, 1980-82, fgn. svc. insp., 1982-83; cons. gen. U.S. Consulate Gen., Leningrad, USSR, 1984-86; spl. asst. to mayor City of San Francisco, 1986-87; dir. Russian lang. ops. U.S. Del. to Negotiations on Nuclear and Space Arms with USSR, Geneva, 1988—; cons. Acad. Arrangements Abroad, N.Y.C., 1987—, Dept. of State, 1989—, Seabourn Cruise Line, San Francisco, 1989—. Lt. USN, 1953-59. Mem. Am. Fgn. Svc. Assn., Harvard Club. Home: 4518 Albemarle St NW Washington DC 20016-2016 also: 123 rue de Lausanne, 1202 Geneva Switzerland

MAGEE, DANA THOMAS, non profit agency administrator, fundraising consu; b. Rahway, N.J., May 13, 1949; s. Raymond Joseph and Edith Frances (Messina) M.; m. Patricia A. Cerkan, Aug. 7, 1971; children: Victoria Hope, Dana T. Jr. BA in Econs. with honors, CUNY, S.I., 1975. Account exec. Joseph Dermer & Assocs., N.Y.C., 1975-77; sr. account exec., exec. v.p. Harold Paul Assocs., N.Y.C., 1977-83; assoc. exec. dir. S.I. Aid, 1983—; mem. adv. bd. Bayley Seton Hosp. Author, co-author numerous books in field; publ. U.S. Cath. Historian, 1983-89; contbr. articles to profl. jours. Bd. dirs. S.I. Child Care Assn., S.I. Aid, Inc.; mem. Community Housing Resource Bd. of S.I., United Way, Execs. of A.I.; past comdr. Am. Legion; vice chmn. S.I. Borough Pres.'s Adv. Com. for Disabled, chmn. youth com. S.I. Community Bd. No. 2; spl. cons. U.S. Cath. Hist. Soc., 1983—; bd. v.p. S.I. Chamber Music Players. With USN, 1967-71. Mem. Nat. Soc. for Fundraising Execs., Soc. for Seamens Children (bd. mgrs.). Home: 62 Ross Ave Staten Island NY 10306-2238 Office: Staten Island Aid 150 Granite Ave Staten Island NY 10303

MAGEE, DEBRA RAHENKAMP, corporate communications professional; b. Pitts., June 10, 1958; d. Richard John and Dorothea Louise (Miller) R.; m. Robert Daniel Magee, Sept. 24, 1983; children: Ryan Patrick, Devin Kendrick. BS in Mktg., Pa. State U., 1980. Sales rep. Procter and Gamble Co., Pitts., 1980-82; regional mktg. mgr. Sambo's Restaurants, Washington, 1982-83; dir. mktg. Redshaw, Inc., Pitts., 1984-87, mgr. corp. communications, 1987—. Contbr. articles to various mags. Mem. exec. bd. PTA Foster Elem. Mt. Lebanon Sch. Dist. Mem. Western Pa. Genealogy Soc., Pa. State Alumni Assn., Delta Gamma Alumni Assn. Republican. Roman Catholic.

MAGEE, WAYNE EDWARD, biochemistry educator, researcher; b. Big Rapids, Mich., Apr. 11, 1929; s. William Fredrick and Elsie E. (Gifford) M.; m. Nannette A. Pierce, June 11, 1951; children: Lawrence, William, John. BA magna cum laude in Chemistry, Kalamazoo Coll., 1951; MS in Biochemistry, U. Wis., 1953, PhD in Biochemistry, 1955. Scientist, then sr. scientist Upjohn Co., Kalamazoo, 1955-71; adj. prof. biology Western Mich. U., 1970-71; prof. life sci. Ind. State U., 1971-74; prof. biology, head div. allied health and life sci. U. Tex.-San Antonio, 1975-80, prof., 1980-81; prof. biochemistry, head dept. bacteriology and biochemistry U. Idaho, 1981-85; dir. div. Life Scis., prof., head dept. biosci. and biotech. Drexel U., Phila., 1985—; Wis. Alumni Found. grad. fellow, 1951-52; NSF predoctoral fellow, 1952-55; Fellow AAAS, Am. Chem. Soc., Am. Inst. Biol. Sci., Am. Soc. Biochemistry and . Molecular Biology, Am. Soc. Microbiology. Contbr. articles and abstracts to profl. jours., chpts. in books. Research on phospholipid membranes, liposomes as drug carriers, immune modulation, monoclonal antibodies. Home: One Independence Pl 241 S 6th St Philadelphia PA 19106 Office: Drexel U Div Life Scis Philadelphia PA 19104

MAGEE-EGAN, PAULIEN CECILIA, psychology and management educator; b. N.Y.C., Feb. 27, 1934; d. John Joseph and Rosina (Sweeney) Magee; m. Patrick Joseph Egan, Aug. 5, 1967; children: Anne, Patrick, Deirdre, John. BS, Fordham U., 1956, MS, 1957, PhD, 1963. Cert. psychologist, N.Y. Rsch. asst. Fordham U., N.Y.C., 1956-58; asst. dir. Bur. Testing and Guidance St. John's U., Jamaica, N.Y., 1958-62, asst. prof. psychology, 1962-78, assoc. prof. mgmt., 1978—; cons. in field, 1962—. Contbr. articles to profl. publs. Bd. dirs. Winston Pres. Sch., N.Y.C., 1989—, St. Vincent's Hosp., Harrison, N.Y. Mem. APA, N.Y. State Psychol. Assn. (past pres. pers., indsl. and orgnl. div.). Home: 321 Avenue C New York NY 10009-1628

MAGENHEIMER, FRED EDWARD, industrial fabric company executive; b. Bklyn., Nov. 29, 1939; s. Fred. E. Sr. and Mary M. (Hottenroth) M.; m. Paula Slawter, Jan. 15, 1964; children: Richard, Jeffrey. BA, Spring Hill Coll., 1961. Sales trainee Internat. Paper Co., N.Y.C., 1964-65; salesman USI Film Products, Phila. and San Francisco, 1965-67; mgr. regional sales USI Film Products, N.Y.C., 1967-70; salesman Rexham Corp., N.Y.C., 1970-74; mgr. nat. sales Herculite Products Inc., N.Y.C., 1974-78, v.p. sales, 1978-82, exec. v.p., 1982-85, pres., 1985—; v.p., bd. dirs. Health-Chem Corp., N.Y.C. Advisor Friends of Arts, 1984-90; mem. alumni bd. Spring Hill Coll. 1st lt. U.S. Army, 1962-64, Korea. Mem. Port Washington Homeowners Assn. (pres. 1974), Indsl. Fabrics Assn. (bd. dirs. 1988—), Internat. Sleep Products Assn. (suppliers council 1985—, bd. dirs. 1988—), U.S. Indsl. Fabric Inst. (bd. dirs.). Roman Catholic. Home: 1055 Wetherburn Dr York PA 17404-1277 Office: Herculite Products Inc PO Box 786 York PA 14705

MAGER, HOWARD M., publishing company executive; b. Bronx, N.Y., Jan. 28, 1948; s. Maurice H. and Jean (Patner) Mager; m. Diane Susan Tamer, Nov. 19, 1971; children: Jennifer, Erica, Jason. BS, Pa. State U., 1969; MBA, Mich. State U., 1970. Dist. mgr. McGraw-Hill, Inc., N.Y.C., 1970-77, advt. sales mgr., 1977-81, assoc. pub. Chem. Week mag., 1981-82, pub., 1982-85; pub. Bus. Travel News, 1985-87; pub. Engring. News Record, 1987-89; v.p., pub. Construction News Pub. Network, 1989-92; v.p. group pub. Constrn. Publs. Group. Bd. dirs. Constrn. Industry Pres. Forum, Internat. Road Fedn. Office: Engring News Record 1221 Ave Of The Americas New York NY 10020-1001

MAGGARD, MARJORIE LOUISE, health, safety and environment supervisor; b. Rhinebeck, N.Y., Sept. 23, 1939; d. John Allen and Marjorie Edith (Traver) Higgs; m. Donald Kendal Maggard, Nov. 28, 1936; children: Joseph Leon, Donald Jr., Viola Marie. Technician Carborundum, Niagara Falls, N.Y., 1965-70; supr. Carborundum, 1970-72, supt., 1972-84, HSEQ, 1984—; advisor safety bd. Niagara County Community Coll., Sanborn, N.Y., 1988--; author Internat. Loss Control Inst., Loganville, Ga., 1986--; bd. dirs. Niagara Falls Hazardous Materials Mgmt. Com., 1985; CPR and first aid instr. Am. Red Cross. Mem. Colonial Village (N.Y.) Presbyn. Ch.; notary pub. State of N.Y. Mem. Am. Soc. Safety Engrs., Internat. Loss Control, Air and Waste Mgmt. Assn. Home: 5893 Garlow Rd Niagara Falls NY 14304-1016

MAGGARD, MICHAEL JAMES, business administration educator; b. Kansas City, Mo., Jan. 3, 1937; s. Francis Henry and Serra (Harte) M.; m. Patricia Ann Steele, Jan. 29, 1966; children: Michael, Andrea. AA, Kans. City (Mo.) Jr. Coll., 1956; BSME, Kans. State U., 1959; MS in Indsl. Engring., U. Mo., 1961; PhD in Bus. Adminstrn., UCLA, 1968. Registered profl. engr., Calif. Engr. Darby Corp., Kansas City, Kans., 1959-60; asst. prof. San Fernando Valley State Coll., Northridge, Calif., 1961-68, U. Tex., Austin, 1968-73; adj. assoc. prof. Overseas Program (Europe) Boston U., 1973-75, assoc. prof., 1975-80; assoc. prof. Northeastern U., Boston, 1980-83, prof., 1983—. Co-author: Computer Models in Operations Management, 1972, 2d edit., 1977, Computer Models in Operations Research, 1974; contbr. articles to profl. jours. Mem. Inst. Indsl. Engrs. (sr., pres. Austin chpt. 1972-73), Decision Sci. Inst. (sec. 1981-83, pres. N.E. region 1982-83), Inst. Mgmt. Sci., Ops. Mgmt. Assn. Home: 105 Parker Rd Wellesley MA 02181-2231 Office: Northeastern U 360 Huntington Ave Boston MA 02115-5096

MAGGIN, BRUCE, communications executive; b. N.Y.C., Apr. 25, 1943; s. Sherwood and Bernice (Lush) M.; m. Jacqueline M. Montagne, Sept. 2, 1973; children: Benjamin M., Daniel M. BA, Lafayette Coll., 1965; JD, Cornell U., 1968, MBA, 1969. Bar: N.Y. 1969. Fin. analyst ABC, N.Y.C., 1970-71, dir. corp. planning, 1974-79, v.p. cost mgmt., 1982-83; sr. v.p. ABC Video Enterprises, Inc. div. Capital Cities/ABC, Inc., N.Y.C., 1983-88; exec. v.p. CC/ABC Video Enterprises, Inc., N.Y.C., 1988—; cons. Irving Trust Co., N.Y.C., 1972-73; v.p. planning, devel. Ziff Corp., N.Y.C., 1979-82; bd. dirs. ESPN, Inc., N.Y.C., Lifetime Cablevision, N.Y.C., Indesys, Inc., Sunnyvale, Calif., Phillips Van-Heusen, N.Y.C., Merchantec Internat., In-Store Advt. Inc., N.Y.C. Home: 8 Lawrence Farms Crsway Chappaqua NY 10514-1210 Office: CC/ABC Inc 77 W 66th St New York NY 10023-6201

MAGGIPINTO, V. ANTHONY, lawyer; b. Tucson, Apr. 15, 1943; s. William Vito and Elizabeth Maria (Rice) M.; m. Maria Teresa Zequeira, Aug. 31, 1976; children: Marshall Albert Nicholas, Spencer William Jonathan. AB cum laude, Southampton Coll., 1970; JD, Fordham U., 1976. Bar: Fla. 1977, N.Y. 1978, U.S. Dist. Ct. (ea. and so. dists.) N.Y. 1979, U.S. Ct. Appeals (2d cir.) 1980. Asst. to pres. Interpub. Group of Cos., N.Y.C., 1965-66; asst. dean of admission Southampton (N.Y.) Coll., 1971-73; investigative aide N.Y. State Com. on Jud. Conduct, N.Y.C., 1974-76; asst. state atty. Dade County State Atty., Miami, Fla., 1977-78; asst. dist. atty. Suffolk Dist. Atty., Hauppage, N.Y., 1978-80; asst. county atty. Suffolk County Atty., Hauppauge, 1980-84; sole practice Riverhead and St. James, N.Y., 1982—; mem. spl. coms. on discovery, civil litigation U.S. Dist. Ct. (ea. dist.) N.Y., Bklyn., 1983-90, arbitrator, 1986—, ea. dist. adv. group. Mem. appeals bd. SSS, 1982—. Served with USN, 1961-65. Recipient Disting. Alumni award L.I. U., 1990. Mem. N.Y. State Bar Assn., Suffolk County Bar Assn., Fla. Bar, U.S. Naval Inst., Navy League, Submarine League, Alexander Hamilton Inn, Am. Inns of Ct. Republican. Roman Catholic. Club: Nissequogue (N.Y.) Golf (counsel 1980—, bd. govs.). Office: 1212 Roanoke Ave Riverhead NY 11901

MAGIDSON, JAY, statistician; b. Chgo., Mar. 18, 1947; s. Samuel and Shirley Arlene (Weininger) M.; m. Elizabeth Katherine Morgan, Oct. 26, 1976; children: Jeremy, Jenna. BA, U. Ill., 1969; MS in Bus., U. Wis., 1971; PhD in Mgmt., Northwestern U., 1976. Sr. analyst Ill. Bell Telephone Co., Chgo., 1971-72; sr. statistician Abt Assocs., Inc., Cambridge, Mass., 1976-81; founder, pres. Statis. Innovations, Inc., Belmont, Mass., 1981—; presenter seminars; cons. A.C. Nielsen Co., Chgo., Nat. Geographic Soc., Washington, 1984—, Beneficial Mgmt. Corp., Peapack, N.J., 1989—; instr. Boston U., Tufts U.; mem. govt. adv. panel USDA, 1984; expert reviewer govt. panel NIH, Washington, 1989, 91, NSF, Washington, 1982, 87. Author: Reforming Schools, 1980; editor: Analyzing Qualitative/Categorical Data, 1978, Advances in Factor Analysis and Structural Equation Models, 1979; designer CHAID market segmentation computer package; contbr. articles to profl jours.; mem. editorial rev. bd. Jour. Direct Mktg., Evanston, Ill., 1988—; computer sect. editor Jour. Mktg. Rsch., 1983-85. Coach youth basketball, baseball and soccer teams. Mem. Am. Statis. Assn., Direct Mktg. Assn. Office: Statis Innovations Inc 375 Concord Ave Belmont MA 02178-3045

MAGILL, JOSEPH HENRY, chemist, educator; b. Drumnabreeze, Ireland, Dec. 16, 1928; came to U.S., 1962; s. Hugh James and Margaret (Gilliland) M.; m. Joyce Elizabeth Morrow, Dec. 17, 1956; children: Annesley Joyce, Aylmer Campbell. BSc, Queens U., Belfast, Ireland, 1952, PhD, 1956; DIC, U. London, 1957; DSc, Queens U., Belfast, 1990. Prof. dept. materials sci. and engring. U. Pitts., 1975—, prof. dept. chem. and petroleum engring., 1980—, adj. prof. dept. chemistry, 1980—; liaison scientist ONR, London, 1991—. adv. bd. Jour. Polymer Sci., 1991—; contbr. 200 papers to profl. publs. Nat. Coal Bd. fellow Imperial Coll. Sci. and Tech., 1956-57; Mellon Inst. fellow, Pitts., 1962-64, 65-68; sr. rsch. fellow Sci. Rsch. Coun., U. Bristol, Eng., 1975-76; sr. awardee Alexander von Humboldt Found., U. Hamburg-Harburg, Germany, 1984-85, Max Planck Inst. Mainz, Germany, 1984-85. Fellow Am. Phys. Soc., Royal Soc. Chemistry; mem. Am. Chem. Soc.

MAGILL, SARASWATHI SUBBIAH, mathematics educator; b. Calicut, Kerala, India, June 18, 1929; came to U.S., 1965; d. Arumugam and Parvathi (Ramalingam) Subbiah; m. Kenneth Derwood Magill Jr., July 8, 1974. MA in Math., Madras (India) U., 1950; MA in Math. Statistics, Columbia U., 1951; PhD in Math., SUNY, Buffalo, 1973; MS in Computer Sci., SUNY, 1982. Asst. prof. Presidency Coll., Madras, India, 1953-63, Queen Mary's Coll., Madras, 1963-65; instr. SUNY, Buffalo, N.Y., 1967-68; asst. prof. Canisius Coll., Buffalo, 1969-73; lectr. SUNY, Buffalo, 1973-82; asst. prof., assoc. prof., chmn. Daemen Coll., Amherst, N.Y., 1977-80; assoc. prof. Daemen Coll., Amherst, 1980-82, chmn., 1982-83, 85-88, prof., 1982—; visiting prof. U. Monash, Australia, 1985. Contbr. over 20 articles to math. jours. Mem. Am. Math. Soc. Home: 209 Orleans St Buffalo NY 14215-2319 Office: Daemen Coll 4380 Main St Buffalo NY 14226-3592

MAGLIOLA, GERTRUDE LOUISE, educator; b. Jamestown, N.Y., May 2, 1933; d. Frank and Frances R. (Ricotta) M. BE, SUNY, Buffalo, 1955; MEd, SUNY, Fredonia, 1961; postgrad., SUNY, U. Pitts., 1979, Pa. State U., 1962-64; cert. adv. studies spl. edn., Syracuse U., 1966; postgrad., Edinboro State Coll., U. Pitts, 1979. Tchr. elem. sch. Jamestown (N.Y.) Pub. Schs., 1955-65, tchr. spl. edn., 1966—; cons. tchr. tng. insvc. Dunkirk Pub. Schs., 1975-77. Chmn. com. exceptional children Jamestown City Coun. PTA; life mem. Carlyle Ring PTA,; mem. adv. bd. State Univ. Coll., Fredonia, 1978-80; bd. dirs. Jamestown Area Learning Ctr., 1972-76, Jamestown Gen. Hosp., 1980, United Cerebral Palsy Chautauqua County, 1980. Mem. ACLD (charter mem., v.p. Chautauqua County chpt.), N.Y. State Assn. for Handicapped Coun. for Learning Disabilities, NEA (life), Coun. for Exceptional Children, Phi Delta Kappa, Delta Kappa Gamma (v.p. 1988-90, pres. 1990—). Home: 153 S Main St Jamestown NY 14701-6818 Office: Rogers Sch 41 Hebner St Jamestown NY 14701-8499

MAGNARELLI, LOUIS ANTHONY, entomologist, microbiologist; b. Syracuse, N.Y., Mar. 27, 1945; s. David and Jennie (Impeciato) M.; m. Sharon Dishaw, June 28, 1969. BS, SUNY, Oswego, 1967; MS, U. Mich., 1968; PhD, Cornell U., 1975. Asst. entomologist Conn. Agrl. Experiment Sta., New Haven, 1975-78, assoc. entomologist, 1978-81, scientist, 1981-87, chief scientist, 1987—, vice-dir., 1992—; Co-inventor in field. Named Edmund Niles Huyck Rsch. fellow, N.Y., 1974.

MAGNESS SENESCHAL, JACQUELYN, planner; b. Balt., Oct. 14, 1957; d. John Henry and Josephine (Spann); m. Phillip G. Seneschal, Oct. 13, 1990. BA, U. Tenn., 1977; MS, Johns Hopkins U., 1985. Planner's asst. Chattanooga-Hamilton County Regional Planning Commn., Tenn., 1975-77; planner Tenn. State Planning Office, Jackson, 1977-81; planner, chief of devel. review Harford County Govt., Bel Air, Md., 1981-86; dir. planning Charles County Govt., LaPlata, Md., 1985—; instr. Charles County Community Coll., LaPlata, Md., 1986—, Harford Community Coll., Bel Air, 1983-85. Bd. dirs. United Way Charles County, 1989—, Associated Cath. Charities Archdiocese of Washington, 1989—.. Mem. Am. Planning Assn. (bd. dirs. Md. chpt. 1986-90), Md. Assn. County Planners (pres. 1988-89). Democrat. Roman Catholic. Office: Charles County Govt PO Box B La Plata MD 20646-0167

MAGOVERN, LINDA LEE, records management consultant; b. Hartford, Conn., July 20, 1957; d. F. Stanley and Nancy E. Phillips; m. Keith R. Magovern, May 20, 1985. BA in Govt., Norwich U., 1979; AS in Criminal Justice, Vt. Coll., 1979; cert., Inst. for Paralegal Tng., Phila., 1979. Litigation paralegal Fish & Neave, P.C., N.Y.C., 1981, Le Boeuf, Lamb, Leiby & MacRae, P.C., N.Y.C., 1981-82, Pennie & Edmonds, P.C., N.Y.C., 1983-85; v.p. Phillips Cons., Inc., Southport, Conn., 1979—; cons. SUNY, Town of Stoney Point, N.Y., 1990—, Iroquois Gas Transmission System, Shelton, Conn., 1991; rep. Primrica Fin. Svcs., Monroe, Conn., 1991—. Bd. dirs. Sausquinaug Assn., Southport, Conn., 1989—, Welcome Wagon Shelton, 1991. Mem. Assn. Records Mgrs. and Adminstrs. Internat., U.S. Recrea-

tional Ski Assn., Sterling Ski Club, Baldwin Yacht Club, Shennecossett Yacht Club. Republican. Home: 128 Princeton Dr Shelton CT 06484-5126

MAGUIRE, MILDRED MAY, chemistry educator, magnetic resonance researcher; b. Leetsdale, Pa., May 7, 1933; d. John and Mildred (Sklarsky) Magura. BS in Chemistry, Carnegie-Mellon U., 1955; MS in Phys. Chemistry, U. Wis., 1960; PhD in Phys. Chemistry, Pa. State U., 1967. Devel. chemist Koppers Co., Monaca, Pa., 1955-58; rsch. chemist Am. Cyanamid Co., Stamford, Conn., 1960-63; asst. prof. chemistry Waynesburg (Pa.) Coll., 1967-70, assoc. prof., 1970-74, prof., 1974—; Leverhulme vis. prof. U. Leicester, Eng., 1980-81, summer 1989; cons. Pitts. Energy Tech. Ctr., summers 1978-86, Oak Ridge Assoc. univs. faculty rsch. participant, summers 1978-80, 82-85. Contbr. articles to sci. jours., chpt. to book. Sec. Waynesburg Women's Club, 1981-82. Recipient Woman of the Yr. award AAUW, Waynesburg, 1983; Cottrell grantee Rsch. Corp. N.Y., 1970-71; Leverhulme vis. fellow U.K., 1980-81; Curie Internat. fellow AAUW, U.K., 1980-81. Mem. AAUP, Am. Chem. Soc. Home: 1550 Crescent Hls Waynesburg PA 15370-1654 Office: Waynesburg Coll College St Waynesburg PA 15370-1318

MAGUIRE, ROBERT WYMAN, JR., publisher; b. Springfield, Vt., Feb. 26, 1944; s. Robert Wyman and Rosamond (Templeton) M.; m. Carol Ann Zeman, Feb. 14, 1989. AA, Champlain Coll., 1964; BS, Husson Coll., 1967. Law enforcement adminstr. Gov's. Crime Commn., Montpelier, Vt., 1971-73; gen. mgr. The Rutland (Vt.) Shopper, 1973-81, pres., pub., 1981—. Bd. dirs. Mendon Meth. Ch., 1985—, Vt. Epilepsy Found., 1971-75; mem. Vt. Rep. State Com., 1969-73; chmn. Windsor County Rep. Com., Vt., 1969-71, Clarendon Rep. Com., 1985-86. Mem. Rutland Region C. of C., Vt. Jaycees (bd. dirs. 1968-69). Home: Windy Ln North Clarendon VT 05759 Office: The Rutland Shopper 98 Allen St Rutland VT 05701-4592

MAHADEVA, WIJEYARAJ ANANDAKUMAR, information industry executive; b. Colombo, Sri Lanka, Aug. 26, 1952; came to U.S., 1976; s. Balakumara and Sundareswari (Tyagaraja) M. BSEE, Cambridge U., 1973, MSEE, 1980; MBA, Harvard Bus. Sch., 1978. Rsch. and devel. engr. British Broadcasting Corp., London, 1973-76; sr. engagement mgr. McKinsey and Co., N.Y.C., 1978-85; corp. dir. AT&T, Bridgewater, N.J., 1985-89, Dun & Bradstreet Corp., N.Y.C., 1989—. Contbr. articles to profl. jours. Home: 201 E 87th St Apt 15 New York NY 10128-3203

MAHAN, ALEXIS ARMSTRONG, JR., insurance company executive; b. Ft. Wayne, Ind., Jan. 8, 1920; s. Alexis Armstrong Sr. and Olive (Gauntt) M.; m. Marjorie Maclachlan, July 24, 1948; children: Gail Mahan Johnson, Douglas Armstrong, Alexander Maclachlan, Gwendolyn Mahan Davey. Student, Boston U., 1938-39; student, U. Miami, 1947-48. Chief Insp. Equifax Co., New Haven, 1942-45; home office rep. Travelers Ins. Co., Hartford, Conn., 1945-47; agt. Provident Life and Accident Ins. Co. of Chattanooge, Boston, 1947, gen. agt., 1948—. Contbr. articles to profl. jours. Town mem. Rep. Party, Hamilton, Mass., 1956-66, 87—; bd. dirs. Hamilton-Wenham Community Svcs., Hamilton, 1955-58, Camp Fleur de Lis, Fitzwilliam, N.H., 1965-76, Camp O-At-Ka, East Sebago Lake, Maine, 1967-76, Hamilton Hist. Soc., 1985; pres. PTA, Hamilton, 1956-58, Wingaersheek Beach Assn., Inc., Gloucester, Mass., 1957-67; chmn., dir. Devel. Com. Hamilton Wenham Community Svcs., 1955-56; mem. fin. com. Town of Hamilton, 1965-68; trustee Hammond Castle Mus., Magnolia, Mass., 1981—, treas., 1982—; adj. apptd. officer Aleppo Temple. With USMC, 1939-41. Mem. Nat. Assn. Life Underwriters (Nat. Quality award 1953—, life and honor roll mem. million dollar round table 1956—, mem. honor roll 1986), Boston Estate Planning Coun., Gen. Agts. and Mgrs. Assn. of Life Underwriters, '76 Club of Boston, Algonquin Club (chmn. membership com. 1979-83), Downtown Club, Boston Madison Sq. Garden Club, Algonquin Club, Crescent Cove Beach Club, Humanaco Club, P.R. Palmas del Mar Club, Masons (local pres. 1960-68), Royal Order of Jesters, Sigma Alpha Elsilon. Episcopalian. Home and Office: 710 Bay Rd W Hamilton MA 01936 Address: Villa 75 Cresent Cove Palmes del Mar Humacao PR 00661

MAHAN, (DANIEL) DULANY, JR., lawyer, real estate developer; b. Hannibal, Mo., Dec. 22, 1914; s. D. Dulany and Sarah (Marshall) M.; m. Eleanor F. Bethea, Sept. 14, 1948 (div. 1953). AB, U. Mo., Columbia; J.D., Harvard U., 1940. Assoc., Office of George M. Clark, N.Y.C., 1940-42; asst. atty. FTC, Washington, 1948-51; assoc. Adams & James, N.Y.C., 1951-68; assoc. Kurnick & Hackman, N.Y.C., 1968—; ptnr. Tall Pines Estates Devel., Jacksonville, Fla., 1971—; atty., prin. Magnolia Grove Real Estate Devel., Dunedin, Fla., 1976—. Served with U.S. Army, 1942-46. Mem. ABA, Internat. Bar Assn., World Assn. Lawyers, N.Y. Bar Assn., Fed. Bar Assn. Republican. Clubs: Harvard (N.Y.C.); Nat. Lawyers (Washington). Home: 98 Ralph Ave White Plains NY 10606-3611 Office: 660 Madison Ave New York NY 10021

MAHAN, KIERAN THOMAS, podiatric surgeon, educator; b. Stamford, Conn., Feb. 13, 1953; s. John Anthony and Evelyn (Riley) M.; m. Blair Marie Wallace, Aug. 21. 1976; children: Sean, Caitlin, Patrick. BS, U. Toronto, Ont., Can., 1974; MS, U. Bridgeport, 1976; D of Podiatric Medicine, Pa. Coll. Podiatric Medicine, Phila., 1980. Diplomate Am. Bd. Podiatric Surgery. Chief resident Dr.'s Hosp., Tucker, Ga., 1982-83; asst. prof. podiatric surgery Pa. Coll. Podiatric Medicine, Phila., 1983-86, assoc. prof., v.p. acad. affairs, 1986—; permanent faculty, founding bd. trustees The Podiatry Inst., Tucker, 1990—; bd. dirs. Nat. Bd. Podiatric Med. Examiners. Contbr. over 50 articles, chpts. to profl. publs. Fellow Am. Coll. Foot Surgeons; mem. Am. Poliatric Med. Assn., Am. Coll. Podopediatrics, Am. Assn. Colls. of Podiatric Medicine (chmn. coun. of deans 1987). Roman Catholic. Office: Pa Coll Podiatric Medicine 810 Race St Philadelphia PA 19107-2406

MAHAR, LAWRENCE WILLIAM, publisher; b. Saratoga Springs, N.Y., July 18, 1928; s. John P. and Edna P. (Krajewski) M.; m. Hazel C. Holmwood, June 7, 1955; children: Michael, Laura, Monica, William, Frances, Daniel, Lawrence, Patrick. BA in English, Siena Coll., 1951. Advt. and pub. rels. dir. Stewart's Ice Cream Corp., Saratoga, 1953-56; mktg. communications mgr. GE, Waterford (N.Y.), Pittsfield, Mass., 1956-71; v.p. Ross Roy/Compton, Inc. Advt., N.Y.C., 1971-81; pres. L & H Mahar Art Publishers, Middle Grove, N.Y., 1981—; cons. Ross Roy/Compton, Inc., N.Y.C., 1981-82. Contbr. articles to profl. jours. Mem. Bd. Edn., Saratoga Springs, 1968-69; publicity chmn. Saratoga County Am. Cancer Soc., Saratoga Springs, 1964-69; adv. com. N.Y. State Legis. Cpl. U.S. Army, 1951-53. Republican. Roman Catholic. Home: 945 Murray Rd Middle Grove NY 12850 Office: L&H Mahar Art Publishers RR 2 Box 502 Middle Grove NY 12850

MAHARAM, LEWIS G., sports medicine physcian; b. Bklyn., Feb. 2, 1955; s. Robert Donald and Jane Barbara (Lowy) M.; m. Marcia Jan Michelson, Dec. 29, 1984; 1 child, Edward Raymond. BA in Biology with honors, Lafayette Coll., 1977; MD, Emory U., 1985. Cert. in sports medicine. Surg. intern Columbia-Presbyn. Med. Ctr., N.Y.C., 1985-86; med. intern Danbury (Conn.) Hosp., 1986-87; med. resident N.Y. Infirmary/Beekman Downtown Hosp., 1987-89; sports medicine fellow Pascack Valley Hosp., Westwood, N.J., 1989-90; dir. sports medicine fellowship program Pascack Valley Hosp., Westwood, 1990-91; med. dir. Sports Medicine Assocs. at Downtown Athletic Club, 1990—; chmn. med. svcs. subcom. Met. Athletics Congress Sports Medicine Team, N.Y.C., 1990-91; med. dir. Nat. Scholastic Track and Field Championship, N.Y.C., 1989-92; vol. med. capt. N.Y.C. Marathon, 1987-92; med. cons. Am. Acad. Sports Dentistry, Maywood, N.J., 1990-92; team physician Emerson (N.J.) High Sch. Football, 1989-90. Author: Maharam's Curve: The Exercise High-How to Get It, How to Keep It, 1992; host Runners Workshop Downtown Athletic Club, N.Y.C.; contbr. articles to profl. jours. Mem. Am. Coll. Physicians, Am. Running & Fitness Assn., Am. Bd. Sports Medicine (chmn. bd. examiners), Nat. Athletic Trainers Assn. (assoc.), Nat. Strength & Conditioning Assn. Home: 401 E 84th St Apt 12A New York NY 10028-6268

MAHER, CAROLYN ALEXANDER, mathematics educator; b. N.J., Jan. 19, 1941; d. John J. and Josephine Claire (Balsewicz) Alexander; m. James A. Maher; 1 child, Steven. BA, Rutgers U., 1962, MEd, 1965, EdD, 1972. Tchr. math. Scotch Plains (N.Y.)- Fanwood High Sch., Matawan Regional, 1962-68; assoc. prof. math., asst. dean Middlesex County Coll., Edison, N.J., 1968-73; vis. prof. math. edn. Rutgers Grad. Sch. Edn., New Brunswick, N.J., 1974-81, chairperson dept. sci. and humanities edn., 1983-85, assoc. prof. math. edn., 1981-91, prof. math. edn., 1992—; acting dir. Rutgers U. Ctr. Math., Sci. and Computer Edn., 1984-85; vis. scholar faculty acad. scholarship program Stanford U., 1987; vis. assoc. prof. dept. devel. and ednl. psychology Tchrs. Coll., Columbia U., 1988; ctr. assoc. U. Wis. Nat. Ctr. Edn. Rsch., Learning/Instrn. Group in Math. Scis. Edn., 1988—; dir. Rutgers-New Brunswick Math. Projects, 1988—, Children with Ptnrs., 1989—, Tchr. Devel. in Math. Rutgers-Schs. Projects, 1988—, Springfield Pub. Schs. Math. Assessment Project, 1989-90. Mem. editorial bd. Teaching Thinking and Problem Solving, 1985-88, Internat. Jour. Applied Engring. Edn., 1986—, Jour. Math. Behavior, 1990—; contbg. author: Math 1 and 2, 1981, 82, Teacher's Guides to Math 1 and 2, 1981, 82, Math 1 and 2 Workbooks, 1989; author: (with J.A. Maher) Applied Statistics, 1973, Statistics for the Beginning Reseacher, 1977; contbr. articles to profl. jours., chpts. to books. Recipient Disting. Svc. award Alumni Assn. Grad. Sch. Edn. Rutgers U., 1990, C. Orswald George prize, 1990, Pioneer in Edn. award for innovative and successful math. tchr. devel. in N.J., Am. Assn. for Higher Edn. and Coll. Bd., 1990. Mem. Internat. Group for Psychology Math. Edn. (pres. North Am. chpt. 1988-90, exec. com. 1986—, program com. 1989—), Am. Soc. Engring. Edn. (elected pres. math. div. 1989-90), Douglass Soc. Assoc. Alumnae Douglass Coll. Rutgers U. Office: Rutgers U Grad Sch Math Sci Computer 10 Seminary Pl New Brunswick NJ 08901

MAHER, CHARLES ANDREW, psychology educator; b. Bayonne, N.J., June 23, 1944. BA, Montclair State Coll., 1966, MA, 1969; profl. diploma in psychology, Kean Coll., 1973; PhD in Psychology, Rutgers U., 1976. Lic. psychologist, N.J.; cert. supt., N.J.; cert. Internat. Bd. Trainers; diplomate Bd. Adminstrv. Psychology. Tchr. of handicapped Southington (Conn.) Pub. Schs., 1966-68; sch. psychologist Kearny (N.J.) Pub. Schs., 1968-73; dir. spl. svcs. Somerville (N.J.) Pub. Schs., 1973-75, asst. supt. schs., 1975-79; assoc. prof. Rutgers U., New Brunswick, N.J., 1979-83, prof., chair dept. applied psychology, 1983—; cons. Wis. Dept. Pub. Instrn., Madison, 1985—, N.J. Dept. Labor, Trenton, 1988—, Chgo. White Sox, N.Y. Yankees, 1989—, Gen. Motors Corp., Rowe Internat.; dir. Inst. Program Planning/Evaluation, Piscataway, N.J., 1991—. Author: Planning and Evaluating Services, 1985, Self Management, 1986; editor Spl. Svcs. jour., 1980—; contbr. articles to profl. jours. Fellow APA (div. v.p. 1986-88, Am. Psychol. Soc., Am. Assn. for Applied and Provacative Psychology. Office: Rutgers U Grad Sch Psychology PO Box 819 Piscataway NJ 08855-0819

MAHER, DANIEL JAY, management consultant; b. Boston, Oct. 11, 1950; s. William and Margaret Mary (Christensen) M. AB, Harvard U., 1984; MBA, Cornell U., 1986. Chef Hayashi Inc., Boston, 1971-74; TV producer/talent KSCI TV, L.A., 1974-75; restaurant mgr. Hayashi Inc., Boston, 1976-84; rsch. assoc. The Harvard Bus. Sch., Cambridge, Mass., 1986-89; cons. The TQM Group Ltd., Cambridge, Mass., 1989—; lectr. in field; dir. ISQA, N.Y.C., The TQM Group (Mexico). Contbr. articles to profl. jours. Republican. Office: The TQM Group Ltd 20 University Rd # 510 Cambridge MA 02138-5756

MAHER, JAMES VINCENT, JR., physics educator; b. N.Y.C., Aug. 25, 1942; s. James Vincent and Anne (Cunneen) M.; m. Angela Beth Braunstein, Aug. 13, 1966; children: Robin, James. BS in Physics, U. Notre Dame, 1964; MS in Physics, Yale U., 1965, PhD in Physics, 1969. Postdoctoral fellow Argonne (Ill.) Nat. Lab., 1968-70; asst. prof. U. Pitts., 1970-74, assoc. prof., 1974-80, prof., 1980—, dept. chair physics and astronomy, 1991—; dir. Scaife nuclear physics lab., 1979-80. Contbr. over 100 articles to profl. jours. Grantee Dept. Energy, NSF. Fellow AAAS, Am. Phys. Soc.; mem. Am. Chrystal Growth Assn. (pres. Pitts. chpt. 1989—, exec. com. 1990—), Sigma Xi. Democrat. Roman Catholic. Home: 1313 Denniston Ave Pittsburgh PA 15217-1330 Office: U Pitts Dept Physics and Astronomy Pittsburgh PA 15260

MAHER, JOHN FRANCIS, physician, educator; b. Hempstead, N.Y., Aug. 3, 1929; s. William Lawrence and Marie Elizabeth (Duffy) M.; m. Margaret Helen Ulincy, Oct. 24, 1953; children: John Michael, Andrew, Mary, George, Paul Duffy. BS, Georgetown U., 1949, MD, 1953. Diplomate Am. Bd. Internal Medicine. Intern Boston City Hosp., 1953-54; resident Georgetown U. Med. Ctr., Washington, 1956-58, fellow in nephrology, 1958-60; instr. medicine Georgetown U., 1960-62, asst. prof., 1962-68, assoc. prof., 1968-69; prof. U. Mo. Med. Ctr., Columbia, 1969-74, U. Conn. Health Sci. Ctr., Farmington, 1974-79, Uniformed Services Univ. Health Scis., Bethesda, Md., 1979—; dir. Georgetown Univ. Med. Ctr. Renal Clinic, 1962-69, Univ. Mo. Med. Ctr. Nephrology Div. and Clin. Research Ctr., 1969-74, Univ. Conn. Health Ctr. Nephrology Div. and Clin. Research Ctr., 1974-79, Uniformed Service Univ. Health Scis. Nephrology Div., 1979—. Author: Uremia, 1961, The Kidney, 1971; editor: Replacement of Renal Function by Dialysis, 1978; contbr. more than 200 articles to profl. jours. Served to capt. USAF, 1954-56. Recipient Karol Marcinkowski award Univ. Poznan, Poland, 1985. Fellow ACP (mem. editorial bd. 1975-78), Royal Coll. Physicians of Ireland (hon.); mem. Am. Soc. Nephrology (audit com. chmn. 1973), Am. Soc. Artificial Internal Organs (pres. 1975-76), Internat. Soc. Nephrology (mem. program com. 1966, nominating com. 1975), Am. Fedn. Clin. Rsch. (editor 1967-69). Republican. Roman Catholic. Home: 8104 Gainsborough Ct E Rockville MD 20854-4271 Office: Uniformed Services U Health Scis 4301 Jones Bridge Rd Bethesda MD 20814-4799

MAHER, JOSEPH PATRICK, mental health professional; b. Phila., July 18, 1934; s. John Patrick and Anna M. (Crowe) M.; m. Rosemary Christine Rybachok, June 23, 1972 (div. Oct. 1974); children: Christopher, Francis; m. Anne Marie Snyder, Nov. 12, 1976; children: Darin, Timothy. BA, LaSalle U., 1961; MEd, Temple U., 1972. Lic. psychologist, Pa. Classification supr. Ea. State Penitentiary, Phila., 1962-69, Pa. Dept. Corrections Graterford (Pa.) Prison, 1969-72; vocat. psychologist Philco-Ford Corp., Phila., 1972-74; counseling dir. Cen. Med. Intake, Inc., Phila., 1974-78, exec. dir., 1978-80; dir. drug treatment svcs. Goldman Clinic, Phila., 1980-81; cons. Phila., 1981-83; career counselor Jewish Employment and Vocat. Svcs., Phila., 1983-88; evening supr. Joseph J. Peters Inst., Phila., 1984-88, assoc. dir., 1988—. Chair bd. dirs. Weavers Way Coop., 1973-75. With USCG, 1953-57. Mem. Am. Psychol. Assn. (assoc.), Pa. Psychol. Assn. Democrat. Office: Joseph J Peters Inst 407 Longfield Rd Philadelphia PA 19118-1340

MAHER, TIMOTHY JOHN, pharmacologist, educator; b. Boston, Nov. 24, 1953; s. Robert Daniel and Veronica Irene (Cody) M.; m. Barbara Jean Walz, Aug. 20, 1977; children: Andrew Michael, Matthew Edward, Elizabeth Irene. BS, Boston State Coll., 1976; PhD, Mass. Coll. Pharmacy, 1980. Asst. prof. Mass. Coll. Pharmacy, Boston, 1980-83, assoc. prof., 1983-87, prof., 1987—, chmn., 1987—; postdoctoral fellow MIT, Cambridge, 1983-88, lectr., 1988—; bd. dirs. Mass. Soc. Med. Rsch., Waltham, 1985—; adv. bd. Mass. Poison Control System, Boston, 1990—. Contbr. 75 articles to profl. jours. Roman Catholic. Office: Mass Coll Pharmacy 179 Longwood Ave Boston MA 02115-5896

MAHER, WILLIAM PATRICK, guidance counselor, educator; b. N.Y.C., Oct. 19, 1936; s. Paul Robert Maher and Marie Josephine (Reilly) McWilliams; m. Elaine Ann Mahar, July 28, 1973; children: Elaine-Marie, Kathryn, Deirdre, John. BA, Marist Coll., 1958; MEd, De Paul U., 1970. Cert. tchr., guidance adminstrn., vocat. edn. adminstrn., Mass. Tchr. Cardinal Hayes High Sch., Bronx, N.Y., 1959-65; tchr. Marist High Sch., Chgo., 1965-67, vice prin., 1967-70; resource tchr. Norwood (Mass.) Jr. High Sch., 1970-71, guidance counselor, 1989—; guidance counselor Henry O. Peabody Sch., Norwood, Mass., 1971-80, dir., 1980-89. Mem. NEA, Mass. Tchrs. Assn., Mass. Vocat. Adminstrs. Assn. Roman Catholic. Home: PO Box 702 Norton MA 02766-0702 Office: Norwood Pub Schs Washington St Norwood MA 02062-1508

MAHINIS, JOHN NICHOLAS, rehabilitation services professional; b. Youngstown, Ohio, June 5, 1961; s. Nicholas Tom and Venice (Diamantis) M.; m. Dianne Bernadette Berry, Jan. 18, 1985; children: Kally Marie, Nicholas John. BA, Youngstown State U., 1981, MS, 1983; PhD, Columbia Pacific U., 1986; MBA, Newport U., 1992. Cert. counselor; lic. social worker and counselor, Ohio. Vocat. evaluator Youngstown Devel. Ctr., Mineral Ridge, Ohio, 1984; caseworker Mahoning County Children Svcs., Youngstown, Ohio, 1984-86; psychotherapist Youngstown, 1984-86, Ea. Mental Health Ctr., Struthers, Ohio, 1986; clin. supr. North Penn Comprehensive Health Svcs., Blossburg, Pa., 1987-88; clin. dir. North Penn Comprehensive Health Svcs., Blossburg, 1988-90; program dir. Allegany Rehab. Assocs., Wellsville, N.Y., 1990-91, Pathways, Inc., Corning, N.Y., 1991—; adj. faculty mem. Newport U., Newport Beach, Calif., 1987—, Columbia Pacific U., San Rafael, Calif., 1986—, Pa. Coll. Tech., Wellsboro, 1989-90; crisis interventionist Tioga County Human Svcs. Agy., Wellsboro, 1987-90; group therapist North Cen. Pa. Vets. Coalition, Covington, Pa., 1989-90; continuing edn. program reviewer Nat. Bd. Cert. Counselors, Alexandria, Va., 1991—; pvt. practice, Hornell, N.Y., 1991—. Chmn. Tigoa County (Pa.) Sexual Abuse Task Force, 1989; speaker Mahoning County Children's Svcs., North Penn and Allegheny Rehab. Assocs., Inc., 1985—. Capt. USAR, 1981—. Recipient Nat. Meritorious Svc. award for acad. excellence U.S. Dept. Def., 1981. Mem. AACD, Nat. Bd. Cert. Counselors, Res. Officers Assn., Allegheny County Mental Health Assn. (bd. mem.), Masons. Greek Orthodox. Home: 418 Hillbrook Ave Elmira NY 14905 Office: Pathways to Learning Day Treatment Program 280 Denison Pkwy Corning NY 14840

MAHLE, CHRISTOPH ERHARD, electrical engineer; b. Stuttgart, Germany, Mar. 7, 1938; came to U.S., 1968; s. Ernst Johannes and Else (Wurth) M.; m. Mary Heavenrich, Mar. 23, 1975; children: Lisa, Charles. Diploma engring., Swiss Fed. Inst. Polytech., Zurich, 1961, D of Sci. Tech., 1966. Rsch. asst. Swiss Fed. Inst. Tech., Zurich, Switzerland, 1961-67; with tech. staff Comsat Labs., Clarksburg, Md., 1968-71, sect. head, 1971-73, dept. mgr., 1973-81, dir., 1981-83, exec. dir., 1983—. Patentee in field; contbr. articles to profl. jours. Fellow IEEE. Office: Comsat Labs 22300 Comsat Dr Clarksburg MD 20871-9475

MAHLE, WALTER STEPHEN, marketing executive; b. Cleve., July 8, 1938; s. Walter Stephen and Florence Agatha (Gerbracht) M.; m. Lynne Marie Miller, Sept. 12, 1959; children: Mary Gretchen, Marcia Anne, W. Stephen, John Lawrence, Jennifer Lynne. BEE, Villanova (Pa.) U., 1961. Nat. systems slaes mgr. Leeds & Northrup Co., North Wales, Pa., 1964-76; dir. ea. region Applicon, Phila., 1976-82; v.p. mktg. Skantek Corp., Warren, N.J., 1982-85; v.p. mfg. ind. mktg. Unisys Corp., Blue Bell, Pa., 1985—. 1st lt. USMC, 1961-64. Mem. Armed Forces Com. Electronics Assn. Home: 188 Gwynedd Manor Rd North Wales PA 19454-2426 Office: Unisys Corp PO Box 500 Blue Bell PA 19424-0001

MAHLER, STEVEN WAYNE, package designer; b. Bklyn., Sept. 7, 1954; s. Marvin Bernard and Vivian (Kahan) M.; m. Heléne Cohn, Oct. 5, 1980; 1 child, Matthew Seth. BS, Rochester Inst. Tech., 1976. Package designer Conpac, Inc., New Orleans, 1976-77; sample maker Wallace Packaging, Maspeth, N.Y., 1977-78; display designer Display Producers, Inc., Springfield Gardens, N.Y., 1978-79; package engr. Queens Group, Woodside, N.Y., 1979-84; freelance package designer N.Y.C., 1984-85; dir. packaging devel. Shorewood Packaging Corp., N.Y.C., 1985—. Designer Barbra Streisand Packaging (Grammy nomination 1992); patentee compact disc package Slidepak. Goalie, coach Canadian Adult Hockey Assn. Recipient Bronze medal Canadian Adult Hockey Assn., 1988, Silver medal, 1989. Office: Shorewood Packaging Corp 10 E 53d St New York NY 10022

MAHN, ANTONY LEROY, television producer; b. Boston, Dec. 31, 1943; s. John Edward and Geneva (Beatty) M. BA, Franklin and Marshall Coll., 1965; cert. in journalism, Columbia U., 1968. Mail clk. Sta. WNET/13, N.Y.C., 1965-67, supr., 1967-68, news assoc., 1968-71, asst. news dir./producer, 1971-73; freelance news producer N.Y.C., 1971-73; assoc. producer MacNeil/Lehrer Prodns., N.Y.C., 1983—. Editor: Guide to Culinary Sources, 1989. Trustee alumni bd. Franklin and Marshall Coll., Lancaster, Pa., 1988-92, mem. pres.'s regional adv. coun., 1992—. Mem. Am. Film Inst., Acad. TV Arts and Scis. (Emmy award nominee 1979-80), Soc. Profl. Journalists, Culinary Historians N.Y. (cons.), James Beard Found. Episcopalian. Home: 309 W 19th St #51 New York NY 10011 Office: MacNeil/Lehrer Prodns 356 W 58th St New York NY 10019

MAHNI, DANIEL EZRA, commodity banker; b. Baghdad, Iraq, June 28, 1945; came to U.S. 1969; BSc summa cum laude, Al-Hikma U., Iraq, 1968; MBA, NYU, 1982; MA, Harvard U., 1972, Harvard U., 1979. V.p. The Chase Manhattan Bank, N.Y.C., 1976-88; sr. v.p. Republic Nat. Bank of N.Y., N.Y.C., 1988—. Contbr. articles to profl. jours.; translator from English to Arabic: F.M. Cornford's Before and After Socrates. Fellow Ctr. for Internat. Affairs, 1974-76. Mem. Internat. Precious Metals Inst., Soc. for Advancement of Mgmt. (pres. 1966-68).

MAHNKEN, THOMAS GILBERT, policy analyst, consultant; b. La Jolla, Calif., Aug. 13, 1965; s. Thomas Elmer Jr. and Madeleine Amelia (Grout) M. BA, U. So. Calif., 1987; MA, Johns Hopkins U., 1989. Policy analyst Heritage Found., Washington, 1987-88; analyst U.S. Dept. Def., Washington, 1988; policy analyst SRS Technologies, Arlington, Va., 1988—. Editor Sch. of Advanced Internat. Studies Rev., 1988; contbr. articles to profl. jours. Regents fellow, 1983, John M. Olin fellow, 1988. Mem. U.S. Naval Inst., Internat. Inst. for Strategic Studies, Phi Beta Kappa, Phi Kappa Phi, Pi Sigma Alpha. Republican. Episcopalian. Office: SRS Technologies 1500 Wilson Blvd Ste 800 Arlington VA 22209-2415

MAHON, ARTHUR JOSEPH, lawyer; b. N.Y.C., Jan. 13, 1934; s. Arthur Logan and Mary Agnes (Craine) M.; m. Myra E. Murphy, Aug. 10, 1957; children—Maura, Madonna, Arthur, Nancy. B.A., Manhattan Coll., 1955; JD, NYU, 1958. Bar: N.Y., Fla., D.C. Adj. prof. law NYU Sch. of Law, N.Y.C., 1964-78; ptnr. Mudge, Rose, Guthrie, Alexander & Ferdon, N.Y.C., 1970—. Trustee Manhattan Col., N.Y., 1988—, Adrian and Jesse Archnold Charitable Trust, N.Y.C., 1976—; mem. joint bd. N.Y. Hosp.-Cornell Med. Ctr., N.Y.C., 1990—; mem. com. on trust and estate gift plans Rockefeller U., N.Y.C., 1984—; bd. dirs. United Way Internat., 1988—, Alexandria, Va.; chmn. planned giving com. lawyers, bankers, and accts. Archdiocese N.Y., N.Y.C., 1985—; vice chmn. bd. overseers Cornell Med. Coll., N.Y.C., 1986-92, chmn., 1992—; dir. Skin Disease Soc., N.Y.C., 1989—, Noel Found., San Francisco, 1990—. Served to capt. USAF, 1958-60. Mem. N.Y. State Bar Assn., Bar Assn. City of N.Y., Fla. Bar Assn., D.C. Bar Assn., Royal Soc. Medicine Found. (bd. dirs. 1977—, pres. 1979—), India House Club (Hanover Sq., N.Y.), Sky CLub (N.Y.C.). Home: 16 Cambridge Dr Madison CT 06443 Office: Mudge Rose Guthrie Alexander & Ferdon 630 5th Ave New York NY 10111-0002

MAHON, WILLIAM MICHAEL, III, college administrator; b. Altoona, Pa., Apr. 24, 1954; s. Wiliam Michael Jr. and Mary Helen (McNally) M. BA in English, Lock Haven State U., 1976. Reporter The Lewistown (Pa.) Sentinel, 1976-81, news editor, 1981-84; asst. mgr. Pa. State U., University Park, 1984, mgr. news bur., 1984-86, dir. pub. info., 1986—. Author: (with others) Teaching How To Work In Groups, 1990; contbr. articles to jours. Vol. William Penn Nursing Ctr., Lewistown, 1981-91; mem. pub. rels. com. Cen. Pa. Festival of Arts, 1988; bd. dirs. Roundhay Ct. Condo Assn., 1990-91. Recipient 1st Pl. Pa. Newspaper Pubs., Harrisburg, 1982, 83, 84, Rebeccca Gross Journalism award Lock Haven U., 1983. Mem. Coll. and U. Pub. Rels. Assn. Pa. (treas. 1987-89, v.p. 1990-91, pres. 1991-93), Coun. for Advancement and Support of Edn., Big Ten News Dirs. Assn., Kappa Tau Alpha (pres. Pa. State U. chpt. 1988-89). Roman Catholic. Home: 9188 Southgate Dr State College PA 16801-4347 Office: Pa State U 312 Old Main University Park PA 16802-1504

MAHONEY, JAMES JOSEPH, library director; b. Bronx, N.Y., Nov. 6, 1946; s. Frank J. and Virginia (Bartlett) M. BA, St. Joseph's Seminary, Yonkers, N.Y., 1970; MLS, Pratt Inst., Bklyn., 1975; MA, Manhattan Coll., 1978. Cert. pub. libr.; lic. real estate broker. Assoc. libr. dir. St. Joseph's Seminary, 1971-79; exec. v.p. The Scholars' Windmill, Ltd., Bklyn., 1979-80; exec. dir. U.S. Cath. Hist. Soc., Yonkers, 1980-85; dir. Sloatsburg (N.Y.) Pub. Libr., 1985-88, The Nyack (N.Y.) Libr., 1988—; mgr. Coldwell Banker Real Estate, Cornwall, N.Y., 1985-87. Editor U.S. Cath. Historian jour., 1980-85. Mem. Rotary, Ramapo Catskill Libr. Dir. (vice chmn. 1988-90), N.Y. Area Theol. Libr. Assn. (com. chmn. 1978), ANSER Automation Coun. (chmn. 1991-92). Democrat. Episcopalian. Office: The Nyack Libr 59 S Broadway Nyack NY 10960-3816

MAHONEY, JAMES VINCENT, corporate tax manager; b. Darby, Pa., Nov. 7, 1956; s. E. Russell and Adeline L. (Zacchie) M.; m. Elizabeth

Serpente, June 4, 1983; 1 child, Karen Elizabeth. AS, Pierce Jr. Coll., Phila., 1980; BS, St. Joseph's U., Phila., 1984; M. in Taxation, Villanova U., 1990. Staff acct. Sun Refining & Mktg. Co., Phila., 1980-86; tax supr. Sun Co., Radnor, Pa., 1986-88; tax mgr. Comcast Corp., Phila., 1988—; tax cons. Martin T. Sarkies Corp., Wayne, Pa., 1989-90. Mem. Tax Execs. Inst., Cable TV Tax Profl. Inst., Cellular Telecommunications Inst. Am. (tax com.), Greater Phila. C. of C. (tax com.). Republican. Roman Catholic. Home: 240 Friendship Rd Drexel Hill PA 19026-5011 Office: Comcast Corp 1234 Market St Philadelphia PA 19107-3727

MAHONEY, JOËLLE KATHERINE, astrological consultant, communications educator; b. Amiens, France, Jan. 6, 1948; came to U.S., 1953; d. Louis James and Regine (LeClercq) Dennis; m. John William Christopher Mahoney, Aug. 14, 1971. AA, Boro Manhattan C.C., 1971; BA, Adelphi U., 1982; MS student, Hofstra U., 1989—. Profl. cert. in astrology; cert. master practitioner neurolinguistic programming. Tri-lingual translator N.A. Bogdan Co., N.Y.C., 1967-71; practicing astrologer Long Island, N.Y., 1971-74; founding pres. Astrological Rsch. Centre and Tng. Inst. Ltd., Mineola, N.Y., 1974-84; internat. astrological cons. Brewster, N.Y., 1984—. Author: Concept I, II and III, 1974, In Search of Time, 1989. Vol. fund raiser Americares, New Canaan, Conn., 1991—, Silver Hill Hosp., New Canaan, 1992—. Mem. Astrologers Guild Am. (pres. 1980-83), Congress of Astrological Orgns. (v.p. 1981-84). Home: 5 Fair Meadow Dr Brewster NY 10509

MAHONEY, MARY JUDITH, educator; b. Bklyn., Dec. 28, 1945; d. Edward Joseph and Kathryn Emily (Phillips) M. BA, St. Elizabeth's Coll., Convent Station, N.J., 1968; MA, U. Scranton, 1974. Cert. tchr., N.J. Tchr. Holy Trinity Elem. Sch., Hackensack, N.J., 1967-70, St. Bridget's Elem. Sch., Jersey City, 1970-72; grad. asst. U. Scranton, Pa., 1972-73; tchr. St. Rose High Sch., Belmar, N.J., 1975—, chair dept. English, 1986—. Mem. NOW, NCEA, Nat. Coun. Tchrs. English, N.J. Coun. Tchrs. English, English-Speaking Union, Jane Austen Soc. N.Am. Office: Saint Rose High Sch 607 7th Ave Belmar NJ 07719-2299

MAHONEY, PATRICK MORGAN, judge; b. Winnipeg, Man., Can., Jan. 20, 1929; s. Paul Morgan and Joan Ethel Tracy (Patrick) M.; m. Mary Alma Sneath, June 28, 1958; children: Michael G., Patrick M., Sheila M., D'Arcy C. B.A., U. Alta., 1950, LL.B., 1951. Bar: Alta. 1952, apptd. Queen's counsel 1972, U.S. Ct. Mil. Appeals (hon.) 1983. Justice trial div. Fed. Ct. Can., Ottawa, Ont., 1973-83; judge Ct. Martial Appeal Ct. Can., Ottawa, 1973-82; chief justice Ct. Martial Appeal Ct. Can., 1982—; pres. Martial Appeal Ct. Can., 1982-83; judge Fed. Ct. Appeal, 1983—; Mem. Parliament for Calgary South, 1968-72, sec. to minister of fin., 1970-71, minister of state, 1972. Mem. Can. Judges Conf. (dir. 1981), Calgary Golf and Country Club, Rideau Club. Home: 3 Coltrin Pl, Ottawa, ON Canada K1M 0A5 Office: Fed Ct Can, Kent & Wellington Sts, Ottawa, ON Canada K1A 0H9

MAHONEY, WILLIAM FRANCIS, editor; b. Joliet, Ill., Jan. 24, 1935; s. Cletus George and Mildred Marie (Ochs) M.; m. Carroll Frances Johnson, June 28, 1958; children: Erin Michele, Kevin William, Megan Ann, Sheila Marie, Nora Aileen. BS in Journalism, Marquette U., 1957. Reporter Ft. Wayne (Ind.) News Sentinel, 1958-59; pub. relations mgr. Motorola, Inc., Franklin Park, Ill., 1959-66; sr. account exec. Young & Rubicam, Inc., Chgo., 1966-68; pub. info. dir. ABA, Chgo., 1969-71; investor relations mgr. Chemetron Corp., Chgo., 1971-76; corp. communications dir. Scott Paper Co., Phila., 1976-80; pub. relations dir. Esmark Inc., Chgo., 1980-81; prin. Mahoney & Mitchell Incorp., Phila., 1981-89; communications cons. Author: Investor Relations: The Professional's Guide to Financial and Marketing Communications, 1991; editor Investor Rels. Update. Mem. Nat. Investor Relations Inst. (pres. Phila. chpt. 1982-84, v.p. 1988—), Pub. Relations Soc. Am. (treas. Phila. chpt. 1979), Vesper Club. Republican. Roman Catholic. Home and Office: 716 S Brandywine St West Chester PA 19382-3511

MAHONY, CHRISTINA HUNT, writing educator; b. Trenton, N.J., Jan. 10, 1949; d. George Joseph and Dorothy Frances (Matheson) Hunt; m. Robert Emmet Mahony, Jan. 20, 1973; 1 child, Nora Matheson. BA, Marquette U., 1970; MA, Univ. Coll., Dublin, Ireland, 1971, PhD, 1988. Lectr. dept. English U. Ill., Chgo., 1975-78, asst. dir. Writing Ctr., 1976-78; lectr. dept. English Cath. U. Am., Washington, 1978—, asst. dir. Ctr. Irish Studies, 1984—; guest lectr. Newberry Libr., Chgo., 1976; editorial cons. Peter Lang Publs., Switzerland, 1991. Contbr. articles to lit. revs., scholarly publs. Mem. MLA, Am. Com. Irish Studies, Internat. Assn. Anglo-Irish Lit., Univ. Coll. Grads. Assn. (pres. 1985-86), Yeats Soc. (com. mem. 1988-89), Joyce Soc. (com. mem. 1985). Democrat. Roman Catholic. Office: Irish Studies Cath Univ Michigan Ave NE Washington DC 20064

MAHOOD, R. WAYNE, educator; b. Maryville, Mo., July 16, 1934; s. Victor E. and Ruth D. (England) M.; m. Barbara Clark, Dec. 29, 1956; children: Bruce Lee, David Clark. AB, Hamilton Coll., 1956; MA, U. Ill., 1962, PhD, 1969. Tchr. social studies York Community High Sch., Elmhurst, Ill., 1959-66; prof. edn. SUNY, Geneseo, 1969—, chair dept. edn., 1980-83. Author: Government USA, 1985, The Plymouth Pilgrims, 1989; contbr. articles prof. jours. Recipient Disting. Social Studies Educator award N.Y. State Coun. for the Social Studies, 1984. Mem. N.Y. State Coun. for Social Studies (pres. 1977-78), Nat. Coun. Social Studies, Phi Delta Kappa.

MAIDENBAUM, ARYEH YEHUDA, psychoanalyst; b. N.Y.C., May 21, 1942; s. Nathan and Esther (Rosenman) M.; m. Judith Covitz, Sept. 5, 1965 (div. Aug. 1985); children: Barak, Leah, Hepzibah; m. Diana Rubin, Feb. 4, 1990. BA, Hofstra U., 1963; MA, NYU, 1969; PhD, Hebrew U., 1977; Diploma, C.G. Jung Inst., 1981. Instr. Hebrew U., 1972-77; exec. dir. C.G. Jung Found. of N.Y., Jerusalem, Israel, 1982—; adj. profl. NYU, 1980—, CUNY, Lehman Coll., 1982—. Co-editor: Lingering Shadows, 1991; contbr. articles to profl. jours. Mem. Internat. Assn. Analytical Psychology, N.Y. Assn. Analytical Psychology. Jewish. Office: C G Jung Found 28 E 39th St New York NY 10016

MAIDMENT, FREDERICK HEROLD, management educator; b. Washington, Nov. 15, 1947; s. Edward and Elinor Juanita (Terheidi) M.; m. Sandra E. Halvorsen, May 24, 1969; children: Katherine, Elizabeth, Frederick Jr., Edward. BS, NYU, 1970; MBA, Baruch Coll., 1972; EdD, U. S.C., 1983. Manual systems analyst Chase Manhattan Bank, N.Y.C., 1970-72; account mgr. NCR Corp., N.Y.C., 1972-76; instr. Western Conn. State Univ., Danbury, 1976-80; asst. prof. Univ. S.C. Columbia, 1980-84; asst. dean So. Ill. Univ., Carbondale, 1984-86; dept. chmn. DeKalb Coll., Clarkston, Ga., 1986-88; assoc. prof. Lebanon Valley Coll., Annville, Pa., 1988-90; asst. prof. Kean Coll. of N.J., Union, 1990—; pres. KEEE Cons., Lebanon, Pa., 1986—; instr., cons. Community Action Agy. Inst., Kirksville, Mo., 1989—, Exec. Devel. Inst., Mt. Gretna, Pa., 1989—, Lake Area Health Edn. Ctr., Erie, Pa., 1991—. Contbr. articles to profl. jours. Membership chmn. Am. Red Cross, Danbury, Conn., 1976-80; speaker Kean Coll. Speakers Bur., Union, 1990—. With USAR, 1968-74. Recipient Cert. of Appreciation, So. Ill. Univ. Alumni Assn., Carbondale, 1986. Mem. ASTD, Am. Mktg. Assn., Assn. for Mgmt. (founding mem.), Assn. for Part-Time Profls., Soc. for the Advancement Mgmt. (faculty advisor), Alpha Kappa Psi, Delta Mu Delta. Office: Kean Coll of N J Morris Ave Union NJ 07083-7117

MAIELLO, THOMAS MICHAEL, college administrator; b. N.Y.C., Apr. 11, 1958; s. Salvatore Alexander and Frances Ann (Tanzillo) M.; m. Pamela T. Downey, Oct. 7, 1989. BA, Bard Coll., 1981; MS, Albany State U., 1989. Dir. student housing, asst. dean Bard Coll., Annandale, N.Y., 1981-84; asst. dir. admissions Columbia-Greene Community Coll., Greenport, N.Y., 1984-88; dir. admissions Ulster County Community Coll., Stone Ridge, N.Y., 1988—; co-chmn. N.Y. State Assn. for Counseling and Devel. Region IV, Kingston, 1989—; treas. SUNY Coll. Admissions Profls., Inc., Stone Ridge, N.Y., 1990—. Contbr. articles to profl. jours. Bd. mem. Am. Heart Assn., Kingston, 1991. Colandra Inst. of CUNY graduate. Mem. Am. Assn. Coll. Registrars and Admissions Officers, N.Y. State Assn. Coll. Admissions Counselors, N.Y. State Assn. Counseling and Devel., Coll. Student Pers. Assn. N.Y., N.Y. State Two-Yr. Coll. Assn.; sister city Assn. for Counseling and Devel., Capital Dist. Assn. for Counseling and Devel. Office: Ulster County Comm Coll Cottekill Rd Stone Ridge NY 12484

MAIER, CHARLES STEVEN, history educator; b. N.Y.C., Feb. 23, 1939; s. Louis and Muriel (Krailsheimer) M.; m. Pauline Alice Rubbelke, June 17, 1961; children—Andrea Nicole, Nicholas Winterer, Jessica Elizabeth Heine. A.B., Harvard U., 1960; postgrad., St. Anthony's Coll., Oxford, Eng., 1960-61; Ph.D., Harvard U., 1967. Instr. history Harvard U., Cambridge, Mass., 1967-69, asst. prof., 1969-73, lectr., 1973-75; vis. prof. U. Bielefeld, Fed. Republic Germany, 1976; assoc. prof. history Duke U., Durham, N.C., 1976-79, prof., 1979-81; prof. history Harvard U., Cambridge, Mass., 1981-91, Krupp Found. prof. European studies, 1991—; rsch. fellow Lehrman Inst., N.Y.C., 1975-76; mem. assoc. staff Brookings Instn., Washington, 1978-84; mem. coun. Fondation Jean Monnet pour l'Europe, Lausanne, Switzerland; mem. joint com. on Western Europe Social Sci. Rsch. Coun. and Am. Coun. Learned Socs., 1978-84, chmn., 1979-81, Am. Acad. Arts and Scis. Author: Recasting Bourgeois Europe, 1975 (Am. Hist. Assn. George Louis Beer award 1976, Herbert Baxter Adams award 1977), In Search of Stability, 1987, The Unmasterable Past, 1988; editor: The Origins of the Cold War and Contemporary Europe, 1978, rev. edit., 1990, (with Dan S. White) The Thirteenth of May and the Advent of de Gaulle's Republic, 1967, (with Leon Lindberg) The Politics of Inflation and Economic Stagnation, 1985, Changing Boundaries of the Political, 1987, The Marshall Plan and Germany, 1991. Fellow NEH, 1977-78, German Marshall Fund, 1980-81, Guggenheim Found., 1984-85; rsch. grantee MacArthur Found., 1988-89. Fellow Woodrow Wilson Ctr. for Scholars (Washington); mem. Council on Fgn. Relations, Am. Hist. Assn., Soc. Italian Hist. Studies, Soc. Historians of Am. Fgn. Rels., Am. Acad. Arts and Scis., Phi Beta Kappa. Home: 60 Larchwood Dr Cambridge MA 02138-4639 Office: Harvard U Ctr for European Studies Cambridge MA 02138

MAIER, EDWARD LOUIS, JR., sales executive, engineer; b. Erie, Pa., Apr. 17, 1955; s. Edward Louis and Mary Jo (Babowicz) M.; m. Debra Ann Loop, July 2, 1978; children: Sara Spencer, Mark Louis, Rebecca Ann. BSME summa cum laude, U. Mich., 1977; MBA, U. Chgo., 1982. Registered profl. engr., Mo. Design engr. Internat. Harvester, Melrose Park, Ill., 1977-81; group leader, stress analysis Nuclear Power Svcs., Chgo., 1981, regional sales mgr., 1981-82; program mgr., tech. Emerson Electric Co., St. Louis, 1982-85, mgr., corp. tech., 1985-86; dir., bus. planning ENI div. Emerson Electric Co., Rochester, N.Y., 1986-88, v.p. sales, ENI div., 1988—; officer, ENI, Inc., Rochester, 1988—. Bd. mem. Mo. Small Bus. Devel. Coun., St. Louis, 1985, 86. Mem. Soc. Automotive Engrs., U. Mich. Alumni Assn., Tau Beta Pi, Beta Gamma Sigma, Pi Tau Sigma. Home: 4 Oak Leaf Ln Pittsford NY 14534-3510 Office: ENI Inc 100 Highpower Rd Rochester NY 14623-3434

MAIER, HENRY B., environmental engineer; b. Yonkers, N.Y., July 11, 1925; s. Henry and Adelaide (Boyce) M.; m. Elizabeth A. Maier, May 4, 1968. BA, Columbia U., 1947; postgrad., Adelphi U., Hofstra U. Prin. Maier Solar Developments, Hempstead, N.Y. Author: Techniques for Seascape Painting. Mem. Am. Chem. Soc., N.Y. Acad. Scis. Home: 6 Sealey Ave Apt 3K Hempstead NY 11550-1231

MAIETTA, DIANE MARIE, writer, production company official; b. Pitts., Apr. 24, 1957; d. Dominic Nicholas Michael and Virginia Lee (Haley) M.; divorced; 1 child, Danielle Nicole Trenney. BA, Point Park Coll., 1982; cert. paralegal, Indiana U. of Pa., 1988. Intern in music rsch. WDVE Radio, Pitts., 1979, asst. pub. rels. mgr. Backstage Spl., 1979-80; acad. counselor Acad. Guidance Svcs., The Ednl. Source, NJ and Apollo, Pa., 1990-91; promotions dir., publicist Tres Chic and Popular Demand Prodns., Pitts., 1991—. Contbr. poems to profl. publs. Leader Girl Scouts U.S.A.; mem. Head Start Parent Group, Apollo, 1989-90; mem. Parents for Rock and Rap, Libertyville, Ill., 1990—. Recipient citation Pa. Ho. of Reps., 1991, Hon. Mention awards World of Poetry, 1988-91, Golden Poet awards World of Poetry, 1988-91, 4th Place award World of Poetry, 1990. Mem. Internat. Soc. Poets, Women's Sports Found. Roman Catholic. Home: PO Box 9 Irwin PA 15642 Office: 525 Grandview Ave Ste 2 Pittsburgh PA 15211

MAIETTE, RALPH LOUIS, program manager, engineer; b. Waterbury, Conn., Nov. 23, 1947; s. Louis and Megan (Davies) M.; m. Sandra Lee Jacobson, July 5, 1969; children: Michelle Lee, Kristie Nicole. Student, Kaynor Tech. Coll., 1965, Post Coll., 1980, 87. Cert. mfg. engr. Tool designer Ivanhoe Corp., Bristol, Conn., 1966-70; machine designer U.S. Baird Corp., Stratford, Conn., 1970-73; project engr. Risdon Corp., Thomaston, Conn., 1973-75; machine designer Bodine Assembly Systems, Bridgeport, Conn., 1975-76; cons. Wolcott, Conn., 1976-77; group mgr. project engring. Unimation, Inc., Danbury, Conn., 1977-83; co-founder, ops. mgr. UAS Automation Systems, Bristol, 1983-89; cons. Forum Assocs., Wolcott, 1990-91; program mgr. Automation Design Concepts, Bridgeport, 1991—. Mem. Soc. Mfg. Engrs. (Robotics Internat. sect., sr. mem., program chmn. 1983-84, sec. 1983-84, chmn. elect 1984-85, chmn. 1986-87, Pres. Club 1987, 10 Yrs. Membership award 1991, Membership Recruitment award 1986). Home: 48 County Rd Wolcott CT 06716-2502 Office: Automation Design Concepts 109 Holland Ave Bridgeport CT 06605-2118

MAILER, NORMAN, author; b. Long Branch, N.J., Jan. 31, 1923; s. Issac B. and Fanny (Schneider) M.; m. Beatrice Silverman, 1944 (div. 1952); 1 dau., Susan; m. Adele Morales, 1954 (div.); children: Danielle, Elizabeth; m. Jean Campbell (div.); 1 dau., Kate; m. Beverly Bentley, 1963 (div.); children: Michael, Steven; m. Carol Stevens (div.); 1 dau., Maggie; m. Norris Church; 1 son, John Buffalo. S.B., Harvard U., 1943; postgrad., Sorbonne, Paris, France. Author: (war novel) The Naked and the Dead, 1948, Barbary Shore, 1951, The Deer Park, 1955 (dramatized 1967), Advertisements for Myself, 1959; (poetry) Deaths for the Ladies and Other Disasters, 1962; The Presidential Papers, 1963, An American Dream, 1965, Cannibals and Christians, 1966, Why are We in Viet Nam?, 1967, The Armies of the Night, 1968 (Nat. Book award, co-winner Pulitzer prize), Miami and the Siege of Chicago, 1968, Of A Fire On The Moon, 1971, The Prisoner of Sex, 1971, Existential Errands, 1972, St. George and the Godfather, 1972, Marilyn, 1973, The Faith of Graffiti, 1974, The Fight, 1975, Some Honorable Men, 1975, Genius and Lust, 1976, A Transit to Narcissus, 1978, The Executioner's Song, 1979 (Pultizer Prize for Fiction 1980), Of Women and Their Elegance, Pieces and Pontifications, 1982, Ancient Evenings, 1983, Tough Guys Don't Dance, 1984, Harlot's Ghost, 1991; film dir.: Wild 90, 1967, Beyond the Law, 1967, Maidstone, 1968, Tough Guys Don't Dance, 1987; editor: Dissent, 1953-69; co-founder: Village Voice, 1955; contbr. to numerous publs. Served with AUS, 1944-46. Recipient 14th ann. award for outstanding service to arts McDowell Colony, 1973, Emerson-Thoreau Medal for lifetime of literary achievement, 1989. Mem. PEN Am. Ctr. (pres. 1984-86). Office: care Random House Author's Mail 201 E 50th St New York NY 10022

MAILLET, MARTIN JOSEPH, SR., police captain; b. Lynn, Mass., Jan. 2, 1933; s. Joseph Maximum and Mary Agnes (Deveau) M.; m. Elizabeth Ann Kasprzak, June 16, 1957; children: Martin Joseph Jr., Lawrence James, Jayne Marie. Student, Bloomberg's St. Law. Boston, 1958-63, Boston U., 1970, North Shore Community Coll., 1974-76; grad., Linotype Sch., Boston, 1954. Cert. secondary tchr., Mass. Linotype operator Willimantic (Conn.) Chronicle, 1954-55; police officer Saugus (Mass.) Police Dept., 1957-64, police sergeant, 1964-73, police capt., exec. officer to chief, 1973—. Dep. sheriff Essex County Sheriffs, 1987—, Mass Police Assn., 1957—. Cpl. U.S. Army, 1950-52, Korea. Democrat. Roman Catholic. Home: 11 Davis St Saugus MA 01906-3517 Office: Saugus Police Dept 6 Taylor St Saugus MA 01906-2299

MAILMAN, HAROLD LEIGH, academic administrator; b. Gowganda, Ontario, Can., Dec. 3, 1926; came to U.S., 1927; s. Clyde Everett and Verna Mae (Crouse) M.; m. Beatrice Alice Heal, June 27, 1948; children: Raymond Lester, Deanne Linda, Cynthia Alice. BS in Indsl. Edn., Gorham State Tchrs. Coll., 1950; MEd, U. Maine, 1962; postgrad., Penn State U., 1968. Tchr. ednl. mfr. U. Maine, Gorham, 1965-81; indsl. edn. tchr. various schs., Maine, 1950-63; state supr., coord. State Dept. Vocat. Edn., Augusta, Maine, 1963-69; dir. No. Maine Tech. Coll., Presque Isle, Maine, 1969-79; dir. continuing edn. Husson Coll., Bangor, Maine, 1981-88; ret., Studio E., 1988—; co-owner, treas. MHR Inc., Bangor, 1985—. Contbr. articles to profl. jours. Chmn. Local Rep. Com., Maine, 1984-86; del. alternate to State Rep. Conv., 1982-90; pres. Rotary Club, Presque Isle, 1976, Jr. C. of C. Madawaska, Maine, 1958. Recipient Disting. Svc. award U. Maine at Presque Isle, 1979; named Harold L. Mailman Constrn. and Mech. Trades Bldg., 1991. Mem.

Am. Vocat. Assn., Kiwanis Club of Hermon. Republican. Home: RR #3 Box 168 Bangor ME 04401

MAIMAN, GEORGE, accountant, finance consultant; b. Hungary, Aug. 30, 1939; s. Al and Anna (Stern) M.; B.A., Concordia U., 1965, Bernard Baruch Coll., City U. N.Y., 1975; m. Edith Schwartz, Nov. 13, 1966; children—Ronald E., Andrew D. Controller, Unimet Corp., N.Y.C., 1973-75, Pickwick Internat. Inc., Woodbury, N.Y., 1975-77; prin. Maiman & Co., C.P.A.'s, N.Y.C., 1977—; cons. C.P.A., N.Y. State. Mem. Am. Inst. C.P.A.'s. Office: 250 W 57th St New York NY 10107-0001

MAIMAN, JULIUS DAVID, law office administrator; b. Bklyn., Nov. 28, 1933; s. Max and Rae (Biller) M.; m. Evelyn Bender, Dec. 25, 1961; children: Jonathan Ira, Nancy H. Maiman Solomon. Student, Cooper Union, 1951-54; BBA in Pers. and Indsl. Rels., CCNY, 1957; MS in Mgmt., Columbia U., 1958. Contracts mgr. TRG, Inc., Syosset, N.Y., 1955-62; bus. mgr., asst. sec. Oceanics, Inc., Plainview, N.Y., 1962-69; v.p. adminstrn., dir. Poseidon Sci. Corp., Hauppauge, N.Y., 1969-74; dir. adminstrn. Serko and Simon, N.Y.C., 1974-79, Guggenheimer and Untermeyer, N.Y.C., 1979-84; dir. adminstrn. N.Y. Finley, Kumble, Wagner, Heine, Underberg, Manley & Casey, N.Y.C., 1984-86; exec. dir. Haight, Gardner, Poor and Havens, N.Y.C., 1986—. Contbr. articles to profl. publs. Scoutmaster, adult vol. Boy Scouts Am., various locations, 1951—, adviser Order of Arrow, Suffolk County coun., 1965-73; trustee, v.p. South Huntington Jewish Ctr., Melville, N.Y., 1968-75; People-to-People del. USSR, 1990. Recipient Vigil Honor, Order of Arrow, Boy Scouts Am., 1969; recipient Shofar award Jewish Com. on Scouting, Medford, N.Y., 1972. Mem. ABA (assoc.), Assn. Legal Adminstrs. (pres. N.Y. chpt. 1984-85, treas. 1982-84, v.p. 1985-87), Columbia Club. Office: Haight Gardner Poor Havens 195 Broadway New York NY 10007-3100

MAIMON, ELAINE PLASKOW, English educator, university dean; b. Phila., July 28, 1944; d. Louis J. and Gertrude (Canter) Plaskow; m. Morton A. Maimon, Sept. 30, 1967; children: Gillian Blanche, Alan Marcus. AB, U. Pa., 1966, MA, 1967, PhD, 1970. Asst. prof. Haverford (Pa.) Coll., 1971-73; lectr. Beaver Coll., Glenside, Pa., 1973-75, asst. prof., dir. writing, 1975-77, assoc. prof., 1977-83, assoc. dean, 1980-84, assoc. v.p., prof. English, 1984-86; adj. assoc. prof. U. Pa., Phila., 1982-83; assoc. dean of coll. Brown U., Providence, 1986-88; dean and prof. English Queens Coll./CUNY, Flushing, N.Y., 1988—; nat. bd. cons. NEH, 1977-81. Co-author: Writing in the Arts and Sciences, 1981; co-editor: Readings in the Arts and Sciences, 1984, Thinking, Reasoning and Writing, 1989. Speech writer Peter Hearn, Dem. for Mayor, Phila., 1990-91. Recipient Lindback award for disting. teaching, 1978; U. Pa. Edn. Alumni Assn. award, 1966. Mem. MLA, Nat. Coun. Tchrs. English (nominating com. 1986-87), Conf. on Coll. Composition Communication (exec. com. 1985-87), Assn. Am. Colls., Phi Beta Kappa. Home: 1701 Newbold Ln Philadelphia PA 19118-1103 Office: Queens Coll 315 Kissena Flushing NY 11367-1252

MAIN, CHARLES LLOYD, small business owner; b. Detroit, Oct. 25, 1954; s. Eugene L. and MoVella (Harris) M.; m. Debra K. Culpepper, Jan. 17, 1976; children: Jeremiah David, Megen Marie. BS in Edn., Cen. Mich. U., 1977; postgrad., Capital Bible Sem., Lanham, Md., 1986—. Millwright local union, Lanham, 1981—; co-owner Main Secretarial Svc., Lanham, 1989—. Dir. Awana Boys & Girls Club, New Carrollton Bible Ch., Lanham, 1987-89, youth group leaders, 1990-92. Office: Main Secretarial Svc 6164 Princess Garden Pkwy Lanham MD 20706

MAIN, DEBRA KAY, small business owner; b. Manchester, Tenn., Mar. 7, 1956; d. Ralph and Maggie Lee (Duncan) Culpepper; m. Charles L. Main, Jan. 17, 1976; children: Jeremiah David, Megen Marie. Student, Cen. Mich. U., 1974-77. Sec. Woodall Corp., Beltsville, Mich., 1986-87, Upjohn Health Programs, Greenbelt, Md., 1987-89; office mgr. Upjohn Health Programs, Greenbelt, 1989-91; co-owner Main Secretarial Svc., Lanham, Md., 1989—. Dir. Awana Boys and Girls Club; dir. New Carrollton Bible Ch., Lanham, 1987-89, youth group leader, 1990-92. Republican. Office: Main Secretarial Svc 6164 Princess Garden Pkwy Lanham MD 20706

MAIN, ROBERT GORDON, JR., state judge; b. Malone, N.Y., May 12, 1951; s. Robert Gordon and Ann Mary (Manson) M. AB, Middlebury (Vt.) Coll., 1973; JD, Albany N.Y.) Law Sch., 1976. Bar: N.Y. 1977, U.S. Dist. Ct. (no. dist.) N.Y. 1977. Assoc. Mullarney & Holland, Malone, N.Y., 1976-79; ptnr. Holland & Main, P.C., Malone, 1980-87; county, surrogate and family ct. judge Unified Ct. Sys.-N.Y. State, Malone, 1988—. Former vice chmn., committeeman Franklin County Rep. Party, Malone; bd. dirs. Alice Hyde Hosp. Assn., Malone, 1988—; pres. Farrar Home, Malone, 1984—; mem. Champlain Valley Physicians Hosp., Plattsburgh, N.Y., 1987—. Mem. N.Y. State Surrogates Assn., N.Y. State Family Ct. Judges Assn., N.Y. State County Judges Assn., Elks. Republican. Roman Catholic. Office: Franklin County Courthouse 63 W Main St Malone NY 12953-1817

MAIOCCHI, CHRISTINE, lawyer; b. N.Y.C., Dec. 24, 1949; d. George and Andreina (Toneatto) M.; m. John Charles Kerecz, Aug. 16, 1980; children: Charles George, Joan Christine. BA in Polit. Sci., Fordham U., 1971, MA in Polit. Sci., 1971, JD, 1974; postgrad., NYU, 1977—. Bar: N.Y. 1975, U.S. Dist. Ct. (so. and ea. dists.), N.Y. 1975, U.S. Ct. Appeals (2nd cir) 1975. Law clk. to magistrate U.S. Dist. Ct. (so. dist.) N.Y., N.Y.C., 1973-74; atty. corp. legal dept. The Home Ins. Co., N.Y.C., 1974-76; asst. house counsel corp. legal dept. Allied Maintenance Corp., N.Y.C., 1976; atty. corp. legal dept. Getty Oil Co., N.Y.C., 1976-77; v.p., mgr. real estate Paine, Webber, Jackson & Curtis, Inc., N.Y.C., 1977-81; real estate mgr. GK Techs., Inc., Greenwich, Conn., 1981-85; real estate mgr., sr. atty. MCI Telecommunications Corp., Rye Brook, N.Y., 1985—. Bd. dirs. League Women Voters, Dobbs Ferry, N.Y., 1988. Mem. ABA, Nat. Assn. Corp. Real Estate Execs. (pres. 1983-84, treas. 1985-86, bd. dirs. 1986), Indsl. Devel. Rsch. Coun. (program v.p. 1985, Pickwick award 1987), N.Y. Bar Assn., Women's Bar Assn. Manhattan, The Corp. Bar (sec. real estate div. 1987-89, chmn. 1990-92), Jr. League Club (Tarrytown, N.Y.), Dobbs Ferry Women's Club (program dir. 1981-92). Home: 84 Clinton Ave Dobbs Ferry NY 10522-3004 Office: MCI Telecommunications 5 International Dr Port Chester NY 10573-1058

MAIONE, THEODORE EDWARD, biochemist; b. Orange, N.J., Oct. 21, 1956; s. Theodore Lincoln and Joan (Leddy) M.; m. Marie Ann McCue, Dec. 3, 1987; children: Sylvana Lisa Maione, Cooper James McCue. BS in Biology, Mich. State U., 1978; PhD in Plant Physiology, Cornell U., 1983. Postdoctoral rsch. assoc. Brandeis U., Waltham, Mass., 1983-85; rsch. scientist Repligen Corp., Cambridge, Mass., 1985-88, prin. investigator, 1988-91, dir. protein therapeutics, 1991—. Reviewer sci. jours. and grant proposals; contbr. articles to profl. jours.; patentee in field. Mem. Am. Chem. Soc., N.Y. Acad. Scis., Am. Soc. for Cell Biology, Am. Soc. for Biochemistry and Molecular Biology, Am. Assn. Cancer Rsch., Am. Soc. for Photobiology. Office: Repligen Corp One Kendall Sq Bldg 700 Cambridge MA 02139

MAIORANA, CHARLIE, computer educator; b. Fredonia, N.Y., Feb. 22, 1942; s. Alfred and Caroline (Bardo) M.; m. Sandra Emrick, 1963 (div. 1973); m. Wendy Bork, Nov. 30, 1975; 1 child, Amanda. BSE in Naval Architecture, U. Mich., 1963; MS in Computer Sci., George Washington U., 1965. Civil servant Dept. of Navy, Washington, 1959-70; asst. prof. George Washington U., Washington, 1967-75; engr. Tetra Tech., Washington, 1970-78, Bolt, Beranek & Newman, Washington, 1978-83; owner Info/Tek, Washington, 1983—; guest lectr. Haystack Sch. of Crafts, Deer Isle, Maine, 1978, U. Mich., Ann Arbor, 1970. Author: (book) Information Resources for Engineers and Scientists, 1992, (video) Sound and Sampling on the Mac, 1991, (video series) Air Force Stinfo Program, 1989-90. Home and Office: 4318 Fessenden St NW Washington DC 20016

MAISANO, DANIEL J., lawyer; b. Wilmington, Del., Mar. 9, 1951; s. Harold E. Peter Maisano and Barbara June (Hudson) Castorani; m. Dawn Marie Gaster, Mar. 2, 1985 (div. Apr. 14, 1988; 1 child, Daniel J. II; m. Patricia Ann Lesniak, Feb. 22, 1991; stepchildren: Scott P. Comegys, Adam J. Comegys. BA in Polit. Sci., U. Del., 1973; JD, Del. Law Sch., Wilmington, 1978. Bar: Pa. 1979, U.S. Ct. Appeals Pa. 1985, U.S. Dist. Ct. (ea. dist.) Pa. 1986, U.S. Supreme Ct. 1979. Sales assoc. Holcomb & Salter

Realty, New Castle, Del., 1974-79; v.p. Conversion Concepts, Ltd., Wilmington, 1979-83; real estae broker, owner Realty Concepts, Kennett Square, Pa., 1985—; sole practitioner Kennett Square, 1984—; adj. prof. Univ. Coll., Widener U., Chester, Pa., 1987-90, Sch. Mgmt. Widener U., 1988-90. Bd. dirs., v.p. ChesPenn Health Svcs., Chester, 1987-91. Republican. Roman Catholic. Office: 115 Marshall St Kennett Square PA 19348

MAISANO, JOHN ALEXANDER, management consultant; b. Somerville, Mass., Feb. 1, 1957; s. Placido Dino and Josephine Mary (Pino) M. BS in Bus. Mgmt. and Acctg., U. Mass., Boston. V.p. fin. P.J. Maisano, Inc., Everett, Mass., 1979-88; systems mgr. City of Boston, 1983-86; cons. KPMG Peat Marwick, Boston, 1989—. Democrat. Roman Catholic. Home: 88 Glen St Somerville MA 02145-4132 Office: KPMG Peat Marwick One Boston Pl Boston MA 02108

MAISANO, PHILLIP NICHOLAS, investment company executive; b. Newark, May 15, 1947; s. Salvatore and Mary (Vella) M.; m. Mary-Alice Yanch, Aug. 10, 1968; children: Phillip, Matthew. BA, Belmont (N.C.) Abbey Coll., 1969; MBA, Iona Coll., 1976; postgrad., NYU Law Sch., 1972-73, Columbia U., summer 1987. CLU. Asst. v.p. The Equitable, N.Y.C., 1969-79; v.p. Manhattan Life Ins. Co., N.Y.C., 1979-81; v.p. MONY Fin. Svcs., Purchase, N.Y., 1981-88, sr. v.p., 1989—; pres. Evaluation Assocs. Inc., Norwalk, Conn., 1988—; chief exec. officer Evaluation Assocs. Inc., 1989—; incorporator New Dartmouth Bank, Hanover, N.H., 1991—; Trustees Belmont Abbey Coll., 1992—. Contbr. articles to profl. publs. V.p. No. Bergen Jr. Football League; bd. dirs. Montvale (N.J.) Athletic League; trustee Belmont Abbey Coll., 1992—. 1st lt. USAR. Roman Catholic. Home: 33 Highland Rd Montvale NJ 07645-2013 Office: 200 Connecticut Ave Norwalk CT 06854-1940

MAISEL, MICHAEL, shoe designer and manufacturer; b. Newark, Oct. 19, 1947; s. Irving and Betty (Markin) M.; m. Arlette Bernstein, Oct. 18, 1980; children: Ian Albert, Alicia Beth, Noah Shawn, Bette Gabrielle. B.S. in Mktg., B.A. in Gen. Bus. Adminstrn., Ariz. State U., 1969. Asst. sales mgr. Mid-Atlantic Shoe Co. div. Beck Industries, N.Y.C., 1969-71; dir. imports Felsway Corp., Totowa, N.J., 1972-73; exec. v.p. Carber Enterprises, N.Y.C., 1973-80; v.p. S.R.O. div. Caressa, N.Y.C., 1980-84; pres. Sandler of Boston, N.Y.C., 1984-85, chmn. bd., 1986—; v.p. Lowell Shoe, Inc., Hudson, N.H., 1992—; cons. in field. Mem. 210 Shoe Industry (life), Nat. Shoe Retailers Assn. (bd. dirs.), Nat. Shoe Mfrs. Assn. Republican. Jewish. Designer Carber's shoe, displayed in Met. Mus. Art; nominated for Coty design award, 1974-78. Office: Lowell Shoe Inc 13 Hampshire Dr Hudson NH 03051

MAISNER, IRWIN GERALD, financial services company executive; b. Bridgeport, Conn., June 14, 1956; s. Abraham and Barbara (Koniger) M.; m. Michele Elaine Ansbache (div. Oct. 1980); m. Anna Polimen, Aug. 6, 1989. BS, U. of So. Fla., 1978. Acct. Pepperidge Farm Corp., Westport and Norwalk, Conn., 1978-80; acct. auditor Gulf United Corp., Jacksonville, Fla., 1980-82; acctg. mgr. Cadbury Schweppes, Stamford, Conn., 1982-84; broker Prudential, N.Y.C., 1984-86; v.p. A. G. Edwards, St. Louis, Mo., 1986—. Mem. Jaycees, Mens Clubs (treas.). Republican. Jewish. Home: 91 Dwight St Fairfield CT 06430 Office: A G Edwards 1229 Post Rd Fairfield CT 06430

MAITLAND, GUY EDISON CLAY, lawyer; b. London, Dec. 28, 1942; (mother Am. citizen); s. Paul and Virginia Francesca (Carver) M. BA, Columbia U., 1964; JD, N.Y. Law Sch., 1968. Bar: N.Y. 1969, U.S. Dist. Ct. (so. and ea. dists.) N.Y. 1969, U.S. Ct. Appeals (2d and D.C. cirs.) 1969. Assoc. Burlingham, Underwood & Lord, N.Y.C., 1969-74; admiralty counsel Union Carbide Corp., N.Y.C., 1974-76; exec. v.p., gen. counsel, dir. Liberian Svcs., Inc., N.Y.C. and Reston, Va., 1976-89, pres., 1990—; del. UN Conf. on Trade and Devel., Manila, 1979, Belgrade, 1983; participant London Conf. on Limitation of Maritime Liability, 1976; mem. legal com. Internat. Maritime Orgn. (UN), London, 1980—; del. UN Conf. on Law of the Sea, 1976-82, London UN Maritime Law Conf., 1984; co-founder The Admiralty-Fin. Forum, N.Y.C., 1986; bd. dir. Four Freedoms Found., 1989—, Empire State Pla. Performing Arts Ctr. Corp., 1989-91; sr. v.p. Internat. Registeries, Inc. Contbr. articles on maritime law, U.S. shipping policy. Del. Rep. Nat. Conv., Kansas City, 1976; sec. N.Y. Rep. County Com., 1976-87, vice chmn., 1988—; co-chmn. Citizens for Reagan, N.Y. State, 1979-80; mem. N.Y.C. Mayor's Port Devel. Coun., 1983—. Named Outstanding Young Man of Am. U.S. Jaycees, 1975; hon. del Rep. Nat. Conv., Dallas, 1984. Mem. ABA, Assn. of Bar of City of N.Y. (chmn. admiralty com. 1982-85), Maritime Law Assn. U.S. (chmn. com. on intergovernmental orgns. 1987—), Maritime Assn. Port of N.Y. (dir. 1984-87), D.C. Bar Assn., Phi Delta Phi, Capitol Hill Club, Univ. Club (Washington), Princeton Club, Down Town Assn. Club (N.Y.C.). Republican. Episcopalian. Office: Pres Liberian Svcs Inc 551 5th Ave New York NY 10176-0001

MAIWURM, JAMES JOHN, lawyer; b. Wooster, Ohio, Dec. 5, 1948; s. James Frederick and Virginia Anne (Jones) M.; m. Wendy S. Leeper, July 31, 1974; children: James G., Michelle K. BA, Coll. Wooster, 1971; JD, U. Mich., 1974. Bar: Ohio 1974, D.C. 1986, Md. 1987, N.Y., 1987. Ptnr. Squire, Sanders & Dempsey, Cleve. and Washington, 1974-90; ptnr., group head Crowell & Moring, Washington, 1990—; gen counsel Adapso Found., 1989-90. Contbr. articles to profl. jours. Mem. ABA, D.C. Bar Assn., Fed. City Coun., Econ. Club Washington, George Mason U. Century Club. Home: 9419 Brian Jac Ln Great Falls VA 22066-2002 Office: Crowell & Moring 1001 Pennsylvania Ave NW Washington DC 20004-2505

MAJCHRZAK, DAVID JOSEPH, artist, printer; b. Buffalo, Aug. 8, 1936; s. Joseph Peter and Charlotte (Radzikowski) M.; m. Nancy Elizabeth Palmer, Sept. 20, 1958 (div. May 1985); children: Gary, Lisa, Glenda; m. Patricia Ann Peganoff, July 11, 1986. Student, SUNY, Buffalo, John Hussian Sch. Art, Phila. Supr. pre-press dept. Case Hoyt Corp., Rochester, N.Y., 1966-86, 87—; journeyman Internat. Colour Svcs. Rochester, 1986-87; tchr. Rochester Schs., 1963-89. One-man show George Frederick Gallery, Rochester, 1979, Artist Showcase, Penfield, N.Y., 1985; 2-man show Austin Harvard Gallery, Rochester, 1988, 3-man show, 1988; exhibited in group shows, 1963—, latest being Downtown Gallery, New Orleans, 1986, Loretta Goodwin Gallery, Birmingham, Ala., Austin Harvard Gallery, 1987, DeBouver Fine Arts, Chgo., 1991; represented in permanent collections various cos., banks, U. Mass., Strong Meml. Hosp., Am. Embassy, Ethiopia. Member Rochester Meml. Art Gallery, Arts Reach of Rochester. With USN, 1955-59. Mem. Arts for Greater Rochester. Republican. Home and Studio: 17 Littlebrook Dr Pittsford NY 14534

MAJERICH, CYNTHIA ANN, engineering specialist; b. North Tonawanda, N.Y., Apr. 12, 1959; d. Andrew John and Helen Joan (Ford) M. AS in Engring., Erie Community Coll., Williamsville, N.Y., 1979; BS in Indsl. Engring., SUNY, Buffalo, 1981. Indsl. engr. Yorktown Industries, Lakewood, N.Y., 1981-82; prodn. supr. Invenex, Grand Island, N.Y., 1982-84; indsl. engr. Invenex, Grand Island and Orlando, Fla., 1984-87; project engring. mgr. Lyphomed, Chgo., 1987-91; facilities engring. supr. Gibco Labs. LTI, Grand Island, 1991—. Mem. Inst. Indsl. Engrs. (sr.), Internat. Soc. Pharm. Engrs. Home: 70 Forestview Dr Williamsville NY 14221 Office: Gibco Labs LTI 3175 Staley Rd Grand Island NY 14072-2090

MAJKRZAK, CHARLES FRANCIS, physicist; b. East Orange, N.J., Mar. 5, 1950; s. Charles Peter and Eleanor (Newman) M.; m. Linda Ann Folena, June 2, 1973; children: Stephen, Matthew. BA in Physics, Montclair State Coll., 1972; PhD in Physics, U. R.I., 1978. Physicist Brookhaven Nat. Lab., Upton, N.Y., 1978-87, Nat. Inst. Standards and Tech., Gaithersburg, Md., 1987—; mem. Brookhaven Reactor Program Adv. Com., Upton, 1990-93. Contbr. articles to profl. jours. Leader Boy Scouts Am., N.Y., 1986-87, Md., 1987—. Mem. Am. Phys. Soc., Smithsonian Instn. (resident assoc.0. Office: Nat Inst Standards and Tech Clopper Rd Gaithersburg MD 20899

MAKAR, ARTHUR, fundraiser; b. Beverly, Mass., June 28, 1950; s. Albert Anthony and Mary (Burkinshaw) M. BA cum laude, Boston Coll., 1972; postgrad., Suffolk U., 1992. Asst. to exec. mgr. Cen. City Opera House Assn., Denver, 1973-74; devel. officer Bentley Coll., Waltham, Mass., 1975-76, Winners, Inc., Boston, 1976-78; dir. devel. East Boston Social Ctrs., 1979-81, Jobs for Youth Boston, 1981-83; corp. fundraiser officer Emmanuel Coll., Boston, 1983-87; dir. devel. Mass. Soc. Prevention of Cruelty to Children, Boston, 1987-88; dir. instnl. advancement N.E. Coll. Optometry, Boston, 1988—. Pres. Neighborhood Arts Ctr., Boston, 1983-85; bd. dirs. Gallery NAGA, Boston, 1982-85. Named one of Outstanding Young Men of Am., 1979; recipient Wizard award Outstanding Fundraising Exec. in Mass. Nat. Philanthropy Day Com., 1990. Mem. Nat. Soc. Fund Raising Execs. Fedn. (dir. 1989—, v.p. 1983-87, pres. Mass. chpt. 1987), Planned Giving Group New Eng., Sisters of Notre Dame, Boston Province (fin. bd. 1985-89), Coun. Advancement and Support Edn. Roman Catholic. Office: New Eng Coll Optometry 424 Beacon St Boston MA 02115-1100

MAKAR, RALPH, marketing professional; b. Cairo, Nov. 10, 1960; came to the U.S., 1966; s. Boshra H. and Nadia (Issa) M. BS in Pharmacy, Rutgers U., 1983; MBA, Columbia U., 1990. Registered pharmacist, N.J. Profl. sales rep. Eli Lilly & Co., Youngstown, Ohio, 1983-85; pharmacy mgr. Rite Aid Corp., Jersey City, N.J., 1985-88; mktg. rsch. intern Merck Sharp & Dohme, West Point, Pa., 1989; asst. product mgr. pool program, pharm. div. CIBA-GEIGY Corp., Summit, N.J., 1990-91, asst. product mgr. pharm. div., 1991-92, product mgr., 1992—; career task force CIBA-GEIGY Corp., 1992—. Mem. alumni coun. Rutgers Coll. Pharmacy, Piscataway, N.J., 1992—; alumni ambassador Columbia Bus. Sch., N.Y.C., 1990—. Mem. Am. Mktg. Assn., Am. Pharm. Assn., N.J. Pharm. Assn. (bd. dirs. 1982-83, award 1983), Beta Gamma Sigma, Phi Lambda Sigma, Delta Sigma Theta. Home: 410 Fairmount Ave Jersey City NJ 07306 Office: CIBA-GEIGY Corp Pharm Div 556 Morris Ave Summit NJ 07901

MAKARI, GEORGE JACK, psychiatrist; b. Plainfield, N.J., July 9, 1960; s. Jack George and Odette (Tamer) M.; m. Arabella Ogilvie, Oct. 7, 1989. BA, Brown U., 1982; MD, Cornell U., 1987. Lic. physician, N.Y. Columnist Washington Tribune, Washington, 1982-83; resident psychiatrist N.Y. Hosp., N.Y.C., 1987-91; Reader's Digest rsch. fellow N.Y. Hosp., 1991—. Contbr. articles to profl. jours. Mem. Am. Psychiatric Assn., History of Psychiatry Sect. of N.Y. Hosp. Home: 435 E 70th St Apt 24L New York NY 10021-5348 Office: N Y Hosp 525 E 68th St New York NY 10021-4873

MAKAROWSKI, WILLIAM STEPHEN, rheumatologist; b. Elmira, N.Y., Dec. 31, 1948; s. William John and Irene (Obuhanich) M.; m. Barbara Ann Payne; children: Elizabeth, Kathleen, Mary Lou. BS cum laude, Saint Bonaventure U., 1970; MD, Loyola-Stritch Coll., 1974; Rheumatology fellow, Cleve. Clinic, 1977-79. Diplomate Nat. Bd. of Med. Examiners, Am. Bd. of Pain Practice Mgmt. Resident in internal medicine Robert Packer Hosp., Sayre, Pa., 1974-77; pvt. practice Erie, Pa., 1984; chief rheumatology div. St. Vincent Hosp., Erie, Pa., 1979-86; med. dir. Musculio Occupational Rehab. Pain Mgmt. program Gt. Lakes Rehab. Hosp., Erie, Pa., 1986—; pres. Great Lakes Rehab. Hosp., Erie, Pa., 1991—; cons. Shriner's Hosp., Erie, 1980—, Metro Health Ctr., 1980—, VA Hosp., 1981—; mem. Hamot Med. Ctr.. Med. Dept., 1979—; pres. med. staff Great Lake Rehab. Hosp.; clin. asst. prof. Gannor U. Columnist: The Joint Achievement newsletter, 1981—. Chmn. med. adv. bd. The Lupus Found., 1987—; advisor Arthritis Discussion Group, 1981-91; mem. bd. of govs. Arthritis Found., 1981-91. Fellow Am. Coll. Rheumatology (founding); mem. AMA, Pa. Med. Soc., Erie County Med. Soc., So. Med. Assn., Am. Pain Soc., Internat. Soc. for Rheumatic Therapy, Can. Pain Soc., Erie Yacht Club, Kahkwa Country Club. Home: 5075 Tramarlac Ln Erie PA 16505 Office: Rheumatology Assocs NW Pa 1781 W 26th St Erie PA 16508-1256

MAKHIJA, MOHAN, nuclear physician; b. Bombay, Oct. 1, 1941; came to U.S., 1969; m. Arlene Zambito, Nov. 11, 1978. MD, Bombay U., 1966. Diplomate Am. Bd. Nuclear Medicine, Am. Bd. Radiology; cert. spl. competence in nuclear radiology. Resident in radiology Morristown (N.J.) Meml. Hosp., 1972-75; resident in nuclear medicine Yale-New Haven Hosp., 1975-76; post-doctoral fellow Yale U. Sch. Medicine, New Haven, 1976-77; jr. attending physician Helene Fuld Med. Ctr., Trenton, N.J., 1977-78; acting dir. dept. nuclear medicine Monmouth Med. Ctr., Long Branch, N.J., 1978, dir. nuclear medicine sect., 1979—, asst. attending radiology, 1978-80, assoc. attending radiology, 1980-83, attending radiologist, 1983—; sr. instr. Hahneman U., Phila., 1978-80, clin. asst. prof., 1980-83, clin. assoc. prof., 1983-91, clin. prof., 1991—. Contbr. articles to profl. jours. Fellow ACP, Am. Coll. Nuclear Physicians (speaker ho. of dels.), Am. Coll. Radiology; mem. Monmouth (N.J.) County Med. Soc. (pres. 1991-92), Radiol. Soc. of N.J. (chmn. nuclear medicine 1988—), Indo-Am. Soc. Nuclear Medicine (pres. 1992—). Home: 5 High Ridge Rd Ocean NJ 07712 Office: Monmouth Med Ctr 300 Second Ave Long Branch NJ 07740

MAKI, JOHN MCGILVREY, educator; b. Tacoma, Wash., Nov. 19, 1909; s. Alexander and Amanda (Bradley) McGilvrey; m. Mary Mariko Yasumura, Oct. 18, 1936 (dec. 1990); children: John Alexander, James Perry. BA, U. Wash., Seattle, 1932; MA, U. Wash., 1936; PhD, Harvard U., 1948; LLD, Hokkaido U., Japan, 1976. Assoc. U. Wash., Seattle, 1939-42; propaganda analyst FCC, Washington, 1942-43; with Office of War Info., Washington, 1943-45; civilian cons. Gen. Hdqrs. Supreme Comdr. for Allied Powers, Tokyo, 1946; from asst. prof. to prof. U. Wash., Seattle, 1948-66; prof. U. Mass., Amherst, 1966-80, vice dean arts and scis., 1967-71, prof. emeritus, 1980—. Author: Japanese Militarism: Cause and Cure, 1945, Government and Politics in Japan, 1962; editor/translator: Court and Constitution in Japan, 1964, Japan's Commission on the Constitution: The Final Report, 1980. Bd. dirs. Hampshire Community United Way, Northampton, Mass., 1981-90. Decorated Order of the Sacred Treasure (Japan). Mem. AAUP, New Eng. Conf. of Assn. for Asian Studies (pres. 1975-76), Assn. for Asian Studies. Home: 44 Hitching Post Rd Amherst MA 01002-1155

MAKOFSKE, FLORENCE LOUISE, tattoo association executive; b. Astoria, N.Y., Sept. 27, 1939; d. Harold Louis and Florence Grace (Bacher) Funk; m. Donald Anthony Makofske, June 21, 1958; children: Donna Louise, Yvonne Marie, Ann Marie, Elizabeth Grace. Dance instr. N.Y., 1955-72; phys. edn. instr. Notre Dame Sch., New Hyde Park, N.Y., 1972-74; sec./treas., co-owner Nat. Tattoo Supplies, New Hyde Park and Allentown, Pa., 1974—; sec./treas. Nat. Tattoo Assn., New Hyde Park and Allentown, Pa., 1974—; conv. coord., Nat. Tattoo Assn., 1985, assn. promoter, 1989. Author, editor, typesetter Nat. Tattoo Assn. newsletter. Leader Girl Scouts Am., New Hyde Park, 1967-76. Office: Nat Tatoo Assn 465 Business Park Ln Allentown PA 18103-9120

MAKOFSKI, ROBERT ANTHONY, science administrator; b. Newport Twp., Pa., Dec. 27, 1930; s. Anthony and Sophia Veronica (Vinarski) M.; children: Richard, David, Stephen, Kathleen. BS, Pa. State U., 1952; MS, U. Va., 1956. Rsch. scientist NACA, Langley Field, Va., 1952-56; rsch. assoc. Calif. Inst. Tech., Pasadena, 1956-57; from tech. staff to asst. dir. Johns Hopkins Applied Physics Lab., Laurel, Md., 1957—; trustee Howard County Gen. Hosp., Columbia, Md., 1982—, chmn., 1991—; cons. U.S. Congl. Office Tech. Assessment, Province of Ontario, Balt. City. Contbr. articles to profl. jours.; inventor lithotripter. Office: Johns Hopkins Applied Physics Lab Johns Hopkins Rd Laurel MD 20810

MAKRIS, CONSTANTINE JOHN, infosystems engineer; b. Chalkis, Greece, Nov. 16, 1927; s. John Constantine and Chryso M.; came to U.S., 1952, naturalized, 1960; radio engring. diploma Inst. Electronic Tech., Athens, Greece, 1951; BEE, N.Y. U., 1958, MEE, 1962; m. Helen Loukaides, 1956; children: John, Nicholas, Dorothy. Research scientist NYU, N.Y.C., 1958-62; product mgr. computer research and devel. Mergenthaler div. Eltra, Plainview, N.Y., 1962-69; mgr. advt. devel. Harris-Intertype, Watchung, N.J., 1969-73; pres. Orthodata Inc., Glen Cove, N.Y., 1973-75; sr. staff mem., project mgr. Network Analysis Corp., Gt. Neck, N.Y., 1976-78; sr. systems engr., asst. sec. Mfrs. Hanover Trust Co., N.Y.C., 1978-88; sr. communications planner networks and telecommunications Grumman Data Systems div. Grumman Corp., Bethpage, N.Y., 1988—; lectr., cons. Vice pres. High Elms Civic Assn., 1968-69, Ch. Council, 1976-77. Served with Greek Air Force, 1949-51. Mem. IEEE, Computer Soc., Communications Soc. Club: Krikos Inc. (v.p. bd. dirs. 1983-86, chmn. L.I. chpt. 1981-83). Contbr. articles to profl. orgns. Home: 42 Old Tappan Rd Glen Cove NY 11542-1210 Office: Grumman Data Systems 1111 Stewart Ave Bethpage NY 11714-3533

MAKSYMOWYCH, ROMAN, scientist, educator; b. West Ukraine, Oct. 15, 1924; s. Andrew and Eudokia (Stecyna) M.; m. Anna Nadia Holowinsky, Oct. 14, 1951; children: Andrew, Alexandra, Nestor, Maria. Student, U. Innsbruck, Austria, 1949; MS in Botany, U. Pa., 1956, PhD in Botany, 1959. Rsch. asst. U. Pa., Phila., 1952-54, 55-57, teaching asst., 1954-55, asst. instr., 1957-58; asst. prof. Villanova (Pa.) U., 1959-62, assoc. prof., 1962-66, prof. biology, 1967—. Author: Analysis of Leaf Development, 1973, Analysis of Growth and Development of Xanthium, 1990; contbr. articles to profl. publs. NSF grantee, 1959-60. Home: 1631 Patricia Ave Willow Grove PA 19090-3721 Office: Villanova U Dept Biology Villanova PA 19085

MALACH, HERBERT JOHN, lawyer; b. N.Y.C., Aug. 3, 1922; s. James J. and Therese (Lederer) M.; m. Patricia Sweeny, Sept. 12, 1953 (dec. 1972); children: Therese, Herbert John, Helen. A.B., Iona Coll., 1951; J.D., Columbia U., 1955. Bar: N.Y. 1957, D.C. 1958, U.S. Dist. Ct. D.C. 1958, U.S. Dist. Ct. (ea. and so. dists.) N.Y. 1958, U.S. Ct. Mil. Appeals 1958, U.S. Ct. Appeals 2d cir.) 1960, U.S. Supreme Ct. 1961, U.S. Dist. Ct. (no. and we. dists. N.Y.) 1988, U.S. Ct. Appeals (fed. cir.) 1988, U.S. Tax Ct. 1988. Pvt. practice N.Y.C., 1957-72, New Rochelle, N.Y., 1960—; lectr. bus. law Iona Coll., New Rochelle, 1957-59, asst. to pres. for community svcs., 1959-62. Vice chmn., exec. dir. Iona Coll. Westchester County Law Enforcement Inst.; spl. counsel N.Y. State Temporary Commn. on Child Welfare; mem. Westchester County Youth Adv. Coun., 1969-73; mem. Law Enforcement Planning. Agy., New Rochelle, 1968-69; adv. counsel Westchester Police Youth Officers Assn.; mem. Westchester County Child Abuse Task Force; mem. New Rochelle Narcotics Guidance Coun., 1972-75; adv. coun. New Rochelle Salvation Army, 1976-79; legal adviser East-End Civic Assn.; law guardian Westchester County Family Ct.; referee New Rochelle City Ct.; arbitrator Civil Ct., Bronx; arbitrator Supreme and County Ct., Westchester. Bd. dirs. Art Inst., Iona Coll., mem. adv. bd. radio activities, adv. bd. criminal justice Iona Coll., bd. dirs. Westchester County Youth Shelter; hon. dep. sheriff Westchester County. Served with AUS, 1942-46. Recipient Patrick B. Doyle award for outstanding service, 1969, William B. Cornelia Founders award, 1976 (both Iona Coll.). Mem. Am. (family law sect.), N.Y. State (com. child welfare, com. family ct.), Bronx County (com. family ct.), Westchester County, New Rochelle Bar assns., Am. Judicature Soc., N.Y. County Lawyers Assn. (family ct. com.), Criminal Cts. Bar Assn. Westchester County, Am. Fedn. Police, Internat. Narcotic Enforcement Officers Assn., Internat. Acad. Criminology, Am. Acad. Polit. and Social Sci., Am. Profl. Soc. on Abuse of Children, Law Guardians Assn. Westchester County (pres. 1987-89, dir. 1989-90), Am. Psychology-Law Soc., Internat., N.Y. State, Bergen County chiefs of police, Nat. Assn. Coun. for Children, Nat. Sheriffs Assn., Am. Soc. Internat. Law, Iona Coll. Alumni Assn., Inc. (pres., chmn. bd. dirs. 1958-60, 62-64, 72-74, 74-76, dir. 1954-58, 68-72, 76-86, v.p. 1966-68). Office: 105 Harding Dr New Rochelle NY 10801-4641

MALACHOWSKI, PHILIP ALEXANDER, civil engineer; b. Scranton, Pa., Apr. 17, 1953; s. Frank P. and Jean F. (Jankowski) M.; children: Philip M., Christopher P. BSCE, Villanova U., 1975, MBA, 1988. Registered profl. engr., Pa. Design engr. Porter & Ripa Assocs., Morristown, N.J., 1975-77, N.H. Bettigole Co., Paramus, N.J., 1977-79, G.S.G.S. & B., Clarks Summit, Pa., 1979-82; sr. design engr. High Steel Structures, Inc., Lancaster, Pa., 1982—; mem. exec. com. Steel Bridge Forum, Washington, 1985—; mem. industry adv. coun. ATLSS Ctr., Lehigh U., Bethlehem, 1986—; mem. fabrication and inspection of metal structures com. Transp. Rsch. Bd., Washington, 1988—; tech. presenter Assn. for Bridge Constrn., Harrisburg (Pa.) chpt. Am. Soc. Hwy. Engrs., Internat. Bridge Conf., 1987, 90. Contbr. articles to Welding Innovation Quar. Recipient merit award Lincoln Arc Welding Found., 1987. Mem. ASCE, NSPE. Office: PO Box 10008 Lancaster PA 17605-0008

MALACHOWSKY, MARTIN NORMAN, physician; b. Glen Ridge, N.J., June 19, 1929; s. Louis and Lena (Sirotkin) M.; m. Zelda L. Rutenberg, Dec. 25, 1951; children: Jeffrey Wayne, Chris Alan. BA, Columbus Coll., 1950; MD, SUNY, 1953. Diplomate Am. Bd. Obstetrics and Gynecology. Intern Mountainside Hosp., Montclair, N.J., 1953-54, resident, 1954-55; physician obstetrics Geisinger Meml. Hosp, Danville, Pa., 1958-60; physician obstetrics Monmouth Med. Ctr., Long Branch, N.J., 1957-58, attending physician ob-gyn.; pvt. practice Long Branch; clin. asst. prof. ob-gyn. Hahnemann Med. Coll. Capt. U.S. Air Force, 1954-57. Fellow Am. Coll. Obstetricians and Gynecologists, Am. Coll. Surgeons; mem. AMA, N.J. Obstetrical and Gynecologic Soc., Soc. Surgeons of N.J., N.J. Med. Soc., Monmouth County Med. Soc., N.J. Acad. Medicine, Am. Fertility Soc., Am. Assn. Gynecologic Laparoscopist. Jewish. Office: Federici Malachowsky Cohen 127 Pavilion Ave Long Branch NJ 07740

MALAMED, SASHA, anatomy educator, cell biologist; b. Bklyn., May 6, 1928; s. Harry and Fannie (Felman) M.; m. Lyanne Schneider, Aug. 12, 1956; 1 child, David. BA, U. Pa., 1948, MS, 1950; PhD, Columbia U., 1955. Rsch. assoc. U. Iowa, Iowa City, 1954-55; instr. CUNY, N.Y.C., 1955; rsch. assoc. Columbia U., N.Y.C., 1955-56; instr. Albert Einstein Coll. of Medicine, Bronx, N.Y., 1958-59, asst. prof., 1959-67; assoc. prof. Robert Wood Johnson Med. Sch. U. Medicine & Dentistry of N.J., Piscataway, 1967-74, prof. Robert Wood Johnson Med. Sch., 1974—; vis. prof. St. Bartholomews Hosp. Med. Sch., London, 1986-87. Contbr. articles to Jour. Biol. Chemistry, Endocrinology, Jour. Cell Biology, Cell Tissue Research. USPHS fellow Columbia U., 1952-54, Case Western Res. U., 1956-58. Office: U Medicine & Dentistry NJ Robert Wood Johnson Med Sch Dept Neurosci/Cell Biology Piscataway NJ 08854

MALAMUD, BARRY EVAN, accountant, auditor; b. Queens, N.Y.C., May 25, 1967; s. Mitchel Lawrence and Karen Lee (Menachem) M. BS, Albright Coll., 1989. CPA, Pa. Sr. assoc. Coopers & Lybrand, Harrisburg, Pa., 1989-92; internal auditor Harsco Corp., Camp Hill, Pa., 1992—. Office: Harsco Corp PO Box 8888 Camp Hill PA 17001

MALAREK, DAVID HARBY, chemist; b. Kearny, N.J., May 15, 1939; s. John and Mavis (Harby) M.; m. Roselynn Stokes, Aug. 6, 1960; children: David Scott, Eric John. BS, Rensselaer Poly., 1960; MS, Seton Hall U., 1965. Scientist Hoffmann-Laroche Inc., Nutley, N.J., 1960-68, 1968—. Mem. Am. Chem. Soc., Internat. Isotope Soc. Home: 334 Franklin Rd Denville NJ 07834-9703 Office: Hoffmann-Laroche Kingsland St Nutley NJ 07110-1310

MALBA, MICHAEL WILLIAM, corporate controller; b. Paterson, N.J., Aug. 3, 1946; s. Vincent Michael and Doris Florence (Magee) M.; m. Nancy Claire Karpiak, Sept. 29, 1968; children: Michael Vincent, Vincent John. AS in Mgmt., Rutgers U., Paterson, N.J., 1970; BS in Acctg., Rutgers U., Newark, N.J., 1972; MBA in Fin., Fairleigh Dickinson, Rutherford, N.J., 1979. Staff acct. Beecham, Inc., Clifton, N.J., 1968-70, Bates Mfg. Co., Inc., Orange, N.J., 1970-73; asst. contr. Theurer, Inc., Newark, N.J., 1973-75; dir. of acctg. Puerto Rico Marine Mgmt., Inc., Elizabeth, N.J., 1975-81; acctg. project mgr. Royal Dutch/Shell Oil, N.Y.C., 1981-86; cons. Eric Andrews Assocs. Inc., N.Y.C., 1987-88; contr. Belcrest, Inc., Clifton, N.J., 1989, Cagiva North Am., Inc., Fairfield, N.J., 1990—. V.p. Clifton (N.J.) Midget League, Inc., pres., 1991, commr., 1982-83, field house com. mem., 1985-88, baseball coach, 1980—, basketball coach, 1982-85, bowling commr., 1985-86; dir. jr. ch. Trinity Ch. of Nazarene, 1988-90. Mem. Am. Legion. Nazarene. Home: 5 Garrabrant Rd Clifton NJ 07013-1511 Office: Cagiva North America 5 Washington Ave Fairfield NJ 07004-3812

MALCARNE, DONALD LEON, retail company executive, lecturer; b. Old Saybrook, Conn., Nov. 24, 1933; s. Leno John and Elizabeth Pauline (Cody) M.; m. Shirley Ann Houghton, Aug. 27, 1955; children: Deborah, Vanessa, Rhonda. BA, U. Conn., 1955; MA in Liberal Studies, Wesleyan U., Middletown, Conn., 1989. In retail mgmt. Montgomery Ward & Co., various locations, 1955-59; in retail mgmt. LaPlace Furniture, Deep River, Conn., 1959—, v.p., bd. dirs., 1962—; lectr. Grad. Liberal Studies Program Wesleyan U., 1991—. Mem. Essex (Conn.) Hist. Soc. (pres. 1990—), Archaeol. Soc. S.E. Conn. (treas. 1990—), Archaeol. Soc. Conn. (bd. dirs. 1990—). Home: 8 Cove Ave Milford CT 06466-0001 Office: LaPlace Furniture 180 Main St Deep River CT 06417-2039

MALCOLM, ANDREW HOGARTH, journalist, writer; b. Cleve., June 22, 1943; s. Ralph Monteith and Beatrice Florence (Bowles) M.; m. Connie D'Amelio, Nov. 28, 1981; children: Christopher, Spencer, Emily, Keddy. BJ, Northwestern U., 1966, MJ, 1967. Clk. The N.Y. Times, N.Y.C., 1967-68, met. reporter, 1969-70; nat. corr. The N.Y. Times, Chgo., 1971-73, San Francisco, 1974-75; fgn. corr. The N.Y. Times, Vietnam, Thailand,

Guam, 1975, Tokyo, 1975-78, Republic of Korea, 1975-78; bur. chief The N.Y. Times, Toronto, Ont., Can., 1978-82, Chgo., 1982-87; 1st asst. nat. editor The N.Y. Times, N.Y.C., 1987-88, nat. affairs corr., columnist, 1988—. Author: Unknown America, 1975, The Canadians, 1985, Final Harvest, 1986, This Far and No More,1987, Someday, 1991, U.S. 1: America's Original Main Street, 1991, The Land and People of Canada, 1991, A Look Back from the Endzone: Football, Fathers and Sons, 1992. Recipient George Polk award L.I. U., 1975, Page One award N.Y. Newspaper Guild, 1975, 83. Office: care New York Times 229 W 43rd St New York NY 10036-3959

MALE, MARY EILEEN, university administrator; b. Schenectady, N.Y., Sept. 22, 1949; d. William John and Dorothy Frances (Hubbard) M. BA, Syracuse U., 1971; MS, Simmons Coll., 1989. Mng. editor Design News Cahners Pub. Co., Boston, 1971-78; supr. employee communications Pub. Svc. Co. N.H., Manchester, 1978-85; mgr. pub. rels. Health NorthEast, Manchester, 1985-90; dir. pub. rels. Notre Dame Coll., Manchester, 1990—. Mem. com. United Way of Greater Manchester, 1990-91. Recipient Graniteer award Advt. Club. N.H., 1987, New Eng. Bell Ringer award Publicity Club Boston, 1984, 88, Touchstone award Am. Soc. for Hosp. Mktg., 1986, award for Disting. Tech. Communication, Soc. for Tech. Communication, 1975. Mem. Pub. Rels. Soc. Am. Office: Notre Dame Coll 2321 Elm St Manchester NH 03104-2213

MALEC, MICHAEL ANTHONY, sociology educator; b. Chgo., Nov. 8, 1940; s. Kazmer T. and Josephine B. (Zemeck) M.; m. Myrna King, June 27, 1965; children: Timothy A., Thomas M. BS, Loyola U., 1962; MS, Purdue U., 1965, PhD, 1968. Instr. Bowdoin Coll., Brunswick, Maine, 1966-68; asst. to assoc. prof. Boston Coll., Chestnut Hill, Mass., 1968—. Editor: Attitude Change, 1971; author: Essential Statistics for Social Research, 1977; editor Jour. of Sport and Social Issues, 1986-92. Mem. Bd. of Aldermen, Newton, Mass., 1981-86, pres., 1985-86. Mem. Am. Sociol. Assn., Alpha Kappa Delta (pres. 1986-88). Democrat. Roman Catholic. Office: Boston Coll Dept Sociology Chestnut Hill MA 02167-3807

MALEKI, NAHID, orthodontist educator; b. Tehran, Iran, Nov. 11, 1945; came to U.S., 1969; d. Husien and Malake Maleki; m. Assad Homayoun, Apr. 1968; 1 child, Aresh. DDS, Tehran U., 1969; MS, Georgetown U., 1977. Clin. instr. Georgetown U., Washington, 1977-79; asst. prof. Georgetown U., 1979-85, assoc. prof., dir. undergrad. studies, 1985—, assoc. prof. tenure, 1986. Contbr. articles to profl. jours. Mem. ADA, Am. Assn. Orthodontists, Mid. Atlantic Soc. Orthodontists, Am. Assn. Dental Schs., Georgetown Club, Omicron Kappa Upsilon (faculty mem.). Home: 8800 Bel Air Pl Rockville MD 20854-1603 Office: Georgetown U Hosp 3800 Reservoir Rd NW Washington DC 20007-2196

MALETSKY, EVAN MERLE, mathematics educator; b. Pompton Lakes, N.J., June 9, 1932; s. Otto and Ethel (Cox) M.; m. Geneva Lucille Moore, June 12, 1954; children: Mark, Kerry, Janine, Lorin. BA, Montclair State Coll., Upper Montclair, N.J., 1953, MA, 1954; PhD, NYU, N.Y.C., 1961. Tchr. math. Pascack Valley Regular High Sch., Hillsdale, N.J., 1956-57; prof. math. Montclair State Coll., Upper Montclair, 1957—. Author: Algebra I and II, 1985, 1985, McGraw Hill Mathematics, 1987, Teaching Mathematics, 1988, Geometry, 1990, Fractals for the Classroom, 1991. With U.S. Army, 1954-56. Home: 34 Pequannock Ave Pompton Lakes NJ 07442-1407 Office: Montclair State Coll Upper Montclair NJ 07043

MALETZ, HERBERT NAAMAN, federal judge; b. Boston, Oct. 30, 1913; s. Reuben and Frances (Sawyer) M.; m. Catherine B. Loebach, May 8, 1947; 1 son, David M. A.B., Harvard, 1935, LL.B., 1939. Bar: Mass. bar 1939, D.C. bar 1952. Mem. staff Truman com. U.S. Senate, 1941-42; atty. anti-trust div. Dept. Justice, 1946-50; with OPS, 1950-53, chief counsel, 1952-53; chief counsel anti-trust subcom. U.S. Ho. of Reps., 1955-61; commr. U.S. Ct. Claims, 1961-67; judge U.S. Ct. Internat. Trade, N.Y.C., 1967-87; vis. judge U.S. Dist. Ct. Md., Balt., 1987—. Served with AUS, 1942-46; lt. col. Res. Office: US Dist Ct Md 101 W Lombard St Baltimore MD 21201-2626

MALEY, PATRICIA ANN, preservation planner; b. Wilmington, Del., Dec. 25, 1955; d. James Alfred and Frances Louise (Fenimore) M.; m. Scott A. Stone, Dec. 7, 1991. AA, Cecil Community Coll., 1973; BA, U. Del., 1975, MA, 1981. Cert. planner: cert. secondary tchr., Del. Analyst econ. devel. City of Wilmington, 1977-78, evaluation specialist, 1978-80, planner II mayor's office, 1980-86, cons. preservation, 1986-87; dir. Belle Meade Mansion, Nashville, 1987-88; dir. planning, devel. Children's Bur. of Del., Wilmington, 1988; prin. preservation planner Environ. Mgmt. Ctr., Brandywine Conservancy, Chadds Ford, Pa., 1988—; cons. cultural resources M.A.A.R. Inc., Newark, Del., 1987, ITC Cons., Wilmington, 1985-86. Contbg. photographer America's City Halls, 1984; author numerous Nat. Register nominations, 1980-86; 88—. Pres., founder Haynes Park Civic Assn., Wilmington, 1977-80; photographer Biden U.S. Senate campaign, New Castle County, Del., 1984; sec. parish council Our Lady Fatima Roman Cath. Ch., 1985-86, choir dir., 1983-87; bd. dirs. Del. Children's Theatre; music dir. St. Elizabeth Ann Seton parish, Bear, Del., 1988—. U. Del. fellow, 1976-77. Mem. Nat. Trust Hist. Preservation, Am. Inst. Cert. Planners, Am. Planning Assn., Nat. Pastoral Musicians Assn., Del. Soc. Architects, Del. Archeol. Soc., Del. Hist. Soc., Chester County (Pa.) Hist. Soc., Am. Inst. Cert. Planners, Pi Sigma Alpha. Democrat. Office: Brandywine Conservancy Environ Mgmt Ctr PO Box 141 Chadds Ford PA 19317-0141

MALHI, BALWINDER SINGH, nuclear pharmacist; b. Ayali Kalan, Punjab, India, Aug. 1, 1944; came to U.S., 1972.; s. Mukhtiar Singh and Bhagwan Kaur Malhi; m. Gurjit Kaur Sangha; children: Sarwinder Kaur, Kirat Kaur. BS in Pharmacy, Panjab U., Chandigarh, 1969, MS in Pharmacy, 1971; MS in Pharmacy, U. Pitts., 1976. Lic. pharmacist, Pa., Fla., Calif. Pharmacist Presbyn.-Univ. Hosp., Pitts., 1975-84, nuclear pharmacist, 1975—; jr. rsch. fellow Panjab U. Sch. of Pharmacy, 1969-71; asst. rsch. officer Pharm. Labs., Ranikhet, 1971-72; lectr. Govt. Med. Coll., Rohtak, 1972; teaching asst. U. Pitts. Sch. of Pharmacy, 1973-76. Trustee Tri State Sikh Cultural Soc., Pitts., 1986-87. Mem. Panjab U. Pharm. Soc. (sec. 1969-70), Am. Soc. Hosp. Pharm., Am. Pharm. Soc., Am. Soc. Nuclear Medicine. Sikh. Home: 142 Regal Ct Monroeville PA 15146-4736 Office: Presbyn U Hosp Cen Imaging Svcs Inc DeSoto at O'Hara Pittsburgh PA 15213

MALIA, PETER JUSTIN, editor; b. New Haven, Conn., July 30, 1951; s. Donald J. and Helen (Walsh) M.; m. Celeste Ann Hurter, July 21, 1978; children: Jason William, Laurie Ann. BA in History, Providence Coll., 1973; MA in Am. History, Trinity Coll., 1975; postgrad., Fordham U., 1975-77. Rsch. assoc. Sleepy Hollow Press, Inc., Tarrytown, N.Y., 1977-81, assoc. editor, 1979-81; mng. editor The Conn. Hist. Soc., Hartford, 1981-84; editor-in-chief Champion Internat. Corp., Stamford, Conn., 1984—. Author: History of West Haven, 1992; editor The Wire, 1987—, Conn. Hist. Soc. Bull. (NEMA award), Conn. Hist. Soc. Press; contbr. articles to profl. jours. Recipient Bicentennial award North Haven Bicentennial Commn., 1976, grad. fellowship Bronx Hist. Soc., 1977. Mem. Conn. Acad. Arts and Scis., Conn. Hist. Soc., Monroe Hist. Soc. Home: 135 Church St Monroe CT 06468 Office: Champion Internat One Champion Plaza Stamford CT 06921

MALIK, HUSSAIN GHULAM, otolaryngologist, facial plastic surgeon; b. Sahiwal Sargodha, Punjab, Pakistan, Dec. 7, 1946; came to U.S., 1970; s. Ghulam Hasan and Aisha (Hasan) M.; m. Aisha Beards, Oct. 3, 1981; children: Ali, Nazneen, Yasmeen, Omar. Grad., Govt. Coll., Sagodha, 1964; MD, King Edward Med. Coll., Lahore, Pakistan, 1969. Diplomate Am. Bd. Otolaryngology and Head and Neck Surgery. Intern Cath. Med. Ctr., Bklyn. and Queens, 1970-71; resident in gen. surgery L.I. Coll. Hosp., Bklyn., 1971-72, resident in otolaryngology, 1975-76; otolaryngologist, facial plastic surgeon Pocono Ear, Nose, Throat and Facial Plastic Surgery Assocs., East Stroudsburg, Pa., 1976—. Mem. AMA, Am. Coll. Surgeons, Am. Soc. Otolaryngology, Am. Cancer Soc., Pa. Med. Soc., Centurion Club for Deafness, Am. Coun. Otolaryngology. Republican. Muslim. Office: Pocono Ear Nose Throat and Facial Plastic Surgery 296 E Brown St East Stroudsburg PA 18301

MALIN, KENNETH WILLIAM, real estate broker, writer, consultant; b. Phila., Mar. 28, 1948; s. Albert A. and Lillian (Trimpol) M.; m. Ellen Donna Fireman, May 24, 1970 (div. Dec. 1981); children: Michael, Julie; m. Toby Marsha Cogan, July 16, 1989; 1 child, Joshua. BBA, Temple U., 1969, postgrad., 1970-72; postgrad., U. Pa., 1991—. Lic. real estate broker, Pa. Gen. mgr. I.W. Levin & Co., Phila., 1973—; v.p. Baseball Analysis Co., Bala Cynwyd, Pa., 1982—; pres. (Residential Div.), 1991, political action chmn., 1990, Phila. Bd. Realtors; pres. Center City Realtors, Phila., 1990. Co-author: Mann/Mallin Fant. Baseball, 1992, Sporting News Basball Guide, 1990; contbr. articles to sports books. Mem. Golden Slipper Club Charities, 1980—. Mem. Mem. Commonwealth, State, Phila. Bd. of Realtors. Democrat. Jewish. Home: 721 Oxford Road Bala Cynwyd PA 19004-2111 Office: IW Levin & Co 716 South St Philadelphia PA 19147

MALINDRETOS, JOHN NIKOLAOU, financial educator; b. Hania, Crete, Greece, Jan. 21, 1954; came to U.S. 1969; s. Nikolaos and Zambia (Giparis) M. BA, Rutgers U., 1976, MA, 1979, PhD, 1986. Asst. prof. econs. Fairleigh Dickinson U., Rutherford, N.J., 1981-84, Ramapo State Coll., Mahwah, N.J., 1984-85; asst. prof. fin. Rider Coll., Lawrenceville, N.J., 1985-88, Fairleigh Dickinson U., Rutherford, 1988-89; assoc. prof. fin. N.J. Inst. Tech., Newark, 1989—; fin. cons. Rider corp. Program; lectr. in field. Contbr. articles to profl. jours. Mem. Ea. Exon. Assn., Ea. Fin. Assn., Internat. Soc. Statis. Sci. in Econs., Fin. Mgmt. Assn., No. Fin. Assn., Decision Sci. Inst., New Eng. Bus. Adminstrn. Assn., Southwestern Fin. Assn. Office: New Jersey Inst Tech Weston Hall Newark NJ 07102

MALING, GEORGE CROSWELL, JR., physicist; b. Boston, Feb. 24, 1931; s. George Croswell and Marjory (Bell) M.; m. Norah J. Horsfield, Dec. 29, 1960; children: Ellen P., Barbara J., Jeffrey C. A.B., Bowdoin Coll., 1954; S.B., S.M., MIT, 1954, Elec. Engr., 1958, Ph.D., 1963. Rsch. asst., postdoctoral fellow MIT, 1957-65; adv. physicist IBM Corp., 1965-71; sr. physicist IBM Corp., Poughkeepsie, N.Y., 1971-92; pres. Empire State Software Systems, Ltd., 1992—; dir. Noise Control Found., Inc., Poughkeepsie, 1975—; chmn. com. Sl-acoustics Am. Nat. Standards Com., 1976-79. Editor Noise/News, 1972-92; assoc. editor: Jour. Acoustical Soc. Am., 1976-83; editor tech. proc.; contbr. numerous articles to profl. jours. Served with U.S. Army, 1955-57. Fellow IEEE, AAAS, Acoustical Soc. Am. (exec. coun. 1980-83), Audio Engring. Soc.; mem. Inst. Noise Control Engring. (bd. dirs. 1972-77, pres. 1975), Internat. Inst. Noise Control Engring. (bd. dirs. 1980-86, 90—). Office: ESSS PO Box 2880 Poughkeepsie NY 12603

MALININ, MIKHAIL VALENTINOVICH, advocate, writer; b. Moscow, Russia, USSR, Jan. 1, 1955; came to U.S., 1988; s. Valentin Mikhailovich Pozdnishev and Alexandra Vladimir Malinina; m. Galina Nikolaevna Sidorova, Jan. 18, 1981 (div. Sept. 1987); 1 child, Alexander Mikhailovich Malinin. Diploma, Moscow U., 1982. Rsch. asst. Regional Plan Assn. City of New York, 1989-90; exec. dir. Am. Soc. (former) Soviet Polit. Prisoners, N.Y.C., 1990—. Editor: (mag.) Sbornik/Documents, 1990—; contbr. articles to various publs. Founder Am. Soc. (former) Soviet Political Prisoners, Inc., 1989. Sgt. Soviet Army, 1973-75. Home: 87-60 113th St #4-C New York NY 11418 Office: Am Soc USSR Polit Prisoners PO Box 8637 New York NY 10116

MALINOSKI, FRANK JOSEPH, general practice physician; b. Troy, N.Y., Sept. 4, 1954; s. Frank and Ruth Elizabeth (Martin) M.; m. Judith Ann Sanders, May 23, 1981; children: Wayne D. Peschel, Matthew C. BA, Colby Coll., Waterville, Maine, 1976; PhD, Rutgers U., 1981; MD, Albany (N.Y.) Med. Sch., 1985. Commd. U.S. Army, 1981, advanced through grades to maj.; intern Brooke Army Med. Ctr., San Antonio, 1985-86; physician U.S. Army Med. Research Inst. Infectious Diseases, Frederick, Md., 1986-92; resigned U.S. Army, 1992; dir. clin. affairs Praxis Biologicals, Rochester, N.Y., 1992—; cons. Frederick Med. Ctr. Clinic, Walkersville, Md., 1987-92; affiliate staff Frederick Meml. Hosp., 1987-92. Contbr. articles to profl. jours. Mem. Frederick County Substance Abuse Coun., 1988-92, Drug Utilization Rev. Bd. of Md., Balt., 1989-92, Instn. Biosafety Com., 1988-92. Nat. Cancer Inst. fellow, 1978-81; Cystic Fibrosis Found. fellow, 1979-80; N.Y. State Health Research Council fellow, 1981-82. Mem. AMA, Am. Soc. Microbiology, Am. Soc. Virology, Am. Soc. Torpical Medicine and Hygiene, Am. Assn. Family Physicians. Republican. Home: 11616 Old Annapolis Rd Frederick MD 21701-3432 Office: Praxis Biologicals 30 Corporate Woods Rochester NY 14623

MALKIEL, BURTON GORDON, economics educator; b. Boston, Aug. 28, 1932; s. Sol and Celia (Gordon) M.; m. Judith Ann Atherton, July 16, 1954 (dec. 1987); 1 child, Jonathan; m. Nancy Weiss, July 31, 1988. BA, Harvard, 1953, MBA, 1955; PhD, Princeton, 1964. Assoc. Smith Barney & Co., N.Y.C., 1958-60; asst. prof. dept. econs. Princeton U., 1964-66, assoc. prof., 1966-68, prof., 1968-81, Rentschler prof. econs., 1969-81, chmn. dept. econs., 1974-75, 77-81; dean Sch. Orgn. and Mgmt., Yale U., 1981-87; Chem. Bank chmn.'s prof. econs. Princeton U., 1988—; mem. Pres.'s Council Econ. Advisors, 1975-77; bd. govs. Am. Stock Exchange; dir. Amdahl Corp., Jeffrey Co., So. New Eng. Telephone Co., Prudential Life Ins. Co. Am., Baker, Fentress & Co., Vanguard Group. Author: The Term Structure of Interest Rates, 1966, (with others) Strategies and Rational Decisions in the Securities Options Market, 1969, A Random Walk Down Wall Street, 1973, 5th edit., 1990, The Inflation-Beater's Investment Guide, 1980. Served to 1st lt. AUS, 1955-58. Mem. Am. Fin. Assn. (dir., pres. 1978). Home: 76 North Rd Princeton NJ 08540-2430 Office: Princeton U Dept Econs Princeton NJ 08544-1021

MALKIN, MOSES MONTEFIORE, employee benefits administration company executive; b. Revere, Mass., Sept. 18, 1919; s. Irving and Annie (Helfant) M.; m. Hannah Lacob, Oct. 11, 1941. AB, U. N.C., 1941; BSME, Columbia U., 1948. Enrolled actuary and chartered life underwriter. Engr. GE, Schenectady, N.Y., 1948-50; engr. Gen. Bronze, Inc., Jersey City, 1950-51; v.p. Malkin Warehouse, Inc., New Haven, 1951-57; pvt. practice actuary New Haven, 1957-72; pres., actuary Profl. Pensions, Inc., East Haven, Conn., 1972—; presenter pension issues at numerous confs., 1970-80. Pres., founder Milford (Conn.), 1962, Milford Child Guidance Clinic, 1966; pres. Clifford Beers Child Guidance, New Haven, 1971, Jewish Family Svc., New Haven, 1973. Mem. Am. Acad. Actuaries, Am. Soc. Pension Actuaries (instr. 1984), Am. Soc. Chartered Life Underwriters, Grads. Club (New Haven), Phi Beta Kappa, Tau Beta Pi. Jewish. Home: Four Tumblebrook Rd Woodbridge CT 06525 Office: Profl Pensions Inc 444 Foxon Rd New Haven CT 06513-2098

MALKIN, STANLEY LEE, neurologist; b. Pitts., Nov. 11, 1942; s. Maurice and Bessie Beatrice (Serbin) M.; m. Karen A. Johnson; BA with honors, U. Pa., 1964; MD, U. Pitts., 1968; children: Justin Ross, Keith Richard. Intern, Montefiore Hosp., Pitts., 1968-69; resident in neurology Columbia-Presbyn. Med. Center, N.Y.C., 1969-72; chief neurology service Wright-Patterson AFB, Dayton, Ohio, 1972-74; practice medicine specializing in neurology, N.Y.C.; attending staff Mt. Sinai Hosp.; former dir. Neuro-Diagnostic Lab, Englewood; asst. clin. prof. neurology Mt. Sinai Sch. of Medicine; founder Bergen-Passaic Tomography Center, Fairlawn, N.J.; neurology cons. Regent Hosp.; med. dir. Pain Suppression Labs., Inc.; med. dir. Efficient Health Systems, Inc.-N.Y.C. Healthline; founder and prin. Hosp. Diagnostic Equipment Corp.; founder Montvale Med. Imaging Assocs. (N.J.), N.Y. Med. Imaging, N.Y.C. Co-mcpl. coord. Ft. Lee Citizens for McGovern, 1972; mem. Edgewater Rent Control Bd., 1978, Nat. Headache Found. Maj. M.C., USAF, 1972-74. Diplomate Am. Bd. Psychiatry and Neurology, Nat. Bd. Med. Examiners. Mem. Am. Acad. Neurology, Am. Assn. Electrodiagnostic Medicine, Am. Soc. Neuro-Imaging (charter), Am. Med. EEG Soc., Am. Assn. for Study of Headache, Nat. Headache Found., Internat. Headache Soc., N.Y. Acad. Scis. Office: 15 Penn Pla 401 7th Ave Ste 189 New York NY 10001-2003 also: 120 W 44th St Ste 701 New York NY 10036

MALLARD, NEWTON JOSEPH, project coordinator; b. Balt., May 27, 1944; s. Newton Joseph and Josephine Mary (Beran) M. Degree in communications engring., Radio Electronics TV Sch., 1965. Remote sta. engr. WITH Radio Sta., Balt., 1964-65; communications tech. AT&T Communications, Balt., 1965-70, installation coord., 1970-82, project coord., 1982—. Mem. Am. Numismatic Assn., B.O. Railroad Mus., KC. Democrat. Home: 4328 Berger Ave Baltimore MD 21206-3649

MALLAY, JAMES FRANCIS, management consultant; b. Morristown, N.J., Dec. 8, 1936; s. Paul Carew and Rachel Reeve (Jones) M.; m. Mary Lou Egert, June 12, 1960; children: Cynthia, Russell. BSME, Lafayette Coll., 1959; MS in Nuclear Engring., MIT, 1961. Registered profl. engr., Ohio, Va. Mgr. performance analysis Babcock & Wilcox, Lynchburg, Va., 1961-82; gen. mgr. Nutech Engrs., San Jose, 1982-83; mgr. engring. mgmt. consulting Mgmt. Analysis Co., San Diego, 1983-88; dir., mktg. Advanced Tech. Engring. Systems, Inc., Reston, Va., 1988-90; cons. The Liberty Cons. Group, Balt., 1990—; lectr. Lynchburg Coll., 1968-72; vis. prof. Internat. Ctr. Theoretical Physics, Trieste, Italy, 1982, Va. State Coll., Petersburg, 1970-71; dir. industry com. to develop procedures guide on probabilistic risk assessment, 1980-83. Capt. U.S. Army, 1962-65. Mem. ASME, Am. Nuclear Soc. (Standards award 1990, chmn. standards steering com. 1980-83, chmn. nuclear power plant standards com. 1976-81), Phi Beta Kappa, Tau Beta Pi. Methodist. Home: RR 1 Box 315 Hamilton VA 22068-9618 Office: The Liberty Cons Group 250 W Pratt St Ste 2201 Baltimore MD 21201-2447

MALLENBAUM, ALLAN ELIYAHU, marketing executive; b. Bklyn., Nov. 26, 1931; s. Arthur I. and Sophie Mallenbaum; m. Irene Bright, Nov. 16, 1953; children: Stephan J., David N., Sandra L., Cheryl D., Lisa G. B in Psychology, NYU, 1952; postgrad., Università Di Padova, Padua, Italy, 1956-60; MBA in Mktg./Internat. Trade, CCNY, 1968. Mktg. rsch. Lennon & Newell Advt., N.Y.C.; mktg. dir. Steifel Labs., Oak Hill, N.Y., Belvac Internat., L.I. City, N.Y.; adminstrv. v.p. Alliance Communication Group, N.Y.C., 1984-86; exec. v.p. Resource Network Internat., N.Y.C., 1986-88; mng. dir./founder Kensington High St. Assocs., Plainview, N.Y., 1988—; arbitrator Better Bus. Bur., N.Y.C. Founder United Zionists of the Americas, N.Y.C.; co-founder Jewish Survival Legion, N.Y.C. With U.S. Army, 1954-56. Mem. Jewish War Vets., Mensa.

MALLERY, ANNE LOUISE, elementary educator, consultant; b. Myersdale, Pa., June 14, 1934; d. Samuel Addison and Ruth Elizabeth (Meehan) M.; m. Richard Gwen Jones, March 9, 1953 (div. 1974); children: Valerie Anne, Joseph Samuel, S. Richard Alan. BS in Edn., Calif. U., Pa., 1970, MEd, 1972; EdD, Pa. State U., 1980. From proficiency coord. to assoc. prof. elem. edn. Millersville (Pa.) U., 1980—; dir. ednl. div. Mobile Vision Tech., Inc., Key Biscayne, Fla., 1990—; editorial bd. Innovative Learning Strategy, Nat. Publ., 1989—; cons. Pequea Valley High Sch, Lancaster, Pa., 1985, Cambridge Adult Edn. Co., 1987, Conawago Elem. Sch., York, Pa., 1991. Contbr. numerous articles to profl. jours. Judge Intelligencer Reg. Spelling Bee, Lancaster, 1990,91. Mem. Assn. Pa. State Coll. and U. Faculty, Internat. Reading Assn., Lancaster Lebanon Reading Assn., Assn. Tchr. Educators, Am. Assn. Colls. Tchr. Edn., Am. Reading Forum. Republican. Presbyterian. Home: 24 Strawberry Ln Lancaster PA 17602-1639 Office: Millersville Univ Stayer Education Ctr Millersville PA 17551

MALLERY, BERRELL, psychologist. BA in Psychology, Hunter Coll., 1975; MS in Psychology, Yeshiva Univ., 1977, Specialist Cert., 1979, PhD in Psychology, 1980. Lic. psychologist, N.Y.; cert. sch. psychologist, N.Y., N.J. Intern N.Y.C. Evaluation and Placement Unit/Bd. Edn., 1975-76, St. Matthew Luth. Sch., N.Y.C., 1976-77; rsch. asst. Montefiore Hosp., 1977-78; intern Bronx (N.Y.) Devel. Svcs./Albert Einstein Coll. of Medicine, 1977-78; NIH internship fellow St. Luke's Hosp. Ctr., N.Y.C., 1978-79; staff psychologist Youth Devel. Clinic of Coll. Medicine and Dentistry of N.J., Newark, 1980-81; sch. psychologist Buckingham Sch., Bklyn., 1981; psychotherapist New Hope Guild Ctr., Bklyn., 1981-84; sr. staff psychologist Staten Island (N.Y.) Mental Health Soc., 1982—; pvt. practice N.Y.C., 1983—; presenter workshops in field. Recipient NIMH fellowship and scholarship, 1976-77. Mem. Am. Psychol. Assn., Ea. Psychol. Assn., N.Y. State Psychol. Assn. (student affiliate steering com. mem., 1976-77), N.Y. Acad. of Scis. Address: 89 Bleecker St Apt 3F New York NY 10012-1526

MALLESON, WILLIAM WALTER, hotel manager; b. N.Y.C., Feb. 8, 1940; s. William W. Jr. and Frances Mary (Wilson) M.; m. Claudia Ann Blumenstock, June 19, 1965; children: Margaret Ann, Mary Kathleen. BS, Pa. State U., 1962. Mgr. Schraffts, Waterby, Conn., 1964-66; sales mgr. The Homestead, Hot Springs, Va., 1966-70; hotel mgr. Callaway Gardens, Pine Mountain, Ga., 1970-77; v.p., gen. mgr. Metro Inns, Little Rock, 1977-82; gen. mgr. RJS Hospitality, Houston, 1982-87; pres., gen. mgr. Pocono Hotel Corp. and Skytop (Pa.) Lodge, 1987—; bd. dirs. Pa. Travel Coun., Harrisburg, Pocono Mountain Vacation Bur., Stroudsburg, Pa., Resort/Hotel Ins. Group, Williamsburg, Va., Pocono Hotels Corp., Wilmington, Del. Capt. U.S. Army, 1962-64. Mem. Am. Hotel Motel Assn. (resort com.). Republican. Roman Catholic. Office: Skytop Lodge # 1 Skytop Skytop PA 18357

MALLET, JACQUES ROBERT, art dealer; b. Paris, Feb. 19, 1945; came to U.S., 1972; s. Jean-Pierre Theodore and Christiane Claire (De Watteville-Berckheim) M.; m. Laurie Helene Belhassen, May 30, 1973 (div. 1985); children: Clementine, Arthur. B in Maths., Lycee Louis-Le-Grand, Paris, 1966; M in Econs., U. Paris, 1971; MBA, Columbia U., 1973. Salesman mut. funds Banque De Neuflize, Schlumberger, Mallet, Paris, 1969; asst. v.p. Kuhn Loeb & Co. Inc., N.Y.C., 1973-78; sr. assoc. corp. fin. ABD Securities Corp., N.Y.C., 1978-80; pres. Mallet Fine Art Ltd., N.Y.C., 1982—. Clubs: Nat. Arts (N.Y.C.); Brooks's (London). Office: Mallet Fine Art Ltd 141 Prince St New York NY 10012-5315

MALLIA, JOSEPH CARMELO, entertainment and media executive; b. Pachino, Sicily, Italy, Mar. 12, 1945; came to U.S., 1951; s. Sebastian and Angelina (DiLorenzo) M.; m. Camille La Ginestra, Dec. 5, 1976; children: Stefanie, Lauren, Andrew. BS, St. John's U., 1967. CPCU, assoc. in risk mgmt. Supervisory underwriter Hartford Ins. Group, N.Y.C., 1971-73; asst. dir., risk mgr. Pinkerton's Inc., N.Y.C., 1973-77; v.p. Shiff-Terhume Inc., N.Y.C., 1977-80; sr. cons. Ebasco Risk Mgmt., N.Y.C., 1980-81; asst. v.p., dir. risk mgmt. Time Warner Inc., N.Y.C., 1981—. 1st lt. U.S. Army, 1968-70, Vietnam. Office: Time Warner Inc Time Life Bldg 41st Fl New York NY 10020

MALLIN, JAY, news editor; b. N.Y.C., Dec. 10, 1927; s. Albert Milton and Cecelia (Jaffe) M.; children: Jay, Linda Anne. AB, Fla. So. Coll., 1949. News editor Havana (Cuba) Herald, 1951-53; stringer corr. Time Mag., N.Y.C., 1956-80; rsch. scientist ctr. for advanced internat. studies U. Miami, 1967-69; editor The Net, Miami, 1974-82; corr. Washington Times, 1982-85; news dir. Radio Marti div. Voice of Am., Washington, 1985-90, news editor TV Marti div., 1991—; cons. to numerous corps.; lectr. in field. Author: Fortress Cuba, 1965, Caribbean Crisis, 1965, Terror in Viet Nam, 1966, (with others) Merc: American Soldiers of Fortune, 1978; editor: Che Guevara on Revolution, 1969, Strategy for Conquest, 1970, Terror and Urban Guerrillas, 1971; contbr. articles to profl. and mil. publs. Home: 1444 Rhode Island Ave NW Washington DC 20005-5427 Office: TV Marti Voice of Am 601 D St NW Washington DC 20547-0001

MALLIN, MICHAEL CURTIS, retail executive; b. N.Y.C., May 8, 1954; s. Joseph and Dorothy (Fae) M.; m. Miriam Pizzaro, Aug. 3, 1987. BS, Baruch Coll., 1976; postgrad., Somerset Coll., 0982-83. Store dir. Laneco Dept. Stores, Easton, Pa., 1981-83; store mgr. McCrorys, Bronx, N.Y., 1983-88; store dir. Toys R Us, Queens, N.Y., 1988—. Inventor: Loss Prevention Log for Retail Shrinkage, 1990. Republican. Home: 635 Castle Hill Ave Bronx NY 10473-1432

MALLIS, BARRY A., marketing executive; b. N.Y.C., Dec. 25, 1946; s. Louis S. and Minnie M.; m. Lourdes Maria Ramirez, Dec. 21, 1969; children: Jesse, Alexander. BA, Oberlin Coll., 1968; MA, Middlebury Coll., 1972; cert., Ecole Jacques Lecoq, Paris, 1977. Tchr. N. Country Sch., Lake Placid, N.Y., 1968-72, Brunswick Sch., Greenwich, Conn., 1972-73, Putney (Vt.) Sch., 1973-84; salesman Micro Svcs. of New Eng., Keene, N.H., 1984-85, gen. mgr., 1985-87; sales mgr. Computer Town, Nashua, N.H., 1987-88; mgr. corp. communications Markem Corps., Keene, 1988-92, internat. mkt. devel. mgr., 1992—; instr. Grad. Sch. of Spanish, Middlebury, Vt., 1973-80; assoc. SES Assocs., Cambridge, Mass., 1977—. Trustee Oberlin (Ohio) Coll., 1968-71; active Maple Valley Ski Patrol, Dummerston, Vt., 1973—; bd. dirs. Monadnock Children's Mus., 1991; referee U.S. Soccer Fedn., N.H., 1991, N.H. Soccer Ofcls. Assn., 1991. Braitmayer fellow, Braitmayer Found., Paris, 1976-77. Home: 127 School St Keene NH 03431-3312 Office: Markem Corp 150 Congress St Keene NH 03431-4373

MALLOCH, THEODORE ROOSEVELT, JR., economist; b. Phila., Sept. 22, 1952; s. Theodore R. and Dorothy J. (Smith) M.; m. Lynette Lockwood, Sept. 29, 1973; children: Ian, Trevor, Nigel. BA, Gordon Coll., 1974; MLitt, U. Aberdeen, Scotland, 1975; PhD, U. Toronto, 1979. Asst. prof. Gordon Coll., Wenham, Mass., 1978-82; sr. internat. econ. U.S. State Dept., Washington, 1982-84; profl. staff U.S. Senate For Rels. Commn., Washington, 1984-85; internat. capital markets Salomon Bros. Inc., N.Y.C., 1985-86; v.p. Wharton-Chase Econometrics, Washington, 1986-88; dep. exec. sec. UN ECE, Geneva, Switzerland, 1988-91; pres. CNN World Econ. Devel. Cong., Washington, 1991—; exec. bd., World Econ. Forum, Assn. for Pub. Justice, Inst. Sec. Studies, Transformation. Author: Beyond Reductionism, 1985, Issues in Trade and Development Policy, 1988; editor: Where Are We Now?, 1982, The State of Political Reflection, 1978. Bush campaign, Dole campaign, Reagan campaign. Recipient Nat. Humanities award, 1982; State Dept. scholar diplomate, 1980. Mem. Am. Polit. Sci. Assn., Am. Econ. Assn. Republican. Episcopalian. Home: 137 Spa View Ave Annapolis MD 21401

MALLOUK, ROBERT SALIM, plastics engineer, developer, researcher; b. Bklyn., Jan. 18, 1926; s. Salim Nicholas and Sarah (Klat) M.; m. Eileen Campbell Mallouk, Oct. 24, 1964; children: Robert, Peter. AB in Chemistry, Princeton U., 1948, MS in Engring., 1950. Rsch. engr. DuPont Co., Wilmington, Del., 1950-58, market devel. specialist, 1958-63, product mgr., 1964-70, market devel. mgr., 1970-80, corp. new bus. devel. mgr., 1980-86; rsch. and devel. assoc. W. L. Gore and Assoc., Elkton, Md., 1986-91. Patentee fluoropolymer products, fluoropolymer ion exchange products and applications; contbr. numerous articles to profl. jours. With U.S. Army, 1944-46, PTO. Recipient Disting. Svc. award Soc. Plastics Engrs., 1980. Mem. Greenville Country Club (pres. 1970), Wilmington Club. Republican. Roman Catholic. Home: 103 Wedgewood Dr Chadds Ford PA 19317

MALLOVE, EUGENE FRANKLIN, science writer, astronautical engineer; b. Norwich, Conn., June 9, 1947; s. Mitchel Noah and Gladys (Alexander) M.; m. Joanne Karen Smith, Sept. 6, 1970; children: Kimberlyn Beth, Ethan Armstrong. SB in Aero./Astronautical Engring., MIT, 1969, SM in Aero./Astronautical Engring., 1970; ScD in Environ. Health Scis., Harvard U., 1975. Cons. engr. Hughes Rsch. Labs., Malibu, Calif., 1970-77; engr. Harvard Air Cleaning Lab., Boston, 1975-77, Analytic Scis. Corp., Reading, Mass., 1977-79; pres., founder Astronomy New England Inc., Holliston, Mass., 1979-85; author, freelance sci. writer Holliston, Mass and Bow, N.H., 1982—; engr. MIT Lincoln Lab., Lexington, 1983-85; sci. writer, broadcaster Voice of Am., Washington, 1985-87; adj. prof. Boston U. Sch. Communication, 1988-90; chief sci. writer news office MIT, Cambridge, 1987-91, lectr. in sci. journalism, 1990—. Author: The Quickening Universe, 1987, The Starflight Handbook, 1989 (Astron. Soc. of Pacific award 1989), Fire From Ice, 1991; contbr. articles to local and national newspapers. Fellow British Interplanetary Soc.; mem. AIAA, AAAS, Nat. Assn. Sci. Writers, Inst. on Religion in an Age of Sci., Sigma Xi, Tau Beta Pi. Republican. Jewish. Home and Office: 171 Woodhill Hooksett Rd Bow NH 03304-5503

MALLOY, JAMES DAVID, publishing executive; b. Passaic, N.J., Oct. 15, 1955; s. Joseph Patrick and Helen (Kozlowski) M. BA, Rutgers U., 1978. Media planner NW Ayer, N.Y.C., 1979-82; mktg. mgr. People Mag.-Time, Inc., N.Y.C., 1982-85; research dir. US Mag., N.Y.C., 1985-86; mktg. research dir. Family Media, Inc., N.Y.C., 1986-88, v.p., dir. rsch., 1988—. Mem. Media Research dirs. Assn., Mag. Pubs. Assn., Advt. Research Found. Democrat. Roman Catholic. Home: 46 Cottage Ln Clifton NJ 07012-2104 Office: Family Media 3 Park Ave New York NY 10016-5902

MALLOY, JOHN FRANCIS, investment management executive; b. Boston, Mar. 16, 1945; s. John F. Sr. and Ann J. (McEachen) M.; m. Mary Alice Sullivan; children: Mark A., Matthew D. BS, State Coll., Fitchburg, Mass., 1969; MBA, Northeastern U., 1977. Trust officer Shawmut Bank Boston, 1972-78; trust officer, asst. v.p. Trust Co. Bank, Atlanta, 1978-80; regional mgr. Equitable Life Assurance Soc., N.Y.C., 1980-83; v.p. David L. Babson & Co., Boston, 1983-86; sr. v.p. Cabot Ptnrs., L.P., Boston, 1986—. Mem. Assn. Investment Mgmt. Sales Execs. Republican. Roman Catholic. Office: Cabot Ptnrs LP 60 State St Boston MA 02109-1803

MALLOY, MICHAEL PATRICK, lawyer, educator, author, consultant; b. Haddon Heights, N.J., Sept. 23, 1951; s. Francis Edward and Marie Grace (Nardi) M.; divorced; 1 child, Elizabeth; m. Susie Pieratos, Jan., 1992. BA magna cum laude (scholar), Georgetown U., 1973, PhD, 1983; JD (scholar), U. Pa., 1976. Bar: N.J. 1976. Research assoc. Inst. Internat. Law and Econ. Devel., Washington, 1976-77; atty. advisor Office Fgn. Assets Control, Dept. Treasury, Washington, 1977-80, Office of Comptroller of Currency, Washington, 1981; spl. counsel SEC, Washington, 1981-82; asst. prof. N.Y. Law Sch., N.Y.C., 1982-83; spl. asst. Office of Gen. Counsel, U.S. Dept. Treasury, Washington, 1985; assoc. prof. Seton Hall U. Sch. Law, Newark, 1983-86, prof., assoc. dean, 1986-87; prof. Fordham U. Sch. Law, N.Y.C., 1987—, dir. grad. studies, 1990—; law lectr. Morin Ctr. Banking Law Studies Boston U. Sch. Law, 1986-90; cons. bank regulation and pvt. internat. law matters . Recipient Spl. Achievement award Dept. Treasury, 1982. Mem. Am. Soc. Internat. Law (exec. council 1986-89), Hegel Soc. Am., L'Association des Auditeurs et Anciens Auditeurs de l'Academie de Droit International de la Haye, Phi Beta Kappa. Author: Corporate Law of Banks (2 vols.), 1988, Economic Sanctions and U.S. Trade, 1990, The Regulation of Banking, 1992; contbr. articles, revs. and comments to profl. jours. Office: Fordham u Sch Law 140 W 62d St New York NY 10023

MALONE, JOSEPH, state treasurer; b. Newton, Mass., Nov. 18, 1954; m. Linda Ploen; 1 child: Joe, Jr. Educated at Harvard Univ. Treas. state of Mass., 1991—. Office: State House Office of Treasurer Rm 227 Boston MA 02133*

MALONE, MONICA, psychologist; b. Camden, N.J., Feb. 28, 1953. BA, La Salle Coll., Phila., 1975; MA, U.S. Internat. U., San Diego, 1976. Diplomate Am. Bd. Profl. Disability Cons.; lic. psychologist, Pa.; cert. rehab. counselor. Drug abuse counselor Rehab. A.I.D., Phila., 1976-77; drug abuse social worker Camden County Drug Abuse Clinic, Camden, N.J., 1977-78; mental health cons. Atlantic Mental Health Ctr., Atlantic City, 1978-83; weight loss counselor Nutrisystem Weight Loss Ctrs., Northfield, N.J., 1983-84; psychologist Woodbine (N.J.) Devel. Ctr., 1984—; pvt. practice, Phila., 1986—; developer, presenter tng. workshops Internat. Lifeline Conv., Melbourne, Australia, tng. programs for other hotlines and adult edn. classes, 1977-84. Pres. Environ. Action Group, Cherry Hill, N.J.; coord. Cherry Hill Recycling Program. President's scholar La Salle Coll., 1971. Mem. APA, Pa. Psychol. Assn., Brigantine Yacht Club. Office: 230 S Broad St 11th Fl Philadelphia PA 19102

MALONE, RICHARD, theology educator; b. Phila., Mar. 31, 1937; s. John and Anne (McDermott) M. STD, Pontifical Lateran U., Rome, 1965; JCL, Pontifical Lateran U., 1971. Ordained priest, 1962. Official Congregation Doctrine of the Faith, Vatican City, Italy, 1966-76; exec. dir. NCCB Com. on Doctrine and Com. for Pastoral Research, Washington, 1976-86; prof. theology Pope John XXIII Nat. Sem., Weston, Mass., 1986—; fellow Cambridge Ctr. Study of Faith and Culture, Cambridge, Mass., 1986—. Editorial bd. Am. Edit. of Communio, 1985; editorial cons. Issues in Law and Medicine; editor: Theology of Priesthood, 1985, The Kung Dialogue, 1980; co-editor: Contemporary Persepctives on Christian Marriage, 1984, John Paul II Speaks to the American Church. Prelate of Honor, Secretariate of State, Vatican City, 1982. Mem. Cath. Theol. Soc. Am., Cath. Bible Soc. Am., Cath. Commn. on Intellectual and Cultural Affairs. Democrat. Roman Catholic. Home and Office: St Charles Seminary Overbrook PA 19096

MALONEY, JAMES HENRY, state senator, lawyer; b. Quincy, Mass., Sept. 17, 1948; s. James Henry Jr. and Katherine Smith (Murphy) M.; m. Mary Angela Draper, Aug. 16, 1980; children: Adele, Anna, Ellen. BA cum laude, Harvard U., 1972; JD, Boston U., 1980. Vol. VISTA, Gary, Ind., 1969-70; exec. dir. Community Action Com. Danbury, Conn., 1974-78; atty. Pinney, Payne, VanLenten, Burrell, Wolfe & Dillman, P.C., Danbury, 1980-86; ptnr. Dice, Maloney, Lenz, & Malloy, P.C., Danbury, 1986—; mem. Conn. Senate, Hartford, 1987—. Chmn. Danbury Community Endowment, 1984—. Recipient Disting. Svc. award Jaycees North Fairfield County, 1984, Community Svc. award Midwestern Conn. Coun. on Alcoholism, 1990; named Legislator of Yr., Caucus Conn. Dems., 1990, Conn. Assn. Ind. Ins. Agts., 1992. Roman Catholic. Office: Conn State Senate State Capitol Bldg Hartford CT 06106 also: Dice Maloney Lenz & Malloy P C 153 White St Danbury CT 06810

MALONEY, MARK JAMES, warehouse distribution manager; b. Trenton, N.J., Feb. 19, 1959; s. James Michael and Helen (Roche) M.; m. Linda Jean Weisgerber, July 31, 1982; children: Kelly Ann, Mark James II. AA in Visual Arts, Mercer County Community Coll., 1979; BS in Bus. Mgmt., Montclair State Coll., 1981. CV supr. Okonite Co., North Brunswick, N.J., 1984-86; from processing supr. to shipping supr. Baker & Taylor Books, Somerville, N.J., 1986-90; mgr. pick/pack Supermart Book Distbrs., Cranbury, N.J., 1990—. Home: 330 Beechwood Ave Trenton NJ 08618 Office: Supermart Book Distbrs 12 S Middlesex Ave Cranbury NJ 08512

MALONEY, MILFORD CHARLES, internal medicine educator; b. Buffalo, Mar. 15, 1927; s. John Angelus Maloney and Winifred Hill; m. Dione Ethyl Sheppard. BS, Canisius Coll., 1947, postgrad., 1947-49; MD, U. Buffalo, 1953. Diplomate Am. Bd. Internal Medicine. Rsch. chemist Buffalo Electrochem. Co., 1947-49; intership Mercy Hosp./Georgetown U., 1953-54; med. residency Buffalo VA Hosp., 1954-56; cardiology fellow Buffalo Gen. Hosp., 1956-57; chmn. dept. medicine Mercy Hosp., 1969—; program dir., internal medicine residency Mercy Hosp., Buffalo, 1972-90; with steering com. Assn. Program Dirs. in Internal Medicine, 1976, cons. mem., 1977-80; clin. prof. medicine SUNY, Buffalo, 1981—; trustee Am. Soc. Internal Medicine, 1984—; edn. leader med. seminar Am. Soc. Internal Medicine, Austria, Switzerland, France, 1987, Argentina, Brazil, Paraguay, 1988; bd. dirs. Internal Medicine Ctr. for Advancement and Rsch. Edn.; pres. Heart Assn. Western N.Y., Buffalo, 1969; sr. cancer rsch. physician Roswell Park Meml. Cancer Inst., 1959-62. Editor (newsletter) N.Y. State Soc. Internal Medicine, 1972-78. bd. dirs. Health Systems Agy. Western N.Y., Buffalo, 1981; exec. com., bd. dirs. Blue Cross Western N.Y., Buffalo, 1987; bd. regents Canisius Coll., Buffalo, 1987—; mem. pres. assocs. SUNY, Buffalo. Capt. M.C., U.S. Army, 1957-59. Recipient Award of Merit N.Y. State Soc. Internal Medicine, 1980, Man of Yr. award Heart Assn. Western N.Y., 1982, Ann. Honoree award Trocai Coll., 1986, Disting. Alumni award Canisius Coll., 1991; named to Sports Hall of Fame, Canisius Coll., 1978. Fellow ACP (Upstate Physician Recognition award 1989), Am. Coll. Cardiology; mem. N.Y. State Soc. Internal Medicine (pres.), Med. Alumni Assn. SUNY (pres. 1975), Med. Soc. County Erie (pres. 1969), Am. Soc. Internal Medicine (trustee 1984—, pres. 1990-91, chmn. long range planning com.), Internal Medicine Purchasing Group of Am. (bd. dirs.), Buffalo Club, Orchard Park Country Club, N.Y. Athletic Club (N.Y.C. Cen. Park S.). Home: 116 Coveport Ln Williamsburg VA 23183 Office: Mercy Hosp Buffalo 565 Abbott Rd Buffalo NY 14220-2095

MALONEY, PAUL JOSEPH, finance director, educator, accountant, business valuation consultant; b. Quincy, Mass., Oct. 9, 1954; s. James H. and Barbara L. (Sullivan) M.; m. Janet A. Witkowski, Nov. 20, 1982; children: Stephanie, James, Matthew, Megan. BS in Econ., Bentley Coll., 1976; MBA in Fin., McGill U., 1978. CPA, R.I. Sr. acct. Comml. Union Assurance Co., Boston, 1978-79; fin. analyst Ea. Gas and Fuel Assn., Boston, 1979-80; asst. prof. Providence Coll., 1980—, chmn. fin. dept., 1988—; pvt. practice Barrington, R.I., 1983—; valuation cons. John S. Renza Jr. CPA, Inc., Cranston, R.I., 1985—; fin. cons. Manisses Communications Group, Providence, 1989—; speaker, discussion leader various nat. confs. Recipient CPA Silver medal R.I. Soc. CPA's, 1983. Mem. AICPA, Am. Soc. Appraisers, Am. Assn. Individual Investors, Inst. Bus. Appraisers, Fin. Mgmt. Assn., R.I. Soc. CPAs. Office: Providence Coll River and Eaton Sts Providence RI 02918

MALOWANY, MOISES SALOMON, pathologist, educator; b. Havana, Cuba, Aug. 10, 1934; came to U.S., 1968; s. Owszyja and Frima Gisia (Bard) M.; m. Rose Camus, Dec. 27, 1961; children: Israel, Daniel. BS, Inst. Vibora, Havana, 1953; MD, U. Havana, 1962. Diplomate Am. Bd. Pathology. Dir. microbiology Univ. Hosp. Aballi, Havana, 1964-66; microbiologist Pinar del Rio (Cuba) Health Dept., 1966-68; dir. microbiology Elmhurst (N.Y.) City Hosp., 1968-72, dir. clin. pathology, 1972-90; assoc. chmn. dept. pathology Booth Meml. Med. Ctr., Flushing, N.Y., 1990—; asst. prof. Mt. Sinai Sch. Medicine, N.Y.C., 1972—. Contbr. articles to sci. jours. Fellow Am. Soc. Clin. Pathologists, Coll. Am. Pathologists; mem. Am. Soc. for Microbiology, N.Y. State Med. Soc., Queens County Med. Soc. Republican. Jewish. Office: Booth Meml Med Ctr 56-45 Main St Flushing NY 11355

MALOY, JOSEPH T., chemistry educator; b. Mt. Pleasant, Pa., Apr. 19, 1939; s. Joseph T. and Helen Maloy; m. Marlene J. Kluska, Sept. 5, 1970; 1 child, Delia Elizabeth. BA, St. Vincent Coll., 1961; MA, U. Tex., 1967, PhD, 1970. Tchr. Mt. Pleasant Area Schs., 1961-65; asst. prof. W.Va. U., Morgantown, 1970-76, assoc. prof., 1976-79; assoc. prof. Seton Hall U., South Orange, N.J., 1979—; rsch. assoc. Aeropropulsion Lab., Wright Patterson Air Force Base, USAF, Dayton, Ohio, 1975-83, F.J. Sieler Lab., USAF Acad., Colorado Springs, Colo., 1988-89, NASA Lewis Rsch. Lab., Cleve., 1991—; cons. AT&T Bell Labs., Murry Hill, N.J., 1984-85; evaluator NIST Office Energy Related Inventions, Washinton, 1984—. Divisional editor Jour. Electrochem. Soc., 1982-89; contbr. more than 40 articles to profl. jours. Active Nat. Eagle Scout Assn., Boy Scouts Am., Ft. Worth, 1972—, Nat. Right to Life Com., Washington, 1979—. Small Bus. Innovation Rsch. Program grantee NSF, 1982; sr. assoc. NRC, 1988-89. Mem. AAAS, Am. Chem. Soc., Soc. Electroanalytical Chem. (pres. 1985-86, sec. 1986—), United Faculty for Life, Sigma Xi. Republican. Roman Catholic. Office: Seton Hall U Dept Chemistry South Orange NJ 07079

MALTBY, FREDERICK LATHROP, engineering executive; b. Bradford, Pa., Dec. 14, 1917; s. Fred Lathrop and Nellie (Brown) M.; m. Mildred Maltby, May 6, 1944; children: Lewis, Laura. BS in Gen. Engring., Grove City Coll., 1940; postgrad., Cornell U., 1940-42; MA in Nuclear Physics, U. Buffalo, 1943. Asst. prof. U. Buffalo, N.Y., 1942-44; tech. dir. and chief project engr. Bristol Co., Waterbury, Conn., 1944-52; tech. dir. Fielden Div. Robert Shaw Controls, Phila., 1952-57; founder Drexelbrook Cons., Jenkintown, Pa., 1957-63; pres. Drexelbrook Engring., Horsham, Pa., 1963-91, chief exec. officer, chmn. bd., 1991—. Recipient Product Advancement award Pollution Engring., 1979, 5 Star award, 1980. Fellow Instrument Soc. Am. (Standards and Practices Honors award 1971); mem. IEEE, Internat. Electrotech. Commn. (CT-31 adv. com.), Am. Phys. Soc., Am. Inst. Physics, Nat. Fire Protection Assn., Sigma Xi. Office: Drexelbrook Engring 205 Keith Valley Rd Horsham PA 19044-1499

MALTBY, PETER FOOTE, SR., engineering executive; b. Meriden, Conn., May 5, 1942; s. Lucius Foote Jr. and Sylvia Faye (Pethick) M.; m. Judith Ann Andrews, Nov. 17, 1962; children: Peter Jr., Daniel Albert. BSEE, U. New Haven, 1978, M in Computer Info. Systems, 1984. Jr. engr./technician Avco-Lycoming, Stratford, Conn., 1967-70; technician Canberra, Meriden, Conn., 1970-72; dr. engring. and rsch. and devel. Branson Ultrasonics, Danbury, Conn., 1972-87; v.p. engring./dir. rsch. and devel. Crest Ultrasonics, West Trenton, N.J., 1987—; instr. Conn. Sch. of Electronics, New Haven, 1979-81. Sgt. USNG, 1962-68. Mem. ASTM, IEEE, Inst. Environ. Scis., Compass Lodge #9 (master 1978). Home: 36 Woodlane Rd Trenton NJ 08648-5542 Office: Crest Ultrasonics Corp Scotch Rd Trenton NJ 08628-2503

MAMANA, JOSEPH, editor; b. Easton, Pa., Sept. 3, 1909; s. Domenico Louis and Maria Filippe (Sacchetti) M.; m. Julia Cericola, Sept. 20, 1935; children: Joseph Jr., James, John, Julianne, June. BS, U. Notre Dame, MA, 1932; postgrad., Muhlenberg Coll., 1932. Cert. tchr., guidance counselor, prin., supt. Tchr. Pocono Sch. for Girls, Pocono Manor, Pa., 1929-30; tchr. U. Notre Dame, Notre Dame, Ind., 1931-32, Easton Sch. Dist., Easton, Pa., 1933-46; guidance counselor Easton Sch. Dist., 1947-50, prin., 1951-72; editor PASSP Schoolmaster Publs., Harrisburg, Pa., 1970—; investment mgr. Boyd Investment Svcs., Easton, 1974—; pres. Easton Edn. Assn., 1957-59; dist. XI commr. Pa. Interscholastic Athletic Assn., Easton High Sch. Assn., 1955-72; pres. Investment Svcs. Cons., 1974—. Contbr. edn. articles to PASSP Jour., 1970—. Edn. chmn. N.C. Am. Cancer Soc., Bethlehem, Pa., 1947-57, N.C. Am. Heart Assn., Bethlehem, 1957-67; mem. bd. 112U.S. SSS, Easton, 1967-73; police commn. mem. to study police brutality, Easton. Named Nat. Prin. of Yr., A.C. Croft Publs., Vision Inc., 1963, to Distg. XI Wrestling Hall of Fame Pa. Interscholastic Athletic Assn., 1981; recipient Medal of Honor (educator) Freedoms Found., Valley Forge, Pa., 1965, Notre Dame U. Alumni award, 1992; named for Joseph Mamana award of merit Prins. Assn. Pa., 1990. Mem. NEA (life, del. 1957-59), Pa. Assn. Secondary Sch. Prins. (life, bldg. chmn. 1980-88), Easton Area Schoolmen's Assn. (life, pres. 1948-72, Schoolman of Yr. 1955, 89), Prins. Assn., Notre Dame Univ. Club (Alumni Svc. award 1992), Investments Club (mgr. 1974-92). Home: 200 Burke St Easton PA 18042-1608 Office: Pa Assn Secondary Sch Prins PO Box 953 Easton PA 18044-0953

MAMELOK, ALFRED EDGAR, ophthalmologist; b. N.Y.C., May 12, 1924; s. Louis and Libby (Livingston) M.; m. Judith Ellen Simon, May 27, 1980; children: Susan Wexler, Jonathan, Edward. AB, Columbia U., 1944; MD, N.Y. Med. Coll., 1946. Diplomate Am. Bd. Ophthalmology. Pvt. practice ophthalmology N.Y.C., 1953—; clin. assoc. prof. ophthalmology Cornell Med. Coll., 1953—; attending ophthalmologist, clinic chief N.Y. Hosp., N.Y.C., 1953—; attending surgeon and dir. Uvetis Clinic, N.Y.C.; chief ophthalmology Beth Israel North Hosp., N.Y.C. Author: Comprehensive Textbook of Psychiatry, 1989; contbr. articles to profl. jours. Capt. U.S. Army, 1948-50. Fellow ACS, N.Y. Acad. Medicine, Am. Acad. Ophthalmology; mem. N.Y. Drs. Club (pres. 1955-59), Harmonie Club, Orchestral Soc. N.Y., Masons. Office: 115 E 61st St New York NY 10021-8172

MAMET, DAVID ALAN, playwright, director; b. Chgo., Nov. 30, 1947; s. Bernard Morris and Lenore June (Silver) M.; m. Lindsay Crouse, Dec. 1977 (div.), m. Rebecca Pidgeon, Sept. 22, 1991. B.A., Goddard Coll., Plainfield, Vt., 1969. Artist-in-residence Goddard Coll., 1971-73; artistic dir. St. Nicholas Theatre Co., Chgo., 1973-75; guest lectr. U. Chgo., 1975, 79, NYU, 1981; assoc. artistic dir. Goodman Theater, Chgo., 1978; assoc. prof. film Columbia U., 1988; chmn. bd. Atlantic Theater Co. Author (plays): The Duck Variations, 1971, Sexual Perversity in Chicago, 1973 (Village Voice Obie award 1976), Reunion, 1973, Squirrels, 1974, American Buffalo, 1976 (Village Voice Obie award, N.Y. Drama Critics Circle award), A Life in The Theatre, 1976, The Water Engine, 1976, The Woods, 1977, Lone Canoe, 1978, Prairie du Chien, 1978, Lakeboat, 1980, Donny March, 1981, Edmond, 1982 (Village Voice Obie award 1983), The Disappearance of the Jews, 1983, The Shawl, 1985, Glengarry Glen Ross, 1984 (Pulitzer prize for drama, N.Y. Drama Critics Circle award), Speed-The-Plow, 1987, Bobby Gould in Hell, 1989, The Old Neighborhood, 1991, Oleanna, 1992; screenplays: The Postman Always Rings Twice, 1979, The Verdict, 1980, The Untouchables, 1986, House of Games, 1986, (with Shel Silverstein) Things Change, 1987, We're No Angels, 1987, Homicide, 1991 (also dir.), Hoffa, 1991; (children's books) Warm and Cold with drawings by Donald Sultan, 1985; (essays) Writing In Restaurants, 1986, Some Freaks, 1989, On Directing Film, 1990, The Cabin, 1992; (poetry) The Hero Pony, 1990; dir. (films) House of Games, 1986, Things Change, 1987, Homicide, 1991. Recipient Outer Critics Circle award for contbn. to Am. theater, 1978; Acad. award nominee for best screen play adaptation, 1983; Rockefeller grantee, 1977; CBS Creative Writing fellow Yale U. Drama Sch., 1976-77.

MAMLET, ROBIN GAIL, college dean; b. Detroit, Mar. 28, 1960; d. Lawrence Norton and Barbara May (Rothman) M. AB, Occidental Coll., L.A., 1982. Asst. dir. admissions Occidental Coll., L.A., 1982-84; assoc. dir. admissions Pomona Coll., Claremont, Calif., 1984-87; dir. admissions Sarah Lawrence Coll., Bronxville, N.Y., 1987-91, dean admissions and fin. aid, 19916. Democrat. Jewish.

MAMO, GEORGE ELIAS, psychiatrist; b. Des Moines, Nov. 27, 1935; s. Elias Jubran and Edna (Debes) M.; m. Myra Jean Malek; children: Anna Jean, Laura Jean. BS with honors, Drake U., 1957; MD, State U. Iowa, 1960. Diplomate Am. Bd. Psychiatry and Neurology. Intern Mercy Hosp., San Diego, 1960-61; residency Western Psychiatric Inst., Pitts., 1963-66; staff psychiatrist St. Francis Hosp., Pitts., 1966-67; consulting psychiatrist Pitts. Poverty Program, 1967-68, Dixmont State Hosp., Pitts., 1967-77; pvt. practice psychiatry Pitts., 1966-71; asst. dir. Latrobe Mental Health Ctr., Latrobe, Pa., 1968-74; med. dir. Latrobe Mental Health Ctr., 1974—; chief dept. psychiatry Latrobe Area Hosp., 1974—; clin. instr. Western Psychiatric Inst., Pitts., 1966-75; lectr. in psychiatry Jefferson Med. Sch., Latrobe, 1977—. Capt. USAF, 1961-63. Univ. honor scholar Drake U., 1957. Fellow Royal Soc. Medicine; mem. Latrobe Acad. Medicine (pres. 1992), Pa. Med. Soc., Westmoreland County Med. Soc., Phi Beta Kappa. Republican. Episcopalian. Home: 4958 Circle Dr Export PA 15632-9349 Office: Latrobe Area Hosp Dept Psychiatry W 2nd Ave Latrobe PA 15650-1166

MANAGO, JOSEPH NICHOLAS, composer, recording artist, educator; b. Bklyn., Jan. 9, 1954; s. Joseph Vincent and Marie Antoinette (Zello) M.; m. Helene Barbara Tenzer, May 13, 1987; children: Louis Michael, John Richard. BS summa cum laude, St. John's U., Jamaica, N.Y., 1975, MS summa cum laude, 1977; postgrad., CUNY, 1977-78, NYU, 1978-81. Instr. L.I. U., Bklyn., 1982-83, York Coll., CUNY, Jamaica, 1983-84; vis. prof. C.W. Post-L.I. U. Grad. Sch. Health/Pub. Svc., Greenvale, N.Y., 1984; adj. prof. grad. div. natural scis. N.Y. Inst. Tech., Old Brookville, 1984; vis. prof. Pratt Inst., Bklyn., 1984-85; adj. prof. Coll. New Rochelle, N.Y., 1985; vis. prof. Downstate Med. Ctr., Rsch. Found. SUNY, Bklyn., 1985; adj. instr. N.Y.C. Tech. Coll., CUNY, Bklyn., 1985-87; music tchr. Music Lessons Studio, Rego Park, N.Y., 1991—; composer Hollywood (Calif.) Artists Record Co., 1991, recording artist, 1992. Composer: Oh Sweet Queens, 1991, Born to be Trans, 1991, Proud to be Gay, 1992; contbr. articles to profl. jours. Pres., founder Manago Ministries, Elmhurst, N.Y., 1983—. Doctoral fellow NYU, N.Y.C., 1978-80, Grad. Ctr., Bklyn. Coll., CUNY, N.Y.C., 1977-78; health careers opportunity grantee Rsch. Found. SUNY, Downstate Med. Ctr., Albany, 1985. Mem. AAAS, N.Y. Acad. Sci., Fedn. Am. Socs. Exptl. Biology, Am. Soc. Cell Biology, Tissue Culture Assn., Am. Chem. Soc. Republican. Office: Joey Manago Music PO Box 7393 Corona-Elmhurst NY 11373

MANBECK, JOHN BYRON, English educator, archivist, author; b. Bklyn., July 11, 1931; s. Jesse Byron and Florence Lillian (Cahill) M.; m. E. Virginia Brooks, June 27, 1964; children: Jessica, Brooks. BA in English, Bucknell U., 1953; MA in Mass Communications, NYU, 1961. Music libr. ABC, N.Y.C., 1953-60; regional mgr. Mercury Records, N.Y.C., 1960; office mgr. IGM Broadcasting Co., N.Y.C., 1961; tchr. English, N.Y.C. Bd. Edn., Bklyn., 1961-65; lectr. English philology Helsinki U., 1965-67; prof. English, Kingsborough Community Coll., CUNY, Bklyn., 19676, dir. journalism program, 1972—; evaluator desktop pub. Union County (N.J.) Coll., 1988-89; cons. Coney Island: The American Experience, PBS, N.Y.c., 1989-91; judge student films Acad. Motion Picture Arts and Scis., Bklyn., 1989—. Author: (monograph) Brooklyn on Film, 1981, Coney Island Kaleidoscope, 1991; editor Jour. Nat. Coun. Adminstrv. Women in Edn., 1986; also articles. Archivist Kingsborough Hist. Soc.; chmn. rsch. com. Bklyn. Borough Pres. Bicentennial Commn., 1975; keynote speaker 50th anniversary Bklyn. Pub. Libr., 1991; panelist St. Francis Coll., Bklyn., 1991. Recipient speaker's award N.Y. Coun. Humanities, 1990; Fulbright scholar Helsinki U., 1965-66. Mem. Soc. Profl. Journalists, Coll. Media Advisers, Archivists Round Table N.Y. Democrat. Baptist. Home: 1330 E 32d St Brooklyn NY 11210 Office: Kingsborough Community Coll 2001 Oriental Blvd Brooklyn NY 11235

MANCHESKI, FREDERICK JOHN, automotive company executive; b. Stevens Point, Wis., July 21, 1926; s. John Stanley and Luella (Zwaska) M.; m. Judith Knox; children: Mary Lou, Laura, Marcia, Bruce, Amy Frederick-a. B.S. in Mech. Engring., U. Wis., 1948. With Timken Roller Bearing Co., Canton, Ohio, 1948-57, McKinsey & Co. (mgmt. cons.), N.Y.C., 1957-63, Echlin Inc., Branford, Conn., 1963—; chmn. bd., chief exec. officer Echlin Inc., 1969—; dir. RB&W Corp., The Conn. Nat. Bank, Portec, Inc. Contbg. author: Turnaround Management, 1974. Former Mem. New Haven Devel. Commn.; former Mem. U.S. Indsl. Council Commn.; former bd. dirs. Quinnipiac council Boy Scouts Am.; trustee Hosp. of St. Raphael, Conn. Hospice, Quinnipiac Coll.; bd. dirs. Jr. Achievement; former trustee Conn. Pub. Expenditure Council. Recipient Gold award Wall Street Transcript, 1985; named Automotive Man of Yr., Automotive Warehouse Distbrs. Assn., 1973, Chief Exec. of Decade (Bronze award), Fin. World, 1989; named to Automotive Hall of Fame, 1985. Mem. Nat. Acad. Engring., World Bus. Council, Young Pres.'s Orgn., Nat. Soc. Profl. Engrs., NAM (former dir.), Conn. Bus. Industry Assn. (former dir.), Greater New Haven C. of C. (former dir.), Sigma Alpha Epsilon. Clubs: Pine Orchard Country (New

Haven), Quinnipiack (New Haven), New Haven Country (New Haven). Home: 10 Old Farm Rd North Haven CT 06473-4431 Office: Echlin Inc 100 Double Beach Rd PO Box 451 Branford CT 06405

MANCINI, ELAINE CAROL, public relations executive; b. Chgo., Sept. 21, 1953; d. Edward A. and Adeline (Renella) M.; m. Alan G. Morrice, Aug. 14, 1974. BA, U. Ill., 1975; MA, NYU, 1977, PhD, 1981. Dir. Film Archive and Film Libr. Svcs., N.Y.C., 1980-86; asst. prof. Sch. Visual Arts St. John's U., CUNY, S.I., N.Y., 1980-86; account exec. Ruder Finn & Rotman, N.Y.C., 1985-86; sr. v.p. GCI Group subs. Grey Advt., N.Y.C., 1986—. Author: The Free Years of the Italian Film Industry, 1985, Luchino Visconti: A Guide to References and Resources, 1986, D.W. Griffith and The Biograph Company, 1986. Fulbright teaching grantee U. Bologna (Italy), 1983. Office: GCI Group 777 3d Ave New York NY 10017

MANCLARK, CHARLES ROBERT, microbiologist, researcher; b. Rochester, N.Y., June 22, 1928; s. Charles and Mary (Powell) M.; m. Doloras Jolly, Dec. 19, 1953; children: Charles Scott, Timothy Brooks. BS in Biology, Calif. Poly. State U., 1953; PhD in Bacteriology, UCLA, 1963. Fellow in microbiology, rsch./teaching asst. UCLA, 1956-61; asst. prof. Calif. State U., Long Beach, 1961-64; rsch. bacteriologist UCLA, 1963-65; asst. prof. U. Calif., Irvine, 1965-67; chief lab. of pertussis Ctr. for Biologic Evaluation and Rsch., Bethesda, Md., 1967—; dir. WHO Collaborating Ctr., Bethesda, 1978—; cons. WHO, UN, Pan. Am. Health Orgn., UNICEF and many fgn. countries worldwide, 1971—. Author of 2 lab. manuals for bacteriology; editor of 9 books on pertussis and pertussis vaccine; contbr. over 100 articles to profl. jours. Patentee in field. Cpl. U.S. Army, 1953-55. Recipient Merit award FDA, 1985, Group Recognition award 1989, medal Institutos de Salud, Lima, Peru, 1980, Disting. Svc. award for biomed. rsch. Dept. HHS, 1992; named Honored Alumnus in Sci. and Math., Calif. Poly. State U., 1992. Fellow Am. Acad. Microbiology; mem. Am. Soc. for Microbiology, Internat. Assn. Biol. Standardization, Sigma Xi, Beta Beta Beta (pres. Epsilon Pi chpt. 1952-53). Home: 503 New Mark Esplanade Rockville MD 20850-2737 Office: Ctr for Biologic Evaluation & Rsch 8800 Rockville Pike Bethesda MD 20892

MANDAVA, NAGEJWARA RAO, surgeon, oncologist; b. India, Nov. 22, 1955; came to U.S., 1968; s. Babu Rao and Vidyadhari (Kakarla) M.; m. Lakshmi Yalamanchili, Aug. 18, 1981; children: Ashok, Sri Vidya, Anupa. MBBS, Andhra (India) U., 1981. Gen. surgical resident Cath. Med. Ctr., Jamaica, N.Y., 1981-86, assoc. dir. surgical oncology, 1989—; surgical oncology fellow Roswell Park Meml. Inst., Buffalo, N.Y., 1986-89.

MANDEL, BARRY IRVING, health club executive; b. Balt., June 17, 1943; s. Milton and Pearl (Adler) M.; m. Arlene Anne Ducat, Feb. 13, 1950; children: Michele, Scott. Grad. high sch., Silver Spring, Md. Mgr. Health Spa, 1964-69; dist. mgr. Health Spa, Washington, 1969-74, v.p., 1974-81, svc. pres., 1982-91; pres. Club Mgmt. Co. Inc. dba Spa Lady, Balt., 1991—. Office: Club Mgmt Co Inc 9610 Deere Co Rd Timonium MD 21094

MANDEL, FRANCINE SHARON, statistician, educator; b. N.Y.C.; d. Benedict and Judith (Abbey) Phillips; m. Alan Ira Mandel, Dec. 3, 1978; 1 child, Judith Elysse. BA, SUNY, Oswego, 1976; MA, MEd, MPhil, Columbia U., 1980, PhD, 1986. Asst. prof. bus. Southampton (N.Y.) Coll., 1981-83; asst. prof. quantitative analysis St. John's U., Queens, N.Y., 1983-90; asst. prof. pub. health Cornell U. Med. Coll., N.Y.C., 1989—; rsch. biostatistician North Shore U. Hosp., Manhasset, N.Y., 1989—; cons., Commack, N.Y., 1978—. Statis. editor: Jour. Pediatrics and Behavioral Medicine, 1990—; reviewer: Decision Line, 1986-90; author: Supplements to Computers: An Introduction, 1989; contbr. articles to profl. jours. Ethel Rollison scholar Tchrs. Coll., 1978. Mem. Am. Psychol. Assn., Am. Statis. Assn., Am. Ednl. Rsch. Assn. Home: 18 Ruth Blvd Commack NY 11725-2105 Office: North Shore U Hosp Div Biostatistics 300 Community Dr Manhasset NY 11030

MANDEL, H(AROLD) GEORGE, pharmacologist; b. Berlin, June 6, 1924; came to U.S., 1937, naturalized, 1944; s. Ernest A. and Else (Crail) M.; m. Marianne Klein, July 25, 1953; children: Marcia Mandel Halgren, Audrey Lynn Mandel Todd. BS, Yale U., 1944, PhD, 1949. Lab. instr. in chemistry Yale U., 1942-44, 47-49; research asso. dept. pharmacology George Washington U., 1949-50, asst. research prof., 1950-52, assoc. prof. pharmacology, 1952-58, prof., 1958—, chmn. dept. pharmacology, 1960—; Advanced Commonwealth Fund fellow Molteno Inst. Cambridge (Eng.) U., 1956; Commonwealth Fund fellow U. Auckland (N.Z.) and U. Med. Scis., Bangkok, Thailand, 1964; Am. Cancer Soc. Eleanor Roosevelt Internat. fellow Chester Beatty Research Inst. London, 1970-71; Am. Cancer Soc. scholar U. Calif., San Francisco, 1978-79; fellow Med. Research Council toxicology unit, Carshalton, Eng., 1986; Burroughs Wellcome Rsch. travel grant, Carshalton, 1988; mem. cancer chemotherapy com. Internat. Union Against Cancer, 1966-73, fellow, Lyon, France, 1989; mem. external rev. com. Howard U. Cancer Research Center, 1972-74 ; cons. Bur. Drugs, 1975-79, EPA, 1978-82; mem. toxicology adv. com. FDA, 1975-78; mem. med. research service merit rev. bd. in alcoholism and drug dependence VA, 1975-78; mem. cancer spl. program adv. com. Nat. Cancer Inst., 1974-78, chmn., 1976-78; mem. Nat. Large Bowel Cancer Project Working Cadre, 1980-84; mem. com. on toxicology NRC-Nat. Acad. Sci., 1978-82; mem. Kettering award selection com. Gen. Motors Cancer Research Found., 1979-81. Editorial bd.: Jour. Pharmacology and Exptl. Therapeutics, 1960-65, field editor, 1978—; editorial bd.: Molecular Pharmacology, 1965-69, Research Communications in Chem. Pathology, Pharmacology, 1972—, Cancer Drug Delivery, Selective Cancer Therapeutics, 1983—, Cancer Research, 1974-76, assoc. editor, 1977-81. Served with AUS, 1944-46. Recipient John J. Abel award in pharmacology Eli Lilly and Co., 1958, Disting. Achievement award Washington Acad. Scis., 1958, Golden Apple Teaching award AMA, 1969, 85. Mem. AAAS, Am. Chem. Soc., Am. Soc. Biochemistry and Molecular Biology, Am. Soc. Pharmacology and Exptl. Therapeutics (pres. 1973-74), Am. Assn. Cancer rsch., Assn. Med. Sch. Pharmacology (pres. 1976-78), Nat. Caucus of Basic Biomed. Sci. Chairs (chmn. 1991—), Internat. Soc. Biochem. Pharmacology, Cosmos Club (Washington), Sigma Xi, Alpha Omega Alpha. Democrat. Home: 4956 Sentinel Dr Bethesda MD 20816-3512 Office: George Washington u Dept Pharmacology 2300 I St NW Washington DC 20037

MANDEL, HERBERT MAURICE, civil engineer; b. Port Chester, N.Y., May 11, 1924; s. Arthur William and Rose (Schmeiser) M.; m. Charlotte Feldman, Aug. 22, 1954; children: Rosanne Mandel Levine, Elliott D., Arthur M. B.S.C.E., Va. Poly. Inst., 1948, M.Engring., Yale U., 1949. Registered profl. engr., N.Y., Conn., Fla., Md., Mich., Minn., Ohio, Pa., R.I., Va., W.Va. Structural engr. Madigan Hyland Co., Long Island City, N.Y., 1949-50; with firm Parsons, Brinckerhoff, Quade & Douglas, Inc., 1950-86; v.p. GAI Cons. Inc., 1986—, project mgr., Atlanta, 1962, N.Y.C., 1963-70, Honolulu, 1970-74, v.p., 1974, sr. v.p., Pitts., 1977-86; faculty Yale U., 1948-49; adj. faculty Bklyn. Poly. Inst., 1956-64, U. Pitts., 1986; gen. chmn. 6th Internat. Bridge Conf., Pitts., 1989. Author tech. papers; prin. works include (prin.-in-charge) Williamstown-Marietta Bridge, W.Va.-Ohio, Dunbar Bridge, W.Va., I-64 Bridge, W.Va., Davis Creek Bridge, Charleston, W.Va., Tygart R. Bridge, W.Va. (project mgr.) Newport Bridge, Narragansett Bay, R.I., (designer/project engr.) Hackensack River Bridge, N.J., Housatonic River Bridge, Conn., Arthur Kill Vertical Lift R.R. Bridge, S.I., N.Y., 62nd St. Bridge, Pitts., Savannah River Cantilever Bridge, Ga., I-84 Bridges, Danbury, Conn., (structural rehab designer) Avondale Bridge, N.J., Lincoln Bridge, N.J., B&O R.R. Bridge, Ind., Hawk St. Viaduct, Albany, N.Y., Congress Ave. Bridge, Austin, Tex., Ohio St. Bridge, Buffalo, Panhandle Bridge, Pitts.; project mgr. Interstate Rt. H-3, Honolulu, 1970-74; project dir. design and constrn. Pitts. Light Rail Transit System, 1977-84; designer Elizabeth R. Tunnel, Norfolk, Va., 1950. Served to 1st lt. U.S. Army, 1943-46, 50-52; ETO. Fellow ASCE, Soc. Am. Mil. Engrs. (pres. Pitts. post 1987-88); mem. Am. Ry. Engring. Assn. (steel structures specifications com., 1974—), Nat. Soc. Profl. Engrs., Profl. Engrs. in Pvt. Practice (vice-chmn. Pa. chpt. 1992—), Internat. Assn. Bridge and Structural Engring., Assn. for Bridge Constrn. and Design, Tau Beta Pi, Chi Epsilon, Omicron Delta Kappa, Phi Kappa Phi, Pi Delta Epsilon, Scabbard and Blade. Jewish. Club: Engineers (Pitts.). Home: 920 Parkview Dr Pittsburgh PA 15243-1116 Office: GAI Cons Inc 570 Beatty Rd Monroeville PA 15146-1300

MANDEL, LEWIS RICHARD, pharmaceutical company executive; b. Bklyn., Nov. 13, 1936; s. Murray and Belle (Teller) M.; m. Rochelle Holtzman, Mar. 27, 1960; children: Beth, Susan, Stefanie. BS, Columbia U., 1958, PhD, 1962. Registered pharmacist, N.Y., N.J., Pa. Lectr. in biochemistry, then asst. prof. pharmacology Columbia U., N.Y.C., 1961-64; rsch. biochemist Merck & Co., Inc., Rahway, N.J., 1964-76, dir. biochemistry, 1976-79, sr. dir. univ. and indsl. rels., 1979-89, exec. dir. indsl. and acad. rels., 1989—. Patentee in field; contbr. articles to profl. pubis. Grantee NIH, 1963-64; recipient Wellcome travel award Burroughs Wellcome, 1963. Mem. Am. Soc. Pharmacology and Exptl. Therapeutics, Am. Soc. Biochemistry and Molecular Biology. Office: Merck and Co Inc PO Box 2000 Rahway NJ 07065-0900

MANDELBROT, BENOIT B., mathematician, scientist, educator; b. Warsaw, Nov. 20, 1924; came to U.S., 1958; s. Charles and Belle (Lurie) M.; m. Aliette Kagan, Nov. 5, 1955; children: Laurent, Didier. Diploma, Ecole Polytechnique, Paris, 1947; MS in Aerospace, Calif. Inst. Tech., 1948; PhD in Math., U. Paris, 1952; D.Sc. (hon.), Syracuse U., 1986, Laurentian U., 1986, Boston U., 1987, SUNY, 1988, U. Bremen, 1968, U. Guelph, 1989, U. Dallas, 1992; DHL (hon.), Pace U., 1989. Jr. mem. and Rockefeller scholar Inst. for Advanced Study, Princeton, N.J., 1953-54; jr. prof. math. U. Geneva, Switzerland, 1955-57, U. Lille and Ecole Polytechnique, Paris, 1957-58; research staff mem. IBM Watson Research Center, Yorktown Heights, N.Y., 1958-74; IBM fellow IBM Watson Rsch. Center, Yorktown Heights, N.Y., 1974—; vis. prof. econs. Harvard U., 1962-63, vis. prof. applied math., 1963-64, vis. prof. math., 1979-80, prof. practice math., 1984-87; vis. prof. engring. Yale U., 1970, prof. math. scis., 1987—; vis. prof. physiology Einstein Coll. Medicine, 1970; Hitchcock prof. U. Calif., Berkeley, 1992; visitor MIT, 1953; also Inst. lectr.; visitor U. Paris, 1966; visitor Coll. de France, Paris, 1973, and various times, Institut des Hautes Etudes Scientifiques, Bures, 1980, Mittag-Leffler Inst., Sweden, 1984, Max Planck Inst. Math., Bonn, 1988; lectr. Yale U., 1970, Cambridge U., 1990, Oxford U., 1990, Imperial Coll., London, 1991; speaker and organizer profl. confs. Author: Logique, Langage et Théorie de l'Information, 1957, Les Objets Fractals: Forme, Hasard et Dimension, 1975, 3rd edit., 1989 (trans. to Italian, Spanish, Basque and Portuguese), Fractals: Form, Chance and Dimension, 1977, The Fractal Geometry of Nature, 1982 (translated to Chinese, German, Japanese, Polish and Spanish), La Geometria della Natura, 1987; contbr. articles to profl. jours. Recipient Franklin medal Franklin Inst., 1986, Alexander von Humboldt Preis, 1987, Caltech. Disting. Svc. award, 1988, Moet-Hennessy prize, 1988, Harvey prize, 1989, Nev. prize U. Nev. System, 1991; Nat. lectr. Sigma Xi, 1980-82; Guggenheim fellow, 1968. Fellow AAAS, IEEE (Charles Proteus Steinmetz medal 1988), Am. Acad. Arts and Scis., European Acad. Arts, Scis. and Humanities, Am. Phys. Soc., IBM Acad. Tech., Inst. Math. Stats., Econometric Soc., Am. Geophys. Union, Am. Statistic Assn.; mem. NAS U.S.A. (fgn. assoc., Barnard medal 1985), Internat. Statis. Inst. (elected), Am. Math. Soc., French Math. Soc. Office: IBM PO Box 218 Yorktown Heights NY 10598-0218 also: Yale U Math Dept New Haven CT 06520

MANDELKER, GERSHON, business educator; b. Dubno, Dec. 12; came to U.S., 1968; s. Isaac and Pearl M.; m. Ester Stock, Jan. 14, 1964; children: Eiran, Sigal. BA, Hebrew U., Jerusalem, 1965; MBA, U. Chgo., 1971, PhD, 1973. Lectr. fin. U. Chgo., 1972-73; asst. prof. indsl. adminstrn. Carnegie-Mellon U., Pitts., 1973-77; prof. bus. adminstrn., fin. U. Pitts., 1977—; cons. fin. and investments, speaker in field. Assoc. editor: Jour. Fin. Rsch., Fin. Rev., Fin. Mgmt., Fin. India, Internat. Rev. Fin., Jour. Small Bus. Fin.; contbr. articles to scholarly jours. Treas. Congregation Dor Hadash. Mem. Am. Fin. Assn., Am. Econ. Assn., Fin. Mgmt. Assn., Western Fin. Assn., Ea. Fin. Assn. (past v.p.). Home: 1323 Murdoch Rd Pittsburgh PA 15217-1236 Office: U Pitts Grad Sch Bus Pittsburgh PA 15260

MANDELLA, DENNIS GEORGE, vocalist, songwriter; b. Worcester, Mass., Aug. 5, 1950; s. Concetta T. (Panebianco) M.; (div.); children: Jamie Dennis, Seth Benjamin, Joel Steven. AA in Liberal Arts, Worcester Jr. Coll., 1972; student, Worcester State Coll., 1972-75. Ordained as minister Community Chs., 1978. Mem. gospel band Living Water Band, New England, 1972-81; mem. N.E. Elders, Manchester, N.H., 1979-86; ministerial coord. Worcester Area Presbytery, 1979-83; owner, pub. D. Mandella Music Pub. Co., Worcester, 1989—; musician, singer Christian music; owner pub. co., mktg. co., 1987—. Artist/co-producer album and video, 1990-92; talk show and media appearances Profiles, 1992. Bd. dirs. Worcester Crisis Ctr., Worcester Bapt. Ch., 1971-73. Mem. ASCAP, Assn. Cert. Liquidators (real estate cert.). Office: D Mandella Music 427 Park Ave Ste 109 Worcester MA 01610-1335

MANDEVILLE, MARY DELEHANTY, communications executive; b. Worcester, Mass., Apr. 12, 1941; d. George Bernard and Catherine Alice (Powers) Delehanty; m. Hubert Carpenter Mandeville, Mar. 2, 1963; children: Tara, Joel, Hubert IV, Catherine. BA, Coll. of New Rochelle, 1963. Dir. mktg. North Dartmouth (Mass.) Mall, 1985-86, Days Inn, New Bedford, Mass., 1986-90; mgr. communications and shareholder rels. Aerovox Inc., North Dartmouth, 1990—. Mem. Corp. Secs. of Am.

MANDL, BETTE, English educator; b. Bklyn., Aug. 19, 1940; d. Frank and Fay (Harap) Greenwald; m. Alexander Ernst Mandl, Nov. 23, 1960; children: Kenneth David, Jeffrey Elliott. BA, Bklyn. Coll., 1961; MA, NYU, 1965; EdD, Boston U., 1981. Tchr. English, N.Y. Pub. High Schs., N.Y.C., 1961-63; instr. lit. Cambridge (Mass.) Ctr. for Adult Edn., 1971—; assoc. prof. English Suffolk U., Boston, 1976-92, prof., 1992—. Contbr. articles to profl. jours. Mem. MLA, Nat. Coun. Tchrs. English, Am. Drama Soc., Phi Beta Kappa. Office: Suffolk U Dept English Beacon Hill Boston MA 02114

MANDL, DAVID, architect; b. N.Y.C., Nov. 8, 1953; s. Otto and Ina (Shulman) M.; m. Anita Boggia, June 6, 1981. BArch, Pratt Inst., 1976. Registered architect, N.Y., N.J. Architect HAUS Internat., Inc., N.Y.C., 1977-79, Welton Becket, N.Y.C., 1979-80; prin. David Mandl Assoc., N.Y.C., 1980—. Prin. works include various buildings, N.Y.C., N.J. Mem. N.Y. Soc. Architects. Office: 688 Ave Of The Americas New York NY 10010-5110

MANDLER, SUSAN RUTH, dance company administrator; b. Kew Gardens, N.Y., Feb. 11, 1949; d. Ernest and Clea (Reisner) M.; m. Robert Morgan Barnett, July 30, 1982. B.S., Boston U., 1971. Asst. mgr. Pilobolus, Inc., Washington, Conn., 1977-80, mgr., 1980—. also: PO Box 388 Washington Depot CT 06794

MANDUJANO, JOHN ANTHONY, computer consultant, writer; b. Chgo., Apr. 11, 1955; s. Anthony and Marie (Guerrero) M.; m. Eileen Sandra Hayes, Sept. 26, 1987. BS, Boston Coll., 1977. Programmer Blue Cross of Mass., Boston, 1981-82, instr., 1982-83; cons. ETA Internat., Inc., Newton, Mass., 1983-84; sr. programmer analyst Interactive Data Corp., Lexington, Mass., 1987; cons. Mandujano Assocs., Brighton, Mass., 1987-91; sr. cons. Boston Computer Assocs., Inc., Syracuse, N.Y., 1991—; ind. cons. various orgns., Boston, 1984-87. Author: The Art and Science of Public Speaking, 1992. Mem. Ctrl. N.Y. Personal Computer Users Group, Boston Computer Soc., Assn. for Computer Machinery. Democrat. Roman Catholic. Office: Boston Computer Assocs Inc PO Box 322 Syracuse NY 13215-0322

MANELA, DAVID, electrical engineering executive, educator; b. Jaffa, Israel, Feb. 14, 1955; came to U.S., 1984; s. Aba and Regina (Waterstein) M.; m. Asnat Schmidt, Apr. 1, 1979; 1 child, Rakia. BSEE, Tel Aviv (Israel) U., 1981; MSEE, CCNY, 1985, PhD, 1987. Engr. Elta Inc., Ashdad, Israel, 1981-84; researcher SCS Telecom, Port Washington, N.Y., 1986-88; asst. prof. CCNY, N.Y.C., 1987—; pres. Madah-Com, Queens, N.Y., 1989—; adj. prof. Bklyn. Coll., 1985-87; cons. Indesys, Sunnyvale, Calif., 1985-87. Patent in enhanced class SM power amplifier, class SM power amplifier, SM method and apparatus. Mem. IEEE, Aircraft Owners and Pilots Assn. Home: 14120 85th Rd Jamaica NY 11435-2549 Office: CCNY 140 Convent Ave New York NY 10031-9127

MANESS, ALAN DEAN, lawyer; b. Greensboro, N.C., Mar. 15, 1956; s. Hugh Burroughs and Maxine Elizabeth (Thompson) M.; m. Jeanne Karen Pettenati, Oct. 25, 1986. BA in Polit. Sci. with highest honors, U. N.C., 1978; JD, Yale U., 1981. Bar: D.C., 1982. Jud. clk. Hon. Patrick E. Higginbotham, Dallas, 1981-82; staff attorney anti-trust div. U.S. Justice Dept., Washington, 1982-85; counsel Senate Com. on Commerce, Sci., and Transp., Washington, 1986-90, sr. minority counsel, 1990—; participant Sr. Mgrs. in Govt. JFK Sch. of Govt., Harvard U., Cambridge, Mass., 1989, congl. adv. coun. mem., 1991—. Mem. Phi Beta Kappa. Republican. Baptist. Office: US Senate Commerce Com 516 Dirksen Bldg Washington DC 20510

MANEVAL, PHILIP AARON, arts administrator, composer; b. N.Y.C., May 16, 1956; s. Raymond Kenneth and Harriet Sue (Kromberg) M.; m. Wendy Cherner, June 17, 1984; children, Jeffrey Mischa, Sarah Kate. MusB, Oberlin Conservatory, 1978; MA, U. Pa., 1982. Co-founder, mgr. Phila. Chamber Music Soc., 1986—; asst. mgr. Marlboro Music Sch. and Festival, Phila., 1982—; co-founder, dir. Waterfront Consortium for the Arts, Phila., 1990—; sec., bd. dirs. Mus. Fund Soc. Phila., 1989—. Composer: Quartet for English Horn and String Trio, 1987 (Pa. Coun. Commn. 1987), Sextet for Strings, 1989 (Phila. Chamber Music Commn. 1989), Landscapes Changing and Unchanged, 1991 (Pa. Coun. for Arts Commn. 1991). Mem. Pi Kappa Lambda. Democrat. Office: Marlboro Sch Music 135 S 18th St Philadelphia PA 19103-5228

MANFRE, FRANK JOHN, pollution control equipment company administrator; b. Cleve., May 31, 1957; s. Louis E. and Angela (DeGaetano) M.; m. Virginia Veazey, Aug. 18, 1979; children: Meryl Ann, Joseph Lewis. BS in Environ. Sci., SUNY, Fredonia, 1979. Jr. environ. engr. Beker Industries, Conda, Idaho, 1979-81; sales engr. Jacoby-Tarbox Corp., Yonkers, N.Y., 1981-84; regional sales mgr. CPAC, Inc., Leicester, N.Y., 1984-89, dir. mktg. communications, 1989-90, ops. mgr., 1990—. Home: 8 Oneida Ave Geneseo NY 14454-9510 Office: CPAC Inc 2364 Leicester Rd Leicester NY 14481-9734

MANGAN, PATRICK JOSEPH, lawyer; b. Newark, June 20, 1958; s. Edward Patrick and Joyce Marina (Trevennen) M.; m. Margaret Ann O'Hare, June 5, 1982; children: Michael John, Jennifer Marie. BA in Polit. Sci., U. S.W. La., 1980; JD, La. State U., 1984. Bar: La. 1984, U.S. Dist. Ct. (we. dist.) La. 1986, U.S. Dist. Ct. (mid. dist.) La. 1987, U.S. Ct. Appeals (5th cir.) 1987, N.J. 1988. Assoc. Losavio & Weinstein, Opelousas, La., 1984-87; ptnr. John Haas Weinstein, APLC, Opelousas, 1989-91; assoc. Shevick, Ravich, Koster, Tobin, Oleckna & Reitman P.A., Rahway, N.J., 1991—. Mem. La. Bar Assn., St. Landry Bar Assn., Assn. Trial Lawyers Am., La. Trial Lawyers Assn., ABA, Fed. Bar Assn., N.J. Bar Assn. Democrat. Roman Catholic. Office: 1743 St Georges Ave Rahway NJ 07065-2092

MANGANARO, JAMES LAWRENCE, chemical engineer; b. Bklyn., Aug. 27, 1939; s. Ralph Thomas and Rose Elizabeth (Lorenzo) M.; m. Patricia Marie Keegan, Sept. 1, 1974; children: Jane, Robert. BS, MIT, 1961, MS, 1962; PhD, Rensellaer Polytechnic Inst., 1965. Chem. engr. Gen. Electric Co., Schenectady, N.Y., 1965-67; asst. prof. Manhattan Coll., Bronx, N.Y., 1967-70; sr. prin. engr. FMC Corp., Princeton, N.J., 1970—; cons. process chem. and biochem. devel., computer simulation, new opportunity devel. Charles Manganaro Engrs., Hackensack, N.J., 1965—. Contbr. articles to profl. jours. Patentee in field. Procter & Gamble fellow, Texaco fellow. Mem. Am. Inst. Chem. Engrs., MIT Alumni Club (v.p. programs). Home: 44 Dodds Ln Princeton NJ 08540-4104 Office: FMC Corp PO Box 8 Princeton NJ 08544-0001

MANGANELLO, SAMUEL JOHN, metallurgical engineer; b. Johnstown, Pa., Jan. 2, 1930; s. John and Mary Catherine (Zito) M.; m. Sara Ann Conley, May 4, 1957; children: Mary Colleen, Sheila, John, Thomas. B-SMetE, U. Pitts., 1951, MSMetE, 1957. Registered profl. engr., Pa. Product engr. Wheeling Steel Co., Steubenville, Ohio, 1951; various positions, now sr. rsch. cons. U.S. Steel Rsch., Monroeville, Pa., 1953—, also instr. co. courses on rolls and plate-steel tech. Contbg. author: Rolls for the Metalworking Industry, 1990; contbr. articles to profl. jours. and conf. procs.; patentee in field. Committeeman Penn Hills (Pa.) Rep. Com., 1972-83; active Home Rule Charter Rev. and Revision Com., Penn Hills, 1981-82; musician several community bands and ensembles, Pitts., 1954—. With U.S. Army, 1951-53. Mem. AIME (chmn. roll tech. com. 1980-81, chmn. editorial adv. com. 1986-89, Leadership and Devoted Svc. award 1988), Am. Soc. for Metals (chmn. Pitts. chpt. 1972-73, President's award 1977), Am. Def. Preparedness Assn. Roman Catholic. Office: US Steel Group USX Corp USS Tech Ctr Monroeville PA 15146

MANGARELLA, JAMES, mill executive; b. New Brunswick, N.J., Aug. 28, 1962; s. Guiseppe Francesco and Mary Louise (Durrenburger) M.; m. Judith Anne Swiderski, Sept. 21, 1985. Student, Middlesex County Coll., 1980-82, Rutgers U., 1982-86. Stockboy, truck driver, salesman Milltown (N.J.) Millwork-North Ea. Lumber, Jamesburg, 1979-83; salesman East Brunswick (N.J.) Lumber Co., 1983-88; owner, mgr. Timber Hardwoods & Millwork, North Brunswick, N.J., 1987—. Mem. New Brunswick C. of C., NRA (life). Republican. Roman Catholic. Home: 28 Cosgrove Ct East Brunswick NJ 08816-5622 Office: Timber Hardwoods & Millwork 120 Georges Rd New Brunswick NJ 08902-3183

MANGER, WILLIAM MUIR, internist; b. Greenwich, Conn., Aug. 13, 1920; s. Julius and Lilian (Weissinger) M.; m. Lynn Seymour Sheppard, May 30, 1964; children: William Muir, Jr., Lilian Wade, Stewart Sheppard, Charles Seymour. BS, Yale U., 1944; MD, Columbia U., 1946; PhD, Mayo Found., U. Minn., 1958. Intern, Presbyn. Hosp., N.Y.C., 1946-47, resident, 1949-50; fellow internal medicine Mayo Found., 1950-57; asst. physician Presbyn. Hosp., 1957—; dir. Manger Rsch. Found., 1961-77; clin. asst. vis. physician Columbia div. Bellevue Hosp., 1964-68; asst. attending physician NYU Bellevue Hosp. 1969-77; assoc. attending physician, 1977-83, attending physician, 1983—; instr. medicine Columbia U. Coll. Phys. and Surg., 1957-66, assoc. medicine, 1966-70, lectr., 1981—; asst. attending physician Presbyn. Hosp., 1966—; asst. clin. prof. medicine N.Y.U. Med. Ctr., 1968-75, assoc. clin. prof. medicine, 1975-83, prof. clin. medicine, 1983—; mem. Internat. Med. Council on Drug Use, 1977—; mem. devel. com. Mayo Clinic, 1981-87; vice chmn. bd. Manger Hotels, Inc., 1957-73. Mem. bd. govs. St. Albans Sch., Washington, 1958-64, 67-73, 83-89, chmn., 1967-69; trustee Found. Rsch. in Medicine and Biology, 1971-77, Buckley Sch., 1975-85, Found. for Advancement Internat. Rsch. in Microbiology, 1977-82, Thyroid Found., 1980-85; mem. bd. visitors Boston U. Med. Sch.; trustee Found. for Depression and Manic Depression, 1978-89, pres., 1980-89; elder Presbyn. Ch., 1968-70, 92—, trustee, 1962-67, 80-84, deacon, 1959-61. Lt. (j.g.) M.C., USNR, 1947-49. Recipient Meritorious Rsch. award Mayo Found., 1955, Disting. Alumnus award, 1992. Diplomate Nat. Bd. Med. Examiners, Am. Bd. Internal Medicine. Fellow ACP, Acad. Psychosomatic Medicine, Am. Geriatric Soc. (coun. on geriatric cardiology), N.Y. Acad. Medicine (admission com. 1976-78, edn. com. 1979—), Am. Coll. Cardiology, Am. Coll. Clin. Pharmacology, Royal Soc. Health, Am. Inst. Chemists; trustee Nat. Hypertension Assn. (chmn. 1977—), AMA, Am. Soc. Internal Medicine, N.Y. State Med. Soc., N.Y. County Med. Soc., Am. Heart Assn. (fellow council on circulation and council for high blood pressure rsch.), Inter-Am. Soc. Hypertension, Internat. Soc. Hypertension, Am. Thoracic Soc., N.Y. Acad. Sci., AAAS, Am. Physiol. Soc., Am. Chem. Soc., Am. Soc. Pharmacology and Exptl. Therapeutics, Am. Soc. for Clin. Pharmacology and Therapeutics, Clin. Autonomic Rsch. Soc., Med. Strollers, N.Y.C., Endocrine Soc., Pan Am. Med. Assn., Harvey Soc., Soc. Exptl. Biology and Medicine, Rsch. Discussion Group (founding mem., sec.-treas. 1958-80), Am. Fedn. Clin. Rsch., Am. Soc. Nephrology, Royal Soc. Medicine (affiliate), Fellows Assn. Mayo Found. (v.p., pres. 1953), Mayo Alumni Assn. (v.p. 1981-82, exec. com. 1981-89, pres. elect 1982-85, pres. 1985-87), Catecholamine Club (founder, sec.-treas. 1967-80, pres. 1981-82), Doctors Mayo Soc. (Disting. Physician-Mayo Alumnus 1992), Albert Gallatin Assos., New Eng. Soc., S.R. (chmn. admissions com. 1959-67, bd. mgrs. 1959-67, 69-70), Soc. Colonial Wars, Sigma Xi, Nu Sigma Nu, Phi Delta Theta, Explorers, Meadow (L.I., N.Y.); Univ.; Yale; N.Y. Athletic (N.Y.C.); Devon Yacht; Southampton Bathing Corp.; Jupiter Island. Co-author: Chemical Quantitation of Epinephrine and Norepinephrine in Plasma, 1959, Pheochromocytoma, 1977; author: Catecholamines in Normal and Abnormal Cardiac Function; editor, contbr. Hormones and Hypertension, 1966; editor: Am. Lecture Series in Endocrinology, 1962-75; guest editor First Irvine H. Page Internat. Hypertension Rsch. Symposium; contbr. articles to profl. and lay jours. Achievements include research on the mechanism of salt-induced

hypertension, on pheochromocytoma. Home: 8 E 81st St New York NY 10028-0201

MANGES, JAMES HORACE, investment banker; b. N.Y.C., Oct. 8, 1927; s. Horace S. and Natalie (Bloch) M.; m. Joan Brownell, Oct., 1969 (div.); m. Mary Seymour, Mar. 28, 1974; children: Alison, James H. Jr. Grad., Phillips Exeter Acad., 1945; BA, Yale U., 1950; MBA, Harvard U., 1953. With Kuhn, Loeb & Co., N.Y.C., 1954-77, ptnr., 1967-77; mng. dir. Lehman Bros., Kuhn Loeb Inc., N.Y.C., 1977-84, Shearson Lehman Hutton, Inc., N.Y.C., 1984-90; adv. dir. Lehman Bros., N.Y.C., 1990—; dir. Baker Industries, Inc., 1967-77; dir., exec. com. Metromedia, Inc. 1970-86. Trustee The Episcopal Sch., 1978—, St. Bernard's Sch., 1985—; trustee Phillips Exeter Acad., 1984-89, mem. trustee's coun., 1989—. Clubs: Bond, Yale (N.Y.C.); City Midday, Century Country (Purchase, N.Y.). Home: 875 Park Ave New York NY 10021-0341 Office: Lehman Bros World Fin Ctr Am Express Tower New York NY 10285

MANGIAFICO, LUCIANO, retired diplomat; b. Siracusa, Sicily, Italy, Dec. 23, 1938; came to U.S. 1956; s. Paolo and Emanuela (Infantino) M.; m. Lina Pellecchia, July 4, 1964; children: Manuela, Paul U., Peter A. BA in Polit. Sci. magna cum laude, U. Hartford, 1968. Vice consul U.S. Embassy, Bridgetown, Barbados, 1970-72, U.S. Consulate Gen., Calgary, Alta., Can., 1972-74; consul U.S. Consulate Gen., Milan, Italy, 1974-77, U.S. Embassy, Bucharest, Romania, 1977-79, U.S. Consulate Gen., Calgary, 1979-82, U.S. Embassy, Manila, Philippines, 1982-85; consul gen. U.S. Embassy, Bridgetown, 1986-89, U.S. Consulate Gen., Palermo, Italy, 1989-91. Author: Contemporary American Immigrants, 1988. With U.S. Army, 1962-68. Mem. Sons of Italy. Roman Catholic.

MANGIAGLI, JOHN CHARLES, JR., technical service specialist, computer consultant; b. Albany, N.Y., Mar. 13, 1954; adopted s. John Charles and Mary Ann (Pezzella) M.; m. Terry Lee Putnam, June 23, 1979; children: Kyle, Patrick. BSME, Worcester Poly. Inst., 1976, MSME, 1979; postgrad., Syracuse U., 1989—. Mfg. engr. Carrier Corp., Syracuse, N.Y., 1976-77; design engr. Steinerfilm, Inc., Williamstown, Mass., 1977-78; lubrication rsch. engr. Texaco, Inc., Beacon, N.Y., 1979-80; tech. svc. engr. Dresser-Rand Co., Painted Post, N.Y., 1980-89, tech. svc. specialist, 1989—. Mem. Soc. Automotive Engrs. Home: 3904 W Hill Rd Painted Post NY 14870-9158 Office: Dresser-Rand Co 100 Chemung St Painted Post NY 14870-1352

MANGIARACINA, LEONARD, municipal government official; b. Bklyn., July 4, 1939; s. Baldasare Mangiaracina and Palma (DiGiovanni) O'Keefe; m. Katherine Eileen Strynkowski, Dec. 26, 1965; children: Susan, Leonard Jr., Gina. BChemE, Poly. Inst. Bklyn., 1961; MChemE, NYU, 1968. Tech. ass.t Phelps Dodge Corp., N.Y.C., 1961-62; design engr. M.W. Kellogg Co., N.Y.C., 1962-64; rsch. engr. Leesona Moos Corp., Great Neck, N.Y., 1964-65; systems engr. Grumman Corp., Bethpage, N.Y., 1965-70; project mgr. Monsanto Biodize Corp., Great Neck, 1970-71; dep. dir. U.S. EPA, Phila., 1971-87; dep. commr. Phila. Dept. Health, 1987-91; dir. office program integration U.S. EPA, 1991—; mdm. Phila. Air Pollution Control Bd., 1987—; chmn. Phila Asbestos Adv. Commn., 1987—, Phila Animal Adv. Bd., 1987—; vice-chmn. Phila Local Emergency Planning Commn., 1987—. Mem. Mt. Laurel (N.J.) Juvenile Conf. Commn., 1979-85, Mt. Laurel Site Plan Rev. Commn., 1979-86; mem., pres. Lenape Band Parents Assn., Medford, N.J., 1981—. Mem. Am. Soc. for Pub. Adminstrn., Am. Inst. Chem. Engrs., Coastal Soc., Am. Motorcycle Assn., KC. Republican. Roman Catholic. Home: 896 Lafayette Dr Mount Laurel NJ 08054-3241 Office: US EPA Region III 841 Chestnut St Philadelphia PA 19107-4427

MANGIERI, SAMUEL A., director of student activities; b. New Castle, Pa., Dec. 17, 1948; s. Samuel and Louise (Gairdo) M.; m. Rhonda Cleon Holyfield, Dec. 16, 1978; 1 child, Brandon Samuel. MA in Student Personnel, Slippery Rock U., Pa., 1977. Recreation dir. Toner Inst., Pitts., 1974-76; grad. employee Slippery Rock U., Slippery Rock, Pa., 1977; real estate sales Realty, Slippery Rock, Pa., 1978-80; counselor Youth Devel. Ctr., New Castle, Pa., 1978-80; asst. dir. student activities Community Coll. of Alleghany County, Pitts., 1980-85, dir. student activities, 1985—; chairperson Student Devel. Svcs. Strategic Planning Com., 1987-88, Permanent Art Com., 1985—, Student Affairs Com., 1988—, Scholarship Com., 1985—; mem. System Strategic Planning Coun., 1987—, Exec. Dean Search Com., 1990, Dean of Homewood Brushton Br. Search Com., 1991, Facilities and Equipment Task Force Systemwide, 1990-91. Recipient Alleghany Campus Merit award, 1985-86, 1989-90. Home: 11 Defoe St Pittsburgh PA 15214-1825 Office: Community College Alleghany County 808 Ridge Ave Pittsburgh PA 15212

MANGINO, MATTHEW THOMAS, lawyer; b. New Castle, Pa., Oct. 3, 1962; s. Thomas Michael and Connie (Frigone) M.; m. Julliann Galmarini, Aug. 6, 1988. BA, Westminster Coll., 1985; JD, Duquesne U., 1988. Bar: Pa., U.S. Dist. Ct. (we. dist.) Pa. Jud. clk. Hon. Francis X. Caiazza, New Castle, 1988-89; asst. pub. defender County of Lawrence, New Castle, 1989; pvt. practice New Castle, 1990—; chmn. New Castle Airport Authority, 1990—; solicitor County of Lawrence, New Castle, 1992—; instr. Pa. State U., 1992—; bd. dirs. Allied Human Svcs., New Castle, Lawrence County Bd. Assistance, New Castle. Columnist, New Castle News, 1989-90; contbr. chpt. to book, article to profl. jours. Mem. campaign staff Dukakis for Pres., Pitts., 1988; del. Dem. Nat. Conv., Atlanta, 1988; com. mem. Lawrence County Econ. Devel. Corp. Mem. ABA, Pa. Bar Assn. (state exec. bd. young lawyers div.), Lawrence County Bar Assn., Assn. Trial Lawyers Am., Greater New Castle C. of C. (bd. dirs. 1990), Eagles. Roman Catholic. Office: 325 E Washington St New Castle PA 16101-4097

MANGIONE, PATRICIA ANTHONY, artist; b. Seattle; d. Mark Livingstone and Ida (Bittle) Anthony; m. W. Robert Evans, Mar. 9, 1939 (div. 1957); 1 child, David Alan; m. Jerre Gerlando Mangione, Feb. 18, 1957. Resident fellow MacDowell Colony, Peterborough, N.H., 1957-76, Va. Ctr. for Creative Arts, Sweet Briar, 1980-88, bd. advisors, 1982—; instr. Fleisher Art Meml., Phila., 1955-66. One woman Shows include Frank Rehn Gallery, N.Y.C., Phila., Rome, St. Paul de Vence, France, Palermo, Italy, 1955-92; Exhibited in group shows at Mus. of Modern Art, N.Y.C., 1975, Albright Knox Mus., 1972, Rochester Meml. Art Gallery, 1976, Phila. Mus. Art, 1983, others; works in pub. collections including Continental Bank & Trust Co., Phila. (mural), Fleisher Art Meml., Phila., Fidelity Bank, Phila., West Chester State Mus., U. Pa. Dental Sch., Phila., Corp. of Yaddo, Saratoga Springs, N.Y., MacDowell Corp., Peterborough, N.H., Va. Ctr. for Arts, Sweet Briar, Noyes Mus., Oceanville, N.J., University City Sci. Ctr., Phila. Mem. Artists Equity Assn. (bd. dirs. Phila. 1954—, award for artistic contbn. to cultural spirit of Phila. 1982), Phila. Sketch Club (medal and 1st prize for oils 1987).

MANGOL, LEONA ALVINA, public broadcasting administrator; b. Fairview, Pa., Dec. 3, 1942; d. Ferdinand Oscar and Julia Catherine (Bausch) Niebauer; m. James L. Mangol, June 26, 1971; children: James Christian, Michael Stephen, (dec.), Matthew Stephen. Student, Erie Bus. Coll., Erie, Pa., 1964, Gannon Coll., 1964-66; postgrad., Ins. Inst. Am., 1965-69. Lic. ins. agt., Commonwealth of Pa. Exec. sec. to exec. v.p. Erie Ins. Exchange, 1960-69; exec. asst., office mgr. Morrow Ins. Agy., Erie, Albion, Pa., 1964-69; exec. sec. to exec. v.p. mktg., corp. sec., office mgr. Systems Capital Corp., Phila., 1969-70; adminstrv. sec., asst. to v.p., sec. bd. Nat. Bd. Med. Examiners, Phila., 1970-77; asst. for info. svcs. Nat. Bd. Med. Examiners, 1977-84, mgr. publs. and the info. office, 1985-88, asst. mgr. publs., 1988-90; asst. sec. bd. dirs., asst. to pres. WHYY, Inc., 1990—. Bd. dirs. Erie Ins. Exchange Activities Assn., 1964-68, sec. bd. dirs., 1964-66, pres. bd. dirs., 1967; bd. dirs. Erie Ins. Credit Union, 1965-69, sec. bd. dirs., 1965-69; chmn. regional heart fund Am. Heart Assn., 1960-69; cert. instr. basic & advanced first-aid ARC, 1966-69; mem. Fairview Centennial Com., 1968, Fairview Vol. Firemen's Aux., 1965-69, St. Vincent Hosp. Aux., 1965-69, Graylady vol. St. Vincent Hosp. Aux., 1966-69. Mem. Internat. Assn. Bus. Communicators. Home: 619 Meadowbrook Ave Ambler PA 19002-4919 Office: WHYY Inc Independence Mall W 150 N 6th St Philadelphia PA 19106-1589

MANILOFF, JACK, biophysicist, educator; b. Balt., Nov. 6, 1938; s. Boris and Edith (Cohen) M.; m. Sandra Sue Steele, Dec. 22, 1960; children: Beth Susan, Eric Steele. BA in Biology, Johns Hopkins U., 1960; MS in Biophysics, Yale U., 1964, PhD in Biophysics, 1965. Research assoc. in chemistry Brown U., Providence, 1964-66; asst. prof. microbiology Sch. Medicine and Dentistry, U. Rochester, N.Y., 1966-71; assoc. prof. Sch. Medicine and Dentistry, U. Rochester, 1971-79, prof., 1979—; lectr. Am. Soc. for Microbiology Found., 1989-90; mem. Internat. Com. on Taxonomy of Viruses, 1975—, mem. exec. com., 1990—; cons. Subcom. on Taxonomy of Mycoplasmatales, Internat. Com. on Systematic Bacteriology, 1978—. Contbr. articles to profl. jours. Recipient Research Career Devel. award USPHS, 1970-75; Fogarty Sr. Internat. fellow, 1987-88; Disting. vis. fellow Christ's Coll., Cambridge, Eng., 1987-88; Lady Margaret lectr. Christ's Coll., 1988. Mem. Biophys. Soc., Am. Soc. Microbiology (chair-elect mycoplasma div. 1992—), Internat. Orgn. Mycoplasmology, Sigma Xi. Office: Univ Rochester Med Ctr Box 672 Dept Microbiology Rochester NY 14642

MANISHIN, GLENN BRETT, lawyer; b. Boston; s. Gerald and Ruth Hariett (Gordon) M.; m. Lourdes Ester Sabi, Sept. 24, 1989. BA cum laude, Brandeis U., 1977; JD, Columbia U., 1981. Bar: Calif. 1982, D.C. 1985. Trial atty. antitrust div. U.S. Dept. Justice, Washington, 1982-85; assoc. Jenner & Block, Washington, 1985-88, ptnr., 1989-90; ptnr. Blumenfeld & Cohen, Washington, 1990—; bd. dirs. Nat. Law Ctr. on Homelessness & Poverty, Washington, 1989—. Mem. Dem. Nat. Com. Mem. ABA, Fed. Communications Bar Assn. Office: Blumenfeld & Cohen 1615 M St NW Ste 700 Washington DC 20036-3214

MANKE, DEAN JOSEPH, publishing executive; b. Chgo., Dec. 11, 1949; s. Edward John and Eleanor Margaret (Senko) M.; m. Patricia Gail Godfrey; 1 child, Matthew. BA, Western Mich. U., 1971; MS, U. Ill., Chgo., 1975. Med. researcher VA West Side Hosp., Chgo., 1973-82; sales rep. W.B. Saunders, Chgo., 1982-84; mktg. mgr. W.B. Saunders, Phila., 1984-85, med. editor, 1985-86, exec. editor, 1986-87, editor-in-chief med. books, 1987-88; v.p. book & looseleaf pubs. J.B. Lippincott, Phila., 1988-90; v.p. sales and mktg. JB Lippincott, Phila., 1991—. contbr. articles to profl. jours. Asst. cubmaster Boy Scouts Am., Burlington County, N.J., 1988—. Mem. Am. Med. Pubs. Assn., Am. Assn. Pubs., Riverton Country Club. Home: 600 Bergen Dr Riverton NJ 08077-4002 Office: JB Lippincott E Washington Ln Philadelphia PA 19144-2009

MANKIN, ROBERT STEPHEN, financial executive; b. N.Y.C., Mar. 26, 1939; s. Samuel Harry Mankin and Dorothy (Rosenblum) Goldstein; m. Joyce Marie Cabel, June 13, 1971; children: Seth Howard, Laura Nicole, Gina Danielle. BA cum laude, Bklyn. Coll., 1961; MBA, Bernard Baruch Coll., 1970; Dr. Profl. Studies with distinction, Pace U., 1982. Mgr. ABC, N.Y.C., 1969-71, Babcock and Wilcox, N.Y.C., 1971-74; v.p. Chase Manhattan Bank, N.Y.C., 1974-84; sr. v.p. 1st Interstate Bank, N.Y.C., 1984-87; sr. v.p., co-head fixed income div., mem. mgmt. com. Nomura Securities Internat., N.Y.C., 1987—; bd. dirs., sec. Nomura Mortgage Capital Corp., N.Y.C. Contbr. articles to profl. jours. Mem. Planning Forum, Assn. for Computing Machinery, Assn. Computer Programmers and Analysts (chmn. bd. 1971). Home: 21 Shield Dr Westwood NJ 07675-8127 Office: Nomura Securities Internat 180 Maiden Ln 38th Fl New York NY 10038

MANKIW, DEBORAH ROLOFF, non-profit organization administrator; b. Wiesbaden, Fed. Republic Germany, July 16, 1958; d. Jerome William and Myrtle Melita (Burrows) Roloff; m. Nicholas Gregory Mankiw, June 16, 1984; 1 child, Catherine Melita. AB, Duke U., 1979; M in City and Regional Planning, Harvard U., 1982. Fin. economist Office of Mgmt. and Budget, Washington, 1982-83; fin. analyst Harvard U., Cambridge, Mass., 1983-84; dir. corp. and found. rels. Nat. Bur. of Econ. Rsch., Cambridge, 1984—. Mem. Nat. Assn. of Bus. Economist, Women in Devel. Home: 45 Chestnut St Wellesley MA 02181-3011 Office: Nat Bur of Econ Rsch 1050 Massachusetts Ave Cambridge MA 02138-5302

MANLEY, CHARLES HOWLAND, food scientist, flavor company executive; b. Acushnet, Mass., Feb. 27, 1943; s. Charles H. and Mabel A. (Ellis) M.; m. Eileen O. Alderson, May 19, 1965; 1 child, Heather. BS in Chemistry, U. Mass., Dartmouth, 1964; MS in Biochemistry, U. Mass., Amherst, 1967, PhD in Food Sci., 1969. Sr. rsch. chemist Givaudan Corp., Clifton, N.J., 1969-73; group leader T.J. Lipton Co., Englewood Cliffs, N.J., 1973-75, mgr. indsl. devel., 1975-79; dir. flavor ops. Nat. Starch & Chem. Co., Bridgewater, N.J., 1979-85; v.p. flavors Quest Internat., East Hanover, N.J., 1985-88; v.p. sci. and tech. Takasago Internat., Teterboro, N.J., 1988—. Editor: Healthy Eating, 1987; also numerous articles. Pres. Ringwood Jaycees, 1975-76. Mem. Inst. Food Technologists (pres. N.Y. sect. 1982-83, nat. exec. com. 1991—, Mem. of Yr. award N.Y. sect. 1989), Flavor and Extract Mfrs. Assn. (v.p., sec.). Office: Takasago Internat 100 Green St Teterboro NJ 07608-1207

MANLEY, JOHN HUGO, computing technology executive, educator; b. Highland Park, Mich., July 9, 1932; s. Hugo Edward and Linda Amelia (Kuure) M.; m. Josephine Theresa Catanzaro, Sept. 3, 1958; children: Lisa Linn, Michele Ann, John David, Marc Darrin. B. Metall. Engring., Cornell U., 1955; MS Indsl. Engring., U. Pitts., 1965, PhD, 1971. Metall. engr. GE, Schenectady, N.Y., 1955-56; commd. 2d lt. USAF, 1956, advanced through grades to lt. col., 1973, ret., 1976; asst. to dir. Johns Hopkins Applied Physics Lab., Laurel, Md., 1976-80; exec. ITT Corp., Stratford, Conn., 1980-83; v.p. Nastec Corp., Southfield, Mich., 1983-85; dir. Software Engring. Inst., Pitts., 1985-87; pres., chmn. Computing Tech. Transition, Inc., Wilmington, Del., 1983—; prof. manufacturing and info. tech. systems engring., dir. mfg. sys. engring. prog. U. Pitts., 1987—; mem. tech. adv. bd. Tartan Labs., Inc., Pitts., 1988-90; bd. dirs. Iconnex Corp., Pitts., Metalworking Tech., Inc., Johnstown, Pa.; mem. com. on Nat. Weather Svc. modernization NRC, 1991—. Editor-in-chief Jour. Systems and Software, 1978-82; contbr. articles to profl. jours. Pres. Point Field Community Assn., Millersville, Md., 1979-80; v.p. Greater Severna Park Coun., Severna Park, Md., 1980. Lt. col. USAF, 1955-76, Vietnam. Decorated Legion of Merit, Bronze Star. Mem. IEEE Computer Soc. (TC exec. bd.), Soc. Mfg. Engrs., Assn. for Computing Machinery, Pitts. Athletic Assn. Republican. Episcopalian.

MANLEY, RICHARD PETER, software design engineer; b. Boston, Sept. 19, 1949; s. Howard Creighton Manley and Hazel Jane (Allen) Smith; m. Susan Leah Spaulding, May 24, 1975 (div. Sept. 1979). BS in Biology/Chemistry, Cumberland Coll., 1976; postgrad., Boston U., 1990—. Software engr. Data Terminal Systems, Maynard, Mass., 1980-82; software design engr. Wang Labs., Lowell, Mass., 1982-85; sr. software design engr. Innovative Micro Systems, Woburn, Mass., 1985-89, Harte-Hanks Data Technologies, Billerica, Mass., 1989—. Active Bedford (Mass.) Hist. Soc., 1985—, Friends of the Job Ln. Ho., Bedford, 1985—, Bedford Minuteman Co., 1985—. Sgt. USAF, 1969-73. Mem. Boston Computer Soc. (OS/2 SIG editor 1989—). Methodist. Home: 84-62 Tennis Plaza Rd Dracut MA 01826-3347

MANN, ALAN EUGENE, physical anthropologist; b. N.Y.C., Sept. 19, 1939; s. Max and Ruth (Newman) M.; m. Michelle Leigh Lampl, May 13, 1982; children: Laura, David. BA, U. Pitts., 1961; postgrad., Columbia U., 1961-64; MA, U. Calif., Berkeley, 1965, PhD, 1968. Acting asst. prof. U. Calif., Berkeley, 1968-69; asst. prof. U. Pa., Phila., 1969-76, assoc. prof., 1976-91, prof. anthropology, 1991—; asst. curator Univ. Mus., Phila., 1969-76, assoc. curator, 1976-91, curator phys. anthropology, 1991—; vis. assoc. prof. Princeton U., 1987, 88, 90; rsch. assoc. Laboratoire d'Anthropologie, U. Bordeaux, France, 1990—; social scis. adv. bd. World Book Ency., Chgo., 1989—; adv. bd. Care Archaeol. Found., London, 1987—; adv. panel on anthropology NSF, Washington, 1977-80; dir. casting program Univ. Mus., Phila., 1975—. Co-author: Human Biology and Behavior, 5th edit. 1990. Recipient Lindback Disting. teaching award, 1980; Ira Abrams Disting. Teaching award, Sch. Arts & Scis., U. Pa., 1985; Fulbright fellow, 1990. Office: Univ of Pa Dept Anthropology Philadelphia PA 19104-6398

MANN, ALFRED KENNETH, physics educator; b. N.Y.C., Sept. 4, 1920; s. David and Belle Aileen (Mann) M.; m. Jayne Pledge Bowers, June 29, 1946; children: Stephen P., Cecile, David T., Brian E. BA, U. Va., 1942, MS, 1946, PhD, 1947. With Manhattan Project, 1942-44; instr. physics Columbia U., N.Y.C., 1947-49; asst. prof. physics U. Pa., Phila., 1949-52, assoc. prof., 1952-57, prof., 1957—; trustee Associated Univs., Inc., 1970-83, Univ. Rsch. Assn., Inc., 1979-84; mem. High Energy Physics Adv. Panel, 1983. Recipient Asahi prize, Japan, 1987, Rossi prize, Am. Astron. Soc., 1989, U.S. Naval Ordnance Devel. award, 1945; Fulbright fellow, 1955-56, NSF Sr. fellow, 1962-63, Guggenheim fellow, 1981-82. Fellow Am. Phys. Soc. (chmn. exec. com. div. particles and fields 1983), Royal Soc. Arts, N.Y. Acad. Sci.; mem. Phi Beta Kappa, Sigma Xi. Office: U Pa 209 S 33d St Philadelphia PA 19104

MANN, KENNETH WALKER, minister, psychologist; b. Nyack, N.Y., Aug. 22, 1914; s. Arthur Hungerford and Ethel Livingston (Walker) M. AB, Princeton U., 1937; STB, Gen. Theol. Sem., N.Y.C., 1942; MS, U. Mich., 1950, PhD, 1956. Ordained priest Episcopal Ch., 1942; diplomate Am. Assn. Pastoral Counselors; lic. clin. psychologist, Calif., Conn.; lic. marriage, family and child counselor, Calif. Vicar in Valley Cottage, Pearl River, N.Y., 1941-43; priest in charge Yonkers, N.Y., 1943-45; dir. youth work and Christian edn. Diocese L.A., 1945-47; curate in Beverly Hills, Calif., 1947-49; counselor Bur. Psychol. Svcs., U. Mich., 1951-52; chaplain, clin. psychologist dept. psychiatry St. Luke's Hosp., N.Y.C., also priest-psychotherapist Cathedral St. John Divine, N.Y.C., psychol. examiner ministerial candidates Diocese N.Y., 1952-58; assoc. chaplain Hosp. Good Samaritan, L.A., 1958-65; exec. pastoral svcs., exec. coun. Episc. Ch. N.Y.C., 1965-70; program officer Acad. Religion and Mental Health, N.Y.C., 1970-72; sr. adviser profl. affairs Inst. Religion and Health, 1972-79; sr. psychol. staff Silver Hill Found., New Canaan, Conn., 1974-84; pres. Rockland County (N.Y.) Mins. Assn., 1942-43; exec. sec. social svc. commn. Diocese N.Y., 1943-45; chmn. div. pastoral svcs. Diocese L.A., 1958-65; field dir. Western region Acad. Religion and Mental Health, 1958-61; assoc. nat. chaplain U.S. Power Squadrons, 1956-57. Author: On Pills and Needles, 1969, Deadline for Survival—A Survey of Moral Issues in Science and Medicine, 1970; contbr. articles to profl. jours. Pres. Adoption Inst. L.A., 1964; mem. edn. com. Calif. Heart Assn., 1962-64; trustee, treas. Acad. Religion and Mental Health, 1954-59, mem. profl. bd., 1960-70; trustee Vis. Nurse Assn. L.A., 1963-65, Children's Home Soc. Calif. in L.A., 1964-65, North Conway Inst., 1966-80. USPHS grantee, 1950-51. Fellow AAAS; mem. APA (chmn. com. rels. between psychology and religion 1956-58), Western Psychol. Assn., Calif. Psychol. Assn., L.A. County Psychol. Assn., N.Y. Acad. Scis., Planetary Soc., Assembly Episc. Hosps. and Chaplains, Upper Nyack Tennis Club, The Club (Diocese N.Y.), Princeton Club N.Y. Republican. Home: 32 Tallman Ave Nyack NY 10960-1606

MANN, OSCAR, physician, internist; b. Paris, Oct. 13, 1934; came to U.S., 1953; s. Aron and Helen (Biegun) M.; m. Amy S. Mann, June 19, 1964; children: Adriana, Karen. AA with distinction, George Washington U., 1958; MD cum laude, Georgetown U., 1962. Diplomate Am. Bd. Med. Examiners, Am. Bd. Internal Medicine, Am. Bd. Internal Medicine subspecialty Cardiovascular Disease; cert. advanced achievement in internal medicine; re-cert. in internal medicine. Intern Georgetown U. Med. Ctr., Washington, 1962-63, jr. asst. med. resident, 1963-64, clin. fellow in cardiology with Proctor Harvey program, 1965-66; sr. asst. resident in medicine Georgetown svc. D.C. Gen. Hosp., Washington, 1964-65; clin. prof. medicine Georgetown U. Sch. Medicine, also regional chmn. Med. Alumni Fund; pvt. practice internal medicine and cardiology, Washington; mem. Med.-Nursing Audit Com., CME adv. com., teaching. adv. com., Opthamology dept. rev. com., surgery dept. rev. com., faculty com., search com. for a new dean for acad. affairs Georgetown U. Med. Ctr.; appointed coun. to the dean Georgetown U. Sch. Medicine, 1977—; mem. Instnl. Self Study Task Force. Contbr. articles to profl. jours. Served with the U.S. Army, 1953-55. Recipient Mead Johnson Postgrad. Scholar ACP, 1964-65, Physicians Recognition award AMA, 1987—, Advanced Achievement in Internal Medicine, 1987. Fellow ACP, Am. Coll. Cardiology, Am. Coll. Chest Physicians; mem. AMA, Am. Soc. Internal Med., Am. Heart Assn. (coun. clin. cardiology), Med. Soc. D.C., Alpha Omega Alpha, Phi Delta Epsilon. Home: 4925 Weaver Ter NW Washington DC 20016-2660 Office: Foxhall Internists PC 3301 New Mexico Ave NW Washington DC 20016-3622

MANN, PREM SINGH, economics educator; b. Punjab, India, Nov. 20, 1947; came to U.S., 1980; s. Malkiat Singh and Darshan Kaur (Gill) M.; m. Sarabjeet K. Bains, May 9, 1975; children: Harpreet K., Kulwinder S., Sukhwinder S. BA, Panjab U., Chandigarh, India, 1968, MA in Econs., 1970; MA in Econs., U. Manchester (Eng.), 1977; PhD in Econs., UCLA, 1988. Tchr. D.S.N. High Sch., Nawanshahr, India, 1970-71; lectr. Panjab U., 1971-75; lectr. Calif. State U., L.A., 1981-82, Fullerton, 1982-86; asst. prof. Ea. Conn. State U., Willimantic, 1986-89, assoc. prof., 1989—. Author: Introductory Statistics, 1992; contbr. articles to profl. publs. Mem. Am. Econ. Assn., Am. Statis. Assn. Sikh. Office: Ea Conn State U Willimantic CT 06226

MANN, RICHARD OTTO, public relations counsulting company executive; b. N.Y.C., July 1, 1933; s. Otto and Ruth (Buchwald) M.; m. Anne Marie Seidenschwang, Apr. 28, 1956; children: Melinda, Susan, Carolyn. BA in History and Polit. Sci., Hofstra U., 1955. Reporter Newsday, Garden City, N.Y., 1951-56; pub. relations v.p., cons. Carl Byoir & Assoc., N.Y.C., 1957-76; v.p. corp. affairs Mack Trucks, Inc., Allentown, Pa., 1976-79; v.p. pub. relations Transway Internat., N.Y.C., 1979-85; pres. Mann Assoc., Mt. Kisco, N.Y., 1985—; track and field official, U.S. Internat. meets, including 1984 Olympics, 1970—. 1st lt. U.S. Army, 1956-57. Mem. Pub. Relations Soc. Am., N.Y. Sales Execs. Club, Mt. Kisco Country Club. Republican. Presbyterian. Home and Office: 37 Indian Hill Rd Mount Kisco NY 10549

MANN, ROGER ELLIS, corporate service executive; b. N.Y.C., Jan. 12, 1948. BA, Wesleyan U., Middletown, Conn., 1971, MAT, 1972; M. Pub. and Pvt. Mgmt., Yale U., 1986. Africa mgmt. cons. and journalist Tanzania, Kenya, Zambia, 1973-84; sr. dir. bus. devel. Marriott Corp., Washington, 1986—, mgr. corp. strategy, 1986-89; dir. bus. devel. Marriott Sports & Entertainment subs. Mariott Corp., Washington, 1990-91; dir. bus. devel. Host Internat., Washington, 1989-90, sr. dir. bus. devel., 1991—; sr. dir. bus. devel. Host Internat., 1991—. Contbr. articles on Africa to profl. jours. Nat. Resource fellow Yale U., 1985-86. Mem. Internat. Assn. Amusement Pks. and Attractions, Am. Assn. Zool. Pks. and Aquariums.

MANN, WILLIAM GEORGE, engineer; b. Tyler, Tex., Nov. 27, 1934; s. Alex and Nora (Syndelis) M.; m. Toby Ann Convissar, Apr. 7, 1962; children: Lesley Beth, Noelle Nora. BCE, Rensselaer Polytechnic Inst., 1956; MBA, Fairleigh Dickinson U., 1973. Registered profl. engr., N.Y., Mich., Ohio, Ala., Maine, Tex. Project engr. trainee Foster Wheeler Corp., N.Y.C., 1956, vessel group engr., 1956-57, vessel and rotating equipment engr., 1957-58, project engr., 1957-61; project engr. Foster Wheeler Corp., London, Eng., 1961-62; field engr. Foster Wheeler Corp., Phila., 1962-63; sr. project engr. Foster Wheeler Corp., Livingston, N.J., 1963-66; design engr. Pfizer Corp., N.Y.C., 1966-71, sr. design engr., 1971-77, project mgr. Ireland, 1977-80, mgr. projects, 1980-82, asst. dir. design engring., 1982-85, dir. design engring, 1985-89, dir. engring. and tech. resources, 1990—; mem. engring. and operating com. Chem. Mfrs. Assn., Washington, 1988-90. Bd. dirs. Day Care Ctr., Boonton, N.J., 1969-77, chmn., 1975-77; alt. mem. Planning Bd., Boonton, 1988—. Cpl. USAF, 1959-67. Mem. Internat. Soc. Pharms. Engrs. Republican. Methodist. Office: Pfizer Inc 235 E 42nd St New York NY 10017

MANNERS, HERBERT CARL, building contractor; b. Punxsutawney, Pa., Oct. 31, 1948; Harold Eugene and Lucille (Lauer) M.; m. Patti Jean Haag, Dec. 13, 1975. A, Pa. State U., 1971. Prin. Manners Contracting, Punxsutawney, 1972—; real estate salesman, Pa. Patentee in tear off shovel and drain check valve. Home: RD # 1 Box 5 Punxsutawney PA 15767

MANNERS, TIMOTHY GEORGE, public relations executive; b. Norwalk, Conn., Oct. 6, 1957; s. David X. and Ruth Ann (Bauer) M.; m. Beth Sydnie Dalis, Sept. 30, 1984. BA in History magna cum laude, Tufts U., 1979. Newscaster Westport (Conn.) Broadcasting Inc., 1979-81; v.p. David X. Manners Co. Inc., Norwalk, 1981-84, pres., 1984—. Editor: The Gundersen Report, N.Y.C.; contbr. articles in field. Cons. Collins for Mayor, Norwalk, 1985, Bruce Babbitt for Pres., 1987-88, John Loeser for U.S. Congress, 1988, 90, St. Sergius High Sch., N.Y.C., 1987-91. Mem. Fairfield County Pub. Rels. Assn. Democrat. Home: 10 Tar Rock Rd Westport CT 06880-6037 Office: David X Manners Co Inc 84 W Park Pl Stamford CT 06901-2211

MANNING, BURT, advertising executive. Chmn., chief exec. officer J. Walter Thompson Co., Worldwide, N.Y.C., 1987—. Bd. dirs. nat. Assn. for Depressive Illness, Nat. Players Co., Advt. Edn. Found.; trustee Neuroscis.

Inst., New Sch. for Social Rsch. Mem. Lotus Club. Office: J Walter Thompson Co 466 Lexington Ave New York NY 10017-3140

MANNING, IRWIN, research physicist; b. Bklyn., Mar. 7, 1929; s. Louis and Nettie (Jaffe) M.; m. Amelia Ann Young, May 24, 1964 (dec. June 1988); children: Emily, Sarah Elizabeth. BS in Maths., MIT, 1951, PhD in Physics, 1955. Rsch. assoc. Syracuse (N.Y.) U., 1955-57, U. Wis., Madison, 1957-59; rsch. physicist Naval Rsch. Lab., Washington, 1959-90; cons., rsch. physicist SFA Inc., Landover, Md., 1990—. Democrat. Jewish. Home: 4506 Dalton Rd Bethesda MD 20815-3733 Office: Naval Rsch Lab Condensed Matter/Radiation Scis Div Washington DC 20375

MANNING, JAMES MATTHEW, biochemistry educator; b. Boston, Jan. 3, 1939; s. Matthew Francis and Mary (Nee) M.; m. Lois Radin, May 9, 1964; children: Robert, Laura. BS in Chemistry, Boston Coll., 1960; PhD in Biochemistry, Tufts U., 1966. USPHS postdoctoral fellow Tufts U., Medford, Mass., 1960-66; NSF postdoctoral fellow U. Rome, Italy, 1966-67; rsch. assoc. Rockefeller U., N.Y.C., 1967-69, asst. prof., 1967-72, assoc. prof., 1972—; cons. Am. Heart Assn., 1976-78, Am. Soc. Biol. Chemists, 1979, NSF, 1979. Contbr. articles to Jour. Biol. Chemistry, Ann. N.Y. Acad. Sci.; contbr. articles to profl. jours. Grantee NIH, 1987. Mem. Am. Soc. Biol. Chemists, Am. Chem. Soc., Am. Soc. Hematology, The Harvey Soc., Soc. Am. Protein Chemists. Office: The Rockefeller U 1230 York Ave New York NY 10021-6341

MANNING, RANDOLPH H., academic administrator; b. Bronx, Dec. 18, 1947; s. Ruthfoy M. and Gertrude (Webber) M.; m. Monica S. McEvilley, May 15, 1972; children: Randolph, Craig, Corey. AA, Suffolk Community Coll., 1969; BA, SUNY, Stony Brook, 1971, MALS, 1975, postgrad. Owner, operator R.H. Manning Enterprises, Coram, N.Y., 1973—; counselor Suffolk County Community Coll., Riverhead, N.Y., 1971-80, prof. psychology and sociology, 1980-85, dean instrn., 1985—; pres. emeritus Spl. Program Personnel Assn., SUNY, 1978-82; ednl. cons. Bds. Coop. Ednl. Svcs., Westhampton, N.Y., 1980; adv. bd. Re-Route Dept. Labor, Suffolk County Sheriff's Dept., 1980—; assoc. commr. N.Y. State Task Force on Race Rels. N.Y.; co-dir. Counsel Internat. Programs, 1990—; Mid. States evaluator, 1990—; cons. to N.J. Dept. Higher Edn., 1990—; curriculum and program evaluator. Pres. N.Y. State Program Personnel Assn., 1978-82; bd. dirs. Gordon Heights FCU, L.I., 1975-82, treas, bd. dirs. L.I. Sickle Cell Inc., Hempstead, 1981—, adv. bd. Suffolk County Farm Coop. Extension. Named one of Outstanding Young Men Am., 1981; recipient Proclamation for Service, County of Suffolk, 1986. Mem. Am. Sociol. Assn., Black Faculty and Staff Assn. Home: 3 Indian Valley Rd East Setauket NY 11733-4037 Office: Suffolk County CC Speonk-riverhea Rd Riverhead NY 11901

MANNING, ROSE THERESE, psychotherapist; b. Bklyn., June 17, 1960; d. Henry Herbert and Audrey Fleur (Linkens) Maturo; m. Thomas Joseph Manning, Dec. 5, 1987. BA, Towson State U., 1982; MS, Johns Hopkins U., 1990. Publicity and prodn. asst. Johns Hopkins Press, Balt., 1982-84; human rels. coord. McCormick and Co., Inc., Hunt Valley, Md., 1984-86; devel. coord. Johns Hopkins U., Balt., 1986-88; asst. dir. devel. Peabody Inst., Balt., 1988-91; counselor Associated Cath. Charities, Balt., 1990—; counselor Greater Balt. Med. Ctr., Towson, 1991—. Bd. dirs. Immaculate Conception Ch., Towson, 1984-87, Towson Promotions Coun., 1988-89; v.p. Towson Jaycees, 1987-89; pres sec. Citizens for Brewster, Towson, 1990. Mem. AACD., Belvedere Ct. Townhouse Assn. Democrat. Roman Catholic. Home: 441 Nicoll Ave Baltimore MD 21212-3151

MANNING, WARREN J., cardiologist; b. Utica, N.Y., Oct. 17, 1957; s. Charles J. and Rita K. Manning; m. Susan G. Rodgin, Sept. 5, 1982; children: Anya, Sara. BS, MIT, 1979; MD, Harvard U., 1983. Intern Beth Israel Hosp., Boston, 1983-84, resident, 1984-86, fellow, 1986-89; asst. prof. medicine Harvard Med. Sch., Boston, 1991—; assoc. dir. cardiac imaging Beth Israel Hosp., Boston, 1990—. Fellow Am. Coll. Cardiology; mem. ACP, Am. Fedn. Clin. Rsch., Soc. Magnetic Resonance Medicine. Office: Beth Israel Hosp 330 Brookline Ave Boston MA 02215

MANNING, WILLIAM GEORGE, manufacturers agency executive; b. Haverhill, Mass., June 10, 1923; s. William George and Annie (Ingram) M.; m. Therese Blanche Chabot (div. 1975); m. Jen Ackerd Lynch; children: William G., Christopher J. Student, Northeastern U., Boston, 1941-42; BS, Mass. Maritime Acad., 1944. Salesman Haverhill (Mass.) Electric Co., 1946-52; regional sales Am. Paper Goods Co., Atlanta, 1952-53, Continental Can Co., Alexandria, Va., 1953-54; pres. Bay Sales, Ltd., Lanham, Md., 1954—. Lt. USNR, 1944-46, ETO, PTO. Mem. Mfrs. Reps. Am. (dir. 1986-89), Mfrs. Agts. Nat. Assn., Army Navy Club. Republican. Roman Catholic. Home: 355 Broadview Ln Annapolis MD 21401-7238 Office: Bay Sales Ltd 9470 Annapolis Rd Ste 310 Lanham Seabrook MD 20706-3022

MANNING, WINTON HOWARD, psychologist, educational administrator; b. St. Louis, Feb. 9, 1930; s. Winton Harry and Jane (Swanson) M.; m. Nancy Mercedes Groves, Aug. 1, 1959; children: Cecelia Groves Tazelaar, Winton H. III. AB with honors, William Jewell Coll., 1947; PhD in Psychology, Washington U., St. Louis, 1959. Instr. psychology William Jewell Coll., Liberty, Mo., 1954-55, asst. prof., acting head dept. psychology, 1955-56; rsch. psychologist Washington U., St. Louis, 1956-58, rsch. assoc., 1958-59; vis. lectr. Washington U., summer, 1961, 62; asst. prof. psychology Tex. Christian U., Fort Worth, 1959-61, assoc. prof., 1961-64, prof., 1964-65, assoc. dir. univ. honors program, 1962-65; assoc. dir. rsch. Coll. Entrance Examination Bd., N.Y.C., 1965-66, dir. program devel., 1966-68, exec. dir. rsch.and devel., 1968-69; dir. devel. rsch. div. Ednl. Testing Svc., Princeton, N.J., 1969-70, v.p., 1970-77, sr. v.p. devel. and rsch., 1977-83, sr. scholar, 1983—; pres. Ednl. Devel. Svc., Princeton, 1983—; pres. Jacques Molle Inc., 1987—; vis. fellow Princeton U., 1982-83; cons. Gallup Internat. Inst., 1990—. Author: The Pursuit of Fairness in Admissions to Higher Education, 1977; Student Manual for Essentials of Psychology, 1960. Contbr. articles on ednl. measurement and psychology of learning to profl. publs. Patentee in field U.S. and Europe. Trustee, Nat. Chicano Coun. on Higher Edn., 1977-85, Assn. for Advancement of Handicapped People, 1975-78, N.J. Arts Festival, 1980-85; vice-chair Found. for Books to China, 1980—; chair bd. trustees Princeton Day Sch., 1981—; trustee Princeton Area Found., Our House Found., 1992—; chair Affordable Housing Bd. of Princeton Borough, 1987-89; sr. warden All Saints Epis. Ch., 1987-89; adv. coun. U. Okla. Ctr. for Rsch. on Minority Edn., 1987—, Ind. Sch. Chmn. Assn., 1987-92; cons. Carnegie Found. for Advancement of Teaching., 1987-89, Coll. Bd., 1988-91; spl. cons. Commn. on Admission to Grad. Mgmt. Edn., 1987-91. Recipient Alumni Achievement citation William Jewell Coll., 1970. Fellow Am. Psychol. Soc. (charter), Eastern Psychol. Assn., Psychometric Soc., Am. Ednl. Rsch. Assn., Nat. Coun. on Measurement in Edn. (mem. com. on legal issues in measurement 1977-79), N.Y. Acad. Scis., Nassau Club, Pendragon Club, Phi Beta Kappa, Sigma Xi. Home: 12 Morven Pl Princeton NJ 08540-3024 Office: Ednl Testing Svc Princeton NJ 08541

MANNINO, ANTHONY COLEGERO, drama director; b. N.Y.C., Dec. 18, 1920; s. Fillipo Minnino and Ninfa Gambino; m. Gail Keith-Jones, 1947 (div. 1952); m. Serena Ballin, 1958; children: Tonianne, Andrew, Elizabeth. Grad., Commerce High Sch., N.Y.; student, Profl. Acting Sch., N.Y., NYU. Acting tchr. Anthony Mannino Studio, N.Y.C., 1941-59; dir., acting tchr. Drama Tree Inc., N.Y.C., 1959—. Appeared on stage in The Playboy of Newark, All You Need Is One Good Break, Flowers and Virtue, Yours A. Lincoln, Spring Again, Tender Offer, So-Ho They Call It; films include Those Lips, Those Eyes, Tattoo, True Blood; TV appearances on All My Children, Saturday Night Live, The Bloodhound Gang, King of America, Guiding Light; narrator Martha Graham major dance concerts. Office: Drama Tree Inc 158 W 15th St New York NY 10011-6727

MANNIX, MARY KATHERINE, library director; b. Long Branch, N.J., July 11, 1960; d. John Francis Xavier and Catherine Alberta (Miles) M. BA, Hood Coll., Frederick, Md., 1982; MA, U. Del., 1984, Mus. Studies cert., 1984. Hist. site surveyer State of Del. Bur. of Archaeology and Hist. Preservation, Dover, 1984; asst. prints and photographs librarian Md. Hist. Soc., Balt., 1985-86; hist. preservation analyst Balt. City Commn. for Hist. and Archtl. Preservation, 1986-88; sr. rsch. asst. PAC Spero & Co., Balt., 1988-89; dir. libr. and rsch. ctr. Howard County Hist. Soc., Ellicott City, Md., 1989—. Art editor Md. Hist. Mag., 1987—. Hood Coll. scholar, 1981; Northeast Mus. Conf. fellow, 1983. Mem. MidAtlantic Regional Archives Conf. Home: 8337B Morven Rd Baltimore MD 21234-4941

MANNO, BRUNO VICTOR, government official; b. Cleve., May 2, 1947; s. Vincenzo and Antoinette (Gattozzi) M. BA with honors, U. Dayton, 1970, MA, 1972; PhD, Boston Coll., 1975. Asst. prof., dir. office moral and religious edn. U. Dayton (Ohio), 1975-78; vis. prof. Cath. Tchrs. Coll., Sydney, Australia, 1978; vis. rsch. assoc. Nat. Opinion Rsch. Ctr., U. Chgo., 1978-79; also vis. fellow Div. Sch.; dir. research, data bank and in-service programs Nat. Cath. Edn. Assn., Washington, 1979-86; chief of staff, dir. planning Office Ednl. Rsch. and Improvement, U.S. Dept. Edn., 1986-89, deputy asst. sec. for policy and planning Office of Ednl. Rsch. and Improvement U.S. Dept. Edn., 1989, acting asst. sec. Office of Policy and Planning, 1991, spl. asst. to sec. and acting asst. Author: How-to Service Students with Federal Education Program Benefits, 1980; co-editor: The Earth is the Lord's: Essays in Stewardship, 1978; conrbr. numerous articles and revs. to religious and scholarly jours. Bd. dirs. U. Dayton, 1982-86. Mem. Coll. Theology Soc., Assn. Profs. and Researchers in Relgious Edn., Nat. Cath. Ednl. Assn., Cath. Theol. Soc. Am., Religious Edn. Assn., Am. Acad. Religion, Polanyi Soc., Phi Sigma Tau. Roman Catholic. Office: US Dept Edn 400 Maryland Ave SW Washington DC 20202-0002

MANOCCHI, JAMES CHARLES, marketing professional; b. New Haven, Mar. 24, 1953; s. Fred and Zoe Anita (Simoncelli) M.; m. Pamela Jean Johnson, June 12, 1976; children: Linnea Caro, Amy Kristin, Lisa Ann, Alex James. BSME, Rensselaer Poly. Inst., 1975; MBA, Lehigh U., 1979. Sr. strategic planner Air Products and Chems., Inc., Allentown, Pa., 1975-80; corp. product dir. Stauffer Chem. Co., Westport, Conn., 1980-85; dir. N.Am. mgmt. cons. and mgr. chems. and plastics unit Arthur D. Little, Inc., Cambridge, Mass., 1986-91; sr. v.p. sales and mktg. Chemfab Corp., Merrimack, N.H., 1991—; presenter in field. Contbr. articles to profl. jours; patentee in field. Mem. Comml. Devel. Assn., Pi Tau Sigma, Sigma Chi. Republican. Home: 38 Pembroke Way Bedford NH 03110 Office: Chemfab Corp 701 Daniel Webster Hwy Merrimack NH 03054

MANOHARAN, THOMAS, pharmacist; b. Vellore, Madras, India, June 5, 1935; came to U.S., 1976; s. Joshua Elias and Annal (David) T. Diploma in compounding, Christian Med. Coll. Hosp., Vellore, 1955, diploma in pharmacy, 1962; B in Pharmacy, Madras Med. Coll., 1966; M in Pharmacy, Nagpur (India) U., 1974. Pharmacist Christian Med. Coll. Hosp., Vellore, 1955-65; asst. chief pharmacist Christian Med. Coll. Hosp., Madras, 1965-76; pharmacist Met. Hosp. Ctr., N.Y.C., 1978-84, asst. dir. pharmacy, 1984—. Author: Manufacturing of Parenteral Fluids in Small Hospital Pharmacy, 1970. Mem. Am. Soc. Hosp. Pharmacists. Home: 92-31 57th Ave # 6M Elmhurst NY 11373 Office: Met Hosp Ctr Pharmacy 1901 First Ave New York NY 10029

MANOR, PHILIP CRAIG, editor, physical chemist; b. Columbus, Ohio, July 20, 1944; s. Paul Anthony and Lola Frances (Riley) M.; m. Barbara Elisat, 1974 (div. 1986); children: Charlotte, Alexander; m. Nancy Patricia Barry, 1991. BSc, Washington and Lee U., 1966; PhD, MIT, 1972. Sr. editor Springer-Verlag, N.Y.C. and Heidelburg, Fed. Republic Germany, 1978-85; editorial dir. Gordon & Breach-Harwood Pubs., N.Y.C., 1987-89; sr. editor John Wiley & Sons, N.Y.C., 1989—; fellow Max-Plank Inst. for Exptl. Medicine, Goettingen, Fed. Republic Germany, 1971-73; rsch. assoc. Princeton (N.J.) U., 1974-78. Translator: Bioprocess Technology, 1988. Alexander von Humboldt Stiftung fellow, 197l. Mem. Coun. Biology Editors, Soc. for Scholarly Pub., Delta Upsilon. Office: John Wiley & Sons 605 Third Ave New York NY 10158

MANOWITZ, PAUL, biochemist, researcher, educator; b. Monticello, N.Y., Dec. 13, 1940; s. Jacob M. and Rose (Levine) M.; m. Joyce L. Swartz, June 16, 1968; children: Neal J., Lauren H. BA in Chemistry with honors, Cornell U., 1962; PhD in Biochemistry, Brandeis U., 1967. Postdoctoral fellow NYU Sch. Medicine, 1967-70, instr., 1970-72; asst. prof. psychiatry U. Medicine and Dentistry N.J. Robert Wood Johnson Med. Sch., Piscataway, 1972-78, assoc. prof. psychiatry, 1978—, assoc. prof. psychiatry and neurology, 1991—; rsch. cons. VA Med. Ctr., Lyons, N.J., 1987—. Editor biochemistry Sci. Matters; contbr. articles to profl. jours. Grantee Nat. Inst. on Alcohol Abuse and Alcoholism, UNICO Found., VA. Mem. AAAS, Am. Soc. for Neurochemistry, Internat. Soc. for Biomed. Rsch. on Alcoholism, Soc. Biol. Psychiatry, Rsch. Soc. on Alcoholism, Soc. for Neurosci., World Fedn. of Socs. Biol. Psychiatry. Home: 7 Guernsey Ln East Brunswick NJ 08816-3506 Office: U Medicine and Dentistry NJ Robert Wood Johnson Med Sch 675 Hoes Ln Piscataway NJ 08854-5635

MANSERGH, GORDON DWIGHT, health education and wellness promotion professional; b. St. Paul, Aug. 7, 1962; s. Gerald Gordon and Nancy Helen (Stuessy) M. BA, Gustavus Adolphus Coll., 1984; MA, Mich. State U., 1986; MEd, Boston U., 1991. Substance abuse counselor NORCAP Lodge, Foxboro, Mass., 1986-87; asst. dir. student affairs Chamberlayne Coll., Boston, 1987; asst. dir. orientation, off-campus svcs. Boston U., 1987-90, founding dir. Wellness Ctr., 1990—; grant writer, adminstr.; dir. PREVENT Consortium, 1991—; drug prevention planning com. U.S. Dept. Edn., 1991—; coord. Project DART, 1990—; mem. Mass. Coun. on Compulsive Gambling Prevention Com.; chair Boston U. Substance Abuse Task Force, 1989—; founding chair Boston AIDS Consortium Coll. Community Edn. Com., 1988-89. Editor, author: Wellnews, 1990—; contbr. articles to profl. jours. Vol. community svc. Aids Action Com. Mass. Honoree Guild of St. Ansgar Gustavus Adolphus Coll., 1984. Mem. Am. Coll. Personnel Assn. (dir. wellness com. 1990—), Am. Coll. Health Assn., Am. Pub. Health Assn., Am. Assn. for Counseling and Devel., Pi Lambda Theta.

MANSFIELD, BRUCE ALEXANDER, professional product consulting firm owner; b. Boston, Apr. 17, 1932; s. Bertram Alexander Mansfield and Prudence Buyrl (Boutilier) Landers; children: Linda Mansfield Carroll, Robert Alexander. AB, Brown U., 1954; BS, Bates Coll., 1978. Sales mgr. Alsco Co., Boston, 1954-59; sales rep. Shell Oil Distributor, Waltham, Mass., 1959-69; prin. Mansfield & Assocs., Newton Lower Falls, Mass., 1954-69; head tennis professional Glen Ellen Country Club, Millis, Mass., 1969-75; gen. mgr. Wimbledon 109 Tennis Club, Inc., Dover, Mass., 1975-77; pres. Dart Tennis Internat. Co., Wellesley Hills, Mass., 1980-84; mem. New Eng. Energy Commn., 1977-84. Author: Another Place Another Time, 1987; inventor dart tennis (Hall of Fame, Newport, R.I. 1975). With USAF, 1951-53, Korea. Mem. Lincoln Group of Boston, Brown U. Sports Found. (charter mem.), Brown U. Boston Club. Episcopalian. Address: PO Box 96 Newton Lower Falls MA 02162-0001

MANSFIELD, EDWARD PATRICK, JR., advertising executive; b. Warren, Pa., Oct. 29, 1947; s. Edward Patrick and Freida (Dahler) M.; m. Norma L. Johnson, Apr. 17, 1971. AS in Acctg., Jamestown Bus. Coll., 1967; BS in Mktg. Advt., Dyke Coll., 1970. Promotion mgr., ad dir. The News-Herald, Lake County, Ohio, 1973-77; dir. advt. The Eagle, Butler, Pa., 1977-78; dir. mktg. Baltimore Mag., 1978-79; dir. advt. The Washingtonian, Washington, 1979—. Founder, chmn. Warm-A-Heart Fund, 1988—; chmn. bd. Columbia Lighthouse for Blind, 1988—, chmn. bd. dirs., 1990—. Home: 347 Cottswold Pl Riva MD 21140-1528 Office: Washingtonian Mag 1828 L St NW Ste 200 Washington DC 20036-5169

MANSFIELD, JOSEPH JOHN, academic official; b. N.Y.C., Jan. 23, 1938; s. Joseph and Catherine (Knock) M.; m. Barbara Hanken, Feb. 23, 1963 (div. 1975); children: Monica, Cynthia, Matthew; m. Deborah L. Bowden, Nov. 19, 1977 (div. 1987); m. Nancy H. Miller, Aug. 5, 1988. BS, Fordham U., 1959; MA, Columbia U., 1960. Asst. dir. alumni rels. Fordham U., Bronx, N.Y., 1960-62; dir. devel. Poly. Inst. Bklyn., 1962-70, Pace U., N.Y.C., 1970-74; exec. dir. devel. N.Y. Infirmary, N.Y.C., 1974-77; dir. devel. Columbia U., N.Y.C., 1977-82; v.p. devel. Pa. State U.,, 1982-84; v.p. univ. devel. U. Buffalo Found., 1984-87, pres., 1987—; bd. dirs. Artpark & Co. Bd. dirs. Episcopal Ch. Home; chmn. clergy compensation com. Episcopal Diocese Western N.Y.; mem. vestry St. Paul's Episcopal Cathedral, Buffalo. Mem. Coun. for Advancement and Support Edn., Nat. Soc. Fund Raising Execs. (bd. dirs. western N.Y. chpt. 1985-90), Fordham U. Alumni Fedn. (nat. chmn. 1974-76), Princeton Club, Saturn Club, Buffalo Club, Phi Delta Kappa. Republican. Episcopalian. Home: 530 Ashland Ave Buffalo NY 14222-1307 Office: U Buffalo Found Inc PO Box 590 Buffalo NY 14231-0590

MANSFIELD, VICTOR NEIL, physics and astronomy educator; b. Norwalk, Conn., May 7, 1941; s. Victor Emanuel and Virginia Louise (Santaniello) M.; m. Elaine Margret Ware, May 18, 1968; children: David, Anthony. BA, Dartmouth Coll., 1963, MS, 1964; PhD, Cornell U., 1972. Prof. physics and astronomy Colgate U., Hamilton, N.Y., 1973—; vis. prof. Cornell U., Ithaca, N.Y., 1976-77; v.p. Odyssey Rsch., Ithaca, 1981-83; dir. Wisdom's Goldenrod Ctr. Philosophic Studies, Burdett, N.Y., 1975-85; vice chmn. Paul Brunton Philosophic Found., Burdett, 1985-90; cons. Borland Internat., Scotts Valley, Calif., 1985-90. Contbr. articles on astrophysics, physics and philosophy and computer sci. to sci. jours. Mem. Internat. Astron. Union, Am. Phys. Soc. Home: 4464 Picnic Area Rd Burdett NY 14818-9716 Office: Colgate U Depts Physics and Astronomy Hamilton NY 13346

MANSHIP, JOHN PAUL, artist, writer; b. N.Y.C., Jan. 16, 1927; s. Paul Howard and Isabel Goshorn (McIlwaine) M.; m. Margaret Carol Cassidy, Oct. 12, 1963. AB magna cum laude, Harvard U., 1948. Author: (biography) Paul Manship, 1989. Mem. Nat. Arts Club, Salmagundi Club, Am. Watercolor Soc., Rockport Art Assn. (pres. 1981-85), North Shore Art Assn., Nat. Soc. Mural Painters (sec. 1971-75), Arts Club Washington. Roman Catholic. Home: 10 Leverett St Gloucester MA 01930-1015

MANSKER, ROBERT THOMAS, press secretary; b. Houston, Jan. 29, 1941; s. A.J. and Anna (Beard) M. AA, Schreiner Coll., 1961; BBA, U. Tex., 1965; MBA, West Tex. State U., 1966; PhD, East Tex. State U., 1976. Instr. Tex. Tech U., Lubbock, 1966-69, Grayson Coll., Sherman, Tex., 1969-71; from instr. to assoc. prof. East Tex. State U., Commerce, 1971-77; adminstrv. asst. Tex. Ho. of Reps., 1975-78; press sec. U.S. Congress, Washington, 1979—. Active Dem. State Exec. Com., 1974-78; elector from Tex., 1992. Mem. Assn. U.S. Ho. Dem. Press Assts. (pres. 1988—). Baptist. Home: 1245 4th SW Washington DC 20024 Office: Congressman Martin Frost 2459 Rayburn Bldg Washington DC 20515

MANSMANN, CAROL LOS, federal judge, educator; b. Pitts., Aug. 7, 1942; d. Walter Joseph and Regina Mary (Pilarski) Los; m. J. Jerome Mansmann, June 27, 1970; children: Casey, Megan, Patrick. B.A., J.D., Duquesne U.; LL.D., Seton Hill Coll., Greensburg, Pa., 1985; PhD, La Roche Coll., 1990. Asst. dist. atty. Allegheny County, Pitts., 1968-72; assoc. McVerry Baxter & Mansmann, Pitts., 1973-79; assoc. prof. law Duquesne U., Pitts., 1973-82; judge west dist. U.S. Dist. Ct. Pa., Pitts., 1982-85; judge 3rd cir. U.S. Ct. Appeals, Pitts., 1985—; mem. Pa. Criminal Procedural Rules Com., Pitts., 1972-77; spl. asst. atty. gen. Commonwealth of Pa., 1974-79; bd. dirs. Pa. Bar Inst., Harrisburg, 1984-90. Mem. adv. bd. Villanova U. Law Sch., 1985-91. Recipient St. Thomas More award, Pitts., 1983, Phila., 1984. Mem. Duquesne U. (bd. dirs 1987—), Nat. Assn. Women Judges, ABA, Pa. Bar Assn., Fed. Judges Assn., Am. JuducatureSoc., Allegheny County Bar Assn., Sewickfey Acad. (bd. dirs. 1988-91), Phi Alpha Delta. Republican. Roman Catholic. Office: US Ct Appeals 1037 US PO & Courthouse 7th & Grant Sts Pittsburgh PA 15219

MANTER, MARGARET CARPENTER, artist; b. Providence, Feb. 20, 1923; d. George William and Lizetta (Higson) Carpenter; m. Wilbur B. Manter, Dec. 20, 1947; children: John, George, Nancy, Berry, Robert. BFA, Syracuse U., 1946. Group Exhibits include Ali Maine Biennial Bordoin Coll., Burnswick, Maine, 1979, Joan Whitney Payson Gallery, Westbrook, Maine, 1981, Maine Women in the Arts, Brick Stone Mus., Kennebonk, Maine, 1986, Mus. of the Hudson Highlands, N.Y., 1986, Rocky Mt. Nat., Golden, Colo., 1987, Nat. Assn. Women Artists, N.Y.C., 1989-90, Watercolor U.S.A., Springfield, Mo., 1991, Fax-Simile: An Invitational, Ill., 1990; one-women shows include Cen. Place Gallery, Bangor, Maine, 1990, and others. *. Mem. Nat. Assn. Women Artists, Deer Isle Art Assn., Soc. Exptl. Artists. Home: 1328 State St Bangor ME 04401-6906

MANTHEY, ROBERT WENDELIN, educator; b. N.Y.C., Dec. 23, 1935; s. Frank A.J. and Josephine (Roth) M.; m. Marcia Christine Dampman; Dec. 27, 1958; children: Catherine, A. David, Jeffrey R. BA, SUNY, Albany, 1957; MA in Teaching, Brown U., 1962. Cert. secondary, sci. tchr., N.Y. Tchr. high. sch. Croton-on-Hudson, N.Y., 1957—. Coord. Boy Scouts Am., Peekskill, N.Y., 1974—; chmn. Conservation Adv. Coun., Peekskill, 1987. Recipient Excellence award Math. Soc. Am., 1953; fellow NSF, 1962; Rsch. Participation grantee Boyce Thompson Inst., Yonkers, N.Y., 1963-64. Mem. Sci. Tchrs. Assn. N.Y. State, N.Y. State Tchrs. Assn., Croton Tchrs. Assn. (v.p. 1972-74, treas. 1976—, exec. com. 1972—), Lions (1st v.p. Peekskill), Elks, KC. Republican. Roman Catholic. Home: 419 Union Ave Peekskill NY 10566-4704

MANTICA, FRANCIS ALBERT, priest; b. Oneonta, N.Y., Nov. 28, 1927; s. Frank Anthony and Mary (Bucci) M. BFA, Syracuse U., 1952; BA, St. Mary's Sem., 1960; MA (hon.), SUNY, Albany, 1979. Tchr. Cath. Cen. High Sch., Troy, N.Y., 1960-63; prin. St. Mary's Sch., Amsterdam, N.Y., 1963-64; dir. and founder Youthville, Oklahoma City, 1965-67; chaplain USAF, Hamilton AFB, Calif., 1968-69; dir. and founder Youthville, Schenectady, N.Y., 1970-71; from vol. adminstr. to dir. of vol. adminstrn. N.Y. State Dept. Mental Hygiene, Albany, 1972-83; dir. and founder Internat. Corological Implosion Rsch., Troy, N.Y., 1984—. Author: Corology-The Phenomenon and Evolution of Love..., 1985, Mankind and Crisis of Puberty, 1987, Person, 1988, The Letter, A True Story..., 1990, Education and Human Sexuality, 1991, The Human Energy to Love and Be Loved..., 1992. Capt. USAF, 1962-63. Mem. Acad. Religion and Psychical Rsch., Kundalini Rsch. Found. of U.S. and Can., Teilhardian Ctr. for Future of Man. Democrat. Roman Catholic. Office: I C I R PO Box 190 North Troy NY 12182-0190

MANTON, THOMAS JOSEPH, congressman; b. N.Y.C., Nov. 3, 1932; m. Diane Schley; children: Cathy, Tom, John, Jeanne. BBA, St. John's U., 1958, LLB, 1962. Mem. N.Y.C. Police Dept., 1955-60; mktg. rep. IBM, 1960-64; practice law, 1964-84; mem. 99th-102nd Congresses from 9th N.Y. Dist., 1984—. Mem. N.Y.C. Council, 1970-84. Served with USMC, 1951-53. Democrat. Office: Ho of Reps 331 Cannon HOB Washington DC 20515

MANTOURA, AMIRA, podiatrist; b. Cairo, Sept. 10, 1962; came to U.S., 1969; d. Magdi F. and Yvette (Farag) M. BS, SUNY, Stony Brook, 1982; D of Podiatric Medicine, N.Y. Coll. Podiatric Medicine, 1986. Resident VA Med. Ctr., New Haven, Conn., 1986-87; assoc. prof. N.Y. Coll. Podiatric Medicine and Foot Clinics of N.Y., N.Y.C., 1988—; resident VA Med. Ctr., West Haven, Conn., 1986-87; mem. staff Stamford (Conn.) Hosp., 1989—, St. Joseph's Med. Ctr., Stamford. Contbr. articles to profl. jours. Recipient Cert. of Appreciation Bergen Pines (N.J.) Hosp. and N.Y. Coll. Podiatric Medicine, 1991. Mem. Am. Podiatric Med. Assn. Roman Catholic. Office: 95 Morgan St Stamford CT 06905-5435

MANUEL, LAU-RENE ANNTWAN, safety and health specialist; b. Bklyn., Mar. 5, 1964; s. William and Patricia Ann (Gregory) M. BS in Indsl. Engring., SUNY, Binghamton, 1987. Student intern Assn. Bldg. Contrs., Binghamton, N.Y., 1985-86; bldg. inspector City of Binghamton, 1986; construction inspector State N.Y., Dept. of Transp., Binghamton, 1986-87; indsl. engr. Dover Electronics, Conklin, N.Y., 1987; assoc. loss control rep. Chubb Group of Ins., White Plains, N.Y., 1988-89; fire/ins. inspector Fast Reports, Inc., Bronx, 1989-90; safety specialist Mayor's office of ops. Citywide Occupational Safety and Health Office, N.Y.C., 1990-91; safety and health specialist Triborough Bridge and Tunnel Authority, N.Y.C., 1991—. Mem. IEEE, Am. Soc. Safety Engrs. Democrat. Roman Catholic. Home: 1191 Anderson Ave Bronx NY 10452

MANUEL, THOMAS ASBURY, research chemist; b. Austin, Tex., Jan. 3, 1936; s. Herschel Thurman and Dorothy (Broad) M.; m. Sally Linn Waddell, June 14, 1958 (div. Sept. 1978); children: Thomas Broad, Elisabeth Linn; m. Nancy Walker Schneider, Dec. 27, 1984. BA, Ohio Wesleyan U., 1957; AM, Harvard U., 1958, PhD, 1961. Rsch. chemist Esso Rsch. and Engring. Co., Linden, N.J., 1960-66; sect. mgr. then mgr. elastomers Exxon Chem., Linden, 1967-76; dir. polymer chems. R&D Air Products and Chems. Inc., Allentown, Pa., 1977-79, gen. sales mgr. polymers, 1980-84, dir. polymer

tech., 1985-86, gen. mgr. chems. tech., 1987-89, gen. mgr. corp. sci. and tech., 1989—. Patentee in field; contbr. articles to profl. jours. Fellow GE, 1958-59, NSF, 1959-60. Mem. Am. Chem. Soc., Soc. Chem. Industry, Tapp I. Office: Air Products & Chems Inc 7201 Hamilton Blvd Allentown PA 18195-9642

MANUEL, VIVIAN, public relations company executive; b. Queens County, N.Y., May 6, 1941; d. George Thomas and Vivian (Anderson) M. BA, Wells Coll., Aurora, N.Y., 1963; MA, U. Wyo.-Laramie, 1965. Mgmt. analyst Dept. Navy, 1966-68; account supr. Gen. Electric Co., N.Y.C., 1968-72, corp. rep. bus. and fin., 1972-76; dir. corp. communications Standard Brands Co., N.Y.C., 1976-78; pvt. cons., N.Y.C., 1978-80; pres. V M Communications Inc., N.Y.C., 1980—. Mem. com. Girls Club N.Y., 1983-84; trustee Wells Coll., 1983-90; mem. adv. bd. Glenholme Sch., 1991—. Mem. AAUW, N.Y. Women in Communications (bd. v.p. 1983-85, chair Matrix awards 1985), Women Execs. in Pub. Rels. (dir. 1985-87, bd. dirs. 1986-88), Women's Econ. Roundtable, N.Y.C. Commn. on Status of Women. Home: 501 E 79th St New York NY 10021-3552 Office: V M Communications Inc 501 E 79th St Ste 17B New York NY 10021

MANVEL, ALLEN DAILEY, fiscal economist; b. Spokane, Wash., June 29, 1912; s. Arthur Orlando and Agnes Louise (Johnson) M.; m. Helen Louise de Werthern, Oct. 9, 1937; children: Sarah Katherine, Bennet. AB in Econs., Occidental Coll., 1934; postgrad., U. Chgo., 1935-36, Harvard U., 1939-40; DSc (hon.), Ohio State U., 1976. Rsch. assoc. Ill. Dept. Fin., Springfield, 1936-41; rsch. dir. Ill. Agrl. Assn., Chgo., 1941-42; state budget supr. Ill. Dept. Fin., Springfield, 1942-43; adminstrv. analyst U.S. Bur. Budget, Washington, 1943-46; chief govts. div. U.S. Bur. Census, Washington, 1946-67; assoc. dir. Nat. Com. on Urban Problems, Washington, 1967-68; asst. dir. Adv. Com. on Intergovt. Rels., Washington, 1968-71; rsch. asst., sr. fellow The Brookings Instn., Washington, 1972-75; econ. cons. Tax Analysts, Inc., Arlington, Va., from 1976; now ret.; lectr. in pub. adminstrn. George Washington U., Washington, 1946-48; cons. Fiscal Div. UN, N.Y.C., 1953, N.Y.C. Commn. on Statis. Programs, 1954-55. Author: (book) Paying for Civilized Society, 1986; co-author: (books) Measuring Fiscal Capacity and Effort, 1971, Monitoring Revenue Sharing, 1975; contbr. numerous articles to profl. jours. Recipient Louis Brownlow award, Nat. Mcpl. League, 1966. Mem. Nat. Tax Assn. (past. bd. dirs.), Cosmos Club, Washington. Democrat. Unitarian. Home and Office: 3001 Veazey Ter NW Apt 126 Washington DC 20008-5455

MANVILLE, STEWART ROEBLING, archivist; b. White Plains, N.Y., Jan. 15, 1927; s. Leo and Margaret (Roebling) M.; m. Ella V. Grainger, Jan. 19, 1972 (dec.). Student U. Wyo., 1944-46; BS, Columbia U., 1962. Various office positions, N.Y.C., 1947-51, 56-58; asst. stage dir. several European opera houses, 1951-55; editor Jas. T. White & Co., N.Y.C., 1959-63; archivist, curator Percy Grainger Library, White Plains, N.Y., 1963—. Mem. CAP. Mem. Hist. House Assn. Am., Nat. Trust Hist. Preservation, Victorian Soc. in Am. (past dir. N.Y. chpt.), Société des Antiquaires de Picardie, Soc. Archtl. Historians, Westchester County Hist. Soc., Titanic Hist. Soc., White Plains Battle Monument Com., Appalachian Trail Conf., Westchester Trails Assn. (past dir.). Quaker. Author: The Manville/Manvel Families in America; contbr. articles and revs. on music to mags. and newspapers. Office: 7 Cromwell Pl White Plains NY 10601-5005

MANYAK, MICHAEL JOHN, urologist, educator, researcher; b. Flint, Mich., Mar. 25, 1951; m. Rebecca Bruning; children: Rachel, Susannah. BA, U. Notre Dame, 1973; MD, U. of East, Manila, 1979. Intern, then resident in gen. surgery Booth Meml. Med. Ctr., Flushing, N.Y., 1980-82; resident in urology George Washington Univ. Med. Ct., Washington, 1982-84, chief resident, 1984-85, instr. urology, 1988-89, asst. prof., 1989-91, assoc. prof., 1991—. Contbr. articles to profl. jours. Fellow Nat. Cancer Inst., 1985-88; scholar Am. Urol. Assn., 1986-88. Office: George Washington Univ Med Ctr 2150 Pennsylvania Ave NW Washington DC 20037

MANZ, AUGUST FREDERICK, welding technology and safety consultant; b. Newark, Mar. 7, 1929; s. August F. and Emma Irene (Nate) M.; m. Irma Hars; children: August F. Jr., Paul C. BSEE, N.J. Inst. Tech., 1957, MSEE, 1959. Devel. engr. Linde div. Union Carbide, Newark, 1957-64, project engr., 1964-69, spl. project engr., 1969-73; project scientist Linde div. Union Carbide, Tarrytown, N.Y., 1973-76; assoc. mgr. regulations tech. Linde div. Union Carbide, Danbury, Conn., 1976-82, mgr. regulations tech., 1982-85; sr. engr. Linde div. Union Carbide, Somerset, N.J., 1985-86; pres. A.F. Manz Assocs., Union, N.J., 1986—; chmn. Z49.1 safety in welding and cutting, ANSI, N.Y.C.; adj. prof. Kean Coll., Union, N.J. Author: Power Supply Handbook, 1973, Welding Processes and Practices, 1988; co-author/contbr. 18 books on welding; patentee in field of welding. With USAF, 1947-54. Named Inventors of Yr., N.J. Inventors Hall of Fame, 1992. Mem. Am .Welding Soc. (chmn. labeling and safe practices, Airco Welding award 1991, William Irrgang award 1990, Samuel Wylie Miller award 1989, Nat. Meritorious award 1988, Plummer Meml. Ednl. Lectr. 1974), Nat. Welding Supply Assn., The Authors Guild, Welding Rsch. Coun. Office: 470 Whitewood Rd Union NJ 07083-8218

MANZ, BETTY ANN, nurse administrator; b. Paterson, N.J., Nov. 30, 1935; d. James Albert and Elsie (Basse) Brown; diploma Newark Beth Israel Hosp. Sch. Nursing, 1955; BSN, Seton Hall U., 1964; m. Roger A. Johnson, Feb. 1988; children: Laura, Richard, Garry. Staff nurse oper. room Newark Beth Israel Hosp., 1955-56, recovery room head nurse, 1956-57, oper. room head nurse, 1957-58, supr. oper. room, 1958-60; substitute tchr. pub. schs. Harding Twp., 1966-70; charge nurse St. Barnabas Med. Ctr., Livingston, N.J., 1965-70, head nurse emergency room, 1970-72; oper. room supr. St. Clares Hosp., Denville, N.J., 1972-77; asst. dir. for oper. rooms and post anesthesia rooms Newark Beth Israel Med. Ctr., 1977-82; asst. dir. nursing oper. room care program Thomas Jefferson U. Hosp., Phila., 1982-84; asst. dir./assoc. nursing dir. oper. room, anesthesia ICU, ambulatory surgery Univ. Hosp., SUNY-Stony Brook, 1984-87 dir. oper. room/post anestesia care ambulatory surgery Med. Ctr. Del., Wilmington and Christiana, Del., 1987-88; practice mgr. Del. Orthopaedic Ctr., Wilmington, 1989—; faculty mem. postgrad. course in microsurgy for Am. Coll. Obstetricians and Gynecologists, Newark, 1982; profl. cons. oper. room products, also health cons. Henry E. Wessel Assocs., Moraga, Calif.; profl. tech. cons., lectr. Surgicot, Inc., Smithtown, N.Y. Dep. dir. Harding Twp. CD, 1967-75. Recipient Service award Essex County Med. Soc., 1979. Mem. AAMI, Nat. Assn. Orthopaedic Nurses, Assn. Oper. Room Nurses, Am. Soc. Post Anesthesia Nurses, Bones Soc. Orthopedic Mgrs., Newark Beth Israel Hosp. Nursing Alumnae Assn., Seton Hall U. Alumnae Assn., Harding Twp. Civic Assn., Am. Field Svc.. Republican. Club: Mt. Kemble Lake Community. Editor operating room sect. SCORE mag. Home: 2620 Lamper Ln Wilmington DE 19808-3808 Office: 2501 Silverside Rd Wilmington DE 19810-3726

MANZI, DANTE ANTHONY, electronic laboratory researcher; b. N.Y.C., May 26, 1937; s. Mathew Leoponte and Mary (Tamburri) M.; m. Patricia Blaicher, Apr. 20, 1961 (div. Sept. 1967); children: Kenneth, Michael. BS, U. Detroit, 1961; MS, Poly. Inst. of Bklyn., 1974. Design/test engr. various positions aerospace industry, 1961-71; author Am. Space Found., Forest Hills, N.Y., 1971-77, sci. researcher, 1979-83; pvt. researcher Columbia U., Manhattan, N.Y., 1983-87; calibration technician Quantum Instruments, Garden City, N.Y., 1987-88; electronic technician Napco Securities, Amityville, N.Y., 1988-89; lab. researcher Wide-Band Products, Manhattan, 1988—; v.p. engring. Barclay's Brokerage, Flushing, 1989—; aircraft pilot Milionaire Flightways, Farmingdale, N.Y., 1987—; lectr. IEEE Engring. in Medicine and Biol. Soc., 9th Ann. Conf., Boston, 1987. Contbr. articles to profl. jours.; patentee in field. Mem. AIAA, Aircraft Owners and Pilots Assn., N.Y. Acad. Sci., Chi Sigma Phi. Republican. Roman Catholic. Home: 154-42 26th Ave Flushing NY 11354

MANZITTI, EDWARD THOMAS, marketing professional; b. N.Y.C., Feb. 3, 1951; s. Edward Ferdinand and Felicia Vita (Bevilacqua) M. BA, SUNY at Buffalo, 1972; PhD, Mich. State U., 1979; cert., NYU, 1983. Asst. prof. SUNY at Oneonta, 1979-81; rsch. dir. Italian-Am. Inst., Flushing, N.Y., 1981-83; staff supr. AT&T, Basking Ridge, N.J., 1983-87; mgr. market rsch. Bell Communications Rsch., Livingston, N.J., 1987—. Author: Data Communications Market Research, 1983-91. Mem. Am. Psychol. Assn., Am. Mktg. Assn. Office: Bell Communications Rsch 290 W Mount Pleasant Ave Livingston NJ 07039

MAPOU, ROBERT LEWIS, neuropsychologist; b. Washington, May 28, 1955; s. Albert and Phyllis Helen (Smul) M.; life ptnr. Michael Jerome Zufall, Jan. 14, 1978. BS, U. Md., 1977; MA, Emory U., 1981, PhD, 1985. Diplomate Am. Bd. Profl. Psychology; lic. psychologist, Md., Mass. Staff neuropsychologist Greenery Rehab. Ctr., Boston, 1986-88; assoc. dir. neuropsychology Am. Neurosci. Ctrs., Gaithersburg, Md., 1988-90; neuropsychology dir. behavioral medicine rsch. program Henry M. Jackson Found. Advancement Mil. Medicine, Washington, 1990—; asst. clin. prof. Tufts U., Boston, 1986-88; ad hoc grant reviewer NIMH, Bethesda, 1989—; adj. asst. prof. Dept. Psychiatry Uniformed Svcs. U. Health Scis., Bethesda, 1991—; clin. assoc. prof. Dept. Neurology and Psychology Georgetown U. Sch. of Medicine, Washington, 1991—; reviewer Psychol. Bull., 1989, Jour. Community Psychology, 1988; presenter at profl. confs. Mem. editorial bd. Jour. of Head Trauma Rehab., 1991—; contbr. articles to profl. publs. Mem. Am. Psychol. Assn., Internat. Neuropsychol. Soc., Assn. Lesbian and Gay Psychologists, Sigma Xi, Phi Beta Kappa, Phi Kappa Phi, Eta Kappa Nu, Phi Eta Sigma. Home: 18331 Leman Lake Dr Olney MD 20832-3015

MAPP, EDWARD CHARLES, educator; b. N.Y.C., Aug. 17, 1929; s. Edward Cameron and Estelle Viola (Sampson) M.; children: Andrew, Elmer, Everett. BA, CCNY, 1953; MS, Columbia U., 1956; PhD, NYU, 1970. Tchr. Bd. Edn., N.Y.C., 1957-64; dir. librs. N.Y.C. Tech. Coll., CUNY, Bklyn., 1964-77; dean of faculty Borough of Manhattan Community Coll., CUNY, N.Y.C., 1977-81; prof. speech and communication Borough of Manhattan Community Coll., CUNY, 1983—; vice chancellor City Colls. of Chgo., 1982-83; commr. N.Y.C. Commn. on Human Rights, N.Y.C., 1987—; treas. U. Faculty Senate of CUNY, 1974-77. Author: Blacks in American Films: Today and Yesterday, 1972; co-author: A Separate Cinema, 1992; editor: Puerto Rican Perspectives, 1974; compiler Books for Occupational Edn. Programs, 1971, Directory of Blacks in the Performing Arts, 1978, 2d edit., 1990; columnist Movie/TV Mktg., Tokyo, 1979—. Bd. dirs UN Assn. of N.Y., 1975-78; mem. Bklyn. Borough Pres. Adv. Panel, 1981-84; trustee N.Y. Met. Ref. and Rsch. Agy., N.Y., 1980-82; exec. com. The Com. for Pub. Higher Edn., N.Y.C., 1978-81. Recipient Founders Day award NYU, 1970. Mem. Archons of Colophon (convenor 1985-86), Black Filmakers Found., Audelco, Theatre Libr. Assn. Democrat. Office: Borough of Manhattan Community Coll CUNY 199 Chambers St New York NY 10007-1006

MARA, JOHN LAWRENCE, veterinarian, consultant; b. Whitesboro, N.Y., May 17, 1924; s. William Edward and Olive Pearl (Brakefield) M.; m. Kathleen Keefe, 1946 (div. 1958); children: William, Michael, Daniel, Patrick; m. Patricia Louise Paulk, 1970; children: Jennifer Lee, Kennon. DVM, Cornell U., 1951. Intern N.Y. State Coll. Vet. Medicine, Cornell U., Ithaca, 1951-52; assoc. veterinarian L.W. Goodman Animal Hosp., Manhasset, N.Y., 1952-55; owner, pres. Mara Animal Hosp., Huntington, N.Y., 1955-79; profl. rep. Hills Pet Products, Topeka, Kans., 1979-80, mgr. profl. rels., 1980-81, dir. profl. affairs, 1981-88, dir. vet. affairs, 1988—. V.p. Huntington United Fund; chmn. Huntington Taxpayers Party, 1968-78, Ch. in the Garden, Garden City, N.Y., 1975-77, trustee, 1975-77. Sgt. U.S. Army, 1943-45, ETO. Mem. L.I. Vet. Medicine Assn., N.Y. State Vet. Medicine Assn., Am. Vet. Medicine Assn., Am. Animal Hosp. Assn.. Republican. Baptist. Home: 130 Buttercup Ln Huntington NY 11743-3006 Office: 130 Buttercup Ln Huntington NY 11743-3006

MARAFIOTI, DOMINICK, small business owner; b. Rochester, N.Y., Apr. 10, 1926; s. Pasquale and Carmela (Parisi) M.; m. Marie Ricciardi, Jan. 19, 1957; children: Mary Ann, Dominic Jr., Bernadette. Mgr. Waring Theatre, Rochester, 1958-60; owner Cleaning Bus., Rochester, 1961—; nat. chief Buck Jones Rangers of Am., Rochester, 1980—. Founder, Boys and Girls Safety Patrol Club, Rochester, 1945. Pfc. U.S. Army, 1943-45. Decorated Bronze Star; recipient Letter of Commendation, Pres. Eisenhower, 1959; Hon. Sheriff Badge, Monroe County Sheriff Dept.; County Medalion and Flag, County of Monroe; Am. Flag, DAR. Home and Office: 15 Alpine Ln Caledonia NY 14423

MARAMOROSCH, KARL, virologist, educator; b. Vienna, Austria, Jan. 16, 1915; came to U.S., 1947, naturalized, 1952; s. Jacob and Stefanie Olga (Schlesinger) M.; m. Irene Ludwinowska, Nov. 15, 1938; 1 dau., Lydia Ann. M.S. magna cum laude in Entomology, Agrl. U., Warsaw, Poland, 1938; student, Poly. U. Bucharest, Rumania, 1944-46; fellow, Bklyn. Bot. Garden, 1947-48; Ph.D. (predoctoral fellow Am. Cancer Soc. 1948-49), Columbia, 1949. Civilian internee in Rumania, 1939-46; asst., then assoc. Rockefeller Inst., N.Y.C., 1949-61; sr. entomologist Boyce Thompson Inst., Yonkers, N.Y., 1961-74, program dir. virology and insect physiology, 1962-74; prof. microbiology Waksman Inst., Rutgers U., New Brunswick, N.J., 1974-85; prof. entomology Cook Coll., Rutgers U., New Brunswick, 1985—, Robert L. Starkey prof., 1983—; vis. prof. agr. U. Wageningen, Netherlands, 1953, Cornell U., 1957, Rutgers U., 1967-68, Fordham U., 1973, Sapporo U., Japan, 1980, Justus Liebig U., Giessen, Ger., 1983; Mendel lectr. St. Peters Coll., Jersey City, 1963; virologist FAO to Philippines, 1960; Disting. Vis. prof. Fudan U., Shanghai, 1982; cons. FAO-UN, World-wide survey, 1963; chmn. U.S.-Japan Coop. Seminar, 1965, 74, 85; mem. panel food and fiber Nat. Acad. Scis., 1966; cons. rice virus diseases AID-IRRI, Hyderabad, India, 1971; cons. UNDP, Bangalore, India, 1978-79; virologist FAO/UNDP, Sri Lanka, 1981, 82, 83, Mauritius, 1985; AIBS lectr., 1970-72, Found. Microbiology Nat. lectr., 1972-73, Fulbright Disting. prof., Yugoslavia, 1972, 78; mem. tropical medicine and parasitology study sect. NIH, 1972-76; chmn. 1st-3d Internat. Confs. Comparative Virology, 1969, 73, 76. Author: Comparative Symptomatology of Coconut Diseases of Unknown Etiology, 1964; editor: Biological Transmission of Disease Agents, 1962, Insect Viruses, 1968, Viruses, Vectors and Vegetation, 1969, Comparative Virology, 1971, Mycoplasma Diseases, 1973, Viruses, Evolution and Cancer, 1974, Invertebrate Immunity, 1975, Legume Diseases in the Tropics, 1975, Invertebrate Tissue Culture: Research Applications, 1976, Invertebrate Tissue Culture: Applications in Medicine, Biology and Agriculture, 1976, Aphids as Virus Vectors, 1977, Insect and Plant Viruses: An Atlas, 1977, Viruses and Environment, 1978, Practical Tissue Culture Applications, 1979, Leafhopper Vectors and Plant Disease Agents, 1979, Vectors of Plant Pathogens, 1980, Invertebrate Systems in Vitro, 1980, Vectors of Disease Agents, 1981, Mycoplasma Diseases of Trees and Shrubs, 1981, Mycoplasma and Allied Pathogens of Plants, Animals and Human Beings, 1981, Plant Diseases and Vectors: Ecology and Epidemiology, 1981, Invertebrate Cell Culture Applications, 1982, Pathogens, Vectors and Plant Diseases: Approaches to Control, 1982, Subviral Pathogens of Plants and Animals, 1985, Viral Insecticides for Biological Control, 1985, Biotechnology Advances in Insect Pathology and Cell Culture, 1987, Mycoplasma Diseases of Crops, 1988, Invertebrate and Fish Tissues Culture, 1988, Biotechnology for Biological Controls of Pests and Vectors, 1991, Viroids and Satellites: Molecular Parasites at the Frontier of Life, 1991, Plant Diseases of Uncertain Etiology, 1992; Methods in Virology, 1964—, Advances in Virus Research, 1972—, Archives of Virology, 1973-78, Intervirology, 1973-77, Advances in Cell Culture, 1979—; editor in chief Jour. N.Y. Entomol. Soc, 1972-84; assoc. editor: Virology, 1964-68, 75-79. Recipient Sr. Research award Lalor Found., 1957; Nat. Ciba-Geigy award in agr., 1976; Wolf prize in agr., 1980; Jurzykowski prize in biology, 1980; Disting. Service award Am. Inst. Biol. Scis., 1983. Fellow AAAS (Campbell award 1958), Entomol. Soc. Am., N.Y. Acad. Scis. (A. Cressy Morrison prize natural sci. 1951, chmn. div. microbiology 1956-60, rec. sec. 1960-61, v.p. 1962-63), Nat. Acad. Scis. India (hon.); mem. Harvey Soc., Growth Soc., Phytopath. Soc., Indian, Japan, Can. phytopath. socs., Leopoldina Acad., Internat. Com. Virus Nomenclature, Electron Microscpe Soc., Am. Soc. Microbiology (Waksman award 1978), Tissue Culture Assn. (pres. N.E. br. 1978-81, pres. history br. 1988-90), Soc. Invertebrate Pathology (founder's lectr., Adelaide 1990), Internat. Assn. Medicinal Forest Plants (pres. 1989—), Sigma Xi (pres. Rugers chpt. 1978). Home: 17 Black Birch Ln Scarsdale NY 10583-7456 Office: Rutgers U Dept Entomology New Brunswick NJ 08903

MARAN, JOE, lawyer; b. Jersey City, Nov. 16, 1933; s. Joseph and Beatrice (Margolin) M.; m. Paula Schwartz, June 15, 1956 (div. Oct. 1979); children: David, Jodi, Erik; m. Joy Breen, July 10, 1980 (div. May 1987); m. Deborah Idol, Nov. 7, 1987. BS, Fairleigh Dickinson U., 1957; LLB, Rutgers U., 1959. Bar: N.J. 1960, U.S. Supreme Ct.; cert. civil trial atty. N.J., Nat. Bd. Trial Adv. Pvt. practice Jersey City, 1960-64, Newark, 1984-87; ptnr. Zarin & Maran, Newark, 1964-83, Maran & Maran, Newark, 1987—. Mem. Essex County Bar Assn., Tau Delta Phi, Kings Bench Frat. Home: Llwellyn Pk West Orange NJ 07052 Office: The Legal Ctr 1 River St Newark NJ 07102-5406

MARANO, ANNAMARIE, health administrator; b. Bklyn., Aug. 30, 1962; d. Antonio and Delia Maria (Picariello) M.; m. Thomas John Farrell, June 1, 1985. BA, Barnard Coll., Columbia U, N.Y.C., 1984; MHA, U. Pitts., 1988, MBA, 1988. Med. asst. Ayerst Labs., N.Y.C., 1984-86; health policy fellow Health Policy Inst., Pitts., 1987-88; adminstrv. resident Staten Island U. Hosp., Staten Island, N.Y., 1988-89, planning, grants mgr., 1989-91, assoc. v.p. geriatrics, 1991—. Researcher, Health Policy Rsch., 1988. Mem. N.Y. Soc. Health Planning, Staten Island Interagency Coun. on Aging. Office: Staten Island Univ Hosp 475 Seaview Ave Staten Island NY 10305-3498

MARANO, ANTHONY JOSEPH, cardiologist; b. White Plains, N.Y., Apr. 14, 1934; s. Anthony Joseph and Mary Antoinette (Perrotta) M.; m. Mary Regina Marbach, Aug. 23, 1958; children—Thomas, Kathryn, Michele. B.A., Williams Coll., 1956; M.D., Cornell Med. Coll., 1960. Diplomate Am. Bd. Internal Medicine, Am. Bd. Cardiovascular Disease. Intern Bellevue Hosp., N.Y.C., 1960-61; resident St. Luke's Hosp., N.Y.C., 1961-63; NIH fellow in cardiology Mt. Sinai Hosp., N.Y.C., 1963-64, research assoc., 1964-75; clin. assoc. in medicine Coll. Physicians and Surgeons, N.Y.C., 1970-86; pres. med. staff White Plains Hosp., 1984-86, chief cardiology, 1985-91, chief cardiology emeritus, 1991—, bd. dirs., 1983-88; cons. in cardiology Burke Rehab. Ctr.; med. dir., founder Paramedic Ambulance, White Plains, 1976-82. Contbr. articles to med. jours. Trustee Pace U., N.Y.C., 1975—, Home Savs. Bank, White Plains, 1973-90; bd. dirs. YMCA, White Plains, 1978—; team physician White Plains High Sch., 1967—; cons. physician Dept. Pub. Safety, White Plains, 1968—. Tyng scholar Williams Coll., 1952-59; recipient Outstanding Achievement award Emergency Med. Services Council, 1982. Fellow ACP, Am. Coll. Cardiology; mem. AMA, Am. Coll. Sports Medicine, Am. Heart Assn., N.Y. State Heart Assn. (bd. dirs. 1982—), Westchester Heart Assn. (v.p. 1983-86, pres. 1987-90), Phi Beta Kappa. Clubs: University (White Plains) (pres. 1970-71); Westchester Country (Harrison, N.Y.). Avocations: tennis, skiing, gardening. Home: 9 Fairway Dr White Plains NY 10605-4107 Office: 20 Old Mamaroneck Rd White Plains NY 10605-2026

MARANO, FRANK NICHOLUS, hair salon executive; b. Jersey City, Oct. 24, 1950; s. Joseph M. and Ann L. Marano; 1 child, Frank Michael. Student, Parrison Beauty Sch., 1971-72, Carpi Hair Sch., 1973, Natural Motion Hair Inst., 1974. Cert. hair dresser, N.J., mgr. operator, N.J. Hair dresser Capri Hair Salon, Clinfton, N.J., 1972-73, Raing Day People, Hackensack, N.J., 1973-74; mgr., tchr. Hair Works, Toms River, N.J., 1974-75; princ., styles dir. Fantasy St. Hair Designs, Leonia, N.J., 1975-80; prin., styles dir. Rainbow St. Hair Designs, Teaneck, N.J., 1980-84; hair dresser Winks, Hackensack, 1984-89; mgr. Scissura Hair, Ridgefield Park, N.J., 1990—; styles dir., owner Fantasy St. Hair Designs; tchr., platform artist, N.J.; profl. model Premier Agy., Wayne, N.J., 1985. Author: Free Movement Haircutting Method, 1979; author numerous poems and songs; actor film Squeeze Play, 1980; patentee anti-hair thinning formula. Fellow Hairdressers Assn. (civit donation award 1973), Writers Guild. Home: 10 Willow Cir Hamburg NJ 07419-1025 Office: 2A Blue Ridge Rd Lodi NJ 07644-2007

MARANO, RICHARD MICHAEL, lawyer; b. Waterbury, Conn., June 22, 1960; s. Albert Nicholas and Angeline Domenica (Viotti) M.; m. Eileen N. Barry. BA, Fairfield U., 1982; JD, Seton Hall U., 1985. Bar: Conn. 1985, U.S. Dist. Ct. Conn. 1985, U.S. Tax Ct. 1986, U.S. Supreme Ct. 1990, U.S. Ct. Appeals (2d cir.) 1991. Assoc. Moynahan, Ruskin, Mascolo & Mariani, Waterbury, 1985-87; ptnr. Marano & Diamond, Waterbury, 1987—; alderman City of Waterbury 1988-90. Co-editor: Counsel for the Defense, 1991—. Bd. dirs. Anderson Boys Club, 1989—; pres. Conn. Young Dems., 1981-82; state coord. McGovern for U.S. Presdl. campaign, 1983-84; campaign mgr. Orman for Congress, 1984; commr. Waterbury Bd. Pub. Assistance, 1986-88; bd. dirs. Italian-Am. Dem. Club, Waterbury, 1988—, Cen. Naugatuck Valley HELP, Inc., 1992—; justice of the peace Waterbury, 1989—; gen. counsel Waterbury Dem. Town Com., 1990—. Mem. ABA, Conn. Bar Assn., Nat. Assn. Criminal Def. Lawyers, Conn. Criminal Def. Lawyers Assn., Conn. Trial Lawyers Assn., Waterbury Bar Assn., New Haven County Bar Assn., Assn. Trial Lawyers Am., Nat. Italian-Am. Bar Assn., Sons of Italy (chpt. v.p. 1989—), Unico Club, K.C., Elks, Alpha Mu Gamma, Pi Sigma Alpha. Roman Catholic. Home: 22 Stephana Ln Waterbury CT 06710-1126 Office: Marano & Diamond 61 Field St Waterbury CT 06702-0309

MARASCIULLO, DAVID LOUIS, clinical psychologist; b. Bklyn., Apr. 24, 1929; s. Joseph and Josephine Elizabeth (Maresca) M.; m. Rosella Margaret Devine, Sept. 1, 1962; children: Paul, Janene, Mark. BA cum laude, Niagara (N.Y.) U., 1957; MA, Fordham U., Bronx, 1959; PhD, St. John's U., Jamaica, N.Y., 1969. Lic. psychologist, N.Y.; sch. psychologist, Pa., N.Y. Asst. prof. psychology Villanova (Pa.) U., 1959-61; rsch. fellow psychology U. Ark., Fayetteville, 1961-62; clin. psychologist Vocat. Adv. Svc., N.Y.C., 1962-63, Bur. Child Guidance, N.Y.C., 1963-68; sr. sch. psychologist USFD #3, Huntington, N.Y., 1968-69; sch. psychologist CHSD #3 Bellmore/Merrick (N.Y.), 1969-86; dir. pupil svcs. Wyandanch (N.Y.) Pub. Schs., 1987-89; supervising psychologist Pederson-Krag Clinic, Huntington, 1990—; cons. psychologist South Oaks Hosp., Amityville, 1970—, Employees Med. Rev., Suffolk County, N.Y., 1986—, Syosset Hosp., 1972-80; adj. clin. instr. Hofstra U., Hempstead, N.Y., 1972-84. Contbr. articles to profl. jours. With U.S. Army, 1953-55. Mem. APA, NASP, N.Y. State Psychol. Assn. (pres. 1988), Suffolk County Psychol. Assn., Nassau County Psychol. Assn. (pres. 1985). Roman Catholic. Home and Office: 18 S Hollow Rd Huntington Station NY 11746-6140

MARASH, STANLEY ALBERT, consulting firm executive; b. Bklyn., Dec. 18, 1938; s. Albert Samuel and Esther (Cunio) M.; m. Muriel Sylvia Sutchin, June 24, 1961; children: Judith Ilene, Alan Scott. Student, Bklyn. Coll., 1956-58; BBA, CCNY, 1961; student, U. Idaho, 1962-63, Boston U., 1964-66; MBA, Baruch Coll., 1970. Registered profl. engr., Calif.; cert. quality engr., reliability engr. Statistician Electric Boat Gen. Dynamics, Groton, Conn., 1961-62; statistician Idaho Nuclear Energy Lab. Electric Boat Gen. Dynamics, Idaho Falls, 1962-63; mgr. quality assurance memory product ops. RCA, Needham, Mass., 1963-65; cons. engr. astroelectronics div. RCA, Princeton, N.J., 1965-66; corp. mgr. quality assurance Ideal Corp., Bklyn., 1966-68; mgr. quality assurance Gen. Instrument, Signalite, Neptune, N.J., 1968; pres. STAT-A-MATRIX, Inc., Edison, N.J., 1968-90; chmn., chief exec. officer STAT-A-MATRIX Group, Edison, 1990—; chmn. bd. STAT-A-MATRIX Inst., Edison, N.J., 1975—; trustee Ellis R. Ott Found., Edison, 1982—; chmn. Quality N.J., 1989—; advisor, quality tech. Middlesex County Coll., Edison, 1970—; vis. prof. U. Sao Paolo, Brazil, 1974, 75, 77, Madrid Poly. U., 1976; expert cons. Internat. Atomic Energy Agy., Vienna, 1974-77; cons. various govt. agys. and pub. and pvt. cos., 1972—; mem. indsl. adv. com. statistics dept. Rutgers U., 1977-78, exec. standard coun. Am. Nat. Standards Inst., N.Y.C., 1979-80. Author: (tng. manual) Statistically Aided Management: What Every Executive Needs to Know, 1987; contbr. numerous articles, manuals and tng. texts. Examiner Malcolm Baldridge Nat. Quality Award, 1990, 91. Fellow Am. Soc. Quality Control (chmn. met. sect. 1966-68, Ellis R. Ott award 1981, chmn. internat. cooperation com. 1989—); mem. IEEE (sr.), ASTM, ASME, Am. Stats. Assn., Am. Soc. Tng. Devel., Am. Nuclear Soc. Office: STAT-A-MATRIX Group 2124 Oak Tree Rd Edison NJ 08820-1059

MARATEA, JAMES MICHAEL, healthcare administrator, editor, consultant; b. Riverside, N.J., Nov. 26, 1946; s. Domenic J. and Martha C. (Moloney) M.; m. Linda Jean Morgan, Sept. 6, 1970; children: Jennifer A., Jill M., Patrick J. BS in Bus. Adminstrn., Trenton (N.J.) State Coll., 1973; MA in Mgmt., Cen. Mich. U., 1977. Staff technologist Del. Valley Hosp., Bristol, Pa., 1966-68; supr. Zurbrugg Meml. Hosp., Riverside, 1968-74; v.p. Maratea Med. Lab., Riverside, 1966-84; rep. Thomas Jefferson U., Phila., 1974-75, lab. mgr., 1975-85, adminstr. dept. clin. and anatomic pathology, 1985—; adminstr. Jefferson Pathology Assn., Phila., 1984—; cons. to maj. league baseball, N.Y.C., 1990—; instr. Thomas Jefferson U., 1985—; mem. Univ. Hosp. Cons. Tech. Adv. Com., Chgo., 1989—. Contbg. author:

Sharpening Management Skills, A Laboratorian's Guide, 1978; contbr. articles to profl. jours. Mem. Camden County (N.J.) Com., 1991—; v.p. Merchantville (N.J.) Rep. Club, 1991, pres., 1992; mem. Bd. Health, Merchantville, 1986—. Recipient MLO Writing award Med. Econs., 1977, 80, 81, 82. Mem. Am. Med. Technologists, Clin. Lab. Mgmt. Assn. (v.p. Delaware Valley 1981-82, pres. 1982-84), Am. Soc. Med. Technologists, Am. Bd. Bionalysts. Roman Catholic. Home: 118 Westminster Ave Merchantville NJ 08109 Office: Thomas Jefferson U 11th and Walnut Sts Philadelphia PA 19107

MARAYNES, ALLAN LAWRENCE, filmmaker; b. N.Y.C., Apr. 26, 1950; s. Harry and Dorothy (Kaufman) M.; m. Bitsy Healy, Oct. 14, 1978; children: Sean, Megan, Matthew. BA, Queens Coll., 1972; MA, Loyola U., L.A., 1974. Assoc. producer CBS News, N.Y.C., 1976-77; producer CBS News-60 Minutes, N.Y.C., 1974-88; pres. Northern Films, N.Y.C., 1988—; exec. producer ABC "SST" program, 1989; producer 20/20 ABC News, N.Y.C., 1990—; lectr. New Sch., N.Y.C., 1979. Writer, dir. CBS News, 60 Minutes, 1976-88; author: (play) A Straight Line to the Market Place, 1975, (screenplay) Warp, 1991. Recipient Emmy award NATAS, 1981, 85, 89 (George Foster Peabody award 1989). Mem. NATAS, Writers Guild Am. Office: ABC News 157 Columbus Ave Ste 600 New York NY 10023-5907

MARBURGER, JOHN HARMEN, III, university president, physics educator; b. S.I., N.Y., Feb. 8, 1941; s. John H., Jr. and Virginia A. (Smith) M.; m. Carol Preston Godfrey, June 12, 1965; children: John Harmen, Alexander Godfrey. B.A. in Physics magna cum laude, Princeton U., 1962; Ph.D. in Applied Physics (NASA trainee), Stanford U., 1967. Physicist Goddard Space Flight Center, NASA, 1962-63; asst. prof. physics and elec. engring. U. So. Calif., Los Angeles, 1966-69, assoc. prof., 1969-75, prof., 1975-80, chmn. physics dept., 1972-75, interim dean Coll. Letters, Arts and Scis., 1976-77, dean Coll. Letters, Arts and Scis., 1977-80; prof. physics and elec. engring., pres. SUNY, Stony Brook, 1980—; cons. laser fusion program Lawarence Livermore Labs., 1972-75; chmn. N.Y. State fact finding panel on Shoreham Nuclear Power Facility, 1983; chmn. bd. trustees Universities Rsch. Assn., 1988—; bd. dirs. N.Y. State Edn. and Rsch. Network, Inc., 1986-88. Contbr. articles to tech. publs. Bd. dirs. Mus. at Stony Brook, 1980—, L.I. Assn., Inc., 1983—, Action Com. for L.I., 1980-83, L.I. Forum for Tech., Inc., 1980—, Rsch. Found. SUNY, 1990—; bd. trustees Princeton U., 1985-89; chmn. N.Y. State Energy Office Rev. Commn., 1980-81, Suffolk County (N.Y.) Task Force on Priorities in Fin., 1980-81; campaign chmn. United Way of L.I., 1991—. Recipient Shuichi Kusaka Meml. Prize Princeton U., 1962. Mem. Assn. of Colls. and Univs. State of N.Y. (pres. 1988-89), Coleman Chamber Music Assn. (bd. dirs. 1969-80). Office: SUNY Office of Pres Stony Brook NY 11794-0701*

MARCATANTE, JOHN JOSEPH, educational administrator; b. N.Y.C., Mar. 3, 1930; s. Joseph and Matilda Clara (Grasso) M. Student, NYU, 1948-50; AB, Bklyn. Coll., 1955; MS in Edn., Hunter Coll., 1958. English tchr. secondary schs. N.Y.C., 1955-72; asst. prin. Astoria Intermediate Sch., N.Y.C., 1967—; instr. Hunter Coll., 1963; lectr. in edn. Grad. Sch., Queens Coll., N.Y.C., 1965-67. Cons., Anglo-Am. Seminar on Grad. Teaching English, Dartmouth Coll., 1966, Anglo-Am. Seminar on Teaching the Disadvantaged, West Midlands Coll., Great Britain, 1968. Author: Identification and Image Stories, 1964, American Folklore and Legends, 1967, (with others) Macmillan Gateway English Series, 1969, Tales from World Epics, 1990; also numerous articles in profl. jours., poetry; editor: Fourteenth Yearbook N.Y. Society for Experimental Study for Education, 1970. Mem. Nat. Coun. Tchrs. English, N.Y.C. Tchrs. English, Coun. Supervisory Assns., Cath. Tchrs. Assn., Columbia Assn. N.Y.C., Poetry Soc. Am. Home: 52 Daffodil Ln Wantagh NY 11793-1802 Office: 34-51 9th St Long Island City NY 11106

MARCELLA, GABRIEL, foreign affairs educator, writer, consultant; b. Farindola, Italy, Aug. 6, 1942; came to U.S., 1952; s. Filippo Biagio and Gilda (Di Francesco) M.; m. Judith Ferraro, Aug. 27, 1966; children: Maria, Sandra, Anna, Philip. BS, St. Joseph's U., Phila., 1964; MA, Syracuse U., 1967; PhD, Notre Dame U., 1973; diploma, Inter-Am. Def. Coll., Washington, 1983. Instr. Temple U., Phila., 1967-69, 73, St. Joseph's, Rosemont, 1968-69, Rosemont, Chestnut Hill and Immaculata Colls., Phila., 1967-68, Ind. U. at South Bend, 1971-72; fgn. affairs analyst Strategic Studies Inst., Carlisle, Pa., 1974-82; prof., dir. Third World studies U.S. Army War Coll., Carlisle, 1983-87, dir. Third World studies, 1989—; internat. affairs advisor U.S. So. Command, Panama, 1987-89. Author numerous articles on Latin Am. affairs. Fulbright-Hays fellow, Ecuador, 1964-65; recipient Meritorious Civilian Svc. award U.S. Army, 1989. Mem. Middle Atlantic Coun. Latin Am. Studies. Democrat. Roman Catholic. Office: US Army War Coll Carlisle PA 17013-5050

MARCELLO, ROSITA LUISA, education educator; b. Caracas, Venezuela, Mar. 12, 1935; came to U.S., 1958; d. Miguel Antonio and Rita Catherine (Cherubin) Valero; m. Robert Marcello, Sept. 24, 1966; 1 child, Joseph Robert. BA, Columbia U., 1962, MA, 1964; PhD, U. Madrid, 1971. Instr. Dean Jr. Coll., Mass., 1964-66; instr. Hunter Coll. CUNY, 1966-68; instr. Manhattan Coll., Riverdale, N.Y., 1970—. Author: (dictionary) Continent Women Writers, 1991; contbr. articles to profl. jours. Mem. Westchester Hispanic Coalition; sec. cultural affairs com. Tuckahoe High Sch., 1990—. Democrat. Roman Catholic. Office: Manhattan Coll Bronx NY 10471

MARCHAM, TIMOTHY VICTOR, pharmacist; b. New Britain, Conn., June 15, 1943; s. John Nelson and Eileen Agnes (Mannings) M. BS in Pharmacy, U. Conn., 1966. Staff pharmacist Kensington (Conn.) Pharmacy, Inc., 1968-72, New Britain Meml. Hosp., 1972-75; cons. pharmacist Health Care Cons. Corp., West Hartford, Conn., 1976-85; staff pharmacist Conn. Dept. Mental Health/Cedarcrest Regional Hosp., Newington, 1978-85; dir. pharmacy Conn. Dept. Mental Health/Cedarcrest Regional Hosp., 1985-91; corporator New Britain (Conn.) Gen. Hosp., 1974—. Radiol. officer, Civil Preparedness/Emergency Mgmt. Div., Town of Plainville, Conn., 1965—; life mem. New Britain Gen. Hosp. Aux.; pres. New Britain Meml. Hosp. Credit Union, 1974-75; provider, SAC officer Health Systems Agy. of North Cen. Conn., 1976-82. Cpt. CAP, 1974—. Fellow Am. Soc. Cons. Pharmacists; mem. Am. Pharm. Assn., Am. Soc. Hosp. Pharmacists, Conn. Pharm. Assn. (awards and scholarship), Conn. Soc. Hosp. Pharmacists, Pharmacy Alumni Assn.-U. Conn. (life). Republican. Episcopalian. Home: 28 Locust St Plainville CT 06062-2321

MARCHAND, JACQUELYN, foundation administrator; b. Rochester, N.Y., Oct. 17, 1961; d. Leo R. and Frances Mary (Popp) M. BA magna cum laude, SUNY, Albany, 1983; postgrad., U. Rochester, 1990—. Devel. asst. Internat. Ctr. Integrative Studies, N.Y.C., 1984-85; nat. mgr. spl. events Nat. Multiple Sclerosis Soc., N.Y.C., 1985-88; devel. officer Christie Sch., Portland, Oreg., 1988-89; assoc. dir. devel. Monroe Community Coll., Rochester, 1989-90; dir. devel. SUNY Coll. at Brockport Found., 1990—. Bd. dirs. Genesee Valley, Inc. coun. Girl Scouts U.S.A., Rochester, 1991—. Mem. Nat. Soc. Fund Raising Execs., Planned Giving Coun. Upstate N.Y., Rochester Women's Network. Office: SUNY Coll at Brockport Found 305 Allen Brockport NY 14420-2263

MARCHAND, NATHAN, electrical engineer, corporation president; b. Shawinigan Falls, Que., Can., June 20, 1916; came to U.S., 1917; s. Harry and Rebecca (Shapiro) M.; m. Ernesta Jaros, Sept. 30, 1938; children: Mary Ann Marchand McLure, Anthony, Babette Marchand Pachence, Bonnie Jean Marchand Thomas. BEE, CCNY, 1937; MEE, Columbia U., 1941; postgrad., Poly. Inst. N.Y., 1949-51. Profl. engr., Conn. Sr. engr. Internat. Tel. & Tel., Nutley, N.J., 1941-45; lectr. Columbia U., N.Y.C., 1943-47; cons. to industry Sylvania, Internat. Tel. & Tel., U.S. Army, USAF, 1945-49; pres. Marchand Electronic Labs., Inc., Greenwich, Conn., 1949—; cons. U.S. Army R & D Command, St. Louis, 1976-86, U.S. Army Troop Support and Aviation Readiness Command, 1976-86, USAF, Cape Kennedy, Fla., 1951-54, various others.; chmn. spl. com. for micro-navigation and position location systems U.S. Army Lab, Ft. Monmouth, N.J. Author: Ultra High Frequency Techniques, 1942, Ultrahigh Frequency Transmission and Radiation, 1947, Frequency Modulation, 1948; author Antenna Section, bd. editors Data for Radio Engrs., Internat. Tel. & Tel. publ., 1st-5th edits., 1943-68—; contbr. numerous tech. papers and articles to profl. jours.;. Lt. (j.g.) USN, 1943. Fellow IEEE (founder, 1st chmn. Info. Theory Group), AAAS; mem. Sigma Xi, Eta Kappa Nu, Tau Beta Pi. Republican. Office: Marchand Electronic Labs 311 Riversville Rd Greenwich CT 06831-3227

MARCHELOS, GEORGE FRANKLIN, historian, educator, genealogist, writer; b. San Diego, May 29, 1937; s. John and Sadie Viola (Ward) M.; m. Beverly Gayle Gillespie, Sept. 3, 1960. BS in Sci., History, U. Fla., 1960, BA in History, Polit. Sci., 1964, MA in History, Anthropology, 1967; Cert. Advanced Grad. Study, Va. Poly. Inst. and State U., 1980; PhD, Columbia Pacific U., 1983; postgrad., Concordia Coll., Forrest Park, Ill., 1986, U. Md., Columbia, Mo. Cert. secondary, adult, devel., community coll. tchr. Div. chmn. Rappahannock Community Coll., Glenns, Va., 1971-73; dean learning resources Harford Community Coll., Bel Air, Md., 1973-77; dean curriculum, instr. El Paso (Tex.) Community Coll., 1977-79; prin. G&M Distbrs., El Paso, 1978-83; asst. to v.p. Reading (Pa.) Area Community Coll., 1980-81; newspaper editor Dept. Army, Bremerhaven, Fed. Republic Germany, 1981-82; sucessively counselor, tchr., asst. prin., counselor Dept. of Def. Schs., Bremerhaven, 1982-91; prof. U. Md., 1986—, Cen. Tex. Coll., 1986—; cons. Govt. of Ajman, Oman, 1975; instr. humanities, math., history at several colls.; guest speaker on Am. history, Halle, Germany; speaker on antiques and collectibles, Europe; lectr. various colls. and univs. Author: Principles of Packaging Instruction Using A-T Methodology, Witness to History: The Ward Family in the South, 1675-1950, Pensacola in the Civil War, History of Pensacola Confederate Post Marks: A Chronology, The Schleswig-Holstein Question, 1864-71, and others; contbr. numerous articles to profl. jours. and newspapers; developer of IBM assisted library check-out system. Fellow U. Fla., 1965. Mem. Md. Community Colls. Assn. (pres. 1976), Nat. Soc. Genealogy, Assn. Ednl. Tech. (presenter of papers 1973-78), Women in Mgmt. (speaker 1973-79), Am. Assn. Secondary Prins., Overseas Edn. Assn., Assn. Devel. Curriculum and Instrn., Am. Philatelic Soc. (life), Am. Numismatic Assn. (life), SAR, Pioneer Families of Fla., Orginal Venetian Family, Phi Delta Kappa.

MARCHESE, PAUL STEPHAN, architect, industrial designer, consultant; b. b. N.Y.C., June 20, 1945; s. Vincent Joseph and Ruhe Louise (Hilsabeck) M.; m. Madeleine Claire Relyea, May 26, 1969. B in Indsl. Design, Syracuse U., 1968; MS, New Sch. for Social Rsch., 1973. Registered architect, indsl. designer. Architect Port Authority N.Y. and N.J., N.Y.C., 1968-74, sr. architect, 1975-80, project architect, 1980-83, mgr. architecture and planning, 1983-85, chief planning, 1985—; cons. indsl. designer and architect, 1969—. Multiple patentee telecommunications designs; architect 1st fully solar house in Conn., 1977. N.Y. regents scholar, 1963; recipient Creative Achievement award in Indsl. Design, Syracuse U., 1968. Mem. AIA, Indsl. Designers Am., Mensa, Old Greenwich Yacht Club, Belle Haven Club. Libertarian. Home: 276 Riversville Rd Greenwich CT 06831 Office: Port Authority NY and NJ One World Trade Ctr New York NY 10048

MARCHESSAULT, THOMAS EDWARD, economist; b. Cambridge, Mass., July 25, 1948; s. Edward George and Ann Regina (Sieverts) M.; m. Sally Sheedy Jackson, July 14, 1979; 1 stepchild, Sean DeGuerre Jackson. BA in Econs., U. Mass., Boston, 1970; postgrad., U. Md., 1970-75. Economist Research & Coordination div. DOT, Washington, 1974-78, Energy Policy div. DOT, Washington, 1978-82, Office Econs., DOT, Washington, 1982—. Recipient Sec.'s Award for Meritorious Achievement, Sec. of Transp., 1985, Asst. Sec.'s Award for Superior Achievement, 1991. Mem. Am. Econs. Assn., Soc. Govt. Economists, Mobility 2000, Intelligent Vehicle-Hwy. Soc. Am. (sec. instl. issues com.). Home: 23 Redding Ridge Dr Gaithersburg MD 20878-2616 Office: US Dept Transp 400 7th St SW Washington DC 20590-0002

MARCHETTI, RONALD ANDREW, telecommunications executive; b. Ely, Nev., Apr. 7, 1947; s. John Robert and Anne (Soley) M.; m. Kathy Margaret Bazar, June 13, 1970; children: Amy, Matt, Michael. BS, U.S. Naval Acad., 1970; MA, Chapman Coll., 1976; MBA, U. Va., 1978. Commd. ensign USN, 1970, advanced through grades to comdr., 1984, ret., 1989; project mgr. MCI Telecommunications Corp., Washington, 1989-90, dir. corp. adminstrn., 1990—; adj. prof. Am. U., Washington, 1981—. Home: 6500 Tiburon Ct Springfield VA 22152 Office: MCI Telecom Corp 1150 17th St NW Washington DC 20036

MARCHI, LORRAINE JUNE, association executive; b. San Francisco, June 5, 1923; d. Leopold Pulverman and Josephine Lillian (Treiber) Heiman; m. Gene Marchi, Apr. 10, 1943 (div. 1973); children—Gene, Jeffrey, Debra, Beth; m. Robert L. Fastie, Oct. 21, 1973. Student Stanford U., 1941-42, U. Calif.-Berkeley, 1942-43. Founder Com. To Aid Visually Handicapped Children, San Francisco, 1954-57; pres. Aid to Visually Handicapped, San Francisco, 1957-59; exec. dir. Nat. Assn. for Visually Handicapped, San Francisco, 1972—; sec. Calif. Conf. for Exceptional and Rehab. Needs, San Francisco, 1955-66; chmn. bd. Langley Porter Neuropsychiat. Inst., San Francisco, 1966-69. Recipient spl. service award Los Angeles County Soc. Ophthalmology, 1971; honor award Am. Acad. Ophthalmology and Otolaryngology, 1971; cert. of appreciation Am. Acad. Ophthalmology, 1978; named Woman of Yr. San Francisco sect. Nat. Council Jewish Women, 1957, one of Ten Disting. Women San Francisco Examiner Bay Area, 1959. Home: 305 E 24th St New York NY 10010-4011

MARCHILDON, MICHAEL BERT, pediatric surgeon; b. Cape Girardeau, Mo., June 16, 1940; s. Clement Angelo and Lorena (Bagley) M.; m. Katherine Agnes Cius, Feb. 23, 1980; 1 child, Patrick Colin. BS in Chemistry summa cum laude, U. Notre Dame, Ind., 1962; MD, Stanford U., 1968. Resident in surgery Johns Hopkins Hosps., Balt., 1968-70; resident, then chief res. surgery NYU Hosp./Bellevue Hosp., N.Y.C., 1970-73; fellow in pediatric surgery Children's Hosp. L.A./U. So. Calif. Med. Ctr., 1973-75; asst. prof. surgery and pediatrics U. Miami/Jackson (Fla.) Meml. Hosp., 1975-81; assoc. prof. surgery and pediatrics Robert Wood Johnson Med. Sch., U. Medicine & Dentistry N.J., Camden, 1981-89, prof. surgery and pediatrics, 1989—; head div. pediatric surgery Cooper Hosp./U. Med. Ctr., Camden, 1981—; bd. dirs. Southern N.J. Perinatal Coop. Contbr. articles to profl. jours. Big brother Big Bros./Big Sisters, Miami, 1978-81. NSF fellow, 1962. Fellow ACS, Am. Acad. Pediatrics; mem. Am. Pediatric-Surgery Assn. (future meetings chmn. 1980-87), Am. Soc. Parenteral/Enteral Nutrition, Soc. Critical Care Medicine, Phila. Acad. Surgery, Alpha Omega Alpha. Home: 132 Heritage Rd Haddonfield NJ 08033-3408 Office: Cooper Hosp/Univ Med Ctr Ste # 411 3 Cooper Plz Camden NJ 08103

MARCHIO, ALBERT NICHOLAS, II, financial executive; b. Plainfield, N.J., Aug. 8, 1952; s. Albert Nicholas and Helene (Chiara) M.; m. Barbara Mitchell, May 26, 1984; 1 child, Christopher M. BA in Econs., Muhlenberg Coll., 1974; MBA in Acctg., Rutgers U., 1975; postgrad., CUNY, 1982. Sr. tax acct. Amerada Hess Corp., Woodbridge, N.J., 1976-82; tax/treasury mgr. J. Crew/Popular Svcs., Inc., Garfield, N.J., 1982-84; tax mgr. Laura Ashley, Inc., Carlstadt, N.J., 1984-86; dir. taxes Laura Ashley, Inc., Mahwah, N.J., 1986-90, treas., 1990-92; treas. A.L. Labs. Inc., Ft. Lee, N.J., 1992—. Chmn. bd. dirs. Plainfield Area YMCA, 1989—. Mem. Fin. Execs. Inst., Inc., Tax Execs. Inst., Inc., U.K./U.S. Treas.' Group, Alpha Tau Omega (pres. alumni bd. govs. Muhlenberg chpt. 1978—). Republican. Roman Catholic. Home: 157 Meadowbrook Dr North Plainfield NJ 07062-2425

MARCOCCIA, LOUIS GARY, accountant, university administrator; b. Syracuse, N.Y., Nov. 6, 1946; s. George A. and Rose J. (Misita) M.; m. Susan Evelyn Miller, June 21, 1974; 1 child: Rachel Kathryn. BS, Syracuse U., 1968, MS, 1969. CPA, N.Y. Acct. Price Waterhouse & Co., Syracuse, N.Y., 1969-75; dir. internal audit Syracuse U., 1975-76, comptroller, 1976-82, v.p., controller, 1982-85, sr. v.p. bus. and fin., 1985—; bd. dirs. Syracuse Bd. Chase Lincoln First Bank N.A., Univ. Hill Corp.; speaker Harvard U. Inst. Ednl. Mgmt., 1984-88, 90-91. Pres. parish coun. St. Michael's Ch., Syracuse, 1985-88, Syracuse U. Theatre Corp., 1987—; bd. dirs Friends of Burnet Park Zoo, 1987—, Syracuse U. Press, 1982—, Syracuse Sports Corp., 1990-91. Mem. AICPA, N.Y. Soc. CPAs, Nat. Assn. Accts., Fin. Execs. Inst., Inst. Internal Auditors. Republican. Roman Catholic. Clubs: Drumlins (pres. 1976—); Century. Home: Hedge Ln Cazenovia NY 13035-9628 Office: Syracuse U Skytop Rd Syracuse NY 13244-5300

MARCONE, JORGE TOBIAS, linguist, hispanist, educator; b. Lima, Peru, Oct. 28, 1959; came to the U.S., 1987; s. Francisco Bartolomé and Betsy Maria (Flores) M.; m. Roxana Alicia Pinglo, Dec. 20, 1986. B in Humanities, U. Catolica de Peru, 1987; PhD in Spanish, U. Tex., 1992. Prof. Assn. Acad. Trener, Lima, 1981-87; asst. instr. U. Catolica del Peru, Lima, 1986-87, U. Tex., Austin, 1987-91; asst. prof. Rutgers U., New Brunswick, N.J., 1991—. Editor: Literatura I: Materiales de Ensenanza, 1988; contbr. articles to profl. jours. Mem. AAUP, MLA, N.E. MLA, Latin Am. Studies Assn. Office: Rutgers U Dept Spanish and Portuguese Douglass Campus New Brunswick NJ 08903-0270

MARCONIS, CAROLYN MARY, lawyer; b. Pottsville, Pa., Dec. 19, 1957; d. Joseph Thomas and Mary (Nickel) M.; m. Christopher C. Wetherill, May 21, 1988. BS, Lehigh U., 1980; JD, Widener U., 1983. Bar: Pa. 1984, U.S. Dist. Ct. (ea. dist.) Pa., U.S. Ct. Appeals (3d cir.). Tax cons. Bankers Trust Co., N.Y.C., 1984-85; assoc. Law Offices Charles A. Bressi, Jr., Pottsville, 1985—. V.p. bd. dirs. Pottsville YWCA; pres. bd. dirs. Hillside Soc. Prevention of Cruelty to Animals, Inc. Mem. ABA, Pa. Bar Assn., Schuylkill County Bar Assn., Assn. Trial Lawyers Am., Allied Artists, Kiwanis, Phi Delta Delta. Home: 330 Macarthur Crest Orwigsburg PA 17961-1624 Office: Law Offices Charles A Bressi 510 Mahantongo St Pottsville PA 17901-3074

MARCOTTE, BRIAN MICHAEL, state agency administrator; b. Lewiston, Maine, May 29, 1949; s. Roland Louis and Eileen Frances (Hopkins) M. BS, Stonehill Coll., 1971; MA, Clark U., 1973; PhD, Dalhousie, Halifax, N.S., Can., 1977; postgrad., McGill U., 1987, U. Maine, 1988. Asst. prof. biology dept. U. Victoria, Can., 1977-80; asst. prof. Inst. Oceanography McGill U., Montreal, Que., Can., 1980-87; dir. marine scis. Maine Dept. Marine Resources, West Boothbay Harbor, 1987—. Author: Invertebrate Zoology Study Guide, 1978, 79, Harpacticoids in the British Museum, 1982, Crustacean Taxonomy and Systematics, 1982; contbr. numerous articles to profl. jours. Linnean Soc. London fellow, 1985. Recipient Pub. Svc. Commendation U.S. Dept. Commerce, 1991. Mem. AAAS, Oceanography Soc., Internat. Assn. Meiobenthologists, Am. Soc. Zoologists, Am. Fisheries Soc., N.Y. Acad. Scis., The Crustacean Soc. (Award for Excellence in Rsch. 1986). Democrat. Roman Catholic. Office: Maine Dept Marine Resources McKown Pt West Boothbay Harbor ME 04575

MARCOTTE, FRANK BASIL, chemical company executive; b. Derry, N.H., June 6, 1923; s. Frank Conrad and Mary Rose (Domingue) M.; m. Bertha Mae Grass, Feb. 2, 1947; 1 child, Jane. BS, U. N.H., 1946, MS, 1948; PhD, U. Rochester, 1951. Instr. U. N.H., Durham, 1947-48; rsch. chemist Celanese Corp., Corpus Christi, Tex., 1951-53, group leader, 1953-54, sect. head, 1954-55, dir. chem. rsch., 1955-60, v.p., tech. dir., 1960-69; dir. rsch. M.W. Kellogg Co., Piscataway, N.J., 1969-71; v.p., dir. rsch. Sonneborn div. Sonneborn div. Witco Corp., N.Y.C., 1972—. Mem. Am. Chem. Soc. Home: 146 Passaic Ave Summit NJ 07901-1232 Office: Witco Corp 520 Madison Ave New York NY 10022-4213

MARCUCELLA, HENRY, psychologist, educator; b. Brookline, Mass., July 12, 1942; s. Henry and Elinor (DiZacomo) M.; m. Jayne Bradley, Apr. 25, 1965; children: Wendy, Henry. AB, Northeastern U., 1965; AM, Boston U., 1967, PhD, 1972. Asst. prof., assoc. prof. Boston U., 1972-90, prof., 1990—; bd. advisors Cambridge (Mass.) Ctr. Behavioral Studies, 1986—; bd. dirs. Greater Boston Phobia Soc., 1987-88. Contbr. chpts. in books and articles to profl. jours. Grantee NSF, Nat. Inst. Alcohol and Alcoholism. Mem. APA, Internat. Soc. Biomed. Rsch. on Alcoholism, Rsch. Soc. on Alcoholism, Psychonomic Soc., Behavioral Pharmacology Soc. Office: Boston U Dept Psychology 64 Cummington St Boston MA 02215-2407

MARCUM, DEANNA BOWLING, university dean; b. Salem, Ind., Aug. 5, 1946; d. Anderson and Ruby (Mobley) Bowling; m. Thomas P. Marcum, June 13, 1974; 1 child, Ursula. BA, U. Ill., 1964; MA, So. Ill. U., 1969; MLS, U. Ky., 1971; PhD, U. Md., 1991. Tchr. Deland-Weldon (Ill.) High Sch., 1967-68; instr. English U. Ky., Lexington, 1969-70, cataloging librarian, 1970-73, asst. to dir., 1973-74; asst. dir. pub. svcs. Joint U. Librs., Nashville, 1974-77; mgmt. tng. specialist Assn. Rsch. Librs., Washington, 1977-80; sr. cons. Info. Systems Cons., Inc., Washington, 1980-81; v.p. Coun. on Libr. Resources, Washington, 1981-89; dean Sch. Libr. and Info. Sch., Cath. U., Washington, 1989—; adv. bd. So. Edn. Found., Atlanta, 1986—; chmn. grants com. Coun. on Libr. Resources, Washington, 1990—. Co-author: (with Richard Boss) The Library Catalog, 1980, On-Line Acquisitions Systems, 1981; contbr. articles to profl. jours. Mem. ALA, Am. Studies Assn., Orgn. Am. Historians, Am. Antiquarian Soc. (adv. bd. 1989—), Beta Phi Mu, Phi Kappa Phi. Home: 911 Malta Ln Silver Spring MD 20901-1136 Office: Cath U Am Marist Hall 228 Washington DC 20064

MARCUM, JAMES BENTON, college dean; b. Cedar County, Mo., June 25, 1938; s. Ralph Emerson and Mary Amanda (Barrett) M.; m. Carol Marlene Brewer, Dec. 26, 1964; children: Eric Bentley, Lara Beth, Sara Bethany. BSAgr, U. Mo., 1960; MS, Cornell U., 1961; MDiv, Midwest Bapt. Sem., 1965; PhD, U. Mo., 1969. Lectr. U. Libya, Tripoli, 1969-71; asst. prof. U. Mass., Amherst, 1971-77, assoc. prof., 1977-85, dept. chmn., 1979-85, prof., assoc. dean Coll. Food and Nat. Resources, 1985—; bd. dirs. Mass. Agr. in the Classroom, Inc., 1985—. Deacon North Leverett (Mass.) Bapt. Ch., 1973—, chmn. deacons, 1975-76, 78-79, 83-84, 87-88, choir dir. , 1972—. Mem. Am. Assn. Higher Edn., Am. Genetic Assn., Am. Soc. Animal Sci., Nat. Assn. Colls. and Tchrs. Agr., Coun. Agrl. Sci. and Tech., Amherst Camera Club (pres. 1977-79), Hampshire Bird Club (pres 1988-91), Sigma Xi, Gamma Sigma Delta, Alpha Zeta. Office: U Mass 111 Stockbridge Hall Amherst MA 01003

MARCUS, ERIC COLTON, social psychologist, organizational consultant; b. N.Y.C., July 18, 1957; s. Peter and Esther (Falkenstein) M.; m. Amy L. Glantzman, Sept. 9, 1987; 1 child, Elli Caroline. BA, SUNY, Binghamton, 1979; MA, Columbia U., 1982, PhD, 1985. Prin. The Marcus Group, N.Y.C., 1985—. Mem. Acad. Mgmt., Am. Psychol. Assn., Orgn. Devel. Network, Human Resource Planning Soc., Internat. Assn. Conflict Mgmt., Soc. Indsl. and Orgnl. Psychology, Met. N.Y. Assn. Applied Psychology, Sigma Xi. Home: 150 Bennett Ave Apt 2K New York NY 10040-3811

MARCUS, ERIC ROBERT, psychiatrist; b. N.Y.C., Feb. 16, 1944; s. Victor and Pearl (Maddow) M.; m Eslee Samberg, Nov. 24, 1985; children: Max Thomas, Pia. AB, Columbia U., 1965; MD, U. Wis., 1969. Diplomate Am. Bd. Psychiatry and Neurology. Intern NYU Med. Ctr. Bellevue Hosp., 1969-70; resident Columbia Presbyn. Med. Ctr.-N.Y. State Psychiatric Inst., 1972-75; dir. St. Marks Free Clinic, N.Y.C., 1971-75; from co-dir. to dir. neuropsychiatric/diagnostic treatment unit Columbia-Presbyn. Med. Ctr., N.Y.C., 1975-84; dir. med. student edn. in psychiatry Columbia U. Coll. Physicians and Surgeons, N.Y.C., 1981—; assoc. clin. prof. psychiatry and social medicine Columbia U. Coll. Physicians and Surgeons, 1981—; mem. faculty Columbia U. Ctr. for Psychoanalytic Tng. and Rsch., 1987—; bd. govs. student health Columbia U., 1986. Author: Psychosis and Near Psychosis, 1992; mem. editorial bd. The Psychoanalytic Study of Society, 1989—; contbr. articles to profl. jours. Grants and edn. com. Am. Cancer Soc., N.Y.C., 1988—. Recipient Weber award Columbia U. Psychoanalytic Ctr., 1991. Fellow Am. Psychiat. Assn. (Roeske award 1991), Am. Psychoanalytic Assn., N.Y. Acad. Medicine. Office: Columbia U Dept Psychiatry 722 W 168th St New York NY 10032-2603

MARCUS, GAIL BOXER, insurance company executive; b. Bklyn., June 26, 1956; d. Maurice Frank and Alice (Schner) Boxer; m. Peter C. Marcus, Sept. 22, 1982. BA, Wesleyan U., Middletown, Conn., 1978; MBA, MSE, U. Pa., 1980. Internal auditor Conn. Gen., CIGNA, Bloomfield, 1979, strategic planner, 1980-81, asst. dir. corp. systems, 1981-83, dir. expense adminstrn., 1983-86; asst. v.p. group pension Conn. Gen., CIGNA, Hartford, 1985-90, asst. v.p. treasury, 1990—. Bd. dirs. Campfire Girls, Hartford. Home: 48 Howey Rd Ashford CT 06278-1013 Office: CIGNA S-256 350 Church St Hartford CT 06152

MARCUS, JEFFREY ARTHUR, clothing company executive; b. N.Y.C., Nov. 1, 1953; s. Stanley and Ruth (Bursuk) M.; m. Jill Elen Braunstein, Sept. 12, 1976; children: Andrew, Michael. BA in Acctg., CUNY, 1977. CPA, N.Y., N.J. Jr. acct. Baron, Bergstein & Weinberg, CPAs, N.Y.C., 1976-78; semi-sr. acct. Vengrove, Zapolsky, Dworkin and McCourt, CPAs, Great Neck, N.Y., 1978; sr. acct. Stephen J. Furst & Co. CPAs, N.Y.C., 1978-81; contr. Andy Johns Fashions, Inc., Clifton, N.J., 1981-86, v.p., contr., 1986-

91, v.p., treas. Mackintosh of New England Co., 1991—; v.p. fin. and adminstrn. Biscayne Apparel, Inc., Clifton, N.J., 1991—. Mem. AICPA, N.J. State Soc. CPAs. Office: Andy Johns Fashions Div Biscayne Apparel Inc 1373 Broad St Clifton NJ 07013-4221

MARCUS, MARIE ELEANOR, pianist; b. Roxbury, Mass., May 25, 1914; d. Frank John and Mary Veronica (McDonough) Doherty; (widowed 1965); children: Jack Brown, Mary Liles, Billy Marcus, Barbara Marcus. Grad. high sch., Roxbury. Freelance jazz pianist various clubs including Venetian Palace, 52d Swing Club, 1933—; freelance jazz pianist for depression era entrepreneurs Dutch Schultz, Frank Costello, 1933—. Performer piano jazz series with Marion McDartland, 1982 (George Foster Peabody medal 1982); featured in book: Alec Wilder and His Friends (Whitney Balliet), 1972, also featured in video about her life, family and career, 1989. Pres. Cape Cod Jazz Soc., Dennisport, Mass., 1983—. Recipient 50th Anniversary in Show Bus. tribute Am. Heart Assn., 1982. Democrat. Roman Catholic. Home and Office: 62 Center St Dennis Port MA 02639-1561

MARCUS, MICHAEL JAY, electical engineer; b. Boston, May 13, 1914; s. Theodore and Mildred (Horowitz) M.; m. Gail Halpern, June 9, 1968. BS, MIT, 1968, ScD, 1972. Project officer USAF, Alexandria, Va., 1972-75; mem. tech. staff Inst. for Def. Analysis, Arlington, Va., 1975-79; chief tech. dir. analysis FCC Office Sci. & Tech., Washington, 1979-87; asst. chief for tech. FCC Field Ops. Bur., Washington, 1987—; cons. Bell Telephone Labs., Murray Hill, N.J., 1966-72. Recipient FCC Engr. award Nat. Soc. Profl. Engrs., 1990. Mem. IEEE, MIT Club Washington (dir. 1974—, pres. 1978). Home: 8026 Cypress Grove Ln Cabin John MD 20818-1003 Office: FCC/ FOB 1919 M St NW Washington DC 20554-0002

MARCUS, RICHARD WARREN, pediatrician, educator; b. Englewood, N.J., Apr. 23, 1955; s. Melvin and Lillian Marcus; m. Deborah J. Fox, Aug. 26, 1982; children: Melanie, Alison. BA, Rutgers Coll., 1977; MD, N.J. Med. Sch., 1982. Diplomate Nat. Bd. Med. Examiners, Am. Bd. Pediatrics. Intern-resident in pediatrics Univ. Medicine and Dentistry of N.J. Children's Hosp. N.J., Newark, 1982-85; assoc. attending physician Clara Maass Med. Ctr., Belleville, N.J., 1985-90; attending physician Clara Maass Med. Ctr., Belleville, 1990-92; assoc. attending physician Mountainside Hosp., Montclair, N.J., 1987-92; pvt. practice pediatrics and adolescent medicine, 1985—; clin. instr. dept. pediatrics U. Medicine and Dentistry of N.J., Newark, 1987; clin. assoc. prof. Seton Hall Grad. Sch. Med. Edn., Orange, N.J., 1990. Bd. dirs. Clifton (N.J.) Jewish Ctr., 1990-92. Named Henry Rutgers scholar Rutgers Coll., New Brunswick, 1977. Fellow Am. Acad. Pediatrics; mem. AMA, N.J. Pediatric Soc. Office: 25 High St Nutley NJ 07110

MARCUSE, WILLIAM, technology transfer executive; b. Fairfield, Conn., Aug. 4, 1924; s. Sidney and Jeanette (Holzmasser) M.; m. Shirley Rozinsky; children: Jason C., Steven M. BA, U. Conn., 1947, MA, 1948; PhD, Columbia U., 1956. Cert. cost analyst. Asst. prof. U. Conn., Storrs, 1948-56; analyst OEG of MIT, Washington, 1956-60; assoc. dept. head Mitre Corp., Bedford, Mass., 1960-69; div. head Brookhaven Nat. Lab., Upton, N.Y., 1969-82; office head Brookhaven Nat. Lab., 1983—; detailee Dept. of Energy, Washington, 1980-82. Capt. USAR, 1944-64. Fellow AAAS; mem. Ops. Rsch. Soc. Am., Am. Econ. Assn., Tech. Transfer Soc. Democrat. Home: 107 Jefferson Ave Prt Jefferson NY 11777-2017 Office: Brookhaven Nat Lab Bldg 475 Upton NY 11973

MARDER, ARNOLD ROBERT, materials science and engineering educator; b. Bklyn., Oct. 24, 1940; s. Charles and Eva (Obludziner) M.; m. Carole Betty Gordon, June 16, 1962; children: Alice Marder Notis, Sara, Tamara. BSME, Poly. Inst. Bklyn., 1962, MSME, 1965; PhD in Met. and Mat. Sci., Lehigh U., 1968. Registered profl. engr., Pa. Engr. Curtiss-Wright Corp., Woodridge, N.J., 1962-65; engr. rsch. dept. Bethlehem (Pa.) Steel Corp., 1965-68, supr. rsch. dept., 1968-80, sr. scientist, 1980-86; assoc. dir. energy rsch. ctr. Lehigh U., 1986—, prof. mat. sci. and engring., 1991—; adj. prof., mat. sci. and engring. Lehigh U., 1982-91. Co-editor: Energy Efficient Electrical Steels, 1981, Phase Transf. In Ferrous Alloys, 1984; contbr. numerous articles to profl. jours.; patentee in field. Fellow Am. Soc. Metals Internat.; mem. ASTM (Villela award 1974), Internat. Metallographic Soc., Soc. Automotive Engrs., Nat. Assn. of Corrosion Engrs., Am. Welding Soc., The Metallurgical Soc./AIME, Sigma Xi, Alpha Sigma Mu. Office: Lehigh U Whittaker Lab Bethlehem PA 18015

MARDER, TOD ALLAN, architectural history educator, editor; b. L.A., June 1, 1947; s. Arthur Jacob and Jan (North) M.; m. Margaret Kuntz, May 21, 1983; 1 child, Hillary Jan. BA with high honors, U. Calif., Santa Barbara, 1969; PhD, Columbia U., 1976. Asst. prof. architectural history Rutgers U., New Brunswick, N.J., 1975-80, assoc. prof., 1980—, chmn. dept. art history, 1984-86; mem. exec. coun. Grad. Sch., Rutgers U., 1984-88. Co-producer (PBS film) More Than Shelter, 1988; contbr. articles to scholarly jours. Gladys Delmas Found. rsch. fellow, Venice, Italy, 1982; Ailsa Mellon Bruce sr. fellow Ctr. for Advanced Study in Visual Arts, Nat. Gallery of Art, Washington, 1989; Graham Found. rsch. grantee, Chgo., 1990-91. Mem. Coll. Art Assn., Soc. Archtl. Historians (bd. dirs., exec. com. 1986-90, editor-in-chief jour. 1987-90). Office: Rutgers U Dept Art History Voorhees Hall New Brunswick NJ 08903

MARETH, PAUL, communications consultant; b. N.Y.C., Nov. 16, 1945; s. Josef Gleicher and Elisabeth (Feitler) Gay; m. Evelyn Heineman, Dec. 26, 1968(div. 1980); children: Leda J., Joanna R. BA, Brandeis U., 1967; MFA, UCLA, 1969. Lectr. U. Pitts., 1976-77; asst. prof. communications Temple U., Phila., 1977-81; vis. faculty fellow in history of sci. Princeton (N.J.) U., 1981-82; founder, owner Projections Co., White Plains, N.Y., 1982—; cons. IBM, RCA, Bell Labs., Ednl. Testing Svc., Children's TV Workshop, Prodigy. Contbr. to Acad. Am. Ency., 1985—, Channels of Communications, 1983-85; editorial advisor IEEE Jour., IEEE Spectrum, 1983-84; contbr. numerous articles to profl. jours. Bd. dirs. Westchester Choral Soc., 1991—, v.p. Grantee WGBH Pub. TV, Boston, 1974, Swedish Film Inst./ Swedish Broadcasting Corp., 1973, Pa. Coun. on the Arts, 1976, 79. Mem. Soc. Motion Picture and TV Engrs., Internat. Interactive Communications Soc. (chmn. program com. 1987-90), Univ. Film/Video Assn. Office: Projections Co 14 Nosband Ave #6D White Plains NY 10605

MARETZO, RICHARD JOSEPH, dentist; b. Bklyn., Dec. 16, 1934; s. Charles Barthelemew and Mildred (Pezzoni) M.; m. Teresa Mary Markey, June 18, 1955; 1 child, Richard Joseph, Jr. BS, Fairleigh Dickinson U., 1961, DMD, 1965. Dentist Suffern, N.Y., 1965—. 2d lt. U.S. Army Res., 1957-68. Holder five world records in benchrest shooting, winner internat. championships, 1983-85, Hall of Fame, 1990. Mem. Am. Dental Assn., Ninth Dist. Dental Soc., Acad. Gen. Dentistry, Rockland County Dental Soc., Good Samaritan Hosp. Staff. Republican. Roman Catholic. Home: 67 Flaming Arrow Rd Mahwah NJ 07430-1354 Office: 29 N Airmont Rd Suffern NY 10901-4221

MARGARITIS, JOHN PAUL, public relations executive; b. N.Y.C., June 8, 1949; s. George H. and Mary (Liakos) M.; m. Charlene Coreman, Feb. 21, 1982. BA in English, Washington and Jefferson Coll., 1971; MA in Media Studies, New Sch. Social Rsch., 1977. Account exec. Hank Boerner & Assocs., Uniondale, N.Y., 1974-76; account exec. Manning, Selvage & Lee, N.Y.C., 1976-77; account supr. Gen. Electric Co., N.Y.C., 1977-79, Burson-Marsteller, Inc., Chgo., 1979-80; v.p., dir. client services Burson-Marsteller, Inc., Los Angeles, 1980-82; exec. v.p., gen. mgr., sr. ptnr. Fleishman-Hillard, Inc., Los Angeles, 1982-88; chmn., chief exec. officer Ogilvy & Mather Pub. Relations, N.Y.C., 1988-92; pres., chief oper. officer Ogilvy Adams and Rinehart, 1992—, also bd. dirs. 1st lt. U.S. Army, 1972-74. Mem. Pub. Rels. Soc. Am. (hons. and awards com. 1986-89, counselors acad. 1985—), Am. Assn. Advt. Agy. (pub. rels. com.), Alpine Country Club. Republican. Greek Orthodox. Home: 38 Hidden Ledge Rd Englewood NJ 07631-5125 Office: Ogilvy Adams and Rinehart 708 3d Ave New York NY 10017

MARGETIAK, CHARLENE JEAN, career counselor; b. Corning, N.Y., Feb. 25, 1954; d. Milton Henry and Loretta Jean (Allen) Stiles; m. Joseph Steven Margetiak, May 28, 1977; children: J. Stefan, Corine Kirsten. AS in Bus. Adminstrn., Pa. State U., Erie, 1979; AS in Sec. Sci., Edinboro U. Pa., 1981, BA in Acctg., 1985, MA in Student Pers. Svcs., 1987; postgrad., Pa. State U. Asst. bookkeeper Overhead Door Co., Du Bois, Pa., 1977-78; acct. Specialty Communications, Erie, 1978-79; clk.-typist Williams and Co., Erie, 1979-80; accounts payable supr. RPS Auto Supply, Erie, 1980-81; student sec. Edinboro U., 1981-82, clk.-typist II, 1982-86, clk.-typist III, 1986-87, office mgr., 1987-88; career counselor Pa. State U., Du Bois, 1988—, elem. keyboarding instr., 1991—; evening peer counselor Edinboro U., 1985-86; grad. intern Pa. State U., Erie, 1986-87; dir. New Horizons, Du Bois, 1989-91. Pres. Choices Program Bell of Pa., Clearfield County, 1990—. With Security Agy., U.S. Army, 1972-76. Mem. ACA, AAUW (bd. dirs.), Nat. Employment Counselors Assn., Nat. Career Devel. Assn., Pa. Coll. Pers. Assn., Human Resource Mgmt. Assn. North Cen. Pa., Am. Coll. Counselors Assn., Clearfield County Coop. Extension-Pa. State U. (master gardener pub. rels. 1991—), DuBois Campus Alumni Soc. Pa. State U. (dir. 1989—). Home: 836 Treasure Lk Du Bois PA 15801-9017 Office: Pa State U DuBois College Pl Du Bois PA 15801

MARGOLIES, GEORGE HOWARD, lawyer, consultant; b. N.Y.C., Feb. 22, 1948; s. Leo and Edith Rose (Kraus) M.; m. Roberta Emanuel, Oct. 8, 1972; children: Janis, Lisa. BA, Am. U., Washington, 1968; JD, 1971. Bar: N.Y. 1973, D.C. 1974, U.S. Dist. Ct. D.C. 1974, Md. 1980. Legis. asst. Nat. Fedn. Fed. Employees, Washington, 1971-72; labor atty. N.Y.C. Bd. Edn., 1972-73; labor counsel D.C. Pub. Schs., Washington, 1973-76, legal counsel to D.C. supt. schs., 1976-89; ad hoc consumer arbitrator Office Consumer Affairs, County of Montgomery, Rockville, Md., 1976-89; ad hoc hearing officer County of Montgomery, 1980-89; ad hoc hearing examiner D.C. Office Human Rights, Washington, 1984—; edn. and labor-mgmt. cons., 1989—; adj. prof. Am. U., 1975-77, 79; bd. dirs. Interages, Inc. Pres. College Gardens PTA, 1985-86, Julius West PTA, 1988-89; chair Montgomery Com. on Children and Youth, 1989-91, Com. for Montgomery, 1991-92. Recipient Disting. Alumni award Am. U., 1984. Mem. D.C. Unified Bar Assn., Am. U. Alumni Assn. (pres. & chmn. 1979-83), Omicron Delta Kappa. Democrat. Jewish.

MARGOLIN, CARL M., psychotherapist; b. N.Y.C., Jan. 23, 1939; s. Samuel and Henrietta (Kressel) M.; B.A., CUNY, 1961; M.S.W., Columbia U., 1965; postgrad. Nat. Psychol. Assn. for Psychoanalysis, 1968-70; m. Susie Echols Watts, Feb. 10, 1964; children—Christopher, Andrew. Sr. psychiat. social worker W.J.C.S., White Plains, N.Y., 1964-76; psychotherapist Whitehill Counseling Service, Yorktown Hights, N.Y., 1973-76; pvt. practice psychotherapy, 1976—; tng. supr. Yeshiva U., 1972-76. Mem. exec. com. No. Westchester Mental Health Council, 1973-79, chmn. planning com., 1975-79. Cert. social worker, N.Y. State. Mem. Nat. Assn. Social Workers (diplomate), Acad. Cert. Social Workers, Soc. Clin. Social Work Psychotherapists (bd. cert. diplomate in clin. social work). Office: 344 E Main St Mount Kisco NY 10549-3027

MARGOLIN, JEAN MADAY, real estate broker; b. N.Y.C., July 27, 1937; d. William Thomas and Beatrice (Fritz) Maday; m. David H. Wolk, Sept. 25, 1960 (div. 1972); children: Richard S., Judith B.; m. Richard H. Margolin, Nov. 16, 1975. BA, NYU, 1959. Sec. Dept. Fin., N.Y.C., 1960-61; energy cons. Honeywell, Inc., N.Y.C., 1972-75; real estate salesman Sammis Real Estate, Cold Spring Harbor, N.Y., 1978-83; real estate broker Daniel Gale Assocs., East Norwick, N.Y., 1983—. Named Top Producer Sammis Real Estate, 1983, Daniel Gale Assocs., 1987, 88, 89. Republican. Home: 687 Donna Dr Oyster Bay NY 11771-4512

MARGOLIN, MILTON, sales and marketing professional; b. Boston, Feb. 26, 1930; s. William and Bessie M.; A.S., Boston U., 1952; m. Roberta Fradin, Oct. 27, 1957; children—Robin Ellen, Susan Beth. Owner, dir. Reliable Metal Co., Randolph, Mass., 1965-68; staff sales rep. Research Inst. Am., N.Y.C., 1968-82; owner, mgr. Reliable Metal Co., Ltd., 1982—; exec. sales cons. Matthew Bender Co., N.Y.C., 1983; br. coordinator consumer direct div. Bose Corp., Framingham, Mass., 1984—; dir. sales and mktg., Best of New Eng. Pubs., Newton, Mass., 1986—; dir. nat. and internat. sales and mktg. Royale Limosine Mfg. Co., Haverhill, Mass., 1987—, pres. Insight Sales and Mktg. Assocs., Randolph, Mass., 1988. Served with USNR, 1950-52. Democrat. Clubs: Dorchester, Roxbury, Mattapan Assn., Enrol Assn., K.P., Knights of Khorassan. Inventor Hulabee and Lost Marbles toys. Home and Office: 5 Mcauliffe Rd Randolph MA 02368-3846

MARGOLIS, DAVID I(SRAEL), corporate executive; b. N.Y.C., Jan. 24, 1930; s. Benjamin and Celia (Kosofsky) M.; m. Barbara Schneider, Sept. 7, 1958; children: Brian, Robert, Peter, Nancy. BA, CCNY, 1950, MBA, 1952; postgrad., NYU, 1952-55. Security analyst Josephthal Co., 1952-56; asst. treas. Raytheon Co., 1956-59; treas. IT&T, N.Y.C., 1959-62; with Coltec Industries Inc. (formerly Colt Industries Inc.), N.Y.C., 1962—, now chmn., chief exec. officer; bd. dirs. Burlington Industries, Offitbank. Mem. bd. trustee Presbyn. Hosp. City N.Y.; bd. overseers NYU Stern Sch. Bus. Mem. Coun. Fgn. Rels. Office: Coltec Industries Inc 430 Park Ave New York NY 10022-3505

MARGOLIS, GERALD JOSEPH, psychiatrist, psychoanalyst; b. Bronx, N.Y., May 7, 1935; s. Max and Sophie (Siegel) M.; A.B., U. Rochester, 1957; M.D., U. Chgo., 1960; postgrad. Inst. Phila. Assn. Psychoanalysis, 1972; m. June Edelman Greenspan, July 13, 1976; children—David J., Peter S., Steven J. Intern, psychiat. resident, Upstate Med. Center, SUNY, Syracuse, 1960-64, instr. psychiatry, 1966-67; from instr. to clin. prof. psychiatry Med. Sch., U. Pa., Phila., 1967—; practice medicine specializing in psychiatry and psychoanalysis, Cherry Hill, N.J.; tng. and supervising analyst Inst. of Phila. Assn. for Psychoanalysis. Served with M.C., USAF, 1964-66. Diplomate Am. Bd. Psychiatry and Neurology. Mem. Am. Psychoanalytic Assn. (cert.), Am. Psychiat. Assn., AMA, Phila. Assn. for Psychoanalysis (tng. and supervising analyst), Phi Beta Kappa. Club: B'nai B'rith. Contbr. articles to profl. pubis. Home: 103 Sussex Dr Riverton NJ 08077-3834 Office: One Cherry Hill Ste 930 Cherry Hill NJ 08002

MARGOLIS, HOWARD, reading educator, special education educator; b. Bklyn., Aug. 27, 1943; s. Benjamin and Sue (Algaze) M.; children: David, Brian, Kelly; m. Marylee McCormick, Nov. 29, 1985. BA, Bklyn. Coll., 1965; MS, Kean Coll. N.J., 1968; EdD, Hofstra U., 1974. Cert. reading specialist, spl. edn. educator, sch. psychologist. Spl. edn. tchr. Newark Bd. Edn., 1965-66, Basking Ridge (N.J.) Bd. Edn., 1966-68, Bd. Coop. Ednl. Svcs., Hicksville, N.Y., 1968-69; reading cons. Connetquot Sch. System, Oakdale, N.Y., 1969-74; coord. R&D program Comprehensive Ednl. Ctr. SUNY, Plattsburgh, 1974-76, assoc. prof. spl. edn., 1976-77; dir. interdisciplinary tng. Developmental Disabilities Ctr. Temple U., Phila., 1977-81; dir. program devel. Star Systems Consultation, Phila., 1981-84; prof. reading CUNY, Flushing, 1984—; cons. N.Y.C. Bd. Edn., 1987-89, Annual Gov.'s Round Table in Developmental Disabilities, Del., 1985; seminar leader Pa. State Hershey Med. Ctr., 1983—, N.J. Sch. Bd. Assn., Trenton, 1986—. Editor Reading and Writing Quar., 1989—, Reading Instructional Jour., 1989-90, Jour. of Ednl. and Psycho. Consultation; contbr. articles to profl. jours. Mem. Internat. Reading Assn., Assn. for Ednl. and Psychol. Consultants (jour. editor 1987—), Learning Disabilities Assn. (Svc. to Children of N.J. award 1990). Home: 1067 Pendleton Ct Voorhees NJ 08043-1809 Office: CUNY Queens Coll 051-PH-DECP Flushing NY 11367-0904

MARGOLIS, LAWRENCE STANLEY, federal judge, educator; b. Phila., Mar. 13, 1935; s. Reuben and Mollie (Manus) M.; m. Doris May Rosenberg, Jan. 30, 1960; children: Mary Aleta, Paul Oliver. B.S.M.E., Drexel U., 1957; J.D., George Washington U., 1961. Bar: D.C. 1963. Patent examiner U. S. Patent Office, Washington, 1957-62; patent counsel Naval Ordnance Lab., White Oak, Md., 1962-63; asst. corp. counsel D.C., 1963-66; atty. criminal div., spl. asst. U.S. atty. Dept. of Justice, Washington, 1966-68; asst. U.S. atty. for D.C., 1968-71; U.S. magistrate U.S. Dist. Ct., Washington, 1971-82; judge U.S. Claims Ct., Washington, 1982—, chmn. alt. dispute resolution, chmn. task force on discovery reform; mem. faculty Fed. Jud. Ctr., 1973—. Editor-in-chief: The Young Lawyer, 1965-66, D.C. Bar. Jour., 1967-73; bd. editor: The Dist. Lawyer, 1978-82. Trustee Drexel U., 1983-89; bd. govs. George Washington U. Alumni Assn., 1978-85. Recipient contbn. award D.C. Jaycees, 1966, svc. award Boy Scouts Am., 1970; Alumni Svc. award George Washington U., 1976, Disting. Alumni Achievement award, 1985; Disting. Alumni Achievement award Drexel U., 1988, Drexel 100 award, 1992; Alt. Dispute Resolution award Ctr. for Pub. Resources, 1988. Fellow Inst. Jud. Adminstrn., Am. Bar Found.; mem. D.C. Jud. Conf., ABA (chmn. jud. adminstrn. div., Disting. Svc. award 1981), Bar Assn. D.C. (bd. dirs. 1970-72, editor-in-chief contbn. award, award young lawyers sect. 1983), Fed. Bar Assn., George Washington U. Nat. Law Assn. (pres. D.C. chpt. 1974-76, pres. 1983-84), ABA Nat. Conf. Spl. Ct. Judges (chmn., Disting. Svc. award 1978), Nat. Lawyers Club, Rotary (bd. dirs. Washington, 1984-90, pres. 1988-89, dist. gov.1991-92, Rotarian of Yr. award 1984, Outstanding Pres. award 1989). Office: US Claims Ct 717 Madison Pl NW Ste 703 Washington DC 20005-1011

MARGOLIS, PHYLLIS, school social worker; b. Bklyn., Mar. 11, 1929; d. Max and Sylvia (Brodsky) Teichberg; m. Sidney O. Margolis, June 24, 1950; children: Jonathan, Dean, Brian. BS cum laude, CUNY, 1949; postgrad., Adelphi U., 1954-55; MSW, NYU, 1972; MA, Coll. of New Rochelle, 1988. Cert. social worker; cert. supr. sch. social workers. Sch. social worker Archdiocese of N.Y., N.Y.C., 1972-77; sch. social worker com. on spl. edn. N.Y.C. Bd. Edn., 1977—. Mem. NASW. Home: 10 W 86th St New York NY 10024 Office: NYC Bd Edn Com on Spl Edn 420 E 106th St New York NY 10029

MARGULIES, HERMAN, artist, educator; b. Boryslaw, Poland, Dec. 7, 1922; came to U.S., 1951; s. Aron and Mina (Rinzler) M.; 1 child, Alan Margulies. Student, Royal Acad. Fine Arts, Brussels, 1947-49. Tchr. pastel painting Washington (Conn.) Studio, 1986—; juror El Paso Tex. Mus. of Art Exhibn. 1989, Kansas Pastel Soc. Nat. Exhibn., Wichita, 1989. Artist: pastel paintings, Bergen, N.J. Mus. (Best in Show 1983), Pastel Soc. of Am. (Exceptional Merit 1983, 1986), Audubon Artists (Isenberg Award 1989); paintings in many collections including Yad Vashem Mus., Mktg. Corp. of Am., Conn. Bank & Trust Co., Xerox, Pepsico. Recipient more than 100 awards including award of Excellence Middlesex Mus., North Brunswick, N.J., 1985, Spaulding award Hudson Valley Art Assn., White Plains, N.Y., 1986, 88, 90. Fellow Am. Artists Profl. League (1st pastel award 1987); mem. Pastel Soc. Am. (bd. dirs. 1983-85, 5 awards, elected Master Pastelist 1985), Hudson Valley Art Assn. (bd. dirs. 1984-89), Knickerbocker Artsists N.Y. (pres. 1985-90, award 1983-84, Gold medal for Disting. Achievement 1991), Allied Artists Am. N.Y. (bd. dirs. 1988—, PSA award 1987, 89), Audubon Artists, Nat. Arts Club, Salmagundi Club (1st pastel award 1991). Home: 32 Revere Rd Washington Depot CT 06793-1007

MARGULIES, JAMES HOWARD, editorial cartoonist; b. Bklyn., Oct. 8, 1951; s. Henry Norman and Miriam Margulies; m. Martha Anne Golub, May 21, 1978; children: Elana, David. BFA, Carnegie-Mellon U., 1973. Editorial cartoonist Jour. Newspapers, Springfield, Va., 1980-84, Houston Post, 1984-90, The Record, Hackensack, N.J., 1990—; syndicated cartoonist various newspapers, 1985—. Author: My Husband is Not a Wimp, 1988; contbr. columns to profl. jours.; cartoons featured on TV programs. Mem. leadership com. Jewish Community Ctr., Houston, 1987, 88. Recipient Best Cartoon award Population Inst., 1985, Global Media award Population Inst., 1985, 2d Place Editorial award Pavillion of Humor, 1985, Judges award World Hunger Media Awards, 1986, Katie award Press Club of Dallas, 1989, Best Black and White Illustration in Advt. and Graphic Arts Addy award Houston Ad Fedn., 1990; named one of Texans Who Made The Eighties winter Ultra Mag., 1990. Mem. Assn. Am. Editorial Cartoonists. Office: The Record 150 River St Hackensack NJ 07601-7110

MARGULIS, THOMAS N., chemist, lawyer; b. N.Y.C., Sept. 7, 1937; s. William and Sonia (Liff) M.; m. Jane Emily Starkman, Sept. 8, 1990; children: Zachary, Jennifer. Bs, MIT, 1959; PhD, U. Calif., Berkeley, 1962; JD, New Eng. Sch. of Law, Boston, 1992. Asst. prof. Brandeis U., Waltham, Mass., 1962-67; prof. chemistry U. Mass., Boston, 1967—; cons. in field; nat. lectr. for Sigma Xi. Contbr. articles on crystallography to profl. jours. Mem. Am. Crystallographic Assn., Sigma Xi. Home: 106 Gibbs St Newton MA 02159-1928 Office: U Mass Dept Chemistry Boston MA 02125-3393

MARIANI, ANGELO, accountant; b. Bronx, Jan. 7, 1963; s. Louis and Marie Mariani; m. Lorraine Giuffra, Apr. 17, 1988; 1 child, Lauren Nicole. BBA in Pub. Acctg. cum laude, Iona Coll., 1985. Sr. acct. IBM, Mt. Pleasant, N.Y., 1985—. Mem. Inst. Mgmt. Accts. Republican. Roman Catholic. Home: 141 Deer Run Chappaqua NY 10514-3722

MARIANI, DAVID FRANK, artist; b. Buffalo, Jan. 19, 1942; s. Guido James and Mable Lucretiam (Pantano) M.; children: Mack David, Todd James. Asst. art dir. Gelia and Wells Advt., Snyder, N.Y., 1967-72; art dir. Rich Advt., Buffalo, 1972-74, Mainspring Advt., Buffalo, 1974-76; freelance illustrator N.Y., 1976-86; sr. artist rsch. and devel. Fisher-Price, East Aurora, N.Y., 1986-88, sr. project artist, 1988—; instr. visual communications SUNY, Buffalo, 1974-78; with editorial dept. Courier-Express, Buffalo, 1982. com. chmn. Elma (N.Y.) Wheat and Barley Festival, 1991. With USAF, 1960-64. Recipient 1st place Addy award Am. Advt. Fedn., 1973. Mem. Graphic Artist Guild Western N.Y. (pres., co-founder 1981-82), Art Dirs. Club Buffalo (best of show, 1978). Republican. Roman Catholic. Home: 2284 Snyder Rd Orangeville NY 14167-9746 Office: Fisher Price R&D 636 Girard Ave East Aurora NY 14052-1824

MARIANS, KENNETH JAY, biochemist, educator; b. Bklyn., Nov. 23, 1951; s. Edward L. and Rose (Joffe) M.; m. Susan Rabbiner, June 8, 1975. BS in Chemistry, Poly. Inst. of Bklyn., 1972; PhD in Biochemistry, Cornell U., 1976. Asst. prof. Albert Einstein Coll. of Medicine, Yeshiva U., Bronx, 1978-83, assoc. prof., 1983-84; assoc. mem. Meml. Sloan-Kettering Cancer Ctr., N.Y.C., 1984-88, mem., 1988—, chmn. molecular biology dept., 1991—; cons. NIH, Bethesda, Md., 1989—. Contbr. articles to profl. jours. NIH grantee, 1978—. Office: Meml Sloan Kettering Cancer Ctr 1275 York Ave New York NY 10021

MARIASCHIN, MARK ARTHUR, management consultant; b. N.Y.C., Oct. 26, 1953; s. Abraham and Mildred (Nevins) M.; m. Karen Robbins, Mar. 13, 1982; children: Jennifer, Melissa. BS, Bklyn. Coll., 1974. Staff acct. Consolidated Edison, N.Y.C., 1974-76; fin. analyst Citibank, N.A., N.Y.C., 1976-79; exec. recruiter A-L Assocs., N.Y.C., 1979-81; pres. Mariaschin & Co., N.Y.C., 1981—.

MARINACCIO, PAUL JOSEPH, consultant; b. Bridgeport, Conn., May 30, 1937; s. Joseph and Jennie (Zielick) M.; m. Eleanor Joanne Nakoneczny, June 20, 1958; children: Mark, Brett, Todd. BS in Chemistry, Fairfield U., 1959; MS in Phys. Chemistry, Purdue U., 1961. Sr. chemist Rexall Chem. Co., Paramus, N.J., 1961-67; rsch. dir. AMF Inc., Stamford, Conn., 1967-85; sr. staff Foster Miller, Inc., Waltham, Mass., 1985-91; cons. Hitek, East Orleans, Mass., 1985—; expert witness on microporous membrane in various law suits world wide, 1985-91. Over 20 patents in field. Bd. dirs. Friends Meeting House Pond, East Orleans, 1992. Mem. AAAS, Am. Chem. Soc., N.Y. Acad. Scis. Roman Catholic. Home and Office: PO Box 1328 East Orleans MA 02643

MARINELLI, JOSEPH MARCELLO, aerospace advisor; b. Phila., Aug. 15, 1948; s. William Marinelli and Lillian (Nicolena) Navarro. Grad. high sch., Phila. Aerospace advisor Rissler Sci. Orgn., Phila., 1982—. Mem. Air Force Assn., U.S. Naval Inst. (life), Navy League (life), Am. Def. Preparedness Orgn. (life), World Futire Soc. (life), Tailhook Assn. (life), Assn. Am. Politics (life), Assn. Naval Aviation (life). Democrat. Roman Catholic. Home: 2141 S 21st St Philadelphia PA 19145-3502

MARINER, DONNA MARIE, art educator, writer; b. Warren, Pa., Aug. 6, 1934; d. Charles James Klenke and Mary Anne (Hackman) Francen; m. Donald William Mariner, Oct. 15, 1955 (dec. Nov. 1989); 1 child, David William. Diploma, U. Minn., 1948, Famous Artists Sch., 1974; cert., Pa. State U., 1983, 84. Artist Warren Art League, 1968—; woodcarver Mariners' Art Studio, Youngsville, Pa., 1969—; antique restorer Mariners' Art Studio, Youngsville, 1972—, glass etcher, 1984—; tchr. art studios and art leagues, Warren, 1977—; poet World of Poetry, Sacramento, 1982—, profl. artist, instr. art, sec., 1991—; writer Youngsville, 1985—; profl. artist, instr. art., sec. art studios, Warren, 1991—; profl. artist, instr. art, 1970—, profl. artist, instr. art own studio, 1970—. Author numerous poems; art works and carvings sold across U.S. Sec., treas. Democrat Club, Youngsville, 1965-67. Mem. Nat. Woodcarvers Assn. Democrat. Roman Catholic. Home: 34 4th St Youngsville PA 16371-1004 Office: PO Box 563 Warren PA 16365-0563

MARINHO, RITA DUARTE, political science educator; b. New Bedford, Mass, Oct. 11, 1942; d. Roger and Hilda (Daniels) M.; m. Robert Moniz, Oct. 21, 1961 (div. Apr. 1990); children: Robert John Moniz, Michael Joseph Moniz, Marc Andrew Moniz; m. Kenneth S. Duarte, Sept. 7, 1990. BA summa cum laude, U. Mass., North Dartmouth, 1974; MA, Brown U., 1975, PhD, 1979. Asst. prof. polit. sci. U. Mass., Dartmouth, 1978-82; assoc. prof. U. Mass., North Dartmouth, 1982-88, prof., 1988—, spl. asst. to pres., 1982-83, dir. women's studies, 1981-84; lectr. Nathan Mayhew Seminars, Martha's Vineyard, Mass., 1976-88; cons., exec. dir. Fall River (Mass.) Regional Task Force, Inc., 1984—; polit. analyst WSMU-TV, New Bedford, 1980. Author: APSA News, 1984; co-author: (book) Politics of Portuguese, 1991; moderator Feminine Forum, Sta. WBSM, New Bedford, Mass., 1980-84; contbr. polit. sci. articles to publs. Councillor, New Bedford City Coun., 1978-80, Dem. com., 1976-84; membership chair Women's Caucus for Polit. Sci., 1978-83; 1st v.p. Nat. Bd. YWCA of U.S.A., N.Y.C., 1984-90, bd. dirs., 1982—. Mellon scholar Wellesley Ctr. Rsch. for Women, 1983-84. Home: PO Box 2854 Edgartown MA 02539-2854 Office: U Mass Old Westport Rd North Dartmouth MA 02747-2512

MARINI, STEPHEN CONRAD, academic dean; b. Phila., Nov. 3, 1949; s. Corradino Joseph and Emma Ruth (Leone) M.; m. Judith Lillian Thomas, June 23, 1978; children: Lauren Elisa, Nicholas Stephen. BS in Biology, Villanova U., 1971; MS in Microbiology, Hahnemann U., 1976; PhD in Microbiology, Pacific Western U., L.A., 1989; D of Chiropractic, Pa. Coll., 1988. Rsch. fellow Hahnemann U., Phila., 1972-75; rsch. specialist Wistar Inst., Phila., 1975-76; med. technologist Hahnemann Med. Hosp., Phila., 1972-80, Children's Hosp., Phila., 1980—; asst. prof. microbiology Pa. Podiatric Coll., Phila., 1975-78; asst. prof. microbiology Pa. Coll. of Straight Chiropractic, Levittown, 1980-81, assoc. prof. microbiology, 1981-88, prof microbiology and biochemistry, 1988—; acad. dean, prof. Pa. Coll. of Straight Chiropractic, Horsham, Pa., 1990; commr. Accreding Agy., Spartanburg, S.C., 1990—; test com. mem. Nat. Bd. Chiropractic Examiners, Greeley, Colo., 1990—; peer rev. cons. Omni Med. Cons., Horsham, 1990—; bd. rev. cons. Irene Gold Assn., Gladwyne, Pa., 1988-90. Contbr. articles to profl. jours. Active Pa. Ballet Co., Phila., 1976—, Morris Animal Refuge, Phila., 1990—, Pony & 4H Club of N.J., South Jersey, 1990—; community health svc. Family Chiropractic Ctr., Phila., 1988—. Presdl. scholarship Villanova U., 1967-71; fellowship Hahnemann U., 1972-75; grantee NIH, 1976-80. Mem. Am. Soc. Microbiology, Internat. Chiropractic Soc., Pa. Chiropractic Fellowship, Pa. Chiropractic Fedn., Am. Coll. Health Assn., Haddonwood Tennis and Health Club. Home: 39 Hartford Rd Sewell NJ 08080-2039 Office: Family Chiropractic Ctr 5001 Oxford Ave Philadelphia PA 19124-2652

MARINICH, VLADIMIR GEORGE, social sciences educator; b. N.Y.C., Sept. 9, 1936; s. Georgi Milosshevich and Lydia Konstantinovna (Globachev) M.; m. Virginia Malone, Jan. 25, 1959 (div. 1989); children: Gregory, Diana, Elizabeth. BA, CCNY, 1958; MA, NYU, 1962; cert. advanced studies, Johns Hopkins U., 1972. Prof. social scis. Howard C.C., Columbia, Md., 1970—; dir. honors program Howard Community Coll., Columbia, Md., 1985—. Contbr. articles to profl. jours. Mem. Md. Collegiate Honors Coun. (sec.-treas. 1989—). Russian Orthodox. Home: 6209 Sutton Ct Baltimore MD 21227-6169 Office: Howard Community Coll Little Patuxent Pky Columbia MD 21044

MARINO, RALPH J., state legislator; b. Rochester, N.Y., Jan. 2, 1928; s. Giacomo and Antoinette (Saraceno) M.; m. Ethel Bernstein, Mar. 11, 1955; children: Judith, James, Robert. BS, Syracuse U., 1951; JD, Fordham U., 1954; Doctor of Civil Law, Dowling Coll., 1989. Sch. bd. clk. Oyster Bay (N.Y.) East Norwich Schs., 1959; housing authority counsel Town of Oyster Bay, 1965, councilman and majority leader, 1967-68; senator N.Y. State Legislature, Albany, 1969—; majority leader, pres. pro tem N.Y. State Senate, 1989—. Contbr. articles to newspapers. Trustee Cornell U., Ithaca, N.Y.; exec. leader Nassau County Rep. Com., Westbury, N.Y., 1966. With U.S. Army, 1946-47. Mem. Nassau County Bar Assn., Am. Legis. Exch. Coun., Italian-Am. Legis., Norwich Rep. Club (exec. leader), Sons Italy, Elks. Republican. Roman Catholic. Office: NY State Senate State Capitol Albany NY 12247 also: Marino Bernstein & La Marca Townsend Sq Oyster Bay NY 11771

MARINO, ROBERT ANTHONY, physics educator; b. Positano, Salerno, Italy, Feb. 19, 1943; came to the U.S., 1955; s. Nicola and Elena Viola (Talamo) M.; m. Carol Ann Forloney, Sept. 30, 1967; children: Andrea Lisa, Nicholas John. BS, CCNY, 1964; PhD, Brown U., 1969. Postdoctoral rsch. assoc. Brown U., Providence, R.I., 1969-70; asst. prof. Hunter Coll. CUNY, N.Y.C., 1970-73, assoc. profc., 1974-81, acting chair dept. physics, 1975-76, chair dept. physics, 1980-84, prof. physics, 1982—; vis. sr. scientist Block Engring., Inc., Cambridge, Mass., 1976-77; vis. prof. U. Geneva, Switzerland, 1985-86. Editor: Physics 101, 1985, 91; contbr. articles to profl. jours. Mem. Am. Phys. Soc., Am. Assn. Physics Tchrs., Internat. Symposium on Nuclear Quadrupole Resonance Spectroscopy (editor newsletter 1989—), Phi Beta Kappa, Sigma Xi. Home: 38 Woodland Ave Syosset NY 11791-2123 Office: Hunter Coll Dept Physics 695 Park Ave New York NY 10021-5085

MARINO, ROCCO ANTHONY, clinical psychologist; b. Leonminster, Mass., Dec. 3, 1952; s. Rocco and Anna (Dicenzo) M.; m. Sheila Ann Botti, July 4, 1981; children: Andrew Davin, Megan Lyn. BA in Psychology with high honors, U. Mass., 1976; MA in Counseling Psychology, Assumption Coll., 1978; specialist degree in Edn. and Psychology, Ctr. for Humanistic Studies, 1982; PhD in Clin. Psychology, The Union Inst., 1985. Lic. psychologist, Mass. Psychotherapist Burbank Hosp., Fitchburg, Mass., 1977-78, Heywood Hosp., Gardner, Mass., 1978-80, Amity Mental Health Clinic, Dearborn, Mich., 1981-82, Stetson Sch., Barre, Mass., 1983-86, Wells Human Svc. Ctr., Southbridge, Mass., 1986-87; psychologist Wing Hosp., Palmer, Mass., 1987-89, Am. Geriatric Svcs., Rockland, Mass., 1989-91; dir. Sturbridge (Mass.) Humann Svcs., 1989-91; lectr. Assumption Coll., Worcester, Mass., 1989; mem. field staff Omni Health Systems, Natick, Mass., 1989-91, Kathleen Greer Assocs., Framingham, Mass., 1990-91, Concern Employee Assistance Program, Cin., 1990-91; adj. prof. Union Grad. Sch., 1992. Mem. APA (mem. div. humanistic psychology), Phi Beta Kappa. Home: 44 Cedar St Sturbridge MA 01566-1353 Office: Sturbridge Human Svcs 258 Main St Sturbridge MA 01566-1282

MARION, KENNETH PHILIP, public relations executive; b. N.Y.C., Sept. 3, 1949; s. Ira Silberstein and Edith Irene (Schoolman) M.; m. Jean Murray, Dec. 23, 1978; children: Rachel Ilana, Alyse Dena, Seth David. BA, CCNY, 1971; MA, CUNY, John Jay Coll., 1976. Rsch. asst. N.Y. State Office Drug Abuse Svcs., N.Y.C., 1972-76, Vera Inst. Justice, N.Y.C., 1977-78; acting dir. program evaluation Manhattan Psychiat. Ctr., N.Y.C., 1978-81; dir. quality assurance Sagamore Children's Psychiat. Ctr., Melville, N.Y., 1981-84; dir. program evaluation Kings Park (N.Y.) Psychiat. Ctr., 1984-88; freelance essayist, 1986—; dir. pub. affairs Kings Park (N.Y.) Psychiat. Ctr., 1988—; guest trainer in time mgmt. employee assistance program Suffolk County, N.Y., 1986—. Author: (children's book) Volunteer Firefighter, 1990. Chair facilities improvement com. Hewlett/Woodmere (N.Y.) Sch. Dist., 1991-92. Office: Kings Park Psychiat Ctr PO Box 9000 Kings Park NY 11754-9000

MARIOTTE, MICHAEL LEE, environmental activist; b. Indpls., Dec. 9, 1952; s. Richard H. and Rozetta Mae (Dorton) M.; m. Lynn W. Thorp, Mar. 3, 1984; 1 child, Nicole Lynn. BA, Antioch Coll., 1978. Editorial asst. ABA, Washington, 1979-81; mng. editor, gen. mgr. City Paper, Washington, 1981-84; editor Nuclear Info. & Resource Svc., Washington, 1985-86, exec. dir., 1986—; dir. Safe Energy Communication Coun., Washington, 1990—. Editor (newsletter) Nuclear Monitor, 1985—. Office: Nuclear Info & Resource Svc 1424 16th St NW # 601 Washington DC 20036-2211

MARISCALO, ROSEMARY JEAN, real estate broker; b. Oyster Bay, N.Y., Dec. 1, 1939. Grad. high sch., Oyster Bay. Translator Baroid Internat., Rome, Italy, 1963-65, U.S. Govt., Rome, 1965-68; ct. reporter Barrister Reporting Svc. Ct., N.Y.C., 1975-83; owner, broker Oyster Bay Real Estate Co. Mem. Oyster Bay C. of C., L.I. Bd. Realtors, Friends of Raynham Hall, St. Bartholomew City Club (N.Y.C.). Office: Oyster Bay Real Estate Co 32 E Main St Oyster Bay NY 11771-2406

MARIWALLA, GOPAL CHETANRAM, project administrator, facilities engineer, cost estimator; b. Karachi, Sind, Pakistan, Aug. 5, 1944; came to U.S., 1983; s. Chetanram L. and Gomi Chetanram (Gomi Kansingh) M.; m. Rajni Gobindram Butani; children: Meena, Jyoti. BSME, Coll. Engring. Poona, Maharashtra, India, 1966. Registered profl. engr., N.Y. Engr. prodn. X.L.O. Ltd., Bombay, 1966-74; mgr. quality control and engring. Globe Steerings Ltd., Bombay, 1974-77; mgr. dy. mktg. Projects and Equipment Corp., New Delhi, 1977-80; project engr. Projects and Equipment Corp., Albeida, Libya, 1980-81; mgr. mktg. Projects and Equipment Corp., New Delhi, 1981-84; resident engr. Castro Blanco Piscioneri Architects, N.Y.C., 1984-86; sr. project mgr. N.Y.C. Health and Hosps. Corp., 1986-89, N.Y.C. Sch. Constrn. Authority, Long Island City, N.Y., 1989—. Office: NYC Sch Constrn Authority 30-30 Thomson Ave Long Island City NY 11101

MARK, BERNARD, telecommunications industry executive, writer, management consultant; b. N.Y.C., Apr. 26, 1932; m. Loretta Mutchnick, Jan. 7, 1956; 3 children. BA, CUNY, 1954. Merchandising exec. The May Co., Balt., Washington, 1956-60; v.p. mktg., sales The John Rider Pub. Co., N.Y.C., 1960-65; pres., chmn. bd. dirs. TCI Telecom. Cons., Inc., Westbury, N.Y., 1965—; sponsor, speaker Bd. of Entrepreneurship L.I., Westbury, 1986. Author: Business Management's Guide and Checklist for the Successful Company Move, 1976, Lifesights: Quick Pathways to the Successful You, 1991. Sgt. U.S. Army, 1954-56. Mem. Am. Legion, N.Y. Inst. Tech. (telecom. adv. coun. of sch. mgmt. 1988—, Outstanding Svc. plaque 1988), L.I. Computer Assn., N.Y. Personal Computer Club, CEO Club (Ctr. for Entrepreneurial Mgmt., Inc.).

MARK, ENID EPSTEIN, artist; b. N.Y.C., June 4, 1932; s. Harry and Miriam (Wolf) E.; m. Eugene Lee Mark, June 13, 1954; children: Peter David, Melanie Ann. BA, Smith Coll., 1954. Represented in permanent collections Israel Mus., The Jewish Mus., Phila. Mus. of Arts, Del. Art Mus., Toledo Mus. of Art, Smith Coll. Mus. of Art, Jane Voorhees Zimmerli Art Mus., Woodmere Art Mus., Mus. of Phila. Civic Ctr., Free Libr. of Phila., U. Del., U. Pa. Law Sch., Beaver Coll., Germantown Friends Sch., RCA Corp., IBM Corp., Hercules Corp., Internat. Chem. Industries, First Pa. Banking & Trust Co., Penn Mutual Ins. Co., Rouse and Co., Warner-Lambert Corp., Houghton Libr., Harvard U., Libr. of Congress Rare Book div., N.Y. Pub. Libr., Princeton U. Libr., Nat. Libr. of Can. Recipient Printmaking award Am. Color Print Soc., 1987, Stella Drabking Meml. award Am. Color Print Soc., 1986, Cheltenham Art Ctr. Print award, 1983, Del. Art Mus. Purchase award, 1981, Beaver Coll. Purchase award, G. Allen Mith Meml. award, 1979, U. Del. Purchase awards, 1978, 74, 70, Donald F. O'Neill award, 1978, Printmaking awards Community Art Ctrs. of Phila., 1977, 76, 70, Printmaking award Mus. of Phila. Civic Ctr., 1973, Copeland Purchase Prize, 1972. Mem. AM. Color Print Soc. (dir.), Print Club of Phila., So. Graphics Council. Home and Office: 210 Sykes Ln Media PA 19086-6337

MARK, LAURENCE PETER, anesthesiology educator; b. N.Y.C., Jan. 30, 1953; s. Lester Charles and Muriel Harriet (Widman) M.; m. Elizabeth Sue Collier, Aug. 29, 1982. BS in Physics, Harvey Mudd Coll., 1975; MD, Columbia U., 1979. Diplomate Am. Bd. Anesthesiology, Nat. Bd. Med. Examiners. Intern surgery St. Vincent's Hosp., N.Y.C., 1979-80; resident anesthesia Mass. Gen. Hosp., Boston, 1980-82; anesthesia fellow Mass. Gen. Hosp., 1982-83; asst. prof. anesthesiology Presbyn. Hosp., Columbia U., N.Y.C., 1983—; med. dir. pre-admission unit Columbia-Presbyn. Med. Ctr., N.Y.C., 1991—; expert witness Kopff, Nardelli & Dopf, N.Y.C., 1988—; article reviewer Anesthesia and Analgesia. Mem. Am. Soc. Anesthesiologists, N.Y. State Soc. Anesthesiologists (speaker closed cir. anesthesiology postgrad. assembly 1988). Democrat. Jewish. Home: 210 W 90th St Apt 9B New York NY 10024-1243 Office: Columbia U 622 W 168th St New York NY 10032-3702

MARK, ROBERT VINCENT, college dean; b. Jamaica, N.Y., Dec. 22, 1942; s. Vincent John and Jean (Steinert) M.; m. Celina Maria de Seixas Correa, Jan. 16, 1988; children: Elizabeth Ann McKoy, Deborah Lynn McKoy, Maria Luiza Lopes de Oliveira. BS in Chemistry, St. John's U., Jamaica, N.Y., 1964, MS in Organic Chemistry, 1966, PhD in Organic Chemistry, 1971. Instr. chemistry SUNY Coll. of Tech., Farmingdale, 1970-74, asst. prof. chemistry, 1974-77, assoc. prof. chemistry, 1977-81, dean Sch. Arts and Scis., 1981—; cons. Estee' Lauder, Melville, N.Y., 1975-77, Pall Corp., Glenn Cove, N.Y., 1975. Contbr. articles to profl. jours.; co-author lab manual: A Lab Manual for General Chemistry, Parts I and II, 1980. Home: 5 Browning Dr Greenlawn NY 11740-3103 Office: SUNY Coll of Tech Nathan Hale Hall Farmingdale NY 11735

MARKEL, GREGORY ARTHUR, lawyer; b. N.Y.C., Aug. 6, 1945; s. Edward and Ann (Larkin) M.; m. Dorothy Flanagan (div. 1979); 1 child, Kimberly; m. Belinda Elizabeth Heym, May 3, 1981; children: Alexis, Amy, William. BA, Columbia U., 1967; MBA, U. Mich., 1968; JD, Yale U., 1972. Bar: N.Y. 1972, U.S. Dist. Ct. (so. and ea. dists.) N.Y. 1974, U.S. Ct. Appeals (2nd cir.) 1975, U.S. Ct. Appeals (3rd cir.) 1978, U.S Dist. Ct. (no. dist.) Calif. 1984, U.S. Ct. Appeals (9th cirs.) 1984, U.S. Ct. Appeals (11th cir) 1987. Assoc. Cravath, Swaine & Moore, N.Y.C., 1972-80; ptnr. Davis, Markel & Edwards, N.Y.C., 1980—. Mem. ABA (antitrust, litigation and ins. coverage sects.), N.Y. State Bar Assn. (fed. litigation and civil practice coms.), Yale Club (N.Y.C.), Mahopac Golf Club (N.Y.). Home: 50 Sutton Pl S New York NY 10022-4167 Office: Davis Markel & Edwards 100 Park Ave New York NY 10017-5516

MARKEL, MERWYN ROBERT, arbitrator; b. Pitts., June 15, 1942. BA, Duquesne U., 1966; MAT, U. Pitts., 1968; LLB, La Salle Ext. U., 1971; MA, St. Francis Coll., Loretto, Pa., 1976. Investigator, fact finder, conciliator Pa. Human Rels. Commn., Pitts., 1968-91; panel mem. Am. Arbitration Assn., N.Y.C., 1991—; arbitrator Arbitration Forums, Inc., Tarrytown, N.Y., 1992—; arbitrator Counsel of Better Bus. Burs., Arlington, Va., 1989—. Wiht U.S. Army Nat. Guard, 1966-72. Mem. Soc. of Profls. in Disputer Resolution. Home and Office: 3000 Swallow Hill Rd #427 Scott Township PA 15220

MARKER, LEONARD K., composer; b. Vienna, Austria; s. Joseph and Erna (Stamm) Kuhmarker; student harmony and counterpoint with Hans Gal; pvt. pupil composition Alban Berg, Vienna, 1930-34; student Acad. Music, Vienna; m. Gertrude Osterer, Oct. 28, 1943; 1 son, James Steven. Came to U.S., 1942, naturalized, 1945. Mem. faculty Hunter Coll., N.Y.C.; composer symphony music, motion picture scores; musicals for stage: Tilted Hat, Max Reinhardt prodn., Ministry is Insulted and Why Do You Lie, Cherie? (7,000 performances in Europe, S.Am.); Twenty-Four Beautiful Hours; The Ant Hill; music for Bobino (play); music for various Erwin Piscator prodns.; also new arrangements of various operas including Wozzeck, Rosenkavalier, Love of Three Oranges. Mem. Broadcast Music Inc.; hon. mem. Alban Berg Soc. Co-author: (with Olin Downes) Ten Operatic Masterpieces; contbr. articles to N.Y. Times, Opera News, Musical Am., others. Address: 150 Claremont Ave New York NY 10027

MARKEY, ARTHUR ANDREW, personnel executive; b. Queens, N.Y., June 17, 1946; s. Arthur A. and Muriel C. (Gerbe) M.; m. Babette E. Vogeley, July 14, 1968. BS in Adminstrv. Sci., SUNY, Binghamton, 1972. Mfg. adminstrv. asst. Ithaco Inc., Ithaca, N.Y., 1972-73; quality control supr. Bendix Corp., Montrose, Pa., 1973-76; mgr. human resources Stow Mfg. Co., Binghamton, 1976-88; dir. human resources Azon Corp., Johnson City, N.Y., 1988—; bd. dirs. SIEBA Inc., Vestal, N.Y.; cons. Armark Assocs., Johnson City, 1986—. Mem. Bd. Coop. Ednl. Svcs. Occupational-Ednl. Adv. Coun., Binghamton; mem. adv. coun. Lourdes Hosp. Pain Clinic, Binghamton; v.p. Two rivers Bus. Health Coalition, Binghamton. Sgt. USAF, 1966-69. Mem. So. Tier Assn. Human Resources (legis. rep. 1991-92), Phi Theta Kappa. Republican. Office: Azon Corp 720 Azon Rd Johnson City NY 13790-1799

MARKEY, EDWARD JOHN, congressman; b. Malden, Mass., July 11, 1946; s. John E. and Christine M. (Courtney) M. B.A., Boston Coll., 1968, J.D., 1972. Bar: Mass. Mem. Mass. Ho. of Reps., 1973-76, 94th-102nd Congresses from 7th Mass. Dist., 1975—, New Eng. Congl. Caucus, N.E.-Midwest Econ. Advancement Coalition, Dem. Study Group, Environ. Study Conf. Freshman Caucus, now chmn. subcom. energy conservation and power. Mem. editorial staff: Boston Coll. Law Rev. Served with USAR, 1968-73. Mem. Mass. Bar Assn. (Mass. Legislator of Year 1975). Club: K.C. Home: 7 Townsend St Malden MA 02148-6322 Office: US Ho of Reps 2133 Rayburn House Office Bldg Washington DC 20515*

MARKHAM, CHARLES RINKLIN, financial executive, investment analyst; b. Travis AFB, Calif., May 13, 1959; s. Charles Whitlow Markham and Helen (Roberson) Williams. BS, MIT, 1984. Assoc. cons. Bain and Co., Boston, 1984-87; cons., 1987-89; investment analyst Hancock Venture Capital, Boston, 1989-91; tax practitioner, fin. cons. in pvt. practice, 1990—; chief fin. officer Dynaflo Systems, Inc., 1991—; dir. Harvard Cooperative Soc., 1980-81, 83-84. Mem. subcom. United Way Citizens Allocation 1982-87; alternate delegate, Republican Nat. Conven., 1984; nat. gov. bd. Common Cause, 1984-85; state gov. bd. Common Cause Mass., 1987—. Mem. Sigma Chi. Home: 85 Brainerd Rd Apt 610 Allston MA 02134-4563 Office: Alewife Capital Mgmt 17 Foch St Cambridge MA 02140-1002

MARKHAM, SISTER M(ARIA) CLARE, chemistry educator, college administrator; b. New Haven, Aug. 12, 1919; d. James J. and Agnes V. (Manning) M. BA in Chemistry, St. Joseph Coll., West Hartford, Conn., 1940, LHD (hon.), 1989; PhD, Cath. U. Am., 1952. Asst. prof. chemistry St. Joseph Coll., West Hartford, Conn., 1952-59, assoc. prof., 1960-67, prof., 1968—, dean grad. div., 1979-87, asst. pres. acad. affairs, 1987-91, dir. inst. rsch., 1991—; chmn. chemistry dept., 1960-70, mem. pres.'s council, 1980—; faculty fellow chem. biodynamics U. Calif., Berkeley, 1967-68, Inst. Tech., Trondheim, Norway, 1967; experimentation chair Sisters of Mercy, West Hartford, 1969-73, councilor, 1969-77; cons. ITT, Madras, India, 1974-77; mem. planning com. Grad. Consortium, Hartford, Conn., 1976-87; under sec. energy State of Conn. Office Planning and Mgmt., 1977-79. Editor: Basic Science Series, 1962-67. Contbr. articles to profl. jours. Mem. White House Conf. on Energy Prodn., Washington, 1978; chmn. adv. bd. Conn. Environ. Mediation Ctr., Hartford, 1982-85; bd. dirs. Conn. Energy Council for Tchrs., Hartford, 1982-87; mem. adv. bd. Conn. Energy Round Table, Hartford, 1982. Research grantee Am. Chem. Soc., NSF, Hartford, 1963-73; faculty fellow NSF, Norway, Berkeley, 1967-78, travel grantee NSF, Madras, India, 1974, 76, 77; sci. edn. grantee NSF, U.S. Dept. Energy, Hartford, 1959-80. Mem. AAAS, Am. Chem. Soc. (councilor 1968-70, 1974-88, chmn. Connecticut Valley sect. 1971-73), Conn. Acad. Sci. and Engring. (chmn. membership com. 1978-79), Sigma Xi (pres. Hartford chpt. 1992—). Office: St Joseph Coll 1678 Asylum Ave West Hartford CT 06117-2700

MARKHAM, WALTER GRAY, political science educator, college dean; b. Washington, Jan. 19, 1926; s. Lemon Pressley and Louise Seale (Walter) M.; m. Martha Leppert, 1956 (div. 1966); children: Martha Louise, Walter Gray (dec.); m. Annette Thompson, Dec. 20, 1966. BA, Westminster Coll., Fulton, Mo., 1948; MA, Boston U., 1964; PhD, U. Pa., 1972. Designated naval aviator. Enlisted U.S. Navy, 1943, commd. ensign, 1948, advanced through grades to lt. comdr., 1960, ret., 1967; mem. faculty U. Hartford, West Hartford, Conn., 1971—, dean arts and scis., 1987-92. Mem. West Hartford Bd. Edn., 1973-81, chmn., 1977. Recipient Edward S. Corwin award Am. Polit. Sci. Assn., 1972. Office: U Hartford Coll Arts and Scis 200 Bloomfield Ave West Hartford CT 06117-1500

MARKLEY, F(RANCIS) LANDIS, aerospace engineer; b. Phila., July 20, 1939; s. Francis L. and Greta T. (Tschan) M.; m. Mary Jane Sheppard, Dec. 21, 1965 (div. 1977); 1 child, Michelle; m. Gail M. Gotsch, July 28, 1978. BS in Engring. Physics, Cornell U., 1962; PhD, U. Calif., Berkeley, 1967. Asst. prof. physics Williams Coll., Williamstown, Mass., 1968-74; computer scientist Computer Scis. Corp., Silver Spring, Md., 1974-78; rsch. physicist U.S. Naval Rsch. Lab., Washington, 1978-85; aerospace engr. NASA Goddard Space Flight Ctr., Greenbelt, Md., 1985—; adj. prof. George Washington U., Washington, 1990—. Mem. editorial bd. Space Tech. Libr., D. Reidel Pub. Co., Dordrecht, The Netherlands, 1985—; assoc. editor Am. Jour. Physics, 1974-76, Jour. Guidance, Control and Dynamics, 1983-85, 1992—. Fellow AIAA (assoc.); mem. Am. Astronautical Soc. (sr.), Am. Assn. Physics Tchrs., Soc. Indsl. and Applied Math. Home: 10317 Wilde Lake Ter Columbia MD 21044-2529 Office: NASA Goddard Space Flight Ctr Code 712 Greenbelt MD 20771

MARKOFF, GARY DAVID, investment executive; b. Brookline, Mass., July 29, 1956; s. Leon Fred and Marylyn Sue (Goldstein) M. BA in Econs., Trinity Coll., Hartford, Conn., 1978. Account exec. E.F. Hutton & Co. Inc., Chestnut Hill, Mass., 1978-83, asst. v.p., 1984-85, v.p., 1986-88; v.p. investments Smith Barney & Co. Inc., Boston, 1988—. Fundraiser Hunger Project, 1985—; active Spl. Olympics, 1988; founding mem. fin. profls. unit B'nai B'rith, 1988. Named one of Best Stockbrokers in Am., Money mag., 1987. Mem. Boston Jaycees. Club: World Runners (San Francisco). Home: Jamaica Pond Estates 100 Pond St Apt 7 Boston MA 02130-2758 Office: Smith Barney & Co Inc Exchange Pl 38th Fl 53 State St Boston MA 02109-2809

MARKOU, PETER JOHN, business educator, business and tax consultant; b. Keene, N.H., Apr. 11, 1940; s. Peter John and Zoe Nicholas (Kussku) M.; m. Ann Corcoran Gibbons, June 25, 1983; 1 child, Justin Peter. BSBA cum laude, Suffolk U., 1964, MSBA, 1965; cert. in taxation, U. Hartford, 1977. Purchasing agt. Fed. Prison Industries, Danbury, Conn., 1965; instr. Becker Jr. Coll., Worcester, Mass., 1967-70; assoc. prof. Post Coll., Waterbury, Conn., 1976-77; asst. prof. bus. North Adams (Mass.) State Coll., 1970-76, assoc. prof., 1977-84, prof., 1984—; bd. dirs. New Products in Mgmt., Inc., North Bennington, Vt., New Directions in Mgmt., Inc., North Bennington. Contbr. articles to small bus. and econ. devel. proc. Pres. North Adams Community Devel. Corp., 1985—, Hardman Indsl. Park Corp., North Adams, 1989—; mem. North Adams Mgmt. Improvement Com., 1987—; mem., sec. Mass. Mus. Contemporary Art Cultural Commn., North Adams, 1988—; bd. dirs., No. Berkshire Community Action, North Adams, 1989—; mem. adv. bd. Salvation Army, North Adams, 1988—. Recipient Disting. Svc. award North Adams State Coll., 1980, 85, Mass. Pride in Performance award Commonwealth of Mass., 1989. Mem. Urban Land Inst. (assoc.), Nat. Soc. Pub. Accts. (educator mem.), Am. Mgmt. Assn., Nat. Assn. Tax Practitioners, Assn. Pvt. Enterprise Edn. Home: PO Box l65 North Adams MA 01247 Office: North Adams State Coll Church St North Adams MA 01247-4100

MARKOVICH, ANNIE MARIE, artist, educator, writer; b. Chgo., Jan. 6, 1947; d. Stephen George and Ann (Boranowskas) M. Student, Northwestern U., 1971-73; BA, So. Ill. U., 1973; postgrad., Art Inst. Chgo., 1973, Royal Coll., London, 1978. Instr. pottery Jane Addams Ctr., Chgo., 1973; art specialist Chgo. Ctr. Urban Opportunity, 1974; muralist, painter CETA Project, Chgo., 1975; mng. editor New Art Examiner, Chgo., 1976-86; tchr. art Ethical Culture Sch., N.Y.C., 1988—, photographer, 1989-90, art cons., 1991; dir. advt. New Art Examiner, N.Y.C., 1987—; artist-in-residence Penlee Mus., Penzance, Eng., 1978-79; lectr. Pori (Finland) Art Mus., 1986; art critic Art Examiner, 1975-86. Exhibited in group show Daley Civic Ctr., Chgo., 1975, Ethical Culture Soc., 1991; mural executed Morningside Adult Ctr., 1978. Grantee Finlandia Found., 1990, Ethical Culture Sch., 1991. Mem. N.Y. Soc. for Ethical Culture, N.Y. Creative Computing Club. Home and Office: 6 Stuyvesant Oval Apt 11C New York NY 10009-2426

MARKOVITS, ANDREI STEVEN, political science educator; b. Timisoara, Rumania, Oct. 6, 1948; came to U.S., 1960, naturalized, 1971; s. Ludwig and Ida (Ritter) M. B.A., Columbia U., 1969, M.B.A., 1971, M.A., 1973, M.Phil., 1974, Ph.D., 1976. Mem. faculty N.Y.U., 1974, John Jay Coll. Criminal Justice, CUNY, 1974, Columbia U., 1975; rsch. assoc. Inst. Advanced Studies, Vienna, Austria, 1973-74, Wirtschafts und Sozialwissenschaftliches Inst., German Trade U. Fedn., Duesseldorf, Fed. Republic Germany, 1979, Internat. Inst. Comparative Social Rsch., Sci. Ctr. Berlin, 1980; asst. prof. govt. Wesleyan U., Middletown, Conn., 1977-83; assoc. prof. polit. sci. Boston U., 1983-92; prof., chair bd. studies in politics U. Calif., Santa Cruz, 1992—; vis. prof. Tel Aviv U., 1986, Osnabruck U., 1987, Bochum U., 1991; sr. rsch. assoc. Ctr. for European Studies, Harvard U., 1975—. Author, editor books and papers in field; TV and radio commentator. Univ. Pres.'s fellow Columbia U., 1969, B'nai B'rith Found. fellow, 1976-77, Kalmus Found. fellow, 1976-77, Ford Found. fellow, 1979, Hans Boeckler Found. fellow, 1982; N.Y. State scholar Columbia U., 1969. Mem. Am. Polit. Sci. Assn., Internat. Polit. Sci. Assn., AAUP. Home: 287 Harvard St Cambridge MA 02139-2336 Office: U Calif Merrill Coll Bd

Studies in Politics Santa Cruz CA 95064 also: Bd Studies in Politics Merrill Coll U Calif Santa Cruz CA 95064

MARKOWITZ, HARRY M., finance and economics educator; b. Chgo., Aug. 24, 1927; s. Morris and Mildred (Gruber) M.; m. Barbara Gay. PhB, U. Chgo., 1947, MA, 1950, PhD, 1954. With research staff Rand Corp., Santa Monica, Calif., 1952-60, 61-63; tech. dir. Consol. Analysis Ctrs., Inc., Santa Monica, 1963-68; prof. UCLA, Westwood, 1968-69; pres. Arbitrage Mgmt. Co., N.Y.C., 1969-72; pvt. practice cons. N.Y.C., 1972-74; with research staff T.J. Watson Research Ctr. IBM, Yorktown Hills, N.Y., 1974-83; Speiser prof. fin. Baruch Coll. CUNY, N.Y.C., 1982—; dir. rsch. Daiwa Securities Trust Co, Jersey City, N.J., 1990—; v.p. Inst. Mgmt. Sci., 1960-62. Author: Portfolio Selection: Efficient Diversification of Investments, 1959, Mean-Variance Analysis in Portfolio Choice, 1987; co-author: SIMSCRIPT Simulation Programming Language, 1963; co-editor: Process Analysis of Economic Capabilities, 1963. Recipient John von Neumann Theory prize Ops. Rsch. Soc. Am. and Inst. Mgmt. Sci., 1989, Nobel Prize in Econs., 1990. Fellow Econometric Soc., Am. Acad. Arts and Scis.; mem. Am. Fin. Assn. (pres. 1982—). Office: CUNY Baruch Coll Sch Bus 17 Lexington Ave New York NY 10010-5526 also: Daiwa Securities 1 Evertrust Plz Jersey City NJ 07302

MARKOWITZ, PHYLLIS FRANCES, case management administrator, psychologist; b. Malden, Mass., Sept. 2, 1931; d. Abraham and Rose (Kaplan) Kalishman; children: Gary Keith, Carol Diane. AB, Harvard U., 1972, EdM, 1974; EdD, Boston U., 1987. Lic. psychologist, social worker, Mass.; cert. sch. psychologist, secondary English and social studies tchr., Mass. Rsch. asst. Boston Coll., Newton, Mass., 1971-73; social worker Combined Jewish Philanthropies, Boston, 1973-74; instr. Harvard U., Cambridge, Mass., 1974-75, counselor, 1974-79; supr. Dept. Social Svcs., Newton and Marlborough, Mass., 1979-87; regional dir. case mgmt. Dept. Mental Health, Boston, 1987—; pvt. practice psychotherapist Brookline, Mass., 1987—; pvt. psychotherapist Bedford, Mass., 1992—; instr. counseling psychology U. Mass., Boston, 1990—; chair com. case mgmt., Dept. Mental Health, Boston, 1987—, regional coord. medically-mentally ill, 1987—, regional trainer case mgmt., 1987—. Grantee Radcliffe Inst., 1972; recipient Rsch. scholar award Boston U., 1981-82. Mem. APA, Mass. Psychol. Assn., Harvard Extension Alumnae Assn. (adv. bd. 1988—). Office: Dept of Mental Health 25 Staniford St Boston MA 02114

MARKOWSKY, GEORGE, computer science educator. BA, Columbia U., 1968; MA, Harvard U., 1969, PhD, 1973. Asst. prof. St. Mary's Coll. Md., St. Mary's City, 1969-72; postdoctoral researcher Harvard U., Cambridge, Mass., 1973-74; rsch. staff mem. IBM, Yorktown Heights, N.Y., 1974-84; chmn. computer sci. U. Maine, Orono, 1984-90, prof. computer sci., 1990—; cons. Kork Systems, Bangor, Maine, 1985—, IBM, Poughkeepsie, N.Y., 1987-88. Author: A Comprehensive Guide to the IBM PC, 1984, The Downeast PC Course, 1991; contbr. more than 60 articles to profl. jours. Dir. Maine Housing Found., Orono, 1990—. Mem. IEEE, Am. Math. Soc., Math. Assn. Am., Assn. Computing Machinery, Bedford Audubon Soc. (pres. 1981-82). Office: U Maine Computer Sci Dept Orono ME 04469

MARKS, BRUCE, artistic director, choreographer; b. N.Y.C., Jan. 23, 1937; s. Albert and Helen (Kosersky) M.; m. Toni Pihl Petersen, Jan. 27, 1966 (dec. May 1985); children: Erik Antony, Adam Christopher, Kenneth Rikard. Student, Brandeis U., 1954-55, Juilliard Sch., 1955-56; DFA (hon.), Wheaton Coll., 1986, Franklin Pierce Coll., 1990. Prof. U. Utah, 1981, 84-86; now artistic dir. Boston Ballet Co., 1985—; mem. dance adv. panel Nat. Endowment for Arts, 1979, chmn. internat. selection com., 1979, chmn. dance adv. panel, 1981, mem. nat. adv. bd. on arts and edn., 1989; bd. dirs. Dance/USA, mem. exec. com., 1989, 92—, chmn., 1990-92, chmn. govt. affairs, 1992—; mem. U.S.-USSR Commn. on Dance and Theatre Studies, Am. Coun. Learned Socs./IREX; mem. jury Internat. Moscow Ballet Competition, 1989. Prin. dancer Met. Opera, 1956-61, Am. Ballet Theatre, 1961-72, Royal Swedish Ballet, 1963, Festival Ballet, London, 1965, Royal Danish Ballet, 1971-76; artistic dir. Ballet West, Salt Lake City, 1976-85; choreographer Eliot Feld Ballet Co., 1970, Royal Danish Ballet, 1972-73, Netherlands Dance Theatre, 1974, Ballet West, 1976-85; artistic fellow Aspen Inst. for Humanistic Studies, 1979—. Bd. dirs. Am. Arts Alliance, 1983-85, Am. Coun. for Arts, 1985—; bd. dirs. Dance U.S.A., 1988, chmn., 1990—; chmn. U.S.A. Internat. Ballet Competition, Jackson, Miss., 1990—, vice chair jury, Helsinki, Finland, 1991; mem. nat. adv. bd. on arts and edn. NEA, 1989-91. Office: Boston Ballet 19 Clarendon St Boston MA 02116-6100

MARKS, COLIN HERBERT, mechanical engineering educator; b. Cardiff, Wales, Oct. 8, 1933; came to U.S., 1946; s. Herbert Marks and Edna (Davies) Wilson; m. Linda Lou Whelan, Jan. 23, 1971; 1 child, Evan. BSME, Carnegie-Mellon U., 1956, MS, 1957; PhD, U. Md., 1965. Instr. mech. engring. U. Md., College Park, 1959-65, asst. prof., 1965-67, assoc. prof., 1967-78, prof., 1978—; vis. scientist Wood Hole (Mass.) Oceanographic Inst., 1967, U.S. Bur. Standards, Gaithersburg, Md., 1988; vis. scholar U. Wash., Seattle, 1978. Contbr. articles to profl. jours. With U.S. Army, 1957-59. Mem. ASME, Combustion Inst. Office: U Md Dept Mech Engring College Park MD 20742

MARKS, DAVID HUNTER, civil engineering educator; b. White Plains, N.Y., Feb. 22, 1939; s. Sidney M. and Jean (Berger) M.; div.; 1 child, Joanna. BCE, Cornell U., 1962, MS in Environ. Engring., 1964; PhD, Johns Hopkins U., 1969. Registered profl. engr., N.Y., Mass.; registered hydrologist, Am. Inst. Hydrology. Sr. sanitary engr. USPHS, Phila., 1964-66; asst. prof. civil engring. MIT, Cambridge, Mass., 1969-72, assoc. prof., 1972-75, prof., 1975—, head dept., 1985-92, dir. program in environ. engring. edn. and rsch., 1991—; bd. dirs. Camp Dresser and McKee, Environ. Engrs., Boston. Office: MIT Dept of Civil Engring Rm 1-290 Cambridge MA 02139

MARKS, EMILY MENLO, non-profit administrator; b. N.Y.C., Jan. 20, 1938; d. Emil and Marie Pauline (Dinkelspiel) M.; m. Burton H. Marks, Dec. 20, 1959; children: Paul, Lisa Marie, Daniel. BA, Smith Coll., 1959; MS, Columbia U., 1978. Asst. adminstr. NYC EPA, 1973-74; v.p. Wildcat Svc. Corp., N.Y.C., 1974-77; assoc. dir. The Vera Inst. of Justice, N.Y.C., 1977-82; cons. Nova Inst., N.Y.C., 1982-84; dep. exec. dir. City Vol. Corps, N.Y.C., 1984-86, acting exec. dir., 1986; exec. dir. United Neighborhood Houses, N.Y.C., 1988—; trustee Settlement Housing Fund, N.Y.C., 1988—; commr. N.Y. State Commn. for the Blind, Albany, 1978-84. Mem. Internat. Fedn. Settlements (v.p. 1989—), Parks Coun. (past pres., trustee 1961—). Office: United Neighborhood Houses 475 Park Ave S New York NY 10016-6901

MARKS, EUGENE MELVIN, physician; b. Buffalo, July 5, 1921; s. Sidney M. and Marcia Maud (Tritchler) M.; m. Edna Mildred Aranibar, Nov. 25, 1943; children: James, Catherine, Joanne, Judith, Elizabeth, Edward. BA in Biology, U. Buffalo, 1943, MD, 1946. Diplomate Am. Bd. Preventive Medicine in Occupational Medicine. Intern E.J. Meyer Meml. Hosp., Buffalo, 1946-47, resident in internal medicine, 1947-48; plant physician E.I. duPont de Nemours & Co., Niagara Falls, N.Y., 1952-58; med. supr. E.I. duPont de Nemours & Co., Buffalo, 1958-68; pvt. practice Alden, N.Y., 1953-64; corp. med. dir. Remington Arms Co., Bridgeport, Conn., 1968-85, contract physician, 1985-89; dist. med. cons. State Div. Rehab. Svcs., Conn., 1968-74, 85—. Mem. Commn. on Aging, Newtown, Conn., 1990, 91. Fellow Am. Coll. Occupational and Environ. Medicine (dir. 1982-85), Am. Coll. Preventive Medicine; mem. Am. Diabetes Assn., Am. Occupational Medicine Assn. (del. 1972-82, 85-89, dir. 1982-85), Conn. Occupational Medicine Assn. (pres. 1973), Am. Lung Assn. Conn., Newtown Rotary (chmn. com. 1969-75). Home: 22 Grand Pl Newtown CT 06470-2114

MARKS, JOEL HOWARD, philosophy educator; b. N.Y.C., Oct. 13, 1949; s. Irving Philip and Rosamonde Elsie (Safier) M.; m. Linda Susan Greer, June 29, 1991; stepchildren: David Novak, Sean Rainey. BA in Psychology, Cornell U., 1972; PhD in Philosophy, U. Conn., 1982. Instr. of psychology and dir. liberal arts Portland (Maine) Sch. of Art, 1973-75; postdoctoral fellow in philosophy U. Rochester (N.Y.), Rochester, N.Y., 1983-84; asst. prof. philosophy U. New Haven, West Haven, Conn., 1984-88, assoc. prof. philosophy, 1988—; chmn. faculty senate U. New Haven, 1989-90; vis. asst. prof. philosophy St. John Fisher Coll., Rochester, 1982-83. Editor: The Ways of Desire, 1986; contbr. articles to profl. jours. Mem. Am. Philos. Assn., Soc. for Asian and Comparative Philosophy, Am. Assn. Philosophy Tchrs., Astron. Soc. New Haven (sec.), Phi Beta Kappa. Office: Dept Philosophy/U New Haven West Haven CT 06516

MARKS, MARVIN LEE, health products executive; b. Balt., May 27, 1936; s. Theodore and Ida Agnes (Blumberg) M.; m. Carol R. Finestone, Nov. 15, 1959 (div. Jan. 1972); children: Jamie, Jonathan, Adam. BA, Duke U., 1957. Trainee S.A. Levyne, Balt., 1957; v.p. sales Doxsee Food Corp., Balt., 1960-76; pres. Ortho-Med Supplies, Inc., Balt., 1976-91; CEO, 1991—; pres. SOS Techs., Inc., Balt., 1977—; bd. dirs. Oxygen Therapy Inst., Memphis, 1987—. Mem. Woodholme Country Club. Democrat. Jewish. Office: SOS Techs Inc 1720 Belmont Ave Baltimore MD 21207-2554

MARKS, PAULINE, hospital administrator; b. N.Y.C., Aug. 21, 1950; d. Arthur and Ruth (Flamberg) M.; m. Ethan D. Scher, Dec. 28, 1980; children: Brooke Kara, Kenneth Louis. BA in Polit. Sci. with honors, NYU, 1972, MPA Health Policy, Planning & Adminstrn., 1975. Ins. cons. Hoffman Assocs., Scarsdale, N.Y., 1973-74; claims account adminstr. Pa. Gen. Agys. of N.Y., Inc., N.Y.C., 1974-75; assoc. dir. profl. svcs. Met. Hosp. Ctr., N.Y.C., 1975-80; assoc. dir. Kings County Hosp. Ctr., Bklyn., 1980-81; asst. v.p. support svcs. United Hosps. Med. Ctr., Newark, 1981-87; v.p. adminstrv. svcs. and ambulatory care Bronx (N.Y.)-Lebanon Hosp. Ctr., 1987—; preceptor field project in mgmt. engring. N.J. Inst. Tech., 1982-87; preceptor Masters program in health care adminstrn. Jersey City State Coll., 1982-87; preceptor residency program in hosp. adminstrn. NYU-Grad. Sch. Pub. Adminstrn., 1988—. Mem. Am. Coll. Healthcare Execs., Greater N.Y. Hosp. Assn. (profl. affairs and hosp. ops. com. 1988—), Fedn. Jewish Philanthropies (ins. policy adv. com. 1988—), Asst. Hosp. Dirs. Assn. N.J. (rep. to N.J. Hosp. Assn. Coun. on profl. practice 1984-87, membership chmn. 1985-86, mem.-at-large to bd. dirs. 1986-87), N.Y. Acad. Medicine. Office: Bronx-Lebanon Hosp Ctr 1650 Grand Concourse Bronx NY 10457-7697

MARKS, RICHARD BEREA, education and training professional; b. Charleston, W.Va.; s. Berea G. and Lillie Mae (Carter) M.; 1 child, Tereza Yvonne Marks. BSBA in Acctg. magna cum laude, Morris Harvey Coll., 1954; MA in Polit. Sci., Marshall U., 1955; MA in Govtl. Adminstrn., George Washington U., 1958. Staff officer and edn. and tng. officer Dept. Def., Washington, 1958-89, ret., 1989; adj. instr. in field. Author: Axioms for the Aspiring Government Bureaucrat, 1988, Adventures in the Brown Shoe Army, 1991; author numerous pub. articles. With U.S. Army, 1955-58. Mem. Kanawha Valley Geneal. Soc. (decendant W.Va. Pioneer Cert. of Recognition), Friends of W.Va. Culture and History.

MARKS, ROBERT E., advertising executive; b. Bklyn., Apr. 27, 1950; s. Herbert and Florence Sadie (Mintz) M.; m. Lynn Susan Eisenberg, Dec. 24, 1973; children: Dana Maris, Heather Leigh. BS in Mgmt., SUNY, Buffalo, 1972; MBA in Mktg., NYU, 1975. Mktg. exec. Newspaper Advt. Bur., N.Y.C., 1972-73; account exec. Doyle, Dane, Berbach Advt., N.Y.C., 1973-77; account supr., v.p. Young & Rubicam Advt., N.Y.C., 1977-81; mgmt. supr., sr. v.p. Geers Gross Advt., N.Y.C., 1981-84; group account dir., sr. v.p. Ephron, Raboy, Tsao, and Kurnit Advt., N.Y.C., 1984-88; dir. account mgmt., sr. v.p. Berenter, Greenhouse & Webster Advt., N.Y.C., 1988—. Democrat. Jewish. Office: Berenter Greenhouse Webster 233 Park Ave S New York NY 10003

MARKS, SPENCER JONATHON, director communicable disease control; b. N.Y.C., Mar. 12, 1950; s. George and Elaine (Weiner) M.; m. Susan Louise Houston, Mar. 28, 1992; children: Austin Lee Hammar, David Houston, Jason Houston. BA in Sociology, SUNY, New Paltz, 1974; MPA, Russell Sage Coll., 1983. Pub. health advisor N.Y. State Dept. Health, Albany, 1974-75; social worker Ulster County Health Dept., Kingston, N.Y., 1975; dir. communicable disease control div. Dutchess County Dept. Health, Poughkeepsie, N.Y., 1975—; mem. med. adv. bd. Planned Parenthood, Poughkeepsie, 1984—; mem. infection control com. Vassar Bros. Hosp., Poughkeepsie, 1984—, St. Francis Hosp., Poughkeepsie, 1984—; mem. Lyme disease adv. bd. West Chester County Health Dept., White Plains, N.Y., 1991—. Office: Dutchess County Health Dept 387-391 Main St Poughkeepsie NY 12601

MARKS, STEPHEN PAUL, law educator; b. San Francisco, June 13, 1943; s. Marion Harris and Ruth Wise (Rosenblum) M.; m. Kathleen A. Modrowski, Feb. 28, 1978; children: Joshua, Emmanuel. BA, Stanford U., 1964; diploma, Inst. Advanced Internat. Studies, Paris, 1972; D Etat, U. Nice, 1979. Researcher, mem. sr. program staff Internat. Inst. Human Rights, Strasbourg, France, 1969-73; sr. program specialist UNESCO, Paris, 1973-83; program officer Ford Found., N.Y.C., 1983-88; prof. law Cardozo Sch. Law, Yeshiva U., N.Y.C., 1989-92, dir. program in internat. law and human rights, 1989-92; asst. to ind. jurst UN Mission for Referendum in Western Sahara, 1992—; chief sect. UN Transitional Authority, Phnom Penh, Cambodia, 1992; lectr. Law Sch., Columbia U., N.Y.C., 1985—, adj. prof. polit. sci., 1989—; Univ. fellow New Sch. for Social Rsch., N.Y.C., 1989—; mem. consultative coun. Lawyers Com. for Nuclear Policy, N.Y.C., 1985—; bd. dirs. Internat. Svc. for Human Rights, Geneva, 1989—; cons. to MacArthur Found., 1992. Bd. dirs. Def. for Children Internat.-USA, N.Y., 1989—, Middle East Watch, 1991—, Media Ctr. for Human Rights, N.Y.C., 1989—. Hague Acad. Internat. Law fellow, 1967, 73, Peaslee fellow Columbia U., 1985. Mem. Acad. Coun. on UN System, Am. Soc. Internat. Law, Am. Polit. Sci. Assn., Internat. Law Assn., Société Française pour Droit Internat., Acad. Polit. Sci., Internat. Studies Assn. Home: Little Cobb Rd Water Mill NY 11976

MARKS, STEVEN WALTER, freelance writer, publisher; b. New London, Conn., Feb. 18, 1953; s. Jack Charles and Mavis Lillian (Arnold) M.; m. Linda Marie Deutch. BA, U. Conn., 1976. Writer, editor various newspapers, 1977-82; freelance writer, 1977—; copywriter Univ. Seminar Ctr., Boston, 1982-85; editorial dir. PT Publs., Palm Beach Gardens, Fla., 1985-89; pub. Tyger Press, New London, 1989—. Author: Gallows Lane, 1988; editor Angry, 1989-91; contbr. articles, essays, poetry.

MARKS, THEODORE LEE, lawyer; b. N.Y.C., Oct. 18, 1935; s. Irving Edward and Isabel (Goodman) M.; m. Benita Cooper, July 13, 1958; children: Eric, Robert, Jennifer. B.S., NYU, 1956, LL.B., 1958. Bar: N.Y. 1959, U.S. Dist. Ct. (so. dist.) N.Y. 1963, U.S. Supreme Ct. 1964, U.S. Ct. Appeals (2d cir.) 1975, U.S. Dist. Ct. (ea. dist.) N.Y. 1978. Assoc. Silver, Bernstein, Seawell & Kaplan, N.Y.C., 1959-65; sole practice N.Y.C., 1965-70; ptnr. Lee, Cash & Marks, N.Y.C., 1970-76, Vogel, Marks & Rosenberg, N.Y.C., 1976-79, Bromberg, Gloger, Lifschultz & Marks, N.Y.C., 1979-85, Epstein Becker Borsody & Green, P.C., N.Y.C., 1985-86, Gelberg & Abrams, 1986-87, Morrison Cohen Singer & Weinstein, 1987—; speaker at meetings of profl. assns. Contbr. articles to profl. jours. Served with Army N.G., 1958-61. Mem. N.Y. State Bar Assn. (mem. real property, banking, corp. and bus. law sects.), N.Y. County Lawyers Assn., Fed. Bar Coun., The Wings Club (N.Y.C.). Office: Morrison Cohen Singer & Weinstein 750 Lexington Ave New York NY 10022-1200

MARKWART, LUTHER ALLAN, association executive; b. Yale, Mich., Dec. 1, 1954; s. Robert William and Audrey Jane (Parker) M. BS in Bus. Adminstrn., Mich. State U., 1977. Tour mgr. Roamer Tours, Reading, Pa., 1978; sales rep. Noxell Corp., Balt., 1978-79; exec. v.p. Farmers & Mfrs. Beet Sugar Assn., Saginaw, Mich., 1979-82, Am. Sugarbeet Growers Assn., Washington, 1982—; cons. Internat. Sugar Agreement, U.S. Govt., Washington/Geneva, 1983, Gen. Agreement on Tariffs and Trade, 1987—, various groups and cos. Contbr. articles to profl. jours. Lutheran. Office: Am Sugarbeet Growers Assn 1156 15th St NW Ste 1101 Washington DC 20005-1704

MARKWOOD, SANDRA REINSEL, program and policy analyst; b. Washington, Aug. 27, 1955; d. Francis Eugene and Delores Jean (Horning) Reinsel-Kahn; m. James Scott Markwood, Aug. 4, 1984; 1 child, Christopher Scott. BA with distinction, U. Va., 1977, M in Urban and Environ. Planning, 1979. Sr. rsch. asst. Nat. League of Cities, Washington, 1979-80; rsch. assoc./ project dir. Nat. Assn. Counties, Washington, 1980-84; asst. to county exec. Albemarle County, Charlottesville, Va., 1984-86; sr. rsch. assoc./ project dir. Nat. Assn. Counties, Washington, 1986—; exec. sec. Nat. Assn. County Aging Programs, Washington, 1986—; com. co-chair Generations United, Washington, 1988-90, intergovtl. liaison Nat. Hwy. Traffic Safety Adminstrn., Washington, 1989-91; chair Aging Needs Assessment Com., Charlottesville, 1985-86. Author: (handbook) Local Officials Guide to Urban Recreation, 1980, (guide) Building Support for Traffic Safety Programs, 1991; co-author (guide) Graying of Suburbia, 1988; contbr. articles to profl. jours. Vol. tchr. St. Louis Cath. Sch., Alexandria, Va., 1980-83, St. Rita's Cath. Sch., Alexandria, 1987-89; coord. Sister Cities Exch. Program, Charlottesville, 1985. Recipient Cert. of Appreciation, Nat. Hwy. Traffic Safety Adminstrn., 1991. Mem. Women's Transp. Seminar, Smithsonian Assocs., Generations United. Roman. Catholic. Home: 3106A Russell Rd Alexandria VA 22305-1742

MARLAND, ALKIS JOSEPH, computer leasing company executive, computer science educator, financial planner; b. Athens, Greece, Mar. 8, 1943; came to U.S., 1961, naturalized, 1974; s. Basil and Maria (Pervanides) Mouradoglou; m. Anita Louise Malone, Dec. 19, 1970; children: Andrea, Alyssa. BS, Southwestern U., 1963; MA, U. Tex., Austin, 1967; MS in Engring. Adminstrn., So. Meth. U., 1971. Cert. in data processing; chartered fin. cons.; cert. fin. planner; enrolled agt. With Sun Co., Richardson, Tex., 1968-71, Phila., 1971-76; mgr. planning and acquisitions Sun Info. Svcs. subs. Sun Co., Dallas, 1976-78; v.p. Helios Capital Corp. subs. Sun Co., Radnor, Pa., 1978-83; pres. ALKAN Leasing Co., Wayne, Pa., 1983—; prof. dept. computer scis. and bus. adminstrn. Eastern Coll., St. David's, Pa., 1985-87; prof. math. Villanova (Pa.) U., 1987-89; bd. dirs. Alkan Leasing Corp., 1983—. Board dirs. Radnor Twp. Sch. Dist., 1987-91, Delaware County Intermediate Unit, 1988-91, Phila. Fin. Assn., 1989—. Mem. IEEE, Assn. Computing Machinery, Data Processing Mgmt. Assn., Internat. Assn. Fin. Planners, Am. Soc. CLUs and ChFC, Am. Assn. Equipment Lessors, Inst. Cert. Fin. Planners, Fin. Analysts Phila., Phila. Fin. Assn. (sec. 1989-92, mem. award 1988), Fgn. Policy Rsch. Inst., World Affairs Coun. Phila., Phila. Union League, Main Line C. of C., Assn. Investment Mgmt. and Rsch., Rotary (pres. Wayne club 1989-90, gov.'s rep. dist. 7450, 1990-91), Masons (32 degree). Republican. Home: 736 Brooke Rd Wayne PA 19087-4709 Office: PO Box 8153 Radnor PA 19087

MARLETTE, DOUGLAS NIGEL, editorial cartoonist, comic strip creator; b. Greensboro, N.C., Dec. 6, 1949; m. Melinda Hartley; 1 child, Jackson Douglas. Student, Fla. State U. Editorial cartoonist The Charlotte (N.C.) Observer, 1972-87, The Atlanta Constn., 1987-89, N.Y. Newsday, N.Y.C., 1989—; syndicated to over 100 newspapers through Creators Syndicate, Inc., L.A., 1988—. Creator syndicated comic strip Kudzu; works reproduced in Time, Newsweek, Christian Century, Rolling Stone, Der Spiegel, Esquire mags., also textbooks and encys.; author: The Emperor Has No Clothes, If You Can't Say Something Nice, Drawing Blood, Kudzu, 1982, Preacher, The Wit and Wisdom of Will B. Dunn, 1984, Just A Simple Country Preacher, 1985, It's a Dirty Job But Somebody Has To Do It, There's No Business Like Soul Business, 1987, Chocolate is My Life, Shred This Book, I Am Not a Televangelist, Doublewide with a View, 1989, In Your Face, A Cartoonist At Work, 1991, (children's book) The Before and After Book, Even While Boys Get the Blues, 1992; co-wrote screenplay "EX"; TV appearances include ABC's Nightline, Good Morning Am., CBS Morning News, Nat. Pub. Radio's Morning Edition; syndicated animated editorial cartoons NBC Today Show. Nieman fellow, 1st for editorial cartoonist, Harvard U.; recipient Nat. Headliners award 1983, 88, Robert F. Kennedy Meml. award 1984, Sigma Delta Chi Disting. Service award 1986, First Amendment award, 1986, 1st Pl. award John Fischetti Editorial Cartoon Competition, 1986, The Golden Plate Acad. of Achievement award, 1991; named to Register of Men amd Women Who Are Changing Am., Esquire Mag., 1984; recipient Pulitzer Prize for editorial cartooning Newsday, 1988. Office: NY Newsday 2 Park Ave New York NY 10016-5603 also: care Creators Syndicate Inc 5777 W Century Blvd Ste 700 Los Angeles CA 90045

MARLEY, MARY LOUISE, psychologist; b. Columbia, Pa., Apr. 18, 1923; d. William Edward and Carrie Cook (Lockard) M. BS in Edn., Millersville (Pa.) State U., 1944; MEd in Psychology and Audiology, Franklin & Marshall Coll., 1952. Lic. psychologist, speech pathologist, audiologist, Pa. Cons. remedial reading Dearborn (Mich.) Elem. Schs., 1944-49; tchr. spl. edn. Hershey (Pa.) Elem. Sch., 1949-52; speech pathologist York (Pa.) County Schs. Office, 1952-55, asst. psychologist, 1955-68; clin. psychologist stroke unit York Hosp., 1968-74; pvt. practice clin. psychology York, 1974—; cons. police depts. York City, York Twp., West York, Hazelton, Pa., Windsor Twp., Red Lion, Gettysburg, Springettsbury Twp., No. Regional, West Manchester, Hanover Boro, Wrightsville, Jackson Twp., Penn Twp., Hellman, Spring Garden Twp., West Manheim Twp., New Oxford Twp., 1983—; cons. fire dept. Spring Garden, Emigsville, Hanover. Author: Organic Brain Pathology and the Bender Gestalt Test, 1982. Mem. Pa. Psychol. Assn., Nat. Assn. Neuropsychology, Nat. Register Clin. Psychology, York County Psychol. Assn. Republican. Methodist. Home: 926 Mckenzie St York PA 17403-3712 Office: 1620 S Queen St York PA 17403-4637

MARLIN, ARTHUR DAVID, executive; b. Cambridge, Mass., Sept. 29, 1934; s. Myer and Blanche (Tobin) M.; m. Lois Ann Bernstein, Sept. 11, 1960; children: Myra Jane, Susan Harriet, Robert Paul. BSBA, Northeastern U., 1960. Jr. acct. Cabot Corp., Boston, 1956-60; sr. acct. Cabot Corp., 1960-62, from credit asst. to corp. credit mgr., 1962-88; exec. v.p. NACM-New Eng., Inc., Arlington, Mass., 1988—; chmn. chem. div. Nat. Chem. Credit Assn., N.Y.C., 1974-75, chmn. internat. div., 1975-76, chmn. exec. bd., 1976-78; chmn. Rubber Industries Credit Assn., N.Y.C., 1972-74, 84-86, Raw Material Credit Assn., N.Y.C., 1987-88; treas. NACM-New England Inc., 1976-78, v.p., 1978-79, pres. 1979-81. Pres. Beth El Temple Ctr., Belmont, Mass., 1975-77. Office: NACM-New Eng Inc PO Box 9103 Arlington MA 02174-9103

MARLIN, JOHN TEPPER, economist, writer, consultant; b. Washington, Mar. 1, 1942; s. Ervin Ross and Hilda (van Stockum) M.; AB cum laude, Harvard U., 1962; BA, Oxford (Eng.) U., 1965, MA, 1969; PhD in Econs., George Washington U., 1968; m. Alice Rose Tepper, Sept. 25, 1971; children: John Joseph Tepper, Caroline Alice Tepper. Fin. economist Fed. Res. Bd., FDIC and SBA, Washington, 1964-69; asst. prof. Baruch Coll., City U. N.Y., 1969-73; founder, pres. Council Mcpl. Performance, N.Y.C., 1973-88; pres. JTM Reports, Inc., 1989—; social auditor Ben and Jerry's Homemade, 1989; dir. Conversion Info. Ctr., Coun. on Econ. Priorities, 1991—; cons. J.M. Kaplan Fund, 1991. Mem. Am. Econ. Assn. (life), Fin. Mgmt. Assn. (life), Economists Against the Arms Race (bd. dirs.), City Club (N.Y.C.), Harvard Club (N.Y.C.), Devon Yacht Club, New Eng. Soc. N.Y., Trinity (Oxford) Soc. U.S.A. (pres.). Author: The Wealth of Cities, 1974, Cities of Opportunity, 1988, Catalogue of Healthy Food, 1990, The Livable Cities Almanac, 1992, (with others) Book of American City Rankings, 1983, Contracting Municipal Services, 1984, Book of World City Rankings, 1986, Soviet Conversion, 1991, Building a Peace Economy, 1992 ; founding editor Jour. Fin. Edn., 1972-73; editor Nat. Civic Rev., 1987-88, Privatization Report, 1986-88. Home: 360 W 22d St New York NY 10011 Office: JTM Reports Inc 30 Irving Pl 9th Fl New York NY 10003

MARLIN, ROBERT LEWIS, pharmaceutical executive; b. Bronx, N.Y., June 28, 1937; s. Leon and Ida (Buchalter) M.; m. Joyce Ann Lyons, Aug. 16, 1959; children: Suzanne Beth, Myron Lawrence. AB, Syracuse (N.Y.) U., 1958, MPA, 1962; PhD, Rutgers U., 1978. Asst. psychology dept. Letchworth Village, Thiells, N.Y., summer 1957, asst., 1958-59; rsch. asst. Sterling Winthrop Rsch. Inst., Rensselaer, N.Y., 1959-62; from regional dist. mgr. to asst. dir. new product devel. Winthrop Labs. Div. Sterling Drug, Inc., N.Y.C., 1962-65; coord. med. affairs and clin. rsch. Knoll Pharm. Co., Orange, N.J., 1965-68; coord. Schering Coop., Bloomfield, N.J., 1968-69; sr. clin. rsch. assoc. Sandoz Pharms., Hanover, N.J., 1969-75; pvt. practice biomed. cons., 1975-83; pres. Careforms, Inc., Parsippany, N.J., 1981—; dir. clin. rsch. Thompson Med. Co., N.Y.C., 1983-90, Slim Fast Foods Co., N.Y.C., 1990—; with Ctr. for Profl. Advancement, New Brunswick, N.J., 1978-83; adj. asst. prof. biomed. sci. Mass. Coll. Pharmacy and Allied Health Sci., 1983-84; adj. asst. prof. dept. pharmacology CUNY, 1986—. Contbr. articles to profl. jours. Mem. Drug Info. Assn. (chmn. publicity and pub. rels. com. 1966-67, 69-70, 73-75, sec. 1968-69, chmn., coord. symposium on adverse drug reactions, Atlantic City, N.J. chpt. 1968, chmn. ann. meeting Phila. chpt. 1970, v.p. 1970-71, chmn. membership com. 1975-77, co-chmn. workshop on drug info., Orlando, Fla. chpt. 1979), Am. Statis. Assn., Biometric Soc., N.Y. Acad. Sci., N.J. Acad. Sci. (editor newsletter), North Am. Assn. Study Obesity (edn. com. 1991—), European Assn. Obes-

ity. Home: 8 Biscay Dr Parsippany NJ 07054-4004 Office: Slim Fast Foods Co 919 3d Ave New York NY 10022-3903

MARMER, ELLEN LUCILLE, pediatrician; b. Bronx, N.Y., June 29, 1939; d. Benjamin and Diane (Goldstein) M.; m. Harold O. Shapiro, June 5, 1960; children: Cheri, Brenda. BS in Chemistry, U. Ala., 1960; MD, U. Ala., Birmingham, 1964. Cert. Nat. Bd. Med. Examiners; diplomate Am. Bd. Sports Medicine, Bd. Pediatrics, Bd. Qualified and Eligible Pediatric Cardiology, Bd. cert. sports medicine. Intern Upstate Med. Ctr., Syracuse, N.Y., 1964-65, resident, 1965-66; fellow in pediatric cardiology Columbia Presbyn. Med. Ctr.-Babies Hosp., N.Y.C., 1967-69; pvt. practice Hartford, Vernon, Conn., 1969—; examining pediatrician child devel. program Columbia Presbyn. Med. Ctr.-Babies Hosp., N.Y.C., 1967, instr. pediatrics, 1967-69; dir. pediatric cardiology clinic St. Francis Hosp., Hartford, 1970-80; asst. state med. examiner, Tolland County, Conn., 1974-79; sports physician Rockville (Conn.) High Sch., 1976—; advisor Cardiac Rehab. com., Rockville, 1984—; mem. bd. examiners Am. Bd. Sports Medicine, 1991—, chmn. credentials com., 1991—. Mem. Vernon Town Coun., 1985-89; bd. dirs. Child Guidance Clinic, Manchester, Conn., 1970—; life mem. Tolland County chpt. Hadassah, v.p., 1969-70, pres., 1970-72, bd. dirs., 1973-74; mem. B'nai Israel Congregation and Sisterhood, Vernon, 1969—, chmn. youth commn., 1970-72. Recipient Outstanding Svc. award Indian Valley YMCA, 1985. Fellow Am. Acad. Pediatrics, Am. Coll. Cardiology; mem. Am. Coll. Sports Medicine (bd. examiners 1991—, chmn. credentials com. 1991—), Conn. Med. Soc., Am. Heart Assn. (mem. coun. cardiovascular disease in young 1969—, chmn. elect New Eng. regional heart com. 1990-91), Conn. Heart Assn. (bd. dirs. 1974-75, 83-84, pres. 1986-88), Heart Assn. Greater Hartford (bd. dirs. 1970-89, mem. exec. com. 1972-73, 79-84, pres. 1982-84), Tolland County Med. Assn. (sec. 1971-72), Rockville Pub. Health Nursing Assn., LWV (state program chairperson Vernon chpt. 1971-73). Democrat. Jewish. Office: 520 Hartford Tpke Vernon CT 06066

MARMORSTEIN, HARRY JOHN, health care administrator; b. Jersey City, Dec. 7, 1954; s. Harry John and Stephanie Marmorstein. BA, Ind. U. of Pa., 1977; MA, Montclair State Coll., 1984. Substance abuse counselor Largo Community Correctional Ctr., Pinellas, Fla., 1977-79; youth counselor Bridge, Inc., West Caldwell, N.J., 1979-80; coord. outpatient svcs. Inter County Coun. on Alcohol and Drug Abuse, Kearny, N.J., 1980-82; coord. of outpatient care Monmouth Chem. Dependency Treatment Ctr., Long Branch, N.J., 1982-84; dir. Passaic County Alcoholism and Drug Abuse, Paterson, N.J., 1984-86; exec. dir. Maryville, Inc., Glassboro, N.J., 1986-91; dir. substance abuse svcs. Kennedy Meml. Hosps.-Univ. Med. Ctr., Cherry Hill, N.J., 1991—; v.p. Passaic County Mental Health Assn., Clifton, N.J., 1984-86; sec. Compulsive Gambling Counselor Cert. Bd., Trenton, N.J., 1988—. Committeeman Boy Scouts Am., South Jersey Area Coun., 1988. Recipient Community Svc. award, Hispanic Info. Ctr. of Passaic County, 1986. Mem. Nat. Assn. Alcoholism and Drug Abuse Counselors, N.J. Assn. Alcoholism Counselors (bd. dirs. 1984-86). Office: Kennedy Meml Hosp-U Med Ctr Chapel Ave and Cooper Landing Rd Cherry Hill NJ 08002

MAROLDA, ANTHONY JOSEPH, management consulting company executive; b. Winthrop, Mass., Sept. 7, 1939; s. Daniel Arthur and Rose Marie (Pagliarulo) M.; m. Maria Theresa Rizzo, Oct. 10, 1970; children: Matthew, Ria. BS in Physics, Northeastern U., 1962; MS in Physics, Northeaster U., 1968; MBA, Harvard U., 1970. Rsch. physicist High Voltage Engrng. Corp., Burlington, Mass., 1962-65; sr. scientist E.G. & G. Inc., Wellesley, Mass., 1965-68; v.p. Arthur D. Little, Inc., Cambridge, Mass., 1970-85; pres. The Winbridge Group, Inc., Cambridge, Mass., 1985—. Inventor Apparatus High Density Plasma, 1965; co-author: Business Problem Solving, 1980, Modern Marketing, 1986. Adv. Waterbury-Leningrad. Intersport, Waterbury, Conn., 1988—. Recipient Hayden Meml. Scholarship, Northeastern U., 1957. Mem. Harvard Club, Harvard Bus. Sch. Alumni Assn. Republican. Roman Catholic. Office: The Winbridge Group Inc 124 Mt Auburn St Cambridge MA 02138

MARON, ALISA JILL, public relations/marketing specialist; b. Manhattan, N.Y., Feb. 1, 1963; d. Neil Simon and Iris Linda (Abrams) Nota; m. Michael George Maron, June 14, 1987. BA, Rutgers Coll., New Brunswick, N.J., 1985. Exhibit mgr. Dept. Health Edn., Rutgers U., New Brunswick, 1983-85; student loan asst. First Atlantic Savs., South Plainfield, N.J., 1985-86; mktg. asst. Rosti (USA) Inc., Kenilworth, N.J., 1986-89; sales promotion specialist The Prudential, Iselin, N.J., 1989—; advt. promotions intern WNBC Radio, N.Y.C., 1985. Editor The Easterner newsletter, 1990—; writer Rsch. and Edn. Assn., Piscataway, N.J., 1991—. Rules com. Indian Head North Homeowners Assn., North Brunswick, N.J., 1991. Recipient award for best catalog design product N.J. Art Dirs. Assn., 1987. Mem. Life Communicators Assn. Home: 95 Aspen Dr North Brunswick NJ 08902-1053

MAROPIS, NICHOLAS, engineering executive; b. Slovan, Pa., May 14, 1923; s. Speros N. and Argero (Skinakis) M.; widowed; children: Samuel, Colin, Janice, Michelle. BA, Washington and Jefferson U., 1949; MS, Pa. State U., 1967. Physicist Naval Ordinance Lab., White Oak, Md., 1950-53; sr. project engr., physicist RM Parsons Inc., Frederick, Md., 1953-55; v.p. engrng. Aeroprojects Inc., Westchester, Pa., 1955-74, UTI Corp., Collegville, Pa., 1972-91; prin. Maropis Tech. Enterprises, Inc. (M-TEI), Baden, Pa., 1991—. Mem. allocations Com. United Way Chester County, Exton, Pa., 1989-90; pres. St. Sophia Greek Orthodox Ch., 1985-87. Sgt. USAAF, 1942-45. Recipient Commendation Atomic Energy Commn., Oak Ridge, Tenn., 1964, NASA, 1968. Mem. Hellenic Ednl. Progressive Assn. (officer 1979-91). Republican.

MAROTTA, CHARLES ANTHONY, neuroscientist, psychiatric researcher; b. N.Y.C., Apr. 12, 1945; s. Joseph and Angelina (Brancato) M.; m. Rosalind Victoria Kearney, Apr. 4, 1981; children: Gianna Christina, Liliana Catherine. BS, CCNY, 1965; MD, Duke U., 1969; MPhilosophy, Yale U., 1972, PhD, 1975. Resident in psychiatry Mass. Gen. Hosp., Boston, 1973-76, dir. neurobiology lab., 1985—, psychobiologist, 1986—; clin. fellow Harvard Med. Sch., Boston, 1974-76, instr. psychiatry, 1976-77, assoc. prof. psychiatry, 1983—; chief molecular neurobiology lab. McLean Hosp., Belmont, Mass., 1982—; dir. Alzheimer Research Program, Boston and Belmont, 1980—; advisor WHO, Geneva, Switzerland, 1985. Editor: Neurofilaments, 1983; contbr. more than 75 articles to profl. jours., 1973—. Advisor Office Career Svcs. Harvard U., Cambridge, 1975—. Recipient MacArthur award MacArthur Found., Chgo., 1981, Neurosci. Devel. award McKnight Found., Mpls., 1985, Alzheimer Research award Wood-Kalb Found., 1985, disting. grant Sandoz Found. for Gerontol. Research, Princeton, N.J., 1988. Mem. Am. Psychiat. Assn., Soc. for Neurosci., Am. Soc. Biochem. and Molecular Biology, Royal Soc. Medicine, Assn. Research Nervous Mental Diseases.

MAROTTA, EDWARD ANTHONY, program director; b. Cleve., Mar. 30, 1947; s. Frank F. and Genieveve Eva (Szychowski) M.; m. Alice Marie Zisk, Feb. 24, 1967; children: Marjorie Ann, Edward Anthony II. BS in Journalism, Ohio U., 1969. News editor, dir. pub. info Rio Grande (Ohio) Coll., 1969-72; dir. col. rels., asst. dir. devel. Waynesburg (Pa.) Coll., 1972-85; dir. pub. info. Washington & Jefferson Coll., Washington, Pa., 1985—; dir. Centerville Clinics Inc., Fredericktown, 1981—; assessor Cen. Greene Tax Assessor, Waynesburg, 1982-91; cons. in field. Editor: Coal and Rural America, 1982, The Second Hundred Years, 1983, W&J Mag., 1985; contbr. articles to profl. jours. Mem. Rotary, Waynesburg, 1982-85, Lions, Waynesburg, 1976-78. Recipient Honorable Mention awards Printing Industry Assn., Pitts., 1986-90, Design Excellence award Internat. Assn. Bus. Communications, Pitts., 1991. Mem. Coun. Advancement and Support Edn., Coll. and Univ. Pub. Rels. Assn. Pa. Republican. Roman Catholic. Home: 305 Park Ave Waynesburg PA 15370-1220

MARPLE, GARY ANDRE, management consultant; b. Mt. Pleasant, Iowa, Feb. 22, 1937; s. Kenneth Lowry and Truma Janice (Cook) M.; m. Ellen I. Metcalf, May 29, 1971 (div. 1981); m. Meredith Ann Rutter, July 23, 1988; children: Brian Edward, Stephen Lowry. BS, Drake U., 1959; MBA, Mich. State U., 1962, DBA, 1963. Postdoctoral fellow mgmt. MIT, 1963; cons. Arthur D. Little Inc., Cambridge, Mass., 1963-82; pres. Commonwealth Strategies, Inc., Lincoln, Mass., 1982—, Oceanus Holding, Ltd., S.W., Harbor, Maine, 1985—; treas. Bramar, Inc., Stow, Mass., 1988—; bd. dirs. M&H Group, Inc., Boulder, Colo., 1987—. Editor, author: Grocery Manufacturing in the U.S., 1968; contbr. to Conquering Government Regulation, 1982.

MARQUARDT, ANN MARIE, small business manager; b. Plainview, N.Y., Oct. 28, 1964; d. Steven Peter Paul and Virginia Ann (Gallo) M. Grad., Harry B. Ward Occupational Ctr, Riverhead, N.Y., 1982; student, Dowling Coll., 1982-84; Assoc. Acctg., Suffolk Community Coll., 1990; postgrad., St. John's U., 1990—. Sec. Dowling Coll., Oakdale, N.Y., 1982-84; sec., office mgr. Pudge, Peteco & Peanuts Corp., Southold, N.Y., 1984-86, Era Albo Agy., Mattituck, N.Y., 1986-87; legal sec. Wickham, Wickham & Bressler, P.C., Mattituck, 1987-89; bus., gen. mgr. Mattituck Laundromat, 1987-89, Gaslight Cafe, Ltd., Mattituck, 1989; office/bus. mgr., bookkeeper accounts payable/receivable Minerva's Tree Svcs. Ltd., Cutchogue, N.Y., 1990—; office/bookkeeping cons. Dickerson's Marine, Mattituck, 1990, Hobby's Plus, Southold. Author poetry and short stories. Mem. Mattituck C. of C. Office: Minervas Tree Svcs Ltd Eastwood Dr Cutchogue NY 11935-2208

MARQUES, DIANE MARIE, clinical psychologist; b. Newark, Mar. 9, 1958; d. Julio and Vitalina (Lopes) M.; m. William T. Oswald, Apr. 9, 1983; children: Elena Victoria, Andrew. BA, Seton Hall U., 1979; MA, U. R.I., 1983, PhD, 1986. Lic. psychologist, Mass.; cert. psychologist, N.H. Intern Children's Hosp. Med. Ctr./Judge Baker Children's Ctr., Boston, 1984-85; staff psychologist South Shore Mental Health Ctr., Quincy, Mass., 1985-86, Alianza Hispana/Alianza Familiar, Roxbury, Mass., 1986-88; psychotherapist North Shore Children's Hosp., Salem, Mass., 1986-87; staff psychologist Children's Hosp. Med. Ctr., Boston, 1988-91; sr. staff psychologist Alianza Hispana/Judge Baker Children's Ctr., Roxbury, 1986-88; instr. psychology dept. psychiatry Harvard U. Med. Sch., Boston, 1988-91; instr. psychology Sch. Human Svcs. Springfield Coll., Manchester, N.H., 1989—; chief child and adolescent psychiatry Lake Shore Hosp., Manchester, 1992—; sch. cons. Human Resource Inst., Malden, Mass., 1987-91; pvt. practice, N.H., 1991—; sr. instr. Cambridge (Mass.) Coll.; presenter workshops on children's responses to grief. Contbr. articles to various publs. Pres. bd. dirs. Alliance for Progress of Hispanic Ams., Manchester, 1990-91; mem. Latin-Am. Ctr., Manchester, 1990—. Clin. fellow in family systems NIMH, U. R.I., 1979-80; clin. fellow in psychology, Harvard U. Med. Sch., 1984-85. Mem. Am. Psychol. Assn., Nat. Hispanic Psychol. Assn., Psi Chi. Office: Lake Shore Hosp 200 Zachary Rd Manchester NH 03109

MARQUEZ, FIDEL, artist, photographer; b. Havana, Cuba, May 13, 1959; came to U.S., 1967; s. Luciano and Inerda (Perez) M. BFA, UCLA, 1980, MFA, 1983. One-man shows include 56 Bleeker Gallery, N.Y.C., 1989, Flamingo East Gallery, N.Y.C., 1991; exhibited in group shows at Hallway Gallery, L.A., 1989, Rempire Gallery, N.Y.C., 1990, Johnson & Johnson Corp. Hdqrs. Gallery, New Brunswick, N.J., 1991, St. Lawrence U., Canton, N.Y., 1991, Mus. in the Community, Charlestown, W.Va., 1991, Gallery at the Ellipse, Arlington, Va., 1991, Sweet Briar (Va.) Coll. Art Gallery, 1991, 1708 East Main Gallery, Richmond, Va., 1992, Del. State Coll. Art Ctr. Gallery, Dover, 1992. Fellow Mid-Atlantic Arts Found., 1990. Home and Studio: 2 Bleecker St New York NY 10012

MARQUIS, GAIL ANNETTE, business analyst, computer programmer, educator; b. N.Y.C., Nov. 18, 1954; d. Salathiel and Geraldine Althea (Matthew) M. BA, Queens Coll. of CUNY, 1980. Registered securities rep. Asst. front office mgr. Hyatt Regency Hotels, Dallas, 1981-83; mortgage processor Anchor Savings Bank, FSB, L.I., N.Y., 1983; retirement plans specialist Dean Witter Reynolds, Inc., N.Y.C., 1984-85, fgn. tax advisor, 1985-87; mgr. retirement svcs. Paine Webber, Inc., Weehawken, N.J., 1987-90; asst. v.p., bus. analyst Paine, Webber, Inc., Weehawken, N.J., 1990—. Advisor, Women With a Future, N.Y.C., 1987—. Recipient Silver medal U.S. Olympic Team Women's Basketball, Montreal, 1976, Silver medal World Univ. Games, Sofia, Bulgaria, 1977, Trophee L'Equipe Palladiam, French Fedn. of Basketball, Paris, 1979; named to Pub. Schs. Athletic League Hall of Fame, 1977. Mem. Am. Mgmt. Assn., Internat. Athletic Assn. Basketball Officials, N.J. Bd. Basketball Officials. Democrat. Lutheran. Office: Paine Webber Inc 3d Fl 1000 Harbor Blvd Weehawken NJ 07087-6727

MARRA, DONALD PAUL, educator, mayor; b. Yonkers, N.Y., Mar. 7, 1948; s. Francis Joseph and Elena (Dichiara) M.; m. Regina Donnelly, June 28, 1975; children: Catharine Elena, Donald Paul Jr. BS, SUNY, Oswego, 1970; MS, Fordham U., 1974. Cert. sch. adminstr. Tchr. Yonkers Bd. of Edn., 1970-73; tchr., internal auditor Irvington (N.Y.) Unified Sch. Dist., 1973—; mayor Village of Dobbs Ferry, N.Y., 1989—, trustee 1982-89, recreation commn. mem. 1980-82. Solid waste adv. coun. mem. N.Y. State Senator Spano, Albany, 1991—. Mem. Phoenix Theater (bd. dirs.). Republican. Roman Catholic. Home: 30 Maplewood Ave Dobbs Ferry NY 10522 Office: Village of Dobbs Ferry 112 Main St Dobbs Ferry NY 10522

MARRA, WILLIAM ANTHONY, education educator; b. Jersey City, Feb. 20, 1928; s. William and Mary (DiMartino) M.; m. Marcelle P. Haricot, Apr. 7, 1958 (dec. Sept. 1982); children: William Regis, Loretta, Joseph, Nicholas; m. Marie Antoinette Duffey, Aug. 3, 1991. PhB, U. Detroit, 1949; MA, Fordham U., 1951, PhD, 1952. Assoc. prof. Fordham U., N.Y.C., 1954—. Author: Happiness & Christian Hope, 1979. Host radio talk show Where Caths. Meet, 1982—. Cpl. U.S. Army, 1952-54, ETO. Roman Catholic. Home: 12 Indian Trail West Milford NJ 07480-3809 Office: Fordham U Lincoln Ctr New York NY 10023

MARRIN, YVETTE, foundation executive; b. N.Y.C., Mar. 28, 1937; m. Albert Marrin, Nov. 22, 1959. BSEd, CCNY, 1958; M, NYU, 1972, PhD, 1985. Tchr. pvt. schs., 1958-64; asst. dir., tchr., adminstr. Marble Hill Nursery Sch., N.Y.C., 1964-70; tchr., cons. Yonkers (N.Y.) Pub. Schs., 1970-85; co-founder, pres. Nat. Cristina Found., Inc., Pelham, N.Y., 1985—. Recipient Citation Md. State Dept. Edn., Balt., 1989, Nat. Orgns. award Nat. Rehab. Assn., 1989. Mem. Coun. for Exceptional Children, Nat. Assn. for Edn. of Young Children, Nat. Rehab. Assn., Phi Delta Kappa (N.Y.C. chpt.). Office: Nat Cristina Found 42 Hillcrest Dr Pelham NY 10803-3306

MARRIOTT, JOHN W., JR., hotel and food service chain executive; b. Washington, Mar. 25, 1932; s. John Willard and Alice (Sheets) M.; m. Donna Garff, June 29, 1955; children: Deborah, Stephen Garff, John Willard, David Sheets. B.S. in Banking and Fin, U. Utah, 1954. V.p. Marriott Hot Shoppes Inc., 1959-64, exec. v.p., bd. dirs., 1964; pres. Marriott Corp., 1964—, chief exec. officer, 1972—, chmn. bd., 1985—; bd. dirs. Outboard Marine Corp., Waukegan, Ill., GM. Trustee Mayo Found., Nat. Geog. Soc., Eisenhower Med. Ctr., Exec. Coun. on Fgn. Diplomats; mem. nat. adv. bd. Boy Scouts Am.; mem. conf. bd. Bus. Coun., Bus. Roundtable. Lt. USNR, 1954-56. Recipient Bus. Leader of Yr. award, Georgetown U. Sch. Bus. Adminstrn., 1984, Svc. Above Self award, Rotary Club at JFK Internat. Airport, 1985, Am. Mgr. of Yr. award, Nat. Mgmt. Assn., 1985, Golden Chain award, Nation's Restaurant News, 1985, Hall of Fame award, Consumer Digest Mag., 1985, Citizen of Yr. award, Boy Scouts of Am., 1986, Restaurant Bus. Leadership award, Restaurant Bus. Mag., 1986, Gold Plate award, Am. Acad. Achievement, 1986, Hall of Fame, Am. Hotel and Motel Assn., 1986, Hall of Fame award, Culinary Inst. of Am., 1987, Hospitality Exec. of Yr. award, Pa. State U., 1987, Bronze winner in Fin. World's Chief Exec. Officers award, 1988, Silver Plate award Lodging Hospitality Mag., 1988, Chief Exec. Officer of Yr. Chief Exec. Officer Mag., 1988, Signature award CA chpt. Nat. Multiple Scelerosis, 1988; named Outstanding Mktg. Exec. Gallagher Report, 1988. Mem. Conf. Bd., U.S. C. of C., Sigma Chi. Mem. LDS Ch. Clubs: Burning Tree (Washington), Met. (Washington). Office: Marriott Corp Marriott Dr Washington DC 20058

MARRO, ANTHONY JAMES, newspaper editor; b. Middlebury, Vt., Feb. 10, 1942; s. Francis James and Esther Martha (Butterfield) M.; m. Jacqueline Helen Cleary, June 5, 1965; 1 child, Alexandria. B.A. in History, U. Vt., 1965; M.S. in Journalism, Columbia U., 1968. Reporter Rutland (Vt.) Herald, 1964-67; Reporter Newsday, L.I., N.Y., 1968-74, chief Washington bur., 1979-81, mng. editor, 1981-86, exec. editor, 1986-87, editor, 1987—; reporter Newsweek, Washington, 1974-76, N.Y. Times, Washington, 1976-79. Co-recipient Pulitzer prizes for Pub. Service Reporting, 1970, 74. Office: Newsday 235 Pinelawn Rd Melville NY 11747-4226

MARRONE, DANIEL SCOTT, business management and data processing educator; b. Bklyn., July 23, 1950; s. Daniel and Esther (Goodman) M.; m. Portia Terrone, Sept. 1, 1979; children: Jamie Ann. BA, Queens Coll., 1972, MLS, 1973; MBA, N.Y. Inst. Tech., 1975; PhD, NYU, 1988; diploma in Quality Engrng., Quality Inst. L.I., 1992. Cert. fellow prodn. and inventory mgmt.; cert. quality auditor; cert. quality engr.; cert. sr. indsl. technologist. Auditor/investigator N.Y. State Spl. Pros., N.Y.C., 1977-78; asst. prof. Delehanty Inst., N.Y.C., 1978-79, Ladycliff Coll., Highland Falls, N.Y., 1979-80, Am. Bus. Inst., Bklyn., 1980-82; asst. dir. Adelphi Inst., Bklyn., 1982-85; asst. prof. Coll. St. Elizabeth, Convent Station, N.J., 1986-88; adj. asst. prof. NYU, 1986-88, Dowling Coll., Oakdale, N.Y., 1989-90; assoc. prof., co-dir. computer mfg., dir. mgmt. tech. SUNY Coll. of Tech., Farmingdale, 1987—. Editor: Research Techniques in Business Education, NYU Doctoral Abstracts, 1981-88, Agnew lecture by P.M. Sapre, 1989, NYU Symposium, 1989. Recipient Paul S. Lomax award, NYU, 1989. Mem. Nat. Assn. Indsl. Tech., Am. Acctg. Assn., Inst. Mgmt. Accts., Am. Prodn. and Inventory Control Soc., Prodn. and Ops. Mgmt. Soc., Am. Soc. for Quality Control, Phi Delta Kappa, Delta Pi Epsilon (Cert. of Merit 1988). Republican. Home: 493 Lariat Ln Bethpage NY 11714-4017

MARRONE-PUGLIA, GAETANA, language and literature educator; b. Salemi, Italy; came to U.S., 1973; d. Francesco and Rosa (Sparacia) Marrone; m. Gerardo Puglia. Doctorate in modern langs./lits., U. Palermo, Italy, 1969; PhD in Italian, Northwestern U., 1976. Conversational asst. U. Warwick, Eng., 1970-73; teaching asst. Northwestern U., Evanston, Ill., 1973-76, lectr., 1981-85; asst. prof. Nazareth Coll., Rochester, N.Y., 1978-81; asst. prof. Princeton (N.J.) U., 1985-91, assoc. prof. dept. romance langs., 1991—. Author: La Drammatica di Ugo Betti, 1988; producer film: Woman in the Wind, 1988. Mem. MLA, Am. Assn. Italian Studies, Internat. Assn. Italian Studies. Office: Princeton U 319 E Pyne St Princeton NJ 08544

MARROW, DOROTHY COMBELLACK, nurse, educator; b. Gardiner, Maine, Mar. 8, 1937; d. James Henry and Esther Phoebe (Morang) Combellack; m. Norman Filmore Marrow, Nov. 27, 1958 (div. July 1982); children: Peter Ward, Gregory James, Jennifer Esther. Nursing diploma, Peter Bent Brigham Hosp., Boston, 1958. Staff nurse, kidney rsch. Peter Bent Brigham Hosp., 1958; staff nurse, psychiatry VA, Togus, Maine, 1958-59, staff nurse, med., surgery, 1960-64, staff nurse, CCU, ICU, 1967-77, nursing instr., 1977—; nursing instr. Mid-State Coll., Augusta, Maine, 1982-85; nursing cons. Loring Air Force Base, Limestone, Maine, 1987; nursing recruiter LPN schs., Maine, 1984-86. CPR instr. Am. Heart Assn., Augusta, 1975-90; nursing chairperson Combined Fed. Campaign, Togus, 1981-82; speaker Girl Scouts USA, Pittston, Maine, 1983, Westbrook (Maine) Community Coll., 1984; mem. bd. dirs. Motivational Svcs., Inc., Augusta, 1987-88. Recipient Makaria Club scholarship, Meth. Ch., Gardiner, Maine, 1955, Peter Bent Brigham Hosp. scholarship, Boston, 1955. Mem. Webber Pond Fish and Game Assn. (sec. 1979-81). Republican. Methodist. Home: PO Box 290 Gardiner ME 04345-0290 Office: VA Togus ME 04330

MARRS, BARRY LEE, science director; b. Newark, Sept. 23, 1942; s. Donald Lee and Goldie (Mack) M.; m. Barbara Abbe Griswold, Aug. 20, 1966; children: Abbe Lea, Gwendolyn. BA, Williams Coll., 1963; PhD, Case Western Res. U., 1968. NSF postdoctoral fellow U. Ill., Urbana, 1967-69; Am. Cancer Soc. postdoctoral fellow Stanford (Calif.) U., 1969-71; rsch. assoc. Ind. U., Bloomington, 1971-72; asst. prof. Sch. Medicine St. Louis U., 1972-75, assoc. prof., 1975-78, prof., 1978-83; sr. rsch. assoc. Exxon Rsch. and Engrng. Co., Clinton, N.J., 1983-85; rsch. mgr. E. I. duPont de Nemours & Co., Wilmington, Del., 1985-90, sci. dir., 1990—. Contbr. over 50 articles to profl. publs. Recipient Career Devel. award NIH, 1973-78. Office: EI duPont de Nemours & Co Experimental Sta Wilmington DE 19880-0173

MARRS, STUART LYNN, percussionist; b. Newark, Sept. 29, 1948; s. Donald Lee and Goldie (Mack) M.; m. Gianna Felix, Apr. 30, 1975. BMus, Ind. U., 1970, MMus, 1984, DMus, 1989. Prin. percussionist Louisville Orch., 1970; prin. percussionist/timp. Nat. Symphony Orch. of Bolivia, La Paz, 1970-71, Nat. Symphony Orch. of Costa Rica, San Jose, 1972-82; prof. percussion Nat. Youth Symphony Program, San Jose, 1972-82; prof. music Nat. U., Heredia, Costa Rica, 1976-82; instr. percussion Ind. U., Bloomington, 1982-84; prof. music U. Maine, Orono, 1985—; soloist on internat. scope, 1971—; founder Costa Rican Sch. Percussion Playing, 1972-82. Contbr. articles to profl. jours. Mem. Percussive Arts Soc. (Maine chpt. pres. 1986—), Pi Kappa Lambda (chpt. pres. 1989—). Office: U Maine 123 Lord Hall Orono ME 04469

MARRUS, LAUREN WINER, publisher; b. Boston, July 12, 1961; d. Howard A. and Nancy A. Winer; m. Michael Edwin Marrus, Sept. 15, 1991. BA magna cum laude, Wellesley (Mass.) Coll., 1983; MBA, Harvard U., 1987. Rsch. assoc. Booz, Allen & Hamilton, N.Y.C., 1983-85; assoc. Bankers Trust Co., N.Y.C., 1987-89; v.p. Cronus Ptnrs., N.Y.C., 1989; jour. publisher Instnl. Investor Inc., N.Y.C., 1989—. Mem. Phi Beta Kappa.

MARSDEN, HERCI IVANA, classical ballet artistic director; b. Omis-Split, Croatia, Dec. 2, 1937; came to U.S., 1958; d. Ante and Magda (Smith) Munitic; m. Myles Marsden, Aug. 10, 1957 (div. 1976); children—Ana, Richard, Mark; m. Dujko Radovnikovic, Aug. 27, 1977; 1 child, Dujko. Student, Internat. Ballet Sch., 1955. Mem. corps de ballet Nat. Theatre, Split, 1954-58; founder Braecrest Sch. Ballet, Lincoln, R.I., 1958—; founder State Ballet of R.I., Lincoln, 1960—, artistic dir., 1976—; artistic dir. U. R.I. Classical Ballet, Kingston, 1966—, lectr., 1966—.

MARSH, BRIAN RICHARD, management executive, playwright; b. Montague, Mass., Nov. 7, 1948; s. Walter Raymond and Elizabeth Hazel (McClary) M.; m. Ljuba Greene, July 25, 1977; children: Alexandra Whitney, Colin Webster. BA, U. Mass., 1970; MA, Bowling Green U., 1971. Pres. Profl. Tng. Inc., Springfield, Mass., 1982—, Almadan Inc., Belchertown, 1984—; producer The Hampshire Shakespeare Co., 1989—. Playwright: This Particular Place, 1988, Play for 21 Voices, 1988, The Church-250 Years, 1987, The Search for Emily, 1988, The Letter from Hope, 1989, Henry David, 1990, The Passenger Pigeon, 1991, Home to Hawley, 1991. Pres. Carriage Towne Players, 1984-87. Mem. Founders of Hartford (Councillor 1986—), Colonial Wars. Episcopalian. Home: 21 Sherwood Dr Belchertown MA 01007-9541

MARSH, DANIEL, clothing store executive; b. Bklyn., Apr. 10, 1924; s. Herbert and Ruth (Gesner) M.; m. Zina Renee Feldman, Dec. 31, 1947 (dec. Sept. 1976); children: Joyce Barbara, Helene Myra, Michael Louis; m. Roberta Jacobs, Jan. 9, 1977. Student, Pratt Inst., 1941-42, NYU, 1946-47. Vice pres. Marsh's Men's & Boys' Shop, Huntington, N.Y., 1945—. Author, editor: Keys To Success, 1966 (cert. of distinction Brand Names Found. 1966). Mem. exec. bd. YMCA, Huntington, 1972-78. Sgt. USAAF, 1942-46, ETO. Decorated Bronze Star with two oak leaf clusters). Mem. Huntington Kiwanis (past pres. 1957), Retail Coun. N.Y., Huntington C. of C. (bd. dirs. 1967-69, treas. 1973-75), Huntington Village Mchts. Orgn. (bd. dirs.). Office: 268-274 Main St Huntington NY 11743-3140

MARSH, DAVID GEORGE, medical educator; b. London, Mar. 29, 1940; came to U.S., 1966; s. Clifford George and Alice (Orr) M.; m. Jeanne E. Harrison, June 2, 1972; children: Stephen, Alexander, Peter. BSc with Honors, U. Birmingham, 1961; PhD, U. Cambridge, 1964; postgrad. Calif. Inst. Tech., 1966-69. Rsch. biochemist Wellcome Rsch. Lab., Beckenham, Eng., 1964-66; asst. prof. medicine Johns Hopkins U., Balt., 1969-75, assoc. prof., 1975-89, prof., 1989—, asst. prof. microbiology, 1972-77; staff mem. Good Samaritan Hosp., Balt., 1970-89; mem. ad hoc grant rev. coms. NIH, 1977—; cons. Allergopharma div. E. Merck, Hamburg, Fed. Republic Germany, 1978-91, Cytel, La Jolla, 1988—; chmn. HLA & Allergy Histocompatibility Workshop, 1991; organizer Allergen Database, 1989—. Contbr. articles to profl. jours. Nat. Inst. Allergy and Infectious Diseases grantee, 1970-88. Fellow Am. Acad. Allergy and Immunology; mem. Am. Assn. Immunology, Am. Soc. Human Genetics, Collegium Internat. Allergology, Sigma Xi. Office: Johns Hopkins Asthma & Allergy 5501 Hopkins Bayview Cir Baltimore MD 21224-6819

MARSH, JOHN LEE, chemistry consultant; b. Washington, Feb. 25, 1916; s. William Judson and Rhoda Olive (Rhea) M.; m. Margaret Durow, 1943

(dec. 1971); children: Alan David, Andrea Beth, Charles Judson; m. Marjorie Ellena Zimmermann, 1972; stepchildren: Frederick Phillip Heitkamp, David Frank, Susan Jane Snyder. BA, U. Rochester, 1938; PhD, U. Ill., 1941. Rsch. chemist Hooker Electro-Chem., Niagara Falls, N.Y., 1941-43; sr. chemist Ciba Pharm. (name now Ciba-Geigy, Summit, N.J., 1943-82; pvt. practice cons. Summit, 1982—. Summit Symphony Orch., clarinetist, 1969-86, pres. 1973-75, dir. 1975—; bd. dirs. ARC, Summit, 1988—, archivist, 1991. Republican. Presbyterian. Home and Office: 108 Beekman Rd Summit NJ 07901-1723

MARSH, ROBERT WILLIAM, marketing communication consultant; b. Mpls., June 23, 1924; s. Ralph A. and Jane Grace (Smith) M.; m. Anne Daviss, Mar. 30, 1951; children: Joan Grace, Barbara Anne, Carol Daviss, William Arthur. BA in Journalism, Pa. State U., 1948. Copy writer, anner WDEL, Inc., Wilmington, Del., 1949-54; advt. asst. DuPont Co., Wilmington, 1954-62; mktg. communication mgr. ICI Ams., Inc., Wilmington, 1962-85; pres. The Mktg. Connection, Inc., Wilmington, 1985—; exec. dir. Assn. Indsl. Metallizers, Coaters & Laminators, Inc., Wilmington, 1986-92; contbg. editor Paper, Film & Foil Converter Mag., 1992—. Author: (novels) MacLaren's Men, 1982, A Taste of Steel, 1983, Code Name: Needlepoint, 1988; contbr. articles to profl. jours. Dir. Kentmere, Wilmington, 1984-86. Sgt. OSS, 1944-45, ETO. Presbyterian.

MARSH, RUTH LORRAINE, editor; b. Rahway, N.J., July 6, 1927; d. Donald F. and Elinore (Williams) M. BA, Fairleigh Dickinson U., 1960. Editor Macmillan Pub. Co., N.Y.C., 1960-62, Silver, Burdett & Ginn, Morristown, N.J., 1962-84; prin. Marsh Editorial Svcs., Ho Ho Kus, N.J., 1984—. Home and Office: Marsh Editorial Svcs 589 W Saddle River Rd Ho Ho Kus NJ 07423-1640

MARSH, WILLIAM LAURENCE, research pathologist executive; b. Cardiff, Wales, Great Britain, Apr. 21, 1926; came to U.S., 1969; s. William and Violet (Hill) M.; m. Jean Beryl Margaret Hill, June 6, 1952; children: Christine Margaret, Nicholas John. Fellow, Inst. Med. Lab. Sci., London, 1954, Inst. Biology, London, 1969; PhD, Columbia Pacific U., 1968; fellow, Royal Coll. Pathologists, London, 1985. Lab. chief Regional Blood Transfusion Ctr., Brentwood, Eng., 1955-69; assoc. investigator N.Y. Blood Ctr., N.Y.C., 1969-79, investigator, 1980-83, sr. investigator, 1984-87; sr. v.p. rsch. Lindsley Kimball Rsch. Inst. of N.Y. Blood Ctr., N.Y.C., 1987—; editorial bd. Transfusion jour., 1979-91, Blood Transfusion and Immunohematology jour., 1980-86; sci. reviewer various jours. Author chpts. on human blood groups in textbooks, 1965-91; contbr. over 250 articles to profl. jours. Recipient Blood Donors award of merit Blood Donor Assn., Eng., 1961. Fellow Inst. Med. Lab. Sci. (Race prize 1976), Inst. Biology, Royal Coll. Pathologists; mem. Internat. Soc. Blood Transfusion, Am. Assn. Blood Banks (Dunsford Meml. award, 1975, Emily Cooley award, 1988, Grove-Rasmussen award, 1990), British soc. Hematology, British Soc. Blood Transfusion. Home: 101 Hillcrest Dr Moneta VA 24121-3003 Office: NY Blood Ctr S310 E 67th St New York NY 10021

MARSHALEK, JEAN RAY, association executive; b. Balt., Nov. 17, 1930; d. Archie Fleming and Ethel Josephine (Donhauser) Ray; m. Melvin Sylvester Marshalek, Sept. 30, 1951; children: Robert Gerald, Cynthia Ann, Randal Fleming, James Kevin, Suzanne Regina, Nancy Antoinette. Grad., Patterson Park High Sch., Balt., 1949. Sec. H.R. Habelson, Balt., 1948-49, Helen Sherry, Atty.-at-Law, Balt., 1949-50; adminstrv. sec. U.S. Govt., Ft. Holabird, 1950-54; pres. Engel's Angels in Humperdinck Heaven Fan Club, 1971—. Editor Cliffdweller newsletter, 1968, The Guardian Engel newsletter, 1971—. Sec. PTA, Carney Elem. Sch., Balt., 1970; pres. Thornewood Park Civic Assn., Balt., 1969-71. Democrat. Roman Catholic. Home and Office: Engels Angels 3024 4th Ave Baltimore MD 21234-3208

MARSHALL, DALE FREDERICK, labor union official; b. Kingston, N.Y., Dec. 18, 1953; s. Stephen and Jacqueline Frances (Temple) M.; m. Cecilia Santiago, Sept. 14, 1979 (div.); 1 child, Christina Ariel. BA, U. Conn., 1974. Asst. comptroller Amalgamated Clothing and Textile Workers' Union, N.Y.C., 1984-89, MIS dir., 1984—, ops. dir., 1989—; shop steward local 153 Office and Profl. Employees Internat. Union, N.Y.C., 1980-84. Mem. Lions (sec. Rahway, N.J. chpt. 1987). Democrat. Office: Amalgamated Clothing and Textile Workers Union 15 Union Sq W New York NY 10003-3316

MARSHALL, DAVID, orthodontist; b. Syracuse, N.Y., Feb. 4, 1914; s. Moses and Fanny (Bagelman) Salutsky; B.S., Syracuse U., 1932-35; D.D.S., U. Md., 1938-42; postgrad. Columbia, 1943-45, Tufts Coll., Northwestern U.; children from previous marriage: Robert Andrew, Howard Randy, Douglas S. (dec.), Susan Beth, Robin (dec.); m. Marjorie Kaufman, Sept. 7, 1973. Practice dentistry specializing in orthodontics, Syracuse, mem. staff St. Joseph's Hosp., Crouse-Irving Hosp., University Hosp., Meml. Hosp.; mem. cons. School Speech, Syracuse U.; orthodontic cons. N.Y. State Health Dept.; lectr. in field, producer sci. exbns., Anat. Mus. Recipient Hektoen medal AMA, 1970. Diplomate Am. Bd. Orthodontists. Mem. Royal Soc. Medicine, ADA, N.Y. Dental Soc., Syracuse Dental Soc., 5th Dist. Dental Soc., Syracuse C. of C., Northeastern (qualifying com.), Am. orthodontists socs., Pierre Fauchard Acad. Contbg. author textbooks dentistry and orthodontics; contbr. articles to dental publs. Home: 5231 Brockway Ln Fayetteville NY 13066-1705 Office: 1124 E Genesee St Syracuse NY 13210

MARSHALL, FRAY FRANCIS, urology educator; b. N.Y.C., Aug. 27, 1944; s. Victor Fray and Barbara (Walsh) M.; m. Lindsay Wheatley, Oct. 6, 1975; children: Wheatley, Brooks. BA, U. Va., 1965, MD, 1969. Asst. prof. Urology Johns Hopkins Hosp., Balt., 1975-79, assoc. prof. Urology, 1979-86, prof. Urology, 1986—, dir. adult Urology, 1990—. Editor (books) Urologic Complication, 1990, Operative Urology, 1991. Office: dept Urology Johns Hopkins Hosp 601 N Wolfe St Baltimore MD 21205

MARSHALL, GARY CHARLES, mailing list company executive; b. Bklyn., Oct. 25, 1943; s. Charles J. and Gladys R. (Walsh) M.; student St. John's U., 1961-64, New Sch. for Social Rsch., 1979; children: Stacey Ann, Kimberly Jane. Circulation mgr. Nat. Rev. mag., N.Y.C., 1967-69; direct mail mgr. Rome Rsch. Co., N.Y.C., 1969-73; gen. mgr. Am. Fulfillment Corp., N.Y.C., 1973-75; v.p. EDP, Hugo Dunhill Mailing Lists, N.Y.C., 1975—. Mem. Republican Nat. Com. With M.P. Corps, U.S. Army, 1965-67. Mem. VFW, Am. Legion, Disabled Am. Vets. Roman Catholic. Home: 135 W 78th St New York NY 10024-6747 Office: Hugo Dunhill Mailing Lists Inc 630 3d Ave New York NY 10017-6705

MARSHALL, JOHN FRANCIS, university administrator; b. Lock Haven, Pa., Oct. 26, 1939; s. John F. and Marian J. Marshall; B.A., Colgate U., 1961; M.A., Columbia U., 1962; Ed.D., Pa. State U., 1969; postdoctoral Harvard U., 1981; m. Margaret Mary Shafer, June 28, 1969; children: Mark John, Wendy Joan. Residence hall coord. Pa. State U., University Park, 1964-66; dean of students Slippery Rock (Pa.) State Coll., 1966-71; v.p. student devel. U. San Francisco, 1971-74; v.p. student, ednl. and adminstrv. svcs. SUNY, Potsdam, 1974-83, v.p. instl. advancement, 1983-88, acting pres., 1988-89; v.p. instl. advancement U. Hartford, West Hartford, Conn., 1989-92; v.p. devel. Belmont (N.C.) Abbey Coll., 1992—. Christian Scientist. Club: Lions (pres. 1979-80) (Potsdam). Office: Belmont Abbey Coll Inst Advancement Belmont NC 28012

MARSHALL, JOHN FRANKLIN, financial officer; b. Phoenixville, Pa., May 1, 1947; s. John L. Marshall and Mary T. (Raquet) Keck; m. Helen M. Wentzel, Mar. 13, 1970; children: Kimberly A., Megan N. BBA, Temple U., 1972; MBA, Drexel U., 1977. CPA, Pa. Auditor Arthur Andersen & Co., Phila., 1972-75; spl. projects analyst ARA Svcs., Inc., Phila., 1975-77; corp. controller Bassett Steel & Tube Co., Inc., King of Prussia, Pa., 1977-84; chief fin. officer Margay Mgmt., Wyomissing, Pa., 1984—. With U.S. Army, 1966-68. Mem. Pa. Inst. CPAs. Roman Catholic. Office: Margay Mgmt Corp 220 N Park Rd Reading PA 19610-2908

MARSHALL, JOHN MAYNARD, training company executive; b. Cin., Dec. 16, 1953; s. Jack Maynard and Sarah Jeannette (Fairo) M.; m. Adrienne Ann Boyd, June 8, 1978; 1 child, John Matthew. BSE, U.S. Mil. Acad., 1978; student, N.H. Coll., 1990. Comd. 2d lt. U.S. Army, 1978; advanced thour grades to capt. 82d Airborne Div., Fayetteville, N.C., 1987; engring. mgr. GTE, Boston, 1987-89; pres. Pilot Leadership Systems, Nashua, N.H., 1989—; cons. in field. Author (software program) Interactive Tng., 1991. Decorated Commendation medal. Mem. ASTD, Smaller Bus. Assn. New Eng., Boston Computer Soc., West Point Soc. N.H. (sec. 1990-91), World Plan (founder, bd. dirs.). Home: 21 Cadogan Way Nashua NH 03062-2254 Office: Pilot Leadership Systems 21 Cadogan Way Nashua NH 03062-2254

MARSHALL, JOHN PATRICK, lawyer; b. Bklyn., July 3, 1950; s. Harry W. and Mary Margaret (Kelly) M.; m. Cheryl J. Garvey, Aug. 10, 1975; children: Kelly Blake, Logan Brooke. BA, Rutgers U., 1972; JD cum laude, N.Y. Law Sch., 1976. Bar: N.Y. 1977, N.J. 1977, U.S. Dist. Ct. N.J. 1977, U.S. Dist. Ct. (so. and ea. dists.) N.Y. 1978, U.S. Ct. Appeals (3rd cir.) 1982, U.S. Dist Ct. (no. dist.) N.Y. 1991. Assoc. Kelley Drye & Warren, N.Y.C., 1976-84; ptnr. Kelley Drye & Warren, N.Y.C. and Parsippany, 1985—; bd. dirs. Am. Foreign Shipping Co., Inc., Westfield, N.J. Editorial bd. N.Y. Law Sch. Law Rev., 1975-76, staffmember, 1974-75. Mem. jud. screening com. N.Y. County Dem. Com., N.Y. County New Dem. Coalition, 1988; v.p. Humanitarian Found. for Nicaragua, 1991. Fellow Am. Bar Found.; mem. ABA, N.Y. County Lawyer's Assn. (sec. 1984-87, mem. com. on Supreme Ct. 1984—, mem. legal edn., admission to bar and lawyer placement com. 1983—), Am. Arbitration Assn. (panel of arbitrators N.Y. and N.J. regions 1991—), Assn. of Bar of City of N.Y. (sec. judiciary com. 1989-92), Plainfield Country Club. Office: Kelley Drye & Warren 101 Park Ave New York NY 10178-0002 also: 5 Sylvan Way Parsippany NJ 07054

MARSHALL, KATHARINE BOEHRINGER, communications executive; b. Reading, Pa., Aug. 12, 1956; d. Charles William and Arlene Mae (Demming) Boehringer; m. John E. Marshall, July 31, 1982; 1 child, Justin Clay. BA in Journalism, Indiana U. of Pa., 1978. Pub. info. officer Alfred (N.Y.) U., 1978-80; assoc. editor Wellsville (N.Y.) Daily Reporter, 1980-81; publs. editor Princeton (N.J.) U., 1981-82; community rels. and internal communications coord. Chase Lincoln First Bank, NA, Rochester, N.Y., 1982-85; editor Burroughs Corp., Detroit, 1985-86, mgr. employee communications, 1986; dir. communications Unisys Corp. (formerly Burroughs Corp.), Blue Bell, Pa., 1987—; instr. Beaver Coll., Glenside, Pa., 1989. Recipient Exceptional Achievement award Coun. for Advancement and Support of Edn., 1982. Mem. INternat. Assn. Bus. Communicators (Gold Quill 1985, Silver Quill 1986), Pub. Rels. Soc. Am., Coun. Communication Mgmt. Home: 123 Heartwood Dr Lansdale PA 19446-1604 Office: Unisys Corp PO Box 500 MS A2-17 Blue Bell PA 19424

MARSHALL, KAY VALERIE, underwriter; b. Bklyn., Mar. 8, 1960; d. Joel Curtis Marshall and Veronica Glendine Browne. Student, Russell Sage Coll., 1978-80; BA in Psychology, Syracuse U., 1982. Cert. N.Y. state agent; lic. broker 1990. Asst. underwriter Empire Allcity Ins. Group, N.Y.C., 1983-85, Home Ins. Group, N.Y.C., 1985-89; account exec. and asst. underwriter Kornreich Ins. Svcs., N.Y.C., 1989-90; comml. underwriter Am. Internat. Group, N.Y.C., 1990—. Mem. Nat. Ins. Industry Assn. Democrat. Episcopalian. Home: 66 E 40th St Brooklyn NY 11203 Office: Am Internat Group 59 John St New York NY 10038

MARSHALL, KENNETH ALLAN, plastic and reconstructive surgeon; b. Boston, Dec. 28, 1938; s. Nathan Harold and Mary (Elizabeth) Creagh; m. JoAnne T. Burrows, Feb. 10, 1968; children: Torrey A., C. Adrian. AB, Harvard U., 1960; MD, Columbia U., 1964. Diplomate Am. Bd. Surgery, Am. Bd. Plastic Surgery. Resident in gen. surgery Harvard Surg. Svc., 1964-66, Boston City Hosp., 1969-72; fellow Shriners Burns Inst., Mass. Gen. Hosp., Boston, 1970; resident in plastic surgery U. Va., Charlottesville, 1973-75; pvt. practice Cambridge and Boston, Mass., 1975—; instr. in surgery Harvard Med. Sch., Cambridge, 1975-83, asst. prof. surgery, 1983—; chief div. of plastic surgery Mt. Auburn Hosp., Cambridge, 1990—. Contbr. articles to profl. jours. Lt. comdr. USNR, 1966-69. Mem. ACS, Am. Soc. of Plastic and Reconstructive Surgery, Am. Burn Assn., Plastic Surg. Rsch. Coun., Mass. Med. Soc., New Eng. Soc. of Plastic Surgery, Northeastern Soc. of Plastic Surgery, Mass. Soc. of Plastic Surgery (sec. 1985-89, pres. 1989-91), Am. Assn. of Hand Surgery, New Eng. Soc. of Plastic Reconstructive Surgery (sec.-treas. 1991—). Office: Drs Office Bldg 300 Mt Auburn St Ste # 306 Cambridge MA 02138

MARSHALL, MICHAEL BORDEN, marketing executive; b. Boston, Mar. 16, 1957; s. Martin Vivan and Rosanne (Borden) M.; m. Susan Diane Parks, June 15, 1991. BA, Oberlin Coll., 1979; MBA, Harvard U., 1983. Analyst Benton & Bowles, Inc., N.Y.C., 1979-80; mktg. mgr. Thor Metal Works, Ltd., Syracuse, N.Y., 1980-81; asst. mgr. Am. Express Co., N.Y.C., 1982; sr. analyst Bank of Boston Corp., 1983-85; cons. John Hancock Mut. Life Ins. Co., Boston, 1985-89; asst. v.p. N.Y. Life Ins. Co., N.Y.C., 1989—; cons. assoc. Bank Mktg. Assn., Boston, 1983-89, N.Y., 1991—; advisor bus. analysis Arthur D. Little, Inc., Cambridge, Mass., 1985—. Author: articles in profl. jours. Mem. adv. bd. Youth Enrichment Svcs. of Boston, 1984-90. Recipient Jerome Davis award Oberlin Coll., 1979, Copeland Sect. award Harvard Bus. Sch., 1982, Corp. Spl. award John Hancock Exec. Com., 1986. Mem. Am. Mktg. Assn. (sr. v.p. 1984—), Mktg. Sci. Inst. (bd. dirs. 1985-89), Life Ins. Mktg. and Rsch. Assn. (devel. bd. 1991—), Coun. on Fin. Competition (adv. bd.), Harvard Club. Episcopalian. Home: RFD 2 Sunset Dr North Salem NY 10560 Office: NY Life Ins Co 51 Madison Ave New York NY 10010-1603

MARSHALL, NATALIE JUNEMANN, university official; b. Milw., June 13, 1929; d. Harold E. and Myrtle (Findlay) Junemann; m. Howard D. Marshall, Aug. 7, 1954 (dec. 1972); children: Frederick S., Alison B.; m. Phillip Shatz, May 27, 1988. A.B., Vassar Coll., 1951; M.A., Columbia U., 1952, Ph.D., 1963. Instr. Vassar Coll., Poughkeepsie, N.Y., 1952-54, 59, 59-60, 63, dean studies, prof. econs., 1973-75, v.p. for student affairs, 1975-80, v.p. for adminstrn. and student services and prof. econs., 1980-91; teaching fellow Wesleyan U., Middletown, Conn., 1955-56; from asst. prof. to prof. SUNY, New Paltz, 1964-73. Editor: (with Howard Marshall) The History of Economic Thought, 1968; Keynes, Updated or Outdated, 1970; author: (with Howard Marshall) Collective Bargaining, 1971. Trustee St. Francis Hosp., 1979-88, Area Fund Dutchess County, 1982-87; trustee Hudson Valley Philharm., 1985—, pres., 1989—. Mem. AAUP, Am. Assn. Higher Edn., Am. Econ. Assn., AAUW (v.p. N.Y. State div. 1964-66), Poughkeepsie Vassar Club (pres. 1965-67). Home: PO Box 2470 Poughkeepsie NY 12603-0882

MARSHALL, PAUL, JR., music educator, composer; b. Cin., Nov. 26, 1927; s. Paul and Addie Mae (Brannon) M.; m. Sylvia Reed, Mar. 15, 1957; children: Elliott, Orrin, David, Jonathan. MusB, Ohio State U., 1954, MA in Music, 1955, BS in Music Edn., 1960. Cert. music tchr., N.Y., Ohio, N.J. Asst. prof. Claflin Coll., Orangeburg, S.C., 1958-59; music instr. pub. schs., Springfield, Ohio, 1961-65, Ringwood, N.J., 1965-68; prof. music Bergen Community Coll., Paramus, N.J., 1968—, chmn. dept. fine arts, 1972-81; composer, arranger Glenn Miller Orch., N.Y.C., 1964-74; arranger, keyboard Muse Records, Englewood, N.J., 1977—; pianist Phoenix Records, N.Y.C., 1978—. Composer: (opera) The Mink Stockings, 1961, (symphony) The Free Spirit, 1963, (song cycle) Soprano and Piano, 1980, (electronic music) Annihilation II, 1992. Bd. trustees John Harms Theater, Englewood, N.J., 1987; dir. High Sch. Equivalency Program, Paramus, N.J., 1969-72. Sgt. U.S. Army, 1947-49. Mem. NAACP, NEA, Am. Fedn. Musicians, Music Educators Nat. Conv., N.J. Edn. Assn. Home: 393 Murray Ave Englewood NJ 07631-1419

MARSHALL, PHYLLIS ELLINWOOD, mental health system executive, consultant; b. Kansas City, Mo., Dec. 20, 1929; d. Herbert Dwight and Mildred (Gillham) Ellinwood; m. John D. Reich, July 1, 1950 (div. 1964); children: Martha Reich Millican, Michael David, Donald Martin; m. C. Randolph Marshall, Nov. 27, 1969. B.A., Washington U., St. Louis, 1951, M.S.W., 1969. Adult program dir. St. Louis YWCA, 1962-64, dir. decentralized programs, 1964-67; alcoholism caseworker Malcolm Bliss Mental Health Ctr., St. Louis, 1968; exec. dir. Cobb County YWCA, Ga., 1969-72; dir. Coastal Area Community Mental Health Ctr., Brunswick, Ga., 1973-77; dir. Mental Health Svcs., Ga. Dept. Human Resources, Atlanta, 1977-84; exec. dir. Integrated Mental Health, Inc., Rochester, N.Y., 1984-92; exec. dir. No. Va. Mental Health Inst., 1992—; cons. NIMH, Washington, 1979-84, So. Regional Ednl. Bd., Atlanta, 1979-84, N.Y. State Office Mental Health, Albany, 1980-84, State of Ill. Dept. Mental Health, 1988, WHO, 1989, Ont., Can., 1990-91, The Netherlands, 1991-92; with mental health programs in Ohio, Mich., Ariz., Md.; co-chair Metro Atlanta Deinstitutionalization Task Force, 1983-85; bd. dirs. Children Have All Rights, Legal, Ednl. and Emotional, Menninger Found. project, Atlanta, 1983-84; bd. dirs. Fingerlakes Health Systems Agy., Rochester, 1985-92, bd. dirs., 1991-92; adviser WHO, 1989; chair Monroe County Adv. Com. on Women's Issues, 1992—, chmn., 1991-92. Contbg. author: Perspectives in Mental Health, 1980, New Directions for Mental Health Svcs., 1988, New Frontiers in Mental Heath, 1989; contbr. articles to profl. publs. Bd. dirs. Human Resources Credit Union, Atlanta, 1982-84. Recipient Boss of Yr. award Brunswick Jaycees, 1977, Good Friend award Brunswick Mental Health Assn., 1977, Community Mental Health award Atlanta U., 1980, Outstanding Achievement award Am. Soc. for Pub. Adminstrn., 1990. Mem. AAUW (chpt. pres. 1978), Assn. Mental Health Adminstrs., Ga. Assn. Community Mental Health Ctrs. (pres. 1975-77), Rochester Women's Network (bd. dirs., treas. 1990-92). Club: Midtown Tennis (Rochester). Avocations: ocean sailing, music, tennis. Office: No Va Mental Health Inst 3302 Gallows Rd Falls Church VA 22042

MARSHALL, ROBERT J., psychologist, psychoanalyst; b. Passaic, N.J., Nov. 15, 1928; s. Joseph S. and Mary (Latosinski) Majuschak; m. Simone Paulette Verniere, Sept. 13, 1953; children: Gabrielle, Annette. BS, Rutgers U., 1950; MS in Edn., CCNY, 1951; PhD, SUNY, Buffalo, 1958; cert. psychotherapy and psychoanalysis, Postgrad. Ctr. Mental Health, N.Y.C., 1964-68. Diplomate Am. Bd. Profl. Psychologists; lic. psychologist, N.Y. Pvt. practice N.Y.C., 1959—; psychologist Lincoln Hall, Lincolndale, N.Y., 1965-75; faculty Ctr. for Modern Psychoanalytic Studies, N.Y.C., 1985—, Derner Inst., Adelphi U., Garden City, N.Y., 1985—. Author: Resistant Interactions, 1983, (with S. Marshall) Transference-Counter Transference Matrix, 1988. 1st lt. USMSC, 1954-59. Home: 300 E 74th St New York NY 10021-3712 Office: 1438 3d Ave New York NY 10028

MARSHALL, SIMONE VERNIERE, psychologist, psychoanalyst; b. Paris, France; came to U.S., 1951; d. Urbain and Sabrielle (Cadiergues) Verniere; m. Robert J. Marshall, Sept. 13, 1953; children: Gabrielle, Annette. Lic. psychology, Sorbonne U., 1948; MA in Devel. Psychology, Columbia U., 1951, PhD in Clin. Psychology, 1959. Cert. in psychoanalysis, White Inst., N.Y.C., 1970. Rsch. sch. psychologist Nat. Bd. of Edn., Paris, 1948-51; child clin. psychologist Children's Hosp., Buffalo, N.Y., 1953-54; clin. psychologist N.J. Dept. of Instns., Trenton, N.J., 1956-58; clin. instr. Rutgers Univ. Psychology Clinic, New Brunswick, N.J., 1958-59; clinician, researcher Children's Village, Dobbs Ferry, N.Y., 1959-60; child therapist Rockland Mental Health Ctr., Monsey, N.Y., 1961-65; pvt. practice psychologist, psychoanalyst Westchester, N.Y., 1960-90, N.Y.C., 1966—; tng. analyst Blanton Peale Inst. Religion & Health, N.Y.C., 1984—; part time cons. Bd. of Edn., Ossining, N.Y., 1960-64; supr. Inst. for Contemporary Psychotherapy, N.Y.C., 1974—; faculty Nassau County Med. Ctr., L.I. Inst. for Psychoanalysis, 1980—; lectr. Union Theol. Sem., N.Y.C., 1983-86. Co-authnor: (with R.J. Marshall) The Transference-Countertransference Matrix, 1988. Coord., founder Croton-Cortlandt Women's Ctr., Croton-on-Hudson, N.Y., 1976-81. Recipient Fullbright scholarship Columbia Univ., 1951-52. Mem. Am. Psychol. Assn., Am. Group Psychotherapy Assn., White Psychoanalytic Soc., Westchester County Psychol. Assn. Home: 300 E 74th St Apt 33D New York NY 10021-3717 Office: 1438 3d Ave New York NY 10028-1978

MARSHALL, STUART ALAN, treasurer; b. Bklyn., Nov. 12, 1946; s. Philip Leon and Norma (Feinstein) M.; m. Joanne Loeffler, June 7, 1969; children: Craig, Bari. BS in Bus. Adminstrn., Monmouth Coll., 1978. Staff acct. Bond Clothes, N.Y.C., 1969-72; asst. contr. Mechanics Fin. Co., Jersey City, N.J., 1972-75; contr., treas. Mainship Corp., Silverton Marine, Marlboro, N.J., 1975-91; pres. Sam & Jam Inc., Neptune City, N.J., 1991—, also bd. dirs. Vol. Silverton First Aid Squad, Toms River, N.J., 1974-78, Cub Scout Pack 92, Toms River, 1979-82. With U.S. Army, 1966-68, ETO. Home: 11 Sage Rd Toms River NJ 08753-2626 Office: Paper Warehouse 11 TFH Plz 3d and Union Ave Neptune City NJ 07753

MARSHALL, THURGOOD, retired U.S. Supreme Court justice; b. Balt., July 2, 1908; s. William and Norma (Williams) M.; m. Vivian Burey, Sept. 4, 1929 (dec. Feb. 1955); m. Cecilia S. Suyat, Dec. 17, 1955; children—Thurgood, John. A.B., Lincoln U., 1930, LL.D. (hon.), 1947; LL.B., Howard U., 1933, LL.D. (hon.), 1954; LL.D. (hon.), Va. State Coll., 1948, Morgan State Coll., 1952, Grinnell Coll., 1954, Syracuse U., 1956, N.Y. Sch. Social Research, 1956, U. Liberia, 1960, Brandeis U., 1960, U. Mass., 1962, Jewish Theol. Sem., 1962, Wayne U., 1963, Princeton U., 1963, U. Mich., 1964, Johns Hopkins U., 1966, Far Eastern Univ., Manila, 1968, Victoria U. of Wellington, 1968, U. Calif., 1968, U. Otago, Dunedin, New Zealand, 1968. Bar: Md. 1933. Practiced in Balt., 1933-37; asst. spl. counsel NAACP, 1936-38; spl. counsel N.A.A.C.P., 1938-50, dir., counsel legal def. and ednl. fund, 1940-61; U.S. circuit judge for 2d Jud. Circuit, 1961-65; solicitor gen. U.S., 1965-67; justice U.S. Supreme Ct., 1967-91; Civil rights cases argued include Tex. Primary Case, 1944, Restrictive Covenant Cases, 1948, U. Tex. and Okla. Cases, 1950, sch. segregation cases, 1952-53; visited Japan and Korea to make investigation of ct. martial cases involving Negro soldiers, 1951; Cons. Constl. Conf. on Kenya, London, 1960; rep. White House Conf. Youth and Children. Recipient Spingarn medal, 1946; Living History award Research Inst. Mem. Nat. Bar Assn., N.Y. County Lawyers Assn., Am. Bar Assn., Bar Assn. D.C., Alpha Phi Alpha. Episcopalian. Club: Mason (33 deg.). Office: US Supreme Ct 1 1st St NE Washington DC 20543

MARSHALL, VERNE MONROE, surgeon; b. Frankfort, N.Y., Mar. 6, 1923; s. Floyd Harry and Ruth Evelyn (Goodale) M.; m. Elizabeth Mather Sill, Apr. 13, 1946; children: Alan Sill, Susan Goodale, Geoffrey Palmer, Wayne Seaverns. BA, SUNY, 1944; MD, Albany Med. Coll., 1947. Diplomate Am. Bd. Surgery. Intern Gen. Hosp. Fresno County, Fresno, Calif., 1947-48; surg. resident Boston City Hosp., 1948-50, Cambridge (Mass.) City Hosp., 1952-54; attending surgeon Geneva (N.Y.) Gen. Hosp., 1954—, chief surgery, 1988-90. Mem. planning bd. City of Geneva, 1972; pres. Finger Lakes coun. Boy Scouts Am., 1962, Geneva Concerts, 1978, Finger Lakes Regional Arts Coun., 1984. Lt. USNR, 1950-52. Fellow ACS; mem. AMA, Soc. Am. Gastrointestinal Endoscopic Surgeons, Med. Soc. State N.Y. (county del. 1985—), Cen. N.Y. Soc. Surgeons (pres. 1986-88), Finger Lakes Squares. Republican. Baptist. Office: 324 W North St Geneva NY 14456

MARSHALL, WAYNE KEITH, anesthesiology educator; b. Richmond, Va., Feb. 9, 1948; s. Chester Truman and Lois Ann (Tiller) M.; m. Dale Claire Reynolds, June 18, 1977; children: Meredith Reynolds, Catherine Truman, Whitney Wood. BS in Biology, Va. Poly. Inst. and State U., 1970; MD, Va. Commonwealth U., 1974. Diplomate Am. Bd. Anesthesiology, Nat. Bd. Med. Examiners. Surg. intern U. Cin., 1974-75, resident in surgery, 1975-77; resident in anesthesiology U. Va. Coll. Medicine, Charlottesville, 1977-79, rsch. fellow, 1979-80; asst. prof. anesthesia Pa. State U. Coll. Medicine, Hershey, 1980-86, assoc. prof., 1986—, assoc. clin. dir. oper. rm., 1982—, dir. pain mgmt. svc., 1984—; moderator nat. meetings. Mem. editorial bd. Anesthesiology Rev., 1987—, Jour. Neurosurg. Anesthesiology, 1988—; contbr. articles and abstracts to med. jours. Recipient Antarctic Svc. medal NSF, 1980. Mem. AMA, AAAS, Soc. Neurosurg. Anesthesia and Critical Care (sec.-treas. 1985-87, v.p. 1987-88, pres. 1989-90, bd. dirs. 1985-91), Assn. Univ. Anesthetists, Am. Soc. Anesthesiologists (del. ASA ho. of dels. 1990-92), Internat. Anesthesia Rsch. Soc., Pa. Soc. Anesthesiology, N.Y. Acad. Scis. Republican. Baptist. Office: Pa State U Dept Anesthesiology PO Box 850 Hershey PA 17033-0850

MARSHELLA, THOMAS JOSEPH, financial analyst; b. Bridgeport, Conn., Mar. 13, 1957; s. Thomas Albert and Dorothy Corrine (D'Elia) M.; m. Linda Elizabeth Humphrey, July 9, 1988; 1 child, Julia Dorothy. BS in Acctg., U. Conn., 1979; MBA in Fin., Tulane U., 1983. CPA, Conn. Staff intern Zolan, Bernstein, Dworken and Klein, CPAs, Bridgeport, 1978; auditor Ernst, Whinney & Young, New Haven, 1979-81; fin. intern, then investment analyst Met. Life Ins. Co., N.Y.C., 1982-85; sr. fin. analyst Moody's Investors Svc., Inc., N.Y.C., 1985-87, asst. v.p. fin. planning and devel., 1987-88; assoc. dir. energy, tech. and communications dept. Pub. Utility Group, N.Y.C., 1988—; speaker at profl. meetings. Pub. rels. vol. Conn. State Spl. Olympics, New Haven, 1980. Mem. AICPA, Wall St. Utility Group. Home: 62 Browns Ln Fairfield CT 06430-5037

MARSIK, FREDERIC JOHN, microbiologist; b. Camden, N.J., June 22, 1943; s. Ferdinand Vincent and Helen (Reidl) M.; divorced; children: Terri Jean, Kristi Ann Marsik McCann. BA, Lebanon Valley Coll., 1965; MS, U. Mo., 1970, PhD, 1973. Diplomate Am. Bd. Med. Microbiology. Asst. prof. Sch. Medicine, U. Va., Charlottesville, 1976-80; tech. dir. microbiology and serology Children's Hosp. Wis., Milw., 1980-84; assoc. prof. microbiology and internal medicine Sch. Medicine, Oral Roberts U., Tulsa, 1984-87; dir. microbiology Crozer-Chester Med. Ctr., Upland, Pa., 1987-88; mgr. media systems Becton Dickinson Microbiology Systems, Cockeysville, Md., 1988—; mem. adv. com. Milw. Area Tech. Coll., Milw., 1983-84, Tulsa Jr. Coll., 1985-87; mem. rev. bd. Clin. Lab. Sci. Publ., Washington, 1990—. Contbr. chpts. to textbooks. Treas. Rose Fire Co. and Ambulance Svc., New Freedom, Pa., 1989—; bd. govs. New Freedom Community Ctr., 1989—; mem. adult edn. com. So. York County Sch. Dist., Glen Rock, Pa., 1989—. Recipient Best Rsch. Project award S.W. Assn. for Clin. Microbiology, 1984. Mem. Am. Soc. Microbiology (mem. lab. practices com. 1990—), Am. Soc. Med. Tech., N.Y. Acad. Scis. Congregationalist. Home: 6 Keesey Rd New Freedom PA 17349-9638 Office: Becton Dickinson 250 Schilling Cir Cockeysville MD 21030

MARSOCCI, VELIO ARTHUR, engineering educator, researcher; b. N.Y.C., June 7, 1928; s. Frank and Jennie (Cioffi) M.; m. Frances Siracusa, Sept. 3, 1955; children: Christopher (dec.), Francesca. BEE, NYU, 1953, MEE, 1955, D of Engring. Sci., 1964. Registered profl. engr., N.Y., N.J. Instr. in elec. engring. NYU, Bronx, 1954-56; asst. prof. elec. engring. Stevens Inst. Tech., Hoboken, N.J., 1956-63, assoc. prof. elec. engring., 1964-65; assoc. prof. elec. engring. SUNY, Stony Brook, 1965-67, prof., 1967—; pvt. practice electronics cons. Contbr. articles to profl. jours. With USN, 1946-49. Grantee NSF, 1985. Mem. IEEE, AAAS, Am. Phys. Soc., Nat. Soc. Profl. Engrs., Am. Soc. Engring. Edn., Eta Kappa Nu, Tau Beta Pi, Sigma Xi. Office: SUNY Dept Elec Engring Stony Brook NY 11794-2350

MARTARELLA, FRANC DAVID, television executive; b. Bklyn., Jan. 23; s. Frank James and Ann (Barbarito) M. BFA, NYU, 1972. Producer/writer/dir. WNYC-TV, 1971-72; unit mgr. ABC News, N.Y.C., 1972-74; prodn. mgr. Feature Films, N.Y.C., 1974-76; prodn. controller WNET/Fin., N.Y.C., 1976-80; prodn. supr. CBS Cable, N.Y.C., 1980; mgr. arts programming for fin. Sta. WNET, N.Y.C., 1981, assoc. dir. bus. affairs, 1982-84, bus. mgr. Prodn. Ctr., 1984-86; dir. co-prodn. financing and prog. adminstrn. Sta. WNET-TV, 1986-89, dir. bus. affairs, 1989—; cons. ABC News, 20/20, Raintree Prodns., Martin Carr Prodns., Office for Telecommunications, U.S. Cath. Conf., Smithsonian Instn., WETA-TV, Cen. TV, London. Contbr. articles to profl. jours. Recipient Emmy Award Certificates, Nat. Acad. TV Arts and Scis., 1982, 86. Mem. Nat. Acad. TV Arts and Sci.

MARTELL, JOHN RAYMOND, JR., orthopaedic surgeon; b. McKeesport, Pa., Feb. 3, 1955; s. John Raymond Sr. and Mary (Rowe) M.; m. Roberta Ann Agosti, May 3, 1975; children: Candice, Nicole, John III. BS, U. Pitts., 1977; MD, Jefferson Med. Coll., 1981. Diplomate Am. Bd. Med. Examiners, Am. Bd. Orthopaedic Surgery. Surg. intern William Beaumont Army Med. Ctr., El Paso, Tex., 1981-82; resident in orthopaedics Dwight G. Eisenhower Army Med. Ctr., Ft. Gordon, Ga., 1982-86; chief orthopaedic svc. Kenner Army Community Hosp., Ft. Lee, Va., 1986-88; mem. attending staff Walter Reed Army Med. Ctr., Washington, 1988-90; orthopaedic surgeon Steele Orthopaedic Ctr., Greenville, Pa., 1990-91, Triangle Orthopedic Assocs., Pitts., 1991—; chief sports medicine svc., quality assurance officer Walter Reed Army Med. Ctr., 1988-90; team physician Duquesne U., Pitts., 1992—. Maj. U.S. Army, 1981-90. Fellow Am. Acad. Orthopaedic Surgeons; mem. AMA (del. Young Physicians sect. 1992), Am. Coll. Sports Medicine, Pa. Med. Soc. (del. Pitts. chpt. 1991, mem. governing coun. Young Physicians sect. 1991—), Allegheny County Med. Soc. (del. Pitts. chpt. 1991), Pa. Orthopaedic Soc., Eastern Orthopaedic Soc. Office: Triangle Orthopedic Assocs 490 E North Ave Ste # 400 Pittsburgh PA 15212

MARTELL, MICHAEL JOSEPH, JR., administration executive, researcher; b. Mpls., May 20, 1932; s. Michael Joseph Sr. and Pearl Elsie (Wester) M.; m. June Elizabeth Pischel, Sept. 30, 1967; children: Karen Jean, Erica Allison. BS in Pharmacy, U. Minn., 1954, PhD in Medicinal, Organic Chemistry 1958; MBA, Fairleigh Dickinson U., 1975. Sloan fellow dept. chemistry U. Minn., Mpls., 1958-59; USPHS NIH fellow dept. chemistry U. Ill., Urbana, 1959-60; rsch. scientist Am. Cyanamid Co., Pearl River, N.Y., 1960-67, sr. rsch. scientist, 1967-70, mgr. internat. product devel., 1970-75, dir. overseas product devel., 1975-82, dir. preclinical planning, 1982-83, project dir., 1983-87, dir. proprietary info. mgmt., 1987—. Contbr. articles to profl. jours.; patentee in field. Recipient Outstanding Alumni Achievement award U. Minn., 1976. Mem. Am. Chem. Soc. Home: 822 Seneca Rd Franklin Lakes NJ 07417-2825 Office: Am Cyanamid Co Rsch Div Middletown Rd Pearl River NY 10965-2611

MARTEN, JAMES F., venture capitalist; b. Liverpool, U.K., Sept. 11, 1931; s. Charles G. and Annie (Clarkson) M.; m. Shirley Barker, Apr. 7, 1953; children: Lewis H., Kay S. PhD, Leeds U., Eng., 1957. Chmn., chief exec. officer Delmed Inc., Canton, Mass., 1983-86, Applied ImmuneSci., Inc., Boston, 1983-86; vice chmn. MedChem, Woburn, Mass., 1985—; dir. Hood Labs. Inc., Pembroke, Mass., 1985—, Navion Biomed. Inc., Canton, 1988—; chmn., chief exec. officer Ultracision Inc., Smithfield, R.I., 1988—; dir. Microspring, Inc., Norwood, Mass., 1989—, Frenenius (USA) Inc., 1992—. Mem. Am. Fedn. U. Leeds (treas., v.p., 1989, bd. dirs.). Home: 78 Nichols Rd Cohasset MA 02025-1121

MARTENS, ALEXANDER EUGENE, technical consultant; b. Schemnitz, Slovakia, Czechoslovakia, June 27, 1923; came to U.S., 1960; s. Eugene and Ann (Naumann) M.; m. Rita M. Wenzel, Oct. 16, 1948; children: Anne, Randolph. BSEE, Tech. U., Breslau, Germany, 1942; MSEE, U. Rochester 1964. V.p. R&D Bausch & Lomb, Rochester, N.Y., 1960-83; tech. cons. Fairport, N.Y., 1983—; adj. prof. Rochester Inst. Tech., 1977-82; adviser High Tech. of Rochester, 1989—. Contbr. articles to profl. jours.; patentee in field. Bd. dirs. Monroe Community Hosp. Aux., 1991; advisor SCORE, SBA, Rochester, 1988—; With German Army. Recipient 2 awards R&D Mag., 1972, 76. Office: 104 Nettlecreek Rd Fairport NY 14450-3056

MARTENS, JOHN DALE, telecommunications company executive; b. Wayne, Nebr., Nov. 12, 1943; s. Leonard William and Irma Bertha (Von Seggern) M.; m. Laura Elizabeth Price, Dec. 28, 1966. BSBA, U. Colo., 1966; MS, Thunderbird Grad. Sch. Internat. Mgmt., 1972; postgrad. Queen Mary Coll., U. London, 1976. Analyst overseas ops. Ford Motor Co., Dearborn, Mich., 1972-73; internat. mktg. ofcl. Agrico Chem. Co., Tulsa, 1973-76; tech. and comml. devel. ofcl. Resource Scis. Co., Tulsa, 1976-78, planning and corp. devel. ofcl., 1978-80; chief exec. officer, pres., treas., dir. Sterling Oil of Okla., Inc., Tulsa, 1980-82; dir. strategic devel. MCI Communications Corp., Washington, 1983-84, v.p. corp. devel., 1984-86; v.p. mktg. So. New Eng. Telecommunications Co. Inc., New Haven, 1986-92; sr. v.p. comml. sales, Williams Telecom. Group, Inc., Tulsa, 1992—. Capt. USAF, 1967-70. Mem. New Haven Country Club. Episcopalian.

MARTH, FRITZ LUDWIG, sports association executive; b. Essen, Germany, Feb. 23, 1935; s. Fritz and Elizabeth (Dietrich) M.; came to U.S., 1952, naturalized, 1959; student pub. schs. Essen; m. Sonja Wiehl, June 17, 1964; children: Fritz Thomas, William Robert. Stock clk. Hamilton Art Metal Co., N.Y.C., 1952-55; with Keystone Metal Finishers, Inc., Secaucus, N.J., 1955—, asst. plant mgr., 1962-66, plant mgr., 1966-83; adminstr. amateur div. U.S. Soccer Fedn., N.J. 1983—. Pres. N.J. State Soccer Assn., 1965-70; sec. So. N.Y. State Soccer Assn., 1972-83; gen. sec. Cosmopolitan Soccer League, 1961—; mem. div. soccer U.S. Olympic Com. With U.S. Army, 1958-59, Korea. Lutheran. Mem. Hoboken (N.J.) Soccer Football. Home: 121 W Passaic Ave Bloomfield NJ 07003-4528 Office: 7800 River Rd North Bergen NJ 07047-6282

MARTIMUCCI, RICHARD ANTHONY, engineering company executive; b. N.Y.C., Sept. 25, 1934; s. Dominic Ernest and Angela (Gentile) M.; m. Claudia Frances Reagan, Nov. 2, 1957; 1 child, Lisa Felice. Student, CCNY, 1952-57; AB, Syracuse U., 1960. Registered profl. engr., Conn., N.Y., N.J., Calif., Pa. Sales engr. Morse-Boulger Inc., N.Y.C., 1960-62; project engr. Nichols Research and Engring., N.Y.C., 1962-65; mgr. ops. Dorr-Oliver, Inc., Stamford, Conn., 1965-72; v.p. Environgenics Systems Chemico div. Aerojet-Gen., El Monte, Calif., 1972-75; pres. RAM Engring., Inc., Wilton, Conn., 1975—. Served with USAF, 1957-59. Mem. ASME, Nat. Soc. Profl. Engrs., Water Pollution Control Assn. Office: 9 Hollyhock Ln Wilton CT 06897-4414

MARTIN, CATHERINE MARIA, educator, nurse; b. Danbury, Conn., May 20, 1948; d. Joseph Michael and Elizabeth Frances (McKeon) Kelly; m. Joseph Robert Martin, Sept. 5, 1970; children: Joseph Robert, Jennifer Hope, Patrick Francis, Kathleen Kelly, Mariah Elizabeth. Diploma, St. Vincent Hosp., N.Y.C., 1969; BA in Psychology, Marymount Manhattan Coll., 1972; MEd, U. Maine, 1980. RN, Maine; cert. tchr., spl. edn. tchr., Maine, Minn. Tchr. Eastern Maine Med. Ctr., Bangor, 1976-78, Hilltop Sch., Waterville, Maine, 1979-80, China (Maine) Nursery Sch., 1980-81, Children's Nursery Sch., Portland, 1981-82, Minn. River Valley Spl. Edn. Coop., New Prague, 1984-85, Mpls. Pub. Schs., 1986-87, Headstart Community Action Agy., Shakopee, Minn., 1987—, Farmington (Minn.) Pub. Sch., 1988-89; nurse Bellevue Maternity Hosp., Niskayuna, N.Y., 1983-84; polit sci. intern Marymount Manhattan Coll., Washington, 1980; spl. edn. tchr. Gray (Maine) New Cloucester High Sch., 1991; liaison Sch. Adminstrv. Dist. 15 Pineland Liaison Spl. Edn., Gray, Maine, 1991—. N.Y. State Regents scholar, 1966-69, Travelers Ins. scholar, 1979-80. Mem. Minn. Assn. Early Childhood Educators, Minn. Tchrs. Assn. Roman Catholic. Home: 1 Beechtree Ln Yarmouth ME 04096-1062 Office: Sch Adminstrv Dist 15 PO Box 1080 14 Shaker Rd Gray ME 04039

MARTIN, DANIEL RICHARD, pharmaceutical company executive; b. Lima, Peru, June 9, 1937; s. James Marion and Clemmy Caroline (Valencia) M.; m. Barbara Artemis Cyrus, June 23, 1962; children: Daniel Richard Jr., John Alexander, Christopher Andrew. BA, Cornell U., 1958; MS, Columbia U., N.Y.C., 1959. Area sales supr. Schering Corp., Bloomfield, N.J., 1960-64; assoc. McKinsey & Co., N.Y.C., 1964-69; treas. Harper & Row, Pubs., N.Y.C., 1969-72; mng. dir. Merck & Co., Rahway, N.J., 1972-77; group v.p. Bell & Howell Co., Chgo., 1977-80; pres. Howland Martin Corp., N.Y.C., 1980-85; pres. Sterling Europe, Middle East, Africa Sterling Drug, Inc., N.Y.C., 1986-89; pres. E-Z-EM, Inc., Westbury, N.Y., 1990—. Pres. Accion Internat., Cambridge, Mass., 1988—; trustee Bangor (Maine) Theol. Seminary, 1991—. Decorated Order of Merit (Ecuador). Mem. Coun. on Foreign Rels., Univ. Club (N.Y.C., Chgo.), Cornell Club (N.Y.C.). Republican. Congregationalist. Home: 2 Dolma Rd Scarsdale NY 10583-4506 Office: E-Z-EM Inc 717 Main St Westbury NY 11590-5021

MARTIN, DARRIS LEE, quality and finance executive; b. Greenville, Miss., June 2, 1950; s. Robert Tllis and L'Vee (Preston) M. BS in Bus. and Fin., Ind. U., 1971; diploma in theology, Gospel Crusade Inc., Bradenton, Fla., 1977. Fin. cons., traveling bible tchr. Gospel Crusade, Inc., 1977-78; estimator Sign Mart Neon Co., Daytona Beach, Fla., 1978-79; with GE, 1971-77, 79—; supr. plant, taxes and expense acctg. GE, Daytona Beach, Fla., 1982-83; specialist reliability & quality assurance program planning GE, Binghamton, N.Y., 1983-84, project leader quality control engring., 1984-85, mgr. quality systems, 1985-87, mgr. ops. planning, 1987-88, mgr. ops. compliance aerospace control systems, 1988-90; mgr. AOD quality programs GE Aerospace Ops. Div., Valley Forge, Pa., 1990—. Formerly vol. supr. Agape Crisis Ctr., active numerous programs including Park Outreach activities for youth, big. brother Halifax Area Youth in Action, counselor, religious instr. Fla. Dept. Corrections. Named MM2 Outstanding Tchr. of Yr., Fla. Dept. Corrections, 1976. Mem. Am. Soc. Quality Control (membership chmn. 1988-89), Zeta Epsilon chpt. Omega Psi Phi (keepr of fin. 1969-71, Man of Yr. 1971). Pentacostal. Home: 26 Lindenwood Dr Exton PA 19341-2135

MARTIN, DAVID, engineering company executive; b. Littleton, N.H., Oct. 25, 1939; s. Cecil William and Rachel (Dodge) M.; m. Barbara Granger Hale, July 20, 1963; children: David Ross, Kristina, Kimberly, Karen. BS, Syracuse U., 1962; MBA, Loyola U., Chgo., 1975. Commd. 2d lt. USAF, 1962, advanced through grades to lt. col., 1981; dir. contracts Saudi AWACS program USAF, Hanscom AFB, Mass., 1981-84; ret., 1984; systems analyst Analytical Systems Engring. Corp., Burlington, Mass., 1984-87, sr. contract adminstr., 1987-89, dir. purchasing, 1989—. Home: 23 Banbury Dr Westford MA 01886 Office: Analytical Systems Engring Corp 5 Burlington Woods Dr Burlington MA 01803

MARTIN, DAVID LEE, neurochemist, educator; b. St. Louis, May 30, 1941; s. Louis Frederick and Ruth Elma (Wilson) M.; m. Sandra J. Bloom, Aug. 20, 1966; children: Laura Eleanor, Rachel Kirsten. BS, U. Minn., 1963; MS, U. Wis., 1965, PhD, 1968. Asst. prof. U. Md., 1968-72, assoc. prof., 1972-80; rsch. chemist Armed Forces Radiobiology Research Inst., Bethesda, Md., 1976-77; rsch. scientist N.Y. State Health Dept., Albany, 1980-83, lab. chief, 1983—; prof. dept. environ. health and toxicology Sch. Pub. Health, SUNY, Albany, 1985—, chmn. dept. environ. health and toxicology, 1989—; cons. NIMH, 1977, NIH, 1981. Author: Molecules in Living Systems, 1978; co-editor: Taurine Functional Neurochemistry, Physiology, and Cardiology, 1990; mem. editorial bd. Jour. Neurochemistry, 1986—; contbr. articles to profl. jours. Grantee NIH, NIMH, 1975—; recipient Merit award NIMH, 1989. Mem. AAAS, Chemistry Assn. Md. (bd. dirs. 1971—), Am. Soc. Biol. Chemists, Soc. for Neurosci., Am. Soc. Neurochemistry, Biochem. Soc. Office: Wadsworth Ctr for Labs and Rsch NY State Health Dept PO Box 509 Albany NY 12201-0509

MARTIN, DAVID O'BRIEN, congressman; b. St. Lawrence County, N.Y., Apr. 26, 1944; s. Edson Albert and Anne (O'Brien) M.; children: Victoria, Kelly, Julia. B.B.A., U. Notre Dame, 1966; J.D., Albany Law Sch., 1973. Mem. N.Y. State Assembly from 112th Dist., 1977-80; mem. 97th-102nd Congresses from 26th N.Y. dist., 1981—. Served to capt. USMC, 1966-70, Vietnam. Mem. ABA, N.Y. State Bar Assn., Am. Legion. Republican. Roman Catholic. Club: Elks. Office: US Ho of Reps Cannon House Office Bldg Rm 442 Washington DC 20515*

MARTIN, DONALD BECKWITH, medical educator, diabetes researcher; b. Phila., July 24, 1927; s. Robert Steen and Florence Margot (Mugnier) M.; m. Anne Jacqueline Holmes, Sept. 8, 1956; children: Jonathan Warren, David Steen, Lydia Anne, Liza Alexandra. AB, Haverford Coll., 1950; MD, Harvard U., 1954; MA (hon.), U. Pa., 1980. Diplomate Am. Bd. Internal Medicine. Intern, resident, chief resident in medicine Mass. Gen. Hosp, Boston, 1954-59; rsch. fellow Nat. Inst. Arthritis and Metabolic Disease, NIH, Bethesda, Md., 1960-61, Nat. Ctr. Sci. Rsch., France, 1962; instr., asst. prof., assoc. prof. Harvard U. Med. Sch., Boston, 1963-79; dir. Rodebaugh Diabetes Ctr., U. Pa., Phila., 1979—, prof. internal medicine, 1979—, assoc. chmn. dept., 1985—; cons. Nat. Inst. Arthritis, Metabolic, Kidney and Digestive Diseases, NIH, 1971—; mem. adv. com. endocrinology and metabolism rev. com. FDA, Rockville, Md., 1974-77; cons. nat. diabetes data group NIH, 1978—; mem. Pa. Diabetes Task Force Commn., Phila., 1980-87. Contbr. numerous articles to sci. jours., chpts. to books. With USNR, 1945-46. Fulbright rsch. scholar, France, 1962; Guggenheim fellow, Switzerland, 1974-75. Fellow ACP; mem. Am. Soc. for Clin. Investigation, Am. Diabetes Assn. (coun. 1973-76). Home: 601 New Gulph Rd Bryn Mawr PA 19010-3650 Office: Hosp of U Pa 3400 Spruce St Philadelphia PA 19104-4220

MARTIN, DONALD LEON, law librarian, legal educator, information resource management analyst, inventor; b. N.Y.C., June 2, 1920; s. Vernie E. and Ruth (Peterson) M.; m. Rose Kocsis, Aug. 23, 1961; 1 child, Virginia Kim. AA, Fairleigh Dickinson U., 1949; BBA, Upsala U., 1950; postgrad. in law, Seton Hall. U., Newark, 1951-53; MS in LS, Columbia U., 1956; LLB, Blackstone Sch. Law, Chgo., 1963. Instr. law, law librarian Seton Hall U., Newark, 1953-61; law librarian U.S. Army Dept. Def., Washington, 1961-68; asst. librarian U.S. Supreme Ct., Washington, 1968-71; law librarian U.S. Dept. Labor, Washington, 1971-88, mgmt. analyst Office Info. Resource Mgmt., 1988—; refrence law librarian (part time) George Washington U. Law Sch., Washington, 1984—. Mem. ARC (recipient Cert. Appreciation 1969, Cert. Honor for Humanitarian Service, 1971-72). Served with U.S. Army, 1942-45, ETO. Decorated Combat Infantry Badge and Bronze Star. Mem. VFW, Am. Legion, Am. Assn. Profs., Am. Soc. Legal Hist., Am. Assn. Law Libraries. Republican. Roman Catholic. Clubs: River Bend Golf and Country (Great Falls, Va.). Home: PO Box 651 Middleburg VA 22117-0651

MARTIN, EDWARD JOSEPH, retired satellite communications executive; b. N.Y.C., Jan. 12, 1932; s. Thomas Francis and Agnes Veronica (Malone) M.; m. Barbara Ann Hayes, July 5, 1958; children: Linda, Deborah, Nancy, Edward Joseph Jr. AB in Math., Fordham U., 1954; MS in Math. and Physics, Northeastern U., 1959. Various tech. and mgmt. positions, 1959-79; v.p., div. mgr. maritime svcs. Comsat Corp., Washington, 1979-83, v.p. internat. ops., 1983-84, v.p. tech., 1985-87, v.p. engring. and ops., 1987-88; ret., 1988; pres. EJM Internat., Rockville, Md., 1988—; mem. Radio Tech. Commn. for Maritime, 1966—; tech. adviser Radio Tech. Commn. for Aeros., 1988—. Mem. IEEE (sr.), AIAA (sr.), Soc. Satellite Profls., Mensa. Home and Office: 7122 Plantation Ln Rockville MD 20852-4452

MARTIN, FRANCIS PAUL, pediatrician; b. N.Y.C., June 3, 1924; s. John Francis and Anna Catherine (Mollers) M.; m. Barbara Elizabeth Kelsey, Sept. 11, 1948; children: Katherine, Therese, Francis, Jeanne, Deborah, James, Thomas, Lawrence, Kenneth, Margaret, Daniel. BS, U. Notre Dame, 1945; MD, NYU, 1948. Diplomate Am. Bd. Pediatrics. Resident pediatrics King County Hosp., Bklyn., 1948-50, Brooke Army Hosp., San Antonio, 1951-52; pvt. practice Lynbrook, Rockville Ctr., N.Y., 1955—; assoc. prof. pediatrics NYU Med. Ctr., N.Y.C., 1966-86; dir. pediatrics Mercy Med. Ctr., Rockville Centre, 1989; cons. in pediatrics Wintrhop U. Med. Ctr., Mineola, N.Y., 1981—; dir. Smith Barney Funds, Inc., N.Y.C. Contbr. articles to profl. jours., chpts. to books. Mem. bishop's com. Rockville Ctr. Diocese Quality of Life, 1987; bd. dirs. Marty Lions Found., 1981—; lector St. Agnes Cathedral, 1956—. Named Man of the Yr. Notre Dame Club of N.Y., 1962; mem. NYU Athletic Hall of Fame, 1990. Fellow Am. Acad. Pediatrics; mem. AMA, N.Y. State Med. Soc., Nassau County Med. Soc. Roman Catholic. Home: 321 N Village Ave Rockville Centre NY 11570-2327 Office: 2000 N Village Ave Rockville Centre NY 11570-1001

MARTIN, FREDERICK WIGHT, physicist, researcher; b. Boston, Feb. 16, 1936; s. Frederick Eastman and Rhoda (Nichols) M.; m. Elizabeth Carey Foltz, Apr. 24, 1965; children: Frederick Nichols, Katharine Eastman. AB, Princeton (N.J.) U., 1957; MS, Yale U., 1958, PhD, 1964. From physicist to sr. physicist Ion Physics Corp., Burlington, Mass., 1963-66; amenuensis I U. Aarhus, Denmark, 1966-68; rsch. assoc., asst. prof. U. Ky., Lexington, 1968-70; asst. prof. U. Md., College Park, 1970-78; pres. Microscope Assocs., Inc., Dedham, Mass., 1978—; adj. assoc. prof. Worcester (Mass.) Polytech. Inst., 1983—; vis. scientist SUNY, Stony Brook, 1975-76. Contbr. over 50 articles to profl. jours. Mem. IEEE, Am. Phys. Soc., Sigma Xi. Office: Microscope Assocs Inc 50 Village Ave Dedham MA 02026-4209

MARTIN, GEOFFREY JOHN, geographer, educator; b. London, Mar. 9, 1934; came to U.S., 1957; s. Charles Walter and Elizabeth Kathleen (Doughty) M.; m. Paula Jean Evans. BSc, London Sch. Econs. & Polit Sci, 1955; GCE, U. London, 1956; MA, U. Fla., 1957; PhD, U. London, 1987. Asst. prof. Eastern Mich. U., Ypsilanti, 1958-65; assoc. prof. Southern Conn. State U., New Haven, 1965-69, prof., 1969—. Author: Mark Jefferson: Geographer, 1968, Ellsworth Huntington: His Life and Thought, 1973, The Life and Thought of Isaiah Bowman, 1980; co-author (with P.E. James): The Association of American Geographer: The First Seventy-Five Years, 1904-1979, 1978, All Possible Worlds: A History of Geographical Ideas, 1981; editor: History of Geog. Jour., 1980—, Geographers: Biobibliographical Studies, 1988; contbr. articles to profl. jours. Scholarship NSF 1984, 89; Outstanding Educator of Yr. award 1973. Mem. Assn. Am. Geographers (archivist 1987—, Honors award 1983), Internat. Geog. Union (U.S. rep. 1987—, dir. of world directory for geog. archives 1989—). Office: So Conn State U 501 Crescent St New Haven CT 06515-1355

MARTIN, GLENN MICHAEL, mortgage banker; b. Pittsfield, Mass., Sept. 13, 1950; s. Thomas Claude and DeLima Rose Marie (Gelinas) M.; m. Dawn Star Schile, Mar. 26, 1983. BS in Biology, Norwich U., 1973; BSBA in Acctg., North Adams State Coll., 1981; postgrad., Air U., Maxwell AFB, Ala., 1983. Cert. tchr., Mass., real estate broker. Sci. tchr. North Adams (Mass.) Middle Sch., 1977-78; sales mgr. Doverbrook Estates, Chicopee, Mass., 1982-83; mortgage officer ComFed Savs. Bank, Leominster, Mass., 1983-85, Bank of Boston, Fitchburg, Mass., 1985-86; v.p. br. mgr. Northeastern Mortgage Co., Inc., Worcester, Mass., 1986-87; br. mgr. First NH Mortgage Corp., Marlboro, Mass., 1988-89; bus. broker VR Bus. Brokers, Leominster, Mass., 1989-90; mktg. dir. Equity Group, Inc., Fitchburg, 1989-90; ops. officer 58th Aerial Port Squadron, USAF Res., Westover AFB, Mass., 1989—. Dep. sheriff Berkshire County Sheriff's Dept., Pittsfield, 1983—; mem. Ashburnham (Mass.) Planning Bd., 1990—. Capt. USAF, 1973-77, maj. Res. Alumni scholar Norwich U., 1969-73. Mem. Res. Officers Assn. (treas. 1983-84), Rotary Internat., Norwich Rugby Club. Roman Catholic. Home: 695 Sunset Isle Dr Sunset Lake Ashburnham MA 01430-1008 Office: USAF Res 58th Aerial Port Squadron Westover AFB Chicopee MA 01022

MARTIN, GREGORY ALLAN, insurance executive; b. Morgantown, W.Va., Nov. 4, 1950; s. Allan Edward and Vivian (Dillon) M. BS, W. Va. U., 1974, MS, 1976. Cert. hazard control mgr. Engr. rep. Aetna Casualty & Surety, Washington, 1976-82; safety cons. Johnson & Higgins, Washington, 1982—. Mem. Am. Soc. Safety Engrs., Nat. Safety Mgmt. Soc., Metro. Constrn. Safety Assn. (sec. 1989-90), The Center Club (bd. advisors 1987—), Demolay (pres. 1968-69). Republican. Office: Johnson & Higgins 1401 I St 350 Washington DC 20005

MARTIN, HARROLD BERT, librarian; b. Cambridge, Pa., Mar. 8, 1916; s. David Hoover and Mary Edna (Wanner) M.; student Temple U., 1940-43; B.A., U. N.Mex., 1947; B.L.S., U. So. Calif., 1947; postgrad. U. Pa., 1949-50, 66, 82, Barnes Found., 1979-82. First asst. curator manuscripts and spl. collections Hist. Soc. Pa., Phila., 1948-62; libr. Phila. City Planning Commn., 1963-79. Served with Spl. Svc. Corp, AUS, 1943-44. Mem. Keats-Shelley Assn. Am., Browning Inst. (Charter), Byron Soc. Am. com., Santa Fe Hist. Found. (life), Friends of Barnes Found. Home: 1515 Sylvania House 1324 Locust St Philadelphia PA 19107-5658

MARTIN, JAMES VICTOR, JR., foreign service officer, writer; b. Tokyo, Nov. 15, 1916; (parents Am. citizens); s. James Victor Sr. and Esther Belle (Ludwig) M.; m. Elizabeth Shaler Smith, June 28, 1941; children: Sarah Martin Brown, Susan Martin Neal, David Ludwig Martin. BA, DePauw U., 1938; MA, Tufts U., 1939, PhD, 1948; postgrad. in Japanese lang., Harvard U., 1941-42, Yale U., 1948-49. Vice consul U.S. Consulate Gen., Bombay, 1946-48; polit. officer, head transl. sect. Office of Polit. Advsier, Tokyo, 1949-50; econ. officer U.S. Consulate Gen., Kobe-Osaka, Japan, 1951-53; prin. officer U.S. Consulate, Fukuoka, Japan, 1953-56; officer-in-charge Japanese Affairs U.S. Dept. State, Washington, 1956-58, personnel planning staff, 1958-61; chief polit. sect. U.S. Embassy, Rangoon, Burma, 1962-64; U.S. polit. adviser Office of U.S. High Commn. to the Ryukyu Islands, Okinawa, 1964-67; polit. counselor U.S. Embassy, Canberra, Australia, 1968-70; country dir. for Australia, N.Z. and Pacific Islands, U.S. Dept. State, Washington, 1970-73; lectr. Far East internat. rels. Am. U., Washington, summer 1961; occasional lectr. U.S. Asian policy U. Md. Extension, Okinawa, 1965-67; cons. Pacific Islands, U.S. Dept. of Interior, Washington, 1973-74. Contbr. articles to profl. jours. Trustee Japan-Am. Soc. Washington, Inc., 1982-89; bd. dirs. Com. for Community Democracies-U.S.A., Washington, 1983-92, v.p., 1986-87; sec., treas. Com. for Community of Democracies (D.C.), Washington, 1985-88. Lt. USN, 1941-46, PTO. Mem. Assn. for Asian Studies, Mid-Atlantic Region Chpt. Assn. for Asian Studies (treas. 1972-76), Washington and Southeast Region Seminar on Japan, Diplomatic and Consular Officers Ret. Methodist.

MARTIN, JANE ROLAND, philosophy educator; b. N.Y.C., July 20, 1929; d. Charles and Sarah (Starr) Roland; m. Michael Lou Martin, June 15, 1962; children: Timothy D., Thomas P. AB, Radcliffe Coll., 1951, PhD, 1961; EdM, Harvard U., 1956. Assoc. prof. philosophy U. Mass., Boston, 1972-81, prof., 1981—. Author: Explaining, Understanding and Teaching, 1970, Reclaiming a Conversation, 1985, The Schoolname, 1992. Bunting Inst. fellow, 1980-81, NSF fellow, 1985-86, Guggenheim Found. fellow, 1987-88. Fellow Philosophy of Edn. Soc. (pres. 1980-81); mem. Am. Philos. Assn., Soc. for Women in Philosophy. Office: U Mass Dept Philosophy Harbor Campus Boston MA 02125

MARTIN, JANET M. DADDINO, educator, consultant; b. Oceanside, N.Y., Aug. 24, 1954; d. Vincent Daddino and Marie Adeline (LoMonaco)

Daddino-Greco; m. Gregory Martin, 1979; children: Sean Vincent, Whitney Marie. BS, SUNY, N.Y.C., 1976; MA, L.I.U., 1979. Cert. elem. tchr., learning disabilities cons. Tchr. of handicapped San Dieguito Sch. Dist., Leucadia, Calif., 1979-81, Newton (N.J.) Pub. Schs., 1981-84; learning cons. Phillipsburg (N.J.) Bd. Edn., 1984-86, Bordentown (N.J.) Regional Schs., 1986-89; ind. cons., 1989—; cons. PACE Assocs. - Clin. Svcs., Princeton, N.J., 1986-89. Mem. Tabernacle (N.J.) Women's Assn., 1986-92. Mem. Learning Disabilities Assn. Republican. Roman Catholic.

MARTIN, JEFFREY LYNN, insurance executive; b. Glendale, W.Va., Nov. 16, 1951; s. Paul A. Sr. and Evelyn Jeanette (Parsons) M.; m. Katheryn Ann Cunningham, Feb. 18, 1972 (div. Nov. 1976); 1 child, Tracy Lynn; m. Cathryn Allyson Baker, Dec. 31, 1977; 1 child, Cara Maureen. Student, W. Liberty State Coll., 1969-71, W.Va. Wesleyan Coll., 1984-86. Asst. program dir. Sta. WEIF Radio, Moundsville, W.Va., 1970-71; air personality Sta. WEIF Radio, 1969-71, Sta. WKWK Radio, Wheeling, W.Va., 1971-73; agt. Equitable Life Ins. Co. Va., Wheeling, 1973-75; sales mgr. Equitable Life Ins. Co. Va., 1975-79; mgr.. Am. Gen. Life Ins. Co., Wheeling, 1979-80; pres. Martin Ins. Agy., Inc., Moundsville, 1980-88; pastor West Buckhannon United Meth. Ch., Buckhannon, W.Va., 1983-86; sales mgr. Monumental Life Ins. Co., Pitts., 1988—. Pres. Teen Age Reps., Moundsville, 1968; candidate Moundsville City Coun., 1975; chairperson coun. on ministries Calvary United Meth. Ch., Moundsville, 1978. Mem. Nat. Assn. Life Underwriters, Elks (local chpt. chaplain 1974-75), Order of DeMolay. Republican.

MARTIN, JOHN CEPHAS, JR., computer marketing professional; b. Dayton, Ohio, June 12, 1958; s. John Cephas and Nancy May (Chayne) M. BA, U. Wash., 1980; MBA, MIT, 1983; program mgmt. cert., Def. Systems Mgmt. Coll., Ft. Belvoir, Va., 1988; cert. in advanced mgmt.-internat. mktg., Babson Coll., 1989. Mktg. cons. Roland Berger & Ptnr. GmbH, N.Y.C., 1983, Visible Systems Corp., Waltham, Mass., 1988-89, ABB Robotics AB, Västerås, Sweden, 1989; exec. asst. to pres. Signatron, Inc. (Sundstrand), Lexington, Mass., 1983-88; mktg. mgr. Stratus Computer, Inc., Marlboro, Mass., 1989—. Mem. Rainier Club (Seattle), Columbia Tower Club (Seattle). Home: 307 Applebriar Ln Marlborough MA 01752-4621 Office: Stratus Computer Inc 55 Fairbanks Blvd Marlborough MA 01752-1298

MARTIN, JOHN GARVIE, III, marketing professional; b. Washington, Sept. 16, 1945; s. John Garvie Jr. and Ellen (Simpson) M.; m. Margaret Wiest, Aug. 22, 1970 (div.); m. Susan Starrett, July 29, 1977; children: John IV, Matthew. BA, Amherst Coll., 1969. Mktg. analyst Reader's Digest, Pleasantville, N.Y., 1969-74, Western Pub. Co., N.Y.C., 1975-76; circulation, list mgr. Brookstone Co., Peterborough, N.H., 1976-81; v.p. Mason and Sullivan, Osterville, Mass., 1981-82, Carroll Reed Ski Shops, Portland, Maine, 1982-84; ind. cons. Cumberland, Maine, 1984—. Cpl. USMC, 1966-68. Home and Office: 11 Oak Ridge Rd Cumberland Center ME 04021-9427

MARTIN, JOHN L., state legislator; b. Eagle Lake, Maine, June 5, 1941; s. Frank and Edwidge (Raymond) M. BA in History and Govt., U. Maine, 1963, postgrad., 1963-64. Tchr. Am. govt. and history Ft. Kent (Maine) Community High Sch., 1966-72; instr. U. Maine, Ft. Kent, 1972—; asst. prof. U. Maine, 1989—; mem. from Eagle Lake and St. Francis dist. Maine Ho. of Reps., 1964—, minority fl. leader, 1970-74, speaker of ho., 1975—; adj. lectr.; mem. intergovtl. rels. com. Nat. Legis. Conf., 1970—; chmn. Maine Land Use Regulation Commn., 1972-73, Maine Bur. Human Rels., 1972, State Legis. Leaders Found., 1979—; mem. exec. bd. Nat. Conf. State Legislatures, chmn. state-fed. assembly, 1985-86, chair task force on reapportionment, 1987-88, vice chmn. budget, fiscal and rules com., 1986-87, v.p., 1988-89, pres.-elect, 1989-90, pres., 1990-91, immediate past pres., 1991-92; mem. exec. com. New Eng. Caucus of State Legislatures, 1978—, chmn., 1982; mem. regional exec. com. Nat. Dem. State Legis. Leaders Assn., 1991—, chmn., 1987—; bd. dirs. Found. for State Legislatures, 1988—; mem. exec. com. Dem. Nat. Com., 1991—. Trustee Eagle Lake Water and Sewer Dist., 1966—, No. Maine Gen. Hosp., Ft. Kent; mem. Rural Health Steering Com. Nat. Acad. for State Health Policy, rural health steering com. Mem. New Eng. Polit. Sci. Assn. Home: PO Box 250 Eagle Lake ME 04739-0250 Office: Maine Ho of Reps State House Augusta ME 04333

MARTIN, JOHN RUSSELL, meteorologist; b. Old Town, Maine, Aug. 14, 1950; s. Albert Joseph and Mary Lina (Cox) M.; m. Susan Marie Anderson, July 11, 1981; children: Robert R., Juliann M. BA, U. Maine, 1972; MS, SUNY, Albany, 1977. Cert. consulting meteorologist. Meteorologist Smith-Singer Assocs., Inc., Amityville, N.Y., 1974-77; meteorologist MES, Inc., Amityville, 1977-81, v.p., 1981-86; v.p. MES Co., Inc., Amityville, 1987—, also bd. dirs., sec., 1987—. Editor: Recommended Dispersion Guide, 1979. Mem. Air and Waste Mgmt. Assn. (chmn. conf. com. N.Y. Metro chpt. 1991), Am. Meteorol. Soc., Wind Energy Rsch. Coun., Phi Beta Kappa, Phi Kappa Phi, Pi Mu Epsilon. Democrat. Roman Catholic. Office: Meteorol Evaluation Svc Co 165 Broadway Amityville NY 11701-2703

MARTIN, KAREN KRAUSCHE, social services administrator, clinical social worker; b. N.Y.C., Sept. 2, 1947; d. John Francis and Gladys Rose (Cure) K.; m. John Charles Martin, Oct. 16, 1977; children: Stacey Elizabeth, Sean Patrick. BA, Sacred Heart U., 1984; MSW, Fordham U., 1985; cert. family therapy, Smith Coll., 1989. Cert. social worker, N.Y., Conn.; cert. sch. social worker, Conn. Social worker United Cerebral Palsy, Bridgeport, Conn., 1983, Norwalk Sch. System, Norwalk, Conn., 1983-84, Cath. Family Services, Bridgeport, 1984-89; pvt. practice social work Ctr. Family Guidance, Stratford, Conn., 1986-90; cons. Apple Tree Nursery Sch., Trumbull, Conn., 1989-91. Cons. Shelton (Conn.) Bd. Edn., 1989—; bd. dirs. Trumbull (Conn.) Counseling Ctr., 1984-89; mem. Reg. Youth Substance Abuse Prevention Coun., Trumbull, 1988-89. Mem. Nat. Assn. Social Workers (register of clin. social work), Conn. Assn. Sch. Social Workers, Acad. Cert. Social Workers. Roman Catholic. Home: 50 Friar Ln Trumbull CT 06611-4014 Office: Shelton Bd Edn Meadow St Shelton CT 06484

MARTIN, KEITH LAMBERT, school counselor; b. Hartford, Conn., Feb. 6, 1956; s. Albert and Elizabeth (Lambert) M. BA in Bus. Adminstrn., Morehouse Coll., 1978; MA in Counseling, Hampton U., 1988; cert. in sch. counseling, Cen. Conn. State U., 1990. Field office mgr. Community Renewal Team, Hartford, 1980-81; underwriter, recruiting cons. Cigna Ins. Co., Hartford-Bloomfield, Conn., 1981-86; employment specialist Greater Hartford C. of C., 1988-90; sch. counselor Bloomfield High Sch., 1990—, vocat. guidance counselor, 1991—; liaison Career Beginnings Program, Bloomfield, 1990—; liaision commonground program, Greater Hartford; mem. planning com. Bloomfield High Mentor Program; mem. planning com. Oasis Program Freshman Orientation. Rep. Conn. Coun. Black Students and Profls., Waterbury, 1989—; cons. family affair, Episc. Ch., Hartford, 1989—. Mem. AACD, Assn. Multicultural Counseling and Devel., Assn. Sch. Counseling, Nat. Career Devel. Assn., Kappa Alpha Psi. Home: 91 Wethersfield Ave Hartford CT 06114-1102 Office: Bloomfield High Sch Huckleberry Ln Bloomfield CT 06002-3132

MARTIN, KENNETH ALBERT, mechanical engineering executive; b. Hyattsville, Md., Sept. 19, 1940; s. Luther Kenneth and Mary Elizabeth (Hartle) M.; divorced; m. Anne Marie Milstead, Aug. 7, 1977; children: Michelle, Jeffrey, Sheri, Sandy. BS in Aero. Engring., Ind. Inst. Tech., Ft. Wayne, 1961. Maintenance engr. Atlantic Research Corp., Gainesville, Va., 1961-62, mech. design engr., 1962-64, rocket assembly process engr., 1964-71; task leader Value Engr. Co., Alexandria, Va., 1971-77; prin. nuclear, cons. engr. Combustion Engring., Inc., Windsor, Conn., 1977-84, cons. engr., 1984-85, mgr. nuclear products, services, 1985—; cons. Dynamic Scis., Inc., Va., 1979-83. Patentee in field. Home: 54 Hollow Brook Rd Windsor CT 06095-1204 Office: Combustion Engring Inc 1000 Prospect Hill Rd Windsor CT 06095-1564

MARTIN, LINDA GAYE, demographer, economist; b. Paris, Ark., Dec. 17, 1947; d. Leslie Paul and Margie LaVerne (Thomas) M. BA in Math., Harvard U., 1970; MPA, Princeton U., 1972, PhD in Econs., 1978. Dir. mgmt. info. bur. purchased social svcs. for adults City of N.Y., 1972-74; rsch. assoc., rsch. dir. U.S. Ho. of Reps. Select Com. on Population, Washington, 1977-79; rsch. assoc. East-West Population Inst., Honolulu, 1979-89, asst. dir., 1982-84; dir. com. on population Nat. Acad. Scis., Washington, 1989—; sr. rsch. scholar dept. demography Georgetown U., Washington, 1989—; asst. prof. econs. U. Hawaii, Honolulu, 1979-81, assoc. prof., 1981-89, prof., 1989; mem. neurosci., behavior and sociology of aging rev. com. Nat. Inst. on Aging, Bethesda, 1991—; mem. tech. evaluation panel on aging in developing countries Bur. of Census, Washington, 1990—; chair panel on aging in developing countries Nat. Acad. Scis., Washington, 1987. Editor: The ASEAN Success Story, 1987; author: (monograph) The Graying of Japan, 1989; contbr. articles to profl. jours. Recipient Fulbright Faculty Rsch. award Coun. for Internat. Exch. of Scholars, 1988. Mem. Gerontol. Soc. Am., Internat. Union for Scientific Study Population, Population Assn. Am. (bd. dirs. 1991—). Democrat. Home: 1948 N Cleveland St Arlington VA 22201 Office: Nat Acad Scis 2101 Constitution Ave Washington DC 20418

MARTIN, LORRAINE B., humanities educator; b. Utica, N.Y., Aug. 18, 1940; d. Walter G. and Laura (Bochenek) Bolanowski; m. Charles A. Martin; children: Denise, Tracy. Student, SUNY, Albany, 1958-60, postgrad.; BA in English and Edn. magna cum laude, Utica Coll. of Syracuse U., 1977; MS in Edn. and Reading, SUNY, Cortland, 1979, CAS in Edn. Adminstrn., 1984; postgrad., Syracuse U., 1990—, SUNY, Albany, 1992—. Cert. elem. tchr., secondary tchr., sch. adminstr. and supr., sch. dist. adminstr., reading specialist, N.Y. Tchr. Poland (N.Y.) Cen. Sch., 1972-80, reading specialist, 1980-84; instr. reading Utica Coll. of Syracuse U., summer 1982-84; adminstr. spl. edn. and chpt. 1 remedial program Little Falls (N.Y.) City Sch. Dist., 1984-85; adminstr. adult and continuing edn. Madison-Oneida Bd. Coop. Ednl. Svcs., Verona, N.Y., 1985-86; dir. gen. programs Herkimer (N.Y.) Bd. Coop. Ednl. Svcs., 1986-88; asst. prof. English and reading Humanities div. Herkimer County Community Coll., Herkimer, 1988—; trainer tchr. performance evaluation program N.Y. State Dept. Edn., Herkimer, 1984, facilitator effective schs. program, 1986-88; cons. Two-Yr. Coll. Devel. Ctr. SUNY, 1985-89, tchr. trainer for the Writing Process; developer summer reading, writing and study skills course for Bridge program. Author: The Bridge Program--Easing the Transition from High School to College, 1990, Tips for Teachers: An Idea Swap, 1989; editor: Research and Teaching in Developmental Education; contbr. to Teaching Writing to Adults. Active Myasthenia Gravis Found., 1988-92, Muscular Dystrophy Assn., 1989-92, Thyroid Found. of Am., 1988-92; advisor Network for Coll. Re-Entry Adults; mem. Profl. Devel. Com. Recipient Leader Silver award for volunteerism 4-H Coop. Extension, Utica, 1980. Mem. Internat. Reading Assn., N.Y. State Reading Assn., Assn. Supervision and Curriculum Devel., Nat. Coun. Tchrs. English, Conf. on Coll. Composition and Communication, N.Y. Coll. Learning Skills Assn., Phi Kappa Phi, Alpha Lambda Sigma. Home: RR2 Box 415B Crooked Brook Rd Utica NY 13502 Office: Herkimer County Comm Coll Reservoir Rd Herkimer NY 13350-1545

MARTIN, LOUIS FRANK, surgery and physiology educator; b. Troy, N.Y., Nov. 7, 1951; s. Eugene Lavern and Lois Jane (Perkins) Martin; m. Deborah Lynn Tjarnberg, Mar. 12, 1977; children: Jesse Tjarnberg, James Casey, Tyler Gene. BA, Brown U., 1973, MD, 1976. Diplomate Am. Bd. Surgery. Resident in gen. surgery U. Wash. Affiliated Hosps., Seattle, 1977-78; resident in gen. surgery U. Louisville, 1978-83, rsch. fellow trauma rsch. and health care ednl. adminstrn., 1980-82; asst. prof. surgery Pa. State U., Hershey, 1983-88, asst. prof. physiology, 1986-88, assoc. prof. surgery and cellular and molecular physiology, 1988—; vis. scientist INSERM, Poste Orange, France, 1990-91. Contbr. articles to newspapers and profl. jours. Recipient Loyal Davis Traveling Surg. scholar ACS, 1990, Clin. Investigator award NIH, 1985-90. Mem. ACS, Am. Coll. Critical Care Medicine, Am. Physiol. Soc., Assn. for Acad. Surgery (councilman 1988-90), Collegium Internat. Chirurgiae Digestivae, Soc. Internat. Chirurgie, Soc. Univ. Surgeons. Home: 44 Primrose Dr Hershey PA 17033-2615 Office: Pa State U Dept of Surgery Milton S Hershey Med Ctr PO Box 850 Hershey PA 17033-0850

MARTIN, LYNN MORLEY, secretary of labor; b. Evanston, Ill., Dec. 26, 1939; d. Lawrence William and Helen Catherine (Hall) Morley; children from a previous marriage: Julia Catherine, Caroline; m. Harry D. Leinenweber, Jan. 1987. B.A., U. Ill., 1960. Former tchr. pub. schs.; mem. Ill. Ho. of Reps., 1977-79, Ill. Senate, 1979-81; mem. 97th-101st Congresses from 16th Ill. Dist., 1981-91; sec. Dept. of Labor, Washington, 1991—. Ill. co-chmn. Bush-Quayle Presdl. campaign, 1988. Named one of Outstanding Young Women in Am., U.S. Jaycees; named Rep. Woman of the Yr., 1989. Mem. AAUW, Jr. League, Phi Beta Kappa (hon. doctorate). Republican. Office: Dept of Labor Office of Sec 200 Constitution Ave NW Washington DC 20210-0002

MARTIN, MALCOLM ELLIOT, lawyer; b. Buffalo, Dec. 11, 1935; s. Carl Edward and Pearl Maude (Elliot) M.; m. Judith Hill Harley, June 27, 1964; children—Jennifer, Elizabeth, Christina, Katherine. A.B., U. Mich., Ann Arbor, 1958, J.D., 1962. Bar: N.Y. 1963, U.S. Ct. Appeals (2d cir.) 1966, U.S. Supreme Ct. 1967. Assoc., Chadbourne, Parke, Whiteside & Wolff, N.Y.C., 1962-73, ptnr., 1974—, now Chadbourne & Parke, 1986; dir., sec. Carl and Dorothy Bennett Found., Inc.; sec., counsel Copper Devel. Assn., Inc.; sec., treas. Jute Carpet Backing Council, Inc. Served with U.S. Army, 1958-60. Mem. ABA, N.Y. State Bar Assn., Assn. Bar City N.Y., St. Andrew's Soc. of State of N.Y., Met. Opera Guild. Clubs: Oratamin (Blauvelt, N.Y.), Nyack (N.Y.) Field, Nyack Boat, Rockefeller Center, Copper (N.Y.C.). Home: 74 S Highland Ave Nyack NY 10960-3602 Office: Chadbourne & Parke 30 Rockefeller Plz New York NY 10112

MARTIN, MALCOLM MENCER, endocrinologist; b. Vienna, Austria, Dec. 10, 1920; came to U.S., 1956; s. Karl H. and Rosa (Glaubach) M.; m. Arline L. Avrick, Apr. 15, 1962; children: Jennifer Ann, Nicholas Robin, Kalman Jeremy. MBBS, Durham U., Newcastle on Tyne, Eng., 1945, MD, 1952; MRCP, Royal Coll. Physicians, London, 1948, FRCP, 1972. Cert. Am. Bd. Internal Medicine. Intern Royal Victoria Infirmary, Newcastle On Tyne, 1946-47; resident Postgrad. Sch. Medicine London U., 1948-49; registrar King's Coll. Hosp., London, 1950-55; rsch. fellow Inst. for Clin. Rsch. Middlesex Hosp., London, 1956; rsch. asst. Johns Hopkins Hosp., Balt., 1956-57; rsch. assoc. Peter Bent Brigham Hosp., Harvard U., Boston, 1957-59; asst. prof. Georgetown U. Med. Ctr., Washington, 1959-63, assoc. prof., 1963-67, prof., 1967—; cons. on drugs, AMA, 1965-66, book reviewer 1966-67; cons. USAF Malcolm Grow Med. Ctr., Andrews AFB, 1967-75. Contbr. over 62 articles to profl. jours. With British Army, 1940-42. Recipient Lund Rsch. fellowship, British Diabetes Assn., London, 1950-51, KIng's Coll. Rsch. grant U. London, 1952-55, Leverhulme Rsch. scholarship, Royal Coll. Physicians, London, 1956, Rsch. fellowship, NIH, Washington, 1957-59, Lederle Faculty award, Lederle Pharm. Found., Washington, 1962-65. Mem. AAAS, Endocrine Soc., Am. Diabetes Assn., Am. Pediatric Soc., So. Soc. for Pediatric Rsch., Am. Fedn. for Clin. Rsch., Am. Soc. for Pediatric Endocrinology. Home: 8501 Seven Locks Rd Bethesda MD 20817-2008 Office: Georgetown U Med Ctr 3800 Reservoir Rd NW Washington DC 20007-2196

MARTIN, MICHAEL FREDERICK, economics educator; b. Detroit, Feb. 20, 1957; s. Darwin Denison Martin and Norah Moncrieff Williams. BA, Mich. State U., 1979; MA, U. Mass., 1984, PhD, 1986. Asst. prof. econs. Madonna Coll., Livonia, Mich., 1985-86, Tufts U., Medford, Mass., 1987-89, Colby Coll., Waterville, Maine, 1989-91; econs. educator Hong Kong Bapt. Coll., 1991—. Mem. Am. Econs. Assn., Assn. Comparative Econ. Studies, Assn. Asian Studies, Union of Radical Polit. Economists.

MARTIN, MICHAEL LEE, accountant, taxpayer's representative; b. New Cumberland, Pa., Aug. 2, 1947; s. John Lee and Miriam G. (Motter) M.; m. Carol Feather, Aug. 26, 1979. BA, Am. U., 1968, MA, 1970; AA in Acctg., Ben Franklin U., 1971; MBA, Am. U., 1973. Lic. pub. acct., D.C.; cert. enrolled agt. IRS. Asst. dean Corcoran Sch. Art, Washington, 1970-71; asst. v.p. for mgmt. Corcoran Gallery Art, Washington, 1971-72; staff acct., dir. mgmt. adv. svcs. Profl. Bus. Mgmt., Washington, 1973-76; ptnr. M & M Tax Seminars, 1990—; pres. Mgmt. and Tax Consulting, Ltd., 1976—; mng. ptnr. Taxpayer Advocates, Ltd., Washington, 1990—. Author: Guide to TRA 1984, 1985, Guide to TRA 1986, 1986, Representing Client before IRS, 1987; contbr. articles on tax and representation to profl. jours. Pres. Dowden TerrACE Civic Assn., Alexandria, Va., 1985, 86, Imperial House Condo, Washington, 1991—. Capt. U.S. Army, 1968-69. Mem. Nat. Assn. Enrolled Agts. (bd. dirs. 1976-78, ednl. found. trustee 1987-90), Assn. Enrolled Agts. (nat. capital area pres. 1976, 78, 80), Washington Inst. Pub. Accts. (pres. 1981-83). Home: 1927 Hawthorne Ave Alexandria VA 22311-1614 Office: Taxpayer's Advs 1601 18th St NW Ste 4 Washington DC 20009-2529

MARTIN, MICHAEL TIMOTHY, internist; b. Springfield, Ohio, Sept. 30, 1960; s. James R. and Veneda (Smith) M. BS, U. Louisville, 1982, MD, 1986. Intern St. Vincent Hosp., N.Y.C., 1986-87, chief resident, 1989-90; attending physician Bellevue Hosp., N.Y.C., 1990—.

MARTIN, MICHAEL TOWNSEND, racing horse stable executive, sports marketing executive; b. N.Y.C., Nov. 21, 1941; s. Townsend Bradley and Irene (Redmond) M.; m. Jennifer Johnston, Nov. 7, 1964 (div. Jan. 1977); children: Ryan Bradley, Christopher Townsend; m. Jean Kathleen Meyer, Mar. 1, 1980. Grad., The Choate Sch., 1960; student, Rutgers U., 1961-62. Asst. gen. mgr. N.Y. Jets Football Club, N.Y.C., 1968-74; v.p. NAMANCO Prodns., N.Y.C., 1975-76; v.p., gen. mgr. Cosmos Soccer Club, N.Y.C., 1976-77; exec. asst. Warner Communications, N.Y.C., 1978-84; owner, operator Martin Racing Stable, N.Y.C., 1983—; pres. Sports Mark, Inc., N.Y.C., 1990—; ptnr. Halstead Property Co., N.Y.C., 1987—; bd. dirs. Juilliard Sch., Varicella Zoster Rsch. Found., Inc.; adv. bd. Night Kitchen, 1992—. Bd. dirs. Very Spl. Arts, 1986—, Phipps Houses, 1986—, Mote Marine Lab., Sarasota, Fla., 1989—; trustee Pennington Sch. With USN, 1963-67. Mem. Athletics Congress (life, cert. official 1984—), U.S. Tennis Assn. (life), Internat. Oceanographic Found. (Miami life mem.), Fla. Thoroughbred Breeders Assn., N.Y. Athletic Club, Quogue Field Club, The Union Club. Republican. Episcopalian. Home: 131 E 69th St Apt 11A New York NY 10021-5158 Office: Ste 1006 575 Madison Ave New York NY 10022

MARTIN, PETER ROSS, broadcast executive; b. Worcester, Mass., July 8, 1940; s. Stuart Thompson and Dorothy (Webster) M.; m. Isabella Macomb Edwards, Nov. 20, 1965; children: Andrew Webster, Pieter Lefferts, Isabella Wetherill. AB in History, Harvard U., 1964. Exec. asst. to Gov. State of Vt., Montpelier, 1970-73; reporter WCAX-TV, Burlington, Vt., 1969-70, v.p. news and pub. affairs, 1973-84, exec. v.p., 1984—. Pres. Greater Burlington YMCA, 1980-83; chmn. bd. Sch. Dirs., Jericho, Vt., 1978-91; bd. dirs. Vis. Nurses Assn., Burlington, 1991-92. Lt. col., USAR 1984—. Episcopalian. Home: Box 235 Field's Ln Jericho VT 05465 Office: Sta WCAX-TV PO Box 608 Burlington VT 05402

MARTIN, REBECCA REIST, librarian; b. Princeton, N.J., Mar. 2, 1952; d. Benjamin A. and Harriet (Nold) Reist; m. Joseph M. Lubow; 1 child, Benjamin R. Martin. BA, U. Calif., Santa Cruz, 1973; MA, San Jose State U., 1975; postgrad., U. So. Calif., L.A., 1990—. Med. librarian VA Med. Ctr., San Francisco, 1975-77, chief libr. svc., 1977-81; head biology libr. U. Calif., Berkeley, 1981-85; assoc. libr. dir. San Jose State U., 1985-90; dir. librs. and media svcs. U. Vt., Burlington, 1990—. Contbr. articles to profl. jours., chpts. to books. Commr. Libr. Commn. of San Jose, 1989-90. Mem. ALA, New Eng. Libr. Assn., Am. Soc. Pub. Adminstrn., Am. Assn. Coll. and Rsch. Librs., Libr. Adminstrn. and Mgmt. Assn. (bd. dirs. 1987-89). Office: U Vt Bailey/Howe Libr Burlington VT 05405

MARTIN, RICHARD CORNISH, priest; b. Phila., Oct. 15, 1936; s. Leon Freeman and Virginia Lorette (Bullock) M. MDiv, Episc. Theol. Sem., Alexandria, Va., 1961; BA in Sci., Pa. State U., 1985; D in Ministry, Howard U., 1988. Ordained to diaconate Episc. Ch., 1961, ordained to priesthood, 1962. Episc. chaplain Pa. State U., University Park, Pa., 1961-64; assoc. rector St. Andrew's Ch., State Coll., Pa., 1961-64; Episc. chaplain George Washington U., Washington, 1964-66; asst. St. Paul's Parish, Washington, 1964-66, assoc. rector, 1966-73, rector, 1989—; rector St. George's Parish, Washington, 1973-89; sec., mem. Standing Com. Diocese of Washington, 1972-82, 1990, chmn. Commn. Ministry, 1966-81; mem. Anglican Internat. Liturgical Consultation. Editor St. Paul's Commentary, 1968-73; editor (books) Studies and Commentaries, Vol. I, 1982, Vol. II, 1984, Vol. IV, 1992. Mem. Foggy Bottom Civic Assn., Washington, 1964-73, Com. on Community Improvement, 1973-80, Hospice, D.C., 1990—; pres. Prevention Blindness Soc., Washington, 1967—; trustee Nashotah House Sem., Wis. Recipient Union of Black Epsics. award, 1989. Mem. Societas Liturgics, Soc. of Mary, Am. Region (superior 1966), Am. Friends Anglican Ctr. in Rome (chmn. 1987), Inter-Ch. Club (pres. 1992—), Vergi Viginti Phila. Home: 957 25th St NW Washington DC 20037-2103 Office: St Paul's Episc Ch 2430 K St NW Washington DC 20037-1797

MARTIN, RICHARD HARRISON, art historian; b. Bryn Mawr, Pa., Dec. 4, 1946; s. Frank Harrison and Margaret Dever M. B.A., Swarthmore Coll., 1967; M.A., Columbia U., 1969, M.Phil., 1971. Instr. William Paterson Coll. of N.J., Wayne, 1972-73; editor Arts Mag., N.Y.C., 1974-88; prof. Fashion Inst. Tech., SUNY, N.Y.C., 1973—, Ednl. Found. for the Fashion Industries, 1991—; exec. dir. Shirley Goodman Resource Center, 1980—; critic-in-residence Md. Inst. Coll. Art, 1985-87; editor, pub. Textile & Text, 1989—; adj. faculty Sch. Visual Arts, N.Y.C., 1975-80; adj. prof. NYU, 1977—, Columbia U., 1987-89, Vt. Coll., 1991—. Author: Fashion and Surrealism, 87, Jocks and Nerds, 1989, The Historical Mode, 1989, The New Urban Landscape, 1990, Giorgio Armani: Images of Man, 1990, Flair: Fashion Collected by Tina Chow, 1992. Mem. Coll. Art Assn. Am., Victorian Soc. Am. (dir. 1980-84, chpt. dir. 1981-83), Soc. Archtl. Historians, Am. Soc. for Aesthetics, Art Libraries Soc. N.Am., N.Y. Hist. Soc., Soc. for History of Tech., Costume Soc. Am. (dir. 1983-89, Region II pres. 1984-87). Home: 235 E 22d St New York NY 10010 Office: Fashion Inst Tech 227 W 27th St New York NY 10001-5902

MARTIN, RICHARD L., insurance executive; b. Franklin, N.J., Feb. 2, 1932; s. Richard Lewis and Elizabeth (Roe) M.; m. Susan Mazuy, June 20, 1970; children: David Cory, Scott Mazuy. BEd, U. Miami, 1958; MA, Columbia U., 1963. Chartered Property Casualty Underwriter. Educator Franklin (N.J.) Sch. Dist., 1958-60; mng. dir. Sparta (N.J.) Sch. Dist., 1960-66; adminstr. Orange (N.J.) Sch. System, 1966-71; chief exec. officer Montague (N.J.) Sch. Dist., 1971-72, Stanhope (N.J.) Sch. System, 1972-73; v.p. Selective Ins. Group, Branchville, N.J., 1973-87; pres., chief exec. officer Med. Malpractice Ins. Assn., N.Y.C., 1987—; chmn. N.J. Anti-Car Theft Com., Trenton, 1980-87; treas. N.J. Ins. News Svc., Newark, 1982-87; chmn. AIA-N.J. State Conf., Trenton, 1983-87. Contbr. several articles to mags. With USMC, 1952-54. Mem. CPCU, Am. Mgmt. Assn., Soc. Ins. Research, Soc. for Corp. Planning, City Midday, Newton Country, Branchville Rotary, Sons of Am. Revolution, Mayflower Soc. Presbyterian. Home: RR 1 Box 60 Augusta NJ 07822-9705 Office: Med Malpractice Ins Assn 110 William St New York NY 10038-3901

MARTIN, RICHARD THEODORE, librarian; b. McKinney, Tex., July 9, 1925; s. Clearence Burl and Asenith M.; children: Richard Jr., Rita H., Martha A. BS, Ea. Carolina U., 1972, MLS, 1979; postgrad., Chapel Hill U., 1979. Enlisted USMC, 1943, advanced through grades to master gunnery sgt., 1967, ret., 1970; media specialist librarian Coastal Carolina Community Coll., Jacksonville, N.C., 1970—. Bd. dirs. Onslow County United Way, Jacksonville, 1972-84. With Tex. N.G., 1942-43. Decorated Purple Heart. Mem. ALA, Assn. for Ednl. Communications and Tech., N.C. Libr. Assn., N.C. Assn. Media Tech., N.C. Learning Resources Assn. Democrat. Lodge: Civitan (pres. Jacksonville club 1975-76, Civitan of Yr. Internat. club 1975-76).

MARTIN, ROBERT FRANCIS, roof maintenance systems company executive; b. Bronx, N.Y., Sept. 16, 1942; s. James Edward and Loretta Rita (Martin); m. Sarah Martin; children: Craig, Keith, Dana; m. Eleanor McGaha, Jan. 11, 1986; children: Paul, Scott, Michael. Student, St. Mary's Coll., Ky., 1960-64; BS in Mktg. Econs., Fordham U., 1967. Cert. roof cons. Mgr. Owens Corning Fiberglass, N.Y.C., 1965-70; gen. sales mgr. Bradco Supply, Avenel, N.J., 1970-73; pres. Roof Maintenance Systems, Farmingdale, N.J., 1973—; mem. teaching staff Ctr. for Profl. Advancement, 1989—. Coach referee Jackson Vics Soccer Club, N.J., 1973-91; coach Holbrook Little League, N.J., 1976-86, Pop Warner Football, N.J., 1979-85; founder Drug Prevention Program for Children, N.Y.C., 1965-69. Mem. Constrn. Specification Inst., Bldg. Owners and Mgrs., Nat. Roofing Contractors, N.E. Roofing Contractors Assn., Bldg. Trades Assn., Single Ply Roofing Inst., Am. Inst. Plant Engrs. (pres. 1987-89, Engr. of Yr. 1981).

Republican. Office: Roof Maintenance Systems 5118 Hwy 33 # 34 Farmingdale NJ 07727-3622

MARTIN, TERRENCE E., investment and financial planning company executive; b. Bronx, N.Y., Jan. 20, 1951; s. Raymond and Marjorie (Plusch) M. BA, Lehigh U., 1973. Registered investment advisor SEC. Account exec. First Investor Corp., Scarsdale, N.Y., 1976-83; prin. Martin Fin. Planning, Hackensack, N.J., 1983—; lectr. Successful Money Mgmt. Seminars, Hackensack, 1986—. Bd. trustees Heightened Independence and Progress (HIP), Englewood, N.J., 1991—; mem. Dial, Clifton, N.J., 1986. Mem. Nat. Assn. Securities Dealers, Masons. Congregationalist. Office: Martin Fin Planning 90 Main St Hackensack NJ 07601-7113 also: Am Cyanamid Co One Cyanamid Plz Wayne NJ 07470

MARTIN, TOM FRANCIS, building maintenance company executive; b. Newark, May 27, 1951; s. Thomas and Ida (Parthymos) M.; m. Kathryn Joyce Martino, June 1, 1975; 1 child, Ryan Thomas. BA in Govt., Manhattan Coll., 1973. Br. mgr. Globe Security Systems, East Orange, N.J., 1973-75; plant mgr. Gen. Mills, Chatham, N.J., 1975-77; br. mgr. ITT Pritchard Svcs., Newark, 1977-81; sr. v.p. ops. Control Bldg. Svcs., Secaucus, 1981—. Mem. Florham Pk. (N.J.) Civic Assn., 1985—. Home: 26 1st St Florham Park NJ 07932-1762 Office: Control Bldg Svcs 333 Meadowlands Pky Secaucus NJ 07700

MARTIN, WALTER JOHN, engineer; b. Lancaster, Pa., Feb. 14, 1932; s. Francis J. and Mary L. (Hannum) M.; m. Rita M. Cosgrove, June 20, 1954; children: Janice, Barbara, William, Laura, Lisa. BS in Mil. Sci. & Engring., U.S. Military Acad., 1954. 2nd lt. U.S. Army, Corps of Engrs., 1954-57; advanced through grades to 1st lt. U.S. Army, 1955, resigned, 1957; engr. Martin Co., Orlando, Fla., 1957-60, Raytheon Co., Portsmouth, R.I., 1960—; cons. Nat. Security Indsl. Agy. Co-inventor: programmable beamformer, 1963, filter, 1973, signal processors, 1974, very high speed integrated circuit chips, floating point multiply accumulate kernel, 1982. Episcopalian. Home: 27 Pheasant Dr Portsmouth RI 02871-1807 Office: Raytheon Co W Main Rd Portsmouth RI 02871

MARTIN, WENDY LYNN, pharmaceutical company executive; b. Aurora, Colo.; d. William and Lois Martin. BS in Bus., U. Colo., 1980; MBA, U. Mich., 1985. Assoc. product mgr. Nat. Farmers Union Ins., Denver, 1980-83; brand asst. Procter & Gamble, Cin., 1985-86; sr. product mgr. Schering-Plough, Inc., Memphis, 1986, Liberty Corner, N.J., 1986—. Adminstrn. dir. Nat. Jr. Achievement Conf., Bloomington, Ind., 1977-89. Republican. Office: Schering-Plough Inc 110 Allen Rd Liberty Corner NJ 07938-9999

MARTIN, WILLIAM JOHN, elementary educator; b. Phila., Dec. 7, 1951; s. Patrick Joseph and Kathleen Claire (Murray) M.; m. Julia Kathrine Ruffner, Nov. 29, 1986; children: Patrick Joseph, William John. BS in Edn., So. Ill. U., 1977. Edn. coord. Atlantic Human Resources, Atlantic City, 1978-80; tchr. Ocean City (N.J.) Bd. Edn., 1980-86, Plesantville (N.J.) Bd. Edn., 1986—; mem. parents adv. bd. A Children's Pl., Ocean City, 1991; mem. planning team South Main St. Sch., Plesantville, 1989-91; adviser Stock Market South Main St., Plesantville, 1988—; mem. facilities rev. com. Marsville Project, Plesantville. Vol. Am. Cancer Soc., Margate, N.J., 1991. With U.S. Army, 1971-72. Recipient 1st Pl. Stock Market Game, South Jersey A.C. Press, Atlantic City, 1990, N.J. Coun. Econ. Edn., 1990. Mem. Smithsonian, Am. Legion, N.J. Assn. Mid. Level. Edn., Atlantic County Bd. Realtors. Republican. Roman Catholic. Home: 315 Simpson Ave Ocean City NJ 08226-4036 Office: South Main St Sch 701 S Main St Pleasantville NJ 08232-3260

MARTIN, WILLIAM JOSEPH, III, lawyer; b. New Brunswick, N.J., Nov. 30, 1953; s. William Joseph, Jr. and Martha Jane (Clay) M.; m. Ann Blom, Aug. 21, 1977; children: William Clay, David John. BA with high honors, U. Del., 1975; JD with honors, Rutgers U., 1978; ML in Taxation, Georgetown U., 1987. Bar: Del. 1978, U.S. Tax Ct. 1979. Assoc. David Nicol Williams, PA, Wilmington, Del., 1978-81; ptnr. Williams, Gordon & Martin, PA, Wilmington, 1981—; speaker Del. Tax Inst., Wilmington, 1987, 89, 91. Bd. dirs. and legal counsel Women and Wellness Found., Wilmington, 1990—; trustee, pres. Concord Presbyn. Ch., Wilmington, 1987-90; mem. staff Del. section Am. Radio Relay League, Wilmington, 1987-88. Mem. ABA (health law sect.), Del. State Bar Assn. (taxation sect.). Home: 719 Burnley Rd Wilmington DE 19803-1730 Office: Williams Gordon & Martin PA Ste 600 One Commerce Ctr 12th and Orange Sts Wilmington DE 19899-0511

MARTIN-BITTMAN, LAWRENCE MICHAEL, educator; b. Prague, Czechoslovakia, Feb. 14, 1931; came to U.S., 1968; s. Ladislav and Andela (Pucentejlova) B.; m. Claire S. Baker, Apr. 30, 1984; children: Katerina, Michael. JD, Charles U., Prague, 1966, MA in Journalism, 1967. Mem. czechoslovak mission Neutral Nations Repatriation Commn., Korea, 1953-54; mem. intelligence officer Czechoslovak Intelligence Svc., Prague, 1954-66; press attaché Czechoslovak Legation, Vienna, Austria, 1966-68; rsch. assoc. Tufts U., Medford, Mass., 1968-70; asst. prof. Boston U., 1972-78, assoc. prof. journalism, 1978-90, prof. journalism Coll. Communication, 1990—; bd. dirs. program for study of disinformation, Boston U., 1986—. Author: The Deception Game, 1972, Spionazni Opratky, 1981, The KGB and Soviet Disinformation, 1985; editor: The New Image Makers, 1988; contbr. articles to profl. jours. Grantee Carthage Found., 1971, Bradley Found., 1986, Olin Found., 1986-90. Mem. AAUP. Office: Boston U 640 Commonwealth Ave Boston MA 02215-2422

MARTINELLI, ROSEMARY, public relations executive; b. Pitts., May 13, 1957. BA summa cum laude, Duquesne U., 1979, MA summa cum laude, 1988. News dir., reporter Sta. WDUQ-FM, Pitts., 1977-78; news and pub. affairs producer Sta. KDKA-AM/WPNT-FM, Pitts., 1978-80; news assignment mgr. and consumer producer WPXI-TV, Pitts., 1980-83, creative dir., publicist, 1983-85; dir. spl. events and publicity Gimbels, Pitts., 1985-86; mgr. community rels. Columbia Gas of Pa., Pitts., 1987—. Mem. corp. com., in-kind svcs. com. Pitts. Ballet Theatre, 1988—; mem. Assocs. Civic Light Opera, Pitts., Pitts. Conv. and Visitors Bur., 1987—, Destination Greater Pitts. Attraction Assn.; mem. tribute to women corp. support com. YWCA, Pitts.; mem. mktg. comm. com. Housing Opportunites, Inc.; mem. Points of Light Found. Pilot Program, Pitts.; mem. fundraising com. Western Pa. Leukemia Soc.; mem. women and heart disease task force Western Pa. Heart Assn.; mem. mktg. communications com. Points of Light Founds., Pitts.; bd. advisors New Options program Calif. U. of Pa.; chair corp. contbns. roundtable Grantmakers of Western Pa. Recipient 1990 Nat. Community Rels. Report Bellringer award, Commitment to Safety of Children award Pa. Chiefs of Police, 1990, Eleanor Polis Capone award for creative writing excellence, 1992 YWCA of Pitts. Tribute to Women award in communications, Scripps Howard award for journalistic excellence. Mem. NAFE, Women in Communications (profl. advisor 1987-88, v.p. programming 1990-91, v.p. mktg. 1991-92, v.p publicity 1992—, Matrix award 1989, 91), Pub. Rels. Soc. Am. (publicity, pub. svc. coms.), Soc. Profl. Journalists (Golden Quill award 1984), Am. Women in Radio and TV (bd. dirs. 1991—), Pitts. C. of C. (publicity com. celebrating women in sports com. 1987-91, publicity chmn. 1989), Women's Press Club Pitts., Exec. Women's Coun. Pitts., Pitts. Radio and TV Club, Press Club Western Pa., Phi Kappa Phi, Kappa Tau Alpha, Omicron Delta Kappa. Office: Columbia Gas of Penn 650 Washington Rd Pittsburgh PA 15228

MARTINEZ, AUGUSTO JULIO, neuropathologist; b. Saint Cruz Sur, Camagüey, Cuba, Apr. 12, 1930; came to U.S., 1962; s. Augusto M. and Aurora (Avila) M.; m. Josephine Bridget O'Donnell, Oct. 15, 1966; children: Killeen Josephine, Bridget Elizabeth, Mary Ondina. BS, Inst. Camagey, 1950; MD, U. Havana, Cuba, 1959. Asst. prof. Med. Coll. of Va., Richmond, 1969-71, assoc. prof., 1974-76; assoc. prof. U. Tenn., Memphis, 1972-74; prof. pathology U. Pitts., 1976—; neuropathologist Presbyn. U. Hosp., Pitts., 1976—, Montefiore U. Hosp., Pitts., 1989—. Author: Freeliving Amebas, 1985. V.p. Spanish Cultural Club, Pitts., 1991—. Named Mem. of Honor Med. Soc. of Cataluna, Barcelona, Spain, 1986, Extraordinary Mem. Soc. of Neuropathologists, Buenos Aires, 1991. Republican. Roman Catholic. Home: 111 Emily Dr Pittsburgh PA 15215-1009 Office: Presbyn Hosp DeSoto and O'Hara Sts Pittsburgh PA 15213

MARTINEZ, BOB, federal official; b. Tampa, Fla., Dec. 25, 1934; s. Serafin and Ida (Carreno) M. BS, U. Tampa, 1957; MA, U. Ill., 1964. Tchr. Hillsborough County, 1957-62, 63-66; exec. dir. Hillsborough County Tchrs. Assn., 1966-75; pres. Cafe Sevilla Spanish Restaurant, 1975-83; mayor City of Tampa, 1979-86; gov. State of Fla., 1987-91; dir. Office Nat. Drug Control Policy, Washington, 1991—; lead gov. on drug trafficking and substance abuse, chmn. so. states energy bd. Nat. Govs. Assn., 1989. Pres. Fla. League of Cities, 1985-86. Office: Nat Drug Control Policy Executive Office of the Pres Washington DC 20500

MARTINEZ, LUIS A., import-export company executive; b. Colombia, S.Am., Apr. 25, 1955; s. Luis H. and Celina (Llamas) de Martinez. AA, Queensborough Community Coll., 1978; BA, Queens Coll., 1981. Pres. Onyx Enterprises, Inc., N.Y.C., 1977—; v.p. Trade N Investments, Ltd., N.Y.C., 1981-84, STV Investments Corp., 1989-91, Goldstone Equities, Inc., N.Y.C., 1991—; pres. Genesis Croup, 1992—; engaged in internat. commodities and financing. Vol. The Lighthouse, Inc., The Fresh Air Found. N.Y.; mem. steering com. N.Y. Cares. Mem. Intrepid Mus. Soc., World Trade Club, Masons, KP. Office: 11 Broadway Ste 1400 New York NY 10004-1302

MARTINEZ, SILVIA JACINTA, bilingual language specialist, special educator; b. Nurnberg, Fed. Republic Germany, Jan. 21, 1955; d. Enrique and Margot (Afanador) M. BA, U. P.R., 1976, MS, 1980; postgrad., Boston U., 1983—; C.A.S., Harvard U., 1990. Cert. speech/language pathologist. Tchr. P.R. Dept. Pub. Instruction, San Juan, 1976-77; bilingual speech pathologist Boston Pub. Schs., 1980-81, bilingual spl. edn. tchr., 1984-86, univ. supr., 1986, evaluation team leader, 1986-87; bilingual supr., coord. Northeastern U., Boston, 1981-84; univ. instr. U. Mass., Boston, 1986-89; bilingual speech pathologist Cambridge (Mass.) Pub. Schs., 1987-90; legis. intern Mass. State House, Cambridge, 1990-91; cons. U. Mass., Boston, 1986-91, Pawtucket (R.I.) Pub. Schs., 1989, Cambridge Pub. Schs., 1990; coop. tchr. Northeastern U., Boston, 1985-86; prof. Lesley Coll., Cambridge, 1989-90, Roxbury Community Coll., 1991—. Author: (curriculum) Culture and Language Awareness Program, 1983. Media coord., fundraiser P.R. Civil Rights Orgn., Boston, 1986-89; vol. rundraiser, cons. Multicultural Edn., Tng. and Advocacy, Somerville, Mass., 1989-90, Centro Presente, Cambridge, Mass., 1988-90; legis. intern Rep. Nelson Merced, Mass., 1990-91; mem. Boston Coalition for Sch. Reform, 1990-91; mem. Cambridge Human Svcs. Commn., 1990—. Doctoral Leadership in Tng. and Rsch. grantee Boston U., 1984, Vocat. Rehab. scholar U. P.R., 1979. Home and Office: 106 Columbia St Apt 2 Cambridge MA 02139-2728

MARTINI, RICHARD K., theatrical producer; b. Bergenfield, N.J., Mar. 11, 1952; s. John F. and June L. (Fenton) M.; m. Susan C. Weaving, Aug. 1, 1981. BA, St. Francis Coll., Loretto, Pa., 1974; MEd, U. S.C., 1975. V.p. Am. Theatre Prodns., N.Y.C., 1975-81; pres. Edgewood Orgn., N.Y.C., 1981-86; pres., owner KL Mgmt., N.Y.C., 1986—; owner, operator Martini Entertainment, Inc., N.Y.C., 1991—. Mem. League of Am. Theatres and Producers. Home: 201 E 37th St New York NY 10016-3159 Office: Martini Entertainment Co Inc 1501 Broadway Ste 1812 New York NY 10036

MARTINO, MICHAEL CHARLES, entertainer, musician; b. Phila., Sept. 10, 1950; s. Salvatore Joseph and Marie Angela (Langone) M. Grad. high sch., Upper Darby, Pa. Spokesperson/rep. Petosa Accordion Co., Seattle, 1979—; featured TV entertainer Mike Martino Show, Delaware County, Pa., 1987-89; accordion tchr. Drexel Hill, Pa., 1989—; entertainer/host/producer St. Jude's Children's Hosp. Marathon, King of Prussia, Pa., 1973; opening act Downingtown, Pa., 1973, Phila., 1981; guest artist/entertainer Internat. Platform Assn. Conv., Washington, 1979; nite club performer Glen Mills, Pa., 1989; actor TV commls., Elkton, Md., 1979, Halloween Spl. KYW-TV, Phila., 1986. Author: (movie script) Forever Fiftys, 1990; composer popular songs. Recipient citation U.S. Ho. Reps., 1989, Proclamation Mike Martino Day Mayor Ward, Del. County, 1988, Danny Thomas Hon. award St. Jude's Hosp., Del. County, 1973. Roman Catholic. Home: 2530 Stoney Brook Ln Drexel Hill PA 19026

MARTINO, PETER DOMINIC, software company executive, military officer; b. N.Y.C., Sept. 21, 1963; s. Rocco Leonard and Barbara Italia (D'Iorio) M.; m. Martha Dorothy Laffey, Sept. 9, 1989; 1 child, Elizabeth Marie. BS, U.S. Naval Acad., 1985. Commd. ensign USN, 1985, advanced through grades to lt., 1989, resigned, 1990; with USNR, 1990—; v.p. mktg. XRT, Inc., Wayne, Pa., 1990, exec. v.p., chief operating officer, 1990—, also bd. dirs.; co-owner, co-founder Computerized Ambulatory Tracking Svcs., Wayne, 1991. Sustaining mem. Rep. Nat. Com., 1981—. Mem. Nat. Corp. Cash Mgrs. Assn., Naval Acad. Alumni Assn., Naval Acad. Athletic Assn., Army Navy Club, Army Navy Country Club, Naval Submarine League. Roman Catholic. Office: XRT Inc 989 Old Eagle School Rd Wayne PA 19087-1704

MARTINO, ROCCO LEONARD, computer systems executive; b. Toronto, Ont., Can., June 25, 1929; s. Domenic and Josephine (DiGiulio) M. BSc, U. Toronto, 1951, MA, 1952; PhD, Inst. Aerospace Studies, 1955; m. Barbara L. D'Iorio, Sept. 2, 1961; children: Peter Domenic, Joseph Alfred, Paul Gerard, John Francis. Dir., Univac Computing Svc. Ctr., Toronto, 1956-59; pres. Mauchly Assos. Can. Ltd., Toronto, 1959-62, v.p. Mauchly Assocs., Inc., Ft. Washington, Pa., 1959-61; mgr. advanced systems Olin Mathieson Chem. Corp., N.Y.C., 1962-64; dir. advanced computer systems Booz, Allen & Hamilton, N.Y.C., 1965-70; pres., chmn. bd. Info. Industries, Inc. and subs.'s, Wayne, Pa., 1965-70; chmn. bd., chief exec. officer XRT, Inc., Wayne, Pa., 1970—; chmn. bd. MBF Computer Ctr. for Handicapped Children; mem. bd. St. Joseph's U., Phila., Gregorian U. Found., N.Y., vice chmn. bd., 1990—; mem. exec. com. Gregorian U., N.Y. and Rome, 1987—, bd. dirs. 1984—, pontifical circle, 1985—, active, 1982—; assoc. prof. math. U. Waterloo, 1959-62, prof. engring., dir. Inst. Systems and Mgmt. Engring., 1964-65; adj. assoc. prof. NYU, 1963-64, adj. prof. math., 1964-65, 66; lectr. on computers mgmt.; chmn. Gov. Ill. Task Force, 1970-71, Ill. Bd. Higher Edn. Task Force, 1971-72, Computer-Use Task Force FCC, 1972-73, Computer-Use Planning Task Force U.S. Postal Svc., 1973-74. Trustee Gregorian Found., N.Y.C. and Rome, 1984—; bd. dirs. St. Joseph's U., 1987—, Cath. League Religious and Civil Rights, 1988-91; chmn. bd. dirs. MBF Ctr. Disabled Children, 1985—; founder Vatican Observatory, 1988—, bd. dirs. Tucson, Rome, 1990—. Mem. Assn. Computing Machinery, Ops. Rsch. Soc. Am., Nat. Italian Am. Found. (bd. dirs. 1991—), Profl. Engrs. Ont., Computing Soc. Can., ITEST (bd. dirs.), Union League Phila., Lions, Overbrook Golf and Country Club, Yacht of Sea Isle City Club (commodore 1973-74, trustee 1975-86, chmn. 1983-86), Commodores Club, Mid-Atlantic Yacht Racing Assn. (commodore 1979-81, sec. 1981-83, officer 1983—), Order St. Gregory the Great (papal knight 1991—), Legatus (bd. dirs. 1988), Papal Knight, Equestrian Order Holy Sepulchre (knight 1986, knight comdr. 1989), KC, Order of Malta, Knights of Malta (knight 1988, knight commdr. 1989) . Author: Resources Management, 1968, Dynamic Costing, 1968, Project Management, 1968, Information Management: The Dynamics of MIS, 1968, MIS-Management Information Systems, 1969, Decision Patterns, 1969, Methodology of MIS, 1969, Personnel Information Systems, 1969, Integrated Manufacturing Systems, 1972, APG-Virtual Application Systems, 1981; contbr. numerous articles on mgmt., computers and planning in profl. publs.; designer, developer Application Program Generator computer system, 1974-75, integrated treasury systems; developer cash mgmt. and on-line internat. trading systems, 1984, local area network systems fault tolerant and disaster tolerant systems for real-time fin. transactions, comml. paper trading systems for global networks. Office: 989 Old Eagle School Rd Wayne PA 19087-1704

MARTINS, PETER, ballet master, choreographer, dancer; b. Copenhagen, Oct. 27, 1946; came to U.S., 1967, naturalized, 1970; m. Lise La Cour (div. 1973); 1 child, Nilas. Pupil of Vera Volkova and Stanley Williams with Royal Danish Ballet. Co-dir. N.Y.C. Ballet, ballet master-in-chief; Tchr. Sch. Am. Ballet, 1975, N.Y.C. Ballet, 1975, ballet master, 1981-83, co-ballet master-in-chief, from 1983, now ballet master-in-chief; artistic adviser Pa. Ballet, 1982—. Mem. Royal Danish Ballet, 1965-67, prin. dancer (including Bournonville repertory), 1967; guest artist N.Y.C. Ballet, 1967-70, prin. dancer, 1970-83; guest artist regional ballet cos. U.S., also Nat. Ballet Can., Royal Ballet, London, Grand Theatre Geneva, Paris Opera, Vienna State Opera, Munich State Opera, London Festival Ballet, Ballet Internat., Royal Danish Ballet; TV appearance in series of Balanchine works, 1974; also has appeared on PBS Dance in America series including A Choreographer's Notebook: Stravinsky Piano Ballets by Peter Martins, 1984; choreographed Broadway musicals including Dream of the Twins (co-choreographer) 1982, On Your Toes, 1982, Song and Dance, 1985; works choreographed include Calcium Light Night, 1977, Tricolore (Pas de Basque sect.), 1978, Rossini Pas de Deux, 1978, Tango-Tango (ice ballet), 1978, Dido and Aeneas, 1979, Sonate di Scarlatti, 1979, Eight Easy Pieces, 1980, Lille Suite, 1980, Suite from Histoire du Soldat, 1981, Capricio Italien, 1981, The Magic Flute, 1981, Symphony No. 1, 1981, Delibes Divertissement, 1982, Piano-Rag-Music, 1982, Concerto for Two Solo Pianos, 1982, Waltzes, 1983, Rossini Quartets, 1983, Tango, 1983, A Schubertiad, 1984, Mozart Violin Concerto, 1984, Poulenc Sonata, 1985, La Sylphide, 1985, Valse Triste, 1985, Eight More, 1985, We Are the World, 1985, Eight Miniatures, 1985, Ecstatic Orange, Tanzspiel, 1988; author: (autobiography) Far from Denmark, 1982. Recipient Dance mag. award 1977, Cue's Golden Apple award 1977, award of merit Phila. Art Alliance, 1985, Liberty award N.Y.C., 1986. Office: NY State Theater NYC Ballet Lincoln Ctr Pla New York NY 10023*

MARTLAND, CARL DOUGLAS, research transportation engineer, consultant; b. Providence, Sept. 22, 1946. BS in Math., MIT, 1968, MSCE, CE, 1972. Rsch. engr. dept. civil engring. MIT, Cambridge, 1972-75, rsch. assoc., 1975-80, prin. rsch. assoc., 1980-91, sr. rsch. assoc., 1991—; cons. in field. Editor: MIT Studies in Railway Operations and Economics, 39 vols., 1972—; also numerous articles on r.r. transp. Clk., bd. dirs. Transporting Handicapped and Elderly in Mass., Cambridge, 1986-88; scoutmaster Boy Scouts Am., Roslindale, 1989. With U.S. Army, 1969-71. Mem. Transp. Rsch. Forum (v.p. program 1984, exec. v.p. 1985, pres. 1986, past pres. 1987, v.p. Found. 1988—, H.O. Whitten award 1991, Conrail Best Paper award 1989-91, Outstanding Paper award 1992).

MARTONI, CHARLES J., dean; b. Pitts., Aug. 24, 1936; s. John and Virginia (Caputo) M. A.A., Community Coll. Allen County, 1969; B.S., California State Coll. (Pa.), 1971, M.A., 1977; M.S., Duquesne U., 1976, M.Ed., 1972; Ph.D., U. Pitts., 1988. Cert. counselor, nat. and Pa. Asst. dir. fin. aid Boyce Campus Community Coll. Allen County, Monroeville, Pa., 1971-73, dir. fin. aid, 1973-76, dir. fin. aid and counseling, 1976-80, dean of students, 1980—; mem. exec. bd. Tri-State Conf. on Steel. Mayor Swissvale, Pa., 1982-90; pres. Coun. Swissvale, 1990, Mon Valley Initiative. With U.S. Army, 1958-60. John Hart scholar, 1970; named Outstanding Alumnus, Boyce Campus, Community Coll. Allen County, 1978. Mem. Pa. Personnel and Guidance Assn., Pa. Mayors Assn., Nat. Assn. Student Personnel Adminstrs., Am. Assn. Counseling and Devel., Nat. Cert. Counselors. Democrat. Roman Catholic. Home: 7114 Church St Pittsburgh PA 15218-2434 Office: City Hall Swissvale PA 15218

MARTORELL, MARIO FRANCISCO, psychologist, educator; b. Guanabacoa, Havana, Cuba, Dec. 3, 1942; came to U.S., 1974; s. Mario Lazaro Inocente and Flor Maria (Borrell) M. MA in Chemistry, Montclair State Coll., 1978; Advanced Cert. in Adminstrn., CCNY, 1980; MS in Edn., L.I. U., 1983; PhD in Sch. Psychology, Fordham U., 1991. Cert. sch. psychologist, tchr., N.Y., N.J. Tchr. Havana Bd. of Edn., 1961-69; dir. comml. dept. Barcelona Import, Inc., Spain, 1972-74; bilingual tchr. of chemistry N.Y.C. Bd. Edn., 1974-79, coord. high sch. prog. Nat. Alliance for Bus., 1979-80, coord., supr. CCOED prog., 1980-84, asst. chmn. com. on handicapped, 1984-85, bilingual sch. psychologist, 1989—; bilingual sch. psychologist Manhattan Regional Bd. Edn., N.Y.C., 1984-86, interim acting clin. supr. of sch. psychologists, 1987-89; prof. psychology Mercy Coll., Dobbs Ferry, N.Y., 1985—; bilingual ednl. cons. N.Y.C. Bd. Edn., 1977—. Author sci. curriculum, 1976. Active the Cuban Am. Nat. Found., Washington, 1990. Recipient scholarship L.I. U., Bklyn. Campus, 1983, Outstanding Achievement award CCNY, 1980, fellowship NSF, Washington, 1979. Mem. Am. Psychol. Assn. (doctoral dissertation award 1991), Nat. Assn. Sch. Psychologists, Am. Ednl. Rsch. Assn., N.Y. State Sch. Psychologist Assn., Ea. Psychol. Assn., Kappa Delta Pi, Psy Chi. Democrat. Roman Catholic. Home: 20 49th St Weehawken NJ 07087-7204 Office: Bd of Edn 660 W 183d St New York NY 10033-3806

MARTUCCI, VINCENT JAMES, composer, pianist; b. Medford, Mass., Oct. 21, 1954; s. Vincent James Sr. and Grace Alice (Giorgio) M.; m. Elizabeth Nicoll Lawrence, Sept. 20, 1981. Student, Berklee Coll. Music, Boston, 1974-75; BA in Music, Colby Coll., 1977; student, Hal Galper, N.Y.C., 1978-80, Dave Holland, Woodstock, N.Y., 1982-84. Lectr. music Alfred (N.Y.) U., 1978-80; registrar, instr. Creative Music Studio, Woodstock, 1980-82; owner, composer, performer Vinnie Martucci Prodns., West Hurley, N.Y., 1987—; free-lance pianist, performer various functions, 1977—; free-lance composer, producer recordings and TV, 1986—; tchr. SUNY, New Paltz, 1991; cons. synthesis and audio technique, 1985—; mem. U.S. Embassy tour concert series, Bogota, Colombia, 1991. Composer, performer The Dolphins, 1987—; arranger radio concert series Karl Berger Composer, 1985; co-author, arranger Adventures of Comander Crumbcake - TV series, 1987; composer: Malayan Breeze, 1991, network theme redesign pkg. lifetime med. TV, 1988, travel channel, 1990, CNN-Daily Menus, 1991; co-composer recording Old World/New World, 1991; author instructional tape series Arranging and Recording Electronic Instruments, 1987. Recipient 2d pl. jazz composition Billboard Mag., 1988. Mem. ASCAP, Am. Fedn. Musicians. Home and Office: Vinnie Martucci Prodn 400 Stone Rd West Hurley NY 12491

MARTUSCELLO, DIANE MATARAZA, arts administrator; b. Poughkeepsie, N.Y., May 12, 1952; d. Michael Morano and Rita (Abbruzzese) M. MusB, Ithaca Coll., 1974; MA, NYU, 1978; Grantsmanship Tng. Cert., U. Del., 1990. Music dir. Chester (N.Y.) Union Schs., 1974-78; asst. dir. music Minisink Schs., Slate Hill, N.Y., 1978-79; acting dir. Dutchess County Arts Council, Poughkeepsie, N.Y., 1980; exec. dir. Dutchess County Arts Council, Poughkeepsie, 1981-84, Alliance of N.Y. State Arts Councils, New Windsor, N.Y., 1985-91; program dir. Nat. Endowment for the Arts, Washington, 1992—; panelist Nat. Endowment for the Arts, Washington, 1988-90, N.J. State Arts Coun., 1990, N.Y. State Gov.'s Arts Awards, N.Y.C., 1987-91; mem. N.Y. State Bus. Coun. Tourism Com., Albany, 1987-91; vice-chmn. N.Y. State Coun. on the Arts Adv. Com., 1983-84; mem. Greater Hudson Valley Coord. Coun., 1991, Art Table, 1990-91. Com. mem. N.Y. State Senate Sub-Com. on Culture, Albany, 1983-85; bd. dirs. State Arts Adv. League of Am., 1988-91; com. mem. Commr.'s Adv. Com., N.Y. State Edn. Dept., 1986-91; assembly steering com. Nat. Assembly of Local Arts Agys., Washington, 1986—. Mem. NYU Alumni Assn., NAFE, Am. Coun. for the Arts, Ithaca Coll. Alumni Assn., Mu Phi Epsilon, Ptnrs. of the Americas. Republican. Roman Catholic. Office: NEA Nancy Hanks Ctr Rm 602 1100 Pennsylvania Ave NW Washington DC 20506-0005

MARTY, ALVIN LEONARD, economist, educator; b. N.Y.C., Jan. 29, 1927; s. Harry and Pearl (Bailin) M. Student, Cambridge (Eng.) U., 1947-50; PhD, U. Calif., Berkeley, 1955; AB, UCLA, 1947. Mem. faculty Northwestern U., Evanston, Ill., 1955-60; prof. econs. CUNY, 1960—; prof. econs. and fin. Ctr. for Study of Bus. and Govt., Baruch Coll., N.Y.C.; visiting prof. U. Chgo., 1962, U. Hawaii, 1973, Columbia U., 1974; Simon rsch. prof. Manchester (Eng.) U., 1975-76. Mem. editorial bd. Am. Econ. Assn.; contbr. articles to profl. jours. Ehrman student Cambridge U., 1947-50; Ford Found. fellow, 1956-57. Home: 545 W End Ave New York NY 10024-2713 Office: Baruch Coll Ctr for Study of Bus & Govt 17 Lexington Ave New York NY 10010-5526

MARVEL, ANDREW SCOTT, songwriter, record company executive; b. Bklyn., Dec. 29, 1962; s. Lawrence Marvel and Sheila Hope (Odesky) Krumholz. Student, Brockport U., 1979, Juilliard Sch. Music, 1980; AAS, Five Towns Coll., 1983. Pres. Ricochet Records, N.Y.C., 1981—, Andy Marvel Music, N.Y.C., 1981—, Andysongs, N.Y.C., 1981—, Bing, Bing, Bing Music, N.Y.C., 1981—, Alyssa Records, N.Y.C., 1983—, Scott Electronics, L.I., N.Y., 1984—, Marvel Home Video, L.I., 1987—. Songwriter CBS-TV, N.Y.C., 1981; scriptwriter ABC-TV shows Roseanne, Who's the Boss, Growing Pains, 1988—; writer Munster's Comics. Mem. ASCAP (awards). Office: PO Box 587 Farmingville NY 11738-0587

MARVIN, JOHN BINGHAM, psychologist; b. Burlington, Vt., Dec. 15, 1935; s. Merrill Morton and Adelia (Johnson) M.; m. Deanna Hart, Sept. 17, 1955; children: Paul, Dawn, Valerie, Timothy, Peter. BA, U. Vt., 1957, MA, 1959; postgrad., Boston U., 1964-68. Lic. psychologist. Asst. dir. mental

health Vt. Dept. Health, Burlington, 1960-62, acting dir. mental health, 1962-63; asst. dir. community svcs. Vt. Dept. Health, Montpelier, 1963-64; psychologist intern Brookline (Mass.) Mental Health Ctr., 1964-65; doctoral fellow Boston U. Human Rels. Ctr., 1965-67; dir. counseling tng. U. Maine in New Eng. Ctr., Durham, N.H., 1967-68; pres. Assocs. Human Resources, Concord, Mass., 1967-74, exec. dir., 1979-85, pres., 1985—; pres., mem. faculty Gestalt Inst. New Eng., Concord, Mass., 1975-79; co-chmn. dept. human behavior Oblate Coll., Natick, Mass., 1972-74; cons. USN Human Resources, Newport, R.I., Digital Equipment Corp., Shrewsbury, Mass., 1987-90; ; mem. task force on prevention compulsive gambling Mass. Coun. on Compulsive Gambling, Boston, 1992—. Mem. APA,, Am. Adoption Congress (life), Nat. Assn. Children Alcholics (state del. 1988-91, bd. dirs. Mass. chpt. 1988—), Assn. Humanistic Psychology (chmn. com.), Nat. Orgn. Men Against Sexism, Orgn. Devel. Network. Home: 20 Nagog Hill Rd Littleton MA 01460-2212 Office: Assocs for Human Resources 191 Sudbury Rd Concord MA 01742-3423

MARVIN, JOHN GEORGE, clergyman, church organization executive; b. Summit, N.J., May 8, 1912; s. George and Caroline (Whitman) M.; B.S., Davidson Coll., 1933; Th.B., Princeton Theol. Sem., 1936; D.D., Coll. of Emporia, 1964; LL.D., Tarkio Coll., 1964; m. Elizabeth Anne Wheater, June 30, 1944; children—Caroline Wheater Dorney, Elizabeth Anne West, Martha Jane Hobbs, Frances Alice Heidel. Ordained to ministry Presbyterian Ch., 1936; pastor, Windsor, N.Y., 1936-37, Montrose, Pa., 1937-44, Lewistown, Pa., 1944-52, Denton, Tex., 1952-61; presbytery exec. Greater Kansas City, Mo., 1961-65; pastor 1st Presbyn. Ch., Bartlesville, Okla., 1965-69; sr. minister Chevy Chase Presbyn. Ch., Washington, 1969-77, pastor emeritus, 1978—; interim sr. minister Catonsville Ch., Balt., 1978, 3d Ch., Rochester, N.Y., 1978-79, 1st Ch., Ft. Worth, 1979-80, Gaithersburg, Md., 1980-81, Westfield, N.J., 1981-82, Ch. of Palms, Sarasota, Fla., 1982-83, Bethel Ch., Balt., 1983-84, Pine Shores Ch., Sarasota, Fla., 1984, Interfaith Chapel, Silver Spring, Md., 1984-87; mem. exec. com. Pa. Council Chs., 1949-52, Tex. Council Chs., 1953-61; mem. exec. com., long range chmn. Greater Kansas City Council Chs., 1962-65; chmn. campus Christian Life Tex. Synod, 1958-61; chmn. nat. mission Pa. Synod, 1949-52; sec. nomination com. Gen. Assembly U.P. Ch., 1955-58, chmn. com. on baptized children, 1969-70, mem. com. of nine on synod bounderies, 1970-72; bd. dirs. Midwest Christian Counseling Ctr., Kansas City, Mo., 1963-69, Presbyn. Homes of Okla., Inc., 1966-69; mem. jud. commn. Synod of Okla.-Ark., 1966-69; mem. strategy com. Bd. Nat. Missions, 1968-70, British-Am. Preaching Exchange, preaching missions to Alaska and Mexico; leader and lectr. on religious heritage tours in Europe, Mid. East, Egypt, Caribbean and Orient, 1972-84. Bd. dirs. Tarkio Coll., 1961-67, Westminster Found., Pa. State U., 1945-52, North Tex. State U., 1952-61; mem. ministerial relations com. Nat. Capital Union Presbytery, 1973-78; bd. visitors Warren Wilson Coll. Mem. Beta Theta Pi. Republican. Club: Rotary. Contbr. articles to religious publs. Home: 14500 Elmhan Ct Silver Spring MD 20906-1839

MARVINNY, CHARLES JOSEPH, retired accountant; b. Jersey City, Dec. 10, 1915; s. Francis J. Sr. and Mary (Mora) M.; m. Elizabeth Garry, Sept. 20, 1945; children; Christopher D., Regina A. BSBA, NYU, 1950. Clk. Internat. Nickel Co., N.Y.C., 1934-40; acct. Colgate Palmolive Co., N.Y., N.J., 1945-77; trustee N.J. Flower and Garden Show, 1985-90. Author: (with others) Gesneriads and How to Grow Them, 1967. With USN, 1940-45. Mem. Am. Gloxinia and Gesneriad Soc. (hon. life) (pres. 1965-68), N.J. State Florists Assn. (treas., sec. 1978—, exec. dir. 1987—), N.J. Plant and Flower Growers Assn. (exec. dir. 1987—, Golden Flower award 1986). Home: 7 Toucan Ct Wayne NJ 07470-3453

MARX, EGON, physicist, researcher; b. Cologne, Germany, Apr. 4, 1937; came to U.S., 1965; s. Erich and Herta Helene (Oberländer) M.; m. Irene Lehmann, Apr. 4, 1965; children: Sonia, Nancy. EE, U. Chile, Santiago, 1959; PhD, Calif. Inst. Tech., 1963. Teaching asst. U. Chile, 1956-59, researcher, 1963-65; teaching and rsch. asst. Calif. Inst. Tech., Pasadena, 1962-63; asst. prof. physics Clarkson U., Potsdam, N.Y., 1965-67, Drexel U., Phila., 1967-72; physicist Harry Diamond Labs., Adelphi, Md., 1972-80, Nat. Inst. Standards and Tech., Gaithersburg, Md., 1980—. Contbr. over 100 articles on field theory and relativistic quantum mechanics, and electromagnetism and applications to profl. jours. Office: Nat Inst Stds and Tech Gaithersburg MD 20899

MARZULLI, FRANCIS NICHOLAS, toxicologist, consultant; b. N.Y.C., Feb. 2, 1917; s. Olindo and Mary Grace (Maccarrone) M.; m. Florence Bushelman, Dec. 4, 1945; children: Catherine Elise, John Francis. BS, St. Peters Coll., 1937; MA, Johns Hopkins U., 1940, PhD, 1941. Aquatic biologist U.S. Fish & Wildlife Svc., Fla., 1941-43; toxicologist Dugway Proving Ground, Toele, Utah, 1946-47; physiologist U.S. Army Chem. Ctr., Edgewood, Md., 1947-52, chief field toxicology, 1953-63; chief dermal toxicology FDA, Washington, 1963-75, sr. scientist, 1975-80; sr. scientist Nat. Acad. Scis./NRC, Washington, 1980-87; pvt. practice cons. toxicologist Bethesda, Md., 1987—; organizer symposia for sci. meetings, 1963—; tchr. in field. Co-editor: Dermatotoxicology, 1977, 2d edit., 1983, 3d edit., 1987, 4th edit., 1991; contbr. articles to profl. jours. Capt. USAF, 1946. Mem. Soc. Toxicology, Am. Coll. Toxicology, Soc. Investigative Dermatology, Assn. for Rsch. in Vision and Ophtahlmology, Polish Dermatology Soc. (hon.), Sigma Xi. Home and Office: 8044 Park Overlook Dr Bethesda MD 20817-2724

MASAITIS, CESLOVAS, retired researcher; b. Kaunas, Lithuania, Mar. 2, 1912; came to U.S., 1949; s. Joshph and Jadvyga (Butkevicius) M.; widowed; 1 child, Nijole. Diploma, U. Kaunas, 1937; PhD, U. Tenn., 1956. Asst. U. Vytautas The Great, Kaunas, 1937-39; sr. asst. U. Vilnius, Lithuania, 1939-44; lectr. Nazareth Coll., Bardstown, Ky., 1950-52, U. Ky., Lexington, 1952-53, U. Tenn., Knosville, 1953-56; mathematician Ballistic Rsch. Lab., Aberdeen, Md., 1956-63, supervisory rsch. math., 1963-80, cons., 1980-84, ret., 1984; lectr. U. Del., Newark, 1957-69, U. Vytautat The Great, 1990; rsch. asst. prof. U. Md. Balt., 1963-76. Contbr. articles to profl. jours. Pres. Alumni of Lithuanian Cath. Orgn., Aux. of Immaculate Conception Convent, 1981—, Lithuanian Christian Dem. Union, Chgo., 1989—. Fellow Ballistic Rsch. Lab. Mem. Am. Math. Assn., Lithuanian Cath. Acad. Sci. (exec. pres. 1984—). Roman Catholic. Home: PO Box 442 Thompson CT 06277

MASCARI, J. BARRY, counseling supervisor, educator; b. Paterson, N.J., Nov. 6, 1948; s. Joseph Edward and Doris Anna (Holmes) M.; m. Aviva Miriam Sanders, Aug. 10, 1980; children: Matthew, Janine. BA, Fairleigh Dickinson U., 1970, MA in Teaching, 1972; MS, U. Bridgeport, 1981; post-grad., Jersey City State Coll., 1986-87. Cert. clin. mental health counselor, drug counselor, nat. counselor. Tchr. Ridgewood High Sch., N.J., 1971-72, Teaneck High Sch., N.J., 1972-80; coord. for Alpha Ctr. Nedac, Inc., Montclair, N.J., 1980-83; exec. dir. N.J. Prevention, Inc., Montclair, 1983-84; prevention specialist Montclair Pub. Schs., 1984-86; special asst. to supt. Clifton Pub. Schs., 1986-89, dir. counseling and student svcs., 1989—; clinical supr. cons. Warren County Drug Abuse, Wash., N.J., 1983-84; mental health cons. West Essex Special Edn. Coop., Caldwell, N.J., 1982-83; chair Profl. Adv. Com. on Alcoholism, Passaic County, N.J., 1989-91, v.p., 1984-89; prof. Kean Coll., Union, N.J., 1984—. Contbr. articles to profl. pubs. V.P. Clifton Against Substance Abuse, 1988; sec. Barnert Temple (Bnai Jeshurin),Franklin Lakes, N.J., 1991; com. mem. Health & Safty Fair, Clifton, 1990. With USARNG, 1969-77. Recipient N.J. Div. Youth & Family Svcs. award for outstanding contbr. to child abuse prevention, 1988; U.S. Drug Enforcement Adminstrn. award for contbr. to drug law enforcement, 1990. Mem. AACD, N.J. and Am. Sch. Counselors Assn., N.J. Profl. Counselors Assn. (pres. 1984-85, Charles Tabler Disting. Profl. Svcs. award, 1990), N.J. Mental Health Counselors Assn. (pres. 1981-83). Jewish. Home: 26 New York Ave Hawthorne NJ 07506-3028 Office: Clifton Pub Schs 745 Clifton Ave Clifton NJ 07013-1885

MASCHIN, DOUGLAS RAYMOND, sales administrator; b. Milw., Oct. 7, 1950; s. Ervin Joseph and Rita Ann (Holzem) M.; m. Gail Louise Miller, Oct. 4, 1980. BBA in Mktg., U. Wis., 1972; postgrad., Keller Grad. Sch., Chgo., 1982-83. Dist. sales rep. Air Products & Chemicals, Inc., St. Louis, 1978-79; area mgr. Cryo-products Air Products & Chemicals, Inc., Trexlertown, Pa., 1979-82; specialty gas specialist Air Products & Chemicals, Inc., Chgo., 1982-83; br. mgr. Air Products & Chemicals, Inc., Milw., 1983-84; dist. mgr. Air Products & Chemicals, Inc., Detroit, 1984-86; mgr. cryo-products dept. Air Products & Chemicals, Inc., Trexlertown, 1986-90; regional mgr. Frigoscanda Food Process Systems Inc., Allentown, Pa., 1990; dir. of sales east zone freezing systems Frigo Scandia Food Process Systems, Inc., Allentown, Pa., 1991—. Author (video tape) Selling Specialty Gas, 1984. Mem. ASHRAE (tech. com. Atlanta chpt. 1988—), Am. Meat Inst., Am. Assn. Meat Packers, Nat. Fisheries Inst., Nat. Frozen Foods Assn., Brookside Country Club (Macungie, Pa.). Republican. Roman Catholic. Home: 2001 Wells Ct Allentown PA 18103-6990

MASEL, WILLIAM H., construction executive, consultant; b. Queens, N.Y., Dec. 11, 1949; s. Herbert George and Dorothy (Beyer) M.; m. Lois Joan Morelli, Aug. 12, 1973; 1 child, William Anthony. A degree, L.I. Tech., Westbury, N.Y., 1974; cert., Union (N.J.) County Coll., 1985. Asst. v.p. Labequipco, N.Y.C., 1974-77; project mgr. Lab. Fumehood Inc., Bklyn., 1977-81; chief of engring. Fiance Assoc., Bronx, 1981-83; project mgr. Rich Assoc. Inc., S.I., 1984-85; v.p. Mariner Ind. Inc., S.I., 1985-90; project mgr. Lacertosa J&C Masonry Inc., S.I., 1990—; owner, cons. Archtl. Svcs. and Planning, S.I., 1984—. With U.S. Army, 1968-74, Vietnam. Decorated Purple Heart. Mem. Vietnam Vets. Am., Nat. 4th Div., S.I. Contractors Assn. Republican. Home: 97 Bennett Ave Staten Island NY 10312-4018 Office: Lacertosa J&C Masonry Inc 20 Kinsey Pl Staten Island NY 10303-1427

MASGAY, THOMAS MICHAEL, driving educator; b. Sanford, Fla., Aug. 8, 1962; s. Stanley Charles and Dorothy Joan (Boegler) M.; m. Nina Diann Malray, June 8, 1991. Driver edn. cert., Keene State Coll., 1985. Profl. driving instr. Hampshire Driving Sch., Nashua, N.H., 1984—; driver improvement instr. Am. Automobile Assn., 1988—; N.H. state licensing examiner State N.H. Motor Vehicle Dept., Concord, 1988—; pub. svc. speaker Hampshire Driving Sch., Nashua, 1984—. Songwriter 16 studio recordings. Office: Hampshire Driving Sch 6 Temple St Nashua NH 03060

MASH, DAVID STEFAN, music educator, dean; b. Detroit, June 25, 1952; s. Jack Burt Mash and Rose Lorraine (Manko) Morgan; m. Erica Marjorie Mack, Aug. 22, 1982; children: Reesa Jamie, Sasha Leah. MusB, Berklee Coll. Music, 1976. Faculty mem. Berklee Coll. Music, Boston, 1976-85, chair music synthesis dept., 1985-90, asst. dean curriculum, 1990—; synthesist Ictus, Boston, 1978-83, Boston Shakespeare Theatre, 1984; cons. Kurzweil Music Systems, Waltham, Mass., 1984-87; clinician KORG, Westbury, N.Y., 1990—. Author: Kurzweil 250 Users Guide, 1988, Computers & The Music Educator, 1991; contbr. articles to profl. jours. Mem. Framingham (Mass.) Action for Edn., 1990—. Composition fellow Mass. Coun. Arts & Humanities, 1980. Mem. Internat. Assn. Jazz Educators, Internat. MIDI Assn., Music Educators Nat. Conf., Nat. Assn. Music Merchants. Office: Berklee Coll Music 1140 Boylston Boston MA 02215

MASHIMO, PAUL AKIRA, dental educator; b. Sakai, Osaka, Japan, Oct. 25, 1926; came to U.S., 1966; s. Eizo and Teruko (Kimura) M.; m. Eunice Kusue Yuasa, Nov. 23, 1955; children: Minoru, Hiroshi. DDS, Osaka Dental U., 1948; PhD, Kyoto (Japan) Med. U., 1955. Instr. dept. oral surgery Osaka Dental U., 1948-50; lectr. dept. microbiology, 1950-54, asst. prof. dept. preventive dentistry, 1955-65; rsch. fellow Columbia U. Sch. Medicine, N.Y.C., 1966-70; asst. prof. Sch. Dentistry SUNY, Buffalo, 1966-70, assoc. prof., 1971-90, mem. faculty Grad. Sch., 1970-90, prof. emeritus, 1990—; vis. prof. Asahi U., Gifu, Japan, 1973, Meikai U., Sakado, Japan, 1988; hon. prof. 4th Mil. Med. U., Xian, People's Republic China, 1988; cons. Sunstar Inc., Osaka and N.Y.C., 1970—, IPD Co. Ltd., Osaka, 1977—, Belmont-Takara Co., Somerset, N.J., 1979—. Co-author: Germ-Free Human Saliva, 1983, Oral Spirochetes, 1983, Oral Microbiology, 1984. Ofcl. interpreter Buffalo-Kanazawa City Affiliation Com., 1969—. John C. Ball fellow, 1955-58, Japan Soc. fellow, 1956-58. Mem. Internat. Assn. Dental Rsch., Am. Soc. for Microbiology, N.Y. Acad. Scis., Osaka Dental U. Alumni Soc., Sigma Xi. Home: 639 Cottonwood Dr Buffalo NY 14221-1355 Office: SUNY Sch Dental Medicine 3435 Main St Buffalo NY 14214-3000

MASHIN, JACQUELINE ANN COOK, federal agency consultant; b. Chgo., May 11, 1941; d. William Hermann and Ann (Smidt) Cook; m. Fredric John Mashin, June 7, 1970; children: Joseph Glenn, Alison Robin. BS, U. Md., 1984. Cert. realtor. Adminstrv. asst. CIA, Washington, 1963-66; asst. to mng. dir. Aerospace Edn. Found., Washington, 1966-74; exec. asst. to asst exec. dir. Air Force Assn., Washington, 1974-79; v.p., ptnrship. owner Discount Linen Store, Silver Spring, Md., 1979-81; asst. regional polit. dir. Office of Pres.-elect, Washington, 1980-81; confidential asst. to dir. Office of Personnel Mgmt. (US), Washington, 1981-83; spl. asst. to dep. dir. Office of Mgmt. and Budget, Washington, 1983-86; dir. internat. communications and spl. asst. to commr. Dept. of the Interior, Washington, 1986-89, cons., 1989—. Pres. Layhill Civic Assn., Silver Spring, Md., 1980; state chmn. Md.'s Reagan Youth Delegation, Annapolis, Md., 1980; state treas., office mgr. Reagan-Bush State Hdqrs. of Md., Silver Spring, 1980; mem. Women's Com. Nat. Symphony Orch. Mem. Air Force Assn. (life), Aux. Salvation Army (life), Am. League Lobbyists, Am. Soc. Pers. Adminstrn., Am. Soc. Pub. Adminstrn., Internat. Platform Assn., Chevy Chase Women's Club (Md.), Capitol Hill Club, Indian Spring Country Club. Republican. Home and Office: 2429 White Horse Ln Silver Spring MD 20906-2243

MASI, J. ROGER, lawyer; b. Bklyn., Jan. 18, 1954; s. John Roger and Evelyn (Teagno) M.; m. Sherrill Alaine Schlett, June 29, 1985; children: Roger C., Christopher J. BA, Franklin & Marshall Coll., 1976; JD, Temple U., 1980. Bar: N.J. 1981, Pa. 1981, U.S. Dist. Ct. N.J. 1981. Assoc. Klinger, Nicolette, Mavroudis & Honig, Oradell, N.J., 1982-86, Gern, Dunetz, Roseland, N.J., 1986-87; ptnr. J. Roger Masi, Esq., Hackensack, N.J., 1987—. Committeeman County Rep., Ridgewood, N.J., 1982-84; mem. Ridgewood Zoning Bd. Adjustment; mem. Commerce and Industry Assn. N.J. Mem. ABA, N.J. State Bar Assn., Bergen County Bar Assn., Rotary. Roman Catholic. Office: 55 State St Hackensack NJ 07601-5426

MASIE, ELLIOTT, training executive; b. N.Y.C., May 13, 1950; s. Harry H. and Dorothy (Gordon) M. BA, SUNY, 1972. Cons. Irish Ministry Health, Dublin, 1972-73; project evaluator N.Y. State Dept. Edn., 1973-76; dir. Nat. Student Leadership Ctr., Raquette Lake, 1977—, pres. Masie Inst., 1991—; cons. Disney, CIA, 1990-91, Dow Chem., NASA, Panama C.Z., Bank of Am., Nat. Assn. Secondary Sch. Prins., Washington, 1985. Author: Computers and Student Activities, 1984, The Computer Training Handbook, 1988, also others. Mem. Assn. Computer Tng. and Support (pres., dir. 1989—, founder 1989—), Nat. Tng. & Computer Projects (bd. dirs., pres. Tools for Tng. 1985—). Democrat. Jewish. Avocation: white water rafting. Home: Camp Uncas Raquette Lake NY 13436 Office: Masie Inst Inc Sagamore Rd Raquette Lake NY 13436

MASLOFF, SOPHIE, mayor; b. Pitts., Dec. 23, 1917; d. Louis and Jennie Friedman; widowed, 1991; 1 child, Linda. Grad. high sch., Pitts. Chief investigator Ct. of Common Pleas, Allegheny County, Pa., 1940—; mem. Pitts. City Council, 1976-88; mayor City of Pitts., 1988—. Alternate del. Dem. Nat. Conv., 1968; del. Dem. Nat. Conf., 1978. Mem. Allegheny County Dem. Women's Guild (sec. 1940—), Pa. Fedn. Dem. Women (sec. 1967—, formerly pres.). Jewish. Lodges: B'nai B'rith, Hadassah. Office: 414 Grant St Pittsburgh PA 15219-2404

MASMAN, GREGGORY ARTHUR, lawyer; b. Wee Waa, N.S.W., Australia, May 18, 1953; came to U.S., 1985; s. Keith Arthur and Lavinia Beatrice Mary (Barton) M.; m. Monica Christopher, June 14, 1986. BA with honors, U. N.S.W., Sydney, Australia, 1977, LLB, 1979; LLM, NYU, 1986. Bar: N.S.W., N.Y. Solicitor Abbott, Tout, Creer & Wilkinson, Sydney, 1980-81; judge's assoc. Fed. Ct. of Australia, Canberra, 1981-82; solicitor Malleson, Stephen & Jaques, Sydney, 1982-85; assoc. Debevoise & Plimpton, N.Y.C., 1986-87, Kelley, Drye & Warren, N.Y.C., 1987—; aide Chief Justice Rep. of the Seychelles, Australia, 1980. Asst. judge Philip C. Jessup Internat. Law Moot Ct. Competition, Canberra, 1984, 85; bd. dirs. Art Gallery Soc. N.S.W., Sydney, 1983-85; bd. dirs., pres. Am. Friends of U. N.S.W., Inc., 1990—. Lasker scholar NYU, 1985, 86. Mem. ABA, N.Y. State Bar Assn., Union Internat. des Avocats, Australia Soc. Office: Kelley Drye Warren 101 Park Ave New York NY 10178

MASON, BRICK See CARUTHERS, DONALD MCILVAINE

MASON, CRAIG WATSON, corporate planning executive; b. Stamford, Conn., June 4, 1954; s. Harry Leeds and Alice Henrietta (Watson) M.; m. Lisa Ellen Boe, Aug. 30, 1980; children: Katherine Anne, Whitney Elizabeth. BA in English, Yale U., 1976. Brand asst. Procter & Gamble Co., Cin., 1976-77; sales trainee Procter & Gamble Co., St. Louis, 1977; asst. brand mgr. Procter & Gamble Co., Cin., 1978-79, Instant Folger's brand mgr., 1979-82, Biz and Mr. Clean brand mgr., 1982-83; dir. brand mgmt. Beecham Products USA, Pitts., 1983-87, dir. bus. planning, 1987-88, dir. bus. and logistics planning, 1988-89; dir. bus. and logistics planning SmithKline Beecham Consumer Brands, 1989—. Editor: The Insiders Guide to the Colleges, 1975; contbr. articles to profl. jours. Class agt. Yale Alumni Fund, 1976—; trustee Peters Twp. (Pa.) Pub. Libr., 1986-90. Mem. Rolling Hills Country Club, Yale Club of N.Y.C. Republican. Episcopalian. Home: 230 King Richard Dr Canonsburg PA 15317-2535 Office: SmithKline Beecham 100 Beecham Dr Pittsburgh PA 15205-9715

MASON, JOHN GROUARD, political science educator; b. N.Y.C., Oct. 31, 1946; s. Edward Gay and Ruth Loring (Warner) M.; m. Catherine Michele Coufleau, Jan. 8, 1983; 1 child, Julia DeForest. BA in History with honors, NYU, 1972, MA in Polit. Sci., 1977; MA in Sociology, Queens Coll., CUNY, 1989; M Phil in Sociology, Grad. Ctr., CUNY, 1991; PhD in Sociology, CUNY, 1992. Lectr. sociology Ramapo (N.J.) State Coll., 1979-84; lectr. polit. sci. William Paterson Coll., 1980—, asst. prof. polit. sci., 1985—; lectr. sociology Queens Coll., CUNY, Flushing, 1985—; press officer Michael Harrington Ctr., Queens Coll., CUNY, 1990-92; resident scholar NYU Inst. for French Studies, 1988-92, NYU Ctr. for European Studies, 1992—; lectr. dept. study of English speaking countries U. Paris VIII, 1984-85; corr. La Fondation Pour Les Etudes de la Defense Nat., Paris, 1986-89. Co-editor: Les Syndicats Francais et Americains face aux mutations technologiques, 1984; contbg. author: French Security Policy in a Disarming World, 1989; editorial assoc. polit. quar. TELOS, N.Y.C., 1982-90, quar. Punto de Contacto/Point of Contact, N.Y.C., 1973-76. Mem. internat. affairs commn. Dem. Socialists Am., 1988—; producer pub. affairs dept. WBAI Radio Pacifica, N.Y.C., 1980-90. Recipient La Bourse Chateaubriand, French Govt., 1984-85; NIH fellow, 1974-77. Mem. Am. Polit. Sci. Assn. (colloquium on European politics and study), Internat. Studies Assn. Democrat. Episcopalian. Home: 240 Sullivan St Apt 8 New York NY 10012-1395 Office: William Paterson Coll NJ Science Hall Wayne NJ 07470

MASON, JOHN HAYES, health science researcher; b. Lynn, Mass., Dec. 25, 1950; s. J. Leo and Marie A. (Hayes) M.; m. Diane Elizabeth Michaud, Aug. 10, 1951; chidren: Diana Marie, John Michael. BA cum laude, St. Michaels Coll., 1972; MA, U. Mass., 1976; PhD, Boston U., 1991. Research coordinator U. Mass., Amherst, 1976-78; research assoc. Boston U. Sch. Medicine, 1978-91, asst. rsch. prof. medicine, 1992—. Assoc. editor: (journal) Arthritis Care and Research, 1988-90; contbr. articles on health issues (Best Research award 1985). Mem. Nahant (Mass.) Hist. Soc., 1986-92, mem. planning bd., 1990—; mem. Friends of Nahant Libr., 1987-89, Safe Waters in Mass., 1984-89; vice-chmn. Mass. chpt. Arthritis Found., Newton, 1989-91, trustee, Atlanta, 1987-91; mem. parish coun. Roman Cath. Ch., 1992. Named Nat., community Vol. of Yr., Arthritis Found., Mass., 1989; recipient rsch. grants NIH, Washington, 1984-87, Arthritis Found., Atlanta, 1979-80, Arthritis Found. So. Calif., 1990-92, fellowship Arthritis Found., Atlanta, 1980-82, Nat. Vol. award Arthritis Found., Atlanta, 1991. Mem. Arthritis Health Professions Assn. (pres. 1988, scholar award 1984, svc. award 1990), Am. Sociol. Assn., Assn. for Health Svcs. Rsch., Arthritis Health Professions Assn. (bd. govs. 1984-89), Boston Area Med. Sociologists. Home: 81 Spring Rd Nahant MA 01908-1203 Office: Bsoton U Sch Medicine Arthritis Ctr 203A Concord St Newton MA 02162-1324

MASON, LUCILE GERTRUDE, fund raiser, consultant; b. Montclair, N.J., Aug. 1, 1925; d. Mayne Seguine and Rachel (Entorf) M. AB, Smith Coll., 1947; MA, NYU, 1968, 76. Editor ABC, N.Y.C., 1947-51; asst. casting dir. Compton Advt., Inc., N.Y.C., 1951-55, dir. and head casting, 1955-65; conf. mgr. Camp Fire Girls, Inc., N.Y.C., 1965-66; exec. dir. Assn. of Jr. Leagues of Am. Inc., N.Y.C., 1966-68; dir. div. pub. affairs Girl Scouts U.S.A., N.Y.C., 1969-71; dir. pub. rels. YWCA of City of N.Y., 1971-73; dir. community rels. and devel. Girl Scout Coun. of Greater N.Y., N.Y.C., 1973-76; dir. devel. Montclair Kimberley Acad., Montclair, N.J., 1976-78, Ethical Culture Schs., N.Y.C. and Riverdale, N.Y., 1978-80; pres. Lucile Mason & Assocs., Montclair, 1980-83; devel. officer founds. and corps. Fairleigh Dickinson U., Rutherford, N.J., 1983-85; dir. devel. Whole Theatre, Inc., Montclair, 1985-86, YMWCA of Newark & Vicinity, 1986-88; v.p. adminstrn. and fin. devel. Inst. Religion and Health, N.Y.C., 1988-90; dir. corp. and found. rels. Upsala Coll., East Orange, N.J., 1990-91; pres. Lucile Mason & Assocs., Montclair, 1991—. Vol. bd. counselors Smith Coll., 1964-74, chmn. theatre com., mem. exec. com., 1969-74; trustee Citizens Com. Presbyn. Meml. Iris Gardens of Montclair, 1992—; v.p. Neighborhood Ctr., Inc., Montclair, 1987—; mem. fund devel. com. Girl Scout Coun. of Greter Essex County, 1986-92. Mem. Am. Women in Radio and TV (pres. N.Y.C. chpt. 1955-56), Community Agys. Pub. Rels. Assn. (membership chmn. 1973-76), Nat. Soc. Fund Raising Execs. (bd. dirs. N.J. chpt 1983-86), Pub. Rels. Soc. Am., Smith Coll. Club of Montclair (bd. dirs. 1986-90). Home: 142 N Mountain Ave Montclair NJ 07042-2350

MASON, MARK EVAN, management educator; b. Norwalk, Conn., May 23, 1955; s. Robert Stanley and Abelle Mason; m. Roslyn Tom, Aug. 12, 1989. BA, Haverford Coll., 1978; MA, Columbia U., 1982; PhD, Harvard U., 1988. Postdoctoral fellow Ctr. for Internat. Affairs, Harvard U., Cambridge, Mass., 1988-90; prof. Sch. of Mgmt. Yale U., New Haven, 1990—, assoc. in rsch. Reischaver Inst., 1990—. Author: American Multinationals and Japan, 1992. Kukin fellow Harvard U., 1988-90, Japan Found. fellow, 1985-86, Nat. Resource fellow U.S. Dept. Edn., 1984-85. Mem. Acad. Internat. Bus., Assn. for Asian Studies, Bus. History Conf., Am. Acad. Polit. and Social Sci., Assn. Japanese Bus. Studies, Internat. House of Japan, Harvard Club N.Y. Office: Yale U Sch of Mgmt 135 Prospect St New Haven CT 06520

MASON, RAYMOND ADAMS, brokerage company executive; b. Lynchburg, Va., Sept. 28, 1936; s. Raymond Watsi and Marion (Adams) M.; married; children: Paige Adams, Pamela Ann, Carter Meade, Morgan Rand. BA in Econs., Coll. William and Mary, 1959. Rep. Mason & Lee Inc., Richmond, Va., 1960-62; founder, pres. Mason & Co. Inc., Newport News, Va., 1962-70; pres. Legg, Mason & Co., Inc., Washington, 1970-73; pres. Legg, Mason Wood Walker, Inc., Balt., 1973—, chmn. bd. dirs.; pres., chmn., chief exec. officer Legg Mason, Inc., 1981—; mem. adv. bd. Potomac Investment Assocs.; bd. dirs. Environ. Elements Corp.; chmn. regional firms com. N.Y. Stock Exchange, 1978-81; chmn. Legg Mason Value Trust; bd. dirs. Legg Mason Value Trust, Legg Mason Masten, Howard Weil Fin., Western Asset Mgmt. Trustee emeritus Endowment Assn., Coll. William and Mary; bd. dir. emeritus William and Mary Sch. Bus. Adminstrn. Sponsors, Inc.; trustee Balt. Mus. Art, Johns Hopkins Hosp.; bd. dirs. Nat. Aquarium, Balt., Johns Hopkins Hosp., Johns Hopkins U.; chmn. bd. sponsors Sch. Bus. and Mgmt., Loyola Coll., Balt., 1980-88; bd. dirs. Greater Balt. Com.; chmn. United Way of Cen. Md., 1985. Mem. Nat. Assn. Securities Dealers (bd. govs. 1971-75, chmn. bd. govs. 1974-75), Securities Industry Assn. (bd. dirs. 1982—, chmn. 1985-86, bd. govs. 1984-88, chmn. bd. govs. 1987). Clubs: Ctr., Mchts., Md., Balt. Country, L'Hirondelle. Home: 1832 Circle Rd Baltimore MD 21204-6415 Office: Legg Mason Wood Walker Inc 111 S Calvert St Baltimore MD 21202-6174*

MASON, ROBERT A., manufacturing executive; b. Glen Falls, N.Y., Apr. 27, 1952; s. Alger Charles and Jane (Mead) M.; m. Anne Therese Shevrovich, Dec. 29, 1973; children: Jennifer, Laurie, Matthew, Elyse. BA in Physics, St. Lawrence U., 1974; MBA, Gannon U., 1981. With GE, Erie, Pa., 1976—, mgr. shop ops., 1984-86; mgr. prodn. plan and control GE, Burlington, Vt., 1986-89, plant mgr., 1989-90; dir. mfg. BF Goodrich-Simmonds Precision, Vergennes, Vt., 1990—. Pres. Homeowners Assn., 1983-84; mem. PTA, 1981—; liturgical min. St. Catherines Parish, Shelburne, Vt., 1987—, instr. religous edn., 1988—. Mem. Am. Prodn. & Inventory Control Soc. Office: Simmonds Presicion Panton Rd Vergennes VT 05491-1033

MASON, SCOTT MACGREGOR, entrepreneur, inventor, consultant; b. N.Y.C., Feb. 11, 1923; s. Gregory Mason and Mary Louise Turner; m. Mildred Davidson, Mar. 13, 1949 (div. 1970); children: Alan Gregory, Phoebe Louise, Caleb; m. Virginia Frances Perkins, May 5, 1970 (dec.

1990). AB, Princeton U., 1943; MS, NYU, 1947. Control chemist Firestone Tire & Rubber Co., Akron, Ohio, 1943-44; R & D chemist Am. Cyanamid Co. Rsch. Labs., Stamford, Conn., 1948-52; mgr. stearate dept. Warwick Chem. div. Sun Chem. Corp., Wood River Junction, R.I., 1952-58; cons., Stonington, Conn., 1958-59; instr. Williams Meml. Inst., New London, Conn., 1959-63; NSF fellow Brown U., Providence, 1963-64; tchr. Moses Brown Sch., Providence, 1964-70; owner, mgr. Innoventures, Wakefield, R.I., 1970—; cons. Greene Plastics Corp., Canonchet, R.I., 1972-80, Dorette Inc., Pawtucket, R.I., 1982-83. Patentee in field. Trustee Pine Point Sch., Stonington, 1956-62, pres. bd., 1959-60. With AUS, 1944-46, ETO. Named Tchr. of Week, Sta. WPRO, Providence, 1968; summer rsch. fellow NSF, U. R.I., 1960. Mem. AAAS, N.Y. Acad. Scis., Dunes Club (founder). Office: Innoventures PO Box 369 Wakefield RI 02880-0369

MASON, SUSAN ELIZABETH, psychologist, academic administrator; b. Glen Ridge, N.J., Sept. 10, 1952. BS in Math., Psychology, Dickinson Coll., 1974; MS in Psychology, Ga. Inst. Tech., 1975, PhD in Psychology, 1977. Asst. prof. dept. psychology Buffalo State Coll., 1977-78, adj. prof. dept. psychology, 1980-82; asst. prof. dept. psychology W.Va. U., Morgantown, 1978-79; asst. prof. dept. psychology Niagara (N.Y.) U., 1979-81, assoc. prof., 1981-85, prof., 1985—, chmn. dept., 1983-87, dean Coll. Arts and Scis., dir. grad. div., 1987—; instr. Multidisciplinary Ctr. for Study of Aging, SUNY-Buffalo, 1978-79; instr. coll. program Attica Correctional Facility, Consortium Niagara Frontier, 1981; cons. in field. Contbr. to profl. publs. Mem. AAAS, Am. Psychol. Assn., Ea. Psychol. Assn., Gerontol. Soc., Sigma Xi, Phi Sigma Iota, Sigma Alpha Sigma, Psi Chi. Office: Coll Arts and Scis Niagara Univ Niagara University NY 14109

MASON, WILLIAM ROBERT, III, college admissions director; b. Newton, Mass., Mar. 26, 1941; s. William R. Jr. and Eleanor (Akeroyd) M.; m. Jennifer Robbins, Feb. 20, 1965; 1 child, Timothy W. BA, Bowdoin Coll., 1963. Asst. dir. admissions Yale U., New Haven, 1967-70, Williams Coll., Williamstown, Mass., 1970-76; dir. admissions Bowdoin Coll., Brunswick, Maine, 1976-91, Coll. of the Holy Cross, Worcester, Mass., 1991—. Mem. bd. trustees Bancroft Sch. Lt. USN, 1964-67. Democrat. Congregationalist. Office: Coll of the Holy Cross 1 College St Worcester MA 01610-2315

MASONE, JINO LEWIS, insurance executive; b. N.Y.C., Mar. 22, 1950; s. Jino Louis and Emily (Lewis) M.; m. Joanne Frances Iararola, June 15, 1974; children: Matthew, Gina. BA, St. Lawrence U., 1972. CLU; chartered property casualty underwriter. Employee benefits rep. Aetna Life and Casualty Co., Utica, N.Y., 1972, 73-74; account exec. Aetna Life and Casualty Co., Hartford, Conn., 1974-79, asst. v.p., 1982-86; gen. mgr. Aetna Life and Casualty Co., Balt., 1986-92; v.p. property and casualty Fidelity and Deposit Cos., Balt., 1992—. Teaching cons. Jr. Achievement, Balt., 1987-88; bd. dirs. Commuter Transp. Ctr., Hanover, Md., 1991-92; appointed mem. Anne Arundel County Mktg. Adv. Com., Annapolis, Md., 1990-92; vice chmn. United Way, Balt., 1989; mem. Conn. CPCU chpt., 1981-86, bd. dirs., 1984-86. Capt. USAR, 1972-73. Mem. Md. Soc. of CPCU, Md. Soc. of CLU, Comml. Casualty Underwriting Assn. (bd. dirs. 1991-92). Republican. Lutheran. Home: 31 Belleview Dr Severna Park MD 21146 Office: Fidelity and Deposit Cos 300 Saint Paul Baltimore MD 21203

MASS, KAREN SUENO, Far Eastern securities research and sales person; b. N.Y.C., Feb. 10, 1964; d. Jeffrey Paul and Kazuko (Miyamori) M. BA, Stanford U., 1985; student, Kansai Gaikokugo Daigaku, Kyoto, Japan. Analyst McKinsey & Co., Inc., Tokyo, 1985-86; rsch., sales staff Jardine Fleming Securities, Tokyo, 1986-88, Robert Fleming, Inc., N.Y.C., 1989—; guest lectr. Stanford U. Bus. Sch., Palo Alto, Calif., 1991. Vol. AIDS and cancer aide Sloane Kettering Meml. Hosp., N.Y.C., 1980-90. Mem. NAFE, Keio Univ. Club. Office: Robert Fleming Inc 1285 Ave of the Americas New York NY 10019

MASSA, MIGUEL SOUZA, III, firefighter; b. Fall River, Mass., Dec. 12, 1950; s. Miguel Souza Jr. and Dolores (Audette) M.; m. Ann Marie Levesque, July 5, 1975. AS, Bristol Community Coll., Fall River, 1987. Supr. School House Candy, R.I., 1976-78; firefighter Fall River Fire Dept., 1978-82, fire prevention officer, arson investigator, 1982-84, lt., 1984—; mcpl. coord. for right to know City of Fall River, 1986—, mem. hazardous materials team, 1986—, 3d party trainer, 1986—; instr. Mass. Fire Acad., Sudbury, 1987. Chmn. Fall River Local Emergency Planning Com., 1987; advisor Boston Dept. Environ. Quality Engring., 1987. Nat. Fire Acad. fellow, 1983. Mem. Internat. Assn. Fire Fighters, K.C. Roman Catholic. Office: Fall River Fire Dept 755 Pine St Fall River MA 02720-5005

MASSA, ROBERT A., diesel manufacturing executive; b. Hartford, Conn., May 13, 1937; s. Anthony John and Catherine (Hagerty) M.; m. Mary Theresa Papp, Nov. 17, 1990; children: Terri Ann Augustine, Lorri Ann, Kimberly Ann. BS, U. Hartford, 1959. Pers. mgr. Jacobs Mfg. Co., West Hartford, Conn., 1961-69; pers. mgr. Am. Standard Products, Hartford, Conn., 1969-72, pers. adminstr., 1972-75, pers. cons., 1975-77; v.p. indsl. rels. Veeder Root Co., Simsbury, Conn., 1977-90; v.p. human rels. Stanadyne Automotive Corp., Windsor, Conn., 1990—; mem. Conn. Bd. Arbitration and Mediation, 1987—. Mem. zoning bd., Old Saybrook, Conn., 1973-78. With USAR, 1959-65. Mem. Conn. Pers. Assn. (v.p. 1988, pres. 1989), Hartford County Pers. Assn. (past pres.). Office: Stanadyne Automotive Corp 92 Deerfield Rd Windsor CT 06095

MASSARUEH, ABDULSALAM YOUSEF, journalist, consultant; b. Taiyiba, Palestine, Dec. 1, 1936; came to U.S., 1964; s. Yousef Abdullatif and Hamdeh (Othman) M.; divorced; children: Joseph, Jeffrey, Samer. BA, Memphis State U., 1969. Editor-in-chief Arab-Am. Media Svc., Washington, 1981—; assoc. editor Jerusalem Press Svc., Washington, 1990—; freelance writer for newspapers and mags. Europe, U.S., Middle East, 1982—. Assoc. editor The Return mag. Mem. Fgn. Corrs. Assn. (pres. 1986—). Democrat. Muslim. Home: 2909 Willston Pl # 101 Falls Church VA 22044-2844 Office: 4400 Macarthur Blvd NW # 305 Washington DC 20007-2521

MASSAUA, JOHN ROGER, retail executive; b. N.Y.C., Aug. 7, 1947; s. George John and Dorothy Regina (Coyle) M.; m. Janice Grace Vroom, Mar. 29, 1970; children: Matthew, Andrew, Meghan. BS, Fordham U., 1969; MBA, Fairleigh Dickinson U., 1973. Mem. staff Supermarkets Gen., Woodbridge, N.J., 1964-73; dist. mgr. Courtesy Drug Stores, Port Washington, N.Y., 1973-75; exec. v.p. Motts Shop Rite Supermarkets, East Hartford, Conn., 1975-80; sr. v.p. Imperial Distbrs., Auburn, Mass., 1980-86; group v.p. ops. Staples Inc., Newton, Mass., 1986-89; pres. Window Rama, Deer Park, N.Y., 1989-91; exec. v.p. ALP Freddy's Ltd., Rochester, N.Y., 1991—. Troop com. chmn. Boy Scouts Am., Northborough, Mass., 1979-89; pres. Minnaseroke Community Assn., 1991. Recipient Sales and Mktg. Achievement award Sales and Mktg. Mag., 1978. Mem. Am. Mgmt. Assn., N.E. Lumberman's Nat. Assn. Chain Drug Stores, Nat. Assn. Remodeling Industry. Roman Catholic. Home: 23 Sutton Pt Pittsford NY 14534 Office: ALP Freddy's Ltd 90 Commerce Dr Rochester NY 14623-3502

MASSEY, MITCHELL VAUGHN, retail manufacturing executive; b. Lexington, Ky., Oct. 9, 1949; s. Robert Lewis and Kathryn Delores (Soulsby) M.; m. Lisa Neven McHugh, Aug. 27, 1983; 1 child, Caitlin. BS in Bus. Mgmt., Berea Coll., 1971. Buyer, store mgr. Federated Dept. Stores, Cinn., 1971-80; v.p. mktg. Talbots, Hingham, Mass., 1980-85; sr. v.p. mktg. Jos. A. Bank Clothiers, Balt., 1985-90; pres. G.H. Bass By Mail, Falmouth, Maine, 1990—; Bd. dirs. Rue de France, Newport, R.I., 1982—, Samuel Roberts, Haverhill, Mass., 1983—. Chmn. United Way Campaign, Maine, 1992. Recipient Retail Ad of Yr. award Nat. Retail Merchants Assn., 1988, 89, 90. Mem. Direct Mktg. Assn. (chmn. 1989—), Creative Guild (N.Y.C.). Republican. Office: G H Bass 360 US Rt 1 Portland ME 04105

MASSEY, THOMAS BENJAMIN, educator; b. Charlotte, N.C., Sept. 5, 1926; s. William Everard and Sarah (Corley) M.; m. Bylee Hunnicutt Massey, July 10, 1968; children: Pamela Ann, Caroline Forest. A.B., Duke U., 1948; M.S., N.C. State U., 1953; Ph.D., Cambridge U., 1968. Assoc. dean students Ga. Inst. Tech., Atlanta, 1950-58; lectr. U. Md. Univ. Coll., 1960-66, asst. dir. London, 1966-69, dir. Toyko, 1969-71, dir. Heidelberg (Fed. Republic of Germany), 1971-76, vice chancellor, 1976-78, chancellor, 1978-88, pres., 1988—; bd. dirs. Internat. Univ. Consortium for Telecommunications in Learning, 1983—. Served with USN, 1943-46. Mem. Am. Assn. Adult and Continuing Edn., Soc. Research in Higher Edn., Nat. Univ. Continuing Edn. Assn., Am. Psychol. Assn., Am. Assn. Higher Edn., Internat. Confs. on Improving Univ. Teaching (chmn., editor Proceedings 1975—). Office: U Md University Blvd at Adelphi Rd College Park MD 20742-1600

MASSLER, HOWARD ARNOLD, lawyer, corporate executive; b. Newark, July 22, 1946; s. Abraham I. and Sylvia (Botwin) M.; m. Randee Elyce Karch, July 1, 1977; children: Justin Scott, Jeremy Ross. BA, U. Pa., 1969; JD, Rutgers U., 1973; LLM in Taxation, NYU, 1977. Bar: N.J. 1974, U.S. Dist. Ct. N.J. 1974, D.C. 1975, U.S. Ct. Appeals (D.C. cir.) 1975, N.Y. 1977, U.S. Dist. Ct. (we. dist.) N.Y. 1977, U.S. Tax Ct. 1977. Counsel house banking, currency and housing com., chmn. sub-com. U.S. Ho. Reps., Washington, 1974-76; tax atty. Lipsitz, Green, Fahringer, Roll, Schuller & James, N.Y.C. and Buffalo, 1977-79; pvt. practice Mountainside, N.J., 1979-89; pres. Bestway Products Inc., A.A. Records Inc., Servor Corp., 1979-85; pres., chief exec. officer, chmn. bd. Bestway Group Inc., Dover, Del., 1985—; gen. ptnr. 26/27 Law Drive Assocs., 1988—; ptnr. Shonageri, Pearce & Massler, Hackensack, N.J., 1989-90, Mott, Pearce, Williams & Lee, Hackensack and Washington, 1990-91, Pearce & Massler, Hackensack, N.J., 1991—; prodn. staff asst. DECCA House Ltd., London, 1968; chief exec. officer Basura Pub., Inc. (afiliated with BMI), 1974-80; arbitrator U.S. Dist. Ct. N.J., 1985—; adj. prof. law Seton Hall U., Newark, N.J., 1988-89, N.J. Inst. for Continuing Legal Edn., 1986; lectr. N.J. Inst. for Continuing Legal Edn., 1986—; assoc. dir. United Jersey Bank/Franklin State Bank, 1987—; del. adv. com. on indsl. trade and econ. devel. U.S./China Joint Sessions, Beijing, People's Republic of China, 1988. Author: QDROs (Tax and Drafting Considerations), 1986, 2nd. ed., 1987; contbr. West's Legal Forms, Vol. 7., 2d edit., 1987, 3d edit., Domestic Relations with Tax Analysis, Contemporary Matrimonial Law Issues: A Guide to Divorce Economics and Practice; tax author: Matthew Bender, NYCP-Matrimonial Actions and Equitable Distribution Actions, 1988; tax author, tax editor: Matthew Bender, Alimony, Child Support & Counsel Fees-Award, Modification and Enforcement, 1988, 2d edit., 1989, 3d edit., 1991, Matthew Bender, Valuation & Distribution of Marital Property, 1988, 89, 91; contbg. author: How to Make Legal Fees Tax Deductible, 1988, Closely Held Corporations, Forms and Checklists, Buy-Sell Agreement Forms with Tax Analysis, 1988, The Encyclopedia of Matrimonial Practice, 1991; author: New York Practice Guide: Negligence, Tax Law of Compensation for Sickness and Injury, 2d edit., 1992; contbg. editor Pensions and Ins. Problems, 1984—, Taxation, 1984—, FairShare, 1984—, Law & Bus., Inc., 1984—; staff contbr., N.J. Law Jour., 1986—; contbr. articles to law revs. and profl. jours. Bd. dirs., legal counsel western N.Y. chpt. Nat. Handicapped Sports and Recreation Assn., 1977-79; counsel Union County, N.J., 1984-85; candidate Springfield (N.J.) Twp. Commn., 1986. Mem. ABA, N.J. Bar Assn. (vice chmn. taxation comm. family law section 1987—), N.Y. Bar Assn. (taxation com., subcom. on criminal and civil penalties), D.C. Bar Assn., Erie County Bar Assn. (sec. taxation com. 1977-79, continuing edn. lectr. taxation 1977—), Essex County Bar Assn. (tax com. 1981—), Union County Bar Assn. (chmn. tax com. 1984—). Republican. Home: 4 Overlook Dr Warren NJ 07059-5144 Office: 25 Main St Hackensack NJ 07601-7025

MASSUMI, MEHRDAD (MIKE), physician; b. Tehran, Iran, Oct. 23, 1957; came to U.S., 1983; s. Majid and Manijeh (Shambayati) M.; m. Eileen Herlihy, Jan. 4, 1986; children: Cameron John, Maryann Elizabeth. MD, Birmingham (Eng.) U., 1982. Diplomate Am. Bd. Phys. Medicine and Rehab. Intern in surgery Queen Elizabeth Med. Ctr., Birmingham, Eng., 1982-83, Dudley Guest Hosp., West Midlands, Eng., 1983; intern in surgery Wash. Hosp. Ctr., 1983-84, resident in surgery, 1984-85; mem. phys. medicine and rehab. staff U. Wash., Seattle, 1985-88; pvt. practice Lutherville, Md., 1988—; dir. divsn. phys. medicine and rehab. Greater Balt. Med. Ctr., 1990—; cons. Am. Bd. Sports Medicine, Inc., Atlanta, 1991—; prse. Mednomics, Inc., Lutherville, 1990—; bd. govs. Balt. County Med. Assn., 1991—; radio and TV appearances on health topics, 1990—. Chairperson Doctor-Lawyer-Tchr. Partnership Against Drugs, Md., 1990—. Fellow Am. Acad. Phys. Medicine and Rehab.; mem. AMA (del. Md. 1991-92), Am. Acad. Pain Mgmt., Am. Acad. Electrodiagnostic Medicine, Med. and Chirugical Faculty Md. Republican. Office: Mike Massumi MD PA 1212 York Rd # A101 PO Box 4775 Lutherville MD 21093

MASTER, STEVEN BRUCE, clinical psychologist; b. Phila., May 27, 1953; s. Hyman and Gertrude (Steiner) M. BA, Muhlenberg Coll., 1975; MS, Villanova U., 1980; PhD, Temple U., 1987. Lic. psychologist, Pa., N.J. Counselor Pottstown (Pa.) Area Drug Rehab. Program, 1979-80, dir. residential treatment, 1980-82; cons. Effective Tng. Cons., Kimberton, Pa., 1980-82; pvt. practice Turnersville, N.J., 1987—, Devon, Pa., 1990—. Contbr. articles to profl. publs. Bd. dirs., pres. Help Counseling, Inc., 1987—; mem. Coventry Canine Search and Rescue, 1989—. Office: 410 Lancaster Ave Ste 208 Devon PA 19333-1588

MASTER-KARNIK, PAUL JOSEPH, art museum director; b. N.Y.C., Nov. 20, 1948; s. Charles Oldrich and Evelyn Theresa (Donnelly) K.; m. Susan Irene Master, Aug. 19, 1973. BA, Rutgers U., 1970, MA, 1971, PhD, 1978. Cert. in mus. studies, 1979. Faculty Rutgers U., New Brunswick, N.J., 1974-78; art critic Newhouse Publs., N.Y.C., 1976-80; faculty NYU, N.Y.C., 1980-83; dir. N.J. Ctr. for Visual Arts, Summit, 1981-84, DeCordova Mus. & Sculpture Pk., Lincoln, Mass., 1984—; bd. dirs. UrbanArts, Inc., Boston,1 988—, Mus. Coun. of N.J., Trenton, 1982-84; adv. bd. Archives of Am. Art, Boston, 1985—; vis. com. Sch. Mus. Fine Arts, Boston, 1987-90. Author: Exhibition Catalogues, 1982—. Recipient Outstanding Svc. award Inst. Mus. Svcs., 1988; Art Critic fellow NEA, 1980, Burns-Marvin fellow Rutgers U., 1971-73. Mem. Assn. Art Mus. Dirs. Office: DeCordova Mus & Sculpture Sandy Pond Rd Lincoln MA 01773-2005

MASTERS, BRIAN WILLIAM, educator; b. Syracuse, N.Y., Apr. 3, 1954; s. William James and Marilyn Virginia (Bowman) M.; m. Susan Eileen Voegele, Apr. 19, 1980; children: Meggan Elizabeth, Marcey Mae, Morgan Aileen. BS, Syracuse U., 1976; postgrad., SUNY, Oswego, 1977, Syracuse U., 1979. Tchr., dir., writer, dramatic coach W. Genesee Sch. Dist., Camillus, N.Y., 1976-77, Jordan-Elbridge Sch. Dist., Jordan, N.Y., 1977—; asst. mgr. Video Libr., Syracuse, 1986-88; shift supr. Video Superstores, Syracuse, 1990-92; clk. Chimney's Video Superstore, DeWitt, N.Y., 1990. Set dir. musical prodn. Wheels, 1984; editor, advisor various sch. publs.; choreographer The Grapevine Connection, 1986. Faculty rep. Jordan-Elbridge PTA/PTC, 1978-85, yearbook adv., 1978-84, sci. adv. com., 1990—. Recipient various awards for publs.; Cayuga-Onondaga Tchr. Ctr. grantee, 1989, 90. Mem. N.Y. State United Tchrs., Cen. N.Y. Ceramic Assn. (hon. mention 1989, 2d place award 1990, 1st place award 1991), Jordan-Elbridge Tchrs. Assn. (treas. 1978-79, v.p. 1980-85, mem. exec. com. 1978—, mem. negotiations team 1982-89, alt. rep. 1982-90, sec. 1987-88, chmn. scholarship com. 1985-87, 88—), Lambda Chi Alpha (presenter, del. gen. assembly 1982, 84, recognition plaque 1986, sec. 1975-76, steward 1975-77, ritualist 1976-77, advisor 1978-86, 89—), Alpha Upsilon (order of merit 1990, internat. order of merit 1992). Republican. Home: 241 Wynnfield Dr Syracuse NY 13219-2952 Office: Jordan-Elbridge Sch Dist Chappell St Jordan NY 13080

MASTERS, EDWARD E., association executive, former foreign service officer; b. Columbus, Ohio, June 21, 1924; s. George Henry and Ethel Verena (Shaw) M.; m. Allene Mary Roche, Apr. 2, 1956; children: Julie Allene, Edward Ralston. Student, Denison U., 1942-43; B.A. with distinction, George Washington U., 1948; M.A., Fletcher Sch. Law and Diplomacy, 1949. Joined U.S. Fgn. Service, 1950; intelligence research analyst Near East Dept. State, 1949-50; resident officer Heidelberg, Germany, 1950-52; polit. officer embassy Karachi, Pakistan, 1952-54; Hindustani lang. and area tng. U. Pa., 1954-55; consul, polit. officer Madras, India, 1955-58; intelligence research specialist South Asia Dept. State, 1958-60; chief Indonesia-Malaya br. Dept. State (Office Research Asia), 1960-61, officer-in-charge Thailand affairs, 1961-63; grad. Nat. War Coll., 1964; counselor for polit. affairs Am. embassy, Djakarta, 1964-68; country dir. for Indonesia Dept. State, 1968-70; dir. Office East Asian Regional Affairs, 1970-71; minister Am. embassy, Bangkok, Thailand, 1971-75; ambassador to Bangladesh, 1976-77, to Indonesia, 1977-81; adj. prof. diplomacy Fletcher Sch. Law and Diplomacy, 1981-82; sr. v.p. Natomas Co., 1982-84; pres. Nat. Planning Assn., 1985—. Mem. Am. Fgn. Service Assn., Phi Beta Kappa, Omicron Delta Kappa, Pi Gamma Mu, Delta Phi Epsilon. Club: Cosmos. Home: 4525 Garfield St NW Washington DC 20007-1165

MASTERS, GARY EVERETT, medical educator, library services educator; b. Fresno, Calif., July 3, 1941; s. Jess Franklin and Lois May (Cain) M.; m. Ella Suzanne Tilson, Dec. 27, 1972. BA, Tex. Tech. U., 1969; MLS, North Tex. State U., 1976, PhD, 1987. Info. specialist CIA, Washington, Vietnam, 1969-75; sci. librarian North Tex. State U., Denton, 1976-87; asst. prof. Uniformed Svcs. U. Health Scis., Bethesda, Md., 1987—. Sgt. U.S. Army, 1965-67. Mem. Soc. Am. Archivists. Democrat. Methodist. Office: USUHS MIM CCRC 4301 Jones Bridge Rd Bethesda MD 20814-4799

MASTERSON, PATRICIA O'MALLEY, publications editor, writer; b. Worcester, Mass., May 15, 1952; d. Paul Francis and Dorothy M. (O'Malley) M. BFA, Emerson Coll., 1974; MA, Goddard Coll., 1980. Reporter, photographer Patriot Newspaper, Webster, Mass., 1975-78; pub. relations dir. Mt. Pleasant Hosp., Lynn, Mass., 1980-84; pubs. editor Ocean Spray Cranberries, Inc., Plymouth, Mass., 1984-89; mktg. communications coord. Groundwater Tech., Norwood, Mass., 1989—; freelance writer newspaper and mag. articles, 1974—. Mem. adv. bd. Ad. Com. mag.; contbr. numerous articles to newspapers, mags.; stringer Hanover (Mass.) Mariner Newspaper, 1987-91. Bd. dirs. Cambridge (Mass.) YWCA; publicity com. United Way, 1987, Healthworks; pres. Abington, Weymouth, Mass., Softball Leagues, 1991-92; col. Rosie's Homeless Shelter, Boston, 1987. Recipient Amy England award YWCA, 1986, Green Eyeshade award Internat. Assn. Bus. Communicators, 1987, Yankee Ingenuity award Internat. Assn. Bus. Communicators, 1991, Employee Pub. 2d Place award Cooperative Info. Fair, 1987, 88, Membership Mag. award Cooperative Info. Fair, 1988; named One of Outstanding Young Women in Am. Jaycees, 1983. Mem. South Shore Ad Club (publicity com., 9th Wave award 1987, 89, 92), Women in Communications, Coop. Communicators Assn. (1st pl. employee publ. award 1987, 3d pl. mag. award 1989), Internat. Assn. Bus. Communicators (Yankee Ingenuity award 1991). Home: 132 Union St Rockland MA 02370-1922

MASTERSON, THOMAS MARSHALL, environmental consulting firm executive; b. San Diego, Feb. 5, 1959; s. Kleber Sanlin Jr. and Sara (Cooper) M.; m. Joumana Bizri. BA, Harvard U., 1980; MD, U. Va., 1984, MS, 1989. Chief exec. officer Alpha Environ. Mgmt. Inc., Washington, 1989—. Contbr. articles to profl. jours. Fellow Am. Cancer Soc., 1986. Mem. Environ. Auditing Roundtable, Am. Coll. Occupational Medicine, Sigma Xi. Home: 404 2d St Alexandria VA 22314 Office: Alpha Environ Mgmt 2020 Penn Ave NW 145 Washington DC 20006

MASTROSIMONE, CLAUDE ANTHONY, publishing executive; b. Pottsville, Pa., Sept. 10, 1937; s. Vito and M. Julia (Rossidivito) M.; m. Candace K. Kozlowski; children: C. Matthew, Marc, Michael, Renee, David John. Student, Rider Coll., 1959-61, Trenton State Coll., 1958-59. Mgr. Safeway Food Stores, Trenton, N.J., 1958-60; fin. clk. U.S. Postal Svc., Trenton, 1060-64; suburban circulation mgr. Times Newspaper, Trenton, 1964-71; parish cons. J.S. Paluch Co., Chgo., 1971-76, east coast regional mgr., 1976-80; pres. Cardinal Pub. Co., Trenton, N.J., 1980—. Contbr. articles to various newsletters and bulletins. Mem. Airport Adv. Commn., Montgomery Twp. N.J.; bd. dirs. Villa Victoria Acad., Trenton; mem. adv. bd. Monitor Newspaper, Trenton; cub scout master Boy Scouts Am., Montgomery Twp. Sgt. USMC, 1956-58. Mem. Greater Mercer County C. of C., Elks, KC. Republican. Roman Catholic. Home: 64 Planters Row Skillman NJ 08558-2201 Office: Cardinal Pub Co PO Box 713 Pennington NJ 08534-0713

MASUBUCHI, KOICHI, naval architect, educator; b. Otaru, Hokkaido, Japan, Jan. 11, 1924; s. Yosaku and Tomi (Ota) M.; m. Fumiko Kaneno, Oct. 24, 1949. BS, U. Tokyo, 1946, MS, 1948, PhD, 1959. Rsch. engr. Transp. Tech. Rsch. Inst., 1948-58; vis. fellow, cons. Battelle Menl. Inst., Columbus, Ohio, 1958-62; rsch. assoc., fellow, tech. adviser Battelle Meml. Inst., 1963-68; chief welding mechanics sect., welding div. Ship Rsch. Inst., 1962-63; assoc. prof. naval architecture MIT, Cambridge, 1968-71; prof. ocean engring. and materials sci. MIT, 1971-89; Kawasaki prof. engring. Mass. Inst. Tech., Cambridge, 1989-. Author: Materials for Ocean Engineering, 1970, Analysis of Welded Structures, 1980; co-author 2 books on residual stresses in weldments; contbr. tech. papers to profl. lit. Recipient Disting. Svc. award Transp. Tech. Rsch. Inst., Ministry Transp., Japan, 1959, Spl. award Min. of Fgn. Affairs, Japan, 1986. Fellow Am. Welding Soc. (life, R.D. Thomas Meml. award 1977, established Prof. Masubuchi/Shinsho Corp. award 1991), Am. Soc. Metals Soc.; mem. Japan Welding Soc. (guest), Soc. Naval Architects and Marine Engrs., Soc. Naval Architects Japan, Sigma Xi. Home: 34 Hamilton Rd Apt 205 Arlington MA 02174-8277 Office: MIT Rm 5-219 Cambridge MA 02139

MASUCCI, CHRISTINA MARIE, university communications specialist; b. Pitts., Aug. 23, 1958; d. James F. and Margaret (Trisch) Romanelli; m. Lawrence J. Masucci, Aug. 18, 1984. Student Bus. Adminstrn., U. Pitts., 1985-. Adminstrv. asst. Moore, Leonard & Lynch, Pitts., 1978-80; account sec. Creamer Inc., Pitts., 1980-81; exec. legal sec., office mgr. William Friedman, Pitts., 1981-82; exec. sec. Wheeling Pitts. Steel Corp., 1982; communications specialist, editorial asst. U. Pitts., 1983—. Roman Catholic.

MASUR, KURT, conductor; b. Brig, Silesia, Poland, July 18, 1927. Grad., Nat. Music Sch., Breslau, Poland, 1944, Leipzig Conservatory, 1948. Repetiteur and conductor Halle Nat. Theatre, 1948-51; conductor Erfurt City Theatre, 1951-53, Leipzig City Theatre, 1953-55, Dresden Philharm., 1955-58; gen. music dir. Mecklenburg Staatstheater, 1958-60; mus. dir. Komische Oper Berlin, 1960-64; chief conductor Dresden Philharm., 1967-72; conductor Leipzig Gewandhaus Orch., from 1970; mus. dir. New York Philharmonic, N.Y.C., 1991—. Tours include Europe, South Am., Japan, U.S., Can., Middle East; conductor: London Philharm. Orch., 1989; recordings include Symphonies by Mendelssohn, Bruckner, Beethoven, Schumann, Tchaikovsky; Prokofiev's Piano Concertos, Beethoven's Missa Solemnis. Office: care NY Philharmonic Avery Fischer Hall 132 W 65th St New York NY 10023-6911 also: Norman McCann Ltd, The Coach House, 56 Lawrie Park Gardens, London SE26 6XJ, England also: Gewandhausorchester Leipzig, Karl-Marx Platz 8, O-7010 Leipzig Federal Republic of Germany*

MASUROVSKY, MARC JEAN, translation services company; b. Neuilly sur Seine, France, Feb. 5, 1956; came to U.S., 1973; s. Gregory and Shirley (Goldfarb) M.; m. Laura Pollard, Jan. 26, 1986; children: Alexander Benjamin, Adam Emile. AB in Communications, Antioch U., 1977; MA in History, Am. U., 1989, postgrad., 1989—. Legal asst. Lawyers Com. for Civil Rights, Washington, 1977-78; tchr., translator Berlitz Sch. Langs., Washington, 1977-78; tchr., project dir. Transemantics, Inc., Washington, 1978-84; cons., historian U.S. Dept. Justice, Washington, 1979-82; prin., v.p. William Gray Enterprises, Inc., Washington, 1984—. Mem. Am. Translators Assn. Office: William Gray Enterprises 1730 K St NW Ste 905 Washington DC 20006

MATARASSO, ALAN, plastic and reconstructive surgeon; b. N.Y.C., Oct. 19, 1953; s. Daniel and Ethel (Hakim) M. BA magna cum laude, Boston U., 1975; MD, U. Miami, Miami, Fla., 1979. Diplomate Nat. Bd. Med. Examiners, Am. Bd. Plastic Surgery. Intern in dept. of gen. surgery Albert Einstein Coll. Med., Montefiore Med. Ctr., Bronx, N.Y., 1979-80, resident in dept. surgery, 1980-82, chief resident dept. of gen. surgery, 1982-83, resident dept. of plastic surgery, 1983-84, chief resident dept. of plastic surgery, 1983-84; fellow aesthetic surgery Manhattan Eye, Ear and Throat Hosp., NYU Med. Ctr., N.Y.C., 1985, asst. attending surgeon, 1985—; clin. asst. prof. plastic surgery Albert Einstein Coll. Med., Montefiore Med. Ctr., 1985—; attending surgeon St. Luke's/Roosevelt Hosp. Ctr., 1986—, N.Y. Eye and Ear Infirmary, 1986—, Doctors Hosp., 1988—. Contbr. chpt. Encyclopedia of Flaps, Clinics in Plastic Surgery, Mastery in Surgery: Plastic Surgery; numerous profl. presentations; contbr. articles to profl. jours. Bd. dirs. Sephardic Home For The Aged, Bklyn. Recipient Physicians Recognition award AMA, 1990. Fellow ACS; mem. Am. Soc. Plastic and Reconstructive Surgery, Northeastern Soc. Plastic Surgeons, Soc. for Acad. Surgeons, Royal Soc. Medicine, Am. Cleft Palate Assn., Pan Am. Med. Soc. Home: 201 E 87th St New York NY 10128-3203 Office: 1009 Park Ave New York NY 10028-0936

MATEO, JULIO CESAR, artist; b. Havana, Cuba, Apr. 16, 1951; came to U.S., 1960; s. Cesar Augusto and Loreto Eulalia (Mirás) M.; m. Raquel Wiltbank, Mar. 17, 1973; 1 child, William Patrick Wiltbank. BFA, U. Fla., 1973; MFA, U. South Fla., 1978. Pub., artist print portfolios The Marriage of Heaven and Earth, 1987, Grace, 19189, Nine Diamonds, 1991; one-man shows Nico Smith Gallery 1985, Stokker-Stikker Gallery 1986, Cathedral Ch. St. John the Divine 1990 (all N.Y.C.); exhibited in group shows Smithsonian Instn., Washington, 1977, Bklyn. Mus., 1985, Mus. Contemporary Hispanic Art, 1985, 86, 88, Bronx (N.Y.) Mus. Art, 1987, 90, P.S. 1 Mus., N.Y.C., 1990; represented in permanent collections N.Y. Pub. Libr., Chase Manhattan Bank, N.Y.C. Fellow Fine Arts Coun. Fla., 1980, Nat. Endowment for Arts, 1989. Home and Studio: 905 Atlantic Ave Brooklyn NY 11238-2704

MATERNA, LINDA SUSAN, Spanish educator; b. Milw., July 23, 1948; d. Robert Leo and Wanda Irene (Gronek) m. Thomas Joseph Newman, Apr. 9, 1978; 1 child, Bryan Thomas. BA in Spanish with honors, Beloit Coll., 1970; MA in Spanish, U. Wis., 1971, PhD in Spanish, 1980. Adjunct asst. prof. Spanish Trenton (N.J.) State Coll., 1981-83; asst. prof. Spanish Trenton State Coll., 1987-88; adjunct asst. prof. Spanish Rider Coll., Lawrenceville, N.J., 1983-87, asst. prof. Spanish, 1988—; lectr. Spanish Princeton (N.J.) U., 1985-87; interpreter Oscar Mayer Co., Madison, Wis., 1977-78, U. Wis. Dept. Rehab., 1978; interpreter, translator Portec Inc., Pioneer Div., Mpls., 1978-79. Contbr. articles to Spanish jours. and chpts. to books. Trustee Pine Knoll Community Orgn., Lawrenceville, N.J., 1985-86, pres., 1987. Recipient Vilas Travel fellowship U. Wis., 1977. Mem. Am. Coun. Tchrs. Fgn. Lang., Am. Assn. Tchrs. Spanish and Portugese, Assn. Internat. de Hispanistas, Fgn. Lang. Educators N.J., Modern Lang. Assn., N.E. Modern Lang. Assn., Twentieth-Century Spanish Assn. Am., Phi Beta Kappa, Phi Beta Delta. Office: Rider Coll 2830 Lawrenceville Rd Trenton NJ 08648-1017

MATERNA, THOMAS WALTER, ophthalmologist; b. Passaic, N.J., Oct. 24, 1944; s. Anthony and Ann (Popowich) M.; m. Jorunn Pauline Aronsen, Aug. 17, 1973; children: Richard C., Barbara L. BA, Coll. Holy Cross, Worcester, Mass., 1966; MD, SUNY, N.Y.C., 1971; postgrad., Rutgers U., Newark, 1990. Diplomate Am. Bd. Ophthalmology. Intern N.Y. Hosp.-Cornell U. Med. Ctr., N.Y.C., 1971-72; resident N.Y. Eye and Ear Infirmary, N.Y.C., 1975-78; pvt. practice ophthalmology San Francisco, 1986; ophthalmologist N.J. Eye Physicians & Surgeons, Newark; pres., chief exec. officer US Try Zub Ent., Inc., Newark. Com. mem. N.J. Sch. for the Arts, Montclair, 1991—. Lt. USN, 1972-74, comdr. USNR, 1974—. Fellow ACS, Am. Acad. Ophthalmology; mem. Rotary, Army-Navy Club. Democrat. Roman Catholic. Home: 87 Lorraine Ave Montclair NJ 07043-2304 Office: NJ Eye Physicians and Surg 16 Ferry St Newark NJ 07105-1420

MATES, ROBERT EDWARD, mechanical engineering educator; b. Buffalo, May 19, 1935; s. Cyril S. and Ruth Elizabeth (Dougan) M.; m. Gail Paxson, June 5, 1960; children: Robert E., Elisabeth, Steven,. BS, U. Rochester, 1957; MS, Cornell U., 1959, PhD, 1963. Instr. Cornell U., Ithaca, N.Y., 1958-61; asst. prof. SUNY, Buffalo, 1962-65, assoc. prof., 1965-69, chmn. mech. and aero. engring., 1967-70, 79-82, prof. mech. engring., 1969—, dir. Ctr. Biomed. Engring., 1989—. Editor various symposium proceedings; contbr. articles to profl. jours. NIH spl. rsch. fellow, 1970-71, 78-79. Fellow ASME (chmn. winter ann. meeting com. 1989—, mem.-at-large bd. communications 1988—), Am. Inst. for Med. and Biol. Engring. (founding); mem. AAUP, Biomed. Engring. Soc. (bd. dirs. 1991—, chmn. awards com. 1991—), Am. Soc. Engring. Edn., Am. Heart Assn., Am. Physiol. Soc. Office: SUNY Dept Mech & Aero Engr 337 Jarvis Hall Buffalo NY 14260

MATESON, PATRICIA HART, environmental management executive, researcher; b. Phila., July 16, 1941; d. Joseph William Hart and Alma Catherine Reagan. BA, St. Joseph's U., 1963; postgrad., Harvard U., 1987, Rutgers U., 1990, U. Mich., 1991. Rsch. asst. Mateson Chem. Corp., Phila., 1980-89; pres. Mateson Environ. Mgmt., Phila., 1989—. Mem. ASTM (com. mem.), ASHRAE (com. mem.), Rotary (environ. rev. com.). Office: Mateson Environ Mgmt Inc 1025 E Montgomery Ave Philadelphia PA 19125-3414

MATEU, ANDREU, economist; b. Reus, Spain, Feb. 14, 1962; came to U.S., 1987; s. Juan Mateu and Montserrat Lamas. BBA, Escuela Superior de Aminstrn. y Direccion de Empresas, Barcelona, Spain, 1984, MBA, 1986. Project mgr. Barcelona Devel. Agy., N.Y.C., 1987-88; dir. indsl. products dept. Comml. Office Embassy Spain, N.Y.C., 1988—. Mem. Roundtable N.Y. Home: 415 E 37th St # 10A New York NY 10016-3200 Office: Embassy of Spain Comml Ofc 44th Fl 405 Lexington Ave New York NY 10174

MATEY, JAMES REGIS, physicist; b. McKeesport, Pa., June 30, 1951; s. John J. and Rita A. (Nuce) M.; m. Alice A. Graff, Aug. 8, 1973; children: Laura, Carolyn, Diana, Andrew. BS in Physics, Carnegie-Mellon U., Pitts., 1973; MS, PhD in Physics, U. Ill., 1978. Mem. tech. staff David Sarnoff Rsch. Ctr., Princeton, N.J., 1977—. Author: Scanning Capacitance Microscopy, 1985, Phonon Propagation in Glassy Metals, 1978; editorial bd. Rev. of Sci. Instruments. Recipient Award for Outstanding Tech. Achievement, David Sarnoff Rsch. Ctr., 1985, 88. Mem. Am. Phys. Soc. (chair instrument and measurement sci. topical group 1989-91), Sigma Xi. Office: David Sarnoff Rsch Ctr CN5300 Princeton NJ 08543-5300

MATHAI, JOSEPH, information scientist; b. Trivandrum, Kerala, India, Mar. 27, 1952; s. Chacko and Aleyamma (John) M.; m. Teresa Louzado, Feb. 12, 1989; 1 child, Michelle. BS, Kerala U., 1973; MBA, Columbia U., 1976. Mgmt. cons. Am. Mgmt. Systems, Arlington, Va., 1976-77; asst. v.p. Paine Weber, N.Y.C., 1977-82; systems mgr. Merrill Lynch Capital Markets, N.Y.C., 1982-85; mng. dir. N.Y. Stock Exch., N.Y.C., 1985-91; chief strategist Instinet Corp., N.Y.C., 1991—. Bd. dirs. Lower East Side Print Shop, N.Y.C. Named to All Star Data Processing/Mgmt. Info. Systems Team, Wall St. Computer Rev., 1989. Home: 15 Evergreen Way Tarrytown NY 10591-1044 Office: Instinet Corp 757 3d Ave New York NY 10017-2013

MATHAMEL, MARTIN STEVEN, chemicals executive, industrial hygienist; b. Hamtramck, Mich., July 16, 1949; s. Flavius Andre and Lila Wanda (Jaszczuk) M.; m. Karen Anne Michels, Sept. 8, 1973 (div. 1980). BS in Chemistry, U. Mich., 1971. Cert. indsl. hygienist, U.S.; registered occupational hygienist, Can. Chemist Flint Ink Corp., Detroit, 1971-72, Tecumseh Products Co., Ann Arbor, Mich., 1972-75; chief chemist Polytechnic, Inc., Chgo., 1975-80; toxicologist Ecology and Environment, Chgo., 1980; corp. dir. health and safety Roy F. Weston, Inc., West Chester, Pa., 1980-85; v.p. Camp Dresser & McKee Inc., Fairfax, Va., 1985-90; corp. dir. health and safety CH2M Hill, Reston, Va., 1990—. Vice pres. communications young profl. group Nat. Multiple Sclerosis Soc., Washington, 1990. Mem. Am. Chem. Soc., Am. Indsl. Hygiene Assn., Internat. Union Pure and Applied Chemists. Home: 3 Washington Cir NW Washington DC 20037 Office: CH2M Hill PO Box 4400 Reston VA 22090

MATHES, CHARLES ELLIOTT, writer, fine and decorative art appraiser; b. Cleve., May 17, 1949; s. Melvin Rothschild Mathes and Elaine (Fisher) Canfield; m. Arlene Graston, Sept. 21, 1985. BA, Webster U., 1973; MFA, Carnegie-Mellon U., 1975. Editor Freelance Mag., St. Louis, 1968-71; assoc. editor St. Louisan Mag., St. Louis, 1972-73; dir. Rodgers & Hammerstein Libr., N.Y.C., 1975-86; pres. Visibles, Inc., N.Y.C., 1986—. Author: The Spirit of America, A State by State Celebration (Introduction by Bob Hope), 1990, Treasures of American Museums, 1991, The Girl With the Phony Name, 1992. Shubert fellow, 1973-75. Assoc. mem. Appraisers Assn. Am.

MATHES, DANIEL BENJAMIN, mathematician, educator; b. Derry, N.H., Feb. 13, 1958; s. Roger Varney and Nancy (Hess) M.; m. Caroline Mudge, May 1, 1982; children: Sarah Hess, Samuel Benjamin, Lindsay Mudge. BA, Middlebury Coll., 1981; PhD, U. N.H., 1988. Postdoctoral fellow Dalhousie U., Halifax, N.S., Can., 1988-90; asst. prof. Colby Coll., Waterville, Maine, 1990—. Contbr. articles to Jour. Operator Theory, Mich. Math. Jour., Jour. Linear Algebra and Applications, Jour. Functional Analysis, Am. Math. Soc. Jour. Mem. Am. Math. Soc. Office: Colby Coll Math Dept Waterville ME 04901

MATHES, KENNETH NATT, electrical engineer, consultant; b. Schenectady, N.Y., June 30, 1913; s. Albert Henry and Etta Mae (Ross) M.; m. Virginia Kelley, July 22, 1940 (dec. June 1990); children: Stanley L., Stephen K. BSEE, Union Coll., 1935. Registered profl. engr., N.Y. Grad. adv. tech. course GE Co., Schenectady, 1935-38; engr. GE Lab., Schenectady, 1937-42, sect. mgr., 1942-50, asst. div. engr., 1950-54, mgr. insulation div. Turbine Lab., 1954-56; cons. maj. staff GE Rsch. Lab., Schenectady, 1956-78; pvt. practice cons. Schenectady, 1978—. Author: (with others) Engineering Design for Plastics, 1964, Engineering Dielectrics, vol. II, 1987. Vol. Literacy Vols. of Am., Schenectady, 1991—; tutor Schenectady City Schs., 1991—. Fellow ASTM (chair com. 1958-62, Merit award 1982), IEEE (Disting. Svc. award 1988, Founders award, 1991), AAAS; mem. Am. Chem. Soc. Home and Office: 2052 Baker Ave Niskayuna NY 12309-4132

MATHES, STEPHEN JON, lawyer; b. N.Y.C., Mar. 18, 1945; s. Joseph and Beatrice M.; m. Michele Marshall, Oct. 22, 1972; children: Aaron, Benjamin. BA, U. Pa., 1967, JD, 1970. Bar: N.Y. 1971, Pa. 1972, U.S. Dist. Ct. (ea. dist.) Pa. 1971. U.S. Ct. Appeals (3d cir.) 1972, U.S. Ct. Appeals (5th cir.) 1985, U.S. Ct. Appeals (4th cir.) 1985, U.S. Supreme Ct. 1978. Law clk. U.S. Ct. Appeals (3d cir.), Phila., 1970-71; asst. dist. atty. Office of Phil. Dist. Atty., Phila., 1975; assoc. Dilworth, Paxson, Kalish & Kauffman, Phila., 1971-74, 76-77, sr. ptnr., 1977-91, mng. ptnr., 1991—, mem. exec. com., 1987-90, co-chmn. litigation dept., 1987-91; ptnr. Hoyle, Morris & Kerr, Phila., 1992—; dir. The Levitt Found., 1990—. Mem. ABA, Pa. Bar Assn., Phila. Bar Assn. (arbitrator), Thanatopsis Soc., Racquet Club, Germantown Cricket Club. Home: 5500 Wissahickon Ave Philadelphia PA 19144-5653 Office: Holye Morris & Kerr One Liberty Pl Ste 4900 Philadelphia PA 19103

MATHEW, MATHEW BOBBY, aeronautical research engineer; b. Podanur, Tamil Nadu, India, Dec. 29, 1958; came to U.S., 1981; s. Kurisumootil and Sosamma (Mathew) M.; m. Mary Anne Vachaparampil, Feb. 9, 1991. BE, U. Madras, India, 1981; MS, Marquette U., 1983; PhD, Rensselaer Poly. Inst., 1987. Rsch. asst. Rensselaer Poly. Inst., Troy, N.Y., 1983-87, postdoctoral fellow, 1987-89; sr. tech. specialist in dynamics Boeing Helicopters, Phila., 1989—. Contbr. articles to profl. jours. Mem. AIAA, Am. Helicopter Soc. Home: 111 Macdade Blvd Apt 109B Folsom PA 19033-2920

MATHEWS, GEORGE MEPRATHU, accounting executive; b. Taiping, Perak, Malaysia, Feb. 23, 1960; came to U.S., 1985; s. Mathews and Annamma Chempanal. B of Commerce, U. Kerala, Trivandrum, South India, 1982; MBA, U. Dallas, 1987. Acctg. asst. AGK Acctg. & Mgmt., Butterworth, Penang, West Malaysia, 1982-83; acctg. officer Sabah Rubber Fund Bd., Kota Kinabula, Sabah, East Malaysia, 1984; acctg./LAN mgr. Karol Media, Wilkes-Barre, Pa., 1988—. Mem. Am. Mgmt. Assn., Sigma Iota Epsilon. Office: Karol Media 350 N Pennsylvania Ave Wilkes Barre PA 18702-4415

MATHEWS, RICHARD STEWART MONTEAGUE, advertising executive; b. Montreal, Que., Can., May 22, 1946; s. William Herbert and Margaret Somerville (Stewart) M.; m. Margaret Larner Ogburn, Oct. 11, 1968 (div. July 1976); 1 child, Alexander Scott. BFA, R.I. Sch. Design, 1968; MFA, Syracuse U., 1969. Asst. art dir. Ted Bates & Co., N.Y.C., 1969-70; art dir. Lintas: Worldwide Advt. Inc., N.Y.C., 1970-72, copywriter, 1972-74, v.p., assoc. creative dir., 1980-84, sr. v.p., assoc. creative dir., 1984-85; sr. v.p. group creative dir., 1985—; sr. copywriter Revlon Inc., N.Y.C., 1974-76, Cosmair Inc., N.Y.C., 1976-78; creative group head Grey Advt. Corp., N.Y.C., 1978-80. Syracuse U. fellow, 1968-69; R.I. Sch. Design European Honors scholar, 1967-68. Mem. Advt. Club N.Y. Episcopalian. Home: 3 Lincoln Ctr New York NY 10023 Office: Lintas NY 1 Dag Hammarskjold Plz New York NY 10017-2201

MATHEWS-ROTH, MICHELINE MARY, medicine educator, microbiology researcher; b. Mineola, N.Y., July 26, 1934; d. John Francis and Micheline Genevieve (Doguereau) Mathews; m. Robert Steele Roth, May 13, 1966; 1 child, John Dogureau. BS magna cum laude, Coll. of St. Elizabeth, Convent Station, N.J., 1956; MD with honors, NYU, 1961. Intern pathology Boston City Hosp., 1962-63; rsch. assoc. in microbiology Harvard U. Med. Sch., Boston, 1965-69, assoc. in microbiology, 1969-71, prin. rsch. assoc. in medicine, 1974-84, assoc. prof., 1984—; jr. assoc. in medicine Peter Bent Brigham Hosp. (now Brigham and Women's Hosp.), Boston, 1977-82, assoc. physician, 1982-92, physician, 1992—; assisting physician in med. microbiology Boston City Hosp., 1973-74. Editor: (with N.I. Krinsky and R.F. Taylor) Carotenoids Chemistry and Biology, 1989; also over 100 articles and revs. Former mem. bd. dirs. Peabody-Mason Music Found., Boston; pres. Mass. State Sci. Fair, Boston, 1989-92, also former mem. bd. dirs. Mem. Am. Soc. for Microbiology, Am. Fedn. for Clin. Rsch., Am. Soc. for Clin. Investigation, Am. Soc. fro Photobiology (assoc. editor Photochemistry and Photobiology 1974-83, councillor 1985-88, pres. 1991-92), Sigma Xi. Office: Channing Lab 180 Longwood Ave Boston MA 02115-5899

MATHEY, CLAIRE KESSINGER, English literature and drama educator; b. Portland, Oreg., Sept. 22, 1950; d. Frederick Albert and Dale (Knox) Kessinger; m. Olivier Henri Mathey. BA, U. N. Mex., 1982; postgrad., NYU, 1986—, MA, 1986. Teaching asst. NYU, 1986-89; tutorial instr. The Cooper Union, N.Y.C., 1987-89; adjunct prof. English Bklyn. Coll., 1989-91, SUNY, Purchase, 1991—. CCD tchr. Corpus Christi Ch., N.Y.C., 1990-91; active Columbia U. Cath. Campus Ministries, 1983-85; dir. plays for community theatre, Croton, N.Y. Mem. MLA, Nat. Coun. Tchrs. of English, Nat. Assn. Scholars, Croton Coun. of the Arts. Democrat. Roman Catholic. Home: 194 Rockledge Ave Buchanan NY 10511-1514 Office: SUNY Purchase 735 Anderson Hill Rd Purchase NY 10577-1402

MATHEY, HORST KARL, engineer; b. Gerolstein, Eifel, Germany, Sept. 28, 1935; s. Johann Heinrich and Anna Luzia (Clemens) M.; m. Rosemarie Burger, Oct. 28, 1960 (div. Aug. 1981); 1 child, Stefanie; m. Katharina Hoesli, Apr. 20, 1983; children: Gabriela, Brigitte. BSME, BSEE, BSMT, Vocat. Tech. dir. yarn clearer div. Loepfe Bros. Ltd., Zurich, 1973-83; tech. sales dir. (nat.) Resimix Co., Whitinsville, Mass., 1985-83; devel. engr. Ashby-Cross Co., Topsfield, Mass., 1985—; cons. in field. Inventor, patentee in field. Office: Ashby-Cross Co 418 Boston St Topsfield MA 01983

MATHIESON, GARRETT ALFRED, insurance company executive; b. Bronxville, N.Y., June 12, 1952; s. William Frederick and Susan (Prager) M.; m. Doris King, June 21, 1980; children: Christine, William. BA, Hobart Coll., 1974; MBA, N.Y. U., 1980. Account rep. Marsh & McLennan, N.Y.C., 1974-77; sr. broker Frank B. Hall & Co., N.Y.C., 1977-78; risk mgmt. cons. Marsh & McLennan, N.Y.C., 1978-80, cons. mgr.-asst. v.p., 1980-82, world cons. div. mgr., 1982-85; mng. cons. Towers Perrin Forster & Crosby, N.Y.C., 1985-86; sr. v.p. Jardine Ins. Brokers, N.Y.C., 1986-90; exec. v.p. Rollins Burdick Hunter, N.Y.C., 1990--; seminar mgr. World Trade Inst., 1982-84, Marsh & McLennan, 1981-85. Contbr. articles to profl. jour. Mem. Ins. Brokers Assn. N.Y., N.Y. Choral Soc., Siwanoy Country Club. Presbyterian. Office: Rollins Burdick Hunter 605 3d Ave New York NY 10158-0180

MATHIESON, KELLY ANNE, money manager; b. Glen Cove, N.Y., Nov. 28, 1965; d. William and Joy Arlene (Marshall) M. BS, SUNY, Binghamton, 1987; MBA, NYU, 1990. Specialist Goldman, Sachs & Co., N.Y.C., 1987-90; assoc. Chase Manhattan Bank, N.Y.C., 1990—. Recipient Marcus Nadler scholarship NYU, 1988-90. Mem. Fin. Woman's Assn. Home: 155 E 29th St Apt 2C New York NY 10016-8121

MATHIESON, MICHAEL RAYMOND, accountant; b. Pontiac, Ill., May 3, 1952; s. Raymond Irving and Dorothy Mae (Yentes) M.; m. Nancy Anne Repa, May 11, 1985; 1 child, Patrick Michael. BS in Acctg., U. Ill., 1974. Sr. mgr. Peat, Marwick, Mitchell & Co., Chgo., 1974-80, N.Y.C., 1980-84; v.p. Becker Paribas, Inc., N.Y.C., 1984-85, Paine Webber Group, Inc., N.Y.C., 1985-89, Chase Manhattan Bank, N.Y.C., 1989-90; asst. contr. Avon Products, Inc., N.Y.C., 1990—. Mem. AICPA, Ill. Soc. CPA's, Westchester Country Club, Alpha Delta Phi. Republican. Presbyterian. Home: 52 Franklin Ave Rye NY 10580-2546 Office: Avon Products Inc 9 W 57th St New York NY 10019

MATHIS, JOHN BERNARD, employee training company executive; b. Binghamton, N.Y., Oct. 21, 1936; s. Joseph and Catherine (O'Shea) M.; m. Martha Schnurbusch, May 31, 1958; children: Michelle, Michael, Mark, Paul, Andrew. Cert. kitchen designer. Salesman Hunphries Kitchens, Binghamton, 1959-60, Modern Kitchens of Syracuse, Binghamton, 1960-66, Quaker Maid Kitchen, Binghamton, 1966-68, Westinghouse Electric, Goshen, Ind., 1968-70, Keyline Co. Inc., Phila., 1970—; bd. dirs. Nat. Kitchen and Bath Assn., 1970s. Author columns on sales and human resource devel. Recipient Bronze award Carlson Learning Co., 1986-87, 90-92, Silver award, 1988. Republican. Roman Catholic. Office: Keyline Co Inc 502 Woodview Dr Exton PA 19341-1799

MATHUR, PERSHOTTAM PRASAD, pharmacologist, researcher; b. Delhi, Jan. 19, 1938; came to U.S., 1963; s. Mukat P. and Batto Mathur. BS, U. Delhi, 1957; PhD, U. Fla., 1968. Rsch. assoc. U. Ga., Athens and Charleston, S.C., 1967-68; NIH fellow St. Luke's Hosp. Ctr., N.Y.C., 1969-72; head clin. chemist St. Barnabas Hosp., Bronx, 1972; sect. head biochemical pharmacology William H. Rorer, Inc., Ft. Washington, Pa., 1972-76; group mgr. cardiovascular lab. A.H. Robins Co., Richmond, Va., 1977-80, sci. coord., 1980-90; group project dir. Organon Inc., West Orange, N.J., 1990—; adj. asst. prof. pharmacology Med. Coll. of Va., Richmond, 1977-82. Chmn., mem. rsch. seminar com. A.H. Robins Co., 1978-80. NIH fellow St. Luke's Hosp. Ctr., 1969-72. Hindu. Home: PO Box 213 West Orange NJ 07052-0213 Office: Organon Inc 375 Mt Pleasant Ave West Orange NJ 07052-2798

MATIJEVIC, EGON, chemistry educator, researcher, consultant; b. Otocac, Croatia, Apr. 27, 1922; came to U.S., 1957; s. Grgur and Stefica (Spiegel) M.; m. Bozica Biscan, Feb. 27, 1947. Diploma in chem. engring., U. Zagreb, 1944, PhD in Chemistry, 1948, Dr. Habil. in Phys. Chemistry, 1952; DSc (hon.), Lehigh U., 1977, M. Curie-Skloslowska U., Lublin, Poland, 1990; DSc. (hon.), V. Clakson U., 1992. Instr. chemistry U. Zagreb, Yugoslavia, 1944-47; sr. instr. phys. chemistry U. Zagreb, 1949-52, privat dozent in colloid chemistry, 1952-54, dozent in phys. and colloid chemistry, 1955-56, on leave, 1956-59; rsch. assoc. Inst. Cinematography, Zagreb, 1948; rsch. fellow dept. colloid sci. U. Cambridge, Eng., 1956-57; vis. prof. Clarkson Coll. Tech., Potsdam, N.Y., 1957-59; assoc. prof. chemistry Clarkson Coll. Tech., Postdam, N.Y., 1960-62; prof. Clarkson U., Postdam, 1962-86, disting. univ. prof., 1986—; assoc. dir. Inst. Colloid and Surface Sci. Clarkson Coll. Tech., 1966-68; dir. inst., 1968-81, chmn. dept. chemistry, 1981-87; vis. prof. Japan Soc. for Promotion Sci., 1973, U. Melbourne, Australia, 1976, Sci. U. Tokyo, 1979, 84; vis. scientist U. Leningrad, USSR, 1977; Internat. Atomic Energy Agy. adviser Buenos Aires, Argentina, 1978, 80; fgn. guest Inst. Colloid and Interface Sci. Sci. U. Tokyo, 1982; lectr. in field; mem. adv. com. Univs. and Space Research Assn.; referee NATO Advanced Study Inst. Author: (with M. Kesler) General and Inorganic Chemistry for Senior High Schools, 11 edits., including Croatian, Macedonian, Hungarian, Italian, 1943-63; translator: Einfuhrung in die Stochiometrie (Nylen and Wigren), 1948; editor: (with Walter J. Weber) Adsorption from Aqueous Solution, 1968, Surface and Colloid Science, vols. 1-14, 1969-87; regional editor Colloid and Polymer Sci., 1966—; contbr. numerous articles to profl. publs. Recipient Gold medal Am. Electroplaters Soc., 1976; guest of honor 56th and 63rd Colloid and Surface Sci. Symposiums, Blacksburg, Va., 1982, Seattle, 1989. Mem. Am. Chem. Soc. (councilor div. colloid and surface chemistry 1982-87, chmn. 1969-70, Kendall award 1972, Langmuir Disting. Lectureship award 1985), Kolloid gesellschaft (Thomas Graham award 1985), Internat. Assn. Colloid Interface Sci. (pres. 1985-87), Chem. Soc. Japan, Inst. Colloid and Interface Sci. of Sci. of Tokyo (hon.), Phalanx Soc., Croatian Acad. Scis. and Arts (fgn.), Am. Ceramic Soc. (hon.), Materials Rsch. Soc. Japan (hon.), Acad. Ceramics (Italy), Croatian Chem. Soc. (Bozo Tezak medal 1991), Sigma Xi (Clarkson Coll. Tech. chpt. award 1972, nat. lectr. 1987-89). Roman Catholic. Office: Clarkson U Potsdam NY 13699-5814

MATLOFF, GREGORY LEE, consulting environmental, space and computer scientist; b. N.Y.C., Mar. 2, 1945; s. Simon and Eudice (Strom) M.; m. Constance Bangs, 1986. B.A., Queens Coll. CUNY, 1965; M.S., N.Y.U., 1969, Ph.D., 1976. Engr. Kollsman Inst. Corp., Elmhurst, N.Y., 1965-67, Grumman Aerospace Co., Bethpage, N.Y., 1967-69; research engr. United Aircraft Research Co., East Hartford, Conn., 1969-70; research assoc. Wesleyan U., Middletown, Conn., 1970-71; asst. editor Am. Inst. Physics, N.Y.C., 1971-72; research asst. N.Y.U., 1972-75, postdoctoral research scientist, 1975-77; cons. staff scientist Systems and Applied Sci. Corp., Riverdale, Md., 1978-81; cons. environ. scientist, Bklyn., 1980—; mem. faculty Pratt Inst., 1980-82, adminstr., 1983-85; mem. faculty N.Y.C. Tech. Coll., 1979—, Baruch Coll. CUNY, 1986-89, St. Hilda's and St. Hugh's Sch., 1988-90. Author: (with E. Mallove) Starflight Handbook, 1989, Urban Astronomer, 1991; contbr. articles to profl. jours. Dir. Astronomy program N.Y.C. Dept. Parks and Recreation, 1987-91. NSF grantee, 1975. Fellow Brit. Interplanetary Soc.; mem. AAAS, Am. Meteorol. Soc., Am. Optical Soc., N.Y. Acad. Scis., Planetary Soc., Sigma Xi. Lodge: K.M. Home: 417 Greene Ave Brooklyn NY 11216-1111

MATLOFF, MARK ALEXANDER, psychologist; b. Bklyn., Feb. 15, 1950; s. Simon and Eudice Rose (Strom) M.; m. Elaine S. Meyers, Oct. 23, 1977; one child, Daniel Aaron. BA, CUNY, 1971; MS, Auburn U., 1974, PhD, 1977. Diplomate Internat. Acad. Behavioral Medicine, Counseling and Psychotherapy. Clin. psychology intern Bradley Ctr. Psychiat. Hosp., Columbus, Ga., 1976-77; clin. psychologist Burwell Psychoednl. Ctr., Carrollton, Ga., 1977-78; staff psychologist Warren (Pa.) State Hosp., 1978-81; pvt. practice psychology Olean, N.Y., 1981-83; program dir. community svcs. team Madison County Dept. Mental Health, Wampsville, N.Y., 1983-85; pvt. practice psychology Syracuse, N.Y., 1985—; cons. POMCO, Syracuse, 1986—, VA, Syracuse, 1988—, Madison County Day Treatment Ctr., Oneida, N.Y., 1983-84; cert. supr. Inst. Rational-Emotive Therapy, N.Y.C., 1989—. Assoc. fellow Inst. Rational-Emotive Therapy, N.Y.C., 1983. Mem. APA, Cen. N.Y. Psychol. Assn. Home and Office: 209 Oakmont Dr Syracuse NY 13214-1533

MATOLYAK, JOHN, physics educator; b. Johnstown, Pa., June 26, 1939; s. Anna (Radak) M.; m. Helen Louise Sida, Aug. 24, 1963; children: Dmitri, Alexander. BS, St. Francis Coll., Loretto, Pa., 1963; MS, Toledo U., 1966; PhD, W.Va. U., 1975. Physicist NASA, Greenbelt, Md., 1963; instr. math and physics St. Francis Coll., 1963-64; prof. physics Ind. U. of Pa., 1966—; cons. Dept. Energy, Morgantown, W.Va., 1978, NASA, Lewis Rsch. Ctr., Cleve., 1981, 82, Night Vision Lab., Alexandria, Va., 1985. Mem. Am. Physical Soc., Sigma Chi Club (v.p. Ind. U. Pa. chpt. 1984-85,. pres. 1985-86). Home: 2541 Melloney Ln Indiana PA 15701-2329 Office: Ind U of Pa Physics Dept Indiana PA 15705

MATSA, LOULA ZACHAROULA, social services administrator; b. Piraeus, Greece, Apr. 16, 1935; came to U.S., 1952, naturalized 1962; d. Eleftherios Georgiou and Ourania E. (Fraguiskopoulou) Papoulias; student Pierce Coll., Athens, Greece, 1948-52; B.A., Rockford Coll., 1953; M.A., U. Chgo., 1955; m. Ilco S. Matsa, Nov. 27, 1953; 1 son, Aristotle Ricky. Cert. clin. social worker. Marital counselor Family Soc. Cambridge, Mass., 1955-56; chief unit II, social service Queen's (N.Y.) Children's Psychiat. Ctr., 1961-74; dir. social services, supr.-coord. family care program Hudson River Psychiat. Ctr., Poughkeepsie, N.Y., 1974-91; supr. social work Harlem Valley Psychiat. Ctr., Wingdale, N.Y., 1991—; field instr. Adelphi, Albany and Fordham univs., 1969—. Fulbright Exch. student, 1952-53; Talcott scholar, 1953-55. Mem. Internat. Platform Assn., Internat. Coun. on Social Welfare, Nat. Assn. Social Workers, Assn. Cert. Social Workers, Pub. Employees Fedn., Pierce Coll. Alumni Assn. Democrat. Greek Orthodox. Contbr. articles to profl. jours.; instrumental in state policy changes in treatment and court representation of emotionally disturbed and mentally ill. Home: 81-11 45th Ave Elmhurst NY 11373 Office: Harlem Valley Psychiat Ctr PO Box 330 Bldg 27 Admission Unit Wingdale NY 12601

MATSEN, JOHN MORRIS, engineer; b. Neenah, Wis., May 30, 1936; s. Morris and Bertha Rowena (Witt) M.; m. Sandra Louise Schwartz, May 8, 1971. BS in Engring., Princeton (N.J.) U., 1957; MS, Columbia U., 1959, PhD, 1963. Instr. Columbia U., N.Y.C., 1959-61; engr. Exxon Rsch. & Engring. Co., Florham Park, N.J., 1961-66, sr. engr., 1966-73, engring. as-

soc., 1973—; mem. tech. com. Particulate Solids Rsch. Inc., Chgo., 1976—. Editor: Fluidization Technology, 1976, Fluidization, 1980; patentee in field; contbr. articles to profl. jours. Member Clinton (N.J.) Twp. Planning Bd., 1976—, chmn., 1978-82; mem. Hunterdon County Agrl. Devel. Bd., N.J., 1982-87; councilman Clinton Twp., 1983—, mayor, 1986; trustee N.J. Symphony Orch. League, N.J., 1966-82, pres., 1973-79. NSF fellow, 1959-60. Mem. Am. Inst. Chem. Engrs., Am. Chem. Soc., Raritan Yacht Club, Princeton Club of N.Y., Rolls Royce Owners Club, Phi Lambda Upsilon. Republican. Home: 39 Sand Hill Rd Annandale NJ 08801-3111 Office: Exxon Rsch & Engring Co PO Box 101 Florham Park NJ 07932-0101

MATSEN, MATTHEW JAMES, export analyst; b. Yonkers, N.Y., Sept. 4, 1969; s. Robert Joseph and Vera Iba (Ippolitio) M. BBA, Iona Coll., 1991. With Gleason Security, Hartsdale, N.Y., 1988; sales clk. Rotiroti Enterprise, Hastings, N.Y., 1989-90; with Ricky's Clam House, Yonkers, N.Y., 1990-91; sales assoc. R.H. Macy's & Co., White Plains, N.Y., 1991-92; export analyst S.G.S. Govt. Programs, Inc., N.Y.C., 1992—. Republican. Roman Catholic. Home: 42 Villard Ave Hastings On Hudson NY 10706

MATSON, SUZANNE MARIE, poet, educator; b. Portland, Oreg., Nov. 12, 1959; d. Carl E. and Kathryn Ruth (Kaufman) M.; m. Joseph Gerard Donnellan, June 15, 1991. BA, Portland State U., 1981; MA, U. Wash., 1983, PhD, 1987. Asst. prof., English dept. Boston Coll., Chestnut Hill, Mass., 1988—; Poetry editor: Seattle REv., 1985-88; author: (book of poems) Sea Level, 1990; contbr. revs. and articles to profl. jours. Recipient award Acad. Am. Poets, 1986, Young Poets award Poetry Northwest Mag., 1983; Susannah McMurphy fellow, U. Wash., 1984, recipient Robert B. Heilman award, 1987. Mem. MLA, Coll. Club (asst. treas. 1989-92). Office: English Dept Boston Coll Chestnut Hill MA 02167

MATSUI, WESLEY TAK, psychologist, human services administrator; b. Chgo., Oct. 15, 1950; s. Takanobu and Tsuyako Florence (Soda) M.; s. Mary Katherine Steidl, Aug. 18, 1979; 1 child, Elena Hanako. BA, Knox Coll., 1972; MS, Hahnemann Med. U., 1977; PhD, Temple U., 1986. Lic. psychologist, N.J. Social therapist Forest Hosp., Desplaines, Ill., 1972-75; clin. instr., psychologist Hahnemann Med. U., Phila., 1977-79; psychology intern Harlen Valley Psychiat. Ctr., Carmel and White Plains, N.Y., 1979-80; adj. lectr. Elizabeth Seton Coll., Yonkers, N.Y., 1980-81; sr. clinician St. Clare's Riverside Med. Ctr., Denville, N.J., 1981-88; dir. admissions N.J. Ctr. for Family Studies, Springfield, 1988-91, mem. faculty, 1986—; exec. dir. N.J. Ctr. for Family Studies, Springfield, 1991—; cons. family therapy Dutton Counseling Ctr., Morristown, N.J., 1985-88. Author: (with others) Interviewing, 1988; contbr. articles to profl. jours.; presenter papers at confs., convs. Mem. APA (div. family psychology), N.J. Psychol. Assn., Assn. for the Advancement Family Therapy (rsch. grantee 1982). Office: 135 Columbia Tpke Ste 3030 Florham Park NJ 07932-2104

MATSUMOTO, TSUTOMU BEN, trademark management company executive; b. Kyoto, Japan, Mar. 6, 1942; came to U.S., 1966; s. Jiro and Hatsue (Oyabu) M.; m. Sanae Haga Matsumoto, Apr. 2, 1973; children: Mia, Rae. BA in Econs., Doshisha U., Kyoto, 1964. Exec. trainee Takashimaya Co., Ltd., Osaka, Japan, 1964-65, Tokyo, 1965-66; buyer, sales mgr. Takashimaya, Inc., N.Y.C., 1966-72; mng. ptnr. Tammy, Inc., N.Y.C., 1972-74, Internat. Bus. Devel., Inc., Wayne, N.J., 1974-76; chief exec. officer Uni Diversified, Inc., River Edge, N.J., 1976—, Unid Network Worldwide, River Edge, 1990—. Fgn. editor: Guinness Book of Records, 1985-89. Mem. Maywood Tennis Club, Santa Barbara Polo & Racket Club. Home and Office: Unid Network 243 Woodland Ave River Edge NJ 07661

MATSUMURA, AKIO, organization executive; b. Aoyama, Tokyo, May 21, 1942; came to U.S., 1978; s. Eseji and Masako (Akima) M.; m. Maki Higuchi, Oct. 10, 1968; 1 child, Keishi. BA in Internat. Econs., Chuo U., Tokyo, 1965. Various positions Taiyo Shipping Co., Tokyo, 1965-72; resource devel. officer western Pacific region Internat. Planned Parenthood Fedn., Tokyo, 1972-74; resource devel. and youth affairs officer Internat. Planned Parenthood Fedn., London, 1974-77; chmn. inter-parliamentary working group project UN Fund for Population and Activities, N.Y.C., 1978-82; spl. advisor to chmn. U.S.-Japan Found., N.Y.C., 1982-85; exec. dir. Global Com. Parliamentarians on Population and Devel., N.Y.C., 1982—, Global Forum Spiritual and Parliamentary Leaders on Human Survival, N.Y.C., 1985—; cons. InterAction Coun. former Heads of Govt., UN Devel. Progamme, Internat. Planned Parenthood Fedn.; organizer numerous workshops on child survival, confs. on population and devel., numerous parliamentary groups; spl. advisor Asian Forum Parliamentarians on Population and Devel., Inter-am. Parliamentary Group on Population and Devel., Africa Parliamentary Coun. on Population and Devel.; sec.-gen. Parliamentary Earth Summit, Rio de Janeiro, 1992. Mem. exec. com. United Earth. Recipient appreciation award Asian Forum Parliamentarians on Population Devel., 1990, John Denver's 1990 Windstar award, 1990. Office: Global Com Parliamentarians 336 E 45th St 10th Fl New York NY 10017

MATT, WALTER J., JR., lawyer, corporate; b. Utica, N.Y., July 11, 1938; s. Walter J. and Kathryn (Kemper) M.; m. Linda Buerk, May 24, 1981. BA, Williams Coll., 1960; Cert. D'Etudes Politiques, Inst. D'Etudes Politiques, Paris, France, 1961; LLB, Columbia U., 1964. Bar: N.Y., 1964. Assoc. Cravath, Swaine & Moore, N.Y.C., 1964-71; asst. atty. gen. N.Y. State Atty. Gen.'s Office, Syracuse, N.Y., 1971-76; asst. gen. counsel Marine Midland Bank, N.A., Buffalo, 1976-85; lawyer Walter J. Matt Jr., Esq., Buffalo, 1985—; pres. Bahawali Assocs. Inc., Buffalo, 1990—; dir. Matt Brewing Co., Inc., Utica, N.Y., 1989—. Mem. Erie County Bar Assn., Cragburn Golf Club, Rotary Club of Buffalo (treas. 1988-89). Home: 8 Soldiers Pl Buffalo NY 14222 Office: Walter J Matt Jr 8 Soldiers Pl Buffalo NY 14222

MATTAR, PHILIP, institute director/editor; b. Haifa, Palestine, Jan. 21, 1944; came to U.S. 1961; m. Evelyn Ann Keith, June 20, 1971; 1 child, Christina. MPhil, Columbia U., 1977, PhD, 1981. Exec. dir. Inst. for Palestine Studies, Washington, 1984—; assoc. editor Jour. Palestine Studies, Washington, 1985—; adj. lectr. history Yale U., 1981; adj. prof. history Georgetown U., 1990, 91. Author: Mufti of Jerusalem, 1988, 2d edit., 1991; co-editor: Encyclopedia of the Modern Middle East, 1993; contbr. articles to profl. jours. Vis. scholar Columbia U., 1984; Fulbright-Hays Rsch. fellow, 1978. Mem. Middle East Studies Assn., Middle East Inst. Office: Inst for Palestine Studies 3501 M St NW Washington DC 20007-2624

MATTERN, GERRY A., engineering consultant; b. Attica, Ind., June 16, 1935; s. George Edward and Wanda Mae (McCann) M.; p. Jane Ann Snell, Dec. 27, 1956; children: Kimberly Kaye, Geoffrey Kurtis, Kamala Anne, Kristin Annette. BSEE, Rose Polytech. Instit., 1958. Registered profl. engr., Penn., W.Va., Ind. With Mattern Electric Co., Attica, 1958; draftsman Yeager Architects, Terre Haute, Ind., 1956-58; application engr. W. Penn. Power Co., Greensburg, 1958-60; indsl. power engr. W. Penn. Power Co., Jeannette, 1960-62; product mgr. Pitts. Reflector Co., Irwin, Penn, 1962-63; owner, operator G.A. Mattern & Assocs., Ligonier, Penn., 1963—; ptnr. Palco, Inc., Greensburg, Penn., 1965—; owner, operator Gay 90's Dairy Queen, Ligonier, Penn., 1972—; instr. Profl. Engr's Review, Penn State U., Am. Instit. of Architects Review Class; adj. prof. Carnegie-Mellon U., Pitts., 1982—; design cons. Pitts. Reflector Co. Inventor infra-red electric furnace; designer electric heating equipment, emergency lighting equipment. Bd. dirs. Ligonier Twp. Planning Commn., 1982, Ligonier Twp. Sewerage Authority, 1991, Westmoreland County Coun. Boy Scouts Am., Heritage United Meth. Ch., Ligonier YMCA; pres. Ligonier C. of C., 1974-78. Recipient of Power-up award Westinghouse Electric Co., 1961. Mem. (life) Ligonier Booster's Club, (life) Fire Co. number 1, (arbitrator) Am. Arbitration Assn. Independent. Club: Tall Cedars (Westmoreland County), Lodge: Masons (Ligonier). Home: RR 1 Box 230 Ligonier PA 15658-9728 Office: GA Mattern & Assocs 205 N Market St Ligonier PA 15658-1258

MATTESON, VICKY LYNN, credit union manager; b. Warren, Pa., Jan. 3, 1957; d. Wayne Eugene and Lois Irene (Saxton) Hammond; m. Thomas P. Matteson, Jan. 7, 1983; children: Julie, Amy, Danny, Michelle. AS in Acctg., Jamestown (N.Y.) Community Coll., 1978. Sec. State Farm Ins., Jamestown, 1975-82; office mgr. Monofrax Employer's Credit Union, Falconer, N.Y., 1979—; mgr., chief exec. officer Jamestown Tchr.'s Credit Union, 1984—. Mem. N.Y. State Credit Union League (asst. treas. Albany, N.Y. chpt. 1988-91, pres. 1992—, Credit Union Mgr. of the Yr. 1988, Outstanding Credit Union Person of the Yr. 1990). Republican. Baptist. Office: Jamestown Tchrs Credit Union 350 E Second St Jamestown NY 14701

MATTEY, JOHN JOSEPH, mortgage and investment company executive, analyst, appraiser, educator; b. Mt. Pleasant, Pa., Nov. 8, 1927; s. John Michael and Dora Ethel (Polcha) M.; m. Betty Ann Jacobs, Aug. 16, 1950; children: Marcia Mattey Cooley, Cynthia Mattey Rager, John D., James, Jerome, Joseph, Jeffrey. Student U.S. Mcht. Marine Acad., 1945, St. Vincent Coll., 1945, U. Pitts., 1953-55, Duquesne U., 1953, Am. U., 1970, Del. U., 1968-76. Mgr. real estate Bi-Lo Stas. Gasoline Co., Lawrenceburg, Ind., 1960-66; exec. v.p. Colonial Investment Co., Ltd., Wilmington, Del., 1967-69; mgr. eastern region real estate Petroleum Cons., Louisville, 1969-73; designated sr. appraiser Jackson-Cross Co., Phila., 1973-78; project dir. valuation of Penn Central real estate taken by ConRail, 1976-77; pres. Del. Bond & Mortgage Co., Wilmington, 1968—, Del. Land and Investment Co., Wilmington, 1977—, Analysts and Appraisers, Inc., 1978—, Mattey Co., 1982—; bd. dirs. Jednota Inc.; lobbyist Del. Senate, Del. Gen. Assembly, 1968—. Founder, bd. dirs. Friends of Lepers, Med. Charity, 1970—; pres. Cath. Men's Club, 1954-55. Fellow Friends of Library of Am. Philos. Soc.; mem. Internat. Right of Way Assn., Sr. Right of Way Assoc., Appraisal Inst., Accredited Appraiser Can. Inst., Mensa, Maritime Soc. Port of Wilmington, Am. Legion (pres., chaplain 1962-65, post vice comdr. 1982—). Republican. Roman Catholic. Home: 1209 Marsh Rd Wilmington DE 19803-3507

MATTHAEI, GAY HUMPHREY, interior designer; b. N.Y.C., Mar. 13, 1931; d. Robert Louis and Ethel Gladys Humphrey; m. Konrad Henry Matthaei, Nov. 16, 1956; children: Marcella, Leslie, Konrad. BA, Mt. Holyoke Coll., 1952; MIA, Columbia U., 1954; MA, cert. Russian Inst. Columbia U., 1954; grad. Parsons Sch. Design, 1970. Lectr., cons. NBC, 1956; dir. Radrick Prodns., Where Time Is a River, 1966-67; cons. N.Y.C. Parks Recreation and Cultural Adminstrn., 1970-72; asso. Pearl R. Mitchell A.S.I.D., 1972-74, owner, 1974-91; owner, mgr. Gay Matthaei Interiors, N.Y.C., 1976-86. Trustee Mt. Holyoke Coll.; mem. Commn. on State Capital Preservation and Restoration, Conn., 1977-82; mem. Nat. Trust for Hist. Preservation. Mem. Am. Soc. Interior Designers, River Club, Mt. Holyoke Club N.Y., Phi Beta Kappa. Restorations include Town Farms Inn, 1978, State Capital of Conn., 1977-78, Pres.'s House, Mt. Holyoke Coll., 1982, Samuel Russell House, Wesleyan Coll., 1984, Courtly Manor, Greenwich, Ct., 1987, Buhl Family Found., 1991, Hillspring Farm, 1991-92. Home: 356 E 69th St New York NY 10021-5706 Office: 505 Park Ave New York NY 10022

MATTHEWS, CHARLOTTE, private school educator; b. Phila., Dec. 29; d. Sammy and Dolly (Herndon) M.; m. R. Sherman (div.); 1 child, Kanisha. BS, LaSalle Coll., 1978. Revenue agt. U.S. Treasury Dept. IRS, Camden, N.J., 1979-83; small bus. cons. Cherry Hill, N.J., 1984-86; controller Dollar Rent-A-Car, Phila., 1986; state, local tax mgr. Siemens Corp., Atlanta, 1987; chief exec. officer, owner Rent A-Temp Inc., Phila., 1988—, Liberty Acad. Bus., Phila., 1988—. Mem. Pa. Assn. Pvt. Sch. Adminstrs., Assn. Vocat. Adminstrs. Home: 19 Woodbury Dr Cherry Hill NJ 08003 Office: Liberty Acad Bus 511 N Broad St Ste 2000 Philadelphia PA 19123

MATTHEWS, CLIFFORD WILLIAM, firefighter, medical technician; b. Rochester, N.Y., May 24, 1947; s. Jacob and Barbara Lorraine (Betty) M.; m. Jo Anne Virginia Pasgenski, Jan. 10, 1970 (div. 1987); children: Clifford William Jr., Jennifer Lynn; m. Marlene Sharon Giffert, June 23, 1989. AAS, Monroe Community Coll., Rochester, N.Y., 1980. Cert. EMT, N.Y. Firefighter, EMT Eastman Kodak Co., Rochester, 1976—; EMT Monroe Ambulance, Rochester, 1990—. Author poems Reflections, 1987, Images, 1989. Vol. firefighter Hilton (N.Y.) Fire Dept., 1972-85, West Webster (N.Y.) Fire Dept., 1986—. With USN, 1965-69. Recipient Golden Poet awards World of Poetry, 1987, 88, 89, 90, 91. Home: 1095 Cane Patch Webster NY 14508

MATTHEWS, DANIEL GEORGE, editorial consultant; b. Lawrenceville, Va., Dec. 18, 1932; s. George Daniel and Evelyn (Goodrich) M.; student George Washington U., 1956-64, U.S. Fgn. Service Inst., 1960-64; m. Linda L. Fink, Oct. 25, 1975; children: Strelka Jamila, Francesca Alina. Analyst, VA, Washington, 1953-54; libr. asst. cataloging U.S. Dept. State, Washington, 1954-63, intelligence and rsch. specialist, 1964-66; editor-in-chief African Bibliog. Ctr., Washington, 1963-83, exec. dir., 1966-83; v.p. Afritec cons. firm, 1983-85; ptnr. The Matthews Assocs., editor Africa Insider, biweekly newsletter on U.S.-African rels., 1984—; editor African Fgn. Affairs, 1985—; editorial cons. Greenwood Press, N.Y.C., 1967—; pres. Washington Task Force on African Affairs, 1969-79, African Communications Liaison Svc., 1979-84; mem. exec. com. coordinating coun. Internat. Ednl. Exch., 1969-87; program dir. So. African Devel. Documentation and Info. Exch., 1979-83; acting Am. dir. U.S./S. Africa Leader Exch. program, 1987-88; dir. Congl. African program Internat. Ctr. for Dynamics of Devel., 1989-90; lectr., cons. to acad. instns. on Africana collections and U.S. fgn. policy toward Africa; N.Am. liaison Orgn. African Unity/UN; mem. Econ. Commn. on Africa's Pan African Devel. Info. System, 1979-82. Bd. dirs. U.S.-South Africa Leader Exch. Program, 1980-90, chmn. exec. com., 1985-87; bd. dirs. Internat. Ctr. for Dynamics Devel., 1985—; dir. ICDD Congressional Africa Program, 1989-90; pres. Internat. Ctr. for Devel. Initiatives, 1991—. With AUS, 1950-53. Mem. ALA, African Studies Assn. (publs. com. 1974), African Heritage Studies Assn. (assoc.; award for outstanding contbn. to Africa 1975), Internat. Inst. Edn. (South African program bd. 1983—). Author: Soviet View of Africa, 1957; A Current Bibliography on Ethiopian Affairs, 1967, 72; editor-in-chief A Current Bibliography on African Affairs, 1963-84, editor emeritus, 1984—; editor: African affairs for General Reader, 1967; Current Themes in African Historical Studies, 1970; editorial bd. African Books in Print, Ife, Nigeria. Home: 9713 Brixton Ln Bethesda MD 20817-1601

MATTHEWS, DANIEL HOBSON, software engineer; b. Salisbury, Md., Dec. 15, 1961; s. Daniel Ernest and Dorothy Maye (Hobson) M.; m. Carolyn Jean Ciborowski, Nov. 12, 1988. BS in Computer Sci., U. Md., 1983. Systems engr. Arbitron Ratings Co., Laurel, Md., 1982-85; software engr. Aeronautical Radio, Inc., Annapolis, Md., 1985-91, mgr. air/ground systems, 1991—. Mem. Holy Trinity Ch. Parish Coun., Glen Burnie, Md., 1990—, chairperson, 1991—; mem. Govs. Youth Adv. Coun., Balt., 1979-84, pres., 1982-83; chairperson Residence Halls Assn., College Park, Md., 1980-82. Named Outstanding Young Man of Am., Jaycees, 1982, 83; Disting. scholar Md. State Scholarship Bd., 1979. Mem. IEEE Computer Soc., Assn. Computing Machinery, USENIX Assn. Home: 706 Carolyn Rd Glen Burnie MD 21061-4510 Office: Aeronautical Radio Inc 2551 Riva Rd Annapolis MD 21401-7435

MATTHEWS, DEBORAH GAIL, non-profit organization executive; b. Detroit, Mar. 22, 1956; d. Leonard Charles and Betty Ruth (Zarder) Matthews; m. Scott Shepard, May 9, 1987; 1 child, Aliana Matthews Shepard. BS, Ga. State U., 1980, postgrad., 1981. Assignment editor Cable News Network, Atlanta, 1980, WXIA-TV, Atlanta, 1980-81, WSB-TV, Atlanta, 1981-86; reporter Atlanta Jour. Constn., 1986-87; press sec. U.S. Rep. Michael Andrews, Washington, 1987-89, U.S. Sen. Wyche Flowler Jr., Washington, 1989-91; dir. communications U.S. Senate Spl. Com. on Aging, Washington, 1991; dep. dir. Sunbelt Inst., Washington, 1991—; cons. Nat. Commn. on Children, Washington, 1991, So. Legis. Conf., Atlanta, 1991. Foster parent Fairfax County, Va., 1987—. Home: 7904 Candlewood Dr Alexandria VA 22306-3218 Office: The Sunbelt Inst 600 Maryland Ave Ste 255 409 Third St S W Ste 202 Washington DC 20024

MATTHEWS, HARRIETT, sculptor, educator; b. Kansas City, Mo., June 21, 1940. BFA, U. Ga., 1962, MFA, 1964. Instr. art U. Okla., Norman, 1964-65; instr. art, asst. prof., assoc. prof., prof. Colby Coll., Waterville, Maine, 1966—; art panel mem. Maine Arts Commn., Augusta, Maine, 1978-83, commn. mem., 1980-83. One person shows at Frick Gallery, Belfast, Maine, 1991, Colby Coll. Art Mus., 1992; exhibited in group shows at Portland Mus. Art, 1990. Mem. Coll. Art Assn. Office: Colby Coll Art Dept Waterville ME 04927

MATTHEWS, JACK, psychologist, speech pathologist, educator; b. Winnipeg, Man., Can., June 17, 1917; s. Samuel and Ellen (Walker) M.; m. Hannah Miriam Polster, Aug. 16, 1942; children: Rachel Sophia, Rebecca. A.B., Heidelberg Coll., 1938, D.Sc., 1976; M.A., Ohio U., 1940; Ph.D., Ohio State U., 1946; student, Vanderbilt U., 1942-43. Asst. dir. speech clinic Purdue U., 1946-48; dir. speech clinic, asst. prof. psychology and speech U. Pitts., 1948-55, dir. speech clinic, dir. div. psychol. services, asso. prof. psychology, 1950-55, prof., chmn. speech dept., 1955—, dean humanities, 1967-68, pres. univ. senate, 1969—; Bd. dirs. Community Hearing Council, Pitts. Hearing Soc.; pres. Am. Bd. Examiners Speech Pathology and Audiology, 1966-67; sec. Speech and Hearing Found., 1964-68; mem. Edn. Commn. States, Nat. Adv. Com. on Handicapped Children; v.p. bd. trustees Western Pa. Sch. for Deaf., 1982—, City Theatre. Asst. editor: Jour. Speech and Hearing Disorders, 1952-54; editorial bd., 1965-69, Speech Monographs, 1951-53, 56-65, Jour. Communications, 1961-64, Deafness, Speech and Hearing pubs.; cons. editor: Today's Speech, 1968- 70, ERIC, 1975—; Contbr. articles to profl. jours. Served as sgt. AC Psychol. Research Unit USAAF, 1942-45. Mem. Am. Speech and Hearing Assn. (pres. 1963-64, asso. editor jours. 1959-62), Am. Assn. Cleft Palate Rehab. (pres. 1957-59), Am. Psychol. Assn., Speech Assn. (mem. adminstrv. council; mem. research bd. 1966-69, chmn. 1967-69), Am. Assn. Mental Deficiency, AAAS, Soc. Psychol. Study Social Issues, Pa. Speech Assn. (pres. 1959-60), Assn. for Communication Adminstrn. (exec. com. 1978-81), AAUP, Sigma Xi, Pi Kappa Delta, Alpha Psi Omega, Tau Kappa Alpha, Sigma Alpha Eta. Home: 825 Old Mill Rd Pittsburgh PA 15238-1711

MATTHEWS, LAWRENCE MILLBOURNE, management consultant; b. Phila., Mar. 5, 1920; s. Lawrence Millbourne and Barbara H. (Moritz) M.; m. Anna Catherine Heck, Apr. 3, 1948; children—Lawrence M., Mark M., Barbara G., James D., Ann E. B.S. in Econs., U. Pa., 1941. Cert. mgmt. cons. Engr., Bendix Corp., Phila., 1941-42; ptnr. mgmt. cons. firm, N.Y.C., 1946-72; prin. Lawrence M. Matthews, mgmt. cons., Phila., 1972—; condr. mgmt. seminars various univs. and bus. groups. Author: Practical Operating Budgeting, 1977; Estimating Manufacturing Costs, 1982. Served to lt. USNR, 1943-46. Mem. Inst. Mgmt. Engrs. (sr.), Inst. Indsl. Engrs. (sr.), Nat. Assn. Accts. (sr.). Republican. Roman Catholic.

MATTHEWS, PAUL CHANDLER, lawyer; b. N.Y.C., May 21, 1926; s. Paul Chandler, Sr. and Mary Louise (Blackman) M.; m. Vera Suzanne Cerstvik, June 18, 1966; children: Paul Chandler III, Barbara Lee Matthews Anderson, Mary Elizabeth Matthews Rhatigan, Timothy J.; stepchildren: Laura Susan Masom Norton, Diana Claire Masom Skerritt, Richard Jeffrey Masom, Stephen Raymond Masom, Andrea Louise Masom. BA, Yale U., 1946; LLB, Columbia U. Law Sch., 1949. Bar: N.Y. 1950, U.S. Dist. Ct. (so. dist.) N.Y. 1951, U.S. Ct. Appeals (2nd cir.) 1952, U.S. Dist. Ct. (ea. dist.) N.Y. 1960, U.S. Dist. Ct. (we. dist.) Tenn. 1968, U.S. Supreme Ct. 1980, U.S. Ct. Appeals (4th cir.) 1983. Law clk. Paul C. Matthews, N.Y., 1949-50, assoc., 1951-68, pvt. practice, 1968—. Justice Village of Nissequogue, L.I., N.Y., 1971-88. Lt. j.g. USNR, 1943-46. Mem. Assn. Trial Lawyers Am., N.Y. State Trial Lawyers Assn., N.Y. County Lawyers Assn., Suffolk County Bar Assn., Maritime Law Assn. of U.S. Home: 39 Thomas Ln New York NY 11733 Office: 107 Washington St New York NY 10006-1815

MATTHEWS, THOMAS EDWARD, college administrator; b. Ogdensburg, N.Y., Jan. 9, 1943; s. Homer Ira and Irene (Fisher) M.; m. Elizabeth Fraser, July 2, 1966; children: Jeffrey Thomas, David Fraser. BS in Edn., SUNY, Plattsburg, 1964, SUNY, Albany, 1965; EdD, U. S.C., 1983. Resident hall dir. SUNY, Brockport, 1965-67; coord. coll. activities SUNY, Geneseo, 1967—; contract negotiations cons. to various colls., 1970—; guest faculty mem. regional and nat. convs. and workshops Nat. Assn. for Campus Activities, 1968—. Contbr. articles to profl. publs. Organizer Geneseo Summerfestival Com., 1980-87; deacon, elder Cen. Presbyn. Ch., Geneseo. Mem. Nat. Assn. Campus Activities (chair bd. dirs. 1975-77, vol./leader, Patsy Morley Outstanding Programmer award 1987, Performing Arts Achievement award 1990, Found. award 1979), Nat. Assn. Student Press Adminstrs., Assn. Coll. Unions Internat., N.Y. State Unified Tchrs. (bd. dirs. 1984—), Assn. Performing Arts Adminstr., SUNY Coll. Union and Campus Activities Professions (pres. 1987-92, leader), United Professions (treas. 1981-88, state exec. bd., 1981—, v.p. for profls. 1992—, pres. SUNY Geneseo chpt. 1987—). Home: 3369 Elm Rd Geneseo NY 14454-9701 Office: SUNY Geneseo MacVittie Union Geneseo NY 14454

MATTHIAS, GEORGE FRANK, educator; b. Greenport, N.Y., Aug. 22, 1934; s. George and Marguerite (Blanchard) M.; B.S., State U. N.Y. at Cortland, 1957; M.S., Syracuse U., 1962; M.A., Conn. Wesleyan U., 1970; m. Mary Jo Avery, Aug. 18, 1956; children: Todd Avery, Tara Lynn. Tchr. secondary earth sci. Belleville (N.Y.) Acad., 1957-58, Croton-Harmon High Sch., Croton-on-Hudson, N.Y., 1961-89; tchr./prin. Raquette Lake (N.Y.) Elementary Sch., 1958-61; mem. N.Y. State Earth Sci. Syllabus Revision Writing Commn., 1967-70, 89-91; coord. Bur. of Sci. Edn., N.Y. State Dept. Edn., 1971-72; instr. Finger Lakes Inst., Alfred U., 1970; guest staff Coll. of St. Rose, summers 1984-85, 88-90; freelance cons. earth science edn.; item writer Nat. Testing Service, Nat. Assessment for Ednl. Progress, 1984; cons. pub. schs. NSF grantee, 1963, 67-70; Shell merit fellow, 1971. Mem. Nat. Assn. Geology Tchrs., Nat. Assn. Research in Sci. Teaching, Sci. Tchrs. Assn. N.Y. State, N.Y. State United Tchrs., Am. Fedn. Tchrs. Author: (with Berey, Higham, Knabel, Maust) Observation and Interpretation in Earth Science, 1972; (with Daley and Higham) Earth Science: A Study of a Changing Planet, 1986; (with Deacon) Plate Tectonics, 1980; developer (with Snyder) Individualized Earth Science Program, 1975-89; (with Snyderetal) Prentice-Hall General Science Series, 1986; also articles. Home and Office: 143 Dutch St Montrose NY 10548-1505

MATTINGLY, ROBERT MARTIN, educator; b. Dayton, Ohio, July 19, 1939; s. Walter Fredrick and Gladys Louise (Martin) M.; m. Ortrun Imgard Saeman, June 2, 1979; children: Mark Martin, Max Martin. BA, U. Dayton, 1973; MA, Columbia U., 1975; EdS, U. Ga., 1989. Dir. radio and TV sta. Don Kemper Co., Dayton, 1963-69; tchr. DODDS, Fulda, Fed. Republic Germany, 1976—; adj. faculty City Colls. Chgo., U. Md. Sgt. USMC, 1957-63. Recipient Excellence in Geography Teaching award Rand McNally Co., 1990, DODDS-Wuerzburg Dist. Tchr. of the Yr. award 1991-92. Mem. ASCD (European dir. coop. learning network and clearinghouse), Am. Polit Sci. Assn., Nat. Coun. for Social Studies, Nat. Coun. for Geog. Edn. (Disting. Teaching Achievement award 1990). Office: Fulda Am High Sch CMR 453 Box 177 APO AE 09146

MATTIOLI, JOSEPH REGINALD, JR., raceway executive, former dentist; b. Old Forge, Pa., Apr. 14, 1925; s. Joseph Reginald Sr. and Mary Elizabeth (Marzzacco) M.; m. Rose Carmella Nocito, July 19, 1927; children: Marilouise, Joseph R. III, Michele Rose. Student, Temple U., 1946-48, DDS, 1952. Pvt. practice dentistry Phila., 1952-62; chief exec. officer, chmn., pres. Mattco, Inc., Bartonsville, Pa., 1962-87, Penn Pocono, Inc., Canadensis, Pa., 1966-87; v.p., dir. Pocono Internat. Raceway, Inc., Long Pond, Pa., 1962-70, chief exec. officer, chmn., 1970—. Bd. dirs. Phila. Council Boy Scouts Am., 1975-87; pres. Auto Racing Frat. Found. Am., Pocono, 1982-87. Served with USN, 1943-46, PTO. Republican. Roman Catholic. Clubs: Downtown (Phila.). Lodge: Lions. Home and Office: Pocono Raceway Long Pond Rd Long Pond PA 18334

MATTISON, DONALD ROGER, dean, physician, military officer; b. Mpls., Apr. 28, 1944; s. Milford Zachary and Elizabeth Ruth (Davey) M.; m. Margaret Rose Libby, Jan. 28, 1967; children: Jon, Amy. BA cum laude in Chemistry and Math., Augsburg Coll., Mpls., 1966; MS in Chemistry, MIT, 1968; MD, Columbia U., 1973. Resident in ob-gyn Presbyn. Hosp., N.Y.C., 1973-75, 77-78; commd. rsch. assoc. USPHS, 1975, advanced through grades to comdr., 1984; rsch. assoc. Nat. Inst. Child Health and Human Devel., NIH, Bethesda, Md., 1975-77, med. officer then chief pregnancy rsch. br., 1978-84; assoc. prof. ob-gyn. U. Ark., Little Rock, 1984-87; prof. U. Pitts., 1987-90, assoc. prof. toxicology, 1984-88, prof., 1988-90, dean Grad. Sch. Pub. Health, prof., 1990—; mem. Bd. Environ. Studies and Toxicology, NRC, NAS, 1988—; mem. sci. adv. bd. Hawaii Heptachlor Edn. and Rsch. Found., 1987—; mem. sci. adv. panel Semicondr. Industry Assn., 1987—; mem. portfolio team United Way Allegheny County and Western Pa., 1990—; mem. pre-screening com. Magee-Women's Hosp., Pitts., 1990—; mem. steering com. Pa. Dept. Health, Harrisburg, 1990—; mem. com. Inst. Medicine, NAS, 1989-91; cons. Women's Vietnam Health Study Protocol Devel., New England Rsch. Inst., 1986-90. Mem. editorial bd. Pediatric Pharmacology, 1980-87, Reproductive Toxicology, 1987—, Devel.

Pharmacology and Therapeutics, Switzerland, 1987—, Reproductive Scis., The Info. Netork, 1989—, Methods in Toxicology, 1989—; guest editor Jour. Symposium on Reproductive Toxicology, Am. Jour. Indsl. Medicine, 1983; contbr. numerous articles, abstracts, letters and editorials to profl. publs. Recipient Am. Chem. Soc. medal Minn. sect. Am. Chem. Soc., 1966, Assn. Am. Publs. award, 1983. Mem. APHA, Soc. Risk Analysis (editorial bd. jour. 1988—), Pitts. chpt. Soc. Risk Analysis, Am. Assn. Cancer Rsch., N.Y. Acad. Sci., Am. Coll. Toxicology, Am. Fertility Soc., Soc. Gynecologic Investigation, Soc. Toxicology. Office: U Pitts Grad Sch Pub Health 130 DeSoto St Pittsburgh PA 15261

MATTONE, JOSEPH MICHAEL, real estate developer; b. Bklyn., Sept. 15, 1931; s. Vincent James and Julia (D'Amato) M.; m. Irene Marie Ficarra, July 14, 1956 (dec. 1989); children: Julia, Irene, Carl, Joseph Jr., Francesca, Teresa, Michael; m. Mary Ann Pessolano, May 18, 1991. BA, St. John's U., N.Y., 1952, LLB, 1955. Bar: N.Y. 1956, U.S. Dist. Ct. (ea., so. dists.) N.Y. 1957. Pvt. practice law Bklyn., 1955-76; real estate developer Mannix and Mattone, Flushing, N.Y., 1963—; sr. ptnr. Mattone, Mattone, Mattone, Megna & Todd, Flushing, 1976—; reps. Citibank N.A., Dime Savs. Bank, Williamsburgh Savs. Bank; counsel Marine Midland. Fund raiser Jackson St. Settlement Assn., C.Y.O., Cerebral Palsy, Muscular Dystrophy, St. Vincent's Home, Am. Cancer Soc., Booth Meml. Hosp.; trustee, Anthropology Mus. People of N.Y.; candidate Supreme Ct. N.Y. 1968; active in gubernatorial campaigns 1974, 78-82; active in mayoral campaigns, 1989; mem. St. Anastasia parish coun., 1977-78; pres. Queens County chpt. Cerebral Palsy, 1989, Queens United Cerebral Palsey, 1990; mem. coun., bd. dirs., sch. law, fund raiser St. John's Univ.; gen. co-chmn. Futures in Edn. Diocese of Bklyn., 1991; gen. chmn. St. John's U. 35th Ann. Ball, 1992. Named Man of Yr. United Cerebral Palsy, 1981, Italian Charities Am., 1983, Flushing Boys Club, 1983, Cath. Youth Orgn., 1985; recipient Top Hat award Am. Cancer Soc., 1989, Legions of Merit award Pres. of Rep. of Italy. Mem. N.Y. State Bar Assn., Queens Bar Assn., Bklyn. Bar Assn., Columbian Lawyers Assn. Queens County (sec. 1985, v.p. 1986, pres. 1989), Columbia Soc. Real Estate Appraisers, Queens County Builders Assn., Delta Theta Pi, KC, Knights Equestrian Order, Holy Sepulchre Jerusalem, Pride of Judea (bd. dirs.), Knights of Malta, Sons of Italy. Office: Mattone Mattone Mattone Mattone Megna & Todd 15918 Northern Blvd Flushing NY 11358-1655

MATTRELLA, ANNE LAURA, educator; b. Waterbury, Conn., Aug. 30, 1954; d. Jack and Victoria (Tomasiello) M. Student, U. Salamanca (Spain), 1975, U. Dijon (France), 1976; BA, U. Conn., 1976, MA, 1979; PhD, Cath. U., Washington, 1985, cert. in adminstrn. and supervision, 1991. Cert. adminstr./supr. Supr. Project Promesa, Waterbury, 1979; translator Embassy of Ecuador, Washington, 1980-81; editor, transcriber Internat. Monetary Fund, Washington, 1982; press analyst Embassy of Japan, Washington, 1982-85; coord. English as a second lang. dept. Southeastern U., Washington, 1985-88; prof. So. Conn. State U., New Haven, 1988—; fgn. lang. instr. Roberto Clemente Mid. Sch., New Haven, 1988—; lectr. for various convs. including Tchrs. of English to Speakers of Other Langs. Nat. Conv., Miami, Fla., 1987, San Juan, 1987-88, Georgetown U., Washington, 1988. Author: An ESL Approach to Hemingway, 1989; contbr. articles to various jours. Mem. exec. bd. Hispanic Cultural Soc. Mem. AAUP, N.E. MLA, S.E. MLA, Nat. Italian Am. Found., Tchrs. of English to Speakers of Other Langs., Conn. Assn. Adult and Continuing Edn., Columbus Day, Inc. Phi Beta Kappa, Phi Kappa Phi, Kappa Kappa Gamma. Republican. Roman Catholic.

MATTSON, CAROL LOUISE, publishing company administrator; b. Elmira, N.Y., June 25, 1952; d. Lloyd William and Retta (Hartman) Moats; m. Steven H. Mattson, Apr. 4, 1972; children: Amy Jo, Barbara. AS in Math., Corning (N.Y.) Community Coll., 1972; BS in Acctg., Ithaca (N.Y.) Coll., 1984. CPA, Pa. Jr. staff acct. Pennypacker & Zeigler, P.C., Wellsboro, Pa., 1984-87; sr. staff acct. Piaker's Lyons, P.C., Vestal, N.Y., 1987-90; controller Divi Hotels, N.V., Ithaca, 1990; corp. acct. United Health Svcs., Inc., Binghamton, N.Y., 1990-91; budget dir. The Haworth Press, Inc., Binghamton, 1991—. Mem. Pa. Inst. CPAs. Office: The Haworth Press Inc 10 Alice St Binghamton NY 13904

MATTSON, CLARENCE RUSSELL, safety engineer; b. Norwood, Mass., Nov. 3, 1924; s. Clarence R. and Jane P. (Dawson) M.; m. Constance W. Towne, June 7, 1953; children: Jennifer Lynn, Sue Ann. AA in Transp., Northeastern U., 1953, BBA, 1956. Cert. safety profl.; registered profl. engr., Calif. Ins. industry safety engr., 1953-62; mgr. accident prevention Dravo Corp., Pitts., 1962-72; corp. mgr. safety and environ. affairs Perini Corp., Framingham, Mass., 1972-84; dir. safety and tng. The Marr Co., South Boston, Mass., 1984; mng. dir. Long Beach-L.A. rail project Transit Ins. Adminstrs.-L.A. County Transp. Commn., 1984-86; v.p. tech. svcs. Fred S. James & Co., Short Hills, N.J., 1987-89; sr. pres. Athena Assocs. Ltd., Safety Mgmt. Cons., 1990—. Deacon Scituate (Mass.) Congl. Ch. Recipient Disting. Svc. award Nat. Safety Coun., 1988. Mem. Am. Soc. Safety Engrs., Nat. Safety Coun. (past gen. chmn. constrn. exec. com., disting. svc. award 1988), Assn. Gen. Contractors Am. (past chmn. safety and health com., safety engrs. adv. com.), Nat. Constructors Assn., Vets. of Safety, Mass. Safety Coun. (bd. dirs.), Elks. Republican. Home and Office: Ll Abigails Way Sandwich MA 02563

MATTSON, DAVID HAROLD, small business owner, sales trainer, consultant; b. East Hampton, Md., Aug. 24, 1963; s. David H. Jr. and Micheala Ann (House) M.; m. Suzanne Lee Parker, May 20, 1989. BSBA in Corp. Adminstrn., U. Conn., 1986. Sales mgr. TEM Assocs., West Hartford, Conn., 1986-88; nat. sales mgr. Sandler Systems, Stevenson, Md., 1988-91, co-owner, 1991—; cons. United Techs., Atlanta, 1990, Telemecanique, Md., 1990, Tex. Instruments, Md., 1991, Hoskyns, London, 1991. Home: 34 Loveton Cir Sparks Glencoe MD 21152-9202 Office: Sandler Systems 10411 Stevenson Rd Stevenson MD 21153-9998

MATTSON, HAROLD FRAZYER, JR., mathematician; b. Ann Arbor, Mich., Dec. 7, 1930; s. Harold Frazyer and Jane Amelia (Reynolds) M.; m. Jeanette Asare, Oct. 2, 1966; children: David Frazyer, Jennifer Elizabeth. AB, Oberlin Coll., 1951; PhD, MIT, 1955; D. (hon.), U. Paul Sabatier, Toulouse, France, 1992. Mathematician Air Force Cambridge Rsch. Lab., Bedford, Mass., 1955-60, Sylvania Applied Rsch. Lab., Waltham, Mass., 1960-69; scientist GTE Sylvania, Needham, Mass., 1969-71; cons. Frazyer Rsch. Co., Cambridge, Mass., 1971-73; prof. Syracuse (N.Y.) U., 1971—; mem. staff Ecole Nat. Supérieure des Télécommunications, Paris, Inst. Nat. pour Recherche en Informatique et Automatique, Rocquencourt, France, 1991-92. Contbr. several articles to profl. jours. Founding mem., pres. S.E. Univ. Neighborhood Assn., Syracuse, 1973-75. Mem. Am. Math. Soc., Math. Assn. Am., IEEE.

MATTSON, MARK EDWARD, psychologist, educator; b. N.Y.C., Feb. 27, 1957; s. Edward Dale and Donna Mae Jeanine (Lintelmann) M.; m. Lauren Perdue, Sept. 10, 1983; 1 child, Adrienne Hope Mattson-Perdue. BA in Psychology, SUNY, Stony Brook, 1979, MA in Psychology, 1983, PhD in Experimental Psychology, 1987. Instr. SUNY, Stony Brook, 1983-86; asst. prof. Clarkson U., Potsdam, N.Y., 1986-89, Fordham U., N.Y.C., 1989—. Contbr. articles to profl. jours. and chpts. to books. Named Eagle Scout Boy Scouts Am., 1974. Mem. Am. Psychol. Assn., Ea. Psychol. Assn., Cognitive Sci. Soc., Sigma Xi (assoc.). Office: Fordham U Div Social Scis New York NY 10023

MATTSON, PETER HUMPHREY, geologist; b. Evanston, Ill., Apr. 3, 1932; s. Bernard Gause and Natalie Nelson (Humphrey) M.; m. Leila Ott, June 13, 1954; children: Andrew, Sarah, Julia. BA, Oberlin Coll., 1953; PhD, Princeton U., 1957. Teaching asst. Princeton (N.J.) U., 1953-57; geologist U.S. Geol. Survey, Washington, 1957-59, Ponce, P.R., 1959-64; asst. prof. Queens Coll., CUNY, Flushing, 1964-65, assoc. prof., 1966-72, prof., 1973—; cons. geologist, Flushing, 1965—. Editor: Fifth Caribbean Geol. Conf., 1971, West Indies Island ARCS, 1977; author three geol. maps, 1968-73; contbr. articles to profl. jours. Mem. Am. Geophys. Union, Geol. Soc. Am., Earthquake Engring. Rsch. Inst., N.Y. Acad. Scis., Seismol. Soc. Am. Home: 13 Linden St Great Neck NY 11021-3841 Office: Queens Coll CUNY Dept Geology Flushing NY 11367

MATUNE, FRANK JOSEPH, lawyer; b. Youngstown, Ohio, Jan. 11, 1948; s. Walter John and Eve (Skiljo) M.; m. Doreen Mary Dolan, June 1, 1974; children: Molly Catherine, John Walter, Kelly Dolan. BA, Ill. Benedictine Coll., 1970; JD, Thomas M. Cooley Law Sch., Lansing, Mich., 1979; LLM, Georgetown U., 1980. Bar: Pa. 1979, U.S. Dist. Ct. (western dist.) Pa. 1982, U.S. Tax Ct. 1980. Tax clk. Bd. Tax Appeals State Mich. Dept. Revenue, Lansing, 1978-79; ptnr. Routman, Moore, Goldstone & Valentino, Sharon, Pa., 1981—. Author: Pennsylvania Tax Service, 1987, Federal Tax Service, 1988. Mem. ABA, Pa. Bar Assn., Mercer County Bar Assn. (treas. 1983-86). Republican. Roman Catholic. Home: 798 Lillian Dr Hermitage PA 16148-1571 Office: Routman Moore Goldstone & Valentino 194 E State St Sharon PA 16146-1701

MATUS, WAYNE CHARLES, lawyer; b. N.Y.C., Mar. 10, 1950; s. Eli and Alma (Platt) M.; m. Marsha Rothblum, Jan. 16, 1982; 1 child, Marshall Scott. BA, Johns Hopkins U., 1972; JD, NYU, 1975. Law clk. Superior Ct. D.C., 1975-76; assoc. Marshall, Bratter, Greene, Allison and Tucker, N.Y.C., 1976-79; assoc. Christy & Viener, N.Y.C., 1979-83, ptnr., 1984—; faculty ABA-Am. Law Inst., 1988. Mem. Assn. Bar City of N.Y. (com. on computer law 1985-88, chmn. com. on state cts., subcom. on motion practice 1982-84), N.Y. State Bar Assn. (comml. and fed. litigation sect., com. on complex civil litigation 1990—), Fed. Bar Council, N.Y. Litigators Club (steering com. 1985—), Johns Hopkins U. Alumni Assn. (bd. dirs. met. N.Y. chpt. 1987—, v.p. 1988—), N.Y. Acad. Scis. Office: Christy & Viener 620 5th Ave New York NY 10020-2402

MATYAS, DIANE CATHERINE, artist, educator; b. Pitts., Nov. 28, 1961; d. Robert Michael and Betty Winsome (Worthen) M. BFA, Cornell U., 1984, MFA, 1989. Asst. prof. Cornell U., Ithaca, N.Y., 1989; program developer Queens (N.Y.) U., 1989; spl. programs instr. Studio in a Sch., Inc., N.Y.C., 1990; artist-in-residence, mus. prog. developer, exhibit designer Staten Island (N.Y.) Children's Mus., 1989—. Exhibited sculpture Desert Pergola, Mesa, Ariz., 1992, Columbus Circle, N.Y.C., 1992, Artist's Space, N.Y.C., 1991, ARC Gallery, Chgo., 1991, Alliance in the Park, Phila., 1987. Rotary scholar, 1979-80; grantee Vt. Studio Sch., 1985, Greater N.Y. ADF grantee Staten Island Zool. Soc., 1988. Home: 1086 Bay St Staten Island NY 10305-4906 Office: SI Childrens Mus 1000 Richmond Terr Staten Island NY 10301

MATYAS, ROBERT MICHAEL, management consultant; b. Hazleton, Pa., Aug. 19, 1926; s. Michael John and Catherine Mary (Mazuroski) M.; m. Betty Winsome Worthen, July 11, 1953; children: Michael L., John R., Carol A., Diane C., Mary E. BArch, Cornell U., 1951. Synchroton engr. lab. nuclear studies Cornell U., Ithaca, N.Y., 1951-54, dir. ops. lab. nuclear studies, 1965-67, exec. officer lab. nuclear studies, 1967-68, asst. v.p., dir. constrn., 1968-74, v.p. ops., 1974-88; supervising engr. nuclear reactor critical facility Westinghouse Corp., Pitts., 1954-62; supr. nuclear core contracts Bettis Lab. div. Westinghouse, Pitts., 1962-65; mgmt. advisor Super Conducting Super Collider, Berkeley, Calif., 1984-85; pvt. practice Facilities for Advanced Tech., 1988—; bd. dirs. Citizens Savs. Bank, FSB, Ithaca, 1975—, Ithaca Gun Co., 1983-86; cons. Superconducting Super Collider, Dallas, 1985—; chmn. investigating panel Collapse of 300' Radio Telescope, Greenbank, W.Va., 1988—. Dir., chmn. Tompkins County Area Devel. Corp., Ithaca, 1974-83. Cpl. USAAC, 1944-46, ETO. Mem. ASME, World Trade Ctrs. Assn. Republican. Roman Catholic. Home: 409 Hanshaw Rd Ithaca NY 14850-2211

MATZ, LEONARD MARVIN, banker; b. Sandusky, Ohio, Dec. 12, 1950; s. Jerome G. and Phyllis (Frankel) M.; m. Carol Sue Ohlemacher, Oct. 14, 1978; children: Emily, Michael, Kevin, Sarah. Student, U. Lancaster, Eng., 1971-72; BA, Case Western Reserve U., 1973. Asst. examiner Fed. Reserve Bank of Cleve., 1973-75, examiner I & II, 1975-78; loan review mgr. Mich. Nat. Bank of Detroit, 1978-79, comml. lender, 1980-82, group v.p. credit adminstrn., 1982-84, sr. v.p. investments, 1984-85; asst. head credit adminstrn. Mich. Nat. Corp., West Bloomfield, 1985-86; exec. v.p. credit policy Equibank, Pitts., 1986-87; exec. v.p. People's Bank of Western Pa., New Castle, 1987—; instr. BAI Grad. Sch. of Banking, 1989-91. Author: Bank Solvency, 1986, Bank Soundness, 1988, Loan Documentation, 1990, Financial Statement Analysis, 1991; contbg. editor Asset Liability Mgmt. newsletter, 1986-90; contbr. numerous articles to trade and consumer mags. Pres. Beth Samuel Jewish Ctr., Ambridge, Pa., 1988-90; vice chmn. Laurence County Israel Bond Com., New Castle, 1991—; treas. Temple Israel, New Castle, 1991—; bd. dirs. Vagabond Repertory Co., New Castle, 1991—, pres. 1992. Mem. Nat. Asset and Liability Mgmt. Assn., Hoyt Inst. Fine Arts. Home: RR 5 Box 635 New Castle PA 16105-9516 Office: People's Bank of Western Pa 27 E Washington St New Castle PA 16101-3899

MATZIORINIS, KENNETH N., economist; b. N.Y.C., May 4, 1954; s. Neocles N. and Penelope (Gregoratos) M.; m. Catherine Marina Astrakianakis, July 27, 1985; children: Anna Maria, Angela, Ellen Rose. BA, McGill U., 1976, MA, 1979, PhD, 1988. Cert. mgmt. cons. Asst. economist Nat. Bank Greece (Can.), Montreal, 1978-81; lectr. econs. McGill U., Montreal, 1977—; prof. econs. John Abbott Coll., Montreal, 1981—; pres. Canbek Econ. Cons., Inc., Montreal, 1983—. Econs. adviser to bd. dirs. Internat. Orgn. Psychophysiology, 1982-89; bd. dirs. Nat. Bank of Greece, Can., 1991—. Author: Introduction to Macro Economics: An Applied Approach, 1988; editor: Vital Graphs of Canadian Economy, 1984; contbr. articles to profl. jours. V.p. Westmount Liberal Riding Assn., Montreal, 1975-77; bd. govs. McGill U., 1978-81; bd. govs. John Abbott Coll., 1988-91; chmn. bd. dirs. Community Service Ctr. St. Louis, Montreal, 1978-80. Mem. Am. Econ. Assn., Am. Hellenic Ednl. and Progressive Assn., Can. Econ. Assn., Que. Inst. Cert. Mgmt. Cons., Nat. Assn. Bus. Economists, Grad. Club Montreal. Greek Orthodox. Home: 615 67th Ave, Laval, Montreal, PQ Canada H7V 3N9

MATZKIN, DONALD ROBERT, architect; b. Phila., Oct. 27, 1940; s. Maurice and Jennie (Goren) M.; m. Arlene Hutton, Oct. 8, 1966; children: Zachary, Aaron. BArch, Cornell U., 1963. Registered architect Pa., N.J., Md. Planner, archtl. intern Murphy Levy Wurman, Phila., 1965-66; archtl. intern Montgomery, Bishop and Arnold, Phila., 1966-67; architect Vincent G. Kline & Assocs., Phila., 1967-70; ptnr. Friday Architects/Planners, Inc., Phila., 1970-87, pres., 1988—; adj. assoc. prof. arch. Drexel U., Phila., 1986—; adj. prof. arch. Temple U., 1974-91; adv. coun. Cornell U. Coll. Arch., 1986-91; vis. critic U. Pa., U. Miami (Fla.), Pa. State U., 1977, 79, 84-86; lectr. in field. Mem. regional svcs. rev. com. United Way, Phila., 1978—; bd. dirs. Community Edn. Ctr., Phila., 1977—, Prints in Progress-Community Arts Program, Phila., 1983—; dir. Relache, Ensemble for Contemporary Arts, Phila., 1985-90. Lt. USNR, 1963-65. Recipient 1991 Urban Design Excellence award Found. for Arch., Phila., 1991, Harry Edling Meml. award Disabled in Action, Phila., 1979. Mem. AIA (Phila. chpt. v.p. 1992—, Design award 1991). Home: 3501 Baring St Philadelphia PA 19104 Office: Friday Architects/Planners 26 S 20th St Philadelphia PA 19103

MATZNER, CHESTER MICHAEL, writer; b. N.Y.C.; s. Sigmund Simon and Rose (Greenberg) M. BS in Physics, L.I. U., 1949; MA in English, Bklyn. Coll., 1954. Tchr. English N.Y.C. Bd. Edn., 1954-59; jr. chemist Nat Synthetic Rubber Co., Louisville; with S. Matzner & Co., N.Y.C. and Mt. Vernon; internat. trade cons. N.Y.C.; fgn. and UN corres. Can. Mil. Jour., Montreal, 1959-79; fgn. corres. The Soldier Illustrated, Manhattan, Kans., 1958-59. Author (plays) Whither Youth?, 1987, Mystic Lady, 1988, The Deceased Embezzler, 1989, Ship Aswirl, 1992, (screenplay) A Warrior's Journey, 1992; producer (documentary films) Margaret Corbin, America's First Heroine, 1989, Caribbeana, 1991, The Pageant of America, 1992; contbr. various mil. jours. County committeeman N.Y. Dem. County Com., 1991. Mem. Am. Fedn. Tchrs., Dramatists Guild, Inc., Authors League of Am., Song Writers Guild of Am., Mus. of Modern Art, Finnish-Am. C. of C. (charter mem.). Office: 521 5th Ave New York NY 10175-0003

MAUCHLY, VIRGINIA ELLEN, college administrator, fund raising consultant; b. Ambler, Pa., Mar. 29, 1954; d. John William and Kathleen (McNulty) M.; m. Guy Lindsey Calcerano, Sept. 21, 1991. BA in Theater, Communications, Temple U., 1976; postgrad. in journalism, communications, Johannes Gutenberg U., Mainz, Fed. Republic Germany, 1979-80; postgrad. ednl. linguistics, U. Pa., 1983-86. Reporter, editorial asst. Sperry Univac, Blue Bell, Pa., 1976-78; editorial asst. Lippincott Pubs., Phila., 1981; editorial asst. U. Pa., Phila., 1982-84, devel. researcher, 1984-86; dir. devel., records, rsch. Franklin & Marshall Coll., Lancaster, Pa., 1987-88; dir. devel., rsch., prospect mgmt. Monmouth Coll., W. Long Branch, N.J., 1988—; devel. cons., 1988—. Democrat. Office: Monmouth Coll West Long Branch NJ 07764

MAUDLIN, ROBERT V., economics and government affairs consultant; b. Washington, June 8, 1927; s. Cecil V. and Eva Jane (Wright) M.; m. Carole M. Jackson, Sept. 3, 1949; children: Lynda C., David V., Tim W.E. Student, MIT, 1945; BS, Am. U., 1951. Ptnr. C.V. & R.V. Maudlin, Washington, 1952-72, owner, 1972—; exec. dir. Joint Govt. Liaison Com., 1973-81; mem. Industry Sector Adv. Com. U.S. Dept. Commerce, Washington, 1975—; sec. Nat. Assn. Scissors and Shears Mfrs., 1970—; mng. dir. Bur. Applied Econs., Washington, 1960—. Contbr. articles to profl. jours. Pres. Forest Hills Citizens Assn., Washington, 1964; chmn. Boy Scouts Am., Washington, 1972. 2nd lt., Corps of Engrs., AUS, 1945-47. Republican. Home: 2906 Ellicott Ter NW Washington DC 20008-1023 Office: CV & RV Maudlin 1511 K St NW Washington DC 20005-1401

MAUL, STEPHEN BAILEY, biotechnology executive; b. Parkersburg, W.Va., Jan. 11, 1942; s. Charles Bailey and Virginia (Stephens) M.; m. Patricia Harbison, June 17, 1967; children: Lydia B., Deborah K., Rachel M. BS in Chemistry, Alilene Christian U., 1963; PhD in Chemistry, U. Tex., 1969. Rsch. assoc. MIT, Cambridge, 1969-70; sr. scientist antibiotic fermentation devel. Eli Lilly & Co., Indpls., 1970-74; mgr. bioengring. Shering Corp., Union, N.J., 1974-76; v.p. Sylvan Spawn Lab., Inc., Kittanning, Pa., 1976-86; pres. Mycorr Tech., Inc., Pitts., 1987—. Patentee in field; contbr. chpts. to books. Rsch. grantee USDA, 1989, 90—. Home: RR 1 Box 282 Worthington PA 16262-9731 Office: Mycorr Tech Inc 440 William Pitt Way Pittsburgh PA 15238-1330

MAULE, JAMES EDWARD, legal educator, lawyer; b. Phila., Nov. 26, 1951; s. Edward Randolph George and Jennie Elisabeth (Zappone) M.; m. Susan Margaret Noonan, June 26, 1982 (div. May 1988); children: Charles Edward, Sarah Margaret; m. Susan K. Garrison, Apr. 7, 1990 (div. 1991). BS cum laude, U. Pa. Wharton Sch., 1973; JD cum laude, Villanova U., 1976; LLM with highest honors, George Washington U., 1979. Bar: Pa. 1976, U.S. Tax Ct. 1986. Atty.-adv. Office of Chief Counsel to IRS, Legis. and Regulations Div., Washington, 1976-78; atty.-adv. judge U.S. Tax Ct., Washington, 1978-80; asst. prof. law Dickinson Sch. Law, 1981-83, lectr. and tax program chmn. continuing legal edn., 1981-83; assoc. prof. Villanova Sch. Law, 1983-86, prof., 1986—; lectr. continuing legal edn. Pa. Bar Inst. Harrisburg, Continuing Legal Edn. Satellite Network, Inc., 1988—; Nat. Merit scholar, 1969-73; lectr. state and local taxes Georgetown U. Law Ctr. Inst., 1992—. Mem. ABA (cons., ex-officio mem. subcom. on state law, S Corp. com., chmn. subcom. on comparison of partnerships, mem. task force on pass-through entities, tax sect., chmn. subcom. manuscripts and unpubl. teaching material, com. teaching tax), Phila. Bar Assn. (lectr. tax sect. state and local tax CLE program 1991), Order of Coif, Beta Alpha Psi. Club: Friars Sr. Soc. (Phila.). Author: Cases and Materials in Federal Income Taxation, 1981, 11th edit., 1991, Materials in Partnership Law and Taxation, 1985, 6th edit., 1991, Materials in Partnership Taxation, 1987, 4th edit. 1991, Materials in Introduction to Taxation, 1987, 2d edit. 1988, Materials in Taxation of Fundamental Wealth Transfers, 1986, 2d edit. 1988, Materials in Tax Consequences of Disposition of Property, 1983, 3d edit., 1985, Materials and Problems in Taxation of Property Disposition I, 1987, 2d edit. 1989, Materials in Tax Planning for Real Estate, 1986, Materials in Estate and Gift Tax, 1983, 3d edit., 1985, Materials in Taxation of Real Estate Transactions, 1986, 2d edit., 1988, 3d edit., 1992, Taxation of Residence Transactions, 1985, S Corporations: State Law & Taxation, 1989, supp. 1989, 90, 91, 92, Materials and Problems in Computer Applications in the Law, 2d edit., 1991, Materials in Tax Policy, 1990, Materials and Problems in Computer Applications in Tax Law, 1991, 2d edit., 1992, (with A Clay) Preparing the 1065 Return, 1992; author Continuing Legal Edn. Publs., 1981-92; contbg. author: Federal Tax Service, Tax Practice Series; contbr. articles to profl. jours. and monographs, chpts. to books; author and developer Computer Assisted Legal Edn. Programs in Taxation; owner, author, editor TaxJEM Inc. (computer assisted tax law instruction); cons. and prin. author ABA Section of Taxation Model S Corporation Income Tax Act and Commentary, 1989; author, editor Report of the Subcommittee on Comparison of S Corporations and Partnerships, 1990, 91; case and comment editor Villanova Law Rev., 1975-76; columnist, mem. editorial adv. bd. S Corps. Jour., 1987-91. Home: 219 Comrie Dr Villanova PA 19085-1402 Office: Villanova U Sch Law Villanova PA 19085

MAULL, GEORGE MARRINER, music director, conductor; b. Phila., Oct. 14, 1947; s. Frederick Dunlap and Helen Norbury (Jordan) M.; m. Marcia Eileen Korn, Aug. 13, 1984. MusB, U. Louisville, 1970, MusM, 1972; postgrad., Julliard Sch. Music, 1976-78. Condr. Louisville Ballet Co., 1971-75; asst. condr. Opera Orch. N.Y., N.Y.C., 1976-78, N.J. Symphony Orch., Newark, 1979-80; music dir., condr. Bloomingdale Chamber Orch., N.Y.C., 1980-83, N.J. Youth Symphony, Summit, 1980—, Philharm. Orch. N.J., Warren, 1987—. Conducting debut Carnegie Hall, N.Y.C., 1989; condr. in Eng., Belgium, The Netherlands, Poland, Romania, Hungary, Germany; featured in WNET mini-documentary Art Effects: Young and Noteworthy, 1988. Mem. Am. Fedn. Musicians, Am. Symphony Orch. League (conducting fellow 1978, Nat. Cert. Merit 1980), Condr's. Guild. Episcopalian. Home: 79 Stone Run Rd Bedminster NJ 07921-1711 Office: Philharm Orch of NJ 67 Mountain Blvd PO Box 4064 Warren NJ 07059

MAUN, MARY ELLEN, communications company analyst; b. N.Y.C., Dec. 18, 1951; d. Emmet Joseph and Mary Alice (McMahon) M. BA, CUNY, 1977, MBA, 1988. Sales rep. N.Y. Telephone Co., N.Y.C., 1970-76, comml. rep., 1977-83, programmer, 1984-86; systems analyst Nynex Svc. Co., N.Y.C., 1987-89, sr. systems analyst, 1990—. Corp. chmn. United Way of Tri-State Area, N.Y.C., 1985; recreation activities vol. Pioneers Am., N.Y.C., 1982—; active Sleepy Hollow Hist. Soc. Recipient Outstanding Community Service award, Calvary Hosp., Bronx, N.Y., 1984. Mem. N.Y. Health and Racquet Club, Road Runners. Democrat. Home: 3 Farrington Ave Tarrytown NY 10591-1302 Office: Nynex Svc Co 1166 Ave of the Americas New York NY 10036-2708

MAUNEY, KEITH JAMES, brokerage house executive; b. Jamaica, N.Y., May 16, 1948; s. Marion Derrill and Ottilie (Hoffmann) M.; m. Virginia Gramm, Sept. 3, 1972 (div. 1987); children: Brian James, Scott Matthew, Alison Lara; m. Gina Giallombardo, May 31, 1987; children: Keith James Jr., Christina Lauren. AB, Princeton U., 1970; MBA, NYU, 1978. Systems coordinator Prudential Ins. Co., Newark, 1971-74; v.p. Smith Barney Harris Upham, N.Y.C., 1974-78; sr. v.p. Petra Capital Corp., N.Y.C., 1978-79; v.p. Goldman, Sachs & Co., N.Y.C., 1979—. With U.S. ANG, 1970-76. Republican. Home: 6 Buchak Cir Princeton Junction NJ 08550-1847 Office: Goldman Sachs & Co 85 Broad St New York NY 10004-2434

MAUNG, MYA, finance educator; b. Kyaiklat, Burma, Jan. 5, 1933; came to U.S., 1954; s. U. Kauk and Day Aye Mayaing; m. Delia Vargas, 1978 (div.); 1 child, Christopher. BA in Econs., U. Rangoon, 1953; MA in Econs., U. Mich., 1957; PhD in Econs., Catholic U., 1961. Dir. rsch. Govt. Burma Asia Found., Burma, 1961-62; assoc. prof. and chmn. econs. dept. Def. Svc. Acad., Maymyo, Burma, 1962-63; asst. prof. econs. Kans. State Tchrs. Coll., Emporia, 1963-64, S.D. State U., Brookings, 1964-66; assoc. prof. fin. Boston Coll. Sch. Mgmt., Chestnut Hill, Mass., 1966-74, full prof. fin., 1975—; rsch. cons. Ctr. Community Econ. Devel., Cambridge, Mass., 1972, Nat. Financiera, S.A., Mex., 1973; rsch. assoc. Fletcher Sch. Law, Medford, Mass., 1969-71, 73, 74. Author: Burma and Pakistan, 1971, The Burma Road to Poverty, 1991. Buddist. Office: Boston Coll Sch Mgmt Fulton Hall Rm 312 Chestnut Hill MA 02167

MAUNSBACH, KAY BENEDICTA, financial analyst, consultant, real estate developer; b. N.Y.C., Apr. 25, 1933; d. Eric and Katherine M. BA, Hunter Coll., 1961; postgrad., NYU, 1961-64. CLU. Jr. fin. analyst Vilas and Hickey, N.Y.C., 1960-62; v.p. investment services Shearson Loeb, Rhoades and Co. Inc., N.Y.C., 1962-73; v.p., dir. corp. communications Manhattan Life Ins. Co., N.Y.C., 1974-80; pres. Atrium Group Ltd., 1979—; gen. ptnr. Prospero Properties, 1982—; gen. ptnr. Prospero Properties II, 1982-89; pres. Atrium Holding Corp., 1982—, Prospero Property II of N.Y., 1985-89, Pegasus Asset Mgmt. Corp., 1985—; v.p. Eaton St. Assn. Fla.,

1986—, Oceanview Owners Inc., 1990—, Shadowood Group, Riverview Assocs. Trustee Art Festival of Continents, Key West, Fla., 1988; commr. Cultural Affairs Soc. of Key West; bd. dirs. Founders Soc. Fellow Fin. Analysts Fedn.; mem. Life Advertisers Assn., Nat. Assn. Bus. Economists, Pub. Relations Council, Am. Council Life Ins., Internat. Assn. Bus. Communicators, Fin. Communications Soc., Pub. Affairs Council, Women's Econ. Roundtable, Life Ins. Council N.Y., N.Y. Soc. Security Analysts, Chartered Life Underwriters, Life Underwriters Assn. N.Y., N.Y. Bd. Realtors, N.Y. Bus. Communicators, World Futurists Soc., N.Y. Soc. Security Analysts.

MAURER, ARTHUR WILLSHIRE, information services executive; b. Rochester, N.Y., July 22, 1940; s. Arthur George and Dorothy Ottilie (Ehrstein) M.; m. Ellen L. Schifferli, Oct. 12, 1963; children: Thomas A., Eric M., Matthew J., Christine M., Jonathan D., Robert A., Peter M. BS in Econs. and Philosophy, Holy Cross Coll., 1962. Mem. staff and ops. Rochester Telephone, 1962-69, dir. info. svcs., 1970-74, dir. engring. and network ops., 1975-81, mktg. dir., 1982-86, dir. info. svcs. planning, 1987—; presenter seminars. Com. chmn. United Way, 1976-86; mem. Greater Rochester Focus, 1987—; mem. exec. com. Data Processing for Disabled People, Rochester, 1988—; pres. United Neighborhood Ctrs. Greater Rochester, 1989—. Mem. IEEE (sr.). Roman Catholic. Office: Rochester Tel 180 S Clinton Ave Rochester NY 14646

MAURER, LUCILLE DARVIN, state treasurer; b. N.Y.C., Nov. 21, 1922; d. Joseph Jay and Evelyn (Levine) Darvin; m. Ely Maurer, Apr. 29, 1945; children: Stephen Bennett, Russell Alexander, Edward Nestor. Student, U. N.C., Greensboro, 1938-40; BA, U. N.C., Chapel Hill, 1942; MA, Yale U., 1945; DH (hon.), Hood Coll., 1984; HLD (hon.), U. Md., 1990. Economist U.S. Tariff Commn., 1942-43; econ. and market research for pvt. firms, 1957-60; cons. Nat. Center for Ednl. Stats., 1969-70; mem. Md. House of Dels., 1969-87, mem. ways and means com., 1971-87, chmn. joint com. on fed. relations, 1983-87; state treas. State of Md., 1987—; mem. intergovtl. adv. coun. U.S. Dept. Edn., 1980-82. Del., Md. Constl. Conv., 1967-68; mem. Montgomery County Bd. Edn., 1960-68; trustee Montgomery Community Coll., 1960-68; vice chmn. nat. planning com., advanced leadership program of seminars on edn. and ednl. policy for state legislators Edn. Commn. of States, 1979-81; mem. exec. com. of edn. com. Nat. Conf. of State Legislatures, 1975-84, chmn., 1978-79, chmn. com. on taxes, trade and econ. devel., 1985-86; mem. adv. com. Servicemems. Opportunity Colls., 1978-82; mem. nat. adv. bd. Inst. for Ednl. Leadership, 1979-81; mem. Nat. Com. on Postsecondary Accreditation, 1974-1979; bd. dirs. Montgomery United Way, 1971-76, 84—; mem. Commn. Higher Edn. of Middle States Assn., 1982-85; mem. Gov.'s Employment and Tng. Coun., 1983—. Recipient Legislator of Yr. award Md. Assn. for Retarded Children, 1972, John Dewey award Montgomery County Fedn. Tchrs., 1972, Hornbook award Montgomery County Edn. Assn., 1972, Legislator of Yr. award Md. Assn. Counties, 1984, Willis award for outstanding service Md. Assn. Bds. Edn., 1984, Louis B. Brandeis Justice in Govt. award Am. Jewish Congress, 1988, Judge Sarah T. Hughes' award for disting. pub. svc. Goucher Coll., 1989, Disting. Pub. Svc. award Md. C. of C., 1989; inductee Md. Women's Hall of Fame, 1990. Mem. LWV (past dir. Montgomery County, past dir. Md.), AAUW (Internat. Women's Yr. award Silver Spring 1975), NOW (Legis. Excellence award 1981), Bus. and Profl. Women's Club (Woman of Yr. 1984), Nat. Assn. State Treas. (v.p. 1989-90, chmn. legis. com. 1989-91, sr. v.p. 1991), Nat. Assn. State Auditors, Comptrs. and Treas. (exec. com. 1988-91, fed./state cash mgmt. reform task force), Women Execs. State Govt. (bd. dirs. 1988-91), Women's Equity Action League, Women's Polit. Caucus, Montgomery County Hist. Soc., Order Women Legislators, Delta Kappa Gamma. Jewish. Office: Goldstein Treasury Bdlg Annapolis MD 21401

MAURICE, ELEANORE INGERSOLL, artist; b. Orange, N.J., Sept. 4, 1901; d. Charles Henry and Eleanore (Bond) Ingersoll; m. Raymond Maurice, Mar. 14; children: Raymond, Gail, Julie. Student, Art Students League, 1922-28. One-woman shows include Nantucket, Martha's Vineyard, Mus. of Bermuda, Boulder, Detroit, So. Va. Art Ctr., Barbizon Pla., Carl Schultz Pk., S.S. Sagasfhord, 1972, Mental Health of N.J., 1985; represented in permanent collections at Montclair Art Mus., Jerswy City Mus., Norfolk Mus., Kansas City Mus. Recipient Audubon Artists Patron's prize, 1975, Nat. Art's Club Bronze medal, SEton Hall Coll. Bronze medal, N.J. Watercolor Soc. Silver medal, 1973, Knickerbocker Artists Bronze medal, A.A.P.L. Gold medal, Bloomfield Art League First prize, 1960, Westfiedl Art Assn. For Their award, 1955, N.J. Watercolor Soc. Nepoc award, 1970.

MAURO, JOSEPH ANTHONY, multi-media producer; b. N.Y.C., Jan. 18, 1951; s. Anthony F. and Rose F. Mauro; m. Janet Karen Diamond, Oct. 2, 1977; children: Sharon, Jillian, Samantha. BS in Psychology, Queens Coll., 1974. Darkroom tech. N.Y.C. Labs., 1974-77; dept. mgr. Photo Labs., Norwalk, Conn., 1977-83; owner TWIN Media, Danbury, Conn., 1983—. Finalist in the Artles, France Photographic Competition, 1974; Bronze award art competition OMNI Mag., 1981; first pl. in A/V Video Publ., Nat. Computer Graphic Competition, 1988. Office: TWIN Media 14 Delmar Dr Brookfield CT 06804

MAURO, RAYMOND VINCENT, cartoonist, illustrator; b. Paterson, N.J., Jan. 27, 1958; s. Rocco and Anne (Favata) M. BA in Visual Communications, Kean Coll., 1976-81. Free-lance comml. artist Clifton, N.J., 1981—; instr., lectr. demonstrator, schs. and assns. in N.J. Cartoons and illustration shown in numerous exhibitions and outdoor shows. Various awards N.J. Art Shows. Mem. Clifton Assn. Artists (bd. dirs.). Democrat. Roman Catholic. Home and Office: Mauro Inc 228 2d St Clifton NJ 07011-2656

MAUSCHBAUGH, ANDREW JOHN, safety engineer; b. Peoria, Ill., Apr. 26, 1963; s. Jack and Beverly (Dudas) M.; m. Melissa Kay Peterson, Apr. 16, 1988. BS, Ea. Ill. U., 1985; MS, Western Ill. U., 1987. Tchr., coach Northwestern High Sch., Sciota, Ill., 1985-86; sr. loss control rep. Florists Mut. Ins. Co., Edwardsville, Ill., 1987—. Named Outstanding Sr., Delta Tau Delta, Charleston, Ill., 1985. Mem. Am. Soc. Safety Engrs., Jaycees. Republican. Lutheran. Home: 657 Worcester St Apt 1603 Southbridge MA 01550-1374 Office: Florists Mut Ins Rt 20 Trolley Crossing Charlton MA 01507

MAUTNER, HENRY GEORGE, chemist; b. Prague, Czechoslovakia, Mar. 30, 1925; came to U.S., 1941, naturalized, 1946; s. Frank Thomas and Maria (Neumann) M.; m. Dorothea Johanna Barkemeyer, Nov. 21, 1967; children—Monica Ann, Matthew Erich, Andrea Christina. B.S., U. Calif. at Los Angeles, 1946; M.S., U. So. Calif., 1950; Ph.D., U. Calif., Berkeley, 1955; M.A. (hon.), Yale U., 1967. Teaching asst. U. Calif., 1951-55; rsch. chemist Productol Co., Santa Fe Springs, Calif., 1950; faculty Yale U., New Haven, 1955-70; prof. dept. pharmacology Yale U., 1967-70, head sect. medicinal chemistry, 1962-70; prof. biochemistry and pharmacology Tufts U. Sch. Medicine, 1970-90, prof. emeritus, 1990—, chmn. depts., 1970-85; vis. scholar Dept. Fine Arts, Harvard U., Cambridge, Mass., 1991—; vis. fellow dept. organic chemistry U. Uppsala, Sweden, 1962; vis. prof. biochemistry Max Planck Inst. Biochemistry, Munich, 1967-68; vis. prof. biochemistry Bio-Ctr., U. Basel, Switzerland, 1985; mem. med. chemistry study sect. NIH, 1968-72, chmn., 1971-72; mem. neurobiology panel NSF, 1977-80; vis. prof. biophys. chemistry U. Bielefeld, Germany, 1987; mem. sci. adv. com. City of Cambridge; sci. chmn. Children's Sch. Sci., Woods Hole, Mass., 1991—; mem. corp. Marine Biol. Lab., Woods Hole. Editorial bd. Jour. Med. Chemistry, 1967-70, 76-81; contbr. articles to profl. jours., chpts. to books. Mem. Am. Chem. Soc., Chem. Soc. (London), Am. Assn. Pharmacology, Am. Assn. Cancer Research, Biophys. Soc., Am. Soc. Biol. Chemists. Home: 183 Ward St Newton MA 02159-1331

MAUZERALL, DAVID CHARLES, research scientist; b. Sanford, Maine, July 22, 1929; s. David James and Jeannette (Morin) M.; m. Miriam I. Jacob, July 31, 1959; children—Denise, Michele. B.S., St. Michael's Coll., 1951; Ph.D. (NSF fellow), U. Chgo., 1954. Mem. faculty Rockefeller U., N.Y.C., 1954-65, 67-69, 69—; prof. biophysics Rockefeller U.; vis. assoc. prof. U. Calif.-San Diego, 1966, now adj. prof. Guggenheim fellow, 1966. Mem. Am. Soc. Biol. Chemists, Biophys. Soc., Am. Chem. Soc. Home: 36 Belden Ave Dobbs Ferry NY 10522-1102 Office: Rockefeller U 1230 York Ave New York NY 10021-6341

MAVROULES, NICHOLAS, congressman; b. Peabody, Mass., Nov. 1, 1929; m. Mary Silva, 1950; children: Debbie, Gail, Brenda. Supr. personnel Sylvania Electronics Corp., 1949-67; ward councillor Peabody, Mass., 1958-61; councillor-at-large Peabody, 1964-65; mayor City of Peabody, 1967-79; mem. 96th-102d Congresses from 6th Mass. dist., 1979—; chmn. armed svc. subcom. on investigations; mem. Nat. Commn. on Drug Free Schs. Recipient David Ben Gurion award State of Israel, James Forrestal award; recognized for efforts to halt nuclear arms race Common Cause. Mem. Mass. Mayor's Assn. Democrat. Greek Orthodox. Lodge: Kiwanis. Office: US Ho of Reps 2334 Rayburn House Office Bldg Washington DC 20515

MAWYER, STAN R., computer company executive; b. Lynchburg, Va., Feb. 1, 1948; s. Alfred R. and Betty A. (Ayers) M.; m. Martha T. Michie, Sept. 9, 1967 (div. Oct. 1975); children: Troy, Kristin; m. Leslie Janet Sheldon, July 21, 1985. BA in Econs., BS in Psychology, Va. Tech., 1970. Sales mgr. C&P Telephone Co., Richmond, Va., 1970-72; staff mgr. C&P Telephone Co., Arlington, Va., 1972-75; dist. mgr. AT&T, Morristown, N.J., 1975-78; regional mgr. AT&T, Silver Spring, Md., 1978-83; v.p. mktg. Uniden Corp., Huntington Beach, Calif., 1984; v.p. sales Communications Group Inc., King of Prussia, Pa., 1985-86; chief oper. officer Maxcom, Waltham, Mass., 1987; mgmt. cons. Digital Equipment Corp., Landover, Md., 1988—. Bd. dirs. Big Bros. Am., N.Y., N.J., 1975-78. Mem. Telecommuting Adv. Coun. Home: 8307 Rising Ridge Way Bethesda MD 20817

MAXCY, EDWARD ELLIS, college dean; b. New Haven, July 2, 1944; s. Ellis Crossman and Margaret (Wise) M. BA, Rollins Coll., Winter Park, Fla., 1966; MS, So. Conn. State U., New Haven, 1973; student, Shakespeare Inst., Stratford, Eng., 1974, 75, 87, U. London, 1992. Tchr. English and drama Hopkins Sch., New Haven, 1967-70; mem. adminstrv. staff Long Wharf Theatre, New Haven, 1970-71; chmn. dept. English, dir. theatre program Internat. Sch., Brussels, Belgium, 1971-77; adminstr., mem. faculty Washington Coll., Chestertown, Md., 1977—, dean students, 1977—, lectr. in English, 1977—, coord. for European admissions, 1992—, pre-law sch. advisor, 1992—. Trustee Rollins Coll., 1990—; bd. dirs. Kent County Arts Coun., Chestertown, Kent County United Way, Chestertown, Kent County Drug/Alcohol Adv. Bd., Chestertown, Kent County Ethics Commn.; mem. Emmanuel Episcopal Ch. Choir, Chestertown, 1989—. Mem. Quinnipiack Club of New Haven, Rollins Coll. Clubs of N.Y. and Washington. Episcopalian. Home: Highcroft Chestertown MD 21620 Office: Washington Coll Chestertown MD 21620

MAXWELL, ANDERS JOHN, brokerage house executive; b. San Francisco, Oct. 3, 1946; s. John L. and Deborah A. Maxwell; m. Alexis S. Collins, June 14, 1975; children: Lauren A., Colin A., Ian W., Erin C. BArch, U. Calif.-Berkeley, 1969; MBA, U. Pa., 1971. Analyst Gen. Electric Co., 1971-73; v.p. Gen. Electric Credit Corp., Stamford, Conn., 1973-83; mng. dir. Dean Witter Reynolds Inc., N.Y.C., 1983-87; v.p. Kidder Peabody & Co., Inc., N.Y.C., 1987-88; prin. L.F. Rothschild & Co., N.Y.C., 1988; v.p. Smith Barney, Harris Upham & Co., Inc., 1989-91, Lazard Frères & Co., N.Y.C., 1991-92; prin. Benedetto, Gartland & Greene, N.Y.C., 1992—. Served to capt. U.S Army, 1971. Office: Benedetto Gartland & Greene Inc 610 Fifth Ave New York NY 10020-2403

MAXWELL, BARBARA SUE, educator, consultant; b. Bklyn., Feb. 22, 1950; d. Vincent and Esther Alice (Hansen) M. BA in Math Edn., Rider Coll., 1972; postgrad., Montclair State U., 1973. Cert. secondary tchr., N.J. Math tchr. Westwood (N.J.) High Sch., 1973-80; programmer Prudential Ins. Co., Roseland, N.J., 1980-81; programmer, analyst Grand Union, Paramus, N.J., 1981-82; project mgr. Info. Sci., Montvale, N.J., 1982-84; cons. Five Techs., Montvale, N.J., 1985-87; cons., project mgr. Info. Sci., Inc., Montvale, N.J., 1987-90; pres. B. Maxwell Assoc., Inc., Westwood, N.J., 1990—; cons. in field, 1984—; guest speaker Info. Sci. Best of Am. Contbr. articles to profl. jours. Trustee Westwood Heritage Soc. Mem. NAFE, Human Resource Systems Profls., N.J. Users of Payroll Pers., Inform. Am. Payroll Assn., Am. Payroll Assn. Republican. Lutheran. Office: PO Box 291 Westwood NJ 07675-0291

MAXWELL, JAMES WEHR, public works administrator; b. Tarrytown, N.Y., Mar. 11, 1950; s. William John and Evelyn Marie (Wehr) M.; m. Elizabeth Moseley Watts, Sept. 30, 1972; 1 child, James Hugh. BS, SUNY, Saratoga Springs, 1990; postgrad., Pace U. Sr. engring. technician Westchester County Pub. Works, White Plains, N.Y., 1973-76, prin. engring. technician, 1977-87; supt. hwys. Town of Mt. Pleasant, Thornwood, N.Y., 1988—, recycling coord., 1989—. Active Thornwood Vol. Fire Dept., 1968—, past chief; commr. Thornwood Fire Dist., 1990—. With U.S. Army, 1970-72. Recipient Ednl. scholarship Westchester County Assn. Mcpl. Pub. Works Adminstrs., 1991. Mem. ASPA, Am. Pub. Works Assn., Inst. Transp. Engrs., Westchester County Assn. Town Supts. Hwys. (pres. 1989-90). Home: 788 Sherman Ave Thornwood NY 10594 Office: Town of Mt Pleasant Columbus Ave Thornwood NY 10594

MAXWELL, ROBERT ALLAN, JR., internist, oncologist, hematologist; b. Leavenworth, Kans., Apr. 2, 1933; s. Robert Allan and Aileen Wyman (Bowers) M.; m. Elsa June Lahr, Aug. 4, 1962; children: Carolyn Lahr, Jennifer Anne, Robert Allan III. BA, Yale U., 1954; MD, U. Louisville, 1958. Diplomate Am. Bd. Internal Medicine, subspecialty med. oncology and hematology. Assoc. physician Abington (Pa.) Meml. Hosp., 1968-82; internship Thomas Jefferson Univ. Hosp., Phila, 1958-59, residency, 1959-62; fellowship in hematology Charlotte Drake Cardeza Found. Thomas Jefferson Univ. Hosp., 1962-63; sr. physician Abington (Pa.) Meml. Hosp., 1982—. Pres. Am. Cancer Soc., Abington br., 1979-81. Capt. USAR, 1963-65. Mem. Montgomery County Med. Soc., St. Andrews Soc. Phila., Huntingdon Valley Country Club. Republican. Episcopalian. Home: 1450 Stocton Rd Meadowbrook PA 19046-1131 Office: Abington Hematology Oncology 1245 Highland Ave Abington PA 19001-3714

MAY, DAVID, university director, consultant, editor; b. Wheeling, W.Va., May 4, 1934; s. Herbert Stanley and Lucille (Bursee) M.; m. Nancy Goodwin Shaw, Feb. 9, 1963; children: Christopher, Andrew, Michael. AB, West Liberty State Coll., 1956; MA, Case Western Res. U., 1958; postgrad., U. Mich., 1958-60, Edinburgh Coll. of Art, Scotland, 1963-64. Designer Toledo Mus. Art, 1961-63; instr. art Bradford (Mass.) Coll., 1964-65; lectr. art, designer U. N.H., Durham, 1965-68; designer Cornell U., Ithaca, N.Y., 1969-71; owner Ithaca Office Communications, 1971-78; dir. publs. Syracuse (N.Y.) U., 1978-87, exec. dir. publs. and printing, 1987—; cons. numerous colls. and univs., 1984—. Editor Syracuse Univ. mag., 1980-85; art dir. Adirondack Life mag., 1976-78; art dir. (books) N.H. Pub. Co., 1968-73; contbr. articles to mags. Mem. Coun. for Advancement and Support of Edn. (chair nat. publs. com. 1985-87), Univ. and Coll. Design Assn., Am. Inst. Graphic Arts. Office: Syracuse U 820 Comstock Ave Syracuse NY 13244-0001

MAY, ERNEST DEWEY, music executive, organist, choirmaster; b. Jersey City, May 8, 1942; s. Ernest Max and Harriet Elizabeth (Dewey) M.; m. Eileen Marie Mayhew, Jan. 29, 1963 (div. 1983); children: Ernest Jr., Beth, Katherine, Caroline, Christopher, Abigail, Deirdre; m. Mary L. Milkey, June 29, 1984. AB, Harvard U., 1964; MFA, Princeton U., 1968, PhD, 1975. Asst. prof. music Amherst (Mass.) Coll., 1969-75; from asst. prof. to prof. music Dept. Music and Dance, U. Mass., Amherst, 1976-88, prof. music, chmn., 1988—; organist, dir. mus. South Congl. Ch., Springfield, Mass., 1983—. Rec.: Music for Trumpet and Organ, 1979; co-editor: J.S. Bach: Neve Ausgabe Samtlicher Werke Vol. 1/20, 1986, J.S. Bach as Organist, 1986; contbr. New Harvard Dictionary of Music, 1986. Mem. Nat. Assn. Schs. Music, Am. Guild Organists, Internat. Music Soc., Am. Musicological Soc. (pres. New Eng. chpt. 1988—). Home: 44 Amherst Rd Amherst MA 01002-9700 Office: U Mass Dept Music and Dance Amherst MA 01003

MAY, GEORGES (CLAUDE), educator, university official; b. Paris, France, Oct. 7, 1920; came to U.S., 1942, naturalized, 1943; s. Lucien and Germaine (Samuel) M.; m. Martha Corkery, Feb. 19, 1949; children: Anne May Berwind, Catherine May Dias. BA, U. Paris, 1937; Licence es Lettres, U. Montpellier, France, 1941; Diplome, d'Etudes Superieures, 1941; PhD, U. Ill., 1947; LHD, U. New Haven, 1990. Asst. U. Ill., 1942-43, 46-47; faculty Yale, 1947—, successively instr., asst. prof., assoc. prof., 1947-56, prof. French, 1956-71; dean Yale Coll., 1963-71, Sterling prof. French, 1971-91, prof. emeritus, 1991—; chmn. dept. French, 1978-79, provost, 1979-81; prof. summers U. Ill., 1946, Middlebury Coll., 1951, 54, U. Minn., 1948, U. Mich., 1952, U. Calif. at Berkeley, 1959; sec. Fourth Internat. Congress Enlightenment, 1975. Author: Tragedie cornélienne, tragedie racinienne, 1948, D'Ovide a Racine, 1949, Quatre Visages de Denis Diderot, 1951, Diderot et La Religieuse, 1954, Rousseau par lui-meme, 1961, Le Dilemme du roman au XVIIIe siecle, 1963, L'Autobiographie, 1979, Les Mille et une nuits d'Antoine Galland, ou le Chef-d'oeuvre invisible, 1986; editor: Corneille's Polyeucte and Le Menteur, 1964, Diderot's Commentary on Hemsterhuis' Lettre sur l'homme, 1964, Diderot's La Religieuse, 1975, Diderot's Sur Terence, 1980; contbr. articles on French lit. to profl. pubs. Trustee Hopkins Grammar Day Prospect Hill Sch., 1970-78; bd. dirs. Am. Council Learned Socs., 1979-89, chmn. bd., 1982-89, chmn. emeritus, 1989—. Served with French Army, 1939-40; Served with AUS, 1943-45. Decorated chevalier French Legion of Honor; Guggenheim Found. fellow, 1950-51, 84-85. Mem. MLA, Am. Acad. Arts and Scis., Am. Philos. Soc., Am. Soc. 18th Century Studies (pres. 1974-75), Internat. Coun. Philosophy and Humanistic Studies (v.p. 1982-84), Am. Assn. Tchrs. French, Union Academique Internationale (bd. dirs. 1983-86, v.p. 1986-89, pres. 1989-92), Assn. des Etudes Francaises, Societe d'Etude du XVIIIe Siecle, Phi Beta Kappa. Home: 177 Everit St New Haven CT 06511-1306

MAY, GITA, French language and literature educator; b. Brussels, Sept. 16, 1929; came to U.S., 1947, naturalized, 1950; d. Albert and Blima (Sieradska) Jochimek; m. Irving May, Dec. 21, 1947. B.A. magna cum laude, Hunter Coll., 1953; M.A., Columbia U., 1954, Ph.D., 1957. Lectr. in French, Hunter Coll., N.Y.C., 1953-56; instr. French, Columbia U., 1956-58, asst. prof., 1958-61, assoc. prof., 1961-68, prof., 1968—, chmn., 1983—, mem. senate, 1979-83, 86-88, chmn. Seminar on 18th Centruy Culture, 1986-89; lecture tour English univs., 1965. Author: Diderot et Baudelaire, critiques d'art, 1957, De Jean-Jacques Rousseau à Madame Roland: essai sur la sensibilité préromantique et révolutionnaire, 1964, Madame Roland and the Age of Revolution, 1970 (Van Amringe Disting. Book award), Stendhal and the Age of Napoleon, 1977; co-editor: Diderot Studies III, 1961; mem. editorial bd. 18th Century Studies, 1975-78, French Rev., 1975-86, Romanic Rev., 1959—; contbg. editor: Oeuvres complètes de Diderot, 1984; contbr. articles and revs. to profl. jours. Decorated chevalier and officer Ordre des Palmes Académiques; recipient award Columbia U. Council for Research in Humanities, 1960, 67, 69, award Am. Council Learned Socs., 1961, award for outstanding achievement Hunter Coll., 1963, Faculty award for Outstanding Teaching Columbia U., 1980; Fulbright research grantee, 1964-65; Guggenheim fellow, 1964-65; NEH, 1971-72. Mem. AAUP, Am. Assn. Tchrs. of French, MLA (del. assembly 1973-75, mem. com. research activities 1975-78, exec. council 1980-83), Am. Soc. 18th Century Studies (pres. 1985-86, 2d v.p. 1983-84, 1st v.p. 1984-85), Société Française d'Etude du Dix-Huitième Siècle, Am. Soc. French Acad. Palms, Phi Beta Kappa. Home: 404 W 116th St New York NY 10027-7202

MAY, HENRY LLOYD, IV, marketing professional; b. Buffalo, Jan. 25, 1941; s. Henry III and Eleanor (Goldsborough) M.; m. Joan Cooley, May 4, 1968; children: Peter, Elizabeth, Alison. BA, SUNY, Buffalo, 1965. Sales exec. Arcata Graphics, N.Y.C., 1971-73, Greater Buffalo Press, N.Y.C., 1973-75; sales exec. World Color Press, Inc., N.Y.C., 1975-82, mgr. comml. sales, 1982-84, v.p. comml. sales, 1984-90, v.p. nat. mktg., 1990—. Mem. Williams Club, Seven Bridges Field Club (pres. 1985). Office: World Color Press Inc 600 3d Ave New York NY 10016

MAY, JAMES, industrial designer; b. Heilbronn, Germany, Feb. 27, 1921; s. Henry and Theka (Saenger-Mai) M.; 1 dau., Vicki Barbara Anderson; came to U.S., 1936, naturalized, 1942. Vice-pres. Perspectives Inc., N.Y.C., 1948-49; dir. Inspire Industrial Design Workshop, N.Y.C., 1950-58; pres. James May Orgn. Inc., N.Y.C., 1959-81; pres. Vienna Workshop Ltd., 1981—, also dir. Exhibited Austrian Inst., N.Y.C., 1982, Mus. Applied Art, Vienna, 1984, Fashion Inst. Technology, N.Y.C., 1984, Williams Coll. Mus. Art, 1985, Mus. Modern Art, N.Y.C., 1986; represented in permanent collections: World Bank, Washington, Library of Congress, Washington, Met. Mus. Art, N.Y.C., Art Inst. Chgo., Research Libraries, N.Y. Public Library, N.Y.C., Germanisches Nat. Mus., Nürnberg ; guest lectr. art and design Kidderminster Coll., Worcester, Eng., Stellenbosch U. Cape of Good Hope Republic South Africa; guest speaker carpet symposium Durban, Republic South Africa, also Frankfurt (Frankfort/Main, Germany) Internat. Trade Fair. Mem. N.Y.C. Mayor's Adv. Council for Interior Furnishings and Design Industry, 1979—. Served to capt., Signal Corps, U.S. Army, 1942-46. Recipient Silver medal of Vienna, 1986. Author: Carpet Printing, 1973; The Vienna Workshop in America, 1982; Vienna Workshop/USA, 1983. Office: Vienna Workshop Ltd 137 E 36th St New York NY 10016-3528

MAY, JOHN FRANKLIN, engineering executive consultant; b. Groton, Mass., Sept. 8, 1929; s. Robert Morse and Virginia Ames (Woods) M.; m. Margaret Gertrude Jackson, Nov. 21, 1961; children: Marsha Jane May Brown, Samuel James, Sandra Phyllis. BSCE, Tufts U., 1952; cert. Bur. Hwy. Traffic, Yale U., 1958. Registered profl. engr., Ill., Pa., N.Y., Conn., R.I., N.H., Calif., Ariz., Mass. Civil engr. Ill. Dept. Hwys., Peoria, 1954-61; dist. traffic engr. Pa. Dept. Hwys., Altoona, 1961-67; field traffic engr. Ill. Dept. Hwys., Springfield, 1967-70; asst. reg. test engr. N.Y. Dept. Transp., Poughkeepsie, N.Y., 1970-77; with Wallace Champagne Assocs., Troy, N.Y., 1977-79; project mgr. Greenman Pedersen Assocs., Sterling, Mass., 1979-81; v.p. Champagne Assocs., 1981-82; pres. Koehrle Traffic Assn., 1982-83; v.p. Green Internat. Affiliates, Medford, Mass., 1984-91; v.p., bd. dirs. Engring. Co., Inc., Boston, 1991—. Bd. dirs. Nashua Valley coun. Boy Scouts Am., chmn. adv. com., 1979-85; mem. Sterling (Mass.) Town Conservation Commn., 1985-87, Town Fin. Com., 1987-89, Town Planning Bd., 1989-91; chmn. standing com. First Ch. of Christ, Lancaster, Mass., 1990—. Lt. comdr. USN, USNR, 1952-61. Recipient Silver Beaver award Boy Scouts Am., 1976, Disting. Eagle award, 1991. Mem. NSPE, Mass. Soc. Profl. Engrs. (pres. chpt. 1989-90, pres. 1990-91), Inst. Transp. Engrs. (life, chpt. pres. 1974-75, dist. chair 1975-76), Masons, Shriners, Chockset Club Sterling (pres. 1985-87). Home: 286 Princeton Rd Sterling MA 01564 Office: Engring Co Inc Ste 600 79 Milk St Boston MA 02109

MAY, JOHN FREDERIC, demographer; b. Elisabethville, Zaire, Mar. 10, 1950; came to U.S., 1987; s. Frederic and Valentine (Van der Vennet) M.; m. Anne Marie Legrand, Oct. 23, 1976; children: Lionel John, Alexandra Anne. BA in Modern History cum laude, U. Louvain, Leuven, Belgium, 1973, diploma in demography cum laude, 1975, MA magna cum laude, 1985; postgrad., U. Paris, 1991—. Assoc. expert in demography UN, Port-au-Prince, Haiti, 1976-79; advisor on demography and population stats. UN, Noumea, New Caledonia, 1979-83; tng. coord. Internat. Union Sci. Study Population, Liege, Belgium, 1985-86; sr. assoc. The Futures Group, Washington, 1987—; vis. scholar Population Reference Bur., Washington, 1991—; cons. UNICEF, Myanmar, 1990—, World Bank, Haiti, Rwanda, 1989—, USAID, Haiti, 1987—, UN Population Fund, Togo, Benin, 1987—; lectr., vis. prof. U. Louvain, 1985—, U. Paris, 1985—, U. Montreal, 1990—, U. Brussels, 1991—. Contbr. articles to profl. jours. Pres. Olivaint Conf. Belgium, Brussels, 1974-75. Andrew W. Mellon Found. vis. scholar, Washington, 1991-92. Mem. Internat. Union Sci. Study Population, Population Assn. Am., Population Reference Bur., Assn. Internat. Démographes Langue Française. Roman Catholic. Home: 10112 Fleming Ave Bethesda MD 20814 Office: Population Reference Bur Ste 520 1875 Connecticut Ave NW Washington DC 20009

MAY, JOHN M., sales and marketing executive, consultant; b. San Diego, Jan. 11, 1948; s. James W. and Ruth I. (Farley) M.; m. Denise L. Blumenthal, June 20, 1971; 1 child, Alicia D. BSME, U.S. Merchant Marine Acad., 1971; MBA, U. New Haven, 1982. Installation and svc. engr. GE, N.Y.C., 1971-72; mgr. Bargain Supply Co., Danielson, Conn., 1972-75; western regional sales mgr. Novenco, Inc., Simsbury, Conn., 1975-78; product mgr. Flakt, Inc., Old Greenwich, Conn., 1978-82; dir. AEC mktg. Pall Corp., Ocala, Fla., 1982-86; owner, mgr. John May Cons., Ocala, 1986-87; mgr. sales and mktg. Gen. Air Div. Zurn Industries, Inc., Erie, Pa., 1987-92; pres. John May Cons., Erie, Pa., 1987—. Editor newsletters, 1984-85, 89—; contbr. articles to profl. jours. Masons, Shriners. Republican. Presbyterian. Home: 5366 Pinehurst Dr Erie PA 16509-3658 Office: John May Cons PO Box 6196 Erie PA 16512-6196

MAY, JOHN M., architect; b. N.Y.C., Jan. 6, 1952; s. Frank Brendan and Margaret (Borza) M. AS, Westchester Community Coll., 1973-75; student, Iona Coll., 1977-78; BArch, Pratt Inst, 1980. Gen. mgr., inventor Top Hat Enterprises/Airamp Ltd., New Rochelle, N.Y., 1973-78; archl. adv., tech. asst. Pratt Inst. Ctr. Community and Environ. Devel., Bklyn., 1978-79; head residential advisor, internat. div. Pratt Inst., Bklyn., 1979-80; resident arch. Tiffany and Co., N.Y.C., 1980-83; arch. Arnold Wile & Assocs., Pleasantville, N.Y., 1984—; tech. dir. Skyhigh Photography, New Rochelle, 1983—; pres. Archs. and Designers Svcs. Unltd., 1987—. Patentee in field. Tech. asst. Vista (Peace Corp.). Mem. U.S. Parachuting Assn., Humane Soc. of U.S., Race Car Club. Republican. Home: PO Box 1380 New Rochelle NY 10802-1380 Office: Arnold Wile and Assocs 34 Marble Ave Pleasantville NY 10570-2992

MAY, JOHN WALTER, chemist; b. London, June 25, 1936; s. Edward May and Eva Susan (Stern) McMaster; m. Maureen Margaret Sexton, July 11, 1964; children: Vivian, Beverly. BA in Chemistry with honors, U. B.C., Vancouver, 1957, MSC, 1960; PhD, Oxford (Eng.) U., 1963. Rsch. assoc. Cornell U., Ithaca, N.Y., 1964-68; rsch. scientist Bartol Rsch. Found., Swarthmore, Pa., 1968-72; rsch. assoc. Eastman Kodak Co., Rochester, N.Y., 1972—. Patentee in field; contbr. articles to profl. jours. Brit. Oxygen Co. fellow, 1960-63; U. B.C. scholar, 1953. Mem. Soc. Photographic Scientists and Engrs. Office: Rsch Labs Eastman Kodak Co Rochester NY 14650-2107

MAY, LEOPOLD, chemistry educator; b. Bklyn., Nov. 26, 1923; s. Louis and Rose H. (Lutz) M.; m. Evelyn Spector, June 29, 1946; children: Kenneth, Ira P. BChemE, CCNY, 1944; MS, Poly. Inst. Bklyn., 1948, PhD, 1951. Instr. chemistry Poly. Inst. Bklyn., 1949-50; rsch. chemist Med. Sch. Columbia U., N.Y.C., 1950-54; lectr. Bklyn. Coll., 1953; rsch. assoc., instr. Psychiat. Inst., Balt., 1954-59; instr. Johns Hopkins U., Balt., 1954-57; asst. to assoc. prof. Cath. U., Washington, 1959-82, prof., 1982—; chemist Lawrence Livermore (Calif.) Nat. Lab., 1987; vis. assoc. prof. Tel-Aviv U., 1972-73; vis. scientist Soreq Nuclear Physics Centre, Yavne, Israel, 1972-73; exch. scientist U.S. and USSR Acads. Sci., Moscow, 1976-78; vis. rsch. prof. Armed Forces Radiobiology Rsch Inst., Bethesda, Md., 1978-82; vis. prof. Hebrew U., Jerusalem, 1984-85. Editor: Spectroscopic Tricks, vols. 1-3, 1967, 71, 74, Introduction to Mössbauer Spectroscopy, 1970; editor-in-chief Applied Spectroscopy Washington, 1961-64. Fulbright sr. lectr., 1980; Navy/Soc. for Engring. Edn. summer faculty rsch. assoc., 1983. Mem. Soc. Applied Spectroscopy (Balt.-Washington sect., Outstanding Mem. award 1972). Office: Cath U Dept Chemistry Washington DC 20064

MAY, RICHARD CAMERON, construction consultant; b. Cornwall, N.Y., Dec. 8, 1939; m. Frances C. May; children: Laurie, John, Jennifer. AAS, Delhi (N.Y.) U., 1959. Field engr., supt. Turner Constrn. Co., N.Y.C., 1959-61; asst. supt./engr. Gilbane Bldg. Co., Providence, R.I., 1961-66; v.p. Aberthaw Constrn. Co., Phila., 1966-76; exec. v.p. Barkan Constrn. Co., Chestnut Hill, Mass., 1976-80; pres., chief operating officer Corcoran Constrn. Corp., East Milton, Mass., 1980-85; pres., chief exec. officer HJP Constrn. Co., Needham, Mass., 1985-87; pres. R.C. May & Assocs., Westwood, Mass., 1987—. Mem. Assn. Builders and Contractors (bd. dirs. 1987-90), Greater Boston Real Estate Bd., Am. Arbitration Assn. Office: 110 Sycamore Dr Westwood MA 02090-3231

MAY, RICHARD WARREN, author, consultant, inventor; b. Marlboro, Mass., Mar. 1, 1944; s. Richard and Lavinia (Crane) M. BS in Psychology, U. Mass., 1968; MA in Humanities and Philosophy, Calif. State U., Dominguez Hills, 1991. Lic. real estate broker. Tchr. Boston Pub. Schs., Boston, 1970-89; pres., founder The Aleph (formerly Promethean Pastimes), Boston, 1975—; adv. bd. mem. and rsch. assoc. Point One Adv. Group, Inc., Madisonville, Ky. Author: (games of strategy) Game of the Gods, 1984, TriHex, 1985; patentee game bd. and pieces TriHex, 1988. Mem. Assn. Advance Ethical Hypnosis, West Orange, N.J., 1974-75, Boston Tchrs. Union, 1984-89, Point One Adv. Group. Fellow Internat. Soc. Philos. Enquiry (asst. historian 1981-82, diplomate); mem. Prometheus Soc. (past first jour. editor, ombudsman 1984—, pres. 1991—), Hoeflin Rsch. Group, The Mega Soc., One-in-Million Soc., Triple Nine Soc. (membership officer 1983-84, regent 1987), Mensa, Cincinnatus Soc., Minerva Soc., Intertel. Office: Point One Adv Group PO Box 1111 Madisonville KY 42431

MAYER, CARL JOSEPH, law educator; b. Boston, Apr. 23, 1959; s. Arno Joseph and Nancy Sue (Grant) M. AB magna cum laude, Princeton U., 1981; JD, U. of Chgo., 1986; LLM, Harvard U., 1988. Bar: N.J. 1986, Mass. 1988, N.Y. 1989, D.C. 1989. Writer for Ralph Nader Washington, 1981-83; law clk. to presiding justice U.S. Dist. Ct., Wilmington, Del., 1986-87; asst. prof. Hofstra Law Sch., Hempstead, N.Y., 1989—; cons. U.S. Senate Com., Washington, 1988-89. Co-author: Public Domain, Private Dominion, 1985; contbr. articles to profl. jours. NYU fellow, 1988-89. Mem. ABA, N.Y. Bar Assn., N.J. Bar Assn., Mass. Bar Assn. Home: 58 Battle Rd Princeton NJ 08540-4902 Office: Hofstra U Sch Law Hempstead NY 11550

MAYER, CHARLES ARTHUR, management consultant; b. Salt Lake City, Oct. 6, 1949; s. Robert C. and Barbara (Arthur) M.; m. Carolyn Familetti, June 21, 1975 (div. June 1989); 1 child, George. BS in Indsl. Mgmt., Purdue U., 1971; MBA, Temple U., 1978. Cert. mgmt. cons. Systems analyst Burroughs Corp., Detroit, 1972-76; cons. Pinkerton Computer Cons., Phila., 1976-79, Coopers & Lybrand, Phila., 1979-82, Deloitte Haskins & Sells, Phila., 1982-85; prin. Mayer Computer Solutions, Merion Station, Pa., 1985—. Pres. Merion Park Civic Assn., Merion Station, Pa., 1979-80. Mem. Inst. Mgmt. Cons. (chpt. pres. 1987-89), Cynwyd Club (treas. 1986—). Office: PO Box 368 Merion Station PA 19066-0368

MAYER, CHARLES JAMES, farmer, Canadian government official; b. Saskatoon, Sask., Can., Apr. 21, 1936; s. Roy Fred and Anna Viola (Anderson) M.; m. Muriel Elaine VanCleave, Dec. 27, 1963; children—Holly Louise, Cheryl Anne, Judith Lenore. B.S. in Agrl. Econs., U. Sask., 1964. Farmer Carberry, Man., Can., 1979—; mem. Can. Ho. of Commons, 1979-87; minister of state Grains and Oilseeds, 1987—, Western Econ. Diversification, 1988—; M.P. for Manitoba riding of Lisgar-Marquette. Progressive Conservative. Presbyterian. Office: Ho of Commons, Parliament Bldgs 175 E Block, Ottawa, ON Canada K1A 0A6

MAYER, HALDANE ROBERT, federal judge, lawyer; b. Buffalo, Feb. 21, 1941; s. Haldane Rupert and Myrtle Kathleen (Gaude) M.; m. Mary Anne McCurdy, Aug. 13, 1966; children: Anne Christian, Rebecca Paige. B.S., U.S. Mil. Acad., 1963; J.D., Coll. William and Mary, 1971. Bar: Va. 1971, U.S. Ct. Appeals (4th cir.) 1972, U.S. Dist. Ct. (ea. dist.) Va. 1972, U.S. Ct. Mil. Appeals, U.S. Army Ct. Mil. Rev. 1973, D.C. 1980, U.S. Supreme Ct. 1977, U.S. Ct. Claims 1984. Law clk. U.S. Ct. Appeals (4th cir.), Richmond, Va., 1971-72; atty. McGuire Woods & Battle, Charlottesville, Va., 1975-77; spl. asst. to chief justice U.S. Supreme Ct., Washington, 1977-80; atty. Baker & McKenzie, Washington, 1980-81; dep., acting spl. counsel U.S. Merit Systems Protection Bd., Washington, 1981-82; judge U.S. Claims Ct., Washington, 1982-87, U.S. Ct. Appeals (Fed. cir.), Washington, 1987—; lectr. U. Va. Sch. Law, 1975-77. Bd. dirs. William and Mary Law Sch. Assn., 1979-85. Served to maj. AUS, 1963-75, lt. col. res. ret. Decorated Bronze Star, two Army Commendation medals, Meritorious Service medal. Mem. West Point Assn. Grads., Army Athletic Assn., West Point Soc. D.C., Omicron Delta Kappa. Republican. Roman Catholic. Office: US Ct Appeals 717 Madison Pl NW Washington DC 20439-0002*

MAYER, JAMES JULIAN, systems analyst; b. Norwalk, Conn., Feb. 2, 1962; s. Paul Edward Jr. and Helen Marie (Hedrick) M.; m. Lisa Ann Hurwitz, May 27, 1990; 1 child, Lauren Elizabeth. Data entry clk. Howe Furniture Corp., Trumbull, Conn., 1980-82, computer operator, 1983-84; programmer Prime Info. Systems, Trumbull, Conn., 1985-86, systems analyst, programmer, 1987-88, programmer supr., 1989-90, sr. systems analyst, 1990-92; info. systems team leader Prime Info. Systems, 1992—. Republican. Episcopalian. Home: 54 Hillcrest Rd Monroe CT 06468 Office: Howe Furniture Corp 12 Cambridge Dr Trumbull CT 06611-0386

MAYER, JAMES WALTER, materials science educator; b. Chgo., Apr. 24, 1930; s. James Leo and Kathleen (Engels) M.; m. Elizabeth Billmire, June 27, 1952; children: James Leo, John William, Frank Charles, Helen Kathleen, William Andrew. BSME, Purdue U., 1952, PhD in Physics, 1960; DSc (hon.), SUNY, Albany, 1988. Tech. staff Hughes Research Lab., Malibu, Calif., 1959-67; prof. Calif. Inst. Tech., Pasadena, 1967-80; master of student houses Calif. Inst. Tech., 1975-80; F. Norwood Bard prof. materials sci. Cornell U., Ithaca, N.Y., 1980-92, Bard prof. emeritus, 1992—; dir. Ctr. for Solid State Sci., Ariz. State U., Tempe, 1992—; scuba instr. Nat. Assn. Underwater Instrs. 1970-80. Author: Backscattering Spectrometry, 1978, Ion Implantation in Semiconductors, 1970, Materials Analysis by Ion Channeling, 1982, Fundamentals of Surface and Thin Film Analysis, 1986, Electronic Materials Science, 1990, Electronic Thin Film Science, 1992; editor: Laser Annealing of Semiconductors, 1982. Served to 1st lt. U.S. Army, 1952-54. Recipient Von Hippel award, Materials Research Soc., Boston, 1981, Silver Medal of U. Catania, Italy, 1986. Fellow Am. Phys. Soc., IEEE; mem. Bohmische Physical Soc., Am. Vacuum Soc., Nat. Acad. Engring. Home: 3355 N Valencia Ln Phoenix AZ 85018 Office: Ariz State U Ctr for Solid State Sci Tempe AZ 85287-1704

MAYER, JEAN, university chancellor; b. Paris, Feb. 19, 1920; s. André and Jeanne Eugenie (Veille) M.; m. Elizabeth Van Huysen, Mar. 16, 1942; children: Andre, Laura, John Paul, Theodore, Pierre. BLitt summa cum laude, U. Paris, 1937, BS magna cum laude, 1938, MS, 1939; PhD in Physiol. Chemistry (Rockefeller Found. fellow), Yale U., 1948; Dr. ès Sc. in Physiology summa cum laude, Sorbonne, 1950; hon. degrees; AM, Harvard U., 1965; MD, J.E. Purkyne Coll. Medicine, Prague, Czechoslovakia, 1968; SD, Wittenberg U., 1975; DSc, Mass. State Coll. at Framingham, 1976; DS, Worcester Poly. Inst., 1977, Ball State U., 1981, Med. Coll. Pa., 1982, U. Medicine and Dentistry N.J., 1983, Tokai U., Tokyo, 1985; D of Pub. Sci. (hon.), Johnson and Wales Coll., 1976; LHD, Northeastern U., 1976, U. Lowell, 1988, Worcester Poly. Inst., 1977, Western New Eng. Coll., 1977, Starr King Sch. for Ministry, 1977, Webster U., 1992; LLD, Curry Coll., 1978; JD, N.E. Sch. Law, 1989; DMus, New Eng. Conservatory, 1990; D honoris causa, Mendeleev Inst. Chem. Tech., Moscow, 1991; DSc (hon.), U. Cape Town, South Africa, 1991; Dr. Pub. Svc. (hon.), U. Health Sci./Chgo. Med. Sch., 1991; DSc, U. Mass., 1992. Fellow Ecole Normale Superieure, Paris, 1939-40, Rockefeller Found. Yale U., New Haven, 1946-48; nutrition officer FAO, UN, 1948-49; from asst. prof. to prof. nutrition Harvard U., 1950-76, lectr. history pub. health, 1961-76; mem. Center for Population Studies, 1968-72, 75-77, co-dir., 1975-76; master Dudley House, 1973-76, hon. master, 1976—; pres. Tufts U., Medford, Mass., 1976-92; chancellor, 1992—; Spl. cons. to Pres. U.S., 1969-70; chmn. White House Conf. on Food, Nutrition and Health, 1969; chmn. nutrition div. White House Conf. on Aging, 1971—; mem. Pres.'s Consumer Adv. Council, 1970-77; mem., vice chmn. President's Commn. on World Food Problems, 1978-80; gen. coordinator U.S. Senate Nat. Nutrition Policy Study, 1974; mem. FAO-WHO Adv. Mission to Ghana, 1959, to Ivory Coast and West Africa, 1960; mem. UNICEF mission to, Nigeria-Biafra, 1969, FAO-WHO Joint Expert Com. on Nutrition, 1961—; mem. protein adv. group UN, 1973-75; dir. Priorities on Child Nutrition UNICEF, 1973-75; bd. dirs. Monsanto Co., 1970-88, Nat. Intergroup, 1980-90, Sta. WGBH, 1976—, Lycée Français N.Y.C., 1984-88, Oppenheimer Fin. Corp., 1987—. Nat. Steel. Adv. bd. Sargent Coll. Boston U., 1955-72; mem. subcom. on med. services U.S. Olympic Com., 1966-70; mem. child health adv. com. Hood Found., 1964-69, chmn., 1968-69; mem. bd. inquiry on hunger in U.S., Citizens' Crusade against Poverty, 1967; chmn. Nat. Council on Hunger and Malnutrition in U.S., 1968-69; mem. food and nutrition bd. Nat. Acad. Scis., 1973-76. Author: Overweight: Causes, Cost, Control, 1968, Human Nutrition, 1972, A Diet for Living, 1975, Food and Nutrition in Health and Disease, 1977, (with J. Goldberg) Diet and Nutrition Guide, 1990; Editor: (with others) Food and Nutrition in Health and Disease, 1972, U.S. Nutrition Policies in the Seventies, 1973, (with W. Aykroyd) Nutrition Terminology, 1973, Health, 1974, World Nutrition: A U.S. View, 1978, Food and Nutrition in a Changing World (with J. Dwyer), 1979, (with J. Goldberg) Dr. Mayer's Diet and Nutrition Guide, 199, 0also numerous sci. articles.; Asso. editor: Nutrition Revs, 1951-54; nutrition editor: Postgrad. Medicine, 1959-71; editorial bd.: Jour. Applied Physiology, 1960-65, Family Health, 1969—, Postgrad. Medicine, 1976-84; cons. editor: Environ. Research, 1967—, Jour. Nutrition Edn, 1968-70, Geriatrics Digest, 1968—; syndicated columnist. Bd. dirs. Action for Boston Community Devel., 1964-70, Am. Kor-Asian Found., 1976-83, French-Am. Found., 1976-83, World Affairs Coun., 1976-86; bd. overseers Shady Hill Sch., Cambridge, Mass., 1965-68; mem. New Eng. Bd. Higher Edn., 1978-92. Decorated Croix de Guerre with two palms, Gold Star and Bronze Star, knight Legion of Honor, Resistance medal, Commdr. de l'Ordre de Merite, Luxembourg, 1989, numerous others; recipient Gold medal City of Paris, 1936, Calvert Smith prize Harvard Alumni Assn., 1961, Alvarenga prize Coll. Physicians Phila., 1968, Atwater prize Agrl. Research Adminstrn., 1971; Presdl. citation AAHPER, 1972; Bradford Washburn prize Boston Mus. Sci., 1975; Golden Door award Internat. Inst., 1975; Poiley Gold medal N.Y. Acad. Sci., 1975; Pub. Edn. award Greater Boston chpt. Am. Heart Assn., 1976; gold medal Franklin Inst., 1978; Lemuel Shattuck medal Mass. Public Health Assn., 1980; numerous lectureships including 1st Charles Francis Adams lectr. Tufts U., 1983, 15th McDougall Meml. lectr. FAO, UN, 1987, Carl Perkins Meml. lectr., D.C., 1989, Lowell lectr. Harvard U., 1989. Fellow Am. Acad. Arts and Scis. (coun. 1970-73), AAAS; fgn. mem. French Acad. Scis., French Acad. Medicine; mem. Am. Inst. Nutrition (coun. 1972-75), Am. Physiol. Soc. (editorial bd. 1960-66), Soc. for Nutrition Edn. (pres. 1974-75), Am. Soc. for Clin. Nutrition, Am. Pub. Health Assn. (chmn. food and nutrition sect. 1972-73), Phi Beta Kappa, Sigma Xi, Beta Beta Beta, Delta Omega. Unitarian (chmn. bd. trustees 1st parish, Sudbury, Mass., moderator 1959-66, vestryman 1970-74, sr. warden King's Chapel, Boston 1974-83). Clubs: Harvard (Boston), Somerset (Boston); Annisquam Yacht (Gloucester, Mass.); University (N.Y.C.). Office: Tufts U Office of Chancellor 755 Atlantic Ave Boston MA 02111

MAYER, JOHN DAVID, psychology educator, researcher; b. N.Y.C., Dec. 6, 1953; s. Arthur Cerf and Edna (Kirschbraun) M. BA, U. Mich., 1975; MA, Case Western Res. U., 1979, PhD, 1982. Writer Sterling Inst., Washington, 1975-77; rsch. assoc. Case Western Res. U., Cleve., 1981-83; asst. prof. SUNY, Purchase, 1985-89, U. N.H., Durham, 1989—; ad-hoc reviewer numerous psychology jours. Contbr. chpts. to books, articles to profl. jours. Recipient Individual Nat. Rsch. Svc. award NIMH, 1983-85, grantee, 1989-91; tng. fellow Pub. Health Svc., 1978-79; postdoctoral scholar Stanford U., 1983-85. Mem. APA, Am. Psychol. Soc. (charter), Ea. Psychol. Assn., Soc. for Personality Assessment, Soc. Exptl. Soc. Psychology. Office: Dept Psychology Conant Hall U NH Durham NH 03824

MAYER, LAWRENCE ARNOLD, economist, editor; b. N.Y.C., Nov. 29, 1918; s. Albert and Emma (Meyer) M.; m. Mary J. Levy, Aug. 28, 1949; children: David J., Elizabeth E. BS in Econs., CCNY, 1940; MA in Econs., NYU, 1951. Staff economist The Conf. Bd., N.Y.C., 1946-52; assoc. editor Fortune, N.Y.C., 1953-69, mem. bd. editors, 1970-76; advisor Fed. Res. Bank N.Y., N.Y.C., 1977; dir. of publs. Joint Coun. Econs. Edn., N.Y.C., 1978-85; editorial and econ. cons. N.Y.C., 1986—. Contbr. chpts. to books. With U.S. Army, 1943-46, ETO. Mem. Am. Econ. Assn., Coun. Fgn. Rels. Home and Office: 65 E 96th St New York NY 10128-0792

MAYER, LEO VERNON, economist; b. Concordia, Kans., Aug. 12, 1936; s. Peter Paul and Georgianna (Martin) M.; m. Elizabeth J. Demarest, Apr. 29, 1979 (div. Apr. 1989); children: Gregory Leo, David Mark, Kelly Lynn, Helen Elizabeth. BS, Kans. State U., 1959, MS, 1961; PhD, Iowa State U., 1967. Rsch. assoc. Iowa State U., Ames, 1962-67, asst. prof., 1967-70, assoc. prof., 1970-72; staff economist Coun. of Econ. Advisors, Washington, 1972-74; sr. specialist Libr. of Congress Congl. Rsch. Svc., Washington, 1974-78; sr. advisor U.S. Trade Rep. Offic, Washington, 1978-79; sr. specialist Libr. of Congress Congressional Rsch. Svc., Washington, 1979-81; assoc. adminstr. Fgn. Agr. Svc. USDA, Washington, 1981-87, dep. asst. sec. Office of Econs., 1987-90; economist Ho. Agr. Com. U.S. Ho. of Reps., Washington, 1990—; negotiator U.S./Can. Trade Agr., Agrl. Sector, 1987. Author: Agricultural Trade, 1979. Fellow Kans. State U. Alumni Assn.; mem. Am. Agr. Econs. Assn., Acad. Polit. Sci. Republican. Home: 5904 Mt Eagle Dr Apt 1216 Alexandria VA 22303-2540

MAYER, RICHARD FREDERICK, neurologist, educator; b. Olean, N.Y., June 2, 1929; s. Frank W. and Rosemond F. (Bush) M.; m. Janet R. Bury, Oct. 10, 1959; children: Kathryn, Andrea, Julianna, Christopher, Randall. BS, St. Bonaventure U., 1950; MD, SUNY, Buffalo, 1954. Diplomate Am. Bd. Psychiatry and Neurology. Fellow in neurology Mayo Clinic, Rochester, Minn., 1955-56; clin. fellow Harvard Med. Sch., Boston, 1956-60, rsch. assoc. in neurology, 1960-66; prof. neurology U. Md., Balt., 1966—; rsch. fellow U. London Nat. Hosp., 1958-59; guest worker NIH, Bethesda, Md., 1975—; mem. Myasthenia Gravis Found., N.Y.C., 198—, Charcot-Marie-Tooth Med. Found., N.Y.C., 1989—. Contbr. rsch. articles to Clin. Neurophysiology, Pathophysiology of the Motor Unit, Studies in Myasthenia Gravis, Pathophysiology of Peripheral Nerve, Treatment in Guillain Barre Syndrome. Lt. USN, 1958-60. Grantee NIH, 1968-75, 85—; recipient cert. of merit Myasthenia Gravis Soc., Md., 1977, VA, Washington, 1982. Fellow Am. Acad. Neurology; mem. Am. Neurol. Assn., Am. Assn. Neuropathologists, Soc. Neurosci. Democrat. Roman Catholic. Office: U Md Med Ctr 22 S Greene St Baltimore MD 21201-1544

MAYER, STEVEN M., accountant; b. Phila., Apr. 15, 1946; s. Max S. and Pearl L. (Levin) M.; m. Miriam Katz, May 10, 1970; children: Jeffrey David, Karen Faye. BS in Acctg., Pa. State U., 1968; M in Taxation, Villanova U., 1985. CPA, Pa. With Max S. Mayer & Co., P C, Bala Cynwyd, Pa., 1968—, now v.p., sec., treas; dir., sec. Davis Advt., Inc., Phila., 1978—. Lodges: Independence, B'nai Brith (pres. 1978-79, 88-89, v.p. 1975-78, treas. 1980—), S.E. Pa. and Del. Coun. B'nai B'rith (treas. 1988-89, 90-91, sec. 1989-90). Office: Max S Mayer & Co 102 10 Presidential Blvd Bala Cynwyd PA 19004

MAYER, SYDNEY L., publisher, historian; b. Chgo., Aug. 2, 1937; s. Sidney L. and Elizabeth Madeleine (Sandorf) M.; m. Charlotte M.W. Bouter, July 10, 1970 (div. Dec. 1988); children: Patrick Michael (dec.). BA, U. Mich., 1962, MA, 1963; student, Yale U., 1963-65, MPhil, 1986. Lectr. in history U. Md., London, Eng., 1966-77; visiting asst. prof. internat. relations U. So. Calif., London, 1969-77; exec. editor History of WWII Purnell Brit. Printing Corp., London, 1968-69; cons. editor History of the Violent Century, Ballantine Books, London, 1969-73; publisher Bison Books, Ltd., London, 1974—; pres. Brompton Books Corp., Greenwich, Conn., 1982—; pres., chief executive officer Twin Books Corp., Greenwich, 1985—; dir. Twin Books (UK) Ltd., London, 1987—. Author: MacArthur, 1971, MacArthur in Japan, 1973; co-editor: The World of Southeast Asia, 1967, The Two World Wars, 1976. Named to Chancellor's Ct. of Benefactors, Oxford U., 1991. Fellow Royal Geog. Soc., Inst. Dirs.; mem. Angell Soc.-U. Mich., Savage Club (London), Yale Club (N.Y.). Republican. Roman Catholic. Home: 643 Bedford Rd Armonk NY 10504-3012 Office: Brompton Books Corp 15 Sherwood Pl Greenwich CT 06830-5606

MAYER, VICTOR, orthopedic surgeon; b. N.Y.C., May 22, 1913. BA with highest honors, Lehigh U., 1934; MD, Jefferson Med. Coll., 1938; postgrad., Columbia Coll., 1946-47, 52. Rotating intern St. Luke's Hosp., Bethlehem, Pa., 1938-39; resident physician Warren Gen. Hosp., 1939-40; asst. resident surgeon Montefiore Hosp., Bronx, N.Y., 1940-41; resident orthopedic surgery Kingsbridge Vet's. Hosp., Bronx, 1946-47, fellow children's orthopedic surgery, 1947-48; asst. surgeon orthopedics Hosp. Spl. Surgery, 1951-82, orthopedic surgeon out-patient dept., 1952-59, assoc. attending orthopedic surgeon, 1970-80, assoc. attending orthopedic surgeon emeritus, 1980-86; surgeon to out patients orthopedics N.Y. Hosp., 1952-58; fellow, orthopedic instr. NYU-Bellevue Med. Ctr., 1953-55; orthopedic cons. children's sect. Inst. Phys. Medicine and Rehab. of NYU-Bellevue Med. Ctr.; asst. surgery Cornell Med. Coll., 1955-56; instr. orthopedic surgery Cornell U. Med. Coll., 1956-58, asst. prof. clin. surgery orthopedic, 1958-60; orthopedic cons. Sullivan County Cerebral Palsy Ctr., 1954, Orange County Cerebral Palsy Treatment Ctr., 1954-60, Richmond County Cerebral Palsy Treatment Ctr., 1954-62, Health Dept. City N.Y. Contbr. articles to profl. jours. With U.S. Army, 1941-46. Recipient Pioneer award Am. Inst. Ultrasound in Medicine, World Fedn. Ultrasound in Medicine and Biology, 1988. Fellow ACS (N.Y. and Bklyn. regional com. on trauma 1965), Am. Acad. Orthopedic Surgeons, N.Y. Acad. Medicine; mem. Am. Inst. Ultrasound in Medicine, N.Y. County Med. Soc., Queens County Med. Soc. (med.-legal com.), Ea. Orthopedic Assn., N.Y. State Soc. Surgeons, N.Y. State Soc. Orthopedic Surgeons, Med. Soc. County Queens (grad. edn. com. 1968-69). Home: 95 Percheron Ln Roslyn Heights NY 11577 Office: 109-20 Queens Blvd Forest Hills NY 11375

MAYER, WOLFGANG ULRICH, marketing and sales executive; b. Munich, Aug. 13, 1937; came to U.S., 1964; s. Ernst Mayer and Baroness Margarete (Von) Mayer-Gaisberg; m. Ursula Augstein, Apr. 5, 1964 (div. June 1976); 1 child, Clementine; m. Isabel Louise Zeoli, Dec. 19, 1981; children: Maxmilian Wolfgang Ludwig, Irmingard Margarete, Louise, Lilo Katharina. Diploma in Bus., P. Ehrlich Inst., Frankfurt, Fed. Republic Germany, 1961; BS in Mgmt. magna cum laude, NYU, 1979, MBA with distinction, 1981; PhD in Bus. Adminstrn., Century U., 1983. Sales corr. Hoechst Chem., Ltd., London and Frankfurt, 1960-63; office mgr. Am. Hoechst Corp., N.Y.C., 1964-69; sr. sales rep. Am. Hoechst Corp., Somerville, N.J., 1970-82; dist. sales mgr. western region Am. Hoechst Corp., L.A., 1983-85; mktg. mgr. Am. Hoechst Corp., Somerville, N.J., 1986-89; nat. accounts mgr. fine chems. Hoechst Celanese Corp., Somerville, N.J., 1989-90; ea. regional mgr. fine chem. Hoechst Celanese Corp., 1990—. Contbr. articles to profl. jours. Mem. alumni fund NYU, 1982—. Mem. Drug Chem. and Allied Trade Assn., Chem. Industry Assn., German Soc. N.Y.C., Internat. Platform Assn., Beta Gamma Sigma. Republican. Clubs: NYU (N.Y.C.); Lake Mohawk Country (Sparta, N.J.). Home: 177 Spring Brook Trail Lake Mohawk Sparta NJ 07871

MAYHALL, DOROTHY ANN, museum director, curator of art; b. Portland, Oreg., May 31, 1925; d. Nelles Harvey and Dorothy (Gray Orton) M. BFA, U. Iowa, 1950, MFA, MA in Art History, 1952; Diplome Doctorat, Ecole Des Beaux-Arts, Paris, 1953. Exec. dir. jr. coun. Mus. Modern Art, N.Y.C., 1961-65; dir. The Aldrich Mus., Ridgefield, Conn., 1965-71, 79-83, Storm King Art Ctr., Mountainville, N.Y., 1971-75, The Nave Mus., Victoria, Tex., 1976-78; dir. of art The Stamford (Conn.) Mus. and Nature Ctr., 1984—. Bd. mem. Stamford (COnn.) Arts Coun., 1984-90, Pub. Art Commn., Stamford, 1986-91; chmn. Mayor's Art Gallery, Stamford, 1986-91; mem. art adv. com. Norwalk Community Coll. 1st lt. WAC, 1952-56. Recipient Fulbright scholar Inst. Internat. Edn., Paris, 1952-53. Office: Stamford Mus 39 Scofieldtown Rd Stamford CT 06903-4096

MAYHEW, ERIC GEORGE, cancer researcher, educator; b. London, Eng., June 22, 1938; came to U.S., 1964; s. George James and Doris Ivy (Tipping) M.; m. Barbara Doe, Sept. 28, 1966 (div. 1976); 1 child, Miles; m. Karen Ann Caruana, Apr. 1, 1978; children: Ian, Andrea. BS, U. London, 1960, MS, 1963, PhD, 1967. Rsch. asst. Chester Beatty Rsch. Inst., London, 1960-64; cancer rsch. scientist Roswell Pk. Meml. Inst., Buffalo, 1964-68, sr. cancer rsch. scientist, 1968-72, assoc. cancer rsch. scientist, 1979—, dep. dir. exptl. pathology, 1988—; assoc. rsch. prof. SUNY, Buffalo, 1979—; ad-hoc mem. NIH study sects., 1982—. Editor jour. Selective Cancer Therapeutics, 1989—; contbr. articles to Jour. Nat. Cancer Inst., Cancer Rsch., other profl. jours. Grantee NIH, Am. Heart Assn., and pvt. industry, 1972—. Mem. Am. Assn. Cancer Rsch., Am. Soc. Cell Biology, N.Y. Acad. Scis. Office: Roswell Park Cancer Inst Elm and Carlton Sts Buffalo NY 14263

MAYHEW, SHANNON JANE, marketing professional; b. Balt., June 30, 1965; d. John Edward and Frances Ann (Messerman) Moore; m. Michael Jeffrey Mayhew, June 18, 1988. BA in English, U. Md., 1987; MA in Publs. Design, U. Balt., 1991. Tech. writer Racal Health & Safety, Inc., Frederick, Md., 1988, promotion asst. I, 1988-89, promotion asst. II, 1989-90; asst. dir. mktg. Stegman & Co., Columbia, Md., 1990-91, mktg. communications mgr., 1991—; writing instr., cons. Nat. Capital Planning Commn., Washington, 1989. Mem. Internat. Assn. Bus. Communicators (award of merit, 1991 winners circle awards 1991), Assn. Acctg. Mktg. Execs., Direct Mktg. Assn. Washington, Affiliated Conf. Practicing Accts. Internat. (mktg. network), Sigma Tau Delta. Home: 5801 Kipling Ct Baltimore MD 21212 Office: Stegman & Co 6851 Oak Hall Ln #300 Columbia MD 21045

MAYMON, GILBERT WILLIAM, telecommunications system engineer; b. Providence, Oct. 12, 1927; s. Howard Barber Maymon and Mabel Ruth (Armstrong) Goff; m. Lois Ruth Brickley, Oct. 11, 1952; children: Howard James, Peter William. AA in Engring., Roger Williams Coll., 1955; BSEE, N.J. Inst. Tech., 1965. With Bell Telephone Labs., Holmdel, N.J., 1955-66; engring. mgr. Graphic Systems div. RCA, Dayton, N.J., 1966-71; project mgr. Automated Bus. System Litton Industries, Pine Brook, N.J., 1971-75; dir. systems integration SWEDA, Internat. Litton Industries, Pine Brook,

1975-79; project mgr. Electronic Assocs., Inc., West Long Branch, N.J., 1979-84; mem. tech. staff Bellcore, Red Bank, N.J., 1984—; Bellcore rep. to Telecommunications Standards Com., 1985-90. Co-author: Software Life-cycle Management, 1984; contbr. papers to profl. confs., articles to tech. publs. Sr. warden, St. Mary's Episcopal Ch., Keyport, N.J., 1975-89, also organist; pres. The Children's Place day care ctr., Keyport, 1987—. With U.S. Army, 1945-46. Mem. IEEE, IEEE Computer Soc., Masons (33 degree), Shriners. Republican. Home: 11 Chestnut Ridge Rd Holmdel NJ 07733-1414 Office: Bellcore 100 Schultz Dr Red Bank NJ 07701-6743

MAYNARD, ANNA MORSE, public health educator, human resources executive; b. Boston, Oct. 24, 1920; d. Charles Warren and Mary Stella (Doherty) Morse; m. Laurence Stratton Maynard, Oct. 11, 1952; children: Margaret, Laurence Jr. BA in Sci., Emmanuel Coll., 1946; MS in Pub. Health, U. N.C., Chapel Hill, 1951. Pub. health educator Suffolk County Dept. Health, Riverhead, N.Y., 1951-53; sr. pub. health educator N.Y. State Dept. Health, Albany, 1967-72; sr. manpower program coord. N.Y. State Dept. Labor, Albany, 1972-81; human resources devel. specialist II N.Y. State Dept. Social Svcs., Albany, 1981—; bd. mem. St. Peters Alcoholism Rehab. Ctr., Albany, 1979-90, Albany Citizens Coun. on Alcoholism; dir. Northeastern Environ. Coun., Albany, 1968-71. Editor: (newletter) Medicaid Update, 1988-89. Bd. mem. Suffolk county Migrant Labor Commn., Riverhead, 1966-67, N.Y. State Migrant Labor Com., 1966-67; mem. thresholds Albany County Jail, 1980-81; fundraiser State AID Assn., Suffolk County, 1966. Recipient Best Community Edn. Project Help Your Environ. award, N.Y. State Joint Legis. Com. on Environ. Mgmt., Albany, 1971, Best Sch. Edn. Project, N.Y. State PTA, Glen Falls, N.Y., 1971; named Woman of Yr. N.Y. State Edn. Dept., Health State, Albany, 1984. Republican. Roman Catholic. Home: 66 Harding St Pittsfield MA 01201-6729 Office: NY State Dept Social Svcs One Commerce Plz Albany NY 12210

MAYNARD, MICHAEL ANTHONY, management consultant; b. North Adams, Mass., Aug. 23, 1953; s. Lloyd Winiford and Rita Anna (Urbano) M.; m. A. Lisa Stockberger, July 21, 1987. BS in Bus. Adminstrn. and Psychology with high honors, North Adams State U., 1975; M in Acctg., Bentley Coll., 1979; postgrad. in bus., Nichols Coll., 1988—. Chief fin. officer Norwood (Mass.) CETA Consortium, 1975-77; systems engr. NCR Corp., Newton, Mass., 1977-79; project mgr., mgr. fin. systems Helix/CTI Tech., Waltham, Mass., 1979-81; pres. Maynard Cons. Services, Stow, Mass., 1981-84, 86—; dir. info. systems ZTEL, Inc., Wilmington, Mass., 1984-85; dir. adminstr., info. systems Encore Computer, Marlboro, Mass., 1985-86; pres. Integrated Mgmt. Resources, 1988—. Columnist Computers and You, 1986-87, Bus. Mag., 1989—. Mem. North Adams Planning Bd., 1975. Mem. Am. Bus. Owners Assn. (bd. adv.), Small Bus. Group, Smaller Bus. Assn. New Eng. (Emerge coun.), N.E. NCA Group (pres. 1985-86), Sales and Mktg. Execs. of Boston, Assn. for Corp. Growth (exec. com.), Speakers U.S.A., Nat. Writers Union, Turnaround Mgmt. Assn., Lexington (Mass.) Golf Club. Home and Office: 119 Adams Dr Stow MA 01775-1085

MAYNE, ALFRED P., JR., sales executive; b. Wilmington, Del., May 25, 1947; s. Alfred Peoples and Alma Mae (McCabe) M.; m. Gretchen Haroy, July 1, 1972; children: Scott Hardy, Elizabeth Grace. Student, Duke U., 1965-67; BA, U. Del., 1970, postgrad., 1970-71. Dist. sales mgr. Nat. Homes Corp., Wilmington, Del., 1971-74; sr. sales exec. Xerox Corp., Wilmington, 1974-79; area sales mgr. Xerox Corp., Lexington, Ky., 1979-80; br. mgr. Xerox Corp., Indpls., 1980-81; dir. sales, mktg. A. Pomerantz and Co., Phila., 1981-83; sr. v.p., gen. mgr. Interspace Inc., Phila., 1983-85; v.p. sales Resource Dynamics Inc., N.Y.C., 1985-87; regional mgr. Am. Seating, Washington, 1987-91; regional sales mgr. Proven Alternative, Wilmington, Del., 1992—. V.p. Brandywine Little League, Wilmington, 1988-91. Mem. Union League Phila., Wilmington Country Club. Republican. Episcopalian. Home: 1518 Turkey Rd Wilmington DE 19803

MAYNE, DAVID RAY, automotive executive; b. Salt Lake City, Aug. 9, 1943; s. John Robert and Willa Mae (Butler) M.; m. Charleen Ruth Wilson, Aug. 5, 1963; children: David Jr., Matthew, Jason, Charée, Jonathan, Mitchell. Student, Brigham Young U., 1961-64, Westminster Coll., 1965-66; BS in Mktg., U. Utah, 1968, MBA, 1969. Instr. in mktg. U. Utah, Salt Lake City, 1968-69; regional field mgr. Lincoln-Mercury, Seattle, 1969-81; v.p., gen. mgr. Seattle Indsl. Controlled Heat, Seattle, 1982-83; regional field mgr. BMW of N.Am., Marina Del Rey, Calif., 1983-84; regional sales mgr. BMW of N.Am., Sterling, Va., 1985-88; nat. logistics planning mgr. BMW of N.Am., Woodcliffe Lake, N.J., 1988; mgr. Eastern region Lexus, Parsippany, N.J., 1988—. LDS. Office: Lexus 205 Jefferson Rd Parsippany NJ 07054

MAYO, GARY ROBERT, insurance broker; b. Concord, N.H., Apr. 7, 1955; s. Robert Edward and Norma Irene (Chateauneuf) M.; m. Cynthia Marie Smart, June 25, 1983; children: Robert, Christine. BA, Dartmouth Coll., Hanover, N.H., 1977. CPCU, CIC, ARM, AIC. Underwriter Chubb & Son, N.Y.C., 1977-78; underwriting supr. NH Ins., Laconia, N.H., 1978-80; account exec. Munsey & Brazil, Laconia, N.H., 1980-82; v.p., treas. A.B. Gile, Inc., Hanover, N.H., 1982—. Campaign chmn. United Way of Upper Valley, Lebanon, N.H., 1989; dir. N.H. Spl. Olympics, Concord, 1988—; reunion chmn. Dartmouth Coll.; panelist Gov.'s Coun. on Volunteerism, Plymouth, 1989. Mem. Profl. Ins. Agts. (named New Eng. Agt. of Yr. 1991), Ind. Ins. Agts., Soc. of CIC, Soc. CPCU. Office: AB Gile Inc PO Box 66 Hanover NH 03755-0066

MAYO, JOHN SULLIVAN, telecommunications company executive; b. Greenville, N.C., Feb. 26, 1930; s. William Louis and Mattie (Harris) M.; m. Lucille Dodgson, Apr. 1957; children: Mark Dodgson, David Thomas, Nancy Ann, Lynn Marie. BS, N.C. State U., 1952, MS, 1953, PhD, 1955. With AT&T Bell Labs., Murray Hill, N.J., 1955—, exec. dir. toll electronic switching div., 1973-75, v.p. electronics tech., 1975-79, sr. v.p. network systems and network svcs., 1979-91, pres., 1991—; mem. N.Y.C. Partnership's High Tech. Com.; adv. bd. Coll. Engring., U. Calif., Berkeley; mem. com. on engring. utilization Am. Assn. Engring. Socs.; bd. dirs. Johnson & Johnson, Poly. U. Corp., Sandia Corp. Contbr. articles to profl. jours.; patentee in field. Named Outstanding Engring. Alumnus N.C. State U., 1977. Fellow IEEE (Alexander Graham Bell award 1978, Simon Ramo medal 1988, C&C prize 1988, Nat. Medal Tech. 1990, IRI medal 1992); mem. Nat. Acad. Engring., Sigma Xi, Phi Kappa Phi. Baptist. Office: AT&T Bell Labs 600 Mountain Ave Murray Hill NJ 07974

MAYO, LOUIS ALLEN, corporation executive; b. Durham, N.C., Nov. 27, 1928; s. Louis Allen and Amy Earl (Overton) M.; student Calif. State Poly. Coll., 1948-50; BA in Criminology, Calif. State Coll., Fresno, 1952; MA in Pub. Adminstrn., Am. U., 1960, PhD in Pub. Adminstrn., 1983; postgrad. U. So. Calif., 1960-62; m. Emma Jean Minshew, Oct. 31, 1953 (div.); children: Louis Allen III, Robert Lawrence, Carolyn Jean; m. 2d, Myrna Ann Smith, Feb. 16, 1980 (div.). Spl. agt. U.S. Secret Svc., Treasury Dept., L.A., 1956-58, 60-63, White House, Washington, 1958-60, 63-66; program mgr. law enforcement Office Law Enforcement Assistance, Justice Dept., 1967-68; acting chief Rsch. Ctr., rsch. program mgr. Nat. Inst. Law Enforcement and Criminal Justice, 1968-74; alternate assoc. mem. Fed. Coun. on Sci. and Tech., White House, 1973-74; dir. tng. and testing div. Nat. Inst. Justice, 1975-87; pres. Murphy, Mayo & Assocs., Alexandria, Va., 1987—; lectr. criminology Armed Forces Inst. Tech., 1954-55; professorial lectr. Am. U., 1974-82. 2d lt. to 1st lt. USAF, 1952-56. Mem. Internat. Assn. Chiefs of Police, Am. Soc. Pub. Adminstrn. (nat. chmn. sect. on criminal justice adminstrn. 1975-76), Am. Probation and Parole Assn., Acad. Criminal Justice Scis., Police Exec. Rsch. Forum, Pi Sigma Alpha. Methodist. Home and Office: 5200 Leeward Ln # 101 Alexandria VA 22310

MAYO, MARTIN, illustrator, entertainer; b. Jersey City, N.J., Feb. 10, 1967; s. Frank and Julie (Caruso) M. BFA, Parsons Sch. Design, 1989. Freelance illustrator The New York Times, 1988, The Boston Globe, 1990, The Nat. Law Jour., 1990, Spin Mag., 1991, The Village Voice, 1990, The Progressive, 1990; freelance Entertainment Weekly, 1992—. Mem. Graphic Artists Guild. Home: 9 Stanford Ave Colonia NJ 07067

MAYO, R. MICHAEL, purchasing executive, publisher; b. Washington, Oct. 14, 1957; s. George William Jr. and Marie Patricia (Brady) M.; m. Nancy Louise Cole, May 3, 1980; children: Emily, Eric. BSBA, Plymouth (N.H.) State Coll., 1979. Ptnr. Mayo & Sons, Meredith, N.H., 1970-79; prodn. contr. Raytheon Co., Waltham, Mass., 1982-84; purchasing mgr. Teradyne Connection Systems, Nashua, N.H., 1984—; owner, pub., columnist NH Events & Activities, Magnet Publs., Bow, 1989—. Mem. East Bear Island Assn., Meredith, 1975—. Capt. U.S. Army, 1979-82. Mem. Nat. Assn. Purchasing Mgmt. (cert.). Republican. Roman Catholic. Home: 21 Timmins Rd Bow NH 03304-4211

MAYOL, ROBERT FRANCIS, pharmaceutical researcher; b. Springfield, Ill., Nov. 11, 1941; s. Alexander Louis and Gertrude Elizabeth (Link) M.; m. Bonnie Jean Meirink, July 26, 1962 (div. July 1981); children: Michele, Matthew, Bryan, Nicole; m. Karen Lee Kastning, Aug. 15, 1985. BA in Chemistry, So. Ill. U., 1964; PhD in Biochemistry, St. Louis U., 1968. Predoctoral fellow St. Louis U., 1964-68; postdoctoral fellow Calif. Inst. Tech., Pasadena, 1968-70; pharm. researcher Bristol-Myers Squibb Co., Evansville, Ind., 1970-87, Wallingford, Conn., 1987—. Contbr. numerous articles to profl. jours.; patentee in field. USPHS fellow, 1964-68, 68-70. Mem. AAAS, Am. Soc. Pharmacology and Exptl. Therapeutics, N.Y. Acad. Sci., Clin. Pharm. Therapeutics, Endocrine Soc., Sigma Xi (pres. Evansville chpt. 1980-85). Home: 56 Green Ln Durham CT 06422-1903 Office: Bristol Myers Squibb Pharm Rsch Inst 5 Research Pky Wallingford CT 06492-1996

MAYO-SMITH, MICHAEL FOX, physician; b. Exeter, N.H., Nov. 20, 1953; s. Richmond and Nancy (Fox) M.; m. Janet Marie Cronin; children: Michael Fox Jr., Leslie Marie. BA in Chemistry, Amherst Coll., 1976; MA, Hahnemann U., 1980; MPH in Epidemiology, Harvard U., 1986. Diplomate Am. Bd. Internal Medicine. Resident in internal medicine Mirium Hosp. Brown U., Providence, 1980-83, chief resident in internal medicine, 1983-84; physician in emergency medicine Carney Hosp., Boston, 1984-85, Cambridge (Mass.) City Hosp., 1985-86, Valley Regional Hosp., Claremont, N.H., 1986-87; physician in internal medicine VA Med. Ctr., Manchester, Mass., 1987—. Contbr. articles to profl. jours. Mem. ACP, Am. Soc. Addiction Medicine, Assn. Med. Edn. and Rsch. in Substance Abuse, Soc. Gen. Internal Medicine, Phi Beta Kappa. Home: 15 Meadowood Dr Franklin NH 03235 Office: VA Med Ctr 718 Smyth Rd Manchester NH 03104

MAZANKOWSKI, DONALD FRANK, Canadian government official; b. Viking, Alta., Can., July 27, 1935; s. Frank and Dora (Lonowski) M.; m. Lorraine Poleschuk, Sept. 6, 1958; children: Gregory, Roger, Donald. Student, pub. schs.; hon. doctorate engring., Tech. U., Nova Scotia. MP Ho. of Commons, 1968—, chmn. com. transp., 1972-74, mem. com. govt. ops., 1976-77, mem. com. trans. and communication, 1977-79; min. of transp., min. responsible for Can. Wheat Bd. Govt. of Can., 1979-80, min. of transp. (re-drafted Nat. Transp. Act), 1984-86, dep. prime min., 1986—, govt. house leader, 1986-88, pres. Privy Coun., 1986-91, pres. Treas. Bd., 1987-88, min. responsible for privatization and regulatory affairs, 1988, min. of agriculture, 1988-91, min. of fin., 1991—. Trustee Vegreville Sch. Bd., 1963-68; mem. Vegreville and Dist. Credit Union; regional dir. Alta. Progressive Conservative Assn., 1962, No. v.p., 1963, No. chmn. orgn., 1964; pres. Vegreville Progressive Conservative Assn., 1963-68. Mem. Commonwealth Parliamentary Assn., Interparliamentary Union, Can. NATO Parliamentary Assn., Can. World Federalist Parliamentary Assn., Vegreville C. of C., Royal Can. Legion (hon.), Alta. Fish and Game Assn., Indian Assn. Alta. Roman Catholic. Club: Vegreville Rotary (past dir.). Lodge: KC. Office: Ho of Commons, Parliament Bldgs, Ottawa, ON Canada K1A 0A6

MAZEL, JOSEPH LUCAS, corporate publications executive; b. Paterson, N.J., Oct. 1, 1939; s. Joseph Anthony and Anne (Kidon) M.; children: Joseph William, Jeanne Eileen; m. Joyce Virginia Kronenberger, Feb. 14, 1992. B.M.E., Newark Coll. Engring., 1960. Mech. engr. Austin Co., Roselle, N.J., 1960-61; engr. Western Electric Co., Newark, Atlanta, 1961-62; asst. assoc., sr. editor Factory mag. McGraw-Hill Publs. Co., N.Y.C., 1962-71, editor-in-chief, sr. editor 33 Metal Producing mag., Newark, Summit, N.J. and N.Y.C., 1971-85, chmn. editorial bd., 1980-82; pub. rels. account supr. Hammond Farrell Inc., N.Y.C., 1985-87; mgr. corp. publs. Siemens Corp., Iselin, N.J., 1987-92; pres. Mazel Editorial Assocs., 1992—; guest lectr. Writers Conf., N.J. Inst. Tech., 1972-83; mem. editorial adv. com. Tech. and Soc. publ., 1981-85. Mem. N.G., 1963-69. Recipient Apolloneer award Gen. Electric Co., 1966; Jesse H. Neal cert. of merit, 1977, 79, 83; Jesse H. Neal Editorial Achievement award, 1979; named to Alumni Achievement Honor Roll, N.J. Inst. Tech., 1979, Steuben Wise Old Owl award U.S. Steel Corp. Mem. Soc. Profl. Journalists, Sigma Delta Chi. Lodge: KC (grand knight 1967-68, trustee); Pitts. Press; Deadline. Home: 40-22 Tierney Pl Fair Lawn NJ 07410

MAZER, SHERRY, hospital administrator, medical technologist; b. Phila., Sept. 1, 1953; d. Samuel Sylvan Weissman and Esther (Green) Weissman-Stone; m. Ned Morton Mazer, June 15, 1980; children: Ross David, Laura Michelle. BA, Adelphi U., 1971; MBA, Rutgers U., 1981. Asst. supr. microbiology lab. Cooper Hosp., Camden, N.J., 1975-76, edn. coord., 1976-78, asst. dir. lab., 1978-79, adminstrv. dir. medicine, 1979-81, dir. patient mgmt., 1980-81, dir. risk mgmt., 1987-88; asst. lab. supr. Kettering (Ohio) Meml. Hosp., 1981-83; dir. quality West Jersey Health Systems, Marlton, N.J., 1988—. Mem. refreshment com. Osage Parent-Faculty Assn., Voorhees, N.J., 1989—; team mother Gibbsboro-Voorhees Athletic Assn., 1990—, Voorhees Soccer Assn., 1990; edn. and meeting coord. Mother's Ctr. South Jersey, Marlton, 1985-86. Mem. Am. Soc. Law and Medicine, N.J. Soc. Healthcare Risk Mgmt., N.J. Assn. Quality Assurance Profls., Nat. Assn. Quality Assn. Profls. (regional rep. fin. com. 1991). Home: 2 Warren Ave Voorhees NJ 08043-1233 Office: West Jersey Health System Brick Rd Marlton NJ 08053-2177

MAZO, MARK ELLIOTT, lawyer; b. Phila., Jan. 12, 1950; s. Earl and Rita (Vane) M.; m. Fern Rosalyn Litman, Aug. 19, 1973; children: Samantha Lauren, Dana Suzanne, Ross Elliott, Courtney Litman. AB, Princeton U., 1971; JD, Harvard U., 1974. Bar: D.C. 1975, U.S. Dist. Ct. D.C. 1975, U.S. Claims Ct. 1975, U.S. Ct. Appeals (D.C. cir.) 1976, U.S. Supreme Ct. 1979. Assoc. Jones, Day, Reavis & Pogue, Washington, 1974-79; assoc. Crowell & Moring, Washington, 1979-81, ptnr., 1981-90; ptnr. Hogan & Hartson, Washington, 1990—. Contbr. articles to profl. jours. White House intern Exec. Office of Pres., Washington, 1972. Capt. USAR, 1971-79. Mem. ABA, Harvard Law Sch. Assn., D.C. Bar Assn., Columbia Country Club, Princeton Club (N.Y.C.), Colonial Club, City Club, Phi Beta Kappa. Republican. Home: 3719 Cardiff Rd Chevy Chase MD 20815-5943 Office: Hogan & Hartson Columbia Sq 555 13th St NW Washington DC 20004-1109 also: Hogan & Hartson, 14 rue Chauveau-Lagarde, 75008 Paris France

MAZOH, JUDITH ANNE, chemist; b. Cleve.. BS, U. Tex., 1982. Geochemist Balcones Rsch. Ctr., Austin, Tex., 1983-86; chemist DuPont, Newark, Del., 1987—. Home: 21 Townsend Rd Newark DE 19711-7903 Office: DuPont Glasgow Site-113 PO Box 6101 Newark DE 19714-6101

MAZOL, THOMAS GEORGE, service executive; b. Flushing, N.Y., July 2, 1947; s. Stanley Anthony and Stella (Sostack) M.; m. Latifa Kharara, Aug. 2, 1973 (div. May 1980); children: Nancy, Magdelene; m. Constance Gargan, July 25, 1980. AS, St. John's U., 1966, BBA, 1968; MS, Fla. Internat. U., 1983; A in Occupational Scis., Johnson and Wales Coll., Providence, R.I., 1984. Auditor Channel Inn Motel, Washington, 1977-78; night mgr. Dolly Madison Hotel, Washington, 1978-80; night chef Pavillion Hotel, Miami, Fla., 1980-83; innkeeper Mountain View Inn, Norfolk, Conn., 1983-84; chef, owner Bradford (N.H.) Inn, 1984—; ind. cons. Bradford Inn Innkeepers, 1984—. Contbr.: Lanier Bed and Breakfast Cookbook 1984, Christmas Cookbook 1985, Country Inn Cookbook 1986. With USN, 1968-77. Mem. N.H. Hospitality Assn., Am. Hotel and Motel Assn., Ind. Innkeepers Assn. Ind. Roman Catholic.

MAZUR, EDWARD JOHN, JR., insurance agent; b. Lowell, Mass., Mar. 5, 1948; s. Edward John Sr. and Mary Annette (Terry) M.; m. Sheila MacDonald, Dec. 13, 1969 (div. Nov. 1984); 1 child, Kristen Leigh; m. Anna Maria Maia, May 18, 1985; children: Edward John III, Kara Maia Mazur. BA in History, U. Lowell, 1969. CLU, Chartered Fin. Cons., Life Underwriters Tng. Coun. Fellow. Agt. John Hancock Mut. Life Ins. Co., Boston, 1973-77, sales supr., 1977-82, field asst., 1982-83, dir. agys., 1983-84; gen. agt. John Hancock Mut. Life Ins. Co., Hartford, 1984-89, Fidelity Union Life, 1990—, Mazur. Fin., 1990—; career mng. gen. agt. Western New Eng. Agy., 1992—; treas. HLUA, 1991. Recipient Raymond T. Wilbur award Mass. Jaycees, 1983, Pres. of Yr., 1983. Recipient Raymond T. Wilbur award, Mass. Jaycees, 1982-83; named President of Yr., Mass. Jaycees, 1982-83, Outstanding Young Men of Am., Mass. Jaycees, 1984. Mem. Million Dollar Round Table, Hartford Life Underwriters Assn. (bd. dirs., edni. chmn. 1987-88, treas. 1991), Life Underwriters Tng. Coun. (chmn. 1988-89, bd. dirs.), Conn. Racquetball Assn. (pres. 1985—), Am. Amateur Racquetball Assn. Home: 58 Parsons Dr West Hartford CT 06117-1308 Office: Mazur Fin 354 Main St Ste 202 Newington CT 06111-2057

MAZUR, MARK STEVEN, mathematics educator; b. Cleve., Jan. 14, 1955; s. Boleslaus Michael and Clare Madeleine (Mazza) M. BS, John Carroll U., 1977, MS, 1979; MS, U. Notre Dame, 1981, PhD, 1984. Asst. prof. Duquesne U., Pitts., 1985-90; assoc. prof. Duquesne U., 1990—; vis. asst. prof. U. Notre Dame, Ind., 1984. Contbr. articles to profl. jours. Arthur J. Schmitt fellow, 1979-80. Mem. Math. Assn. Am., Am. Math. Soc., Phi Mu Epsilon, Alpha Sigma Nu. Democratic. Roman Catholic. Home: 5931 Wellesley Ave Pittsburgh PA 15206 Office: Duquesne U 600 Forbes Ave Pittsburgh PA 15282-0202

MAZUR, ROBERT ANDREW, healthcare executive; b. Passaic, N.J., Jan. 14, 1949; s. Stanley and Jane (Molinski) M.; m. Linda L. Ryburn, Dec. 17, 1971; children: Jeffrey, Maryann. BA, Fairleigh Dickinson U., 1970; MA, U. Tulsa, 1972. Pers. coord. Columbus Hosp., Great Falls, Mont., 1972-73; asst. dir. pers. Elizabeth (N.J.) Gen. Med. Ctr., 1973-79, dir. pres., 1979-88, v.p. human resources, 1988—. sec. Bd. Adjustment, Wallington, N.J., 1973-79; commr. Union County (N.J.) Hosp. Softball League, 1976—; team mgr. Toms River (N.J.) Little League, 1987-88. Mem. Am. Soc. Healthcare Human Resource Adminstrn. (outstanding chpt. contribution award 1991), N.J. Soc. for Healthcare Human Resource Adminstrn. (v.p. 1991—, chmn. N.J. pers. group 1988—), Ea. Union County C. of C. Office: Elizabeth Gen Med Ctr 925 E Jersey St Elizabeth NJ 07201-2789

MAZYCK, REAVEN ELAINE, data processor; b. Moncks Corner, S.C., Feb. 14, 1954; d. Ceaser and Azerlee (Glover) M.; 1 child, Ibrahim. BBA, Pace U., 1987. Researcher maternity and infant care Dept. Health; with EDP systems tech. support dept. CUNY; researcher maternity and infant care U. Md., 1972; fin. analyst Clove Market, S.I., N.Y., 1984-86. Author: (essays) From the Memoirs of Orrie Brown Mazyck. Mem. S.I. Coun. on Arts. Mem. N.Y. Metro Clipper Users Group, CUNY Women's Coalition.

MAZZA, COSMO, process control engineer; b. Medford, Mass., Feb. 4, 1966; s. Louis Anthony and Carol Ann (Cummings) M.; m. Janice M. Goggin, Oct. 6, 1990. BS in Indsl. Tech., U. Lowell, Mass., 1988, M in Mfg., 1991. Quality assurance engr., intern Lockheed, Nashua, N.H., 1987-88, quality assurance engr., 1988-89, mfg. engr., 1989-90, continuous quality improvement specialist, 1990; sr. statis. process control engr. M/A-COM, Burlington, Mass., 1990—; guest speaker Am. Soc. Quality Control, Lowell, Mass., 1988—. Recipient George Mason Scholarship for Advancement of Quality Control, Am. Soc. for Quality Control, 1988. Mem. Soc. Mfg. Engrs., Am. Soc. Quality Control. Roman Catholic. Office: MA COM 43 Savin St Burlington MA 01803-2209

MAZZACANE, JOHN ROYAL, health care facility administrator; b. New Haven, Conn., Apr. 4, 1940; s. James Vincent and Lena (Ciarleglio) M.; m. Alyce Paecht, May 12, 1962 (div. Oct. 1975); 1 child, Michael; Maureen Gayle Cameron, Aug. 25, 1990; children: Kelly, Kevin. Cert. in Respiratory Therapy Scis., Yale New Haven Med. Ctr., 1962; AA, South Cen. Community Coll., New Haven, Conn., 1980; BA, So. Conn. State U., 1985. Registered Nat. Bd. for Respiratory Care. Staff therapist Yale-New Haven Med. Ctr., 1963-66, asst. chief therapist, 1966-67; instr. Hosp. of St. Raphael/Sch. of Respiratory Care, New Haven, 1967-68, chief instr., 1968-80, chief therapist, 1980-83; asst. dir. dept. respiratory care VA Med. Ctr., West Haven, Conn., 1983-85, dir., Respiratory Care Ctr., 1985—; accreditation inspector Join Rev. Commn. for Respiratory Therapy, Lenecka, Kans., 1981—. Chmn. 3rd Dist. Young Reps., Hamden, Conn., 1976, Christian Social Problems, St. Paul's Ch., West Haven, 1978-82; parlimentarian West Haven Young Reps., 1971-77; publ. chmn. West Haven Town Com., 1975-80. Recipient Rahman Excellence in Edn. award Hosp. of St. Raphael Alumni Com., New Haven, 1975. Mem. Conn. Soc. of Cardiopulmonary Technologists (pres. 1975-78), Am. Assn. Phys. Assts. (cert. 1975—). Roman Catholic. Office: VA Med Ctr 950 Campbell Ave West Haven CT 06516-2700

MAZZAGLIA, ALFIO JOSEPH, podiatric surgeon; b. Lawrence, Mass., Aug. 16, 1932; s. Domenic T. and Rose E. (Ferrante) M. Student, Tufts U., 1949-51; D Podiatric Medicine, Ill. Coll. Podiatric Medicine, 1955. Diplomate Am. Bd. Podiatric Surgery, Am. Bd. Podiatric Orthopedics, Am. Bd. Quality Assurance & Utilization Rev. Chief surgery, dir. interns, clin. prof. surgery Ill. Coll. Podiatric Medicine and Surgery, Chgo., 1955-59, guest lectr., 1971; pvt. practice, Lawrence, Mass., 1961—; assoc., 1st surg. asst. Dr. Henri L. DuVries, Chgo., 1955-59; dir. surg. seminar courses New Eng. Coll. Foot Surgeons, 1960-61; adj. faculty clinician Ohio Coll. Podiatric Medicine, 1983; physician reviewer Mass. PRO, 1989—; chmn. coord. foot screening program 131st ann. conv. Am. Dental Assn., 1990; mem. med. staff St. John's Lowell Gen. Hosps., St. Joseph's Hosp., Lowell, Lawrence Gen. Hosp., Cath. Med. Ctr., Manchester, Mass.; lectr. on foot surgery, local anesthesia and surg. wound irrigation to local and nat. orgns.; lectr. U. Mass. Med. Sch., Orthopedic Dept., 1989-90. Contbg. author: Principles and Practice of Podiatry; also numerous articles; innovator operative procedures for intractable plantar keratosis, hammer toe, ingrown nail, hallux abductovalgus. Named hon. citizen City of Lowell, 1975; recipient citation Mass. Senate, 1988; Italian Coll. club scholar Sons of Italy, 1949. Fellow Am. Assn. Hosp. Podiatrists, Am. Acad. Podiatric Microsurgery, Am. Acad. Ambulatory Foot Surgery, Am. Soc. Podiatric Med., Am. Coll. Foot Surgery, Am. Acad. Podiatric Laser Surgery; mem. Am. Podiatric Med. Assn. (pres. Northeastern divsn. 1981-83, chmn. 1992—, state pres. 1987-88, com. on hosps. 1988-89, com. on health systems 1990-92, mem. ho. of dels. 1988-91). Home and Office: 338 Ames St Lawrence MA 01841-4113

MAZZARESE, MICHAEL LOUIS, human resources executive; b. S.I., Jan. 25, 1941; s. Louis John and Helen Ermenia (Mazzei) M.; m. Maureen Ann Starace, Oct. 3, 1970; children: Lauren, Adrienne. BA, St. Joseph's Sem. and Coll., 1962; MS, CUNY, 1971, profl. dipl., 1973; PhD, Fordham U., 1980. Tchr. high sch. N.Y. and Maine, 1963-73; prof. CUNY, 1973-78; asst. dir. med. edn. St. Barnabas Med. Ctr., Livingston, N.J., 1978-79; staff supr. AT&T, Bedminster, N.J., 1979-84; mgr. Johnson and Johnson, New Brunswick, N.J., 1984-86; dir. EQUICOR, N.Y.C., 1986-87; exec. dir. Dun and Bradstreet, Murray Hill, N.J., 1987-92; v.p. Hoechst Celanese Corp., Somerville, N.J., 1992—. Translator: Letters from Paris (Teilhard J. Chardin), 1966. Recipient Excellence in Human Resources Devel. award Brigham Young U., 1985. Mem. Am. Psychol. Assn., Am. Soc. Tng. and Devel., Am. Evaluation Assn., Am. Evaluation and Rsch. Assn., Soc. Human Resource Mgmt., Human Resources Planning Soc. Home: 330 Benson Pl Westfield NJ 07090-1302 Office: Dun & Bradstreet Info Svcs 1 Diamond Hill Rd Murray Hill NJ 07974

MAZZASCHI, ANTHONY JOSEPH, scientific society executive; b. Laconia, N.H., Nov. 21, 1955; s. Albert John and Priscilla Frances (Whedon) M.; m. Harlie Gene Sponaugle, Apr. 24, 1980; 1 child, Andrew Homer Sponaugle. BA, Mich. State U., 1976. Legis. asst. U.S. Senator Thomas McIntyre, Washington, 1976-79; exec. asst. to pres. Nat. Ocean Industries Assn., Washington, 1979-82; profl. staff mem. U. S. House Oceanography Subcom., Washington, 1982-86; pres. Mazzasachi-Sponaugle Assocs., Arlington, Va., 1986—; pub. affairs liaison Fedn. Am. Socs. for Experimental Biology, Bethesda, Md., 1988-90; dir. pub. affairs Am. Soc. Pharmacology and Exptl. Therapeutics, Bethesda, 1990—. Mem. Sci. Curriculum Com., Arlington County Sch. Bd., 1989-90. Democrat. Office: Am Soc Pharmacology and Exptl Therapeutics 9650 Rockville Pike Bethesda MD 20814-3998

MAZZIE, SANDRA ANNE, hospital administrator; b. Buffalo, Oct. 12, 1951; d. Laverne Edward and Carol Ann (Matthews) Myers; m. A. Vincent, May 19, 1973. BS in Nursing, SUNY, Brockport, 1973; MA, NYU, 1978; postgrad., Columbia U., 1986—. Staff nurse VA Hosp. Castle Point, Beacon, N.Y., 1973-74, rehab. nurse, 1974-78; rehab. program dir., clin. nurse specialist St. Francis Hosp., Poughkeepsie, N.Y., 1978-82, dir. patient care services, 1982-86, div. dir., 1986-88, dir. bus. planning and devel., 1988;

dir. nursing St. Luke's Hosp., Newburgh, N.Y., 1988-91, v.p. patient care svcs., 1991-92; cons. SAM Assocs., 1992—; nursing expert witness H.U.M. Ins. Co., White Plains, N.Y., 1978—; clin. assoc. Sch. Allied Health Profls., Ithaca, N.Y., 1986—; preceptor Pace U., White Plains, N.Y., 1986-91, W. Conn. U., 1990-92. Mem. program coun. Am. Heart Assn., 1982-86; bd. dirs. Holden Home of Newburgh. Mem. ANA (cert. advanced nursing adminstr.), Mid-Atlantic Regional Nursing Assn., N.Y. State Nurses Assn. (v.p. 1986, chmn. coun. on legis. 1980-82, dist. v.p. 1985), Am. Orgn. Nurse Execs., Ea. Orange C. of C. (bd. dirs. 1991—), Nat. League for Nursing, Sigma Theta Tau. Roman Catholic. Office: SAM Assocs 77 Balmville Rd Newburgh NY 12550

MAZZOCCO, ANGELO, educator; b. Isernia, Italy, May 13, 1936; s. Giuseppe and Ida (Rotolo) M.; m. Elizabeth Hunt Davis, Oct. 7, 1990; children: Michael Ray, Marco Angelo. BS, BA, Ohio State U., 1959, MA, 1963; PhD in Romance Langs. and Lits., U. Calif., Berkeley, 1973. Instr. Spanish John Carroll U., Cleve., 1962-65; teaching asst. Italian U. Calif., Berkeley, 1966-69; asst. prof. Italian No. Ill. U., DeKalb, 1970-75; asst. prof. Spanish and Italian Mt. Holyoke Coll., South Hadley, Mass., 1975-78, assoc. prof., 1978-83, prof., 1983—. Author: Linguistic Theories in Dante/Humanists, 1992; contbr. chpts. in books and articles to profl. jours. Mem. MLA (exec. com. Medieval and Renaissance Italian Lit. 1981-85, assembly del. 1875-87), Dante Soc. Am., Medieval Acad., Renaissance Soc. Am., Internat. Assn. Neo-Latin Studies, Internat. Assn. History Lang. Socs., Assn. Internat. Studi di Lingua e letteratura italiana. Office: Mt Holyoke Coll Dept Spanish/Italian South Hadley MA 01075

MAZZOLA, ANTHONY THOMAS, editor, art consultant, designer; b. Passaic, N.J., June 13, 1923; s. Thomas and Jennie (Failla) M.; m. Michele Morgan, Nov. 18, 1967; children: Anthony Thomas II, Marc Eden, Alisa Morgan. Grad., Cooper Union Art Sch., N.Y.C., 1948. Art dir. Street & Smith Publs., N.Y.C., 1948, Town and Country mag. (pub. by Hearst Corp.), N.Y.C., 1948-65; editor-in-chief Town and Country mag. (pub. by Hearst Corp.), 1965-72; now editor-in-chief Harpers Bazaar, 1972—; Pres. Anthony Mazzola Design Corp., N.Y.C., 1963—; cons. designer United Nations Childrens' Fund, Assn. Jr. Leagues Am., Columbia Pictures Corp., Sells Spltys., Gen. Foods, Paramount Pictures, Princess Marcella Borghese, Inc., Huntington Hartford, Ltd., N.Y. World's Fair, 1965. Exhibited, Art Dirs. Club. N.Y., ann. exhbns., 1948—. Served with AUS, 1943-46. Decorated Knight Officer of Order of Merit Italy; recipient Certificate of Merit awards N.Y. Art Dirs. Club; medal Art Dirs. Club N.Y.C., 1955. Office: Harper's Bazaar 1700 Broadway Rm 3718 New York NY 10019-5905

MAZZOLA, CLAUDE JOSEPH, physicist, small business owner; b. Newton, Mass., May 24, 1936; s. Gradinola and Anne (Cicconi) M.; m. Helen Alamanos, July 25, 1965; children: Peppina, Jean-Claude. BS in Physics, Boston Coll., 1959; postgrad. in Physics, MIT, 1961-62. Jr. engr. Lab. for Electronics, Boston, 1959-61; scientist AVCO R&D, Wilmington, Mass., 1961-62; engr. Space Scis., Waltham, Mass., 1962-63, BBN, Cambridge, Mass., 1963-72; staff engr. Edo, College Point, N.Y., 1972-82; engr. Sperry, Great Neck, N.Y., 1982-89; sole proprietor Namlak, Mamaroneck, N.Y., 1989—. Patentee Magnetic Storage Device (floppy disc), 1963; contbr. articles to profl. jours., papers to sci. confs. and meetings. Mem. IEEE. Republican. Roman Catholic. Home: 106 Lawn Ter Mamaroneck NY 10543-4023 Office: Namlak 206 Lawn Ter # 804 Mamaroneck NY 10543-4025

MAZZONE, A. DAVID, federal judge; b. Everett, Mass., June 3, 1928; s. A. Marino and Philomena M.; m. Eleanor G. Stewart, May 10, 1951; children: Margaret Clark, Andrew David, John Stewart, Jan Eleanor, Martha Ann, Robert Joseph, Carolyn Cook. B.A., Harvard U., 1950; J.D., DePaul U., 1957. Bar: Ill. 1957, Mass. 1959, U.S. Supreme Ct. 1964. Asst. dist. atty. Middlesex County, Mass., 1961; asst. U.S. atty. Mass., 1961-65; partner firm Moulton, Looney & Mazzone, Boston, 1965-75; asso. justice Superior Ct., Boston, 1975-78; U.S. dist. judge Boston, 1978—. Served with U.S. Army, 1951-52. Mem. ABA, Mass. Trial Lawyers Assn., Am. Law Inst., Mass. Bar Assn., Boston Bar Assn., Middlesex Bar Assn., Fed. Bar Assn. Democrat. Roman Catholic. Office: US Dist Ct McCormack PO & Courthouse Rm 2001 Boston MA 02109*

MAZZONE, JAMES VINCENT, sales and marketing manager, consultant; b. White Plains, N.Y., May 30, 1938; s. Jack Giacinto and Florence (Russo) M.; m. Nancy Dorothy Durec, Apr. 8, 1967; children: James Vincent Jr., Michelle Durec Mazzone. BA, The Citadel, 1960; MBA, Fairleigh Dickinson U., 1987. Br. mgr. Gen. Foods Corp., White Plains, 1964-69; regional mgr. Kitchens of Sara Lee, Chgo., 1969-72; nat. field sales mgr. Durkee Foods, Cleve., 1972-83; sales mgr. Anchor Food Svc., Chgo., 1984-91; ind. mktg. and sales cons. Randolph, N.J., 1984—; sales and mktg. dir. Corby Hall Inc., Rockaway, N.J., 1992—. Cub master Boy Scouts Am., Ramsey, N.J., 1984-87. 1st lt. USMC, 1960-63, CBI. Named Cub Master of the Yr., Boy Scouts Am., 1985. Mem. The Citadel Alumni Assn. (pres. N.Y.C. chpt. 1989—), Fairleigh Dickinson U. Alumni Assn. Home: 14 Drake Ct Randolph NJ 07869

MAZZUCCHELLI, LOUIS JOSEPH, JR., computer techonolgist, executive; b. Providence, Jan. 3, 1956; s. Louis Joseph Sr. and Thelma (Dilibero) M.; m. Susan Grace Paffrath, 1984; 1 child, Elizabeth Ann. AB, Brown U., 1977. Mgr., software support Internat. Data Scis., Providence, 1977-79; sr. staff cons. Yourdon inc., N.Y.C., 1979-82; founder, v.p., chief technical officer Cadre Technologies Inc., Providence, 1982—; cons. Sailcomp Industries, Newport, R.I., 1979. Contbr. articles to profl. jours. Recipient R.I. Govs. Technological Achievement award, 1991. Mem. AIAA, Assn. Computing Machinery, Computer Mus. (founding mem.). Office: Cadre Technologies Inc 222 Richmond St Providence RI 02903

MAZZUCELLI, COLETTE GRACE, educator; b. Bklyn., Nov. 26, 1962; d. Silvio Anthony and Adeline Marie (De Ponte) M. BA, U. Scranton, 1983; MA of Law and Diplomacy, Fletcher Sch. Law & Diplomacy, 1987; postgrad., Georgetown U., 1991—. Instr. European Integration Sch. of Summer and Continuing Edn. Georgetown U., Washington, 1990—; rsch. fellow Inst. fuer Europaeische Politik und Deutsche Gesellschaft fuer Auswaertige Politik, Bonn. Asst. editor: The Evolution of an International Actor: Western Europe's New Assertiveness, 1990. Swiss Univ. grantee Inst. Internat. Edn., 1984-85; Grad. scholar Rotary Found., 1987-88, Fulbright scholar Inst. Internat. Edn., 1991; Jean Monnet fellow Am. Coun. for Jean Monnet Studies, Inc., 1992, Robert Bosch Found. fellow, 1992—. Mem. Atlantic Coun. U.S., Am. Polit. Sci. Assn., Alpha Sigma Nu (student pres. 1984), Pi Gamma Mu (chpt. sec. 1983-84, Frank C. Brown scholarship medal 1984), Phi Sigma Tau (founder), Phi Alpha Theta, Pi Sigma Alpha, Alpha Mu Gamma, Delta Tau Kappa. Home: 1864 74th St Brooklyn NY 11204 Office: Georgetown U 37th and O Sts Washington DC 20057

MAZZUKI, MICHAEL ROBERT, financial executive; b. Columbus, Ga., Sept. 30, 1960; s. Robert Neil and Patricia Eileen (McKay) M.; m. Suzanne Silletto. BS in Math. Ops. Rsch. and Systems Analysis, U.S. Mil. Acad., 1982; MS in Systems Mgmt., U. So. Calif., 1986. Commd. 2d lt. U.S. Army, 1982, advanced through grades to capt.; officer 902d Engr. Co. U.S. Army, Ft. Belvoir, Va., 1986; co. comdr. 802d Engring. Bn. U.S. Army, Korea, 1986; ops. officer Recruiting Bn. U.S. Army, Houston, 1987; resigned U.S. Army, 1988; chief fin. officer Bellatrix Internat. Inc., Denville, N.J., 1988-90; pres. Practical Advice Systems, Hawley, Pa., 1990-91; fin. cons. Merrill Lynch, S.I., N.Y., 1991—. Roman Catholic. Office: Merrill Lynch 2555 Richmond Ave Staten Island NY 10314-5848

MCABEE, DOROTHY READING, moving and storage company executive; b. Easton, Pa., Aug. 6, 1963; d. John S. and Audrey (Reading) McA. AA, Churchmans Coll., 1982; BS cum laude, Ft. Lauderdale Coll., 1983. Store mgr. Pools & Trains, Bangor, Pa., 1979-80; receiving clk. Losey, Easton, Pa., 1980-81; crew person Wendy's Old Fashioned Hamburgers, Easton, 1981-82; mgr. trainer Wendy's of South Fla., Ft. Lauderdale, 1982-83; asst. sales mgr. Deichman Walker Chevrolet, Easton, 1983-85; fin. mgr. Kelly Buick, Allentown, Pa., 1985; sales rep. Faulkner Oldsmobile/Cadillac/Subaru, Bethlehem, Pa., 1985-88; acct. rep. Paychex, Inc., Allentown, 1988-91; nat. acct. rep. Diehl Moving & Storage, Allentown, 1991—. V.p. Ar thritis Found., Lehigh Valley, 1990-91. Mem. Jaycees (Allentown chpt., Jaycee of Yr. 1990), Kiwanis (treas. Palmer twp. club 1990-91), LeTip (pres.). Republican. Lutheran. Office: Diehl Moving & Storage 2655 Moravian Ave Allentown PA 18103-5523

MCADAM, WILL, electronics consultant; b. Wheeling, W.Va., Oct. 22, 1921; s. Will and Elizabeth Margaret (Wickham) McA.; m. Evelyn Virginia Warren, Sept. 22, 1945; children: Elizabeth Ruth, Margaret Evelyn. BSEE, Case Inst. Tech., 1942; MSEE, U. Pa., 1959. Registered control engr., Calif. Rsch. technologist Leeds & Northrup Co., Phila., 1945-57; head elec. sect. R&D dept. Leeds & Northrup Co., North Wales, Pa., 1957-68, assoc. dir. rsch. ops., 1968-75, mgr. devel. and engring. adv. devel., 1977-79, prin. scientist rsch. dept., 1979-82, ret., 1982; cons. in electronics, 1982—. Contbr. articles to profl. jours., chpts. to handbooks; 30 patents in field. 1st lt. AUS, 1942-45, ETO. Decorated Bronze Star. Fellow IEEE (life; chmn. subcom. on elec. and high frequency measurements 1957-59, com. indsl. electronic and control instruments 1961-65, Prize Paper award 1958). Republican. Presbyterian. Home: PO Box 470 Worcester PA 19490-0471

MCAFEE, NAOMI JONES, engineering executive; b. Hart County, Ky., Oct. 27, 1934; d. Charles Thomas and Emma Florence (Cobb) Jones; m. George Henry McAfee, Aug. 22, 1958. BS in Physics, Western Ky. State Coll., 1956. With electronic systems group Westinghouse Electric Corp., Balt., 1956—, dir. reliability, maintainability and supportability, 1987—; chair Concurrent Engring. Task Group Computer-Aided Acquisition and Logistics Support/Concurrent Engring. Industry Steering Group, 1988—. Editor: Reliability Training text, 1958; contbr. articles to profl. publs. Mem. Army Sic. Bd., Washington, 1983-90; active Pres.'s Commn. on the Nat. Medal of Sci., 1981-84. Fellow Soc. Women Engrs. (nat. pres. 1972-74); mem. IEEE (pres. reliability soc. 1984-86), Am. Soc. Quality Control (electronic div. award 1977, Edwards medal 1980, Ralph Evans award 1991). Republican. Baptist. Home: 13 Seminole Ave Baltimore MD 21228-5638

MCALEER, JOHN JOSEPH, English literature educator; b. Cambridge, Mass., Aug. 29, 1923; s. Stephen Ambrose and Helen Louise (Collins) McA.; m. Ruth Ann Delaney, Dec. 28, 1957; children: Mary Alycia, Saragh Delaney, Seana Caithlin, John Joseph, Paul Bernard, Andrew Stephen. AB, Boston Coll., 1947, MA, 1949; PhD, Harvard U., 1955. Teaching fellow Boston Coll., 1947-48, English and Latin instr., 1948-50; teaching fellow gen. edn. Harvard U., 1953-55; from asst. prof. to prof. Boston Coll., 1955—; vis. fellow Durham (Eng.) U., 1988-89. Author: Ballads and Songs Loyal to the Hanoverian Succession, 1962, Theodore Dreiser: A Biography, 1968, Artist and Citizen Thoreau, 1971, (with M. Tjader) Notes On Life: The Philosophical Writings of Theodore Dreiser, 1974, Justice Ends at Home: The Early Crime Fiction of Rex Stout, 1977, (with others) Rex Stout: An Annotated Primary and Secondary Bibliography, 1980, (with Billy Dickson) Unit Pride, 1981, Royal Decree: Conversations with Rex Stout, 1983, Ralph Waldo Emerson: Days of Encounter, 1984, Queens Counsel: Conversations with Ruth Stout, 1986, Coign of Vantage, 1988; editor-in-chief: Rex Stout Jour., 1979—, Thorndyke File, 1981—; assoc. editor: Best Sellers, 1965-85, Shakespeare newsletter, 1959-71, Armchair Detective, 1978-82; cons. editor: Dreiser Studies, 1971—. Mem. adv. bd. Walden Woods Project, 1990-92, Parents Choice, 1980—. Sgt. U.S. Army, 1942-46. Recipient Cath. Press. Assn. award, 1969, New Eng. Hist. Soc. award, 1985, Humanities award Boston Coll. Alumni Assn., 1991. Mem. Thoreau Soc., Mystery Writers Am. (v.p., dir. 1979-89, Edgar Allan Poe award 1978), R. Austen Freeman Soc. (pres. 1981—), Jane Austen Soc. (Burke award 1991), Internat. Dreiser Soc. (founding mem. 1991—), Boston Authors Club (pres., dir. 1982-92), Tavern Club (Boston). Democrat. Roman Catholic. Home: 121 Follen Rd Lexington MA 02173 Office: Boston Coll Dept English Carney 435 Chestnut Hill MA 02167

MCALEVEY, JOHN FRANCIS, lawyer; b. Bklyn., Jan. 18, 1923; s. John F. and Florence (McVarish) McA.; m. Hazel Edna Hansen, June 11, 1949 (dec. Dec. 1969); children: Peter, Benedict, Catherine, John, Thomas, Birgitta, Jane; m. Marlene Rotbert, July 7, 1976; stepchildren: Mitchell Rotbert, Clifford Rotbert. Student, Manhattan Coll., 1941-42, 46-47; LLB, Columbia U., 1950. Bar: N.Y., 1951, U.S. Supreme Ct. Assoc. Root, Ballantine, Harlan, Bushby and Palmer, N.Y.C., 1950-51; counsel Bur. Accident and Health Underwriters, N.Y.C., 1951-56; asst. gen. counsel Health Ins. Assn. Am., N.Y.C., 1956-66; ptnr. Glickman and McAlevey, N.Y.C., 1976-91; lawyer solo practice, 1992—; lectr., cons. in field of land use and planning; Amtrak Commuter Svcs. Corp. Mayor Village of Sloatsburg, N.Y., 1957-63; supr. Town of Ramapo, N.Y., 1966-73; del. Dem. Nat. Conv., 1988; atty. Village of Suffern, N.Y., 1989—. Decorated Air medal with 2 oak leaf clusters. Mem. Rockland County Bar Assn. Home: 145 Stillwater Ave Orono ME 04473-1017 Office: 120 N Main St New City NY 10956-3717

MCALLISTER, JOHN DAVID, insurance broker; b. Nov. 20, 1949; s. John D. and Doretha Alberta (Alford) McA.; m. Marcelle, Feb. 19, 1983. BA, Coll. of Ins., N.Y.C., 1975, MBA, 1978. Account exec. Johnson & Higgins, N.Y.C., 1975-80; founder, pres. McAllister & Assocs., N.Y.C., 1980; asst. v.p. Marsh & McLennan, N.Y.C.; pres. McAllister & Johnson, Inc., N.Y.C., 1988—; founder, chmn. N.Y. Consortium of Minority Brokers, Inc., N.Y.C.; founding mem., bd. dirs. Nat. Ins. Industry Assn., N.Y.C. Mem. 100 Black Men, N.Y.C., 1975—; 1st v.p. Rosetta Gaston United Dem. Club, Bklyn., 1980—. Mem. N.Y. C. of C., Bklyn. C. of C., U.S. Hispanic Women's C. of C. Democrat. Baptist. Home: 121 Brooklyn Ave Brooklyn NY 11213-1512 Office: McAllister and Johnson Inc 230 W 55th St New York NY 10019

MCALLISTER, PAUL ROBERT, statistician; b. Camden, N.J., Oct. 10, 1952; s. Charles S. and Lorraine S. (Weber) McA.; m. Terri Ruth Simcox, Jan. 13, 1973; children: David Mark, Michael Scot, Heather Rai. BS, Rutgers U., 1975; MS, Temple U., 1978, PhD, 1980. Analyst CHI Computer Horizons, Inc., Cherry Hill, N.J., 1976-80, rsch. statistician, 1980-84; sr. statistician Rohm and Haas Rsch. Labs., Springhouse, Pa., 1984-86; quality support statistician Rohm and Hass DVI Phila. Plant, Phila., 1986-89; mgr. of tng. Rohm and Haas DVI Bristol Plant, Bristol, Pa., 1989—. Author: (computer software) Nested, 1990; contbr. articles to profl. jours. Foster parent Div. Youth and Family Svcs., 1987. Mem. Am. Statis. Assn., Am. Soc. Quality Control. Home: 18 Cooper St Collingswood NJ 08108-2305 Office: Rohm and Haas DVI PO Box 219 Tullytown PA 19007-0098

MCANULTY, THOMAS, sculptor; b. Phila., Feb. 28, 1942; s. John and Monica (O'Toole) McA.; m. Mary Moore, Aug. 21, 1970; children: Stephen, Kathleen. BFA, Phila. Coll. of Art, 1971; MFA, Ind. U., 1976. Vis. artist Ind. U., Bloomington, 1976, Phila. Coll. of Art, 1982; prof. art Adelphi U., Garden City, N.Y., 1987—; lectr. in field. One-man show includes Jan Weiss Gallery, N.Y., 1989, 90, 91, Plohn Gallery, Bridgeport, Conn., 1990. Recipient Sculpture prize Showhegan Sch., 1971. Home: 115 W 96th St # 5 New York NY 10025-6417 Office: Adelphi U Garden City NY 11530

MCARDLE, FRANK BRIAN, employee benefit and compensation legislative consultant; b. N.Y.C., Aug. 20, 1946; s. Francis Joseph and Lucy Agnes (Trionfi) McA.; m. Jennifer Ann Eastman, Sept. 10, 1972 (div. Dec. 1985). BA summa cum laude, Fordham U., 1969; PhD, U. Va., Charlottesville, 1974. Pub. health ofcl. Thomas Jefferson Dist. Health Dept., Charlottesville, 1974-76; spl. asst. to commr. U.S. Social Security Adminstrn., Washington, 1976-81; mem. profl. staff U.S. Senate Spl. Com. on Aging, Washington, 1981-83; edn. and communications dir. Employee Benefit Rsch. Inst., Washington, 1983-88; mng. ptnr. Hewitt Assocs., Washington, 1988—; writer, researcher Pres. Commn. on Pension Policy, Washington, 1980; cons. expert White House Conf. on Aging, Washington, 1981; speaker throughout U.S. and Europe. Author: Altopascio, 1978; editor: Changing Health Care Market, 1987; producer award-winning documentary Coming to Terms, 1990; contbr. articles to profl. jours. Expert staff Ofcl. U.S. Social Security delegation to Europe, 1979; tutor Literacy Action D.C., Washington, 1980-81; mem. adv. bd. Human Resources Yearbook, 1986-92; vol. Hand on Housing, 1990-92. Woodrow Wilson Found. fellow, 1972-73; Fulbright fellow, Florence, Italy, 1972-73; recipient Spl. Achievement award U.S. Social Security Adminstrn., Washington, 1980. Mem. Nat. Acad. Social Ins., Nat. Press Club, Coll. and Univ. Pers. Assn., Phi Beta Kappa. Roman Catholic. Home: 4918 Albemarle St NW Washington DC 20016-4348 Office: Hewitt Assocs 2121 K St NW Ste 620 Washington DC 20037-1801

MC ARTHUR, JANET WARD, endocrinologist, educator; b. Bellingham, Wash., June 25, 1914; d. Hyland Donald and Alice Maria (Frost) McA. A.B., U. Wash., 1935, M.S., 1937; M.B., Northwestern U., 1941, M.D., 1942; Sc.D., Mt. Holyoke Coll., 1962. Diplomate: Am. Bd. Internal Medicine. Intern Cin. Gen. Hosp., 1941-42, asst. resident in medicine, 1942-43; asst. resident, rsch. fellow in medicine H.P. Walcott fellow clin. medicine Mass. Gen. Hosp., Boston, 1943-47, assoc. physician, 1959-84, assoc. children's svc., 1968-84; instr. Harvard U., 1955-57, asst. prof., 1960-64, assoc. prof., 1964-73, prof., 1973-84, prof. emeritus, 1984—; clin. prof. medicine Boston U. Sch. Medicine, 1984—; adj. prof. Sargent Coll. Allied Health Scis. Boston U., 1982—; mem. reproductive biology study sect. NIH, 1974-78, Com. on Population Studies, 1980-84; co-dir. Vincent Meml. Rsch. Lab., 1977-79; sr. scientist U. London, 1985-86. Author: (with others) Functional Endocrinology from Birth Through Adolescence, 1952; editor: (with Theodore Colton) Statistics in Endocrinology, 1970; contbr. articles to profl. jours. Fellow ACP; mem. AMA, AAAS, Endocrine Soc., Am. Fertility Soc., Am. Assn. Clin. Endocrinologists, Boston Obstet. Soc., Phi Beta Kappa, Sigma Xi, Alpha Omega Alpha. Home: 19 Brimmer St Boston MA 02108-1025 Office: Boston U 4th Fl 635 Commonwealth Ave Boston MA 02215-1610

MCARTHUR, ROBERT PAUL, university administrator, philosophy educator; b. San Mateo, Calif., Feb. 18, 1944; s. John P. and Julia A. (Monahan) McA.; m. Shannon L. White, Aug. 12, 1967; 1 child, Lauren. BA, Villanova U., 1967, MA, 1968; PhD, Temple U., 1972; MA (hon.), Colby Coll., 1984. Asst. prof. philosophy Colby Coll., Waterville, Maine, 1972-78, assoc. prof., 1978-84, prof., 1984—, v.p. for acad. affairs, 1988—; vis. prof. Univ. Coll., Cork, Ireland, 1986-87. Author: Tense Logic, 1975, From Logic to Computing, 1991; contbr. articles to profl. jours. Overseer Mid Maine Med. Ctr., Waterville, 1987—; vol. Big Bros./Big Sisters. Am. Coun. of Edn. fellow, 1975-76. Mem. Am. Philos. Assn., Rotary Internat. Office: Colby Coll Waterville ME 04901

MCATEE, CHARLES PATRICK, research biochemist; b. Mt. Vernon, Ill., Aug. 5, 1955; s. William Nelson and Clara Nadine (Roth) McA.; m. Jennifer Anne Durham, June 21, 1986. BS, U. Ill., 1978; MS, So. Ill. U., 1986; PhD, U. Chgo., 1989. Rsch. virologist Inst. for Molecular Virology, St. Louis, 1978-79; rsch. assoc. U. Ill., Urbana, 1979-81, vis. rsch. biochemist, 1981; rsch. biochemist Monsanto Rsch. Ctr., St. Louis, 1982-83; NEI fellow So. Ill. U., Carbondale, 1983-85; NRSA predoctoral fellow U. Chgo., 1985-87, J. Kennedy fellow, 1987-89; rsch. scientist Baxter Diagnostics Internat., Miami, Fla., 1989-91; sr. rsch. biochemist Am. Cyanamid Co., Pearl River, N.Y., 1991—; cons., collaborator Protein Chemistry Facility, Yale U., New Haven, 1991—; collaborator Kennedy Rsch. Ctr., U. Chgo., 1989—; adj. prof. Meml. Sloan Kettering, N.Y.C., 1992—, Fla. Internat. U., Miami, 1990-91. Contbr. articles to profl. jours.; author (patent) disclosure) purification of tumor markers and recombinant DNA-derived biopharms. Mem. Am. Chem. Soc., Alpha Phi Omega (v.p. 1978), Phi Mu Alpha Sinfonia (pres. 1978), Alpha Chi Sigma (chmn. alumni fund 1981). Presbyterian. Office: Am Cyanamid Co Middletown Rd Pearl River NY 10965

MCAULIFFE, EUGENE VINCENT, retired diplomat and business executive; b. Boston, Oct. 25, 1918; s. Thomas Joseph and Charlotte Philippine (Metzger) McA.; m. Winifred Marie Gallivan, Aug. 17, 1946; children: Eugene Vincent Jr., Paul, Lawrence, Marie, Stephen, Terence, Patricia, John. AB cum laude, Boston Coll., 1940; postgrad., Boston U., 1940-42, Nat. War Coll., 1962-63. Spl. agt. Mass. Bonding & Ins. Co., Boston, 1940-42; vice consul, exec. sec. Office of High Commn. for Germany, Berlin, 1948-54; with U.S. Dept. State, Washington, 1954-58, 63-68; 1st sec. Am. Embassy, Mexico City, 1958-62; minister, dep. chief of mission Am. Embassy, Madrid, 1968-70; ambassador Am. Embassy, Budapest, Hungary, 1975-76; minister counselor, internat. advisor SHAPE, Casteau, Belgium, 1970-72; minister counselor, dep. chief of mission U.S. Mission to NATO, Brussels, 1972-75; asst. sec. def. for internat. security affairs Dept. Def., Washington, 1976-77; pres. United Tech. (Europe) Inc., Brussels, 1977-83. Capt. U.S. Army, 1942-47. Decorated Bronze Star, Croix de Guerre, Belgian Govt., 1945. Mem. Am. Fgn. Svc. Assn., Acad. Polit. Sci., Assn. Diplomatic Studies, SHAPE Officers Assn., Nat. War Coll. Alumni Assn., Boston Coll. Alumni Assn., Boston Latin Sch. Assn., Internat. Inst. Strategic Studies (London), Fgn. Affairs Retirees New Eng. (pres. 1985-86), Ambs. Coun. World Affairs Boston, DACOR House. Roman Catholic. Home: 80 Flint Locke Dr Duxbury MA 02332-4807

MCAUSLAND, RANDOLPH M., art association administrator; b. Phila., Oct. 9, 1934; s. John Randolph and Helen (Neal) McA.; m. Marilyn Kemp (div. 1976); children: Andrew, Sean; m. Jan E. Tribbey, May 8, 1986. AB, Princeton U., 1957. Pres. Design Publs. Inc., N.Y.C., 1982-89; dir. Design Mgmt. Inst., Boston, 1986-88, Design Arts Program, NEA, Washington, 1989-90; dept. chmn. Design Arts Program NEA, Washington, 1990—; founder, dir. Design History Found., N.Y.C., 1988-89. Author: Supermarkets: History of an American Institution, 1980; contbr. articles to profl. jours. Recipient Bronze Apple award Indsl. Design Soc., 1987. Mem. Am. Ctr. For Design (hon.), Princeton Club. Home: 3020 Tilden St NW Washington DC 20008-3019 Office: Nat Endowment For Arts 1100 Pennsylvania Ave NW Washington DC 20506-0005

MCAVADDY, JOHN PATRICK, direct marketing specialist; b. Atlantic City, N.J., Mar. 17, 1966; s. John James and Martha Ann (Gormley) McA. BS in Fin., Seton Hall U., 1988, MBA in Mktg., 1990. Transfer student advisor Seton Hall U. Stillman Sch. Bus., South ORange, N.J., 1988-90; acct. exec. Market Support Internat. Bus., Mt. Olive, N.J., 1990-91, accts. supr., 1991—; adj. instr. Seton Hall U., 1989—. Republican. Roman Catholic. Home: 80 Riggs Pl West ORange NJ 07052 Office: Market Support Internat 600 International Dr Mount Olive NJ 07828

MCAVOY, THOMAS JAMES, judge. AB, Villanova U., 1960; JD, Union U., 1964. Bar: N.Y. 1964, U.S. Dist. Ct. (no. dist.) N.Y. 1964. Assoc. Hinman, Howard & Kattell, Binghamton, N.Y., 1964-69, Kramer, Wales, & McAvoy, Binghamton, 1969-84, McAvoy & Hickey, P.C., Binghamton, 1984-85; judge U.S. Dist. Ct. (no. dist.) N.Y., Binghamton, 1986—. With USMC, 1958. Office: US Dist Ct/No Dist NY 225 Courthouse & Fed Bldg 15 Henry St Binghamton NY 13901

MCBRIAN, ANDREW KIMBEL, psychologist; b. Peoria, Ill., Sept. 15, 1954; s. Anne Jane (McCaffrey) McB.; m. Elizabeth Pierce Hetzler, June 18, 1988; 1 child, Sarah Frances Hetzler. BA, Yale Coll., 1977; MEd, Harvard U., 1984, EdD, 1989. Lic. psychologist. Account exec. McCaffrey & McCall, Inc., N.Y.C., 1977-78; researcher Ctr. for Food and Farm Rsch., Salisbury, Conn., 1980-81; spl. needs tchr. Pine Cobble Sch., Williamstown, Mass., 1981-83; psychology intern mental health clinic Boston U., 1987-88; psychology intern Eliot Community Mental Health, Concord, Mass., 1988-89; psychologist Milton (Mass.) Acad., 1989—; pvt. practice as psychologist, Cambridge, Mass., 1991—, as ednl. therapist, 1984—; asst. dir. Salisbury Summer Sch. for Reading and English, 1984—, tchr., dept. head, 1976-84; ednl. cons. St. Mark's Sch., Southboro, Mass., 1985-88, Roxbury (Mass.) Latin Sch., 1985, Tufts Summer Reading Program, Medford, Mass., 1984; freelance cartoonist, 1984—. Recipient numerous acad. prizes Suffield Acad., 1970-73, Harvard U. Book prizes, i972. Mem. Learning Disabilities Network, Am. Assn. for Counseling and Devel., Yale Club N.Y.C., Small Point Club. Home: 44 Chestnut St Dedham MA 02026 Office: Milton Acad Counseling Ctr 170 Centre St Milton MA 02186-3397

MCBRIDE, PAUL WILBERT, history educator; b. Youngstown, Ohio, May 23, 1940; s. Wilbert B. and Frances L. (Fleisher) McB.; m. Joanne L. Biscan, June 9, 1962; children: Paula Jo McBride Gates, Paul Joseph, Marc Alan. BA, Youngstown (Ohio) U., 1963; MA, Kans. State U., 1965; PhD, U. Ga., 1972. High sch. tchr. Jackson-Milton High Sch., North Jackson, Ohio, 1962-63; instr. history and philosophy Augusta (Ga.) Coll., 1966-67; prof. history Ithaca (N.Y.) Coll., 1970—; editorial adv. bd. Ethnic Groups, 1982—. Author: Culture Clash: Immigrants and Reformers, 1975, Italians in America, 1975; contbr. articles to profl. jours. Centennial lectr. Ithaca Centennial Commn., 1986. 1st lt. U.S. Army, 1965-67. Summer Rsch. award Nat. Endowment for the Humanities, 1980. Mem. Immigration History Assn., Italian-Am. Hist. Assn., Phi Kappa Phi, Phi Alpha Theta. Democrat. Roman Catholic. Office: Ithaca Coll Dept History Danby Rd Ithaca NY 14850-5736

MCBRIDE, RODNEY LESTER, investment counselor; b. Denver, Sept. 1, 1941; s. Laurence Thomas and Harriet Alvina (Primmer) McB.; m. Nancy Faye Davenport, Mar. 21, 1964 (div. June 1984); children: Douglas L., Cheryl L. BS in Mktg., U. Colo., 1963; MBA, U. Calif., Berkeley, 1976. Chartered investment counselor Investment Counsel Assn. Am., Fin. Analyst Fedn. Indsl. salesman Fibreboard Corp., San Diego and San Francisco, 1963-66; investment counselor Shuman, Agnew & Co., San Francisco, 1966-71; investment counselor, co-founder capital counseling svc. Bank of Am., San Francisco, 1971-75; investment counselor Scudder, Stevens and Clark, San Francisco, 1975-76; sr. v.p., office mgr. Crocker Investment Mgmt. Corp., Los Angeles, 1977-84; sr. v.p., dir. portfolio mgmt., chmn. equity strategy com. Crocker Investment Mgmt. Corp., San Francisco, 1984-86; v.p., sr. portfolio mgr., chmn. equity strategy com. Chancellor Capital Mgmt., Inc. (formerly Citicorp Investment Mgmt. Corp.), N.Y.C., 1986—. Pres., coach Palos Verdes (Calif.) Basketball Assn., 1982-83; mem. 2d Congregational Ch.; bd. dirs. Greater N.Y. couns. Boy Scouts Am. Mem. L.A. Soc. Fin. Analysts (sec., bd. dirs. 1984, treas. 1983, chmn. seminar com. 1982-83), N.Y. Soc. Fin. Analysts, Assn. Investment Mgmt. and Rsch. (charteed fin. analyst), Western Pension Conf., U. Colo. Alumni Assn., U. Calif. Alumni Assn., Stanwich Country Club, Alpha Kappa Psi (treas. 1963). Republican. Home: 11 Ridgebrook Rd Greenwich CT 06830 Office: Chancellor Capital Mgmt Inc 153 E 53d St New York NY 10022-4611

MCBRIEN, JOHN ROBERT, federal government official; b. Alton, Ill., Feb. 11, 1944; s. John Low and Harriet Louise (Ash) McB.; m. Sallie Douglas Wallace, Jan. 7, 1983; children: Kelly Leigh, John Wallace Ash. BA in Govt., So. Ill. U., 1966; JD, St. Louis U., 1969; disting. grad., Nat. War Coll., 1977. Bar: Mo. 1969, U.S. Ct. Appeals (8th cir.). Atty. U.S. Dept. Justice, Washington, 1970-72; adviser U.S. Dept. Treasury, Washington, 1972-76, spl. asst., 1977-80, dep. to asst. sec., 1980-86, chief internat. programs office fgn. assets control, 1987—; vis. scholar Ctr. for Strategic and Internat. Studies, Washington, 1986-87. Contbr. chpts. to books and articles to newspapers. Bd. dirs. River Farms Homeowners Assn., Alexandria, Va., 1990-92, treas., 1991-92. Mem. ABA, Fed. Bar Assn., Mo. Bar Assn. Episcopalian. Office: US Dept Treasury Office Fgn Assets 1500 Pennsylvania Ave NW Washington DC 20220

MC BRYDE, FELIX WEBSTER, geographer, ecologist, consultant; b. Lynchburg, Va., Apr. 23, 1908; s. John McLaren and Flora O'N. (Webster) McB. B.A., Tulane U., 1930, LL.D. (hon.), 1967; Ph.D., U. Calif., Berkeley, 1940; postgrad. (rsch. fellow) U. Colo., 1930-31, Clark U., 1931-32; m. Frances Van Winkle, July 23, 1934; children: Richard Webster, Sarah Elva, John McLaren. Geographer-photographer 4th Tulane Expdn. across Cen. Am. Maya Area, 1927-28; geology teaching asst. Tulane U., 1929-30, U. of Utah-Smithsonian Uinta Ute Expdn., No. Utah, 1931; field fellow Clark U.-Carnegie Inst., Washington, Guatemala, 1932; rsch. fellow Middle Am. Rsch. Inst., Tulane U., 1932-33; teaching asst. geography U. Calif., Berkeley, 1933-35, 37; predoctoral field fellow social sci. Social Sci. Rsch. Coun. N.Y., Guatemala and El Salvador, 1935-36; instr. geography Ohio State U., 1937-42, UCLA, 1940; field fellow in natural scis.NRC, Washington, also Berkeley, Guatemala, Mexico, 1940-41; expert cons., sr. geographer M.I., War Dept., Washington, 1942-45; lectr. geography Western Res. U., 1944; dir. Peruvian office Inst. Social Anthropology, Smithsonian Instn., Washington, Lima, 1945-47; dir., organizer and writer of curriculum Inst. Geography, U. San Marcos, Lima, 1945-47; spl. rep. Inst. Andean Rsch., Lima, 1947-48; lectr. Fgn. Svc. Inst., Dept. State, 1949-53; prof. geography U. Md., 1948-59, cons. prof., 1959-63; chief geographer office of coord. Internat. Stats. U.S. Bur. Census, Washington and Latin Am., 1948-56; geographer com. on 1950 Census of Ams., Inter-Am. Statis. Inst., cons. all Am. nations, 1948-51; chief U.S. Census Mission, tech. advisor 1st Nat. Census of Ecuador, Quito, 1949-51; dir. regional planning Gordon A. Friesen Assos., Inc., Washington and San Jose, Costa Rica nat. master hosp. plan, 1956-58; on contract to Exec. Rsch. Inc., N.Y.C., presdl. campaign advisor Pres. Villeda Morales, Honduras, 1957; U.S. rep., electoral advisor to Pres. Ydigoras Fuentes, Guatemala, 1958-64; pres. F.W. McBryde Assocs., Inc., Washington and Guatemala, 1958-64; founder-pres. Inter-Am. Inst. Modern Langs., Guatemala, 1962-66; Latin Am. cons. Inst. Modern Langs., Washington, 1962-66; chief phys. and cultural geography br., natural resources div. Inter-Am. Geodetic Survey, U.S. Army, Fort Clayton, C.Z., 1964-65; field dir. Bioenviron. Program, Atlantic-Pacific Interoceanic Sea-Level Canal Studies in Panama and Colombia (AEC contract), 1965-70, field dir. U.S. Army, Natick, Mass., Andean ecology project, S.Am., 1967-69, dir. project devel. program, Cen. Am. and Mex., 1968-69; cons. in ecology Battelle Meml. Inst., Columbus, Ohio, 1970—; founder-dir. McBryde Ctr. for Human Ecology, 1969—; cons. in human ecology and Latin Am., Transemantics, Inc., Washington, 1970—; with UN Devel. Program, ecologist (tourism), expert Jamaica, W.I., 1971; hydrology ecologist, expert Parana River Nav. Improvement Project, Argentina, 1972; ecol. cons. Battelle Meml. Inst., Panama and Brazil, 1972; U.S. Bur. Census geography adviser to Govt. of Honduras on cartography for 1973 population census, 1972; Battelle cons., procedural analysis in internat. project devel., 1972; ecologist World Bank environ. impact analysis Bayano River Hydroelectric Project, one-man mission to Panama; Battelle cons., ecologist, prin. investigator and field coord., environ. impact study Darien Gap Hwy., Panama-Colombia for U.S. Dept. Transp., 1973; cons. Enviro Plan. Chesapeake Bay ecology; expert ecologist (biology) Engr. Agy. for Resources Inventories, C.E., U.S. Army, Washington, 1974; dir. recruitment, dir. internat. bus. intelligence, 1975-80, dir. Geog. Rsch. div. Transemantics, Inc., Washington, 1975—; cons. geographer Census Office, Govt. of Honduras, 1981; cons. ecologist UN Tech. Cooperation and Devel., Cerro Colorado Copper Mine, Panama, 1981. Mem. nat. adv. bd. Am. Security Coun.; state advisor U.S. Congl. Adv. Bd., Am. Security Coun. Found.; charter founder Ronald Reagan Rep. Ctr., Washington, 1988, founder PrTrust Rep. Nat. Com., 1988; charter mem. Pres. Bush's Rep. Presdl. Task Force, 1989; charter mem. Rep. Presdl. Trust, 1992; Fellow Explorers Club (life); mem. Am. Anthrop. Assn., AAAS, Am. Cartographic Assn., Am. Congress on Surveying and Mapping, Am. Geog. Soc., Assn. Am. Geographers (formerly Am. Soc. for Profl. Geographers founding pres., sec.(1 yr.), treas., meetings coord., editor publs. 1943-45, creator 8 regional divs. in U.S., now 9 quasi-socs. in U.S. and Can.), Am. Geophys. Union (life), Am. Inst. Biol. Scis., Conf. Latin Americanist Geographers, Arctic Inst. N.A., Assn. Tropical Biology, Chesapeake Bay Found., Am. Soc. Photogrammetry and Remote Sensing, Ecuadorian Inst. Anthropology and Geography (founder dir. 1950-52, hon. dir. 1952—), Inter-Am. Coun. (organizing sec. 1953-59, pres. 1959-62), N.Y. Acad. Scis., Washington Acad. (adv. bd. 1981—), Lima Geog. Soc., Oceanography Soc. (charter mem.), Soc. Am. Archeology, Soc. Am. Mil. Engrs., Soc. for Med. Anthropology, N.Am. Cartographic Info. Soc., Guatemalan Soc. Geography and History, Internat. Oceanographic Found., Nature Conservancy Internat. Program, Mexican Soc. Geography and Stats., U.S. Naval Inst., World Wildlife Fund, Nat. Wildlife Fedn. (world assoc.), Phi Beta Kappa, Sigma Nu, others. Episcopalian. Author: Solola, 1933; Cultural and Historical Geography of Southwest Guatemala, 1947, Spanish , 1969, 2 vols. transl. by Francis Gall, Guatemala, 1969, Greenwood reprint (English), 1971; (with P. Thomas) Equal-Area Projections for World Statistical Maps, 1949; founding editor Profl. Geographer; contbr. numerous articles to profl. jours. Achievements include patent for equal-area designs and methods of constructing original projections for world maps, wherein median representations between true overall global linear scale (equidistance), true azimuth (indicated by directional bearings of intersecting graticule lines, hence shape of terrestrial features), and equivalence (or true relative size of land and water bodies on the map) are plotted to attain the closest similarity to earth features in all dimensions, which are completely true only on the spherical surface of the terrestrial globe; discovery of origin of beans phaseolus vulgaris and p. lunatus in western Guatemala and Chiapas, of maize variety, zea mays; development of new system of biological/ecological classification keyed to environmental factors, of new micro-geodemographic planning techniques employing data graphics plotted on thematic maps, especially useful in hospital, health, and economic surveys; research in Mayan and Andean archeology, ecology, on tectonic and seismic determinants and geomorphology. Home: 10100 Falls Rd Rockville MD 20854-4106

MCBRYDE, SARAH ELVA, art librarian; b. Columbus, Ohio, July 2, 1942; d. Felix Webster and Frances (Van Winkle) McB. Student, Syracuse U., 1960-61; BFA, Washington U., 1964; postgrad., Skowhegan Sch. Painting, 1964; MFA, Am. U., 1976. Freelance portrait painter Specialty Children, Potomac, Md., 1957-65; gallery asst. Esther Stuttman Gallery, 1966-67; art libr. Martin Luther King Meml. Library, Washington, 1968—. Represented in pub. and pvt. collections including mural at Hotel Las Palmeras, San Blas Islands, Republic of Panama, 1966, Panamanian-Am. Inst., 1967, Nat. Trust for Hist. Preservation, Washington, 1972, Urdong's of Georgetown, Washington, 1974, Nat. Zoo Bookstore/Gallery, Washington, 1976-83, Martin Luther King Meml. Library, Washington, 1988, 89, Artist's Equity Awards Exhbn., 1989; commissioned works Portrait of Giambattista Vico, Vico Inst. of N.Y., 1989, drawings of Gaimbattista Vico, Naples, Italy. Recipient cash award design for logo Nat. Library Assn., Washington, 1982. Mem. Artists Equity, Kappa Kappa Gamma. Episcopalian. Home: 10130 Falls Rd Rockville MD 20854-4106

MCCABE, CHARLES T(HOMAS), environmental and safety consultant; b. Troy, N.Y., Mar. 28, 1950; s. Charles J. and Elaine (Ogden) McC. Cert. safety specialist; registered environ. property assessor. Hazard communications specialist Monsey Products, Waterford, N.Y., 1980-88; pres. Material Safety System Inc., Latham, N.Y., 1987-88; v.p. Material Safety Systems, Latham, 1988-90; project mgr. Entek Environ. & Tech. Svcs., Inc., Troy, 1989—. Co-chmn. Watervliet (N.Y.) Bicentennial Parade Com., 1975. Mem. ASTD (Hudson/Mohawk chpt.), Am. Indsl. Hygiene Assn. (affiliate), Am. Soc. Safety Engrs., World Safety Orgn. (affiliate), Elks. Democrat. Roman Catholic. Home: 17 Lansing Ln Cohoes NY 12047 Office: Entek Environ & Tech Svcs 125 Defreest Dr Troy NY 12180-8361

MCCABE, EDWARD FRANCIS, III, bank executive; b. Bklyn., Aug. 13, 1942; s. Edward Francis Jr. and Anna Catherine (Kennedy) McC.; m. Monica Therese McEnroe, Oct. 21, 1967; children: Edward Francis IV, William, Melissa, Brendan. BBA, St. Francis Coll., 1965; MBA, NYU, 1971. Various mgmt. positions Chem. Bank, N.Y.C., 1965-72, mgr. letter of credit, dep. to internat. oper. group head, 1972-74; chief adminstrv. officer holding co. Chem. Bank, Rochester, N.Y., 1974-76; v.p., group head staff svcs. Chem. Bank, N.Y.C., 1976-79, v.p., dir. employee rels., 1979-86; sr. v.p., human resources dir. Horizon Bancorp (now Chem. Bank N.J.), Morristown, N.J., 1986-88, Chem. Bank N.J., East Brunswick, 1989—. Mem. exec. com. fin. employee rels. study group Wharton Sch. Fin., Phila., 1983—; mem. exec. com. Indsl. Rels. Soc., N.Y.C., 1980-86; trustee Sta. WNET Channel 13 Edn. and Community Outreach Subcom., Newark, 1991—; active Ridgewood Baseball Assn., Ridgewood Soccer Assn. With U.S. Army N.G., 1966-71. Mem. Am. Inst. Banking (pres. N.Y. chpt. 1985-86, trustee Garden State chpt. 1987—), N.J. Bankers Assn. (human resources com. 1987-89, chmn. 1991—). Roman Catholic. Home: 187 Bellair Rd Ridgewood NJ 07450-4123 Office: Chem Bank NJ Two Tower Ctr East Brunswick NJ 08816-1093

MCCABE, FRANK LACEY, service executive; b. N.Y.C., Nov. 20, 1943; s. Edwin Howard and Marie Florence (Ryan) McC.; m. Patricia Leann Varner, June 27, 1970; children: Dawn Lacey, David Lloyd, Jack Howard. BS, Cornell U., 1967. From gen. mgr. to purchase mgr. Hospitality Motor Inns, Cleve., 1967-74; v.p. ops. and devel. Crown Am. Corp., Johnstown, Pa., 1974-88; pres. High Hotels, Ltd., Lancaster, Pa., 1988—. Bd. dirs. Pa. Dutch Conv. Vis. Bur., Lancaster, 1988. Mem. Cornell Soc. Hotelment (v.p. 1984-85). Republican. Presbyterian. Home: 2645 Hazelwood Rd Lancaster PA 17601-4850 Office: High Hotels Ltd 1853 William Penn Way Lancaster PA 17601-6741

MCCABE, JAMES FREELAND, JR., service company executive, consultant; b. Salisbury, Md., Aug. 16, 1950; s. James Freeland and Eunice Elizabeth (Lewis) McC.; m. Diane Lucy Ercole (div. 1984); 1 child, Jennifer; m. Arlene Gale Musselman, Oct. 18, 1991; 1 child, Kelly. BA, Western Md. Coll., 1972; MPA, U. Balt., 1979. Merchandiser Montgomery Ward Catalog Div., Balt., 1973-74; buyer, inventory control mgr. Towson (Md.) State U., 1974-77, ops. mgr., 1977-79; sr. acct. exec. Balt. Conv. Ctr., 1979-80; asst. dir. Balt. Arena, 1980-82; mktg. cons. Scollon Mgmt. Group, Reisterstown, Md., 1982-83; exec. dir. Towson Ctr./Minnegan Stadium Towson (Md.) State U., 1983-87; bus. and econ. devel. ctr. mgr. Essex Community Coll., Balt., 1988-91; dir. conv. svcs. CES Security, Inc., Balt., 1991—; adjunct prof. Towson (Md.) State U., 1985-87, Essex Community Coll., Balt., 1988-90; pres. JAM Prodns., Cockeysville, Md., 1990—; travel cons. Falls Rd Travel, Balt., 1991—. Mem. Balt. County C. of C., Phi Alpha Alpha. Home: 10317-K Malcolm Cir Cockeysville MD 21030

MCCABE, JAMES PATRICK, library director; b. Phila., May 24, 1937; s. Felix and Josephine (Murtaugh) McC. BA, Niagara U., 1963; MA, U. Mich., 1964, MA in LS, 1965, PhD, 1968. Libr. dir. Allentown Coll., Center Valley, Pa., 1968-89; acting libr. dir. Muhlenberg Cedar Crest Colls., Allentown, Pa., 1989-90; dir. univ. libr. Fordham U., N.Y.C., 1990—. Author: Critical Guide to Catholic Reference Books, 3d edit., 1989. Bd. dirs. Pa. Shakespear Festival, Center Valley, 1990—. Office: Fordham U Libr Bronx NY 10458

MCCAFFERTY, JAMES ARTHUR, sociologist; b. Columbus, Ohio, Jan. 1, 1926; s. James A. and Marjorie Agatha (Gilchrist) McC.; m. Jane Roush, June 13, 1948 (dec. Oct. 1984); children: Lucinda Jane Martin, James Stanley Thomas, Bridget Anne Roush Green; m. Carolyn Ring Bradley, Nov. 7, 1987 (div. Apr. 1992). BS, Ohio State U., 1948; MA, 1954; postgrad. Am. U. Social rsch. analyst Ohio State Dept. Pub. Welfare, 1948-51; criminologist U.S. Bur. Prisons, Washington, 1951-63; asst. chief div. info. systems Adminstrv. Office of U.S. Cts., Washington, 1963-77, chief statis. analysis and reports div., 1977-86, ret.; vis. lectr. American U., 1959, 62-64; adj. instr. Fordham U., 1978-89. Editor: Capital Punishment, 1972; contbr. articles on criminology to profl. jours. Life mem. Md. State PTA; pres. Potomac area coun. Camp Fire Girls of U.S., 1966-67; v.p. Prince George's County (Md.) Coun. of PTAs, 1964-65; chmn. Prince George's County Youth Commn., 1970-72; mem. Hypoglycemia Assn.; pres. Interfaith Community Action Coun., Inc. With USAAF, 1944-46. Mem. AAUP, Md. Soc. SAR (pres.), Am. Sociol. Assn., Am. Correctional Assn. (life), Assn. Correctional Rsch. and Info. Mgmt., Am. Statis. Assn., Prince George's County Geneal. Soc. (past pres.), Ohio Geneal. Soc. (Nat. Capital Buckeye chpt., editor newsletter), Judicature Soc., Am. Soc. of Criminology, Md. State Beekeepers Assn., DAV (life), Sons of Union Vets. Civil War. Am. Legion. Presbyterian. Home: 613 Rosier Rd Fort Washington MD 20744-5554

MCCAFFREY, DEBORAH, educator; b. Princeton, N.J., Mar. 28, 1941; d. John and Dorothy Elizabeth (Hunt) McNutt; m. Charles Borromeo McCaffrey, Jan. 13, 1967 (div. 1989); 1 child, Kevin Cullen. BS in English, West Chester (Pa.) Coll., 1963; postgrad., Pa. State U., 1965-69, U. Pa., 1985. Health, phys.edn. tchr. Chester (Pa.) Sch. Dist., 1963; tchr. English Sun Valley Sch. Dist., Brookhaven, Pa., 1963-70, Garnet Valley Sch. Dist., Concordville, Pa., 1970-74, Barclay Psychiatric Inst., Chgo., 1977, Central Bucks Sch. Dist., Doylestown, Pa., 1981-82; humanities tchr. gifted prog. Bucks County Intermediate Unit, Doylestown, 1982-84; tchr. 6th grade Plymouth Meeting Friends, Pa., 1985-86; tchr. English, sci. Phila. Sch. Dist., 1987-88; tchr. English gifted and talented program Pennsauken (N.J.) Sch. Dist., 1988—. Designer, writer humanities curriculum guides, 1982-84. Coord. Soc. Friends ann. meeting weekend progs., Phila., 1985-86, overseas com. mem., 1988—, pastoral care of meeting mems.; organizer Recycling prog., Phila., 1987—; vol. on Barkintine Sailing Ship, Gazella. Mem. NEA, N.J. Edn. Assn., Pa. Assn. Gifted Educators, Phila. Sketch Club, Fleisher Art Meml., Ship Preservation Guild. Soc. of Friends. Home: 2403 South St Philadelphia PA 19146-1035 Office: Pennsauken Bd Edn Hylton Rd Pennsauken NJ 08110-1386

MCCAFFREY, DONNA THERESE, history educator; b. N.Y.C., Nov. 29, 1949; d. Raymond A. and Virginia Teresa (Forster) McC. BA in Psychology and History, Dominican Coll. of Blauvelt, N.Y., 1971; MA in History, Providence Coll., 1973, PhD in History, 1983, MA in Religious Studies, 1987. Author: The Origins and Early History of P.C., 1985; contbr. articles to profl. jours. U. Notre Dame fellow, 1973. Mem. AAUP, Cath. Hist. Assn., R.I. Hist. Assn., Phi Alpha Theta. Democrat. Office: Providence Coll Dept History River and Eaton Sts Providence RI 02918

MCCAFFREY, EDWARD MICHAEL, JR., estate tax specialist; b. Rockville Centre, N.Y., Sept. 23, 1958; s. Edward Michael and Patricia Hope (Tunney) McC.; m. Laura Ann Meccariello, May 31, 1986; 1 child, Brian Edward. AS, SUNY, Farmingdale, 1979; BA, U. Richmond, 1981. Asst. br. mgr. Thomas Meadows, Ltd., Boston, 1981-83; mgr. Dreyfus Direct Dreyfus Corp., Garden City, N.Y., 1983-85; mut. fund coord. Nathan & Lewis Securities, N.Y.C., 1985-87; estate tax specialist McCaffrey & Assocs. Ltd., Massapequa, N.Y., 1987—; pension cons. George H. Adams, Ltd., Jamaica, N.Y., 1990—, R.G.S. X-Ray, Freeport, N.Y., 1989—. Mem. Internat. Assn. Fin. Planning, The Am. Coll. (assoc.), Oppenheimer Leaders' Club, Phi Theta Kappa. Roman Catholic. Office: McCaffrey & Assocs Ltd PO Box 149 Massapequa Park NY 11762-0149

MCCAFFREY, JOHN ANTHONY, brokerage house executive; b. Bklyn., June 16, 1944; s. Bernard and Ann Florence (Sweeney) McC.; m. Cynthia Elizabeth Bushek, Nov. 6, 1965; children: Tara, Heather. BBA, Pace U., 1975. Asset liability mgr. Bank of Montreal, N.Y.C., 1964-77; mgr., corp. bond trader Midland Doherty, Inc., N.Y.C., 1977-78; corp. bond trader Burns, Fry & Timmons, N.Y.C., 1978-81; 1st v.p. Cantor, Fitzgerald, Inc., N.Y.C., 1981-87; exec. v.p. Brokerage Corp. of Am., N.Y.C., 1987-89; 1st v.p. Cantor, Fitzgerald, Inc., N.Y.C., 1989—. Mem. Vols. for Wildlife, Cold Spring Harbor, N.Y., 1985-92, Greenpeace, 1988-92. Cpl. USMC, 1965-67, Vietnam. Mem. K.C., Am. Legion. Republican. Roman Catholic. Home: 32 Marilyn Blvd Plainview NY 11803-1945

MCCAHILL, BARRY WINSLOW, federal public affairs official; b. Glen Ridge, N.J., May 25, 1947; s. William Francis and Frances (Elliott) McC.; m. Margaret Anne Bonnes, Feb. 8, 1980; children: Jennifer, Kimberly, Erin, Meghan; 1 stepchild, Rob White. BA in English, U. Va., 1969, postgrad., 1974-76. Lic. U.S. Coast Guard capt. Account exec. Whyte Berry Price, Advt. & Pub. Rels., Washington, 1967-69; publs. mgr. Nat. Telephone Coop. Assn., Washington, 1972-74; visual info. specialist U.S. Customs Svc., Washington, 1974-76; pub. affairs specialist IRS, Washington, 1976-79; mgr. radio and TV news Nat. Hwy. Traffic Safety Adminstrn., U.S. Dept. Transp., Washington, 1979-85, dep. dir. Office Pub. and Consumer Affairs, 1985—. Loaned exec. Combined Fed. Campaign United Way, Washington, 1983. 1st lt. U.S. Army, 1969-72. Recipient Blue Pencil award Nat. Assn. Govt. Communicators, 1975, 88, Adminstrs. award for exceptional achievement Nat. Hwy. Traffic Safety Adminstrn., 1983, Sec.'s Honor award Sec. of Treasury, 1983, Sec.'s award for meritorious achievement Sec. of Transp., 1985. Mem. Washington Automotive Press Assn., Cobbosseecontee Yacht Club (Manchester, Maine), Pi Kappa Alpha. Roman Catholic. Home: PO Box 2057 Middleburg VA 22117-2057 Office: Nat Hwy Traffic Safety Adminstrn 400 7th St SW NOA-40 Washington DC 20590

MCCALEB, MICHAEL LYLE, scientist; b. Lubbock, Tex., Apr. 16, 1953; s. Russell Haeber and Martha Lee (Adams) McC.; m. Hilary Anne Thompson; children: Rachel, Megan, Victoria. BS, Ariz. State U., 1975; MS, Purdue U., 1977, PhD, 1979. Post-doctoral fellow Sloan Kettering Inst., N.Y.C., 1979-81; post-doctoral fellow U. Rochester (N.Y.) Med. Ctr., 1981-83, sr. instr., 1983-84; rsch. assoc. Ayerst Labs., Princeton, N.J., 1984-86; sr. rsch. assoc. Wyeth-Ayerst Rsch., Princeton, 1986-88, rsch. fellow, 1988-92; prin. staff scientist Miles, Inc., West Haven, Conn., 1992—. Contbr. articles to profl. jours.; patentee in field. Mem. AAAS, N.Y. Acad. Scis., Am. Diabetes Assn., Endocrine Soc., Internat. Diabetes Fedn. Office: Miles Inc 400 Morgan Ln West Haven CT 06516

MCCALLEY, ROBERT B(RUCE), JR., retired mechanical engineer.; b. Miami, Fla., Dec. 17, 1922; s. Robert Bruce and Ida (Castles) McC.; B.S. magna cum laude, U. S.C., 1947; M.C.E., Cornell U., 1949; Ph.D., 1952; m. Anita Baker, July 4, 1951. Rsch. assoc. Cornell U., 1948-51; engr. Applied Physics Lab., Johns Hopkins U., 1951-55; structural engr. Knolls Atomic Power Lab., Gen. Electric Co., 1955-57; reactor containment engineer AEC, 1958-59; cons. engr., 1960-63, mgr. stress analysis, 1963-68; mgr. structural mechanics Aircraft Engine group Gen. Electric Co., 1968-71, mgr. tech. ops., machinery apparatus ops., 1971-75, mgr. engring. support, 1976-87; ret. Served to 2d lt. AUS, 1943-46. Registered profl. engr., N.Y., Md. Mem. ASCE, ASME, N.Y. Acad. Scis., Phi Beta Kappa, Tau Beta Pi, Phi Kappa Phi. Episcopalian. Contbr. articles to profl. jours. Home: 826 Karenwald Ln Niskayuna NY 12309-6414

MCCALLISTER, LARRY DWAYNE, military officer, civil engineer, educator; b. Rolla, Mo., Nov. 21, 1955; s. Paul Lloyd and Della Mae (Anderson) M.; m. Lynn Weiss, May 19, 1979. BS in Civil Engring., U. Mo., Rolla, 1978, MS in Civil Engring., 1979; PhD in Civil Engring., U. Tex., Arlington, 1990. Registered profl. engr., Va., Tex. Platoon leader/staff officer, 293rd engr. bn. U.S. Army, Baumholder, West Germany, 1980-83; project mgr./engr., Ft. Worth Dist. U.S. Army, Ft. Worth, 1983-85; co. comdr. E co., 2nd engr. bn. U.S. Army, Camp Pelham, Korea, 1985-87; ops. officer, 20th engr. brigade (Desert Storm) U.S. Army, 1991, Saudia Arabia; asst. prof. U.S. Military Acad., 1990—. Contbr. engring. articles to numerous profl. jours. Music dir. West Point Bapt. Ch., 1990-91. Mem. Soc. Am. Military Engrs. (membership chmn. 1984-85), ASCE. Republican. Baptist. Home: 567 Connor Loop # C West Point NY 10996-1207 Office: Civil & Mech Engring West Point NY 10996

MCCALLY, RUSSELL LEE, physicist; b. Marion, Ohio, Sept. 27, 1940; s. Charles Lee and Jean Violet (Brillhart) McC.; m. Mary Louise Schade, June 17, 1961; children: Kaye Louise, Karen Elizabeth. BSc, Ohio State U., 1964; PhD, Johns Hopkins U., 1991. Assoc. physicist Applied Physics Lab. Johns Hopkins U., Laurel, Md., 1965-76, sr. staff physicist, 1976-91, prin. staff physicist, 1991—. Contbr. articles to Jour. of Physiology (London), Exptl. Eye Rsch., Jour. of the Optical Soc. of Am. A and Jour. of Applied Physics. William S. Parsons fellowship Johns Hopkins U. Applied Physics Lab., 1979-80. Mem. Am. Phys. Soc., Assn. for Rsch. in Vision and Ophthalmology. Office: Applied Physics Lab Johns Hopkins U Johns Hopkins Rd Laurel MD 20723-6099

MCCANDLESS, J(ANE) BARDARAH, religion educator; b. Dayton, Ohio, Apr. 16, 1925; d. J(ohn) Bard and Sarah Catharine (Shuey) McC. BA, Oberlin Coll., 1951; MRE, Bibl. Sem., N.Y.C., 1953; PhD, U. Pitts., 1968. Dir. Christian edn. Wallace Meml. United Presbyn. Ch., Pitts., 1953-54, Beverly Heights United Presbyn. Ch., Mt. Lebanon, Pa., 1956-61; instr. religion Westminster Coll., New Wilmington, Pa., 1961-65, asst. prof., 1965-71, assoc. prof., 1971-83, prof. religion, 1983—, chair dept. religion and philosophy, 1988—; leader Christian edn. workshops Presbytery of Shenango, Presbyn. Ch. (U.S.A.), 1961—, Synod of Trinity, 1972, 76. Author: An Untainted Saint...Ain't, 1978; contbr. articles to profl. jours., Harper's Ency. Religious Edn. Mem. session New Wilmington Presbyn. Ch., 1977-79. Mack grantee Westminster Coll., 1962-63, Faculty rsch. grantee, 1972, 78, 90. Mem. Religious Edn. Assn., Assn. Profs. and Researchers in Religious Edn. (mem. exec. com. 1978-80), Soc. for Sci. Study Religion, Phi Beta Kappa, Pi Lambda Theta. Office: Westminster Coll Dept Religion and Philosophy New Wilmington PA 16172

MCCANDLESS, WILLIAM HOWARD, JR., child psychologist; b. Elizabeth, N.J., May 30, 1955; s. William Howard and Doris May (Paton) McC. BA, NYU, 1978, MA, 1981, MS, 1991; PhD, Columbia U., 1985. Lic. psychologist, N.Y. Rsch. asst. dept. child psychiatry NYU Med. Ctr., N.Y.C., 1979-82; child psychology intern Columbia Presbyn. Med. Ctr. N.Y. State Psychiat. Inst., N.Y.C., 1982-83; psychologist dept. child psychiatry Columbia Presbyn. Med. Ctr., N.Y.C., 1984-86; psychologist Shield Inst. for the Mentally Retarded and Devel. Disabled, N.Y.C., 1983-84; chair dept. psychology Manhattan childrens psychiat. ctr. N.Y. State Office Mental Health, N.Y.C., 1986—, dir. Project Assist and Mobile Mental Health Treatment Teams, 1986—; chmn. Lower East Side Child and Adolescent Svcs. Commn., N.Y.C., 1989—; co-chmn. Lower East Side Mental Health Consortium, N.Y.C., 1989—; cons. N.Y.C. Bd. Edn., 1983—, Child Welfare Adminstrn., N.Y.C., 1988—, Ednl. Alliance, 1991—; policy and program devel. com. N.Y. State Office Mental Health, N.Y.C. Dept. Mental Health, 1988—; speaker numerous mental health confs. and seminars. Contbr. articles to profl. jours. Active Manhattan Child and Adolesence Svcs. Commn., N.Y.C., 1982—, Manhattan Inter Hosp. Child Protection Commn., N.Y.C., 1989—. NIMH grantee, 1982. Mem. APA (assoc.), Assn. for Advancement Behavior Therapy, Soc. Pediatric Psychology, N.J. State Psychol. Assn., Ea. Psychol. Assn. Home: 5601 Boulevard E Apt 8I West New York NJ 07093-3546 Office: Manhattan Childrens Psychiatric Ctr Wards Island New York NY 10035

MCCANN, CHARLES PAUL, computer consultant; b. Mineola, N.Y., Mar. 21, 1954; s. Harry Ellis and Mildred Katherine (Burgemeister) McC.; m. Robin Kelly, Feb. 12, 1977. AB in Math., Dartmouth Coll., 1976.

Tchr., chmn. math. dept. Marvelwood Sch., Cornwall, Conn., 1976-78; sr. ednl. specialist Digital Equip. Corp., Lanham, Md., 1978-80; prin. software specialist Digital Equip. Corp., Burlington, Mass., 1983-84, software cons., 1984-86, sr. software cons., 1986-91, prin. cons., 1991—; sr. telecommunication specialist GE Co., Burlington, Vt., 1980-83. Vol. Vt. Spl. Olympics, Burlington, 1982, Vt. Ednl. TV, 1983, Boston Pub. TV, 1992. Mem. Assn. for Image and Info. Mgmt., Digital Equip. Corp. Users Soc. (sec.-treas. 1981-83), WGBH Leadership Circle, Atlantic Cetacean Rsch. Ctr. Home: 2 Poe Rd Billerica MA 01821-2844 Office: Digital Equipment Corp 1 Burlington Woods Dr Burlington MA 01803

MCCANN, DAVID STEWART, security engineer, consultant; b. Dundee, Angus, Scotland, Dec. 11, 1945; arrived U.S., 1978; s. Henry James and Daisy May (Conn) McC.; m. Evelyn Margaret Ferris, June 27 (div. Jan. 1987); children: Jillian, Keith, Gail; m. Colette Kendal Sherba, Apr. 22, 1989. BSc in Econs., London U., 1967, BSc in Computing, 1968. Account mgr. Honeywell Info. Systems, London, 1969-71; group systems mgr. Beaverbrook Newspapers Ltd., London, 1971-73; sr. cons. Unilever Ltd., London, 1973-76; v.p. Digital Computer Controls, Fairfield, N.J., 1976-77; dir. internat. Computer Labs., Greensboro, N.C., 1977-80; v.p. Wheelock Signals, Long Branch, N.J., 1980-82; pres. Wellesley Internat., Inc., Ocean, N.J., 1982—; bd. dirs. Sen Electronics, Geneva, 1976-78; cons. Uniqey Am. Inc., N.Y.C., London, 1986-88, SIAT Inc., L.I., 1985—, Classified Security. Elder Our Good Shepherd Luth. Ch., Point Pleasant, N.J., 1990—; asst. fin. sec., 1991. Lt. RAF, 1963-69. Mem. IEEE, Nat. Fire Protection Assn., Internat. Mgmt. Assn., British Inst. Mgmt. Office: Wellesley Internat Inc 3321A Doris Ave Ste #8 Ocean NJ 07712

MCCANN, EDWARD, investment banker; b. San Diego, June 22, 1943; s. Edward F. and Anna Marie (McKay) McC.; m. Sara Sheffield Hall, Nov. 15, 1980; children: Sheffield Hall, Henry Howland, Edward Brewster. BS, U.S. Naval Acad., 1965, MSEE, 1965; postgrad., MIT, 1970. Staff mem. Rsch. Lab. Electronics MIT, Cambridge, Mass., 1968-70; program mgmt. exec. Westinghouse Corp. Rsch. Lab., Churchill, Pa., 1971-73; chief planner Chevron Shipping Co., San Francisco, 1973-77, div. mgr., 1977-79; corp. planning and acquisition staff exec. Standard Oil Co. Calif., San Francisco, 1979-83; dir. strategic planning, def. sector Sperry Corp., N.Y.C., 1983-85, with merger team, 1986; v.p. corp. fin. Eberstadt Fleming Inc., N.Y.C., 1986-88; sr. v.p. investment banking, dir. aerospace and tech. group Robert Fleming Inc., London and N.Y.C., 1988-90; prin. investment banking Hambrecht & Quist, Inc., N.Y.C., 1990—; bd. dirs. Am. Def. Preparedness Assn., L.I. Biol./Cold Spring Harbor Lab., 1988—. Mem. long-range planning coun. United Way, L.I., 1983-86; treas. Oyster Bay Youth and Family Counseling Agy., 1984-86; trustee Oyster Bay Community Found., 1984—. Recipient class prize systems engring. and naval weaponry, S.R. and Daus. of Am. Colonists awards, 1965. Mem. Coun. Fgn. Rels., Soc. Naval Architects and Marine Engrs., Am. Soc. Naval Engrs., Assn. Old Crows, Navy League, Naval Inst., Assn. Naval Aviators, Naval Acad. Alumni Assn., Am. Def. Preparedness Assn. (bd. dirs. 1988—), Bohemian Club, Seawanhaka Corinthian Yacht Club, Cold Spring Harbor Beach Club. Episcopalian. Home: 191 Oyster Bay Rd Oyster Bay NY 11771 Office: Hambrecht & Quist Inc 230 Park 21st Ave New York NY 10169-0005

MCCANN, GERALD R., mayor, certified public accountant; b. Jersey City, Mar. 20, 1950; s. Roy Gerald and Elizabeth Jane (Feeley) McC.; m. Maureen Curtin, Aug 10, 1973; children: Tara, Lauren. Grad., St. Peter's Coll., 1972. Acct. Arthur Young, Newark; acct., ptnr. Donohue & McCann, Jersey City, 1975-81; councilman City of Jersey City, 1977-81, mayor, 1981-85, 89—. Chmn. Hudson County Dem. Org., N.J., 1991; active Urban Mayor's Conf. Mem. N.J. Soc. CPAs. Roman Catholic. Office: City of Jersey City 280 Grove St Jersey City NJ 07302

MCCANN, MICHAEL F., industrial hygienist; b. Toronto, Ont., Can., Jan. 19, 1943; s. Jack Francis McCann and Bertha Alice (Singleton) Maher; m. Lois Kaggen, Sept. 26, 1984. BSc with honors, U. Calgary, 1964; PhD in Chemistry, Columbia U., 1972. Sci. tchr. St. Anne's Episc. Sch., Bklyn., 1971-72; sr. technical writer, product safety coord. GAF Corp., N.Y.C., 1973-75; dir. Art Hazards Resource Ctr. Found. for Community of Artists, N.Y.C., 1975-77; founder, exec. dir. Ctr. for Safety in Arts (formerly Ctr. Occupational Hazards), N.Y.C., 1977—; adj. faculty N.Y. State Sch. Indsl. and Labor Rels., Cornell U., N.Y.C., 1978, 79; lectr. environ. scis., Sch. Pub. Health, Columbia U., N.Y.C., 1981—; instr., U. Man., Winnipeg, Can., 1982, 83; adviser, task force on toxicity of art materials, Am. Soc. Testing and Materials, 1980-82; mem. ad hoc com. on heal hazards of arts and crafts materials, Can. Dept. Nat. Health and Welfare, 1981—; mem. adv. bd., Mt. Sinai Occupational Health Clinic, N.Y.C., 1987—. Author: Health Hazards Manual for Artists, 1975, 3d edit., 1985, Artist Beware, 2d edit., 1991, Lights! Camera!, Safety, 1990; contbr. articles on art materials hazards to various publs.; editor profl. publs.; writer, narrator videotape, Art Safety: Hazards and Precautions, 1988. Presenter testimony on labeling of art materials, U.S. Ho. of Reps., 1980, N.Y. State Assembly, 1981. Mem. Am. Acad. Indsl. Hygiene, Am. Indsl. Hygiene Assn., Am. Chem. Soc. (chem. health and safety div.), N.Y. Com. Occupational Safety and Health (exec. bd. 1977-87, treas. 1980-85), Soc. Occupational and Environ. Health, Internat. Arts-Medicine Assn. Office: Ctr for Safety in Arts 1030 5 Beekman St New York NY 10038-2206

MCCARGAR, JAMES GOODRICH, diplomat, writer; b. San Francisco, Apr. 20, 1920; s. Jesse B. and Addie May (Goodrich) McC.; m. Geraldine Claudia Cooper-Key, Aug. 2, 1948 (div. 1954); m. Emanuela Butculescu, Dec. 22, 1973. BA, Stanford U., 1942. U.S. fgn. svc. officer Moscow, 1942, Vladivostok, 1942-43, Moscow, 1943, Santo Domingo, 1943-44; sec. of legation, chief polit. sect. Budapest, 1946-47; vice consul Genoa, 1948; chief div. Southeastern European Affairs Office of Policy Coordination, Washington, 1948-50; sec. of embassy, mem. U.S. Del. to Allied Coordinating Com., Paris, 1950-53; asst. to v.p. Free Europe Com., Inc., N.Y.C., 1955; European dir. polit. ops. Free Europe Com., Inc., Paris, 1956-58; cons. to pres. Free Europe Com., Inc., 1959-60, 71-76; spl. asst. to chmn. NEH, Washington, 1978-82; U.S. del. UNESCO confs., 1978, 80, 82, Sem. on Funding of Culture, Madrid, 1982; U.S. observer UNESCO European Regional Conf., Oslo, 1991; cons. BBC-TV, London, 1984, Nat. Dem. Inst. Internat. Affairs, Washington, 1984, African-Am. Labor Ctr., Washington, 1984-85, Am. Inst. Free Labor Devel., Washington, 1985, Dept. Internat. Affairs, AFL-CIO, Washington, 1986—; editorial adv. Interco Press, Washington, 1988—; bd. dirs. Ams. for Universality of UNESCO, Washington, 1985—; U.S. observer UNESCO European Regional Conf., Oslo, 1991. Author: A Short Course in the Secret War, 1963, rev. edit., 1988, 3d edit., 1992, El Salvador and Nicaragua: The AFL-CIO Views on the Controversy, 1985; co-author: Three-Cornered Cover, 1972, Lost Victory, 1989; contbr. articles and book revs., 1940-70. Co-founder, sec. Ams. Abroad for Kennedy, Paris, 1960. Ensign USNR, 1944-46. Decorated Officer's Cross Order Hungarian Republic; Knight First Class Royal Norwegian Order St. Olav, 1983; recipient Cert. of Appreciation Internat. Ctr. for Free Trade Unions in Exile, 1958, Fed. Outstanding Performance award NEH, 1979, 81, Silver Medallion of the Hungarian Parliament, 1991, Officer's Cross Order of the Hungarian Republic, 1992. Mem. Polish Inst. Arts and Scis. Am. (elected), Diplomatic and Consular Officers Retired, Chevaliers du Tastevin (France), Vets. of OSS (hon.), Authors' Guild. Democrat. Home and Office: Apt 1207 W 4201 Cathedral Ave NW Washington DC 20016-4901

MCCARLEY, ROBERT WILLIAM, psychiatrist, educator; b. Mayfield, Ky., Aug. 17, 1937; s. Robert Smith and Mary Agnes (McGill) McC.; m. Alice Margaret Bowen, Aug. 10, 1968; children: Robert Vinton, Scott William. AB summa cum laude, Harvard U., 1959, MD, 1964. Intern Peter Bent Brigham Hosp., Boston, 1964-65; resident in psychiatry Mass. Mental Health Ctr., Boston, 1965-68; instr. psychiatry Harvard Med. Sch., Boston, 1970-75, asst. prof. psychiatry, 1975-78; co-dir. lab. neurophysiology Mass. Mental Health Ctr., Harvard Med. Sch., Boston, 1975-85, assoc. prof. psychiatry, 1978-84, dir. lab. neurosci., 1985—, prof. psychiatry, 1984—; chair rsch. com. dept. psychiatry Harvard Med. Sch., Boston, 1991—; co-dir. clin. rsch. tng. program Harvard Med. Sch., 1980—; assoc. chief dept. psychiatry Brockton VA Med. Ctr., 1985—; cons. Mass. Rehab. Commn., Boston, 1976—, Commonwealth Rsch. Ctr., Boston, 1986; chmn. clin. neurosci. rev. com. NIMH, 1992—. Author: Neuronal Activity in Sleep, 1974, Brainstem Control of Wakefulness & Sleep, 1990; contbr. over 100 articles on neurophysiology of sleep and schizophrenia. Neurophysiology research grantee NSF, 1979-84; career devel. grantee NIMH, 1980-85, neurophysiology research grantee, 1984—, schizophrenia research grantee, 1986—, Va. med. research grantee, 1986—. Mem. AAAS, Am. Psychiat. Assn., Soc. for Neurosci., Sleep Rsch. Soc. (exec. sec. 1987-90, pres. 1991), Assn. Profl. Sleep Socs. (vice chair 1987-91), Harvard Club, Neighborhood Club. Democrat. Methodist. Office: Harvard Med Sch/Brockton VAMC 940 Belmont St # 116A Brockton MA 02401-5596

MC CARRICK, THEODORE EDGAR, archbishop; b. N.Y.C., July 7, 1930; s. Theodore Egan and Margaret (McLaughlin) McC. Student, Fordham U., 1950-52; AB, St. Joseph's Sem., 1954, AM, 1958; MA, Cath. U., 1960, PhD, 1963; LLD, Mt. St. Vincent Coll., 1967; STD, Inter-Am. U., 1969; STD (hon.), Niagara U., 1982; LHD (hon.), St. John's U., 1974, St. Peter's Coll., 1987. Ordained priest Roman Cath. Ch., 1958. Asst. chaplain Cath. U. Am., Washington, 1959-61, dean students, 1961-63, asst. to rector, dir. univ. devel., 1963-65, instr. dept. sociology, 1961-65; domestic prelate, 1965; pres. Cath. U. P.R., 1965-69; assoc. dir. edn. Archdiocese of N.Y., 1969-71; sec. to Cardinal-Archbishop N.Y., 1971-77; titular bishop of Rusubisir, aux. bishop N.Y., 1977-81; 1st bishop Diocese of Metuchen, N.J., 1981-86; 4th archbishop Newark, 1986—; mem. policy bd. Washington Consortium, Peace Corps, 1962-63, Pontificial Commn. for Migrants and Refugees, 1987; chmn. U.S. Bishops Com. on Migration, 1986-89 ; pres. Nat. Coun. for Spanish-Speaking People, 1961-65; chmn. Gov.'s Commn. for Higher Edn. in P.R., 1968, P.R. Adv. Coun. on Tech. and Vocat. Edn., 1968-69. Mem. Fed. Commn. for Study of Migration and Econ. Devel., 1989—; Episcopal promoter, Apostleship of the Sea, 1989—. Named knight grand cross Holy Sepulchre. Clubs: K.C, Am. Assn. Knights Malta (chaplain 1978-82). Office: 31 Mulberry St Newark NJ 07102-5296

MCCARROLL, WILLIAM HENRY, chemistry educator, researcher; b. Bklyn., Mar. 19, 1930; s. Joseph Allen and Elva Jeanette (Hill) McC.; m. Chantal Sonja Gleanzer, Oct. 25, 1958; children: Monique, Marthe, Marc, Marianne. BS, U. Conn., 1953, PhD, 1957. Mem. tech. staff RCA Labs., Princeton, N.J., 1956-67; asst. prof. chemistry Rider Coll., Lawrenceville, N.J., 1967-72, assoc. prof., 1973-79, prof., 1979—; rsch. assoc. Rutgers U., Piscataway, N.J., 1982—. Mcpl. chmn. Lawrence Twp. Rep. Orgn., Lawrenceville, 1967-69; councilman Twp. Lawrence, Mercer County, N.J., 1976. Mem. Am. Chem. Soc. (chmn. Trenton sect. 1978-79, 83-84, nat. councillor 1986—). Presbyterian. Office: Rider Coll PO Box 6400 Trenton NJ 08648-0400

MCCARRON, PAUL J., art dealer; b. Mason City, Iowa, June 15, 1933; s. Ralph Noble and Margaret (Mogan) McC. BFA, Art Inst., Chgo., 1958, MFA, 1959. Owner Paul McCarron Fine Prints and Drawings, N.Y.C., 1970—. Author: Catalogue Raisonne of Prints by Martin Lewis. With U.S. Army, 1953-55. Mem. Internat. Fine Print Dealers Assn. Democrat. Roman Catholic. Office: 1014 Madison Ave New York NY 10021-0103

MCCARRON, ROBERT ANDREW, physician; b. Bayonne, N.J., June 22, 1949; s. James Patrick and Marie Louise (Sheppard) McC.; m. Patricia Ann Marie Amabile, June 8, 1991; children: Robert Andrew Jr., Brianna Maria. BS, St. Peters Coll., Jersey City, N.J., 1982; MD, SUNY, Bkyln., 1988. Intner The Brookdale Hosp., Bklyn., 1988-89; resident Jersey Shore Med. Ctr., Neptune, N.J., 1991, physician dept. internal medicine, 1991—. Sgt. USAF, 1968-72. Mem. Vietnam Vets. N.J. Roman Catholic. Home: 727 Avenue C Bayonne NJ 07002-2813 Office: The Jersey Shore Med Ctr 1945 Corlies Ave Neptune NJ 07753-4859

MC CARTER, THOMAS N., III, investment counseling company executive; b. N.Y.C., Dec. 16, 1929; s. Thomas N., Jr. and Suzanne M. (Pierson) McC.; student Princeton, 1948-51. Sales exec. Mack Trucks, Inc., N.Y.C., 1952-59; ptnr. Kelly, McCarter, D'Arcy Investment Counsel, N.Y.C., 1959-62; v.p., sec., dir. D'Arcy, McCarter & Chew, N.Y.C., 1962-66; v.p., dir. Trainer, Wortham & Co., Inc., N.Y.C., 1967-71, exec. v.p., 1971-75; chmn. bd., dir. Island Security Bank Ltd., 1976-78; pres. Knottingham Ltd., N.Y.C., 1976-84; gen. ptnr. W.P. Miles Timber Properties, New Orleans; exec. v.p., Yorke McCarter Owen & Bartels, Inc., N.Y.C., 1985-89, also bd. dirs.; fins. cons. Laidlaw Holdings, Inc., 1990—; pres., bd. dirs., Mentor Mgmt. Group, Inc. N.Y.C., 1986-90; chmn. bd. dirs. Ramapo Land Co., Sloatsburg, N.Y., 1990—. Chmn. bd. trustees Christodora Found., Inc., N.Y.C.; charter trustee Dalton Sch., N.Y.C., 1968-76, v.p., 1972-76; pres., trustee Civil War Library and Mus., Phila., 1985-92, Nat. Symphony Orch., Washingtono; chmn. trustee Am. Soc. Prevention Cruelty to Animals; chmn. Loyal Legion Found., N.Y.C.; trustee Children's Aid Soc. N.Y.C., Joffrey Ballet, Found. for Am. Dance, 1973-77; pres., trustee N.Y.C. Marble Cemetery Assn.; mem. Com. for Preservation of the U.S. Treasury Bldg., 1988-92; trustee Nat. Symphony Orch. Chartered investment counselor. Mem. Loyal Legion U.S. (comdr. N.Y. State 1964-66, nat. comdr. in chief 1977-81), Racquet and Tennis Clubs, Brook Club, Links Club, River Club, St. Nicholas Soc., Pilgrims of U.S. (N.Y.C.), Meadow Club (Southampton, N.Y.), Ivy Club (Princeton, N.J.). Home: 823 Park Ave New York NY 10021-2849 Office: Laidlaw Holdings Inc 275 Madison Ave New York NY 10016-1101

MCCARTHY, ALBERT HENRY, human resources executive; b. Worcester, Mass., May 17, 1944; s. Albert H. and Rosemary (Sheehan) McC.; m. Ann F. Arseneault, 1965; children: Erin Marie, Caitlin Ann. BA in Sociology, Coll. Holy Cross, Worcester, Mass., 1968, Cert. Indsl. Rels., 1975; postgrad., Assumption Coll., Worcester, Mass. Recruiter Data Gen. Corp., Southborough, Mass., 1972-73, personnel adminstr., 1973-74, personnel supr., 1974-76; New Eng. dist. personnel mgr. Digital Equip. Corp., Waltham, Mass., 1976-78; mgr. staffing systems and programs Honeywell Info. System, Inc., Waltham, Mass., 1978-80; dir. human resources NEC Info. Systems, Inc., Boxborough, Mass., 1980-84, v.p. human resources, 1984—; speaker, panelist Japan External Trade Orgn./Bus. Wk. Symposium, 1989. Author: Personnel Journal, 1989, 91. Capt. USAF, 1968-71. Recipient Best Practice: Recruitment Category Personal Recruitment Program award Human Resource Exec. mag., 1992. Mem. Soc. Human Resource Mgmt. (Yoder Heneman Creative Application award 1990), N.E. Human Resources Assn., Boxborough Bus. Assn. (founding mem.), Toastmasters. Home: 466 Burncoat St Worcester MA 01606-1418 Office: NEC Technologies Inc 1414 Massachusetts Ave Boxboro MA 01719-2298

MCCARTHY, BARRY WAYNE, clinical psychologist; b. Chgo., Sept. 7, 1943; s. Edward Joseph and Dorothy (Small) McC.; B.A., Loyola U., Chgo., 1965; Ph.D., So. Ill. U., 1969; m. Emily Jeannette McCabe, Nov. 19, 1966; children: Mark, Kara, Paul. Intern, Wood VA Hosp., Milw., 1968-69; psychology cons. Mt. Vernon Ctr. for Community Mental Health, Alexandria, Va., 1970-73; mem. faculty Am. U., Washington, 1969—, prof. psychology, 1978—; ptnr. Washington Psychol. Ctr., 1977—. Diplomate Am. Bd. Profl. Psychology; cert. sex therapist. Mem. Am. Psychol. Assn., Assn. for Advancement of Behavior Therapy, Am. Assn. Sex Educators, Counselors and Therapists, Am. Assn. Marital and Family Therapists. Author: (with M. Ryan and F. Johnson) Sexual Awareness: A Practical Approach, 1975; What You Still Don't Know About Male Sexuality, 1977; (with wife) Sexual Satisfaction After Thirty, 1981, (with wife) Sexual Awareness: Sharing Sexual Pleasure, 1984, Male Sexual Awareness: Increasing Sexual Pleasure, 1988, (with wife) Female Sexual Awareness: Achieving Sexual Fulfillment, 1989, (with Emily Jeannette McCarthy) Couple Sexual Awareness: Building Sexual Happiness, 1990. Home: 126 Gills Neck Rd Lewes DE 19958-1407 Office: 4201 Connecticut Ave NW Washington DC 20008-1158

MCCARTHY, DANIEL WILLIAM, management consultant; b. Syracuse, N.Y., Apr. 15, 1952; s. William Cornelius and Ruth Francis (Geller) McC.; m. Mary Coleen Kisil, Jan. 27, 1987; children: Katherine M., Kevin D. BA in Polit. Sci., SUNY, Geneseo, 1974; MBA, NYU, 1982. Asst. buyer Abraham & Straus, Bklyn., 1976-78; buyer Lord & Taylor, N.Y.C., 1978-80; cons. Touche Ross, Newark, 1982-87; sr. mgr. Deloitte & Touche, N.Y.C., 1987—. Author: Point of Sale - Current Trends and Beyond, 1986; contbr. articles to profl. jours. Mem. Nat. Retail Fedn., Inst. Mgmt. Cons. Roman Catholic.

MCCARTHY, EDWARD DAVID, JR., financial planner and consultant; b. Providence, Feb. 20, 1955; s. Edward David and Anne (McDonald) McC.; m. Diane Winkleman, Aug. 18, 1979. BA, U. R.I., 1979; M in Internat. Bus., U. S.C., 1981; postgrad., U. Conn., 1991—. Cert. fin. planner. Fin. planner Goluses & Co. CPA's, Providence, 1988-91; rsch. asst. U. Conn., Storrs, 1991—; 1990-91; instr. U. R.I., Kingston, 1987—, Bryant Coll., Smithfield, R.I., 1990-91; pub. R.I. Rate Monitor, 1990-91; rsch. asst. U. Conn., 1991—. Contbr. articles to profl. jours. Mem. Inst. Cert. Fin. Planners (v.p. nat. bd. dirs. 1990).

MCCARTHY, FREDERICK WILLIAM, investment banker; b. Boston, Nov. 25, 1941; s. Frederick William and Josephine Leona (Pannier) McC.; children: Daniel Arthur, Frederick William III, Kathryn Elizabeth. BA magna cum laude, Harvard U., 1963, MBA with high distinction, 1967. Mgmt. cons. Booz Allen & Hamilton, Inc., Chgo., 1967-70; 1st v.p. investment banking Shearson, Hammill & Co., Inc., N.Y.C., 1970-72, Chgo., 1972-74; mng. dir. Drexel Burnham Lambert, Inc., Boston, 1974-90, The Boston Corp. Fin. Group Inc., 1990—; bd. dirs. Fairchild Corp., Seminole Kraft Corp., Stone Savannah River Pulp & Paper Co. Inc., The Westwood Group Inc., Rexnord Holdings Inc., NutraMax Products Inc. Mem. bd. govs. Haifa U., Israel. 1st lt U.S. Army, 1963-65. Home: Palm Beach FL 33480-3050 Ofice: One Post Office Sq 37th Fl Boston MA 02109

MCCARTHY, JAMES JADIDI, bank executive; b. N.Y.C., Sept. 5, 1965; s. Nasser B. Jadidi and Jean McCarthy; m. Haleh Milani, Dec. 30, 1989. BA in Internat. Politics with honors, NYU, 1986, MBA in Fin./Internat. Bus., 1989. Liaison officer Liberal Internat. (Internat. Arm of Liberal Party U.K.), London, 1985-86; legal asst. Vladeck, Waldman, Elias & Engelhard, N.Y.C., 1986-88; mgr. corp. accounts, asst. v.p. Toronto-Dominion Bank, N.Y.C., 1989—. Treas., bd. dirs. Gabe Velez Found. for the Constrn. and Renovation of Recreational Facilities for City Kids, N.Y.C., 1991—; capt. NYU Squash Team, 1989—. Fgn. Lang./Area Studies award Dept. of Def., Princeton U., 1984, Dept. of Def., Columbia U., 1986; Grad. fellow for the study of politics and Near Eastern studies NYU, 1986. Mem. Met. Squash Racquets Assn., U.S. Squash Raquets Assn. Home: 153 E 32d St # PHE New York NY 10016 Office: Toronto Dominion Bank 31 W 52d St New York NY 10019

MCCARTHY, JAMES JOSEPH, oceanography educator, museum director; b. Ashland, Oreg., Jan. 25, 1944; m. 1969, 2 children. B.S., Gonzaga U., 1966; Ph.D., Scripps Inst. Oceanography, U. Calif.-San Diego, 1971. Research assoc. biol. oceanography Chesapeake Bay Inst., Johns Hopkins U., 1971-72, assoc. research scientist, 1972-74; asst. prof. Harvard U., 1974-77, assoc. prof., 1977-80, prof. biol. oceanography, 1980—, assoc. dean faculty Arts and Scis., 1986-90; dir. Agassiz Mus. Comparative Zoology, 1982—. Editor: Global Biogeochemical Cycles, 1986-90. Chmn. Internat. Coun. of Scientific Unions, Scientific Com. Internat. Geosphere-Biosphere Program, 1987—. Fellow AAAS, Am. Acad. Arts and Scis.; mem. Phycol. Soc. Am., Am. Soc. Limnology and Oceanography, Am. Geophys. Union. Office: Mus Comparative Zoology 26 Oxford St Cambridge MA 02138-2902

MCCARTHY, JOHN PATRICK, registrar, political science educator; b. Gary, Ind., Oct. 31, 1921; s. Daniel Joseph and Sadie (Sweeney) McC.; m. Sally Anne O'Neil, June 9, 1962; children: John, Eileen, Sheila, Maura. BA, Ind. U., 1946; MA, U. Chgo., 1947. Asst. prof. polit. sci. The Cath. U. of Am., Washington, 1956—, asst. dean Sch. Arts and Scis., 1970-85, registrar, 1985—. Sgt. U.S. Army, 1943-46, ETO. Mem. Am. Assn. Collegiate Registrars and Admissions Officers. Roman Catholic. Office: The Cath U of Am Washington DC 20064

MCCARTHY, JOHN ROBERT, real estate firm officer; b. Carlisle, Pa., May 29, 1945; s. James Francis and Eleanor Marie (Harrington) McC.; m. Cathleen Ann Rice, Oct. 25, 1975; children: Kevin James, Michael John. BA in Bus. & Polit. Sci., St. Leo Coll., Fla., 1969. Mktg. rep. R.H. Donnelley Corp., N.Y.C., 1969-70; employee benefits rep. Marsh & McLennan Corp., N.Y.C., 1970-73; overseas sales rep. AMF, Inc., White Plains, N.Y., 1973-79; ptnr., sr. v.p. Rostenberg-Doern Co., White Plains, 1979-90; ptnr. pres. McCarthy-O'Callaghan Co Inc, White Plains, 1990—. Mem. Con Edison Sports Hall of Fame Com., White Plains, 1982—, St. Agnes Hosp. Children's Com., 1983—; bd. dirs. Am. Diabetes Assn. Westchester, 1987—; mem. Cardinals Com. of Laity Westchester. Mem. Exch. Club (hon., past pres. Downtown chpt.), Friendly Sons St. Patrick (officer Westchester chpt. 1984—, pres. 1990-91, bd. stewards 1991—), Orienta Beach Club (chmn. children's com. 1987—), Winged Foot Golf Club. Roman Catholic. Home: 16 Ridgeway Cir White Plains NY 10605-4119 Office: 1 N Broadway White Plains NY 10601

MCCARTHY, JOSEPH JUSTIN, academic administrator; b. Washington, Aug. 3, 1949; s. Joseph Justin and Mary Lourdes (Riley) McC.; m. Marina Alexandra Chukayeff, Sept. 16, 1972; children: Kevin Justin, Natasha Alexandra. BA, Boston Coll., 1972, MA, 1974; Cert. Adv. Study, Harvard U., 1983, EdM, 1990, EdD, 1991. Cert. tchr. of English, social studies, sec. adminstr., Mass. Tchr. secondary English, social studies, math various schs., U.S.A., Greece and Holland, 1972-82; lectr. English Boston Coll., Chestnut Hill, Mass., 1982-86; cons. Coalition of Essential Schs. Brown U., Providence, 1985-87; teaching fellow, rsch. asst. Grad Sch. Edn. Harvard Univ., Cambridge, Mass., 1982-87, spl. asst. Office Acad. and Student Svcs., 1984-86; fellowr, expository writing program Harvard Coll., Cambridge, Mass., 1986-87; study group leader Inst. of Politics Harvard Univ., Cambridge, Mass., 1987-90, exec. asst. to dean Kennedy Sch. of Govt., 1989-90; asst. dean for acad. planning Office Acad. Affairs Faculty of Arts and Scis., Harvard U., 1990—; bd. dirs. Harvard Law Sch. Child Care Ctr., 1989-90; cons. in field. Contbr. articles to profl. jours. Organizer polit. campaigns, Mass.; affiliate Dudley House, Harvard U. Recipient Herold Hunt fellowship Harvard U., 1985, Jessie Smith Noyes fellowship, 1984-86. Mem. Harvard Club, Phi Delta Kappa. Democrat. Roman Catholic. Home: 23 Pine St Belmont MA 02178-2765 Office: Harvard U Univ Hall 9 Cambridge MA 02138

MC CARTHY, JOSEPH MICHAEL, historian, educator; b. Lynn, Mass., Oct. 2, 1940; s. Joseph Donald and Johanna (Downing) Mc C.; A.B., St. John's Sem., 1961, postgrad., 1961-63; A.M., Boston Coll., 1968, Ph.D., 1972; m. Kathleen Frances Wright, July 30, 1966; children—Joanna, Kristenmarie, Erika, Joseph Michael. Tchr., Bishop Fenwick High Sch., Peabody, Mass., 1964-67; asst. dir. student fin. aid Boston Coll., 1967-69, 70-71; asst. dir. Inst. Human Scis., Chestnut Hill, Mass., 1969-70; lectr. in edn. Boston Coll., 1971-73, adj. lectr., 1974, 90; prof. edn., grad. program coord., dir. leadership programs Suffolk U., 1973—; adj. lectr. Merrimack Coll., 1975, Boston U., 1973; gen. editor Garland Pub., 1979—. Recipient Hearn scholarship, 1959-61, fellowship, 1961-63. Mem. Assn. Ancient Historians, Am., Cath. Hist. assns., East European Rsch. Inst., Soc. for Medieval and Renaissance Philosophy, Soc. Romanian Historians, East European Rsch. Inst., Medieval Acad. Am., Mass. Coll. Personnel Assn., Mass. Assn. of Student Fin. Aid Adminstrs., Phi Alpha Theta, Phi Delta Kappa. Author: An International List of Articles on the History of Education, Published in Non-Educational Serials, 1965-74, 1977; Guinea-Bissau and Cape Verde Islands: A Comprehensive Bibliography, 1977; Humanistic Emphases in the Educational Thought of Vincent of Beauvais, 1976; Pierre Teilhard de Chardin, 1981; Training School Administrators: The Principal, 1984; Training School Administrators: The Supervisor, 1984; assoc. editor The Urban and Social Change Rev., 1969-72; asst. editor occasional papers series The Bureaucrat, Inc., 1974-76; contbr. to numerous scholarly jours. Home: 344 West St Box 1193 Duxbury MA 02331-1193 Office: Suffolk U Beacon Hill Boston MA 02114

MCCARTHY, JUSTIN MILTON, marketing professional; b. St. Paul, Feb. 9, 1924; s. Frederic Donough and Florence Ruth (Milton) McC.; m. Inez Victoria Jensen, June 25, 1949; children: Patricia E. McCarthy Graham, Daniel V., John D., Anne Marie McCarthy Brosko. B in Med. Sci., U. Minn., 1949, MA, 1954; DO (hon.), Am. Coll. Gen. Practice, Arlington Heights, Ill., 1982. With Wyeth Labs., 1950—; dir. profl. rels. Wyeth-Ayerst Labs., Radnor, Pa., 1979—; bd. dirs. Trade Show Bur., Denver, 1986—. Co-author: Job Loss, 1981; contbr. numerous articles to profl. jours. Bd. dirs., past chmn. Nat. Osteopathic Found., Chgo., 1963—; past pres. Del. County chpt. Am. Heart Assn.; campaign chmn. Rep. Com., Radnor, 1979, 83, 87, 91. Pfc. Med. Svc., 1943-46. Recipient Hon. Citizenship, City of New Orleans, 1964; named Main Line Person of Yr., Lions, Wayne, 1971, Man of Yr., Pa. Police Chiefs, Harrisburg, 1970. Mem. Am. Coll. Ob/Gyn. (cons.

task force on cancer 1985—), Am. Cancer Soc. (bd. dirs., past pres. Delaware County unit), Am. Acad. Family Physicians Found. (trustee 1986—, Award of Merit 1984), Healthcare Conv. and Exhibitors Assn. (bd. dirs., past pres.), Found. for Advances in Clin. Medicine (bd. dirs.), Exhibit Industry Edn. Found. (bd. dirs. 1988—), Harris County Med. Soc. (hon.). Republican. Roman Catholic. Home: 125 Cornwall Ln Saint Davids PA 19087

MCCARTHY, KATHLEEN D., educator; b. Hollywood, Fla., Feb. 19, 1949; d. Daniel D. and Joan McC.; m. Christopher K. Olander, May 20, 1975 (div. 1988). BA, U. Ill., 1972; MA, U. Chgo., 1973, PhD, 1980. Instr. Roosevelt U., Chgo., 1978-79; vis. rsch. fellow Rockefeller Found., N.Y.C., 1980-82; cons. NEH, N.Y.C., 1982-83; asst. sec. Metro. Life Found., N.Y.C., 1983-86; assoc. prof. and dir. Ctr. for Study of Philanthropy Grad. Sch. and Univ. Ctr., CUNY, 1986—. Author: Women's Culture: American Philanthropy and Art, 1830-1930, 1991, Noblesse Oblige: Charity and Cultural Philanthropy in Chicago, 1849-1929, 1982; editor: Lady Bountiful Revisited: Women Philanthropy and Power, 1990, Philanthropy and Culture: The International Foundation Perspective, 1984; contbr. articles to profl. jours. Recipient numerous grants to develop Ctr. for Study of Philanthropy. Office: Ctr for Study Philanthrophy Rm 1525 GB 33 W 42d St New York NY 10036

MCCARTHY, KEVIN PAUL, beverage products executive; b. Rockville Ctr., N.Y., Apr. 13, 1957; s. Charles Joseph and Mary Bridget (O'Sullivan) McC.; m. Valerie Ross, Sept. 6, 1985; children: Alison Michelle, Kevin Charles. BS, Bradley U., 1979. Asst. rte. sales mgr. Pepcom Industries, Garden City, N.Y., 1980-84, rte. sales mgr., 1980-81, food svc. mgr., 1981-84; area sales mgr. Sunkist Soft Drinks, inc., Atlanta, 1984-86; account sales mgr. Seven-Up Co., St. Louis, 1986-87; account sales mgr. Dr Pepper/Seven-Up Co., Dallas, 1987-88, spl. account mgr., 1988—. Recipient Disting. Sales award from Sales and Mktg. Exec. Internat., 1989. Office: Dr Pepper/Seven-Up Co 216 Roosevelt Ave Freeport NY 11520

MCCARTHY, MARGARET WILLIAM, music educator; b. Brockton, Mass., Nov. 20, 1931; d. William Francis and Julia Margaret (O'Brien) McC. MusB, Manhattanville Coll., Purchase, N.Y., 1953; MusM, Pius XII Inst., Florence, Italy, 1954; MusD, Boston U., 1965. Joined Sisters of St. Joseph of Boston, 1954. Music specialist St. Thomas Sch., Jamaica Plan, Mass., 1959-61; music prof. Regis Coll., Weston, Mass., 1961—; adv. bd. Sisters of St. Joseph Office of Peace & Justice, Brighton, Mass., 1987-89. Editor: More Letters of Amy Fay, 1986; contbr. articles to profl. jours. Active Weston (Mass.) Arts Coun., 1989—, Beyond War, Wellesley, Mass., 1990-92, Found. for a Global Community, 1992—. Radcliffe Rsch. Support grantee Radcliffe Coll., 1987, 83, Mass. Coun. on Arts & Humanities grantee, 1984, Travelto-Collection grantee NEH, 1987, Summer Seminar grantee, 1975. Mem. Music Critics Assn., Sonneck Soc., Am. Musicological Soc., Internat. Soc. for Music Edn., Sigma Alpha Iota. Democrat. Roman Catholic. Home and office: 235 Wellesley St Weston MA 02193-1505

MCCARTHY, PAUL JAMES, chemistry educator; b. Rochester, N.Y., June 15, 1924; s. Patrick James and Margaret Catherine (Schwan) McC. AB, Spring Hill Coll., 1950; MS, Holy Cross Coll., Worcester, Mass., 1952; PhD, Clark U., 1955; STL, Woodstock Coll., 1958. Instr. chemistry Regis High Sch., N.Y.C., 1950-51, St. Peter's Coll., Jersey City, 1959-60; instr. chemistry Canisius Coll., Buffalo, 1960-62, asst. prof., 1962-68, assoc. prof., 1968-72, prof., 1972—; vis. prof. York U., Downsview, Ont., Can., 1974, U. Bern (Switzerland), 1982-83. Author, editor: (with K. Nakamoto) Spectroscopy and Structure of Metal Chelate Compounds, 1968; contbr. articles to profl. jour.s. Recipient Niagara sect. award Soc. Applied Spectroscopy, Buffalo, 1968; fellow NATO, Copenhagen, Denmark, 1966-67. Mem. Am. Chem. Soc. Roman Catholic. Office: Canisius Coll 2001 Main St Buffalo NY 14208-1098

MCCARTHY, RAYMOND LAWRENCE, chemist; b. Jersey City, N.J., Sept. 6, 1920; s. Francis Robert and Catherine Clare (Flannery) McC.; m. Gloria Ison, Sept. 11, 1943; children: Raymond Jr., Kevin, Sharon, Maureen. AB in Math., Fordham U., 1941, MA in Physics, 1942; MS in Physics, Yale U., 1947, PhD in Physics, 1948. Rsch. scientist E.I. DuPont, Wilmington, Del., 1948-52, rsch. mgr., 1952-56, asst. lab. dir., 1956-60; mfg. supt. E.I. DuPont, Pennsville, N.J., 1960-64; lab. dir. E.I. DuPont, Wilmington, 1964-74, tech. dir., 1974-85; pres. Lenape Cons., Westtown, Pa., 1985—; chmn. Internat. Flurocarbon Panel, Washington, 1972-80; adj. prof. physics U. Del., Newark, 1968-72; faculty selection com. Harvard U., Cambridge, Mass., 1974-76. Contbr. 16 articles to profl. jours. Del. UN Environ. Program, Amsterdam, Copenhagen, 1976-80; pres. West Chester (Pa.) Sch. Bd., 1954-76; chmn. Chester County Youth Expo, West Chester, 1990-91; chmn. Chester County ARC, 1987-91; bd. dirs. Chester County Hist. Soc., 1985-91, Chester County YMCA, 1988-91. Lt. (j.g.) USN, 1942-45. Mem. Am. Phys. Soc., Rotary (chmn. dist. 745 conv. 1989, bd. dirs. West Chester chpt. 1983). Republican. Roman Catholic. Home: PO Box 35 Westtown PA 19395-0035 Office: Lenape Cons Lenape Westtown PA 19395

MCCARTHY, ROBERT E., mental health counselor; b. Newark, Sept. 5, 1949; s. Edward Francis and Elise Jean (Litcholt) McCarthy; m. Carolyn Grace Laginestra, Aug. 16, 1970; children: Edward, Theresa, Roc Alan. AA, Rockland Community Coll., 1969; BA in Psychology, Fairleigh Dickinson U., 1971; MA in Clin. Psychology, St. John's U., Queens, N.Y., 1972; PhD in Counseling Psychology, Columbia Pacific U., 1987. Diplomate and fellow Am. Bd. Psychotherapy, Am. Bd. Stress Practitioners. Staff psychologist Letchworth Devel. Ctr., Thiells, N.Y., 1972-73, Barnert Meml. Hosp., Paterson, N.J., 1973-74, Orange County Community Mental Health Ctr., Goshen, N.Y., 1974-77; dir. behavior modification unit Harlem Valley Psychiat. Ctr., Wingdale, N.Y., 1976-77; supervising psychologist Goshen Secure Ctr., 1977-84, Tryon Secure Ctr., Johnstown, N.Y., 1984-88; program coord. mobile mental health team Capital Dist. Psychiat. Ctr., Albany, N.Y., 1988-90; exec. dir. Saratona Clin. Assocs., Saratoga Springs, N.Y., 1990—; adj. faculty mem. Ctr. for Distance Learning, Empire State Coll., Saratoga Springs, 1987-91; mem. faculty Columbia Pacific U., San Rafael, Calif., 1987—; psychol. cons. Pius XII Youth and Family Svc., Chester, N.Y., 1983-84; cons. Falkirk Psychiat. Hosp., Central Valley, N.Y., 1972-84; adj. faculty mem. Orange County Community Coll., Middletown, N.Y., 1981-82, asst. prof., 1979-80; adj. faculty mem. Bergen County Community Coll., Paramus, N.J., 1973-76. Contbr. articles to profl. publs. Recipient Profl. Svc. award AMHCA, 1990, 91. Fellow Internat. Acad. Behavioral Medicine, Counseling and Psychotherapy, Inc. (diplomate), Am. Assn. Profl. Hypnotherapists, Am. Bd. Med. Psychotherapy; mem. AACD, Nat. Computer Systems, Am. Mental Health Counselors Assn. (Counselor Of Yr. 1991), N.Y. State AACD, N.Y. State Mental Health Counselors Assn., Assn. Advancement Psychophysiology and Biofeedback, Biofeedback Soc. N.Y., Am. Assn. Behavioral Therapists, Soc. for Personality Assessment, Nat. Acad. Cert. Mental Health Counselors (approved clin. supr.), Chi Sigma Iota, Psi Chi. Roman Catholic. Home: 65 Brackett Ln Gansevoort NY 12831-1776 Office: Saratoga Springs Clin Assoc 376 Broadway Ste 7L Saratoga Springs NY 12866-3115

MCCARTHY, SUSAN STACY, financial analyst; b. China Lake, Calif., Aug. 8, 1962; d. Paul Fenton Jr. and Sandra Sue (Williams) McC. BA in Econs. and Chinese Studies, U. Calif., San Diego, 1986; M of Pub. Fin. Mgmt., Am. U., 1992. Exec. v.p. Calif. Designers Delivery, Vernon, Calif., 1986-88; fin. mgr. office of comptr. U.S. Dept. Navy, Washington, 1988-91; fin. analyst def. subcom., appropriations com. U.S. Senate, 1991-92; fin. mgt. strategic nuclear forces and sealift Office of Navy Comptroller, 1992—. Active Habitat for Humanity, So Others Might Eat, ARC; sponsor World Visions, Sponsor Plan Internat. With USNR, 1990—. Mem. Am. Soc. Mil. Comptrs. Republican. Episcopalian. Home: 100 Century Dr Apt 7309 Alexandria VA 22304-5795

MCCARTHY, TIMOTHY FRANCIS, financial services company executive; b. San Mateo County, Calif., Sept. 19, 1951; s. Timothy Daniel and Helen Josephine (Sinnott) McC.; m. Kirsten Hydorn, Sept. 13, 1981; children: Priscilla, Madeleine, Timothy. BA in Econs. and Internat. Rels., U. Calif., Davis, 1973; MBA with highest acad. honors, Harvard U., 1978. Officer Chem. Bank, N.Y.C., Frankfurt, Germany, 1973-76; pres. McCarthy Internat., San Francisco, 1978-82; v.p. Merrill Lynch, N.Y.C., 1983-87; pres. NFIS-Fidelity Investments, Boston, 1987—; key speaker Securities Industry Assn., N.Y.C., 1990-91, Global Trading Symposium, N.Y.C., 1991-92. Bd. dirs. World Affairs Coun., Boston, 1989—; chmn. small bus. campaign United Way, Boston, 1991. Baker scholar Harvard U., 1978. Home: 21 Garden Rd Wellesley MA 02181 Office: NFIS-Fidelity Investments 82 Devonshire L3 B Boston MA 02109

MC CARTNEY, ROBERT CHARLES, lawyer; b. Pitts., May 3, 1934; s. Nathaniel Hugh and Esther Mary (Smith) McC.; m. Janet Carolyn Moore, June 16, 1956; children: Ronald K., Sharon S., Carole J. AB, Princeton U., 1956; JD, Harvard U., 1959. Bar: D.C. 1959, Pa. 1960, U.S. Dist. Ct. (we. dist.) Pa. 1960, U.S. Ct. Appeals (3d dist.) 1960, U.S. Supreme Ct. 1966. Assoc. Eckert, Seamans, Cherin & Mellott, Pitts., 1959-64, ptnr., 1965—; sec., gen. counsel Ryan Homes, Inc., Penn Beaver Veneer Corp.; gen. counsel Edn. Mgmt. Corp.; bd. dirs. United Meth. Found. of Western Pa., 1972—, v.p., 1981-85, chmn., 1985-86. Solicitor North Pitts. Community Devel. Corp., 1968-76, alt. dir., 1968-80; mem. McCandless Twp. Govt. Study Commn., 1973-74; solicitor, asst. sec. McCandless Indsl. Devel. Authority, 1972—; mem. exec. com. Princeton U. Alumni Coun., 1966-70, 76-85, vice chmn., 1981-83, chmn., 1983-85; trustee Otterbein Coll., 1975-83; corp. bd. North Hills Passavant Hosp., 1976—; chmn. conf.-wide endowment program United Meth. Conf. Western Pa., 1985-87; bd. dirs. Pitts. Civic Light Opera Assn., 1986—, v.p., 1987—; bd. dirs., gen. counsel The Ireland Inst. Pitts., 1991—; mem. No. Ireland Partnership, 1991—, Golden Triangle YMCA. Princeton fellow Harvard U., 1956-59. Mem. ABA, Pa. Bar Assn., Allegheny County Bar Assn., Princeton U. Alumni Assn. West Pa. (pres. 1976-78), Harvard-Yale-Princeton Club, Allegheny Club, Duquesne Club, Princeton Club (N.Y.C.). Republican. Home: 9843 Woodland Rd Pittsburgh PA 15237-4362 Office: 600 Grant St USX Tower 42d Fl Pittsburgh PA 15219

MCCARTY, HARRY DOWNMAN, tool manufacturing company executive; b. Balt., Aug. 30, 1946; s. H. Downman and Melissa (Dunham) McC.; m. Helen Hilliard, May 13, 1948; children: Cormac Downman, Henning Hilliard. BA, Johns Hopkins U., 1968. Math. instr. Gilman Sch., Balt., 1970-71; sales mgr. Balt. Tool Works Inc., Balt., 1971-79, pres., 1979—; bd. dirs. Tool Ins. Co., Ltd., Hamilton, Bermuda. Co-chmn. Robert Nicolls scholarship fund Friends Sch., Balt., 1986—. 1st lt. U.S. Army, 1968-70. Recipient Barton Cup winner for campus leadership, Johns Hopkins U., 1968, 1st Team All-Am.-Lacrosse, 1968. Mem. Hand Tools Inst. (bd. dirs. 1985-86, 1990—), Am. Hardware Mfg. Assn., Am. Supply and Machinery Mfg. Assn., Specialty Tools and Fastener Distbn. Assn., Am. Soc. Metals, Md. Club, L'Hirondelle Club (bd. dirs. 1989—), ODK Hon. Soc. Republican. Episcopalian. Office: Balt Tool Works Inc 110 W West St Baltimore MD 21230-3725

MCCARTY, KATHRYN SHANE, information services executive; b. Syracuse, N.Y., Oct. 22, 1954; d. Clifford John and Mary Katherine (Eckel) Shane; m. Kevin S. McCarty, Aug. 13, 1983; children: Shane, Katelyn. BA, Denison U., 1976; MPA, U. Washington, 1983. Dir. community devel. P.E.A.C.E., Inc., Syracuse, N.Y., 1976-77; dir. community svcs. City of Alexandria's (Va.) Econ. Opportunity Commn., 1977-78; tng. coord. Am. Pub. Welfare Assn., Washington, 1978-79; asst. project dir. Section 504 Compliance Project Nat. League of Cities, Washington, 1979-81; exec. asst. Office of the King County Exec., Seattle, 1982-83; adminstrv. asst. (dep. dir.) Kirkland (Wash.) Dept. Fin. and Adminstrn., 1984; dir. adminstrn. and program devel. Consumer Energy Coun. of Am., Washington, 1984-86; dir. info. svcs. Nat. League of Cities, Washington, 1986—; staff liaison Women in Mcpl. Govt., Washington. Office: Nat League Cities 1301 Pennsylvania Ave NW Washington DC 20004

MCCARTY, LUANN, public relations executive; b. Hammonton, N.J., Apr. 26, 1960; d. Michael Joseph and Anna Marie (Donio) Pajic; m. Terrance James McCarty, Oct. 6, 1984; children: Lindsay Anne, Daniel James. Bachelors, Trenton State Coll., 1982, Masters, 1990. Adminstr. pub. affairs RCA Labs., Princeton, N.J., 1982-87; asst. v.p., assoc. dir. UJB Fin. Corp., Princeton, 1987-91; dir. pub. rels. Helene Fuld Med. Ctr., Trenton, N.J., 1991—. Mem. United Way of Delware Valley, Trenton, 1991—; mem. golf com. Am. Heart Assn., 1985-87. Mem. Pub. Rels. Soc. Am., Internat. Assn. Bus. Communicators, Am. Hosp. Assn., Pub. Rels. Soc. N.J., N.J. Hosp. Assn. Pub. Rels. and Mktg., C. of C. of Princeton, Mercer County C. of C. Office: Helene Fuld Med Ctr 750 Brunswick Ave Trenton NJ 08638-4174

MCCARTY, RICHARD EARL, biochemist, biochemistry educator; b. Balt., May 3, 1938; s. Maclyn and Anita (Davies) McC.; m. Kathleen Connolly, June 17, 1961; children—Jennifer A., Richard E., Jr., Gregory P. A.B., Johns Hopkins U., 1960, Ph.D., 1964. Postdoctoral assoc. Pub. Health Research Inst., N.Y.C., 1964-66; asst. prof. Cornell U., Ithaca, N.Y., 1966-72, assoc. prof., 1972-77, prof., 1977-90, prof., chmn., 1981-85; dir. biotech. program Cornell U., Ithaca, 1988-90; prof., chmn. Johns Hopkins U., Balt., 1990—; mem. editorial bd. Jour. Biol. Chemistry, Bethesda, Md., 1978-88, assoc. editor, 1981-82; mem. panel NSF, Washington, 1985—. Author: (with D. Wharton) Experiments and Methods in Biochemistry, 1972; contbr. articles to profl. jours. Career Devel. award NIH, 1968-73. Mem. AAAS, Am. Soc. Biochemistry and Molecular Biology, Am. Soc. Plant Physiologists. Home: 2204 Dalewood Rd Lutherville Timonium MD 21093-2701 Office: Johns Hopkins U Dept Biology Baltimore MD 21218

MCCARTY, VIDA FINCH, office manager; b. Atlantic City, Feb. 27, 1945; d. Walter G. and Mary Adele (Roberts) Finch. AA, Catonsville Community Coll., Balt., 1965; BS, U. Md., 1968. Exec. trainee Hutzlers, Balt., 1968-69, asst. buyer, 1969-70; employment counselor Guilford Persolnal, Balt., 1970-72; interior designer Hochschilds, Balt., 1972-75; office mgr., bookkeeper McCarty & McCarty Law Firm, Catonsville, 1976—. Program, hospitality, involvement in action com. Catonsville Presbyn. Ch., 1990—, deacon. Mem. Parliamentary Edn. Assn., Catonsville Community Coll. Alumni Assn. (pres. 1975-76), Bent Twig Federated Garden Club (pres. 1989-91), Federated Women's Club of Catonsville (1st v.p. 1990—). Home: 1606 Frederick Rd Baltimore MD 21228-5087 Office: McCarty & McCarty 1606 Frederick Rd Baltimore MD 21228-5087

MC CAUGHEY, ANDREW GILMOUR, corporate executive; b. Montreal, Que., Can., Dec. 8, 1922; s. Andrew Gilmour and Mary Doris (Sheldon) McC.; m. Lorraine Baltera; children: Jennifer H., Andrew John, Matthew James. B.Com. with honors in Econs, McGill U., 1949. Chartered acct. Auditor Clarkson, Gordon & Co., Montreal, Que., and Toronto, Ont., 1949-53; with Can. Marconi Co., 1953-67, exec. v.p. fin. and adminstrn., 1967-80; sr. v.p. fin. The Molson Cos. Ltd., 1980-88; dir., pres., chief exec. officer N.Am. Life Assurance Co., Toronto, 1988-89; chmn. bd. Grayrock Shared Ventures, Toronto, 1989-92; chmn., chief exec. officer Scott's Hospitality, Inc., Toronto; bd. dirs. Toromont Industries, Ltd., Molson Cos. Ltd. Global Govt. Plus Fund, Monal Internat., Inc., Aquaterra Corp. Bd. dirs. Tim Horton Childrens Found. Pilot RCAF, 1941-45. Mem. Inst. Chartered Accts. of Que. and ONt., Fin. Execs. Inst. of Toronto (pas pres. Montreal chpt.), Toronto Club, Univ. Club, Roayl Canadian Yacht Club, Royal Canadian Mil. Inst., Lambton Gold and Country Club, Goodwood Club (Toronto), RAF Club (London), Met. Club (N.Y.C.). Conservative. Anglican. Office: Scotts Hospitality Inc, 1 Dundas St W, Toronto, ON Canada M5G 1Z3

MCCAULEY, FLOYCE REID, psychiatrist; b. Braddock, Pa., Dec. 30, 1933; d. John Mitchel and Irene (Garner) Reid; m. James Calvin McCauley, July 15, 1955; children: James Stanley, Lori Ellen. BS in Nursing, U. Pitts., 1956; D.O., Coll. Osteopathic Medicine, Phila., 1972. Bd. eligible in child and adult psychiatry. Intern Suburban Gen. Hosp., Norristown, Pa., 1972-73; resident in adult psychiatry Phila. State Hosp. and Phila. Mental Health Clinic, 1973-75; fellow Med. Coll. of Pa. and Ea. Pa. Psychiat. Inst., Phila., 1975-78; Chief child psychiatry inpatient unit Med. Coll. Pa., Phila., 1978-80; med. dir. Carson ValleySch., Flourtown, Pa., 1980-82; dir. outpatient psychiat. clinic Osteopathic Med. Ctr. Phila., 1980-86; staff psychiatrist Kent Gen. Hosp., Dover, Del., 1986-89; psychiat. cons. Del. Guidance Svcs. for Children, Dover, 1986-91; clin. dir. children's unit HCA Rockford Ctr., Newark, 1991—; mem. Mental Health Code Rev. Com. for Del., 1991; inducted into the Chapel of Four Chaplains, Phila., 1983; psychiat. cons. Seaford (Del.) Br. of New Eng. Fellowship for Rehab., Cath. Charities Day Treatment Program for 3-6 Yr. Olds, Dover, Del., 1990—; cons. Del. Guidance Day Treatment Program, 1990—. Mem. Mayor's Com. for Mental Health, Phila., 1983. Mem. Am. Osteopathic Assn., Am. Coll. Neuropsychiatrists, Am. Psychiat. Assn., Am. Acad. Child Psychiatrists (Del. br.). Democrat. Methodist.

MCCAULEY, H(ENRY) BERTON, retired public health dentist; b. Duluth, Minn., Dec. 20, 1913; s. Henry Berton and Flora Agnes (Bourassa) McC.; m. Claire Ann Wolff, Dec. 20, 1937. DDS, U. Md., 1936. Lic. dentist, Md. Instr. oral roentgenology U. Md., Balt., 1936-40; Carnegie fellow in dentistry U. Rochester, N.Y., 1940-43, asst. prof. dentistry, 1943-45; dir. dental care Balt. City Health Dept., 1949-75; health advisor, liaison officer Office of Mayor, Balt., 1975-80; pres. Am. Acad. History of Dentistry, Balt., 1990-91. Contbr. more than 50 articles to profl. jours. Pres. North Balt. (Mental Health) Ctr., Balt., 1980. Comdr. USCG and USPHS, 1945-49. Fellow APHA, AAAS, Am. Coll. Dentists (J. Ben. Robinson award 1991), Internat. Coll. Dentists; mem. ADA (life, coun. on dental therapeutics 1943-48, chmn. sect. on pub. health 1968), Internat. Assn. Dental Rsch., Md. State Dental Assn. (Disting. Svc. award 1986), Am. Acad. History of Dentistry (Hayden-Harris award 1988), Md. Hist. Soc., Balt. City Life Mus., Am. Assn. Pub. Health Dentistry, Walters Art Gallery, Nat. Mus. Dentistry (v.p. 1991—), Mil. Order World Wars, Sigma Xi, Omicron Kappa Upsilon. Roman Catholic. Home: 3804 Hadley Sq E Baltimore MD 21218-1807

MCCAULEY, ROSEMARIE GAROSSINO, business education educator; b. Jersey City, N.J., Apr. 10, 1935; d. Primo and Anna (Bullerdick) Garossino; m. Robert F. McCauley, June 21, 1958; 1 child, Roseanne. BS, Trenton State Coll., 1957; MA, Seton Hall U., 1964; EdD, Fairleigh Dickinson U., 1984. Cert. bus. edn. tchr., N.J. Tchr., bus. edn., dept. chmn. Rutherford (N.J.) High Sch., 1957-67; prof. Montclair State Coll., Upper Montclair, N.J., 1967—, dept. chmn., 1984-90; cons. Pa. Sch. Dist., 1990-91; speaker, workshop coord., panelist in field. Author: Professional Reference for the Office, 1987, Word Processing on the Job, 1987, Mini Sims Temporary, Vols. I and II, 1979; co-author: Business Spelling and Word Power, 2d and 3d edits., 1988, 91; editor Nat. Assn. Bus. Tchr. Educators' Rev., 1985-87, Bus. Edn. Index, 1977-89. Mem. Benevolent Guild, Weehawken, N.J., 1958—, pres., 1963-64; mem. Stevens Inst. of Tech. Parents Assn., Hoboken, N.J., 1982-86, U.S. Power Squadron, Palisades Squadron, 1980—. Recipient Cooperative Edn. Faculty award Montclair State Coll., 1986. Mem. N.J. Bus. Edn. Assn. (pres. 1990-91), Ea. Bus. Edn. Assn. (Collegiate Educator of Yr. 1990), Nat. Bus. Edn. Assn. (Collegiate Educator of Yr. 1989), Assn. Record Mgrs. and Adminstrs., N.J. Bus. Edn. Assn., N.J. Edn. Assn., Curriculum and Adminstrs. Assn., Office Systems Rsch. Assn., Kappa Delta Pi, Pi Omega Pi. Home: 58 Liberty Pl Weehawken NJ 07087-7056 Office: Montclair State Coll BEOSA Dept Upper Montclair NJ 07043

MCCAULEY, WILLIAM, actor; b. Wayne, Pa., Nov. 20, 1947; s. William Stevens and Florence (Enz) Wiley. BS, Northwestern U., Evanston, 1969. Mus. dir. Goodman Theatre, Chgo., 1972-73. Entertainer St. Regis Hotel, N.Y.C., 1975-77, Mildred Pierce, N.Y.C., 1983-85, Ealdorf-Astoria Hotel, N.Y.C., 1986; actor "Chicago", 77 U.S. Cities, 1979-82, "Edwin Prood", N.Y.C., Sacramento, Calif., 1987-88, Tamara, N.Y.C., 1988-91. Recipient Anna Moffo Vocal award Anna Moffo, 1965. Mem. Chi Psi.

MCCAULEY-GRIFFIN, ROSEANNE, gas and electric utilities company executive; b. Hoboken, N.J., Oct. 23, 1964; d. Robert F. and Rosemarie (Garossino) McCauley; m. Daniel P. Griffin, June 24, 1989. B in Engring., Stevens Inst. Tech., 1986; MS, Fairleigh Dickinson U., 1990, Exec. MBA, 1992. Assoc. engr. Pub. Svc. Electric and Gas Co., Newark, 1986-87, engr., 1987-89, lead engr., 1989-91; prin. staff bus. systems analyst Pub. Svc. Electric and Gas Co., 1991—. V.p. Benevolent Guild of Weehawken, N.J., 1991—. Office: Pub Svc Electric & Gas Co 80 Park Plz # 10B Newark NJ 07102-4106

MCCAW, W(ILLIAM) RALPH, psychologist, retired educator; b. Hallowell Twp., Ont., Canada, Oct. 8, 1927; came to the U.S., 1960; s. William James and Eva (Robinson) McC.; m. Grace G. Linney, Aug. 27, 1955; children: Sharon E., Daniel W., Joan C. BA, U. Western Ont., 1951; MA, Northwestern U., 1953, PhD, 1956. Cert. elem. tchr., Ont. Tchr. Garafrax Twp., Belwood, Ont., 1943-46, Manvers Twp., Pontypool, Ont., 1946-49; tchr. Bd. Edn., Toronto, Ont., 1949-50, Sarnia, Ont., 1951-52; tchr. Sr. Sch., Etobicoke, Ont., 1955-57; sch. psychologist TSA 1, Thornhill, Ont., 1957-58, Child Guidance Svc., Toronto, 1958-60; prof. Jersey City State Coll., 1960-90, ret., 1990. Contbr. articles to profl. jours. V.p., pres. Bloomfield (N.J.) Com. for Quality Schs., 1968-70, 75-76. Mem. Am. Psychol. Assn., N.J. Assn. Sch. Psychologists, Am. Assn. Sch. Psychologists, AFT. Democrat. Episcopalian. Home: 140 Demarest Ave Bloomfield NJ 07003-4507

MCCAWLEY, AUSTIN, psychiatrist, educator; b. Greenock, Scotland, Jan. 17, 1925; came to U.S., 1954; s. Austin and Anna Theresa (McBride) McC.; m. Gloria Klein, Feb. 15, 1958; children: Joseph, Tessa. MBCHB, U. Glasgow, 1948. Diplomate Am. Bd. Psychiatry and Neurology; DPM Royal Coll. London. Intern Glasgow Royal Infirmary, Scotland, 1948; resident Inst. Living, Harford, Conn., 1954-57, clin. dir., 1960-66; med. dir. Westchester br. St. Vincent's Hosp., N.Y.C., 1966-72; dir. psychiatry St. Francis Hosp., Hartford, 1972-88; prof. psychiatry U. Conn. Med. Sch., Farmington, 1983—; pvt. practice, West Hartford, Conn., 1988—. Co-author: The Physician, 1983; contbr. articles to profl. jours. Chmn. Bd. Mental Health, State of Conn., 1981-84, Search Com. for Commr. Mental Health, Conn., 1981; mem. Gov.'s Spl. Task Force on Mental health Policy, Conn., 1982. With RAF, 1948-50. Fellow Am. Psychiat. Assn., Am. Coll. Psychiatry (charter fellow, founder); mem. Conn. Psychiat. Soc. (pres. 1978-79), Hartford Golf Club. Democrat. Roman Catholic. Home: 128 Westmont St West Hartford CT 06117-2932 Office: 18 N Main St West Hartford CT 06107-1903

MCCLAFFERTY, STEVEN JOSEPH, controller; b. Poughkeepsie, N.Y., Sept. 15, 1957; s. Floyd Joseph and Mildred Constance McC.; m. Christine F. Keegan, Apr. 3, 1982; children: Meghan Ariana, Maura Helen, Katherine Theresa. AAS, Dutchess Community Coll., 1977; BS, Northeastern U., Boston, 1980; MBA, U. Mass., 1986. Supr. ARC, Boston, 1980-81; analyst New Eng. Life Ins. Co., Boston, 1981-84; acct. Ea. Exclusives, Boston, 1984-85; sr. acct. Univ. Hosp., Boston, 1985-88; asst. dir. fiscal svc. St. Joseph's Hosp., Lowell, Mass., 1988—; group leader gen. ledger/accounts payable Muse-N.E. Region, Boston, 1991—. Home: 4 Dick Dr Merrimack NH 03054 Office: St Josephs Hosp 220 Pawtucket St Lowell MA 01854

MCCLAIN, TOMEY VAN, minister; b. Dallas, June 10, 1952; s. George Tomey McClain and Charlcie Van (Allen) Perry; m. Nancy Ruth Parsons, Aug. 13, 1977; children: Amber Rachel, Vanessa Ruth, Tommy Marshall. BA, Dallas Bapt. U., 1974; MDiv, Southwestern Bapt. Theol. Sem., 1977, PhD, 1985. Ordained to gospel ministry So. Bapt. Ch., 1979. Minister music, youth Cen. Bapt. Ch., Weatherford, Tex., 1979-81; asst. pastor LaPrada Bapt. Ch., Garland, Tex., 1981-83; interim pastor Chapel of the Lake, Wills Point, Tex., 1983-85; pastor First Bapt. Ch., Quinlan, Tex., 1985-89, Calvary Bapt. Ch., Kemp, Tex., 1989; interim pastor Floyd (N.Y.) Bapt. Ch., 1989-90, Long Falls Bapt. Ch., Carthage, N.Y., 1991—; asst. prof. O.T. and Hebrew Mid-Am. Bapt. Theol. Sem., N.E. br., Schenectady, 1989—. Author: Tawakoni News, 1987. Mem. Hunt Bapt. Assn. So. Bapts. for Life (founder 1987), Tawakoni Ministerial Assn. (pres. 1987-89), Hunt Bapt. Assn. (chmn. Christian Life 1987-89), Kiwanis (dir. 1987). Home: 9 Fawn Dr Schenectady NY 12302-3001 Office: Mid-Am Bapt Theol Sem 2810 Curry Rd Schenectady NY 12303-3463

MCCLAIN, WILLIAM THOMAS, lawyer; b. Louisville, June 4, 1926; s. George Lee and Catherine (Spalding) McC.; m. Wanda Barry, Feb. 28, 1949; children: Nina, Catherine, Ann, William, Mary. BS in Metall. Engring., U. Ky., 1948; JD, Loyola U., New Orleans, 1958. Bar: Ill. 1960, D.C. 1988. Engr. Shell Oil Co., Deer Park, Tex., 1948-55; asst. prof. U. Houston, 1951-55; sales engr. Pacific Valves, Inc., New Orleans, 1955-58; assoc. Wilson, Greene & Nelson, New Orleans, 1958, Amoco Corp., Chgo., 1959-86, Finnegan, Henderson, Farabow, Garrett & Danner, Washington, 1987—. With USN, 1944-46. Mem. ABA (chmn. 1987—), Am. Intellectual Property Law Assn. (dir., treas. 1986-90). Republican. Office: Finnegan Henderson et al 1300 I St NW Washington DC 20005-3314

MCCLANAHAN, PRESTON MOORE, III, artist, educator; b. Charleston, W.Va., Dec. 23, 1933; s. Preston Moore Jr. and Katherine McKee (Pierson) McC.; m. Magdalena Maria Michels, May 16, 1959; children: Peter Burke, Noel Martin, Eve Ann. Student, Cin. Art Acad., 1952-55, Columbia U., 1964-65. Designer Pub. Libr. Cin. Hamilton County, 1957-59, George Nelson Co., N.Y.C., 1959; graphic designer Lester Beall, Inc., Brookfield, Conn., 1959-60, Columbia Records, N.Y.C., 1960; prof. R.I. Sch. of Design, Providence, 1972—, program head graphic design, 1987-89; design cons. Mus. of Primitive Art, N.Y.C., 1959-64, N.Y. Med. Coll., N.Y.C., 1959-64, N.Y. Med. Coll., N.Y.C., 1966-72, Harcourt, Brace, Jovanovich, N.Y.C., 1965-66; design assoc. Ladislav Sutnar, Sutnar Design, N.Y.C., 1964-67; designer exhbns. The Am. Mus. Natural History, 1960-71. Producer, dir.: (documentary film) Zardis, 1985-89; contbr. articles to art jours.; exhibited at group shows at Mus. of Modern Art, N.Y., The Whitney Mus. Am. Art, The Smithsonian Inst., Washington, Stedelijk Van Abbemuseum, Netherlands, Howard Wise Gallery, N.Y., The Arts Coun. of G.B., Walker Arts Ctr., Mpls., The Contemporary Arts Ctr., Cin., Inst. Contemporary Art, Phila. and Boston, Contemporary Arts Mus., Houston, Arts Coun. WM/YWHA, Phila., Nat. Autonomous U. Mex., Cleve. Art Mus., R.I. Sch. Design, Woods-Gerry Gallery, Providence Opera Theatre; commd. works include for IBM, Textron, Inc., Mus. Primitive Art, Mus. Art R.I. Sch. Design, PM Films, R.I. Dept. Health, Brown and Sharpe, Inc., Graphic Design Dept. R.I. Sch. Design, Procter and Gamble, Cin. Art Mus., Chase Manhattan Bank, Pepsi Cola Corp., Foster Parents Nat. Office, Providence Pub. Libr., Whitney Mus. Am. Art, Contemporary Arts Ctr. Cin., Champion Paper, New Repub. Mag., Rosenthal Publ. Co., Standard Oil N.J., William S. Merrill Co., Baldwin Piano Co. Grantee R.I. Com. for the Humanities, 1988, R.I. State Coun. on the Arts, 1987, 88, faculty devel. fund R.I. Sch. of Design, 1986, 87; recipient Famous Person award Kanawha County Bicentennial, Charleston, W.Va., 1988. Mem. Am. Inst. Graphic Arts. Home: 74 Blue Gentian Rd Cranston RI 02921 Office: RI Sch of Design 2 College St Providence RI 02903-2707

MCCLEARY, BENJAMIN WARD, investment banker; b. Washington, July 9, 1944. AB, Princeton U., 1966. Mng. dir. Shearson Lehman Hutton Internat., London, 1987-88, Shearson Lehman Hutton, Inc., N.Y.C., 1988-89; ptnr. McFarland Dewey & Co., N.Y.C., 1989—. Office: McFarland Dewey & Co 230 Park Ave Ste 1450 New York NY 10169-1450

MCCLELLAN, BION WALTON, photography company executive; b. Buffalo, Sept. 11, 1933; s. William Walton and Hazel Emma (Rich) McC.; m. Marilyn Fairfield Gray, Aug. 26, 1956; children: Scott R., Denise L. B Mech. Engring., Cornell U., 1957; MS in Mech. Engring., U. Rochester, 1962, MBA, 1973. Devel. engr. Eastman Kodak Co., Rochester, N.Y., 1957-65, bus. devel. dir., 1985—; engring. supr. Xerox Corp., Rochester, 1965-69, engring. mgr., 1969-73, product planning mgr., 1973-84. Patentee in field. Mem. Beta Gamma Sigma. Home: 4 Tiffany Ct Pittsford NY 14534 Office: Eastman Kodak Co 343 State St Rochester NY 14650

MCCLELLAND, RICHARD LEE, dentist; b. Pitts., May 18, 1927; s. William Noble and Pauline Elizabeth (Lee) McC.; m. Elizabeth Anne Michon, Dec. 6, 1958; children: Richard Scott, William Alfred, Robert Craig. BA, Princeton U., 1950; DDS, U. Pa., 1954. Pvt. practice Princeton, N.J., 1958-92; clin. instr. U. Pa. Dental Sch., Phila., 1958-62; mem. exec. com. Med. Ctr. Princeton, 1971-72, past chmn. dental dept. Lt. Dental Corps, USNR, 1954-57, capt., ret. Fellow Am. Coll. Dentists, Internat. Coll. Dentists, Acad. Gen. Dentistry, Acad. Dentistry Internat.; mem. ADA, Am. Prosthodontic Soc., Fedn. Dentaire Internat., Res. Officers Assn., Nassau Club, Princeton Club (N.Y.C.), Rotary (pres. Princeton 1978-79). Republican. Episcopalian.

MCCLEMENTS, ROBERT, JR., oil company executive; b. Phila., Dec. 1, 1928; s. Robert and Emma (Connor) McC.; m. Barbara Joan Rose, Dec. 20, 1952; children: Kathleen, Mary Anne. BCE, Drexel U., 1952; Advanced Mgmt. Program, Harvard U., 1977. Project engr. Foster-Wheeler Co., Livingston, N.J., 1952-54; project mgr. Catalytic Constrn. Co., Phila., 1956-65; plant mgr., v.p. Sun-Great Can. Oil, Ft. McMurray, Alta., Can., 1965-71; dir., materials mgr. Sun Co., Inc., Phila., 1971-72, dir. engring., 1972-74; v.p. energy ventures Sun Co., Inc., Dallas, 1974-75, pres. Sunoco Energy Devel. Co., 1975-77; exec. v.p. Sun Co., Inc., Radnor, Pa., 1977-81, pres., 1981-86, chief exec. officer, 1985—, chmn. bd., 1987—, also pres., dir.; dir. Core States Fin. Corp.; bd. dirs. Bethlehem Steel Corp., Unisys Corp. Trustee Drexel U., Grove City Coll.; mem. United Way, Greater Phila. First Corp., Phila. Orch., Local Initiatives Support Corp., Phila. Policy Bd. With U.S. Army, 1954-56. Mem. Am. Petroleum Inst. (bd. dirs.), Am. Productivity Ctr., Greater Phila. C. of C., Nat. Indsl. Adv. Coun., Pa. Bus. Roundtable, Urban Affairs Partnership. Clubs: Union League (Phila.); Aronimink Golf (Newtown Square, Pa.). Home: 773 Sugartown Rd Malvern PA 19355-3331 Office: Sun Co Inc 100 Matsonford Rd Wayne PA 19087-4527*

MCCLINTIC, HOWARD GRESSON, foundation executive; b. Pitts., Feb. 27, 1951; s. Stewart and Pamela Mary (Gresson) McC.; m. Katherine Davis Foss, Sept. 14, 1948; children: Margaret Gresson, Katherine Davis, Henry Stewart. BA in Polit. Sci./Econs., George Washington U., 1973. Legis. asst. U.S. Sen. Howard H. Baker, Washington, 1973-75; assoc. cons. Energy Decisions, Inc., Washington, 1975-78; energy policy analyst Chem Systems, Inc., N.Y.C., 1978-80; sr. cons. Coal Use Group, Inc., Washington, 1980-83; staff officer Nat. Acad. Scis., Washington, 1983-87; exec. dir. The Jefferson Energy Found., Washington, 1987—; spl. cons. Nat. Acad. Scis., 1973-74, Law Offices of Dudley & Warner, N.Y.C., 1979, Internat. Bus. Counsellors, Washington, 1982, Japan Nat. Oil Co., Washington, 1983. Co-editor: NAS Com. Rpt., Oceans in Year 2000, 1974, staff coordinator rpts., 1984, 86; exec. producer energy films: Everything Starts with Energy, Energy Policy on Trial, Future Energy Sources, Double Jeopardy, Access to Public Lands and Waters, Nuclear Waste and the West, The Emerging National Energy Strategy. Co-founder The Decade Soc., Washington, 1979-83; coordinator Washingtonians for Bush, 1983; subcom. chmn. U.S. Dept. Energy, 1988; study participant energy Atlantic Council of U.S., Washington, 1989; assoc. mem. Naval War Coll. Found. Mem. Internat. Assn. Energy Economists, Atlantic Council U.S., Am. Energy Assurance Council (advisor 1988—), Rolling Rock Club, Mid-Ocean Club (Bermuda), Gibson Island Club, Chevy Chase Club, Potomac Boat Club. Republican. Episcopalian. Home: 5275 Partridge Ln NW Washington DC 20016-5338 Office: The Jefferson Energy Found 1101 16th St NW Washington DC 20036-4803

MCCLOSKEY, FRANCIS GERARD, priest; b. N.Y.C., Sept. 20, 1939; s. Francis and Sheila C. (Brennan) McC. Student, Cath. U. Am., 1959-63. Ordained priest Roman Cath. Ch., 1963. Instr. St. Patrick's High Sch., Catskill, N.Y., 1963-65; assoc. pastor Annunciation Ch., Ilion, N.Y., 1965-66; chaplain Albany (N.Y.) Med. Ctr., 1966-70; pastor St. Bridget's Ch., Copake Falls, N.Y., 1977-81; founding pres. Christian Ireland Ministries, Albany, 1983—; exec. dir. No. Ireland News Svc., Albany, 1985—; v.p. The Sinaitic Conf., Monsey, N.Y., 1991—. Author software packages. Office: No Ireland News Svc PO Box 11057 Albany NY 12211-0057

MCCLOSKEY, JOHN L., academic administrator, marketing educator; b. Phila., Dec. 29, 1920; s. Edward A. and Anna M. (Fay) McC.; m. Elizabeth A. Patton, Oct. 3, 1943; children: John R., James E., Catherine, Daniel. BS in Acctg., La Salle U., 1948; MBA in Mktg., Temple U., 1957; cert. in econs., Case Inst., Cleve., 1963. Campus store mgr. La Salle U., Phila., 1946-54, asst. prof. mil. sci., 1950-52, asst. to pres., 1955-58, assoc. prof. mktg., 1957—, v.p. pub. affairs, 1959-86, dir. pub. affairs, 1986-88, asst. v.p. devel., 1988—; faculty advisor James L. Fisher Award Com. Dist. II, 1987-90. Bd. dirs. James Finnegan Found., Harrisburg, Pa., 1977-91; bd. dirs., chair pers. com. Catholic Social Svcs., 1980-91, St. Francis Home for Boys, 1980-91; v.p. bd. St. Gabriel's Protectory, 1980-91; chair Mayor's City Scholarship Com., Phila., 1981—; cons. Catholic Life 2000, St. Christophers Parish, Phila., 1992. 1st lt. U.S. Air Corps, 1942-45. Recipient John J. Finley Alumni award, 1972, Coun. for Advancement of Edn. Svc. award, 1986, Dep. of the Army Commdr.'s award, 1986; Republic Steel fellow, 1963. Mem. Am. Mktg. Assn., Phila. Pub. Rels. Assn., Friendly Sons of St. Patrick, Phila. Quartette Club. Democrat. Roman Catholic. Home: 1102 Warwick St Philadelphia PA 19116

MCCLOSKEY, WILLIAM DONALD, manufacturing company executive; b. Phila., July 29, 1930; s. J. Carroll and Helen (Campbell) McC.; B.S. in Mech. Engring., Drexel U., 1952; m. Rosemarie Seydel, June 27, 1953; children—Mary Ann Jacqueline, Colleen, Patricia, Sheila, Eileen. In various engring. and mktg. positions ITT Nesbitt Co., Phila., 1952-72; v.p. mktg. Balt. Aircoil Co., Inc. subs. Amsted industries, Inc., 1972-74, exec. v.p., 1974—, v.p., gen. mgr. Pacific Pumping Co. div., Oakland, Calif., 1974-79, also dir. 6 Balt. Aircoil Co.-related cos.; active Thermal Storage Applications Rsch. Ct. adv. coun. U. Wis., adv. bd. to chancellor U. Md. Served with U.S. Army, 1953-55. Mem. Am. Refrigeration Inst., ASHRAE, Mech. Contractors Am. (Mfg./MCAA Liaison com.), Air conditioning and Refrigeration Inst. (bd. dirs.), Cooling Tower Inst., Hydraulic Inst.—Pump Assn., Balt. Irish Festival (pres.). Republican. Roman Catholic. Home: 2200 Old Frederick Rd Baltimore MD 21228-4808 Office: PO Box 7322 Baltimore MD 21227

MCCLUNG, KENNETH AUSTIN, JR., training executive, consultant; b. Decatur, Ga., Apr. 11, 1947; s. Kenneth Austin Sr. and Marianne (Conklin) McC.; m. Christina June Palensar, Mar. 21, 1975. BA, North Ga. Coll., 1969; MS, EdD, U. So. Calif., 1976. Commd. 2d lt. U.S. Army, 1969, advanced through grades to maj., 1980; lt. col. USAR; cons. in field Suffern, N.Y., 1980-81; sr. ptnr. Instrl. Design Group, Inc., Morristown, N.J., 1981—; bd. dirs. Nat. Productivity Ctr., Boulder, Colo.; author/mgr. more than 100 mgmt., sales, and tech. tng. programs for major corps. Author: Microcomputers for Medical Professionals, 1984, Microcomputers for Legal Professionals, 1984, Microcomputers for Investment Professionals, 1984, Microcomputers for Insurance Professionals, 1984, Personal Computers for Executives, 1984, French edit. 1985; co-author: Sales Training Handbook, 1989. Mem. ASTD, Nat. Soc. Performance Instruction (pres. N.J. chpt. 1986-88, N.E. regional cons. 1989-90, nat. nomination chmn. 1990-91, nat. emerging tech. chmn. 1991-92). Office: Instrnl Design Group Inc 144 Speedwell Ave Morristown NJ 07960-3850

MCCLURE, CHARLES ROBERT, information studies educator, consultant; b. Syracuse, N.Y., May 24, 1949; s. Robert C. and Doris C. (Gordon) McC.; m. Victoria A. Jones, Dec. 30, 1971; 1 child, Gwendolyn A. BA in Spanish, Okla. State U., 1971, MA in History, 1972; MLS, U. Okla., 1973; PhD in Info. Studies, Rutgers U., 1977. Head govt.-history dept. U. Tex. Libr., El Paso, 1972-73; instr. Sch. Libr./Info. Scis., Rutgers U., New Brunswick, N.J., 1974-76; prof. Sch. Libr./Info. Scis., U. Okla., Norman, 1977-86, Sch. Info. Studies, Syracuse U., 1986—; pres. Info. Mgmt. Cons. Svcs. Inc., Manlius, N.Y., 1986—; cons. U.S. Congress Office of Tech. Assessment, Washington, 1990-91, U.S. Govt. Printing Office, Washington, 1989-90. Author: Federal Information Policies in the 1980s, 1988 (Best Book of Yr. in info scis. Am. Soc. for Info. Sci. 1988), Public Access to Government Information, 1989, The National Research and Education Network, 1991 (Best Rsch. Paper of Yr. in libr./info. scis. ALA 1990); author, editor: U.S. Scientific and Technical Information Policies, 1990. Mem. ALA (cons. 1986-88), Am. Soc. for Info. Sci., Assn. Libr. and Info. Sci. Educators. Office: Syracuse U Sch Info Studies Syracuse NY 13244

MCCLURE, JAMES FOCHT, JR., judge; b. Danville, Pa., Apr. 6, 1931; s. James Focht and Florence Kathryn (Fowler) McC.; m. Elizabeth Louise Barber, June 14, 1952; children: Holly McClure Kerwin, Kimberly Ann Pacala, Jamee McClure Sealy, Mary Elizabeth Hudec, Margaret McClure Persing. AB, Amherst Coll., 1952; JD, U. Pa., 1957. Bar: D.C. 1957, Pa. 1958, U.S. Dist. Ct. D.C. 1957, U.S. Dist. Ct. (ea. and mid. dist.) Pa. 1958, U.S. Ct. Appeals (3d cir.) 1959. Atty., advisor Dept. State, Washington, 1957-58; assoc. Morgan, Lewis & Bockius, Phila., 1958-61; atty. Merck & Co., Inc., N.Y.C., 1961-65; ptnr. McClure & McClure, Lewisburg, Pa., 1965-77, McClure & Light, Lewisburg, 1978-84; pres., judge Ct. Common Pleas, 17th Jud. Dist. Pa., Lewisburg, 1984-90; dist. judge U.S. Dist. Ct. (mid. dist.) Pa., Williamsport, Pa., 1990—; dist. atty. Union County, Lewisburg, 1974-75. Pres. bd. sch. dirs. Lewisburg Area Sch. Dist., 1969-74. Cpl. U.S. Army, 1952-54. Mem. ABA, Pa. Bar Assn., Union County Bar Assn., Bucknell U. Golf Club, Susquehanna Valley Chorale, Order of Coif, Phi Beta Kappa. Republican. Presbyterian. Home: 63 University Ave Lewisburg PA 17837-2111 Office: US Dist Ct 240 W 3d St # 1448 Williamsport PA 17701-6438

MCCLURE, MARK STEPHEN, entomologist; b. Northbridge, Mass., Oct. 27, 1948; s. Lionel Alfred and Helen Constance (Zicko) McC.; m. Laura Marie Arbia, Aug. 20, 1971; children: Jason Mark, Evan Daniel. BA in Biology, U. Mass., 1970; MS, U. Ill., 1973, PhD in Entomology, 1975. Teaching asst. U. Ill., Urbana, 1971-75; asst. scientist Conn. Agrl. Experiment Sta., New Haven, 1975-79, assoc. scientist, 1979-81, full scientist, 1981-87; chief scientist Conn. Agrl. Experiment Sta., Windsor, 1987—; recipient Bd. Control Lectureship, Conn. Agrl. Expt. Sta., New Haven, 1981. Co-editor: Variable Plants and Herbivores in Natural and Managed Systems, 1983. Rsch. grantee NSF, Japan, 1984, Conn. Nurserymen's Assn., Japan, 1984, U. Ill., Costa Rica, Cen. Am., 1973. Mem. Entomol. Soc. Am., Ecol. Soc. Am., Conn. Nurserymen's Assn., Conn. Tree Protective Assn. (pres. 1991, bd. dirs. 1986—). Office: Conn Agrl Expt Sta PO Box 248 Windsor CT 06095-0248

MCCLURE, ROBERT LYNCH, military officer; b. Chattanooga, Dec. 16, 1953; s. Milton Dallas and Patricia Ellen (Lynch) McC. BS, U.S. Mil. Acad., 1976; MS in System Mgmt., U. So. Calif., 1981; MPA, Harvard U., 1988. Registered profl. engr., Va. Commd. 2d lt. U.S. Army, 1976, advanced through grades to maj.; co. comdr., staff officer 12 Engr. BN U.S. Army, Dexheim, Fed. Republic Germany, 1977-81; aide-de-camp to commanding gen. U.S. Army, Ft. Belvoir, Va., 1981-83; co. comdr. 42nd Engr. Co./Berlin Bde. U.S. Army, West Berlin, 1985-87; asst. prof. dept. social scis. U.S. Mil. Acad., West Point, N.Y., 1989; with 23d Engr. Bn., Friedberg, Germany, 1989—. Named Olmsted Scholar, George Olmsted Found., Arlington, Va., 1982. Mem. Soc. Am. Mil. Engrs., U.S. Mil. Acad. Assn. of Grads., Nat. Eagle Scout Assn., Rotary Internat.

MCCLURE, WILBERT JAMES, management consultant; b. Toledo, Oct. 29, 1938; s. Wilbert Jesse and Evalyn (Wiley) McC.; m. Barbara Bridges, Oct. 16, 1962 (div. Aug. 1975); 1 child, Karen Christine. B. Edn., U. Toledo, 1961; MEd, Wayne State U., 1968, PhD, 1973. Profl. boxer Toledo, 1961-68; owner McClure Sewing Machine Sales/Svc., Detroit, 1964-67; tchr. Detroit Pub. Schs., 1968-70, guidance cons., 1970-71; assoc. dir. Wayne State U., Detroit, 1971-73; prof. Northeastern U., Boston, 1973-80; pres. McClure & Assocs., Chestnut Hill, Mass., 1980—. Contbr. articles to profl. jours. Bd. mgrs. YMCA, Boston, 1991—. With U.S. Army, 1961-63. Recipient gold medal-boxing Internat. Olympic Com., 1960, Pan Am. Games, 1959; named Boston Black Achiever, 1978. Mem. Am. Arbitration Assn., AACD, U.S. Amateur Boxing Fedn. Inc. (judge), Kappa Alpha Psi. Home: 57 Broadlawn Park # 26 Chestnut Hill MA 02167

MCCLUSKEY, NEIL GERARD, gerontologist, educator, literary agent; b. Seattle, Dec. 15, 1920; s. Patrick John and Mary Genevieve (Casey) McC.; m. Elaine Lituchy, June 5, 1977. AB, Gonzaga U., 1944, MA, 1945; Lic. in Sacred Theology, Gen. Theol. Union, Berkeley, 1952; PhD, Columbia U., 1957. Assoc. editor Am. (Nat. Cath. Weekly), N.Y.C., 1955-60; dean sch. edn. Gonzaga U., Spokane, 1960-62, dir. hons. program, 1963-65, v.p. acad., 1963-66; prof. U. Notre Dame, South Bend, Ind., 1966-71; dean, dir. Inst. Studies in Edn. U. Notre Dame, South Bend, 1968-71; prof., dean profl. studies Lehman Coll. CUNY, 1971-75; dir. Ctr. Gerontol. Studies CUNY Grad. Sch., 1975-81; exec. dir. BHRAGS Social Svcs. Ctr., Bklyn., 1981-84; sr. cons. Retirement Advisors, Inc., N.Y.C., 1985—; sr. tutor Empire State Coll., SUNY, 1989—; edn. coord. Mutual of N.Y., Teaneck, N.J., 1990—; pres. Westchester Lit. Agy., 1991—; mem. adv. bd. Springer Series on Adulthood and Aging, N.Y.C., 1979. Author: Public Schools and Moral Education, 1958, Catholic Viewpoint on Education, 1959 (Cath. Book of Yr. 1960), Catholic Education Faces Its Future, 1969; author, editor: Aging and Retirement, 1981. Bd. dirs. Cath. Big Bros. N.Y., 1985—; editorial bd. Rsch. on Aging, Seattle, 1980—; mem. task force in higher edn. State of N.Y., 1985—, com. Mayor's Second Careers Program, 1983—; del. White House Conf. on Aging, 1981. Mem. Gerontol. Soc., N.Y. Acad. Sci., Religious Edn. Assn. (bd. dirs. 1957—), N.Y. State Assn. Gerontologist Educators (bd. dirs. 1985—), Nat. Coun. on Religion and Pub. Edn. (pres. 1974-78). Home: 50 E Hartsdale Ave Hartsdale NY 10530-2725

MCCLYMONT, ELEANOR JEAN, educational administrator, pathologist; b. Newark, July 5, 1938; d. Michael Joseph and Selena (Gilchrist) Gargan; m. William James McClymont, June 20, 1959; children: Scott William, Lisa Eleanor McClymont Chowansky. BA, Montclair State Coll., 1960, MA, 1975; prin.-supr. cert., Kean Coll., 1982. Speech and lang. pathologist Saddle Brook (N.J.) Bd. Edn., 1960-61, Vis. Nurse Assn., Plainfield, N.J., 1963-65; speech and lang. pathologist Scotch Plains (N.J.) Fanwood Bd. Edn., 1969-83, chair dept. speech and lang., 1983-86, supr. spl. edn., 1986-90; dir. spl. edn., 1990—. Mem. Jaycetts, Scotch Plains, 1968-72; v.p. Fanwood Jr. Women's Club, 1964-65; mem. bd. deacons First Bapt. Ch., Somerville, N.J., 1988-89, chair presch. com., 1980-90, choir mem., 1975—. N.J. State Dept. Edn. grantee, 1986, 87-88, 88. Mem. Assn. for Supervision and Curriculum Devel., N.J. Prins. and Suprs. Assn., N.J. Speech and Hearing Assn., Coun. for Exceptional Children. Republican. Home: 292 Goldfinch Dr Bridgewater NJ 08807-1106 Office: Office of Pupil Svcs 721 Westfield Rd Scotch Plains NJ 07076-2197

MCCOLLUM, GARY WAYNE, Spacelab program manager; b. Mineral Wells, Tex., Apr. 14, 1939; s. Buster Len and Edna Sue (Fowler) McC.; m. Sonja Dru Woodham, May 27, 1960 (div. 1973); children: Scott, Greg, Cynthia; m. Barbara Jean Millican, Sept. 16, 1978. BS in Biology, East Tex. State U., 1962, MS in Biology, 1963. Quarantine control officer Lunar Receiving Lab., Apollo Program to Moon, Houston, 1969-71; mgr. med. surveillance officer Apollo Flight Crew Health Stabilization Program, Houston, 1971-72; mgr. med. surveillance office Skylab Flight Crew Health Stabilization Office, Houston, 1972-74; life wcis. ground ops. mgr. NASA Life Sci. project Div., Houston, 1974-78; discipline mgr., Life Sci. NASA Life Sci. Project Div., Houston, 1978-83; payload integration mgr. NASA Space Shuttle Program Office, Houston, 1983-88; program mgr. NASA Hdqrs. Office of Space Sci. & Applications, Washington D.C., 1988—. 1st lt. USAF, 1963-66. Mem. Am. Inst. Aero. and Astronautics (sr. mem.). Home: 15504 Vine Cottage Dr Centreville VA 22020-3750 Office: NASA Hdqs Mail Code SM 600 Independence Ave SW Washington DC 20546-0002

MCCOLLUM, RANDALL HAMPTON, retail executive; b. Houston, Dec. 13, 1944; s. Herbert Hampton and Verna (Duke) McC.; m. Gretchen McCollum (div. Dec. 1975); m. Nancy Dennis McCollum, Nov. 24, 1979; children: Derek, Kyle, Tyler. BS, Lamar U., 1968, MEd, 1969. Area sales mgr. Xerox Corp., Houston, 1970-79; regional mgr. O.C. Tanner Co., Houston, 1979-82; exec. v.p. Texas Arai, Inc., Houston, 1982-84; pres., chief exec. officer Hampton Energy Corp., San Antonio, 1984-88; v.p. Tiffany & Co., N.Y.C., 1988—. Bd. dirs. Camelot Found., San Antonio, 1988-89; advisor San Antonio Airport Bd., 1988-89. Mem. Dominion County Club Golf Assn. (bd. dirs. 1987-89), Kingwood Country Club. Home: 13426 Vista Del Rey San Antonio TX 78216-2233 Office: Tiffany & Co Fifth Ave New York NY 10011-8800

MCCOLM, ROBERT BRUCE, human rights organization executive; b. Sept. 30, 1950. AB cum laude, Williams Coll., 1972; M in Theol. Studies, Harvard U., 1974; postdoctoral, U. Chgo., 1974-76. Founder, dir. documentary film co. N.Y.C., 1976-79; resident scholar Freedom House, N.Y.C., 1980-82; dir. Ctr. Caribbean and Cen. Am. Studies, 1982-86; deputy dir. Freedom House, 1987-88, exec. dir., 1988—; U.S. Nat. to Inter-Am. Commn. on Human Rights of Orgn. of Am. States, 1983-87; spl. cons. to U.S. Senate Observer Group to monitor the Cen. Am. Peace Accords; bd. dirs. nat. com. Social Democrats, U.S.A., League for Indsl. Democracy, East-West Round Table, Latin Am. Labor Inst.; editorial bd. Assn. Libro Libre; adv. bd. Inter-Am. Ctr. for Electoral Promotion & Assistance. Contbr. articles to Wash. Post, N.Y. Times, Wall Street Jour., Newsweek and others. Home: 21 S Peak St Highlands NJ 07732 Office: Freedom House 48 E 21st St New York NY 10010-7223

MCCONNAUGHEY, JAMES WALTER, economist; b. Washington, May 8, 1951; s. William Eugene and Eunice (Ensor) McC.; m. Rosemarie Fuchs, June 23, 1984. BS in Econs. with high honors, U. Md., 1973; MA in Econs., George Washington U., 1979; MPA with high honors, Harvard U., 1992. Industry economist FCC Common Carrier Bur., Washington, 1973-80, sr. economist, 1981-83; sr. assoc. Bolter and Nilsson, Bethesda, Md., 1983; mgr. rsch. studies div. Bethesda Rsch. Inst., 1983-89; sr. economist office policy analysis and devel. U.S. Dept. Commerce Nat. Telecommunications and Info. Adminstrn., Washington, 1989—. Author: (with others) Telecommunications Policy for the 1980's: The Transition to Competition, 1984, Telecommunications Policy for the 1990's and Beyond, 1990, U.S. Telecommunications in a Global Economy: Competitiveness at a Crossroads, 1990. Campaign worker, contbr. nat. and local elections; coach Bowie (Md.) Boy's Club; mem. Neighborhood Open Space Com.; worker, contbr. numerous environ. and consumer orgns.; wards evaluator Ford Found./Harvard U. Innovations in State and Local Govt. Program, 1992. Recipient certs. of appreciation for leadership Prince George's County (Md.) Pub. Sch. System, 1986, Nat. Found. Cancer Rsch., 1990; Robert Seamans tech. fellow, Lucius Littauer fellow John F. Kennedy Sch. Govt., Harvard U., 1991-92. Mem. Am. Econ. Assn., Pub. Utilities Group of Am. Econ. Assn., Ea. Econ. Assn., So. Econ. Assn., Soc. Govt. Economists, Indsl. Orgn. Soc., Phi Eta Sigma, Omicron Delta Epsilon, Beta Gamma Sigma, Phi Kappa Phi. Home: 8380 Sweet Cherry Ln Laurel MD 20723-1062

MCCONNELL, JOHN HOWARD, personnel management consultant, writer; b. Highland Park, Mich., June 18, 1933; s. Melvin William and Dorothy Marie (Miller) McC.; m. Dolores Ann Cooper, Oct. 29, 1955; children: Keith Ernest, Brian Howard, Eric William. BS, Wayne State U., 1957, MEd, 1963. Tchr. Detroit Bd. Edn., 1957-59, Highland Park Bd. Edn., 1959-60; personnel mgr. Wolverine Tube Co., Allen Park, Mich., 1960-69; personnel dir. Garan, Inc., N.Y.C., 1970-71; cons. Morristown, N.J., 1971-74; cons. human resource mgmt., pres. McConnell, Simmons & Co., Inc., Morristown, 1974—; bd. dirs. Circus Royale, Inc., Morristown. Author: How To Audit, 8 vols., 1974-85, Introduction to Human Resources, 1982; contbr. articles to various publs. Pres. Morristown Civic Assn., 1980. Mem. Am. Psychol. Assn., Am. Mgmt. Assn., Acad. Magical Arts, Magic Castle Club (L.A.), Circus Hist. Soc., Masons. Democrat. Methodist. Home: One Skyline Dr Morristown NJ 07960 Office: 73 E Hanover Ave Morristown NJ 07960-3147

MCCONOMY, THOMAS ARTHUR, chemical company executive; b. Wilmerding, Pa., July 26, 1933; s. Thomas Michael Murray and Catherine Elizabeth (Herbert) McC.; m. Eileen Adele Cerutti, June 22, 1956; children: Thomas E., Robert M., Karen E. BSChemE, Carnegie Mellon U., 1955. Svc. engr. Calgon Corp., Pitts., 1955-60; staff engr. Calgon Carbon Corp., Pitts., 1960-67, nat. accounts mgr., 1967-70, div. internat. mgr., 1972-74, environ. bus. dir., 1974-75, div. dir., 1975-78, div. gen. mgr., 1978-79, v.p., 1979-85, pres., chmn., chief exec. officer, 1985—; mgr. Calgon Inter-Am. Corp., Caracas, Venezuela, 1970-72; bd. dirs. Pitts. Nat. Bank, Equitable Resources. Contbr. tech. articles and papers on indsl. water treatment. Vice chmn. Carnegie Mellon U., Pitts., 1988; bd. dirs. Jr. Achievement S.W. Pa., Pitts., 1988, United Way Allegheny County, 1989, Pitts. High Tech. Coun. Mem. Greater Pitts. C. of C. (bd. dirs. 1990), Montour Heights Country Club (Coraopolis, Pa.), Edgeworth Club (Sewickley, Pa.), Duquesne Club (Pitts.). Office: Calgon Carbon Corp PO Box 717 Pittsburgh PA 15230-0717

MCCOOK, JAMES MARSHALL, banking consultant; b. Jersey City, N.J., May 30, 1952; s. James Felix and Catherine Uriel (Rogall) McC.; m. Louise Ann Shesniak, June 30, 1973; children: Jason. Tory, Katelyn. Banker, ATM mgr. Perth Amboy (N.J.) Savings Inst., 1971-84, First Atlantic Savings, South Plainfield, N.J., 1984-91; cons. JMM Consulting, Neptune, N.J., 1991—; pres. Treas. Users Group, New Brunswick, N.J., 1985-86, advisor, 1986-89; mem. bd. advisors NCR Tristate Users Group, Phila., 1989-90; advisor MAC Users Group, Phila., 1989-90. Buddy Hyacinth Found., New Brunswick, 1992; treas. Atonement Luth. Ch., Asbury Park, N.J., 1988-92, feed-the-hungry, 1990-91. Home and office: 207 Durand Rd Neptune NJ 07753

MCCOOL, HELEN BUNTING, counselor; b. Selbyville, Del., Feb. 25, 1948; d. Eugene and Mary (Gray) Bunting; m. Ronald William McCool, Oct. 8, 1989; 1 child by previous marriage, Robert Earl Bunting. AA, Del. Tech. and Community Coll., 1981; BA, Salisbury State U., 1984, MEd, 1986. Interior designer Georgetown, Del., 1970-81, Custom Craft Builders, Ocean View, Del., 1981-83; counselor Turnabout Counseling Ctr., Seaford, Del., 1983-90, clin. dir., 1990—; staff supr. Seaford House Residential Treatment Ctr., 1988-89, asst. dir., 1990-91; mem. Gov.'s Task Force on Suicide

Prevention, Dover, 1989-90. Mem. Georgetown Bus. and Profl. Women (pres., sec. 1984-87). Methodist. Office: Turnabout Counseling Ctr 350 Virginia Ave Ste 1 Seaford DE 19973-1516

MCCORD, ARLINE FUJII, university administrator, educator; b. Nahcotta, Wash., May 16, 1935; d. George and Mary (Murakami) Fujii; m. Ted T. Sakuma, Nov. 10, 1952 (div. Dec. 1970); m. William McCord, May 8, 1971; children: Karen, Ted, Michael, William, Elinor. BA, U. Wash., 1960, MA, 1965, PhD, 1968. High sch. tchr. Seattle (Wash.) Pub. Schs., 1960-63; asst. prof. Calif. State Univ., Fullerton, 1967-68, Syracuse (N.Y.) Univ., 1968-71; asst. to assoc. prof. Hunter Coll., N.Y.C., 1971-85, chair dept., 1983-85; prof. and dean social scis. CCNY, N.Y.C., 1985-89; assoc. provost Yale Univ., New Haven, 1989—; researcher, cons. Eisenhower Commn. on Causes and Prevention of Violence, Washington, 1968-69. Co-author: Black Students on White College Campuses, 1972, Urban Social Conflict, 1977, American Social Problems, 1977, Power and Equity, 1977, Paths to Progress, 1986. Cons. Edn. Policy Rsch. Ctr., Syracuse (N.Y.) Univ., 1968-69; dir. Rosenberg/Humphrey Inst. Pub. Affairs, 1985-89, Bus. and Internat. Edn. Program, CCNY and Harlem Third World Trade Inst., 1987-89. Office: Yale U Office of the Provost New Haven CT 06520

MCCORD, JOAN, sociologist, researcher; b. N.Y.C., Aug. 4, 1930; d. Robert and Mildred Lucile (Stern) Fish; m. William Maxwell McCord, Mar. 17, 1951 (div. 1965); children: Geoffrey Sayre McCord, Robert Maxwell McCord; m. Carl Avrom Silver, June 24, 1970. BA, Stanford U., 1952, PhD, 1968. Tchr. Concord (Mass.) Pub. Schs., 1952-55; rsch. asst. Harvard U., Cambridge, Mass., 1955-56; rsch. assoc. Stanford (Calif.) U., 1959-65; asst. prof., prof. Drexel U., Phila., 1968-87; prof. Temple U., Phila., 1987—; sr. assoc. U. Montreal, Quebec, 1987—, Johns Hopkins U., Balt., 1986—. Author (article in book) Straight and Devious Pathways From Childhood to Adulthood, 1990, At The Threshold: The Developing Adolescent, 1990; editor: Facts, Frameworks and Forecasts: Advances in Criminological Theory, 3, 1992; contbr. articles to profl. jours. Recipient Josiah Royce fellow Harvard U., 1957, Stanford Wilson fellow Stanford U., 1962-63, fellow NIMH, 1965-68, Am. Soc. Criminology, 1982, Internat Soc. for Rsch. on Aggression, 1984. Mem. NSF (adv. bd. mem. 1987-91), NAS (vice-chair Nat. Rsch. Coun., law and justice com. 1990—), Internat. Soc. Criminology (bd. dirs.), Am. Soc. Criminology (pres. 1988-89), Am. Sociol. Assn. (chmn. sect. on crime, law, and deviance 1989-90, Herbert Block award 1991), Soc. for Life History Rsch. (chair 1990—). Home: 623 Broad Acres Rd Narberth PA 19072-1510 Office: Temple U Philadelphia PA 19122

MCCORD, MAXWELL LAURENT, health club manager; b. Houston, Oct. 12, 1965; s. William Maxwell and Kirsten Laurent (Andersen) McC. Asst. mgr. Form and Figure, Farum, Denmark, 1983-84; gen. mgr. Nautilus/Sci. Fitness Club, Copenhagen, 1984-85; owner/pres. Studio Fitness, Farum, 1985-88; cons./owner Studio Designs, Farum, 1987-88; gen. mgr. Body Works, West Nyack, N.Y., 1988-89, Am. Superspas, Scarsdale, N.Y., 1989—. Author/editor (newsletter) Science Applied to Tanning, 1985. Home: 189 Main St # 131 White Plains NY 10601-3101 Office: Am Superspas 696 White Plains Rd Scarsdale NY 10583-5008

MCCORD, MICHAEL JAMES, bank executive; b. Hartford, Conn., Oct. 29, 1961; s. Donald Robert and Myrna Barbara (Maynard) McC.; m. Janet Elaine Schenk, June 25, 1983. BS, Roger Williams Coll., 1982; grad., Nat. Sch. Fin. and Mgmt., 1989. Mgmt. trainee Keene (N.H.) Savs. Bank, 1985-86, asst. contr., 1986-87; contr. Granite Bank, Amherst, N.H., 1987-89; contr. Granite State Bankshares, Inc., Keene, 1989-91, v.p., contr., 1991—. mem. Windom World Affairs Coun., Brattleboro, Vt., 1990. Mem. Lions Internat. Home: 133 Bay State Rd # 3 Boston MA 02215-1716 Office: Granite State Bankshares 122 W St Keene NH 03431

MC CORISON, MARCUS ALLEN, librarian, cultural organization administrator; b. Lancaster, Wis., July 17, 1926; s. Joseph Lyle and Ruth (Mink) McC.; m. Janet Buckbee Knop, June 10, 1950; children: Marcus Allen II, Judith McC. Gove, Andrew Buckbee, Mary McC. Rosenbloom, James Rice, Peter Gardner. AB, Ripon Coll., 1950; MA, U. Vt., 1951, LittD, 1992; MS, Columbia U., 1954; LHD (hon.), Assumption Coll., Worcester, Mass., 1987, Coll. of the Holy Cross, 1992; LittD (hon.), Clark U., 1992. Librarian Kellogg-Hubbard Library, Montpelier, Vt., 1954-55; chief of rare books dept. Dartmouth Coll. Library, Hanover, N.H., 1955-59; head spl. collections dept. State U. Iowa Libraries, 1959-60; librarian Am. Antiquarian Soc., Worcester, Mass., 1960-91; dir. Am. Antiquarian Soc., 1967-89; pres. Am. Antiquarian Soc., Worcester, Mass., 1989-92, pres. emeritus, 1992—; editor Procs. Am. Antiquarian Soc., 1960-67; mem. internat. and N.Am. steering coms. 18th Century Short Title Catalogue, 1977—; mem. Com. for a New Eng. Bibliography, 1968-90, treas., 1970-77; trustee Old Sturbridge Village, 1981—; mem. adv. com. Eleutherian Mills-Hagley Found., 1971-74, 87-89; trustee Fruitlands Mus., 1978-89; mem. adv. coun. Princeton U. Libr., 1988—; bd. govs. Rsch. Librs. Group, 1980-91, chmn. preservation com., 1982-85, governance com., 1989-91, chmn. The Writings of James Fenimore Cooper, 1991—; trustee Hist. Deerfield, Inc., 1991—. Author: Vermont Imprints 1778-1820, 1963, The 1764 Catalogue of the Redwood Library, 1965; contbr.: The Pursuit of Knowledge in the Early American Republic, 1976; Editor: History of Printing in America by Isaiah Thomas, 1970. Served with USNR, 1944-46, AUS, 1951-52. Recipient Samuel Pepys medal Ephemera Soc., London, 1980, Disting. Alumni award Ripon Coll., 1989. Fellow Pilgrim Soc.; mem. Am. Antiquarian Soc., Mass. Hist. Soc., Coll. and Rsch. Librs. Assn. (chmn. rare books sect. 1965-66), Biblog. Soc. Am. (pres. 1980-84, del. to Am. Coun. Learned Socs. 1985—), Vt. Hist. Soc. (trustee 1956-66), Worcester Hist. Mus. (exec. com. 1967-80), Ind. Rsch. Librs. Assn. (chmn. 1972-73, 78-80), Ctr. for Rsch. on Vt. (assoc.), Assn. Internat. de Bibliophilie, NE Am. Soc. 18th Century Studies (pres. 1978-79), Colonial Soc. Mass. Congregationalist. Democrat. Clubs: Odd Volumes, Grolier (councillor 1979-82, 83-84), St. Botolph, Century. Home: 4 Military Rd Worcester MA 01609-1627 Office: Am Antiquarian Soc 185 Salisbury St Worcester MA 01609-1634

MCCORKLE, BARBARA BACKUS, map curator; b. N.Y.C., Sept. 9, 1920; d. Northup Richard and Helen M. (Stoddard) Swanton; B.A., Hunter Coll., 1942; M.L.S., Emporia (Kans.) State U., 1968; m. Oswald Prentiss Backus, III, Apr. 9, 1944 (dec. July 8, 1972); children—Mary Elizabeth, Frances Dudley, Robert Henry, Oswald Prentiss IV, Anthony Stoddard, Richard Swanton; m. George Maston McCorkle, Apr. 13, 1974. With Macy's, N.Y.C., 1942-47; instr. in English, U. Kans., Lawrence, 1961-66, assoc. libr.rare books, 1968-74; sr. reference libr. Yale U., New Haven, 1974-75, curator maps, sr. reference librarian, 1979-87, curator maps, 1988—; sr. reference librarian Purdue U., West Lafayette, Ind., 1976-79; lectr. history of cartography Yale U.; cons. to de Menil Found., 1981. Lilly Library research grantee, 1977; Spl. Libraries Assn. research grantee, 1981—. Mem. Soc. for History of Discoveries (sec.-treas. 1979-91), ALA, Spl. Library Assn., Am. Printing History Assn., Internat. Soc. for History of Cartography, Grolier Club. Editor: Books and Libraries at the University of Kansas, 1970-74; contbr. articles to profl. jours. Home: 45 Mill Rock Rd Hamden CT 06517-4021 Office: Yale U Map Collection New Haven CT 06520

MCCORMACK, GRACE, retired microbiology educator; b. Rochester, N.Y., Feb. 16, 1908; d. Walter and Maud (Brimacomb) McC. AB, U. Rochester, 1941; MS, U. Md., 1951. Technician U. Rochester Sch. Medicine and Dentistry and Atomic Energy, 1942-48; bacteriologist Dept. Interior U.S. Fish and Wildlife Svc., Coll. Park, East Boston, 1948-53, Md. State Dept. Health, Balt., 1953-55, VA Hosp., Canandaigua, N.Y., 1955-66; asst. to assoc. to microbiology prof. Monroe Community Coll., Rochester, N.Y., 1966-77; prof. Community Coll. of the Finger Lakes, Canandaigua, 1982-86, 88. Fellow Am. Inst. of Chems., Am. Biog. Inst. (hon. mem. rsch. bd. of advisors 1987, Outstanding Educator of Yr. 1987), Royal Soc. of Health (Eng.), Intercontinental Biog. Assn. (Eng.); mem. Am. Soc. Microbiologists, N.Y. State Pub. Health Assn., Am. Inst. of Food Technologists, Nat. Found. of Infectious Diseases. Home: 162 Raleigh St Rochester NY 14620-4148

MCCORMALLY, KEVIN JAY, editor; b. Boston, Mar. 13, 1950; s. John Patrick and Marguerite Louise (Wichert) McC.; m. Anne Louise Long, May 27, 1972; children: Niamh Anna, Patrick Henry. BA with honors, U. Iowa, 1972. Area editor Burlington (Iowa) Hawk Eye, 1969-70; city editor Daily Iowan, Iowa City, 1971-72; press sec. U.S. Rep. Edward Mezvinsky, Washington, 1972-77; assoc. editor Changing Times Mag., Washington, 1977-85, sr. editor, 1985-90; exec. editor Kiplinger's Personal Fin. Mag. (formerly Changing Times), Washington, 1991—; commentator Nightly Bus. Report PBS. Author: Successful Tax Planning, 1988, Sure Ways to Cut Your Taxes, 1989, 90, 91; co-author: A Term to Remember, 1977; editor: Get More for Your Money, 1981. Mem. Nat. Press Club (best consumer journalism award 1986, 88), Sigma Delta Chi. Democrat. Roman Catholic. Home: 161 D St SE Washington DC 20003-1809 Office: Kiplingers Personal Fin Mag 1729 H St NW Washington DC 20006

MCCORMICK, CHARLES CLAIR, retail company executive; b. Ashland, Pa., Dec. 3, 1946; s. C. Clair and Catherine B. (McCaffery) McC.; children: Sean C., Patrick M.; m. Beth Ann Barry, Mar. 17, 1992. Student, Keystone Jr. Coll., La Plume, Pa., 1965-66; BA in Bus. Adminstrn., Lycoming Coll., 1969. Mktg. rep. Mobil Oil Corp., Harrisburg, Pa., 1969-71; adminstrv. analyst Mobil Oil Corp., Phila., 1971-73; sr. adminstrv. analyst Mobil Oil Corp., Atlanta, 1973-76; v.p., gen. mgr. Huntingdon (Pa.) Oil Co., 1976-80; gen. sales mgr. Way Oil Co., Lancaster, Pa., 1980-82, v.p., gen. mgr., 1982-83, pres., 1983-84; pres. P. Lebzelter & Son Co., Lancaster, 1983—; Adv. bd. Mobil Oil Distributor, Phila. 1983; mem. Goodyear Dealer Council, Phila., 1986. Bd. dirs. Lancaster County United Way, Goodwill Industries of Southeastern Pa.; bd. dirs. Lancaster County Easter Seal Soc., 1984—, chmn., 1990-91; bd. dirs., sec. Goodwill Industries of Lancaster, 1988—; cons. Jr. Achievement, Lancaster, 1986-88; chmn. evaluation com., mem. exec. com. United Way of Lancaster County; mem. pub. rels. com. Pa. State Easter Seal Com. Named Outstanding Young Man of Am., U.S. Jaycees, 1978, 79, 80. Mem. Lancaster C. of C., Pa. Dutch Visitors Bur. Republican. Roman Catholic. Home: 1301 Clayton Rd Lancaster PA 17603-2401 Office: P Lebzelter & Son PO Box 7865 Lancaster PA 17604-7865

MCCORMICK, DOUGLAS JESS, industrial psychologist; b. L.A., Aug. 28, 1949; s. James Lincoln and Esther Veronica (Mayo) McC. BA, U. Calif., Santa Barbara, 1971; MA, U. So. Calif., 1979, PhD, 1983. Pers. analyst III L.A. County Pers. Dept., 1982-83; staff mgr. AT&T Selection and Testing Div., Morristown, N.J., 1983—. Contbr. articles to profl. jours. Mem. APA (div. 5 measurement), Am. Psychol. Soc., Am. Ednl. Rsch. Assn., Assn. for Computing Machinery, Soc. for Indsl. and Orgnl. Psychology, Psychometric Soc. Democrat. Home: 7 E Grand St Hampton NJ 08827 Office: AT&T PO Box 1937 Morristown NJ 07962-1937

MCCORMICK, EDWARD THEODORE, JR., educational systems company executive; b. Washington, Dec. 29, 1939; s. Edward Theodore and Ione (Reese) McC.; m. Joanne Ochs Findlay, Dec. 31, 1960; children: Edward Theodore III, Richard William. Student, Duke U., 1961. Specialist's clk. Am. Stock Exch., N.Y.C., 1958-63; self-employed ins. cons. N.Y.C., 1963-67; tchr., sales Dan/Ro, Inc., N.Y.C., 1967-71; pres., owner Modern Ednl. Systems, Inc., Ridgefield, Conn., 1971—; cons. Higher Edn. Opportunity Program, N.Y., 1966-72, Dist. #1 Archdiocese N.Y., N.y.C., 1972-73. Dir. Cub Scouts, Tarrytown, n.Y., 1968-71; coach Little League, Ridgefield, 1971-75, Townies Basketball, Ridgefield, 1978-81; chmn. Youth Commn., Ridgefield, 1981-86; started 2d Safe Rides Program in U.S., 1982—. Player, U.S. Olympic Field Hockey Tng. Team, 1965-67. Mem. Alpha Kappa Psi (treas. 1960-61). Roman Catholic. Home and Office: 15 Limestone Ter Ridgefield CT 06877

MC CORMICK, JAMES HAROLD, academic administrator; b. Indiana, Pa., Nov. 11, 1938; s. Harold Clark and Mary Blanche (Truby) McCormick; m. Maryan Kough Garner, June 7, 1963; children: David Harold, Douglas Paul. BS, Indiana U. of Pa., 1959; MEd, U. Pitts., 1961, EdD, 1963, postdoctoral, 1966; postdoctoral, Columbia U., U. Mich., 1966-67, Harvard U., 1982. Tchr. Punxsutawney (Pa.) Area Joint Sch. Dist., 1959-61; adminstr. Baldwin-Whitehall Schs., Pitts., 1961-64; grad. asst. U. Pitts., 1962-63; asst. supt. instrn. Washington (Pa.) City Schs., 1964-65; prof. dept. edn. and psychology, asst. dean acad. affairs, acting dean acad. affairs, acting dean tchr. edn., asst. to pres., v.p. adminstrn. and fin. Shippensburg (Pa.) U., 1965-73; pres. Bloomsburg (Pa.) U., 1973-83, pres. emeritus, 1983—; chancellor Pa. State System Higher Edn., 1983—; Falk intern in politics, 1959; mem. adv. bd. Pa. Ednl. Policy Seminar, Nat. Ctr. for Study Sport in Soc.; mem. Gov.'s Econ. Devel. Partnership Bd.; mem. higher edn. adv. coun. pa. State Bd. Edn.; commr. Edn. Commn. of the States. Contbr. articles profl. jours. Recipient Ten Outstanding Young Men of Yr. award Pa. Jr. C. of C., 1974, Young Leaders in Edn. award Phi Delta Kappa, 1981, Disting. Alumnus award Indiana U. of Pa., 1981, Outstanding Alumni award Bloomsburg U., 1984, Outstanding Alumnus, U. Pitts., 1985, Adler award Pa. State Edn. Assn., 1992. Mem. Am. Assn. State Colls. and Univs. (Pa. state rep. 1988—, former chmn. acad. and student pers. com., mem. com. on state rels. and task force on ednl. equity), Am. Coun. on Edn. (commn. on women in higher edn.), Commn. State Colls. and Univs. (mem. and past chmn. govt. rels. and student rels. coms.), Assn. Governing Bds. (adv. coun.), Am. Assn. for Affirmative Action, Am. Assn. Higher Edn., Am. Assn. Sch. Adminstrs., Am. Assn. Univ. Adminstrs., Pa. Assn. Colls. and Univs. Pers. Assn., Bloomsburg Area C. of C. (pres. 1983), Rotary (bd. dirs.), Urban League Harrisburg (bd. dirs.), Phi Delta Kappa. Presbyterian. Home: PO Box 28 Lemoyne PA 17043-0028 Office: Pa State System Higher Edn PO Box 809 301 Market St Harrisburg PA 17108

MCCORMICK, JOHN PATRICK, psychologist; b. N.Y.C., Aug. 21, 1945; s. John James and Marie (Murray) McC.; m. Linda L. Puertas, May 25, 1967 (div. Jan. 1988); children: Melissa Louise, Danielle Marie; m. Carmen Patricia Otoya, Jan. 29, 1988. BS, SUNY, 1983; MA, Columbia U., 1980, EdM, 1982, EdD, 1987. Lic. psychologist, N.Y.; cert. drug and alcohol counselor. Electrician IBEW Local, Flushing, N.Y., 1967-87; psychologist Priorities, Inc., N.Y.C., 1987-91; psychologist, pvt. practice N.Y.C., 1991—; psychologist Ctr. for Family Devel., Bronxville, N.Y., 1987-91, Inst. for Contemporary Psychotherapy, N.Y.C., 1983—. With USN, 1962-66. Mem. Am. Psychol. Assn. Office: 315 Central Pk W Apt 5W New York NY 10025-7656

MCCORMICK, JOSEPH FRANCIS, SR., inventor; b. Westfield, Mass., Sept. 7, 1933; s. Francis Prendergast and Margaret (O'Brien) McC.; m. Ruth Mary Walden, Apr.25, 1987. BSME, Lowell (Mass.) Inst. Tech., 1962. Program mgr. Aerojet Gen. Corp., Sacramento, 1963-64; applied scientist Gen. Dynamics, Inc., Rochester, N.Y., 1964-66; product mgr. Helicoil Corp., Brewster, N.Y., 1966-72; pres. McCormick Systems, Danbury, Conn., 1972—. Inventor in field. Office: McCormick Systems Inc PO Box 2490 Holyoke MA 01041-2490

MCCORMICK, KENNETH JAMES, computer specialist; b. Olney, Md., Dec. 23, 1951; s. Gerald James McCormick and Margaret Lillian (Saunders) Saulpaugh. BS in Math., U. Md., 1974. Computer scientist Smithsonian Instn., Washington, 1974—. Author: (game) 3-Player Chess, 1987. Mem. Nat. Capital Velo Club Inc (treas. 1981—), Boy Scout Troop 933 (treas. 1990—). Home: 3821 Monte Vista Dr Alexandria VA 22309-1454 Office: Smithsonian Instn A & I 2310 Washington DC 20560

MCCORMICK, PAMELA ANN, artist, sculptor; b. Grand Rapids, Mich., Jan. 7, 1948; d. William Albert McCormick and June (Wente) Schuster; m. William K. Scarvie, Mar. 19, 1965 (div. Jan. 1972); children: Wil, Jeffrey. BA in Art, San Jose (Calif.) State U., 1972, MA in Art Sculpture, 1974; postgrad., Stanford U., 1975-76. Instr. art Am. River Coll., Sacramento, 1976; dir. Children's Art Studio, N.Y.C., 1981-84; prodn. mgr. Precision Imaging Corp., N.Y.C., 1986-88; cons. desktop pub. various pub. cos., N.Y.C., 1988-90; set design Color Story Chaparral, N.Y., 1992, Living Theatre prodn. Sixth Book, N.Y., 1991; solo exhbn. sculpture and photography Mus., N.Y., 1991. Prin. works include Quatrain sculpture Cen. Park, N.Y.C., 1986-89, Flying Light Flushing Park, Queens, N.Y., 1986, Channeling, Erie Barge Canal, Lockport, N.Y., 1988, numerous floating sculptures for Cen. Park, N.Y.C., 1989, set design for Ice Theatre of N.Y., 1989, set and costume design Carmen Beuchat Dance Co., N.Y., 1990, Sixth Book, Living Theater, 1991, Ice Theater of N.Y., 1991, Living Theater, 1991, Color Story, Chaparral, N.Y., 1992; one-person exhbn. of sculpture & photography N.Y.C. Mus. 1991. Recipient award of distinction Audubon Naturalist Soc., 1986; fellow Nat. Endowmentfor Arts, 1974; grantee Pollock Krasner Found., Inc., 1990. Mem. ARtists Representing Environ. Art, Internat. Sculpture Orgn., Arts and Sci. Collaborations Inc. Democrat. Studio: 97 Wooster St New York NY 10012

MCCORMICK, ROBERT H., chemical engineering educator, consultant; b. Potters Mill, Pa., Apr. 28, 1914; s. George H. and Nellie C. (Mingle) McC.; m. Isabel Bradford, Aug. 19, 1939; 1 child, George M. BSChemE, Pa. State U., 1935, MSChemE, 1942. Rsch. asst. Pa. State U., University Park, 1935-44, from asst. prof. to assoc. prof. chem. engring., 1944-64, prof., 1964-79, prof. emeritus, 1979—; tech. specialist Pa. Tech. Assitance Program, 1971-79, resource advisor, mem. adv. coun., 1979—; bus. counselor Pvt. Industry Coun. of Centre County, State Coll., Pa. 1981-91; v.p., co-founder Svc. Corps. Retired Execs., 1991—. Author: (with others) Introduction to Separation Science, 1973, volume 2, 1988, Food Analysis: Principles and Techniques, 1987; co-author: Separation Processes in Practice, 1961; contbr. articles to profl. jours. Bd. dirs. Am. Cancer Soc., Centre County, Pa., 1957—, exec. com., 1958-87, adminstrv. com., 1970-87, pres., 1958-61, chmn. County Crusade, 1957-58, mem. program coms., 1958—; active United Way, Centre County; adult leader, com. mem., Boy Scouts Am.; Hosp. Bldg. Fund Campaign, Centre County; active Youth Projects, 1958-70; precnct chmn., 1957-77, county exec. com., 1960-68, bd. elections judge, 1978-82, minority inspector, 1982-89. Recipient Nat. Recreation Assn. award Outstanding Contbr. to recreation Movement if Am., 1958; Benjamin Rush award Centre County Med. Soc., 1964; Meritous Work citation Pa. United Cerebral Palsy, 1966; Outstanding Svc. award Am. Cancer Soc., 1960, Volunteer of Year award, 1970, Bronze Metal Nat. award, 1971, Sword of Hope award, 1976; fellow Am Inst. Chem. Engrs., 1976, Am. Inst. Chemists, 1976. Fellow Am. Inst. Chem. Engrs. (chmn. nat. student chpts. com. 1968-69, student contest program 1968, 69, nat. student chpt. pres. workshop 1967, 68, nat. admissions com. 1981-90, advisor Pa. State U. student chpt. 1959-70), Am. Inst. Chemists (patent com. 1981-90), Am. Assn. Univ. Profs., Am. Chem. Soc. (life), Am. Soc. Engring. Edn., Phi Lambda Upsilon, Sigma Xi.

MCCORMICK, THOMAS JAY, infosystems engineer; b. Pitts., Nov. 23, 1946; s. Thomas Jay and Marion (Smith) McC.; m. Patricia Michelle McCormick, Dec. 1, 1990; 1 child, Randall James. BA, Dickinson Coll., 1968; MS, Troy State U., 1976; MA, Boston U., 1985. Tech. officer U.S. Army Units, various cities, 1968-78; army research & devel. coord. BETA Joint Program Office, Washington, 1978-80; student officer Armed Forces Staff Coll., Norfolk, Va., 1981; branch exec. officer Defense Intelligence Agy., Washington, 1981-83; ground forces branch chief Defense Liaison Detachment, Bonn, Germany, 1983-86; army operational test officer Army Operational Test and Evaluation AGy., Washington, 1986-87, chief, intelligence systems branch, 1987-88; intelligency systems specialist GTE Govt. Systems Corp., Chantilly, Md., 1988—. co-author: Notes and Cases in Military Management, 1976. Council pres. St. Thomas More Parish, Bonn, Germany, 1985-86. Recipient Disting. Svc. award Crofron Civic Assn., 1983. Mem. Internat. Test and Evaluation Assn., Armed Forces Communications Electronics Assn., Nat. Mil. Intelligence Assn., Kiwanis (sec. 1982-83), Theta Chi. Republican. Methodist. Home: 306 Leafcup Rd Ste 607 Gaithersburg MD 20878-2651 Office: GTE Govt Systems Corp 15000 Conference Center Dr Chantilly VA 22021-3800

MCCORMICK, WILLIAM, inventor, management consultant; b. Oaks, Pa., Feb. 17, 1942; s. William and Mary Catherine (Jones) McC.; m. Marjorie Alice Milani, June 27, 1969. BS in Engring. Sci., Penn State U., State Coll., 1964; PhD in Biophysics, Mass. Inst. Tech., Cambridge, 1968; MBA, Harvard U., Boston, 1973. Sr. rsch. fellow Merck & Co. (R&D Labs), Rahway, N.J., 1968-71; dir. R&D Becton Dickinson Co., Rutherford, N.J., 1973-76; pres. McCormick Assocs., Inc., Lowell, Mass., 1976—, McCormick Labs., Inc., North Chelmsford, Mass., 1979-90, MBO Labs., Inc., North Chelmsford, 1990—; assoc. Pharmacol., Harvard Med. Sch., Boston, 1976-78; cons. Dept. Radiation Therapy, U. Pa. Med. Sch., Phila., 1985-86. Patentee in field. Mem. Carlisle Edn. Found., Mass., 1990—; corporator Ctr. for Blood Rsch., Boston, 1991—. Home: 65 Hickory Ln Carlisle MA 01741-1139 Office: McCormick Assocs Inc PO Box 948 110 Middlesex St North Chelmsford MA 01863

MCCOWN, WAYNE GORDON, religion educator; b. Compton, Calif., Mar. 9, 1942; s. George Arnold and Lewise Daisy (Nasby) McC.; m. Darlene Elizabeth McCown, June 14, 1962; children: Mark Wayne, Peter Lewis. BA, Seattle Pacific U., 1963; BD, Asbury Theol. Sem., Wilmore, Ky., 1966; MA, U. Wash., 1967; ThM, Union Theol. Sem., Richmond, Va., 1968, PhD, 1970. Ordained elder Free Meth. Ch., 1964. Asst. prof. Seattle Pacific U., 1970-73; prof., dean Western Evang. Sem., Portland, Oreg., 1973-85; supt. So. Calif.—Ariz. conf. Free Meth. Ch. N.Am., L.A., 1985-88; sr. v.p., provost Roberts Wesleyan Coll., Rochester, N.Y., 1988—; supt. So. Calif.-Ann. Conf. Free Meth. Ch., 1985-88; sec. study commn. on doctrine Free Meth. Ch., Indpls., 1985—. Editor: God's Word Interpreted for Today's World, 1979; contbr. articles to religious jours. Supt. So. Calif.-Ariz. Conf. Free Meth. Ch., 1985-88; asst. pastor North City Free Meth. Ch., 1963-64, 66-67, 70-72; coord. Faith and Life Free Meth. Ch., 1976-77; interim pastor Lebanon Free Meth. Ch., 1977; asst. dir. John Wesley Sem. Found., 1972-85; ptnr. Western Evang. Sem., 1973—; mem. study commn. on doctrine Free Meth. Ch., 1978-85. Recipient Alumni Medallion award Seattle Pacific U., 1981; fellow Roberts Wesleyan Coll., Seattle Pacific U. Mem. Soc. Bibl. Lit., Wesleyan Theol. Soc. (pres. 1980-81), Alpha Kappa Sigma, Theta Phi. Office: Roberts Wesleyan Coll 2301 Westside Dr Rochester NY 14624-1997

MCCOY, EILEEN CAREY, academic dean; b. Jersey City; d. James Bernard and Nan (Dalton) Carey; m. Thomas James McCoy; children: Thomas James III, Mary Eileen McCoy Whang. BA, Coll. St. Elizabeth, Convent Station, N.J., 1954; MA, Fairleigh Dickinson U., 1969, EdD, 1983; postgrad., Harvard U., 1985. Mem. faculty County Coll. Morris, Dover, N.J., 1970-75; dir. community relations Raritan Valley Community Coll., Somerville, N.J., 1977-79, dean continuing, community edn. and svcs., 1979—. Author: The Community Education Component of the Community College: New Jersey in Comparative Perspective, 1983. Mem. Morris County Bd. Freeholders, 1975-77; founding chmn. Somerset County Commn. on Women, 1985-88; mem. adv. coun. Somerset County Office on Aging, 1987—; bd. advisors Somerset County United Way; bd. dirs. Somerset County Mental Health Assn. Recipient Righteous Gentile award Jewish Fedn. Somerset, Hunterdon and Warren Counties, 1989, Somerset County Tercentennial award, 1989. Mem. Nat. Coun. Continuing Edn. and Community Svc. (bd. dirs. and region rep. 1987—, Person of Yr. region 2 1989), Greater Somerset County C. of C. (v.p. and bd. dirs. 1988-92, Outstanding Woman in Business and Industry 1982), Rotary (pres. Branchburg, N.J., club 1989-90). Republican. Roman Catholic. Office: Raritan Valley Commun Coll PO Box 3300 Somerville NJ 08876-1265

MCCRARY, EUGENIA LESTER (MRS. DENNIS DAUGHTRY MCCRARY), civic worker, writer; b. Annapolis, Md., Mar. 23, 1929; d. John Campbell and Eugenia (Potts) Lester; m. John Campbell Howard, July 15, 1955 (dec. Sept. 1965); m. Dennis Daughtry McCrary, June 28, 1969; 1 child, Dennis Campbell. AB cum laude, Radcliffe Coll.-Harvard U., 1950; MA, Johns Hopkins U., 1952; postgrad., Harvard U., 1953, Pa. State U., 1953-54, Drew U., 1957-58, Inst. Study of USSR, Munich, 1964. Grad. asst. dept. Romance langs. Pa. State U., 1953-54; tchr. dept. math. The Brearley Sch., N.Y.C., 1954-57; dir. Sch. Langs., Inc., Summit, N.J., 1958-69; trustee Sch. Langs., Inc., Summit, 1960-69. Co-author: Nom de Plume: Eugenia Campbell Lester, (with Allegra Branson) Frontiers Aflame, 1987. Dist. dir. Eastern Pa. and N.J. auditions Met. Opera Nat. Coun., N.Y.C., 1960-66, dist. dir. publicity, 1966-67, nat. vice chmn. publicity, 1967-71, nat. chmn. public rels., 1972-75, hon. nat. chmn. pub. rels., 1976—; bd. govs., chmn. Van Cortlandt House Mus., 1985-90. Mem. Nat. Soc. Colonial Dames Am. (bd. mgrs. N.Y. 1985-90), Met. Opera Nat. Coun., Soc. Mayflower Desc. (former bd. dirs. N.Y. soc., chmn. house com. 1986-89), Soc. Daus. of Holland Dames (bd. dirs. 1982-87, 3d directress gen. 1987-92, directress gen. 1992—), L'Eglise du Saint-Esprit (vestry 1985-88, sr. warden 1988-90), Huguenot Soc. Am. (governing coun. 1984-90, asst. treas. 1990-91, sec. 1991—), Colonial Dames Am., Colony Club (bd. govs. 1988—). Republican. Episcopalian. Home: 24 Central Pk S New York NY 10019-1632

MCCRAVEN, STEPHEN, drummer; b. Washington, Aug. 7, 1954; s. Marcus Rollins and Marguerita (Mills) McC.; m. Agnes Zsigmondi, Feb. 2, 1985; children: Makaya, Kinga. Student, Berklee Coll. Music. Instr. Git La Coeur Sch. Dance and Music, Paris, 1981-83; asst. instr. tap program Am. Ctr., Paris, 1982-83; dir. drum dept. Community Music Sch. of Springfield, Mass., 1989—; asst. tchr. U. Mass., Amherst, 1990-91. Albums include Wooley the Newt, Intertwining Spirits, Up from the Skies, International

World; other recordings with Marion Brown, Sonny Grey, Jemeel Moondoc, Calvin Newborm, Sam Rivers, Archie Shepp, Yusef Lateef. Home: 7 Cone St Northampton MA 01060

MCCRAW, EDWARD LEE, communications executive; b. Roanoke, Va., Nov. 8, 1951; s. James Edward and Clara Louise (Childress) McC.; m. Connie Martin, June 23, 1974. BA in Mass Communications, U. South Fla., 1974, BA in English, 1974. Pub. rels. writer GTE Corp., Tampa, 1977-78, pub. affairs adminstr., 1978-81, mgr. communications, 1981-89; mgr. editorial and fin. communications svcs. GTE Corp., Stamford, Conn., 1989—; advisor Fla. High Tech. Coun., Tallahassee, 1987-88. Bd. dirs. Tampa Urban League, 1988-89; mem. pres. coun. U. South Fla., Tampa, 1988-89. Home: 18 Fairfax Ave Wilton CT 06897-4016 Office: GTE Corp 1 Stamford Forum Stamford CT 06901-3516

MCCREADY, SAM, theatre educator, actor, director; b. Belfast, No. Ireland, Nov. 22, 1936; s. David James and Sarah Elizabeth (Howlett) McC.; m. Joan Carslake, Mar. 16, 1962; children: Marcus Diarmuid Julian, Richard Alastair. MA, U. N. Wales, U.K., 1976. Advt. mgr. Berkshire Internat., No. Ireland, 1961-63; head dept. theatre Orangefield Boys Sch., Belfast, 1963-67, head English dept., 1967-69; lectr. U. N. Wales, Bangor, 1969-78; artistic dir. Lyric Theatre, Belfast, 1980-81; head dept. theatre Stranmillis Coll., Belfast, 1978-83; assoc. prof. theatre U. Md., Catonsville, 1984—; artistic dir. Shakespeare On Wheels, 1985—; examiner Guildhall Sch. Music and Drama, London, 1969—; trustee Lyric Theatre, Belfast, 1978-82. Author: Lucille Lortel: The Queen of Off-Broadway, 1992; adaptor, dir. play: Spring's Awakening, 1987 (Best Dir. award 1987), No Country for Old Men, 1985, Picture of Dorian Gray, 1988, Salome, 1989; contbr. articles to profl. jours. Named Outstanding Dir., Am. Coll. Theatre Festival, 1986, 87. Mem. Brit. Actors Equity, E. Cen. Theatre Conf. Episcopalian. Office: U Md Dept Theatre Catonsville MD 21228

MCCREIGHT, SUSAN BUCKLEY, human resources executive; b. Oakland, Calif., Feb. 19, 1946; d. Milton Chester and Virginia Jean (Kincaid) Buckley; m. John A. McCreight, May 18, 1985 (div. Feb. 1989). BS in Social Sci. summa cum laude, Fordham U., 1983. Flight attendant Am. Airlines, N.Y.C., 1969-73, analyst flight svc., 1973-76, sr. analyst flight svc., 1976-78, mgr. flight svc. procedures, 1978-79; mgr., adminstrn. and spl. projects ABC, Inc., N.Y.C., 1979-81, mgr. fair employment practices, 1981-84; dir. personnel Chilton Co., Radnor, Pa., 1984-85; dir. human resources Cahners Pub. Co., N.Y.C., 1987-89; v.p. human resources Warner Pub., Inc., N.Y.C., 1990—. Mem. Soc. for Human Resources Mgmt., N.Y. Personnel Mgmt. Assn., Phi Kappa Phi. Republican. Episcopalian. Home: 104D Heritage Hill Rd New Canaan CT 06840-4623 Office: Warner Pub Inc 666 5th Ave New York NY 10103-0001

MCCREVAN, ROSEMARY ANN, contingency planning consultant; b. Boston, Aug. 1, 1952; d. George Patrick and Mary (Joyce) McC. BS in Mgmt., Boston State Coll., 1981; MBA, Babson Coll., 1988. With Hawaii Nat. Bank, Honolulu, 1973, U.S. Trust Co., Milton, Mass., 1973-78, Shawmut Bank, Boston, 1978-88, Bank of Boston, 1988-89, Strohl Systems, Tampa, Fla., 1989-90; ind. cons. Milton, Mass., 1990-91; pres. Bus. Continuation Svcs., Inc., Milton, Mass., 1991—. Mem. No. New Eng. Disaster Recovery Info. X-Change. Mem. Info. Systems Security Assn., Contingency Planning Exchange, DECUS, Psi Chi. Home: 50 St Agatha Rd Milton MA 02186-4364 Office: Bus Continuation Svcs Inc PO Box 145 Milton MA 02186-0002

MCCROSSAN, JOHN PATRICK, bank executive; b. N.Y.C., Apr. 8, 1943; s. John Patrick and Sarah Jane (McKeon) McC.; m. Mary Rose Esmiol; children: Deborah Ann, John Patrick III. Data processing mgr. Pepsico Leasing Inc., Purchase, N.Y., 1970-73; mgr. data ctr. ops. Citicorp/Citibank, N.Y.C., 1974-78; dir. data ctr. ops. Citicorp Retail Svcs., Englewood, Colo., 1979-80; dir. data ctr. ops. Citibank, S.D., 1981-84, Nev., 1984-86; dir. group data svcs. Citicorp U.S. Card Products, N.Y.C., 1987—; developer, implementator Citicorp Command Ctr., 1987. With U.S. Army, 1961-63, ETO. Roman Catholic. Home: 19007 Hunt Pass Ct Parkton MD 21120 Office: Citicorp US Card Products 200 International Cir Hunt Valley MD 21030

MCCUAN, WILLIAM PATRICK, real estate company executive; b. Muskogee, Okla., Oct. 28, 1941; s. Lee L. and LaRee A. (Beverage) McC.; m. Jill Pamela Thomas, May 5, 1982; children: LaRee, Megan. Student, U. Tulsa, 1961-62; BA in Psychology, Baylor U., 1965; MRE, So. U., Louisville, 1967; MS, U. Louisville, 1969; postgrad., U. Md., 1971-73. Prof., asst. dean grad. sch. U. Md., Balt., 1969-73; lobbyist, cons. Washington, 1973-76; chmn. bd. KMS Group, Inc., Columbia, Md., 1976-84; chief exec. officer, pres. McCuan Devel. Group, Inc./K&M Devel. Corp., Columbia, Md., 1985—; adj. prof. Community Coll. Balt., 1969-72, U. Md., College Park, 1969-71; lectr. Univ. Coll.-Univ. Md., Balt., 1970-71, Howard Community Coll., Columbia, 1987-88; chmn. Pet Holiday, Inc., Toledo, 1973—; bd. dirs. Howard Vocat. Constrn. Co.; non-lawyer mem. Atty. Grievance Commn. Md., 1990—. Contbr. to numerous publs. Chmn. United Way, Howard County, Md., 1984; fin. chmn. Repub. Cen. Com., Howard County, 1988-91; chmn. Am. Presdl. Inaugural Com., Md., 1988, Howard County Community Partnerships; trustee Columbia Found., Howard County, 1979-80, Mental Health Assn. Howard County; mem. Pres.' Commn. on Food, Nutrition and Health, Washington, 1970, Howard County Environ. Affairs Bd., Indsl. Edn. Alliance Howard, Columbia Archives Com.; mem. bus. adv. coun. Howard Community Coll.; bd. dirs. Congl. Commn. on Mental Health of Children, Washington, 1973-75, Human Svcs. Inst. for Children & Families. Mem. Nat. Assn. Home Builders (bd. dirs. 1979-87, fed. govt. affairs com.), Md. Builders Assn. (pres. 1981-82), Home Builders Assn. Md. (bd. dirs. 1977-82, Award of Honor 1979, Award of Excellence 1980, Presdl. award 1982), Atty. Grievance Commn. of Md., Howard County Home Builders Assn. (pres. 1978-80), Howard County C. of C. (pres. bd. dirs. 1984-86). Mem. Reformed Ch. Home: 11838 Farside Rd Ellicott City MD 21042-1526 Office: McCuan Devel Corp/K&M Devel Corp K&M Lakefront Bldg Ste 312 5550 Sterrett Pl Columbia MD 21044

MCCUE, ARTHUR BERNARD, city government official; b. Providence, June 27, 1926; s. Daniel Lawrence and Mary Ellen (O'Malley) McC.; m. Helen Elizabeth Flynn, Apr. 24, 1954; children: Gerald, Brian, Timothy, Julie, Joan, Marie, Joseph, Jeanette. BS, Boston Coll., 1950; LLB, Boston U., 1953; LLM, Suffolk U., 1961; MEd, U. Mass., Boston, 1985. Bar: Mass. 1955, U.S. Dist. Ct. (fed. dist.) 1957, U.S. Ct. Appeals (1st cir.) 1959, U.S. Supreme Ct. 1959, U.S. Ct. Claims 1960, U.S. Ct. Mil. Appeals 1969. Enlisted U.S. Army, 1944; advanced through grades to lt. USNR, 1965—; trial counsel Md. Casualty Co., Boston, 1968-78, chief trial counsel, 1978-86; asst. city clk. City of Somerville, Mass., 1986-88, city clk., 1988—. Mem. Mass. Def. Lawyers Assn., Def. Rsch. Inst. Roman Catholic. Home: 21 Bromfield Rd Somerville MA 02144-1311 Office: Somerville City Clk 93 Highland Ave Somerville MA 02143-1794

MCCUE, ARTHUR HARRY, artist, educator; b. N.Y.C., Sept. 27, 1944; s. Raymond Noel and Alice (Cassidy) McC. BFA, Pratt Inst., N.Y.C., 1967; MFA, U. Colo., 1969. Instr. art SUNY, Geneseo, 1969-72; instr. printmaking and drawing Ithaca (N.Y.) Coll., 1973-77, chmn. dept. art, 1977—. One-man shows include Univ. Club, Boulder, Colo., 1968, David Gallery, Rochester, N.Y., 1973, Ithaca Coll., 1977, 79, Art Gallery Adelphi U., Garden City, N.Y., 1980, Wagner Gallery, Lodi, N.Y., 1983, Ithaca House Gallery, 1984, 85, Schwein Furth Meml. Mus., Auburn, N.Y., 1986, Johnson Mus. Art, Ithaca, 1987; two-person shows: Harry McCue/David Smyth, Ithaca House, Ithaca, N.Y., 1980, Hackworth/McCue, U. Pa., Edinboro, Grippi/McCue, Handwerker Gallery, Ithaca; group shows: Internat. Gallery, Denver, 1969, Double U Gallery, N.Y.C., 1977; Upstairs Gallery, Ithaca, 1978, 83, Handwerker Gallery, Ithaca Coll., 1980, 82, 84, 85, 86, 87, 89, 90, Upstairs Gallery, 1983—, Everson Mus., Syracuse, N.Y., (2d prize printmaking 1987), New Visions Gallery, Ithaca, 1987, 88, 89, 90, Elmira Coll., 1991; nat. exhbns.: Fall River Art Show, Mass., 1973, 74, 76, Marietta Coll., Ohio, 1974, 76, Arnot Mus., Elmira, N.Y., 1977, Ft. Hays State U., 1984, U. Maine, 1985, Everson Mus., 1985, U. Maine, 1992; included in book The American History Supply Catalogue, 1983, N.Y. Art Rev., 3rd Edit.; invited spl. guest at spl. showing Christie's Auction House, N.Y.C., 1984, Roch Meml. Art Gallery, 1991; commissioned by Cornell U./Statler Hotel to Design art work for hotels, 1988. Lodestar grantee, 1984. Home: RR 2 Lodi NY 14860-9802 Office: Ithaca Coll Dept Art Danby Rd Ithaca NY 14850-5736

MCCUE, BERNICE, office manager; b. Pitts., July 25, 1960; d. Bernard John McCue Jr. and June Clarice (Hargrove) Wiefling; m. Robert Francis Brace, Apr. 12, 1980. AS in Corrections Adminstrn., Pitts. Community Coll., 1985; BSBA, Robert Morris Coll., 1989. Lab. technician Koppers Co., Inc., Monroeville, Pa., 1978-84; office mgr. MovExpress, Sharpsburg, Pa., 1990-92. Mem. Nat. Parks and Conservation Assn.

MCCUE, KENNETH RUSSELL, investment banker; b. Bryan, Tex., Apr. 4, 1946; s. Robert Leslie and Ella (Yeager) McC.; m. Helen Blair, Jan. 25, 1970; children: Erin Christine, Ashley Lynne. BS in Nuclear Engring., Tex. A&M U., 1969; MS in Nuclear Engring., Purdue U., 1972, MS in Indsl. Mgmt., 1973, PhD, 1978; APC in Fin., N.Y.U., 1988. Cons. Stone & Webster Mgmt. Cons., N.Y.C., 1973-79; mgr. mktg. Transnuclear, White Plains, N.Y., 1979-82; v.p., regional mgr. Nuexco, Stamford, Conn., 1982-85; v.p. corp. fin. Dean Witter Reynolds, N.Y.C., 1985-88; mng. cons. Cresap, McCormick and Paget, N.Y.C., 1988-91; assoc. dir. Barclays Bank PLC, N.Y.C., 1991—. Mem. Nat. Assn. Securities Dealers (registered rep.). Home: 116 Michael Rd Stamford CT 06903-3021 Office: Barclays Bank PLC 222 Broadway New York NY 10038-2510

MCCUEN, PETER BURTON, publishing executive; b. New Britain, Conn., Nov. 18, 1934; s. Burton Arthur and Mary Ruth (Cook) McC.; m. Lorraine Iris Gorges, Apr. 30, 1960; children: Tracey Ann, Samantha Ann. BA, Albright Coll., Reading, Pa., 1956. Various positions Sweets div. McGraw-Hill Info. Systems Co., N.Y.C., 1958-78, v.p., gen. mgr., 1978-79, sr. v.p. devel., 1979-83; group v.p. product info. group McGraw-Hill Inc., N.Y.C., 1983-85; group v.p. communications info. group McGraw-Hill Inc., 1985-87, group v.p. Sweets group, 1987-88; v.p. pub. devel. R.R. Bowker, 1988-90; pres. The Ea. Rsch. Corp., Parsippany, N.J., 1990-91; v.p. sales and corp. planning Nelson Publs., Port Chester, N.Y., 1992—. Trutee, chmn. devel. com., mem. exec. com. Albright Coll., 1980—. Recipient Disting. Alumnus award Albright Coll., 1985. Home: 6 Old Ln Scarsdale NY 10583-1502 Office: Nelson Publs One Gateway Plz Port Chester NY 10573

MCCULLEN, MICHAEL JOHN, advertising executive; b. Phila., Aug. 12, 1937; s. Joseph Thomas and Sara Ellen (Berryman) McC.; m. Kathleen Carol Flynn, Sept. 14, 1968; 1 child, Kelly Ann. BS in Mktg., Temple U., Phila., 1963. Creative liaison Phila. Inquirer, 1963-66; artist/writer The Phila. Bull., 1966-71; pres. Creative Creatures, Inc., Phila., 1971-79; advt. mgr. Eckerd Drug Co., Newark, Del., 1979-83; advt./sales promotion mgr. Eljo Products, Inc., Pennsauken, N.J., 1983—. Mem. Rep. Nat. Com., Washington, 1985-86. With USN, 1957-59. Mem. Am. Soc. Advt. and Promotion, Nat. Assn. Desktop Pubs., Mktg. Color Group, Phila. Advt. Club. Republican. Roman Catholic. Home: 268 Grisscom Ct Marlton NJ 08053-2011 Office: Eljo Products Inc 6940 Central Hwy Merchantville NJ 08109-4110

MCCULLOCH, ANNA MARY KNOTT, pharmacy technician; b. Riverdale, Md., Aug. 29, 1964; d. Samuel Eugene and Jean M. (Schildt) Knott; m. Richard Sears, Nov. 6, 1988. Student, W.Va. U., 1982-84; cert., Children's Inst. Lit., 1987. Pharmacy technician Montgomery Gen. Hosp., Olney, Md., 1981—; med. asst., sec. Dr. Arthur Lomant, Eldersburg, Md., 1986-87; pharmacy technician Frederick (Md.) Meml. Hosp., 1991—. Mem. Assn. Pharmacy Technicians, Stringband Am., Inc. (v.p. Eldersburg chpt. 1989-90). Roman Catholic. Home: 109 Woodside Ave Thurmont MD 21788-1932

MCCULLOM, CORNELL, JR., professional association executive; b. Gary, Ind., Apr. 5, 1932; Cornell Leamon and Gussie (Dixon) McC.; m. Berta Gholson, June 4, 1957; children: Cornell III, Kevin B., Michele D., Scott B. BS in Engring., U.S. Mil. Acad., 1957; BS in Meteorology, U. Utah, 1963, MS in Meteorology, 1964; MBA, L.I. Univ., 1976. Commd. 2d lt. U.S. Army, 1957, advanced through grades to col., 1978; served in Vietnam, 1967-68; staff, faculty U.S. Mil. Acad, 1969-73; dep. chief of staff communications-electronics U.S. Army Support Command, Thailand, 1973-74; post comdr. U.S. Mil. Acad. STAS, 1974-78; ret. U.S. Army, 1978; mgr. personnel Fed. Express Corp., Newburgh, N.Y., 1979-80; dir. human resources YMCA Greater N.Y.C., 1980-81; sr. mgr. ITT Corp./U.S. Transmission Systems, Corp., Secaucus, N.J., 1981-85; v.p. Nat. Action Council Minorities Engring., Inc., N.Y.C., 1985-89; pres. CMC Assocs., Salisbury Mills, N.Y., 1989—; adj. faculty U. Alaska, Fairbanks, 1965-67, U. Md., Gelnhausen, Germany, 1958-60. Mem. Am. Assn. Engring. Socs. (bd. govs. 1986-89), Jr. Engring. Tech. Soc. (bd. dirs. 1987-89), West Point Soc. N.Y. (bd. govs. 1989—), Am. Mgmt. Assn., Armed Forces Communications Elec. Assn., Am. Mil. Assn., Am. Soc. Engring. Educators. Office: CMC Assocs PO Box 316 Salisbury Mills NY 12577-0316

MCCURN, NEAL PETERS, federal judge; b. Syracuse, N.Y., Apr. 6, 1926. LL.B., Syracuse U., 1952, J.D., 1960. Bar: N.Y. 1952. Ptnr. Mackenzie Smith Lewis Mitchell & Hughes, Syracuse, 1957-79; judge U.S. Dist. Ct. (no. dist.) N.Y., 1979-88; chief judge U.S. Dist. Ct. (no. dist.), N.Y., 1988-; del. N.Y. State Constl. Conv., 1976; mem. 2d Cir. Jud. Council. Pres. Syracuse Common Coun., 1970-78. Mem. ABA, N.Y. State Bar Assn. (chmn. state constn. com.), Onondaga County Bar Assn. (past pres.), Am. Coll. Trial Lawyers, Am. Judicature Soc. (bd. dirs. 1980-84). Office: US Dist Ct 100 S Clinton St Rm 33 Syracuse NY 13260-0001

MCCURRACH, JAMES CRAMPTON, professional squash player; b. Bklyn., June 8, 1934; s. James C. and Margaret (Means) McC.; m. Lynn Zabriskie (dec.); children: James C. III, Peter Zabriskie. V.p. Bankers Trust Co., N.Y.C., 1965-80; pres. Boxes Restaurant Inc., N.Y.C., 1980-82; exec. placement office Fanning, Inc., N.Y.C., 1982-84; recreation mgr. Printing Ho. Recreation, N.Y.C., 1984-90; assoc. recreational staff NYU, N.Y.C., 1989—; squash profl. Cape Cod Recreation, Inc., 1991—; pres. McCurrach Enterprises, Inc., Provincetown, Mass., 1991—. Mem. U.S. Squash Racquets Assn. (top five U.S. vets., 1979-83, #4 in U.S. 1986—), Met. Squash Racquets Assn. (ranked #1 Vet., Sr., N.Y.C., N.Y. State 1979—). Club: Univ. (N.Y.C.). Home: PO Box 1529 81 Province Lands Rd Provincetown MA 02657-1163 Office: McCurrach Enterprises 10 Thistlemore Rd Provincetown MA 02657

MCCUTCHEN, WILLIAM WALTER, JR., management educator; b. Hamlet, N.C., Aug. 26, 1940; s. William Walter and Edith Wall (Rucker) McC.; m. Irene Katherine Lilly, June 16, 1962; 1 child, William Walter III. BS in Civil Engring., Duke U., 1962; MBA, Harvard U., 1967; PhD, Ind. U., 1988. Sales rep. Eli Lilly and Co., San Francisco, 1967-69; analyst econ. studies Eli Lilly and Co., Indpls., 1969-70; mgr. econ. studies Eli Lilly and Co., 1970-72, mgr. personnel (mktg.), 1972-73; dir. nat. sales Elizabeth Arden, N.Y.C., 1973-76; mng. dir. Lilly Industries Pty. Ltd., Sidney, Australia, 1976-79; dir. corp. communications Eli Lilly & Co., Indpls., 1980-83; asst. prof. mgmt. Baruch Coll., CUNY, N.Y.C., 1988—. Capt. USMC, 1962-65. Mem. Acad. Mgmt., Am. Econ. Assn., Woodstock Club, Univ. Club, Phi Delta Theta, Beta Gamma Sigma. Presbyterian/Congregationalist. Office: CUNY Baruch Coll 17 Lexington Ave New York NY 10010-5526

MCCUTCHEON, ALLAN LEE, sociology educator; b. Clarinda, Iowa, Mar. 15, 1950; s. Merle Marvin and Margaret Lucille (Larabee) McC.; m. Nancy Ann Cooper, June 13, 1970 (div. May 1975); 1 child, Jennifer; m. Elisabeth Jean Crockett, May 25, 1985. BS, Iowa State U., 1972; MA, U. Chgo., 1977, PhD, 1982. Asst. prof. Sociology U. Del., Newark, 1982-88, assoc. prof. Sociology, 1988—, assoc. chair dept. Sociology, 1989—; cons. Disaster Rsch. Ctr., Newark, 1986-88; vis. scientist Max Planck Inst., Freiburg, Germany, 1988-89; dozent U. Cologne (Germany), 1989; instr. European Consortium for Polit. Rsch. U. Essex (Eng.), 1990—. Author (book) Latent Class Analysis, 1987; editor (newsletter) States and Societies, 1988—; contbr. articles to profl. jours. Resource cons. Leadership Del. United Way, Wilmington, 1991-92. U. Chgo. rsch. fellow, 1974-77; Deutscher Akademischer Austauschdienst scholar, 1990. Mem. World Assn. for Pub. Opinion Rsch., Coun. for European Studies, Am. Assn. for Pub. Opinion Rsch., Am. Statis. Assn., Am. Sociol. Assn., Sigma Xi. Office: Dept of Sociology U Del Newark DE 19716

MCCUTCHEON, IRENE, elementary school educator; b. N.Y.C., Feb. 21, 1940; d. Allen Robert and Margaret (Geoghegan) McC. BS in Edn. cum laude, Dominican Coll. Blauvelt, N.Y., 1963; MEd, LaSalle U., 1986, MA in Theology, 1986; MA in Guidance and Counseling, Loyola U., Balt., 1991. Tchr. Mother Seton Sch., Emmitsburg, Md., 1965-74, Portsmouth (Va.) Elem. Sch., 1974-75, St. Dominic's Elem. Sch., Balt., 1975-78; tour guide Seton Shrine Ctr., Emmitsburg, 1978-79; tchr., social dir. St. Ann's, Hyattsville, Md., 1979-80; parish min. St. Mary's Parish, Greensboro, N.C., 1980-83; pastoral assoc. Immaculate Conception Parish, Balt., 1983-85; tchr. Balt. County Sch. System, Catonsville, Md., 1986—, grade level chairperson, 1990-91; dir. religious edn. Immaculate Conception Parish, 1983-85, parish rep. to Md. food bank, 1983-85. Active parish coun. Immaculate Conception Parish, 1983-85, Ch. of Ascension, Halethorpe, Md., 1991—. Recipient Mayor's Citation for Pub. Svc., Balt., 1985. Mem. Tchrs. Assn. Balt. County (rep. 1991—), Md. State Tchrs. Assn., NEA, Am. Assn. for Counseling and Devel. Roman Catholic. Office: Catonsville Elem Sch 615 Frederick Rd Baltimore MD 21228-4683

MC DADE, JOSEPH MICHAEL, congressman; b. Scranton, Pa., Sept. 29, 1931; s. John B. and Genevieve (Hayes) McD.; children: Joseph, Aileen, Deborah, Mark; m. Sarah Scripture, May 1988; 1 child, Jared. B.A. in Polit. Sci. with honors, U. Notre Dame, 1953; LL.B., U. Pa., 1956; LL.D. (hon.), St. Thomas Aquinas Coll., 1968, U. Scranton, 1969, Misericordia Coll. and Kings Coll., 1981, Mansfield State Coll., 1982; H.H.D., Kings Coll. Bar: Pa. bar 1957. Clk. to fed. judge, 1956-57; pvt. practice law Scranton, 1957—, city solicitor, 1962; mem. 88th-102nd Congresses, 10th Dist. Pa., 1963—, mem. appropriations com., small bus. com. Mem. Am., Pa., Lackawanna County bar assns., Scranton C. of C. Republican. Roman Catholic. Clubs: K.C; James Wilson Law (Phila.). Office: US Ho of Reps 2370 Rayburn House Office Bldg Washington DC 20515

MCDANIEL, C.J., III, sales executive; b. Knoxville, Tenn., Mar. 2, 1945; s. Charles Jackson Jr. and Norma (Rice) McD.; m. Patricia Alice Van Beveren, May 14, 1977; children: Caitlin Elise, Christopher Jon. Student, USAF Acad., 1963-64; BS, East Tenn. State U., 1969. Golf profl., 1969-74; dir. sports programs British Caledonian Airways, Santa Monica, Calif., 1970-74; sales trainee Hyatt Worldwide, L.A., 1975; sales mgr. Hyatt Wilshire, L.A., 1976-78; dir. sales Hyatt Rickeys, Hyatt Palo Alto, Calif., 1978-81; dir. sales and mktg. Hyatt Regency Knoxville, 1981-82; dir. mktg. PGA Am., Palm Beach Gardens, Fla., 1983-86; exec. v.p. Cornerstone Sports, Dallas, 1986-91; v.p. sales and mktg. Bobby Jones Div. Hickey Freeman Co., Rochester, N.Y., 1991—; cons. City of Glen Rose, Tex., 1990, City of Fredericksburg, Tex., 1990. Bd. dirs. Project Shelter, Dallas, 1990; scoutmaster Cub scouts Boy Scouts Am., Plano, Tex., 1990. Recipient Phoenix award Sigma Alpha Epsilon, 1969. Republican. Baptist. Home: 4613 Adrian Way Plano TX 75024 Office: Hickey Freeman Co 1155 Clinton Ave N Rochester NY 14621

MCDANIEL, NORWOOD ALLAN, insurance broker; b. Pitts., Dec. 16, 1928; children: Norwood Jr., Cherie Suzanne, Thomas Cavin. Student, Washington and Lee U., 1948-50. Gen. ins. broker Pitts., 1949—; adv. bd. Union Nat. Bank, Pitts. Asst. treas. Community Coll. Allegheny County, 1986-90. Recipient citation Pa. Senate, 1987, Pa. Ho. of Reps., 1987, tribute Congl. Record, Pres. Ronald Reagan, 1987; inducted into Pa. Sports Hall of Fame, 1973. Mem. Fellows Club, City Club, Ins. Club Pitts., Profl. Ins. Agts. Assn., Amen Corner, Masons, Shriners (potentate Syria Temple Shrine 1978), Variety Club (chief barker), The Shrine Treas. Assn. N.Am. (sec.-treas. 1985—). Home and Office: 423 Greentree Rd Pittsburgh PA 15220

MCDERMOTT, JOHN JAMES, education educator; b. Wyoming, Pa., Oct. 20, 1933; s. James Aloysius and Isabel (Williams) McD.; m. Karen Scott, Apr. 6, 1953; children: John, Elisabeth, Matthew, Meaghan. BS in Edn., Shippensburg U., 1955; MEd in Natural Scis., U. Del., 1960; postgrad., Ohio State U., 1960-65. Sci. tchr. Greencastle (Pa.)- Antrim High Sch., 1955-59; tchr./coord. Carlisle (Pa.) Area Schs., 1959-66; rsch. assoc. Ohio State U., Columbus, 1964-66; sr. sci. adviser Pa. Dept. Edn., Harrisburg, 1966-88; assoc. prof. edn. Wilson Coll., Chambersburg, Pa., 1988—; adj. prof. Dickinson Coll., Carlisle, 1959-60; established Pa. Nuclear Sci. Program, 1981; founder Pa. Gov.'s Sch. for Scis., Pitts., 1985; regional dir. Pa. Sci. Olympiad, Chambersburg. Mem. Am. Nuclear Sci. Tchrs. Assn. (exec. dir. 1967-89, hon. exec. dir. 1989—), Pa. Jr. Acad. Sci. (Disting. Svc. award 1974, 75), Pa. Sci. Suprs. Assn. (Disting. Svc. award 1989), Fedn. State Cultural and Ednl. Profls. (pres. 1985-88). Office: Wilson Coll 1015 Philadelphia Ave Chambersburg PA 17201-1285

MCDERMOTT, SUSAN JEAN CASSI, business executive; b. Astoria, N.Y., Mar. 1, 1953; d. Walter George and Jean Louise (Krivicich) Cassi; m. Michael I. McDermott, Apr. 13, 1980. AA in Liberal Arts and Spanish, Nassau Community Coll., Garden City, N.Y., 1973; BA in Speech and Communications, SUNY, Oneonta, 1975. With advt. sales dept. N.Y. Daily News, N.Y.C., 1975-78, mgr. circulation dept., 1978-82; sales rep. Radio Relay, Hicksville, N.Y., 1983; with circulation ops. dept. USA Today, Bayside, N.Y., 1983-85; exec. dir. AHHS Neighborhood Press Coalition, Rockaway, N.Y., 1985-86; dir. devel. Threshold Svcs. Inc., Kensington, Md., 1989—. Contbg. editor Newspix mag., 1982. Mem. Silver Spring C. of C. Democrat. Roman Catholic. Home: 9009 2d Ave Silver Spring MD 20910 Office: Threshold Svcs Inc 10920 Connecticut Ave Kensington MD 20895-1613

MCDIARMID, LUCY, English educator, author; b. Louisville, Mar. 29, 1947; m. Harris B. Savin, Oct. 13, 1984; children: Emily Clare, Katharine Eliza. BA, Swarthmore (Pa.) Coll., 1968; MA, Harvard U., 1969, PhD, 1972. Asst. prof. Boston U., 1972-74; from asst. prof. to assoc. prof. Swarthmore Coll., 1974-81; asst. prof. U. Md. Balt. County, Catonsville, 1982-84; prof. Villanova (Pa.) U., 1984—. Author: Saving Civilization: Yeats, Eliot, and Auden Between The Wars, 1984, Auden's Apologies for Poetry, 1990; co-editor: Selected Writings of Lady Gregory, 1994, High and Low Moderns: Literature and Culture, 1889-1939, 1993; contbr. articles to profl. jours. NEH fellow, 1981-82; ACLS grantee, 1976. Home: 1931 Panama St Philadelphia PA 19103-6609 Office: Villanova U Dept of English Villanova PA 19085

MCDONALD, BONNIE LYNN TERESA, administrative assistant, registrar; b. Bridgeport, Conn., Jan. 17, 1951; d. John R. and Julie (Potak) Banas; m. James E. McDonald II, Oct. 3, 1970; children: James E. III, Eric John, Kimberly L. (dec.). Student, Community Coll. Vt., White River Junction, 1990—. Pvt. sec. St. Vincent Hosp., Bridgeport, 1967-70; regional claims clk. Hartford Ins., Fairfield, Conn., 1970-73; exec. sec. Jim & Sons Electronics, Milford, Conn., 1975-85; nurse's aide St. Joseph Manor/Wandas/Hanover Terr., Trumbull, Conn., Bradford, Vt., 1983-87; sr. sec., adminstrv. asst., registrar Dartmouth Coll., Hanover, N.H., 1987—; tchr., educator Office of Continuing Edn., Employee Health Clinic, Dartmouth-Hitchcock Med. Ctr., Lebanon, N.Y., 1988—. Den leader Boy Scouts Am., Milford, also Vershire, Vt., 1981-83, 90; pres. Vershire Elem. Sch. PTO, 1984-87; notary pub. Orange County, 1983-88. Mem. NAFE. Home: 133C Vershire Rd Vershire VT 05079

MCDONALD, CHRISTOPHER JOHN, naval officer; b. Urbana, Ill., Feb. 27, 1961; s. James Robert and Sharon Lee (Chalfant) McD.; m. Pamela Lee Mitchel, Aug. 4, 1984; children: Caitlin, Robert. AB, Dartmouth Coll., 1982; postgrad., Def. Intelligence Coll., 1988; postgrad. Nat. Law Ctr., George Washington U., 1988—. Commd. ensign USNR, 1983; with USN, 1989—, advanced through grades to lt., 1987; main propulsion asst. USS Francis C. Hammond, Yokosuka, Japan, 1984-86, combat info. ctr. officer, 1986-87; senate liaison officer Office of Legis. Affairs, Washington, 1987; action officer Office of the CNO, Washington, 1988-90; combat systems officer USS Samuel B. Roberts, Newport, R.I., 1991—; USN del. US-USSR Emerging Leaders Conf., Sochi, Russia, 1990. Decorated Navy Commendation medal. Mem. U.S. Naval Inst., Appalachian Trail Conf., Sierra Club. Home: 2862 Baylis Dr Ann Arbor MI 48108 Office: USS Samuel B Roberts (FFG-58) FPO AE 09586

MCDONALD, DENNIS PATRICK, college official; b. Albany, N.Y., Apr. 23, 1954; s. Edmund Raynsford and Anna Mae (Hughes) McD.; m. Jeanne Marie O'Connor, Jan. 21, 1978; 1 child, Christine Marie. AAS, Hudson Valley Community Coll., Troy, N.Y., 1975; BA, Coll. of St. Rose, Albany, 1977, MS in Edn., 1991. Dir. youth ministry Roman Cath. Diocese of

Albany, 1977-85; dir. confs. and spl. events Coll. of St. Rose, 1985-88, asst. dean for residence, 1988-90, assoc. dean students, 1990—; co-chmn. Capital Dist. Consortium on Alcohol, Albany, 1990-92. Vice pres. St. Vincent's Parish Coun., Albany, 1990-92. Mem. Am. Coll. Pers. Assn., Coll. Student Pers. Assn. (legis. affairs rep. 1991-92). Office: Coll of St Rose 432 Western Ave Albany NY 12203-1490

MCDONALD, GEORGE THOMAS, human service executive; b. South Orange, N.J., Apr. 28, 1944; s. John Crawford and Helen (Storminger) McD.; m. Harriet Louise Karr, Oct. 20, 1987; children: John, Andrea, Abigail, Ashley. Student, Fairleigh Dickenson U., 1963. V.p. mktg. McGregor Sportswear, Inc., N.Y.C., 1963-71; exec. v.p. Warnaco, Inc., N.Y.C., 1971-75; owner, pres. McDonald Apparel, Inc., N.Y.C., 1975-79; dir. N.Y. state vols. Presdl. Primary Sen. Edward Kennedy, N.Y.C., 1979-80; founder, pres. The Doe Fund, Inc., N.Y.C., 1980—. Dem. Congl. Candidate, N.Y., 1988; active N.Y.C. Civil Rights Coalition, 1989—, City Coun.'s Legis. Commn. on Homeless, 1990—, Mayor's Adv. Commn. on Single Homeless, 1990—, N.Y.C. Commn. on Homelessness. Home and Office: The Doe Fund Inc 232 E 84th St New York NY 10028

MCDONALD, JOE, photographer, writer; b. Wilkes-Barre, Pa., Aug. 26, 1952; s. Patrick James and Margarete (Quinn) McD.; m. Carol Hilda Demkee, Nov. 3, 1979 (div. 1990); m. Mary Ann Biddle, June 29, 1991. BS in Biology, Indiana U. Pa., 1974, MEd, 1976; cert. in edn., Lehigh U., Bethlehem, Pa., 1978. Biology tchr. Whitehall (Pa.) High Sch., 1978-83; freelance photographer McClure, Pa., 1983—. Author: A Practical Guide to Photographing American Wildlife, 1984, The Wildlife Photographers Field Manual, 1992, The Complete Guide to Wildlife Photography, 1992. Mem. Pa. Outdoor Writers Assn. (Best Published Photos award 1989, 90, 91), Outdoor Writers Assn. Am. (Best Color Photos award 1985, 86, 88),. Home and Office: Wildlife Photography RR 2 Box 1095 McClure PA 17841-9340

MCDONALD, JOHN FRANCIS PATRICK, electrical engineering educator; b. Narberth, Pa., Jan. 14, 1942; s. Frank Patrick and Lulu Ann (Hegedus) McD.; m. Karen Marie Knapp, May 26, 1979. B.S.E.E., MIT, 1963; M.S. in Engring., Yale U., 1965, Ph.D., 1969. Instr. Yale U., New Haven, 1968-69, asst. prof., 1969-74; assoc. prof. Rensselaer Poly. Inst., Troy, N.Y.,1974-86, prof., 1986—; founder Rensselaer Ctr. for Integrated Electronics, 1980—. Contbr. articles to 154 profl. publs. Patentee in field. Recipient numerous grants, 1974—. Mem. ACM, IEEE, Optical Soc., Acoustical Soc., Vacuum Soc. Office: Rensselaer Poly Inst Ctr for Integrated Electronics Troy NY 12181

MCDONALD, WILLIAM NAYLOR, III, public relations executive; b. Gloversville, N.Y., Sept. 28, 1913; s. Hugh Marshall and Bessie Maria (Loadwick) McD.; m. Ruth Seely Berry, Nov. 28, 1942; children: William Naylor IV, Patricia Berry. AB, Cornell U., 1936. Reporter Binghamton (N.Y.) Sun, 1936-38, Syracuse (N.Y.) Herald, 1938-39; assoc. editor Jour. of Commerce, N.Y.C., 1939-41; asst. dir. Puerto Rican News Bur., San Juan, 1941-42; dir. pub. rels. AMF, N.Y.C., 1946-69; account exec. Doremus & Co., N.Y.C., 1969-76; dir. corp. communications Flight Safety Internat., Flushing, N.Y., 1976—. Lt. USN, 1942-46; PTO. Episcopalian. Home: 131 Manor Ln Pelham NY 10803-2410 Office: Flight Safety Internat LaGuardia Airport Flushing NY 11371

MCDONEL, MICHAEL EUGENE, designer; b. Mechanicsburg, Pa., July 27, 1946; s. Russel Lewis and Kathlene (Sober) McD. BS in Art Edn., Kutztown U., 1968; MA in Fine Arts, U. Notre Dame, 1972. Cert. tchr. art edn., Pa. Tchr. studio art U. Notre Dame, 1972; asst. prodn. Galactica 1980 Universal Studios, Hollywood, Calif., 1979; toy designer Marvin Glass and Assocs., L.A., 1981; media specialist E-Systems, Ohio U., Saudi Arabian mil., Taif, Saudi Arabia, 1983—; appeared on NBC-TV Network "Today" Show, 1991. Home: PO Box 695 Mechanicsburg PA 17055-0695

MCDONELL, ROBERT TERRY, magazine editor, novelist; b. Norfolk, Va., Aug. 1, 1944; s. Robert Meinard and Irma Sophronia (Nelson) McD.; m. Joan Raffeld Hitzig, June 15, 1981; Robert Nicholas Campbell, Thomas Hunter Campbell. Student, U. Calif., Berkeley, 1962-63, San Jose State U., 1963-64; BA in Art, U. Calif., Irvine, 1967. With AP, N.Y.C., 1970-72; reporter Los Angeles Weekly, 1972-73; asso. editor San Francisco mag., 1974-76, City mag., San Francisco, 1976-77; sr. editor San Francisco mag., 1977, Outside mag., San Francisco, 1978-79; founding editor Rocky Mountain mag., Denver, 1979-80; mng. editor Rolling Stone mag., N.Y.C., 1980-83; asst. mng. editor Newsweek Mag., N.Y.C., 1983-86; founder Smart mag., N.Y.C., from 1986; now editor-in-chief Esquire mag., N.Y.C. Author: California Bloodstock, 1980, paperback edit., 1989; screenwriter: Miami Vice, China Beach. Office: Esquire Mag 1790 Broadway New York NY 10019-1412

MCDONOUGH, EUGENE FRANCIS, JR., surgeon; b. Boston, Oct. 19, 1930; s. Eugene Francis and Abigail Julia (Barry) McD.; m. Ingrid Anna Barrett, June 8, 1974; 1 child, Eugene Francis III. Student, Harvard Coll., 1952; MD, Tufts U., 1955, MS in Surgery, 1960. Resident surgery Boston City Hosp., 1955-56, 59-62, Meml. Sloan Kettering Cancer Ctr., N.Y.C., 1962-65; instr. surgery Harvard Med. Sch., Boston, 1966-72, asst. prof. clin. surgery, 1972—; mem. surg. staff Faulkner Hosp., Boston, 1966—, New Deaconess Hosp. Contbr. surg. articles to profl. jours., chpt. to book. Fellow ACS (pres. Mass. chpt. 1991), Soc. Surg. Oncology, New Eng. Surg. Soc., Boston Surg. Soc. (v.p. 1989). Home: 23 Bemis Rd Dedham MA 02026 Office: 1658 Centre St West Roxbury MA 02132

MCDONOUGH, MICHAEL RICHARD, architect, artist; b. Boston, July 12, 1951; s. Thomas Michael and Ethlyn Patricia (Barry) McD.; m. Kristin Lee Johnson, Aug. 24, 1985 (div. Nov. 1986). BA in English, U. Mass., 1974; MArch, U. Pa., 1983. Registered architect, N.Y. Assoc. SITE, Inc., N.Y.C., 1976-78; prin. Michael McDonough, Architect, N.Y.C., 1984—; faculty NYU, 1978-81, Parsons Sch. of Design, N.Y.C., 1984—. Editor: VIA 4, 1980; contbg. author: Architects Unnoticed Avant-G, 1983; contbg. editor: ID Mag., Met. Home Mag.; contbr. articles to profl. jours. Recipient Annual Designer's Choice award ID Mag., 1989, winner 2001 Competition Design Explorations, 1991. Mem. AIA. (Design award 1990). Home and Office: 131 Spring St New York NY 10012-5209

MCDONOUGH, PAUL DIAZ, accountant; b. Needham, Mass., Apr. 14, 1967; s. John Coleman and Iris Velma (Schofield) McD. BSBA, Merrimack Coll., 1989. Regional collections analyst Cullinet Software, Westwood, Mass., 1988; sr. staff acct. John T. Chipman & Co. CPAs, Norwood, Mass., 1989—. Mem. Needham (Mass.) Town Rep. Com., 1990. Republican. Roman Catholic. Home: 173 Fairfield St Needham MA 02192-4527 Office: John T Chipman & Co CPAs 955 Washington St Norwood MA 02062-3428

MCDONOUGH, THOMAS PATRICK, writer; b. Jersey City, N.J., June 2, 1949; s. Thomas Michael and Helen (Glendon) McD.; m. Joann Lalicata, Aug. 26, 1972; children: Tara, Thomas John. BA in History, William Paterson Coll., 1971; postgrad., NYU, 1974. Sales/svc. coord. Oscar Meyer & Co., Ft. Lee, N.J., 1971-78; freelance writer, 1978—; reporter The Record, Hackensack, N.J., 1980-81; mgr. employee publs. Am. Internat. Group, N.Y.C., 1981-88; sr. publs. editor Chemical Bank, N.Y.C., 1988-92. Contbr. poems, fiction and articles to gen. interest mags.

MCDONOUGH, WILLIAM EUGENE, public relations executive, writer; b. Chelsea, Mass., June 22, 1957; s. William J. and Dorothy A. (Teevens) McD.; m. Ellen M. Wirzburger, Sept. 26, 1981; children: Eamonn, Keely, Devon, Conor. BS, Colo. State U., 1980. Copywriter Merrill Assocs., Kingston, N.H., 1985-87; account exec. SGM & Co., Norwell, Mass., 1987, Conrad & Co., Hingham, Mass., 1987-88; v.p. Graham Communications, Quincy, Mass., 1988—. Author articles for various publs. Publicity dir. St. Mary's Bldg. Com., Hanover, Mass., 1989-92. Winner 2 Graniteer awards N.H. Ad Club, 1987, Ninth Wave award South Shore Ad Club, 1990, 92, Laurel award Cadillac Motor div., 1986. Office: Graham Communications 40 Oval Rd Quincy MA 02170

MCDOUGALL, BARBARA JEAN, Canadian government minister; b. Toronto, Ont., Can., Nov. 12, 1937; d. Robert James and Margaret Jean (Dryden) Leamen; m. Peter McDougall, Sept. 6, 1963 (dec.). B.A. in Polit. Sci. and Econs. with honors, U. Toronto, 1960. Chartered Fin. Analyst. Econ. analyst Can. Imperial Bank Commerce; market research analyst Toronto Star Ltd.; mgr. portfolio investments N.W. Trust Co., Edmonton, Alta., Can., 1974-76; v.p. A.E. Ames and Co. Ltd., 1976-81, Dominion Securities Ames Ltd., 1981-82; exec. dir. Can. Council of Fin. Analysts, 1982-84, 88—; cons. govt. cabinet minister Can. Ho. of Commons, Ottawa, Ont., 1984—, minister of state for fin., 1984-86, minister of state for privatization, minister responsible for regulatory affairs, 1986-88, minister responsible for status of women, 1986-90, minister of employment and immigration, 1988-91, sec. of state for external affairs, 1991—. Fin. columnist Chatelaine mag.; fin. commentator CBC Take 30; bus. columnist City Woman mag.; bus. journalist CITV Edmonton, Vancouver Sun. Chmn. City of Toronto Salvation Army 1984 Red Shield Appeal; bd. dirs. Community Occupational Therapy Assocs., chmn., 1982-84; bd. dirs. Enoch Turner Schoolhouse, Second Mile Club; counsellor Oakhalla Province Prison for Women; vice chmn. Elizabeth Fry Soc.; past pres. Rosedale Progressive Conservative Assn. Office: House of Commons, Parliament Bldgs, Ottawa, ON Canada K1A 0A6

MCDOW, PATRICIA DIANA, image consultant; b. Bklyn., Apr. 26, 1953; d. William and Catherine (George) McD. Exchange student, U. Ife, Ile-Ife, Nigeria, 1974; BS, SUNY, New Paltz, 1975; MA, C.W. Post, 1978. Cert. tchr., N.Y. Speech pathologist Northport (N.Y.) VA, 1977, Central Islip (N.Y.) Psychiat. Ctr., 1978-80, Rockland Children's Psychiat. Ctr., Orangebury, N.Y.; pres. Tricia Beauty and Fashion Cons., White Plains, N.Y., 1980—; educator OPI Products, Inc., North Hollywood, Calif., 1988—. Author: Let's Do Nails, 1990. Active Redeeming Love Christian Ctr. Mem. Nat. Nail Technician Group (N.Y. state del. 1989—, Mem. of Yr. award 1990), Assn. of Image Cons. Internat., Delta Sigma Theta (Corresponding sec. 1986-90). Democrat. Office: Tricia Beauty and Fashion Conss 405 Tarrytown Rd Dept 598 White Plains NY 10607-1349

MCDOWALL, ROBERT HUGH, anesthesiologist, educator; b. Akron, Ohio, May 4, 1956; s. Robert H. and Julia V. (Chuchu) McD. BA, Coll. Wooster, 1978; MD, U. Cin., 1982. Diplomate Am. Bd. Anesthesiologists, Am. Bd. Pediatrics. Clin. fellow Nat. Cancer Inst., Cin., 1979; resident pediatrics Columbia U. Coll. Physicians and Surgeons, N.Y.C., 1982-85; resident anesthesiology Columbia U. Sch. Physicians and Surgeons, N.Y.C., 1985-87, fellow pediatric anesthesiology and critical care, 1987-88; asst. clin. mem. Meml. Sloan-Kettering Cancer Ctr., N.Y.C., 1989—, dir. pediatric anesthesia, 1992—; asst. prof. anesthesiology Cornell U. Med. Ctr., N.Y.C., 1989—. Contbr. articles to profl. jours., chpts. to books. Fellow Mus. Modern Art, N.Y.C., 1988—. Fellow Am. Acad. Pediatrics; mem. Am. Soc. Anesthesiologists, Internat. Anesthesia Rsch. Soc., Soc. Pediatric Anesthesia, Soc. Pediatric Critical Care Medicine, Soc. Critical Care Medicine.

MCDOWELL, DAVID JAMISON, clinical psychologist; b. Pitts., Jan. 11, 1947; s. David Emerson and Auleene Marley (Jamison) McD.; m. Nancy Annis, Jan. 13, 1973; children: Sasha, Christopher. BA, Princeton U., 1968; PhD, U. Maine, 1980. Predoctoral intern clin. psychology Worcester (Mass.) State Hosp., 1976-77, admissions officer, 1979-82; instr. dept. psychology Coll. Holy Cross, Worcester, 1977-78; lectr. dept. psychology and edn. Assumption Coll., Worcester, 1978-79; clin. dir. Milford (Mass.) Assistance Program, 1978-80; asst. prof. psychiatry and pediatrics U. Mass. Med. Ctr., Worcester, 1980-83; clin. dir. Newton-Wellesley-Weston-Needham (Mass.) Multi-Service Ctr., 1983-84; dir. Lancaster (Mass.) Assocs., 1987—; ptnr. Worcester County Counseling Assocs., Bolton, Mass., 1980-87; allied profl. staff St. Vincent Hosp., Worcester, 1985—; clin. cons. Mass. Dept. Youth Svcs., Worcester, 1986-87, 89-90; lectr. and cons. in field. Author: (with others) The Mental Health Industry, 1978; contbr. articles to profl. jours. Mental Health fellow U. Maine, 1973-75. Fellow Mass. Psychol. Assn. (legis. com. 1985-86), Am. Orthopsychiat. Assn.; mem. Am. Psychol. Assn., Soc. for Clin. and Experimental Hypnosis. Office: Lancaster Assocs North County Health Ctr 136 High Street Ext Lancaster MA 01523-2026

MCDOWELL, MICHAEL HAMILTON COULTER, journalist; b. Belfast, No. Ireland, Mar. 5, 1952; came to U.S., 1988; s. Hamilton Coulter and Pat (Irwin) McD. BA, Trinity Coll., Ireland, 1973. Journalist Belfast Telegraph Newspapers, 1973-78; Nieman fellow Harvard U., Cambridge, Mass., 1978-79; sr. assoc. Carnegie Endowment for Internat. Peace, N.Y.C., 1979-80; reporter, social issues writer, fgn. affairs writer The Globe and Mail, Toronto, Ont., Can., 1981-84; reporter, producer British Broadcasting Corp., 1981—; fgn. affairs producer Canadian Broadcasting Corp., Toronto, 1984-88; dep. dir. in the U.S. and sr. producer Canadian Broadcasting Corp., Washington, 1988—; spl. lectr. Inst. Politics, Kennedy Sch. Govt. Contbr. articles to various newspapers and jours. Former dir. Ireland Fund of Can., Toronto, 1983-87. Home: 250 10th St SE Washington DC 20003-2117 Office: Can Broadcasting Corp Nat Press Bldg Ste # 500 Washington DC 20045

MCDUFFIE, DAVID WAYNE, investment banker; b. Buffalo, Feb. 7, 1960; s. Horace Jr. and Fannie (Gibson) McD.; m. Alena Hutchins, Mar. 27, 1982 (div. Oct. 1986); m. Patricia L. Bell, Sept. 9, 1987. BA in Econs., Fredonia (N.Y.) State Coll., 1981. Tchr. Buffalo Pub. Schs., 1981-84; gen. agt. Buffalo Bus. and Estate Planning Corp., 1982-83; tax acct. Control Data Corp., Balt., 1984; fin. mgr. Merrill Lynch, Balt., 1984-88; investment rep. The Chapman Co., Balt., 1988-89; pres. David Alexander Group, Columbia, Md., 1989—; contr., corp. sec. The Eatman Co., Inc., Balt., 1991—; corp. treas. D. Williams, Inc., Balt., Pusch, Inc., Balt.; bd. dirs. Execucorp, Inc., Data Connections, Inc., Balt., Penn-North Devel. Corp. Editor Chess Jour., 1981-83. Bd. dirs. Balt. Ctr. for Victims of Sexual Assault, 1985—, NAACP Balt. Br., 1987—, Balt. Urban League, 1988—, Balt. Mus. Art, Joshua Johnson Coun., 1989—; co-founder Friends of Sheila Dixon-Smith, Balt.; mem. Morgan State U. Found., Balt., 1985—; ways and means dir. Young Dems., Balt., 1986-87. Mem. Jaycees (Md. dir. 1986—), U.S. Chess Fedn., N.Y. State Chess Assn. (bd. dirs. 1981-83), Buffalo Inner City Chess Club (mgr. 1981-84), Balt. Exch. Club. Republican. Office: JW Gant Investment Bankers 10451 Mill Run Cir Owings Mills MD 21117

MCDUFFIE, MICHAEL ANTHONY, portfolio manager, investment broker; b. Buffalo, May 1, 1954; s. Horace Jr. and Fran (Gibson) McD.; m. Deborah L. Blann, Mar. 18, 1989. AAS, Canton (N.Y.) Agrl. and Tech. Coll., 1974; BS, SUNY, Geneseo, 1976; cert., Am. Inst. Banking, Buffalo, 1987. Underwriter Aetna Life and Casualty Ins. Co., Buffalo, 1976-77; fin. counselor Bank Am. Corp., Buffalo, 1977-81; soccer, track coach Buffalo State Coll., 1981-85; credit counselor Goldome Fin. Savs. Bank, Buffalo, 1985-86; agt. Equitable Fin. Cos., Buffalo, 1986; soccer coach Hilbert Coll., Hamburg, N.Y., 1987-89; portfolio investment broker Advest, Inc., 1989; investment mgmt. cons. Saperston Fin. Group, Buffalo, 1989—; v.p. David Alexander Group, 1987, Data Connections. 3d v.p. no. region Black Polit. Caucus, Buffalo, 1987; mem. United Negro Coll. Fund Com., 1987, corp. campaign com. 1989, golf com., western N.Y. chpt. bd. dirs., 1989—, co-chair golf, 1990; bd. dirs. Niagara Pioneer Soccer League, 1989-91, Niagara Police Athletic Soccer Club, Acad. Fin. Lafayette High Sch., 1990, mem. adv. bd., 1988-89; vol. Am. Heart Assn., 1990; co-chair football com. World Univ. Games, 1990; mem. World Cup Buffalo Com., 1990; panelist Arthritis Found.; mem. coaching staff, instr. Buffalo and We. N.Y. Dist. League, 1990; rep. Buffalo State Found., Burchfield Art Ctr., 1992; mem. ad hoc com. 100 Black Men of Am. Named one of Outstanding Young Men Am., 1985-86. Mem. Life Underwriter Assn., Buffalo C. of C., U.S. Soccer Fedn., Nat. Soccer Coaches Assn., Buffalo Urban League. Democrat. Baptist. Home: 1370 Sheridan Dr Buffalo NY 14217-1253

MCEACHERN, WILLIAM ARCHIBALD, economics educator; b. Portsmouth, N.H., Jan. 4, 1945; s. Archibald Duncan and Ann Teresa (Regan) McE.; m. Patricia Leonardo, Aug. 18, 1973. AB in Econs., Holy Cross Coll., 1967; MA in Econs., U. Va., 1969, PhD in Econs., 1975. Asst. prof. U. Conn., Storrs, 1973-78, assoc. prof., 1978-84, prof. econs., 1984—, dir. grad. studies, 1981-87; econ. cons. U.S. Dept. Labor, 1977-79, FTC, 1979-82, Conn. Conf. on Municipalities, New Haven, 1975-76, 87-88; dir. Bipartisan Commn. on Conn. Finances, Hartford, 1982-83. Author: Managerial Control and Performance, 1975, Economics: A Contemporary Introduction, 2d edit., 1991; editor: Quarterly Report on Conn. Economy; founding editor The Teaching Economist; contbr. articles to profl. jours. 1st lt. U.S. Army, 1969-71. Nat. Def. fellow U. Va., 1967-69, 72-73. Mem. Nat. Tax Assn., Am. Econ. Assn., Northeast Bus. and Econs. Assn. (founder, assoc. editor 1978-81), Pub. Choice Soc., So. Econ. Assn., Western Econ. Assn. Office: U Conn Dept Econs U 63 341 Mansfield Rd Storrs Mansfield CT 06268

MCEACHRON, DONALD LYNN, biology educator, researcher; b. Erie, Pa., Nov. 8, 1953; s. Karl Boyer and Marjorie (Blalock) McE.; m. Barbara Anne O'Donnell, Aug. 14, 1987. BA with highest honors, U. Calif., 1977, PhD, 1984. Lab. technician psychiatry VA Med. Ctr., La Jolla, Calif., 1978-82; rsch. technician cell biology U. Tex. Health Sci. Ctr., Dallas, 1983-84; sci. dir. Imaging and Computer Vision Ctr. Drexel U., Phila., 1984-88, vis. asst. prof. Dept. Biosci., 1986-88, rsch. asst. prof. Biomed. Engring. and Sci. Inst., 1989—; dir. life sci. Image Processing Ctr. Imaging and Computer Vision Ctr., Phila., 1988—; vis. asst. prof. Dept. Psychology Haverford (Pa.) Coll., 1987; lectr. U. Pa., Phila., 1986—; adj. asst. prof. Thomas Jefferson U., Phila., 1989—; cons. Hoffman-La Roche, Nutley, N.J., 1984-86; mem. adv. bd. BioAutomation, Inc., Bridgeport, Pa., 1988—. Editor: Functional Mapping in Biology and Medicine, 1986; contbg. editor Diversity in Biomed. Imaging, 1989, Progress in Imaging in the Neurosciences using Microcomputers and Workstations, 1990; mem. editorial bd. Computerized Med. Imaging and Graphics, 1988—, NeuroImage, 1990. Mem. Fishtown Civic Assn., Phila., 1989. 1st lt. USAR, 1987—. Regent's fellow U. Calif., 1979. Mem. AAAS, Internat. Soc. Chronobiology, Soc. for Study of Evolution, N.Y. Aca. Sci., Animal Behavior Soc. Republican. Office: Drexel U Imaging and Computer Vision Ctr Rm 128 Philadelphia PA 19104

MCELROY, FREDERICK WILLIAM, economics educator, consultant; b. Dublin, Ireland, May 18, 1939; came to U.S., 1963; s. Herbert John and Annie Maureen (McDowell) McE.; m. Kathleen Child, Sept. 8, 1964; children: Dominique, Hugh. BA, Nat. U. of Ireland, Dublin, 1960; MA, U. Coll. Dublin, 1961; PhD, Georgetown U., 1967. Asst. prof. econs. SUNY, Buffalo, 1967-68; asst. prof. econs. Georgetown U., Washington, 1968-71, assoc. prof. econs., 1971-77, prof. econs., 1977—; cons. in antitrust cases; cons. Grocery Mfrs. of Am., Washington, 1976—. Contbr. articles to profl. jours. Trustee, treas. Help the Aged, Washington, 1982-86; bd. dirs. Oxfam-Am., Boston, 1976-79. Mem. Am. Econs. Assn., Phi Beta Kappa, Alsph Sigma Nu. Democrat. Roman Catholic. Home: 5013 Brookdale Rd Bethesda MD 20816-1709 Office: Georgetown U Dept Econs Washington DC 20057

MCELVEEN, JOSEPH JAMES, JR., public broadcasting executive; b. Sanford, Fla., Feb. 23, 1939; s. Joseph James Sr. and Genevieve (Stoll) McE.; m. Idris Baker, Aug. 14, 1965 (div. 1975); m. Mary Louise Young, Aug. 18, 1979; 1 child, Ryan Leighton. BA, Furman U., 1961; MA, U. S.C., 1968. Editor, pub. West Ashley News, Charleston, S.C., 1951-57; reporter, photographer Charleston Post, 1955-57; tchr. English and journalism St. Andrew's Parish High Sch., Charleston, 1961-65; dir. info. Columbia Coll., S.C., 1965-68; prof. journalism U. S.C., Columbia, 1968-79; staff pub. affairs FCC, Washington, 1979-81; dir. pub. affairs adminstrn. Nat. Cable TV Assn., Washington, 1981-87; dir. internal communications Corp. for Pub. Broadcasting, Washington, 1987-92, dir. program adminstrn., 1992—; ombudsman, columnist Alexandria (Va.) Gazette, 1981-88. Author: Introduction to Creative Writing, 1963, Modern Communications, 1964; contbr. chpt. to International Biography (Mencken), 1986. Mem. Orgn. of News Ombudsmen, Soc. Profl. Journalists, Mencken Soc. Democrat. Episcopalian. Office: Corp for Pub Broadcasting 901 E St NW Washington DC 20004-2037

MCELVEEN-MCKNIGHT, KERAN ELAINE, credit union executive; b. Kingstree, S.C., Sept. 1, 1968; d. Isiash William and Bertha Mae (McFadden) McElveen; m. Jammie McKnight, Apr. 28, 1987. Student, Ctr. of Degree Studies, Scranton, Pa., 1987—. Relief mgr. Wawa Food Mkt., Croydon, Pa., 1987-90; supr. Tel-One Telemktg., Horsham, Pa., 1990-91; svc. rep. Spiegel Catalog, Phila., 1990-91, Navy Fed. Credit Union, Willow Grove, Pa., 1991—; bookkeeper McElveen Trucking, New Zion, S.C., 1986—. Sec. Refuge Holy Temple, Bristol, Pa., 1991-92; ch. worker Social Svcs. for Children, 1991. Democrat. Baptist. Home: 315 Thunder Cir Bensalem PA 19020

MCENROE, CHRISTOPHER PADRAIC, counselor; b. Syosset, N.Y., Sept. 10, 1966; s. Robert William and Alice McEnroe. BA, SUNY, Albany, 1988. Resdl. counselor North Suffolk Mental Health Assn., Chelsea, Mass., 1990—. Author: Blue Eyes at the White Trash Cafe, 1991, Anatomy of an Angry Moment, 1992. Home: 213 Summer St #2R Somerville MA 02143 Office: North Suffolk Mental Health 25 Procter Ave Revere MA 02151

MCENROE, HARRY DAMIAN, lawyer; b. Orange, N.J., Apr. 25, 1960; s. Harry Aloysius and Margaret (Harte) McE. BA, Washington Coll., Chestertown, Md., 1982; JD, Seton Hall U., 1985. Bar: N.J. 1985. Asst. prosecutor Essex County, Newark, 1985-88; assoc. Shanley & Fisher, P.C., Morristown, N.J., 1988—; adj. prof. Sch. Law, Seton Hall U. Editor Seton Hall Legis. Jour., 1984-85. Mem. ABA, N.J. Bar Assn., Essex County Bar Assn. Office: Shanley & Fisher PC 131 Madison Ave Morristown NJ 07960-6009

MCENTEE, WILLIAM JOSEPH, JR., advertising executive, art director; b. Brockton, Mass., Jan. 18, 1952; s. William Joseph and Mary Margaret (Kent) McE. BFA, Mass. Coll. of Art, 1975. Freelance portrait artist, designer, muralist various locations, Mass., 1979-82; graphics dir. Brockton Assembly of God, 1980; mech. artist, illustrator Auld Assoc. Advt., South Weymouth, Mass., 1981; graphic designer Ariel Design, Westwood and Norwood, Mass., 1983-86; art dir. Matthew Steven and Assoc., Inc., North Easton, Mass., 1986-88; prin. McEntee Design, North Easton, 1988-90; art dir. Sunday River Ski Resort, Bethel, Maine, 1991—. Recipient grant for 10 paintings Images of Easton, Easton Coun. for the Arts, 1985-87. Home: RR 2 Box 20052 Bethel ME 04217-9802 Office: Sunday River Ski Resort Bethel ME 04217

MCEVOY, SHARLENE ANN, business law educator; b. Derby, Conn., July 6, 1950; d. Peter Henry Jr. and Madaline Elizabeth (McCabe) McE. BA magna cum laude, Albertus Magnus Coll., 1972; JD, U. Conn., West Hartford, 1975; MA, Trinity Coll., Hartford, 1980, UCLA, 1982; PhD, UCLA, 1985. Bar: Conn., 1975. Pvt. practice Derby, 1984—; asst. prof. bus. law Fairfield (Conn.) U. Sch. Bus., 1986—; adj. prof. bus. law, polit. sci. Albertus Magnus Coll., New Haven, Conn., 1978-80, U. Conn., Stamford, 1984-86; acting chmn. polit. sci. dept. Albertus Magnus Coll., 1980; assoc. prof. law Fairfield U., 1992—; Chmn. Women's Resource Ctr., Fairfield U., 1989-91. Staff editor Jour. Legal Studies Edn., 1989—; reviewer Am. Bus. Law Assn. jour., 1988—; contbr. articles to profl. jours. Mem. Derby Tercentennial Commn., Derby, 1973-74; bd. dirs. Valley Transit Dist., Derby, 1975-77, Justice of Peace, City of Derby, 1975-83. Recipient rsch. grant Fairfield U., 1989, 91, Best Paper award N.E. Regional Bus. Law Assn., 1990, Best Paper award Tri-State Regional Bus. Law Assn., 1991. Mem. ABA, Conn. Bar Assn., Am. Bus. Law Assn., Assn. Trial Lawyers Am., Mensa (coord. SINISTRAL spl. interest group 1977—). Democrat. Roman Catholic. Office: Sharlene A McEvoy Atty at Law 198 Emmett Ave Derby CT 06418-1258

MCEWEN, MARY LOUISE, nurse; b. Cambridge, Mass., Apr. 10, 1960; d. James Keith and Mary Elizabeth (Arapoff) McE. BSN, Salem State Coll., 1982; MBA, U. Maine, 1987. RN, Mass., Maine; cert. med.-surg. nurse, psychiat. nurse, nursing adminstr. ANA. Staff nurse USAF Hosp., Beale AFB, Calif., 1982-85; staff devel. officer Maine Air NG, Bangor, 1985-91, chief nurse, 1991—; head nurse Bangor Mental Health Inst., 1987-89, asst. dir. nursing, 1989—. Recipient Presidential Achievement award, U. Maine, 1986, Maine Commendation award, Maine Air NG, 1988. Mem. NAFE, Air N.G. Nursing Assn., Air N.G. of Maine Assn., Sigma Theta Tau. Roman Catholic.

MCEWEN, ROBERT JOSEPH, economist, educator; b. Boston, June 6, 1916; s. Robert John and Mary Ellen (Aherne) McE. AB, Boston Coll., 1940; Lic., Weston Sch. Philosophy, 1941; AM, Fordham U., 1943; STL, Weston Sch. Theology, 1947; PhD, Boston Coll., 1957. Instr. mktg. Boston Coll., 1942-43, instr. econs., 1948-51, asst. prof. econs., 1952-56, assoc. prof., chmn. econs., 1957-67, prof., 1968—; vis. prof. Loyola U., L.A., 1963; founder, 1st pres. Consumer Fedn., Washington, 1968-69; 1st chmn. Adv. Cons. Coun. to Atty. Gen., Mass., 1958-63, State Consumer's Coun., Mass.,

1964-65; chmn. Ford Motor-Consumer Appeals Bd., New Eng., 1983-88, Consumer Adv. Panel AT&T, Basking Ridge, N.J., 1989-90, mem., 1975—; chmn. Home Rec. Rights Com. Washington, 1981—. Contbr. articles to profl. jours. Recipient Consumer Tribune award Better Bus. Bur., 1973. Mem. Am. Coun. on Consumer Interests (pres. 1965-67), Assn. Mass. Consumers (pres. 1971-77), Conf. Cons. Orgns. (vice chmn. 1973-85, chmn. 1985—). Roman Catholic. Home: 140 Commonwealth Ave Chestnut Hill MA 02167-3801 Office: Boston Coll Dept Econs 140 Commonwealth Ave Chestnut Hill MA 02167-3801

MCFADDEN, JAMES J., educational administrator; b. Altoona, Pa., Dec. 1, 1919; s. James and Elizabeth (Canole) McF.; m. Helen Ann Nieters, July 12, 1944; children: James, Helen, Elizabeth, William, Patrick, Peter, Christopher. BA, U. Notre Dame, 1942. Staff rep. NLRB, Boston, 1943-45, 46, 49, Textile Workers Union, N.Y.C., 1945-46; labor dir. Greater N.Y. Found., 1950; dir. labor devel. Dem. State Com., N.Y.C., 1950-52; commr. N.Y.C. Dept. Labor, 1953-65; pres. Manpower Edn. Inst., N.Y.C., 1966—; dir., organizer various affordable housing projects, N.Y.C., 1955—. Chmn. labor coms. various presdl. campaigns, N.Y.C., 1948-68. Recipient Leadership award Minority Bus. Coun., 1978; named Outstanding Contbr. N.J. Dept. Edn., 1974. Mem. Am. Arbitration Assn. (arbitrator 1954—). Roman Catholic. Home and Office: 715 Ladd Rd Bronx NY 10471

MC FADDEN, JAMES PATRICK, publisher; b. Youngstown, Ohio, Sept. 25, 1930; s. Francis Jerome and Recelba Katherine (Onorato) McF.; m. Faith Abbott, Apr. 18, 1959; children—Robert Arthur, Maria James, Patrick Abbott, Regina Laudis, Christina Luke. B.A., Youngstown Coll., 1953. Reporter Youngstown Vindicator, 1952-54; with Nat. Rev. mag., N.Y.C., 1956-89; assoc. pub. Nat. Rev. mag., 1971-83, cons. to editor, 1983-89; pres. Communications Distbn., Inc., N.Y.C., 1968—; v.p. Ultra Arts, Inc., N.Y.C., 1960-80; pres. Ultra Arts, Inc., 1980—; chmn. The Ad Hoc Com in Def. of Life, Inc., N.Y.C., 1973—. Editor Human Life Rev., 1975—, Lifeletter, 1973—, Cath. Eye, 1983—. Pres. Human Life Found., 1974—; chmn. Nat. Com. Cath. Laymen, 1977—. Served with CIC AUS, 1954-56. Roman Catholic. Home: 1050 Park Ave New York NY 10028-1031 Office: 150 E 35th St New York NY 10016-4178

MCFADDEN, PETER WILLIAM, mechanical engineering educator; b. Stamford, Conn., Aug. 2, 1932; s. Kenneth E. and Marie (Gleason) McF.; children: Peter, Kathleen, Mary. B.S. in Mech. Engring, U. Conn., 1954, M.S., 1956; Ph.D., Purdue U., 1959. Registered profl. engr., Ind. Asst. instr. U. Conn., 1954-56, prof. mech. engring., 1971—, dean Sch. Engring., 1971-85, dir. devel., 1985-88, provost, v.p., 1988, exec. asst. to pres., exec. sec. to bd. trustees, 1989—; mem. faculty Purdue U., 1956-71; prof. mech. engring., head Purdue U. (Sch. Mech. Engring.), 1965-71; postdoctoral research Swiss Fed. Inst., Zurich, 1960-61; cons. to industry, 1959—. Mem. ASME, Am. Soc. Engring. Edn. Office: U Conn Gulley Hall U-48 352 Mansfield Rd Storrs Mansfield CT 06268

MCFADDEN, THOMAS, academic administrator; b. N.Y.C., Nov. 12, 1935; m. Monica A. Dowdall; children—Monica, David. B.A., Cathedral Coll., 1957; S.T.L., Gregorian U., 1961; S.T.D., Cath. U., 1963. Asst. prof. St. Joseph's Coll., Bklyn., 1963-66; chmn. theology dept. Cathedral Coll., Douglaston, N.Y., 1966-68; asst. prof. Loyola Coll., Balt., 1968-69; prof. St. Joseph's U., Phila., 1970-82, dean Coll. Arts and Scis., 1982-87; acad. v.p. St. John Fisher Coll., Rochester, N.Y., 1987-92; pres. Marymount Coll., Calif., 1992—; vis. prof. Cath. U., Washington, 1967-68, LaSalle U., Phila., summer 1974-79. Author, editor: New Cath. Ency., 1974, 79. Editor, Dictionary of Religion, 3 vols., 1979; editor: Liberation, Revolution and Freedom, 1975, America in Theological Perspective, 1976. Recipient Disting. Teaching award Lindback, 1978, N.Y. State Excelsior award Bd. Examiners, 1991; HEW grantee, 1972; CAPHE grantee, 1985. Mem. AAUP, Coll. Theology Soc. (chmn. pubs. com. 1973-77). Democrat. Roman Catholic. Office: Marymount Coll Rancho Palos Verdes CA 90274

MCFARLAND, DAVID E., university official; b. Enid, Okla., Sept. 25, 1938; s. Eugene James McF. and Lydia May (Catlin) Lawson; m. Marcia Ruth Lake, Nov. 27, 1958 (div. 1978); children—Jennifer, Jeffrey, Jon, Julie; m., Susan Kaye Siler, Mar. 3, 1979; 1 child, Matthew Chapple. B.S., Wichita State U., 1961, M.S., 1964; Ph.D., U. Kans., 1967. Stress analysis engr. Boeing Co., Wichita, Kans., 1957-64; instr. U. Kans., Lawrence, 1964-67; asst. v.p., dean Wichita State U., 1967-81; dean. sch. tech., Pittsburgh State U., Kans., 1981-85; provost, v.p. acad. affairs Cen. Mo. State U., 1985-88; pres. Kutztown U. of Pa., 1988—. Author: Mechanics of Materials, 1977; Analysis of Plates, 1972. Contbr. articles to tech. jours. Office: Kutztown U of Pa Office of Pres Kutztown PA 19530

MCFARLAND, EDWARD PAUL, JR. (ED MCFARLAND), management consultant; b. Boston, Jan. 6, 1954; s. Edward Paul and Margaret M. (Delaney) McF.; m. Janice Lee Blomberg, Nov. 18, 1989; 1 child, Colin Edward. Assoc. Communications, Grahm Jr. Coll., Boston, 1979; BS in Econs., Northeastern U., 1986; MBA, Suffolk U., 1991. Mgr. Lafayette Home Electronics, West Roxbury, Mass., 1979-80; shipper Mass. Auto Supply Co., Roxbury, 1981-82; dispatcher New Eng. Telephone, Waltham, Mass., 1982-83; warehouse mgr. Cablevision of Boston, 1983-84; control specialist Bank of Boston, 1985-89; prin. The McFarland Group, Boston, 1989—; chmn. New Eng. Latin Am. Bus. Coun., Boston, 1991—. Coach Parkway Youth Hockey, West Roxbury, 1971-84, Parkway Little League, West Roxbury, 1971-82; treas. Amateur Hockey Assn. Commonwealth Mass., Boston, 1974-91; counselor U.S.A. Hockey Olympic Tng., Lake Placid, Mass., 1980-90; bd. dirs. Hyde Park Community Devel. Corp., 1991—. Named Outstanding Contbr., Amateur Hockey Assn. Commonwealth Mass., 1988. Mem. North Shore C. of C., Internat. Trade Coun., Greater Boston C. of C., Interant. Trade Coun. Home and Office: 175 Clare Ave # C-7 Hyde Park MA 02136-2260

MCFARLAND, HENRY BERNARD, economist; b. Jersey City, Aug. 18, 1951; s. Henry Bernard and Margaret Etta (Flaherty) McF.; m. Mary Ann McDonough, June 21, 1980; children: Bridget, Matthew, Brendan, Eileen. BA, Georgetown U., 1973; MA, Northwestern U., 1975, PhD, 1978. Economist antitrust div. U.S. Dept. Justice, Washington, 1977-80, 84-89; economist U.S. Internat. Trade Commn., Washington, 1980-84; sr. economist Economists Inc., Washington, 1989—; referee Rev. of Econs. and Statistics, Cambridge, Mass., 1988—. Contbr. articles to profl. jours. Pres. Dominion Hills Civic Assn., Arlington, Va., 1986-87, bd. dirs., 1988. Mem. Am. Econ. Assn. Office: Economists Inc 1233 20th St NW # 600 Washington DC 20036-2345

MC FEELEY, JOHN JAY, chemical engineer; b. Bklyn., Aug. 15, 1945; s. John Joseph and Maude May (Irvine) McF.; m. Jacquelyn Anne Ratzin, Oct. 30, 1971; children: Christine, John Jay. BS, Poly. Inst. Bklyn., 1966, MS, 1967, Phd, 1972. Engr. Polaroid Corp., Cambridge, Mass., 1971-72, sr. engr., 1972-74, sr. scientist, 1974-77, prin. engr. research and devel., 1977-79, tech. mgr. chem. engring. devel., 1979-83, sr. mgr. chem. engring., 1983—. Mem. water supply study com. Town of Norfolk (Mass.), 1976-77, mem. adv. bd., 1979-81, mem. bicentennial com., 1975-76, chmn. adv. bd., 1980-81, selectman, 1981-84, chmn., 1983-84; registrar of voters, 1991—; mem. Dem. Town Com., 1981—, vice-chmn., 1988—. NDEA fellow, 1969-71; NSF fellow, 1968-69, teaching fellow, 1967-68, rsch. fellow, 1966-67. Mem. AAAS, Am. Chem. Soc., Am. Inst. Chem. Engrs., N.Y. Acad. Scis., Lions (pres. 1977-78, 89-90), Tau Beta Pi, Sigma Xi, Omega Chi Epsilon, Phi Lambda Upsilon. Democrat. Roman Catholic. Contbr. articles in field to profl. jours. Home: 10 Chicatabut Ave Norfolk MA 02056-1164 Office: 1 Upland Rd Norwood MA 02062

MCGANN, JAMES GERARD, management consultant; b. Phila., Jan. 8, 1955; s. John T. and Mary C. (Handlon) McG.; m. Emily Mira Cohen, June 14, 1987. BA, LaSalle U., Phila., 1977; MSW in Non-Profit Adminstrn., Temple U., Phila., 1980; MA, U. Pa., Phila., 1989, PhD, 1991. Planning assoc. United Way Of Southeastern Pa., Phila., 1980-83; program officer Pew Charitable Trust, Phila., 1983-88; asst. dir. Harvard U. KSG Inst. of Politics, Cambridge, Mass., 1989; sr. v.p. Exec. Coun. on Fgn. Diplomats, Armonk, N.Y., 1989-90; sr. cons. Internat. Trading Group, Phila., 1991—; cons. Harvard U. Kennedy Sch. Govt., The Atlantic Coun. U.S., Cambridge, Mass., 1990—. Author: The Competition for Scholars, Dollars and Influence In the Public Policy Research Industry, 1991. Mem. Phila. Com. on City Policy, 1984—. Mem. Phila. Com. of Fgn. Rels., Una Chapman Cox Found., Atlantic Coun. of the U.S. Home: 8811 Wainwright Rd Philadelphia PA 19118-1445

MCGANN, JOHN RAYMOND, bishop; b. Bklyn., Dec. 2, 1924; s. Thomas Joseph and Mary (Ryan) McG. Student, Cathedral Coll. Immaculate Conception, 1944, Sem. Immaculate Conception, Huntington, 1950; LL.D., St. Johns U., 1971; L.H.D., Molloy Coll., 1977, Niagara U., 1983, St. Joseph's Coll., 1983, Adelphi U., 1985. Ordained priest Roman Cath. Ch., 1950, ordained bishop, 1971. Asst. priest St. Anne's, Brentwood, 1950-57; asst. chaplain St. Joseph Convent, Brentwood, 1950-54; tchr. religion St. Joseph Acad., 1950-54; assoc. Cath. chaplain Pilgrim State Hosp., 1950-57; asst. chancellor Diocese of Rockville Centre, 1957-67, vice chancellor, 1967-71; sec. to Bishop Kellenberg, 1957-59; elevated to papal chamberlain, 1959; sec. to Bishop Kellenberg, 1959-70; apptd. titular bishop of Morosbisdus and aux. bishop Diocese of Rockville Centre, 1970-76, bishop, 1976—; Del. Sacred Congregation for Religious to Marianists, 1973-76; theol. cons. Nat. Conf. Cath. Bishops, Rome, 1974, treas. 1984-87; mem. adminstrv. com., 1977-79; Anglican/Roman Cath. task force on pastoral ministry of bishops, 1978-81, nat. adv. coun. U.S. Cath. Conf., 1969-70, 81-83, treas. 1984-87; mem. health affairs com., 1972-75, adminstrv. bd., 1976-79, sem. admissions bd. Diocese Rockville Centre, 1971-76, diocesan boundary commn., 1971-76, Tri-Conf. Religious Retirement Project, 1985-88; mem. Papal visit, 1986-87. Bd. Diocesan Svcs., Inc., 1971-76; com. that established Consultation Svcs. for Religious, 1972-74; vicar gen. Diocese Rockville Centre, 1971-76, Episc. vicar, Suffolk County, 1971-76; mem. N.Y. State Cath. Conf. Com. on Prison Apostolate, 1971-74, U.S. Bishops' Com. for Apostolate to Laity, 1972-76, Rockville Centre Diocesan Bd. Consultors, 1969-76; Episc. mem. N.Y. State Cath. Com., 1974-78; chmn. N.Y. State Bishops' Com. on Elective Process, 1974—, Com. Religious Studies in Pub. Edn., 1975-79; mem. com. on ednl. concerns, com. on priests senates and couns. N.Y. State Cath. Conf.; bd. dirs. Good Samaritan Hosp., West Islip, N.Y., 1972-76, chmn., 1976—; trustee Cath. Charities Diocese of Rockville Centre, 1971-76; trustee St. Charles Hosp., Port Jefferson, N.Y., 1972-76, chmn., 1976—; pres. Mercy Hosp., St. Francis Hosp., Diocesan Commodities, Inc., 1976—; chmn. Consolation Residence, 1976—; bd. advisers Sem. Immaculate Conception, 1975—; treas. Nat. Conf. Cath. Bishops U.S. Cath. Conf., 1984-87, ad hoc com. on stewardship, 1988—, tri-conf. commn. on religious life and ministry, 1988—; mem. Papal Visit, 1986-87, Tri-Conf. Religious Retirement Project., 1985-88; chmn. Nat. Conf. Cath. Bishops/U.S. Cath. Conf. Telecommunications Network Am., 1990; mem. adminstrv. bd. Nat. Conf. Cath. Bishops, 1991—. Office: 50 N Park Ave Rockville Centre NY 11570-4184

MCGARRITY, GERARD JOHN, microbiologist; b. Bklyn., Oct. 9, 1940; s. Joseph Francis and Mary Abigail (Montague) McG.; m. Beverly J. Odgers, June 20, 1964; children: Gerard John, Meridith. BS, St. Joseph Coll., Phila., 1962; MS, Jefferson Med. Coll., Phila., 1964; PhD, Thomas Jefferson U., Phila., 1970. Rsch. assoc. Coriell Inst. for Med. Rsch., Camden, N.J., 1965-70, asst. mem., 1970-72; head dept. microbiology Cornell Inst. for Med. Rsch., Camden, N.J., 1971-91, assoc. mem., 1972-83, v.p. sci. affairs, 1984-86, pres., 1986-91; v.p., dir. devel. Genetic Therapy Inc., Gaithersburg, Md., 1991—, v.p., 1991—; adj. prof. Thomas Jefferson U. Coll. Medicine, Phila., 1984—, Robert Wood Johnson Med. Sch., Piscataway, N.J., 1985-91; chmn. NIH Recombinant DNA Adv. Com., Bethesda, Md., 1988-91; bd. trustees Thomas Jefferson U., 1989—; delegation leader People to People Internat., 1984, 87. Contbr. over 100 articles to profl. jours., 33 chpts. to books; editor Med. Rsch. Books, 1978—. Recipient Disting. Alumnus award, Thomas Jefferson U., 1986. Mem. Internat. Assn. Cell Cultures (pres. 1987-91), Union League Phila., Sunday Breakfast Club. Office: Genetic Therapy Inc 19 Firstfield Rd Gaithersburg MD 20878-1703

MCGARRY, JOHN PATRICK, JR., advertising agency executive; b. Elizabeth, N.J., Nov. 22, 1939; s. John Patrick and Elizabeth (Weber) McG.; m. Gilda R. Spurio, Oct. 24, 1964; children: Victoria Elizabeth, John Patrick, III. B.S. in Mktg. Econs, Villanova U., 1961. Salesman Exxon Corp., Elizabeth, 1961-64; advt. exec. Young and Rubicam Inc., N.Y.C., 1965-69, sr. v.p., mgmt. supr., 1969-87, pres., mem. ops. com., advt. exec. com., 1987—; vice chmn. Young and Rubicam Advt. Worldwide, N.Y.C., 1990—; chmn. Client Svcs. Worldwide, N.Y.C., 1987—; bd. dirs. Caramoor. Bd. dirs. New Youth Performing Theatre, Bedford, N.Y., Regional Rev. League, Westchester, 4 A's, Louisville Opera Assn., 1981-83, Dominican Coll., Dropout Prevention Fund; head Parents Fund St. Lawrence U. With USNG, 1963-69. Mem. Internat. Advt. Assn. (pres. U.S./Can.), Proprietary Assn. (bd. dirs.), Bedord Club, Golf and Tennis Club. Democrat. Roman Catholic. Home: Cantitoe Rd Bedford NY 10506 Office: Young & Rubicam Inc 285 Madison Ave New York NY 10017-6401*

MCGARRY, ROBERT ALAN, university administrator; b. Passaic, N.J., Dec. 23, 1965; s. Thomas R. and Irene (Crawford) McG. MusB, Bucknell U., 1988; M. Music Edn., Hartt Sch. Music, Hartford, Conn., 1990. Cert. tchr. music. Area coord. Carnegie Mellon U. Office of Residence Life, Pitts., 1990—. Mem. Mid Atlantic Assn. Coll. and Univ. Housing Officers (presenter 1992), Am. Coll. Pers. Assn. (presenter 1990—). Home and office: 1060 Morewood Ave Pittsburgh PA 15213

MCGARVEY, MARY HEWITT, writer; b. Phila.; s. Raymond John and Beatrice (Hewitt) McG. BA summa cum laude, CUNY, 1983; MA cum laude, New Sch. for Social Research, 1986. Author: (books) Walking to Camden, 1984, Floating to Broadway, 1987. Mem. Classical Assn. of the Empire State, Jung Found., The Met. Mus. Art, South St. Seaport Mus., Internat. Soc. Dramatists, Exploration Soc. Am., Am. Mus. Natural History, Nat. Trust Hist. Preservation. Roman Catholic. Home and Office: 319 E 14th St New York NY 10003-4242

MCGEADY, SISTER MARY ROSE, religious organization administrator, psychologist; b. Hazelton, Pa., June 28, 1928; d. Joseph James and Catherine Cecilia (Mundie) McG. BA in Sociology, Emmanuel Coll., 1955; MA in Clin. Psychology, Fordham U., 1961; DHL (hon.), St. John's U., Queens, N.Y., 1982, Coll. New Rochelle, N.Y., 1991, Fordham U., 1991, Niagara U., 1991, Coll. St. Rose, Albany, N.Y., 1991, DePaul U., 1991. Joined Daus. of Charity St. Vincent De Paul, Roman Cath. Ch., 1946. Dir. Astor Home Clinics, Rhinebeck, N.Y., 1961-66; exec. dir. Nazareth Child Care Ctr., Boston, 1966-71; dir. mental health Cath. Charities Bklyn., 1971-79, assoc. exec. dir., 1987-90; dir. Kennedy Child Study Ctr., N.Y.C., 1979-81; provincial supr. Daus. of Charity St. Vincent DePaul, Albany, 1981-87; pres., chief exec. officer Covenant House, N.Y.C., 1990—; bd. dirs. Cardinal Cooke Health Care Ctr., N.Y.C., Good Samaritan Hosp., Pottsville, Pa., Ctr. for Human Devel., Washington. Author: Catholic Special Education, 1979. Mem. N.Y. State Mental Health Svcs. Coun., Albany, 1983-90, N.Y. State Mental Health Planning Coun., Albany, 1986-91, Cath. Charities USA, 1966—. Recipient svc. award N.Y.C. Dept. Mental Health, 1988, Encouragement award Cath. U. Am., 1991. Home: 75 Lewis Ave Brooklyn NY 11206-7097 Office: Covenant House 346 W 17th St New York NY 10011-5002

MCGEE, DOROTHY HORTON, author, historian; b. West Point, N.Y., Nov. 30, 1913; d. Hugh Henry and Dorothy (Brown) McG.; ed. Sch. of St. Mary, 1920-21, Green Vale Sch., 1921-28, Brearley Sch., 1928-29, Fermata Sch., 1929-31. Asst. historian Inc. Village of Roslyn (N.Y.), 1950-58; historian Inc. Village of Matinecock, 1966—. Author: Skipper Sandra, 1950; Sally Townsend, Patriot, 1952; The Boarding School Mystery, 1953; Famous Signers of the Declaration, 1955; Alexander Hamilton-New Yorker, 1957; Herbert Hoover: Engineer, Humanitarian, Statesman, 1959, rev. edit., 1965; The Pearl Pendant Mystery, 1960; Framers of the Constitution, 1968; author booklets, articles hist. and sailing subjects. Chmn., Oyster Bay Am. Bicentennial Revolution Commn., 1971—; historian Town of Oyster Bay, 1982—; mem. Nassau County Am. Revolution Bicentennial Commn.; hon. dir. The Friends of Raynham Hall, Inc.; treas. Family Welfare Assn. Nassau County, Inc., 1956-58; dir. Family Service Assn. Nassau County, 1958-69. Recipient Cert. of award for outstanding contbn. children's lit. N.Y. State Assn. Elem. Sch. Prins., 1959; award Nat. Soc. Children of Am. Revolution, 1960; award N.Y. Assn. Supervision and Curriculum Devel., 1961; hist. award Town of Oyster Bay, 1963; Cert. Theodore Roosevelt Assn., 1976. Fellow Soc. Am. Historians; mem. Soc. Preservation L.I. Antiquities (hon. dir.), Nat. Trust Hist. Preservation, N.Y. Geneal. and Biol. Soc. (dir., trustee), Oyster Bay Hist. Soc. (pres. 1971-75, chmn. 1975-79, trustee), Theodore Roosevelt Assn. (trustee), Townsend Soc. Am. (trustee). Republican. Address: Box 142 Locust Valley NY 11560

MCGEE, JAMES PATRICK, information industry executive; b. N.Y.C., Dec. 27, 1941; s. James Edward and Norah Elizabeth (Russell) McG.; m. Roseann Marie Carmody, Feb. 20, 1966; children: James Patrick, Richard Carmody. BBA, CUNY, 1965; MBA, Baruch Coll. N.Y., 1972; PMC, Iona Coll. of New Rochelle, 1974; MS in Computer Sci., Poly. Inst. N.Y., 1978, PhD in computer sci. Southwestern U. Ariz., 1982, PhD in Info. Sci., Walden U. Minn., 1984. Cert. quality engr., records mgr., data processor, computer programmer, info. systems mgr., data mgr., systems profl. Programmer N.Y. Med. Coll., N.Y.C., 1964-65; sr. programmer Shell Oil Co., N.Y.C., 1968-70, sr. systems analyst/rsch. staff mem. IBM T.J. Watson Rsch. Ctr., Yorktown, 1970—; info. systems mgr. IBM, Somers, N.Y., 1990—; program mgr. IBM Worldwide Mgmt. Cons. Practices Tech., White Plains, N.Y., 1992—; lectr. Baruch Coll. of CUNY, 1973-75; ednl. coordinator Assn. Computing Machinery, N.Y.C., 1975-76; lectr. in field. Contbr. articles to profl. jours. Bd. dirs. White Pond Community Ctr., Stormville, N.Y., 1975, Internat. Tech. Inst., 1985-88, Tech. Transfer Soc., 1986-88; leader, instr. Explorer Scout Troop, White Plains, 1973-74. Served with U.S. Army, 1965-67. Decorated Bronze Star. Mem. Am. Assn. Artificial Intelligence, Am. Nat. Standards Inst. (Data Base Systems Study Group adv. group), Assn. Computational Linguistics, Assn. for Computing Machinery, Spl. Interest Group for Mgmt. Data, Assn. of Inst. Certification of Computer Profls., Assoc. Info. Mgrs., Am. Mgmt. Assn., Assn. Records Mgrs. Adminstrs., Assn. for Systems Mgmt., Am. Soc. Quality Control, Data Adminstrn. Mgmt. Assn., Data Entry Mgmt. Assn., Data Processing Mgmt. Assn., Electronic Data Processing Auditors Assn., IEEE, Internat. Tech. Inst. (bd. dirs.), Vietnam Vets. of Am. (life), VFW (life), Omicron Delta Epsilon. Republican. Roman Catholic. Home: Mey Crescent Rd Stormville NY 12582-5624

MCGEE, JOHN JOSEPH, police sergeant; b. Newark, Jan. 27, 1946; s. Bernard John and Stephanie Josephine (Yurkiewicz) McG.; m. Barbara Lee Marzoli, June 6, 1970; 1 child, Brian Scott. AS, Morris County Coll., 1974; BS, William Paterson Coll., 1976. Police officer Parsippany (N.J.) Police Dept., 1968—, police sgt., 1990—. Basketball coach P.A.L., Parsippany, 1976-78; baseball coach Little League, Parsippany, 1986-90; post advisor Boy Scouts Am. Explorers, Denville, N.J., 1990—. Sgt. U.S. Army, 1965-71. Mem. N.J. Police Benevolent Assn. (v.p. 1978-80), Superior Officers Assn. Roman Catholic. Home: 5 Ionic Ct Parsippany NJ 07054 Office: Parsippany Troy Hills Police Dept 3339 Rt 46 Parsippany NJ 07054

MCGEHEE, JAMES OLIVER, JR., systems analyst, consultant; b. Balt., Jan. 13, 1946; s. James Oliver and Elizabeth Margaret (Kuhn) McG.; m. Valerie D. Bowen, June 9, 1968 (div. 1989); children: Stacie Ann McGehee Lawson, James Patrick, Matthew Ryan; m. Linda Lorraine Robinson, Oct. 5, 1990. Student, Anne Arundel Community Coll. Cert. systems analyst. Systems analyst Dept. of Defense, Ft. Meade, Md., 1969-88; engr. mgr. Ford Aerospace Corp., Hanover, Md., 1988-89; cons. Coact, Inc., Elkridge, Md., 1989-91; govt. program mgr. ACC Systems, Columbia, Md., 1991—; pres. Coact, Inc., Elkridge, 1989-91. Author, pub. (poems) The Feelings of Life, 1992. Pres. Linthicum (Md.) Youth Athletic Assn., 1972-76; scoutmaster Boy Scouts Am., Linthicum, Brooklyn Park, Md. Cpl. USMC, 1966-69, Viet Nam. Decorated Purple Heart. Methodist. Home: 6256 Ducketts Ln Elkridge MD 21227 Office: ACC Systems 8320 Guilford Rd Ste G Columbia MD 21046

MC GHAN, WILLIAM FREDERICK, pharmacist, educator; b. Sacramento, July 6, 1946; s. Roy William and Nelleen (Zischang) McG.; children: Monica, Matthew, Brian, Brent; m. Marilyn Dix Smith. Community scholar, U. Calif.-San Francisco, 1966-70; Pharm.D., U. Calif., San Francisco, 1970; Ph.D., U. Minn., 1979. Pharmacy intern U. Calif. Med. Center, San Francisco, 1969-70; pharmacy resident U. Calif. Med. Center, 1970-71; pharmacy coordinator Appalachian Student Health Project, summer 1970; staff dir. Student Am. Pharm. Assn., Washington, 1971-74; chmn. community health Student Am. Pharm. Assn., 1969-70; staff dir. Project SPEED, nat. drug edn. program, 1971-73; assoc. dir., 1973-74; staff dir. Acad. Pharm. Scis., Washington, 1974-76; mem. pub. policy com. Acad. Pharm. Scis., 1974-78, chmn. publs. com., 1975-76; grad. fellow, instr. Coll. Pharmacy, U. Minn., 1976-78; asst. prof. Sch. Pharmacy, U. So. Calif., 1978-82; prof., coord. div. adminstrv. and behavioral scis. Coll. Pharmacy U. Ariz., Tucson, 1982-89; prof., chmn. dept. pharm. practice and adminstrn., exec. dir. Inst. for Pharm. Econs. Phila. Coll. Pharm. & Sci., 1989—; mem. membership com. Nat. Coord. Coun. for Drug Edn., 1974-75; mem. steering com. Am. Pharm. Assn. Drug Interactions Program, 1973-76; Acad. Pharm. Scis. liaison to NAS-NRC, 1975-76. Editor: Student Am. Pharm. Assn. News, 1971-73; mng. editor, 1973-74; editor: Acad. Reporter, 1974-76. Recipient Archambault award Am. Soc. Cons. Pharm. Fellow Am. Found. for Pharm. Edn.; mem. Am. Pharmacy Assn., Acad. Pharm. Rsch. and Sci. (chmn. econ., social, and adminstrv. scis. sect. 1987-88, pres. 1988), Am. Soc. Hosp. Pharmacists, Am. Assn. Colls. Pharmacy (chmn. pharm. adminstrn. sect. 1989-90, Lyman award), Am. Assn. Pharm. Sci. (chmn. econs. sect. 1988), Delta Sigma Phi, Rho Chi, Phi Kappa Phi, Sigma Xi. Democrat. Methodist. Office: Phila Coll Pharmacy and Sci Inst for Pharm Econs 600 S 43d St Philadelphia PA 19104-4495

MCGHEE, SAMUEL TIMOTHY, college admissions director; b. Jersey City, May 29, 1940; s. Samuel Timothy and Lucile (Bitten) McG.; m. Connie Bentley, May 1, 1983; children: Darren, Elissa, Samuel III, Jeffrey. BA, Jersey City State Coll., 1962; MA, Seton Hall U., 1965. Tchr. history Jersey City Pub. Schs., 1962-69; asst. dir. students Jersey City State Coll., 1969-70, assoc. dir. admissions, 1970-76, dir. admissions, 1976—. Pres. of bd. trustees WBGO Pub. Radio in Newark, 1991—. Mem. NAACP, Omega Psi Phi (asst. keeper of fin.). Democrat. Home: 1548 Maple Ave Hillside NJ 07205-1437 Office: Jersey City State Coll 2039 Kennedy Blvd Jersey City NJ 07305

MCGILL, ALLYSON FAITH, English educator, researcher; b. Manchester, Conn., Nov. 20, 1953; d. Thomas S. and Barbara Faith (Swanson) McG.; m. Michael James O'Brien, Mar. 31, 1990. AA, Hartford (Conn.) Coll. Women, 1973; BA magna cum laude, Wheaton Coll., 1976; MA, Ind. U., 1983, PhD, 1989. Assoc. instr. Ind. U., Bloomington, 1977-82, 84-85; editorial asst. Victorian Studies Jour., Bloomington, 1982-83, mng. editor, 1983-84; editor Sch. of Music Ind. U., Bloomington, 1987-89; program coord. Leadership Bloomington, 1987-89; editor Chadwyck-Healey, Inc., Alexandria, Va., 1989-90; vis. asst. prof. St. Mary's Coll. of Md., St. Mary's City, 1990-92. Author: The Swedish Americans, 1988; contbr. articles to profl. jours. and publs. Vol. The Source Theatre, Washington, 1985-86, Bloomington Vols., 1986, WILPF, Bloomington, 1987-89, Ind. Peace Network, Bloomington, 1987-89. Ind. U. grantee, 1984. Mem. AAUW, MLA, Nat. Coun. Tchrs. English, Wheaton Coll. Alumni Assn. (Wash. chpt.). Democrat. Roman Catholic. Home: 9016 Bowler Dr Fairfax VA 22031-2058

MC GILLICUDDY, JOHN FRANCIS, banker; b. Harrison, N.Y., Dec. 30, 1930; s. Michael J. and Anna (Munro) McG.; m. Constance Burtis, Sept. 9, 1954; children: Michael Sean, Faith Burtis Benoit, Constance Erin Mc Gillicuddy Mills, Brian Munro, John Walsh. A.B., Princeton, 1952; LL.B., Harvard, 1955. With Mfrs. Hanover Trust Co. subs. Mfrs. Hanover Corp., N.Y.C., 1958-91, v.p., 1962-66, sr. v.p., 1966-69, exec. v.p., asst. to chmn., 1969-70, vice chmn., dir., 1970, pres., 1971-91, chmn., chief exec. officer, 1979-91; chmn. bd., chief exec. officer Chem. Banking Corp., N.Y.C., 1992—; bd. dirs. USX Corp., Continental Corp., UAL Corp. Bd. dirs. Nat. Multiple Sclerosis Soc.; trustee N.Y. Hosp., N.Y. Pub. Libr.; trustee emeritus Princeton U. Lt. (j.g.) USNR, 1955-58. Mem. Assn. Res. City Bankers, Bus. Council, Bus. Roundtable. Roman Catholic. Clubs: Westchester Country (Rye, N.Y.); Blind Brook (Port Chester, N.Y.); Princeton (N.Y.C.). Office: Chem Banking Corp 270 Park Ave New York NY 10017-2014

MCGINLEY, JOSEPH PATRICK, brokerage house executive; b. Phila., Mar. 17, 1947; s. Joseph Robert and Kathaleen (Brennan) McG.; m. Linda L. Irvin, May 15, 1970 (div. 1981); children: Lisa C., Andrew S.; m. Sharon A. Malloy, Sept. 7, 1984; 1 child, Christopher J. BSBA, Villanova U., 1965-69. Sr. v.p. Dean Witter, Phila., 1974—; bd. dirs. Tara Investments Ltd., Phila., Orion Assoc., Phila., Florence Ave. Corp., Phila. Mem. Union League Yacht Club (flag officer), Union League of Phila., Cynwyd Club.

Republican. Roman Catholic. Office: Dean Witter Reynolds 2 Logan Sq Philadelphia PA 19103-2707

MCGINN, DONALD JOSEPH, English educator; b. Indian Lake, N.Y., Apr. 1, 1905; s. James and Mary Elizabeth (McCarthy) McG.; m. Margaret Mary Howley, June 27, 1940 (dec. 1979); children: Kathleen McGinn Spring, Donald J. Jr. AB, Cornell U., 1926, MA, 1929, PhD, 1930. Tchr. Rutgers Prep., New Brunswick, N.J., 1930-36, Rutgers U., 1936-73; prof. English Georgian Court Coll., Lakewood, N.J., 1945—. Author: Shakespeare's Influence on the Drama of His Age, 1938, The Admonition Controversy, 1949, (with George Howerton) Literature as a Fine Art, 1959, John Penry and the Marprelate Controversy, 1966, Thomas Nashe, 1981. Home: 2 President Ave Lavallette NJ 08735-2148 Office: Georgian Ct Coll English Dept Lakewood NJ 08701

MCGIVNEY, WILLIAM DAVID, new products marketing company executive; b. N.Y.C., Jan. 7, 1934; s. Michael Joseph and Margaret Mary (Delaney) McG. BSBA summa cum laude, St. John's U., 1957. Account supr., v.p. Compton Advt., N.Y.C., 1957-66; exec. v.p., account mgr. Wells Rich Greene, N.Y.C., 1966-86; pres. Precision Mktg., Palisades, N.Y., 1987—; cons. Goya Foods, Secaucus, N.J., 1986-87, Paula Green Advt., N.Y.C., 1986-87; mktg. cons. Lonestar Cafe, N.Y.C., 1986-87; participant Exporting to Japan seminar, Tokyo. Designer athletic and therapeutic footwear and socks. Mem. ad hoc com. for advt. and fund raising Nat. Dem. Com., Washington, 1976. With USN, 1951-54. Mem. Am. Diabetes Assn. (profl.), Am. Arthritis Assn. (profl.), Am. Mgmt. Assn., Am. Pedorthic Assn., Footwear Inst. Am., Direct Mktg. Assn., Sporting Goods Mfg. Assn., Nat. Sporting Goods Assn. Office: Precision Mktg 227 Washington Spg Rd Palisades NY 10964

MCGLYNN, JOHN FRANCIS, prosecutor; b. Bklyn., Oct. 24, 1941; s. John Francis and Rita (White) McG.; m. Jo Moran, May 22, 1976; children: Patrick, Michael. BS, St. Peter's Coll., 1963; JD, St. Johns U., 1971; LLM, NYU, 1981. Bar: N.Y. 1972. Assoc. appellate counsel Legal Aid Soc., N.Y.C., 1972-86; asst. dist. atty. Nassau County Dist. Atty., Mineola, N.Y., 1986—. With U.S. Army, 1964-66. Mem. Assn. of Bar of City of N.Y., N.Y. County Lawyers Assn. Office: Nassau County Dist Atty 262 Old Country Rd Mineola NY 11501

MCGOLDRICK, WILLIAM PATRICK, academic administrator; b. N.Y.C., Nov. 17, 1946; s. William Patrick and Mary Margaret (Flanagan) McG.; m. Elizabeth Margaret Coyne, July 5, 1969; 1 child, Margaret. BA, Siena Coll., Loudonville, N.Y., 1968; MA, Syracuse U., 1973. Dir. pub. rels. Harrisburg (Pa.) Area Community Coll., 1971-74; asst. to pres. for pub. rels. SUNY, Oswego, 1974-77; dir. of major gifts Coll. of William and Mary, Williamsburg, Va., 1977-80; dir. of devel. Rensselaer Poly. Inst., Troy, N.Y., 1980-85, v.p. inst. rels., 1985—. Bd. dirs. Big Bros., Albany, N.Y., 1980-83, Harrisburg Boy's Club, 1971-74, Oswego C. of C., 1974-77, Samaritan Hosp., Troy, N.Y., 1989—. Mem. Siena Coll. Alumni Assn. (bd. dirs. 1983-85). Roman Catholic. Home: 16 Carriage Hill Dr Latham NY 12110-4947 Office: Rensselaer Poly Inst 110 8th St Troy NY 12180-3522

MCGONIGLE, JAMES GREGORY, consultant; b. Bklyn., Nov. 17, 1945; s. William John and Helen Bernadette (Dennin) McG.; m. Francine Anne Falango, May 27, 1972; children: MarieElena, Lauren Anne. AAS in Acctg., CUNY, 1972; BS in Fin. summa cum laude, L.I. U., 1980. Cert. fin. planner Internat. Bd. Cert. Fin. Planners. Account exec. Coburn Credit Corp., Rockville Centre, N.Y., 1965-66; asst. credit mgr. UNI-CARD, Greatneck, N.Y., 1966-68; accounts receivable mgr. Granite Leasing Corp., Garden City, N.Y., 1968-73; v.p. Citicorp., N.Y.C., 1973-88; cons. O/E Learning, Inc., Detroit, 1988-90; regional dir. Ednl. Techs., Inc., Troy, Mich., 1989—. Vol. Family Svc. Assn., Nassau, N.Y., 1981-84, Better Bus. Bur., Farmingdale, N.Y., 1987—; vol., career advisor L.I. U., Brookville, N.Y., 1990—; treas. W. Tresper Clarke Friends of Arts, 1988-89. Mem. Fin. Mgmt. Assn., Internat. Assn. Fin. Planning (cert.), Adelphi Soc. Certified Fin. Planners, Internat. Assn. Registered Fin. Planners (speakers bur.), Nat. Assn. Life Underwriters, Nat. Panel Consumer Arbitrators, Nat. Ctr. for Fin. Edn., Inst. Cert. Fin. Planners (bd. dirs. L.I. 1989—), N.Y. State Assn. Cert. Fin. Planners, Delta Mu Delta. Republican. Roman Catholic. Home: 2167 Plum Tree Rd N Westbury NY 11590-6029 Office: 33 Willis Ave Mineola NY 11501-4411

MCGOUGH, JOHN PAUL, conveyor and power transmission company executive; b. Pitts., June 14, 1935; s. Patrick J. and Adelean R. (Skillen) McG.; m. Alice M. Gase, Feb. 15, 1958 (div. Dec. 1974); children: Mary G., Paul, Daniel J., Timothy F.X. Student, St. Vincent Coll., Latrobe, Pa., 1953-57; BA, DePaul U., Chgo., 1966; MA, Montclair State Coll., 1973. Sales rep. Shields Rubber Corp., Pitts., 1957-62; dist. mgr. Fabreeka Products Co., Skokie, Ill., 1962-67; regional mgr. Fabreeka Products Co., Wayne, N.J., 1967-75, Continental Rubber Works, Erie, Pa., 1975-76; dir. mktg. Daneline Inc., Kenilworth, N.J., 1976-80; exec. v.p., chief exec. officer Volta Internat., Livingston, N.J., 1980-83; vice chmn. J. E. Rhoads & Sons Inc., Newark, Del., 1983—. Mem. county com. Wayne Dem. Orgn., 1968-72; vice chmn. Wayne Dem. Club, 1969-70 . With U.S. Army, 1957-62. Mem. Pitts. Athletic Club. Unitarian.

MCGOVERN, DEIRDRE JOAN, public relations executive; b. N.Y.C., May 17, 1963; d. Alfred Tully and Barbara (Woisin) Robbins; m. Mark Gerard McGovern, Aug. 13, 1988. BA in Mktg., Iona Coll., 1986. Sr. acct. exec. Nichol & Co., N.Y.C., 1986-89; pub. rels. mgr. Wamsutta/Pacific Home Products, N.Y.C., 1989—. Mem. Pub. Rels. Soc. Am., Internat. Furnishings Design Assn., Am. Printed Fabrics Coun. Office: Wamsutta-Pacific 1285 Ave of the Americas New York NY 10019-6028

MCGOVERN, JOHN HUGH, urologist, educator; b. Bayonne, N.J., Dec. 18, 1924; s. Patrick and Mary (McGovern) McG.; m. Mary Alice Cavazos, Aug. 2, 1980; children by previous marriage: John Hugh, Robert, Ward, Raymond. BS, Columbia U., 1947; MD, SUNY, Bklyn., 1952. Diplomate Am. Bd. Urology. Rotating intern Bklyn. Hosp., 1952-53; asst. resident in surgery Bklyn. VA Hosp., 1953-54; with urology N.Y. Hosp., 1954-56; exchange surg. registrar West London Hosp., Eng., 1956-57; resident in urol. surgery N.Y. Hosp., 1957-58, rsch. asst. pediatric urology, 1958-59, asst. attending surgeon James Buchanan Brady Found., 1959-61, assoc. attending surgeon, 1961-66, attending surgeon, 1966—; asst. in surgery Med. Coll. Cornell U., 1957-59, asst. prof. clin. surgery, 1959-64, assoc. prof., 1964-72, prof., 1972—; attending staff in urology Lenox Hill Hosp., 1969—, in-charge urology, 1969-83; cons. urology Rockefeller Inst., St. Vincent's Hosp., Mercy Hosp., Phelps Meml. Hosp.; chmn. coun. on urology Nat. Kidney Found., 1982. Contbr. articles to profl. jours., chpts. to books. Lt. M.C., U.S. Army, 1942-45. Recipient Conatvoy mos medal Chile, 1975, Tree of Life award Nat. Kidney Found., 1990; named Huesped de Honor, Mimunicipalidad de Guayaquil (Ecuador), 1976; award in urology Kidney Found. N.Y., 1977, Sir Peter Freyer medal, Galway, Ireland, 1980. Fellow N.Y. Acad. Medicine (exec. com. urol. sect. 1968-72, chmn. 1972), ACS (credentials com. 1991-92), Am. Acad. Pediatrics; mem. AMA (diagnostic and therapeutic tech. assessment bd. 1991—, diagnostic and therepautic tech. assessment program panel 1991, DATTA panel 1991-92), N.Y. State Med. Soc. (chmn. urol. sect. 1975), Med. Soc. County N.Y., Am. Urol. Assn. (pres.-elect 1988, pres. 1989-90, pres. N.Y. sect. 1979-80, N.Y. rep. exec. com. 1982-87, socioecons. com. 1987, chmn. fiscal affairs rev. com. 1987, chmn. awards com. 1990, time and place com. 1989-90), N.Y. State Urol. Soc. (exec. com. 1982—), Pan Pacific Surg. Assn., Am. Assn. Clin. Urologists (pres.-elect 1987, pres. 1988-89, bd. dirs. 1984—, mem. interpersonal rels. com. 1975—, govt. rels. com. 1989-90, program com. 1989-90, nominating com. 1989-90), Assn. Am. Physicians and Surgeons, Pan Am. Med. Assn. (diplomate 1981—), Société Internationale d'Urologie, Urol. Investigators Forum, Soc. Pediatric Urology (pres.-elect 1979-80, pres. 1980-81), Am. Trauma Soc., Kidney Found. (med. adv. bd. N.Y. sect., trustee, 1979) Société Internationale d'Urologie (exec. com. U.S. sect.); hon. mem. Sociedad Peruana de Urología, Sociedad Guatemala de Urologia, Sociedad Ecuadoriana de Urología, Royal Coll. Surgeons (London). Home: 969 Park Ave New York NY 10028-0322 Office: 53 E 70th St New York NY 10021-4962

MCGOVERN, MICHAEL P., investment company executive; b. N.Y.C.. BA in Econs., Iona Coll., New Rochelle, N.Y., 1980. V.p. Vestron Inc., Stamford, Conn., 1983-90; prin. Credit Investors, Orange, Conn., 1990—. Republican. Office: Credit Investors Corp PO Box 1213 845 Hillcrest Rd Orange CT 06477

MCGOWAN, ANDREW JOHN, video and radio production distribution company executive; b. N.Y.C., Sept. 28, 1939; s. Patrick Joseph and Bridget (Duggan) McG.; m. Judith Ellen May, June 29, 1963; children: Ian, Peter, Sean. BA, CCNY, 1962, postgrad. in bus. adminstrn., 1962-67; cert. in film prodn., NYU, 1973. Producer, moderator Talk Back show Sta. WBAI-FM, N.Y.C., 1967-68; v.p. Markhouse Corp. Communications, N.Y.C., 1968-71; mgr. pub. rels. St. Luke's Hosp. Ctr., N.Y.C., 1971-76; v.p. Planned Communication Svcs., N.Y.C., 1976-88, pres., 1988—; instr. pub. rels. Sch. Visual Arts, N.Y.C., 1986-91. Co-author: The Underground Church, 1968, New Technology in Public Relations, 1986. Mem. Pub. Rels. Soc. Am. (accredited, bd. dirs. N.Y. chpt. 1980-91), W.B. Yeats Soc. N.Y. (founder, pres. 1989—), Phi Kappa Theta (bd. dirs. nat. found. 1973—). Democrat. Home: 281 W 254th St Bronx NY 10471 Office: PCS Broadcast Svcs 1 Robinson Ln Ridgewood NJ 07450

MCGOWAN, GEORGE VINCENT, public utility executive; b. Balt., Jan. 30, 1928; s. Joseph H. and Ethna M. (Prahl) McG.; m. Carol Murray, Aug. 6, 1977; children by a previous marriage: Gregg Blair, Bradford Kirby. BS in M.E., U. Md., 1951; LHD (hon.), Villa Julie Coll., 1991, Loyola Coll., Md., 1992. Registered profl. engr., Md. Project engr. nuclear power plant Balt. Gas & Electric Co., 1967-72, chief nuclear engr., 1972-74, pres., chief operating officer, 1980-87, chmn. bd. dirs, 1988—, mgr. corp. staff services, 1974-78, v.p. mgmt. and staff services, 1978-79; bd. dirs. Balt. Life Ins. Co., McCormick & Co., Life of Md. Inc., Am. Gas Assn., UNC Inc., Orgn. Resources Counselors, Inc., MNC Fin., Inc., Assn. Edison Illuminating Cos. Bd. dirs. Am. Nuclear Energy Coun., Washington, 1982—, U. Md. Med. System, United Way Cen. Md., Pride of Balt.; chmn. bd. regents U. Md. System; chmn. Gov.'s Vol. Coun. State of Md.; trustee Walters Art Gallery, Balt., 1982—; dir. Southeastern Elec. Exch.; chmn. bd. dirs. Balt. Symphony Orch., CollegeBound Found. Recipient Disting. Alumnus award U. Md. Coll. Engring., 1980, U. Md., 1987, Disting. Marylander award Advt. and Profl. Club Balt., 1992, Disting. Citizen award U. Md., 1991, Dist. Citizen of Yr. award Boy Scouts Am. Balt. Coun., 1991. Mem. ASME, Am. Nuclear Soc., U.S. Energy Assn. of the World Energy Conf., Engring. Soc. Balt. (Founders Day award 1988), Md. C. of C. (bd. dirs.), Caves Valley Golf Club, The Ctr. Club (bd. govs.), U. Md. M Club, Talbot Country Club, Annapolis Yacht Club, Md. Club. Presbyterian. Office: Balt Gas & Electric Co PO Box 1475 Baltimore MD 21203-1475

MCGOWAN, JOAN YUHAS, development researcher; b. Trenton, N.J., Feb. 13, 1955; d. Bernard Joseph and Estelle (Gray) Yuhas; children: Matthew Sheehan, Allison Joo Ok. BA summa cum laude, Trenton State Coll., 1977. Cert. tchr., N.J. Tchr. Blessed Sacrament Sch., Trenton, 1977; intake officer Mercer County Juvenile Ct, Trenton, 1978-82; rsch. dir. Audits and Surveys, Princeton, N.J., 1982-85; project dir. The Gallup Orgn., Princeton, 1985-86, Hase/Schannen Rsch. Assocs., Princeton, 1986; devel. researcher Trenton State Coll., 1986—; guest lectr., Thomas Jefferson U., Rutgers U., Helene Fuld Sch. Nursing; guest speaker local television programs. Author: Waiting: The Hopes and Frustrations of a Childless Couple, 1983; contbr. articles to various publs. Pres. Resolve, Inc., Phila, 1982; mem. Holt Internat. Children's Svcs., Trenton, 1984-85, Incarnation Altar Rosary Soc., Trenton, 1988—, Holy Name Soc., Trenton, 1989—. Recipient Think and Suggest award State of N.J., 1977, Meritorious award Trenton State Coll., 1989. Mem. Am. Fedn. Tchrs., Am. Prospect Researchers Assn., New Eng. Devel. Researchers Assn., Villa Park Civic Assn. Democrat. Roman Catholic. Home: 941 Lyndale Ave Trenton NJ 08629-2409 Office: Trenton State Coll Hillwood Lakes CN 4700 Trenton NJ 08650

MC GOWIN, WILLIAM EDWARD, artist; b. Hattiesburg, Miss., June 2, 1938; s. William Edward and Emily (Ratliff) McG.; m. Claudia DeMonte, May 28, 1977; children: Leah, Jill. B.S., U. So. Miss., 1961; M.A., U. Ala., 1964. prof. art SUNY, Old Westbury, 1978—, Coll. Old Westbury; mem. faculty Corcoran Gallery Art, 1966-77, head sculpture dept., 1967-74; lectr. in field. One-man shows include Corcoran Gallery Art, Washington, 1962, 71, 75, Martha Jackson Gallery, N.Y.C., 1968, Am. Cultural Center, Paris, 1974, Museum Modern Art, Paris, 1978, Brooks Jackson Gallery Iolas, N.Y.C., 1978-80, Fendrick Gallery, Washington, 1977-80, U. Colo., New Orleans Contemporary Art Ctr., 1982, Project Studios 1, L.I., N.Y., Cranbrook Acad., Bloomfield Hills, Mich., 1983, Art Park, Lewiston, N.Y., 1984, Gracie Mansion Gallery, N.Y.C., 1985, 86, 89, Mus. Fine Arts, Miami, Jones-Troyer Gallery, Washington, 1987, 89, Boca Raton (Fla.) Mus., 1991, Margulis-Taplin Gallery, Miami, Fla., 1991, Hokin-Kauffman Gallery, Chgo., 1991; group shows include, Contemporary Mus., Houston, Miss. Mus. Art, Whitney Mus., N.Y.C., Detroit Inst. Art, Guggenheim Mus., Speed Mus., Ky., Cologne (Fed. Republic Germany) Art Fair, Zurich (Switzerland) Art Fair; represented in permanent collections, Phillips Collection, Washington, Indpls. Mus. Art, Addison Mus. Art, Andover, Mass., Corcoran Gallery Art, Nat. Collection Fine Arts, Washington, New Orleans Mus. Art, Whitney Mus. Am. Art, N.Y.C., Guggenheim Mus., N.Y.C., Hirshhorn Gallery and Sculpture Garden, work reviewed in numerous newspapers, jours. and books. Mem. pub. outdoor sculpture commn. VA, 1985. Recipient Oscar for painting, 1977, Painting prize 9th Internat. Painting Festival, prize Cagnes-sur-Mer, France, 1977, Miss. Arts and Letters award for visual arts, 1980; Nat. Endowment for Arts grantee, 1967-68, 79-80, GSA grantee, 1978-79, Pub. Outdoor Sculpture grantee Nat. Endowment, 1977, 79, Cassandra Found. grantee, 1972—. Home and Office: 96 Grand St New York NY 10013-2633

MCGRATH, CAROLINE C., pharmaceutical company executive; b. Manchester, Eng., Aug. 31, 1952; came to U.S. 1972; d. Basil and Constance C. (Beesley) McGrath; m. Parrilla, June 1, 1981; 1 child, Alexander. AA with honors, CUNY, 1983, BS cum laude, 1985; MPS, N.Y. Inst. Tech., 1989. Adminstrv. asst. Fiat Motor Sales, Ltd., London, 1977-78, UK Mission to UN, N.Y.C., 1978-80; info. officer Brit. Info. Svcs., N.Y.C., 1980-81; adminstrv. asst. to travel commr. N.Z. Tourist Office, N.Y.C., 1981-82; sectl. scis. instr. Project ReDirect, N.Y.C., 1982-83; typing instr. N.Y. Sch. Med. & Dental Assts., 1983-84; ind. pharm. rep. N.Y.C., 1987—. Mem. Phi Theta Kappa, Psi Chi.

MCGRATH, DORN CHARLES, JR., urban and regional planning educator, consultant; b. Bradford, Pa., May 16, 1930; s. Dorn Charles and Dorothy (Henline) McG.; m. Susan Allen, June 14, 1955 (div. Dec. 1981); children: Dorn Charles III, Martha Winston; m. 2d, Leila Iris Baskin, Oct. 3, 1982. B.A., Dartmouth Coll., 1952; M. City Planning, Harvard U., 1959. Prin., The Planning Services Group, Cambridge, Mass., 1961-64; dir. project planning and engring. U.S. Urban Renewal Adminstrn., Washington, 1964-66; dir. div. met. area analysis HUD, Washington, 1966-68; prof. city and regional planning, chmn. dept. urban and regional planning George Washington U., Washington, 1968-84; dir. Inst. for Urban Devel. Rsch., 1984—; dir. Nat. Urban Coalition, Washington, 1981—; mem. adv. panel Office Tech. Assessment, Washington, 1974—. Author, editor: Urban Waterfront Lands, 1980. Trustee, Washington Ctr. for Met. Studies, 1974-78; chmn. Inter-univ. adv. com. on Comprehensive Plan for the Nat. Capital, Washington, 1983; chmn. Com. of 100 on Fed. City, Washington, 1986—. Served to lt. comdr. CEC, USN, 1953-57. Recipient Order of Most Disting. Services, Govt. Peru, 1980. Mem. Am. Inst. Planners (pres. 1971-73, disting. service award 1973), Urban Land Inst., Lambda Alpha (bd. govs. George Washington chpt.). Democrat. Home: 2710 Brandywine St NW Washington DC 20008-1040 Office: George Washington U Washington DC 20052

MCGRATH, GARY MICHAEL, telecommunications manager; b. Ottawa, Ill., Mar. 7, 1950; s. Edmund Thomas Jr. and Mary Lorraine (Corcoran) McG.; m. Deborah Ann Bower, Mar. 13, 1976; children: G. Michael, Stephen E., Mark P., Kevin W. BS, U. Ill., 1972; MBA, Ind. U., 1974. Banking rep. No. Trust Co., Chgo., 1974-76; fin. analyst Jos. Schlitz Brewing Co., Milw., 1976-77; mgr. treasury ops. Universal Foods Corp., Milw., 1977-80; mgr. treasury svc. Bandag Inc., Muscatine, Iowa, 1980-84; group mgr. treasury ops. GTE Corp., Stamford, Conn., 1984—. Pres., dir. Am. Youth Soccer Orgn., Monroe, Conn., 1988—; dir. Monroe Soccer Club, 1992—. Mem. Fairfield County Treasury Mgmt. Assn. Republican. Roman Catholic. Office: GTE Corp One Stamford Forum Stamford CT 06904

MCGRATH, JAMES ALOYSIUS, Canadian provincial official; b. Buchans, Nfld., Can., Nov. 1, 1932; s. Patrick and Mary (Cole) McG.; m. Margaret Smart, Sept. 4, 1960; children: Kathleen, Caroline, Margaret-Moira, Joanna, Sean, Sheilagh. LLD (hon.), St. Francis Xavier U. Provincial sec. Prog. Conservative Party, St. John's, Nfld., 1955-57, pres., 1965-68; m.p. from St. John's East Ho. of Commons, 1957-61, 68-86, parliamentary sec. to minister mines and tech. surveys, 1962, exec. asst. leader opposition, 1963-65, ofcl. opposition spokesman on consumer and corp. affairs, regional and econ. expansion, labour, consumer affairs, housing and urban affairs, 1968-79, mem. Queen's privy council, minister fisheries and oceans, 1979-80, ofcl. spokesman opposition health and welfare, housing, employment and immigration, mem. joint senate and house com. Can. constitution, 1980-84, chmn. spl. com. reform ho. commons, mem. trilateral commn., internat. council parliamentarians global action, 1984-86; lt. gov. Nfld., 1986—; speaker in field. Served with RCAF, 1950-55. Recipient Queen's Jubilee Medal, Humanitarian award Boys and Girls Clubs Can. Mem. Commonwealth Parliamentary Assn. (vice chmn. Can. br. 1984-86). Lodges: Knights of Malta. Office: Office of Lt Gov, Govt House/Military Rd, Saint John's, NF Canada A1C 5W4

MCGRATH, RAYMOND J., congressman; b. Valley Stream, N.Y., Mar. 27, 1942; m. Joanne Coady, 1967; 1 son, Timothy. B.S., SUNY, Brockport, 1963; M.A., NYU, 1968. Tchr. SUNY, Farmingdale, 1969; lectr. Hunter Coll., N.Y.C., 1969; mem. N.Y. State Assembly, 1976-80; dep. commr. Hempstead Twp. Parks and Recreation; mem. 97th-102nd Congresses from 5th Dist. N.Y., 1981—, mem. Ho. ways and means com., 1981—; mem. curriculum adv. coms. Nassau Community Coll., C W Post Coll. Contbr. articles on recreation of handicapped to profl. jours. Named Man of Yr. Nassau Suffolk L.I. chpt. Cystic Fibrosis Found., 1980. Mem. Ancient Order Hibernians, Naral Club, Elks,, K.C., Holy Name Soc., Am. Irish Congress. Republican. Clubs: Ancient Order Hibernians, Elks, KC, Holy Name Soc, Am. Irish Congress. Office: US Ho of Reps 431 Cannon House Office Bldg Washington DC 20515

MCGRATH, WALTER JOSEPH, advertising executive; b. Jersey City, July 20, 1939; s. Walter Joseph and Amelia Mary (Richardson) McG.; m. Sally A. Cushing, Sept. 29, 1977; children: Patrick J., Michael J., William J., Charles W., Linda M. BA in Econs., Fordham U., 1961; MS in Indsl. Mgmt., Ga. Inst. Tech., 1972; mil. arts, Armed Forces Staff Coll., 1978. From comdr. to dir. indsl. ops. U.S.Army, 1963-83; security, partner CAP-EQ, Inc., Bethlehem, Pa., 1983-86; gen. ptnr. 196 Devel. Group, Tobyhanna, Pa., 1986-91; v.p. closed circuit TV advt. New Image Network Corp., 1991—; govt. funding cons. W.J. McGrath Assocs., Tobyhanna, 1984-90. Author: Olympic Pin Blue Book, 1990; contbr. articles to profl. jours. Sch. bd. mem. Pocono Cen. Cath. Sch., Cresco, Pa., 1989—; bd. dirs. Pocono Mtn. Industries, Stroudsburg, Pa., 1985-88. Mem. VFW, KC, Pocono Mtns. C. of C. (bd. dirs. Econ. Devel. com.). Republican. Roman Catholic. Home: 16 Park Drag Tobyhanna PA 18466-8970 Office: 196 Devel Group Rt 196 Tobyhanna PA 18466

MCGRAW, LAVINIA MORGAN, former retail company executive; b. Detroit, Feb. 26, 1924; d. Will Curtis and Margaret Coulter (Oliphant) McG. AB, Radcliffe Coll., 1945. Mem. Phi Beta Kappa. Home: 2501 Calvert St NW Washington DC 20008-2620

MCGRAW-LEWICKI, M(ARJORIE) LEE, small business owner; b. Englewood, N.J., Jan. 18, 1957; d. John L. and Marjorie (Peddy) McGraw; m. Matthew E. Lewicki, Oct. 1, 1983. BBA, Stetson U., 1979; postgrad., Fairleigh Dickinson U., 1982-83. Promotion asst. McGraw-Hill, Inc., N.Y.C., 1979-81, mktg. communication assoc., 1981-82, mktg. communications mgr., 1982-85; pres., owner The Gift Basket, Inc., Sudbury, Mass., 1987—. Bd. advs. Stetson U. Sch. Bus., Deland, Fla., 1984—. Episcopalian. Office: The Gift Basket Inc 6 Craig Ln Sudbury MA 01776-1274

MCGRAY, MARY JENNIFER, accountant; b. Boston, Dec. 22, 1966; d. Elton G. and Carolyn (Higgins) McG. BA in Mgmt., Simmons Coll., 1988; postgrad., Northeastern U., 1991—. CPA, Mass. Accounts payable asst. Treas. Office Simmons Coll., Boston, 1986-88, computer cons. computer facilities, 1985-88; tax specialist, intern BDO Seidman, Boston, 1988; sr. auditor small bus. group Coopers and Lybrand, Boston, 1988-91; acct. W.R. Grace, Lexington, Mass., 1991—. Creator 4 inventions. Vol. Spl. Olympics, Peabody, Mass. Mem. Lynn Photographic Assn. Republican. Roman Catholic. Home: 7 Irving St Peabody MA 01960-4224

MCGREGOR, DUNCAN DOUGLASS, process engineer, consultant; b. Wadesboro, N.C., Sept. 1, 1930; s. Duncan Hardy and Sallie Berry (Douglass) McG.; m. Anne Harmon, Nov. 22, 1952; children: Sally Ann McGregor Rivers, Jane Elizabeth. Student, Presbyn. Coll., Clinton, S.C., 1947-49; BSCE, Clemson U., 1952; MSCE, Purdue U., 1956; cert. mgmt. devel., U. Tex., 1974. Constrn. engr. DuPont Co., Aiken, S.C., 1952; staff engr. Aluminum Co. Am., Badin, N.C., 1956-60; prodn. engr. Aluminum Co. Am., Point Comfort, Tex., 1961-62; electrode supt. Aluminum Co. Am., Point Henry, Australia, 1962-65; project engr., engring. mgr. Aluminum Co. Am., Rockdale, Tex., 1965-73, plant mgr., 1973-76, works mgr., 1976-77; chief process engr. Aluminum Co. Am., Pitts., 1977-92; ret., 1992; v.p. Alcoa Generating Corp., Pitts., 1980-84. Co-inventor patented smelting process, 1984. Mem. Rockdale Tex. Sch. Bd., 1969-77, Tex. Chem. Council, Austin, 1974-77. Served to 1st lt. U.S. Army, 1952-56. Recipient Cert. of Achievement, Inter Am. Geodetic Survey, Panama Canal Zone, 1956. Mem. Am. Inst. Metall. Engrs. Republican. Presbyterian. Home: 8800 West Ct # 204 Allison Park PA 15101-2731

MCGREGOR, WALTER, medical products company designer, inventor, consultant, educator; b. Kiew, Ukraine, Nov. 2, 1937; came to U.S., 1957; s. William and Lydia (Aplass) McG.; m. Helen McGregor, July 18, 1965; children: Roxanne, Walter. BS, Fairleigh Dickinson U., 1973, MBA, 1975. Sect. leader Ethicon Inc., Somerville, N.J., 1965-68, supr., 1968-76, mgr., 1976-83, dir. surg. products devel. and materials engring., 1983-92, dir. of tech., 1992—; guest cons. Wilmer Inst., Johns Hopkins Hosp. Rsch. Lab., Balt., 1965-70; guest lectr. dept. plastic surgery U. Va. Med. Sch., Charlottesville, 1986—. Contbr. articles to profl. jours. Patentee surg. instruments. Life mem. Rep. Presdl. Task Force, Washington, 1984—; mem. Rep. Nat. Com., 1991. Fellow Soc. for Advancement of Med. Instrumentation; mem. Am. Med. Informatics Assn. (founding). Home: 104 Hoffman Rd Flemington NJ 08822 Office: Ethicon Inc US Rt 22 Somerville NJ 08876

MCGRIFF, RICHARD BERNARD, chemist; b. St. Petersburg, Fla., July 15, 1935; s. Walter Lee Sr. and Beatrice (Green) McG.; m. Brenda Jordan Riley, May 24, 1969; children: Alison J., Tara B. BS, Fla. A&M U., 1955; MS, Calif. Inst. Tech., 1959; PhD, U. Wis., 1967. Chemist Riker Labs., Northridge, Calif., 1959-62; rsch. chemist Hercules, Inc., Wilmington, Del., 1967-73; sr. chemist Xerox, Webster, N.Y., 1973—. Contbr. articles to profl. jours. Mem. Urban League of Rochester, N.Y., 1983—. Mem. NAACP, Am. Chem. Soc., Am. Soc. for Mass Spectroscopy, N.Am. Thermal Analysis Soc. Presbyterian. Home: 886 Independence Dr Webster NY 14580-2659 Office: Xerox 139-64A 800 Phillips Rd Webster NY 14580-9791

MCGRORY, NANCY RUTH, advertising executive; b. Elmira, N.Y., Dec. 10, 1960; d. Matthew and Leah Winnifred (Hafleigh) Paton; m. John McGrory Jr., Aug. 1, 1987. BA in Communications/Journalism, Shippensburg U., 1982; postgrad., Drexel U., 1988-90. Jr. account exec. Al Paul Lefton, Phila., 1982-84; mktg. and communications exec. TACT Technology, Phila., 1984-86; advt. mgr. Internat. Mobile Machines, King of Prussia, Pa., 1986-90; owner Creatively done, Drexel Hill, Pa., 1990-91, Info. Works, Phila., 1991—. Pub. rels. chairperson Habitat for Humanity, Phila., 1989—. Mem. NAFE, Nat. Assn. Profl. Saleswomen, Delaware County C. of C. Democrat. Presbyterian. Home: 3825 Plumstead Ave Drexel Hill PA 19026 Office: Zeewy Design 914 S 111th St 2d Fl Philadelphia PA 19147

MCGUIGAN, THOMAS J., engineering company executive; b. Toronto, Ont., Can., Jan. 3, 1942; s. Thomas F. and Priscilla M (Robitaille) McG.; m. Ileana Petrie, Aug. 3, 1968; children: Andrea, Mark. BSc., U. Toronto, Can., 1963. Project engr. Litton Systems Can. Ltd., Etobicoke, Ont., 1963-71, dir. advance programs, 1971-81, v.p. mktg., 1981-86, pres., 1986—; v.p.

Litton Industries, L.A., 1988—. Office: Litton Systems Can Ltd, 25 City View Dr, Etobicoke, ON Canada M9W 5A7

MCGUINESS, EDWARD J., telephone company executive; b. Bronx, Apr. 18, 1931; s. John B. and Agnes E. (Woodward) McG.; m. Rose A. Shimko, Oct. 12, 1957; children: Tracey Ann, Robin Marie, Karen Lee. EE, Bridgeport Engring. Inst., Conn., 1961, Computer Programmer, 1985. Quality control technician Perkin-Elmer Corp., Norwalk, Conn., 1954-57; project engr. Barnes Engring. Co., Stamford, Conn., 1957-66; asst. dept. head Kollmorgan Corp., Northampton, Mass., 1966-69; owner retail liquor store Norwalk, Conn., 1969-81; air pollution engr. Health Dept., City of Norwalk, 1972-77; engring. adminstr. Spadone Machine Co., Norwalk, 1977-86; gen. mgr. Tele-Products Co., Norwalk, 1986—; owner, cons. M & M Assocs., Norwalk, 1985—. Co-founder, pres. Meals on Wheels of Norwalk, 1970-80, bd. dirs.; com. chair Sea Scout Ship 6, Norwalk, 1970-83. With USN, 1950-54. Mem. Ancient Order of Hibernians (state bd. sec. 1987—, div. fin. sec. 1989—), KC (pres. 1976-79). Democrat. Roman Catholic. Home: 263 East Ave Norwalk CT 06855-1924

MC GUINNESS, FRANK JOSEPH, construction company executive; b. Trenton, N.J., Aug. 1, 1928; s. Frank J. and Catherine C. (Campbell) McG.; B.S.C.E., Rutgers U., 1953; m. June Atkins; children by previous marriage—Kathleen, Edward, Anne, Mary, Frank. Civil engr. N.J. Hwy. Dept., Trenton, 1951-53; dist. engr. Lehigh Portland Cement Co., Allentown, Pa., 1956-68; exec. v.p. Knott Industries, Balt., 1968-78; pres. The Knott Co., Balt., 1978—; dir. Knott Industries, Inc. Mem. Greater Balt. Com., 1979—. Served to 1st lt., Ordinance Corps, U.S. Army, 1953-56. Registered profl. engr., N.J. Mem. Assn. Builders and Contractors, Nat. Soc. Profl. Engrs., Am. Concrete Inst., Nat. Assn. Office and Indsl. Parks (v.p. 1976-78), Urban Land Inst. Democrat. Roman Catholic. Club: Hon. Order of Ky. Cols. Office: 1825 Woodlawn Dr Baltimore MD 21207-4080

MCGUINNESS, JOHN SEWARD, management consultant, actuary; b. Kingston, Pa., Mar. 12, 1922; s. John P. and Mary (Bogert) M.; m. Shirley Paige Campbell, Nov. 23, 1957; children: Brian B., Ann B., Lauren K. Student, U. Wash., 1941-43, U. Pitts., 1943-44; BS, U. Calif., Berkeley, 1948, MBA, 1949; postgrad., U. Zurich, Switzerland, 1949-50; PhD, Stanford U., 1955; grad., U.S. Army War Coll, 1971. Ins. clk., underwriter, 1939-43; chief automotive svc. br. EUCOM Exch. System, 1946-47; assoc. actuary Allstate Ins. Co., 1955-58; casualty actuary MacArthur Ins. Group, 1958-61; budget dir., actuary Glens Falls Ins. Group, 1961-64; pres. John S. McGuinness Assocs., Scotch Plains, N.J., 1964—; bd. dirs. RLI Corp. Author: Top-Management Organization and Control of Insurance Companies, 1954; contbr. articles to profl. jours. Elder Presbyn. Ch. With AUS, 1943-46; col. Res. ret. Decorated Knight (Sovereign Mil. Order of Temple of Jerusalem); named to Hon. Order of Ky. Cols. Fellow Casualty Actuarial Soc., Can. Inst. Actuaries (emeritus), Soc. for Advancement Mgmt. (internat. v.p. 1972-74, internat. pres. 1979-80, internat. chmn. bd. 1980-81); mem. AAAS, Am. Acad. Actuaries (charter), Internat. Actuarial Assn., Assn. Actuarial Studies in Non-Life Ins., Assn. Actuarial Approach to Fin. Risks, Am. Statis. Assn., Ins. Soc. N.Y., Soc. C.P.C.U.s, Soc. Ins. Rsch. (nat. pres. 1972), Ops. Rsch. Soc., Res. Officers Assn. (nat. treas. 1984-86), Confédération Internationale des Officiers de Res., Swiss Assn. Actuaries, Order Ky. Cols., Lloyd's of London, Internat. Ins. Soc., Willow Grove Swimming Club, Union Club, Lloyd's Yacht Club, Beta Gamma Sigma, Alpha Kappa Psi, Delta Tau Delta. Republican. Office: 15 Kevin Rd Scotch Plains NJ 07076-2211

MCGUINNESS, MARGARET MARY, religious historian; b. Providence, R.I., Aug. 23, 1953; d. Daniel Leo and Margaret Mary (Coleman) McG.; m. William Wayne Shipley, Mar. 31, 1984; children: William McGuinness, Erin Elizabeth. AB in Am. History and Civilization, Boston U., 1975, M in Theol. Studies, 1979; MPhil, Union Theol. Sem., N.Y.C., 1984; PhD, Union Theol. Sem., 1985. Asst. archivist Archdiocese Boston, 1979-80; field archivist Seton Hall U., South Orange, N.J., 1980-83; editor Union Sem. Quarterly Rev., 1982-85; asst. prof. religion Cabrini Coll., Radnor, Pa., 1985-92, assoc. prof., 1992—; cons. archives Archdiocese Phila., 1988; book rev. editor Am. Cath. Hist. Soc., Phila. 1988—. Birth buddy Franklin Maternity Hosp., Phila. 1986-88; adv. bd. children's sch. Cabrini Coll., 1987—; mem. PTA A Child's Place, Strafford, Pa., 1990-91. Mem. Am. Hist. Assn., Am. Soc. Ch. History. Office: Cabrini Coll 610 King of Prussia Rd Wayne PA 19087-3698

MCGUIRE, E(DWARD) PATRICK, safety researcher; b. Jersey City, Mar. 17, 1932; s. Edward and Kathryn (Comes) McG.; m. Kathryn Judith Honecker, Apr. 5, 1953; children: Timothy, Colleen, Megan, Kerry, Erin. BS, Rutgers U., 1962; MS, Greenwich U., 1991; MA, Norwich U., 1992. Cert. crane safety profl., indsl. safety profl. OSHA. Tech. svcs. rep. Swift & Co., Chgo., 1954-59; tech. svcs. mgr. The Borden Co., N.Y.C., 1958-69; exec. dir. rsch. The Conf. Bd., Inc., N.Y.C., 1969-90; pres. Padric Assocs., Inc., Bernardsville, N.J., 1965—; sr. cons. U.S. Consumer Product Safety Commn., Washington, 1980-82, NSF, Washington, 1990-91. Author 34 books; contbr. articles to profl. jours. With USCG, 1950-51. Mem. Am. Soc. Safety Engrs., Am. Indsl. Hygiene Assn., Nat. Safety Coun., Nat. Fire Protection Assn., Human Factor Soc. Roman Catholic. Office: Padric Assocs Inc 80 Mountaintop Rd Bernardsville NJ 07924-1122

MCGUIRE, JAMES EDWARD, history and philosophy of science educator; b. London, Ont., Can., Oct. 29, 1931; came to U.S., 1971; s. John H. McGuire and Madelin Gibbs; m. Penelope Gore, Apr. 15, 1962 (div. July 1975); 1 child, Dominic. BA, U. Western Ont., 1956; postgrad, Oxford U., 1958-60. Lectr. U. Leicester, England, 1961-63, U. Leeds, England, 1963-71; prof. U. Pitts., 1971—; Silverman prof. Tel Aviv U., Israel, 1991. Author: (with others) Hermeticism and Scientific Revolution, 1977, Certain Philosophical Questions, 1983; cons. editor Studies in History and Philosophy of Sci., 1972—; editor How Things Are, 1984.

MCGUIRE, JAMES RICHARD, sales executive; b. Glens Falls, N.Y., June 30, 1964; s. Eleanor (Martin) McG. Student, Adirondack Community Coll., 1982-83; grad., Dale Carnegie Inst., 1991. Front office mgr. Queensbury Hotel, Glens Falls, 1985-88, asst. mgr., 1988-89, dir. of catering, 1989-90, exec. sales mgr., 1990—. Mem. Soc. Assn. Execs. Upstate N.Y., Inc., Adirondack Regional C. of C., Albany County C. of C. Democrat. Roman Catholic. Office: Queensbury Hotel 88 Ridge St Glens Falls NY 12801

MCGUIRE, JOHN FRANCIS, JR., construction company executive; b. N.Y.C., May 28, 1941; s. John Francis and Ann Helena (Hoey) McG.; m. Dorann Rastetter (dec. July 1968); 1 child, Sean Philip; m. Jan Barbara Close, Oct. 18, 1969; 1 child, Seth Adrian. Student, Marist Coll., Poughkeepsie, N.Y., 1976, Dutchess Community Coll., Poughkeepsie, 1976, 90—. Founder, owner, mgr., pres. McGuire Constrn. Co., Rhinebeck, N.Y., 1966—; mem. Rhinebeck Town/Village Shared Svcs. study com., 1991. Co-author Rhinebeck and Hyde Park Fire Codes. Trustee Rhinebeck Theater Soc., asst. treas., chmn. fin. com.; bd. dirs., v.p., mem. fin. com., chmn. phys. plant & grounds Wilderstein Preservation Inc.; coach, instr., referee, umpire Rhinebeck Little League Baseball, Jr. League Baseball, Girls Softball League; co-founder, coach Rhinebeck Soccer League, 1972-85; former vice chmn. sch. bldg. needs com. Rhinebeck Cen. Sch. Dist.; chief fire officer Hillside Fire Dist., 1963-75; asst. to mgr. Dutchess County Fair, 1976-85; co-chmn. Rhinebeck Bicentennial, 1974-77; chmn. Rhinebeck Rep. Com.; mem. coord. coun. Dutchess County Criminal Justice; mem. Friends of Clermont, Mills Mansion. Named to Hall of Fame, Dutchess County Sports Mus., Poughkeepsie, 1989. Mem. Rhinebeck C. of C. (bd. dirs. 1968—), Huguenot Hist. Soc., Quitman Resource Ctr., Rotary. Home and Office: 13 Ackert Hook Rd Rhinebeck NY 12572-2600

MCGUIRE, JOSEPH EDWARD, lawyer; b. Worcester, Mass., Nov. 30, 1926; s. Joseph A. and Julia E. (Kenney) McG.; m. Sheila Whitewood Bennett, June 17, 1967; 1 child, Kristine Nelson McGuire Forzley. BS, Georgetown U., 1947, JD, 1950. Bar: Mass. 1950, U.S. Dist. Ct. Mass. 1951, U.S. Supreme Ct 1969. Ptnr. McGuire & McGuire, Worcester, 1950—; instr. Inst. Labor and Mgmt., Holy Cross Coll., Worcester, 1972-85; mem. jud. nominating coun. Commonwealth of Mass., 1983-86; commr. Mass. Indsl. Accident Bd., 1959-65. Nominee for lt. gov. Mass. Dem. party, 1966; mem. Dem. City Com., Worcester, 1950—; regent Georgetown U., Washington, 1979—; mem. Worcester Rent Control Bd., 1951-53; mem. bd. dirs. Nat. Soc. to Prevent Blindness, 1979—, chmn. Mass. affiliate, 1979—. Lt. comdr. USNR, ret. Mem. ABA, Mass. Acad. Trial Lawyers, Am. Judicature Soc., Mass. Bar Assn. (mem. workers compensation com. 1950—), Worcester County Bar Assn. (chmn. legis. com. 1982), Internat. Assn. Indsl. Accident Bds. and Commns. (vice chmn. legis. affairs com. 1963-65, cons. 1978—), Megansett Yacht Club, Plaza Club, Ward Room Club. Home: 12 Schussler Rd Worcester MA 01609-2214 Office: McGuire & McGuire PC 340 Main St Worcester MA 01608-1601

MCGUIRE, MARTIN CYRIL, economics educator; b. Shanghai, People's Republic of China, Dec. 12, 1933; came to U.S., 1939; s. Martin Cyril and Margaret (Walsh) M. BS, U.S. Mil. Acad., 1955; BA, Oxford U., England, 1958; PhD, Harvard U., 1964. Commd. 2nd lt. U.S. Army, 1955, advanced through grades to capt., 1961, ret., 1961; analyst Office Sec. Defense, 1964-65; dir. program analysis U.S. Commerce Dept., 1965-67; prof. econs. U. Md., College Park, 1967—. Author: Secrecy and the Arms Race, 1965; contbr. articles to profl. jours. Rhodes scholar, 1955, Fulbright scholar, 1988. Mem. Cosmos Club. Office: U Md Dept Econs College Park MD 20742

MCGUIRE, MAVIS LOUISE, professional society administrator; b. Sioux Falls, S.D., Oct. 6, 1948; d. Francis and Beverly Beatrice McG.; m. Kenneth Chatzinoff, May 22, 1983. BSN, U. Iowa, 1974, MA in Nursing, 1976. Cert. pediatric nurse practitioner. Pediatric nurse practitioner Children & Youth Project, Davenport, Iowa, 1976-77; dir. pediatric nurse practitioner program Gwynedd Mercy Coll., Gwynedd Valley, Pa., 1977-84; exec. dir. Nat. Assn. Pediatric Nurse Assocs. & Practioners, Cherry Hill, N.J., 1981—; bd. dirs. Pa. Nurses Assn. Dist. Level, 1978-80; cons. in field. Mem. edit. bd. Jour Pediatric Health Care, 1986—. Fellow Nat. Assn. Pediatric Assocs. and Practitioners; mem. NAFE, Nat. Assn. Assn. Execs., Sigma Theta Tau. Home: 2 Greenbriar Ln Riverton NJ 08077-3876 Office: Nat Assn Pediatric Nurse Assocs and Practitioners 1101 Kings Hwy N # 206 Cherry Hill NJ 08034-1912

MCGUIRE, THERESE BENEDICT, art history educator; b. Jersey City; d. John Joseph and Anna Marie (Coddington) McG. BA, Chestnut Hill Coll., 1962; MFA, Cath. U. Am., 1972; PhD, NYU, 1986. Joined Sisters of St. Joseph, Roman Catholic Ch., 1944; cert. tchr. English, art, art history, Pa.; cert. tchr., N.Y. Tchr. Hallahan High Sch., Phila., 1959-62; tchr. fine arts, English Notre Dame High Sch., Easton, Pa., 1962-76; tchr. fine arts Hubert's High Sch., Phila., 1976-80; assoc. prof. art history and studio art Chestnut Hill Coll., Phila., 1980—. Contbr. articles to profl. jours. Mem. Women in Arts Nat. Mus. (charter), Internat. Soc. Hildegard Bingen Studies, Coll. Art Assn., Phi Delta Kappa. Office: Chestnut Hill Coll Northwestern and Germantown Aves Philadelphia PA 19118-2695

MCGUIRE, WALTER GARY, college dean; b. Martinez, Calif., Feb. 1, 1943; s. Walter Henry and Elizabeth Ann (Doyle) McG.; (div. Jan. 1989); children: Christopher Michael, Timothy Andrew, Elizabeth Lee. BA, SUNY, Buffalo, 1967, MEd, 1969; DEd, Pa. State U., 1979. Asst. dean of students Augustana Coll., Rock Island, Ill., 1969-72; asst. dir. Quad-Cities Grad. Ctr., Rock Island, 1972-73; dir. spl. programs Mohawk Valley Community Coll., Utica, N.Y., 1975-80; dean lifelong learning Niagara County Community Coll., Sanburn, N.Y., 1980—; cons. Pa. Dept. Higher Edn., 1985. Bd. dirs. Eastern Niagara ARC, Lockport, N.Y., 1991—, Lewiston Trail coun. Boy Scouts Am., Lockport, 1991—, N.Y. Dept. Social Svcs., Niagara Falls, 1991—. Recipient numerous grants. Mem. Niagara County Pvt. Industry Coun. (bd. dirs. 1991—), Lions (pres. Rock Island chpt. 1982-83). Roman Catholic. Home: 474D South St Lockport NY 14094-3946

MCGUIRK, JAMES GERARD, mental health services professional, psychologist; b. Wappinger Falls, N.Y., Apr. 27, 1955; s. Joseph and Rosemary (Milner) McG.; m. Mary Elizabeth McGuirk, June 19, 1976; 1 child, Sean. BA, SUNY, Albany, 1977, PhD in Psychology, 1985. Lic. psychologist, N.Y. Crisis counselor Middle Earth Crisis Ctr. SUNY, Albany, 1974-77; child care worker St. Catherines Ctr. for Children, 1977, houseparent, child care worker Hubbard House, 1977-78, house coord. Hubbard House, 1978-79; intern Astor Home for Children, Rhinebeck, N.Y., 1982-83, clin. coord., 1984-86, program dir., 1986—; pvt. practice Rhinebeck, 1986—; mem. Mental Health Adv. Com. for Children and Youth; mem. mental health com. N.Y. State Cath. Charities Dirs.; presenter to numerous orgns., 1981—. Author: For Want of a Child: A Psychologist and his Wife Explore the Emotional Effects and Challenges of Infertility, 1991. Mem. Coalition Residential Treatment Facilities (sec. 1991—, chair tng. com., mem. program com.). Roman Catholic. Home: 12 Platroon Pl Glenmont NY 12077 Office: Astor Home for Children 36 Mill St Rhinebeck NY 12572-1495

MCGUIRK, RONALD CHARLES, banker; b. Balt., Dec. 9, 1938; s. Charles F. and Grace E. (Delcher) McG.; m. Katherine Sauer, Oct. 1, 1960; children: Frank D., Ann E. Student St. John's Coll., Annapolis, Md., 1956-59. Sr. data processing officer 1st Nat. Bank, Balt., 1966-72, v.p. data processing, 1972-76, v.p. mktg., 1976-80, sr. v.p. mktg., 1980-90, sr. v.p. corp. plan, chief of staff to chief exec. officer, 1990—. Bd. dirs. North Arundel Hosp., Glen Burnie, Md., 1974—, Internet, Inc., 1990—, Annapolis Symphony, 1991-92; mem. adv. bd. Hist. Annapolis, 1982-85, dir., 1985-90; chmn. Annapolis Boundary Commn., 1983-84; mem. Anne Arundel County Coun., 1974-82, Anne Arundel County Libr. Bd., 1974-84; pres. Anne Arundel County Scholarship for Scholars/Bd. Edn., 1983-85, treas., 1985-88; mem. Anne Arundel County Charter Rev. Commn., 1986, Anne Arundel County Govt. Salary Commn., 1985, 89; chmn. Anne Arundel County Impact Fee Study Task Force, 1987; pres. Anne Arundel County YMCA, 1987-89, bd. dirs. 1982-87, 89-90; mem. Commn. for Ednl. Excellence, 1988-90; vice chmn. Ft. Meade Coordinating Coun., 1989-91, CAC on Sch. System Mgmt., 1992—; mem. Citizens Adv. Commn. Sch. System Mgmt., 1991—, Exec. Commn. Md. Bus.-Industry PACm 1991—, Anne Arundel County Charter and Orgn. Transition Group, 1991—; corp. ptnr. Sch. bus. and Mgmt. Morgan State U., 1991—. Mem. Ctr. Club. Democrat. Roman Catholic. Office: 1st Nat Bank Md PO Box 1596 Baltimore MD 21203

MCGURL, MAUREEN KATHLEEN, human resources executive; b. Peckville, Pa., Feb. 18, 1948; d. Michael F. and Stephany (Peko) McG. BA in Math., Marywood Coll., Scranton, Pa., 1969; grad. mgmt. program, Harvard U., 1975. Various positions Pathmark div. Supermarkets Gen. Corp., Woodbridge, N.J., 1973-79, v.p. human resources, 1979-83, corp. v.p. human resources and orgn. planning, 1983—; mem. adv. bd. food industry mgmt. prog. home study div. Cornell U., 1980-83; chmn. Human Resources Adv. Com., Food Mktg. Inst., 1988. Mem. Am. Soc. for Tng. and Devel, Human Resource Planning Soc., Harvard Bus. Sch. Club Greater N.Y. Democrat. Roman Catholic. Office: Supermarkets Gen Corp 301 Blair Rd Woodbridge NJ 07095

MCHALE, THOMAS JOSEPH, construction products executive; b. Pawtucket, R.I., Feb. 10, 1938; s. Francis Austin and Jane Mary (Meehan) McH.; m. Sheila Ann Sartini, June 3, 1961; children: Alan, Kim, Melissa. BS, U. Notre Dame, 1959. Staff Western Union Telegraph Co., N.Y.C., 1959-62; pres. PRM Concrete Corp., Pawtucket, 1962—. Active YMCA, Children's Mus. R.I. With USAR, 1960-66. Mem. Nat. Ready Mixed Concrete Assn. (bd. dirs., chmn. 1992), C. of C. (pres. 1986-87), R.I. Builders Assn. Republican. Home: 45 Tanglewood Dr Cumberland RI 02864-4127 Office: PRM Concrete Corp 775 School St Pawtucket RI 02860-5710

MCHUGH, BRIAN JOSEPH, priest; b. Lowell, Mass., Aug. 22, 1959; s. Robert Joseph and Jane Marie (Golen) McH. BA cum laude, U. Lowell, 1981; MDiv, St. John's Sem., Brighton, Mass., 1988. Ordained priest Roman Cath. Ch., 1988; cert. secondary history tchr., Mass. Jr. high sch. tchr. St. Charles Parish, Woburn, Mass., 1981-83; deacon Immaculate Conception Ch., Salem, Mass., 1987-88; priest St. Francis Xavier Ch., South Weymouth, Mass., 1988—. Mem. U. Lowell Honor Soc. in Edn., K.C. Democrat. Home and Office: 261 Pleasant St Weymouth MA 02190-2598

MCHUGH, DOREEN COLLINS, counselor, psychology educator; b. N.Y.C., Apr. 21, 1966; d. John James and Margaret (Weber) Collins; m. Robert James McHugh, Nov. 11, 1989. Student, St. Clare's Hall, Oxford, Eng., 1986; BA, Manhattanville Coll., 1988; MA, Anna Maria Coll., 1991. Teaching asst. Mamaroneck (N.Y.) Sch., 1987-88; counselor, dir. housing Becker Coll., Leicester, Mass., 1988-90; coord. counseling svcs. Becker Coll., Leicester and Worchester, Mass., 1990—; instr. psychology Becker Coll., Worcester, 1991—; tchr. Coll. Gate Program, Worcester, summer 1989; coord. alcohol/drug edn. Worcester Consortium for Higher Edn., 1988—. Mem. AACD, Am. Mental Health Counselors Assn., Am. Sch. Counselors Assn., Am. Coll. Counseling Assn., Mass. Mental Health Counselors Assn. Home: 250 Lebanon Hill Southbridge MA 01550 Office: Becker Coll 3 Paxton St Leicester MA 01550

MCHUGH, JAMES LENAHAN, JR., lawyer; b. Pitts., June 28, 1937; s. James Lenahan and Annette (Dalton) McH.; m. Amry-Ann Curto, Feb. 16, 1963 (div. 1988); children: Angela Dalton, Hillary Lenahan; m. Rosa Lamoreaux, Sept. 8, 1991. BA, Duquesne U., 1959; LLB, Villanova U., 1962. Bar: D.C. 1963. Law clk. U.S. Dist. Ct. (ea. dist.) Pa., Phila., 1962-63; law clk. to Assoc. Justice Tom C. Clark, U.S. Supreme Ct., Washington, 1963-64; assoc. Steptoe & Johnson, Washington, 1967-71, ptnr., 1971—; mem. bd. consultors Villanova Law Sch., Pa., 1973—; dir. Higher Achievement Program, Washington, 1984-87; coordinator Washington Lawyers' Project, Robert F. Kennedy Meml. Found., Washington, 1972-75. Editor-in-chief Villanova Law Rev., Vol. VII, 1961-62; chmn. editorial adv. bd. Fed. Communications Law Jour., 1981-84. Bd. dirs. Columbia Hosp. for Women Found., Washington, 1985—, Children's Radio Theatre, Washington, 1983-86; chmn. exec. giving Archbishop's Appeal, Archdiocese of Washington, 1982-84; bd. visitors Ctr. fir Study of Orgns. and Mgmt., U. Md. Univ. Coll., 1987—; chmn. bd. dirs. Human Rsch. Orgn., Inc., 1978—, chmn., 1991—; mem. bd. advisors Inst. for Conflict Analysis and Resolution, George Mason U. Mem. ABA, D.C. Bar Assn., Choral Arts Soc. Washington, Order of Coif. Home: 4112 Fessenden St NW Washington DC 20016-4227 Office: 1330 Connecticut Ave NW Washington DC 20036-1704

MCHUGH, JAMES T., bishop; b. Orange, N.J., Jan. 3, 1932. Educated at Seton Hall Univ., Immaculate Conception Sem. (Darlington, N.J.), Fordham Univ., Catholic Univ., Angelicum (Rome). Ordained priest, 1957; consecrated bishop, 1988. Asst. dir. Family Life Div., U.S. Cath. Conf., 1965-67, dir., 1967-75; dir. Office for Pro-Life Activities, Nat. Conf. Cath. Bishops, 1972-78; titular bishop Morosbisdo, 1987-89; aux. bishop Newark, 1987-89; bishop Diocese of Camden, N.J., 1989—. Home: Marywood PO Box 577 Blackwood NJ 08012 Office: Camden Diocesan Ctr PO Box 709 Camden NJ 08101-0709*

MCHUGH, JOHN MICHAEL, state senator; b. Watertown, N.Y., Sept. 29, 1948; s. Donald and Jane (O'Neill) McH. BA in Polit. Sci., Syracuse U., 1970; MPA, Nelson A. Rockefeller Grad. Sch. Pub. Affairs, 1977. Confidential asst. Watertown City Mgrs. Office, 1971-76; chief of research, liaison with local govts. Office of N.Y. State Senator, 1976-84; U.S. senator from N.Y., 1984—; chmn. Joint Legis. Commn. on Dairy Industry Devel., Albany, N.Y., 1987—. Mem. Legis. Commn. on Modernization of the Tax Code, Nat. Conf. State Legis., Commerce & Econ. Devel. Com., Commerce, Labor and Regulation Com. of the State Fed. Assembly, Coun. State Govt. Eastern Regional Conf. Com. on Fiscal Affairs. Recipient 40 Outstanding Alumni awards Syracuse U., Individual Achievement award N.Y. State Dept. Econ. Devel.; named to Hon. First Citizen, City of Watertown, 1976. Mem. Legis. on State Legislators (nat. conf. state legislators), Nat. Conf. State Legislators (vice chmn. agrl. and internat. trade com. State-Fed. Assembley), Am. Soc. Young Polit. Leaders. Republican. Roman Catholic. Office: NY State Senate 814 Legislative Office Bldg Albany NY 12247

MCHUGH, MATTHEW F., congressman; b. Phila., Dec. 6, 1938; s. Peter F. and Margaret M. (Whalen) McH.; m. Eileen Alanna Higgins, 1963; children: Alanna, Kelli, Meg. B.S., Mt. St. Mary's Coll., 1960; J.D., Villanova U., 1963. Bar: N.Y. 1964. Practiced N.Y.C.; pros. atty. City of Ithaca, N.Y., 1968; dist. atty. Tompkins County, N.Y., 1969-72; mem. 94th-98th Congresses from 27th N.Y. Dist., 98th-102nd Congresses from 28th N.Y. Dist. Active numerous civic orgns. Mem. Am., N.Y. State, Tompkins County bar assns. Democrat. Office: 2335 House Office Bldg Washington DC 20515

MCHUGH, ROBERT ERNEST (BOB MCHUGH), pianist, composer; b. Kearny, N.J., July 20, 1946; s. Edward William and Marie (Spinello) McH.; m. Jane Regina Belli, June 27, 1970; children: Erik Bernard, Meredith Jane. BA, Jersey City State Coll., 1971. Cert. music tchr. N.J. Keyboardist The Duprees, N.Y.C., 1978; pianist, keyboardist Perception Records, N.Y.C., 1979; keyboardist The Chatterband, N.Y. and, N.J., 1980-84; pianist Billy Battison Quartet, Long Branch, N.J., 1985; music dir. Bob McHugh Trio Pratos, Carlstadt, N.J., 1986-91; composer Frank Chacksfield, Eros BBC, London, 1989-91; rec. artist Outstanding Records, Huntington Beach, Calif., 1991—; lectr. in field; music tchr. gifted and talented Fairview (N.J.) Schs., 1986-91; pres. Jarob Pub., Pompton Plains, N.J., 1989—. Composer, performer (jazz composition) Lincoln Center, 1975, (mus. composition) Am. Song Festival, 1978 (Cash prize), WNBC Hometown Album, 1979. Teacher summer music program Christ the King Ch., Jersey City; performer Jazz Mass, North Jersey and N.Y. Chs.; performer, tchr. Pequannock (N.J.) Twp. Sch. Music Programs. Mem. ASCAP, NEA, Am. Fedn. Musicians, N.J. Edn. Assn. Home: 21 Voorhis Pl Pompton Plains NJ 07444-1839

MCILHONE, JOHN THOMAS, educational administrator; b. Montreal, Que., Can., Jan. 26, 1911; s. Robert Emmett and Ellen Eva (O'Rourke) McI.; B.A., Loyola Coll., Montreal, 1933; M.A., U. Montreal, 1939, B.Ed., 1940, Ph.D., 1942; m. Dorothy Agnes Quinn, June 20, 1942; children—Anne Marie (Mrs. R. Marc Huberdeau), Quinn. Prof. edn. St. Joseph's Coll., Montreal, 1939-40, 45-48; dir. English schs. Montreal Cath. Sch. Bd., 1948-69, dep. dir. gen., 1967-73; dir. gen. Mt. St. Patrick Corp., Montreal, 1973—. Ednl. cons. Montreal Cath. Sch. Commn., 1973—; mem. Royal Commn. Enquiry into Edn., 1961-66. Active charity campaigns; trustee Loyola Coll., Concordia U.; bd. dirs. Canadian Cath. Trustees; bd. dirs. Mt. St. Patrick Inc., pres., 1985. Served to comdr. RCAF, 1940-45. Decorated comdr. Cross of Merit, Order of Malta. Recipient Coronation medal Govt. Can., 1952, Centennial medal, 1967; named comdr. Order of Sch. Merit, Que. Province, 1956. Mem. Can. (life), Nat. Cath. edn. assns., Can. Coll. Tchrs., Phi Delta Kappa. Club: Mount Stephen (Montreal). Contbr. articles to profl. jours. Home: 1440 Laird Blvd, Town of Mount Royal, PQ Canada H3P 2T4

MCILRAITH, MARY ANN F., human resources firm executive, consultant; b. Bklyn., Mar. 8, 1957; d. David John and Josephine McClellan; m. John Patrick McIlraith, Dec. 13, 1975; 1 child, Dawn Michelle. BA, Century U., 1980. Programmer-analyst project mgr. Occidental Petider, Houston, 1977-81; sr. devel. mgr. In Sci-Info. Sci. Inc., Montvale, N.J., 1981-84; exec. tech. cons. Cullinet Software, Washington, 1984-89; pres. Maximum Potential, Rockville, Md., 1989—; bd. advs. Maxwell MacMillan, 1990—. Bd. advs. Bldg. Drug-Free Community, Rockville, Md., 1989-90, Office Econ. and Devel., 1992; v.p. Women Bus. Owners, Wash Metro, Md., 1991—. Mem. Am. Soc. Tng. Devel. (co-chmn. 1991—), Human Resource Systems Profls. Roman Catholic. Office: Maximum Potential 4216 Flower Valley Dr Rockville MD 20853-1808

MCILRATH, THOMAS JAMES, physicist, educator; b. Dowagiac, Mich., May 10, 1938; s. William Fredrick and Leora (Lewis) M.; m. Valerie Hoy, June 30, 1962; children: Christine, Laura. BS, Mich. State U., 1960; PhD, Princeton, 1966. Rsch. fellow Harvard Coll. Obs., Cambridge, Mass., 1967-70; rsch. assoc. and lectr. Harvard U., Cambridge, 1970-73; assoc. prof. U. Md., College Park, 1973-81, prof. physics, 1981—; physicist Nat. Inst. Standards and Tech., Gaithersburg, Md., 1974—; cons. Princeton (N.J.) Plasma Physics Lab., 1984—, AT&T Bell Labs., Murray Hill, N.J., 1985—. Editor: Laser Techniques for Extreme UV Spectroscopy, 1982; contbr. over 10 articles to books; contbr. over 70 articles to profl. jours. Recipient silver medal Dept. Commerce, 1980, Indsl. Rsch. 100 award Indsl. Rsch mag., 1981. Fellow Am. Phys. Soc., Optical Soc. Am.; mem. Sigma Xi. Office: U Md Inst Phys Sci & Tech College Park MD 20742

MCILVAINE, ALICE NICOLSON, retired state department official, civic worker; b. Washington, Feb. 19, 1924; d. Llewelyn Dudley and Edith (Vance) Nicolson; m. Robinson McIlvaine, Sept. 18, 1961; children: Ian, Katherine. AB, Sweet Briar Coll., 1945. Office dir. Brit. Airways, Washington, 1945-49; with advt. dept. Sunset Mag., San Francisco, 1949-50; adminstrv. asst. Dept. State, Washington, Germany and Eng., 1951-61; wife of

ambassador to Africa Dept. State, Benin, Guinea, Kenya, 1961-75. Bd. dirs. Thrift Shop, Columbia Hosp. Women's Bd.; active McLean fgn. policy discussion group; docent Octagon House, Washington, 1987—. Mem. Chevy Chase Club (Md.).

MC ILVEEN, WALTER, mechanical engineer; b. Belfast, Ireland, Aug. 12, 1927; s. Walter and Amelia (Thompson) McI.; came to U.S., 1958, naturalized, 1963; M.E., Queens U., Belfast, 1948; H.V.A.C., Borough Polytechnic, London, 1951; m. Margaret Teresa Ruane, Apr. 17, 1949; children: Walter, Adrian, Peter, Anita, Alan. Mech. engr. Davidson & Co., Belfast, 1943-48; sr. contract engr. Keith Blackman Ltd., London, 1948-58; mech. engr. Fred S. Dubin Assos., Hartford, Conn., 1959-64; chief mech. engr. Koton & Donovan, West Hartfor, Conn., 1964-66; prin., engr. Walter McIlveen Assos., Avon, Conn., 1966—. Mem. IEEE, ASME, ASHRAE, Illuminating Engring. Soc., Hartford Engring. Club, Conn. Engrs. in Pvt. Practice. Mem. Ch. of Ireland. Home: 3 Valley View Dr Weatogue CT 06089-9714 Office: 195 W Main St Avon CT 06001

MCILWAIN, JOHN KNOX, lawyer; b. N.Y.C., Nov. 9, 1943; s. Knox and Emily Edey (Woods) McI.; m. Wende Lillian Sheffield, Oct. 28, 1972; 1 child, Knox. AB, Princeton U., 1966; JD, NYU, 1970. Bar: N.Y. 1970, D.C. 1979. Assoc. Dewey, Ballantine, Bushby, Palmer & Wood, N.Y.C., 1970-73; dep. dir. Maine State Housing Authority, Augusta, 1976-77; exec. asst. to asst. sec. for housing Fed. Housing Commn., HUD, Washington, 1977-79; ptnr. Cohen & Uretz, Washington, 1979-84; sr. v.p. Nordheimer Bros. Co., Arlington, Va., 1984-85; ptnr. Powell, Goldstein, Frazer & Murphy, Washington, 1985—, mng. ptnr. Washington Office, 1988-92. Bd. dirs. Ctr. for Housing Policy, 1981—; Nat. Housing Conf., Washington, 1980-90, treas., 1985-90, vice chmn., 1990—; vestryman St. Mark's Episcopal Ch., Washington, 1986-91; bd. dirs., v.p. Nat. Housing and Rehab. Assn., Washington, 1988—; bd. dirs., mem. exec. com. Washington Area Housing Partnership, 1991—, Coun. for Ct. Excellence in Govt., 1989—. Mem. ABA, D.C. Bar Assn. (steering com. real estate sect. 1980-82), Seawanaka Corinthian Yacht Club (Oyster Bay, N.Y.). Democrat. Home: 3605 Underwood St Bethesda MD 20815-4107 Office: Powell Goldstein Fraser & Murphy 1001 Pennsylvania Ave NW Washington DC 20004-2505

MCINDOE, DARRELL BRUCE, SR., communications executive; b. San Antonio, Mar. 28, 1957; s. Darrell Winfred and Carole Jean (McClain) McI.; m. Deborah Louise Clarkson, Aug. 4, 1982; children: Darrell Bruce Jr., Garrett Adam. BS in Physics, Allegheny Coll., 1979; MS in Computer Sci., Johns Hopkins U., 1984. Mem. tech. staff Computer Scis. Corp., Silver Spring, Md., 1979-82; pres. CSSI, Columbia, Md., 1982—. Mem. IEEE, Assn. Computing Machinery, Wash. Tech.'s Fast 50 Club, Assn. Old Crows. Office: CSSI 10260 Old Columbia Rd Columbia MD 21046

MCINNES, HAROLD A., manufacturing company executive; b. Groton, Conn., 1927. B.S.M.E., MIT, 1949. With Delco Appliance div. Gen. Motors Corp., 1949-55, Tracerlab, Inc., 1955-60, Reed Rolled Thread Die Co., 1960-62, Dresser Industries, Inc., 1962-65, AMP, Inc., Harrisburg, Pa., 1965—; mfg. mgr. packaging components AMP, Inc., 1966-70, mgr. automach div., 1970-73, group dir. gen. products, 1973-78, v.p. mfg. resources planning, 1978-79, corp. v.p. engring. and tech. resources, 1979-81, pres., 1981-86, vice chmn., bd. dirs., 1986-90, chmn., chief exec. officer, 1990—; bd. dirs. PPG Industries, Pitts. Bd. dirs. U.S. Coun. on Competitiveness, Conf. Bd. Mem. Nat. Assn. Mfrs., Am. Electronics Assn., Elec. Mfrs. Club. Office: AMP Inc 470 Friendship Rd Harrisburg PA 17111-1203

MCINNIS, JAMES MILTON, publishing company executive; b. Repton, Ala., Jan. 8, 1934; s. Clarence W. and Ada Mae (Owens) McI.; m. Joan Horton, May 17, 1953; children: Deborah Lynn, Cynthia Jane, Daniel Paul, Brenda Joyce. BA, Am. U., 1959, LLB, 1962, JD, 1963. Gen. agt., ins. broker, 1958-61; staff asst. U.S. Senate, Washington, 1961-62; with FBI, 1962-63; jr. atty. So. Ry. System, Washington, 1964-65; mgmt. exec. Public Utilities Reports, Arlington, Va., 1965—, advt. sales mgr., 1965-68, asst. gen. mgr., asst. v.p., 1968-69, v.p., asst. sec., treas., 1970-72, v.p. adminstrn., 1972-76, v.p. ops., 1976-79, exec. v.p., gen. mgr., 1980-81, pres., chief exec. officer, 1981—; mem. Washington legal com. Am. Bus. Press, Washington; substitute instr. U. Tubingen (Germany), 1955; past chmn. Assn. Paid Circulation Publs. Officer, Arlington County (Va.) PTA, 1973-75; mem. adv. com. Arlington County Sch. Bd., 1973-75; bd. deacons First Bapt. Ch., Washington, 1969—; bd. dirs. Arlington Heart Assn. Served with U.S. Army, 1953-55. Mem. Delta Theta Phi. Republican. Clubs: Nat. Potomac Yacht (vice commodore), Arlington Forest, Admirals. Contbr. articles to Life Ins. Salesman mag.; top ins. salesman in U.S., Mut. and United of Omaha Life Ins. Co., 1961.

MCINNIS, JUDY BREDESON, foreign language educator; b. Roseau, Minn., Sept. 22, 1943; d. Ervin Oliver and Elsie Mae (McFarlane) Bredeson; m. Clay W. McInnis, July 15, 1967; children: Meghan Emily, Clay W., Ian O. BS, Bemidji (Minn.) State U., 1964; PhD, U. N.C., 1974. Instr. U. Del., Newark, 1971-74, asst. prof., 1975-82, assoc. prof., 1982—. NEH fellow, 1979; AAUW scholar, 1963-64, Bemidji State U. scholar, 1961, 62, NDEA scholar, 1966-69. Mem. AAUP, MLA, Mid-Atlantic Coun. on Latin Am., Am. Assn. Tchrs. Spanish and Portuguese (nat. dir. Spanish Exams 1985-91). Office: U Del Dept Fgn Langs Newark DE 19716

MCINTOSH, JAMES BOYD, JR., insurance company executive; b. Boston, Nov. 9, 1950; s. James Boyd Sr. and Frances (Glading) McI.; m. Louise Lindenberg Kent, May 26, 1973; children: Elena Lindenberg, Kathryn Boyd, Margaret Kent. AB, Lafayette Coll., 1973; MBA, Capital U., 1980. From claims supr. to rsch. analyst Motorists Ins. Co., Columbus, Ohio, 1974-80; sr. fin. analyst Republic Steel Svcs. Group, Inc., Cleve., 1980-82; cons., adminstrv. asst. Bankers and Shippers Ins. Co. of N.Y., Burlington, N.C., 1982-84; asst. v.p. Charter Security Life Ins. Co., Jacksonville, Fla., 1984-85, Metlife Security Life Ins. Co., N.Y.C., 1985-89; dir. quality mgmt. Met. Life Ins. Co., N.Y.C., 1989—. Mem. govtl. affairs com. N.J. Assn. for Retarded citizens, East Brunswick, 1988-91; pers. com. mem. U.S. Assn. for Retarded Citizens, Arlington, Tex., 1988—; pres./chmn. bd. trustees Plan/NJ, Middlesex, chmn. pers. com., chmn. planning com. Mem. Internat. Svc. Quality Assn. (mem. planning com.), Am. Soc. Quality Control. Republican. Episcopalian. Home: 109 Beechwood Rd Summit NJ 07901-2104 Office: Met Life Ins Co 72 Eagle Rock Ave East Hanover NJ 07936

MCINTYRE, CARL HENRY, JR., lawyer; b. Washington, May 9, 1958; s. Carl Henry and Joyce Lee (Booker) McI. BA cum laude, Am. U., 1980; JD, Howard U., 1984. Bar: Pa. 1985, U.S. Ct. Appeals (D.C. cir.) 1986, U.S. Ct. Appeals (9th cir.) 1987, U.S. Ct. Appeals (5th cir.) 1988, U.S. Ct. Appeals (10th cir.) 1989, U.S. Ct. Appeals (7th, 1st and 3 cirs.) 1991, U.S. Supreme Ct. 1990, D.C. 1991. Motions atty. Ct. Appeals (D.C.), 1984-85; atty., advisor U.S. Labor Dept., Washington, 1985-86; clk. to presiding justice Ct. Appeals (D.C.), 1986-87; trial atty. civil div. U.S. Dept. Justice, Washington, 1987—; voting del. Jud. Conf. D.C., 1988-92; profl. musician trumpet, flugelhorn; toured with Gladys Knight and the Pips; performed with Temptations, Four Tops, Dells, Manhattans, O'Jays, Thad Jones and Mel Lewis Big Band; prin. trumpet Internat. Festival Orch., Internat. Festival of Youth Orch., Aberdeen, Scotland, Lond, 1974. Assoc. editor Howard Law Jour., 1983-84. Active Friends of the Kennedy Ctr., Washington, 1988—, Washington Area Tennis Patrons Found., 1988-90; bd. dirs. Takoma Park Symphony Orch., St. Augustine Cath. Ch. Instrumental Music Program. D.C. Youth Orch. Trumpet scholar, 1974; recipient Civil Div. Meritorious award U.S. Dept. Justice, 1989, Spl. Achievement award, 1990, 91. Mem. ABA, Nat. Bar Assn., Internat. Platform Assn. Democrat. Roman Catholic. Home: 3900 16th St NW Apt 631 Washington DC 20011-8326

MCINTYRE, JAMES PHILIP, academic administrator; b. Malden, Mass., Feb. 27, 1934; s. Peter Philip and Ann Francis (Halloran) McI.; m. Monica Flatley, Nov. 24, 1962; children: Mary, Peter, James, Ann, Karalyn, David. BA, Boston Coll., 1957, MEd, 1961, EdD, 1967. Asst. dir. admissions and fin. aid Boston Coll., Chestnut Hill, Mass., 1959-66; exec. asst. v.p. for student affairs Boston Coll., Chestnut Hill, 1966-68, v.p. for student affairs, 1968-76, v.p. for univ. rels., 1976-86, sr. v.p., 1986—; instl. del. Coll. Entrance Examination Bd. and Coll. Scholarship Svc., 1966—. Contbr. articles to profl. jours. Chair feasibility com. Girls'Cath. High Sch., Malden, Mass., 1985; mem. fin. com. Immaculate Conception Parish, Malden, 1986—; mem. Clover Club, Boston, 1989—. With U.S. Army, 1957-59. Mem. Am. Assn. Higher Edn., Am. Assn. Univ. Adminstrs. (bd. dirs. 1977-84, selection and rev. com., v.p. 1980-81), Am. Coll. Pers. Assn., Coun. Student Pers. Assn. (rep. Am. Jesuit Colls. and Univs., commn. on current and developing issues in student life, 1969, ethics commn. 1969—), Nat. Assn. Coll. Aux. Svcs. (editorial bd. 1973—), Nat. Assn. Student Pers. Adminstrs. (local arrangement co-chmn. for nat. conv. 1969-70, editorial bd. 1972-75), Nat. Assn. Jesuit Student Pers. Adminstrs., others. Roman Catholic. Office: Boston Coll 78 College Rd Chestnut Hill MA 02167-3837

MCINTYRE, JAMES RUSSEL, JR., infosystems specialist; b. Detroit, Apr. 1, 1941; s. James R. and Irene McI.; m. Betsy Davis, June 22, 1963; children: David W., Carol L. BSEE, U. Mich., 1967; MBA, Fla. Inst. Tech., 1982. Electronics engr. USN, 1976-84; pres. Info. & Edn. Svcs., Co., Hudson, N.H., 1985—; software, svcs., hardware and product mktg. DEC, Merrimack, N.H., 1987—. Contbr. articles to profl. jours. Office: Info & Edn Svcs Co 24 Brook Dr Hudson NH 03051-5102

MCINTYRE, KAYE, non-profit organization executive, consultant; b. Hartford, Conn., Oct. 13, 1950; d. Richard Arthur and Helen Marie (von Richter) Tillotson; m. Daniel Brian McIntyre, Feb. 21, 1969 (div. Dec. 1979). AS in Human Svcs., N.W. Conn. Community Coll., 1983; BSBA, Charter Oak Coll., 1985; MA in Liberal Studies, Wesleyan U., 1990. Counselor McCall House, Torrington, Conn., 1979-80; freelance photographer, 1980—; exec. dir. Warner Theatre, Torrington, 1982-84, Elderly Health Screening Svc., Inc., Waterbury, Conn., 1982—; cons. in field. Asst. coord. Conn. Earth Action Group, Litchfield, 1971; regional coord. Conn. Citizens Action Group, Litchfield County, Conn., 1971-72; pres. N.W. Conn. Assn. for the Arts, Inc., Torrington, 1981-84; bd. dirs. Torrington Trust for Hist. Preservation, Inc., 1981-85; 6th dist. coord. Office of Protection and Advocacy for the Handicapped and Developmentally Disabled, Litchfield County, 1982; chairperson adult programming com. YWCA of Waterbury, 1985-87; v.p. Thomaston Opera House Found., 1985-88. Recipient citation Conn. Soc. Prevention of Blindness, 1984, Conn. Gen. Assembly, 1984, 86, 92, Project Health award U.S. Dept. HHS Adminstrn. Aging, 1986, Secs. Excellence award U.S. Dept. HHS Community Health Promotion Program, 1986. Mem. NAFE, AAAS, Am. League Hist. Theatres, N.Y. Acad. Scis., Community Assocs. of Conn., Inc. (bd. dirs.), Am. Pub. Health Assn., Nat. Assn. Fundraising Execs., Am. Soc. on Aging, Gerontological Soc. Am., Nat. Coun. on Aging, N.Y. Acad. Scis., Conn. Assn. Hist. Theatres (pres. 1984—), Internat. Platform Assn., Nat. Trust for Hist. Preservation, Mensa (Litchfield County coord. 1979-84). Republican. Taoist. Office: Elderly Health Screening Svc Inc 24 Central Ave Waterbury CT 06702-1205

MCKAY, DONALD ARTHUR, mechanical contractor; b. Providence, June 10, 1931; s. Benjamin Arthur and Florence (Heeney) McK.; m. Janette Capellaro, Dec. 30, 1978; children by previous marriage: Susan Kelly, Barbara Albury, Laura Lower, Douglas. AB, Harvard U., 1952. Registered profl. engr., Mass. Sales engr. C.P. Blouin, Cambridge, Mass., 1955-60; contract mgr. to v.p. Limbach Co., Boston, 1960-68; exec. v.p. Tougher Heating & Plumbing Co., Albany, N.Y., 1968-74; chmn., chief exec. officer Tougher Industries, Albany, 1986—, pres., 1974-86; v.p. Spunduct Inc. Pres. Fifty Group of Columbia County, 1972-74; mem. corp. gifts com. Albany Med. Ctr., 1978-84; chmn. 25th reunion fund raising com. of upstate N.Y., Harvard Class '52; mem. curriculum adv. bd. Hudson Valley Community Coll.; trustee Coll. St. Rose; bd. dirs. Empire State Aeroscis. Mus., Ctr. for Econ. Growth, Albany Meml. Hosp. (chmn. 1988-91). With USN, 1951-54; mem. U. Albany Found. Mem. ASHRAE, NSPE, Am. Soc. Sanitary Engrs., Am. Soc. Plumbing Engrs., Mech. Contractors Assn. Am. (pres. capital dist. 1981-82, pres.-elect 1988, pres. 1989-90), Mech. Contractors Assn. N.Y. State (v.p. 1981-82, pres. 1981-82), Subcontrators Assn. N.Y. (bd. dirs.), Aircraft Owners and Pilots Assn., Exptl. Aircraft Assn., U.S. C. of C. (small bus. coun.), Albany-Colonie C. of C. (bd. dirs.). Congregationalist. Clubs: Harvard (pres. N.E. N.Y. chpt. 1987-88), Pvt. Industry Coun., Ft. Orange (Albany), Masons (Dorchester, Mass.), Wolferts Roost Country, Schuyler Meadows. Home: 6 Park Ridge Albany NY 12204-2233 Office: Tougher Industries PO Box 4067 175 Broadway Albany NY 12204-0067

MCKAY, JACK ALEXANDER, electronics engineer; b. Alhambra, Calif., Apr. 3, 1942; s. Gordon Alexander and Helen Leona (Lappin) McK.; m. Emily Gantz, July 3, 1965. BS in Physics, Stanford U., 1964, MSEE, 1967; MS in Physics, Carnegie-Mellon U., 1969, PhD in Physics, 1974. Rsch. physicist Naval Rsch. Lab., Washington, 1974-84; rsch. scientist Phys. Scis. Inc., Alexandria, Va., 1984-91; scientist Rsch. Support Instruments, Cockeysville, Md., 1991—. Home: 3200 19th St NW Washington DC 20010-1006 Office: Rsch Support Instruments 10610 Beaver Dam Rd Cockeysville Hunt Valley MD 21030-2288

MCKAY, JAMES ROBERT, psychology educator, researcher; b. Coronado, Calif., June 9, 1955; s. George Robert and Bobbie (Squires) McK.; m. Rachel Kabasakalian, Apr. 21, 1990. BA, Loyola U., 1983; MA, Harvard U., 1986, PhD, 1987. Lic. psychologist, Mass., Pa. Intern in clin. psychology Harvard U./McLean Hosp., Belmont, Mass., 1987-88; postdoctoral fellow Brown U., Providence, 1988-90; investigator, asst. prof. Addiction Rsch. Ctr. dept. psychiatry U. Pa., Phila., 1990—; cons. dept. epidemiology Harvard U., Boston, 1990. Contbr. articles to profl. jours. G & C Naumberg Fund scholar, 1986. Mem. APA, Assn. for Advancement of Behavior Therapy. Office: U Pa Addiction Rsch Ctr 3900 Chestnut St Philadelphia PA 19104-3109

MCKAY, STEVEN FRANK, actuary; b. Balt., Sept. 10, 1950; s. Ellsworth F. and Ruth E. (Strong) McK.; m. Mary Elizabeth Sabine, May 30, 1981; children: Steven M., Christine E. BS in Applied Math., MIT, 1972; MBA in Econs., Loyola Coll., Balt., 1986. Actuary Social Security Adminstrn., Balt., 1973-79, supervisory actuary, 1979—. Author: Long-Range Estimates for Old-Age, Survivors, and Disability Insurance, 1980, Short-Range Actuarial Projections for the Old-Age, Survivors, and Disability Insurance Program, 1988. Fellow Soc. Actuaries; mem. Nat. Acad. Social Ins., Internat. Actuarial Assn. Office: Social Security Adminstrn 6401 Security Blvd Baltimore MD 21235

MCKEE, CLYDE DAVID, JR., political science educator; b. Brimingham, Ala., Dec. 4, 1929; s. Clyde D. and Hattie Mae (Parker) McK.; m. Mary Gwudz, Dec. 26, 1953; children: Roxane, Valerie, Clyde D., Deanne, Cornelius, Ralph. BA, Wesleyan U., 1952, MAT, 1959; postgrad., U. Chgo., 1952-53, Harvard U., 1959; MA/PhD, U. Conn., 1967. Pub. sch. tchr., 1959-61; with Univ. of Conn. Fgn. Adminstr.'s Tng. Prog., 1964-65; polit. sci. educator Trinity Coll., Hartford, Conn., 1965—; rsch. prof. Univ. East Anglia, Norwich, Eng., 1986; vis. prof. Trinity Rome Campus, Italy, 1986; guest lectr. New Eng. Mcpl. Clk.'s Inst., 1973—, various colls. Author: New England Political Parties, 1983, Perspectives of a State Legislature, The Connecticut General Assembly, 1978, 2nd edit. 1980; contbr. articles to profl. jours. Active Dem. party all levels, pres. Young Dems., 1963, mem. town com. 1964-67, mem. Jimmy Carter's Conn. Campaign com. 1975-76. With USAF, 1953-57. Recipient Disting. Svc. awards, Conn. Gen. Assembly, 1976, 79, 80, Conn.'s Disting. Adminstr. award/The Karl Bosworth Meml. award 1978, Outstanding Citizen award New Era newspaper, 1961; Pub. Adminstrn. fellow, Washington, 1971-72. Mem. Am. Soc. Pub. Adminstrn. (founder Conn. chpt. 1967, pres. 1968-69, coun. mem. 1968-76), Am. Polit. Sci. Assn. (Leonard D. White award 1967), New Eng. Polit. Sci. Assn. (pres. 1985-86, exec. coun. 1983-89, other offices), AAUP (mem. legis. com. 1978). Home: 68 Crescent St Hartford CT 06106-3119 Office: Trinity Coll Polit Sci Dept Summit St Hartford CT 06106-3149

MCKEE, CRAIG LLOYD, lawyer; b. Royal Oak, Mich., Nov. 4, 1960; s. Lloyd Edwin and Helen Elizabeth (Vivian) McK. Student, London Sch. Econs., 1980-81; BA, Kalamazoo Coll., 1982; MA in Econs., U. Mich., 1986, JD, 1986. Bar: Mich. 1986. Intern economist Data Resources, Inc., Lexington, Mass., 1981; teaching asst. dept. econs. U. Mich., Ann Arbor, 1985; assoc. Miller, Canfield, Paddock & Stone, Detroit, 1986-88; atty. office of gen. counsel U.S. Internat. Trade Commn., Washington, 1988-91; assoc. O'Melveny & Myers, Washington, 1991—. Sponsoring mem. Phillips Gallery of Art, Washington, 1988-91; mem. World Affairs Coun., Washington, 1988-91, Am. Friends of London Sch. Econs., McLean, Va., 1983-91. Wilson scholar Kalamazoo Coll., 1981. Mem. ABA, Am. Econ. Assn., Mich. State Bar Assn., Fed. Bar Assn. Presbyterian. Home: 1600 N Oak St Apt 1731 Arlington VA 22209-2770 Office: 555 13th St NW Washington DC 20004

MCKEE, DANIEL J., police officer; b. Yonkers, N.Y., Sept. 22, 1950; s. James Russell and Anne (Thornton) McK.; m. Elizabeth Helena Firlus, May 10, 1975 (div. Aug. 1990); children: Melissa, Daniel, Kristyna. AAS, Ocean County Coll., Toms River, N.J., 1971; BA, Richard Stockton State U., 1973. Police officer Trenton (N.J.) Police Div., 1973-80, sgt., comdr. communications dept., 1980-84, lt., comdr. crime scene investigations unit, 1984-87, detective lt., comdr. homicide unit, 1987-90, comdr. spl. and tech. sect., 1990—. Named Employee of Yr. City of Trenton, 1988. Home: 25 Plymouth St Trenton NJ 08638 Office: Trenton Police Div 225 N Clinton Ave Trenton NJ 08609

MCKEE, FRANCIS JOHN, association executive, lawyer; b. Bklyn., Aug. 31, 1943; s. Francis Joseph and Catherine (Giles) McK.; m. Antoinette Mary Sancis; children: Lisa Ann, Francis Dominic, Michael Christopher, Thomas Joseph. AB, Stonehill Coll., 1965; JD, St. John's U., 1970. Bar: N.Y. 1971. Assoc. Samuel Weinberg, Esquire, Bklyn., 1970-71, Finch & Finch, Esquire, Long Island City, N.Y., 1971-72; staff atty. Med. Soc. of State of N.Y., Lake Success, N.Y., 1972-77; prin. Francis J. McKee Assocs., Clinton, N.Y., 1984—; exec. dir. Suffolk Physicians Rev. Orgn., East Islip, N.Y., 1977-81, N.Y. State Soc. Surgeons, Inc., Clinton, N.Y., 1981—, N.Y. State Soc. Orthopaedic Surgeons, Inc., Clinton, 1981—, Upstate N.Y. chpt. ACS, Inc., Clinton, 1981—, N.Y. State Ophthalmol. Soc., 1984—, N.Y. State Soc. Obstetricians and Gynecologists, 1985—, Orthopac of N.Y., 1986—, Nat. Com. for the Preservation Orthopaedic Practice, Clinton, 1989—. With U.S. Army, 1966-68. Mem. Oneida County Bar Assn., N.Y. State Bar Assn., Am. Soc. Assn. Execs., Am. Assn. Med. Soc. Execs., Engine Eleven Club, Nightstick Club (Utica), Skenandoa Club (Clinton). Republican. Roman Catholic. Home: 19 Mulberry St Clinton NY 13323-1532 Office: 40 Chenango Ave Box 308 Clinton NY 13323-0308

MCKEE, LAURIS ANNETTE, anthropology educator; b. Crosbyton, Tex., Feb. 21, 1931; d. Robert McBride and Rebecca Virginia (Williams) McK.; m. Joseph Beyda, Sept. 15, 1950 (div. 1972); children: Kent, David, Katherine, Adam; m. Robert Laurence Moore, July 26, 1987. BA with honors, George Washington U., 1972; MA, Cornell U., 1975, PhD, 1980. Lectr. Cornell U., Ithaca, N.Y., 1980-81, rsch. assoc., 1982-85; asst. prof. Franklin & Marshall Coll., Lancaster, Pa., 1985-89, assoc. prof., 1990—; adj. asst. prof. SUNY Cortland, Ithaca, 1982-85. Contbg. editor: Nuevas Investigaciones Antropologicas, Ecuatorianas, 1988; editor jour. Med. Anthropology; contbg. editor jour. in field; direction and script five video documentaries, 1984-86. Recipient pre-doctoral fellowship NIMH, Ecuador, 1975-78, postdoctoral rsch. grantee NSF, 1982-85, Fulbright Found., 1982-83, film-making grant Nat. Archeol. Mus. of Ecuador, Quito, 1984. Fellow Am. Anthrop. Assn.; mem. Soc. for Cross-Cultural Rsch. (rep. for anthropology 1988-91), Soc. for Psychol. Anthropology, Soc. for Visual Anthropology (Film award for Excellence 1988), Soc. Med. Anthropology, Soc. for Latin Am. Anthropology. Democrat. Home: 150 N Sunset Dr Ithaca NY 14850-1460 Office: Dept Anthropology Franklin & Marshall Coll PO Box 3003 Lancaster PA 17604-3003

MCKEE, MARGARET JEAN, federal agency executive; b. New Haven, June 20, 1929; d. Waldo McCutcheon and Elizabeth (Thayer) McKee; A.B., Vassar Coll., 1951. Staff asst. United Rep. Fin. Com., N.Y.C., 1952; staff asst. N.Y. Rep. State Com., N.Y.C., 1953-55; staff asst. Crusade for Freedom (name later changed to Radio Free Europe Fund), N.Y.C., 1955-57; researcher Stricker & Henning Research Assocs., Inc., N.Y.C., 1957-59; exec. sec. New Yorkers for Nixon (name later changed to N.Y. State Ind. Citizens for Nixon Lodge), N.Y.C., 1959-60; asst. to Raymond Moley, polit. columnist, N.Y.C., 1961; asst. campaign com. Louis J. Lefkowitz for Mayor, N.Y.C., 1961; research programmer, treas. Consensus, Inc., N.Y.C., 1962-67; spl. asst. to U.S. Senator Jacob K. Javits, N.Y., 1967-73, adminstrv. asst., 1973-75; dep. adminstr. Am. Revolution Bicentennial Adminstrn., 1976, acting adminstr., 1976-77; chief of staff Perry B. Duryea (minority leader) N.Y. State Assembly, 1978; public affairs cons., 1979-80; dir. govt. relations Gen. Mills Restaurant Group, Inc., 1980-83; exec. dir. Fed. Mediation and Conciliation Service, 1983-86; mem. Fed. Labor Rels. Authority, 1986-89, chmn., 1989—; bd. dirs. Interam. Life Ins. Co., 1979-86. Mem. N.Y. State Bingo Control Commn., 1965-72, U.S. Adv. Commn. on Public Diplomacy, 1979-82; pres. Bklyn. Heights Slope Young Rep. Club, 1955-56; co-chmn. Bklyn. Citizens for Eisenhower-Nixon, 1956; chmn. 2d Jud. Dist. Assn. N.Y. State Young Rep. Clubs, Inc., 1957-58, vice-chmn., mem. bd. govs., 1958-60, v.p., 1960-62; pres., 1962-64; mem. exec. com. Fedn. Women's Rep. Clubs N.Y. State, Inc., 1960-64, mem. council, 1964-70; mem. exec. com. N.Y. Rep. State Com. 1962-64; co-chmn. spl. assts. Rockefeller for Pres. Nat. Campaign com., N.Y.C., 1964; co-dir. N.Y. Rep. State Campaign Com., 1964; asst. campaign mgr. Kenneth B. Keating for Judge Ct. Appeals, N.Y., 1965; dir. scheduling Gov. Rockefeller campaign, 1966, Sen. Charles E. Goodell campaign, 1970; dir. scheduling and speakers' bur. N.Y. Com. to Re-elect the Pres., 1972; dir. planning and strategy, Conn. Reagan-Bush campaign, Hartford, 1980. Mem. bd. govs. Women's Nat. Rep. Club, N.Y.C., 1963-66. Mem. Jr. League of Bklyn. (past dir.), Exec. Women in Govt. (chmn. 1986), Nat. Women's Edn. Fund (mem. bd.), Am. Newspaper Women's Club, Nat. Soc. Colonial Dames Am. Episcopalian. Club: Vassar (past dir.) (Bklyn.). Home: 3001 Veazey Ter NW Washington DC 20008-5407

MCKEEVER, BRIAN EVANS, banker; b. N.Y.C., Sept. 28, 1949; s. Charles F. and Margaret (Evans) McK.; m. Frances Patricia Somers, Aug. 2, 1975; children: Brian, Michael, Patrick, John. BA in History, St. John's U., 1971, MA in History, 1972; MBA, NYU, 1978. Econ. analyst Morgan Guaranty Trust Co., N.Y.C., 1973-76; rep. Bank of N.S., N.Y.C., 1976-79; asst. v.p. Marine Midland Bank, N.Y.C., 1979-82; sr. v.p.-head of fin. instns. group, dep. head of N.Y. mktg. Nat. Westminster Bank PLC, N.Y.C., 1982—. Home: 118 Weyford Ter Garden City NY 11530-2514 Office: Nat Westminster Bank PLC 175 Water St New York NY 10038-4918

MCKELDIN, WILLIAM EVANS, management consultant; b. Richmond, Va., Aug. 14, 1927; s. Robert A.W. and Mary E. (Burke) McK.; BS in Bus. Adminstrn., Temple U., 1951, postgrad., 1951-53; postgrad. U. Pitts., 1953-54; m. Phyllis Shellhase, Jan. 23, 1982; children by previous marriage: William Evans, Roberts E. Various employee relations and mgmt. positions with Westinghouse Corp., Pitts., 1950-62, Farrel Corp., Rochester, N.Y., 1963-66, Gen. Signal Corp., Norwalk, Conn. and Watertown, N.Y., 1966-71, Copperweld Steel Co., Warren, Ohio, 1971-75, Tenn. Forging Steel, Knoxville, 1975-77, Val Bradley Assocs., West Chester, Pa., 1977-79; pres. and owner McKeldin Assocs., West Chester, 1979—. Bd. dirs. United Fund, YMCA, ARC, Rochester Inst. Tech., Jefferson Community Coll., Kent State U. Served with USAAF, 1945-47. Mem. Inst. Mgmt. Cons., Am. Soc. Safety Engrs., Am. Soc. Personnel Adminstrn., C. of C. (dir.). Republican. Presbyterian. Clubs: Masons, Rotary. Contbr. articles to trade jours. Address: McKeldin Assocs 125 Willowbrook Ln West Chester PA 19382

MCKELLIPS, DAVID ALLAN, transportation company executive; b. Neenah, Wis., Aug. 11, 1943; s. Allan David and Gretta Margaret (Taft) McK.; m. Mary Lee Swentner, July 10, 1965 (div. Jan. 3, 1977); children: Scott Allan, Steven John, Timothy Paul. BA in English, U. Wis., Oshkosh, 1966. Salesperson Am. Can Co., Mpls., 1965-70; tng. mgr. Pitney Bowes, Phila., 1971-76; dir. tng. Ingersoll-Rand Co., Woodcliff Lake, N.J., 1976-80; prin. Excalibur Tng. Assn., Charlotte, N.C., 1980-86, Briarpatch Tng. R & D, Atlanta, 1986-90; dir. corp. devel. New Eng. Motor Freight, Elizabeth, N.J., 1990—; cons. ITT Worldwide Dirs., Amsterdam, Netherlands, 1987-88, Time Mag., Singapore, 1988, Jones Truck Lines, Springdale, Ariz., 1986-87; writer Harcourt Brace Jovanovich, Orlando, Fla., 1989. Author/editor: TASK, 1977; author: The Inner Game of Selling, 1989, MarketMaster, 1986. Home: 320 Ocean Park Ave Bradley Beach NJ 07720-1419 Office: New Eng Motor Freight 1-71 North Ave E Elizabeth NJ 07201

MCKELVEY, JOHN PHILIP, physics educator; b. Ellwood City, Pa., Nov. 9, 1926; s. Dennis Benedict and Regina Elizabeth (Fletcher) McK.; m. Elaine Clark Buechner, Aug. 26, 1950; children: Edward Andrew, Alexandra Anne. BS in Physics, Pa. State U., 1949, MS in Physics, 1950; PhD in Physics, U. Pitts., 1957. Rsch. physicist, supervising physicist Westinghouse Rsch. Labs., Pitts., 1951-62; assoc. prof. to prof. physics Pa. State U.,

University Park, 1962-74, asst. dean Coll. of Sci., 1969-72; prof. physics Clemson (S.C.) U., 1974-87, head dept. physics and astronomy, 1974-82; adj. prof. physics Pa. State U., University Park, 1989—; vis. prof. physics Va. Poly. Inst. and State U., Blacksburg, 1987-88. Fellow Am. Phys. Soc.; mem. Am. Assn. Physics Tchrs. Home: 410 S Gill St State College PA 16801-3964 Office: Pa State U Dept Physics 104 Davey Lab University Park PA 16802-6300

MCKENNA, BARBARA LOUISE, travel and tourism educator, consultant; b. Pomona, Calif., Nov. 25, 1928; d. Carl Frederick Williamson and Nellie Marguerite (Funkhouser) Fitken; m. Quentin Carnegie McKenna, Sept. 12, 1948 (div. 1984); children: Candace Mylet, Megan Greve, Carl Carnegie McKenna, Erin McKenna. Student, Pomona Coll., 1946-48; BS, U. Pitts., 1983; MA, George Washington U., 1989. Travel agt. Pa., Mo., Del., 1983—; dir. travel and tourism program Columbia (Mo.) Coll., 1985-89, Widener U., Chester, Pa., 1989—; instr. Travelco, Wilmington, Del., 1989—; instr. summer program Johnson & Wales, Oxford, Eng., 1990; bd. dirs. Chester County Tourist Bur., West Chester, Pa., 1990—; chairperson transp. and hospitality Asian Pacific Conf. on Arts Edn., Columbia, 1988-89. Chmn. housing com. Ojai (Calif.) Tennis Tournament, 1968-74; sexual assault counselor Women's Svcs. Westmorland County, Greensburg, Pa., 1980-85, The Shelter, 1986-89; bd. govs. Ligonier (Pa.) Valley Endowment, 1982-84; vol. Ft. Ligonier, 1983-84. Mem. 99's Internat. Women Pilots, Soc. Travel and Tourism Educators (v.p. 1991—), bd. dirs. 1989—, program chair conf. 1989), Am. Soc. TravelAgts., Inst. Cert. Travel Agts. (cert. travel counselor). Republican. Episcopalian. Home: 7419 Society Dr Claymont DE 19703-1775

MCKENNA, FAY ANN, electrical manufacturing company executive; b. Bennington, Vt., Jan. 7, 1944; d. George Francis and Barbara Mae (Youngangel) Hoag; m. James Dennis McKenna, Sept. 3, 1963 (div. 1983); children: Russell (dec.), Laura, James, Sean, Michael. Student, Mercy Coll. Key punch operator N.Y. State Taxation and Fin. Dept., Albany, 1960-61; receptionist Trine Mfg./Square D Co., Bronx, 1972-76; clk. Square D Co., Bronx, 1976-78, exec. sec., 1978-79, personnel mgr., 1979-86; mgr. mktg. adminstrn. Trine Products Corp., 1986-89, adminstrv. mgr., 1989—. Mfg. Fund raiser YMCA, Bronx, 1979—; mem. Community Bd. #9, Bronx, 1984—. Recipient Svc. to Youth award YMCA, 1985. Mem. Adminstrv. Mgmt. Soc. Republican. Roman Catholic. Avocations: physical fitness, reading, interior decorating. Home: 410020 Hutchinson River Pky E Bronx NY 10475-4746 Office: Trine Products Corp 1430 Ferris Pl Bronx NY 10461-3699

MCKENNA, FRANK JOSEPH, Canadian politician, lawyer; b. Apohaqui, N.B., Can., Jan. 19, 1948; s. Durward and Olive (Moody) McK.; m. Julie Friel; children: Toby, Tina, Jamie. BA with honors, St. Francis Xavier U., 1970; postgrad., Queen's U., 1970-71; LLB, U. N.B., 1974. Spl. asst. to pres. Privy Council, 1971; mem. orgn. and policy coms. N.B. Liberal Party, Chatham, 1974-81, leader, 1985; v.p. U. N.B. Faculty of Law Liberal Assn., Fredericton, 1974; pres. Chatham Const. Liberals, 1981-82; premier Province of N.B., Fredericton, 1987—; ptnr. Martin, Lordon, McKenna & Bowes, Chatham, 1974-87; chief returning officer, mem. steering com. Leadership Conv., 1982. Former pres. Chatham C. of C.; founder, 1st pres. Chatham Downtown Mchts. Recipient Vanier award, 1988. Mem. Can. Bar Assn. (mem. coun. N.B. chpt.), N.B. Bar Assn. Liberal. Office: PO Box 6000, Fredericton, NB Canada E3B 5H1

MCKENNA, JOHN JOSEPH, psychology educator, clinical psychologist; b. Harrisburg, Pa., Jan. 21, 1940; s. John Joseph and Elizabeth Carmelita (Sculley) McK.; m. Jacquelyn Helen Willette, May 25, 1974. STM, Andover Newton Theol. Sch., 1972; PhD, U. Vt., 1987. Lic. clin. psychologist, Vt. Tng. coord. Alcohol & Drug Abuse Div., Waterbury, Vt., 1972-73; project dir. Alcohol & Drug Abuse Div., Montpelier, Vt., 1973-74; intern. Vt. State Hosp., Waterbury, Vt., 1979-80, Behavior Therapy & Psychotherapy Ctr., Burlington, Vt., 1980-83; intern Wright House, Colchester, Vt., 1985-88; pvt. practice Colchester, Vt., 1988—; from instr. to assoc. prof. Trinity Coll., Burlington, Vt., 1974—; presenter profl. devel. seminar Vt. State Hosp., Waterbury, May 1990; cons.mediator Habitat for Humanity, Burlington, 1989—; coord. of Assessment, Trinity Coll., 1990—. Recipient Sears Roebuck Found. Teaching Excellence and Campus Leadership award Trinity Coll., 1990, Wye faculty fellow Wash. U., 1989. Mem. APA, New Eng. Psychol. Assn., Vt. Psychol. Assn. Home: 157 Rivermount Ter Burlington VT 05401-1115 Office: Trinity Coll 208 Colchester Ave Burlington VT 05401-1422

MCKENNA, QUENTIN CARNEGIE, tool company executive; b. Claremont, Calif., Sept. 2, 1926; s. George Alexander and Lillian Frances (Street) McK.; m. Barbara Louise Williamson, Sept. 12, 1948 (div. 1984); children: Candace, Megan, Carl, Erin; m. Barbara K. Somogye, Mar. 18, 1989. B.A. cum laude, Pomona Coll., 1948; postgrad., Stanford U. (Hewlett Packard fellow), 1948-50, U. So. Calif., 1951-53, UCLA, 1968-69. Mem. tech. staff guided missile div. Hughes Aircraft Co., 1950-52; with Indsl. Electronics, 1952-55; with Hughes Aircraft Co., 1955-78, asst. group exec. missile systems group, 1977-78; with Kennametal, Inc., Latrobe, Pa., 1978—, chmn. bd., chief exec. officer, 1989-91; ret.; bd. dirs. Interlake Corp., Pitts. Nat. Bank, PNC Fin. Corp.; adj. prof. indsl. adminstrn. Grad. Sch. Indsl. Adminstrn., Carnegie-Mellon U., 1990—. Patentee in field. Trustee St. Vincent Coll., 1981-89; mem. com. bd. trustees Buhl Sci. Ctr., Carnegie Inst., 1989. Recipient Eli Whitney Meml. award, Soc. Mfg. Engrs., 1983. Mem. Phi Beta Kappa, Sigma Xi. Episcopalian.

MCKENNEY, MICHAEL ALLEN, career army officer; b. Portland, Oreg., Nov. 23, 1954; s. Allen Edwin and Thelma Lue (Jarrell) McK.; m. Frances Aiko Nose, Mar. 22, 1983; children: Christopher, Leia. BA, Loyola U., 1977; MBA, Case Western Reserve U., 1985. Commd. 2d lt. U.S. Army, 1977, advanced through grades to maj., 1979—. Mem. Boston Computer Soc. Home: 755 SE Third Ave Hillsboro OR 97123

MCKENZIE, ANDRÉ, academic administrator, educator; b. Chgo., May 4, 1955; s. Alberta Chisholm. BS, Ill. State U., 1977, MS, 1979; MEd, Columbia U., 1985, EdD, 1986. Assoc. residence hall dir. No. Ill. U., DeKalb, 1979-82; asst. dir. student activities Northeastern Ill. U., Chgo., 1982-84; assoc. dean of students St. John's U., Jamaica, N.Y., 1986-89, dir. opportunity programs, 1989-91, asst. v.p., 1991—; tng. specialist Anti-Defamation League, N.Y.C., 1989—; cons. on coll. black Greek letter orgns., 1988—; mem. N.Y State policy bd. Higher Edn. Opportunity Program, 1990-92; facilitator leadership skills workshops, 1986—. Contbr. articles to profl. jours. Mem. N.Y. Urban League, Jamaica, 1990, 100 Black Men, N.Y.C. Edn. Policy fellow Inst. for Ednl. Leadership, 1990-91. Mem. Assn. for Humanistic Edn. and Devel. (pres. area II 1992—), Nat. Assn. Student Pers. Adminstrs. (mem. adv. bd. region II 1988-91), Am. Coll. Pers. Assn., Alpha Phi Alpha (Bro. of Yr. Eta Tau chpt. 1976). Office: St Johns U St John Hall 134 Jamaica NY 11439

MCKENZIE, GEORGE FRANCIS, real estate manager; b. Newark, N.J., July 16, 1955; s. George Francis and Lenore Loretta (Flynn) McK.; m. Deborah Lee Marlin, June 17, 1978; children: Catherine, Heather, Patrick. BS, U.S. Naval Acad., 1977; MBA, U. R.I., 1985. Commd. ensign U.S. Navy, 1977, advanced through grades to lt. cmdr., 1985; served as naval aviator U.S. Navy, various, 1977-85; v.p. asset mgmt. Prudential Realty Group, Newark, Washington, 1985—. Mem. KC. Republican. Roman Catholic. Home: 11621 Moorestown Pl Gaithersburg MD 20878 Office: Prudential Realty Group 1100 15th St NW #400 Washington DC 20005

MCKENZIE, GWENDOLYN VERON, marketing business development and public relations executive; b. Durham, N.C.; d. Lionel Wilfred and Blanche (Veron) McK. BS, U. Rochester, 1977; MEd, Harvard U., 1982. Adminstrv. asst. Kennedy Sch. Govt., Cambridge, Mass., 1981; mktg. coord. Payette Assocs., Boston, 1983-86; mktg. mgr. Profl. Designs Inc., Boston, 1986, Staats Internat., Boston, 1987-89, Arrowstreet Inc., Somerville, Mass., 1990—. Vol. John Kerry for Senator, Boston, Nat. Alliance for Mentally Ill, Boston, 1989. Mem. Internat. Assn. Corp. Real Estate Execs. (exec. v.p. New Eng. chpt. 1992—), Boston Soc. Architects, New Eng. Women in Real Estate, Harvard Club (Boston). Office: Arrowstreet Inc 212 Elm St Somerville MA 02144-2946

MCKEON, MICHAEL KEARNEY, admissions director; b. Peekskill, N.Y., Sept. 6, 1955; s. Matthew Joseph and Phyllis Virginia (McNearny) McK.; m. Cheryl Ann Krocker, June 15, 1985; 1 child, Seamus Michael. BS summa cum laude, SUNY, Oneonta, 1978; MA, Adelphi and Hofstra Univs., 1985. Asst. dir. admissions Adelphi U., Garden City, N.Y., 1979-82; assoc. then dir. admissions Alfred (N.Y.) U., 1982-89; dir. admissions SUNY, Cortland, 1989—. Author: (book) The Robeson Riots: Two Incidents Which Foreshadowed the Rise of McCarthyism, 1985. Mem. ACLU, Nat. Assn. Coll. Admission Counselors, Nat. Assn. Fgn. Student Affairs, N.Y. State Assn. Coll. Admission Counselors (newsletter editor, mem. exec. bd.), SUNY Coll. Admissions Pers., Amnesty Internat., Omicron Delta Epsilon, Phi Alpha Theta. Democrat. Roman Catholic. Office: SUNY Graham Ave Cortland NY 13045-2424

MCKEON, WARREN HOWARD, environmental consultant; b. Ossining, N.Y., Mar. 21, 1922; s. Robert A. and Edna S. (O'Dasha) McK.; m. Anne Louise Manning, Apr. 10, 1945; 1 child, Diana H. BS, Fordham U., 1948; MS, Cornell U., 1951. Cert. wildlife biologist. Wildlife biologist N.Y. State Dept. Environ. Cons., Rochester, Poughkeepsie, 1951-60; regional supr. fish and wildlife N.Y. State Dept. Environ. Cons., New Paltz, N.Y., 1960-71, regional dir., 1971-76; sr. scientist Ecol. Analysts, Middletown, N.Y., 1976-79; consulting biologist New Paltz, 1979—; exec. dir. The Hudson River Environ. Soc., New Paltz, 1980—. Co-editor Hudson River Ecology, 1976, 80, 85, 89. mem. environ. conservation com. Town of New Paltz, 1982-91, zoning bd., 1984-91, master plan com., 1987-90; bd. mem. Stony Kill Found., Fishkill, N.Y., 1983-91. Lt. USNR, 1942-66. Recipient Disting. Svc. award Mohonh Cons., New Paltz, 1989. The Wildlife Soc. (pres. N.Y. State chpt. 1978-79), Nat. Historic Trust. Home: PO Box 535 New Paltz NY 12561-0535 Office: Hudson River Environ Soc 9 High Pasture Rd New Paltz NY 12561-3707

MCKEOWN, MARTIN, manufacturing executive; b. Glasgow, Scotland, Sept. 28, 1943; came to U.S., 1968.; s. Martin and Marion (Cameron) M.; m. Anne Campbell, Dec. 30, 1967. Degree in mech. engrng., Stow Coll., Glasgow, 1964; BSc, U. Strathclyde, Glasgow, 1966. Cert. mfg. engr. Apprentice Rolls Royce Aero Engine, Glasgow, 1960-66; methods engr. No. Electric, Toronto, Ont., Can., 1966-67; mfg. engr. nuclear fuel div. Westinghouse Electric Corp., Pitts., 1968-72; tool engrng. specialist steam turbine div. Westinghouse Electric Corp., Winston-Salem, N.C., 1972-79; mgr. mfg. devel. elevator div. Westinghouse Electric Corp., Randolph, N.J., 1979-81, mgr. mfg. tech. elevator div., 1981-83, mgr. devel. engrng. elevator div., 1983-84; mfg. devel. mgr. transp. div. Westinghouse Electric Corp., West Mifflin, Pa., 1984-86, mgr. ops. program mgmt. transp. div., 1986, product line mgr. transp. div., 1986-88; product line mgr. AEG Westinghouse Transp. Systems, Pitts., 1988-89; mfg. mgmt. advisor AEG Westinghouse Transp. Systems, Berlin, 1990-91; mgr. product line AEG Westinghouse Transp. Systems, 1991—. Mem. Inst. Prodn. Engrs., Robotics Internat. Roman Catholic.

MCKEOWN, RONALD PAUL, JR., restaurant company executive, consultant; b. N.Y.C., July 27, 1951; s. Ronald Paul Sr. and Margaret (Kelly) McK. BA, Walsh Coll., 1972; MS, U. Dayton, Ohio, 1974; MA, Coll. of New Rochelle, N.Y., 1975; MBA, Hartford (Conn.) U., 1985. Dir. disaster and safety programs Am. Nat. Red Cross, Fairfax, Va., 1972-73; instr. Westchester Community Coll., Valhalla, N.Y., 1973-74; constrn. coord. McKeown/Matheson Inc., N.Y.C., 1974; tchr. Archdiocese of N.Y., Westchester City, 1975-77; freelance writer Pelham, N.Y., 1977-80; dir. of devel. FFMP Architects, Hartford, 1981-84; v.p. Healthwoods, Ltd., Wallingford, Conn., 1984-85; cons. Conn. Health Systems, Meriden, 1985-86; exec. v.p., bd. dirs. Diversified Hospitality Group, Inc., Milford, Conn., 1986—; cons. Nat. Aquatic Assn., Washington, 1978-82, Conn. Hist. Commn., Hartford, 1984-86; bd. dirs. Toddle Home Restaurants Inc., Milford. Writer, columnist syndicated column. Mem. Middlefield (Conn.) Planning & Zoning Commn., 1982-87, Middlefield Devel. Commn., 1983-84, Rep. Senatorial Inner Circle, Washington, 1987-92; chmn. Selective Svc. System, Conn., 1985-92; bd. dirs. Conn. Preservation Trust, Hartford, 1984-92. Mem. Friendly Sons of St. Patrick, Conn. Trust Historic Preservation. Roman Catholic. Office: Diversified Hospitality Group Inc 540 New Haven Ave Milford CT 06460

MCKERNAN, JOHN RETTIE, JR., governor of Maine; b. Bangor, Maine, May 20, 1948; s. John Rettie and Barbara (Guild) McKernan; 1 son, Peter Alexander. B.S., Dartmouth Coll., 1970; J.D., U. So. Maine, 1974. Bar: Maine. Atty. Verrill & Dana, Portland, Maine, 1976-82, Sterns & Finnegan, Bangor, Maine, 1974-76; mem. 98th-99th Congresses from 1st Dist. Maine, 1983-87; gov. State of Maine Augusta, 1987—. Mem. Pres. Commn. on Presidential Scholars, 1981. Republican. Office: Office of Gov State House Sta 1 Augusta ME 04333*

MCKIBBON-TURNER, BAMBI, economic development director; b. Columbus, Ohio, Apr. 12, 1947; d. Alfonso Jackson and Myra Josephine (Kelley) McKibbon; (div. 1972); children: John M. III, Linda M., Lisaj D. BS in Human Svcs., N.H. Coll., 1989, MS in Community Econ. Devel., 1989. Caseworker Office of Congressman Don J. Pease, Washington, 1977-79, fed. grant specialist, 1979-89, econ. devel. and fed. grant specialist, 1989-90, legis. asst. and econ. devel. specialist, 1990-91, econ. devel. dir., 1991—; pres., chief exec. officer McKibbon Mgmt., Inc., Washington, 1987-90, Arlington, Va., 1991—. Mem. No. Va. Dem. Club, Arlington, 1991. Named Outstanding Young Woman of Am., 1983; recipient Outstanding Congl. Black Assocs. Worker award, 1984. Mem. Am. Mgmt. Assn., Coalition of 100 Black Women (charter mem. Nat. City chpt. 1983), Nat. Assn. Women Bus. Owners, Orgn. Caribbean Bus. Persons. Office: Congressman Don J Pease 2410 Rayburn Housing Office Washington DC 20515

MCKIE, W. GILMORE, human resources executive; b. Marquette, Mich., Aug. 25, 1927; s. Walter G. and Amy Gertrude (Larson) McK.; m. Elenore R. MacNally, Sept. 9, 1950 (div. Nov. 1962); 1 child, Janet; m. Mary Simmons, Mar. 21, 1964 (dec. Aug. 1970) 1 child, Gwen DeBuck; m. Eunice Winifred Curtis, July 10, 1971; children: Ellen Sheive, Norrine Halvorsen. BS in Econs., U. Rochester, 1951. Employment interviewer Taylor Instruments Cos', Rochester, N.Y., 1951-60; employment mgr. Graflex, Inc., Rochester, 1960-62, Gen. Railway Signal Co., Rochester, 1962-67; dir. human resources The Singer Co., N.Y.C. and Rochester, 1967-77, Norwich-Eaton Pharms., Norwich, N.Y., 1977-80; personnel mgr. Ness Automatic Machine Products, Rochester, 1980-84; v.p. human resources Marine Midland Bank, N.A., Rochester, 1984-89; pres. HRM Cons., Inc., Rochester, 1989—; mgmt. adv. bd. Cornell U. Extension div., Rochester, 1984-90. Adv. bd. Salvation Army, Rochester, 1986—, N.Y. State div. of Human Rights, Rochester, 1987—; bd. dirs. Ralph Bunche Scholarship Fund, Rochester, 1990—, Youth at Risk, Rochester, 1988—; bd. govs. N.Y. State Fingerlakes Regional Edn. Ctr. for Econ. Devel., Rochester, 1984—; exec com. United Negro Coll. Fund, Rochester, 1986—; adv. bd. chmn. Coll. of Continuing Edn. Rochester Inst. Tech., 1985-90; chmn. Loftus C. Carson Human Rights Awards Luncheon, Rochester, 1991. Mem. Soc. for Human Resource Mgmt. (dist. dir. N.Y. state 1985-89, pers. rsch. com. 1989—, pres. Genesee Valley chpt. 1982-84, chmn. bd. 1984-87, founder 1982). Republican. Lutheran. Home and Office: HRM Cons Inc 2854 St Paul Blvd Rochester NY 14617-3740

MCKILLIP, PATRICIA CLAIRE, operatic soloist; b. Milw., Apr. 28; d. Lester J. and Ruth J. (Lohneis) McK.; m. Mark Richard McKillip, June 16, 1990. BA in English-Drama, Creative Writing, Lit., Alverno Coll., 1980; MusB in Applied Music, Alverno Coll., Milw., 1981; postgrad., Wis. Conservatory of Mus., 1981-82, U. Wis., Milw., 1982, The Juilliard Sch., 1982-84, Am. Acad. Dramatic Arts, 1983-84, Adelphi U., 1984. Soloist Amadeus Opera Co.; instr. vocal music seminars various high schs., N.Y.; co-founder, co-dir. The Masque Consort, N.Y.C., 1990-91, exec. v.p., 1991; v.p., co-founder Creative Learning Assocs. Performed with numerous opera cos. including The Florentine Opera Co., Music Under the Stars Prodns., Milw. Opera Co., Westchester Lyric Opera Co., Profl. Opera Workshop at Lincoln Ctr., Met. Opera Co., N.Y. Grand Opera Co., Monteverdi Opera Guild Prodns., Republic Opera Co., La Puma Opera Co., and other chamber, theater and folk groups; puppeteer, costumer, designer Puppet Art Troupe; performed in over 50 mus. shows and prodns., 6 solo recitals, also medieval concerts, choruses, orchestras, oratorio; 42 other recitals. Exec. v.p. Masque Consort, a multi-media theatrical orgn. Music dept. scholar Alverno U. Mem. AFTRA, SAG, Nat. Assn. Music Tchrs., Music Educators Nat. Conf. (treas.), Internat. Platform Assn., Wis. Fedn. Music Clubs, Music Clubs Am., Am. Guild Mus. Artists, Q'ahal-Liturgical Music Soc., Delta Omicron (v.p., chaplain, warden Gamma Gamma chpt., WMA State and Regional Vocal award 1978, Star of Delta Omicron award 1980, 40 music medals from state and dist. WSMA), Alpha Sigma Tau. Democrat. Roman Catholic. Home: 425 E 76th St Apt 1C New York NY 10021-2511

MCKINLEY-HAAS, MARY, artist; b. St. Louis; d. Lee Carrington and Florence (Dowden) McK.; m. Saul Haas; children: Christopher, Matthew. BA, Smith Coll.; student, Art Students League, 1973-74, Nat. Acad. Design, 1965-66, Studio and Forum Stage Design. Head costume design dept. ABC-TV, NYC, 1968-73. One women shows include Tarlowe Gallery, Westhampton Beach, N.Y., 1974, Fontbonne Gallery, St. Louis, 1977, Gallery Yssa, N.Y.C., 1979, Vered Internat. Gallery, East Hampton, N.Y., 1981, Netherlands Bank & Ludlow-Hyland Gallery, N.Y.C., 1981, U. Tex., Austin, 1988, RVS Fine Art, Southampton, N.Y., 1990, TSS Gallery, N.Y.C., 1992, U. Tex., Austin, 1992; exhibited in group shows at Vered Gallery, 1985, Works II Gallery, 1986, RVS Fine Art, 1987, Marymount Manhattan Gallery, 1988, Nabisco Brands Gallery, 1989, Lincoln Ctr., 1990, Queens Coll., 1991, others; costumer designer for Broadway and TV shows. Mem. United Scenic Artists, Women in the Arts. Office: 280 Lafayette St Loft 5B New York NY 10012-3313

MCKINNEY, CAROL ANN, marketing professional; b. L.A., Feb. 16, 1950; d. Thomas Alexander Jr. and Phyllis Ann (Aston) Cowen; m. John Adams McKinney Jr., Dec. 22, 1970; children: John A. McKinney III, Thomas A. McKinney. BA, Principia Coll., 1970. Elem. tchr. Williamsburg-James City (Va.) County Schs., 1971-73, West Windsor (N.J.)/Plainsboro Sch., 1973-75; investor support rep. Michael Marcus, Princeton, N.J., 1976-82; campaign mgr. Melamed for Mayor, Shaker Heights, Ohio, 1982-83; bus. adminstr. S.E. Investments, Inc., Cleve., 1983-84; dir. mktg./fin. New Horizon Press, Fall Hills, N.J., 1984-85; pub. rels. dir. The Morris Mus., Morristown, N.J., 1986-87; asst. dir./pub. rels. Raritan Valley Community Coll., Somerville, N.J., 1987; mgr. community rels. United Way of Morris County, Morristown, 1987-89; devel. dir. Children's Ctr., Morris Plains, N.J., 1989—. Producer (film) The Other Side, 1988. Chair state coun. of N.J. Jr. Leagues, 1990-91; task force Morris 2000, Project 90, Morris County, 1990—; bd. dirs. Jersey Battered Women's Svcs., Morris County, 1986-87; adv. bd. First Call for Help, Morris County, 1991—; trainer/cons. Assn. of Jr. League Internat., N.Y., 1987-91; adv. bd. Govs. Conf. on Cultural Tourism, Trenton, N.J., 1986-87; pub. rels. com. N.J. Gives, Morristown, 1988—; exec. bd. mem. Jr. League of Morristown, 1987-88; trustee NORWESCAP, 1992—; mem. Friends of Morris Mus., Leadership Morris; com. mem. United Way, trainer. Mem. Nat. Soc. of Fund Raising Execs. Office: Children's Ctr 260 State Rt 53 Morris Plains NJ 07950-2697

MCKINNEY, DAVID BROOKS, geology educator; b. Colorado Springs, Colo., Oct. 7, 1952; s. Isaac Harding and Mary Ruth (Kimrey) McK.; m. Patricia Joy Blakeslee, Sept. 18, 1981; 1 child, Courtney Brooke. BSc, Beloit Coll., 1975; MA, Johns Hopkins U., 1984, PhD, 1985. Geologist Anaconda Co., Salt Lake City, 1975-78; prof. geology Hobart and William Smith Colls., Geneva, N.Y., 1984—. Mem. Geol. Soc. Am., Mineral. Soc. Am., Sigma Xi. Office: Hobart and William Smith Colls Dept Geosci Geneva NY 14456

MCKINNEY, HENRY DANIEL, dermatologist; b. N.Y.C., Oct. 16, 1936; s. Owen and Kathleen (Malloy) McK.; m. Barbara C. Nacovsky, June 20, 1964; children: Ronald M., Christian M., Lauren E., Brendan J. BS, Fordham U., 1959; MD, U. Bologna (Italy), 1969. Diplomate Am. Bd. Dermatology. Intern Geisinger (Pa.) Med. Ctr., 1970-71, resident in dermatology, 1971-74; pvt. practice Altoona, Pa., 1974%; chief dermatology Altoona Hosp., 1974—; cons. physician in dermatology Mercy Hosp., Altoona, VA Hosp., Altoona, Nason Hosp., Roaring Spring, Pa., 1974—. Mem. AMA, Pa. Med. Assn., Blair County Med. Assn., Am. Acad. Dermatology, Am. Acad. Cosmetic Surgeons, Pa. Acad. Dermatology. Office: 1800 Grant Ave Altoona PA 16602-4508

MCKINNEY, JOHN EDWARD, physicist; b. Altoona, Pa., Apr. 6, 1925; s. Clayton A. and Katie Ellen (Kessler) McK.; m. Ursula Katherine Guttstadt, Aug. 16, 1958. BS, Pa. State U., 1950; postgrad., U. Md., 1952-58. Physicist Nat. Inst. Sci. and Tech. (formerly Nat. Bur. Standards), Gaithersburg, Md., 1949-89, cons., 1989—; guest scientist Nat. Physics Lab., Teddington, Eng., 1964. Author handbook: Density and Compressibility of Liquids, 1972; contbr. chpt. to book. Chmn. transp. com. East Bethesda (Md.) Citizens Com., 1975-79. With U.S. Army, 1943-45, ETO. Recipient Bronze medal U.S. Dept. Commerce, 1983. Mem. Soc. Rheology, Internat. Assn. Dental Rsch. Home: 9124 Mcdonald Dr Bethesda MD 20817-1942 Office: NIST Gaithersburg MD 20899

MCKINNEY, WILLIAM, academic administrator, sociologist; b. Salem, Mass., Mar. 14, 1946; s. William J. and Mary A. (O'Leary) McK.; m. Linda Roberts, Sept. 7, 1968. BA, Colby Coll., 1968; MA, Hartford (Conn.) Sem., 1970, MDiv, 1971; PhD, Pa. State U., 1979. Ordained to ministry United Ch. of Christ, 1971. Rsch. dir. United Ch. Bd. for Homeland Ministries, N.Y.C., 1974-85; dean, prof. Hartford Sem., 1985—; pres. Religious Rsch. Assn., N.Y.C., 1983-84; mem. Project Team for Congl. Studies, 1980—; trustee Alban Inst., Washington, 1991—. Co-author: Religion's Public Presence, 1982, Varieties of Religious Presence, 1984, Handbook for Congregational Studies, 1986, American Mainline Religion, 1987. Fellow Hartford Sem., 1972, Colby Coll., 1974. Office: Hartford Sem 77 Sherman St Hartford CT 06105-2260

MCKINNON, FLOYD WINGFIELD, textile executive; b. Columbus, Ga., Dec. 1, 1942; s. Malcolm Angus and Sarah C. (Bullock) McK.; m. Barbara Evans Roles, June 18, 1966; children—James Wingfield, Sarah Elizabeth, Robert Kent. A.B., Washington and Lee U., 1964. V.p. Cotswold Industries, Inc., N.Y.C., 1966—, also bd. dirs.; v.p., corp. sec. Cen. Textiles, Inc., S.C., 1984—, also bd. dirs.; arbitrator Am. Arbitration Assn., 1983—. Pres. Berkley-n-Scarsdale Assn., 1980; admissions rep. Washington and Lee U., 1979-89. Mem. St. Andrews Soc. N.Y., Ch. Club N.Y. Republican. Episcopalian. Clubs: Union League (bd. govs. 1974-77, 88-91, sec. 1981-83) (N.Y.C.); Scarsdale Golf (bd. govs. 1983—, pres. 1990-91) (Hartsdale, N.Y.); Bras Coupe (exec. com. 1980—) (Maniwaki, Can.). Home: 26 Taunton Rd Scarsdale NY 10583-5610 Office: Cotswold Industries 10 E 40th St New York NY 10016

MCKINNON, ROGER HUGH, telecommunications executive; b. Ft. Eustis, Va., May 28, 1950; s. Hugh and Kathleen (Case) McK.; m. Debra Ann Huff, Nov. 8, 1984; children: Shannon Leigh Briggs, Robert Howard Briggs III, Lauren Kathleen. AS, Thomas Nelson Community Coll., 1972; BS, William and Mary Coll., 1976. Indsl. engrng. technician Naval Air Rework Facility, Norfolk, Va., 1977-78, indsl. systems mgmt. analyst, 1978-79; computer specialist Naval Regional Data Auto. Ctr., Norfolk, 1979-81; project leader telecommunications Naval Regional Data Auto. Ctr., 1981; telecommunications cons. CIGNA, Voorhees, N.J., 1981-82; sr. tech. project mgr. CIGNA, 1982-84, sr. telecommunications cons., 1984-85; sr. telecommunications cons. ARA Svcs., Inc., Phila., 1985-88, dir. telecommunications, 1988—. With USNR, 1967-73. Mem. Internat. Communication Assn., Communication Mgrs. Assn., Nat. MCI User's Group (steering com.). Methodist.

MCKISSICK, MICHAEL LANDON, transportation consultant; b. Clearfield, Pa., June 12, 1950; s. Robert Charles and Ruby Delores (Landon) McK. AS in Mech. Design, Pitts. Tech. Inst., 1979, AS in Computer System Mgmt., 1985. Inventory control coord. Aerotech, Inc., Pitts., 1974-75; owner, operator No. Photographic Svcs., Warren, Pa., 1975-77; drafter bearings div. TRW, Falconer, N.Y., 1979; proposal engr. Blaw Knox F&MM Co., Pitts., 1979-80; instr. Pitts. Tech. Inst., 1980-82, v.p., 1982-85; instr. Carnegie Mellon U., Pitts., 1981-82; cons. Pa. Dept. Transp., Trout Run, 1985—; mem. Pitts. Tech. Inst. Bd. Advs., 1985—; speaker in field. Author: (book) Computer Aided Drafting and Design, 1987. Mem. Intergraph Users Group. Home and Office: RR 1 Box 186B Trout Run PA 17771-9801

MCKOWN, RICHARD GEORGE, artist, educator; b. Cambridge, Mass., Nov. 30, 1947; s. Joseph Maxwell and Miriam (Barker) McK.; m. Deborah J. Berry, Aug. 10, 1969. BA in Studio Arts, U. N.H., 1969; MA in Photography, U. Iowa, 1971, MFA in Photography, 1972. Dir. media svcs. Emerson Coll., Boston, 1973-75; acting dir. Provincetown (Mass.) Group Gallery, 1976; real estate broker Foster and Foster, Inc., Acton, Mass., 1979-81; photography instr. Decordova Mus. Sch., Lincoln, Mass., 1979-81; artist-in-residence Cultural Edn. Collaborative Inst. for the Arts, Boston, 1983-88; photography instr. Middlesex Community Coll., Bedford, Mass., 1984—, No. Essex Community Coll., Haverhill, Mass., 1988—. One-man shows include Abbott Meml. Libr., Emerson Coll., Boston, 1974, 75, Tirca Karlis Gallery, Provincetown, Mass., 1976, Photoworks Gallery, Boston, 1977, Photographic Gallery, Mid. Tenn. State U., Murphreesboro, 1978, Grey Gallery, Antioch Coll., Yellow Springs, Ohio, 1979, 417 Gallery, Prairie State Coll., Chgo. Heights, Ill., 1980, Concord (Mass.) Free Pub. Libr., 1981, Andover (Mass.) Gallery, 1985, Meridien Hotel, Boston, R.J. Grey Art Gallery, Acton, 1988, New East End Gallery, 1989; group shows include Danforth Mus., Framingham, Mass., 1987, J.L. Becker East End Gallery, Provincetown, Mass., 1988, Hudson River Mus., Yonkers, N.Y., 1989, No. Essex Community Coll., Haverhill, Mass., Middlesex Community Coll., Burlington, Mass., Inst. de Bachillerato Federico Garcia Lorca, Granada, Spain, 1990, Berta Walker Gallery, Provincetown, 1990, U. N.H. Art Gallery, Durham, 1990; films and multimedia prodns. include Autobiographical Film, 1969, Bellybutton, 1969, Marianne in Morning, 1970, December Observations, 1971, My Hillside--A Day in June, 1971, A History of American Landscape Photography, 1972, A Nightmare, 1972, Primary, 1973, Annum, 1974; appeared in numerous publs. Finalist Mass. Artists' Found. fellow Program, 1979, 82; recipient Purchase prize McDonald's Corp. Fine Arts Collection Competition, Oakbrook, Ill., 1984; U. Iowa fellow, 1970-71. Home: 672 Massachusetts Ave Acton MA 01720-2233

MCLANE, SUSAN NEIDLINGER, state legislator; b. Boston, Sept. 28, 1929; d. Lloyd Kellock and Marion (Walker) Neidlinger; m. Malcolm McLane, 1948; children: Susan B., Donald W., Deborah, Alan, Ann Lloyd. Ed., Mt. Holyoke Coll.; LLD (hon.), New England Coll., 1983, Franklin Pierce Coll., 1988. Mem. N.H. Ho. of Reps., Concord, 1969-80; chmn. ways and means com. N.H. Ho. of Reps., 1976-80; mem. N.H. State Senate, Concord, 1980—, chmn. ways and means, 1990—; del. Rep. Nat. Conv., 1976; pres. N.H. Coun. Affairs, 1976-80. Office: NH State Senate State Capitol Concord NH 03301 also: 205 Mountain Rd Concord NH 03301

MCLAREN, FELICIA (IRIS) DIBLE, volunteer; b. Plum Boro, Pa., Dec. 22, 1924; d. George Featherston and Susan Louise (Koch) Dible; (widowed Mar. 1977). Student, U. Pitts. Check writer Nat. Union Fire Ins. Co., Pitts., 194-53; sec. Nat. Union Fire Ins. Co., San Francisco, 1953-55, Old First Presbyn. Ch., San Francisco, 1955-56; sec., audio visual supr. Cokesbury Book Store, San Francisco, 1956-59; sec. McIndoes (Vt.) Acad., 1967-68. Reporter, compiler State Grange Newspaper, 1979-83. Clk. of session Barnet Ctr. (Vt.) Presbyn. Ch., 1984-89; buyer, chmn. hosp. gift shop NVRH, St. Johnsbury, Vt., 1979-89; mem. com. on ministry Presbytery of No. New Eng., Haverhill, Mass., 1988-89, voting del. to gen. assembly Presbyn. Ch., 1988; chmn. Fall Foliage Festival, Town of Barnet, Vt., 1963—; chmn. Shepherd Pomona Food Booth, Caledonia County Fair, Lydonville, Vt. Mem. Barnet Hist. Soc. (pres. 1985-88), Lakeview Grange, Shepherd Pomona Grange (master 1983-88). Republican. Home: RR 1 Box 32 East Ryegate VT 05042-9710 also: care George F Dible 315 Repp Rd RFD #2 New Kensington PA 15068

MCLAUGHLIN, ALBERT HOWARD, dentist; b. Bridgeport, Conn., Apr. 14, 1924; s. Albert Augustine and Edna Frances (Howard) McL.; m. Jeannette Cecile Keller, Sept. 11, 1948; children: Maureen, Laurence, James, Kevin, Meghan, Brendan. AA, Jr. Coll. Conn., Bridgeport, 1942-43; Student, Trinity Coll., Hartford, 1943-44; DDS, U. Pa. Sch. of Dentistry, 1948. Pvt. practice Bridgeport, Conn., 1948-50, Woodbury, Conn., 1952—; dir. Dental Assisting Nat. Bd., Chgo., 1987—; mem., cons. North East Regional Bd. of Dental Examiners, Washington, 1973—. Editor: (jour.) Connecticut State Dental Association, 1976-85. Pub. health coun. State of Conn., 1971-73, dental commn., 1972-77; moderator Town of Woodbury, 1982—; chmn. Rep. Town Com., Woodbury, 1968-70, 86-92. Capt. USAF, 1951-52. Recipient Svc. award Pub. Health Coun. State of Conn., 1966, Conn. Acad. Gen. Dentistry, 1982. Mem. Am. Dental Assn. (appeals bd., commn. on dental edn. accreditation 1990—), Dental Soc. Greater Waterbury (pres. 1972-73), Conn. State Dental Assn. (Horace Hayden award 1985, pres. 1965-66, speaker ho. of dels. 1968-70, 90—), Am. Assn. Dental Examiners (pres. 1983-84). Republican. Roman Catholic. Home: 155 Good Hill Rd PO Box 593 Woodbury CT 06798-2502 Office: 357 Main St S Woodbury CT 06798-3408

MCLAUGHLIN, BRIAN JOHN, retail executive; b. Boston, Sept. 21, 1946; s. James H. and Mary (Fitzgerald) McL.; m. N. Jeanne Upham, Feb. 1, 1966; children: Keith, Kyle, Kerry, Brian Jr., Conor. Chief exec. officer D'Angelo, Inc., West Bridgewater, Mass., 1978—. Bd. dirs. Key Program, Framingham, Mass., 1983—, Genesis Fund, Brighton, Mass., 1985—; coord. Program Opportunity, Easton, Mass., 1987-88. Roman Catholic. Office: DAngelo Inc 321 Manley St West Bridgewater MA 02379-1096

MCLAUGHLIN, EDWARD MANUS, dean; b. Wilkes-Barre, Pa., Mar. 4, 1934; s. Edward Manus and Josephine Loretta (Haggerty) McL.; m. Irene Loftus, June 22, 1957; children: Daniel, Sean, Mary Jo, Michael. BA in Econs., King's Coll., 1955; MBA, Marywood Coll., 1985. Secondary tchr. Montgomery County, Silver Spring, Md., 1955-56; nat. security agy. Fed. Govt., Fort Meade, Md., 1956-60; computer div. Honeywell Inc., Wellesley Hills, Pa., 1960-65; dir. of EDP Luzerne County Courthouse, Wilkes-Barre, Pa., 1965-69; bus. mgr. Wyo. Valley Sanitary Authority, Wilkes-Barre, Pa., 1969-78; exec. dir. Mountaintop Sewer Authority, Mountaintop, Pa., 1978-81; dean bus. Luzerne County Community Coll., Nanticoke, Pa., 1981—. Treas. King's Coll. Alumni; bd. dirs. United Rehab. Svcs., Wilkes-Barre, 1962-69, New Options, Wilkes-Barre, 1988-92; exec. bd. Bishop Hoban High Sch., Wilkes-Barre, 1984-88. Mem. Data Processing Mgmt. Assn. (v.p., bd. dirs., pres. 1965-69), King's Coll. Alumni Assn., Marywood Coll. Alumni Assn. Roman Catholic. Office: Luzerne County Community Coll 1333 S Prospect St Nanticoke PA 18634

MCLAUGHLIN, JOSEPH MICHAEL, religious order administrator; b. Boston, Aug. 16, 1943; s. Joseph M. and Mary E. (O'Hare) McL. AB, St. Michael's Coll., 1966; MDiv., U. St. Michael's, 1969; AM, St. Michael's Coll. U. Toronto, 1972. Ordained May 16, 1970. Gen. councilor Soc. St. Edmund, Burlington, Vt., 1976-82, treas. gen., 1982-86, superior gen., 1986-90; dir. sem. St. Basil's Coll., Toronto, 1972-76; assoc. prof. St. Michael's Coll., Winooski, 1978—; v.p. Edmundite So. Missions, Inc., Selma, Ala., 1986-90. Author: From Pontigny, 1978. Chmn. Prudential Com. Town of Colchester, Vt., 1982-87, clk., 1979-85; mem. Burlington Community Land Trust, 1983—; trustee, sec. St. Michael's Coll., Winooski, 1979-90, chmn. bd. trustees, 1986-90; active Armagh Hist. Soc. Mem. Am. Conf. for Irish Studies, Am. Cath. Hist. Assn. Roman Catholic. Home and Office: St Michael's Coll Winooski Pk Colchester VT 05439

MCLAUGHLIN, JUDITH BLOCK, educator; b. Gainesville, Fla., Dec. 13, 1948; d. Seymour Stanton and Gertrude (Hecht) Block; m. Edward F. McLaughlin, June 14, 1975; children: Kerry Ann, Peter James. AB, U. N.C., 1970; MAT, Harvard U., 1971, EdD, 1983. Tchr. social studies Newton (Mass.) High Sch., 1970-72; residence hall dir. Boston U., 1972-74; dean student affairs Wheelock Coll., Boston, 1974-76, Mt. Vernon Coll., Washington, 1976-79; exec. dir. Nat. Acad. Edn., Cambridge, Mass., 1980-83; rsch. assoc. Harvard U., Cambridge, Mass., 1983-91, instr., 1984-86, lectr., 1986—; ednl. chmn. Harvard Seminar for New Pres., Cambridge, 1990—; dir. Field Experience Program, Harvard U., Cambridge, 1991—; adv. bd. Acad. Search Cons. Svc., Washington, 1990—. Cons. editor ASHE-Eric Higher Edn. Series, 1987-88; contbr. articles to profl. jours.; author: Choosing a College President, 1990, An Education of Value, 1984. Vol. Planned Parenthood, Alexandria, Va., 1977-79; co-chmn. after sch. enrichment program High Rock Sch., Needham, Mass., 1990—; vol. Common Cause, Boston, 1974-76. Recipient Howard W. Odum award U. N.C., 1970. Mem. Am. Assn. Higher Edn., Phi Beta Kappa. Jewish. Office: Harvard U Appian Way Cambridge MA 02138-3704

MCLAUGHLIN, LARRY W., chemistry educator; b. Seattle, Oct. 27, 1950; s. Wendell Lloyd and Nildred Elizabeth (Reitz) M.; m. Jean Leask Franklin, Dec. 30, 1972; children: Martin John, Mareika Leask. BS, U. Calif., Riverside, 1968-72; PhD, U. Alberta, Edmonton, Alta Can., 1979. Group leader Max-Planck Inst., Göttingen, Germany, 1981-85; asst. prof. Boston Coll., 1985-89, assoc. prof., 1989-91, chemistry prof., 1991—; cons. Integrated DNA Tech., Iowa City, 1988-89, Schering-Plough, Bloomfield, N.J., 1990—; mem. NIH Div. of Rsch. Grants, Bethesda, Md., 1990-94. Contbr. over 66 articles to profl. jours. NIH Rsch. grantee, 1986—, NSF, 1986—; Am. Cancer Soc. Faculty Rsch. award, 1991-95. Mem. Am. Chemistry Soc., Nat. Assoc. Advanced Sci. Office: Boston Coll Chemistry Dept 140 Commonwealth Ave Chestnut Hill MA 02167-3801

MCLAUGHLIN, RICHARD WARREN, retired insurance company executive; b. Boston, Nov. 25, 1930; m. Marilyn Slye, 1956; children: Kathleen, Richard Warren Jr., Thomas, Judy. B.S., Boston Coll., 1952; grad. Advanced Mgmt. Program, Harvard U., 1979. Trainee Travelers Ins. Co., Hartford, Conn., 1956, asst. sec., 1966-69, sec., 1969-70, 2d. v.p., 1970-73, v.p., 1973-81, sr. v.p., 1981-85; exec. v.p. Travelers Corp., Hartford, Conn., 1985-91; pres. Travelers Ins. Co., Hartford, Conn., 1991—; chmn. Travelers Indemnity Co., Hartford, 1991—; bd. dirs. Health Ins. Assn. Am., Washington. Corporator St. Francis Hosp. Capt. USAF, 1952-56, Korea. Mem. Eastward Ho Club (Chatham, Mass.), Hawks Nest Club (Vero Beach, Fla.). Home: PO Box 947 Eastham MA 02642 Office: Travelers Corp 1 Tower Sq Hartford CT 06183-0001

MCLAUGHLIN, WALTER JOSEPH, actuary; b. N.Y.C., Dec. 7, 1931; s. Walter Joseph Sr. and Margaret Mary (Lynch) M.; m. Helen Joan Knecht, Sept. 5, 1955; children: John, Philip, Clare (dec.), James, Michael. AB in Econs., Fordham U., 1953. Cons., actuary Cons. Actuaries Internat., 1966-68, Stone, Young & Co., 1968-70, Marsh & McLennon, 1970-73; rev. actuary Buck Cons., Inc., 1973—; instr. pensions Rockland Community Coll., Monsey, N.Y., 1979-80. Pub. Buck Mortality Table 1989. Recipient Disting. Svcs. to Youth award Rockland County High Sch. Basketball Coaches, 1982. Fellow Soc. Actuaries (enrolled actuary, chmn. pub. rels. com. 1976-78, mem. joint exam. com. for enrollment of actuaries 1978-81, com. on retirement plans 1990—), Conf. Consulting Actuaries; mem. Internat. Actuarial Assn., Am. Acad. Actuaries, Am. Pension Conf., Actuarial Soc. Greater N.Y. (panel moderator, pension com. 1980-83), Am. Arbitration Assn. (panel of arbitrators), PCIC (mem. malpractice avoidance com.), Rockland County 2000 Com. Republican. Roman Catholic. Office: Buck Cons 500 Plaza Dr Secaucus NJ 07094-3602

MCLEAN, IAN WILLLIAM, ophthalmic pathologist, researcher; b. Durham, N.C., Sept. 21, 1943; s. I. William and Brita (Rosenqvist) McL.; m. Susan R. Gabler, June 14, 1987; children: Elenor Lee, Rebecca Ann, January D. BS, U. Mich., 1965, MD, 1969. Diplomate in anatomic pathology Am. Bd. Pathology. Pathology intern U. Colo. Med. Ctr., Denver, 1969-70, resident in pathology, 1970-73; staff pathologist, dept. ophthalmic pathology Armed Forces Inst. Pathology, Washington, 1973-83, acting chmn. dept. ophthalmic pathology, 1983-86, chmn. dept., 1986—. Contbr. more than 100 articles to sci. jours. Col. USA, 1973—. Recipient Gold medal U. Sao Paulo, 1988. Mem. Assn. for Rsch. in Vision and Ophthalmology, Eastern Ophthalmic Pathology Soc., Am. Acad. Ophthalmology, Am. Assn. Ophthalmic Pathologists, Verhoeff Soc. Office: Dept Ophthalmic Pathology Armed Forces Inst Pathology Washington DC 20306-6000

MCLEAN, ROBERT BRENNAN, physician; b. Hazleton, Pa., Dec. 27, 1935; s. Laird Brennan and Julia Elizabeth (Schuetrumpf) McL.; m. Jane Cecelia Altmiller, Apr. 16, 1960. BA, U. Pa., 1957, MD, 1961; MHA, Baylor U., 1974. Diplomate Am. Bd. Surgery. Med. officer, advanced through grades to col. U.S. Army, Washington, 1960-90; corp. med. dir. Nat. Passenger R.R. Corp. (AMTRAK), Washington, 1990, chief med. officer, 1990—. Decorated Bronze Star, Legion of Merit medal; recipient Superior Svc. medal Dept. Def., 1986. Fellow ACS, Am. Coll. Physician Execs.; mem. Assn. Am. R.R.'s, D.C. Med. Soc. Home: 8205 Hensley Ct Alexandria VA 22308-1529 Office: Nat Passenger RR Corp (AMTRAK) 60 Massachusetts Ave NE Washington DC 20002-4225

MCLEAN, RONALD WILLIAM, university administrator; b. Ilion, N.Y., Nov. 11, 1927; s. William Roberts Cuthbert and Bessie (Soutar) McL.; m. Helen Francis Finnigan, June 12, 1947; children: Eric, David, Janice, Jeffrey, Mary Ellen. BS in Pharmacy, Albany Coll. of Pharmacy, 1951; MS in Edn., SUNY, Albany, 1980. Staff pharmacist Fox Drug Co., Carthage, N.Y., 1951-52; owner McLean Pharmacy, Newport, N.Y., 1952-76; ptnr. Maple Dale Pharmacy, Banneveld, N.Y., 1968-73; asst. dir. div. of extension svcs. Albany Coll. of Pharmacy, Union U., 1976-78, dir. div. of extension svcs., 1976—; cons. pharmacist St. Margarets Home for Babies, Albany, 1982—; mem. N.Y. State Bd. Pharmacy, 1982-89, disciplinary officer, 1989—. Bd. pres. Interfaith Partnership for Homeless, Albany, 1986-88; bd. dirs. Am. Cancer Soc., Syracuse, N.Y., 1985-87. Staff sgt. USAF, 1945-47. Recipient Disting. Achievement in Pharmacy award Merk Sharpe-Dohme, 1989; named Disting. Alumnus Am. Coll. Pharmacy Alumni Assn., 1983. Mem. Am. Assn. of Colls. of Pharmacy (chair sect. of continuing profl. edn. 1990-91), Pharm. Soc. State of N.Y. (ednl. cons. 1989—), Honey Hill Country Club (pres.). Office: Albany Coll Pharmacy Union U 106 New Scotland Ave Albany NY 12208

MCLEAN, WILLIAM GEORGE, engineering education consultant; b. Scranton, Pa., Mar. 15, 1910; s. Michael and Matilda Marie (Geueke) McL.; B.S. in Elec. Engring., Lafayette Coll., 1932; M.S., Brown U., 1933. Head math. dept. West Scranton (Pa.) High Sch., 1934-37; asst. prof. mech. engring. Lafayette Coll., Easton, Pa., 1937-44; asst. to supr. spl. products div. Eastman Kodak Co., Rochester, N.Y., 1944-46; prof., head engring. sci. Lafayette Coll., 1946-75, dir. engring., 1962-75; cons. in field, 1950—; mem. Pa. Registration Bd. Profl. Engrs., 1981-87. Chmn. Hugh Moore Park Commn., 1969—; v.p. United Neighborhood Ctrs., Lackawanna County, Pa.; mem. Am. Nat. Metric Practice Group, 1974—. Fellow ASME (nat. v.p. 1953-55, 70-72, mem. various bds., Codes and Standards medal 1977, Performance Test Codes medal 1984); mem. Nat. Soc. Profl. Engrs. (pres. Pa. 1965-66), Am. Soc. Engring. Edn., Sigma Xi, Phi Beta Kappa, Tau Beta Pi, Eta Kappa Nu, Pi Tau Sigma, Kappa Delta Rho. Democrat. Roman Catholic. Author: (with E.W. Nelson) Engineering Mechanics, 1952, 4th editn., 1988; (with C.L. Best) Engring. Mechanics, 1965. Home and Office: 333 5th Ave Scranton PA 18505-1022

MCLEAN, WILLIAM RONALD, electrical engineer, consultant b. Bklyn., Mar. 26, 1921; s. Harold W. and Helena Winifred (Farrell) McL.; m. Cecile L. Mills, Aug. 17, 1946 (div.); m. 2d, Evelyn Hupfer, Nov. 29, 1968. BA, Bklyn. Coll., 1980, BS, 1981. Chief electrician U.S. Mcht. Marine, 1942-64; elect. designer, engr., 65-76; sr. elect. engr. Rosenblatt & Son, Inc., N.Y.C., 1976-86; cons., 1986—. Mem. Soc. Naval Architects and Marine Engineers, IEEE, Am. Soc. Naval Engrs. Home and Office: 45 Grace Ct Brooklyn NY 11201-4187

MCLEER, LAUREEN DOROTHY, marketing professional; b. N.Y.C., Feb. 5, 1955; d. William Myers and Una Lee (Massey) McL. BS, Columbia U., 1977; MBA, U. London, 1981. RN, N.Y.; state registered nurse Eng., Wales. Staff nurse NYU Med. Ctr., N.Y.C., 1977-78; charge nurse Scripps Clinic and Rsch. Found., La Jolla, Calif., 1979-80; clin. researcher Ayerst Labs., N.Y.C., 1982-83; sales rep. Pfizer, Inc., N.Y.C., 1983-87, Cahners Pub. Co., N.Y.C., 1988-89; dir. bus. devel. Pro Clinica, N.Y.C., 1990-91; account supr. Salthouse Torre Norton, Inc., Rutherford, N.J., 1992—. Chmn. Help Our Neighbors Eat Yr. 'Round, N.Y.C., 1987-89; trustee Murray HIll Com., N.Y.C., 1988-90; bd. dirs. East Midtown Svcs. for Older People, 1987—. Mem. Pharm. Advt. Coun., Healthcare Bus. Women's Assn. Home: 137 E 38th St New York NY 10016-2622 Office: Salthouse Torre Norton Inc Meadows Office Complex 301 Rt 17 N Rutherford NJ 07070

MCLELLAN, LAWRENCE PHILLIP, cartoonist, graphic designer, artist; b. Waterville, Maine, Oct. 18, 1944; s. Claude Robert and Beatrice Emogene (Chipman) McL.; m. Nancy Lee Frappier, Apr. 3, 1965; children: Larry, Marie. Student, Famous Artist Sch., Westport, Conn., 1969-71; art student, U. Maine, 1982. Author, illustrator: (comic book) Captain Cult, 1990-91, (comic strip) Beane; designer, pub. (mags.) Neon After Dark, Coffee Light; contbr. editorial cartoons and print advt. to various publs. Artist First Baptist Ch., Fairfield, Maine, 1980-92, Boy Scouts Am., Benton, Maine, 1982, Waterville (Maine) Police Dept., 1976. With U.S. Army, 1966-69. Republican. Baptist. Home and Studio: 12 Osborne St Fairfield ME 04937

MCLENNAN, BERNICE CLAIRE, human resources professional; b. Malden, Mass., Dec. 26, 1936; d. Ralph Cyril Worth and Alice Seaman (Hunter) Worth Barrett; m. Hubert Earle McLennan, Oct. 28, 1961; 1 child, Cynthia Alice. Student, Moody Bible Inst., 1958, Salem State Coll., 1988, Bentley Coll., 1989. Youth dir. Faith Evangelical Ch., Melrose, Mass., 1971-77; adminstrv. asst. Boston (Mass.) Redevel. Authority, 1977-85, adminstr. coord., 1985-87, asst. sec. to the authority, 1981—, dir. human resources, 1989—; moderator Faith Evangelical Ch., Melrose, 1985-88, Christian edn. chair, 1973-76. Sec. Melrose (Mass.) Sch. Com., 1983-85; vol. Boston (Mass.) Youth Campaign, 1989, 90. Mem. Internat. Pers. Mgmt. Assn., Assn. Affirmative Action Profls. Home: 31 Botolph St Melrose MA 02176-1126 Office: Boston Redevel Authority 33 3d Ave Charlestown MA 02129

MCLEOD, GERALD ALAN, management consultant; b. Worcester, Mass., Oct. 18, 1930; s. Archibald Linton and Evelyn Louise (Barnes) McL.; m. Margaret Alice Steeves, Oct. 6, 1962; children: Cheryl Lee McLeod Le Geyt, Catherine Jean, Heather Page. BS, U. Md., 1961; MA in Internat. Rels., Am. U., 1967. Cert. credit adminstr. Assoc. The Penn Mutual Life Ins. Co., Wellesley and Boston, 1965-70; adminstr. The Worcester Sci. Ctr. and Natural History Mus., Mass., 1970-73; dist. mgr. The Rsch. Inst. of Am., N.Y.C., 1973-76; dir. devel. Internat. Order St. Luke, Rochdale, Mass., 1976-78; assoc. Robert Half Inc., Hartford, Conn., 1979-87, Credit Solutions, Inc., Rocky Hill, Conn., 1987-91; mng. ptnr. McLeod & McLeod, Mgmt. Cons., Southington, Conn., 1991—. Contbr. articles to profl. jours. Mem. Charter Commn., Northboro, Mass., 1969-70; regional coord. various campaigns for U.S. Senate, other statewide offices Rep. Party; charter mem., trustee Rep. Presdl. Task Force, 1985—; vestryman, commn. chmn. asst. treas., fundraiser, lay reader Episcopal Ch.; active Ministry of Christian Healing through Internat. Order of St. Luke the Physician, N.Am. devel. dir. and lay missioner. With U.S. Army, 1948-52. Commended by Atty. Gen. of Mass., 1964. Home and Office: McLeod & McLeod 42 North Rd Southington CT 06489-1831

MCLINN, HARRY MARVIN, facial orthopaedic educator, consultant; b. Huntsville, Ala., Oct. 31; s. Benjamin and Clara (Derrick) McL.; m. angela Louise Jones, Aug. 1, 1944; children; Teloca, Marvin, Jenol. DDS, Howard U., 1944; cert., Columbia U., 1947. Diplomate Am. Bd. Orthodontics. Pvt. practice Pa., N.Y., 1950-73; med. officer U.S. Civil Svc., 1973-76; Louise Ball fellow Columbia U., N.Y.C., 1947; dept. head orthodontics Howard U., 1948-50; pvt. practice N.Y.C., 1950-73; assoc. prof. orthodontics U. Medicine Dentistry of N.J., Newark, 1973-85; facial orthopedic cons. Englewood, N.J., N.Y.C., 1985—; dept. head orthodontics Howard Dental, Washington, 1948-50; health cons., N.J., N.Y.C., 1975—. Contbr. articles to profl. jours. Mem. Englewood Bd. Health, N.J., 1970's; panel mem., cons. handicapped children, N.Y.C., 1955-70; planning bd. Englewood Hosp., N.J., 1976-82. Capt. U.S. Army, 1944-46. Fellow Internat. Coll. Dentists; mem. ADA, Am. Assn. Orthodontics, AAUP, Omega Kappa Upsilon, Lambda Kappa. Office: 433 Mt View Rd Englewood NJ 07631

MCLOONE, J. MARK, health facility administrator; b. Phila., Mar. 16, 1954; s. John Cornelius and Jane Mary (Bradley) McL.; m. Martha Alice McDonald; children: Angela, J. Mark. BA, LaSalle U., 1976; MBA, St. Joseph's U., 1984. Mgr. housekeeping and laundry Mercy Hosp., Wilkes-Barre, Pa., 1977-79; unit mgr. emergency rm. Einstein Med. Ctr., Phila., 1979-81, adminstr. anesthesiology and rsch., 1981-84, asst. adminstr., 1984-87; assoc. adminstr. duPont Inst., Wilmington, Del., 1987—. Coach Berwyn (Pa.)-Paoli Little League, 1977; mentor Multicultural Student Mentor Program, Phila., 1991-92; asst. coach Paoli (Pa.) Wildcats Girls Basketball, 1991-92. Recipient award of excellence Svc. Master Industries, 1978. Mem. Am. Coll. Health Care Execs., Am. Hosp. Assn., Assn. Del. Hosps., Del. Valley Hosp. Coun. Roman Catholic. Office: A I duPont Inst 1600 Rockland Rd Wilmington DE 19899

MCMAHON, EILEEN MARIE, artist's agent; b. Jersey City, July 15, 1953; d. William John and Marie Rita (Stringer) M. BA in Art, Jersey City State Coll., 1974; postgrad., Rutgers U., 1974-76, New Sch. for Social Research, 1976-77, Sch. of Visual Arts, 1976. Asst. curator Jersey City Mus., 1975-77; curator Ian Woodner Family Collection, N.Y.C., 1977-78; assoc. rep. Artist's Assocs., Inc., N.Y.C., 1978-81; sr. rep. Gerald and Cullen Rapp, Inc., N.Y.C., 1981-86; mktg. dir. Corey Chaloner Millen, N.Y.C., 1986-88; assoc. rep. John Locke Studios Inc., N.Y.C., 1988—. Co-author, designer: mus. catalog, August Will: Scenes of Old Jersey City, 1976. Office: John Locke Studios Inc 15 E 76th St New York NY 10021-1719

MCMAHON, NEIL MICHAEL, real estate executive; b. N.Y.C., Oct. 12, 1953; s. Thomas Joseph and Catherine Margaret (Lane) M.; m. Debra Brylawski, Oct. 2, 1982; children: Alexa Lauren, Brendan Patrick. BA, Loyola Coll., Balt., 1975; MBA, U. Notre Dame, 1980. Staff acct. Coopers & Lybrand, Balt., 1975-77; sr. assoc. Korn/Ferry Internat., Chgo., 1980-84; mgr. real estate fin. Prudential Ins. Co., Washington, 1984-87, gen. mgr. real estate devel., 1987-88; mng. dir. Capital Ptnrs. Inc., Washington, 1988—. Bd. dirs. Lawrence Hall Sch. for Boys, Chgo., 1981-84. Named Sesquicentennial Scholar State of Md., 1971-75. Mem. Nat. Assn. Indsl. and Office Parks, Real Estate Group, Mortgage Bankers Assn., Notre Dame Club. Republican. Roman Catholic. Home: 3548 Winfield Ln NW Washington DC 20007-2368 Office: Capital Ptnrs Inc Ste 600 2300 N St NW Washington DC 20037

MCMAHON, THOMAS ARTHUR, applied mechanics and biology educator; b. Dayton, Ohio, Apr. 21, 1943; s. Howard Oldford and Lucille (Nelson) McM.; m. Carol Ehlers, June 20, 1965; children: James Robert, Elizabeth Kirsten. B.S., Cornell U., 1965; S.M., MIT, 1967, Ph.D., 1970. Postdoctoral fellow Harvard U., Cambridge, Mass., 1969-70, lectr. bioengring., 1970-71, asst. prof., 1971-74, assoc. prof., 1974-77, prof. applied mechanics and biology, 1977—; cons. numerous industries, legal firms. Author: (novels), Principles of American Nuclear Chemistry, 1970, McKay's Bees, 1979, Loving Little Egypt, 1987; (non-Fiction) Muscles, Reflexes and Locomotion, 1984; (with others) On Size and Life, 1983. Grantee NIH; System Devel. Found., Sloan Found.; recipient Richard and Hinde Rosenthal award Am. Acad. and Inst. Arts and Letters, 1988. Mem. Biomed. Engring. Soc., Am. Physiol. Soc., N.Y. Acad. Scis., PEN. Home: 65 Crest Rd Wellesley MA 02181-4620 Office: Harvard U Dept Applied Scis Pierce Hall Cambridge MA 02138

MCMANAMON, DANIEL THOMAS, real estate executive, developer; b. Schenectady, N.Y., Mar. 13, 1952; s. Daniel Joseph and Mary Wilimenia (Flanagan) McM.; m. Mary Elizabeth Marsolais, Mar. 17, 1983; 1 child, Daniel Francis. BS, Union Coll., 1976. Equity mktg. specialist. Asst. photographer Siciliano Studios, Schenectady, 1976-79; account exec. Prudential Bache, Albany, 1979-81, E.F. Hutton, Albany, 1981-84, Tucker Anthony & R.L. Day, Albany, 1984-86; sr. account exec. H. Linn Cushing, Albany, 1986-88; v.p., sec. McVan Asset Mgmt., Inc., Clifton Park, N.Y., 1987—; assoc. broker Realty U.S.A. Comml., Albany, 1988—. Active Saratoga County Hist. Soc., Ballston Spa, N.Y. Mem. ASCE (assoc.), Nat. Coun. Exchangers, Comml. Investment Real Estate Bd., N.Y.State Assn. Realtors, N.Y. State Comml. Investment Div., Albany County Bd. Realtors, Saratoga Soaring Assn., So. Saratoga County C. of C., Albany-Colonie C. of C., Latham C. of C., Adirondack C. of C. Home: 6 Kingswood Dr Clifton Park NY 12065 Office: Realty USA Comml 17 Computer Dr East Albany NY 12205

MCMANMON, JOHN JOSEPH, English educator; b. Evanston, Ill., July 26, 1932; s. John Joseph and Mary Ellen (Hickey) McM.; m. Nancy Joan Kline, Aug. 8, 1982; children: Willa Mae, Stephen Thomas. BA in Philosophy, U. Notre Dame, 1955, MA in English, 1962; MA in Theology, Holy Cross Coll., 1959; PhD in English, U. Chgo., 1965. Asst. prof. English U. Notre Dame, Ind., 1964-66, UCLA, 1966-68; assoc. prof. English SUNY, Geneseo, 1968-69, Calif. State U., Northridge, 1969-71; prof. English Indiana U. Pa., 1971—; editorial adviser New Growth Arts Rev., Indiana, Pa., 1987—. Co-translator: On Plot in Tragedy, 1971; contbr. poetry to lit. mags., articles to scholarly publs. Founder, exec. dir. New Growth Arts Festival, Indiana, Pa., 1972-74; co-dir. Heart Fund, Indiana County, 1977.

Grantee Am. Philos. Soc., 1970. Mem. MLA, Eighteenth Century Scottish Soc., Christianity and Lit. Office: Indiana U Pa Leonard Hall 209 D Indiana PA 15705-1094

MCMANMON, THOMAS ARTHUR, JR., oil industry executive; b. Boston, Sept. 10, 1943; s. T. Arthur and Maura (Sullivan) M.; m. Suzanne Cole, Nov. 17, 1973; children: Katherine, Suzanne, Thomas III. BA in History, U. Notre Dame, 1966; MBA, Dartmouth Coll., 1968. V.p. N.E. Merchants Bank, Boston, 1968-77; sr. v.p. Entwistle Corp., Hudson, Mass., 1977-78, Global Petroleum Corp., Waltham, Mass., 1978—; dir. Griffith Consumers Corp., Cheverly, Md., 1985—, Atlantic Petroleum Corp., Chelsea, Mass., 1989, Montello Oil Corp., Waltham, Mass., 1980, Carl King, Dover,Del., 1985, Nimrod Nat. Gas, Tulsa. Dir. New England Fuel Inst., Watertown, Mass., 1980—. Mem. Marion-Beverly Yacht Club, Sippican Tennis Club, Boston Algonquin Club, Brookline Country Club. Office: Global Petroleum Corp 800 South St Waltham MA 02154-1439

MCMANUS, JOHN STEPHEN, tax accountant; b. Middletown, N.Y., July 12, 1967; s. John Joseph Mcmanus and Regina Marie (Comer) Noble; m. Joy Ann Orlosky, July 28, 1990. BS, Pa. State U., 1989. CPA, Md. Tax sr. Arthur Andersen & Co., Washington, 1989—. Mem. AICPA, Md. Assn. of CPAs, Delta Upsilon Alumni Assn. (bd. dirs. 1990—). Democrat. Roman Catholic. Home: 2909 Brinkley Rd # T-2 Temple Hills MD 20748-6060 Office: Arthur Andersen & Co 1666 K St NW Washington DC 20006-2803

MCMANUS, KEVIN PATRICK, industrial hygienist; b. Lynn, Mass., Nov. 1, 1953; s. Lawrence R. and Barbara C. (Long) McM. BS, Boston Coll., 1975. Indsl. hygienist U.S. Dept. Labor, Boston, 1975-80, U.S. Pub. Health Svc., Boston, 1980—; exec. v.p. Nat. Treasury Employees Union, Boston, 1985—. Contbr. articles to profl. jours. Counselor Camp Fatima Exceptional Childrens Week, N.H., 1970—; coord. St. Joseph's Religious Edn., Lynn, Mass., 1971—; v.p., dist. commr., Babe Ruth Baseball, 1983—. Named Outstanding Young Men of Am., Jaycees, 1983; recipient Regional Dirs. award U.S. Govt., Boston, 1984, Oustanding Community Svc award Fed. Exec. Bd., Boston, 1986. Mem. Am. Indsl. Hygiene Assn., Am. Acad. Indsl. Hygiene, Am. Conf. of Govtl. Indsl. Hygienists, Knights of Columbus, Order of Hibernians, Nat. Assn. Sports Officials, Mass. Baseball Umpires Assn. Democrat. Roman Catholic. Office: US Pub Health Svc 1401 JFK Federal Bldg Boston MA 02203

MCMANUS, MICHAEL JOHN, religion columnist; b. Springfield, Ohio, June 11, 1941; s. John Grever and Ruth (Fisher) McM.; m. Harriet Ecker, Oct. 16, 1965; children: Adam Joseph, John Ecker, Timothy Michael. AB, Duke U., 1963. Layman St. Paul's Episcopal Ch., Darien, Conn., 1971-87, Fourth Presbyn. Ch., Bethesda, Md., 1987—; radio commentator Dobson's Family News in Focus, 1990—; syndicated columnist Bethesda and Stamford, Conn., 1977—. Author: 1350 weekly columns, Ethics and Religion, 1981—, also Solutions, 1977-91, 40-page introduction to Final Report of Atty. Gen.'s Commn. Pornography, 1986 (Media Awareness award Religious Alliance Against Pornography): syndicated columnist in over 100 newspapers (Wilbur award of Religious Pub. Rels. Coun. 1985, 89). Exec. dir. Choices for '76, Regional Plan Assn., N.Y.C., 1970-74; founder Northeast Gov.'s Coalition and Northeast-Midwest Congl. Coalition. Mem. Religion Newswriters Assn. Home and Office: 9500 Michaels Ct Bethesda MD 20817-2214

MCMANUS, WALTER L(EONARD), JR., real estate officer; b. Balt., July 21, 1942; s. Walter Leonard and William (Ziegler) McM.; m. Cynthia Ford, Dec. 20, 1970; children: Walter III, Jill. BA, Washington & Lee U., 1964. Credit analyst Md. Nat. Bank; v.p., bd. dirs. CEM Securities Corp.; pres., bd. dirs. Castlewood Realty Co. Inc., Balt.; bd. dirs. Bank of Md., Balt.; chmn. Towson (Md.) Bank, Danis Co., Brokerage House, Balt. Bd. dirs. YMCA. Mem. Md. Horse Breeders Assn., Balt. Country Club. Office: Castlewood Realty Co Inc 204 E Joppa Rd # PH3 Baltimore MD 21204

MCMANUS, WILLIAM RAYMOND, JR., transportation executive; b. Bklyn., June 14, 1967; s. William Raymond and Margaret Ann (Coady) McM. BBA, St. Johns U., Jamaica, N.Y. Crew coord. TWA, Jamaica, N.Y., 1987-88; mgr. TWA, Jamaica, 1988-89, ops. controller, 1989-90; mgr. ops., 1990—. Republican. Roman Catholic. Home: 1538 E 32d St Brooklyn NY 11234 Office: TWA Hanger 12 JFK Airport Jamaica NY 11430

MCMICKLE, ROBERT HAWLEY, utility company executive, physics researcher educator; b. Paterson, N.J., July 30, 1924; s. Levi Battersby and Bessie Margaret (Hawley) McM.; m. Gwendolyn Ann Gill, Aug. 27, 1949; children—Douglas, Alan, Kathleen, Barry, Margaret. B.A., Oberlin Coll., 1947; M.S., U. Ill., 1948; Ph.D., Pa. State U., 1952. Research physicist B.F. Goodrich Research Ctr., Brecksville, Ohio, 1952-59; faculty mem., chmn. dept. physics Robert Coll./Bogazici U., Istanbul, Turkey, 1959-79; prof. physics Schreiner Coll., Kerrville, Tex., 1979-80, Luther Coll., Decorah, Iowa, 1980-81; sr. lectr. physics Memphis State U., 1981-83; adminstrv. asst. Pub. Service Co. of N.H., Seabrook, 1983—; cons. Innovative Systems Research Co., Pennsauken, N.J., 1976. Served with USNR, 1943-46. Brit. Council grantee Internat. Conf. on Lab. Teaching, Oxford U., 1978; Am. Petroleum Inst. fellow, 1950-52. Mem Am. Phys. Soc., Am. Assn. Physics Tchrs., Turkish Phys. Soc., Sigma Xi. Methodist. Contbr. articles to profl. lit. Address: 36 Granite Dr North Hampton NH 03862

MCMILLAN, ROBERT RALPH, lawyer; b. N.Y.C., May 21, 1932; s. Harry and Vivian (Beatty) McM.; m. Jane Gail Arbo, June 7, 1958; children: Robin, Karen, Kenneth. Student, Adelphi U., 1951-52, 55-56; JD, Bklyn. Law Sch., 1960. Bar: N.Y. 1960. Spl. asst. staff of Richard M. Nixon, N.Y., Washington, 1960, 64-65; counsel Senator Kenneth B. Keating, Washington, 1960-62; govt. rels. advisor Mobil Oil Co., N.Y.C., 1962-63, 65-68; v.p. Avon Products, N.Y.C., 1973-78, 79-85; sr. v.p. A&S Dept. Stores, N.Y.C., 1978-79; counsel Rivkin, Radler, Bayh, Hart & Kremer, Uniondale, N.Y., 1986-91; ptnr. McMillan, Rather, Bennett & Rigano, P.C., Melville, N.Y., 1991—; bd. dirs. Lumex, Inc., Bayshore, N.Y., Beauty Labs., Inc., Hauppauge, N.Y.; bd. dirs. Panama Canal Commn., 1989—. Commentator TV News 12, 1989. Trustee Adelphi U., 1984-89; bd. dirs. L.I. Assn., N.Y., 1984-90, chmn. L.I. Housing Partnership, 1988—. 1st lt. U.S. Army, 1952-54. Decorated Bronze Star. Mem. Nassau County Bar Assn., Suffolk County Bar Assn. Republican. Office: McMillan Rather Bennett & Rigano PC 394 N Service Rd Melville NY 11747 also: McMillan Rather Bennett & Rigano PC 395 N Service Rd Huntington Station NY 11747

MCMILLEN, MARVIN ALLAN, surgeon, educator; b. Tonawanda, N.Y., Dec. 24, 1948; s. Wilford Beecher and Margarita Verna (Werth) McM.; m. Victoria Althea Elliot, June 24, 1988. BA, SUNY, Buffalo, 1971, MD, 1975. Diplomate Am. Bd. Surgery, Sub-Bd. Critical Care. Intern, resident dept. medicine SUNY, Buffalo, 1975-77, intern, resident dept. surgery, 1977-79; resident, fellow dept. surgery U. Minn., Mpls., 1979-83; ast. prof. surgery SUNY Downstate Med. Ctr., Bklyn., 1983-87; assoc. prof. surgery Yale U., New Haven, 1987—; dir. surg. ICU, VA Med. Ctr., West Haven, Conn., 1987—; v.p. Exec. Source Internat., N.Y.C., 1986—. Contbr. articles to profl. jours. Mem. Youngstown (N.Y.) Yacht Club, Yale Club of N.Y.C. Office: West Haven VA Med Ctr Dept Surgery 950 Campbell Ave West Haven CT 06516-2700

MCMILLEN, (CHARLES) THOMAS, congressman; b. Elmira, N.Y., May 26, 1952. BS, U. Md., 1974; BA, MA, Oxford U., 1978. Profl. basketball player Buffalo Braves, 1975-77, N.Y. Knicks, 1977, Atlanta Hawks, 1977-83, Washington Bullets, 1983-86; mem. 100th-102nd Congresses from 4th Md. dist., Washington, 1987—. Rhodes scholar; named to U.S. Olympic Team, 1972. Office: US Ho of Reps Office of House Mems Washington DC 20515*

MCMILLER, ANITA WILLIAMS, army officer, transportation professional, educator; b. Chgo., Dec. 23, 1946; d. Chester Leon and Marion Claudette (Martin) Williams; m. Robert Melvin McMiller, July 29, 1967 (div. 1980). BS in Edn., No. Ill. U., 1968; MBA, Fla. Inst. Tech., 1979; M of Mil. Arts and Sci., U.S. Army Command & Gen. Staff Coll., 1990. Social worker County of Cook, Chgo., 1968-69; recruiter, dir. personnel, analyst State of Ill., Chgo., 1969-75; commd. 1st lt. U.S. Army, 1975, advanced through grades to lt. col., 1991; platoon leader, motor officer, exec. officer 155th Transp. Co., Ft. Eustis, Va. and Okinawa, Japan, 1976-78; S-1 pers. and adminstrn. officer 38th Transp. Bn., Ft. Eustis, 1978-79; installation transp. officer, fin. mgr. 3d Armor Div., Hanau, Fed. Republic Germany, 1979-82; transp. co. comdr. 3d Armor Div., Hanau, 1982-83; transp. plans officer Mil. Traffic Mgmt. Command, Falls Church, Va., 1983-85; tour with Sea Land Corp., Menlo Park, N.J., 1985-86; dep. comdr., ops. officer Bremerhaven (Fed. Republic Germany) Terminal, 1986-89; staff officer logistics The Pentagon, Arlington, Va., 1990-91; comdr. Mil. Traffic Mgmt. Command, U.K. Terminal, Eng., 1991—; instr. Cen. Tex. Coll., Hanau, Fed. Republic Germany, 1981-83, Phillips Bus. Coll., Alexandria, Va., 1983-84, City Colls. Chgo., 1987-89. Contbr. articles to profl. jours. Child advocate, foster mother Army Community Service, Hanau, 1980-83; tutor Parent-Tchr. Club Hanau Schs., 1981-83; vol. Vis. Nurses Assn. No. Va., 1983-85; coordinator, English tutor Adopt-a-Sch. Project, Washington, 1983-85; treas. Bremerhaven Girl Scouts Coun., 1987-89. Mem. Nat. Def. Transp. Assn., Assn. U.S. Army, Fedn. Bus. Profl. Women, Alpha Kappa Alpha. Office: Mil Traffic Mgmt Command UK Terminal PSC 53 Box 4900 APO AE 09497 also: MIMC-UK, 2 Parker Ave, Felixstowe IP11-84F, England

MCMILLIN, HARVEY SCOTT, English language educator; b. Pitts., June 29, 1934; s. Harvey Scott and Elizabeth (Bradley) McM.; m. Sally Ann Hyde, May 11, 1957; children: David, Paul, Andrew. BA, Princeton U., 1956; MA, George Washington U., 1960; PhD, Stanford U., 1965. Prof. English Cornell Univ., Ithaca, N.Y., 1964—. Author: Sir Thomas More and the Elizabethan Theatre, 1987, Shakespeare in Performance: Henry IV, Part One, 1991; editor Restoration and 18th Century Comedy, 1972; contbr. articles to various publs. Organizer Cornell Faculty Against Apartheid, Ithaca, N.Y. Lt. USN, 1957-60. Fellow Am. Philosophical Soc., Washington, 1972-73; grantee Nat. Endowment for Humanities, Washington, 1968, 87. Mem. Shakespeare Assn. Am. (trustee 1988-91), Modern Language Assn., Am. Soc. for Theatre Rsch. Home: 507 N Tioga St Ithaca NY 14850-3647

MCMINN, WILLIAM SCOTT, employee benefits consulting firm executive; b. Pitts., Jan. 27, 1956; s. William John and Margaret (Byars) McM.; m. Teresa Marlene Olander, Nov. 11, ,1978; children: William John II, Bryan Paul, Shannon Leigh. BS, W.Va. Wesleyan U., 1977. Mgr. Mut. of Omaha, Orlando, Fla., 1978-81; cons. Babb, Inc., Pitts., 1981-83; mgr. Godwins Inc. (formally Frank B. Hall Cons.), Pitts., 1983-86, v.p., 1986-88, regional dir., 1988—; bd. dirs. Bell Fed. Savs. and Loan Assn., Pitts. Coach Upper St. Clair (Pa.) Athletic Assn., 1989—; bd. dirs. Delta Gamma chpt. Theta Chi, 1986—. Mem. Pitts. Personnel Assn., Pitts. Assn. Group Execs. Republican. Methodist. Home: 1657 Red Mill Dr Upper Saint Clair PA Office: Godwins Inc 4 Ppg Pl Ste 500 Pittsburgh PA 15222-5404

MCMULLEN, JOHN HENRY, JR., manufacturing company executive, educator; b. Phila., Sept. 9, 1944; s. John Henry and Clara (Johnson) McM.; m. Evelyn Corrine Lawson, July 19, 1964; children: Yolanda, John III, Yvette, Yvonne. BS, Tuskegee U., Ala., 1969; MBA, Anna Maria Coll., 1984. Asst. program planner Ingall's Shipbldg., Pascagoula, Miss., 1969-71; indsl. engr. supr. Luken's, Coatesville, Pa., 1971-76; mgr. mfg. engring. Newport News (Va.) Shipbldg., 1976-78; gen. supr. Polaroid Corp., Cambridge, Mass., 1978-85; mfg. mgr. Keene Corp., East Providence, Mass., 1985-86; master scheduler Prime Computer, Natick, Mass., 1987-89; small bus. and small disadvantaged bus. liaison officer GTE Govt. Systems Corp.-C3, Needham Heights, Mass., 1989—; instr. Anna Maria Coll., Paxton, Mass., 1983-86. Ct.-apptd. spl. advocate Suffolk County Juvenile Ct., Boston, 1983; bd. dirs. Mattapan (Mass.) Community Health Ctr., 1983—, treas., 1984-86, pres., 1987-91; treas. ADAPT, Inc., Roxbury, Mass., 1986-88, v.p., 1988-89; active Urban League Eastern Mass., 1987-91; pres., founder Alpha Phi Alpha Edn. Found., 1983-87. Recipient Vice-Commandants award USAF, 1965; U.S. Dept. Edn. grantee, 1966; NAACP scholar, 1962. Mem. Afro-Am. Cultural Assn. Sharon (founder 1980), Polaroid Found., Inst. Indsl. Engrs., Exec. MBA Assn. of Anna Maria (bd. dirs. 1983-86), Nat. Black MBA Assn. (co-founder, treas. Boston chpt. 1985-87), Tuskegee Alumni Club (chpt. fin. sec. 1985-91, asst. fin. sec. 1988-90, asst. regional dir. 1990—, Outstanding Alumni award 1988), Elks, Shriners, Alpha Phi Alpha (chpt. pres. 1981-86, Alpha Man of Yr. 1986). Home: 8 Pine St Sharon MA 02067-1616 Office: 17 A St Needham MA 02194-2806

MCMURTRY, ARTHUR WILLIAM, educator; b. Cambridge, Mass., Jan. 12, 1910; s. Louis Frederick and Selma Florence (Svenson) McM.; m. Erma June Ramsdell, Aug. 15, 1940; 1 child, Pamela Ann. BA, Mass. Coll. Art, 1932, BS, 1934; postgrad., Boston U., 1939. Supr. art Yarmouth-Dennis-Brewster (Mass.) Sch., 1934-37; head drawing dept. Wethesfield (Conn.) Sch., 1938; curriculum dir. Cambridge (Mass.) Sch. Dept., 1940-75; ret., 1975; designer, Stanley Instrument Corp., Chestnut Hill, Mass., 1941-45; mem. staff, Mass. Sch. Art, Harvard U., Tufts U., Cambridge Indsl. Sch., Cape Cod Edn. Found.; lectr. in field. Illustrator for maj. pub. cos. including Macmillan, Prentiss Hall; represented in maj. corps. and pvt. collections in U.S. and abroad. Art dir. for non-profit orgns., hosps. Mem. Church of England. Home: 95 Wild Hunter Rd Dennis MA 02638-1113

MCMURTRY, CARL HEWES, ceramic scientist; b. Wellsville, N.Y., Dec. 6, 1931; s. Walter Rice and Edna (Hewes) McM.; m. Virginia L. Downing, June 9, 1955; children: Paul H., Karen A., Amy L. BS in Ceramic Engring., Alfred U., 1953, MS in Ceramic Engring., 1958. Rsch. assoc. Alfred (N.Y.) U., 1953-58; engr., scientist The Carborundum Co., Niagara Falls, N.Y., 1958—; mem. U.S. Commerce Dept. MTL Tech. Adv. Com., 1987—. Contbr. articles to profl. jours. Committeeman, scoutmaster Boy Scouts Am., Niagara Falls, 1958-75. Named Western N.Y. Inventor of Yr., Western N.Y. Patent Law Assn., 1979, 82. Fellow Am. Ceramic Soc.; mem. ASTM, Can. Ceramic Soc., The Metall. Soc., Western N.Y. Ceramic Soc. (chmn.), Ducks Unltd. (area chmn. 1973—). Home: 3939 Lower River Rd Youngstown NY 14174-9702 Office: The Carborundum Co PO Box 832 Niagara Falls NY 14302-0832

MCNABB, JOSEPH WILLIAM, vice president, dean of academic affairs; b. Springfield, Mass., Mar. 6, 1949; s. Joseph William and Helen (Stathis) M.; m. Helen Margaret May (div. Dec. 1988); children: Ryan, Kelley, Colin. BA, Boston U., 1972, MA, 1975; postgrad, Northeastern U., Boston, 1975—. Faculty mem. Mass. Bay Community Coll., Wellesley, Mass., 1975-78; dept. head Mass. General Hosp., Boston, 1975-79; cons./faculty Northeastern U., Boston, 1980—; v.p., dean Laboure Coll., Boston, 1979—; dir. Mass. Down Syndrome Congress, 1984—, Access Unlimited, 1989—; mem. adv. com. City of Boston, Madison Park Highschool, Hubert Humphrey Resource Ctr., 1987—. Mem. town meeting Town of Milton, 1984—; adv. for homeless Lemuel Shattuck Shelter, Boston, 1990—. Recipient: Excellence in Teaching Award, Northeastern U., 1991. Democrat. Roman Catholic. Office: Laboure Coll 2120 Dorchester Ave Dorchester MA 02124-5698

MCNAIR, FRANK CORNELIOUS, data processing specialist, consultant; b. Plymouth, N.C., Oct. 25, 1946; s. Cornelious and Gertrude (Worsley) McN.; m. Annie Hill, Oct. 12, 1968; children: Kevin, Kenneth, Yolanda. BA, CUNY, 1975; postgrad., Rutgers U., 1983-85. With CIGNA Corp., Phila., 1978—, sr. ops. mgr., 1984-85, asst. dir., 1985—. Bd. dirs. Christian Tabernacle Acad., Phila., 1988-89. Mem. Clergical Coun. (pres. Phila. chpt. 1989—). Office: CIGNA 401 White Horse Rd Voorhees NJ 08043-2699

MCNAIR, JOHN CALDWELL, judge; b. Fredericton, N.B., Can., Jan. 24, 1923; s. John Babbit and Marion M. (Crocket) McN.; m. Marion M. Morrison, Aug. 1, 1950; children: Jean, John, Kathleen. BA, U. N.B., Fredericton, 1944, MA, 1947; postgrad., U. London, 1947-48; LLB, Dalhousie U., Halifax, Can., 1951. Lectr. U. N.B., Fredericton, 1946-47, asst. prof., 1948-49; pvt. law practice Winslow, Hughes & Dickson, Fredericton, 1952-53, McNair & McNair, Fredericton, 1953-55; sole practitioner law Fredericton, 1955-83; judge Fed. Ct. Can., Ottawa, Ont., 1983-91. 2d lt. Can. Army, 1945, PTO. Lord Beaverbrook Overseas scholar, 1947-48. Mem. Can. Bar Assn., Fredericton Shrine Club, Soc. St. Andrew, Royal Can. Legion, Masons, Shriners. Presbyterain.

MCNALLY, TERRENCE, playwright; b. St. Petersburg, Fla., Nov. 3, 1939; s. Hubert Arthur and Dorothy Katharine (Rapp) McN. B.A., Columbia U., 1960. Stage mgr. Actors Studio, N.Y.C., 1961, tutor, 1961-62; film critic The Seventh Art,, 1963-65; asst. editor Columbia Coll. Today, N.Y.C., 1965-66. Author: (plays) And Things That Go Bump in the Night, 1965, Next, 1969, Sweet Eros, 1969, Noon, 1969, Where Has Tommy Flowers Gone, 1971, Bad Habits, 1973, The Ritz, 1974, The Golden Age, 1975, Broadway, Broadway, 1978, The 5:48, 1980, The Rink, 1984, It's Only a Play, 1986, Frankie and Johnny in The Clair de Lune, 1988, The Lisbon Traviata, 1989, Up in Saratoga, 1990, Kiss of the Spider Woman, 1990, Andre's Mother (Emmy award), 1990, Lips Together, Teeth Apart, 1991, (screenplay) Frankie and Johnny, 1991. Recipient Obie award, 1974, Dramatists Guild Hull-Warriner award, 1973, 88, 90; Guggenheim fellow, 1966, 69. Mem. Am. Acad. Arts and Letters, Dramatists Guild (v.p. 1981—). Office: care Gilbert Parker William Morris Agy 1350 Ave Of The Americas New York NY 10019-4701*

MCNAMARA, DENNIS LOUIS, sociology educator; b. Portage, Wis., Mar. 11, 1945; s. Louis Vincent and Lucille Mary (O'Connell) McN. BA, St. Louis U., 1969; MA, Fordham U., 1974; MDiv, Jesuit Sch. Theology, Berkeley, 1976; PhD, Harvard U., 1983. Lectr. Sogang U., Seoul, Korea, 1969-72; instr. sociology Marquette U., 1976-77; postdoctoral fellow Inst. East Asian Studies, U. Calif., Berkeley, 1983-84; prof. sociology Georgetown U., Washington, 1984—; cons. Fgn. Svc. Inst., Washington, 1986—, Bus. Coun. for Internat. Understanding, Washington, 1987—. Author: Colonial Origins of Korean Enterprise, 1990; contbr. articles to profl. jours. Fulbright fellow Coun. for Internat. Exchange of Scholars, 1987; U. Calif.-Berkeley fellow, 1983; NSF fellow, 1991; Fulbright-Hayes fellow (Korea), 1992. Mem. Am. Sociol. Assn. Assn. for Asian Studies, Internat. Sociol. Assn., Fulbright Alumni Assn. Roman Catholic. Office: Georgetown U Dept Socioloty Washington DC 20057

MCNAMARA, ELIZABETH TAYLOR, education researcher; b. Milw., Oct. 21, 1953; d. Samuel Joseph and Louise Patricia (Burress) Taylor; m. Laurence Henry McNamara, Aug. 23, 1991. BA, SUNY, Albany, 1974, MA, 1976, EdD, 1979. Dir. instnl. rsch. Regents Coll., Albany, 1981-86; assoc. dean Schenectady County Community Coll., Schenectady, 1986-88; asst. N.Y. State Edn. Dept., Albany, 1979-81, cons. on edn. rsch., 1986-88, assoc., 1988—. Trustee Mohawk Opportunities for Mental Health, Schenectady, 1992—. Office: NY State Edn Dept 860 Edn Bldg Addition Albany NY 12234

MCNAMARA, JOHN JEFFREY, advertising executive; b. N.Y., Jan. 31, 1937; s. John Joseph and Alexandra (Salem) M. BA, N.Y. Law Sch., 1963. Asst. v.p. Albert Frank Guenther Law Inc., N.Y., 1959-66; acct. supr., v.p. Doremus and Co., N.Y., 1966-74; v.p., exec. v.p. Wiley Kiernan Inc Charles Barker Ayer, N.Y., 1974-76; v.p. acct. supr. Tinker Campbell Ewald, N.Y., 1976-78; pres., chmn. John McNamara Advt. Inc., N.Y., 1978—; corr. cons. Hamilton College Alumni, Clinton, N.Y., 1978-88. Republican. Presbyterian. Home: 420 Majors Path Southampton NY 11968-2402 Office: 74 Broad St New York NY 10004-2210

MCNAMARA, JOHN MICHAEL, sales executive; b. Boston, June 26, 1957; s. William Patrick and Angela Marie (Casey) McN.; m. Lisa Anne Duffy, Oct. 2, 1982; children: Tricia, Kaitlin, Christopher, Ryan, Erin. BS in Mktg. Mgmt., Stonehill Coll., 1979. Asst. buyer William Filenes Sons, Boston, 1979-81; sales rep. Chaps by Ralph Lauren div. C.F. Hathaway, N.Y.C., 1981-86, Christian Dior div. C.F. Hathaway, Boston, 1986-87, Izod LaCoste div. Crystal Brands, Boston, 1987-88; regional sales mgr. Reliable Automatic Sprinkler Co., Inc., Boston, 1988—. Mem. Nat. Fire Protection Assn., Nat. Fire Sprinkler Assn. (sec. Boston chpt. 1992—), Fire Safety Assn. Mass. (treas., v.p. 1990-91, pres. 1991—). Roman Catholic. Office: Reliable Automatic Sprinkler Co 488 State Rd Ste 3 Plymouth MA 02360-5153

MCNAMARA, JOHN STEPHEN, painter, educator; b. Cambridge, Mass., Feb. 16, 1950; s. John Stephen and Mary (Adams) McN. BFA in Painting, Mass. Coll. Art, Boston, 1971, MFA in Painting, 1977. Tchr. Mus. Fine Arts Sch., Boston, 1983; undergrad. and grad. painting tchr. Mass. Coll. Art, Boston, 1988; undergrad. painting tchr. Boston Archtl. Ctr., Boston, 1977; color fundamentals tchr. Mass. Coll. Art, Boston, 1987, undergrad. drawing, 1975-88. One-man shows include Stavaridis Gallery, Boston, 1985, Bess Cutler Gallery, 1986, Mass. Coll. Art, 1986, Honolulu Acad. Fine Art, 1987, Nielson Gallery, 1990, 92; exhibited in group shows at Boston Collects, Mus. Fine Arts, Stavaridis Gallery, 1986, Bess Cutler Gallery, N.Y.C., 1987, Am. Painters and Sculptors, Met. Mus. Art, N.Y.C., 1988, Resonant Abstraction, Fuller Mus. Art, Brockton, Mass., 1989-90. Mass. Art and Humanities grantee, 1980, 83, 86, 89, Award in the Visual Arts grantee, 1982, Nat. Endowment Arts grantee, 1981. Home: 1140 Washington St Boston MA 02118

MCNAMARA, KEVIN JOHN, research institute executive; b. Abington, Pa., Oct. 6, 1957; s. John Kerwin and Dolores Ann (Auchinleck) McN; m. Juliane Cary Roebuck, July 17, 1982; children: Hilary Megan, Whitney Morgan. BA, Temple U., 1989. Journalist Calkins Newspapers Inc., Doylestown, Pa., 1981-85; congl. aide U.S. Rep. R. Lawrence Coughlin, Washington, 1985-88; asst. dir. Fgn. Policy Rsch. Inst., Phila., 1988—, rapporteur, 1990—. Contbg. editor Directors and Boards, 1988-89, Orbis: A Journal of World Affairs, 1990—; contbr. articles to profl. jours. Co-chmn. Marty Laub for State Rep., 1992, Craig Snyder for Congress, 1992; vol. Fox/Mele Rep. Team, 1991, George Bush for Pres. Com., 1987-88, Snyder for State Ho. Com., 1990; cons. Coughlin for Congress Com., 1986; bd. dirs. Abington Free Libr., 1992—. Mem. Am. Polit. Sci. Assn., World Affairs Coun. Phila., Abington High Sch. Alumni Assn. (v.p. 1984). Republican. Episcopalian. Office: Fgn Policy Rsch Inst 3615 Chestnut St Philadelphia PA 19104-6006

MCNAMEE, JOYCE MARIE, educator; b. Waterloo, Iowa, Dec. 14, 1934; d. Theory Gaven Jr. and Vera Louise (Morse) McN. B in Religious Edn., Bapt. Bible Sem., 1957; MS in Elem. Edn., SUNY, Cortland, 1963. Cert. elem. edn., N.Y., Ohio, Pa., secondary edn. Ohio. Dir. Christian edn. Immanuel Bapt. Ch., Fort Wayne, Ind., 1957-60; acad. tchr. Syracuse (N.Y.) State Sch., 1960-62; dir. Christian edn. Northfield (Ohio) Bapt. Ch., 1962-64; tchr., elem. and secondary edn. Bapt. Christian Sch., Cleve., 1964-76; assoc. prof. Bapt. Bible Coll. of Pa., Clarks Summit, Pa., 1976—; chair dept. Christian sch. edn. Bapt. Bible Coll. of Pa., Clarks Summit, 1986-91; chair Dept. Christian Sch. Edn. Bapt. Bible Coll. of Pa., 1991—. Mem. Nat. Coun. Tchrs. English. Home: Tall Timbers Box 89 Factoryville PA 18419 Office: Bapt Bible Coll of Pa PO Box 800 Clarks Summit PA 18411-0800

MCNEELY, TORI LEIGH, personnel manager; b. Jacksonville, N.C., Sept. 25, 1956; d. Arch Henry and Alyce Elisabeth (Stanley) Poeppel; m. Charles Ray McNeely Jr., July 5, 1980; children: Richard Raymond, Charles Ray III, Dustin Charles. Student, Cumberland County Coll., 1987-88. Pers. mgr. Val Mode Lingerie, Inc., Bridgeton, N.J., 1975—. Author: (poem) My Little Donnie, 1988 (Golden Poet award 1991). Vol. March of Dimes (Vol. of Yr. 1991). Val Mode Mut. Benefit Assn. (pres. 1986—), Bridgeton Quarterback Club (v.p. 1989—). Republican. Home: 222 Belmont Ave Bridgeton NJ 08302-4007 Office: Val Mode Lingerie Inc 45 Rosehayn Ave Bridgeton NJ 08302

MCNEIL, EDWARD WARREN, real estate executive; b. Alhambra, Calif., Jan. 5, 1942; s. Murray Charles and Helen Katherine (Curtis) McN.; m. Jutta Bocking, Apr. 1, 1941; children: Anja Britt, Bradley Stuart. Student civil engring., U. Calif., Berkeley, 1960-63. Structures engr. Peter Kiewit Sons Co., various cities, Calif., 1961-63; project engr. Huntington Harbour, Sunset Beach, Calif., 1963-64; project supt. Coordinated Realty, Inc., Anaheim, Calif., 1964-65; field ops. mgr. Lear Siegler, Saigon, Vietnam, 1965-67; project engr. Constructora Emkay, Rio Blanco, Chile, 1968-69; ptnr. The Pyramid Cos., Syracuse, N.Y., 1969-75, The Pioneer Group, Syracuse, 1975—. Chmn., bd. dirs. Crouse Irving Meml. Hosp. Found., Syracuse, 1986—; trustee Everson Mus. of Art, Syracuse, 1981—; past vice chmn.; bd. dirs. Syracuse Stage, 1981—, past chmn. and vice chmn.; trustee Adirondack chpt. Nature Conservancy, 1991—, Adirondack Land Trust, 1991—. Recipient award for svc. to the arts, Cultural Resource Coun., Syracuse, 1987. Mem. Aircraft Owners and Pilots Assn., Seaplane Pilots Assn., Slocum Soc., Century Club, Royal Cornwall Yacht Club (Eng.).

Republican. Methodist. Office: The Pioneer Group 500 S Salina St Syracuse NY 13202-3302

MCNEIL, JAMES H., JR., loss prevention consultant; b. Williamsport, Pa., Aug. 3, 1945; s. Chester Allen and Charlotte May (Eslick) Matters; m. Fay Ann Derr, Dec. 28, 1965; children: Beverly Ann, Shawn Gregory. BA in Bus., Columbia (Mo.) Coll., 1976. Probation and parole officer Northumberland County, Sunbury, Pa., 1983-87; loss prevention cons. PMA Group, Lemoyne, Pa., 1987—. With U.S. Army, 1963-83. Decorated Purple Heart, Bronze Star with V. Mem. Am. legion, Am. Soc. Safety Engrs., Non-Commd. Officers Assn. Republican. Roman Catholic. Home: RR 2 Box 370 Watsontown PA 17777-9405 Office: PMA Group PO Box 604 Lemoyne PA 17043-0604

MCNEIL, KENNETH MARTIN, chemical engineer, educator; b. Edinburgh, Scotland, Oct. 20, 1941; came to U.S., 1965; s. George Martin and May Hood (Wardlaw) McN. BSc summa cum laude, U. Edinburgh, 1962; PhD, U. Cambridge, England, 1966. Registered profl. engr., Pa. Sr. project chem. engr. Amoco Chems. Corp., Whiting, Ind., 1965-70; asst. prof. chem. engring. Drexel U., Phila., 1970-76; cons. chem. engr. Kenneth M. McNeil & Assoc., Phila., 1976-81; chmn. dept. chem. engring. Widener U., Chester, Pa., 1982—; cons. Sun Oil Co., Marcus Hook, Pa., 1972-84, Catalytic, Inc., Phila., 1973-78, Du Pont Co., Wilmington, Del., 1990—. Contbr. articles to profl. jours. Recipient Shell prize Shell Oil Co., 1961; Carnegie Found. scholar, 1962-65. Mem. Inst. Chem. Engrs., Am. Inst. Chem. Engrs., Am. Chem. Soc., Am. Soc. Engring. Edn., Sigma Xi. Home: 969 E 20th St Chester PA 19013-5615 Office: Widener U Dept Chem Engring Chester PA 19013

MCNEIL, MICHAEL BREWER, metallurgist; b. Houston, July 26, 1938; s. Brewer Taylor and Anne Caroline (Smith) McN.; m. Carol Beth Elizabeth Beckman, Dec. 21, 1960; 1 child, Brewer Taylor. BA, Rice U., 1959, MA, 1962; PhD, U. Mo., 1966. Postdoctoral fellow Wills Lab., Bristol U., U.K., 1966-67; assoc. physicist Midwest Rsch. Inst., Kansas City, Mo., 1967-68; vis. assoc. prof. Iowa State U., Ames, 1969; assoc. prof. Miss. State U., State College, 1968-72; metallurgist Nat. Bur. Standards, Gaithersburg, Md., 1972-77; program mgr. Dept. Energy, Washington, 1977-82; materials scientist NRC, Washington, 1982-87; supervisory physicist Naval Coastal Systems Ctr., Panama City, Fla., 1987-91; materials scientist NRC, Washington, 1991—; Nat. Acad. Sci. vis. lectr. to Bucharest and Cluj, Romania, 1971. Co-author: Waste Heat Management Guidebook, 1977; contbr. articles to profl. jours. NSF fellow, 1959-60; AEC spl. fellow, 1964-66. Fellow Phys. Soc., Instn. of Metallurgists (treas. 1972-76). Home: 9501 Aspenwood Pl Gaithersburg MD 20879 Office: NRC Office of Rsch Washington DC 20555

MCNEILL, ALFRED THOMAS, JR., construction executive; b. Elizabeth, N.J., Dec. 21, 1936; s. Alfred T. and Mary Ellen (Byrne) McN.; m. Dorothy J. Keidat, Oct. 4, 1982; children: Mary McNeill Ivanoski, Gabrielle McNeill Hensley, Matthew, Christopher, Peter, Bartholomew, Elizabeth McNeill Downes, Catherine, Gwyneth Elizabeth. BSCE, Lehigh U., 1958. Registered profl. engr., Ohio, N.Y. With Turner Constrn. Co., 1958-86; field engr. Turner Constrn. Co., N.Y.C., 1958; supt. Turner Constrn. Co., Cin., 1961, gen. supt., 1969; corp. v.p. ops. Turner Constrn. Co., N.Y.C., 1973; v.p., gen. mgr. Turner Constrn. Co., Phila., 1975, regional sr. v.p., 1981; pres., chief exec. officer Turner Constrn. Co., N.Y.C., 1985; pres. The Turner Corp., N.Y.C., 1986-89, chmn. bd., chief exec. officer, 1989—; chmn. State of Ohio Apprenticeship Coun., Cin., 1970-73; mem. nat. collective bargaining com. Associated Gen. Contractors, 1970-75, nat. dir., 1986-87; mem. labor policy com. Gen. Bldg. Contractors Assn., 1975-80, bd. dirs., 1978-84; bd. dirs. Tchrs. Properties, Inc., Rouse-Tchrs. Properties; adv. bd. Liberty Mut. Ins. Co.; mem. Constrn. Industry Pres.'s Forum; mem. civil engring. adv. bd. Lehigh U. Co-author: Construction Management for the General Contractor, 1974. Mem. chmn.'s circle USA-ROC Econ. Coun. 2d lt. U.S. Army, 1959, capt. Res. Recipient award Nat. Associated Gen. Contrators, 1974, De La Salle medal Manhattan Coll., 1991; cert. of recognition Harvard Bus. Sch., 1982. Mem. Am. Inst. Constructors (constructor), Regional Plan Assn. (bd. dirs. 1985-87), Econ. Club N.Y., Aronimink Country Club (Newtown Square, Pa.), The Sky Club (N.Y.C. v.p., bd. govs.), Blind Brook Club (Purchase, N.Y.), Ocean Reef Club (Key Largo, Fla.). Roman Catholic. Office: The Turner Corp 375 Hudson St New York NY 10014

MCNEILL, ANDREA, violin maker; b. Sussex, Eng., May 25, 1964; came to U.S., 1988; Diploma in violin making, 1991. Prin. Music Printing Bus., Brighton, Eng., 1984-85, Child Care Bus., Sydney, Australia, 1986; clk. Texaco Offices, London, 1986, Middlesex Hosp., London, 1987, Associated Bd. of Music, London, 1988; artist Boston, 1988—. Mem. Nature Conservancy, Sierra Club (resident artist 1990—).

MCNEILL, CORBIN ASAHEL, JR., utility executive; b. Santa Fe, July 6, 1939; s. Corbin Asahel and Madeline (Thielen) McN.; m. Dorice Schiller, June 16, 1962; children: Michele, Corbin IV, Kevin, Alicia, Timothy. BS in Marine Engring., U.S. Naval Acad., 1962; postgrad., Naval Nuclear Power Sch., Mare Island, Md., 1962-63, U. Calif., Berkeley, 1975-76, Syracuse U., 1983-84. Commd. ensign USN, 1962, advanced through grades to comdr., 1981, ret., 1981; sr. v.p. nuclear generation N.Y. Power Authority, White Plains, 1981-85, Pub. Service Electric & Gas Co., Hancocks Bridge, N.J., 1985-88; exec. v.p. nuclear div. Phila. Electric Co., 1988-90, pres., chief operating officer, 1990—. Trustee The Meml. Hosp. of Salem County (N.J.) Inc., 1986; chmn. TeamWalk March of Dimes, Salem, 1986; bd. dirs. Oswego (N.Y.) C. of C., 1982-83. Mem. Am. Nuclear Soc., Nuclear Utility Mgmt. and Resources Com. Office: Phila Electric Co 2301 Market St S26 1 Philadelphia PA 19101

MCNELIS, JOHN, surgeon; b. N.Y.C., June 13, 1957; s. Edward Joseph and Katerina (Toumpopoulou) McN.; m. Maribeth Slevin, Dec. 27, 1991. BA, NYU, 1979; MD, U. Buffalo, 1983. Intern N.Y. Med. Coll., Valhalla, 1983-84, resident, 1984-88, chief resident, 1988-89, clin. instr., 1989-90; attending physician, emergency rm. Westchester Sq. Med. Ctr., Bronx, N.Y., 1989; fellow cardiothoracic surgery Newark (N.J.) Beth Israel Med. Ctr., 1990-91; staff surgeon Raritan Bay Med. Ctr., Pearth Amboy, N.J., 1991—. Mem. AMA.

MCNERNEY, JAMES EDWARD, JR., podiatrist, educator; b. Binghamton, N.Y., Nov. 25, 1946; s. James E. and Catharine (Hurley) McN. AB, King's Coll., 1968; D Podiatric Medicine, Pa. Coll. Podiatric Medicine, 1972. Diplomate Am. Bd. Podiatric Health, Am. Bd. Foot Surgeons, Am. Bd. Podiatric Orthopedics. Asst. prof. clin. edn. and community health Pa. Coll. Podiatric Medicine, Phila., 1978, assoc. prof. orthopedics and surgery, 1978—. Fellow Am. Coll. Podiatric Orthopedics.

MCNERNEY, JOHN CORNELIUS, medical consultant; b. Southington, Conn., Dec. 8, 1902; s. Cornelius and Mary M. (Martin) McN.; m. Evelyn Fay (dec. 1950); m. Katherine J. Gallagher, July 21, 1956. MD, Jefferson Med. Sch., 1927. Diplomate Am. Bd. Surgery. Resident Jefferson Hosp., Phila., 1927-30; fellow Crile Clinic, Cleve., 1935-36; asst. mem. staff in neurol. surgery Jefferson Hosp., Phila., 1938-41; instr. in neurol. surgery Temple U., Phila., 1941-42; commd. lt. comdr. USNR, 1942; advance through grades to capt. USN, 1946, ret., 1951; chief neurol. surgery Nat. Naval Med. Ctr., Bethesda, Md., 1948-51; asst. prof. neurol. surgery Women's Med. Coll., Phila., 1951-52; cons. St. Joseph's Hosp., Stamford, Conn., 1953—. Fellow ACS, Internat. Coll. Surgeons; mem. AMA, Am. Assn. Neurosurgeons, Army Navy Club, Rotary Club. Home and Office: 111 Fourbrooks Rd Stamford CT 06903-4629

MCNICOL, SHARON-ANN GOPAUL, psychologist; b. Trinidad and Tobago, Oct. 6, 1958; came to U.S., 1979; d. St. Elmo and Monica (Pantor) Gopaul; m. Ulric McNicol, Jan. 6, 1979; 1 child, Monique. BA in Psychology, NYU, 1981; MA in Devel. Psychology, Columbia U., 1982; MS in Gen. Psychology, Hofstra U., 1984, PhD in Clin. Psychology, 1986. Lic. psychologist, N.Y.; cert. sch. psychologist, N.Y. Psychologist Nassau County Dept. Drug and Alcohol Addiction, L.I., N.Y., 1985-86, Creedmore Psychiat. Ctr., N.Y.C., 1986-87; exec. dir. Multicultural Ednl. and Psychol. Svcs. P.C., Hempstead, N.Y., 1987—; psychol. cons. N.Y.C. Edn. Edn., 1987—, L.I. Bd. Edn., 1987—; adj. asst. prof. St. John's U., N.Y.C., 1989—; cons. to Caribbean polit. parties, W.I., 1989—, Trinidad and Tobago Tchrs. Union, Ministry Edn. in Caribbean, Caribbean Commonwealth Consuls Gen. Author: (with T. Thomas and G. Irish) Immigrant Handbook on Some Educational and Social Issues in the United States, 1991; also articles. Grad. fellow Columbia U., 1981-82, Hofstra U., 1983-86. Mem. APA, N.Y. State Assn. Black Psychologists, Nassau County Psychol. Assn. Democrat. Roman Catholic. Home: 109 Holly Ave Hempstead NY 11550-5209

MCNIEL, KENNETH LAURENCE, psychologist; b. Orange, N.J., Jan. 26, 1955; s. Kenneth Edwin and Laurette (Connors) McN.; m. Mary Kate Hauck, June 26, 1982; children: Kevin, Brian. BA, U. Pa., 1977, MS, 1977; PhD, U. Louisville, 1988. Tchr., coach Montville (N.J.) Twp. High Sch., 1978-82; clin. dir. Beadleston Sch., Clark, N.J., 1987-90; prin. clin. psychologist Adult Diagnostic and Treatment Ctr., Avenel, N.J., 1990—. Mem. APA, Assn. for Advancement of Family Therapy (bd. dirs. 1990-91), N.J. Psychol. Assn. Democrat. Unitarian. Home and Office: 39 Canoe Brook Pky Summit NJ 07901-1401

MCNIFF, CHRISTINE MARIE, personnel manager; b. Concord, Mass., July 13, 1946; d. John Nicholas and Anna Elizabeth (Casey) D'Errico; m. John Thomas McNiff, June 20, 1970; children: Lisa Ann, Sean Patrick. AS in Bus. Adminstrn., Boston U., 1986, BS in Human Resource Mgmt., 1990. Designer, trainer Digital Mgmt. Edn., Bedford, Mass., 1978-84; sr. pers. cons. Digital Equipment Corp., Nashua, N.H., 1984-86, tng. mgr., 1986-87; human resource mgr. Digital Equipment Corp., Maynard, Mass., 1987-88, pers. mgr., 1988—. Vol. Concord Family Svcs. Young Parent Program; tchr. Confraternity of Christian Doctrine. Mem. Organizational Devel. Network, Soc. Human Resource Mgrs. Office: Digital Equipment Corp 146 Main St Maynard MA 01754-2504

MCNULTY, MICHAEL ROBERT, congressman; b. Troy, N.Y., Sept. 16, 1947; s. John J. McN. Jr.; m. Nancy Ann Lazzaro; children: Michele, Angela, Nancy, Maria. Grad., St. Joseph's Inst., Barrytown, N.Y., 1965, Loyola U. Rome Ctr., 1968, Hill Sch. Ins., N.Y.C., 1970; B.A. in Polit. Sci., Coll. Holy Cross, 1969. Town supr. Town of Green Island, N.Y., 1969-77, mayor, 1977-82; mem. N.Y. State Assembly, 1982-88, chmn. subcom. on town and village elections, mem. legis. commn. on rural resources, 1982-88, asst. dir. adminstrv. regulations rev. commn., 1977-82, mem. com., 1977-82; past chmn. planning com. Capital Dist. Transp. Com.; mem. 101st-102nd Congresses from 23rd N.Y. dist., 1989—; past chmn. task force for constrn. Troy-Green Island Bridge; chmn. United Way campaign, 1982. Mem. staff com. on edn. N.Y. State Constl. Conv., 1967; del. Dem. Nat. Conv., 1972; campaign mgr. John J. McNulty Jr. for Sheriff of Albany County, N.Y., 1973; participant 1974 polit. campaign mgmt. inst. Kent State U., Ohio; mem. Albany County Dem. Com.; chmn. Green Island Dem. Com.; mem. N.Y. State Dem. Com. Office: US Ho of Reps Office House Mems Washington DC 20510*

MCNULTY, NANCY G(ILLESPIE), business writer, editor, management consultant; b. Greenville, Pa., May 1, 1919; d. Stanley A. and Bess (Anthony) Gillespie; m. Arthur P. McNulty, July 16, 1942 (dec. 1961); 1 child, Terence. BA, Thiel Coll., 1940; MA, NYU, 1948. Industry analyst Equity Corp., 1940-42; writer, researcher Time Inc., N.Y.C., 1942-45; internal cons., 1957-68; founder, dir. Internat. Survey of Mgmt. Edn., N.Y.C., 1968—; cons. Chase Bank World Info. Svc., Japan Soc., Am. Mgmt. Assn., Inst. for Advancement of Economy, Austria, The Conf. Bd., UN Dept. of Tech. Coop. for Devel., N.Y. State Commn. on Edn., Time Inc.; editor, writer, cons. mgmt. edn., 1968—. Editor: Training Managers-The International Guide, 1969, Management Education Programs-The World's Best, 1980, The International Directory of Executive Education, 1985; contbr. numerous articles to profl. jours. Ford Found. scholar, 1968, 78. Fellow Internat. Acad. Mgmt. (hon.); mem. N.Am. Mgmt. Coun. (v.p., editor newsletter 1990—), Internat. Cons. Found., European Found. Mgmt. Devel., Internat. Found. Action Learning, Acad. Internat. Bus., Acad. Mgt., Yale Club of N.Y.C. Episcopalian. Home and Office: 55 W 89th St New York NY 10024-2028

MCPARTLON, JAMES PETER, III, ambulance service executive; b. Niagara Falls, N.Y., Mar. 28, 1959; s. James Peter McPartlon Jr. and Anne Kathryn (O'Connor) Brown; m. Diana Williams, May 9, 1987; 1 child, James Peter IV. BSBA, Niagara U., 1985. Adminstrv. dir. Mohawk Ambulance Svc., Schenectady, N.Y., 1984-86, v.p., gen. mgr., 1986—; bd. dirs. Schenectady Local Devel. Corp. Mem. adv. bd. Drug Abuse Resistance Edn. Program, Schenectady, 1991—; bd. dirs. Schenectady County Traffic Safety Bd., 1992. Mem. Elks (esquire 1988-89, 2d place award 1989), Kiwanis Club of Schenectady (pres. 1991-92). Republican. Roman Catholic. Home: 1015 DiBella Dr Schenectady NY 12303 Office: Mohawk Ambulance 793 State St Schenectady NY 12307

MC PHEE, JOHN ANGUS, writer; b. Princeton, N.J., Mar. 8, 1931; s. Harry Roemer and Mary (Ziegler) McP.; m. Pryde Brown, Mar. 16, 1957; children: Laura, Sarah, Jenny, Martha; m. Yolanda Whitman, Mar. 8, 1972; stepchildren: Cole, Andrew, Katherine, Vanessa Harrop. AB, Princeton U., 1953; postgrad., Magdalene Coll., Cambridge (Eng.) U., 1953-54; LittD (hon.), Bates Coll., 1978, Colby Coll., 1978, Williams Coll., 1979, U. Alaska, 1980, Coll. William and Mary, 1988, Rutgers U., 1988; ScD, Maine Maritime Acad., 1992. TV playwright for Robert Montgomery Presents, N.Y.C., 1955-56; contbg. editor, assoc. editor Time mag., 1957-64; staff writer The New Yorker mag., 1965—; Ferris prof. journalism Princeton U., 1975—. Author: A Sense of Where You Are, 1965, The Headmaster, 1966, Oranges, 1967, The Pine Barrens, 1968, A Roomful of Hovings, 1968, Levels of the Game, 1969, The Crofter and the Laird, 1970, Encounters with the Archdruid, 1971, The Deltoid Pumpkin Seed, 1973, The Curve of Binding Energy, 1974, Pieces of the Frame, 1975, The Survival of the Bark Canoe, 1975, Coming into the Country, 1977, Giving Good Weight, 1979, Basin and Range, 1981, In Suspect Terrain, 1983, La Place de la Concorde Suisse, 1984, Table of Contents, 1985, Rising From the Plains, 1986, The Control of Nature, 1989, Looking for a Ship, 1990. Recipient award in lit. Am. Acad. and Inst. Arts and Letters, 1977, Woodrow Wilson award Princeton U., 1982, John Wesley Powell award U.S. Geol. Survey, 1988. Fellow Geol. Soc. Am.; mem. Am. Acad. and Inst. Arts and Letters.

MCPHERSON, ROBERT WESLEY, anesthesiology educator; b. Pocahontas, Ark., June 12, 1947; s. Raymond and Ruby Faye (Waltrip) McP.; m. Sarah Jane Roberts, Jan. 23, 1969; children: Kelly Allison, Adrienne Michelle. MD, U. Ark., 1973. Intern Brooke Army Med. Ctr., Ft. Sam Houston, Tex., 1973-74, resident in anesthesiology, 1974-77; staff Walter Reed Army Med. Ctr., Washington, 1977-80; asst. prof. anesthesiology Uniform Svc. Med. Sch., Bethesda, Md., 1978-80; asst. prof. Anesthesiology Johns Hopkins Hosp., Balt., 1980-85, assoc. prof. Anesthesiology, 1985—; bd. dirs. Johns Hopkins Hosp., Balt. Author 15 book chpts.; contbr. articles to profl. jours. Rsch. grantee NIH, Bethesda, 1992. Home: 1512 Applecroft Ln Cockeysville MD 21030 Office: Meyer 8-138 Johns Hopkins Hosp 600 N Wolfe St Baltimore MD 21205

MCQUAID, JOSEPH WOODBURY, newspaper executive; b. Manchester, N.H., Feb. 12, 1949; s. Bernard John and Margaret (Griffin) McQ.; m. Signe Karin Anderson, Nov. 2, 1975; children—Katharine, Brendan. Student, U. N.H., 1967-69. Reporter Union Leader, Manchester, N.H., 1969-71; Sunday editor N.H. Sunday News, Manchester, N.H., 1971-76; mng. editor Union Leader-Sunday News, Manchester, N.H., 1976-82, editor-in-chief, 1982—, v.p., 1986—; dir. Union Leader Corp., Manchester. Sec. Manchester Indsl. Council, 1974-84. Roman Catholic. Home: 256 N Bay St Manchester NH 03104-2324 Office: Union Leader Corp 100 William Loeb Dr Manchester NH 03109-5309

MCQUAID, SARAH LINN ALLEN, musician; b. Madrid, May 19, 1966; came to U.S., 1968; d. Jose Jardiel and Jane Addams Allen; m. Noel Martin McQuaid, May 28, 1988. Diploma, U. Strasbourg, France, 1986; BA in Philosophy magna cum laude, Haverford Coll., 1987. Tchr. music D.C. Pub. Schs. Summer Program, Washington, 1982; mgr. Vintage Instruments, Phila., 1987—; freelance musician Phila., 1987—. Musician record album Carnloch, 1990; co-author entry on musical instruments Anness Law Encyc. of Antiques, 1991; contbr. articles to newspapers. Bd. dirs. Phila. Ceili Group, 1989-90. Mem. Phila. Folk Song Soc. Democrat. Unitarian. Home: 37 W Durham St Philadelphia PA 19119 Office: Vintage Instruments 1529 Pine St Philadelphia PA 19102

MCQUILLEN, JEREMIAH JOSEPH, distribution executive; b. Buffalo, Jan. 7, 1941; s. Joseph Bernard and Marca Rita (Ammerman) McQ.; m. Maureen Elaine Brett; children: Michael, Karen, Kathleen. BS, Canisius Coll., 1962. Nat. sales mgr. Birge Wallcoverings, Buffalo, 1973-74, v.p., gen. mgr., 1976-79; v.p. mktg. Reed Decorative Products, Toronto, 1974-76; exec. v.p. Atlanta, 1979-81; exec. v.p. Northeastern Wallcoverings, Boston, 1981-88, pres., 1989-91; pres. comml. wallcoverings Forbo Wallcoverings Inc., 1991-92; exec. v.p. Hytex Industries, 1992—. Served to 1st lt., U.S. Army, 1962-64. Mem. Wallcovering Distbrs. Assn. (sec., treas. 1987—, v.p. 1988, pres. 1989-90), Wallcovering Info. Bur. (pres. 1980), Wallcovering Mfg. Assn. (v.p. 1980). Republican. Roman Catholic. Home: 3 Nauset St Medfield MA 02052-3006

MCQUILLEN, MICHAEL JOHN, academic dean, history educator; b. Buffalo, June 24, 1944; s. Harold Jerome and Mary Anne (O'Conner) McQ.; m. Joy Carol Knoll, June 15, 1968; children: David Michael, Daniel Michael, Carolyn Joy. BA, Canisius Coll., 1966; PhD, U. Va., 1973. From asst. to assoc. prof. Mercyhurst Coll., Erie, Pa., 1971-83, prof., 1983—, acad. dean, 1988—. Author: Best Known Name in Paper: Hammermill, A History of the Company, 1986, A Legacy of Love: A History of the Dr. Gertrude Barber Center, 1991. Mem. Arms Control Assn., Kiwanis, Phi Beta Kappa. Democrat. Roman Catholic. Home: 2334 Wintergreen Dr Erie PA 16510-4042 Office: Mercyhurst Coll 501 E 38th St Erie PA 16546-0001

MCSHANE, MICHAEL ALBERT, telecommunications executive; b. New Bedford, Mass., Apr. 26, 1947; s. Albert and Nina Elizabeth (Terry) McS.; m. Carole Brooks Webster, June 19, 1970; children: Christopher Michael, Andrew Albert. BA in Social Sci., U. So. Fla., 1972; MA in Indsl. Rels., U. Minn., 1974. Mgr. organizational planning Xerox Corp., Rochester, N.Y., 1977-79; mgr. hdqrs. personnel Xerox Corp., Rochester, 1983-87; mgr. personnel ops. Xerox Corp., Lexington, Mass., 1979-81; mgr. region personnel Xerox Corp., Phila., 1981-83; dir. human resources Sibson & Co., Princeton, N.J., 1987-89; v.p. human resources Contel ASC, Rockville, Md., 1989—. Contbr. articles to profl. jours. Coach, asst. commr. Howard County (Md.) Youth Programs, 1991. 1st lt. U.S. Army, 1967-70. Mem. Soc. Human Resources Mgmt., Forest Hills Country Club, Phi Kappa Phi. Home: 4034 Dado Ct Ellicott City MD 21042-5310 Office: GTE Spacenet 1700 Old Meadow Rd Mc Lean VA 22102-4304

MCSHEA, ROBERT JOSEPH, JR., data processing executive; b. Phila., Aug. 8, 1940; s. Robert Jospeh and Anne Elizabeth (Carroll) McS. BS in Econs., Villanova (Pa.) U., 1962; MBA, Ind. U., 1964. Data processing analyst Chgo. Transit Authority, 1963-67; sr. computer systems designer Pa., N.J., Md. Internconnection, Valley Forge, Pa., 1968—; treas. Tempo, Phila., 1978-86; sec. Computer Systems Subcom., Phila., 1987—; mem. Inter Utility Data Exch. Consortium Tech. Subcom., 1988—. Mem. Historic Preservation Soc. of Norristown, Pa., 1986—. Mem. COMMON, SHARE, Nat. Assn. Rwy. Passengers. Roman Catholic. Home: 635 W Main St Norristown PA 19401-4511 Office: Pa NJ Md Interconnection 955 Jefferson Ave Eagleville PA 19403-2497

MCSWEENEY, LINDA H., library director; b. Elizabeth, N.J., Jan. 19, 1956; d. Walter L. and Mary E. (Hatten) Howatt; m. D. Thomas McSweeney, Aug. 20, 1977. BS, Dickinson Coll., 1977; MLS, Rutgers U., 1982. Reference libr. Rutgers U., New Brunswick, N.J., 1982-84; head of reference Dept. of Librs., Montpelier, Vt., 1984-88; libr. dir. Vt. Tech. Coll., Randolph Center, 1988—. Mem. ALA, Vt. Libr. Assn. (pres. 1991—), Beta Phi Mu. Home: 9 Prospect St Northfield VT 05663-1417 Office: Vt Tech Coll Hartness Libr Randolph Center VT 05061

MCTAGGART, TIMOTHY THOMAS, mathematics/computer science secondary educator; b. Danville, Pa., Dec. 8, 1949; s. Thomas Francis and Mary Elizabeth (Russial) McT. BS, Bloomsburg (Pa.) U., 1971; MDiv, St. Vincent Coll., Latrobe, Pa., 1974; MEd, Millersville (Pa.) U., 1980; EdD, Pacific Western U., Honolulu, 1991. Cert. in secondary edn., Pa. Math. tchr. Lancaster (Pa.) Cath. High Sch., 1978-85, Columbia (Pa.) Sr. High Sch., 1985—; head track coach Columbia High Sch., 1986—. Mem. Pa. Athletic Assn. (football ofcl.), K.C. (knight 4th deg.). Home: 728 Sharon Dr Mount Joy PA 17552 Office: Columbia High Sch 901 Ironville Pike Columbia PA 17512

MCTEAGUE, LINDA BRAGDON, preservation planner, consultant; b. Rahway, N.J.; d. Lyle M. and Garnet (Gowdy) Cooper; m. John W. Bragdon; children: David A., Lucinda J. AB, Rutgers U., 1966, M of City and Regional Planning, 1984. Tchr. secondary history and Eng. Rahway High Sch. and The Vail Deane Sch., Elizabeth, N.J., 1966-84; preservation planner Union County, N.J., 1984—; adj. prof. Rutgers U., New Brunswick, 1986-88; advisor N.J. State Hist. Preservation Plan, 1987-88; cons. in field. Editor, author: Preserving New Jersey, 1986, rev. edit., 1987; editor: Rediscovery of Rahway, 1976; contbr. articles to profl. jours. State planner Washington Inaugural Bicentennial Project, 1988-89; bd. trustees Union County Arts Ctr. Mem. Am. Planning Assn., Nat. Trust for Hist. Preservation, Am. Assn. for State and Local History. Home and Office: 1208 Pierpont St Rahway NJ 07065-3231

MC TIGUE, JOHN FRANCIS, financial executive; b. Jersey City, N.J., Dec. 30, 1960; s. John F. Sr. and D. Joan (Ashmore) Mc T.; m. Elizabeth Adis, June 11, 1983 (div. Oct. 1987); m. Cynthia Jo Campo, Apr. 23, 1988. BS in Acctg., Seton Hall U., 1982, postgrad., 1989-91. CPA, N.J. Acct. Navresso, S.I., 1980-82, Rothstein Kass & Co CPAs, Roseland, N.J., 1983-89; chief fin. officer Daw Spl. Systems, Stamford, Conn., 1989-90; chief fin. officer, treas. Dawn Spl. Systems/Dawn Capital, Stamford, 1991—. Mem. AICPA, N.J. Inst. CPAs, Inst. of Mgmt. Accts. Home: 10 Greenview Dr Pequannock NJ 07440-1705 Office: Dawn Capital Corp & Subs 29 Elm Ave Mount Vernon NY 10550

MCVEIGH, KAREN HENDRIKA GEERTE, sales, marketing executive; b. The Hague, The Netherlands, Sept. 18, 1961; d. Hendrik J.L. and Maarje (Brouwer) Schuurmans; m. David McVeigh, June 3, 1989. BS, Rider Coll., Lawrenceville, N.J., 1983. Mktg. coord. CBS Inc., N.Y.C., 1983-87; pub. sales/book mktg. mgr. and advt./circulation mgr. Am. Found. for the Blind, N.Y.C., 1987—. Mem. Assn. Am. Pubrs. Republican. Presbyterian. Office: Am Found for the Blind 15 W 16th St New York NY 10011-6390

MCVEY, JAMES PAUL, fisheries biologist, aquaculturist; b. Evansville, Ind., Aug. 5, 1943; s. Donald Francis and Virginia Mae (Beckquist) McV.; m. Eileen Marie Keep, Aug. 16, 1970; children: Colleen Marie, Christopher James. BS, U. Miami, 1965; MS, U. Hawaii, 1967, PhD, 1970. Fishery aid Bur. Comml. Fisheries, Gulf Breeze, Fla., 1963-65; rsch. biologist Lockheed Aircraft Svc. Co., Kaneohe, Hawaii, 1966-67; rsch. asst. Bur. Sports Fisheries, U. Hawaii, Honolulu, 1967-70, teaching asst., 1969; fishery biologist Trust Ter. Pacific, Koror, Palau, 1970-72, chief Micronesian Mariculture Ctr., 1973-77; chief aquaculture div. SE Fisheries Ctr. Nat. Marine Fisheries Svc NOAA, Galveston, Tex., 1977-82; supervisory fishery biologist AID, Am. Embassy, Jakarta, Indonesia, 1982-84; dir. aquaculture program nat. sea grant program NOAA, Silver Spring, Md., 1984—; program chmn., chmn. U.S.-Japan Natural Resources Panel, Washington, 1986—; vice chair U.S. Joint Subcom. on Aquaculture, Washington, 1987—. Editor: CRC-Handbook of Mariculture, Vol. I, 1983, Vol. II, 1991; also articles. Vol. Internat. Exec. Svc. Corps, Egypt, 1981, Panama, 1988; coach Montgomery County Soccer Assn., Rockville, Md., 1984-90; leader Boy Scouts Am., Rockville, 1985—. Recipient spl. commendation Govt. of Indonesia, 1984, Outstanding Performance award NOAA, 1990; numerous rsch. grants, 1972-77. Mem. Nat. Aquaculture Assn., Nat. Shellfish Assn., Western Soc. Naturalists, World Aquaculture Soc. (bd. dirs. 1990—), Caribbean Aquaculture Soc., Pacific Aquaculture Assn. Methodist. Office: NOAA Nat Sea Grant Coll Program 1335 East-West Hwy Silver Spring MD 20910

MCWILLIAMS, BAYARD TAYLOR, forensic engineer. BSME, Pa. State U., 1948; MS in Aero. Engring., Bklyn. Poly. Inst., 1951; MBA cum laude, U. Wash., 1959. Registered profl. engr., N.J., Pa. Indsl. engr. group leader Boeing Aerospace Co., 1948; co-owner, chief engr. W.P. Damon Corp.; rsch.. engr. United Aircraft Co.; design test, sales and field engr. Curtiss-Wright Corp.; chief engring. devel. div., program mgr. Army Aviation Material Command, St. Louis, 1969-63; engring. group mgr. Naval Air Propulsion

Ctr., 1963-74, tech. cons. to comdg. officer, 1975-82; pres. McWilliams Engrng. Inc., Yardley, Pa., 1971—; chmn. 8 nat. confs. on environ. effects on aircraft and propulsion systems; grad. instr. Newark Coll. Engring., 1972; guest lectr. U. Tenn. Space Inst., 1976; advisor mech. engring. dept. Mercer County Community Coll.; advisor dept. electronics engring. tech. and dept. mech.-indsl. tech. Trenton (N.J.) State Coll. Fellow AiAA (assoc.), ASME (v.p. bd. profl. practice and ethics 1983-84), ; mem. NSPE, N.J. Soc. Profl. Engrs. (chmn. employer accreditation com., trustee 1981-82, Am. Assn. Engring. Socs. (chmn. engring. affairs coun. 1988—), AAAS, Am. Soc. Safety Engrs., Nat. Acad. Forensic Engrs. (diplomate), Nat. Fire Protection Assn., Am. Helicopter Soc. (sect. chmn.), Cen. Jersey Engring. Coun. (chmn. 1975-77), Profl. Engrs. Soc. Mercer County (trustee 1974, pres. 1981, Engr. of Yr. award), Franklin Inst. Office: PO Box 177 Yardley PA 19067

MCWILLIAMS, HARRY KENNETH, advertising executive; b. Middlesboro, Ky., July 20, 1907; s. John William and Mattie S. (Bayliss) McW.; student U. Colo., 1927, numerous spl. courses Denver Sch. Tech., 1925-26; m. Rosa di Giulio, June 3, 1936 (dec. Jan. 1988); children: Rosanne McWilliams Ulmer, Harry Kahle, Sarah Jane Fuller (Mrs. Gijs Van Stavern). Sales mgr. Acme Films, N.Y.C., 1930-32; owner Advt. Flag Co., 1930-37; publicity mgr. numerous chains, including Harry E. Huffman theatres and Paramount Publix Theatres, N.Y.C., Toledo, Denver, Dallas, 1926-30; advt. and publicity dir. Cin. Summer Opera, 15 seasons, also publicity mgr. concert booker number leading personalities including violinist Rubinoff, and radio program, mgr. Benton and Bowles, Ted Bates, Inc., also advance agt. San Carlo Opera Co., Legitimate Theatre Corp., USO Camp Shows, 1937-45; dir. exploitation Columbia Pictures Corp., N.Y.C., 1945-53; dir. advt. and pub. relations Screen Gems, Inc., 1953-54; pres., sales mgr. Air Programs, Inc., 1954-55; asst. dir. advt. and pub. Ben-Hur at MGM, 1959; coordinator advt. and pub. King of Kings, 1960; dir. advt. and pub. Pepe at Columbia Pictures, 1960; dir. community relations U. Cin., 1961-62; pvt. pub. relations counsellor, N.Y.C., promotion, publicity co-ordinator 1959, 60, 61, Acad. Awards Telecast, Motion Picture Assn. Am., Inc.; asst. advt. and pub. dir. Magna Theatres Corp.; advt. exec. 20th Century Fox Film Corp.; asst. gen. mgr. The Original Amateur Hour; pres., gen. mgr. Original Amateur Hour de Mexico, S.A., pres., gen. mgr. Harry K. McWilliams Assos., Inc., 1964-75; owner, gen. mgr. Pyramid Press, 1966-75; pres., owner MCW Orgn., Inc., N.Y.C., 1975—; world-wide distbr. fine arts films; pub. relations cons. Nat. Assn. Theatre Owners. Bd. dirs. Carolina Theatre. Recipient Silver Anvil award Am. Pub. Relations Assn., 1960. Mem. Assn. Theatrical Press Agt. and Mgrs. (gov., exec. com. 1955), Asso. Motion Picture Advertisers, Inc. (pres. 1950-52; dir., dean, founder sch. Showmanship, 1952-54), Pub. Rels. Soc. Am. Club: Travelers Century (life, gold card), Circumnavigator (N.Y.C.).

MEACHAM, JOHN ALLEN, psychology educator; b. Buffalo, Oct. 4, 1944. BA, Stanford U., 1966; MA, U. Mich., 1967, PhD, 1972. Vol. Peace Corps, Turkey, 1967-69; prof. psychology SUNY, Buffalo, 1972—, assoc. chmn. dept. psychology, 1984-86, assoc. vice provost for undergrad. edn., 1990—. Editor: The Developing Individual in a Changing World, 1976, Social Development in Youth, 1981, On the Development of Developmental Psychology, 1983, Family and Individual Development, 1985, Interpersonal Relations, 1987, Human Development, 1978-87, The Genetic Epistemologist, 1990—, (monograph series) Contributions to Human Development, 1980-88. Fellow Am. Psychol. Assn., Am. Psychol. Soc.; mem. AAUP, Jean Piaget Soc. (pres. 1991-93), Soc. for Rsch. in Child Devel. Office: SUNY Dept Psychology Buffalo NY 14260

MEACHIN, DAVID JAMES PERCY, investment banker, import-export executive; b. Teignmouth, Devon, Eng., Jan. 1, 1941; came to U.S., 1969; s. James Alfred and Ena Annie Meachin; m. Barbara Marshall Maxwell, Sept. 25, 1971; children: Jonathan J.M., Philip D.M. BS in Physical Sci., U. Natal, Republic South Africa, 1960; BSChemE, U. Cape Town, Republic South Africa, 1963; MS in Petroleum Engring., French Petroleum Inst., Paris, 1965; diploma in Indsl. Mgmt., Cambridge (Eng.) U., 1966; MBA with distinction, Harvard U., 1971. Project engr. Humphreys and Glasgow Ltd., London, 1966-69; 2d v.p. investment banking Smith Barney and Co. Inc., N.Y.C. and Tokyo, 1971-75; v.p., gen. mgr. internat. corp. fin. Salomon Bros., N.Y.C. and London, 1975-81; mng. dir. investment banking Merrill Lynch Capital Markets, N.Y.C., 1981-91; chmn., chief exec. officer Cross Border Enterprises Inc., 1991—; gen. ptnr. Meachin, Rath & Co., 1991—; bd. dirs. Ground Round Restaurants. Chmn. British Am. Ednl. Found.; elder Brick Presbyn. Ch., N.Y.C., 1988—; bd. dirs., vice-chmn. U. Cape Town Found., N.Y.C., 1985—; mem. UN Assn. Coun. of Fellows. Mem. Misquamicut Club (gov.), Watch Hill Yacht Club, Hurlingham Club, United Oxford and Cambridge Club, Jupiter Island Club, Harvard Club, Union Club, Sky Club (N.Y.C.). Home: 1105 Park Ave New York NY 10128-1200 Office: Cross Border Enterprises Inc 441 Lexington Ave New York NY 10017

MEADER, JOHN DANIEL, judge; b. Ballston Spa, N.Y., Oct. 22, 1931; s. Jerome Clement and Doris Luella (Conner) M.; m. Joyce Margaret Cowin, Mar. 2, 1963; children: John Daniel Jr., Julia Rae, Keith Alan. BA, Yale U., 1954; JD, Cornell U., 1962. Bar: N.Y. 1963, U.S. Dist. Ct. (no. dist.) N.Y. 1963, U.S. Ct. Appeals (2d cir.) 1966, U.S. Supreme Ct. 1967, U.S. Ct. Mil. Appeals 1973, Ohio 1978, U.S. Dist. Ct. (no. dist.) Ohio 1979, Fla. 1983. Sales engr. Albany (N.Y.) Internat. Corp., 1954-59; asst. track coach Cornell U., 1959-62; asst. sec., asst. to pres. Albany Internat. Corp., 1962-65; asst. atty. gen. State of N.Y., Albany, 1965-68; ops. counsel, attesting sec. GE, Schenectady, 1968-77; gen. counsel, asst. sec. Glidden div. SCM Corp., Cleve., 1977-81; chmn. bd., pres. Applied Power Tech. Co., Fernandina Beach, Fla., 1981-84; pres. Applied Energy, Inc., Ballston Spa, 1984-88; judge N.Y. State Workers Compensation Bd., Albany, 1988—; dir. Saratoga Mut. Fire Ins. Co. Author: Labor Law Manual, 1972, Contract Law Manual, 1974, Patent Law Manual, 1978. Candidate U.S. Ho. of Reps., 29th Dist. N.Y., 1964, N.Y. Supreme Ct., 1975, 87. Col. JAGC, USAR, 1968—, dep. staff judge adv. 3d U.S. Army & Cen. Command, 1984. Nat. AAU High Sch. 1000 Yard Indoor Track Champion, 1949, Nat. AAU Prep. Sch. 440 and 880 Yard Indoor Track Champion, 1950, Nat. AAU Outstanding Performer award, Melrose Games Assn., 1950, Heptagonal Track 880-Yard Champion 1954. Mem. ABA, N.Y. State Bar Assn., Fla. Bar, Amelia Island Plantation Club, Cyprus Temple Club, Yale Club Jacksonville (pres.), Masons. Republican. Presbyterian. Home: 271 Round Lake Rd Ballston Lake NY 12019-1714 Office: NY State Workers Compensation Bd 100 Broadway Albany NY 12241-0001

MEADOR, CHARLES LAWRENCE, infosystems systems consultant, educator; b. Dallas, Oct. 7, 1946; s. Charles Leon and Dorothy Margaret (Brown), m. Diane E. Collins, May 18, 1985. BSME with honors, U. Tex., 1970; MSME, MS in Mgmt., MIT, 1972. Mem. engring. staff Union Carbide Corp., Houston, 1967-68; instr. Alfred P. Sloan Sch. Mgmt. MIT, Cambridge, 1972-75, asst. dir. Ctr. Info. Systems Rsch., 1976-78, lectr. Sch. Engring., co-dir. Macro-Engring. Rsch. Group, 1978—; founder, pres. Decision Support Tech., Inc., 1974-92; co-founder, vice chmn., dir. Software Productivity Rsch., Inc., 1985-87; pres., dir. The Softbridge Group, 1989-92; pres., dir. Mgmt. Support Tech. corp., 1992—; cons. to govt. and industry. Editor: How Big and Still Beautiful? Macro-Engineering Revisited, 1980, Macro-Engineering: The Rich Potential, 1981, Macro-Engineering and the Future: A Management Perspective, 1982, Macro-Engineering: Global Infrastructure Solutions, 1992; mem. editorial adv. bd. Computer Communication, 1979-91; mem. editorial bd. Communicacion e Informatica, 1980—; contbr. papers in field. Wilfred Lewis fellow, 1971; Draper Lab. fellow, 1974; NSF trainee, 1970. Mem. Computer Soc. of IEEE (vice chmn. Eastern Hemisphere and Latin Am. area com. 1977-83), Ops. Rsch. Soc. Am., Cosmos Club, St. Botolph's Club, Sigma Xi, Tau Beta Pi, Pi Tau Sigma. Home: 3 Windy Hill Ln Wayland MA 01778-2612 Office: MIT Rm 3-282 Cambridge MA 02139

MEADOW, LYNNE (CAROLYN MEADOW), theatrical producer and director; b. New Haven, Nov. 12, 1946; d. Frank and Virginia R. Meadow. BA cum laude, Bryn Mawr Coll., 1968; postgrad., Yale U., 1968-70. Dir. Theatre Communications Group, 1978-80; adj. prof. SUNY, Stony Brook, 1975-76, Yale U., Circle in the Sq., 1977-78, 89-91, NYU, 1977-80; theatre and music/theatre panelist Nat. Endowment for Arts, 1977-88; artistic advisor Fund for New Am. Plays, 1988-90. Artistic dir. Manhattan Theatre Club, N.Y.C., 1972—; guest dir. Nat. Playwrights Conf., Eugene O'Neill Theatre Ctr., 1975-77, Phoenix Theatre, 1976; dir. Ashes for Manhattan Theatre Club and N.Y. Shakespeare Festival, 1977; producer off-Broadway shows Ain't Misbehavin', 1978, Crimes of the Heart, 1981, Miss Firecracker Contest, 1984, Frankie and Johnny, 1987, Eastern Standard, 1988, Lisbon Traviata, 1989, Lips Together, Teeth Apart, 1991; dir. Principia Scritoriae, 1986, Woman in Mind, 1988 (Drama Desk award), Eleemosynary, 1989, Absent Friends, 1991; dir. Broadway prodn. A Small Family Business, 1992; co-producer off-Broadway and Broadway show Mass Appeal, 1981. Recipient Citation of Merit Nat. Coun. Women, 1976, Outer Circle Critics award 1977, Drama Desk award, 1977, Obie award for Ashes, 1977, Margo Jones award for Continued Encouragement New Playwrights, 1981, Critics Circle award Outstanding Revival on or off Broadway for Loot, 1986, Lucille Lortel award for Outstanding Achievement, 1987, Spl. Drama Desk award, 1989, N.y. Drama Critics Circle award Best Fgn. Play for Aristocrats, 1989, Torch of Hope award, 1989; named Northwood Inst. Distinq. Woman of Yr., 1990. Office: Manhattan Theatre Club 453 W 16th St New York NY 10011-5896

MEADOWS, GREGORY PAUL, graphic designer; b. Oneonta, N.Y., June 5, 1962; s. Paul Owen and Marthe-Marie (Methot) M. AAS, Mohawk Valley Community Coll., 1982; BA, SUNY, Fredonia, 1984. Graphic designer Roger White Advt., Binghamton, N.Y., 1984-85; art dir. Design for Industry, Inc., Buffalo, 1985—; lectr. art SUNY, Fredonia, 1986—, Villa Maria Coll., Buffalo, 1988-89. Mem. Am. Inst. Graphic Arts, Art Dirs. Club. Home: 31 Livingston St Buffalo NY 14213-1942

MEADS, DONALD EDWARD, management services company executive; b. Salem, Mass., Sept. 23, 1920; s. Laurence G. and Gertrude F. M.; m. Jane Lightner, June 15, 1943; children: Edward G., Robert C., Laurence G., Judith C. Antrim, Suzanne M. O'Neil, Clifford L., Nancy Chapin. A.B. in Pre-Law, Dartmouth Coll., 1942; M.B.A. in Fin., Harvard U., 1947. Vice-pres., vice-chmn. investment com. N.Y. Life Ins. Co., N.Y.C., 1947-61; v.p. fin., chmn. investment com. Investors Diversified Services Inc., Mpls., 1961-65; pres., chief exec. officer Internat. Basic Economy Corp., N.Y.C., 1965-67, chmn., chief exec. officer, 1967-71; exec. v.p., dir., chief fin. officer, chmn. investment com. INA Corp., Phila., 1971-74; chmn. bd., chief exec. officer CertainTeed Corp., Valley Forge, Pa., 1974-78, dir., 1973-78; chmn. Mateer-Burt Co., Inc., Plymouth Meeting, Pa., 1984-87; chmn. Phila. First Group Inc., 1982-90; chmn. Carver Assocs., Inc., Plymouth Meeting, 1978—; dir. Perdue Farms, Inc., Salisbury, Md.; hon. life trustee Valley Forge Mil. Acad. & Coll., Wayne Pa., trustee emeritus Thomas Jefferson U., Phila.; bd. dirs. Independence Hall Assn., Phila.; hon. dir. Marine Corps Scholarship Found., Princeton, N.J.; mem. Phila. Com. on Fgn. Relations; bd. dirs. World Affairs Council Phila. Served to capt. USMC, 1942-45. Decorated D.F.C., Air medals (6). Mem. Harvard Club of N.Y.C., Sunday Breakfast Club, Union League (Phila.), Rockefeller Ctr. Club (N.Y.C.).

MEAGHER, ROBERT STEPHEN, advertising director; b. Balt., Dec. 17, 1958; s. Mark Joseph and Patricia Ann (Essex) M.; m. Patricia Ann Acerenza, Oct. 2, 1982; children: Kyle Louis, Patrick Robert. BS, Am. U., 1982. Sales rep. Sawyer Fergusen Walker Co., Boston, 1983-86; N.Y. sales mgr. USA Weekend Mag., N.Y.C., 1986-88; sales rep. Reader's Digest, N.Y.C., 1988-89; v.p., midwest mgr. Fin. World Mag., Chgo., 1989-90; v.p., ea. advt. dir. Fin. World Mag., N.Y.C., 1990—. Mem. Newspaper Advt. Sales Assn. (sec. 1984-86), Ad Club N.Y., Agate Club Chgo., Exch. Club of Edison, N.J. Office: Fin World Mag 1328 Broadway New York NY 10001-2121

MEAKIN, JOHN DAVID, university research executive, educator; b. Nottingham, Eng., Feb. 11, 1934; came to U.S., 1958, naturalized, 1972; s. Claude Edwin and Hilda May (Storer) M.; m. Katharine Sadie Glover, July 21, 1956; children: Robert Nicholas, David Harry, Ian James, William Edwin, Andrew John. B.Sc. in Metallurgy, Leeds (Eng.) U., 1955, Ph.D., 1957. Vis. asso. Franklin Inst., Phila., 1958-59; research fellow U. Durham, Eng., 1960-62; sr. rsch. scientist Franklin Inst., 1962-65, prin. scientist, 1965-70, mgr. lab., 1970-74; prof. mech. engring. U. Del., 1974—, chmn. mech. engring. dept., 1987—, sr. scientist Inst. Energy Conversion, 1974—; vis. prof. U. Del., 1966, U. Murdoch, 1983. Contbr. articles to profl. jours. Yorkshire Copper Works (Eng.) Research scholar, 1955; Dept. Sci. and Indsl. Research scholar, 1956-57; Imperial Chem. Industries sr. research fellow, 1961, 62. Mem. IEEE (sr.). Home: 905 Baylor Dr Newark DE 19711-3127

MEALEY, MICHAEL PALMER, publishing company executive; b. Oakland, Calif., May 16, 1940; s. Thomas Rowan and Mary Patricia (Palmer) M.; m. Judith Marion Seaverns, May 14, 1970; children: Thomas Michael, Elizabeth Ann. Grad. high sch., Concord, Calif., 1958. Copy boy, sports reporter San Francisco Examiner, 1958-59; reporter Concord Transcript, 1959-61, Oakland Tribune, 1961-64, 66-67; reporter, Saigon bur. chief Pacific Stars and Stripes, Tokyo, Saigon, 1964-65; bur. chief McGraw-Hill World News, Tokyo, 1968-76; sr. corr. McGraw-Hill World News, Washington, 1976-79; mng. editor Andrews Publs., Inc., Edgemont, Pa., 1979-83; pres. Mealey Publs., Inc., Wayne, Pa., 1984—; bd. dirs. Prog. Bus. Publs., Berwyn, Pa., 1991—. Trustee Acad. Notre Dame du Namur, Villanova, Pa., 1989—. With U.S. Army, 1964-65, Tokyo/Vietnam. Decorated Bronze Star. Mem. Newsletter Pubs. Assn. (bd. dirs. 1989—), Pacific Stars and Stripes Alumni Assn. (pres. 1991—), Overbrook Golf Club. Republican. Home: 38 Dunminning Rd Newtown Square PA 19073 Office: Mealey Publs Inc 512 Lancaster Ave Wayne PA 19087

MEANS, ELIZABETH ROSE THAYER, lawyer, contracts manager, financial consultant; b. N.Y.C., Aug. 29, 1960; d. Cyril Chesnut and Rosaline (Limtucio) M. BS, Chatham Coll., 1983; JD, Samford U., 1989; LLM, Boston U., 1990; Cert. in Comparative Law, Heidelberg U., 1988. Bar: Mass., 1991, Pa., 1991. Dancer The N.Y.C. Ballet Co., 1971, Balanchine Cast for PBS "The Nutcracker Suite", N.Y.C., 1971; docent The Hammond Castle Mus., Gloucester, Mass., 1982-85; asst. mgr. The Gallery, Rockport, Mass., 1979-83; cons. The Galleries, Ltd., Wellesley, Mass., 1988; legal intern U. Ala. Health Svcs. Found., Birmingham, 1988-89; loan officer UN/UNFCU, N.Y.C., 1984-86; contracts mgr. for Eastern Region Unisys Corp., Berkeley Heights, N.J., 1990-92; fin. cons. Innovatech, Lexington, Mass., 1992—; chairwoman Cordell Hull Speakers' Forum, Birmingham, 1988-89; alumnae class sec. Chatham Coll. Class of 1980s, Pitts., 1983-88. Recipient Cert. of Appreciation 1990 Alumni award Cumberland Sch. Law, 1990; named to Nat. Dean's List, 1989-90. Mem. DAR, The Federalist Soc. Cumberland Chpt. (treas. 1988-89, adv. bd. 1988, sec. 1987-88), The Menzies Clan Soc., Princeton Club. Republican. Episcopalian. Home: Brier Neck 13 Salt Island Rd Gloucester MA 01930 Office: Innovatech 6 Abbott Rd Lexington MA 02173

MEANS, FRED ERNEST, dean; b. Pacolet, S.C.; s. Fred Sr. and Lemor E. (Tucker) M.; m. Helen Pryor; children: Vincent, Marc, Chad. BS, NYU, 1959; MA, Trenton State Coll., 1963; MEd, Rutgers U., 1973, EdD, 1975. Cert. tchr., N.Y., N.J. Tchr. PS 621, N.Y.C., 1959-60, Dayton Elem. Sch., Newark, 1960-65; tchr., title coord. South Side High Sch., Newark, 1965-70; lectr., program dir. Rutgers U., New Brunswick, N.J., 1970-71, dir., 1970-75; dir. Jersey City State Coll., 1975-78, dir., asst. dean, 1978-85, dean, 1985—; prin. Cleveland Head Start, Newark, summers 1968, 69, 70; bd. dirs. Newark Bd. Edn., 1973-76, Rsch. for Better Schs., 1983—. Chmn. Newark-Essex Congress Racial Equality, 1964-65; bd. dirs. United Community Corp. Newark Anti-Poverty Agy., 1966, Bus. Indsl. Coord. Coun., Newark, 1967-69, Action for Sickle Cell, Hudson County, N.J., 1982-89; pres. Orgn. Negro Edn., Newark, 1967-70; com. chair Nat. Alliance Black Sch. Edn., 1974-75. With U.S. Army, 1953-56. Mem. ASCD, N.J. Assn. Black Educators (Outstanding Black Educator 1987), Nat. Alliance Black Sch. Educators (com. chair 1974-75), N.J. Coun. Edn. (bd. dirs. 1991), Assn. Tchrs. Educators (presenter 1991), Am. Assn. Colls. for Tchrs. Educators (presenter 1990, 92), Am. Edn. Rsch. Assn. (presenter 1980), Alpha Phi Alpha, Phi Delta Kappa. Democrat. Baptist. Office: Jersey City State Coll 2039 Kennedy Blvd Jersey City NJ 07305

MEBUS, CHARLES ALBERT, veterinarian; b. Paterson, N.J., Sept. 10, 1932; s. Charles Albert and Mary (Ponstingel) M.; m. Sept. 10, 1955; children: Jane C., Patricia A., Charles A. DVM, N.Y. State Vet. Coll., 1956; MS, Kans. State U., 1962, PhD, 1963. Diplomate Am. Coll. Vet. Pathologists. Gen. practice Dover, Del., 1958-60; NDEA staff asst. Kans. State U., Manhattan, 1960-63, assoc. prof., 1963-65; prof. U. Nebr., Lincoln, 1965-77; rsch. leder Agrl. Rsch. Svc. USDA, Greenport, N.Y., 1977-88; chief Animal and Plant Health Inspection Svc. USDA Foreign Animal Disease Diagnostic Lab., Greenport, N.Y., 1988—. Trustee Ea. Long Island Hosp., Greenport; vestry Holy Trinity Ch., Greenport. 1st lt. U.S. Army, 1956-68. Mem. AVMA, U.S. Animal Health Assn., Am. Assn. Vet. Diagnosticians. Episcopalian. Office: USDA Diagnostic Lab PO Box 848 Greenport NY 11944-0848

MECCA, JOSEPH NICHOLAS, manufacturing company executive; b. Passaic, N.J., May 8, 1947; s. Danta Virgilio and Theresa Ann (Digangi) M.; m. Margaret Diane Cooper, Jan. 7, 1969; children: Joseph Jr., Anthony, Margaret. BS in Ops. Mgmt., Thomas Edison State Coll., 1981, BS in Human Resouce Mgmt., 1981. Dept. mgr. W.T. Grant, Paterson, N.J., 1964; dept. supr. Popular Svcs. Club, Passaic, 1970-71; gen. mgr. K-Mart Apparel Corp., North Bergen, N.J., 1971-82; v.p. ops. Fortunoff, Wayne, N.J., 1982-84, Commodore Bus. Machines, Inc., West Chester, Pa., 1984—; v.p. worldwide transp. and internat. trade adminstrn. GM US Ops., Mfg. Pres. Pop Warner Football, Marlboro, N.J., 1983, 84; head coach, Jr. All Am. Football, Garden Grove, Calif., 1974-79; mgr. Little League Baseball, Garden Grove, 1975, Marlboro, 1980-81; treas. St. Columbus Parents Club. With USN, 1965-70, Vietnam, lt. comdr. USNR. Recipient Commendation and Achievement medals, USN Seabees, Vietnam Service medals. Mem. Am. Mgmt. Assn., Mgmt. Assn. Del Valley, Soc. Am. Mil. Engrs., Naval Res. Assn., Am. Soc. Transp. and Logistics, VFW, Am. Legion. Republican. Home: 807 Nathan Hale Dr West Chester PA 19382-7053 Office: Commodore Internat Ltd 1200 Wilson Dr West Chester PA 19380-4251

MECH, TERRENCE FRANCIS, library director; b. Birdorup Park, Wiltshire, Eng., Feb. 24, 1953; s. Emil Paul and Madelyn (Tremmel) M. BS, U. Wis., Stevens Point, 1975; MS, Ill. State U., 1978; MLS, Clarion U., 1979. Pub. svcs. libr. Tusculum Coll., Greensville, Tenn., 1979-80; libr. dir. Coll. of the Ozarks, Clarksville, Ark., 1980-82, King's Coll., Wilkes-Barre, Pa., 1982—; bd. dirs. Northeastern Pa. Bibliographic Ctr., 1982—; mem., officer Coun. Pa. Libr. Networks, 1984-89, chair, 1987-89. Contbr. chpts. to books and articles to profl. jours. Mem. ALA, Pa. Libr. Assn. (bd. dirs. 1986-87, various coms. 1985—). Office: Kings Coll 14 W Jackson St Wilkes Barre PA 18701-2010

MECHANIC, DAVID, social sciences educator; b. N.Y.C., Feb. 21, 1936; s. Louis and Tillie (Penn) M.; children—Robert Edmund, Michael Alexander. B.A., CCNY, 1956; M.A., Stanford U., 1957, Ph.D., 1959. Faculty U. Wis., Madison, 1960-79; prof. sociology U. Wis., 1965-73, John Bascom prof., 1973-79; dir. U. Wis. (Center for Med. Sociology and Health Services Research), 1971-79, chmn. dept. sociology, 1968-70; prof. social work and sociology Rutgers U., New Brunswick, N.J., 1979—; acting dean faculty arts and scis. Rutgers U., 1980-81, Univ. prof., dean faculty arts and scis., 1981-84, Univ. prof. and Rene Dubos prof. behavioral scis., 1984—, dir. Inst. for Health, Health Care Policy and Aging Research, 1985—; mem. panel on health svcs. rsch. Pres.'s Sci. Adv. Com., 1971-72; mem. treatment com. on reduction of cancer mortality Nat. Cancer Inst., 1984; vice-chmn. com. pain, disability and chronic illness behavior Inst. Medicine-Nat. Acad. Scis., 1985-86, mem. panel on prevention of disability, 1989—; coordinator panel Pres.'s Commn. Mental Health, 1977-78; mem. Nat. Adv. Council Aging, NIH, 1982-86; expert adv. panel on mental health, WHO, 1984-89; mem. health adv. bd. GAO, 1987—; mem. nat. com. on vital and health statistics HHS, 1988—; mem. commn. on behavioral and social scis. and edn. NRC, 1989—, commn. on med. edn. Robert Wood Johnson Found., 1990—. Author: Students Under Stress, 1962, 2d edit., 1978, Medical Sociology, 1968, rev. edit., 1978, Mental Health and Social Policy, 1969, rev. edit., 1980, 89, Public Expectations and Health Care, 1972, Politics, Medicine and Social Science, 1974, (with Charles E. Lewis and Rashi Fein) A Right to Health, 1976, Growth of Bureaucratic Medicine, 1976, Future Problems in Health Care, 1979, From Advocacy to Allocation: The Evolving American Health Care System, 1986, Painful Choices: Research and Essays on Health Care, 1989; author, editor: Symptoms, Illness Behavior and Help-Seeking; editor: Handbook of Health, Health Care and the Health Professions, 1983, Improving Mental Health Services: What the Social Sciences Can Tell Us, 1987; Co-editor: (with Robert Houser, Archibald Haller and Tess Hauser) Social Structure and Personality, 1982, (with Linda Aiken) Applications of Social Science to Clinical Medicine and Social Policy, 1986; Paying for Services: Promises and Pitfalls of Capitation, 1989; (with Marian Osterweis and Arthur Kleinman) Pain and Disability: Clinical Behavior and Public Policy Perspectives, 1987, (with Carl Taube and Ann Hohmann) The Future of Mental Health Services Research, 1989. Fellow Ctr. for Advanced Study in Behavioral Scis., 1974-75, NIMH rsch. fellow, 1956-66, Ford Behavioral Sci. fellow, 1956-57, Guggenheim fellow, 1977-78; recipient Ward medal CCNY, 1956, Med. Sociologist award Am. Sociol. Assn., 1983, Carl Taube award Am. Pub. Health Assn., 1990, Disting. Investigator award Assn. for Health Svcs. Rsch., 1991, Disting. Contbn. award mental health sect. Soc. for Study of Social Problems, 1991, Emily Mumford medal Columbia U., 1991. Fellow AAAS (chmn. sect. social, econ. and polit. scis. 1985); mem. Am. Sociol. Assn. (governing coun. 1977-78, chmn. med. sociol. sect. 1969-70, chmn. publs. com. 1989—), Inst. Medicine-Nat. Acad. Scis. (governing coun. 1972-74), Nat. Acad. Scis., Hogg Found. Mental Health (nat. adv. coun. 1987), Phi Beta Kappa. Office: Rutgers U Inst Health Care Policy and Aging Rsch 30 College Ave New Brunswick NJ 08903

MECKLOSKY, MORTON MATHEW, educator; b. N.Y.C., Apr. 13, 1932; s. Abraham Jack and Ida (Applebaum) M.; m. Lorraine Kaufman, May 24, 1952; children: Carolyn, Robert. BA, CUNY, 1959; MA, Profl. Diploma, ABD, Columbia U., 1961; MA, Rutgers U., 1964. Tchr. N.Y.C. Pub. High Sch., 1959-62; prof. Suffolk Coll., Selden, N.Y., 1963-87, prof. emeritus, 1987—; lectr. Stony Brook (N.Y.) U., 1968-72, producer radio, 1988—; cons. in student retention, logic, math. edn. and critical thinking; producer, host radio shows Critique, Unfinished Bus., 1989—. Author: Patterns and Proof, 1968. Grantee NSF 1960-65, NDEA. Mem. Nat. Coun. Tchrs. Math., Math. Assn. Am., Theodore Gordon Fly Fishers, Fedn. Fly Fishers. Home: 35 Shelbourne Ln Stony Brook NY 11790-3175

MEDEIROS, PETER WILLIAM, state official, consultant; b. Providence, Dec. 29, 1946; s. Peter and Dorothy Irene (Cunha) M.; m. Arlene F. Casey, Oct. 29, 1980 (div. 1983); children: Christopher, Melissa. BS, Johnson & Wales Coll., 1975, MBA, 1989. Auditor Gov.'s Justice Commn. State of R.I., West Warwick, 1975-78; sr. acct. Controller's Office State of R.I., Providence, 1978-83; bus. mgr. State of R.I. Dept. Corrections, Cranston, 1983—; cons. SBA, Providence, 1974-75. Vol. R.I. Ct. Appointed Spl. Advocate, Providence, 1985. With USAF, 1967-70. Recipient Sr. Faculty award Johnson & Wales Coll., 1974, 75. Mem. Soc. Govtl. Accts. and Auditors (v.p. 1990-92), New Eng. Regional Correctional Industries Assn., Eagles Club, Phi Delta Alumni Assn. Office: RI Dept Corrections One Howard Ave Cranston RI 02920

MEDEN, ROBERT PAUL, interior design educator; b. Cleve., Jan. 24, 1950; s. Paul Joseph and Irene Theresa (Chuey) M.; m. Maryellen Hudak, June 22, 1979; children: Christina Rose, Patrick Michael. BArch, Kent State U., 1973, MArch, 1975; DArch, Cath. U. Am., 1989. Registered architect, Ohio, Md., Va., D.C., Ind. Planner, draftsman John Roush, Architects, Cleve., 1975; hist. sites restoration coord. hist. preservation div. N.Y. State, Office of Parks and Recreation, Albany, 1976-77; designer, draftsman Robert C. Gaede, Cleve., 1977; interior design instr. Sch. Family and Consumer Studies Kent (Ohio) State U., 1977-79; asst. prof. interior design Mt. Vernon Coll., Washington, 1979-82; asst. prof. architecture Ball State U., Muncie, Ind., 1982-85; dir. preservation programs The Am. Inst. Architects, Washington, 1985; assoc. prof. interior design Marymount. U. Sch. Arts and Scis., Arlington, Va., 1986-90; prof. Marymount U. Sch. Arts and Scis., Arlington, Va., 1990—, program chair, 1989—; hist. architect U.S. Dept. Interior Tech. Preservation Svcs., Washington, 1980; architect Turner Renovations, Inc., Washington, 1979-82, Suburban Contractors, Inc., Vienna,Va., 1986-87; architect, preservation specialist Browning, Day, Mullins, Dierdorf, Inc., Indpls., 1984-85; condr. numerous seminars and presentations. Author: Architectural Character Study of the Buckeye Road District, 1975; co-author and illustrator: History of Housing and Furnishings Handbook, 1977; editor and illustrator: Access to Historic Buildings for the Disabled, 1981. Asst. to dir. Mayfield (Ohio) Recreation Com., 1968-73; basketball coach St. Mary's Ch., Cath. Youth Orgn., Albany, 1976-77, basketball coach St. Lawrence Ch., Cath. Youth Orgn., Muncie, 1982-83, woman's varsity soccer coach Marymount U., 1986-88. Recipient ASID Scalamandre Hist. Preservation

award, 1978, Dora Brahms award, 1980, 83, Nat. Endowment for Arts, Design Arts Program, Entering Profl. award, 1981; grantee The Cleve. Found., 1979, The Nat. Endowment for the Arts Design Arts Program, 1981. Mem. AIA, Am. Soc. Interior Designers, Interior Design Educators Coun., Internat. Assoc. Lighting Designers. Roman Catholic. Home: 6013 27th St N Arlington VA 22207-1232 Office: Marymount U 2807 N Glebe Rd Arlington VA 22207-4224

MEDINA, DAVID, publishing company executive; b. Bklyn., June 2, 1948; s. Frederick and Louise (Acevedo) M.; m. Leta G. Hillman, June 13, 1971; children: Jason Philip, Charles Louis, Daniel James. BA, Northeastern U., Boston, 1971; MEd, Boston State Coll., 1972; MA, Hofstra U., 1976. Elem. sch. tchr. Freeport (N.Y.) Pub. Schs., 1972-73; bilingual tchr. Roosevelt (N.Y.) Pub. Schs., 1973-75; adj. prof. State U. N.Y., Old Westbury, 1975-76; asst. to project dir. Bd. Coop. Edn. Svcs., Westbury, N.Y., 1975-76, pres., 1977-78; asst. to pres. Hillman Publ. and Distdn. Corp., Glen Cove, N.Y., 1976-77, v.p., 1978-89, pres., 1989—; with HMS Graphic Svcs., Inc., Oldsmar, Fla.; project dir., bilingual summer aide, dir. Villa Alegre project Roosevelt Pub. Schs., 1974; project cons. rsch. and devel. Bd. Coop. Edn. Svcs., Roosevelt, 1974. U.S. Office Edn. fellow, 1975. Office: HMS Graphic Svcs Inc 231 Douglas Rd E # 5 Oldsmar FL 34677

MEDINA, LEILANI, accountant; b. Pasay City, The Philippines, Dec. 3, 1967; came to U.S., 1969; d. Teodoro Gadi and Idelila (Palma) M. BSBA magna cum laude, W.Va. U., 1989. CPA, Pa. Med. asst. Dr. Teodoro Medina, Bridgeport, W.Va., 1984-85; salesperson Lerner, Bridgeport, Morgantown, W.Va., 1985-89; ins. asst. W.Va. U., Morgantown, 1988-89; aerobics instr. Mountaineer Nautilus, Morgantown, 1988-89; acct. Deloitte & Touche, Pitts., 1989—; tax preparer, cons., Pitts., 1990—. Participant United Way, Pitts., 1990; coord. Jr. Achievement, Pitts., 1991, Spl. Olympics, Morgantown, 1990. Mem. Pa. Inst. CPAs, Golden Key, Phi Kappa Phi, Beta Gamma Sigma, Beta Alpha Psi. Home: 360 Camelot Dr Pittsburgh PA 15220-2515 Office: Deloitte & Touche 2 Oliver Plz Pittsburgh PA 15222-2705

MEDLAND, MARY ELIZABETH, writer, marketing executive; b. Alexandria, Va., June 13, 1952; d. Francis Frederic and Stephanie (Uhriniak) M.; m. Jack Lawrence Gohn, Sept. 24, 1988; 1 child, Matthew Nicholas. BA in Visual Arts, Goucher Coll., 1974. Prodn. coord. Johns Hopkins U. Press, Balt., 1980-83; advt. mgr. U. Nebr. Press, Lincoln, 1983-85; mktg. dir. U. Press Va., Charlottesville, 1985-86, Island Press, Washington, 1986-88; freelance writer Balt., 1988—; mktg. dir. The Sidran Press, Balt., 1992—. Mem. Balt. Writers' Group, The In-Print Group (founder). Democrat. Roman Catholic. Home: 743 McHenry St Baltimore MD 21230

MEDLEY, MARC ALLEN, marketing executive; b. Paterson, N.J., Aug. 17, 1962; s. James Allen and Jane Alden (Bernard) M.; m. Jean Trenice Joye, June 15, 1985; 1 child, Aria Monique. BABA, William Paterson Coll., 1984. Tchr. Passaic City Tech. & Vocat. High Sch., Wayne, N.J., 1983-85; mktg. staff supr. AT&T, Basking Ridge, N.J., 1985. Publicist com. to re-elect Albert Rowe, Paterson, 1986, Bill Pascrell for N.J. State Assembly, 1992; bd. trustees, organist, tchr. St. Luke Bapt. Ch. With U.S. Army Nat. Guard, 1987—. Recipient USAF medal of achievement, Recognition award Tri-State United Way, 1987, award Paterson City Coun. Mem. William Paterson Coll. Alumni Assn., Alpha Phi Alpha (sec. 1987-91, pres. 1991). Home: 678 14th Ave Paterson NJ 07504-1810 Office: AT&T 295 N Maple Ave Basking Ridge NJ 07920-1025

MEDLIN, TERRY, data processing executive; b. Paducah, Ky., Aug. 4, 1947; s. Jere W. and Carrie (Pearson) M.; m. Carol Krewinghaus, Sept. 6, 1969; children: Julie, Kathy. BA in Chemistry, Vanderbilt U., 1969; MS in Computer Sci., U. Md., 1972. Sect. chief NIH, Bethesda, Md., 1971-80; v.p. Gejac, Inc., Laurel, Md., 1981-83, Survey Sampling, Fairfield, Conn., 1984—; RSX SIG chair DECUS, Marlboro, Mass., 1983-85, DECUServe chair, 1987-89. Pres. Men's Club, Meth. Ch., Fairfield, 1986-88. Republican. Home: 90 Northwood Rd Fairfield CT 06432-1641 Office: Survey Sampling One Post Rd Fairfield CT 06430

MEDVE, RICHARD JOHN, biology educator; b. California, Pa., Jan. 28, 1936; s. Andrew D. and Marian E. (Bardelli) M.; m. Mary Lee, Nov. 26, 1958; children: Pamela, Steven, Kenneth, Kathleen, David. BS in Edn., California (Pa.) U., 1957; MA, Kent State U., 1958; PhD, Ohio State U., 1969. Tchr. Willoughby (Ohio) South High Sch., 1959-66; prof. Slippery Rock (Pa.) Univ., 1966—. Author: Edible Wild Plants of Pennsylvania and Neighboring States, 1990; contbr. articles to profl. jours. Named Tchr. Laureate Slippery Rock U., 1969; recipient Disting. Acad. Svc. award Commonwealth of Pa., 1983, Disting. Faculty award Slippery Rock U., 1982. Mem. Torrey Bot. Club, Pa. Acad. Sci., Ohio Acad. Sci., Nat. Assn. Biology Tchrs., Western Pa. Conservancy. Office: Slippery Rock U Slippery Rock PA 16057

MEEHAN, GERRY, professional hockey team executive; b. Toronto, Ont., Can.; m. Mirella Meehan; children: Danny, Adam, Katie. Grad., Canisius Coll.; JD, U. Buffalo, 1982. Professional hockey player Toronto Maple Leafs, 1968, Phila. Flyers, 1969; professional hockey player Buffalo Sabres, 1970-74, asst. gen. mgr., 1984-86, gen. mgr., 1986—; player Vancouver (Can.) Canucks, 1975, Atlanta Flames (now Calgary Flames), 1975, Washington Capitals, 1976-79; atty. Cohen Swados Wright Hanifin Bradford Brett, Buffalo, 1984. Home: Amherst NY Office: Buffalo Sabres Meml Auditorium Buffalo NY 14202

MEEHAN, ROBERT HENRY, utilities executive, human resources executive, instructor; b. Hakensack, N.J., June 19, 1946; s. Horace Miles and Pauline Jeannette (Pente) M.; m. Ruth Ann Auletta, Sept. 28, 1969; children: Robert Michael, Brian John. BA, Montclair State Coll., 1968; MA magna cum laude, Fairleigh Dickinson U., 1972; postgrad., Pace U., 1985—. Cert. secondary sch. tchr. of social studies, N.J., compensation profl. Job analyst Citicorp, N.Y.C., 1969-70, sr. job analyst, 1970-72, ofcl. asst., 1972, project specialist pers. practices/policy review, 1973, project specialist attitude surveys, 1973-75, pers. officer nat. banking group, 1975-76; asst. dir. pers. N.Y. Power Authority, White Plains, N.Y., 1976-84; dir. compensation N.Y. Power Authority, White Plains, 1984—; instr. Am. Compensation Assn., Scottsdale, Ariz., 1986—; mem. N.Y. Power Pool Salary com., 1990—. Sr. author: Managing a Direct Pay Program, Cert. Course 4A, 1991, Determining Compensation Costs: An Approach to Estimating and Analyzing Expense, 1991; contbr. articles to profl. jours. Scoutmaster, Boy Scouts Am., Ridgefield Park, N.J., 1968; also scouting coordinator, Maywood, N.J., 1982-83; vestryman, sr. warden St. Martin's Episcopal Ch., Maywood, 1977-84. Mem. Am. Compensation Assn. (cert. instr. 1986—, cert. and currency com. 1990-91, chmn. dir. compensation com. 1992), Soc. for Human Resource Mgmt., Human Resources Planning Soc., Doctoral Students Assn. Pace Univ., Acad. Mgmt., Order DeMolay (master councilor 1962-65, scribe, adv. bd. 1965-68, Meritorious Svcs. award 1965), Psi Chi, Delta Mu Delta. Episcopalian. Office: NY Power Authority 2162 Brookside Ave Wantagh NY 11793-3850

MEEK, AMY GERTRUDE, retired educator; b. Frostburg, Md., Jan. 3, 1928; d. Arthur Stewart and Amy Laura (Brain) M. BS, Frostburg State U., 1950; MEd, U. Md., 1956; postgrad., Columbia U., 1964, Am. U., 1968-70. Cert. tchr., Md. Tchr. elem. sch. Prince Georges County Schs., Bradbury Heights, Md., 1950-51; tchr. elem. sch. Allegany County Schs., Cumberland, Md., 1951-60, Frostburg, 1960-84; now ret. Author: (with others) Stir Into Flame, 1991; contbr. articles to hist. publs. Mem. Frostburg Hosp. Aux., 1987—; bd. dirs. Frostburg Hist. Mus., 1988, Coun. of Alleghenies, 1991; sec. Braddock Estates Civic Assn., Frostburg, 1988; mem. bldg. com. Frostburg Libr., 1989; tchr. Ch. Conf. Schs. Missions, 1970; vol. tutor, 1986—; pres. Ch. Women United, Frostburg, 1989; trustee Frostburg United Meth. Ch.; pres. Cumberland-Hagerstown dist. United Meth. Women, 1985-89, chmn. fin. interpretation Balt. Conf., 1990—. Mem. AAUW (past pres., treas. Md. div. 1974, Woman of Yr. award Frostburg br. 1980). Republican.

MEEK, PHILLIP JOSEPH, newspaper publisher; b. Los Angeles, Nov. 17, 1937; s. Joseph Alcinus and Clara Amy (Phillips) M.; m. Nancy Jean LaPorte, June 25, 1960; children: Katherine Amy, Brian Joseph, Laurie Noel. B.A. cum laude, Ohio Wesleyan U., 1959; M.B.A., Harvard U., 1961. Fin. analyst Ford Motor Co., 1961-63, supr. capacity planning, 1963-66, supr. domestic scheduling, 1966, controller mktg. services, 1966-68; on loan as pres. Econ. Devel. Corp. Greater Detroit, 1968-70; pres., pub. Oakland Press Co., Pontiac, Mich., 1970-77; exec. v.p., gen. mgr. Ft. Worth Star-Telegram, 1977-79, pres., editorial chmn., 1980-82, pres., pub., 1982-86; sr. v.p., pres. pub. group Capital Cities/ABC Inc., N.Y.C., 1986—. Past mem. Pontiac Stadium Bldg. Authority; pres. United Way Pontiac-North Oakland, 1977; pres. Tarrant County United Way, 1982-83, chmn., 1983-84; bd. dirs. Arts Council of Ft. Worth and Tarrant County; chmn. North Tex. Commn., 1983-84; bd. dirs. Tex. Ind. Coll. Fund; trustee Ohio Wesleyan U., 1984—. Mem. Am. Newspaper Pubs. Assn., So. Newspaper Pubs. Assn., Tex. Daily Newspaper Assn. (pres. 1984), Ft. Worth C. of C. (dir. 1980-83); Mem. Phi Beta Kappa, Omicron Delta Kappa, Sigma Delta Chi, Pi Delta Epsilon, Phi Gamma Delta. Methodist. Clubs: Stanwich (Conn.); Crystal Downs (Mich.); Rivercrest (Tex.). Office: Capital Cities/ABC Inc 77 W 66th St New York NY 10023-6201

MEEKER, GUY BENTLEY, banker; b. Calcutta, India, Nov. 4, 1945; (parents Am. citizens); s. Lincoln Voght and Fortune Helen (Bentley) M.; m. Lavenia Yale Nelson, Apr. 27, 1967 (div. 1979); children: G. Bentley Jr., Melissa Anne ; m. Marcia Lee Zink, Nov. 4, 1984. BSBA, Georgetown U., 1967; MBA, George Washington U., 1970. Cons. OAS, Washington, 1971-73; v.p. The Deltec Banking Corp., Nassau, Bahamas & N.Y.C., 1973-78, Comml. Credit Internat. Banking Corp., Balt., 1978-82; sr. v.p., gen. mgr. Union Planters Internat. Bank, N.Y.C., 1982-84; exec. v.p., gen. mgr. Worthen Bank Internat., N.Y.C., 1984-86; exec. v.p. and chief exec. officer N.Am. Bank Cen. Asia, N.Y.C., 1984—. Contbr. articles, monographs in field. Mem. Bankers Assn. Fgn. Trade (internat. adv. com. 1992—), Inst. Internat. Bankers (legis. and regulatory com. 1992—), Asia Soc. (corp. coun. 1987—), River Club, Coffee House Club, Dutch Treat (N.Y.C.) Club, Melrose (S.C.) Club. Roman Catholic.

MEEKER, MURRAY M., lawyer; b. L.A., Nov. 22, 1946; s. Russell Clinton and Elizabeth Esther (Chickering) M.; m. Diana Marie Corser, Oct. 22, 1982; children: Nicholas Russell, Danielle Elizabeth. AB, Stanford U., 1969; JD, U. Calif., Hastings, 1972. Bar: Calif. 1972, U.S. Supreme Ct. 1979, U.S. Ct. Appeals (5th cir.) 1983. Atty. U.S. Civil Svc. Commn., Washington, 1972-79; sr. atty. U.S. Office Personnel Mgmt., Washington, 1980—; staff atty. EEO Coordinating Com., Washington, 1972-73. Author Fed. Garnishment Regulations, 1977—. Rep. U. Calif. Program for Congl. Support, Washington, 1988. Dofflemyer scholar Stanford U., 1967-69. Mem. Washington Tennis Fedn., Mid-Atlantic Tennis Assn., U.S. Tennis Assn. Home: 6313 Hillcrest Pl Alexandria VA 22312 Office: US Office Pers Mgmt 1900 E St NW Washington DC 20415

MEE-LEE, DAVID, psychiatrist, consultant; b. Brisbane, Queensland, Australia, Aug. 9, 1949; came to U.S., 1974; s. Alfred and Ora Marjorie (Hon) Mee-Lee; m. Marcia Ruth Corrigan, Dec. 10, 1972; children: Miya, Taylor, Mackenzie. MD, U. Queensland, 1972; MS in Psychiatry, Ohio State U., 1976. Dir. ins. edn. for human svcs. New Eng. Meml. Hosp., Stoneham, Mass., 1977-81, asst. chief psychiatry, 1980-85, dir. addictions treatment unit, 1981-85; v.p. Monarch Health Corp., Marblehead, Mass., 1985-87; assoc. med. dir. Parkside Med. Svcs. Corp., Park Ridge, Ill., 1987—; psychiat. cons. New Eng. Telephone, Boston, 1986— cons. Norcap Ctr., Norfolk, Mass., 1987—. Contbr. articles to profl. jours. Chmn. Drug Rehab. Adv. Bd., Boston, 1989-92. Mem. Am. Soc. Addiction Medicine (regional bd. dirs. 1987-91), Am. Psychiat. Assn., Mass. Med. Soc., Mass. Psychiat. Soc., Am. Acad. Psychiatrists in Alcoholism and Addictions. Adventist. Office: Parkside Med Svcs Corp Little Harbor Marblehead MA 01945

MEENAN, JAMES RONALD, foreign service officer, accountant; b. Providence, Dec. 23, 1941; s. James Joseph and Angie May (Richmond) M.; m. Vera Helena Barretto de Carvalho Lima, May 3, 1968; children: Patrick Allen, John Edward. BBA, Woodbury Coll., 1962; grad., Legis. Inst., 1991. Cert. internal auditor. Acct. Jonathan Club, L.A., 1961-63; prodn. cost analyst USAF Auditor Gen., Santa Monica, Calif., 1963-65; supervisory acct., auditor USAID to Vietnam and Brazil, Saigon and Rio de Janeiro, 1965-68; sr. budget analyst Strategic Systems, USN, Washington, 1968-69; supervisory auditor USAID to Chile and Panama, Santiago and Panama, 1969-74; program devel. mgr. USAID to Africa Bur., Sri Lanka, Philippines, Asia, Near East Europe Bur., Washington, Colombo, Manila and Washington, 1974-90; legis. asst. Internat. Trade and Econ. Devel., U.S. Senator Max Baucus, Washington, 1987%; mem. governing bd. Internat. Sch., Manila, 1985-86. Mem. Fairfax (Va.) Hosp. Assn. Found., 1986—, Dem. Nat. Com., Washington, 1987—; mem. governing bd. Internat. Sch., Manila, 1985-86. Decorated Svc. award (Vietnam). Mem. Am. Fgn. Svc. Assn. (treas. 1977-78, rep. Colombo, Sri Lanka 1979-83), Soc. for Internat. Devel. (exec. bd. Sri Lanka chpt. 1980-83), L.A. C. of C., Sri Lanka Hill Club, Mantua Swim and Tennis Club, Elks, K.C. Roman Catholic. Home: 3317 Albion Ct Fairfax VA 22031-3001 Office: US Senator Max Baucus Hart Senate Office Bldg Rm 706 Washington DC 20510

MEER, AMEENA BIBI, editor, journalist; b. Boston, May 29, 1965; d. Syed Ahmed and Arshiya Bibi (Rauf) M. BA, U. Calif., Santa Cruz, 1985. Adminstrv. and editorial asst. Harper's Mag., N.Y.C., 1985-86; mng. editor East Village Eye, N.Y.C., 1986-87; copy editor, book editor PAPER Mag., N.Y.C., 1989-90; mng. editor BOMB Mag., N.Y.C., 1988—; contbg. writer India Mag., New Delhi, 1987—, Times of India, New Delhi, 1987—; book editor PAPER Mag., N.Y.C., 1990-91. Author (short stories) Indian-Am. mag., 1991; contbr. articles to various mags. Selection com. Asian-Am. Film Festival, N.Y.C., 1991, 92; caseworker Sakhi for Women, N.Y.C., 1991—; Salman Rushdie defense Pen-Am. Ctr., N.Y.C., 1989. Mem. Nat. Writers Union, Asia Soc. Democrat. Muslim. Office: BOMB Mag 594 Broadway New York NY 10012

MEGLEY, SHEILA, university executive, administrator, English educator; b. Binghampton, N.Y., Feb. 16, 1938; d. John Edward and Ann (Feely) M.; BA in Math., Philosophy, and Edn., Rosary Coll., River Forest, Ill., 1961; MA in Theology, St. Xavier Coll., Chgo., 1968; MA in English Lit, U. Chgo., 1970; PhD, U. Nebr., 1974; MS in Fin. Mgmt., Acctg., Salve Regina U., 1989. Tchr. math. Holy Child High Sch., Waukegan, Ill., 1961-64, Immaculate Heart of Mary High Sch., Westchester, Ill., 1964-65; resident hall dir., instr. math. St. Xavier Coll., Chgo., 1965-69; instr. in English, U. Nebr., 1970-74; prof. English, acad. dean, dean of students Salve Regina U., 1974-76, v.p., acad. dean, dean. of students, 1976-80, v.p. instrn. and curriculum, acad. dean, 1980-85, provost, v.p. instrn. and curriculum, 1985-88, exec. v.p., provost, 1988-92; pres. Regis Coll., Weston, Mass., 1992—; chmn. exec. com. Mercy Higher Edn. Colloquim; mem. secretariat Nat. Assn. Ind. Colls. and Univs.; mem. exec. com. Neylan Commn., Assn. Cath. Colls. and Univs. Chmn. R.I. Equal Ednl. Opportunity Task Force, 1974-76; mem. R.I. Com. Humanities, 1980-87; trustee Trinity Rep Theater, Providence; mem. Citizens Adv. Com. City of Newport, R.I., 1989—. Mem. AAUW, Am. Assn. Coll. Deans. Office: Regis Coll Weston MA 02193

MEGNA, JEROME FRANCIS, academic administrator, educator; b. Bklyn., Mar. 11, 1939; s. James G. and Irene (Bodkin) M.; m. Doreen Ann Filippi, Dec. 23, 1973; 1 child, Donna Marie. BA, St. Francis Coll., 1966; MA, NYU, 1968; PhD, Ball State U., 1972. Tchr. English Franciscan Bros., Bklyn., 1959-69; instr. English Ball State U., Muncie, Ind., 1969-71; prof. edn. CUNY, Bklyn., 1971-88; dean of edn. Rider Coll., Lawrenceville, N.J., 1988—. Author: Study Guide on Italian Americans, 1978; contbr. articles to profl. jours. Democrat. Roman Catholic. Office: Rider Coll 2083 Lawrenceville Rd Trenton NJ 08648-3099

MEHANDRU, SUSHIL KUMAR, internist, nephrologist; b. Jullundur, Punjab, India, Jan. 20, 1947; m. Urmila Mehandru. Premed. studies, DAV Coll. Punjab, 1964; BA, Punjab U. Coll., 1966; MD with Distinction in Physiology, Christian Med. Coll., 1972. Diplomate Am. Bd. Internal Medicine, Am. Bd. Nephrology. Resident in internal medicine L.I. Jewish Med. Ctr., Stonybrook U., New Hyde Park, N.Y., 1972-75; fellow in clin. nephrology Thomas Jefferson U. Hosp., Phila., 1975-76; fellow in clin. nephrology and renal physiology Temple U. Hosp., Phila., 1976-77, attending physician in medicine, 1977-78; instr. medicine Temple U. Sch. Medicine, 1977-78, clin. asst. prof., 1978-83, clin. assoc. prof., 1983—; chief nephrology VA Hosp., Wilmington, Del., 1977-78; dir. dept. nephrology and dialysis Jersey Shore Med. Ctr., Neptune, N.J.; cons. in nephrology Point Pleasant (N.J.) Hosp.; pres. Prime Manhattan Inc. Contbr. book chptrs. and articles to profl. jours. Recipient Best Research Publ. award Jersey Shore Med. Ctr., Rutgers Med. Sch., 1982-83, Outstanding Clin. Pulb. award Jersey Shore Med. Ctr., Rutgers Med. Sch., 1984, Outstanding Tchr. of Yr. award Rutgers Med. Sch., 1984; honored by Senate of N.J. for outstanding extensive med. research, 1985; N.J. State Pistol Champion, Finalist for U.S. Olympic Team, 1984, 88. Fellow ACP; mem. Internat. Soc. Nephrology, Am. Soc. Nephrology, Internat. Soc. Artificial Internal Organs. Hindu. Home: 1732 Belmar Blvd Belmar NJ 07719-3953 Office: 1925 Hwy 35 Belmar NJ 07719-3581

MEHLMAN, EDWIN STEPHEN, endodontist; b. Hartford, Conn., Nov. 30, 1935; s. Sol Abraham and Rose (Slitt) M.; m. Lesley Judith Lunin, June 13, 1959; children: Jeffrey Cole, Brian Scott, Erik Van. BA, Wesleyan U., 1957; DDS, U. Pa., 1961; cert. endodontics, Boston U., 1965. Diplomate Am. Bd. Endodontists. Instr. oral medicine Sch. Dental Medicine Harvard U., Boston, 1965-67; clin. instr. endodontics Sch. Dental Medicine Tufts U., Boston, 1968-70; lectr. endodontics Sch. Dental Medicine Harvard U., Boston, 1970-72, asst. clin. prof. endodontics Sch. Dental Medicine, 1972—; staff assoc. Forsyth Dental Ctr., Boston, 1965—; pvt. practice Providence, 1965—; vis. lectr. dental hygiene U. R.I., Kingston, 1965-71, Community Coll. R.I., Lincoln, 1990—; cons. com. on accreditation of Dentists and Dental Aux. Edn. Programs, 1974-78. Contbr. articles to profl. jours. Pres. Temple Habonim, Barrington, R.I., 1968-70, Bur. Jewish Edn. of R.I., 1980-84; area v.p. Jewish Fedn. R.I., 1975-78; mem. R.I. Legis. Commn. to Study Malpractice Crisis, 1985-86; chmn. R.I. Dental Polit. Action Com., 1987-90. Capt. USAF, 1961-63. Fellow Am. Coll. Dentists, Internat. Coll. Dentists, Pierre Fauchard Acad. (Award of Merit); mem. ADA (coun. on govt. affairs and fed. dental svcs. 1988-92, vice chmn. 1991-92), Am. Assn. Endodontists (dir. 1988-91), R.I. Dental Assn. (pres. 1986-87), Alpha Omega. Jewish. Home: 6 Ridgeland Rd Barrington RI 02806-4028 Office: 130 Waterman St Providence RI 02906-2010 also: 1090 New London Ave Cranston RI 02920

MEHLMAN, MYRON A., environmental and occupational medicine educator, environmental toxicologist; b. Poland, Dec. 21, 1934; m. Sept. 4, 1960; children: Mara, Hope, Alison. BS, CCNY, 1957; PhD, MIT, 1964. Prof. biochemistry Rutgers U., Newark, 1965-69; prof. biochemistry Coll. of Medicine U. Nebr., Omaha, 1967-71; chief biochem. toxicology FDA, Washington, 1972-73; spl. asst. toxicology dept. HEW, Washington, 1973-75; interagy. liaison officer NIH, Bethesda, Md., 1975-77; dir. toxicology Mobil Oil, Princeton, N.J., 1977-89; prof. U. Medicine and Dentistry of N.J., Piscataway, 1990—. Editor Jour. Environ. Pathology & Toxicology, 1977-81, Jour. Toxicology and Indsl. Health, 1975-78, Jour. Clean Tech. and Environ. Sci., 1989—; contbr. over 100 articles to profl. jours.; edited over 60 books. 1st lt. U.S. Army, 1958-60. Fellow Acad. Toxol. Soc., Am. Coll. Toxicology, Collequim Ramazzinic (bd. dirs.). Home: 7 Bouvant Dr Princeton NJ 08540-1208 Office: U Medicine and Dentistry NJ 675 Hoes Ln Piscataway NJ 08854-5635

MEHLMAN, STEVEN, public relations and communications executive; b. Bronx, N.Y., Dec. 15, 1942; s. Philip and Ethel (Crasnick) M.; m. Mary Ann Burskey, May 10, 1975; 1 child, Sandra Lynn. BA, Am. U., 1965. Accredited in pub. rels. Intern Congl. Quar., Washington, 1964; staff reporter The Courier-News, Plainfield, N.J., 1967-69; press sec. to Congressman Robert N. Giaimo Washington, 1969-71; mgr. editorial svcs./spl. asst. AARP, Washington, 1971-91; exec. loaned exec. program AARP/Children's Def. Fund, 1992; creator Nat. Press Found. Seminar on Aging for Journalists, 1987-89. Co-author: Career in Public Affairs, 1988. Pres. Crofton Commons Homeowners Assn., Crofton, Md., 1987-88; disting. pres. Kiwanis Club and Found., 1989-90; co-chmn. Save the Caps Com., Washington, 1982; bd. dirs. Greater Crofton Substance Abuse Ctr., 1989-91; del. nominating conv. Anne Arundel County Bd. Edn., 1990. Recipient Cert. of Appreciation, Nat. Press Found., 1988-90. Mem. Pub. Rels. Soc. Am., Nat. Press Club. Home: 1506 Flynt Pl Crofton MD 21114-1520 Office: AARP 601 E St NW A9-200 Washington DC 20049

MEHRABIAN, ROBERT, academic administrator; b. Tehran, Iran. Former prof. MIT, U. Ill., Urbana; dean Coll. of Engring. U. Calif., Santa Barbara, until 1990; past dir. Ctr. Materials Sci. Nat. Bur. of Standards; pres. Carnegie-Mellon U., Pitts., 1990—. Office: Carnegie-Mellon U Office of Pres Pittsburgh PA 15213

MEHRPORE, ABDUL RAUF, radio broadcasting editor; b. Mazar-i-Sharif, Afghanistan, Mar. 18, 1948; came to U.S. 1978; s. Abdul Rahman and Hajera (Fazl) M.; m. Nafisa Insaf, Apr. 13, 1976; children: Jalil, Lila. BA, Am. U. Beirut, 1975; MPA, SUNY, Albany, 1980. Mgr. Anglo-Afghan Trade Ctr., Kabul, Afghanistan, 1976-78; radio broadcaster Voice of Am., Washington, 1981-85, editor, broadcaster, 1985—; political analyst-commentator, bd. dirs. Ariana Afghan TV, Washington, 1990—. Democrat. Muslim. Home: 7758 Epsilon Dr Rockville MD 20855-2555 Office: Voice of Am 330 Independence Ave SE Washington DC 20547-0001

MEHRTENS, SUSAN EMILY, research company executive; b. Elmhurst, N.Y., Sept. 27, 1945; d. William Frederic, and Pauline (Kaufmann) M.; m. Edwin M. Davis, May 31, 1981 (div. Apr. 1984). BA, Queens Coll, 1967; MPhil, Yale U., 1969, PhD, 1973. Asst. prof. Queens Coll., Flushing, N.Y., 1971-77; assoc. prof. Coll. of Atlantic, Bar Harbor, Maine, 1977-87; pres., chief exec. officer Potlatch Group Inc., Bear, Del., 1987—; cons. Family Care Am., Phoenix, 1991; instr. Mt. Desert (Maine) Island Adult Edn., 1977-87, U.S. Power Squadron-Sewanaka, Freeport, N.Y., 1975-77. Author: Earthkeeping, 1974, Being Human in the West, 1991, Ecoguide, 1991, Revisioning Science, 1991; contbr. articles to profl. publs. Grantee Am. Philos. Soc., 1974, 86, Am. Coun. Learned Socs., 1974; Yale U. fellow, 1967-69. Mem. Phi Beta Kappa. Home and Office: 239 Garwick Blvd Mineola NY 11501

MEHTA, DWIREF R., surgeon; b. Bombay, May 3, 1952; came to U.S., 1976; s. Rashmikant and Prafullaben Mehta; m. Yvonne Pêna; 1 child, Jonathan. M.B.B.S., G.S. Med. Coll., Bombay, 1974. Asst. attending Bklyn. Hosp., 1982—; dir. surg. clinics, asst. attending Meth. Hosp., Bklyn., 1983—. Fellow ACS. Home: 15 Treeview Dr Melville NY 11747 Office: 294 1st St Brooklyn NY 11215

MEHTA, MAHARSHI P., industrial hygienist, safety engineer, consultant; b. Bhavnagar, India, Apr. 4, 1955; came to U.S., 1984; s. Padmakant L. and Rudrabala (Vora) M.; m. Gangotri Mehta, Nov. 17, 1986; 1 child, Sagar. BS, Saurashtra U., India, 1975; MS, U. Cin., 1986. Cert. indsl. hygienist, safety profl. Safety officer Tata Chem., India, 1975-80; safety engr. Dodsal GmbH, Bahrain, 1981-86; indsl. hygienist intern Proctor and Gamble, Cin., 1985-86; program mgr. N.J. State Health Dept., 1986-89; corp. indsl. hygienist Witco Corp., Woodcliff Lake, N.J., 1990—; instr. Orange County Community Coll., Middletown, N.Y., 1991. Author: Predicting Concentrations for Indoor Chemical Spills, 1987. Mem. Am. Indsl. Hygiene Assn., Am. Bd. Indsl. Hygienists. Home: RR 1 Box 211A Chester NY 10918-9717 Office: Witco Corp 155 Tice Blvd Westwood NJ 07675-7664

MEHTA, NARINDER KUMAR, marketing executive; b. Lahore, Punjab, India, Feb. 18, 1938; came to U.S., 1959; s. Puran Chand and Raj Rani Mehta; m. Narayanaswamy Sampath; children: Kiren, Ravi. B of Commerce, U. Delhi, India, 1958; MA, U. Minn., 1961. Program dir. All India Mgmt. Assn., New Delhi, India, 1963-67; with Am. Express Co., Chgo., 1968-82; nat. sales dir. Am. Express Co., N.Y.C., 1975-80, v.p. sales, 1980-82; sr. v.p. Shearson Lehman/Am. Express, Boston, 1982-85, Capital Credit Corp., Fairfield, N.J., 1985—; sr. v.p. Temporary Investment Funds, 1982-85, Trust for Short Term Fed. Securities, 1982-85, Mcpl. Fund for Calif. Investors, 1983-85; conducted seminars for profl. assns., colls. and univs. Contbr. articles to profl. jours. Nat. v.p. Muscular Dystrophy Assn., N.Y.C., 1984-86; student body pres. U. Delhi, India, 1958-59. Recipient 1st prize inter-coll. debate, 1958. Mem. Am. Mgmt. Assn., Tau Kappa Epsilon. Office: Capital Credit Corp 492 Route 46 Fairfield NJ 07004-1970

MEHTA, PRAVIN K., optostructural mechanist; b. Palanpur, Gujarat, India, Dec. 4, 1935; came to U.S., 1960; s. Kalidas R. and Lilaben K.

(Zaveri) M.; m. Joan Ann Kanca, Sept. 6, 1969; children: Marc, Milan, Neil. BSc with honors, U. Bombay, 1957; diploma, Madras (India) Inst. Tech., 1960; MS, Pa. State U., 1962, PhD, 1966. Asst. prof. Pa. State U., University Park, 1966-67; from sr. engr. to sr. staff engr. Perkin-Elmer Corp., Wilton, Conn., 1967-79; from mgr. engring. dept. to sr. scientist Perkin-Elmer Corp., Danbury, Conn., 1980-89; sr. scientist Hughe Danbury Optical Systems, 1989-91, sr. prin. scientist, 1991—. Contbr. articles to profl. jours. Mem. Am. Acad. Mechanics (founding mem.). Office: Hughes Danbury Optical 100 Wooster Heights Rd Danbury CT 06810-7589

MEHTA, RAKESH KUMAR, physician, consultant; b. Gidderbaha, Punjab, India, Aug. 18, 1952; came to U.S., 1985; s. Parkash Chander and Sheela (Thukral) M.; m. Anita Gupta. MB BS, Med. Coll., Amritsar, Punjab, 1975; MD, Postgrad. Inst. Med. Edn., Chandigarh, 1979. Diplomate Am. Bd. Internal Medicine. Intern Victoria Jubilee, Amritsar, 1975; resident in medicine Hosp. Postgrad. Inst., Chandgarh, India, 1976-78, sr. resident in medicine, 1978-79; sr. resident in medicine All India Inst. of Med. Scis., New Delhi, 1979-81, U. Alta., Edmonton, Can., 1981-83; clin. fellow in oncology Cross Cancer Inst., Edmonton, 1984-85, N.Y. Med. Coll., N.Y.C., 1985-86; cons. med. oncologist Vets. Affairs, Castle Point, N.Y., 1986-92; clin. asst. prof. medicine N.Y. Med. Coll., Valhalla, 1992—; chief oncology program Vets. Affairs Med. Ctr., Castle Point, 1986—. Contbr. articles to professional jours. Fellow ACP, Royal Coll. Physicians and Surgeons of Can., Am. Coll. Internat. Physicians; mem. Am. Soc. of Clin. Oncologists, Can. Assn. Med. Oncologists. Office: Vets Affairs VA Med Ctr Castle Point NY 12511

MEHTA, ZULEKHA SAIFUDDIN, psychologist; b. Bombay, June 26, 1942; came to U.S., 1969; d. Saifuddin and Sara (Kagalwala) Mehta; m. Bijan Rabenou, July 3, 1976; 1 child, Ramin Rabenou. BA in Psychology with honors, U. Bombay, 1964, MA in Clin. Psychology, 1966; MA in Exptl. Psychology, Roosevelt U., 1973; PhD in Human Cognition, U. Okla., 1975; cert., Inst. for Rational Emotive Therapy, 1983. Lic. psychologist, N.Y. Rsch. psychologist Indian Coun. Med. Rsch. King Edward Meml. Hosp., Bombay, 1966-67; clin. psychologist Child Guidance Clinic Nayar Hosp., Bombay, 1967-68; intern Rock County Health Care Ctr., Janesville, Wis., 1971-72; grad. teaching and rsch. asst. dept. psychology U. Okla., Norman, 1972-75; coord. clin. svcs. Kenosha (Wis.) Achievement Ctr., 1975-82; program dir. Nat. Ctr. for Protection Children, Tehran, Iran, 1977-79; asst. prof. dept. social scis. Damavand Coll., Tehran, 1979-80; staff clin. psychologist Tng. Retarden in Useful Svcs., N.Y.C., 1984-86, Fed. Employment and Guidance Svc., N.Y.C., 1986-87; adj. asst. prof. psychology dept. social scis. Queensborough Community Coll., N.Y.C., 1987-88; staff psychologist Optifast Program Cath. Med. Ctr. of Bklyn. and Queens, N.Y.C., 1988-90; dir. psychol. svcs. Assn. Advancement of Blind and Retarded, N.Y.C., 1988-91; pvt. practice N.Y.C., 1988—; supr. psychol. svcs. L.I. (N.Y.) Assn. for Children with Learning Disabilities, 1990—; cons. psychologist Working Orgn. for Retarded Children, N.Y.C., 1988—; presenter in field. Fellow Am. Psychol. Assn.; mem. Assn. for Behavior Analysis (supporting), N.Y. State Assn. for Behavior Analysis (supporting). Home: 84-21 122d St Kew Gardens NY 11415

MEI, HENRY LONG, research chemist, engineer; b. Shanghai, China, Mar. 5, 1946; came to U.S., 1981; s. Harry J. and Lucy Y. (Bao) M.; m. Jean J. Xi, Apr. 3, 1971; children: Margaret, Victor. BS in Chem. Engring., East China Inst. Chem. Tech., Shanghai, 1967; MS in Organic Chemistry, NYU, 1983; MS in Polymer Sci. and Engring., Poly. U., Bklyn., 1986, PhD in Polymer Chem., 1989. Chem. engr. Zhon San Chem. Inc., Nanking, China, 1967-73, tech./prodn. mgr., 1973-81; rsch. chemist, engr. Hercules Inc., Rsch. Ctr., Wilmington, Del., 1988—. Contbr. articles to profl. jours.; inventor in field. Mem. Am. Chem. Soc. (polymer chemistry div., polymer materials sci. and engring. div., speaker nat. meeting 1991), Soc. Plastic Engrs. Office: Hercules Inc Research Ctr Wilmington DE 19894

MEIER, GEORGE HENRY, vascular surgeon; b. Atlanta, Sept. 11, 1954; m. Margaret Connifey; 3 children. BA, Rice U., 1976; MD, Emory U., 1980. Resident in gen. surgery Mass. Gen. Hosp., Boston, 1980-85, resident in vascular surgery, 1985-86, asst. in surgery, 1986-87; attending surgeon, dir. non-invasive vascular lab. West Haven (Conn.) VA Med. Ctr., 1987—, Yale-New Haven Hosp., 1987—; asst. prof. surgery Sch. Medicine Yale U., New Haven, 1987—. Welch Found. scholar, 1974-75; NSF grantee, 1975; preceptorship Am. Soc. Anesthesiologists, 1978. Mem. ACS, AMA, AAAS, Assn. Acad. Surgeons, N.Y. Acad. Scis., Internat. Soc. Cardiovascular Surgeons, New Eng. Soc. Vascular Surgeons. Home: 45 Morse St Hamden CT 06517-3211 Office: Yale U Sch Medicine 333 Cedar St # 137 New Haven CT 06510-3289

MEIJER, BARBARA ELIZABETH, banker; b. Paterson, N.J., Nov. 27, 1964; d. Robert John and Barbara Ann (Campbell) Nash; m. Robert Craig Meijer, June 24, 1989. BS in Fin. cum laude, Boston U., 1986; MBA in Fin., NYU, 1990. Asst. treas. Investment Mgmt. Group Bankers Trust, N.Y.C., 1986-89; asst. v.p. corp. fin. Sumitomo Trust & Banking Co., Ltd., N.Y.C., 1990—. Mem. N.Y. Cares, N.Y.C., 1991. Arthur Moynihan scholar Boston U., 1985. Mem. Fin. Women's Assn., Golden Key, Lock Honor Soc. (pres. 1986), Beta Gamma Sigma. Home: 31 Godfrey Ave Roseland NJ 07068-1332 Office: Sumitomo Trust & Banking Co 527 Madison Ave New York NY 10022-4304

MEIKSIN, ZVI H., electrical engineering educator; b. 1926. BSEE, Israel Inst. Tech., Haifa, 1950, Dipl. Ing., 1951; MSEE, Carnegie Mellon U., 1953; PhDEE, U. Pitts., 1959. Registered profl. engr., Pa. Design engr. McGraw Edison, Cannonsburg, Pa., 1953-54; sr. project engr. Westinghouse Electric Corp., Pitts., 1956-59; prof. dept. elec. engring. U. Pitts., 1959-91; pres. Internat. Sensor Corp., Pitts., 1989—; cons. engr. 28 orgns., U.S., Europe, 1959—; vis. prof. Israel Inst. Tech., Haifa, 1969, Sacramento State U., 1968-69. Author: Thin & Thick Films, 1976, Active Filter Design, 1990; co-author: Electronic Design, 1980, 84, Microprocessor Based Design, 1986; jour. referee profl. publs., 1970—; contbr. articles to profl. jours.; inventor, patentee 5 patents. Fellow IEEE (award coms.); mem. Eta Kappa Nu, Sigma Xi. Office: Internat Sensor Corp 675 Wm Pitt Way Pittsburgh PA 15238

MEILLER, MORRIS, physician; b. Lima, Peru, July 18, 1931; came to U.S., 1960; s. Abraham and Bertha (Pait) M.; m. Maria Elvira Santaella, Dec. 20, 1963 (div. Aug. 1991); 1 stepchild, Bryan Alan; m. Nelida Beatriz Houriett, Dec. 20, 1991; stepchildren: Andres, Martin. BS, U. San Marcos, 1952; MD, U. San Marcos Sch. Medicine, 1960. Resident Sheppard and Enoch Pratt Hosp., Towson, Md., 1963-64; asst. psychiatrist Johns Hopkins Hosp. Phipps Clinic, Balt., 1963-64; staff psychiatrist Spring Grove Hosp. Ctr., Catonsville, Md., 1970-75, St. Elizabeth's Hosp., Washington, 1979-83; chief mental hygiene clinic VA Outpatient Clinic, Orlando, Fla., 1975-77; staff psychiatrist Springfield Hosp. Ctr., Sykesville, Md., 1985-91; psychiatrist, unit dir. Walter P. Carter Ctr., Catonsville, 1991—; cons. in field. Mem. Am. Psychiat. Assn., Md. Psychiat. Soc. Home: 16420 Old Frederick Rd Mount Airy MD 21771 Office: Walter P Carter Ctr Catonsville Unit PO Box 3235 Catonsville MD 21228

MEINDL, JAMES RICHARD, psychology educator; b. Naha, Okinawa, Japan, Mar. 16, 1952; came to U.S., 1952; s. John Baptist and Yasuko (Nishimura) M.; m. Roberta Leslie Schatten, June 23, 1980; children: Jeremy Kim, Kevin James. BA in Psychology/Sociology, U. Rochester, 1974; MA in Social Psychology, U. Waterloo, 1978, PhD in Social Psychology, 1981. Postdoctoral fellow, vis. scholar dept. bus. adminstrn. U. Ill., Champaign, 1980-81; asst. prof. orgn. Sch. of Mgmt. SUNY, Buffalo, 1981-87, assoc. prof. orgn. Sch. of Mgmt., 1987—. Editor: Advances in Information Processing in Organizations; editorial bd. Adminstrv. Sci. quarterly, 1983-89, Acad. of Mgmt. Jour., 1986-90, Acad. of Mgmt. Rev., 1990—; contbr. articles to profl. jours./publs. Mem. Am. Psychol. Assn., Acad. Mgmt., Soc. for Exptl. Social Psychology. Office: Sch of Mgmt SUNY/Buffalo Buffalo NY 14260

MEINEL, CURT ROBERT, photographic studio executive, photographer; b. Manhattan, N.Y., June 8, 1949; s. Curt R. and Dorothy L. (Rydzeski) M.; m. Patricia A. Acritani, May 27, 1972; children: Curt R. III, Morgan Leigh. BFA, N.Y. Inst. Tech., 1971. Mgr. CLM Photography Inc., Huntington, N.Y., 1971-73; v.p. CLM Photography Inc., Huntington, 1973-76; mgr. N.Y. Photographic, Mt. Vernon, N.Y., 1977-80; pres. Westchester Photography Inc., Ossining, N.Y., 1981-86, CPM Photography, Inc., Ossining, 1986—; pres. Sunbeam Car Club, Ossining, 1976-86. Mem. Profl. Photographers Am., Profl. Photographers N.Y., Profl. Photographers Westchester. Republican. Roman Catholic. Home and Office: 2 Tavano Rd Ossining NY 10562

MEINHOLD, CHARLES BOYD, health physicist; b. Boston, Nov. 1, 1934; s. Russell and Jane (Boyd) M.; m. Anne Elizabeth DuVally, Oct. 20, 1956; children: Anne Frances, Patricia Marie, Michael John, Peter Russell, Catherine Louise. BS in Physics, Providence Coll., 1956; postgrad., U. Rochester, 1956-57. Staff scientist health physics div. Brookhaven Nat. Lab., Upton, N.Y., 1957-72, head, sr. health physicist safety and environ. div., 1972-88, sr.scientist, div. head, 1988-91; sr. scientist radiol. scis. div. Dept. Nuclear Energy, Upton, 1991—; pres. Nat. Coun. on Radiation Protection and Measurement, Bethesda, Md., 1991—; mem. Internat. Commn. on Radiol. Protection, 1978—; mem. Nat. Commn. on Radiol. Protection, 1977—; cons. Consol. Edison Co., 1984—. pres. South Haven Bd. Edn., Brookhaven, N.Y., 1965-87. Fellow Health Physics Soc.; mem. Internat. Radiation Protection Assn. (v.p. 1988-92, pres. 1992—). Roman Catholic. Home: 41 Old South Country Rd Brookhaven NY 11719-9526 Office: Dept Nuclear Energy Radiol Sci Div Bldg 703m B Upton NY 11973

MEINKE, ALAN KURT, surgeon; b. Eaton Rapids, Mich., May 25, 1952; s. Richard Keydel and Kaarina Elli (Ranta) M.; m. Lori Anne Alley, Sept., 1985; children: Christopher Richard, Mary Elizabeth. BA, Albion (Mich.) Coll., 1974; MD, Wayne State U., 1978. Intern Mayo Clinic, Rochester, Minn., 1978, resident gen. surgery, 1978-82, chief resident, 1982-83; assoc. attending physician Norwalk (Conn.) Hosp., 1983—; ptnr. Surg. Assocs., Westport, Conn., 1985—; med. dir. Wilton Vol. Ambulance Corp., 1983—; mem. med. adv. com. Fairfield-Westchester Crohn's and Colitis Found., 1992—; cons. U.S. Surg. Corp. Contbr. articles to profl. jours. Active med. sect. United Way of Westport and Weston, 1989—. Fellow ACS (credentials com. Conn. chpt. 1991—), Priestly Soc.; mem. AMA, Internat. Microsurg. Soc., Soc. Am. Gastrointestinal Endoscopic Surgeons, Am. Coll. Sports Medicine, Conn. Med. Soc., Norwalk Med. Soc., Fairfield County Med. Soc., Phi Beta Kappa. Office: Surg Assocs PC The Willows # 125 Westport CT 06880-2428

MEIROWITZ, CLAIRE CECILE, public relations executive; b. Frankfurt, Fed. Republic Germany, Jan. 14, 1934; came to U.S., 1939; d. Karl and Margot (Herrmann) Bier; m. Richard Meirowitz, Sept. 12, 1954 (div., July, 1969); children: Diane, Laura, Linda; m. Joseph Spiegel, Apr. 20, 1975. AA, Nassau Community Coll., 1971; BA magna cum laude, Hofstra U., 1976; postgrad., N.Y. Inst. Tech., 1987—. Pres., owner, editor, writer Profl. Editing Svcs., Massapequa Park, N.Y., 1972-76; editorial asst. United Technical Publs., Garden City, N.Y., 1976-77; publs. assoc. N.Y. Inst. Tech., Old Westbury, N.Y., 1977-79; asst. dir. coll. rels., dir. publs. SUNY, Old Westbury, 1979-87, dir. of community rels. and publs., 1987—; pres. SUNY Coun. for Univ. Affairs and Devel., 1987-89; cons. Guarino Graphics, Greenvale, N.Y., 1985—, editor, copywriter, 1986—. Manuscript editor: Journal of Collective Negotiations in Public Sector, 1972—; editor: art catalog, South Africa/South Bronx, 1981 (art excellence award, 1982); author: New Student Prospectus, The Coll. at Old Westbury, 1979, Labor-Management Relations Among Government Workers, 1983; co-editor: Strategies for Impasse Resolution, 1992; contbr. articles to jours. v.p., treas., sec., Taxpayers Edn. Assn., Hicksville, N.Y., 1962-68; mem. The Nature Conservancy, Cold Spring Harbor, N.Y., 1980—. Recipient Excellence in Profl. Svc. award SUNY at Albany, 1987, Disting. Svc. award SUNY Coun. Univ. Affairs, 1989, award for excellence in communications SUNY Westbury Alumni Assn., 1992, award for disting. leadership L.I. Women's Coun. for Equal Edn., Employment and Tng., 1992. Mem. L.I. Communicators Assn., Internat. Assn. of Bus. Communicators. Democrat. Jewish. Home: 325 Ocean Ave Massapequa Park NY 11762-1814 Office: SUNY 223 Store Hill Rd Old Westbury NY 11568-1706

MEISEL, MARTIN, English and comparative literature educator; b. N.Y.C., Mar. 22, 1931; s. Joseph and Sally (Rössler) Mörsel; m. Martha Sarah Winkley, Dec. 22, 1957; children—Maude Frances, Andrew Avram, Joseph Stoddard. A.B., Queens Coll., 1952; M.A., Princeton U., 1957, Ph.D., 1960; postgrad., U. Rome, 1959. Instr. English Rutgers U., New Brunswick, N.J., 1957-58; instr., asst. prof., assoc. prof. Dartmouth Coll., Hanover, N.H., 1959-65; prof. English U. Wis., Madison, 1965-68; prof. English and comparative lit. Columbia U., N.Y.C., 1968—, Brander Matthews prof. dramatic lit., 1987—, chmn. dept., 1980-83, acting v.p. arts and scis., 1986-87, v.p. arts and scis., 1989—; trustee Columbia U. Press, 1990. Author: Shaw and the 19th Century Theater, 1963, Realizations: Narrative, Pictorial, and Theatrical Arts in 19th Century England (George Freedley Meml. award Theater Library Assn. 1984; Barnard Hewitt award Am. Theatre Assn. 1984), 1983; mem. editorial and adv. bds. Jour. Victorian Studies, PMLA, Jour. Contemporary Lit., Bull. Research in the Humanities. Served with U.S. Army, 1954-56. Fellow Guggenheim Found., 1963-64, 1987-88, Am. Council of Learned Socs., 1970-71, Inst. for Advanced Studies in the Humanities, Edinburgh, 1977, Huntington Library and Art Gallery, 1978, 80, 83, Nat. Humanities Ctr., 1983-84, Wilson Ctr., Smithsonian Instn., 1987-88. Mem. MLA, Acad. Lit. Studies, Am. Soc. Theatre Rsch. Home: 18 Bacon Hill Rd Pleasantville NY 10570-3502 Office: Columbia U 208 Low Libr New York NY 10027

MEISNER, LORA DENISE, association executive; b. Chgo., Feb. 28, 1952; d. Kenneth Russell and Helen Lorraine (Vodnansky) M. BA in Liberal Arts, Coll. Notre Dame, Balt., 1986; MA in Internat. Devel., Am. U., 1989. Sales mgr. Amfac Hotels, Albuquerque, 1980-81; dir. sales Park Cen. Hotel/Omni Internat. Hotel, Washington, 1981-83; program coord. Nat. Assn. Treasurers, Silver Spring, Md., 1983-85, 86—. Mem. Silver Spring Transp. Adv. Com., 1988-89; commr. Commn. on Landlord/Tenant Affairs, Takoma Park, Md., 1991—. Mem. Am. Mgmt. Assn., Am. Soc. Assn. Execs. Roman Catholic. Home: 8308 Flower Ave Apt 505 Takoma Park MD 20912-6756 Office: Nat Assn Treas 8824 Cameron St Silver Spring MD 20910

MEISTAS, MARY THERESE, endocrinologist, diabetes researcher; b. Grand Rapids, Mich., July 22, 1949; d. Frank Peter and Anne Therese (Karsokas) M. MD, U. Mich., 1975. Diplomate Am. Bd. Internal Medicine, Am. Bd. Endocrinology. Intern, then resident in internal medicine Cleve. Clinic Hosp., 1975-78, endocrinology fellow, 1978-79; fellow in pediatric endocrinology Johns Hopkins Hosp., Balt., 1979-81; diabetes researcher Joslin Diabetes Ctr., Boston, 1981-86; assoc. in medicine Brigham and Women's Hosp., Boston, 1981-86; asst. in medicine, diabetes researcher Mass. Gen. Hosp., Boston, 1986—. Contbr. articles to profl. jours. Mem. ACP, Am. Diabetes Assn., Am. Fedn. Clin. Research, Endocrine Soc. Office: Emerson Hosp John Cuming Bldg Level One Concord MA 01742

MEISTER, MICHAEL WILLIAM, art educator; b. West Palm Beach, Fla., Aug. 20, 1942; s. Charles Michael and Dorothy May (Beaver) M.; m. Norma Jean Chatfield, Aug. 17, 1970 (div. June 1974); m. Adele Naude Santos. BA, Harvard U., 1964, MA, 1971, PhD, 1974; MA (hon.) U. Pa., 1979. Asst. prof. art U. Tex., Austin, 1974-76; asst. prof. U. Pa., Phila., 1976-79, assoc. prof., 1979-87, prof., 1988—; bd. dirs. Am. Com. of S. Asian Art, 1976-79, 83-86; mem. art com. Am. Inst. Indian Studies, Chgo., 1978—; bd. scholars S. Asia Religious Art Studies, Reading, Eng., 1982—. Editor: Encyclopaedia of Indian Temple Architecture, 1983, 86, 88, 91, Discourses on Siva, 1984, Making Things in South Asia, 1988; contbr. articles to profl. jours. Grantee Fulbright Found., 1964-66, NEH, 1980-91, AIIS, 1987; Fulbright scholar, 1976-77. Mem. Assn. Asian Studies, Coll. Art Assn. Democrat. Unitarian. Home: 2009 Naudain St Philadelphia PA 19146-1316 Office: U Pa Dept History of Art 3440 Market St Fl 560 Philadelphia PA 19104-3339

MELBOURNE, BERTRAM LLOYD, religious educator; b. John's Hall, St. James, Jamaica, May 13, 1948; came to U.S., 1982; s. James Ishmael and Vida May (Panther) M.; m. Cavel Andrea Beckford, OCt. 17, 1971; children: Yolande Almarie, Maurice Anthony, Launice Andrea. BTh, West Indies Coll., Mandeville, Jamaica, 1968; MA, Andrews U., 1976, PhD, 1986. Vice prin., bible tchr. Savanna-La-mar (Jamaica) High Sch., 1968-70; pastor/evangelist West Jamacia Conf. of S.D.A., Montego Bay, 1970-74, youth and edn. dir., 1974-78; campus ministries dir. West Indies Coll., 1978-82, asst. prof., 1980-82, chair, asst. prof. theology, 1980-82; assoc. prof. Columbia Union Coll., Takoma Park, Md., 1985-89, prof. religion, 1989-90, chair dept. religion, 1990—; lectr. Howard U. Div., Washington, 1990—. Author: Slow to Understand: The Disciples in Synoptic Perspective, 1988; contbr. articles to profl. jours. Dir. Pathfinder Club, Savanna-La-mar, 1968-70, White Hill, 1972-74, Western Jamaica, 1974-78. Recipient Thomas and Violet Zapara award for teaching excellence, 1991. Mem. Soc. Bibl. Lit., Am. Acad. Religion, Andrews Soc. for Religious Studies. Mem. Seventh Day Adventist. Office: Columbia Union Coll 7600 Flower Ave Silver Spring MD 20912-7796

MELCHER, JAN LOUISE, counselor; b. Reading, Pa., Sept. 27, 1953; d. Herbert R. and Lois June (Enders) Melcher; m. Francis Edward Lenich, Dec. 24, 1974. BS, Pa. State U., 1975; MS, Calif. U. of Pa., 1990. Tchr. Washington County Head Start, Washington, Pa., 1977-79; group supr. Washington County Day Care, Canonsburg, Pa., 1979-81; owner, operator Farmers' Daus., Bentleyville, Pa., 1981-84; cons. Cosmopolitan Club, Charleroi, Pa., 1984-88; grad. asst. California U. of Pa., 1988-89; intern Centerville Clinics, Inc., Fredericktown, Pa., 1989-90; cons. Fayette County MH/MR Program, Uniontown, Pa., 1990—, Frazier Area Sch. Dist., Perryopolis, Pa., 1991—; counselor Chestnut Ridge Counseling Svcs., Inc., Uniontown, Pa., 1990—; group facilitator and speaker's bur. Pitts. Ednl. Network for Eating Disorders, 1989—. Mem. Pitts. Insight, 1990—. California U. of Pa. Presdl. scholar, 1990. Mem. Am. Assn. for Counseling and Devel., Pa. Counseling Assn., Pitts. Ednl. Network for Eating Disorders. Democrat. Office: Chestnut Ridge Counseling 100 New Salem Rd #116 Uniontown PA 15401

MELCONIAN, LINDA JEAN, state senator, lawyer; b. Springfield, Mass.; d. George and Virginia Elaine (Noble) Melconian. B.A., Mt. Holyoke Coll., 1970; M.A., George Washington U., 1976, J.D., 1978. Bar: Mass. Chief legis. asst. to Ho. of Reps. Speaker Thomas P. O'Neill, Jr., U.S. Congress, Washington, 1971-80; pros. atty. Hampden County Dist. Atty., Springfield, Mass., 1981-82; state senator Mass. Gen. Ct., Boston, 1983—; instr. Western New Eng. Coll., Springfield, 1978-82; Our Lady of the Elms Coll., Springfield, 1982-83. Chmn., Heart Fund Ball, Western Mass., 1983; incorporator Springfield Coll., 1982—; ex officio trustee Ella T. Grasso Found., Conn., 1982—; active Democratic State Com., Mass., 1983, Hampden County Dems. Recipient Appreciation award Vietnam Vets. of Greater Springfield, 1983; Equal Edn. for All Children award Bilingual Parents of Springfield, 1983; Appreciation award Vets.-Hampden County Council, 1984. Mem. Hampden County Bar Assn., Zonta. Club: Mt. Holyoke. Home: 257 Ft Pleasant Ave Springfield MA 01108-1521 Office: Mass State Senate Rm 213-B Boston MA 02133

MELE, GREGG CHARLES, computer programmer; b. Hackensack, N.J., May 4, 1965; s. Charles Archangelo and Jennie (Johobowska) M. BS cum laude, Montclair State Coll., 1986; MS, Steven Inst. Tech., 1988. Lab. asst. Montclair (N.J.) State Coll., 1984-86; computer programmer Bac Data Med. Info. Systems, Wayne, N.J., 1985-86; computer programmer/analyst corp. hdqrs. AT&T, Somerset, N.J., 1986-90; computer programmer/analyst corp. trust The Bank of N.Y., N.Y.C., 1990—. Author: The Best in the Business, 1983, Baker's Dozen, 1987. Garden State scholar Montclair State Coll., 1984; finisher in N.Y.C. Marathon, 1991. Roman Catholic. Home: 58 Meadow Rd Edison NJ 08817-5547 Office: The Bank of NY 101 Barclay St New York NY 10286-0001

MELICKIAN, GARY EDWARD, trade association executive; b. L.A., Apr. 2, 1935; s. Ara Harry Melickian and Virginia Anne (Gargan) Jardine; m. Greta Gail Rasbury, Aug. 20, 1955 (div. 1972); children: Mark Stanley, Lynn Anne; m. Sharon Anne McDaniel, July 28, 1989. Student, UCLA, 1953-55; EM, Colo. Sch. Mines, 1959; postgrad., U. So. Calif., 1961-67, Calif. Poly. Inst., 1969-71. Lic. geologist, Calif., Alaska, engring. geologist, Calif.; cert. profl. geologist. Geologist Humble Oil & Refining Co., L.A., 1959; civil engr. L.A. County Flood Control Dist., L.A., 1960; geophysicist Dames & Moore, L.A., 1961, project geologist, 1962-64, mgr. pers., 1965-66, mgr. pub. rels., 1967-69, ptnr., 1970-84; dir. mining Dames & Moore, Denver, 1970-80; dir. tech. svcs. Dames & Moore, Bethesda, Md., 1980-84; pres., bd. dirs. Consultation Networks, Inc., Washington, 1985-90, Expert Witness Network, Washington, 1985-90; dir. indsl. mktg. Am. Gas Assn., Arlington, Va., 1990—; bd. dirs. Allcom, Inc., La Canada, Calif., 1986—; presenter in field. Contbr. articles to profl. jours. Fellow Geol. Soc. Am. (editor Engring. Geology newsletter 1966-67); mem. NSPE, ASME, Am. Inst. Profl. Geologists (pres. Calif. sect. 1971, bd. dirs. 1972-73, sec.-treas. 1982, Cert. of Merit 1982, 83), Soc. Mining Engrs. (bd. dirs. 1972-74, chmn. Peele award com., publs. com., program com.), Assn. Engring. Geologists, Am. Assn. Petroleum Geologists, Hist. Earth Sci. Soc., Am. Soc. Metals, Tech. Assn. Pulp and Paper Industry, Assn. Iron and Steel Engrs. Office: Am Gas Assn 1515 Wilson Blvd Arlington VA 22209-2402

MELIGNANO, CARMINE (EMANUEL MELIGNANO), video engineer; b. N.Y.C., Dec. 19, 1936; s. Salvatore and Lita (Poggialli) M.; m. Eileen Kinzie; children: Lori Ann, Robert, Michael. BS in Elec. Engring., Stevens Inst. Tech., Hoboken, N.J., 1959; postgrad., William Paterson Coll., 1978, Pace U., 1979. Registered profl. engr., N.J. Quality contr. Isomet Corp., Palisades Park, N.J., 1959-63; sales engr. RCA Service Corp., Camden, N.J., 1963-73; video engr. N.J. Sports and Expn. Authority, East Rutherford, 1974-77; chief engr. Price Waterhouse, N.Y.C., 1978—; engring. cons. Passaic County Vocat. Edn. High Sch., Wayne, N.J., 1971-77, Meadowlands Racetrack, East Rutherford, 1973-77, Royal Sound, Eatontown, N.J., 1984-86. Bd. trustees N.Y.C. chpt. Leukemia Soc., 1981-86, pres., 1987-90, nat. bd. trustees, 1990—. Recipient Emmy award NATAS, 1985, Outstanding Svc. award Leukemia Soc. Nat. Bd., 1986, Vincent T. Lombardi Humanitarian award, 1990, Pres.' award Leukemia Soc. Am., 1991, People's award, 1991. Mem. Soc. Motion Picture and TV Engrs. (sec., treas. elect N.Y.C. chpt. 1984-86), Nat. Sports Com., Nat. Performing Arts Com. (vice chmn. 1985—), Friar's Club Internat. (N.Y.C., profl. mem., mem.-elect). Republican. Roman Catholic. Lodge: KC. Home: PO Box 3 Lodi NJ 07644-0003 Office: CarMel Prodns 10 Dell Glen Ave Lodi NJ 07644-1740 also: Carmel Home Entertainment Ltd 641 Lexington Ave 21st Fl New York NY 10022

MELIKIAN, MARY, painter, art teacher; b. Worcester, Mass., Nov. 19, 1927; d. Earle and Armenouhi (Keljikian) M.; m. Warren Edward Haynes, June 28, 1979; stepchildren: Hayward, Christine, Elizabeth. BFA, R.I. Sch. Design, 1955; postgrad., Columbia U., 1957-60. Asst. designer Fuller Fabrics, N.Y.C., 1956; art tchr. Nutley (N.J.) Schs., 1957-60; asst. dir. Grand Ctrl. Moderns, N.Y.C., 1960-61; dir. pub. rels. Grand Ctrl. Art Galleries, N.Y.C., 1961-68; freelance artist N.Y.C., 1955—. Exhibited paintings include "Exodus", Ctr. for Human Rights, UN, "Roses", Worcester Mus. of Art, "Gramercy Park", Mint Mus., Charlotte, N.C., others. Bd. dirs. Women's Bible Soc., N.Y.C., 1987—; alumni trustee R.I. Sch. Design, 1970-73. Mem. Parrish Art Mus., Guild Hall, Nat. Arts Club. Episcopalian. Home and Studio: 429 E 52nd St New York NY 10022

MELILLO, JOSEPH VINCENT, producer, performing arts; b. New Haven, Conn., Nov. 15, 1946; s. Vincent and Viola (Fucci) M. BA, Sacred Heart U., 1968; MFA, Cath. U. Am., 1972. Adminstr. City Ctr. Music and Drama, N.Y.C., 1972-75; mktg. dir. The Walnut St. Theatre, Phila., 1975-76; dir. FEDAPT, N.Y.C., 1976-80; gen. mgr. New World Festival of Arts, Miami, Fla., 1982; dir. Next Wave Festival, N.Y.C., 1983-89; artistic dir. N.Y. Internat. Festival, N.Y.C., 1990—; producing dir. Bklyn. Acad. Music, 1991—; bd. trusteesEnGarde Arts, N.Y.C., 1991—; v.p. bd. dirs. Assn. Performing Arts Presenters, Washington, 1991—; cons.-specialist Opera Am., Washington, 1991—. Editor: Market the Arts, 1980. Democrat.

MELISSINOS, ADRIAN CONSTANTIN, physicist, educator; b. Thessaloniki, Greece, July 28, 1929; came to U.S., 1955, naturalized, 1970; s. Constantin John and Olympia (Abbott) M.; m. Mary Joyce Mitchell, June 7, 1960; children: Constantin John, Andrew William. Student, Royal Naval Acad., Greece, 1945-48; M.S., Mass. Inst. Tech., 1956, Ph.D., 1958. Naval cadet Greek Navy, 1945-48, commd. ensign, 1948, advanced through grades to lt., 1951; ret., 1954; teaching and research asst. Mass. Inst. Tech., 1955-58; instr. U. Rochester, N.Y., 1958-60; asst. prof. physics U. Rochester, 1960-63, assoc. prof., 1963-67, prof., 1967—, chmn. dept. physics and astronomy, 1974-77; vis. scientist CERN European Center for Nuclear Research, 1968-

69, 77-78, 89-90; cons. Brookhaven Nat. Lab., 1970-72, 75-79. Author: Experiments in Modern Physics, 1966, (with F. Lobkowicz) Physics for Scientists and Engineers, 1975; (with A. Das) Quantum Mechanics, 1985, Principles of Modern Technology, 1990. Decorated Swedish Order of Sword. Fellow Am. Phys. Soc.; mem. Greek Nat. Acad. (corr.). Home: 177 Whitewood Ln Rochester NY 14618-3223 Office: Dept Physics U Rochester Rochester NY 14627

MELLA, ARTHUR JOHN, insurance company executive; b. New York, N.Y., Sept. 25, 1937; s. Anthony Arthur and Angela Helen (Morrongiello) M.; m. Louise Vetere, May 5, 1962; children: Douglas James, Gregory Arthur. BS, Fordham U., 1959. CPCU. Supr. Liberty Mut. Ins. Co., N.Y.C., 1960-70; v.p. The Home Ins. Co., N.Y.C., 1970-80, Skandia Am. Reinsurance Co., N.Y.C., 1980-85; sr. v.p. Reliance Reinsurance Corp., Phila., 1985—. With USNG, 1960-63. Mem. Fedn. Ins. and Corp. Counsel, Excess Surplus Lines Claims (pres. 1988-89, v.p. 1987-88, bd. dirs. 1986-87), Broker and Reins. Underwriting, Soc. CPCU. Republican. Roman Catholic. Office: Reliance Reinsurance Co 1 Penn Center Plz Philadelphia PA 19103-1801

MELLAN, OLIVIA JULIE, psychotherapist; b. Bklyn., Oct. 14, 1946; d. Eli N. and Sara Blossom (Tepper) M.; m. Anand Mundra (div. 1984); children: Aniel; m. Michael Shapiro, May 17, 1987. BA in French cum laude, Mt. Holyoke Coll., 1968; MS in French, Georgetown U., 1973, post-grad. Sec., bur. chief Wall St. Jour., Washington, 1972-74; pvt. practice psychotherapy Washington Therapy Guild, Washington, 1975—; cons., trainer psychology Olivia Mellan Assocs. Inc., Washington, 1982—; keynote speaker nat. and regional confs. for fin. planners, 1986-91; trainer therapists; vol. Psychologists for Social Responsibility, Washington, 1986—. Author: 10 Days to Money Harmony: A Guide for Individuals and Couples, 1989, (audiocassette) Finding Balance in Your Money Life: Money Harmony for Individuals and Couples, 1988. Mem. AACD, ASTD, Am. Assn. Transpersonal Psychology, Washington Ethical Soc., Phi Beta Kappa. Democrat. Jewish. Office: Olivia Mellan & Assocs Inc 2607 Connecticut Ave NW Washington DC 20008

MELLEN, JOAN, educator; b. N.Y.C.. BA, Hunter Coll., 1962; MA, CUNY, 1964, PhD, 1968. Prof. Temple U., Phila., 1967—. Author: The Battle of Algiers, 1972, Marilyn Monroe, 1973, Women and their Sexuality in the New Film, 1974, Voices from the Japanese Cinema, 1975, The Waves at Genji's Door, 1976, Big Bad Wolves: Masculinity in the American Film, 1978; editor: The World of Luis Buñel, 1978, Privilege: The Enigma of Sasha Bruce, 1980, Natural Tendencies: A Novel, 1981, Bob Knight: His Own Man, 1988. Home: PO Box 359 Pennington NJ 08534-0359 Office: Temple U Anderson Hall Dept English Philadelphia PA 19122

MELLER, GEORGE MIECZYSLAW JERZY, international trade consulting company executive; b. Lwow, Poland, Apr. 11, 1935; s. Ludwik and Natalia (Holsztyn) M.; (div. 1982); children: Kristin Cecile, Paul Ludwik, Mark Antony. BS in Engring., London U., 1956; MBA, Harvard U., 1978. Chmn., founder George Meller Ltd., London, Eng., Holland, Middle East, Fed. Republic Germany, Spain, 1960-81; chief exec. officer Polmark Group, N.Y.C., Toronto, London, Moscow, 1982—; mem. Lloyds of London, 1973—; co-owner Pvt. Bank & Trust N/A, Miami; lectr. internat. trade in USSR. Co-author: Ethnic Influence in International Trade, 1982. Fellow Inst. of Dirs. of Eng., Royal Can. Yacht Club. Home: 3839 Leafy Way Miami FL 33133

MELLETT, JAMES SILVAN, geology educator; b. N.Y.C., July 12, 1936; s. Harry James and Evelyn Emaline (Reynolds) M.; m. Dorothy Ann Ashworth, Apr. 8, 1961; children: Jeanne-Marie, Claudine. BS in Biology, Iona Coll.; MA in Geology, Columbia U., PhD in Geology. Asst. prof. biology Iona Coll., New Rochelle, N.Y., 1963-67, acting chmn. dept. biology, 1966-67; asst. prof. NYU, N.Y.C., 1967-71, assoc. prof., 1971—, chmn. dept. geology, 1971-73; cons. Bur. of Land Mgmt., U.S. Dept. of Interior, Grand Junction, Colo., 1981-83; natural history cons. F.S. Gula Assocs., 1975-77, 79-81, dir. rsch., 1986—, ednl. cons. Challenger Ctr., 1987-89; geol. cons. Enviro-Sci., Rockaway, N.J., 1974-80; cons. seismic and volcanic risk maps Nat. Geographic Soc., 1985; pres., chief exec. officer Subsurface Cons. Ltd., New Fairfield, Conn., 1987—. Contbr. numerous articles to profl. jours. Member Concerned Citizens of New Fairfield, 1991—; justice of the peace State of Conn., 1972—; mem. bldg. com. New Fairfield Free Pub. Libr., 1973-80; chmn. Bicentennial Commn., 1974-76; chmn. interlocal agreement commn. for water diversion project City of New Fairfield, 1983-87; chmn. Zoning Bd. Appeals, 1972-81. Recipient awards and citations various police depts., FBI; grantee NSF, 1966, NYU, 1967-70, 75, Am. Mus. Natural History, 1967-75. Mem. AAAS, Am. Inst. Profl. Geologists, Am. Geol. Inst., Geol. Soc. Am., Soc. Vertebrate Paleontology, Sigma Xi. Home: 22 Curtis Ave New Fairfield CT 06812-4507 Office: NYU Dept Biology 1009 Main Washington Sq New York NY 10003

MELLIN, GILBERT WYLIE, pediatrics educator, consultant; b. Manorville, Pa., Sept. 22, 1925; s. Willard Colby and Hazel Naomi (Wylie) M.; m. Suzanne Naomi Seeds, Dec. 28, 1955; children: Deborah Louise, Sarah Agnew. BS summa cum laude, Bethany Coll., 1945; MD, Johns Hopkins U., 1949. Diplomate Am. Bd. Pediatrics. Intern in gen. medicine U. Pitts. Med. Ctr., 1949-50; jr., sr. and chief resident in pediatrics Bellevue Hosp., N.Y.C., 1950-53; instr. NYU Med. Sch., N.Y.C., 1952-53; jr. assoc. Children's Hosp., Washington, 1953-55; instr., assoc. in pediatrics Columbia U. Coll. Physicians and Surgeons, N.Y.C., 1955-58, asst. prof., 1958-67, assoc. prof., 1967—, acting chmn. dept., 1970-71; clin. instr. Georgetown U. Med. Sch., Washington, 1953-55; asst. pediatrician Babies Hosp. and Vanderbilt Clinic, Presbyn. Hosp., N.Y.C., 1955-57, asst. attending, 1957-67, assoc. attending, 1967—, acting dir. pediatric svc. 1970-71, dir. quality assurance, 1977—; mem. adv. bd. Assn. for Mentally Ill Children in Manhattan, 1961—; mem. tech. adv. com. on cleft palate N.Y.C. Dept. Health, 1961—; mem. hosp. rev. com. New York County Health Svcs. Rev. Orgn., 1977—, bd. dirs., 1982—; also others. Contbr. articles to med. jours. With USNR, 1943-46; sr. surgeon USPHS, 1948, 53-55. Fellow APHA (program area com. on drugs 1967-68); mem. AAAS, Am. Acad. Pediatrics, Am. Pediatric Soc., Harvey Soc., Soc. for Pediatric Rsch., Teratology Soc. (charter), Johns Hopkins U. Med. and Surg. Assn. Presbyterian. Home: 494 Ridgeland Ter Leonia NJ 07605-1017 Office: Columbia U Coll Phys & Surg 630 W 168th St New York NY 10032-3702

MELLIN, NORMAN, professional society executive, music educator; b. Pitts., Oct. 22, 1953; s. Robert Oscar and Hetti K.V. (Biederman) M. B Music Edn., U. Cin., 1976; Master's equivalency, Bowling Green State U., 1982. Exec. sec. Nat. Sch. Orch. Assn., Pitts., 1985—; clinician on old-time fiddling Mass. All-State Conf., Boston, 1989, Pa. All-State Conf., Harrisburg, 1989, U. So. Miss., Hattiesburg, 1990, N.Y. State SMA Summer Conf., Rochester, 1991. Author: (book) Incorporating Traditional Fiddling into the School Orchestra Curriculum, 1991. Mem. Nat. Sch. Orch. Assn., Music Educators Nat. Conf. Home and Office: 801 Louisville Rd Starkville MS 39759-3723

MELLINGER, MICHAEL VANCE, ecologist, environmental manager; b. Harrisburg, Pa., Dec. 21, 1945; s. Vance Charles and Arlene Francis (Berrier) M.; m. Karen Jane Solliday, Aug. 10, 1968; children: Scott, Christopher. BA, Bloomsburg (Pa.) U., 1967; PhD, Syracuse U., 1972. Registered environ. mgr.; cert. sr. ecologist. Sr. scientist Sargent & Lundy Engrs., Chgo., 1972-80; project mgr. Roy F. Weston, Inc., West Chester, Pa., 1980-85; cons. Mellinger Environ. Cons., Exton, Pa., 1985-86, 88-89; project mgr. Rollins Environ. Svcs. Inc., Chadds Ford, Pa., 1986-88; environ. mgr. Rohm & Haas Co., Bristol, Pa., 1989—. Contbr. articles to profl. jours. Bd. dirs. Lionville (Pa.) Youth Assn., 1982-87. NDEA fellow Syracuse U., 1970-72. Mem. Sigma Xi. Home: 122 Baker Dr Exton PA 19341-1506 Office: Rohm & Haas Bristol Rsch Park PO Box 219 Bristol PA 19007-0028

MELLON, W. GILES, economics educator; b. Chgo., Mar. 7, 1931; s. Walter Jackson and Julia Adele (Krengel) M.; m. Kathryn O'Connell, June 20, 1964; children: Joshua, Christopher, Jonathan. BA, U. Va., 1953; MA, Princeton U., 1956, PhD, 1962. Instr. Princeton U., 1956-60; fin. economist Chase Manhattan Bank, N.Y.C., 1960-66; assoc. prof. Grad. Sch. Mgmt. Rutgers U., Newark, 1966-69, prof., 1969—, dir. exec. MBA program, 1988—, chmn. econs. and fin. depts., 1970-88; dir. Daily Income Fund, N.Y.C., others; cons. in field. Contbr. articles to profl. jours. Mem. Phi Beta Kappa. Democrat. Episcopalian. Office: Rutgers U Grad Sch Mgmt 180 University St Newark NJ 07102

MELLOR, BARBARA LOUISE, educator, librarian, counselor consultant; b. Fall River, Mass., Jan. 27, 1945; d. Ernest and Dorothea Vera (Phelps) M.; m. Joseph John Cabaup, June 26, 1965 (div. 1986); children: Joseph Ernest, Jean Marie. AA, Sch. Lifelong Learning, Durham, N.H., 1981, BGS in Libr./Media, 1983; MEd, Plymouth State Coll., 1988. Cert. media generalist, guidance counselor, N.H. Tchr., libr. Littleton (N.H.) Jr.-Sr. High Sch., 1980—. Author: (books and tchr. guide) Activities for the Occupational Outlook Handbook (3 grade levels), 1989. Mediator Youth and Family Mediation Program, Littleton, 1988—; bd. trustees Bethlehem (N.H.) Pub. Libr., 1977—. Mem. NEA, AACD (N.H. chpt.), N.H. Sch. Counselors Assn., N.H. Career Devel. Assn., N.H. Ednl. Media Assn., Phi Delta Kappa. Home: RFD 1 Box 138 Bethlehem NH 03574 Office: Littleton High Sch School St Littleton NH 03561-1226

MELLORS, ROBERT CHARLES, pathologist; b. Dayton, Ohio, 1916; s. Bert S. and Clementine (Steinmetz) M.; m. Jane K. Winternitz, Mar. 25, 1944; children: Alice J., Robert Charles, William K., John W. Ph.D., Western Res. U., 1940; M.D., Johns Hopkins, 1944. Diplomate: Am. Bd. Pathology in path. anatomy. Intern Nat. Naval Med. Ctr., Bethesda, Md., 1944-45; rsch. fellow medicine Meml. Center Cancer and Allied Diseases, N.Y.C., 1946-50; rsch. fellow pathology Meml. Ctr. Cancer and Allied Diseases, 1950-53, asst. attending pathologist, 1953-57, assoc. attending pathologist, 1957-58; sr. fellow Am. Cancer Soc., 1947-50; sr. clin. rsch. fellow Damon Runyon Meml. Fund, 1950-53; asst. attending pathologist Meml. Hosp., N.Y.C., 1953-57, assoc. attending pathologist, 1957-58; asst. attending pathologist Ewing Hosp., N.Y.C., 1953-57, assoc. attending pathologist, 1957-58; instr. biochemistry Western Res. U., 1940-42; rsch. assoc. Poliomyelitis Rsch. Ctr. and Dept. Epidemiology Johns Hopkins U. Sch. Hygiene, 1942-44; asst. prof. biology Meml. Ctr. Cancer and Allied Diseases, N.Y.C., 1952-53; asst. prof. pathology Sloan Kettering div. Cornell U., 1953-57, assoc. prof., 1957-58; prof. pathology Cornell U. Med. Coll., 1961-90, prof. emeritus, 1990—; assoc. attending pathologist N.Y. Hosp., 1961-72, attending pathologist, 1972-86; pathologist-in-chief, dir. labs., 1958-84, emeritus, 1984-85, hon. staff, 1986—; assoc. dir. rsch. Hosp. for Spl. Surgery, N.Y.C., 1958-69, dir. rsch., 1969-84, emeritus, 1984-85, scientist emeritus, 1986—; mem. rsch. adv. com. NIH, 1962-66; adv. com. Nat. Inst. Environ. Health Sci., 1966-69; com. nomenclature and classification of disease Coll. Am. Pathologists, 1960-64. Author: Analytical Cytology, 1955, 2d edit., 1959, Analytical Pathology, 1957. Served as lt. (j.g.), M.C. USNR, 1944-46. Recipient Kappa Delta award Am. Acad. of Orthopedic Surgeons, 1962. Fellow Royal Coll. Pathologists, Am. Soc. Clin. Pathology; mem. Am. Assn. Pathologists, Am. Assn. Immunologists, Am. Soc. Biochemistry and Molecular Biology, Am. Coll. Rheumatology, Am. Orthopedic Assn. (hon.). Home: 3 Hardscrabble Cir Armonk NY 10504-2222

MELLOTT, CLOYD ROWE, lawyer; b. McConnellsburg, Pa., Feb. 16, 1923; s. Wesley William and Alice (Cutshall) M.; m. Lois M. Williams, Aug. 16, 1952; children: Christopher R., Deborah L. BSEE, Carnegie Inst. Tech., 1947; LLB, U. Pitts., 1950, JD, 1968. Bar: Pa. 1951, U.S. Dist. Ct. (we. dist.) Pa. 1951, U.S. Ct. Appeals (3d cir.) 1952, U.S. Supreme Ct. 1968, various U.S. cts. appeal and U.S. dist. cts. Law clk. U.S. Dist. Ct. (we. dist.) Pa., Pitts., 1951-53; assoc. Smith, Buchanan, Ingersoll, Rodewald & Eckert, Pitts., 1953-58; ptnr. Eckert, Seamans, Cherin & Mellott, Pitts., 1958—; mem. lawyers adv. com. U.S. Ct. Appeals for 3d Cir., 1984-86, chmn., 1986, permanent mem. U.S. 3d cir. jud. conf. chmn., 1989; chmn. Fund for Bicentennial Celebration of Common Pleas Ct. of Allegheny County, 1987-88. Trustee U. Pitts., 1979—; bd. visitors, Sch. Law, U. Pitts., 1978—, Sch. Engring., U. Pitts., 1979—; mem. various bds. and divs. of Pitts. Presbytery, Fox Chapel Presbyn. Ch., Pitts. 1st Lt. USAF, 1942-45, ETO. Decorated D.F.C., Air medal with three oak leaf clusters, Purple Heart; recipient Medallion of Distinction U. Pitts. Mem. ABA, Am. Judicature Soc., Pa. Bar Assn., Allegheny County Bar Assn. (chmn. civil lit. sect. 1981-82, fed. ct. sect. 1987-88), Duquesne Club, Pitts. Field Club, Allegheny Club (Pitts.), Lakewood Country Club (St. Petersburg, Fla.), Am. Legion. Republican. Office: Eckert Seamans Cherin & Mellott 42d Fl 600 Grant St Pittsburgh PA 15219-2701

MELMAN, ISRAEL J., technology and information systems executive; b. N.Y.C., Apr. 18, 1920; m. Esther; children: Martin, Daniel, Barry. BS, Bklyn. Coll., 1941; Student, Yale U., 1943, Polytechnic Inst. of Bklyn., 1946-47, Rochester (N.Y.) U., 1966-67. Chief engr. CBS-Columbia, Queens, N.Y., 1950-56, Fairchild Camera and Inst. Corp., Syosset, N.Y., 1956-59; gen. mgr. Electro-Optical div. Servo Corp., Hicksville, N.Y., 1959-65; mgr. facsimile systems Xerox Corp., Rochester, N.Y., 1965-69; mgr. corp. devel. Sanders Assocs., Nashua, N.H., 1969-71; pres. Lexan Assocs., Lexington, Mass., 1971—; chmn. of the bd. Telebase Systems Inc., Bryn Mawr, Pa., 1985—; mem. Nat. TV Systems Com., 1950-56. Office: Lexan Assocs 2 Paddock Ln Lexington MA 02173-5899 also: Telebase Systems Inc 435 Devon Park Dr Wayne PA 19087

MELMED, MATTHEW ELIOTT, non-profit organization executive; b. Bklyn., Mar. 31, 1954; s. Murray M. and Thelma (Rettig) M.; m. Deborah A. Rozell, Aug. 16, 1981; children: Andrew Zachary, Jeremy David. BA, Harpur Coll., 1975; JD, SUNY, Buffalo, 1978. Staff atty. Conn. Legal Svcs., Bridgeport, 1978-80, project dir., 1979-80, mng. atty., 1981-82; exec. dir. Conn. Assn. for Human Svcs., Hartford, 1982—; dir. Food Rsch. and Action Ctr., Washington, 1983—, Community Mediation Program, New Haven, 1988—. Recipient Gofstein award Conn. Assn. Dirs. Health, 1990, Child Advocacy award Collaboration for Conn. Children, 1986, Lewis Hine award Nat. Child Labor Com., 1985, others. Mem. Phi Beta Kappa. Democrat. Jewish. Office: Conn Assn for Human Svcs 880 Asylum Ave Hartford CT 06105-1901

MELNGAILIS, JOHN, physicist; b. Riga, Latvia, Feb. 4, 1939; arrived in U.S., 1949; s. John and Jakobine (Zile) M.; m. Susan Toye, Jan. 23, 1967 (div. July 1982); children: Ilze, Sarma; m. Michaele Weissman, Nov. 7, 1982; 1 child, Noah. BS in Physics, Carnegie Mellon Inst., 1960, MS in Physics, 1962, PhD in Physics, 1965. Researcher Westinghouse Rsch., Pitts., 1960-65; postdoctoral fellow Max Planck Inst., Stuttgart, Fed. Republic Germany, 1965, CNRS, Bellevue, France, 1966; mem. staff Lincoln Lab., Lexington, Mass., 1967-79; prin. rsch. scientist MIT, Cambridge, Mass., 1979-90, sr. rsch. scientist, 1990—; U.S. chmn. workshop on focused ion beam tech. NSF, Osaka, Japan, 1987; co-chair workshop NATO, Cargese, France, 1987. Contbr. chpt. to VLSI Handbook, 1991, also numerous articles to profl. publs. Grantee NSF, DARPA, U.S. Army. Mem. IEEE (sr.), Am. Phys. Soc. Home: 47 Page Rd Newton MA 02160-1534 Office: MIT Rm 39-427 Cambridge MA 02139

MELNICK, EDWARD LAWRENCE, statistician, educator, consultant; b. Ann Arbor, Mich., Dec. 21, 1938; s. Daniel and Alice (Lupatin) M.; m. Virginia Mayer, June 23, 1963; children: Karen Ruth, John Ronald. B.A., Lehigh U., 1960; M.S., Va. Poly. Inst., 1963; Ph.D., George Washington U., 1969. Math. statistician U.S. Census Bur., Washington, 1963-69; prof. stats. NYU, 1969—; prin. E. Melnick Statis. Cons., N.Y.C., 1969—. Speaker in field. Assoc. editor Jour. of Forecasting; contbr. numerous articles to profl. jours. Recipient Great Tchr. award NYU, 1983, 88, 89, 90. Fellow Royal Stats. Soc.; mem. Am. Stats. Assn., Inst. Math. Stats. Home: 100 Bleecker St # 17A New York NY 10012-2202 Office: NYU 40 W 4th St Rm 519 New York NY 10012-1106

MELON, CANDY A., recording industry executive, fan club promoter; b. Rochester, N.Y., Jan. 20, 1967; d. Abe and Mary (Cob) M. With Mirror Records Inc., Rochester; mgr., promoter Armand Schaubroeck Steals Fan Club, 1970—, Immaculate Mary Fan Club, 1990—. Office: Mirror Records Inc 645 Titus Ave Rochester NY 14617

MELOON, DANIEL THOMAS, JR., chemistry educator; b. Buffalo, Aug. 13, 1935; s. Daniel Thomas and Ruth Eleanor (Rand) M.; m. Laura June Newell, June 13, 1959; children: Jeanette Marjorie, Daniel III, Stephen Paul. BA, U. Buffalo, 1957, MA, 1960; PhD, SUNY, Buffalo, 1963. Sr. chemist Carborundum Co., Niagara Falls, N.Y., 1963-66; from asst. prof. to assoc. prof. Buffalo State Coll., 1966-80, prof., 1980—. Author: (manual) Experiments for General Chemistry, 1971, 2d edit., 1986, Instrumental Analysis Laboratory Experiments, 1978, 2d edit., 1985, 3d edit., 1992. Mem. Am. Chem. Soc., Creation Rsch. Soc. Republican. Baptist. Office: Buffalo State Coll 1300 Elmwood Ave Buffalo NY 14222-1095

MELTER, ROBERT ALAN, mathematics educator, researcher; b. N.Y.C., Mar. 20, 1935; s. George I. and Hattie (Eisenstein) M.; m. Therese Balavoine, Oct. 10, 1965; 1 child, Vanessa. AB, Cornell U., 1956; AM, U. Mo., 1960, PhD, 1962. Asst. prof. math. U. R.I., Kingston, 1962-64, U. Mass., Amherst, 1964-67; assoc. prof. math. U. S.C., Columbia, 1967-71; dir. sci. div. L.I. U., Southampton, N.Y., 1986-88, prof. math., 1971—. Assoc. editor: Math. Revs., 1973-74; translator Problems in Combinatorics, 1985, Combinatorial Configurations, 1988; contbr. articles to profl. jours. NAS Exch. fellow, 1981; Fulbright prof., 1985. Mem. Am. Math. Soc. Office: LI U Dept Maths Southampton NY 11968

MELTON, EDWARD MADISON, recycled paperboard manufacturer; b. Waycross, Ga., Apr. 21, 1955; s. Mitchell and Frances Jeanette (Thrift) M.; m. Judy Darnell Shelton, Aug. 16, 1980; 1 child, Frances Elizabeth. BS in Paper Technology, N.C. State U., 1977. Mgmt. trainee Sonoco Products Co., Hartsville, S.C., 1977-78; prodn. asst. Sonoco Products Co., Hartsville, 1978-80; quality control supr. Sonoco Products Co., Munroe Falls, Ohio, 1980; shift supr. Sonoco Products Co., Downingtown, Pa., 1980-84; mill supt. Sonoco Products Co., Downingtown, 1984-86; plant mgr. Natick (Mass.) Paperboard Corp., 1986-87, Haverhill (Mass.) Paperboard Corp., 1987-89; gen. mgr. Newark Boxboard Corp., 1989—. Mem. TAPPI, PIMA, N.C. State U. Alumni Assn., N.C. State U. Pulp and Paper Found. Methodist. Home: 354 Whispering Hills Rd Annandale NJ 08801-3402 Office: Newark Boxboard Corp 20 Jackson Dr Cranford NJ 07016-3609

MELTZER, ALLAN H., economist, educator; b. Boston, Feb. 6, 1928; s. George B. and Minerva I. (Simons) M.; m. Marilyn Ginsburg, Aug. 27, 1950; children: Bruce Michael, Eric Charles, Beth Denise. A.B., Duke U., 1948; M.A., UCLA, 1955, Ph.D., 1958. Lectr. econs. U. Pa., Phila., 1956-57; mem. faculty Carnegie Mellon U. Grad. Sch. Indsl. Adminstrn., Pitts., 1957—; prof. econs. Carnegie Mellon U. Grad. Sch. Indsl. Adminstrn., 1964—, Maurice Falk prof. econs. and social sci., 1970-80, John M. Olin univ. prof. polit. economy and pub. policy, 1980—; acting dean Grad. Sch. Indsl. Adminstrn. Carnegie Mellon U., 1972-73; vis. prof. U. Chgo., 1964-65, Fundacao Getulio Vargas, Rio de Janeiro, 1976-79, City U., London, 1979-86; vis. fellow Hoover Instn., 1977-78; vis. scholar Am. Enterprise Inst., Washington, 1989—; co-chmn. Shadow Open Market Com., 1974-89, chmn., 1989—; cons. U.S. Treasury, Joint econ. com. U.S. Congress, 1960; com. on banking and currency U.S. Ho. of Reps., 1963-64; mem. Pres.'s Econ. Policy Adv. Bd, 1988—; acting mem. Coun. Econ. Advisors, 1988-89; cons., bd. govs. FRS, FDIC; dir. Cooper Tire & Rubber Co.; hon. advisor Inst. Monetary Studies Bank Japan, 1987—; bd. dirs. Sarah Scaife Found., Commonwealth Found., Global Econ. Action Inst. Author: (with Karl Brunner) An Analysis of Federal Reserve Monetary Policymaking, 1964, (with Karl Brunner) Monetary Economics, 1989, Keynes's Monetary Theory: A Different Interpretation, 1988, (with Alex Cukierman and Scott Richard) Political Economy, 1991; editor: (with Karl Brunner) Carnegie-Rochester Conf. Series, 1976-89, (with Charles Plosser), 1989—; contbr. articles to profl. jours. Recipient Award for Outstanding Achievement UCLA, 1983; Social Sci. Research Council fellow, 1955-56; Ford Found. fellow, 1962-63. Mem. Am. Econ. Assn. (v.p. 1990), Western Econ. Assn. (pres. 1985-86), Am. Fin. Assn., Phila. Soc. (v.p. 1981-83), Cosmos Club. Office: Carnegie Mellon U Dept Econs Pittsburgh PA 15213

MELTZER, EVAN FREDERICK, podiatrist, consultant; b. Rochester, N.Y., May 12, 1946; s. Harold S. and Shirley (Gold) M.; m. Linda Blazek, Aug. 5, 1989; children: Wendy R., Peter J. BA, Mich. State U., 1968; MS, U. Colo., 1970; DPM, Pa. Coll. Podiatric Medicine, 1977. Diplomate Am. Bd. Podiatric Surgery; lic. podiatrist, N.Y., Colo., Md., D.C. Instr. in organic, gen. chemistry and phys. sci. Agrl. and Tech. Coll. SUNY, Canton, 1970-73; chief podiatry svc. orthopedic dept. Kimbrough Army Community Hosp., Ft. George G. Meade, Md., 1977-81; pvt. practice podiatrist Silver Spring, Md., 1981-82, Ithaca, N.Y., 1982—; podiatric cons. Gannett Health Ctr. Cornell U., Ithaca, 1988—; mem. staff Tompkins Community Hosp., Ithaca, N.Y., mem. laser com., mem. operating rm. com., mem. utilization and rev. com. With U.S. Army, 1977-81. NSF grantee Lake George Water Rsch. Inst. Rensselaer Poly. Inst., 1971, Inst. Arctic and Alpine Rsch. U. Colo., 1972. Fellow American College of Foot Surgeons; mem. Am. Podiatric Med. Assn., N.Y. State Podiatric Med. Assn. (v.p. Southern Tier divsn.), Am. Acad. Podiatric Sports Medicine, Adirondack Mountain Club, Ithaca Yacht Club. Office: Tompkins Foot Care Ctr 201 Dates Dr Ste 201 Ithaca NY 14850-1335

MELTZER, JACK, consultant, retired college dean; b. Bayonne, N.J., Aug. 21, 1921; s. Louis and Debbie (Gold) M.; m. Rae Libin, June 26, 1944; children: Richard, Marc, Ellen. B.A., Wayne State U., 1941; M.A., U. Chgo., 1947. Dir. planning Michael Reese Hosp., Chgo., 1953-54; S.E. Chgo. Commn. and U. Chgo., 1954-58; propr. Jack Meltzer Assos. (planners), 1958-63; acting dir. Am. Soc. Planning Ofcls., 1967-68; prof., dir. Center Urban Studies, U. Chgo., 1963-71; prof. div. social scis., prof. Sch. Social Service Adminstrn., 1965-83; prof., dean Sch. Social Scis. U. Tex.-Dallas, 1983-86; pvt. practice cons., 1986—; cons. to govt. and industry, 1945—. Author book revs., articles, books. Village trustee, Park Forest, Ill., 1950-52, mem. plan commn., 1949; Served to capt. USAAF, World War II. Mem. Am. Soc. Planning Ofcls. (past treas.), Am. Inst. Planners (past v.p. pvt. practice dept.), Nat. Assn. Housing and Renewal Ofcls., Am. Soc. Pub. Adminstrn., Lambda Alpha. Home: 4550 North Park Ave # 803 Chevy Chase MD 20815

MELTZER, JEFF MATTHEW, film editor, producer, writer; b. N.Y.C., Feb. 14, 1957; s. Paul and Rosalie (Abouaf) M.; m. Fonda Lifrak, Nov. 25, 1984; children: Rachel, Emily. BA, U. Md., 1979. Film editor Jenkins/Covington Prodns., N.Y.C., 1979-80; asst. film editor Nuchow Editorial, N.Y.C., 1980-85; editor, pres. Jeff Meltzer Films, Inc., N.Y.C., 1985—; pres. Go Direct TV, Inc., N.Y.C., 1989-90, TV Salvage & Recovery, Inc., N.Y.C., 1992—; film editor Time Warner, Gen. Foods, Procter & Gamble, Lever Bros., Warner Lambert, Panasonic, RKO, Learning Channel, Hearst Publs. Film editor Ad Coun., Eye Bank, Epilepsy Found., Homeless Coalition, Planned Parenthood, 1982—. Recipient Clio award, 1986. Mem. Hastings Arts Coun. Office: Jeff Meltzer Films Inc 575 Lexington Ave 729 7th Ave New York NY 10019

MELTZER, PETER CLAUDE, scientist; b. Johannesburg, South Africa, Jan. 29, 1949; came to U.S., 1977; s. Daniel and Lily (Chiat) M.; m. Lynn J. Segal, Dec. 3, 1972; children: Colin J., Dan L. BSc with honors, U. of the Witwatersrand, Johannesburg, 1972, PhD, 1976. Jr. lectr. U. of the Witwatersrand, 1971-76, rsch. assoc., 1976-77; rsch. assoc. MIT, Cambridge, 1977-78; group leader Sisa Pharm. Lab., Cambridge, 1978-83; v.p. R&D H.G. Pars Pharm. Labs. Inc., Cambridge, 1983-86; pres. Organix Inc., Woburn, Mass., 1986—; cons. Nat. Inst. of Drug Abuse, Nat. Inst. Medicine Chem., Nat. Inst. Child Health and Human Devel. Assoc. editor The Nucleus, 1981-83; contbr. articles to profl. jours.; patentee in field. Scholarship CSIR, 1972; Senate Rsch. grant U. Witwatersrand, 1975. Mem. Am. Chem. Soc. (Northeastern sect. medicine chmn. 1983—, nominating com. 1987-88, long range planning com., 1990). Jewish. Office: Organix Inc 65 Cummings Pk Woburn MA 01801-2124

MELUCCI, RICHARD CHARLES, research institute administrator; b. Oceanside, N.Y., July 17, 1946; s. Richard Joseph and Marcia Jane (Lockwood) M.; B.S., Adelphi U., 1968, M.B.A., 1971; m. Rosanne Alice Kessel, Dec. 15, 1968; children—Christine Ann, Donna Marie, Richard Paul, Robert Joseph, John Charles. Planning engr. Sperry Gyroscope Co., Great Neck, N.Y., 1967-70; planning adminstr. PRD Electronics, Inc., Syosset, N.Y., 1970-73, program adminstr., 1973-74; sr. staff asst. dept. physics Brookhaven Nat. Lab., Upton N.Y., 1974-79, adminstr. dept. applied sci., 1979—; adj. assoc. prof. computer info. systems Dowling Coll., Oakdale, N.Y., 1978—; vis. prof. SUNY at Oswego, 1982—. Recipient Cert. Inst. Certification of Computer Profls. Office: Brookhaven Nat Lab Bldg 179A Upton NY 11973

MELVILLE, R. JERROLD, executive; b. Rochester, N.Y., May 9, 1953; s. Ronald Frederick and Joan (Kearney) M.; m. Christie Meagley, June 4, 1978 (div.); children: Alison, Craig. AA, Monroe Community Coll., 1975; BA, SUNY, 1978; MSW, Syracuse U., 1982, MPA, 1982. Cert. social worker, N.Y. Psychiat. aide Strong Meml. Hsop., Rochester, N.Y., 1975-76; houseparent St. Catherine's Child Care Ctr., Albany, N.Y., 1978-79; program dir. Oneida County ARC, Utica, N.Y., 1982-83, Oswego County Opportunities, Fulton, N.Y., 1983-85; health planner Cen. N.Y. Health Systems Agy., Syracuse, N.Y., 1985-87; exec. dir. So. Tier Environs. for Living, Helmuth, N.Y., 1988—. Mem. Assn. Community Living Agys. Mental Health (we. N.Y. regional dir. 1989—). Home: 29 Euclid Ave Jamestown NY 14701-3160

MELVILLE, ROBERT SEAMAN, chemist; b. Worcester, Mass., Nov. 20, 1913; s. Carey Eyster and Maud Tesmer (Seaman) M.; m. Eleanor Elisabeth Vogel, Mar. 6, 1942; children: Robert Andrew, John Frederick, Margaret Ellen, Emily Jean, Martin Carroll. AB in Chemistry, Clark U., 1937; PhD in Biochemistry, State U. Iowa, 1950. Chief chemist St. Luke's Hosp., Chgo., 1950-54; chief biochemist VA Hosp., Iowa City, 1954-63; chief biochemist, lab. requirement specialist VA Cen. Office, Washington, 1963-65; health sci. adminstr. Nat. Inst. Gen. Med. Scis., NIH, Bethesda, Md., 1965-67, chief automated clin. lab. program, 1967-77, spl. asst. to dir. of biomed. engring., 1977-81; dir. In Vitro Diagnostic Device Standards div. Bur. Med. Devices, FDA, Silver Spring, Md., 1981-82; cons. in clin. scis., 1983—; clin. prof. pathology George Washington U. Med. Ctr., Washington, 1977—; pres. Trans-Tech. Biomed., 1983—. Contbr. articles on clin. lab. automation to profl. publs. With U.S. Army, 1942-46. Fellow AAAS, Am. Chem. Soc., Am.. Assn. Clin. Chemistry (Joseph H. Rowe award 1972, Nat. Fisher award 1976, pres. 1969-70), Instrument Soc. Am., Assn. for Advancement of Med. Instrumentation; mem. Am. Bd. Clin. Chemists (pres. bd. dirs. 1978-81), Am. Inst. Chemists (chmn. cert. commn. in chem. engring. and chemistry 1981-84, 87-91, cert. chemist 1989—), Alpha Chi Sigma (Profl. Chemist award 1990), Lambda Chi Alpha. Unitarian. Club: Cosmos. Lodge: Masons. Home and Office: 11112 Kenilworth Ave PO Box 56 Garrett Park MD 20896

MELVIN, PETER JOSEPH, astrophysicist, educator; b. Seattle, Mar. 12, 1944; s. William Leopold and Virginia (Stevens) M.; m. Alice Sue Pfiester, May 25, 1975; children: Robert Dennis, Chloe Ann. B.A., Western Wash. State Coll., 1965; M.S., U. Ill., 1966, Ph.D., 1970. NASA trainee U. Ill., Urbana, 1966-68, instr. phys. sci., 1970-72, asst. prof., 1972-77; sr. engr. Martin-Marietta Aerospace Co., Denver, 1977-80, staff engr., 1980-83; sr. specialist engr. engring. tech. applications div. Boeing Computer Services, Seattle, 1983-86; astrophysicist U.S. Naval Research Lab., Washington, 1986—; vis. faculty Applied Math. Div., Nat. Bur. Standards, Boulder Labs., Colo., 1977. Recipient Berman Publ. award Naval Rsch. Lab., 1988, 89, 92. Mem. AIAA, Am. Math. Soc., Soc. Indsl. and Applied Math., Am. Geophys. Union. Contbr. articles to profl. jours.

MELVIN, T. STEPHEN, manufacturing company executive; b. Winter Haven, Fla., Mar. 12, 1938; s. Talmage Stephen and Doris Louise (Walker) M.; m. Beverly Sue Sauls. BIE with hons., U. Fla., 1960. Registered profl. engr., Fla. With Gen. Electric, various locations, 1960-70; v.p. mfg. Armor Elevator/A.O. Smith, Louisville, 1970-73; v.p. ops. Hamilton Std. div. United Technologies Corp., Windsor Locks, Conn., 1973-76; v.p., gen. mgr. Turbo Power & Marine/United Tech. Corp., Farmington, Conn., 1976-79; pres. Elliott Turbomachinery/United Tech. Corp., Jeannette, Pa., 1979-82; pres. mfg. div. Pratt & Whitney div. United Techs. Corp., East Hartford, Conn., 1982-86; pres. aerospace div. AMCA Internat., Newington, Conn., 1986-87; pres. Smith & Wesson, Springfield, Mass., 1987-91. Mem. Springfield C. of C. (vice chmn.), Suffield (Conn.) Country Club, Callawassie (S.C.) Country Club, Alpha Tau Omega. Republican. Episcopalian.

MENA, DANILO J., financial services company executive; b. San Jose, Costa Rica, Jan. 8, 1937; came to U.S., 1941; s. Luis and Consuelo (Reuben) Mena-Solorzano; m. Betsy Alice Gimpel, Dec. 9, 1972; children: Charles Bradford, Sarah Elizabeth, William Andrews. BME, Bklyn. Poly. Inst., 1960; MBA, Adelphi U., 1968. Design engr. Syska & Hennessy, N.Y.C., 1962-64; staff engr. Am. Standard, N.Y.C., 1964-66; account exec. IBM Corp., N.Y.C., 1966-70, customer exec. instr., 1970-74; industry mgr. IBM Corp., Armonk, N.Y., 1974-77; dir. mktg. Itel Corp., N.Y.C., 1977-79; pres. Williams Equity Group Ltd., Chappaqua, N.Y., 1979—. Chmn. New Castle Rep. Com., Chappaqua, N.Y., 1990—, N.Y. State Rep. Nat. Hispanic Assembly; dist. leader Westchester County Rep. Com., 1980; chmn. Westchester Rep. Nat. Hispanic Assembly, 1988—; dist. leader New Castle Rep. Town Com., 1979—; bd. dirs., sec. United Way Westchester and Putnam Counties, White Plains, N.Y., 1989-92; trustee Presbyn. Ch., Mt. Kisco. Mem. ASME, Univ. Glee Club N.Y.C. (pres. 1985-87), Rotary (program chmn. Chappaqua), Univ. Club (N.Y.C.) (chmn. musical affairs com.), Met. Opera Club (N.Y.C.).

MENAGH, CHARLES MOLESWORTH, non-profit foundation executive; b. Newark, Jan. 4, 1920; s. Percy Bowne and Helen Marius (Moles) M.; m. Betty Jane Goodman, May 3, 1947; children: Melissa Marius, Melanie Campbell Menagh-Mills. ABA, Nichols Coll., 1940; BS, NYU, 1951. Asst. sec. Standard Oil Co. (N.J.), N.Y.C., 1964-70, Esso Edn. Found., N.Y.C., 1964-70; exec. dir. Edna McConnell Clark Fund, N.Y.C., 1970-72, Sperry Hutchinson Found./Prospect Hill Found., N.Y.C., 1972, Beineke Found./Skerry Vore Found., N.Y.C., 1972, F.W. Beineke Found., N.Y.C., 1972; v.p. John O'Donnell Co., N.Y.C., 1973; exec. dir. Geraldine Rockefeller Dodge Found., Morristown, N.J., 1974; pvt. practice cons. N.Y.C., 1975—; organizer Corps. Adv. Group, N.Y.C., 1964-70. Bd. dirs. ARC, Somerville, 1989, United Way, Somerville, 1989, Tri-State United Way of N.Y., N.Y.C., 1989. With USNR, 1941-45. Mem. Soc. Colonial Wars, Sons on the Revolution (bd. dirs.), St. Nicholas Soc. N.Y.C., Nat. Soc. Fundraising Execs. (bd. dirs. N.Y.C. and Washington chpts. 1975-80). Republican. Episcopalian.

MENAGIAS, ELIAS DENNIS, educator; b. Kefalonia, Greece, Feb. 28, 1949; came to U.S., 1953; s. Dennis G. and Nike D. M. BS in Indsl. Tech. Edn., CCNY, 1974, MS in Spl. Edn., 1980. Cert. tchr. indsl. tech. and spl. edn., N.Y. Instr. electricity and ceramics N.Y.C. Bd. Edn., 1974-76, instr. graphic arts, 1976-78; instr. indsl. tech. State of N.Y. Office of Mental Health, Bronx, 1978—. Mem. N.Y.C. Tech. Edn. Assn., N.Y. State Tech. Edn. Assn., Internat. Tech. Edn. Assn., Am. Vocat. Assn., Coun. for Exceptional Children. Democrat. Greek Orthodox. Home: 96-41 46 Ave Corona NY 11368-2717 Office: Bronx Children's Hosp 1000 Waters Pl Bronx NY 10461-2701

MENAKER, RONALD HERBERT, banking executive; b. N.Y.C., Dec. 17, 1944; s. Harold L. Menaker and Gladys (Bleiberg) Ross; m. Kathleen Sager Thomas, Sept. 11, 1966; children: Meredith E., Kyri D. Student, Queen's Coll., 1965-66. Sr. v.p. J.P. Morgan & Co., Inc., N.Y.C., 1966—; pres. J. P. Morgan Svcs., Wilmington, Del., 1989—. Vice chmn., trustee N.Y. Downtown Hosp., N.Y.C., 1991—; exec v.p. The Dog Mus., St. Louis, 1989—; trustee Morris Animal Found., Englewood, Colo. Sgt. Army Security Agy., 1962-65. Mem. Westminster Kennel Club (show chmn. 1990—). Office: J P Morgan & Co Inc 60 Wall St New York NY 10260

MENARD, EDITH, English educator, artist, poet, actress; b. Washington, Dec. 5, 1919; d. Willis Monroe and Edith Berncenia (Gill) M. BS summa cum laude, Miner Tchrs. Coll., Washington, 1940; MA in English, Howard U., 1942; postgrad., NYU, 1944-46; MA in Teaching English, Columbia U., 1952; postgrad. in edn., George Washington U., 1966-79, 89-92, doctoral candidate, 1992—. Instr. English and speech Howard U., Washington, 1946-53; high sch. tchr. English D.C. Pub. Schs., Washington, 1953-73; chmn. dept. English Woodrow Wilson High Sch., Washington, 1972-73; adj. asst. prof. English fundamentals U. D.C., 1988-90; founder, dir. Miss Menard's Exclusive English Tutorial Svc., 1991—; substitute tchr. D.C. and Montgomery County (Md.) pub. schs. Contbr. articles and poetry to various publs. Reader poetry to civic orgns. Recipient Golden Poet award World of Poetry, 1988, Silver Poet award, 1989; Julius Rosenwald fellow Yale U., 1943-44. Mem. Smithsonian Assocs. Episcopalian. Home: Rittenhouse Apts 6101 16th St NW # 916 Washington DC 20011

MENCER, GLENN EVERELL, federal judge; b. Smethport, Pa., May 18, 1925; s. Glenn Hezekiah and Ruth Leona (Rice) M.; m. Hannah Jane Freyer, June 24, 1950; children—Ruth Ann, Cora Jane, Glenn John. B.B.A., U. Mich., 1949, J.D., 1952. Bar: Pa. 1953, U.S. Dist. Ct. (we. dist.) Pa. 1953, U.S. Supreme Ct. 1958. Sole practice Eldred, Pa., 1953-64; dist. atty. McKean County, Pa., 1956-64; judge 48th Jud. Dist. Ct., Smethport, 1964-70, Commonwealth Ct. of Pa., Harrisburg, 1970-82, U.S. Dist. Ct., Erie, Pa., 1982—. Served with U.S. Army, 1943-45, ETO. Mem. Fed. Judges Assn., Pa. Bar Assn., McKean County Bar Assn. Republican. Methodist. Lodge: Masons (33 degree). Home: 30 W Willow St Smethport PA 16749-1524 Office: US Dist Ct PO Box 1820 Erie PA 16507-0820

MENCHER, PETER MILTON, psychiatrist; b. N.Y.C., Sept. 22, 1946; s. Hymen and Mae (Berman) M.; m. Mary-Jo Adams, Apr. 3, 1982; children: Samuel, Nicholas. AB, Boston U., 1969, MD, 1969; MPH, Harvard U., 1989. Diplomate Am. Bd. Med. Examiners, Am. Bd. Psychiatry and Neurology. Intern George Washington Med. Svc., D.C. Gen. Hosp.; resident in adult psychiatry Boston U. Med. Ctr.; psychiatrist Brockton Multiservice Ctr., West Bridgewater, Mass., 1973-74, Met. State Hosp., Waltham, Mass., 1974-78; psychiatrist, chief psychiatrist Greater Lawrence (Mass.) Mental Health Ctr., 1978-82; psychiatrist Ctr. for Life Mgmt., Salem, N.H., 1982-85; pvt. practice, Winchester, North Andover, Mass., 1986—; chief psychiatry Winchester Hosp., 1991—. Mem. Amnesty Internat., Cambridge, Mass., 1986. Mem. Am. Psychiatric Assn., Am. Pub. Health Assn., Mass. Psychiatric Soc., Mass. Med. Soc., Physicians for Human Rights. Home and Office: 20 Maxwell Rd Winchester MA 01890-2919

MENDE, ROBERT GRAHAM, retired engineering association executive; b. Newark, Dec. 4, 1926; s. Herman Ernest and Etta (Hillenbrand) M.; m. Joan B. Tamlyn, Apr. 12, 1958; children: Lisa Anne, Robert Graham Jr. Student, Mass. Inst. Tech., 1944-45; degree, N.Y. State Maritime Acad., 1947; B.S., Webb Inst. Naval Architecture, 1951. Project engr. Foster Wheeler Corp., N.Y.C., 1953-56; dist. mgr., naval architect Bird-Johnson Co., N.Y.C., 1956-62; sr. naval architect J.J. Henry Co., Inc., N.Y.C., 1962-69; exec. dir. Soc. Naval Architects and Marine Engrs., 1969-91; mem. marine engring. coun. Underwriters Labs., Inc., 1969-91; ad hoc vis. com. Engrs. Coun. for Profl. Devel., 1970-72. Bd. dirs. Friends of World Maritime U., 1987-91; trustee Webb Inst. Naval Architecture, 1987-91. Lt. USNR, 1951-53. Fellow Royal Inst. Naval Architects, Soc. Naval Architects and Marine Engrs. (hon. life v.p., chmn. N.Y. sect. 1968-69, Vice Admiral E.S. Jerry Land medal 1991); mem. ASME, Am. Soc. Naval Engrs., Am. Soc. Assn. Execs., Coun. Engring. and Sci. Soc. Execs. (bd. dirs. 1988-91), Maritime Coll. Assn., N.E. Coast Inst. Engrs. and Shipbuilders, Webb Alumni Assn. (pres. 1970-72).

MENDELOWITZ, ALLAN IRWIN, federal agency administrator; b. Middletown, Conn., May 1, 1943; s. Madeline Sylvia (Shlien) M.; m. Shereen Lee Lawall, June 18, 1967; children: Eitan G., Rina Y. AB, Columbia U., 1966; MA, Northwestern U., 1969, PhD, 1971. Asst. prof. econs. Rutgers U., New Brunswick, N.J., 1970-75; econ. policy fellow Brookings Inst., Washington, 1975-76; asst. dir. U.S. GAO, Washington, 1976-80, assoc. dir., 1980-88, dir., 1988—. Contbr. articles to profl. jours. Mem. Am. Econ. Assn. Jewish. Home: 1507 Blue Meadow Rd Rockville MD 20854-2621 Office: US GAO 441 G St NW Rm 5492 Washington DC 20548-0002

MENDELSON, HAIM, artist, educator, art gallery director; b. Siemiatycze, Bielsk, Poland, Oct. 15, 1923; s. David Cemach and Frieda (Konopiati) M.; m. Lita Joan Gordon, Mar. 30, 1955 (div. June 1966); children: Paul, Jan. Student, Am. Artists Sch., 1938-41, Saul Baizerman Sch. Art, 1940-43, Ednl. Alliance Art Sch., 1946. Tchr. Ednl. Alliance, N.Y.C., 1956-61; instr. CCNY, 1961-64; tchr. Columbia Grammar Sch., 1963-64, City and Country Sch., N.Y.C., 1964-91; dir. Hudson Guild Art Gallery, N.Y.C., 1971—. One-man shows, Creative Galleries, N.Y.C., 1954, Caravan Gallery, N.Y.C., 1957, Chase Gallery, N.Y.C., 1960, Hudson Guild Art Gallery, N.Y.C., 1961, 76, 79, 82, Yellow Poui Art Gallery, Grenada, W.I., 1973, 76, 79, 82, Ednl. Alliance, N.Y.C., 1976, Berkshire Artisans Gallery, Pittsfield, Mass., 1987; group shows include, Mus. Modern Art, N.Y.C., 1940-41, Pa. Acad. Fine Arts, 1965, Butler Inst. Am. Art, Ohio, 1965, 67, St. Paul Art Center, 1961, 66, NAD, N.Y.C., 1965, 68, 75, 77, 90, Bronx Mus. Arts, 1976, Prints U.S.A., 1982, Gallery Assn. N.Y. State, 1975-78; represented in permanent collections, N.Y. Public Library, Minn. Mus. Art, Edward Ulrich Mus., Wichita, Kans., St. Vincent Coll., Latrobe, Pa., Griffiths Art Center, Canton, N.Y., Manhattan Coll., Riverdale, N.Y., Flint (Mich.) Inst. Fine Arts; (portfolio drypoint engravings) Grass, 1963, The Artist and His Dead, 1975. Recipient numerous awards, prizes. Mem. Fedn. Modern Painters and Sculptors, Audubon Artists, Print Consortium, Am. Soc. Contemporary Artists. Home: 234 W 21st St New York NY 10011-3446

MENDELSON, LEONARD M., lawyer; b. Pitts., May 20, 1923; s. Jacob I. and Anna R. M.; m. Emily Solomon, Dec. 2, 1956; children: Ann, James R., Kathy S. AB, U. Mich., 1947; JD, Yale U., 1950. Bar: Pa. 1951, U.S. Supreme Ct. 1955. Mem. Hollinshead, Mendelson, Delle Donne, Bresnahan & Nixon, P.C., Pitts., chmn. bd., 1974—; chmn. Lawyer-Realty Joint Com., Pitts., 1971-72. Mem. Pitts. Bd. Pub. Edn., 1975-76. Mem. ABA, Pa. Bar Assn., Allegheny County Bar Assn. Office: 230 Grant St Pittsburgh PA 15219-2105

MENDER, MONA SIEGLER, music educator; b. Jersey City, May 24, 1926; d. George and Freda (Steierman) Siegler; m. Irving M. Mender, Aug. 25, 1946; children: Donald Matthew, Judith J. Mender. BA, Mt. Holyoke Coll., 1947. Instr. piano and music theory, Fair Lawn, N.J., 1947-75; state edn. chmn. N.J. Symphony Orch., Newark, 1980-82, state chmn. bd. regents, 1983-84, bd. dirs., 1983-91. Author: Music Manuscript Preparation: A Concise Guide, 1991. Recipient Women's Network commendation Sen. Bill Bradley, 1984. Mem. Mountain Ridge Country Club (West Caldwell, N.J.), Williams Coll. Faculty Club (Williamstown, Mass.), Taconic Golf Club, Plantation Golf and Country Club (Venice, Fla.).

MENDERS, CLAUDE EMANUEL, architect; b. Neuvic, Correze, France, Mar. 1, 1944; came to U.S. 1958, naturalized 1965; s. Lothar Mendershausen and Beatrice (Lebenheim) M. BArch, Carnegie-Mellon U., 1967. Registered architect, Mass. With MIT Planning Office, Cambridge, 1970-71; architect Davies, Wolf & Bibbins, Architects, Inc., Mass., 1971-75; ptnr., v.p. Davies, Bibbins Menders Architects, Inc., 1976-78; pres. Claude Emanuel Menders Architects, Inc., Boston, 1979—; Peace Corps architect, Grenada, W.I., 1967-70. Contbr. articles to profl. jours. Mem. adv. bd. Mass. Exec. Energy Office, Boston, 1984—. Pitts. Plate Glass traveling scholar, 1966; recipient Lighting Design award Illuminating Engring. Soc. N.Am., 1980. Mem. AIA, Boston Soc. Architects, Boston Archtl. Ctr. Address: 59 Commercial Wharf Boston MA 02110

MENDES, GEORGE MICHAEL, marketing professional; b. Lima, Ohio, Nov. 3, 1961; s. Isidro Silva and Mariana Menitra (Leal) M.; m. Christine Ann Harnishfeger, July 20, 1985. BSBA, Bowling Green State U., 1984; MBA, Duke's Fuqua Sch. Bus., 1989. Systems analyst Marathon Oil Co., Findlay, Ohio, 1983; jr. programmer IBM, Cary, N.C., 1984-85, assoc. programmer, 1985-86, software designer, 1986-87, sr. assoc. programmer, 1987-88; software devel. project lead, 1988-89, product mgr., staff programmer, 1989, account mktg. rep., 1989—; participant IBM/Software Devel. Tech. Achievers Forum, Ft. Lauderdale, Fla., 1986. Mgr. Disaster Svcs. Shelter Wake County Red Cross, Raleigh, 1985-89; vol. U.S. Olympic Festival, Raleigh, 1986-87; arbitrator Better Bus. Bur., 1991—; mem. Nat. Panel of Consumer Arbitrators; English tutor Literacy Coun. of Montgomery County, 1991-92; employee charitable contbn. campaign corp. canvasser United Way, 1991. Recipient IIS/SD Tech. Appreciation award, IBM, 1986. Mem. Bowling Green State U. Alumni Assn. (exec. bd., founding mem. N.C./S.C. chpt. 1988-89), Cary Athletic Club (adv. bd. 1988-89), Beta Gamma Sigma, Beta Alpha Psi, Omicron Delta Kappa. Roman Catholic. Home: 13213 Trumpet Pl Silver Spring MD 20904-6880 Office: IBM Corp 6705 Rockledge Dr Bethesda MD 20817

MENDES, ROBERT WARNER, pharmaceutical educator and company executive; b. Fall River, Mass., Apr. 6, 1938; s. Manuel John and Ethel (Potter) M.; m. Catherine Burgess, Aug. 27, 1960; 1 child, Cheryl Ann. BS in Pharmacy, Northeastern U., 1960; MS, U. N.C., 1964, PhD, 1966. Lic. pharmacist, Mass., N.C. Prof., chair pharmaceutics and indsl. pharmacy Mass. Coll. Pharmacy, Boston, 1965-92; v.p. regulatory affairs, dir. new technologies Ascent Pharms. Inc., Billerica, Mass., 1992—; cons. in field, 1971—; mem. editorial adv. bd. Pharm. Tech.; presenter in field. Contbr. articles to profl. publs., chpts. to books. Mem. Mansfield (Mass.) Planning Bd., 1967-73, chair, 1969-73; mem. Southeastern Regional Planning and Econ. Dept. Commn., Mass., 1968-73, chair, 1970; mem. Mansfield Charter Commn., 1972. Mem. Am. Assn. Pharm. Scientists, Soc. Cosmetic Chemists (chair New Eng. chpt. 1980), Am. Assn. Colls. of Pharmacy. Office: Ascent Pharms Inc 9 Linnell Cr Billerica MA 01821-3902

MENDEZ, ALBERT ORLANDO, industrialist, financier; b. Bogota, Colombia, Sept. 7, 1935; came to U.S., 1960; naturalized, 1968; s. Angelino Benjamin and Ana Isabel (Gutierre de Cetina) M.; children: Nicole C., Eric A. BS in Nuclear Physics, N.C. State U., 1961, MS in Nuclear Engring., 1963; MBA, U. Hartford, 1970. Physicist, mgr. mfg. Combustion Engring. Co., Windsor, Conn., 1963-67; mgr. corp. devel. and planning Gulf Oil Corp., Pitts., 1967-71; v.p. mktg., controller for Latin Am. Xerox Corp., Stamford, Conn., 1971-76; exec. v.p., chief operating officer, bd. dirs. Ogden Corp., N.Y.C., 1976-84; chmn., chief exec. officer, prin. shareholder Am. Indstl. Corp., Stamford, 1984—; chmn., chief exec. officer, prin. Argo-Tech Corp., Aerospace, Cleve., 1986-89; bd. dirs. Catalyst Energy Co., N.Y.C., 1st Prin. corp., N.Y.C., Demag, AG, Hamburg, Germany; gen. ptnr. Agnem Holdings Ltd. Partnership, New Canaan, Conn., 1984—; pres., chief exec. officer, bd. dirs., prin. shareholder Agnem Investment Co., New Canaan, 1983—; pres., chief exec. officer, prin. shareholder AM World Trade Corp., West Palm Beach, Fla. Contbr. articles to profl. jours. Mem. Internat. Platform Assn., Am. mgmt. Assn., Assn. of Corp. Dirs., The Conf. Bd., Am. Nuclear Soc., Palm Beach (Fla.) Polo Club. Office: 131 Pequot Ln New Canaan CT 06840-2023

MENDIK, BERNARD H., real estate developer; b. Glasgow, Scotland, May 24, 1929; came to U.S., 1930; s. Michael and Yetta (Brownleader) M.; m. Annette Silverstein, Mar. 30, 1955 (div. Mar. 1979, dec. June 1981); children: Laurie Jill, Kevin Russell, Todd Lansing; m. Susan Carol Batkin, Feb. 25, 1979; 1 child, Alexander Michael. BBS, CCNY, 1954; LLB, NYU, 1958. Bar: N.Y. 1958. Chmn. Mendik Co., N.Y.C., 1957—; gov., chmn. Real Estate Bd. of N.Y., N.Y.C., 1982—; assoc. prof. NYU, 1960-87. Editor NYU Law Sch. Jour., 1958. Mem. Legis. Adv. Com. on Homeless, N.Y.C., 1991—; chmn., trustee N.Y. Law Sch., 1989—; trustee Citizens Budget Commn., N.Y.C., 1964—, Jewish Guild for the Blind, N.Y.C., 1974—, Character and Fitness Com. of N.Y. Bar, 1st Dept., Appellate Div., 1985-91, Montefiore Med. Ctr., Bronx, 1985—, Bronx High Sch. of Sci., 1984—; regent St. John the Devine Cathedral, 1984—, Hobart & William Smith Colls., 1990; vice chmn. Fifth Ave. Assn., N.Y.C., 1982—; co-chmn. 34th St. Bus. Improvement Dist., N.Y.C., 1991—. Sgt. Gen. Staff Corps U.S. Army, 1950-53. Recipient Teaching Excellence award NYU, 1981. Mem. Palm. Beach Country Club, Atlantic Country Club. Office: Mendik Co 330 Madison Ave New York NY 10017-5001

MENDLER, ALLEN NEIL, school psychologist; b. N.Y.C., Oct. 21, 1949; s. Harold and Ida (Zimmer) M.; m. Barbara Klein, June 6, 1971; children: Jason, Brian, Lisa. BA, Queens (N.Y.) Coll., 1971; MA, Alfred (N.Y.) U., 1973; PhD, Union Inst., Cin., 1981. Cert. sch. psychologist, N.Y. Sch. psychologist Rush-Henrietta Schs., Henrietta, N.Y., 1973-81, Webster (N.Y.) Schs., 1985-90, City Sch. Dist., Rochester, 1983-85; psychol. cons. N.Y.State Div. for Youth, Rochester, 1982—, United Cerebral Palsy, Rochester, 1982—, Mary Cariola Children's Ctr., Rochester, 1982—, Discipline Assocs., Rochester, 1980—. Author: What Do I Do When? How To Achieve Discipline with Dignity in the Classroom, 1992. Mem. Assn. for Supervision and Curriculum Devel., Nat. Assn. Sch. Psychologists, Am. Psychol. Assn. Home: 146 Locust Hill Dr Rochester NY 14618-5416

MENDOLIA, JOSEPH C., construction executive, management consultant; b. Camden, N.J., Sept. 13, 1949; s. Joseph and Velia Marie (Chierici) M.; m. Deborah Anne Gall, Nov. 22, 1985; 1 child, Dina Kristin. A, Gloucester County Coll., 1970; B, Glassboro State Coll., 1980. Contr., v.p. Winslow Mech. Contractors, Williamstown, N.J., 1969-78; contr., asst. v.p. J.E. Brenneman, Phila., 1978-81; v.p. Ehret, Inc. and Constrn. Mgmt. Systems, Princeton, N.J., 1981-84; owner, pres. Mendolia & Co.,Inc., West Deptford, N.J., 1984-91; dir. constrn. N.J. Sports and Exposition Authority, East Rutherford, 1992—; cons. constrn. mgmt. various orgns. Recipient Alumnus of Yr. award Gloucester County Coll., 1990, Career Excellence award N.J. Jr. Colls., 1991. Office: 395-F Breakneck Rd Mullica Hill NJ 08062

MENEGON, LUCIO, musician, writer, producer; b. Greenwich, Conn., Dec. 31, 1962; s. Benito Arnaldo and Lea Cesira (Fachin) M. BA in Econs. cum laude, St. Lawrence U., Canton, N.Y., 1985. Freelance musician, 1985—; with E.U. Wurlitzer Music, Boston, 1989-90; assoc. Supply Planning Assocs., Old Greenwich, Conn., 1991-92; owner/producer Kingtone Studios and Records, Old Greenwich, Conn., 1991—; tchr. guitar, Old Greenwich, 1991—. Author/artist: Manatee "Tons", 1991, Manatee "Unlikely Mermen", 1988; author/artist/producer: "The Kingtone Sampler", 1992. Midget football coach Old Greenwich/Riverside Community Ctr., 1986-87. Mem. Sigma Alpha Epsilon.

MENEY, GEORGE HARLOW, educational administrator; b. London, Ky., July 24, 1947; s. Benjamin F. and Martha (Whiting) M.; m. Joyce Muriel Wylie, Jan. 24, 1970; 1 child, Seth Aaron. BS, U. Del., 1970, MEd, 1976; EdD in Ednl. Leadership, Nova U., 1988. Instr. dept. phys. edn. U. Del., Newark, 1970-71; dir. youth Faith Bapt. Ch., Wilmington, Del., 1971-75; tchr. William Penn High Sch., New Castle, Del., 1975-77, asst. prin., 1977-78; instrnl. supr. New Castle County Sch. Dist., New Castle, 1978; prin. George Read Mid. Sch., New Castle, 1978-89; asst. supt. schs. Colonial Sch. Dist., New Castle, 1989—. Mem. Stage Road Community Assn., Newark; commr. Del. Amateur Softball Assn.; coach, mgr. Newark Nat. Little League. Recipient Order of Excellence, Del. Bd. Edn., 1986; named Del. Prin. of Yr., 1986-87. Mem. Am. Assn. Sch. Adminstrs., Nat. Assn. Secondary Sch. Prins. (In Honor of Excellence award 1986), Assn. for Supervision and Curriculum Devel., Nat. Mid. Sch. Assn., Del. Assn. Sch. Adminstrs., Del. Prins. Acad., Phi Delta Kappa. Republican. Baptist. Office: Colonial Sch Dist 318 E Basin Rd New Castle DE 19720

MENG, HEINZ KARL, biology educator; b. Baden, Republic of Germany, Feb. 25, 1924; came to U.S., 1929; s. Richard Ludwig and Elise (Merkel) M.; m. Elizabeth Agnes Metz, June 20, 1953; children: Robin Elizabeth, Peter-Paul. BS, Cornell U., 1947, PhD, 1951. Cert. tchr. ornithology, entomology, vertebrate zoology. Biology prof. SUNY, New Paltz, 1951—; dir. No. Am. Falconers' Assn., 1967-76. Author: Falcons Return, 1975; pioneer in field of in-captivity breeding of Peregrine falcons. Grantee SUNY, 1957, 58, 61, NSF, 1967, IBM, 1980, 82, 83, 85, 86, 87, 88, 91. Fellow Explorers Club; mem. Am. Ornithologists Union, Wilson Ornithological Soc., Cooper Ornithological Soc., New Paltz Peregrine Falcon Found. (pres. 1977—), Wildlife Soc. Home: 10 Joalyn Rd New Paltz NY 12561-2115 Office: SUNY New Paltz NY 12561

MENG, JOHN JOSEPH, educational administrator; b. N.Y.C., June 10, 1942; s. John Joseph and Marjorie (Brunini) M.; m. Christine Fall, Dec. 6, 1989; children: John, Ann, Catherine. BA, Cath. U., 1964; JD, Columbia U., 1967; LHd (hon.), Mercy Coll., 1979. Instr. Cath. U. P.R., Ponce, 1967-68; asst. to chancellor CUNY, N.Y.C., 1968-70, dean of students, 1970-72, vice chancellor, 1972-78; pres. Culinary Inst. Am., Hyde Park, N.Y., 1978-79; dean Antioch Law Sch., Washington, 1980; v.p. Boston U., 1980-91; pres. Meng Group, 1991—. Office: 31 Bay State Rd Boston MA 02215-1783

MENGEL, PHILIP R(ICHARD), investment banker; b. Memphis, Oct. 30, 1944; s. John P. and Marjorie Ann M.; m. Jayne E. Frutig, Dec. 20, 1980; 1 child, Jill Kathryn. AB, Princeton U., 1968; cert., Woodrow Wilson Sch. Pub. & Internat. Affairs, 1968. With Fiduciary Trust Co. N.Y., N.Y.C., 1968-77, mem. exec. com., 1973-77, v.p., 1970-77; pres., dir. Fiduciary Investment Corp., N.Y.C., 1973-77; founder, pres., dir. Mengel & Co., Inc. (formerly Mengel, McCabe & Co., Inc.), N.Y.C., 1978—; chmn., pres. Mengel & Co., Inc., N.Y.C., 1983-90; pres., chief exec. officer Glen-Gery Corp., Wyomissing, Pa., 1990—, also bd. dirs.; bd. dirs. Brick Inst. Am.; speaker Practising Law Inst., various investment confs. Trustee St. Stephen's Sch., Rome, 1976-88, chmn. bd. 1978-82; co-chmn. Graham Windham Childcare Benefit, 1986-88. With USNR, 1962-64. Mem. Racquet and

Tennis Club, The Brook, Racquet Club of Phila., Tuxedo Club (gov. 1988—). Episcopalian. Office: 1166 Spring St Reading PA 19604-2238 also: 9 Three Kings Yard, London England

MENGES, CARL BRAUN, investment banker; b. N.Y.C., Sept. 17, 1930; s. Hermann and Alice (Braun) M.; m. Cordelia Sykes, Apr. 24, 1965; children: James C., Benjamin W., Samuel G. B.A., Hamilton Coll., 1951; M.B.A., Harvard U., 1953. Salesman Owens Corning Fiberglas Corp., 1954-59, mktg. mgr., 1959-63; with instl. sales dept. Model Roland Co., N.Y.C., 1963-65; with instnl. sales dept., syndicate mgr., dir. internat. Donaldson, Lufkin & Jenrette Inc., 1965-77, mng. dir., 1972—, chmn. fin. services group, 1984-87, vice chmn. of bd., 1987—; chmn., pres., chief exec. officer Wood, Struthers & Winthrop, money mgmt. div. Donaldson, Lufkin & Jenrette, 1989—; pres., chmn. bd. Winthrop Focus Fund, 1986—, Neuwirth Fund, 1986—; pres., dir. Pine St. Fund, 1986—; bd. dirs. Whitbreads, N. Am., Med. Indemnity Assurance Corp. Hosp. for Spl. Surgery, The Greenwall Found. Treas., bd. dirs., trustee Assn. Homemaker Services, N.Y.C., 1971-73; trustee Hosp. for Spl. Surgery, 1977—, Hamilton Coll., Clinton, N.Y., trustee 1985—; v.p., treas., trustee The Allen-Stevenson Sch., N.Y.C., 1979-86, Security Industry Assocs. Internat. Com., 1986; bd. dirs. Boys Club of N.Y. Clubs: Union, Maidstone (gov. 1969-86, pres. 1982-86), National Golf Links America, Regency Whist, Union, Bond of N.Y., Leash, L.I. Wyandanch. Office: Donaldson Lufkin & Jenrette Securities Corp 140 Broadway New York NY 10005-1101

MENKE, THOMAS BRADLEY, educational administrator; b. Bklyn., May 25, 1947; s. Henry Joseph and Adelaide Ainsley (Lloyd) M.; m. Joanne Maree Ferriera, July 17, 1974; children: Avery Thomas, Leandra. BS, Cornell U., 1981; MS, SUNY, Brockport, 1986. Cert. tchr., N.Y. Rsch. technician Cornell U., Ithaca, N.Y., 1979-81; supt. Breezy Point Golf Course, Waterport, N.Y., 1981; tchr. Albion (N.Y.) Correctional Facility, 1982-85; edn. supr. Groveland Correctional Facility, Sonyea, N.Y., 1985—, accreditation mgr., 1987-89, mem. crisis response team, 1987—, data liaison, 1989-90. Contbr. articles to profl. publs. Scout master Boy Scouts Am., Dansville, N.Y., 1990. With U.S. Army, 1967-69, Vietnam. Mem. Am. Vocat. Assn., Am. Correctional Assn., Correctional Edn. Assn., Phoenix Lodge (jr. deacon 1990-91, sec. 1992). Republican. Home: 3 N Elizabeth St Dansville NY 14437-1107

MENN, JULIUS JOEL, scientist; b. Danzig, Free City (now Poland), Feb. 20, 1929; came to U.S., 1950, naturalized, 1959; s. David Gregory and Regina (Ajzenstadt) M.; m. Alma Roma Zito, Aug. 31, 1952 (div. 1981); children: Leslie, David (dec.), Diana (dec.); m. Dianne R. Sagner, Apr. 17, 1992. BS, U. Calif., Berkeley, 1953, MS, 1954, PhD, 1958. Dir. biochem. and insecticide rsch. Stauffer Chem. Co., Mountain View, Calif., 1957-79; dir. agrichem. research Zoecon Corp., Palo Alto, Calif., 1979-85; nat. program leader crop protection Agrl. Rsch. Svc., USDA, Beltsville, Md., 1985-88, assoc. dep. area dir. Beltsville Agrl. Rsch. Ctr., 1988—; chmn. Gordon Rsch. Conf., 1989; adj. prof. environ. toxicology San Jose State U., Calif., 1979-84; adj. prof. entomology U. Md., College Park, 1986—; mem. U.S./USSR Team on Environ. Pollution, 1974-85. Editor: Insect Juvenile Hormones, 1972, Insect Neuropeptides, 1991, 8 other tech. books; contbr. over 100 articles to profl. jours.; pioneered pesticide metabolism studies and pioneered research on selective insect control agents including juvenile hormones and neuropeptides; patentee in field. Recipient Bussart Meml. award Eastern Br. Entomol. Soc. Am., 1990, Ciba-Geigy Recognition award, Eastern Br. Entomol. Soc. Am. 1991. Mem. Am. Chem. Soc. (fellow pesticide chem. div. 1973, councilor 1981-89, adv. bd. books dept. 1991—, Burdick & Jackson Internat. award 1979), Internat. Soc. Study Xenobiotics (councilor 1983-86), Cosmos Club. Office: USDA ARS Plant Scis Inst Bldg 003 Beltsville MD 20705-2351

MENTZ, LAWRENCE, lawyer; b. N.Y.C., Nov. 5, 1946; s. Joseph Walter and Audrey Cecilia (Armstrong) M.; m. Barbara Antonello, Nov. 10, 1973; children: Kathleen Elizabeth, Lawrence Goodwin. BS in Physics, Rensselaer Poly. Inst., 1968; JD, U. Notre Dame, 1973. Bar: N.Y. 1973; Washington 1974. Assoc. Condon & Forsyth, N.Y.C., 1973-80, ptnr., 1981-89; ptnr. Biedermann, Hoenig, Massamillo & Ruff, N.Y.C., 1990—; counsellor at law; speaker Worldwide Airlines Customer Rels. Assn. Conf., Singapore, 1983, 2d Cir. Speakers Bur., Com. on BiCentennial of U.S. Constn., 1987; arbitrator U.S. Dist. Ct. (ea. dist.) Bklyn., 1986—. With USNR, 1969-70. Mem. ABA, Fed. Bar Coun., N.Y. State Bar Assn. (exec. com. sect. on comml. and fed. litigation, com. Supreme Cts.), Assn. of Bar of City of N.Y. (com. on aeronautics law), Wings Club. Roman Catholic. Office: Biedermann Hoenig Massamillo & Ruff 733 3d Ave New York NY 10017

MEOTTI, MICHAEL PATRICK, state legislator, lawyer; b. New Britain, Conn., Oct. 30, 1953; s. Joseph John Sr. and Margaret Mary (O'Brien) M.; m. Pamela Goldman, June 16, 1990. BS in Fgn. Service cum laude, Georgetown U., 1975, JD cum laude, 1978. Atty. Updike, Kelly & Spellacy, P.C., Hartford, Conn., 1978-80; gen. counsel Ins. Assn. Conn., Hartford, 1980-85; counsel The Travelers Cos., Hartford, 1985—; mem. Conn. State Senate, Hartford, 1987—; chmn. environment com. gen. assembly State of Conn., Hartford, 1987-89, transp. com., 1989—. Mem. Bd. Edn., Glastonbury, Conn., 1979-83; mem. Town Council, Glastonbury, 1983-86, majority leader, 1985-86. Mem. Georgetown U. Alumni Club Conn. (pres. 1984-89). Democrat. Roman Catholic. Home: 56 Heather Glen Rd Glastonbury CT 06033-4161 Office: Travelers Ins Co Law Dept 1 Tower Sq Hartford CT 06183-0001 also: Conn Senate State Capitol Hartford CT 06106

MERCURIO, LAURA DEUBLER, textile designer; b. Akron, Ohio, Feb. 14, 1953; d. Lawrence Philip and Ruth Dale (Winders) Deubler; m. Joseph Michael Mercurio Jr., Sept. 23, 1979. Student, U. Ga., 1971-73; BS, Ga. Inst. Tech., 1976. Textile designer Maharam Fabric Corp., Hauppauge, N.Y., 1976-83; dir. product design J.M. Lynn, Inc. div. Adam James Textiles, Smithtown, N.Y., 1984-87; pres. Deubler Mercurio Color Design Cons., St. James, N.Y., 1987—; nd. dirs. Color Mktg. Group, 1991—; vice chmn. edn. com. Color Mktg. Group, Richmond, Va., 1984-86; chmn. edn. com., 1987—. Recipient IBD Gold award Inst. Bus. Designers, 1979, Roscoe award Resources Council, 1985, Product Design award Corp. Design Mag., 1987. Mem. NAFE, Color Assn. U.S., Assn. Contract Textiles, Am. Soc. Textiles and Materials.

MERCURIO, PETER, playwright, actor; b. Queens, N.Y., June 23, 1968; s. Sam and Louise (Bello) M. BA, Montclair State Coll., 1990. Box office mgr. Garden State Ballet, Newark, 1990; prodn. coord. Words and Pictures Creative Svc., Inc., Park Ridge, N.J., 1991; artistic dir. Seventh Seal Ensemble, Upper Montclair, N.J., 1992—; v.p. Life Repertory Co., Montclair, 1991-92. Playwright: The Garage Sale, 1986 (Excellence in Writing award 1986), Water Signs, 1991, Anchors, Talk Shows, Love and Poetry, 1991, Unpredictable Spirits, 1992. Recipient Svc. award Lambda Pi Eta, Upper Montclair, 1990. Assoc. mem. The Dramatists Guild. Home: 36 5th Ave Westwood NJ 07675

MEREDITH, ANNE LEBLANC, equine services firm executive; b. Miami, July 12, 1968; d. Spencer Barrett and Georgina (LeBlanc) M. BA in Polit. Sci., Mt. Holyoke Coll., 1990. Cert. equine sports massage therapist. Case team asst. Bain & Co., Inc., Boston, 1990-91; ptnr. Meredith-Irwin Equine Enterprises, Boston and Tampa, Fla., 1991—; mgr., trainer Meredith Arabians, Tampa, 1992—. Vol. Animal Protection League of Hillsborough County, Inc., Tampa, 1992. Mem. Internat. Arabian Horse Assn., Am. Horse Shows Assn. Republican. Home: 5902 Birchwood Dr Tampa FL 33625 Office: Meredith-Irwin Equine Enterprises PO Box 19 Boston MA 02113

MEREDITH, GEORGE (MARLOR), association executive, writer; b. Somerville, N.J., Apr. 21, 1923; s. Gilbert Judson and Dorothea (Pope) M. m. Elizabeth Jean Moore, Nov. 15, 1955; children: Gilbert Judson III, Scott Arthur. Student, Columbia U., 1940-41. Mng. editor Mast, 1944-47; editor Premium Practice, 1947-55; ptnr., editorial dir. Meredith Assocs., 1955-67, pres., 1967-88, chmn., 1989-91; pres. Meredith Rsch. Corp., 1962-74; mng. dir. Meredith & Henry, 1977-92, chmn., 1992—; exec. sec. Assn. Incentive Mktg., 1957-67, exec. dir., 1967-74, pub. rels. dir., 1972—; mng. dir. Eastman Editorial Rsch., 1979-87; exec. sec. Nat. Assn. Food Equipment Mfrs., 1957-59; exec. dir. Nat. Premium Mfrs. Reps., 1963-66, dir. rsch. programs, 1964-67; dir. Mktg. New Bur., Red Bank, N.J., 1973—; exec. dir. Trading Stamp Inst. Am., Assn. Retail Mktg. Svcs., 1979-89, editorial dir., 1991—, mng. dir., 1981-85, exec. dir. N.Y. chpt., 1981-82. Author: Effective Merchandising with Premiums, 1962, Creative Application of Sales Incentive Plans, 1972; (film) The Caine Coil, 1973; Incentives in Marketing, 1977, Incentives in Marketing & Motivation, 1992; editor: Premiums in Marketing, 1971; exec. editor, rsch. dir. Incentive Marketing Facts, 1968-87; rsch. dir. Incentive Mag., 1988—; editor, pub. Sales Motivation Letter, 1973-74; editor The Register, 1979—, The Communicator, 1982-85, Creative Mktg. newsletter, 1989—; contbr. articles to profl. publs. Coord., moderator Premiums and Incentives Conf. NYU, 1972; pub. rels. dir. Soc. Incentive Travel Execs., 1974-79. Recipient Premium Man of Yr. award Nat. Premium Mfrs. Reps., 1973, Nat. Premium Sales Execs. Past Pres.'s award, 1966, Disting. Achievement award Premium Advt. Assn. Am., 1963. Mem. Overseas Press Club, Am. Soc. Assn. Execs., Incentive Fedn. (vice chmn. 1984-88, 89—, chmn. 1988-89), Assn. Incentive Mktg., Premium Merchandising Club N.Y., Lions. Home: 3 Caro Ct Red Bank NJ 07701-2315

MEREDITH, ORSELL MONTGOMERY, radiobiologist, government official; b. Jamestown, N.Y., Oct. 19, 1923; s. Orsell Montgomery and Bernardine Elva (Goggin) M.; m. Martha Linnea Helbon, Jan. 29, 1949; 1 child, Michael Wayne. BS, U. Chgo., 1948; MS, U. So. Calif., 1951, PhD, 1953; MS, Am. U., 1974. Asst. prof. nuclear medicine and biophysics UCLA, 1953-61; rsch. scientist Lockheed Missiles and Space Co., Palo Alto, Calif., 1961-66; radiol. biologist Naval Radiol. Def. Lab., San Francisco, 1966-68; ops. rsch. analyst Naval Ordnance Lab., Silver Springs, Md., 1968-76; health scientist adminstr. Nat. Cancer Inst., NIH, Washington, 1976—. Contbr. articles to sci. jours. Lt. (j.g.) USNR, 1943-46, PTO. Mem. Am. Soc. for Pharmacology and Exptl. Therapeutics, Radiation Rsch. Soc., N.Y. Acad. Scis. Home: PO Box 4135 Rockville MD 20849-4135 Office: Nat Cancer Inst NIH 5333 Westbard Ave Bethesda MD 20892-0001

MEREDITH, PAMELA LOUISE, corporate executive; b. Montreal, Aug. 27, 1956; d. William C.J. and Liv (Mithassel) M.; m. James J. Rohacik, Apr. 11, 1988; children: Andrew J. LLM, McGill U., Montreal, 1983; JD, U. Oslo, Norway, 1981. Bar: N.Y. 1983. Space law cons. Law Office of Martin Rothblatt, Washington, 1983-85, Latham & Watkins, Washington, 1985-87; pres. Space Conform, Washington, 1987—; adj. prof. law Am. U., Washington, 1989—. Contbr. articles to profl. jours. Mem. ABA, AIAA (co-chmn. com. on space debris 1989—), Fed. Bar Assn., Nat. Space Club. Home: 700 New Hampshire Ave NW Washington DC 20037-2406 Office: Space Conform 600 New Hampshire Ave NW # 140 Washington DC 20037-2403

MEREDITH, WILLIAM (MORRIS MEREDITH), poet, English language educator; b. N.Y.C., Jan. 9, 1919; s. William Morris and Nelley (Keyser) M. A.B., Princeton U., 1940, Woodrow Wilson fellow, 1946-47. Copy boy, reporter N.Y. Times, 1940-41; instr. English, creative writing Princeton U., 1946, 47-48, 49-50; asst. prof. English U. Hawaii, 1950-51; mem. faculty Conn. Coll., 1955—, prof. English, 1965-83; mem. faculty Bread Loaf Sch. English, 1958-62; dir. Conn. Coll. Humanities-Upward Bound program, 1964-68; poetry cons. Library of Congress, 1978-80; Chancellor Acad. Am. Poets, from 1964; mem. Conn. Commn. Arts, 1963-65. Author: poems Love Letter From an Impossible Land, 1944, Ships and Other Figures, 1948, The Open Sea and Other Poems, 1958, Shelley, 1962, The Wreck of the Thresher and Other Poems, 1964, Winter Verse, 1964, translation Alcools, 1964, Earth Walk: New and Selected Poems, 1970, Hazard, The Painter, 1975, The Cheer, 1980, Partial Accounts: New and Selected Poems, 1987, (Pulitzer Prize 1988); libretto The Bottle Imp, 1958; ed.: Shelley, 1962, Univ. and College Poetry Prizes, 1960-66, 1966, (with Mackie L. Jarrell) Eighteenth Century Minor Poets, 1968, Poets of Bulgaria, 1986. Served with USAAF, 1941-42; to lt. USNR, 1942-46, PTO; to lt. comdr. USNR, Korea. Decorated Air medal with oak leaf cluster; recipient Loines prize Nat. Inst. Arts and Letters, 1966; Van Wyck Brooks award, 1971; Internat. Nicola Vaptsarov prize in lit., Sofia, Bulgaria, 1979, L.A. Times prize, 1987. Mem. Nat. Inst. Arts and Letters. also: care Dept of English Conn Coll 270 Mohegan Ave New London CT 06320*

MERENBLOOM, ROBERT BARRY, hospital and medical school administrator; b. Balt., July 13, 1947; Philip William and Florence Ruth (Surosky) M.; B.A., U. Md., 1969; M.S., Morgan State U., 1973; M.B.A., U. Balt., 1980. Mem. staff Mayor Balt. Office Manpower Resources, 1972-73; assoc. staff mem. Office Dean, U. Md. Med. Sch., 1976-80; adminstrv. officer rsch. and devel. Balt. VA Med. Ctr., 1974-80; assoc. adminstr. dept. medicine Johns Hopkins U. Sch. Medicine, Balt., 1980-84, adminstr. dept. medicine Johns Hopkins Hosp., 1984-88, assoc. Sch. Hygiene and Pub. Health, 1984-88; lectr. dept. medicine Bowman Gray Sch. Medicine Wake Forest U., 1988—, asst. chmn. Dept. Medicine, 1988-91; assoc. chmn. Dept. Medicine, 1991—; instr. sociology U. Balt., 1973-76; adj. faculty Weekend Coll., Coll. Notre Dame, Balt., 1980—. Exec. dir. J. Paul Sticht Ctr. on Aging. Recipient Hon. Corpsmen Leader award Office Mayor Balt., 1973; Outstanding Performance award Balt. VA Med. Ctr., 1975, Superior Performance award, 1980. Mem. Am. Gerontology Soc., So. Gerontology Soc., Soc. Rsch. Adminstrs., Nat. Coun. Univ. Rsch. Adminstrs., Adminstrs. Internal Medicine, Assn. Am. Med. Colls. (group on bus. affairs), Am. Hosp. Assn., Am. Pub. Health Assn., Am. Coll. Healthcare Adminstrs., Soc. Gen. Internal Medicine, John Hopkins Club, Piedmont Club.

MERION, RICHARD DONALD, construction company executive; b. Northampton, Mass., Jan. 28, 1936; s. H. Davis and Tacy (Walton) M.; m. Jeanette T. Martinkus, Jan. 27, 1944; children: Renee, Mark. BS, West Chester U., 1959, MEd, 1969; MPH, U. Mich., 1967; grad., U.S. Army War Coll., 1978. Field and hosp. sanitarian Pa. Dept. of Health, West Chester, 1959-66, supervising sanitarian, 1966-68; dir. environ. health Chester County Health Dept., West Chester, 1968-70; mcpl. mgr. Borough of Malvern, Pa., 1970-76; pres. Land Devel. Svcs., Ltd., West Chester, 1976-86, Chester County Devel. Svcs., West Chester, 1986—; dir. Barnegat Bay Trading Co., Manhawkin, N.J., 1987—, Chester County Utilities, West Chester, 1976—, Franklin Water Co., West Chester, 1979—, Onyx Constrn. Co., West Chester, 1978—. Tax collector West Whiteland Twp., Exton, Pa., 1985—; pres. Chester County Assn. of Boroughs, 1975; bd. dirs. Paoli Meml. Assn., Malver, 1971-77, USO Phila., 1989—; chmn. S.E. Pa. Com. for Support of Guard and Res., 1985—, dep. state chmn. 1991; com. Rep. Com., Chester County, 1975—. Brig. gen. USAR, 1957-87. Decorated Legion of Merit. Mem. SAR, Am. Acad. Sanitarians, Civil Affairs Assn. (dir. Washington 1983—, Disting. Svc. award 1983), Mil. Order of World Wars, Ret. Officers Assn., Res. Officers Assn., West Chester U. Alumni Assn. (v.p. 1988—, pres. 1990-91), Union League, Washington Crossing Soc., Am. Legion, Chapel of Four Chaplains (Legion of Honor award 1990, comdr. Vets. Guard Phila. 1992), Brit. Officers Club, Rotary, Mason, Moose. Republican. Office: Chester County Devel Svcs 420 W Market St West Chester PA 19382-2839

MERKEL, PAUL BARRETT, chemist, consultant; b. Rochester, N.Y., May 14, 1945; s. Paul A. and Jeanette B. M. BS, St. John Fisher Coll., 1967; PhD, U. Notre Dame, 1970. Postdoctoral rsch. Univ. Calif., Riverside, 1970-71; rsch. chemist Eastman Kodak Co., Rochester, N.Y., 1971—. Patentee in field; contbr. articles to profl. jours. Mem. Am. Chem. Soc., Sigma Xi. Home: 525 Westfield St Rochester NY 14619-2134 Office: Eastman Kodak Rsch Labs Bldg 82 Rochester NY 14650

MERKEL-KELLER, CLAUDIA ELISABETH, educational planning and evaluation specialist; b. Viernheim, Fed. Republic Germany, Aug. 27, 1948; came to U.S., 1953; d. Karl Wilhelm and Else Elisabeth (Sommer) Merkel; m. Walter J. Keller Jr., June 20, 1970; 1 child, Jessica Merkel. BA, Douglass Coll., 1970; MEd, Rutgers U., 1971, EdD, 1974. Cert. elem., secondary math. tchr., N.J., supr., prin., N.J., adminstr., N.J. Info. analyst Ednl. Testing Svc., Princeton, N.J., 1970-72; rsch. asst. N.J. Dept. Edn., Trenton, 1972-73, asst. dir., 1977-78, acting dir., 1978, dir., 1979-83, planning assoc., 1983—; rsch. evaluation specialist Edn. Improvement Ctr., Morris Plain, N.J., 1973-74, rsch. evaluation coord., 1974-77; cons. Nat. Prevention Evaluation, Madison, 1980-82; adv. panel Resource Network Northeast Regional Ednl. Lab.-Evaluation Program, Portland, 1983-85; lectr. in field. Contbr. articles to profl. jours. Bd. dirs. Glen Ridge Swim Club, Bridgewater, N.J., 1985-89; rep. Van Holten PTO, Bridgewater, 1988; mem. Far Hills (N.J.) Country Day Schs. Parents Assn., 1990—. Recipient Disting. Svc. award Grad. Sch. Edn. Rutgers U., New Brunswick, 1991. Mem. APA, Nat. Coun. Tchrs. Math., Am. Edn. Rsch. Assn., Nat. Coun. Measurement in Edn., Epsilon Pi Tau (exec. com., past pres., v.p., sec., treas.), Phi Delta Kappa (exec. com., newsletter editor 1982-83). Home: 383 Rolling Knolls Way Bridgewater NJ 08807-1971 Office: NJ State Dept Edn 225 W State St Trenton NJ 08608-1001

MERKER, EDWARD, internist; b. N.Y.C., Jan. 29, 1940; s. Moe and Anne (Fisher) M.; m. Laura Ruth Schaefer, June 12, 1966; children: Melody Larissa, Daniel Edward Schaefer. AB in Math. cum laude, Harvard U., 1961; MD, NYU, 1965. Diplomate Am. Bd. Internal Medicine, Am. Bd. Endocrinology and Metabolism. Intern Barnes Hosp., St. Louis, 1965-66; med. officer USPHS Indian Hosp., San Carlos, Ariz., 1966-67, Winnebago, Neb., 1967-68; resident Mt. Sinai Hosp., N.Y.C., 1968-70, fellow, 1970-72; pvt. practice N.Y.C., 1972—; chief endocrinology div. St. Clares Hosp., N.Y.C.; asst. clin. prof. medicine (endocrinology and metabolism) Mt. Sinai Sch. Medicine; attending physician Cabrini Hosp.; assoc. attending physician Lenox Hill Hosp. Mem. AMA, Am. Diabetes Assn., N.Y. State Med. Soc., N.Y. County Med. Soc., N.Y. State Soc. Internal Medicine, Endocrine Soc., Harvard Club (mem. schs. com.). Home: 1 Lincoln Plz New York NY 10023 Office: 35 E 85th St New York NY 10028

MERKLE, DALE GORDON, science education educator; b. Bay City, Mich., Nov. 11, 1933; s. Emil Henry and Jane Marie (Brown) M.; m. Mary Lynn Raymond, June 11, 1960; chidlren: D. Gordon, Christopher R., Sarah Lynn. BS, Mich. State U., 1955, MAT, 1962, PhD, 1969. Tchr. Caro (Mich.) Community Schs., 1957-63, Port Huron (Mich.) Jr. Coll., 1963-64, Essexville (Mich.)-Hampton Schs., 1964-67; prof. sci. edn. Shippensburg (Pa.) U., 1969—. With U.S. Army, 1955-57, Germany. Mem. Nat. Sci. Tchrs. Assn., Pa. Sci. Tchrs. Assn., Nat. Assn. for Rsch. in Sci. Teaching, Assn. Edn. Tchrs. Sci. Office: Shippensburg U FSC 109 Shippensburg PA 17257

MERLE, H. ETIENNE, restaurateur; b. N.Y.C., July 8, 1944; s. Pierre and Josephine Merle. BS, Cornell U., 1969. Mgr. food and beverages DiviDivi Beach Hotel, Aruba, 1969-70; restaurant mgr., chmn. food dept. Tng. Resources for Youth, N.Y.C., 1971; gen. mgr. L'Auberge du Cochon Rouge, Ithaca, N.Y., 1971-92; v.p. Pascale Wine Bar and Restaurant, Syracuse, N.Y., 1982—; ops. cons. Merle & Roy Assocs., N.Y.C., 1975—. Mem. Cornell Soc. Hotelmen, Chefs de Cuisine Assn. Am., Soc. Culinaire Philanthropique, Vatel Club, L'Union Francaise (pres. 1975, 76, 86, 91—), N.Y. Athletic Club. Home and Office: 1152 Danby Rd Ithaca NY 14850-9406

MERLINO, ANTHONY FRANK, orthopedic surgeon; b. Providence, Jan. 21, 1930; s. Anthony Frank and C. Mildred (Campagna) M.; m. Dolores Mary Aucello, Nov. 22, 1956; children: Christa Marianne, Paula Nicole. BS, Providence Coll., 1951; MS, U. Conn., 1952; MD, Jefferson Med. Coll., 1956. Diplomate Am. Bd. Orthopedic Surgery. Intern St. Joseph Hosp., Providence, 1956-57; resident orthopedic surgery VA Hosp., Phila., 1959-63; pvt. practice medicine specializing in orthopedic surgery, Phila., 1963-68, Providence, 1968—; attending orthopedic surgeon St. Joseph Hosp., Providence, pres. med. staff, 1974-75, trustee, 1973-76, med. staff/trustee joint conf. com. 1982; attending orthopedic surgeon Our Lady of Fatima Hosp., North Providence, R.I.; vis. orthopedic surgeon R.I. State Hosp., Howard, 1968-75; asst. orthopedic surgery Hahnemann Med. Coll., Phila., 1965-69; pediatric orthopedic surg. cons. Crippled Children's Program of R.I., 1968-86; cons. orthopedic surgeon Roger Williams Gen. Hosp., Providence, 1969-89; v.p. R.I. Orthopedic Group, Inc., Providence, 1969-83; pres., 1983—; team physician hockey and basketball teams Providence Coll., 1968-87; mem. R.I. Gov.'s Med. Malpractice Commn., 1975-77, R.I. Bd. Examiners in Chiropractic, 1977-80; mem. study commn. R.I. Med. Rev. Bd., 1977-85; mem. corp. Blue Cross/Shield R.I., 1976-87; physician-adv. R.I. Assn. Med. Assts., 1979-84; mem. R.I. Workers' Compensation Adv. Panel, 1978-88; mem. adv. bd. Cath. Social Svcs., 1981-84; police surgeon Am. Law Enforcement Officers' Assn., 1980; cons. orthopedic surgery Am. Assn. Medicolegal Cons., 1980-90; pres. Hindle Bldg. Assocs., 1983—. Contbr. articles to profl. jours. Mem. med. splty. adv. bd. Medical Malpractice Prevention, 1985-90. Capt., M.C., USAF, 1957-59. Recipient Dr. William McDonnell award Providence Coll. Alumni Assn., 1981. Fellow Am. Acad. Orthopedic Surgeons, ACS, (pres. R.I. chpt. 1982-84), Internat. Coll. Surgeons, Latin Am. Soc. Orthopedics and Traumatology; mem. AMA, Orthopaedic Rsch. and Edn. Found. (life), Am. Coll. Legal Medicine, Am. Fracture Assn., Pan-Pacific Surg. Assn., New Eng., R.I. (sec.-treas. 1978-80, v.p. 1980-82, pres. 1982-84), Ea. Orthopedic Socs., Jefferson Orthopaedic Soc., R.I. Med. Soc. (commr. profl. rels. 1976, ho. of dels. 1976-82, commr. internal affairs 1982), Providence Med. Assn., Am. Profl. Practice Assn., Am. Acad. Compensation Medicine, Am. Coll. Sports Medicine, Am. Orthopedic Soc. for Sports Medicine, Am. Med. Photography Assn., Internat. Soc. Orthopedics and Traumatology, Internat. Soc. Rsch. in Orthopedics and Trauma, Am. Soc. Law and Medicine, Thomistic Inst. Drs. Guild, R.I. Hist. Soc., Boston Orthopedic Club, Mal Brown Club, The 100 of R.I. Club. Roman Catholic. Home: 2 Countryside Dr Providence RI 02904-3419 Office: 655 Broad St Providence RI 02907-1444

MERMER, IRA, finance educator; b. Bronx, N.Y., June 20, 1924; s. M. Tobias and Frieda Charlotte (Besell) M.; m. Rose Akawie, June 19, 1948; children: Brion, Teri. Student, NYU, 1949-53. Mgr. Ea. Seaboard Credit Interchange Bur., N.Y.C., 1953-62; sec. New Eng. Assn. Credit Execs., Boston, 1962-66; mgr. Fgn. Credit Interchange Bur.-Nat. Assn. Credit Mgmt., N.Y.C., 1966-79, dir. world-wide collections, 1972-79; treas. Credit Rsch. Found., Lake Success, N.Y., 1980-88; dir. adminstrn. Grad. Sch. Credit Fin. Mgmt., Lake Success, 1980-88. Editor: Fgn. Credit Interchange Bur. Weekly Bull. and Minutes Monthly conf., 1966-80. With USMC, 1943-45. Mem. Am. Soc. Tng. and Devel., Masons. Republican.

MERNER, PETER W., security analyst; b. Boulder City, Nev., Oct. 17, 1935; s. Herbert Kenneth and Marjorie (Mullarkey) M.; m. Marta Wavra, May 15, 1990. AB in Physics, U. Calif., Berkeley, 1958. Researcher Lockheed Aircraft, Palo Alto, Calif., 1959-63, Link Aviation, Binghamton, N.Y., 1963-64; stock broker Glore Forgan & Co., N.Y.C., 1964-70, Philips Apel & Walden, N.Y.C., 1970-73; security analyst L.F. Rothschild & Co., N.Y.C., 1973-82, Merner Research, N.Y.C., 1982—. Pvt. 1st class U.S. Army, 1958-59. Mem. N.Y. Soc. Security Analysts, Nat. Assn. Securities Dealers. Office: Merner Rsch 77 Bleecker St New York NY 10012

MERRELL, JESSE HOWARD, writer; b. Shelby, Ala., Dec. 9, 1938; s. James Walton and Emma Thelma (Davis) M.; m. Betsy Lee Davis, Jan. 11, 1964 (div. 1979); children: Sandra, Mark, Brad, Carolyn, Gwen. Grad., Shelby High Sch., Columbiana, Ala., 1957. Pitcher Cin. Redlegs, 1958-62; reporter, news dir. WHAP Radio, Hopewell, Va., 1963; writer/editor Hopewell News, 1963-65; state editor Daily Progress, Charlottesville, Va., 1965-68; assoc. editor Transport Topics, Washington, 1968-75; spl. asst. to pres. Am. Trucking Assn., Washington, 1975-76; editor Transport Topics, Washington, 1976-77; pres. Merrell Ent., Washington, 1977—; pub. rels. cons. Am. Movers Conf., Washington, 1969-72; instr. Dale Carnegie courses, Washington, 1974-81; cons. Middle Atlantic Conf., Riverdale, Md., 1981-82, Contract Carrier Conf., 1977-82; speechwriter ICC, Washington, 1982. Author: (novel) A Christmas Gift, 1979; syndicated columnist Religion and the Times, Washington Welter. With U.S. Army, 1961-62. Recipient Liberty award Congress of Freedom, Jackson, Miss., 1970, 71, Honor Cert., Freedoms Found., 1972, 1st place editorial writing Va. Press Assn., 1965, 1st place news writing, 1966. Office: Merrell Ent 2610 Garfield St NW Washington DC 20008

MERRIAM, GEORGE RENNELL, JR., ophthalmologist; b. Harrisburg, Pa., May 22, 1913; s. George Rennell and Harriet (Lombard) M.; m. Martha Hildegarde Carlson, Sept. 5, 1936; children: George, John, Charlotte, Susan. AB, Brown U., 1934; MD, Columbia U., 1941. Diplomate Am. Bd. Ophthalmology. Instr. in ophthalmology Coll. of Physician and Surgeons/Columbia U., N.Y.C., 1949-54, assoc. in ophthalmology, 1955-58, asst. prof. of clin. ophthalmology, 1959-63, assoc. prof. clin. ophthalmology, 1964-73, prof. clin. ophthalmology, 1973-78, prof. emeritus, 1978—; ophthalmologist Francis Delafield Hosp., N.Y.C., 1949-75; dir. surgical svc. Edward S. Harkness Eye Inst., N.Y.C., 1960-78; cons. ophthalmologist, Meml. Hosp., N.Y.C., 1949-69; cons. Harlem Hosp., N.Y.C., 1970-87. Contbr. articles to profl. jours. Capt. Med. Corps, 1942-45, ETO. Mem. AMA, ACS, Am. Ophthal. Soc., Am. Acad. of Ophthalmology, Am. Radium Soc., N.Y.

Ophthal. Soc., N.Y. Acad. Medicine. Republican. Prebyterian. Office: 635 W 165th St New York NY 10032-3701

MERRICK, CRAIG RUSSELL, executive; b. East Orange, N.J., Aug. 23, 1941; s. Frank Medford and Helen (Burdick) M.; m. Joan Jamison, June 24, 1964 (div. 1972); children: Glenn, David; m. Jill Ann Montgomery, Sept. 5, 1987; children: Rachael, Chelsea. BS, Rutgers U. Coll. Pharmacy, 1963. Registered pharmacist. Pharmacist Mountain Lakes (N.J.) Pharmacy, 1964-67; sales mgr. Eli Lilly & Co., Indpls., 1967-72; v.p. sales & mktg. Erika Div. N.M.C., Englewood Cliffs, N.J., 1972-76; med. product group Kendall & Co., Boston, 1976-79; founder, chief exec. officer The Hilton Search Group, Beverly Hills, Calif., 1979-90; exec. dir. N.H. Pharmacists Assn., Concord, 1990—; mem. Orange Coast Venture Group, Irvine, Calif.; apptd. to Congl. Healthcare Task Force, 1992; del. A. Pha. Ho. Reps., Washington, 1991-92. Founding mem. N.H. HEalth & Human Svcs. Drug Task Force, Concord. Mem. Nat. Coun. State Pharm. Execs., Am. Soc. Assn. Execs. Home: PO Box 385 Derry NH 03038-0385 Office: NHPA 76 S State St Concord NH 03301-3520

MERRIFIELD, ROBERT BRUCE, biochemist, educator; b. Ft. Worth, July 15, 1921; s. George E. and Lorene (Lucas) M.; m. Elizabeth Furlong, June 20, 1949; children: Nancy, James, Betsy, Cathy, Laurie, Sally. B.A., UCLA, 1943, Ph.D., 1949. Chemist Park Research Found., 1943-44; research asst. Med. Sch., UCLA, 1948-49; asst. Rockefeller Inst. for Med. Research, 1949-53, assoc., 1953-57; asst. prof. Rockefeller U., 1957-58, assoc. prof., 1958-66, prof., 1966—, John D. Rockefeller prof., 1984—; Developed solid phase peptide synthesis; completed (with B. Gutte) 1st total synthesis of an enzyme, 1969. Assoc. editor: Internat. Jour. Peptide and Protein Research; contbr. articles to sci. jours. Recipient Lasker award biomed. research, 1969; Gairdner award, 1970; Intra-Sci. award, 1970; Nichols medal, 1973; Alan E. Pierce award Am. Peptide Symposium, 1979; Nobel prize in chemistry, 1984. Mem. Am. Chem. Soc. (award creative work synthetic organic chemistry 1972, Hirschmann award in peptide chemistry 1990), NAS USA, Am. Soc. Biol. Chemists, Sigma Xi, Phi Lamda Upsilon, Alpha Chi Sigma. Office: Rockefeller U New York NY 10021

MERRILL, AUBREY JAMES, systems and electrical engineer; b. Dover-Foxcroft, Maine, Apr. 3, 1948; s. George A. and Gladys M. (Carey) M. Student, Colby Coll., 1966-68; BSEE, U. Maine, 1976, MSEE, 1978. Mem. tech. staff digital multiplex div. AT&T Bell Labs., Holmdel, N.J., 1978-86, mem. tech. staff electronic switch div., 1988-92, mem. tech. staff ops. planning div., 1992—; mem. tech. staff edn. div. AT&T Bell Labs., Middletown, N.J., 1986-88; chair adapted toys for disabled children com. Telephone Pioneers of Am., AT&T Bell Labs., Holmdel, 1991-92. With U.S. Army, 1968-71. Mem. IEEE, N.Y. Acad. Scis., Phi Kappa Phi, Tau Beta Pi, Sigma Xi (assoc.). Home: PO Box 240 Holmdel NJ 07733-0240 Office: AT&T Bell Labs RM # 2J-421 101 Crawford Corner Rd Holmdel NJ 07733

MERRILL, DALE MARIE, sales executive; b. Melrose, Mass., Feb. 21, 1954; d. Richard Paul and Rosemarie Reine (Porelle) M. BA in English, U. of Lowell, Mass., 1976; MA in Am. Studies, Boston Coll., 1983; CSS in Mgmt., Harvard U., 1989; MBA, Boston Coll., 1992. Sales rep. A-Copy Inc., Natick, Mass., 1976-77; sales mgr. Jan Optical Co., Waltham, Mass., 1977-78; market researcher Decision Rsch. Co. div. Temple, Barker & Sloane, Lexington, Mass., 1979-81; sales rep. Henco Software Co., Waltham, 1981-82; account mgr. Univ. Computing Co., Chgo., 1982-83; regional sales mgr. CompuServe Data Techs. (formerly Software House), Cambridge, Mass., 1983-89; internat. sales mgr. Hypersoft Corp., Cambridge, 1989—; dir. sales Info. Mapping, Waltham, 1990—; bd. dirs. M.T. Corp., Woburn, Mass. Author: How to Buy Software: Avoiding the Traps Salespeople Set, 1989; author, editor: Seeds mag. (Poetry award 1972), 1971-72; contbr. poetry to mags. Organizer 18x72 project, Stoneham, Mass., 1970-71; bd. dirs. Stoneham Hist. Commn., 1976-77. Recipient Top Sales award A-Copy Inc., 1976-77, Interviewer award Decision Rsch. Co., 1981, Triple Crown Sales award, 1985, 86, 87, Million Dollar Sales Club award, 1987, 88. Mem. NAFE, NOW, Digital Equipment Co. User Soc., Boston Computer Soc. Democrat. Home: PO Box 2586 Woburn MA 01888-1186 Office: Info Mapping 303 Wyman St Waltham MA 02154-1217

MERRILL, EDWARD WILSON, chemical engineering educator; b. New Bedford, Mass., Aug. 31, 1923; s. Edward Clifton and Gertrude (Wilson) M.; m. Genevieve de Bidart, Aug. 19, 1948; children—Anne de Bidart, Francis de Bidart. A.B., Harvard, 1945; D.Sc., Mass. Inst. Tech., 1947. Research engr. Dewey & Almy div. W.R. Grace & Co., 1947-50; mem. faculty Mass. Inst. Tech., 1950—, prof. chem. engring., 1964—, Carbon P. Dubbs prof., 1973—; cons. in field, 1950—; cons. in biochem. engring. Harvard U. Health Services, 1982—. Author articles on polymers, rheology, med. engring. Pres. bd. trustees Buckingham Sch., Cambridge, 1969-74; trustee Browne and Nichols Sch., Cambridge, 1972-74, hon. trustee, 1974—. Fellow Am. Inst. for Med. and Biol. Engring., Am. Acad. Arts and Scis.; mem. Am. Chem. Soc., Am. Inst. Chem. Engrs., Soc. for Biomaterials. Home: 90 Somerset St Belmont MA 02178-2010

MERRILL, GARY FRANK, physiologist; b. Afton, Wyo., Dec. 28, 1947; s. Frank Lester and Colleen Esther (Tippetts) M.; m. Marlene Haderlie, June 17, 1966; children: Rory, Justin, Travis, Angela, Bart, Jared, Britney, Stacey, Sean. BS, Weber State U., 1971; MS, Mich. State U., 1973, PhD, 1975. Grad. rsch. asst. dept. physiology Mich. State U., East Lansing, 1973-75; postdoctoral fellow dept. physiology La. State U. Med. Ctr., New Orleans, 1975-76; asst. prof. physiology Rutgers U., New Brunswick, N.J., 1976-82; assoc. prof. physiology dept. biol. scis. Rutgers U., New Brunswick, 1982—; cons. Biodynamics, Inc., East Millstone, N.J., 1989—, Anaquest Pharm., Murray Hill, N.J., 1990—, Miles Pharm., West Haven, Conn., 1980-84. Editor: Adenosine & Neurohumors, 1983; contbr. articles to profl. jours. Speaker Rutgers U. Speakers Bur., New Brunswick, 1989—, Am. Heart Assn., 1991—; pub. affairs dir. Fed. Am. Soc. Exptl. Biology, Bethesda, 1985—. NIH cardiovascular pre/postdoctoral fellow Mich. State U., 1973-75, La. State U., 1975-76. Mem. Am. Physiol. Soc., Am. Soc. Pharmacological Exptl. Therapeutics, Coun. on Circulation Am. Heart Assn., N.Y. Acad. Scis., N.J. Assn. Biomed. Rsch. (bd. trustees 1990—). Home: 522 Halsey Rd North Brunswick NJ 08902-2617

MERRILL, GEORGE VANDERNETH, lawyer, investment executive; b. N.Y.C., July 2, 1947; s. James Edward and Claire (Leness) M.; m. Janice Anne Humes, May 11, 1985; 1 child, Claire Georgina. AB, Harvard U., 1968, JD, 1972; MBA, Columbia U., 1973. Bar: N.Y. 1973, U.S. Dist. Ct. (so. and ea. dists.) N.Y. 1974, U.S. Ct. Appeals (2d cir.) 1974. Assoc. Cleary, Gottlieb, Steen & Hamilton, N.Y.C., 1974-77, Hawkins, Delafield & Wood, N.Y.C., 1977-79; v.p. Irving Trust Co., N.Y.C., 1980-82; v.p., gen. counsel Listowel Inc., N.Y.C., 1982-84, bd. dirs., exec. v.p., gen. counsel, 1984—, also bd. dirs. Pres. Arell Found., N.Y.C., 1985—, also bd. dirs.; pres. Northfield Charitable Corp., N.Y.C., 1986—; v.p., sec. Brougham Prodn. Co., N.Y.C., 1986—, bd. dirs., sr. v.p., sec., 1990—; v.p., sec. Marinetics Inc., N.Y.C., 1988-90, sr. v.p., sec., 1991—, also bd. dirs., 1989—; v.p. Sci. Design and Engring. Co., Inc., N.Y.C., 1987-88, bd. dirs., exec. v.p., 1989—. Recipient Detur award Harvard U., 1968, John Harvard scholar. Mem. ABA, Am. Mgmt. Assn., Assn. of Bar of City of N.Y., The Brook, Union Club, Down Town Assn., Knickerbocker Club, Racquet and Tennis Club, Players Club, Pilgrims of U.S. Home: 50 Glenbrook Rd Stamford CT 06902-2969 Office: Listowel Inc 2 Park Ave New York NY 10016-5603

MERRILL, JOHN THOMAS, atmospheric scientist/meteorologist; b. Oakland, Calif., May 29, 1946; s. Gordon T. and Dorothea (Rohrer) M.; m. Kathleen I. Gremel, June 12, 1976; children: Mathew, Karen. BA, U. Calif., Berkeley, 1968; MS, U. Ill., 1970; PhD, U. Colo., 1976. Postdoctoral fellow, asst. prof. U. Miami Sch. Marine & Atmospheric Sci., Miami, 1976-81; assoc. marine scientist, assoc. rsch. prof. Grad. Sch. Oceanography, U. R.I., Narragansett, 1981-86, assoc. prof., 1991—. Mem. Am. Meteorol. Soc., Am. Geophys. Union. Office: U RI Ctr Atomspheric Chem Study Grad Sch Oceanography Narragansett RI 02882

MERRILL, WENDY JANE, university official; b. Waterbury, Conn., Dec. 4, 1961; d. David Kenneth and Jane Joy (Nevius) M. BA in Journalism, George Washington U., St. Louis, 1981; postgrad. in mgmt., Cornell U., 1990-92. Intern in edn. HEW, Washington, summer 1978, writer, summer 1979; rsch. asst. dep. health svcs. adminstrn. George Washington U., Washington, 1979-81; sec. Nat. Assn. Beverage Importers, Washington, 1981; account exec. Staff Design, Washington, 1982; adminstrv. aide Internat. Food Policy Rsch. Inst., Washington, 1983-86; program assoc. Acad. for Ednl. Devel., Washington, 1986-87; pvt. practice cons. Washington, 1987-88; adminstrv. mgr. food and nutrition policy program Cornell U., Ithaca, 1988-92; cons., editor George Washington U., 1986; cons., rapporteur Internat. Food Policy Restaurant Inst., Washington and Copenhagen, Denmark, 1987; cons., adminstr. Hansell & Post, Washington, 1987-88, Cornell U., Washington and Ithaca, 1988. Sponsor Worldvision, Tanzania, 1988-91. George Washington U. scholar, 1979-81. Mem. NAFE, Am. Mgmt. Assn. (assoc.), Sigma Delta Xi (scholar 1980). Democrat. Episcopalian. Home: 104 Sharlene Rd Ithaca NY 14850-6316

MERRISS, PHILIP RAMSAY, JR., corporate banker; b. N.Y.C., June 7, 1948; s. Philip Ramsay and Elisabeth (Paine) M.; m. Janet Henry Hylan, Oct. 27, 1973. AB in Econs. magna cum laude, Lafayette Coll., 1970, MBA with high distinction, Dartmouth Coll., 1972. Assoc. corp. fin. dept. A.G. Becker and Co. Inc., N.Y.C., 1972-73; fin. analyst corp. banking dept. Chase Manhattan Bank, 1973, asst. treas. N.Y.C. dist., 1974-75, 2d v.p. mining and metals div., 1976-78, 2d v.p. petroleum div., 1978-79, v.p. global petroleum div., 1979-86, client exec., v.p. pub. utilities component, 1986-87, client exec., v.p. global energy component, 1987-89, credit supervising officer, div. exec., v.p. U.S. pvt. banking, 1989—. Served to capt. U.S. Army, 1978. Tuck scholar Dartmouth Coll., 1972. Mem. Am. Econ. Assn., Fin Mgmt. Assn., Aircraft Owners and Pilots Assn., N.Y. Road Runners Club, Weston Gun Club, Yale Club, Fairfield County Fish and Game Club, Phi Beta Kappa. Republican. Episcopalian. Home: 100 Hillspoint Rd Westport CT 06880-5111 Office: Chase Manhattan Bank 1211 Ave of the Americas New York NY 10036-8701

MERRITHEW, GERALD S., Canadian government official; b. St. John, N.B., Can., Sept. 23, 1931; m. Gloria McLean; 6 children. Grad. Tchrs. Coll., Frederickton; B.A., B.Ed., U. N.B. Tchr., prin. various schs., St. John; minister edn. N.B. Legislature, 1974-76, minister commerce and devel., 1975-82, minister of natural resources, 1982; mem. Ho. of Commons, Ottawa, Ont., Can., 1984—, former minister of state forestry, from 1984, now minister vet. affairs. Mem. youth adv. bd. Can. Red Cross; bd. dirs. United Fund. Served with Can. Army. Mem. Can. Inf. Assn., N.B. Rifle Assn., Black Powder Assn. Office: House of Commons, Parliament Bldgs, Ottawa, ON Canada K1A 0A6

MERRITT, CHARLES, JR., chemist; b. Lynn, Mass., Mar. 15, 1919; s. Charles and Sarah Jane (Collins) M.; m. Barbara Ann Keilty, Oct. 11, 1942 (div. Jan. 1981); children: Paul S. (dec.), Ann M., Patricia J.; m. Mary Alice Lyness, Nov. 16, 1984. AB, Dartmouth Coll., 1941; MS, U. Vt., 1948; PhD, MIT, 1953. Chemist GE, Lynn, Mass., 1941-46; instr. chemistry U. Vt., Burlington, 1946-49; rsch. chemist Nat. Bur. Standards, Washington, 1953; asst. prof. chemistry Poly. Inst. Bklyn., 1953-56; head analytical chemistry lab. U.S. Army Labs., Natick, Mass., 1956-83; lectr. Grad. Sch. Northeastern U., Boston, 1953-74; adj. prof. U. Mass., Amherst, 1975-85. Editor 4 books; contbr. articles to profl. jours. Mem. Mt. Washington Valley Arts Assn., North Conway, N.H., 1989—, Marblehead (Mass.) Arts Assn., 1992—. Recipient R.A. Isker award Rsch. and Devel. Assocs., Chgo., 1966, Rsch. and Devel. Achievement award Dept. of Army, Washington, 1979. Mem. Am. Chem. Soc., Corinthian Yacht Club, Swampscott Yacht Club, Wentworth Golf Club. Home: PO Box 478 Glen NH 03838-0478

MERRITT, WILLIAM THOMAS, anesthesiologist, consultant, researcher; b. Easton, Md., Aug. 12, 1946; s. William Tholmas and Marie (LaBeau) M.; m. Helen M. Bunker, Oct. 30, 1981; children: William, Ryan, Caitlin. BS in Chemistry, Biology, Mt. St. Mary's Coll., 1968; MD, U. Md., Balt., 1972. Pediatric intern U. Md. Hosp., Balt., 1972-73, pediatric resident, 1976-78; fellow pediatric infectious disease Walter Reed Army Med. Ctr., Washington, 1978-80; head pediatric infectious disease Naval Regional Med. Ctr., Oakland, Calif., 1980-82; anesthesiology resident Johns Hopkins Hosp., Balt., 1982-84, critical care anesthesiology, 1984-85, chief liver transplant anesthesia, 1986—; cons. Modular Instruments, Malvern, Pa., 1987—. Contbr. articles to profl. jours. Coach Naval Acad. Sailing Squadron, Annapolis, Md., 1976—. With USN, 1978-82, 88-90. Mem. ASA, IARS, Internat. Liver Transplantation Soc. (sec./treas. 1989—). Roman Catholic. Office: Johns Hopkins Hosp Dept Anesthesiology Tower 711 600 N Wolfe St Baltimore MD 21205

MERTON, ROBERT K., educator, sociologist; b. Phila., July 5, 1910. A.B., Temple U., 1931, LL.D. (hon.), 1956; M.A., Harvard U., 1932, Ph.D., 1936, LL.D. (hon.), 1980; L.H.D. (hon.), Emory U., 1965, Loyola U., Chgo., 1970, Kalamazoo Coll., 1970, Cleve. State U., 1977, U. Pa., 1979, Brandeis U., 1983, SUNY-Albany, 1986; Dr. honoris causa, U. Leyden, 1965, Jagiellonian U., Cracow, Poland, 1989; LL.D. (hon.), Western Res. U., 1966, U. Chgo., 1968, Tulane U., 1971, U. Md., 1982; Litt.D. (hon.), Colgate U., 1967, SUNY, 1984, Columbia U., 1985, SUNY, Albany, 1986, Oxford U., 1986; Dr. Social Sci. (hon.), Yale, 1968; D.Sc. in Econ. (hon.), U. Wales, 1968; Ph.D. (hon.), Hebrew U. of Jerusalem, 1980; PhD (hon.), U. Oslo, Norway, 1991. Tutor, instr. sociology Harvard U., 1934-39; prof., chmn. dept. Tulane U., 1939-41; asst. prof. to prof. sociology Columbia U., 1941-63, Giddings prof., 1963-74, univ. prof., 1974-79, spl. service prof., 1979-84, Univ. prof. emeritus, 1979—; assoc. dir. Bur. Applied Social Rsch., 1942-71; adj. faculty Rockefeller U., 1979—; George Sarton prof. hist. sci. U. Ghent, Belgium, 1986-88; adv. editor sociology Harcourt Brace Jovanovich, 1947—; ednl. adv. bd. Guggenheim Found., 1963-79, chmn., 1971-79. Author: Science Technology and Society in 17th Century England, 2d edit., 1970, Mass Persuasion, 2d edit, 1971, Social Theory and Social Structure, rev. edit, 1968, On The Shoulders of Giants, 1965, vicennial edit., 1985, On Theoretical Sociology, 1967, The Sociology of Science, 1973, Sociological Ambivalence, 1976, Sociology of Science: An Episodic Memoir, 1979, Social Research and the Practicing Professions, 1982; co-author: The Focused Interview, rev. edit, 1956, 3d edit., 1990, Freedom to Read, 1957; Co-editor, co-author: Continuities in Social Research, 1950, Social Policy and Social Research in Housing, 1951, Reader in Bureaucracy, 1952, The Student-Physician, 1957, Sociology Today, 1959, Contemporary Social Problems, 4th edit, 1976, The Sociology of Science in Europe, 1977, Toward a Metric of Science, 1978, Qualitative and Quantitative Social Research: Papers in Honor of Paul F. Lazarsfeld, 1979, Sociological Traditions from Generation to Generation, 1980, Continuities in Structural Inquiry, 1981; co-editor Internat. Ency. of the Soc. Scis., vol. 19, 1991, Social Sci. Quotations, 1992. Trustee Center Advanced Study Behavioral Scis., 1952-75, Temple U., 1964-68, Inst. Sci. Info., 1968—. Recipient prize disting. scholarship humanities Am. Coun. Learned Socs., 1962, Commonwealth award for Disting. Svc. to Sociology, 1979, award Meml. Sloan-Kettering Cancer Ctr., 1981; Guggenheim fellow, 1962, MacArthur Prize fellow, 1983-88, Russell Sage Found. resident scholar, 1979-90, Found. scholar, 1990—. Fellow Am. Acad. Arts and Scis. (Talcott Parsons prize 1979); mem. Nat. Acad. Scis., Am. Philos. Soc., Sociol. Rsch. Assn. (pres. 1968), Nat. Acad. Edn., Nat. Inst. Medicine, Am. Sociol. Soc. (pres. 1957, Disting. Scholarship award 1980), Eastern Sociol. Soc. (pres. 1969), History Sci. Soc., World Acad. Arts and Scis., Soc. Social Studies of Sci. (pres. 1975, Bernal prize, Royal Swedish Acad. Scis. (fgn.), Academia Europaea (fgn.), Century Assn. (N.Y.C.). Office: Columbia U 415 Fayerweather Hall New York NY 10027

MERTZ, FRANCIS JAMES, academic administrator; b. Newark, Sept. 24, 1937; s. Frank E. and Marian E. (Brady) M.; m. Gail Williams, Apr. 11, 1964; children: Lynn, Christopher, Suzanne, David, Amy, Jonathan. BA, St. Peter's Coll., 1958; JD, NYU, 1961; LLD (hon.), Felician Coll., 1984, Stevens Inst. Tech., Hoboken, N.J., 1988. Bar: N.J. 1967. Exec. v.p. St. Peter's Coll., Jersey City, 1972-78; v.p.,chief fin. officer N.Y. Med. Coll., Valhalla, 1978-79; dir. adminstrn. Sage Gray Todd and Sims, N.Y.C., 1979-81; pres. Ind. Coll. Fund N.J., Summit, 1981-90, Assn. Ind. Colls. and Univs. N.J., Summit, 1982-90, Fairleigh Dickinson U., Rutherford, N.J., 1990—; bd . dirs. UJB Fin., Princeton, N.J., Gibraltar Corp., N.Y.C. Mem., officer Bd. Edn., Watchung, N.J., 1982-85; trustee, sec. St. James Found., Westfield, N.J., 1987—; bd. dirs. Found. for Ind. Higher Edn., Stamford, Conn., 1990—, Tri County Scholarship Fund, Paterson, N.J., 1992—. Mem. N.J. State Bar Assn., N.J. Assn. Colls. and Univs. (vice chmn. 1990—), University Club (N.Y.C.). Home: 60 Bayberry Lan Watchung NJ 07060 Office: Fairleigh Dickinson U 233 Montross Ave Rutherford NJ 07070

MERTZ, KENNETH GEORGE, II, investment officer; b. Harrisburg, Pa., June 14, 1952; s. Kenneth George and Edna Laura (Rhan) M.; m. Shirley Rae Greer, Nov. 20, 1976; children: Leigh Anne, Kenneth Douglas. BA in Econs., Millersville U., 1974. Charterd fin. analyst, Pa. V.p. Dauphin Deposit Bank, Harrisburg, 1975-85; chief investment officer Pa. State Employees' Retirement System, Harrisburg, 1985—; mem. adv. bd. APA-Fostin Pennad Venture Capital Fund, Phila, 1987—. Mem. coun. St. Peter's Luth. Ch., 1952—, pres. 1984-89. Fellow Fin. Analyst Fedn.; mem. Cen. Pa. Investment Mgt. Assn. (pres. 1985-87, chmn. 1987-89), Inst. Chartered Fin. Analysts, Assn. Investment Mgmt. and Rsch. Home: 803 Wilhelm Rd Harrisburg PA 17111-2106 Office: Pa State Employees Retirement System 909 Green St Harrisburg PA 17102-2999

MERVYN, LOIS WINNER, foreign service officer; b. Great Falls, Mont., Sept. 2, 1932; d. Herbert A. and Dorothy (Stone) Winner; (div. 1972); children: Robin Lois, Jason Hunter. BA, U. Idaho, 1951; MA, Wash. State U., 1965; PhD, U. Ariz., 1976. Cert. secondary adminstr., Ariz. From instr. to asst. prof. U. Ariz., Tucson, 1968-77; assoc. prof. U. So. Colo., Pueblo, 1977-78; fgn. svc. officer U.S. Info. Agy., Madrid, London, Managua, 177890, Lahore, Pakistan, 1991—; chief ctrs. mgmt. U.S. Info. Agy., Lahore, 1989-91; English teaching fellow coord. U.S. Info. Agy., Washington, 1989-90; Editor: The American Epic, 1976. Mem. transatlantic coun. Boy Scouts USA, Madrid and London, 1979-84. Mem. Phi Beta Kappa. Democrat. Episcopalian. Office: US Info Agy 301-4th SW Rm 304 Washington DC 20547

MESA-LAGO, CARMELO, economist, educator; b. Havana, Cuba, Aug. 11, 1934; s. Rogelio M. and Ana Maria (Lago); m. Elena Mesa-Gross, Sept. 3, 1966; children: Elizabeth, Ingrid, Helena. LL.B., U. Havana, 1956; Doctorate, U. Madrid, 1958; M.A. in Econs., U. Miami, 1965; Ph.D., Cornell U., 1968. Asst. prof. Cath U. Villanueva, Havana, Cuba, 1956-57, 59-61; research assoc. U. Miami, Fla., 1962-65; asst. prof. U. Pitts., 1968-71, assoc. prof., 1971-76, prof., 1976-81, disting. prof. econs. and Latin Am. affairs, 1981—; dir. Ctr. Latin Am. Studies, 1974-86; vis. prof. Oxford U., 1977; regional advisor Econ. Commn. Latin Am., Santiago, Chile, 1983-84; rsch. assoc. Max-Planck-Inst., Munich, 1991-92; vis. prof. Inst. Univ. Ortegay Gasset, 1990-91; cons. in field. Author: Cuba in the 1970's, 1974, 2d edit., 1978, Social Security in Latin America, 1978, The Economy of Socialist Cuba, 1981 (a.P. Whitaker 1982), The Crisis of Social Security and Health Care: Latin American Experiences and Lessons, 1985, Ascent to Bankruptcy: Financing Social Security in Latin America, 1989; former editor: Yearbook Cuban Studies. Recipient numerous rsch. grants, 1986—, Alexander von Humboldt sr. rsch. prize, 1990-91. Mem. Latin Am. Studies Assn. (pres. 1980), Caribbean Studies Assn. (exec. council 1973-74), Am. Econ. Assn., Assn. Comparative Econs., Internat. Assn. Labor Law and Social Security, Coun. on Fgn. Rels. Democrat. Roman Catholic. Club: Spanish Cultural (Pitts.) (v.p.). Office: U Pittsburgh Dept Econs 4M38 Forbes Quadrangle Pittsburgh PA 15260

MESCHES, ARNOLD, artist; b. Bronx, N.Y., Aug. 11, 1923; s. Benjamin and Anna (Grosse) M.; m. Sylvia Snetsky, Apr. 8, 1945 (div. 1972); children: Paul Elliot, Susan Jean; m. Jill Karen Ciment, Mar. 19, 1983. Student, Art Ctr. Sch., 1943-45, Jepson's Art Inst., 1945, Chouinard's Art Inst., 1945. Instr. painting U. So. Calif., L.A., 1950; instr. painting and drawing Kann Inst. Art, L.A., 1950-55, New Sch. of Art, L.A., 1955-58, Otis Art Inst., L.A., 1963-67, U. Calif., L.A., 1972-77, Otis/Parsons Art Inst., L.A., 1975-84; instr. advanced painting and drawing Parsons Sch. Design, N.Y.C., 1986; guest prof. grad painting Rutgers U., New Brunswick, N.J., 1985; instr. grad. painting and drawing NYU, N.Y.C., 1988—; art dir. Frontier mag., L.A., 1954-60; ct. room artist Walter Cronkite Program, CBS, L.A., 1966. One-man shows include Civilian Warfare Gallery, N.Y.C., 1984, 85, Hallwalls, Buffalo, 1985, Marsh Gallery, U. Richmond, 1986, Haines Gallery, San Francisco, 1988, 91, Jack Shainman Gallery, N.Y.C., 1985, 86, 89, Castellani Art Mus., 1988, Burchfield Art Ctr., Buffalo, 1988, Madison Art Ctr., 1989, Carlo Lamagna Gallery, 1989, East Hampton Ctr. for Contemporary Art, 1990, Robert Berman Gallery, Santa Monica, 1990, E.M. Donahue Gallery, N.Y.C., 1991, Brody's Gallery, Washington, 1992. Grantee John F. and Anna Lee Stacey Sch. Fund, 1954, 56, NEA, 1982, N.Y. Found. for Arts, 1991; Ford Found. Faculty grantee, 1979-80. Home: 254 E 7th St # 15-16 New York NY 10009-6053

MESCHINO, JOSEPH ALBERT, drug development executive; b. Cranston, R.I., Aug. 23, 1932; s. Albert and Frances (Ialongo) M.; m. Gloria Cora Capuano, Aug. 14, 1954; children: Joseph A. Jr., David, Paul. ScB, Brown U., 1954; PhD, Rice U., 1958. Sr. scientist McNeil Labs., Phila., 1959-61; group leader McNeil Labs., Ft. Washington, Pa., 1961-67, chem. dept. dir., 1967-79; dir. internat. sci. affairs McNeil Pharm., Springhouse, Pa., 1980-83; dir. life scis. Univ. Patents, Westport, Conn., 1983-86; pres. Pharmacepts Assocs., Fairfield, Conn., 1986-91; chief pharm. and regulatory affairs Nat. Inst. Allergy and Infectious Diseases, Bethesda, Md., 1991—; dir. industry liaison U. Va., Charlottesville, 1987-91; cons. Mitsui Pharms., N.Y.C., 1986-91, Ortho Pharms., Raritan, N.J., 1986-87. Contbr. articles to profl. publs.; patentee in field. Pres. Lions Club, North Wales, Pa., 1970-71. NIH fellow, 1958-59. Mem. Am. Chem. Soc. Home: 9709 Days Farm Dr Vienna VA 22182-7304 Office: NIAID 6003 Executive Rd Bethesda MD 20892

MESELSON, MATTHEW STANLEY, educator, biochemist; b. Denver, May 24, 1930; s. Hymen Avram and Ann (Swedlow) M.; m. Jeanne Guillemin, 1986; children: Zoe, Amy Valor. Ph.B., U. Chgo., 1951, D.Sc. (hon.), 1975; Ph.D., Calif. Inst. Tech., 1957; Sc.D. (hon.), Oakland Coll., 1964, Columbia, 1971, Yale U., 1987, Princeton U., 1988. From research fellow to sr. research fellow Calif. Inst. Tech., 1957-60; asso. prof. biology Harvard U., 1960—, prof. biology, 1964-76, Thomas Dudley Cabot prof. natural scis., 1976—. Recipient prize for molecular biology NAS, 1963, Eli Lilly award microbiology and immunology, 1964, Alumni medal U. Chgo., 1971; Lehman award 1975, Presidential award 1983, N.Y. Acad. Scis., 1975; Alumni Disting. Svc. award Calif. Inst. Tech., 1975; Leo Szilard award Am. Phys. Soc., 1978; MacArthur fellow, 1984-89. Fellow AAAS (Sci. Freedom and Responsibility award); mem. NAS, Inst. Medicine, Am. Acad. Arts and Scis., Fedn. Am. Scientists (chmn. 1986-88, Pub. Svc. award 1972), Coun. Fgn. Rels., Accademia Santa Chiara, Am. Philos. Soc., Royal Society (London), Académie des Sciences (Paris). Office: Harvard U Fairchild Biochem Bldg 7 Divinity Ave Cambridge MA 02138-2092

MESKILL, THOMAS J., federal judge; b. New Britain, Conn., Jan. 30, 1928; s. Thomas J. M.; m. Mary T. Grady; children—Maureen Meskill Heneghan, John, Peter, Eileen, Thomas. B.S., Trinity Coll., Hartford, Conn., 1950, LL.D., 1972; J.D., U. Conn., 1956; postgrad., Sch. Law, NYU; LL.D., U. Bridgeport, 1971, U. New Haven, 1974. Bar: Conn., Fla, D.C., U.S. Supreme Ct. Former mem. firm Meskill, Dorsey, Sledzik and Walsh, New Britain; mem. 90th-91st Congresses 6th Conn. Dist.; gov. Conn., 1971-75; judge U.S. Ct. Appeals (2d cir.), New Britain, Conn., 1975—, chief judge, 1992—. Pres. New Britain Council Social Agys.; Asst. corp. council City of New Britain, 1960-62, mayor, 1962-64, corp. counsel, 1965-67; mem. Constl. Conv., Hartford, 1965. Served to 1st lt. USAF, 1950-53. Recipient Distinguished Service award Jr. C. of C., 1964, Jud. Achievement award Assn. Trial Lawyers Am., 1983. Mem. Fla. Bar Assn., Conn. Bar Assn., Hartford County Bar Assn., New Britain Bar Assn., K.C. Republican. Office: US Ct Appeals 114 W Main St New Britain CT 06051-4223

MESKILL, VICTOR PETER, educator, college president; b. Albertson, N.Y., May 9, 1935; s. James Joseph and Ida May (Pfalzer) M.; m. Gail Heidinger King, 1986; children by previous marriage—Susan Ann, Janet Louise, Gary James, Glenn Thomas, Kenneth John, Matthew Adam. B.A., Hofstra U., 1961, M.A. (grad. scholar), 1962; Ph.D., St. John's U., 1967; postgrad. insts., Ohio State U., 1968, Harvard U., 1972, NYU, 1973. Lab. asst., instr. biology Hofstra U., 1960-62; N.Y. State teaching fellow St. John's U., 1962-63; instr. biology Nassau (N.Y.) Community Coll., 1963-64; tchr. sci. Central High Sch. Dist. 2, Floral Park, N.Y., 1963-64; lectr. biology C.W. Post Coll., Greenvale, N.Y., 1963-64, instr. biology, 1964-67, asst. prof., 1967-68, assoc. prof., 1968-74, assoc. dir. Inst. for Student Problems, supr. student tchrs., 1967-68, asst. dean Coll., dean summer sch., coordinator

Admissions Office, coordinator adult and continuing edn. programs, 1968-69; dean adminstrn. C.W. Post Ctr. of L.I. U., 1969-70, v.p. adminstrn., 1970-77, prof. biology, 1975-77; pres. Dowling Coll., Oakdale, L.I., 1977—; cons. in edn. and biology.; chem. technician, detective Tech. Research Bur., Nassau County Police Dept., 1958-63, mem. sci. adv. com., 1970; mem. adv. coun. Aerospace Edn. Coun. Inc. N.Y., 1968; trustee Commn. Ind. Colls. and Univs.; mem. evaluation teams Middle States Assn., 1971—; mem. higher edn. adv. com. N.Y. State Senate; mem. state legis. com. Commn. on Ind. Colls. and Univs.; mem. Nassau-Suffolk Comprehensive Health Planning Coun.; cons. higher edn. and sci. Author book; contbr. articles to profl. jours. Founding mem., vice chmn. bd. trustees Nassau Higher Edn. Consortium; bd. dirs. Suffolk County coun. Boy Scouts Am.; mem. N.Y. State Energy Rsch. and Devel. Authority, Town of Islip Devel. Commn.; chmn. bd. trustees L.I. Regional Adv. Coun. Higher Edn.; chmn. L.I. Mid Suffolk Bus. Action; bd. dirs. Southside Hosp., N.Y.; v.p. L.I. Forum for Tech. NSF rsch. grantee, 1967-69; Named Tchr. of Year, Aesculapius Med. Arts Soc., C.W. Post Coll. of L.I. U., 1967; Disting. Faculty Mem. of Year, C.W. Post Ctr. L.I. U., 1977; recipient George M. Estabrook award Hofstra U., 1978, Higher Edn. Leadership award Corning Glass Works, 1987, Disting. Leadership award L.I., 1989. Mem. AAAS, Council Advancement and Support of Edn., Am. Assn. Collegiate Registrars and Admissions Officers, Am. Assn. Higher Edn., Am. Inst. Biol. Scis., Am. Soc. Zoologists, Am. Assn. Univ. Adminstrs., Nat. Assn. Biology Tchrs., Nat. Sci. Tchrs. Assn., Soc. Protozoologists, N.Y. Acad. Scis., Met. Assn. Coll. and Univ. Biologists (founder, mem. steering com.), Oakdale C. of C. (founding mem., dir.), L.I. Assn. Commerce and Industry (v.p. edn., dir.), Sigma Xi., Beta Beta Beta, Alpha Eta Rho, Delta Mu Delta, Kappa Delta Rho. Club: University (N.Y.C.). Office: Dowling Coll Office of the Pres Oakdale NY 11769-1999

MESNER, MAX HUTCHINSON, aerospace engineer, retired; b. Meadville, Mo., Apr. 16, 1912; s. Merle Lynd and Etta Belle (Hutchinson) M.; m. Ethel Gertrude Vietren, Oct. 10, 1938; 1 child, Barbara Sue Mesner Howard. AS, Kansas City (Mo.) Jr. Coll., 1932; BSEE, U. Mo., 1940. Rsch. engr. RCA Labs., Princeton, N.J., 1940-58; mgr. space TV systems RCA Astro Div., Hightstown, N.J., 1958-77; adj. lectr. Rutgers U., New Brunswick, N.J., 1948-61; cons. Burns Rsch., San Jose, Calif., 1981; welfare dir. Cranbury Twp., Cranbury, N.J., 1986—. Patentee in field; contbr. articles to profl. jours. Fellow IEEE, AIAA (assoc.); mem. SPIE, Lions Internat., Sigma Xi, Tau Beta Pi, Etta Kappa Nu. Republican. Presbyterian. Home: South Rossmoor 677B Yarborough Way Jamesburg NJ 08831

MESROP, ALIDA YOLANDE, college dean; b. N.Y.C., Dec. 23, 1931; d. Umberto and Jessica (Subrizi) R.; m. Alden Mesrop, Nov. 25, 1954; children: Andrea Francesca, Alison Bianca, Claudia Anne. BA cum laude, Hunter Coll., 1952. Freelance writer-cons., 1960-66; prodn. asst. Today Show, Nat. Broadcasting System, N.Y.C., 1952-54; pub. rels. coord. Tonight Show, Nat. Broadcasting System, N.Y.C., 1954-59; pub. rels. dir. Sta. WPIX-TV, N.Y.C., 1959-60; spl. asst. to pres. Coll. for Human Svcs., N.Y.C., 1966-79, dean, 1979—. PTA com. chair, Pelham, N.Y., 1969-79; rep. Dem. Party, Pelham, 1977-80; pub. rels. dir. Coalition on Environment, Pelham, 1978-82. Mem. Exec. Women in Human Svcs., Phi Beta Kappa. Office: Audrey Cohen Coll 345 Hudson St New York NY 10014-4502

MESSAM, LEROY ANTHONY, accountant; b. Kingston, Jamaica, West Indies, July 24, 1923; came to U.S., 1951; s. David A. and Irene Beatrice (Patterson) M.; m. Ruby Patricia Jackson, July 25, 1964; children: LeRoy Jr., Andrea, Conrad, Mahalia. BA in Bus. Adminstr., Bryant & Stratton, Boston, 1958; MEd, Cambridge Coll., 1983; DD, Free Anglican Ch. in Am., 1979; DBA, Southland (Lassell) U., Pasadena, Calif., 1986; grad., Harvard U., 1980. CPA; accredited Accreditation Coun. for Accountancy. Prin. Leroy A. Messam, Pub. Acct., Boston, 1962—; bishop St. John's Episcopal Ch., Mattapan, Mass., 1986—. Author: Resource Handbook for Black & Minority Entrepreneurs, 1983; co-author Pub. Adminstrn. of Our Nat. Economy, 1983. Treas. NAACP, Boston, 1962; coord. Boy Scouts Am., Boston, 1984—; del. White House Conf. on Small Bus., Washington, 1986; bd. dirs. Mass. Dept. Social Svcs., Boston, 1987; chmn. Jamaican Hurricane Relief, 1988—. Recipient Community Svcs. award Boston Soc. Vulcans Inc., Black Profl. Fire Fighters, 1989. Fellow Reg. Pub. Accts. of Jamaica (v.p. 1975-76); mem. Nat. Soc. Pub. Accts., Mass. Assn. Pub. Accts., Jamaican Culture Soc. (pres. 1962-73), The Friends of BOAF (sec. 1989—). Republican. Episcopalian. Home: Blue Castle Dr Mashpee MA 02649-3770 Office: 96 Greenfield Rd Mattapan MA 02126-3203

MESSANO, ALBERT FRANCIS, JR., electrical engineer, consultant; b. Teaneck, N.J., Oct. 5, 1949; s. Albert F. Messano and Frances M. Poretta; m. Diane M. Onny, Oct. 6, 1980; children: Wendy Lauren, Eric Alan. B Eng. in Elec. Engring., Stevens Inst. Tech., 1971; MS in Indsl. Engring., Poly. Inst. N.Y., 1976; MSEE, Fairleigh Dickinson U., 1990. Various positions in engring. and ops. Bklyn. Union Gas Co., 1971-75, dir. purchasing svcs., 1975-77; engring. mgr. Orange and Rockland Utilities, Pearl River, N.Y., 1977-85; gen. mgr. Nynex Mobile Communications, Pearl River, 1985-87; pres. Raynor Assocs., Inc., Dumont, N.J., 1987—; mem. Integrated System Digital Network working group for Nat. Tech. Info. Svc. Mem. IEEE (sr., exec. com. 1990-93, speaker electro conv. 1989), Instrument Soc. Am., Soc. Photo-Optical Instrumentation Engrs. (fiber optics working group), Ind. Computer Cons. Assn. Office: Raynor Assocs Inc 175 Washington Ave Dumont NJ 07628-2302

MESSENGER, DONALD B. W., lawyer; b. Federalsburg, Md., Sept. 11, 1935; s. Henry B. and Esther (White) M.; m. Barbara Beard Beall, Aug. 15, 1960; children: Colleen Beall Baldwin, Melanie Dorsey. BA, Washington Coll., 1957; LLB, LLD, Washington & Lee U., 1960; postgrad., Georgetown U., 1985. Bar: Md., 1960, D.C., 1964. Atty. Duckett, Orem & Christie, Hyattsville, Md., 1960-64, Burgess, Cassidy & Messenger, Upper Marlboro, Md., 1964-68, Messenger & Lynch, Beltsville, Md., 1968-75, Messenger, Lynch & Miller, Beltsville, 1975-80, Messenger, Lynch, Hills & Miller, Beltsville, 1980-85, Messenger & Assocs., P.A., Beltsville, 1985—; pres., gen. counsel Consumer Real Estate Title, Inc., Beltsville, 1984—; faculty Prince George's Community Coll., Largo, Md., 1975-85; chmn. Consumer Protection Agy., Upper Marlboro, 1972-76; atty. Prince George's Election Bd., Upper Marlboro, 1968-70. Chmn. Howard County Rep. Cen. Com., Ellicott City, Md., 1980-84; mem. Prince George's Cen. Com., Upper Marlboro, 1966-72; sec.-treas. Laurel-Beltsville Community Hosp., 1984-86; chmn. Ronald Reagan Campaign, Howard County, 1980. Sgt. U.S. Army, 1960. Mem. Beltsville Rotary (pres. 1991-92), Eastern Shore Soc. (historian, v.p. 1985-92, pres.-elect 1992—), Am. Legion, Corridor C. of C. Republican. Roman Catholic. Home: 10497 Graeloch Rd Laurel MD 20723-1116 Office: Messenger & Assocs PA 4743 Sellman Rd Beltsville MD 20705-2573

MESSER, STANLEY BERNARD, psychology educator; b. Montreal, Que., Can., Nov. 28, 1941; s. Nathan Harry and Sylvia (Hamovitch) M.; m. Donna Rebecca Ann Evin, Dec. 29, 1966; children: Elana, Leora, Tova. BSc, McGill U., Montreal, 1962; MA, Harvard U., 1966, PhD, 1969. Lic. psychologist, N.J. Asst. prof. Rutgers U., New Brunswick, N.J., 1968-74, assoc. prof., 1974-80, prof., 1980—. Co-editor: Psychoanalytic and Behavior Therapy: Is Integration Possible?, 1984, Hermeneutics and Psychological Theory, 1988, History of Psychotherapy: A Century of Change, 1992. Bd. dirs. B'nai Brith Hillel Found., Rutgers U., 1980—. Grant N.J. Coun. on the Humanities, 1985. Fellow Am. Psychol. Assn.; mem. Soc. for Psychotherapy Rsch., Soc. for the Exploration of Psychotherapy Integration, Eastern Psychol. Assn. Office: GSAPP Rutgers U PO Box 819 Piscataway NJ 08855-0819

MESSIER, DONALD WILMORE, educational administrator, financial planner; b. Waterbury, Conn., Oct. 5, 1937; s. René Wilmore and Mary Louise (Garlando) M.; m. Doris Ann Jones, Mar. 25, 1968; children: Matthew Eric, Stephen Elliot. BA in Edn., Providence Coll., 1959; MA in Adminstrn. and Supervision, Fairfield U., 1963. Cert. supt. schs., K-12 prin., Vt. Tchr. pub. schs., watertown, Conn., 1959-63; asst. prin. Frankfurt (Germany) High Sch., 1963-70, Essex Junction (Vt.) High Sch., 1970-77; prin. Winooski (Vt.) Sch. Dist., 1977-78, supt., 1978-84; sales mgr. N.Y. Life, Winooski, 1984-88, Mut. N.Y., Burlington, Vt., 1988-89, New Eng. Ins. Co., Burlington, 1989-91; prin. Addison Cen. Sch., Vergennes, Vt., 1991—. Assoc. trustee St. Michael's Coll., 1984-89; mem. Ednl. TV Citizen Adv. Coun., Colchester, Vt., 1985—. Fellow NDEA, 1966-68. Mem. NAESP, Rotary, KC (4th degree), Phi Delta Kappa (pres. Karlsburg, Germany 1969-70, v.p. Burlington 1974-76). Republican. Roman Catholic. Home: 46 Foothills PO Box 330 Jericho VT 05465 Office: Addison Cen Sch RR 1 Vergennes VT 05491

MESSINA, BARBARA ANN, artist; b. Hudson, N.Y., July 27, 1940; d. Joseph and Helen Marie (Krein) Stafkey; 1 child, Mary Theresa. Student, Albany Coll. Pharmacy, 1959-60, Rensselaer County Coun. Arts, Troy, N.Y., 1973-76, Art Students League, Woodstock, N.Y., 1977-78. Contbg. artist, designer mural City of Pittsfield, Mass., 1987; one-woman shows include Saratoga (N.Y.) Performing Arts Ctr. Hall of Springs, 1980, Columbia-Greene C.C., 1980, 92, The Arts Ctr, Southbridge, Mass., 1987, Spencertown (N.Y.) Acad., 1990, Inst. of Man and Sci., Rensselaerville, N.Y., 1984, 88, Simon's Rock of Bard Coll., Great Barrington, Mass., 1987, others; exhibited at group shows at Cooperstown Nat. Exhbn., 1990, Conn. State House, Hartford, 1988; represented in permanent collection Columbia-Greene Community Coll., Hudson, N.Y., Westbridge Assocs., West Stockbridge, Mass., Peat, Marwick, N.Y.C., Eddy Meml. Found., Troy, N.Y. Assoc. mem. Nat. Assn. Painters in Casein and Acrylic (exhibitor Nat. Arts Club 1991); mem. Sheffield Art League (exhibitor Invitational for Prizewinners 1991), Adirondack Mountain Club (one-woman show at hdqtrs. 1991). Democrat.

MESSINA, JOSEPH R., JR., artist; b. Newark, 1904; s. Joseph Messina and Grace (Grazia) Catania; widowed; children: Joanna (dec.), Maryanna (dec.), Bernice Messina Gates. Grad., Fawcett Art Sch., Newark, 1920; student, Nat. Acad. Design, N.Y.C., 1923, George B. Bridgeman, 1924, Arts Student League, N.Y.C. guest artist Bayonne (N.J.) Art Mus. Art Gallery. First portrait commd. at age 15; work has been featured on TV shows, in newspapers and mags.; exhibited in group shows at South Pines, N.C., Nat. Miniature Art Exhbn. (1st place award), Festa Italiana Garden State Arts Ctr. (1st place award), Bosque Farms, N.Mex. (1st and 2d place awards), Salmagundi Club, 1991, Art Expo, Jacob Javits Conv. Ctr., N.Y.C., 1992; commd. to do numerous portraits, both on ivory and canvass. Recipient first prize N.J. Garden State Art Ctr., 1984, 85, numerous art awards. Studio: 71 Valley St South Orange NJ 07079

MESSING, GORDON MYRON, educator; b. Toledo, Mar. 4, 1917; s. Samuel Meyer and Selma (Silberberg) M.; m. Florence Evelyn Hope, Mar. 16, 1946; children—Hope Candida (Robbins), Faith Erica (Winters), Daniel Peregrine, Seth Jeremy. A.B., Harvard, 1938, A.M., 1940, Ph.D., 1942. Asst. prof. classics, chmn. dept. comparative philology U. Wis.-Madison, 1946-47; mem. diplomatic staff State Dept. (various internat. locations), 1947-65; attache Am. embassy, Athens, Greece, 1955-60; attache, polit. officer Am. embassy, Reykjavik, Iceland, 1962-65; asso. prof. classics Cornell U., N.Y., 1967-71; prof. classics and linguistics Cornell U., 1971-87, emeritus, 1987—. Editor: Smyth's Greek Grammar, 1956, A Glossary of Greek Romany as Spoken in Agia Varvara (Athens), 1988; contbr. articles to profl. jours. Served with AUS, 1942-46, ETO. Decorated Bronze Star.; Nat. Endowment Humanities sr. fellow, 1973-74. Mem. Linguistic Soc. Am., Am. Philol. Assn. Home: 135 Graham Rd Ithaca NY 14850-1122

MESSING, PAUL DAVID, composer, artist; b. N.Y.C., Oct. 9, 1949; s. Jess Benjamin and Muriel Virginia (Habas) M.; m. Sally Ann Stalker, Dec. 27, 1974. Student, Phila. Coll. Art, 1968-71. Prodn. dir. WMMR-FM Radio Sta., Phila., 1970-72; v.p., creative dir. Radio Band Am., N.Y.C., 1972-77; freelance composer Bala Cynwyd, Pa., 1983—. Writer, producer radio commercials, music for TV, 1973-80; composer animated films, 1986—, Ballet for Pa. Ballet, 1989; cartoonist greeting cards, 1980. Recipient Clio awards, 1973-80. Mem. ASCAP, AFTRA. Home and Office: 426 Tregaron Rd Bala Cynwyd PA 19004

MESSING, RICHARD DAVID, rabbi; b. Montreal, Jan. 4, 1941; s. Joseph Harvey and Sarah (Goldberg) M.; m. Gilda Mostovitch, Dec. 5, 1964 (div. 1977); children: Alisa Ruth, Cheryl Deborah, Pamela Tamar; m. Paulette Merle Lambert, June 10, 1986. BA, Concordia U., Montreal, 1962; BHL, Hebrew Union Coll., Cin., 1965, MA in Hebrew Lit., 1968. Rabbi, 1968. Rabbi Temple Beth Israel, Plattsburgh, N.Y., 1968-73, Spring Hill Ave. Temple, Mobile, Ala., 1973-77, Temple Sholom, Vancouver, B.C., 1977-82; dir. sales and mktg. Slumber Lodge Devel. Corp., Vancouver, B.C., 1982-84; rabbi Temple Beth Shalom, Vero Beach, Fla., 1984-88, Temple Israel, Brockton, Mass., 1988—; founder Jewish-Christian Dialogue Group, Mobile, 1975-77. Compiler, editor: Creative Worship Svcs., 1968—. Named Young Clergyman of the Yr. Jaycees, Mobile, 1975; recipient Masada award State of Israel Bonds, Mobile, 1975. Mem. Cen. Conf. Am. Rabbis, Rotary. Office: Temple Israel 184 W Elm St Brockton MA 02401-4399

MESSING, SIMON DAVID, anthropologist, retired; b. Franfurt on Main, Germany, July 13, 1922; came to U.S., 1940; s. Jacob and Helen (Friedler) M.; m. Denise Messing, July 25, 1967; 1 child, Jacqueline. BS, CCNY, 1949; PhD, U. Pa., 1957. Asst. prof. Paine Coll., Augusta, Ga., 1956-58; assoc. prof. Hiram (Ohio) Coll., 1958-60, U. So. Fla., Tampa, 1960-61, 63-64; foreign svc. USAID, Addis Ababa, Ethiopia, 1961-63, 64-67; prof. So. Conn. State U., New Haven, 1968-89; researcher pub. health USAID-Ethiopia, 1961-63, 64-67. Author: Target of Health in Ethiopia, 1972, The Story of the Falashas of Ethiopia, 1982, Highland Plateau Amhara of Ethiopia, 1985. With U.S. Army, 1942-44. Recipient Harrison fellowship, U. Pa., 1950-51, Ford Found. grant, 1954. Fellow Am. Anthrop. Assn., African Studies Soc., Soc. for Applied Anthropology, Soc. for Med. Anthropology; mem. APHA.

MESSNER, RICHARD STEPHEN, school system administrator; b. N.Y.C., Nov. 8, 1939; s. Blasius and Anna (Kuti) M.; m. Eugenia Mancuso, Oct. 22, 1968 (div. 1974); 1 child, Stephanie; m. Mary Theodorakis, May 28, 1976' stepchildren: Paul, Nicole. BS, Alderson-Broaddus Coll., 1961; MBA, Fairleigh Dickinson U., 1972; MEd, Rutgers U., 1980. Acctg. mgr. McGraw-Hill, Hightstown, N.J., 1968-71; bus. coord. Fairleigh Dickinson U., Rutherford, N.J., 1971-73; dep. treas. County of Somerset, Somerville, N.J., 1973-78; asst. dir. of adminstrv. svcs. Somerset County Vo-Tech, Bridgewater, N.J., 1978-82; dir. adminstrv. svcs. Somerset County Vocat. Tech., Bridgewater, 1982-85, asst. supt. for bus., 1985—, acting supt., 1987-88, supt. of schs., 1992—. Dep. mayor Franklin Twp., N.J., 1975, mayor, 1975-76; commr. Urban Enterprize Zone Authority, N.J., 1984—; treas. Somerset County Reps., 1985—. With U.S. Army, 1962-64. Mem. Am. Soc. Bus. Officers Internat. (chmn. purchasing com. Reston, Va. chpt. 1986-88, legis. com. 1988—), N.J. Assn. Bus. Ofcls. (chmn. legis. com. Bordentown, N.J. chpt. 1985—), Somerset County Bus. Ofcls. (v.p. Somerville chpt. 1991—), N.J. Edn. Assn. (adv. com. 1984—), VFW, Masons, Phi Delta Kappa. Baptist. Home: 32 Pin Oak Rd Skillman NJ 08558

MESZOELY, CHARLES ALADAR MARIA, biology educator; b. Szekesfehervàr, Hungary, Apr. 24, 1933; came to U.S., 1951; s. Karoly and Sarolta (Erdelyi) M.; m. Janice Massie, Apr. 10, 1961; children: Ingrid, Greta. BS, Northeastern U., Boston, 1961; MS, Boston U., 1963, PhD, 1967. Instr. Boston U., 1966-68; assoc. prof. Northeastern U., 1970-84, prof., 1984—. Contbr. articles to profl. jours. Active Conservation Commn., Mansfield, Mass., 1970-84. Capt., U.S. Army, 1968-70. Mem. Soc. Vertebrate Paleontologists. Roman Catholic. Office: Northeastern University Dept of Biology Boston MA 02115

METAXAS, JOHN C., producer, lawyer; b. N.Y.C., Feb. 26, 1958. BA, Columbia Coll., 1980; MS, Columbia U., 1983, JD, 1984. Bar: N.Y. 1984. Prodn. coord. ABC Sports, N.Y.C., L.A., 1984-85; staff reporter The Nat. Law Jour., N.Y.C., 1985-87, legal editor, 1987; reportorial producer ABC News, N.Y.C., 1987-90; corr. CNBC, N.Y.C., 1990—. Chmn. WKCR Alumni Adv. Bd., Columbia U., 1986—. Greek Orthodox.

METCALF, BRIAN WALTER, pharmaceutical industry executive; b. Perth, Australia, July 13, 1945; came to U.S., 1978; s. Walter Bell and Audrey (Begent) M.; m. Heather Dawn, Jan. 31, 1970. BSc with honors, U. Western Australia, 1966, PhD, 1970. Scientist Merrell Dow, Strasbourg, France, 1973-78, head chemistry dept., 1978-83; dir. med. chemistry Smith Kline & French, Phila., 1983-87; v.p. chem. rsch. Smith Kline & Frencia, Phila., 1987-89; v.p. chem. and biol. sci. Smith Kline Beecham, Phila., 1989—. Contbr. numerous articles to profl. jours.; numerous patents in field. Mem. Am. Chem. Soc. (Phila. sect. award 1988). Office: Smith Kline Beecham 709 Swedeland Rd Swedeland PA 19671

METCALF, HAROLD R., government administrator; b. Covington, Ky., May 4, 1947; s. Maurice D. and Elise (Donnell) M.; m. Linda Dehnel, Aug. 7, 1982; children: Christopher, Jennifer, Andrew. AAS, No. Va. Community Coll., Annandale, 1969; BA, George Washington U., 1970, MBA, 1974. Grad. Fed. Exec. Inst.; lic. pilot. Budget analyst FAA, Washington, 1970-72, nat. budget system mgr., 1972-81; mgmt. and budget officer Washington Nat. and Dulles Internat. Airports, Washington, 1981-85; fin. systems and budget mgr. Fed. Transit Adminstrn., U.S. DOT, Washington, 1985—. Designer computer systems. Rep., Mt. Vernon Coun., Alexandria, Va., 1986-88; bd. dirs. Riverside Estates, Alexandria, 1986-88; bd. dirs., treas. Tartan Village, Alexandria, 1981-85. Recipient Silver medal, 1991. Mem. Aircraft Owners and Pilots Assn. Presbyterian. Office: Fed Transit Adminstrn 400 7th St SW Rm 9424 Washington DC 20590-0002

METCALF, JAMES RICHARD, orthodontist; b. Troy, N.Y., Aug. 2, 1950; s. James M. and Ruth Amy (Metcalf) Sunukjian; m. Cynthia A. Komatinsky, Aug. 25, 1973; children: Jeffrey, Jennifer. BA, SUNY, Oswego, 1972; DMD, U. Pitts., 1976, M in Dental Sci., 1980. Resident Strong Meml. Hosp., Rochester, N.Y., 1977; orthodontist Northeastern Dental Assocs., Schenectady, N.Y., 1980-81, Orthodontic Assocs., Lowell, Mass., 1981—. Contbr. articles to profl. jours. Mem. Cen. Congl. Ch. (fin. com. 1988—). Mem. ADA, Am. Assn. Orthodontists (award 1976), Mass. Soc. Orthodontists, Mass. Dental Soc., Greater Lowell Dental Soc. (pres. 1987-88), Nat. Rifle Assn. (cert. instr. pistol, rifle, shotgun, home firearms responsibility and personal protection courses), State Rifle and Pistol Assn. Mass., New Eng. Wood Carvers, Nat. Wood Carvers, Am. Radio Relay League, Westford (Mass.) Sportsmens Club, Tewksbury (Mass.) Rod and Gun Club, Omicron Kappa Upsilon. Home: 63 Thomas Dr Chelmsford MA 01824-2061 Office: Orthodontic Assocs 517 Rogers St Lowell MA 01852-3897

METCALF, MARSHA LINDA, civic worker; b. Camp Lejune, N.C., Apr. 10, 1947; d. George Francis and Helen (Orechwo) G.; m. James Edward Metcalf, Sept. 18, 1976; children: Vanessa Gwynne, Benjamin James. BS, Bluefield State U., 1970. Cert. elem. tchr., Mass. Acct. payable clk. Hoffman Mfg. Co., Boston, 1970-71; prodn. mgr. Cahners Pub. Co., Boston, 1971-76; tchr. Child Garden Nursery Sch., Exeter, N.H., 1976-77. Vol. Am. Found. for the Blind, 1986, 87, Outreach Program Our Lady of Miraculous Medal Ch., Hampton, N.H., 1990—, Sacred Heart Sch., 1988—; vol. Fish of Hampton, Inc., 1982—, chmn., 1986—; mem. N.H.Adv. Com. for Blind, 1984—. Recipient Community Citizen award Ocean Side Grange, 1990. Mem. Seacoast Community Women (chmn. presch. vision and hearing screening program 1987-90), Am. Coun. Blind (N.H. coun. pres. 1984-86), Retinitis PIgmentosa Foun. (Boston chpt. sec. 1972-74). Republican. Roman Catholic. Home: 63 Edgewood Dr Hampton NH 03842-3926

METCALF, MICHAEL WARREN, state senator, educator; b. Wareham, Mass., Apr. 4, 1946; s. William G. and Elizabeth (Carpenter) M.; m. Mary Lee Merrill, Apr. 4, 1970; children: Chase G., Keyes M. AB in Am. History, Colby Coll., 1968; MA in Internat. Rels., U. Ark., 1974. Tchr. Hazen Union Sch., Hardwick, Vt., 1974—; state senator Vt. State Legislature, Montpelier, 1989—. Selectman Town of Greensboro, 1984—, justice of the peace, 1984—. Capt. USAF, 1969-74. Jimmy Doolittle fellow, 1986; finalist Tchr. in Space NASA, 1985. Republican. Congregationalist. Home: RFD Box 1390 Greensboro VT 05841 Office: Vt State Senate State Capitol Montpelier VT 05602

METCALF, TIMOTHY CLARE, computer software development manager; b. Cleve., Dec. 15, 1951; s. Jack Logan and Claire Gizella (Revus) M.; m. Madeline Sue Kelley, July 24, 1976; 1 child, Christopher Michael. BS, Cornell U., 1974; MS, SUNY, Binghamton, 1980. Tech. profl. IBM, Owego, N.Y., 1974-80, system software mgr., 1980-83, applications mgr., 1983-84, sr. programmer mgr., 1984-85, tech. planning mgr., 1985-86; programming cons. IBM, Purchase, N.Y., 1986-88; program mgr. IBM, Endicott, N.Y., 1988—. Asst. cubmaster Boy Scouts Am. Mem. Assn. for Computing Machinery. Home: 1331 Allen Glen Rd Owego NY 13827-3427

METCALFE, DEAN DARREL, medical research physician; b. Medford, Oreg., June 27, 1944; s. Darrell S. and Lucille E. (Moore) M.; m. Joan I. Peterson, Dec. 21, 1977; children: Justin, Jonathan, Elisabet. BS, No. Ariz. U., 1966; MS in Microbiology, U. Mich., 1968; MD, U. Tenn., 1972. Medicine residency Univ. Mich. Hosps., Ann Arbor, 1972-74; clin. assoc. NIH, Bethesda, Md., 1974-77; Rheum fellow Harvard Med. Sch. and Hosp., Boston, 1977-79; clin. investigator NIH, Bethesda, 1979-85; head mast cell physiology lab. of clin. investigation Nat. Inst. of Allergy and Infectious Diseases, Bethesda, 1985—; co-dir. Allergy-Immunology Tng. Program, NIAID/NIH, Bethesda, 1979—; dir. Am. Bd. Allergy-Immunology, Phila., 1990—. Capt. USPHS, 1979—. Recipient Commendation medal USPHS, 1985, Outstanding Svc. medal, USPHS, 1991. Fellow Am. Acad. Allergy and Immunology, Am. Rheumatism Assn.; mem. Am. Fedn. for Clin. Rsch., Am. Soc. for Clin. Investigators, Assn. Am. Physicians. Office: NIH Bldg 10 Rm 11C210 Bethesda MD 20892

METCALFE, MURRAY ROBERT, venture capitalist; b. Toronto, Feb. 3, 1954; s. Marvin Earl and Joan Evelyne (Pepper) M.; m. Nancy Therese Lukitsh, Oct. 12, 1985. B Applied Sci., U. Toronto, 1977; MS, Stanford U., 1979, PhD, 1983. Mgmt. cons. McKinsey & Co., N.Y.C., 1983-87; v.p., gen. ptnr. The Sprout Group, Donaldson, Lufkin & Jenrette, Boston, 1987—. Episcopalian. Home: 12 Ross Rd Belmont MA 02178-2115 Office: Donaldson Lufkin & Jenrette 75 State St Boston MA 02109-1807

METZ, CRAIG HUSEMAN, lawyer; b. Columbia, S.C., Aug. 26, 1955; s. Leonard Huseman and Annette (Worthington) M.; m. Karen Angela McCleary, Aug. 11, 1984. BA, U. Tenn., 1977; JD, Memphis State U., 1986; cert., U.S. Ho. of Reps. Rep. Leadership Parlimentary Law Sch., 1987. Bar: U.S. Supreme Ct., U.S. Ct. Appeals (4th cir.). Intern U.S. Senator Strom Thurmond, Washington, summer 1976, Congressman Floyd Spence, Washington, summer 1977; canvass coord., liaison Campaign to Re-elect Congressman Floyd Spence, 1978; del., chmn. Shelby County Del. to 1983 Tenn. Young Rep. Fedn. Conv.; vice chmn. Shelby County Young Reps., 1983-84, chmn., 1984-85; Shelby County adminstr., asst. to Tenn. state exec. dir. Reagan-Bush Campaign, 1984; field rep. Campaign to Re-elect Congressman Floyd Spence, 1986; spl. asst. to Congressman Floyd Spence, 1986-88; counsel com. on labor and human resources U.S. Senate, 1988-90; commr.'s counsel U.S. Occupational Safety and Health Rev. Commn., Washington, 1990-91; acting dir. office legis. and congl. affairs U.S. Dept. Edn., Washington, 1991—; lawyers for Bush-Quayle, 1988. Judge nat. writing competition U.S. Constn. Bicentennial, S.C., 1987-88; active Friends of Kennedy Ctr.; resident assoc. Smithsonian Instn.; bd. dirs. 3rd tier Memphis Symphony Orch., 1984-86; dist. rep. steering com. Rep. Party of Shelby County, 1983-85. Recipient award of merit Rep. Party of Shelby County, 1985, Outstanding Leadership award Shelby County Young Reps., 1985. Mem. ABA, Fed. Bar Assn., S.C. Bar, Inter-Am. Bar Assn., Bar Assn. D.C., Bar of Supreme Ct. of U.S., Bar of U.S. Ct. Appeals 4th Cir., Am. Soc. Internat. Law, Am. Judicature Soc., Rep. Nat. Lawyers Assn. (state chmn. S.C. chpt. 1987-90), Federalist Soc., Am. Soc. Legal History, Orgn. Am. Historians, U.S. Capitol Hist. Soc., Freedoms Found. Valley Forge, U. So. Caroliniana Soc., S.C. Hist. Soc., Capital Region Assoc. of the Nat. Trust for Hist. Preservation, SAR, Newcomen Soc., St. David's Soc., St. Andrew's Soc. of Washington, Mil. Soc. of War of 1812, Vet. Corps. Arty. of State of N.Y., Gen. Soc.of War of 1812, Mil. Order of Loyal Legion of U.S., Confederate Meml. Assn., Sons of Confederate Vets., Mil. Order Stars and Bars, Nat. Cathedral Assn., Nat. Trust for Scotland, U. Tenn. Nat. Alumni Assn. Washington, Nat. Lawyers Club, Sigma Alpha Epsilon Found., Phi Alpha Delta (v.p. McKellar chpt., Outstanding Svc. award 1983). Republican. Episcopalian. Office: US Dept Edn Office Legis and Congl Affairs 400 Maryland Ave SW Washington DC 20202-3100

METZ, DONALD JOSEPH, scientist; b. Bklyn., May 18, 1924; s. Emil Arthur and Madeline Margaret (Maas) M.; m. Dorothy Gurman, Aug. 30, 1947. BS, St. Francis Coll., Bklyn., 1947; DSc (hon.), St. Francis Coll., 1984; MS, N.Y. Poly. U., 1949, PhD, 1955. From lectr. to prof. St. Francis Coll., 1947-76; from assoc. to sr. scientistsci. edn. Brookhaven Nat. Lab., Upton, N.Y., 1957—. With U.S. Army, 1943-46, ETO. Roman Catholic.

Home: 147 Southern Blvd East Patchogue NY 11772 Office: Brookhaven Nat Lab Upton NY 11973

METZ, HELEN CHAPIN, Middle East analyst; b. Beijing, China, Apr. 13, 1928; d. Selden and Mary Paul (Noyes) Chapin; m. Ronald Irwin Metz, July 14, 1951; children: Mary Selden Metz Evans, Helen Winchester Metz Ketchum, Grace Chapin Metz. AB, Vassar Coll., 1949; MA, Am. U., Beirut, 1954; postgrad., Berkeley Div. Sch. of Yale U., 1966-69. Hostess to The Honorable Selden Chapin, U.S. Amb. to the Netherlands, The Hague, 1950; instr. Beirut Coll. for Women (now Beirut Univ. Coll.), 1954-55, Madeira Sch., Greenway, Va., 1959-60; rsch. analyst Arabian Am. Oil Co., Dhahran, Saudi Arabia, 1956-58, 63-66; administrv. asst. Office Anglican Archbishop, Jerusalem, 1969-75; instr. Mercyhurst Coll., Erie, Pa., 1977-79; exec. dir. Internat. Inst., Erie, 1978-81; dep. head, devel. officer Brent Internat. Sch., Baguio, Philippines, 1981-82; analyst, sr. analyst Fed. Rsch. div. Libr. of Congress, Washington, 1983-87, supr. Middle East, North Africa, 1987-90, supr. Middle East, Africa, Latin Am., 1990—. Editor: Libya: A Country Study, 1989, Iran: A Country Study, 1989, Iraq: A Country Study, 1990, Israel: A Country Study, 1990, Jordan: A Country Study, 1991, Egypt: A Country Study, 1992, Nigeria: A Country Study, 1992. Mentor Edn. for Ministry St. Margaret's Ch., Washington, 1984—; mem. mission devel. adv. com. Diocese Washington, 1987-90, mem. evangelism com., 1990—. Vassar Coll. fellow, 1954-55. Mem. Middle East Studies Assn., Middle East Inst., Phi Beta Kappa (prize, 1949). Democrat. Episcopalian. Home: 3001 Veazey Ter NW Apt 334 Washington DC 20008-5455 Office: Libr of Congress Fed Rsch div 2d and C Sts SE Washington DC 20540

METZ, MARGARET ELIZABETH, medical transcriptionist; b. Elizabeth, N.J., Apr. 22, 1949; d. Whitman Joseph Dickson and Marilyn Doris (Shea) Hill; separated; 1 child, Michelle Elizabeth. High sch. grad., Scotch Plains, N.J. Sec. to pres. Parker Wholesale Florist, Inc., Scotch Plains, 1965-70; sec. Richards Ins., N. Plainfield, N.J., 1970-71; sec. to internat. sec.-treas. Phi Alpha Theta, Allentown, Pa., 1971-79; legal sec. Atty. Wm. G. Sherr, Allentown, Pa., 1979-92; medical transcriptionist pathology dept. Lehigh Valley Hosp., Allentown, 1992—. Fund raiser Lehigh Christian Acad., 1984-90, Lehigh Valley Crisis Pregnancy Ctr., 1989—, Lehigh Valley Christian High Sch., 1990-91, Whitehall Music Parents Assn., 1991—; sec. Trinity Bapt. Ch. Republican.

METZ, RONALD IRWIN, retired priest, addictions counselor; b. Walthill, Nebr., Aug. 11, 1921; s. Harry Elmer and Emma Rilla (Howe) M.; m. Helen Chapin, July 14, 1951; children: Mary Selden Metz Evans, Helen Winchester Metz Ketchum, Grace Chapin. BA in Chinese and Far Ea. Studies, U. Calif., Berkeley, 1945; MA in Mid. Ea. Studies, Am. U., Beirut, 1954; M Div., Yale U., 1969, STD, 1975. Ordained priest Episcopal Ch., 1969. Intelligence officer various govtl. intelligence agys., Far East and Washington, 1944-52; exec. Arabian/Am. Oil Co., Dhahran and Riyadh, Saudi Arabia, 1954-66; deacon Grace Cathedral, San Francisco; priest St. George's Cathedral, Jerusalem, 1969; exec. asst. to archbishop Jerusalem and Mid. East Archbishopric, 1969-75; rector Ch. of the Holy Spirit, Erie, Pa., 1976-81; chaplain Brent Sch., Baguio, Philippines, 1981-82; counselor of chemically dependent Washington, 1982—; addictionologist, vol. New Beginnings Treatment Ctr., P.I.W. Hosp., Washington, 1989-90, Found. Next Step Outpatient Treatment Ctr., Washington, 1991-92; adj. clergy St. Margaret's Ch., Washington; mem. D.C. Diocesan Commn. on Alcohol and Drug Abuse, Washington, 1982-89. Bd. dirs. Mid. East Inst., Washington, 1959-60, Pub. Broadcasting System, n.w. Pa., 1976-81; mem. adv. bd. Children's Aid Internat., 1988-89. Served to col. U.S. Army, 1942-45, CBI, OSS. Decorated Bronze Star. Mem. Iran Diocesan Assn. U.S.A, Phi Beta Kappa, Sigma Chi (chaplain D.C. alumni assn. 1982—). Democrat. Home: # 334 3001 Veazey Ter NW Washington DC 20008

METZ, VERNON WAHL, educator; b. Zelienople, Pa., Oct. 25, 1917; s. Lester Cameron and Alma (Wahl) M.; A.B., Capital U., 1938; M.Litt., U. Pitts., 1940. Chmn. speech dept., dir. advanced placement and student activities North Hills Sch. Dist., Pitts., 1939-69; prin. North Hills Intermediate High Sch., 1969-73; instr. speech Pa. State U., U. Pitts.; speech cons. Pitts. Savs. & Loan, Industry (Pa.) Dept. Pub. Instrn. Served with AUS, 1943-45. Recipient Freedoms Found. medal, 1960, Pa. Dept. Pub. Instrn. citation, 1967. Mem. NEA, Pa. Edn. Assn., Am. Speech Assn., Ea. States Speech Assn., Pa. Speech Assn., Nat. Forensic League (nat. dir.), Tau Kappa Alpha, Phi Alpha Theta, Phi Delta Kappa. Republican. Lutheran. Clubs: Masons, K.T., Rotary. Author: Primary Sources in Teaching and Interpreting American History, 1967. Home: 810 Harden Dr Pittsburgh PA 15229-1109 Office: Pa State U Beaver Campus Monaca PA 15061

METZBOWER, MICHAEL FRANCIS, banker; b. Balt., Mar. 4, 1962; s. William Edward and Evelyn Louise (Senkyr) M.; m. Cynthia Lee Riordon, Aug. 14, 1984; children: Michael Jr., Matthew, John. BSBA, Towson (Md.) State U., 1985; MA in Sci., Johns Hopkins U., 1990. Mktg. analyst Signet Bank/Md., Balt., 1985-88; mktg. officer Merc. Safe Deposit & Trust Co., Balt., 1988—. Mem. Am. Mktg. Assn. Republican. Roman Catholic. Home: 4213 Euclid Ave Baltimore MD 21229 Office: Merc Safe Deposit/Trust Co Ste # 800 409 Washington Ave Towson MD 21204

METZER, PATRICIA ANN, lawyer; b. Phila., Mar. 10, 1941; d. Freeman Weeks and Evelyn (Heap) M.; m. Karl Hormann, June 30, 1980. BA with distinction, U. Pa., 1963, LLB, 1966. Bar: Mass. 1966, D.C. 1972, U.S. Tax Ct. 1988. Assoc., then ptnr. Mintz, Levin, Cohn, Glovsky and Popeo, Boston, 1966-75; assoc. tax legis. counsel U.S. Treasury Dept., Washington, 1975-78; shareholder, dir. Goulston & Storrs, P.C., Boston, 1978—; lectr. program continuing legal edn. Boston Coll. Law Sch., Chestnut Hill, Mass., spring 1974; mem. adv. com. NYU Inst. Fed. Taxation, N.Y.C., 1981-87; mem. practitioner liaison com. Mass. Dept. of Revenue, Mass., 1985-90; speaker in field. Author: Federal Income Taxation of Individuals, 1984; contbr. chpts. to books and articles to profl. jours. Bd. mgrs. Barrington Ct. Condominium, Cambridge, Mass., 1985-86; bd. dirs. University Road Parking Assn., Cambridge, 1988—; trustee Social Law Libr., Boston, 1989—. Mem. ABA (tax sect., chmn. subcom. allocations and distbns. partnership com. 1978-82, vice chmn. legis. com. govt. submissions 1991—), Mass. Bar Assn., Boston Bar Assn. (coun. 1987-89, chmn. tax sect. 1989-91), Fed. Bar Assn. (coun. on taxation, chmn. corp. taxation com. 1977-81, chmn. com. partnership taxation 1981-87), Boston Estate Planning Coun. (exec. com. 1975, 79-82). Office: Goulston & Storrs PC 400 Atlantic Ave Boston MA 02110-3333

METZGER, DIANE HAMILL, paralegal, poet; b. Phila., July 23, 1949; d. David Alexander Sr. and Eunice (Shelton) Hamill; m. Frank Allen Metzger, Aug. 29, 1969; 1 child, Jason Frank. AA in Bus. Adminstrn. magna cum laude, Northampton Coll., 1980; BA in Polit. Sci. magna cum laude, Bloomsburg U., 1987; paralegal cert., Pa. State U., 1988. Statistician Am. Viscose div. FMC Corp., Phila., 1967-72; research asst. Temple U., Phila., 1972-73; clk. II State Correctional Instn. at Muncy, Pa., 1977—; freelance writer, 1964—, paralegal, 1989—. Author: (poems) Coralline Ornaments, 1980; lyricist: Come Now, Shepherds, 1979, Sleep Now, My Baby, 1986; poetry pub. in numerous mags., publs. including Phila. Poets, The Grit, The Long Islander, Inside/Out, Working Parents, South Coast Poetry Jour., Pearl (featured poet 1989), ANIMA: A Jour. of Human Experience, Collages and Bricolages. Recipient numerous awards for poetry including 2d place award Phila. Writers Conf., 1969, 1st prize PEN Writing Awards, 1985, 2d prize Carver Prize Essay Competition, 1986; also Citation for Outstanding Achievement Pa. Ho. of Reps., 1988, Citation for Outstanding Achievement Pa. Senate, 1988. Mem. ASCAP, NAFE, Poetry Soc. Am., Am. Humanist Assn., Laubach Lit. Coun., Mensa. Democrat. Home: 313 Barker St Ridley Park PA 19078-3501 Office: SCIM # 005634 PO Box 180 Rt 405 Muncy PA 17756

METZGER, HENRY, federal research institution administrator; b. Mainz, Germany, Mar. 23, 1932; came to U.S., 1938; naturalized, 1945; s. Paul Alfred and Anne (Daniel) M.; m. Deborah Stashower, June 16, 1957; children: Eran D., Renée V., Carl E. MD, Columbia U., 1957. Chief med. officer chem. immunology sect. Nat. Inst. Arthritis & Musculoskeletal & Skin Disease/NIH, Bethesda, Md., 1973—; br. chief USPHS, Bethesda, 1983—, sci. dir., 1987—, med. officer grade VI, 1975—; Carl Prausnitz Meml. lectr., 1982; Ecker Meml. lectr. Case Western Res. U., Cleve., 1984; Harvey Soc. lectr., 1984; Eli Nadel Meml. lectr. St. Louis U., 1987. Editor: Fc Receptors & the Action of Antibodies, 1990; assoc. editor Ann. Rev.Immunology, 1982—; contbr. numerous articles to profl. jours.; mem. editorial bd. numerous sci. jours. Recipient Meritorious Svc. award USPHS, 1978, Disting. Svc. award, 1985, Joseph Mather Smith prize Columbia U., 1984. Fellow AAAS, Am. Acad. Allergy and Immunology; mem. NAS, Am. Assn. Immunologists (pres. 1991-92), Am. Soc. Biol. Chemists, Am. Soc. Cell Biology, Am. Rheumatism Assn., Internat. Union Immunological Soc. (pres. 1992—), Found. for Advanced Edn. in the Scis. (pres. 1990-92), Alpha Omega Alpha. Home: 3410 Taylor St Bethesda MD 20815-4024 Office: NIH Bldg # 10 Rm # 9N228 Bethesda MD 20892

METZGER, THOMAS ANDREW, mathematics educator; b. Paterson, N.J., July 14, 1944; s. Andrew and Elizabeth Catherine (Boyle) M.; m. Judith Ann Bearss, Aug. 8, 1970; children: Beth Ann, James T., Pamela M., Katie, Bill. BS, Seton Hall U., 1965; MS, Creighton U., 1967; PhD, Purdue U., 1971. Asst. prof. math. Tex. A&M U., College Station, 1971-73; asst. prof. math. and statistics U. Pitts., 1973-80, assoc. prof., 1981—. Author: BMOA on Riemann S., 1987; contbr. articles to profl. jours. Capt. U.S. Army, 1965-73. Mem. Am. Math. Soc., Math. Assn. Am. Office: U of Pitts Dept of Math/Stats Pittsburgh PA 15260

METZLER, KIMBERLY ANN, accountant; b. Lewisburg, Pa., Mar. 24, 1967; d. Terry William and Sherry Ann (Boney) M. BS, Bloomsburg (Pa.) U., 1989. Staff acct. KPMG Peat Marwick, Harrisburg, Pa., 1989-90, Herring and Roll, Sunbury, Pa., 1990—. Home: 88 Queen St Northumberland PA 17857-1922 Office: Herring and Roll 41 S 5th St Sunbury PA 17801-2866

METZNER, CHARLES MILLER, judge; b. N.Y.C., Mar. 13, 1912; s. Emanuel and Gertrude (Miller) M.; m. Jeanne Gottlieb, Oct. 6, 1966. A.B., Columbia U., 1931, LL.B., 1933. Bar: N.Y. 1933. Pvt. practice, 1934; mem. Jud. Council State N.Y., 1935-41; law clk. to N.Y. supreme ct. justice, 1942-52; exec. asst. to U.S. atty. gen. Herbert Brownell, Jr., 1953-54; mem. firm Chapman, Walsh & O'Connell, 1954-59; judge U.S. Dist Ct. (so. dist.) N.Y., 1959—. Mem. Law Revision Commn. N.Y. State, 1959; chmn. com. adminstrn. magistrates system U.S. Jud. Conf. Chmn., Columbia Coll. Council, 1965-66. Pres. N.Y. Young Republican Club, 1941; Trustee Columbia U., 1972-84, trustee emeritus, 1984—; bd. dirs. N.Y.C. Ctr. Music and Drama, 1969-74. Recipient Lawyer Div. of Joint Def. Appeal award, 1961, Columbia U. Alumni medal, 1966, Founders award Nat. Coun. U.S. Magistrates, 1989. Mem. ABA, Am. Law Inst., Fed. Bar Coun. (cert. Disting. Jud. Svc. 1989). Lodge: B'nai B'rith. Office: US Courthouse Foley Sq New York NY 10007-1501

MEURIN, DAWN ADELE, magazine publisher, professional billiards player; b. Brockton, Mass., June 12, 1960; d. Daniel Anetol Edward Meurin and Doris E. (Ryder) Worrell. Various office positions various cos., 1979-87; pub., editor, photographer All About Pool Mag., Pomona, N.J., 1990-92; founder, promoter, organizer Men's All About Pool Tour, New Eng., 1990-92, Women's All About Pool Tour, New Eng., 1991-92, Men's Tri-State Tour, N.Y., N.J., Pa., 1991-92, Women's Tri-State Tour, N.Y., N.J., Pa., 1992. Named Player of Yr., Women's All About Pool Tour, 1991, N.Y. State Women's Champ, 1991, N.H. State Women's Champ, 1991, R.I. State Women's Champ, 1991, New Eng. States Women's Champ, 1990, all sanctioned by Profl. Billiards Tour Assn. Mem. Women's Profl. Billiard Assn. Home and Office: PO Box 93a Pomona NJ 08240

MEURVILLE, FRANCOIS X, leasing company executive; b. Dijon, Cote D'or, France, Feb. 16, 1960; came to U.S., 1990; s. Jean-Claude and Marguerite M. (Lignier) M.; m. Vicki D. Isenberg, June 25, 1985; 1 child, Alexis. Master's, École Supérieure de Commerce, Dijon, 1983. Big tickets asst. mgr. LocaFrance, Paris, 1984-86, asst. v.p., 1989-90; dep. gen. mgr. Afribail, Abidjan, Ivory Coast, 1986-89; treas.-sec. LCA Holding Corp., N.Y.C., 1990—. Mem. Found. for Acctg., Met. Mus. Art, Smithsonian Inst. Roman Catholic. Home: 200 E 82d St # 27D New York NY 10028

MEUSE, KIMBERLY RAE, computer graphics illustrator; b. Des Moines, June 9, 1956; d. Mace A. and Ruth Arlene (Foote) Coolley; m. James David Meuse, Sept. 17, 1983; 1 child, Justin Richard. BA in Advt. Design, Iowa State U., 1978. Art dir. Sta. WMUR-TV, Manchester, N.H., 1979-83; computer graphics illustrator Sanders Assocs., Nashua, N.H., 1983-87, Imagebuilder Design, Hartford, Conn., 1987-89; freelance computer graphics illustrator Conn., N.Y., N.J.; cons. Dugban Prodns., N.Y.C. Illustrator (cover) AV Video Mag., 1986, 88 (Best Cover 1988), Dicomed, 1985 (1st Pl. 1985). Mem. Copley Soc., Conn. Classic Art Assn. Home: 715 Wilcoxson Ave Stratford CT 06497-4241

MEUSEL, THOMAS HUBERT, marketing executive; b. Binghamton, N.Y., May 18, 1964; s. Hubert Alois and Susan Ava (Engel) M. BA, Potsdam Coll., 1986; MBA, Northeastern U., 1991. Materials coord. Cable Data, Braintree, Mass., 1986-87; from sales rep. to sales mgr. MicroCAD Inst., Cambridge, Mass., 1987-88; account rep. Boston CADD Systems, 1988-89; mktg. rep. IBM Corp., Boston, 1989-91, account mktg. rep., 1991—; cons. V.J. Enterprises, Fishkill, N.Y., 1991—. Patentee in field. Mem. Boston Computer Soc., Sierra Club, Northeastern U. Alumni Assn., Potsdam Coll. Alumni Assn. Roman Catholic. Home: 18 Melbourne Ave Newtonville MA 02160 Office: IBM Corp One Copley Pl Boston MA 02116

MEVERS, FRANK CLEMENT, state archivist, historian; b. New Orleans, Oct. 10, 1942; s. Lloyd F. and Mary Ashley (Collins) M.; m. Kathryn Ann Hayes, Dec. 23, 1967; children: John F., Lauren K. BA in History, La. State U., 1965; PhD in Am. History, U. N.C., 1972; MA, La. State U., 1967. Editor Papers of James Madison, Charlottesville, Va., 1972-74, Papers of Josiah Bartlett, Concord, N.H., 1974-77, Papers of William Plumer, Concord, 1977-79; state archivist State of N.H., Concord, 1979—. Editor, author: New Hampshire: State That Made US a Nation, 1989. Mem. Pub. Libr. Bd. Trustees, Concord, 1979—. With U.S. Army, 1967-69, Korea. Episcopalian. Home: 29 Bradley St Concord NH 03301-6432 Office: NH State Archives 71 S Fruit St Concord NH 03301-2410

MEYER, ANDREW C., JR., lawyer; b. N.Y.C., June 28, 1949; s. Andrew and Myra Meyer; m. Kathleen A. Sullivan, May 7, 1982; children—Joshua Andrew, Daniel Gregory, Jessica Kathleen. B.S., C.W. Post Coll., 1971; J.D., Suffolk U., 1974. Bar: Mass. 1974, U.S. Dist. Ct. Mass. 1974, U.S. Ct. Appeals (1st cir.) 1974. Ptnr. Lubin & Meyer, P.C., Boston, 1974—. Contbr. articles to law jours. Mem. Mass. Bar Assn. (chmn. trial practice com. 1983-84, award 1984, seminar speaker, 21st Century Club award 1984, Continuing Legal Edn. Faculty award 1984), Mass. Acad. Trial Attys., Boston Bar Assn. Office: Lubin & Meyer PC 141 Tremont St Boston MA 02111-1209

MEYER, ANDREW R., manufacturing executive; b. Phila., Feb. 15, 1956; s. Herbert C. and Joan (Freedman) M.; m. Constance B. Goldberg, Dec. 20, 1981; children: Jacob Abraham Meyer, Gabrielle Taryn Meyer. BBA, U. Miami, 1977; degree, Gemological Inst. Am., Santa Monica, Calif., 1978. Cert. gemologist, registered supplier, Am. Gem. Soc., Calif. V.p. Oxford Jewelry, Inc., Wyncote, Pa., 1978-80, Bookend Jewelry Inc., Jenkintown, Pa., 1980-84; pres. Andrew Meyer Jewelry, Inc., Fort Washington, Pa., 1985—. Coach Upper Dublin (Pa.) Soccer Club, 1990—. Mem. Am. Gem. Soc. (chmn. regional guilds 1990—, bd. dirs. 1990—), Meadowlands Country Club, Temple Sinai, Debeers Christmas Collection Program. Republican. Jewish. Office: PO Box 100 Fort Washington PA 19034-0100

MEYER, CORD, columnist; b. Washington, Nov. 10, 1920; s. Cord and Katharine (Thaw) M.; m. Mary Pinchot, Apr. 19, 1945 (div. July 1958); children: Quentin, Mark; m. Mary Starke Patteson, Jan. 8, 1966. BA summa cum laude, Yale U., 1942; postgrad., Harvard U., 1946-47, 49-51. Spl. asst. to H. Stasser U.S. Del. to Founding Conf. of U.N., San Francisco, 1945; pres. United World Federalists, N.Y.C., 1947-49; with CIA, Washington, 1951-77, asst. dep. dir. for ops., 1967-73; dir. for ops. CIA, London, 1973-76; columnist Washington, 1978—. Author: Peace or Anarchy, 1947, Facing Reality, 1980. Pres. United World Federalists, N.Y., 1947-49. Capt. USMC, 1942-45. Decorated Bronze star USMC, Guam, 1945, Purple Heart, USMC, Guam, 1945, Presdl. citation USMC, Guam, 1945, three Disting. Intelligence medals CIA, Washington. Mem. Coun. on Fgn. Rels., Washington Inst. on Fgn. Affairs, Met. Club. Democrat. Home: 1523 34th St NW Washington DC 20007 Office: 529 14th St NW Washington DC 20045

MEYER, EDWARD HENRY, advertising agency executive; b. N.Y.C., Jan. 8, 1927; s. I.H. and Mildred (Driesen) M.; m. Sandra Raabin, Apr. 26, 1957; children: Margaret Ann, Anthony Edward. B.A. with honors in Econs, Cornell U., 1949. With Bloomingdale's div. Federated Dept Stores, 1949-51, Biow Co. (agy.), 1951-56; with Grey Advt., Inc., N.Y.C., 1956—; exec. v.p. Grey Advt., Inc., 1963-68, pres., chief exec. officer, 1968—, chmn. bd., 1970—; bd. dirs. May Dept. Stores Co., Inc., Harman Internat. Industries, Inc., Trans-Lux Corp.; bd. dirs., trustees 18 mut. funds Merrill Lynch Asset Mgmt., Inc. Trustee Am. Film Inst., Am. Mus. Natural History, Film Soc. of Lincoln Ctr.; bd. overseers NYU Schs. Bus., trustee, bd. dirs., NYU Med. Ctr., Guggenheim Mus. With USCGR, 1945-47. Mem. Econ. Club (N.Y.C.), Century Country Club, Harmonie Club (N.Y.C.), Univ. Club (N.Y.C.). Office: care Grey Advt Inc 777 3d Ave New York NY 10017

MEYER, FRANK, journalist; b. Port Chester, N.Y., Jan. 1, 1936; s. Moses and Jennie (Marcus) M.; m. Michele Jean Landers, Dec. 31, 1980; children: Jana Beth, Ryan Marc. AB in Philosophy, U. Miami, 1959. Acting dir. English programs Israel Broadcasting Authority, Jerusalem, 1971-72; pvt. practice Miami, 1972-74, 81-82; publicity dir. Fla. Philharm., Miami, 1989-81; reporter Variety, N.Y.C., 1974-75, music editor, 1975-80, spl. sects. dir., 1982-83, mng. editor, 1983-88, editor spl. projects, 1988-90; mng. editor, agt. to mgr. variety, N.Y.C., 1991—; freelance writer-editor, 1991—. With U.S. Army, 1955-58. Democrat. Jewish. Home: 45 Brevoort Rd Chappaqua NY 10514-3503

MEYER, HANS PAUL, brokerage house executive; b. Vienna, Austria, July 8, 1928; came to U.S., 1938; s. Leo and Julie (Feldman) M.; m. Myrna Spencer, Aug. 22, 1959; children: Robert, Bruce. Student, N.Y. Inst. Arts & Scis., 1947, CCNY, 1948-49, Columbia U., 1951-53, N.Y. Inst. of Fin., 1963-68. Cert. Fin. Planner. Pres. Custom Covers, Inc., New Rochelle, N.Y., 1948-68, Sport Tech., Inc., New Rochelle, N.Y., 1948-68, Air Tech. Industries, Clifton, N.J., 1955-68; v.p. Paine Webber, Inc., N.Y.C., 1968-84, Prudential Securities, Inc., Mount Kisco, N.Y., 1984—; assoc. prof., dir. of program, Adelphi U., Garden City, N.Y., 1977-85. Inventor: inflatable structures (8 patents), 1955-62, automated garage (5 patents), 1973; designer: N.J. Expo Pavilion (2nd prize), 1964, curriculum for AdelphiU. Cert. Fin. Planner degree, Garden City, N.Y., 1977; cons. Prentice Hall's Income Tax Text Book, 1978. Active Charitable Trust, Rockefeller U., N.Y.C., 1978, White Plains (N.Y.) Hosp., White Plains (N.Y.) Sch. Bd., Am. Diabetes Assn., N.Y.C., 1980. Office: Prudential Securities Inc 83 S Bedford Rd Mount Kisco NY 10549

MEYER, IRWIN STEPHAN, lawyer, accountant; b. Monticello, N.Y., Nov. 14, 1941; s. Ralph and Janice (Cohen) M.; children: Kimberly B., Joshua A. BS, Rider Coll., 1963; JD, Cornell U., 1966. Bar: N.Y. 1966; CPA, N.J. Tax mgr. Lybrand Ross Bros. & Montgomery, N.Y.C., 1966-71; mem. Ehrenkranz, Ehrenkranz & Schultz, N.Y.C., 1971-74; prin. Irwin S. Meyer, 1974-77, 82—; mem. Levine, Honig, Eisenberg & Meyer, 1977-78, Eisenberg, Honig & Meyer, 1978-81, Eisenberg, Honig, Meyer & Fogler, 1981-82. With U.S. Army, 1966-71. Mem. ABA, N.Y. Bar Assn., Am. Assn. Atty.-CPAs, N.Y. Assn. Atty.-CPAs, AICPA, N.J. Soc. CPAs. Office: 1 Blue Hill Plz Ste 1006 Pearl River NY 10965-8663

MEYER, LAWRENCE GEORGE, lawyer; b. East Grand Rapids, Mich., Oct. 2, 1940; s. George and Evangeline (Boerma) M.; children from previous marriage: David Lawrence, Jenifer Lynne; m. Linda Elizabeth Buck, May 31, 1980; children: Elizabeth Tilden, Travis Henley. BA with honors, Mich. State U., 1961; JD with distinction, U. Mich., 1964. Bar: Wis., 1965, Ill. 1965, U.S. Supreme Ct. 1968, D.C. 1972. Assoc. Whyte, Hirschboeck, Minahan, Hardin & Harland, Milw., 1964-66; atty. antitrust div. U.S. Dept. Justice, Washington, 1966-68; legal counsel U.S. Senator Robert P. Griffin, Mich., 1968-70; dir. policy planning FTC, Mich., 1970-72; ptnr. Patton, Boggs & Blow, Washington, 1972-85, Arent, Fox, Kintner, Plotkin & Kahn, Washington, 1985—. Contbr. articles on antitrust and trial practice to law jours.; asst. editor. U. Mich. Law Rev., 1960-61. Recipient Disting. Svc. award FTC, 1972. Mem. ABA, D.C. Bar Assn., Wis. Bar Assn., Ill. Bar Assn., U.S. Senate Ex S.O.B.'s Club, City Tavern Club, Congl. Country Club, Pisces Club, The Bayhill Club. Home: 8777 Belmart Rd Potomac MD 20854-1610 Office: 1050 Connecticut Ave NW Washington DC 20036-5303

MEYER, MARION M., editorial consultant; b. Sheboygan, Wis., July 14, 1923; d. Herman O. and Viola A. (Hoch) M. BA, Lakeland Coll., 1950; MA, NYU, 1957. Payroll clk. Am. Chair Co., Sheboygan, 1941-46; tchr. English and religion, dir. athletics Am. Sch. for Girls, Baghdad, Iraq, 1950-56; mem. edn. and publ. staff United Ch. Bd. for Homeland Ministries, United Ch. Press/Pilgrim Press, 1958-64, sr. editor, 1965-88, ret., 1988; cons. to individuals and orgns. on editorial matters and copyrights. Editor: Penney Retirement Community Newsletter, 1990—; writer (hymns) Look to God, Be Radiant, 1989, Be Still, 1990; contbr. articles to various publs. Incorporating mem. Contact Phila., Inc., 1972, bd. dirs., 1972-75, v.p., chmn. com. to organize community adv. bd., chmn. auditing com., editor newsletter, 1972-74, pres., 1974-75, assoc. mem., 1977—; mem. ofcl. bd. Old First Reformed Ch., Phila., 1984-89; deacon United Ch. Christ, 1984—, Mid.-East Com. of Pa. SE Conf. United Ch. Christ, 1986-88. Honored as role model United Ch. of Christ, 1982, 85. Mem. AAUW, Nat. Mus. Women in the Arts (charter mem.). Home: PO Box 656 Penney Farms FL 32079

MEYER, MARY-LOUISE, art gallery executive; b. Boston, Feb. 21, 1922; d. Alonzo Jay and Louise (Whitledge) Shadman; m. Norman Meyer, Aug. 9, 1941; children: Wendy C., Bruce R., Harold Alton, Marilee, Laurel. BA, Wellesley Coll., 1943; MS, Wheelock Coll., 1965. Head tchr. Page Sch., Wellesley Coll., Mass., 1955-60; instr. early childhood edn. Pine Manor Coll., Brookline, Mass., 1960-65; chaplain/counselor Charles St. Jail, Boston, 1974-79; Christian Sci. practitioner, Wellesley, Mass., 1974—; owner Alpha Gallery, Boston, 1972-87; cons. Living & Learning Centers, Boston, 1966-69; 2d reader Christian Sci. Ch., 1979-82. Contbr. articles to profl. jours. Overseer Sturbridge Village, 1981—, trustee, 1986; visitor Am. Decorative Arts dept. Mus. Fine Arts, Boston, 1973—; chmn. Wellesley Voters Rights Com., 1983-84; state organizer Ednl. Channel 2 Group, Boston, 1960; cofounder Boston Assn. for Childbirth Edn., 1950; overseer Strawberry Banke Living Mus., 1987; trustee Maine Coast Artists, Rockport, Maine, 1991; incorporator Bay Chamber Concerts, Rockport, 1990. Mem. Mus. Trustees Assn., Farnsworth Mus., Waldoboro Hist. Soc., Soc. for Pres. New Eng. Antiquities, Wellesley Coll. Club.

MEYER, MICHAEL, automobile company executive; b. Derby, Conn., Sept. 15, 1958; s. Samuel and Margaret Lorraine (Slivinski) M. BA, U. Conn., 1980; MBA, Coll. of William and Mary, 1982. Auditor supr. Anheuser Busch Entertainment, Williamsburg, Va., 1981-82; dist. mgr. Ford Motor Co., Falls Church, Va., 1982-85; reg. consumer svc. mgr. BMW of N.Am., Inc., Woodcliff Lake, N.J., 1985-90; nat. owner rels. mgr. Rolls-Royce Motor Cars, Inc., Lyndhurst, N.J., 1991—. Democrat. Home: 54 Woodledge Ct Rockaway NJ 07866-2245 Office: Rolls-Royce Motor Cars Inc Lyndhurst NJ 07071

MEYER, MICHELE JEAN (MIKKI MEYER), marriage and family therapist; b. Coral Gables, Fla., June 10, 1949; d. Bernard and Cynthia (Kuowitt) Landers; m. Frank Meyer; children: Jana Beth, Ryan Marc. Student, U. South Fla., 1967-70; BS in Early Childhood Edn., Fla. Internat. U., 1972, MS in Counseling, 1981. Cert. counselor; cert. family life educator; lic. marriage and family therapist, Fla. Co-owner, operator Famous Restaurant, Miami Beach, Fla., 1970-78; producer Richard Boone Repertory Co. of fla., Miami, 1978-80; asst. dir. Intensive Counseling State Svcs., Miami, 1981-82; dir. social svcs. Pius XII Youth and Family Svcs., Bronx, N.Y., 1982-87; site supr. PINS Mediation and Diversion, N.Y.C., 1987—; coord. Peace Program, N.Y.C., 1991—; pvt. practice Chappaqua, 1982—, N.Y.C., 1982—; coord. Parent Edn. and Custody Effectiveness, N.Y.C., 1991. Chmn. Drug Abuse Prevention Coun., New Castle, N.Y., 1987—; mem. adolescent adv. bd. Regent Hosp., N.Y.C., 1990—; mem. N.Y.C. Mayor Policy Com., PINS, N.Y.C., 1987—; adv. bd. Student Assistance Programs. Mem. APGA, ASCD, Am. Assn. for Marriage and Family Therapy (mem. coun.), Nat. Coun. on Family Rels. (cert. family life edu-

cator), Nat. Bd. Cert. Counselors, N.Y. Assn. for Marriage and Family Therapy (pres. Westchester County/Mid-Hudson chpt. 1988—), Kappa Delta Pi. Home: 45 Brevoort Rd Chappaqua NY 10514-3503 Office: PINS Mediation and Diversion 60 Lafayette St # 422F New York NY 10013-4048

MEYER, RICHARD ALAN, songwriter, stage designer; b. New Rochelle, r, N.Y., Sept. 6, 1952; s. Charles Herbert and Anne (Bordon) M. BA, U. Bridgeport. Author of songs, 1983—; songwriter (albums) Laughing/Scared, The Good Life!; editor: Fast Folk Musical mag., N.Y.C., 1985—; resident designer East Coast Arts, New Rochelle, 1986-91, Berkshire Pub. Theatre, Pittsfield, Mass., 1983-91. Office: Fast Folk Mus Mag PO Box 938 Village St New York NY 10014

MEYER, STEPHEN ALAN, federal banking official; b. Washington, Feb. 28, 1949; s. Morton Allan and Miriam Janet (Blevins) M.; m. Frances Ann Katzman, Aug. 21, 1971; children: Alyssa Rachel, Julia Katharine. AB, Oberlin Coll., 1970; MA, M.Phil., Yale U., 1972, PhD, 1979. Lectr. in fin. U. Pa., Phila., 1974-79; asst. prof. fin. U. Pa., 1979-84; sr. economist Fed. Res. Bank Phila., 1980-84, rsch. advisor, 1984-87, v.p., assoc. dir. rsch., 1987—; adj. asst. prof. fin. U. Pa, Phila, 1984-86, adj. assoc. prof. fin., 1986-89, adj. prof. fin., 1989—. Contbr. articles to profl. jours. NSF grad. fellow, 1971-74, resch. fellow Rodney L. White Ctr. for Fin. Rsch., Phila., 1975, 79. Mem. Am. Econ. Assn., Am. Fin. Assn., Phila. Coun. Bus. Economists. Office: Fed Res Bank Phila 10 Independence Mall Philadelphia PA 19106

MEYER, WOLFGANG EBERHARD, mechanical engineering educator, retired; b. Berlin, Aug. 2, 1910; came to U.S., 1937; s. Alfred and Martha M.; m. Ann Nachouk, June 15, 1946; 1 child, Frances L. Anderson. BSME, U. Stuttgart, Fed. Republic Germany, 1933; MSME, U. Hannover, Fed. Republic Germany, 1935. Rsch. engr. Daimler-Benz AG, Gaggenau, Germany, 1935-37; head, diesel lab. Am. Bosch Corp., Springfield, Mass., 1938-40; rsch. engr. Yale U., New Haven, Conn., 1940-43; project engr. Bulova Watch Co., Woodside/L.I., N.Y., 1944-45; chief engr. Rsch. Engring. Corp., New Haven, Conn., 1945-47; prof. of mech. engring. Pa. State U., University Park, 1947-76; dir. automotive rsch. Pa. Transp. Inst. of Pa. State U., 1958-76; vis. rsch. prof. Chevron Rsch. Ctr., Richmond, Calif., 1961; pvt. cons. Editor: Frictional Interaction of Tire and Pavement, 1983, Surface Characteristics of Roadways, 1990; patentee in field. Recipient MetroLife award on Accident Prevention, Nat. Safety Coun., 1968, Outstanding Rsch. award Pa. State Engring. Soc., 1978. Fellow ASTM (com. chmn. 1970-76, award of merit 1978, Shelburne award 1983), Soc. Automotive Engrs. (transport rsch. bd., com. chmn. 1970-76). Republican. Office: Pa Transp Inst 230 Research Office Bldg University Park PA 16802

MEYERS, ABBEY SUE, foundation administrator; b. Bklyn., Apr. 11, 1944; d. Herbert and Blossom (Ruben) Feldman; m. Jerrold B. Meyers, Oct. 23, 1966; children: David, Adam, Laura. AAS, N.Y.C. Community Coll., 1962. Comml. artist various advt. agys., N.Y.C., 1962-65; dir. patient svcs. Tourette Syndrome Assn., Bayside, N.Y., 1980-85; exec. dir., founder Nat. Org. for Rare Disorders, New Fairfield, Conn., 1985—; U.S. commr. Nat. Commn. on Orphan Diseases, Washington, 1986-89; mem. subcom. Human Gene Therapy NIH, Bethesda, Md., 1989—; mem. Health Care Payor Adv. Commn. of Conn. Commn. on Hosps. and Health Care, 1992—. Author: (with others) Orphan Drugs and Orphan Diseases: Clinical Reality and Public Policy, 1983, (with others) Cooperative Approaches to Research and Development of Orphan Drugs, 1985, (with others) Tourette Syndrome: Clinical Understanding and Treatment, 1988, (with others) Physicians Guide to Rare Diseases, 1992. Bd. dirs. Nat. Orphan Drug and Device Found., N.Y.C., 1982-85; leader Coalition to Pass Orphan Drug Act of 1983, 1979-82. Recipient Pub. Health Svc. award HHS, 1985, Commr.'s Spl. citation FDA, 1988. Mem. Nat. Health Coun. (bd. dirs. 1989—), Alliance of Genetic Support Groups (bd. dirs. 1987-89). Office: Nat Org for Rare Disorders PO Box 8923 Fairwood Profl Bldg New Fairfield CT 06812

MEYERS, GEORGE EDWARD, plastics company executive; b. N.Y.C., June 26, 1928; s. Sol and Ethel (Treppel) M. Student, Sampson Coll., 1948-49, Columbia U., 1949-50; m. Marianna Jacobson, Dec. 8, 1955; children: Deborah Lynn, Joanne Alyssa. Technician Manhattan Project, 1944; tech. rep. Mearl Corp., 1952-56; sales mgr. Rona Labs., Bayonne, N.J.1956-59; v.p. Dimensional Pigments Corp., Bayonne, 1959-60; pres. Plastic Cons. Internat., Inc., Dix Hills, N.Y., 1959—, Tech. Machinery Corp., Plainview, N.Y., 1963-69; pres. Extrudyne, Inc., Amityville, N.Y., 1970-77, also bd. dirs.; bd. dirs. rsch. and devel. Homeland Industries, Bohemia, N.Y., 1977-80; bd. dir. ops. Aqua-Sol, Inc., Deer Park, N.Y., 1980-85; tchr., staff cons. N.Y.C. Bd. Higher Edn., Bronx Community Coll., 1966-70; lectr. NYU, Technion, Haifa, Israel. Served with CIC, AUS, 1946-48. Mem. Soc. Plastics Engrs. (sr. mem., v.p. N.Y. sect. 1967-68), Soc. Plastics Industry (profl. mem.), Am. Ordnance Assn., Aircraft Owners and Pilots Assn, NRA (life mem., cert. instr.), Am. Chem. Soc., Internat. Assn. Housing Sci. (charter mem.), Internat. Assn. Soilless Culture. Contbr. articles to profl. jours. Patentee in field; lectr.; seminar conductor in plastics and hydroponics and seminar leader Modern Plastics Mag. courses. Avocations: flying, numismatics, pistol shooting, antique collector, tech. expert to legal firms and qualified expert witness in state and federal courts. Home and Office: 25 Penn Dr Dix Hills NY 11746-8500

MEYERS, PETER L., banker; b. Syracuse, N.Y., Mar. 19, 1939; s. Edwin Clark and Phyllis (Schiess) M.; m. Teresa Maley, Mar. 4, 1963; children: Gary, Gregory, Cheryl. BBA, Syracuse U., 1974. With Merchants Nat. Bank & Trust Co., Syracuse, N.Y., 1963—, v.p., comml. loan officer, 1975-78, v.p., sr. loan officer, 1978-79, sr. v.p., 1979, exec. v.p., 1980-88, exec. v.p., chief operating officer, 1988, pres., chief exec. officer, 1988—; vice chair, dir. N.Y. Bus. Devel. Corp. Bd. dirs. Met. Devel. Assn., Syracuse, Syracuse Housing Partnership, United Way Cen. N.Y., Mus. Sci. and Tech. Found.; trustee Erie Canal Mus.; bd. regents LeMoyne Coll.; mem. Syracuse Onondaga County Youth Bd. Mem. Am. Inst. Banking, Syracuse C. of C. (bd. dirs.), Syracuse U. Alumni Assn., Century Club, Onondaga Golf and Country Club. Office: Mchts Nat Bank & Trust 216220 S Warren St Syracuse NY 13202

MEYERS, WILLIAM FRANCIS, brokerage house executive; b. Bklyn., Apr. 26, 1947; s. William Thomas and Catherine (Walsh) M.; m. Patricia Ann Meehan, Oct. 23, 1971; children: Tracy Elizabeth, Paul Corbett. BS, Fordham U., 1969, MBA, 1975. Bond trader Eastman Dillon, N.Y.C., 1969-71; mcpl. broker MKI Securities Corp., N.Y.C., 1971-75, v.p. corp. bonds, 1975-78, sr. v.p. corp. bonds, 1978-82, exec. v.p., 1982-88, now bd. dirs.; exec. v.p. MKI Eurocurrencies Inc., 1982-84, pres., 1984-86, also bd. dirs.; exec. v.p. MKI Money Markets Inc., N.Y.C., 1982-84, pres., 1984-86; mng. dir. Meyers & Morgan Inc., 1988-90; pres. Meyers and Morgan Inc., 1990—. Mem. Met. Mus. Art. Mem. Nat. Soc. for Hist. Preservation, Westchester Country Club (Rye, N.Y.), St. James Club (London). Republican. Roman Catholic.

MEYERSON, MARTIN, aerospace engineer; b. East Orange, N.J., Oct. 22, 1927; s. Max and Anna (Slobodin) M.; children: Mark Lawrence, Jann Lesley Sidorov, Jack David. BSEE, N.J. Inst. Tech., 1948, MSEE, 1951. Asst. project engr. Kay Electric Co., Pinebrook, N.J., 1949-50; program mgr. U.S. Army Signal Engring. Labs., Fort Monmouth, N.J., 1950-57; with Martin Marietta Corp., 1957-79; dir. programs Martin Marietta Corp., Balt., 1977-79; dep. program dir. Fairchild Rep. Co., Farmingdale, N.Y., 1979-87; dir. bus. analysis Allied Signal Aerospace Co., Arlington, Va., 1987-88; dir. bus. planning Ford Aerospace Corp., McLean, Va., 1988-90; asst. to pres., dir. bus. devel. Elec. Systems div. Grumman Corp., Great River, N.Y., 1990—; mem. faculty, lectr. Dept. Def. Weapon Systems Mgmt. Ctr., Dayton, Ohio, 1967-71; mem. study panel, cons. Congl. Commn. on Govt. Procurement, Washington, 1971-72; mem. seminar team on environ. quality U.S. Dept. Commerce, Prague, Czechoslovokia, 1972; chmn. environ. quality Md. Gov.'s Science Adv. Coun., Annapolis, Md., 1957-77. Author articles, reports in field. Mem. by-laws com. Admiralty Bd. dirs., Bay Shore, N.Y., 1983-85. Fellow AIAA (assoc.), IEEE (sr.). Republican. Jewish. Home: 187 Captains Way The Admiralty West Bay Shore NY 11706 Office: Grumman Corp Elec Systems Div Sunrise Hwy # A38 043 Great River NY 11739 also: The Promenade 5225 Pooks Hill Rd Bethesda MD 20814

MEYERSON, MORTON, communications executive; b. N.Y.C., Jan. 16, 1935; s. Rachel (Lochmond) M.; m. Roberta, Jan. 3, 1959; children: James, William, Jennifer, Alexander. BA, NYU, 1956. Reporter, editor Fairchild News Svc., N.Y.C., 1956-58, AP, N.Y.C., 1958-59; assoc. editor Biddle Survey, N.Y.C., 1961-65; editor, writer Eastman Dillon, N.Y.C., 1965-66; dir. communications Coopers & Lybrand, N.Y.C., 1966-83, Arthur Young, N.Y.C., 1983-89; dir. communications Ernst & Young, N.Y.C., 1989—, bd. dirs. With USAFR, 1952-59. Mem. Overseas Press Club. Home: 21 Canterbury Rd Great Neck NY 11021-2123 Office: Ernst & Young 787 7th Ave New York NY

MEZA, PEDRO THOMAS, history educator; b. N.Y.C., Sept. 2, 1941; s. Louis Carlos and Elizabeth Jane (Gibson) Meza De Leon; m. Rose Ethel Althaus, Dec. 24, 1946; children: Winifred Elizabeth, Wallis Ethel. AB, NYU, 1962, MA, 1963, PhD, 1967. Teaching asst. NYU, 1965-66; lectr. CUNY, 1966-67; asst. prof. Queens Borough Community Coll., CUNY, 1967-74, assoc. prof., 1974-82, prof., 1982—. Editor: Readings in Western Civilization, 1970; contbr. articles to profl. jours. Mem. AAUP, Soc. for History of Technology. Democrat. Office: Queensborough Community Col 56th Ave & Springfield Blvd Bayside NY 11364

MEZEI, MIHALY, chemist; b. Budapest, Hungary, June 17, 1944; came to U.S., 1973; s. Arpad and Eva (Erdely) M.; m. Katalin Agnes Bencsath, July 2, 1970. Diploma, Eötrös Lorand U., Budapest, Hungary, 1966, PhD, 1972. Systems programmer Hungarian Chem. Industries, Budapest, Hungary, 1966-72, Young & Rubican Internat. Inc., N.Y.C., 1973-74; postdoctoral fellow NYU, N.Y.C., 1974-76; sr. rsch. assoc. Hunter Coll., CUNY, N.Y.C., 1976-86, adj. assoc. prof., 1976-78, 88-90, mgr. biomolecular computing, 1987—; rsch. assoc. prof. Mt. Sinai Sch. Medicine, CUNY, N.Y.C., 1991—; mem. grad. chemistry faculty CUNY, Grad. Ctr., N.Y.C., 1989—. Contbr. over 70 sci. papers to profl. publs. Bd. dirs. Westerly Tenants' Assn., N.Y.C., 1980—. Grantee CUNY, 1988-91; recipient Shannon award NIH, 1991-93. Mem. Am. Chem. Soc., N.Y. Acad. Scis., Sigma Xi. Office: CUNY Mt Sinai Sch of Medicine Dept Physiology & Biophysics New York NY 10029

MFUME, KWEISI, congressman; b. Balt., Oct. 24, 1948; children: Donald, Kevin, Keith, Ronald, Michael. BS, Morgan State U.; MA, Johns Hopkins U., 1984. Mem. Balt. City Council, 1979-87, 100th-102d Congresses from 7th Md. dist., Washington, 1987—; former asst. prof. polit. sci. Morgan State U., Balt. Office: US Ho of Reps 217 Cannon House Office Bldg Washington DC 20515

MIALE, JOSEPH NICOLAS, chemist; b. Johnston, R.I., May 9, 1919; s. Francesco Candido and Incoronata (Granieri) M.; m. Margaret Amelia Woodburn, Aug. 6, 1955; children: Joanne, Joseph Francis, Ruth Constance. BS in Chemistry, Providence Coll., 1940; MS in Chemistry, Tex. A&M U., 1947. Instr. chemistry Tex. A&M U., College Station, 1946-47; rsch. chemist Mobil R & D Corp., Paulsboro, N.J., 1947-61; sr. rsch. chemist Mobil R & D Corp., Princeton, N.J., 1962-84; ret. Contbr. articles to profl. jours.; co-author: Red Rail Fence, 1980. Mem., v.p. Lawrence Twp. Conservation Adv. Com., Lawrenceville, N.J., 1966-71; mem. adv. com. Mercer County 4-H, Trenton, 1972—; mem. Mercer County Bd. Agr., Trenton, 1978—; guide Bowman's Hill Wild Flower Preserve, Washington Crossing, Pa., 1983—; vol. N.J. Network (TV), Trenton. Maj. U.S. Army, 1941-46, USAR, 1947-59. Recipient Disting. Svc. Natural Resource Conservation award Mercer County Soil Conservation, 1970. Mem. Am. Chem. Soc. (emeritus), Nat. Audubon Soc., Trenton Naturalist Club, Lawrence Five Sr. Club, Exploring Nature 4-H Club (leader). Roman Catholic. Home: 25 Merritt Dr Trenton NJ 08648-3131

MICCICHE, ALPHONSE SALVATORE, photographer; b. Maynard, Mass., May 21, 1942; s. R. Samuel and Marion (Terrasi) M.; m. Helen M. Ferguson, Apr. 30, 1966; children: Lisa Micciche Murray, Thomas. Grad., N.Y. Inst. Photography, 1961. Photographer, studio adminstr. Samuels Studio Photography, Maynard, 1961—. Mem. Profl. Photographers Assn. Am. (master of photography 1987, craftsman photographer 1990, contbr. to loan collection book 1991), Profl. Photographers Assn. New Eng. (Hastings award), Profl. Photographers Assn. Mass., Indsl. Photographers New Eng. (past pres.), Elks. Office: Samuels Studio Inc PO Box 201 Maynard MA 01754-0201

MICEK, KATHERINE DANLEY, physician, retired; b. Phila., Dec. 27, 1925; d. Hollis Lapp and Marian Earl (Scholes) Danley; m. Edward William Micek, Sept. 3, 1950; 1 child, Andrea Madelaine. AB, Gettysburg Coll., 1945; MD, Temple U., 1950. Diplomate Am. Bd. Family Practice. Anesthesia resident Temple U., 1951-54; anesthesiologist, chief dept. Shriners Hosp., Phila., 1960-63, mem. staff, 1964-70; mem. med. liaison dept. Merck Sharp & Dohme Med. Rsch. Div., West Point, Pa., 1961-65; pvt. practice Phila., 197-75, 82-89; student health physician U. Pa., Phila., 1975-78; asst. dir. med. dept. Septa Transp. System, Phila., 1978-81; staff physician Inglis House, Phila., 1987-89; retired from pvt. practice, 1989. Republican.

MICHAEL, EUGENE RICHARD, professional baseball team executive; b. Kent, Ohio, June 2, 1938; children: Sandra, Mark, Matthew. BS, Kent State U. Baseball player various minor league teams, 1959-66, Pitts. Pirates (Maj. Leagues), 1966, Los Angeles Dodgers, 1967, N.Y. Yankees, 1968-74, Detroit Tigers, 1975; with Boston Red Sox, 1976; mgr. Columbus Clippers (N.Y. Yankees Farm System), 1979; with N.Y. Yankees, 1980-86, gen. mgr., 1980, mgr., 1981, 82, scout, 1981, 82, 83, 88, coach, 1984-86, now v.p., gen. mgr.; mgr. Chgo. Cubs, 1986-87. Office: NY Yankees Yankee Stadium E 161st St and River Ave Bronx NY 10451*

MICHAEL, MILES REGAN, II, messenger; b. N.Y.C., Oct. 9, 1955; s. Miles Regan and Laura Laurestie (Bonnemere) M. Student, John Jay Coll., 1972-75, 77-79. Provisional housing asst. N.Y.C. Housing Authority, 1977; bank teller Cen. Savs. Bank, N.Y.C., 1979, Midlantic Bank, Tenafly, N.J., 1979-80; kennel keeper Pet Lodges of Am., N.Y.C., 1980-81; messenger Archer Courier Systems, Inc., N.Y.C., 1981—. Team capt. N.Y. Gay Pool League, Manhattan, N.Y., 1990-91, 91-92. Office: PO Box 554 Ansonia Station 1980 Broadway New York NY 10023

MICHAEL, SANDRA DALE, reproductive endocrinology educator, researcher; b. Sacramento, Calif., Jan. 23, 1945; d. Gordon G. and Ruby F. (Johnson) M.; m. Dennis P. Murr, Aug. 12, 1967 (div. 1974). BA, Calif. State Coll., Sonoma, 1967; PhD, U. Calif., Davis, 1970. NIH postdoctoral fellow U. Calif., Davis, 1970-73, asst. rsch. geneticist, 1973-74; asst. prof. SUNY, Binghamton, 1974-81, assoc. prof., 1981-88, prof. reproductive endocrinology, 1988—, dept. chair, 1992—; mem. NIH Reproductive Endocrinology Study Sect., 1991—; cons., presenter in field; grant reviewer NIH, NSF, USDA and others. Contbr. articles to profl. jours. Vice chair Tri Cities Opera Guild, Binghamton, 1987-90, chair 1990—; mem. Harpur Forum, Binghamton, 1987—, SUNY Found., Binghamton, 1990—. Grantee NIMH, 1976-79, Nat. Cancer Inst., 1977-80, 83-87, Nat. Inst. Environ. Health Scis., 1979-80, NSF, 1981-83, NIH, 1987—. Mem. Endocrine Soc., Soc. for the Study of Reprodn., Soc. for Study of Fertility, Am. Soc. for Immunology of Reprodn., Women in Endocrinology (sec.-treas. 1992—), Soc. for Exptl. Biology and Medicine, N.Y. Acad. Sci., Sigma Xi. Office: SUNY Dept Biol Scis PO Box 6000 Binghamton NY 13902-6000

MICHAEL, SANDRA MARIE, athletics director; b. Phila., Feb. 13, 1953; d. Domenic and Mary Jo (Joseph) Stumpo; m. Robert Steven Michael, June 26, 1976; children: Brian, Julie. BS in Phys. Edn., Temple U., 1975. Tchr.'s instructional cert., Pa. Dir. phys. edn. Nazareth Acad. Grade Sch., Phila., 1974—; health instr. Phila. Sch. Bd., 1975-76; dir. health edn., phys. edn. instr. Nazareth Acad. High Sch., Phila., 1976-81; dir. athletics Holy Family Coll., Phila., 1985—; dir. game day ops. Phila. Spirit U.S. Basketball League, 1991—; pres. Keystone Athletic Conf., Phila., 1988—. Asst. softball coach Torresdale Boy's Club, Phila., 1990—. Nat. Assn. Intercollegiate Athletics (chair. dist. 19 women's basketball 1989—, chair women's softball 1991—, Athletic Adminstr. of Yr. award 1991). Office: Holy Family Coll Grant and Frankford Aves Philadelphia PA 19114

MICHAELIS, ARTHUR FREDERICK, health care company executive; b. N.Y.C., July 24, 1941; s. Paul F. and Rose (Landsberry) M.; m. Judith Anne Gordy, June 7, 1964; children: Bradley, Jennifer. BS, Bucknell U., 1963; MS, U. Wis., 1965, PhD, 1967; MBA, Fairleigh Dickinson U., 1976. Dir. quality control Sandoz, Inc., E. Hanover, N.J., 1970-71, dir. pharmacy and analytical chemistry, 1971-77, dir. pharm. devel., 1977-79; pres., applied tech. div. KV Pharm. Corp., St. Louis, 1979-80; dir., rsch. and devel. McNeil Consumer Products, Ft. Washington, Pa., 1980-81; v.p., rsch. and devel. Menley and James Lab, Phila., 1981-85; pres. Controlled Therapeutics, Malvern, Pa., 1985-91; founder, CEO, chmn. bd. Gt. Valley Pharms., Inc., Malvern, 1991—; chmn., dir. Polysystems Healthcare Ltd., East Kilbride, Scotland, 1986-91, Controlled Therapeutics-Scotland, 1985-91; pres., dir. Advanced Med. Techs., 1989-91. Contbr. articles to profl. jours.; editorial bd.: Analytical Profiles of Drug Substances. Capt. U.S. Army, 1968-69. Fellow Am. Inst. Chemists; mem. AAAS, Am. Pharm. Assn., Acad. Pharm. Scis., N.J. Pharm. Quality Control Assn., N.Y. Acad. Scis., Chester Valley Golf Club (Malvern, Pa.), Morris County Golf Club (Convent Station, N.J.). Office: Great Valley Pharms Inc Ste 160 10 Great Valley Pky Malvern PA 19355

MICHAELS, ADLAI ELDON, retired chemistry educator; b. Alma, Wis., Nov. 22, 1913; s. Frederick William and Olga (Wald) M.; m. Josephine Blake, Mar. 16, 1941 (dec. Mar. 1969); children: Carol Michaels Price, Lee F.; m. Opal Carfrey, June 4, 1971. BS in Chemistry, U. Wis., 1935; PhD in Chemistry, Ohio State U., 1939; DSc (hon.), Washington & Jefferson Coll., 1984. Asst. Ohio State U., Columbus, 1935-39; instr. U. Tenn., Knoxville, 1940-43; rsch. chemist Esso Rsch. and Engring. Co., Linden, N.J., 1943-59; from asst. prof. to prof. Chemistry Washington and Jefferson Coll., Washington, Pa., 1959-83; ret., 1983; cons. to mem. U.S. Ho. Reps., Washington, 1970-83. Author lab. manuals; patentee in field. Advisor Delta Tau Delta, 1964-83; sec., bd. dirs. Indsl. Devel. Authority of Washington County, Pa., 1982—. Mem. Air Pollution Assn. S.W. Pa., Elks (lectr., leading knight). Home: 73 Crestvue Rd Washington PA 15301-2919

MICHAELS, CRAIG ADAM, psychologist; b. N.Y.C., Mar. 2, 1954; s. Melvin A. and Helen (Courtney) M.; m. Susan Jane Knowles; children: Noah Lynn, Alana Rose, Esther Leor. BFA, San Francisco Art Inst., 1976; MA in Spl. Edn., NYU, 1979, ABD, 1990. Cert. rehab. counselor, 1990. Reading specialist Stephen Gaynor Sch., N.Y.C., 1978-80; vocat. program coord. Endeavor Learning Ctr., Silver Springs, Md., 1981-85; sr. learning disability specialist Nat. Ctr. on Employment and Disability, Albertson, N.Y., 1985-86, coordinator learning disability project, 1986-87, sr. coord. learning disability projects, 1987-88, sr. coord. spl. rehab. projects, 1988—. Author, editor: From High School to College, 1988, How to Succeed in College, 1988; contbr.: Dyslexia: A Neuropsychological and Learning Perspective, 1988; author, editor: Social Skills for the World of Work and Beyond, 1991, Gateways to the Working World, 1991. Mem. Nat. Rehab. Assn., Am. Ednl. Rsch. Assn., Learning Disabilities Assn. Am., Am. Assn. for Counseling and Devel., Coun. on Exceptional Children. Office: Nat Ctr For Disability Svcs 201 I U Willets Rd Albertson NY 11507-1599

MICHAELS, PAUL See MICHALOVSKY, PAUL M.

MICHAELS, THOMAS JOSEPH, construction executive; b. Bklyn., May 2, 1957; s. Thomas and Margaret (Buonincontri) Macaluso; m. Anne Mary Dash, Oct. 1, 1984; 1 child, Thomas Joseph Jr. BS, St. Joseph's Coll., 1979; MBA, Manhattan Coll., 1984. Ast. dir. N.Y.C. Health & Hosps. Corp., Bklyn., 1980-84; dir. ops. N.Y.S. Div. Housing and Community Renewal, 1984-86; dist. mgr. City of N.Y., 1986-88; dep. exec. dir. Plumbing Found. City of N.Y. Inc., 1988-90; exec. dir. N.Y.C. One Call Ctr., Queens, 1990—. Contbr. articles to profl. jours. Chmn. Marine Park Civic Assn., Bklyn., 1986—; v.p. New Era Dems., Bklyn., 1987—; adv. bd. Congress Italian Am. Orgns., Bklyn., 1987—; trustee Flatianos Vol. Ambulance Corps, Bklyn., 1986-90. U.S. Dept. Energy grantee, 1978; recipient Col. J. Gardner Conroy Philosophy award St. Joseph's Ch., 1979, Cert. of Merit N.Y. State Federated Appeal Program, 1985. Mem. N.Y.C. One Call Users Coun. (sec. 1988-91), Am. Pub. Works Assn., One Call Internat. Com. Roman Catholic. Office: NYC One Call Ctr 36-35 Bell Blvd Bayside NY 11361

MICHAELSON, BENJAMIN, JR., lawyer; b. Annapolis, Md., May 30, 1936; s. Benjamin and Naomi Madora (Dill) M.; m. Frances Means Blackwell, Apr. 12, 1986; children: Benjamin, Robert Wendell. BA, U. Va., 1957; JD, U. Md., 1962. Bar: Md. 1962, U.S. Dist. Ct. Md. 1976. Assoc. Goodman, Bloom & Michaelson, Annapolis, 1962-63; pvt. practice, Annapolis, 1963-73; sr. ptnr. Michaelson & Christhilf, P.A., Annapolis, 1973-77, Benjamin Michaelson, Jr., P.A., Annapolis, 1977-81, Michaelson & Simmons, P.A., Annapolis, 1982-86, Michaelson & Newell, P.A., 1987-88, Michaelson, Krause & Ferris, P.A., 1988-91; pvt. practice law, 1991—; gen. counsel, dir. Annapolis Fed. Savs., 1965—; bd. dirs. Security Title Guarantee Corp. Balt., Md. Svc. Corp.; bd. dirs., gen. counsel Annapolis Bancorp Inc. Counsel Anne Arundel County (Md.) Bd. Edn., 1966-76. Lt. U.S. Army, 1957-59. Named one of Outstanding Young Men Am., Severna Park chpt. U.S. Jaycees, 1965. Fellow Am. Coll. Mortgage Attys.; mem. ABA, Md. Bar Assn. (chmn. real property, planning and zoning sect. council 1982-84, grievance commn. inquiry panel 1976-85, vice-chmn. 1983-85, grievance commn. rev. bd. 1985-88), Anne Arundel County Bar Assn., Jaycees (Md. state legal counsel 1964-65, nat. dir. 1965-66), Sailing Club of Chesapeake (commodore 1982), N.Y. Yacht Club, Annapolis Yacht Club, Rotary (pres. 1975-76, Paul Harris fellow), Delta Theta Phi. Republican. Episcopalian. Home: 3 Southgate Ave Annapolis MD 21401-2709 Office: 80 West St Ste 110 Annapolis MD 21401-2401

MICHALEK, BERNARD JOSEPH, management education educator, accountant; b. Pitts., Dec. 9, 1934; s. Stanislaus Joseph and Magdalen (Warzynska) M.; m. Mary Eleanor Newman, July 3, 1957; children: Tawnya Lou Hartberger, Mary Magdalen Capp, Gregory Edward M. BBA, U. Pitts., 1961, MBA, 1971. CPA, Pa. Office mgr. Virginia Erection Corp., Pitts., 1960-62; audit mgr. Main Lafrentz (now Peat Marwick), Pitts., 1962-67; v.p. fin., sec., treas. Anvil Products, Inc., Allison Park, Pa., 1967-86; pvt. practice Pitts., 1986—; asst. prof. La Roche Coll., Pitts., 1987—. Elder Reorganized Ch. of Jesus Christ, Pitts., 1965—, elder, pastor, 1986-88, seminar leader, New Hamburg, Pa., 1987-91. Staff sgt. USAF, 1953-57, ETO. Mem. AICPA, Nat. Assn. for Preservation of Storytelling, Pa. Inst. CPAs (com. on rels. with schs. and colls. Pitts. chpt. 1989—), Inst. Mgmt. Accts., Masons, Delta Sigma Pi (treas. 1980—). Democrat. Home: 1066 Waldwick Dr Pittsburgh PA 15237-4056 Office: La Roche Coll 9000 Babcock Blvd Pittsburgh PA 15237-5898

MICHALIK, EDWARD FRANCIS, construction company executive; b. Hartford, Conn., Apr. 4, 1946; s. Edward S. and Helen A. (Sito) M.; m. Dianne E. Del Cegno, 1967 (div. 1978); children: Marc Edward, Michael Donald; m. Cecilia C. Zoltanski, 1987; children: Alexander Edward, Gabrielle Therese. BBA, Nichols Coll., Dudley, Mass., 1969. Cost auditor Wigton-Abbott Corp., Plainfield, N.J., 1969-70; dir. cost control The John W. Cowper Co., Inc., Buffalo, 1970-73; v.p. Titan Group Inc., Paramus, N.J., 1973-76; exec. v.p. Harrison Western Corp., Denver, 1976-85; pres. The John W. Cowper Co., Inc., Buffalo, 1985-88, Adrian Devel., Inc., Buffalo and Denver, 1988—; pres., chief exec. officer, bd. dirs. Sunburst Excavation, Inc., Denver, 1991—. Member: Soc. Am. Mil. Engrs., Associated Gen. Contractors of Am., The Beavers. Republican.

MICHALOVSKY, PAUL M. (PAUL MICHAELS), investment banker, stock broker; b. Scarsdale, N.Y., June 16, 1965; s. Isaac and Myrna (Shapiro) M. Student, Tulane U. Lic. stock broker. Buyer and seller of exotic automobiles, 1983-86; assoc. mem. corp. fin. dept. Emanuel and Co., N.Y.C., 1986-88; founder, exec. v.p. Global Capital Group Inc., 1988-89; founder, operator Telemktg. Concepts, Inc., 1989-90; regional dir. Garden City office Kimbridge & Co. N.Y., 1990; officer, registered rep. Lew Lieberbaum & Co., Inc., 1990—; pres., chief exec. officer, dir., gen. ptnr. Classicar Ptnrs. Inc., N.Y.C., 1990—. Bd. dirs. New Directions Br. Am. Cancer Soc., 1991—. Mem. Elmwood Country Club. Home: 370 E 76th St B707 New York NY 10021 Office: Classicar Ptnrs Ste 330 600 Old Country Rd Garden City NY 11530

MICHALOWICZ, JOSEPH VICTOR, mathematician, physicist; b. Washington, Oct. 23, 1941; s. Joseph Casimir and Louise (Anselmo) M.; m. Karen Dee Shuman, June 8, 1963; children: Joleen, Michael. BA, Cath. U. Am., 1963, PhD, 1967. Asst. prof. math. Cath. U. Am., Washington, 1967-73; rsch. mathematician Harry Diamond Labs., Adelphi, Md., 1973-85; rsch. physicist Naval Rsch. Lab., Washington, 1985—; cons. Rsch. Analysis

Corp., McLean, Va., 1967-70; lectr. in elec. engring. Cath. U. Am., 1973-74. Contbr. numerous articles to profl. jours. Office: Naval Rsch Lab 4555 Overlook Ave SW Washington DC 20375

MICHALOWSKI, DANIEL RICHARD, zoological park director; b. Rochester, N.Y., Aug. 22, 1938; s. John T. and Pauline (Cieslinski) M.; m. Beverly Ann Merkel, Aug. 26, 1961; children: Linda Ann, Cheryl Ann. BA, St. John Fisher Coll., 1960. Nature specialist Rochester Dept. Parks and Recreation, 1960-62; zoologist Monroe County Dept. Parks, Rochester, 1962-68; zoo curator Monroe County Dept. Parks, 1968-78, zool. park dir., 1978—. Contbr. articles to zool. publs. Nature dir., Rochester area Boy Scouts Am., 1958-60, merit badge counselor, 1958-82. Sgt. U.S. Army, 1961-62. Fellow Am. Assn. Zool. Parks and Aquaria (bd. dirs. 1974-77, Disting. Svc. award 1977); mem. Internat. Soc. Zooculturists, Am. Soc. Ichthyologists and Herpetologists, Herpetologists' League, Polish Falcons Am. (Silver Star award 1988), Polish Civic Assn. Republican. Office: Seneca Park Zoo 222 St Paul St Rochester NY 14604-1120

MICHALS, GEORGE FRANCIS, multi-industry company executive; b. Hungary, Sept. 14, 1935; came to Can., 1956, naturalized, 1961; s. Todor and Ilona (Sinkovich) Mihalcsics; m. Patricia Elizabeth Hoffman, June 18, 1971; children: Katherine, Julie, Elizabeth, Georgina. BComm, Sir George Williams U., Montreal, 1961; CA, McGill U., 1963. Chartered acct. McGill U., Montreal, 1963. Acct. Coopers & Lybrand, Montreal, 1963-68; from treas. to exec. v.p. Dominion Textile Co. Ltd., 1969-74; v.p. fin., sr. v.p., then exec. v.p. Genstar Corp., San Francisco, 1974-86; exec. v.p., chief fin. officer Can. Pacific Ltd., Montreal, 1987-90; pres. Baymont Capital Resources Inc., Toronto, 1990—; chmn. Armbro Enterprises Inc., 1992—; mem. adv. bd. Ctr. for Real Estate and Urban Econs., Berkeley, Calif. Mem. Urban Land Inst., Mount Royal Club, Bankers Club. Home: RR 5, Orangeville, ON Canada L9W 2Z2 Office: Baymont Capital Resources Inc, 141 Adelaide St W Ste 1506, Toronto, ON Canada M5H 3L5

MICHAUD, ALPHEE MARTIAL, retail executive; b. St. Quentin, N.B., Can., Nov. 13, 1938; s. Napoleon and Alpheda (Deschenes) M.; M.D., Laval U., 1965; postgrad. in econs. McGill U., 1973; m. Claudette Gingras, July 4, 1964; children—Harold, Isabelle. Intern, Hotel-Dieu and Hosp. St. Sacrement, Quebec City, Que., 1964-66; resident in internal medicine Hosp. St. Sacrement, Quebec City, 1966-67; gen. practice medicine, Caraquet, N.B., 1968-71; pres., owner Les Pharmacies Populaires Ltd., Caraquet, 1971-88; pres. Les Entreprises Ami Ltd., Caraquet, 1972—; pres., sec. Radio-Acadie Ltd., Caraquet, 1976—; pres., owner Malofilm, 1991—; pres., owner weekly newspapers; dir. N.B. Devel. Corp., 1973-79. Bd. dirs. Tracadie Assn. Mental Disease, 1973-76, N.B. Indsl. Devel. Bd., 1979-86; pres. Le Festival Acadien Caraquet, 1974-76. Mem. Can., N.B. med. assns., Assn. Med. De Langue Francaise, Caraquet Bd. Trade, Atlantic Provinces Bd. Trade (chmn.), Canadian C. of C. (dir. 1980-82). Roman Catholic. Med. editor weekly newspaper Le Voilier, 1972-76; pub. weeklies Levoilier/Le Point, 1983-87, Week-End, 1983-87. Home: PO Box 990, Caraquet, NB Canada E0B 1K0 Office: Place Caraquet, Caraquet, NB Canada E0B 1K0

MICHEL, HAROLD GUSTAVE, insurance marketing executive; b. West Haven, Conn., Sept. 29, 1926; s. Joseph Gustave and Dorothy (Petersen) M.; m. Joyce Hudson, June 10, 1948 (div. 1971); children: Kathleen Elizabeth, Stephen Joseph, Brian Harold, Nancy Ann; m. Shirley Dahlgard, May 8, 1971. Student, U. New Haven, 1945-47. Pres. Joseph G. Michel & Sons, Inc., West Haven, Conn., 1940-80; exec. sec. Nat. Assn. Plumbing, Heating, Cooling Contractors Group Ins., West Haven, Conn., 1980-84; pres. Michel & Co., West Haven, Conn., 1984—; mem. Conn. adv. bd. Bank of Boston, 1983-91. Contbr. articles to profl. jours. Bd. dirs. West Haven (Conn.) C. of C., 1960-88 (named Man of Yr. 1986); pres., bd. dirs. Lausanne Condominium Assn., Naples, Fla., 1988—; dir. scholarship com. U. New Haven (Conn.), 1986—; mem. Rep. Senatorial Com., Washington, 1980—; mem. West Haven Libr. Bd., v.p. 1964-72, chmn. Bldg. Com. 1970-71. Mem. Nat. Assn. Plumbing, Heating, Cooling Contractors (bd. dirs. 1964-66), Conn. Assn. Plumbing, Heating, Cooling Contractors (bd. dirs. 1949—, pres. 1965-66, chmn. ins. com. 1984—, named Contractor of the Yr. 1975, Assoc. Mem. of the Yr. 1985), Lions Club (bd. dirs. 1975-80), Country Club of Naples (Fla.). Republican. Home: Apt 605N 3215 Gulfshore Blvd Naples FL 33940 Office: Michel & Co 28 Atwood Ave West Haven CT 06516-5298

MICHEL, PAUL REDMOND, federal judge; b. Phila., Feb. 3, 1941; s. Lincoln M. and Dorothy (Kelley) M.; m. Sally Ann Clark, 1965 (div. 1987); children: Sarah Elizabeth, Margaret Kelley; m. Elizabeth Morgan, 1989. BA, Williams Coll., 1963; JD, U. Va., 1966. Bar: Pa. 1967, U.S. Supreme Ct., 1970. Asst. dist. atty. Dist. Atty's Office, Phila., 1967-71, dep. dist. atty. for investigations, 1972-74; asst. spl. prosecutor Watergate investigation Dept. Justice, Washington, 1974-75, dep. chief pub. integrity sect., Criminal div. and prosecutor "Koreagate" investigation, 1976-78, assoc. dep. atty. gen., 1978-81, acting dep. atty. gen., 1979-80; asst. counsel intelligence com. U.S. Senate, 1975-76, counsel and adminstrv. asst. to Sen. Arlen Specter, 1981-88; judge U.S. Ct. Appeals (Fed. cir.), Washington, 1988—. 2d lt. USAR, 1966-72. Office: US Ct Appeals Fed Cir 717 Madison Pl NW Ste 808 Washington DC 20439-0002

MICHEL, RICHARD CHRIS, retired economist; b. Rochester, N.Y., Dec. 25, 1945; s. James Peter and Dina (Noun) M. AB, Syracuse U., 1967; MPA, U. Pa., 1975. Assoc. analyst Congl. Budget Office, Washington, 1975-76; sr. rsch. assoc. Urban Inst., Washington, 1976-77, 79-91; dir. Income & Benefits Policy Ctr., (formerly Income Security & Pension Policy Ctr.), Washington, 1983-91; sr. economist Office Sec. HEW, 1977-79. Contbr. articles to profl. publs. Mem. Am. Econ. Assn., Western Econ. Assn., Assn. Pub. Policy and Mgmt., Wharton Alumni Club, Syracuse Alumni Club (Washington chpt.). Democrat. Mem. Greek Orthodox Ch. Home: 7512 Rambling Ridge Dr Fairfax VA 22039-2911

MICHELE, ROBERT CHARLES, investment management, portfolio manager; b. Phila., Nov. 19, 1959; s. Charles Theodore and Evelyn (Witol) M.; m. Katherine Mary Elizabeth Lyons, Oct. 1, 1988; children: Charles Theodore II, William Keane. BA, U. Pa., 1981; CFA, Inst. Chartered Fin. Analysts, Charlottesville, Va., 1988. Investment mgr. Bankers Trust Co., N.Y.C., 1981-85; dep. mgr. Brown Bros. Harriman & Co., N.Y.C., 1985—. Mem. N.Y. Soc. Security Analysts, U. Pa. Alumni Club Fairfield County (admissions com.), St. Anthony Hall Club Phila. Republican. Episcopalian. Home: 19 Stephanie Ln Darien CT 06820-2722 Office: Brown Bros Harriman Co 59 Wall St New York NY 10005

MICHELINI, ALEX J., reporter; b. Englewood, N.J., July 31, 1937; s. Anthony and Jenny Michelini; m. Janet Alberghina, June 20, 1976. BS, Temple U., 1959. Reporter UPI, Phila., 1959-61; reporter UPI, Newark, 1961-63, bur. chief, 1963-66, N.J. state mgr., 1967-68; reporter N.Y. Daily News, N.J., 1968-74, N.J. state editor, 1974-78; assoc. city editor N.Y. Daily News, N.Y.C., 1978-82, city hall bur. chief, 1983-84, reporter supreme ct., 1984-87, reporter fed. ct., 1987—; reporter, commentator Radio Sta. WOR, N.Y. Councilman, Ft. Lee, N.J., 1965-67. Recipient N.Y. Rep. Assn. Byline award, 1966, Gold Typewriter award N.Y. Press Club, 1982, 89. Democrat. Roman Catholic. Office: NY Daily News 220 E 42d St New York NY 10017

MICHELS, DOUG, world architect; b. Seattle, June 29, 1943; s. Robert W. and Caroline (Burkhard) M. BArch, Yale U., 1967; MA, Harvard U., 1986. asst. prof. Dept. Architecture Cath. U., 1967; vis. prof. Coll. Architecture U. Houston, 1969; workshop dir. Sch. Architecture Rice U., 1972, vis. prof., 1979; vis. critic Grad. Sch. Architecture U. Calif., 1982, Coll. Architecture Tex. A&M U., 1987. Exhibited in one man shows at Corcoran Gallery, 1967, Washington Gallery of Modern Art, 1967, Paris Biennial, 1969, Houston Contemporary Art Mus., 1974, San Francisco Mus. Art, 1977, A.I.A. Octagon Mus., 1986, OKC Air and Space Mus., 1987; prin. works include Cadillac Ranch, Tex., 1974, Dolphin Embassy, Australia, Project Bluestar, 1986, New America, Washington, D.C., 1990, The Hyperion Project, Japan, 1991, numerous others. Office: Doug Michels Architecture 1409 21st St NW Washington DC 20036-5952

MICHELSEN, CHRISTOPHER BRUCE HERMANN, surgeon; b. Boston, Aug. 18, 1940; s. Jost Joseph and Ingeborg Elizabeth (Dilthey) M.; B.A., Bowdoin Coll., 1961; M.D., Columbia U., 1969; children: Heidi Elizabeth, Matthew Christopher, Joshua Jost. Intern Columbia Presbyn. Med. Center, N.Y.C., 1969-70, resident, 1970-71; orthopedic resident N.Y. Orthopedic Hosp., N.Y.C., 1971-73, jr. Anne C. Kane fellow, 1973-74, sr. Anne C. Kane fellow and hip fellow, 1974-75, traveling fellow, 1975-76; postgrad. fellow in biomechanics, instr. biomed. engring. Case-Western Res. U.; assoc. prof. clin. orthopaedic surgery Columbia Coll. Physicians and Surgeons; co-dir. combined orthopaedic neuro surg. spine svc.; chief orthopaedic spine surgery svc. Col. USAR, 1961-63. Diplomate Am. Bd. Orthopaedic Surgery. Fellow A.C.S., N.Y. Acad. Medicine, Am. Assn. for Surgery of Trauma, Am. Orthopaedic Assn., N.Am. Spine Soc., Am. Acad. Orthopaedic Surgeons; mem. AMA, Orthopaedic Research Soc., Am. Soc. for Bone and Mineral Research, Royal Soc. Medicine (affiliate). Home: 10257 Shearwater Ct E Jersey City NJ 07305-5419 Office: 5141 Broadway New York NY 10034-1199

MICHELSON, DAVID TODD, training and development consultant; b. Newton, Mass., May 24, 1961; s. Alan Phillip and Saundra (Sklar) M. BS in Econs., Dickinson Coll., 1983; MS in Human Resource Devel., Am. U., 1990. Cons. assoc. Bart Ludeman Assocs., Signal Hill, Calif., 1984-85; supr. mgmt. and orgn. devel. Great Western Bank, Chatsworth, Calif., 1984-87; cons. Consultative Resources Corp., Darien, Calif., 1988-91; pres. Career Successing, Brookline, Mass., 1991—; prin. Michelson Con., Brookline, 1991—, World Creations Music, Brookline, 1984—. Mem ASTD (communications mktg. dir. 1991-92). Home: 77 Thorndike St # 1 Brookline MA 02146 Office: Career Successing PO Box 1265 Brookline MA 02146

MICHENFELDER, JOSEPH FRANCIS, public relations executive; b. Webster Groves, Mo., Mar. 30, 1929; s. Albert Aloysius and Ruth Josephine (Donahue) M.; m. Audrey Laurine Glynn, Aug. 8, 1970. BA, N.Y. State U., N.Y.C., 1951, STB, 1954, MRE, 1955; MS in Journalism, Columbia U., 1958. Projects dir. Maryknoll Headquarters, Ossining, N.Y., 1955-57; communications dir. Maryknoll Headquarters, Ossining, 1958-62; dir., chief exec. officer Noticias Aliadas, S.A., Lima, Peru, 1962-69; pub. rels. dir. Pub. Affairs Analysts, Inc., N.Y.C., 1970-72; exec. v.p. Pub. Affairs Analysts, Inc., 1973-89; sr. v.p. Napolitan Assocs./PAA, Inc., N.Y.C., 1989—; pres. IDOC/N. Am., Inc., North Am., Inc., N.Y.C., 1976—. Mng. Editor (polit. quarterly) POLITEIA, 1970-73; co-producer: TV documentary A Quiet Revolution, 1987. Cons. UNESCO World Health Orgn., Bogota, Lima, 1964-66; bd. dirs. Jobs for Youth, Inc., N.Y.C., 1978-84. Mem. Internat. Pub. Relations Assn., Internat. Assn. Polit. Cons., Columbia U. Journalism Alumni Fed. (pres. 1971-74), Ovrses Press Club, Columbia Club. Democrat. Office: Napolitan Assocs/PAA Inc 55 5th Ave New York NY 10003-1007

MICHIELLI, DONALD WARREN, exercise physiology educator; b. Queens Village, N.Y., Aug. 15, 1934; s. James and Marie (LaBelle) M.; m. Donna Covello, Dec. 23, 1989. BS, Springfield Coll., 1957; MA, Ohio State U., 1961, PhD, 1965. Asst. prof. L.I. U., Bklyn., 1966-70; prof. Bklyn. Coll., 1971—; adj. assoc. prof. NYU, CUNY; reviewer Jour. Applied Physiology, Bethesda, Md., 1989, 91. Author: Spectral Analysis of the Acoustical Characteristics of Human Skeletal Muscle, 1989; contbr. chpts. to books on exercise physiology, skeletal muscle; contbr. articles to profl. publs. With U.S. Army, 1957-59, Korea. Grantee HEW, 1974-75. Fellow Am. Coll. Sports Medicine (v.p. mid-Atlantic chpt., 25 Yr. Meritorious Svc. award); mem. AAAS, N.Y. Acad. Scis., Am. Heart Assn. (exercise com.), Sigma Psi (treas. Bklyn. Coll. chpt. 1990—). Office: Bklyn Coll Bedford Ave and Ave H Brooklyn NY 11210

MICOLO, ANTHONY MICHAEL, human resources executive; b. Bklyn., Mar. 3, 1949; s. Antonio and Mildred (Lapolla) M.; m. Susan Lynn Ross; children: Steven, Julie. BBA, Baruch Coll., N.Y.C., 1971; postgrad., Queens Coll., Flushing, N.Y., 1972-73. Personnel mgr. Emerald Electro Products, Jamaica, N.Y., 1974-80; tech. recruiter Am. Electric Power Service Corp., N.Y.C., 1980-83; instr. St. John's U., Jamaica, 1983-84; personnel mgr. Group Health, Inc., N.Y.C., 1984-86; mgr. subs. personnel The Dime Savings Bank of N.Y. FSB, Garden City, 1986-88; human resources officer, mgr. employment and tng. The Dime Savings Bank of N.Y. FSB, Uniondale, N.Y., 1988-89; v.p. human resources The Dime Savings Bank of N.Y. FSB, 1989—. Author: Practical Supervision: How to Organize for Effectiveness; contbr. articles to profl. jours. N.Y. State Bd. of Regents scholar, 1966. Mem. Am. Soc. Personnel Adminstrn., Am. Compensation Assn., Human Resource Systems Profls., Employment Mgmt. Assn. Office: The Dime Savs Bank of NY FSB EAB Plz East Tower 10th Fl Uniondale NY 11556-0128

MICZEK, KLAUS ALEXANDER, psychology educator; b. Burghausen, Bavaria, Germany, Sept. 28, 1944; came to U.S., 1967; s. Erich and Irene (Wirthl) M.; m. Christiane Baerwaldt, Aug. 8, 1970; 1 child, Nikolai A. Tchrs. cert., Paedagogische Hochschule, Berlin, 1966; PhD, U. Chgo., 1972. Asst. prof. Carnegie-Mellon U., Pitts., 1972-74, assoc. prof., 1974-79; assoc. prof. Tufts U., Medford, Mass., 1979-83, prof., 1983—; cons. Duphar v.b., Weesp, The Netherlands, 1984—, Nat. Inst. Drug Abuse, Rockville, Md., 1984—; Boerhaave prof. U. Leiden, The Netherlands, 1987; mem. panel on violence, NAS, 1989—. Editor: Ethopharmacology, 1983, Ethopharmacological Addression Research, 1984; field editor, coord. editor Behavioral Pharmacology, Jour. Psychopharmacology; contbr. articles on psychopharmacology, 1973—. Research grantee Nat. Inst. Drug Abuse, 1973—, Nat. Inst. Alcoholism and Alcohol Abuse, 1981—. Fellow Am. Psychol. Assn. (program chmn. 1981, pres. div. psychopharmacology 1990-91), Behavioral Pharmacological Soc. (pres. 1992-94), Internat. Soc. for Rsch. on Aggression (councilor 1987); mem. Soc. Neurosci., N.Y. Acad. Scis., Internat. Primatol. Soc. Office: Tufts U Dept Psychology 490 Boston Ave Medford MA 02155-5532

MIDANEK, DEBORAH HICKS, portfolio manager, director; b. N.Y.C., Nov. 30, 1954; d. Frederick Stevens and Mary Leavenworth (Barnes) H.; m. James Ira Midanek, Sept. 29, 1985; children: Benjamin Abraham, Thomas Hicks. AB, Bryn Mawr Coll., 1975; MBA, U. Pa., 1980. Asst. dir. admissions Bryn Mawr (Pa.) Coll., 1975-78; asst. v.p. Bankers Trust, N.Y.C., 1980-84; v.p. Drexel Burnham Lambert, N.Y.C., 1984-90; chief exec. Solon Asset Mgmt. Corp., N.Y.C., 1990—; bd. dirs. Drexel Burnham Lambert Group, Debtor in Possession, Tricapital Ltd., Bermuda, MB Holdings, Inc. Trustee DBL Found., 1992—; bd. dirs. Pelham (N.Y.) Art Ctr., 1988-91, Mgmt. Decision Lab. Stern Sch. Bus., NYU, 1991, United Way of Pelham, 1991; mem. exec. bd. exploring div. Greater N.Y. Coun. Boy Scouts Am., 1991—. Mem. Bryn Mawr Coll. Club of N.Y. (pres. 1991—), Econ. Club of N.Y. Republican. Home: 49 Hillcrest Dr Pelham NY 10803-3305 Office: Solon Asset Mgmt Corp Ste 2100 1000 Main St New Rochelle NY 10801

MIDDENDORF, ALICE CARTER, volunteer; b. Balt., Dec. 7, 1940; d. John William and Alice Temple (Carter) M. BA, Wellesley Coll., 1963, Oxford U., England, 1972. Librarian Boston Athenaeum Libr., 1963-66; editor Houghton Mifflin Co., Boston, 1966-69; bd. dirs. Balt. Zool. Soc., 1976; cons. Nat. Zoo, Washington, 1976-77, G. Ward & Assocs., Ridgefield, Conn., 1976-79; from bd. dirs. to bd. govs. Nat. Aquarium in Balt., 1976-88, sec. bd. govs., 1987-88, chmn. animal policy com., 1982-88; bd. dirs. Total Health Care (merger Constant Care Med. Ctr. and West Balt. Constant Health Ctr.), Balt., 1981—, sec. bd. dirs., 1990—; advisory bd. Nat. Aquarium in Balt., 1989—; bd. dirs. Constant Care Med. Ctr., Balt., Park Heights State Acad., Balt., sec., 1988—; pres. Fulmar Corp., Cayman Islands, British West Indies, 1991—. Recipient Pres.'s Citation, Pres. City Coun. Balt., 1974, 76, Award of Appreciation, Mayor of Balt., 1981. Mem. Am. Assn. Zool. Parks and Aquariums. Home and Office: 1301 Hillside Rd Stevenson MD 21153

MIDDLEMAN, RAOUL FINK, artist; b. Balt., Apr. 3, 1935; s. Paul B. and Elizabeth (Fink) M.; m. Pat Bird Forget (div.); m. Ruth Katherine Channing, Dec. 2, 1971; children: Raphael Bachrach, Benjamin Jacob, Nathaniel John. BA, Johns Hopkins U., 1955; postgrad., Penn. Fine Arts, 1959-61, Bklyn. Mus., 1961. Faculty Md. Inst. Coll. of Art, Balt., 1961-85; vis. critic Vt. Studio Sch. Summer Program,1 985; resident dir. Summer Landscape Painting Program, Md. Inst. Coll. of Art, 1981-83; vis. artist Artists for Environment Found., Walpack Ctr., 1977-81; artist-in-residence Hoffberger Sch. of Painting, 1973-76; lectr. for Figurative Alliance, Studio Sch., N.Y.C., Nat. Gallery in Edinborough, Yale Norfolk, 1980, Md. Inst. Coll. of Art, 1985. One-man shows include Swanston Fine Arts, 1988, Allan Stone Gallery, 1985, 1981,1975, 1972, 1969, 1968, Grimaldis Gallery, 1984, 1981, 1979, 1978, William Capro Gallery, 1983, The Water Gap Art Gallery, 1982, The Md. Inst., Coll. of Art, 1974, Krasner Gallery, 1966; exhibited in groups shows at Nat. Acad. Design, 1990, Md. Inst., 1989-90, Gaumann Cicchino Gallery, 1989, Ingber Gallery, 1989, Bendann Gallery, 1989, Swanston Fine Arts, 1988, Haus der Kunst, 1986, Kornbluth Gallery, 1985 and others. Recipient Robert and Rochelle Phillipp prize Nat. Acad. Design, 1990.

MIDDLETON, DAWN E., education educator; b. Pottstown, Pa.; d. William H. and Sara G. Bowman; m. Stephen R. Mourar, June 1983; children: William Middleton, Shelly Mourar. AA in Early Childhood Edn., Montgomery Community Coll., 1972; BS in Elem. Edn., West Chester State Coll., 1974; MA in Edn. Curriculum and Instrn. Edn., Pa. State U., 1982, EdD, 1984. Instr. Continuing Edn. Pa. State U., University Park; dir. specialized early childhood programs and svcs. Wiley House, Bethlehem, Pa.; dir. Children's Sch. of Cabrini Coll., Radnor, Pa.; dept. chmn., asst. prof. edn. Cabrini Coll., Radnor. Home: 208 Bethel Rd Spring City PA 19475-9720

MIDDLETON, ELLIOTT, JR., physician; b. Glen Ridge, N.J., Dec. 15, 1925; s. Elliott and Dorothy (Thoman) M.; m. Elizabeth Blackford, Sept. 25, 1948; children: Elliott III, Ellen Alice, Blackford, James Jay. A.B., Princeton U., 1947; M.D., Columbia U., 1950. Diplomate: Am. Bd. Internal Medicine, Am. Bd. Allergy and Immunology. Intern Presbyn. Hosp., N.Y.C., 1950-51; resident in medicine Presbyn. Hosp., 1951-52; asst. in medicine immunochem. lab. Coll. Physicians and Surgeons, Columbia U., 1952-53; clin. assoc. Nat. Heart Inst., 1953-55; fellow in allergy R.A. Cooke Inst. Allergy, Roosevelt Hosp., N.Y.C., 1955-56; practice medicine Montclair, N.J., 1956-69; dir. clin. services and research Children's Asthma Research Inst. and Hosp., Denver, 1969-76; asso. clin. prof. medicine U. Colo., 1969-76; prof. medicine and pediatrics, dir. allergy div. Sch. Medicine, SUNY, Buffalo, 1976—; attending physician Buffalo Gen. Hosp.; cons. in allergy Children's Hosp., VA Hosp., Buffalo. Editor-in-chief Allergy: Principles and Practice, 1978, 3d edit., 1988; editor Jour. Allergy and Clin. Immunology, 1983-88; contbr. numerous articles to jours. chpts. to books. Served with M.C. USNR, 1944-50; Served with M.C. USPHS, 1950-55. Fellow Am. Acad. Allergy and Immunology (pres. 1972, Disting. Svc. award 1991); mem. AAAS, Am. Assn. Immunologists. Episcopalian. Home: 36 Hodge Ave Buffalo NY 14222-2016 Office: Buffalo Gen Hosp 100 High St Buffalo NY 14203-1154

MIDDLETON, STEVEN TRAVIS, utility company financial management consultant; b. Winona, Miss., May 13, 1951; s. James Travis and Irene (Fullilove) M.; m. Frances Christensen, June 11, 1977; children: Ellen, Peter. BSME, U.S. Naval Acad., 1974; MSA in Indsl. Mgmt., George Washington U., 1982. Commd. ensign USN, 1974, advanced through grades to lt., 1978, resigned, 1980; sr. engr. Balt. Gas and Electric Co., 1980-88; v.p. Riley Natural Gas Co., Milford, W.Va., 1988-90; pres. Utility Cost Mgmt. Co., Severna Park, Md., 1990—. Coach local youth soccer. Mem. ASME, Assn. Energy Engrs., Anne Arundel Trade Coun., USNA Class of 1974 (pres. 1990—). Office: Utility Cost Mgmt Co PO Box 1405 Severna Park MD 21146

MIDDOUR, JAY WENGER, aerospace engineer; b. Waynesboro, Pa., Aug. 3, 1958; s. Joseph Francis and Janice L. (Wenger) M.; children: Tessa Ann, Rebecca Lynn. BS, Pa. State U., 1981; MS, George Washington U., 1987. Aerospace engr. Locus, Inc., Alexandria, Va., 1981-87, Naval Rsch. Lab., Washington, 1987—. Contbr. articles to profl. jours. Mem. AIAA (sec. astrodynamics tech. com. 1991—), Am. Astro. Soc.

MIDLARSKY, ELIZABETH RUTH STECKEL, psychologist educator; b. Brooklyn; d. Abraham Allan and Frances Lucille Rae (Wiener) Steckel; m. Manus Issachar Midlarsky, June 25, 1961; children: Susan Rachel, Miriam Joyce, Michael George. BA, CUNY, 1961; MA, Northwestern U., 1966, PhD, 1968. Lic. psychologist, Colo., Mich. Asst. prof. psychology U. Denver, 1968-73; dir. research and evaluation Park East Mental Health Ctr., Denver, 1973-75; assoc. prof., dir. psychology training prog. Met. State Coll., Denver, 1975-77; chmn. dept. psychology U. Detroit, 1978-81, dir. ctr. for study devel. aging, 1981-90, assoc. prof., 1977-83, prof. psychology, 1983-90; prof. psychology Tchrs. Coll. Columbia U., N.Y., 1990—, dir. Ctr. for Lifespan and Aging Studies, 1992—; initial rev. group mem. NIMH, Bethesda, Md., 1976-82; mem. site rev. groups Nat. Heart, Lung and Blood Inst., Bethesda, 1985-86, study sect. NIH, Bethesda, 1986-91, mem. Nat. Reviewer's Res., 1991—. Editor: Acad. Psychology Bull., 1982-86; co-editor: Humboldt Jour. of Social Relations, 198-5-86; contbr. articles to profl. jours. Grantee Nat. Inst. Aging, 1982-85, 87-90, AARP Andrus Found., 1982-83, 88-89; AAUW fellow, 1974-75. Fellow Am. Psychol. Soc., Am. Orthopsychiatric Assn.; mem. Gerontol. Soc. Am. (exec. com. of prog. com. 1983-84), Soc. Psychol. Study Social Issues, Mich. Psychol. Assn. (exec. council mem). Jewish. Avocations: singing; playing piano; writing poetry; walking; riding horses. Home: 3 Falcon Rd East Brunswick NJ 08816-2716

MIDURA, EDMUND MICHAEL, mass communication educator; b. Utica, N.Y., Oct. 25, 1935; s. Genevieve (Midura) MacMaster; m. Patricia Ann Mulhall, Aug. 19, 1961; children: Christopher, Jennifer K., Jonathan C., Abigail K. BS, Syracuse U., 1957; MA, Pa. State U., 1966; PhD, U. Iowa, 1969. Sports editor Oneida (N.Y.) Daily Dispatch, 1958-60; copy editor Milw. Jour., 1962-63; asst. prof. journalism U. Md., College Park, 1969-72; asst. prof. communication U. Wis., Milw., 1972-75; features copy desk chief Phila. Inquirer, 1975-77; assoc. prof. communication U. Miami, Coral Gables, Fla., 1980-85; asst. prof. Towson (Md.) State U., 1985—; disting. vis. cons. Am. U., Cairo, 1977-80; exchange prof. Sungkyunkwan U., Seoul, Republic of Korea, 1988; publs. cons. UNESCO, 1978-80. Editor: Blacks and Whites: The Urban Communication Crisis, 1970. Trustee Wilde Lake Village Bd., Columbia, Md., 1972-73, Dorsey's Search Village Bd., Columbia, 1987-88. Grantee Fulbright Found., 1986, USIA, 1988. Mem. Assn. for Edn. in Journalism and Mass Communication. Home: 3 Southerly Ct Unit 407 Baltimore MD 21204-2778 Office: Towson State U Dept Speech & Mass Communication Towson MD 21204

MIDWINTER, THOMAS RICHARD, insurance company official; b. Bklyn., Nov. 7, 1938; s. Thomas Francis and Marie (Pfeiffer) M.; m. Geraldine K. Faber, Sept. 8, 1962; children: Doreen, Kevin, Michele, Brian. BBA, St. John's U., 1960. Claim rep. Liberty Mut. Ins. Co., Rego Park, N.Y., 1962-65; claim examiner Kemper Ins. Group, Plainview, N.Y., 1965-69, St. Paul Fire & Marine Ins. Co., Jericho, N.Y., 1969—. With U.S. Army, 1960-62. Mem. N.Y. State Claim Mgrs. Coun. (pres. 1982-83), Nassau/Suffolk Claims Mgr. Coun. Roman Catholic. Office: St Paul Fire & Marine Ins 1 Jericho Plz Jericho NY 11753

MIEKKA, RICHARD GEORGE, manufacturing company executive; b. Pontiac, Mich., Oct. 18, 1933; s. George Erhard and Hazel Frances Miekka; m. Jeanette Ann Lambe, June 22, 1958; children—James, Frederick, Cynthia. B.S. in Chemistry, B.S. in Chem. Engring., U. Mich., 1956; M.S. in Chem. Engring., MIT, 1958, Sc.D., 1961. Mgr. chem. research Amicon Corp., Cambridge, Mass., 1962-63; research physics chemist Gen. Electric Corp., Lynn, Mass., 1963-64; research sect. head Dennison Mfg. Co., Framingham, Mass., 1964-73, mgr. chem. research div., 1973-82, mgr. tech. devel., 1982—. Patentee in field. Gomberg fellow in chemistry U. Mich., 1955; Arthur O. Little fellow MIT, 1960; U.S. Atomic Energy grantee, 1958. Mem. N.Y. Acad. Scis., Am. Vacuum Soc., Am. Chem. Soc., Tech. Assn. Pulp and Paper Industry, Sigma Xi. Republican. Lodge: Masons. Avocations: golf; fishing; camping; classical music. Office: Dennison Mfg Co 300 Howard St Framingham MA 01701

MIELE, JOEL ARTHUR, SR., civil engineer; b. Jersey City, May 28, 1934; s. Jene Gerald Sr., and Eleanor Natale (Bergida) M.; m. Faith Roseann Trombetta, July 21, 1952 (div. 1954); m. 2d Josephine Ann Cottone, Feb. 14, 1959; children: Joel Arthur, Jr., Vita Marie, Janet Ann. B.C.E., Poly. Inst. Bklyn., 1955. Registered profl. engr., N.Y., N.J.; profl. planner, N.J. Civil engr. Yudell & Miele, Queens, N.Y., 1955-57; chief engr. Jene G. Miele Assocs., Queens, 1960-68; prin., chief exec. officer Miele Assocs., Queens, 1968—. Patentee masonry wall constrn. Commr. N.Y.C. Planning Commn., 1990—; pres. bd. visitors Creedmoor State Hosp., 1979—; pres., bd. dirs. Peninsula Hosp. Ctr., 1990—, Peninsula Nursing Home, 1990—; chmn. Community Bd. 10, Queens, 1978-90; trustee, treas. Queens Pub. Communications Corp., 1983—; trustee, treas. Queens Borough Pub. Libr.,

1979—; pres., bd. dirs. Queen County Overall Econ. Devel. Corp., 1989—; exec. v.p. Queens coun. Boy Scouts Am., 1991—. Lt. (j.g.) USN, 1958-60; capt. USNR, 1960-88. Named Italian-Am. of Yr. Ferrini Welfare League, Queens, 1980; recipient Outstanding Community Leader award Boy Scouts Am., 1987, Pride of Queens award, 1990. Fellow ASCE; mem. ASTM, NSPE (trustee polit. action com. 1988—), N.Y. State Soc. Profl. Engrs. (v.p. 1984-86, pres. 1988-89, nat. dir. 1987-90, Engr. of Yr. 1983, pres. Queens chpt. 1980-82), Soc. Am. Mil. Engrs., N.Y. State Assn. of Professions (founding), Ozone Howard C. of C. (pres. 1980-84, 86—), Am. Parkinson Disease Assn. (dir. 1985—, exec. com. 1987—). Democrat. Congregationalist. Office: Miele Assocs 81-01 Furmanville Ave Middle Village NY 11379

MIFFLIN, THEODORE EDWARD, clinical biochemistry educator; b. Zion, Ill., Aug. 4, 1946; s. Edward Kenneth and Doris (Kleeb) M.; m. Mary Louise Epperson, May 19, 1973; children: Jonathon, Jennifer, Christopher. BS in Chemistry, Weber State Coll., 1968; PhD in Biochemistry, Utah State U., 1984. Cert. clin. chemist Nat. Registry in Clin. Chemistry. Chemist Southwest Bioclin. Lab., San Antonio, 1974-77; grad. rsch. asst. Utah State U., Logan, 1977-83; rsch. fellow med. ctr. U. Va., Charlottesville, Va., 1983-86; rsch. asst. prof. med. ctr. U. Va., 1986-90; assoc. prof. U. Pitts. Med. Ctr., 1991—; instr. Utah State U., Logan, 1980; dir. molecular probe lab., med. ctr. U. Va., Charlottesville, 1988-90; sect. chief molecular diagnostic unit clin. chem. div. Presbyn. U. Hosp., Pitts., 1991—. Author: Use of Nucleic Acid Probes in the Clinical Laboratory, 1988; contbr. articles to profl. jours.; mem. editorial adv. bd. Clin. Chem. News, 1987-92. With U.S. Army, 1968-73, staff sgt., 1972-73. Recipient Young Invest award Acad. Clin. Lab. Physicians and Scientists, 1986. Mem. Am. Assn. for Clin. Chemistry (E. Cotlove award 1985), AAAS, Am. Chem. Soc. Home: 266 Joseph St Pittsburgh PA 15237 Office: Presbyn U Hosp Rm 5845 Main Tower Desoto At O'Hara Sts Pittsburgh PA 15213

MIGEON, BARBARA RUBEN, pediatrician, geneticist; b. Rochester, N.Y., July 31, 1931; d. William Saul and Sara (Gitin) Ruben; m. Claude Jean Migeon, Apr. 2, 1960; children: Jacques Claude, Jean-Paul, Nicole. BA, Smith Coll., 1952; MD, SUNY, Buffalo, 1956. Diplomate Am. Bd. Pediatrics; cert. in med. genetics. Pediatric residency The Johns Hopkins U., Balt., 1956-59; fellow in endocrinology Harvard U. Med. Sch., Boston, 1959-60; fellow in genetics The Johns Hopkins Sch. Medicine, Balt., 1960-62, assoc. prof. pediatrics, 1970-79, joint appointment in biology, 1978—, prof. in pediatrics, 1979—, dir. PhD program in genetics, 1979-89; mem. Genetics Study Sect., NIH, Bethesda, Md., 1975-77, Mammalian Genetics Study Sect., NIH, Bethesda, 1977-79, Human Genome Study Sect., NIH, Bethesda, 1991—, editorial bds. Cancer Rsch., Somatic Cell Genetics, Trends in Genetics, Cytogenetic and Cell Genetics. Assoc. editor Jour. Exptl. Zoology; contbr. more than 100 rsch. papers to profl. publs. Named Prin. Investigator NIH grant, 1970—; recipient Outstanding Woman Physician award Med. Coll. Pa.; Vis. investigator Carnegie Instn. of Washington, 1975, Exch. prof. Guys Hosp., 1986. Mem. Am. Pediatric Soc., Am. Soc. Human Genetics, Genetics Soc. Am. Office: Ctr for Med Genetics CMSC 10-04 The Johns Hopkins U Baltimore MD 21205

MIGEON, CLAUDE JEAN, medical educator; b. Lievin, Pas-De-Calais, France, Dec. 22, 1923; came to U.S., 1950, naturalized, 1967; s. André and Pauline (Descamps) M.; m. Barbara Lou Ruben, Apr. 2, 1960; children: Jacques, Jean-Paul, Nicole. M.D., Sch. Medicine, U. Paris, 1950. Fellow dept. pediatrics Sch. Medicine, Johns Hopkins U., 1950-52, asst. prof., 1954-60, asso. prof., 1960-71, prof. pediatrics, 1971—; instr. biochemistry U. Utah, 1952-54; pediatrician Johns Hopkins Hosp., 1954—; mem. diabetes and metabolism tng. grants com. NIH, 1963-67, gen. clin. research centers com., 1968-71, mem. endocrinology study sect., 1974-78; cons. Med. Research Council Can., 1969-85, others; vis. prof. Maadi Armed Forces Hosp., Cairo, 1985, Guy's Hosp., London, 1986. Mem. editorial bd.: Johns Hopkins Med. Jour., 1970-72, Jour. Clin. Endocrinology and Metabolism, 1971-77, Hormone Rsch., 1979—; contbr. articles to profl. jours. Fulbright fellow, 1950; Am. Field Service fellow, 1950-51; Andre and Bella Meyer fellow, 1951-52; recipient research career award NIH, 1964-85. Fellow AAAS; mem. Endocrine Soc. (coun. 1971-74, chmn. pub. affairs com. 1974-91, Ayerst award, Williams award), Soc. Pediatric Rsch. (emeritus), Am. Pediatric Soc., Lawson Wilkins Pediatric Endocrine Soc. (founding pres. 1972), Am. Soc. Clin. Investigation (emeritus), Am. Physiol. Soc., Japanese Pediatric Endocrine Soc. (hon.), Found. for Am. Meml. Hosp. (bd. dirs. 1985—), Soc. Francaise d'Endocrinologie (fgn. corr. mem.). Home: 502 Somerset Rd Baltimore MD 21210-2720 Office: CMSC 3-110 Johns Hopkins Hosp Baltimore MD 21205

MIGLIACCIO, JOHN NICHOLAS, communications company executive; b. Bronx, N.Y., Sept. 17, 1949; s. Nicholas Joseph and Antonina (Martella) M.; m. Ann Dorothy Sonneville, Mar. 10, 1974; children: Renee, Joseph. BS in Psychology/Philosophy cum laude, Boston Coll., 1971; MEd, Columbia U., 1974, PhD, 1992. Sr. counselor Postgrad. Ctr., N.Y.C., 1974-77; cons. Achievement Concepts, N.Y.C., 1977-80; dir. spl. projects Retirement Advs. Div./Hearst, N.Y.C., 1980-89, v.p., 1989-92; pres. Maturity Mark Svcs., White Plains, N.Y., 1992—. Contbr. articles to profl. jours. Bd. advisors U.S. Adminstrn. on Aging, Washington, 1990—; adv. bd. Mainstream, SUNY, Westchester, Valhalla, 1984—. Mem. Am. Soc. on Aging (bd. dirs. San Francisco, 1987-92, cert. of award 1988, 92, chair bus. forum on aging 1990-92), Nat. Assn. for Sr. Living (bd. dirs. Annapolis 1985—, cert. of award 1987), Internat. Soc. of Retirement Planners (editor jours. 1987-90, award 1991), Metro N.Y. Assn. Applied Psychology, Internat. Soc. for Near Death Studies (bd. dirs. 1978-85), Nat. Found. for Retirement Living (cert. award 1990). Office: Maturity Mark Svcs 55 Springdale Ave Ste 100 White Plains NY 10604-2309

MIHAILESCU, MANUELA, marketing executive; b. Bucharest, Romania, May 25, 1950; came to U.S. 1980; d. Luca and Elena Livia (Papadopol) M.; m. Jon Dogar Marinesco, June 17, 1980. Student, U. Bucharest, 1969-71; MA, Film/Theater Inst., Bucharest, 1974; MBA, CUNY, 1988. Dir. mktg./advt. Theater I. Creanga, Bucharest, 1974-79; v.p. mktg. Point Blank, Inc., N.Y.C., 1988—. Contbr. articles to profl. jours. Recipient lst prize award 18th ann. Philip Morris Mktg./Communications Competition, 1987. Mem. Beta Gamma Sigma. Eastern Orthodox. Office: Point Blank Inc 27 W 20th St # 605 New York NY 10011-3707

MIHALSKI, TIMOTHY I., engineer; b. Pottsville, Pa., Feb. 16, 1950; s. Edmund F. and Gladys (Snyder) M.; m. Nanci M. Mayer, June 12, 1982. AS in Engring., Pa. State U., 1970; BS in Engring., Widener U., Chester, Pa., 1985. Draftsman E.I. Du Pont de Nemours & Co., Wilmington, Del., 1970-76, designer, 1976-83, sr. engr. designer, 1983-85, sr. engr., 1985-89, project engr., 1989—. Bd. dirs. Wellington Hills Civic Assn., Hockessin, Del., 1991. Mem. Nat. Inst. for Cert. Engring. Technicians. Republican. Roman Catholic.

MIHALSZKI, JOHN STEVEN, avionics engineer, physicist; b. Newark, Oct. 20, 1957; s. John and Magdolna (Juhasz) M. BS in Physics, Seton Hall U., 1979; postgrad., U. Ky., 1979-86. Sr. engr. Singer Corp., Wayne, N.J., 1984-89; staff engr. Boeing Helicopters, Ridley Park, Pa., 1989—. Mem. AIAA, IEEE Computer Soc., Inst. Navigation, Soc. Computer Simulation.

MIHM, MARTIN CHARLES, JR., pathologist, dermatologist; b. Pitts.; s. Martin Charles and Cecilia Matilda (Hepp) M. AB, Duquesne U., 1955; MD, U. Pitts., 1961; MA (with honors), Harvard U., 1989. Diplomate Am. Bd. Dermatology, Am. Bd. Pathology. Intern Mt. Sinai Hosp., N.Y.C., 1961-62, resident in medicine, 1963-64; resident in dermatology Mass. Gen. Hosp., Boston, 1964-67, resident in Pathology, 1968-72, chief dermatopathology, 1973—; asst. prof. pathology Harvard U. Med. Sch., Boston, 1972-75, assoc. prof., 1975-79, chief dermatopathology, 1982—; prof. pathology Mass. Gen. Hosp.-Harvard U., Boston, 1980—; adj. prof. pathology Vanderbilt U, 1989—; chmn. pathology com. Intergroup Melanoma Study, 1983—; pathologist Malignant Melanoma Coop. Group, 1972-77; chief sr. adminstr. Wellman Labs., Mass. Gen. Hosp., 1985—; cons. WHO, 1985—, chmn. pathology standing com., 1991—. Author: Primer of Dermatopathology, 1984, Problematic Pigmented Lesions, 1990; editor: Lymphoproliferative Disorders of the Skin, 1986, Pathbiology and Recognition Malignant Melanoma, 1988; contbr. articles to med. jours. Served to comdr. USPHS, 1967-69. Fellow ACP, Am. Acad. Dermatology, Am. Soc. Dermatopathology; mem. AMA (Harvard Med. Sch. rep. to med. sch. sect. 1991), Harvard Dermatology House Officer's Assn. (pres. 1982), Harvard Club (Boston, N.Y.C.), Alpha Omega Alpha, Pi Gamma Mu. Democrat. Roman Catholic. Home: 100 Memorial Dr Apt 87A Cambridge MA 02142-1330 Office: Mass Gen Hosp Fruit St Boston MA 02114-2620

MIHRAM, GEORGE ARTHUR, systemic scientist; b. Norman, Okla., Sept. 21, 1939; s. Russell George and Ella Lee (Stanaland) M.; m. Danielle Redibaum, Dec. 22, 1965. BS summa cum laude, U. Okla., 1960; postgrad., Wash. State U., Pullman, 1960-61; MS, Okla. State U., 1962, PhD, 1965. Operational researcher Ops. Rsch., Inc., Silver Spring, Md., 1965-66; systems analyst Joint Chiefs Staff, Washington, 1966-68; asst. prof. U. Pa., Phila., 1968-74; mem. faculty U. So. Calif., University Park, 1978-79; cons. IBM Corp., East Fishkill, N.Y., 1973, Acad. Ntural Scis., Phila., 1970-71, Office Asst. Sec. Def., 1969, Hdqrs. USAF, 1968-69. Author: Simulation: Statistical Foundations and Methodology, 1972, An Epistle to Dr. Benjamin Franklin, 1975, A Critique of World Models, 1975; co-author: Human Knowledge: Role of Models, Metaphors, and Analogy, 1974, Religion: Man's Earliest Science, 1978, Credibility: Every Computer Programme is a Simulation Model, 1985, Tele-cybernetics: Implications for the International Marketplace, 1988; assoc. editor: Simulation, 1973-75, Internat. Jour. Gen. Systems, 1973—, Modeling and Simulation, 1974. Mem. peer rev. panels NSF, Washington, 1974, 82. Capt. U.S. Army, 1966-68. Decorated Joint Svcs. Commendation medal; recipient award Conf. Simulation of Large Systems, Bielefeld, Fed. Republic Germany, 1980; Fulbright scholar U. Sydney, Australia, 1964-65; NSF rsch. initiation grantee, 1970-72, internat. travel grantee, 1975, NATO grantee, 1977. Mem. AAAS (profl. socs. ethics group), Internat. Assn. Statis. Computing, Internat. Soc. Systems Sci., Soc. Computer Simulation (chmn. tech. com. on verification and validation 1974-75), Soc. Lit. and Sci., Internat. Assn. Cybernetics, Am. Math. Soc., Am. Statis. Assn., Assn. Computing Machinery, Ops. Rsch. Soc. Am. (ethics and profl. practice com.), Math. Assn. Am., Sigma Xi, Pi Mu Epsilon, Phi Eta Sigma, Phi Beta Kappa. Home and Office: PO Box 1188 Princeton NJ 08542-1188

MIKELS, RICHARD ELIOT, lawyer; b. Cambridge, Mass., July 14, 1947; s. Albert Louis and Charlotte Betty (Shapiro) M.; m. Deborah Gwen Katz, Aug. 29, 1970; children: Allison Brooke, Robert Jarrett. BS in Bus. Adminstrn., Boston U., 1969, JD cum laude, 1972. Bar: Mass. 1972, U.S. Dist. Ct. Mass. 1974, U.S. Ct. Appeals (1st cir.) 1978. Legal examiner ICC, Washington, 1972-74; ptnr. Riemer & Braunstein, Boston, 1974-80; ptnr., chmn. comml. law sect. Peabody & Brown, Boston, 1980-88; mem., chmn. comml. law sect. Mintz, Levin, Cohn, Ferris, Glovsky and Popeo, P.C., Boston, 1988—. Contbr. articles to profl. jours. Tng. adv. com. Jewish Vocat. Svc., Boston, 1991. Fellow Am. Coll. Bankruptcy; mem. ABA, Am. Bankruptcy Inst., Assn. Comml. Ins. Attys., Comml. Law League Am., Mass. Bar Assn., Boston Bar Assn. Home: 1 Louis W Farley Dr Framingham MA 01701 Office: Mintz Levin Cohn Ferris Glovsky and Popeo PC 1 Fin Ctr Boston MA 02111

MIKLAUCIC, MICHAEL JAMES, international relations and foreign policy program administrator; b. Long Beach, Calif., June 17, 1954; s. Arwayne F. and Sonia (Brochetejn) M.; m. Antoinette Pauline Moon, Jan. 12, 1982. BA, U. Calif., Santa Cruz, 1976; MSc, London Sch. Econs., 1981; Cert., Internat. Law Inst., Washington, 1986, Salzburg (Austria) Seminar, 1987. Acad. analyst U. Calif., Santa Cruz, 1976-77; dep. editor Millennium Jour. of Internat. Studies, London, 1980-81, London-Washington Report, Washington, 1982-83; researcher Woodrow Wilson Ctr., Washington, 1983-84; project dir. AMIDEAST, Washington, 1984-90; dir. devel. Internat. Law Inst., Washington, 1991—. Contbr. articles to profl. jours. Rapporteur Salzburg Seminar on U.S. Fgn. Policy, 1988. Mem. Internat. Inst. Strategic Studies, Am. Soc. Internat. Law, Internat. Law Assn., Am. Polit. Sci. Assn., Mid. East Studies Assn., Internat. Polit. Sci. Assn., Internat. Law Inst. (fellow). Office: Internat Law Inst 1615 New Hampshire Ave NW Washington DC 20009

MIKOLAJCZAK, BOLESLAW, computer science educator, researcher, consultant; b. Poznan, Poland, June 30, 1946; came to U.S., 1986; s. Walenty and Maria (Piechocka) M; m. Urszula Hajdrowska, Aug. 14, 1971; children: Maciej, Wojciech Rafal. MS in Control Engring. summa cum lauda, Tech. U., Poznan, 1970, PhD, 1974, Dr.Habilitis in Computer Sci., 1979; MS in Math., Adam Mickiewicz U., Poznan, 1972. Lectr. Inst. Control Engring., Poznan, 1970-74, asst. prof., 1974-79, assoc. prof., 1980-85; assoc. prof. Computer Sci. Ctr., Poznan, 1985-86; vis. lectr. dept. computer sci. Southea. Mass. U. (now U. Mass.), Dartmouth, 1986-87, assoc. prof., 1987-91; assoc. prof. dept. computer and info. sci. U. Mass. (formerly Southeastern Mass. U.), Dartmouth, 1991—; sci. cons. Elana, Torun, Poland, 1980-85, Tekoma, Warsaw, Poland, 1982-84, Lenin's Steelwork, Cracow, Poland, 1984-85, Mercomp, Warsaw, 1985-86; vis. scholar Cornell U., Ithaca, N.Y., 1976-77. Author: Transformations of Automata and Computational Complexity of Some Problems in Automata Theory, 1988, Algebraic and Structural Automata Theory, 1989, others; contbr. articles to profl. jours.; patentee in field. Active Polish Tchrs. Assn., 1964-80, Trade Union Solidarnosc, 1980—. Recipient award Ministry of Sci. and Tech., 1980, Gen. Tech. Orgn., 1980, Polish Acad. Scis., 1981, 84, Ministry of Higher Edn., 1982. Mem. Am. Math. Soc., Computer Soc. of IEEE, Polish Math. Soc., Assn. for Computing Machinery, Polish Computer Soc., Mass. Tchrs. Assn., Math. Revs. (reviewer 1976—). Roman Catholic. Office: U Mass Old Wesport Rd Dartmouth MA 02747

MIKULSKI, BARBARA ANN, senator; b. Balt., July 20, 1936; d. William and Christina Eleanor (Kutz) M. B.A., Mt. St. Agnes Coll., 1958; M.S.W., U. Md., 1965; LL.D. (hon.), Goucher Coll., 1973, Hood Coll., 1978. Tchr. Mt. St. Agnes Coll., 1969; tchr. Community Coll. Balt., 1970-71, VISTA Tng. Ctr., 1965-70; with Balt. Dept. Social Services, 1961-63, 66-70, York Family Agy., 1964, Assoc. Catholic Charities, 1958-61; mem. Balt. City Council, 1971-76; mem. 96th-99th Congresses from 3d Md. Dist., 1979-87, mem. interstate, fgn. commerce, mcht. marine coms.; U.S. senator from Md., 1987—, mem. appropriations, labor and numan rels., small bus. coms.; mem. Congl. Steel Caucus, Congresswomen's Caucus, Democratic Study Group, Environ. Study Conf., Mems. Congress for Peace Through Law; cons. Nat. Ctr. Urban Ethnic Affairs, others. Contbr. articles to mags. and newspapers. Bd. dirs. Valley House; nat. bd. dirs. Urban Coalition; mem. Polish Women's Alliance, Polish Am. Congress, Citizens Planning and Housing Assn., S.E. Community Orgn.; chmn. com. community devel. Archdiocesan Urban Commn.; mem. nat. com. Muskie for Pres., 1971-72; chmn. com. del. selection and party structure Dem. Nat. Com.; Dem. nominee U.S. Senate, 1974, Ho. of Reps., 1976; mem. Dem. Nat. Strategy Council. Named Woman of Yr. MS. mag., 1987; first woman apptd. to U.S. Ho. Reps. energy and commerce com.; elected to represent Dem. Party in both houses of Congress; first Dem. woman elected to U.S. Senate in her own right. Mem. Nat. Women's Polit. Caucus, Nat. Bus. and Profl. Women's Assn., Am. Fedn. Tchrs., Nat. Assn. Social Workers, LWV. Office: US Senate 320 Hart Office Bldg Washington DC 20510-2003*

MIKUS, ELEANORE ANN, artist; b. Detroit, July 25, 1927; d. Joseph and Bertha (Englot) M.; m. Richard Burns, July 6, 1949 (div. 1963); children: Richard, Hillary, Gabrielle. Student, Mich. State U., 1946-49, U. Mex., summer 1948; B.F.A., U. Denver, 1957, M.A., 1967; postgrad., Art Students League, 1958, NYU, 1959-60. Asst. prof. Cornell U., Ithaca, N.Y., 1979-80, assoc. prof., 1980-92, prof. art, 1992—; asst. prof. art Monmouth Coll., West Long Branch, N.J., 1966-70, prof. Cornell, Rome, 1989; vis. lectr. painting Cooper Union, N.Y.C., 1970-72, Central Sch. Art and Design, London, 1973-77, Harrow (Eng.) Coll. Tech. and Art, 1975-76. Exhibited in 14 one-person shows at, Pace Gallery, N.Y.C. and O.K. Harris Gallery, N.Y.C., Baskett Gallery, Cin., 1982, 84, 85; represented in permanent collections including, Mus. Modern Art, N.Y.C., Whitney Mus., N.Y.C., Los Angeles County Mus., Cin. Mus., Birmingham (Ala.) Mus. Art, Indpls. Mus. Art, Nat. Gallery Art, Washington, Victoria and Albert Mus., London, Library of Congress, Washington; subject of book Eleanore Mikus, Shadows of the Real (by Robert Hobbs and Judith Bernstock), 1991. Guggenheim fellow, 1966-67; Tamarind fellow, summer 1968; MacDowell fellow, summer 1969; grantee Cornell U., 1988. Mem. AAUP. Home: PO Box 6586 Ithaca NY 14851-6586 Office: Cornell U Dept Art Tjaden Hall Ithaca NY 14853

MIKUTOWICZ, MICHAEL ANTHONY (MICKY TOWIICZ), musician; b. Adams, Mass., Dec. 12, 1958; s. Walter John and Jacqueline Virginia (Brooks) M.; m. Margie Marie Melillo, May 31, 1986. Grad. high sch., Chesire, Mass. Musician, drummer Strut, 1988-89; singer Loudcrowd, 1990—. Singer with Strut on album: Unlimited Access, 1988. Mem. Forest Pk. Country Club and Golf Course (Class B Club champ 1987). Office: Loudcrowd PO Box 512 Adams MA 01220

MIKVA, ABNER JOSEPH, federal judge; b. Milw., Jan. 21, 1926; s. Henry Abraham and Ida (Fishman) M.; m. Zoe Wise, Sept. 19, 1948; children: Mary, Laurie, Rachel. JD cum laude, U. Chgo., 1951; DL (hon.), U. Ill., Am. U., Northwestern U.; DHL (hon.), Hebrew U. Bar: Ill. 1951, D.C. 1978. Law clk. to U.S. Supreme Ct. Justice Sherman Minton, 1951; ptnr. firm Devoe, Shadur, Mikva & Plotkin, Chgo., 1952-68, D'Ancona, Pflaum, Wyatt & Riskind, 1973-74; lectr. Northwestern U. Law Sch., Chgo., 1973-75, U. Pa. Law Sch., 1983-85, Georgetown Law Sch., 1986-88, Duke U. Law Sch., Durham, N.C., 1990-91, U. Chgo. Law Sch., 1992—, 1992—; mem. Ill. Gen. Assembly from 23d Dist., 1956-66, 91st-92d Congresses from 2d Dist. Ill., 94th-96th Congresses from 10th Dist. Ill., ways and means com., judiciary com.; chmn. Dem. Study Group; resigned, 1979; judge U.S. Circuit Ct. Appeals D.C., 1979-91; chief judge, 1991—; chmn. Ill. Bd. Ethics, 1973. Author: The American Congress: The First Branch, 1983. Served with USAAF, World War II. Recipient Page One award Chgo. Newspaper Guild, 1964; Best Legislator award Ind. Voters Ill., 1956-66; named One of Ten Outstanding Young Men in Chgo. Jr. Assn. Commerce and Industry, 1961. Mem. ABA, Chgo. Bar Assn. (bd. mgrs. 1962-64), D.C. Bar Assn., Am. Law Inst., Phi Beta Kappa, Order of Coif. Office: US Ct Appeals 3d & Constitiution Ave NW Washington DC 20001

MIKVA, ZOE WISE, development director; b. St. Louis, Apr. 4, 1928; d. Harry and Minnie (Laventhal) Wise; m. Abner J. Mikva, Sept. 19, 1948; children: Mary, Laurie, Rachel Mikva Rosenberg. BA, U. Chgo., 1947, MA, 1951. Cert. tchr. Ill., D.C. Adminstrv. asst. ACLU Ill. Div., 1950-51; legis. cons. Friends Commn. on Legis., Washington, 1951-52; office mgr. United Steelworkers PAC-3rd Congrl. Dist., Ill., 1952, 54; tchr. D.C. Pub. Schs., Washington, 1968-72, 80-82, Evanston (Ill.) Pub. Schs., 1972-79; state affairs coord. Nat. Hwy. Traffic Safety Adminstrn., Washington, 1979-80; bus. owner The Hill Co., Washington, 1982-91; dir. devel. Advocacy Inst., Washington, 1986—; chmn. fin. com. Micah House Inc., Washington; organizer Progressive Fundraisers Roundtable, Washington. V.p. D.C. Chpt. Women's Equity Action League, Washington, 1986-90. Mem. Older Women's League, Clearinghouse on Women's Issues. Democrat. Jewish. Office: Advocacy Inst 1730 Rhode Island Ave NW Washington DC 20036-3101

MILAI, KIMBERLY IVY, music teacher; b. Pitts., July 2, 1958; s. Ahmed Samuel and Barbara (Arrington) M. Student, Ind. U. of Pa., 1976-79; MusB, Baldwin Wallace Coll., 1981; MusM, Eastman Sch. Music, 1984. Tchr. Kodaly Third St. Music Sch., N.Y.C., 1986-89; music tchr. Bklyn. (N.Y.) Music Sch., 1988-90; music tchr. Kodaly Little Red Sch. House, N.Y.C., 1989-91, Greenwich House Music Sch., N.Y.C., 1989—; music tchr. Yung Wing Sch. Pub. Sch. 124, N.Y.C., 1988—; drummer, percussionist Raw Mgmt., N.Y.C., 1988-90; drummer Antoinettes, N.Y.C., 1982-88. Composer: The Girls Can't Help It, 1984; illustrator in field. Mem. N.Y. Flute Club, Am. Harp Soc. Bahai. Office: Yung Wing Sch Pub Sch 124 40 Division St New York NY 10002-6705

MILANI, VICTOR JOHN, science educator; b. Mount Vernon, N.Y., Sept. 26, 1945; s. Victor John and Sonia (Iandoli) M.; m. Joanne Elizabeth Armbruster, June 22, 1973; children: Victor John III, Valerie Jean. BS, CCNY, 1967; MS, NYU, 1971, PhD, 1973. Teaching assoc. NYU, N.Y.C., 1967-72; asst. prof. CUNY, N.Y.C., 1972-73; rsch. assoc. Manhattan Coll., Bronx, N.Y., 1972-74; prof. sci./law Bay Path. Coll., Longmeadow, Mass., 1974—; sr. acad. instr. Mass. Criminal Justice Tng. Coun., State of Mass., 1979—. Recipient citations gov., sec. of state, Commonwealth of Mass., 1983, Mass. Ho. of Reps., 1986, U.S. Marshal Svc., 1990; recipient Citizen of Yr. award Quaboag C. of C., 1986. Mem. Am. Soc. Microbiology. Office: Bay Path Coll 588 Longmeadow St East Longmeadow MA 01106-2292

MILARDO, TERRENCE JOHN, lawyer; b. Middletown, Conn., Mar. 4, 1941; s. Salvatore Joseph and Rose Ann (Tracy) M.; m. Mary Ann Overend, Oct. 7, 1961 (div. June 1976); children: Cheryl, Terrence Jr., Michelle. AA, Middlesex Community Coll., 1981; BS in Econs., Central Conn. State U., 1985; JD, U. Bridgeport, 1989. Bar: Conn. 1990. Mfg. engr. Pratt & Whitney Aircraft Co., Middletown, 1967-77, group supr., 1977-79, foreman, 1979-84, analyst, 1984-90; ret., 1990; pvt. practice, East Haddam, Conn., 1990—; music tchr. Conn., 1960-67. Pres. Middletown Young Democrats, 1963-65. Mem. Jaycees (state rep. Middletown, 1961-64). Home and Office: 110 Boardman Rd East Haddam CT 06423-1339

MILAS, LAWRENCE WILLIAM, foundation executive, lawyer; b. Milw., June 29, 1935; s. George and Leah (Kahn) M.; m. Marjorie Helene Weiser, Jan. 17, 1958; children: Scott Charles, Betsy Nan, Wendy Beth. BSBA, Babson Coll., 1958; LLB, Columbia U., 1963; DFA (hon.), Roanoke Coll., 1985; DHL (hon.), Whitman Coll., 1988. Bar: N.Y. 1963. Assoc. Wynn & Blattmachr, N.Y.C., 1963-68; ptnr. Wynn, Blattmachr Campbell & Milas, N.Y.C., 1968-76; ptnr. Baer Marks & Upham, N.Y.C., 1976-88, of counsel, 1988—; asst. v.p. F.W. Olin Found., Inc., N.Y.C., 1974-76, v.p., 1976-83, counsel, 1974-83, pres., 1983—, also bd. dirs. With U.S. Army, 1954-55. Recipient Babson medal Babson Coll. Alumni Assn., 1988. Mem. ABA, N.Y. State Bar Assn., Assn. Bar City N.Y., Northport Yacht Club (N.Y.), Princeton Club. Office: FW Olin Found Inc 780 3d Ave Ste 3403 New York NY 10017

MILASKI, JOHN JOSEPH, marketing, systems consultant; b. Johnson City, N.Y., Sept. 16, 1959; s. John Walter and Nellie Joan (Panaro) M. AAS, Broome Community Coll., 1979; BSEE, Rochester Inst. Tech., 1984; MBA, Syracuse U., 1989. Registered engr., N.Y. Design engr. IBM, Endicott, N.Y., 1979-84; systems engr. IBM, Endicott, 1984-85, mktg. cons., 1985-91; CIM cons. C&WNY, Endicott, 1992—; Mem. IEEE (sr.) ASME (Sr.), Computer and Automated Systems Assn., Am. Prodn. and Inventory Control Soc. (sr.), IBM 100 Percent Club (Nat. Mktg. award 1987-89), IBM Systems Engring. Tech. Symposium (1989), US. C. of C. Inventor. Recipient Utilities Industry Mktg. Excellence award, 1989. Mem. IEEE (sr.), ASME (sr.), Computer and Automated Systems Assn., Am. Prodn. and Inventory Control Soc. (sr.), IBM 100 Percent Club (Nat. Mktg. award 1987, 87), U.S. C. of C. Republican. Roman Catholic. Home: 214 Cornell Ave Endicott NY 13760-2724

MILBERGS, EGILS, academic administrator; b. Lubeck, Fed. Republic Germany, Aug. 7, 1946; s. Adolph and Cita Vija (Tuperins) M.; m. Cynthia Modisett, Sept. 16, 1972; 1 child, Stephanie Kambar. AB, Harvard U., 1968. Program analyst Office Mgmt. and Budget, Washington, 1968-72; mem. staff Pres.'s Adv. Coun. Exec. Orgn., Washington, 1970; dir. program devel. Stanford Rsch. Inst. (SRI), Menlo Park, Calif., 1972-80; dep. asst. sec. U.S. Dept. Commerce, Washington, 1980-84; exec. dir. Pres's Commn. Indsl. Competitiveness, Washington, 1985, Am. Fedn. Info. Processing Socs., Reston, Va., 1986-87; pres., chief operating officer Inst. for Ill., Washington and Chgo., 1988—; mem. Nat. Adv. Coun. for Counseling Edn., Washington, 1984, exec. com. Nat. Conf. for Advancement Rsch., Washington, 1985; bd. dirs. Ill. Coalition. Mem. Harvard Club Washington, City Club Washington. Office: Inst for Ill Washington and Chgo 409 3rd St SW Washington DC 20024-3212

MILDER, JAY, artist; b. Omaha, May 12, 1934; s. Leo and Jeanette M.; children: Rachael, Rifka, Joshua, Isobella. Student, U. Nebr., Omaha, 1953-54, Sorbonne, Paris, 1954-56, Art Inst. of Chgo., 1956-57, Hans Hofmann Sch., Provincetown, Mass., 1958-62. tchr. art Dayton Art Inst., 1963-65, N.Y. Inst. Tech., N.Y.C., 1965, Pratt Inst., Bklyn., 1966, Brandeis Inst., Santa Susana, Calif., 1967-68, Md. Art Inst., Balt., 1969, Chrysler Mus. Sch., Norfolk, Va., 1970, CUNY, 1971-89, Vt. Studio Sch., Johnson, 1989. Numerous one man shows at various mus. and galleries including Harcourts Contemporary, San Francisco, 1987, Richard Green Gallery, N.Y.C., 1987, Gallery Jupiter, Little Silver, N.J., 1988, eleonore Austerer Fine Art, San Mateo, Calif., 1988, Girgis & Klym Gallery, Australia, 1988, Anton Gallery, Washington, 1989, Yares Gallery, Scottsdale, Ariz., 1989; nomerous group shows including Galerie Helen Grubair, Miami, Fla., 1988, Newport Art

Mus., 1988, Unipas Gallery, N.Y.C., 1988, many others. Home and Office: 108 Wooster St New York NY 10012-5205

MILES, CHRISTINE MARIE, museum director; b. Madison, Ind., Mar. 2, 1951; d. Leland Weber and Mary Virginia (Geyer) M.; B.A., Boston U., 1973; M.A., George Washington U., 1982; postgrad. Mus. Mgmt. Inst., 1985. Curatorial asst. Mus. of the City of N.Y., 1973-75; art gallery dir. South Street Seaport Mus., N.Y.C., 1975-77; researcher AIA Found., Washington, 1978-80; dir. Fraunces Tavern Mus., N.Y.C., 1980-86, Albany (N.Y.) Inst. History and Art, 1986—; bd. dirs. SUNY-Albany Found., Lower Manhattan Cultural Council, Hist. Albany Found., Fedn. Hist. Services, SUNY at Albany Found.; pres. Gallery Assn. N.Y. State; council mem. N.Y. State Assn. Museums; mus. aid panel N.Y. State Council on Arts, 1985-88;. Author, writer/coordinator, compiler of catalogs in field. Mem. Am. Assn. Mus. Office: Albany Inst History & Art 125 Washington Ave Albany NY 12210-2296

MILES, EDWARD HARRY, optometrist; b. Bklyn., Feb. 16, 1936; s. Bernard Ralph and Esther (Ungarten) M.; m. Ina Beth Goldberg, June 4, 1970; children: Bradley Samuel, Jamie Lauren, Michael Jared. Student, Bklyn. Coll., 1957-59, L.I. U., 1959, NYU, 1959, Roosevelt U., 1962; BS in Optics, Ill. Coll. Optometry, 1962, D in Optometry, 1962; postgrad., N.Y. Tech. Coll., 1981. Mem. staff orthopedic ward Baimbridge (Md.) Hosp., 1955, dir. med. sick call rm., 1955-57; pvt. practice N.Y.C., 1964—; contract physician Health Ins. Plan Greater N.Y., 1975—; sec.-treas. Comprehensive Profl. Systems, N.Y., 1980—, United Dental Systems, N.Y., 1989—, Comprehensive Purchasing Group, N.Y., 1990—; mem. legis. com. Local 408 Optical Workers Union, N.Y., 1986—. Author: Chauffers Badges and Auto-Related Badges of the World, Keychain Tag News-Many License Plate Collectors newsletter. Mem. Nassau Civic Club, N.Y., 1986—, Bnai Brith Teamsters Lodge, N.Y., 1986—; bd. dirs. N.Y. Consumer Assembly, Greater N.Y. Safety Coun. With USN, 1954-57. Mem. Execs. Assn. Greater N.Y., State Revenue Soc. (bd. dirs. 1980-92), Am. Revenue Assn., N.Y. State Optometric Assn., Automobile License Plate Collectors Assn. (editor newsletter). Home and Office: 888-8th Ave New York NY 10019

MILES, HERMAN WILBUR, data processing executive; b. Vandergrift, Pa., Dec. 10, 1924; s. Charles Abraham and Bertha Alma (Collins) M.; m. Bertha Dorcas Henson, Apr. 12, 1947; children: Herman Jr., Sterling, Clyde, Phyllis, Gordon, Deborah, Sharon, Steven, Lorie. BSBA, Am. U., 1955; diploma, Indsl. Coll. of the Armed Forces, 1972; M of Sci. Adminstrn., George Washington U., 1972. Lic. real estate broker Md., D.C., Va. Survey statistician Armed Svcs. Tech. Info. Agy., Arlington Hall Station, Va., 1946-59; chief systems & programming Def. Tech. Info. Ctr., Cameron Station, Va., 1959-67, dir. devel., 1967-73, dep. adminstr., 1973-80; gen. mgr. NASA Sci. & Tech. Info. Ctr., Linthicum, Md., 1980-84; v.p. Planning Rsch. Co., McLean, Va., 1984-88, Kendrick & Co., Washington, 1988-89; owner Superior Realty Co., Temples Hills, Md. and Fairfax, Va., 1955—. Recipient Sr. Exec. Svc. award U.S. Civil Svc., Washington, 1979. Mem. ACM, Am. Soc. for Info. Scis. Home: 9105 Wexford Dr Vienna VA 22182-2152 Office: Superior Realty Corp 9916 Main St # B Fairfax VA 22031-3901

MILES, MITCHELL SCOTT, clergy member, educator; b. Mishawaka, Ind., Aug. 28, 1954; s. John Henry and Clarice Susanne (Kindig) M.; m. Judith Kay Zink, July 24, 1976; children: Michelle Renee, Wesley Scott. BA, Bethel Coll., 1976; MA in Theology, Fuller Theol. Sem., 1980. Ordained to ministry Brethren in Christ Ch., 1986. Youth pastor Bethany Missionary Ch., Elkhart, Ind., 1976-77, Faith Missionary Ch., Pomona, Calif., 1977-78; min. edn. Avalon Missionary Ch., Ft. Wayne, Ind., 1980-82; assoc. pastor, leader devel. Brethren in Christ Ch., Lancaster, Pa., 1982-85; sr. pastor Brethren in Christ Ch., Abilene, Kans., 1985-88; assoc. pastor for Christian edn. Brethren in Christ Ch., Waynesboro, Pa., 1988—; ch. edn. cons. in field. Author: Families Growing Together, 1990, Unwrapping God's Gift, 1990, The Goodness of God Among Us, 1990, Confronting a World Gone Wrong, 1992, Peace Is: Family Camp Program, 1992; contbr. articles to ministry periodicals. Recipient Alumni Achievement award Bethel Coll., 1992. Mem. Profl. Assn. Christian Educators, Sesquehanna Valley Christian Edn. Assn. Republican. Home: 11612 Westminster Dr Waynesboro PA 17268

MILES, REBECCA STEPEK, clinical psychologist; b. Pitts., Apr. 24, 1950; d. Stephen and Mary Ann (Kaelin) Stepek; m. David K. Miles, Apr. 12, 1980. BA, U. Pitts., 1974; PhD, Duquesne U., 1986. Lic. psychologist, Pa. Therapist Rehab. Inst. Pitts., 1975-81; pvt. practice, 1984—; asst. prof. psychology Duquesne U., 1986-87; clin. coord. Pitts. Cancer Inst., 1989—; mem. Profl. Psychology Consultation Group, Pitts.; mem., originator Profl. Women's Study Group, 1991—. Mem. APA, Pa. Psychol. Assn. Office: Cathedral Mansions 4716 Ellsworth Ave Pittsburgh PA 15213-2851

MILES, RICHARD BRYANT, mechanical and aerospace engineering educator; b. Washington, July 10, 1943; s. Thomas Kirk and Elizabeth (Bryant) M.; m. Susan McCoy, May 14, 1983; children: Thomas, Julia. BSEE, Stanford U., 1966, MSEE, 1967, PhD in Elec. Engring., 1972. Rsch. assoc. elec. engring. dept. Stanford (Calif.) U., summer 1972; asst. prof. mech. and aerospace engring. dept. Princeton (N.J.) U., 1972-78, assoc. prof., 1978-82, prof., 1982—, chmn. engring. physics program, 1980—; lectr. Northwestern Poly. U., Xian, China, 1987. Contbr. articles to profl. publs., chpt. to book Advances in Fluid Mechanics Measurements, 1989; patentee in field. Bd. dirs. Fannie and John Hertz Found., Livermore, Calif., 1989—. Fannie and John Hertz Found. fellow, 1969-72; NSF summer trainee, 1972. Mem. AIAA (sr.), IEEE (sr.), Am. Phys. Soc., Optical Soc. Am. Office: Princeton U Mech & Aerospace Engring D-414 Eng Quad Olden St Princeton NJ 08544

MILGRAM, MORRIS, integrated housing developer; b. N.Y.C., May 29, 1916; s. Benjamin and Fannie (Gladstone) M.; m. Grace B. Smelo, June 26, 1937 (div. Mary. 1969); chliden: Gene, Elizabeth S.; m. Jean Babcock Gregg, Apr. 21, 1967 (div. Nov. 1975); m. Lorna Scheide, Dec. 13, 1975 (dec. Aug. 1987); m. Frances Johnson Drevers, June 11, 1988. BA in Econs., Rutgers U., 1939; LHD, Starr-King Sch. for Ministry (Unit.), 1967. Pres. Smelo-Peters-Milgram, Inc., Phila., 1950-53; exec. v.p. Concord Park Homes, Inc./Greenbelt Assocs., Inc., Phila., 1954-57, Princeton (N.J.) Housing Assocs., 1957-59; pres. Modern Community Developers and Planned Communities, Inc., 1958-69; mgr. Mut. Real Estate Investment Trust, N.Y.C., 1965-69; gen. ptnr. Ptnrs. in Housing, Phila., 1969—; pres. Choice Communities Inc., Phila., 1969-77, co-chmn. 1977—; pres. Fund for an Open Soc., Phila., 1975—. Author: Good Neighborhood, The Challenge of Open Housing, 1977, 79; (with Roger N. Beilenson) Racial Integration in Housing, 1968; contbr. articles to profl. jours.; patentee in field. Trustee Rutgers U., New Brunswick, N.J., 1968-74; bd. dirs. Rural Advancement Fund, Charlotte, N.C., 1979-85, Bucks County Housing Devel. Corp., Doylestown, Pa., 1987-89; mem. Pa. adv. com. U.S. Commn. on Civil Rights, 1985—. Recipient 1st Ann. Walter White award Nat. Com. vs Discrimination in Housing, 1965, 1st Nat. Human Rights award HUD, 1968, Ernest Siler award Nat. Neighbors, 1984, Clarence Farmer award Phila. Commn. on Human Rels., 1990. Mem. Nat. Assn. Housing and Redevel. Ofcls., Citizens Housing and Planning Coun. N.Y., Am. Jewish Com. Home: 290 Winchester Ave Apt 220 Langhorne PA 19047-2230 Office: Fund for an Open Soc 311 S Juniper St # 400 Philadelphia PA 19107-5804

MILGROM, FELIX, immunologist, educator; b. Rohatyn, Poland, Oct. 12, 1919; came to U.S., 1958; naturalized, 1963; s. Henryk and Ernestina (Cyryl) M.; m. Halina Miszel, Oct. 15, 1941; children: Henry, Martin Louis. Student, U. Lwow, Poland, 1937-41, U. Lublin, Poland, 1945; MD, U. Wroclaw, Poland, 1947; MD (hon.), U. Vienna, Austria, 1976, U. Lund, Sweden, 1979, U. Heidelberg, Fed. Republic Germany, 1979, U. Bergen, Norway, 1980; DSc (hon.), U. Med. Dent., N.J., 1991. Rsch. assoc., prof. dept. microbiology Sch. Medicine U. Wroclaw, 1946-54, chmn. dept., 1954; prof., head dept. microbiology Sch. Medicine, Silesian U., Zabrze, Poland, 1954-57; rsch. assoc. Svc. de Chime Microbienne, Pasteur Inst., Paris, 1957; rsch. assoc., prof. dept. bacteriology, immunology Sch. Medicine, U. Buffalo, 1958-62; assoc. prof., then prof. and disting. prof. microbiology Sch. Medicine, SUNY, Buffalo, 1962—, chmn. dept., 1967-85. Author: Studies on the Structure of Antibodies, 1950; co-editor: International Convocations on Immunology, 1969, 75, 79, 85, Principles of Immunology, 1973, 2d edit., 1979, Principles of Immunological Diagnosis in Medicine, 1981, Medical Microbiology, 1982; editor in chief Internat. Archives of Allergy and Applied Immunology, 1965—; contbg. editor Vox Sanguinis, 1965-76, Transfusion, 1966-73, Cellular Immunology, 1970-83, Transplantation, 1975-78; contbr. numerous articles to profl. jours. Recipient Alfred Jurzykowski Found. prize, 1986, Paul Ehrlich and Ludwig Darmstaedter prize, 1987. Mem. Am. Assn. Immunologists, Transplantation Soc. (v.p. 1976-78), Am. Acad. Microbiology, Coll. Internat. Allergologicum (v.p. 1970-78, pres. 1978-82), Sigma Xi. Home: 474 Getzville Rd Buffalo NY 14226-2555

MILICEVIC, JELENA, health science specialist; b. Skopje, Macedonia, Yugoslavia, Jan. 1, 1939; came to U.S., 1972; d. Miladin and Hedy (Hem) M.; m. Ernst Anzbock, Dec. 14, 1959 (div. 1971); children: Harald, Evelyn; m. Ranko Caric, Nov. 3, 1973 (div. 1980); 1 child, Peter. Student, Molloy Coll., 1979-81, L.I. U., 1981-82, Rockland Community Coll., 1985, Vt. Coll., 1985-86, Orange County Community Coll., 1988, Empire State Coll., 1990—. Ordained to ministry Universal Spiritualist Assn. U.S.A., 1985; lic., real estate agt., N.Y.; registered and cert. reflexologist, N.Y. Owner Walter's Bake Shop, 1973-79; nurse's aide Hillside Manor, 1980; clerical worker Molloy Coll., 1980-81, L.I. U., 1981-82; chiropractor asst. Steven R. Siegel D.C., 1982; owner Linden Motel, 1983; lectr. on Shiatsu and reflexology New Age Ctr., 1985-86; v.p., min. Universal Ctr. New Age Consciousness, Inc., Milford, Pa., 1985—; with Abatelli Realty, 1988; gen. agt. Intern Cons. Exchange, San Diego, Calif., 1986. Mem. Am. Massage Therapy Assn., Alliance of Massage Therapists, Inc., Universal Spiritualist Assn., N.Y. State Soc. Med. Massage Therapists, Internat. Platform Assn., Warwick Art League. Home: 119 Wickham Ave Middletown NY 10940 Office: Universal Ctr New Age 313 Broad St Milford PA 18337-1322

MILLAR, ROBERT JAMES, social science educator; b. Abington, Pa., Feb. 15, 1951; s. Robert Eugene and Louise Ruth (Mitsch) M.; m. Lynn C. Harding, May 18, 1974; children: Nancy, Reed, Scotty. BS in Social Studies, Kutztown U., 1973, MEd in Social Studies, 1978. Tchr. social studies Hatboro (Pa.)-Horsham Sch. Dist., 1973-75, Fleetwood (Pa.) Area Sch. Dist., 1975-77; adj. prof. social sci. Reading (Pa.) Area Community Coll., 1977—; instr. archaeology Kutztown (Pa.) U., 1985—; instr. social sci. Alvernia Coll., Reading, 1986-88; resource person in anthropology and archaeology Berks County Intermediate Unit, Reading, 1984—; cons. archaeologist Borough of Shillington, Pa., 1985—. Producer, host local TV program, ACLU Presents, 1981-88, Alternative News Show, 1991—; editor: Prehistoric Artifacts of the Schuylkill Valley, 1983. Bd. dirs. Health Systems Coun. S.E. Pa., Allentown, 1982-86; chmn. pub. affairs com. Planned Parenthood Ea. Pa., Reading, 1987—; vice chmn. Sierra Club Berks County, Kutztown, 1988—; chmn. Dem. Socialists Club; v.p. Dem. Coun. Berks County, 1987-89; pres. Berks County sect. ACLU, 1981-84, 86-92, bd. dirs. Pa. chpt. 1980-84; mem. Berks County Planning Commn., 1991—. Mem. Soc. Pa. Archaeology (bd. dirs. 1981-86), Schuylkill Valley Archaeology Soc. (pres. 1976-77, 81-87), Eastern States Archaeol. Fedn., Archaeol. Soc. N.J., N.Y. Archaeol. Soc. Unitarian. Home: 19 Spring Ln Fleetwood PA 19522-1035 Office: Reading Area Community Coll PO Box 1706 Reading PA 19603-1706

MILLARD, JAMES KEMPER, marketing executive; b. Lexington, Ky., Oct. 28, 1948; s. Lyman Clifford and Cora (Carrick) M.; m. Madelyn Hooper, Nov. 26, 1983; children: Lyman Clifford III, Sean Duffy, James Kemper Jr., Caroline Carrick. BA, Transylvania U., Lexington, Ky., 1971. Writer AP, Lexington, 1970-71; asst. news. dir. Sta. WLEX-TV, FM, Lexington, 1971-76; producer Ky. Dept. Pub. Info., Frankfort, 1973; dir. univ. rels. Transylvania U., Lexington, 1973-79; acct. supr. Abbott Advt., Inc., Lexington, 1979-85; mktg. dir. Steak N' Shake, Inc., Indpls., 1985; field mktg. mgr. Blue Bell, Pa., 1985-86; field mktg. dir. Nutri/System Inc., Blue Bell, Pa., 1986-88, v.p. communications, 1988-90, sr. v.p. mktg., 1990-91; pres. Mktg. Communications Overview, Inc., Exton, Pa., 1991—; mem. acad. adv. com. Ea. Ky. U., Richmond, 1983-87; treas. Bluegrass Integrated Pest Mgmt., Lexington, 1983-85; case study speaker Radio Advertisers Bur., 1989, 90. Author: C&O Streamliners, 1988. Advertising officer Chesapeake & Ohio Rwy. Hist. Soc., Alderson, W.Va., 1983—, ann. fund officer, 1989—; mem., comdr.-in-chief Leadership Circle, 1990—; pres. Swan Kitchen Car Co., 1990—; mem. Am. Assn. Pvt. R.R. Car Owners, 1990—; mem. R.R. Passenger Car Alliance, 1990—; mem. Hon. Order Ky. Cols., Louisville, 1976—, Kidney Found. Ind.; deacon Cen. Christian Ch., Lexington, 1984-86; cons. Jr. Achievement Project Bus. Lexington, 1984-85. Recipient Great Menu award Nat. Restaurant Assn., 1982, Key Man award Jerrico Inc., 1981, Silver and Bronze ADDY Awards Lexington Advt. Club, 1982, Gold Award Fla. Restaurant Assn., 1984. Mem. Columbia Club Indpls., Whitford Country Club, Exton, Pa., Internat. Platform Assn., Colonial Williamsburg Assocs., Delta Sigma Phi (sec., historian 1961-71). Democrat. Mem. Disciples of Christ. Address: 270 Watch Hill Rd Exton PA 19341

MILLER, ALAN, software executive, management specialist; b. Bklyn., Apr. 20, 1954; s. Michael and Lillian Charlotte (Garment) M.; m. Zelda Sara Bochlin, Nov. 16, 1974; children: Michael Glenn, Dana Jennifer. BS in Computer Sci. magna cum laude, SUNY, 1975; MBA in Mgmt. with honors, Adelphi U., 1982. Tech. svcs. mgr. Guardian Life Ins. Co., N.Y.C., 1977-81; project mgr. Mfrs. Hanover Trust Co., N.Y.C., 1981-83; asst. v.p. Bankers Trust Co., N.Y.C., 1983-86; v.p., MIS dir. Bank Am. Trust Co. of N.Y., N.Y.C., 1986-87; assoc. John Diebold and Assocs., N.Y.C., 1987-89; mgr. banking practice AGS Info. Svcs., N.Y.C., 1989-90; v.p. bus. devel. and spl. projects BIS Banking Systems, N.Y.C., 1990—. Chmn. Sch. Dist. Adv. Com., Plainview, N.Y., 1981-83; exec. producer Oklahoma prodn. Patio Players, Plainview, 1990-91; bd. dirs., mem. men's club Plainview Jewish Ctr., 1986—. Mem. Delta Mu Delta. Jewish. Home: 21 Beaumont Dr Plainview NY 11803-2507 Office: BIS Banking Systems 900 3d Ave New York NY 10022-4728

MILLER, ALAN M., editor, educator, writer; b. N.Y.C., July 24, 1934; s. Philip and Sylvia (Lubash) M.; m. Roberta B. Brody, Sept. 2, 1956 (div. 1977); children—Neil, Peter, Stephanie, Douglas; m. Ferne Mayer Steckler, Jan. 13, 1978 (div. 1985). A.B., Syracuse U., 1955, LL.B., 1958, J.D., 1968. Commr., Village of Woodsburgh, N.Y., 1980; asst. counsel 3 joint legis. coms. N.Y. State Legislature, 1968-70; counsel to minority Nassau County Bd. Suprs., 1974-75; legal editor West Pub. Co., Westbury, N.Y., 1985—; adj. prof. Hofstra U. Law, 1978-85, Emory U., 1982, Touro Coll. Law, 1983-85; N.E. regional faculty mem., sect. leader Nat. Inst. Trial Advocacy, 1978-85, mem. nat. teaching team, 1982; adj. faculty N.Y. State Inst. Tech., 1974-75, Nassau Community Coll., 1978-80; anchor, regular panelist Joe Franklin TV Show, WWOR-TV and cable, 1990—; mem. faculty screenwriting and writing Hofstra U., 1990—, Discovery Ctr., 1990—, N.Y. Inst. Tech., Old Westbury, 1987-89. Assoc. editor: Plaintiff's Adv., 1961-62, Trial Lawyers Quar., 1962-63, Nassau Lawyer, 1964-65; columnist South Shore Record, Woodmere, N.Y., "Another Viewpoint" 1985— (awards N.Y. Press Assn., 1988, 89), "Single-Minded", 1991—, N.Y. Bowler, 1991— (award 1991), Nostalgia Mag., 1990-91 (2 awards 1992); contbr. numerous articles to various publs. including N.Y. Times, Newsday Mag. Assembly dist. leader N.Y. State Democratic Com., 1965-76. Mem. Nat. Writer's Club. Jewish. Office: 17 Crest Rd E North Merrick NY 11566

MILLER, ALBERT, physician, researcher; b. N.Y.C., July 28, 1936; m. Elaine Grant, June 6, 1959; children: Dina, Jeffrey, Neil, Michele. BA, U. Wis., 1955, MD, 1959. Diplomate Am. Bd. Internal Medicine, Am. Bd. Pulmonary Medicine; cert. expert pneumoconiosis Am. Bd. Radiology, Nat. Inst. Occupational Safety and Health. From assoc. clin. prof. to clin. prof. medicine Mt. Sinai Med. Ctr., N.Y.C., 1981—, clin. prof. community medicine, 1981—. Editor, chief author: Pulmonary Function Tests in Clinical & Occupational Lung Disease, 1986, Pulmonary Function Tests: A Guide for The Student & House Officer, 1987; contbr. over 75 articles to profl. jours. Comdr. USPHS, 1962-64. Fellow ACP, Am. Coll. Chest Physicians; mem. Am. Thoracic Soc., Am. Pub. Health Assn., Phi Beta Kappa, Alpha Omega Alpha. Office: Mt Sinai 1 Gustave L Levy Pl # 1232 New York NY 10029-6504

MILLER, ALLEN R., psychologist; b. Madison, W.Va., July 16, 1951; s. Rush and Catherine (McCarthy) M.; m. Wanda Lefevre, Aug. 18, 1990. BA, Millersville U., 1973, MS, 1981; PhD, Union Inst., 1989. Probation officer Lancaster (Pa.) County Cts., 1974-76; dir. Impaired Drivers Program, Lancaster, 1984-90; clin. supr. Family Svcs. of York, Pa., 1989—; clin. dir. York (Pa.) Hosp., Substance Abuse Ctr., 1990—; pvt. practice psychologist Lancaster, 1981—. Mem. Am. Psychol. Assn., Pa. Psychol. Assn., Lancaster-Lebanon Psychol. Assn. Office: PO Box 8247 247 N Shippen St Ste 12 Lancaster PA 17604

MILLER, ANNE SMALL, retired educator; b. Calhan, Colo., Sept. 15, 1907; d. Richard Webster and Florence (Blower) Small; m. Purviance Miller, Aug. 14, 1932; 1 child, Judith Anne. BA with honors, Colo. Coll., 1926; MA, Smith Coll., 1927. Tchr. tng., 1928; tchr. lang., lip reading, and sex edn. Clarke Sch. for Oral-Aural Deaf, Northampton, Mass., various positions; tchr. Clarke Sch. Summer Inst., Northampton, ret., 1974; lectr. Internat. Congress for Deaf, Manchester, England, 1958, Northampton, 1967, Stockholm, Sweden, 1970; panel mem. and lectr. various profl. confs.; TV appearances; conducted workshops on language, speech, curriculum, sex edn. at various profl. functions in U.S.; summer camp work with hearing children; speech-reading classes for adults and children, demonstrations at Rockport, Mass. Art Assn. Contbr. articles to profl. jours. Smith Coll. Trustee fellow, 1927-28. Mem. Teachers Union, Phi Beta Kappa. Unitarian. Home: 4 Cathedral Ave Rockport MA 01966-1147

MILLER, ARTHUR, scientist; b. N.Y.C., Apr. 3, 1930; s. Joseph Charles and Mary (Widom) M.; m. Arlene Lillian Katz, June 11, 1961; children: Michael Alan, Neil Irvin, Adrienne Sari. BS, Poly. U., 1951; PhD, Calif. Inst. Tech., 1957. Technician Brookhaven Nat. Labs., Upton, N.Y., 1950; rsch. asst. Brookhaven Nat. Labs., Upton, 1951, Los Alamos (N.Mex.) Sci. Lab., 1952; mem. tech. staff RCA Labs., Princeton, N.J., 1956-83; sr. mem. tech. staff RCA Labs., Princeton, 1983-87, Sarnoff Rsch. Ctr., Princeton, 1987—. Contbr. chpt. to book and articles to profl. jours.; patentee in field. Mem. Am. Phys. Soc., Princeton Folk Music Soc. (pres. 1987-89), Phi Lambda Upsilon, Sigma Xi. Home: 2 University Way Princeton Junction NJ 08550-1618 Office: David Sarnoff Rsch Ctr CN5300 Princeton NJ 08543-5300

MILLER, ARTHUR ROCKWELL, physical oceanographer; b. Boston, Aug. 6, 1915; s. Mora Luther and Madeline (Hansen) M.; m. Florence Estella Tee, Nov. 18, 1941; children: Carole Ann, Richard Howard. Cert. in phys. oceanography, Woods Hole Oceanographic Inst. Scientist technician Woods Hole (Mass.) Oceanographic Instn., 1946-51, rsch. assoc., 1951-61, phys. oceanographer, 1961-80; founder, pres. Associated Scientists at Woods Hole, 1979-89, treas., 1989—; rsch. specialist Rutgers U., Bivalve, N.J., 1951-52; adviser U.S. Weather Bur., Washington, 1955; mem. Internat. Com. on Bibliography Phys. Oceanography, Helsinki, Finland, 1960; mem. Indian Ocean Expedition Planning Com., Washington, 1961; designated expert on phys. oceanography of Mediterranean Sea; UN adviser to govt. of Greece. Lead author: Red Sea Hot Brines, 1970, Mediterranean Atlas, 1970; author: Hurricanes, Storm Surges, 1955; editor Recent Accessions and References, Woods Hole, 1955-64; contbr. articles to profl. jours. Asst. dist. commr. Upper Cape Cod coun. Boy Scouts Am., 1955; mem. town meeting Town of Falmouth, Mass., 1958—; chmn. Falmouth Flood Plain Study Com., 1975. CPO USNR, 1942-45. Mem. Am. Geophys. Union, Am. Soc. Limnology and Oceanography, Bermuda Biol. Sta. Rsch., N.Y. Acad. Scis., Oceanographic Soc., Explorers Club. Republican. Episcopalian. Home: 175 Lakeview Ave Falmouth MA 02540-2835

MILLER, BARRY, academic administrator, psychologist; b. N.Y.C., Dec. 25, 1942; s. Jack and Ida (Kaplan) M.; m. Susan Hallermeier; children: Eric, Arianne, Kristina, Barrie. BS in Psychology, Bklyn. Coll., 1965; MS in Psychology, Villanova U., 1967; PhD in Psychiatry, Med. Coll. Pa., 1971. Instr. psychology Villanova (Pa.) U., 1971-73; asst. dir. dept. behavioral sci., med. rsch. scientist Ea. Pa. Psychiatric Inst., Phila., 1971-73, sr. med. rsch. scientist, 1973-80; assoc. prof. psychiatry Med. Coll. Pa., Phila., 1981-90, rsch. assoc. prof. medicine, 1983-90, assoc. dean for rsch., 1981-90; dir. for rsch. devel. Albert Einstein Med. Ctr., Phila., 1990—; dir. Pa. Bur. Rsch. and Tng., Harrisburg, 1973-81; asst. prof. psychology U. Pa. Med. Sch., Phila., 1975-78, clin. asst. prof. , 1978—.; mem. sci. and tech. task force Pa. Econ. Devel. Partnership, Harrisburg, 1987—; mem. adv. com. Clin. Rsch. Ctr. Psychopathology of Elderly, Phila., 1985-88; mem. cancer control program Pa. Dept. Health, 1984; adj. assoc. prof. psychiatry Med. Coll. Pa., Phila., 1990—, vis. rsch. assoc. prof. medicine, 1991—; rsch. assoc. prof. psychiatry Temple U. Sch. Medicine, 1990—. Contbr. articles to profl. jours.; mem. editorial bd. Jour. Mental Health Adminstrn., 1988—, assoc. editor, 1989—. Bd. dirs. Community Mental Health Ctr. 6A, Phila., 1969-73, Northwest Jewish Youth Ctrs., Phila., 1974-75; mem. Lafayette Hill Civic Assn., 1973-86, Citizens Coun. Whitemarsh (Pa.) Twp., 1975-86. Grantee HHS, NIH. Fellow Pa. Psychol. Assn.; mem. Am. Psychol. Assn., Ea. Psychol. Assn., AAAS, Assn. Mental Health Adminstrs. Office: Albert Einstein Med Ctr York and Tabor Rds Philadelphia PA 19141

MILLER, BERNARD, chemist, educator; b. Monticello, N.Y., Sept. 1, 1931; s. Isidore and Sarah (Mandelbaum) M.; divorced; children: Judith Rosalind, Laura Alison. BS, CCNY, 1951; MA, Columbia U., 1953, PhD, 1955. Rsch. chemist Am. Cyanamid Co., Stamford, Conn., 1957-60; sr. rsch. scientist Am. Cyanamid Co., Princeton, N.J., 1960-67; assoc. prof. chemistry U. Mass., Amherst, 1967-71, prof., 1971—. Author: Organic Chemistry: The Basis of Life, 1980; contbr. articles to profl. jours; patentee in field. Tremain scholar CCNY, 1949-50; univ. fellow Columbia U., 1954; postdoctoral fellow U. Wis., NSF, 1956, NIH, 1957. Mem. Am. Chem. Soc., Sigma Xi, Phi Lambda Upsilon. Home: 3 Webster Ct Amherst MA 01002-2833 Office: U Mass Dept Chemistry Amherst MA 01003

MILLER, BRADLEY ADAM, economist; b. Plainfield, N.J., Sept. 14, 1959; s. H. Glen and Betty (Woodruff) M. BS Physics, Computer Sci., Purdue U., 1981; MS Pub. Policy Analysis, U. Rochester, 1983; PhD in Econs., U. Calif., Berkeley, 1988. Teaching asst. dept. physics Purdue U., W. Lafayette, Ind., 1980-81; vis. rsch. fellow Lunar & Planetary Inst, NASA, Houston, 1980, 81; dept. instr. dept. polit. sci. U. Rochester, Rochester, N.Y., 1982; grad. rsch. resident Argonne Nat. Lab., Washington, 1982, 83; regulatory impact analyst U.S. Dept. Energy, Washington, 1983-84; grad. rsch. asst. dept. econs. law sch. U. Calif., Berkeley, 1985-88, grad. student instr. dept. econs., 1986; ind. cons. Berkeley, 1984-88; sr. assoc. Charles River Assocs., Boston, 1988—. Co-author: Oil Import Quotas in the Context of the International Energy Agency Sharing Agreement, 1988; author several conf. papers. Flood fellow U. Calif., Berkeley, 1984-85, grad. student fellow U. Rochester, 1982-83, pub. svc. fellow U.S. Dept. Edn., 1981-82. Mem. Internat. Assn. Energy Econs., Am. Econ. Assn., Ops. Rsch. Soc. Am., Sigma Pi Sigma. Office: Charles River Assocs 200 Clarendon St Boston MA 02116-5021

MILLER, BRENDA, artist; b. Bronx, N.Y., Nov. 14, 1941; d. Abe and Florence (Kramer) M. Cert., Parsons Sch. Design, N.Y.C., 1963; BFA, U. N.Mex., 1965; MFA, Tulane U., 1967. Tchr. Newcomb Coll., Tulane U., New Orleans, 1965-67; tchr. Cooper Union, N.Y.C., 1967-68; tchr. SUNY, Stony Brook, 1972-74, Old Westbury, 1975; tchr. Cooper Union, N.Y.C., 1980; artist, 1980—; guest lectr. Sarah Lawrence Coll., Bronxville, N.Y., 1983, NISDA, 1975, Newhouse Gallery, Snug Harbor, Staten Island, N.Y., 1986. One-woman shows include Whitney Mus. Am. Art, 1975, Sperone Westwater, Fischer, Inc., N.Y.C., 1977-80; exhibited in group shows Islip Art Mus., East Islip, N.Y., 1989, Fine Arts Ctr., U. R.I., 1989, Cable Gallery, N.Y.C., 1988, AC Project Room, N.Y.C., 1992, Louise Ross Gallery, New, N.Y.C., 1992. Nat. Endowment for the Arts fellow, 1976, 79, 87, 88, Guggenheim fellow, 1978. Mem. Am. Abstract Artists. Home: 36 W 26th St New York NY 10010-2010

MILLER, CAROLE ANN, human resource development specialist, consultant; b. Jersey City, N.J., Apr. 23, 1941; d. Jack and Helen (Chary) Gordon; m. Robert H. Miller, June 11, 1960 (div. 1987); children: Randi Lyn Walter, Jill Marlin Miller, Loren Kim Miller. BA, William Paterson Coll., 1966; MA, Montclair State Coll., 1976; EdD, Rutgers U., 1983. Spl. edn. tchr. Paramus (N.J.) Bd. Edn., 1964-66; spl. edn. tchr. Parsippany (N.J.) Bd. Edn., 1971-74, adult edn. tchr., 1972-75; council dir. B'nai B'rith Youth Orgn., Newark, 1962-67; counseling psychologist B'nai B'rith Career and Counseling Ctr., Union, N.J., 1973-75; instr. County Coll. of Morris, Randolph, N.J., 1975-90; cons., instr. Rutgers U., New Brunswick, N.J., 1976-89, Bergen Community Coll., Paramus, N.J., 1975—; pres., counselor, cons. The Humanex Group, Teaneck, N.J., 1976—; bd. dirs. N.J. Assn. Lifelong Learning, 1981-87; pres. N.J. Assn. for Specialists in Group Work,

1978. Co-author: (counseling model) Miller/Morgan Career Development Model, 1976; inventor: (assessment instrument) Miller Occupational Stress Survey, 1984. Mem. N.J. Network Bus. and Profl. Women (bd. dirs. 1988-92, sec. 1991-92), NJAWBO, NAWBO, N.J. Assn. Tng. and Devel. (bd. dirs. 1978-81, named Oustanding Mem. 1989), N.J. ALL (recipient Outstanding Contribution award 1986), N.J. Assn. Counseling and Devel., Nat. Assn. Counseling and Devel., N.J. Assn. Women Bus. Owners, Nat. Assn. Women Bus. Owners, N.J. Assn. Lifelong Learning. Office: The Humanex Group Atrium at Glenpointe 400 Frank W Burr Blvd Teaneck NJ 07666-6803

MILLER, CHARLES JAY, dentist; b. Pitts., Nov. 10, 1924; s. I. Franklin and Ella (Abrams) M.; m. Barbara Thorpe, May 30, 1975; children: Sandi, Wayne, Wendy, John Thorpe. BS, U. Pitts., 1948, DDS, 1950. Diplomate Am. Acad. Osseointegration. Dentist Miller, Werrin, Gruendel, P.A., Pitts., 1950—; chmn. Council Dental Health, Odontological Soc. Wester Pa., Pitts., 1974; clin. prof. fixed partial prosthodontics Grad. Sch. Dental Medicine, U. Pitts., 1981—. Author: Inlays, Crowns and Bridges, 1962 (translated into German, Portuguese and Spanish, 1965-67); editor: Restorative Dentistry, 1972, (with others) Electrosurgery, 1989, Cosmetic Dentistry, 1987. Bd. dirs. United Jewish Fedn., Pitts., 1981-83; chmn. alumni giving fund U. Pitts., 1990—. 1st lt. USAAF, 1944-45, ETO. Decorated Air medal with 5 silver oak leaf clusters, Presdl. Citation, European campaign ribbon, Victory ribbon; recipient Disting. Alumnus award U. Pitts., 1988. Fellow Am. Coll. Dentists, Internat. Coll. Dentists; mem. Greater N.Y. Acad. Prosthodontics, Internat. Congress Oral Implantologists, Am. Acad. Esthetic Dentistry (charter), Concordia Club (pres. 1984-86), Kiwanis (pres. Pitts. 1965). Democrat. Office: 3506 5th Ave Pittsburgh PA 15213-3386

MILLER, CHRISTINE LEE, psychotherapist; b. New Orleans, Oct. 13, 1948; d. Leo Miller and Janice (Mathews) Pizzolato; m. Harold Butler, Nov. 22, 1969 (div. 1980); m. Michael Kevin Brown, Mar. 26, 1983; 1 child, Elizabeth Miller. Student, Hollins Coll., 1966-69; BA, La. State U., 1970; MEd, Boston U., 1972. Cert. mental health counselor. Administrv. asst. psychiat. pavilion St. Elizabeth's Hosp., Brighton, Mass., 1970-72; juvenile group supr. Hillcrest Juvenile Hall, Belmont, Calif., 1973; counselor, tchr. cons. Manchester (N.H.) Sch. Dept., 1973-74; dir. social svcs. Manchester Family Planning, 1974-77; dir. Child & Family Svcs. Group Home, Concord, N.H., 1980-87; pvt. practice Manchester, 1989—; adj. faculty N.H. Tech. Inst., Concord, New England Coll., Henniker, N.H., 1977-84; cons. Bedford (N.H.) Schs., 1991-92, Resolve, Inc., N.H., 1990-92; grant reviewer U.S. Dept. HHS, Washington, 1984—. Elected del. Dem. Nat. Conv., N.Y.C., 1992; city chair Clinton for Pres., Concord, 1992; vol. N.H. Nat. Abortion Rights Action League, Concord, 1985—. Mem. Nat. Acad. Cert. Clin. Mental Health Counselors, AACD. Episcopalian. Office: 1361 Elm St Ste 202 Manchester NH 03101

MILLER, CLIFF, engineer; b. Griffin, Ga., Aug. 8, 1958; s. Isaiah and Marline Miller; m. Charlotte Lenoir Free, Aug. 9, 1986. BS in Gen. Engring., U.S. Mil. Acad., 1982. Commd. 2d lt. U.S. Army, 1982, advanced through grades to capt., 1985; resigned, 1987; mgr. level 1, Procter & Gamble, Mehoopany, Pa., 1987-91, mgr. level 2, 1991—. Mem. Saddle Lake Homeowners Assn., Tunkhannock, Pa., 1987—; diversity trainer By Visions, Boston; leader Black Mgrs. Work Team, Mehoopany, 1988-89. Mem. Northeastern Networking, Tunkhannock Jaycees. Baptist. Home: 1 Eastwoods Rd Tunkhannock PA 18657 Office: Procter & Gamble RR 87 Box 32 Mehoopany PA 18629

MILLER, CORBIN RUSSELL, investment banker, director; b. Huntington, W.Va., Apr. 6, 1948; s. Corbin Russell and Ernestine (Thorne) M.; m. Kathryn Ann Anderson, Sept. 16, 1978. AB cum laude, Princeton (N.J.) U., 1971. Trainee Morgan Guaranty Trust Co., N.Y.C., 1972-74, asst. treas., 1974-77; assoc. Wm. Sword & Co. Inc., Princeton, 1977-79; v.p. J. Henry Schroder Corp., N.Y.C., 1979-83, J. Henry Schroder Bank & Trust, N.Y.C., 1983-87; sr. v.p. IBJ Schroder Bank & Trust Co., N.Y.C., 1987-90; chmn. Koala Techs. Corp., Pleasanton, Calif., 1990-91; mng. dir. Regent Ptnrs. Inc., N.Y.C. and Denver, 1991—; bd. dirs. Lombard Investments, Inc., San Francisco, Koala Techs. Corp., Carey Internat., Inc., Washington, Evcon Industries, Inc., Wichita, Kans. Assoc. Manhattan Inst. for Policy Rsch., N.Y.C., 1989—; patron Met. Opera Assn., N.Y.C., 1989—. Mem. Met. Opera Club (pres. 1992—), Knickerbocker Club, Rockaway Hunting Club, Racquet and Tennis Club, Princeton Club of N.Y. Republican. Episcopalian. Home: 1165 5th Ave New York NY 10029-6931 Office: Regent Ptnrs Inc 555 Madison Ave # 700 New York NY 10022-3301

MILLER, D. ARLENE, health care executive; b. Johnson County, Iowa, June 25, 1930; d. Frank G. and Erma M. (Swartzendruber) Eash; m. Mervin Miller, Aug. 21, 1954; children: Kim Edward, Dirk Andrew, Emily R., Ann E. BSN, Goshen Coll., 1954; MSN, U. Pitts., 1987. Cert. community health nurse, Pa. Staff nurse Frick Community Hosp., Mt. Pleasant, Pa., 1964-68; community health nurse Pa. Dept. of Health, 1968-76, 77-85, pub. health dir., 1985—; sch. nurse Southmoreland Sch. Dist., Scottdale, Pa., 1976-77; mem. adv. bd. Child and Adolescent Svc. System Program, Fayette County, Pa., 1989—; facilitator for support group for persons with HIV infection, 1992. Editor quar. news update FATF Community Update, 1991—. Bd. dirs. Fayette AIDS Task Force, 1988—; active Southwestern Pa. AIDS Coalition, Pa. Community-Based AIDS Orgns.; mem. Exec. Com. Agy. Coordination, 1990; mem. Bd. of Contract Mgmt., 1991—. Mem. Fayette County Mental Health Assn. Mennonite. Home: RR 1 Box 308 Scottdale PA 15683-9529 Office: State Health Ctr 100 New Salem Rd Uniontown PA 15401-8936

MILLER, D(ALE) MERRILY, educational consultant; b. Yonkers, N.Y., Mar. 3, 1943; d. Stanley and Pearl Sylvia (Colin) Dulman; children: Logan, Sloan, Dane. A.B. cum laude, Vassar Coll., 1965; M.A., Memphis State U., 1968; Ed.M., Columbia U., 1972, Ed.D., 1974. Tchr., Yonkers (N.Y.) Bd. Edn., 1968-72; mem. faculty Fairleigh Dickinson U., Teaneck, N.J., 1972-73; coordinator ednl. services Massive Econ. Neighborhood Devel. Corp., N.Y.C., 1973-74; dir. ednl. research The Door, N.Y.C., 1974-75; asst. prof. dept. psychology, edn., and services Grad. Sch. Edn., Fordham U., Tarrytown, N.Y., and Lincoln Center, N.Y.C., 1976-83, assoc. prof. 1986-88; pvt. practice ednl. cons., ednl. therapy, Katonah, N.Y., 1981—; faculty Coll. New Rochelle, 1984-86; adj. assoc. prof. Fordham U. Grad. Sch. Edn., 1986-88; assoc. prof. Mt. St. Mary Coll., 1988—; cons. in field specializing in curriculum based assessment and ednl. consultation, collaborative consultation, behavior mgmt., instructional adaptations for main streaming at the secondary level; cons. N.Y. State Dept. Edn., Office for Educating Children with Handicapping Conditions. Mem. Council for Exceptional Children, Am. Psychol. Assn., Learning Disabilities Assn., N.Y. Educators of Emotionally Disturbed, Assn. Women Adminstrs. of Westchester County, Assn. for Psychol. and Ednl. Cons., Conn. Ednl. Cons. Network, Coalition for Family Justice. Home and Office: 57 Jay St Katonah NY 10536-9738

MILLER, DANIEL, psychiatrist, psychoanalyst; b. N.Y.C., May 4, 1918; s. Max and Sarah (Hershman) M.; m. Edith Wolfe, June 23, 1945; children: Marc William, Karen Joyce Miller Orlando, Richard Judd. AB, NYU, 1940, MD, 1943. Intern Jewish Hosp. Bklyn., 1944; resident psychiatry VA Hosp., Lyons, N.J., 1946-48; asst. chief dept. psychiatry VA Hosp., Bklyn., 1949-55; pvt. practice psychiatry N.Y.C., 1956-58, 59-82, 83—; attending psychiatrist Nassau County Med. Ctr., East Meadow, N.Y., 1970-90; mem. founding faculty, tng. and supervising analyst L.I. Inst. Psychoanalysis, 1977—. 1st lt. Med. Corps, AUS, 1944-46. Fellow Am. Psychiat. Assn., Am. Acad. Psychoanalysis; mem. Nassau Psychiat. Soc. (pres. 1969-70), Nassau County Med. Soc., N.Y. State Med. Soc. Democrat. Jewish. Office: 520 Franklin Ave Garden City NY 11530-5801

MILLER, DAVID, mathematician, educator; b. Denver, Jan. 11, 1965; s. Barry and Helen (Schubert) M. AB, Columbia Coll., 1986; PhD, NYU, 1991. Asst. prof. Swarthmore (Pa.) Coll., 1991—. Democrat. Office: Swarthmore Coll Dept Maths 500 College Ave Swarthmore PA 19081-1110

MILLER, DAVID EMANUEL, physics educator, researcher; b. Bethel, Vt., Aug. 30, 1943; s. Manuel Southworth and Lucille (Shurtleff) M. BA, U. Vt., 1965; MA, SUNY, Stony Brook, 1967, PhD, 1971; Habilitation in Theoretical Physics, U. Bielefeld, Fed. Republic Germany, 1978. Instr. physics SUNY, Stony Brook, 1970-71; Wissenschaftlicher asst. Freie U., Berlin, 1972-75; scientist U. Bielefeld, 1975-78, privat dozent, 1978-83, univ. prof., 1987—; asst. prof. of physics Pa. State U., Hazelton, 1983-86, assoc. prof., 1986—; mem. faculty senate, 1988—. Mem. Am. Phys. Soc., Am. Assn. Physics Tchrs., Deutsche Physikalische Gesellschaft, Deutscher Hochschulverband, N.Y. Acad. Sci., Am. Math. Soc., Phi Beta Kappa, Sigma Xi. Home: PO Box 611 Conyngham PA 18219-0611 Office: Pa State U High Acres Hazleton PA 18201

MILLER, DAVID FREDRICK, sales executive; b. Rochester, N.Y., June 30, 1959; s. Ivan W. and S. Jean (Kriegh) M. AS in Chemistry and Math., Monroe Community Coll., 1980; BA in Biology, Boston U., 1982. Sales mgr. Ivan Miller, Inc., Rush, N.Y., 1982-85; sales rep. Harris Moran Seed Co., Hayward, Calif., 1985-89; mgr. tech. sales. Petoseed Co., Inc., Saticoy, Calif., 1989—. Mem. Atlantic Seedmens Assn., Mid Atlantic Food Processors Assn., N.J. Vegetable Growers Assn., Pa. Vegetable Growers Assn., Md. Vegetable Growers Assn., N.Y. Vegetable Growers Assn., New Eng. Vegetable Growers Assn., Va. Vegetable Growers Assn. Republican. Lutheran. Home: 109 Leland Dr Clarks Summit PA 18411

MILLER, DAVID JERGEN, insurance executive; b. Rochester, N.Y., Dec. 2, 1933; s. Harry Jacobs and Beatrice Lucille (Crippen) M.; m. Luanne Ashton Zahniser (div. 1980); children: Frances Z. Miller Kinney, David Stewart; m. Doris Elaine Reibsome, 1981. BA, Ohio Wesleyan U., 1956; postgrad., Plymouth State Coll., 1983. Agt., brokerage mgr. Conn. Mut. Life Ins. Co., Rochester, N.Y., 1958-65; br. mgr. Continental Assurance Co., Rochester, 1965-70; gen. agt. Continental Casualty Co., Rochester, 1970-77, Manhattan Life Ins. Co., Rochester, 1970-77; regional supt. agys. Standard Security Life Ins. Co. N.Y., N.Y.C., 1979-80; regional v.p. Maine Fidelity Life Ins. Co., Keene, N.H., 1980-88; nat. mktg. dir. Colonial Life and Accident Ins. Co., Columbia, S.C., 1988-89; mng. gen. agt. Capitol Bankers Life Ins. Co., Milw., 1989—. Contbr. articles to profl. jours. Board dirs. Walpole (N.H.) Hist. Soc., 1983-86; chmn., bd. dirs. Town Congl. Soc., 1983-86. With U.S. Army, 1956-58. Fellow Life Mgmt. Inst.; mem. Am. Soc. CIUs and Chartered Fin. Cons., Voluntary Employee Benefit Bd. (exec. com. 1986-88). Methodist. Home and Office: 403 E 4th St Bloomsburg PA 17815-1915

MILLER, DAVID JOHN, psychologist, director of clinical training; b. St. Louis, Aug. 22, 1956. BA in Psychology, U. Mo., 1978, MA in Psychology, 1980, PhD in Psychology, 1983. Lic. psychologist, Pa. Intern VA Med. Ctr., Palo Alto, Calif., 1983; coord. psychiatry VA Med. Ctr., Pitts., 1984-87, dir. clin. tng., 1987—; asst. prof. U. Pitts. Sch. Medicine, 1989—. Editor: Research Fraud, 1990; contbr. articles to profl. jours. Mem. APA, Pa. Psychol. Assn., Am. Assn. Preventive Psychology. Office: VA Med Ctr Highland Dr # 116B Pittsburgh PA 15206-1297

MILLER, DAWN MARIE, meteorologist, marketing communications specialist; b. Hartford, Conn., Sept. 17, 1963; d. Eugene E. Miller and Audrey E. (Flagg) Laurel; m. Dennis James Miller, Sept. 9, 1989. BS in Meteorology, SUNY, Oneonta, 1985. Customer support specialist WSI Corp., Bedford, Mass., 1985-87; in media (TV) mktg. WSI Corp., Billerica, Mass., 1987-91, media (TV) and industry mktg. rep., 1991-92, mktg. communications specialist, 1992—. Mem. Am. Meteorol. Soc., Oneonta Alumni Assn., Nat. Arbor Day Found., Am. Film Inst. Republican. Episcopalian. Home: 10 Hartford Ln Nashua NH 03063-1904 Office: WSI Corp 4 Federal St Billerica MA 01821-3593

MILLER, DONALD KEITH, asset management executive; b. Akron, Ohio, Feb. 2, 1932; s. Clinton Raymond and Hazel Elizabeth (Curl) M.; m. Barbara Dewees Duff, Sept. 25, 1971 (div. 1983); children: Prescott Clinton, Barclay St. John; m. Priscilla Corwith Barker, Sept. 17, 1989. BS, Cornell U., 1954; MBA, Harvard U., 1959. Asst. treas. Chase Manhattan Bank, N.Y.C., 1959-62; asst. to v.p. Electric Bond & Share, N.Y.C., 1962-66; gen. ptnr. G.H. Walker & Co. Inc., N.Y.C., 1966-74; sr. v.p. White Weld & Co., N.Y.C., 1974-77; mng. dir. Blyth Eastman Paine Webber Inc., N.Y.C., 1978-86; chmn. Greylock Fin., N.Y.C., 1987—, Christensen Boyles Corp., Salt Lake City, 1987—; chmn., chief exec. officer Thomson Adv. Group L.P., Stamford, Conn., 1990—; bd. dirs., chmn. audit com. RPM, Inc., Medina, Ohio, 1972—, Huffy Corp., Dayton, Ohio, 1988—, bd. dirs., mem. exec. com. 1st lt. U.S. Army, 1954-57. Home: 588 Round Hill Rd Greenwich CT 06831 Office: Thomson Adv Group One Station Pl Stamford CT 06902

MILLER, DONALD KENNETH, engineering consultant; b. St. Louis, Oct. 18, 1925; s. Henry Edward and Ernestine Elizabeth (Schmeer) M.; m. Arline Louise Heckman, Feb. 27, 1953; children: Garry Edwin, Kristine Louise Miller Morris. BSChemE, Mo. U., 1950. Registered profl. engr., Pa. Application engr. York Corp., St. Louis, Houston, York, 1951-62; mgr. quality control York Div. Borg Warner Corp., 1962-65, chief engr., 1965-85; refrigeration specialist York Internat. Corp., 1985-88; pres. MDK Engring. Corp., York, 1988—. Author: (with others) Plant Engineering Handbook, 1959, ASHRAE, 1981-94, Applied Thermal Design, 1989; contbr. articles to profl. jours.; inventor desuperheater control in a refrigeration apparatus. With USNR, 1944-46. Mem. Cen. Pa. Chpt. ASHRAE (life, sec. 1972-73, treas. 1973-74, v.p. 1974-75, pres. 1975-76), Nat. Soc. Profl. Engrs., Pa. Soc. Profl. Engrs., Internat. Inst. Refrigeration. Republican. Presbyterian. Home: 1749 Prescott Rd York PA 17403-4607 Office: MDK Engring Corp 391 Greendale Rd York PA 17403-4627

MILLER, DONALD L., artist; b. Summerfield, Chapleton, Jamaica, June 30, 1923; came to U.S., 1924; s. Claude C. and Rhena Jane (Newman) M.; m. Julia Alcina Guitano, June 8, 1952; children: Eric Wentworth, Craig Louis. Cert. grad., Cooper Union, 1949. Graphic artist Glaberman Studios, N.Y.C., 1959-50; art dir. Dunay & Rader Advt., N.Y.C., 1950-52, Black Star & Gorham, N.Y.C., 1952-56; illustrator, graphic artist, painter Montclair, N.J., 1956-81, 82—; tchr., graphic art Jacaranda Inc., Lagos, Nigeria, 1981-82; tchr. illustration Edna Manley Sch. Art, Kingston, Jamaica, 1987-89; tchr. mural painting Newark Sch. Fine & Indsl. Art, 1989—. Illustrator 40 children's books; painter murals, portraits, other works for pvt. and pub. collections. Commr. Martin Luther King Commn., N.J., 1988—; pres. bd. trustees Pub. Libr., Montclair, 1968-72; mem. adv. bd. arts & culture Essex County, N.J., 1964-70, mem. exec. coun. NAACP, Montclair, 1962-75 (Arts award 1984). With U.S. Army, 1943-46. Mem. Soc. Illustrators. Home: 14 Stanford Pl Montclair NJ 07042-5010

MILLER, DONALD ROSS, management consultant; b. Huntington, N.Y., Aug. 5, 1927; s. George Everett and Ethel May (Ross) M.; m. Constance Higgins, 1948 (div. 1955); children: Donald Ross Jr., Cynthia Lynn, Candace Lee; m. Janet Heyman Behr, Apr. 15, 1965; children: Jeffrey Lawrence, Wendy Lorraine. BS/BEA, MIT, 1950. Cert. mgmt. cons. Inst. of Mgmt. Cons. Staff engr. Stop & Shop, Inc., Boston, 1950-56; v.p., dir. Cresap, McCormick and Paget, Inc., N.Y.C., 1956-76; mng. dir. Donald R. Miller Mgmt. Cons., Forest Hills, N.Y., 1977—; bd. dirs. Nash Finch Co., Mpls. Author: Management Practices Manual, 3 vols., 1963, (booklet) Management of Managerial Resources, 1969. Bd. dirs. Queens Mus. Art, Flushing, N.Y., 1982—, pres., 1988-92; pres. Lexington House, Forest Hills, 1984-92. With U.S. Maritime Svc., 1945-46, ETO, U.S. Army, 1946-48. Mem. Nat. Assn. Corp. Dirs., Inst. Mgmt. Cons. (cert. com. 1986—), Sky Club. Episcopal. Home: 68-10 108th St Forest Hills NY 11375 Office: PO Box 649 Forest Hills NY 11375

MILLER, DONALD SPENCER, geologist, educator; b. Ventura, Calif., June 12, 1932; s. Spencer Jacob and Marquerite Rachael (Williams) M.; m. Carolyn Margaret Losee, June 12, 1954; children: Sandra Louise, Kenneth Donald, Christopher Spencer. BA, Occidental Coll., 1954; MA, Columbia U., 1956, PhD, 1960. Asst. prof. Rensselaer Poly. Inst., Troy, N.Y., 1960-64, assoc. prof., 1964-69, prof., 1969—, chmn. dept. geology, 1969-76, 80-90; research assoc. geology Columbia U., 1960-63; research fellow geochemistry Calif. Inst. Tech., Pasadena, summer 1963; NSF Sci. Faculty fellow U. Bern, Switzerland, 1966-67; sci. guest prof. Max-Planck Inst. Nuclear Physics, Heidelberg, Fed. Republic Germany, 1977-78, vis. prof., summer 1979, guest scientist, Aug. 1979, 80, 81, 82; vis. prof. Isotope Geology Lab., U. Berne, summer 1979; participant NATO exchange program Demokritos Inst., Athens, Greece, Sept. 1983, 85; vis. rsch. fellow U. Melbourne, Australia, summer 1988; mem. nat. screening com. Inst. Internat. Edn., 1988-91. Pres., treas. Troy Rehab. and Improvement, Inc., 1968-74; mem. Troy Zoning Bd. Appeals, 1970-85. Fellow Geol. Soc. Am.; mem. Am. Geophys. Union, Geochem. Soc., Nat. Assn. Geol. Tchrs., Sigma Xi, Sigma Pi Sigma. Home: 2198 Tibbits Ave Troy NY 12180-7015 Office: Rensselaer Poly Inst Dept Earth & Environ Scis Troy NY 12181

MILLER, DOUGLAS KENNETH, biochemist, researcher; b. Devils Lake, N.D., Dec. 8, 1947; s. Kenneth Earl and Adeline Christine (Metzler) M.; m. Carol Louise Healey, Jan. 27, 1978; children: Kieran Eric, Ryan Kenneth, Christopher Kittredge. BS in Chemistry, U. N.D., 1970; MA, Harvard U., 1971, PhD, 1975. Rsch. assoc. Tufts U./New Eng. Med. Ctr., Boston, 1975-78; sr. rsch. biochemist Merck & Co., Rahway, N.J., 1982-85, rsch. fellow, 1985-90, sr. rsch. fellow, 1990—; adj. asst. prof. Robert Wood Johnson Med. Sch., Piscataway, N.J., 1978-82. Contbr. articles to profl. jours. and chpts. in books; patentee in field. Trustee, v.p. Employees Ctr. for Young Children, Rahway, 1986-90. Woodrow Wilson Found. fellow, 1970, NSF fellow, 1970-72. Mem. Am. Soc. Biochemistry and Molecular Biology, Am. Assn. for Cell Biology, Soc. for Complex Carbohydrates, Phi Beta Kappa. Office: Merck & Co Inc 126 E Lincon Ave PO Box 2000 Rahway NJ 07065

MILLER, DUANE KING, health and beauty care company executive; b. N.Y.C., Mar. 1, 1931; s. Henry Charles and Helen Marion (King) M.; A.B. in Econs. and Fin., NYU, 1951; m. Nancy L. Longley, June 6, 1954; children—Cheryl L., Duane L. Vice pres. mktg. Warner-Chilcott div. Warner Lambert Co., Morris Plains, N.J., 1970-72, pres. div., 1973-77, exec. v.p. Am. Optical div. and pres. Am. Optical Internat. div., Southbridge, Mass., 1978; pres. biol. and proprietary products divs., v.p. Revlon Health Care Group, Revlon Corp., Tuckahoe, N.Y., 1978-80, pres. ethical, proprietary and vision care divs., 1981-82, corp. v.p. parent co., 1982, pres. Revlon Health Care Group, 1983-92, corp. exec. v.p. parent co., 1984-92, pres. Revlon Health Beauty Care and Internat. Group, 1988-92, ret., 1992; pres. DKL Properties, health care cons. Promedex Techs., 1992—. Mem. Republican Nat. Com. Mem. Pharm Mfrs. Assn. (bd. dirs.), Nat. Pharm. Council, Am. Mgmt. Assn., Am. Mktg. Assn. (pres. N.J. chpt. 1967-68), Sales Exec. Club N.Y. Clubs: Princeton N.Y.; Cripple Creek (Del.) Golf; Clubs of Ocean Pines (Md.); Masons, Shriners. Author: (with others) Marketing Planning for Chief Executives and Planners, 1966. Home: 8 Western Dr Colts Neck NJ 07722 Office: Bldg 3 48 1 Bethany Rd Hazlet NJ 07730

MILLER, EDMUND CHARLES, III, English educator; b. Queens, N.Y., Aug. 18, 1943; s. Edmund Charles Jr. and Eugenia Marie (Andreani) M. BA, L.I. U., 1965; MA, Ohio State U., 1969; PhD, SUNY, Stony Brook, 1975. Asst. prof. L.I. U., Brookville, N.Y., 1981-86, assoc. prof., 1986-90, prof. English, 1990—. Author: Drudgerie Divine: The Rhetoric of God and Man in Goerge Herbert, 1979, poetry little mags. and chapbooks; editor: (newsletter) Cross-Bias: The Newsletter of the Friends of Bermerton, 1985—; co-editor: (book with Robert DiYanni) Like Season'd Timber: New Essays on George Herbert, 1987; contbr. articles in the Libr., English Lang. Notes, Renaissance and Reformation. Mem. Modern Lang. Assn. (life), Conf. on Christianity and Lit. (pres. N.W. region 1985), Lewis Carroll Soc. N.Am., Milton Soc. N.Am. (life). Home: 43-55 Kissena Blvd Apt 3D Flushing NY 11355 Office: LI U CW Post Campus Brookville NY 11355

MILLER, EDWARD JEREMY, theology educator, consultant; b. Phila., Sept. 17, 1940; s. Edward P. and Mary (Collins) M.; m. Kathleen Stevens, May 21, 1983; children: Brian, Kevin. BA, Providence Coll., 1963; MA, St. Stephens Inst., Dover, Mass., 1965; PhD, U. Louvain, Belgium, 1975, STD, 1982. Prof. Ohio Dominican Coll., Columbus, Ohio, 1968-71, Emory U., Atlanta, 1975-85; program officer Nat. Endowment for Humanities, Washington, 1986-87; dean Coll. of New Rochelle (N.Y.), 1987-92; prof. theology Gwynedd Mercy Coll., Phila., 1992—; edn. cons. Various U.S. Coll., 1987—; v.p. Coll. Theology Soc., 1976-78. Author: John Henry Newman on Idea of Church, 1987; contbr. articles to profl. jours. Vol. Meals on Wheels, City of New Rochelle, 1987—. Recipient postdoctoral fellowship, U. Chgo., 1981-82. Mem. Coll. Theology Soc., Cath. Theology Soc. Am., Am. Acad. Religion, Coun. Grad. Schs., Internat. Newman Soc. Office: Sumneytown Pike Gwynedd Mercy Coll Gwynedd Valley PA 19437

MILLER, EDWIN HAVILAND, English educator; b. Johnstown, Pa., Sept. 2, 1918; s. Louis G. and Lucinda (Haviland) Miller; m. Rosalind Schnitzer, June 25, 1946; 1 child, Pamela Price Miller Ness. BA, Lehigh U., Bethlehem, Pa., 1940; MA, Pa. State U., 1942; PhD, Harvard U., 1951. Teaching asst. Pa. State U., State College, 1940-42, 45-46; instr. to prof. English Simmons Coll., Boston, 1947-61; prof. NYU, 1961-86, prof. emeritus English, 1986—. Author: Walt Whitman's Poetry: A Psychological Journey, 1968, Melville - A Biography, 1975, Salem is My Dwelling Place: A Biography of Nathaniel Hawthorne, 1991; editor: Correspondence of Walt Whitman, 6 vols., 1961-77, A Century of Whitman Criticism, 1969, Walt Whitman's Song of Myself: A Mosaic of Criticism, 1989. Guggenheim fellow, 1967, 78, Coun. of Am. Learned Socs. fellow, 1959. Mem. MLA, Phi Beta Kappa. Home: 4642 Waldo Ave Bronx NY 10471-3000

MILLER, ELIJAH LEWIS, JR., deputy public defender; b. Trenton, N.J., July 12, 1944; s. Elijah Lewis and Hattie Mae (Everson) M.; m. Carmen N. Quiñones, May 27, 1982; children: Kristen Brandy, Alyssa Kari. BA, Rutgers Coll., 1968; JD, Rutgers U., 1971; cert., Northwestern U., 1974. Bar: N.J. 1971, D.C. 1971, U.S. Dist. Ct. N.J. 1971, U.S. Supreme Ct. 1977. Assoc. Shanley & Fisher, Newark, N.J., 1970-73; asst. dept. pub. defender Office of Pub. Defender N.J., Passaic County, 1973-86; dep. pub. defender Office of Pub. Defender N.J., Union County, 1987—; trustee Union County Legal Svcs. Corp., Elizabeth, 1989—; mem. fugitive warrants com. Supreme Ct., New Brunswick, N.J., 1991—. Poll watcher Com. for Kenny Gibson Mayoral Campaign, Newark, 1968-69. Capt. U.S. Army, 1968-76. Mem. Assn. Criminal Def. Lawyers of N.J. (trustee 1989—), Union County Bar Assn. Democrat. Methodist. Home: 536 River Rd Westwood NJ 07675-6337 Office: Office of Pub Defender NJ 65 Jefferson Ave Elizabeth NJ 07201-2425

MILLER, ELIZABETH JANE, historian; b. Pitts., Sept. 21, 1953; d. Albert and Phyllis (Lewandowski) M. BA in Am. Studies and History, Am. U., 1975; MA in Am. Studies, George Washington U., 1977. Curator Columbia Hist. Soc., Washington, 1977-84, dir., 1984-85; dir. Maine Hist. Soc., Portland, 1985—; adj. prof. New Eng. Studies Program, U. So. Maine; cons. curator NAS, Washington, 1983-84. Co-author exhbn. pamphlet: Lighthouse of the Sky, 1983; contbr. articles to profl. jours. Mem. Am. Assn. Mus., Am. Assn. for State and Local History (grantee 1983), New England Mus. Assn. Office: Maine Hist Soc 485 Congress St Portland ME 04101-3401

MILLER, ERNEST ARTHUR, religious organization officer; b. Burlington, Iowa, May 29, 1925; s. John Arthur and Frieda (Maurer) M.; m. Mary June Klaas, June 13, 1949. MusB, Northwestern U., 1949. Music sec. cen. region Salvation Army, Chgo., 1963-70, pub. rels. sec., 1970-74; dir. nat. pub. affairs Salvation Army, Washington, 1974—, dir. World Svc. Office, 1977-81, cons., 1981-90.

MILLER, ERNEST CHARLES, management consultant; b. Bronx, N.Y., July 14, 1925; s. Ernest Philip and Elizabeth (Hellwig) M.; m. Edith Grosvenor Porterfield, Nov. 11, 1947 (div. Oct. 3, 1963); children: Laura Lee, Marcy Rogers, Ernest Charles; m. Tung-fen Lin, Jan. 8, 1985. A.B., Yale U., 1945; M.A., U. Pa., 1949. Lic. psychologist, N.Y. Instr. U. Pa., 1947-51, cons., 1950-53; br. mgr., bd. dirs. Richardson, Bellows, Henry & Co., Inc., 1953-55; mgr. personnel tech. Am. Standard, Inc., 1955-59; mng. prin. Hellwig, Miller & Assos., Westport, Conn., 1959-61; sr. assoc. Cresap, McCormick & Paget, Inc., N.Y.C., 1961-63; with Am. Mgmt. Assns., N.Y.C., 1964-83; pres. AMACOM div. Am. Mgmt. Assns., 1978-81, group v.p. AMA Publs. Group, 1981-83; pres. Miller, Hellwig Assocs., 1984—. Author works in strategic planning, orgn. devel., human resources, exec. compoensation and mgmt. Bd. dirs., pres. Lincoln Towers Community Assn., 150 West End Ave. Owners Corp., La Jolla Inst. for Allergy and Immunology; mem. Columbia U. All-Univ. Seminar, China Internat. Bus., Orgn. and Mgmt., Labor Rels. NEH fellow, 1980. Mem. Am. Psychol. Assn., Japan Soc., Soc. Indsl. and Orgnl. Psychology, Inc. Episcopalian. Office: Miller Hellwig Assocs 150 W End Ave New York NY 10023-5702

MILLER, EVANGELINE LYNN, international consulting firm executive; b. Harvey, Ill., Mar. 2, 1949; d. George Peter and Athena Lula (Drivas) Melonas (Miller); m. Thomas Stephan Couston, Oct. 24, 1970 (div. June

1981); children—George Peter, Stephan Thomas, Elaine Anastasia. B.S. in Communications, Northwestern U., 1969. Asst. editor World Book div. Field Enterprises Ednl. Corp., Chgo., 1969-70; claims and rates agt. traffic dept. Solo Cup Corp., Chgo., 1970-71; sr. cons., asst. to mgmt. Bus. Men's Clearing House subs. Gen. Employment Enterprises Corp., Chgo., 1973-81; pres., chief exec. officer, owner, founder ELC Internat. Corp., Chgo., 1982—, Fas-Claim Corp., Chgo., 1983—. Active Spl. Olympics, Spl. Children's Charities; mem. Chgo. Council Fgn. Relations, Art Inst. Chgo., Lincoln Park Conservation Assn., Lincoln Park Zool. Soc. Mem. Iron and Steel Soc. of AIME, Internat. Bus. Council Mid-Am., Pres.'s Assn. of Am. Mgmt. Assn., Women in Internat. Trade, Hellenic Profl. Soc. Greek Orthodox. Club: Executives (youth com., speakers' table com.) (Chgo.). Home: 175 N Harbor Dr Apt 2511 Chicago IL 60601-7362 Office: Australian Investments Ltd Ste 900 601 Pennsylvania Ave NW Washington DC 20004

MILLER, FAY A., university dean; b. N.Y.C., Feb. 17, 1945; d. Joseph and Helen (Kyprion) Miller. BSN, Niagara U., 1966; MA Adult Psychiat.-Mental Health Nursing, NYU, 1970, PhD in Nursing Sci., 1984. RN, Conn. Nurse adminstr., clinician Tremont Crisis unit Bronx (N.Y.) Psychiat. Ctr.; coord. BSN program Medgar Evers Coll., Bklyn.; chmn. dept. of nursing, assoc. prof. Cleve. State U.; dean Sch. Profl. Studies, So. Conn. State U., New Haven; supr. family therapy program Albert Einstein Coll. Medicine. Contbr. articles to profl. publs. Recipient Helena Rubenstein scholarship 1979, NIMH scholarship, 1968-70; named Involved Nurse, Greater Cleve. Nurses Assn., 1984. Mem. ANA, AACN, Conn. Nurses Assn. (pres. dist. IV), Nat. League for Nursing, Conn. League for Nursing (mem. conv. planning com.), Deans and Dirs. Coun.

MILLER, FREDERICK WILLIAM, molecular immunologist; b. Troy, Ohio, Jan. 25, 1951; s. Frederick William and Frances Marie (Klosterhuber) M.; m. Lori A. Love, Sept. 14, 1986. BA, Miami U., Oxford, Ohio, 1973; MD, PhD, Case Western Res. U., 1979. Intern Emory U. Sch. Medicine, Atlanta, 1979-80, fellow in clin. rsch., 1980-81; resident Stanford (Calif.) U. Sch. Medicine, 1981-83; staff fellow NIAMS, NIH, Bethesda, Md., 1983-90; officer Ctr. for Biologics Evaluation and Rsch., FDA, Bethesda, 1990—. Contbr. articles to profl. jours. Lt. comdr. USPHS, 1991—. Fellow Am. Coll. Rheumatology; mem. AAAS, Am. Assn. Immunologists, Am. Fedn. for Clin. Rsch., ACP, D.C. Rheumatism Soc., Internat. Soc. Cryptozoology. Home: 3518 Astoria Ct Kensington MD 20895-1434 Office: CBER/FDA NIH 29 507 Bethesda MD 20892

MILLER, GEORGE MCCORD, JR., aerospace marketing manager; b. Schenectady, N.Y., Sept. 18, 1957; s. George McCord and Ethel (Waldron M.; m. Susan Boyles, Oct. 8, 1983; 1 child, Katharine Hannah. BSME, Duke U., 1979; MBA, Tulane U., 1981. Tech. mktg. engr. GE, Schenectady, N.Y., 1981-85; application engr. Morganite, Inc., Dunn, N.C., 1985-88; mktg. mgr. Clevite Seals, Morrisville, N.C., 1988-90, EG&G Pressure Sci., Inc., Beltsville, Md., 1990—. Mem. ASME (assoc. mem.). Republican. Methodist. Office: EG&G Pressure Sci Inc 11642 Old Baltimore Pike Beltsville MD 20705-1294

MILLER, GERALD RAY, chemistry educator; b. Milw., Nov. 13, 1936; s. Victor Hugo and Erma Emma (Luebke) M.; m. Claire Ellen Holtzen, June 21, 1958; children: Karin Miller O'Callaghan, Russell Bruce. Student, Oberlin Coll., 1954-55; BS in Chemistry, U. Wis., 1958; MS, U. Ill., 1960, PhD, 1962. Asst. prof. dept. chemistry U. Md., College Park, 1965-71, assoc. prof., 1971-85, prof. dept. chemistry and biochemistry, 1985—, acting dean undergrad. studies, 1986-88, chair Campus Senate, 1991-92; assoc. dir. fellowships Nat. Acad. Sci.-Nat. Rsch. Coun., Washington, 1974-76. Contbr. articles to profl. jours. Capt. U.S. Army, 1963-65. Recipient Bronze medal Am. Inst. Chemists, 1958; NSF fellow, 1958-61, 61-63. Mem. AAAS, Am. Chem. Soc., Am. Phys. Soc., Royal Soc. Chemistry, Internat. Soc. Magnetic Resonance, Sigma Xi, Phi Beta Kappa. Lutheran. Office: U Md Dept Chemistry/Biochemistry College Park MD 20742-2021

MILLER, (RICHARD) GUY, sculptor, retired military officer, educator; b. Pitts., Oct. 27, 1917; s. John Thomas and Florence Ann (Sohner) M.; BA in Chemistry, U. Conn., 1956; postgrad. Heatherley Sch. of Fine Arts, also City and Guilds of London Art Council, London, 1958, Art Students League, N.Y.C., 1961-63; MFA, Pratt Inst., 1965; 1 son, Richard Guy. Commd. 2d lt. USAF, 1943, advanced through grades to lt. col. USAF, 1955; engring. officer U.K. and Europe, 1943-49; assoc. prof. AFROTC, U. Conn., 1950-54; exec. officer, dep. chief staff installations 3d Air Force, London, 1955-59; airbase engr. Stewart AFB, N.Y., 1960-63, ret., 1963; instr. sculpture Pratt Inst., Bklyn., 1965, West Long Br. Monmouth (N.J.) Coll., 1966-69; artist-in-residence Friends World Coll., Huntington, N.Y., 1977-78; one-man shows of sculpture include: Pratt Inst., Bklyn., 1965, Caravan Gallery, N.Y.C., 1967, 68, Shelter Rock Library, 1972, Syosset (N.Y.) Library, 1972, Manhasset (N.Y.) Pub. Library, 1976, Ward-Nasse Gallery, N.Y.C., 1976-78, Ctr. for Arts, Bath, Maine, 1986, Eau Gallie Library, Melbourne, Fla., 1986-91; commd. works include: New Sch. for Social Research, N.Y.C., 1977, Hall of Fame, L.I., N.Y., 1979, Birchwood Devel. Corp., Elhurst, N.Y., 1979, John T. Mather Hosp., Port Jefferson, N.Y., 1981, Birchwood Devel. Corp., Jericho, N.Y., 1985, Buckingham Towers, Ft. Lee, N.J., 1987; group shows include: Royal Soc. Water Colorists, London, 1956, Bethlehem Art Gallery, New Windsor, N.Y., 1960, El Paso, Tex., 1962, State U. Coll., New Paltz, N.Y., 1963, Monmouth Coll., 1967, 68, Selected Artists Gallery, N.Y.C., 1970, Maury Mark Gallery, Great Neck, N.Y., 1970, Patrick Galleries, P.R., 1973, Nantucket Gallery, 1973, Trianon Gallery, N.Y.C., 1975, Lever House, N.Y.C., 1976, Parish Mus., Southampton, N.Y., 1976, Elsen Gallery, N.Y.C., 1976, Himelfarb Gallery, Watermill, N.Y., 1977, Caumsett Park, Huntington, N.Y., 1978, Lincoln Center, N.Y.C., 1978, Guild Hall, East Hampton, N.Y., 1979, 80, 83, Betty Parsons Gallery, N.Y.C., 1980, Parish Mus., Southampton, N.Y., 1980, Elain Benson Gallery, Bridgehampton, N.Y., 1980-81, Stanford Art Festival, Stanford, Conn., 1981, Ctr. for Arts, Bath, 1982, Galeria Mesa Exhbn., Ariz., 1986, Cochise Coll., Douglas, Ariz., 1987, Hockaday Ctr. for Arts, Kalispell, Mont., 1988, Novelty Garden Folk Gallery, Maimi Beach, Fla., 1989, Orr's-Bailey Arts Assn. Ann. Exhibits, Orr's Island, Amine, 1989-91, Bowdoin Coll., Brunswick, Maine, 1991; represented in permanent collections: Pratt Inst., State U. N.Y., New Paltz, Jericho (N.Y.) Pub. Library, Betty Parsons Gallery, N.Y.C., New Sch. Library, Manhasset Pub. Libr., N.Y.C., Art Expo, N.Y.C., 1980, Artist Forum, Centerport, N.Y., 1981, A New Hope Gallery, 1982, Ctr. for the Arts, Bath, Maine, 1986, Missoula Mus. Art, Mont., 1988, also pvt. collections. Louis Comfort Tiffany Found. grantee, 1966; MacDowell Colony fellow, 1968; Sculpture award Guild Hall, 1980; cert. tchr., N.Y. State. Mem. Art Students League (life), Orrs-Bailey Art Assn. (chmn. bd. Maine chpt. 1989—). Address: PO Box 95 Orrs Island ME 04066-0095

MILLER, HARVEY S. SHIPLEY, medical company executive; b. Phila., Sept. 28, 1948; s. Frank Leroy and Betty Charlotte (Elfont) M. BA, Swarthmore Coll., 1970; JD, Harvard U., 1973. Bar: N.Y. 1973. Assoc. Debevoise & Plimpton, N.Y.C., 1973-75; curator and dir. dept. collections and spl. exhbns. Franklin Inst., Phila., 1975-81; v.p. Energy Solutions, Inc., N.Y.C., 1982-84; pres., chief exec. officer, dir. Daltex Med. Scis., Inc., N.Y.C., 1983-86, chief operating officer, vice chmn., 1986-91, pres., chief operating officer, 1991—. Author: Milton Avery: Drawings and Paintings, 1976; It's About Time, 1979; author, editor: New Spaces: Exploring the Aesthetic Dimensions of Holography, 1979; co-author: Rapid Inactivation of Infectious Pathogens by Chlorhexidine-coated Gloves, 1992. Mem. vis. com. on photography George Eastman House, Rochester, N.Y., 1976-78; trustee Milton and Sally Avery Arts Found., N.Y.C., 1983—; assoc. trustee U. Pa., 1981—; trustee Phila. Mus. Art, 1985—; bd. govs. Print Club, Phila., 1976-87; bd. overseers U. Pa. Sch. Nursing, 1981—, Edith C. Blum Art Inst. Bard Coll., 1984-87; bd. dirs., mem. corp. MacDowell Colony, N.Y.C., 1982-85; exec. bd. dirs. Fabric Workshop, Phila., 1976-86; mem. prints and drawings and photographs trustees adv. com. Phila. Mus. Art, 1974—, trustee, 1985—, investment com., 1989—; bd. assocs. Swarthmore Coll. Librs., Phila., 1978-86; treas. Arcadia Found., Norristown, Pa., 1981—; chmn. adv. bd. Inst. Contemporary Art U. Pa., 1982-84; trustee, vice chmn. coms. on instrn. Pa. Acad. Fine Arts, 1982-91, trustee emeritus, 1991—, chmn. collections and exhbns. comm., 1985-87; trustee N.Y. Studio Sch., 1974-80, U. of the Arts, 1979-86; mem. exec. bd. Citizens for Arts in Pa., 1980, Friends of Moore Coll., 1981-83; bd. dirs. Once Gallery, Inc., 1974-75; mem. Mayor's Cultural Adv. Coun., Phila., 1987-91; bd. dirs. Wildlife Preservation Trust Internat., Inc., 1990—; mem. collections com. Hist. Soc. Pa., 1991—, councillor-elect, 1992. Mem. ABA, Assn. of Bar of City of N.Y., Athenaeum, Libr. Co. Phila., Am. Philos. Soc., Hist. Soc. Pa. (collections com. 1991—), Phila. Art Alliance, Union League of Phila., Harvard Club of N.Y.C., Swarthmore Club Phila., Phi Sigma Kappa. Republican. Episcopalian. Home: Moorhope Mathers Ln Fort Washington PA 19034 Office: Daltex Medi-Scis Inc 50 Kulick Rd 2d Fl Fairfield NJ 07004

MILLER, HENRY FRANKLIN, lawyer; b. Phila., May 19, 1938; s. Lester and Bessie (Posner) M.; m. Barbara Ann Gendel, June 20, 1964; children: Andrew, Alexa. AB, Lafayette Coll., 1959; LLB, U. Pa., 1964. Bar: Pa. 1965. Law clk. U.S. Dist. Ct. Del., Wilmington, 1964-65; assoc. Wolf, Block, Schorr & Solis-Cohen, Phila., 1965-71, ptnr., 1971—. Pres. Soc. Hill Synagogue, Phila., 1978-79, Big Brothers/Big Sisters Assn. of Phila., 1980-81, Jewish Family & Children's Agy., Phila., 1986-88. 1st lt. U.S. Army, 1959-60. Mem. Am. Coll. Real Estate Lawyers. Office: Wolf Block Schorr Solis-Cohen 12th Fl 15th and Chestnut Sts Philadelphia PA 19118-3743

MILLER, HENRY GEORGE, transportation executive, consultant; b. Uniontown, Ohio, Apr. 30, 1924; s. Rollie C. and Fannie P. Miller; m. Martha Jane McGee, June 12, 1948; children: Barbara Susan, Rodney Charles. AB, Baldwin Wallace Coll., 1944; postgrad., Columbia U., 1946-48. Distbr. mgr. Dow Chem. Co., Freeport, Tex., 1948-56, Midland, Mich., 1956-64; gen. mgr. distbr. Diamond Crystal Salt Co., St. Clair, Mich., 1964-78; dir. distbr. Lubrizol Corp., Wickliffe, Ohio, 1978-85; exec. dir., cons. Shippers for Competitive Ocean Transp., Washington, 1986—. Lt. (j.g.) USN, 1943-46, PTO. Mem. Coun. Logistics Mgmt. (Oak Brook, Ill., nat. pres. 1969), Chem. Mfrs. Assn. (chmn. ocean and internat. com., distbr. com. 1982-85). Republican. Episcopalian. Home: 10615 Hunters Chase Ln Damascus MD 20872-2191

MILLER, IRIS ANN, landscape architectural consultant, urban designer; b. Pitts., Jan. 6, 1938; d. Bernard and Sadye (Topel) Ress; m. Lawrence Alan Miller, Jan. 24, 1959; children: Bradley Stuart, Richard Lyle, Stefan Ress. BS cum laude, U. Pitts., 1959, MEd in Secondary Edn., 1961; post-grad. in psychology and counseling, U. Md., 1962-68; MArch, Cath. U. Am., 1979. Tchr. various pub. and pvt. schs., Pitts., Monroeville, Pa., Montgomery County, Md., 1959-61, 63-64; free lance landscape design Washington, 1965-81; architecture design and research O'Neil and Manion Architects, Bethesda, Md., 1979, 81; architecture design and drawing Frank Schlesinger Architects/Planners, Washington, 1979-80, Georgetown Day High Sch. landscape design, Washington, 1988, W.Va. Wesleyan Coll. Campus plan for religious and arts ctr., 1992; pvt. residence landscape projects, 1982—; cons. architecture, landscape and urban design Washington, 1982—; vis. lectr. Cath. U. Am., Washington, 1983-86, vis. asst. prof., 1987-92, dir. landscape and architecture studies, 1986-89; urban design cons. Techworld, Washington, 1984-86; devel. dir. Tech 2000 Mus., 1985-86; developer, presenter lectr. series resident assoc. program Smithsonian Instn., Washington, 1982, 83, 85, 87, 89; dir., founder 7th, 8th, and 9th Sts. Group Streetscape project, Washington, 1986—, others; Charrette urban design seminar, Washington, Dallas, Alexandria, Va., St. Louis and Cleve., 1982-89; initiator, participant Sarasota (Fla.) Regional Urban Design Assistance R/UDAT team, 1983, seminar Nat. Gallery Art, Washington, 1984, Nat. Arboretum, 1988, symposia Cath. U. of Am., 1987-92; dir., mem. steering com. numerous confs. in field; speaker in field. Author, co-editor (book): Urban Design: Visions and Reflection, 1991, (map and booklet) Visions of Washington: Composite Plan of Urban Interventions, 1991; contbr. articles to profl. pubs.; curator, author exhbn. and catalogue Sumner Sch. Mus., 1987, 92; co-curator, author exhbn. and catalogue Octagon Mus., 1987; project dir., curator Paris-Washington Exhbn., 1987—; recent landscape projects include Nesse, Lewis Residence, Silver Spring , Md., 1992, Friedman Residence, Washington, 1992, Drysdale Hershon Residence, Washington, 1991, Miller Residence, Washington, 1990-92, Sexton Residence, Kenwood, Chevy Chase, Md., 1990, Romano Residence, Fairfax Station, Va., 1989, Mushinski Residence, Bethesda, Md., 1989, 8th St. Mall Washington, 1987-88, Mishkin, Jennis Residence, Bethesda, 1988Cramer Residence, Bethesda, 1988. Co-chmn. stamp com. Bicentennial Washington, 1987-90; founding mem. Washington Network, 1986-89; mem. adv. panel L'Enfant Forum, Washington, 1987-90, Hist. Georgetown Found., 1989—; trustee John J. Sexton Fund for Local Govt. Studies, Sch. Pub. Affairs, U. Md., College Park, 1983—; dir., founder Pub.-Pvt. Partnership and Univ. Scholarship Outreach Inner-City High Sch. Program, Cath. U. Am., Washington Pub. Schs., 1985—; dir., founder Intern Exch. Program Landscape, France-U.S.A., Cath. U. Am., U. Va., 1991—; historic landscape com. U.S/ Internat. Coun. on Monuments and Sites, 1990—; active Cultural Alliance Greater Washington, Nat. Trust for Historic Preservation, Ikebana Internat., Hist. Soc. Washington, Nat. Mus. for Building Arts, alumni coun. Sch. Architecture and Planning, Cath. U. Am., 1986—. Travel rsch. grantee Cath. U. Am., 1978, 79, Rsch. grantee Govt. France, 1985; grantee NEA, 1982, grantee D.C. Commn. on Arts, 1991, 92; recipient Program Devel. award Cath. U. Am., 1978. Mem. APA, U.S.-Internat. Coun. on Monuments and Sites (program speaker 1987, 92, hist. landscapes com.), Friends Vieilles Maisons Francaise (program speaker 1987—), AIA (assoc., regional urban design com., chmn. edn. subcom 1987—, chmn., founder data base on design edn., chmn. edn. conf. 1983, edn. com. D.C. chpt. 1981-83, Charrette co-chmn., program devel. award 1982), Assn. Collegiate Schs. Architecture (speaker N.E. region conf. 1989, speaker ann. meeting 1n. panel 1989, 90, 91, 92, chair collegiate exhbn. for excellence in urban design, 1990, 91, 92, author conf. procs. 1991, 92), Am. Soc. Landscape Architects (assoc.), Gem, Lapidary and Mineral Soc., Inst. Urban Design, Friends of Vieilles Maisons Francaises, Alpha Epsilon Phi (pres. D.C. alumni 1965-67). Home: 3820 52d St NW Washington DC 20016 Office: 914 11th St NW Washington DC 20001-4408

MILLER, ISADORE, television executive, consultant; b. Montreal, Quebec, Can.; s. Michael S. and Mollie (Becker) M.; m. Lilly, Nov. 10, 1952; children: Laura Lee, Elise Wendy Debra. BBA, CCNY, 1952, MBA, 1957; LLB, LaSalle Extension U., 1970. Various positions CBS, N.Y.C., 1954-70; mgr. spl. projects Entertainment div. CBS, N.Y.C., 1970-72, assoc. dir. bus. affairs, 1972-77, dir. children's programming, 1977-80; mgr. prodn. ctr. Operations div. CBS, N.Y.C., 1980-81; v.p. bus. adminstrn. D'Arcy Masius Benton & Bowles, N.Y.C., 1981-88; sr. v.p. Riverview Prodns. Inc. subs. D'Arcy Masius Benton & Bowles, N.Y.C., 1983-88; bd. dirs. Riverview Prodns., Inc., 1985-88; cons. various orgns., N.Y.C. and L.A., 1980-88; pres. Izzy Miller Enterprises, Inc., 1988—, Millinnium III, Inc., 1991. Vol. Jewish Family Service of No. Middlesex County, Edison, N.J., 1983— (cert. of Appreciation for Outstanding and Dedicated Service 1986). Served with U.S. Army, 1952-54, Korea. Mem. NATAS (gov. N.Y. chpt. 1984, 91—, trustee 1985-90, nat. treas. 1986-90, 1st v.p. 1987-88, head nat. fin. com., nat. award com.), Internat. Radio and TV Soc., B'nai B'rith, Am. Jewish Congress, Mus. Broadcasting, Zimerli Mus. Democrat. Jewish. Home: 30 S Adelaide Ave Highland Park NJ 08904-1606

MILLER, ISRAEL, rabbi, university administrator; b. Balt., Apr. 6, 1918; s. Tobias and Bluma (Bunchez) M.; m. Ruth Joan Goldman, Oct. 16, 1945; children: David, Michael, Deborah, Judith. B.A. magna cum laude, Yeshiva Coll., 1938, D.D., 1967; M.A., Columbia U., 1949. Ordained rabbi, 1941. Rabbi Kingsbridge Heights Jewish Center, Bronx, 1941-68; rabbi emeritus Kingsbridge Heights Jewish Center, 1968—; asst. to pres. Yeshiva U., N.Y.C., 1968-70; v.p. Yeshiva U., 1970-80, sr. v.p., 1980—; counselor B'nai B'rith Hillel Found., Hunter Coll., Bronx, 1951-60; lectr. homiletics Yeshiva U., 1954-55; prof. applied rabbinics Rabbi Isaac Elchanan Theol. Sem., 1968—. Editor: Sermon Manual, 1951. V.p. Bronx Coun. Am. Jewish Congress, 1954-60, Bronx Coun. Jewish Edn., 1964-68; pres. Rabbinical Coun. Am., 1964-66, hon. pres., 1966-68; mem. exec. com. World Zionist Orgn., 1971-76; chmn. Am. Jewish Conf. on Soviet Jewry, 1965-67, Am. Zionist Council, 1967-70; pres. Am. Zionist Fedn., 1970-74, hon. pres., 1974—; v.p. Religious Zionists Am., 1966-68; religious cons., retreat master Dept. Def. in, Europe, 1954, 63-64, Alaska, 1958, Japan, 1960; Vice chmn. Conf. Pres.'s Am. Jewish Orgns., 1969-74; chmn. Conf. Pres.'s Major Am. Jewish Orgns., 1974-76; vice chmn. N.Y. Jewish Community Rels. Coun., 1976—; exec. com. Bronx coun. Boy Scouts Am., 1951-58; mem. Nat. Citizens Com. Community Rels., 1946—; bd. dirs. Nat. Jewish Welfare Bd., v.p., 1969—; chmn. Commn. Jewish Chaplaincy, 1962-65; bd. dirs. Bd. Jewish Edn. N.Y.C., Nat. Jewish Community Relations, United Israel Appeal, 1968—; bd. dirs., acting pres. Conf. on Jewish Material Claims Against Germany, 1983, pres., 1984; pres. Conf. on Jewish Material Claims Against Austria, 1984; sec. Meml. Found. for Jewish Culture, 1973—; bd. govs. Jewish Agy. for Israel, 1971-76; vice chmn. Am. Israel Pub. Affairs Com., 1983; mem. Jerusalem Com., 1990—; bd. dirs. The Jerusalem Found., 1985—; hon. chmn. Jewish Nat. Fund. Served as chaplain USAAF, 1945-46. Recipient Bernard Revel award Yeshiva Coll. Alumni Assn., 1961, Nat. Rabbinic Leadership award Union of Orthodox Jewish Congregations, 1966, 81, Shofor award Boy Scouts Am., 1965, Frank L. Weill award Nat. Jewish Welfare Bd., 1972; Man of Year award Nat. Council Young Israel, 1976; Dr. Harris J. Levine award B'nai Zion, 1979; others. Mem. Jewish War Vets. (nat. chaplain 1962-63), Assn. Jewish Chaplains Armed Forces (pres. 1955-56), Rabbinic Alumni Yeshiva U. (pres. 1960-62). Home: 2619 Davidson Ave Bronx NY 10468-4103 Office: Yeshiva U 2540 Amsterdam Ave New York NY 10033-2807

MILLER, J(AMES) GORMLY, retired librarian, emeritus educator; b. Rochester, N.Y., Jan. 5, 1914; s. James Billings and Marian (Robinson) M.; m. Mildred Catharine Bevan, Sept. 6, 1939; children: Susan Miller Milligan, James Gormly, Paul B. A.B., U. Rochester, 1936; B.S. in L.S, Columbia U., 1938. Asst. librarian Rochester Pub. Library, 1938-42; research asst. Bur. Adult Edn., N.Y. State Dept. Edn., 1946; librarian Cornell U.-N.Y. State Sch. Indsl. and Labor Relations, 1946-62, assoc. prof., then prof., 1949-70, 74-77, asst. dir. personnel and budget univ. libraries, 1962-70, libraries dir., 1975-79, librarian, 1979-80, prof. emeritus, 1980—; acting Univ. librarian Cornell U., 1985-86; dep. chief central library and documentation br. ILO, Geneva, 1970-74; trustee Finger Lakes Library System, 1967-69; pres. bd. trustees South Central Research Library Council, 1980-83, v.p., 1984-85; cons. in field. Author profl. articles, reports. Alderman Ithaca (N.Y.) Common Council, 1959-63, 68; commnr. Ithaca Civil Service Commn., 1964-67. Served with U.S. Army, 1943-46. Mem. Am. Soc. for Info. Sci., ALA, N.Y. State Library Assn., Indsl. Relations Research Assn. Democrat. Anglican. Home: 7-D Wildflower Dr Eastwood Commons Ithaca NY 14850 Office: Cornell U 331 Ives Hall Ithaca NY 14853

MILLER, JANET, archivist; b. Pitts., May 28, 1954; d. Robert C. and Ruth (Erb) M. BA, Chatham Coll., 1976; MA, Am. U., Washington, 1978; MS, Columbia U., 1986. Archivist, registrar anthropology dept. Field Mus. Natural History, Chgo., 1986-89; dir.-archivist Archives & Spl. Collections Women in Medicine Med. Coll. Pa., Phila., 1989—; advisor Acad. Natural Scis., Phila., 1990-93; trustee Alumnae Assn. Spl. Trust Fund, Phila., 1991—. Editor Hue Points, 1986; author: AAUW Chi: One Hundred Years, 1989. Curator Celebrating our Diversity: An Exhbn. Honoting Harold Washington, Oak Woods Cemetery Assn., Chgo., 1988. Mem. Soc. Am. Archivists (local arrangements com. 1990-91, historian Chgo. br. 1989, outstanding svc. award). Office: Med Coll Pa 3300 Henry Ave Philadelphia PA 19129-1191

MILLER, JEAN MARIE, graphic designer, consultant; b. Meriden, Conn., Dec. 10, 1951; d. Charles Avery Sr. and Dorothy Jeannie (Keyes) M. Grad., cert. in wildlife mgmt., N.Am. Sch. Conservation, 1972; student, Bible Inst. New Eng., 1972-73; cert. in comml. art, Art Instrn. Sch., 1971; student, Conn. Inst. Fine Arts, 1977. Layout and paste-up artist Step Saver, Southington, Conn., 1973-76, art dir., 1976-78; cartographer, designer T-Sq. Graphics, Plainville, Conn., 1978-79; comml. artist Bozzuto's, Inc., Cheshire, Conn., 1980-84; graphic designer Speedprint, Meriden, 1985-86; graphic designer Hull Printing Co., Meriden, 1986-89, dir. creative svcs., 1989-91; artistic cons. 1st United Meth. Ch., Wallingford, Conn., 1973—. Mem. Nat Wildlife Fedn., First United Meth. Bd. Global Missions. Democrat.

MILLER, JEANNE-MARIE ANDERSON (MRS. NATHAN J. MILLER), English educator, academic administrator; b. Washington, Feb. 18, 1937; d. William and Agnes Catherine (Johns) Anderson m. Nathan John Miller, Oct. 2, 1960. BA, Howard U., 1959, MA, 1963, PhD, 1976. Instr. dept. English Howard U., Washington, 1963-76, asst. prof., 1976-79, assoc. prof., 1979-92, prof., 1992—, also asst. dir. Inst. Arts and Humanities, 1973-75, asst. acad. planning office, v.p. for acad. affairs, 1976-90; cons. Am. Studies Assn., 1972-75, Silver Burdett Pub. Co., Nat. Endowment for Humanities, 1978—; adv. bd. D.C. Libr. for Arts, 1973—, John Oliver Killens Writers Guild, 1975—, Afro-Am. Theatre, Balt., 1975—. Editor, Black Theatre Bull., 1977-86; Realism to Ritual: Form and Style in Black Theatre, 1983; assoc. editor Theatre Jour., 1980-81; contbr. articles to profl. jours. Mem. Washington Performing Arts Soc., 1971—, Friends of Sta. WETA-TV, 1971—, Mus. African Art, 1971—, Arena Stage Assos., 1972—, Washington Opera Guild, 1982—, Wolf Trap Assocs., 1982—. Ford Found. fellow, 1970-72; So. Fellowships Fund fellow, 1972-74; Howard U. research grantee, 1975-76; Am. Coun. Learned Socs. grantee, 1978-79; Nat. Endowment Humanities grantee, 1981-84. Mem. Nat. Coun. Tchrs. of English, Coll. English Assn., Am. Studies Assn., Am. Theatre Assn., AAUP, AAUW, D.C. LWV, Common Cause, ACLU, Am. Acad. Polit. and Social Sci., Coll. Lang. Assn., MLA, Am. Assn. Higher Edn., Nat. Assn. Women Deans, Adminstrs. and Counselors, Friends Kennedy Ctr. for Performing Arts, Pi Lambda Theta. Democrat. Episcopalian. Home: 504 24th St NE Washington DC 20002-4818

MILLER, JOHN FREDERICK, meteorologist, consultant; b. L.A., Mar. 24, 1928; s. Charles William and Cerlestia (Kerr) M.; m. Carlotta Ann Firm, Aug. 7, 1954; children: Cynthia Ann, John Francis, Diane Elizabeth, Carla Marie. AB, UCLA, 1951. Forecast meteorologist Fleet Weather Cen., U.S. Navy Sta., Dept. Navy, Norfolk, Va., 1959-62; rsch. meteorologist Office of Hydrology, Nat. Weather Svc., Washington, 1953-59, 62-64; chief spl. studies br. water mgmt. info. div. Office of Hydrology, Nat. Weather Svc., Silver Spring, Md., 1964-71, chief water mgmt. info. div., 1971-85; cons. meteorologist Rockville, Md., 1985—. Author: Manual for Estimation of Probable Maximum Precipitation, 1986; author: (with others) Engineering Meteorology, 1982; contbr. to numerous reports. Comdr. USNR, 1946—. Mem. Am. Meteorol. Soc., Am. Geophys. Union. Home and Office: 13420 Oriental St Rockville MD 20853-3055

MILLER, JOHN PAUL, sales executive; b. Saratoga Spring, N.Y., Oct. 22, 1948; s. John Paul and Mary Lou (DiFebo) M.; m. Kathryn Christianson, Dec. 29, 1989 ; children from previous marriage: Meghan E. Heather L., Caitlin S. BS in Biology, Siena Coll., 1971. Sales rep. Clay Adams, Boston, 1971-80, Deseret, Syracuse, N.Y., 1976-80, Ivac, Syracuse, 1980-81; ops. mgr. Ivac, San Diego, Calif., 1981-84; regional mgr. Ivac, Boston, 1984-86; eastern regional mgr. Nellcor, Hayward, Calif., 1986-88; nat. sales mgr. Advanced Video Products, Concord, Mass., 1988-89; founder, pres. New Eng. Mktg. Assoc., Haverhill, Mass., 1989—; cons. New Care Med., Inc., Andover, Mass., 1988, New Eng. Wound Care, Inc., Salem, N.H., 1989, Gemini Tech. Svcs., Londonderry, N.H., Novametrix, Wallingford, Conn., A.F. Assocs., Northvale, N.J., Advanced Techs., Berlin, N.H. Republican. Roman Catholic. Home: 62 Perkins Ct Haverhill MA 01832-1185 Office: New Eng Mktg Assoc 62 Perkins Ct Haverhill MA 01832-1185

MILLER, JOHN PETER (JACK MILLER), journalist; b. Peterborough, Ont., Can., Aug. 3, 1928; s. Wesley and Margaret (Baker) M.; ed. Welland and Toronto, Ont.; m. Helen DeMars, July 30, 1949; 1 son, Gregory (dec.). Sports editor to front page editor Welland Evening Tribune, 1949-53; with Hamilton (Ont.) Spectator, 1953-71, radio and TV columnist, 1955-71; radio and TV columnist Toronto (Ont.) Daily Star, 1971-78, communications editor, 1979-85, sci. columnist, 1982-85, sci. writer, 1985-89, sci. editor, 1989-91, sci. corr., 1991—; frequent TV and radio appearances. Recipient writing awards CSWA 1985 (2), 87, 88 (2), 89. Mem. AAAS, Can. Sci. Writers Assn., Nat. Sci. Writers Assn., Internat. Sci. Writers Assn., Scientists' Inst. for Pub. Info., Chgo. Journalistic Soc., Sigma Delta Chi. Contbr. stories to mags. Home: 198 Dalhousie Ave, Saint Catharines, ON Canada L2N 4X9

MILLER, JOHN R., accountant; b. Wilkes-Barre, Pa., Nov. 28, 1946; s. John Turner and Elsie May (Johns) M.; m. Cathy Lynn Redstone, July 27, 1968; children: Stephen, Jo-El. BS in Commerce and Fin., Wilkes U., 1968. CPA. Audit exec. Com. of Pa., Harrisburg, 1971-73; sr. acct. KPMG Peat Marwick, Phila., 1968-71; mgr. KPMG Peat Marwick, Harrisburg, 1973-76; sr. mgr. KPMG Peat Marwick, N.Y.C., 1976-79, ptnr., 1979—; chmn. govt. acctg. and auditing com. AICPA, Washington, 1987-90, chmn. audit quality, 1991—; mem. U.S. Auditing Standards Adv. Coun., Washington, 1990—, Govtl. Acct. Standards Adv. Coun., Norwalk, Conn., 1987-91. Bd. dirs. Rye (N.Y.) YMCA, 1988—, Osborn Retirement Community; mem. Nat. Civic League, Denver, 1985—; trustee Citizens Budget Commn., N.Y.C., 1985—; Prin. Coun. for Excellence in Govt., Washington, 1987—. Mem.

AICPA, Pa. Inst. of CPAs (Leadership award 1968), N.Y. State Soc. of CPAs, Masons, Marco Polo Club, Coveleigh Club. Episcopalian. Office: KPMG Peat Marwick 345 Park Ave New York NY 10154

MILLER, JOHN T., JR., lawyer, educator; b. Waterbury, Conn., Aug. 10, 1922; s. John T. and Anna (Purdy) M.; children: Kent, Lauren, Clare, Miriam, Michael, Sheila, Lisa, Colin, Margaret. AB with high honors, Clark U., 1944; JD, Georgetown U., 1948; Docteur en Droit, U. Geneva, 1951; postgrad., U. Paris, 1951. Bar: Conn. 1949, D.C. 1950, U.S. Ct. Appeals (3d cir.) 1958, U.S. Ct. Appeals (D.C. cir.) 1952, U.S. Ct. Appeals (5th cir.) 1957, U.S. Supreme Ct. 1952. With Econ. Cooperation Adminstn. Am. Embassy, London, 1950-51; assoc. Covington & Burling, 1952-53, Gallagher, Connor & Boland, 1953-62; pvt. practice Washington, 1962—; adj. prof. law Georgetown U. Law Ctr., Washington, 1959—; mem. Panel on Future of Internat. Ct. Justice. Co-author: Regulation of Trade, 1953, Modern American Antitrust Law, 1948, Major American Antitrust Laws, 1965; author: Foreign Trade in Gas and Electricity in North America: A Legal and Historical Study, 1970, Energy Problems and the Federal Government: Cases and Material, 1979, 6th edit. 1991; contbr. articles, book revs. to legal publs. Trustee Clark U., 1970-76; bd. advs. Georgetown Visitation Prep. Sch., 1972—; former fin. chmn. troop 46 Nat. Capital Area coun. Boy Scouts Am. 1st lt. U.S. Army, 1943-46, 48-49. Recipient 10 yr. teaching award Nat. Jud. Coll., 1983. Mem. ABA (coun., chmn. adminstrv. law sect. 1972-73, ho. dels. 1991—), D.C. Bar Assn., Fed. Energy Bar Assn. (pres. 1990-91), Internat. Bar Assn., Internat. Law Assn., AAUP, Internat. Club, Congl. Country Club, Palm-Aire Country Club., Prettyman-Leventhal Am. Inn of Ct. (master), Sovereign Mil. Order of Malta (knight). Republican. Roman Catholic. Home: 4721 Rodman St NW Washington DC 20016-3234 Office: 1001 Connecticut Ave NW Washington DC 20036-5504

MILLER, J(OHN) WESLEY, III, lawyer, author; b. Springfield, Mass., Oct. 3, 1941; s. John Wesley Jr. and Blanche Ethel (Wilson) M. AB, Colby Coll., Waterville, Maine, 1963; AM, Harvard U., 1964, JD, 1981. Bar: Mass. 1984, U.S. Dist. Ct., 1984. Instr. English Heidelberg Coll., Tiffin, Ohio, 1964-69; teaching asst. U. Wis., 1970-73; real estate broker, 1977-84; founder Miller Family Papers, Vt., Madison (Wis.) People's Poster and Propaganda Collection. Author: The Millers of Roxham, 1959, Giroux Genealogy, 1959, Symphonic Heritage, 1959, Aunt Jennie's Poems, 1986; editor: Hein's Reprints of Legal Poetry, 1985, The Curiosities and Law of Wills, 1989, The Lawyers Alcove, 1990, Famous Divorces, 1991, Law Libr. Microform Consortium Legal Poetry Collection, 1991; exhibitor and creator A Salute to Street Art, State Hist. Soc. Wis., 1974; contbr. Collection Building Reader, 1992; also numerous articles on Am. street lit., bibliography, ethics, history, edn., law, librarianship, mgmt. of archives. Mem. MLA, Am. Philol. Assn., Milton Soc., New Eng. Historic Geneal. Soc., Vt. Hist. Soc., Social Law Library, Pilgrim Soc., Ancient and Hon. Arty. Co., Mayflower Soc., Soc. Colonial Wars, Sons and Daus. of the Victims of Colonial Witch Trials, Mensa. Office: 5 Birchland Ave Springfield MA 01119-2708

MILLER, JUDITH SCANNELLA, school placement administrator; b. Trenton, N.J., Sept. 10, 1952; d. Anthony Michael and Lucy Theresa (Di Paola) Scannella; m. Bruce Noble Miller, Aug. 5, 1978; 1 child, Amanda Kathryn. BA, Rider Coll., 1974. Food program specialist United Progress Inc., Trenton, N.J., 1975-77, dir. summer food program for children, 1975-77; investigator State of N.J., Office Pub. Advocate, Office Pub. Defender, Hackensack, 1977-79; customer svc./sales rep. Manpower Temp. Svcs., Paramus, N.J., 1981-82; customer svc. rep., office mgr. Western Temp. Svcs., Paramus, 1981-82; polit. cons. Bergan County Dem. Orgn., Hackensack, 1979—; regional pers. asst. Lane Bryant Inc., Secaucus, N.J., 1982-83; placement dir. Nat. Edn. Ctr. Radio Electronic TV Sch. Campus, Nutley, N.J., 1983-89, Phillips Bus. Sch., Paterson, N.J., 1991—. Author: Job Placement Handbook, 1989 (Honorable Mention award 1989). Mem. NOW, Hackensack, 1989, LWV, Glen Rock, N.J., 1990, N.J. Fedn. Dem. Women, Trenton, 1974. Mem. NAFE. Home: 44 Bergen St Glen Rock NJ 07452 Office: Phillips Bus Sch div CareerCom Inc 8 Mill St Paterson NJ 07501

MILLER, JUDY LYNN, engineer; b. Goshen, N.Y., July 16, 1952; d. Albert Henry and Emeline (Harvath) M. BS, Boston U., 1974; MS, MIT, 1979. Tech. staff Charles Stark Draper Lab., Cambridge, Mass., 1976-79, task leader, 1979-81, tech. dir., 1981-85, prog. mgr., 1985—. Draper fellow C.S. Draper Lab., 1979, MIT fellow MIT Ctr. for Space Rsch., 1974. Mem. IEEE, AIAA, Soc. Women Engrs., N.Y. Acad. Sci., Inst. Navigation, Boston Downtown Alumni Club, Air Force Assn., Sigma Xi, Tau Beta Pi. Jewish. Office: Charles Stark Draper Lab 555 Technology Sq Cambridge MA 02139-3563

MILLER, KAREN, judge; b. Okmulgee, Okla., Nov. 18, 1944; d. Moses Paul and Rosalie (Genn) Braverman; widowed. BS cum laude, NYU, 1974; JD, N.Y. Law Sch., 1977. Bar: N.Y. 1978, U.S. Dist. Ct. (so. dist., ea. dist.) N.Y. 1978, D.C. 1979. Atty.-advisor U.S. Dept. HEW, Newark, 1977-79; chief adminstrv. law judge City of N.Y. Dept. Consumer Affairs, N.Y.C., 1979—. Mem. N.Y. State Bar Assn., N.Y. County Lawyers Assn., D.C. Bar Assn., Civil Svc. Bar Assn. (trustee welfare fund 1987—). Home: 301 E 21st St New York NY 10010-6534 Office: Dept Consumer Affairs Adjudication Div 42 Broadway New York NY 10004-1617

MILLER, KENNETH HULL, automotive executive; b. Rockville Center, N.Y., May 24, 1946; s. Wendell Hull and Madeleine (Park) M.; m. Judith Ann D'Esti, Feb. 21, 1970; children: Sarah, Joshua, Margaret. BA, Colgate U., 1968; MBA, Syracuse U., 1970. Mgr. Miller Motor Car Corp., Binghamton, N.Y., 1970-76; v.p. Miller Motor Car Corp., 1976—; sec. Miller Presision Car Corp., Vestal, N.Y., 1988—; pres. Miller Motor Car Of Syracuse (N.Y.), Inc., 1988—. Chmn. Celebrity Hockey Classic, Broome County, 1984—; bd. dirs. Broome County YMCA, 1986-91. Named Dealer of Distinction, Sports Illustrated, 1989. Mem. Am. Internat. Auto Dealers (vice chmn. 1986-89), N.Y. State Automobile Dealers (dist. v.p. 1979—), Broome County Auto Dealers (pres. 1978-85), Honda Nat. Dealer Coun. (zone rep. 1981-83), Live Wire Club (pres. 1986), Harper Forum, Broome County C. of C. (chmn. 1987-88), Rotary. Republican. Episcopalian. Office: Miller Motor Car Corp 4455 Vestal Pky Vestal NY 13850

MILLER, KENNETH IRVIN, financial executive; b. Arlington, Va., June 7, 1956; s. Robert Irvin and Joanne (Daugherty) M.; m. Karen Diane Henry, Nov. 17, 1979 (div. Jan. 1990); children: Killian Zachary, Kelly Brent. BS, Va. Poly. Inst. and State U., 1978. CPA, Va. Staff acct., sr. acct. to acctg. mgr. Arthur Andersen & Co., Washington, 1978-85; sr. v.p., chief fin. officer Johnston Lemon Group, Inc., Washington, 1986—. Tchr. Project Bus., Fairfax, Va., 1984. Mem. AICPA, Va. Soc. CPAs, N.Y. Stock Exchange, Beta Alpha Psi. Office: Johnston Lemon Group Inc 1101 Vermont Ave NW Washington DC 20005

MILLER, KENNETH MERRILL, computing services company executive; b. Lowell, Mass., Dec. 13, 1930; s. Harry Dow and Marjorie Louise (Morris) M.; m. Mary Jo Putnam, June 8, 1952 (div. Aug. 1979); children: Debra, Pamela, Carol; m. Eileen Anne Durnin, Feb. 4, 1980; 1 child, Andrew. BS, Am. U., 1964; MBA, Syracuse U., 1966. Commd. 2d lt. U.S. Army, 1953, advanced through grades to col., 1974; assigned to France, Fed. Republic Germany, Korea, Vietnam; ret., 1978; v.p. Robert W. Baird & Co., Inc., Milw., 1978-79; sr. v.p. Automatic Data Processing, Inc., Roseland, N.J., 1979—. Decorated Legion of Merit with three oak leaf clusters, Bronze Star, Purple Heart. Mem. Ont. Club (Toronto). Office: ADP Inc, 4 King St W, Toronto, ON Canada M5H 1B6

MILLER, L. MARTIN, accountant, financial planning specialist; b. N.Y.C., Sept. 17, 1939; s. Harvey and Julia (Lewis) M.; m. Judith Sklar, Jan. 21, 1962; children: Philip, Marjorie. BS, Wharton Sch., U. Pa., 1960. CPA; accredited fin. planning specialist. Jr. acct. Deloitte, Haskins & Sells, N.Y.C., 1960-62, sr. acct., Phila., 1962-64; mng. partner Cogen Sklar Levick, Phila., 1964—; treas. Coronet Container Co., Inc., Phila., Val Mar Realty Corp., N.Y.C.; dir. Penn Internat. Trading Co., Phila.; mng. dir. CPA Tax Forum, 1966-69; underwriting mem. Lloyds of London, 1978—, chmn. Mid-Atlantic region, 1991—; vis. prof. Wharton Sch. U. Pa., 1992—; lectr., discussion leader on fin. and taxation; columnist Montgomery and Bucks County Dental News. Mem. Phila. Rep. com., 1963-67; chmn. Lower Merion Twp. scholarship fund, 1975-78; bd. dirs. Penn Valley Civic Assn., 1973-79; mem. Lower Merion Planning Commn., 1978-82; mem. Gov.'s Tax Study Commn.; pres. Mensa Edn. and Rsch. Found., 1984-86; mem. SEC Forum on Small Bus. Capital Formation, 1983; apptd. to Pa. State Bd. Accountancy, 1985—, chmn., 1990-91. Served with U.S. Army, 1961-62. Recipient Outstanding Achievement award Germantown Civic Assn., 1965. Mem. Pa. Inst. CPAs (edn. com. 1975-78, bd. dirs. 1979-81, by-laws chmn. 1980-83), Nat. Assn. State Bds. Accountancy (edn. com. 1987, nominating com. 1989, experience com. 1990), AICPAs (nat. tax commn. 1979-82, exec. com. self regulation div. for CPA firms 1984-87, acctg. and rev. services com. 1985-88, ethics div. 1985-88, specialization bd. 1989-90, ethics exec. com. 1990—), Little 10 Acctg. Assn. (edn. chmn. 1980-84), Mensa (internat. fin. officer 1970-74), Beta Alpha Psi. Clubs: Masons (past master) Plays and Players (treas. 1978-79). Author: Accountants Guide to S.E.C. Filings, 1968; contbr. articles to profl. jours. Home: 204 Dove Ln Haverford PA 19041-1902 Office: Cogen Sklar Levick 150 Monument Rd Bala Cynwyd PA 19004

MILLER, LEONARD MARTIN, manufacturing executive; b. Oceanside, N.Y., Aug. 26, 1941; s. Jacob T. and Rose (Shear) M.; m. Sandra Rochelle Weiss, Jan. 14, 1967; children: Robin Lisa, Karen Beth, Tracey Sara. BBA, St. John's U., N.Y.C., 1964. Inventory controller R.H. Macy & Co., N.Y.C., 1965-66; with Superior Insulated Wire Corp., Stony Point, N.Y., 1966—, pres., 1983-84, pres., chief exec. officer, 1985—. Republican. Jewish. Office: Superior Insulated Wire Washburn Ln Stony Point NY 10980

MILLER, LINDA PATTERSON, English educator; b. Detroit, Jan. 27, 1946; d. Harold LeRoy and Inez (Peterson) Patterson; m. Randall M. Miller, Aug. 3, 1968; 1 child, Nathaniel. BA, Hope Coll., 1968; MA, Ohio State U., 1972; PhD, U. Del., 1979. Prof. Pa. State U.-Ogontz, Abington, Pa., 1980—; scholarly cons. Am. Playhouse, PBS Broadcasting, N.Y.C., 1985-89. Editor: Letters from the Lost Generation, 1991; contbr. articles on Am. lit. to Am. Transcendental Quar., Jour. Modern Lit., Renascence, others. Lilly Found. postdoctoral fellow, 1982-83; Danforth Found. assoc., 1982-88. Mem. Ernest Hemingway Soc. (past officer), Ernest Hemingway Found. (bd. dirs. 1987-90). Home: 244 Sagamore Rd Upper Darby PA 19083-3912 Office: Pa State U Ogontz 1600 Woodland Rd Abington PA 19001-3918

MILLER, LORING ERIK, insurance agent, broker; b. N.Y.C., Apr. 6, 1951; s. Martin and Frances (Kaufman) M.; m. Ilene Jane Cook, Dec. 18, 1983; children: Justin, Jennifer, Mallory. BBA, L.I. U., 1972; diploma, GM Sch. Dealership Mdse./Mgmt., 1977. Treas. Dial Chevrolet Inc., Westbury, N.Y., 1970-77; v.p., owner Dial Chevrolet Inc., Westbury, 1977-88; pres. Middle Country Brokerage Inc., Westbury, 1984-87, Loring E. Miller Agy. Inc., Melville, N.Y., 1978—. Bd. dirs., exec. v.p. Nassau County Police Res. Assn., 1985—; mem. N.Y.C. Police Res. Assn., 1986—; trustee N.Y. State Fraternal Order Police. Mem. Profl. Ins. Agts. N.Y., Rotary. Home and Office: PO Box 1358 331 Mt Misery Rd Melville NY 11747

MILLER, LORRAINE MARIE, tariff and rate specialist; b. Newark, July 8, 1941; d. John M. Ostachowski (dec.) and Helen H. (Stawiarz) Yurechka; (div. 1976); 1 child, Leigh M. Druckenmiller. AA, Fairleigh Dickinson, 1961, BA, 1965. Internat. tariff specialist Maritz Travel, White Plains, N.Y., 1988—; cons., owner CorpoRATES, Scarsdale, N.Y., 1990—; internat. rate desk standardization com. Maritz Travel, St. Louis, 1991—. Author: (manuals) Business Travelers' Guide to Lower Internat. Airfares, 1990, Travel Strategies, 1991. Fellow NAFE, Westchester Exec. Network, World Found. Successful Women. Roman Catholic. Home: 372 Central Park Ave 3E Scarsdale NY 10583 Office: CorpoRATES PO Box 1342 Scarsdale NY 10583

MILLER, LYNN, biology educator; b. McCook, Nebr., Nov. 6, 1932; s. Dale Miller and Edythe (Rupp) Ovesen; m. Jean Douglas, June 21, 1957; children: Ivor Lynn, Craig Douglas. BS, San Francisco State Coll., 1957; PhD, Stanford U., 1962. NIH postdoctoral fellow Hopkins Marine Sta., Stanford U., Pacific Grove, Calif., 1962-64; NIH postdoctoral fellow genetics and microbiology dept. U. Wash., Seattle, 1964-65, vis. scholar, 1975; asst. prof. biology Am. U. Beirut, 1965-68, Adelphi U., Garden City, N.Y., 1968-70; assoc. prof. Hampshire Coll., Amherst, Mass., 1970-74, prof., 1974—. Contbr. articles to sci. jours. Office: Hampshire Coll Sch Natural Sci Amherst MA 01002

MILLER, LYNNE EWING, physician; b. Chgo., Mar. 1, 1938; d. Frank Daugherty and Ruth Helen (Wild) Ewing; m. John Pindyck Miller, Apr. 17, 1965; children: Saam Anthea, Inness Alden. BA, Middlebury Coll., 1960; diploma, Juilliard Sch. Music, 1966; MD, Albert Einstein Coll. Medicine, 1985. Diplomate Am. Bd. Internal Medicine. Intern U. Conn. Health Ctr., Farmington, 1985-86, resident, 1986-87; resident Danbury (Conn.) Hosp., 1987-88; pvt. practice in internal medicine Brewster, N.Y., 1988—. Office: 601 Village Dr Brewster NY 10509-1306

MILLER, MARA (MARGARET MARY MILLER), philosophy, Asian studies educator; b. Scranton, Pa., Feb. 3, 1952; d. Lee L. and Mary (Hosie) M.; m. Scott Paul Robertson, Oct. 29, 1981. BA, Cornell U., 1973; MA, U. Mich., 1976; PhD, Yale U., 1987. Lectr. Kwassui Jr. Coll., Nagasaki, Japan, 1977-78; asst. prof. art history Franklin & Marshall Coll., Lancaster, Pa., 1987-91; dir. Asian studies, asst. prof. philosophy Drew U., Madison, N.J., 1991—; rsch. assoc. Internat. Soc. for Eighteenth Century Studies, Paris, 1990, Ctr. for Hist. Analysis, Rutgers U., New Brunswick, N.J., 1990-92, East-West Ctr., Honolulu, 1990—. Contbr. chpts. to books and articles to profl. jours. Named fellow Folger Libr., Washington, 1986-87; recipient NEH summer stipend Aston Magna Acad., 1989, Yale/Mellon West European Grant-in-aid-of Rsch., 1988; rsch. grantee Drew U., 1991-92, Franklin and Marshall Coll., 1987-90, grands for grad. study and rsch. U. Mich., 1975-76, Yale U., Yale Ctr. for Brit. Art, 1979-84, Smithsonian Instn., 1984. Mem. Am. Philos. Assn., Am. Soc. for Aesthetics (steering com. Ea. div. 1989-92, program chair Ea. div. 1991), Assn. for Asian Studies, Soc. for Cross- Cultural Rsch., Coll. Art Assn., Japan Soc., Asia Soc. Home: 31 S Middlebush Rd Middlebush NJ 08873 Office: Drew U SWB Madison NJ 07940

MILLER, MARGERY STAMAN, educator; b. Uniontown, Pa., Mar. 6, 1945; d. Harry and Bernice (Arnheim) Staman; m. Leland G. Miller. BA, Simmons Coll., Boston, 1967; MS, U. Pa., 1968, EdD, 1976. Reading, lang. arts tchr. Vanguard Middle Sch., Paoli, Pa., 1968-70; reading cons. Lower Merion Sch. Dist., Ardmore, Pa., 1970-73; prof. reading edn. Lesley Coll., Cambridge, Mass., 1973—, dir. reading progs., 1980—, acting dean edn./spl. edn. depts., 1987; acting dir. PhD programs Lesley Coll., Cambridge, spring, 1992. Co-author: Reading the Newspaper, 1987-88, Integrating Computers into Elementary, High School and Middle School Curriculum, 1987; contbr. articles to profl. jours. Lesley Coll. grantee, 1986—, Bd. Regents Mass. grantee, 1987—. Mem. Greater Boston Reading Coun., Mass. Reading Assn. (exec. bd.), Mass. Assn. Coll. and U. Reading Educators (pres. 1990-92), Internat. Reading Assn., Nat. Coun. Tchrs. English. Office: Lesley Coll 29 Everett St Cambridge MA 02138-2790

MILLER, MARVIN EDWARD, building materials company executive; b. Far Rockaway, N.Y., Jan. 28, 1929; s. Philip J. and Dorothy B. (Verby) M.; m. Beverly Kolikof, June 7, 1953; children: Lisa, Deborah, James. BS, Ind. U., 1949; MS, Columbia U., 1950. Salesman M. Verby Co., Jamaica, N.Y., 1953-56; pres. Miller Supply Corp., White Plains, N.Y., 1956-74, chmn. bd., 1975—; pres. Grip-Rite Ltd., Hong Kong, 1979—; chmn., co-chief exec. officer PrimeSource, Inc., 1990—. Bd. dirs., v.p. Westchester Jewish Community Svcs., Hartsdale, N.Y., 1985. With AUS, 1951-53. Mem. Masons, Shriners. Republican. Home: Woodlands Rd Harrison NY 10528-1416 Office: PrimeSource Inc 2900 Westchester Ave Purchase NY 10577-2551

MILLER, MARY JEANNETTE, office management specialist; b. Washington, Sept. 24, 1912; d. John William and David Evengeline (Hill) Sims; m. Cecil Miller, June 17, 1934 (dec.); children: Sylvenia Delores Doby, Ferdi A., Cecil Jr. Student, Howard U., 1929-30, U. Ill., 1940-42, Dept. Agr. Grad. Sch., 1957-59, U. Md., 1975; cert. in Vocat. Photography, Prince George's Community Coll., 1986. Chief mail processing unit Bur. Reclamation, Washington, 1940-57; records supr. AID, Manila, Korea, Mali, Guyana, Dominican Republic, Indonesia, Laos, 1957-71; office engr. Bechtel Assocs., Washington, 1976-79; real estate assoc; tchr. English as 2d lang. Ministry of Edn., Seoul, Korea, 1960-61, Ministry of Fin., Laos, 1968-70; cons. to Ministry of Fin. Royal Lao Govt., 1971-74; cons. AID missions to Yemen, Sudan, Somalia, 1982; records mgmt. cons. AID, Monrovia, Liberia, 1980-81, Sri Lanka, 1984; docent Mus. African Art Smithsonian Inst., Washington, 1986-89; circulation asst. Prince George County Meml. Libr. System, Hyattsville, Md., 1987-91, ret.; mem. Friends of Internat. Edn. Com., 1985—. Author handbooks on office mgmt. Mem. Mayor's Internat. Adv. Coun. Mem. Soc. Am. Archivists, Am. Mgmt. Assn., Montgomery County Bd. Realtors, Am. Fgn. Svc. Assn., Nat. Trust Hist. Preservation, Assn. Am. Fgn. Svc. Women's Writer Group, Zeta Phi Beta. Roman Catholic. Home: 14200 Pimberton Dr Hudson FL 34667

MILLER, MELVIN HOWARD, state legislator; b. Bklyn., July 24, 1939; s. Henry and Frieda (Chaiet) M.; m. Elizabeth Mohr, 1961; children: Susan, Lawrence. BA, Bklyn Coll., 1961; LLB, NYU Sch. Law, 1964. Assoc. O'Dwyer & Bernstein, N.Y.C., 1964-67, Joseph Keller, 1967-69, Bluestone, Kleigman & Israel, 1969-71; ptnr. Sherman, Adolf & Miller, 1971-91; assemblyman 44th assembly dist. N.Y. State, 1971; Speaker of the House N.Y. State Assembly, Albany, 1987, mem. rules com. Mem. Flatbush Com. for Youth, Midwood Community Coun. With U.S. Army, 1957. Mem. N.Y. County Bar Assn., Fidelity Lodge, KofP. Democrat. Jewish. Office: House Speaker State Capitol Albany NY 12224

MILLER, MELVIN ORVILLE, JR., artist; b. Balt., May 16, 1937; s. Melvin and Edith Amelia (Schmier) M. Diploma, Md. Inst. Art, 1959. mem. Six Realists Gallery of Balt., 1962-63; participant Art in Embassies Program, Freetown, Sierra Leone, 1986-88. One man shows include I.F.A. Galleries, Washington, 1970, Center Club, Balt., 1980, 92; exhibited in numerous group shows Washington, Balt., Ohio, Mass., Va., N.Y.C., Conn., R.I., Calif., Fla., N.J., Wash.; exhibited in shows at Karachi, Pakistan, 1970s, Port-Au-Prince, Haiti, 1970s; represented in numerous pvt. collections in Eng., Germany, Greece, Brazil, other fgn. countries. With USAFR, 1959-65. John F. and Anna Lee Stacey scholar, 1965. Mem. Grand Cen. Art Gallery, Am. Soc. Marine Art (charter), Charcoal Club (Balt.). Democrat. Home: 2001 Alto Vista Ave Baltimore MD 21207-5245 Studio: 2007 Fleet St Fell's Pt Baltimore MD 21231

MILLER, MICHAEL BARBREE, investment company executive; b. Los Angeles, Sept. 14, 1938; s. Keith S. and Dorothy (Barbree) McHugh; student U. Calif., 1955-56, Poly. Inst. N.Y., 1959-61; m. Diane W. Wolf, Dec. 10, 1991; 1 child from earlier marriage, Kim Elizabeth. V.p. Citicorp., 1961-68; v.p. portfolio mgr. Faulkner, Dawkins & Sullivan, Inc., N.Y.C., 1968-70; pres., founder Adv. Dynamics, Inc., N.Y.C., 1970-74; v.p. William D. Witter, Inc., N.Y.C., 1974-76; v.p. Loomis Sayles & Co., Washington, 1977-79; sr. v.p., chief investment officer Am. Security Bank, N.A., Washington, 1979-86; pres., dir., chief investment officer ASB Capital Mgmt., Inc., Washington, 1983-86; sec., treas., dir. Susan C. Miller Assocs., Inc., Washington, 1986-87; exec. v.p. Sigma Mgmt., Inc., Wilmington, Del., 1987—; exec. v.p., dir., chief investment officer Provident Mut. Mgmt. Co., Inc., Wilmington, 1987—. Vice chmn. Found. for Phys. Therapy, Washington, 1979-86; pres. John Dickson Home, Washington, 1980-86, Elizabeth R. Shoemaker Home, Washington, 1981-86, Henry and Annie Hurt Home for Blind. Served with USMC, 1956-59. Mem. Wilmington Fin. Analysts (cfp), Inst. Chartered Fin. Analysts, N.Y. Soc. Security Analysts, Washington Soc. Security Analysts, Nat. Economists Club, Congl. Country Club. Office: Provident Mut Mgmt Co 220 Continental Dr Newark DE 19713-4304

MILLER, MICHAEL FRANCIS, mechanical engineer, consultant; b. Springfield, Mass., Feb. 9, 1948; s. Robert A. and Kathleen A. (McIntyre) M.; m. Ann Carol Amodeo, June 15, 1973; children: Tara, Allison. BSME, U. New Haven, 1970. Lic. profl. engr., Conn. Engring. draftsman Cahn Engrs., New Haven, 1967-68; draftsman, technician Charles Brewer, Architect, New Haven, 1968-69, Roche, Dinkeloo & Assocs., New Haven, 1969; engring. technician Cahn Engrs., New Haven, 1970, design engr., 1970-72; project engr. Flaherty-Giavara Assocs., West Haven, Conn., 1972-76; prin. Miller Group, North Haven, Conn., 1976-86; ptnr. Spectrum Engring. Group, Cheshire, Conn., 1986—. Author: Classical Greek and Roman Coins, 1971. Named Hon Maitre d' Leukemia Soc., Celebrity Waiters Luncheon, Cheshire, 1989-90. Mem. ASME, Am. Soc. Civil Engrs., Am. Soc. Safety Engrs., Soc. Automotive Engrs., Human Factors Soc., Am. Boat and Yacht Coun., Astron. Soc. New Haven, Assn. for the Advancement of Automotive Medicine, Assn. Lunar and Planetary Observers, Duck Island Yacht Club, Nautical Rsch. Guild. Office: Spectrum Engring Group 1111 S Main St Cheshire CT 06410-3432

MILLER, NAIRN LOCKWOOD, small business owner, engineer; b. N.Y.C., Mar. 4, 1922; s. Clyde Kennedy and Leah (Ingraham) M.; m. Evelyn Rickey, Mar. 21, 1948 (div. Ept. 1965); children: Nancy Rickey, Bruce Campbell. BS in Aero. Engring., Rensselaer Poly. Inst., 1943; MBA, Columbia U., 1950. Engr. N.Am. Aviation, Inc., L.A., 1944, 46-48; mgr. GE, N.Y.C., Phila., 1950-62; v.p. mktg. Franklin Electric, Co., Bluffton, Ind., 1962-65, Itek Corp., Rochester, N.Y., 1965-68, Baker Industries, N.Y.C., 1968-69; pres. Lockwood Ford Tractor, Inc., Springfield, Mass., 1969-73, N.L. Freedman, Inc., Springfield, 1973—. Inventor 6 component balance system, twin electric circuit breaker. Mem. Better Bus. Bur., Springfield, 1982—, bd. dirs., 1988—. Lt. USN, 1944-46. Mem. C. of C. Republican. Home: 1757 E Mountain Rd Westfield MA 01085-1458 Office: NL Freedman Inc 850 Berkshire Ave # 3143 Springfield MA 01151-1306

MILLER, NANCY JANET, insurance agent; b. Champaign, Ill., Sept. 14, 1954; d. Allan Stephen and Janet Margaret (Worth) M.; m. David W. Sanborn, Nov. 24, 1990. BA cum laude, U. Mass., 1976. CLU, Chartered Fin. Cons. Spl. agt. Prudential Ins. Co. Am., East Longmeadow, Mass., 1976—; broker various ins. cos., East Longmeadow, 1980—. Recipient Nat. Sales Achievement award for 10 yrs. Nat. Assn. Life Underwriters, 1989; selected one of 125 Univ. of Mass. grads. to watch. Mem. Am. Soc. CLUs, Am. Soc. Chartered Fin. Cons., Springfield Assn. Life Underwriters (v.p. 1985-86, pres. 1987-88), Springfield C. of C. (Breakfast Club com. 1986-89), East Longmeadow C. of C. (clk. 1989-90, pres. 1991-92). Office: Prudential Ins Co 200 N Main St East Longmeadow MA 01028-2326

MILLER, NEAL ELGAR, psychologist, emeritus educator; b. Milw., Aug. 3, 1909; s. Irving E. and Lily R. (Fuenfstueck) M.; m. Marion E. Edwards, June 30, 1948; children: York, Sara. B.S., U. Wash., 1931; M.S., Stanford U., 1932; Ph.D., Yale U., 1935; D.Sc., U. Mich., 1965, U. Pa., 1968, St. Lawrence U., 1973, U. Uppsala, Sweden, 1977, LaSalle Coll., 1979, Rutgers U., 1985. Social sci. research fellow Inst. Psychoanalysis, Vienna, Austria, 1935-36; asst. research psychologist Yale U., 1933-35; instr., asst. prof., research asst. psychol. Inst. Human Relations, 1936-41, assoc. prof., research assoc., 1941-42, 46-50, prof. psychology, 1950-52, James Rowland Angell prof. psychology, 1952-66; fellow Berkeley Coll., 1955—; prof. Rockefeller U., N.Y.C., 1966-81; prof. emeritus Rockefeller U., 1981—; research affiliate Yale U., 1985—; expert cons. Am. Inst. Research, 1946-62; spl. cons. com. human resources Research and Devel. Bd., Office Sec. Def., 1951-53; mem. tech. adv. panel Office Asst. Sec. Def., 1954-57; expert cons. Ops. Research Office and Human Resources Research Office, 1951-54; bd. of sci. counsellors Nat. Inst. of Aging, 1987-90; bd. gov.s and mem. of exec. com. N.Y. Acad. of Scis., 1987. Author: (with J. Dollard et al) Frustration and Aggression, 1939, (with Dollard) Social Learning and Imitation, 1941, Personality and Psychotherapy, 1950, Graphic Communication and the Crisis in Education, 1957, N.E. Miller: Selected Papers, 1971; contbr. chpts. to psychol. handbooks; editor: Psychological Research on Pilot Tng., 1947. Chmn. bd. sci. dirs. Roscoe B. Jackson Meml. Lab., Bar Harbor, Maine, 1962-76, hon. trustee, 1980—; bd. sci. counsellors NIMH, 1957-61; fellowship com. Founds. Fund for Research in Psychiatry, 1956-61; mem. central council Internat. Brain Research Orgn., 1964; v.p. bd. dirs. Foote Sch., 1964-65; chmn. NAS/NRC Com. on Brain Scis., 1969-71; bd. sci. counsellors Nat. Inst. Child Health and Human Devel., 1969-72; v.p. Inst. for Advancement of Health, 1982-90. Maj. USAAC., 1942-46; officer in charge research, Psychol. Research Unit 1, Nashville 1942-44; dir. psychol. research project Hdqrs. Flying Tng. Command, Randolph Field, Tex. 1944-46. Recipient Warren medal for exptl. psychology, 1954, Newcomb Cleveland prize, 1956; Nat. medal of Sci., 1964, Kenneth Craik Research award U. Cambridge, 1966, Wilbur Cross medal Yale U., 1966, Alumnus Summa Laude Dignitatus U. Wash., 1967, Disting. Alumnus award Western Wash. State Coll., Gold medal award Am. Psychol. Found., 1975, Mental Health Assn. rsch. achievement award, 1978, Inst. for Advancement of Health Sci. and Art of

Health award, 1988, Disting. Scholar award Internat. Soc. for Behavioral Medicine, 1990. Fellow Am. Acad. Arts and Scis. (council 1979-83), Brit. Psychol. Soc. (hon. fgn.); mem. Am. Philos. Soc., N.Y. Acad. Scis. (hon. life), Spanish Soc. Psychology (hon.), Am. Psychol. Assn. (council reps. 1954-58, pres. exptl. div. 1952-53, pres. 1960-61, pres. div. health psychology 1980-81, Disting. Sci. Contbn. award 1959, award for Disting. Contbns. to Knowledge 1983, citation for Outstanding Lifetime Contribution to Psychology 1991), Eastern Psychol. Assn. (pres. 1952-53), NRC (div. anthropology and psychology 1950-53, chmn. 1958-60), Nat. Acad. Sci. (chmn. sect. psychology 1965-67, chmn. com. brain sci. 1969-71, sr. fellow Inst. of Medicine 1983—, bd. mental health and behavioral medicine 1980—), German Soc. of Behavioral Medicine and Behavior Modification (hon.), Soc. Exptl. Psychologists, AAAS, Soc. Neurosci. (pres. 1971-72), Biofeedback Soc. Am. (pres.-elect 1983, pres. 1984, Outstanding Rsch. award 1987), Acad. Behavioral Medicine Research (pres. 1978-79, Neal E. Miller New Investigator award established 1989), Sigma Xi (pres. Rockefeller U. chpt. 1968-69), Phi Beta Kappa. Club: Mory's (New Haven). Office: Yale U Dept Psychology PO Box 11A Yale Sta New Haven CT 06520

MILLER, NEIL S., financial officer, advertising executive; b. N.Y.C., July 30, 1958; s. Irving Israel Maltz and Lenore (Goldstein) M.; m. Karen Joyce Salomon, Nov. 22, 1987; 1 child, Lindsay Alexandra. BS, SUNY, Buffalo, 1980; MBA, SUNY, Binghamton, 1982. CPA, N.Y. Staff auditor Peat Marwick Mitchell & Co., N.Y.C., 1982-83; ops. auditor Gulf & Western Industries, N.Y.C., 1983-84; spl. projects acct. Mickelberry Corp., N.Y.C., 1984-86; v.p. fin. Ptnrs. & Shevack Inc. (subs. Mickelberry Corp.), N.Y.C., 1986-87, sr. v.p. fin., 1987-89, exec. v.p., chief fin. officer, 1989—. Mem. AICPA, N.Y. State Soc. CPAs (com. chief fin. officers and advt.), Advt. Agy. Fin. Mgmt. Group. Home: 594 W Saddle River Rd Upper Saddle River NJ 07458 Office: Ptnrs & Shevack Inc 1211 Ave of the Americas New York NY 10019-4701

MILLER, PATRICIA ANN, writer; b. Abington, Pa., June 22, 1957; d. Albert Anthony and Doris Patricia (Robinson) Maida; m. Walter George Miller, Aug. 2, 1980 (div. Aug. 1989). BA in English Lit., West Chester U., 1982. With VA, Phila. and West Chester, Pa., 1979-82; freelance writer, photographer, 1981—; specification typist Phila. Naval Shipyard, Phila., 1984-89; customer svc. rep. various, 1989-91. Editor newspaper Phila. Naval Shipyard, 1987; author poetry, (books) The Story of the Cornerstone of Pennsylvania, Marcus Hook, 1986, Marcus Hook, Pennsylvania-A Pictorial History, 1992. Alt. del. St. Paul's Episcopal Ch., Elkins Park, Pa., 1991. With U.S. Army, 1976-78, Korea. Home: 1806 Beech Ave Philadelphia PA 19126-1011 Office: 111 Tasg Bldg 300 Willow Grove PA 19090

MILLER, PAULA ANN, insurance company executive; b. Syracuse, N.Y., July 27, 1958; d. Donald Paul and Sarah (Harabedian) M. AAS in Bus. Adminstrn., SUNY, Alfred, 1978; BSBA, LeMoyne Coll., Syracuse, 1982. Account clk. Fayette Ins. Agy., Fayetteville, N.Y., 1982-83; comml. lines rater Great Am. Ins. Co., Syracuse, 1983-84; comml. lines rater Excelsior Ins. Co., Syracuse, 1984-86, group leader comml. lines rater, 1986, asst. supr., 1986-88; supr. comml. lines casualty rating Hanover Ins. Cos., Liverpool, N.Y., 1988-89; asst. account rep. Young Ins. Agy., Inc., 1989—. Mem. Syracuse Ins. Women's Assn., Ins. Inst. Am., Am. Mktg. Assn. Republican. Roman Catholic. Home: 4285 Virgo Crse Liverpool NY 13090-1919

MILLER, RENE HARCOURT, aerospace engineer, educator; b. Tenafly, N.J., May 19, 1916; s. Arthur C. and Elizabeth M. (Tobin) M.; m. Marcelle Hansotte, July 16, 1948 (div. 1968); children: Christal L., John M.; m. Maureen Michael, Nov. 20, 1973. B.A., Cambridge U., 1937, M.A., 1954. Registered profl. engr., Mass. Aero. engr. G.L. Martin Co., Balt., 1937-39; chief aero. and devel. McDonnell Aircraft Corp., St. Louis, 1939-44; mem. faculty aero. engring. MIT, Cambridge, 1944—, prof., 1957-86, Slater prof. flight transp., 1962-86; head dept. aeros. and astronautics MIT, 1968-78, prof. emeritus, 1986—; v.p. engring. Kaman Aircraft Corp., Bloomfield, Conn., 1952-53; mem. tech. adv. bd. FAA, 1964-66; mem. Aircraft panel Pres.'s Sci. Adv. Com., 1960-72, Army Sci. Adv. Panel, 1966-73; chmn. Army Aviation Sci. Adv. Group, 1963-73; mem. Air Force Sci. Adv. Bd., 1959-70; com. on aircraft aerodynamics NASA, 1960-70. Contbr. articles to profl. jours. Recipient U.S. Army Decoration for Meritorious Civilian Service, 1967, 70; recipient L.B. Laskowitz award N.Y. Acad. Scis., 1976. Fellow Am. Helicopter Soc. (hon. tech. dir. 1957-59, editor jour. 1957-59, Klemin award, Hon. Nikolski lectr. 1983), AIAA (hon., pres. 1977-78, Sylvanus Albert Reed award), Royal Aero. Soc. (Great Britain); mem. Nat. Acad. Engring., Internat. Acad. Astronautics, Academie National de L'Air et de L'Espace France. Home: San Jose New Rd, Penzance Cornwall TR18 4PN, England Office: MIT Dept Aeros and Astronautics 33-411 Cambridge MA 02139

MILLER, RHONDA LORI, occupational psychologist; b. Phila., Jan. 13, 1955; m. Stephen John Selwyn, Oct. 15, 1977; children: James Selwyn, Alec Selwyn. BA in Psychology, Franklin and Marshall Coll., 1976; MA in Occupational Psychology, U. Sheffield, Eng., 1981. Pers. officer Alcan Aluminum (U.K.) Ltd., Banbury, Eng., 1977-79; sr. psychologist Brit. Post Office, London, 1981-85; cons. London, N.Y., 1985-87; mgr. people planning and devel. N.Y. Power Authority, White Plains, 1987—. Recipient Women in Govt. award State of N.Y., 1990. Fellow Brit. Psychol. Soc. (assoc.). Home: 84 1st Pl # 3 Brooklyn NY 11231-4248 Office: N Y Power Authority 2162 Brookside Ave Wantagh NY 11793-3850

MILLER, RICHARD BRUCE, electronics company executive; b. Bryn Mawr, Pa., Jan. 2, 1947; s. Robert and Kathryn (Marks) M; m. Nedra Lynn Herbert, Aug. 28, 1971; children: Sean Patrick and Ryan Cameron. BA in Polit. Sci., Shippensburg State U., 1969, MA in Polit. Sci., 1975. Asst. city mgr. City of Chambersburg, Pa., 1970-72; city mgr. City of New Cumberland, Pa., 1972-76, Montgomery Twp., N.J., 1976-78; internal control mgr. Xerox Corp., Harrisburg, Pa., 1978-79, credit mgr., 1979-80, controller, 1980-83; field adminstrn. ops. mgr. Xerox Corp., Stamford, Conn., 1983-85; ctr. mgr. N.Y.C., 1985-88; transition mgr. bus. ops. Stamford, Conn., 1988-89; mgr., ops. support Ea. region, 1989-90; mgr. quality/customer satisfaction Xerox Corp., Stamford, 1990-91; mgr. customer svc. ops. Xerox Corp., Stamford, Conn., 1991-92; mgr. systems products adminstrn. Xerox Corp., Rochester, N.Y., 1992—; mem. All Star Club, Xerox Corp., 1982-83, 85-86, 87-88, 88-89, 89-90, grad. Astronaut VII, 1987. Bd. dirs. So. Conn. Child Guidance Ctr., 1988-90, Child Care Ctrs., Stamford, 1990-92. Republican. Roman Catholic. Home: 60 Vineyard Hill Fairport NY 14450 Office: Xerox Corp Xerox Sq 100 Clinton Ave S Rochester NY 14644

MILLER, RICHARD JEROME, bank executive; b. Erie, Pa., May 8, 1939; s. Richard A. and Irene (Strahl) M.; children by previous marriage: Edward Scott, Lisa Ann, Sondra Lynn; m. Suzanne Marie Johnson, Oct. 22, 1983. BS, Lehigh U., 1961; MA, New Sch. N.Y.C., 1964; postgrad. NYU, 1964-68. With Chase Manhattan Bank, N.Y.C., 1961-82, v.p., 1974-82; v.p. E.F. Hutton Credit Corp./Chrysler Capital Corp., Greenwich, Conn., 1982-88, The CIT Group, N.Y.C., 1988-90; prin. Miller/Davis & Assocs., 1991—; v.p. Nat. Westminster Bank, 1991—. Mem. Waldwick Bd. Edn., N.J., 1968-72, v.p., 1971-72. Mem. Am. Econ. Assn., Western Fin. Assn., Fin. Mgmt. Assn. Democrat. Roman Catholic. Club: NYU (N.Y.C.). Office: Miller/Davis & Assocs 275 W 96th St Apt 2E New York NY 10025-6264

MILLER, RICHARD KERMIT, biologist, professor; b. Scranton, Pa., Oct. 17, 1946; s. Roland Kermit and Vera (Edwards) M.; m. Judith Ann Berens. AB in Biology, Dartmouth Coll., 1968; PhD in Pharmacology, Toxicology, Dartmouth Med. Sch., 1973; postgrad., Jefferson Med. Coll., Phila., 1972-74. Asst. prof. sch. medicine and dentistry U. Rochester, N.Y., 1974-80, assoc. prof., 1980-88, prof. ob.-gyn., toxicology, 1988—; dir. div. rsch. U. Rochester, 1978—, dir. PEDECS, 1987—; prof. reproductive biology U. Paris VI, 1983; mem. bd. scientific counselors Nat. Toxicology Program NIH, 1988—; chair panel on pregnancy biomarkers Nat. Rsch. Coun. Nat. Acad. Medicine, 1986-89; mem. scientific rev. bd. NIH/TERIS, 1988—; mem. com. teratology Nat. Libr. Medicine, 1987—; cons. FDA, NIEHS, EPA, 1988—; advisor World Health Orgns. Program Rsch. Devel. in Human Reproduction, 1990—. Editor-in-chief Trophoblast Research, 1982—; editorial bd. Teratology, 1979-87, Placenta, 1980—, Reproductive Toxicology, 1986—, Procs. of Soc. for Exptl. Biology and Medicine, 1991—. Sr. internat. fellow NIH/Fogarty, 1983, fellow Smith Kline and French, 1972-74, NIH, 1968-74; named Disting. Prof. Fulbright Program, 1988. Mem. Am. Soc. for Pharmacology and Exptl. Therapeutics, European Teratology Soc., Neurobehavioral Teratology Soc. (councilor 1986-89), Soc. for Gynecologic Investigation, Teratology Soc. (pres. 1991-92, chair pub. affairs 1985-88), Sigma Xi. Office: U Rochester Med Ctr Dept Obs-Gyn 601 Elmwood Ave Rochester NY 14642-8668

MILLER, RICHARD LEROY, JR., manufacturing company executive; b. Lebanon, Pa., July 30, 1951; s. Richard Leroy and Rena (Biely) M.; m. Vohnie Burrows, July 14, 1973; children: Andrew Richard, Brooke Rene. BA Bus. Adminstrn., Math., Houghton Coll., 1973. Staff. acct. Quaker Alloy div. Harsco Corp., Myerstown, Pa., 1973-74; mgr. acctg., 1974-77; div. controller Quaker Alloy div. Harsco Corp., 1977-80, v.p. investment casting ops., 1980-83; pres. Penna Precision Cast Parts, Inc., Myerstown, 1983—; bd. dirs. Peoples Nat. Bank, SETCO (local JTPA), Harrisburg, Pa.; co-chmn. small bus. adv. com. Lebanon Valley C. of C., Lebanon, 1988-89, chmn.-elect, 1991, chmn., 1992. Bd. dirs. Am. Cancer Soc., Lebanon, 1986, Grace Community Life Care Community, Myerstown, 1987—; chmn. Grace Christian Sch. Bd., Myerstown, 1978-89. Named Small Bus. Person of Yr. Lebanon Valley C. of C., 1989, Small Bus. Person of Yr. for Pa. SBA, 1990. Republican. Mem. Brethen Ch. Home: PO Box 152 4 Lantern Ave Myerstown PA 17067 Office: Penna Precision Cast Parts PO Box 282 Myerstown PA 17067-0282

MILLER, RICHARD MCDERMOTT, sculptor; b. New Philadelphia, Ohio, Apr. 30, 1922; s. J. Harry and Clela Belle (McDermott) M.; m. Audrey F. Miller, 1942; 1 dau., Sue Ann (Mrs. Kenneth Hartz); m. Gloria B. Bley, Mar. 18, 1961. Student, Cleve. Inst. Art, 1940-42, 49-51. Prof. emeritus Queens Coll., CUNY. One man shows at, Peridot Gallery, N.Y.C., 1964, 66, 67, 69, Washburn Gallery, N.Y.C., 1971, 74, 75, 77, Canton (Ohio) Art Inst., 1980, 20 yr. retrospective, Artists Choice Mus., N.Y.C., 1984, Springfield Mus. Art, Mo., 1985, Friends of Figurative Sculpture Gallery, N.Y.C., 1987-92, Philharm Ctr., Naples, Fla., 1991; represented in numerous pub. and pvt. collections.; author: Figure Sculpture in Wax and Plaster, 1971. Served with AUS, 1942-46. Mem. Sculptors Guild, NAD (pres. 1989-92), Century Assn. Address: 53 Mercer St New York NY 10013

MILLER, RICHARD WESLEY, electronics company executive; b. Buffalo, Nov. 22, 1940; s. John Irwin and Rose Mary (Mirco) M.; m. Sharon Ann Betzler, Jan. 28, 1967; children: Barbara Ann, Thomas Andrew. B.B.A., Case Western Res. U., 1967; M.B.A., Harvard U., 1970. With Nat. City Bank, Cleve., 1961-68, credit officer, 1966-68; with Penn Central Corp., N.Y.C., 1970-82; v.p. fin., then exec. v.p. subs. Penn Central Corp. (Arvida Corp.), Boca Raton, Fla., 1972-79, corp. sr. v.p. fin., chief fin. officer, 1979-82; exec. v.p., chief fin. officer RCA Corp., N.Y.C., 1982-85, exec. v.p. consumer products and entertainment, 1985-86; sr. v.p. consumer electronics bus. Gen. Electric Co., 1986-88; pres., chief exec. officer Thomson Consumer Electronics, 1988; ptnr. Am. Indsl. Ptnrs., 1988-89; pres. Wang Labs., 1989—, chief oper. officer, 1989-90, chmn., chief exec. officer, 1990—; tchr. Interracial Council Bus. Opportunity, N.Y.C., 1971-72. Pres. Econ. Council Palm Beach County, Fla., 1977-78; trustee Fla. Atlantic U., 1977-79, bd. advisors, 1975-79; mem. Gov. Fla. Com. on Energy, 1976; chmn. Housing Adv. Bd. Boca Raton, 1977-78; bd. dirs. South Fla. Coordinating Council, 1977-79; mem. vis. com. Harvard U., 1981-86. Named Bus. Man of Yr. Palm Beach County, 1978. Mem. Urban Land Inst. (chmn. recreational devel. coun. 1979), Harvard U. Bus. Sch. Assn. (pres. 1980, exec. coun.), Electronics Industries Assn. (bd. govs. 1987-88), Greenwich Country Club. Home: 415 Nashawtuc Rd Concord MA 01742-1616 Office: Wang Labs Inc 1 Industrial Ave Lowell MA 01851-5106

MILLER, RICHARDS THORN, naval architect, engineer; b. Jenkintown, Pa., Jan. 31, 1918; s. Herman Geistweit and Helen Buckman (Thorn) M.; B.S. in Naval Architecture and Marine Engring., Webb Inst. Naval Architecture, 1940; Naval Engr., MIT, 1951; m. Jean Corbat Spear, Sept. 13, 1941; (dec.); children: Patricia (Mrs. Charles G. Fishburn), Linda (Mrs. John X. Carrier); m. 2d, Alice Johnson Houghton, May 19, 1984. Commd. ensign U.S. Navy, 1940, advanced through grades to capt., 1960; specialized work design oceanographic research ships, mine sweepers, torpedo boats, destroyers; ret., 1968; mgr. ocean engring. Oceanic div. Westinghouse Electric Corp., 1969-75, adv. engr., 1975-79; cons. naval architect and engr., 1968—; mem. com. naval architecture Am. Bur. Shipping, 1960-63, mem. tech. com., 1978—, mem. ship structure com., 1966-68. Decorated Navy Legion of Merit; recipient William Selkirk Owen award Webb Alumni Assn., 1983. Fellow Soc. Naval Architects and Marine Engrs. (chmn. S.E. sect. 1965-66, chmn. marine systems com. 1970-77, chmn. tech. and rsch. steering com. 1977-78, chmn. small craft com. 1983-87, v.p. tech. and rsch. 1979-81, hon. v.p. (life), 1981—, mem. coun. 1976—, mem. exec. com. 1977-81; Capt. Joseph H. Linnard prize 1964, Disting. Svc. award 1988); mem. Am. Soc. Naval Engrs. (mem. council 1976-78), U.S. Naval Inst., N.Y. Yacht Club, Annapolis Yacht Club, Sailing Club of the Chesapeake, Sigma Xi. Author: (with R.G. Henry) Sailing Yacht Design, 1963, (with K.L. Kirkman) Sailing Yacht Design-A New Appreciation, 1990; also sects. in books, articles. Home and Office: 957 Melvin Rd Annapolis MD 21403-1315

MILLER, RITA, personnel consultant, diecasting company executive; b. Bklyn., Jan. 15, 1925; d. Joseph and Etta M.; BA, Bklyn. Coll., 1947; MA, Boston U., 1949; children: Erika Greenwald, Roy Barnet Glickman. Personnel officer, sec. to pres. Marine Elec. Corp., Bklyn., 1943-47; script writer Song Debut, Boston, 1949-50; dir. Writers' Workshops, interviewer pub. opinion surveys, New Rochelle, N.Y., 1962-64; mgr. employee relations Dynacast div. Coats & Clark, Inc., Yorktown Heights, 1966-89. Mem. Am. Soc. Personnel Adminstrn., Westchester Personnel Mgmt. Assn. (dir.), Personnel Council New Rochelle, Bus. and Profl. Women U.S.A., Nat. Sociology Hon. Soc. Editor: The Management Consultant (George Kenning), 1965; contbr. articles to profl. jours. Home: 280 Clove Rd New Rochelle NY 10804-3506

MILLER, ROBERT CLEMENS, chemical engineering consultant, actor; b. Jersey City, Mar. 9, 1943; s. Clemens Joseph and Martha Phillips (Rowlands) M.; m. Beverly Haviland Nelson, June 26, 1965; children: Christopher Robert, Andrew Clemens. BSChemE, Newark Coll. Engring., 1965. Registered profl. engr., N.J. Project engr. Am. Chicle Co., N.Y.C., 1965-67; sr. engr. Nabisco, Inc., Fair Lawn, N.J., 1967-74; rsch. specialist Cornell U., Geneva, N.Y., 1974-77; project leader Borden, Inc., Syracuse, N.Y., 1977-80; cons. Robert C. Miller, Cons. Engr., Auburn, N.Y., 1980—; advisor Inst. Food Sci. Cornell U., Ithaca, N.Y., 1986—, Ctr. for Advanced Food Tech. Rutgers U., New Brunswick, N.J., 1985, faculty Ctr. for Profl. Advancement, 1985. Contbg. author: Breakfast Cereals and How They Are Made, 1990, Food Extrusion Science and Technology, 1992; contbr. articles to profl. jours.; composer music for children's plays; appeared in feature film December, 1991, summer stock mus. and TV advts.; patentee in field. Bd. dirs. Community Action Coun., Ringwood, N.J., 1971-74, Cayuga County Arts Coun., Auburn, 1990—; mem. Conservation Commn., Ringwood, 1972-74, Auburn Players Community Theatre, 1976—. Mem. Am. Inst. Chem. Engrs. (Profl. Devel. award 1985, 90), Am. Soc. Agrl. Engrs., Am. Assn. Cereal Chemists (faculty 1986—), Tech. Club Syracuse, Inst. Food Technologists, R & D Assocs. for Mil. Food and Packaging Systems. Democrat. Home: RR 2 Box 413 Auburn NY 13021-9647

MILLER, ROBERT EDVIN, environmental education specialist, researcher; b. Lancaster, Pa., May 8, 1935; s. Grant Edvin and Regina (Keller) M.; m. Nancy Jean Gustafson, May 29, 1982; children: Lenore Ruth, David Robert, Robert E. Jr., Stacy JoAnn, Regina Louise. B.S., U. Millersville, 1966; M.S., U. Md., 1976. Tchr. pub. schs., Lancaster, Pa., 1966-68, Pottstown, Pa., 1968-70; faculty research asst. U. Md., Solomons, 1970-76; environ. specialist III, U. Md., Cambridge, 1971-81, environ. specialist IV, 1981—; fisheries biologist Horn Point Environ. Labs., Cambridge, 1981—; prof. Wor-Wic Tech. Nursing Sch., Cambridge, 1981-83; referee Fishery Bull., Cambridge, 1982-83, Bull. of Marine Sci., Cambridge, 1983—. Narrator and cons. ednl. film Chesapeake Blues, 1974 (Golden Eagle award 1975). Contbr. articles to profl. jours. Mem. ways and means com. United Fund of Dorchester County, Cambridge, 1981-83; trustee Reach, Inc., Cambridge, 1982-85; tchr. Dorchester County Adult Edn. and Queen Anne County Adult Edn., Kent Island, Md., 1983. Grantee Power Plant Siting Program, 1979-81, Univ. Md., 1983-84, Waddell Found., 1983. Mem. Roddy Sci. Soc. (pres. 1965), Atlantic Estuarine Research Soc. (membership com. 1973), Estuarine Research Soc., Nat. Marine Edn. Assn., Nat. Sci. Tchrs. Assn. (communication com., evaluation com.). Republican. Home: 5531 White Hall Rd Cambridge MD 21613 Office: Horn Point Environ Labs PO Box 775 Cambridge MD 21613-0775

MILLER, ROBERT EMIL, college administrator; b. Guilford, Conn., Nov. 7, 1930; s. Emil Augustus and Alice Mary (Walsh) M.; m. Sylvia Ellen McCorrison, Sept. 19, 1954; children: Robert, Anne, Paul, Crista, Daniel. BA, U. Conn., 1952, MA, 1958, PhD, 1966. Supt. Conn. Gen. Life Ins. Co., Bloomfield, 1952-60; asst. dean of men U. Conn., Storrs, 1960-68; assoc. adminstr. Conn. Commn. for Higher Edn., Hartford, 1968-69; acad. officer Conn. Community Coll. System, Hartford, 1969-71; pres. (founding) Quinebaug Valley Community Coll., Danielson, Conn., 1971—; adj. prof. U. Conn., Storrs, 1971—; commr. New Eng. Assn. Schs. and Colls. Bd. dirs. Conn. Coalition on Literacy, Hartford, 1989—, N.E. Conn. Econ. Alliance, Danielson, 1987—; v.p. Ea. Conn. Found. Pub. Giving, Norwich, 1988—. With U.S. Army, 1953-55. Recipient Disting. Alumni award U. Conn. Alumni Assn., 1978, Civic Achievement award Killingly-Brooklyn (Conn.) C. of C., 1984, Thomas J. Peters Nat. Leadership award, U. Tex., 1989. Mem. New Eng. Bd. Higher Edn. (bd. dirs., past chmn.), Alpha Sigma Phi (nat. pres. 1970-74, disting. svc. award 1988). Roman Catholic. Office: Quinebaug Valley CC 742 Upper Maple St Danielson CT 06239-1440

MILLER, ROBERT KEITH, sales executive, business owner; b. Bath, N.Y., May 9, 1940; s. George Deyo and Irma Dorothy (Applegate) M.; m. Patricia Anne Dinkel, June 23, 1962; children: Kevin Andrew, Kimberly Anne, Kristopher Allen. BS in Edn., Oswego State U., 1963; MS in Edn., Cortland State U., 1965. Tchr. Owego (N.Y.) Bd. Edn., 1963-81; with sales staff Nat. Small Bus. Assn., Washington, 1981-82, Brass & Things, Binghamton, N.Y., 1981-83, Tioga Indsl. Supply, Binghamton, N.Y., 1983-85, Curtis Assocs., Ithaca, N.Y., 1985-91; owner, salesperson R & P Assocs., Friendsville, Pa., 1991—. Republican. Methodist. Home and Office: Main and Lake Sts PO Box 33 Friendsville PA 18818

MILLER, ROBERT LEO, water conditioning company executive; b. McSherrystown, Pa., June 26, 1932; s. Leo Paul and Helen Anne (Eline) M.; m. Doris McIntyre, June 9, 1932; children: Sandrae L., Victoria M., Susan E., Robert Leo II, Samantha A. M Hydro-Geology, Columbia Pacific U., 1983. Owner Miller & Assocs., Hanover, Pa., 1951-68; sales and account exec. Rustcraft Greeting Cards Inc., Dedham, Mass., 1968-81; chief exec. officer Aqua Budget Conditioning Co., Hanover, Pa., 1981—. With U.S. Army, 1951-55, PTO, Korea. Mem. Elks. Home: 4655 Grandview Rd Hanover PA 17331-9754 Office: 445 Grandview Rd Hanover PA 17331-9540

MILLER, ROSEMARY MARGARET, accountant; b. Jersey City, Jan. 3, 1935; d. Joseph John and Marguerite (Delatush) Corbin; m. James Noyes Orton, 1956 (div. 1977); m. Julian Allen Miller, Oct. 14, 1978; children: Alexandria Lynn Hayes, Jennifer Ann Orton Cole. Student Barnard Coll., 1953-54, Rutgers U., Newark, 1954-56, Howard U., 1962-63, No. Va. Community Coll., 1976-83; AA, Thomas A. Edison State Coll., 1981; BS in Acctg., U. Md., 1987; cert. H & R Block, 1981. Bookkeeper Gen. Electronics, Inc., Washington, 1970-73; cost acct. Radiation Systems, Inc., Sterling, Va., 1973-80; acct. Bilsom Internat., Inc., Reston, Va., 1980-83; sales mgr. Bay Country Homes, Inc., Fruitland, Md., 1984; sr. staff acct. Snow, Powell & Meade, Salisbury, Md., 1985-86; acct. Meadows Hydraulics, Inc., Fruitland, Md., 1987-88; acct. Porter & Powell CPAs, Salisbury, 1988—; owner, prin. RCOM Cons., acctg., bookeeping, taxes, Princess Anne, Md. Mem. Accreditation Council for Accountancy (accredited 1981), Nat. Soc. Public Accts., Nat. Acct. Assn., Inst. Mgmt. Assn., Nat. Student Bus. League, Alpha Kappa Mu. Democrat. Lutheran. Home: 30531 Bardwell Dr Princess Anne MD 21853 Office: PO Box 153 107 High St Salisbury MD 21803

MILLER, ROSS LINCOLN, English educator; b. Bklyn., Feb. 12, 1946; s. Kermit and Frances (Resnick) M.; m. Julia Wang, June 22, 1969; 1 child, Alexandra Wang. AB, U. Mich., 1968; MA, Cornell U., 1970, PhD, 1972. Asst. prof., assoc. prof. U. Conn., Storrs, 1972-89, prof., 1990—; vis. prof. Trinity Coll., Hartford, Conn., 1986-87; vis. critic Yale U. Sch. Architecture, New Haven, 1982—. Author: American Apocalypse: The Great Fire and the Myth of Chicago, 1990; co-editor: Spring: A Journal of Architecture and Culture, Storrs, 1988—; contbg.editor: Progressive Architecture, Stamford, Conn., 1990—; contbr. articles to profl. jours. sr. rsch. fellow Ctr. for Humanities Wesleyan U., Middletown, 1986, Chgo. Inst. for Architecture and Urbanism, 1991, Yale U., New Haven, 1982-83. Mem. Soc. Archtl. Historians. Office: U Conn PO Box 25 Storrs Mansfield CT 06269-0001

MILLER, SALLY, public relations professional; b. N.Y.C., Dec. 6, 1925; d. Samuel and Marion Levy; m. Merle Roy Miller, Dec. 26, 1946; children: Terry L., Laurie Farr, Deborah Burke, Wendy Adams. MA, SUNY, Stony Brook, 1982. Adminstr., tchr. Dists. 3 and 7, Oyster Bay, Huntington, N.Y., 1957-68; copywriter and Broadway theatre reviewer Sta. WGSM, Huntington, 1968-69; program and publicity coord., dir. public relations Half Hollow Hills Community Library, Dix Hills, N.Y., 1969-81; public relations specialist Sally Miller Enterprises, Huntington, 1981—; lectr. C.W. Post Library Sch., 1978, Suffolk Co. Library Assn., 1974, ALA, 1974, Huntington Historical Soc., 1974; producer t.v. comml. Parachute Prodns., 1989; cons. Nassau/Suffolk Library Inst. Editor: DATA, Suffolk Co. Library Assn., 1966-67. Pres. Library Pub. Relations Coun., 1977-78, Suffolk Co. Library Assn., 1980-81. Recipient John Cotton Dana award, 1973. Mem. ALA (pub. rels. sect. cert. of recognition 1990). Home and Office: Sally Miller Enterprises 157 E Pulaski Rd Huntington Station NY 11746-1855

MILLER, SAMUEL CLIFFORD, museum director; b. Roseburg, Oreg., May 6, 1930; s. Loren and Blanche (Baron) M.; m. Nell Schoellkopf Ely, 1966 (dec.); m. Rosetta Averill, May 7, 1977. BA, Stanford U., 1951; postgrad., NYU Inst. Fine Arts, 1962-64; DFA (hon.), Seton Hall U., South Orange, N.J., 1976; LittD (hon.), Rutgers U., 1983. Photograph researcher Associated Press, N.Y.C., 1954-55; asst. to dir. Nat. Serigraph Soc. and Meltzer Gallery, N.Y.C., 1955-62, Albright-Knox Art Gallery, Buffalo, 1962-67; dir. Newark Mus., 1968—. Mem. art com. Port Authority of N.Y. and N.J.; mem. bd. Newark Preservation and Landmarks Com. With U.S. Army, 1951-53, PTO. Recipient Brotherhood award Nat. Conf. Christians and Jews, 1982, Katherine Coffey award Mid-Atlantic Assn. Mus., 1991, Trustees award N.J. Inst. Tech., 1989; named Outstanding Citizen N.J. N.J. Advt. Club, 1980. Mem. Assn. Art Mus. Dirs., Am. Assn. Mus., N.E. Mus. Conf., Mus. Coun. N.J. Home: 375 Mt Prospect Ave Newark NJ 07104-2134 Office: Newark Mu PO Box 540 49 Washington St Newark NJ 07101

MILLER, STEVEN RICHARD, lawyer; b. N.Y.C., Nov. 11, 1953; s. Arnold and Beatrice Miller. BA summa cum laude, NYU, 1974, M of Urban Planning, JD, 1977. Bar: D.C. 1978, N.Y. 1979, U.S. Supreme Ct. 1981. Intern U.S. Energy Rsch. and Devel. Adminstrn., Washington, 1977; intern U.S. Dept. Energy, Washington, 1977-78, atty.-advisor, 1978-91, dep. asst. gen. counsel for environ., 1991—. Contbr. articles to profl. jours.; assoc. editor NYU Rev. of Law and Social Change, 1977. CPR program chmn. Adas Israel Synagogue Men's Club, Washington, 1985—, mem. exec. bd., 1986-88, bd. dirs., 1985-86, 88—; rec. sec. Adas Israel Singles Aux., Washington, 1986-88; chair Adas Israel Sr. Citizens Seder, Washington, 1985. Recipient award for chairing and organizing sr. citizen Passover seder Adas Israel Synagogue, Washington, 1985, Recognition Vol. Svc. award Folger Shakespeare Theater, Washington, 1990, Yasher Koach award Adas Israel Men's Club, 1990, Pres.'s Point of Light award, 1992. Mem. ASME (mixed waste com.), Fed. Bar Assn. (chairperson energy law com. 1988-91, chair sect. on energy, environment and natural resources 1991—, award for sustained leadership 1989), Am. Nuclear Soc. (chair session orgn. 1984-88, exec. com. mem. environ. sci. div. 1984-86), Phi Beta Kappa. Jewish.

MILLER, SUE BARRICK, counseling facility director; b. Pitts., Aug. 26, 1955; d. Eugene Edwin and Shirley Ann (Abbott) B.; m. David John Miller, Mar. 23, 1985; 1 child, Alexander Zachary. B Psychology, Edinboro State Coll., 1977, M Profl. Psychology, 1978; PhD in Counselor Edn., U. Pitts., 1988. Staff therapist Harborcreek Sch. for Boys, Erie, Pa., 1975-78; drug and alcohol therapist Myriad Project-D&A Program, Jeannette, Pa., 1979-80; staff psychologist Harmarville Rehab. Ctr., Pitts., 1980-86, supervising psychologist, 1986-87, program coord., 1987-89, dir. behavioral svcs., 1989-90; exec. dir. The Caring Pl., Inc., Monroeville, Pa., 1989—; cons. Beulah

Christian Presch., Pitts., 1989—. Contbr. articles to profl. jours. Sandoz Pharm. Co. grantee, 1987. Mem. APA, Pa. Psychol. Assn., Greater Pitts. Psychol. Assn. (mem. newsletter com. 1984-85). Office: The Caring Pl Inc Parkvale Bldg Ste 504 Monroeville PA 15146

MILLER, TERRI ANN, materials manager; b. Luzna, Poland, Sept. 6, 1953; came to U.S., 1962; d. Walter John and Helena Victoria (Raczkowska) Mandel; m. Brian Bernard Miller, May 12, 1979; children: Kristin Nicole, Emily Corrine, James Daniel. AS, Ea. Conn. State Coll., 1975; BS, Fairfield (Conn.) U., 1977; MBA, N.H. Coll., 1983. Dept. supr. Barkers Dept. Store, Westport, Conn., 1969-77; assoc. materials mgr. GTE Products Corp., Stamford, Conn., 1977-78; supr. prodn. control GTE Info. Systems, Anaheim, Calif., 1978-79; materials mgr. Hendrix Electronics Corp., Manchester, N.H., 1980-82, cons., 1982-84; materials mgr. Kalwal Corp., Manchester, 1986-88, Pitco Frialator, Concord, N.H., 1988—; cons. Hendrix Electronics Inc., 1982-84. Fellow Am. Prodn. and Inventory Control Soc. Office: Pitco Frialator PO Box 501 Concord NH 03302-0501

MILLER, THOMAS EDGAR, college administrator, consultant; b. Pottsville, Pa., Nov. 25, 1948; s. Edgar Jason and Wilhelmina Mary (Peischl) M.; m. Carol Lesher, July 2, 1971; children: Andrew, Justin. BS, Muhlenberg Coll., Allentown, Pa., 1970; MS, Ind. U., 1972, EdD, 1979. Coord. for residence life Ind. U., Bloomington, 1974-77, asst. to dean for student svcs., 1977-79; dean of students Canisius Coll., Buffalo, 1979-87, v.p. for student affairs, 1988—; dir. Higher Edn. Consortium on Retention, Buffalo, 1986-91; chmn. adv. bd. Nat. Consortium for Acads. and Sport, 1991; cons. to various colls., assns., pub. cos. Mem. editorial bd. NASPA Jour., 1990—; contbr. articles to profl. jours. Pres. Higher Edn. Consortium on Substance Abuse, Buffalo, 1987—; mem. adv. com. and campaign devel. com. Western N.Y. Against Drugs, Buffalo, 1986—. Recipient Disting. Alumnus award Ind. U. Higher Edn. and Student Affairs Program, 1989. Mem. Nat. Assn. Student Pers. Adminstrs. (v.p. 1983-85), Am. Assn. for Higher Edn., Assn. for Instl. Rsch., Nat. Assn. Coll. and Univ. Bus. Officers, Eastern Assn. Coll. Deans (pres. 1991), Phi Kappa Tau, Alpha Sigma Nu, Beta Gamma Sigma. Office: Canisius Coll 2001 Main St Buffalo NY 14208-1098

MILLER, TIMOTHY ALAN, automotive executive; b. N.Y., Jan. 25, 1956; s. William Henry Miller and Elizabeth (Bessey) Berry; m. Lora Jean Ventrella, Apr. 26, 1975; children: Crystal Lynn, Julie Ann. Grad. high sch., Rochester, N.Y. Asst. mgr. Ky. Fried Chicken, Rochester, 1972-74; machinist Micro Instruments, Rochester, 1974, Gleason Works, Rochester, 1974-75; inspector Eastman Kodak Co., Rochester, 1975-79; owner, pres. Tim's Trim, Inc., Rochester, 1977—. Mem. devel. com. St. Lawrence Sch., Rochester, 1987-91. Mem. Specialty Equipment Market Assn., Nat. Mobility Equipment Dealers Assn., Rochester Claims Assn. Republican. Roman Catholic. Home: 119 Hincher Rd Hilton NY 14468-8918 Office: Tim's Trim Inc 30 Bermar Pk Rochester NY 14624-1541

MILLER, TIMOTHY EARL, planning company executive; b. Johnstown, Pa., Dec. 21, 1952; s. Gene E. and Ives (Stibich) M.; m. Donna Marie Tiffany, Sept. 22, 1985. BS in Environ. Resource Mgmt., Pa. State U., 1974. Project mgr. Earth Metrics, Inc., Palo Alto, Calif., 1975-77; asst. dir. mktg. Environ. Sci. Assn., San Francisco, 1977-81; sr. planner Wagstaff-Brady, Berkeley, Calif., 1981-82; regional dir. ESA-Urbitran, N.Y.C., 1982-84; pres. Hudson Ptnrship., Inc., N.Y.C. and New Brunswick, N.J., 1984-86; prin., pres. Tim Miller Assocs., Inc., Cold Spring, N.Y., 1986—; sec. Hawthorne Petroleum Investments, Inc. Contbr. articles to profl. jours. Active Big Bros./ Big Sisters, San Francisco, 1980-82, Bklyn. Heights Assn., 1985-87. Mem. Am. Inst. Cert. Planners (cert.), Am. Planning Assn., N.Y. State Planning Fedn., Regional Plan Assn., Urban Land Inst. Democrat. Office: 15 Main St Cold Spring NY 10516-3211

MILLER, VIRGINIA M., medical-surgical nurse; b. Pottsville, Pa., Feb. 28, 1955; d. Joseph and Marguerite F. (Knorr) Yourshaw; children: Leslie, Justin. Student, Allentown Hosp. Sch. Nursing, 1976. Staff nurse Lehigh Valley Hosp. Ctr., Allentown, Pa.; staff nurse, asst. supr. Phobe Home Inc., Allentown; program dir ICF MR Facility; facility dir., asst. project dir. Luther Ridge; pulmonary nurse coord. Miner's Clin; asst. project dir., adminstrn. Luther Ridge Personal Care Facility; staff nurse Good Samaritan Regional Med. Ctr. Office: Good Samaritan Regional Med Ctr E Norwegian St Pottsville PA 17901

MILLER, WALTER RICHARD, JR., banker; b. N.Y.C., Nov. 20, 1934; s. Walter Richard and Ann M. (Phelan) M.; m. Joan M. Groark; children: Kathryn A., Margaret E., Jennifer M., Walter Richard III. AB, Dartmouth Coll., 1955; MBA, Columbia U., 1957; PhD, NYU, 1965. Dir. mktg., v.p. Mellon Nat. Corp., Pitts., 1965-78; sr. v.p. First Atlanta Corp., 1979-81; exec. v.p. Norwest Corp., Mpls., 1981-86; pres., chief exec. officer First Constn. Fin. Corp., New Haven, 1987—, also bd. dirs.; pres., chief exec. officer First Constn. Bank, New Haven; also bd. dirs., pres., CEO Fin. Mktg. and Planning Corp., New Haven; exec.-in-residence Quinnipiac Coll.; pres. CIRRUS System, Inc.; pres., ceo Fin. Mktg. and Planning co.; exec.-in-residence Quinnipiac Coll. Contbr. articles, chpts. to profl. pubs. Bd. dirs. St. Paul Chamber Orch., Minn. Pub. Radio, Sci. Mus. Minn., Quinnipiac Coll., Hamden, Conn., Quinnipiac Coun. Boy Scouts Am., The Mus. of AM. Theatre; chmn. bd. Orchestra New England. With USAF, 1958. Teaching fellow NYU, N.Y.C., 1960; Ford Found. fellow NYU, 1962. Mem. Interbank Card Assn. (internat. chmn., bd. dirs.), Am. Mktg. Assn. (contbg. editor), Bank Mktg. Assn. (bd. dirs., chmn. mktg. planning council, chmn. mktg. mgmt. council), Somerset Club, New Haven County Club, Quinnipiack Club, Lawn Club. Home: 2 Marshall Rd Hamden CT 06517-3505 Office: Financial Mktg-Planning Corp New Haven CT 06517

MILLER, WAYNE, telecommunications executive; b. Orange, N.J., Nov. 5, 1950; s. Charles John and Virginia (Caruso) M.; m. Joan Marie Stabile, June 2, 1973; children: David John, Alyse Marie. BS in Engring., N.J. Inst. Tech., Newark, 1972, MS in Engring., 1974; MBA, Nova U., 1986. Registered profl. engr., N.J. Nat. account exec. Pennwalt Corp., Clifton, N.J., 1975-81; from dir. nat. accounts to asst. v.p. Mitel, Inc., Boca Raton, Fla., 1981-91; nat. mktg. mgr. Panasonic Communications & Systems Co., Secaucus, N.J., 1991—. Teaching fellow N.J. Inst. Tech., 1972-74. Mem. Woodfield Country Club.

MILLER, WAYNE DUNBAR, speech pathologist, audiologist; b. Brockton, Mass., Dec. 26, 1934; s. Wilford Eugene and Doris Mae (Dunbar) M.; m. Helen Louise Grant; children: Valerie-Gail, Wilford Gordon. BA in Speech Pathology, Staley Coll., Brookline, Mass., 1958; ME in Counseling, Psychotherapy, Suffolk U., 1971. Certs. in clin. competence speech pathology, lang. pathology and audiology; lic. speech pathologist, audiologist, Mass. Tchr. English Mendon (Mass.) High Sch., 1958-59; acad. clin. practicum in aphasiology Holy Ghost Hosp., Cambridge, Mass., 1959-61; pvt. practice speech pathology, 1961—; supr. speech therapy and hearing Paul A. Dever State Sch., Taunton, Mass., 1961-70; neuro-audiology and aphasiology specialist Goddard Meml. Hosp., Stoughton, Mass., 1966—; mem. allied med. staff Sturdy Meml. Hosp., Attleboro, Mass., 1970—; speech pathologist Attleboro Pub. Schs., 1970—; founder Speech, Lang. and Hearing Clinic Morton Hosp., 1968. Deacon Covenant Congl. Ch., North Easton, Mass., 1979-81, 87; mem. profl. adv. bd. and utilization rev. com. Stoughton Pub. Health Com., 1980—; sustaining mem. Rep. Nat. Com., 1981—. With Army N.G., 1953-61. Clin. fellow Parson (Kans.) State Hosp., 1964. Fellow Am. Acad. Audiology; mem. NEA, Am. Speech and Hearing Assn., Am. Audiology Soc., Mass. Speech and Hearing Assn., Mass. Edn. Assn., Attleboro Edn. Assn., U.S. Naval Inst., Am. Legion, Masons, Shriners, DeMolay (chpt. adv. coun. 1980-89, rainbow adv. bd. 1987-89). Home and Office: 76 Short St South Easton MA 02375-1019 also: Goddard Meml Hosp 909 Sumner St Stoughton MA 02072

MILLER, WILBUR HOBART, business diversification consultant; b. Boston, Feb. 15, 1915; s. Silas Reuben and Muriel Mae (Greene) M.; m. Harriett I. Harmon, June 20, 1941; children: Nancy Iber Miller Harray, Warren Harmon, Donna Sewall Miller Davidge. B.S., U. N.H., 1936, M.S., 1938; Ph.D., Columbia U., 1941. Rsch. chemist Am. Cyanamid Co., Stamford, Conn., 1941-49, Washington tech. rep., 1949-53, dir. food industry devel., 1953-57; tech. dir. products for agr. Cyanamid Internat. Am. Cyanamid Co., N.Y.C., 1957-60; sr. scientist Dunlap & Assos., Darien, Conn., 1960-63, sr. assoc., 1963-66; coord. new product devel. Celanese Corp., N.Y.C., 1966-67, mgr. comml. rsch., 1967-68, dir. corp. devel., 1969-84; bus. diversification cons., 1984—; lectr. on bus. and soc. Western Conn. State Coll., 1977-79. Contbr. sci. papers to profl. jours.; patentee in field. Chmn. Stamford Forum for World Affairs, 1954-87, hon. chmn. 1987—; mem. adv. bd. Ctr. for the Study of the Presidency, 1980—; bd. dirs. Stamford Symphony, 1974-80, v.p., 1978-80; bd. dirs. Stamford Hist. Soc., 1988, v.p., 1991—; pres. Coun. for Continuing Edn., Stamford, 1962, bd., 1960-70; elder United Presbyn. Ch., nominating com., 1960-63; pres. Interfaith Coun. of Stamford, 1973; internat. fellow U. Bridgeport, 1985—; mem. pres.'s coun. U. N.H., 1982—. Recipient outstanding achievement award Coll. Tech., U. N.H., 1971, Am. Design award, 1948, Golden Rule Award J.C. Penney & Co., 1986; Univ. fellow Columbia U., 1940-41. Fellow AAAS, Am. Inst. Chemists (councillor N.Y. chpt. 1984-85); mem. Am. Chem. Soc. (news svc. adv. bd., 1948-53), N.Y. Acad. Scis., Société de Chimie Industrielle (v.p. fin. Am. sect. 1980-84, dir. 1984—), Inst. Food Tech., Soc. for Internat. Devel., Am. Acad. Polit. and Social Scis., Stamford Hist. Soc., Chemists Club (N.Y.C., treas. 1982-84), Sigma Xi, Alpha Chi Sigma, Phi Kappa Phi. Home: 19 Crestview Ave Stamford CT 06907-1906

MILLER, WILLIAM JACOB, public relations executive; b. Providence, R.I., Apr. 28, 1952; s. Gerald Howard and Eunice Ruth (Gomberg) M. BS, Emerson Coll., 1974. Theatrical publicist Cameron Mackintosh, Inc., N.Y.C., to date; mgr. Theatre of Performing Arts, Miami Beach, Fla., 1986-87; adv. dir. Same Time, Next Year touring prodn. 1978, 79; press rep. numerous theatrical prodns. including The Phantom of the Opera, 1991—, Les Miserables, 1988—, Cats, 1987-88, Sugar Babies, 1979, 82-85, Colette, 1982, Fiddler on the Roof, 1981-82, Lolita, 1980-81, Shanghai Acrobatic Theatre, 1980, Deathtrap, 1980, others. Mem. Assn. Theatrical Press Agts. and Mgrs. Home: 47 Perry St Apt 1D New York NY 10014-2763

MILLER, WILLIAM MARSHALL, JR., automobile dealership executive; b. Phila., Dec. 28, 1943; s. William Marshall and Gertrude Virginia (Hoff) M.; m. Peggy Lee Hoch; children: William Marshall III, Kristine Lynn. Student, Harrisburg Area Ctr., 1962, Messiah Coll., Grantham, Pa., 1965. Salesman Sunderland Chevrolet, Lemoyne, Pa., 1966-69, sales mgr., 1970-77; owner, mgr. Bill Miller Ford-Mercury, Elizabethtown, Pa., 1977-84; ptnr. Carlisle (Pa.) Collector Car Flea Market, 1974—, Love Chevrolet, Downingtown, Pa., 1985-87, Caren Chevrolet-Olds-Geo, Woodbine, N.J., 1988-90, Win Chevrolet-Olds-GEO, 1990—, Varsity Volkswagen, Carlisle, 1988—. Author: Salesperson's Policy and Procedure Guide, 1978, Sales-managers Policy and Procedure Guide, 1978. Bd. dirs. Two West Penn, retirement home, Carlisle, 1988-91. Mem. Pa. Automobile Dealers Assn. (bd. dirs. 1979-81), Pa. Automotive Assn. (bd. dirs. 1981-83), Antique Automobile Club Am. (Hershey, Pa.), Kaiser Frazer Owners Club, Cushman Club of Am., Vintage Motor Bike Club, Ocean City Fishing Club. Republican. Methodist. Office: Carlisle Prodns 1000 Bryn Mawr Rd Carlisle PA 17013-1500

MILLER, WILLIAM MCELWEE, JR., aeronautical company executive; b. Meshed, Mazandaran, Iran, Mar. 30, 1926; s. William McElwee and Isabelle Pennock (Haines) Miller. BA, Princeton (N.J.) U., 1953; STB, N.Y. Theol. Sem., 1956; ThM, Princeton Theol. Sem., 1964. Staff worker fgn. students Inter-Varsity Christian Fellowship, Manhattan, N.Y., 1957-60; pres. Aereon Corp., Princeton, 1967—, pres., treas., 1970—. inventor V/Stol aircraft, airborne surveillance platform. Trustee Scripture Union, USA, Phila., 1965; corp. mem. Children's Ministries, Inc., Pitts., 1970. Lt. (j.g.) USN, 1944-49. Republican. Presbyterian. Office: Aereon Corp 20 Nassau St Princeton NJ 08542-4509

MILLER, WILLIAM RUSSELL, medical and data collection equipment manufacturing executive; b. Bklyn., Dec. 16, 1928; s. William Albert and Claudia Anna (Ballagh) M.; m. Marlene Christine Sullivan, July 21, 1961; children: Claudette Patrice, Kathleen Brenda. BS, MIT, 1952, MS, 1952. Registered profl. engr., Pa. Engr. GE, Erie, Pa., 1954-62, supr. devel. engring., 1962-65, mgr. advance engring., 1965-66, mgr. product engring., 1966-71, mgr. engring., 1971-72; gen. mgr. systems div. Am. Sterilizer Co., Erie, 1972-75, v.p. rsch. and devel., 1975-87; chief corp. devel. officer Welch Allyn, Inc., Skaneateles Falls, N.Y., 1988—; bd. corporators, mem. planning com. St. Vincent Health Ctr., 1970-88; mem. engring. adv. bd. Gannon U., 1976-88, co-chmn., 1977; chmn. tech. focus panel Syracuse Met. Devel. Authority; bd. dirs. N.Y. Photonics Devel. Corp.; grant reviewer N.Y. Sci. & Tech. Found., 1991. With USAF, 1952-54, capt., 1959. Home: PO Box 717 Skaneateles NY 13152-0717 Office: PO Box 50 Skaneateles Falls NY 13153-0050

MILLER-BERNAL, LESLIE JEAN, sociology educator; b. N.Y.C., Apr. 12, 1946; d. Vincent and Mary Frances (Reilly) Dunkel; m. Daniel John Miller, Aug. 20, 1966 (div. Mar. 1979); 1 child, Adam; m. Martin Gardiner Bernal, Mar. 10, 1979; 1 child Patrick. BA summa cum laude, SUNY, Stony Brook, 1969, MA, 1970; PhD, Cornell U., 1978. Rsch. assoc. Cornell Univ., Ithaca, N.Y., 1970-72; asst. to full prof. Wells Coll., Aurora, N.Y., 1975—; part time lectr. Elmira (N.Y.) Coll., 1971-72, 75; vis. scholar Cambridge (Eng.) Univ., 1981-82, 88-89. Client adv. Tompkins County Task Force for Battered Women, Ithaca, 1985-87; community mem. Women's Studies Exec. com., Cornell Univ., Ithaca, 1990—. Mem. Am. Sociol. Assn., Sociologists for Women in Soc., Ea. Sociol. Soc., N.Y. State Sociol. Assn. Democrat. Home: 105 Cornell St Ithaca NY 14850-4827 Office: Wells Coll Rt 90 Aurora NY 13026

MILLER-HOUCK, NANCY JOAN, nurse, psychotherapist, consultant, educator; b. Newton, Mass., May 20, 1947; d. Harold Max and Selma Irma (Finkelstein) Gerrish; divorced, 1974; m. Douglas Houck, July 13, 1991. BA in Sociology, C. W. Post Coll. L.I. U., 1968; postgrad., Mich. State U., 1969; RN diploma, Jackson Meml. Hosp., 1977; MS in Mental Health Counseling, Barry U., 1989. Cert. psychiatric RN, specialist in adult mental health nursing. Social worker Suffolk (N.Y.) County Social Svcs., 1968-71; social worker, counselor Met. Dade County, Miami, Fla., 1971-74; charge nurse Newton Wellsley Hosp., Newton Upper Falls, Mass., 1977-78; head nurse substance abuse Humana Hosp. Biscayne, Miami, Fla., 1978-80; charge nurse Mt. Zion Hosp., San Francisco, 1980-81; staff nurse mental health unit Marin Gen. Hosp., Greenbrae, Calif., 1981-84; clin. coord. Humana Hosp. Biscayne, Miami, Calif., 1984-86; head nurse, dir. treatment svcs. addiction Victoria Hosp., Miami, 1986-87; per diem nurse Highland Park Hosp., Miami, 1987-89; staff nurse med./surg. Blue Hill (Maine) Meml. Hosp., 1989; pvt. practice Blue Hill, 1989-91, Lahana, Hiwaii, 1992—. HIV/AIDS Teaching grantee State of Maine, 1990, Social Svcs. Program grantee State of Fla., 1974. Mem. AACD, ANA (cert. psychiat. nurse, clin. nurse specialist). Office: Lahaina Shopping Ctr Ste 206 PO Box 11348 Lahaina HI 96761-6348

MILLER-JACOBS, SANDRA MARCIA, educator; b. N.Y.C., Dec. 25, 1945; d. Harold M. and Clara Miller; m. Harold H. Jacobs, Sept. 16, 1973; children: Shira Fay, Rena Lee. BA, Queens Coll.-CUNY, 1967; MEd, Boston U., 1971; DEd, Boston Coll., 1979. Spl. educator Wakefield (Mass.) Jr. High Sch., 1968-69, Community Clin. Nursery Sch., South Boston, Mass., 1969-73; prof., chmn. dept. spl. edn. Fitchburg (Mass.) State Coll., 1973—; presenter at nat. confs. Contbr. articles to profl. jours. Chair youth com. Temple Emunah, Lexington, Mass., 1990-91; bd. dirs. Camp Ramah of New Eng., 1991—. Recipient citation, Commonwealth of Mass., 1989. Mem. Coun. for Exceptional Children (pres. 1986-88, gov. 1988-91, v.p. 1991—), Phi Delta Kappa. Office: Fitchburg State Coll 160 Pearl St Fitchburg MA 01420-2697

MILLERS, EDIE (EDIE BAZZANO), children's clothing designer; b. Riga, Latvia, Feb. 15, 1938; came to U.S., 1951; d. Roberts and Sofija (Svite) M.; m. Rudolf Valdmanis, Oct. 3, 1964 (div. 1970); 1 child, Marita; m. Pat Bazzano, Nov. 21, 1976. BA, Fashion Inst. Tech., 1960. Designer Little Fashion, N.Y.C., 1961-63, Pemay, N.Y.C., 1963-70, Doe Spun, N.Y.C., 1970-72, Thomas Textile, N.Y.C., 1972-75; pres. Play Pen Set, Hastings On Hudson, N.Y., 1975—. Bd. dirs. Gallery at Hastings, Hastings On Hudson, 1987, Am. Field Svc. Hastings On Hudson, 1984—. Mem. Fashion Group, Westchester Assn. Women Bus. Owners, NAFE. Lutheran. Office: Play Pen Set 40 Amherst Dr Hastings On Hudson NY 10706-3302

MILLES, SAUL STEVEN, company medical director, physician; b. N.Y.C., Feb. 16, 1931; s. Benjamin and Fanny (Benimovich) M.; m. Sandra Faythe Cohen, Dec. 19, 1953; children: Karen, Douglas, Beth. Student, Cornell U., 1948-51; MD, U. Rochester, 1955. Diplomate Am. Bd. Internat. Medicine. Resident internal medicine Maimonides Hosp., N.Y.C., 1955-57; fellow internal medicine Yale U., New Haven, Conn., 1959-61, clin. asst. prof. internal medicine, 1964-68, clin. assoc. prof. internal medicine, 1968—; attending physician Yale Med. Ctr., New Haven, 1961-84; assoc. med. dir. GE, Fairfield, Conn., 1984-89, med. dir., 1989—; mem. Deans Adv. Coun. Yale U., 1989—; pres. staff Yale Med. Ctr., 1972. Fellow ACP; mem. Am. Soc. Internal Medicine (pres. 1970), Am. Occupational Med. Assn. Jewish. Home: 304 Hotchkiss Rd Orange CT 06477 Office: GE 3135 Easton Tpke Fairfield CT 06431-0001

MILLET, JOHN BRADFORD, retired surgeon; b. Buffalo, Aug. 8, 1916; s. John Alfred Parsons and Alice Jeannette (Murrell) M.; m. Constance Hopkins Dallas, Nov. 1974; children: John Bradford Jr., David Francis, Polly Watson. BS, Harvard U., 1938, MD, 1942. Diplomate Am. Bd. Surgery. Surg. intern Mass. Gen. Hosp., Boston, 1942-43, surg. resident, 1946-49; chief thoracic surgery, partner Slocum Dickson Clinic, Utica, N.Y., 1949-55; pvt. practice medicine specializing in surgery Utica, 1955—; sr. attending surgeon St. Luke's Meml. Hosp. Ctr., Utica, 1955-81, chief dept. surgery, 1969-70; sr. attending surgeon St. Elizabeth's Hosp., 1955—, Faxton Hosp., 1979-86; ret., 1985; asst. to pres. Mohawk Metal Products Inc., 1989-91; former cons. surgeon Herkimer Meml. Hosp., Rose Hosp., Rome, N.Y., Marcy (N.Y.) State Hosp.; former med. adv. to Vis. Nurse Assn.; former dir. Health Systems Agy. Cen. N.Y., Med. Securities Fund, 1964-65, Med. Funds Mgmt. Corp., 1964-65, Digimetrics Inc., M.V. Hockey Inc., Millwheel Inc., IEX Inc., JDC Resources, Inc., B.F.I. Telecommunications Co. Inc., Utica Disposables Inc., Input Specialists Inc., LJB Ventures Inc.; pres. White Birch Home of Utica, Inc. Former med. adv. com. Planned Parenthood of Mohawk Valley; pres. Midstate Com. on Area Wide Health Planning, 1966-72; co-chmn. citizens com. on devel. of med. sch. in Utica area; co-developer Brookside Racquet Club, Wedgewood Apartments, Treadway Resort, Meadows. Maj. M.C. AUS, 1943-46. Fellow ACS, Am. Coll. Chest Physicians; mem. AMA, Am. Thoracic Soc., Coll. Angiology, Central N.Y. Surg. Soc., Mohawk Valley Surg. Soc. (pres., 1968-69), Central N.Y. Acad. Medicine, Oneida County (chmn. edn. com., 1968-69), N.Y. State Soc. Surgeons (bd. dirs. 1970-85), N.Y. State Med. Soc. (com. for homeless), Pan-Am. Med. Assn., Pan Pacific Surg. Assn., Utica Med. Club (pres. 1960-61), Med. Soc. N.Y. State (com. on homeless), Night Stick Club (chief 1965-66), Harvard Club of Mohawk Valley (pres. 1951-66), Harvard Coll. Alumni Club (Fund area chmn.), Ft. Schuyler Club, Sadaquada Golf Club, Adirondack League Club, Ideal Flying Club, Rotary, Masons, Shriners (potentate 1981-82). Republican. Episcopalian. Home: RR 1 Box 736 Forestport NY 13338-9776

MILLETT, CAROLINE DUNLOP, real estate developer, consultant; b. Kansas City, Mo., Feb. 14, 1939; d. Henry Shirley and Anne (Alexander) M. Student, U. Edinburgh, Scotland, 1959-60; BA, U. Wis., 1961; MA, Stanford U., 1963. Cert. tchr., Calif. Tchr., counselor pub. schs., Calif., 1961-64; fgn. svc. officer USIA, Sao Paulo, Brazil, 1965-68; cultural attaché USIA, Brazilia, Brazil, 1969-70; v.p. Pub. Mgmt. Corp., N.Y.C., 1971-72, U. Arts, Phila., 1984-85; gen. ptnr. Real Estate Devel. Partnership, Washington, 1973-82; pres. Millett Enterprises, Phila., 1986—; chief exec. officer CDM Contracting Corp., Bensalem, Pa., 1991—; advisor on arts USIA, Washington, 1973-80; asst. advisor on arts Dept. State, Washington, 1990-91. Trustee Wilma Theater, Phila., 1988-90, Preservation Coalition Greater Phila., 1989—; v.p. Powelton Village Civic Assn., Phila., 1988-90. Mem. West Phila. Coalition Bus. Office: 317 N 33d St Philadelphia PA 19104

MILLETT, JOHN EDWARD, retired state government executive; b. Bronx, N.Y., Feb. 27, 1934; s. Russell Clare and Christine (Cavaliere) M.; m. Beverly Jane Cole, July 10, 1955; children: Robert J., Russell C. III, Beth M. BS in Agrl., U. Ga., 1957; M in Govt. Adminstrn., U. Pa., 1968. Entomologist Pa. Dept. Agr., Harrisburg, 1957-63; personnel analyst Pa. Dept. Welfare, Harrisburg, 1963-64; from asst. personnel dir. to personnel dir. Pa. State Police, Harrisburg, 1964-68; personnel dir. Pa. Dept. Banking, Harrisburg, 1968-69; dep. dir. civil svc. Pa. Civil Svc. Commn., Harrisburg, 1969-77, exec. dir. civil svc., 1977-88; sec.-treas. Nat. Assn. State Personnel Execs., Lexington, Ky., 1978-79, pres., 1979-80; mem. exec. coun. Internat. Personnel Mgmt. Assn., 1986-88. Author: (workshop) Towards Human Effectiveness: Baseline Motivation, 1977. Vestry man All Saints Episc. Ch., Hanover, Pa., 1972-75, '89-91, sr. warden, 1986-88, property warden, 1990. Recipient Recognition plaque Nat. Assn. State Personnel Execs., Lexington, 1988. Mem. Am. Arbitration Assn. (cert. labor panel arbitrator), Indsl. Rels. Rsch. Assn., Internat. Pers. Mgmt. Assn. (exec. coun. 1986-88, Appreciation plaque 1988, Frank A. Densler award ea. region 1990). Democrat. Home: 575 Cedar Rd New Oxford PA 17350-9776

MILLHEIM, JOHN EDWARD, religious organization administrator, educator; b. Phila., Nov. 9, 1934; s. William L. and Frances (Bookout) M.; m. Esther Fredia Steinbruck, June 25, 1955; children: Debby L., Daniel J., Diana L. BA, Houghton Coll., 1957; MDiv, Faith Theol. Sem., 1960; ThM, Princeton Sem., 1975; D of Ministry, Faith Theol. Sem., 1988, ThD, 1992. Pastor Park Community Ch., Riverside, N.J., 1957-60, Calvary Bapt. Ch., Norwalk, Ohio, 1960-64; gen. sec. Am. Coun. of Christian Chs., N.Y.C., 1964-71; dir. pub. rels. Bapt. Bible Ch., Clarks Summit, Pa., 1971-74; v.p., dir. Bapt. Bible Theol. Sem., Clarks Summit, Pa., 1974-85; prof. ch. history Faith Theol. Sem., Phila., 1986—; assoc. sec. Internat. Coun. Christian Chs., Collingswood, N.J., 1986—; gen. sec. Associated Missions, Collingswood, N.J., 1990—; educator various sems., 1986—; mem. press Gen. Assn. Regular Bapt. Chs.-Internat. Coun. Christian Chs., The Associated Missions, 1965—. Author: (booklet) The Ecumenical Movement and the Roman Catholic Church, 1984, Jonathan Edwards Evangelistic Passion, 1983; editor: Let Rome Speak for Herself, 1985; contbr. articles to profl. jours. Mem. Informissions (exec. com. 1975—), Interface (exec. com. 1976—). Home: 120 Spring St Clarks Summit PA 18411-2510 Office: Associated Missions 756 Haddon Ave Collingswood NJ 08108-3712

MILLHOLLAND, RUSSELL BRUCE, human resources executive; b. Waltham, Mass., Dec. 15, 1945; s. Thomas Knox and Marion (Gordon) M.; m. Janice Favreau, June 19, 1970; children: John, Peter. BSBA in Fin., Suffolk U., Boston, 1970; MBA, Suffolk U., 1971; Sr. Exec. Program, MIT, 1990. Supr. cost acctg. Norton Co. Materials Div., Worcester, Mass., 1977-78, mgr. mfg. acctg., 1978-79, supr. prodn. planning., 1979-80, acting plant mgr., 1981, materials mgr., 1981-84; mgr. info. resources Norton Co. Advanced Ceramics, Worcester, 1984-88, mgr. orgn. devel., 1988; dir. adminstrn. R&D Norton Co. Advanced Ceramics, Northboro, Mass., 1988-90; dir. human resources Norton Co. Saint-Gobain Indsl. Ceramics, 1991—. Chmn. Cable TV Commn., Town Govt. Study Commn., Indsl. Devel. Commn., Southboro, 1976-90; mem. Town Planning Bd., Southboro, 1976-90. Mem. ASTD, Am. Soc. for Quality Control, Am. Mgmt. Assn. Office: Norton Co Goddard Rd Northborough MA 01532-1546

MILLIAN, KENNETH YOUNG, chemical company executive; b. Washington, Sept. 29, 1927; s. John Curry and Myrtle (Young) M.; m. Alva Randolph Clarke, Sept. 10, 1949; children: John R., Kenneth Y. Jr., Kathleen M. Gilbert, Elizabeth W. Allen. BA, U. Md., 1951; MA in Internat. Rels., George Washington U., 1969; Diploma, Nat. War Coll., Washington, 1969; MS in Bus., Columbia U., 1980. Officer U.S. Fgn. Svc., 1951-76; corp. exec. W.R. Grace & Co., N.Y.C., 1976—; corp. v.p., dir. govt. rels. W.R. Grace & Co., Washington, 1982-88; corp. v.p., dir. environ. policy W.R. Grace & Co., N.Y.C., 1988—; bd. dirs. Nat. Fgn. Trade Coun., N.Y.C.; adb. bd. Parvus Co., Washington; pres. Found. for Pres.'s Pvt. Sector Survey on Cost Control, 1986—. Labor columnist Japan Times, 1955-57. Bd. govs. Wesley Sem., Am. U., Washington, 1988—. Democrat. Methodist. Office: WR Grace & Co One Town Center Rd Boca Raton FL 33486-1010

MILLIGAN, JASON MICHAEL, playwright; b. Corpus Christi, Tex., July 23, 1961; s. Jack Roland Milligan and Alice Henlon (Tankersley) McCormick; m. Stefanie Vogel, Oct. 3, 1986. BFA in Theatre Arts, U. Miss., 1983. Dir. spl. projects The Dramatists Guild Inc., N.Y.C., 1990—; artistic dir. Silver Lining Prodns., N.Y.C., 1987-90; lit. mgr. Cab Theatre Co., Inc., N.Y.C., 1985-87. Author: (audition monologues) Going Solo, 1992, (collections of plays) Southern Exposures, 1990, New York Stories, 1992, (play) And the Rain Came to Mayfield 1992. Mem. The Dramatists

Guild, Inc. Office: Dramatists Guild Inc 234 W 44th St New York NY 10036

MILLIGAN, MELVIN LEE, banker; b. Boston, May 15, 1948; s. Melvin Lee Milligan and Nancianna (Brenneman) Crandell; m. Priscilla Alden Phipps, Dec. 22, 1968 (div.); children: Aaron Blackford, Timothy Seeds; m. Mary Elizabeth Egner, Aug. 17, 1986; children: Mercedes Morier, Louise Stoll. BA in German Lit., Harvard U., 1970; B of Edn., U. New Brunswick, 1976; MBA, INSEAD, Fontainebleau, France, 1984. Bookkeeper Artel Inc., Laval, P.Q., Can., 1970-71; mental retardation aide supr. Southbury (Conn.) Tng. Sch., 1971-74; fin. mgr. The Bin Ladin Orgn., Dubai, U.A.E., 1976-83; asst. v.p. Lloyds Bank Internat., N.Y.C., 1985-86, v.p., 1987-90; v.p., mgr. The Daiwa Bank, Ltd., Balt., 1990—. Mem. Greater Balt. Com., 1990-91, Balt. Coun. on Fgn. Affairs, 1991. Mem. BMW Car Club of Am., Downtown Athletic Club, The Nature Conservancy. Home: 7001 Kenleigh Rd Baltimore MD 21212-1904 Office: The Daiwa Bank Ltd 10 E Baltimore St Ste 1402 Baltimore MD 21202-1642

MILLIKEN, CHARLES BUCKLAND, lawyer; b. New Haven, June 2, 1931; s. Arthur and Susan Lord (Buckland) M.; m. Sandra Stewart, July 6, 1957; children: Susan S., Andrew S. BA, Yale U., 1952; JD, Harvard U., 1957. Bar: Conn. 1957. Assoc., Shipman & Goodwin, Hartford, Conn., 1957-60, ptnr., 1961—; lectr. law corp. taxation U. Conn.; dir. Acromold Products Corp. Trustee Westminster Sch., Simsbury, Conn., 1969—, sec., 1970-74, chmn., 1974-80; bd. dirs. Hartford Symphony, 1959-74, 1980—, sec., 1960-62, pres., 1962-64; bd. dirs. Greater Hartford Arts Council, 1971-90; trustee Hartt Sch. Music, 1980—, chmn., 1988-90; regent U. Hartford, 1988. With U.S. Army, 1952-54. Fellow Am. Coll. Trust and Estate Counsel, Am. Coll. Tax Counsel; mem. ABA, Conn. Bar Assn. (chmn. tax sect. 1979-82), Hartford County Bar Assn. Contbr. articles on law to profl. jours. Home: 56 Ely Rd Farmington CT 06032-1707 Office: 1 American Row Hartford CT 06103-2833

MILLMAN, JODE SUSAN, lawyer; b. Poughkeepsie, N.Y., Dec. 28, 1954; d. Samuel Keith and Ellin Sadenberg (Bainder) M.; m. Michael James Harris, June 20, 1982; children: Maxwell, Benjamin. BA, Syracuse U., 1976, JD, 1979. Bar: N.Y. 1980, U.S. Dist. Ct. (so. and ea. dists.) N.Y. 1982, U.S. Supreme Ct. 1983. Asst. corp. counsel City of Poughkeepsie, 1979-81; assoc. Law Office of Lou Lewis, Poughkeepsie, 1981-85; pvt. practice Poughkeepsie, 1985—; staff counsel City of Poughkeepsie Office of Property Devel., 1990—. Contbg. author: Kaminstein Legislative History of the Copyright Law, 1979. Pres. Dutchess County (N.Y.) Vis. Bur., 1980-82; bd. dirs. Poughkeepsie Ballet Theater, 1982, Jewish Community Ctr., 1988; mem. assigned counsel program Dutchess County Family Ct., 1985—; trustee Greater Poughkeepsie Libr. Dist., 1991—. Mem. ABA, N.Y. State Bar Assn., Dutchess County Bar Assn. (chmn. pub. rels. 1991—), Mid-Hudson Women's Bar Assn. Democrat. Jewish. Office: 367 Main Mall Poughkeepsie NY 12601-3140

MILLMAN, SANDY KEITH, public relations executive; b. Poughkeepsie, N.Y., Mar. 23, 1940; s. Morris and Rosalie (Josephson) M.; m. Ellin Bainder, Aug. 30, 1965; children: Jode, Stuart. AB in Publicity, U. Miami, 1962; postgrad., SUNY, New Paltz, 1963, New Sch. Social Rsch., New Paltz, 1965; MA, NYU, 1987. With div. intelligence svcs. U.S. State Dept., 1960; dir. pub. rels. Far East Golf, Tokyo, 1964-70, Japan External Trade Commn., Tokyo, 1960-68; cons. in pub. rels. Honduras UN Trade Commn., N.Y.C., 1968-70; dir. pub. rels. Hudson Valley Radio, Inc., Poughkeepsie, 1970-73; pres. Sandy Millman Publicity, N.Y.C., 1973—. Author: Defensive Driving, 1978, Hard Core Publicity, 1987; contbr. articles to Hudson Valley Travel mag., 1985; patentee golf gloves. Mem. Pub. Rels. Soc. Am., Publicity Club N.Y., Overseas Press Club, Travel Soc., Nat. Profl. Journalism Soc., Golf Writers Assn. Am. Home: 7 Adriance Ave Poughkeepsie NY 12601-4901 Office: 201 E 28th St New York NY 10016-8538

MILLS, CAROL ANN BERGFELD, psychology educator, researcher, consultant; b. St. Charles, Mo., Feb. 2, 1948; d. Fred Henry and Lucille Anna (Buenemann) B.; m. Judson Ridgway Mills, Dec. 27, 1970; 1 child, Ridgway. BS, U. Mo., 1970; postgrad., U. Tex., 1970-71; MA, U. Md., 1973, PhD, 1976. Dir. Human Factors Lab. Sci. Application Inc., Rossyln, Va., 1976-77; postdoctoral fellow Gallaudet Coll., Washington, 1977-78; instr. U. Md., College Park, 1979-83; rsch. psychologist Army Rsch. Inst., Alexandria, Va., 1984-85; rsch. scientist U. Md., College Park, 1984-85; sr. rsch. scientist Am. Inst. for Rsch., Washington, 1985-91; prof. psychology Goucher Coll., Towson, Md., 1986—. Contbr. 25 articles to profl. jours.; inventor convertible doll and sleeping bag. Mem. Psychonomic Soc., Human Factors Soc., Am. Psychol. Soc., Am. Psychol. Assn. (psych info. adv. com. 1990—), Psi Chi. Home and Office: Goucher Coll Psychology Dept Towson MD 21204

MILLS, CHARLES GARDNER, lawyer; b. Griffin, Ga., Feb. 29, 1940; s. Charles G. and Marguerite (Powell) M. AB, Yale U., 1962; JD, Boston Coll., 1967. Bar: N.Y. 1967, U.S. Dist. Ct. (so. and ea. dists.) 1972, U.S. Ct. Appeals (2d cir.) 1975, U.S. Supreme Ct., 1977, U.S. Ct. Claims 1991. Assoc. Smart & McKay, N.Y.C., 1967-68, Smart & Mills, N.Y.C., 1969-71, Eaton & VanWinkle, N.Y.C., 1971-82, Payne, Wood & Littlejohn, Glen Cove, Melville, N.Y., 1982-91. With U.S. Army, 1962-64, ETO. Mem. Nassau County Bar Assn., N.Y. State Bar Assn., Assn. of the Bar of the City of N.Y., Rotary (pres. Glen Cove club 1989-90), Am. Legion (comdr. Locust Valley, N.Y. post 1988-90, vice-comdr. Nassau County com. 1990-91). Republican. Roman Catholic. Office: 56 School St Glen Cove NY 11542-2512

MILLS, CLAUDIA ELISE (ELKEMA), accountant; b. Paterson, N.J., Feb. 12, 1964; d. Harry Philip and Barbara Ann (Garcia) E. BS in Acctg., St. John Fisher Coll., Rochester, N.Y., 1986. CPA. Staff acct. Bonadio, Insero & Co., Rochester, 1986-89; fin. acctg. mgr. Roadway Motor Plazas, Inc., Rochester, 1989-91; controller Lifetime Stainless Steel Corp., Rochester, 1991—. Mem. com. Teddi Project Dance Marathon, Rochester, 1984-86; mem. Humane Soc. Rochester, 1986—. Mem. AICPA, Nat. Assn. Accts., St. John Fisher Coll. Acctg. Alumni Com. Office: Lifetime Stainless 12 Railroad St Fishers NY 14453-9999

MILLS, GEORGE MARSHALL, state official, insurance executive; b. Newton, N.J., May 20, 1923; s. J. Marshall and Emma (Scott) M.; m. Dorothy Lovilla Allen, Apr. 21, 1945; children: Dianne (Mrs. Thomas McKay III), Dorothy L.A. (Mrs. Edward Sphatt). BA, Rutgers U., 1943; MA, Columbia U., 1951. profl. cert., 1952. CLU; CPCU; chartered fin. cons. Pres. George M. Mills Inc., North Brunswick, N.J., 1946-75; pres. CORECO, Inc., Newark, 1960-78; risk mgr. N.J. Hwy. Authority, Woodbridge, 1978—; cons. Govs.'s Com. on Bus. Efficiency in Pub. Schs., 1979-80. Bd. dirs. Alpha Chi Rho Ednl. Found., vice-chmn. 1991—; workshop Easter Seal Soc.; mem. Gov.'s Task Force on Sound Mcpl. Govt., 1981-82; pres. Nat. Interfrat. Conf., 1979-80. With USNR, 1943-46. Mem. Am. Coll. Life Underwriters, Am. Coll. Property Liability Underwriters, Internat. Bridge Tunnel and Turnpike Assn. (chmn. risk mgmt. com., mem. bus. ins. risk mgmt. bd. 1988—, Matthew J. Lenz Jr. medal 1989), New Brunswick Hist. Soc., English Speaking Union, Alpha Chi Rho (nat. councillor 1964-70, nat. pres. 1970-73, nat. treas. 1975-87), Kappa Kappa Psi, Tau Kappa Alpha, Phi Delta Phi. Rutgers U. Alumni-Faculty Club (New Brunswick, N.J.). Mem. Reformed Ch. Am. Home: 1054 Hoover Dr N Brunswick NJ 08902-3244 Office: US Rt 9 Woodbridge NJ 07095

MILLS, GREGORY DOUGLAS, podiatry educator; b. Belleville, N.J., June 25, 1963; s. Robert Donald and Nance Rose (Carnevale) M.; m. Susan Theresa Lazaro, Mar. 7, 1987. Student, Columbia U., 1981-85, Pa. Coll. Podiatric Medicine, 1985-89. Clin. instr. dept. orthopedics Pa. Coll. Podiatric Medicine, Phila., 1990—; mem. staff Our Lady of Lourdes Med. Ctr., Camden, N.J., 1990—, West Jersey Hosp., Camden, 1990—, Kennedy Meml. Hosp., Cherry Hill, N.J., 1990—. Mem. Am. Podiatric Medicine Assn., N.J. Podiatric Med. Assn., Cherry Hill C. of C., Lions, K.C. Home: 827-D Sutton Towers Collingswood NJ 08107 Office: 1930 E Rte # 70 Cherry Hill NJ 08003

MILLS, JAMES THOBURN, association executive; b. Balt., Nov. 30, 1923; s. Victor Garfield and Beatrice M. (Moore) M.; m. Frances Clagett Keller, June 16, 1951; children—Elizabeth R. Mills Durkee, Hilary F. Mills Lambert, Frances T. Mills Wonnell, Margaret K. B.A., Princeton U., 1947; LL.B., Yale U., 1950. Bar: N.Y. 1951. Assoc. Burke & Burke, N.Y.C., 1950-51; assoc. Mudge, Stern, Baldwin & Todd, N.Y.C., 1951-56; with Sperry & Hutchinson Co., N.Y.C., 1956-80; pres. Sperry & Hutchinson Co., 1978-80, chmn. bd., chief exec. officer, 1980-81, also dir.; pres. The Conference Board, Inc., N.Y.C., 1982-88; bd. dirs. Union Camp Corp., Wayne, N.J. Pres. Montclair (N.J.) Art Mus., 1990—. 1st lt. U.S. Army, 1943-46. Decorated Bronze Star medal, Purple Heart. Clubs: University (N.Y.C.); Montclair Golf (N.J.). Home: 102 Inwood Ave Montclair NJ 07043-2317 Office: Montclair Art Mus 102 Inwood Ave Montclair NJ 07043 also: Art Mus 3 S Mountain Ave Montclair NJ 07042

MILLS, JONATHAN CLARKE, international cultural exchange executive; b. Bayshore, N.Y., May 4, 1954; s. Robert Laurence and Elise (Ackley) M. AB, Brown U., 1976; MBA, Columbia U., 1979. Fin. analyst Citibank, N.A., N.Y.C., 1978-80, account officer, 1980-82; exec. dir. Friendship Ambs. Found., Upper Montclair, N.J., 1982-91, pres., 1991—. Chmn. bd. dirs. L'Ensemble Chamber Music Ctr., Albany, N.Y., 1984—. Mem. Brown U. Club N.Y. Home and Office: Friendship Ambs Found 273 Upper Mountain Ave Montclair NJ 07043-1015

MILLS, JOSHUA REDMOND, financial executive; b. Lynn, Mass., Aug. 30, 1936; s. Joshua and Adelaide (Redmond) M.; m. Annette Aliferis Perillo, May 29, 1965; children: Carlotta, Anastasia. AB, Harvard U., 1957; postgrad., NYU, 1960-65. Cert. employee benefits specialist. With Chase Manhattan Bank, N.Y.C., 1960-63, Continental Bank Internat., N.Y.C., 1963-66; v.p. Amerconsult Corp., N.Y.C. and Peru, 1966-74; pres. Joshua Mills & Co., Greenwich, Conn., 1974—, Fin. Counsel Corp., Montvale, N.J., 1984—. Chmn. strategy com., mem. gen. council Presbytery of N.Y.C., 1976-81; rep. to Town Meeting, Greenwich, Conn., 1981-83; mem. steering com. Tri-State Urban Conf., Fairfield County 2000 Task Force (conf.). Mem. Harvard Club, Landmark Club (Stamford, Conn.). Republican. Office: PO Box 339 Montvale NJ 07645-0339

MILLS, KARIN MAHLBERG, public relations consultant; b. Upper Darby, Pa., Sept. 1, 1949; d. Roy Francis and Lillian (Larson) Mahlberg; m. Larry Kenneth Mills, Mar. 16, 1971; children: Courtney, Eric. BA, Northwestern U., 1971. Account asst. N.W. Ayer & Son Pub. Relations, N.Y.C., 1971-73; pub. relations assoc. Benton & Bowles, Inc., N.Y.C., 1973-74, pub. relations mgr., 1974-76; pub. relations dir. Seventeen Mag., N.Y.C., 1976-81, Panorama Mag., N.Y.C., 1980-81; cons. pvt. practice Montclair, N.J. Author (booklet) Guide to Business Careers in Mag. Pub., 1985. Bd. dirs. Jr. League of Montclair, Newark, 1989-90, 92—, Montclair Arts and Cultural Alliance, 1990—. Named Vol. of the Yr. Jr. League of Montclair, 1990. Mem. Pub. Relations Soc. Am. (com. chmn. 1975-78, bd. dirs. 1978-81). Home and Office: 121 Essex Ave Montclair NJ 07042-4127

MILLS, WILLIAM STEWARD, manufacturing executive; b. Chattanooga, Feb. 22, 1920; s. William Joseph and Mary Margaret (Steward) M.; m. Janet Elizabeth Patten; children: Ann Elizabeth, Norma Fleury, Manker Patten, Mary Steward, William Joseph. BA, U. Chattanooga, 1941. Sec. D.M. Steward Mfg. Co., Chattanooga, 1939-57, pres., 1957; pres. Nat. Ceramic Co., Trenton, N.J., 1957-58, W.S. Mills, Inc., Trenton, 1958-85; sec. W.J. Mills Inc., Trenton, 1985—; chmn. Pennington Wholesale, Trenton, 1987. 1st lt. U.S. Army, 1953-56. Decorated Bronze Star. Mem. Am. Ceramic Soc., Mountain City Club. Republican. Roman Catholic. Office: Pennington Wholesale 4th Ave Trenton NJ 08619-3213

MILMAN, DOUGLAS SCOTT, psychologist; b. Balt., July 12, 1953; s. Donald Stuart and Marilyn Martha (Holstein) M. BA, Bard Coll., 1976; MA, Adelphi U., 1978, PhD, 1983. Lic. psychologist, N.Y. Psychologist SUNY, Farmingdale, 1980—, Baldwin (N.Y.) Coun. Against Drug Abuse, 1981—; pvt. practice Baldwin, 1987—. Author: Are You Normal?, 1983. Mem. Am. Psychol. Assn., Adelphi Soc. for Psychotherapy and Psychoanalysis, United U. Profls., Nassau County Psychol. Assn., N.Y. State Psychol. Assn., Nat. Register Health Svc. Providers. Office: 1914 Grand Ave Baldwin NY 11510-2454

MILMAN, PATRICIA ELLEN, professional society administrator, consultant; b. N.Y.C., Mar. 17, 1950; m. Irving M. Milman; children: John H. Haman, Lori B. Haman. BA cum laude, CUNY, 1983. Chief statis. div. Nat. Assn. Mut. Savs. Banks, N.Y.C., 1976-84; dir. adminstrn. Am. Med. Women's Assn., Inc., N.Y.C., 1985-88, acting exec. dir., 1986; mgr. governance ops. ASME, N.Y.C., 1989-90, dir. bd. ops., 1990-91; mktg. and sales cons. Lightning Up, Inc., N.Y.C., 1988-90; healthcare mktg. and fundraising cons. Concepts in Art, Hackensack, N.J., 1992; fundraising cons. Am. Sportscasters Assn., N.Y.C., 1991. Mem. Am. Soc. Assn. Execs., N.Y. Soc. Assn. Execs., N.Y. Soc. Fundraising Execs., Nat. Soc. Fundraising Execs., Chinese Shar-Pei Club Am., Shar-Pei Club N.E. (com. mem. Rescue League 1987—).

MILNE, GEORGE MCLEAN, JR., pharmaceutical company executive; b. Port Chester, N.Y., Dec. 29, 1943; s. George McLean and Janet (Odell) M.; m. Carol Todd, June 19, 1965; children: George Todd, Adam Durant. BSc, Yale U., 1965; PhD, MIT, 1974. Postdoctoral fellow Stanford (Calif.) U., 1969-70, Med. Coll. Va., Richmond, 1975; rsch. scientist Pfizer Cen. Rsch., Groton, Conn., 1970-73, sr. rsch. scientist, 1973-74, project leader, 1974-78, mgr., 1978-81, dir., 1981-84, exec. dir., 1984-85, v.p., 1985-88, sr. v.p., 1988—; bd. dirs. Thames Sci. Ctr., New London, Conn., 1987—, Am. Type Culture Collection, Rockville, Md., 1991—; sci. bd. Ventures Med., Houston, 1987—. Contbr. articles to profl. jours.; patentee in field. Apothecary bd. dirs. Fla. A&M U., Tallahassee, 1989—, Summer Music, New London, 1991—; mem. citizen bd. Project Oceanology, Groton, 1984—. Mem. N.Y. Acad. Sci., Am. Soc. Microbiology, Am. Chem. Soc., Yale Club of Ea. Conn. (bd. dirs. 1984—), The Explorers Club (fellow), Sigma Xi. Office: Pfizer Ctrl Rsch Eastern Point Rd Groton CT 06340

MILNE, TEDDY (MARGARET THEODORA MILNE), writer; b. Delaware, Ohio, Oct. 17, 1930; d. Philip Frederick and Emily (Powell) Mayer; m. Alexander W. Milne, Apr. 24, 1965 (dec. 1982); children: Timmon, Peter, James. Student, U. Paris, 1953-54; BA, Boston U., 1951. Reporter, copy editor Daily Hampshire Gazette, Northampton, Mass., 1961-67, columnist, 1989—; editor Alumni News Northampton Sch. for Girls, 1967-68; editor Laser, Northampton, 1982-89, Compassion Mag., Northampton, 1987-89, Peace Devel. Fund newsletter Peace Devels., Amherst, Mass., 1984-86. Author: Be Your Own Boss, 1982, Choose Love, 1986, Anthony, 1986, Peace Porridge One, 1987, Peace Porridge Two, 1987, Shambala Warriors, 1987, War is a Dinosaur, 1987, The Candy Puzzle, 1989, Money, Power and Responsibility, 1990, Solo Publishing, 1990, Is War Okay?, 1991; contbr. articles and stories to mags. and newspapers. Clk. publs. com. Friends Gen. Conf., 1989-91. Recipient awards Obadiah Brown Fund, 1983, Topsfield Found., 1985, Woodbridge Fund, 1987. Mem. Quakers Uniting in Publ. Office: Pittenbruach Press PO Box 553 Northampton MA 01061-0553

MILNER, CHARLES FREMONT, JR., manufacturing company executive; b. Durham, N.C., July 21, 1942; s. Charles Fremont and Eloyse (Sargent) M.; B.A., Guilford Coll., 1963; M.B.A., Harvard, 1965; m. Molly Franc Wakefield, Aug. 28, 1965; children: Bernadette Ann, Eloyse Lee. Asst. to comptroller Harvard, 1965-66; instr. Northeastern U., Boston, 1965-66; with Burlington Hosiery Co. div. Burlington Industries (N.C.), 1966-71, asst. v.p., 1970-71; exec. v.p. Parklane Hosiery Co., Inc., New Hyde Park, N.Y., 1971-74, also dir.; pres. Rudin & Roth, Inc. div. NCC Industries, N.Y.C., 1974-75, also dir.; v.p. apparel group M. Lowenstein and Sons, N.Y.C., 1975-76; pres., chief exec. officer BBC Inc. and Camp Industry divs. Genesco Inc., 1976-80, gen. mgr. Johnston and Murphy Shoe Co. div., 1979—, gen. mgr. footwear mktg. and mfg. Genesco Inc., 1980-81, v.p., 1981-82; pres., chief exec. officer Hope Hosiery Mills and C.M. Industries, Inc., Adamstown, PA, 1983—. Trustee Friends Acad., Locust Valley, N.Y., 1974-79, Guilford Coll., 1982—, vice-chmn., 1989, chmn., 1990—; mem. class chief fund agt. Harvard Bus. Sch., 1986-91, alumni bd. 1992—. Mem. Nat. Assn. Hosiery Mfrs. (dir. 1978-82, 87—, exec. com. 1989—, 2nd vice chmn. 1991-92, vice chmn. 1992—), Lancaster Country Club, Hamilton Club, Moselem Springs Golf Club. Home: 158 Hamilton Rd Lancaster PA 17603-4734 Office: Box 487 Adamstown PA 19501

MILNOR, WILLIAM ROBERT, physician; b. Wilmington, Del., May 4, 1920; s. William Robert and Virginia (Sterling) M.; m. Gabriella Mahaffy, Aug. 19, 1944; children—Katherine Alexander, William Henry. A.B., Princeton U., 1941; M.D., Johns Hopkins U., 1944. Diplomate: Am. Bd. Internal Medicine. Intern, resident Johns Hopkins Hosp., 1944-46; research fellow Nat. Heart Inst., 1949-51; physician-in-charge heart sta. Johns Hopkins Hosp., 1951-60, physician, 1952—; mem. faculty Johns Hopkins Med. Sch., 1951—, prof. physiology, 1969—; vis. fellow St. Catherine's Coll., Oxford (Eng.) U., 1968; mem. med. adv. panel Am. Inst. Biol. Scis., 1971—; assessor Nat. Med. Research Council of Australia, 1976—. Author: Hemodynamics, 2d edit., 1989, Cardio-vascular Physiology, 1990; contbr. articles to med. textbooks, med. jours. Served to capt. M.C. USAAF, 1946-48. Fellow A.C.P.; mem. Am. Physiol. Soc., Am. Fedn. Clin. Research, Biomed. Engrng. Soc., Am. Heart Assn. (chmn. research com. 1966), Heart Assn. Md. (past pres.). Clubs: L'Hirondelle, Princeton, 14 W Hamilton St. Office: Johns Hopkins Med Sch 725 N Wolfe St Baltimore MD 21205-2105

MILO, GENNARO DOMENICK, medical psychotherapist, educator; b. Bklyn., Apr. 26, 1946; s. Domenick and Harriet (Anderson) M. AA, Kingsborough Community Coll., Bklyn., 1972; BA in English, CUNY, Bklyn., 1974; MS in Guidance and Counseling, L.I. U., 1980, grad. cert. in family counseling, 1986; post-grad. cert. in behavior therapy, Behavior Therapy Inst., Creedmore Psychiat. Ctr., Queen's Village, N.Y., 1987; PhD in Counseling Psychology, Columbia Pacific U., 1987. Cert. tchr., N.Y. Tchr. English, music, coord. multicultural programs Sarah J. Hale High Sch., Bklyn., 1978—; counselor Gramercy Pk. Counseling Ctr., N.Y.C., 1984-85, Creedmoor Psychiat. State Hosp., Queen's Village, 1985-86; pvt. practice Bklyn., 1985—; counselor L.I. U., 1986; tchr. curriculum and instrn. NYU, 1987-88. Author monograph: An Investigation Into the Possible Relationship Between Attitudes Towards Homosexuality and Academic Discipline of a Select Group of New York City High School Teachers, 1989; contbr. poems to anthologies. Fellow Am. Assn. Profl. Hypnotherapists; mem. APA, Am. Acad. Pain Mgmt. (diplomate), Am. Assn. Counseling and Devel., Am. Bd. Med. Psychotherapists (clin. assoc.), Am. Fedn. Tchrs., Am. Mental Health Counselors Assn., Am. Orthopsychiat. Assn., Assn. Advancement Behavior Therapy, Doctorate Assn. N.Y. Educators, N.Y. Acad. Scis., N.Y. Neuropsycology Group, Internat. Psycho-Oncology Soc., Inst. Advancement Health, Internat. Acad. Behavioral Medicine, Counseling and Psychotherapy (diplomate). Libertarian. Humanist. Home and Office: 8223 Bay Pky Brooklyn NY 11214-2664

MILONAS, MINOS, artist, designer, poet; b. Heraklion, Crete, Greece, Apr. 28, 1936; came to U.S., 1964; s. Stavros and Maria (Kaplantzis) M.; m. Arlene Watson, Dec. 23, 1963 (div. 1970); m. Sarah Brown, Dec. 1973 (div. 1974); m. Elaine Mauceli, May 26, 1988. BA, Calif. State U., Northridge, 1970; MFA, U. Wash., Seattle, 1972. Freelance writer and poet Athens, 1960-64; freelance artist L.A., 1964-66; instr. U. Wash., 1971-72, Studio Milonas, 1972-76; artist Studio Milonas, N.Y.C., 1977—, textile designer, 1984—. One man shows include Second Story Gallery, Seattle, 1971, Henry Art Gallery, Seattle, 1972, Polly Friedlander Gallery, Seattle, 1973, Stavrakakis Gallery, Crete, Greece, 1977, West Broadway Gallery, N.Y.C., 1979, 81, 82, Heraklion Art Gallery, Crete, 1983, Kreonides Gallery, Athens, 1983, 84, Doma Gallery, N.Y.C., 1988, Hellenic Cultural Ctr., N.Y., 1990, Cypriot Consulate, N.Y.C., 1990; exhibitions in group shows at Calif. State U., Northridge, 1968-69, Mcpl. Art Gallery, L.A., 1969, U. Wash. Libr., Seattle, 1971, 72, Panaca Gallery, Bellevue, Wash., 1973, Mercer Island Art Gallery, Seattle, 1973, Henry Art Gallery, Seattle, 1973, Tacoma Art Mus., 1973, 75, N.W. Watercolor Soc., 1974, Gordon Woodside Gallery, Seattle, 1974, Coll. of the Cisciyous, Calif., 1975, Laguna Gloria Art Mus., Austin, Tex., 1975, Redmonds (Wash.) Arts Festival, 1975, Univ. Dist. Arts Festival, Seattle, 1976, Bellevue art Mus., 1976, Sunne Savage Gallery, Boston, 1976, Cretan Artists, Stavrakakis Gallery, Heraklion, Crete, 1978, Internat. Drawing Biennale, Cleveland, Eng., 1981-82, Haggin Mus., Stockton, Calif., 1985-86, U. N.D., Grand Forks, 1987, Greek Cultural Ctr., Springfield, Mass., 1987, 89, Del Bello Gallery, Toronto, Ont., Can., 1987, Ball State U., Muncie, Ind., 1989, Morin-Miller Galleries, N.Y.C., 1989-90, Columbia (Md.) Coll., 1989, Grand Prospect Hall, Bklyn., 1990; author: The Small Caravan, 1962; videos include Multimedia Artist, 1988, 500 Definitions--Art Is, 1991. Recipient 4 Sculpture awards Summer Art Festivals, 1970-76, 2 Merit awards Greek Cultural Ctr., 1987; U. Wash. grantee, 1970; U. Wash. scholar, 1971. Mem. Nat. Artists Equity Assn., Inc., N.Y. Artists Equity Assn., Inc. Democrat. Home and Office: 790 11th Ave Apt 39A New York NY 10019-3521

MILROD, EVE MEREDITH, product manager; b. N.Y.C., Nov. 8, 1962; d. Burton Sidney and Rosalind Lee (Fishman) M. AB, Smith Coll., 1984; MBA, Columbia U., 1989. Analyst, cons. Johnson & Higgins, N.Y.C., 1984-85; analyst Towers Perrin, N.Y.C., 1985-87; mgr. Chemical Bank, N.Y.C., 1989--. Mem. Smith Coll. Class (sec. 1989-94), N.Y. Smith Club. Office: Chem Bank Rm 738 55 Water St New York NY 10041-0002

MIL'SHTEIN, SAMSON, semiconductor physicist; b. Vinitza, USSR, Aug. 6, 1940; came to U.S., 1982; s. Khaim and Golda (Tzukerman) M.; married; children: Mark, Valery. MS, State U., Odessa, USSR, 1963; PhD, U. Jerusalem, 1976. Lectr. Jr. Coll., Kherson, USSR, 1963-65; mem. staff Inst. Marine Engrs., Odessa, 1965-67, Inst. Solid State Physics, Moscow, 1967-72; lectr. U. Jerusalem, 1974-76; sr. lectr. Ben-Gurion U., Beer-Shera, Israel, 1976-82; vis. scientist Bell Labs., Murray Hills, N.J., 1982-83; sr. scientist Semiconductors Group, Cabot Corp., Billeria, Mass., 1984-86; prof. elec. engrng. U. Mass., Lowell, 1987—, dir. Advanced Electronic Tech. Ctr., 1990—; adj. prof. physics U. Mass., Boston, 1985—. Contbr. over 100 articles to profl. jours., confs. Recipient 1st prize for sci. achievements Inst. Solid STate Physics of Acad. Scis. USSR, 197l. Mem. IEEE, Materials Rsch. Soc., Elec. Micros. Soc. Jewish. Home: 6 Warwick Dr Chelmsford MA 01824-3768

MILTON, PHILIP LAFAYETTE, chemical engineer; b. Alexandria, Va., Oct. 19, 1964; s. Philip Smallwood and Barbara Ann (Ryan) M. BS in Chem. Engring., Tufts U., 1986. Chemist Versar Inc, Springfield, Va., 1986-88; environ. auditor Versar Inc, Springfield, 1988-89; chem. engr. US EPA, Washington, 1989—. Recipient Bronze medal U.S. EPA, 1991. Mem. Am. Inst. Chem. Engrs., Am. Chem. Soc. Roman Catholic. Home: 6461 Frenchmens Dr Alexandria VA 22312-1657 Office: US EPA (EN-342) 401 M St SW Washington DC 20460-0002

MILWAY, JAMES THOMAS, purchasing executive; b. Orange, N.J., Apr. 12, 1935; s. James Thomas Sr. and Helen Loretta (Driscoll) M.; m. Mary Jane Theresa Hayde, May 6, 1961; children: Laura Ann Milway Hyde, Colleen Theresa, Timothy John, Kerry Anne Milway Mault, Jennifer Marie. BS, Seton Hall U., 1957, MBA, 1968. cert. purchasing mgr. Nat. Assn. Purchasing Mgmt. Mgr. purchasing AT&T Western Electric, Burlington, N.C., 1968-69; dist. mgr. quality assurance AT&T Western Electric, Springfield Gardens, N.Y., 1970-72; dist. mgr. purchasing staff AT&T Western Electric, N.Y.C., 1972-73; resident mgr. purchasing AT&T Western Electric, Kearny, N.J., 1974-83; dir. purchasing Bell Communications Rsch., Inc. (Bellcore), Piscataway, N.J., 1983—; adj. prof. Bloomfield (N.J.) Coll., 1986-90; advisor Bloomfield Coll. Materials Mgmt. Inst., 1980—. Bd. dirs. New Humanity Movement Bur. Economy and Work, N.Y.C., 1988—. 1st lt. Signal Corps, U.S. Army, 1957-59. Mem. Nat. Assn. Purchasing Mgmt. N.J. Inc. (pres. 1990-92). Democrat. Roman Catholic. Office: Bellcore 8 Corporate Pl Piscataway NJ 08854-4120

MILZA, CHERYL ANNE, mechanical engineer; b. Hackensack, N.J., Nov. 8, 1966; d. Ronald Patrick and Rosemarie Josephine (Graziano) M. BSME, Drexel U., 1990. Mech. engr. Phila. Naval Shipyard, 1987—. Scholar Dept. Navy, 1988-90. Mem. AIAA, ASME. Office: Phila Naval Shipyard Philadelphia PA 19112

MINARD, JOANNE SHALHOUB, financial consultant; b. Englewood, N.J., Nov. 27, 1950; d. Mary Ann Gissubel; m. Paul A. Hunt, July 18, 1970 (div. Dec. 1980); children: Travis, Sarah; m. Phillip Lee Minard, Aug. 4, 1989. BLS, U. Evansville, 1987. Cashier supr. E.F. Hutton, Cin., 1980-82; ops. mgr. Merrill Lynch, Cin., 1982-83; with sales dept. Prudential, Cin., 1983-84; mgr. Credithrift Fin., Evansville, Ind., 1985-88; with sales dept. Weichert Realtors, Morristown, N.J., 1989-90, Metlife Fin. Svcs., Florham Park, N.J., 1989-91; fin. cons. Beardslee and Assocs., Fairfield, N.J., 1991—.

Fellow Life Underwriters Tng. Coun.; mem. Nat. Assn. Life Underwriters, Nat. Assn. Women Bus. Owners (estate planning coun.), Nat. Assn. Realtors, N.J. Assn. Realtors, N.J. Assn. Women Bus. Owners. Office: Beardslee and Assocs Inc 710 Rt 46 Fairfield NJ 07004-1540

MINASI, ANTHONY, software company executive; b. N.Y.C., July 9, 1948; s. Dominic H. and Mary (De Rosa) M.; m. Patricia Ann Gallagher, Oct. 3, 1976; children: Christopher, Marie Elizabeth. BA, Hunter Coll., 1971; MBA, Pace U., 1982, postgrad., 1988. Bus. analyst Am. Internat. Group, N.Y.C., 1971-75; systems mgr., officer Fiduciary Trust Co., N.Y.C., 1975-79; systems mgr. Flexivan Leasing, N.Y.C., 1979-84; group mgr., v.p. Drexel Burnham, N.Y.C., 1984-89; group mgr. Vista Concepts, Inc., N.Y.C., 1989—. Mem. Micro Mgrs. Assn., OS/2 Users Group. Office: Vista Concepts 5 Hanover Sq New York NY 10004

MINASY, ARTHUR JOHN, aerospace and electronic detection systems executive; b. N.Y.C., July 19, 1925; s. John and Esther (Horvath) M.; B.S. in Adminstrv. Engring., N.Y. U., 1949, M.S. in Indsl. and Mgmt. Engring., 1952; postgrad. Case Inst. Tech., 1953-55; m. Jayne Marion Leary, June 29, 1946; children: Karen Lynn, Keith Leary, Kathy Jayne. Asst. gen. mgr. Def. div. Bulova Watch Co., Maspeth, N.Y., 1950-53; chief indsl. engr. Standard Products Co., Cleve., 1953-55; gen. mgr. ops. Gruen Industries, Cin., 1955-57; mgmt. cons. Booz-Allen and Hamilton, N.Y.C., 1957-60; mfg. mgr. Sperry Gyroscope Co., Great Neck, N.Y., 1960-62; v.p. ops. Belock Instrument Co., College Point, N.Y., 1962-64; pres. Detection Devices, Inc., Woodbury, N.Y., 1963—; chmn., chief exec. officer KNOGO Corp., Hauppauge, N.Y., 1966—; founder, pres. Internat. Electronic Articles Surveillance Mfrs. Assn., Brussels, 1989; bd. dirs. KNOGO Italia S.r.l., Milan, Italy, KNOGO SA, Belgium, KNOGO Caribe Inc., Cidra, P.R., KNOGO Australia, KNOGO The Netherlands B.V., KNOGO Switzerland S.A., KNOGO France S.A., KNOGO Denmark APS, KNOGO Deutschland GMBH, KNOGO Scandinavia AB, KNOGO UK Ltd., KNOGO Iberica SA; prin. Arthur J. Minasy Assocs., Mgmt. Cons., 1957-62; adv. bd. Abilities, Inc.; also lectr. in sci. law enforcement and detection systems. Dir., mem. adv. bd. Human Resources Found.; trustee Rehab. Inst. Served with AUS, 1943-46. Decorated Commdr. of Order of the Crown, King of Belgium, 1992; recipient Humanitarian of Yr. award Am. Cancer Soc.; named L.I.'s Entrepeneur of Yr., Inc. Mag., 1990; inductee to Smithsonian Nat. Mus. Am. History, 1991. Mem. Am. Inst. Indsl. Engrs., Internat. Electronic Article Surveillance Mfgrs. Assn. (founder, pres. 1989), Am. Ordnance Assn., Am. Mgmt. Assn., Tau Beta Pi, Alpha Pi Mu. Patentee in field. Home: 15 Hunting Hill Rd Woodbury NY 11797-1403 Office: KNOGO Corp 350 Wireless Blvd Hauppauge NY 11788-3927

MINDELL, JODI ANN, psychology educator; b. Bklyn., Oct. 11, 1962; d. Irwin W. Mindell and Roberta S. (Bernard) Stewart. BA, SUNY, Binghamton, 1984; MA, SUNY, Albany, 1986, PhD, 1989. Licensed clin. psychologist. Asst. prof. psychology St. Joseph's U., Phila., 1989—. Mem. Am. Psychol. Assn., Assn. for Advancement of Behavior Therapy, Assn. Profl. Sleep Soc. Office: St Joseph's U Philadelphia PA 19131

MINDLIN, PAULA ROSALIE, educator; b. N.Y.C., Nov. 27, 1944; d. Simon S. and Sylvia (Naroff) Bernstein; m. Alfred Carl Mindlin, Aug. 14, 1965; 1 child, Spencer Douglas. BA in Edn., Bklyn. Coll., 1965; MS in Edn., Queens Coll., 1970, Specialist Sch. Adminstrn, 1973. Cert. sch. dist. adminstr., prin., asst. prin., spl. edn. supr., ednl. adminstr. Tchr. Dist. 16 Pub. Sch., Bklyn., 1965-68; reading tchr. Dist. 29 Pub. Sch. and Dist. 16, Bklyn., 1968-85; instr. coll., inservice courses Community Sch. Dist. 29, Queens Village, N.Y., 1984—; reading coordinator Reading/Communications Arts Program, Community Sch. Dist. 29, Queens, N.Y., 1985-90; dir. reading Community Sch. Dist. 29, Queens, 1990—; adj. lectr. York Coll., 1989. Mem. ASCD, Internat. Reading Assn., Nassau Reading Coun., Queensboro Reading Coun. (v.p., bd. dirs.). Office: Pub Sch 37 Dist 29 Queens Reading/Communication Arts 17937 173rd Ave Jamaica NY 11434-4625

MINER, JACQUELINE, political consultant; b. Mt. Vernon, N.Y., Dec. 10, 1936; d. Ralph E. and Agnes (McGee) Mariani; B.A., Coll. St. Rose, 1971, M.A., 1974; m. Roger J. Miner, Aug. 11, 1975; children—Laurence, Ronald Carmichael, Ralph Carmichael, Mark. Ind. polit. cons., Hudson, N.Y.; instr. history and polit. sci. SUNY, Hudson, 1974-79. Rep. county committeewoman, 1958-76; vice chmn. N.Y. State Ronald Reagan campaign, 1980; candidate for Rep. nomination for U.S. Senate, 1982; co-chair N.Y. state steering com. George Bush for Pres. campaign, 1986-88; vice chmn. N.Y. State Rep. Com., 1991—; chmn. Coll. Consortium for Internat. Studies; mem. White House Outreach Working Group on Central Am.; co-chmn. N.Y. State Reagan Roundup Campaign, 1984-86; mem. nat. steering com. Fund for Am.'s Future, 2d cir. Hist. Com. Mem. U.S. Supreme Ct. Hist. Soc., P.E.O. Address: RD 2 Box 110E Hudson NY 12534

MINER, JOHN BURNHAM, industrial relations educator, writer; b. N.Y.C., July 20, 1926; s. John Lynn and Bess (Burnham) M.; children by previous marriage: Barbara, John, Cynthia, Frances; m. Barbara Allen Williams, June 1, 1979; children: Jennifer, Heather. AB, Princeton U., 1950, PhD, 1955; MA, Clark U., 1952. Lic. psychologist, N.Y. Rsch. assoc. Columbia U., 1956-57; mgr. psychol. svcs. Atlantic Refining Co., Phila., 1957-60; faculty mem. U. Oreg., Eugene, 1960-68; prof., chmn. dept. orgnl. sci. U. Md., College Park, 1968-73; rsch. prof. Ga. State U., Atlanta, 1973-87; pres. Orgnl. Measurement Systems Press, Buffalo, 1976—; prof. Human Resources SUNY, Buffalo, 1987—; chmn. dept. orgn. and human resources, 1989—; cons. McKinsey & Co., N.Y.C., 1966-69; vis. lectr. U. Pa., Phila. 1959-60; vis. prof. U. Calif., Berkeley, 1966-67, U. South Fla., Tampa, 1972; researcher on orgnl. motivation, theories of orgn., human resource utilization, personnel mgmt., bus. policy and strategy, entrepreneurship. Author many books and monographs including Personnel Psychology, 1969; Personnel and Industrial Relations, 1969, 73, 77, 85; The Challenge of Managing, 1975; (with Mary Green Miner) Policy Issues in Personnel and Industrial Relations, 1977; (with George A. Steiner) Management Policy and Strategy, 1977 (James A. Hamilton-Hosp. Adminstrs. Book award 1982, 86), (with M.G. Miner) Employee Selection Within the Law, 1978; Theories of Organizational Behavior, 1980; Theories of Organizational Structure and Process, 1982; People Problems: The Executive Answer Book, 1985; The Practice of Management, 1985; Organizational Behavior: Performance and Productivity, 1988, Industrial-Organizational Psychology, 1992; contbr. numerous articles, papers to profl. jours. Served with AUS, 1944-46, ETO. Decorated Bronze Star, Combat Infantryman's Badge; named Disting. Prof. Ga. State U., 1974. Fellow Acad. Mgmt. (editor Jour. 1973-75, pres. 1977-78), Am. Psychol. Assn., Soc. for Personality Assessment; mem. Indsl. Rels. Rsch. Assn., Princeton Club, Transit Valley Country Club. Republican. Home: 11054 Howe Rd Akron NY 14001-9743 Office: SUNY Dept Orgn and Human Resources Jacobs Mgmt Ctr Buffalo NY 14260

MINER, KAREN MILLS, executive; b. Callicoon, N.Y., July 21, 1947; d. Kenneth James and Phyllis (Parker) M.; m. James David Miner, Aug. 19, 1972; children: Jeffrey, Jason. BA in Chemistry, SUNY, Plattsburgh, 1969; PhD in Biochemistry, U. Md., 1974. Postdoctoral fellow Case Western Res. U., Cleve., 1974-75; asst. prof. Kent (Ohio) State U., 1975-76, Lake Erie Coll., Painesville, Ohio, 1976-77, Sam Houston State U., Huntsville, Tex., 1977-79; postdoctoral fellow U. Calif., Irvine, 1979-82; sr. rsch. scientist Merck Sharp & Dohme, Rahway, N.J., 1982-84; sr. lit. scientist Lederle Labs., Pearl River, N.Y., 1984-87; pres. Biomed. Info. Ctr. Inc., Ridgewood, N.J., 1987—. Contbr. articles to profl. jours. Mem. Jr. League of Bergen County, N.J., 1984—, State Pub. Affairs Com., Bergen County, N.J., 1987-88. Mem. Am. Soc. for Cell Biology, Assn. Ind. Info. Profls., Drug Info. Assn., Am. Med. Writers Assn., Sigma Xi. Office: Biomed Info Ctr Inc PO Box 1298 Ridgewood NJ 07451-1298

MINER, MARK ALAN, public relations manager; b. Pitts., June 29, 1961; s. Odger Wayne and Constance Irene (Jagerski) M. BS in Journalism, West Va. U., 1983. Jr. acct. exec. Hill and Knowlton, Inc., Pitts., 1983-84; freelance writer Koppers Co., Inc., Pitts., 1985; pub. rels. asst. Michael Baker Corp., Beaver, Pa., 1985-86, staff editor, 1987-90, pub. rels. mgr., 1991; media and pub. rels. mgr. Buchanan Ingersoll Profl. Corp., Pitts., 1991—; communications task force Airport Area Devel. Adv. Commn., Pitts., 1990-91; lectr. hist. topics, 1988—. Contbr. articles to hist. publs. Bd. dirs. United Way, Beaver, Pa., 1986-88; econ. devel. conf. com. County of Beaver, 1987. Recipient Community Citation Merit award County of Allegheny, Pa., 1991, Communications Excellence award Employee Stock Assn. Am., 1989, Communicators Recognition award Internat. Assn. Bus. Communicators/United Way., 1987. Mem. Cons. Engrs. Coun. (pub. rels. com. 1986-91), Profl. Svcs. Mgmt. Assn. (pub. rels. com. 1988-91). Office: Buchanan Ingersoll Profl Cp USX Tower 58th Fl 600 Grant St Pittsburgh PA 15219-2701

MING, SI-CHUN, pathologist, educator; b. Shanghai, China, Nov. 10, 1922; came to U.S., 1949, naturalized, 1964; s. Sian-Fan and Jan-Teh (Kuo) M.; m. Pen-Ming Lee, Aug. 17, 1957; children—Carol, Ruby, Stephanie, Michael, Jeffrey, Eileen. M.D., Nat. Central U. Coll. Medicine, China, 1947. Resident in pathology Mass. Gen. Hosp., Boston, 1952-56; assoc. pathologist Beth Israel Hosp., Boston, 1956-67; asst. prof. pathology Harvard U. Med. Sch., 1965-67; assoc. prof. U. Md., 1967-71; prof. Temple U., 1971—, acting chmn. dept. pathology, 1978-80, dep. chmn. dept. path., 1980-86; mem. Internat. Study Group on Gastric Cancer; U.S. rep. WHO Collaborating Ctr. for Evaluation of Methods of Diagnosis and Treatment of Stomach Cancer. Author: Tumors of the Esophagus and Stomach, 1973, supplement, 1985, Precursors of Gastric Cancer, 1984, Pathology of the Gastrointestinal Tract, 1992. Nat. Cancer Inst. sr. fellow Karolinska Inst., Stockholm, 1964-65. Mem. Internat. Acad. Pathology, Am. Assn. Pathologists, AAAS, N.Y. Acad. Scis., Am. Gastroenterol. Assn. Office: 3400 N Broad St Philadelphia PA 19140-5196

MINGUS, NANCY BLUMENSTALK, computer training company executive, educator; b. Schenectady, N.Y., May 21, 1956; d. Louis Charles and Myrtle Lucy (Thompson) Blumenstalk; m. Michael Robert Mingus, Nov. 10, 1979; children: Marissa Marie, Paige Allison. BS, Oneonta (N.Y.) State Coll., 1977; MS in Edn., Alfred (N.Y.) U., 1982. Acad. programmer Alfred U., 1978-81; programmer/analyst Worthington/McGraw Edison, Wellsville, N.Y., 1981-83; instructional designer M&T Bank, Buffalo, 1983-87; systems analyst Moog Inc., East Aurora, N.Y., 1987-90; pres. Mingus Assocs., Inc., Williamsville, N.Y., 1989—; instr. in geology Alfred U., 1981; instr. Allegany County BOCES, Belmont, 1982-83; trainer Sch. of Mgmt., SUNY, Buffalo, 1984-89, instr. Millard Fillmore Coll., 1987-89. Contbr. articles to DATAPRO, Computerworld, Today's Parts Manager, and others. Mem. Assn. for Computer Tng. and Support, Assn. for Systems Mgmt. (pres. Buffalo chpt. 1991-92), Upstate N.Y. Performance Support Users Group (chmn. 1987-90), Western N.Y. Data Processing Trainers (co-founder). Office: Mingus Assocs Inc 34 Hirschfield Dr Williamsville NY 14221

MINI, LOUISE ANN, psychologist; b. Bklyn., Apr. 28, 1949; d. Enrico H. and Anna Marie (Ventrice) M. BA, CUNY, Bklyn., 1971, MS, 1973; MA, Hofstra U., 1977, PhD, 1979. Cert. sch. psychologist N.Y., 1973, psychologist N.Y. 1981. Psychologist in tng. N.Y.C. Bur. Child Guidance, 1974-75, psychologist, 1976; coll. instr. dept. behavioral scis. N.Y. Inst. Tech., N.Y.C., 1976-77; teaching asst. Hofstra U., Hempstead, N.Y., 1977, adj. lectr. psychology dept., 1978-79, field supr., 1982-83; intern S.E. Nassau Guidance Ctr., Lynbrook, N.Y., 1977-78; cons. sch. psychologist New Hyde Park Sch. Dist., Lynbrook, 1979-80; psychologist St. Christopher's Residential Treatment Ctr., Lynbrook, 1977-80, cons. psychologist ICF/MR Programs, 1981-83; chief psychologist, childhood unit coordinator The Shield Inst. for the Developmentally Disabled and Mentally Retarded, Lynbrook, 1980-81; psychologist, dir. spl. services Hewlett Consultation Ctr., Lynbrook, 1981—; cons. psychologist N.Y. State Dept. Social Services Office of Disability Determination, 1982—, N.Y. State Office Vocat. Rehab., 1983—, Hearing & Speech Ctr. L.I. Jewish Hosp., 1983-85; pvt. practice psychotherapy Hewlett (N.Y.) Cons. Svc.; cons. Shapiro & Siegel Law Firm, Conn., 1983—. Intern Brookdale Hosp. Comprehensive Child Care Ctr., 1971-72, Coney Island Hosp. Dept. Child Psychiatry, 1973; therapist Nassau Psychol. Services Inst., 1982-86. Mem. APA (assoc. 1974—), Nassau County Psychol. Assn., N.Y. State Psychol. Assn., Bklyn. Psychol. Assn. Office: Hewlett Cons Ctr 255 Broadway Lynbrook NY 11563-3243

MINICK, ROBERT DALE, psychologist, consultant; b. Carmel, Calif., Dec. 25, 1946; s. Paul Leroy and Betty Jo (Souply) M.; m. Esther Ruth Hammer, Mar. 23, 1983; children: Cassandra Lee, Alysia Kim. BA, Colgate U., 1969; MS, Boston Coll., 1977; PhD, St. Louis U., 1979. Lic. psychologist, Va. Dir. Together, Inc., Marlboro, Mass., 1972-74; cons. Mass. Dept. Pub. Welfare, Boston, 1979-80; evaluation specialist GAO, Washington, 1981-87, mgr., 1987-88; rsch. assoc. Litigation Scis. Inc., Phila., 1988-90; dir. Litigation Scis. Inc., N.Y.C., 1991—. Contbr. articles to profl. jours. War Meml. scholar Colgate U., 1964-68. Mem. APA. Home: Apt 3G2 PO Box 307 Scarborough NY 10510 Office: Litigation Scis Inc 9 W 57th St New York NY 10019

MINICUCCI, ANTHONY JOHN, import company executive; b. Chgo., July 21, 1962; s. Ronald Michael and Shirley Ann (Wadzinski) M. Grad. high sch., Schaumburg, Ill. Sous chef Marriot Hotel, Atlanta, 1978-79, Ritz Carlton Hotel, Atlanta, 1979-80; pres. Prince and the Pauper Catering, Sarasota, Fla., 1980-81; gen. mgr. Oriental Mdse. Assoc., Inc., Md., 1981-84; pres. Mini Doro Enterprises, Inc., New Britain, Conn., 1984—. Home: 1347 Bower Hill Rd Pittsburgh PA 15243-1307 Office: Mini Doro Enterprises Inc 1798 N Highland Rd Pittsburgh PA 15241-1206

MININI, DONALD JOSEPH, marketing consultant; b. N.Y.C., Feb. 14, 1934; s. Joseph Aloysius and Anna Winifred (La Plante) M.; m. Patricia Ann Di Chiara, May 14, 1960; 1 child, Maria Catherine. BA, Cornell U., 1955; postgrad., Pace U., 1964. Sales trainee IBM, Buffalo, 1955-56; supr. N.Y. Reservations Am. Airlines, N.Y.C., 1956-61; mgr. devel. Am. Airlines, Briarcliff Manor, N.C., 1961-67; dir. EDP Mohawk Airlines, Utica, N.Y., 1967-71; v.p. Greenwich Data Systems, Inc., McLean, Va., 1971-75; dir. cybernetics Cyber Svcs. Control Data Corp., Rockville, Md., 1974-75; v.p. Securities Industry Automation Corp., N.Y.C., 1975-82, Bedford Assocs. Inc., Norwalk, Conn., 1982-90; pres. Excalibur Assocs., Greenwich, Conn., 1990—; exec. v.p. mktg. Computer Systems Software & Cons. Inc., Nutley, N.J., 1991—. Fund raiser Rollins Coll., Conn., 1985-89. Mem. Ind. Computer Consultants Assn., Air Cargo Assn., Cornell Club in Fairfield County (scholarship com.), Bklyn. Tech. Alumni Assn. Republican. Roman Catholic. Home and Office: Excalibur Assocs 46 Dandy Dr Cos Cob CT 06807-2203

MINIO, PETER ALAN, systems consulting company executive; b. N.Y.C., June 12, 1951; s. Peter and Mary (Ferrara) M.; m. Jacqueline E. Rothstein, Nov. 19, 1972; children: Peter James, James Alan. BS, St. Francis Coll., Bklyn., 1972. Actuarial trainee Met. Life, N.Y.C., 1972-74, programmer, 1973-74; programmer, analyst Bradford Securities, N.Y.C., 1974-76, Computer Horizons Corp., N.Y.C., 1976-77; software project mgr. J.C. Penney Co., N.Y.C., 1976-79; cons. Compucore Co., South Salem, N.Y., 1979—. Mem. Ind. Computer Cons. Assn. (cons. 1984—, publicity com. 1990—). Republican. Home and Office: Rt 4 Dr # 14 South Salem NY 10590

MINK, GARY STUART, investment consultant; b. Rochester, N.Y., June 1, 1953; s. Jack and Louise (Littner) M. BA in Politics with honors, N.Y.U., 1974. Agt. Mass Mutual Life Ins. Co., Rochester, N.Y., 1974-76; brokerage mgr. Can. Life Ins. Co., Rochester, 1976-78; acct. exec. Fred S. James, Rochester, 1979-82, mgr. employee benefits, 1981-82; pres. Mink Orgn., Rochester, 1982—; advisor Compensation and Benefits Mgmt., N.Y.C., 1984-87. Found chmn. commerce and industry, United Way, 1981. Mem. Rochester Life Underwriters (assoc.), Internat. Assn. Fin. Planners. Democrat. Jewish. Clubs: Midvale Country, Order Ky. Cols. (hon.). Office: Mink Orgn Ltd 815 Sibley Tower Rochester NY 14604

MINKOFF, JACK, economics educator; b. N.Y.C., Jan. 29, 1925; s. Isidore and Yetta (Fine) M.; m. Anne B. Johnson, June 19, 1948; children—Ellen, Paul. A.B., Cornell U., 1948; A.M., Columbia U., 1950, Ph.D. (Ford Found. fellow), 1960. Instr. econs. Western Res. U., 1952-53; instr. econs. Sarah Lawrence Coll., 1959-60; prof. econs., chmn. dept. social sci. Pratt Inst., Bklyn., 1960—; acting dean Sch. Liberal Arts and Scis. Pratt Inst., 1985-86, dean, 1986—. Served with USAAF., 1943-45. Fellow Social Sci. Research Council, 1950-51. Mem. Phi Beta Kappa. Home: 57 Ruxton Rd Great Neck NY 11023-1528 Office: Pratt Inst Brooklyn NY 11205

MINKOW, EDWARD, manufacturing executive, consultant; b. Bklyn., Mar. 21, 1937; s. Sidney and Sadye (Sperling) M.; m. Roberta Zivilik (div. June 1969); children: Rochelle Minkow Wilson, Eric; m. Diane Leslie Silvers, May 1, 1970; children: Adam, Andrea. BS in Chemistry, Clarkson U., 1958; MBA, NYU, 1962; MS, Rutgers U., 1978. V.p. Super Corrugated, N.Y.C., 1959-67, Bradley Container, Jersey City, 1960-62, Cardinal Container, Bklyn., 1962-63; exec. v.p. Am. Packaging, Jersey City, 1967-80; pres. Nat. Contract Packaging, Jersey City, 1972-80; pres., chief exec. officer Rampac Industries, Livingston, N.J., 1980—; assoc. Mark Marpet & Assocs., Chester, N.J., 1990. Coach Chester Little League, 1986-88. Lt. U.S. Army, 1958-59. Named to Honorable Order of Ky. Cols., 1973. Mem. Packaging Inst. USA, N.J. Packaging Exec. Club, Chester Optimist Club, Masons. Office: Rampac Industries 513 W Mt Pleasant Ave Livingston NJ 07039-1721

MINNELLI, LIZA, singer, actress; b. Los Angeles, Mar. 12, 1946; d. Vincente and Judy (Garland) M.; m. Peter Allen, 1967 (div. 1972); m. Jack Haley, Sept. 15, 1974 (div.); m. Mark Gero, Dec. 4, 1979 (div. 1992). Appeared in Off-Broadway revival of Best Foot Forward, 1963; recorded You Are For Loving, 1963, Tropical Nights, 1977, Liza Minelli at Carnegie Hall, 1987; appeared with mother at London Palladium, 1964; appeared in Flora, the Red Menace, 1965 (Tony award), The Act, 1977 (Tony award), The Rink, 1984; nightclub debut at Shoreham Hotel, Washington, 1965; films include Charlie Bubbles, 1967, The Sterile Cuckoo, 1969, Tell Me That You Love Me, Junie Moon, 1970, Cabaret, 1972 (Oscar award), That's Entertainment, 1974, Lucky Lady, 1975, A Matter of Time, 1976, Silent Movie, 1976, New York, New York, 1977, Arthur, 1981, Rent A Cop, Arthur on the Rocks, 1988, Stepping Out, 1991; albums include: Results, 1989; appeared on TV in own spl. Liza With a Z, 1972 (Recipient Emmy award); other TV appearances include Goldie and Liza Together, 1980, Baryshnikov on Broadway, 1980, The Princess and the Pea, Showtime, 1983, A Time to Live, 1985, Sam Found Out, 1988; internat. tour with Frank Sinatra, Sammy Davis Jr., 1988. Also awarded the Brit. equivalent of the Oscar for Best Actress, 1972, Italy's David di Donatello award (twice), the Valentino award. Office: care PMK 1776 Broadway, 8th Floor New York NY 10019-2002

MINNICH, HANS, astronomy educator; b. Mt. Vernon, N.Y., Mar. 31, 1949; s. John and Sava (Domenis) M.; m. Ngoc Diem Nguyen, Oct. 10, 1981 (div. Mar. 1983). BS, Lehman Coll., 1970; MA, Hunter Coll., 1978. Prof. astronomy Physics dept. Fordham U., Bronx, N.Y., 1980—. Vietnamese linguist. Sgt. USAF, 1970-74. Roman Catholic. Office: Fordham U Rose Hill Campus Bronx NY 10458

MINNO, DEREK FRANK, venture capital investor; b. Pitts., Nov. 2, 1959; s. Alexander Mackey and Frances Patricia (Fraher) M.; m. Elizabeth Ward Connell, Oct. 7, 1989; 1 child, Mary Christian. BS in Civil Engring., Vanderbilt U., 1981; MBA, Carnegie-Mellon U., 1985. Chartered Fin. Analyst. Engr. Shell Oil Co., Houston, Tex., 1981-83; fin. supr. AT&T Communications, Oakton, Va., 1984; cons. Enterprise Corp., Pitts., 1985; investment officer Mellon Bank, Pitts., 1985-88; gen. ptnr. Point Venture Ptnrs., Pitts., 1989—; bd. dirs. Swan Techs., State Coll., Pa., City Pride Bakery, Pitts. Vol. Guild for the Blind, Pitts., 1988-91, Make A Wish Found., 1988; mem. Major Gifts Com. Carnegie-Mellon U., Pitts., 1991. Mem. Pitts. Venture Capital Assn., Nat. Venture Capital Asssn., Soc. Petroleum Engrs., Assn. for Investment Mgmt. and Rsch. Roman Catholic. Office: Point Venture Ptnrs 600 Grant St Pittsburgh PA 15219-2701

MINO, MICHAEL GEORGE, engineering executive, plastic welding manufacturer; b. Buffalo, Oct. 9, 1954; s. George Michael and Rita Cecilia (DiGennaro) M.; m. Lynn Ann Barone, Apr. 12, 1986. BSEE, Rensselaer Polytechnic Inst., 1975, MSEE, 1976; MBA in Fin., Rochester Inst. Tech., 1978. Registered profl. engr., N.Y. Engr., supr. Eastman Kodak Co., Rochester, N.Y., 1974-82; exec. v.p., founder Ormec Systems Corp., Rochester, 1982-90; also bd. dirs.; exec. v.p., gen. mgr. Vinton Inc., Henrietta, N.Y., 1990—; mem. investment review com. Tech Ventures. vice-chmn. Rensselaer Exec. Bd., Troy, N.Y., 1976; coord. Kodak Jr. Achievement, Rochester, 1980-82. Mem. Rensselaer Alumni Assn. (pres. 1980-83), Jaycees (vice-chmn. Rochester br. , Key Leader award), Phalanx, Tau Beta Pi, Eta Kappa Nu. Home: 92 Brentwood Ln Fairport NY 14450-2227 Office: Vinton Inc 1001 Lehigh Station Rd Henrietta NY 14467-9389

MINOR, ANN LAMBERT, clinical nurse; b. Norwich, Conn., Mar. 10, 1955; d. Albert Francis and Rosemay (Colburn) Lambert; m. Mark Edward Minor, Oct. 23, 1976; children: Heather Ann, Rebecca Jane. RN, Hartford Hosp. Sch. Nursing, Conn., 1976; postgrad., St. Joseph Coll., West Hartford, 1989—. RN, Conn. Staff nurse kidney transplant unit Hartford Hosp., 1976-81; staff nurse maxi-care unit Bristol (Conn.) Hosp., 1981-84, staff nurse ob/gyn unit, 1984-89, clin. nurse ambulatory surgery unit, 1989-90, clin. nurse II ambulatory surgery unit, 1990—; adv. bd. and psychoednl. sexual abuse program group facilitator Wheeler Clinic, Plainville, Conn., 1989—; corporator Wheeler Clinic. Adv. bd. St. Joseph Coll., 1990—; officer Bingham Sch. PTO, Bristol, 1987, 88. Recipient The Ethel E. Brooks award Hartford Hosp. Sch. Nursing, 1976. Mem. ANA, Am. Soc. Post-Anesthesia Nurses, Conn. Soc. Post-Anesthesia Nurses, Conn. Nurses Assn., Internat. Assn. for Near Death Studies, Nurse Healers Profl. Assocs., Am. Holistic Nurses Assn. Congregationalist. Home: 1725 Perkins St Bristol CT 06010-8909 Office: Bristol Hosp Brewster Rd Bristol CT 06010-5160

MINSKY, HYMAN PHILIP, economic researcher; b. Chgo., Sept. 23, 1919; s. Sam and Dora (Zakon) M.; m. Esther DePardo; children: Diana, Alan. BS, U. Chgo., 1941; MPA, Harvard U., 1947, PhD, 1954. Instr. Carnegie Tech., Pitts., 1947; from asst. to assoc. to prof. Brown U., Providence, 1949-57, U. Calif., Berkeley, 1955-65; prof. Washington U., St. Louis, 1965-90; disting. scholar Jerome Levy Econ. Inst. Bard Coll., Annandale On Hudson, N.Y., 1990—; Advisor, bd. dir. Mark Twain Banks, St. Louis, 1968-90. Author: John Maynard Keynes, 1975, Can It Happen Again, 1982, Stabilizing an Unstable Economy, 1986. Cpl. AUS, 1943-46, ETO. Office: Bard Coll Jerome Levy Econ Inst Annandale On Hudson NY 12504

MINSTER, LAWRENCE R., bank executive; b. Altoona, Pa., Jan. 16, 1953; s. Roy C. and Genevieve A. (Wolf) M.; m. Rose A. Himes, Sept. 1, 1973; 1 child, Lawrence R. Jr. B., Pa. State U., 1973. CPA, N.Y. Auditor Price Waterhouse, N.Y.C., 1973-76; staff acct. Chase Manhattan, N.Y.C., 1976-81; contr. Chase Bank Internat., Newark, 1981-87; chief fin. officer Chase Bank of Fla., St. Petersburg, 1987-89, Chase Lincoln First, Rochester, N.Y., 1989—. Office: Chase Lincoln First 1 Lincoln Tower Rochester NY 14643

MINSTER, SHIRLEY MARION RICE, educational administrator; b. Portland, Maine, Oct. 19, 1953; d. Richard Nash and Edith Luella (Meserve) Rice; m. Donald Blair, June 24, 1973. BS in Edn. cum laude, U. So. Maine, 1979, MEd in Counsling Edn., 1984. Lic. counselor, elem. tchr., Maine. Tchr. Greater Portland Christian Sch., South Portland, 1979-83, 84-87, mem. edn. com., 1983, 88; counselor Minster Counseling, Gray, Maine, 1987—; ednl. cons. Minster-Moitozo, Lewiston, Maine, 1988-89; ednl. cons., prin., founder North Atlantic Regional Schs., Inc., Auburn, Maine, 1989—; dir. edn. svcs. Home Sch. Assocs., 1989—; bd. dirs. Edn. Today, Inc.; nat. speaker on ednl. issues, including home sch. Mem. Am. Assn. Counseling and Devel., Am. Mental Health Counselors Assn., Mil. Educators and Counselors Assn., Maine Assn. Counseling and Devel., Maine Homeschool Assn. (bd. dirs. 1988-90). Republican. Office: North Atlantic Regional Schs 116 3d Ave Auburn ME 04210

MINTER, JAMES FRANKLIN, assistant director of admissions; b. Milledgeville, Ga., Jan. 14, 1952; s. M.F. and Elizabeth (Chandler) M. BA, Columbia U., 1973, MA, 1974. Tchr. of classics Bollingbrook Sch., Petersburg, Va., 1978-80, Chapin Sch., N.Y.C., 1980-85; asst. dir. coll. admissions Columbia U., N.Y.C., 1985—; nat. chmn. Nat. Jr. Classical League, Oxford, Ohio, 1983-85. Treas. Front Runners, N.Y.C., 1988-89. Mem. Am. Classical League. Democrat. Home: 65 Park Terrace E # C78 New York NY 10034-1447 Office: Columbia U Columiba Coll Admissions 212 Hamilton Hall New York NY 10027

MINTER, KENDALL ARTHUR, lawyer; b. N.Y.C., May 24, 1952; s. William Arthur and Jerolyn (Johnson) M.; m. Revola Fontaine, Sept. 29, 1954; children: Kamali, Namik. BA, Cornell U., 1974, JD, 1976; postgrad.

Wharton Sch., 1977. Bar: N.Y. 1977, D.C. 1978, U.S. Dist. Ct. (ea. and so. dists.) N.Y. 1978. Disc jockey, newscaster, salesman, dir. black affairs dept. WKTO and WVBR-FM, 1970-76; founder, chmn. bd. Full Circle Enterprises, Inc., 1972-76; corp. counsel, dir. broadcasting Fairchild Industries, Inc., Germantown, Md., 1976-78, Burns, Jackson, Miller, Summit and Jacoby, N.Y.C., 1978-80; sole practice, N.Y.C., 1980-88; ptnr. Minter and Gay, P.C., N.Y.C., 1988—; legal advisor Black Music Assn. Bd. dirs. Am. Youth Hostels, met. N.Y. council and nat. council, bd. dirs. 100 Black Men. Mem. Internat. Bar Assn., ABA (forum com. on entertainment and sports industry), Fed. Communications Bar Assn., Black Entertainment Lawyers Assn. (founding mem., exec. dir.), N.Y. State Bar Assn., Assn. Bar City of N.Y. Avocations: scuba-diving, water-skiing, camping, traveling, skiing. Office: Minter and Gay 111 Broadway New York NY 10006-1901

MINTO, CLIVE, retail company executive; b. Cardiff, Wales, Aug. 17, 1945; arrived in Can., 1969; s. Clifford and Doris (Parkhouse) M.; m. Frances Betty Lloyd, Sept. 23, 1967; children: Anna, Emma. B.S. in math. and stats. with honors, U. Birmingham, Eng., 1966. Mktg. exec. Rank Xerox (Europe), London, 1966-69; account exec. Maclaren Advt., Toronto, Ont., Can., 1969-70; mgr. personal products div. Lever Detergents, Toronto, 1970-77; dir. mktg. Pepsi-Cola Can. Ltd., Toronto, 1977-80, pres., chief exec. officer, 1983-87; mng. dir. Pepsi-Cola Africa, Johannesburg, Republic of South Africa, 1980-81; v.p. No. European region Pepsico Internat., London, 1981-83; exec. v.p. Can. Tire Corp. Ltd., Toronto, 1987—. Office: Can Tire Corp Ltd, 2180 Yonge St, Toronto, ON Canada M4P 2V8

MINTO, KARL DEAN, research electrical engineer; b. Minden, Ont., Can., Apr. 2, 1958; came to U.S., 1986; s. Robert Andrew and Margaret Jean (Kerr) M.; m. Shelley Ann Jones, Dec. 4, 1957; children: Heather, James, Keren. BA in Sci., U. Waterloo (Ont.), 1981, MA in Sci., 1983, PhD, 1985. Rsch. scientist GE Corp. R & D Ctr., Schenectady, 1986—. Contbr. articles to profl. jours.; author software. Mem. IEEE, AIAA, Control System Soc. (chmn. Schenectady br. 1989—). Home: 5 Nolan Rd Ballston Lake NY 12019-2020 Office: GE Corp R & D Ctr River Rd Schenectady NY 12345-6002

MINTZ, FRED, acoustical engineer; b. N.Y.C., June 30, 1918; s. Sam and Dora Mintz; m. Shirley Pomerantz, Aug. 14, 1942 (dec. Nov. 1973); children: Susan Ellen Mintz Super, Robert Edward; m. Elaine Joyce Katsh Prensky, Feb. 22, 1976. Student, CCNY, 1933-37; BS in Engring., George Washington U., 1940, ME, 1946; ME, UCLA, 1965. Registered profl. engr., Ill. Physicist Taylor Model Basin USN, Washington, 1940-49; acoustician, mech. engr. Armour Rsch. Found. IIT, Chgo., 1949-55; various managerial and tech. positions Lockheed Aircraft Corp., Burbank, Calif., 1955-73; environ. scientist EPA, Washington, 1973-81; staff noise cons., 1985—. Author: (with others) Shock and Vibration Control, 1960, Experimental Stress Analysis, 1947. Bd. dirs., v.p., sec. Elizabeth Condo, Chevy Chase, Md., 1978-92. Fellow Acoustical Soc. Am. Home: 4601 N Park Ave Apt 908 Bethesda MD 20815-4522 Office: EPA 401 M St SW Washington DC 20460-0002

MINTZ, M. J., lawyer; b. Phila., Oct. 29, 1940; s. Arthur and Lillian (Altenberg) M.; divorced; children—Robert A., Christine L.; m. Judith E. Held. B.S., Temple U., 1961, J.D., 1968. Bar: D.C.; C.P.A., Pa., D.C. Atty. adv. to judge U.S. Tax Ct., Washington, 1968-70; asst. gen. counsel Cost of Living Council, Washington, 1971-73; ptnr. Dickstein, Shapiro & Morin, Washington, 1973—; adj. prof. George Mason U. Law Sch., Va., 1974-78; adv. Employee Retirement Income Security Act of 1974, Adv. Council, Washington, 1982-85. Contbr. articles to profl. jours. Apptd. by Pres. Reagan to advisory com. Pension Benifit Guaranty Corp., 1987; reapptd. and designated chmn. by Pres. George Bush; rep. candidate Fairfax County Bd. of Suprs., 1971. Fellow Nat. Assn. Watch & Clock Collectors; mem. ABA, Am. Inst. C.P.A.s, Antuquarian Horological Soc. (London). Clubs: Cosmos, Belle Haven Country, Met. Club of Washington, Chappaquiddick Beach, Capitol Hill. Avocations: antiquarian horologist.

MINTZ, NORBETT LAWRENCE, psychologist; b. Bklyn., Mar. 17, 1931; s. Henry and Gertrude Miriam (Glaser) M.; m. Sophie Baran, Agu. 14, 1960 (wid. Feb. 1982); m. Carol Imelda Purdy, Nov. 26, 1983. BA, Rollins Coll., 1952; MA, U. N.Mex., 1954; PhD, Brandeis U., 1957. Lic. psychologist, Mass.; diplomate Am. Bd. Psychotherapy, Am. Bd. Medical Psychotherapists, Nat. Register Health Svc. Providers. Instr. in social rels. Harvard U., Cambridge, Mass., 1958-61; asst. prof. Brandeis U., Waltham, Mass., 1961-64; chmn. dept. psychology U. Mass., Boston, 1966; lectr., from asst. prof. to assoc. Harvard Med. Sch., Boston, 1965—; psychologist McLean Hosp., Belmont, Mass., 1964-83, attending psychologist, 1983—; prof. Mass. Sch. Profl. Psychology, Dedham, Mass., 1974—; clin. assoc. prof. Boston U. Sch. Social Work, 1978-81. Co-author two books, numerous scientific papers. Recipient career devel. award NIMH, 1966-72. Fellow Am. Psychol. Assn., Am. Acad. Psychotherapy, Mass. Psychol. Assn. (Ezra Saul Psychol. Svc. award),. Office: Mass Sch Profl Psychology 322 Sprague St Dedham MA 02026-5250

MINTZ, STEPHEN ALLAN, real estate company executive, lawyer; b. N.Y.C., May 21, 1943; s. Irving and Anne (Medwick) M.; m. Dale Leibson, June 19, 1966; children: Eric Michael, Jaclyn Leibson. AB, Cornell U., 1965; JD cum laude, Harvard U., 1968. Bar: N.Y. 1969. Assoc. Proskauer, Rose, Goetz & Mendelsohn, N.Y.C., 1968-76, ptnr., 1976-80; v.p. Integrated Resources, Inc., N.Y.C., 1980-84, 1st. v.p., 1984-86, sr. v.p., 1986-89, exec. v.p., 1989—; chmn. Resources Hotel Mgmt. Svc. Div., 1986—. Mem. ABA, N.Y. State Bar Assn., Assn. of Bar of City of N.Y., Urban Land Inst. Democrat. Jewish. Home: 11 Eve Ln Rye NY 10580-4113 Office: Integrated Resources Inc 10 Union Sq E New York NY 10003-3314

MINUTILLO, PATRICK MICHAEL, detective services official; b. Hoboken, N.J., Apr. 1, 1949; s. Mario Matthew and Anne Elizabeth (Quagliano) M. Grad., Mommouth County (Police) Acad, 1973; BS in Criminal Justice, Jersey City State Coll., 1978. Police officer Matawan Township Police Dept., Aberdeen Township, N.J., 1973-74, Wood-Ridge (N.J.) Police Dept., 1974-76; detective, lt. Harrison (N.J.) Police Dept., 1976—; notary pub. Hudson & Morris County, N.J., 1991—; tng. officer Am. Soc. Law Enforcement Instrs., N.J., 1990—; terminal agy. coord. N.J. State Police, 1989—; instr. (black belt martial arts/self defence) County Coll. Morris, Randolph. N.J., 1988—. Contbr. articles to profl. jours. Mem. LAw Enforcement Exec. Forum, Hudson-Essex County, N.J., 1991—. With USN, 1968-72, Vietnam. Mem. Internat. Narcotics Enforcement Officers Assn., Nat. Assn. Chief of Police, Am. Soc. Notaries, Nat. Assn. Bunco Investigators, Ea. Armed Robbery Conf., N.J. Narcotic Enforcement Officers Assn., N.J. Crime Prevention Officers Assn., N.J. Vehicle Theft Investigators Assn. Roman Catholic. Home: 223 Lake Shore Dr Lake Hiawatha NJ 07034-1603 Office: Harrison Police Dept 318 Harrison Ave Harrison NJ 07029-1796

MIODUCKI, JOHN FRANK, financial services company executive; b. Schenectady, N.Y., Jan. 11, 1954; s. Sigmud F. and Hazel M. (Whitney) M.; m. V. J. Gonzenbach, Feb. 5, 1977 (div. 1981); m. Gail J. Jurczynski, May 21, 1983. Grad., Linton High Sch., Schenectady, 1972. Mktg. rep. Benche Inc./Union Book, Schenectady, 1974-76, Nat. Graphics, Albany, N.Y., 1976-80, OCE Industries, Chgo., 1980-81; v.p. sales Acme Press/Tyhelen Corp., Schenectady, 1983-90; pres. GC Radcorp, Talahassee, Fla., 1990—; ptnr. PFH Assocs., Scotia, N.Y., 1990—; pres. The Marz Group, Scotia, N.Y., 1990—; chief operating officer TMF Systems Inc., Scotia, N.Y., 1990—; pres., chmn. bd. J.M. Marz, Inc., Scotia, N.Y., 1989—. com. mem. Bus. Platform com. Adv. to the City Coun., Schenectady, 1985. Mem. Univ. Club of Albany, The Mohawk Club (chmn. pubs. com. 1988-89). Republican. Roman Catholic. Office: JM Marz Inc 123 Saratoga Rd # 313 Schenectady NY 12302-4181

MIODUSZEWSKI, JAMES FRANCIS, controller; b. Engelwood, N.J., Feb. 25, 1954; s. Joseph and Matilda (Klimek) M.; m. Catherine Ann Whitaker, May 7, 1983; children: James Robert, William Joseph. BA in Acctg., William Paterson Coll., 1977. Acctg. mgr. Buitoni Foods Corp., South Hackensack, N.J., 1978-86; fin. analyst Crum & Forster, Inc., Morristown, N.J., 1986-87; contr. Am. Instants, Inc., Stanhope, N.J., 1987—. Auditor United Meth. Ch., Dover, N.J., 1987—; coach Little League Baseball, Dover, 1991. Mem. Moose Lodge. Office: Am Instants Inc PO Box 536 Stanhope NJ 07874-0536

MIRABELLA, GRACE, magazine publishing executive; b. Maplewood, N.J., June 10, 1930; d. Anthony and Florence (Belfatto) M.; m. William G. Cahan, Nov. 24, 1974. BA, Skidmore Coll., 1950. Mem. exec. tng. program Macy's, N.Y.C., 1950-51; mem. fashion dept. Saks Fifth Ave., N.Y.C., 1951-52; with Vogue mag., N.Y.C., 1952-54, 56-88; assoc. editor Vogue mag., 1965-71, editor-in-chief, 1971-88; publ. dir. Mirabella mag., 1988—; mem. pub. relations staff Simonetta & Fabiani, Rome, Italy, 1954-56; hon. bd. dirs. Catalyst; lectr. New Sch. Social Research. Adv. bd. Columbia U. Sch. Journalism. Decorated cavalier Order of Merit Republic of Italy; recipient Outstanding Grad. Achievement award Skidmore Coll., 1972; Fashion Critics award Parsons Sch. Design, 1985; Woman of Distinction award Birmingham-So. Coll., 1985, Girl Scouts Am. Leadership award, 1987, Excellence in Media award Susan G. Komen Found., 1987, Equal Opportunity award NOW, 1987; officer Order of Merit, Republic of Italy, 1987; Mary Ann Magnin award, 1988; Achievement award Am. Assn. Plastic and Reconstructive Surgery, 1988; Spl. Merit award Coun. Fashion Designers Am., 1989. Mem. Women's Forum N.Y. Office: Mirabella Mag 200 Madison Ave New York NY 10016-3903

MIRABELLE, GARY JOHN, sculptor; b. New Rochelle, N.Y., June 16, 1951; s. Richard and Edith (Beladino) M.; m. Raquel Rios, Dec. 13, 1978. BFA in Sculpture, SUNY, New Paltz, 1976; postgrad., Art Student League, 1976-78. Sculptor Carolina Enterprises, N.Y.C., 1979-80; pvt. practice N.Y.C., 1980-83, 89—; sculptor, designer MJM Studios, South Kearny, N.Y., 1983-89.

MIRAGLIOTTA, ANTHONY, lawyer; b. Passaic, N.J., Mar. 17, 1954; s. Carmelo and Josephine (Aria) M.; m. Kathryn Jane Colca, Sept. 8, 1979; 1 child, Michela. BA, Fairleigh Dickinson U., 1976; JD, Temple U., 1979. Bar: N.J. 1981. Pers. mgmt. analyst N.J. Dept. Civil Svc., Trenton, 1979-81; rules analyst N.J. Office of Adminstrv. Law, Trenton, 1981-84, statewide rules monitor, 1984-88, asst. dir. rules & publs., 1988—; instr. Rutgers U., Newark, 1988-90, Cert. Pub. Mgrs. Program, Trenton, 1986—. Co-author, editor: N.J. Rulemaking Manual, 1984. Mem. KC. Home: 31 John Alden St Clifton NJ 07013-2557 Office: Office of Adminstrv Law 9 Quakerbridge Plz CN-049 Trenton NJ 08625

MIRANDA, MYRA, pharmacist; b. Bklyn., Apr. 18, 1968; d. Mario and Elsa (Medina) M. B., St. John's U., 1991. Lic. pharmacist. Pharmacy clk./intern Village Pharmacy, Queens Village, N.Y., 1986-91; pharmacist, lectr. CVS Pharmacy, Northbergen, N.J., 1991—; lectr. CVS Pharmacy, Northbergen, 1991—. Acad. grantee St. John's U., 1986; Local 102 scholar Teamsters Local 102, Queens, N.Y., 1986. Mem. NAFE, Am. Pharm. Assn. (Patient Counseling Runner-up award 1991), Pharm. Soc. of the State of N.Y., Campus Ministry of St. John's U. (fundraising Oxfam Fund 1987-91), Intersorority Coun. of St. John's U. (rush chairperson 1989-90), Theta Phi Alpha (pres. 1989-91, bd. dirs. rep. 1987-88, Most Active Collegiate award 1989, 90). Roman Catholic. Office: CVS Pharmacy 9018 Bergenline Ave Northbergen NJ 07047

MIRANDA, ROBERT NICHOLAS, publishing company executive; b. Bklyn., July 9, 1934; s. John and Florence Miranda; m. Marilyn H. Pils, May 25, 1958; children—Marilyn, Robert, Susan, Lori, Jennifer. A.A. in Acctg. and Bus. Adminstrn., SUNY-Farmingdale. Pres. Pergamon Press, Inc., Elmsford, N.Y., 1965-92; chmn., chief exec. officer Cognizant Communication Corp., Elmsford, 1992—; dir. exec. v.p., vice chmn. Soc. and Assoc. Service Corp., McLean, Va., 1979-92. Served with USNR, 1954-59. Mem. ALA, Spl. Library Assn., Council Sci. Editors. Office: Cognizant Communication Corp 90 Fairview Park Dr Elmsford NY 10523-1520

MIRSEN, THOMAS ROBERT, neurology educator; b. Buenos Aires, Argentina, May 14, 1957; came to U.S., 1965; s. Stefan and Maria (Kunowski) M. AB in Biochemistry cum laude, Princeton U., 1978; MD cum laude, SUNY, Bklyn., 1982. Diplomate Am. Bd. Psychiatry and Neurology. Intern Albert Einstein & Jacobi Hosps., Bronx, N.Y., 1982-83; resident in neurology NYU-Bellevue Med. Ctr., 1983-86; clin. rsch. fellow U. Western Ont., London, Can., 1986-89; neurol. coord. N.Am. Symptomatic Carotid Endarterectomy Robarts Rsch. Inst., London, Can., 1989-90; asst. prof. neurology Cooper Hosp., U. Medicine and Dentistry of N.J., Camden, 1990—; ad hoc reviewer Jour. Neurol. Scis., Winston-Salem, N.C., 1991. Author: (with others) Epidemiology and Classification of Vascular and Multi-Infarct Dementia, 1988, Changing Concepts of Vascular Dementia, 1988; contbr. articles to profl. jours. Mem. stroke coun. Am. Heart Assn., 1989. Grantee Alzheimer's Disease and Related Disorders Assn., 1990-91. Mem. Soc. for Clin. Trials, Alpha Omega Alpha. Home: 38 Walnut St Haddonfield NJ 08033-1853 Office: Cooper Hosp/Univ Med Ctr 3 Cooper Plz Camden NJ 08103

MIRSKI, MICHAEL D. SVIATOPOLK, retired economist, Sovietologist; b. Boczsa, Russia, Mar. 24, 1904; came to U.S., 1940; s. Dimitri Sviatopolk and Mary A. (De Bellegarde) M.; m. Mary A. Bouteneff, Feb. 4, 1940 (dec. Jan. 1973); children: Mary Mirski Haile, Elisabeth S. BA and Scs., Gymnasium No. 2, Chisinau, Bessarabia, 1921; LLM, U. Czernowitz (Romania), 1925; D Jurisprudence, U. Paris, 1929. Dir., insp., organizer Polish Clearing Office and Exports Control, Warsaw, 1935-40; instr. econs. Bklyn. Coll., 1943; lectr. contemporary civilization dept. econs. Columbia U., N.Y.C., 1943-48; sr. fellow Hoover Inst., Stanford, Calif., 1948-49; prof., head Russian lang. dept. U.S. Mil. Acad., West Point, N.Y., 1949-57; prof. Russian history U. Md., Balt., 1960-61; economist Social Security Adminstrn., Balt., 1957-74; ret., 1974. Author: Monetary Crisis in Poland, 1929, Private Debt after Inflation, 1929; patentee optics field. Lt. col. U.S. Army, 1949-57, Korea. Decorated Cross of Merit (Poland); recipient appreciation award Nat. ARC, 1946, 47; fellow Stanford U., 1948-49. Mem. Am. Econ. Assn., Am. Assn. for Advancement Slavic Studies, Am. Assn. Tchrs. Slavic and Ea. European Langs. Home: 4633 Schenley Rd Baltimore MD 21210-2525

MIRZA, HUMAYUN, banker; b. Poona, India, Dec. 9, 1928; came to U.S., 1956; s. Iskander and Rifaat M.; m. Marilia Cleci; children: Zareen, Samia. Grad., Chartered Ins. Inst., London, 1953; MBA, Harvard U., 1958. Resident insp. for Pakistan Alliance Assurance Co. Ltd., London, 1951-54; dir. ins. Pakistan Indsl. Devel. Corp., Karachi, Pakistan, 1954-56; fin. analyst, ops. officer World Bank, Washington, 1958-70, chief Nigerian div., 1970-73; chief resident mission World Bank, Lagos, Nigeria, 1973-76; chief Brazil div. World Bank, Washington, 1977-83, chief Cen. Am. div., 1983-86, sr. advisor to v.p., 1986-88; internat. cons. Mirza Assocs. Internat., Bethesda, Md., Pakistan, 1988—. Advisor to Prime Minister of Pakistan, Washington and Karachi, 1968-70; bd. dirs. Internat. Eye Found. Mem. Harvard Club Washington, Harvard U. Bus. Sch. Club. Home and Office: 8508 Thornden Ter Bethesda MD 20817-6810

MISER, HUGH JORDAN, operations research—systems analyst, consultant; b. Fayetteville, Ark., June 23, 1917; s. Wilson Lee and Nellie (Pyle) M.; m. Josephine Spence Lehmann, June 24, 1944; children: James Spence, Wendel Lee, Andrew Lehmann, Emily Margaret. BA magna cum laude, Vanderbilt U., 1938; MS, Ill. Inst. Tech., 1940; PhD, Ohio State U., 1946. Tchr. math. Ill. Inst. Tech., Chgo., 1938-40, 42-44, Ohio State U., Columbus, 1940-42, 45-46; acting chmn. dept. math. Lawrence Coll., Appleton, Wis., 1944; ops. analyst Hdqrs. 20th Air Force, Washington and Guam, 1945; asst. prof. math. Williams Coll., Williamstown, Mass., 1946-49; ops. analyst Hdqrs. USAF, Washington, 1949-59, dep. asst. ops. analysis, 1951-59, acting asst. for ops. analysis, 1958-59; dir. operational scis. lab. Rsch. Triangle Inst., Durham, N.C., 1959-60; dir. applied sci. div. ops. evaluation group MIT, Cambridge, Mass., 1960-62; asst. to dir. systems planning and rsch. Mitre Corp., Bedford, Mass., 1962-65; v.p. Travelers Rsch. Ctr., Inc., Hartford, Conn., 1965-69; with U. Mass., Amherst, 1969—, prof. indsl. engring. and ops. rsch., 1969-80, acting head dept. indsl. engring. and ops. rsch., 1975-76, head dept., 1976-79, prof. emeritus, 1980—; leader craft of systems analysis, exec. editor publs. Internat. Inst. Applied Systems Analysis, Laxenburg, Austria, 1979-82, acting head communications, 1980-81; cons., sec., chief of staff USAF, 1967-68; cons. ops. analysis office hdqrs. USAF, 1968-71; mem. NAS Evaluation Panel for Inst. Applied Tech., Nat. Bur. Standards, 1969-72, Evaluation Panel for Tech. Analysis Div., 1967-69, 72-73, chmn. 1969-72; mem. commerce tech. adv. bd. Panel on Noise Abatement, 1968-71; cons. info. systems programs NSF Office Sci. Info. Svc., 1969-74, Ctr. for the Environment and Man Inc., Hartford, 1970-79, Rensselaer Poly. Inst. of Conn., Hartford, 1970, Am. Acad. Arts and Scis., Cambridge, 1983-85; chmn. rsch. adv. com. Ins. Inst. for Hwy. Safety, Washington, 1967-69; cons., mem. systems and program analysis panel Gen. Acctg. Office, Washington, 1972-76; mem. internat. advisory com. Systems Practice jour. Co-author: Basic Mathematics for Engineers, 1944; Basic Mathematics for Science and Engineering, 1955; co-editor; Handbook of Systems Analysis, Vol. 1, 1985, Vol. 2, 1988. Moderator 1st Ch. of Christ, Congl., Farmington, Conn., 1986-88; pres. New World Chamber Ensemble, Inc., Simsbury, Conn., 1986-88, 90—. Recipient Arthur S. Flemming award U.S. Jr. C. of C., 1952. Fellow AAAS; mem. Ops. Rsch. Soc. Am. (founding mem. 1952, sec. 1958-61, v.p. 1961-62, pres. 1962-63, rep. to NRC 1967-73, editor Bull. 1959-61, editor Ops. Rsch. 1968-74, George E. Kimball medal 1975), Inst. Mgmt. Scis., Can. Operational Rsch. Soc. (Harold Larnder prize 1990), Am. Math. Soc., Math. Assn. Am., Soc. for Indls. and Applied Math., Inst. Math. Stats., Am. Statis. Assn., Conn. Acad. Sci. and Engring. (founding mem. 1976), Ops.-Rsch./Mgmt.-Sci. Found. Inc. (pres. 1987-91), Operational Rsch. Soc., Assn. Pub. Policy and Mgmt., Phi Beta Kappa, Sigma Xi. Home and Office: 199 South Rd Farmington CT 06032-2522

MISERANDINO, MARIANNE, psychology educator; b. Rockville Centre, N.Y., July 1, 1960; d. Dominick Alfred and Catherine Margaret (Healy) M.; m. Raymond Joseph Folven, July 13, 1991. BA, U. Rochester, 1982; PhD, Cornell U., 1987. Teaching asst., statis. cons. Cornell U., Ithaca, N.Y., 1983-87; asst. prof. psychology Hobart and William Smith Colls., Geneva, N.Y., 1987-90; rsch. assoc. U. Rochester, N.Y., 1990-92; asst. prof. Beaver Coll., Glenside, Pa., 1992—; adj. faculty Tompkins-Cortland Community Coll., Dryden, N.Y., 1986-87. Contbr. articles to profl. jours. Mem. Am. Psychol. Assn. (div. teaching of psychology, div. social and personality), Am. Psychol. Soc. Office: Beaver Coll Dept Psychology Glenside PA 19038

MISHNE, JONATHAN MICHAEL, guitarist, composer; b. Cleve., May 4, 1958; s. Robert Daniel and Judith (Marks) M.; m. Rosa Maria D'Jesus Esparza, Sept. 9, 1985 (div. 1987). Student, U. Maine, 1982-83, Aspen Music Sch., 1985, Centro de Flamenco, Cordoba, Spain, 1986; MusB, New Eng. Conservatory, 1988. Tchr. New Eng. Conservatory Extension, Boston, 1986-87, Powers Music Sch., Belmont, Mass., 1991—; dir. Spring Strings Chamber Music Series, Easthampton, N.Y., 1987-90; lead guitarist, composer, leader, mgr. Boccherini Ensemble, Boston, 1989—; lead guitarist Blues Syndicate, Boston, 1991—; quartet in residence with Boccherini Ensemble Powers Music Sch., Belmont, 1991—; producer Boccherini Recordings, Boston, 1989-92; creative cons. film on my life , 1990—. Composer, performer, producer: (albums) A New Direction, 1990, J Darc, 1992, Fandango, 1992; producer, performer, composer Attica (N.J.) State Prison Benefit, 1991; performer Internat. Red Cross Benefit, Geneva, 1990; performer, producer Maine State Prison Benefit, Thomaston, 1990. Mem. ASCAP, New Eng. Conservatory Alumni. Democrat. Jewish. Home and Office: Boccherini Ensemble 66 Woodlawn St Jamaica Plain MA 02130

MISIANO, FRANK, long term care facility administrator; b. Bklyn., Feb. 6, 1949; s. Frank Amedio and Rose (Chuisano) M.; m. Leslie Joan Wiegan, Aug. 19, 1973; children: Jason, Dana. BA in Social Psychology, Queens Coll., Flushing, N.Y., 1976; MPA, L.I. U., Greenvale, N.Y., 1985. Lic. nursing home adminstr., N.Y., Fla. Hosp. adminstr. Chester Bus. Svc., N.Y.C., 1976-85; asst. adminstr. Hillside Manor HFR, Jamaica, N.Y., 1986-87; adminstr. Hollis (N.Y.) Park Manor, 1986-87, Little Neck (N.Y.) Nursing Home, 1987—; adj. prof. L.I.U. C.W. Post Campus 100 Nursing Home Course, Greenvale, N.Y., 1985, 89. Mem. Am. Coll. Health Care Adminstrs., Pi Alpha Alpha. Democrat. Home: 139 Celler Ave New Hyde Park NY 11040-2016 Office: Little Neck Nursing Home 26019 Nassau Blvd Flushing NY 11362-2294

MITCHAM, CARL, humanities educator; b. Dallas, Sept. 20, 1941; s. J.T. and Betty (Clapp) M.; m. Marylee Daniel, Mar. 26, 1965; children: Mark, Jessica, Emilie, Anna. BA in Philosophy magna cum laude, U. Colo., 1967, MA in Philosophy, 1969; PhD, Fordham U., 1988. Instr. philosophy Berea Coll., Ky., 1970-72, lectr. philosophy and social sci. St. Catharine Coll., Ky., 1972-82; assoc. prof. humanities Poly. U., Bklyn., N.Y., 1982-89; assoc. prof. philosophy and sci. tech. soc. Pa. State U., 1989—. Rev. and bibliography editor: Research in Philosophy and Tech., 1976-85; author: Philosophy and Technology: Readings in the Philosophical Problems of Technology, 1972, reprinted edit., 1983. Theology and Technology: Essays in Christian Analysis and Exegesis, 1984, Philosophy and Technology II: Information Technology and Computers in Theory and Practice, 1986, Qué es la Filosofía de la Techologia, 1989; contbr. articles to profl. jours. Grantee NSF, 1975-78, NEH, 1978-80, Am. Council of Learned Socs., 1981, Ky. Humanities Council, 1981-82, Franklin J. Matchette Found. and Goethe House N.Y., 1983, Exxon Edn. Found., 1984-88, JM Found., 1986, NSF, 1988, MacArthur Found., 1988. Mem. Am. Cath. Philos. Assn., Humanities and Tech. Assn., Inst. for Theol. Encounter with Sci. and Tech., N.Y. Acad. Scis., Soc. for Philosophy and Tech. (bd. dirs. 1980-85, co-editor Newsletter 1982-84), Soc. for History of Tech. (Abbot Payson Usher prize 1974). Office: Pa State U Philosopy Dept Sparks 240 University Park PA 16802

MITCHEL, IRENE, art educator; b. Askam Peely, Pa.; d. John Michel and Anna (Petruska) M. BS in Art cum laude, Kutztown U., 1954; MS in Art, Pa. State U., 1959, DEd in Art, 1968. Tchr. art, supr. Alfred I. duPont Sch., Wilmington, Del., 1954-55, Hanover Twp. Sch. Dist., Lee Park, Pa., 1955-61; instr. Pa. State U., Scranton, 1967-69; prof. art East Stroudsburg (Pa.) U., 1961—, chmn. art dept., 1968-72, 82-86; instr. art Jewish Community Ctr., Wilkes-Barre, Pa., 1956-61, Playground Recratin Ctr., Wilkes-Barre, 1957-61. Mem. Nat. Art Edn. Assn., Pa. Art Edn. Assn., Eastern Arts Assn., Internat. Soc. Edn. Through Art, Kappa Delta Pi. Home: 148 Marguerite St East Stroudsburg PA 18301-2711 also: 728 Hazle St Ashley PA 18706

MITCHELL, ALICE ANN, personnel administrator; b. Plainfield, N.J., Mar. 10, 1956; d. John D. and Dorothy M. (Maier) M. BMus, Heidelberg Coll., 1978; MA, Bowling Green State U., 1982. Admissions counselor Heidelberg Coll., Tiffin, Ohio, 1978-80; residence hall dir. Ohio Northern U., Ada, 1980-82; career counselor Allegheny Coll., Meadville, Pa., 1982-89; student devel. educator Longwood Coll., Farmville, Va., 1989-90; doctoral fellow U. Md., College Park, 1990—. Contbr. articles to profl. jours. Mem. Am. Coll. Personnel Assn. (dir. commn. IX 1990—, govtl. rels. liaison 1991—, ethics and profl. practice com. 1991—), Nat. Assn. Student Personnel Adminstrs., Am. Edn!. Rsch. Assn., Am. Assn. Higher Edn. Office: U Md 3214 Benjamin Bldg College Park MD 20742

MITCHELL, ANDREA, journalist; b. N.Y.C., Oct. 30, 1946; d. Sydney and Cecile Mitchell. B.A., U. Pa., 1967. Polit. reporter KYW Newsradio, Phila., 1967-76; polit. corr. Sta. KYW-TV, Phila., 1972-76; corr. Sta. WTOP-TV, Washington, 1977-78; gen. assignment and energy corr. NBC News, Washington, 1978-81; White House corr. NBC News, 1981-88, chief congl. corr., 1989—; instr. Gt. Lakes Colls. Assn., 1974-76; co-anchor Summer Sunday, USA, NBC-TV News, 1984, substitute anchor Meet the Press, 1988—. Overseer Coll. Arts and Scis. U. Pa., 1989—. Recipient award for public affairs reporting Am. Polit. Sci. Assn., 1969, Public Affairs Reporting award AP, 1976; AP Broadcast award, 1977; named Communicator of the Yr., Phila. chpt. Women in Communications, 1976, Woman of the Yr., Phila. chpt. Am. Women in Radio and TV, 1989. Mem. Sigma Delta Chi (award for broadcast reporting Phila. chpt. 1975). Club: Nat. Press, White House Corrs. Assn. Office: 4001 Nebraska Ave NW Washington DC 20016-2795*

MITCHELL, BRENDA K., secretary of the Commonwealth of Pennsylvania; married; 1 child, Corrie Nelson. BA, Fordham U., 1973; MA in Urban Affairs, Hunter Coll., 1974; PhD in Pub. Adminstrn., Nova U., 1981. Dir. community econ. revitalization project City Ventures Corp., 1980-83; bus. mgr. Control Data Corp. Bus. Tech. Ctr., 1983-87; spl. asst. to gov., dep. sec. for policy, planning, adminstrn. and program mgmt. Dept. of Commerce, Pa., since 1987; now sec. of the Commonwealth of Pa. Pa. Dept. of State; alternate rep. Appalachian Regional Commn., Washington; gov.'s liaison Dept. of Community Affairs, Labor and Industry; mem. Gov.'s Adv. Commn. on African Am. Affairs. Former v.p. Phila. Regional Port Authority, West Parkside Phila. Bus. Assn.; co-founder. former v.p. Nat. Forum for Black Pub. Adminstrs.; former bd. dirs. West Phila. c. of C., Ben Franklin Partnership Advanced Tech. Ctr. for Southeastern Pa., Phila. Fund Community Devel.; former trustee United Way of Southeastern Pa. Office: PA State Dept N Office Bldg Harrisburg PA 17120

MITCHELL, CAROL ANN, lawyer; b. New Bedford, Mass., Sept. 2, 1957; d. John E. and Edith A. (Mogensen) M. AB, Vassar Coll., 1979; JD, William and Mary Coll., 1982. Bar: D.C. 1983, U.S. Ct. Appeals (Fed. cir.) 1988, U.S. Ct. Internat. Trade 1986. Atty.-advisor Benefits Rev. Bd., Washington, 1982-83; import compliance specialist Internat. Trade Adminstrn. U.S. Dept. Commerce, Washington, 1983-85; assoc. Collier, Shannon & Scott, Washington, 1985-90, Akin, Gump, Strauss, Hauer & Feld, Washington, 1990-91, Dewey, Ballantine, Washington, 1991—. Mem. ABA, Women in Internat. Trade, Vassar Club. Office: Dewey Ballantine 1775 Pennsylvania Ave NW Washington DC 20006

MITCHELL, CHARLES ARCHIE, financial planning consultant, engineer; b. Kodia Kanal, Madras, India, May 3, 1926; came to U.S., 1932; s. Charles Archie and Ethel Blanche (Nutter) M.; m. Betty Louise Johnson, June 15, 1947; children: Cynthia E., Charles Archie Jr., Susan L. BSEE, Worcester (Mass.) Poly. Inst., 1946; MBA, Harvard U., 1954; cert., Coll. of Fin. Planning, 1974. Sales engr. Johnson Steel & Wire Co., Worcester, 1947-50; dist. sales mgr. GE, Plainville, Conn., 1954-61; v.p. mktg. Dictograph Co., Danbury, Conn., 1962-63; dir. corp. planning GCA Corp., Bedford, Mass., 1963-65; div. mgr. Polaroid Corp., Cambridge, Mass., 1965-66; rep. Hayden Stone, Inc., Boston, 1966-69; div. mgr. Westamerica Fin. Corp., Boston, 1971-77; officer, dir. MHA Mgmt. Corp., Braintree, Mass., 1977-89; pres., dir. Mitchell Fin. Corp., Falmouth, Mass., 1989—. Contbr. articles to profl. jours. Instr. Northeastern U., Boston, 1962-66, Mass. Dept. of Edn., Cambridge, 1966-69. Lt. USN, 1943-47, Korea. Mem. Internat. Assn. Fin. Planners (treas., bd. dirs. 1975-76), Inst. Cert. Fin. Planners (ea. v.p. nat. bd. dirs. 1974-79), Nat. Assn. Life Underwriters, Cape Cod Estate Planning Coun., Cape Cod Curling Club, Woods Hole Golf Club, Woods Hole Yacht Club, Masons, Shriners. Office: PO Box 550 Falmouth MA 02541-0550

MITCHELL, CHARLES HILL, farmer, tax consultant; b. Wilmington, Del., May 11, 1924; s. Henry Burton and Florence Sparks (Hill) M.; m. Cecilia Ann King, June 27, 1953; children: Linda Ann, Charles William II, John Burton. Student, U. Del., 1942, 45-48. Mgr. Mission Feed Co., Millsboro, Del., 1948-53; farmer Millsboro, Del., 1948—, tax cons., 1948—; chmn. adv. bd. So. States Br. Brasure & Smith, Millsboro, 1954-55. Bd. dirs. Selective Svc. System, 1989—; sec.-treas. Millsboro Pub. Libr., 1976; dist. chmn. Del-mar-va coun. Boy Scouts Am., 1986-91, mem. exec. bd., 1986—; active Grace United Meth. Ch., Little League; pres. Millsboro PTA, 1965; pres. bd. edn. Indian River Sch. Dist., Frankford, Del., 1966-86; pres. Del. Sch. Bds. Assn., 1982, Dover, Del.; bd. dirs. Sussex County Vocat.-Tech. Sch. Dist., Georgetown, Del., 1986—. With U.S. Army, 1942-45. Recipient Disting. Svc. award Del. Sch. Bds. Assn., 1987, Order of Merit award Boy Scouts Am., 1978, Silver Beaver award 1982, Legion of Honor award Chapel of Four Chaplains, 1991; named Vol. of Yr. Little League, State of Del., 1991. Mem. Disabled Am. Vets. (Disting. Svc. award 1977), Scouting Heritage Soc., U.S. Naval Acad. Athletic Assn., American Legion, Sussex Pines Country Club, Sigma Nu. Democrat. Home and Office: Rt 24 W PO Box 456 Millsboro DE 19966

MITCHELL, DAVID FRISCH, environmental scientist; b. Wilmington, Del., Dec. 28, 1953; s. John Young Stock and Mary Elizabeth (Frisch) M.; m. Carol Ellen Bolduan, Sept. 24, 1988; 1 child, Matthew David. BA, Brandeis U., 1975; MS, U. Oreg., 1979; PhD, Cornell U., 1986. Cert. profl. lake and reservoir mgr. Cons. Ichthyologicla Assocs., Ithaca, N.Y., 1985-86; sr. scientist Baystate Environ. Cons., East Longmeadow, Mass., 1986-88, assoc., 1988-91; environ. mgr. Battelle Meml. Inst., Windsor, Conn., 1991—; adj. prof. Springfield (Mass.) Coll., 1986—; invited lectr. Cornell U., Holyoke Community Coll., Springfield Coll., others, 1984-90; reviewer ecology program NSF, Washington, 1987-89; trainer workshop Mass. Congress of Lake & Pond Assns., Worcester, Mass., 1987-88; workshop developer Con-Test, East Longmeadow, Mass., 1991. Author: (with others) Lake and Pond Management, 1990; editor: Recreational Ponds, 1991; contbr. articles to profl. jours. Campaign worker Robert Markel Mayoral Campaign, Springfield, 1991. Faculty fellow Cornell U., 1984-85; grantee Andrew W. Mellon Found., 1982, Nat. sigma Xi., 1982, 83. Mem. Am Soc. Limnology and Oceanography, N.Am. Lake Mgmt. Soc., Nat. Assn. Environ. Profls., Soc. Wetland Scientists. Democrat. Office: Battelle Meml Inst 1 Univac Ln Windsor CT 06095

MITCHELL, ELLEN CLABAUGH, investment executive; b. Omaha, Mar. 2, 1942; d. Joseph Franklin and Dorothy (Newton) Carpenter; m. Dixon L. Mitchell, Aug. 25, 1962; 1 child, Lara Ellen. BS in Fin. & Econs., U. Nebr., Omaha, 1965; MBA, Va. Poly. Inst., 1983. Chartered Fin. Analyst. Asst. v.p. Firstier Fin., Omaha, 1965-69, 1971-75; asst. v.p. Bridges Investments, Omaha, 1970-71; analyst U.S. Securities and Exchange Commn., Washington, 1983-85; v.p. Nat. Bank of Washington, 1985-87, Foxhall Investment Mgmt., Washington, 1987—. Mem. Washington Soc. Investment Analysts, Inst. Chartered Fin. Analysts, Garden Club (v.p., treas. 1980). Episcopalian. Home: 2017 Turtle Pond Dr Reston VA 22091-4045 Office: Foxhall Investment Mgmt 815 Connecticut Ave NW Washington DC 20006-4004

MITCHELL, ERIC IGNATIUS, orthopedic surgeon; b. Washington, Aug. 1, 1948; s. Ignatius and Pearlene (Jackson) M.; m. Norma Alicia Romero, Nov. 26, 1983; children: Justin Ignatius, Marcus Alexander. BS, St. Joseph's U., 1971; MD, U. Pa., 1974. Cert. Arthroscopy Bd. N.Am. (bd. dirs. 1989—). Rotating internship Phila. Gen. Hosp., 1974-75; fellowship in orthopaedic research Pa. Sch. Medicine, Phila., 1975-76; resident in orthopaedic surgery Hosp. U. Pa., Phila., 1976-79, fellowship in sports medicine program dept. orthopaedic surgery, 1979-80; practice medicine in orthopaedic surgery, sports medicine Phila., Camden, N.J., 1980—; preceptor med. student program The Hahnemann Med. Coll. and Hosp., Phila., Temple U. Sch. Medicine, Phila., 1982—, McCarrie Schs. Health Scis. and Tech., Phila., 1984—, Hosp. U. Pa., 1987—; instr. Hahnemann Med. Coll. and Hosp., 1983—; sports medicine subcom. Gov.'s Council Physical Fitness and Sports, 1979-82; east coast cons. Pop Warner Football, Phila., 1981—; orthopaedic cons. to State Surgeon Gen., Pa. Army NG, 1984—; team physician and drug testing chief, Athletics Congress of USA, Indpls., 1985—; physician Olympic Tng. Ctr., Colorado Springs, Colo., 1988. Bd. dirs. Urban League Pa., 1970-74, 89—; trustee Easter Seal Soc., Phila., 1981-84; mem. pres.'s coun. St. Joseph's U., Phila., 1982-86, bd. dirs. 1986—; chmn. Sports Medicine Div. Franklin Sq. Hosp., 1992. Mem. Keystone State Med. Soc. (pres. 1983-85), Med. Soc. Ea. Pa. (pres. 1984-86, outstanding service award), Shaffrey Med. Soc. (pres. 1985-86), Student Nat. Med. Assn. (sec. 1972-73), D. Hayes Agnew Surg. Soc. (pres. 1972-74). Roman Catholic. Office: Franklin Sq Hosp 5th Fl 201 N 8th St 2115 South S Philadelphia PA 19106

MITCHELL, GEORGE FREDERICK, association executive; b. N.Y.C., Oct. 18, 1937; s. Joseph Michael and Ruth Ann (McEvoy) M.; m. Lorraine Wanda Nalwak, Nov. 3, 1962; children: Michael A., Susan A., Karen L., Kathleen A. BS, Syracuse U., 1970; postgrad., Boston U., 1971. Cert. assn. exec. Asst. mgr. underwriting Utica (N.Y.) Mut. Ins. Co., 1962-68; dir. pub. rels. and publs. Soc. Chartered Property and Casualty Underwriters, Media, Pa., 1971-75; exec. dir., treas. Northeastern Loggers' Assn., Old Forge, N.Y., 1976—; mem. regional adv. bd. Norstar Bank of Utica, 1985—; dir. Am. Hardwood Export Coun., Washington, 1986—; guardian Nat. Fedn. Ind. Bus. N.Y., Albany, 1986—. Contbr. articles to trade jours. Trustee, treas. Old Forge (N.Y.) Libr. Assn., 1978-86; mem., pres. Sch. Bd., Town of Webb Union Free Sch. Dist., Old Forge, 1979-87. With USAF, 1956-62. Mem. Nat. Coun. Forestry Assn. Execs. (pres. 1989-90), Am. Soc. Assn. Execs., Nat. Assn. Expo Mgrs., N.Y. Forest Owners' Assn. (dir., membership ssec. 1980-86). Roman Catholic. Office: Northeastern Loggers Assn PO Box 69 Old Forge NY 13420-0069

MITCHELL, GEORGE JOHN, lawyer, senator; b. Waterville, Maine, Aug. 20, 1933; s. George J. and Mary (Saad) M.; 1 child, Andrea. B.A., Bowdoin Coll., 1954; LL.B., Georgetown U., 1960. Bar: Maine 1960, D.C. 1960. Trial atty. anti-trust div. U.S. Dept. Justice, Washington, 1960-62; exec. asst. Senator Edmund Muskie, 1962-65; ptnr. Jensen, Baird, Gardner & Henry, Portland, Maine, 1965-77; U.S. atty. Maine, 1977-79; U.S. dist. judge, 1979-80, U.S. senator from Maine, 1980—, mem. environ. and pub. works com., 1980—, mem. vet. affairs com., fin. com., 1981—, mem. nat. ocean policy study group, arms control observer group, ex officio mem. intelligence com.; elected majority leader U.S. Senate, Washington, 1988—; chmn. Dem. Senatorial Campaign Com., 1984-86; chmn. Maine Democratic Com., 1966-68; nat. committeeman, Maine, 1968-77; asst. county atty. Cumberland County, 1971. Served with U.S. Army, 1954-56. Office: US Senate 176 Russell Senate Bldg Washington DC 20510

MITCHELL, JAMES EDWIN, architect, educator; b. N.Y.C., July 27, 1942; s. Edward Elbert Mitchell and Marian Tompkins (Cowles) Botsford; m. Catherine Fairbank, Aug. 28, 1963; 1 child, Natasha. BA cum laude, Harvard U., 1965, MS, 1967; MArch, U. Pa., 1973. Registered architect, Pa., N.J., N.Y. Staff architect Robert Gorman, Architect, Phila., 1974-75; assoc. dir. Ednl. Futures, Inc., Phila., 1975-76; assoc. Robert D. Lynn Assoc. Architects, Phila., 1976-79; prin. James E. Mitchell, AIA, Phila., 1979-81; founding ptnr. Jordan, Mitchell, Inc., Phila., 1981-88; assoc. prof. Drexel U., Phila., 1988—, interim dept. head civil and archtl. engring., 1991-92, assoc. dean for undergrad. affairs Coll. of Engring., 1992—. Prin. works include Ctr. for Study of Adult Devel., 1979, Columbia Med. Ctr., 1983, Spring Garden Health Ctr., 1984, TJo Sports Medicine Ctr., 1988. Bd. dirs. Better Bus. Bur. Phila., 1987-88, The Phila. Sch., 1985—. With USPHS, 1987-89. Mem. AIA (treas. Phila. chpt. 1982-84), ASHRAE, ASCE, Nat. Soc. Archtl. Engrs. (charter), Constrn. Specifications Inst., Am. Soc. Engring. Edn. Office: Drexel U Dept Civil & Archtl Engring Philadelphia PA 19104

MITCHELL, JAMES NICOLA, manufacturing executive; b. Libby, Mont., Aug. 4, 1931; s. James and Bessie Ella (Heppe) M.; m. Marianne Peters, Sept. 21, 1952; children: James Nicola Jr., Monty Richard. BA in Bus., U. Wash., 1953; MBA, U. Oreg., 1969. Traffic supr. Gen. Mills., Inc., Tacoma, Wash., 1953-56; distbn. supr. Crown Zellerbach Corp., Portland, Oreg., 1956-62; v.p. distbn. P & E Tool Co., Milwaukie, Oreg., 1962-68; pres. Proto Tools of Can., Ltd., London, Ont., Can., 1968-72; nat. sales mgr. Proto Tool Co., L.A., 1971-72; pres. Millers Falls Co., S. Deerfield, Mass., 1972-80, Milford Products Corp., Branford, Conn., 1980—; bd. dirs. Deerfield (Mass.) Plastics Co., Prototype Plastic Mold Co., Middletown, Conn., Milford Saws Ltd., Banbury, Eng. Commr. police Town of Madison, Conn., 1990-91. Mem. Am. Supply and Machinery Mfrs. Assn. (pres. 1988, bd. dirs. 1985-91), Quinnipiack Club. Republican. Lutheran. Office: Milford Products Corp 30 Thompson Rd Branford CT 06405-2842

MITCHELL, JEFFREY THOMAS, emergency health educator; b. Bklyn., Oct. 19, 1948; s. Loren Pierce and Rita (O'Rourke) M. BA, St. Mary's Sem., Balt., 1971; MS, Loyola Coll., Balt., 1975, cert., 1977; PhD, U. Md., 1983. Tchr. Our Lady of Victory Sch., Balt., 1971-74; regional coord. Md. Inst. for Emergency Med. Svcs., Balt., 1974-79; instr. dept. emergency health svcs. U. Md., Catonsville, 1980-83, asst. prof., 1983-90, clin. assoc. prof., 1990—; therapist Adult and Child Counseling Ctr., Balt., 1978-82, Psych Assocs., Balt., 1980-83; paramedic, fire fighter Arbutus (Md.) Vol. Fire Dept., 1972-79; cons. in field, 1983—. Author: Emergency Services Stress, 1990, Emergency Response to Crisis, 1981; directed videotapes on Critical Incident Stress and Disaster Psychology, 1985. Democrat. Roman Catholic. Office: Am Critical Incident Stress PO Box 204 Ellicott City MD 21041-0204

MITCHELL, JOHN DAVID, journalism educator; b. Chgo., Jan. 22, 1924; m. Mila Agnes Johnston, Sept. 12, 1947 (div. 1981); children: Justin, Alexandra. AB, Oberlin Coll., 1950; MS in Journalism, Kans. State U., 1959. Reporter/desk man Rockford Morning Star, Ill., 1950-52, Lima News, Ohio, 1952-56; temp. instr. Kans. State U., 1956-58; asst. prof., assoc. prof. Univ. Colo., 1958-73; mag. dept. acting chair Newhouse Sch., Syracuse Univ., N.Y., 1973-79; newspaper dept. chair Newhouse Sch., Syracuse Univ., 1973-83, journalism div. acting asst. dean, 1980-81, journalism prof., 1983—; Fulbright lectr. Thammasat Univ., Bangkok, 1962-63; exec. sec. N.Y. State Soc. of Newspaper Editors, Syracuse, 1973-80. Co-author: (book) Mass Communication Resources in Thailand, 1965; contbr. articles to profl. jours. Mem. Assn. for Edn. in Journalism and Mass Communication (charter mem. newspaper div., head 1976-79, minorities and communications div. charter mem., sec. 1977-79), Soc. Profl. Journalists, Syracuse Press Club (Svc. award 1984). Democrat. Home: 101 Sun Harbor Dr Liverpool NY 13088-4323 Office: Syracuse U Newhouse Sch Syracuse NY 13244

MITCHELL, JOHN DIETRICH, theatre arts institute executive; b. Rockford, Ill., Nov. 3, 1917; s. John Dennis Royce and Dora Marie (Schroeder) M.; m. Miriam Pitcairn, Aug. 25, 1956; children: John Daniel, Lorenzo Theodore, Barbarina Mitchell Heyerdahl. BSS, Northwestern U., 1939, MA, 1941; EdD, Columbia U., 1956; HHD (hon.), Northwood Inst., 1986. Dir., producer Am. Broadcasting Co., N.Y.C., 1942-46; assoc. editor Samuel French, Publ., N.Y.C., 1946-48; assoc. prof. Manhattan Coll., N.Y.C., 1948-58; pres. Inst. for Advanced Studies in the Theatre Arts, N.Y.C., 1958—; bd. dirs. Beneficia Found., Jenkintown, Pa.; trustee Northwood Inst., Midland, Mich., 1972-91. Mem. Players Club (N.Y.), Nippon Club (N.Y.), N.Y. Athletic Club. Home: 703 Eaton St Key West FL 33040 Office: Inst for Advanced Studies in Theatre 12 West End Ave #304 New York NY 10023

MITCHELL, KEITH PHILLIP, electrical engineer; b. Balt., Oct. 7, 1944; s. Phillip Francis and Sarah Estelle (Streett) M.; m. Mary Ann Mays, Apr. 23, 1983. BSEE, Johns Hopkins U., 1978, MS in Computer Sci., 1983, MSEE, 1986. Registered profl. engr., Md., Pa. Broadcast engr. WCBC-FM, Catonsville, Md., 1964-65; sr. lab. tech. Comsat Labs., Clarksburg, Md., 1969-72; project engr. Gen. Instrument Corp., Hunt Valley, Md., 1972-80; dir. sys. engring. Electronic Modules Corp., Hunt Valley, 1980-87; sr. engr. Noise Cancellation Tech., Columbia, Md., 1987—. With U.S. Army, 1965-69. Mem. Audio Engring. Soc., Am. Legion, Am. Radio Relay League. Home: 138 E Nicodemus Rd Westminster MD 21157-7514 Office: Noise Cancellation Tech 1015 W Nursery Rd Linthicum Heights MD 21090-1200

MITCHELL, LOUIS LIVINGSTON, consortium executive; b. Bronxville, N.Y., Mar. 12, 1930. BA in History and Sociology, Columbia U., 1953; MA in Theology, Va. Theol. Sem., 1958. Ordained to ministry Episcopal Ch., 1958. Clergyman N.Y. State, 1958-60, Birmingham, Ala., 1960-63; so. field rep. U.S. Commn. on Civil Rights, 1963-65; dep. regional dir. for North Africa, Near East, South Asia U.S. Peace Corps, 1965-69; country dir. U.S. Peace Corps, Afghanistan, 1969-73; sr. mgmt. advisor to prime ministry Govt. of Afghanistan, 1973-77; pres. TransCentury Corp., Arlington, Va., 1977-88; chief exec. officer Pvt. Agys. Collaborating Together, Inc., Washington, 1989—. Capt. USMC, 1953-58. Office: PACT Ste 501 1901 Pennsylvania Ave NW Washington DC 20006

MITCHELL, MYRON JAMES, ecologist, educator; b. Denver, Apr. 11, 1947; s. James Walter and Lillian Constance (Mack) M.; m. Deborah Gabel, Apr. 7, 1973; children: Charlotte Angele, Michael James. BA, Lake Forest Coll., 1969; PhD, U. Calgary, Alberta, Can., 1974. Post-doctoral fellow U. British Columbia, Vancouver, Can., 1974-75; asst. prof. Coll. Environ. Sci. & Forestry SUNY, Syracuse, N.Y., 1975-82; assoc. prof. Coll. Environ. Sci. & Forestry SUNY, Syracuse, 1982-84, prof., 1984—; vis. scholar, U. Calgary, Alberta, Can., 1983. Editor: (book) Microfloral and Faunal Interactions; contbr. 100 articles to profl. jours. Recipient Undergrad. Rsch. scholarship, Nat. Sci. Found., Oak Ridge, Tenn., 1968, Fulbright Travel fellowship, New Zealand, 1983-84. Fellow AAAS; mem. Nat. Sci. Found. (ecology panel), Upstate Freshwater Inst. N.Y., (bd. dirs.), Ecol. Soc. Am., British Ecol. Soc., Soil Sci. Soc. Am. Democrat. Episcopalian. Home: 100 Woodberry Ln Fayetteville NY 13066-1746 Office: SUNY Coll Environ Sci Forestry 1 Forestry Dr Syracuse NY 13210-2778

MITCHELL, PETER KENNETH, JR., educational association administrator; b. Bklyn., June 12, 1949; s. Peter Kenneth and Joan Marie (Hayes) M.; m. Susan Veitch Mitchell, June 25, 1983; 1 child, Elyse Alexandra. BA, SUNY, Geneseo, 1970; MS in French, L.I. U., 1975; cert. of French lang. proficiency, U. de Neuchatel, Switzerland, 1969. Tchr. French and Spanish Middle Country Sch. Dist., Selden, N.Y., 1972-81; tech. asst. to dir. internat. affairs dept. Am. Fedn. Tchrs., Washington, 1981-82; asst. to gen. sec. Internat. Fedn. of Free Tchrs. Unions, Amsterdam, 1982-90; exec. dir. Internat. Reading Assn., Newark, Del., 1990-91; owner Insights Out Assocs., Newark, Del., 1992—. Del. Dem. Nat. Conv., N.Y.C., 1980. Mem. ACLU, Am. Edn1. Rsch. Assn., Am. Soc. of Assn. Execs., N.Y. State United Tchrs., Washington U. Club. Office: Insights Out Assocs PO Box 9652 Newark DE 19714-9652

MITCHELL, PHILIP MICHAEL, aerospace engineer, air force officer; b. Mobile, Ala., Feb. 12, 1953; s. Philip Augustus and Betty J. (Hardy) M. BS in Aeros. magna cum laude, Embry-Riddle Aero. U., Daytona Beach, Fla., 1980, MS in Aeros., 1987. Radar systems engr. ITT, Van Nuys, Calif., 1980-82; commd. 2d lt. USAF, 1982, advanced through grades to capt., 1986; bomber br. chief 42d Orgnl. Maintenance Squadron, Loring AFB, Maine, 1983-86; officer-in-charge weapons br. 520th Aircraft Generation Squadron, RAF Upper Heyford, Eng., 1986; asst. maintenance supr. 20th Equipment Maintenance Squadron, RAF, RAF Upper Heyford, 1986-87, 88-90; weapons safety officer 20th Tactical Fighter Wing, RAF Upper Heyford, 1986-87; chief standardization and tng. div. 42d Bomb Wing, Loring AFB, 1990-91; maintenance supr. 42d Maintenance Squadron, Loring AFB, Maine, 1991—; adj. prof. European div. Embry-Riddle Aero. U., 1988-90; aerospace cons., 1987—. Fellow Brit. Interplanetary Soc.; mem. AIAA (sr.), Air Force Assn., Royal Scottish County Dance Soc. Anglican. Home: 3690 River Rd Caribou ME 04736-1741 Office: 42d Maintenance Squadron/LGMS PO Box 505 Loring AFB ME 04751-0505

MITCHELL, RICHARD BOYLE, advertising executive; b. St. Louis, June 20, 1947; s. Samuel West and Blair (Boyle) M.; m. Deborah Mead Boas, June 1, 1968; children: Rebecca, Jessica. BS in Mktg., NYU, 1969. Account exec. D.L. Blair Corp., N.Y.C., 1967-70, NW Ayer Advt. Agy., N.Y.C., 1970-74; sr. account exec. Ted Bates Agy., N.Y.C., 1974-75; sr. v.p. DKG Advt., N.Y.C., 1975-81, McCaffrey/McCall, N.Y.C., 1981-86; pres., CEO Marshall Jaccoma Mitchell Advt., N.Y.C., 1986—. Commr. Wilton (Conn.) Police Dept., 1984—. Served with USAR, 1969-75. Democrat. Roman Catholic. Club: Wilton Riding. Home: 43 Collinswood Rd Wilton CT 06897-1811 Office: Marshall Jaccoma Mitchell Advt 41 Madison Ave 32d Fl New York NY 10010

MITCHELL, ROSS EDOUARD, systems consultant, consumer electronics executive; b. Rockville Centre, N.Y., Jan. 28, 1952; s. Martin Jacob and Anita (Zeman) Berman; m. Mary Eleanor Fussa, May 21, 1980; children: Joseph, Melissa. Grad. high sch., Elwood, N.Y., 1969. Ops. supr. Call-A-Computer, Melville, N.Y., 1969-70; cons. Gen. Time Share, Brussels, 1970-73, Line Data, Paris, 1974-78; producer The Fantasticks, Paris, 1978; owner, cons. Systems Cons., Newton, Mass., 1979—; pres. Acclimator Time Corp., Newton, 1991—. Patentee jet lag watch. Office: The Jet Lag Watch Co 1193 Walnut St Ste # 8 Newton MA 02161

MITCHELL, SALLY HAYDEN, English educator; b. San Antonio, Oct. 8, 1937; d. Gilbert and Marion (Comstock) Hayden. BA, U. Colo., 1959; MA, U. Wis., Milw., 1972; DPhil, Oxford U., Eng., 1977. Asst. then assoc. prof. Temple U., Phila., 1979-91, dir. Women's Studies, 1987-89, prof. English, 1991—. Author: The Fallen Angel, 1981, Dinah Mulock Craik, 1983; editor: Victorian Britain: An Encyclopedia, 1988. Fulbright scholar Oxford U., 1972-73; fellow Danforth Found. Oxford U., 1975-76. Fellow Soc. for Values in Higher Edn.; mem. Temple Assn. U. Profls. (v.p. 1987-91), Nat. Women's Studies Assn., Modern Lang. Assn., Rsch. Soc. Victorian Periodicals (pres. 1987-89). Office: Temple U English Dept Philadelphia PA 19122

MITCHELL, THOMAS EDWARD, personnel executive; b. Watertown, N.Y, Oct. 19, 1946; s. Harold Edward and Ann (Owen) M.; m. Judith Mary Jones, Sept. 19, 1970; children: Kelly Suzanne, Lindsay Ann. B. Indsl. and Labor Rels., Cornell U., 1969. Personnel interviewer/personnel adminstr. Mohawk Data Scis. Corp., Herkimer, N.Y., 1969-73; mgr. employment Sperry-Univac, Utica, N.Y., 1973-75; sr. personnel adminstr. Value Engring. Co., Alexandria, Va., 1976-78; employment rep., personnel mgr. Tracor Applied Scis., Inc., Groton, Conn., 1978—; treas. Southeastern Area Com. on Employment of Disabled, Groton, 1982—; dir. JWR Ent., Inc., Groton. Bd. dirs. Child & Family Agy. of Southeastern Conn., New London, 1989—, 1st v.p., 1992—; adv. bd. Easter Seal Rehab. Ctr. Southeastern Conn., Norwich, 1982—. Vol. of Yr., Inst. Human Resource Devel., Glastonbury, 1990. Mem. Ea. Conn. Pers. Assn. (treas. 1986-91, pres. 1991—), Lions (dir. 1988-90). Home: 1 Applewood Common East Lyme CT 06333-1444

MITCHELL, W. GARRY, management consultant; b. Medicine Hat, Alta., Mar. 22, 1938; came to U.S., 1964; s. Archibald Hugh and Isobel Lucille (Barber) M.; m. Valerie Nield, Dec. 16, 1967; 1 child, Heather McCall. BE, U. Alta., 1962; MA, CUNY, 1975; PhD, NYU, 1989. Broadcaster various cos., N.Y.C. and Can., 1958-80; tchr. Edmonton (Alta.) Pub. Schs., 1962-64; actor, performer N.Y.C., 1964-72, sales and mktg. various cos., 1972-76; prof. Nassau Community Coll., N.Y.C., 1976-82; pvt. practice mgmt. cons. N.Y.C., 1980—; cons. Am. Mgmt. Assn., worldwide, 1980—, Dun & Bradstreet, 1982—, Negotiation Inst., worldwide, 1988—, Standard & Poors, worldwide, 1988—. Author: The Trainer's Handbook, 1987, 2d revised edit., 1992, Heart of the Sale, 1991, (textbooks) How to Interview Effectively, 1982, Total Time Management, 1984, How to Motivate for Superior Performance, 1985. Mem. ASTD, N.Y. Acad. Sci., Internat. Soc. Gen. Semantics. Home and Office: 68 E 86th St New York NY 10028

MITCHELL, WALTER ROY, composer, arranger, consultant; b. Connellsville, Pa., Oct. 8, 1961; s. John Dale and Mary Louise (Kunkle) M.; m. Phyllis Anne Sander, Aug. 24, 1991. Student, Duquesne U., 1979-82; BA in Jazz Studies, Ind. U. Pa., 1989. Composer, arranger Indiana, 1989—; staff arranger Complex One Recording Studios, Indiana, 1987—. Composer jazz suite for tuba and jazz trio. Mem. Phi Mu Alpha Sinfonia. Home and Office: 4901 Lucerne Rd Indiana PA 15701

MITCHELL, WILLIAM ALEXANDER, food consultant; b. Raymond, Minn., Oct. 21, 1911; s. Ernst Michael and Florentina (Fletter) M.; m. Ruth Chilla Cobbey, Sept. 3, 1938; children: William, Charles, Michael, John Jan, Steven, Cheryl. BA, Nebr. Wesleyan U., 1935; MS, U. Nebr., 1938; DS (hon.), Nebr. Wesleyan U., 1980. High sch. sci. tchr. Belvidere, Nebr., 1935-36; chemist Experimental Sta., Univ. Nebr., Lincoln, 1937-38; organic chemist Eastman Kodak Co., Rochester, N.Y., 1939-41; project leader to rsch. scientist Gen. Foods Corp., Hoboken to Tarrytown, N.J., N.Y., 1941-76; pvt. practice, food cons. Lincoln Park, Shelburne, N.J., Vt., 1976—. Contb. articles to profl. jours.; patentee in field. Sch. bd. to v.p. Lincoln Park, 1953-61. Mem. Am. Chem. Soc., Cereal Chemist. Lutheran.

MITCHELL, WILLIAM GRAHAM CHAMPION, lawyer; b. Raleigh, Dec. 24, 1946; s. Burley Bayard and Dorothy Ford (Champion) M.; children: William Graham, Margaret Scripture. AB, U. N.C., 1969, JD with highest hons., 1975. Bar: N.C. 1975, U.S. Dist. Ct. (ea., mid. and we. dists.) N.C. 1976, U.S. Ct. Appeals (4th cir.) 1978. Ptnr. Womble, Carlyle, Sandridge & Rice, Winston-Salem, 1975-87; sr. v.p. for external affairs RJR Nabisco, Atlanta, 1987-89; exec. v.p. R.J. Reynolds Tobacco Co., Winston-Salem, 1988-89; ptnr. Howrey & Simon, Washington, 1990—. Contbr. articles to profl. jours. Mem. Pres.'s Export Coun., Washington, 1990-91, Pres.'s Adv. Com. on Trade Policy and Negotiations, Indsl. Policy Adv. Com., Washington, 1991—; mem. exec. com. Nat. Assn. Mfrs., Washington, 1988-89, Nat. Fgn. Trade Coun., 1988-89; chmn. Tobacco Inst., Washington, 1988-89; dir. Washington Performing Arts Soc., 1988—; vice chmn. Bush/Quayle 1992 Com. Lt. USN, 1969-72. Mem. ABA (vice chmn. antitrust sect., pvt. litigation com. 1987-89, chmn. subcom. of FTC com. 1986), Georgetown Club, City Club of Washington, Forsyth Country Club, Order of the Coif. Office: Howrey & Simon 1730 Pennsylvania Ave NW Washington DC 20006-4706

MITCHELL, WILLIAM PATRICK, anthropology educator, researcher; b. Bklyn., Aug. 30, 1937; s. Edward J. and Catherine (Dorsey) M.; children: Sean, Nick. BA, CUNY, 1961; PhD, U. Pitts., 1972. Asst. prof. anthropology Monmouth Coll., West Long Branch, N.J., 1968-73, assoc. prof., 1973-78, prof., 1978—, Freed prof. Social Sci., 1986—; chmn. seminar on ecol. systems Columbia U., N.Y.C., 1978-80; founding pres. Global Studies Consortium N.J. Colls. and Univs., Princeton, 1985-87; vis. prof. Cath. U., Lima, Peru, 1987-88. Author: Peasants on the Edge, 1991; co-editor: Irrigation at High Altitudes, 1992; assoc. editor Latin Am. Anthrop. Rev., 1988—. Trustee ACLU N.J., Newark, 1982-86, Monmouth People for Peace and Disarmament, Red Bank, N.J., 1991—. Summer grantee NEH, 1977, rsch. grantee NSF, 1983; Fulbright fellow, Lima, 1987-88. Fellow Am. Anthropol. Assn.; mem. N.Y. Acad. Scis. (vice-chmn., chmn. anthropology 1990—), Inst. Andean Studies, Phi Beta Kappa, Sigma Xi. Office: Monmouth Coll Anthropology Dept West Long Branch NJ 07764

MITMAN, STEWART PHIPARD, retired purchasing officer; b. Huntington, N.Y., Feb. 2, 1925; s. Samuel Thomas and Marie Louise (Phipard) M.; m. Anne Carruthers Cochrane, Aug. 15, 1953; children: Suzanne Marie, Nanette Louise, Lucille Anne. BSBA, Lehigh U., 1949. Cert. pub. purchasing officer. Engring. sales rep. Gen. Cable Corp., N.Y.C., 1949-59; dir. purchasing County of Suffolk, Riverhead, N.Y., 1960-72; adminstrv. officer grants Town of Huntington, N.Y., 1972-79; dir. purchasing SUNY, Stony Brook, 1979-88; ret., 1988; part-time instr. Nat. Inst. Govtl. Purchasing, Falls Church, Va., 1988—. Contbg. author: Public Purchasing and Materials Management, 1983. Flight officer USAAF, 1943-45, ATO. Mem. Nat. Inst. Govtl. Purchasing (bd. dirs. 1968-72,, 82-88, life mem., Disting. Svc. award 1990).

MITNICK, HAROLD, lawyer, mediator; b. Balt., Oct. 8, 1923; s. Henry and Adeline (Ehrlich) M.; children: Hilary D., Judith Sue. JD, U. Balt., 1952. Bar: Md. 1953, D.C. 1973; cert. effectiveness trainer, creative divorce instr. Title abstractor, 1949-53; sole practice, Bethesda, Md., 1953—; mediator family matters, 1970—; pres. Marital Mediation Service Agy., Inc.; vis. prof. Bowie State Coll.; tchr. creative divorce Montgomery Coll., Prince Georges Community Coll, George Mason U.; mediator Cir. Ct. Montgomery County. Former post comdr. VFW. Served with U.S. Army, 1943-46; ETO. Mem. Md. Bar Assn. (family and juvenile sect. mediator for alt. dispute resolution com.), ABA (family law sect., mediation and arbitration com.), D.C. (family law sect.), Montgomery County Bar Assn. (family law sect., arbitration com., discovery rev. com.). Author: How to Handle Your Divorce, Step by Step, 1981; contbr. articles to mags. Office: 8315 Frontwell Cir Gaithersburg MD 20879-4922

MITOFSKY, WARREN JAY, organization executive; b. N.Y.C., Sept. 17, 1934; s. Howard Bernard and Elsie (Sonderling) M.; m. Dolores Evelyn Kilgore, Sept. 17, 1956 (div. Sept. 1971); children: Bryan Dean, Elisa Lynn; m. Ronda Shaw Rubinoff, July 22, 1990. BS, Guilford Coll., 1957; postgrad., U. N.C., 1957-58, U. Minn., 1958-60, 62-64. Br. chief Census Bur., Washington, 1960-62, 64-67; exec. producer CBS News, N.Y.C., 1967-90; exec. dir. Voter Rsch. & Surveys, N.Y.C., 1990—; cons. Coll. Physicians and Surgeons, Columbia U., N.Y.C., 1970—, Fintec, N.Y.C., 1987—, Summit (N.J.) Analytics, 1991—. Editor: Campaign '76, 1977, Campaign '78, 1979, History of American Association for Public Opinion Research, 1992. Fellow Am. Statis. Assn.; mem. Am. Assn. Pub. Opinion Rsch. (pres. 1988-89), Nat. Coun. Pub. Polls (pres. 1981-84). Jewish. Office: Voter Rsch & Surveys 533 W 57th St New York NY 10019

MITORAJ, SUZANNE OGORZALEK, English educator; b. Middletown, Conn., June 19, 1945; d. Stanley Joseph and Regina (Lojewski) Ogorzalek; m. Steven Edward Mitoraj, June 17, 1967. BA, U. Hartford, 1967; MA, Trinity Coll., Hartford, Conn., 1971; Cert. of Advanced Study, Wesleyan U., Middletown, 1980; PhD, U. Conn., 1991. Cert. ednl. adminstr., English tchr. English tchr. Bd. Edn., Wallingford, Conn., 1967-75; adj. instr. U. Conn., Storrs, 1975—; chair English dept. Bd. Edn., Wallingford, 1975—; site researcher U. Conn., Storrs, 1986, 87, 90; critical reviewer Harcourt Brace Jovanovich, Orlando, Fla., 1980-84; doctoral rsch. fellow U. Conn., 1989. Co-author: Elements of Literature Teacher's Guide, 1989. Bd. dirs. Briar Bank Assocs., Ogunquit, Maine, 1991, Mattabasset Condominiums, Meriden, Conn., 1983-86. Mem. ASCD, NEA, Nat. Coun. Tchrs. English, New Eng. Assn. Tchrs. English, Conn. Coun. Tchrs. English, Conn. Heads of English Depts. (pres. 1989—), Phi Delta Kappa. Democrat. Home: 64 Mattabasset Dr Meriden CT 06450-7431 Office: Sheehan High Sch 142 Hope Rd Wallingford CT 06492

MITRA, SHASHANKA SHEKHAR, electrical engineering educator; b. Calcutta, India, Oct. 19, 1933; came to U.S., 1955; s. Khagendra N. and Labanya P. (Buxy); m. Sheila M. Milton, June 15, 1960 (div. 1975); children: Nila, Shaibal. BS, U. Allahabad, India, 1951, MS, 1953; PhD, U. Mich., 1957. Corning Found. fellow U. Mich., Ann Arbor, 1955-57; postdoctoral fellow Nat. Rsch. Coun., Ottawa, Ont., Can., 1957-59; sr. rsch. fellow U. Allahabad, 1959-60; rsch. scientist Ont. Rsch. Found., 1960-62; sr. rsch. scientist IIT Rsch. Inst., Chgo., 1962-66; prof. elec. engring. U. R.I., Kingston, 1966—; co. dir. R.I. Ctr. for Thin Film & Interface Rsch., Kingston, 1988—; dir. Advanced Study Inst., NATO, Freiburg, Germany, 1966, Delft, The Netherlands, 1968, 70, U. R.I., 1974; vis. scientist Lab. Haute Pression, Bellevue, France, 1972-73; chmn. Intewrnat. Conf. Optical Properties of Highly Transparent Solids, Waterville Valley, N.H., 1975, also others; disting. vis. prof. Indian Inst. Sci., Bangalore, 1984-85; cons. Argonne Nat. Labs. Editor: Optical Property of Solids, 1969, Far Infrared Property of Solids, 1970, Physics of Structurally Disordered Solids, 1976, Fiber Optics, Advances in Research and Development, 1979, Physics of Fiber Optics, 1981; contbr. over 250 articles to profl. jours. Mem. Dem. exec. com., South Kingstown, R.I., 1985—. Grantee NSF. Fellow Am. Phys. Soc., Optical Soc. Am.; mem. IEEE (sr.), AAUP (pres. R.I. chpt. 1980-82), Lions Club (sec. 1987-89, chair raffle 1987-89). Home: 108 Biscuit City Rd Kingston RI 02881-1632 Office: U RI Kingston RI 02881

MITSCHELE, MICHAEL DOUGLAS, concrete and aggregate company executive; b. Orange, N.J., May 15, 1956; s. Herbert James Jr. and Joyce Francis (Weber) M.; m. Elaine June Sperun, Dec. 13, 1975; children: Melissa, Dawn, Daniel. Student, Seton Hall Coll., South Orange, N.J., 1974, 75. Owner Mitchele's Stables, Livingston, N.J., 1971-77, North Jersey Auto Ent., Parsippany, N.J., 1976-78; ops. mgr. Robert J. Baer, Inc., Roseland, N.J., 1975-82; chief operating officer Robert J. Baer, Inc., 1982-87, pres., 1987—; pres. Baer Aggregates, Inc., Carpentersville, N.J., 1986—; chmn. N.J. Concrete Awards, 1985, 86; mem. adv. coun. The Summit Trust Co., Roseland, N.J., 1987—; pres. Odd-A-See Enterprise, 1991—. Vice chmn. Roseland Recreation Com., 1981-86, soccer coach, 1990, 91; chmn. bd. Roseland First Aid Squad, 1987-88, 91—; bd. dirs. Nat. Truck Wt. Adv. Coun., 1988—. Mem. N.J. Concrete & Aggregate Assn. (charter bd. dirs. 1989), Am. Concrete Inst., U.S. C. of C., N.J. Bus. and Ind. Assn., N.J. State Police Col.'s Club, Rotary (pres. 1986-87, gov.'s rep. 1988-89, Paul Harris fellow 1987, 89, chmn. dist. 747 conf. 1991). Republican. Roman Catholic. Office: Robert J Baer Inc 117 Harrison Ave Roseland NJ 07068-1218

MITTERMEIER, RUSSELL ALAN, conservation executive, educator; b. N.Y., Nov. 8, 1949; children: John, Michael. AB summa cum laude, Dartmouth Coll., 1971; MA in Biol. Anthropology, Harvard U., 1973, PhD in Biol. Anthropology, 1977. Teaching asst. dept. anthropology Dartmouth Coll., 1971; teaching fellow dept. anthropology Harvard U., 1972-73; conservation assoc. N.Y. Zool. Soc., 1976-77, fellow in primate ecology, 1977-79; adj. asst. prof. dept. anat. scis. SUNY, Stony Brook, 1977-83, adj. assoc. prof. dept. anat. scis., 1983-90, adj. prof. dept. anat. scis., 1990—; adj. asst. prof. dept. anthropology SUNY-Stony Brook, 1983—; pres. Conservation Internat., 1989—; bd. advisors Primarily Primates, Inc., Belize Zoo; mem. sci. adv. bd. FUNATURA, Brazil, 1986—, The Digit Fund, 1986-89; mem. sci. coun. Peruvian Conservation Found., 1985—; cons. Internat. Union for Conservation of Nature & Natural Resources, World Conservation Union, 1983—. Editor Primate Conservation newsletter, 1981—; mem. editorial bd. Biology and Conservation, 1990, Zoo Biology, 1990—, Revue de Zoologie Africaine, Jour. Med. Primatology, 1979—; mem. editorial adv. bd. Orion Nature Quarterly, 1980—; cons. editor Am. Jour. Primatology. Recipient grant NSF, 1974-76, fellowship NSF, 1972-75, fellowship NIH, 1971-72, Dartmouth Reynolds scholar, 1967, Dartmouth Gen. fellow, 1967, Dartmouth Sr. fellow, 1967, Diploma of Merit for Nature Protection, Govt. State of Minas Gerais, Brazil, 1985 (1st fgn. recipient in history of award). Mem. Internat. Primatological Soc. (conservation com. 1977—), Am. Soc. Primatologists (conservation com. 1977—), Linnean Soc. London, N.Y. Zool. Soc. (sci. fellow 1988—), Phi Beta Kappa. Office: Conservation Internat 1015 18th St NW Ste 1000 Washington DC 20036

MITTLER, JOAN MORGAN, psychotherapist, educator, counselor; b. Plainfield, N.J., Dec. 10, 1941; d. John McClement and Villette (Voss) Morgan; m. William Alfred Mittler, June 27, 1978; 1 child, Maggy. Student, The Juilliard Sch., N.Y.C., 1962-64; AB, Wilson Coll., 1974; MA, NYU, 1991; grad. women bus. owners' program, Fashion Inst. Tech., 1991. Cert. Rubenfield Synergist, Active Parenting group leader. Adminstrv. asst. Dept. of Edn. Mus. Modern Art, N.Y.C., 1967-76, Lincoln Ctr. Inst., N.Y.C., 1976; frelance dir. paintings exhbn. West Broadway Gallery, N.Y.C., 1979, 81; devel. asst. The Dance Notation Bur., N.Y.C., 1982; co-founder, adminstrv. dir. The Ctr. for Integrated Recovery, N.Y.C., 1987-90; pvt. practice N.Y.C., 1990—; dance program cons. NYU, N.Y.C., 1973-75; tutor, cons. Empire State Coll. SUNY, N.Y.C., 1974. Researcher, author: (catalog) The Kitchen Center for Video Music, 1976. Recipient Mike Bender award NYU, 1986; Joseph Papp scholar NYU, 1985. Mem. AACD, Am. Mental Health Counselors Assn., Inst. Advancement of Health. Episcopalian. Office: 104 W 17th St Ste 4E New York NY 10011-5418

MITTY, LIZBETH, artist, educator; b. N.Y.C., Oct. 28, 1952; d. Sol and Anne (Ross) M.; m. David W. James, Aug. 27, 1976; children: Maris Mitty, Dana Mitty. Student, SUNY, Stony Brook, 1969-71; BS, U. Wis., 1973, MFA, 1975. Instr. painting SUNY, New Paltz, 1991—; lectr. Lake Erie Coll., Painesville, Ohio, 1975-76, Ohio State U., Columbus, 1976-77, U. Ga., Athens, 1978-79, Atlanta Coll. Art Extension, 1979, Find Art Workshop, N.Y.C., 1981-82, Gt. Neck (N.Y.) Schs., 1981-82, Nassau Community Coll., Garden City, N.Y., 1981-83, also others; vis. artist Riker's Island State Prison, N.Y.C., 1982, Skidmore Coll., Saratoga Springs, N.Y., 1983, Mus. at Stony Brook, 1991, Mus. Modern Art Edn. Dept., 1991. One-woman shows Image Gallery, Athens, 1978, Heath Gallery, Atlanta, 1978, Rosa Esman Gallery, N.Y.C., 1982, 83, 85; exhibited in group shows Jay Gallery, N.Y.C., 1988, 90, 91, Bronx Mus., 1989, Assoc. Am. Artists Gallery, N.Y.C., 1989, Mus. Nat. Arts Found., N.Y.C., 1989, Berkshire Mus., Pittsfield, Mass., 1989, Mus. at Stony Brook, 1990, Tom Cugliani Gallery, N.Y.C., 1990, also others; represented in permanent collections Met. Mus. Art, Mint Mus., Newark Mus., Chem. Bank. Fund raiser Pub. Sch. 234, N.Y.C., 1989-91. Home and Studio: 165 Church St Apt 5N New York NY 10007

MIU, PATRICK, computer software developer. chief exec. officer Trident Computing, Inc., N.Y. Inventor pen-based Chinese, Japanese ideograph recognition software. Office: Trident Computing Inc 173 Cold Spring Rd Syosset NY 11791-2204

MIYASAKI, GAIL YOTSUE, television production company executive; b. Paauilo, Hawaii, Apr. 9, 1949; d. Herbert Yoshiki and Akiko (Matsumoto) M.; m. Charles Raphael Husson, Jan. 17, 1986; 1 child, Lani Keiko. AB, U. Calif., Berkeley, 1971; MEd, U. Hawaii, 1976. Lectr. ethnic studies U. Hawaii, Honolulu, 1971-73; feature writer Hawaii Herald, Honolulu, 1973-76; promotion dir. Hawaii Pub. TV, Honolulu, 1976-82, publ. editor, 1976-80, assoc. producer. writer, 1980-82; copywriter MCA TV, N.Y.C., 1982-84; writer Showtime/The Movie Channel, N.Y.C., 1982-85; promotion dir. Reading Rainbow Pub. Broadcasting System, N.Y.C., 1984-85; dir. corp. relations Children's TV Workshop, N.Y.C., 1985—. Editor: (anthology) Talk Story, 1978; contbr. chpts. to anthology and textbook. Bd. dirs. YWCA of Oahu, Honolulu, 1978-80. Mem. N.Y. Women in Communications. Office: Children's TV Workshop 1 Lincoln Plz New York NY 10023

MIZEJEWSKI, GERALD JUDE, research scientist; b. Pitts., Aug. 1, 1939; s. Edward Lenard and Ann Veronica (Barnosky) M.; m. Darlene Diana Dietrich, June12, 1965; children: Steven Michael, James Gerald, William Matthew, Susan Marie, Gerald Jude Jr., Michael Christopher. BS in Biology, Duquesne U., 1961; MS in Zoology, U. Md., 1965, PhD in Zoology, 1968; post doctoral, U. Mich., 1970. Rsch. asst. vetinary science dept. U. Md., College Park, 1967-68; rsch. assoc. internal medicine dept. U. Mich., Ann Arbor, 1968-70, instr. sch. pub. health, 1970-71, rsch. physiologist VA hosp., 1970-71; asst. prof. biology dept. U. S.C., Columbia, 1971-74; rsch. scientist N.Y. State Health Dept., Albany, 1974-79; sr. rsch. scientist Wadsworth Ctr. Labs., Albany, 1979—; assoc. prof. SUNY, Albany, 1988—, Albany Med. Coll., 1980—, Rensselaer Poly. Inst., Troy, N.Y., 1986—, Union Coll., 1990—. Author numerous books; contbr. articles to profl. jours. Youth leader YMCA Indian Guides, Clifton Park, N.Y., 1978-84; pack leader Boy Scouts of Am., Clifton Park, 1976-86. Ensign USMC, 1961-66. Named Rsch. fellow Nat. Science Found., 1963; grantee Nat. Cancer Inst., Bethesda, Md., 1990. Mem. N.Y. Acad. Sci., Am. Fedn. Clin. Rsch. Office: Wadsworth Ctr NYS Health Dept Empire State Plz Albany NY 12201

MIZRUCHI, SUSAN LAURA, English educator; b. Cortland, N.Y., July 13, 1959; d. Ephraim Harold and Ruth (Trachtenberg) M.; m. Sacvan Bercovitch, Dec. 31, 1988; 1 child, Alexander Philip. BA in English, BA in History, Washington U., St. Louis, 1981; MA in English, Princeton U., 1983, PhD in English, 1985. Lectr. English, Princeton (N.J.) U., 1985-86; asst. prof. English, Boston U., 1986-92, assoc. prof., 1992—; lectr., cons. USIA, Washington, 1986; reader, cons. Princeton U. Press, 1987—; panelist, reviewer NEH, Washington, 1989—; rsch. affiliate Woodrow Wilson Ctr., smithsonian Instn., Washington, 1990-91. Author: The Power of Historical Knowledge, 1988; contbr. short stories to literary mags., articles to Am. and European jours. Harold S. Dodds fellow Princeton U., 1984-85, jr. humanities fellow Boston U., 1988-89, fellow NEH, 1990. Mem. Modern Lang. Assn., Am. Lit. Assn., Northeastern Modern Lang. Assn., Am. Studies Assn., Harvard U. Seminar for Am. Lit. Scholars. Jewish. Office: Boston U 236 Bay State Rd Boston MA 02215-1403

MIZUSAWA, BERT KAMEAALOHA, lawyer; b. Honolulu, Jan. 31, 1957; s. George Tsuneji and Theodora (Berghuis) M. BS, U.S. Mil. Acad., 1979; M in Pub. Policy, Harvard U., 1989; JD, Harvard Law Sch., 1989; postgrad., Harvard U., 1989—. Bar: N.Y. 1990, Washington 1990. Commd. 2d lt. U.S. Army, 1979, advanced through grades to maj., 1985; various assignments 1-509th Airborne Bn. Combat Team, Vicenza, Italy, 1980-83; student Inf. Officer Advanced Course, Ft. Benning, Ga., 1983-84; comdr. Joint Security Force, UN Command, Panmunjom, Republic of Korea, 1984-85; PhD fellow Harvard U., 1985-89, MacArthur fellow internat. securities, 1988-90; assoc. Sullivan & Cromwell, Washington, 1990—. Pres. VA Harvard U., 1987-89. Decorated Bronze Star; Order of Merit (Republic of Korea): recipient Polit. Sci. award Soc. Fgn. Wars, 1979; named Mass. Jr. Officer of Yr., Army Resolution Com., Res. Officer Assn., 1989, Nat. Finalist White House fellow, 1989. Phi Kappa Phi. Office: Sullivan & Cromwell 1701 Pennsylvania Ave, NW Washington DC 20006

MOAKLEY, JOHN JOSEPH, congressman; b. Apr. 27, 1927; m. Evelyn Duffy, 1957. LLB, Suffolk U., 1956. Bar: Mass. 1957. Practice Boston, 1957-72; mem. 93d-102nd Congresses from 9th Mass. dist., 1973—, chmn. com. on rules. Chmn. com. on rules Mass. Senate, 1964-70; mem. Boston City Coun., 1971-72, chmn. com. on appropriations and fin. With USNR, 1943-46. Address: US Ho of Reps 235 Cannon House Office Bldg Washington DC 20515

MOAK-MAZUR, CONNIE J., investment consultant, marketing professional; b. Ft. Worth, Feb. 5, 1947; d. David Clark and Dorothy Carol (Jackson) Moak; m. Jay Mazur, May 31, 1987. BBA, N. Tex. State U., 1969. Cert. bus. edn. tchr. V.p. Lionel D. Edie & Co., N.Y.C., 1969-77; mgr. Peat, Marwick, Mitchell & Co., N.Y.C., 1977-80; v.p. Shaw Data, N.Y.C., 1980, Fred Alger Mgmt., N.Y.C., 1980-82; ptnr. Glickenhaus & Co., N.Y.C., 1982—; speaker in field. Contbr. articles to profl. jours. Mem. Fin. Women's Assn., Am. Pension Conf., Internat. Found. Employee Benefit Plans, Assn. Investment Mgmt. Sales Execs. (bd. dirs., pres.-elect). Home: 150 E 69th St Apt 19C New York NY 10021-5704 Office: Glickenhaus & Co 6 E 43rd St New York NY 10017-4609

MOBASSERI, BIJAN GHOLAMREZA, electrical engineering educator; b. Tehran, Iran, Jan. 16, 1953; s. Yousef and Alieh (Taghavi) M.; m. Fatemeh Aleyassin, Aug. 29, 1982; children: Armin, Ramin, Shervin. BSEE, Purdue U., 1973, MSEE, 1974, PhD in Elec. Engring., 1978. Rsch. fellow Lab. for Applications of Remote Sensing, West Lafayette, Ind., 1978-79; faculty elec. engring. Telecommunication U., Tehran, 1979-84; prof. elec. engring. Villanova (Pa.) U., 1984—; tech. reviewer NSF, Washington, 1989, IEEE, 1990. Pa. Ben Franklin Program grantee, 1990-91; Villanova U. Rsch. awardee, 1987, 90. Mem. Sigma Xi, Eta Kappa Nu, Phi Kappa Phi. Office: Villanova U Dept Elec Engring Villanova PA 19085

MOBILIA, PAMELA ANN KRISTIN, economics educator, researcher; b. Buffalo, Jan. 18, 1956; d. Anthony John and Geraldine Dorthea (Prelosky) M. Student, SUNY, Buffalo, 1974-77, Julliard Sch., 1978-79, 86—; BA, CUNY, 1982, MPhil, 1989, PhD, 1990; MA, NYU, 1986. Dir. mktg. Cable Holdings, N.Y.C., 1979-82; mgr. nat. markets Showtime/The Movie Channel, N.Y.C., 1982-84; v.p. Sage Entertainment, N.Y.C., 1984; asst. prof. econs. Bklyn. Coll. CUNY, 1987—; cons. to bd. The Basic Theatre, N.Y.C., 1990—. Contbr. articles to profl. jours. Vol. Bus. Vols. for Arts, N.Y.C., 1986—, Jr. League, N.Y., 1990—. Named Favorite Tchr., Bklyn. Coll. Students, 1991; univ. fellow State of N.Y., 1986-88. Mem. Nat. Bur. Econ. Rsch., Am. Econ. Assn., N.Y. State Econ. Assn., Ea. Econ. Assn., Arts and Bus. Coun. Office: CUNY Bklyn Coll Econs Dept Ave H and Bedford Ave Brooklyn NY 11210

MOBLEY, ROBERT, insurance company professional; b. Winter Haven, Fla., July 24, 1953; s. Mernith Reylands and Francis (Woods) M.; m. Cecilia Jane Mobley, Jan. 5, 1979 (div. Apr. 1986); m. Diane M. Barber, July 7, 1990. AS in Mgmt., Polk Community Coll., Winter Haven, 1973; AA in Mktg., Polk Community Coll., 1973; BS, Fla. Atlantic U., 1975, MEd, 1976. Instr. Clewstion High Sch., Clewiston, Fla., 1975-76; instr., dept. chmn. South Tech. Ctr., Boynton Beach, Fla., 1976-79; curriculum coord. Marshall U., Huntington, W.Va., 1979-80; mktg. rep. Progressive Casualty Co., Charleston, W.Va., 1980; agt. State Farm Ins. Cos., Marmet, W.Va., 1980-87; agy. mgr. State Farm Ins. Cos., Wilmington, Del., 1988—; bd. dirs. M-W Auto Parks, Inc., Chickamauga, Ga.; ptnr. M & B Fin. Svcs., Wilmington, 1990—; v.p. market planning M & W Aviation Svcs., Wilmington, 1990—. Author: Auto Parts Marketing, 1978, Education in America: Myth or Reality, 1980, Statical Approaches to Needs Analysis, 1990, Issues in Agency Recruitment, 1990. Republican. Home: 323 Sheringham Dr Hockessin DE 19707-1928 Office: 5209 W Woodmill Dr Wilmington DE 19808-4068

MOCCIO, JOHN RAYMOND, guidance counselor; b. Mt. Vernon, N.Y., Mar. 5, 1947; s. Anthony Louis and Jeanne Rose (Terraciano) M.; 1 child, Melanie Patricia; m. Ann Marie Camerone, June 22, 1991. BA in History and Edn., Marist Coll., 1969; MA in Spl. Edn., NYU, 1971; student, U. Bridgeport, 1973; MA, CUNY, 1992. Cert. counselor and spl. edn. tchr., N.Y. Tchr. emotionally disturbed Mt. Vernon Sch. Dist., 1969-73, tchr. spl. edn., 1984-88, coord. vocat. ednl. svcs. for individuals with disabilities, 1988—, guidance counselor, 1988—; behavior specialist Charlotte County Schst., Port Charlotte, Fla., 1975; tchr. Lee County schs., Ft. Myers, Fla., 1974; tchr. exceptional children Broward Coutny Schs., Ft. Lauderdale, Fla., 1977-84, program monitor exceptional children, 1981-82; adj. prof. Nova U., Ft. Lauderdale, 1982; cons. in field. Author: Cosmic Humanism, 1978; (column) Mt. Vernon Times newspaper. Bd. dirs. Westchester County Youth Shelter, Mt. Vernon, 1987—; mem. Mayor's Task Force on Drugs, Crime Blight, Mt. Vernon, 1987-089; mem. state com. drug addiction and alcoholism N.Y. State Senate Adv. Com., Albany, 1988—. Mem. Mt. Vernon Italian Civic Assn. (chmn. ICA scholarship com. 1988, 89, 92, mem. sch. improvement com. 1988-89, chaplain I.C.A. 1990-91, officer). Roman Catholic. Office: Mt Vernon Sch Dist 165 N Columbus Mount Vernon NY 10553

MOCHEL, MYRON GEORGE, mechanical engineer, educator; b. Fremont, Ohio, Oct. 9, 1905; s. Gustave A. and Rose M. (Minich) M.; m. Eunice Katherine Steinicke, Aug. 30, 1930 (dec. Dec. 1982); children: Kenneth R., David G., Virginia June. BSME, Case Western Res. U., 1929; MSME, Yale U., 1930. Registered profl. engr. N.Y., Mass., Pa. Devel. engr. nitrogen div. Allied Chem. Corp., Hopewell, Va., 1930-31; devel. engr. R&D dept. Mobil Corp., Paulsboro, N.J., 1931-37; design and devel. engr. gearing div. Westinghouse Electric Corp., Pitts., 1937-43; rsch. assoc. underwater sound lab. Harvard U., Cambridge, Mass., 1943-45; supr. of tng. steam turbine div. Worthington Corp., Wellsville, N.Y., 1945-49; prof. mech. engr. Clarkson U., Potsdam, N.Y., 1949-71; prof. emeritus Clarkson U., Potsdam, 1971—; lect. U. Pitts., 1938-43, N.Y. State U. Adult Edn., Wellsville, 1946-49, Oswego, 1965, N.Y. State High Sch. Enrichment Program, Potsdam, 1962-71; cons. Designers for Industry, Cleve., 1953, rsch. engr. Morris Machine Works, Baldwinsville, N.Y., 1954, design engr. Racquette River Paper Co., Potsdam, 1955. Author: Fundamentals of Engineering Graphics, 1960, Pre-Engineering and Applied Science Fundamentals, 1962, Fortran Programming, Programs and Schematic Storage Maps, 1971; co-author: (with Eunice S. Mochel) Funds For Fun, 1983, (with Donald H. Purcell) Beyond Expectations, 1985; contbr. articles to profl. jours. Officer, vol. St. Lawrence Valley Hospice, 1983; pres. Mayfield Tenants Assn., 1989-91. Mem. ASME, Am. Soc. Engring. Edn. (advt. mgr. Jour. Engring. Graphics 1963-66, sec. 1966-67, high schs. laision on engring. graphics 1962-65, awards com. chmn. 1965-66), Am. Assn. Ret. Persons (founder St. Lawrence County chpt., income tax counselor 1988-89, medicare/medicaid assistance program counselor 1988—, pres. 1989-90). Republican. Home and Office: 9C-1 Mayfield Apts May Rd Potsdam NY 13676-1309

MOCK, CHARLES A., sales executive; b. Easton, Md., Apr. 26, 1945; s. Carlton Richard and Adeline (Simpson) M. BA in History, Washington Coll., Chestertown, Md., 1968; student, Duke U., 1963-65. Sales rep. Equitable Life Assurance Soc. U.S., Phila., 1968-69, Prices Tire Ctr., Inc., Easton, Md., 1971-72; sales rep./sales mgr. West Chem. Products, Inc., Richmond, Va., 1972-78; sales rep. Monroe Sys. for Bus., Easton, 1978-83, Carey Machinery & Supply Co., Inc., Balt., 1984-87, Conveyor Handling Co., Inc., Jessup, Md., 1987—. Mem. Dorchesher Heritage, Inc., Cambridge, Md., 1980—, pres., 1989. With U.S. Army, 1969-71. Decorated Army Commendation medal. Mem. Am. Soc. Safety Engrs. (sec.-treas. 1990-91), Am. Inst. Plant Engrs. (chpt. treas. 1987-89), Delmara Safety Assn. (pres. 1988-89), Soc. Mfg. Engrs., Lions (pres. 1979, 85, 89, leadership devel. co-chmn. 1990—, multiple dist. 22 train-the-trainer/leadership devel. chmn. 1992—, recipient Internat. Leadership award 1989). Republican. Home: 4205 Cabin Rd Hurlock MD 21643 Office: Conveyor Handling Co Inc 7175 Montevideo Rd Jessup MD 20794-9373

MOCK, ROBERT CLAUDE, architect; b. Baden, Fed. Republic of Germany, May 3, 1928; came to U.S., 1938, naturalized, 1943; s. Ernest and Charlotte (Geismar) M.; m. Belle Carol Bach, Dec. 23, 1952 (div.); children: John Bach, Nicole Louise; m. Marjorie Reubenfeld, Dec. 20, 1964. B.Arch., Pratt Inst., 1950; M. Arch., Harvard U., 1953. Registered architect, N.Y., Conn., N.J., Nat. Council Archtl. Registration Bds. Architect George C. Marshall Space Center, Huntsville, Ala., 1950-51; archtl. critic Columbia Sch. Architecture, N.Y.C., 1953-54; dir. facility design Am. Airlines, N.Y.C., 1955-60; founder Robert C. Mock & Assocs. (architects and engrs.), N.Y.C., 1960—; mem. Mayor's Panel of Architects, N.Y.C. Prin. works include: Shine Motor Inn, Queens, N.Y., 1961 (recipient 1st prize motel category Queens C. of C. 1961), temporary terminal bldg. Eastern Air Lines , La Guardia Airport, N.Y.C., 1961, cargo bldgs United Airlines and Trans World Airlines, Kennedy Airport, N.Y.C., Bridgeport (Conn.) Airport, 1961, Eastern Air Lines Med. Ctr., Kennedy Airport, 1962, ticket office Trans World Airlines Fifth Ave., N.Y.C., 1962, terminal bldgs. Eastern Air Lines and Trans World Airlines , La Guardia Airport, N.Y.C., 1963, 7 bldgs. Mfrs. Hanover Trust Co. , 1964-66, kitchen and commissary bldg. Lufthansa German Airlines, 1964, Ambassador Club, La Guardia Airport, 1964, Happyland Sch., N.Y.C., 1965, cargo bldgs. Alitalia and Lufthansa German Airlines, Kennedy Airport, 1965, FAA-Nat. Prototype Air Traffic Control Tower, 1966; Lufthansa German Airlines; Irish Internat. Airlines, El Al Israel Airlines, Varig Brazilian Airlines; passenger terminals Kennedy Airport, 1970; Swiss Air Cargo Terminal, Lufthansa German Airlines, cargo terminals El Al Israel airline cargo terminal, Kennedy Airport, 1972, passenger terminal Aerolineas Argentina, 1974, N.Am. hdqrs. Aerolineas Argentinas, N.Y.C., 1974, corp. hdqrs. Am. Airlines, 1977, N.Am. hdqrs. Varig Brazilian Airlines, N.Y.C., 1977, Norel-Ronel Indsl. Pk., Hollywood, Fla., 1979, N.Am. hdqrs. Irish Internat. Airlines , N.Y.C., 1979, corp. hdqrs. Bankers Trust Co., N.Y.C., 1980, cargo terminal Air India, cargo terminal Flying Tiger, Kennedy Airport, 1982, 2 flight kitchen bldgs. Ogden Food Corp., Kennedy Airport, 1984, 88 and LaGuardia Airport, 1987, Greenwich Assn. Retarded Citizens Sch., 1983, passenger terminal extension Varig Brazilian Airlines , 1985, 3 restaurants La Guardia Airport, 1987, residences Palm Beach, Fla., 1989-91. Recipient United Way Vol. of Yr. award, 1984. Mem. Am. Arbitration Assn. Clubs: City, Harvard, Admirals Cove. Office: 185 Byram Shore Rd Greenwich CT 06830-6909

MOCKNICK, DAVID LEE, writer, security specialist; b. Phila., Aug. 11, 1958; s. Peter John and Jane Marie (Potter) M. Student, Abraham Lincoln Coll., 1977, Neshaminy Adult Edn., 1985, Pa. State U., 1989—. Store mgr. Nat. Shirts, Inc., Bensalem, Pa., 1977-83; mail order operator D. L. Mocknick Enterprises, Levittown, Pa., 1982-86; security specialist Guardsmark, Inc., Phila., 1987-90, Atlantic Inc., Bensalem, 1991—. Author: To

Love Is To Die, 1987, Attrigis, 1988, (screenplays) Program V-X, 1991, A Place To Go, 1991, Another Day in Philly, 1991, Peace at Last, 1992; also articles. Democrat. Roman Catholic. Home: 3566 Stouton St Philadelphia PA 19134-2026

MOCKOVIAK, JOHN WADE, trust company executive; b. North Bergen, N.J., Mar. 9, 1944; s. John Samuel and Elsie Marion (Steinel) M.; m. Virginia Mary Livelli, Nov. 5, 1946; children: John Wade, Michael James. BBA, Fairleigh Dickinson U., 1966; MBA, Loyola Coll., 1981. Asst. v.p. The Bank of N.Y., N.Y.C., 1966-77; sr. v.p. Md. Nat. Bank, Balt., 1977-88; exec. v.p. Security Trust Co., Balt., 1988—; chmn. exec. com. Fiduciary Services div. ABA, Washington, 1985-86; chmn. nat. conf. Nat. Trust Operations Conf. ABA, San Diego, 1984; bd. dirs. ASB Capital Mgmt. Co. Pres. Meals on Wheels, Balt., 1985—; adv. bd. Community Found. Greater Balt., 1986—. Mem. Assn. of Trust Mgrs., Balt. Cashiers Assn. Home: 13311 Falls Rd Cockeysville Hunt Valley MD 21030-1421 Office: Security Trust Co NA PO Box 987 Baltimore MD 21203-0987

MODERACKI, EDMUND ANTHONY, educator, conductor; b. Hackensack, N.J., July 18, 1946; s. Edmund Joseph and Helen Theresa (Fisher) M. BA, Montclair State Coll., 1968, postgrad., 1970-71; MA, Hunter Coll., 1970, postgrad., 1970-72; postgrad., Newark State Coll., 1969-70, Seton Hall U., 1970, Rutgers U., 1976-78, Ctr. for Understanding Media, 1973. Tchr. music pub. schs. River Vale, N.J., 1968—; asst. condr. Ridgewood (N.J.) Symphony Orch., 1969-80, assoc. condr., 1980—, trustee, pres., 1986-87; tuba soloist Rutherford Community Band, Ridgewood Village Band, Waldwick Band, Ridgewood Concert Band, bd. dirs., 1985-91; condr. Waldwick Band, 1978—, Ridgewood Concert Band, 1983—; guest condr., 1985, 86, 88. Bergen County PTA fellow, 1976, recipient Exec. Vol. award, 1991, Tchr. Recognition award Gov. of State of N.J., 1990. Mem. NEA, Music Educators Nat. Conf., N.J. Orch. Assn. (trustee 1981-85), N.J. Edn. Assn. (del. assembly alt. 1983—), River Vale Edn. Assn. (pres. 1981-83, 88—), Ednl. Media Assn. N.J., Brigade Am. Revolution (bd. dirs. at large 1991—), River Vale Town Historian, Phi Mu Alpha Sinfonia, Kappa Delta Pi. Home: 531 Westwood Ave Westwood NJ 07675-5526 Office: Woodside Sch River Vale NJ 07675

MODERY, RICHARD GILLMAN, marketing and sales executive; b. Chgo., Sept. 20, 1941; s. Richard Gustave Modery and Betty Jane (Gillman) Perok; m. Kay Francis Whitby, July 31, 1966 (div. July 1977); children: Stacey Lynn, Marci Kay; m. Anne-Marie Lucette Arsenault, Feb. 27, 1979. Student, Joliet (Ill.) Jr. Coll., 1959-61, Aurora (Ill.) Coll., 1963-65, Davenport Bus. Coll., Grand Rapids, Mich., 1969-71, Northwestern U., Evanston, Ill., 1987. Mktg. products mgr. Rapistan, Inc., Grand Rapids, 1964-75; mgr. estimating, project mgmt., customer svc. E.W. Buschman Co., Cin., 1975-78; exec. v.p. Metzgar Conveyor Co., Grand Rapids, 1979-84; mng. dir. Metzco Internat (cen. and S.Am.), Grand Rapids, Mich., 1981-84, Transfer Technologies, Inc., Grand Rapids, 1984-87; gen. ptnr., pres., chief exec. officer Nat. Monument Co., Grand Rapids, 1986—; v.p. Translogic Corp., Denver, 1987-88; corp. officer, v.p. mktg., field ops. and sales S.I. Handling Systems, Inc., Easton, Pa., 1988-91; v.p. mktg., sales and engring. Integrated Material Handling Co., Tomkins Industries, Inc., Oshkosh, Wis., 1991—; speaker and cons. in field. Patentee in field. Commr. City of East Grand Rapids, Mich. Traffic Commn., 1983-86. Served with USNG, 1963-69. Mem. Internat. Material Mgmt. Soc., Am. Mgmt. Assn., Material Handling Inst. Am., Material Handling Inst. (speaker nat. confs.), Am. Mktg. Assn., Conveyor Equipment Mfrs. Assn., Material Handling Equipment Distbrs. Assn., Masons (32 degree). Home: 2411 Newport Ct Bethlehem PA 54904 Office: Integrated Material Handling Co 3255 Medalist Dr Oshkosh WI 54901-7123

MODEST, MICHAEL FRITZ, mechanical engineering educator; b. Berlin, Mar. 1, 1944; came to U.S., 1969; s. Fritz Ulrich and Ella (Weiss) M.; m. Ellen J. Peterson, June 1974 (div. 1979); m. Monika Klara Graf, Aug. 11, 1984; children: Mara Claudia, Michelle Rebecca. Diploma in engring., Tech. U. Munich, 1968; MS, U. Calif., Berkeley, 1972, PhD, 1972. Postdoctoral rsch. asst. Johnson Space Ctr. NASA, Houston, 1972-74; lectr. in engring. San Francisco State U., 1974-75; from asst. to assoc. prof. engring. Rensselaer Poly. Inst., Troy, N.Y., 1975-80; from assoc. prof. to prof. mech. engring. U. So. Calif., L.A., 1980-86; prof. mech. engring. Pa. State U., University Park, 1987—; cons. Lawrence Berkeley Lab., 1975, GE, Schenectady, N.Y., 1975-76, 80-84, HUD, Albany, N.Y., 1978, and others. Author: Radiative Heat Transfer; editor several conf. proc.; contbr. articles to profl. jours. Rsch. grantee NSF, NASA, NIH, Dept. Energy, and others. Fellow ASME; mem. AIAA, Laser Inst. Am., Sigma Xi. Office: Pa State U 211 Hallowell Bldg University Park PA 16802

MODIGLIANI, FRANCO, economics and finance educator; b. Rome, June 18, 1918; came to U.S., 1939, naturalized, 1946; s. Enrico and Olga (Flaschel) M.; m. Serena Calabi, May 22, 1939; children: Andre, Sergio. D. Jurisprudence, U. Rome, 1939; D. Social Sci., New Sch. Social Rsch., 1944; LLD (hon.), U. Chgo., 1967; D. honoris causa, U. Louvain, Belgium, 1974, Istituto Universitario di Bergamo, 1979, Hartford U.; LHD (hon.), Bard Coll., 1989; HLD (hon.), Brandeis U., 1986, New Sch. Social Research, 1989, Mich. State U., 1989; D. (hon.), U. Ill., 1990; D (hon.), U. Valencia, Spain, 1992. Instr. econs. and statistics N.J. Coll. Women, New Brunswick, 1942; instr., then asso. econs. and statistics Bard Coll., Columbia, 1942-44; lectr., asst. prof. math. econs. and econometrics New Sch. Social Rsch., 1943-44, 46-48; rsch. asso., chief statistician Inst. World Affairs, N.Y.C., 1945-48; rsch. cons. Cowles Commn. Rsch. in Econs. U. Chgo., 1949-54; asso. prof., then prof. econs. U. Ill., 1949-52; prof. econs. and indsl. adminstrn. Carnegie Inst. Tech., 1952-60; vis. prof. econs. Harvard U., 1957-58; prof. econs. Northwestern U., 1960-62; vis. prof. econs. MIT, 1960-61, prof. econs. and finance, 1962—, Inst. prof., 1970-88, Inst. prof. emeritus, 1988—; Fellow polit. economy U. Chgo., 1948; Fulbright lectr. U. Rome, also, Palermo, Italy, 1955. Author: The Debate Over Stabilization Policy, 1986, Il Caso Italia, 1986, The Collected Papers of Franco Modigliani, 3 vols., 1980, 4th and 5th vols., 1989; co-author: National Incomes and International Trade, 1953, Planning Production, Inventories and Work Forces, 1960, The Role of Anticipations and Plans in Economic Behavior and Their Use in Economic Analysis and Forecasting, 1961, New Mortgage Designs for Stable Housing in an Inflationary Environment, 1975, (with Frank J. Fabozzi) Capital Markets: Institutions and Instruments, 1991—. Mem. macro econs. policy group Ctr. for European Policy Studies, 1985—. Recipient Nobel prize in econ. sci., 1985; Cavaliere Di Gran Groce Repubblica Italiana, 1985, Premio Coltura for Econs., Repubblica Italiana, 1988, Premio APE award, 1988, Graham and Dodd award, 1975, 80, James R. Killian Jr. Faculty Achievement award, 1985, Lord Found. prize, 1989, Italy Premio Columbus, 1989, Italy Premio Guido Dorso, 1989, Italy Premio Stivale D'oro, 1991. Fellow NAS, Am. Econ. Assn. (v.p. 1975, pres. 1976), Econometric Soc. (coun. 1960, v.p. 1961, pres. 1962), Am. Acad. Arts and Scis., Accademia Dei Lincei, Internat. Econ. Assn. (v.p. 1977-83, pres. 1983—); mem. Am. Fin. Assn. (pres. 1981). Office: 25 Clark St Belmont MA 02178

MODLIN, HOWARD S., lawyer; b. N.Y.C., Apr. 10, 1931; s. Martin and Rose Modlin; m. Margot S., Oct. 18, 1956; children: James, Laura, Peter. AB, Union Coll., Schenectady, 1952; JD, Columbia U., 1955. Bar: N.Y. 1956, D.C. 1973. Assoc., Weisman, Celler, Spett & Modlin, N.Y.C., 1956-61, ptnr., 1961-76, mng. ptnr., 1976—; sec., dir. Fedders Corp., Peapack, N.J., Gen. DataComm Industries, Inc., Middlebury, Conn.; dir. Trans-Lux Corp., Norwalk, Conn., Am.-Book-Stratford Press, Inc., N.Y.C. Chmn. bd. dirs. Daus. of Jacob Geriatric Ctr., Bronx, N.Y. Mem. ABA, Assn. Bar City N.Y., D.C. Bar Assn. Office: Weisman Celler Spett & Modlin 445 Park Ave New York NY 10022-2606

MOE, ALDEN JOHN, university dean; b. Cookston, Minn., Apr. 9, 1939; s. Melvin Truman and Martha Mathilde (Njus) M.; m. Margery Elizabeth Sharbono, Aug. 1959 (div. 1983); m. Elayne Ackerman, Jan. 2, 1984; children: Christine Marie, Perry Wayne. BS, U. Minn., 1963; MA, Clarke Coll., Dubuque, Iowa, 1967; PhD, U. Minn., 1971. Tchr. St. Anthony Village, Minn., 1963-66; instr. Clarke Coll., 1967-69, U. Minn., 1969-71; from asst. to assoc. prof. Purdue U., West Lafayette, Ind., 1971-82; prof. La. State U., Baton Rouge, 1982-85, assoc. dean, 1985-88; dean of edn. Lehigh U., Bethlehem, Pa., 1988—. Author: Vocabulary of First Grade Children, 1982, Ginn Word Book for Teachers, 1983, Analytical Reading Inventory, 4th edit., 1989, Occupational Literacy Education, 1986. Mem. Internat. Reading Assn. (bd. dirs. 1980-83), Am. Ednl. Rsch. Assn., nat. Conf. Rsch. in English. Democrat. Home: 5606 Meadow Dr Orefield PA 18069-9027 Office: Lehigh U Dean of Edn Bethlehem PA 18015

MOECKEL, HENRY THEODORE, architect; b. Waterbury, Conn., May 13, 1918; s. Henry Theodore and Anna Gertrude (Vest) M.; m. Beryl Bronson (div. 1949); children: Holly, Steven, Cathy, Jeffery, Henry T. III.; m. Marjorie Hollis, Nov. 2, 1963. BArch, Rensselaer Poly. Inst., 1940. Registered architect, Conn. With Henry T. Moeckel & Son, Architects, Naugatuck, Conn., 1945-60, Henry T. Moeckel & Assocs., Architects, Naugatuck, Conn., 1960-70; pres. Moeckel & Oris, Architects, Naugatuck, Conn., 1970—. Prin. works include sch. bldgs., libraries, firehouses, town halls, housing projects for elderly, chs. Mem. AIA. Republican. Congregationalist. Lodge: Rotary (pres. 1950, dist. gov. 1955). Home: 994 Main St S Woodbury CT 06798-3801 Office: Moeckel & Oris Architects 305 Church St Naugatuck CT 06770-2836

MOELLER, FRANCIS XAVIER, JR., investment officer; b. Mineola, N.Y., Oct. 19, 1948; s. Francis Xavier and Eleanor V. (Molinet) M.; m. Carol Lynn Schindler, May 28 1972; children: Brian, Kevin, Dennis. BBA in Fin., Hofstra U., 1977. V.p., investment officer Nat. Westminster Bank USA, N.Y.C., 1972-87; chief investment officer KWFS, Rockville Centre, N.Y., 1987-88; v.p., chief investment officer 1st Am. Bank N.Y., N.Y.C., 1988—. Asst. coach East Meadow (N.Y.) Soccer Club, 1988; leader Cub Scouts Am., Westbury, N.Y., 1988-90; trustee, com. mem. Boy Scouts Am., Westbury, 1990-91; v.p. fundraising Temple Sholomon, Westbury, 1990-91. Jewish. Home: 727 Kensington Dr Westbury NY 11590-5814

MOELLER, MARY ELLA, home economist, educator, radio commentator; b. Southampton, N.Y., Mar. 11, 1938; d. Harry Eugene and Edith Leone (Reester) Parsons; m. James Myron Moeller, Aug. 5, 1961; 1 child, Mary Beth. B.S. in Home Econs., U. Nebr., 1960; M.L.S., SUNY-Stony Brook, 1977. Tchr. home econs. Port Jefferson Schs., N.Y., 1960-70; home econs. program asst. Suffolk County Coop. Extension of Cornell U., Riverhead, N.Y., 1972-82; tchr. home econs. Eastport High Sch., Riverhead, 1982-85, South County Schs., Bellport Middle Sch., N.Y., 1985—; host Ask Your Neighbor, Sta. WRIV, Riverhead, 1982-87; trainer Home Econs. Entrepreneurship N.Y. State Edn. Dept., 1986—; mem. home and career skills regional team N.Y. State Edn. Dept., 1984-86; mem. consumer homemaking adv. bd. Bd. Coop. Edn. Contbr. monthly articles to consumer publs. Mem. N.Y. State Home Econs. Assn., Am. Home Econs. Assn. (cert. home economist), Suffolk County Home Econs. Assn., DAR (historian 1985), Eastern Star (matron 1970). Home: PO Box 377 Miller Place NY 11764-0377 Office: Bellport Mid Sch Kreamer St Bellport NY 11713-2307

MOERDLER, CHARLES GERARD, lawyer; b. Paris, Nov. 15, 1934; came to U.S., 1946, naturalized, 1951; s. Herman and Erna Anna (Brandwein) M.; m. Pearl G. Hecht, Dec. 26, 1955; children: Jeffrey Alan, Mark Laurence, Sharon Michele. BA, L.I.U., 1953; JD, Fordham U., 1956. Bar: N.Y. 1956, U.S. Supreme Ct. 1962. Asso. firm Cravath, Swaine & Moore, N.Y.C., 1956-65; spl. counsel coms. City of N.Y. and judiciary N.Y. State Assembly, 1960-61; commr. bldgs. City of N.Y., 1966-67; sr. partner, chmn. litigation dept. Stroock & Stroock & Lavan, N.Y.C., 1967—; cons. housing, urban devel. and real estate to Mayor of N.Y.C., 1967-73; mem. com. on character and fitness of applicants for admission to Bar, Appellate div. 1st Dept., N.Y., 1977—; commr. N.Y. State Ins. Fund, 1978—, vice chmn., 1986—. Mem. editorial bd. N.Y. Law Jour., 1985—; assoc. editor Fordham Law Rev., 1956. Asst. dir. Rockefeller nat. presdl. campaign com., 1964; adv. bd. Sch. Internat. Affairs Columbia U., 1977-80; bd. govs. L.I.U., 1966, trustee, 1985-91; chmn. Community Planning Bds. 8 and 14, Bronx County, 1977-78; nat. bd. govs. Am. Jewish Congress, 1966; bd. overseers Jewish Theol. Sem. Am., 1983—; trustee St. Barnabas Hosp., Bronx, N.Y., 1985—. Recipient Walker Metcalf award L.I. U., 1966. Mem. Am. Bar Assn., N.Y. State Bar Assn., N.Y. County Lawyers Assn., Internat. Bar Assn. of City of N.Y., Free Sons of Israel, World Trade Ctr. Club, Metro. Club. Home: 7 Rivercrest Rd Bronx NY 10471-1236 Office: Stroock Stroock & Lavan 7 Hanover Sq New York NY 10004-2616

MOFFETT, BECKY MAY, advertising executive; b. Havre de Grace, Md., Dec. 31, 1963; d. Frances (Williams) Wheeling. Degree in Bus., Harford Coll., 1983. Exec. sec. The Wolff Co. Advt., Balt., 1983-86; media planner/buyer Trahan, Burden & Charles, Balt., 1987—. Office: Trahan Burden & Charles 1030 N Charles St Baltimore MD 21201

MOFFETT, ROY JAMES, importing company executive, consultant; b. Plainfield, N.J., Dec. 7, 1947; s. Roy Vincent and Estelle (Hartz) M.; m. Elaine Margaret Farley, Jan. 30, 1968; children—Lori, Mary Margaret. Student Union Coll., Cranford, N.J., 1965-66, L.I. U., Bklyn., 1969; A.A., Newark State U., 1971. Pres., Estelle Uniform Shops, N.J., 1971-83, Burnham Motors, Inc., Morristown, N.J., 1980-82; cons. IPCO Corp., N.J., N.Y., 1983-84; pres. Quest Importing Co., Italy and N.Y.C., 1984—, John L. Cook Co., Argentina and U.S., 1989; mng. ptnr. Palm Canyon Assoc. Real Estate Devel., Palm Springs, Calif., 1989-92; pres. John L. Cook Clothing Co., 1992—; U.S. sales dir. Guy LaRoche Pour Enfants of Can., 1989; cons. Italian Mrs. Assn., Florence, 1985, dir., cons. Assoc. Store Fixture Co., Old Bridge, N.J., 1985; dir. Amazon Clothing Co., 199-92; cons. in field. Campaign dir. Office of Councilman, New Providence, N.J. Reps., 1973. Served with USCGR, 1967-71. Roman Catholic. Avocations: skiing, swimming, sailing, writing. Home: 410 Roanoke Rd Westfield NJ 07090-2922 Office: Quest Importing Co PO Box 1598 Cranford NJ 07016-5598

MOFFITT, PHILLIP WILLIAM, magazine editor; b. Kingsport, Tenn., Sept. 11, 1946; s. Wallace and Claire Matilda (Allen) M. BS, U. Tenn., 1968, MS, 1971. Co-founder 13-30 Pub. (now Whittle Communications), Knoxville, Tenn., 1971, editor, 1971-79, pres., 1976—; editor-in-chief 13-30 Publs. Group, Knoxville, Tenn., 1979-86; editor, pres. Esquire Magazine, N.Y.C., 1979-84, editor-in-chief, pres., 1984-86; chmn. Lightsource Computer Images, Inc., 1989—. Co-author: The Power to Heal, 1990; contbr. columns to Esquire Mag., 1979-88. Bd. dirs. C.J. Jung Found. Mem. Mag. Pubs. Assn. (bd. dirs. 1984—). Home and Office: 1 Pelican Point Rd Belvedere Tiburon CA 94920-2456

MOFFITT, VIRGINIA LYNN, association executive; b. Somers Point, N.J., Apr. 2, 1949; d. Ralph Fuller and Alice Elizabeth (Dean) Ames; m. William Thomas Moffitt, Feb. 1, 1969; children: Kevin Thomas, Glenn Allen. Grad. high sch., Christiansted, St. Croix, V.I. Clk. Christiansted Imports, 1966-67; fgn. exch. First Nat. City Bank N.Y., Christiansted, 1967-68; returns clk. Board Walk Nat. Bank, Pleasantville, N.J., 1968-69; br. mgr. Sarah Coventry, Tuckahoe, N.J., 1971-74; bookkeeper, teller First Nat. Bank Tuckahoe, 1971-81; receptionist Adam Schwartz & Co., Ocean City, N.J., 1981-84; sec. Upper Twp. Bd. Edn., Tuckahoe, 1984-87; fleet maintenance person Trump Castle, Atlantic City, 1987-90; exec. dir. Bowling Proprietor's Assn. N.J., Marmora, 1990—. Pres. Upper Twp. (N.J.) PTA, 1977-81; coord. Upper Twp. Minor League, 1981. Home: 15 Mcdonald Dr Ocean View NJ 08230-1209 Office: Bowling Proprietors Assn NJ PO Box 809 Marmora NJ 08223-0809

MOFFLY, JOHN WESLEY, IV, magazine publishing executive; b. Phila., Aug. 5, 1926; s. John W. III Moffly and Audrey (Kane) Chancellor; m. Donna Jeanette Clegg, July 11, 1959; children: Jonathan Wesley, Audrey Kane. BA, Princeton U., 1949. Advt. sales rep. Woodrow Wilson Sch. Time Inc., Cleve., 1954-62; N.Y. advt. mgr. House & Home Mag. Time Inc., N.Y.C., 1962-66, category mgr. LIFE mag., 1967-73, v.p. selling areas mktg. divsn., 1973-87; pub., owner GREENWICH (Conn.) mag., 1987—. Bd. dirs. Greenwich Hist. Soc., 1989—, Boys and Girls Club Greenwich, 1991—, Community Answers, Greenwich, 1987-91; mem. Ambassador's Round Table- Forum World Affairs. With USAAF, 1944-45. Mem. Greenwich C. of C. (bd. dirs. 1992—, Small Businessman of Yr. 1991), Exch. Club Greenwich, Riverside Yacht Club, Cruising Club Am. Republican. Episcopalian. Home: 100 Meadow Rd Riverside CT 06878 Office: GREENWICH mag 39 Lewis St Greenwich CT 06830

MOGAN, GLEN R., gastroenterologist; b. N.Y.C., Oct. 1, 1949; s. Harry H. and Elsie (Beck) M.; m. Diane Susan Hoberman, Jan. 22, 1972; children: Grant, Craig, Douglas. BA, Case Western Res. U., 1971; MD, Upstate Med. Sch., 1975. Intern, resident, fellow Mt. Sinai Hosp., N.Y.C., 1975-80; pvt. practice West Orange, N.J., 1980—; chief sect. gastroenterology St. Barnabas Med. Ctr., West Orange, N.J., 1980—. Author: Digestive Diseases, Constipation-Elderly. Fellow Am. Coll. Physicians; mem. Am. Gastroent. Assn., Am. Soc. Gastrointestinal Endoscopy, Alpha Omega Alpha. Jewish. Office: Glen R Mogan MD 101 Old Short Hills Rd West Orange NJ 07052

MOGELEVER, BERNARD, public relations executive; b. Newark, Oct. 15, 1940; s. Louis J. and Kate (Rosenblatt) M.; m. Diane Hinkley, Feb. 1966; children: Elisa, Jonathan G. BA, Rutgers U., New Brunswick, N.J., 1962. News & feature writer S.I. Advance, N.Y., 1965-66; pub. rels. writer The Nat. Found., N.Y.C., 1966-68; exec. A.A. Schechter Assocs., N.Y.C., 1968-73; sr. v.p. Harshe-Rotman & Druck, Inc., N.Y.C., 1973-82; exec. v.p. Ruder Finn & Rotman, N.Y.C., 1982-85; sr. v.p. Burson-Marsteller, 1985-91; pres. Mogelever Comm., Inc., N.Y.C., 1991—. Lt. USAF, 1962-65.

MOGENSEN, CHARLES RAY, JR., food service administrator; b. Elizabeth, N.J., May 7, 1946; s. Charles Ray Sr. and Hellen Oakley (Holland) M.; m. Linda Diane Friezer, Apr. 25, 1970; children: Charles Ray III, Jason C., Eric S., Lindsey H. Student, Middlesex County Vocat. Coll., 1972. Cert. food executive, 1979, 1987. Chef St. Elizabeth Hosp., Elizabeth, N.J., 1969-70; dir. food svcs. Cornell Hall Conv. Ctr., Union, N.J., 1970—; pres. C.R.M. Food Enterprises, Ltd., Kenilworth, N.J., 1971-89. Author: (recipes) Escargots Without Shells, 1979 (citation merit 1979). Mem. Rep. Nat. Com., Washington, 1988; mem. adv. bd. Episcopalian Program for Homeless, Elizabeth, 1990, Union County (N.J.) Coalition for Homeless, 1991. Cpl. USMC, 1964-68, Vietnam. Named N.Y. Dist. winner Gen. Foods Corp., 1981; recipient Cert. of Appreciation Roselle Park (N.J.) First Aid Squad, 1986, award of merit USNR, 1990. Mem. VFW, Vets. of Vietnam War, Am. Legion, Masons, Internat. Food Svc. Exec. Assn. (pres. 1977, 79, 85, 86, bd. dirs., treas. 1989-91, Royal Order of Skillet 1987, Humanitarianism award 1987). Home: 30 N 19th St Kenilworth NJ 07033-1658 Office: Mega Care Cornell Hall 234 Chestnut St Union NJ 07083-9409

MOGENSEN, PAUL ROBERT, artist; b. L.A., Dec. 3, 1941; s. Edmund Svend and Grethe (Nielsen) M.; children: Kirsten O., Elise S. Student, Yale U., 1962; BFA, U. So. Calif., 1963. One-person exhbns. include Bykert Gallery, N.Y.C., 1967, 68, 69, 75, Tex. Gallery, Houston, 1975, Esman Gallery, N.Y.C., 1976, 77, Weinberg Gallery, San Francisco, 1977, 80, Mary Boone Gallery, N.Y.C., 1978, Houston Mus. Fine Art, 1978-79, Janus Gallery, L.A., 1980, Edward Thorp Gallery, N.Y.C., 1987; displayed in pub. collections Mus. Modern Art, N.Y.C., Houston Mus. Fine Art, Walker Art Ctr., Mpls., High Mus., Atlanta, Wadsworth Atheneum, Hartford, Conn. Grantee Guggenheim Found., 1976, NEA, 1980, Pollock-Krasner Found., 1988.

MOGLIA, PAUL LOUIS, psychologist; b. N.Y.C., Oct. 16, 1954; s. John Joseph and Frances Bernadette (McLarnon) M.; m. Jean Ann Busi, Nov. 25, 1988; 1 child, Eugenia. BA, Cathedral Coll., Douglaston, N.Y., 1976; MA, Fordham U., 1980, Boston Coll., Chestnut Hill, Mass., 1984; PhD, Boston Coll., Chestnut Hill, Mass., 1988. Lic. psychologist, N.Y. Tchr. Cathedral Prep. Sem., N.Y.C., 1977-79, Loyola Sch., N.Y.C., 1979-80; lectr. religious studies Mercy Coll., Dobbs Ferry, N.Y., 1980-82; lectr. English, Regis Coll., Weston, Mass., 1984-86; teaching fellow Boston Coll., 1984-88; clin. fellow Harvard Med. Sch., Cambridge, Mass., 1988; coord. behavioral medicine 5th pathway program faculty ethicist St. Joseph's Med. Ctr., Yonkers, N.Y., 1988—; cons. psychologist St. Joseph's Sem., Yonkers, 1989—; cons. to pvt. med. and mental health practitioners, N.Y.C., 1988—, to legal firms, 1990—; reviewer profl. jours., 1990—; lectr. on psychology and religion. Author: John: Apostle and Friend, 1980; also articles. Recipient rsch. award Fordham U., 1980, study grant, 1979; teaching fellow Boston U., 1982-86. Mem. APA, Soc. Behavioral Medicine, Soc. Tchrs. Family Medicine, Nat. Register Health Svc. Providers, Cath. Bibl. Soc., N.Y. State Psychol. Assn. (city rep.), Westchester Psychol. Assn., Phi Delta Kappa, Alpha Sigma Nu. Home: 17 Edwards St Roslyn Heights NY 11577-1117 Office: St Joseph's Med Ctr 127 S Broadway Yonkers NY 10701-4080

MOGRO-CAMPERO, ANTONIO ALBERTO, physicist; b. Liverpool, Eng., Aug. 25, 1940; s. Antonio Mogro-Moreno and Olga Campero-Mealla; m. Patricia Estenssoro-Terrazas, Aug. 30, 1966; children: Patricia, Cynthia, Cristina. BSEE, Columbia U., 1963; MS in Physics, U. Chgo., 1967, PhD in Physics, 1970. Rsch. assoc. Enrico Fermi Inst., U. Chgo., 1970-73; rsch. physicst, lectr. U. Calif., San Diego, 1974-75; physicist GE R & D Ctr., Schenectady, N.Y., 1975—. Contbr. articles to profl. publs. (award 1982, 86, 90); patentee in field. Mem. Am. Phys. Soc., Materials Rsch. Soc. Office: GE R&D Ctr PO Box 8 Schenectady NY 12301-0008

MOHAN, MRS. JOHN T., JR. See POSTHUMUS, CAROL LAYTHAM

MOHL, NORMAN DAVID, dental educator; b. Paterson, N.J., May 15, 1931; s. Irving and Fannie (Weiss) M.; m. Eldene Jaffe, Dec. 27, 1953; children: Ilana, Lawrence, Daniel, Steven. DDS, U. Buffalo, 1956; MA, SUNY, Buffalo, 1968, PhD, 1971. Dentist, pvt. practice Buffalo, 1958-67; asst. prof. dentistry SUNY, Buffalo, 1963-67, assoc. prof., 1970-71; prof. SUNY, 1971—; dir. oral sci. grad. program SUNY, Buffalo, 1977—; bd. dirs., mem. coun. on dental materials, instruments and equipment ADA, Chgo., 1987-92, NIH, Washington, 1988—, FDA, Washington, 1989—. Author: A Testbook of Occlusion, 1988; contbr. articles to profl. publs. Lt. USNR, 1956-58. Mem. IADR Neuroscis. TMD-Orofacial Pain Programs (pres. 1991-92), Am. Coun. on Edn. (fellow Acad. Adminstrn. 1975-76). Home: 242 Wedgewood Dr Buffalo NY 14221-1401 Office: SUNY 3435 Main St Buffalo NY 14214-3000

MOHN, GEORGE WILLIAM, JR., manufacturing company executive, engineer; b. Pottstown, Pa., Sept. 3, 1935; s. George William Sr. and Bernice Florence (Bechtel) M.; m. Nancy Lee Wilhelm, Dec. 1, 1956; children: Tarra Lynn Mohn Slater, Allyson Michelle Mohn DeVesty. BA in Commerce & Engring., Drexel U., 1958. Applications engr. Link Belt Co., Phila., 1956-58, F.J. Stokes Co., Phila., 1959-64; sales engr. F.J. Stokes Co., Warminster, Pa., 1964-66; dist. sales mgr. Pennwalt Corp., Oak Brook, Ill., 1966-72; area sales mgr. Key Industries, Rolling Meadows, Ill., 1972-76; v.p. Key Industries, Englishtown, N.J., 1976-81; v.p., gen. mgr. Key II Industries, Inc., Englishtown, 1981-85; v.p. mfg. Key Internat., Inc., Englishtown, 1985—; staff lectr. Ctr. for Profl. Advancement, East Brunswick, N.J., 1987—; reviewer tabletting specification manual Am. Pharm. Assn., Washington, 1990. Trustee United Meth. Ch., Middletown, N.J., 1984-87. Capt. inf. U.S. Army, 1958-66, USAR, 1966—. Mem. Masons. Republican. Home: 17 Adele Ct Red Bank NJ 07701-5243 Office: Key Internat Inc 480 Rt # 9 Englishtown NJ 07726

MOHRFELD, RICHARD GENTEL, heating oil distributing company executive; b. Camden, N.J., Dec. 30, 1945; s. Herbert Henry and Elizabeth Weldon (Gentel) M.; m. Ann Bacon, June 20, 1971 (div. 1975); m. Janice Lee Strickland, July l, 1978; children: Kathryn Elizabeth, Christopher Hall. BSc in Geology, Dickinson Coll., 1971. Staff geologist Temple U., Phila., 1971-74; pres. Mohrfeld Inc., Collingswood, N.J., 1974—; bd. dirs. South Jersey Savs. & Loan Assn., Turnersville, N.J., MedQuist Inc., Gibbsboro, N.J. Bd. dirs. Boy Scouts Am., Camden County, N.J., 1985—; trustee, treas. Knight Park trustees, Collingswood, 1986—; bd. dirs. Rep. Execs. Fin. Club, Camden County, 1987—. Sgt. USAF, 1969-71. Mem. Air Conditioning Contractors Am. (pres. 1986-88), Fuel Mchts. Assn. N.J. (pres. 1992—), Rotary (pres. Collingswood 1980-81). Episcopalian. Office: 24 Lees Ave Collingswood NJ 08108-1926

MOILY, JAYA PADUBIDRI, manufacturing management educator; b. Padubidri, India, June 14, 1951; s. Ishwara M. and Sathyu D. Moily. B in Engring., U. Mysore, 1973; grad. diploma, Indian Inst. of Sci., 1974; MBA, U. Wis., 1978, PhD, 1982. Engr. Indian Oil Corp., India, 1974-77; teaching asst., lectr. U. Wis., Madison, 1978-82; asst. prof. Syracuse (N.Y.) U., 1982-87, assoc. prof., 1987-89; assoc. prof. U. Balt., 1989—; cons. Am. Potato Co., Wis., 1981; project cons. Health Scis. Dept. SUNY, Syracuse, 1986, CASE Ctr./IBM Syracuse U., 1986; rev. Mgmt. Sci., 1985, 87-88, Naval Rsch. Logistics Quarterly, 1988, Decision Scis., 1989, Ops. Rsch., 1989, European Jour. Ops. Rsch., 1989; participant nat. and internat. profl. conf.

proceedings, profl. conf. track chairperson; seminar panelist on internat. trade. Co-author: Structured Systems Analysis and Design: A Case-Based Approach, 1987; author computer game Man/Man: The Manufacturing Management Game; contbr. articles to profl. jours. IBM Expert Help System Project grantee, 1986, Syracuse U. Senate Rsch. grantee; recipient Jawaharlal Nehru Meml. award, 1975, Indian Inst. Engrs. award, 1975, Karnataka State Govt. award, 1975. Mem. Inst. of Mgmt. Sci., Am. Assn. for Artificial Intelligence, Ops. Rsch. Soc. of Am., Inst. of Indsl. Engrs., Ops. Mgmt. Assn., Beta Gamma Sigma. Home: 2382 Nutmeg Ter Baltimore MD 21209-4626 Office: U Balt Merrick Sch of Bus 1420 N Charles St Baltimore MD 21201-5720

MOIR, RONALD BROWN, JR., museum director; b. Romulus, N.Y., Dec. 18, 1953; s. Ronald Brown and Tia Mary (Dangler) M.; m. Antoinette Czekanski, Apr. 11, 1981; children: Jesse Emrys, Ryan Brown, Brady Matthew. BA, Hampshire Coll., 1977; MST, Antioch U., 1979. Tchr., naturalist Habitat Inst. for the Environment, Belmont, Mass., 1977-78; program dir. Antrim (N.H.) Conservation Commn., 1979; asst. scientist Sea Edn. Assn., Woods Hole, Mass., 1979-80; tchr. sci. Jaffery-Rindge (N.H.) Mid. Sch., 1981, Pike Sch., Andover, Mass., 1981-84; curator of natural history Peabody Mus., Salem, Mass., 1984-92; exec. dir. The Discovery Mus., Acton, Mass., 1992—; narrator-naturalist New Eng. Aquarium, Boston, 1981-82; cons. whale project Meml. U., St. Johns, Newfoundland, 1982-83; naturalist Dirigo Cruises, Rockland, Maine, 1982-83, Mass. Audubon Soc., Lincoln, 1982-89. Editor: (intro.) The Sea Is All About Us, 1987; contbr. articles to profl. jours. Mem. Com. Salem Partnership, 1988-92; subcom. chair adv. group on environ. edn. State of Mass., Boston, 1989—; chair christian concern com. Second Congl. Ch., Boxford, Mass., 1990—; bd. dirs. Cambridge Sch. System, Weston, Mass., 1987—. Mem. Nat. Marine Educators Assn. (bd. dirs. 1984-87, James Centorino award 1988), Mass. Environ. Edn. Soc., Gulf of Maine Educators Assn. (pres. 1984-85), Essex County Ornithological Club (pres. 1986—). Office: The Discovery Mus 177 Main St Acton MA 01720

MOK, CARSON KWOK-CHI, structural engineer; b. Canton, China, Jan. 17, 1932; came to U.S., 1956, naturalized, 1962; s. King and Chi-Big (Lum) M.; B.S. in Civil Engring., Chu Hai U., Hong Kong, 1953; M.C.E., Cath. U. Am., 1968; m. Virginia Wai-Ching Cheng, Sept. 19, 1959. Structural designer Wong Cho Tong, Hong Kong, 1954-56; bridge designer Michael Baker Jr., Inc., College Park, Md., 1957-60; structural engr., chief design engr., asso. Milton A. Gurewitz Assos., Washington, 1961-65; partner Wright & Mok, Silver Spring, Md., 1966-75; owner Carson K.C. Mok, Cons. Engr., Silver Spring, 1976-81, pres., 1982—; facility engring. cons. Washington Met. Area Transit Authority, 1985-86; pres. Transp. Engring. and Mgmt. Assocs., P.C., Washington, 1986—; adj. asst. prof. Howard U., Washington, 1976-79, adj. assoc. prof., 1980-81; bd. dirs. U.S. Pan Asian Am. C. of C. Sec., N.Am. bd. trustees, China Grad. Sch. Theology, Wayne, Pa., 1972-74, pres., 1975-83, v.p., 1984—; elder Chinese Bible Ch. Md., Rockville, 1978-80; chmn. Chinese Christian Ch. Greater Washington, 1958-61, 71, elder, 1972-76. Recipient Outstanding Standard of Teaching award Howard U., 1980; registered profl. engr., Md., D.C. Mem. ASCE, ASTM, Constrn. Specification Inst., Nat. Assn. Corrosion Engrs., Concrete Reinforcing Steel Inst., Am. Concrete Inst., Am. Welding Soc., Prestressed Concrete Inst., Post-Tensioning Inst., Soc. Exptl. Mechanics., Internat. Assn. Bridge and Structural Engring. Contbr. articles to profl. jours. Home: 4405 Bestor Ct Rockville MD 20853-2137 Office: 9001 Ottawa Pl Silver Spring MD 20910-2257

MOK, PETER PUI KWAN, clinical pharmacist; b. Burma, May 30, 1938; came to U.S., 1961, naturalized, 1974; s. Chi-Wing and Sze-Ying Leung M.; B.A. in Zoology, UCLA, 1966; B.Sc. in Pharmacy, Phila. Coll. Pharmacy and Sci., 1969; Pharm.D., U. Mich., 1971; m. Drosa Y. C. Chang, Jan. 4, 1969; children—Mimi Elizabeth, Oliver Jacob. Clin. pharmacy resident U. Mich. Hosps. and Med. Ctr., 1970-71; instr. preventive and community medicine Albany Med. Coll. (N.Y.), 1971-76, clin. asst. prof., 1976—; dir. clin. pharmacy services, chmn. quality assurance Whitney Young Health Ctr., Albany, 1971—; assoc. clin. prof., clin. preceptor Albany Coll. Pharmacy, 1971—. Bd. dirs. Chinese Community Ctr. of Albany-Schenectady, Rensselaer-Saratoga areas 1979-82. Cited for excellence of clin. practice Pharmacy Practice Inst., Albany Coll. Pharmacy, Union U., 1978. Mem. Am. Soc. Hosp. Pharmacists, Am. Chinese Pharm. Assn., Am. Pharm. Assn. Contbr. articles to profl. jours., papers to confs. Address: PO Box 99 Guilderland NY 12084 Office: Whitney Young Health Ctr Lark Dr Albany NY 12210-2632

MOKOTOFF, MICHAEL, pharmaceutical sciences educator; b. Bklyn., Jan. 23, 1939; s. Jack Israel and Pauline (Hochberg) M.; m. Bonnie Faith Arieff, Apr. 22, 1967; children: Jeffrey David, Naomi Joy, Jay Daniel. BS in Pharmacy, Columbia U., 1960; MS, U. Wis., 1963, PhD, 1966. Cert. pharmacist, N.Y. Postdoctoral staff fellow NIH, Bethesda, Md., 1966-68; asst. prof. U. Pitts., 1968-72; vis. scientist Weizmann Inst. Sci., Rehovot, Israel, 1978; assoc. prof. medicinal chemistry U. Pitts., 1972-85, assoc. prof. pharm. scis., 1985—; mem. Pa. Drug, Device and Cosmetic Bd., Harrisburg, 1990—. Editor, author: (with others) Pharmacokinetics and Pharmacodynamics Vol. 3: Peptides, Peptoids and Proteins, 1991; contbr. articles to Jour. Protein Chemistry, Jour. Heterocyclic Chemistry, Internat. Jour. Peptide Protein Rsch., Jour. Medicinal Chemistry. Mem. Am. Assn. Colls. Pharmacy, N.Y. Acad. Scis., Am. Chem. Soc., Am. Assn. Cancer Rsch., Am. Assn. Phar. Scientists. Office: U Pitts 529 Salk Hall Pittsburgh PA 15261-1905

MOLD, FREDERICK, JR., clergyman; b. Jersey City, June 17, 1926; s. Frederick and Wilhemena Fredica (Sterl) M.; m. Doris Gertrude Sethman, June 6, 1953; children: Caryn Jeanne, David Frederick, Lynn Doris. AB cum laude, Muhlenberg Coll., 1950; MDiv cum laude, New Brunswick Theol. Sem., 1955; cert. in marriage and family counseling, Presbyn. Synod of N.J., 1974. Ordained to ministry Reformed Ch., 1955. Dir. religious edn. Old Bergen Reformed Ch., Jersey City, 1951-52; minister Reformed Ch. of Middletown, N.J., 1955-58, Reformed Ch. of Freehold, N.J., 1958-79; v.p. New Brunswick (N.J.) Sem., 1979-85, adj. prof., 1980—; stated clk. Classis of New Brunswick/Reformed Ch. in Am., 1957-92, Synod of the Mid-Atlantics, New Brunswick, 1990—; minister Reformed Ch. of Tinton Falls (N.J.), 1986-91; v.p. Bd. of N.Am. Missions, N.Y.C., 1964-67; sec. Synod Found., Inc., Synod of the Mid-Atlantics/Reformed Ch., New Brunswick, 1990—; moderator Commn. on Jud. Bus./Reformed Ch., N.Y.C., 1988—. Mem. Manasquan Beach Improvement Assn. With USN, 1944-46. Mem. Assn. Retarded Citizens, Muhlenberg Coll. Alumni Assn., New Brunswick Sem. Alumni Assn. Home and Office: Synod of Mid Atlantics 564 Pompano Ave Manasquan NJ 08736-3923

MOLDOVER, EDWARD DAVID, lawyer; b. Albany, N.Y., Feb. 21, 1926; s. Abraham and Lilly (Sanders) M.; m. Nancy H. Helpern, July 22, 1956. AB, Cornell U., 1945, MA, 1946; JD, Harvard U., 1949. Bar: N.Y. 1949, U.S. Supreme Ct. 1961. Assoc. Demov & Morris, N.Y.C., 1949-50, Lynton & Saslow, N.Y.C., 1950-57; assoc., sr. Wien Lane & Malkin, N.Y.C., 1957-68; sr. ptnr. Moldover Hertz Cooper & Gidaly, N.Y.C., 1968—. Author: Proprietorships, Partnerships and Corporations, 1970, 80. Chmn. Com. for Pub. Higher Edn., N.Y.C., 1974-78; co-counsel N.Y. Com. Pub. Edn. and Religious Liberty, N.Y.C., 1967-88; chmn. Com. on Structure of Govt. City Club, N.Y.C., 1973-76; pres. 201 E. 79th St., N.Y.C., 1990-92; trustee Brit. Mus. Nat. History Internat. Found., Inc., 1992—; del Gov.'s Conf. on Edn., N.Y., 1970. Mem. ABA (sec. on individual rights and responsibilities), Am. Jewish Com. (life, exec. bd. N.Y. chpt., pres. 1969-72, human rels. award 1976), N.Y. County Lawyers Assn., Assn. Bar City N.Y., Harvard Club N.Y. Democrat. Jewish. Home: 201 E 79th St New York NY 10021-0830 Office: Moldover Hertz Cooper & Gidaly 750 3d Ave Ste 2400 New York NY 10017

MOLDOVER, MICHAEL ROBERT, physicist; b. N.Y.C., July 19, 1940. BS, Rensselaer Poly. Inst., 1961; MS, Stanford U., 1962, PhD, 1966. Asst. prof. U. Minn., Mpls., 1967-72; rsch. physicist Nat. Inst. Standard and Tech., Gaithersburg, Md., 1972-89, group leader, 1989—. Contbr. over 80 articles to profl. jours. Mem. Am. Phys. Soc., Am. Assn. Physics Tchrs., Acoustical Soc. Am., Sigma Xi. Office: Nat Inst Stds & Tech Bldg 221 Rm A 105 Gaithersburg MD 20899

MOLENKAMP, RENÉ JOHN, priest, psychotherapist; b. Haarlem, The Netherlands, Apr. 19, 1960; came to U.S., 1986; s. Martinus and Johanna Carolina (Tangermann) M. Student, Hochschüle for Philosophie, 1984-86; MDiv, Jesuit Sch. Theology, Berkeley, Calif., 1989; MS in Pastoral Counseling, Loyola Coll., 1990, postgrad., 1990—. Ordained priest Roman Cath. Ch., 1990. Pastoral counselor Arundul Hospice, Millersville, Md., 1989-90; inpatient therapist Saint Luke Inst., Suitland, Md., 1990-91; counselor Cath. U. Am., Washington, 1991-92; campus min. Trinity Coll., Washington, 1991-92; retreat dir. "Om Vuur" Jesuit Retreat House, Deventer, The Netherlands, summers, 1987—; min. Jesuit Vol. Corps., Oakland, Calif., 1987-88; bd. mem. Beginning Experience, Oakland, 1987-88, dir. screening, 1987-89. Interviewee: (book) Jezuieten in Nederland, 1988; contbr. articles to profl. jours. Mem. AACD (student mem.), Assn. for Religius and Values Issues in Counseling (student mem.), Assn. for Specialists in Group Work (student mem.), Am. Psychol. Assn. (student mem.). Roman Catholic. Home: 1225 Otis St NE Washington DC 20017

MOLETTE, CARLTON WOODARD, fine arts educator; b. Pine Bluff, Ark., Aug. 23, 1939; s. Carlton William and Evelyn Adele (Richardson) M.; m. Barbara Jean Roseburr, June 15, 1960; children: Carla Evelyn, Andrea Rose. BA, Morehouse Coll., 1959; MA, U. Iowa, 1962; PhD, Fla. State U., 1968. Designer, tech. dir. Des Moines Community Playhouse, 1962-63; asst. prof. drama Howard U., Washington, 1963-64; asst., assoc. prof. theatre Fla. A&M U., Tallahassee, 1964-69; assoc. prof. theatre Spelman Coll., Atlanta, 1969-75, chair div. fine arts, 1974-75; dean sch. communications Tex. So. U., Houston, 1975-84; dean coll. arts & scis. Lincoln U., Jefferson City, Mo., 1985-87; v.p. for academic affairs Coppin State Coll., Balt., 1987-91, prof., 1987—; pres. Communication Matrix, Inc., Balt., 1991—. Co-author: (with Barbara Molette) Black Theatre: Premise and Presentation, 1986, (play) Rosalee Pritchett, 1970, (play) Doctor B.S. Black, 1971. Bd. dirs. Young Audiences of Md., Balt., 1990—. Mem. Nat. Conf. on African Am. Theatre, Dramatists Guild, Assn. for Theatre in Higher Edn. Home: 255 W Lanvale St Baltimore MD 21217-4124 Office: Coppin State Coll 2500 W North Ave Baltimore MD 21216-3698

MOLINA, JOHN FRANCIS, chemist; b. Jamaica, N.Y., Jan. 4, 1950; s. Joseph Robert and Lee Marie (Salvatore) M.; m. Leslie Barbara Swartz, Jan. 8, 1973; children: Joseph Robert II, Lisa Nicole. BS in Chemistry, Northeastern U., Boston, 1973; PhD in Chemistry, U. New Orleans, 1977. Rsch. chemist Celanese Rsch. Co., Summit, N.J., 1979-81; group leader analytical svcs. Apollo Techs., 1981-83; mgr. lab. ops. At Sea Incineration, 1983-85; mgr. field analytical svcs. OH Material Corp., Findlay, 1985-86; exec. v.p. ops., dir. lab. Hager Labs., Englewood, Colo., 1987-89; v.p. Lab. Testing Svcs., Inc., N.Y. Testing Labs., Inc., 1990-92, sr. v.p., 1992—; chem. cons. Booz Allen & Hamilton, Florham Park, N.J., 1979-81, N.Y. Testing, Westbury, N.Y., 1983-85. Crime watch coord. Tuxedo Park Neighborhood Assn., South Orange, N.J., 1979-83; mgr. Findlay Youth Baseball League, 1985. Mem. Am. Chem. Soc., Soc. for Applied Spectroscopy, Am. Inst. Chemists, N.Y. Acad. Scis., Alpha Theta Epsilon (award of honor 1976). Republican. Roman Catholic. Home: 36 Melbourne St Oyster Bay NY 11771

MOLINARI, GUY VICTOR, municipal official; b. N.Y.C., Nov. 23, 1928; m. Marguerite Wing, 1956; 1 dau., Susan. B.A., Wagner Coll., 1949; LL.B., N.Y. Law Sch., 1951. Bar: N.Y. 1953. Sole practice N.Y.C., from 1953; mem. 97th-100th Congresses from 14th Dist. N.Y., 1981-89; now pres. borough S.I. N.Y.C. Founder, chmn. bd. United Activities Unltd.; active YMCA, S.I. Roller Hockey League, Pee Wee Football League; mem. N.Y. Ho. of Reps., 1974-80. Served to sgt. USMC, 1951-53. Recipient Disting. Service award Richmond County Women's Com. for Cerebral Palsy, 1975; recipient Continuous Service award Italian-Am. Alliance for Progress; named Man of Yr. S.I. chpt. N.Y. Assn. Learning Disabled, 1977, Man of Yr. Richmond County Conservative Party, 1980, Outstanding Citizen of Yr. Richmond County chpt. Am. Legion, 1982. Mem. Richmond Bar Assn. (dir.), VFW. Republican. Office: Office Borough Pres Borough Hall 10 Richmond Ter Staten Island NY 10301-1954

MOLINARI, SUSAN K., congresswoman; b. S.I., N.Y., Mar. 27, 1958; d. Guy V. and Marguerite (Wing) M.; m. John Lucchesi. BA, SUNY, Albany, 1980, MA, 1982. Former intern for State Senator Christopher Mega; former rsch. analyst N.Y. State Senate Fin. Com.; former fin. asst. Nat. Rep. Gov.'s Assn.; ethnic community liaison Rep. Nat. Com., 1983-84; councilwoman N.Y.C., 1986-90; mem. 101st, 102nd Congresses from N.Y. 14th Dist., 1990—. Roman Catholic. Office: 315 Cannon HOB Washington DC 20515-3214*

MOLINARO, MARIO ANDRE, psychotherapist; b. Cosenza, Italy, Feb. 19, 1952; s. Elimio and Theresa Molinaro. BA in Psychology, CUNY, 1974, MA in Forensic Psychology, 1983; postgrad., Pace U., 1976-79. Psychotherapist Clin. Consultation Ctrs., Bronx, 1982—; psychotherapist, instr. Bronx Mcpl. Hosp. Ctr., N.Y.C., 1974-83; psychotherapist Urban Health Plan, Bronx, 1988—. Mem. N.Y.S. Assn. Counseling and Devel., Am. Bd. Med. Psychotherapists, Am. Assn. Counseling and Devel., Am. Criminal Justice Ass., Psi Chi, Alpha Lambda Epsilon. Home: 1144 Lydig Ave Bronx NY 10461-1707 Office: 1540 Pelham Pky S Bronx NY 10461-1106

MOLINE, HAROLD EMIL, research plant pathologist; b. Frederic, Wis., Nov. 13, 1939; s. Thorsten and Agnes Virginia (Johnson) M.; m. Bonnie Gay Larson, Mar. 5, 1965; children: Jenel, Christopher. BS, U. Wis., 1967; PhD, Iowa State U., 1972. Plant pathologist USDA-Agrl. Rsch. Svc., Brookings, S.D., 1972-73; rsch. plant pathologist USDA-Agrl. Rsch. Svc., Beltsville, Md., 1974—; adj. prof. George Washington U., 1981-85, Howard U., Washington, 1977—. Co-author: Postharvest Phsyiology of Vegetable, 1987; editor: Postharvest Pathology of Fruits and Vegatables, 1984; contbr. articles to profl. jours. Founder Bowie-Croften (Md.) Garden Club, 1980—. With USN, 1958-62. Mem. Am. Phythopathl. Soc., Toastmasters Internat. (pres. 1975-86), Sigma Xi. Lutheran. Office: USDA-ARS Bldg 002 BARC-W Beltsville MD 20705

MOLINO-BONAGURA, LORY JEAN, neurobiologist; b. Quezon, The Philippines, Mar. 1, 1964; came to U.S., 1967; d. Lorenzo Daban and Carmelita (Jason) M.; m. Anthony Francis Bonagura, Aug. 10, 1991. BS, SUNY, Brockport, 1986; MA, NYU, 1989. Rsch. asst. dept. psychology SUNY, Brockport, 1985-86; rsch. asst. dept. psychology NYU, N.Y.C., 1986-87, rsch. asst. dept. biology, 1987-88; tech. rsch. specialist dept. psychiatry SUNY, Stony Brook, 1988-90; asst. scientist cardiovascular biology dept. Rhone-Poulenc Rorer Pharms., Phila., 1991—. Presenter N.Y. Acad. Sci., 1989, Soc. for Neuroscience, 1989; contbr. articles to profl. jours. Mem. AAAS, Assn. for Women in Scis., N.Y. Acad. Scis., Soc. for Neurosci., Internat. Brain Orgn. Republican. Home: 4562 Fleming St Philadelphia PA 19128-4719

MOLL, CLARENCE RUSSEL, university president emeritus, consultant; b. Chalfont, Pa., Oct. 31, 1913; s. George A. and Anna A. (Schmidt) M.; m. Ruth E. Henderson, Nov. 19, 1941; children: Robert Henderson, Jonathan George. BS, Temple U., 1934, EdM, 1937; LHD, Pa. Mil. Coll., 1949; PhD, NYU, 1955; LLD, Temple U., 1963; ScD, Chungang U., Seoul, Korea, 1969; LLD, Swarthmore Coll., 1970, Gannon U., 1981; LittD, Delaware Valley Coll., 1976; PedD, Widener U., 1981. Instr. physics and chemistry Conshocken (Pa.) High Sch., 1935-37; instr. sci. Freehold (N.J.) High Sch., 1937-38; instr. physics, chemistry Memorial High Sch., Haddonfield, N.J., 1938-42; instr. electronics and radar U.S. Navy, Phila., 1942-43; asso. prof. physics Pa. Mil. Coll., Chester, Pa., 1943-45; registrar, coordinator engring. program Pa. Mil. Coll., 1945-47, dean admissions, student personnel, prof. edn., 1947-56, v.p., dean personnel services, 1956-59, pres. coll., 1959-72; pres. Widener U. (formerly PMC Colls.), 1972-81, chancellor, 1981-88, pres. emeritus, 1988—; pres. RC Assocs., Inc., 1981—; instr. electronics Temple U., 1944-46; headmaster Pa. Mil. Prep. Sch., 1945-47; bd. dirs. Fedders Corp., Ironworkers Savs. Bank, RDC, Inc. Author: numerous mag. articles. History of Pennsylvania Military College. Chmn. Pa. Commn. Ind. Colls., 1969, Found. for Ind. Colls. Pa., 1970; chmn. Com. for Financing Higher Edn. in Pa., 1975; bd. dirs. Tyler Arboretum, Crozer Chester Med. Ctr.; trutee Pa. Inst. Tech.; mem. Am. Assn. Homes for Aging, Continuing Care Accrediting Commn. Recipient Horatio Alger award, 1962, Disting. Alumnus award Temple U., 1964, B'nai B'rith Citizen Service award, 1966, Distinguished Citizen award, 1971, Themis award Del. County Bar, 1976, Good Citizenship award Phila. Bar, 1976, Exec. of Yr. award Soc. Advancement Mgmt., 1978. Mem. Assn. Mil. Colls. and Schs. (pres. 1969), Pa. Assn. Colls. and Univs. (pres. 1970), Am. Soc. Engring. Edn., Masons, Springhaven Club (Wallingford, Pa.), Racquet Cub, Sunday Breakfast (Phila.), University Club (Wilmington, Del.), Tau Beta Pi, Phi Delta Kappa, Alpha Sigma Lambda, Phi Kappa Phi. Lutheran. Home: 1960 Dog Kennel Rd Media PA 19063-1008 Office: Widener U Chester PA 19013

MOLLO-CHRISTENSEN, ERIK LEONARD, oceanographer; b. Bergen, Norway, Jan. 10, 1923; came to U.S., 1951, naturalized, 1955; s. Axel and Helga (Holmboe) Mollo-C.; m. Johanna D. Waller, Nov. 20, 1948; children—Jan E., Peter E., Anne. S.B. in Aero. Engring, Mass. Inst. Tech., 1948, S.M., 1949, Sc.D., 1954. With Norwegian Def. Research Establishment, 1949-51, sr. sci. officer, 1951; grad. student, then research assoc. Mass. Inst. Tech., 1951-55, prof. aeronautics, 1955-84, prof. meteorology, 1964-73, prof. oceanography, 1973-84; prof. oceanography NASA/Goddard Space Flight Ctr., 1983-90, assoc. dir. earth scis., 1990-91, ret., 1991; Cons. to industry, 1955—. Guggenheim fellow, 1957. Mem. AIAA (Von Karman award 1970), Am. Phys. Soc., Am. Meteorol. Soc., Am. Geophys. Union, Am. Acad. Arts and Scis. Home: 10 Barberry Rd Lexington MA 02173-8026

MOLLOY, JAMES DENNIS, lawyer; b. Bklyn., July 16, 1943; s. John Lawrence and Viola (Heslin) M.; m. Donna Feustal, July 28, 1974; children: Maura, Megan, Dennis, Patrick. BA, Mt. St. Mary's Coll., Emmitsburg, Md., 1965; JD, Antioch Sch. Law, Washington, 1983. Bar: D.C. 1984, Va. 1986. Dir. labor rels., v.p. Met. Hosp. Ctr., N.Y.C., 1970-77, v.p. labor div., 1977-85; sr. v.p., assn. counsel Printing Ind. of Am., Alexandria, Va., 1985-89; prin., ptnr. Hanson & Molloy, Washington, 1989—; U.S. gen. counsel, dir. United Ins. Co. Ltd., Hamilton, Bermuda. Author: Controlling a Work Stoppage, 1988, Health Care Practices, 1980. Gen. counsel, trustee, exec. condr., mem. U.S. Capitol Hist. Soc., Arlington Nat. Cemetery Hist. Soc.; gen. counsel PIA, Ltd., Hamilton, Bermuda. With U.S. Army, 1967-69. Mem. VFW, Am. Legion, Bermuda Bio. Soc. for Rsch., Phi Delta Phi. Republican. Roman Catholic. Home: 2931 Ft Lee St Herndon VA 22071-1813 Office: Hanson & Molloy Ste 1210 1225 I St NW Washington DC 20005

MOLMED, STEPHEN JEFFREY, engineer; b. N.Y.C., Mar. 2, 1954; s. Leon and Pearl (Diener) M. BSEE, Wentworth Inst. Tech., 1977. Registered profl. engr., N.Y. Engr. Indsl. Valley Controls, Conshohocken, Pa., 1977-80, Engrs. Inc., Newark, 1980-82; project mgr. Mariano D. Molina, P.C., N.Y.C., 1982-86; chief engr. James T. Kelly, P.C., Kingston, N.Y., 1986-88; pres. S.J.M. Assoc., West Shokan, N.Y., 1988—. Mem. Catskill Ctr., Arkville, N.Y., 1988—. Mem. N.Y. Soc. for Profl. Engrs., Sierra Club, Nature Conservancy, Am. Mus. of Natural History, Nat. Fire Protection Assn. Office: SJM Assoc 58 Private Rd # 11 West Shokan NY 12494-5403

MOLNAR, LAWRENCE, lawyer; b. Czygand, Hungary, Apr. 14, 1927; came to U.S., 1954; s. Alexander and Marie (Vavra) M.; m. Karla Lehmann, Jan. 8, 1955. Juris Utriusque Candidatus, Charles U., Prague, Czechoslovakia, 1951; JD, NYU, 1962; LLM, LLD (hon.), Charles U., 1991. Bar: N.Y. 1962, U.S. Dist. Ct. (so. and ea. dists.) N.Y. 1970, Czechoslovakia, 1991. Mem. intelligence staff U.S. Govt., Berlin, 1951-54; with Lansen, Naeve Corp., N.Y., 1955-56; asst. mgr. export traffic Intra-Mar Shipping Corp., N.Y., 1957-58; mgr. export traffic Melchior, Armstrong, Ridgefield, N.J., 1958-59; assoc. Hamburger, Weinschenk, N.Y.C., 1963-69; ptnr. Hamburger, Weinschenk & Molnar, N.Y.C., 1969—. Mem. ABA, Assn. of Bar of City of N.Y., Consular Law Soc. (v.p. 1980—), Fgn. Law Assn., Queens Bar Assn. Office: Hamburger Weinschenk Molnar & Busch 36 W 44th St New York NY 10036-8102

MOLTER, LYNNE ANN, electrical engineering and physics educator, researcher; b. Pitts., Sept. 8, 1957; d. John R. and Marilyn Jean (Vogel) M.; m. Andrew S. Orr, Apr. 12, 1980; children: David Molter Orr, Shawn Molter Orr. BS in Engring. and BA in Math., Swarthmore Coll., 1979; MSEE, MIT, 1983, ScDEE, 1987. Product engr. Hewlett Packard, Santa Clara, Calif., 1979-81; rsch. asst. MIT, Cambridge, 1981-87; asst. prof. Swarthmore (Pa.) Coll., 1987—; cons. Electronic Tech. and Devices Lab., U.S. Army, Ft. Monmouth, N.J., 1988—; mem. alumni coun. Swarthmore Coll., 1990-93, mem. faculty procedures, 1991-93; reviewer Fellowships for Dept. Def., 1987—. Contbr. articles to profl. jours.; reviewer articles for profl. jours. Advisor on E/M fields from power lines Swarthmore Borough Coun., 1991. NSPE scholar 1975-79; Newport Rsch. Corp. fellow, 1984-85. Mem. NSF (mem. adv. com. elec. and communications div. 1991, reviewer 1987—, Presdl. Young Investigator award 1988-94), IEEE (reviewer jour. 1987—), AAUP, Optical Soc. Am. (mem. ednl. coun. 1991-94, scholarship 1984), Sigma Xi, Tau Beta Pi. Office: Swarthmore Coll 500 College Ave Swarthmore PA 19081-1397

MOLYNEAUX, MARGARET MARY, think tank employee; b. Davenport, Iowa, Dec. 24, 1961; d. Daniel Anthony and E. Katherine (Spaeth) M. BA in Fin., Iowa State U., 1984; MA in Internat. Rels., Am. U., 1987. Adminstrv. asst. Am. Enterprise Inst., Washington, 1988-90, mgr. Gulf War Project, 1991—; media and program coord. Com. for Peace and Security in the Gulf, Washington, 1990-91; cons. Beaconsfield Corp., Washington, 1990—. Republican. Roman Catholic. Office: Am Enterprise Inst 1150 17th St NW Washington DC 20036-4603

MONACO, JAMES FREDERICK, publisher, writer; b. Flushing, N.Y., Nov. 15, 1942; s. George C. and Susanne (Hirschland) M.; m. Susan R. Schenker, Oct. 24, 1976; children: Andrew, Charles, Margaret. BA, Muhlenberg Coll., 1963; MA, Columbia U., 1964. Pres., founder Baseline II, Inc., Beverly Hills, Calif., Zoetrope Inc.; bd. dirs. Interactive Svcs. Assn.; former commentator for Nat. Pub. Radio and many other radio and tv networks; faculty mem. New Sch. or Social Rsch., Columbia U., CUNY, and others. Author: Who's Who in American Film Now, Alain Resnais, The New Wave: Truffaut, Godard, Chabrol, Rohmer, Rivette, Media Culture, How to Read a Film: The Art, Technology, Language, History and Theory of Film and Media, The French Revolutionary Calendar, The Connoisseur's Guide to the Movies, Celebrity, American Film Now: The People, The Power, The Money, The Movies, The Encyclopedia of Film, The Movie Guide. Office: Baseline 838 Broadway New York NY 10003-4812

MONAGHAN, W(ILLIAM) PATRICK, immunohematologist, retired naval officer, health educator, consultant; b. Ashtabula, Ohio, June 24, 1944; s. Paul E. and June E. (Sober) M. m. Mary Lou Gustafson, Mar. 15, 1976; children: Ian Patrick, Erin Kelly. BS, Old Dominion U., Va., 1968; MS in Biology, Bowling Green State U., Va., 1972, PhD, 1975. Enlisted U.S. Navy, 1961, commd. ensign Med. Service Corps, 1969, advanced through grades to comdr., 1983; staff med. technologist officer Nat. Naval Med. Ctr., Bethesda, Md., 1969; clin. lab. and blood bank officer USS Sanctuary Nat. Naval Med. Ctr., Bethesda, Md., S. Vietnam, 1969-70; clin. lab. officer Nat. Naval Med. Ctr., Charleston, S.C., 1970-72; blood bank fellow U.S. Army Med. Rsch. Lab., Ft. Knox, Ky., 1972-73; head blood bank Nat. Naval Med. Ctr., 1975-85; faculty and course dir. for immunohematology med. tech. Nat. Naval Med. Ctr., Ft. Knox, S.C., S. Vietnam, 1976-84, dir. blood bank, 1976-84; asst. prof. pathology George Washington U. Sch. Medicine, Washington, S.C., 1976-83; assoc. prof. George Washington U. Sch. Medicine, Washington, 1983-88; mem. faculty Walter Reed Army Med. Ctr., Washington, 1976-88; dep. asst. dean grad. and continuing edn. Uniformed Svcs. U. of Health Sci., Washington, 1984-88, ret., 1988; v.p. Met. Washington Blood Banks, 1976-81, ex officio mem. bd. dirs. 1981-87; cons. D.C. chpt. Hemophiliac Found., 1977-78; spl. USN rep. Am. Soc. Med. Tech., 1976-88; dir. N.E. area blood system Navy Blood Program, 1978-88; mem. tri-service blood bank com. Dept. Def. Blood Program, 1978-88; faculty and program adv. com. ARC, Washington, 1978-84, Johns Hopkins Med. Sch., Balt., 1978-85; faculty U. Tenn. Center for Health Scis., Memphis, 1978, U. Ill. Sch. Medicine, Peoria, 1978-79; guest lectr. NIH Blood Bank, 1978-84; adj. assoc. prof. Bowling Green State U., Ohio, 1981-89; bd. dirs. Exam, Inc., Rockville, Md. Navy editor Procs. Armed Forces Med. Lab. Scientists, 1976, 79, 80, editor-in-chief, 1982-85; assoc. editor Am. Jour. Med. Tech., 1978—, Jour. Allied Health; Navy editor History of the Blood Program of the U.S. Military Services in Vietnam and S.E. Asia, 1976-84; contbr. articles to profl. jours. Active, Big Bros., 1976-85. Decorated various combat and

service medals; USN grantee, 1977, 78, 79. Mem. Am. Soc. Med. Technologists (chmn. immunohematology task group 1976), Am. Blood Commn. (task force 1976, regionalization), Am. Assn. Blood Banks (sci. assembly 1976—, adminstrv. sect. 1976—, blood component therapy com. 1977-79, edn. com. 1976-83), AAAS, Am. Soc. Clin. Pathologists, Soc. Mil. Surgeons, Naval Inst., Sigma Xi, others. Home: 14116 Parkvale Rd Rockville MD 20853-2526

MONAHAN, EDWARD CHARLES, academic administrator, marine science educator; b. Bayonne, N.J., July 25, 1936; s. Edward C. and Helen G. (Lauenstein) M.; m. Elizabeth Ann Eberhard, Aug. 27, 1960; children: Nancy Elizabeth, Carol Frances, Eilis Marie. B of Engring. Physics, Cornell U., 1959; MA, U. Tex., 1961; PhD, MIT, 1966; DSc, Nat. U. Ireland, Dublin, 1984. Rsch. asst. Woods Hole (Mass.) Oceanographic Inst., 1964-65; asst. prof. physics No. Mich. U., Marquette, 1965-68; asst. prof. oceanography Hobart and William Smith Coll., Geneva, N.Y., 1968-69; asst. prof. dept. meteorology, oceanography U. Mich., Ann Arbor, 1969-71, assoc. prof. dept. atmosphere and ocean sci., 1971-75; dir. edn. and rsch. Sea Edn. Assn., Woods Hole, 1975-76; statutory lectr. phys. oceanography U. Coll., Galway, Ireland, 1976-86; prof. marine scis. U. Conn., Avery Point, 1986—; dir. Conn. Sea Grant Coll. Program, Avery Point, 1986—. Editor: Oceanic Whitecaps and Their Role in Air-Sea Exchange Processes, 1986, Climate and Health Implications of Bubble-Mediated Sea-Air Exchange, 1989; contbr. over 200 articles to profl. jours. Recipient more than 80 rsch. grants, 1966—. Fellow Royal Meteorol. Soc.; mem. AAUP, Am. Geophys. Union, Am. Meteorol. Soc. (profl.), Am. Soc. Limnology and Oceanography, Internat. Assn. Theoretical and Applied Limnology, Irish Meteorol. Soc., Acoustical Soc., The Oceanography Soc. (life).

MONAHAN, GAYLE, interior designer, educator; b. Gainesville, Tex., Jan. 3, 1941; d. Walton Edward and Willie Grace (Hobbs) Wilfong; m. John Patrick Monahan Jr., Dec. 1, 1973; children: Sean Thomas, Kristen Ames, John Roger Ames Jr. BA, U. Okla., 1965. Cert. interior designer, Conn. Pvt. practice Houston, Darien, Newtown, Tex., Conn., 1965-84; asst. interior designer Neuhaus & Taylor, Architects, Houston, 1973; designer Henry Dick & Son, Inc., Danbury, Conn., 1984-86; prin. Monahan Design Assocs., Newtown, 1986—; pvt. tutor Darien, Conn., 1989, tchr. Albertus Magnus U., Danbury, 1990, Danbury Bd. Edn., 1990. Cover designer various publications, 1987—. Mem. Newtowners Opposed to Pipeline Exploitation, 1990, St. John's Roman Cath. Ch. pancake breakfast, 1976-78; leader, recruiter Girl Scouts USA, Houston, 1971-72; vol. Newtown Vis. Nurse Assn., 1982-84. Mem. Am. Soc. Interior Designers (sec. Conn. chpt. 1991—, chmn. hospitality 1989—, award for excellence 1990, presdl. citation 1989, 90), Nat. Coun. Interior Design Qualification. Home and Office: Monahan Design Assocs 24 Butterfield Rd Newtown CT 06470-1009

MONAHAN, THOMAS ANDREW, JR., accountant; b. Erie, Pa., Jan. 23, 1920; s. Thomas Andrew and Margaret (McEnery) M.; m. Patricia Tompkins, Sept. 4, 1948 (div. June 1983), m. Rita Fargo, Sept. 3, 1985; children—Kathleen, Thomas P., Kevin, Margaret, Daniel. B.S., U. Pitts., 1942. C.P.A., Pa. Jr. acct. Price Waterhouse & Co., Pitts., 1942-43; sr. acct. Coopers & Lybrand, Phila., 1944-48; lectr. acctg. U. Pitts., 1948-49; pvt. practice acctg., Erie, Pa., 1949—; lectr. Gannon U., Erie, 1965-78. Contbr. articles to C.P.A. jour. Mem. AICPA (coun. mem. 1981-83), Pa. Inst. CPAs (v.p. 1971-72, coun. mem. 1968-71). Club: Kahkwa Country (treas. Erie chpt. 1978-90). Home: 628 Delaware Ave Erie PA 16505-4602 Office: 1202 State St Erie PA 16501

MONAN, JAMES DONALD, college president; b. Blasdell, N.Y., Dec. 31, 1924; s. Edward Roland and Mary Gertrude (Ward) M. AB, Woodstock Coll., 1948, PhL, 1949, STL, 1956; PhD, U. Louvain, 1959; post-doctoral research, Munich, Oxford, Paris; LHD (hon.), Le Moyne Coll., 1973, St. Joseph's Coll., 1973, New Eng. Sch. Law, 1975, Northeastern U., 1975; LLD (hon.), Harvard U., 1982, Loyola U., Chgo., 1987, Nat. U. Ireland, 1991. Prof. philosophy Le Moyne Coll., Syracuse, N.Y., 1960-68; v.p., acad. dean Le Moyne Coll., 1968-72; pres. Boston Coll., Chestnut Hill, Mass., 1972—; cons. to N.Y. Jesuit Provincial for Higher Edn., 1966-72; dir. First Nat. Bank Boston, Bank of Boston Corp. Author: The Philosophy of Knowing, 1952, A Prelude to Metaphysics, 1967, Moral Knowledge and Its Methodology in Aristotle, 1968. Chmn. edn. div. Boston United Way, 1974; chmn. steering com. of coll. pres. under phase II of ct.-ordered desegregation, Boston Pub. Sch. System, 1975-76; bd. dirs. Boston 200 Corp., 1974-76, Coun. for Aid to Edn., 1985—, The Partnership, 1984—, Sr. Thea Bowman Black Cath. Ednl. Found., 1989—; trustee Le Moyne Coll., 1961-69, Fordham U., 1969-75, Boston Coll., 1972—, Sta. WGBH, 1972—, Canisius Coll., 1976-82, Georgetown U., 1978-84; mem. Mass. bd. regents higher edn., Task Force on Student Fin. Aid, 1987-88, com. Rev. and Implement the Apostolic Constn., 1991—, Nat. One to One Bd., 1991—, adv. bd. Peter F. Drucker, 1990—; co-chair Greater Boston One to One. Mem. Assn. Jesuit Colls. and Univs. (dir., chmn. exec. com. 1983-86), Assn. Ind. Colls. and Univs. Mass. (exec. com. 1988-91, chmn. 1977-78), Nat. Assn. Ind. Colls. and Univs., Harvard Bd. Overseers (com. to visit grad. sch. bus. adminstrn., 1987—), Nat. Collegiate Athletic Assn. (pres.'s commn. 1984-88), Metaphys. Soc. Am., Jesuit Philos. Assn., Soc. Phenomenology and Existential Philosophy, Soc. Ancient Greek Philosophy. Home: Boston Coll Chestnut Hill MA 02167

MONCHICK, LOUIS, research chemist; b. Bklyn., Dec. 27, 1927; s. Jack and Victoria (Waschler) M.; m. Carol Dexter Jansen, May 28, 1966. BA, Boston U., 1948, MA, 1951, PhD, 1954. Rsch. assoc. Air Force Cambridge Rsch. Ctr., Boston, 1953-54, U. Notre Dame (Ind.) Radiation Lab., 1954-56; chemist G.E. Knolls Atomic Power Lab., Schenectady, 1956-57, Johns Hopkins U. Applied Physics Lab., Laurel, Md., 1957—; asst. prof. dept. chemistry Johns Hopkins U., Balt., 1968-69, lectr. dept. chmn. engring., 1979-90, Wm. S. Parsons prof., 1975, 82; vis. scientist ZIFF, Universitat Bielefeld, German Fed. Republic, Huygens Laboratorium, Universiteit Leiden, The Netherlands, 1980. Mem. editorial bd. APL Tech. Digest, 1989—; contbr. more than 75 articles to profl. jours. Named to Collegium of Disting. Alumni, Boston U., 1974. Mem. Am. Phys. Soc., Am. Chem. Soc., Phi Beta Kappa. Office: Applied Physics Lab Johns Hopkins U Johns Hopkins Rd Laurel MD 20723-6099

MONDANI, THOMAS PATRICK, SR., educational association administrator; b. Deep River, Conn., Aug. 6, 1934; s. Frank J. and Ellen A. (Campbell) M.; m. Henrietta Bloch, Nov. 19, 1960; children: Thomas P. Jr., James F. BA, U. Conn., 1956; MEd, U. Hartford, 1962. Salesperson Napier Co., Meriden, Conn., 1958-59; tchr. social studies and English Hale-Ray Sch., East Haddam, Conn., 1959-63; dir. rsch. Conn. Edn. Assn., Hartford, Conn., 1963-71, exec. dir., 1971—; trustee Farmers and Mechanics Savings Bank, Middletown, Conn.; mem. adv. coun. Horace Mann Ins. Co., Springfield, Ill., 1981—. Author: Manual for Teacher Negotiations, 1966. State senator Conn. Gen. Assembly, Hartford, 1970-72, state rep., 1966-70. With U.S. Army, 1956-58. Recipient Friend of Edn. award Student Edn. Assn., 1972; named to Valley Regional High Sch. Hall of Fame, Deep River, 1985. Mem. NEA (life), Nat. Edn. Employees Asst. Fund, Edn. Commn. of the States, Bd. Govs. for Higher Edn. Democrat. Home: 120 Timms Hill Rd Haddam CT 06438-1041 Office: Conn Edn Assn 21 Oak St Ste 500 Hartford CT 06106-8001

MONDELLO, JOHN PAUL, financial consultant; b. N.Y.C., Aug. 9, 1948; s. Salvatore Carmelo and Mary (Monaco) M.; m. Catherine Mary Seyfried, Sept. 12, 1970; children: Lynn Marie, Timothy. BA in Econs., LeMoyne Coll., Syracuse, N.Y., 1971; MS in Fin. Svcs., Am. Coll., Bryn Mawr, Pa., 1986. CLU, Chartered Fin. Cons. Fin. cons. Comprehensive Fin. Svcs., East Meadow, N.Y., 1972—; instr. estate planning Am. Soc. CLU & ChFC, Garden City, 1990—. 1st lt. U.S. Army N.G., 1971-77. Recipient Victor Goldberg Svc. award, Nassau County Life Underwriters, 1989. Mem. N.Y. State Life Underwriters (membership chmn.), Nassau County Life Underwriters (past pres., nat. committeeman), Am. Soc. CLU/Chartered Fin. Cons. (pres.), John Hancock Chmn.'s Coun., Million Dollar Round Table (life), John Hancock Pres.'s Cabinet. Office: John Hancock Life Ins 1900 Hempstead Tpke Ste 206 East Meadow NY 11554-1720

MONDLIN, MARVIN, antiquarian book dealer; b. Bklyn., July 1, 1927; s. Samuel and Thelma (Schultz) M.; m. Phyllis Grossman, Oct. 23, 1962 (div. 1968); 1 child, Gerri; m. Irene Szmulewicz, Sept. 4, 1970. Student, Cornell U., 1945; studies in Aesthetic Realism with Eli Siegel, 1945-68; student, CCNY, 1948, Bklyn. Coll., 1969-71. Clk. Strand Book Store, N.Y.C., 1951; ptnr. Amory Books, N.Y.C., 1953-59; estate book buyer Strand Book Store, N.Y.C., 1959-71, 74-76; sr. exec. v.p. Strand Book Store, 1976—; bus. mgr. Definition Press., N.Y.C., 1957; cataloger U. Cath. de Louvain, Belgium, 1972. Proofreader, copy editor Dover Publs., N.Y.C., 1958; editor Yearbook of Internat. Assocs., 1974. Mem. Antiquarian Booksellers Assn. Am., Appraisers assn. Am., Bibliographical Soc. Am., Am. Photog. Hist. Soc., European Soc. History of Photography. Home: 889 Broadway New York NY 10003-1212 Office: Strand Book Store 828 Broadway New York NY 10003-4805

MONDORE, PATRICIA ANNE, health facility administrative assistant; b. Syracuse, N.Y., Feb. 8, 1956; d. George Gillis and Margaret Elaine (Lehmann) Wilson; m. Robert Jesse Mondore, May 20, 1989. BS in Music Edn., Houghton Coll., 1978; MA in Mus., Syracuse U., 1981. Cert. music tchr., N.Y. Choral music tchr. Fabius (N.Y.)-Pompey Cen. Schs., 1978-81; mgr. music dept. Sacred Melody Bookstore, Syracuse, N.Y., 1981-89; coord. residency program dept. pediatrics SUNY Health Sci. Ctr., Syracuse, 1989—; dir. choral clinic Sacred Melody Bookstore, Syracuse, 1988; choir dir. Univ. Hills Ch., Syracuse, 1982-88, LaFayette (N.Y.) Alliance Ch., 1988-89; singer various chs., meetings, coffee houses, 1982—; talk show guest WMHR Radio, Syracuse, 1988, 89, WTVH Channel 5, Syracuse, 1987, Rocumentary Video-Newchannels, TV, Syracuse, 1988. Author of poems; composer numerous songs; contbr. articles to profl. pubs. Organizer community mall choir concerts, Syracuse, 1985-88, choral clinics, N.Y., 1982-89; singer, speaker various prison ministries, 1983—, mus. mission concerts, Austria and Czeckoslovakia, 1988, 89. Mem. Internat. Concerts of Prayer, Jorstadt Internat. Ministries (music leader 1983), Nat. Right to Life, Christian Women's Clubs (speaker, soloist). Republican. Home: PO Box 123 Jamesville NY 13078-0123 Office: SUNY Health Sci Ctr Pediats 750 E Adams St Syracuse NY 13210-2306

MONESSON, HARRY S., writer; b. N.J., Mar. 1, 1935; s. Louis and Marian Bernice (Selbin) M. Diploma, USAF Tech. Sch., Sheppard AFB, Tex., 1953, Jet Engine Sch., Eglin AFB, 1958, Ocean County Vocat. Sch., Toms River, N.J., 1964. Author: Knibblers in the Sands, Sand Sharks in the Pines, 1988, Up a Cranberry Tree, 1990, Tales of the New Jersey Pines, 1992, The World's Biggest Tummy, 1992. Sgt. USAF, 1953-61. Mem. Archaeological Soc. N.J., Lenni Lenape Hist. Soc., Liberty Lobby Bd. of Policy.

MONGAN, MARIE MADELINE, adult education educator, hypnotherapist; b. San Diego, Feb. 1, 1933; d. Patrick John and Marie Yvonne (Bonneau) Flanagan; m. Eugene Francis Mongan, May 23, 1970; children: Wayne, Brian, Maura, Shawn. BEd, Plymouth State Coll., 1954, MEd, 1970; cert., Am. Inst. Hypnotherapy, Santa Ana, Calif., 1991. Cert. hypnotherapist; cert. secondary sch. tchr., N.H. Tchr. Town of Lincoln (N.H.) Schs., 1954-55; tchr. Town of Franklin (N.H.) Schs., 1956-57, bus. edn. dept. chair, 1957-63; English instr. Pierce Coll. for Women, Concord, N.H., 1963-64, dean, 1964-70; asst. chief of staff N.H. Div. of Welfare, Concord, 1970-73; owner, dir. The Thomas Sch. of Bus., Concord, 1973—; lectr. and workshop leader various AGCYS Orgns., 1973—; cons. State of N.H., Concord, 1975; weight loss clinic dir., Concord, 1989—; birthing educator Hypnobirthing Found., Concord, 1990—; diplomat Bridges for Peace Found., Moscow, 1991. Author: Achieving Your Ideal Weight, 1989, Birth Fulfillment through Hypnobirthing, 1990, Essentials of Business English, 1988. Town chair Chichester (N.H.) Dem. Com., 1991; bd. dirs. Community Svcs. Coun., Concord, 1988—, Merrimack County, 1988—; mem. Robert Frost Contemporary Am. Award com., 1986-89. Recipient N.H. Ednl. Leader award Harvard U., 1966. Mem. Plymouth State Coll. Alumni Assn. (bd. dirs., Outstanding Achievement award 1982), Am. Bd. Hypnotherapists, Nat. Guild of Hypnotherapists (conv. chair 1990-91, Disting. Svc. award 1990, 91), Am. Bus. Women's Assn., N.H. Hosp. Assn., Bus. and Prol. Women's Club. Democrat. Unitarian. Home: RR # 2 Box 1250 Burnt Hill Rd Chichester NH 03263 Office: The Thomas Sch of Bus 146 Sheep Davis Rd Suncook NH 03275-3711

MONGELLI, THOMAS GUY, broadcast executive, radio personality; b. Jersey City, Sept. 14, 1952; s. Thomas A. and Marie (Trevelise) M.; m. Sandra F. Castoro, Apr. 4, 1987; children: Thomas John, Jaclyn Amber. BA in Mass Communications, Rutgers U., 1974. Adv. salesman Sta. WNJR, Union, N.J., 1974-75; asst. sales mgr. Dispatch Pub. Co., Union City, 1975-78; N.Y. dist. sales mgr. Aquarian Pub. Co., Montclair, N.J., 1979-82; assoc. editor Bergen News Pub. Co., Palisades Park, N.J., 1982-84; producer, host Jazz 'n More Sta. WDHA-FM, Dover, N.J., 1981—; program dir., entertainment editor, air talent Sta. WMTR, Morristown, N.J., 1984-91; reporter, radio engr., Shadow Broadcast Svcs., Rutherford, N.J., 1988-91; air talent Sta. WKXW-FM, Trenton, N.J., 1991—; audio producer MJI Broadcasting, N.Y.C., 1991—; sr. v.p. mktg. and promotion Music Am., Inc., Wayne, N.J., 1992—; co-founder Maxx Communications Ltd., 1989;. Originator various programs. Recipient Best Pub. Svc. Series award N.J. Broadcasters Assn., 1990, Recognition of Svc. award Big Bros./Big Sisters of Morris County, N.J., 1989-91. Home: 8302 2D Ave North Bergen NJ 07047 Office: Sta WDHA-FM 55 Horsehill Rd Cedar Knolls NJ 07927-2003

MONGIOVI, GARY VINCENT, economist; b. Bklyn., Oct. 23, 1957; s. Daniel Vincent and Carmela (Longobardi) M.; m. Christine Rider, Apr. 6, 1991. BS, St. John's U., 1978; MA, NYU, 1981; PhD, New Sch. for Social Rsch., 1988. Fin. analyst Mfrs. Hanover Trust Co., N.Y.C., 1980-81; assoc. prof. St. John's U., Jamaica, N.Y., 1984—; editorial cons. Edward Elgar Pub., Cheltenham, U.K.; referee for various jours. Editor: Macroeconomic Theory: Diversity and Convergence, 1991; contbr. articles to profl. jours. Vol. New Sch. Archive Project, N.Y.C., 1991—. Mem. Royal Econ. Soc., History of Econs. Soc., Can. Econ. Soc., Econ. History Assn., Econ. History Soc., Eastern Econ. Assn. Roman Catholic. Office: St John's U Econs Dept Jamaica NY 11439

MONHEIT, ALAN GOODMAN, obstetrician, gynecologist; b. Phila., Apr. 5, 1949; s. Richard S. and Jane G. Monheit; m. Deborah Monheit; children: Robin, Jeffrey, Daniel. BSc, Muhlenberg Coll., 1971; MD, U. Pa., 1975. Intern U. Calif., San Diego, 1975-76, resident physician dept. ob-gyn., 1975-79, fellow maternal/fetal medicine, 1979-81; attending physician/clin. assoc. prof. SUNY, Stony Brook, 1981—; tchr. medicine, specialist in high risk pregnancy SUNY, Stony Brook, 1981—. Contbr. articles to profl. jours. Asst. coach Three Village Soccer Club, Stony Brook, 1991. Recipient Faculty Teaching award Dept. Ob-Gyn., SUNY, Stony Brook, 1982, 88. Mem. Am. Coll. Ob-Gyn., Assn. Profs. Ob-Gyn., Soc. Perinatal Obstetricians (poster prize 1987), L.I. Perinatal Soc., Suffolk County Ob-Gyn. Soc., Phi Beta Kappa. Office: SUNY Dept Ob-Gyn HSC T-9 Stony Brook NY 11794

MONIUS, DAVID ANTHONY, structural engineer; b. Balt., July 31, 1956; s. John Francis and Margaret Rita (Boland) M.; m. Eileen Jo Tully, May 16, 1981. AA, Essex Community Coll., 1976; BSME, U. Md., 1982; M in Engring., U. Va., 1990. Registered engr. Md.; cert. Nuclear Medicine Techs. cert. bd., Am. Registry Radiologic Techs. Nuclear medicine intern Johns Hopkins Med. Inst., Balt., 1976; nuclear medicine tech. VA, Washington, 1976-78, Prince Georges Gen. Hosp., Cheverly, Md., 1978-82; assoc. engr. Dominion Engring., McLean, Va., 1982-86; structural engr. Swales and Assocs., Beltsville, Md., 1986-91; sr. structural engr. EER Systems Corp., Seabrook, Md., 1991—. Co-author: Improved Methods for Removal and Replacements of BWR Control Rod Drives, 1985. Mem. AIAA, Soc. Naval Architects and Marine Engrs., Tau Beta Pi. Home: 12033 Beltsville Dr Beltsville MD 20705

MONNING, RICHARD FRANK, education educator, small business owner; b. Pitts., Nov. 16, 1946; s. Walter Hanes and Lucille (Mancuso) M.; m. Linda Ann Beggs, Nov. 24, 1972; children: Ashley Brennan, Drew Richard. BS, Duquesne U., 1969; MEd, U. Pitts., 1971. Commd. 2d lt. U.S. Army, 1969, advanced through grades to capt., 1975, resigned, 1977; educator Chartiers Valley Sch. Dist., Bridgeville, Pa., 1969—; cons. various bus. enterprizes, 84 Lumber Corp.; owner, operator Resort Furnishings, Somerset, Pa., 1989—, retail furniture store. Mem. Democratic Com., Upper St. Clair, 1983-85; mem. PTSO, Upper St. Clair, 1981—; longhouse officer YMCA Indian Guide Program, Upper St. Clair, 1986—. Capt. U.S. Army, 1969-77. Profl. grantee U. Pitts., 1972. Mem. Am. Fedn. Tchrs., Pa. Sch. Bd. Assn., Pa. Student Council Assn., Allegheny County Edn. Forum, Nat. Assn. Secondary Sch. Prins., Scabbard and Blade Mil. Honor Soc., Lions, Rotary (ednl. observer Allegheny County), Somerset C. of C., Sigma Chi Theta. Democrat. Presbyterian. Home: 2441 Broadlawn Dr Pittsburgh PA 15241-2407 Office: Chartiers Valley Sch Dist 50 Thoms Run Rd Bridgeville PA 15017-2832 also: Resort Furnishings Rte 31 Somerset PA 15501

MONRAD, E(RNEST) SCOTT, physician, health facility administrator; b. Ft. Knox, Ky., Aug. 8, 1953; s. Ernest E. and Elizabeth A. (Haffenreffer) M.; m. Paule Couture, July 30, 1977; children: Ernest Jean-Marc, Catherine Andree, Julia Sondra. BA, Harvard U., 1975; MD, CM, McGill U., Montreal, Que., Can., 1979. Intern, then resident New England Med. Ctr., Boston, 1979-82; fellow in cardiology Beth Israel Hosp., Boston, 1982-85; rsch. fellow Univ. Hosp., Zurich, Switzerland, 1985-86; dir. cardial carterization lab. Hosp. of Albert Einstein Coll. Medicine, Bronx, N.Y., 1986—. Contbr. articles to profl. jours. Office: Hosp Albert Einstein Coll Medicine 1825 East Chester Rd Bronx NY 10461

MONROE, CARL DEAN, III, lawyer; b. Birmingham, Ala., Sept. 15, 1960; s. Carl D. and Martha Jo M. BA, Birmingham-So. Coll., 1982; JD, Georgetown U., 1985. Bar: Ala. 1986, U.S. Ct. Appeals (11th cir.) 1988. Scheduler Siegelman for Atty. Gen., Montgomery, 1986; legal rsch. aide Office of Sec. of State State of Ala., Montgomery, 1986; asst. atty. gen., adminstrv. asst. Office of Atty. Gen., Montgomery, 1987-89; atty.-advisor Office Gen. Counsel, U.S. Dept. Energy, Washington, 1989—; mem. panel of judges Georgetown Law Ctr. Moot Ct., 1991, 92. Mem. panel of judges Ala. YMCA Youth Legislature, Montgomery, 1979, 87, 88, 89; office coord. blood dr. ARC, Montgomery, 1987, 88; com. mem. Georgetown Alumni Admissions, Washington, 1986-91; mem. Nat. Trust for Hist. Preservation. Mem. ABA, Acad. Polit. Sci., Ala. Bar Assn., Birmingham-So. Alumni (alumni leader 1986—), Smithsonian Assocs., Phi Beta Kappa. Democrat. Presbyterian. Home: 1121 Arlington Blvd # 848N Arlington VA 22209 Office: 1000 Independence Ave SE Washington DC 20585-0001

MONROE, ROSE MARIA MASK, reading specialist, educator; b. Newport News, Va., Nov. 1, 1955; d. Curtis Van and Mary Ella (Pearson) M.; m. Marke A. Monroe, Sept. 6, 1986; children: Monteece C., Jamila T. BA, Utica Coll. Syracuse U., 1976; MS, Morgan State U., 1984. Cert. tchr., N.Y., Ohio, Md. Asst. Liberty Street Day Care, Newburgh, N.Y., 1969; jr. counselor Neighborhood Youth Corps, Newburgh, 1974; tutor, counselor Higher Edn. Opportunity Program, Utica, N.Y., 1976; tchr. English Balt. Pub. Schs., 1977-79; agt. Balt. Police Dept., 1979-88; instr. Bowie (Md.) State U., 1988-91; asst. prof. New Community Coll. of Balt., 1991—; tutor reading Utica Free Acad., 1975; tutor English Utica Coll., Syracuse, N.Y., 1976; reading clinician Towson (Balt.) State U., 1984; instr. Reading Community Coll. Balt., 1987-91. Counselor Utica YWCA, 1974. Recipient Merit Sonitrol Security Systems award, 1983; grantee Ottawa Found., 1973, Utica Coll. Higher Edn. Opportunity Program, 1973. Mem. NAACP, Vanguard Justice Soc. (sec. 1980-82), Alpha Kappa Alpha. Democrat. Baptist. Office: 2901 Liberty Heights Ave Baltimore MD 21215

MONROE, WILLIAM JOHN, computer science educator; b. Livonia, Mich., Jan. 26, 1964; s. William John and Margaret Elizabeth (Shaw) M. BA, Houghton Coll., 1986; MS, Rochester Inst. Tech., 1989. Asst. prof. Roberts Wesleyan Coll., Rochester, N.Y., 1987—; dir. acad. computing Roberts Wesleyan Coll., Rochester, N.Y., 1987—; dir. acad. computing Roberts Wesleyan Coll., Rochester, 1990-92. Nat. Merit scholar, 1982, Elk's Nat. scholar Benevolent and Protective Order of Elks, 1982. Mem. Assn. for Computing Machinery, Spl. Group for Computer Sci. Edn. Republican. Methodist. Home: 4325 Buffalo Rd North Chili NY 14514-1203 Office: Roberts Wesleyan Coll 2301 Westside Dr Rochester NY 14624-1997

MONTANA, PAUL BERNARD, oil company executive; b. Hudson, N.Y., Mar. 3, 1947; s. Paul Robert and Louise (Whitaker) M.; m. Carol Ann DeAngelo, Jan. 15, 1949; children: Thomas Henry, Sarah Jane Elizabeth, Joseph Paul. BS in Pub. Relations, Syracuse U., 1970. Asst. dir. admissions Syracuse U., Utica, N.Y., 1970-71, dir. alumni, 1971-74; dir. continuing edn. Columbia Greene Community Coll., Hudson, N.Y., 1974-75, dir. coll. services, 1975-78, asst. to pres., 1978-80; pres. Valley Oil Co., Inc., Claverack, N.Y., 1980—; v.p. The Creative Team, Hudson, N.Y., 1978—; pres. Miller-Wilkins, Valatie, N.Y., 1980—, Monbeck Enterprises, Claverack, N.Y., 1983—; mem. adv. coun. Exxon Distbrs./NE, N.Y.C., 1981-83, Mobil Distbrs/NE Region, 1984—, N.Y. Brand Chmn. Citgo Distbrs., 1985-89, Citgo Nat. Coun., 1987—; bd. dirs. Empire State Petroleum Assn., Elmsford, N.Y. Pres. Columbia County Young Reps., Hudson, 1978-83, state committeeman, Hudson, 1986-90; bd. dirs. United Way, Columbia County, 1982. Mem. Columbia County C. of C. Republican. Roman Catholic. Club: A.B. Shaw Fire (pres. 1978-80). Office: Valley Oil Co Inc RR 9 Claverack NY 12513

MONTEIRO, GEORGE, English educator; b. Cumberland, R.I., May 23, 1932; s. Francisco José and Augusta (Temudo) M.; m. Lois Ann Hodgins, Aug. 14, 1958 (div. 1992); children: Katherine, Stephen, Emily. AB, Brown U., 1954; AM, Columbia U., 1956; PhD, Brown U., 1964. Instr., asst. prof., then assoc. prof. Brown U., Providence, 1961-72, prof. English, 1972—; vis. prof. Providence Coll., 1967-68; Fulbright prof. Am. lit. U. Sao Paulo, 1969-71. Author: Henry James and John Hay: The Record of a Friendship, 1965, The Coffee Exchange: Poems, 1982, Robert Frost and the New England Renaissance, 1988; editor: The Man Who Never Was: Essays on Fernando Pessoa, 1982, The Correspondence of Henry James and Henry Adams, 1877-1914, 1992; translator: A Man Smiles at Death with Half a Face, 1991. Decorated Order of Prince Henry the Navigator, govt. of Portugal, 1989. Office: Brown U Dept English Providence RI 02912

MONTEITH, WALTER HENRY, JR., utility company executive; b. Framingham, Mass., Sept. 9, 1930; s. Walter H. and Ann (Sullivan) M.; m. Jane Marceau, Aug. 14, 1954; children: Deborah, Diane, Karen. B.A., Amherst Coll., 1952. With So. Eng. Telephone Co., New Haven, 1954—, asst. comptr., 1966-68, asst. v.p., div. ops. mgr., 1968-70, v.p. staff, 1970-79, exec. v.p. adminstrn. and fin., 1979-82, pres., 1982-84, pres., chief exec. officer, 1984—, chmn., 1985—; now also chmn., pres., chief exec. officer So. New Eng. Telecommunications, New Haven; bd. dirs. Conn. Nat. Bank, Hartford, Kaman Corp., Bloomfield, Conn. Bd. dirs. Long Wharf Theater, New Haven, 1978, Yale New Haven Hosp., 1985. Mem. Conn. World Trade Assn. (bd. dirs. 1987—). Clubs: New Haven Country, Quinnipiack (New Haven). Office: So New England Tel Co 15th Fl 227 Church St New Haven CT 06506

MONTERO, FERNAN GONZALO, advertising executive; b. Buenos Aires, May 22, 1948; came to U.S., 1952; s. Adolfo and Donne (Strang) M.; m. Cheryl Bowman, Dec. 30, 1976. BBA, U. Wis., 1971; M. Journalism in Advt., Northwestern U., 1972. With Young & Rubicam Inc., 1972-82; pres. Young & Rubicam Argentina, Buenos Aires, 1982-85; dep. area mgr. Young & Rubicam Latin Am., Sao Paulo, Brazil, 1985-87; sr. v.p., dir. bus. devel. Young & Rubicam Inc., N.Y.C., 1987-91, exec. v.p., area dir. Latin Am., worldwide account dir., 1991—. Mem. Internat. Advt. Assn., Am. Assn. Advt. Agys. (mem. internat. com., co-chmn. L.Am. sub-com. 1990—), Coun. of the Ams. (adv. bd. dirs. 1992—). Office: Young & Rubicam 285 Madison Ave New York NY 10017

MONTESANO, GAIL JEAN, hairdresser, cosmetologist, consultant; b. Newark, Jan. 29, 1948; d. Constant John and Mary (Di Vincenzo) M. Course in cosmetology, Masters' Beauty Sch., Passaic, N.J., 1967; student, Maria Pole' Inst., Short Hills, N.J., 1975, Montclair State Coll., 1983, European Acad., Union, N.J., 1987. Hairdresser Delores' Hair Fashions, Nutley, N.J., 1966-70, Paul McGregors, N.Y.C., 1970-72; cons. Conair Corp., Edison, N.J., 1977-80; cons., technician Clairol, Inc., N.Y.C., 1977—, mgr. product evaluation Salon Test Ctr., 1987—; esthetician Skin Care Co., Nutley, N.J., 1975—; haircolorist, cosmetologist Hair Co., Nutley, 1972—; platform artist Internat. Beauty Show, N.Y., 1975-76, 81; artist internat. shows Clairol Hosftra U., N,Y , 1977; chief exec. officer Skin Care Co., Inc., Nutley, 1975—; pres. Natural Hair and Skin Care Co., Inc., Nutley, 1975—; founder Skin Care Assn. Am., Ft. Lee, N.J., 1975; hon. mem. Clairol Presdl. Haircolorists Council, 1981. Contbr. articles to profl. jours. Sponsor, participant 32 Hr. Cut-A-Thon for Kidney Found., Nutley, 1972; participant 48 Hr. Marathon for Charity 5, Monmouth College, N.J.,

1974; vol. hairdresser Mt. St. Joseph's Children Ctr., Totowa, 1979-85. Recipient Disting. Service award Nutley Jaycees, 1984. Mem. Nat. Hairdressers and Cosmetologists Assn., Bergen County Hairdressers and Cosmetologists Assn. (v.p., bd. dirs. 1980, Merit award 1980). Roman Catholic. Office: Hair Co PO Box 540 Nutley NJ 07110-0540 also: Clairol Inc Salon Test Ctr 345 Park Ave New York NY 10154

MONTGOMERY, GEORGE CRANWELL, lawyer, former ambassador; b. Chattanooga, Aug. 24, 1944; s. George Donaldson and Mary Elizabeth (Cranwell) M.; m. Carol Lanfear, 1 child, Erynn Elizabeth. BA, U. Va., 1966; JD, Vanderbilt U., 1975. Bar: U.S. Ct. Appeals (D.C. cir.) 1976. Mem. legis. staff Senator Howard Baker, Washington, 1975-80; spl. counsel Senate Majority Leader, Washington, 1980-85; U.S. amb. to Oman, 1985-89; ptnr. Baker, Worthington, Crossley, Stansberry & Woolf, Washington, 1989—. Mem. Coun. for Excellence in Govt. With USN, 1966-72, capt. Res. Mem. ABA, D.C. Bar Assn., Sigma Chi. Office: Baker Worthington Crossley Stansberry & Woolf 801 Pennsylvania Ave NW Ste 800 Washington DC 20004-2615

MONTGOMERY, HUGH EVERETT, JR., civilian military employee; b. Jackson, Miss., July 9, 1944; s. Hugh Everett and Clara (Neelly) M.; m. Liller Markel, May 19, 1966; children: Melinda Dawn, Michelle Elise. BS in Physics and Math., Miss. Coll., 1966; MS in Physics, U. Tenn., 1969, postgrad., 1969-70; diploma, Kennedy Sch. Govt. Harvard U., 1989. Rsch. physicist Naval Surface Warfare Ctr., Dahlgren, Va., 1966-72, dir. tech. br., 1972-79; dir. rsch. Naval Sea Systems Command, Washington, 1979-80; dir. planning and programming Office Naval Tech., Washington, 1980-81; industry R & D mgr. Office Chief Naval Material, Washington, 1981-84; tech. dir. tech. assessment div. Office Chief Naval Ops., Washington, 1985-86, dep. dir. sci. and tech. div., 1986-90, dir. sci. and tech. requirements div., 1990—; exec. dir. Navy sci. and tech. requirements com. Office Chief Naval Ops., 1989—, chmn. Navy sci. and tech. working group, 1985—; chmn. Navy industry R & D bd. Office Chief Naval Material, 1982-84. Patentee in field; contbr. articles to profl. jours. Organizer, leader Sea Walker's Quartet, Fredericksburg, Va., 1979—; spokesman Friends of the Rappahannock, Fredericksburg, 1986—, North Ferry Farm Civic Assn., Fredericksburg, 1972-80, Fredericksburg Environ. Group, 1974-78; deacon Ferry Farm Bapt. Ch., 1986—, tchr., 1974—. Mem. Fed. Exec. Inst. Alumni Assn., River Bluffs Civic Assn., Audubon Soc., Fredericksburg Sister City Assn., Miss. Soc. Washington, Sigma Pi Sigma. Home: 3 River Oak Pl Fredericksburg VA 22407 Office: Office Chief Naval Ops OP-911 Pentagon Rm 5C678 Washington DC 20350-2000

MONTGOMERY, WILLIAM LAYTON, music educator; b. Waco, Tex., Mar. 28, 1934; s. Layton Edmond and Fey Ruth (Fomby) M.; children: Layton Howard, Scott Lewis, Claudia Cathleen. B Mus. Edn., Cornell Coll. Iowa, 1953; postgrad., Curtis Inst. Music, 1953-54; MusM, Cath. U. Am., Washington, 1957, PhD, 1975. Prin. flutist Nat. Gallery of Art Orch., Washington, 1965-88, Theater Chamber Players of Kennedy Ctr., Washington, 1968—; prof. music U. Md., College Park, 1964—; bd. advisors Flute Talk Mag., Northbrook, Ill., 1982—, Instrumentalist Mag., Northbrook, 1978—; adv. cons. Libr. Congress, Music Div., Washington, 1978, 79, 84. Mem. U.S. Marine Band, 1954-63. Mem. Nat. Flute Assn. (pres. 1976-77), Flute Soc. Washington (pres. 1978-80, 82-84), Arts Club Washington (music chmn. 1990—). Home: 4614 Harvard Rd College Park MD 20740-3753 Office: U Md Music Dept College Park MD 20742

MONTLACK, EDITH, artist; b. N.Y.C., Dec. 30, 1921; d. Jospeh Montlack and Sarah Hilleowitz. Student, Met. Art Sch., N.Y.C.; student, Art Students League, N.Y.C., Nat. Acad., N.Y.C. Author: Painting: A New Approach; exhibited in group shows at Parrish Gallery, N.Y.C., Riverside Mus., N.Y.C. Grand Cen. Art Gallery, N.Y.C., Knickerbocker Artists, N.Y.C., Natural Arts Club Gallery, N.Y.C., Hall of Art, N.Y.C., Jason Gallery, N.Y.C., Leges Gallery, N.Y.C., Norval Gallery, N.Y.C., Nat. Acad., Nat. Arts Club Gallery, Catherine Lorillard Wolfe Art Club, Gallerie Internat., Pietrantonio Gallery, Crespi Gallery, Hammond Mus. Recipient Emil Kohn medal, St. Gaudens medal, 1st prize Nat. Assn. Women Artists, Grumbacher award. Mem. Royal Soc. Arts (London, life), Hammond Mus. Home: 90 Taymil Rd New Rochelle NY 10804-2802

MONTONI, MARIO ENRICO, podiatrist, pharmacist; b. Bronx, N.Y., June 2, 1962; s. Peter and Gina (Palmieri) M.; m. Annette N. Savone, Sept. 2, 1989. BS in Pharmacy, St. John's U., Jamaica, N.Y., 1985; D Podiatric Medicine, N.Y. Coll. Podiatric Medicine, 1989. Pharmacist Genovese Drug Store, Ardsley, N.Y., 1989-90; pvt. practice, Yonkers, N.Y., 1991—. Mem. Am. Coll. Foot Surgeons (assoc.), Am. Podiatric Med. Assn. (assoc.), Sport Medicine Assn. (assoc.), Sons Italy, Rho Chi, Pi Delta. Republican. Roman Catholic. Office: 657 Yonkers Ave Yonkers NY 10704-2653

MONTPETIT, CHRISTOPHER MARK, entertainment manager; b. Niagara Falls, N.Y., May 23, 1965; s. Marcel Joseph and Claudette Sue (Burns) M. BA, Niagara U., 1987; MFA, Columbia U., 1990. Asst. stage mgr. ABC/Capital Cities, Inc., N.Y.C., 1987; prodn. svcs. asst. ABC/Capital Cities, Inc., New Orleans, 1988; gen. mgr. Horace Mann Theatre, N.Y.C., 1987-89; press asst. N.Y. Shakespeare Festival, N.Y.C., 1989; asst. Gatchell & Neufeld, Ltd., N.Y.C., 1989-90; bus. and pers. mgr. "The Attix", N.Y.C., 1989—; box office and gen. mgr. Alma Schapiro Theatre Ctr., N.Y.C., 1990-92; house mgr. Kathryn Bache Miller Theatre, N.Y.C., 1991-92; info. mgr. Monty Prodns., N.Y.C., 1992—. Gen. mgr., Off-Off Broadway rock musical "The Book", N.Y.C., 1990-91. Mem. Columbia U. Sch. Arts Alumni Assn. (bd. com. 1991). Democrat. Roman Catholic. Home: 203 W 109th St # 2E New York NY 10025-2311 Office: Monty Prodns PO Box 1846 New York NY 10025-1846

MONTVILLE, THOMAS JOSEPH, food microbiologist, educator; b. Somerville, N.J., Jan. 10, 1953; s. Frank Vincent and Elisabeth (Para) M.; m. Nancy Helen Shiffner, June 6, 1976; children: Christopher, Rebecca, Matthew. BS cum laude, Rutgers U., 1975; PhD, MIT, 1979. Rsch. asst. food sci. dept. MIT, Cambridge, 1975-80; rsch. microbiologist USDA, Ea. Region Rsch. Ctr., Phila., 1980-84; assoc. prof. food sci. dept. Rutgers U., New Brunswick, N.J., 1984-91, prof. food sci. dept., 1991—; cons., lectr. in field 1985—; editorial bd. Jour. Food Protection, 1985-92, Applied & Environ. Microbiology, 1980-83; bd. editors Food & Nutrition Press, 1988—. Editor: Food Microbiology, vol. 1, 2, 1987; co-editor Jour. Food Safety; contbr. articles to profl. jours. Recipient McGraff lectureship, Long Island U., 1991, Cert. Merit, USDA, 1983. Fellow Am. Acad. Microbiology; mem. AAAS, Internat. Assn. Milk Food and Environ. Sanitarians, Am. Soc. Microbiology, Inst. Food Technologists (chmn. biotech. div. 1991-92), Soc. Indsl. Microbiology, Soc. Applied Bacteriology, Phi Tau Sigma. Office: Rutgers U Food Sci Dept PO Box 231 New Brunswick NJ 08903-0231

MOODHE, JOSEPH PATRICK, lawyer; b. Bklyn., June 24, 1955; s. Frank E. and Maureen P. (Gallagher) M.; m. Carole Lysaght, Aug. 16, 1980; children: Janine, Nicole. AB, Columbia U., 1977; JD, Harvard U., 1980. Bar: N.Y. 1982, U.S. Dist. Ct. (so. and ea. dists.) N.Y. 1983, U.S. Tax Ct. 1987. Law clk. to hon. judge Lloyd F. MacMahon U.S. Dist. Ct. N.Y., N.Y.C., 1980-81; assoc. Debevoise & Plimpton, N.Y.C., 1981-90; ptnr. DeBevoise & Plimpton, N.Y.C., 1990—. Author: (with others) Communications Law, 1984-91; editor Harvard U. Law Rev., 1978-80. Mem. ABA, Assn. of Bar of City of N.Y., Mchts. Club. Office: Debevoise & Plimpton 875 3d Ave New York NY 10022-6225

MOODIE, DOUGLAS ROME, educator, researcher; b. Edinburgh, Scotland, Sept. 9, 1951; came to U.S., 1985; s. Alan Rome and Catherine Catriona (Murray) M.; m. Ginny Zhan, 1992. BS, Bristol U., Eng., 1973; MS, MBA with distinction, Cornell U., 1989. Process engr. British Petroleum, London, 1969-85; design engr. Johnson Wax, London, 1986; rsch. assoc. Hewlett Packard, Palo Alto, Calif., 1987; teaching asst. Sch. Mgmt., Syracuse U., 1990—. Capt. awarded Territorial Decoration in Royal Engrs. Mem. AIME (assoc. mem.). Mem. Ch. of Scotland. Home: 101 Comstock Pl Apt 2 Syracuse NY 13210-2021

MOODIE, WALTER TAYLOR, banker; b. North Bay, Ont., Can., Dec. 6, 1943; came to U.S., 1981; s. William and Florence E. (Johnson) M.; m. Anne Meintje van Dassen, July 6, 1968; children: William T., Jason B., Jonathan M.F. BA, Queens U., Kingston, Ont., 1967. Chartered acct., Can. Auditor Touche Ross & Co., Montreal, Que., Can., 1966-71; asst. mgr. Royal Bank Can., Halifax, N.S., Can., 1971-76; lending head office Royal Bank Can., Montreal, 1976-78; sr. mgr. Royal Bank Can., London, 1978-81; sr. mgr. Royal Bank Can., N.Y.C., 1981-82, v.p. S.E., 1983-89, v.p. N.Y. br., 1989—. Republican. Episcopalian. Office: Royal Bank Can Financial Sq 23d Fl New York NY 10005-3531

MOODY, BARBARA, art educator, college executive administrator; b. Elizabeth, N.J., Nov. 27, 1946; d. Russell W. and Beverly S. (Shepard) Cloer; m. William B. Moody, July 8, 1967; children: Nathaniel, Elizabeth. Diploma, Montserrat Coll. Art, Beverly, Mass., 1971; BFA, Syracuse U., 1983; postgrad., Vt. Studio Colony, 1986, 89; cert. Inst. Ednl. Mgmt., Harvard U., 1990, postgrad., 1991. Assoc prof. Montserrat Coll. Art, 1975—, dir. gallery, 1978-83, chmn. painting dept., 1983-88, asst. dean, 1987-88, acting pres., 1989, dean, v.p. acad. affairs, 1988—; prof. Art Inst. Boston, 1982-83; participant Alliance Ind. Colls. Art Symposium, 1990. Exhibited in one woman shows Orphanos Gallery, Boston, 1987, Akin Gallery, Boston, 1989, Brush Gallery, Lowell, Mass., 1990, and throughout New England. Mem. Nat. Assn. Women Deans, Adminstrs. and Counselors, Coll. Art Assn., Nat. Coun. of Art Adminstrs., Nat. Art Edn. Assn. Office: Montserrat Coll Art PO Box 26 Beverly MA 01915-0026

MOODY, FLORENCE ELIZABETH, education educator, college dean; b. Penn Yan, N.Y., Sept. 29, 1932; d. James William Southby and Rebecca (Worrall) M.; B.S., SUNY, Geneseo, 1954; M.S., Syracuse (N.Y.) U., 1961; Ed.D. (NDEA fellow), U. Rochester (N.Y.)., 1969. Elem. sch. tchr., N.Y. State, 1954-64, 66-68; coord. profl. devel. Eastern Regional Inst. Edn., Syracuse, 1969-71; mem. faculty SUNY, Oswego, 1971—, prof. elem. edn., 1978—, assoc. dean profl. studies, 1980-86, dean, 1986—; mem. N.Y. State Tchr. Edn. Cert. and Practice Bd., 1983-89; mem. Tchr. Edn. Conf. Bd., 1982-84. Nat. sec. Nat. Women's Party, 1974-76; bd. dirs. Oswego County Extension Service, 1974-76. Danforth asso., 1978—. Mem. Am. Assn. Colls. Tchr. Edn. (pres. N.Y. State chpt. 1983-84), Assn. Tchr. Educators, Assn. Supervision and Curriculum Devel., Am. Ednl. Research Assn., N.Y. State Assn. Tchr. Educators (sec., exec. bd. 1976-78), Kappa Delta Pi, Pi Lambda Theta, Phi Delta Kappa, Delta Kappa Gamma. Presbyterian. Club: Order Eastern Star. Author reports, curriculum materials in field. Home: 5143 Franklin Ave Oswego NY 13126-1711 Office: SUNY Div Profl Studies Oswego NY 13126

MOODY, JAMES L., JR., retail food distribution company executive; b. Manchester, N.H., 1931; married. AB, Bates Coll., 1953. With Gen. Electric Co., 1955-59; with Hannaford Bros. Co., Scarborough, Maine, 1959—; treas. Hannaford Bros. Co., 1961-69, pres., 1969-84, chief exec. officer, 1973—, chmn., 1984—, also bd. dirs.; dir. Penobscot Shoe Co., UNUM Corp., Sobey's Stores Ltd., Can., Hills Dept. Stores, Mass., Colonial Group of Funds, Mass. Served with U.S. Army, 1953-55. Office: Hannaford Bros Co 145 Pleasant Hill Rd Scarborough ME 04074-8768

MOODY, LAURA BETTYE, computer and financial consultant; b. Nashville, Oct. 13, 1944; d. Roy Frederick and Granville Allene (Pettus) M. BA in Econs., Transylvania U., 1966; MA in Econs., NYU, 1973. Staff economist Domestic div. Morgan Guaranty Trust Co., N.Y.C., 1966-69; account rep. time-sharing div. GE Corp., N.Y.C., 1969; sales mgmt. group fixed income F.S. Smithers & Co., Inc., N.Y.C., 1969-70, Drexel Firestone, Inc., N.Y.C., 1970-71; computer cons. N.Y.C., 1971-72; fixed income portfolio mgr., v.p. The Colonial Group, Inc., Boston, 1972-90; cons. Boston, 1990—.

MOODY, LORI HANLEY, video producer; b. Clarksburg, W.Va.; d. Charles and Agnes (Harkins) Hanley; m. Charles F. Moody; children: Chip, Lisi, David. BS in Speech, Northwestern U., Evanston, Ill.; MBA, U. Conn. Exec., producer N.W. Ayer & Son, Inc., N.Y.C., 1961-67; project mgr., producer Conn. Yankee Internat., Darien, Conn., 1986-88; owner, exec. producer MVP Video Prodns., Darien, 1988—; Pres. Yale House Corp., Yale U., New Haven, 1989-90, SBL Corp., Darien, Conn., 1989—. Recipient Clios, Am. TV Comml. Festival, N.Y.C., 1962, 65, Bravo award, Detroit, Internat. Broadcasting award, L.A., Quasar award finalist Mercomm, Inc., N.Y.C., 1990. Mem. Conn. Press Club (treas. 1989-90, 1st v.p. 1991—, award 1989), NMTA (mem. chmn.), Pi Beta Phi Alumnae Club (v.p. 1989—). Republican. Roman Catholic.

MOODY, ROBERT ELBRIDGE, historian; b. Rushville, N.Y., Apr. 20, 1897. s. Edward Lincoln Moody and Alice Stearns; m. Edith Johncox, Oct. 19, 1921 (dec. Oct. 1962); children: Priscilla Saxby, Jante Merriman, Edward Lewis; m. Oneta Hayes Hawkins, May 28, 1966. AB, Cornell U., 1918. Tchr. history and English, Rushville High Sch., N.Y., 1928-39; tchr. history Middlesex Valley Central, Rushville, 1939-62; civil service commr. County of Ontario, Canandaigua, N.Y., 1942-63; supr. Town of Gorham, N.Y., 1966-70, town historian, 1971—. Author: Poetic Plays on Iroquois Confederacy, Hiawatha, 1956, Dekanawida, 1957, Outline of Rushville's History, 1976, America's First Rushville, 1991; editor: Town of Gorham Scrapbook, 1976. Address: 4034 Rts 245 and 247 Rushville NY 14544

MOON, CLARENCE NORMAN, insurance company executive, safety engineer; b. Gadsden, Ala., Feb. 3, 1934; s. Lee O. Sr. and Beecie P. (Gentry) M.; m. Rita McCann, June 5, 1958; children: Gregory, Mary, Kathleen, Suzanne, Christopher. B in Indsl. Mgmt., Auburn U., 1959. Profl. safety engr., Calif.; cert. safety profl., assoc. in risk mgmt. Safety engr. Liberty Mut. Ins. Co., Atlanta, 1959-63, sr. safety engr., 1963-64; sect. engr. Liberty Mut. Ins. Co., Albany, N.Y., 1964-67; loss prevention mgr. Liberty Mut. Ins. Co., Syracuse, N.Y., 1967-72; tech. dir. Liberty Mut. Ins. Co., Pitts., 1972-76, asst. div. mgr., 1976-84; mgr. adminstrn. and pers. Liberty Mut. Ins. Co., Boston, 1984-87, asst. v.p. and mgr., 1987—; co-chmn. East N.Y. Safety Conf., Albany, 1965-66; com. mem. Western Pa. Safety Assn., Pitts., 1977-83. Solicitor Am. Heart Assn., Atlanta, 1963. With U.S. Army, 1952-55, Taiwan, 1960-62, Korea; 2d lt. USAR. Mem. Am. Soc. Safety Engrs. (treas., 1st and 2d v.p. Albany chpt. 1964-67). Republican. Roman Catholic. Office: Liberty Mut Ins Co Dept LP PO Box 140 Boston MA 02117-0140

MOON, DUDLEY GEORGE, physiology and biology educator; b. Niagara Falls, N.Y., June 22, 1950; m. Deborah B. Moon, Nov. 27, 1970; four children. MS, SUNY, Binghamton, 1979; PhD, Albany Med. Coll., 1983. Postdoctoral fellow Cleve. Clinic Found., 1983-85; rsch. asst. prof. Albany (N.Y.) Med. Coll., 1985-89, asst. prof., 1989-91; assoc. prof. Albany Coll. Pharmacy, 1991—. Contbr. articles to profl. jours. and books. Co-chmn. sci. edn. com. Selkirk (N.Y.) Sch. Dist., 1991—. Recipient FIRST award NIH, 1990—; Am. Heart Assn. grantee, 1988. Mem. Internat. Soc. Thrombosis and Haemostasis, Electron Microscopic Soc. Am., Histochem. Soc., Am. Physiol. Soc., Am. Soc. Cell Biology. Office: Albany Coll Pharmacy 106 New Scotland Ave Albany NY 12208-3492

MOON, FRANCIS RICHARD, aerospace engineer; b. Huntington, N.Y., Dec. 9, 1965; s. Frank Vincent and Dolores Antoinette (Englert) M. BS in Aerospace Engring., Poly. U., Farmingdale, N.Y., and Bklyn., 1987. Design engr. UTC-Sikorsky Aircraft, Stratford, Conn., 1989—; freelance designer, Huntington, 1986-89, engr., rsch. scientist. On-call donor L.I. Blood Svcs., Melville, N.Y., 1983-89. Recipient Silver award Poly. U. SGO, 1987. Mem. AIAA (student br. pres. 1986-87, recipient spl. citation, 1987-89, coun. advisor 1988—, student activities chmn. 1988-89), Planetary Soc. Republican. Roman Catholic. Office: Sikorsky Aircraft MS S313A2 6900 Main St Stratford CT 06497-1361

MOON, JAMES CLARK, social services administrator, foundation administrator; b. Fountain Inn, S.C., Aug. 11, 1938; s. Jimmie Lee and Lillie (Owens) M.; m. Ruby Reese, Oct. 20, 1960; children: Ruby Reese Jr., Jamesa Clarke. BA in Agr. Chemistry, S.C. State Coll., 1958; M in Adminstrn., Morgan State U., 1967; PhD in African Studies, Howard U., 1976; cert. in theology, Georgetown U., 1991. Mgr. Pilgrim Health & Life Ins. Co., Augusta, Ga., 1958-59; tchr. Pub. Schs. State Ga., Greenboro, 1959-63, Balt. City Pub. Schs., 1963-65, Washington Pub. Schs., 1965-71; chief adminstr. U.S. Dept. Health and Human Svcs., Bethesda, Md., 1971-83, sr. exec. adminstr., 1987—; founding dir. African studies Georgetown U., Washington, 1978-85; pres. NIH Blacks in Govt., Bethesda, 1991—; v.p. United Black Fund, Washington, 1975—; exec. dir. Internat. United Black Fund, Washington, 1981—. Author: The Problem of Designing African American Studies in U.S. Public School: A Case Study of D.C.P.S., 1991, The Physical Qualities of Life in Subsaharan Africa: A Survey of Twenty-Two Nations; contbr. articles to profl. jours. Pres. So. Christian Leadership Conf., Rockville, Md., 1991-92. Recipient Key to City, Rockville, 1992; rsch. grantee Md. Humanities Coun., 1988-90. Mem. Blacks in Govt. (chair Nat. Agy. Watch 1985—), Masons (chair Soc. Action 1990—), Alpha Phi Alpha (life mem., dir. pub. info. 1988-91). Democrat. Home: 1204 Potomac Valley Rd Rockville MD 20850 Office: NIH 9000 Rockville Pike Bethesda MD 20892

MOON, PETER STEVENSON, librarian; b. Washington, Feb. 22, 1953; s. Alfred Evans and Doris (Pender) M.; m. Mary Gemmel, May 26, 1979. BS, Syracuse U., 1977, MLS, 1980; cert. libr., SUNY, 1980. Reference libr. Countway Libr. Med., Harvard U., Boston, 1980-85, Health Ctr., U. Conn., Farmington, 1987, Aetna Life & Casualty, Hartford, Conn., 1988; libr. svcs. coord. New Eng. Jour. Medicine, Waltham, Mass., 1985-86; info. prof. Donahue & McCaughtry, Inc., Wethersfield, Conn., 1987-88; mgr. tech. resource ctr. Hartford Steam Boiler Inspection and Ins. Co., 1988—; libr. profl. Gov.'s Conf. on Libr. and Info. Svcs., Waterbury, Conn., 1990. Compiler bibliography Countway Mini-Guide, 1982, editor, 1983-84; assoc. editor newsletter The Pulse, 1985-86. Mem. county com. 19th Election Dist. of Oyster Bay, N.Y., 1971. Recipient cert. of appreciation Rep. Lester Wolff, 1970. Mem. ALA, Spl. Librs. Assn. (chmn. employment com. Conn. Valley chpt. 1989—), Am. Soc. Info. Sci., New Eng. Online Users Group, Soc. Competitive Intelligence Profls. Home: 82 Mallard Dr East Hartford CT 06118-2918 Office: Inspection and Ins Co 8th Fl 1 State St Hartford CT 06102-3001

MOONEY, CHRISTOPHER FRANCIS, theologian, lawyer, religious studies educator; b. Bayonne, N.J., Feb. 23, 1925; s. Christopher James and Frances Mary (Behan) M. BA, Loyola U., Chgo., 1950, MA, 1955; STD, Cath. U., Paris, 1964; MLS, Yale U., 1975; JD, U. Pa., 1978; DHL (hon.), Jewish Theol. Sem. Am., N.Y.C., 1972, Rockhurst Coll., 1991. Joined S.J., 1944; ordained priest Roman Cath. Ch., 1957. Asst. prof. Canisius Coll., Buffalo, 1959-60, St. Peters Coll., Jersey City, 1960-61; prof. Fordham U., Bronx, N.Y., 1964-69, dept. chair, 1965-69; pres. Woodstock Coll., N.Y.C., 1969-74; asst. dean Law Sch. U. Pa., Phila., 1978-80; acad. v.p. Fairfield (Conn.) U., 1980-87, prof., 1980—. Author: Teilhard de Chardin and Mystery of Christ, 1966 (Nat. Cath. Book award 1966), The Making of Man, 1971, Man Without Tears, 1975, Religion and the American Dream, 1977, Inequality and the American Conscience, 1982, Public Virtue, 1986, Boundaries Dimly Perceived, 1990. Mem. ABA, Am. Acad. Religion, Soc. Sci. Study of Religion, Cath. Theol. Soc. Am. Democrat. Roman Catholic. Home and Office: Fairfield U Fairfield CT 06430

MOONEY, LORI, county official; b. Atlantic City, Aug. 22, 1929; d. Joseph Aloysius and Alice Marie Inemer; m. Charles H. Calvi (div.); children: Joseph P., Stephen C., Christina L.; m. Thomas Christopher Mooney; children: Thomas C., Timothy C. Service rep. Bell Telephone Co., Atlantic City, 1950-58; sr. evaluator U.S. Census Bur., N.J., 1960-63; coordinator Nat. Small Bus. Com. for Johnson and Humphrey, Washington, 1964; owner, mgr. Lori Mooney & Co., Realtors, Atlantic County, N.J., 1965-77; commr. Atlantic County Bd. Elections, from 1970, also chmn. 5 yrs.; county clk. County of Atlantic, Mays Landing, 1978—; mem. Active Corps Execs., Nat. SBA; chmn. county clk. liaison com. N.J. Supreme Ct., 1984-86. Del. Dem. Nat. Conv., 1972, 76, 84, 88; mem. congl. liaison com. Acad. for State and Local Govts., 1989—; mem. U.S. Senator Bill Bradley's Citizen Adv. Com. Recipient Woman of Achievement award N.J. Fedn. Bus. and Profl. Women, 1985, Role Model award The Sun newspaper, 1989. Mem. Internat. Assn. Clks., Recorders, Election Ofcls. and Treas. (N.J. dir. 1988—), Atlantic County Realtors Assn., Bus. and Profl. Women Atlantic County (scholarship chmn. 1982-85), County Officers Assn. N.J. (bd. dirs. 1978—, pres. 1991-92), N.J. Assn. County Clks. (chmn. 1984-86), N.J. Assn. Realtors, Nat. Assn. Realtors, N.J. League Municipalities, Assn. Records Mgrs. and Adminstrs., Atlantic City Women's C. of C. Home: 100 Carol Rd Linwood NJ 08221 Office: Atlantic County Clks Office Main St Mays Landing NJ 08330-1702

MOONEY, MICHAEL JOSEPH, artist; b. Albany, N.Y., Sept. 24, 1950; s. Robert Edward and Patricia Rose (Margaria) M.; m. Deborah Lee Garner, Sept. 4, 1976. B.Profl. Studies, Empire State Coll., 1980; MA, SUNY, Albany, 1982, MFA, 1983. Exhibited in shows E.M. Donahue, N.Y.C., 1988, 89, 91, Borgenicht Gallery, 1988, Ruth Siegel Gallery, N.Y.C., 1983-86. Home: 194 Warren St Brooklyn NY 11201-6114

MOONEY, ROBERT MICHAEL, ophthalmologist; b. Mt. Vernon, N.Y., July 25, 1945; s. Robert Michael and Marie Evelyn (sabatini) M.; m. Dorothy May Kazmaier, Feb. 21, 1981. BS in Biology, Fordham U., 1966; MD, U. Bologna, Italy, 1972. Diplomate Am. Bd. Ophthalmology. Intern Grasslands Hosp., Valhalla, N.Y., 1972-73; resident in surgery Grasslands Hosp., 1973-74; resident in ophthalmology N.Y. Med. Coll., Valhalla, 1974-76; chief resident ophthalmology N.Y. Med. Coll., 1976-77; acting dir. dept. ophthalmology Westchester County Med. Ctr., Valhalla, 1980-86; pvt. practice Katonah-Mt. Kisco, N.Y., 1979—; asst. clin. prof. ophthalmology N.Y. Med. Coll., Valhalla, 1982—. Fellow Am. Acad. Ophthalmology, Am. Coll. Surgeons; mem. Med. Soc. State of N.Y., Westchester County Med. Soc., Westchester Acad. Medicine (chmn. sect. ophthalmology 1987-89), MENSA. Republican. Roman Catholic. Office: 51 Bedford Rd Katonah NY 10536-2135

MOORE, ALLAN BARON, lawyer; b. Boston, July 21, 1964; s. Roger Allan and Barbara Lee (Wildman) M.; m. Vivian Margaret Sogor, Aug. 4, 1990. BA, Harvard U., 1986, JD, 1990. Bar: Mass. 1991, D.C. 1991, U.S. Ct. Appeals (9th cir.) 1991, U.S. Ct. Appeals (D.C. cir.) 1992. Mem. nat. adv. com. for juvenile justice U.S. Dept. Justice, Washington, 1982-85; fin. analyst Trammell Crow Co., Dallas, 1986-87; asst. gen. counsel Rep. Nat. Conv., New Orleans, 1988; jud. clk. U.S. Ct. Appeals (9th cir.), Portland, Oreg., 1990-91; assoc. Covington & Burling, Washington, 1991—. Recipient Barrett Wendell prize Harvard Coll., 1989. Mem. Rep. Nat. Lawyers Assn. Anglo-Catholic. Office: Covington & Burling 1201 Pennsylvania Ave NW Washington DC 20004

MOORE, ANDREW GIVEN TOBIAS, II, state supreme court justice; b. New Orleans, Nov. 25, 1935; m. Ann Elizabeth Dawson, June 5, 1965; children—Cecily Elizabeth, Marianne Dawson. B.B.A., Tulane U., 1958, J.D., 1960. Bar: La. 1960, Del. 1963. Law clk. to chief justice Del. Dover, 1963; assoc. firm Killoran & Van Brunt, Wilmington, Del., 1964-70; partner Killoran & Van Brunt, 1971-76; partner firm Connolly, Bove & Lodge, Wilmington, 1976-82; justice Del. Supreme Ct., Wilmington, 1982—; mem. Del. Bd. Accountancy, 1965-72, Del. Bd. Bar Examiners, 1975-82, Del. Jud. Selection Commn., 1977-82; mem. Del. Gen. Corp. law com., 1969-83; chmn. joint com. Del. Bar Assn.-Del. Bankers Assn., 1978-79; chmn. Del. Jud. Proprieties Com., 1983—, Del. Bench and Bar Conf., 1988—; trustee Del. Bar Found., 1984—; faculty Tulane Inst. European Legal Studies, Paris; adj. prof. law Georgetown U. Law Ctr., Widener U. Sch. Law, U. Iowa Coll. of Law; guest lectr. law Tulane U., U. Toronto, Can., U. Tex., Villanova U., Washington U., St. Louis, U. Iowa, Geo. Mason U.; mem. pres's. coun. Tulane U., 1990—; chmn. Tulane Corp. Law Inst., 1988—. Trustee Del. Home and Hosp. for Chronically Ill, Smyrna, 1966-70, chmn., 1966-69; mem. New Castle County Hist. Rev. Bd., Wilmington, 1974-82; mem. Del. Long Range Cts. Planning Com., 1982—; dean's coun. Tulane U. Law Sch., 1988—; bd. visitors Walter F. George Sch. Law, Mercer U., 1985-91, chmn., 1988-90. With JAGC, USAFR, 1960-63. Mem. ABA, La. Bar Assn., Del. Bar Assn. (v.p. 1976-77, exec. com. 1982-83), Am. Judicature Soc. (bd. dirs. 1982-86), Order Barristers, Phi Delta Phi, Delta Theta Phi (hon.), Omicron Delta Kappa. Democrat. Presbyterian. Home: 11 Red Oak Rd Wilmington DE 19806-1247 Office: Supreme Ct Del PO Box 1997 Wilmington DE 19899-1997

MOORE, CATHLEEN TURNER, psychology educator, consultant; b. Pretoria, Transvaal, Republic South Africa, Oct. 18, 1944; came to U.S., 1970; d. James William and Kathleen Elizabeth (Diamond) Turner; m. Dan Houston Moore, Feb. 25, 1975. Transvaal diploma, Coll. Edn., Republic

South Africa, 1964; BA, Rutgers U., 1974; MEd, Temple U., 1975, EdD, 1979. Assoc. prof. psychology Phila. Coll. Pharmacy and Sci., 1981—; pvt. practice, cons. in human rels. and resources, 1980—; vis. prof. U. Durban-Westville, S.Am. Contbr. articles to profl. jours. Cons., trainer Polish Found. Bus. Sch., Vilnius U., Lithuania. Mem. APA, Ea. Psychol. Assn., Pa. Psychol. Assn., Psychologists for Social Responsibility, Orgn. Devel. Inst. (profl.). Home: 515 S 46th St Philadelphia PA 19143-2101 Office: Phila Coll Pharmacy and Sci 600 43d St Philadelphia PA 19104

MOORE, DANIEL EDMUND, psychologist, educator, retired educational administrator; b. Pitts., Dec. 31, 1926; s. John Daniel and Alma Helen (Goehring) M.; m. Rose Marie Blunkosky, Nov. 11, 1949; children: Catherine, Claire Marie Moore Caveney, Mary Moore Brilmyer, Suzanne Moore Gray, Elizabeth Moore Sullivan. BSEd, Duquesne U., 1949, MEd, 1952; postgrad., California (Pa.) State Coll., 1954-56, U. Pitts., 1958-59, Mt. Mercy Coll., 1959-60, Cath. U. Am., 1966, W.Va. U., 1970-72. Lic. psychologist. Tchr. math. Cecil Twp. Sch. Dist., McDonald, Pa., 1949-52, Pitts. Public Schs., 1952-53; with Mt. Lebanon Twp. (Pa.) Sch. Dist., 1953-88, psychologist, 1954-71, dir. pupil personnel svcs., -88; psychol cons. Peters Twp.Sch. Dist., McMurray, Pa., 1961-88, Blackhawk Sch. Dist., Beaver, Pa., 1989—, Quaker Valley Sch. Dist., Sewickley, Pa., 1989-90; lectr., supr. Grad. and Undergrad. Sch. Edn.Duquesne U.; lectr. ednl. psychology Grad. Sch. Edn., Duquesne U., 1957—, supr. student tchrs., 1989—; ednl. cons. St. Francis Schs. Nursing, New Castle and Pitts., 1959—; mem. test adv. bd. Ednl. Records Bur., 1976-86; hearing officer Right to Edn. Office, Dept. Edn., Harrisburg, Pa., 1975—; in-svc. adv. bd. Pa. Dept. Edn. Hearing Officers. Mem. Chartiers Valley Sch. Dist. Bd., 1963—, pres. 1971, v.p., 1991; mem. Pkwy. West Tech. Sch. Bd., 1965-67; bd. dirs. secondary sch. rsch. program Ednl. Testing Svc., Princeton, 1971-85; bd. dirs. Robert E. Ward Home for Children, 1975-87, St. Agatha Parish Coun., 1988—, Pathfinder Sch., 1989, v.p., 1990—; vol. Bridgeville Area Food Bank, 1988—; chairperson Parish 100 Jubilee Ceremony. Served with USNR, 1945-48. Henry C. Frick grantee, 1970, 73; named Jaycee Educator of Yr. for South Hills Area, Ward Home Outstanding Community Leader, 1984. Mem. Am., Pa. psychol. assns., Coun. Exceptional Children (pres. 1957), Phi Delta Kappa (pres. chpt. 1974-75, chmn. lay awards com. 1979—, Svc. Key award 1985). Roman Catholic. Home: 213 Station St Bridgeville PA 15017-1806 Office: Pvt Psychologist 428 Forbes Ave Pittsburgh PA 15219-1603

MOORE, DAVID AUSTIN, pharmaceutical company executive, consultant; b. Phoenix, May 8, 1935; s. Harry Theodore and Helen Ann (Newport) M.; m. Emily J. McConnell, Jan. 26, 1991; children by previous marriage: Austin Newport, Cornelia Christina, Christopher Robinson. Grad. high sch., Glendale, Ariz.; study opera and voice with Joseph Lazzarini, 1954, 55, 57-64; studies with Joseph Lazzarini, U.S., 1954-55, 57-64; studied opera and voice, Italy, 1955-56; study with Clarence Loomis, 1958-60. Pres., owner David A. Moore, Inc., Phoenix, 1969-71, Biol. Labs. Ltd., Phoenix, 1972-78; pres., co-owner Am. Trace Mineral Rsch. Corp., Phoenix, 1979-83; pres., owner Biol. Mineral Scis., Ltd., Phoenix, 1979-82; rsch. dir., pres., owner Nutritional Biols. Inc., Phoenix, 1979-83; nutritional dir.-owner Nutritional Biol. Rsch. Co., Phoenix, 1984-85; rsch. dir., product formulator Nutrition and Med. Rsch., Scottsdale, Ariz., 1986—; biochem. cons. Nutripathic Formulas, Scottsdale, 1975-88; introduced di Calcium Phosphate free concept and 100 percent label disclosure, 1979-83. Pub. NMR Newsletter. Inventor first computerized comprehensive hair analysis interpretation, 1976. Recipient Plaque Am. Soc. Med. Techs., 1982, Mineralab Inc., 1976. Home and Office: PO Box 98 Barnesboro PA 15714

MOORE, HERBERT BELL, headmaster; b. Glen Cove, L.I., N.Y., July 30, 1926; s. Lewis Kingsley and Thelma Morton (Bell) M.; m. Martha Marie Fay, June 22, 1951; children: Jeffrey, Janice, Stephen, Susan, Elizabeth, Charles. B.A., Bowdoin Coll., 1947; M.A., Boston U., 1953; Ed.M., Harvard, 1958. Tchr. math., coach Berkshire Sch., Sheffield, Mass., 1947-51; history tchr., coach, pub. relations dir., fund sec. Belmont (Mass.) Hill Sch., 1951-58; headmaster Tilton (N.H.) Sch., 1958-65, Holland Hall Sch., Tulsa, 1965-74, Kent-Denver Country Day Sch., Englewood, Colo., 1974-80; dir. schs. Cranbrook Ednl. Community, Mich., 1980-82; headmaster Tilton (N.H.) Sch., 1982-87, assoc. headmaster, 1987—; past pres. Ind. Sch. Assn. S.W., Colo. Assn. Ind. Schs. Assn. No. New Eng.; trustee Derryfield Sch., Manchester, N.H., Iona Savs. Bank, Tilton; search cons. Carney, Sandoe & Assocs., Boston. Recipient Educator of Yr. award Bowdoin Coll., 1969. Mem. Country Day Sch. Headmasters Assn., Headmasters Assn., Cum Laude Soc. (registrar gen.). Home: RFD # 1 Box 302 Winona Rd Ashland NH 03217

MOORE, JAMES ALFRED, chemist, educator; b. Bklyn., Aug. 30, 1939; s. Joseph Alfred and Henrietta (Utzig) M.; m. Lotte Wiechert, Jan. 15, 1966; children: Martina, Christopher. BS, St. John's U., 1961; PhD, Poly. Inst. Bklyn., 1967. Postdoctoral fellow U. Mainz, Fed. Republic of Germany, 1967-68; rsch. assoc. U. Mich., Ann Arbor, 1968-69; asst. prof. Rensselaer Poly. Inst., Troy, N.Y., 1969-75, assoc. prof., 1975-84, prof., 1984—; cons. Arco Chem. Co., Newtown Square, Pa., 1990—. Contbr. articles to more than 150 profl. jours. Mem. Am. Chem. Soc. Office: Rensselaer Poly Inst Dept Chemistry Troy NY 12180-3590

MOORE, JANET RUTH, nurse, educator; b. Bridgeport, Conn., Sept. 19, 1949; d. Robert Hartland and Florence (Merritt) Bessom; m. William James Moore, Sept. 5, 1971; children: Jeffrey, Gregory. AA, Green Mountain Coll., 1969; diploma, Mass. Gen. Hosp., 1974; BS in Nursing, Am. Internat. Coll., 1980; postgrad., U. Mass., 1990—. RN, Mass. Nurse's aide Lynn (Mass.) Hosp., 1967-69, staff nurse, 1972-73; nursing asst. U.S. Army Hosp., Ft. Polk, La., 1971-72; staff nurse Ludlow (Mass.) Hosp., 1980-85; staff edn. instr. Springfield (Mass.) Mcpl. Hosp., 1985-88; dir. staff edn. Jewish Nursing Home, Longmeadow, Mass., 1988—; nurse Camp Wilder, Springfield, 1981-84; clin. instr. Holyoke (Mass.) Community Coll., 1990. Mem. Jr. League of Springfield, 1981-88, Community Health Edn. Council for Children and Adolescents; bd. dirs. Mass. Soc. for Prevention of Cruelty to Children, Springfield, 1985-90, Coun. of Chs., chairperson, Div. on Aging, 1989-90. Mem. Am. Nurses' Assn. (cert. gerontol. nurse), Wilbraham (Mass.) Jr. Women's Club, Alpha Chi. Home: 104 Burleigh Rd Wilbraham MA 01095-2620 Office: Jewish Nursing Home 770 Converse St East Longmeadow MA 01106-1786

MOORE, JOHN DAVID, computer company office manager; b. Cambridge, Mass., Aug. 13, 1952; s. John Melvin and Barbara Ann (Powers) M.; m. Marianne Szlyk, Oct. 31, 1986. BS, SUNY, Albany, 1987. Lib. svc. researcher Walking Ency., Eugene, Oreg., 1986-88; acctg. asst. Chelsea Pictures, Inc., N.Y.C., 1990-91; office mgr., Marcus Computer Svcs., Inc., N.Y.C., 1991—. Editor Alphonse Dance New Eng., Boston, 1992. Recipient Letter of Commendation Boston Police Dept., 1980. Mem.Boston Computer Soc., Dance Friday (co-founder), Mensa. Democrat. Buddhist. Home: PO Box 426 Brookline MA 02146 Office: Marcus Computer Svcs Inc 243 Riverside Dr #S-103 New York NY 10025

MOORE, JOHN LEE, III, arts administrator; b. Winston-Salem, N.C., Feb. 27, 1953; s. John Lee Moore and Florence (Nekoda) Sherard; m. Delisa Kay Saunders, July 13, 1985; 1 child, Derek Duone Anthony. BA in Theatre Arts, Morgan State Coll., 1975; MA in Performing Arts Mgmt., Sangamon State U., 1983. Actor N.Y.C., 1975-76; dir. youth, outreach and community devel. YMCA's, Washington and Greensboro, 1976-79; field rep. N.C. Cultural Arts Coalition, Raleigh, 1980-81; dir. devel. N.C. Shakespeare Festival, High Point, N.C., 1984-85; assoc. dir. devel. L.A. (Calif.) Theatre Ctr., 1985-86; dir. devel., assoc. dir. Washington Project for the Arts, 1987-91; pres., dir. African Continuum Theatre Coalition, Washington, 1989—; bd. dirs. League of Washington (D.C.) Theatres, Everyday Theatre Youth Ensemble, Washington. Recipient Arts Mgmt. fellowship Nat. Endowment for the Arts, 1982; named Outstanding Young Man in Am., 1984. Mem. Charlin Jazz Soc., TransAfrica, Omega Psi Phi. Office: African Continuum Theatre Coalition 410 8th St NW 5th Fl Washington DC 20004

MOORE, JOHN MORRISON, retired administrator, educator; b. Denver, Colo., July 21, 1904; s. John Fraser and Nannie D. (Love) M.; m. Margaret Elizabeth Whiteside, Aug. 20, 1930; children: Nancy Elizabeth Moore Ruskin, Eleanoe Mary Moore Barr. AB, Park Coll., 1925; BD, Union Theol. Sem., 1933; AM, Harvard U., 1933; PhD, Columbia U., 1938. Instr. Park Coll., Parkville, Mo., 1926-27; field sec. Student YMCA, S.W. Region, 1927-28; asst. Union Theol. Sem., N.Y.C., 1930-32; from asst. prof. to assoc. prof. philosophy & religion Hamilton Coll., Clinton, N.Y., 1933-43; from assoc. prof. to prof. Swarthmore (Pa.) Coll., 1943-73, assoc. dean and registrar, 1945-71, acting dir. Friends Hist. Libr., 1971-73, prof. emeritus; exec. dir. Nat. Coun. Religion in Higher Edn., Swarthmore, Pa., 1943-48, bd. dirs. 1948-60; mgr., bd. dirs. Pendle Hill, Wallingford, Pa., 1955-75. Author: Theories of Religious Experience, 1938, The Vitality of the Christian Tradition, 1944; (with others) Liberal Theology, An Appraisal, 1941; editor: Friends in the Delaware Valley, 1981; co-editor: Seeking the Light, 1986. Mem. Friends Hist. Assn. (editor Quaker Hist. 1973-80, pres. 1980-86). Democrat. Mem. Soc. of Friends. Home: 400 N Walnut St West Chester PA 19380-2487

MOORE, JOHN RUNYAN, academic dean, economic consultant; b. Columbus, Ohio, Sept. 30, 1929; s. Lawrence Levi and Hazel Marie (Runyan) M.; m. Marjorie Ann Coy, June 14, 1953; children: Lee, Andrew. BSc in Agrl., Ohio State U., 1951; MSc in Agrl. Econs., Cornell U., 1955; PhD in Agrl. Econs., U. Wis., Madison, 1959. County 4-H Club agent Ohio Coop Ext. Svc., Steubenville, 1951; grad. rsch. asst. Cornell U., Ithaca, N.Y., 1953-55, U. Wis., Madison, 1955-58; asst. prof. Mich. State U., East Lansing, 1958-62; assoc. prof. to prof. U. Md., College Park, 1962—; mktg. specialist Ford Found., New Delhi, 1968-70; asst. dean Internat. Program U. Md., College Park, 1979—; econ. cons. FTC, Washington, 1963-64, Ford Found., New Delhi, 1968-70, World Bank, India and Nigeria, 1971-74, USAID, Indonesia, Malawi, Haiti, Liberia and Egypt, various yrs., FAO, Beijing, 1990. Co-author: (book) Market Structure of Agriculture Industries, 1964, U.S. Investment In Latin American Food Processing, 1966, Indian Food Grain Market, 1972. Lt. USNR, 1951-53. Recipient Internat. Honor awrd USDA, Washington, 1985, Cert. of Appreciation, 1986, Internat. Disting. Faculty Svc. award U. Md., 1992. Mem. Am. Agrl. Econ. Assn. (Thesis award 1960), Am. Econ. Assn., Internat. Agrl. Econ. Assn., Assn. U.S. U. Dirs. Internat. Agrl. Program (chmn. lobby com. 1982-84, bd. dir. 1989—), College Park Rotary (bd. dir.).

MOORE, JOHN SPAETH, JR., civil engineer; b. Drexel Hill, Pa., Aug. 23, 1950; s. John Spaeth and Matilda (Atchison) M.; m. Mary Ellen Connell, May 26, 1973; children: Megan, Brendan. BCE, U. Del., 1972. Registered profl. engr., Pa. Engr. Phila. Electric Co., Phila., 1972-84, sr. engr. quality control, 1985-87, asst. supt., 1988, sr. project mgr., 1989-90, br. mgr., 1991—. Mem. exec. bd. Woodbury (N.J.) Jr. and Sr. High Sch. PTSA, 1990-91. Mem. ASCE, Am. Welding Soc. Home: 343 Delaware St Woodbury NJ 08096-5876 Office: Phila Elec Co 955-965 Chesterbrook Blvd 63B-1 Wayne PA 19087

MOORE, JOHN WILLIAM, educator; b. Brookeville, Pa., Mar. 7, 1928; s. John Thompson and Josie May M.; m. Laura Phillipine Battenberg, Aug. 25, 1961; children: William A., Laura Josie, Virginia Kathleen. BS, Clarion (Pa.) State Tchrs.Coll, 1948; MEd, Pa. State U., 1956, EdD, 1959. Tchr. math. Brookville (Pa.) Area Schs., 1948-58; grad. asst. Coll. Edn. Pa. State U., University Park, 1958-59; dir. rsch. dept. edn. Bucknell U., Lewisburg, Pa., 1959-61, assoc. prof. edn., 1961-63, prof. and dept. head, 1963—. Co-author: Conditioning and Instrumental Learning, 1977; contbr. articles to profl. jours. Ruling elder First Presbyn. Ch., Lewisburg, Pa., 1984-87. Carnegie Found. grantee, 1964-65, U.S. Office Edn. grantee, 1968-69; recipient Lindback Award for disting. teaching, Bucknell U., 1978; named one of 70 Most Disting. Educators, Assn. Tchr. Educators, 1990. Mem. Pa. Ssn. Coll. and Tchr. Educators (bd. dirs. 1981-89), Am. Ednl. Rsch. Assn. Office: Bucknell U Dept Edn Lewisburg PA 17837

MOORE, JOYCE KRISTINA, financial services representative; b. Phila., June 19, 1955; d. Oscar Herbert Hariu and Virginia Wilson (Guss) Leas ; m. William Burns Moore, June 20, 1980 (div. 1990); children: William Patrick, Kristofer Sean. Student, Beloit Coll., 1973-74, U. Pa., 1974-75, Lafayette Coll., 1984-88. With photographic sales staff MacCallum Stores, Ardmore, Pa., 1974-77; photographer Clair Pruett Studios, Drexel Hill, Pa., 1977-80; photographic cons. Dan's Camera City, Allentown, Pa., 1980-81; contr., co-founder BioService, Inc., Bethlehem, Pa., 1985-89; contr. Mega Video Inc., Easton, Pa., 1989-91; spl. rep. John Hancock Fin. Svcs., Allentown, Pa., 1990—. Former mem. Warren County Dem. Com., Phillipsburg, N.J., 1981-83; overseer Religious Soc. Friends, 1986-92; bd. dirs. Spring Garden Children's Sch., Easton, Pa.; den leader Cub Scout Pack 31, Williams Twp., Pa.; councilwoman Glendon Borough. Mem. LWV (bd. dir. Easton area 1987-91, pres. 1989-90), Balloon Fedn. Am., Gt. Ea. Balloon Assn., Nat. Assn. Life Underwriters. Office: John Hancock Fin Svcs 1259 S Cedar Crest Blvd Allentown PA 18103-6206

MOORE, JULIA ALICE, non-profit executive; b. Jersey City, N.J., Sept. 10, 1950; d. John Richard and Jean (Alexander) M.; mm. Harry C. Blaney III, Feb. 14, 1976. BS in Frgn. Svc., Georgetown U., Washington, 1972. Analyst Washington Analysis Corp., Washington, 1972-73; assoc. dir. Joseph S. White & Assoc., Washington, 1973-75; dep. dir. Arms Control Assn., Washington, 1982-84; legis. & pub. affairs officer U.S. Dept. of State, Washington, 1975-86; v.p. communications World Wildlife Fund, Washington, 1986-90; sr. assoc. Ogilvy & Mather Pub. Affairs, Washington, 1990-91; exec. dir. Physicians for Social Responsibility, Washington, 1991—; bd. dirs. Scoville Fellowships, Washington, Profls. Coalition for Nuclear Arms Control. Author: OP-EDS. Named Rusk Fellow, Georgetown U., 1985. Mem. Nat. Press Club, Internat. Inst. for Strategic Studies, Arms Control Assn. Roman Catholic. Home: 4700 Connecticut Ave NW Washington DC 20008-5629 Office: Physicians for Social Responsibility 1000 16th St NW Washington DC 20036-5705

MOORE, KEVIN WAYNE, marketing executive; b. Clarion, Pa., Feb. 16, 1951; s. Thomas D. Moore and Patricia Seigworth Rhoads; m. Patricia Magrini, Aug. 7, 1971; children: Lori Ann, Paul Thomas, Jeffrey Agustine. Student, Coll. William and Mary, Williamsburg, Va., 1973. Sales rep. Senco Products Inc., Pitts., 1973-78; area sales mgr. Senco Products Inc., Holliston, Mass., 1978-80; sales/mktg. tng. Senco Products Inc., Cin., 1980-83; sales rep. Matthews Internat. Corp., Pitts., 1983-85; reg. sales mgr. Matthews Can. Ltd., Burlington, Ont., 1985-88; sales/mktg. mgr. Matthews Internat., Pitts., 1988-90, mgr. C&I products, 1991—. Office: Matthews Internat Corp 6515 Penn Ave Pittsburgh PA 15206-4407

MOORE, MARILYN BRACEY, career and adult education educator, consultant; b. Alexandria, Va., Apr. 10, 1944; d. Arthur Woodrow and Miriam (Robinson) Bracey; m. Lewis Preston Moore Jr., Dec.27, 1965 (div. 1978); children: Constance Michele Moore-Jones, Lewis Stefan. BS, Va. State U., 1965; MEd, Howard U., 1976; postgrad., U. D.C., 1973, Trinity Coll., 1974, Southeastern U., 1978, Johns Hopkins U., 1987, Howard U. Fishery aide tech. U.S. Dept. Interior, Oxford, Md., 1965; sci. tchr. Muscogee Sch. System, Columbus, Ga., 1967; biology tchr. D.C. Pub. Schs., 1968-72, tchr.-coord., 1972-85, tchr. employability skills/entrepreneurship skills, 1986—, computer lab instr., 1990—; sales agt. World Book Ency., Washington, 1971-72; GED sci. instr. U. D.C., 1977; cons., facilitator Potomac Electric Power Co., 1982-84. Mem. Randall Estates Civic Assn., Alexandria, 1978-91. LaVerne B. Noyes fellow Howard U., 1974-76. Mem. AACD, NCDA, Nat. Employment Counselors Assn., Assn. for Multicultural Counseling and Devel., Assn. for Providers of Employment and Tng., Earthwatch, Va. State U. Alumni Assn., Future Bus. Leaders of Am., Alpha Kappa Alpha. Home: 7023 Jube Ct Alexandria VA 22307 Office: Howard Dilworth Woodson High Sch 55th & Eads Sts NE Washington DC 20019

MOORE, MARSHA LYNN, elementary school educator; b. Washington, May 19, 1946; d. Marshall Alexander and Doris Virginia (Diggs) M. BA, Howard U., 1967; MEd, U. Md., 1973. Cert. elem. sch. counseling. Counselor Balt. County Schs., Towson, Md., 1972-77; fashion coord., mgr. Wallach's Ladies' Store, Nanuet, N.Y., 1977-80, Livingston, N.J., 1977-80; adult edn. cons., counselor East Orange (N.J.) Adult High Sch., 1980-83; minority counselor Essex County Community Coll., Newark, 1984-85; equal opportunity fund counselor, instr. Kean Coll., Union, N.J., 1985-87; elem. tchr. Washington Pub. Schs., 1967-72, 87—; coord. counselor Summer Youth Employment Program, East Orange, 1982, career fair coord. East Orange Adult High Sch., 1981, Essex County Community Coll., 1985, math. tutorial coord., sch. newspaper coord. Brookland Sch., Washington, 1990-91. Chmn. Teen Lift, N.J., Delteens, Washington. Mem. Am. Fedn. Tchrs., Howard U. Alumni Assn. (coord. 1980-87, v.p. 1989-91, pres. 1991—), Delta Sigma Theta. Epsicopalian.

MOORE, MARY JULIA, educator; b. Pitts., Oct. 10, 1949; d. Edward Henry and Julia Ann (Polkabla) Sauer; 1 child, Jason Michael Sauer; m. John Harold Moore, Oct. 27, 1990. BS in Art Edn., Edinboro State Coll., 1971; MS in Spl. Edn., Clarion State Coll., 1980; postgrad. U. Pitts., 1988—. Cert. art tchr., spl. edn. tchr. for mentally retarded. Tchr. Polk (Pa.) State Sch. & Hosp., 1971-72; vol. VISTA, Bath, N.Y., 1972-73; tchr. Polk Ctr., 1973-80, program specialist, 1980-92; residential svc. supr., qualified mental retardation profl. Polk (Pa.) Ctr., 1992—; lectr., speaker, video on local TV on history of Polk Ctr., 1987. Patentee beer bottle shaper cake pan; cakes displayed in TV videos and in various mags.; creator history video Polk Ctr. Mem. Internat. Cake Expn. Soc. Democrat. Roman Catholic. Home: RD # 3 Box 232-AI Franklin PA 16323

MOORE, NANCY ANN (GARDNER), vocational school director, school counselor; b. Altoona, Pa., June 10, 1941; d. Willard A. and Helen Catherine (Zeek) Gardner; m. Thomas I. Moore, June 1, 1963; children: James T., Melissa A. BS in Edn., Ind. State Coll., 1963; MEd, Ind. U. Pa., 1965; cert. in guidance, Ind. & State U. Pa., 1967; cert. dir. vocat. edn., Pa. State U., 1981. Cert. counselor. Bus. edn. tchr., guidance counselor Altoona Area Sch. Dist., 1963-76; guidance counselor, supr. vocat. evaluation ctr. Altoona Area Vocat.-Tech. Sch., 1976—; mem. Blair County Drug & Alcohol Adv. Com., Altoona. Mem. NEA, ACA, Am. Sch. Counselors Assn., Pa. Sch. Counselors Assn. (chair membership com.), Am. Vocat. Assn. (life), Pa. Vocal. Assn. (life, exec. bd., Vocat. Educator of Yr. 1992), Pa. Edn. Conf. Planning Com., State Adv. Coun. for Vocat. Edn. (chair 1984-85), Pa. State Edn. Assn., Altoona Vocat. Tchrs. Soc. (Educator of Yr. 1991-92). Office: Altoona Area Vocat-Tech Sch 1500 4th Ave Altoona PA 16602-3695

MOORE, PATRICIA ANNE, funeral director; b. Montclair, N.J., Feb. 5, 1956; d. John Michael and Regina (D'Amelio) Josephs; m. Robert C. Moore, IV, 1980; 1 child, Robert C. V. BS, Montclair State Coll., 1980; funeral service studies, Mercer County Community Coll., N.J., 1987. Lic. life insur. agt., N.J. N.J. Sanitary Inspector Grade 1 Wayne & Paramus, N.J., 1981-87; funeral dir. Moore's Home for Funerals, Wayne, N.J., 1987—. Eye enucleator N.J. Lions Eye Bank, Newark, 1989. Mem. Nat. Funeral Dirs. Assn., N.J. Funeral Dirs. Assn., Passaic County Funeral Dirs. Assn. (treas. 1988—), Zonta Internat. Democrat. Roman Catholic. Office: Moore's Home for Funerals 1591 Alps Rd Wayne NJ 07470-3641

MOORE, POWELL ALLEN, former government official, consultant; b. Milledgeville, Ga., Jan. 5, 1938; s. Jere N. and Sarah (Allen) M.; m. Katherine Southward, Oct. 14, 1961; children: Frances Moore Preston, Powell Allen Jr. B.A. in Jounalism, U. Ga., 1959. Press sec. to Richard Russell, U.S. Senate, Washington, 1966-71; dep. dir. pub. info. Dept. Justice, Washington, 1971-72; dep. spl. asst. to Pres. for legis. affairs The White House, Washington, 1973-75, dep. asst. to Pres. for legis. affairs, 1981-82; cons. pub. affairs Washington, 1975-81; asst. sec. for congl. rels. Dept. State, Washington, 1982-83; v.p. legis. affairs Lockheed Corp., Washington, 1983-85, Ginn, Edington, Moore and Wade, Washington, 1985-90; pres. ASL Internat., Washington, 1990—. Dir. press Com. to Re-elect the Pres., Washington, 1972; cons. Pres. Ford Com., 1976, Reagan-Bush Com., 1980. Served to capt., inf. U.S. Army, 1959-62. Mem. Belle Haven Country Club, Capitol Hill Club, Met. Club. Republican. Episcopalian.

MOORE, RICHARD HORACE, government official; b. Trenton, N.J., Feb. 12, 1950; s. Clifford Roscoe and Carolyn Marguerita (Davenport) M.; m. Aug. 21, 1972 (div. 1986); 1 child, Taj. BA, Antioch Coll., Yellow Springs, Ohio, 1972; EdM, Harvard U., 1975; MBA, U. Pa., 1987. V.p. Infinity Plus Svcs., Springfield, Ohio, 1966-70; commrs. asst. Balt. City Bd. Sch. Commrs., 1970-71; dir. rsch. and program devel. Homestead-Montebello Ctr., Antioch Coll., Balt., 1971-72; mgmt. intern U.S. Dept. HEW, Washington, 1974-77; asst. to the asst. sec. Asst. Sec. for Planning & Evaluation, U.S. HEW, Washington, 1977-78, dep. exec. officer, 1978-79, dir. planning and spl. studies, 1979-80; mgr. planning and policy devel. Energy Info. Adminstrn., U.S. Dept. Energy, Washington, 1980-84, mgr. evaluation and spl. programs, 1984—. Author (poetry book): When Morning Wakes to a Lullaby of Drums..., 1973. Bd. dirs. Towson (Md.) Unitarian Universalist Ch., 1990; historian Blacks in Govt., 1990-91; commr. Md. Commn. for Women, 1986-90; chmn. Balt. Exptl. High Sch. Trustees, 1977-86; co-founder Sojourner-Douglass Coll., Balt., 1972. Recipient Spl. Merit, Md. Women's History Project, 1990, Outstanding Leadership award Combined Fed. Campaign, 1986. Mem. Antioch Network Alumnai (reunion com. coord. 1990—). Office: US Dept Energy EI-23.1 1000 Independence Ave SE Washington DC 20585-0001

MOORE, RICHARD LAWRENCE, structural engineer, consultant; b. Rocky Ford, Colo., Feb. 7, 1934; s. Lawrence and Margaret Kathryn (Bolling) M.; m. Donna St. Clair, Mar. 26, 1972 (div. 1983); 1 child, Andrew Trousdale; m. Margaret Ann Guthrie, May 4, 1984. BSCE, U. Colo., 1957; MS, Princeton U., 1963; PhD, Calif. Western U., Santa Ana, 1975. Registered profl. engr., Mass., Maine, Colo., Pa., Iowa, Nebr., N.Mex., Wyo., Ill., Ark., Mo., N.D., Mich., Okla. Structural engr. Cameron Engrs., Denver, 1964-66; v.p. Moore Internat., Jeddah, Saudi Arabia, 1967-78; asst. to pres. C.H. Guernsey Co., Oklahoma City, 1979-82; pres. R.L. Moore Co., Boston, 1983—; v.p., dir. Isolink Ing., Basel, Switzerland, 1990—; nat. chmn. Roof Cons. Inst., Raleigh, N.C., 1988—; prof. Episcopal Sch. Theology, Denver, 1967-71. Patentee in field. Member Mound City (Mo.) Libr. Bd., 1963-64; pres. Dist. Rep. Party, Boston, 1988—; sr. warden St. John Chrysostom Epis. Ch., Denver, 1966-71. Danforth Found. scholar, 1962. Mem. ASCE, NSPE, Am. Concrete Inst., Nat. Forensic Ctr. Home and Office: RL Moore Co 534 E Broadway Boston MA 02127-4407

MOORE, RICHARD LEROY, II, engineering scientist; b. Trenton, N.J., June 18, 1948; s. Richard Leroy and Dorothy Estelle (Holtzhammer) M.; m. Linda Elizabeth Young, Feb. 24, 1968, (div. Jan. 1980); children: Michele, Christopher; m. Mary Elizabeth Quinty, Oct. 5, 1983. AA, Mercer County Coll., 1971; BA, Trenton State Coll., 1973. Cert. secondary tchr., N.J. Engring. asst. Princeton (N.J.) U., 1968-80; tchr. II Youth Correctional Inst., Bordentown, N.J., 1973-74; sr. lab scientist Perkin-Elmer Corp., Edison, N.J., 1980-91; sr. analyst Evans East Inc., Plainsboro, N.J., 1991—. Contbr. numerous articles to profl. jours.; patentee in field. Mem. Am. Ceramic Soc., Am. Vacuum Soc., Am. Soc. for Materials (chmn. analytical instruments and techniques 1986—). Democrat. Home: 2158 Monmouth Junction Rd Monmouth Junction NJ 08852-2613 Office: Evans E Inc 666 Plainsboro Rd Ste 1236 Plainsboro NJ 08536-3046

MOORE, RICHARD THOMAS, state legislator; b. Milford, Mass., Aug. 7, 1943; s. Thomas James and Helen Eliza (Andrew) M.; m. Joanne Bednarz, May 26, 1979. BA, Clark U., 1966, postgrad.; MA, Colgate U., 1967; postgrad., U. Mass. Assoc. dean students Assumption Coll., Worcester, Mass., 1967-69; asst. to pres. Bentley Coll., Waltham, Mass., 1969-76; state rep. Mass. Ho. of Reps., Boston, 1976—; chmn. Mass. Dem. Leadership Coun., Inc., Boston, 1990—; bd. dirs. Mass. Found. for Humanities, South Hadley, Mass., 1988—. Selectman Bd. of Selectmen, Hopedale, Mass., 1970-78; pres. Mass. Selectmen's Assn., Boston, 1975-76; chmn. Blackstone Nat. Heritage Corridor Commn., Uxbridge, Mass., 1988-90; chmn. Ho. Com. on Taxation, Boston, 1983-84, chmn. Ho. Com. Election Laws, 1992. Named Legislator of Yr. Mass. Bar Assn., 1984, Animal Rescue League, Inc., 1982; recipient Ann. Preservation award Mass. Hist. Commn., 1987; U.S./U.K. Exchange fellow U.S. Nat. Park Svc., 1988. Mem. Am. Soc. for Pub. Adminstrn. (bd. dirs. Mass. chpt. 1979-82, Dist. Svc. award 1984). Democrat. Roman Catholic. Home: 235 Williams St Uxbridge MA 01569-1130 Office: Ho of Reps State House - Rm 171 Boston MA 02133

MOORE, ROBERT ERIC, artist; b. Manchester, N.H., Oct. 13, 1927; s. George Anthony and Verna Winona (Blaisdell) M.; m. Margaret Doherty, June 2, 1950; children: Deirdre, Bridget, Michael O'Doherty. Student, New England Sch. Art, 1949-51, U. N.H., 1953. One-man shows include Alerbescht Gallery, Telford, Pa., Bayberry Art Gallery, Southern Pines, N.C., Benbow Gallery, Newport, R.I., Copley Soc., Boston, Doll and Richards, Boston, Frost Gully Gallery, Portland, Maine, The Gallery, Spartenburg, S.C., Guild of Boston Artists, Hancock Coll. Art, Santa Maria, Calif., Hobe Sound Galleries North, Portland, John Black Gallery, Cold Spring Harbor,

N.Y., Loft Gallery, Princeton, N.J., Munson Gallery, New Haven, Conn., Ogunquit (Maine) Gallery, and others; exhibited in numerous group shows; represented in several permanent collections. Juror Audubon Artists 49th Annual Exhbn., N.Y.C., 1991, Annual New England Watercolor Exhbn., Boston, 1989, Audubon Artists 47th Annual Exhbn., N.Y.C., 1989, Adirondacks Nat. Exhbn Am. Watercolor, 1988; nat. juror 118th Annual Am. Watercolor Soc. Exhbn., N.Y.C., 1985. Recipient Garnet award Adirondacks Nat. Exhbn. Am. Watercolors, 1991, Pulsifer award, 1987, William Kowalsky prize, 1983, Dick Blick award La. Watercolor Soc., 1987, High Winds medal 118th Annual Am. Watercolor Exhbn., 1985, St. Vincent's Hosp. award Watercolor Soc. Ala., 1981, Griffey's TV award Nat. Watercolor Soc., 1978, Arches Paper award, 1977, Watercolor award N.Mex. Art League, 1978, Copley prize Copley Soc. Boston, 1967, Yankee Mag. award, 1967, Cavanaugh award Springfield Mus. Art, 1962, and others. Fellow Am. Watercolor Soc. (Winsor and Newton award 1984, Dale Myers Cooper medal 1985, Internat. Waters travel exhbn. award 1991-92); mem. Nat. Acad. Design (assoc. 1991, Adolph and Clara Obrig prize 1991), Allied Artists Am. (David Soloway Meml. award 1989, Dr. Clifford W. Mills award 1986, Orion Nova Ltd. award 1982, Grumbacher Artists Materials Co. silver medal 1982), Audubon Artists (Grumbacher Gold medallion 1987). Home: 111 Cider Hill Rd York ME 03909-5213

MOORE, ROBERT FRANCIS, bottle gas distribution company executive; b. Westfield, Mass., Oct. 20, 1952; s. Ralph Barnard and Mary (Buchanan) M.; m. Maura Ann Crowley, Nov. 11, 1978; children: Rachel, Courtney, Patrick. BS, Am. Intern. U., 1975; MBA, Plymouth State Coll., 1984. CPA, Mass. Asst. gen. mgr. L.E. Belcher, Inc., Springfield, 1975-76; staff acct. Wakeman Industries Inc., West Springfield, Mass., 1976-77; asst. comptr. Wakeman Industries Inc., Claremont, N.H., 1977-84, comptr., 1984—, treas., 1985—, v.p. fin., 1991—. Mem. Nat. Assn. Accts., Crown Point Country Club. Republican. Office: Wakeman Industries Inc RR 2 Box 243 Claremont NH 03743-9217

MOORE, ROBERT JOHN, JR., minister; b. Abington, Pa., May 28, 1948; s. Robert John Sr. and Florence (Fleming) M.; m. Nancy Marie Benbow, June 10, 1972; children: Kevin Robert, Jeremy Peter, Kimberly Joy. BA in History, Ursinus Coll., 1970; MDiv cum laude, Trinity Evang. Div. Sch., Deerfield, Ill., 1973; postgrad., Western Conservative Bapt. Sem., Portland, Oreg., 1981. Ordained to ministry Bapt. Ch. Pastoral asst. Glenview (Ill.) Presbyn. Ch., 1972-73, Wharton Bapt. Ch., Glenside, Pa., 1973-74; pastor Grace Bapt. Ch., Ambler, Pa., 1974-82, First Bapt. Ch., Bayonne, N.J., 1982-88; sr. pastor Calvary Bapt. Ch., Flemington, N.J., 1988—; pres. Brookdale Christian Sch. Parent-Tchr. Fellowship, Bloomfield, N.J., 1985-87. Pres. Concerned Citizens Against Pornography, Hunterdon County, N.J., 1990-91. Mem. Conservative Bapt. Assn. N.J. (ordination adv. com. 1990-91, rec. sec. 1991—), Rotary (Flemington chpt., prayer com., food distbn. com. 1990-91, Rotarians in need com. 1991—). Republican. Home and Office: Calvary Bapt Ch 262 S Main St Flemington NJ 08822-1798

MOORE, SANDRA, architect, environmental designer, educator; b. Charleston, S.C., June 30, 1945. B.A. in Architecture, Tuskegee Inst., 1967; M.Environ. Design, Yale U., 1973; Doctorate, Harvard U., 1982. Architect Clauss and Nolan, Architects, Planners, Trenton, N.J., 1968-72; founder, exec. dir. Trenton Design Ctr., 1970-73; asst. prof. Schs. Architecture and Edn., U. Wis.-Milw., 1973-75; dir. ctrs. for environ. edn. Edn. Devel. Ctr., Cambridge, Mass., 1975-76; asst. prof. environ. design Mass. Coll. Art, Boston, 1975-76; assoc. Alexander Cooper & Assocs., N.Y.C., 1976; adminstr. Dept. Housing Preservation and Devel., N.Y.C., 1978-79; asst. prof., asst. dean Sch. Architecture, Fla. A&M U., Tallahassee, 1979-82; assoc. prof., assoc. dean Sch. Architecture, N.J. Inst. Tech., Newark, 1982-83, assoc. prof., 1983—; chmn. housing task force mayoral transition team City of Newark, 1986-87; community advisor, Newark, 1987—. Co-editor Many Faces of Architecture, 1988. Mem. policy panels Nat. Endowment for Arts, Nat. League Cities; cons. design arts program N.J. State Council on the Arts, 1987—; mem. Nat. Def. Exec; mem. architecture adv. commn. Mercer County Community Coll., 1987—; mem. community reinvestment act adv. bd. Midlantic Nat. Bank, Edison, N.J., 1987—. Recipient Pub. and Inst. Svc. award N.J. Inst. Tech., 1989; named Alumnus of Yr. Tuskegee U. Dept. Architecture, 1987; Nat. Endowment Arts fellow, 1984, 85. Mem. N.J. Soc. Architects (bd. dirs., citation award 1983).

MOORE, SONIA, theatre administrator, researcher; b. Gomel, USSR, Dec. 4, 1902; came to U.S., 1940; d. Evser and Sophie (Pashershtnik) Shatzov; m. Leon Moore, May 11, 1926 (dec. Mar. 1957); 1 child, Irene Moore Jaglom. Degrees, Reale Conservatorio Di Musica Santa Cecilia, Rome, 1939, Reale Accademia Filarmonica, Rome, 1939; student, U. Kiev, U. Moscow, Studio Moscow Art Theatre. Dir. Sonia Moore Studio of the Theatre (accredited Nat. Assn. Schs. Theatre), N.Y.C., 1961—; founder, pres. Am. Ctr. for Stanislavski Theatre Art Inc., 1964—; artistic dir. Am. Stanislavski Theatre, N.Y.C., 1970—; tchr. Sonia Moore Studio, N.Y.C., 1961—; guest artist lectr.-demonstrator numerous univs. in U.S. and Can., 1978—; vis. prof. U. Mo., Kansas City, 1981; TV and radio interviews, 1961—; convs. presenter, 1982—; keynote speaker Theater USSR, U. S.C.; lectr. Fordham U., 1991, U. N.C., 1989. Dir. numerous off-Broadway plays, 1960-90, Anna Christie, N.Y.C., 1989, A View from a Bridge, 1990; translator, editor: Stanislavski Today, 1973, Logic of Speech on Stage, 1976; author: The Stanislavski Method, 1960, Training an Actor: The Stanislavski system in class, 1979, The Stanislavski System, 1984, Stanislavski Revealed: The Actor's Complete Guide to Spontaneity on Stage, 1991; contbr. articles to Ency. Britannica, Theatre Jour., Drama Rev., Secondary Sch. Jour., Players Mag.; 10 cassette lectures on Stanislavski System; videocassette interview by Julie Harris. Founding mem. Nat. Mus. Women in the Arts; charter mem. Battle of Normandy Mus. Recipient Am. Heritage award JFK Library for Minorities, N.Y.C., 1974. Mem. ALA, Authors Guild, Soc. Stage Dirs. and Choreographers, Am. Theatre Assn., Internat. Biog. Assn., Smithsonian Instn., Assn. for Theatre in Higher Edn. (lectr. convs. N.Y.C. 1989, Chgo., 1990), Seattle, 1991, Nat. Trust for Hist. Preservation. Home: 485 Park Ave New York NY 10022-1228 Office: Am Ctr for Stanislavski Theatre Art Inc 485 Park Ave New York NY 10022-1228

MOORE, THOMAS WILLIAM, educator; b. Detroit, Oct. 8, 1940; s. Thomas Benjamin and Mary Virginia (Owens) M.; 1 child, Siobhan. BA, DePaul U., 1967; MA, U. Mich., 1969, U. Windsor, 1972; PhD, Syracuse U., 1975. Asst. prof. Glassboro (N.J.) State Coll., 1975-76, So. Meth. U., Dallas, 1976-81; psychotherapist pvt. practice, Amherst, Mass., 1985-91, West Stockbridge, Mass., 1985-91; prof. Lesley Coll., Cambridge, Mass., 1987—. Author: The Planets Within, 1982, Rituals of the Imagination, 1985, A Blue Fire, 1989, Dark Eros, 1990, Care of the Soul, 1992. Fellow Dallas Inst. Humanities and Culture. Office: 50 Boylston St Brookline MA 02146

MOORE, TYRONE BRADLEY, college official; b. Erie, Pa., Oct. 8, 1949; s. Essie James and Maebelle (Pope) M.; m. Charlise Butler, Aug. 24, 1974; 1 child, Monica Lynn. MEd in Secondary Edn. Guidance, Edinboro (Pa.) U., 1975; postgrad., Mercyhurst Coll., 1982, Gannon U., 1984; BS in Secondary Edn., Edinboro (Pa.) U., 1972. Cert. secondary social sci. tchr., guidance and counseling, Pa. Supr. game-time unit Mayor's Office Community Affairs, Erie, 1970-73, asst. dir. pupil incentive program, 1972-73; tchr. social sci. Erie Sch. Dist., 1972-74; guidance counselor upward bound program Gannon U., Erie, 1974-75; asst. dir. PACE program Mercyhurst Coll., Erie, 1974-80, dir. counseling and career svcs., 1977-80, asst. dir. student svcs., 1980—, dir. career svcs., coop. edn. and internship programs, 1980—, guest lectr. criminal justice, also mem. faculty senate; evaluator and proposal reviewer coop. edn. br. U.S. Dept. Edn.; mem. Hotel Restaurant and Instnl. Mgmt. Adv. Bd. Bd. dirs. Foodbank Erie County, Human Rels. Commn., Family Svcs., Inc., Erie City-Erie County Libr., Minority Health Edn. Delivery Systems; trustee 2d Bapt. Ch., Erie; mem. exec. bd. Black Assocs. Erie, Inc.; chmn. bd. Greater Erie Community Action Com. Mem. NEA, APGA, Coop. Edn. Assn. Pa. (exec. bd.), Mid Atlantic Assn. Sch., Coll. and Univ. Staffing (pres.), Assn Sch., Coll. and Univ. Staffing, Mid Atlantic Placement Assn., N.W. Pa. Pers. Assn., Coll. Placement Coun., Coop. Edn. Assn., Black Conf. on Higher Edn., Nat. Soc. Internships and Experiential Edn., Elks (exec. bd. Erie), Omega Psi Phi. Democrat. Home: 4428 Koehler Rd Erie PA 16510-3928 Office: Mercyhurst Coll Career Svcs Glenwood Hills Erie PA 16546

MOORE, VIRGINIA BRADLEY, librarian, educator; b. Laurens, S.C., May 13, 1932; d. Robert Otis Brown and Queen Esther (Smith) Bradley; m. David Lee Moore, Dec. 27, 1957 (div. 1973). B.S., Winston-Salem State U., 1954; M.L.S., U. Md., 1970. Cert. in libr. sci. edn. Tchr. John R. Hawkins High Sch., Warrenton, N.C., 1954-55, Happy Plains High Sch., Taylorsville, N.C., 1955-58, Young and Carver elem. schs., Washington, 1958-65; libr. Davis and Minor elem. schs., Washington, 1965-72, Ballou Sr. High Sch., Kramer Jr. High Sch., Washington, 1972-75, 78-80, Anacostia Sr. High Sch., Washington, 1975-77, 80—; class, club sponsor, 1975— chmn. competency-based curriculum D.C. Pub. Schs., 1978—; speaker, presenter Ch. and Synagogue Libr. Assn., 1975, 80, 83; dir. ch. libr. workshops Asbury United Methodist Ch., Washington, 1972-74, 76; mem. 1st libr. and info. sci. del. to People's Republic China, 1985. Author: (bibliography) The Negro in American History, 1619-1968, 1968, (with Helen E. Williams) Books By African-American Authors and Illustrators for Children and Young Adults, 1991; TV script for vacation reading program, 1971, sound/slide presentation D.C. Church Librs.' Bicentennial Celebration, 1976; video script and tchr.'s guide for Nat. Libr. Week Balloon Launch Day, 1983; bibliography Black Literature/Materials, 1987; contbr. articles to profl. jours. Rec. sec. Washington Pan-Hellenic Coun., 1975; libr. Mt. Carmel Bapt. Ch., Washington, 1984; co-chair nat. libr. involvement com. Martin Luther King, Jr. Fed. Holiday Commn., 1989—; coord. White House Conf. on Libr. and Info. Svcs., 1989-91. Recipient certs. of award D.C. Pub. Libr., 1980, D.C. Pub. Schs., 1983; NDEA scholar Central State Coll., Edmond, Okla., 1969, U. Ky., 1969; scholar Ball State U., 1969; grad. fellow U. Md., 1969. Mem. NEA (life), ALA (councilor-at-large 1983-91), LWV, Internat. Assn. Sch. Librs., Am. Assn. Sch. Librs. (coms. 1973-83, 87—), D.C. Assn. Sch. Librs. (pres. 1971-73, citation 1973, newsletter editor 1971-75, 83, Soc. Sch. Librs. Internat., Internat. Assn. Sch. Librs., Freedom to Read Found., Intellectual Freedom Roundtable (bd. dirs., exec. com. 1989-91), D.C. Libr. Assn., Md. Ednl. Media Orgn., Internat. Platform Assn., Prince Georges County LWV, S.E. Neighbors Club, Zeta Phi Beta (v.p. chpt. 1972-74), Delta Kappa Gamma (v.p. Alpha chpt. 1990-92, pres. 1992—, membership chair 1991-92). Democrat. Home: 2100 Brooks Dr Apt 721 District Hts MD 20747-1016 Office: Anacostia Sr High Sch 16th and R Sts SE Washington DC 20020

MOORHEAD, THOMAS BURCH, lawyer, pharmaceutical company executive; b. Evanston, Ill., May 3, 1934; s. John William and Jane (Hendrich) M.; m. Christie Barnard, Dec. 31, 1966; children: Merrell Hendrich, Hannah Christie, Rachel McGill. BA, Yale U, 1956; postgrad., The Hague Acad. Internat. Law, 1958; JD, U. Pa., 1959; LLM, NYU, 1964. Bar: N.Y. 1960, Conn. 1971. Assoc. Milbank, Tweed, Hadley & McCloy, N.Y.C., 1959-63; assoc. counsel, asst. sec. Hooker Chem. Corp., N.Y.C., 1963-68, dir. indsl. rels., 1968-69, v.p. indsl. rels., 1969-72; v.p. employee rels. Champion Internat. Corp., N.Y.C., 1972-74; v.p. adminstrn. Beker Industries Corp., Greenwich, Conn., 1974-76; v.p. corp. affairs Estée Lauder, Inc., N.Y.C., 1976-84, sr. v.p., 1984-87; v.p. human resources Carter-Wallace, Inc., N.Y.C., 1987—; bd. dirs., vice chmn. Transaction Billing Resources, Inc., 1991—. Mem. New Canaan (Conn.) Rep. Town Com., 1980-85; elected to New Canaan Town Coun., 1985—, vice chmn., 1989—; appointed to Conn. oversight commn. Metro-North Commuter R.R., 1985-89; U.S. del. ILO, 1985; bd. dirs. Yale U. Alumni Fund, 1987—A Nat. Choral Coun., 1988—, United Way Tri-State, Inc., 1986-89, bd. dirs. United Way New Canaan, 1983-89, pres., 1986-87; bd. dirs. Les Amis d'Escoffier Soc., 1990—, Les Amis D'Escoffier Found., 1990—. Mem. ABA, Assn. of Bar of City of N.Y., Am. Soc. Internat. Law, Met. Club, New Canaan Country Club, Gridiron Club of New Canaan (pres. 1990—), Yale (N.Y.C.). Home: 148 Ramhorne Rd New Canaan CT 06840-3007 Office: 1345 Ave Of The Americas New York NY 10105-0099

MOOS, EDWARD A., securities company executive; b. N.Y.C., July 17, 1937; s. Henry H. and Dorothy E. (Warren) M.; m. Louise E. Wheadon, Dec. 26, 1964; children: Philip, Antonia. BA in History, Houghton Coll., 1959, D of Commerce, 1991; postgrad. Sch. Fgn. Affairs, George Washington U., 1959-60, Grad. Sch. Bus., NYU, 1961-63; D of Comml. Sci., Houghton Coll., 1991. With Smith Barney, N.Y.C. 1961-63; exec. v.p. Weeden Co., N.Y.C. 1963-77, mem. exec. com. 1975-77, mgr. mcpl. bond dept., U.S. govt. bond dept. and internat. bond dept., 1977-78; chmn. bd., chief exec. officer E.A. Moos & Co. Inc., Summit, N.J., 1978—. Bd. dirs. Cheshire Home, A. Gary Shilling and Co.; mem. United Way Millburn, Short Hills, N.J. Served with U.S. Army, 1960-61. Mem. Pub. Securities Assn., Mcpl. Bond Club N.Y. (gov.), Short Hills Club. Republican. Home: 19 Moraine Pl Short Hills NJ 07078-1956 Office: 350 Springfield Ave Summit NJ 07901-4602

MOOSBRUKER, JANE BARBARA, organization development consultant; b. Jamaica, N.Y., Oct. 29, 1938; d. Raymond Andrew and Evelyne (Ross) M.; m. Robert Charles Silvia, Feb. 17, 1990. BA in Psychology, Adelphi U., 1960; MA, Radcliffe Coll., 1962; PhD in Social Psychology, Harvard U., 1965. Bd. cert. psychologist, Mass. Asst. prof. Tufts U. Sch. Dental Medicine, Boston, 1964-66, Boston Coll., Chestnut Hill, Mass., 1966-70; cons. orgn. devel. Bolton, Mass., 1970—; rsch. assoc. Harvard Sch. Dental Medicine, Boston, 1967-70, lectr., 1970-82; cons. Honeywell, Inc., Mpls. and Lexington, Mass., 1973-89, Harvard Community Health Plan, Cambridge, Mass., 1983-85, Nashua (N.H.) Meml. Hosp., 1980-86, 91, Digital Equipment Corp., Maynard, Mass., 1984—. Author: (with others) Team Building Blueprints for Productivity and Satisfaction, 1987; contbr. articles to profl. jours. and books. Chair Bolton Conservation Commn., 1991—, mem., 1987—; mem., sec. mental health sect. Mass. Pub. Health Assn., Boston, 1977—; program chair Mass. Psychol. Assn., Boston, 1963-64; researcher Cardinal's Commn. on Human Rights, S.E. Mass. Region, 1967; mem. Planned Parenthood Fedn. Am. Recipient Best Paper on Psychol. Topic award Mass. Mental Health Ctr., 1963. Mem. Nat. Tng. Labs. (mem. coms.), Soc. for Psychol. Study of Social Issues, Orgn. Devel. Network, Acad. Mgmt., Walden Earthnet (bd. dirs. 1991), Nat. Audobon Soc., Union Concerned Scientists.

MORAKIS, JAMES ANTHONY, oil company executive; b. Cambridge, Mass., Aug. 12, 1934; s. Anthony and Netsa Morakis; m. Betty Dimitrion, Jan. 26, 1958; children: Lee, Todd, Jay. BS in Pub. Rels., Boston U., 1956, M in Pub. Rels., 1961. Pub. rels. asst. Western Electric Co., N.Y.C., 1961-62; pub. rels. rep. Exxon Rsch. and Engring. Co., Linden, N.J., 1962-64; pub. rels. coord. Enjay Chem., NY.C., 1964-66; pub. rels. mgr. Esso Pappas, Athens, Greece, 1966-68; pub. affairs analyst Esso Middle East, N.Y.C., 1968-69; sr. pub. affairs advisor Exxon Chem., N.Y.C., 1969-74; press rels. mgr. to pub. info. mgr. to ops. mgr. Pub. Affairs Exxon Corp., N.Y.C., 1974-86; ops. mgr. Corp. and Pub. Affairs Exxon Corp., N.Y.C., 1986-90; pub. affairs mgr. Exxon Co. Internat., Florham Park, N.J., 1990—; bd. trustees Media Inst., Washington, 1988—. Lt. USN, 1956-60. Mem. Am. Petroleum Inst., World Environment Ctr. (communications com.), Media Inst. (trustee), Internat. Pub. Rels. Roundtable.

MORALES, CARLOS ALBERTO, retail company executive, financial consultant; b. Managua, Nicaragua, Dec. 14, 1946; came to U.S., 1976; s. Silvio Morales-Etienne and Elsa Molina; m. Jo Anne Worley, Sept. 19, 1969; children: Susan, Robin, Carlos. BS in Engring., U. Calif., Berkeley, 1969; MBA in Fin., Fordham U., 1981. Mgr. ops. Aceitera Corona, S.A., Managua, 1970-76; dir. ops. Chiquita Brands Internat., N.Y.C., 1976-88; fin. cons. CAM Cons., Jackson, N.J., 1989-90; fin. councillor R.H. Macy & Co., Inc., N.Y.C., 1991—; outside cons. Black & Decker Latin Am., Miami, Fla., 1989-90, Rhône Poulenc Inc.. (USA), Princeton, N.J., 1990-91. Roman Catholic. Home: 3 Florida Pl Jackson NJ 08527 Office: RH Macy & Co Inc 151 W 34th st New York NY 10001

MORALES, DAVID, banking administrator, accountant; b. Ceiba, P.R., Nov. 14, 1947; s. Jesus and Fabiana (Feliciano) M.; divorced; children: David, Alexis. BS in Bus. Adminstrn., Iona Coll., 1990; AAS in Bus. Acctg., Bronx Community Coll., 1992. Teller Citibank N.A., N.Y.C., 1968-74, auditor, 1974-76, ops. supr., 1976-81, ops. mgr., 1982-84, sales mgr., 1985-88, br. dep. mgr., 1989—. Mem. Jamaica Hill Community Assn., 1992. With U.S. Army N.G., 1969-75. Mem. Nat. Soc. Pub. Accts. (assoc.). Home: 84-49 168th St Apt 1K Jamaica Hill NY 11432

MORALES, PEDRO, accountant; b. San Juan, P.R., Nov. 19, 1947; came to U.S., 1959; s. Pedro and Juanita (Delgado) M.; m. Barbara Morales, Mar. 17, 1969 (div. May 1975); children: Peter, Paul. BS in Acctg., Bklyn. Coll., 1974; MBA in Acctg., Pace U., 1980. Salesperson Nabisco Inc., Bklyn., 1970-74; acctg. mgr. Alcoa Steamship Co. Inc., N.Y.C., 1974-87; asst. treas. Shipcentral Ltd. Co., N.Y.C., 1987-91; treas. A.L. Burbank & Co. Ltd., N.Y.C., 1991—. Mem. Bay Ridge Dem. Club, Bklyn., 1988-90. Recipient Vol. Recognition award Nat. Multiple Sclerosis Soc., 1989. Mem. Nat. Soc. Tax Profls., Nat. Assn. Tax Practitioners, Inst. Cert. Tax Practitioners, N.Y. Soc. Ind. Accts., N.Y. Cycle Club. Home: 760-67th St Brooklyn NY 11220 Office: AL Burbank & Co Ltd 41 E 42d St New York NY 10017-5202

MORAN, JEFFREY WILLIAM, safety engineer; b. Sewaren, N.J., Mar. 3, 1954; s. Raymond A. and Margaret J. (Allen) M.; m. Karen M. Anderson, Oct. 15, 1988. BS, Morningside Coll., 1976; AAS, Middlesex County Coll., 1988. Rscher. Woodbridge (N.J.) Twp., 1977-79; safety technician, rscher. Selective, Inc., East Brunswick, N.J., 1979-82; safety engr., fire chief U.S. Metals Refining, Carteret, N.J., 1982; fire protection, safety cons. J.H. Merritt, N.Y.C., 1982-85; occupational safety cons. N.J. Dept. Labor, Trenton, 1985-89; firefighter Woodbridge Fire Dept., 1989—; guest lectr. N.J. State Fire Coll., Cranford, 1986-87. Vice-pres. Woodbridge G.O.P. Club, 1987-88; county com. Middlesex County Rep. Party, 1989; exec. officer Woodbridge Emergency Squad, 1977-88. Mem. Nat. Fire Protection Assn., Am. Soc. Safety Engrs., Am. Assn. Indsl. Hygienists, N.J. State Safety Coun., N.J. Indsl. Fire Chiefs, Internat. Soc. Fire Svc. Instrs. Republican. Episcopalian. Home: 70 Caroline St Woodbridge NJ 07095-2824 Office: Woodbridge Fire Hdqrs 418 School St Woodbridge NJ 07095-2935

MORAN, JOHN DOUGLAS, investment banker; b. Phila., Oct. 24, 1926; s. William Bailey and Florence Dorothy (Hildenbrand) M.; m. Ann Biddle, Feb. 10, 1960 (div. 1984); children: J. Douglas, James Biddle; m. Barbara T. McNeel, May 13, 1990. BS, U. Pa. Wharton Sch. of Bus., 1951; MA, U. Pa., 1955. Trainee Fed. Res. Bank, Phila., 1951-53; credit analyst Fidelity Bank, Phila., 1953-60; asst. v.p. Indsl. Valley Bank, Phila., 1961-68; v.p. Mgmt. Data Corp., Phila., 1968-69; dir. corp. fin. Suplee-Mosley, Inc., Phila., 1969-74; sr. v.p. Danes, Cooke & Keleher, N.Y.C., 1975-76; sr. ptnr. J.D. Moran Assocs., Phila., 1976-84, 86—; v.p. Boenning & Scattergood, Phila., 1985; pres. Windsor Fin. Corp., Flemington, N.J., 1986. With USN, 1944-46, Philippines. Mem. Phila. Cricket Club, Princeton Club of N.Y. Republican. Episcopalian. Home: 7101 Chew Ave Philadelphia PA 19119-1815 Office: J D Moran Assocs 7101 Chew Ave Philadelphia PA 19119-1815

MORAN, JOHN PATRICK, JR., publishing executive, marketing consultant; b. N.Y.C., June 6, 1943; s. John Patrick and Evelyn (Dowdy) M.; m. Mary Alice Silton, Sept. 28, 1973; children: John P. III, Sarah Alice. BSBA, Boston U., 1969. Sales rep., key account mgr. Datagraphix, N.Y.C. and Los Angeles, 1969-73; nat. sales rep. Sta. NBC-TV, N.Y.C., 1973-75; consumer account rep. Wall Street Jour., N.Y.C., 1975-77; sr. account rep. U.S. News and World Report, N.Y.C., 1977-79; category mgr. Time, Inc., N.Y.C., 1979-82; assoc. pub. CDM Communications, N.Y.C., 1982-84; exec. v.p., assoc. publ., 1984-85; pres., chief exec. officer, group pub. CDM Communications, N.Y.C.; exec. v.p., pub. CDM Communications/CDM Publs., N.Y.C., 1983-85; pres. chief exec. officer Group Pubs. CDM Communications/CDM Publs., 1986—; pres., chief exec. officer CDM Group, 1989—; chmn. C.O.M. Mfrs. Assocs., N.Y.C., 1971-72; mktg. cons. 21 Brands, Inc., N.Y.C., 1980—, Bell Atlantic/Ketchum Advt., 1986-87. Publ., founder America's Cup Challenge Mag., 1985, Performance Sailing Mag., 1986, America's Cup Defense Mag., 1987. Com. U.S. Olympic Sailing Team, Greenwich, Conn., 1986, chmn., 1987-88, 89-90; chmn. C.O.M. Mfrs. Assn., 1971-72. With USNR, 1962-64. Mem. U.S. Yacht Racing Union (industry rels. com. L.I. chpt., 1977—, Spl. Achievement award 1978), N.Y. Yacht Club, Am. Yacht Club, Storm Trysail Club, Block Island Raceweek Com., 1983, 85, 87, 89, Ft. Worth Boat, Royal Hawaiian Ocean Racing Club, Antigua Yacht Club. Republican. Presbyterian. Office: CDM Group 100 5th Ave New York NY 10011-6903

MORAN, JULIE LUMPKIN, lawyer; b. Madrid, Spain, July 22, 1963; d. Lee R. and Mona Fay (Long) L.; m. Sean Michael Moran, June 11, 1988; children: Katherine Elizabeth, Sean Michael Jr. Student, Scripps Coll., 1981-83; BA magna cum laude, SUNY, Binghamton, 1984; JD, Fordham U., 1988. Bar: Conn. 1989, N.Y. 1989. Summer assoc. Cahill, Gordon & Reindel, N.Y.C., 1987; assoc. Townley & Updike, N.Y.C., 1988-90; freelance writer Pelham, N.Y., 1990—; pvt. practice law Yonkers, 1990—; in-house counsel, bd. dirs. Pelhamdale Ave. Owner's Corp., Pelham, 1990—; researcher for book for dean Fordham U. Law Sch., 1986. Articles editor Forham Environ. Law Reporter, 1987-88; contbr. articles to various consumer publs. Pro bono atty. N.Y. County Lawyer's Assn. Programs, 1990-91. Mem. ABA, Westchester Women's Bar Assn., Assn. of Bar of City of N.Y. (com. on bar admission and legal edn.), Fordham Law Rev., Phi Beta Kappa. Episcopalian. Home: 71 Margaret Ave Yonkers NY 10707 Office: 71 Margaret Ave Yonkers NY 10707

MORAN, MARTIN JOSEPH, fund raising company executive; b. Bklyn., Nov. 3, 1930; s. Dominick and Mary (Lydon) M.; m. Mary Therese Schofield, June 5, 1954; children: Martin Joseph, John P., Maureen M., Thomas S., Robert P., William M., Maria M. BA, St. John's U., 1952. Profl. fund raising cons., 1956—; founder Martin J. Moran Co., Inc., N.Y.C., 1964, pres., 1964-74, chmn. bd., 1974—. Mem. Cardinal's Com. for Edn., N.Y.C., 1970-79, Cardinal's Com. for Laity Archdiocese N.Y., 1979—, Am. Revolution Bicentennial Commn., Oyster Bay, N.Y.; mem. Massapequa Park (N.Y.) Bd. Zoning Appeals, 1972-84, chmn., 1978-84; mem. Massapequa Park Ethics Commn., 1969-72; trustee Notre Dame Coll., S.I., 1969-72, La Salle Acad., N.Y.C., 1971-87; mem. pres.'s council Cath. U.P.R., Ponce, 1966-71. Served as aviator USNR, 1952-56. Decorated knight Order Holy Sepulchre, Pope Paul VI, 1968, Knight of Malta, Pope Paul VI, 1973; recipient Pietas medal St. John's U., N.Y., 1988; bd. councillors, sec., treas. Equestrian Order Holy Sepulchre of Jerusalem, 1990—. Mem. Navy League, Navy Hist. Assn., St. John's U. Alumni Assn. (pres. 1987—), Am. Assn. Fund Raising Counsel (bd. dirs. 1970—), Nassau County Hist. Soc., Friendly Sons of St. Patrick. Roman Catholic. Club: Madison Square Garden (N.Y.C.); Lost Tree Village Golf (North Palm Beach, Fla.), Old Port Yacht Club. Lodge: KC. Home: 1300 Lakeshore Dr Massapequa Park NY 11762-1755 also: 677 Village Rd North Palm Beach FL 33408 Office: Martin J Moran Co One Penn Plz New York NY 10119

MORAN, M(ICHAEL) MARCUS, JR., retail executive; b. Fitchburg, Mass., Apr. 19, 1943; s. M. Marcus Sr. and Claire Paulette (Aubuchon) M.; m. Tonia Francavilla, July 29, 1966; children: Marcus III, Coutney L., Justin M. BBA, Nichols Coll., 1966; MBA, Babson Coll., 1967. Prof. North Shore Community Coll., Beverly, Mass., 1967-70; pers. mgr., treas., v.p. W. E. Aubuchon Co., Inc., Westminster, Mass., 1970—, also bd. dirs.; bd. dirs., chmn. investment com. I-C Fed. Credit Union, Fitchburg, Mass., 1987—; past instr. acctg. and fin. Fitchburg State Coll., Boston U., North Shore Community Coll., Mt. Wachusett Community Coll. Author: Business Mathematics, 1969. Pres., bd. dirs. United Way, Fitchburg, 1984-88; trustee Fitchburg State Coll./FTC Found., 1978—; past trustee Nichols Coll.; bd. dirs. Julie Country Day Sch., Leominster, Mass., 1980, Cushing Acad., Ashburnham, Mass., 1989—; chmn. bus. edn. fund, Monty Tech. Vocation Sch. Recipient Key to City-Life Saving, City of Fitchburg, 1965, Fitchburg State Coll. Community Leadership award, 1991. Mem. Fay Club (past dir., pres. 1970—), Beta Gamma, Zeta Alpha Phi. Republican. Roman Catholic. Home: Round Meadow Pond Westminster MA 01473 Office: W E Aubuchon Co Inc 95 Aubuchon Dr Westminster MA 01473

MORAN, PHILIP DAVID, lawyer; b. Lynn, Mass., June 3, 1937; s. J. Francis and Margaret M. (Shanahan) M.; m. Carole A. Regan, May 12, 1962; children: Maura F., Philip David. A.B., Holy Cross Coll., 1958; Ed.M., Salem State Coll., 1961; J.D., Suffolk U., 1968. Bar: Mass. 1968, U.S. Dist. Ct. Mass., 1972, U.S. Supreme Ct., 1988. House counsel Viatron Computer Systems Corp., Burlington, Mass., 1968-71; ptnr. Kane & Moran, Lynn, Mass., 1972-78; pvt. practice law Salem, Mass., 1978—; asst. dist. atty. Essex County (Mass.), 1974-78. Bd. dirs. Nat. Right to Life Inc., 1977-83, 87—, treas., 1981-83; mem. Salem Conservation Commn., 1980-89, chmn., 1982-89; mem. pres.'s coun. Holy Cross Coll., 1985—; mem. Nat. Inst. Trial Advocacy U. Colo., 1973. W with U.S. Army, 1960-66. Mem. Mass. Bar Assn., Salem Bar Assn., Lynn Bar Assn., Am. Trial Lawyers Assn., Nat. Acad. Elder Law Attys. Roman Catholic. Avocations: swimming, reading, gardening, boating. Home: 415 Lafayette St Salem MA 01970-5337 Office: 32 Lynde St Salem MA 01970-3447

MORAN, RICARDO JULIO, economist, consultant; b. Havana, Cuba, Sept. 4, 1939; came to U.S., 1960; s. Jose Ricardo and Maria Luisa (Forcade) M.; m. Mayra Buvinic, Dec. 24, 1973 (div. 1981); m. Mary Louise Fox, Apr. 25, 1987. BA, Tulane U., 1963; MA in Econs., U. Calif., Berkeley, 1966, postgrad., 1968. Prof., sr. rsch. assoc. Universidad Catolica de Chile, Santiago, 1967-70; pvt. practice Washington, 1970-73; v.p. Moran Equities, Inc., Miami, Fla., 1973; economist The World Bank, Washington, 1973-90; prin. Moran Internat., Washington, 1990—; cons. Interam. Devel. Bank, Washington, 1990-91, Govt. of Ecuador, Quito, 1991. Co-author: Declining Births in Chile, 1972, Brazil, 1981; contbr. articles to profl. jours. Fellow Latin Am. Teaching Program Tufts U., 1957, Ford Found., 1965, OAS, 1963-65. Mem. Am. Econ. Assn. Home and office: 2910 Cortland Pl NW Washington DC 20008-3429

MORAWETZ, CATHLEEN SYNGE, mathematician; b. Toronto, Ont., Can., May 5, 1923; came to U.S., 1945, naturalized, 1950; d. John Lighton and Elizabeth Eleanor Mabel (Allen) Synge; m. Herbert Morawetz, Oct. 28, 1945; children: Pegeen Ann, John Synge, Lida Joan, Nancy Babette. B.A., U. Toronto, 1945; S.M., M.I.T., 1946; Ph.D., NYU, 1951; hon. degree, Eastern Mich. U., 1980, Smith Coll., 1982, Brown U., 1982, Princeton U., 1986, Duke U., 1988, N.J. Inst. Tech., 1988. Research assoc. Courant Inst., NYU, 1952-57, asst. prof. math., 1957-60, assoc. prof., 1960-65, prof., 1965—, assoc. dir., 1978-84, dir., 1984-88. Editor Jour. Math. Analytical Applications, Communications in PDE, Advanced Applicationa Math., Comm. in Pure and Applied Math.; contbr. articles on applications of partial differential equations, especially transonic flow and scattering theory, to profl. jours. Trustee Princeton U., 1973-78, Sloan Found., 1980—. Guggenheim fellow, 1967, 79; Office Naval Rsch. grantee, until 1990. Fellow AAAS; mem. NAS, Am. Math. Soc. (term trustee), Am. Acad. Arts and Scis., Soc. Indsl. and Applied Math. Office: 251 Mercer St New York NY 10012-1185

MORDFIN, LEONARD, mechanical engineer; b. Bklyn., June 23, 1929; s. Samuel and Margaret (Flyer) M.; m. Norma Marcia Reich, Oct. 10, 1954; children: Stephen Jay, Theodore Gary, Robin Ilene. B of Mech. Engring., Cooper Union, N.Y.C., 1950; PhD, U. Md., 1966. Mech. engr. Nat. Bur. of Standards, Gaithersburg, Md., 1950-67; aerospace engr. Nat. Bur. of Standards, Gaithersburg, 1969-76; phys. sci. adminstr. A.F. Office of Aerospace Rsch., Arlington, Va., 1967-69, Nat. Bur. Standards, Gaithersburg, 1976-90; group leader for mechanical testing Nat. Inst. Standards and Tech., Gaithersburg, 1990—. Editor: Mechanical Relaxation of Residual Stresses, 1988, N.D.E. Reliability, 1986, Critical Issues in Materials Engineering, 1982, Nondestructive Testing Standards--Present and Future, 1992; contbg. author: Materials and Processes, 1985, ency. chpt., 1986. U.S. del. to com. on nondestructive testing Internat. Orgn. for Standardization, 1983—. Recipient Bronz medal Dept. of Commerce, 1983. Fellow ASTM (award of merit 1989, Charles W. Briggs award 1992). Jewish. Office: NIST B144 Materials Bldg Gaithersburg MD 20899

MORDUCHOW, MORRIS, engineering educator; b. Rogachev, USSR, Sept. 25, 1921; came to U.S., 1923, naturalized, 1932; s. Benjamin and Lisa (Greenfield) M.; m. Arlene J. Gottesman, June 15, 1975. B.A., Bklyn. Coll., 1942; B.Ae.E., Poly. Inst. Bklyn., 1944, M.Ae.E., 1945, D.Ae.E., 1947. Research assoc. Poly. Inst. Bklyn., 1944-47, instr. aero. engring., 1947-50, asst. prof. applied math., 1950-53, assoc. prof., 1953-61, prof. applied mechanics, 1961-76, prof. mech. and aerospace engring. Poly. Inst. N.Y., 1976—, prof. Aerospace Engring, 1988—; adj. prof. math. Bklyn. Coll., 1971-73. Contbr. articles in fluid and solid dyn and numerial anal, stability of shock waves to profl. jours. Recipient I.B. Laskowitz award N.Y. Acad. Scis., 1980; 40-Yr. Service award Poly. Inst. N.Y., 1983. Assoc. fellow AIAA (cert. 1969, 79); mem. ASME (cert. 1968, 73), Am. Math. Soc., Math. Assn. Am., Soc. Indsl. and Applied Math., AAAS, Sigma Xi, Tau Beta Pi, Pi Mu Epsilon. Avocations: reading; bridge. Office: Poly Inst NY 333 Jay St Brooklyn NY 11201-2990

MOREAU, BERNARD CLAUDE, social club administrator; b. Neuilly, Hauts de Seine, France, May 13, 1947; s. André George Moreau and Denise (Magnan) LeBoucher; m. Kazumi Suzuki, Oct. 2, 1981. Student art schs., Paris. Graphic artist Galeria de Arte Moderno, Rio de Janeiro, 1968-70; maitre d'hotel Biltmore Hotel and Olive Mill Bistro, Santa Barbara, Calif., 1970-72, Norweigian Am. Line, U.S.A.-Europe, 1972; ship photographer M/S Sagaford and Vistaford, U.S.A.-Europe, 1973-77; filmmaker B. Moreau Prodns., Haiti, 1978-80, Gaumont Press, Calif., 1980; restaurant mgr. Watergate Hotel, Hay Adams Hotel, Washington, 1982-86; gen. mgr. Century Assn., N.Y.C., 1987—; freelance photographer Explorer Agy., Sipa Press, others, Paris, 1978-81; filmmaker Am. Film Festival, Brit. Acad. TV Art, London, 1978. Author: (multimedia) Noble Savage, 1987; editor: (catalog) Noble Savage, 1989; painter: Primitive Expressions, 1991; filmmaker: (Noble Savage), 1989; one-man show in multimedia Nat. Arts Club & Union League Club, 1992. Mem. Nat. Arts Club N.Y.C., Sketch Club N.Y.C., Century Assn. N.Y.C. (gen. mgr. 1987—). Home: 529 W 42d St # 4S New York NY 10036 Office: Century Assn 7 W 43d St New York NY 10036

MOREAU, JAMES WILLIAM, stuntman; b. Old Town, Maine, May 2, 1948; s. Clement Joseph and Madilene Daisy (Trask) M.; m. Peggy Louis Hatch, Feb. 2, 1974 (div. 1975); 1 child, Tina Marie. Student, Mattanawcook Acad., Lincoln, Maine, 1963-64. Prop. person Joie Chitwood Thrill Show, Tampa, Fla., 1965; stuntman/clown, motorcyclist Buddy Wagners Lucky Hell Drivers, Phila., 1966-69, 71; stuntman King Kovas Auto Daredevils, Ft. Lauderdale, Fla., 1970; stunt coord. Death Riders Motorcycle Danville, Ill., 1972-73; stuntman, stunt coord. The Death Riders Motorcycle Thrill Show, Danville, 1972-75; stuntman Johnny Olson Daredevils, Poughkeepsie, N.Y., 1978; producer, owner Internat. Danger Angels, Bangor, Maine, 1978; dynamite act World Series of Thrills, Bellefontaine, Ohio, 1980; stuntman, thrill show clown Bill Siros Thrill-A-Rama, Houston, 1979, 81-84; stuntman Jack Kochman Hell Drivers, Winston-Salem, N.C., 1985; stuntman, human torch Jake Plumsteads All Am. Stunt Team, Mt. Holly, N.J., 1986; stuntman, coord., cons. Can. Auto Circus, Montreal, Que., 1989-90; prin., stuntman Crash Prodns. Death Drivers, Bangor, Maine, 1990—; mem. Hurrican Hell Drivers, Tampa, 1973; stuntman Am. Motor Sports, Milw., 1991-92, Motorsports Promotions, St. Paul, Minn., 1992; stuntman, stunt coord. Am. unit Can. Auto Circus, Renfrew, Pa., 1991. Stuntman (TV series documentary) Thrill Seekers, 1972, (documentary film) Death Riders, 1974, (film) Death Driver, 1975, Crash Prodns., 1991. Named Rookie Stuntman of Yr., Internat. Stuntman's Assn., Phila., 1966. Mem. World Fedn. Internat. Daredevils. Democrat. Roman Catholic. Home: 7 Railroad St Lincoln ME 04457-1411 Office: Crash Prodns PO Box 40 Bangor ME 04402-0040

MOREAU, STEPHEN JOHN, insurance broker; b. Burlington, Vt., Sept. 22, 1944; s. Omer Louis and Dorothy Mary (Martell) M.; m. Dayle Anne Aiken, May 9, 1970; children: Sean Eric, Stephanie Anne. BA, U. Vt., 1968. Real estate broker Pomerleau Real Estate, Burlington, Vt., 1968-70, ins. agt., 1970-72, ins. agt., office mgr., 1972-78; ins. broker, co-owner Mroeau Agy. Inc., South Burlington, Vt., 1978-89; ins. broker, v.p. Pomerleau Agy. Inc., 1989-91, sr. v.p., 1991—; br. chmn. personal lines PACER CNA Ins. Co., Farmington, Conn., 1992—. Dir. Ethan Allen Club, Burlington, 1986-89. Mem. Profl. Ins. Agts. Vt. (bd. dirs., steering com. 1988-92), Sigma Alpha Epsilon (bd. dirs. 1971-85, chmn. 1985-92). Republican. Roman Catholic. Home: 16 Marble Island Rd Colchester VT 05446

MOREHOUSE, JOHN FARLEY, financial analyst; b. New Hartford, N.Y., Nov. 22, 1964; s. Henry Daniel and Nancy (Bremer) M. BS, Siena Coll., 1987. With GE, 1987—; svcs. analyst Internat. Power Systems div. GE, Schenectady, N.Y., 1991—. Fellow Mohawk Valley Hockey Assn., Steuben Athletic Club. Office: GE 1 River Rd Bldg 513W-1st Schenectady NY 12345

MOREHOUSE, WARD, human rights organization executive, publisher; b. Evanston, Ill., Mar. 26, 1929; s. Edward Ward and Anna (Ely) M.; m. Cynthia Thomas, Oct. 3, 1953; children: John T., Andrew E. AB in History and Anthropology, Yale U., 1950; AM, Asia Inst., 1953; postgrad., NYU, 1953-59. Exec. sec. Internat. Conf. on Asian Problems, N.Y.C., 1952-54, Conf. on Asian Affairs, Inc., N.Y.C., 1954-57; instr. dept. govt. NYU, 1956-57; ednl. dir. Asia Soc., N.Y.C., 1957-62; UNESCO fellow in South and Southeast Asia, 1962-63; dir. Ctr. for Internat. Programs and Comparative Studies Univ. of the State of N.Y., 1963-76; pres. Coun. on Internat. and Pub. Affairs, N.Y.C., 1976—; chmn. Intermediate Tech. Devel. Group N.Am., 1979—; pub. The Apex Press, 1988—; rsch. assoc. So. Asia Inst., Soc. Internat. Affairs, Columbia U., 1977—; cons. in field; vis. prof. U. Lund, Sweden, 1976-77, Adminstrv. Staff Coll. of India, Hyderabad, 1969-70. Author: (with M. Arun Subrasanias) The Bhopal Tragedy: What Really Happened and What It Means for American Workers and Communities at Risk, 1986, Building Sustainable Communities: Tools and Concepts for Self Reliant Economic Change, 1989, Abuse of Power: The Social Performance of Multinational Corporations, 1990, (with Lucinda Wykel and David Dembo) Worker Empowerment in a Changing Economy, 1991, others; contr. articles to profl. jours., chpts. to books. Trustee Coun. on Internat. and Pub. Affairs, 1954—, Ctr. for Devel. Policy, Washington, 1979-82; mem. steering com. Ctr. for Study of Expanded Capital Ownership, Washington, 1984-87; mem. Citizens Comn. on Bhopal, 1985-87, Corod. Com. on Toxics and Drugs, 1981-86; mem. adv bd. Croton Housing Task Force, Croton-on-Hudson, N.Y., 1988-90; bd. dirs. Croton Community Land Conservancy, Inc., 1990—; mem. state com. Liberal Party of N.Y. State, 1973—, mem. policy com., 1990—, others. Mem. Assn. for Asian Studies, Internat. Group for Grass Roots Initiatives (bd. dirs. 1986—), Oil Chem. and Atomic Workers (chief steward Local 8-149 1991—). Unitarian. Home: RR 1 Box 348 Croton On Hudson NY 10520-9801 Office: 777 United Nations Plz # 3C New York NY 10017-3521

MORELLA, CONSTANCE ALBANESE, congresswoman; b. Somerville, Mass., Feb. 12, 1931; d. Salvatore and Mary Christine (Fallette) Albanese; m. Anthony C. Morella, Aug. 21, 1954; children: Paul, Mark, Laura; guardians of: Christine, Catherine, Louise, Rachel, Paul, Ursula. AA, Boston U., 1950, AB, 1954; MA, Am. U., 1967, D of Pub. Svc. (hon.), 1988; D of Pub. Svc. (hon.), Norwich U. and Dickinson Coll., 1989. Tchr. Montgomery County (Md.) Pub. Schs., 1956-60; instr. Am. U., 1968-70; prof. Montgomery Coll., Rockville, Md., 1970-86; mem. Md. Ho. Dels., Annapolis, 1979-86, 100th Congress from 8th Md. dist., 1987—; adv. bd. Am. Univ., Washington; trustee Capitol Coll. Laurel, Md. Trustee Capitol Coll, Laurel, Md., 1977—; mem. P.O. and Civil Svc. com. (ranking mem. subcom. on civil svc.), Select Com. on Aging, Sci., Space, and Tech.; coun. mem. Montgomery County United Way; adv. coun. Montgomery County Hospice Soc.; hon. bd. mem. Nat. Kidney Found; active Human Rights Caucus, Congressional Caucus Women's Issues, Black Caucus; chair Arms Control and Fgn. Policy Cacus and others. Office: US Ho of Reps 1024 Longworth House Office Bldg Ste 302 11141 Georgia Ave Silver Spring MD 20902

MORENO, CARLOS SANCHEZ, aerospace engineer; b. East Point, Ga., Sept. 28, 1964; s. Hugo Sanchez and Alida (Smith) M.; m. Genevieve Lucy Fairbrother, June 22, 1991. BS, MIT, 1986, MS, 1988. Teaching asst. MIT Aeronaautics & Astronomics Dept., Cambridge, Mass., 1986; staff engr. NASA Jet Propulsion Lab., Pasadena, Calif., 1988-90, C.S. Draper Lab. Inc., Cambridge, Mass., 1990—. Editor concepts & tech. catalog, 1990. Summer fellow, U. Space Rsch. Assn., NASA, 1986, Draper fellow, 1987. Mem. AIAA, Sigma Gamma Tau, Tau Beta Pi.

MORENO, JOSE GUILLERMO, psychiatrist; b. Bogota, Colombia, Sept. 6, 1951; came to U.S., 1976; s. Guillermo and Olga (Herrera) M.; m. Anne Dorothea Novitt, Dec. 17, 1978; children: Christina, Andrew, Michael. MD, Javeriana U., Bogota, 1973. Intern Javeriana U., Bogota, 1973-74; asst. dir. Mental Health Hosp., Armero, Colombia, 1975-76; resident psychiatry N.J. Med. Sch., Newark, 1976-79; attending psychiatrist St. Joseph's Hosp., Paterson, N.J., 1979—, St. Michael's Hosp., Newark, 1979—, Chilton Meml. Hosp., Pompton Plains, N.J., 1980—; chief psychiat. inpatient unit St. Joseph's Hosp. and Med. Ctr., Paterson, 1981-85, chmn. dept. psychiatry, 1985—; pres. Jose G. Moreno, MD, P.A., Chester, N.J.; chief resident dept. psychiatry N.J. Med. Sch., Newark, 1978-79; assoc. prof. sch. grad. med. edn. Seton Hall U., 1989—. Mem. Am. Psychiat. Assn., N.J. Psychiat. Assn., U.S. Naval Inst. Republican. Roman Catholic. Office: 205 Ridgedale Ave Florham Park NJ 07932-1349

MORENO, VALERIE LUCILLE, educator, artist; b. Bklyn., Oct. 15, 1939; d. Harry J. and Vivian L. (Buttacavoli) Trivisonno; m. Michael Vetri, Sept. 2, 1961 (div. 1970); children: Jan E., Scott M.; m. Charles J. Moreno (div. 1983). BA, Coll. of New Rochelle, 1961; postgrad., Bklyn. Coll., 1976; postgrad. in counseling, Montclair State Coll., 1988—; student, Art Students League, 1984. Tchr. art N.Y.C. Bd. Edn., S.I., N.Y., 1968; pvt. practice art therapy, 1983—; art therapist NYU Med. Ctr., N.Y.C., 1983—; tchr. Summit (N.J.) Community Sch., 1982-86, Watchung Hills Regional Sch., Warren, N.J., 1982; lectr. art, therapy Bayview Correctional Instn. for Women, N.Y.C., 1981; judge N.J. Teen Arts Festival, 1987, 91, 92. Recipient 1st place for oils S.I. Art Exhibit, 1972. Mem. N.Y. State Art Tchrs. Assn., Nat. Mus. for Women in Arts, N.J. Ctr. for Visual Arts, Short Hills Arts Assn. Home: 96 Salem Rd New Providence NJ 07974-2346

MORENON, ELISE, artist; b. Paris, June 26, 1939; d. Ernest E. and Elizabeth (Leland) M. BS, Northwestern U., 1961; postgrad., Sch. Mus. of Fine Arts, Boston, 1962-63, Yale U., 1964-65, Art Students League, N.Y.C., 1967-80. Scenic artist summer theater in N.Y. and Mass., 1955-64; scenic designer Berkshire Playhouse, Stockbridge, Mass., 1962-64; display artist Norman Morris Corp., N.Y.C., 1966-78, Omega Watch Corp., N.Y.C., 1978-86; free lance artist, 1986—; instr. Sch. Visual Arts Alumni Program, N.Y.C., 1978-85, Teaneck (N.J.) Community Edn. Ctr., 1991—; watercolorist, demonstrator, juror. Group shows include Nat. Assn. Women Artists, Israel, Egypt, 1981-82, N.Y.C., 1991, Audubon Artists, N.Y.C., 1982, 91, Allied Artists Am., N.Y.C., 1986, 87, 89, Watercolor U.S.A., 1991; pvt. collections. Recipient Grumbacher Silver medal, 1982, 90, Jurors Spl. Choice award Nat. Art Club, N.Y.C., 1985. Mem. Am. Watercolor Soc., Midwest Watercolor Soc. (awards 1978, 82), Nat. Assn. Women Artists (awards 1978, 81, 83, 86, 89), Knickerbocker Artists (award 1979), others. Home: 420 Fairview Ave Fort Lee NJ 07024

MORETZ, ROGER CLARK, cell biologist; b. Warren, Ohio, July 4, 1942; s. Rodney Russell and Ruth Elizabeth (Gurganious) M.; m. Carol Marilynn Taylor, Aug. 12, 1967; children: Brenda Lynn, Heather Dawn. BA in Physics, Greenville Coll., 1964; MS in Radiol. Health, Rutgers U., 1965; PhD in Biophys Sci., SUNY, Buffalo, 1973. Rsch. asst. Tam div. Nat. Lead Co., Niagara Falls, N.Y., 1966-67; rsch. scientist Roswell Pk. Meml. Inst., Buffalo, 1967-72; postdoctoral fellow U. Colo., Boulder, 1972-74; rsch. assoc. Peter B. Brigham Hosp., Boston, 1974-76; rsch. scientist N.Y. State Inst. for basi Rsch., S.I., 1976-89; sr. prin. scientist Boehringer Ingelheim Pharms., Ridgefield, Conn., 1989—; lectr. Coll. Med. and Dentistry N.J., Piscataway, 1978-80. Contbr. chpts. to books and articles to profl. jours. Elder, music dir. New Durham Chapel, Piscataway, N.J., 1978-89; v.p. PTO Arbor Sch., Piscataway, 1979-80; pres. Parent-Tchr. Fellowship Timothy Chrsitan Sch., Piscataway, 1984-86. NIH fellow, 1972. Mem. AAAS, Electron Microscopy Soc. Am., N.Y. Acad. Scis., Conn. Electron Microscopy Soc., Microbeam Analysis Soc. (met. sect., sec.-treas. 1988-89). Office: Boehringer Ingelheim Pharms 900 Ridgebury Rd Ridgefield CT 06877

MOREY, DAVID EDWARD, consultant; b. Morristown, N.J., Jan. 14, 1956; s. Charles Harold and Dorothy (Holmes) M. BSc, U. Pa., 1978; postgrad., Princeton U., 1979; MSc, London Sch. Econs., 1982. Freelance writer, stringer various publs, London and Houston, 1981-82; fgn. policy adviser U.S. Senator John Glenn, Washington, 1982-84; sr. assoc. D.H. Sawyer & Assocs., N.Y.C., 1984-86; dir. internat. affairs J.E. Seagran, N.Y.C., 1986-88; exec. dir. East-West Forum, N.Y.C., 1986—; adj. prof. internat. policy, Columbia U., N.Y.C., 1987—; pres. David Morey & Co., a strategic consultig group; cons. to Pres. Corazon Aquino, Manila, Philippines, 1986. Author: America and Europe, 1984; contbr. to profl. publs. Named All-Am. in track and field for decathlon NCAA, 1974, 75, 76, 77, 78. Mem. Fgn. Policy Assn., Friends of LSE, Nat. Policy Inst., Coun. Fgn. Rels., Internat. Inst. Statis. Studies, Friends of London Sch. of Econs., Wharton Club, Centurian Club, N.Y. Athletic Club. Democrat. Presbyterian. Office: Ste 202 3426 16th St NW Washington DC 20010

MOREY, ROBERT THOMAS, publisher; b. Amsterdam, N.Y., May 7, 1933; s. Andrew Thomas and Frances Theresa (Duell) M. BSME, Rensselaer Poly. Inst., Troy, N.Y., 1955; postgrad., Boston U.; 1956-58. Staff MIT, Cambridge, 1956-59; account exec. McCann-Erickson Advt., L.A., 1962-65; freelance indsl. writer, photographer various cos. incl. Eastman Kodak, Nat. Cash Register, 1962-71; seminar leader Tech. Transfer Inst., Tokyo, 1984; pubr. Advanced Battery Tech., Cooperstown, N.Y., 1965—; owner Robert Morey Assocs., Cooperstown, 1986—. With USAR, 1955-63. Mem. Cooperstown C. of C., Battery Council Internat. Home: Chicken Farm Rd Cooperstown NY 13326 Office: Robert Morey Assocs PO Box 30 Cooperstown NY 13326-0030

MORGAN, BRUCE CURTIS, educational administrator; b. Montclair, N.J., Oct. 4, 1939; s. Lester Elvert and Ruth Vianna (Winters) M.; m. Judith Peterson, May 12, 1984; children: Christine Michelle, Kathleen Mary. BA, Montclair State Coll., 1961, MA, 1966. Lic. pers. and guidance supr. Tchr. Roselle (N.J.) Sch. System, 1961-63, Scotch Plains (N.J.)-Fanwood Sch., 1963-66; counselor Parsippany (N.J.)-Troy Hills Sch., 1966-67, Whippany (N.J.) Park High Sch., 1967-77; coord. guidance/testing Haddonfield (N.J.) Meml. Schs., 1977—. bd. mem. Am. Liver Found., Delaware Valley chpt., Phila., 1978—. Recipient Disting. Svc. award Nat. Career Devel. Assn., 1982. Mem. AACD, Nat. Assn. Coll. Admissions Counselors, N.J. Assn. Coll. Admissions Counselors, N.J. Assn. Counseling and Devel., N.J. Career Guidance Assn. (pres. 1979-80), Morris County Guidance Assn. (pres. 1970-71), Camden County Guidance Assn. (pres. 1980-81, Counselor of Yr. 1985). Home: 11 Lenape Rd Cherry Hill NJ 08002-1313 Office: Haddonfield Pub Schs Haddonfield Meml High Sch Haddonfield NJ 08033

MORGAN, BRUCE HARRY, physics educator, retired; b. Sharon, Pa.; s. Harry A. and Ruth M. (Shank) M.; m. Olivia Denniston, 1958 (dec. 1989); children: Julia, Elaine. AB, Harvard U., 1953; MS, Calif. Inst. Tech., 1954; JD, George Washington U., 1968. Bar: Md. 1969. Assoc. prof. physics U.S. Naval Acad., Annapolis, Md., 1957-92. Mem. Am. Assn. Physics Tchrs., Am. Solar Energy Soc., Phi Beta Kappa, Sigma Xi (assoc.). Christian Scientist. Office: US Naval Acad Dept Physics Michelson Hall Annapolis MD 21402

MORGAN, CHARLES ROBERT, chemist, researcher; b. Kingston, Pa., July 18, 1934; s. Charles Henry and Ann Elizabeth (Kvashnak) M.; m. Virginia Dahan, Aug. 10, 1968; children: Denise Elizabeth, Kevin Daniel. BS, Pa. State U., 1956; PhD, MIT, 1963. Postdoctoral fellow MIT, Cambridge, 1963-65; rsch. chemist W.R. Grace & Co., Columbia, Md., 1965-72, sr. rsch. chemist, 1972-75, mgr., 1975-87, sr. rsch. assoc., 1987—. Contbr. articles to sci. jours.; numerous patents in U.S. and fgn. countries. Mem. Am. Chem. Soc., Inter-Am. Photochem. Soc., Internat. Electronics Packaging Soc., N.Am. Membrane Soc. Home: 19108 Holberton Ln Brookeville MD 20833-2634 Office: WR Grace & Co 7379 State Rt 32 Columbia MD 21044-4098

MORGAN, CHRISTOPHER B., advertising professional; b. St. Paul, May 21, 1964; s. Harry Wayne Morgan and Catherine Howard (Johnston) Westlake. BA in Polit. Sci., Marlboro Coll., 1986. Asst. media planner Arnold & Co., Boston, 1986-89; sr. media planner Altschiller Reitzfeld Tracy Locke, N.Y.C., 1989—.

MORGAN, DENISE WILLIAMS, family therapist; b. Scranton, Pa., Oct. 25, 1952; d. Eldon E. and Doris (Gumble) Williams; m. Robert M. Morgan, June 15, 1974; children: Justin, Hillary, Zachary. BS, St. Lawrence U., 1974; diploma in respiratory therapy, U. Chgo., 1976; MA, Marywood Coll., 1990. Respiratory therapist St. Luke's Hosp., Bethlehem, Pa., 1974-79; resort mgr. Nemanie Lodge, Paupack, Pa., 1979-85; respiratory therapist Wayne Meml. Hosp., Honesdale, Pa., 1985-89; program coord. Head Injury Recovery Ctr. at Hillcrest, Milford, Pa., 1989—. Active Paupack United Meth. Ch., 1966—; group leader Freedom from Smoking/Am. Lung Assn., 1984—; instr. Winter Emergency Care, Ea. Pa., 1990—; basic patroller Nat. Ski Patrol. Mem. AACD, Am. Assn. Respiratory Care, Nat. Bd. Respiratory Care, Marywood Counseling Assn. (chmn. bus. com. 1989-90), Nat. Head Injury Found. (founder tri-state chpt. 1991), Chi Sigma Iota. Republican. Home: HCI Box 1857 Tafton PA 18464 Office: Head Injury Recovery Ctr at Hillcrest 404 E Harford St Milford PA 18337-1099

MORGAN, DENNIS ALAN, federal official; b. St. Joseph, Mo., Feb. 1, 1947; s. John Frederick and Eunice L. (Seiter) M.; m. Linda Terrell James, June 22, 1968 (div. 1983); 1 child, Tracey Melinda. BA, U. Mo., 1969; MS, U. So. Calif., 1973; PhD, Pacific Western U., 1991. With Dept. of Navy, Washington, 1969—, dir. bus. and fin. mgmt., 1984—, also chmn. mgmt. com.; lectr. in field. Author: The Pechora Intercept, 1988, Act of Contrition, 1991. Curators scholar U. Mo., 1965. Mem. SAR, IEEE, Mensa, Internat. Platform Assn., Time Mag. Editor's Circle Adv. Panel, East Barcroft Assn. (bd. dirs. 1985—), Nat. Geographic Soc., Earthwatch, Nat. Parks and Conservation Assn., Lambda Chi Alpha. Republican. Home: 914 S George Mason Dr Arlington VA 22204-1557

MORGAN, JAMES ORVAL, non-profit company executive; b. Albia, Iowa, Nov. 4, 1933; s. Orval M. and Agnes (Howie) M.; m. Wanda B. Busby, Oct. 23, 1954; children: Terri Lea, Kathleen Anne, Martha Lyn. AB, Lincoln (Ill.) Christian Coll., 1955, MA, 1957; AB, So. Nazarene Coll., Bethany, Okla., 1962; MA, U. Okla., Norman, 1966. Prof. lang. Manhattan Christian Coll., Manhattan, Kans., 1965-74; v.p. devel. Manhattan Christian Coll., 1969-74; assoc. prof. Kans. State U., Manhattan, 1968-73; v.p. devel. World Neighbors, Oklahoma City, 1974-76; pres., chief exec. officer World Neighbors, 1977-83; exec. dir. Rodale Inst., Emmaus, Pa., 1983-87; v.p. Rodale Inst., 1987—; cons. in field. Contbr. articles to profl. jours. Mem. Rotary (bd. dirs. 1968—). Presbyterian. Home: 3547 Pleasant Ave Allentown PA 18103-9734 Office: Rodale Inst 222 Main St Emmaus PA 18098-0099

MORGAN, JOHN ANDREW, JR., political science educator; b. Cary, N.C., May 26, 1935; s. John Andrew and Elsie Florence (Farthing) M.; m. Anne Louise Desautels, June 19, 1958; children: Vicki Anne, John Andrew III, Sarah Catherine. BA magna cum laude, Stetson U., 1957; MA, Duke U., 1959, PhD, 1963. Social sci. analyst U.S. Commn. on Civil Rights, Washington, 1959; instr. polit. sci. U. Southwestern La., Lafayette, 1960-62; instr. polit. sci. Duke U., Durham, N.C., 1962-64, rsch. assoc., summers 1963-64, vis. rsch. assoc., summer 1965; asst. prof. polit. sci. George Washington U., Washington, 1964-68, assoc. prof. polit. sci., 1968-74, prof. polit. sci. and pub. affairs, 1974—; cons. Spl. Action Office for Drug Abuse Prevention, Washington, 1973-75, NIMH, Bethesda, Md., 1971-73, Cabinet Com. on Edn., Washington, 1970. Manuscript reviewer various pubrs., 1965—; co-author: The Politics of Mental Health, 1968; contbg. author chpts. in books; contbr. articles to profl. jours. Woodrow Wilson fellow, 1957-58; So. Fellowships Fund fellow, 1957-60; recipient Citation for Disting. Svc. George Washington U. Faculty Senate, 1978, 84. Democrat. Episcopalian. Home: 8802 Parliament Dr Springfield VA 22151 Office: George Washington U Dept Polit Sci Washington DC 20052

MORGAN, JOHN BLACK, securities company executive, educator; b. Suffolk, Va., May 1, 1938; s. John Black and Mildred Mae (Brinkley) M.; m. Mary Ann Theil, Sept. 18, 1970; 1 child, John B. IV. MusB, U. Mich., 1960, MusM, 1962; MBA in Fin., Adelphi U., 1982; JD, William Howard Taft U., Fountain Valley, Calif., 1990. Bar: Calif. 1990; lic. securities prin., arbitrator Nat. Assn. Securities Dealers. Tchr. music, dir. bands, supr. instrumental music parochial and pub. schs., 1961-76; account exec. Advest, Inc., Syracuse, N.Y., 1976-77, Merrill Lynch, Pierce, Fenner & Smith, Inc., Syracuse, 1977-79, Shearson, Lehman Bros., N.Y.C., 1979-80; dir. compliance, corp. sec. Muriel Siebert & Co., Inc., N.Y.C., 1980-82; sr. compliance assoc. Lehman Bros. Kuhn Loeb, Inc., N.Y.C., 1982-84; dir. compliance Asiel & Co., N.Y.C., 1984—; adj. prof. fin. Adelphi U., Garden City, N.Y., 1983; instr. Securities Tng. Corp., N.Y.C., 1986—, N.Y. Inst. Fin. N.Y.C., 1987-89; mem. compliance and legal div. Securities Industry Assn. Contbr. articles to music jours. Vestryman St. Lawrence of Canterbury Episcopal Ch., Dix Hills, N.Y., 1983-89, St. Patrick's Episcopal Ch., Deer Park, N.Y., 1992—. Mem. ABA, State Bar of Calif., Am. Contract Bridge League, Met. Opera Guild, Am. Mus. Natural History, U. Mich. Alumni Assn. (bd. dirs. 1991—), U. Mich. Band Alumni Assn., U. Mich. Club L.I. (pres. 1984-90), U. Mich. Club 1st Dist. (N.Y., New Eng., N.J. and Ont., sec. 1987-89, pres. 1989-91, dist. dir. 1991—), N.Y. Philharmon. Soc., Phi Mu Alpha. Democrat. Home: 34 Merle Pl Deer Park NY 11729-1819 Office: Asiel & Co 20 Broad St New York NY 10005-2601

MORGAN, JOHN SMITH, writer; b. Cleve., Mar. 20, 1921; s. Clyde Spencer and Mariem (Smith) M.; m. Virginia Lucille Willis, Feb. 15, 1947; children: Penelope, Patricia M. Berger, Medeleine M. Fackler. BA, Yale U., 1943. Managing editor Steel Mag., Cleve., 1947-64; cons. GE, N.Y.C., 1964-74; dir. employee communication Rockwell Internat. Corp., Pitts., 1974-80; owner Advocacy Communications, Pitts., 1980—. Author: Getting Across to Employees, 1964, Practical Guide to Conference Leadership, 1966, Managing the Young Adults, 1967, Improving Your Creativity on the Job, 1968, Managing Change, 1972, Noah Webster, A Biography, 1975, Robert Fulton, A Biography, 1977, The Wolf Strikes, 1981, How Executives Solve Problems, 1987, Interpersonal Skills for the Manager, 1987, Getting a Job After 50, 1988, Organizational Development To Meet Changing Needs, 1989, and others; contbr. articles to profl. jours. Sgt. Med. Dept., 1943-46. Mem. Coun. Communication Mgmt. (bd. dirs. 1970-74), U. Club Pitts. (bd. dirs. 1988-90). Republican. Presbyterian. Home: 302 Fox Chapel Rd Apt 516 Pittsburgh PA 15238-2338

MORGAN, JOHN STEPHEN, state representative, materials science researcher; b. Washington, Dec. 23, 1963; s. James Donald and Virginia Louise (Hendrickson) M. BS, Loyola Coll., Balt., 1984; MS in Engring., Johns Hopkins U., 1988, PhD, 1990. Rsch. assoc. Johns Hopkins U., Balt., 1986-90; postdoctoral fellow Applied Physics Lab. Johns Hopkins U., Laurel, Md., 1990—; mem. Md. Gen. Assembly, Annapolis, 1991—. Chmn. adv. com. Bd. Edn. Howard County, Md., 1989-90; chmn. voter registration Howard County Rep. Party, 1987-89. Recipient Charles Miller award Howard County Rep. Party, 1988. Mem. Am. Phys. Soc., Materials Rsch. Soc., Elkridge Jaycees, Kiwanis. Lutheran. Home: 9070-A Stebbing Way Laurel MD 20723 Office: Md Gen Assembly Lowe House Office Bldg Annapolis MD 21401

MORGAN, KAREN JOHNSON, food company executive, consultant; b. Watseka, Ill., Feb. 22, 1945; d. Howard Edgar and Margaret Lucille (Dilling) Johnson; m. Fred William Morgan, Jr., Aug. 26, 1967 (div. June 1974); 1 child, Todd Anthony; m. Rick Elam, Nov. 19, 1979; 1 stepchild, Paula Helene. B.S., Purdue U., 1967; M.S., Mich. State U., 1968; Ph.D., U. Mo., 1977. Instr. nutrition assessment and food policy research U. Mo., Columbia, 1973-74, grad. research asst., 1974-77, asst. prof., 1981-83, assoc. prof., 1983-86; asst. prof. Mich. State U., East Lansing, 1977-81; dir. consumer affairs Nabisco Brands, Inc., East Hanover, N.J., 1987-90; sr. dir. nutrition and consumer affaris Nabisco Foods Group, 1991—; cons. numerous food industries and pub. relation firms, 1979-87. Author: Nutrients in Foods, 1983; computerized nutrient data bank at Mich. State U., 1979 (yearly updates). Editor Nutrition Data Bank Conf. Proc., 1980. Contbr. articles to profl. jours. Grantee USDA, HHS. Fellow Am. Coll. Nutrition; mem. Am. Inst. Nutrition, Nat. Acad. Scis. (com. foods additives survey data), Am. Agrl. Econs. Assn., Inst. Food Technologists, Am. Home Econs. Assn. Avocations: downhill skiing, reading. Office: Nabisco Foods Group Nutrition and Consumer Affairs 7 Campus Dr Parsippany NJ 07054

MORGAN, LEWIS B., counseling education educator; b. Fountain Springs, Pa., May 23, 1934; s. Burgess S. and Marion R. (Lewis) M.; m. Irene L. Morgan, Dec. 30, 1960; children: Jennifer, David. BS in Edn., Kutztown State Coll., 1960; EdM in Counseling, Rutgers U., 1963; PhD in Counseling, U. Conn., 1970. Lic. psychologist, N.J. Tchr. Triton Regional High Sch., Runnemede, N.J., 1960-61; tchr., counselor Overbrook Regional High Sch., Clementon, N.J., 1961-63; counselor Pennsauken (N.J.) High Sch., 1963-64; registrar Kutztown (Pa.) State Coll., 1964-66; guidance dir. Bolton (Conn.) Pub. Schs., 1966-70; prof. counselor edn. Villanova (Pa.) U., 1970—; pvt. practice counselor, 1970—; cons. local sch. dists., 1970—. Author: A Casebook for School Counselors, 1974; contbr. articles on counseling to profl. publs. Mem. NEA, AACD, Am. Psychol. Assn., Assn. Specialists in Group Work, Phi Kappa Phi, Kappa Delta Pi. Democrat. Episcopalian. Office: Villanova U Dept Edn and Human Svcs Villanova PA 19085

MORGAN, MARY LOUISE FITZSIMMONS, fund raising executive; b. N.Y.C., July 22, 1946; d. Robert John and Mary Louise (Gordon) Fitzsimmons; m. David William Morgan, Aug. 7, 1971; children: Mallory Siobhan, David William. BA, Marquette U., 1964; MA, Catholic U., Wash., 1966. Asst. prof. Monmouth Coll., West Long Branch, N.J., 1966-69; campaign dir. United Way, N.Y.C., 1969-80; pres. Morgan Communications, N.Y.C., 1980-82; capital campaign dir. YMCA of Greater N.Y., 1982-85; dir. devel. N.Y. Med. Coll., Valhalla, 1985-88; counsel Challenger Ctr., Va., 1988—; v.p. Ctr. Molecular Medicine & Immunology, Newark, 1989—, Garden State Cancer Ctr., Newark, 1990—; dir. Casita Maria Inc., N.Y.C. 1975—; pres., founding dir. Achievement Rewards for Coll. Scientists Inc., N.Y.C. 1978-80. Sec. Darien (Conn.) Dem. Town Com., 1984—, vice chmn. Darien nominating com. 1986—. Recipient 50th Anniversary award Casita Maria Inc., N.Y.C., 1984, Iris award Bus. Communicators of Am., 1991. Mem. Nat. Soc. Fund Raising Execs., Nat. Soc. Hosp. Adminstrn., Spring Lake (N.J.) Bath and Tennis Club. Democrat. Roman Catholic. Home: 14 Anthony Ln Darien CT 06820-5001 Office: Garden State Cancer Ctr Ctr Molecular Medicine 1 Bruce St Newark NJ 07103-2709

MORGAN, MICHAEL SCOTT, marketing educator; b. Detroit, Mar. 21, 1953; s. Rodney Scott and Janet Elizabeth (Moss) M.; m. Gilda Marie Narciso, May 23, 1987; 1 child, Gerry. BA magna cum laude, U. Tex., 1976; MS, U. Tex./Dallas, Dallas, 1990; PhD, U. Tex., Dallas, 1990. Dir. ops. Bruyea-Pond Motels, San Diego, 1980-84; rms. div. mgr. Sheraton Mockingbird, Dallas, 1984-85; rooms div. mgr. Lincoln Hotel Corp., Dallas, 1985-87; teaching asst. Sch. Mgmt. U. Tex., Dallas, 1987-90; asst. prof. Sch. Hotel Adminstrn. Cornell U., Ithaca, N.Y., 1990—; cons. Savitz Rsch. Ctr., Dallas, 1989—. Mem. Soc. for Math. Psychology, Operators Rsch. Soc., The Inst. for Mgmt. Scis., Am. Mktg. Assn. Episcopalian. Home: 100 Graham Rd # 10F Ithaca NY 14850-1137 Office: Cornell U Sch of Hotel Adminstrn 545-A Statler Hall Ithaca NY 14853

MORGAN, PAMELA ANTOINETTE, English educator; b. Sayre, Pa., Dec. 28, 1947; d. Roland Evert and Rosanne A. (Faulkner) M. BS, Mansfield (Pa.) U., 1971. Cert. secondary edn. tchr., Pa. Tchr. Towanda (Pa.) Area Sch. Dist., 1971—; workshop presentor in field, 1988—. Mem. Nat. Coun. Tchr.'s of English, NEA, Pa. State Edn. Assn., Towanda Area Edn. Assn., Assn. for Supervision and Curriculum Devel. Home: PO Box 242 PO Box 242 Canton PA 17724-0242 Office: Towanda Area Sch High Sch Dr Towanda PA 18848

MORGAN, PAMELA YVONNE, human resource specialist; b. Allentown, Pa., Jan. 23, 1961; d. Carl Robert and Elizabeth Dorethy (Campbell) Ruggles; m. Charus T. Morgan, June 28, 1985 (div. Feb. 1990). Student, Post Coll., 1979-81. Conf. coord. New Seabury Corp., Hyannis, Mass., 1984-87; dir. pers. The Flatley Co., Hyonnis, Mass., 1987-90; dir. human resource The Flatley Co., Framingham, Mass., 1990—. Vol. The Am. Heart Assn., Falmouth, Mass., 1990, The Falmouth Fireworks Com., 1990-91. Mem. Soc. Human Resource Mgmt., Northeast Human Resource Assn., Metrowest Human Resource Mgmt. Assn. (bd. dirs.). Home: PO Box 1619 North Falmouth MA 02556-1619

MORGAN, ROBIN EVONNE, author, journalist, activist, editor; b. Lake Worth, Fla., Jan. 29, 1941; 1 child, Blake Ariel. Grad. with honors, The Wetter Sch., 1956; student, pvt. tutors, 1956-59, Columbia U.; DHL (hon.), U. Conn., 1992. Free-lance book editor, 1961-69; editor Grove Press, 1967-70; editor, columnist World column Ms. Mag., N.Y.C., 1974-87, editor in chief, 1990—; vis. chair and guest prof. women's studies New Coll., Sarasota, Fla., 1973; disting. vis. scholar, lectr. Ctr. Critical Analysis of Contemporary Culture, Rutgers U., 1987; invited spl. cons. UN com. UN Conv. to End All Forms Discrimination Against Women, Sao Paulo and Brasilia, Brazil, 1987; mem. adv. bd. ISIS (internat. network women's internat. cross-cultural exch.); spl. advisor gen. assembly conf. on Gender UN Internat. Sch., 1985-86; free-lance journalist, lectr. cons., editor, 1969—; invited speaker numerous confs., orgns., acad. meetings, U.S. and abroad. Author, compiler, editor: Sisterhood Is Powerful: An Anthology of Writings From the Women's Liberation Movement, 1970, Swedish edit. 1972, Sisterhood Is Global: The International Women's Movement Anthology, 1984, U.K., 1985, Spanish ed., 1992; author: (nonfiction) Going Too Far: The Personal Chronicle of a Feminist, 1978, German edit. 1978, The Anatomy of Freedom: Feminism, Physics and Global Politics, 1982, fgn. edits. U.K. 1984, Germany, 1985, Argentina, 1986, The Netherlands, 1988, Portugal, 1991, The Demon Lover: On the Sexuality of Terrorism, 1989, fgn. edits. U.K. 1989, Japan, 1992, The Word of A Woman: Selected Dispatches 1968-91, 1992; (fiction) Dry Your Smile: A Novel, 1987, U.K. edit. 1988, The Mer-Child: A New Legend, 1991, (poetry) Monster: Poems, 1972, Lady of the Beasts: Poems, 1976, Death Benefits: Poems, 1981, Depth Perception: New Poems and a Masque, 1982, Upstairs in the Garden: Selected and New Poems, 1968-88, 1990, (plays) In Another Country, 1960, The Duel, 1979; co-editor: (with Bunch and Weeks) The New Woman: Anthology, 1969; contbr. numerous articles, essays, book revs., poems to various publs.; presenter poetry readings univs., poetry ctrs., radio, TV, others, 1970—. Mem. 1st women's liberation caucus CORE, 1965, Student Nonviolent Coordinating Com., 1966; organizer 1st feminist demonstration against Miss Am. Pageant, 1968; founder, pres. The Sisterhood Fund, 1970; founder, pres. N.Y. Women's Law Ctr., 1970; founder N.Y. Women's Ctr., 1969; co-founder, bd. dirs. Feminist Women's Health Network, Nat. Battered Women's Refuge Network, Nat. Network Rape Crisis Ctrs.; bd. dirs. Women's Fgn. Policy Coun.; adv. trustee Nat. Women's Inst. for Freedom of Press; founding mem. Nat. Mus. Women in Arts; co-founder Sisterhood is Global Inst. (internat. think-tank), 1984, sec., 1989—, co-organizer, U.S. mem. official visit Coalition of Philippines Women's Movement, 1988; chair N.Y. state com. Hands Across Am. Com. for Justice and Empowerment, 1988. Recipient Front Page award for disting. journalism, Wonder Woman award for internat. peace and understanding, 1982, Feminist of Yr. award Fund for Feminist majority, 1990; writer-in-residence grantee Yaddo, 1980; grantee Nat. Endowment for Arts, 1979-80, Ford Found., 1982, 83, 84. Mem. Feminist Writers' Guild, Media Women, N.Am. Feminist Coalition, Pan Arab Feminist Solidarity Assn. (hon.), Israeli Feminists Against Occupation (hon.). Office: Ms Mag 230 Park Ave New York NY 10169-0005

MORGAN, RODGER F., manufacturing company executive; b. Bklyn., Jan. 21, 1944; s. Rodger F. and Laura (Whalen) M.; m. Connie Lee Heil, 1963 (div. 1968); children: Christine Kelly, Kathleen Dawn; m. Angela, Dec. 5, 1972; children: Rodger Erick, Anthony Joseph, Lynn Marie. Student in graphic arts, N.Y.C. Community Coll. Svc. technician Chemco Photoproducts, Nassau, N.Y., Fabcon, Nassau; ornamental iron worker and supr. IAOBSOIW Local 580, Manhattan, N.Y.; with Ricanlynn Svcs., Inc., Hunter, N.Y. Leader Boy Scouts Am., Lindenhurst, N.Y. Mem. C. of C. Office: Ricanlynn Svcs Inc PO Box 566 Hunter NY 12442-0003

MORGAN, SISTER RUTH, educator; b. Elizabeth, N.J., Aug. 1, 1938; d. Joseph Southers and Marie Helen (Trepain) M. BA, Douglass Coll., 1959; MEd, Rutgers Univ., 1964; MA, Rider Coll., 1976. Cert. educator, supr., adminstr. Tchr. South Plainfield (N.J.) Pub. Schs., 1960-61; tchr. Piscataway (N.J.) Pub. Schs., 1961-80; sec. Cathedral Grammar Sch., Trenton, N.J., 1980-81; office mgr. Diocese of Metuchen, N.J., 1983-84; prin. Cathedral Grammar Sch., Trenton, N.J., 1984-90; assoc. dir. family life office Archdiocese of Newark, Irvington, N.J., 1990-92; pastoral assoc. St. Mary of the Assumption Ch., Elizabeth, N.J., 1992—. Mem. Sisters of Mercy of N.J., Nat. Cath. Edn. Assn., Delta Pi Epsilon (pres. 1986-88). Roman Catholic. Home: 1600 Martine Ave Scotch Plains NJ 07076-2995 Office: St Mary of Assumption Ch 155 Washington Ave Elizabeth NJ 07202

MORGAN, SAMUEL P(OPE), physicist, applied mathematician; b. San Diego, July 14, 1923; s. Samuel Pope and Beatrice Marie (Summers) M.; m. Mary Caroline Annin, Jan. 23, 1948; children: Caroline Gail, Lesley Anne, Alison Lee, Diane Elizabeth. B.S., Calif. Inst. Tech., 1943, M.S., 1944, Ph.D. in Physics, 1947. Mem. tech. staff AT&T Bell Labs., Murray Hill, N.J., 1947-59; head dept. math. physics AT&T Bell Labs., 1959-67, dir. computing tech., 1969-70, dir. computing sci. research center, 1967-82, disting. mem. tech. staff, 1982—. Research, publs. on electromagnetic theory, applied math., queueing theory. Fellow IEEE; mem. Am. Phys. Soc., Assn. Computing Machinery, AAAS, Sigma Xi. Home: 9 Raleigh Ct Morristown NJ 07960-2535 Office: AT&T Bell Labs Murray Hill NJ 07974-0636

MORGAN, THOMAS BRUCE, broadcast executive, author, press secretary; b. Springfield, Ill., July 24, 1926; s. David Edward and Mabel Ariel (Wolfe) M.; m. Joan T. Zuckerman, Oct. 3, 1950 (div. 1972); children: Katherine Tarlow, Nicholas David; m. Mary Clark Rockefeller, May 4, 1974 (div. 1988); stepchildren: Geoffrey, Michael, Sabrina Strawbridge; m. Hadassah Teitz Brooks, Aug. 19, 1990; stepchildren: Shoshone, Goldhill, Benjamin. BA, Carleton Coll., 1949. Assoc. editor Esquire Mag., N.Y.C., 1949-53; sr. editor Look Mag., N.Y.C., 1953-58; freelance writer N.Y.C., 1958-69, 80—; press sec. Mayor John V. Lindsay, N.Y.C., 1969-73; sr. editor New York Mag., 1974-75; editor The Village Voice, N.Y.C., 1975-76, Politicks mag., N.Y.C., 1976-79; novelist, freelance writer, 1980-90; pres. WNYC Comm. Group, N.Y.C., 1990—; press sec. Stevenson for Pres., 1960, McCarthy for Pres., 1968. Author: Friends and Fellow Students, 1956, Self Creations, 1965, This Blessed Shore, 1966, Among the Anti-Americans, 1967, Snyder's Walk, 1987; screenwriter: (feature film) Albert Schweitzer, 1958; contbr. numerous articles to jours. and mags. Trustee Carleton Coll., Northfield, Minn., 1975-79, 80—. With AC, U.S. Army, 1945. Mem. PEN, Author's Guild, Century Club. Democrat. Jewish. Home: 1155 Park Ave New York NY 10128 Office: WNYC Comm Group 1 Centre St New York NY 10007

MORGAN, THOMAS JOSEPH, physicist; b. Bklyn., Oct. 20, 1943; s. James Patrick and Mary Elizabeth (Colgan) M.; m. Janet Isabelle Head, Mar. 23, 1968; children: Brian Keith, Brent Thomas. AB, Carroll Coll., 1965; BS, Mont. State U., 1966; MS, U. Calif., Berkeley, 1968, PhD, 1971. Univ. fellow Queen's U. of Belfast, No. Ireland, 1971-73; asst. prof. Wesleyan U., Middletown, Conn., 1973-80, assoc. prof., 1980-86; vis. prof. U. Paris, Orsay, 1986, prof. physics, 1986-90, dean of the scis., 1990—; cons. Oak Ridge (Tenn.) Nat. Lab., 1976—; Moshinsky vis. prof. U. Mex., Mexico City, 1984. Editor: Aps New England Newsletter, 1978-81; contb. over 50 articles to profl. jours. Vis. fellow Joint Inst. Lab. Astrophysics, 1982; sr. fellow Chem. Inst., U. Western Ont., 1990. Mem. Am. Phys. Soc., Conn. Acad. Arts & Scis., Sigma Xi. Office: Physics Dept Wesleyan U Sci Tower Middletown CT 06459-0155

MORGAN, TODD BYERS, financial and management consultant; b. Pitts., Jan. 16, 1956; s. Robert Arthur and Betty (Byers) M.; m. Maria Michelon. BS in Bus. Adminstrn., Susquehanna U., 1978; MBA, Marshall U., 1979. Assoc. Booz Allen & Hamilton, Inc., Lexington Park, Md., 1979-85; chmn. bd. Eagan, McAllister Assocs., Inc., Lexington Park, 1985—; instr. Community Coll. St. Mary's, Lexington Park, 1980—, Embry-Riddle Aero. U., 1981-83, 92—, univ. coll. U. Md., Lexington Park, 1984—. Active Com. to Elect Ronald Reagan, 1979-80, fundraiser, 1983-84; active Bush for Pres. Campaign, 1988; v.p. Wildewood Homeowners Assn., California, Md., 1985-86, pres., 1986-91; treas. Eagan for County Commr. Campaign, 1987, 90; mem. com. Boy Scouts Am., 1988—; mem. Nat. Eagle Scout Assn.; vestry mem. Ch. of Ascension. Mem. Masons. Republican. Episcopalian. Home: 121 Chestnut Ridge Dr Leonardtown MD 20650-4501 Office: Eagan McAllister Assocs Inc PO Box 986 Lexington Park MD 20653-0986

MORGAN, WANDA BUSBY, health care executive, educator; b. Cromwell, Okla., Aug. 27, 1930; d. Charles C. and Gladys J. (Beaty) Busby; m. James O. Morgan, Oct. 23, 1954; children: Terri, Kathleen, Martha. BA, Lincoln (Ill.) Christian Coll., 1954; MA, Kans. State U., 1973; postgrad., Cen. State U., Edmond, Okla., 1977-79, U. Okla., 1980-84, Purdue U., 1983. Prof. Manhattan (Kans.) Christian Coll., Manhattan, 1970-74; instr. Seminole (Okla.) Jr. Coll., 1978-80; prof. Bethany (Okla.) Nazarene Coll., 1980-84; instr. Moravian Coll., Bethlehem, Pa., 1984-85, Allentown Coll., Center Valley, Pa., 1985-88; edn. coordinator Sacred Heart HealthCare System, Allentown, Pa., 1985-87; v.p. Sacred Heart Health Care System, Allentown, Pa., 1987—; cons. Communication Arts, Ltd., Allentown, 1978—; advisor Okla. Dept. Edn., Oklahoma City, 1981; tchr., cons. U. Okla. Dept. Edn., Norman, 1980—, Okla. Writing Project, 1980—. Author: Bridging the English Gap, 1983; co-author: Grammar, Ltd., 1983. Mem. adv. bd. Lehigh County (Pa.) Human Svcs. Dept., 1986-89, chmn., 1988-89. Fellow U. Okla., 1980. Mem. Am. Soc. Healthcare Mktg. and Pub. Rels., Hosp. Assn. Pa. (mem. pub. rels. and mktg. div.), Okla. Coun. Tchrs. of English (vice chair coll. sect. 1983-84). Democrat. Presbyterian. Office: Sacred Heart Hosp 421 W Chew St Allentown PA 18102-3490

MORGANROTH, JOEL, cardiologist, educator; b. Detroit, Oct. 29, 1945; m. Gail Morrison, June 25, 1972. BS, U. Mich., 1967, MD, 1970. Diplomate Am. Bd. Cardiology, Am. Bd. Internal Medicine. Intern, asst. resident Beth Israel Hosp., Boston, 1970-72; resident, fellow Nat. Heart and Lung Inst., NIH, Bethesda, 1972-74, U. Pa. Med. Sch., Phila., 1974-75; asst. prof. medicine U. Pa., Phila., 1975-78; assoc. prof. Jefferson Med. Sch., Phila., 1978-82; prof. medicine and pharmacology Hahnemann U., Phila., 1982-89; dir. Nat. Cardiovascular Rsch. Ctr., Haddonfield, N.J., 1982-89,sudden death prevention program Likoff Cardiovascular Inst., Phila., 1982-88, cardiac rsch. and devel. The Grad. Hosp., Phila., 1987—; dir. edn., rsch. Presbyn. Med. Ctr., 1992—, Phila. Heart Inst., 1992—; cons. to bus. Author/editor 20 books; contbr. over 300 articles to med. jours. Mem. editorial bd. Am. Jour. Cardiology, Jour. Am. Coll. Cardiology, Circulation, others. Fellow Am. Coll. Cardiology, ACP, Am. Coll. Chest Physicians, Am. Coll. Clin. Pharmacology; mem. Phila. Acad. Cardiology (pres. 1985), S.E. Pa. Heart Assn. (pres. 1986). Home: 1040 Stony Ln Gladwyne PA 19035-1197 Office: Phil Heart Inst 39th and Market St Philadelphia PA 19104

MORGANSTERN, BARRY FRASIER, communication educator; b. Manchester, N.H., Aug. 21, 1948. BS, So. Ill. U., 1970, MS, 1974; PhD, U. Mo., 1977. Instr. Mascoutah (Ill.) Community High Sch., 1970-73; asst. prof. W.Va. U., Morgantown, 1977-81; assoc. prof. William Paterson Coll., Wayne, N.J., 1981—; cons. in field. Author: Nonverbal Teacher Behavior, 1978 (Top Three award 1978); (film scripts) Senior Citizen Service, 1990, For the Homeless, 1990; actor (French script) Taxi, 1984. V. chmn. bd. dirs., chmn. pub. rels. Passaic County Lit. Coalition, Paterson, N.J., 1991—; mem. Leadership Paterson, 1992—. N.J. Dept. Higher Edn. grantee, 1984; N.J. Consortium Global Edn. Project fellow, 1990-91. Office: William Paterson Coll. 300 Pompton Rd Wayne NJ 07470

MORGENS, WARREN KENDALL, lawyer; b. Oklahoma City, May 25, 1940; s. Alvin Gustav and Helen Alene (McFarland) M. Student, Westminster Coll., Fulton, Mo., 1958-60; BSBA, Washington U., St. Louis, 1962, JD, 1964. Bar: Mo., 1964, D.C., 1981. Atty. gen. counsel's office SEC, Washington, 1968-69; asst. atty. gen. State of Mo., St. Louis, 1969-72; ptnr. Park, Craft & Morgens, Kansas City, Mo., 1973-76; pvt. practice law Kansas City, 1976-81; mng. atty. Hoskins. King, McGannon & Hahn, Washington, 1981-85; spl. ptnr. Barnett & Alagia, Washington, 1985-89; of counsel Anderson, Hibey, Nauheim & Blair, Washington, 1989—; bd. dirs. George Washington Nat. Bank, Alexandria, Va., George Washington Banking Corp. Patron Nat. Symphony, Washington, 1966-68, 81-85, Washington Performing Arts Soc., 1989—, Kansas City Philharmonic, 1974-80, Supreme Ct. Hist. Soc., Washington, 1982—, The Williamsburg (Va.) Found., 1982—. Named one of Outstanding Young Men Am., 1977. Mem. Mo. Bar Assn., D.C. Bar Assn., Univ. Club (St. Louis). Republican. Presbyterian. Home: #201 Crystal Park 5 Crystal Dr Arlington VA 22202 Office: Anderson Hibey Nauheim & Blair 1708 New Hampshire Ave NW Washington DC 20009-2586

MORGENSTERN, HANS GEORGE, consulting engineer; b. Berlin, Germany, May 29, 1936; came to U.S., 1949; s. Oskar Adolph and Wally Marie (Prothmann) M. SB in Chem. Engring., MIT, 1958. Project engr. Bethlehem Steel Corp., Sparrows Point, Md., 1958-66, Edgewood Arsenal, Md., 1966-69; cons. engr. Md. Equities, Ltd., Towson, N.D., 1969-75; pres. HGM Assocs., Edgewood, 1975—. Mem. Rep. Nat. Com., Washington, 1960—; mem. Am. Security Coun., Boston, Va., 1963—; mem. Nat. Com. to Preserve Social Security and Medicare, Washington, 1970—; mem. Ideas for America's Future, Wilmington, Del. Maj. U.S. Army, ret. Mem. Am. Inst. Chem. Engrs., World Safety Assn., Nat. Assn. Self Employed, Internat. Airline Passenger Assn., KC (3d deg.). Roman Catholic. Office: PO Box 65 Edgewood MD 21040-0065

MORGENSTERN, STEPHEN, developmental optometrist; b. Bklyn., Mar. 2, 1940; s. Abraham and Yetta (Steiger) M.; B.S. in Pharmacy, Bklyn. Coll. Pharmacy, 1961; B.S., Pa. Coll. Optometry, 1969, O.D., 1970; m. Marcia Mandel, Oct. 11, 1970; children: Andrew Seth, Rebecca Jill, Lauren Dayna. Instr., Bklyn. Coll. Pharmacy, 1961; registered pharmacist, 1961-62; resident orthoptics and vision tng. Optometric Center N.Y., 1970, engaged in myopia research project, 1970; developmental optometrist N.Y. Center Learning Disorders, 1970-71; pvt. practice developmental optometry, East Northport, Coram, N.Y., 1970—; dep. examiner N.Y. State Bd. Optometry, 1985-90; examiner N.E. Regional Clin. Optometric Assessment Testing Svc., 1990—; optometrist staff mem. Suffolk County Assn. Retarded Children, 1973-80; cons. in field. Author manual, Handwriting Skills for Left Handed Children. Served to 1st lt. USAF, 1962-65. Fellow Coll. Optometrists in Vision Devel.; mem. Am., N.Y. State, Suffolk County optometric assns., Optometric Extension Program (clin. asso.), Internat. Myopia Prevention Assn., Assn. Children with Learning Disorders, Coun. Exceptional Children, N.Y. Assn. Brain Injured Children, Suffolk County Mental Health Assn., KP. Home: 6 Norman Ct Huntington Station NY 11746-5812 Office: 554 Larkfield Rd East Northport NY 11731-4205 also: 248 Middle Country Rd Coram NY 11727

MORGENTHAL, BECKY HOLZ, aerial photography company executive; b. Altadena, Calif., Aug. 5, 1947; d. E. William and Elizabeth (DeLong) Holz; m. Roger Mark Morgenthal, Aug. 12, 1972. AA, Goldey Beacom Coll., 1967; grad., Wilson Coll., 1990. Clk. Hercules, Inc., Wilmington, Del., 1969-71; acct. Beth Products, Lebanon, Pa., 1971-72; adminstrv. asst. Legal Services, Inc., Carlisle, Pa., 1973-76; office mgr. CEMI Corp., Carlisle, 1976-77; acct. Tressler Luth. Services, Camp Hill, Pa., 1978-79, Benatec Assocs., Inc., Camp Hill, 1979-82; fin. analyst Electronic Data Systems, Camp Hill, 1983-87; owner BHM Bus. Svcs., Carlisle, 1982—; pres. Legal Eye Aerial Photography. Pres. Carlisle Jr. Civic Club, 1979-80, v.p., 1978-79; active Diocese of Harrisburg, Pa., 1985-89, chmn. pro-life com., 1988-89; mem. Council of Cath. Women, Carlisle, 1986—. Republican. Home: 1311 Windsor Ct Carlisle PA 17013-3562

MORIN, BRUCE LEO, mechanical engineer, researcher; b. Springfield, Mass., Feb. 15, 1963; s. Leo Edward and Wanda (Furlani) M. BSME, Western New England Coll., 1985; MSME, Rensselaer Poly. Inst., 1988. Asst. rsch. engr. United Techs. Rsch. Ctr., East Hartford, Conn., 1985-89, assoc. rsch. engr., 1989-91, rsch. engr., 1991—. Recipient Mech. Engring. Dept. award Western New England Coll., 1985, United Techs. Rsch. Ctr. Spl. award, 1992. Mem. AIAA, ASME (Book award Weston New Eng. Coll., 1985). Office: United Techs Rsch Ctr Silver Ln East Hartford CT 06108

MORIN, GASTON JEAN FRANCOIS, former municipal officer, land surveyor; b. Chisholm, Maine, July 12, 1938; s. Frank and Monique Josephine (Croteau) M.; m. Patricia Murray Soule, Feb. 7, 1969 (div. Feb. 1982); children: Timothy Eric, Joshua Stephen. BS in Civil Engring., U. N.H., 1974. Chief draftsman Housing Authority City of Manchester, N.H., 1965-74, subdiv. officer City Planning Dept., 1974-90; land survey crew chief John Gillis (now Gillis Engring. Corp.), 1973—; prof. surveying N.H. Vocat. Tech. Coll., 1985—. Served with U.S. Army, 1958-61. Libertarian.

MORIN, ROLAND L., nurse practitioner; b. Auburn, Maine, Dec. 29, 1944; m. Doris J. Bolduc; children: Paul, Michelle. AS, North Shore Community Coll., Beverly, Mass., 1970; cert. pediatric nurse practitioner, Northeastern U., 1974. Family nurse practitioner, founder Health Care Today, South Portland, Maine, 1965-90; occupational health nurse Bass Shoe, Wilton, Maine, 1964-65; pediatric nurse practitioner Bon Secours Hosp., Methuen, Mass., 1974-76, Michael Kellum, Caribou, Maine, 1976-78; dir. nursing, physician's asst. Plummer Meml. Hosp., Dexter, Maine, 1978-80; family nurse practitioner Sacobee Valley Health Ctr., Kezar Falls, Maine, 1991—. Vol. St. Martin's of the Poors, Lewiston, Maine, 1991—. Mem. Maine Med. Practice Mgmt. Assn. Roman Catholic. Home: 120 Gill St Auburn ME 04210-6612 Office: Sacopee Valley Health Ctr Maine St Kezar Falls ME 04047

MORING, JOHN FREDERICK, lawyer; b. Farmville, Va., Oct. 30, 1935; s. Scott O'Ferrall and Margaret Macon (Mitchell) M.; m. Margaret Ann Clarke, Mar. 30, 1959; children: Martha, Elizabeth, Scott, Lee. BS, Va. Poly. Inst., 1957; JD, George Washington U., 1961. Bar: Va. 1961, D.C. 1962, U.S. Supreme Ct. 1964. Assoc. Morgan, Lewis & Bockius, Washington, 1961-68, ptnr., 1969-78; ptnr. Jones, Day, Reavis & Pogue, Washington, 1978-79, Crowell & Moring, Washington, London, Newport Beach, Calif., 1979—. Columnist Nat. Gas Jour., 1989—; monthly contbr. Natural

Gas Jour., 1989—. Pres. Sterling Citizens Assn., Alexandria, Va., 1971-77; Rep. candidate 23d Dist./Va. Gen. Assembly, Alexandria, 1973; chmn. Alexandria Rep. Com. on Candidate Recruitment, 1974; bd. govs. St. Stephen's and St. Agnes Sch., Alexandria, 1989—; pres. St. Stephen's Found., Inc., 1990—; sr. warden Immanuel Ch. on the Hill, Alexandria, 1988, 89. 2d lt. U.S. Army, 1958. Mem. ABA (natural resources law sect. 1982-86, coun.); mem. Fed. Energy Bar Assn. (sec. 1963-66, pres. 1982-83), Belle Haven Country Club, Univ. Club (Washington). Episcopalian. Home: 509 Canterbury Ln Alexandria VA 22314-4747 Office: Crowell & Moring 1001 Pennsylvania Ave NW Washington DC 20004-2505 also: 4675 MacArthur Ct Ste 4675 Newport Beach CA 92660-1851 also: One Sergeants Inn, ECAY ILL London England

MORIN-MILLER, CARMEN ALINE, writer; b. Montreal, Quebec, Can., Dec. 20, 1929; came to U.S., 1983; d. J. Gabriel Morin and Marie-Jeanne (Guay) Vincent; m. Benoit H. Massicotte, July 28, 1951 (div. 1975); children: Andree, Chantal, Joane Claude, Anne; m. Jack Conway Miller, Sept. 9, 1983. Diploma, U. Laval, Quebec, 1950, C.I.M., 1974; Diploma in Art, Charles-Huot Sch., Quebec, 1978. Freelance writer, 1954—; info. officer Ministere des Communications of Quebec, Quebec City, 1974-83; gallery owner Morin-Miller Galleries, N.Y.C., 1985-90, Equity Art Svcs., Collegeville, Pa., 1991—; dir. Amities Culturelles, Beauport, Quebec City, 1968-75. Author: Lumiere, 1988, Conspiration, 1977; contbr. articles to Perspectives mag., other mags., newspapers. Pres. Assn. des Parents, Beauport, 1964-74. Mem. Am. Rhododendron Soc., Clud des Journalistes (pres. com. 1967-69).

MORISHIMA, AKIRA, physician, director, educator, consultant; b. Tokyo, Apr. 18, 1930; came to U.S., 1955; s. Azusa and Toshiko (Tezuka) M.; m. Hisayo Oda, June 3, 1961; children: Amy, Alyssa. MD, Keio U., Tokyo, 1954, PhD, 1963. Postdoctoral fellow Columbia U., N.Y.C., 1958-61, instr. in pediatrics, 1961-63, assoc. in pediatrics, 1963-65, asst. prof. pediatrics, 1965-66; asst. prof. pediatrics U. Calif., San Francisco, 1966-68; assoc. prof. pediatrics Columbia U., N.Y.C., 1968—, dir. div. pediatric endocrinology, 1969—; assoc. attending physician Presbyn. Md. Ctr., N.Y.C., 1968—, Englewood (N.J.) Hosp., 1991—; cons. Overlook Hosp., Summit, N.J., 1978—; hon. cons. St. Luke's Roosevelt Hosp. Ctr., N.Y.C., 1988—. Contbr. over 55 articles to profl. jours. Mem. Health Planning Bd., Bronx, 1974-76; v.p., treas. Dist. 10 Community Sch. Bd., N.Y.C., 1974-80; chmn. com. Community Bd. # 8, N.Y.C., 1977-85. Fulbright scholar U.S. Edn. Commn., 1955-57; grantee NIH; recipient Citation, City Coun. of N.Y., 1985. Mem. AAAS, AAUP, Acad. Pediatrics, Am. Pediatrics Soc., Environ. Mutagen Soc., Soc. for Study of Reprodn., Soc. Human Genetics, Endocrine Soc., Soc. for Pediatric Rsch., N.Y. Japanese/Am. Lions. Republican. Presbyterian. Office: Columbia U Coll Physicians & Surgeons 622 W 168th St New York NY 10032-3702

MORITZ, MILTON EDWARD, telephone company executive; b. Reading, Pa., Sept. 5, 1931; s. Edward Raymond and Anna May M.; m. Elizabeth Ann Walls, June 6, 1952; children: Betsy Ann Moritz Koppenhaver, Stephen Edward, Sandra E. Student, U. Md., 1950-51, Fla. State U., 1959-60. Enlisted U.S. Army, 1949, chief warrant officer 3, 1968, spl. agt. M.I.; ret., 1970; safety and security dir. Harrisburg (Pa.) Hosp., 1970-72; security mgr. United Tel. Systems, Carlisle, Pa., 1972—; lectr., instr. Harrisburg Area Community Coll.; mem. Indsl. Security Adv. Coun. Pres. Greater Harrisburg Crime Clinic, 1974. Decorated Bronze Star with oak leaf cluster. Mem. Am. Soc. Indsl. Security (past pres., chmn. bd. dirs.), Assn. Former Intelligence Officers, Internat. Narcotic Enforcement Officers Assn., Pa. Crime Prevention Assn. (bd. dirs.). Republican. Lutheran. Home: 7723 Avondale Ter Harrisburg PA 17112-3805 Office: 1201 Walnut Bottom Rd Carlisle PA 17013-0905

MORITZ, ROGER HOMER, mathematics educator; b. Cleve., Mar. 11, 1937; s. Homer Charles and Hertha Caroline (Schimke) M.; m. Lois Blanche Menegay, Jan. 4, 1986; children: Scott, Dawn, Brad, Susan. B.S. in Elec. Engring., Valparaiso U., 1959; M.S. in Math., U. Pitts., 1961, Ph.D., 1964. Sr. engr. Goodyear Atomic, Waverly, Ohio, 1962-64; research mathematician Cornell Aero. Lab., Buffalo, 1964-70; asst. prof. math. Alfred U., N.Y., 1970-72, assoc. prof., 1973-79, prof., 1980—, chmn. dept. math., 1970—, Cole prof. applied math., 1985—. Author: Statistical Inference for Engineers, 1977; contbr. articles to profl. jours. Mem. Math. Assn. Am., Am. Math. Soc. Avocations: chess, tennis, running, reading. Episcopalian. Home: 61 Sayles St Alfred NY 14802-1325 Office: Alfred U Alfred NY 14802

MORLOK, EDWARD KARL, engineering educator, consultant; b. Phila., Nov. 3, 1940; s. Edward Karl and Anna Marie (Kurtz) M.; m. Ottilia Angela Husz, Dec. 14, 1968 (div. July 1984); 1 child, Jessica Angela; m. Patricia Jane Conboy, Mar. 23, 1991. BE, Yale U., 1962; PhD, Northwestern U., 1967; MA, U. Pa., 1973. Civil engr., transp. U.S. Dept. Commerce, Washington, 1966-67; from asst. prof. civil engring. to assoc. prof. Northwestern U., Evanston, Ill., 1967-73, asst. dir. rsch., transp. ctr., 1969-73; 1907 Found. assoc. prof. U. Pa., Phila., 1973-75, chmn., transp. grad. group, 1983-86, UPS found. prof. transp., 1975—, chair systems grad. program, 1986—; cons. nat. transp. policy study commn., Washington, 1978-79. Author: Analysis Transportation Technology and Network Structure, 1969, Introduction to Transportation Engineering and Planning, 1978; assoc. editor Transp. Rsch. Jour., 1975—; consulting editor series in transp. for McGraw-Hill Publ. Co., 1980—; contbr. more than 50 articles to profl. jours. Mem. Nat. Assembly Engring. panel on innovation in transp., Washington, 1979-80, panel on hazardous material transp., Washington, 1980-81. Recipient U.S. Sr. Scientist award Alexander von Humboldt Found., 1980-81; rsch. grantee Commonwealth of Pa., Consol. Rail Corp., U.S. Dept. Transp., NASA. Mem. ASCE, Transp. Rsch. Forum (v.p. 1974-75, pres. 1975-76, bd. disting. mems. 1983), Transp. Rsch. Bd. (rev. com. of coun. of univ. transp. ctrs., 1985-88, coun. mem. 1988-90). Lutheran. Office: U Pa Dept Systems/SEAS 220 S 33d St Philadelphia PA 19104

MORNINGSTAR, ROBERT DAVID, computer company executive; b. Bluefields, Nicaragua, Oct. 18, 1948; s. Ludovico Bottner and Ines (Gomez) Echeverri. BS in Psychology, Fordham U., 1974; postgrad., Hunter Coll., 1973-75, China Inst. Am., 1977-78. Asst. mgr. Wittenberg Surg. Supply Co., N.Y.C., 1970-73; dir. dance and Oriental studies Metaphorms, Inc., N.Y.C., 1977-80; bilingual instr. China Inst. Am., 1977-78; Tai Chi master, lectr. N.Y. State Office Parks, Recreation and Hist. Preservation, N.Y.C., 1980-81; dance critic In-Step: The N.Y. Dancer, N.Y.C., 1983-84; Tai Chi instr. to physical therapy staff Internat. Ctr. for Disabled, N.Y.C., 1985-86; pres. M.A.R.S., Inc., N.Y.C., 1986—; lectr. Ctr. of Influence USAFR, 1986; coach Lifesport Gymnastics, N.Y.C., 1983—. Inventor "Light Painting" solar lighting panels. Mem. Boston Tai Chi Sch., 1988—; founding mem. Challenger Found.; dir. gymnastics program Bank Streeet Coll. Sch. Edn., 1989-92. Regents scholar Fordham U., 1967-74. Mem. N.Y. C. of C., Aircraft Owners and Pilots Assn., Air Force Assn., Aerospace Edn. Found., N.Y. Fedn. Police (assoc.), N.Y. State Assn. Chiefs Police (assoc.), Internat. Platform Assn., Nat. Trust for Hist. Preservation, Hamburg Tai Chi Club (founder 1991). Office: Computers from MARS 214 W 92d St Ste 3E New York NY 10025

MORPEAU, WILLIAM ANTOINE, small business owner; b. Cayes, Haiti, Sept. 15, 1937; came to U.S., 1967; s. Daniel and Emily (Morpeau) Leon; m. Mirielle Gornail, Dec. 9, 1965; children: Myriam, Michael, Martine. Owner Shell Gas Sta., Bklyn., 1968-70; mechanic Internat. Havester Co., L.I., 1970-75; owner Willie's Auto, Rosedale, N.Y., 1975-87; Inventor dribbler master, random substitute, Big Apple Success & Tragedy board game; patentee. Inventor dribbler master, random substitute, Big Apple Success & Tragedy board game. Home: 216-14 113th St Queens Village NY 11429

MORRESSY, JOHN, writer, educator; b. Bklyn., Dec. 8, 1930; s. John Emmett and Jeanette Agnes (Geraghty) M.; m. Barbara Turner, Aug. 11, 1956. BA in English, St. John's U., 1953; MA in English, NYU, 1961. Instr. St. John's U., Bklyn., 1962-66; asst. prof. Monmouth Coll., West Long Branch, N.J., 1966-67; assoc. prof., prof., writer-in-residence Franklin Pierce Coll., Rindge, N.H., 1968—. Novelist: The Blackboard Cavalier, 1966, A Long Communion, 1974, Frostworld and Dreamfire, 1977, A Remembrance for Kedrigern, 1990, others; contbr. articles to various publs. Me. Authors Guild, Sci. Fiction Writers Am. Republican. Roman Catholic. Office: Franklin Pierce Coll Rindge NH 03461

MORRILL, BERNARD, retired engineering educator; b. Boston, May 31, 1910; m. Bernice Bernstein, May 29, 1940; 1 child, Richard Anthony. BSME, MIT, 1947; MME, U. Del., 1949; PhD, U. Mich., 1959. Instr. Swarthmore (Pa.) Coll., 1947-48, asst. prof., 1948-62, prof., 1962-75, emeritus prof., 1975—. Author: Mechanical Vibrations, 1957, Equilibrium Thermodynamics, 1972. NSF fellowship U. Mich., 1958, Imperial Coll., London, 1964. Home: 1014 Strath Hvn Swarthmore PA 19081-2222

MORRILL, DEXTER GEORGE, music educator; b. June 17, 1938; m. Barbara Dodds, 1962; children: Jennifer, Allison. BA, Colgate U., 1960; MA, Stanford U., 1962; MusD, Cornell U., 1970. Fellow Ford Found., University City, Mo., 1962-64; resident composer Kans. State Tchrs. Coll., Emporia, 1966; instr. in music St. John's U., N.Y.C., 1966-68; asst. prof. music, assoc. prof. Colgate U., 1969-72, 72-80, dept. chmn., 1971-74, prof. music, 1980-88, Charles A. Dana prof. music, 1988—; vis. prof. music SUNY, Binghamton, 1982-83, Stanford U., 1984. Author: A Guide to the Big Band Recordings of Woody Herman 1936-87, 1990; also articles; works include Three Lyric Pieces, 1969, Fantasy Quintet, 1977, Six Dark Questions, 1978, Disco, 1979, TARR, 1981, Quartet, 1984, Roxbury Preludes, 1986, Sketches for Invisible Man, 1987, Walden Nocturnes, 1990; recorded numerous works. grantee Colgate U. Rsch. Coun., 1970-86, Herman and Bessie Adler Found., 1973, Nat. Endowment for Arts, 1978-81. Mem. Broadcast Music Inc., Am. Music Ctr., Computer Music Assn., AAUP (pres. local chpt. 1973-74, 78-79). Home: 20 Montgomery St Hamilton NY 13346-1007

MORRILL, JAMES AGRIPPA, paper company executive; b. Newburyport, Mass., Dec. 7, 1946; s. Frank Forrest and Frances (Robert) M.; m. Penny Chittim, July 12, 1969; children: Jackson, Julia. BA, Tulane U., 1969; MS in Govt. Adminstrn., George Washington U., 1976. Tchr. Episcopal Acad., Phila., 1969-72; dist. mgr. U.S. Rep. Jim Collins, Dallas, 1972-73; buyer Tex. Instruments, Dallas, 1973-74; legis. asst. U.S. Dept. Housing & Urban Devel., Washington, 1974-76; staff asst. U.S. House Appropriations Ctr., Washington, 1976-78; dir. house liaison Nat. Assn. Realtors, Washington, 1978-80; v.p. govt. and community rels. Scott Paper Co., Washington, 1980—. Asst. scoutmaster Boy Scouts Am., McLean, Va., 1986—. Mem. Bus. Govt. Rels. Coun. Office: Scott Paper Co 1726 M St NW Ste 901 Washington DC 20036-4502

MORRILL, JOHN HUGH, energy efficiency executive, researcher; b. Fall River, Mass., Apr. 9, 1960; s. John Hugh and Ruth Gail (Hixon) M.; lm. Maureen Murtha, Feb. 15, 1986. BA, Clark U., 1982. Rsch. asst. Clark U., Worcester, Mass., 1981-83; instr. English OTC, Inc., Nagoya, Japan, 1988-90; rsch. assoc. Am. Coun. for An Energy-Efficient Economy, Washington, 1983-88, bus. mgr., 1990—. Co-author: Residential Indoor Air Quality & Energy-Efficiency, 1989, Consumer Guide to Home Energy Savings, 1991; contbg. editor Energy Auditor & Retrofitter mag., 1987. Mem. Am. Planning Assn., Assn. Energy Engrs., Phi Beta Kappa. Office: Am Coun for Energy Efficient Economy 1001 Connecticut Ave NW # 801 Washington DC 20036

MORRIS, ARLENE MYERS, marketing professional; b. Washington, Pa., Dec. 29, 1951; d. Frank Hayes Myers and Lula Irene (Slusser) Kolcan; m. John L. Sullivan, Feb. 17, 1971 (div. July 1982); m. David Wellons Morris, July 27, 1984. BA, Carlow Coll., 1974; postgrad., Western New England Coll., 1981-82. Sales rep. Syntex Labs., Inc., Palo Alto, Calif., 1974-77; profl. sales rep. McNeil Pharm., Spring House, Pa., 1977-78, mental health rep., 1978-80, asst. product dir., 1981-82, dist. mgr., 1982-85, new product dir., 1985-87, exec. dir. new bus. devel., 1987-89, v.p. bus. devel., 1989—. Mem. Found. of Ind. Colls., Phila., 1989. Mem. Am. Diabetes Assn., Am. Acad. Sci., Healthcare Bus. Womens Assn., Licensing Execs. Soc. Home: 289 Stormfield Dr Harleysville PA 19438 Office: McNeil Pharm Spring House PA 19438

MORRIS, BARBARA LOUISE, English educator; b. Niskayuna, N.Y., June 4, 1947; d. Edward Lawrence and Mary (Havelka) M. BA, St. John's U., 1969; MA, Columbia U., 1971, EdD, 1977; LLD, Niagara U., 1987. Asst. to dean for acad. devel. St. John's U., Jamaica, N.Y., 1969-71, asst. to exec. v.p., 1971-72, asst. to exec. v.p. and dir. acad. planning, 1972-75, asst. to exec. v.p. and dean for acad. planning, 1975-80, v.p. for acad. planning and compliance officer, 1980-86, acad. v.p., 1986-92, prof. English, 1992—. Recipient Pres.'s medal St. Jhn's U., 1986. Mem. AAUW, Am. Assn. Higher Edn., Soc. for Coll. and Univ. Planning, Tau Kappa Alpha, Omicron Delta Epsilon. Office: St Johns U Grand Central and Utopia Jamaica NY 11439

MORRIS, BARRY STEPHEN, residence life director; b. St. Louis, Feb. 25, 1948; s. Roy William Morris and Winifred (Slaight) Lewis. BA, So. Meth. U., 1970; MA, Coll. of William & Mary, 1975, EdS, 1982; postgrad., U. Pitts., 1982—. Asst. mgr. Wharf Restaurant, Yorktown, Va., 1975-76; area coord. Coll. of William & Mary, Williamsburg, Va., 1976-79; asst. dir. housing ops. U. Dayton, Ohio, 1979-84; dir. residence life Clarion (Pa.) U., 1984—; adviser U. Dayton Jaycees, 1983-84, Sigma Phi, Clarion, 1986-89, Clarion Internat. Assn., 1988-91. Member disaster com. ARC, Clarion, 1991—; bd. dirs. Consumer Buying Club, Clarion, 1990-91. Clarion U. Found. grantee, 1986, 91; recipient Citizenship Svc. award Commonwealth of Pa., 1991. Mem. Am. Coll. Pers. Assn., Am. Coll. and Univ. Housing Officers Internat. (presentor conf. workshop Milw. chpt. 1990), Nat. Assn. Student Pers. Adminstrs., Kiwanis. Office: Clarion U 228 Egbert Hall Clarion PA 16214

MORRIS, BERNARD ROSS, television producer, writer; b. Tacoma, June 4, 1932; s. Bernard R. and Helen Elmira (Hoover) M.; m. Ellen Marie Peterson, Oct. 8, 1966. AB, Willamette U., 1954; MA, Wash. State U., 1958. Corr., editor AP, Seattle and Juneau, Alaska, 1956-60, Time Mag., N.Y.C., 1960-62; producer, writer ABC News, N.Y.C., 1962-66, Sta. WNBC-TV, N.Y.C., 1966-72; dir. U.S. Commn. on Civil Rights Office Info. & Publs., Washington, 1972-73; speech writer IBM World Trade Corp., N.Y.C. and Paris, 1973-76; producer, writer N.J. Network, Newark, 1976-81; freelance producer and writer, 1981-84, 88—; dir. N.J. Office of Cable TV, Newark, 1984-88; commr., vice chmn. N.J. Pub. Broadcasting Authority, Trenton, 1981-84. Producer, writer numerous TV documentaries. Sec. Short Hills (N.J.) Assn.; pres. N.J. Jazz Soc., 1981—; trustee Millburn Free Pub. Libr., 1991—. Recipient 3 Emmy awards N.Y. chpt. Acad. TV, Arts and Scis., 1964-71, Edward R. Morrow award Radio & TV Dirs. Assn., 1968, TV award N.J. Bar Assn., 1980, Cine Golden Eagle award Coun. on Internat. Non-Theatrical Events. Mem. TV Acad., Nat. Acad. Cable Programming (judge 1989-91), Overseas Press Club, Short Hills Club. Republican. Episcopalian. Home and Office: 12 Lake Rd Short Hills NJ 07078-3208

MORRIS, CORDELL YVONNE, communications company executive; b. Richmond, Va., Sept. 12, 1944; d. Louis Avaughn Morris and Laura Ophelia (Jones) Pressey. BA, Marymount Coll., 1988. Employment recruiter N.J. Bell Co., Newark, 1967-71; plant sch. instr. N.J. Bell Co., 1971-74, staff asst., 1974-78, asst. mgr., 1978-79, mgr., 1979—. Mem. adv. coun., Ret. Sr. Vol. Program Essex County, Orange, N.J., 1986—; trustee, The Bd. Mem. Inst. N.J., Orange, 1988—, sec., 1989. Named N.J. Black Achiever, YMWCA of Newark and Vicinity, 1988. Mem. Coalition 100 Black Women (bd. dirs. N.J.), Nat. Assn. Negro Bus. and Profl. Women's Clubs (sec. 1985-86; named Bus. Woman of Yr. 1984). Democrat. Baptist. Office: NJ Bell Rm 900 540 Broad St Newark NJ 07102-3178

MORRIS, CYNTHIA TAFT, economics educator; b. Cin., Apr. 28, 1928; d. Charles Phelps and Eleanor Kellogg (Chase) Taft; m. Donald Richard Morris, Sept. 18, 1955 (div. 1984); children: David Taft Morris, Michele Taft Morris. BA, Vassar Coll., 1949; MSc in Econs., London Sch. Econs., 1951; PhD, Yale U., 1959. Econ. analyst Info. Sect. Mutual Security Agy., Paris, 1951-53; tutor, fellow Kirkland Ho., Harvard U., Cambridge, 1955-57; rsch. fellow AAUW, Washington, 1958-59; asst. prof. econs. Am. U., Beirut, 1961-62; assoc. prof. econs. Am. U., Washington, 1964-69, prof. econs., 1969-83; Charles N. Clark profl. econs. Smith Coll., Northampton, Mass., 1983—; coord. Washington Area Econ. History Seminar, 1981—; cons. Office of Program and Policy Coordination Agy. for Internat. Devel., Washington, 1962-69; cons. electricity power com. Econ. Commn. of Europe, Geneva, 1960. Co-author: The Evolution of Wage Structure, 1956, Society, Politics and Economic Development, 1967, Economic Growth and Social Equity, 1973, Comparative Patterns of Economic Development, 1850-1914, 1988. Rsch. grantee NSF, 1965-73, 80-82. Mem. Econ. History Assn. (v.p. 1984-85), Cliometric Soc., Am. Econ. Assn. Democrat. Home: 64 Kensington Ave Northampton MA 01060-2920 Office: Smith Coll Northampton MA 01063

MORRIS, DANIEL HYMAN, investment company executive; b. N.Y.C., Dec. 31, 1948; s. Marvin Morris and Norma (Lifshen) Toorock; m. Robin H. Hausman, May 14, 1975; children: Sabrina, Jesse, Tyler, Paul (quadruplets). BSBA, Babson Coll., 1970. Pres. Lake Motors Inc., Bayshore, N.Y., 1973-81; investment cons. E.F. Hutton & Co., N.Y.C., 1981-83; assoc. dir. Bear Stearns Inc., N.Y.C., 1983-87; 1st v.p. Paine Webber Inc., White Plains, N.Y., 1987—. Vice pres. Bay Shore C. of C., 1977-81; bd. trustees Babson Coll., 1971-73, Sinai Reform Temple, Bay Shore, 1978-81; 1st v.p. Rotary Internat., Bay Shore, 1981. Jewish. Office: Paine Webber Inc 11 Martine Ave White Plains NY 10606

MORRIS, DANIEL JOSEPH, research astrophysicist; b. Mpls., Oct. 19, 1951; s. Thomas Daniel and Elizabeth Mae (Cowette) M. SB in Physics, MIT, 1973; PhD in Physics, U. Md., 1982. Teaching asst. U. Md., College Park, 1973-76, rsch. asst., 1976-82; NRC rsch. fellow Nasa Marshall Space Flight Ctr., Huntsville, Ala., 1982-84; rsch. scientist U. N.H., Durham, 1984—; co-investigator gamma ray telescope and satellite, 1991. Mem. Am. Phys. Soc., Sigma Xi. Democrat. Office: U NH Sci and Engring Rsch Bldg Durham NH 03824

MORRIS, DAVID WOOLLARD, lawyer; b. Albany, N.Y, Aug. 9, 1935; s. Ernest Brougham and Elizabeth (Woollard) M.; m. Eleanor Utter, Nov. 22, 1955 (div. 1968); children: David J., Nancy A. Flores, Kathleen M. Hinckley, Karen E. Kowalczyk, Caroline K.; m. Brenda Schuttenheim, Mar. 9, 1968; children: Suzanne M., Jennifer A. BA, Union Coll., 1958; JD, Albany Law Sch., 1961. Ptnr. Wood, Morris, Sanford & Hatt, Albany, N.Y., 1961-67; ptnr. Schrade, Morris & Roche, Albany, 1967-73; pres. Saratoga Harness Racing, Inc., Saratoga Springs, N.Y., 1973-87; pvt. practice Saratoga Springs, 1987—; adv. bd. Norstar Bank Upstate N.Y., Saratoga Springs, 1986-91; chmn. adv. bd. Empire State Youth Theatre Ins., Albany, 1987-89. Bd. dirs. Saratoga C. of C., Saratoga Springs, 1976-78, Harness Tracks Am., Morristown, N.J., 1973-87, U.S. Trotting Assn., Columbus, Ohio, 1980-87, State U. Found., Albany, 1984-87; bd. dirs., chmn. Saratoga Conv. & Tourism Bur., Saratoga Springs, 1985-90; mem. Rotary Internat., Saratoga Springs, 1985-88. With U.S. Army, 1955. Mem. Saratoga County Bar Assn., N.Y. State Bar Assn., Schuyler Meadows Club (Loudonville, N.Y.), Pasadena Yacht & Country Club (St. Petersburg, Fla.). Republican. Presbyterian. Home: 23 Longwood Dr Saratoga Springs NY 12866-2823 Office: 526 Maple Ave Saratoga Springs NY 12866-5509

MORRIS, EDWARD LOUIS, rheumatologist; b. Balt., Mar. 14, 1947; s. Moses and Eleanor (Oppenheimer) M.; children: Jacqueline Leigh, Benjamin Jay;m. Barbara Rudich; stepson: Justin Flax. BS, U. Md., 1969, MS, 1971, MD, 1975. Intern U. Md. Med. Ctr., Balt., 1975-76, resident, 1976-78; fellow Johns Hopkins Med. Sch., Rheumatology, Balt., 1978-80; pvt. practice rheumatology Balt., 1980—; mem. nat. profl. edn. com. Am. Rheumatism Assn., Atlanta, 1988-89; chmn. profl. edn. com. Arthritis Found., Balt., 1987-89. Contbr. articles to profl. jours. Bd. dirs. Lupus Found. of Md., Balt., 1986-91, 1st v.p. 1990-91, Arthritis Found. of Md., Balt., 1984—, sec. of bd. dirs. 1990-91, 91-92 (Vol. of Yr. 1987, Nat. Vol. Svc. Citation 1991); mem. Men's Occupational Rehab. Tng., Balt., 1985—, Md. Med. Chiurgical Soc. Legis. Com., Balt., 1987-89. Recipient Merck Manual award, 1977. Fellow Am. Coll. Physicians, Am. Coll. Rheumatology; mem. AMA, Am. Soc. Internal Medicine, Md. Soc. Rheumatology (pres. 1987-88), Alpha Omega Alpha. Office: 4000 Old Court Rd Ste 300 Baltimore MD 21208-2840

MORRIS, ELIZABETH JOHNSON, vocational educator, nurse; b. Somerville, Mass., Jan. 22, 1937; d. Harold Adams and Theresa Margaret (Pretty) Short; m. Roger E. Johnson, Sept. 10, 1960 (dec. 1979); m. George Frederick Morris, July 24, 1981; children: Eric E., Jeffrey D., Wendy E. Dipl. in nursing, N.E. Deaconess Sch. Nursing, 1957; BS in Health Edn. and Psychology, U. Lowell, 1981, MEd, 1984. RN, Mass. Staff nurse N.E. Deaconess Hosp., Boston, 1957-58; head nurse Boston Lying-In Hosp., 1958-60; office nurse Longwood Pediatrics, 1960-65; pvt. duty nurse N.E. Deaconess Hosp. and Mass. Gen. Hosp., 1965-81; instr. continuing edn. Middlesex Community Coll., Bedford, Mass., 1981-89, Newbury Jr. Coll., Lowell, Mass., 1983; dir. retention program U. Lowell, 1983-88; instr. health tech. Shawsheen Valley Tech. High Sch., Billerica, Mass., 1988—; cons. Learning to Learn Inc., Cambridge, Mass., 1985; workshop presenter freshman yr. conf. U. S.C., Columbia, 1985-87; judge Nat. Vocat. Indsl. Clubs Am. Skills Olympics, Tulsa, 1989. Rep. town meeting Billerica, 1963-69. Mem. NEA, Vocat. Indsl. Clubs Am., Mass. Tchrs. Assn., U. Lowell Alumni Assn., N.E. Deaconess Sch. Nursing Alumnae Assn., Shufflin' Shoes Square Dance Club (sec. 1976-77), Order Ea. Star, Pi Lambda Theta.

MORRIS, JACK, retired military officer; b. Columbus, Ohio, Aug. 5, 1923; s. Philip Henry and Mildred Esther (Davis) M.; m. Harriett Louise Edwards, Aug. 31, 1947; children: Brian L., Beth A., Bruce E., Brent N. BSBA, Ohio State U., 1948. Chief accounts receivable Bonney-Floyd Steel Co., Columbus, 1948-50; exec. sec. Hilltop Bus. Assn., Columbus, 1950-51; commd. 2d lt. USAF, 1951, advanced through grades to sr. col., 1981, ret., 1983; cons. Betac Corp., Washington, 1983—. Cubmaster Boy Scouts Am., Ohio, Washington, 1959-62, 66-69, dist. dir., Hawaii, 1963-66, scoutmaster, 1969-72, regional com., 1972-85; dir. Nat. Hist. Intelligence Mus., Washington, 1990—; trustee Intelligence Scholarship Found., Washington, 1990—. Mem. Nat. Mil. Intelligence Assn. (bd. dirs. 1989—, pres. 1989—), Sons Am. Revolution, Ret. Officers Assn., Assn. Former Intelligence Officers, Ohio State U. Alumni Assn., 749th Tk. Bn. Assn., Masons, Lions. Methodist. Home: 866 Waterside Ln Bradenton FL 34209

MORRIS, JAMES MALACHY, lawyer; b. Champaign, Ill., June 5, 1952; s. Walter Michael and Ellen Frances (Solon) M.; m. Mary Delilah Baker, Oct. 17, 1987; children: James Malachy Jr., Elliot Rice Baker. Student, Oxford U. (Eng.), 1972; BA, Brown U., 1974; JD, U. Pa., 1977. Bar: N.Y. 1978, U.S. Dist. Ct. (so. and ea. dists.) N.Y. 1978, Ill. 1980, U.S. Tax Ct. 1982, U.S. Supreme Ct. 1983; admitted to Barristers Chambers, Manchester, Eng., 1987. Assoc. Reid & Priest, N.Y.C., 1977-80; sr. law clk. Supreme Ct. Ill., Springfield, 1980-81; assoc. Carter, Ledyard & Milburn, N.Y.C., 1981-83; sole practice N.Y.C., 1983-87; counsel FCA, Washington, 1987—; acting sec., gen. counsel FCS Ins. Corp., McLean, Va., 1990—; cons. Internat. Awards Found., Zurich, 1981—, Pritzker Architecture Prize Found., N.Y.C., 1981—, Herbert Oppenheimer, Nathan & VanDyck, London, 1985—. Contbr. articles to profl. jours. Mem. ABA, Ill. Bar Assn., N.Y. State Bar Assn., N.Y. County Lawyers Assn., Assn. Bar City N.Y., Brit. Inst. Internat. and Comparative Law, Lansdowne Club (London), Decatur (Ill.) Club. Office: Georgetown Sta PO Box 25723 Washington DC 20007-8723

MORRIS, JAMES MCGRATH, publisher; b. Washington, Sept. 28, 1954; s. Stephen V.C. and Persis Warren (Masson) M.; m. Patricia McGrath, Dec. 19, 1981; children: Stephanie, Benjamin, Alexander. Reporter Ithaca (N.Y.) Jour., 1983-85; editor Cornell U., Ithaca, 1985-86, Vineyard & Winery Mag., Watkins Glen, N.Y., 1986-87; pub. Seven Locks Press, Inc., Washington, 1987—. Editor: T. Jefferson's European Travel Journals, 1987. Home: 1421 N Highland St Arlington VA 22201-5006 Office: Seven Locks Press Inc 7307 Macarthur Blvd Bethesda MD 20816-1036

MORRIS, JANET ELLEN, policy analyst, consultant; b. Boston, May 25, 1946; d. Cecil R. and Hannah Anne (Fromm) Freeman; m. Christopher Crosby Morris, Oct. 31, 1970. Student, Boston Mus. Sch. Fine Arts, 1963, NYU, 1965-66. Freelance novelist, 1975-85; Mid. East expert Nat. Intelligence Study Ctr., Washington, 1985-88; project dir. U.S. Global Strategy Coun., Washington, 1989-90, rsch. dir., 1990—; cons. advanced conventional weapons Lawrence Livermore (Calif.) Nat. Lab., 1991—; cons. competitive strategies and resources Office Sec. Def. Pentagon, Washington, 1991—; cons. Los Alamos (N.Mex.) Nat. Lab., 1989-91; chmn. bd. dirs. US Intertech., Inc., Arlington, Va., 1992—. Author: Cobra, 1990; co-author: The 40 Minute War, 1985 (Helva award 1986), Non Lethality, 1991, Warrior Class, 1991. Inst. for Polit. Studies fellow, 1990.

MORRIS, JOHN E., lawyer; b. N.Y.C., Sept. 30, 1916; s. John and Honora C. (Long) M.; m. Patricia E. Grojean. A.B., CCNY; A.M., Columbia U.; J.D., Harvard U. Bar: N.Y. 1942, U.S. Dist. Ct. (so. and ea. dists.) N.Y. Trial lawyer Clarke & Reilly, 1946-50; ptnr. Morris & Duffy, N.Y.C., 1950—. Served to lt. USCG, 1942-46; ETO. Mem. ABA, N.Y. State Bar Assn., N.Y. County Lawyers Assn. (mem. judiciary com.), Airplane Owners & Pilots Assn., Internat. Assn. Ins. Counsel. Roman Catholic. Clubs: Harvard, N.Y. Athletic (N.Y.C.), Great Dane Club Am. (bd. dirs.). Office: 18th Fl 233 Broadway New York NY 10279-0130

MORRIS, JOHN LUNDEN, international transportation executive; b. Wilmington, Del., Feb. 26, 1943; s. Arthur Lunden and Carolyn Wilson (Bickell) M.; m. Sally Carolyn Wheeler, Mar. 9, 1967; children: Christopher Wheeler, Kevin Arthur. BA, U. Del., 1965; postgrad., Rutgers U., 1968-71. Ocean container specialist E.I. DuPont de Nemours & Co., Inc., N.Y.C., 1968-72; mgr. pricing U.S. gulf Seatrain Lines, Inc., Weehauken, N.J., 1972-73; dir. pricing Europe Seatrain Lines, Inc., Rotterdam, Holland, 1973-75; dir. market planning, advt. Seatrain Lines, Inc., Weehauken, 1975-76; dir. pricing Seatrain Agys., Inc., N.Y.C., 1976-80; dir. mktg. Prudential Lines, Inc., N.Y.C., 1980-85; dir. mktg. and rsch. Trans Atlantic Associated Freight Confs., N.Y.C., 1985-87; exec. dir. U.S. Atlantic and Gulf Venezuela Conf., Jersey City, 1987-91; chief exec. officer Inter-Am. Freight Conf., Jersey City, 1987—; pres. Inwood Assocs. Transp. Cons., Upper Montclair, N.J., 1985—; mem. Twp. Transp. Adv. Com., Montclair, N.J., 1982-85; mem. U.S. Commerce Fgn. Trade Data Users Group, Washington, 1986—; electronic systems adv. com. U.S. Customs Svc., Washington, 1988—; study com. Fed. Maritime Commn., Washington, 1989. Mem. adv. com. Ward 1 Montclair, Upper Montclair, N.J., 1980—; chmn., cubmaster Upper Montclair area Boy Scouts Am., 1982-88. Mem. Christian Bus. Men's Club (N.Y.C.), Whitehall Club (N.Y.C.), Montclair YMCA. Presbyterian. Office: Inter Am Freight Conf Harborside Fin Ctr 806 Plz II Jersey City NJ 07311-3980

MORRIS, J(OSEPH) ANTHONY, health science association administrator; b. nr. Marboro, Md., Sept. 6, 1918; s. Charles Lafayette and Essie (Stokes) M.; B.S., Cath. U. Am., 1940, M.S., 1942, Ph.D., 1947; m. Ruth Savoy, Nov. 1, 1942; children—Carol Ann, Marilyn T., Joseph A., Larry A. Asst. scientist Josiah Macy, Jr. Found., N.Y.C., 1943-44; virologist, Depts. Agr., Interior, Laurel, Md., 1944-47; virologist, chief hepatitis virus research Walter Reed Army Inst. Research, Washington, 1947-56; virologist, asst. chief, dept. virus and rickettsial diseases U.S. Army Med. Command, Japan, 1956-59; virologist chief sect. respiratory viruses, div. biologics standards NIH, Bethesda, Md., 1959—, dir. slow, latent and temperate virus br. FDA, Bethesda, 1972-76; lectr. dept. microbiology U. Md., College Park, 1977-79; vice-chmn. Bell of Atri, Inc., College Park, 1979-82, chmn., 1983; cons. Commn. on Influenza, Armed Forces Epidemiologic Bd., 1960—, Nat. Inst. Neurol. Diseases and Blindness, 1962—. Mem. Soc. Tropical Medicine and Hygiene, Soc. Am. Microbiologists, Soc. Exptl. Biology and Medicine, Am. Assn. Immunologists, N.Y. Acad. Sci. Discoverer of respiratory sycytial virus; research on infectious hepatitis, respiratory diseases of virus etiology and zoonosis. Home: 23E Ridge Rd Greenbelt MD 20770-0714

MORRIS, KENNETH DONALD, lawyer; b. Montclair, N.J., Apr. 5, 1946; s. Thomas Almerin and Katherine Louise (Jacobs) M.; m. Susan Sauer, May 1, 1976; children: Ian, Jennifer. BA, Ohio Wesleyan U., 1968; MBA, George Washington U., 1971, JD, 1972. Bar: Pa. 1973, N.J. 1975, D.C. 1989. Atty. Westinghouse Electric, Pitts., 1972-74, Tenneco Chems., Inc., N.J., 1974-76; asst. corp. counsel Ronson Corp., Bound Brook, N.J., 1976-78; assoc. Walder, Sondak, Berkley & Brogan, Newark, 1978-81; sec., gen. counsel, mem. mgmt. com. NOR-AM Chem. Co. subs. Schering AG, Wilmington, Del., 1981—, environ. com., 1987—, mem. fiduciary com., 1988—. Incorporator, pres. Charter Oaks Assn.; mem. Gov.'s Internat. Trade Coun., Del. Wolcott Found. scholar, 1969. Mem. ABA (antitrust sect., tort and ins. sect., corp. counsel com., banking and bus. law sect., multinational corps. subcom.), Am. Arbitration Assn. (panel arbitrators), Del. Bar Assn., Am. Corp. Counsel Assn. (dir. Delvacca chpt.), Def. Rsch. Inst. (corp. counsel com.), George Washington U. Sch. Govt. and Bus. Adminstrn. Alumni Assn. (Phila. chpt.), George Washington U. Nat. Law Ctr. Alumni Assn., European-Am. Gen. Counsel Assn., Fed. Bar Assn. (corp. counsel com.), Nat. Agrl. Chem. Assn. (vice chmn. law com.). Republican. Presbyterian. Office: NOR-AM Chem Co 3509 Silverside Rd Wilmington DE 19810-4904

MORRIS, LESLIE R., librarian; b. Sewickley, Pa., Dec. 18, 1935; s. Harry and Elizabeth (Saperstein) M.; children: Hallie, Lee. BS, Geneva Coll., Beaver Falls, Pa., 1957; MS, Duquesne U., 1961; MLS, U. So. Miss., 1985. Cataloger St. Francis Coll., Loretto, Pa., 1961-63; head cataloger East Stroudsburg (Pa.) U., 1963-69; head tech. svc. SUNY, Fredonia, 1969-75; head libr. Xavier U., New Orleans, 1973-85; dir. librs. Niagara U., Niagara Falls, N.Y., 1985—. Editor: Choosing a Bibliographic Utility, 1988, Interlibrary Loan Policies Directory, 4th edit., 1991; editor Jour. Interlibrary Loan and Info. Supply, 1990. Fellow Molesworth Inst.; mem. ALA, Assn. Coll. and Rsch. Librs. Office: Niagara U Libr Niagara University NY 14109

MORRIS, MARK, choreographer; b. Seattle, Wash.. Studied with, Verla Flowers and Perry Brunson. Choreographer Monaie Dance Group (now Mark Morris), Brussels and N.Y.C., 1988—; performed with Lar Lubovitch Dance Co., Hannah Kahn Dance Co., Laura Dean Dancers and Musicians, Eliot Feld Ballet, Koleda Balkan Dance Ensemble. Choreographer, White Oak Dance Project, 1990, Monnaie Dance Group, BAM Majestic Theater, 1990, BAM Opera House, 1990, Boston Ballet, Joffrey Ballet, Am. Ballet Theater, Paris Opera Ballet, others. Office: Mark Morris Dance Group Ste 504 225 Lafayette New York NY 10012-4015*

MORRIS, MELVIN LEWIS, dentist, educator, researcher; b. N.Y.C., Nov. 28, 1914; s. David and Rose (Harris) M.; m. Muriel Liebling, Sept. 19, 1943; children—Barry, Stephen, David. B.S., CCNY, 1934; M.A., Columbia U., 1937, D.D.S.,1941. Diplomate Am. Bd. Periodontology. Intern in dentistry Mt. Sinai Hosp., N.Y.C., 1941-42, chief periodontia clinic, 1947-52; periodontist Polyclinic Hosp., 1946-47; instr. periodontia Columbia U., N.Y.C., 1950-53, asst. clin. prof. dentistry, 1953-58, assoc. clin. prof., 1958-69, clin. prof., 1969-84, clin. prof. emeritus dentistry, 1985—; practice dentistry specializing in periodontics, N.Y.C., 1946—; asst. attending dentist Presbyterian Hosp., N.Y.C., 1974-75, assoc. attending dentist, 1975-85, cons. in dentistry, 1985—; cons. periodontia VA Franklin D. Roosevelt Hosp., 1953-59, VA Castle Point Hosp., 1953-56; lectr. in field. Author: (with Baer) Periodontics, 1977; also chpts., numerous articles on periodontal healing, 1941—. Served as capt. Dental Corps, U.S. Army, 1942-46, ETO. Recipient Isidor Hirschfeld Meml. award NE Soc. Periodontics, 1979, Disting. Alumnus award Columbia U. Dental Sch., 1984, Townsend Harris medal CCNY, 1984. Mem. ADA, Am. Acad. Periodontology, Internat. Assn. Dental Research, AAAS, Sigma Xi, Omicron Kappa Upsilon. Jewish. Avocations: tennis; opera. Home: 750 Kappock St Bronx NY 10463-4612 Office: 30 E 60th St New York NY 10022-1008

MORRIS, PATRICIA ANNE, academic administrator, language educator; b. Jamaica, N.Y., Jan. 6, 1931; d. Canice Joseph and Beatrice Marie (McGillivray) M. BA, St. John's U., Jamaica, N.Y., 1953; MA, Cath. U. Am., 1968; PhD, CUNY, 1978. Cert. French and Spanish tchr., N.Y. Elem. tchr. various schs. L.I., 1956-62; tchr. St. Agnes High Sch./Seaford High Sch., L.I., 1962-70; instr. in French Molloy Coll., Rockville Centre, N.Y., 1970-74, asst. prof. French, 1974-78, assoc. prof. French, 1978-85, v.p. acad. affairs, 1980—, prof. French, 1985—; originator, coord. freshman studies program Molloy Coll., 1988—; cons. Bayamon Cen. U., P.R., fall 1987. Contbr. articles to profl. jours. Originator Programs for Russian Immigrants, Molloy Coll., L.I., 1987—; speaker Rotary, Glen Cove and L.I., 1991. Recipient Disting. Svc. medal Molloy Coll., 1987. Mem. Am. Assn. Higher Edn., Inst. for Cross-Cultural and Cross Ethnic Studies (adv. bd. 1982—), Mid. States Assn. Colls. and Schs. (coll. rels. com. 1987—), PhD Alumni Assn. (1st v.p. 1983—), Alpha Mu Gamma, Delta Epsilon Sigma, Phi Alpha Theta, Lambda Iota Tau. Home and Office: Molloy Coll 1000 Hempstead Ave Rockville Centre NY 11570-1199

MORRIS, PHILIP JOHN, aerospace engineering educator; b. Llandudno, Wales, Apr. 21, 1946; came to U.S., 1973; s. William Garnet and Dora (Butterworth) M.; m. Brenda Mary English, Aug. 24, 1968; children: Nicola Carol, Karen Elizabeth, Anthony Richard. BSc with honors, Southampton (Eng.) U., 1967, MSc, 1969, PhD, 1972. Registered profl. engr., Ont., Can. Rsch. assoc. U. Toronto, Ont., 1971-73; rsch. engr. Lockheed-Ga. Co., Marietta, 1973-77; asst. prof. Pa. State U., University Park, 1977-80; assoc. prof. Pa. State U., 1980-86, prof., dir. computational fluid dynamic studies, 1986—, Boeing prof. aerospace engring., 1992—; cons., Lockheed Ga. Co., 1977-88. Contbr. to tech. publs. Mem. AIAA (aeroacoustics tech. com. 1981-84, 89—), State College (Pa.) Soccer Club (coach 1988—), State Coll. (Pa.) Youth Ice Hockey Assn. (bd. dirs. 1991—). Office: Pa State U 153D Hammond Bldg University Park PA 16802

MORRIS, ROBERT, educator; b. Akron, Ohio, Nov. 21, 1910; s. Joseph and Katherine (Spielberger) Schmaltz; m. Sara Goldman, Dec. 20, 1940. AB, U. Akron, 1931; MSc, Western Res. U., 1935; DSW, Columbia U. Sch. Social Work, 1959; D of Humane Letters (hon.), Brandeis U., 1984. Prin. welfare officer UNRRA, 1945; regional dir. social services VA, Chgo., 1946-48; social planning cons. Council Jewish Fedns. and Welfare Funds, N.Y.C., 1948-58; prof. social planning Brandeis U., Waltham, Mass., 1959-68, Kirstein prof. planning, 1968-79; Cardinal Medeiros lectr. U. Mass., Boston, 1983—, lectr. Harvard U. Sch. Pub. Health, 1974-88; prof. Inst. Health Professions, Mass. Gen. Hosp., 1980-83; mem. adv. com. Aging Research, U.S. Dept. of Health, Edn. and Welfare, 1971, Helen Keller Internat. Found. on the Overseas Blind, 1971-74; mem. spl. med. adv. group VA, Washington, 1969-71; cons. on Geriatric Research, Nat. VA, 1974-78, U.S. Office of Human Devel. Services, 1978-79; v.p. Vis. Nurses Assn., Boston, 1979—; mem. Fed. Adv. Council on Aging Research, Mass. State Health Co-ordinating Council, 1984-85; vice-chmn. Mass. Health Data Consortium, 1979-89; chmn. Internat. Rev. Com. Brookdale Inst. for Gerontology and Adult Human Devel., Israel, 1982-83, cons. 1984-85; chmn. Am. Found. for the Blind Com. on Geriatric Blindness, 1969-74. Author: Feasible Planning for Social Change, 1966, Urban Planning and Social Policy, 1968, Centrally Planned Change, 1964, Trends and Issues in Jewish Social Welfare in the U.S., 1966, Encyclopedia Social Work and Social Welfare, 1971, Toward a Caring Society, 1974, Centrally Planned Change: A Re-Examination of Theories and Concepts, 1974, Social Policy of the American Welfare State, 1979, 2nd edit. 1985, Allocating Resources for the Aged and Disabled, 1981, Rethinking Social Welfare: Why Care for the Stranger, 1986, Retirement Reconsidered, 1988, Economic Roles for the Elderly, 1987, Testing The Limits: International Perspectives on Social Welfare Changes in Nine Countries, 1988; editor-in-chief Jour. of Social Work, 1960-72; editor Jour. Aging and Social Policy. Cons. NIMH, 1964-70; chmn. adv. bd. Mass. Dept. Welfare, 1968-69; profl. adv. com. Easter Seal Soc., 1971-80; mem. Mass. Gov.'s Commn. on Nursing Homes, 1962-67, on Aging, 1962-67, on Hosp. Costs, 1967, Mass. Soc. Prevention Blindness, 1971-75. With AUS, 1943-44. Fulbright award, Italy, 1965-66, 68, Ford Found. fellow, U.K., 1969-70; recipient rsch. awards Ford Found. 1960-65, Treuhaft Found., 1964, 72, Max and Anna Levinson Fund, 1970-72, U.S. Pub. Health Svcs., 1957, 59, 65, NSF, 1975-78. Fellow AAAS, APHA; mem. Nat. Gerontol. Soc. Am. (Kent award 1988, pres. 1966-67), Mass. Pub. Health Assn. (Lemuel Shattuck medal 1976), Ctr. for Applied Gerontology (Heritage award 1987), Commonwealth of Mass. and Assn. for Gerontology in Higher Edn. (Spl. Recognition award 1987). Home: 3801 Canterbury Rd Apt 801 Baltimore MD 21218 Office: U Mass Boston MA 02125

MORRIS, ROBERT, reinsurance analyst; b. Cambridge, Mass., Apr. 20, 1923; s. Henry Winthrop and Alice May (Bartlett) M.; m. Sigrid Margarete Henker, June 18, 1948; children: Elaine Antoinette, Susan Jeanette, Steven Walter. Diploma, Dalhousie Comml. Coll., Can., 1942; BA, MA, U. Pa., 1964. CPCU. Enlisted U.S. Army, 1942, advanced through grades to sgt. maj., 1949, ret., 1962; ins. adjustor Ins. Co. N.Am., Phila., 1962-65, asst. underwriter, 1965-71; asst. v.p. Am. Mut. Reinsurance Co., Chgo., 1971-73, v.p. regional sales, 1973-80, v.p. underwriting, 1980-83, sr. v.p. underwriting, 1983-85; v.p. U.S. Reinsurance Corp., Boston, 1985-89; reins. analyst, advisor, Beverly, Mass., 1989—; instr. Ins. Soc. Phila., 1966-71; reinsurance cons., Chgo., 1985. Dir. Gulph Mills (Pa.) Civic Assn., 1971-76, v.p., 1972-73. Mem. Soc. CPCU (chmn. edn. com. Phila. chpt. 1966-80, mem. reinsurance sect. Boston chpt. 1982—), Retired Officers Assn. (life), Am. Legion. Republican. Clubs: Chgo. Athletic Assn., Princeton of N.Y., Ambassadors (Kansas City, Mo.) (life). Lodge: Masons, Shriners. Home and Office: 14 Driscoll Ln Beverly MA 01915-1471

MORRIS, ROBERT ERWIN, financial executive; b. N.Y.C., Aug. 18, 1945; s. Erwin Francis and Jane Covert (O'Brien) M.; m. Regina Marie Sullivan, Oct. 19, 1968; children: Robert E., Kathleen A., Stepehn J. (dec.), Kara A., Timothy J., Kieran A. BS, Fordham U., 1966; MBA, Loyola U., Chgo., 1976; cert., Williams Coll., 1979. Midwest region credit mgr. Union Carbide Corp., Chgo., 1976-81; mgr. cen. credit dept. Union Carbide Corp., N.Y.C. and Danbury, Conn., 1981-85; mgr. credit, chems. and plastics Union Carbide Corp., Danbury, 1985-86, mgr. money and banking ops., 1986—; instr. fin. Chgo. Inst. Credit, 1981; instr. econs. Project Bus., Jr. Achievement, Danbury, 1985; adviser, evaluator N.Y. Regents Nat. Program Non-Collegiate Sponsored Instrn.; speaker at profl. confs. Sec. Sch. Bd. St. James Sch., Glen Ellyn, Ill., 1980-81; past pres. St. Joseph's Home and Sch. Assn., Danbury, 1982-84; past pres., mem. parents adv. bd. Immaculate High Sch., Danbury, 1985—. 1st lt. U.S. Army, 1966-68, Vietnam. Mem. Nat. Assn. Credit Mgmt., Nat. Chem. Credit Assn., Fairfield County Treasury Mgmt. Assn., Nat. Corp. Cash Mgmt. Assn. Republican. Roman Catholic. Home: 25 Kilian Dr Danbury CT 06811-3434

MORRIS, ROBERT LESTER, university dean; b. Dillsburg, Pa., Feb. 7, 1932; s. Raymond Lester and Helen Lucille (Twigg) M.; m. C. Ruth Schenley, Oct. 4, 1958; children: Karen Sue, Gregg Lawrence. BA, Lycoming Coll., 1955; MA, Columbia U., 1960; PhD, W.Va. U., 1965. Cert. tchr. history and Russian, Pa. Tchr. pub. schs., Williamsport, Pa., 1955-61; prof. history Frostburg (Md.) State Coll., 1961-62; prof. history Indiana U. Pa., 1962-66, dir. Ctr. for Internat. Studies, 1966-88, dean internat. programs, 1988—; exec. dir. Ptnrs. in Bus., Inc., Indiana, 1990—. Contbr. articles to profl. jours. Bd. dirs. Indiana Free Libr., 1986, Pitts. Roundtable Internat. Bus., 1988. With U.S. Army, 1951-53. Recipient 1st ann. Disting. Prof. award Indiana U. Pa., 1965; Commonwealth fellow Pa. System Higher Edn., 1976. Mem. Assn. Overseas Educators (exec. dir. 1984-91), VFW, Indiana Country Club. Home: 545 Oak St Indiana PA 15701-1974 Office: Ind U Pa Ctr for Internat Studies Indiana PA 15705

MORRIS, RONALD ANTHONY, county official; b. Wilmington, Del., Nov. 8, 1946; s. Elwood and Sophia (Ptak) M.; m. Barbara Marie Szostkowski, July 16, 1976; 1 child, David. BS, U. Balt., 1970; MBA, Widener U., 1975. Cost acct. Atlas Chem. Industries, New Castle, Del., 1966-67; sr. cost acct. Bethlehem Steel Corp., Balt., 1967-70; sr. acct. J.K. Lasser & Co., CPAs, Wilmington, 1970-71; dep. dir. fin. City of Wilmington, 1971-74; acctg. supr. New Castle County, 1974-75, controller, 1975-80, budget and acctg. mgr., 1980—. Recipient Achievement award Nat. Assn. Counties, 1990, Award of Excellence Nat. Assn. County Info. Officers, 1989. Mem. Del. Assn. Govtl. Fin. Officers (v.p. 1990—), Am. Soc. for Pub. Adminstrn., Del. Assn. for Pub. Adminstrn. (councilman 1980-82), Govt. Fin. Officers Assn. U.S. and Canada (com. mem. 1989-91, Fin. Reporting Achievement award 1981-90, Disting. Budget Presentation award 1991), Am. Acctg. Assn., Nat. Assn. Accts. Home: 904 Wawaset St Wilmington DE 19806-3244

MORRIS, SARA, artist, writer; b. Shelby, N.C., May 21, 1955; d. William Monroe and Nydia (Early) M.; m. William Swetcharnik. Grad., Schuler Sch. Fine Art, 1978, postgrad., 1978-79; student, Art Students League, N.Y.C., 1979-81. resident Va. Ctr. Creative Arts, 1990. Author: (short story) The Dogwood Tree, 1991 (1st Pl. 1991); one-person show Catepetl Gallery, Frederick, Md., 1977; two-person shows include Genesis Arts, Frederick, 1978, Eikon Fine Arts, Frederick, 1979, Weinberg Ctr. for Arts, Frederick, 1980, Mt. St. Mary's Coll., Emmitsburg, Md., 1981, Christ Ch., Tarrytown, N.Y., 1982, Landon Sch. Gallery, Bethesda, Md., 1990, Frederick (Md.) Community Coll. Gallery, 1992, Acarroll Community Coll., Westminster, Md., 1992; exhibited in group shows including Miniature Painters, Sculptors and Gravers Soc., Washington (1st Pl. in Sculpture 1976), others. Fulbright fellow 1988-89; Schuler Sch. Fine Arts scholar, Art Students League scholar. Office: Swetcharnik-Morris Art 7044 Woodville Rd Mount Airy MD 21771-7934

MORRIS, STEPHEN BRENT, mathematician; b. Dallas, Mar. 28, 1950; s. Jack Brent and Maxene (Peek) M.; m. Nancy Marie Turner, May 22, 1971; children: Terrance Brent, Mary Patricia. BS, So. Meth. U., 1971; AM, Duke U., 1973, PhD, 1974; MS, Johns Hopkins U., 1980. Instr. math. Duke U., Durham, N.C., 1972-75; mathematician Dept. Def., Washington, 1975—; lectr. elec. engring. and computer sci. Johns Hopkins U., Balt., 1979-85. Mem. editorial bd. Scottish Rite Jour., 1989—; contbr. articles to profl. jours.; co-inventor method for accessing in dynamic memories, fast parallel sorting processor. Chmn. edn. com. Scottish Rite Charitable Found. Inc., Balt., 1983—. Fellow Philalethes Soc. (exec. sec. 1975-85); mem. Am. Math. Soc. (mem. joint com. employment opportunities 1988—, chair 1992-93), Math. Assn. Am. (com. on mathematicians outside academia 1990—, gov. 1991—, vis. lectr. 1991—), Assn. Computing Machinery (lectr. 1990—), Masons (33 degree), Patmos Lodge (master 1979-80), Grand Lodge Md. (grand dir. ceremonies 1980-81). Republican. Methodist. Home: 5088 Lake Cir W Columbia MD 21044-1442

MORRIS, TRISHA ANN, librarian; b. Canton, Ohio, Dec. 15, 1941; d. James Warren and Anna Marie (Packa) Lamoreaux; m. Kenneth F. Whitmer, June 5, 1962 (dec. 1971); children: Erica M., Tess A., Clifford K.; m. Nick D. Morris, Oct. 4, 1973; children: Aaron D., Shawn K., Tasha T. BA, Kent State U., 1973, MLS, 1977. Dir. libr. So. Ohio Coll. N.E., Akron, 1985-87; asst. libr. Prestonsburg (Ky.) Community Coll., 1987-90; dir. libr. Pa. State U., Du Bois, 1990—. Author: (index) Appalachian Heritage, 1991; contbr. entries Ency. Ky., 1990; columnist Floyd County Times, 1987-90. Mem. ALA, AAUW (editor newsletter 1991), Pa. Libr. Assn., Appalachian Writers Assn., Du Bois Area Librs. (editor union list 1991). Office: Pa State U Du Bois Campus Coll Pl Du Bois PA 15801

MORRISON, ALVIN CONSTANTINE, clergyman; b. St. Mary, Jamaica, Feb. 11, 1928; came to U.S., 1974; s. Nehemiah Nathiel and Josephine Morrison; m. Una May Tyrell, Sept. 9, 1933 (div. 1975); m. Ensthyn Iona Andrews, Feb. 12, 1976; children: Micheal, Jennifer, Desirie, Christopher, Gary. BS, St. Francis Coll., Bklyn., 1979; MDiv, Theol. Sem., New Brunswick, N.J., 1984. Ordained as pastor Nazarene Ch., 1984. Life underwriter Dominion Life Ins. Co. Can., Jamaica, 1962-69; dep. dir. Cobala Youth Camp Youth Devel. Agy., Kingston, Jamaica, 1969-74; pastor Stirling United of Jamaica and Caymah, 1974-80; assoc. pastor Nazarene United Ch. of Christ, Bklyn., 1984—. Bd. dirs. New Communities, Bklyn., 1986—, New Prospects, Bklyn., 1987—, New Initiative, Bklyn., 1987—. Mem. St. Francis Coll. Alumni Assn., New Brunswick Theol. Sem. Alumni Assn. Democrat. Home: 709 Logan St Brooklyn NY 11208-4419 Office: Interboro Inst 450 W 56th St New York NY 10019-3602

MORRISON, BART WILLIAM, record company executive; b. Wichita, Dec. 29, 1951; s. Melvin and Anna Catherine (Green) M.; m. Marguerite Eleanor Howard, Sept. 22, 1984; 1 child, William Loomis Howard Morrison. BA, U. Tex., 1974; MBA, U. Pa., 1976. Fin. analyst Chase Manhattan Bank, N.Y.C., 1977; fin. analyst CBS Television Stas., N.Y.C., 1977-78, mgr. mktg. profitability analysis, 1978-80; dir. planning CBS Radio, N.Y.C., 1980-82; dir. planning and rsch. CBS/Fox Video, N.Y.C., 1982-84, v.p. strategic analysis, 1984-88; v.p. fin. Bertelsmann Music Group Distbn., N.Y.C., 1988-92; sr. v.p. fin. and adminstrn. PolyGram Group Distbn., N.Y.C., 1992—. Fund raising Arts and Entertainment Dist. Explorer Scouts, N.Y.C., 1989— (dist. award of merit 1992). Mem. N.Y. Tex. Execs. (U. Tex. Alumni chpt. pres. 1984-86), The Wharton Club, Phi Beta Kappa. Episcopalian. Office: PolyGram Group Distbn Inc Worldwide Pla 825 Eighth Ave New York NY 10019

MORRISON, CRAIG MICHAEL, psychologist; b. N.Y.C., Sept. 16, 1958; s. Frederick and Sondra (Skriloff) M.; m. Theresa Lorraine Nitti, June 17, 1989. PhD, Hofstra U., 1985. Lic. psychologist, N.Y. Pvt. practice Rockville Centre, N.Y., 1986—; psychologist Booth Meml. Med. Ctr., Queens, N.Y., 1987—; Island Park (N.Y.) Unified Free Sch. Dist. Island Park (N.Y.) UFSO, 1986—; vol. psychologist Nassau Psychol. Svcs. Inst., Hempstead, N.Y., 1987-89. Mem. APA, Nassau County Psychol. Assn. Office: 66 Lincoln Ct Rockville Centre NY 11570-5743

MORRISON, DONALD FRANKLIN, statistician, educator; b. Stoneham, Mass., Feb. 10, 1931; s. Daniel Norman and Agnes Beatrice (Packard) M.; m. Phyllis Ann Hazen, Aug. 19, 1967; children: Norman Hazen, Stephen Donald. B.S. in Bus. Adminstrn, Boston U., 1953, A.M., 1954; M.S., U. N.C., 1957; Ph.D., Va. Poly. Inst. and State U., 1960; M.A. (hon.), U. Pa., 1971. Mem. staff Lincoln Lab., M.I.T., 1956; cons. math. statistician NIMH, Bethesda, Md., 1956-63; mem. tech. staff Bell Labs., Holmdel, N.J., 1967; mem. faculty, dept. stats. Wharton Sch., U. Pa., 1963—, prof. stats., 1973—, chmn. dept., 1978-85. Author: Multivariate Statistical Methods, 3d edit., 1990, Applied Linear Statistical Methods, 1983; editor: The American Statistician, 1972-75; assoc. editor: Biometrics, 1972-74; contbr. articles to profl. jours. Served with USPHS, 1956-58. NSF grantee, 1966. Fellow Am. Statis. Assn., Inst. Math. Stats.; mem. Internat. Statis. Inst., Biometric Soc., Royal Statis. Soc., Psychometric Soc., B&M R.R. Hist. Soc., Nat. R.R. Hist. Soc. Democrat. Home: 118 E Brookhaven Rd Media PA 19086-6327 Office: U Pa Wharton Sch Philadelphia PA 19104-6302

MORRISON, GORDON MACKAY, JR., investment company executive; b. Boston, Jan. 18, 1930; s. Gordon Mackay and Alice (Blodgett) M.; m. Barbara J. Lee, June 15, 1954; children: Lee, Leighton, Faith. AB, Harvard U., 1952, MBA, 1954. Regional mgr. Bankers Leasing Corp., Boston, 1965-68; portfolio mgr. Loomis, Sayles and Co., Boston, 1969-71; sr. v.p. Ft. Hill Investors Mgmt., Boston, 1972-75; chmn. bd. Bradford Gordon, Inc., Boston, 1976—; trustee East Boston Savs. Bank, 1962-91, Meridian Mut. Holding Co., 1991—. Bd. dirs. The New Eng. Hosp., 1961—. Republican. Congl. Club: Harvard. Lodge: Masons. Home: 32 Old Orchard Rd Sherborn MA 01770-1037 Office: Bradford Gordon Inc 50 Congress St Boston MA 02109-4002

MORRISON, H. ROBERT, writer, editor; b. Pitts., Apr. 7, 1938; s. Hugh and Gertrude Mary (Gehenio) M.; m. Meredith Wollenberg, Dec. 8, 1979; children: Hugh Robert Jr., Justin William. BA in English, Howard U., 1969. Writer Nat. Geog. Soc., Washington, 1969-73, editor ednl. filmstrips, 1973-77, sr. writer, 1977-88, mng. editor nat. geography bee, 1988-89. Contbg. author to numerous books including America's Seashore Wonderlands, 1985, America's Wild Woodlands, 1985, Exploring America's Valleys, 1984, America's Hidden Corners, 1983, America's Magnificent Mountains, 1980, America's Majestic Canyons, 1979, Mysteries of the Ancient World, 1979, The Ocean Realm, 1978, As We Live and Breathe, 1971; co-author: America's Atlantic Isles, 1981. Vice chmn. Falls Church (Va.) Dem. Com., 1988—. With U.S. Army, 1961-64. Mem. St. Andrew's Soc. Washington. Home: Bonnie Briar 502 Walden Ct Falls Church VA 22046-2628 Office: Nat Geog Soc 17th and M Sts NW Washington DC 20036

MORRISON, IAN ALASTAIR, human services executive; b. Glasgow, Scotland, Apr. 22, 1924; came to U.S., 1932, naturalized, 1937; s. William John and Alexandrina (Smith) M.; m. Naida Brown, Apr. 19, 1946; children: Craig William, Sheila Elise. BA, Wagner Coll., S.I., N.Y., 1948, LHD, 1968; MA, Columbia U., 1950, MS, 1958, EdD, 1961; LHD, Bard Coll., 1968. Assoc. prof. history, dean students Wagner Coll., 1949-56; exec. Inter Royal Corp., N.Y.C., 1956-57; exec. sec. Greer Sch., Millbrook, N.Y., 1958-61; exec. dir. Greer Sch., Millbrook, 1961-72; pres. Greer-Woodycrest Children's Svc., N.Y.C., 1972-89; pres. Greer Crest retirement community, N.Y.C., 1984-89, pres. emeritus, 1989—; pres. Greer Inst., Bank of Millbrook, 1974-91. Author: Higher Education in World War II, 1950, American Political Parties, Political Science Handbook, 1953, Foster Care in the United States, 1975; editor NAHC Pub. Affairs Bull., 1975-87, Continuing Care Retirement Communities: Social, Political and Financial Issues; pub. Resdl. Group Care quar.; contbr. articles to profl. jurs.; author pub. affairs newsletter. Pres. Eastchester (N.Y.) Bd. Edn., 1962-66, Unionvale (N.Y.) Bd. Edn., 1969-87; mem. adv. coun. Dutchess County Coll.; mem. long-range com. Columbia U. Div. Geriatrics and Gerontology; trustee emeritus St. Francis Hosp., Poughkeepsie, N.Y., 1981-90, chmn., 1990; bd. dirs. Millbrook, 1980-85. With AUS, World War II, ETO, POW, Germany. Decorated Purple Heart with oak leaf cluster, Prisoner of War medal, Bronze Star; Grad. fellow 1948 Wagner Coll., 1948. Mem. N.Y. State Assn. Child Care Agencies (pres. 1969), N.Y. State Assn. Children's Inst. (chmn. edn. com. 1961-68, pres. 1968), Nat. Assn. Homes for Children (hon. life mem.,

dir. 1975-89, pres. 1977-79, chmn. pub. affairs com. 1975-87, bd. dir. 1975-84, author code of ethics), Nat. Assn. Sr. Living Industry (founding mem.), Child Welfare League Am., Fgn. Policy Assn., St. Andrews Soc., Caledonia Soc., Nat. Assn. Homes for Children, Am. Assn. Homes for Aged, Nat. Assn. Fundraising Execs., Union League Club (N.Y.C.), Millbrook Golf and Tennis Club, Columbia U. Club (N.Y.C.).

MORRISON, J. KENT, university dean; b. Mpls., Sept. 1, 1940; s. James Leo and Elsie (Tascher) M.; m. Jeanne Darke, Dec. 29, 1977; children: Michael, Mark, Malcolm. BA, U. Va., 1962; MA, Eastern N.Mex. U., Portales, 1965, U. Wash., 1966; PhD, U. Wash., 1970. Prof. polit. sci. U. Utah, Salt Lake City, 1970-89, assoc. dean, 1987-89; dean Grad. Sch. U. R.I., Kingston, 1989—; vis. prof. Inst. Internat. Rels., Beijing, China, 1984, Chinese Acad. Social Scis., Beijing, 1984-85, U. Hamburg (Germany), 1977; Fulbright prof. Zhong Shan U., Guangzhou, China, 1983-84; dir. Intermountain-Pacific Rim Trade Project, Salt Lake City, 1986-89. 1st lt. USAF, 1962-65. NSF fellow, Taiwan and Hong Kong, 1968-70. Office: U RI Grad Sch 204 Quinn Hall Kingston RI 02881

MORRISON, JAMES FREDERICK, flavor and fragrance company executive, accountant; b. Evanston, Ill., Aug. 12, 1933; s. Paul Leslie and Carolyn Lola (Rosemeier) M.; m. Myra Val Wokoun, June 22, 1957; children: Myra Hollie Morrison Nielsen, Cynthia Leslie Morrison Karlsson. BA, Northwestern U., 1955, MBA, 1958. CPA, Wis. Accounting mgr. Froedtert Malt Corp., Milw., 1958-61; asst. controller, asst. v.p. Northwestern Nat. Ins. Co., Milw., 1961-65; controller Eutectic Welding Alloys Corp., Flushing, N.Y., 1965-68; internal auditor Sterling Drug, N.Y.C., 1968-69; controller Internat. Flavors and Fragrances, N.Y.C., 1970-76; mng. dir., v.p. Europe Internat. Flavors and Fragrances, London, 1977-80; v.p. new bus. group U.S. Internat. Flavors and Fragrances, N.Y.C., 1981-84; v.p. export and communications U.S. Internat. Flavors and Fragrances, Hazlet, N.J., 1984—. Mem. Manhasset (N.Y.) Bd. Edn., 1970-75, v.p., 1975; bd. dirs. United Way Monmouth County, 1991—. 1st lt. USAF, 1955-57. Mem. AICPA, Fin. Execs. Inst. (pres. L.I. chpt. 1975-76), Internat. Trade Facilitation Coun. (vice-chmn. 1991—), Wis. Soc. CPA's, Internat. Commerce Club N.J., Systems and Procedures Assn. (pres. Milw. chpt. 1965), Beta Gamma Sigma. Presbyterian. Home: 14 Circle Dr Rumson NJ 07760 Office: Internat Flavor & Fragrances 600 State Hwy 36 Hazlet NJ 07800

MORRISON, JOHN BENNETT, cardiologist, educator; b. White Plains, N.Y., Apr. 6, 1938; s. Frederick A. and Louise (Feldt) M.; m. Barbara Ann Otto, June 12, 1970; children; Donna E., Gregory J. BS, St. Lawrence U., Canton, N.Y., 1960; MD, Cornell U., 1964. Intern L.A. County Gen. Hosp., 1964-65; resident North Shore Univ. Hosp., Manhasset, N.Y., 1967-69; cardiology fellow N.Y. Hosp., N.Y.C., 1969-71; asst. prof. medicine Cornell U. Med. Coll., N.Y.C., 1971-76, assoc. prof. medicine, 1976—; co-chief div. cardiology North Shore Univ. Hosp., Manhasset, 1981—; mem. NHLBI, Ischemic Myocardium, Bethedsa, Md., 1976, steering com. NIH Thrombolysis in Myocardial Infarction Contract, 1986-90. Contbr. articles to profl. jours. Pres. L.I. Heart Coun., Hicksville, N.Y., 1991—. Lt. U.S. Army, 1965-67. Mem. Coun. on Clin. Cardiology, Harvey Soc., Am. Heart Assn. (chpt. pres. 1986-88). Office: North Shore Univ Hosp 300 Community Dr Manhasset NY 11030-3800

MORRISON, KENNETH ALLEN, publishing executive, consultant; b. Lancaster, Pa., Apr. 10, 1940; s. Jay Harlan and Sarah Idalice (Smith) M.; m. Alice Rose Gordon, Aug. 12, 1972; 1 child, Megan Alice. Grad. high sch., Lancaster. With Lancaster Press, Inc., 1958—, foreman, 1972-84, supt., 1984—; cons. G.E. Richards, Landisville, Pa., 1984—. Mem. Susquehanna Litho Club, Lions (tail twister Quarryville, Pa. chpt. 1986-87). Presbyterian. Home: 5 Elk Cir New Providence PA 17560-9703 Office: Lancaster Press Inc Prince & Lemon Sts Lancaster PA 17603

MORRISON, MARK DENNIS, banker; b. Methuen, Mass., July 11, 1959; s. Augustine Daniel and Mary Elizabeth (Sullivan) M.; m. Mary-Bligh Quigley, Aug. 18, 1989; 1 child, Mark Augustine. BA in History, Siena Coll., 1981; postgrad., Stonier Grad. Sch. Banking, 1992. Exec. mgmt. program assoc. Key Bank of N.Y. N.A., Albany, N.Y., 1981-82; customer svc. officer Key Bank N.A., Albany, N.Y., 1982-83, comml. credit officer, 1983-84, mgr. asset-based lending, 1984-85, loan officer asset-based lending, 1985-86, asst. v.p. comml. loans, 1986-88; v.p. corp. lending Key Bank of N.Y., Albany, 1988-90; sr. v.p. Key Bank of Ea. N.Y., Albany, 1991—. Bd. dirs. Am. Heart Assn., Albany, 1986—, ARC, Albany, 1987—; chmn. Albany Med. Ctr. Bus. & Industry Fund, 1991—. Named Vol. of the Yr. Am. Heart Assn., 1990. Mem. Am. Inst. Banking, Robert Morris Assocs., Comml. Fin. Assn., Bank Mgmt. Inst. (bd. dirs. 1989—), Siena Coll. Alumni Assn. (bd. dirs. 1987—), Steuben Athletic Club, Wolferts Roost Country Club. Roman Catholic. Home: 10 Sky Hollow Dr Menands NY 12204 Office: Key Bank of NY 66 S Pencl St 66 S Pearl St Albany NY 12207

MORRISON, MURRAY ALLAN, orthopaedic surgeon; b. Columbus, Ohio, Dec. 6, 1939; s. Benjamin Gerald and Mildred (Jacobs) M.; m. Susan Gail Kobren, July 30, 1967; children: Jennifer Anne, Sarah Elise. AB, Harvard U., 1961; MD, NYU, 1965. Diplomate Am. Bd. Orthopaedic Surgery. Surg. intern U. Mich. Med. Ctr., Ann Arbor, 1965-66, asst. resident surgery, 1966-67; orthodaedic resident Hosp. of U. of Pa., Phila., 1967-70; attending surgeon Bridgeport (Conn.) Hosp., 1970—; sr. attending surgeon Bridgeport Hosp., Phila., 1980—; clin. instr. Yale U. Sch. of Medicine, New Haven, 1985—; dir. Ralston Orthopedic Libr., U. Pa. Dept. of Ortho-surgery, Phila., 1984—. Fellow Am. Coll. Surgeons, Am. Acad. Orthopaedic Surgeons, Eastern Orthopaedic Assn., Conn. State Med. Soc. Office: Orthopaedic Specialty Group DC 325 Reed Rd Fairfield CT 06430

MORRISON, PERRY ERWIN, real estate management company executive; b. Long Beach, N.Y., May 18, 1929; s. Morris M. and Florence (Stone) Goldberg; m. Beatrice Jean Epstine, Aug. 7, 1960; children: Lesa, Abby. AB, Columbia Coll., 1949; MS, Columbia U., 1950. CPA, N.Y. Mem. staff Arthur Young & Co., N.Y.C., 1953-58; contr. May Stern & Co., Pitts., 1958-60, v.p., treas., 1960-71, pres., 1971—; dir. Comnet Corp., Greenbelt, Md., 1988-92, now adv. dir.; trustee Lehman-Epstine Charitable Trust, Pitts., 1960—, The Morrison Found. Bd. dirs., Y Music Soc., Pitts., 1962—, also past pres.; bd. dirs. Montefiore Hosp., Pitts., 1984-90, Eye and Ear Inst., Pitts., 1991—; mem. Hist. Dist. Local Rev. Commn., Pitts., 1989—. 1st lt. U.S. Army, 1951-53, Korea. Mem. AICPA, N.Y. State Soc. CPAs, Duquesne Club, Concordia Club (Pitts.). Office: 914 Penn Ave Pittsburgh PA 15222-3713

MORRISON, ROY DENNIS, II, philosophy, religion, and science educator; b. Marshall, Tex., Dec. 30, 1926; s. Roy Dennis and Louise (Smith) M.; m. Margaret Cornelia Johnson, July 18, 1959; 1 child, Sylvia Louise. BA, Howard U., 1947; BD, North Bapt. Theol. Seminar, Chgo., 1950; MA, U. Chgo., 1969, PhD, 1972. Asst. prof. New Collegiate Div., U. Chgo., 1970-73, Divinity Sch., U. Chgo., 1970-73; prof. philosophy, epistemology, religion and sci. Wesley Theol. Sem., Washington, 1973—. Contbr. articles to profl. jours. Mem. Am. Acad. of Religion, N.Am. Paul Tillich Soc. (pres. 1985), Inst. on Religion in an Age of Sci. (acad. fellow 1991). Unitarian Universalist. Home: 2611 Evans Dr Silver Spring MD 20902 Office: Wesley Theol Sem 4500 Massachusetts Ave NW Washington DC 20016

MORRISON, WILLIAM GAMBLE BOYD, III, graphic designer; b. Seal Beach, Calif., Nov. 13, 1952; s. William Gamble Boyd Jr. and Pamela (Rosser) M.; m. Patrice Angela Moser, Aug. 29, 1987; 1 child, William Gamble Boyd IV. BS, La. State U., 1976. Freelance designer and illustrator La., 1976-77, London, 1977-78, L.A., 1979-80; project designer Herman & Lees Assocs., Cambridge, Mass., 1982-84; dir. graphic design Steffian Bradley Assocs., Boston, 1984-87; assoc. Selbert Design, Cambridge, 1987-90; dir., owner Gamble Design, Portsmouth, N.H., 1991—; team mem. USA Rugby Football Union, 1977-80; chmn. Nat. Clubs Com., 1992—; guest lectr. Monserrat Coll. Art, 1989, Boston Archt. Ctr., 1989. Design dir. (book) Design Primer for Cities and Towns, 1989. Pro bono advisor Planning Dept. City Portsmouth, 1991-92; mem. Leadership Seacost, Class 1992; bd. dirs. POrtsmouth Advocates, 1992—. Mem. Soc. for Environ. Graphic Design (N.E. profl. rep. 1988-90), Am. Ctr. Design, Am. Inst. Graphic Arts, Environ. Design Rsch. Assn., PLAN N.H., Boston Rugby Football Club (pres. 1988-90), Sigma Chi. Office: Gamble Design 9 Sheafe St Portsmouth NH 03801

MORRISSEY, ALICE, accountant; b. Huntingdon Valley, Pa., July 2, 1967; d. James David and Mary Alice (Fasy). BS in Acctg., Villanova U., 1989, postgrad., 1991—. Acctg. clerk James D. Morrisey, Inc., Phila., 1981-89; staff acct. Enrst Whitney, Phila., 1988, Peat Marwick, Phila., 1989-91. Republican. Roman Catholic. Home: 1328 Old Ford Rd Huntingdon Valley PA 19006-8106

MORRISSEY, KATHLEEN DAVIS, managed health care plan administrator; b. Phila., Jan. 4, 1947; d. Francis J. and Florence K. (Hillebrand) Davis; m. William Leonard Morrissey, June 1, 1968; children: William L. Jr., Brian Edward. RN, Mercy Cath. Med. Ctr., 1967; BS, Phila. Coll. Textiles & Sci., 1981; MBA, Temple U., 1983. Med.-surg. nurse several hosps. Pa., Mass., 1967-77; health adminstrv. cons. Duane, Morris & Heckschure, Phila., 1983-85; dir. value assurance Family Health Plan, King of Prussia, Pa., 1985-87; v.p. Ethix Mid-Atlantic (formerly Family Health Plan), Wayne, Pa., 1987—; guest lectr. MBA program, Temple U., 1984—. Mem. Temple U. Health Adminstrn. Alumni Assn. (pres. 1990-92). Office: Ethix Mid Atlantic Valley Forge Office Ct Ste 201 530 E Swedesford Rd Wayne PA 19087

MORRISSEY, LEO, artist; b. Phila., Aug. 22, 1958; s. Leo and Jane (Thomas) M.; m. Nancy Blair. BFA with honors, U. Fla., 1983; MFA, Rutgers U., 1985. Rep. Gallery Vicent Bernat, Barcelona, Spain, 1991—. Exhibited in group shows including Z Gallery, N.Y.C., 1991, Vicent Bernat Gallery, Barcelona, Spain, 1991, Masterworks Gallery, Auckland, 1990, Cartoon Gallery, Barcelona, 1990; represented in permanent collections including Jane Voorhees Zimmerli Mus., King Stephen Mus., Hungary, Glass Mus., Ebeltoft, Denmark, Can. Postal Mus., Ottawa. Grantee Pollack-Krasner Found., 1987. Mem. Coll. Art Assn. Home: PO Box 1794 New Brunswick NJ 08903-1794

MORRIS-YAMBA, TRISH, educational and social service association director; b. Binghamton, N.Y.; d. Maurice and Lillian (Flippen) Walker; divorced; 1 child, Lae D.; m. A. Zachary Yamba, Apr. 11, 1987; stepchildren: Zachary, Soukaina, Mailissa. BA, Livingston Coll., 1972; MEd, Rutgers U., 1973. Adminstr. Community Action Tng., Inc., Trenton, 1968-70; exec. dir. Coun. for Higher Edn. in Newark, 1973-81, Newark Day Ctr., 1981—; host, producer sta. WWHT TV, Newark, 1982-86, current ednl. cons. Pres. Fedn. Youth Services, 1984—. Recipient Community Service award Senator Bill Bradley, 1984, N.J. Transit Community Service award, 1988, Outstanding Svcs. Children of N.J., 1988, Bronze shield for Community Svc., 1989. Mem. Nat. Polit. Congress Black Women (pres. met. Newark chpt. 1988—), Negro Bus. and Profl. Women, Inc. (Profl. Woman of Yr. 1982), Essex County Coll. Women's Ctr. (mem. adv. bd. 1986—). Baptist. Office: Newark Day Ctr 43 Hill St Newark NJ 07102-2649

MORRONE, EDWARD P., state senator, insurance and real estate company executive; b. Westerly, R.I., Mar. 17, 1950; s. Anthony Joseph and Elizabeth E. (Mermes) M.; m. Deborah A. Morrone, Sept. 18, 1971; children: Darrell E., Kerri Lynn, Courtney Beth. BA, U. R.I., 1972. State rep. Dist. 57, Westerly-New Shoreham, 1980-84; state senator Dist. 26, Westerly-New Shoreham, 1988—; pres. Capalbo & Morrone Agy. Ins. & Real Estate Inc., Westerly. Pres. Westerly-Pawcatuck C. of C., 1986. Mem. Westerly Lions, Fraternal Order Police. Home: 16 Pasadena Ave Westerly RI 02891 Office: 90 High St PO Box 526 Westerly RI 02891

MORROW, GREGORY WILLIAM, naval officer; b. Greencastle, Ind., Feb. 23, 1963; s. William Lockhart Morrow and Peggy Ann Eutsler; m. Su-Ling Morrow, Mar. 22, 1989; 1 child, Davina Mei-Ling. BS in Engring. Mgmt., U.S. Naval Acad., 1985; MBA, U. Md., 1991. Comnd. ensign USN, 1985; advanced through grades to lt. jr. grade, 1987; communications officer USS Doyle FFG-39, Jacksonville, Fla., 1985-87; ordnance officer USS Doyle FFG-39, Jacksonville, 1987-88; contract specialist Bur. Naval Pers., Washington, 1988—, total quality advisor, 1988-91. Coun. Logistics Mgmt. scholar, 1990. Mem. U.S. Naval Acad. Alumni Assn., Am. Legion. Home: 6405 Blarney Stone Ct Springfield VA 22152-2105 Office: Bur of Naval Pers Arlington Annex Rm 1608 Washington DC 20370-5000

MORROW, JON STANLEY, pathology educator, medical scientist; b. Ft. Wayne, Ind.. BS, Ind. U., 1969, PhD, 1974; MD, Yale U., 1976. Prof. pathology Yale Med. Sch., New Haven, Conn., 1989—; chmn. pathology dept. Yale Med. Sch., New Haven, 1990—; chief pathology Yale-New Haven (Conn.) Hosp., 1990—. Office: Yale U Sch Medicine Dept Pathology 310 Cedar St New Haven CT 06510-3218

MORROW, SCOTT DOUGLAS, choreographer, educator; b. N.Y.C., Jan. 29, 1954; s. Alfred Lionel and Lorraine (Power) M. Grad., High Sch. Performing Arts, N.Y.C., 1972; BFA in Dance, SUNY, Purchase, 1976; MA in Choreography, UCLA, 1986. Prin. instr. Phil Black Dance Studio, N.Y.C., 1969-77; dir. dance div. No. Ill. U., DeKalb, 1976-78; artistic dir., resident choreographer No. Ill. Repertory Dance co., 1976-78; artistic dir. Scott Morrow Dance Theatre Co. and Sch., L.A., 1978-85; prin. instr. Mary Tyler Moore Los Angeles Dance Ctr., 1979-80; resident dance master South Coast Repertory Acting Conservatory, Calif., 1979-82; vis. prof. Wright State U., Ohio, 1981; ballet master, resident choreographer Empire State Ballet, Buffalo, 1984-85; asst. prof. U. Kans., Lawrence, 1985-88; resident choreographer Kans. U. Dance Co., Lawrence, 1985-88; choreographer Morrow Dance Theatre-in-residence, U. Kans., 1985-88, 92d St. Dance Ctr., YMHA and YWHA, N.Y.C., 1989; assoc. dir., dir. edn. pub. sch. dance programs K-12, Bronx Dance Theatre, N.Y.C., 1990—; mem. faculty Internat. Summer Sch. Royal Acad. Dancing, N.Y.C., 1991—, State Edn. Dept. Summer Inst. on Assessment in Arts, N.Y., 1992—. Choreographer: (musical theater) Broadway Musical Classics on International Tour, (film musicals) Chestnuts, Rainbows End, (teleseries) Adventures of Hans Christen Andersen, (indsl. show) Le Parfum Salvador Dali; world premieres presented at numerous festivals including Morningside Dance Festival, N.Y.C., Mid Am. Dance Festival, L.A. Dance Kaleidoscope Festival, Smithsonian Instn.'s Duke Ellington Festival, Washington, Marche Internat. de Disque et de l'Edition Musicale, Cannes, France; creator over 40 ballets. Nat. Festival for the Performing Arts Choreographers fellow, 1989; named Choreographer of Yr., Kaymore Found. for Arts, 1984, Master Educator and Disting. Fellow, Am. Bd. Master Educators, 1987; Alvin Ailey scholar, Sch. Am. Ballet scholar, Harkness House for Ballet Arts scholar; recipient Grand Prize for Choreography, Ann. Internat. Artistic Impression Competition, 1991; grantee numerous founds., corps., univs. Office: Lorraine Prodns 2269 Ocean Ave Brooklyn NY 11229-3198

MORROW, WALTER EDWIN, JR., electrical engineer, university laboratory administrator; b. Springfield, Mass., July 24, 1928; s. Walter Edwin and Mary Elizabeth (Ganley) M.; m. Janice Lila Lombard, Feb. 25, 1951; children—Clifford E., Gregory A., Carolyn F. S.B., M.I.T., 1949, S.M., 1951. Mem. staff Lincoln Lab., MIT, Lexington, Mass., 1951-55, group leader, 1956-65; head div. communications MIT Lincoln Lab., 1966-68, asst. dir., 1968-71, asso. dir., 1972-77, dir., 1977—. Contbr. articles to profl. publs. Recipient award for outstanding achievement Pres. M.I.T., 1963, Edwin Howard Armstrong Achievement award IEEE Communications Soc., 1976. Fellow IEEE, Nat. Acad. Engring. Office: Lincoln Lab 244 Wood St PO Box 73 Lexington MA 02173

MORSE, FRANCIS, aerospace engineering educator; b. Pittsfield, Mass., Sept. 8, 1917; s. Harold Francis and Rosamond (Hull) M.; m. Carmen Gloria Flory, July 28, 1945; children: Diana, Emily, Harold, Elizabeth. B in Engring., Yale U., 1939; MS, Calif. Tech. Inst., 1940. Registered profl. engr., Mass. Liaison engr. Lockheed Aircraft, Burbank, Calif., 1940-42; design engr. Goodyear Aircraft, Akron, Ohio, 1942-45, GE, Pittsfield, 1946-55; prof. Boston U., 1958-82, prof. emeritus, 1982—; cons. USN, Newport, R.I., 1971-72, Dao Bros. Engring. Co., San Marino, Calif., 1979-80. Author: How Big & Still Beautiful, 1980; contbr. articles to profl. jours. Chairman United World Federalists, Framingham, Mass., 1962—; mem. Dem. Town Com., Wayland, Mass., 1968—. Mem. AIAA. Home: 18 Reservoir Rd Wayland MA 01778-3713

MORSE, JAMES HAROLD, video producer, consultant; b. Providence, Apr. 26, 1939; s. George Harold and Grace Catherine (Prendergast) M. MDiv, St. John's Coll., Boston, 1967; MEd, U. N.C., Charlotte, 1971. Mental health cons. Corrigan Mental Health Ctr., Fall River, Mass., 1970-75; assoc. dir. Ctr. for Human Devel., Washington, 1976-86, dir., 1986-88; supervising producer CTNA HealthNet, Washington, 1989—; pres. Communications Resource Group, Washington, 1990—. Producer (video tng. tapes) Self Knowledge, 1984, Peer Counseling Skills, 1987, Leadership Skills, 1987; TV producer Prolonging Life Decision, 1990, Values and Ethics in Healthcare Mission, 1991, Graying of America, 1992. Mem. Am. Coll. Healthcare Execs., Am. Hosp. Assn., Assn. Healthcare Adminstrs., New Eng. Assn. Healthcare Cons. Office: CTNA HealthNet 3211 4th St NE Washington DC 20017-1106

MORSE, J(OSIAH) MITCHELL, retired English educator; b. Columbia, S.C., Jan. 14, 1912; s. Josiah and Etta (Ferguson) M.; m. Frances Belkin, June 28, 1936; children: Jonathan Irving, Carolyn Herman. AB, U. S.C., 1932, MA, 1933; PhD, Pa. State U., 1952. Reporter Columbia (S.C.) Record, 1933-34; mng. editor Am. Banker, N.Y.C., 1934-43; asst. editor The Nation, N.Y.C., 1943-45; U.N. corr. Free Press India, N.Y.C., 1945-47; from instr. to prof. Pa. State U., University Park, 1948-67; prof. English, Temple U., Phila., 1967-79. Author: The Sympathetic Alien, 1959, Matters of Style, 1968, The Irrelevant English Teacher, 1972, Prejudice and Literature, 1976; book rev. editor Jour. Gen. Edn., University Park, 1960-67; editorial advisor Jour. Modern Lit., Phila., 1969—. Advanced grad. fellow Am. Assn. Learned Socs., 1951. Mem. Modern Lang. Assn. (editorial bd. PMLA 1970-74), Am. Jewish Congress, Anti Defamation League B'nai B'rith, Franklin Inn Club (Phila.).

MORSE, RICHARD ALAN, accountant; b. Newburgh, N.Y., Mar. 2, 1954; s. Wesley Benjamin and Louise Barbara (Spinner) M. BS, Ill. State U., 1977. CPA, N.Y. Pvt. practice acctg. N.Y.C., N.Y., 1977—. Actor in various plays, films and TV shows. Mem. N.Y. State Soc. CPAs, AFTRA, Screen Actor's Guild, Actor's Equity Assn.

MORSE, STEPHEN SCOTT, virologist, immunologist; b. N.Y.C., Nov. 22, 1951; s. Murray H. and Phyllis Morse; m. Marilyn Gewirtz, Feb. 1991. BS, CCNY, 1971; MS, U. Wis., 1974, PhD, 1977. NSF trainee dept. bacteriology U. Wis., Madison, 1971-72, rsch. asst., 1972-77; rsch. fellow Nat. Cancer Inst.-Med. Coll. Va./Va. Commonwealth U., Richmond, 1977-80, instr., 1980-81; asst. prof. microbiology Rutgers U., New Brunswick, N.J., 1981-85; rsch. assoc. Rockefeller U., N.Y.C., 1985-88, asst. prof., 1988—; cons. U.S. Congress Office Tech. Assessment, Washington, 1989-90; chair conf. on emerging viruses NIH, 1989; cons. Inst. Medicine-Nat. Acad. Scis., com. mem. microbial threats to health, chair subcom. on viruses, 1990—. Mem. Am. Soc. Microbiology, Am. Assn. Pathologists, Am. Assn. Immunologists, Marine Biol. Lab., Sigma Xi. Office: Rockefeller U 1230 York Ave New York NY 10021-6399

MORSE, WILLIAM MICHAEL, physicist; b. Portland, Maine, May 16, 1947; s. Donald Richard and Eileen Marie (Bartlett) M.; m. Sara Ellen Troyer, Aug. 19, 1973; children: Andrew, Kathleen, David, Rachel. BS, SUNY, Stony Brook, 1969; PhD, Purdue U., 1976. Physicist Brookhaven Nat. Lab., Upton, N.Y., 1976—. Mem. Am. Phys. Soc. Methodist. Office: Brookhaven Nat Lab Physics Dept Upton NY 11973

MORSTAIN, BARRY ROLAN, public policy educator, agency consultant; b. Toledo, July 12, 1944; s. Harold C.L. and Sarah G. (Yourist) M.; m. Jeri D. Metallo, Oct. 19, 1984; m. Jacqueline F. Spelman, Aug. 15, 1967 (div. 1975). BS, Bowling Green State U., 1966; MA, Kent State U., 1968; PhD, U. Calif., Berkeley, 1972. Rsch. asst. NSF Bowling Green State U., 1963-64; rsch. counselor Vocat. Rehab. Ctr., Akron, Ohio, 1967-68; rsch. assoc. Project for Undergrad. Edn., Berkeley, Calif., 1968-70, Ednl. Testing Svc., Berkeley, Calif., 1970-71; from dir. academic planning to assoc. prof. U. Del., 1971—; pres. Micro League Sports, Inc., Newark, Del., 1982-89, Devel. Rsch. Assocs., Chadds Ford, Pa., 1977—; cons. various pub. sector agencies, 1979—. Author numerous profl. articles, 1971—. Baseball coach Police Athletic League, WIlmington, Del., 1990—. S. Frohman scholar Bowling Green State U., 1964-65, Solen E. Summerfield scholar, 1965-66; Nat. Inst. Edn. grantee U. Del., 1977-79. Mem. AAUP, Internat. Personnel Mgmt. Assn., Internat. Assn. Chiefs Police, Internat. Fire Chiefs Assn. Office: U Del Graham Hall Coll of Urban Affairs and Public Policy Newark DE 19716 Cons Office: 500 Kennett Pike Chadds Ford PA 19317

MORTENSEN, EUGENE PHILLIPS, hospital administrator; b. N.Y.C., Mar. 28, 1941; s. Eugene Phillips and Mary (Hogarty) M.; m. Ellen Louise McDavitt, Aug. 8, 1964; children: Jeffrey Phillips, Jennifer-Kristin McDavitt. BA, Seton Hall U., 1963; MS in Mgmt., Frostburg State U., 1974; M in Profl. Studies, Cornell U., 1976. Commd. 2d lt. U.S. Army, 1963, advanced through grades to maj., 1971; med. budget advisor Office Army Surgeon Gen., Cholon, Vietnam, 1968-69; chief materials mgmt. br. and test and standards Office of Compt., Office Surgeon Gen., Washington, 1969-71; chief systems div. and health care system br. U.S. Army Health Svcs. Data Systems Agy., Ft. Detrick, Md., 1971-74, resigned, 1974; asst. adminstr. for gen. svcs. St. Joseph's Hosp. and Med. Ctr., Paterson, N.J., 1976-79, for clin. svcs., 1979-83, v.p. clin. svcs., 1983-89, exec. v.p., chief operating officer, 1989-92; sr. v.p. for operation, chief oper. officer Jersey City Med. Ctr., 1992—. Mem. editorial bd. Perinatal Newsletter, 1984-92. Coach Upper Saddle River (N.J.) Soccer Assn., 1986—; webelos den leader Cub Scouts Am., Upper Saddle River, 1986-90; asst. scoutmaster Boy Scouts Am., 1990—; trustee N.J. Vis. Health Svcs., Totawa, 1988-92; trustee, mem. adv. bd. Passaic Valley Hospice, Totawa, 1986-92. Decorated Bronze Star. Fellow Am. Coll. Healthcare Execs. (coun. regents); mem Am. Hosp. Assn., N.J. Hosp. Assn. (coun. on govt. rels. 1992—), Paterson C. of C. (bd. dirs. 1989—). Republican. Roman Catholic. Home: 8 Iron Latch Ct Upper Saddle River NJ 07458-2005 Office: Jersey City Med Ctr 50 Baldwin Ave Jersey City NJ 07304

MORTLAND, DONALD FRANK, English educator; b. Searsport, Maine, Jan. 20, 1927; s. Ralph Irving and Annie Rolfe (Buck) M.; m. Jacqueline Alice Currier, Aug. 23, 1956; children: Deborah, Pamela. AB, Bowdoin Coll., 1950; AM, Yale U., 1953; D of New Eng. Lit. (hon.), Unity Coll., 1980. English tchr. Potter Acad., Sebago, Maine, 1950-52, Pemetic High Sch., Southwest Harbor, Maine, 1953-56, South Portland (Maine) High Sch., 1956-57, Searsport High Sch., 1957-59, New Hampton (N.H.) Sch., 1959-66; prof. English Unity (Maine) Coll., 1966—. Editor: Sea Stories, 1987; contbr. article, story to profl. pubs. Speaker Unity Union Ch., 1990. Staff sgt. U.S. Army, 1945-46. Mem. Phi Beta Kappa. Republican. Methodist. Home: PO Box 63 Unity ME 04988-0063 Office: Unity Coll Quaker Hill Unity ME 04988

MORTLOCK, ROBERT PAUL, microbiologist, educator; b. Bronxville, N.Y., May 12, 1931; s. Donald Robert and Florance Mary (Bellaby) M.; m. Florita Mary Welling, Sept., 1954; children—Florita M., Jeffrey R., Douglas P. B.S., Rensselaer Poly. Inst., N.Y., 1953; Ph.D., U. Ill., Urbana, 1958. Asst. prof. microbiology U. Mass., Amherst, 1963-68, assoc. prof. microbiology, 1968-73, prof. microbiology, 1973-78; prof. microbiology Cornell U., Ithaca, N.Y., 1978—. Editor: Microorganisms as Model Systems for Studying Evolution, 1984, The Evolution of Metabolic Function, 1992. Served to 1st lt. U.S. Army, 1959-61. Fellow Am. Acad. Microbiology; mem. AAAS, Am. Soc. Microbiology, Northeastern Microbiologists, Physiology, Ecology and Taxonomy (pres. 1984-91). Office: Cornell U Sect Microbiology Wing Hall Ithaca NY 14853

MORTON, EDWARD JAMES, insurance company executive; b. Ft. Wayne, Ind., Nov. 8, 1926; s. Clifford Leroy and Clara Marie (Merklein) M.; m. Jean Ann McClernon, Apr. 30, 1949; children: Marcia Lynn, Anne; m. Matthild Schneider, Sept. 19, 1986; 1 child, Katharine. BA, Yale U., 1949. With John Hancock Mut. Life Ins. Co., Boston, 1949—, v.p., then sr. v.p., 1967-74, exec. v.p., 1974-82, pres., chief operating officer, 1982-86, chmn., chief exec. officer, 1987-91; bd. dirs. John Hancock Mutual Life Ins. Co., M/A-COM, Inc. Trustee Gettysburg Coll.; trustee, chmn. Egyptian and Ancient Nr. Ea. Art, mem. corp. adv. com. Mus. Fine Arts; bd. overseers Boston Symphony Orch.; hon. life overseer Children's Hosp.; mem. Boston Pub. Libr. Partnership; hon. dir. Nat. Scoliosis Found.; bd. dirs. Greater Boston Arts Fund, John F. Kennedy Ctr. for Performing Arts, Washington;

chmn. 1991 Boston Geog. Savs. Bonds Campaign. Fellow Soc. Actuaries; mem. Nat. Assn. Security Dealers (prin.), Actuaries Club Boston, Comml. Club of Boston, Algonquin Club of Boston, Phi Beta Kappa. Office: John Hancock Mut Life Ins Co PO Box 111 Boston MA 02117-0111

MORTON, ELAINE LESLIE, political scientist; b. N.Y.C., Aug. 9, 1937; d. Lewis Matthias and Miriam (Bidner) Morton; m. Allan Shale Krass, July 16, 1961 (div. 1971); 1 child, Caroline Diane. BA with great distinction, Stanford U., 1959; MA, Fletcher Sch. Law & Diplomacy, Medford, Mass., 1960; PhD, Stanford U., 1972. Asst. prof. Rutgers U., New Brunswick, N.J., 1971-74; spl. asst. to dir. Bur. of Intelligence and Rsch. Dept., Washington, 1974-78; mem. policy planning staff Dept. of State, Washington, 1978-85; mem. nat. security coun. staff Exec. Office of the Pres., Washington, 1985-86; sr. policy advisor Office of the Legal advisor, Dept. of State, Washington, 1986-90; vis. sr. fellow Ctr. for Strategic & Internat. Studies, Washington, 1990—. Recipient Commendation Pres. of U.S., 1982, Morris Abrams prize Morris Abrams Found., Chgo., 1970; Woodrow Wilson fellow, 1960, NRC/ACDA fellow, 1970-71. Mem. Phi Beta Kappa. Home: 4620 N Park Ave Apt 1504W Chevy Chase MD 20815 Office: Ctr Strategic & Internat 1800 K St NW Washington DC 20006-2202

MORTON, ROBERT ALLEN, small business owner; b. Boston, Oct. 18, 1954; s. Ralph A. and A. Louise (Dibblee) M.; m. Cynthia Walpole, Apr. 19, 1980; children: Angela Walpole, Jared Walpole. Grad. high sch., Walpole. Machinist Foxboro (Mass.) Co., 1972-73, Bird Machine Co., South Walpole, 1973-75; v.p., treas. A&W Instruments, Inc., Walpole, 1976-88, pres., 1988—. Member Nat. Arbor Day Found., 1985—, Mass. Audubon Soc., 1988—, Nat. Parks & Conservation Assn., 1990—; sustaining mem. Rep. Nat. Com., 1991—. Mem. Nat. Fedn. of Ind. Bus. (guardian mem. 1981—), Neponset Valley C. of C. Roman Catholic. Office: A&W Instruments Inc 405 Street St Walpole MA 02081-0109

MORTON, ROBERT JOHN, newspaper editor in chief; b. Kingsport, Tenn., Apr. 19, 1949; s. Stephen Andrew Jr. and Mary Cooper (Hill) M.; m. Choon Boon Shin, July 1, 1982; 1 child, Laurene Sunmee. BS in Math., Milligan (Tenn.) Coll., 1971; MA in Communications, U. Tex., 1977. Investigative reporter News World, N.Y.C., 1977-78, Tokyo corr., 1978-80, internat. editor, 1980; editor in chief, v.p. N.Y. City Tribune, 1980-91; corp. editor Washington Times Corp., 1991—; mng. editor Global Affairs, Washington, 1986-90; editor Free Press Internat. Report, N.Y.C., 1980-91. Mem. Overseas Press Club, Am. Soc. Newspaper Editors, East Side Conservative Club. Office: Washington Times Corp 3600 New York Ave NE Washington DC 20002-1996

MORTON, WILLIAM GILBERT, JR., stock exchange executive; b. Syracuse, N.Y., Mar. 13, 1937; s. William Gilbert and Barbara (Link) M.; m. Margaret Halleron, Nov. 26, 1982; children: Andrew Baker, William Gilbert III, Sarah Ellsworth, Kate Spencer. BA, Dartmouth Coll., 1959; MBA, NYU, 1965. Asst. v.p. Discount Corp. N.Y., 1960-67; co-mgr. trading, sr. v.p., dir. Mitchell Hutchins Inc., 1967-79; mng. stock exchange floors, sr. v.p., dir. Dean Witter Reynolds Inc., 1979-85; chmn., chief exec. officer Boston Stock Exchange Inc., 1985—; chmn. allocation com. N.Y. Stock Exchange, floor official, 1976-81, various working coms. 1970-85; bd. dirs. Tandy Corp., Ft. Worth. Bd. dirs. Vt. Acad., Saxtons River; trustee search com. Dartmouth Alumni Coun., 1988-91; bd. Overseers Boys & Girls Club Boston. With USMC, 1959-65. Mem. Field Club Greenwich (Conn., bd. dirs.), Algonquin Club (Boston), Racquet and Tennis Club N.Y.C., N.Y. Stock Exch. Luncheon Club, Stratton Mt. Country Club (Vt.), Colo. Arlberg Club (Winter Park), Boston Econ. Club, Theta Delta Chi. Republican. Presbyterian. Office: Boston Stock Exch 1 Boston Pl Boston MA 02108-4401

MOSACK, MARGUERITE ANN, psychologist, educator; b. Garfield Heights, Ohio, May 14, 1951; d. Anthony Joseph and Christine Clarice Mosack. BA, U. Dallas, 1973; MA in Psychology, Duquesne U., 1984. Lic. psychologist, Pa. Psychotherapist Duquesne U. Counseling & Testing Ctr., Pitts., 1985-87; psychol. evaluator Pitts. Assessment and Consultation Ctr., 1985-87; psychology intern Staunton Clinic at Sewickley (Pa.) Valley Hosp., 1987-88; psychologist Northeastern Pa. Counseling Ctr., Kingston, 1988-91; pvt. practice Wilkes-Barre, Pa., 1991—; instr. psychology Community Coll. Allegheny County, Pitts., 1986, Pa. State U., Lehman; grad. instr. mental health referral Inst. Formative Spirituality, Duquesne U., Pitts., 1988; instr. grad. mgmt. Misericordia Coll., Dallas, Pa., 1990; lectr., cons. We Are Remembered Ministry Diocese of Pitts., 1986-87; presenter women's spirituality Luzerne County Women's Conf., Wilkes-Barre, 1989-90; presenter psychol. issues of elderly Misericordia Coll. Conf., 1989; presenter stress mgmt. ARC, Persian Gulf Support Groups, 1991; instr. assertiveness tng. for educators Pa. State U., 1991. Mem. APA, Northeastern Pa. Psychol. Assn., Pa. Psychol. Assn., Luzerne County Women's Network.

MOSBACHER, GEORGETTE PAULSIN, cosmetics executive; b. Hammond, Ind., Jan. 16, 1947; d. George Michael and Dorothy (Bell) Paulsin; m. Robert Mosbacher Sr., Mar. 1, 1985. BS, Ind. U., 1969; DFA (hon.), Internat. Fine Arts Coll., 1990; DBA (hon.), Bryant U., 1992. Chief exec. officer, chmn. La Prairie, Inc., N.Y.C.; v.p. licensing Faberge, Inc., N.Y.C.; CEO Georgette Mosbacher Enterprises, N.Y.C.; past chmn. La Prairie, Inc., N.Y.C. Bd. dirs. Houston Gran Opera Exec. Com., Am. Hosp. in Paris, Ind. U. Found., Statute of Liberty/Ellis Island Commn., Am. Art Alliance, M.D. Anderson Hosp.; mem. adv. bd. Ctr. for Strategic Internat. Studies; bd. dir. Child Help U.S.A. Mem. Women's Econ. Alliance.

MOSBY, DEWEY FRANKLIN, art museum administrator; b. San Augustine, Tex., Jan. 2, 1942; s. Dewey and Jessie Evelyn (Jones-Garner) M.; B.S., Lamar U., 1963; M.A., UCLA, 1969; Ph.D., Harvard U., 1973; children: Christopher D., Veronique. Asst. prof. SUNY, Buffalo, 1973-74; vis. asst. prof. Harvard U., 1974; curator European art The Detroit Inst. Arts, 1974-81; dir. The Picker Art Gallery Colgate U., 1981—; mem. policy panel NEA Mus. Program, 1977-81; panelist NEH programs, 1979-82. Served with U.S. Army, 1964-66. Decorated chevalier Ordre des Arts et des Lettres, 1979, Order Costantiniano di St. Giorgio Neapolitan decoration, 1981. Mem. Coll. Art Assn. Am., Am. Assn. Mus., Societe de l'Histoire de l'Art Francais. Author: Alexandre Gabriel Decamps 1803-1860, 1977, Henry Ossawa Tanner, 1991; contbr. articles to profl. jours. Office: Colgate U The Picker Art Gallery Hamilton NY 13346

MOSCATELLI, JOHN JOSEPH, public relations executive; b. Phila., Mar. 15, 1944; s. P.J. and Charlotte (Migliore) M.; m. Gerry A. Gerew, July 3, 1965; children: Ann Marie, John Andrew. BS in History, St. Joseph's U., 1965. Commd. 2d lt. USAF, 1965, advanced through grades to maj., 1981; ret., 1986; account exec. Kalish & Rice, Phila., 1986-87; account supr. Earle Palmer Brown, Phila., 1987-89; v.p. pub. rels. Earle Palmer Brown & Spiro, Phila., 1989-91, sr. v.p. pub. rels., 1991—; mem. adj. faculty communications dept. Glassboro (N.J.) State Coll., 1988—. Bd. dirs. Utility Emergency Svcs. Fund, Phila., 1990—. Recipient EPIC award Internat. Assn. Bus. Communicators, 1988, 91. Mem. Pub. Rels. Soc. Am. (accredited, pres.-elect Phila. chpt. 1992—, Bronze Anvil award 1988, 91), Air Force Assn. Office: Earle Palmer Brown & Spiro One Liberty Pl 1650 Market St Philadelphia PA 09103-7301

MOSE, JEFFREY LEE, marketing administrator; b. Hagerstown, Md., Feb. 9, 1953; s. Terry Lee and Arlene Kay (Eichelberger) M.; m. Melisa Lea Paye, June 7, 1991. AA, Hagerstown Jr. Coll., 1984; BS, Towson State U., 1986; MS, Syracuse (N.Y.) U., 1987. Sales exec. Brooks Robinson Sporting Goods, Balt., 1976-77, Nike, Annapolis, Md., 1977-79; sales mgr. H.W. Wright & Co., Ltd., Balt., 1979-82; sports dir. Antietam Cable TV, Hagerstown, 1983-85; talent/producer Md. Pub. TV, Owings Mills, 1985-86; announcer Sta. WAER-FM, Syracuse, 1986-88; sr. account exec. Sta. WCNY-TV/FM, Syracuse, 1987-88; sr. mgr. mktg. Sta. WPBT2, Miami, Fla., 1988-90; dir. of mktg. Sta. WJHU-FM, Balt., 1990—. Vol. Lady Md. Found., Balt., 1992—. With USN, 1971-74. Recipient Leadership award Hagerstown Jr. Coll., 1984, Tolbert award Towson State U., 1985, Patrick J. O'Connell award, 1985. Mem. Devel. Exch., Am. Legion, Syracuse U. Alumni Greater Balt. (pres. 1992—), Omicron Delta Kappa. Home: 6814 Bonnie Ridge Dr # 102 Baltimore MD 21209

MOSELEY, CHRIS ROSSER, marketing executive; b. Balt., Apr. 13, 1950; d. Thomas Earl and Fern Elaine (Coleman) Rosser; m. Thomas Kenneth Moseley. BA with honors, The Coll. of Wooster, 1972. Asst. dir. advt. and promotion Sta. WBAL-TV, Balt., 1972-74; dir. pub. rels. Mintz & Hoke Advt. Inc., Hartford, Conn., 1974-75; promotion mgr. Sta. WFSB-TV, Hartford, 1975-77; audience promotion mgr. Sta. WTVJ-TV, Miami, Fla., 1977-78; pres. CMA Mktg. Cons., Hyde Park, N.Y., 1979-82; promotion mgr. Ind. Network News-Sta. WPIX-TV, N.Y.C., 1982-84; sr. v.p., mgmt. supr. Christopher Thomas Muller Jordan Weiss, N.Y.C., 1984-89, Earle Palmer Brown/N.Y., N.Y.C., 1989-90; sr. v.p. mktg. and communications Discovery Networks, Bethesda, Md., 1990—. Recipient Emmy award local broadcasting, 1977, Bronze medal Internat. Film and TV Festival, 1983, Merit award N.Y. Art Dirs. Club, 1984, Best Business-to-Business award Art Direction mag., 1984. Mem. CTAM, BPME/BDA, WIC, AWNY. Democrat. Home: PO Box 418 Riderwood MD 21139-0418 Office: Discovery Networks 7700 Wisconsin Ave Bethesda MD 20814-3578

MOSENTHAL, PETER BOOTH, language educator; b. Passaic, N.J., Dec. 6, 1947; s. Andreae Waters and Barbara (Gunschel) M.; m. Randie Lynn Davidson, Aug. 16, 1979; children: Beth Rebecca, Lauren Andreae. BA, Coll. of Wooster, 1969; MA, Ohio State U., 1971, PhD, 1975. Rsch. cons. Battelle Meml. Labs., Columbus, Ohio, 1973-75; asst. prof. SUNY, Geneseo, 1975-77; assoc. dir. Ctr. for Literacy Studies SUNY, Albany, 1977-80; prof. Syracuse (N.Y.) U., 1980-84, 85—, dir. Literacy Consultation Ctr., 1991—, chmn. reading and lang. arts ctr., 1991—; vis. rsch. scientist IBM Yorktown Heights (N.Y.) Rsch. Ctr., 1984-85; literacy cons. BOCES, Syracuse, 1991, Fla. Inst. Edn., Jacksonville, 1987-89, edtl. testing svc., 1988-92. Mem. editorial adv. bd. Reading Research Quar., Elem. Sch. Jour., Jour. Ednl. Psychology, Review of Edn. Fellow Nat. Coun. Researchers in English; mem. Internat. Reading Assn., Am. Acad. Scis., Am. Psychol. Assn., Nat. Coun. Tchrs. English, Nat. Reading Conf. Office: Syracuse U 170 Huntington Rd Syracuse NY 13244-0001

MOSER, ANN BOODY, biochemist; b. Wakefield, Mass., Feb. 7, 1940; d. Philip Cutler and Esther (Hanson) Boody; m. Hugo Wolfgang Moser, Dec. 28, 1963; children: Karen Maria, Lauren Esther. BA, Radcliffe Coll., 1961. Rsch. technician McLean Hosp., Belmont, Mass., 1961-63, Mass. Gen. Hosp., Boston, 1963-68, Eunice Kennedy Shriver Ctr., Waltham, Mass., 1968-76; sr. technician Kennedy Inst., Balt., 1976—; asst. in neurology Johns Hopkin's U./Kennedy Inst., Balt., 1982-91, rsch. assoc. neurology, 1991—. Author: (chpt.) The Metabolic Basis of Inherited Disease, Techniques in Diagnostic Human Biochemical Genetics, 1991; contbr. numerous articles to profl. jours. Member choir Univ. Bapt. Ch., Balt., 1984—, mem. music com., 1986—. Mem. LWV, Am. Soc. Neurochemistry, Am. Soc. Human Genetics. Home: 100 Beechdale Rd Baltimore MD 21210-2209 Office: Kennedy Inst 707 N Broadway Baltimore MD 21205-1832

MOSER, DONALD BRUCE, magazine editor; b. Cleve., Oct. 19, 1932; s. Donald Lyman and Kathryn (McHugh) M.; m. Penny Lee Ward, Dec. 20, 1975. B.A., Ohio U., 1957; postgrad., Stanford U., 1975-58, U. Sydney, 1959-60. With Life mag., 1961-72, West Coast bur. chief, 1964-65, Far East bur. chief, 1966-69, asst. mng. editor, 1970-72; free-lance writer, 1972-77; exec. editor Smithsonian mag., Washington, 1977-80; editor Smithsonian mag., 1981—. Author: The Peninsula, 1962, The Snake River Country, 1974, A Heart to the Hawks, 1975, Central American Jungles, 1976, China-Burma-India, 1978; contbr. articles to numerous mags., jours. Served with U.S. Army, 1953-55. Stegner fellow, 1957-58; Fulbright scholar, 1959-60. Mem. Phi Beta Kappa. Office: Smithsonian Mag 900 Jefferson Dr SW Washington DC 20560-0001

MOSER, M(ARTIN) PETER, lawyer; b. Balt., Jan. 16, 1928; s. Herman and Henrietta (Lehmayer) M.; m. Elizabeth Kohn, June 14, 1949; children—Mike, Moriah, Jeremy. A.B., The Citadel, Charleston, S.C., 1947; LL.B., Harvard U., 1950. Bar: Md. 1950, U.S. Supreme Ct., U.S. Ct. Appeals (4th cir.), U.S. Dist. Ct. Md. Asst. states atty. City of Balt., 1951, 53-54; assoc. Blades Rosenfeld, Balt., 1950, 53-54; ptnr. Frank, Bernstein, Conaway & Goldman and predecessor firms, Balt., 1955-90, co-chmn. firm, 1983-86; counsel, 1991-92, Piper & Marbury, 1992—; instr. U. Balt. Law Sch., 1954-56, 86, U. Md. Law Sch., 1986-87. Contbr. articles to profl. jours. Del., chmn. local govt. com. Md. Constl. Conv., 1967-68; mem. Balt. City Planning Commn., 1961-66, Balt. Regional Planning Council, 1963-66, Md. Commn. to Study Narcotics Laws, 1965-67, Mayor's Task Force on EEO, 1966-67, Met. Transit Authority Adv. Council, 1962, Com. to Revise Balt. City Planning Laws, 1962, Com. to Revise Balt. City Charter Provision on Conflicts of Interest, 1969-70; mem. Citizens Adv. Com. on Dist. Ct., chmn., 1971, Dist. Adv. Bd. for Pub. Defender System for Dist. 1, 1973-85; mem. Atty. Grievance Commn. of Md., 1975-78, chmn. 82-86; chmn. Md. State Ethics Commn., 1987-89; bd. dirs. Sinai Hosp., 1983—, Ct. of Appeals Comm. to Study the Model Rules, 1983-86. Served with JAGC, U.S. Army, 1951-53. Fellow Am. Bar Found., Md. Bar Found.; mem. ABA (ho. of dels. 1978—, treas.-elect 1992—, bd. govs. 1984-87, 92—, ethics com. 1981-84, 87-90, chmn. 1981-82, 87-90, scope and cor. com. 1987-92, chmn. 1990-91), Md. State Bar Assn. (pres. 1979-80), Balt. Bar Assn. (pres. 1971-72), Assn. Trial Lawyers Am., Fed. Bar Assn., Am. Law Inst. Democrat. Jewish. Clubs: Wednesday Law, Lawyers' Round Table, Hamilton St. Office: Frank Bernstein Conaway & Goldman 300 E Lombard St Ste 19 Baltimore MD 21202-3226

MOSES, ALFRED HENRY, lawyer; b. Balt., July 24, 1929; s. Leslie William and Helene Amelia (Lobe) M.; m. Carol Whitehill, Nov. 24, 1955; Barbara, Jennifer, David, Amalie. BA, Dartmouth, 1951; student, Woodrow Wilson Sch., Princeton U., 1951-52; JD, Georgetown U., 1956. Bar: D.C. 1956. Assoc. Covington & Burling, Washington, 1956-65, ptnr., 1965—; special advisor, special counsel Pres. Jimmy Carter, Washington, 1980-81; legal advisor minority rights Dem. Nat. Com., Washington, 1969, DC Commision on Urban Renewal, 1972; lectr. Am. Law Inst., ABA, New Orleans, 1970, Am. Inst. CPAs, ABA, Washington, 1969, Georgetown U. Law Ctr., 1971, Tax Exec. Inst., Washington, 1967-68, Tulane Tax Inst., New Orleans, 1971; commr. Pub. Housing, Fairfax County, Va., 1971-72. Contbr. articles, commentaries to jours. Co-chmn. legal div. United Givers Fund, Wahsington, 1975-76; mem. Coun. Fgn. Rels., N.Y.C., 1977—; bd. dirs. Paralysis Cure Rsch. Found., 1978-81; trustee Phelps Stokes Fund, N.Y.C., 1978-84; pres. Nat. Children's Island, Washington, 1975-76; trustee Jewish Publ. Soc., 1989—, Haifa U., 1988-90; pres. Am. Jewish Com., 1991—; mem. bd. regents Georgetown U., 1986—. Mem. ABA, D.C. Bar Assn., Golda Meir Assn. (pres. 1986-88, nat. chmn. 1988—), City Club (gov. 1986—), Met. Club. Democrat. Jewish. Home: 7710 Georgetown Pike Mc Lean VA 22102-1412 Office: Covington & Burling PO Box 7566 1201 Pennsylvania Ave NW Washington DC 20044

MOSES, HAMILTON, III, neurology educator, hospital executive; b. Chgo., Apr. 29, 1950; s. Hamilton Jr. and Betty Anne (Theurer) M.; m. Elizabeth Lawrence Hormel, 1977 (dec. 1988); m. Alexandra MacCollough Gibson, 1992. BA in Psychology, U. Pa., 1972; MD, Rush Med. Coll., Chgo., 1975. Intern in medicine Johns Hopkins Hosp., Balt., 1976-77, resident in neurology, 1977-79, chief resident, 1979-80, assoc. prof. neurology, 1986—, vice chmn. neurology and neurosurgery, 1980-86, v.p., 1988—, dir. Parkinson's Ctr., 1984—. Editor, major author: Principles of Medicine, 1985-88; editor newsletter Johns Hopkins Health, 1988—; contbr. numerous articles to med. jours. Mem. com. on med. ministries Episcopal Diocese Md., Balt., 1987; bd. dirs. Valleys Planning Ct. Mem. Am. Acad. Neurology (sec. 1989—), Am. Neurol. Assn., Md. Neurol. Soc. (pres. 1984-86), Movement Disorders Soc., Md. Club, Green Spring Valley Hunt Club (Garrison, Md.). Republican. Office: Johns Hopkins Hosp 600 N Wolfe St Baltimore MD 21205-2104

MOSES, JOHNNIE, JR., microbiologist; b. N.Y.C., May 24, 1939; s. Johnnie Moses and Lillie Ann (Williams) Dillahunt; m. Mirian Louise Mosely, Aug. 16, 1958; children: Nicholas G., Adrianne D. BA, Fordham U., 1978; MA, NYU, 1982. Lic. clin. lab. tech. Lab. technologist Harlem Hosp. Ctr., N.Y.C., 1962-68, sr. lab. technologist, 1968-80, lab. microbiologist, 1980-90, lab. microbiology cons., 1980—, assoc. microbiology, 1990—; hematology isntr. Mandl Med. Asst. Sch., N.Y.C., 1983-85; Am. history prof. Malcolm-King Coll., N.Y.C., 1983-88. Adv. mem. N.Y. State Assembly, N.Y.C., 1988; treas., exec. Addicts Rehab. Ctr., 1975—; treas. Manhattan Christian Reformed Ch., 1975—. Recipient Cert. of Appreciation, Harlem Hosp. Pathology Dept., 1990. Mem. Internat. Soc. Clin. Lab. Tech. (certs. of merit 1982, 91), Fordham U. Alumni Assn., NYU Alumni Assn. Democrat. Home: 990 Tinton Ave Bronx NY 10456-7106 Office: Harlem Hosp Ctr 506 Lenox Ave New York NY 10037-1802

MOSES, LOUIS JEFFREY, career officer; b. Wilmington, Del., Aug. 31, 1943; s. Conrad E. and Rhoda (Seitz) M.; m. Vesna Krondorff, Aug. 12, 1980; 1 child, Iris Ina. BA, Coe Coll., 1967; MBA in Transp. Econs., U. Tenn., 1979; postgrad., Nat. War Coll., 1983. Col., strategy and plans analyst Pacific Air Forces, Honolulu, 1969-73; strategy and analysis officer Directorate of Plans USAF, The Pentagon, Washington, 1973-77, spl. asst. to the undersec., 1979-80; spl. asst. to the chmn. joint chiefs of staff The Pentagon, Washington, 1980-82; sr. fellow Nat. War Coll., Washington, 1982-83; dir. strategy analysis U.S. European Command, Stuttgart, Fed. Republic of Germany, 1983-87; comdr. Hellenikon Air, 7206 Air Base Group, Athens, Greece, 1987-89; base spl. asst., dir. plans Hdqrs., USAF, The Pentagon, Washington, 1989—. Author: The Call for Joint Chiefs of Staff Reform, 1973, (with others) Military Strategy, 1973. Decorated Bronze Star, Legion of Merit, Superior Svc. medals. Mem. Beta Kappa Phi. Home: 7876 Newport Glen Pass Annandale VA 22003-1554

MOSES, NANCY, public relations executive; b. Pitts., Mar. 19, 1948; d. Allen I. and Janet (Baer) M.; m. Myron A. Bloom, Aug. 26, 1974; 1child, Nella Moses Bloom. AB, George Washington U., 1970, MA, 1974. Program chief NEH, Washington, 1972-74; nat. devel. officer Sta. WQED, PBS, Pitts., 1974-75; pres. Moses, Epstein, Wiseman Inc., Washington, 1975-78; assoc. dir. Ctr. for Phila. Studies, U. Pa., Phila., 1978-80; planning dir. Century IV Celebration, City of Phila., 1981-82; mng. dir. Collaborations, Inc., Phila., 1983—. Bd. dirs. Pub. Interest Law Ctr. Phila., 1986-89, Internat. Visitors Ctr., Phila., Phila. Soc. for Preservation Landmarks; com. mem. Greater Phila. Econ. Devel. Coalition, 1989—; mem. Green Platform Com., Phila., 1990-91; del. U.S.-USSR Emerging Leaders Summit, 1990. Recipient spl. achievement award U.S. Govt., 1974. Mem. Forum Exec. Women. Office: Collaborations Inc Ste 308 New Market Philadelphia PA 19147

MOSES, WILSON JEREMIAH, history and English educator; b. Detroit, Mar. 5, 1942; s. William Heard and Ida Mae (Johnson) M.; m. Maureen Connor, Nov. 30, 1963; children: William, Jeremiah. BA, Wayne State U., 1965, MA, 1967; PhD, Brown U., 1975. Asst. prof. U. Iowa, Iowa City, 1971-76; assoc. prof. So. Meth. U., Dallas, 1976-80; assoc. prof. Brown U., Providence, 1980-86, prof. history and English, 1986-88; prof. history and English, dir. AfroAm. studies Boston U., 1988—. Author: Golden Age of Black Nationalism, 1978, Black Messiahs Uncle Toms, 1982, Alexander Crummell, 1989, Wings of Ethiopia, 1990. Mellon Found. fellow, 1978-79, Fulbright fellow, 1983-84, 1987-88, Ford Found. fellow, 1983-84, NEH fellow, 1988. Mem. Alpha Phi Alpha. Roman Catholic. Office: Boston U 138 Mountfort St Brookline MA 02146

MOSHER, FREDERICK KENNETH, engineering consultant; b. Middletown, N.Y., Aug. 25, 1943; s. Fred J. and Ruth M. (Werlau) M.; student N.Y.U., 1970-72, Lafayette U., 1973-74; m. Gail J. Berry, Jan. 24, 1968; children—Scott, Kerri, Dean. With Mayo, Lynch & Assos., Architect & Engrs., Hoboken, N.J., 1962-64, designer, 1964-69; mech. designer Louis Goldberg & Assos., Metuchen, N.J., 1969-74, assoc., 1975; partner Brownworth, Mosher & Doran, Piscataway, N.J., 1976-90, Mosher & Doran, Edison, N.J., 1990—. Pres., St. Luke's Luth. Ch., Washington, N.J., 1975-81; mem. Warren County Uniform Constrn. Code Bd. Appeals. Served with Security Agy., U.S. Army, 1965-71. Recipient Mem. Recognition award Cons. Engrs. Coun. N.J., 1990. Fellow Am. Soc. Cert. Engring. Technicians, Am. Cons. Engring. Coun. (Nat. Award for Engring. Excellence 1979); mem. N.J. Cons. Engrs. Coun. (chmn. engring. excellence com.), Am. Soc. Mil. Engrs., IEEE, ASHRAE (3d pl. award for alternative or renewable energy utilization 1982), Nat. Soc. Profl. Engrs., Constrn. Specification Inst. Lutheran. Home: 21 Oak Ridge Rd Washington NJ 07882-1503 Office: Ste 300 3090 Woodbridge Ave Edison NJ 08818

MOSHER, GREGORY DEAN, director; b. N.Y.C., Jan. 15, 1949; s. Thomas Edward and Florence Christine M. Student, Oberlin Coll., 1967-69; B.F.A., Ithaca Coll., 1971; postgrad., Juilliard Sch., 1971-74. Dir. Stage 2, Goodman Theatre, Chgo., 1974-77, artistic dir., 1978-85; dir. Lincoln Ctr. Theater, 1985-92, resident dir., 1992—; producer new works by Tennessee Williams, Studs Terkel, David Mamet, John Guare, Michael Weller, Wole Soyinka, Elaine May, David Rabe, Mbongeni Ngema, Edward Albee, Spalding Gray, Arthur Miller, Leonard Bernstein, Stephen Sondheim, Richard Nelson, Jerome Robbins; producer: Samuel Beckett's first directing work in U.S., Krapp's Last Tape, 1979, Endgame, 1980; dir.: Glengarry Glen Ross (David Mamet), Broadway, 1984-85, (premieres of Mamet's) Am. Buffalo, 1975, A Life in the Theatre, 1977, Edmond, 1982; dir., prodr.: Speed-the-Plow (David Mamet), Danger: Memory! (Miller premiere), 1987, Broadway, 1988, London, 1989, Our Town (50th Anniversary prodn., Thornton Wilder), Broadway, 1988, (BBC/Sta. WNET co-prodn.) Uncle Vanya, 1990, (Elaine May premiere) A Streetcar Named Desire, Broadway, 1992.

MOSHER, LOREN RICHARD, psychiatrist; b. Monterey, Calif., Sept. 3, 1933; s. Harold and Anne (O'Brien) M.; m. Irene Carleton, May 26,1 961 (div. 1972); children: Hal, Tim, Missy; m. Judy Schreiber, Apr. 10, 1988. AB, Stanford U., 1956, postgrad., 1956-58; MD, Harvard U., 1961. Diplomate Am. Bd. Psychiatry and Neurology, Nat. Bd. Med. Examiners. Asst. prof. psychiatry Yale U., New Haven, 1967-68; chief Ctr. Studies of Schizophrenia, div. extramural rsch. NIMH, Rockville, Md., 1968-80; prof. psychiatry U.S. U. Health Sci., Bethesda, Md., 1981-88; assoc. dir. Dept. Addiction, Victim and Mental Health Svcs. County of Montgomery, Rockville, Md., 1988—; clin. prof. U.S. U. Health Sci., Bethesda, Md., 1988—; cons. Va. Dept. Mental Health, Richmond, 1983-88. Co-author: Community Mental Health Principles and Practice, 1989; editor books; editorial adv. bd. Contemporary Family Therapy, Internat. Jour. Therapeutic Communities, Schizophrenia Bull., Psychosocial Rehab. Jour.; contbr. articles to profl. jours. Capt. USPHS, 1974-88. Mem. Mem. Am. Family Therapy Assn. (program com.), Am. Orthopsychiat. Assn. (chair inst. com. 1985-88, mem. program com. 1988—). Home: 3327 Rittenhouse St NW Washington DC 20015-1671 Office: Montgomery County DAVMHS 401 Hungerford Dr Ste 500 Rockville MD 20850-4155

MOSKAL, ANTHONY JOHN, management and education consultant; b. South Amboy, N.J., May 31, 1946; s. Anthony Joseph and Jennie (Salamon) M.; m. Kathryn Jean Coakley, July 8, 1978; 1 child, Nicole Elizabeth. AB, Villanova (Pa.) U., 1968, MA, 1972; MEd, Ga. State U., 1974; PhD, Columbia Pacific U., San Rafael, Calif., 1987. Research mgr. Blue Cross and Blue Shield, Columbus, Ga., 1972-74; sales rep. J.C. Penney Co., Parlin, N.J., 1974-76; dean students Alliance Coll., Cambridge Springs, Pa., 1976-77; tchr. Sayreville (N.J.) pub. schs., 1977-79; county 4-H agt. Rutgers U., New Brunswick, 1979-86; pres. Eagle Assocs., South Amboy, N.J., 1985—; adj. faculty Georgian Ct. Coll., Lakewood, N.J., 1987—, U.S. Army Command and Gen. Staff Coll., Ft. Leavenworth, Kans., 1990—, Nat. Def. U., Washington, 1991; cons. in field; liaison officer U.S. Mil. Acad., 1984—. Contbr. articles to profl. jours. Dir. religious edn. Sacred Heart Parish, South Amboy, N.J., 1988—; counselor Thomas A. Edison coun. Boy Scouts Am., 1982—. With U.S. Army, 1969-71, 90-91, maj., USAR. Decorated Army Commendation medal, Meritorious Svc. medal; United Way of Central Jersey grantee, 1984, others. Mem. N.J. Assn. 4-H Agts. (pres. 1985-86, Outstanding Svc. citation 1981, 87), Nat. Assn. Extension 4-H Agts., Assn. for Supervision and Curriculum Devel., Am. Fedn. Police (Award of Merit 1989, J. Edgar Hoover Meml. medal 1991), Res. Officers Assn., Holy Name Soc., Kiwanis, K.C. Republican. Roman Catholic. Home: 166 Luke St South Amboy NJ 08879-2231 Office: Eagle Assocs PO Box 231 South Amboy NJ 08879-0231

MOSKI, GREGORY EDWARD, university administrator; b. Erie, Pa., Oct. 11, 1953; s. Edward F. and Jeanette E. (Priester) M.; m. Karen Mary Connell, Sept. 20, 1985. BA in Law Enforcement, Mercyhurst Coll., Erie, 1976; MA in Pub. Adminstrn., Edinboro U. of Pa., 1980. Clk. FBI, Washington, 1976-78; grad. asst. Edinboro U of Pa., 1978; grad. intern Pa. Dept. Community Affairs, Erie, 1980; rsch. specialist, rsch. assoc. Mgmt. Engrs. Inc., Reston, Va., 1979-80; coord. projects with industry Dr. Gertrude

Barber Ctr., Erie, 1981-85; job devel. specialist Control Data Corp., Erie, 1984-85; program/job developer Erie Pvt. Industry Coun., 1985-87; grants coord. Edinboro U. of Pa., 1987—; lectr. Edinboro U. of Pa., 1987—. Author, co-author, contbr. numerous grants for acad. and community svc. Vol. United Way Agys. of Erie County, Erie, 1990-91; vol. tutor Edinboro U. of Pa., 1990-91; mem. Erie Community Data Base Task Force, 1989; mem. Erie Excellence Coun. Mem. Am. Assn. State Colls. and Univs. (liaison officer), Continuing Edn. Assn. Pa., Erie Area C. of C. Democrat. Roman Catholic. Home: 480 Moorheadville Rd North East PA 16428-2323 Office: Edinboro U of Pa Taylor House Edinboro PA 16444

MOSKOWITZ, ELLEN S., marketing executive; b. N.Y.C., Mar. 15, 1955; d. Paul and Frances (Green) M.; m. Douglas Ray Sussman, Nov. 18, 1984. Student, Vassar Coll., 1973-75; BA in Geography summa cum laude, Clark U., 1978; M in Mgmt., Yale U., 1984. Rsch. assoc. Clark U., Worcester, Mass., 1978-79; dir. Ethnic Studies Inst. Queens Coll., CUNY, 1979-82; asst. acct. exec. Ogilvy & Mather Direct, N.Y.C., 1983; mktg. dir. Am. Express TRS, N.Y.C., 1984—. Mem. Am. Mktg. Assn., Product Devel. and Mgmt. Assn., Phi Beta Kappa. Jewish. Office: Am Express TRS World Fin Ctr 34th Fl New York NY 10285

MOSKOWITZ, SHIRLEY EDITH, artist; b. Houston, Aug. 4, 1920; d. Joseph Lewis and Flora (Susnitsky) M.; m. Jacob William Gruber; children: Ruth Ellen, Frank, Samuel. BA, Rice U., 1941; MA, Oberlin (Ohio) Coll., 1942; postgrad., Morris Davidson Sch. of Art, 1943, 48, Phila. Coll. of Art, 1974-76. Asst. art dir. Houston Pub. Schs., 1943-46; art supr. Oberlin Pub. Schs., 1946-47. Exhibited in group shows at various mus., U.S., Italy and New Zealand, 1941-91; represented in pub. collections William Penn Mus., Free Libr. of Phila., Museo di Roma, Nat. Mus. of Am. Jewish History, Phila. Mus. of Art, Arco Corp., Bell Atlantic. Recipient Oil Painting prize Houston Mus. of Fine Arts, 1944, Sculpture prize Cheltenham (Pa.) Art Ctr., Woodmere Mus., 1962, IBM Printing prize Phila. Civic Ctr., 1979, Watercolor prize Artist Equity Triennial, 1981. Mem. Am. Color Print Soc., Pa. Acad. Fine Arts, Norristown Art League (pres.), Phila. Watercolor Club (sec. 1968-70), Artist Equity of Phila. (sec. 1980-82). Home: 1530 Locust St Philadelphia PA 19102-4401 Summer Studio: c/o Gruber, 05020 Morre/Morruzze Italy

MOSLEHI, FARID, fluid dynamicist; b. Arak, Iran, Feb. 28, 1959; s. Mohammad Taghi and Fatemeh (Taghavi) M. BS in Aerospace Engring., U. Okla., MS in Aerospace Engring., PhD in Mechanical Engring. Instr., sci. U. Conn. Health Ctr., Farmington, 1988-91; asst. prof., anesthesiology U. Conn. Health Ctr., 1991—. Contbr. articles to profl. jours. and trade jours. Mem. AIAA, Math. Assn. Am., ASME, IEEE. Home: PO Box 655 Farmington CT 06034-0655

MOSS, ALFRED ALFONSO, JR., education educator; b. Chgo., Mar. 2, 1943; s. Alfred Alfonso Sr. and Ruth (Watson) M.; divorced; 1 child, Daniel Clement. BA with honors, Lake Forest Coll., 1965; MDiv, Episcopal Divinity Sch., Cambridge, Mass., 1968; MA, U. Chgo., 1972, PhD, 1977. Asst. minister Episcopal Ch. of the Holy Spirit, Lake Forest, Ill., 1968-70; assoc. chaplain Episcopal Chaplaincy U. Chgo., 1970-75; instr. dept. history U. Md., College Park, 1975-77, asst. prof. dept. history, 1977-83, assoc. prof., 1983—. Author: American Negro Academy, 1981; co-author: Looking at History, 1986, From Slavery To Freedom, 1988; co-editor: The Facts of Reconstruction, 1991. Episcopalian. Office: U Md Dept History College Park MD 20742

MOSS, ANDREA, fundraiser, community service volunteer; b. Balt., Feb. 19, 1943; d. Manuel and Sylvia (Fox) Schwartz; m. Paul Moss, Oct. 23, 1966; Danielle Lea, Kevin Scott, Shara Alyse. BS, U. Md., 1965. Restaurant critic and writer: Gastronome, 1987; bd. advisors Insider's Guide to Florida Restaurants. Pres. Svc. League, Monmouth Med. Ctr., Long Branch, N.J., 1971-73; corr. sec., ball chmn. Ruth Newman Shapiro Cancer & Heart Fund, Atlantic City, N.J., 1977—, bd. dirs, fine arts com. Congregation Beth Israel, Northfield, N.J., 1977—; mem. Atlantic City Med. Ctr. Aux.; co-chmn. Shore Chpt. World Affairs Coun. Phila., Atlantic City, 1985—; nat. bd., founder, chmn. Atlantic County Chpt. Am. Assocs. Ben Gurion U. of the Negev, 1986—; co-chmn. Pro-Am LPGA Atlantic City Classic Golf Tournament, 1985—; Nat. Hostess Com. The Miss America Pageant, Atlantic City, 1989—; mem. nat. gastronome advt. com. Chaine des Rotisseurs, 1990—; com. Save Our Strength, 1988; mem. spl. gifts com. United Way of Atlantic County, 1989-90; host Dine for Dimes March of Dimes; mem. devel. com. Noyes Mus.; mem. Jewish Agy. Com. Atlantic County, Breast Health Inst., Phila., Hadassah and Nat. Coun. Jewish Women, Ashbury Park, N.J., 1971-75; chmn. Gala for RNS Designer Show House, 1992. Named Showstopper of the Year, The Sun Newspaper, Atlantic City, 1985; officer chargé de presse La Chaine des Rotisseurs, 1991, L'Ordre Mondial. Mem. AAUW, Sigma Delta Tau (chpt. historian). Republican. Home: 204 Arbor Ct E Linwood NJ 08221-2152

MOSS, ARTHUR HENSHEY, lawyer; b. Reading, Pa., July 26, 1930; s. John Arthur and Christine Bracken (Henshey) M.; m. E. Leslie Fritz, Feb. 1982; 1 child by previous marriage, John Arthur. AB, Williams Coll., 1952; JD, U. Pa., 1955. Bar: Pa. 1956. Assoc. Montgomery, McCracken, Walker & Rhoads, Phila., 1960-69, ptnr., 1969—. Chmn. Radnor-Haverford-Marple Sewer Authority, 1968-83: pres. Wayne Civic Assn., 1964-65; steward, deacon Wayne Presbyn. Ch., 1963-66, ruling elder, 1966-72, 79-84, 86—, clk. of session, 1971, 78-89, trustee, 1987—; commr. Gen. Assembly Presbyn. Ch. (U.S.A.), 1983; dir. John Bartram Assn., 1987—, treas. 1989—; trustee Presbytery of Phila., 1984. Lt. USN, 1955-60. Mem. ABA, Pa. Bar Assn., Phila. Bar Assn., Radnor Hist. Soc. (dir., sec. 1978-90), The Athanaeum of Phila., Broadacre Trouting Assn., Merion Golf Club, Edgemere Club. Editor: U. Pa. Law Rev., 1954-55. Contbr. articles to profl. jours. Home: 200 Walnut Ave Wayne PA 19087-3423 Office: 20th Fl 3 Parkway Philadelphia PA 19102

MOSS, JACK, print shop executive, textile chemist, consultant; b. Bklyn., Aug. 29, 1928; s. Sol and Rose (Cohen) M.; m. Phyllis Y. Resnick, June 29, 1952; children: William, Michael A. BS in Chemistry, Southeastern Mass. U., 1951. Plant supt. Vitromar Piece Dye, Paterson, N.J., 1951-58; supt. Sudamtex de Uruguay, Colonia, Uruguay, 1958-61; rsch. chemist GAF Corp., Easton, Pa., 1961-66; tech. rep. Sandoz, Inc., East Hanover, N.J., 1966-70, Ventron Corp., Beverly, Mass., 1970-77; cons. Whittaker Textiles, Marysville, N.B., Can., 1977-78; sales mgr., asst. to pres. Apex Chem Corp., Elizabeth, N.J., 1975-77; pres. Jack-B-Quick, Inc., Millburn, N.J., 1978—; chmn. bd. JBQ Printing Svcs., Inc., Livingston, N.J.; cons. in field. Contbr. material on disperse dyes, fiber blends to Chem. Encyc., 1965. Mem. Nat. Assn. Quick Printers, N.J. Assn. Quick Printers (sec., advt. mgr.), C. of C., Masons (master of lodge 1992). Office: Jack B Quick Inc 299 Millburn Ave Millburn NJ 07041-1608

MOSS, JOE FRANCIS, sculptor, painter; b. Kincheloe, W.Va., Jan. 26, 1933; s. Thomas R. and Audra (Frazier) M.; m. Jean Elizabeth Marcrum, July 1, 1952 (dec.); children: Joe Marcrum, Jon Eric, Jay Keith; m. Daphne Nittis Brauner, 1992. BA in Art, W.Va. U., 1955, MA in Art, 1960. Tchr. art Morgantown (W.Va.) High Sch., 1956-60; assoc. prof. art W.Va. U., Morgantown, 1960-70; prof. art U. Del., Newark, 1970—. One-man shows of sculpture Washington Gallery Modern Art, 1967, Russell Mus., Great Falls, Mont., 1973, Sculpture Now Gallery, N.Y.C., 1975, CUNY Grad. Center, 1975, J.B. Speed Mus., Louisville, 1977, Madison Sq. Park, N.Y.C., 1980, Marian Locks Gallery and Marian Locks East, Phila., 1981, Fine Arts Gallery U.M.B.C., Balt., 1986; 20-yr. retrospective Edison Fine Arts Gallery, Ft. Myers, Fla., 1985; exhibited in numerous group shows including, Mus. Modern Art, N.Y.C., 1966, Fischbach Gallery, N.Y.C., 1966, Fellows of the Center Exhbn., M.I.T., 1978, Sculpture Now, N.Y.C., 1979, Laumeier Sculpture Park, St. Louis, 1979, Neuberger Mus., Purchase, N.Y., 1981, Kunsthalle, Hamburg, Fed. Republic Germany, 1985, Robert Moses Plaza, N.Y.C., 1985-86, MIT, 1986 Lights Orot, Yeshiva U., N.Y.C., 1988-89, St. Mary's Coll., South Bend, Inc., 1989—, Hist. and Fine Arts Mus., Anchorage, 1987, Montreal, Can. 1988; traveling exhibits include Multiple Interaction, MIT, also Phila., N.Y.C., L.A., Sculpture 75 Exhbn., Phila., 1975, invitational exhibit, U. Tenn., Chattanooga, 1971; represented in permanent collections Arts and Humanities Council Huntington (W.Va.) Galleries, Polaroid Corp., Cambridge, Mass., Martin Fine Villa, Miami, Fla., Cedarcrest Coll., Allentown, Pa., Johnson Mus., Ithaca, N.Y., Urban Am., Washington, Bloomsburg (Pa.) State Coll., St. Louis Art Mus., Del. Art Mus., others, also pvt. collections; one-man shows of paintings Pa. State U., 1965, Pitts. Playhouse Gallery, 1965, W.Va. U., 1965; exhibited in group shows, Fifty Artists Fifty States, Burpee Mus., Rockford, Ill., 1965, Am. Fedn. Art, 1966-68, Bocour Collection, Keene (N.H.) State Coll., 1974, others, interviews, WTOP-TV, Washington, 1967, Voice of Am, 1967; speaker Internat. Sculpture Conf. Kans. U., Lawrence, 1974; feature CNN including Sci. Week in Rev. Grantee W.Va. U., 1963, 67, 68, U. Del. Research Found., 1971, 72, Dimer Found., 1976-77; vis. research fellow Ctr. for Advanced Visual Studies MIT, Cambridge, 1973, Nat. Endowment for Arts fellow, 1980-81, Del. State Arts Council fellow, 1980-81; recipient 1st prize Nat. Show Huntington Galleries Mus., 1963, Environmental Sculpture award Three Rivers Exhbn., 1968, sculpture award Appalachian Corridors Exhibit, 1968. Home: 801 Valley Rd Newark DE 19711-2585

MOSS, JOEL, medical researcher; b. Bklyn., Nov. 27, 1946. BA, Brandeis U., 1967; MD and PhD, NYU, 1972. Intern, then resident Johns Hopkins Hosp., Balt., 1972-74; rsch. assoc., pulmonary fellow Nat. Heart, Lung and Blood Inst., Bethesda, Md., 1974-77, staff investigator, 1977-79, head molecular mechanisms sect., 1979—, dep. chief lab., 1986—. Office: NIH Rm 5N-307 Bldg # 10 Bethesda MD 20892

MOSS, JUSTIN LESLIE, opera/musical theatre producer; b. San Francisco, Dec. 2, 1947; s. William T. and Ruth (Mitchell) M.; m. Troy-Jjohn Bromberger, Nov. 19, 1978. BA in Lit., Westmont Coll., 1969. Dir. devel. Va. Opera Assn., Norfolk, 1982-86; dir. devel. Balt. Opera Co., 1986-89, acting gen. mgr., 1989; gen. dir. Boston Lyric Opera, 1989—. Office: Boston Lyric Opera 114 State St Boston MA 02109-2402

MOSS, LAWRENCE CRAIG, lawyer; b. N.Y.C., Oct. 16, 1952; s. Sanford Graham and Eleanore (Freedman) M. AB with honors, Brown U., 1973; JD (Calif. State scholar), Stanford U., 1976. Bar: Wash. 1977, N.Y. 1980. Trial atty. Seattle Pub. Defender, 1976-78; assoc. Fried, Frank, Harris, Shriver & Jacobson, N.Y.C., 1979-80; pvt. practice law N.Y.C., 1981—; of counsel Kayser & Jaffe, N.Y.C., 1987-90; of counsel Lawyers Com. for Human Rights, N.Y.C., 1979—; gen. mgr. Sta. WBRU-FM, Providence, 1971-72; pub. affairs dir. Sta. WBRU, 1969-71. Co-author: A Handbook for Bicycle Activists, 1976; editor: Materials on Human Rights and the Rule of Law in El Salvador, 1980, Materials on Human Rights and The Rule of Law in Nicaragua, 1980. Elected mem. N.Y. State Dem. Com., 1990—; vice chmn. New Dem. Coalition, N.Y.C., 1986-88, chmn., 1988-90; pres. Downtown Ind. Dems., 1985-88; del. N.Y. County Jud. Conv., 1983, 85, 86. Harvey M. Baker fellow Brown U., 1973. Mem. ABA, Assn. of Bar of City of N.Y. (coun. on Internat. Affairs 1990—, com. on Internat. Human Rights 1979-83, com. on Inernat. arms Control and Security Affairs 1986-89), Lawyers Alliane Nuclear Arms Control (steering com. 1989-91), Lawyers Alliance for World Security (steering com. 1991—) Transp. Alternatives (bd. dirs. 1990-91, adv. com. 1991—), Lawyers Com. Human Rights, Phi Beta Kappa. Democrat. Office: 1 Madison Ave 30th Fl New York NY 10010

MOSS, ROGER WILLIAM, JR., historian, writer, administrator; b. Zanesville, Ohio, Jan. 31, 1940; s. Roger William and Dorothy Elizabeth (Martin) M.; m. Gail Caskey Winkler, 1981; children by previous marriage: Elizabeth deHaven, Victoria Stiles. BS in Edn., Ohio U., 1963, MA, 1964, postgrad., summer 1966; PhD, U. Del., 1972. Curator of rare books Ohio U., 1962-64; lectr., dept. history U. Del., 1966-68, U. Md., 1967-68; exec. dir. Athenaeum of Phila., 1968—; adj. assoc. prof. architecture U. Pa., Phila., 1981—. Publs. include Morgan Collection, 1965, Master Builders, 1972, Century of Color, 1981, Biographical Dictionary of Philadelphia Architects, 1985, Philadelphia, 1986, Victorian Interior Decoration, 1986, Victorian Exterior Decoration, 1987 , Lighting for Historic Buildings, 1988 (Joel Polsky prize 1989), The American Country House, 1990; gen. editor Athenaeum Libr. of Nineteenth-Century Am. series, 1975—; contbr. to profl. jours. Bd. dirs., sec. Ludwick Edn. Found., 1969—; bd. dirs., sec., treas. Victorian Soc. in Am., 1969-88; assoc. Nat. Preservation Inst., 1982—; bd. dirs. Hist. House Assn. Am., 1978-83, Com. for Preservation of Archtl. Records, 1978-80, Phila. Area Cultural Consortium (treas.), 1977-82, Mus. Council Phila., 1976-78; Conservation Ctr. for Art and Hist. Artifacts, 1984—, Hopkinson House Council (sec.), 1982—, Clivden Council, Nat. Trust for Hist. Preservation, 1974-81, 84-86, Harriton House, 1969-81, Friends of Laurel Hill, 1978-83, Franklin Inn Club, 1976-79, Woodlands Cemetery Co., 1990—; exec. com. Phila. Area Consortium Spl. Coll. Librs., 1988—. NEH grantee, 1983-85. Fellow Royal Soc. Arts; mem. Soc. Archtl. Historians, Furniture History Soc., Soc. Preservation New Eng. Antiquities, Hist. Soc. Pa., Libr. Co. Office: Athenaeum of Phila 219 S 6th St Philadelphia PA 19106-3719

MOSS, STEPHEN EDWARD, lawyer; b. Washington, Nov. 22, 1940; s. Morris and Jean (Sober) M.; m. Abigail Deady, Dec. 19, 1964; children: Aubrey, Hilary. BBA, Baldwin-Wallace Coll., 1962; JD with honors, George Washington U., 1965, LLM, 1968. Bar: D.C. 1966, Md. 1971. Assoc. Cole & Groner, Washington, 1965-70; pvt. practice law Bethesda, Md., 1971-80; pres. Stephen E. Moss, P.A., Bethesda, 1981-89; ptnr. Moss, Strickler and Weaver, P.A., 1989—. Fellow Am. Acad. Matrimonial Lawyers (cert.); mem. Montgomery County Bar Assn. (chmn. family law sect. 1981). Office: 4550 Montgomery Ave Ste 805 Bethesda MD 20814-3304

MOSSE, PETER JOHN CHARLES, travel services executive; b. Mtarfa, Malta, Sept. 8, 1947; came to U.S., 1977; s. John Herbert Charles and Barbara Haworth (Holden) M. BA, Oxford U., 1969; MBA, U. Pa., 1971; MA, Oxford U., 1989. Bank officer N.M. Rothschild & Sons Ltd., London, 1971-76; spl. projects officer banking Bumiputra Mcht. Bankers Berhad, Kuala Lumpur, Malaysia, 1976-77; v.p., treas., sec. NMR Metals Incorp., N.Y.C., 1977-79, exec. v.p., 1979-83; sr. v.p. Rothschild, Inc., N.Y.C., 1983-90; v.p., chief fin. officer The Arista Group Inc., N.Y.C., 1991—. Mem. Gold Inst. (co. rep., bd. dirs. 1985-90), Silver Inst. (co. rep., bd. dirs. 1989-90), Newcomen Soc. U.S., St. George's Soc. N.Y., Oxford Soc. (v.p. N.Y. br. 1991—), Copper Club. Episcopalian. Home: 353 E 72d St 33D New York NY 10021 Office: Arista Travel Svcs Worldwide New York NY 10010-4589

MOST, CHARLES JOHANNES, clinical psychologist; b. Bklyn., Sept. 26, 1952; s. Charles Thomas and Rose Marie (Vacarro) M.; m. Christine Ann Loughnane, June 26, 1976; children: Colin, Allison. BA, NYU, 1974; MS, Fort Hays Kans. U., 1976; PsyD, Ill. Sch. Profl. Psychology, 1983. Psychologist Ea. Nebr. Human Svcs., Omaha, 1976-78, Englewood Health Svcs., Chgo., 1979-83, Warren County Family Guidance, Washington, N.J., 1983-86; dir. psychology N.J. Dept. Corrections, Skillman, 1983-86; psychologist Warren Counseling Ctr., Phillipsburg, N.J., 1986—; dir.psychology Easton Nursing Home Praxis Alzheimers Unit, 1992—; dir. Employee Assistance Program, Flexco Microwave, Port Murray, N.J., 1988-90; chmn. adv. com. Warren County Spl. Svcs. Dist., Washington, N.J., 1990—; lectr. in field. Contbr. articles to newspapers. Mem. Clinton (N.J.) Bd. Adjustment, 1987. Mem. APA, N.J. Psychol. Assn., Psi Chi, Phi Kappa Phi. Lutheran. Office: Warren Counseling Ctr Coventry Centre D-1 Phillipsburg NJ 08865

MOST, JACK LAWRENCE, lawyer, consultant; b. N.Y.C., Sept. 24, 1935; s. Meyer Milton and Henrietta (Meyer) M.; children: Jeffrey, Peter; m. Irma Freedman Robbins, Aug. 8, 1968; children: Ann, Jane. BA cum laude, Syracuse U., 1956; JD, Columbia U., 1960. Bar: N.Y. 1960, U.S. Dist. Ct. (so. and ea. dists.) N.Y. 1963. Assoc. Hale, Grant, Meyerson and O'Brien, N.Y.C., 1960-66; dep. assoc. dir. OEO, Exec. Office of The Pres., Washington, 1965-67; asst. to gen. counsel C.I.T. Fin. Corp., N.Y.C., 1966-70; corp. counsel PepsiCo, Inc., Purchase, N.Y., 1970-71; v.p. legal affairs Revlon, Inc., N.Y.C., 1971-76; asst. gen. counsel Norton Simon, Inc., N.Y.C., 1976-79; ptnr. Rogers Hoge and Hills, N.Y.C., 1979-86; ptnr. Finkelstein Bruckman Wohl Most & Rothman, N.Y.C., 1986—, mng. ptnr., 1990—; corp. sec. Requa, Inc., Flowery Beauty Products, Inc., 1987—. Contbr. articles to profl. jour. and mags. Bd. dirs. Haym Salomon Home for Aged, 1978-91, pres., 1981-92; bd. advisors Touro Coll. Health Scis., 1989-90; bd. dirs. Haym Salomon Geriatric Found., 1992—. Mem. ABA (fed. regulation of securities com., food, drug and cosmetic law com., trademark and unfair competition com.), N.Y. State Bar Assn. (food, drug and cosmetics com., 1989—, corp. sec.), Am. Soc. Pharmacy Law, YRH Owners Corp. (bd. dirs., pres. 1989—), Lords Valley Country Club (bd. govs. 1984-90, 1st v.p. 1987-88, 2d v.p. 1988-90), Zeta Beta Tau, Omicron (trustee Syracuse chpt. 1988-91). Jewish. Home: 1175 York Ave New York NY 10021-7169 Office: Finkelstein Bruckman Wohl Most & Rothman 575 Lexington Ave New York NY 10022-6102

MOST, JOSEPH MORRIS, chemistry educator; b. N.Y.C., Apr. 24, 1943; s. Emanuel and Helen Claire (Blum) M.; m. Rochelle Harriet Stulzaft, Dec. 26, 1965; children: Steven Benjamin, Sharon Rebecca. AB, Rutgers U., 1964, PhD, 1974; MS, N.J. Inst. Tech., 1989. Chemist NL Industries, Inc., Hightstown, N.J., 1964-66; instr. Rutgers U., New Brunswick, N.J., 1971-74; asst. prof. Upsala Coll., East Orange, N.J., 1974-82, assoc. prof., 1982-89, prof., 1989—; assoc. Danforth Found., 1980. Mem. AAUP, Computer Soc. of IEEE, Am. Chem. Soc., Assn. for Computing Machinery, Cognitive Sci. Soc. Office: Upsala Coll PO Box 1186 East Orange NJ 07019-1186

MOSTILLO, RALPH, medical association administrator; b. Newark, Apr. 11, 1944; s. Joseph and Antoinette (Cipriano) M. BA in Chemistry magna cum laude, Rutgers U., Newark, 1972; MA in Biochemistry, Princeton U., 1974, PhD in Biochemistry, 1978. NIH rsch. fellow Princeton (N.J.) U., 1972-78; sr. scientist drug regulatory affairs Hoffmann-La Roche, Inc., Nutley, N.J., 1979-85; founder, chmn., chief exec. officer Am. Cancer Assn., Nutley, 1986—. Assoc. editor U.S. Pharmacopoeia XX-Nat. Formulary XV, 1980-85. With USN, 1962-66, Vietnam. Mem. Am. Chem. Soc., Am. Mgmt. Assn., Am. Mktg. Assn., N.Y. Acad. Scis., Am. Legion, Phi Beta Kappa. Home: 85 Union Ave Nutley NJ 07110-3307 Office: Am Cancer Assn PO Box 87 Nutley NJ 07110-0087

MOTE, NANCY STAMMELBACH, educator, consultant; b. Pitts., Dec. 6, 1940; d. Albert Edmond and Kathryn (Wain) S.; m. Kenneth Lewis Hoffman, Sept. 3, 1966 (div.); m. James Curtis Mote, Jan. 1, 1977. BA, Grove City Coll., 1962; MEd, Pa. State U., 1965; postgrad., Rutgers U., 1973-81. Tchr. East Orange (N.J.) Bd. Edn., 1962-70; science coordinator, environ. edn. coordinator Livingston (N.J.) Bd. Edn., 1970-86; ednl. cons. McGraw-Hill Book Co., Hightstown, 1988-89, Macmillan/McGraw-Hill, Riverside, N.J., 1989—; dir. Livingston Student Devel. Program, 1974-79; cons. Delta Edn., Nashua, N.H., 1980-86, State Dept. Edn., Trenton, N.J., 1985, McGraw-Hill, Hightstown, N.J., 1986-87. Trustee Hilltop Montessori Sch., Sparta, N.J., 1978-82, Pocono Environ. Edn. Ctr., 1987—. Mem. Nat. Sci. Tchrs. Assn. (exec. com.), N.J. Sci. Tchrs. Assn. (chmn. Elementary Sch. Sci. sect.), Nat. Sci. Suprs. Assn., N.J. Sci. Suprs. Assn. (treas. 1977-78), Assn. for Supervision and Curriculum Devel. Home: Starbuck Hill Rd PO Box 700 Chestertown NY 12817 Office: MacMillan-McGraw-Hill Sch Pub Co Riverside NJ 08520

MOTLEY, CONSTANCE BAKER (MRS. JOEL WILSON MOTLEY), federal judge, former city official; b. New Haven, Sept. 14, 1921; d. Willoughby Alva and Rachel (Huggins) Baker; m. Joel Wilson Motley, Aug. 18, 1946; 1 son, Joel Wilson, III. A.B., N.Y. U., 1943; LL.B., Columbia U., 1946. Bar: N.Y. bar 1948. Mem. Legal Def. and Ednl. Fund, NAACP, 1945-65; mem. N.Y. State Senate, 1964-65; pres. Manhattan Borough, 1965-66; U.S. dist. judge So. Dist. N.Y., 1966-82, chief judge, 1982-86, sr. judge, 1986—. Mem. N.Y. State Adv. Council Employment and Unemployment Ins., 1958-64. Mem. Assn. Bar City N.Y. Office: US Dist Ct US Courthouse Foley Sq New York NY 10007-1501

MOTOLO, PAUL LEON, small business owner; b. Syracuse, N.Y., Feb. 4, 1964; s. Francis Raymond and Jeannine Anne (Liberty) M. Student, Onondaga Community Coll., Syracuse, 1982-84. Salesman Decker Motor Car Co., Inc., Syracuse, 1983-85, bookkeeper, 1984-85; owner-mgr. Paul-Rich Motors, Syracuse, 1985—; ptnr. Garcia's Automotive Parts, Syracuse, 1987-92; owner-mgr. Paul Motolo Real Estate, Syracuse, 1988—. Supporter religious edn. St. Charles Sch., Syracuse, 1982, U.S. Army Recruiting Command, Syracuse, 1986; active polit. campaigns, 1986—. Republican. Roman Catholic. Home: 207 King Ave Syracuse NY 13209-2127 Office: Paul-Rich Motors 2001 Milton Ave Syracuse NY 13209-1540

MOTRONI, HECTOR JOHN, manufacturing executive; b. Havana, Cuba, Dec. 2, 1943; came to U.S., 1956; s. Marco Antonio and Lilia Ines (Suarez) M.; m. Myra Helene Egan, Aug. 9, 1969; children: Marcus Alan, Melissa Aimee. BA, Dartmouth Coll., 1966, BE, 1967, ME, 1968. Engr. USPHS, Bethesda, Md., 1969-71; various positions Xerox Corp., Stamford, Conn., 1971-91; v.p. quality, customer satisfaction and orgnl. effectiveness Xerox Corp., Stamford, 1991—. Trustee Temple Israel, Westport, Conn., 1981-84. Lt. USPHS, 1969-71. Mem. Dartmouth Soc. Engrs. (pres. 1977-85), Dartmouth Coll. Alumni Coun. (chmn. communications 1983-88), Coun. of the Ams. (adv. bd. 1983-89). Office: Xerox Corp Box 1600 Stamford CT 06904

MOTT, EDWARD RAYMOND, education educator, consultant; b. Oil City, Pa., Feb. 16, 1928; s. Clifford and Madeline (Rapp) M.; m. Joan Weidle, Aug. 10, 1953; children: Suzanne Mott Bieryla, Timothy E. BS in Edn., Grove City (Pa.) Coll., 1950, Clarion U. Pa., 1952; MEd, Pa. State U., 1954, EdD, 1957. Cert. tchr., prin., Pa. Tchr. Franklin (Pa.) Schs., 1952-53; prin. Butler (Pa.) Schs., 1953-54, Centre County Schs., State College, Pa., 1954-56; prof. edn. Indiana U. Pa., 1956—; ednl. cons. to schs. and colls., Pa., 1970—. Vice pres. Mental Health Assn., Indiana, 1970-75. With U.S. Army, 1946-48, Korea. Mem. Lions (v.p. Indiana 1973-79). Office: Ind U Pa Indiana PA 15705

MOTTA, RICHARD ALLEN, industrial engineer; b. Fall River, Mass., Feb. 10, 1955; s. Joseph F. and Rosalina (Caetano) M.; m. Brenda J. Laliberte, Aug. 24, 1974; children: Kristin, Peter, Thomas. BS, U. Mass., 1976. Chief engr. Trina Inc., Fall River, Mass., 1975-88; corp. chief engr. Richman Bros./ Anderson-Little, Fall River, Mass., 1988—. Treas. East Freetown (Mass.) Sports Assn., 1990-92; dir. Needle Trades Action Project, Fall River, 1982-86; mem. allocations com. Fall River United Way, 1990-92. Recipient Chmns. Vol. Svc. award Woolworth Corp., 1990. Mem. Inst. Indsl. Engrs. (sr.). Roman Catholic. Home: 27 Parker Dr W East Freetown MA 02717

MOTYL, ALEXANDER JOHN, political science educator; b. N.Y.C., Oct. 21, 1953; s. Alexander and Maria Victoria (Bojczuk) M.; m. Irene Helene Mudretzkyj, June 30, 1979; 1 child, Katherina. BA summa cum laude, Columbia Coll., 1975; MIA, Sch. Internat. Affairs, 1979; M of Philosophy, Columbia U., 1983, PhD, 1984. Asst. prof. Columbia U., N.Y.C., 1985-90, assoc. prof., 1990-92, dir. nationality and siberian studies program, 1988-92; assoc. dir. Harriman Inst., 1992—; cons. RFE-RL, Inc., Washington, 1989-90. Author: The Turn to the Right, 1980, Will the Non-Russians Rebel?, 1987, Sovietology, Rationality, Nationality, 1990; editor: Thinking Theoretically about Soviet Nationalities, 1991, Dilemmas of Independence, 1992, The Post-Soviet Nations, 1992; editor Westview Press Series on Post-Soviet Republics, 1990—; assoc. editor Nationalities Papers, 1988—. Mem. Am. Assn. for the Advancement of Slavic Studies, Am. Polit. Sci. Assn., Phi Beta Kappa. Greek Catholic. Office: Columbia U New York NY 10027

MOTZ, JOHN FREDERICK, federal judge; b. Balt., Dec. 30, 1942; s. John Eldered and Catherine (Grauel) M.; m. Diana Jane Gribbon, Sept. 20, 1968; children: Catherine Jane, Daniel Gribbon. AB, Wesleyan U., Conn., 1964; LLB, U. Va., 1967. Bar: Md. 1967, U.S. Ct. Appeals (4th cir.) 1968, U.S. Dist. Ct. Md. 1968. Law clk. to Hon. Harrison L. Winter U.S. Ct. Appeals (4th cir.), 1967-68; Assoc. Venable, Baetjer & Howard, Balt., 1968-69; asst. U.S. atty. U.S. Atty.'s Office, Balt., 1969-71; assoc. Venable, Baetjer & Howard, Balt., 1971-75, ptnr., 1976-81; U.S. atty. U.S. Atty.'s Office, Balt., 1981-85; judge U.S. Dist. Ct. Md., Balt., 1985—. Trustees Friends Sch., Balt., 1970-77, 1981-88, Sheppard Pratt Hosp., 1987—. Mem. ABA, Md. State Bar Assn., Balt. Bar Assn., Am. Bar Found., Am. Law Inst., Am. Coll. Trial Lawyers. Republican. Quaker. Office: US Dist Ct 101 W Lombard Rm 510 Baltimore MD 21201-2682

MOTZ, LLOYD, physicist, researcher, writer; b. Susquehanna, Pa., June 5, 1910; s. Solomon and Minnie (Seltzer) M.; m. Minne R. Motz, June 14, 1934; children: Robin O., Julie Ann. BS, CCNY, 1930; PhD, Columbia U., 1935. Prof. astronomy Columbia U., N.Y.C., 1950-78. Author: The Constellations, 1988, The Atomic Scientists, 1989, The Unfolding Universe, 1989, The Story of Physics, 1989, Conquering Mathematics, 1991; contbr. numerous articles to profl. jours. Recipient Gravity Rsch. award Gravity

Rsch. Found., 1960. Fellow AAAS, Am. Phys. Soc., Royal Astron. Soc., N.Y. Acad. Sci. (pres. 1970, Sci. award 1972), World Acad. Arts and Scis. Home: 140 Cabrini Blvd Apt 86 New York NY 10033-3433

MOUCHA, NANCY SUSAN, public relations specialist; b. Washington, Sept. 16, 1960; d. Louis Anton Moucha and Vera Irene (Kovarik) Moucha-Sanborn; m. Stephen T. Aust. BA in Gen. Social Studies, Providence Coll., 1982. Acct. exec. Communications Ink, Albany, N.Y., 1982-84; press sec. Rep. Nat. Com., Washington, 1984-87; program dir. The Canzeri Co., Washington, 1987; communications dir. Exec. Office of the Pres. of U.S., Washington, 1987-88; media advisor Retired Chief Justice Warren Burger, Washington, 1988; dir. pub. and environ. affairs Dorf & Stanton Communications, N.Y.C., Washington, 1989—; media cons. Willie Shoemakers Farewell Tour, L.A., 1989; forum mem. Rene DubosCtr., N.Y.C., 1991; environ. cons. Joint Industry Com. Solid Waste, Washington, 1990—. Mem. Am. Horse Coun., Washington, 1988—, Westport Hist. Soc., 1988-92. Republican. Roman Catholic. Home: 34 Rayfield Rd Westport CT 06880-4525 Office: Dorf & Santon Communications 111 5th Ave New York NY 10003-1005

MOULTHROP, ROBERT WALLACE, marketing executive; b. Fall River, Calif.; s. Richard Wallace Moulthrop Gwendolyn May (Beaver) Scott; m. Jewel Garill, Mar. 27, 1971; children: Peter, William, Daniel. BA, Brandeis U., 1961; MA, Cath. U. Am., 1966. Dir. news bur., then acctg. dir. univ. rels. CUNY, N.Y.C., 1967-75; dir. pub. rels. and mktg. Ednl. Testing Svcs., Princeton, N.J., 1975-82; mkt. dir. Deloitte Haskins & Sells, N.Y.C., 1982-88; sr. mkt. dir. KPMG Peat Marwick, N.Y.C., 1988—. Author: (short stories) San Jose Studies, 1990 (Best Fiction award granted by bd. dirs. San Jose (Calif.) Studies, San Jose State U., 1990). Pres. Dance Mag. Found., N.Y.C., 1985-88; chmn. leadership bd. Nat. Found. for Advancement of Arts, 1986-90. Recipient Fellowship for prose fiction N.J. State Coun. on Arts, 1991-92. Mem. Pub. Rels. Soc. Am., Am. Mktg. Assn., Internat. Assn. Bus. Communicators. Office: KPMG Peat Marwick 345 Park Ave New York NY 10154-0004

MOUNT, CHARLES MORRIS, interior designer; b. Troy, Ala., Mar. 6, 1942; s. Charles Madison and Fannie Ruth (Carnes) M. B.Interior Design with honors, Auburn U., 1964. Designer Finch, Alexander, Barnes, Rothschild and Paschal, Atlanta, 1964-67; project dir. Interior Space Design, N.Y.C., 1967-70; dir. interiors George Nelson & Co., N.Y.C., 1970-72; pres. Charles Morris Mount Inc. (now Silver & Ziskind/Mount), N.Y.C., 1972—. Author: Residential Interiors: A Global Perspective, 1992; kitchen and restaurant designs featured in numerous mags. Recipient numerous awards in design including Nat. Restaurant Instn. Mag. Design awards, 1971, 75, 76, 81, Lumen Design awards, 1971, 75, 76, Restaurant and Instns. Interior Design awards, 1984, 85, award Am. Soc. Interior Designers, 1984, Gold Key award Am. Hotel Assn., 1987, 89, Sign of the Times awards, 1987, 89, Restaurants and Instns. Design award, 1987, Dupont Antron award, 1989, Am. Olean Tile Co. award, 1989, SEGD award, 1989, Designing N.Y. award, 1991. Mem. Am. Inst. Wine and Food, Symposium on Am. Cuisine. Avocations: photography, music, gardening, travel, antiques. Home: 300 W 108th St New York NY 10025-2757 Office: Silver & Ziskind/Mount 4th Fl 233 Park Ave S New York NY 10003-1656

MOUNT, DONALD RAYMOND (RAY MOUNT), clinical psychologist; b. Camden, N.J., July 17, 1946; s. Donald Rider and Carolyn (Bauer) M.; m. Heather K. Snell, Aug. 2, 1969 (div. 1974); 1 child, Damien Arthur. BS in Biology, Wagner Coll., S.I., 1968; MS in Biology, Villanova U., 1973; MEd in Counseling, Boston State Coll., 1982; PhD in Psychology, Hofstra U., 1986. Lic. psychologist Mass. Mktg. rep. Millipore Corp., Bedford, Mass., 1973-79; mental health worker McLean Hosp., Belmont, Mass., 1980-82; psychol. asst. Danvers State Hosp., Hawthorne, Mass., 1986-88; program design staff Ctr. for Nutritional Rsch., Boston, 1988-90; psychologist in pvt. practice Lynnfield, Mass., 1988—; cons. Melrose Wakefield Hosp., 1991—. Contbr. articles to profl. jours. With U.S. Army, 1968-71. Mem. APA, Mass. Psychol. Assn. (referral com. 1990-91), New Eng. Psychol. Assn., Rotary. Home: 12 Bourbon St Peabody MA 01960 Office: 55 Salem St Lynnfield MA 01940-2645

MOUNT, RICHARD EDWARD, economist; b. Bklyn., May 10, 1947; s. Richard A. and Elizabeth (Burl) M.; m. Kathryn S. Favorito, Aug. 30, 1969, (wid. Dec. 1988); children: Kristen, Gregory. BS, St. Peter's Coll., 1969; MA, New Sch. for Social Rsch., N.Y.C., 1972, ABD, 1980. Dir. rsch. MacKay-Shields Econs., N.Y.C., 1978-80; mgr. housing constrn., regional rsch. Merrill Lynch Econs., N.Y.C., 1980-88; pres., chief economist Mount Econ. Cons., Middletown, N.J., 1987—. Mem. Nat. Assn. Bus. Economists. Roman Catholic. Home: 121 Marcshire Dr Middletown NJ 07748-3104

MOWAT, WILLIAM HENRY, JR., insurance executive; b. Somerville, Mass., Feb. 13, 1940; s. William Henry Sr. and Ellen Aileen (Crossman) M.; m. Jacqueline Ann O'Connor, Feb. 19, 1966; children: Jennifer, Pamela, William Henry III. BA, Baldwin-Wallace Coll., 1962; MBA, NYU, 1967. Fin. analyst Chase Manhattan Bank, N.Y.C., 1962-66; asst. treas. Richardson-Merrell Inc., N.Y.C., 1966-69; controller Richardson-Merrell GmBH, Gross Gereu, Fed. Republic of Germany, 1970-73; fin. dir. Richardson-Merrell Ltd., London, 1973-77; v.p. fin. Richardson-Vicks Inc.-Internat., Westport, Conn., 1977-85, Richardson-Vicks-U.S. Health Care, Wilton, Conn., 1985-88; sr. v.p., chief fin. officer N.Y. Life Worldwide, N.Y.C., 1989—; bd. dirs. New World Life Worldwide Ltd., Hong Kong, Windsor Group Ltd., Telford, Eng., N.Y. Life Worldwide Holding, N.Y.C.; rep. bd. dirs. N.Y. Life Ins. of Korea, Seoul. Pres. Twin Ridge Homeowners Assn., Ridgefield, Conn., 1985; chmn. bd. trustees First Congl. Ch., Ridgefield, 1989-90. Sgt. USAR, 1962-68. Mem. Nat. Assn. Corp. Treas., Am. Coun. Life Insurers (internat. com.), Life Ins. Market Rsch. Assn. (internat. com.), Fin. Exec. Inst. Office: NY Life Ins 51 Madison Ave New York NY 10010-1603

MOWBRAY, ROBERT NORMAN, government agricultural and natural resource development officer, forest ecologist; b. Warren, Pa., Feb. 26, 1935; s. Leonard Kelly and Jean Elizabeth (Lowes) M.; m. Sonia de los Angeles Baquerizo, June 7, 1969; children: Norma Mercedes, Elizabeth Lanning. BA, Dartmouth Coll., 1957; M of Forestry, Yale U., 1963; postgrad., Duke U., 1966-68. Rsch. asst. forest ecology Duke U., Panama, 1967, Ecuador, 1968-70; research asst. forest ecology U. Tenn., Knoxville, 1970-71; research asst. ecology Oak Ridge (Tenn.) Nat. Labs., 1971-72; reclamation crew chief Tenn. Mountain Mgmt., Knoxville, 1972; assoc. dir. Peace Corps, Asunción, Paraguay, 1972-78; agrl. devel. officer A.I.D., San Jose, Costa Rica, 1978-80, Kingston, Jamaica, 1980-83, Washington, 1983-88, 90—, Quito, Ecuador, 1988-90; forestry vol. Peace Corps, Ecuador, 1963-66, editor tech. newsletter, 1964-66. Author: (with others) Natural Resource Management and Conservation of Biodiversity and Tropical Forests in Ecuador-A Strategy for USAID, 1989; contbr. articles to profl. jours. Mem. World Wildlife Fund. 1st lt. USMC, 1958-61. Mem. Nature Conservancy, Assn. for Tropical Biology, Internat. Soc. Tropical Foresters, Friends of the Nat. Zoo, Nat. Coun. Returned Peace Corps Vols.

MOWRER, TONY ALAN, music educator; b. Valdosta, Ga., Oct. 16, 1956; s. Dwight P. and Marcia June (Smith) M.; m. Linda J. Burks, July 23, 1977; children: Nathan Alan, Kendra Dawn, Andrea Elizabeth. AA, Northeastern Christian Coll., 1976; BA, Lubbock Christian U., 1979; MA in Music History, West Chester (Pa.) U., 1985; postgrad., Temple U., 1989—. Dir. Gander Brook Christian Camp, Poland Springs, Maine, 1982-85, 88-90; v.p. for student svcs. Northeastern Christian Jr. Coll., Villanova, 1989-90, asst. prof. music, 1979-91; asst. prof. music Faulkner U., Montgomery, Ala., 1992—. Mem. Am. Choral Dirs. Assn., Music Tchrs. Nat. Assn., Pa. Music Educators Assn., Alpha Chi. Mem. Ch. of Christ. Office: Faulkner U 5345 Atlanta Hwy Montgomery AL 36193

MOYED, RALPH SAM, columnist, editorial writer; b. Phila., Aug. 26, 1930; s. Edward M. and Elizabeth (Hartz) M.; m. Myra S. Snyder, Mar. 13, 1957; 1 stepchild, Mark Goldberg, 1 child, Nancy Leah Dunlap. Student, Temple U., 1948-50, NYU, 1952-53, Northwestern U., 1971. Copyboy Evening Bull., Phila., 1948-50; pub. info. aide USN, N.Y.C., 1951-54; copywriter Yardis Advt. Co., Phila., 1955; reporter Intelligencer-Jour., Lancaster, Pa., 1956-61; reporter News Jour., Wilmington, Del., 1961-68, 71-78, columnist, 1978—; pub. relations dir. Rep. State Com., Wilmington, 1969-71; commentator WAMS Radio Sta., Wilmington, 1987-90. Named Journalist of Yr. Temple U. Journalism Sch., 1979; recipient Pub. Service award AP Mng. Editors Assn., 1972. Mem. Investigative Reporters and Editors. Jewish. Home: 5213-8 Le Parc Dr Wilmington DE 19809-2705 Office: News Jour Co PO Box 15505 Wilmington DE 19850

MOYER, CHARLES FREDERICK, health services administrator, deputy sheriff; b. Canadaigua, N.Y., June 4, 1930; s. Kenneth Randall and Helen Mary (Tate) M.; children: Kimberle Adele, Kregg Aaron, Kevin Aric. BS, Ithaca Coll., 1955; MSS, U.S. Sports Acad., 1983; postgrad., Calif. U. Cert. athletic trainer. Chief phys. therapy Del. Valley Hosp., Walton, N.Y., 1955-57; indsl. phys. therapist Indsl. Clinic GE, Schenectady, N.Y., 1957-59; chief phys. therapy FF Thompson Hosp., Canadaigua, 1959-86; mgr. phys. medicine Lancaster (Ohio)-Fairfield Hosp., 1986-87, United Health Svcs. Hosp., Binghamton, N.Y., 1987—; assoc. prof. phys. edn. dept. C. C. Finger Lakes, 1974-86; clin. instr. numerous phys. therapy programs, 1974-86; sch. instr. NRA; mem. Bd. Phys. Therapy Examiners, N.Y. State Edn. Dept.; cons. profl. conduct N.Y. State Edn. Dept. Mem. Mayor's Commn. on Higher Edn., Canandaigua, 1963; bd. dirs. Am. Heart Assn.; mem. Ont. County Bd. Suprs. Environ. Com. Lt. Col. U.S. Army, 1992. Recipient Pres.'s award Jaycees, 1963, Disting. Svc. award N.Y. chpt. Am. Phys. Therapy Assn., 1972. Mem. NRA (life) (Nat. Pistol Record award 1975, 80), Nat. Athletic Trainers Assn., Nat. Sheriffs Assn., Nat. Marine Investigators Assn., Mil. Surgeons Assn., Internat. Shooting Coaches Assn., Vestal Rotary Club, Alpha Phi Omega (life). Republican. Episcopalian. Home: 28 James St Apt B Binghamton NY 13903

MOYER, DAVID LEE, veterinarian; b. Reading, Pa., May 7, 1940; s. Robert Bretz and Helen Verna (Lutz) M.; m. Ann Marie DeGarmo, Aug. 8, 1964 (div. Sept. 1979). BS, Pa. State U., 1962; postgrad., Temple U., 1967; VMD, U. Pa., 1968; psychology, Kutztown U., 1980. Lic. doctor vet. medicine, Pa. Veterinarian Antietam Valley Animal Hosp., Reading, 1969-76, Kutztown Animal Hosp., Dryville, Pa., 1976-83; meat and poultry inspection supr., vet. med. officer U.S. Dept. Agr., Food Safety and Inspection Svc., Fredericksburg, Pa., 1983-88; veterinarian Exeter Animal Hosp., Birdsboro, Pa., 1983—; cons. City of Reading, 1969-80, Humane Soc. Berks County, Reading, 1970-72, Animal Rescue League SPCA, Reading, 1970—. Advisor Boy Scouts Am., Reading, 1969-74. Mem. Am. Vet. Med. Assn., Am. Animal Hosp. Assn., Pa. Vet. Med. Assn., Keystone Vet. Med. Assn., Schulykill Vet. Med. Assn., Lehigh Vet. Med. Assn., Western Vet. Conf., Vet. orthopedic Soc., Am. Soc. Vet. Ophthalmology, Am. Assn. Feline Practitioners (charter), Cornell Feline Health Ctr., Internat. Vet. Ophthalmology, Am. Soc. Vet. Nutrition, Am. Assn. Food Hygiene, Am. Assn. Avian Pathologists, Vet. Cardiology Soc. (pres. 1983), Am. Vet. Dental Soc., Toastmasters (pres. 1983). Democrat. Lutheran. Home and Office: 6800 Daniel Boone Rd Birdsboro PA 19508

MOYER, JAMES WALLACE, physicist, consultant; b. Syracuse, Aug. 16, 1919; s. Wallace Earl and Viola (Hook) M.; m. Nedra Blake, Sept. 10, 1940; children—Jeffry Mark, Elaine, Virginia, Julia. A.B., Cornell U., 1938; postgrad. Rutgers U., 1938-41; Ph.D., U. Rochester, 1948. Insp. ordnance U.S. Army, 1941-42; physicist Radiation Lab., U. Calif., Berkeley, 1942-43; sr. physicist Tenn. Eastman, Oak Ridge, 1943-46; research assoc. Gen. Electric Research, Knolls Atomic Power Lab., Schenectady, N.Y., 1948-55; cons. engr. Gen. Electric Microwave Lab., Palo Alto, Calif., 1955-57; mgr. phys. sci. Gen. Electric Tempo, Santa Barbara, Calif., 1957-60; research dir. Sperry Rand Research Ctr., 1960-61; research dir. Servo Mechanisms, Inc., 1961-63; dir. applied research Autonetics div. N.Am. Aviation, Anaheim, Calif., 1963-65; dir. phys. scis. Northrop Space Lab., 1965-67; dir. engring. Northrop Corp., Beverly Hills, Calif., 1967-70; mgr. phys. systems So. Calif. Edison, Rosemead, 1976-84; cons., 1984—; cons. Nat. Bur. Standards, 1956-62; mem. panel Nat. Acad. Sci., 1967-70, 71. Mem. IEEE (sr.), Am. Phys. Soc., Sigma Xi. Home: 143 Campbell Ave Ithaca NY 14850-2057

MOYER, RALPH OWEN, JR., chemist, educator; b. New Bedford, Mass., May 19, 1936; s. Ralph Owen and Annie (Brown) M. BS, U. Mass., Dartmouth, 1957; MS, U. Toledo, 1963; PhD, U. Conn., 1969. Devel. engr. Union Carbide Corp., Fostoria, Ohio, 1957-64; asst. prof. chemistry Trinity Coll., Hartford, Conn., 1969-76, assoc. prof., 1976-86, prof., 1986-91, Scovill prof. chemistry, 1991—; vis. lectr. U. West Indies, Kingston, Jamaica, 1985; rsch. collaborator Brookhaven Nat. Lab., Upton, N.Y., 1977-78. Contbr. articles and chpt. to profl. pubs. With U.S. Army, 1959. Mem. Am. Chem. Soc. (chmn. Connecticut Valley sect. 1984), N.Y. Acad. Scis., Sigma Xi (pres. Hartford chpt. 1990-91). Home: 9 Grandview Ter Wethersfield CT 06109-3240 Office: Trinity Coll 300 Summit St Hartford CT 06106-3100

MOYERMAN, ROBERT MAX, chemist; b. Atlantic City, N.J., Sept. 14, 1925; s. Harry and Rosalind (Ephraim) M.; m. Shirley Mazer, May 6, 1951; children: Maxine Frances, Judith Ann, David Robert. BS in Chemistry, Rutgers U., 1949; MS in Chemistry, U. Ala., 1951. Chemist Nuclear Devel. Assocs., White Plains, N.Y., 1951-52; assoc. chemist Applied Physics Lab. Johns Hopkins U., Silver Spring, Md., 1952-55; rsch. investigator Am. Smelting and Refining Co., South Plainfield, N.J., 1955-58; sr. rsch. chemist, sect. head analytical dept. Ansul Co., Marinette, Wis., 1958-65; sr. chemist Scholler Bros., Phila., 1965-68; group leader Sun Chem. Corp., Wood River Junction, R.I., 1968-70; tech. svc. dir. Organic Chem. Corp., East Providence, R.I., 1970-72; asst. to tech. dir. Dexter Chem., Bronx, N.Y., 1972-73; mgr. R & D Hydrolabs, Paterson, N.J., 1974-75; owner Warwick (R.I.) Labs., 1970—. Chmn. govt.-social svcs. subcom. Menominee (Mich.) Community Study Group, 1962-65; v.p. Boswell Elem. Sch. PTA, Menominee, 1963-64. Staff sgt. USAAF, 1943-45, PTO. Naval Rsch. grantee, 1950. Mem. Am. Chem. Soc. (sec.-treas. N.E. Wis. sect. 1964, chmn. elect 1965), Am. Microchem. Soc., Am. Assn. Textile Chemists and Colorists, Air Force Assn., Sigma Xi. Office: Warwick Labs 118 Edmond Dr Warwick RI 02886-8545

MOYLAN, DAVID JOHN, III, radiation oncologist, educator; b. Phila., Nov. 28, 1951; s. David John Jr. and Virginia (Hippenstiel) M.; children. Matthew, Elizabeth Anne, Tara Patricia, Lauren Victoria. SB, MIT, 1973; MD, Georgetown U., 1977. Intern Bryn Mawr (Pa.) Hosp., 1977-78, resident in internal medicine, 1978-79; resident in radiation oncology Thomas Jefferson U. Hosp., Phila., 1979-82; asst. prof. Jefferson Med. Coll., Phila., 1982-85, Pa. State Hershey Med. Sch., 1986—; med. dir. Schuylkill Cancer Ctr., Pottsville, Pa., 1985—, Mahoning Valley Cancer Ctr., Lehighton, Pa., 1988—. Mem. Am. Soc. Therapeutic Radiology and Oncology (mem.-at-large, bd. dirs. 1991—), Am. Soc. Clin. Oncology, Radiation Rsch. Soc. Office: Schuylkill Ctr 1 Norwegian Plz Pottsville PA 17901-3056

MOYLAN, JAY RICHARD, medical products executive; b. Greenfield, Mass., Dec. 20, 1950; s. Richard J. and Margaret M. (McCarthy) M.; m. Sharon J. Slater, June 18, 1976; children: Jaimee, Shauna. AA in Liberal Arts, Greenfield Community Coll., 1972; AS in Respiratory Therapy, Springfield Tech. Community C., 1975; BS in Health Care Mgmt., U. Mass., 1983. Staff respiratory therapist Mercy Hosp., Springfield, Mass., 1973-74; respiratory therapy supr. Brattleboro (Vt.) Meml. Hosp., 1974-75; dir. cardiopulmonary svc. Farren Meml. Hosp., Turners Falls, Mass., 1975-83; cardiopulmonary sales rep. Erich Jeager, Inc., Rockford, Ill., 1983-85; cardiovascular sales rep. Electro Catheter Corp., Rahway, N.J., 1985-86; cardiopulmonary sales specialist Sensor Medics Corp., Yorba Linda, Calif., 1986—; chmn. Coun. Pulmonary Svc. Mgrs., Springfield, 1980-81. Chmn. Cath. Stewardship Appeal Holy Trinity Parish, Greenfield, 1989; bd. dirs. cen. Mass. chpt. Am. Lung Assn., 1981-83; treas. FMH Credit Union, 1980-83. Recipient Achievement award Mass. Soc. Respiratory Care, 1989. Mem. Coun. Pulmonary Svc. Mgrs. (Lifetime Mem. award), Am. Coll. Sports Medicine, Am. Assn. Respiratory Care (registered, rev. com. 1991), Am. Registry Diagnostic Med. Sonographers (registered), Nat. Bd. Respiratory Care (cert.), Nat. Soc. Cardiopulmonary Tech. (cert.), Mass. Thoracic Soc., Mass. Lung Assn. Home: 53 Meadow Ln Greenfield MA 01301-9703

MOYLAN, RICHARD JOHN, cemetery executive; b. Bklyn., Aug. 7, 1954; s. Joseph and Eleanor (Klimczak) M.; m. Gloria Elizabeth Reyes, Aug. 24, 1991. BA, Hunter Coll., 1980; JD, N.Y. Law Sch., 1984. Bar: N.Y. 1986. Supr. The Green-Wood Cemetery, Bklyn., 1977-84, asst. sec., 1985-86, exec. v.p., 1986-88, pres., 1989—; dir. N.Y. State Assn. Cemeteries, N.Y.C., 1989—. Mem. ABA, N.Y. State Bar Assn., Vol. Lawyers for the Arts, Bklyn. Bar Assn. Office: The Green-Wood Cemetery 1 Hanson Pl Brooklyn NY 11243-0101

MOYNE, JOHN ABEL, computer scientist, linguist, educator; b. Yezd, Iran, July 6, 1920; s. Abul Kasim and Sogra (Afshar) M.; came to U.S., 1956, naturalized, 1965; B.A., Georgetown U., 1959, M.A., 1960; Ph.D., Harvard U., 1970; m. Claudia Wienert, July 4, 1963; children—David, Nicholas, Parvin. With Brit. Govt., Iran and India, 1943-52, market research officer, Tehran, 1952; linguist U.S. Govt., Cyprus, 1953-56; rsch. assoc. Georgetown U., Washington, 1960-63; mgr. applied linguistics dept. IBM Corp., Cambridge, Mass., 1963-71; prof., chmn. computer sci. dept. Queens Coll., CUNY, Flushing, 1971-81, chmn. div. math. and natural scis., 1978-81, chmn. univ. faculty for Ph.D. in Computer Sci., 1978-82, exec. officer Grad. Sch. Ph.D. Program in Linguistics, 1983-88; prof. linguistics and computer sci. CUNY, 1971-91, prof. emeritus linguistics and computer sci., 1991—. Grantee, EURATOM, AEC, NSF, City U. N.Y. Mem. Linguistic Soc. Am., N.Y. Acad. Scis., Assn. Computing Machinery, Brit. Inst. Engring. Technology, Sigma Xi. Democrat. Episcopalian. Author: Hafiz of Shiraz, 1946; Life in India, 1949; Open Secret, 1984; Understanding Language: Man or Machine, 1985; Unseen Rain, 1986, Rumi: These Branching Moments, 1988; This Longing: Poetry, Teaching Stories, and Letters of Rumi, 1988, LISP: A First Language for Computing, 1991; contbr. articles to profl. jours., chpts. to books. Home: 40 Prospect Ave Sea Cliff NY 11579-1029 Office: CUNY PhD Program Linguistics Grad Ctr 33 W 42d St New York NY 10036-8003

MOYNIHAN, DANIEL PATRICK, senator, educator; b. Tulsa, Mar. 16, 1927; s. John Henry and Margaret Ann (Phipps) M.; m. Elizabeth Therese Brennan, May 29, 1955; children: Timothy Patrick, Maura Russell, John McCloskey. Student, CCNY, 1943; BA cum laude, Tufts U., 1948; MA, Fletcher Sch. Law and Diplomacy, 1949, PhD, 1961, LLD (hon.), 1968; Fulbright fellow, London (Eng.) Sch. Econs. and Polit. Sci., 1950-51; AM (hon.), Harvard U., 1966; LLD (hon.), La Salle Coll., 1966, Seton Hall Coll., 1966, Cath. U. Am., 1968, Ill. Inst. Tech., 1968, New Sch. Social Rsch., 1968, Duquesne U., 1968, St. Louis U., 1968, U. Calif., 1969, U. Notre Dame, 1969, Fordham U., 1970, St. Bonaventure U., 1972, Ind. U., 1975, St. Anselm's Coll., 1976, Boston Coll., 1976, Ohio State U., 1976, Adelphi U., 1976, Hebrew U., 1976; D Pub. Adminstrn. (hon.), Providence Coll., 1967; LHD (hon.), U. Akron, 1967, Hamilton Coll., 1968; DSc (hon.), Villanova U., 1968; DH (hon.), Bridgewater State Coll., 1972; DSc (hon.), Mich. Tech. U., 1972; numerous other hon. degrees. With Internat. Rescue Com., 1954; successively asst. to sec., asst. sec., acting sec. to gov. State of N.Y., 1955-58, mem. tenure commn., 1959-60, dir. Syracuse U. govt. rsch. project, 1959-61, spl. asst. to sec. labor, 1961-62, exec. asst. to sec., 1962-63, asst. sec. labor, 1963-65; dir. Joint Ctr. for Urban Studies MIT and Harvard U., 1966-69; prof. edn. and urban politics Kennedy Sch. Govt., Harvard U., 1966-73, sr. mem., 1966-77, prof. govt., 1973-77; asst. for urban affairs to Pres. U.S., 1969-70; counsellor to Pres. U.S., mem. Cabinet, 1969-70, cons. to Pres. U.S., 1971-73; mem. U.S. del. 26th Gen. Assembly, UN, 1971, Pres.'s Sci. Adv. Com., 1971-73; ambassador to India New Delhi, 1973-75; U.S. permanent rep. to UN, N.Y.C., 1975-76; U.S. senator from N.Y., 1977—; vice chmn. Pres.'s Temp. Commn. on Pennsylvania Avenue, 1964-73; chmn. adv. com. traffic safety dept. HEW; fellow Ctr. Advanced Studies, Wesleyan U., 1965-66; hon. fellow London Sch. Econs. and Polit. Sci., 1970—; sec. pub. affairs com. N.Y. State Dem. Com., 1958-60; del. Dem. Nat. Conv., 1960, 76. Author: Maximum Feasible Misunderstanding, 1969, The Politics of a Guaranteed Income, 1973, Coping: On the Practice of Government, 1974, A Dangerous Place, 1978, Counting Our Blessings, 1980, Loyalties, 1984, Family and Nation, 1986, Came the Revolution: Argument in the Reagan Era, 1988, On the Law of Nations, 1990; co-author: Beyond the Melting Pot, 1963; editor: The Defenses of Freedom, 1966, On Understanding Poverty, 1969, Ethnicity: Theory and Experience, 1975, others; editorial bd. Pub. Interest; contbr. articles to profl. jours. Vice chmn. Woodrow Wilson Internat. Ctr. for Scholars, 1971-76; chmn. bd. trustees Joseph H. Hirshhorn Mus. and Sculpture Garden, 1971-85; mem. bd. regents Smithsonian Instn., 1987—. With USN, 1944-47. Recipient Centennial medal Syracuse U., 1969. Mem. AAAS (vice chmn. 1971, dir. 1972-73), Am. Philos. Soc., Nat. Acad. Pub. Adminstrn., Am. Acad. Arts and Scis. (chmn. seminar on poverty), Century Club, Harvard Club. Office: US Senate 464 Russell Senate Bldg Washington DC 20510

MOYNIHAN, DAVID STANTON, lawyer; b. Worcester, Mass., Oct. 16, 1942; s. John Joseph and Eleanor Mary (Toomey) M. BS in History, Coll. of the Holy Cross, Worcester, 1964; JD, New Eng. Sch. Law, Boston, 1981. Bar: Mass.; U.S. Cir. Ct. Appeals (9th and 10th cirs.); U.S. Supreme Ct. Hearing officer Comm. of Mass., Boston, 1975-81; trial atty. antitrust U.S. Dept. Justice, Washington, 1981-83, trial atty. tax div., 1983-85; criminal asst. atty. U.S. Atty's. Office, Las Vegas, 1985-87, civil asst. atty., 1987-89, chief civil sect., 1990—. Coordinating editor New Eng. Law Rev., 1980-81. 1st lt. U.S. Army, 1968-70. Democrat. Roman Catholic. Home: 425 8th St NW Washington DC 20004 Office: Office Legal Edn 601 D St NW #10332 Washington DC 20530

MOYNIHAN, ROBERT DUNCAN, English educator; b. Denver, June 26, 1936; s. Charles John and Maxine Gladys (Hallenbeck) M.; m. Carolyn Marie Filchak, Mr. 17, 1963 (div. 1984); children: Moira, Brigit. BA, Regis Coll., 1958; MA, U. Colo., 1962; PhD, U. Ariz., 1969. Instr. English U. Ariz., Tucscon, 1962-67; from asst. prof. to assoc. prof. English SUNY, Oneonta, 1967-87, prof. English, 1987—. Author, editor: The Necessary Learning, 1989, A Recent Imagining, 1987; contbr. articles to profl. jours. Scholarship Aspen Inst., 1954; postdoctoral grantee NEH, Yale, UCLA, 1973, 79, 85, 91; Andrew Mellon fellowship Clark Libr., 1979-80. Mem. MLA. Home: Stanwell Main St # 66 Unadilla NY 13849 Office: SUNY Oneonta NY 13820

MOZELESKI, PETER A., publishing executive, education consultant; b. Chicopee, Mass., May 9, 1940; s. Peter Sr. and Rita (Nadeau) M.; m. Janet Oulos; children: Jeffrey, Glenn, Anthony, Paul, Dean. Assoc. degree, Springfield (Mass.) Tech. C.C., 1987. CEO, pub. Mozeleski Cons. and Project Devel., Wilbraham, Mass., 1992—; Author: (with Paul Mozeleski) The Rubber Bros. Comics, 1987, When Aids Strikes, 1989. Author: The Rubber Bros. Comics, 1987, When AIDS Strikes, 1989. Roman Catholic. Home: PO Box 431 Wilbraham MA 01095-0431 Office: 131 Johnson St Springfield MA 01108-1806

MRAZEK, ROBERT J., congressman; b. Newport, R.I., Nov. 6, 1945; s. Harold Richard and Blanche Rose M.; m. Catherine Susan Gurick, Mar. 31, 1971; children: Susannah Rose, James Nicholas. BA in Govt., Cornell U., 1967. Spl. asst. to U.S. Senator Hartke Washington, 1969-71; spl. projects coordinator Town of Huntington, N.Y., 1971; legislator Suffolk County, Hauppauge, N.Y., 1975-82, minority leader, 1979-82; mem. 98th-102nd Congresses from 3d N.Y. dist., 1983—. Bd. dirs. Youth Devel. Assn. Huntington Village, N.Y., 1971-76, pres. 1972-74. Mem. DAV. Democrat. Methodist. Office: 143 Main St Huntington NY 11743-6957*

M-ROBLIN, JOHN, publishing company executive, art director; b. Syracuse, N.Y., Apr. 9, 1958; s. John Membery and Mary Pauline (Hayes) Roblin; m. Patricia Mastroianni, Jan. 3, 1981. BS in Graphic Design, SUNY, Buffalo, 1980. Artist Quick Fox Pub. Co., N.Y.C., 1980-81, Music Sales Corp., N.Y.C., 1980-82; art dir. Grosset & Dunlap Pubs., N.Y.C., 1981-82, Hayden Book Co., Hasbrouck Heights, N.J., 1983-86; dir. art and desktop pub. Garland Pub. Co., N.Y.C., 1986—; owner, mgr. Square One Graphics, Baldwin, N.Y., 1981—, Miehoumme Studio, Baldwin, 1989—. Contbr. articles to profl. jours. Mem. Nat. Assn. Desktop Pubs., Amnesty Internat., Greenpeace. Democrat. Episcopalian. Office: Garland Pub 717 5th Ave New York NY 10022-8101

MROSZCZYK, ROSE VICTORIA, guidance counselor, educator; b. Waltham, Mass., Dec. 20, 1945; d. Henry Edward and Nandina Louise Mroszczyk; m. William J. McDonald, Dec. 29, 1976; children: Dylan, Alex, William Henry. BA in French, Brandeis U., 1967; MS in Edn., Bank St. Coll. Edn., 1969; MA in Counseling Psychology, Antioch U., 1978. Tchr. Newton (Mass.) Pub. Schs., 1968-70, Lab. Kindergarten Nursery Brandeis U., Waltham, 1970-73, Shady Hill Sch., Cambridge, Mass., 1973-75; therapist alcohol and individual therapy Mental Health Svcs. of Southeastern Vt., White River Junction, 1976-77; child and family therapist United Coun-

seling Svc., Bennington, Vt., 1977-78; family therapist Alternatives for Human Growth and Devel., West Lebanon, N.H., 1979-81; guidance counselor Hartford (Vt.) Mid. Sch., 1989—. Mem. NEA, Am. Assn. Counseling and Devel., Vt. Assn. Counseling and Devel. (bd. dirs. 1989—).

MROZ, JOHN EDWIN, political scientist; b. Lowell, Mass., May 1, 1948; s. Edwin T. and Margaret Mary (Little) M.; m. Karen Linehan, June 17, 1972; children: Jonathan E.R., Jessica, Jeffrey. BA, cert. Soviet and East European studies, U. Notre Dame, 1970; A.M., Northeastern U., 1972; M.A., M.A.L.D., Tufts U., 1974. Exec. sec. UN Assn. Greater Boston, 1971-73; exec. v.p., dir. Middle East Studies, Internat. Peace Acad., Inc., N.Y.C., 1976-81; pres. Inst. East-West Security Studies, N.Y.C., 1981—; cons., U.S. Govt. intermediary in Middle East, U.S. Dept. State, 1981-82; cons. Fgn. Svc. Inst., Dept. State, 1977-81; cons. Coun. of Europe, Strasbourg, Fed. Republic Germany, 1989—, East European govts., 1990—. Author: Beyond Security: Private Perceptions Among Arabs and Israelis, 1980. Contbr. articles to profl. jours. Teaching fellow NSF, 1971-72. Decorated Officer's Cross of Order of Merit Fed. Republic of Germany, 1991. Mem. Coun. on Fgn. Rels., Internat. Inst. Strategic Studies. Republican. Roman Catholic. Avocations: tennis, reading, classical music. Office: Inst East-West Security Studies 360 Lexington Ave New York NY 10017-6502

MROZIK, HELMUT, chemist; b. Habelschwerdt, Silesia, Germany, Oct. 23, 1931; came to U.S., 1959; s. Herbert and Gretel (Zimmerman) M.; m. Hannelore Hofmann, Oct. 22, 1957; children: Susanne, Patricia. PhD, U. Basel, Switzerland, 1958. Postdoctoral rsch. asst. Columbia U., N.Y.C., 1959-60; with Merck, Sharp and Dohme Rsch. Labs., Rahway, N.J., 1960—, sr. rsch. chemist, 1960-65, rsch. fellow, 1965-71, sr. rsch. fellow, 1971-78, sr. investigator, 1978-85, now sr. scientist, 1985—. Contbr. articles, revs. to profl. publs.; patentee in field. Home: 159 Idlebrook Ln Matawan NJ 07747-1744 Office: Merck Sharp Dohme Rsch Lab PO Box 2000 Wickatunk NJ 07765-9998

MRUK, CHARLES KARZIMER, agronomist; b. Providence, Sept. 23, 1926; s. Charles and Anna (Pisarek) M. BS in Agr., U. R.I., 1951, MS in Agronomy, 1957. Soil scientist soil conservation svc. Dept. Agr., Sunbury, Pa., 1951; insp. Charles A. McGuire Co., Providence, 1952; claims insp. R.R. Perishable Inspection Agy., Boston, 1953-55; asst. in agronomy U. R.I., 1955-57; agronomist Hercules Inc., 1957-79, tech. salesman, 1957-79; sr. tech. sales rep. BFC Chems., Inc., 1981-82; are devel. supr. Ea. States, 1982-84, ret., 1984; cons. turf maintenance Olympic Stadium and grounds, Mexico City, 1968, Fenway Park, Boston, 1963-70. author and editor articles on turf culture and fertilizers, 1979-81. Mem. Rep. Ward Com., Providence, 1963-76. With USN, 1944-46. U.S. Golf Assn. Green Sect. grantee, 1955-57. Mem. Am. Soc. Agronomy, R.I. Golf Course Supts. Assn., Mass. Turf and Lawn Grass Coun. (dir., mem. planning com., chmn. fin. com., 1987, pres., 1987-89), VFW, Am. Registry Cert. Profls. in Agronomy (cert. agronomist), Sigma Xi, Alpha Zeta. Mem. Polish National Ch. Home: 75 Burdick Dr Cranston RI 02920-1517

MRUK, EUGENE ROBERT, marketing professional, urban planner; b. Buffalo, Sept. 12, 1927; s. Stanley and Lucy Ann (Wolanski) M.; m. Florence Helen Guzy, Apr. 15, 1950; children: Linda, Lawrence, Edith, Ginny. AA in Engring., U. Buffalo, 1966, BA in Sociology, 1970, MA in Econs., 1974. Asst. dir. planning City of Buffalo, 1958-70; commr. planning Erie County, N.Y., Buffalo, 1970-74; dir. socioecon. studies Ecology and Environment, Inc., Buffalo, 1974-79, dir. transp. system studies, 1979-81, dir. bus. devel., 1981-86, v.p. sales and mktg., 1986-90, sr. v.p. sales and mktg., 1990—; pvt. practice planning cons. Buffalo area, 1950-64; v.p. rsch. and planning coun. WNY, 1971-74; mem. indsl. adv. bd. dept. chem. engring. SUNY, Buffalo. Author various mcpl. govt. plans. Coord. Econ. Devel. program, Buffalo, 1966; exam. cons. Civil Svc. Commn. City of Buffalo, 1974; grand marshal Gen. Pulaski Parade com., Buffalo, 1972; trustee Villa Maria Coll. Buffalo, 1992—. Named Man of Yr. in Govt. Am-Pole Eagle newspaper, 1970. Mem. Am. Assn. Cert. Planners, Am. Planning Assn. (Disting. Leadership award N.Y. upstate chpt. 1992), Profl. Businessmen's Assn. Democrat. Roman Catholic. Home: 3 Dennis Ln Buffalo NY 14227-1301 Office: Ecology and Environment Inc Buffalo Corp Ctr 368 Pleasant View Dr Lancaster NY 14086-1397

MRYKALO, FRANK MICHAEL, psychology educator; b. Scranton, Pa., Oct. 1, 1943; s. Daniel and Helen (Primich) M.; m. Jill Ann Hubert, Nov. 19, 1966; children: Frank Michael Jr., Marci Sarah. BA, U. Scranton, 1965, MS, 1967; EdD, Lehigh U., 1975. Lic. psychologist; cert. sch. psychologist. Asst. prof. psychology Broome Community Coll., Binghamton, N.Y., 1966-69; sr. clin. psychologist Binghamton State Hosp., 1966-69; asst. prof. Luzerne Community Coll., Nanticoke, Pa., 1969-70; prof. Marywood Coll., Scranton, Pa., 1970—; cons. United Cerebral Palsy, Scranton, Pa., 1970-75; psychologist pvt. practice Forum Psychol. Assocs., Scranton, Pa., 1975—. Named Tchr. of the Yr., Sears Roebuck, 1991. Mem. APA, Pa. Psychol. Assn. Democrat. Roman Catholic. Home: 2227 Hollister Ave Scranton PA 18508-2087

MTEWA, MEKKI, foundation administrator; b. Sungo, Mangochi, Malawi, Apr. 13, 1946; 1 child, Natasha. BA, Chapman Coll., 1974; MA in Polit. Sci., Calif. State U., Fullerton, 1975; postgrad., Miami U., Oxford, Ohio, 1975-76; diploma in exec. law and leadership studies, LaSalle Extension U., Chgo., 1977; PhD in Pub. Adminstrn. and Pub. Policy, Claremont Grad. Sch., 1979; postdoctoral in legal studies, Vrije U., Brussels, 1985-86. Regional adminstrv. sec. Agrl. Devel. and Mktg. Corp., Limbe, Malawi, 1964-66; adminstrv. sec. United Transport (Malawi) Ltd., Blantyre, 1966-67; legal asst. Lilley, Wills & Co., Limbe, 1968-70; exec. dir., founder Assn. for Advancement Policy, Research and Devel. in the Third World, 1981—; exec. v.p., dep. dir. POS Inst., Washington, 1982—; chmn., chief exec. officer Internat. Devel. Found. Inc., 1984—; chmn. Malawi Inst. Internat. Affairs, 1987—; research asst. Calif. State U., Fullerton, 1974-75, adj. prof., spring 1978-79; research asst. Polit. Sci. Dept. Miami U., Oxford, Ohio, 1975-76; adj. asst. prof. polit. sci. and mgmt. U. D.C., 1982-85; asst. prof. polit. sci. Howard U., Washington, 1979-85; cons. in field; lectr. in field. Author: Public Policy and Development Politics: The Politics of Technical Expertise in Africa, 1980, The Consultant Connexion: Evaluation of the Federal Consulting Service, 1981, Malawi Democratic Theory and Public Policy: A Preface, 1986; editor: Science Technology and Development: Options and Policies, 1982, Perspectives in International Development, 1986, Contemporary Issues in African Administration and Development Politics, 1987, International Development and Alternative Futures: The Coming Challenges, 1988, Internat. Science and Technology: Theory, Philosophy and Policy, 1990; contbr. articles to profl. jours., chpts. to books; mem. adv. bd. CHANGE: The Internat. Tech. newspaper; guest editor Jour. Ea. African Research and Devel.; various TV and radio appearances; subject of articles. Dep. br. sec. Malawi Congress party, 1965-66; com. chair S.W. Scholarship Fund, S.S. Neighborhood Assembly, Washington; chair election com. Rosemary Coop. Housing project. Grantee Sci. and Tech. in So. Africa Devel. Coordination Conf., 1982, Peace Corps Coll. project, 1982; fellow Midwestern U. Consortium, Miami U., Alpha Assn. Phi Beta Kappa Alumni in So. Calif.; recipient Seminar award Fgn. Student Council. Mem. Internat. Services Assn. (bd. dirs.), Sci. Soc. Chile (bd. dirs.), Lions, Phi Sigma Alpha. Office: Internat Devel Found PO Box 70257 Washington DC 20024-0257

MUCCI, GARY LOUIS, lawyer; b. Buffalo, Nov. 12, 1946; s. Guy Charles and Sally Rose (Battaglia) M.; m. Carolyn Belle Taylor, May 4, 1991. BA cum laude, St. John Fisher Coll., 1968; JD, Cath. U., 1972. Bar: N.Y. 1972. Law clk. to Hon. John T. Curtin U.S. Dist. Ct., Buffalo, 1972-74; assoc. atty. Donovan Leisure Newton & Irvine, N.Y.C., 1974-75; assoc. atty. Saperston & Day P.C., Buffalo, 1975-80, sr. ptnr., 1980—. Chmn. bd. Buffalo Philharmonic Orch., 1985-86; pres. Hospice Buffalo, 1986-87; mem. N.Y. State Coun. on the Arts, 1987—; chmn. Citizens Com. on Cultural Aid, Buffalo, 1992. Recipient Brotherhood award Nat. Conf. Christians & Jews, Buffalo, 1983; named Man of Yr. William Paca Soc., 1984. Mem. Erie County Bar Assn., N.Y. State Bar Assn. Home: 27 Tudor Pl Buffalo NY 14222 Office: Saperston & Day PC One Fountain Plz Buffalo NY 14203

MUCCI, LOUIE (LOUIS DAVID MUCCIOLO), music composer and manager; b. Jamaica, N.Y., Apr. 16, 1958; s. Louis Cosmo and Mary Michelina (Galante) M.; m. Lindsey Anne Howes, Sept. 16, 1990. BA, CUNY, Flushing, 1980. Acct. Palex Securities, Ltd., N.Y.C., 1980-81, Drexel Burnham Lambert, Inc., N.Y.C., 1981-83; tchr., asst. prin. N.Y. Bus. Sch., 1984-89; musical dir., performer N.Y. Rhythm, Glendale, 1981-91; disc jockey U.R.S.-DJ's, Glendale, N.Y., 1986—; owner GAL Pub., Glendale, 1990—; mgr., pub. G-n-A, Glendale, 1989—; music producer, cons. Fun Little Movies, N.Y.C., 1988—. Music producer, composer, performer (TV show soundtrack) Nothing Upstairs, 1990 (short film soundtrack) Seeing is Believing, 1992, (TV comm.) Private Eyes, 1989; composer song G-n-A TV Appearance, 1991. Mem. ASCAP, Nat. Music Pubs. Assn. Democrat. Roman Catholic. Home and Office: GAL Pub (ASCAP) 69-39 67th Pl Glendale NY 11385-6624

MUCCI, PATRICK JOHN, financial consultant; b. Albany, N.Y., July 5, 1947; s. Philip and Angeline (Patrella) M.; m. Beverly Ann Scully, June 8, 1968; children: Philip Michael, Angelina Maria. AAS, Hudson Valley Community Coll., Troy, N.Y., 1967; BS, SUNY, Albany, 1977; MBA, Fairleigh Dickinson U., 1979. Cert. review appraiser; registered mortgage underwriter. Adminstrv. asst. Nat. Savs. Bank, Albany, 1973-76; asst. v.p. Heritage Savs. Bank, Kingston, N.Y., 1976-78, Home Savs. Bank, Albany, 1978-81; v.p. Home Savs. Bank, 1981, Home & City Savs. Bank, Albany, 1981-83; sr. v.p. lending Home & City Savs. Bank, 1983-90; pres., chmn. bd., founder Greenbush & Assocs., Inc., East Greenbush, N.Y., 1990—. Active Italian-Am. Community Ctr.; mem. City of Albany Stratigic Planning Com., 1986; treas., bd. dirs. Theater Voices, 1990; bd. dirs. Albany League Arts, Discovery Ctr. Capital Region, 1990, N.Y. State Mus. Inst., Capital Affordable Housing Funding Com., Albany County Affordable Housing Corp. Staff sgt. USAF, 1969-72. Mem. Nat. Assn. Mortgage Brokers, N.Y. State Mortgage Brokers Assn., Capital Region Execs., N.Y. State Assn. Comml. and Indsl. Brokers, Soc. Internat. Financiers. Home: 157 Luther Rd East Greenbush NY 12061-1009

MUCCIA, JOSEPH WILLIAM, lawyer; b. N.Y.C., May 31, 1948; s. Joseph Anthony and Charlotte (Mohring) M.; m. Margaret M. Reynolds, June 29, 1985. BA magna cum laude, Fordham U., 1970, JD, 1973. Bar: N.Y. 1974, U.S. Dist. Ct. (so. dist.) N.Y. 1974, U.S. Dist. Ct. (ea. dist.) N.Y. 1980, U.S. Ct. Appeals (2d cir.) 1974, U.S. Ct. Appeals (D.C. cir.) 1980, U.S. Supreme Ct. 1980. Assoc. Cahill Gordon & Reindel, N.Y.C., 1973-82; ptnr. Corbin Silverman & Sanseverino, N.Y.C., 1973-82, 1983—. Assoc. editor Fordham Law Rev., 1972-73. Mem. ABA (litigation sect.), N.Y. County Lawyers Assn., Fed. Bar Coun., N.Y. State Bar Assn. (com. litigation sect.), Phi Beta Kappa, Pi Sigma Alpha. Office: Corbin Silverman & Sanseverino 805 3rd Ave New York NY 10022-7513

MUCHA, JOHN FRANK, data processing professional; b. Ludlow, Mass., Sept. 12, 1950; s. Joseph Walter and Sophie (Chrusciel) M.; m. Anne Virginia Casey, Sept. 1, 1973 (div. Feb. 1989). BA in Polit. Sci., U. Mass., 1972; MBA in Tech. and Profl. Communications, Frostburg State U., 1985. Cert. in data processing. Computer programmer IRS, Washington, 1974-79, computer systems programmer, 1979-81; computer systems programmer IRS, Martinsburg, W.Va., 1981-86; staff systems programmer fed. systems div. IBM, Gaithersburg, Md., 1986-87; chief tech. support IRS Martinsburg Computing Ctr., 1987-91; staff asst. to projects dir. info. systems devel. IRS, Washington, 1991-92, computer specialist transition mgmt. office, 1992—. Contbr. articles to profl. jours. Team mem., sec. Beginning Experience of Balt., 1989—; pres. Cath. Single Again Coun. of Balt., Inc., 1991—. Mem. Data Processing Mgmt. Assn. (bd. dirs.), Assn. of the Inst. for Certification of Computer Profls., Moose. Democrat. Roman Catholic. Home: 2482 Warm Spring Way Odenton MD 21113-1542

MUCHNICK, RICHARD STUART, ophthalmologist; b. Bklyn., June 21, 1942; s. Max and Rae (Kozinsky) M.; BA with honors. Cornell U., 1963, MD, 1967; m. Felice Dee Greenberg, Oct. 29, 1978; 1 child, Amanda Michelle. Intern in medicine N.Y. Hosp., N.Y.C., 1967-68, now assoc. attending ophthalmologist, chief Pediatric Ophthalmology Clinic; resident in ophthalmology, 1970-73; practice medicine, specializing in ophthalmology, notably strabismus and ophthalmic plastic surgery N.Y.C., 1974—; attending surgeon, chief Ocular Motility Clinic, Manhattan Eye, Ear and Throat Hosp., N.Y.C.; clin. assoc. prof. ophthalmology Cornell U., N.Y.C., 1984—. Served with USPHS, 1968-70. Recipient Coryell Prize Surgery Cornell U. Med. Coll., 1967. Diplomate Am. Bd. Ophthalmology, Nat. Bd. Med. Examiners. Fellow A.C.S., Am. Acad. Ophthalmology; mem. Am. Soc. Ophthalmic Plastic and Reconstructive Surgery, Am. Assn. Pediatric Ophthalmology and Strabismus, Internat. Strabismological Assn., N.Y. Soc. Clin. Ophthalmology, AMA, N.Y. Acad. Medicine, Manhattan Ophthal. Soc., N.Y. Soc. Pediatric Ophthalmology and Strabismus, Alpha Omega Alpha, Alpha Epsilon Delta. Clubs: Lotos, 7th Regt. Tennis. Clin. researcher strabismus, ophthalmic plastic surgery, 1973—. Office: 69 E 71st St New York NY 10021-4213

MUCKLOW, NIGEL BIGGLES, textiles executive; b. Stratford upon Avon, Eng., Nov. 14, 1957; came to U.S., 1979; s. Samuel and Judy (Biggles) M.; 1 child, Alexa; m. Claudia Shouter Wolfmüller, June 1, 1987; 1 child, Dominic B. BA in Sci., Cambridge (Eng.) U., 1978; MBA, Münich U., 1982. Dept. head Du Pont, Del., 1986-88; dir. U.K. Monsanto, Eng., 1988-89; pres. New Eng. F.C. Plc., Eng., U.S., Germany, 1989—. Inventor loom over shuttle drive. Dist. chmn. Nat. Front, London, 1979. Named ICI Textile Newcomer London Coun., 1989. Home: N Greenbush Rd Charlotte VT 05945

MUDAR, M(ARIAN) JEAN, biologist, environmental scientist; b. Albany, N.Y.; d. Michael and Jean (Hnyda) M. BS in Biology, SUNY, Albany, 1973, MS in Biology Edn., 1976; MS Urban/Environ Studies summa cum laude, Rensselaer Poly. Inst., 1981, PhD in Urban/Environ. Studies cum laude, 1991. Cert. tchr., N.Y. With N.Y. State Environ. Facilities Corp., Albany, 1981—, indsl. waste program analyst, 1981-86, program analyst, 1986-91, environ. scientist, 1991—; mem. adv. panel Congl. Office Tech. Assessment, 1986; mem. editorial adv. bd. Govt. Insts., Inc., Rockville, Md., 1986-91; mem. adv. bd. Nat. Roundtable of State Pollution Prevention Programs, Mpls., 1990-92; mem. coordinating com. Forum on State and Tribal Toxics Action, Washington, 1991—; project lead Pollution Prevention Project, Washington, 1991—; mem. team of scientists and engrs. to conduct joint Indo-U.S. workshop on indsl. wastewater recycling and reuse Govt. of India, 1986. Author, editor materials in field; editor: (pamphlet) Guide to Household Hazardous Wastes, 1988. Mem. Cousteau Soc. (founding), Athletics Congress, Internat. Marina Inst. (rsch. assoc.), Boat/U.S., World Wildlife Orgn., Air and Waste Mgmt. Assn.

MUDER, ROBERT RICHARD, physician, epidemiologist; b. Pitts., June 11, 1951; s. Richard Edward and Gemma (Lombardi) M.; m. Janet D. Vlha, June 4, 1977; children: Jane Elizabeth, Michael Richard. BA, Oberlin (Ohio) Coll., 1973; MD, U. Pitts., 1977. Diplomate Am. Bd. Internal Medicine. Intern, then resident in medicine Mercy Hosp., Pitts., 1977-81, asst. coord. med. edn., 1983-84, coord. med. edn., 1984-86, assoc. program dir., 1986-89, fellow in infectious disease, 1981-83; asst. prof. medicine U. Pitts., 1989—; chief infection control Pitts. VA Med. Ctr., 1986—. Contbr. articles to profl. jours. Mem. ACP, Am. Soc. for Microbiology, N.Y. Acad. Scis., Soc. for Hosp. Epidemiology Am., Phi Beta Kappa, Alpha Omega Alpha. Office: Pitts VA Med Ctr University Dr C Pittsburgh PA 15240-1002

MUDGE, RICHARD RAGSDALE, economist, consultant; b. Norristown, Pa., May 2, 1945; s. Richard Bachelder and Nina (Ragsdale) M.; m. Ilene Lafer, June 29, 1969; children: Rachel, Jared. BA, Columbia U., 1968; MA, U. Pa., 1970, PhD, 1972. Rsch. assoc. Wharton Sch., Phila., 1970-72; dir. Econ. Devel. Studies N.Y.C. Rand Inst., 1972-75; from prin. analyst to chief of pub. investment unit Congl. Budget Office, Washington, 1975-86; v.p., co-founder Apogee Rsch. Inc., Bethesda, Md., 1986-87; co-pres. Apogee Rsch. Inc., Bethesda, 1987—. Co-author: Financing Infrastructure, 1987, Airports and Airways, 1987. Recipient Fast 50 award Washington Tech., 1991, 92, Inc. 500, 1991. Mem. Nat. Acad. Sci. (Transp. Rsch. Bd. mem., Finance, Aviation Econs. com. mem.). Office: Apogee Rsch Inc 4350 E-W Hwy Bethesda MD 20854

MUDRY, MICHAEL, pension and benefit consultant; b. Lucina, Czechoslovakia, Dec. 5, 1926; (parents Am. citizens); s. John Zaleta and Helen (Molchan) M.; m. Kendall Archer, June 17, 1960; children: F. Goodrich Archer, Benjamin Kendall. BA, U. Conn., 1951. Sr. v.p. Hay/Huggins Co. Inc., Phila., 1956—; actuary Ch. Pensions Conf. Contbr. articles to profl. jours. Bd. mem. Com. Gift Annuities, Dallas, 1978—. With U.S. Army, 1945-46. Fellow Soc. Actuaries, Conf. Cons. Actuaries; mem. Am. Acad. Actuaries, Internat. Actuarial Assn., Internat. Assn. Cons. Actuaries, Union League Club. Democrat. Home: 749 Mancill Rd Wayne PA 19087-2004 Office: Hay/Huggins Co Inc 229 S 18th St Philadelphia PA 19103-6144

MUELLER, DENNIS CARY, economics educator; b. Milw., June 13, 1940; s. Anthony John and Catherine Pearl (Engelhardt) M.; m. Lillian Sandra Johnson (div. 1974); children: Laurance James, Holly Kay; m. Judith Lee Murphy; children: Jacob Lincoln, Adrienne Llyn. BS, Colo. Coll., 1962; PhD, Princeton U., 1966. Assoc. prof. Cornell U., Ithaca, N.Y., 1970-76; postdoc. fellow Va. Polytechnic Inst., Blacksburg, 1972-73; sr. rsch. fellow Internat. Inst. Mgmt., Berlin, 1974-77; rsch. contract FTC, Washington, 1978-81; fellow Internat. Ins. Mgmt., Berlin, 1981-83, dir., 1982-83; prof. econs. U. Md., College Park, 1977—; guest scholar Internat. Monetary Fund, Washington, 1986; vis. prof. Monash U., Australia, 1986. Author: Public Choice II, 1989, Profits in the Long Run, 1986, The Modern Corporation, 1986; editor: The Determinants and Effects of Mergers, 1980; editorial bd.: Internat. Jour. of Indsl. Orgn., Coventry, Eng., 1982—, Antitrust Law and Econs. Rev., Vero Beach, Fla., 1985—, Social Justice Rev., Ontario, Can., 1986—, Constitutional Political Economy, Fairfax, Va., 1988—. Mem. Pub. Choice Soc. (pres. 1984-86), Indsl. Orgn. Soc. (pres. 1985), So. Econ. Assn. (pres. 1987), Am. Econ. Assn., European Assn. for Rsch. Indsl. Econs. (pres. 1989-91). Home: 7512 Rhode Island Ave College Park MD 20740-3527 Office: U Md Dept Econs College Park MD 20740

MUELLER, JAMES PAUL, engineer; b. Freeport, N.Y., July 25, 1956; s. Paul Arthur and Elizabeth Wooten (Henry) M.; m. Cynthia Lois Warren, Apr. 30, 1986. BS, Bklyn. Polytech, 1977. Sr. engr. Grumman Space and Electronics, Princeton, N.J., 1977—. Mem. "Otta" Sights and Sounds (art dept. 1991-92). Office: Grumman 4 Independence Way Princeton NJ 08540

MUENCH, DONALD LEO, mathematics educator; b. Rochester, N.Y., Jan. 31, 1934; s. Oswald John and Jean (Sponenberg) M.; m. Marilyn Brady; children: Anne, David, Stephen, Gregory. BS, St. John Fisher Coll., 1955; ArtsD, Idaho State U., 1974. Asst. prof. math. U.S. Naval Acad., Annapolis, Md., 1960-66; prof. math., computer sci. St. John Fisher Coll., Rochester, N.Y., 1966—; Reviewer in field. Contbr. articles to profl. jours. Mem. Am. Math. Soc., Math. Assn. Am., Assn. Computing Machinery (Rochester chpt. vice chmn. 1989-91). Home: 16 Smallwood Dr Pittsford NY 14534-3434 Office: St John Fisher Coll Rochester NY 14618

MUENTER, ANNABEL ADAMS, research chemist; b. N.Y.C., Dec. 3, 1944; d. Richard Miller and Annabel (Van Winkle) Adams; m. John Stuart Muenter, Aug. 24, 1968; 1 child, Annabel Helen. BS in Chemistry, U. Mich., 1966; PhD in Chem. Physics, Harvard U., 1972. Sr. rsch. chemist Eastman Kodak Co., Rochester, N.Y., 1970-77, rsch. assoc., 1977-90, sr. rsch. assoc., 1990—; mem. Ctr. for Photo-induced Charge Transfer, U. Rochester, 1989—. Contbr. articles to profl. jours. Fellow Soc. for Imaging Sci. & Tech.; mem. Am. Chem. Soc., Sigma Xi (treas. local sect. 1986-90). Home: 9 Park Pl Rochester NY 14625-2163 Office: Eastman Kodak Co Kodak Park # B-2 Rochester NY 14652-3208

MUESING ELLWOOD, EDITH ELIZABETH, writer, researcher, publisher, editor; b. N.Y.C., Sept. 18, 1947; d. Carl Earl and Elsbeth (Bushbeck) Muesing; m. William Adonis Ellwood, Sept. 15, 1980; children: Jeanie, Colin, Caroline. BA, Fordham U., 1969; MA, NYU, 1971. Adminstrv. asst. The English Speaking Union, N.Y.C., 1979; freelance writer, researcher The Acad. Rsch. Group, Rutherford, N.J., 1975-78, 80-82; pres. Colin-Press, Bklyn., 1984-88; editor Ellwood Editing Svc., 1990—. Author: U.S. Democracy: Myth vs. Reality, 1985, The Alternative to Technological Culture, 1986; contbr. haiku poems and sketches to mags., newsletters and anthologies, 1979—, articles to jours., mags., tabloids and newsletters. Active Nat. Trust for Hist. Preservation, Washington, 1980—, Friends of Central Park, N.Y.C., 1980-86, South St. Seaport Mus., N.Y.C., 1974-83, 90—; founding mem. Nat. Mus. Women in Arts, Washington, 1985-88; mem. Environ. Def. Fund, 1973—, Nature Conservancy, 1986—, Nat. Chronic Pain Outreach Assn., 1991—; contbg. mem. Dem. Nat. Com., 1991—; founding patron Katharine Houghton Hepburn Fund, Planned Parenthood, 1989—. Mem. NOW, Nat. Writers Cub, Internat. Women's Writing Guild, Women in Scholarly Pub. (editor column in newsletter 1990), Am. Acad. Poets (contbr.), Interstitial Cystitis Assn., Nat. Writers Union. Democrat. Roman Catholic. Home and Office: 229B Pond Way Staten Island NY 10303-1645

MUESSIG, ROBERT ANDREW, manufacturing executive; b. Newark, June 13, 1928; s. August Charles and Adelaide Dorothy (Noll) M.; m. Frances Joan Flynn, June, 1954 (div. Dec. 1976); 1 child, David; m. Patricia Ann O'Dell, Mar. 19, 1977. ME, Stevens Inst. Tech., 1953, MS, 1958. Registered profl. engr., N.J., N.Y. Plant/process engr. GM Corp., Linden, N.J., 1953-58; salesman Binks Mfg. Co., Long Island City, N.Y., 1959-69; br. mgr. Binks Mfg. Co., Moonachie, N.J., 1970-78; regional mgr. Binks Mfg. Co., Pine Brook, N.J., 1979—. With U.S. Army, 1946-48, ETO. Mem. Overseas Automotive Club (dir. 1991—). Home: 15 Harwich Rd Morristown NJ 07960-2639 Office: Binks Mfg Co 1 Chapin Rd PO Box 696 Pine Brook NJ 07058

MUGAN, DANIEL JOSEPH, educational association executive; b. N.Y.C., Dec. 10, 1933; s. James and Ellen Lena (O'Callaghan) M.; m. Rosa Ines Salinas, Dec. 24, 1969. BA, Bklyn. Coll., 1962, MA, 1966; PhD, NYU, 1990. Pres. Assn. of Tchrs. of Latin Am. Studies, N.Y.C., 1972—; cons. Bklyn. Mus., McGraw Hill Co., Del Mar, Calif., 1983, N.Y.C. Bd. Edn., 198—, Acad. for Ednl. Devel., Washington, 1980—, N.Y. State Dept. Edn., 1980—. Author: Latin America: History Culture People, 1980; author film: Latin America, 1983. U.S. Dept. Edn. grantee, 1964, 68, 72, 73, 83, 85, 86, 89, 92, Tinker Found. grantee, 1984. Mem. Americas Soc., Acad. Polit. Sci., Am. Assn. Polit. Sci. Democrat. Roman Catholic. Home and Office: ATLAS 1st Level 252-58 63d Ave Flushing NY 11362-2406

MUHA, DENISE BOUSTEAD, trade association administrator; b. Aliquippa, Pa., Apr. 9, 1959; d. Wenzel Dean and Patricia (McNally) Boustead; m. Christopher David Muha, Oct. 10, 1981. BA, Thiel Coll., 1981. Dir. sales Ramada Hotels, Coraopolis, Pa., 1984-85; dir. membership Nat. Leased Housing Assn., Washington, 1985-88, exec. dir., 1988—. Bd. dirs. Nat. Low Income Housing Coalition, Washington, 1988—; vol. Christmas in Apr., Washington, 1988-91. Mem. Am. Soc. Assn. Execs., Women in Housing and Fin. Presbyterian. Office: Nat Leased Housing Assn 2300 M St NW # 260 Washington DC 20037-1434

MUHAMMAD, KHALIL ABDUL, professional association administrator; b. Phila., Oct. 19, 1962. MA, Lincoln (Pa.) U., 1986; postgrad., U. Sarasota. Cert. secondary tchr., Fla. Owner Cert. Paralegal Assocs., Phila.; exec. dir. Nat. Assn. Profl. Word Processing Technicians, Phila. Mem. reception com. University City Rep. Com., Phila. Recognized at Buckingham Palace by Her Majesty Queen Elizabeth II, 1974. Mem. ABA, Phila. Bar Assn., Nat. Lawyers Guild (bd. dirs.).

MUI, JIMMY KUN, architect; b. Hong Kong, Sept. 1, 1958; came to U.S., 1971; s. Yuk-on and Kum-Ngor (Yuen) M.; m. Soo N. Yew, Sept. 23, 1989; 1 child, Deborah Yoke-Kit. BArch, SUNY, Buffalo, 1982, postgrad., 1982-84. Architecture aide City of N.Y. Dept. of Health, 1978; intern architect Niagara Frontier Transp. Authority, Buffalo, 1983; architect, drafter Bradley Corp. Park, Blauvelt, N.Y., 1984-85; asst. architect City of N.Y. Dept. of Housing Preservation and Devel., 1985-87, N.Y.C. Bd. Edn., 1987-91; design cons. J.K. Mui Design, Bronx, N.Y., 1989—; project coord. N.Y.C. Pub. Schs., 1991—. Vice chmn. bd. dirs. Hong Kong Students Assn. N.Y. Inc., 1989-91, chmn., 1987-89, pres., 1986. Recipient N.Y. State Regent Scholarship award, 1977-81, Husted Eward Scholarship award SUNY, 1980. Roman Catholic. Home: 2237 Haviland Ave Bronx NY 10462-5202 Office: NYC Pub Schs Div Sch Facilities 28-11 Queens Plz N Rm 534C Long Island City NY 11101

MUILENBURG, ROBERT WILLIAM, electric utility executive; b. San Fernando, La Union, Philippines, Aug. 7, 1933; came to U.S., 1951; s. Cornelius William and Anne Amelda (Jackola) M.; m. Phyllis Jean Wier-

enga, June 8, 1955; children: Pamela, Robert II. AB, Hope Coll., Holland, Mich., 1955; MS in Journalism, Northwestern U., 1957. Edn. dir. Am. Seating Co., Grand Rapids, Mich., 1960-65, pub. rels. mgr., 1965-71; group pub. rels. mgr. Babcock & Wilcox, Barberton, Ohio, 1971-76; mgr. corp. communications Jersey Cen. Power & Light, Morristown, N.J., 1976-82, v.p. communications, 1982—. Vice chmn. Alliance for Action, Woodbridge, N.J., 1988—; chmn. N.J. for a Clean Tomorrow, Woodbridge, 1989-91. Lt. comdr. USNR, 1957-58. Recipient Eagle award Alliance for Action, 1986. Office: Jersey Ctrl Power & Light 300 Madison Ave Morristown NJ 07960-6118

MUIR, BROCKETT, lawyer; b. Washington, Apr. 21, 1905; s. Charles Stothard and Carlotta (Brockett) M.; m. Helen Cassin Dapray (dec.); children: Brockett Jr., Helen Muir Bertke, John Dapray, Stephen Cassin, Marilyn Calvert Smith. Student, George Washington U., 1923-24, Brown U., 1924-25, Georgetown Fgn. Service Sch., 1927-28; LLB, Nat. U., 1932. Bar: D.C. 1934, Md. 1946. Founder Potomac Title Co., Bethenda, Md., 1946; sole practice Chevy Chase, Md., 1946—. Patentee disposable flashlight. Served as comdr. USNR, 1942-46. Republican. Roman Catholic. Club: Chevy Chase. Home: 5100 Dorset Ave Bethesda MD 20815-5465

MUIR, MALCOLM, federal judge; b. Englewood, N.J., Oct. 20, 1914; s. John Merton and Sarah Elizabeth (Stabler) M.; m. Alma M. Brohard, Sept. 6, 1940 (dec. 1985); children: Malcolm, Thomas, Ann Muir Weinberg, Barbara (dec.), David Clay. B.A., Lehigh U., 1935; LL.B., Harvard U., 1938. Sole practice Williamsport, Pa., 1938-42, 45-49; mem. firm Williamsport, 1949-70; judge U.S. Dist. Ct. (mid. dist.) Pa., 1970—. Active charitable orgns., Williamsport, 1939-70. Mem. ABA, Pa. Bar Assn. (pres.-elect 1970). Office: US Dist Ct PO Box 608 Williamsport PA 17703-0608

MUKAI, CROMWELL DAISAKU, chemist; b. Bostonia, Calif., Apr. 13, 1917; s. Thomas Tasaburo and Fusae (Tsujino) M.; m. Kyoko Hoshiga, Oct. 26, 1944; children: Robert Lawrence, Thomas Victor, David Daisaku, Margret Kyoko. BS, U. Calif., Berkeley, 1943; MS, NYU, 1949, PhD, 1955. Devel. chemist Gelatin Products Corp., Detroit, 1944-46; rsch. assoc. Boyle-Midway, Cranford, N.J., 1946-75; lab. mgr. Polychrome Corp., Yonkers, N.Y., 1975-80; rsch. mgr. Deleet Merchandising Corp., Newark, 1980-91; pvt. practice chem. cons. Exec. Resource Assocs., Berkeley Heights, N.J., 1991—. Patentee in field. Mem. Japanese Am. Citizens League, N.Y.C., 1960—. Recipient Achievement award Polychrome Corp., 1976, Extraordinary Accomplishment, 1977. Mem. AAAS, Am. Chem. Soc., Smithsonian Instn., U. Calif.-Berkeley Alumni Assn., Sigma Xi, Phi Lambda Upsilon. Methodist. Home and Office: 26 Brook St Berkeley Heights NJ 07922-1814

MUKAMAL, STEVEN SASOON, lawyer; b. Bagdad, Iraq, Aug. 5, 1940; s. Abaraham and Mary (Murad) M.; m. Nancy Barst, Aug. 3, 1963 (div. Mar. 1983); children: Wendy, Betsy, Thomas; m. Kathleen Nanowsky, Nov. 25, 1983; children: Theodore Douglas, Andrew John. BA, Mich. State U., 1962; JD, Bklyn. Law Sch., 1965. Bar: N.Y. 1966, U.S. Dist. Ct. (so. dist.) N.Y. 1967, (ea. dist.) N.Y., U.S. Ct. Appeals (1st, 2nd and 3rd cirs.) 1968, U.S. Supreme Ct. 1975. Sr. ptnr. Barst & Mukamal, N.Y.C., 1965—; pres. Immigration Info. System, Hong Kong. Mem. editorial bd. Transnational Immigration Lawyer Reporter, 1978—; contbr. articles to profl. jours. Exec. dir., spl. immigration counsel Nat. Com. for Furtherance of Jewish Edn., 1980—; mayor Village of Woodsburg, N.Y., 1975-78. Recipient Internat. Humanitarian award Nat. Com. for Furtherance of Jewish Edn., 1981. Mem. Am. Immigration Lawyers Assn. (chair com. cert. 1991, life mem. bd. dirs., lectr. 1970—, chmn. ann. conf. 1967-81, treas. 1974-75, 1st v.p. 1975-76, 2d v.p. 1976-77, pres. 1977-78). Office: Barst & Mukamal 2 Park Ave New York NY 10016-5603

MUKASEY, MICHAEL B., district judge; b. 1941. AB, Columbia U., 1963; LLB, Yale U., 1967. Assoc. Webster Sheffield Fleishchmann Hitchcock & Brookfield, 1967-72, Patterson, Belknap, Webb & Tyler, 1976-88; asst. U.S. atty. U.S. Dist. Ct. (so. dist.) N.Y., 1972-76, dist. judge, 1988—. Contbr. articles to profl. jours. Mem. Assn. of Bar of City of N.Y. (fed. cts. com. 1979-82, communications law com. 1983-86). Office: US Dist Ct US Courthouse Foley Sq New York NY 10007-1581

MUKHERJEE, MARGARET REED, college director; b. Troy, N.Y., Oct. 25, 1934; d. Harvey Lewis and Jessie (Dixon) Reed; m. Ben Mukherjee, Aug. 1, 1964; children: David, Brian. BS, Cornell U., 1956; MA, Mich. State U., 1961; PhD, Rutgers U., 1978. Asst. county 4-H Club agt. Saratoga Springs, N.Y., 1957-59; grad. asst. Mich. State U., 1959-61, ext. clothing specialist, 1961-65; from instr. to prof. dept. of home economics Montclair (N.J.) State Coll., 1965—, special asst. to the dean sch. profl. studies, 1984-86, dir. grad. studies, 1986—. Author: (with others) Introduction to Research in Home Economics, 1982, (workbook 1985). Coun. mem. Twp. Governing Body, Montclair, N.J., 1988-92, dept. mayor, 1990-92; commr. Redevelopment Agy., Montclair, 1984-88; pres. Montclair Mainstreet Project, 1986-88. Margaret Mukherjee Scholarship named in her honor, Women of Montclair State Coll., 1991. Mem. Rotary (bd. dirs. 1991-92). Home: 281 Highland Ave Montclair NJ 07043-1009 Office: Montclair State Coll Office of Grad Studies Montclair NJ 07043

MUKHOPADHYAY, NIKHILES, chemical company executive, environment consultant; b. Calcutta, India, July 6, 1944; came to U.S., 1966; s. Suniles Mukherji and Smrity (Dasgupta) M.; m. Dolly Chattopadhyay, Feb. 3, 1969; 1 child, Camellia. BS in Chemistry (honors), Calcutta U., 1962; BSChemE, Jadavpur U., Calcutta, 1966; MSChemE, U. Colo., 1968. Prodn. mgr. Tenneco Chems. Inc., Fords, N.J., 1968-74; sr. project engr. C.F. Braun & Co., Murray Hills, N.J., 1974-75; sr. chem. engr. Sherwin Williams Chems., Cin., 1975-78; staff engr. Ciba-Geigy Corp., Cranston, R.I., 1978-83; dir. mfg./environ. Ciba-Geigy Corp., Hawthorne/Ardsley, N.Y., 1983-91; mgr. process and environ. svcs. Baker Environ. Inc., Coraopolis, Pa., 1991—. Treas. Indian Students' Assn., Boulder, Colo., 1967-68; mem. Cultural Assn. of Bengal, Pelham Manor, N.Y., 1983—; mem. Bengal Assn., Pitts., 1991—. Named King's Scout, Boy Scouts of India, 1957; recipient Dow scholarship and teaching assistantship, U. Colo., 1967. Mem. Am. Inst. Chem. Engrs., Air and Waste Mgmt. Assn. Hindu. Home: 105 Freedom Ct Coraopolis PA 15108-9020 Office: Baker Environ Inc 420 Rouser Rd Bldg 3 Coraopolis PA 15108-2750

MULA, FRANK M., financial company executive; b. Bklyn., Mar. 28, 1955; s. Frank A. and Frances (Castello) M.; m. Vera Cheverino, Nov. 14, 1976; children: Francis Vincent, Christopher Vincent. AA, Elizabeth Seton Coll., 1985. Asst. v.p. Pershing & Co., Inc., Jersey City, N.J., 1974-83; v.p. Sequor Group, N.Y.C., 1983—. Mgr. Howell (N.J.) Cen. Little League, 1991. Fellow Security Industry Assn., Internat. Ops. Assn., Dividend Div. Roman Catholic. Office: Sequor Group 127 John St New York NY 10038-3604

MULCAHY, JOHN, lawyer; b. White Plains, N.Y., Sept. 28, 1950; s. Thomas John and Jane Catherine (Ryan) M.; m. Christine Mayne Heath, Aug. 2, 1975; children: Thomas, Megan, Anne, Jane. BA cum laude, Tufts U., 1972; JD, Georgetown U., 1977. Bar: Mass. 1978, N.Y. 1979, U.S. Dist. Ct. (so. dist.) N.Y. 1979, U.S. Dist. Ct. (ea. dist.) N.Y., 1990, U.S. Ct. Appeals (2d cir.) 1984, U.S. Supreme Ct. 1984. Asst. dist. atty. N.Y. County Dist. Atty. Office, N.Y.C., 1978-86; spl. asst. U.S. atty. So. Dist. N.Y., N.Y.C., 1982-85; ptnr. White, Fleischner & Fino, N.Y.C., 1986-91, White, Fleischner, Fino & Wade, N.Y.C., 1991—. Mem. N.Y. County Lawyers Assn. Home: 5 Incognito Ln Ossining NY 10562-2504 Office: White Fleischner Fino Wade 195 Broadway New York NY 10007-3100

MULCKHUYSE, JACOB JOHN, energy conservation-environment consultant; b. Utrecht, the Netherlands, July 21, 1922; came to U.S., 1982; s. Lambertus D. and Aagje (Van Geyn) M.; m. Cornelia Jacoba Wentink, Jan. 17, 1953; children: Jacobien, Hans, Dieuwke, Linda, Marlies. MSc, U. Amsterdam (the Netherlands), 1952, PhD, 1960. Dir. Chemisch-Farmaceutische Fabriek Hamu, the Netherlands, 1951-57; tech. asst. mgr. Polak & Schwarz (now IFF), the Netherlands, 1957-60; asst. tech. mgr. Albatros Superphosphate Fabrieken, the Netherlands, 1960-61; tech. mgr. for overseas subsidiaries Verenigde Kunstmestfabrieken, the Netherlands, 1961-64, gen. mgr. process engring. dept., 1964-70; dept. head process engring. dept. Unie van Kunstmestfabrieken, the Netherlands, 1970-82; sr. chem. engr. World Bank, Washington, 1982-83, sr. cons. chem. engr., 1983-87; ind. cons. World Bank and several cons. firms, 1987—. Author: (with Heath and Venkataraman) The Potential for Energy Efficiency in the Fertilizer Industry, 1985, (with Gamba and Caplin) Industrial Energy Rationalization in Developing and Constraints in Energy Conservation, 1990, Process Safety Analysis: Incentive for the Identification of Inherent Process Hazards; editor: Environmental Balance of the Netherlands, 1972. Mem. Am. Inst. Chem. Engrs., Royal Dutch Chem. Soc., Fertilizer Soc. (pres. 1969-70), Internat. Inst. for Energy Conservation (bd. dirs. 1990—), Rotary. Home: 53 Ponderosa Ln Palmyra VA 22963

MULDER, ELIZABETH A., psychotherapist, weight management consultant; b. Englewood, N.J., July 10, 1936; d. Charles Arthur and Emma (Leswing) Jones; m. Jerrold H. Mulder, Apr. 8, 1961 (div. June 1989); children: Todd, Bradford, Steven. BS, Bucknell U., 1958; MSW, NYU, 1979. Diplomate Nat. Assn. for Social Workers; cert. social worker; credentialled alcoholism counselor. Psychiat. social worker St. Vincent's Hosp., N.Y.C., 1980-84; psychotherapist Assn. for Psychotherapy, N.Y.C., 1982-85; counselor Bklyn. Friends Sch., 1984-88; pvt. practice psychotherapy N.Y.C., 1984—. Candidate for Kings County Assembly, Bklyn., 1963; ann. ball chmn. Jr. League of Bklyn., 1972; chmn. ann. dinner Nat. Audubon Soc., N.Y.C., 1977. Mem. Nat. Assn. for Social Workers, Nat. Psychol. Assn. for Psychoanalysis (in-tng.). Presbyterian. Home and Office: Ste 10B 130 E 63d St New York NY 10021

MULDOON, FRANCIS CREIGHTON, judge; b. Winnipeg, Manitoba, Canada, Aug. 3, 1930; s. William John and Laura Grace (Meredith) M.; m. M. Lucille Shirtliff, Aug. 6, 1955; 2 children. BA, U. Manitoba, 1952, LLB, 1956. Cert. barrister, solicitor, notary pub. Lawyer Monnin, Grafton, Deniset & Co., Winnipeg, Man., 1956-70; chmn. Manitoba Law Reform Commn., Winnipeg, 1970-77; v.p. Law Reform Commn. Can., Ottawa, 1977-78, pres., 1978-83; judge Fed. Ct. Can., Ottawa, 1983—, Ct. Martial Appeals Ct., Ottawa, 1983—; Bencher Law Soc. Manitoba, Winnipeg, 1968-71. Contbr. articles to profl. jours. President Children Aid Soc. Winnipeg, 1969-70, Manitoba Medico-Legal Soc., Winnipeg, 1973-77. Lt. Can. Army, 1952-60. Disting. Svc. Manitoba Bar Assn., 1987. Mem. Med. Legal Soc. Ottawa-Carleton (founder), St. Paul's Coll. (hon.). Roman Catholic. Office: Fed Ct Can, Kent & Wellington Sts, Ottawa, ON Canada K1A 0H9

MULDROW, CHARLES NORMENT, chemical company executive; b. Washington, Dec. 27, 1930; s. Charles Norment and Mary Pauline (Hearon) M.; m. Nancy Gerda Fugelso, June 14, 1958; children: James Norment, Ralph Charles, Robert William. BS in Chemistry, Coll. of Charleston, 1950; MA in Phys. Chemistry, U. N.C., 1954; PhD in Phys. Chemistry, U. Va., 1958. Teaching asst. U.N.C., Chapel Hill, 1951-52; rsch. chemist Shell Devel. Co., Emeryville, Calif., 1958-59; sect. head Am. Enka Co., Enka, N.C., 1959-76; sr. scientist NL Industries, Hightstown, N.J., 1976-82; project leader Wellman Inc., Johnsonville, S.C., 1982; v.p. product devel. Shamrock Chemicals, Newark, 1982-84; tech. dir. Princeton Polymer Labs., Plainsboro, N.J., 1985-89; sr. cons. Arthur D. Little, Cambridge, Mass., 1989-91; dir. product devel. XMX Corp., Burlington, Mass., 1991—. Patentee in field. Mem. East Windsor (N.J.) Rep. Club, 1992. With USN, 1953-55. Dupont fellow, Charlottesville, Va., 1957, NSF fellow, Charlottesville, 1957-58. Mem. Am. Chem. Soc. (chmn. cen. subsect., North Jersey 1987-89), N.J. Inst. Chemists (v.p. 1988-89), Am. Inst. Chemists (mem. nat. ethics coms. 1989—), Soc. Plastics Engrs., Soc. Coatings Tech., Soc. for Advancement of Materials and Process Engring., N.Y. Acad. Scis., Sigma Xi. Home: 5 Knollwood Dr East Windsor NJ 08520 Office: XMX Corp Ste 400 6 Executive Park Burlington Mall Rd Burlington MA 01803

MULFORD, THOMAS JAMES, operations executive; b. Rochester, N.Y., Oct. 17, 1943; s. Eldon James and Ines Mae M.; m. Virginia Anne Capron, June 25, 1966; children: Deborah Anne, Michael Thomas, Brian Thomas. BSME, Union Coll., 1966, AB in Econs., 1966; MBA in Mktg., U. Rochester, 1968. Lic. profl. engr., N.Y. Unit mgr. GE, Schenectady, N.Y., 1966-73; mgr. mfg. Taycor Instrument/Sybron, Rochester, N.Y., 1973-79; dir. mfg. Taylor Instrument/Sybron, Rochester, 1979-84; v.p. ops. Anastar/Kodak, Rochester, 1984-87, IBI/Kodak, Rochester, 1987-89, Holotek, Ltd., Rochester, 1989—; dir. Hill Sci., Inc., New Haven, 1989—, CYP Youth Basketball, Pittsford, N.Y., 1984-88; bd. dirs. Holotexk, Rochester, 1989—. Vol. Head Start, Schenectady, N.Y., 1972-73; coach Youth Soccer of Pittsford. Mem. Am. Mgmt. Assn. Home: 29 Harper Dr Pittsford NY 14534-3116 Office: Holotek Ltd 300 E River Rd Rochester NY 14623-1214

MULHARE, EILEEN MARGARET, social scientist; b. Norwalk, Conn., Jan. 18, 1953; d. Francis Carroll and Mirta Teresita (de la Torre) Mulhare. BA in Anthropology, Carlow Coll., 1972; PhD in Anthropology, U. Pitts., 1986. Instr., researcher U. Pitts., 1972-80; patient accounts supr. Community Home Health Svcs., Phila., 1981-82; sr. devel. assoc. Lawrence Inst. Tech., Southfield, Mich., 1982-87; dir. grants, devel. libraries Wayne State Univ., Detroit, 1988-90; rsch. assoc. Colgate U., Hamilton, N.Y., 1990—; researcher, translator U. Kans. Biomed. Project, Saltillo, Mexico, 1974; cons. L.P. Campbell Assoc., Pitts., 1976; contract grant writer Social Rsch. Application Corp., Wash., 1977. Mem. adv. Allegheny County Indochinese Refugee Resettlement Task force, Pitts., 1975-76. Rsch. fellow Fulbright-Hays, Puebla, Mex., 1978-89, Orgn. Am. States, Puebla, 1979. Fellow Soc. Applied Anthropology, Am. Anthropol. Assn.; mem. Nat. Soc. Fund Raising Execs. Home: RR 2 Box 38 Hamilton NY 13346-9802 Office: Colgate U Dept Sociology Anthropology Alumni Hall Hamilton NY 13346

MULHAUSER, KAREN, management and public affairs consultant; b. Burlington, Vt., Nov. 5, 1942; d. Harold H. and Leta H. Webber; B.A. in Biology, Antioch Coll., 1965; m., Aug. 18, 1968; 1 child, Christopher. Research assoc. Albert Einstein Coll. of Medicine, Bronx, N.Y., 1965-67; sci. tchr. Cambridge Sch., Weston, Mass., 1967-70; family planning trainer/educator HEW Region X, Seattle, 1970-73; lobbyist Nat. Abortion Rights Action League, Washington, 1973-75, exec. dir., 1975-81; polit. cons., 1982; exec. dir. Citizens Against Nuclear War, Washington, 1982-87; exec. dir. Ctr. for Edn. on Nuclear War, Washington, 1982-87; ptnr., cons. Mulhauser, Yanofsky & Assocs., 1989-90; cons. Mulhauser & Assocs., Washington, 1990—; trustee Antioch U.; bd. dirs. Internat. Devel. Conf., Am. Forum, Scoville Peace Fellowship; bd. dirs. Ind. Action, Nat. Ctr. Careers in Pub. Life; former chmn. Women for a Meaningful Summit, 1985—; former bd. dirs. exec. com. Nuclear Weapons Freeze Campaign. Mem. Planned Parenthood Met. Washington, past pres., bd. dirs.; former bd. dirs. Ctr. for Population Options; sec., mem. exec. com. Voters for Choice; mem. exec. com. Friends of Family Planning; chair bd. dirs. Am. Security Info. Coun.; pres. Antioch Coll. Alumni Assn. Democrat. Office: 1225 15th St NW Washington DC 20005-2844

MULL, CHARLES LEROY, II, travel agency executive; b. Reading, Pa., Dec. 30, 1927; s. Charles Leroy and Harriet Jane (MacMullen) M.; m. Sara Louise Tooke, July 19, 1952; children: Deborah Louise, Carol Lynn Mull-Taggart, Charles Wesley. BS in Marine Engring., U.S. Naval Acad., 1950; BS in Engring. Electronics, U.S. Naval Postgrad. Sch., 1957. Commd. ensign USN, 1950; advanced through grades to capt., 1970; shore electronics engring. officer U.S. Naval Ship Repair Facility, Yokosuka, Japan, 1964-67; nuclear guided missile cruiser combat system project officer U.S. Naval Ship Engring. Ctr., Washington, 1967-70; comdg. officer U.S. Naval Electronics Engring. Ctr., Charleston, S.C., 1970-73; tech. dir. U.S. Naval Guided Missile Frigate Project, Washington, 1973-76; supr. shipbldg., overhaul and repair USN, Bath, Maine, 1976-81; ret., 1981; pres. Stowe Travel Internat., Inc., Brunswick, Maine, 1981—. Monthly travel columnist Pejepscot Cryer, Brunswick, 1985—. Corporator Mid Coast Hosp., Brunswick, 1986—; campaign chmn. Bath-Brunswick Area United Way, 1986; pres. United Way Mid Coast Maine, 1989-91. Decorated Legion of Merit, Meritorious Svc. medal with oak leaf cluster; recipient Joshua Chamberlain award Bath-Brunswick Mil. Community Coun., 1981; named (with wife Sally) Co-Citizens of Yr., Brunswick Area C. of C., 1992. Mem. Am. Soc. Travel Agts., Assn. Retail Travel Agts., U.S. Naval Inst., Navy League U.S. (pres. Casco Bay, Maine coun. 1988-90), Brunswick Area C. of C. (chmn. retail devel. task force 1991—), Nat. Trust Hist. Preservation, Pejepscot Hist. Soc., Ret. Officers Assn., U.S. Naval Acad. Alumni Assn., Brunswick Rotary (Pres.'s award Bath Rotary 1978), Masons, Shriners. Republican. Episcopalian. Office: Stowe Travel Internat Inc 9 Pleasant St Brunswick ME 04011-2253

MULLEN, BRIAN, psychology educator; b. Syracuse, N.Y., July 7, 1955; s. Terrence Patrick and Sophie Rose (Potish) m.; m. Mary Lou Porter, Mar. 21, 1979; 1 child, Darcy. BA in Psychology, Siena Coll., 1977; PhD in Social Psychology, SUNY, 1982. Asst. prof. North Cen. Coll., Naperville, Ill., 1981-83, Murray (Ky.) State U., 1983-85; asst. prof. Syracuse (N.Y.) U., 1985-88, assoc. prof., 1988—; dir. social psychology grad. program Syracuse U., 1988—; rsch. cons. (grantee) USN, U.S. Army, USAF, NASA, 1986—. Mem. Am. Psychol. Assn., Soc. Experimental Soc. Psychologists, Soc. Personality & Soc. Psychology, European Assn. Experimental Soc. Psychology, Psychol. Soc. Ireland. Office: Syracuse U Dept Psychology Syracuse NY 13244-2340

MULLEN, DANNY WALTER, educator, actor, writer; b. Buffalo, July 30, 1954; s. Harrison and Addie Mae (Outline) M.; m. Alfreda Taylor, June 15, 1977; children: Derrick, Tiffany, Alexander, Danny II. BA in Sociology, Buffalo State U., 1981. Cert. social studies tchr. Tchr. Buffalo Pub. Schs., 1985—. Author, actor: (screenplay) Wilfred, 1985, (play) President-General Marcus Garvy, 1990. Recipient Operation Discovery award Langston Hughes Ctr., Buffalo, 1986. Home: 413 Riley St Buffalo NY 14208-2149

MULLEN, ROBERT LEE, electrical engineer; b. Muncie, Ind., Aug. 29, 1948; s. Robert Larkin and Bernice Thelma (Day) M.; m. Cherryll Ann Tuttle, Apr. 26, 1968; children: Sally Elizabeth, John Larkin. BS in Elec. Engring., U. South Fla., 1974; MS in Elec. Engring., Johns Hopkins U., 1983. Narte Cert. Engr. Repairman, technician U.S. Army Signal Branch, 1968-71; rsch. engr. I.I.T. Rsch. Inst., Annapolis, Md., 1974—; cons. Electromagnetic Compatibility Analysis Ctr., Annapolis, Md., 1974—. Mem. Federal Towne Civic Assn., Annapolis, Md., 1974—. With U.S. Army, 1968-71. Mem. Assn. Old Crows, Inst. Elec. and Electronic Engrs., Tau Beta Pi Nat. Engring Honor Soc. Office: IIT Rsch Inst 185 Admiral Cochrane Dr Annapolis MD 21401

MULLER, ALFRED, videotape editor; b. Templin, Germany, Feb. 14, 1940; came to U.S., 1963; s. Alfred and Martha (Klauschen) M.; m. Joann Rake, Jan. 20, 1979; children: Christine, Nicole. BSEE, Engr. Funk & Fernmeldewesen, Berlin, 1961. Videotape editor Reeves Video Svcs., N.Y.C., 1966-68; dir. post prodn. Lewron TV, N.Y.C., 1968-71; videotape editor EUE/Screen Gems, N.Y.C., 1971-77; pres. Nexus Prodns., Inc., N.Y.C., 1977—. Videotape editor TV program: Pueblo, 1973 (Emmy award). Treas. Pocantico Lake Civic Assn., Mt. Pleasant, N.Y., 1985. Mem. Soc. Motion Picture and TV Engrs., Dirs. Guild Am. (bd. dirs.). Republican. Presbyterian. Office: Nexus Prodns Inc 10 E 40th St New York NY 10016-0200

MULLER, CHARLES WILLIAM, administrative law judge; b. N.Y.C., Jan. 21, 1930; s. Charles John and Mary Alice (Martin) M.; m. Patricia Jane Sheridan, Aug. 10, 1957; children: Reid Thomas, Roger Sheridan. BA, Fordham U., 1951, JD, 1956; ML, NYU, 1963. Bar: N.Y. 1956. Assoc. counsel Equitable Life Assurance Soc. U.S., N.Y.C., 1956-88; adminstrv. law judge N.Y.C. Taxi & Limousine Commn., 1989—; arbitrator Am. Arbitration Assn., 1992—. Col. USAFR, 1951-82. Roman Catholic. Home and Office: 14 Stuyvesant Oval 12-B New York NY 10009-2225

MULLER, EUGENE WILLIAM, psychologist; b. Teaneck, N.J., Oct. 23, 1956; s. Eugene Harry and Emily M.; m. Ju-Nie Shen, Mar. 26, 1984. BS in Psychology, Ramapo Coll., 1978; MA in Psychology, Columbia U., 1982, MA in Computing in Edn., 1984, EdD in Psychology, 1985. Lic. psychologist, N.Y. Data mgr. Tchrs. Coll. Columbia U., N.Y.C., 1983-85; test specialist N.Y.C. Bd. Edn., 1985-86; sr. psychometrician N.Y. Stock Exch., N.Y.C., 1987-88; pres. Indsl. and Ednl. Measurement, Montvale, N.J., 1988—; adj. prof. CUNY, Queens, 1985-87; cons. Nat. Assn. Purchasing Mgmt., Tempe, Ariz., 1987—. Author: (with others) Changes in Science Education, 1990, Handbook of Test Validity, 1991; editor: CPM Diagnostic Kit, 1988. Mem. APA, Am. Ednl. Rsch. Assn., Nat. Coun. on Measurement in Edn., Met. Assn. Applied Psychologists, Kappa Delta Pi, Phi Delta Kappa. Office: 7 Terkuile Rd Montvale NJ 07645-1213

MULLER, FREDERICK ARTHUR, legal editor, publisher; b. Center Moriches, N.Y., Dec. 18, 1937; s. Frederick Henry and Estelle May (Reeve) M.; m. Ellen Ruth Willard, Sept. 8, 1962; children: John F., Matthew R. BA, U. Rochester, N.Y., 1960; JD, U. Chgo., 1963. Bar: Ill. 1963, N.Y. 1964, U.S. Ct. Mil. Appeals 1965, U.S. Dist. Ct. (we. dist.) N.Y. 1971. Law clk. to judge N.Y. State. Ct. Appeals, 1968-69, 72; assoc. Hodgson, Russ, Andrews, Woods & Goodyear, Buffalo, 1969-72; asst. consultation clk. N.Y. State Ct. Apls., 1973-82; dep. state reporter State of N.Y., 1982-90, state reporter, 1990—; cons. staff atty. N.Y. State Ct. on Judiciary, 1973; chmn. supervisory com. Stewart AFB Fed. Credit Union, 1964-65. Editor N.Y. State Official Style Manual, 1985, 87. Mem. budget and allocations com. United Way Northeastern N.Y., Inc., 1975-80, bd. advisors law sch. U. Chgo., 1988—. Served with JAGC USAF, 1964-67. Mem. ABA (com. on appellate style manual 1987—), Nat. Assn. Reporters of Jud. Decisions (sec. 1988-89, v.p. 1989-90, pres. 1990-91), N.Y. State Bar Assn., U. Chgo. Club (chmn. alumni schs. com., 1984-89, bd. dirs. 1986—), Phi Beta Kappa, Phi Delta Phi. Baptist. Club: Tri-City Racquet (Latham, N.Y.). Home: RD # 1 Box 52 Swift Rd Voorheesville NY 12186 Office: One Commerce Ave Ste 1750 Albany NY 12210

MULLER, HENRY JAMES, journalist, magazine editor; b. Garmisch-Partenkirchen, Germany, Feb. 10, 1947; came to U.S., 1953; s. Henri Jacques and Helga (Mensch) M.; m. Maggie McComas, June 19, 1968. BA, Stanford U., 1968. Tchr. U.S. Peace Corps, Ethiopia, 1968-70; chief Vancouver (B.C., Can.) bur. Time mag., 1971-73; European econ. corr. Time mag., Brussels, 1973-77; chief Paris bur. Time mag., 1977-81; world editor Time mag., N.Y.C., 1982-85, chief of corrs., 1986-87, mng. editor, 1987—; faculty mem. profl. pub. course Stanford (Calif.) U., 1989—. Trustee Stanford U., 1991—, Carnegie Corp., 1992—. Recipient David Brower Environ. Journalism award Sierra Club, 1990. Mem. Am. Soc. Mag. Editors (bd. dirs. 1991—). Office: Time Mag Time & Life Bldg Rockefeller Ctr New York NY 10020

MULLER, MIKLOS, biochemist, educator; b. Budapest, Hungary, Nov. 24, 1930; came to U.S. 1964; s. Pal and Ilona (Marsovszky) M.; m. Noemi Mezei, Apr. 28, 1959 (div. 1969); children: Judit, Daniel Amos David; m. Janet Sue Keithly, June 24, 1973. MD, Budapest Med. U., 1955. Asst. prof. Budapest Med. U., 1955-64; rsch. assoc. Rockefeller U., N.Y.C., 1964-65, asst. prof., 1966-68, assoc. prof. biochem. parasitology, 1968—; guest investigator Carlsberg Laboratorium, Copenhagen, Denmark, 1965-66; adj. assoc. prof. Cornell U. Med. Coll., 1975-87; steering com. mem. WHO, Geneva, 1977-82; study group mem. NIH, Bethesda, 1984-87; sci. coun. mem. Internat. Inst. Cellular & Molecular Pathology, Brussels, 1985-90. Contbr. numerous articles in sci. jours.; founding editor Molecular & Biochem. Parasitology Jour., 1980-87. Mem. Am. Hungarian Found. (bd. dirs. 1990—), Soc. of Protistologists (pres. 1982-83, S.H. Hutner prize 1977), Hungarian Soc. Parasitologists (hon.). Office: Rockefeller U 1230 York Ave New York NY 10021-6341

MULLER, REID THOMAS, physician; b. N.Y.C., Aug. 17, 1960; s. Charles William and Patricia Jane (Sheridan) M.; m. Shelley Ann Gilroy, Sept. 19, 1987; 1 child, Aislinn Patricia. BS, Rensselaer Polytechnic Inst., 1980; MD, Ross U. Sch. Medicine, 1984. Diplomate Am. Bd. Internal Medicine. Resident Meth. Hosp., Bklyn., 1984-87, fellow in cardiology, 1987-89; mem. staff Community Meml. Hosp., Hamilton, N.Y., 1989—, Crouse-Irvine Meml. Hosp., Syracuse, N.Y., 1990—, Oneida (N.Y.) City Hosp., 1991—; dir. cardial lab. Community Meml. Hosp., Hamilton, 1989—, dir. ICU, 1989—; dir. cardiac lab. Oneida City Hosp., Oneida, 1991—. Contbr. articles to profl. jours. Fellow ACP, Am. Coll. Chest Physicians, Am. Coll. Cardiology. Office: Hamilton Med Specialists PC 150 Broad St Hamilton NY 13346

MULLETTE, JULIENNE PATRICIA, health center administrator, television personality and producer, author; b. Sydney, Australia, Nov. 19, 1940; came to U.S., 1953; d. Ronald Stanley Lewis and Sheila Rosalind Blunden (Phillips) M.; m. Fred Gillette Sturm, Nov. 24, 1964 (div. Dec. 1969); m. Kenneth Walter Gillman, Dec. 27, 1971 (div. Dec. 1978); children: Noah Khristoff Mullette-Gillman, O'Dhaniel Alexander Mullette-Gillman. B.A., Western Coll. for Women, Oxford, Ohio, 1961; postgrad., Harvard U., 1964, U. Sao Paulo, Brazil, 1965, Inst. do Filosofia, Sao Paulo, 1965, Miami U.,

Oxford, 1967-69. Tchr. English, High Mowing Sch., Wilton, N.H., 1962-64, Stoneleigh-Prospect Hill Sch., Greenfield, Mass., 1964; seminar dir. Western Coll., Oxford, Ohio, 1967-69; pres. Family Tree, The Home Univ., Montclair, N.J., 1978-80; dir. Pleroma Holistic Health Ctr., Montclair, 1980—; dir. Astrological Rsch. Ctr., Sydney, Australia, 1983; hostess (radio talk show) You and the Cosmos Sta. WFMU, East Orange, N.J., 1985, Sta. WJFF, Jeffersonville, N.Y., 1992—, The Juliette Mullette Show, Connections TV, Newark, 1985—, The Juliette Mullette Show Sta. WFDU, Fairleigh Dickinson U., N.J., 1986—; founder Spiritual Devel. Rsch. Group 1986—; pvt. astrology counselor, 1962—; lectr., speaker worldwide, 1968—; guest on radio and TV shows, U.S. and Can., 1962—; host syndicated radio talk show The Juliette Mullette Show, N.Y., N.J., 1987—; owner, pres. Moonlight Pond, Woodbourne, N.Y., 1988—; founder The Spiritual Devel. Ctr., 1986—, Pleroma Found. for Astrological Rsch. and Studies, 1990; breeder, trainer llamas, alpacas and other exotic animals. Author: The Moon-Understanding the Subconscious, 1973; also articles, 1968—; founding editor KÓSMOS mag., 1968-78, The Jour. of Astrological Studies, 1970; contbg. columnist I Love Cats, 1988—. Founder local chpt. La Leche League, Montclair, 1974. Mem. AAUW (chair cultural affairs Montclair chpt.), Spiritual Devel. Group (founder 1987), Internat. Soc. Astrological Research (founding pres. 1968-78), Am. Fedn. Astrologers (cert.), Société Belge d'Astrologie, Am. Assn. Humanistic Psychology, AAUW (dir. cultural affairs 1987—), NAFE, Internat. Llamas Assn. Avocations: competitive tennis, local theatre, singing.al theatre, singing. Home: 89 Star Rt Woodbourne NY 12788

MULLIGAN, ROBERT FRANCIS, JR., economist, civil engineer; b. Westbury, N.Y., May 29, 1961; s. Robert F. and Helen Christine (Romano) M. BSCE, Ill. Inst. Tech., 1983; MA, SUNY, Binghamton, 1989, postgrad., 1989—. Resident advisor Ill. Inst. Tech., Chgo., 1982-83. Contbr. articles to profl. publs. Capt. USAF, 1983-87. Mem. Am. Econ. Assn., Internat. J.A. Schumpeter Soc., Mil. Order World Wars (v.p. Spokane chpt. 1981-82). Roman Catholic. Home: 504 E Main St Apt 5 Endicott NY 13760-4679 Office: SUNY PO Box 6000 Plattsburgh NY 12901-0298

MULLINIX, EDWARD WINGATE, lawyer; b. Balt., Feb. 25, 1924; s. Howard Earl and Elsie (Wingate) M.; m. Virginia Lee McGinnes, July 28, 1944; children: Marcia Lee (Mrs. R. David Hoffelt), Edward Wingate. Student, St. John's Coll., 1941-43; JD summa cum laude, U. Pa., 1949. Bar: Pa. 1950, U.S. Supreme Ct. 1955. Assoc. Schnader, Harrison, Segal & Lewis, Phila., 1950-55; ptnr. Schnader, Harrison, Segal & Lewis, 1956—; mem. adv. bds. Antitrust Bull., 1970-81, BNA Antitrust and Trade Regulation Report, 1981—; mem. Civil Justice Reform Act of 1990 adv. group U.S. Dist. Ct. for the Ea. Dist. Pa., 1991—; mem. adv. com. U. Pa. Law Sch. Ctr. on Professionalism. Trustee Sta. KYW-TV Project Homeless Fund, 1985-86. Served with USMCR, 1943-44; to lt. (j.g.) USNR, 1944-46. Fellow Am. Bar Found. (life), Am. Coll. Trial Lawyers (mem. complex litigation com. 1980-91, vice-chmn. com. 1981-83); mem. ABA (spl. com. complex and multidist. litigation 1969-73, co-chmn. com. 1971-73, coun. litigation sect. 1976-80), Pa. Bar Assn., Phila. Bar Assn. (hon. trustee Campaign for Qualified Judges 1985—), Am. Judicature Soc., Juristic Soc., Hist. Soc. U.S. Dist. Ct. for Ea. Dist. Pa. (bd. dirs. 1984—, pres. 1991—), Hist. Soc. U.S. Ct. Appeals for Third Cir. (bd. dirs. 1991—), Assn. Profl. Responsibility Lawyers, Order of Coif, Lawyers Club (Phila.), Union League (Phila.), Socialegal Club (Phila.), Down Town Club (Phila.), Aronimink Golf Club (Newtown Sq., Pa.). Republican. Presbyterian. Home: 251 Chamounix Rd Saint Davids PA 19087-3605 Office: 1600 Market St Ste 3600 Philadelphia PA 19103-4252

MULLINIX, JOSEPH PHILIP, university official; b. Balt., Nov. 12, 1942; s. Thomas Henry and Maurine Roselynn (Reich) M.; m. Kathleen Patricia Mullin, June 18, 1966; children: Jonathan Thomas, David Joseph, Brendan Philip. Student, Harvard U., 1969-72; AB, Georgetown U., 1964; MBA, U. Chgo., 1965. Auditor Arthur Young and Co., N.Y.C., 1965-66, 68-69; sr. cons. Urban Systems, Inc., Cambridge, Mass., 1970-71; mgmt. cons., Cambridge, 1971-72; sr. budget examiner Office Mgmt. and Budget, Exec. Office of Pres., Washington, 1972-76, chief Justice-Treasury br., 1976-78, dep. assoc. dir., 1978-81; sr. fin. analyst Goldman, Sachs and Co., N.Y.C., 1981-83; vice provost Columbia U., N.Y.C., 1983-84, sr. v.p., 1984—. Bd. dirs. Community Impact, N.Y.C., 1988—. 1st lt. U.S. Army, 1966-68. Home: 279 Bellair Rd Ridgewood NJ 07450-4127 Office: Columbia U Office Sr VP New York NY 10027

MULLINS, BETTY KAYE, accounting educator; b. Great Falls, Mont., Dec. 17, 1942; d. Bill and Kathryn (McDonald) Baker; m. Gerald V. Mullins, Jan. 12, 1962; children: Christine, Michael, Cathy Lee. BSBA, U. So. Miss., 1983. Def. contract auditor Def. Contract Audit Agy., Burlington, Mass., 1986; fin. counselor U.S. Army, Ft. Devens, Mass., 1987-89; bus. instr. Hesser Coll., Nashua, N.H., 1986-87; acctg./bus. tchr. State of N.H. VoTech, Nashua, 1984—; acctg. instr. Daniel Webster Coll., Nashua, 1984—; cons. in field; owner Wooden Tulip, Nashua, 1988—; dir. bus. and industry tng. Nashua Tech. Coll. Recipient Dept. Army Commendation awds., 1988. Mem. Fed. Womens Prof., Am. Soc. Women Accts. Republican. Office: Daniel Webster Coll Nashua NH 03063

MULREED, ELLEN MARIE, telecommunications executive; b. New Brunswick, N.J., Jan. 21, 1963; d. Joseph Michael and Kathryn Mary Fallon; m. Thomas Paul Mulreed, Apr. 6, 1991. BS cum laude, Kean Coll. of N.J., 1989. With conf. planning AT&T Support Svcs., Somerset, N.J., 1985-86; adminstrv. asst. AT&T Support Svcs., South Plainfield, N.J., 1986-87; lead operator AT&T Contract Svcs. Orgn., Piscataway, N.J., 1987-89; asst. mgr. AT&T Consumer Direct Products and Svcs., Basking Ridge, N.J., 1990—. Mem. NAFE. Roman Catholic. Home: 68 Highland Ave Bridgewater NJ 08807 Office: AT&T Consumer Direct Products and Svcs 295 N Maple Ave Basking Ridge NJ 07920

MULRONEY, (MARTIN) BRIAN, prime minister of Canada; b. Mar. 20, 1939; s. Benedict and Irene (O'Shea) M.; m. Mila Pivnicki, 1973; 4 children. B.A., St. Francis Xavier U., LL.D. (hon.), 1979; LL.L., U. Laval, Que.; LL.D. (hon.), Meml. U., 1980. Ptnr. Ogilvy, Renault, Montreal, Que., 1965-76; pres. Iron Ore Co. of Can., 1976-83; mem. Parliament Can. from Central Nova, Nova Scotia, Ottawa, Ont., 1983-84; mem. Parliament Can. from Manicouagan, 1984-88, mem. Parliament Can. from Charlevoix, 1988—, leader of Her Majesty's Loyal Opposition, 1983-84; prime minister Can., 1984—; royal commr. Cliche Commn. investigating violence in Que. constrn. industry, 1974; mem. internat. adv. council Inst. Internat. Studies. Author: Where I Stand, 1983. Clubs: Mt. Royal (Montreal); Albany (Toronto); Garrison (Quebec). Office: Ho of Commons, Office of Prime Min, Ottawa, ON Canada K1A 0A6

MULRONEY, JOHN PATRICK, chemical company executive; b. Phila., 1935; married. BS, U. Pa., 1957, MS, 1959. With Rohm and Haas Co., Phila., 1958—; group leader engring. dept. Rohm & Haas Co., Phila., 1962-64, dept. head, 1964-67, asst. dir. rsch., 1967-71, pres., chief oper. officer, 1986—; asst. gen. mgr. Filital, Milan, 1971-73, gen. mgr., 1973-75; bus. mgr. AG Chem., Europe, 1975-77, regional dir. Europe, 1977-78; v.p. polymers, resins, monomers Indsl. Chem., 1978-80, v.p. tech., 1980-82, v.p. corp. bus., from 1982, also bd. dirs., 1982—; bd. dirs. Aluminum Co., Am. Teradyne Inc. Mem. Am. Inst. Chem. Engrs., Am. Chem. Soc. Office: Rohm and Haas Co Independence Mall W Philadelphia PA 19105

MULVANEY, MARY FREDERICA, systems analyst; b. N.Y., Nov. 27, 1945; d. Michael Joseph and Mary Catherine (Clapper) M. BA, Marymount Coll., 1967; MA, U. Va., 1968. Cert. data processor Inst. Certification of Computer Profls., Ill. Computer systems analyst Dept. of Def., Ft. Meade, Md., 1968-74; sr. programmer analyst Planning Rsch. Corp., McLean, Va., 1974-83; mem. tech. staff Fed. Systems Group TRW Inc., Fairfax, Va., 1983-90; sr. mem. tech. staff GTE Govt. Systems Corp., Rockville, Md., 1990—. Mem. Data Processing Mgmt. Assn., Computer Measurement Group, Digital Equipment Corp. Users Soc. Roman Catholic. Office: GTE Govt Systems Corp 1700 Research Blvd Rockville MD 20850

MULVEY, WILLIAM W., publishing executive; b. Schenectady, Apr. 26, 1916; s. Peter J. and Laura (Walsh) M.; m. Marcelle Clark, Oct. 11, 1946; children—Christopher Clark, William Walsh. Grad. Union Coll., Schenectady, 1938. Copywriter Batten, Barton, Durstine & Osborne; successively copy supr., account exec., mktg. exec., account supr. Maxon, Kenyon & Eckhardt, until 1954; with Cunningham & Walsh, N.Y.C., 1954-61, v.p., then exec. v.p., mem. exec. com., mem. fin. com., dir.; pres. Wilmar (investments), 1958-70; sr. v.p. McCann Erickson, N.Y.C., 1960-64, exec. v.p., mem. exec. com., 1964-70, chmn. exec. com., 1969-70; pres. Interpub. Mgmt. Corp. 1970-73; treas., chmn. Horizons Communications Corp., 1971; pres. William Mulvey Inc., pubs. Bull's-Eye Books. Co-author novel: A Dangerous Woman. Vol. Cath. Archdiocese, N.Y., 1991—. Mem. Cardinal's Com. of Laity, Roman Catholic Ch., N.Y.C.; trustee Union Coll. Mem. Delta Upsilon. Club: Union League. Office: William Mulvey Inc 26 Vitti St New Canaan CT 06840-4823

MULVOY, THOMAS F., JR., newspaper editor, journalist; b. Boston, Feb. 4, 1943; s. Thomas Francis and Julia Frances (Harrington) M.; m. Anastasia Vakina Coulianos, June 1, 1985; children: Stephen Tasos, Michael Thomas. AB in Philosophy, Boston Coll., 1964. News dir. Sta. WPLM AM/FM, Plymouth, Mass., 1965-66; copy editor The Boston Globe, 1967-74, asst. sports editor, 1974-76, news editor, 1976-79, asst. mng. editor, 1979-83, dep. mng. editor, 1983-86, mng. editor, 1986—. Stanford U. fellow, 1983. Roman Catholic. Office: Boston Globe Newspaper PO Box 2378 Boston MA 02107-2378

MUMFORD, WILLARD ROYAL, engineering educator, educational consultant; b. McMinnville, Oreg., Aug. 1, 1933; s. Edgar Royal and Violet (Coe) M.; m. Elaine Virginia (Lineback), Aug. 20, 1955; children: Laura, Amy, David. BS, U. Md., 1956; BSME with honors, So. Meth. U., 1964; MSME, Tex. A&M U., 1969. Commd. 2d lt. USAF, 1956, advanced through grades to lt. col., 1974; assigned to Vietnam, 1969-70; chief reliability and value engring. Ogden (Utah) Air Logistics Ctr., 1971-75, chief logistics systems mgmt. dir., 1975-76; prof. aerospace studies Angelo State U., San Angelo, Tex., 1976-79; dep. dir. Electro Magnetic Compatibility Ctr., Annapolis, Md., 1979-81; ret., 1981; prof. engring., chmn. engring. and tech. div. Anne Arundel Community Coll., Arnold, Md., 1981—; cons. N.J. Bd. Edn., Princeton, 1987-88, NSF, Washington, 1990-91; mem. Md. Task Force on Engring. Edn., Annapolis, 1990-91. Editor Civil War Token Soc. Jour., 1980—, Md. Token and Medals Soc. Jour., 1987—. Dist. chmn. Boy Scouts Am., Balt., 1980-83; advisor Jr. Engring. Tech. Soc., Arnold, 1985—; bd. dirs., v.p. Anne Arundel County Trust for Hist. Preservation, Annapolis, 1986—; pres. Anne Arundel County Hist. Soc., 1987—; elder Presbyn. Ch. Decorated Bronze Star, Air medal; recipient George Washington Honor medal Freedoms Found., 1978. Mem. Armed Forces Communications and Electronics Assn. (pres. 1979), Am. Assn. for Engring. Edn., Md. Assn. for Higher Edn. (pres. 1988-89, editor Jour. 1987-90, Outstanding Svc. award 1990), Md. Coun. on Engring. and Techs. (founder, bd. dirs. 1989—), Soc. Old Crows, Rotary (bd. dirs. Annapolis 1984-86), Tau Beta Pi, Phi Kappa Phi, Pi Tau Sigma, Tau Alpha Pi. Home: 987 Sherwood Forest Rd Annapolis MD 21401-6432 Office: Anne Arundel CC 101 College Pky Arnold MD 21012-1895

MUNASINGHE, MOHAN, development economist; b. Colombo, Sri Lanka, July 25, 1945; s. Peter Munasinghe and Flower Wickramasinghe; m. Sria Gooneratne, May 8, 1970; children: Anusha, Ranjiva. BA with honors, Cambridge (Eng.) U., 1967, MA, 1968; SM, MIT, 1969, EE, 1970; PhD in EE, McGill U., Montreal, Can., 1973; MA in Econs., Concordia U., 1975. Rsch. officer Ceylon Inst. Sci. and Indsl. Rsch., Colombo, 1968-70; asst. dir. Internat. Inst. Quantitative Econs., Montreal, 1973-75; div. chief World Bank, Washington, 1975—; vis. prof. Am. U., Washington, 1977-81, Inst. Tech. Policy in Devel., SUNY, 1982-88, Energy Ctr. U. Pa., Phila., 1988—; sr. advisor to pres. Office of Pres. Sri Lanka, Colombo, 1982-87, chmn. computer and info. tech. coun., 1983-86; sr. rsch. fellow Ctr. Internat. Devel. and Conflict Mgmt., U. Md., College Park, 1987-90; pres.-emeritus Sri Lanka Energy Mgmt. Assn., Colombo, 1985—, pres., 1983-85. Author: 40 books including Economics of Power System Reliability and Planning, 1979, Energy Economics, Demand Management and Pricing, 1983, Rural Electrification for Development, 1987, Integrated National Energy Planning and Management, 1988, Computers and Informatics in Developing Countries, 1989, Energy Analysis and Policy, 1990, Electric Power Economics, 1990, Water Supply and Environmental Management, 1992, Energy Modelling and Policy, 1992; author over 150 tech. papers. Recipient Prize for Outstanding Achievement Latin Am. and Caribbean Energy Conf., 1988, Exceptional Contributions award Internat. Assn. of Energy Econs., 1987, Outstanding Scientists Gold medal Lions Internat., 1985; Grass fellowship MIT, 1968. Fellow Nat. Acad. Scis. (Sri-Lanka), Inst. Elec. Engrs. (UK, Beauchamp award 1967), Inst. Engrs. (Sri Lanka); mem. IEEE, Am. Econ. Assn., Am. Phys. Soc., Sri Lanka Assn. Adv. Sci., Sri Lanka Econ. Assn. Home: 4201 E West Hwy Bethesda MD 20815-5910 Office: World Bank 1818 H St NW Washington DC 20433-0002

MUNDY, CARL EPTING, JR., commandant of the marine corps; b. Atlanta, July 16, 1935; s. Carl Epting Sr. and Anne Louise (Dunn) M.; m. Linda Stringfield Sloan, Nov. 28, 1957; children: Elizabeth Anne, Carl Epting III, Timothy Sloan. BS, Auburn U., 1957; MS, Naval War Coll., 1977. 2d lt. USMC, 1957, advanced through grades to gen.; comdt. USMC, Washington. Decorated Legion of Merit, Bronze Star, Purple Heart, Navy Commendation medal. Mem. Phi Kappa Tau. Office: USMC Office of Lt Gen Norfolk VA 23515-5001*

MUNDY, JEAN, playwright, psychotherapist, author; b. St. Louis, July 17, 1930; d. John and Mary (Kuszynski) M. BS, St. Louis U., 1951, MS, 1952; PhD, Cath. U., Washington, 1960. Lic. in psychology, N.Y. Pvt. practice psychotherapy N.Y.C., 1960—; prof. L.I. U., Greenvale, N.Y., 1964-85; prof. emeritus L.I. U., Green Valley, N.Y., 1985—. Author: Let's Talk: Western Psychological Service, 1991: (play) Believe Me, 1989; contbr. articles. Dir., producer conf. Ending Sexism, N.Y.C., 1970; speaker NOW, N.Y.C., 1975. Home: 33 Windward East Hampton NY 11937 Office: 105 W 13th St New York NY 10011

MUNICH, ADRIENNE AUSLANDER, English educator; b. Detroit, Mar. 13, 1939; d. Irving and Mildred (Abramsky) Auslander; m. Richard Lee Munich, June 18, 1961; children: Edwin Seth, Matthew Aaron. BA, Brandeis U., 1960; MAT, Yale U., 1961; PhD, CUNY, 1976. Lectr. Yale U., New Haven, 1979-81; asst. vis. prof. English Wesleyan U., Middletown, Conn., 1977-79; asst. prof. SUNY, Stony Brook, 1982-88, assoc. prof., 1988—; bd. dirs. Women's Studies Program, SUNY, 1990—, Browning Inst., N.Y.C., Florence, Italy, 1978—. Author: Andromeda's Chains, 1989; editor: Arms and the Woman, 1989, Robert Browning: Critical Essays, 1979; editor Jour. Victorian Lit. and Culture, 1982—. Dir. Ctr. Ind. Study, New Haven, 1981. Rsch. fellow N.Y. Rsch. Found., 1982, 84; fellow Yale Ctr. Brit. Art, 1986, Lilly Found., 1987. Mem. MLA, Nat. Women's Studies Assn., N.E. Victorian Studies Assn. (program com.). Office: SUNY Women's Studies Program Stony Brook NY 11794-3456

MUNIER, WILLIAM BOSS, medical service executive; b. Corning, N.Y., Dec. 8, 1942; s. John Hammond and Marguerite (Boss) M.; m. Sandra Lorraine Koerber, 1965 (div. 1976); m. Ann Elizabeth Wessel, 1980; children: Michael, Andrew, Laura. BA, U. Pa., 1964; MD, Columbia U., 1968; MBA, Harvard U., 1973. Diplomate Nat. Bd. Med. Examiners; lic. physician, surgeon, N.Y. Surg. intern Roosevelt Hosp., N.Y.C., 1968-69; profl. staff HEW, Washington, 1969-71, 73-75, dir. Office Quality Standards, , 1975-77, dir. Office Health Practice Assessment,, 1977-79; exec. v.p. Mass. Med. Soc., Boston, 1979-84; prin. Ernst & Whinney, Boston, 1984-85; pvt. practice mgmt. cons. Wellesley, Mass., 1985-86; pres. Quality Standards in Medicine, Inc., Boston, 1986—; vis. prof. Harvard Sch. Pub. Health, Boston, 1980—. Contbr. articles to profl. jours. Mem. human services com. Town of Wellesley, 1984-85. Served with USPHS, 1969-79. Mem. AMA, Mass. Med. Soc. Republican. Episcopalian. Clubs: St. Botolph, Harvard; Capitol Hill.

MUNITZ, MILTON KARL, philosophy educator; b. N.Y.C., July 9, 1913; s. Samuel and Anna (Blumberg) M.; m. Lenore Deborah Bloom, Dec. 22, 1946; children: Charles, Andrew. BA, CCNY, 1933; MA, Columbia U., 1935, PhD, 1939. Instr. and lectr. philosophy CCNY, Queens, 1935-46; prof. philosophy NYU, 1946-73, head dept. philosophy, 1968-73; disting. prof. philosophy CUNY, 1973-83, disting. prof. emeritus philosophy, 1983—; vis. lectr. Princeton U., 1952; vis. disting. prof. philosophy Brockport State Coll., SUNY, 1967-68; vis. prof. philosophy Bar Ilan U., Israel, 1972, 84, U.S. Mil. Acad., West Point, 1981-82; sec. Conf. on Methods in Philosophy and Sci., 1950; chmn. Fulbright Screening Com., 1965-69; organizer Internat. Philosophy Yr., Brockport Coll., 1967-68. Mem. editorial bd. Philosophia, 1969—; cons. editor NYU Press, Dover Publs.; author: The Moral Philosophy of Santayana, 1939, Space, Time, and Creation: Philosophical Aspects of Scientific Cosmology, 1957, The Mystery of Existence, 1965, Existence and Logic, 1974, The Ways of Philosophy, 1979, Contemporary Analytic Philosophy, 1981, Cosmic Understanding, 1986, The Question of Reality, 1990; editor: Theories of the Universe, 1957, Identity and Individuation, 1971, Logic and Ontology, 1973, Philosophy and Semantics, 1974, others; contbr. articles to profl. jours. 2nd lt. USAF, 1943-45. Recipient Nicholas Murray Butler medal Columbia U., 1963; Faculty fellow Ford Found. Fund for the Advancement of Edn., 1954-55, Fulbright Sr. Rsch. fellow, 1960-61, Guggenheim fellow, 1960-61, Einstein Vis. fellow Israel Acad. Scis. and Humanities, 1984-85; Resident scholar Rockefeller Found., 1972. Mem. Am. Philosophical Assn. Home and Office: PO Box 354 Scarborough NY 10510

MUNN, JACOB, real estate and manufacturing executive; b. Bklyn., May 29, 1951; s. Abraham and Roza (Rybaizen) M.; m. Diane Judith Westreich, Aug. 27, 1972; children: Jeremy, Marissa. BS in Archtl. Tech., N.Y. Inst. Tech., 1972; MArch, Ohio U., 1974. Registered architect, N.Y. Jr. architect Feldman-Mistopolous Assn., N.Y.C., 1974-76, Max Wechsler Assocs., N.Y.C., 1976-77; project architect Drexel Burnham, N.Y.C., 1977-78; v.p., gen. mgr. Abe Munn Picture Frames, Inc., Long Island City, N.Y., 1978-84; pres. Abe Munn Picture Frames, Inc., Long Island City, 1984—; ptnr. A.M.J. Realty Co., Long Island City, 1978—. Trustee Temple Beth Sholom, Flushing, N.Y., 1988-89, v.p., 1989-91; bd. dirs. L.I. City Bus. Devel. Corp., 1989—. Mem. Profl. Picture Framers Assn. (cert. picture framer), Am. Philatelic Assn., Lionel Operating Train Soc. Office: Abe Munn Picture Frames Inc 51-02 21st St PO Box 1189 Long Island City NY 11101

MUNN, KATHERINE TRACY, psychologist, psychotherapist; b. Oakland, Calif., Oct. 2, 1959; d. Richard Condit and Julia (Bartholomew) M. BA summa cum laude, Princeton U., 1982; MA, U. Mich., 1986, PhD, 1989. Lic. psychologist, Mass. Staff psychologist Boston Coll., Univ. Counseling Svcs., Chestnut Hill, Mass., 1989—; pvt. practice, psychotherapist Cambridge, Mass., 1991—; dept. assoc., dept. psychology Univ. Mich., Ann Arbor, 1987-89. Named Regents fellow Univ. Mich. Bd. Regents, Ann Arbor, 1984-88. Mem. Am. Psychol. Assn., Mass. Assn. Psychoanalytic Psychologists, Appalachian Mt. Club. Home: 195 Park Dr Apt 41 Boston MA 02215-4734 Office: Boston Coll Gasson Hall Rm #108 Chestnut Hill MA 02167

MUNN, RICHARD THOMAS, accountant; b. Norwood, Mass., Aug. 19, 1967; s. Patrick Joseph and Joan Marie (Fynn) M. BA in Econs. and Acctg., Coll. of Holy Cross, 1989. Sr. acct. Price Waterhouse, Boston, 1989—. Mem. KC. Roman Catholic. Home: 8 Philip Ln Foxboro MA 02035-1223 Office: Price Waterhouse 160 Federal St Boston MA 02110-1700

MUÑOZ, CARLOS RAMÓN, bank executive; b. N.Y.C., Dec. 8, 1935; s. Alejandro and Gladys Helena (Judah) M.; m. Wilhelmina Elaine North, June 8, 1957; children: Carla Christine, Kyle Alexander. BA, Columbia U., 1957, MA, 1961. Insp., ofcl. asst. Citibank, N.A., N.Y.C., 1959-64, asst. mgr., then mgr. in Dominican Republic and P.R., 1965-70, asst. v.p., N.Y.C., 1971-72, v.p., dept. head, 1972-78, sr. v.p., regional mgr. and dir. Citicorp. USA, San Francisco, 1978-81, sr. v.p., mem. Credit Policy Com., 1982—. Bd. dirs. Episcopal Mission Soc., N.Y.C., 1974—, chmn. exec. com., 1990—; bd. dirs. Inner City Scholarship Fund, 1984—, Corp. for Relief Widows and Orphans of Protestant Episcopal Clergymen in State N.Y., 1974-79; mem. nat. advisory bd. Ctr. for Am. Cultures Studies, 1990—. Served as 1st lt. USAR, 1958-64. Recipient Productivity award State Senator Diane Watson, Los Angeles, 1981; named Fairfield County Alumnus of Yr., 1989-90. Mem. Columbia Univ. Alumni Assn. (bd. dirs. 1983—, treas. 1988-92, v.p. 1992—). Republican. Office: Citibank NA 399 Park Ave 3rd Fl Zone 16 New York NY 10043

MUNOZ, HECTOR JOSE, banker; b. Elizabeth, N.J., Nov. 2, 1967; s. Hector and Rita (Chavez) M. AAS, Union Coll., 1990. Sales rep. Twinkle Inpt Corp., Bronx, N.Y., 1986-87; dir. Ea. mktg. Lime Light Corp., Elizabeth, 1987-89; ops. mgr. City Fed. Bank, Union, N.J., 1989-90; community bank rep. First Fidelity Bank Nat., New Providence, N.J., 1990—. treas. St. Michaels Youth Assn., Elizabeth, 1987, Sam Rode for Mayor, Elizabeth, 1988; pres. Cuban Youth Assn., Elizabeth, 1988-89. Mem. Eliz Cubananos, Lions, Am. Mgmt. Assn. Republican. Roman Catholic.

MUNRO, ELIZABETH BENNETT (BETTY MUNRO), artist; b. Spokane, Apr. 8, 1919; d. Howard J. and Florence Louise (Hanan) B.; m. John Willoughby Munro, July 2, 1949; children: Thomas Bennett, Elizabeth Alice. BS, U. Wis., 1942; MA, Columbia U., 1949. Lic. tchr. Wis. Art supr. pub. schs., Wausaw, Wis., 1942-44; art tchr. high Sch., Janesville, Wis., 1944-46; art dept. head Deerfield Shields High Sh., Highland Park, Ill., 1946-49; represented in permanent collection Everson Mus. Art (Purchase prize Mr. & Mrs. Mark S. Wilder Meml. 1971), nat. and juried art shows throughout N.E. and included in pub. and pvt. collections in Chgo. and Washington area, N.Y., Fla., Ariz., Wis. One-woman shows include Syracuse Civic Ctr., 1976, 86, Community Arts Ctr., Old Forge, N.Y., Syracuse C. of C., 1991; 3-artist show Oswego (N.Y.) Civic Arts Ctr., Ft. Ontario Park, 1982, Munson Williams Proctor Inst., Utica, N.Y., also nat. and juried shows throughout N.E; 14 watercolors in Changing Impressions of Syracuse, 1990. Active Preservation Assn. Cen. N.Y.; bd. dirs. Landmarks Cen. N.Y., Syracuse. Mary Garrison Meml. Prize Cooperstown Nat., 1982, N.Y. State Purchase Prize FairPermanent Collection, 1982. Mem. PEO (state conv. delegate, chpt. officer, 1968—), Nat. League of Am. Pen Women (treas., sec.), Associated Artists of Syracuse (John Detore Meml. prizes 1976, 81). Home: 6810 Dutch Hill Rd Fayetteville NY 13066-1717

MUNRO, HAMISH NISBET, biochemist, educator; b. Edinburgh, Scotland, July 3, 1915; came to U.S., 1966, naturalized, 1973; s. Donald and Margaret (Nisbet) M.; m. Edith E. Little, Apr. 5, 1946 (dec. 1987); children: Joan Bruce, Colin Scott, Andrew Fraser, John Michael. B.Sc., U. Glasgow, Scotland, 1936, M.B., 1939, D.Sc., 1956; M.D. with honors, U. Glasgow, 1983; Docteur honoris causa, U. Nancy, France, 1982. Physician, pathologist Victoria Infirmary, Glasgow, 1939-45; lectr. physiology U. Glasgow, 1946-47, sr. lectr., reader biochemistry, 1948-63, prof. biochemistry, 1964-66; prof. physiol. chemistry MIT, Cambridge, 1966-90; prof. medicine and of nutrition Tufts U., Boston, 1979—; dir. USDA Human Nutrition Research Center on Aging, Tufts U., Boston, 1979-84, sr. scientist, 1984—. Editor: Mammalian Protein Metabolism, vols. 1-4, 1964-70, Nutrition, Aging and the Elderly, 1989; contbr. articles in field of protein metabolism, molecular biology of iron storage to profl. jours. Recipient Osborn Mendel award Am. Inst. Nutrition, 1968, Borden award, 1978; Bristol-Myers award for disting. achievement in nutrition research, 1981, Rank prize for significant advances in nutrition, 1982, Corson medal of Franklin Inst. Phila., 1988; named to Agr. Research Service Sci. Hall of Fame, 1988. Fellow Royal Soc. Edinburgh, Am. Acad. Arts and Scis., Royal Coll. Physicians London (hon.); mem. Nat. Acad. Sci. U.S., Am. Soc. Biol. Chemists, Am. Inst. Nutrition (pres. 1978-79), Brit. Biochem. Soc. Presbyterian. Home: 159 Concord Ave Cambridge MA 02138-2325 Office: USDA Human Nutrition Rsch Ctr on Aging 711 Washington St Boston MA 02111-1524

MUNRO, JOSEPH BARNES, JR., lawyer, human resources consultant; b. Providence, Jan. 7, 1930; s. Joseph Barnes and Ruth Baker (Hodgkins) M.; m. Marilyn Poland Fish, Dec. 26, 1952; children: Joseph Barnes III, Charles Fish, Edward Addison. BS in Physics, Brown U., 1952; MS in Indsl. Mgmt., U. R.I., 1960; JD, Bridgeport U., 1983. Bar: Conn. 1983. U.S. Dist. Ct. Conn. 1990. Rsch. and devel. engr. Electric Boat div. Gen. Dynamics Co., Groton, Conn., 1956-60, salary adminstr., 1960-66; personnel mgr. corp. hdqrs. Gen. Dynamics Co., N.Y.C., 1966-68; mgr. compensation and benefits Quincy (Mass.) Shipbldg. div. Gen. Dynamics Co., 1968-73; staff cons. Orgn. Resources Counsellors, N.Y.C., 1973-76; compensation mgr., legal counsel ITT, N.Y.C., 1976-87; ptnr. Munro & Munro, Westport, Conn., 1983—; pres., owner Munro Assocs., Westport, 1987—; instr. Thames Valley State Tech. Inst., Norwich, Conn., 1960-62; instr. extension program U. R.I., Providence, 1962-66; lectr. various orgns., Boston and N.Y.C., 1966—; seminar organizer, presenter, 1987—. Author: Basic Sales Incentive

Compensation, 1986, Basic Compensation Cookbook, 1987, Salary Position Evaluation Plan, 1987; inventor Flexigrid (c), FlexEval (c), Flexiplan (c). Lt. USNR, 1952-56. Mem. ABA, Conn. Bar Assn., Westport Bar Assn., Assn. Trial Lawyers Am., Conn. Trial Lawyers Assn., Am. Compensation Assn. Home: 45 Washington Ave Westport CT 06880-2549 Office: PO Box 418 Greens Farms CT 06436

MUNSCHAUER, JOHN LATHROP, writer; b. Buffalo, Mar. 30, 1919; s. Edwin Adam and Louise (Lathrop) M.; m. Grace Wood, May 24, 1952 (dec. 1961); children: Susan, Lynne; m. Barbara York, Jan. 31, 1962 (dec. 1971); stepchildren: Amy York, Thomas York; m. Joyce Robinson, Feb. 1, 1979; stepchildren: Gregory Robinson, Bruce Robinson. AB, Cornell U., 1940. Sales corres. Nat. Gypsum Co., Buffalo, 1940-41; dir. Cornell Career Ctr., Ithaca, N.Y., 1946-84, dir. emeritus, 1984—; career cons. J. Munschauer & Assocs., Ithaca, 1984—; employment cons. U.S. Govt., 1951, 61, various corps. Author: Jobs for English Majors and Other Smart People, 1991; contbr. articles to profl. jours. Trustee DeWitt Hist. Soc., Ithaca, 1991. 1st Lt. U.S. Army, 1941-46. Decorated Bronze Star. Mem. Cornell Emeritus Profs. Assn. (dir. 1990—), Rotary. Roman Catholic.

MUNSELL, MONROE WALLWORK, chemical consultant; b. New London, Conn., Jan. 8, 1925; s. Paul Weston and Vivienne Elaine (Elwood) M.; m. Jean Harrison Townsend, Nov. 6, 1954; children: Keith Albert, Cynthia Ann. BS in Chemistry, Carnegie Mellon U., 1947, MS in Organic Chemistry, 1950, PhD in Organic Chemistry, 1955. Rsch. chemist Esso Chem., Linden, N.J., 1955-60; sr. rsch. chemist Enjay Labs., Linden, 1966-67; group head Esso Chem. U.K., Abingdon, 1966-67; rsch. assoc. Esso Chem. S.A., Brussels, 1967-69, Exxon Chem. Co. Japan, Tokyo, 1969-72, Exxon Chem Co., Linden, 1972-86; cons. Monroe W. Munsell, Inc., Berkeley Heights, N.J., 1986—. Contbr. articles to profl. jours.; patentee in field. Lt. (s.g.) USNR, 1944-46, 51-53. Mem. Am. Philatelic Soc., Lighthouse Point Yacht Club. Republican. Methodist. Home: 180 Sutton Dr Berkeley Heights NJ 07922-2536

MUNSON, HOWARD G., federal judge; b. Claremont, N.H., July 26, 1924; s. Walter N. and Helena (O'Halloran) M.; m. Ruth Jaynes, Sept. 17, 1949; children: Walter N., Richard J., Pamela A. B.S. in Economics, U. Pa., 1948; LL.B., Syracuse U., 1952. Bar: N.Y. With Employers' Assurance Corp., Ltd., White Plains, N.Y., 1949-50; mem. firm Hiscock, Lee, Rogers, Henley & Barclay, Syracuse, N.Y., 1952-76; judge U.S. Dist. Ct. No. Dist. N.Y., Syracuse, 1976—. Mem., pres. Syracuse Bd. Edn.; bd. dirs. Sta. WCNY-TV; chmn. ethics com. Onondaga County Legislature. Served with U.S. Army, 1943-45, ETO. Decorated Bronze Star, Purple Heart. Mem. Am. Coll. Trial Lawyers, Nat. Assn. R.R. Trial Counsel, Am. Arbitration Assn., Justinian Soc., Alpha Tau Omega, Phi Delta Phi. Office: US Dist Ct US Courthouse 100 S Clinton St Syracuse NY 13260-0001

MUNSON, NANCY KAY, lawyer; b. Huntington, N.Y., June 22, 1936; d. Howard H. and Edna M. (Keenan) Munson. Student, Hofstra U., 1959-62; JD, Bklyn. Law Sch., 1965. Bar: N.Y. 1966, U.S. Supreme Ct. 1970, U.S. Ct. Appeals (2d cir.) 1971, U.S. Dist. Ct. (ea. and so. dists.) N.Y. 1968. Law clk. to E. Merritt Weidner Huntington, 1959-66, sole practice, 1966—; mem. legal adv. bd. Chgo. Title Ins. Co., Riverhead, N.Y., 1981—; bd. dirs., legal officer Thomas Munson Found. Trustee Huntington Fire Dept. Death Benefit Fund; pres., trustee, chmn. bd. Bklyn. Home Aged Men Found. Mem. ABA, N.Y. State Bar Assn., Suffolk County Bar Assn., Bklyn. Bar Assn., NRA, DAR, Soroptimists (past pres.). Republican. Christian Scientist. Office: 197 New York Ave Huntington NY 11743

MUNSON, RONALD DUANE, international operations executive; b. Waterloo, Iowa, Feb. 8, 1943; s. Cecil Wallace and Doris Nadine (Johnson) M.; m. Delynn J. Hoag, Jan. 7, 1977 (div. Feb. 1982); children: Vanessa and Mercedes (twins); m. Mary Hollander, Mar. 19, 1983. BS, U. Minn., 1968. Inside sales rep. The Dow Chem. Co., Boston, 1968-69; sales rep. The Dow Chem. Co., Moorestown, N.J., 1969-73; various product mgr. positions The Dow Chem. Co., Midland, Mich., 1973-78; regional sales mgr. The Dow Chem. Co., Houston, 1978-83; dir. mktg. Chems. div. Church & Dwight Co., Inc., Piscataway, N.J., 1983-85; dir. sales Chems. div. Church & Dwight Co., Inc., Princeton, N.J., 1985-86, gen. mgr. agrl. products, 1986-88, v.p., gen. mgr. agrl. products, 1988-89, v.p., gen. mgr. specialty products, 1989-91, v.p. internat. ops., 1991—. Mem. Coun. of the Ams., N.Y.C., 1991. With U.S. Army, 1966-72. Office: Church and Dwight Co Inc 469 N Harrison St Princeton NJ 08540-3510

MUNSTER, ANDREW MICHAEL, medical educator, surgeon; b. Budapest, Hungary, Dec. 10, 1935; came to U.S., 1965; s. Leopold S. and Marianne (Barcza) M.; m. Joy O'Sullivan, Dec. 7, 1963; children—Andrea, Tara, Alexandra. M.D., U. Sydney (Australia), 1959. Diplomate Am. Bd. Surgery. Research fellow Harvard U. Med. Sch., Boston, 1966-67; asst. prof. surgery U. Tex.-San Antonio, 1968-71, assoc. prof. surgery Med. U. S.C., Charleston, 1971-76; assoc. prof. Johns Hopkins U., Balt., 1976-85, prof. surgery, 1985—; dir. burn ctr. Balt. City Hosp., 1976—; v.p. Chesapeake Physicians, Balt., 1978-84. Author: Surgical Anatomy, 1971; Surgical Immunology, 1976; Burn Care for House Officers, 1980; contbr. numerous articles to med. jours. Pres., Chesapeake Ednl. Research Trust, Balt., 1980-84, Charleston Symphony, 1974-75, Charleston TriCounty Arts Council, 1975-76. Served to lt. col. U.S. Army, 1968-71. Recipient John Hunter prize U. Sydney, 1959; named Hunterian prof. Royal Coll. Surgeons, 1974. Fellow Royal Coll. Surgeons of Eng., Royal Coll. Surgeons of Edinburgh (Scotland), Am. Assn. Surgeons of Trauma, Colombian Coll. Surgeons (hon.); mem. Soc. Surg. Assn., Soc. Univ. Surgeons, Am. Surg. Assn. Office: Balt City Hosps 4940 Eastern Ave Baltimore MD 21224-2780

MUNSTER, MARY CATHERINE, safety specialist; b. Ashland, Pa., Oct. 8, 1966; d. Christopher Eugene and Anna Elizabeth (Hogan) McGee; m. Jeffrey Scott Munster, Aug. 25, 1990. BS, Millersville U., 1988. Safety asst. Kellogg's, Lancaster, Pa., 1988; assoc. indsl. hygienist Lancaster Labs, Inc., 1988-89, safety specialist, 1989—; mem. workers' compensation rev. task force Lancaster County C. of C., Lancaster, 1991. Tech. advisor: (video tape) Laboratory Conditions: Using Chemicals Safety, 1990. Bd. dirs. Lancaster County Indsl. Safety Coun., 1991—. Mem. Am. Indsl. Hygiene Assn., Am. Soc. Safety Engrs. (scholar 1987). Roman Catholic. Office: Lancaster Labs Inc 2425 New Holland Pike Lancaster PA 17601-5994

MUNT, JANE ANN, academic administrator, consultant, educator; b. Batavia, N.Y., July 1, 1956; d. John Frank and Dolores Marie (Krause) M.; 1 child, Bethany Jane. BA in Secondary Edn., State U. Coll., Oswego, 1978; MS in Reading Edn., SUNY, Brockport, 1984. Tchr. French East Rochester (N.Y.) Mid. Sch., 1979-81; mem. reading and study faculty Rochester (N.Y.) Inst. Tech., 1981-86, coord. study skills project, 1986-88, staff chair study skills dept., 1988—; cons. in field, Rochester, 1981—; adj. instr. Monroe Community Coll., Rochester, 1989—. Co-author (instructional video tapes) Learning Power, 1989. Mem. steering com. Rochester Inst. Tech., United Way, 1987-91; tng. advisor United Way of Greater Rochester, 1990-91, co-chair tng. adv. com., 1991; lector St. Thomas More Cath. Ch., Rochester, 1990-91. Rochester City Sch. Dist. grantee, 1991. Mem. N.Y. State Coll. Learning Skills Assn. Roman Catholic. Home: 33E Clintwood Dr Rochester NY 14620-3343 Office: Rochester Inst Tech 1 Lomb Memorial Dr Rochester NY 14623-5603

MUNZER, JEAN GRUEN, hypnosis consultant, educator; b. Passaic, N.J., Nov. 27, 1934; d. Siegfried and Clara (Lehr) Gruen; m. Hugo Harry Munzer, June 24, 1956 (div. June 1987); children: Laura, Diane, Jane. BA with high honors, Rutgers U., 1956; postgrad., Seton Hall U., 1956, Montclair Coll., 1957. Tchr. Paterson (N.J.) Pub. Sch. System, 1956-57; adult sch. tchr. Paramus (N.J.) Community Sch., 1975—, Pompton Lakes (N.J.) Adult Sch., 1974—, Wayne (N.J.) Adult Sch., 1976—, Ft. Lee (N.J.) Adult Sch., 1989—; hypnosis cons. Oakland, N.J., 1981—; lectr. various community and bus. orgns., 1974—. Creator tapes on personal growth; lyricist Douglass Coll. Alma Mater, 1955. Mem. Metaphys. Ctr. N.J. (bd. dirs. 1976—, dir. 1978—, hon. plaque 1988, 91), Assn. to Advance Ethical Hypnosis, Assn. Rsch. and Enlightenment, Phi Beta Kappa. Home and Office: 10 Pequot Path Oakland NJ 07436-3815

MUNZNER, ROBERT FREDERICK, biomedical engineer; b. Balt., July 3, 1936; s. Robert F. Munzner and Catherine E. (Appel) Gay; m. Jo Ann Goettee, Sept. 2, 1960 (div. 1980); children: Elizabeth Mae, Robert Victor, Ann Catherine. BS in Physics, Loyola Coll., Balt., 1963; PhD in Biomed. Engrng., U. Va., 1976. Aerospace engr. Westinghouse Def. and Space, Balt., 1963-69; rsch. assoc. Johns Hopkins U., Balt., 1975-77; chief, neurol. devices br. U.S. FDA, Rockville, Md., 1977—; exec. sec. neurol. device adv. panel. Contbg. author: Cerebellar Stimulation for Spasticity, 1984; contbr. articles to profl. jours. Recipient postdoctoral fellowship Johns Hopkins U., Balt., 1975, Univ. fellowship U. Va., Charlottesville, 1972-73, Thornton fellowship, 1971. Mem. IEEE, Biomed. Engrng. Soc., AAAS, Sigma Xi. Office: FDA Device Evaluation 1390 Piccard Dr HFZ-450 Rockville MD 20850

MURABITO, STEPHEN JOSEPH, English educator; b. Oswego, N.Y., Feb. 21, 1956. BA in English/Writing Arts, SUNY, Oswego, 1981; MFA in Writing, U. Pitts., 1986. Rsch. asst. English dept. U. Pitts., 1985, tutor, master tutor The Writing Workshop, 1985, teaching asst., 1986-88; asst. prof. U. Pitts., Greensburg, 1988—. Assoc. poetry editor The Pa. Rev., 1985; author: Brooklyn Review, 1989, Lake Effect, 1990; contbr. essays, revs. and poetry to profl. jours. Recipient finalist award Brittinahm Poetry Prize Competition, 1990; Endowment Arts fellow in poetry, 1991. Home: PO Box 170 Slickville PA 15684-0170

MURASHIGE, ALLEN, defense analysis executive; b. Lihue, Hawaii, Mar. 20, 1946; s. Fred A. and Evelyn Y.T. M.; m. Rae Ann Sears, June 7, 1981; children: Lance, Danielle. BS in Aero. Engrng., U. Washington, 1968; MS in Statistics/Ops. Rsch., U. Denver, 1973; postgrad. Program for Execs. in Nat. Security, Harvard U., 1989. Aero. engr. Air Force Western Test Range, Vandenberg AFB, Calif., 1968-70; aero. engr. Space & Missile Test Ctr., Vandenberg AFB, 1970-73, ops. analyst, 1973-77; ops. analyst Hdqrs. USAF in Europe, Ramstein AFB, Germany, 1977-84; chief current ops. div. Hdqrs. USAF in Europe, Ramstein AFB, 1985-87; sci., tech. advisor Air Force Studies and Analysis, Washington, 1987—; U.S. rep. and com. chmn. NATO Adv. Group for Aero Rsch. & Devel., Paris, 1987—; mem. Joint Tech. Coord. Group Sr. Adv. Bd., 1989—; mem. DOD Simulation Validation Sr. Steering Com., 1990—; bd. dirs. Air Force Incentive Awards Bd., Pentagon, Washington, 1987—; rep. Dept. of Def. C3I Test and Evaluation Steering Com., Pentagon, 1989-91, DOD Modeling and Simulation Policy Group, 1990-92. Author tech. reports in field. Air Force nominee Dept. of Def. Disting. Civilian Svc. award, 1990, Air Force Meritorious Civilian Svc. award, 1986, Fellowship for Grad. Study in Ops. Rsch., 1972. Mem. AIAA, Mil. Ops. Rsch. Soc., Air Force Assn., Am. Def. Preparedness Assn., Porsche Club of Am. Office: Air Force Studies/Analysis Hdrs USAF/SAG Washington DC 20330

MURATORE, ROBERT, physicist; b. N.Y.C., Jan. 19, 1957; s. Albert and Modestina (DiGiacomo) M.; m. Doris Jean Benter, Oct. 13, 1990. B Engrng. Sci., Johns Hopkins U., 1979; MS Engrng., Princeton U., 1985; PhD in Biophysics, Syracuse U., 1988. Tech. staff Hughes Aircraft Co., El Segundo, Calif., 1979-80; project dir. Space Studies Inst., Princeton, N.J., 1981; rsch. assoc. Syracuse (N.Y.) U., 1989, Nat. Rsch. Coun., Bethesda, Md., 1989-91; asst. prof. physics SUNY, Geneseo, 1991—. Author: (with others) Antiproton Science and Technology, 1988, Advances in Neurology, vol. 54, 1990; contbr. articles to profl. jours. Univ. fellow Syracuse U., 1986-88. Mem. Am. Phys. Soc., N.Y. Acad. Scis. Home: 108 Point Pleasant Rd Rochester NY 14622-1637 Office: SUNY Dept Physics Geneseo NY 14454-1401

MURAWINSKI, DANIEL JUDE, air force officer; b. Jersey City, Sept. 18, 1949; s. John Stanley and Ann Marie (DeMarco) M.; m. Nancy Ellen Schwalm, June 5, 1971; children: Heather, Rebecca, Daniel. BS cum laude in Physics, Stevens Inst. Tech., 1971; MS cum laude in Lasers/Optics, Air Force Inst. Tech., 1977. Commd. 2d lt. USAF, 1971, advanced through grades to col., 1991; asst. prof. physics USAF Acad., Colorado Springs, Colo., 1977-81; chief pilot, asst. ops. officer 37th Tactical Airlift Squadron, Rhein Main Air Base, Fed. Republic Germany, 1982-85; long range planner Air Staff, Pentagon, Washington, 1985-88, Air War Coll., Maxwell AFB, Ala., 1988-89; arms control force structure and strategic def. initiative Joint Staff, Pentagon, Washington, 1989—; speaker, cons. in field. Leader, Boy Scouts Am., Hoboken, N.J., 1970-71; mem. Orange Hunt Estates Civic Assn., Springfield, Va., 1987—; eucharistic minister St. Mary's of Sorrows Ch., Fairfax, Va., 1988. Named to Outstanding Young Men of Am., 1978. Mem. Air Force Assn., Arnold Air Soc., Pentagon Officers Athletic Club, Army and Navy Club, Order of Daedalians, Tau Beta Pi. Republican. Roman Catholic. Home: 6813 Reynard Dr Springfield VA 22152-2728 Office: Joint Staff J-5 Policy Div Pentagon Washington DC 20318-5000

MURBACH, DAVID PAUL, horticulturist; b. N.Y., July 19, 1952; s. J. Frederick and Ragna M. (Samuelsen) M. BS, U. Ariz., 1974; AAS, SUNY, Farmingdale, 1981; MS, U. Del., 1988. Cert. in Mus. Studies. Mgr. gardens div. Rockefeller Ctr. Mgmt. Corp., N.Y.C., 1985—; computer cons. Murbach, Inc., N.Y.C., 1989—; chmn. bd. dirs. Metro Hort. Group, N.Y.C., 1988-90; adj. asst. prof. urban landscape architecture program Sch. Architecture and Environ. Studies CUNY, 1990. Author: (booklet) Directory of Computer Use in Plant Record Keeping, 1984; contbr. articles on plants and drought to profl. jours. DuPont-Longwood fellow, 1984. Mem. Hort. Soc. N.Y., Am. Assn. Bot. Gardens and Arboreta (chmn. computer svc. com. Wayne, Pa. 1988-90). Office: Rockefeller Ctr Mgmt Corp 1230 Ave of the Americas New York NY 10020-1513

MURCHISON, DAVID CLAUDIUS, lawyer; b. N.Y.C., Aug. 19, 1923; s. Claudius Temple and Constance (Waterman) M.; m. June Margaret Guilfoyle, Dec. 19, 1946; children—David Roderick, Brian, Courtney, Bradley, Stacy. Student, U. N.C., 1942-43; A.A., George Washington U., 1947, J.D. with honors, 1949. Bar: D.C. 1949, Supreme Ct. 1955. Asso. Dorr, Hand & Dawson, N.Y.C., 1949-50; partner Howrey, Simon, Baker & Murchison, Washington, 1956—; legal asst. under sec. army, 1949-51; counsel motor vehicle, textile, aircraft, ordnance and shipbldg. divs. Nat. Prodn. Authority, 1951-52; asso. gen. counsel Small Def. Plants Adminstrn., 1952-53; legal adv. and asst. to chmn. FTC, 1953-55. Chmn. So. Africa Woldlife Trust. Served with AUS, 1943-45. Mem. ABA (chmn. com. internat. restrictive bus. practices, sect. antitrust law 1954-55, sect. adminstrv. law, sect. litigation), Fed., D.C., N.Y. bar assns., So. Africa Wildlife Trust (chmn.), Africa Safari Club Washington (pres.), Order of Coif, Phi Delta Phi. Republican. Clubs: Metropolitan, Chevy Chase. Home: 5409 Spangler Ave Bethesda MD 20816-1847 Office: 1730 Pennsylvania Ave NW Washington DC 20006-4706

MURDOCH, DAVID ARMOR, lawyer; b. Pitts., May 30, 1942; s. Armor M. and N. Edna (Jones) M.; m. Joan Wilkie, Mar. 9, 1974; children: Christina, Timothy, Deborah. AB magna cum laude, Harvard U., 1964, LLB, 1967. Bar: Pa. 1967, U.S. Dist. Ct. (we. dist.) Pa. 1967, U.S. Ct. Mil. Appeals 1968, U.S. Supreme Ct. 1990, U.S. Ct. Appeals (3d cir.) 1991. Assoc. Kirkpatrick & Lockhart, Pitts., 1971-78, ptnr., 1978—. Co-author: Business Workouts Manual. Vice pres., bd. dirs. Avonworth Sch. Dist., 1977-83; chmn. bd. dirs. Pitts. Expt., 1980-82, mem. 1988—, chmn., 1989-91; mem. Pa. Housing Fin. Agy., 1981-88, vice chmn., 1983-87; alt. del. Rep. Nat. Conv., 1980; mem. coun. legal advisors Rep. Nat. Com., 1981—; elder The Presbyn. Ch. of Sewickley, 1986-92. Capt. U.S. Army, 1968-71. Fellow Am. Coll. Bankruptcy; mem. ABA (mem. bus. bankruptcy com., chmn. subcom. on bankruptcy coms., trust indentures and claims trading 1991—), SAR, Pa. Bar Assn., Allegheny County Bar Assn., Duquesne Club, Harvard-Yale-Princeton Club, Edgeworth Club. Republican. Office: Kirkpatrick & Lockhart 1500 Oliver Pittsburgh PA 15222-2404

MURDOCH, MARTIN H., contractor; b. Neptune, N.J., Sept. 10, 1946; s. Martin H. and Eleanor M. (Blakeman) M.; m. Paula Joan Sabosik, Oct. 2, 1965; children: Robert E., Jennifer M. AS in Bus., Ocean County Coll., 1972. Foreman Newark Parquet Flooring, 1965-72; owner M.E. Sabosik Assoc. Inc., Point Pleasant, N.J., 1972—. Mem. Floor Covering Installation Contractors Assn. (com. chmn. Dalton, Ga. chpt. 1988-92). Office: ME Sabosik Assoc Inc 2319 Bridge Ave Point Pleasant NJ 08742

MURDOCH, ROBERT WHITTEN, lawyer; b. Pitts., Mar. 21, 1937; s. Thomas and Julia (Whitten) M.; m Eleanore L. Uram, Sept. 26, 1967; 1 child, Robert John. BA, U. Pitts., 1960; pvt. law study, 1963-67. Bar: Pa. 1967, U.S. Dist. Ct. (we. dist.) Pa. 1968, U.S. Ct. Appeals (3d cir.) 1978, U.S. Supreme Ct. 1978, U.S. Ct. Appeals (8th cir.) 1983, U.S. Ct. Appeals (11th cir.) 1986. Ptnr. Jones, Gregg, Creehan & Gerace, Pitts., 1967-85, Grogan, Graffam, McGinley & Lucchino, P.C., Pitts., 1985—. Author: Pfeifer: The Supreme Court on The Longshoremen's and Harbor Workers Compensation Act and Inflation, 1983, 84. 2d lt. U.S. Army, 1960-61. Mem. ABA, Pa. Bar Assn., Allegheny County Bar Assn., Maritime Law Assn. U.S., Def. Rsch. Inst., Pa. Def. Inst., Acad. Trial Lawyers Allegheny County, Nat. Assn. R.R. Trial Counsel, Pa. Claims Assn. (assoc.), Pitts. Claims Assn. (assoc.), Pitts. Fire Loss Conf. (assoc.), Avanti Owners' Assn., Internat., SAR, Descs. Colonial Clergy, Sons Union Vets. Civil War, Nat. Soc. Sons Colonial New Eng., Am. Soc. Law and Medicine, Hon. Order Blue Goose Internat., W. Pa. Risk Mgmt. Assn., The Sea Heritage Found., Clan Donald, Studebaker Drivers Club, Pitt Varsity Letter Club, 65 Roses Club (cystic fibrosis), Rivers Club, Pitt. Golden Panthers, St. Andrews Soc. Pitts., Plymouth Hereditary Soc., Caledonian Soc., Phi Alpha Delta. Republican. Presbyterian. Office: Grogan Graffam McGinley & Lucchino Three Gateway Ctr 22d Fl Pittsburgh PA 15222

MURDOCK, KEITH CHADWICK, chemist; b. Garfield, Utah, Feb. 5, 1928; s. Keith Murdock and Marjorie (Miles) Welty; m. Martha Allen, June 22, 1953; children: Keith Allen, Neil Collins. BA, U. Utah, 1948, MA, 1950; PhD, U. Ill., 1953. Rsch. chemist Am. Cyanamid Co., Bound Brook, N.J., 1953-54; prin. rsch. chemist Am. Cyanamid Co., Pearl River, N.Y., 1956-91. Contbr. numerous articles to profl. jours. With U.S. Army, 1954-56. Mem. Am. Chem. Soc., Phi Lambda Upsilon, Alpha Chi Sigma. Office: Am Cyanamid Co Lederle Labs Middletown Rd Pearl River NY 10965-2611

MURDOCK, WILLIAM JOHN, librarian; b. N.Y.C., Nov. 19, 1942; s. William and Catherine T. (Ryan) M.; m. Barbara Tyra, Nov. 24, 1968. BS, Manhattan Coll., 1964; MLS, Pratt Inst., 1966; MA, NYU, 1972. Librarian N.Y. Pub. Libr., N.Y.C., 1964-67; serials librarian Manhattan Coll., Riverdale, N.Y., 1967-70; asst. prof. CUNY-Lehman Coll., Bronx, N.Y., 1970-77, chief circulation libr., 1970-77; dir. librs. Pace U., Pleasantville, N.Y., 1977—; chmn. Coun. of Librarians, N.Y.C., 1988-89. Contbr. articles to profl. jours. Candidate for bd. trustees Mt. Kisco, N.Y., 1991; mem. Republican. Nat. Com., 1989—; mem. Cath. Big Bros., Westchester, 1983—. Mem. ALA, N.Y. Libr. Assn., Westchester Libr. Assn. (treas. 1981-83), Westchester Assn. Libr. Dirs. (sec. 1986-87), AAUP, Assn. Coll. and Rsch. Librarians, Am. Legion. Office: Pace U 861 Bedford Rd Pleasantville NY 10570-2799

MURDZA, DEANNA CAROL, market research analyst; b. Holyoke, Mass., May 13, 1966; d. William Renato Mezzetti and Virginia Marie (Tighe) LaMarche. BS in Bus. Mgmt., Westfield State Coll., 1988. Interviewer 1st Nat. Supermarkets, Windsor Locks, Conn., 1988-89, asst. analyst, 1989-90, market rsch. analyst, 1990—. Mem. NAFE. Roman Catholic. Office: 1st Nat Supermarkets Inc 500 North St Windsor Locks CT 06096-1198

MURIANA, JOSEPH PAUL, university administrator, lawyer; b. N.Y.C., Mar. 22, 1953; s. Joseph Vincent and Letitia (Magnatta) M. BS, Fordham U., 1975, JD, 1989. Bar: N.Y., N.J. Profl. community organizer N.W. Bronx Community & Clergy Coalition, 1975-83, exec. dir., 1983-85; asst. dir. govt. rels. and urban affairs Fordham U., Bronx, 1985-88, dir. govt. rels. and urban affairs, 1988—. Pres., bd. dirs. Univ. Neighborhood Housing Program, Bronx, 1986—; bd. dirs. Kingsbridge Hts. Neighborhood Assn., 1989—, Belmont Italian Am. Playhouse, Bronx, 1991, Belmont Arthur Local Devel. Corp., Bronx, 1987—; bd. dirs., vice chair Selective Svc. System Local Bd., Bronx, 1986—; vol. Bread for the World, Washington, 1975—. Recipient Community Crime Prevention award Bronx Dist. Atty., 1984. Mem. ABA, Nat. Lawyers Guild, N.Y. State Bar Assn., Bar of the State of N.J. Amnesty Internat., Green Peace. Democrat. Roman Catholic. Office: Fordham U Office Govt Rels Bronx NY 10458

MURIEL, AMADOR CRUZ, physicist; b. Marikina, Philippines, Nov. 24, 1939; came to the U.S., 1963; s. Amado and Lucena (Cruz) M.; children: Anna Christina, Rosemarie. MA, SUNY, Stony Brook, 1965, PhD, 1968. Assoc. prof. Hostos Community Coll., Bronx, N.Y., 1972-79, acting dean, 1979-80; v.p. Burlington County (N.J.) Coll., 1980-81; project mgr. Citibank, N.Y.C., 1981-82; assoc. prof. CUNY-Baruch Coll., N.Y.C., 1982-85; pres. Data Transport Systems, N.Y.C., 1985—; cons. UN, N.Y.C., Geneva, Austria, 1985—. Editor: Stellar Dynamics I, II, 1980, Stellar Evolution, 1980; contbr. articles to Phys. Rev., Physica, Physics Letters. Rockefeller Found. scholar, 1965-68, All Nations Women's Group scholar, 1957, Fulbright scholar, 1963. Mem. Am. Phys. Soc., AAAS. Home: 347 E 62d St New York NY 10021 Office: Data Transport Systems 347 E 62d St New York NY 10021

MURNAGHAN, FRANCIS DOMINIC, JR., federal judge; b. Balt., June 20, 1920; m. Diana Edwards; children: Sheila H., George A., Janet E. B.A., Johns Hopkins U., 1941; LL.B., Harvard U., 1948. Bar: Md. 1949. Asso. firm Barnes Dechert Price Smith & Clark, Phila., 1948-50; staff atty. Office of Gen. Counsel, U.S. High Commr. for Ger., 1950-52; asst. atty. gen. State of Md., 1952-54; asso. firm Venable Baetjer & Howard, Balt., 1952-57; partner Venable Baetjer & Howard, 1957-79; judge U.S. Ct. Appeals for 4th Circuit Balt., 1979—. Chmn. Balt. Charter Rev. Commn., 1963-64; trustee Walters Art Gallery, 1961, v.p. 1961-63, pres. 1963-80, chmn. 1980-85, chmn. emeritus, 1985—; pres. Balt. Sch. Bd., 1967-70; trustee Johns Hopkins U., 1976—. Lt. USNR, 1942-46. Mem. ABA, Md. Bar Assn., Balt. Bar Assn., Am. Coll. Trial Lawyers. Office: US Ct Appeals 4th Cir 101 W Lombard St Baltimore MD 21201-2626

MURO, MICHAEL JOHN, manufacturing systems executive; b. New Haven, Conn., Aug. 5, 1949; s. Anthony Louis and Mary Louise (Trotta) M.; m. Cynthia Joan Baldesari, Oct. 18, 1975; 1 child, Mary Ann. BA, U. Conn., 1971. Office mgr. Good Humor Corp., Hartford, Conn., 1967-76; with corp. loss control dept. Good Humor Corp., Englewood, N.J., 1976-78; material mgr. Good Humor Corp., Balt., 1978-81; project devel. mgr. Md. Cup Corp., Owings Mills, Md., 1981-84; project leader Westinghouse Electric Corp., Hunt Valley, Md., 1984—; bar code technology leader Westinghouse Electric, 1985-86. Coach Hampstead (Md.) Little League, 1986-92. With U.S. Army, 1971-73. Mem. Am Prodn. and Inventory Control Soc. (pres. 1988-90, exec. v.p. 1986-88, bd. dirs. 1990—), Mut. Investment Club Hampstead. Roman Catholic. Home: 4610 Lower Beckleysville Rd Hampstead MD 21074-2612 Office: Westinghouse Electric 111 Schilling Rd Cockeysville Hunt Valley MD 21031-1205

MUROYAMA, PAUL MICHIHISA, business and political consulting firm executive; b. Yokosuka, Kanagawa, Japan, Mar. 9, 1950; came to U.S., 1982; s. Iwao and Nobuko Muroyama; m. Janet R. Hunziker, Sept. 27, 1952; children: Andrew D., Alexander P. BA, Gakushuin U., 1972, MA, 1974. Internat. researcher Japan Fedn. Employers' Orgns., Tokyo, 1974; mgr. Japan Overseas Enterprises Assn., Tokyo, 1975-81; econ. and trade analyst Wald Harkrader & Ross, Washington, 1982-84; account exec. Gray & Co., Washington, 1985-86; sr. account exec. Hill & Knowlton, Inc., Washington, 1987-88; pres., chief exec. officer Paul Muroyama & Assocs., Inc., Washington, 1988—. Coun. mem. Holy Trinity (Cath.) Ch., Washington, 1982—. Home: 7824 Custer Rd Bethesda MD 20814-1346 Office: Paul Muroyama & Assocs Inc 1000 16th St NW Ste 800 Washington DC 20036-5705

MURPHY, ANDREW PHILLIP, JR., lawyer; b. Swampscott, Mass., Sept. 27, 1922; s. Andrew Phillip and Irene Mary (O'Connell) M.; m. Ann Marie O'Hagan, Feb. 13, 1954; children: Sean Francis, Andrew Phillip III, Chrystal Ann, James Byrne, Paul Clarke. AB, Harvard Coll., 1943; LLB, Boston U., 1949. Bar: Mass. 1949, D.C. 1957. Assoc. Hannan and Mayo, Lynn, Mass., 1949-50; atty. Econ. Stabilization Agy., Wage Stabilization Bd., Washington, 1951-52, R.R. and Airline Wage Bd., Washington, 1952; mem. chief counsel Nat. Enforcement Commn., Washington, 1952-53; labor rels. counsel, asst. legis. counsel Nat. Assn. Home Builders, Washington, 1954-60; pvt. practice Washington, 1960—; gen. counsel Western Mortgage Investors, Boston, 1964-83, Southeastern Mortgage Investors, Charlotte, N.C., 1963-70, Universal Investors Trust, Miami, Fla., 1970-72, First Gen. Real Estate Trust, Washington, 1962-78; trustee, counsel Found.for Constitution, N.Y.C., 1987—; counsel Found. for Friends of Museums, Balt., 1990. Co-editor: Research and Development Procurement Law, 1958; editor in chief

Fed. Bar Jour., 1954-60. Mem. labor rels. com. U.S. C. of C., Washington, 1956-60; alt. mem. Constrn. Industry Stabilization Com., Washington, 1974-75; mem. Collective Bargaining Com. in Constrn., Washington, 1975-76; mem. Coun. Constrn. Employers, Washington, 1972-76. Lt. (j.g.) USN, 1943-46. Mem. Metropolitan Club (Washington), Metropolitan Club (N.Y.C.), Gibson Island (Md.) Club, Farmington Country Club (Charlottesville, Va.), Eastern Yacht Club (Marblehead, Mass.). Roman Catholic. Office: 1100 Connecticut Ave NW Washington DC 20036-4101 also: 271 Skywater Rd Gibson Island MD 21056

MURPHY, AUSTIN JOHN, congressman; b. North Charleroi, Pa., June 17, 1927; s. Austin John and Evelyn Frances (Spence) M.; m. Eileen Ramona McNamara, Feb. 7, 1953; children: Colleen, Brian, Sheila, Erin, Holly, Maureen. B.A., Duquesne U., 1949; J.D., U. Pitts., 1952. Bar: Pa. 1952. Gen. practice law; solicitor for 10 municipalities; auditor, councilman Borough of Speers, 1952-56; asst. dist. atty. Washington County, 1957; mem. Pa. Ho. of Reps., 1959-70, Pa. Senate, 1970-76, 95th-102nd Congresses from 22d Pa. dist., 1977—; Mem. Pa. Local Govt. Commn.; mem. Charleroi Sch. Dist., 1956, Monongahela Democratic Com., 1952. Mem. law rev. staff: U. Pitts, 1965. Served with USMCR, 1944-46. Recipient Thomas Chrostwaite award Pa. Assn. Boroughs, 1973. Office: US Ho Reps 2210 Rayburn Ho Office Bldg Washington DC 20515*

MURPHY, BARBARA MACDONALD, English educator; b. Chgo., Aug. 15, 1927; d. William Buttercase and Gladys Ruth (Thomas) MacDonald; m. Raymond Murphy, July 17, 1952 (div. 1959); children: James William, Daniel Thomas. BA, Grove City (Pa.) Coll., 1949; MA, U. Rochester, 1961. Cert. supr., N.Y. English tchr. Truxton (N.Y.) Cen. Sch., 1949-51, Sherwood (N.Y.) Cen., 1958-60; English dept. chmn. Fairport (N.Y.) High Sch., 1960-85; effective writing tchr. Cornell Sch. Labor Rels., Rochester, N.Y., 1986—; English instr. St. John Fisher Coll., Rochester, N.Y., 1988—; memoir writing tchr. Athenaeum, Rochester, 1987—; supr. English student tchrs. Nazareth Coll., 1990—; speaker Kodak Geneology, Rochester, Rochester Geneology Club, 1990; cons. Rochester Inst. Tech., 1989. Treas. Fairport Reps., 1986—, Perinton Reps., 1987-88; mem. North Bank Study, Fairport, N.Y., 1985, Zoning Bd., Fairport, 1982—. Congregational. Home: 6 Lewis St Fairport NY 14450-2414

MURPHY, CAROLINE ANN, economics educator; b. Worcester, Mass., June 25, 1938; d. John Henry and Helen Louise (Crowe) M. BA, Regis Coll., 1960; MA, Clark U., 1963, PhD, 1971. Lectr. Becker Jr. Coll., Worcester, 1960-64; instr. Westfield (Mass.) State Coll., 1964-66, Coll. of the Holy Cross, Worcester, 1970-71; prof. Fitchburg (Mass.) State Coll., 1971—. Bd. dirs. Montachusett Opportunity Coun., Leominster, Mass., 1983-85; fin. com. Montachusett coun. Girl Scouts U.S., 1990-91. Fellow NSF, Clark U., Worcester, 1967-70. Home: 136 Lancaster Ave Lunenburg MA 01462-1508 Office: 160 Pearl St Fitchburg MA 01420-2697

MURPHY, CHARLES HENRY, aeronautical engineer; b. Chgo., Sept. 1, 1927; s. Charles Henry and Dorothy (Berrey) M.; m. Elizabeth Ann Brown, Aug. 16, 1952; children: Christopher K., Michael T., Sharon E., Virginia K., Deirdre L., Megan G. BS cum laude, Georgetown U., 1947; MA, Johns Hopkins U., 1948, MS in Engring., 1952, PhD, 1957. Instr. U. Hawaii, Honolulu, 1949-50; engr. U.S. Army Ballistic Rsch. Lab., Aberdeen Proving Ground, Md., 1950-70, chief LFD, 1970—.

MURPHY, CLARENCE JOHN, chemistry educator, researcher; b. Manchester, N.H., Apr. 20, 1934; s. Clarence Francis and Elsie Frieda (Schmidt) M.; m. Elizabeth Schuler, Sept. 23, 1960; children: Elizabeth Ann, Kathleen Diane, Constance Greta. BS, U. N.H., 1955, MS, 1957; PhD, SUNY, Buffalo, 1962. Rsch. assoc. MIT, Cambridge, 1960-61; from asst. prof. to assoc. prof. dept. chemistry Ithaca (N.Y.) Coll., 1961-69, chmn. dept., 1961-66; prof. dept. chemistry East Stroudsburg (Pa.) U., 1969—, chmn. dept., 1969-84; NSF vis. rsch. prof. St. Anselm Coll., Manchester, 1986-87; rsch. scientist Lehigh U., Bethlehem, Pa., 1981—. Contbr. articles to profl. jours., also numerous book revs. in field; patentee in field. Mem. Monroe County Emergency Planning Commn., Stroudsburg, 1985—; bd. dirs. Monroe County Hist. Assn., 1992—. Mem. Am. Chem. Soc. (sect. chmn. 1973-74), Pa. Acad. Sci. (rec. sec. 1991—), History of Sci. Soc., Soc. Applied Spectroscopy, Soc. Plastics Engrs., Sigma Xi. Office: East Stroudsburg U Dept Chemistry East Stroudsburg PA 18301

MURPHY, DANIEL IGNATIUS, lawyer; b. Phila., Mar. 14, 1927; s. John Anthony Murphy and Irene Cooper (Thorn) Lister; m. Jeanne B. Genetti, July 28, 1956 (div. Aug. 1978); children: Jewel A., Daniel I. Jr.; m. Barbara Ann Uncles, Jan. 1, 1979. BS in Econs., U. Pa., 1950; LLB, Yale U., 1953. Bar: Pa. 1954, U.S. Dist Ct. (ea. dist.) Pa. 1954, U.S. Ct. Appeals (3d cir.) 1954, U.S. Tax Ct. 1956, U.S. Supreme Ct. 1959. Assoc. Evans, Bayard & Frick, Phila., 1953-55; asst. city solicitor City of Phila., Pa., 1956-59; ptnr. Cavanaugh, Murphy & Kalodner, Phila., 1958-64, Shapiro, Stalberg, Cook, Murphy & Kalodner, Phila., 1964-66, Takiff, Bolger & Murphy, Phila., 1966-72, Waters, Gallagher, Collins & Masterson, Phila., 1972-80, Stradley, Ronon, Stevens & Young, Phila., 1980—; tchr. Am. Soc. CLU's, Villanova, Pa., 1956-57; mem. exec. com. Phila. Estate Planning Coun., 1958—; lectr. Pa. Bar Inst., Harrisburg, 1974—, Pa. Coll. Orphans Ct. Judges, Harrisburg, 1978, Pitts., 1991. Editor: Phila. Bar Assn. Mag. The Shingle, 1958-67; contbr. chpts. to manuals and articles to profl. jours. Mem., chmn. Phila. Chpt. Am. Cancer Soc., 1956-63; mem. Com. of 70, Phila., 1968—, chmn., 1972-74; mem., pres. Inst. for Cancer & Blood Diseases, Phila., 1975—; trustee Hahnemann Univ., Phila., 1983-86. With USN, 1945-46. Fellow Pa. Bar Found; mem. ABA, Assn. Trial Lawyers Am., Pa. Bar Assn., Phila. Bar Assn. (vice chmn. com. censors 1971), Union League Phila., Phila. Country Club, Pa. Soc. SAR. Democrat. Roman Catholic. Office: Stradley Ronon Stevens & Young 2600 One Commerce Sq Philadelphia PA 19103

MURPHY, DONN BRIAN, theater educator; b. San Antonio, July 21, 1930; s. Arthur Morton and Claire Frances (McCarthy) M. BA, Benedictine Coll., 1954; MFA, Catholic U., 1956; PhD, U. Wis., 1964. Prof. Georgetown U., Washington, 1954—; exec. dir. Nat. Theatre Corp., Washington, 1985—; tech. theater liaison The White House, Washington, 1961-65. Author: A Director's Guide to Good Theatre, 1968, Stage for a Nation, 1985, (plays) Creation of the World, 1970, Something of a Sorceress, 1971, Tyger/Tyger, 1977, (with others) Eleanor: First Lady of the World, 1984. Cpl. U.S. Army, 1950-52. Recipient Outstanding Svc. award Am. Theatre Assn., 1984, Forrest Roberts award No. Mich. U., 1977; Ford Found. fellow, 1963. Democrat. Roman Catholic. Home: 2401 S Kenmore St Arlington VA 22207-4938

MURPHY, DOUGLAS EDWARD, illustrator; b. Passaic, N.J., Jan. 31, 1964; s. Gerald Edward and Laura Elizabeth (Duffy) M. BA, Montclair State Coll., 1987. Designer Motor Club Am. Ins. Co., Newark, 1986-87, David A. Block Advt., Inc., Montclair, N.J., 1987-88, Skylight Graphics, Inc., Hackensack, N.J., 1988-89; illustrator Whitman Studio, Inc., Clifton, N.J., 1989-90; freelance illustrator Clifton, 1990—; tchr. illustration techniques, Clifton, 1990—. Semi-finalist Internat. Typeface Corp., 1987; recipient travel award for poster design Am. Airlines, 1991. Mem. Phi Kappa Phi. Roman Catholic.

MURPHY, EVA THOMPSON, educator; b. Whiteville, N.C., Feb. 2, 1936; d. Willie J. and Fannie (King) Thompson; m. Berkley Murphy, Apr. 21, 1957; 1 child, Linnea P. BS, Allen U., Columbia, S.C., 1971; postgrad., NYU, 1975; MS, SUNY, New Paltz, 1977, CAS, 1978. Tchr. bus. Middletown (N.Y.) Pub. Schs., 1970-84, asst. prin., 1971-76, tchr. secondary English, 1976-84; asst. prin. minority student affairs Ithaca (N.Y.) City Sch. Dist., 1984—. V.p. NAACP, Middletown, 1973-82; mem. Zoning Bd. of Appeals for Village of Dryden, N.Y., 1990. Recipient Citizen of Yr. award, 1982. Mem. Women in Ednl. Leadership, N.Y. State United Tchrs., Tompkins County Mental Health Assn. (v.p. 1987-89). Democrat. Presbyterian. Home: 20 Hilton Rd Dryden NY 13053-9709

MURPHY, EVELYN FRANCES, former state official, economist; b. Panama Canal Zone, May 14, 1940; d. Clement Bernard and Dorothy Eloise (Jackson) M. AB, Duke U., 1961, PhD, 1965; MA, Columbia U., 1963; hon. degrees, Regis Coll., 1978, Curry Coll., Northeastern U., Simmons Coll., Wheaton Coll., Anna Maria Coll., Bridgewater State Coll., Salem State Coll., Emmanuel Coll.; hon. degree, Suffolk U. Pres. Ancon Assocs., Boston, 1971-72; ptnr. Llewelyn-Davies, Weeks, Forrester-Walker & Bor, London, 1973-74; sec. environ. affairs Commonwealth of Mass., Boston, 1975-79, sec. econ. affairs, 1983-86, lt. gov., 1987-91; mng. dir. Brown Rudnick Freed and Gesmer, Boston, 1991—; vis. pub. policy scholar Radcliffe Coll., 1991; vice-chmn./chmn. Nat. Adv. Com. on Oceans and Atmosphere (Presdl. apptd.), 1979-80. Recipient Disting. Svc. award Nat. Sierra Club, 1978, Nat. Govs. Assn. 1978, Outstanding Citizen award Mass. Audubon Soc., 1978; Harvard U. fellow, 1979-80. Mem. Women Execs. in State Govt. (chair 1987). Democrat. Office: Brown Rudnick Freed and Gesmer 1 Financial Ctr Boston MA 02111-2621

MURPHY, GERARD DANIEL, police officer; b. Worcester, Mass., Sept. 30, 1949; s. Timothy Joseph and Mary Theresa (White) M.; m. Bridget M. Korp, Oct. 3, 1970. BS in Criminal Justice, Clark U., 1982; MA in Law Enforcement, Anna Maria Coll., 1983. Staff sgt. Mass. State Police, Boston, 1972—; pvt. practice accident reconstrn. cons. Worcester, 1985—; instr. Mass. Criminal Justice Tng., Needham, 1983—; adj. faculty U. North Fla. Inst. Police Tech. and Mgmt., Jacksonville, 1984—; mem. panel for reconstrn. tng. standards Nat. Hwy. Traffic Safety Adminstrn., Northwestern U., 1986; mem. commn. accident reconstrn. cert. bd. Accreditation Commn. for Traffic Accident Reconstrn., Denver, 1990—. Mem. Internat. Assn. Accident Reconstruction Specialists (bd. dirs. 1983—), Soc. Accident Reconstruction Specialists, Soc. Automotive Engrs. (affiliate). Home: 52 Dick Dr Worcester MA 01609-1141 Office: Mass State Police Acad 470 Worcester Rd Framingham MA 01701-5390

MURPHY, GERARD NORRIS, trade association executive; b. Washington, July 10, 1950; s. Maurice J. and Marguerite (Norris) M.; m. Jacqueline F., May 26, 1973; children: Anne Marie, Michael Jonathan, Kathleen Elizabeth. BA, U. Md., 1972, MA, 1975; JD, George Mason U., 1980. Mgmt. trainee Automotive Trade Assn. Nat Capital Area, Rockville, Md., 1972-74, asst. chief exec. officer, 1974-82, pres., chief exec. officer, 1982—; bd. dirs. Internat. Credit Assn. Greater Washington, Silver Spring, Md., 1991, Coun. Ct. Excellence, Washington, 1990—; bd. dirs., chmn. Met. Washington Better Bus. Bureau, 1989—; chmn. Nat. Capital Area Transp. Fedn., Washington, 1990—. Co-founder, past chmn. Washington Regional Alcohol Program, Silver Spring, 1983-86; trustee Greater Washington Bd. Trade Polit. Action Com. for Md., 1989—; bd. dirs., exec. Boys & Girls Clubs Greater Washington, Silver Spring, 1987—; v.p. Fairfax Vocat. Edn. Found., Fairfax County Pub. Schs., Va., 1990—. Recipient Govs. citation, Gov. William Donald Schaefer, 1990. Mem. ABA, Am. Soc. Assn. Execs. (cert., com. chmn. 1989-90, fellow 1991—), Dist. Columbia Bar Assn., Automotive Trade Assn. Execs. (bd. dirs. 1987-88), Greater Washington Soc. Assn. Execs., Rotary Club, Delta Theta Phi, Delta Tau Delta. Democrat. Roman Catholic. Office: Automotive Trade Assn Nat Capital Area 15873 Crabbs Branch Way Rockville MD 20855-2610

MURPHY, GLORIA WALTER, novelist; b. Hartford, Conn., Feb. 22, 1940; d. Frank and Elizabeth (Lemkin) Walter; m. Joseph S. Murphy; children: William Gitelman, Laurie Gitelman, Daniel Gitelman, Julie Gitelman, Caitlin Murphy. Student, No. Essex Community Coll., Haverhill, Mass., 1979-81, Boston U., 1981-82. Columnist Pandora's Box The Peabody (Mass.) Times, 1975; columnist Murphy's Law The Methuen (Mass.) News, 1979. Author: Nightshade, 1986, Bloodties, 1987, Nightmare, 1987, The Playroom, 1987, Cry of the Mouse, 1991, Down Will Come Baby, 1991, A Whisper in the Attic, 1992. Mem. Mystery Writers Am., Authors Guild. Address: Box 670 Ringwood NJ 07456

MURPHY, GRATTAN PATRICK, mathematics educator; b. Parsons, Kans., Sept. 15, 1935; s. Frank John and Fidelis Margaret (Brown) M.; m. Barbara Ann Hallisy, June 10, 1961; children: Theresa, Timothy, Richard, Patricia. BS, Rockhurst Coll., 1957; MS, St. Louis U., 1962, PhD, 1966. Asst. in math. St. Louis U., Cahokia, Ill., 1957-59; instr. St. Louis U., 1961-65; tech. analyst McDonnell Aircraft, St. Louis, 1959-61; asst. prof. U. Maine, Orono, 1965-69, assoc. prof., 1970-80, prof., 1980—, chmn. math. dept., 1986—. Mem. Am. Math. Soc., Math. Assn. Am. (chmn. N.E. sect. 1976, vice-chmn. 1975, assoc. editor Math. Monthly 1968-71), Soc. Indsl. and Applied Math. Democrat. Roman Catholic. Home: 40 Peters St Orono ME 04473-1750 Office: U Maine Orono ME 04469

MURPHY, JAMES JOSEPH, physics educator; b. N.Y.C., Apr. 29, 1938; s. James Joseph and Kathleen Ann (Finnegan) M.; m. Francine Cranny, Aug. 26, 1961; children: Ellen Marie Brown, James J. III, Daniel Liam. BS, St. Joseph's U., Phila., 1959; MS, Fordham U., 1961, PhD, 1971. Instr. physics Iona Coll., New Rochelle, N.Y., 1961-64; asst. prof., 1964-72, assoc. prof., 1972-76, prof., 1976—, chmn. dept. physics, 1967-76, 87-90; chmn. dept. physics, 1991-92; dir. sci. and tech., 1982-86; adj. faculty Fordham U., 1962, Bergen C.C., 1968-76, Upsala Coll., 1969-70; curriculum cons. Trenton State Coll., C.C. Morris, Felician Coll., St. Peter's Coll., 1986-88. Coauthor: Physics Quiz Book; contbr. articles to profl. jours.; speaker in field. Active Our Lady of Victories Ch., Harrington Park, N.J., 1979-82. Recipient academic sholarship St. Joseph's Coll., 1955-59; research fellow N.J. Inst. Tech., 1986-87, NSF fellow, 1960, 65, 73. Mem. AAAS, Am. Assn. Physics Tchrs., Nat. Sci. Tchrs. Assn., Soc. Coll. Sci. Tchrs., Humanities and Tech. Assn. (pres. 1991—), Sci. Tchrs. Assn. N.Y. State, Nat. Assn. Sci. Tech. and Soc. (v.p. 1992—). Roman Catholic. Office: Iona Coll 715 North Ave New Rochelle NY 10801-1890

MURPHY, JEFFERSON (CHARLES), carpenter, mason, contractor, poet, songwriter; b. Balt., Aug. 25, 1947; s. Charles Jefferson and Mada (Gail) M.; m. Olivia Tsen, 1974 (div. 1982); 1 child, Charles Jefferson III; m. Virginia Lena, June 12, 1982; children: Jesse Lena-Murphy, Gabriella Lena-Murphy. Student, N.E. La. State Coll., 1966-67, West Community Coll., 1970-71, Empire State Sch., 1984-85. Pvt. practice gen. contractor, 1970-81; carpenter Children's Village, Dobbs Ferry, N.Y., 1981-85; maintenance mechanic Oss Bd. Edn., 1988-91. Producer: (record album) Meant to Be, (video cassette, album) Sal Mancuso Memorial Concert, 1990; author: Poems for the Latter Days, vols. 1, 2. With U.S. Army, 1967-70, Vietnam. Decorated Nat. Def. Svc. medal, Vietnam Svc. medal, Vietnam Campaign medal, Army Commendation medal, Good Conduct medal U.S. Army, South Vietnam, 1969-70. Mem. ASCAP, Vietnam Vets of Am. (chpt. 49). Seven Day Adventist. Home: PO Box 718 Baldwin Place NY 10505-0718

MURPHY, JOHN ANTHONY, marketing executive; b. Westport, Conn., June 12, 1939; s. William Francis and Alice (Vivien) M. BS in Econs., Belmont Abbey Coll., 1961. Copywriter Sears Roebuck & Co., Charlotte, N.C., 1961-66; dir. advt. Cato Stores, Inc., Charlotte, 1966-69, Belk Stores Services, Charlotte, 1969-72; dir. retail Newpaper Advt. Bur., N.Y.C., 1972-78; v.p. mktg. Nat. Retail Merchants Assn., N.Y.C., 1978-87; sr. v.p. retail Knight-Ridder Newspaper Sales, N.Y.C., 1987—. Editor, pub. of mktg. books. Mem. Inst. Store Planners, Retail Mktg. Soc., Retail Advt. and Mktg. Assn. (Chgo.), Nat. Retail Fedn., Internat. Coun. of Shoppng Ctrs., Overseas Press Club. Republican. Roman Catholic. Home: 137 Riverside Dr New York NY 10024-3702 Office: Knight-Ridder Newspaper Sales 280 Park Ave New York NY 10017-1216

MURPHY, JOHN CORNELIUS, physicist, educator; b. Wilmington, Del., Feb. 28, 1936; s. John Cornelius and Madeline Mary (Taggart) M.; m. Marie Allison Scully, June 14, 1958; children: Kathleen, Sheila, Margaret, John, Michael, Daniel, Patricia. BA, Cath. U., 1957, PhD, 1971; MS, U. Notre Dame, 1959. Assoc. physicist Applied Physics Lab., Johns Hopkins U., Laurel, Md., 1959-68, sr. physicist, 1968-82, prin. physicist, 1982—, supr., 1988—; rsch. prof. materials sci. dept. Johns Hopkins U., Balt., Md., 1987-90, part-time prof. biomed. engring. dept., 1990—; Fitzgerald Dunning prof. Johns Hopkins U., Balt., 1983; bd. dirs. Hopkins Ctr. for NDE, Balt., 1985—; chmn. Conf. on PHotoacoustic and Photothermal Phenomena, Balt., 1989. Editor: Photothermal Phenomena II, 1990; contbr. over 100 articles to profl. publs., chpt. to book Fundamentals of Thermal Imaging, 1991; patentee in field. Chmn. Howard County (Md.) Bd. Edn., 1974-76; mem. Commn. on Secondary Edn., Md., 1981-84; mem. Responser to Nation at Risk, Md., 1984; mem. Howard County Parks and Recreation Bd., 1977-81. Mem. Am. Phys. Soc., Materials Rsch. Soc. Republican. Roman Catholic. Office: Johns Hopkins U Applied Physics Lab Johns Hopkins Rd Laurel MD 20723

MURPHY, JOHN JOSEPH, surgeon, urologist; b. Scranton, Pa., Oct. 2, 1920; s. John Joseph and Ida Josephine (Neher) M.; m. Alice Joan McHale, Sept. 18, 1944; children: Madeline, John, Patricia, Peter, Alice Marie, Genevieve. BS, Scranton (Pa.) U.; MD, U. Pa. Diplomate Am. Bd. Surgery, Am. Bd. Urology. Intern, gen. surgery resident Hosp. U. Pa., Phila., 1945-52; resident in urology Hosp. U. Mich., Ann Arbor, 1952-53; sr. instr. surgery U. Mich., Ann Arbor, 1952-53; Harrison fellow in urologic surgery, Am. Cancer Soc. fellow Dept. Urology, U. Mich., Ann Arbor, 1952-53; assoc. in urology Hosp. U. Pa., Phila., 1953-56, asst. prof. urology, 1956; assoc. prof. urology and dir. div. urology Grad. Hosp. and Grad. Sch. Medicine, U. Pa., 1958; prof. urology and dir. div. urology Hosp. U. Pa. and Grad. Hosp. U. Pa., 1964-80; attending urologist VA Hosp., 1953-62; cons. urology VA Hosp., 1962-80, Rehab. Ctr. Hosp. of U. Pa., Children's Seashore House, Atlantic City, Div. Urology, Children's Hosp. of Pa., 1967—; cons. surgeon in urology Pa. Hosp., 1968—; cons. staff urologist Mercy Cath. Med. Ctr., Darby, Pa., 1969—; cons., lectr. Phila. Naval Hosp., 1972-76; sr. attending physician Dept. Urology, Phila. Gen. Hosp., 1973-78. Contbr. more than 168 articles to profl. jours.; cons. editor Urology Digest, 1965-75, Science, 1964-67, Urol. Survey, 1976, Jour. of Trauma, 1962—; editorial bd. Jour. Urology, to 1986. Capt. U.S. Army, 1946-52. Fellow ACS; mem. Urologic Investigators Forum, Urol. Assn. Pa., Soc. Univ. Surgeons, Soc. Univ. Urologists, Societe International D'Chirurgie, Societe Internationale D'Urologie, Phila. Urol. Assn., Phila. Physiol. Soc., Phila. County Med. Soc., Phila. Acad. Surgery, Pa. Med. Soc., N.Y. Acad. Sci., Am. Urol. Assn. (chpt. pres. 1974-75), John Morgan Soc., Halsted Soc., Assn. of Am. Med. Colls., Am. Surg. Assn., Am. Soc. Exptl. Pathology, Am. Assn. Genitourinary Surgeons, many others. Republican. Roman Catholic. Home: 941 Wooton Rd Bryn Mawr PA 19010-2227 Office: Mercy Fitzgerald Med Office Bldg 1501 Lansdowne Ave Darby PA 19023-1333

MURPHY, JOSEPH JAMES, chiropractic physician; b. Newark, N.J., July 30, 1956; s. Joseph P. and Roberta (Nittolo) M.; m. Rebecca Lynn Swanson, June 21, 1986; 1 child, Joseph Raymond. BA in Biology, Rider Coll., 1978; D in Chiropractic Medicine, Palmer Coll., 1984. Diplomate Nat. Bd. Chiropractic Examiners; cert. N.J. State Bd. Med. Examiners. Rsch. chemist Mallinkrodt, Inc., Englewood, N.J., 1979-81; staff physician Mid-Isalnd Chripractic, Levittown, N.Y., 1984; dir., chief exec. officer Suburban Chiropractic Ctr., Chatham, N.J., 1984—. Advisor Chatham High Sch. Key Club, 1986-87. D. D. Palmer scholar, 1981, 82, 83. Mem. APHA, AAAS, Am. Assn. Cereal Chemists, Am. Chiropractic Assn., N.J. Chiropractic Soc. (bd. dirs. 1987—, chmn. inter profl. rels. com. 1989—, editor-in-chief Jersey Jour. 1986—, Meritorious Svc. award 1986, Disting. Svc. award 1987, 88, 89, 90), N.Y. Acad. Sci., Internat. Soc. Food Technologists, Morris County Chiropractic Soc. (pres. 1987—), Chatham C. of C. (chmn. profl. rels. com. 1988-92, pres. 1989-92), Kiwanis (bd. dirs. Chatham club 1986-89), Tri Beta. Republican. Presbyterian. Home: 139 Woods End Basking Ridge NJ 07920 Office: Suburban Chiropractic Ctr 301 Main St Chatham NJ 07928

MURPHY, JOSEPH KEMP, psychologist; b. Augusta, Maine, Feb. 2, 1951; s. John Kemp Murphy and Florence (Berube) Dodge; m. Barbara Carruthers, June 11, 1977. BA, McGill U., 1976; MA, La. State U., 1980, PhD, 1985. Instr. Med. Coll. Ga., Augusta, 1983-84; asst. prof. U. Tenn., Memphis, 1984-89; asst. prof. psychiatry Brown U., Providence, 1989—; mem. staff div. behavioral medicine Miriam Hosp., Providence, 1989—; grant reviewer Nat. Inst. Drug Abuse, Rockville, 1989—; presenter at profl. confs. Contbr. sci. articles to profl. publs. Grantee Nat. Inst. Drug Abuse/NIH, 1989, Nat. Heart, Lung and Blood Inst., 1989—. Mem. Am. Heart Assn., Am. Psychol. Assn., Am. Psychosomatic Soc., Am. Soc. Hypertension, Assn. Advancement Behavior Therapy, Internat. Soc. Hypertension in Blacks, Soc. Behavioral Medicine. Office: Div Behavioral Medicine Miriam Hosp 164 Summit Ave Providence RI 02906-2894

MURPHY, KEVIN GEORGE, novelist; b. Albany, N.Y., Feb. 29, 1952; s. Matthew George and Kathleen Mary (Dvorak) M.; m. Cathy Ann Clampett, July 14, 1973 (div. 1975); m. Judith Marion Chester, Jan. 9, 1987. Student, Empire State Coll., 1972-74. Novelist Scott Meredith Literary Agy., N.Y.C., 1984—, Barbara Bauer Lit. Agy., N.J., 1990. Author: The Dawn Run, 1986, Let Freedom Ring, 1986, In Someone Else's World, 1987, The Small Adventures of a Quiet Man, 1989, Humanform 2891, 1990, The Short Stories of Kevin George Murphy, 1991, Laura and the Abyss, 1991, Emergency, 1991, others; (poetry) Though Villages May Sleep, 1989, Her Hands Untied the Sun, 1991; contbr. to mags. and jours. Participant anti-nuclear marches, N.Y., Washington, 1977, anti-Klan march, Albany, 1991. Mem. Mental Health Assn. (plaque 1986), Amnesty Internat. Democrat. Mem. Soc. of Friends. Home and Office: 548 Madison Ave Apt 1 Albany NY 12208

MURPHY, KEVIN KEITH, management consultant; b. Bellefonte, Pa., Oct. 6, 1962; s. Raymond O. and Violet Marie (Carver) M.; m. Kimberly Jo Pedersen, Mar. 15, 1986. BA in Speech Communication, Bus. Adminstrn., Pa. State U., 1984. Asst. exec. dir. Cornwall (Pa.) Manor Found. Inc., 1984-85, exec. dir., 1985, v.p. pub. rels., devel., 1985-86, v.p. pub. rels., devel., mktg., 1986-90; spl. asst. to sec. and press sec. Pa. Dept. of Aging, 1990-91; v.p. The Bricker Group, 1991—; cons. Hershey, Pa., 1986-91; seminar instr. Pa. State U., 1988-90. Mem. pub. rels. com. Pa. Assn. Nonprofit Homes for Aging, 1986-90; pub. rels. task force, fund devel. task force United Meth. Assn. Health Welfare Ministries, 1985-90, sec., 1988-90; mem. pers. com. St. Paul's United Meth. Ch., 1982-83, adminstrv. bd., 1980-83; chmn. Golden Cross Fund Ea. Pa. Conf. United Meth. Ch., 1986-89, Greater Harrisburg Renaissance Scholarship Com., 1987-90, Pa. State Class 1984 Gift Fund; mem. mktg. com. Pa. Easter Seal Soc., 1992—, bd. dirs. Lebanon County chpt., 1987-90, strategic planning com., 1989-90. Mem. Nat. Soc. Fund Raising Execs. (bd. dirs. 1986-90), Pa. State Alumni Assn. (bd. dirs. 1985-91), Mt. Nittany Soc., Mensa, Pa. State Club (Lebanon, Harrisburg), Pa. State Lion Ambs., Pi Kappa Phi (chpt. advisor 1988-91, alumni corp. pres. 1991—), Alpha Sigma Alpha. Democrat. Home: 1103 Limerick Ct Hummelstown PA 17036-9024 Office: The Bricker Group 1525 Oregon Pike Ste 602 Lancaster PA 17601-4374

MURPHY, MARIE ANN, educator; b. Boston; d. Albert Leslie and Mary (Holland) Fish; children: Thomas Paul. BA, Regis Coll., Weston, Mass., MA; MA, Boston Coll.; MEd, Curry Coll., Milton, Mass. Tchr. Canton (Mass.) High Sch., Milton, 1964-69; edn. coord. St. Thomas Parish, Millis, Mass., 1970-73; instr. edn. Oblate Coll. & Sem., Natick, Mass., 1970-73; psycho-edn. diagnostician Carney Hosp., Dorchester, Mass., 1975-83; dir., sch. psychologist Marsalin Inst., Halliston, Mass., 1976-79; assoc. prof. Curry Coll., Milton, Mass., 1978—; prisn edn. cons. Mass Correctional Inst., 1987—; cons. in field; conductor workshops in field. Author/designer various sch. curriculums. Mem. ASCD, AAUP, Mass. Assn. Handicapped Students, New Eng. Assn. Tchrs. of English, Correctional Edn. Assn., Phi Delta Kappa. Roman Catholic. Home: 87 Farm St Millis MA 02054-1425

MURPHY, MARK JOSEPH, marketing executive; b. Rockville Centre, N.Y., Aug. 5, 1960; s. John Stephen and Barbara Ann (Seeney) M.; m. Annamaria Martin, July 19, 1986; 1 child, Dana Martine. BS in Econs. and Fin., St. John's U., 1983. Sr. tech. clk. St. John's U., Jamaica, N.Y., 1979-83; systems engr. trainee Property and Liability Br. IBM Corp., N.Y.C., 1983-84, systems engr. N.Y. Ins. Br., 1984-86, mktg. rep. Manhattan Ins. Br., 1986-89, adv. mktg. staff Eastern Area, 1989, mktg. mgr. N.Y. banking, 1990—. Bus./mktg. advisor The Times Sq. Project Common Ground Community HDFC, Inc., N.Y.C. Mem. Am. Mgmt. Assn. Home: 18 North St West Islip NY 11795-3010 Office: IBM Corp 14th Fl 33 Maiden Ln New York NY 10038-4518

MURPHY, BROTHER MICHAEL ANTHONY, juvenile counselor; b. Omaha, June 23, 1939; s. Joseph Frances and Margaret Lillen (Gillen) M. BBA, St. Mary's U., San Antonio, 1966; MS, U. Dayton, 1990. Bus. mgr., fin. mgr. Nolan High Sch., Ft. Worth, 1966-69; supt. bldg. and grounds Chaminade Coll. Prep. St. Louis, 1969-74; asst. adminstr. temporal affairs St. Mary's High Sch., St. Louis, 1974-78; dir. ctr. and Marianist community Marianist Apostolic Ctr., Glencoe, Mo., 1978-84; dir. vocation svcs. Marianist Vocation Svc., 1984-88; practicum student Dayton (Ohio) Correctional Instn., 1988-90; acting dir. Marianist Community, Rockaway Park, N.Y., 1990-92; dir. Marianist Community, Rockaway Park, 1992—; religious edn., drug and alcohol edn. liaison St. John's Home, Rockaway Park, N.Y., 1991—; chmn. adv. bd. Marianist Apostolic Ctr.; trustee Sisters of St. Joseph's Retirement Community; mem. adv. bd. St. Louis

Archdiocesan Vocation Office; founder, chmn. St. Louis Archdiocesan Retreat Dirs. Assn.; intern, Ranchi, India, 1990. Mem. AACD, Assn. Multicultural Counseling and Devel., Assn. Religious and Value Issues in Counseling, Internat. Assn. Addictions and Offender Counselors, Am. Mental Health Counselors Assn., Assn. Specialists in Group Work. Democrat. Home: 144 Beach 111th St Far Rockaway NY 11694-2592 Office: St John's Home for Boys 144 Beach 111th St Far Rockaway NY 11694-2592

MURPHY, MICHAEL MCKAY, food company executive; b. Fayetteville, N.C., Aug. 13, 1946; s. Charles Lawrence M.; m. Gwendolyn Lillian Fergeson; 1 child, L. Mark. BS in Commerce, St. Louis U., 1968. Life underwriter John Hancock Life Ins. Co., St. Louis, 1968-71; bus. mgmt. specialist Fort Mtr. Co., Waltham, Mass., 1971-75; dir. consumer affairs Dunkin Donuts, Inc., Randolph, Mass., 1975—. Bd. dirs. United Svc. Orgn., Boston, 1991; chmn. Bd. Health, Canton, Mass., 1991; councilor Gov.'s Coun., Commonwealth of Mass., 1990; past pres. Blue Hill Civic Assn. Mem. Nat. Restaurant Assn., Phi Beta Sigma. Republican. Home: 8 Flintlock Ln Canton MA 02021-2426 Office: Dunkin Donuts Inc 14 Pacella Park Dr Randolph MA 02368-1700

MURPHY, NORA SHARKEY, public relations executive; b. Bronx, N.Y., July 21, 1940; d. Peter Paul and Cornelia Hart (Keane) Sharkey; m. Michael Gerard Murphy, June 18, 1972; 1 child, Michael Timothy. BS, Fordham U., 1961; MA, Manhattan Coll., 1971. Editorial asst. Dell Pub. Co., N.Y.C., 1961-62; pub. rels. asst. St. Vincent's Hosp., N.Y.C., 1963-63; english tchr. Maria Regina High Sch., Hartsdale, N.Y., 1963-70; assoc. editor The Cath. News, Mt. Vernon, N.Y., 1970-75; adj. instr. dept. communications Coll. Mt. St. Vincent, Riverdale, N.Y., 1979-85; pub. rels. cons. Cath. Charities Archdiocese N.Y., N.Y.C., 1979—; pub. rels. counsel Calvary Hosp., Bronx, N.Y., 1980-82; dir. pub. rels. Supt. Schs. Archdiocese N.Y., N.Y.C., 1981—; bd. dirs. St. Ursula Learning Ctr. Editor: Fordham Univ. Alumni News, 1970-74, Cath. Charities Archdiocese N.Y. Annual Reports, 1979—. Mem. exec. bd. Tuckahoe PTA, Eastchester, N.Y., 1981-87, co-pres., 1985-87, named hon. life mem., 1988; chair pub. rels. adv. bd. Tuckahoe Bd. Edn., 1983-87; mem. communications bd. Town of Eastchester; chair parish coun. St. Joseph's Parish, Bronxville, 1989-90. Mem. Nat. Cath. Edn. Assn. (chmn. Washington pub. rels. com. 1988), Cath. Press Assn., Nat. Sch. Pub. Rels. Assn., Publicity Club N.Y., Fordham U. Sch. Edn. Alumni (bd. dirs.), St. Catharine Acad. Alumnae Assn. (Bronx, N.Y., v.p. 1988—). Democrat. Office: Archdiocese of NY Office Supt of Schs 1011 1st Ave New York NY 10022-4134

MURPHY, PATRICIA A, speech and language pathologist, social worker; d. Michael and Nora (Dennehy) M. BA in Speech Pathology and Audiology, Hunter Coll., 1968; MA in Communication Scis., NYU, 1970, MA in Learning Disabilities and Reading, 1977; postgrad. in Ednl. Psychology, Columbia U., 1983-86; MSW, NYU, 1989. Lic. speech lang. pathologist; cert. social worker. Speech-lang. pathologist Goldwater Meml. Hosp./NYU Med. Ctr., N.Y.C., 1970-78; lang. learning specialist in child and adolescent psychiatry Met. Hosp., N.Y.C., 1980-90; cons. speech-lang. pathologist Mary Manning Walsh Nursing Home, N.Y.C., 1974—. Clin. social worker St. Luke's Comprehensive Alcohol Treatment Program, 1990—. Mem. NASW, N.Y. State Soc. Clin. Social Work Psychotherapists, Inc., N.Y. Fedn. Alcohol Counselors, Am. Speech.-Lang. and Hearing Assn., Hunter Coll. Alumni Assn., Appalachian Mountain Club, Am. Small Craft Assn., U.S. Power Squadron. Home: 1619 3d Ave Apt 3CE New York NY 10128

MURPHY, PATRICK, department head, artist; b. Allentown, Pa., Feb. 17, 1946; s. Thomas William and Mary Evelyn (Bickert) M.; m. Susan Elizabeth Gregory, Mar. 20, 1971; children: Jessica Dara, Aaron Matthew. BA, King's Coll., 1972; MS in Edn., Parsons Sch. of Design/Bank St. Coll., 1988. Illustrator, cons. Ed Media Tech., Wilkes-Barre, Pa., 1975-79; instr. Luzerne County Community Coll., Nanticoke, Pa., 1976-79; assoc. prof. art Pa. Coll. of Tech., Williamsport, 1979-90, head dept. communication arts, 1990—; mem. editorial adv. bd. Collegiate Press, Alta Loma, Calif., 1991—. Editorial reviewer (book) Technical Illustration, 1984. Bank St. Coll. fellow, 1987. Mem. Internat. Graphic Arts Edn. Assn. Office: Pa Coll of Tech 1 College Ave Williamsport PA 17701-5799

MURPHY, ROBERT BLAIR, management consulting company executive; b. Phila., Jan. 19, 1931; s. William Beverly and Helen Marie (Brennan) M.; B.S., Yale, 1953; children: Stephen, Emily, Julia, David, Catherine. Indsl. engr. DuPont Corp., Aiken, S.C., 1953-55; mgr. sales can div. Reynolds Metals Co., Richmond, Va., 1955-69; gen. mgr. corrugated div. Continental Can Co., N.Y.C., 1969-73; v.p. and gen. mgr. beverage div. Am. Can Co., Greenwich, Conn., 1973-75; asso. Heidrick & Struggles, Inc., N.Y.C., 1976-78, v.p., 1978; v.p., mng. dir. Stamford office Spencer Stuart & Assocs., 1978-84, ptnr., 1982-84; co-founder Sullivan-Murphy Assocs., 1984—. Clubs: Riverside Yacht (Greenwich); Yale (N.Y.C.); Merion Cricket (Haverford, Pa.). Home: 11 Indian Mill Rd Cos Cob CT 06807-1315 Office: 6 Landmark Sq Stamford CT 06901

MURPHY, ROBERT P., physician; b. Aug. 11, 1943; m. Emily Ying Chew, Oct. 11, 1986; children: Alison Anne Chew Murphy, Emma Elizabeth Ying Murphy, Erica Lynn Chew Murphy. BS, St. Louis U., 1965; MD, Northwestern U., 1969. Intern Milw. County Gen. Hosp., 1969-70; resident internal medicine U. Calif., Irvine, 1972-75; resident ophthalmology Stanford (Calif.) U. Med. Ctr., 1975-78; asst. prof. Sch. of Medicine Johns Hopkins U., Balt., 1980-84, assoc. prof. Sch. of Medicine, 1984-91; pvt. practice Retina Ctr. St. Joseph Hosp., Towson, Md., 1991—. Mem. Am. Acad. Ophthalmology, Assn. Rsch. in Vision and Opthalmology, Macula Soc., Retina Soc., Pan-Am. Assn. Ophthalmology, Md. Soc. Eye Physicians and Surgeons. Office: St Joseph Hosp Retina Ctr O'Dea Med Arts Bldg 7505 Osler Dr Ste 103 Baltimore MD 21204

MURPHY, SHAUN EDWARD, bank executive; b. London, June 3, 1961; came to U.S., 1962; s. John Joseph and Annie (Coyle) M.; m. Angela Mary Murphy, July 19, 1986. BSBA, Villanova U., 1983; MSc, London Sch. Econs., 1984. Rating analyst Fireman's Fund Ins. Co., N.Y.C., 1978-83; corp. officer Marine Midland Bank, N.A., N.Y.C., 1985-88; v.p., mgr. Nat. Bank Washington, 1988-89, Riggs Nat. Bank, Washington, 1989—; chief credit officer Riggs AP Bank, London, 1991; cons. Michael S. O'Meara Corp., Annapolis, Md., 1988—. Senate mem. U. London Convocation, 1984—; exec. Cath. Charities Washington, 1988—. Mem. Am. Friends of London Sch. Econs., Assn. Corp. Growth, Army and Navy Club. Republican. Roman Catholic. Home: 1045 31st St NW Washington DC 20007-4407 Office: Riggs Nat Bank 800 17th St NW Washington DC 20006-3910

MURPHY, STEPHEN VINCENT, investment banker; b. Bklyn., Oct. 15, 1945; s. Robert A. and Virginia (Still) M.; m. Vicki Sorg, Dec. 13, 1969; children: Bryan F., S. Gannon. BSBA, Georgetown U., 1967; MBA, Columbia U., 1968. Mng. dir. The First Boston Corp., N.Y.C., 1978-88, Merrill Lynch Capital Markets, N.Y.C., 1988-90; pres. S.V. Murphy & Co., Inc., Oyster Bay, N.Y., 1990—. Treas. Peoples' Symphony Concerts, N.Y.C., 1980—; vice chmn. Nat. Ctr. for Disability Svcs., Albertson, N.Y., 1991. Served to lance cpl. USMC, 1968-72. Roman Catholic.

MURPHY, THOMAS FRANCIS (TODD MURPHY), wholesale distribution company executive; b. Burlington, Vt., Sept. 11, 1942; s. Edmund Joseph and Rosella (Juve) M.; A.B.A., Champlain Coll., 1964; OPM, Harvard Bus. Sch., 1983; m. Jane Christie, Apr. 30, 1966; children—Kara, Glenn. Brian. Pres., Burlington News Agy., Inc., Burlington, 1964—, Lake Champlain Yacht Sales, Inc., Burlington, 1971-76, European Auto, Inc., 1972-74, owner Bookglenn, 1968-72; pres. Daytona News, Inc., Daytona Beach, Fla., 1976—, Plattsburgh News Co., 1982—; dir. Mchts. Nat. Bank. Chmn. Burlington St. Commn., 1972-75; chmn. Burlington Water Pollution Control Bd., 1972-75; trustee emeritus Champlain Coll.; mem. Bank of Vermont Council, 1974—. Mem. Atlantic Coast Ind. Distbrs. Assn. (dir. 1966-85). Roman Catholic. Clubs: Ethan Allen, Mallets Bay Boat. Home: 5 Driftwood Ln Burlington VT 05401-2720 Office: Hercules Dr Colchester VT 05446-1548

MURPHY, THOMAS FRANCIS, federal judge; b. N.Y.C., Dec. 3, 1905; s. Thomas Michael and Susan Anne (White) M.; m. Katherine F. Hotaling, June 28, 1957. A.B., Georgetown U., 1927; LL.B., Fordham, 1930; LL.D., St. Joseph's Coll., 1950. Bar: N.Y. bar 1930. Asst. U.S. atty. So. Dist., N.Y., 1942-50; police commr. N.Y.C., 1950-51; U.S. dist. judge, 1951—. Decorated knight Equestrian Order of Holy Sepulchre of Jerusalem. Mem. Friendly Sons St. Patrick. Club: Sharon Country. Office: US Dist Ct PO Box 756 Sharon CT 06069-0756

MURPHY, THOMAS JAMES, accountant; b. Utica, N.Y., May 15, 1956; s. Edward John and Eileen Patracia (Rousch) M.; m. Margot A. Pajares, July 7, 1980. BS, Towson State U., 1978; MBA, Loyola Coll., 1989. CPA, Md. Cost acctg. mgr. State Use Industries, Balt., 1978-79; asst. contr. Jim Walter Plastics Div., Balt., 1979-81; contr. Joseph Camac Co., Balt., 1982-85, Microtec Plastics Co., Balt., 1986-88; pvt. practice Balt., 1988—, Thomas Murphy & Assoc., Jacksonville, Fla., 1991—. Mem. AICPA, Nat. Soc. Tax Profls. Republican. Roman Catholic. Office: 4005 Seven Mile Ln Baltimore MD 21207

MURPHY, THOMAS S., media company executive; b. Bklyn., May 31, 1925; married. B.S., Cornell U., 1945; M.B.A., Harvard U., 1949. With Kenyon & Eckhardt, 1949-51; with Lever Bros. Co., 1951-54; with Capital Cities ABC Inc. (formerly Capital Cities Communications Inc.), N.Y.C., 1954—, exec. v.p., 1961-64, pres., 1964-72, chief exec. officer, 1966-90, chmn., 1966—, also bd. dirs.; dir. Gen. Housewares Corp., Texaco Inc., Johnson & Johnson, Internat. Bus. Machines Corp. Served with USN. Office: Capital Cities/ABC Inc 77 W 66th St New York NY 10023-6201

MURRAH, JUDITH ANN, marketing executive; b. Providence, Mar. 11, 1958; d. John Anthony and Julia Gloria (Santoro) Silvestri; m. Lance Edward Murrah, July 9, 1983. BS in Indsl. Engring., U. R.I., 1980; MBA, Harvard U., 1985. Indsl. engr. summer intern Texas Instruments, Attleboro, Mass., 1978, Eastman Kodak, Rochester, N.Y., 1979; indsl. engr. Kaiser Aluminum, Oakland, Calif., 1980-83; product mgr. Symbol Technologies, Bohemia, N.Y., 1985-87; sr. product mgr. Symbol Technologies, 1987-88, product line mgr., 1988-89, sr. market mgr., 1989—. Mem. Phi Kappa Phi, Tau Beta Pi, Sigma Kappa. Home: 15 Elberta Dr East Northport NY 11731-5641

MURRAY, ANDREW, social studies educator; b. Roanoka, Va., June 25, 1942; s. Max Andrew and Dorothy (Garst) M.; m. Teresa Kathleen Robinson, June 22, 1963; children: Kristin Alease, Kimberly Garst. AB, Bridgewater (Va.) Coll., 1964; MDiv, Bethany Theol. Sem., Oak Brook, Ill., 1968, DMin, 1980. Ordained to ministry Ch. of Brethren, 1968. Pastor Peace Ch. of Brethren, Portland, Oreg., 1968-71; campus min. Juniata Coll., Huntingdon, Pa., 1971-85, asst. prof. religion, 1973-85, assoc. prof. peace and conflict studies, 1986—, dir. peace and conflict studies, 1975—, dir. Baker Inst., 1986—; cons. to numerous colls. and univs. in U.S. and Can., 1975—; Staley disting. lectr. Staley Found., 1981, 88; vis. scholar Pa. State U., 1990; mem. Internat. Assn. Univ. Pres./UN Commn. on Arms Control, N.Y.C., 1991—. Author: PACS as Applied Liberal Arts, 1984; writer, performer, producer rec. Just As I Am, 1991, also others. Mem. Pa. Commn. on Ministry in Higher Edn., 1979-86. Recipient Beechley award for disting. acad. svc. Juniata Coll., 1991. Mem. Nat. Peace Studies Assn. (charter, chmn. exec. com. 1988—), Nat. Pastors Assn. (pres. 1975). Democrat. Home: RR 4 Box 3 Huntingdon PA 16652-9707 Office: Juniata Coll Huntingdon PA 16652

MURRAY, ANITA JEAN, data processing executive, consultant; b. Pitts., May 22, 1943; d. Julius and Nancy (Betza) Czujko; m. Christopher H. Murray, Apr. 6, 1968 (div. 1976), m. 2d, May 1, 1989. BS in Psychology, U. Pitts., 1964; MS in Stats., Stanford U., 1967. Cert. data processor. Systems analyst Pan Am. World Airways, N.Y.C., 1967-69; asst. contr. Bunge Corp., N.Y.C., 1969-79; prin. nat. office Arthur Young & Co., N.Y.C., 1979-82; v.p. mgmt. info. systems Murjani Internat. Ltd., Saddle Brook, N.J., 1982-85; pres. Amston Mgmt., Inc., N.Y.C., 1985—; seminar leader Am. Mgmt. Assn., N.Y.C., 1979-82. Author: Minicomputer Bus. Solutions, 1981. Pres. Married Ams. for Tax Equality, N.Y.C., 1973-76; chmn. office mgmt. com. Community Bd. 1, N.Y.C., 1983. Mem. Tax Watch Assn., Skating Club of N.Y., Lincoln Harbor Yacht Club, Collier Athletic Club. Office: Amston Mgmt Inc 52 Laight St New York NY 10013-2016

MURRAY, CHARLES ALAN, social scientist; b. Newton, Iowa, Jan. 8, 1943; s. Alan Benton and Frances Bradburn (Patrick) M.; m. Suchart Dej-Udom, Aug. 19, 1966 (div. 1980); children: Narisara, Sarawan; m. Catherine Bly Cox, July 29, 1983; children: Anna, Bennett. BA, Harvard U., 1965; PhD, MIT, 1974. Scientist Am. Insts. for Rsch., Washington, 1974-79, chief scientist, 1979-81; fellow Manhattan Inst., N.Y.C., 1981-90; Bradley fellow Am. Enterprise Inst., Washington, 1990—. Author: Losing Ground, 1984, In Pursuit, 1988, Apollo, 1989. Office: Am Enterprise Inst 1150 17th St NW Washington DC 20036-4603

MURRAY, CHRISTINE MARIE, psychotherapist, addictions counselor; b. N.Y.C., Oct. 26, 1949; d. William Brown and Gloria Ann (Rodrigo) Rodriguez; m. William Patrick Murray, June 7, 1975; children: Jennifer, Jessica. BS in Social Sci./Psychology, St. Thomas Aquinas Coll., 1975; MS in Community Mental Health Counseling, L.I. U., 1982; EdS in Marriage & Family Therapy, Seton Hall U., 1992. Nat. cert. addiction counselor, nat. cert. alcohol and drug counselor, cert. addiction specialist, cert. alcohol and drug counselor, N.J. Adolescent counselor The Shire, Mendham, N.J., 1986-88; family therapist The Shire, Mendham, 1988-90; family program coord. The Steps Recovery Ctr., Mendham, 1990-91; therapist Affiliated Psychotherapists, Long Valley, N.J., 1990-91; clinician Alcohol and Substance Abuse Program Newton (N.J.) Meml. Hosp., 1991—. Mem. Am. Assn. Marriage and Family Therapists, Nat. Assn. Alcohol and Drug Abuse Counselors, Nat. Cert. Reciprocity Consortium, Am. Acad. Health Care Providers in the Addictive Disorders, N.J. Assn. Alcoholism and Drug Abuse Counselors, N.J. Assn. Marriage and Family Therapists. Roman Catholic. Office: ASAP Newton Meml Hosp 175 High St Newton NJ 07860

MURRAY, DAVID AUSTIN, interior designer; b. Germantown, Pa., Mar. 2, 1943; s. Henry Kedward and Ethel Beatrice (Rairigh) M.; m. Henya Berman, July 10, 1977 (div. Jan. 1983); m. Deborah Dahl Eisenberg, June 29, 1983; children: Megan, Ariel, Rachael, Sara, Galen. Student, East Stroudsburg U., 1962-64, Fairfield U., 1981-83, Norwalk Tech. Coll., 1989-91. Pres. Murray Office Interiors, Westport, Conn., 1970—; cons. Apple Computers - Applications for Interior Design and Architecture, 1989—. Mem. Am. Soc. Interior Designers (bd. dirs. 1990—, top comml. design award 1989, 90), Conn. Coalition Interior Design. Home and Office: 39 Cross Hwy Westport CT 06880-2139

MURRAY, EDWARD LEO, priest, psychologist, educator; b. Ambridge, Pa., Feb. 17, 1920; s. Michael D. and Catherine C. (Cosgrove) M. BA in Philosophy, St. Vincent Coll., 1941, MA in Philosophy, 1945; MA in Psychology, Duquesne U., 1964, PhD in Psychology, 1968. Lic. psychologist, Pa.; ordained priest, Roman Cath. Ch., 1945. Faculty Psychology Dept., Duquesne U., Pitts., 1964—, chmn., 1970-75, prof., 1983—; acad. v.p. Duquesne U., Pitts., 1975-82, acting pres., 1976-77; chmn., bd. dirs. Simon Silverman Phenomenology Ctr., Duquesne U., Pitts., 1985—. Author: Life of Christ, 1948, Imaginative Thinking and Human Existence, 1986; editor/author chpt.: Imagination and Phenomenological Psychology, 1987; contbr. 25 articles to profl. jours. Mem. APA, Pa. Psychol. Assn., Greater Pitts. Psychol. Assn. Democrat. Roman Catholic. Home: 801 Bluff St Pittsburgh PA 15282-0001 Office: Duquesne U Coll Hall Psychology Dept Pittsburgh PA 15282

MURRAY, EDWARD ROCK, insurance broker; b. Bklyn., Jan. 31, 1947; s. Garrett Francis and Anne M. (Rock) M.; m. Barbara Marie Robotti; children: Pamela Jean, Stephanie Elise. BA in Bus. Adminstrn., St. Bonaventure U., 1968. Claims examiner N.Y.C., 1970-72; agt. and mgr. John Hancock Life Ins., Albany, N.Y., 1972-76; regional dir. Colonial Life Insur, Albany, 1976-80; ptnr. Murray & Zuckerman, Inc., Schenectady, N.Y., 1980—; bd. dirs. Am. Med. Ins., Hicksville, N.Y., 1988—, Northeast Mgmt. Forum, 1990—; mem. adv. bd. William Penn Life Ins. Co. 1st lt. U.S. Army, 1968-70, Vietnam. Roman Catholic. Office: Murray & Zuckerman Inc 670 Franklin St Schenectady NY 12301

MURRAY, HARRY LAWRASON, III, transportation executive, federal official; b. Ft. Jackson, S.C., Mar. 28, 1942; s. Harry Lawrason Jr. and Helen Jean (Ray) M.; m. Laura Hearne Croom, June 17, 1972. AB, Princeton U., 1969; MBA, U. North Fla., 1974. Student auditor Peat, Marwick, Mitchell & Co., N.Y.C., 1970-71; traveling auditor Fla. Nat. Banks of Fla., Inc., Jacksonville, 1971-72; transp. specialist Fed. Maritime Commn., Washington, 1975—. 1st lt. U.S. Army, 1963-67. Mem. Princeton Club of Washington. Episcopalian. Home: 2112 Salt Kettle Way Reston VA 22091-4124 Office: Fed Maritime Commn 1100 L St NW Washington DC 20573-0001

MURRAY, JAMES DOYLE, accountant; b. Rochester, N.Y., July 24, 1938; s. William Herbert and Mildred Frances (Becker) M.; m. Mary Louise Goodyear, June 22, 1962; children: William Doyle, Robert Goodyear. B.S., U. Rochester, 1961. CPA, N.Y. With Ernst & Whinney, Rochester, N.Y., 1963—, ptnr., 1977-86; pvt. practice Rochester, 1986—; mem. faculty Found. for Acctg. Edn., N.Y.C., 1979—. Contbr. articles to profl. jours. Treas. William Warfield Scholarship Fund, 1987—; active fund raising Boy Scouts Am., Rochester Philharm., Rochester Mus. and Sci. Ctr.; bd. dirs., treas. Downstairs Cabaret, 1985; mem. Eagle bd. of rev. Boy Scouts Am.; elder Presbyn Ch., 1987—; pres. Egypt Vol. Fire Dept., 1975. Lt. USN, 1961-63. Mem. AICPAs, N.Y. State Soc. CPAs (pres. Rochester chpt. 1982-83), Nat. Assn. Accts. (bd. dirs. 1978-80). Republican. Presbyterian. Home: 42 Blackwatch Trail Fairport NY 14450-3702 Office: 2060 Fairport-Nine Mile Point Rd Ste 400 Penfield NY 14526

MURRAY, JAMES VINCENT, III, chemical company executive, lawyer; b. Charleston, W.Va., Sept. 10, 1942; s. James V. Jr. and Audrey E. (Norris) M.; m. Merrie C. Little, Sept. 9, 1967; children: Leanne, Michael, Meredith. AB, Georgetown U., 1964; JD, Fordham U., 1967. Bar: N.Y. 1967, U.S. Dist. Ct. (so. dist.) N.Y. 1972, U.S. Ct. Appeals (2d cir.) 1972. Atty. Union Carbide Corp., N.Y.C., 1971-78; dir. regional pub. affairs Union Carbide Corp., Danbury, Conn., 1978-90; dir. govt. affairs Union Carbide Corp., Washington, 1990—; dir. Pub. Affairs Coun., Washington, 1990—, State Govt. Affairs Coun., Washington, 1989-91. Capt. USMC, 1968-71. Mem. ABA. Office: Union Carbide Corp 1100 15th St NW # 1200 Washington DC 20005-1707

MURRAY, JENNIFER JAYNE, retirement services executive; b. Newport, Vt., Jan. 10, 1963; d. Earle Edward, Jr. and Marilyn Elizabeth (Leavitt) Hulburd; m. Thomas Joseph Murray, June 25, 1988. B in Econs., Holy Cross Coll., 1985; student, Bentley Coll. Cert. employee benefits and pension specialist. Sales mgr. Jordan Marsh Co., Boston, 1985-86; account mgr. Fidelity Investments, Boston, 1986-88, asst. mgr., 1988-90, mktg. mgr., 1990-91, asst. v.p., 1991—. Mem. Holy Cross Club of Greater Boston.

MURRAY, JOEL ANTHONY, software development company executive; b. Balt., Apr. 13, 1948; s. Clifton Scott and Ethel Minerva (Grant) M.; children: Nicolle Yvette, Joel Anthony Jr.; m. LaVern Anita Williams, Sept. 8, 1990; 1 child, Brennan Anthony. Student, Morgan State Coll., Balt., 1964-69. Programmer, analyst Comml. Credit Corp., Balt., 1969-72, Cen. Info. Processing Corp., Balt., 1972-73; systems rep. Honeywell Info. Systems, Inc., Columbia, Md., 1973-76; mgr. data processing Wilkens-Rogers, Inc., Ellicott City, Md., 1976-78; sr. analyst Marriott Corp., Bethesda, Md., 1978-79; pres. Jam Systems, Inc., Columbia, 1979-82; v.p. Comp-3 Systems, Inc., Columbia, 1982-85; pres. Applications Plus, Inc., Columbia, 1985—; instr. Comml. Credit Computer Corp., Balt., 1970-72, Montgomery County Adult Edn., Rockville, Md., 1976-77. Mem. Balt. City Vocational Edn. Adv. Com. on Data Processing, 1974. Office: Applications Plus Inc 9200 Old Annapolis Rd Ste 206 Columbia MD 21045-1842

MURRAY, JOSEPH EDWARD, plastic surgeon; b. Milford, Mass., Apr. 1, 1919; s. William Andrew and Mary (DePasquale) M.; m. Virginia Link, June 2, 1945; children—Virginia, Margaret, Joseph Link, Katharine, Thomas, Richard. A.B., Holy Cross Coll., 1940, D.Sc., 1965; M.D., Harvard, 1943; D.Sc., Rockford (Ill.) Coll., 1966, Roger Williams Coll., 1986. Diplomate: Am. Bd. Surgery, Am. Bd. Plastic Surgery (chmn. 1969). Chief plastic surgeon Peter Bent Brigham Hosp., Boston, 1951-86, chief plastic surgeon emeritus, 1986—; chief plastic surgeon Children's Hosp. Med. Center, Boston, 1972-85, emeritus, 1985; prof. surgery Harvard Med. Sch., 1970—. Served to maj. M.C. AUS, 1944-47. Recipient Gold medal Internat. Soc. Surgeons, 1963, hon. award Am. Acad. Arts and Sci., 1962, Nobel prize in medicine, 1990. Hon. fellow AAAS, AMA, Royal Australasian Coll. Surgeons, Royal Coll. Surgeons of Eng., Royal Coll. Surgeons Ireland, Royal Coll. Surgeons Edinburgh; mem. ACS (regent 1970-79, v.p. 1983), Am. Surg. Assn. (v.p. 1979), New Eng. Surg. Soc. (pres. 1986-87), Boston Surg. Soc. (pres. 1975), Soc. U. Surgeons, Am. Assn. Plastic Surgeons (hon. award 1969, pres. 1964-65), Harvard Med. Sch. Alumni Council (pres. 1984), Alpha Omega Alpha. Clubs: Badminton and Tennis, Wellesley Country. Home: 108 Abbott Rd Wellesley MA 02181-6104

MURRAY, LAWRENCE, management consultant; b. N.Y.C., May 10, 1939; s. Gilbert and Edna (Blatt) M.; m. Jennifer Lynn Gustavson, Dec. 2, 1990; children: Robert, David, Daniel, Abigail. BA, Cornell U., 1961; MBA, U. Okla., 1966. Account exec. Merrill Lynch, Paramus, N.J., 1965-69; chmn., pres. Murray, Lind & Co., Inc., Jersey City, 1969-72; dir. investor rels. IU Internat. Corp., Phila., 1972-73, dir. spl. projects, 1974-75; dir. fin. communications ARA Svcs., Inc., Phila., 1975-78; chmn., chief exec. officer Century Mgmt. and affiliated cos., West Chester, Pa., 1976-82, Creative Mgmt. Corp., Bala Cynwyd and West Chester, Pa., 1982-87; underwriter Jefferson Standard Life Ins. Co., Greensboro, N.C., 1982-83; chmn., chief exec. officer Fin. Mgmt. Profl. Corp., West Chester, 1983-89; chmn. bd. dirs. Venture Frontiers Co., Denver, 1984-89; chmn. bd., chief exec. officer Fin. Intelligence Corp., West Chester, 1989—; lectr. bus. orgn. and mgmt. Bergen Community Coll., 1971-72. Author: The Organized Stockbroker, 1970; A New Era in Mergers and Acquisitions, 1974; Communications: Management's Newest Marketing Skill, 1976; contbr. articles to profl. jours. Pres., Congregation Beth Israel, Media, Pa., 1977-78, Parents Without Partners, Valley Forge, Pa., 1982-83; v.p. Cornell U. Class of 1961, 1981-86. Served to 1st lt. arty., U.S. Army, 1963-64. Mem. Nat. Investor Rels. Inst. (pres. Phila. chpt. 1976-78), Internat. Coun. Shopping Ctrs. Home and Office: 924 Hollyview Ln West Chester PA 19380-1376

MURRAY, LOWELL, Canadian senator; b. New Waterford, N.S., Can., Sept. 26, 1936; s. Daniel and Evelyn (Young) M.; m. Colleen Elaine MacDonald; children: William, Colin. BA, St. Francis Xavier U., Antigonish, N.S., Can.; MA in Pub. Adminstrn., Queen's U., Kingston, Ont., Can. Chief of staff Minister of Justice and Minister of Pub. Works Can., Ottawa, Ont., Senator M. Wallace McCutcheon, Ottawa, Ont.; leader of opposition Can., Ottawa, Ont.; dep. minister Premier N.B. (Can.); mem. Senate of Can., Ottawa, Ont., 1979—, co-chmn. joint Senate-House of Commons com. ofcl. langs., 1980-84; chmn. standing Senate com. on banking, trade and commerce Senate of Can., 1984-86; trustee Inst. Rsch. Pub. Policy, 1984-86, mem. Trilateral Commn., 1985-86. National campaign chmn. gen. election Progressive Conservative Party Can., 1977-79, 81-83; sworn of the privy coun., appointed Leader of the Govt. in the Senate, 1986—, Minister of State Fed. and Provincial Rels., 1986-91, Minister Responsible for the Atlantic Can. Opportunities Agy., 1987-88. Roman Catholic. Office: The Senate, Ottawa, ON Canada K1A 0A6

MURRAY, ROBERT GRAY, sculptor; b. Vancouver, C., Can., Mar. 2, 1936; s. John Gray and Vera (Meakin) M.; m. Cintra Wetherill Lofting, Jan. 23, 1971; children: Rebecca and Megan (twins), Claire, Hillary. Student, U. Sask., 1956-58. One man shows Betty Parsons Gallery, N.Y.C., 1965, 66, 68, David Mirvish Gallery, Toronto, 1967, 68, 72, 73, 74, 75, Jewish Mus., N.Y.C., 1967, Hammarskjold Plaza, N.Y.C., 1971, Paula Cooper Gallery, N.Y.C., 1974, Janie Lee Gallery, Houston, 1977, Hamilton Gallery, N.Y.C., 1977, 79, 80, Klonaridis Inc., Toronto, 1979, 81, 82, Rice U., 1978, Dayton Mus., 1979, Columbus Mus., 1979, Lamont Gallery, Phillips Acad., Exeter, N.H., 1983, Art Gallery Greater Victoria, 1983, Gallery One, Toronto, 1985, Culturale Canadese Roma, 1985, Gallery 291, Atlanta, 1986, Richard Greene Gallery, N.Y.C.,1986, L.A., 1987, Del. Art Mus., Wilmington, 1990, Muhlenberg Coll., Allentown, Pa., 1992; exhibited in group shows at Whitney Mus. Am. Art, N.Y.C., 1964-66, Tibor de Nagy Gallery, N.Y.C., 1965, Musée cantonal des Beaux Arts, Lausanne, Switzerland, 1966, World House Gallery, N.Y.C., 1966, Betty Parsons Gallery, 1966, Sch. Visual Arts, N.Y.C., 1967, Los Angeles County Mus., 1967, Nat. Gallery Can., Toronto,

1967, Inst. Contemporary Art, Boston, 1967, U. Toronto, 1967, Guggenheim Mus., N.Y.C., 1967, Inst. Torcuato Di Tella, Buenos Aires, 1967, Musée d'Art Moderne, Paris, 1968, Whitney Mus., 1967, Walker Art Gallery, 1969, X Sao Paulo Biennial, Brazil, 1969, Boston City Hall, 1971, Artist and Fabricator, Amherst, Mass., 1975, Met. Mus., N.Y.C., 1983, Del. Art Mus., 1990; represented in permanent collections, Montreal Mus. Fine Arts, Nat. Gallery Can., Joseph Hirshhorn Collection, Art Gallery Ont., Larry Aldrich Mus., Ridgefield, Conn., New Brunswick Mus., Whitney Mus. Am. Art, Met. Mus., N.Y.C., Columbus Mus., Dayton Art Inst., Storm King Art Centre, Del. Art. Mus., Wilmington, others; major commns. include, Everson Mus., Syracuse, N.Y., Fredonia (N.Y.) State Coll., Canadian Dept. External Affairs, Ottawa, Ont., U. Mass., U. Toronto, Ont., State Ct. Bldg., Juneau, Alaska, Honeywell Corp., Mpls., also others. Office: 66 Grand St New York NY 10013-2217

MURRAY, RONALD, small business owner; b. N.Y.C., Nov. 21, 1931; s. Adolph and Rhea Evelyn (Wadden) Ansorge; m. Ruth Knecht, June 1951 (div. 1956); children: Robin, Rhea; m. Sallie Susanne Smith, 1970; children: LeeAnn, Lynnette, Todd, Andrew George; 1 stepchild, Jeff Moser. BSBA, Lehigh U., 1953. Analytical reporter Dun & Bradstreet, Allentown, Pa., 1953-56; purchasing agt. R.E. Moyer, Inc., Catasauqua, Pa., 1956-59; salesman United Fund, Allentown, 1959; mgr. mdse. Hess Bros., Allentown, 1959-64; mgr. nat. sales Talens & Son, Union, N.J., 1964-69; ptnr. The Blue Victorian, Allentown, 1970—; mgr., owner Fountain Park & Shop, Allentown, 1970—; owner Gallery Downtown Parking, Allentown, 1988—; ptnr. Corporate Downtown Parking, 1991—. Sec. Neighbors in Common Endeavor, Allentown, (pres. 1977-80); v.p. Community Neighborhood Orgn., Allentown, 1980; mem. Housing Rev. Bd., Allentown, 1986—. Mem. Lehigh County Constables Assn. (treas. 1984-88, sec. 1988-90, v.p. 1991—), Swain Lacrosse Club (founder 1988, coach 1989—). Republican. Lutheran. Home: 945 E Walnut St Allentown PA 18102-4864 Office: Fountain Park & Shop 945 W Walnut St Allentown PA 18102-4864

MURRAY, SHAWN MICHAEL, small business owner; b. Phila., June 28, 1956; s. Bruce F. and Rose (Sylvester) Murray. Student, Rutgers U., 1976. Lic. real estate agt., N.J. Acquisitions mgr. Kaselaan & D'Angelo Assocs., Inc., Haddon Heights, N.J., 1986-90; ptnr., gen. mgr. Blue Chip Leasing, Inc., Haddon Heights, 1986-91; founder, owner, photographic art pub. Bruce Murray Collection, Cherry Hill, N.J., 1990—. Mem. Ea. Pa. Sports Collectors Club, N.J. Bd. Realtors, Am. Assn. Equipment Lessors. Home: 2606 Church Rd Cherry Hill NJ 08002

MURRAY, STEPHEN JAMES, lawyer; b. Phila., Jan. 27, 1943; s. Paul Martin and Hannah (Smith) M.; m. Linda Sanders, June 20, 1970; children: Gordon Joshua, Cara Sanders. AB cum laude, Brown U., 1963; LLB, Harvard U., 1966; LLM, George Washington U., 1967. Bar: N.Y. 1968, U.S. Ct. Appeals (2nd cir) 1971, U.S. Dist. Ct. (so. and ea. dists.) N.Y. 1972, U.S. Ct. Claims 1974, U.S. Supreme Ct. 1975, Conn. 1988, U.S. Dist. Ct. Conn. 1988. Spl. asst. SEC, Washington, 1966-67, Maritime Adminstrn., Washington, 1967-68; assoc. Hill, Betts & Nash, N.Y.C., 1970-76; transp. atty. Union Carbide Corp., N.Y.C., 1976-78, sr. transp. atty., 1978-85; chief transp. counsel Union Carbide Corp., Danbury, Conn., 1985—, group counsel, 1986—; real estate counsel, 1992—; speaker at profl. seminars. Contbr. articles to profl. jours. Lt. JAGC, USN, 1968-70. Mem. ABA, Maritime Law Assn., U.S. Transp. Lawyers Assn., N.Y. State Bar Assn., Westchester-Conn. Corp. Counsel Assn., Conn. Maritime Assn., Harvard Club, Brown Club. Home: 14 Pilgrim Ln Weston CT 06883-2412 Office: Union Carbide Corp Law Dept 39 Old Ridgebury Rd Danbury CT 06817

MURRAY, TERENCE RODNEY (TERRY), professional hockey team coach; b. Shawville, Que., Can., July 20, 1950; m. Linda Murray; children: Megan, Lindsey. Hockey player Calif. Golden Seals, 1972-75, Phila. Flyers, 1975-77, 78-81, Detroit Red Wings, 1977; hockey player Washington Capitals, 1981-82, asst. coach, 1982-88, head coach, 1990—; head coach Balt. Skipjacks, 1988-90. Named to 3 Am. Hockey League all-star teams; named most valuable defenseman Am. Hockey League, 1978, 79. Office: Washington Capitals Landover MD 20785*

MURRAY, WILLIAM MICHAEL, lawyer; b. Buffalo, Dec. 21, 1953; s. William Joseph and Mary Ann (Lichtenthal) M.; m. Antoinette Ioco, Aug. 12, 1978; children: Colleen Elizabeth, William Michael Jr., Caitlin Anne. BA, U. Notre Dame, 1975; JD, U. Detroit, 1978. Bar: N.Y. 1978, U.S. Dist. Ct. (we. dist.) N.Y. 1980. Asst. county atty. Erie County, Buffalo, 1978-79; ptnr. Stamm & Murray, Williamsville, N.Y., 1979—. Mem. Amherst (N.Y.) Rep. Com., 1980—; chmn. Amherst Zoning Bd. Appeals, 1986—. Mem. N.Y. State Bar Assn., Erie County Bar Assn., Williamsville Bus. Assn. (bd. dirs., v.p. 1985—), Rotary (pres. Williamsville 1989—). Roman Catholic. Home: 433 Tiburon Ln East Amherst NY 14051-1447 Office: 5555 Main St Buffalo NY 14221-5430

MURRELL, CARLTON DECOURCEY, artist, shipping coordinator; b. Bridgetown, Barbados, July 17, 1945; s. Charles Herbert and Albertha Clarissa Murrell; m. Hazel Adams, Mar. 31, 1969 (div. Mar. 1987); 1 child, Jacqueline. Student, Art Students League, N.Y.C., 1968-70; diploma, Pels Art Sch., N.Y.C., 1972-75. Acctg. clk. Gen. Adjustment Bur., N.Y.C., 1970-74; comml. artist Graphic Engravers, N.J., 1974-75; expediter Colonial Hardware, N.J., 1975-79; shipping coord. Codelco Inc., N.Y.C., 1979—; tchr. art Bklyn. Truth Ctr., 1988—; tchr. art Ft. Green Sr. Citizens Ctr., Bklyn. Exhibited oil paintings at Flushing Art League (2d prize), 1979, Fulton Art Fair (1st prize), 1982, (1st prize), 1984, Salamagundi Art Club, 1982. Set designer Caribbean Theater Workshop, Bklyn., 1975; art cons. Caribbean African Am. Coun. N.Y., Bklyn., 1986-88. Mem. Bklyn. Watercolor Soc. Mem. First Ch. Religious Sci. Home: 543 E 21st St # 8A Brooklyn NY 11226-6868

MURTAGH, LIANE RENÉE, personnel professional; b. N.Y.C., Aug. 9, 1962; d. Jack Leo and Sonya Harriet (Hamburger) Schaffer; m. Michael Paul Murtagh, May 6, 1990. Student, U. Madrid, Spain, 1982-83; BA, U. Del., 1984. Overseas adminstrn. and compensation asst. Associated Merchandising Corp., N.Y.C., 1984-85, pers. communications asst., 1985-86; adminstrv. asst. Coopers and Lybrand, N.Y.C., 1986-87, nat. recruiting specialist, 1987-89, pers. supr., 1989—. Mem. external affairs com. Independence Harbor Condominium Assn., Edgewater, N.J., 1991; Coopers and Lybrand coord. United Way, 1989, 90. Mem. Middle Atlantic Placement Assn., Toastmasters Internat. (edn. v.p. 1988-89), Sigma Delta Pi, Psi Chi. Office: Coopers and Lybrand 1301 Ave of the Americas New York NY 10019-6022

MURTHA, JOHN PATRICK, congressman; b. New Martinsville, W.Va., June 17, 1932; s. John Patrick and Mary Edna (Ray) M.; m. Joyce Bell; three children. B.A. in Econs., U. Pitts., 1961; postgrad., Indiana U. of Pa., 1962-65; H.H.D. (hon.), Mt. Aloysius Jr. Coll. Mem. 93d-102nd Congresses from 12th Pa. Dist., 1974—; chmn. ho. appropriations subcom. on def., 1989, chmn. ho. steel caucus, co-chmn. ho. coal group; mem. Pa. Ho. of Reps., 1969-73. Served to lt. USMC, 1952-55, as maj. 1966-67, Vietnam; ret. col. Res. Decorated Bronze Star, Purple Heart (2); Cross of Gallantry Vietnam; Pa. Disting. Svc. award, 1978, Pa. Meritorious Svc. medal, numerous service awards for work during Johnstown flood, 1977, Iron Mike award Marine Corps League, 1988, Disting. Am. award Nation's Capital chpt. Air Force Assn., 1989, Outstanding Veteran award Vets. Caucus of Am. Acad. Physician Assts., 1989, Man of Steel award Cold Finished Steel Bar Inst., 1989; named Man of Yr. Johnstown Jaycees, 1978. Office: US Ho of Reps 2423 Rayburn House Office Bldg Washington DC 20515*

MURTHA, MARYANN KATHRYN, legislative assistant; b. Rockville Centre, N.Y., Apr. 24, 1966; d. Joseph Warren and Agnes Cecilia (Stamm) M. BA, Marymount Coll., 1987. Staff asst. U.S. Congressman Raymond J. McGrath, Washington, 1989-90, legis. asst., 1990—. Editor (newsletter) Capitol Hill Restoration Soc. News, 1991—. Bd. dirs. Capitol Hill Restoration Assn.; lector St. Joseph's Roman Cath. Ch.; publicity chair Capitol Hill House and Garden Tour, 1992. Mem. House Legis. Assts. Assn., Hist. Soc. Washington, Congl. Staff Club, Am. Legion Aux. Republican. Office: Rep Raymond J McGrath 205 Cannon House Office Bldg Washington DC 20515

MURTHY, SRINIVASA K., electrical engineer; b. Bangalore, Karnataka, India, June 12, 1949; came to U.S., 1979; s. Ramaswamy and Gowramma Kadur. BS in Physics, Bangalore U., India, 1967; MS in Physics, Bangalore U., 1969; MSEE, Mysore U., India, 1971. Mgr. project engring. Indian Space Rsch. Orgn., Bangalore, 1971-79; asst. prof. Calif. State U., Pomona, 1979-80, Fullerton, 1981-82; mgr. project Systems and Applied Scis. Corp., Anaheim, Calif., 1980-83; dir. div. IMR Systems Corp., Arlington, Va., 1983-84; mgr. systems engring. GE, Portsmouth, Va., 1984-85; bus. mgr. AT&T Bell Labs, Holmdel, N.J., 1985—; bd. advisors IMR Systems Corp., Roslyn, Va., 1988—. Contbr. articles to profl. jours. Recipient Disting. Achievement award Dept. Space, Indian Govt., 1975. Mem. IEEE (sr. mem., bd. dirs. 1986—, standards bd. 1986—, bd. dirs. Electronics and Aerospace Systems conf. 1983-84, editorial bd. dirs. Network Jour 1986—, area activities bd. and tech. activities bd. 1988, Computer Soc. 1987—, lectr. India, Singapore, Austalia 1989, South Am. 1990, numerous other coms.), Engring. Mgmt. Soc. of IEEE (bd. govs. 1986—). Home: 5 Polo Club Dr Eatontown NJ 07724-3823 Office: AT&T Bell Labs Rm 2N437 Crawford Corner Rd Holmdel NJ 07733

MURVIN, HARRY JAMES, educator; b. Coatesville, Pa., Dec. 19, 1944; s. Harry Arthur and Evelyn (Randow) M.; m. Tersilla P. Robino, Sept. 28, 1974 (div. 1991); 1 child, Harry J. II. BS, Pa. State U., 1966, MEd, 1968; MBA, Widener U., Chester, Pa., 1982, MS in Taxation, 1989. Bus. tchr. Balt. County Pub. Schs., Towson, Md., 1968-70; v.p. ops. Primo's Italian Foods, Wilmington, Del., 1980-86; assoc. prof. bus. adminstrn. Widener U., Chester, 1970—; fin. cons. Tax Masters, Wilmington, 1970—. Co-author (with Richard L. Price): Managerial Accounting Student Workbook Manual and Computer Applications, 1991, Federal Taxes Student Workbrook, 1991, Financial Accounting Student Workbook Manual and Computer Applications, 1990; contbr. articles to profl. jours. Bd. govs. Malta Home for the Aging, Granville, Pa., 1991; dist. com. Chester County coun. Boy Scouts Am., 1970—, chmn. troop 65, Wilmington, 1989—. Widener U. grantee, 1990. Mem. Nat. Assn. Accts., Nat. Bus. Edn. Assn., Tchrs. of Acctg. in Two-Yr. Colls., Am. Auto Racing Writers and Broadcasters Assn., Interstate Developmental Educators Assn., Pa. Knights of Malta (grand comdr. 1990-91), Knights of Malta (comdr. 1980-90). Baptist. Home: 2632 Skylark Rd Wilmington DE 19808-1634 Office: Widener Univ Chester PA 19013

MURZYCKI, JOHN VINCENT, marketing professional; b. Milford, Mass., July 30, 1953; s. John F. and Pauline A. (Parente) M.; m. Carol A. Raymond, Sept. 8, 1979; 1 child, Jessica. BS in Polit. Sci., Boston U., 1975, MS in Communications, 1978; MBA, Babson Coll., 1987. Editorial asst. PR Reporter, Exeter, N.H., 1976-77; dir. community rels. Am. Water Works, Westwood, Mass., 1977-84; mktg. communications mgr. LTX Corp., Westwood, 1984-89, Sequoia Systems, Inc., Marlboro, Mass., 1989—; pub. rels. counsel New England Water Works, Westwood, 1980. Contbr. articles to profl. jours. Campaign asst. Larry DiCara for Boston City Coun., 1975, Jack Backman for State Senate, 1974. Mem. Pub. Rels. Soc. Am. Office: Sequoia Systems Inc 400 Nickerson Rd Marlborough MA 01752-4696

MUSCHIO, HENRY MICHAEL, JR., biology educator; b. N.Y.C., Apr. 25, 1931; s. Henry M. and Katherine (Diorio) M.; m. Lucy DeRea; children: Henry M. III, Joseph P., Edward C., Laura M. AB in Biology, Syracuse U., 1952; MS in Biology, Fordham U., 1957, PhD in Biology, 1963. Instr. Fairleigh Dickinson U., Madison, N.J., 1958-62; asst. prof. Montclair State Coll., Upper Montclair, N.J., 1962-66; prof., dept. head allied health and biol. scis. Dutchess Community Coll., Poughkeepsie, N.Y., 1966-93; ret., 1993—; cons. Choice - Pub. of Assn. of Coll. & Rsch. Libr., 1967—. HEW grantee 1985-88, NSF grantee 1979-82, March of Dimes grantee, 1975-80. Mem. N.Y. State Assn. two Yr. Colls. (pres. 1987-89, named Outstanding Mem. 1986), Rotary (bd. dirs. 1988-89). Republican. Office: Dutchess CC 53 Pendell Rd Poughkeepsie NY 12601-1595

MUSGRAVE, R. KENTON, judge; b. 1927. Student, Ga. Inst. Tech., 1945-46, U. Fla., 1946-47; BA, U. Wash., 1948; JD with distinction, Emory U., 1953. Asst. gen. counsel Lockheed Internat., 1953-62; v.p., gen. counsel Mattel, Inc., 1963-71; mem. firm Musgrave, Welbourn and Fertman, 1972-75; asst. gen. counsel Pacific Enterprises, 1975-81; v.p., gen. counsel Vivitar Corp, 1981-85; v.p., dir. Santa Barbara Applied Rsch., 1982-87; judge U.S. Ct. Internat. Trade, N.Y.C., 1987—. Trustee Morris Animal Found., DIGIT Fund, Dolphins of Sharks Bay (Australia); hon. trustee Pet Protection Soc.; mem. United Way, South Bay-Centinela Svc. Orgn., Save the Redwoods League; active LWV, Legal Aid, Palos Verdes Community Assn. Mem. ABA, Internat. Bar Assn., Pan Am. Bar Assn., State Bar Calif. (chmn. corp. law sect. 1965-66, del. 1966-67), L.A. County Bar Assn., State Bar Ga., Fng. Trade Assn. So. Calif. (bd. dirs.), Sierra Club. Office: US Ct Internat Trade 1 Federal Plz New York NY 10007

MUSIC, JOHN FARRIS, performance consultant; b. Childress, Tex., Oct. 5, 1921; s. Rondo William and Madeline Callie (Hanson) M. m. Barbara Ellen Isett, Sept. 20, 1942; children: Barbara Helen, Elizabeth Ann. BA in Chemistry with honors, U. Tex., 1946, PhD in Phys. Chemistry with honors, 1951. With Gen. Electric Co., Richland, Wash., 1951-60; rsch. scientist rsch. and devel. mgmt. Gen. Electric Co., Schenectady, 1960-62; implementing cons. for def., space and info. systems groups Gen. Electric Co., King of Prussia, Pa., 1962-71; pres. MacroOps., Inc., 1971—, The Performance Cons. Group, 1989—; also speaker. Author: The Logic of Business Success...And How to Apply It, 1978, Power and Recognition, 1987. Mem. Am. Chem. Soc., Am. Phys. Soc., Inst. Mgmt. Scis., Sigma Xi, Phi Beta Kappa, Phi Lambda Upsilon. Address: 239 E King Lancaster PA 17602

MUSKIE, EDMUND SIXTUS, lawyer, former secretary of state, former senator; b. Rumford, Maine, Mar. 28, 1914; s. Stephen and Josephine (Czarnecki) M.; m. Jane Frances Gray, May 29, 1948; children—Stephen O., Ellen Muskie Allen, Melinda Muskie Stanton, Martha, Edmund Sixtus. A.B. cum laude, Bates Coll., 1936; LL.B., Cornell U., 1939; hon. degrees, U. N.B., Middlebury Coll., St. Anselm's Coll., William and Mary Coll., U. Md., Alliance Coll., U. N.H., Northeastern U., John Carroll U., Providence Coll., Boston U., Syracuse U., U. Maine, Suffolk U., Bowdoin Coll., Colby Coll., Lafayette Coll., U. Notre Dame, Hanover Coll., George Washington U., U. Buffalo, Nasson Coll., Husson Coll. Bar: Mass. 1939, Maine 1940, U.S. Dist. Ct 1941, N.Y. State 1981, U.S. Supreme Ct. 1981. Practice law Waterville, Maine, 1940, 45-55; gov. of Maine, 1955-59, U.S. senator from Maine, 1959-80; chmn. senate budget com., mem. fgn. relations com., U.S. Senate, chmn. subcom. on intergovtl. relations of senate govt. affairs com., subcom. environ. pollution of environment and pub. works com., subcom. on arms control, asst. majority whip; sec. of state of U.S., 1980-81; ptnr. Chadbourne & Parke, Washington, 1982—; former mem. Adv. Commn. Intergovtl. Relations; nat. exec. dir. Amvets, 1951; dist. dir. OPS, Maine, 1951-52; Maine chmn. citizens com. for Hoover report, 1950; chmn. Roosevelt Campobello Internat. Park Commn. Author: Journeys, 1972; co-author (with McGeorge Bundy) Presidential Promises and Performances, 1980. Mem. Maine Ho. of Reps., 1948-51, Democratic floor leader, 1949-51; mem. Dem. Nat. Com., 1952-55, Dem. candidate for vice pres. U.S., 1968. Served to lt. USNR, 1942-45. Recipient Laetare medal Notre Dame U., 1981, Presdl. Medal of Freedom, 1981, Former Mems. Congress Disting. Service award, 1981. Mem. Maine Bar Assn., Kennebec County Bar Assn., Waterville Bar Assn., Am. Legion, VFW, Amvets, Phi Beta Kappa, Phi Alpha Delta.

MUSSER, CHARLES HENRY, secondary music educator; b. West Chester, Pa., Mar. 15, 1943; s. Henry O. and Bertha E. (Kraft) M.; m. Patricia Irene Murphy, Aug. 22, 1964; children: Jennifer Lynn Musser Grill, Douglas Charles. BA in Music Edn., Glassboro (N.J.) State Coll., 1965, MA in Teaching of Music, 1975. Cert. tchr., supr., prin., N.J. Tchr. music Madison Twp. Pub. Schs., Old Bridge, N.J., 1965-66, Pennsville (N.J.) Pub. Schs., 1969—; camp dir. YMCA of Salem County, Carneys Point, N.J., 1986—; tchr. life guard tng. inst. Salem County chpt. ARC, Carneys Point, 1985—; music dir. Salem County Brass Soc., 1988—, pres., 1974—; music dir. Union Presbyn. Ch., 1978—, Salem Community Coll. Oak Singers, 1991—. Lt. USNR, 1966-69. Mem. NEA, N.J. Edn. Assn., Music Educators Nat. Conf., Am. Guild of English Handbell Ringers, Presbyn. Assn. Musicians, Choristers Guild, Salem County Sportsman Club, Washington Club. Presbyterian. Home: 8 Pinewood Ave Carneys Point NJ 08069

MUSTIN, LLOYD MONTAGUE, II, small business owner; b. Jacksonville, Fla., Feb. 9, 1959; s. Henry Croskey and Lucy Jane (Holcomb) M. BS in Bus. Adminstrn., U. Richmond, 1981; postgrad., Johns Hopkins U., Balt. Founder, exec. dir. Hunter Temporary Svcs. and Hunter Med. Svcs., Vienna, Va., 1987-88, XL Assocs., Inc., Washington, 1988—; co-founder NCMA Mentor Program, 1989—. Contbr. articles to profl. jours. Chmn. Combined Fed. Campaign, 1987; mem. carpenter Shelter, Washington, 1987—, Habitat for Humanity, Washington, 1987—; vol. Mary Pickford Theatre in the Libr. of Congress, 1987—, Friends of the Kennedy Ctr., 1987—. Lt. USN, 1982-87; lt. comdr. USNR, 1987—. Mem. The Smithsonian Assocs., Nat. Contract Mgmt. Assn., Nat. Trust for Historic Preservation, Army Navy Club, Army Navy Country Club. Episcopalian. Home: 1005 Massachusetts Ave NE Washington DC 20002 Office: XL Assocs Inc 121 13th St NE Unit 103 Washington DC 20002

MUSTO, RONALD GERALD, publisher; b. N.Y.C., May 24, 1948; s. Pasquale Louis and Gloria Ann (Casolaro) M.; m. Eileen Gardiner, Aug. 2, 1970. BA in History, Fordham U., 1969; MA in History, Columbia U., 1970, PhD in History, 1977. Vis. lectr. history NYU, N.Y.C., 1976; fellow Am. Acad. Rome, Italy, 1978-79; vis. prof. Columbia U., N.Y.C., 1980; asst. prof. history Duke U., Durham, N.C., 1980-81; writer, editor Humanities Ref., N.Y.C., 1981-85; editor Overseas Assignment Directory, N.Y.C., White Plains, 1983-86, Renaissance News & Notes, N.Y.C., 1988; pubr. Italica Press, Inc., N.Y.C., 1985—; cons. film Ciné Soleil, Haitian Project, N.Y.C., Newport, R.I., 1989—; mem. Book Award com. Pax Christi, USA, Erie, Pa., 1989—; lectr. in field. Author: The Catholic Peace Tradition, 1986 (Best Book of 1986 Cath. Press Assn.), The Peace Tradition in the Catholic Church, An Annotated Bibliography, 1987, Liberation Theologies: A Research Guide, 1991; editor: Petrarch, The Revolution of Cola di Rienzo, 1986, Theoderich, Guide to the Holy Land, 1987, Pierre Gilles, The Antiquities of Constantinople, 1987, (with John Monfasani) Renaissance Society and Culture: Essays in Honor of Eugene F. Rice, Jr., 1991; contbr. articles to profl. jours. Pres. bd. dirs. Roosevelt Island Community Libr., N.Y.C., 1989-90, bd. dirs., 1986-90. Andrew W. Mellon Found. fellow, 1980-81, NEH fellow, 1978-79, Renaissance Soc. Am. fellow in manuscript rsch., 1974, N.Y. State Teaching fellow, 1969-74. Mem. Am. Hist. Assn., Am. Cath. Hist. Assn., Medieval Acad. Am., Renaissance Soc. Am., Am. Acad. in Rome, Soc. of Fellows. Democrat. Roman Catholic. Office: Italica Press Inc 595 Main St Apt 605 New York NY 10044-0045

MUSTONE, AMELIA P., state legislator; b. Salem, Mass., July 16, 1928; d. Udo A. and Alberta (Durand) Poppey; m. John J. Mustone, 1950; children: John, Lisa, Mary Ellen, Paul, Anastasia, Jessica. B.A., Goddard Coll., Vt. Pres., Meriden Bd. Edn., Conn., 1974-78; mem. Conn. State Senate from 13th Dist., 1979—, dep. majority leader, 1987—. Mem. Nat. Conf. State Legislators, Council on State Govts., Caucus New Eng. State Legislators, Conn. Women's Polit. Caucus, Conn. Student Loan Found.; mem. Martin Luther King Jr. Commn.; active YMCA. Recipient Citizen of Yr. award Civitan Club, 1978, 1st Eleanor Roosevelt award NOW. Mem. AAUW, Meridan LWV, Latin Am. Soc. (hon.), Am. Assn. Retail Persons, NAACP. Roman Catholic. Lodge: Soroptimist Internat. Home: 34 Tunxis Cir Meriden CT 06450-7401

MUSZYNSKI, ROMAN, systems engineer; b. Bydgoszcz, Poland, June 15, 1956; came to U.S., 1980; s. Jerzy and Agnieszka (Galinowska) M.; m. Miriam Falzon, Nov. 27, 1991. BS in Math. and Computer Sci., U. Warsaw, Poland, 1979; MS in Math., U. Cin., 1982; MS in Applied Math., U. So. Calif., L.A., 1984, postgrad., 1985. Sci. programmer Bently Nev. Corp., Minden, 1981, 84; data base programmer Lift Engring. Co., Carson City, Nev., 1982; application programmer U. So. Calif., 1983-85; instr., lectr. Norton U., L.A., 1984-85; software engr. Allen-Bradley Co., Cleve., 1986-87; software systems engr. Ohmart Corp., Cin., 1987-89; sr. systems cons. Booz-Allen & Hamilton, Inc., Bethesda, Md., 1989—; cons. SRA, Sydney, Australia, 1989-91, Conrail Corp., Phila., 1990-92. Mem. IEEE, Math. Assn. Am., Transp. Rsch. Forum, C User's Group, Deans Club. Home: 10320 Westlake Dr # E404 Bethesda MD 20817 Office: Booz Allen & Hamilton Inc 4330 E West Hwy Bethesda MD 20814

MUTI, RICCARDO, orchestra and opera conductor; b. Naples, Italy, July 28, 1941. Edn., Milan Conservatory; MusD (hon.), U. Pa., Curtis Inst. Music U. Bologna, Mt. Holyoke Coll.; LLD (hon.), Warwick U., Eng.; Doctor Honoris Causa, Westminster Choir Coll., Princeton, N.J. Prin. condr. Orch. Maggio Musicale Florentino, Florence, Italy, 1969-80; guest condr. numerous orchs., Europe and U.S.; music dir. Philharmonia Orch., London, 1973-82; prin. guest condr. Phila. Orch., 1967-78, music dir., 1980-92, laureate condr., 1992—; music dir. La Scala, 1986—, prin. condr., 1973-82; concerts at Salzburg, Edinburgh, Lucerne, Flanders, Vienna and Berlin Festivals; condr. operas at Vienna, Salzburg, La Scala, Milan, Munich. Decorated officer of merit Republica Tedesca, Commendatore and Grand Ufficiale Della Republica Italiana; winner Guido Cantelli prize, 1967; recipient Verdienst Kreuz, Fed. Republic of Germany; hon ambassador by UN High Commr. for refugees; recipient numeours internat. prizes for recordings. Hon. mem. Royal Acad. Music, Acad. Santa Cecilia, Acad. Luigi Cherubini. Office: Phila Orch 1420 Locust St Ste 400 Philadelphia PA 19102-4297 also: Orch del Teatro alla Scala, Via dei Filodrammatici, I-20121 Milan Italy

MUUSS, ROLF EDUARD, psychologist, educator; b. Tating, Germany, Sept. 26, 1924; came to U.S., 1953; s. Rudolf A. and Else (Osterwald) M.; m. Gertrude Louise Kremser, Dec. 22, 1953; children: Michael John, Gretchen Elise. Diploma, Tchr. Coll., Flensburg, Germany, 1951; student, U. Hamburg, Germany, 1951, Central Mo. State Coll., 1951-52, Columbia Tchrs. Coll., 1952; M.Ed., Western Md. Coll., 1954; Ph.D., U. Ill., 1957. Tchr. pub. sch. Germany, 1945-46, 51, 52-53, substitute prin., 1952-53; tchr. trainee U.S. Office Edn., 1951-52; houseparent Child Study Center, Balt., 1953; grad. asst. U. Ill., 1954-57; research assoc. prof. Iowa Child Welfare Research Sta., State U. Iowa, 1957-59; research cons., 1960, 61; mem. faculty Goucher Coll., 1959—, prof. edn., 1964—, chmn. dept., 1972-75, dir. spl. edn., 1977—, Elizabeth C. Todd disting. prof., 1980-85, chmn. dept. sociology and anthropology, 1983-85; rsch. assoc. edn. Johns Hopkins, 1962-63; part-time or summer tchr. U.B.C., 1962, Johns Hopkins, 1962, 65, U. Del., 1965, Towson State Coll., 1967, U. Ill., 1967; teaching assoc. Sheppard and Enoch Pratt Hosp., 1969-80; guest lectr. Tchrs. Coll., Kiel, Fed. Republic Germany, 1977-78. Author: First-Aid for Classroom Discipline Problems, 1962, Theories of Adolescence, 1962, 5th edit., 1988, Grundlagen der Jugendpsychologie, 1982; also numerous articles; editor: Adolescent Behavior and Society: A Book of Readings, 1971, 4th edit., 1990. Served with German Air Force, 1942-45. Recipient award for disting. scholarship Goucher Coll., 1979; grantee Andrew W. Mellon Found., 1976-77. Fellow Am. Psychol. Soc., Am. Psychol. Assn., Md. Psychol. Assn. (treas. 1971-73); mem. Balt. Psychol. Assn. (chmn. membership com. 1966, v.p. 1970-71), Soc. Rsch. Child Devel., Soc. Rsch. on Adolescence, Kappa Delta Pi (v.p. Alpha chpt. 1956-57), Phi Delta Kappa. Home: 1540 Pickett Rd Lutherville Timonium MD 21093-5822 Office: Goucher Coll Towson MD 21204

MUZYKA, DONALD RICHARD, specialty metals executive, metallurgist; b. Northampton, Mass., Aug. 23, 1938; s. Stephen S. and Mary (Paul) M.; m. Eileen J. Hannigan, June 10, 1961; children: Steven Richard, James Paul, David Joseph. Supr. high temperature alloy research Carpenter Tech. Corp., Reading, Pa., 1966-73, mgr. alloy research and devel., 1973-76, mgr. high temperature alloys research, 1975-76, gen. mgr. research and devel. labs., 1976-77, gen. mgr. distbn., 1977-79, v.p. tech. div., 1979-82; dir. tech. Cabot Corp., Boston, 1982-85; gen. mgr. refractory metals Cabot Corp., Boyertown, Pa., 1985-87, gen. mgr. elec. and refractory metals, 1987-88; v.p., gen. mgr. Cabot Corp., Boyertown, 1988-89; v.p. rsch. and devel. Cabot Corp., 1989; pres. Spl. Metals Corp., New Hartford, N.Y., 1990—. Contbr. articles to profl. jours.; patentee in field. Bd. dirs. Wilson Sch. Bd., West Lawn, Pa., 1960-63, Montessori Country Day Sch., Wyomissing, Pa., 1960-63. Recipient Engring. Alumni award U. Mass., 1984. Fellow Am. Soc. Metals (trustee 1982-84, Bradley Stoughton award 1981); mem. The Metall. Soc., Indsl. Research Inst., Am. Ceramic Soc., Am. Soc. Quality Control. Republican. Roman Catholic. Home: RR 4 449E Reservoir Rd Clinton NY 13323 Office: Spl Metals Corp Middle Settlement Rd New Hartford NY 13413-9558

MYER, CHARLES RANDOLPH, venture capitalist; b. Elizabeth, N.J., June 6, 1921; s. Pettit Alonzo and Jessie Maud (Winans) M.; m. Nancy Ellen McCloud, Aug. 4, 1943; children: C. Randolph III, Bentley McCloud, Colin Winans. BS in Aero. Engring., Princeton U., 1943. Gen. mgr. Elgin (Ill.) Nat. Industries, 1951-58; pres., chief exec. officer Indsl. Supply Corp., Aurora, Ill., 1958-64; sr. v.p. Diversey Corp., Chgo., 1964-66; v.p., chief ops. officer Loctite Corp., Newington, Conn., 1966-68, also bd. dirs.; mng. dir. Heidrick & Struggles, Boston, 1968-86; pres. Myer Enterprises, Inc., Manchester, Mass., 1986—; chmn. bd. dirs. Indsl. Supply Corp.; mem. exec. com. Elgin Nat. Industries, 1955-58. Patentee in field. Bd. dirs. local Congl. Ch., Allendale Sch. for Boys; twp. chmn. Ill.; active local sch. bd. Lt. (j.g.) USN, 1943-46, ETO. Mem. Cruising Club Am., Myopia Hunt Club (Hamilton, Mass.), Chgo. Club, Chgo. Commonwealth Club, Manchester Yacht Club. Republican. Home: 15 Forster Rd Manchester MA 01944-1421 Office: Myer Enterprises Inc PO Box 621 Manchester MA 01944-0621

MYERS, ALFRED FRANTZ, state education official; b. Crooked Creek State Park, Pa., Feb. 19, 1936; s. Jacob Alfred Jr. and Ida Gertrude (Schaeffer) M. BA, Lehigh U., 1958, MA, 1966; postgrad. George Peabody Coll., 1971-72. Instr., Grand River Acad., Austinburg, Ohio, 1966, Culver (Ind.) Mil. Acad., 1966-68, Kiskiminetas Springs Sch., Saltsburg, Pa., 1968-71; asst. prof. social studies Ind. State U., Terre Haute, 1972-73; div. trainer Ency. Britannica, Rochester, N.Y., 1973-75; mgr. Rupp's, Kittanning, Pa., 1976-77; criminal justice system planner Pa. Commn. on Crime and Delinquency, Harrisburg, 1977-80; rsch. assoc. Pa. Dept. Edn., Harrisburg, Pa., 1980-89, basic edn. assoc., 1989—. Social work Dominican Rep., 1958. 1st lt. USAF, 1958-63. Mem. ACLU, AAUP, ASCD, Nat. Coun. Social Studies, Am. Acad. Polit. and Social Sci., Am. Evaluation Assn., Am. Ednl. Rsch. Assn., Am. Hist. Assn., Caribbean Studies Assn., Acad. Polit. Sci., Conf. Latin Americanist Geographers, Mid. States Coun. for Social Studies (pres. 1987-88), Nat. Braille Assn., People for Am. Way., Am. Legion, Orgn. Am. Historians, Phi Beta Kappa, Phi Delta Kappa. Home: PO Box 11604 Harrisburg PA 17108-1604

MYERS, ALLEN RICHARD, medical school dean, rheumatologist; b. Balt., Jan. 14, 1935; s. Ellis Benjamin and Rosina (Blumberg) M.; m. Ellen Patz, Nov. 26, 1960; children: David Joseph, Robert Todd, Scott Patz. BA, U. Pa., 1956; MD, U. Md., 1960. Diplomate Am. Bd. Internal Medicine. Intern Univ. Hosp., Balt., 1960-61; resident in medicine Univ. Hosp., Ann Arbor, Mich., 1961-64; fellow in rheumatology Mass. Gen. Hosp. and Harvard Med. Sch., Boston, 1966-69; dir. clin. tng. rheumatology U. Pa. Sch. Medicine, Phila., 1969-72, chief rheumatology sect., 1972-78; dep. chair medicine Temple U. Sch. Medicine, Phila., 1978-84, acting chmn. medicine, 1984-86, dean, 1991—, prof. medicine, 1978—; vis. prof. Cardiothoracic Inst., U. London, 1988; med. adv. bd. Scleroderma Rsch. Found., Santa Barbara, Calif., 1986. Editorial bd. Arthritis & Rheumatism, 1985-90, Brit. Jour. Rheumatology, 1989—; editor: Systemic Scleroderma, 1985, Medicine, 1986. Exec. com. Phila. Health Congress, 1990—; adv. com. Pa. Lupus Found., 1976—. USPHS, 1964-66. Recipient Margaret Whitaker prize U. Md. Sch. Medicine, 1960, Lindback Found. award Temple, 1981; named Physician of Yr. Temple U. Hosp., 1986. Fellow Phila. Coll. Physicians, ACP, Am. Coll. Rheumatology; mem. Phila. Rheumatism Soc., Am. Fedn. Clin. Rsch., N.Y. Acad. Scis., Brit. Soc. Rheumatology. Office: Temple U Sch Medicine 3400 N Broad St Philadelphia PA 19140

MYERS, CHARLES FRANCIS, accountant; b. N.Y.C., Sept. 28, 1941; s. Frank J. and Beatrice (Miller) M.; m. Lorraine Alice, Dec. 28, 1963; children: Debra Lynn, David Charles. BS, Fordham U., N.Y.C., 1963. CPA, N.J. Audit mgr. Ernst & Whinney, N.Y.C., 1963-73; asst. v.p., head internal audit G&W Industries, N.Y.C., 1973-75; exec. v.p., chief fin. officer Simon & Schuster, N.Y.C., 1975-80; owner Charles F. Myers, CPA, Haworth, N.J., 1981—; dir. G&H Soho, N.Y.C. Mem. AICPA, N.Y. State Soc. CPAs, Closter C. of C. (pres., treas. 1985-90), Ridgewood Country Club. Home: 35 Grant St Haworth NJ 07641-1918

MYERS, CHRISTINE MCCARRICK, fundraiser; b. Washington, Oct. 24, 1961; d. James Patrick and Patricia (Milmoe) McCarrick; m. Eric Tipton Myers, Oct. 6, 1990. BA, Holy Cross Coll., 1983. Asst. to sec. Dept. Labor, Washington, 1983-85; asst. dir. pvt. sect. init. The White House, Washington, 1985-86, assoc. dir. scheduling, 1986-88; regional dir. mktg. Am. Cons., N.Y.C. and Washington, 1989-90; dir. mktg. and devel. Am. Enterprise Inst., Washington, 1990—. Republican. Roman Catholic.

MYERS, DAVID RICHARD, youth organization financial executive; b. Plainfield, N.J., Oct. 5, 1948; s. George Kelsall and Margaret (Story) M.; m. Loretta Margaret D'Angelo; 1 child, Christina Marie. BS in Bus. Adminstrn., U. Kans., 1971; MBA in Fin., U. Mo., 1981. Check processor No. Trust Bank, Chgo., 1971; officer trainee Commerce Bank Kansas City (Mo.), 1973-74; sales mgr. Sun Life of Can. Ins. Co., Kansas City, 1974-75; with Boy Scouts Am., 1975—; dist. exec. Boy Scouts Am., Des Moines, 1975-78, Kansas City, 1978-81; dir. fin. svcs. Boy Scouts Am., N.Y.C., 1981-84; dir. fin. and mktg. Boy Scouts Am., Phila., 1984-89; scout exec. Green Mountain Coun. Waterbury, Vt., 1989—; guest lectr. Iowa State U., Ames, 1976-78, Pace U., N.Y.C., 1982-84; tech. 10 nat./regional meetings Boy Scouts Am., 1977-80, leader 3 overseas trips. Producer 10 in-house booklets, contbr. monthly in-house publs. Boy Scouts Am. Area chmn. United Way Phila., 1986-87; mem. Congl. redistricting com., 1980; bd. dirs. Jaycees, Iowa, Mo., 1972-81. Served to 1st. lt. USMC, 1971-72. Recipient Eagle Scout award Boy Scouts Am., 1962, Medal of Peace Govt. Egypt, 1984; named Man of Yr. Beta Theta chpt. Phi Kappa Tau, 1969, Keyman Kansas City Jaycees, 1974. Mem. Nat. Soc. Fund Raising Execs. (pub. rels. com. 1986), Phila. Ad Club, Boy Scouts Am. (4 Disting. Exec. awards, Good Scout award 1984), U. Kans. Alumni Assn. N.Y. (treas. 1982-84), U. Mo. Kansas City Alumni Assn., Rotary. Republican. Epsicopalian. Home: 340 Harford Rd Somerdale NJ 08083-2518 Office: Boy Scouts Am Green Mountain Coun Rte 2 PO Box 557 Waterbury VT 05676

MYERS, DONALD, lawyer; b. Bklyn., June 9, 1930; s. Lewis Gene and Claire Vivian (Meyerowitz) M.; m. Elaine Kesselhaut, Feb. 20, 1955; children: Jeffrey Myers, Amy Friedman. BS, Seton Hall U., S. Orange, N.J., 1952; LLB, Seton Hall U., Newark, 1955, JD, 1969. Bar: N.J. 1955, U.S. Supreme Ct. 1960. Pvt. practice law Elizabeth, N.J., 1955—; prosecutor Roselle, N.J., 1964-69, judge, 1971-73; county atty. Union County, N.J., 1969-72, county adjuster, 1970-72. Vice chmn. Union County Welfare Bd., 1971-72; chmn. United Fund, Union County, 1961-63, State of Israel Bonds, Linden, N.J., 1978— (Jerusalem award 1975); pres. Suburban Jewish Ctr., 1970-76; v.p. Rutgers U. Hillel Bd., 1981—; v.p. N.J. United Synagogue of Am., 1978-82. Recipient Americanism award B'nai B'rith, 1976, 77, 78, Shofar award, Boy Scouts Am., 1979. Mem. B'nai B'rith (pres. dist. three 1979-80, internat. v.p. 1984-88). Republican. Office: Donald Myers Esq 1139 E Jersey St Elizabeth NJ 07201-2436

MYERS, DONALD G(ROMEL), university administrator, consultant; b. DuBois, Pa., Oct. 18, 1946; s. Delmar Knisley and Carolyn Elnora (Gromel) M.; m. Susan Berry Finkbeiner, June 23, 1973. BA, Washington & Jefferson Coll., 1968; MS, Boston U., 1972. History educator Coun. Rock Intermediate Sch., Richboro, Pa., 1968; asst. admissions officer Culver (Ind.) Mil. Acad., 1969-71; communications dir. Choate Rosemary Hall, Wallingford, Conn., 1972-76; asst. prin. Emma Willard Sch., Troy, N.Y., 1976-81; dir. devel. Bennington (Vt.) Coll., 1981-82; dir. devel. U. Pa. Law Sch., Phila., 1982-90, asst. dean, 1990—; cons. Vanderbilt Law Sch., Nashville, 1989—, William Mitchell Law Sch., St. Paul, 1990. Bd. dirs. Dance Conduit, Phila., 1987-90, Cedar Park Neighbors, 1989, Hudson Mohawk Indsl. Gateway, Troy, 1978-82; treas. Friends of Chamber Music, Troy, 1979-82. Mem. Nat. Soc. Fund Raising Execs. Democrat. Home: 116 Dartmouth Rd Bala Cynwyd PA 19004-2213 Office: U Pa Law Sch 3400 Chestnut St Philadelphia PA 19104-6204

MYERS, DUANE GEORGE, accountant; b. Phila., Dec. 7, 1954; s. George and Pauline (Friend) M.; m. Ruth Smith, Oct. 16, 1987; 1 child, Joshua Quincy. BS in Acctg., Bus. Adminstrn., Widener U., 1976, postgrad., 1992—. CPA. Sr. acct. Stockton Bates & Co. CPAs, Phila., 1978-80; sr. auditor Arthur Young & Co. CPAs, Phila., 1980-82; acctg. specialist sr. projects Chase Manhattan Bank, Wilmington, Del., 1982-83; acctg. systems officer Mfrs. Hanover Corp., N.Y.C., 1983-86; div. controller Bankers Trust - N.Y. Co., N.Y.C., 1986-91; pvt. practice, Hainesport, N.J., 1978—. Vol. tax preparer low income families, Widener U., Chester, Pa., 1976; co-founder, Widener U. Acctg. Soc., sec. 1975-76. Mem. AICPA (tax. div., personal fin., planning div.). Home and office: 415 Laurel Ridge Rd PO Box 718 Hainesport NJ 08036

MYERS, EDITH MAE, secondary education educator, retired; b. Sandy Lake, Pa., Sept. 9, 1924; d. Leroy and Mamie (Price) Everitt; m. Leon H. Myers, Dec. 26, 1962; children: Rita, Karol, Rhonda, Richard. BS, Ind. U. of Pa., 1946; MEd, Pa. State U., 1958; postgrad., Thiel Coll., Westminster, 1954, Alaska U., 1978. Cert. tchr. vocat. home econs. Cafeteria mgr., home econs. tchr. Stoneboro (Pa.) Sch. Dist., 1946-54, Lakeview Sch. Dist., Stoneboro, 1954-84; mem. adv. bd. Penn Power Co. Pres. Lakeview Edn. Assn., 1968, 75, Lakeview Sch. Dist. PTA, 1975, Stoneboro Women's Club, 1974; county pres. Mercer County Fedn. of Women's Clubs, Mercer, Pa., 1986-87; vol. Helping Hands, 1984—; bd. dirs. Childrens Aid Soc., 1984—, Mental Retardation and Mental Health Bd., 1984—, others. Recipient Forrester scholarship Delta Kappa Gamma, 1958. Mem. Pa. Home Econs. Assn. (com. chmn. 1961—, state councilor 1962-65), Am. Vocat. Assn. (com. chmn. 1974), Pa. State Edn. Assn. (county chmn. 1981, life mem.), Nat. Home Econs. Vocat. Assn. (pres. 1958), Phi Lambda Theta, Delta Kappa Gamma. Republican. Presbyterian. Home: 377 Paxton Rd Sandy Lake PA 16145

MYERS, ERNEST RAY, human resources development educator, consultant; b. Middletown, Ohio; s. David I. Sr. and Alma (Harper) M.; m. Carole Elaine Ferguson. BA, Howard U., 1962, MSW, 1964; PhD, Union Inst., 1976. Lic. ind. clin. social worker, D.C. Dir. Community Evaluation Office U. D.C., Washington, 1969-71; program dir., expert cons. servicemen's early ednl. counseling program Bur. Higher Edn. U.S. Office of Edn., Washington, 1971, program dir., assoc. prof. community psychology program, 1972-78; assoc. prof. counseling and mental health dept. U. D.C., Washington, 1979-86, dept. chmn., prof. human resource devel. dept., 1986-89, prof., 1989—; pres. ERM Cons. Corp., Washington, 1980—; dept. chmn. U. D.C., Washington, 1992—; free lance cons., community psychology mgmt. organization and staff devel., 1971—; cons. Pres.'s Task Force Against Poverty, Washington, 1964-65; program officer U.S. HUD, Washington, 1967-68; regional program field officer VISTA, OEO, Washington, 1965-67; dept. mgr. Westinghouse Learning Corp., Bladensburg, Md., 1968-69. Author: The Community Psychology Concept, 1977; author, editor: Race & Culture in Mental Health in the Delivery Systems, 1981, The Refugee Crisis, 1983; contbr. numerous articles to profl. jours. Mem. Kiwanis, Washington, 1985; mem. bd. advisors Zest Inc., Washington, 1989—; bd. dirs. D.C. Mental Health Assn., Washington, 1976-82, Wider Opportunity for Women, Washington, 1982-85; nat. asst. dir. Nat. Urban League, Washington, 1968; bd. trustees Wooley Halfway House, Washington, 1985—. Mem. NASW (grievance com. D.C. chpt.), Assn. Black Psychologists (pres. D.C. chpt. 1975), Acad. Cert. Social Workers, Am. Psychol. Assn. Democrat. Home: 5315 Colorado Ave NW Washington DC 20011-3622 Office: U DC 4200 Connecticut Ave NW Washington DC 20008-1174

MYERS, HAROLD EMMET, executive consultant, retired state administrator; b. Siddonsburg, Pa., Nov. 7, 1926; s. Chanley Ellsworth and Viola (Eppley) M.; m. Reba Lorena Keller, June 8, 1949; children: Beverly Byers, Marjorie Rittner, Maria Strickler, Darla Boyle. Student, Pa. State U., 1945. Advanced rec. clk. Pa. Dept. Hwys., Harrisburg, 1955-56, asst. twp. engr., 1956-58, dist. mcpl. svc. supr., 1958-63, asst. dir., 1963-69; bd. dirs. Pa. Dept. Transp., Harrisburg, 1969-85; retired Pa. Dept. of Transp., 1985. Mem. Salvation Army, Harrisburg, 1991, Nat. Rep. Com., Washington, 1991. Mem. Am. Pub. Works Assn. (life), Am. Soc. Hwy. Engrs. (life). Home: 914 Thornton Dr Mechanicsburg PA 17055-5751

MYERS, HOWARD, systems analyst, aerospace scientist; b. N.Y.C., Jan. 27, 1928; s. Howard G. and Sally (Kline) M.; m. Lois Marie Lowe, July 19, 1948 (dec. Apr. 1969); m. Joan Cerwin, May 29, 1976; children—Susanna, William, Sally Joy. Ph.B., U. Chgo., 1948, B.S., 1950, M.S., 1956. Scientist, Hughes Research Labs., Culver City, Calif., 1953-57; tech. specialist Douglas Aircraft Co., Santa Monica, Calif., 1957-61; program mgr. Aerospace Corp., El Segundo, Calif., 1961-66; mem. tech. staff TRW Inc., Redondo Beach, Calif., 1966-69; sr. tech. specialist McDonnell Douglas, St. Louis, 1969-80; sr. systems analyst Gen. Electric Corp., King of Prussia, Pa., 1981—; pres. CPRL, Paoli, Pa., 1968—. Contbr. articles to profl. jours. Patentee elastometer. Mem. AAAS, N.Y. Acad. Sci., Am. Chem. Soc., Am. Geophys. Union, Math. Assn. Am., Sigma Xi. Democrat. Home: 699 N Valley Rd Paoli PA 19301-1006 Office: CPRL 699 N Valley Rd Paoli PA 19301

MYERS, JACK CHARLES, advertising executive; b. Utica, N.Y., Oct. 12, 1947; s. David Sanford and Gert (Grossman) M.; m. Janice Lee Stieber, July 2, 1970; children: Andrew, Ariele, Daniel. BS in Communications, Syracuse U., 1969; MA in Media, NYU, 1976. Dir. civic survey Syracuse (N.Y.) U., 1969-70; account exec. Metromedia, N.Y.C., 1970-73; sales mgr. ABC Radio, N.Y.C., 1973-76, Sta. WCBS-TV, N.Y.C., 1976-79; dir. mktg. CBS-TV, N.Y.C., 1979-81; pres. Myers Mktg. & Rsch., Parsippany, N.J., 1981—, Infomktg., Inc., Parsippany, 1983—; chmn. Worldwide Mktg. Leadership Panel. Editor, pub. (newsletter) Myers Report, 1981-87; contbr. articles to profl. jours. Pres. Worldwide Mktg. Leadership Panel; bd. dirs. Sight Savers Internat., Washington. Recipient Svc. award Dayton (Ohio) Advt. Club, 1981. Mem. Retail Advt. Conf., Cable TV Advt. Bur., Advt. Rsch. Found., Am. Media Coun. (chmn. 1984—), Norther N.J. Ad Club, Internat. Radio and TV Soc., Internat. Biographical Soc. (dep. dir. gen.), Cable TV Adminstrs. and Mktg. Assn. Club: Pine Brook Jewish Ctr. Men's (pres. 1983-85). Office: 322 Route 46 Parsippany NJ 07054-2340

MYERS, JEFFREY, pathologist; b. Phila., Feb. 8, 1932; s. William Lee Myers and Roberta Appel; m. Dorothy Lois Meyer, Feb. 6, 1960 (div. 1966); m. Diane Helen Heisner, May 3, 1969; 1 child, William. AB, U. Pa., 1953; MD, Temple U., 1957, MS, 1962; PhD, McGill U., 1965. Intern Phila. Gen. Hosp., 1957-58; resident Temple U. Hosp., Phila., 1958-62; asst. pathologist Allentown (Pa.) Hosp., 1965-66; pathologist Phila. Gen. Hosp., 1966-73, chief div. surg. pathology, 1973-77; chief dept. pathology Meml. Hosp. of Burlington County, Mt. Holly, N.J., 1977—; asst. prof. pathology U. Pa. Sch. Medicine, Phila., 1966-77; med. dir. Sch. Med. Tech., Burlington County Coll., 1983—. Contbr. articles to profl. jours. USPHS fellow, 1962-65. Fellow Coll. Am. Pathologists; mem. N.Y. Acad. Scis., Med. Soc. N.J., Burlington County Med. Soc., South Jersey Soc. Pathologists (sec. 1990-91), Phila. Pathol. Soc. Office: Meml Hosp Burlington County 175 Madison Ave Mount Holly NJ 08060-2099

MYERS, JOHN EDMUND, III, musician, ethnomusicologist; b. Balt., Sept. 26, 1951; s. John Edmund Jr. and Marjorie (Tyler) M.; m. Alice Chin, Oct. 13, 1974; children: Anna, Lisa. BA in Philosophy, Towson State U., 1973, BA in Music, 1977; MusM, Howard U., 1979; PhD in Ethnomusicology, U. Md., Balt., 1987. Instr. applied music, guitar Towson State U., Balt., 1977-87, Howard C.C., Columbia, Md., 1981-87; instr. applied music, guitar U. Md. Baltimore County, Balt., 1981-87, teaching asst., 1983-87; assoc. prof. dept. music Simon's Rock Coll. of Bard, Great Barrington, Mass., 1987—, chmn. dept. music, 1992—; leader, composer jazz group Realtime, Mass., N.Y. and Conn., 1981—. Composer: Jazz at the Rock, 1991; author: Way of the Pipa, 1992; contbr. articles, revs. to profl. jours. Nat. Endowment of Humanities fellow, 1988, 92; Nat. Coun. Learned Socs. fellow, 1990. Mem. Soc. Ethnomusicology, Assn. Chinese Music Rsch., Am. Fedn. Musicians. Office: Simons Rock Coll Alford Rd Great Barrington MA 01230

MYERS, JOHN HOLT, lawyer; b. Washington, Feb. 28, 1923; s. Paul Forrest and Mae Clare (Holt) M.; m. Eleanor Brown, Dec. 18, 1948; children: John Holt Jr., Julie, Lynn, Pamela. AB, Princeton U., 1943; JD, U. Mich., 1949; LLM, Georgetown U., 1955. Bar: U.S. Dist. Ct. D.C. 1950, U.S. Dist. Ct. Md. 1952, Md. 1954, U.S. Claims Ct. 1957, U.S. Tax Ct. 1958, U.S. Supreme Ct. 1960, U.S. Ct. Appeals 1984. Ptnr. Williams, Myers and Quiggle, Washington, 1949-88, Ross, Marsh, Foster, Myers & Quiggle, Washington, 1988—; adj. prof. George Washington U., 1974-80, Law Ctr. U. Miami (Fla.), 1976-80. Author: (with others) Guide to the Administration of Charitable Remainder Trusts, 1978; contbr. over 75 articles to jours. and seminars. Lt. USN, 1943-46. Recipient Disting. Svc. to Higher Edn. award Am. Coll. Pub. Rels. Assn., 1970. Mem. ABA (chair subcom.), Md. Bar Assn., D.C. Bar Assn., Nat. Assn. Coll. & Univ.Attys. (Disting. Svc. award 1988), Cosmos Club, Chevy Chase Club. Democrat. Lutheran. Home: 102 E Melrose St Bethesda MD 20815-3304 Office: Ross Marsh Foster Myers & Quiggle 888 16th St NW Ste 400 Washington DC 20006-4137

MYERS, LINDA SUSAN, management consultant; b. N.Y.C., June 5, 1954. BA, Goucher Coll., Towson, Md., 1976; MA, Columbia U., 1977; PhD, Harvard U., 1991. With adminstrn. State of Md., Marlboro, 1978-81; group HR planner Squibb Corp., Princeton, N.J., 1983-86; mgr. HR Savin Corp., Stamford, Conn., 1986-88; mng. dir. Harvard Cons. Group, Princeton, 1988—. Office: Harvard Cons Group PO Box 1357 50 Princeton Ave Princeton NJ 08540

MYERS, MARK ALAN, fine arts dealer; b. St. Joseph, Mo., Nov. 12, 1953; s. Bob Buford and Barbara Fay (Burnett) M.; m. Melissa Ann Milkovich, Sept. 18, 1982; 1 child, Marina Amanda. BA, Dartmouth Coll., 1975; postgrad, U. Pa., 1977. East Coast mgr. Am. Design. Ltd., Denver, 1976-82; pres. Atlantic Arts Inc., Annapolis, Md., 1982—. Mem. Columbus Cup Com., Balt., 1989, 90, 91. Mem. Annapolis Yacht Club. Office: Atlantic Arts Inc 433 4th St Annapolis MD 21403-3212

MYERS, PAUL JOHN, mortgage banker; b. Detroit, Nov. 8, 1945; s. John Watt and Reva (Nemoff) M.; m. P. Judy L. Feinberg; children: Jennifer, Zachary, Joshua. BS in Polit. Sci, Am. U., 1968. Pres. D-M Pharm. Inc., Rockville, Md., 1968-79, Securities Fin. Group Inc., Bethesda, Md., 1979—. Bd. dirs. Cath. Univ. Summer Opera Theatre; organizer, tchr. Literacy Coun. Montgomery County, Wheaton, Md., 1987—; fund raiser Sunshine Found., Washington, 1988—. Republican. Office: Securities Fin Group Inc 4919 Hampden Ln Bethesda MD 20814-2913

MYERS, ROBERT CHARLES, foreign service officer; b. Emporia, Kans., Sept. 19, 1939; s. Clovis D. and Oleva (Morrison) M.; m. Dianne Wertz, Aug. 1, 1966; 1 child, Debbie Aileen. BA in History, Park Coll., 1961; postgrad., Duke U., 1961-62. Rental agt. Avis Rent-A-Car, Washington, 1966, Hertz Car Rental, Washington, 1966-67; pers. officer U.S. Embassy, Manila, Philippines, 1967-70; budget and mgmt. officer Dept. State, Washington, 1970-73; bus. mgr. U.S. Embassy, Bucharest, Romania, 1974-75; chief transp. Dept. State, Washington, 1976—. With U.S. Army, 1962-65. Mem. Am. Mgmt. Assn., Coun. of Logistics Mgmt., Nat. Railroad Hist. Soc., Nat. Def. Transp. Assn., Transp. Rsch. Forum, Nat. Trust for Hist. Preservation, Delta Nu Alpha. Presbyterian. Home: 4600 Duke St Apt 506 Alexandria VA 22304-2518

MYERS, ROBERT JAY, aerospace company executive; b. Bklyn., Oct. 15, 1934; s. John J. and Clara S. (Martinsen) M.; m. Carolyn Erland, Aug. 10, 1963; children—Susan, Kenneth. BCE, NYU, 1955, postgrad., 1957-65; P.M.D., Harvard U., 1972. With Grumman Aerospace Corp., Bethpage, N.Y., 1964—, v.p. resources, 1980-83, sr. v.p. bus. and resource mgmt., 1983-85; sr. v.p. corp. svcs. Grumman Corp., Bethpage, N.Y., 1985-86; pres. Grumman Data Systems Corp., Bethpage, 1986-90; pres., chief operating officer, bd. dirs. Grumman Corp., 1991—; mem. sci. adv. coun. Ala. Space and Rocket Ctr., 1986-91. Mem. adv. panel on econ. devel. N.Y. State Project 2000, 1985-86; mem. L.I. Project 2000; mem. adv. bd. L.I. Youth Guidance, 1986-91; bd. dirs. Huntington Hosp., Poly. U., 1991—. 1st lt. U.S. Army, 1955-57. Fellow Poly. U., 1987, Disting. Alumni award, 1989. Mem. Aerospace Industries Assn. (procurement and fin. coun. 1979-86), Am. Def. Preparedness Assn. (bd. dirs. 1992), Nat. Space Club (bd. govs. 1986-89), Huntington Country Club. Lutheran. Home: 7 Heather Ln Huntington NY 11743-1011 Office: Grumman Corp 1111 Stewart Ave Bethpage NY 11714-3533

MYERS, ROLLAND GRAHAM, investment counselor; b. St. Louis, Aug. 30, 1945; s. Rolland Everett and Lurilien (Graham) M. Diploma, St. Louis Country Day Sch., 1963; AB cum laude in History and Lit., Harvard U., 1966; postgrad. Faculties of Social Scis. and Law, U. Edinburgh, Scotland, 1966-67; postgrad. Fondation Nationale des Sciences Politiques and Faculte de Lettres et des Sciences Humaines, U. Paris, 1967-68. Trainee global credit dept. The Chase Manhattan Bank, N.A., N.Y.C., 1968-69, mem. 32nd spl. devel. program, 1969, strategic planner internat. dept., 1969-70, securities analyst, mktg. rep., fiduciary investment dept., 1970; assoc. Smith, Barney & Co., Inc., N.Y.C., 1971, account exec. N.Y. sales dept., 1971-72, instl. account exec. N.Y. internat. sales dept., 1972-74, 2nd v.p., stockholder, 1975-76; v.p., stockholder Smith Barney, Harris Upham & Co., Inc. (subs. SBHU Holdings, Inc.), N.Y.C., 1976-78; prin. W.H. Graham & Sons, family investment office, 1977-82, investment counsel, 1982—; ltd. ptnr. Croke Patterson Campbell, Ltd., Denver, 1975—; joint founder, gen. ptnr. Mansion Disbursements, Denver, 1979—; pres., chmn. exec. com., bd. dirs. Fifty-Five Residents Corp., N.Y.C., 1980-84; bd. dirs. Fifty-Six Danbury Rd. Assn., Inc., New Milford, Conn. Trustee, mem. corp. Bishop Rhinelander Found. (Episcopal chaplaincy at Harvard and Radcliffe Colls.), Cambridge, 1973-75; v.p., treas., bd. dirs. The Whitehill Graham Found., St. Louis, 1976—; bd. dirs., mem. corp. The Pratt Ctr.: Your Connection with the Natural World, New Milford, 1987—; treas., bd. dirs., mem. corp. Kent (Conn.) Land Trust, Inc., 1989—; project financier Restoration of 1851 Samuel Curtiss Hosford House, Nat. Register Historic Dist., Falls Village, Conn., 1984-86; commr. Housatonic River Commn., Warren, Conn., 1985—, vice chmn., 1986-88, chmn., 1988—; commr., vice chmn. Conservation, Inland Wetlands and Watercourses Commn., Kent, 1988—; mem. schs. and scholarships com., Office of Admissions and Fin. Aid, Harvard and Radcliffe Colls., 1991—. Mem. Cum Laude Soc., St. Louis Country Day Sch. Alumni Assn., Harvard Alumni Assn., Capitol Hill Club (Washington), Harvard Club (N.Y.C.), Hasty Pudding-Inst. of 1770 (Cambridge). Republican. Episcopalian. Home: 251 Kent Rd Kent CT 06757-1409 Office: W H Graham & Sons Investment Counsel 56 Danbury Rd New Milford CT 06776-3412

MYERS, RONALD KOSTY, manufacturing executive, inventor; b. Mercer, Pa., Aug. 31, 1946; s. Cecil Charles and Mildred Elma (Hrisak) M.; m. Carol Lee Hunter, July 31, 1964; children: Tammy Lynn, Ronald K., Thomas Christopher. Mailbox painter Hermitage, Pa., 1960-61; drive in usher Hickory Drive In, Hermitage, 1961-63; clk. Oscars Drive Thru, Masury, Ohio, 1963-64; gas station shift leader Kayo Oil Co., Warrenton, Va., 1967-68; clk. Erie R.R., Ferrona, Pa., 1968-70; diesel mechanic Sharon Steel Corp., Farrell, Pa., 1969-70, craneman, 1970—; roofer contractor R&R Roofing, Sharon, Pa., 1978-79; asst. wrestling coach Sharon High Sch., 1979-85; chief exec. officer Flick It Mfg., Sharon, 1991—; clk. B&O R.R., Youngstown, Ohio, 1973; coord. tour guide Army Security Agy., Va., 1967-68. Author: How to Flick It, 1991. Chmn. activities Hartford Apple Festival, 1988—. With U.S. Army, 1964-69. Mem. F.H. Buhl Club. Democrat. Roman Catholic. Home and Office: 440 N State Line Rd Sharon PA 16146

MYERS, RUSSELL DAVIS, vocational school educator; b. Dighton, Mass., Mar. 22, 1938; s. Russell Bruce and Gwendolyn (Davis) M.; m. Anne Weld Lincoln, Jan. 28, 1961; children: Scott, Kimberly, Todd. B. Marine Sci., Maine Maritime Acad., 1958. Registered engr. Draftsman Nactor, Taunton, Mass., 1954-55; plumber Russell B. Myers & Sons and Churchfuel, Taunton, Mass., 1961-78; vocat. instr. Bristol Plymouth, Taunton, Mass., 1978—. Mem. Raynham (Mass.) Fin. Com., 1976-78; cooperator Bristol County Savings Bank, Taunton. Lt. USN, 1958-61. Republican. Home: 106 Leonard St Raynham MA 02767-1110

MYERS, SYLVIA JEAN, gift planning specialist; b. Uniontown, Pa., Oct. 28, 1948; d. Charles Albert and Jean Rose (Durant) Schiffbauer; 1 child, Kevin Charles. BS in Comunications, California U. of Pa., 1974, MEd in Reading, 1982, MA in English, 1977; law student, Duquesne U., Pitts., 1980-84. Sec. tchr. of English and communication Albert Gallatin Area Sch. Dist., Point Marion, Pa., 1974-76; dir. devel., pub. and alumni affairs California Univ. of Pa., 1976-85; fin. and estate planning cons. Pitts., 1985—; gift planning specialist Sewickley Valley Hosp., Pa., 1987—; gift planning specialist charitable and instl. trust dept. Pits Nat. bank, 1991—. Co-author book series: Smart Marketing for Non-P rofits, 1986, 87; co-author workbook: Smart Marketing for Non-Profits, 1987; contbr. articles to profl. jours. Officer The Pitts. Planned Giving Coun., 1986—, program chmn. 1990—; mem. Estate Planning Coun. of Pitts., 1986—. Consortium for Internat. Edn. scholar, 1977; named Outstanding Female Exec. Leader, Westmoreland County Community Coll., 1989. Mem. Assn. for Healthcare Philanthropy, Nat. Com. on Planning Giving (liaison for Pitts. region), Nat.

Assn. Women Bus. Owners (bd. dirs. 1987-89). Home: The Tower at Chatham Ctr 3H Pittsburgh PA 15219 Office: C and I Trust Pittsburgh PA

MYERS, THERESE JOSEPHINE, publishing executive; b. Albany, N.Y., July 2, 1956; d. Thomas Wayne and Josephine Ann (Dottino) M. BA, Mary Washington Coll., 1978; MPA, SUNY, Albany, 1981. Editorial asst. Clarity Pub. Co., Albany, 1979-80; tchr. Petersburg (Va.) High Sch., 1981-82; editor Ayco Corp., Albany, 1983—, mgr. editing dept., 1984-86; mgr. corp. communications Norstar Bancorp, Albany, 1986-87; mgr. corp. publs. and internal communications Fleet/Norstar Fin. Group, Providence, 1987-88; asst. v.p. Fleet/Norstar Fin. Group, 1988-91; v.p. Fleet Fin. Group, 1991—; instr. bus. writing Katharine Gibbs Sch., 1991—; freelance copy editor MacMillan, 1990—. Todd Meml. fellow SUNY, Albany, 1980-81. Mem. Internat. Assn. Bus. Communicators (newsletter editor 1986-87, program chmn. 1987-88, bd. dirs. at-large 1986-88), Pub. Rels. Soc. Am., Assn. Bus. Communicators, Freelance Editorial Assn. Office: Fleet Fin Group 111 Westminster St Providence RI 02903-2305

MYERSON, RALPH MAYER, physician; b. New Britain, Conn., July 21, 1918; s. Benjamin and Idah Sarah (Fineberg) M.; m. Loretta Francis Walsh, Aug. 7, 1943; children: Patricia Ann Huntington, Paul Andrew. BS summa cum laude, Tufts Coll., Medford, Mass., 1938; MD cum laude, Tufts Med. Coll., Boston, 1942. Diplomate Am. Bd. Internal Medicine. Intern Boston City Hosp., 1942-43, resident, 1946-48; staff physician VA Hosp., Wilmington, Del., 1948-53; asst. chief medicine VA Hosp., Phila., 1953-58, chief med. svc., 1958-72, chief of staff, 1972-75; group dir. Smithkline & French Labs., Phila., 1975-80, cons., 1980-85; freelance writer Phila., 1985-90; assoc. dean grad. med. edn. Med. Coll. Pa., Phila., 1990—; v.p. Dickson-Gabbay Corp., Berwyn, Pa., 1990—. Contbr. 150 articles to profl. jours.; author 7 textbooks on medicine. Capt. U.S. Army Med. Corps, 1943-46. Fellow ACP, Am. Gastroenterology Assn., Am. Coll. Gastroenterology; mem. AMA, Pa. Soc. Medicine, Phi Beta Kappa, Alpha Omega Alpha. Home: 310 Maplewood Rd Merion Station PA 19066-1031 Office: Dickson-Gabbay Corp 1205 Westlakes Dr Ste 150 Berwyn PA 19312-2405

MYGATT, SUSAN HALL, lawyer; b. Stamford, Conn., Sept. 29, 1947; d. Eben Clarke and Jane Elizabeth (Terhune) Hall; m. Samuel G. Mygatt, June 11, 1977; children: Elizabeth, Jenny, Catherine. BA, Smith Coll., 1969; JD, Boston U., 1977. Bar: Mass. 1977. Adminstrv. asst. HUD, Washington, 1969-73; exec. asst. Urban Devel. Corp., N.Y.C., 1973-74; ptnr. Goodwin, Procter & Hoar, Boston, 1977—. Mem. ABA, Mass. Bar Assn., New Eng. Women in Real Estate. Office: Goodwin Procter & Hoar Exchange Pl Boston MA 02109-2808

MYLES, DIANE JACQUELINE, academic administrator; b. Croydon, Surrey, Eng., Nov. 8, 1964; d. Emry George and Muriel Elaine (Williams) M. BA in Cultural Anthropology, Premedicine, Columbia U., 1987, MBA in Fin., Pub. and Non-Profit Mgmt., 1991. Tchr. math. and physics Immaculate Conception high, Kingston, Jamaica, 1988-89; instr. Upward Bound program Double Discovery Ctr., N.Y.C., 1989-91; regional coord. Mercury Communications Ltd., London, 1990; cons. Dohr Computer Ctr., N.Y.C., 1990-91; asst. bus. mgr. Columbia U. Devel., N.Y.C., 1991; asst. dir. talent search program Double Discovery Ctr., N.Y.C., 1991—; pvt. tutor, Bklyn.,. Mem. Highland Ch. Jacoby scholar Columbia U., 1985-87. Mem. N.Y. Coalition of 100 Black Women. Office: Double Discovery Ctr 402 Ferris Booth Hall New York NY 10027

MYLONAKIS, STAMATIOS GREGORY, chemist; b. Athens, Greece, Aug. 18, 1937; came to U.S., 1963; s. Gregory and Vassiliki (Charalampopoulos) M.; m. Pamela H. Morton, May 15, 1965 (dec. Mar. 1978); 1 son, Gregory John. BS in Chemistry, U. Athens, 1961; MS in Phys. Organic Chemistry, Ill. Inst. Tech., 1964; PhD in Phys. Organic Chemistry, Mich. State U., 1971. Research scientist Brookhaven Nat. Lab., Upton, N.Y., 1965-68; instr. U. Calif., Berkeley, 1971-73; group leader Rohm and Haas Co., Springhouse, Pa., 1973-76; supr. DeSoto Inc., Des Plaines, Ill., 1976-79; staff scientist Borg-Warner Chems., Inc. Des Plaines, 1979-81, research and devel. mgr., 1981-87, dept. head EniChem Ams. Inc., Princeton, N.J., 1988— . Author numerous research papers; assoc. editor Jour. Applied Polymer Sci.; patentee in polymer synthesis and applications fields. Mem. tech. adv. bd. Case Western Res. U.; mem. PhD thesis adv. com. Lehigh U., mem. adv. bd. NSF Ctr. Polymer Interfaces; mem. rev. panel NSF. Served as lt., Greek Army, 1961-63. Ill. Inst. Tech. fellow, 1963-64; Mich. State U. fellow, 1968-71. Mem. Am. Chem. Soc., Sigma Xi. Office: EniChem Ams Inc 2000 Princeton Pk Monmouth Junction NJ 08852

MYLROIE, GERALD RICHARD, real estate executive; b. Salt Lake City, June 30, 1945; s. Robert Joseph and Grace (Sill) M.; m. Elizabeth Alma Silsby, Sept 1, 1979; children: Robert Peter, John Myles, Jacqueline Marie. BS in Environ. Design, Calif. State Poly. U., Pomona, 1968; M in Planning, U. So. Calif., 1970; MBA, U. Chgo., 1986. Am. Inst. Cert. Planners. City planner City of La Puente, Calif., 1967-68, City of Montclair, Calif., 1968-70; urban planner, cons. Wilsey & Ham, Los Angeles, 1970-71; sr. staff dir. Am. Inst. Planners, Washington, 1971-76; study dir. U.S. Congl. Commn., Washington, 1976-77; devel. planner, mgr. U.S. Dept. Commerce, Washington, 1977-82; devel. planner, mgr. of mgmt. and budget U.S. Exec. Office of the Pres., Washington, 1979-80; v.p. 1st Nat. Bank of Chgo., 1982-86; sr. v.p., corp. dir. mgmt. services group Cushman & Wakefield, Inc., N.Y.C., 1986-89, sr. v.p., dir. govt. svcs. group, 1989-90; sr. v.p., dir. portfolio mgmt. The O'Connor Group, N.Y.C., 1990—; cons. UN Internat. Youth Conf. on the Human Environment, Hamilton, Can., 1975; mem. White House Inter-Agy. Task Force on Energy Impact Assistance, Washington, 1977-82, Interdisciplinary Council on Environ. Design, Washington, 1971-76. Author: California Environmental Law, 1970, 4th edit., 1973; contbr. articles to profl. jours. Bd. dirs. Citizens Coordinating Com. on Friendship Heights, Chevy Chase, Md., 1973-80; pres. Chevy Chase Gardens Citizens Assn., 1971-76; mem. Dem. Nat. Com., Domestic Affairs Task Force Com. on Urban Problems, Washington, 1975-76, Montgomery County (Md.) Growth Policy Task Force, 1976, mem. Bright New City Com. Chgo, 1983-86, Cen. Area Com. Task Force, Chgo., 1983-86, Burnham Park Planning Bd., Chgo. 1985-86. Served to staff sgt. USMC, 1963-64. Mem. Am. Inst. Cert. Planners, Am. Planning Assn. (com. chmn. Washington 1980-82, chmn. city planning and mgmt. div. 1988-90, founder ann. Am. City Quality Week 1989—, exec. dir. 1990—), Com. of 100 on the Fed. City, Urban Land Inst., Sierra Club, Nature Conservancy, Common Cause, Midday Club Chgo., Univ. Club N.Y.C., Innis Arden Golf Club. Democrat. Methodist. Office: The O'Connor Group 200 Park 51st Ave New York NY 10166-0005

MYRES, KAREN W., healthcare manager; b. Hampton, Va., Aug. 9, 1944; d. Walter D. and Pauline E. (Werwinski) Withka; m. Jay Bradley Myres, Oct. 2, 1971 (div. 1990); 1 child, Jason. BA, Rosemont Coll., 1966; MAS, Johns Hopkins U., 1989. Program coord. USAID, Montevideo, Uruguay, 1968; pub. info. officer Ptnrs. of Ams., Washington, 1968-71; writer, editor Dorchester News, Cambridge, Md., 1972, Daily Banner, Star-Democrat, Easton, Md., 1973-82; press sec. Sen. Porter Hopkins, Easton, 1982; dir. communications Meml. Hosp. Easton, 1983-85, dir. health edn. ctr., 1985-91; dir. edn. svcs. Sewickley (Pa.) Valley Hosp., 1991—; free-lance publicist, 1972—. Mem. Talbot County AIDS Task Force, 1987—. Fulbright fellow, 1966-68. Mem. Easton CommunityTelevision Inc. (v.p. 1986-91), The Chem. People, Tidewater Performing ARts Soc. (bd. dirs. 1989—), Soroptomists (bd. dirs. 1976-82). Democrat. Roman Catholic. Home: 705 Duncan Ave Pittsburgh PA 15237-5867 Office: Sewickley Valley Hosp Dept Edn Sewickley PA 15143

MYRON, WILLIAM PAUL, systems analyst; b. Pitts., Sept. 19, 1966; s. Thomas Leo and Kathleen Regina (Lynch) M.; m. Michele Marie Pituch, Apr. 6, 1991; 1 child, Maria Kathryn. BA in Math. and Computer Sci., St. Francis Coll., Loretto, Pa., 1987; MBA in Acctg., MS in MIS, U. Pitts., 1989. Applications analyst Aluminum Co. Am., Pitts., 1989-90, systems analyst, 1990—. Home: 492 Sylvania Dr Bridgeville PA 15017 Office: Aluminum Co Am 1501 Alcoa Bldg Pittsburgh PA 15219

MYSEN, BJORN OLAV, scientist; b. Oslo, Norway, Dec. 20, 1947; came to U.S., 1971; s. Martin T. and Randi M. (Fosser) M.; m. Susana Laya, Feb. 22, 1975; children: Joanna, Christopher. BS, U. Oslo, 1969, MA, 1971; PhD, Pa. State U., 1974. Fellow Carnegie Instn., Washington, 1974-77, sr. scientist, 1977—; lectr. Johns Hopkins U., Balt., 1975-76. Author: Structure and Properties of Silicate Melts; editor: Physico Chemical Principles of Rock-Forming Materials, 1986, Phase Diagrams for Ceramists, 1990; contbr. over 180 articles to profl. jours. Recipient Reusch medal Geol. Soc. Norway, 1979. Fellow Mineral. Soc. Am.; mem. Am. Geophys. Union, Geochem. Soc. (F.W. Clarke medal 1977), Royal Norwegian Acad. Arts and Letters. Office: Geophys Lab 5251 Broad Branch Rd NW Washington DC 20015-1305

MYSLINSKI, NORBERT RAYMOND, medical educator; b. Buffalo, Apr. 14, 1947; s. Bernard and Amelia Joan (Lesniak) M.; m. Patricia Ann Byrne, June 19, 1970 (dec. 1980). BS in Biology, Canisius Coll., Buffalo, 1965-69; PhD in Pharmacology, U. Ill., Chgo., 1973. Research assoc. Tufts U., Boston, 1973-75; asst. prof. U. Md., Balt., 1975-80; assoc. prof. physiology U. Md., 1980—, co-dir. Facial Pain Clinic, 1980-84, instr. nursing, 1982-84; research fellow U. Bristol, Eng., 1984-85; instr. Community Coll. Balt., 1980-82; dir. grad. prog. dept. physiology U. Md., 1981—; cons. in field; reviewer profl. jours. Editor newsletter Med. Soc. Med. Rsch., 1977-82; contbr. articles to profl. jours. and books on pharmacology and neurosci.; inventor in field. Rep. Task Force on Aging, U. Md., 1979-84; instr. Am. Heart Assn., Balt., 1978—, ARC, Balt., 1977-83. Capt. U.S. Army, 1969-77. Grantee, NIH, various drug cos., founds. Mem. European Brain and Behavior Soc. (hon.), Internat. Brain Rsch. Orgn., Md. Soc. Med. Rsch. (exec. com., bd. dirs. 1978-86), Internat. Assn. Dental Rsch. (advisor 1980-81), Am. Physiol. Soc., Soc. for Neurosci. (pres. Balt. chpt. 1990-92), Sigma Xi. Democrat. Roman Catholic. Home: 108 Rockrimmon Rd Reisterstown MD 21136-3214 Office: U Md Physiology Dept 666 W Baltimore St Baltimore MD 21201-1586

MYTELKA, ARNOLD KRIEGER, lawyer; b. Jersey City, July 24, 1937; s. Herman Donald and Jeannette (Krieger) M.; m. Rosalind Marica Kaplan, Dec. 17, 1961; children: Andrew Charles, Daniel Sommer. AB, Princeton U., 1958; LLB cum laude, Harvard U., 1961; postgrad., London Sch. Econs., 1961-62. Bar: N.J. 1961, U.S. Dist. Ct. N.J. 1963, U.S. Supreme Ct. 1970, U.S. Ct. Appeals (3d cir.) 1978, U.S. Dist. Ct. (so. and ea. dist.) N.Y. 1983. Law sec. Chief Justice N.J. Supreme Ct., Newark, 1962-63; assoc. Clapp & Eisenberg, Newark, 1963-68, ptnr., 1968—; lectr. Rutgers Law Sch., Newark, 1973; mem. Am. Law Inst., Phila., 1989—; founding trustee Newark Legal Svcs. Project, 1965-68; trustee Edn. Law Ctr., 1974-75; chmn. dist. V ethics com. Supreme Ct. N.J., 1983-84; trustee Legal Svcs. Found. Essex County, 1982—, pres., 1990-92. Mem. editorial bd. N.J. Law Jour., 1991—; contbr. legal articles to profl. jours. Chmn. bd. trustees Ramapo Coll. N.J., 1979-80. Frank Knox Meml. fellow Harvard U., London Sch. Econs. and Polit. Sci., 1961-62. Mem. N.J. State Bar Assn. (chmn. appellate practices study com. 1977-79, chmn. land use sect. 1984-85). Home: 56 Hall Rd Chatham NJ 07928-1723 Office: Clapp & Eisenberg One Newark Ctr Newark NJ 07102

NABATOFF, ROBERT ALLAN, vascular surgeon, educator; b. N.Y.C., Nov. 19, 1918; s. Abraham Louis and Emma (Goldin) N.; m. Joan Herman, Sept. 11, 1955; children: Diane, Richard, Ross. BA, U. Mich., 1939; MD, SUNY, N.Y.C., 1943. Intern in surgery Mt. Sinai Hosp., N.Y.C., 1943-44, resident in surgery, 1945-46, Dazian pathology fellow, 1944-45; Rosenstock Found. fellow in cardiovascular surgery Presbyn. Hosp., N.Y.C., 1948-49; asst. clin. prof. in vascular surgery Mt. Sinai Hosp., N.Y.C., 1972-74, assoc. clin. prof. in vascular surgery, 1974-79, clin. prof. vascular surgery, 1978—, attending vascular surgeon, 1979—, dir. ambulatory surg. svc., 1982—; cons. Jewish Hosp. and Home for Aged, N.Y.C., 1978—. Author 3 book chpts.; contbr. over 60 articles to profl. jours.; inventor 6 surg. devices. Recipient Hon. Medallion, Keio Sch. Medicine, Japan, 1962, Medallion of Honor, Mt. Sinai Alumni Assn., 1965. Fellow AMA, ACS, N.Y. Acad. Medicine; mem. N.Y. State Med. Soc., N.Y. County Med. Soc., N.Y. Soc. for Cardiovascular Surgery, N.Y. Surg. Soc., Pan Am. Med. Assn. (pres. vascular surgery sect.). Office: Medical Office 1020 Park Ave New York NY 10028

NABIRAHNI, MOHAMMAD ALI (DAVID NABIRAHNI), chemist, educator; b. Tehran, Iran, July 10, 1956; came to U.S., 1979; Dakhil and Shokat (Hajizadeh) N.; m. Fariba Eshaghzadeh, Mar. 14, 1979; children: Azad, Bobak. BS, Nat. U. Iran, 1979; MS with honors, Ea. N.Mex. U., 1980; PhD, U. New Orleans, 1985. Chmn. and English tchr. Armaghan Tarbiat Sch., Tehran, 1975-79; teaching and rsch. asst. Ea. N.Mex. U., Portales, 1979-80; from teaching and rsch. asst. to sr. rsch. chemist U. New Orleans, La., 1981-86; asst. prof. analytical chemistry Pace U., Pleasantville, N.Y., 1986-89, assoc. prof., 1990-92, prof., 1992—, dir. ctr. applied analytical chemistry, 1988—, adj. prof. environ. law, 1992—; adj. rsch. chemist, Am. Health Found., Valhalla, N.Y., 1987; adj. assoc. prof. chemistry Manhattanville Coll., Purchase, N.Y., 1990—; vis. prof. Inst. Analytical Chemistry, U. Florence, Italy, 1990; vis. scientist IBM T.J. Watson Rsch. Ctr., Yorktown Hts., N.Y., 1991-92. Contbr. articles to profl. jours. Environ. advisor to congresswoman Nita M. Lowey, 1990--. Mem. Am. Chem. Soc., Am. Assn. Clin. Chemistry, Perisan Am. Chemists Assn. (founder, chmn., sec. bd. dirs. 1988—, ran for chmn. N.Y. sect. 1991, chmn. Westchester div. 1991), Soc. Electroanalytical Chemistry, N.Y. Acad. Sci., Sigma Xi. Muslim. Office: Pace U Dept Chemistry Pleasantville NY 10570

NACKNOUCK, JAMES DOMINIC, management executive; b. Newark, May 7, 1950. BS, Montclair State Coll., 1972; MBA, Fairleigh Dickinson U., 1984. Asst. art dir. Markal Corp., Montclair, N.J., 1972-75; art educator Phillipsburg (N.J.) Pub. Sch., 1975; prodn. mgr. Landmark Assocs. Ltd., Orange, N.J., 1975-77; graphic designer Exxon Rsch. and Engring. Co., Florham Park, N.J., 1977-81, supr. graphic design, 1981-88; unit head accounts payable Exxon Central Svcs., Florham Park, 1988-92; process control leader Exxon Rsch. and Engring. Co., Florham Park, 1992—; pres. The Users Group, N.J., 1986-88. Mem. Am. Mgmt. Assn. Home: 48 Washburn Pl Caldwell NJ 07006-5935 Office: Exxon Rsch and Engring Co 180 Park Ave Florham Park NJ 07932-1093

NADEL, FRED S., financial consultant; b. Hamburg, Germany, May 13, 1936; came to U.S., 1939.; s. Eric and Irma (Baruch) N.; m. Doris Mae Kitzberger, Dec. 30, 1967. BSChemE, MIT, 1958; MBA, Stanford, 1960. CPA, N.Y. Engr. Monsanto, St. Louis, 1960-64; asst. to pres. KV Pharmacal, St. Louis, 1964-66, Rachael Labs (Subs Inter Rectfr.), Long Beach, Calif., 1966-68; mfg. mgr. New Ventures div. Xerox Corp., Pasadena, Calif., 1968-70; audit mgr. Occidental Petroleum, Grand Island, N.Y., 1970-71; fin. mgr./contr. Sierra Research Corp., Buffalo, 1970-76; owner Fred S. Nadel & Assoc., Buffalo, 1976—; v.p. BizComp Inc., Buffalo, 1984—; bd. dirs. Rosa Coplon Nursing Home, Buffalo, 1987—. V.p., pres. Amherst (N.Y.) Symphony Orch., 1984-90, 90-92. Mem. Rotary (treas. 1983-84, sec. 1984-85, v.p. 1985-86, pres. 1986-87), MIT Alumni Club of WNY (treas. 1978—). Home: 175 Hunters Ln Buffalo NY 14221-4551 Office: Fred S Nadel & Assoc 175 Hunters Ln Buffalo NY 14221-4551

NADEL, KAY CHANEY, advertising and public relations executive; b. Charleston, Ill., Apr. 2, 1945; d. Jack and Eleanor (Gardner) C.; m. Brown Harris, II (div. 1972); 1 child, Brown; m. Ed Nadel, 1984. AA, Stephens Coll., 1965; BS, U. Mo., Columbia, 1967; MS, U. Mo., Kansas City, 1976. Tchr. curriculum writer, adminstr. St. Louis and Kansas City, 1968-74; dir. alumnae programs Stephens Coll., Columbia, Mo., 1974-78; v.p. univ. rels. U. Charleston, W.Va., 1978-79; v.p. McCluney/Brewer Advt., Kansas City, 1979-80; sr. v.p. Hickerson/Powell Advt., Kansas City, 1980-82; pres., owner Harris & Assocs., Kansas City, 1982-85, C-N Communications, Inc., N.Y.C., 1985—; lectr. in field. Contbg. writer: The Best of CASE Currents: A Marketing Approach to Student Recruitment, 1979, 3d edit. 1985; Sourcebook, Guide to Alumnae Admissions program, 1976. Board dirs. Family Svc. Westchester, United Way, Colombia, 1976-78, YWCA of Kansas City, 1981; charter mem. Columbia Ambs., 1976; vol. Girl Scouts U.S., 1980-83; adv. bd. dirs. Rsch. Med. Ctr., Kansas City, 1982; hon. trustee Truman Med. Ctr., Kansas City, 1982; mem. pers. and fundraising com. Cen. Exch., Kansas City, 1981—; mem. coun. N.Y. Hosp.-Cornell Med. Ctr., 1989—. Recipient Best of Class award for advt. Mo. Gov.'s Conf., 1978, Pres.'s award Am. Soc. Interior Design, 1982. Mem. Pub. Rels. Soc. Am., Coun. for Advancement and Support Edn. (Nat. Merit award 1978), Westchester Assn. Retarded Citizens (bd. dirs.). Roman Catholic. Home: Pleasant Ridge Rd Harrison NY 10528-1004

NADELBERG, ERIC PAUL, brokerage house executive; b. Providence, R.I., Dec. 14, 1947; s. Arnold and Sandra (Schwartz) N.; m. Evelynne Luberoff, Dec. 12, 1968; children: Amanda, Ariel. BA, Bklyn. Coll., 1973; postgrad., Sch. of Journalism, N.Y.U., 1976-77. Registered commodities rep. News analyst The Wall Street Jour., N.Y.C., 1973-76; reporter Reuters Ltd., N.Y.C., 1976-77; sr. analyst E.F. Hutton & Co., Inc., N.Y.C., 1977-79, v.p., 1983-85; v.p. Gill & Duffus Svcs., Inc., N.Y.C., 1979-81, Rudolf Wolff Futures, Inc., N.Y.C., 1981-83; pres. Tropical Trader, Inc., Hoboken, N.J., 1985-90; v.p. Tropical Trader Group Merrill Lynch Inc., N.Y.C., N.J., 1990—. Contbr. Barrons Fin. Mag., 1976-79; contbg. editor Commodity Rsch. Bur., 1986—; columnist Cotton Mag., Memphis, Tenn., 1977-88. With U.S. Army, 1968-71. Mem. Caledonian, Knights of Pythias. Democrat. Office: Merrill Lynch Inc 2 World Fin Ctr New York NY 10080

NADELMANN, ETHAN AVRAM, lawyer, educator; b. N.Y.C., Mar. 13, 1957; s. Ludwig and Judith (Wolpert) N.; m. Donna Lynn Sherman, Sept. 14, 1986. BA, Harvard U., 1979, JD, 1984, PhD in Polit. Sci., 1987; MSc in Internat. Relations, London Sch. Econs., 1980. Bar: Mass. 1985. Teaching asst. Dept. Govt. Harvard U., Cambridge, Mass., 1982-87; asst. prof. politics and pub. affairs Princeton (N.J.) U., 1987—; lectr. U.S. and internat. drug policies and problems. Contbr. articles to profl. jours. cons. Bur. Internat. Narcotics Matters, U.S. Dept. of State, Washington, 1984-85, Ford Found., N.Y.C., 1986-87. NSF grad. fellow, 1980-84; grad. research fellow Nat. Inst. Justice, 1984-85; John M. Olin fellow in internat. security Ctr. Internat. Affairs, 1986-87; NOMOS fellow, 1985-86; fellow, grantee Harvard U., 1985-87. Mem. ABA, Am. Soc. Internat. Law, Am. Polit Sci. Assn., Law and Soc. Assn., Drug Policy Found. (bd. dirs.). Jewish. Home: 54B Western Way Princeton NJ 08540-7206 Office: Princeton U Woodrow Wilson Sch Princeton NJ 08544

NADICH, JUDAH, rabbi; b. Balt., May 13, 1912; s. Isaac and Lena (Nathanson) N.; m. Martha Hadassah Ribalow, Jan. 26, 1947; children: Leah N. (Mrs. Aryeh Meir), Shira A. (Mrs. James L. Levin), Nahma M. Nadich (Mrs. David Belcourt). B.A., CCNY, 1932; M.A., Columbia U., 1936; rabbi, M.H.L., Jewish Theol. Sem. Am., 1936, D.H.L., 1953, D.D. (hon), 1966. Rabbi Temple Beth David, Buffalo, 1936-40; co-rabbi Anshe Emet Synagogue, Chgo., 1940-42; lecture tour U.S., South Africa and Rhodesia, 1946-47; rabbi Kehillath Israel Congregation, Brookline, Mass., 1947-57; rabbi Park Ave. Synagogue, N.Y.C., 1957-87, rabbi emeritus, 1987—; conducted first Bat Mitzvah in People's Republic of China, 1990. Author: Eisenhower and the Jews, 1953, Jewish Legends of the Second Commonwealth, 1983; Editor, translator: (Menachem Ribalow) The Flowering of Modern Hebrew Literature, 1959; editor: (Louis Ginzberg) Al Halakha v'Aggada, 1960. Pres. Rabbinical Assembly, 1972-74; pres. Jewish Book Council Am., 1968-72; bd. dirs., exec. com. Jewish Theol. Sem. Am.; formerly bd. dirs., mem. exec. com. Nat. Jewish Welfare Bd., Fedn. Jewish Philanthropies N.Y.; mem. hospice com. Beth Israel Med. Ctr.; mem. N.Y.C. Holocaust Meml. Com.; v.p. bd. dirs. Jewish Braille Inst.; past pres. Assn. Jewish Chaplains Armed Forces. Served to lt. col. as chaplain AUS, 1942-46, ETO. Decorated Order Brit. Empire; Croix de Guerre France; Ittur Lohamai Hamdinah Israel; fellow Herbert Lehman Inst. Talmudic Ethics, 1958. Mem. Mil. Chaplains Assn., Phi Beta Kappa. Lodge: Masons. Home: 1040 Park Ave New York NY 10028-1032 Office: Park Ave Synagogue 50 E 87th St New York NY 10128-1099

NADLER, PAUL STEPHEN, banking educator, columnist; b. N.Y.C., Apr. 2, 1930; s. Marcus and Cecilia (Sachs) N.; m. Beverly Goldsmith, Nov. 4, 1990; children: Julie, Margaret, David, Saul. AB, Brown U., 1951; MA, U. Wis., 1953; PhD, NYU, 1958. Prof. Rutgers U., Newark, 1958-61, 69—. Author: Commercial Banking in the Economy, 1968-85, Paul Nadler Writes About Banking, 1973, The Banking Jungle, 1985; contbg. editor Am. Banker, 1959—, Banking Monthly, 1963—, Secured Lender, 1970—, Commercial Lending Review, 1975—. Home: 14 Friar Tuck Cir Summit NJ 07901-3713 Office: Rutgers U 92 New St Newark NJ 07102-1818

NADLEY, HARRIS JEROME, accountant, educator, author; b. Phila., July 6, 1926; s. Michael and Celia (Millman) N.; BS, U. Pa., 1950; MA, PhD, Harvard U., 1952; m. Barbara A. Malone, June 28, 1953; children—Jennifer Beth, Amy Jane, Adam Christopher. Asst. trust officer Provident Trust Co., Phila., 1949; exec. trainee Merrill, Lynch, Pierce, Fenner & Smith, N.Y.C., 1950; ptnr. Michael Nadley Co., CPAs, Phila., 1952—. Teaching fellow Harvard, 1952; instr. fin. Wharton Sch., Phila., 1953-54; adj. prof. bus. adminstrn. St. Joseph's Coll., Phila., Acad. Food Mktg., Pa. Inst. CPAs, N.J. Soc. CPAs, AICPA; cons. Control Data Corp., 1971; participant Current Strategy Forum, Naval War Coll., 1978, Naval War Coll. Found., 1979. Gen. chmn. Marine Corps Birthday Ball, Phila., 1973. Bd. dirs. Montgomery County Assn. for Retarded Children, Cruiser Olympia Assn., ea. Pa. chpt. Arthritis Found.; trustee Lesley Coll., Cambridge, Mass.; pres. adv. council Wharton Sch., U. Pa., 1950; del. White House Conf. on Small Bus., 1986; mem. pres.'s council Chestnut Hill Coll.; mem. Benjamin Franklin Assocs., U. Pa.; chmn. bd. advisors USMC Tun's Tavern Commn., 1991. Served with USMCR, 1944-46; PTO. Mem. Am. Radio Relay League, Fraternal Order Police (hon.), Econometric Soc., Am. Econ. Soc., Mil. Order Fgn. Wars, Preservation Soc. Newport County, St. Joseph's Coll. Acad. Food Mktg. (founder), Quarter Century Wireless Assn., Marine Corps Res. Officers Assn., Sixth Marine Div. Assn., Marine Raiders Assn., Navy League, Pa. Soc., Beta Gamma Sigma, Pi Gamma Mu, Beta Sigma Rho. Clubs: Masons, Union League, Harvard, Harvard Faculty, Mercedes-Benz, Urban (Phila.). Author: A Covey of Peacocks, 1969. Contbr. articles to profl. jours.; fin. columnist Phila. mag., Welcomat Newspaper, Phila. Bus. Jour.; cons. Fin. News Network, Phila. Home and Office: 325 S 3d St Philadelphia PA 19106

NADOLINK, RICHARD HUGHES, scientist; b. Worcester, Mass., Feb. 13, 1943; s. Louis and Evelyn (Hughes) N.; m. Janet Ann Stepenovitch, Apr. 2, 1966; 1 child, Erik David. BS in Physics, U. Mass., 1965, MS in Civil Engring., 1967; PhD in Engring. Physics, U. Calif., San Diego, 1986. Rsch. asst. Civil Engring. Lab. U. Mass., Amherst, 1965-67; mech. engr. U.S. Naval Torpedo Station, Newport, R.I., 1967-75; head fluid mechanics branch U.S. Naval Underwater Systems Ctr., Newport, 1975-83, head weapon tech. div., 1983—, chair in hydrodynamics, 1987—; owner Neport Sci. and Engring. Co., Portsmouth, R.I., 1988—. Contbr. articles to profl. jours. Bd. dirs. Newport Hosp. Corp., 1991. Recipient Navy Spl. Achievement awards in sci. Naval Underwater Systems Ctr., 1972, Disting. Chair award in Sci. and engring. Naval Underwater Systems Ctr., David Bushnell award, 1989. Mem. Am. Def. Preparedness Assn. (Millbury Mass. Man of Distinction 1991). Roman Catholic. Home: 540 Sandy Point Ave Portsmouth RI 02871-3514

NAEGLE, MADELINE ANNE, mental health nurse, educator; b. Penn Yan, N.Y., Feb. 2, 1942; d. Lester Lawrence and Nona Caroline (Muir) N.; m. James Michael McGowan, Aug. 6, 1966 (div. 1984); children: Amanda Allen, Benjamin Logan. BS, Nazareth Coll. Rochester, 1964; MA, NYU, 1967, PhD, 1980. Staff nurse Syracuse (N.Y.) Meml. Hosp., summer 1964; staff nurse, asst. head nurse Payne Whitney Clinic, N.Y.C., 1964-65; instr. nursing Herbert H. Lehman Coll., Bronx, N.Y., 1972-75, part-time instr. nursing, 1975-78; asst. clin. prof. Sch. Nursing U. Pa., Phila., 1979-83; pvt. practice N.Y.C., 1980—; assoc. prof. Leinhard Sch. Nursing Pace U., Pleasantville, N.Y., 1983-85; assoc. prof. div. nursing NYU, N.Y.C., 1985—; cons. The Day Sch., 1980-84, State Nurses Assn. Peer Assistance Program, 1986—; mem. N.Y. State Gov.'s Health Care Adv. Bd., 1991—. Author: (with others) Nursing Process with Clients Using Drugs, 1990, Patterns of Substance Abuse, 1991; author, editor: (model curriculum) Substance Abuse Education in Nursing, 1991; editor Addictions Nursing Network, 1988—; contbr. articles to profl. jours. USPHS fellow, 1978-79; grantee Nat. Inst. of Alcohol Abuse and Alcoholism, Nat. Inst. of Drug Abuse, 1989-90, Office of Substance Abuse Prevention, 1990; recipient Presdl. Citation award N.Y. County RN Assn., 1986; inductee Acad. Women Achievers, YWCA, 1991. Fellow Am. Acad. of Nursing; mem. ANA (com. chair 1987-89, com. on addiction 1990), N.Y. State Nurses Assn. (chair com. on impaired nursing nursing practice 1986-88, pres. 1989-91, pres. 1989-91). Nat. League for Nursing, Sigma Theta Tau (Upsilon chpt.). Democrat. Office: NYU Div Nursing 50 W 4th St New York NY 10003

NAGAMIYA, SHOJI, physicist; b. Mikage-shi, Hyogo-Ken, Japan, May 24, 1944; came to U.S., 1973; s. Takeo and Masako Nagamiya; m. Tae Nagamiya, Nov. 9, 1969; children: Masahiko, Kenji. BSc, U. Tokyo, 1967; DSc, Osaka (Japan) U., 1972. Rsch. assoc. U. Tokyo, 1972-75; staff scientist

Lawrence Berkeley (Calif.) Lab., 1975-82; assoc. prof. U. Tokyo, 1982-88; prof. Columbia U., N.Y.C., 1986—, chmn. dept. physics, 1991—; chmn. Internat. Conf. on Quark Matter, Lennox, Mass., 1987-88. Author: Advances in Nuclear Physics, 1984, Annual Review of Nuclear & Particle Science, 1984; mem. editorial bd. Il Nuovo Cimento, 1989—, Jour. Phys. Soc. Japan, 1984-86; mem. adv. com. Jour. Phys. G., 1992—, Internat. Jour. Modern Phys. E., 1992—. Mem. evaluation com. Swedish Natural Rsch. Coun., 1987; mem. vis. com. Lawrence Berkeley Lab., Oak Ridge (Tenn.) Nat. Lab., and others; chmn. Nuclear Physics Com. of Japan, 1985-87. U.S. Dept. of Energy grantee, 1986—, Yamada Sci. Found. grantee, 1989-91; recipient Inoue prize, 1992. Fellow Am. Phys. Soc. Home: 24 Victor Dr Irvington NY 10533-1923 Office: Columbia U Dept of Physics W 120th St New York NY 10027

NAGANO, PAUL TATSUMI, artist; b. Honolulu, May 21, 1938; s. Don Sakae and Masako (Imamoto) N. BA in English, Columbia Coll., 1960; postgrad., Pa. Acad. Fine Arts, 1963-67. Art dir. Pucker Safrai Gallery, Boston, 1967-89. One man shows include Pucker Safrai, 1976-88, Art Complex Mus., Duxbury, Mass., 1982, Indonesian Idylls, Jakarta, Indonesia, 1990; two-person shows include Honolulu Acad. of Arts, 1988, Neka Mus., Ubud, Bali, 1992; contbr. articles to profl. jours. Lt. (j.g.) USN, 1960-63. Recipient Packard prize Pa. Acad. Fine Arts, 1964, Lewis S. Ware prize Pa. Acad. Fine Arts, 1967. Mem. Japan Soc. of Boston. Home and Studio: Fenway Studio 406 30 Ipswich St Boston MA 02215-3616

NAGELL, RAYMOND H., geologist, consultant; b. Rochester, N.Y., Apr. 10, 1927; s. Raymond H. and Julia Adel (Bartholomew) N.; m. Doris F. Worth, June 13, 1949 (dec. Apr. 1983); 1 child, Raymond H.; m. Elaine Marilyn Krogstad, June 9, 1984. BA, U. Rochester, 1951, MS, 1952; PhD, Stanford U., 1958. Geologist Cerro de Pasco Corp., Morocha, Peru, 1952-55, Cia Minera Cuprum, S.A., Mex., 1956-57, Shenon and Full, Salt Lake City, 1961-63, U.S. Geol. Survey, Pakistan and Brazil, 1963-70; chief geologist ICOMI, Brazil, 1957-61; sr. geologist Bethlehem Steel Corp., Spain, Brazil and Australia, 1970-85; pvt. practice cons. Bethlehem, Pa., 1985—. Author various geol. studies. Cpl. U.S. Army, 1945-47. Recipient Meritorious Achievement award U.S. AID, 1974. Mem. AIME, Soc. Econ. Geologists. Home and Office: 357 Carver Dr Bethlehem PA 18017-4716

NAGLE, DENNIS CHARLES, engineer, researcher; b. Dolgeville, N.Y., Jan. 13, 1945; s. John Daniel and Marguerine Bridget (Murphy) N.; m. Patricia Elaine Kiesell, Mar. 22, 1969; children: Melissa, Matthew, Eric, Jason, Kristen. BS in Ceramic Engring., Alfred (N.Y.) U., 1967; PhD, Pa. State U., 1972, postgrad., 1973. Sr. engr. United Techs. Corp., South Winzer, Conn., 1973-76; sr. scientist Martin Marietta Labs., Balt., 1976-80, staff scientist, 1980-87, prin. engr., 1987—. Contbr. articles to profl. jours.; holder 32 patents in field. Mem. Am. Ceramics Soc. (officer 1984-88). Home: 10148 Tanfield Ct Ellicott City MD 21042-5808 Office: Martin Marietta Labs 1450 S Rolling Rd Baltimore MD 21227

NAGLE, GEORGE, JR., state mental health administrator; b. Bklyn., July 8, 1932; s. George and Elizabeth (Gaffney) N.; m. Marcia Elynore Moran, July 2, 1964; 1 child, Kristen. BA in Govt. and Bus. magna cum laude, Lehigh U., 1955. Jr. mgmt. trainee Dept. Def., 1956-57, exec. officer, 1959-66; dep. dir. adminstrn. Nathan Kline Inst. for Psychiat. Rsch. NYU, Orangeburg, N.Y., 1966—; exec. dir. Internat. Com. Against Mental Illness, N.Y.C., 1966—; treas. N.J. Rsch. Found. for Mental Hygiene, 1966—; instr. psychiatry dept. NYU Med. Ctr., N.Y.C., 1979—; mem. adv. bd. refugee assistance program Adelphi U., 1987; cons. Bus. Counselors, Inc., N.Y.C., 1966-72. Mem. planning and adv. bd. Hampton's Hosp. Fund, Inc., 1968-74; bd. dirs. Assn. for Study Man-Environ. Relations, 1969-75, Research Found. for Mental Hygiene, Inc., N.Y.C., 1971—, Friends North Castle Library; mem. zoning bd. Town of North Castle. Served to 1st lt. U.S. Army, 1956-58. Mem. Assn. Mental Health Adminstrs. (cert.), Nat. Coun. Univ. Rsch. Adminstrs., Soc. for Rsch. Adminstrs., N.Y. State Orgn. Mgmt. Confidential Employees, Big Bros., Lehigh Club (N.Y.), Westhampton Beach Yachting Club (past commodore), North Cove Yacht Club, Pi Gamma Mu, Phi Alpha Theta. Democrat. Home: 92 Byram Ridge Rd Armonk NY 10504-1212 Office: Nathan S Kline Inst Orangeburg NY 10962

NAGORNIAK, JOHN JOSEPH, investment company executive; b. Buffalo, Dec. 16, 1944; s. Alphonso and Marie Theresa (Scheuerle) N.; m. Jill Diane Hampton, Sept. 7, 1969; children: Peter, Joy. AB, Princeton U., 1966; MS, Mass. Inst. Tech., 1970. Actuarial trainee John Hancock Life Ins. Co., Boston, 1966-68, rsch. officer, 1970-73, dir. computer applications, 1973-79; v.p. State St. Bank & Trust Co., Boston, 1979-81, sr. v.p., 1981-82; pres., chief exec. officer Franklin Portfolio Assocs., Boston, 1982—; co-chmn. Investment Tech. Symposium, N.Y.C., 1978. Contbr. articles to profl. jours. Chmn. ann. giving Princeton (N.J.) U., 1988-90. Mem. Inst. Chartered Fin. Analysts, Boston Security Analysts Soc. (bd. dirs. 1990—), Princeton Assn. New Eng. (bd. dirs. 1983—), Assn. Investment Mgmt. and Rsch., Boston Security Analysts Soc. (bd. dirs. 1990—). Home: 31 Shoreline Dr Foxboro MA 02035-1116

NAGY, ROY ALAN, association executive; b. Boston, Nov. 5, 1951; s. John P. and Florence (Horton) N.;m. Kendra Ann Gavin, Sept. 18, 1982; stepchildren: Annette Obey, Richard Obey, Glenn Obey. BS in Speech, Emerson Coll., 1973. Assoc. dist. exec. Boston Coun. Boys Scouts Am., Boston, 1974-75; dir. Project-Link Boy Scouts of Am.-Boys Clubs of Am., Boston, 1975-78; devel. officer Mass. Bay Federated Couns. of Boy Scouts Am., Peabody, Mass., 1979; exec. dir. Boys and Girls Club of Lynn, Mass., 1979—. Chmn., founder Emerson Coll. Athletic Trust Fund, Boston, 1984—. Recipient Citation Mass. Ho. of Reps., 1989; recipient Outstanding Alumni award Emerson Coll., 1987. Mem. Lynn Area C. of C., Mass. Soc. Fund-Raising Execs., Boys and Girls Clubs Profl. Assn., Boys and Girls Clubs of Met. Boston (chmn. 1987-89), Rotary (pres. 1990-91). Democrat. Roman Catholic. Home: 129 Fairmount Ave Saugus MA 01906-1415 Office: Boys and Girls Club Lynn 25 N Common St Lynn MA 01902-4391

NAHABEDIAN, CHARLES EDWARD, telecommunications executive; b. Boston, Mass., Apr. 6, 1940; s. Sarkis and Lucy (Demirjian) N.; m. Barbara Ann Sielinski, Jan. 21, 1967; children: Cynthia Ann, Christina Marie. BSEE, Northeastern U., Boston, 1963, MSEE, 1965; MBA, Seton Hall U., S. Orange, N.J., 1987. Supr. Bell Telehone Labs., Holmdel, N.J., 1967-78; mgr. AT&T, Basking Ridge, N.J., 1978-82; dir. AT&T, Morristown & Parsipany, N.J., 1982-87; pres. and co-founder Fonetek Corp., Basking Ridge, 1987-88, Atlantic Video Systems, Inc., Mendham, N.J., 1988-90, Charles Edward Assocs., Mendham, N.J., 1988-91; program dir. Fidelity Capital, Boston, 1990-91, sr. prin., 1991—; cons. Pub. Telecommunications Systems Partnership, Denver, 1990-91. Inventor in field. Chmn. St. Mary Armenian Ch., Livingston, N.J., 1983, treas., 1982; mem. choir Hilltop Presbyn. Ch.; chmn. Parent Coun., Hilltop Sch., Mendham, N.J., 1980-81; sec. Lindcroft First Aid Squad, 1976, chmn., 1974-75. 1st lt. U.S. Army, 1965-67. Recipient Outstanding Svc. award, Lincroft First Aid Squad, 1976. Mem. IEEE, Knights of Vartan (comdr. 1975-78). Republican. Office: TSC 205 N Michigan Ave Ste 1500 Chicago IL 60601

NAHAPETIAN, ARA TOONNAZ, biotechnologist, nutritional biochemist; b. Isfahan, Iran, May 4, 1942; came to U.S., 1967; s. Yervand and Katharina (Nazloomian) N.; m. Beta B. Martinian; children: Eta, Katherine. BSc, Am. U. of Beirut, Lebanon, 1965, MSc, 1967; ScD, MIT, 1971. From asst. to assoc. prof. Shiraz (Iran) U., 1971-80; vis. scientist MIT, Cambridge, 1978-79, rsch. scientist, 1980-85; sr. rsch. scientist Dupont, Wilmington, Del., 1985-91, DuPont Merck Pharm. Co., Wilmington, 1991—. Contbr. numerous articles to profl. jours. Fulbright Hays fellow MIT, 1978-79; AID scholar Am. U. Beirut, 1961-65. Mem. AAAS, Am. Inst. Nutrition, Tissue Culture Assn., Sigma Xi. Home: 209 Paddock Ln Wilmington DE 19803-1918 Office: DuPont Merck Pharm Co 500 S Ridgeway Ave Glenolden PA 19036-2398

NAHAS, GABRIEL GEORGES, pharmacologist, educator; b. Alexandria, Egypt, Mar. 4, 1920; came to U.S., 1947, naturalized, 1962; s. Bishara and Gabrielle (Wolff) N.; m. Marilyn Cashman, Feb. 13, 1954; children: Michele, Anthony, Christiane. BA, U. Toulouse, France, 1937, MD, 1944; MS, U. Rochester, 1949; PhD, U. Minn., 1953; DSc (hon.), U. Uppsala, 1988. Rockefeller Found. fellow U. Rochester, 1947-48; Mayo Found. fellow Mayo Clinic, 1949-50; research fellow U. Minn., 1950-53, mem. faculty, 1955-57; staff Walter Reed Army Inst. Research, 1957-59; faculty George Washington U. Med. Sch., 1957-59; faculty Columbia Coll. Physicians and Surgeons, 1959—, prof. anesthesiology, 1962-92; rsch. prof. anesthesiology NYU, 1992—; prof. anesthesiology NYU Med. Ctr., 1992—; Fulbright scholar, 1966; adj. prof. anesthesiology (research) U. Paris, 1968-71; Fellow Council Circulation and Basic Sci., Am. Heart Assn., 1961—; com. on trauma NRC, 1964-66; adv. bd. Cousteau Soc.; cons. U.N. Commn. on Narcotics. Author: Marihuana, Deceptive Weed, 1973, 2d edit., 1984, Keep Off the Grass, 1976, 5th edit., 1990, Cocaine: The Great White Plague, 1989; editor: (with W.D.M. Paton) Marihuana: Biological Effects, 1979, (with H.C. Frick) Drug Abuse in the Modern World, 1981, Physiopathology Addictive Drugs, 1991, Manual on Drug Dependence, 1992. Spl. agt. French Underground, 1941-44; 1st lt. M.C., French Army, 1944-45. Decorated Presdl. Medal of Freedom with gold palm U.S.; comdr. Legion of Honor, Croix de Guerre with 3 palms (France), Order Brit. Empire, Order Orange Nassau Netherlands, Silver medal City of Paris; recipient Medal of Honor, Statue of Liberty Centennial, 1986. Fellow AAAS, N.Y. Acad. Sci.; mem. Am. Physiol. Soc., Harvey Soc., Am. Soc. Pharmacology and Exptl. Therapeutics, Am. Soc. Clin. Pharmacology, Soc. Physiol. Langue Française, French Acad. Medicine (laureate), Brit. Pharm. Soc., Sigma Xi. Home: 114 Chestnut St Englewood NJ 07631-3033 Office: NYU Med Ctr Dept Anesthesiology 550 First Ave New York NY 10016

NAHIGIAN, ROBERT JOHN, real estate development broker; b. Boston, Feb. 24, 1956; s. John Moses and Theresa (Zeytoundjian) N. BA cum laude, Lehigh U., 1978; MS in Urban Planning, Columbia U., 1980. Property mgr. Auburndale (Mass.) Realty Co., 1972-77; jr. planner Bethlehem (Pa.) Redevel. Authority, 1978; planner, tech. analyst Perkins & Will Archtl. Firm, N.Y.C., 1978-80; city planner, econ. developer City of Bowie, Md., 1980-81; v.p. The Norwood Group, Inc., Burlington, Mass., 1981-88; v.p., dir. The Robbins Group, Cambridge, Mass., 1988-89; pres. Auburndale Realty Co., Newton, Mass., 1989—; dir., lectr. real estate studies Northeastern U., Boston, 1982—; lectr. real estate Lehigh U., Harvard Grad. Sch. Design, Grad. Sch. MIT, The Exch. Club, Maynard (Mass.) C. of C., assessing dept. City of Boston, N.H. Realtor's C.I. div., N.E. Constrn. show, So. Calif. Constrn. Show, Soc. Indsl. and Office Realtors, Mass. Assn. Realtors, profl. orgns., 1984—. Contbr. articles to profl. jours. Mem. Wang Ctr. for the Performing Arts, Boston, 1985. Recipient Cert. of Appreciation, Northeastern U., 1987, 90, Soc. Indsl. and Office Realtors, 1990, 91, The Exch. Club, 1991, N.E. Constrn. show, So. Calif. Constrn. show. Mem. Nat. Assn. Realtors, Soc. Indsl. and Office Realtors (Cert. of Appreciation, cert. profl. edn. com., instr.'s com. and office mktg. forum, office leasing handbook taskforce, property evaluation forum, expert roundtable com.), Am. Planning Assn., Nat. Assn. Indsl. Office Parks, Nat. Trust for Hist. Preservation, Lehigh Club (pres.), Algonquin Club. Republican. Mem. Armenian Apostolic Ch. Home: 85 Hosmer St Apt 6B Acton MA 01720-5425 Office: Auburndale Realty Co 335 Auburn St PO Box 125 Newton MA 02166

NAIDER, FRED ROBERT, chemistry educator; b. N.Y.C., Jan. 31, 1945; s. Leonard and Molly (Schwebel) N.; m. Anita Joy Serle, Dec. 23, 1967; children: Avraham, Shoshana, Rachel, Elana. BSChemE, MSChemE, Cornell U., 1966; PhD, Poly Technic Inst., 1970. Postdoctoral fellow Weizmann Inst. Sci., Rehovot, Israel, 1971-73; asst. prof. CUNY, 1973-75; assoc. prof. Coll. S.I., 1976-79; Michael fellow Weizman Inst. Sci., Rehovot, 1980-81; prof. Coll. S.I., 1980—, chmn. dept. chemistry, 1986—; prof. Grad. Sch. Univ. Ctr. CUNY, 1973—; cons. Bioresearch Inc., Farmingdale, N.Y., 1973—; mem. adv. bd. Biopolymers. Contbr. over 105 articles to profl. jours. Fulbright fellow, 1989-90; grantee NIH, 1975-80, Am. Cancer Soc. Jewish. Office: Coll SI Dept Chemistry 50 Bay St Staten Island NY 10301-2511

NAIM, JOHN O., research scientist; b. Bklyn., Dec. 20, 1954; s. Osman John and Angela (Rella) N.; m. Joan Theresa McCormick, Aug. 16, 1975; children: Jennifer, Emily. BS, SUNY, Geneseo, 1977; MT, Gen. Hosp. Sch. Med. Tech., 1978; MS, Rochester Inst. Tech., 1983; PhD, SUNY, Buffalo, 1991. Surg. rsch. technologist Rochester (N.Y.) Gen. Hosp., 1978-81, surg. rsch. assoc., 1981-88, surg. rsch. scientist, 1988-91, dir. laser surgery rsch. lab., 1991—; mem. radiation safety com. Rochester Gen. Hosp., 1989—, mem. institutional animal care and use com., 1992—. Author: (with others) Progressi Clinice: Chirurgia LaChirurgia Conservitiva Della Milza, 1985; contbr. articles to profl. jours. Fellow Am. Soc. Laser Medicine and Surgery; mem. AAAS, Am. Soc. Clin. Pathologists, Acad. Surg. Rsch., N.Y. Acad. Sci., Am. Soc. Microbiology. Office: Rochester Gen Hosp Laser Ct 1425 Portland Ave Rochester NY 14621

NAIMAN, ADELINE LUBELL, educational administrator; b. Boston, Oct. 27, 1925; d. Joseph and Jennie Rachel (Samuel) Lubell; m. Mark Lewis Naiman, July 3, 1947; children: Joris, Alaric, P. Kieron. BA, Radcliffe Coll., 1946. Editor Little, Brown Co., Boston, 1945-48; freelance script writer Coronet Films, Chgo., 1948-51; freelance editor J.B. Lippincott Co., Phila., 1954-57; editor-in-chief Elem. Sci. Study, Newton, Mass., 1964-71; dir. publs., asst. to pres. Edn. Devel. Ctr., Newton, 1970-79; mng. dir. Tech. Edn. Rsch. Ctrs., Cambridge, Mass., 1979-82; software dir. Human Rels. Media, Pleasantville, N.Y., 1982-88; dir. publs. Nat. Scis. Resources Ctr., Washington, 1988; dir. edn. The Computer Mus., Boston, 1988-90; acad. dir. Mass. Corp. for Edn. Telecommunications, Cambridge, 1990—; trustee Lesley Coll., Cambridge, 1975—; vice-chair Mass. Ednl. Tech. Adv. Coun. Co-author: Practical Guide to Computers for Administrators, 1985; author: Microcomputers in Education: An Introduction, 1981; contbg. editor BCS Update, Personal Computing; contbr. articles to profl. jours. Bd. dirs. Mus. Inst. for Teaching Sci. Home: Moccasin Hill Lincoln MA 01773 Office: 38 Sidney St Ste 300 Cambridge MA 02139-4160

NAIMARK, GEORGE MODELL, advertising executive; b. N.Y.C., Feb. 5, 1925; s. Myron S. and Mary (Modell) N. B.S., Bucknell U., 1947, M.S., 1948; Ph.D., U. Del., 1951; m. Helen Anne Wythes, June 24, 1946; children: Ann, Richard, Jane. Rsch. biochemist Brush Devel. Co., Cleve., 1951; dir. quality control Strong, Cobb & Co., Inc., Cleve., 1951-54; dir. sci. svcs. White Labs., Inc., Kenilworth, N.J., 1954-60; v.p. Burdick Assocs., Inc., N.Y.C., 1960-66; pres. Rajah Press, Summit, N.J., 1963—; pres. Naimark and Barba, Inc., N.Y.C., 1966—. With USNR, 1944-46. Fellow AAAS, Am. Inst. Chemists; mem. Am. Chem. Soc., N.Y. Acad. Scis., Edinburgh (Scotland) Bibliog. Soc., Am. Mktg. Assn., Pharm. Advt. Coun., Med. Advt. Agy. Assn. (bd. dirs.). Author: A Patent Manual for Scientists and Engineers, 1961, Communications on Communication, 1971, 3d edit., 1987; patentee in field; contbr. articles in profl. jours. Home: 87 Canoe Brook Pky Summit NJ 07901-1404 Office: Naimark & Barba Inc 248 Columbia Tpke Florham Park NJ 07932-1210

NAIMI, SHAPUR, cardiologist; b. Tehran, Iran, Mar. 28, 1928; s. Mohsen and Mahbuba (Naim) N.; came to U.S., 1959, naturalized, 1968; M.B., Ch.B., Birmingham (Eng.) U., 1953; m. Amy Cabot Simonds, May 11, 1963; children—Timothy Simonds, Susan Lyman, Cameron Lowell. House physician Royal Postgrad Med. Sch. London, 1955; sr. house officer Inst. Diseases of the Chest, London, 1956; fellow in grad. tng. New Eng. Med. Center and Mass. Inst. Tech., 1961-64; cardiologist Tufts New Eng. Med. Center, Boston, 1966—, dir. intensive cardiac care unit, 1973—, asso. prof. Med. Sch., 1970—. Recipient Distinguished Instr. award, 1972, Teaching citation, 1976, Excellence in Teaching award, 1982 (all Tufts Med. Sch.); diplomate Royal Coll. Physicians London, Royal Coll. Physicians Edinburgh, Am. Bd. Internal Medicine (subsplty. bd. cardiovascular disease). Fellow Royal Coll. Physicians (Edinburgh), A.C.P., Am. Coll. Cardiology; mem. Am. Soc. Exptl. Biology and Medicine, Am. Heart Assn., Mass. Med. Soc. Clubs: Country Brookline; Cohasset Yacht. Contbr. to profl. jours. Home: 265 Woodland Rd Chestnut Hill MA 02167-2204 Office: 171 Harrison Ave Boston MA 02111-1854

NAIR, BALA RADHAKRISHNAN, engineer; b. Belgaum, Mysore, India, Feb. 14, 1936; came to U.S., 1967; s. Cherukatt Balakrishnan and Malamal Parvathy Nair; m. Indira Rajagopal Menon, Dec. 9, 1963; children: Nandita, Sarita. BS in Mech. Engring., U. Madras, 1959; MS in Indsl. Engring., Kansas State U., 1969. Jr. engr. Larsen & Toubro, Ltd., Bombay, 1959-60; trainee AEC, Bombay, 1960-61, scientific officer, 1961-64; asst. engr. Voltas Ltd., Bombay, 1964-67; sr. engr. Crane Co., Chgo., 1969-72; design engr. Rockwell Internat., Pitts., 1972-74; sr. prin. engr. Westinghouse Electric Corp., Pitts., 1984-78, engring. mgr., 1979—. Patentee in field; contbr. articles to profl. jours. Recipient grand prize Excellence in Design, Design News Mag., Chgo., 1988. Mem. Am. Soc. Mech. Engrs., Am. Nuclear Soc., Titanium Devel. Assn.. Republican. Hindu. Home: 610 Charles Dr Irwin PA 15642-1941 Office: Westinghouse Electric Corp PO Box 158 Madison PA 15663

NAIR, K. AIYAPPAN, computer science educator; b. Trivandrum, Kerala, India, Jan. 7, 1936; came to U.S., 1966; s. U. Karunakaran and Giourikutty (Amma) N.; m. K. B. Lalitha Kunjamma, May 30, 1966; children: Hari, Devi. BSc, U. Travancore, India, 1956; MSc, U. Kerala, 1958; PhD, SUNY, Buffalo, 1970. Lectr. U. Kerala, 1960-66; prof. Edinboro U. of Pa., 1971—. Mem. Am. Statis. Assn., Assn. Computing Machinery. Democrat. Hindu. Office: U Pa Dept Math and Computer Sci Edinboro PA 16444

NAIR, PADMANABHAN PADMANABHAN, biochemistry educator, researcher; b. Singapore, Nov. 9, 1931; came to U.S., 1960; s. Padmanabhan Krishna and Kunjulakshmy (Amma) N.; m. Prasanna Nair, July 12, 1959; children: Balagopal, Jaygopal, Ramgopal. BS, U. Coll., Trivandrum, India, 1951; MS, Bombay U., 1954, PhD, 1956. Rsch. officer ICMR project Inst. of Sci. Bombay U., 1956-58; rsch. officer All-India Inst. Med. Sci., New Delhi, 1958-60; rsch. assoc. McCollum-Pratt Inst. Johns Hopkins U., Balt., 1960-62, Fulbright scholar dept. biology, 1960-63, lectr. in medicine Sch. of Medicine, 1972-86; asst. prof. Sch. Hygiene & Pub. Health Johns Hopkins U., 1980-88, adj. assoc. prof. Sch. of Hygiene & Pub. Health, 1991—; rsch. assoc. biochemistry rsch. div. Sinai Hosp. of Balt., Inc., 1962-63, dir. biochemistry rsch. div., 1964-83; rsch. chemist human Nutrition Rsch. Ctr., Beltsville, Md., 1983—. Editor (treatise) The Bile Acids, vol. 2, 3, 4, 1971-88; contbr. and co-contbr. numerous articles to scholarly jours. Mem. AAAS (coun. Washington chpt. 1966-72, consortium internation programs 1979—), Am. Oil Chemists Soc. (assoc. editor LIPIDS 1974-84), Am. Inst. Nutrition, Am. Soc. Biochemistry and Molecular Biology, Am. Chem. Soc. Office: Lipid Nutrition Lab 10300 Baltimore Ave Beltsville MD 20705-2325

NAIR, VELUPILLAI KRISHNAN, cardiologist; b. Kerala, India, Dec. 30, 1941; came to U.S., 1973; s. Veupillai and Bharathy Nair; m. Sathy Nair, Apr. 22, 1971; children: Parvathy, Pradeep. BSc, Kerala U., Trivandum, India, 1961, MB BS, 1965, MD, 1971. Diplomate Am. Bd. Internal Medicine, Am. Bd. Cardiology. Asst. prof. N.Y. Med. Coll. Lincoln Hosp., Bronx, 1978-80; cardiologist, dir. cardiology svc. Somerset (Pa.) Hosp., 1980—, chief of med. dental staff, 1990—. Former pres. Somerset County divsn. Am. Heart Assn. Fellow Am. Coll. Cardiology; mem. AMA, Pa. Med. Soc., Somerset County Med. Soc. (former pres.), Soc. Hypertension, Soc. Echocardiography, Cardiac Club (advisor). Office: 223 S Pleasant Ave Somerset PA 15501

NAJMAN, RONALD, director media relations; b. N.Y.C., Mar. 13, 1948; s. Joseph and Emilie (Virgens) N. BA, Middlebury (Vt.) Coll., 1976. Asst. editor Saturday Rev. of the Arts, San Francisco, 1973-74; publicist corp. rels. ABC, Inc., N.Y.C., 1974-75; mgr. pub. rels. ABC News, Inc., N.Y.C., 1975-78; mgr. info. svcs. CBS News, Inc., N.Y.C., 1978-80; dir. news info. NBC News/NBC, N.Y.C., 1980-83; dir. media rels. Nat. Gay and Lesbian Task Force, N.Y.C., 1984-86, SUNY Health Sci. Ctr., Bklyn., 1987—. Contbr.: (AIDS manual) A Guide for Health Care Administrators National Health Publishing, 1988. Mem. King's County Dist. Atty. Community Adv. Bd., Bklyn., 1990—; vol. AIDS Med. Foun. (now Am. Found. for AIDS Rsch.), N.Y.C., 1983; v.p. Boerum Hill Neighborhood Assn., Bklyn., 1989—; bd. dirs. Hetrick-Martin Inst., Inc., N.Y.C., 1985-89. Democrat. Lutheran. Home: 210 Wyckoff St Brooklyn NY 11217-2229 Office: SUNY Health Sci Ctr 450 Clarkson Ave Brooklyn NY 11203-2098

NAKAI, YOSHIRO, aeronautical engineer, educator; b. Osaka, Japan, June 29, 1952; came to U.S., 1975; s. Victoria Ann Houle, Dec. 17, 1977; children: Mary Elizabeth, Katherine Eileen. B of Engring. in Aeronautics and Astronautics, Tokai U., Kanagawa, Japan, 1975; M of Engring in Aeronautical Engring., Rensselaer Poly. Inst., 1977. Lic. tech. translator in mech. engring. and applied physics Nat. Translation Inst. Sci. and Tech. of Japan. Rsch. asst. MIT Energy Lab., Cambridge, 1978-79; aerodynamics engr. Lockheed Ga. Co., Marietta, 1979-82, sr. aerodynamics engr., 1982-84; staff systems engr. Singer Link Corp., Binghamton, N.Y., 1984-88; project engr. CAE Link Corp., Binghamton, 1989—; instr. So. Tech. Inst., Marietta, 1983-84; speaker, 1990; evaulator Area II Contest, 1989. Rsch. grantee NSF, 1976; winner photo contest State of Maine Publicity Bur., 1991. Mem. AIAA (sr., award chmn. 1986, 90, sec. So. Tier 1988-90, 91—, Toastmasters (treas. Nat. Link Club 1986, ednl. v.p. 1987, pres. 1988), Susquehanna Club, Sigma Xi. Home: RR 7 Box 327 Binghamton NY 13904-9622 Office: PO Box 1237 Binghamton NY 13902-1237

NAKASONE, ROBERT C., retail toy and game company executive; b. 1947; married. BA, Claremont Coll., 1969; MBA, U. Chgo., 1971. With Brighams Ice Cream Parlor & Sandwich Shops, 1979-82; v.p., gen. mgrs. Jewel Food Stores, 1982-84; Midwest stores v.p. Toys R Us Inc., 1986-89; pres., vice-chmn. Toys R Us, USA, 1989—; pres. Toys R Us Worldwide Toy Stores; also bd. dirs. 1st lt. U.S. Army, 1979-82. Office: Toys R US Inc 461 From Rd Paramus NJ 07652 also: 395 W Passaic St Rochelle Park NJ 07662*

NAKAYAMA, TADASHI, treasurer; b. Shanghai, China, Oct. 3, 1932; came to U.S., 1968; s. Naoji and Yae (Egawa) N.; m. Shizue Yamada, Apr. 4, 1965; children: Kyoko, Manabu. BA in English Lit., Doshisha U., Kyoto, Japan, 1959. Asst. treas. The Mitsui Bank, Ltd., Osaka, Japan, 1952-55; asst. mgr. The Mitsui Bank, Ltd., Kyoto, 1955-59; mgr. The Mitsui Bank, Ltd., Tokyo, 1959-66, Nagoya, Japan, 1966-68, N.Y.C., 1968-73; dep. treas. UN, N.Y.C., 1974-83, treas., 1983—. Mem. Japanese Ednl. Inst. N.Y. (bd. dirs. 1983—). Home: 13510 Grand Central Pky Apt 109 Jamaica NY 11435-1051 Office: UN Hdqs New York NY 10017

NAKAZAWA, PAUL WESLEY, architect; b. Chgo., Feb. 8, 1951; s. Yoshio and Yuri Lilly (Takahashi) N.; m. Maria Laura Rocha, Jan. 24, 1951; children: Natalia, Marie-Nicole, Isabella. BA, U. Chgo., 1973, MBA, 1974; MArch, Harvard U., 1979. Registered architect Ill., N.J., N.Y., Conn., Mass., N.C. Archtl. designer Yosh Nakazawa & Assocs., Inc., Evanston, Ill., 1968-75, Edward Larabee Barnes, N.Y.C., 1979; mgr. fin. and adminstrn. B.A. Capital Corp., N.Y.C., 1979-81; exec. v.p. Nakazawa Corp., Charlotte, N.C., 1982-87; adj. to chmn. acquisitions, corp. strategic planning and fin., corp. sec. Office of Chmn. Tribble Harris Li Inc., Charlotte, 1987-90; mng. prin. Clark Tribble Harris & Li Architects, P.A., N.Y.C., 1989-90, Moshe Safdie & Assocs., Inc., Boston, 1990—; lectr. (studio) in Architecture U. N.C., Charlotte, 1982; mem. designer selection bd. Commonwealth Mass., 1991-93. Mem. AIA, N.Y. State Assn. Architects, Am. Phys. Soc., N.Y. Acad. Scis., Constrn. Specifications Inst., Am. Assn. for Artificial Intelligence, ASTM, Am. Arbitration Assn. (comml. panel).

NAKHLA, ATIF MOUNIR, biochemist; b. Cairo, Oct. 23, 1946; came to the U.S., 1981; s. Mounir and Afifa (Nagib) N. BS in Biochemistry, Cairo U., 1967, MS, 1971, PhD, 1975. Instr., lectr. Cairo U., 1967-80, assoc. prof., 1980-85; rsch. scientist Columbia U., N.Y.C., 1985—; postdoctoral fellow Aarhus (Denmark) U., 1976-79; fellow in residence Rockefeller U., N.Y.C., 1981-85. Contbr. articles to profl. jours. Fellow Danish Internat. Devel. Agy., 1976, World Health Orgn., 1981. Mem. AAAS, Am. Soc. Biochemistry and Molecular Biology, Endocrine Soc. U.S.A., Am. Recorder Soc., Egyptian Biochem. Soc., Sigma Xi. Home: PO Box 7917 Jersey City NJ 07307-0917

NAKOVICH, FRANK, electrical equipment manufacturing company executive; b. Marianna, Pa., Feb. 3, 1947; s. John and Margaret (Demko) N. B.S. in Physics, Washington and Jefferson Coll., 1969; M.B.A., Cleve. State U., 1983. Engring. asst., lab. technician Bethlehem Steel Corp., 1967-69; quality control technician Combustion Engring. Inc., Floreffe, Pa., 1970-72, quality control engr., Lancaster, Ohio, 1972-74; quality assurance engr./mgr. Halmar Electronics, Inc., Columbus, Ohio, 1974-77; sr. quality assurance engr., auditor Ocean Systems div. Gould Inc., Cleve., 1977-84; adminstr. quality assurance Govt. Systems div. RCA, Camden, N.J., 1984-87; supr. quality assurance research and devel. programs Allied-Signal Bendix Flight Systems Div., 1987—. Mem. Soc. Mfg. Engrs., Am. Soc. for Quality Control

(cert. quality engr., exec., Com. Phila. sect. 1984-86). Home: PO Box 1947 South Hackensack NJ 07606-0547 Office: Allied Signal Bendix Flight Systems Div Rte 46 Teterboro NJ 07608

NAKROSIS, STEPHEN M., newspaper editor; b. Newark, N.J., Feb. 12, 1965; s. John Daniel and Elena Mary (Miskewitz) N. BS in Mass Communication, Emerson Coll., 1987. Reporter Suburban Newspapers of North N.J., Paramus, 1987-88; editor West Hudson Pub., Kearny, N.J., 1989—. Mem. Kearny Emergency Mgmt. Bd., 1991. Mem. N.J. Pica Club (award 1988). Roman Catholic. Office: West Hudson Pub 531 Kearny Ave Kearny NJ 07032-2786

NALLY, THOMAS JOHN, urban planner; b. Brockton, Mass., Mar. 22, 1949; s. Frederick Ross and Alice Phyllis (Guidinas) N.; m. Susan Brownlee, July 22, 1983. BArch, Cornell U., 1972; MArch in Advanced Studies, MIT, 1977, M in City Planning, 1977. Registered architect, Mass. Designer Peirce, Pierce and Kramer, Boston, 1972-74; urban designer City Devel. Authority, Lowell, Mass., 1975; planner Massport, Boston, 1976; designer, planner Wallace, Floyd, Ellenzweig, Moore Inc., Cambridge, Mass. 1977-78; architect, planner, 1978-84; adminstrv. asst. to dep. commr. Mass. Div. Capital Planning and Ops., Boston, 1984-86, spl. unitcoordinator, 1986-87, spl. unit dep. dir., 1987-89; planning dir. Artery Bus. Com., Boston, 1989—; instr., thesis advisor Boston Archtl. Ctr., 1978-88; mem. alumni adv. panel dept. urban studies and planning MIT, 1988—. Recipient Urban Design award, Progressive Architecture Mag., 1979, Design for Transp. award, U.S. Dept. Transp./Nat. Endowment Arts, 1981. Mem. Am. Planning Assn. Democrat. Home: 17 Cushing Rd Brookline MA 02146-7553 Office: Artery Bus Com 13th Fl 600 Atlantic Ave Boston MA 02210

NAMBA, TATSUJI, physician, researcher; b. Changchun, China, Jan. 29, 1927; came to U.S., 1959, naturalized, 1968; s. Yosuke and Michino (Hinata) N. M.D., Okayama U., Japan, 1950, Ph.D., 1955. Asst., lectr. medicine Okayama U. Med. Sch. and Hosp., 1955-62; research assoc. Maimonides Med. Ctr., Bklyn., 1959-66; dir. neuromuscular labs. Maimonides Med. Ctr., 1966-70, dir. neuromuscular disease div., head electromyography clinic, 1966—; instr., asst. prof., assoc. prof. medicine State U. N.Y., Bklyn., 1959-76; prof. State U. N.Y., 1976—; mem. med. adv. bd. Myasthenia Gravis Found., 1968—. Recipient commendation for rsch. and clin. activities on insecticide poisoning Minister Health and Welfare, Japanese Govt., 1958; Fulbright scholar, 1959-62. Fellow ACP, Royal Soc. Medicine; mem. AMA, Am. Acad. Neurology, Am. Soc. Pharmacology and Exptl. Therapeutics, Am. Soc. Clin. Pharmacology and Therapeutics, Am. Assn. Electrodiagnostic Medicine. Office: 4802 10th Ave Brooklyn NY 11219-2999

NAMEROW, DAVID M., pediatrician; b. N.Y.C., Dec. 12, 1947; s. Nathan and Claire (Goodstein) N.; m. Pearila Brickner, June 14, 1981; children: Jordan Ilana, Evan Gabrielle, Zoe Alexandra. BS, CCNY, 1968; MD, U. Louisville, 1972. Pediatric intern Children's Hosp. Med. Ctr., Cin., 1972-73, resident in pediatrics, 1973-75; fellow in adolescent medicine U. Md. Hosps., Balt., 1975-77; pediatrician Plaza Med. Assocs., Flanders, N.J., 1977-79; dir. adolescent medicine St. Joseph's Hosp. Med. Ctr., Paterson, N.J., 1977-81; founder, pediatrician PediatriCare Assocs., Fair Lawn, N.J., 1979—; attending pediatrician Valley Hosp., Ridgewood, N.J., 1979—; adj. asst. clin. prof. pediatrics N.Y. Hosp.-Cornell Med. Ctr., N.Y.C., 1979—. Fellow Am. Acad. Pediatrics; mem. Soc. for Adolescent Medicine, Ambulatory Pediatric Assn. Office: PediatriCare Assocs 2020 Fairlawn Ave Fair Lawn NJ 07410

NANCE, FRANCIS CARTER, health facility administrator, educator, surgeon; b. Manila, Jan. 1, 1932; s. Dana Wilson and Anna (Boatner) N.; m. Patricia L. Terry, Feb. 14, 1959; children: Ellen, Michael, Catherine, John. Pre-med, Vanderbilt U., 1949-52, U. Tenn., 1952-53; MD and MS in Physiology, U. Tenn., 1959. Diplomate Am. Bd. Surgery, Nat. Bd. Med. Examiners. Intern U. Chgo. Clinics, 1959-60; asst. resident Hosp. of U. of Pa., 1960-64, chief resident in surgery, 1964-65; Harrison fellow dept. surg. rsch. U. Pa., 1960-65; instr. La. State U., New Orleans, 1965-67, asst. prof., 1967-69, assoc. prof. surgery and physiology, 1969-73; prof. surgery and physiology La. State U. Med. Ctr., New Orleans, 1973-85; chief burn svc. La. State U. Surg. Svc. Charity Hosp. of La., New Orleans; chmn. dept. surgery St. Barnabas Med. Ctr., Livingston, N.J.; clin. prof. surgery U. Medicine & Dentistry of N.J./N.J. Med. Sch., Newark; profl emeritus La. State U. Med. Ctr.; researcher in field. Contbr. numerous articles to profl. jours. Am. Cancer Soc. fellow, 1962-63, 63-64; grantee NSF, 1957-59, USPHS, 1964, Edward G. Schleider Edn. Found., 1967, 68, Parke-Davis Co., 1968, 69, Marion Labs., 1970, Eaton Labs., 1970, NIH, 1972, 74, Upjohn Co., 1974, 78, Lilly Co., 1976, McGraw Labs., 1977, Ethicon Co., 1979, Davis and Geck, 1985, 86, Johnson and Johnson, 1987. Mem. AAAS, ACS, Am. Assn. for Surgery of Trauma, Am. Burn Assn., Am. Coll. Emergency Physicians, Am. Gastroent. Assn., Am. Surg. Assn., Assn. Acad. Surgery, Assn. for Gnotobiotics, Assn. Program Dirs. in Surgery, Soc. Internat. Chirurgiae Digestivae, Soc. Surgery of the Alimentary Tract, Soc. Univ. Surgeons, Southern Med. Assn., Southern Soc. Clin. Surgeons, Southern Surg. Assn., Southeastern Surg. Congress, Surg. Assn. La., Surg. Infection Soc., N.J. Acad. Medicine, N.J. Gastroenterology Soc., N.J. Med. Soc., New Orleans Surg. Soc., Orleans Parish Med. Soc., Ravdin-Rhoads Surg. Soc., Soc. Internat. de Chirurgiae Digestivae, Soc. for Surgery of Alimentary Tract, Soc. for Univ. Surgeons, Southeastern Surg. Congress, So. Med. Assn., So. Soc. Clin. Surgeons, So. Surg. Assn., Surg. Assn. La., Surg. Infection Soc. Office: St Barnabas Med Ctr 94 Old Short Hills Rd Livingston NJ 07039

NANCE, MARJORIE GREENFIELD, educator; b. Brookline, Mass., Jan. 30, 1949; d. J. George and Bertha (Lotten) Greenfield; (div. Feb. 1991); 1 child, Rachel. BA, U. Mass., 1970; MEd, Boston State Coll., 1975, Lesley Coll., 1987. Cert. in elem. edn., spl. needs edn., and computer edn. Spl. needs tchr. Boston Pub. Schs., 1970-71, 4th grade tchr., 1971-73, 1st grade tchr., 1973-79, spl. needs tchr., 1980—. Parent rep. Milton (Mass.) Acad. Lower Sch. Parents' Assn., 1985-87, sec., 1987-88, v.p., 1988-89, pres., 1989-90; mem. core com. Multicultural Parents Assn. of Milton Acad., 1988-90; parent rep. Milton (Mass.) Acad. Upper Sch., 1992—; tri-chmn. Milton Acad. Parents for Diversity, 1991—. Impact II grantee, 1987, Horace Mann grantee, 1989, Boston Pub. Schs. Mem. ASCD, Coun. Spl. Educators. Home: 642 Brush Hill Rd Milton MA 02186-1306 Office: James W Hennigan Sch 200 Heath St Jamaica Plain MA 02130-1198

NAPARSTEK, NATHAN, school psychologist; b. Forest Hills, N.Y., Aug. 1, 1956; s. Chaim and Chana N.; m. Denise Kerman, May 1, 1983; children: Eli, Rachel, Joseph. PhD, SUNY, Albany, 1988. Lic. psychologist. Sch. psychologist Beacon City Schs., N.Y., 1981-83, Schenectady City schs., 1984—; adj. prof. Coll. St. Rose, 1989—; pvt. practice, Schenectady, 1991—. Mem. APA, NASP, N.Y. Assn. Sch. Psychologists. Home: 165 Glenridge Rd #a Schenectady NY 12302-4500

NAPIER, AUSTIN, physicist, educator; b. Jenkins, Ky., Aug. 18, 1947; s. Carl and Lena Thelma (Sergent) N.; m. Linda Elizabeth Cerveny, Dec. 6, 1972. BS in Physics, MIT, 1969, PhD in Physics, 1979. Rsch. assoc. high-energy physics Tufts U., Medford, Mass., 1979-80, asst. prof. physics, 1980-86, assoc. prof., 1986—; guest scientist Fermi Nat. Accelerator Lab., 1988-89. Contbr. articles to physics jours. Served with U.S. Army, 1971-73. NDEA fellow, 1973-76. Mem. AAUP, Am. Phys. Soc., Div. of Particles and Fields of Am. Phys. Soc., Computer Soc. of IEEE, Sigma Xi. Office: Tufts U Dept Physics Stacey Way # 4 Weymouth MA 02190-2653

NAPLES, RICHARD FRANCIS JOSEPH, JR., auto leasing consultant; b. New Britain, Conn., Oct. 21, 1957; s. Richard J. and Carol (Moore) N.; m. Debra L. Hanson, June 24, 1978; children: Christopher, Kelly-Marie. Cert. of Achievement, Wilson Learning, 1987. Cert. fin. planner. Auto lease mgr. Hoffman Enterprises, Avon, Conn., 1984-85; regional mgr. Shawmut Nat. Bank, Boston, 1987-88; regional sales mgr. auto lease div. Tammac Corp., Wilkes-Barre, Pa., 1986-90; pres. R & D Enterprises, Plainville, Conn., 1990—. Author: To Buy or Lease: A Simple Consumer Guide to the World of Automobile Leasing, 1991. Mem. Nat. Vehicle Leasing Assn., Nat. Orgn. Camps, Resort Camplands Internat. Office: R & D Enterprises 25 Chester St # 611 Plainville CT 06062-2409

NAPLES, SHARON J., advertising agency executive; b. Wilkes-Barre, Pa., June 14, 1952; d. John Joseph Jr. and Marguerite (Romik) Rodgers; m. Gary James Naples, May 10, 1980; 1 child, Sabrina Nichole. BFA, Wilkes Coll., 1974. Advt. artist Pomeroy's Dept. Store, Wilkes-Barre, Pa., 1975-76; creative dir. Sheldon Vale Assocs., Wilkes-Barre, 1976-82; owner, ptnr. Freelance Assocs., Kingston, Pa., 1982—. Active communications com. United Way of Wyoming Valley, Wilkes-Barre, Pa., 1985—, chairwoman communications and mktg. com., 1989, leadership vol., bd. dirs. Named Prominent Woman in Advt. H. Whitney McMillan Co., Sauk Rapids, Minn., 1983-84; recipient Gold, Silver, and Bronze Effective Retail Mktg. awards Retail Mktg. Group, Memphis, 1983, Bronze Telly award United Way of Wyo. Valley, 1992. Mem. Am. Inst. Graphic Artists. Democrat. Roman Catholic. Office: Freelance Assocs 471 Northampton St Wilkes Barre PA 18704-4559

NAPOLEON, DONALD PAUL, grocery store executive; b. Niagara Falls, N.Y., Apr. 10, 1954; s. Vincent Dominic and Lucy Ann (Manuse) N.; m. Justine Ann Wieszczyk, May 7, 1977; children: Rachel Marie, Rebecca Ann, Paul Vincent John. Assoc., Nat. Radio Inst., Washington, 1979. Night mgr. Tops Friendly Markets, Niagara Falls, 1972-76, asst. mgr., 1976-80, grocery mgr., 1980—; owner, prin. Cataract Refrigeration Co., Niagara Falls, 1979—. Mem. Niagara Coun. of Arts, 1989; mem. Parent Network, Buffalo, 1989; recording sec. United Cerebral Palsy Assn. of Niagara, Inc., 1989—. Mem. Refrigeration Svc. Engrs. Soc., Moose. Republican. Roman Catholic.

NAPOLITAN, GENE JOSEPH, JR., insurance company executive; b. Jamaica, N.Y., July 27, 1935; s. Gene Joseph and Ann Rita (Spinelli) N.; m. Erin Ann Gallagher, Oct. 23, 1965; children: Jessica Kate, Danielle Meg. BME, Stevens Inst. Tech., 1958. Field engr. Fire Ins. Rating Bur. N.J., Newark, 1958, 60-62, Mut. Svc. Office, Paterson, N.J., 1962-64; v.p., mgr. tech. lines Am. Internat. Underwriters/Am. Internat. Group, N.Y.C., 1964—. With U.S. Army, 1958-60. Home: 1013 Franklin Tpke Allendale NJ 07401-1315

NAPPER, ALVER WOODWARD, JR., advertising company executive, marketing manager; b. Greenwich, Conn., Sept. 23, 1943; s. Alver Woodward Sr. and Berenice (Norwood) N.; m. Katherin Kerns Elder, July 10, 1965 (div. July 1979). BFA in Advt. Design, Syracuse (N.Y.) U., 1965. Art dir. Owen, Mastro & Paul, Syracuse, 1965; dir. curriculum materials Devel. Ctr. Crusade for Opportunity, Syracuse, 1965-67; art dir. Ednl. Communications Ctr., SUNY, Stony Brook, 1967-68; project dir. Ednl. Communications Ctr., SUNY, Albany, 1968-73; prin. Woodward Assocs., Albany, 1971—; sr. group head, art dir. R.T. Blass Inc., Old Chatham, N.Y., 1983-84; v.p. Outreach Inc., Loudonville, N.Y., 1984-86; founder, mng. ptnr. Interlink, The Creative Network, Loudonville, 1990—; mem. adj. faculty Jr. Coll. of Albany, div. Russell Sage Coll., 1975, '87-89. Designer corp. logos. Mem. Ad Club (Newspaper award 1970, 71, Sales Promotion award 1973, 3 Nori awards 1992), Creative Club, Hudson River Club, Syraucse U. Alumni Assn. Home and Office: Woodward Assocs/Interlink 79A Wertman Ln Loudonville NY 12211

NAPPI, MAUREEN A., computer and video artist; b. Phila., May 1, 1951; d. Michael Pasquale and Quintina Marie (Marziani) N. BFA, NYU, 1976, MA, 1978. Video dir. Pop Network, N.Y.C., 1980-81; producer, dir. Ind. Prodn., 1981-82; graphic designer Satellite News Channel, 1982-83, MTV Network, N.Y.C., 1983-84; art dir. VCA Teletronics, Inc., N.Y.C., 1984, dir. computer graphics, 1984-85; ind. artist, dir. Maureen Nappi, Inc., N.Y.C., 1985—. Exhibiting artist at Tokyo Cen. Mus., 1991, Bronx Mus. of the Arts, 1991, Dallas Pub. Libr. Dist., 1990, Mus. of Modern Art, N.Y.C., 1989; contbr. articles to profl. jours. Organizer Media Consortium Against the War, 1991. Recipient Spl. Jury Gold award Houston Internat. Film Festival, 1990; recipient Broadcast Design Assn. award, 1990, Image du Futur Art award Cite des Arts et Nouvelle Technologia de Montreal, 1990. Mem. N.Y. State Coun. of the Arts (media prodn. panelist 1987-88), Women's Caucus for the Arts, Women Who Make Moves (bd. dirs. 1983-84), ACM/SIGGRAPH (bd. dirs., chmn. exhbn. com. 1990—). Home and Office: 229 W 78th St # 84 New York NY 10024-6638

NAPPY, NICHOLAS J., company owner; b. Bklyn., July 17, 1946; s. Nicholas and (Murena) N.; m. Clara Ines, Sept. 2, 1972; children: Nicole, Christina, Nicholas. AAS, N.Y.C. Community Coll.; BS, Pratt Inst. Owner, pres. Long Island Cho Factory, Northport, N.Y. Founder, pres. Nat. Jr. Baseball League, Northport, 1988. 1st lt. U.S. Army, 1969-70. Office: LI Cho Factory 395 Ft Salonga Rd Northport NY 11768-3099

NAPURANO, VIRGINIA, human resource specialist; b. Spangler, Pa., June 12, 1939; d. Michael and Mary (Sidwar) Salamanchuk; m. Frank W. Napurano, Oct. 19, 1957. BBA, Rider Coll., 1984, postgrad., 1985-86. Mgr. facility svcs. Squibb Corp., Princeton, N.J., 1982-84, mgr. adminstrn., 1984-85, dir. human resources, 1985-87, v.p. human resources, 1987-89; v.p. human resources Bristol Myers Squibb Co., Princeton, 1989-90; pres. The Learning Curve, Sergeantsville, N.J., 1990—. Contbr. articles to profl. jours. Chmn. Am. Diabetes Assn. Mercer, Princeton, 1988; sec. Delaware Twp. Environ. Assn., Sergeantsville, N.J., 1980-85. Mem. ASTD, Alpha Sigma Lambda. Office: The Learning Curve PO Box 232 Sergeantsville NJ 08557-0232

NARAD, JOAN STERN, psychiatrist; b. N.Y.C., June 21, 1943; d. Victor and Grete (Metzger) S.; m. Richard M. Narad; children: Christine, Laurie, Michael. BA, NYU, 1964; MD, Woman's Med. Coll., Pa., 1968. Diplomate Am. Bd. Psychiatry, Am. Bd Child Psychiatry. Intern pediatrics Stanford (Calif.) U. Hosp., 1968-69; resident adult psychiat. Med. Coll., Phila., 1969-71, chief resident in child psychiatry, 1971-73; grad. in psychoanalysis and child psychoanalysis Phila. Psychoanalytic Inst., 1978; practice medicine specializing in child and adolescent psychiatry Westport, Conn., 1979—; chief Adolescent and Young Adult Svc., Silver Hill Found., New Canaan, Conn., 1980-84, 89—; cons. Cath. Home Girls, Phila., 1971-78, Germantown Friends Sch., 1973-79; asst. prof. Child Psychiat. Med. Coll. Pa., 1975-79; asst. clin. prof. Yale Child Study Ctr., 1979-92, assoc. clin. prof., 1992—. Fellow NIMH, 1968. Fellow Am. Acad. Child and Adolescent Psychiat.; mem. Am. Psychiat. Assn., AMA, Alumnae Assn. Med. Coll. Pa., Am. Psychoanalytic Assn., Western New Eng. Psychoanalytic Soc., Conn. Coun. Child Psychiatry. Home: 3 Colony Rd Westport CT 06880-3703 Office: Silver Hill Hosp 280 Valley Rd New Canaan CT 06840-3812

NARAD, RICHARD M., safety engineer; b. Niagara Falls, N.Y., July 7, 1935; s. Marian F. and Mary (Blum) N.; m. Faye Erhard, June 16, 1962 (dec. 1977); children: Christine, Laurie; m. Joan Gabrielle Stern, June 2, 1978; 1 child, Michael. BS, U. New Haven, 1976. Safety engr. Aetna Life & Casualty, Buffalo, Boston, 1962-71; corp. safety mgr. Scovill Mfg. Co., Waterbury, Conn., 1971-77; dir. safety Brinks, Inc., Darien, Conn., 1977-79; dir. indsl. safety, hygiene and security Gulf & Western, N.Y.C., 1981-86; dir. corp. safety Wickes Cos., Inc., N.Y.C., Santa Monica, 1986-88; owner R.M. Narad & Assocs., Westport, Conn., 1988—; cons. in field; aj. instr. U. New Haven, 1975-81. With USAF, 1954-58. Mem. Nat. Safety Mgmt. Soc., Nat. Fire Protection Assn., Am. Soc. Safety Engrs. Address: 3 Colony Rd Westport CT 06880

NARATIL, WILLIAM ALBERT, educational media specialist; b. Palmerton, Pa., Oct. 10, 1936; s. William Anthony and Geraldine (Ruch) N.; m. Feb. 13, 1965; children: Joanna Mary, Elizabeth Ann, William Gregory. BS in Library Sci., BS in History, Kutztown State Coll., 1961, MLS, 1973; postgrad., Lehigh U., 1962. Libr. Pen Argyl (Pa.) High Sch., 1961-62, Hackettstown (N.J.) High Sch., 1963—. Bd. dirs. Hackettstown Pub. Libr., 19756, Warren County Audio-Visual Commn., 1966-68; day camp supr. Boy Scouts Am., 1990-91; committeeman Rep. party, Mansfield Twp., 1990-91. With USN, 1954-58. Named Coach of Yr. Hackettstown Gazette, 1985, N.J. Herald, Newton, 1990; named to Hall of Fame, N.J. State Coaches Assn., Robbinsville, N.J., 1989. Mem. ALA, NEA, N.J. Edn. Assn., Hackettstown Edn. Assn., Warren County Edn. Assn., NRA, UBNJ. Roman Catholic. Office: Hackettstown High Sch Warren St Hackettstown NJ 07840-2216

NARAYAN, K(RISHNAMURTHI) ANANTH, biochemist; b. Secunderabad, India, Oct. 1, 1930; came to U.S., 1954, naturalized, 1970; s. Ananthnarayan and Rukmani (Sreenivasan) Krishnamurthi; m. Suhasini Naik, Sept. 3, 1961; children—Krishnamuthi, Sheila. B.S. in Chemistry, Christian Coll., India, 1949; M.S. in Chem.Tech., Osmania U., India, 1951; Ph.D. in Food Tech., U. Ill., 1957. Research assoc. Wash. State U., Pullman, 1957-61; asst. prof. U. Ill., Urbana, 1962-71; research biochemist U.S. Army Natick Research and Devel. Ctr., Mass., 1971—. Contbr. chpts. to books. Grantee NIH, 1966-70, Am. Cancer Soc., 1968-70, Am. Heart Assn., 1967-71. Mem. Am. Oil Chemists Soc., Am. Inst. Nutrition, N.Y. Acad. Scis., Biochem. Soc., Soc. Exptl. Biologists. Hindu. Avocations: photography; woodworking; jogging. Home: 84 Indian Head Rd Framingham MA 01701-7920 Office: US Army R and D Ctr Food Engring Directorate Natick MA 01760-5020

NARAYAN, VISWANATHAN, social worker, educator; b. Bangalore, Mysore, India, Apr. 16, 1931; came to U.S., 1966; s. Krishnan and Visalakshi Narayan; m. Nalini Rangnekar, Mar. 31, 1963; children: Bhamati, Aditi. BA, Hislop Coll., Nagpur, India, 1950; MA, Delhi U., India, 1952; MS, Columbia U., 1957, PhD, 1961. Lectr. Sch. Social Work, Madras, India, 1952-54; dir. Inst. Social Work, Colombo, Sri Lanka, 1954-56; lectr. Tata Inst. Social Sci., Bombay, India, 1962-65; assoc. prof. U. Ill., Chgo., 1966-75; prof. Adelphi U., Garden City, N.Y., 1975—. Editor: Human Edge: Information Technology and Helping People, 1986; contbr. articles to profl. jours. Founder Carnatic Music Soc. N.Am., N.Y.C., 1976; bus. adv. coun. mem. Young Adult Inst., N.Y.C., 1985—. Fellow Columbia U., 1956, Asia Found. 1956-61, Nat. Acad. Scis. 1979. Hindu. Home: 215 Oyster Rd Locust Valley NY 11560 Office: Adelphi U Garden City NY 11530

NARDI RIDDLE, CLARINE, superior court judge; b. Clinton, Ind., Apr. 23, 1949; d. Frank Jr. and Alice (Mattioda) Nardi; m. Mark Alan Riddle, Aug. 15, 1971; children: Carl Nardi, Julia Nardi. AB, Ind. U., 1971, JD, 1974; LHD (hon.), St. Joseph Coll., 1991. Bar: Ind. 1974, Conn. 1979, U.S. Supreme Ct. 1980, U.S. Dist. Ct. Ind. 1974, Fed. Dist. Ct. Conn. 1980, U.S. Ct. Appeals (2d cir.) 1986; Cert. tchr., Ind. Staff atty. Ind. Legis. Svc. Agy., Indpls., 1974-78, legal counsel, 1978-79; dep. corp. counsel City of New Haven, 1980-83; counsel to atty. gen. State of Conn., Hartford, 1983-86, dep. atty. gen., 1986-89, acting atty. gen., 1989, atty. gen., 1989-91; judge Superior Ct., 1991—; asst. counsel state majority Conn. Gen. Assembly, Hartford, 1979, legal rsch. asst. to prof. Yale U., New Haven, 1979; legal counsel com. on law revision Indpls. State Bar Assn., 1979; mem. Chief Justice's Task Force on Gender Bias, Hartford, 1988-90; mem. ethics and values com. Ind. Sector, Washington, 1988-90; judge Superior Ct., State of Conn., 1991—. Bd. visitors Ind. U., Bloomington, 1974—; mem. Gov.'s Missing Children Com., Hartford, Conn. Child Support Guidelines Com., Gov.'s Task Force on Justice for Abused Children, Hartford, 1988-90. Named Conn. History Maker Women's Bur. & Permanent Commn. on Status of Women, U.S. Dept. Labor, 1989; recipient Citizen award Nat. Task Force on Children's Constl. Rights. Mem. ABA, Conn. Bar Assn. (chair com. on gender bias, Citation of Merit women and law sect. 1989), Nat. Assn. Attys. Gen. (chair charitable trusts and solicitation 1989-90), New Haven Neighborhood Music Sch. (bd. dirs.). Democrat. Presbyterian.

NARVEKAR, PRABHAKAR RAMKRISHNA, international financial agency official; b. Bombay, Jan. 5, 1932; came to U.S., 1951; s. Ramkrishna M. and Indira (Borekar) N.; m. Meera P. Rao, Jan. 21, 1959; children: Medha, Nirmal. Student, Sydenham Coll., Bombay, 1947-51, BCom, 1951; MA, Columbia U., 1953. Various positions IMF, Washington, 1953-85, dep. dir. European dept., 1979-80, dir. Asian dept., 1986-91, spl. advisor to mng. dir., 1991—. Contbr. articles to econ. jours. Home: 4701 Willard Ave Bethesda MD 20815

NASH, DAVID, physician; b. Syracuse, N.Y., Oct. 15, 1929; s. Sam and Pearl Nash; m. Ellen C. Nash, Sept. 2, 1956; children: Stephen, Robert. BA magna cum laude, NYU, 1950, MD, 1953. Diplomate Am. Bd. Internal Medicine. Intern Mt. Sinai, N.Y.C.; asst. resident in medicine Univ. Hosp., Syracuse; resident in medicine Mt. Sinai, N.Y.C.; med. rsch. fellow in cardiology Beth Israel Hosp. and Harvard Med. Sch., Boston; clin. prof. medicine Upstate Med. Ctr., Syracuse; mem. staff St. Joseph's Hosp., Syracuse; pres. DTN Clin. Rsch. Lab. Ltd., Syracuse, 1975—; manuscript reviewer JAMA, Annals of Internal Medicine, Am. Jour. Cardiology, Jour. of the Am. Coll. of Cardiology, Postgrad. Medicine, Geriatrics; presented papers at Am. Heart Assn., Am. Coll. Cardiology, N.Y. Acad. Medicine, Hugh Lofland Annual Conf. on Arterial Wall Metabolism, Cardiovascular Risk Factor Internat. Meeting. Contbr. over 120 articles to profl. jours. Maj. USAF, 1955-57. Fellow ACP, Am. Coll. Cardiology, Am. Coll. Nutrition, Am. Heart Assn. (coun. on arteriosclerosis, coun. on epidemiology), Onondaga County Med. Soc. Office: 600 E Genesee St Syracuse NY 13202-3108

NASH, DAVID BRET, physician; b. N.Y.C., Nov. 15, 1955; s. Albert J. and Charlotte Nash; m. Esther Jean Nash; children: Rachel and Leah (twins), Jacob. BA, Vassar Coll., 1977; MD, U. Rochester, 1981; MBA, U. Pa., 1986. Internship The Graduate Hosp., U. Pa., 1981-82, residency, 1982-84; med. dir. Health Evaluation Ctr., Hosp. U. Pa., Phila., 1988-90; dir. health policy and clin. outcomes Thomas Jefferson U. Hosp., Phila., 1990—. Editor: Future Practice Alternatives, 1987, Providing Quality Care, 1989. Bd. dirs. Delaware Valley Child Care Coun., Phila., 1988—. Fellow ACP; mem. Phi Beta Kappa. Office: Thomas Jefferson U 621 Curtis Bldg 1015 Walnut St Philadelphia PA 19107-5005

NASH, HOWARD ALLEN, biochemist, researcher; b. N.Y.C., Nov. 5, 1937; s. Harvey and Harriet (Ratner) N.; m. Dominie Maria Shortino, Aug. 31, 1963; children: Janet Elisabeth, Emily Julia. BS, Tufts U., 1957; MD, U. Chgo., 1961, PhD, 1963. Intern U. Chgo. Clinics, 1963-64; rsch. assoc. NIMH, Bethesda, Md., 1964-68, med. officer (res), 1968-84, chief, sec. molecular genetics, 1984—; chmn. Gordon conf. on Nucleic Acids, New Hampton, N.H., 1988; organizer work shop on Site-specific Recombination and Transp., Woods Hole, Mass., 1990. Assoc. editor Cell jour., 1985-91. Lt. comdr. USPHS, 1964-68. Recipient Superior Svc. award USPHS, 1985, Disting. Svc. award HHS, 1990. Fellow Am. Acad. of Arts & Sci.; mem. NAS, Am. Soc. for Biochemistry and Molecular Biology, Am. Soc. for Microbiology. Office: Lab Molecular Biology 9000 Rockville Pike Bethesda MD 20892-0036

NASH, JOHN N., professional basketball team executive; b. Phila., Nov. 28, 1946; s. John N. and Rosemary K. (Noon) N.; m. Anne Kelly (div.); children: Andrea, Carolyn; m. Ann Raley, Oct. 27, 1979; children: Brian, Barbara; stepchildren: Elizabeth, Meridyth. 1975-81. Dir. group sales Phila. 76ers, 1969-71, asst. gen. mgr., 1981-86, gen. mgr., 1986-90; ticket mgr. athletic dept. U. Pa., Phila., 1971-72, Phila. Blazers, 1972-73, Phila. Flyers, 1973-75; exec. sec. Big 5 Basketball, 1975-81; asst. gen. mgr., bus. mgr. Phila. 76ers, 1981-86, gen. mgr., 1986-90; v.p. and gen. mgr. Washington Bullets, 1990—. Office: Washington Bullets Capital Centre Landover MD 20785

NASH, JONATHAN DAVID, marketing professional, consultant; b. White Plains, N.Y., Sept. 27, 1955; s. Malcolm David and Phyllis Elaine (Van De Carr) N. BBA in Mgmt., Mercy Coll., 1977; MBA in Mktg., L.I. U., 1980. Sales mgr. Games Mgmt. Svcs., Valhalla, N.Y., 1978-85; freelance sports mktg. and bus. cons. Ossining, N.Y., 1985—. Editor (newsletter) Hudson Valley Navigator, 1989-91. World cup event organizer Internat. Orienteering Fedn., Fahnestock State Park, N.Y., 1986. Mem. U.S. Orienteering Fedn. (bd. dirs. mktg. and pub. rels. com. 1984—), Hudson Valley Orienteering (pres. bd. dirs. 1984—), Mercy Coll. Alumni Assn. (pres. 1986-88). Office: US Orienteering Fedn PO Box 1444 Forest Park GA 30051-1444

NASH, KAREN MARSTELLER, international manufacturer, designer; b. Washington, Aug. 30, 1943; d. Frederick Arell and Ruth Mary (Quinn) M.; m. Christian W. Myers, Oct. 4, 1963 (div. 1973); children: Christian W. III, Meredith Kennedy. Student, U. Va., Fredericksburg, 1961-63. Boatbuilder Solna Corp., Newport, 1974-75; boatbuilder, purchase mgr. Coddington Yachts, Jamestown, R.I., 1975-77; real estate assoc. Heritage Newport, 1978-84; boatbuilder, purchase mgr. Williams & Manchester Shipyard, Newport, 1983-87; boatbuilder, dir. purchasing Shannon Boat Co., Bristol, R.I., 1987-89, Aries Powercraft Ltd., Fall River, Mass., 1989-90; systems designer, mgr. Ronaco Internat. Inc., Fall River, Mass., 1990—, Guatemala and Nicaragua, 1990—; designer, cons. The Grand Design, Newport, 1975—; rsch. costume designer The R.I. Shakespeare Theatre, Newport, 1978—, Am. Renaissance Theatre, N.Y.C., 1982-84; design and systems cons. Blue Pelican Jazz Club,

Newport, 1983—. Bd. dirs. The R.I. Shakespeare Theatre, Newport, 1981-84, Cultural Affairs Commn., Newport, 1982-84, The Hill Assn., Newport, 1983-85. Recipient Rhody award Providence Jour., 1984; U.S. Dept. Interior grantee, 1978. Democrat. Episcopalian. Home: The Gothic Cottage 104 John St Newport RI 02840 Office: Wildcat Consulting 104 John St Newport RI 02840-3108

NASH, WILLIAM ARTHUR, civil engineer, educator; b. Chgo., Sept. 15, 1922; s. William A. and Rose (Keck) N.; m. Verna Lucile Baer, Aug. 8, 1953; children: Rebecca Ann, Phillip Arthur. B.S. in Civil Engring, Ill. Inst. Tech., 1944, M.S., 1946; Ph.D., U. Mich., 1949. Research engr. David W. Taylor Model Basin, Navy Dept., Washington, 1949-54; mem. faculty U. Fla., Gainesville, 1954-67; head dept. engring. mechanics U. Fla., 1964-67; prof. civil engring. U. Mass., Amherst, 1967—; cons. to govt. and industry; hon. prof. Shanghai Inst. Tech., 1985. Author: Theory and Outline of Strength of Materials, 2d edit, 1973, Statics and Mechanics of Materials, 1991, also 105 rsch. articles; editor: Internat. Jour. Nonlinear Mechanics, 1967—. Recipient Humboldt U.S. Sr. Scientist award to Fed. Republic Germany, 1986; named Outstanding Sr. Faculty Mem. in Engring., U. Mass., 1987. Fellow ASME; mem. Internat. Assn. Shell and Spatial Structures, Am. Soc. Engring. Edn. (Curtis W. McGraw Research award 1961), AIAA, Earthquake Engring. Research Inst. Congregationalist. Office: 235 Marston Hall U Mass Amherst MA 01003

NASLUND, HOWARD RICHARD, geology educator, researcher; b. Green Hills, Ohio, Nov. 25, 1950; s. Howard Walter and Marjorie Ann (Brenneman) N.; m. Cheryl Jackson Terrass, June 9, 1979; children: Sterling Terrass, Skye Jackson, Neelam Prarthana. BS in Geology, U. Ill., 1972; MS in Geology, U. Oreg., 1977, PhD in Geology, 1980. Predoctoral fellow Carnegie Inst., 1975-77; asst. prof. Dartmouth Coll., 1979-87; assoc. prof. SUNY, Binghamton, 1987—; assoc. chmn. dept.of geol. scis. SUNY, 1987-88, dir. grad. studies dept. geol. scis., 1988-92; chmn. dept. SUNY, Binghamton, 1992—; leader East Greenland Expeditions, 1985, 86, 88, 89, mem. 1974, 76, 81; scientist JOIDES-Ocean Drilling Program-LEG 140, 1991. Contbr. numerous articles and abstracts to profl. jours. Recipient NSF Rsch. grants, 1982-85, 88-91, 90-91, 90-92, NASA, 1985-88. Mem. Am. Geophys. Union, Geol. Soc. Am., Mineral. Soc. Am., Soc. for Mining, Metallurgy and Exploration, Mineral. Assn. Can. Unitarian. Home: 305 Brooks Ave Vestal NY 13850-2672 Office: SUNY Geol Scis Dept Binghamton NY 13902-6000

NASON, F(REDA) LEE, bank executive; b. Bridgeport, Conn., July 5, 1944; d. Walter Gustav and Ruth Mathilda (Fohrenbach) Mayer; m. Paul Harris Nason, Jan. 25, 1963 (div.); 1 child, George Harris; m. Donald Joseph Hunt, June 27, 1982 (div.). BS, Northeastern U., 1973; MArch, MIT, 1977. Lic. constrn. supr., Mass. Project mgr. real estate ops. New Eng. Tel. & Tel., Boston, 1971-82, dist. mgr. real estate ops., 1982-90; v.p. Shawmut, Inc., 1990—. Original sponsor Proposition 2-1/2, Mass., 1980; conv. credentials committeeperson Libertarian Nat. Party, 1978-80, chmn. Mass., 1978; dir. Ballot Access New England. Mem. Nat. Assn. Women in Constrn., Assn. Libertarian Feminists (treas. 1983—, editor, 1983-89), Internat. Facilities Mgmt. Assn. (treas. Boston chpt. 1987-91, v.p. 1992), New England Constrn. Users Coun. (pres. 1991—).

NASON-CRUZ, SALLY AURELIA, psychologist; b. Vieques, P.R., Jan. 1, 1946; d. Theodore Albers and Flor de Osiris (Cruz) Nason. BS, Inter-Am. U. P.R., 1969; MS, Inst. Psicológico P.R., 1972; PhD, Caribbean Ctr. Postgrad. Studies, San Juan, 1987. Lic. psychologist, N.Y. With Psychol. Services P.R., Caguas, 1971-73; clin. psychologist Agencia Sobre Problemos Adicción a Drogas, Santurce, P.R., 1972-73, Eastside Methadone Maintenance Service, N.Y.C., 1974-76; supr. Hispanic Research Ctr., N.Y.C., 1980-82; clin. psychologist Luth. Mental Health Ctr., N.Y.C., 1980-83; sch. psychologist N.Y. Bd. Edn., N.Y.C., 1984—; group therapist dept. employment Commonwealth P.R., 1972; instr. Universidad del Sagrado Corazon, San Juan, 1973; researcher Tchr.'s Coll., Columbia U., 1979; psychotherapist Behaviorial Coun. Assocs. Ft. Lee, N.J., 1988—. Contbr. articles to profl. jours. Mem. Nichren Shoshu Am., 1984. Commonwealth P.R. scholar, 1971, Presdl. scholar Fordham U., 1978. Mem. Nat. Assn. Sch. Psychologists, Delta Tau Gamma. Buddhist. Home and Office: 32 Valley Pl Edgewater NJ 07020-1312

NASR, SALAH, sales manager; b. Alexandria, Egypt, May 31, 1952; came to U.S., 1972; s. Nasreldin and Fawzia (Shahata) Mohamed; m. Chris Assini (div. 1981); m. Elizabeth A., July 15, 1982; children: Adam K., Amanda E., Adrian S. Student, Alexandria U. Commerce, Egypt, 1968-72. Waiter Theodore's Restaurant, N.Y.C., 1974-75; waiter, mgr. Astera Food's, N.Y.C., 1975-77; free-lance photographer N.Y.C., 1977-78; mgr. Jay Dee Restaurant, Troy, N.Y., 1979-80; sales rep. Cooley VW Corp., Rensselaer, N.Y., 1980-84; sales mgr. Paine Webber, Albany, N.Y., 1984-90; chmn. Alexandria Group of N.J. Corp., Princeton, 1987—. Appearances on local TV fin. talk shows, 1986-88. Fund raising vol. March of Dimes, Albany, 1988-89, Princeton, 1988-89, bd. dirs., N.E. chpt. Mem. Owl Creek Club. Republican. Moslem. Home: 2 Shore Dr Waretown NJ 08758-9339 Office: Alexandria Group NJ Corp 19A-1594 Rt 9 Toms River NJ 08755

NASRA, GEORGE YOUSEF, banker; b. Bethlehem, Jordan, Aug. 19, 1947; came to U.S., 1986; s. Yousef Antoine and Victoria (Touchie) N.; m. Diana Mitri Madanat, Dec. 26, 1977; children: Tala, Anas, Mais. BA in Econs., U. Jordan, 1970; postgrad., U. Houston, 1985, MIT, 1987. Credit officer Grindlays Bank, Amman, Jordan, 1971-76; asst. mgr. credit and mktg. Chase Manhattan Bank, Amman, 1976-79; dep. head internat. banking group Nat. Bank Kuwait, Kuwait City, 1979-85; dep. gen. mgr. Nat. Bank Kuwait, N.Y.C., 1986-88, gen. mgr., 1988—. Mem. Inst. Internat. Bankers (bd. dirs.). Office: Nat Bank Kuwait 299 Park Ave New York NY 10171-0002

NASSAU, KURT, material science consultant, freelance author; b. Stockerau, Austria, Aug. 25, 1927; came to U.S., 1948; s. Julius and Frieda (Hauser) N.; m. Julia Wechsler, June 21, 1949. BS with honors, U. Bristol, Eng., 1948; PhD, U. Pitts., 1959. Rsch. and devel. chemist Glyco Products, Inc., Williamsport, Pa., 1948-54; rsch. scientist Walter Reed Army Med. Ctr., Washington, 1954-56, AT&T Bell Labs., Murray Hill, N.J., 1959-89; vis. prof. Princeton (N.J.) U., 1989-90; pres. Nassau Cons., Lebanon, N.J., 1990—; mem. bd. govs. Gemological Inst. Am., Santa Monica, Calif., 1975—. Author: (book) Gems Made by Man, 1980, The Physics and Chemistry of Color, 1983, Gemstone Enhancement, 1984, (article Colour) Ency. Britannica, 1988; contbr. over 350 articles to profl. jours. With U.S. Army, 1954-56. Fellow Am. Ceramic Soc., Am. Mineral. Soc.; mem. Am. Chem. Soc., Am. Optical Soc., Am. Crystallographic Assn., Phi Lambda Upsilon (pres. 1958-59). Home and Office: 154A Guinea Hollow Rd Lebanon NJ 08833

NATALIE, ANDREA LEIGH, cartoonist, publisher; b. Norwich, N.Y., Feb. 12, 1958; d. Barbara Violanda (Natali) Silverman. Student, Cornell U., 1976-78. Nationally syndicated cartoonist, 1989—; pres. Venus Press, Guttenberg, N.J., 1990—; pres., founder Lesbian Cartoonist Network, Guttenberg, 1990—. Author: Stonewall Riots, 1990 (Lambda Literary award finalist 1990). Named Reader's Choice Favorite, Hot Wire Mag., 1991. Office: Venus Press 7100 Boulevard E West New York NJ 07093-4717

NATANSOHN, SAMUEL, research chemist; b. Rzeszow, Poland, June 18, 1929; came to U.S., 1949; s. Saul Natansohn and Rose (Teitelbaum) Weinbach; m. Sidonia Schwimmer, June 20, 1951; children: Deborah Linda, Rena Bella, Sharon Fay, Saul. Student, U. Frankfurt, Fed. Republic of Germany, 1948-49; BA in Chemistry, Bklyn. Coll., 1955, MA in Phys. Chemistry, 1959. Various positions GTE Labs. (predecessor firms Sylvania Basic Rsch. Labs.), Bayside, N.Y., 1955-85; sr. staff scientist GTE Labs., Waltham, Mass., 1985—. Inventee in field; contbr. articles to profl. jours. President GTE Labs. Sigma Xi chpt., Waltham, 1979-80, Temple Israel, Sharon, Mass., 1980-81, 85-86, The 25 Yr. Club of GTE Labs., Waltham, 1986-87. Named Man of the Yr., Brotherhood of Temple Israel, 1982. Mem. ASTM, Am. Ceramic Soc., Am. Chem. Soc., Metall. Soc. Home: 5 Briggs Pond Way Sharon MA 02067-3009 Office: GTE Labs 40 Sylvan Rd Waltham MA 02154-1168

NATHAN, KURT, consulting engineer; b. Essen, Ger., June 27, 1920; s. Ludwig and Emmy (Meyer) N.; m. Barbara Enid Wilson, July 17, 1948; 1 child, Bernard David. BS, Cornell U., 1946, MS, 1948; BSAE, Rutgers U., 1955. Registered profl. engr., N.J.; profl. land surveyor, N.J. Teaching asst. Cornell U., Ithaca, N.Y., 1946-48; asst. prof. Del. Valley Coll., Doylestown, Pa., 1948-51; rsch. assoc. to prof. engring. Rutgers - The State U. of N.J., New Brunswick, 1951-82; pres. Conservation Engring., P.A., Somerset, N.J., 1981—; mem. adv. com. tech. manual for stream encroachment N.J. Dept. Environ. Protection, Trenton, 1981-84, N.J. Dept. Agr., Stds. for Erosion Control, Trenton, 1973-87. Co-author: Site Engineering for Landscape Architects, 1985; author: Basic Site Engineering for Landscape Designers, 1975; contbr. articles to profl. jours. Pres. Franklin Twp. Bd. Edn., Somerset, N.J., 1962, 63. NSF grantee, 1966, 71. Mem. NSPE (chpt. pres. 1968-69), ASCE, Am. Soc. Agrl. Engrs. (life sr. mem.), Am. Water Resources Assn., Sigma Xi, Phi Kappa Phi. Jewish. Home: 144 Dayton Ave Somerset NJ 08873-1966

NATHAN, PHYLLIS KLEINFELD, educator; b. Bklyn., Jan. 2, 1947; d. Ely Eric and Renee (Mertik) Kleinfeld; m. H. Ronald Nathan, Aug. 27, 1967; children: Edward Eric, Corey Scott. BA cum laude, Bklyn. Coll., 1967; MS in Edn., Richmond Coll., 1973. Cert. early childhood educator, N.Y. Kindergarten tchr. P.S. 14, Staten Island, N.Y., 1967-69, P.S. 29, Staten Island, 1973-80, P.S. 60, Staten Island, 1980—; music workshop leader N.Y.C. Bd. Edn. Dist. 31, Staten Island, 1988-89. Editor: (newsletters) ThORTfully Yours, 1980-83, Dutchman 200, 1985—. Equipment mgr. Manalapan (N.J.) Little League, 1982-85. Mem. Staten Island Early Childhood Assn. (music cons. 1988), Erasmus Hall High Sch. Alumni Assn. (exec. bd. 1985—), Hadassah (life mem.), Kappa Delta Pi. Home: 15 Scott Ln Englishtown NJ 07726-2916 Office: Alice Austen Sch PS 60 55 Merrill Ave Staten Island NY 10314-3397

NATHANS, DANIEL, biologist; b. Wilmington, Del., Oct. 30, 1928; s. Samuel and Sarah (Levitan) N.; m. Joanne E. Gomberg, Mar. 4, 1956; children: Eli, Jeremy, Benjamin. B.S., U. Del., 1950; M.D., Washington U., 1954. Intern Presbyn. Hosp., N.Y.C., 1954-55; resident in medicine Presbyn. Hosp., 1957-59; clin. assoc. Nat. Cancer Inst., 1955-57; guest investigator Rockefeller U., N.Y.C., 1959-62; prof. microbiology Sch. Medicine, Johns Hopkins, 1962-72, prof., dir. dept. microbiology, 1972-82, Univ. prof. molecular biology and genetics, 1982—; sr. investigator Howard Hughes Med. Inst., 1982—. Recipient Nobel prize in physiology or medicine, 1978. Fellow Am. Acad. Arts and Scis.; mem. NAS, Pres.'s Coun. Advisers on Sci. and Tech. Office: Johns Hopkins U Dept Molecular Biology & Genetics 725 N Wolfe St Baltimore MD 21205-2105

NATHANSON, BENJAMIN, chemist, educator; b. N.Y.C., Jan. 9, 1929; s. Morris and Clara (Crystal) N. BS, CCNY, 1947; MA, Columbia U., 1949; PhD, NYU, 1965. Instr. dept. chemistry Finch Coll., N.Y.C., 1966-67; asst. prof. dept. chemistry Pratt Inst., N.Y.C., 1967; lectr. dept. chemistry Pace Coll., N.Y.C., 1967-68; sr. chemist N.Y.C. Dept. Environ. Protection, 1968—; adj. asst. prof. dept. chemistry Cooper Union, 1976, 85. Contbr. articles to profl. jours. Mem. Am. Chem. Soc. Home: 470 W 24th St Apt 7G New York NY 10011-1210 Office: NYC Dept Environ Protection 51 Astor Pl Rm 643 New York NY 10003-7184

NATION, JOHN ARTHUR, electrical engineering educator, researcher; b. Bridgwater, Eng., Aug. 8, 1935; came to U.S., 1965; naturalized, 1991.; s. Arthur John and Doris Edith (Rides) N.; m. Sally Gillian Leeds, May 31, 1961; children—Philip David, Robert James. B.Sc., Imperial Coll., London, 1957; Ph.D., Imperial Coll., 1960. Cons. Comitato Nazionale per L'Energia Nucleare, Frascati, Italy, 1960-61; staff physicist Central Electricity Generating Bd., Leatherhead, Eng., 1962-65; elec. engring. faculty Cornell U., Ithaca, N.Y., 1965—; prof. Cornell U., 1978—, dir. Sch. Elec. Engring., 1984-89; cons. miscellaneous cos., 1965—. Contbr. articles to profl. jours. Fellow Am. Phys. Soc., IEEE (plasma scis. exec. com. 1985-89, chair com. 1987-88, Centennial medal 1984). Home: 1041 Hanshaw Rd Ithaca NY 14850-2741 Office: Cornell U 325 Engring & Theory Ctr Ithaca NY 14853

NAUGHTON, ANN ELSIE, educator; b. N.Y.C., Apr. 27, 1942; d. George and Wilma (Lubitz) Bruning; m. Gerald Richard Naughton, Dec. 26, 1965 (dec. Apr. 1983); 1 child, Jonathan. BA, CUNY, 1963; MA, Columbia U., 1965; postgrad., Greenburgh Inst. Tchrs. Social worker div. child and family welfare Westchester County, Yonkers, N.Y., 1963-64; tchr. Hastings On Hudson (N.Y.) Pub. Schs., 1965—; tchr. Lincoln Ctr. Inst., N.Y.C., 1986—. Mem. Hastings Tchrs. Union (mem.-at-large exec. com. 1982—, state facilitator and trainer N.Y. parent tchrs. confs. 1988—, exec. com. 1982-88, corr. sec. 1989—), N.Y. Zool. and Ecol. Habitat (trainer 1991—). Home: 31 Walbrooke Rd Scarsdale NY 10583-2743 Office: Hastings On Hudson Pub Schs Hastings On Hudson NY 10706

NAUGHTON, JAMES, actor; b. Middletown, Conn., Dec. 6, 1945; s. James Joseph and Rosemary (Walsh) N.; m. Pamela Parsons, Oct. 1968; children: Gregory J., Keira P. BA, Brown U., 1967; MFA, Yale U., 1970. Broadway appearances include Edmund in Long Day's Journey Into Night, 1971 (Theatre World award, N.Y. Drama Critics award, Vernon Rice award 1971), Stone in City of Angels (Tony award 1990, Drama Desk award), I Love My Wife, 1977, Whose Life Is It Anyway, 1980; (feature films) Paper Chase, 1972, Glass Menagerie, 1986, Good Mother, 1988.

NAUMANN, HANS JUERGEN, manufacturing company executive; b. Fed. Republic Germany, May 5, 1935; came to U.S., 1960; s. Herbert and Elfriede (Heydenreich) N.; m. Edith Huempel; children: Irene, Michelle, Jacqueline, John. MME, U. Hamburg, Fed. Rep. Germany, 1960; MBA, Rochester (N.Y.) U., 1965. Registered profl. engr., N.Y. Mgr. engring. Farrell Corp., Rochester, 1961-66; exec. v.p. Hegenscheidt Corp., Troy, Mich., 1966-70; pres., chief exec. officer, stockholder Hegenscheidt GmbH, Erkelenz, Fed. Republic Germany, 1970-82; chmn., chief exec. officer Internat. Knife Corp., Erlanger, Ky., 1982-84; chmn. bd., chief exec. officer, stockholder Simmons Machine Tool Corp., Albany, N.Y., 1984—. Author: Tool and Manufacturing Engineering Handbook, 1976; patentee roller finishing and deep rolling. Bd. dirs. U. Albany Fund, Inc., 1986—. Mem. ASME, SAE, Am. Inst. Mgmt. (pres.'s coun.), Am. Mgmt. Assn., Am. Pub. Transit Assn., Verein Deutscher Ingenieure, Soc. Mech. Engrs., Capital Region Tech. Devel. Coun., Capital Region World Trade Coun., Assn. for Mfg. Tech. (formerly Nat. Machine Tool Builders Assn.), Albany Colonie Regional C. of C., Rwy. Supply Assn., N.Y. R.R. Club Inc., Lions (past pres.). Home: 26 Folmsbee Dr Albany NY 12204-1206 Office: Simmons Machine Tool Corp 1700 Broadway Albany NY 12204-2793

NAVA, ELOY LUIS, clothing executive; b. N.Y.C., May 19, 1942; s. Eloy and Dolores Nava; m. Diane Margret Binder, Dec. 21, 1968; children: Alyson Beth, David Eloy. BMgmt Engring., Rensselaer Poly. Inst., 1964, BMech. Engring., 1965, MSMgmt., 1970. Indsl. engr. Johnson & Johnson Inc., Troy, N.Y., 1965-66; nuclear project engr. and chief nuclear test engr. to ops. analysis project mgr. Electric Boat Div., Gen. Dynamics Corp., Groton, Conn., 1966-78; ptnr., chief fin. officer Collado Ozamiz Co., N.Y.C., 1978-88; pres., chmn. bd. JB Apparel Corp., N.Y.C., 1984—; bd. dirs. Jose Blanco Inc., Santo Domingo, Dominican Republic; mgmt., fin. cons. various orgns. in Dominican Republic. Chmn. water, sewer com. City of Waterford, Conn., 1975-77; mem. Rep. Nat. Com.; swimming ofcl. YMCA, USS. Mem. Midwest Decoy Collectors Assn., NRA, Am. Philatelic Soc., Country Club of Darien (Conn.). Roman Catholic. Home: 15 Pasture Ln Darien CT 06820-5618

NAVARRO, BELTRAN, management consultant; b. Port of Spain, Trinidad, Sept. 6, 1945; s. Rafael and Isabel (Gonzalez) N.; m. Young Mi Kim, May 24, 1979. Licenciado Chemistry, UCV, Caracas, Venezuela, 1972; MEd, Ind. U., 1977, MS in Chemistry, 1979; degree in bus., IESA, Caracas, 1981; degree in project mgmt., Fubd Getulio Vargas, Rio de Janeiro, 1982; degree in pub. adminstrn., UNDP, Caracas, 1983. Head gen. studies IUTET, Valera, Venezuela, 1979-80; dep. dir. Mersifrica, Caracas, 1980-81; dir. acads. Politecnico Luis C. Mejias, Caracas, 1981-84; dir. Navarro, Kim & Assocs., Balt., 1984—; bd. dirs. Colegio Venezeula de Productores de Seguros, Caracas, Venezuela, 1988-89; cons. Congress of Venezuela, Caracas, 1979—. Recipient Briscoe award Ind. U. Bloomington, Ind., 1976, 27th of June Order Venezuelan govt., Caracas, Venezuela, 1983. Mem. Venezuelan-Am. Club of Md., D.C. and Va. (pres. 1991).

NAVAS, WILLIAM ANTONIO, JR., military officer, civil engineer; b. Mayaguez, P.R., Dec. 15, 1942; s. William Antonio Sr. and Ethel Ines (Marin) N.; m. Wilda Margarita Cordova Navas, Aug. 7, 1965; children: William Antonio III, Gretchen Maria. BSCE, U. P.R., 1965; MS in Engring. Mgmt., U. Bridgeport, 1979. Registered profl. engr., P.R. Commd. 2d. lt. U.S. Army, 1966, advanced through grades to maj. gen., 1990; served in U.S. Army Corps of Engrs., 1966-70; with Interamerican Def. Coll., Washington, 1981-82; dir. ops. P.R. Army Nat. Guard, San Juan, 1982-84, 84-87; comdr. Engr. Task Force, Panama, 1984; dep. dir. N.G. Bur., Washington, 1987—; vice chief Nat. Guard Bur., 1990; project engr. Empresas Navas, Inc., Mayaguez, P.R., 1970-72; ptnr., prin. W.A. Navas Jr. & Assoc., Mayaguez, 1972-80; dir. Navas & Moreda, Inc., Mayaguez, 1973-81; chmn. Dept. of Army Hispanic Employment Commn., Washington, 1988. Mem. Nat. Guard Assn. of the U.S. (del. 1980-86), Nat. Guard Assn. of P.R., Soc. of Am. Mil. Engrs. Republican. Roman Catholic. Home: Qtrs # 16A Fort Myer VA 22211 Office: NG Bur The Pentagon Washington DC 20013

NAVASKY, VICTOR SAUL, magazine editor; b. N.Y.C., July 5, 1932; s. Macy and Esther Blanche (Goldberg) N.; m. Anne Landey Strongin, Mar. 27, 1966; children: Bruno, Miri, Jenny. A.B., Swarthmore Coll., 1954; LL.B., Yale U., 1959. Spl. asst. to Gov. G. Mennen Williams, Mich., 1959-60; editor-in-chief, pub. Monocle Mag., 1961-65; editor N.Y. Times mag., 1970-72; editor-in-chief The Nation mag., N.Y.C., 1978—; vis. scholar Russell Sage Found., 1975-76; Ferris prof. journalism Princeton U., 1976-77. Author: Kennedy Justice, 1971 (Nat. Book Award nominee), Naming Names, 1980 (Am. Book award 1981), rev. edit., 1991; editor: (with C. Cerf) The Experts Speak, 1984. Mem. bd. mgrs. Swarthmore Coll., 1991—. Served with U.S. Army, 1954-56. Guggenheim fellow, 1974-75. Mem. Author's Guild Coun., PEN (exec. com.), Com. to Protect Journalists (exec. com.), Phi Beta Kappa. Democrat. Jewish. Office: Nation 72 5th Ave New York NY 10011-8004

NAVKAL, SHREE HARI, information services executive, financial planner; b. Bombay, India, Dec. 27, 1946; came to U.S., 1968; s. Harirao K. and Shanta H. (Meena) N.; m. Mary L. Smith, Nov. 29 (div. Oct. 1983); 1 child, Vaishali. BS in Mech. Engring., Indian Inst. Tech., Bombay, 1968; MS in Indsl. Engring. and Mgmt., Okla. State U., 1971. Systems mgr. Computer Logistics Corp., Chgo., 1969-73; sect. mgr. Western Union Teleprocessing Inc., Mahwah, N.J., 1973-75; sr. project mgr. Morgan Stanley & Co., N.Y.C., 1975-82; v.p. Chase Manhattan Bank, N.Y.C., 1982-84, Decision Strategies, Inc., Hasbrook Heights, N.J., 1984-86; sr. v.p., MIS dir. Putnam Investor Svc., Boston, 1986-88; v.p. First Boston Corp., N.Y.C., 1988—. Home: 356 Fairmount Rd Ridgewood NJ 07450 Office: First Boston Corp 5 World Trade Ctr New York NY 10048

NAVROZOV, LEV, writer, columnist; b. Moscow, Nov. 26, 1928; came to U.S., 1972; s. Andrei and Dina (Mintz) N.; m. Muza Levit, Jan. 2, 1956; 1 child, Andrei. BA, Moscow Inst. Fgn. Langs., 1953. Columnist N.Y.C. Tribune, 1981—; also, freelance writer. Author: The Education of Lev Navrozov, 1975; contbr. numerous articles to publs. Pres. Ctr. Survival of Western Democracies, 1978—, Alternatives to N.Y. Times Com., 1978—. Home: 3419 Irwin Ave Riverdale NY 10463

NAWY, EDWARD GEORGE, civil engineer, educator; b. Baghdad, Iraq, Dec. 21, 1926; came to U.S., 1957, naturalized, 1966; s. George M. and Ava (Marshall) N.; m. Rachel E. Shebbath, Mar. 23, 1949; children: Ava Margaret, Robert M. DIC, Imperial Coll. Sci. and Tech., London, 1951; CE, MIT, 1959; D of Engring., U. Pisa, Italy, 1967. Registered profl. engr., N.J., N.Y., Pa., Calif., Fla. Head structures Israel Water Planning Authority, Tel-Aviv, 1952-57; mem. faculty Rutgers U., New Brunswick, N.J., 1959—; mem. grad. faculty Rutgers U., 1961—, prof. civil engring., 1966-72, Distinguished prof. (prof. II), 1972—, chmn. dept. civil and environ. engring., dir. grad. programs, 1980-86; chmn. Coll. Engring. Del. Assembly, 1969-72; mem. Univ. Senate, 1973-80, also mem. exec. com.; also faculty rep. mem. bd. govs. and trustee; Guest prof. Nat. U. Tucuman, Argentina, summer 1963, Imperial Coll. Sci. and Tech., summer 1964; vis. prof. Stevens Inst. Tech., Hoboken, 1968-72; hon. prof. Nanjin Inst. Tech., China, 1987; mem. N.J. Chancellor Higher Edn. Com. for Higher Edn. Master Plan; mem. bridge com., Rutgers U. rep. Transp. Research Bd.; cons. to industry; U.S. mem. commn. on cracking Comité EuroInternat. du Beton; mem. Civil Engring. Tech. Adv. Council N.J., 1966-72; concrete systems cons. FAA, Washington; cons. energy div. U.S. Gen. Accounting Office, Washington; gen. chmn. Internat. Symposium on Slabs and Plates, 1971; mem. hon. presidium RILEM Internat. Conf., Budapest, 1977. Author: Reinforced Concrete, 1985, 2d edit., 1990, Simplified Reinforced Concrete, 1986, Prestressed Concrete, 1989; contbr. over 115 articles to profl. publs. Vice pres. Berkeley Twp. Taxpayers Assn., Ocean City, N.J., 1966-70. Recipient merit citation and award N.J. Concrete Assn., 1966; C. Gulbenkian Found. fellow, 1972. Fellow ASCE (mem. joint com. on slabs), Instn. Civil Engrs. (London), Am. Concrete Inst. (pres. N.J. chpt. 1966, 77-78, chmn. nat. com. on cracking 1966-73, bd. com. chpts. 1969-72, ACI rep. internat. commn. fractures, H.L. Kenneday award 1972, award of recognition N.J. chpt. 1972, chpt. activities award 1978, chmn. nat. com. on deflection 1989—); mem. NSPE, AAUP (chmn. budget and priorities com Rutgers U. chpt. 1972), Am. Soc. Engring. Edn., Prestressed Concrete Inst. (Bridge Competition award 1971, mem. tech. activities com.), N.Y. Acad. Scis., N.J. Bldg., Tall Bldgs. Coun., Contractors Assn. (cons. ednl. com.), Rotary, Sigma Xi, Tau Beta Pi, Chi Epsilon (hon.). Office: Rutgers State U of NJ Civil Engring Dept New Brunswick NJ 08855

NAYERAHMADI, HABIB, psychologist; b. Tehran, Iran, Apr. 4, 1949; came to U.S., 1975; s. Younes Nayerahmadi and Nasimeh (Sheikhzadeh) Tavassoli; m. Mitra Farzaneh, Aug. 6, 1979; children: Kooshan, Poorya. BA in Psychology, Pars Coll., Tehran, 1973; MA in Clin. Psychology, Ball State U., 1978; PhD, U. Pa., 1989. Psychologist, counselor Imperial Iranian Air Force, Tehran, 1973-75; rsch. asst. U. Pa., Phila., 1980-82; rsch. cons. CON-RAIL, Phila., 1986-87; cons. psychologist Uni-Marts, Inc., Phila., 1981-88; sr. clin. psychologist North Princeton (N.J.) Devel. Ctr., 1988—. Author: Development of a Homesickness Scale for Iranian Population, 1989, others. Mem. Am. Psychol. Assn., Am. Ednl. Rsch. Assn. Home: 13 Covered Bridge Path Philadelphia PA 19115-2123 Office: North Princeton Devel Ctr PO Box 1000 Princeton NJ 08543-1000

NAYLON, BETSY ZIMMERMANN, artist; b. Buffalo, Jan. 27, 1934; d. Gerard M. and Marion G. (McDonald) Zimmermann; m. Bernard M. Naylon, Aug. 11, 1956; children: Lisa, Bernard, Claire. BA, Rosary Hill Coll., 1955; postgrad., Daeman Coll., 1976; studied with, William Paden, N.Y.C., 1986. instr. Daeman Coll., Buffalo, 1969-70, SUNY, Buffalo, 1974-79, Niagara U., 1981-83, Trinity Ch., 1990-91, Niagara Falls Soc. Artists, 1992; art exhbn. judge Internat. Children's Art Exhibit, Niagara Falls, Ont., Can., 1991, Lewiston Art Festival, Buscaglia-Castellani Art Gallery, Niagara U., Grand Island Art Group Exhibit, Niagara on the Lake, Ont. Commd. artworks CECOS Internat. Inc., 1981, Browning Ferris Industries, Niagara Falls, N.Y., 1982, Mader Corp., Buffalo, 1983, Synder Tank Co., Internat. Harvester Co., Ohio, 1985, Peller & Mure Co., Buffalo, 1985, Carborundum Abrasives, Niagara Falls, Ohio, Va., 1984, Bantam, Doubleday Dell Publ. Co., 1989, 90, Studio Arena Theater, 1988, 92, Martha W. Bennett, 1991, J. & M. Broderick, 1990; exhbns. Albright-Knox Gallery, Buffalo, 1980, Burchfield Art Ctr., Buffalo, 1981, O'Keefe Ctr., Toronto, Can., 1982, AAO Galleries, Buffalo, 1984; various solo exhibits. Mem. Nat. Assn. Women Artists (traveling printmaking exhibit U.S. 1987-89, traveling painting exhibit India 1989-90), Nat. League Am. Penwomen (1st Place award 1991, Merit award 1989), Nat. Mus. Women in the Arts, Nat. Women's Caucus for Art, Niagara Coun. Arts (bd. dirs. 1983-84), Niagara Frontier Watercolor Soc. (Painting award 1989). Home: 4116 Washington St Niagara Falls NY 14305-1558 Studio: 537 3d St Niagara Falls NY 14303

NAZARIAN, JOHN, academic administrator, mathematics educator; b. Pawtucket, R.I., Sept. 6, 1932; s. Zakie and Amenia (Nahas) N. EdB, R.I. Coll., 1954; AM, Brown U., 1956; MA, U. Ill., 1961; PhD, NYU, 1967. Instr. math. R.I. Coll., Providence, 1954-58, asst. prof., 1958-67, assoc. prof., 1967-71, prof., 1971—, assoc. dean Arts and Scis., 1970-72, spl. asst. to pres., 1971-77, v.p. adminstrn. and fin., 1977-90, pres., 1990—. Chmn., vice-chmn. Arabic Ednl. Found., Pawtucket, 1966-72; chmn. Sargeant Rehab. Ctr, Providence, 1983-86, Diocesan Pastoral Coun., West Newton, Mass.,

1974-78. Recipient Cross of Jerusalem, Patriarch of Melkite Ch., 1976. Office: RI Coll 600 Mt Pleasant Ave Providence RI 02908-1924

NAZZ, JAMES, artist; b. N.J., Jan. 2, 1951; s. Edward F. and Betty (Davis) Nass; m. Barbara E. Brown, June, 17; 1 child, Theodore. Student, DuCret Sch. Arts, N.Y., 1971-72, Nat. Acad., N.Y.C., 1973, Art Students League, N.Y.C., 1974, Sch. Visual Arts, N.Y.C., 1974. contbg. artist Image Bank, N.Y.C., 1990—. Prin. works appeared in numerous publs. including Time, Newsweek, Fortune, Forbes, Psychology Today, others. Gardener 10th St. Block Assn., N.Y.C., 1980—. Recipient Merit awards Dimensional Illustrators, 1990, 91. Mem. Graphic Artists Guild. Home: 159 2d Ave New York NY 10003 Office: 41 Union Sq New York NY 10003

NAZZARO, JAMES RUSSELL, college vice president; b. N.Y.C., June 5, 1931; s. James Vincent Nazzaro and Eva (Rajotte) Schroeder; m. Jean Nelson, Aug. 1955 (div.); children: Jessica, Valerie; m. Carol Wright. BA, CUNY, 1957; AM, Columbia U., 1958, PhD, 1961. Psychology chair, Mary Washington Coll. U. Va., Fredericksburg, 1961-69; psychology chair Calif. State U., Chico, 1969-71; adminstv. officer edn. APA, Washington, 1971-76; dir. biostatistics AHPA, Washington, 1977-79; psychology chair U. North Fla., Jacksonville, 1979-81; dean Arts and Humanities U. Bridgeport, Conn., 1981-88; v.p. acad. affairs Stockton State Coll., Pomona, N.J., 1988—. Contbr. articles to profl. jours. Cpl. U.S. Army, 1951-53, Korea. Fellow APA. Office: Stockton State Coll Jimmy Leeds Rd Pomona NJ 08240-9999

NEAL, JAMES PRESTON, state senator, project engineer; b. Cin., July 1, 1935; s. James Preston and Desha Frank (Thompson) N.; m. Nancy Joan Tyner, June 11, 1961; children: Leslie Helen, Karen Desha, James V. BSME, U. Ill., 1960. Registered profl. engr., Del. Tech. svc. engr. DuPont Co., Parlin, N.J., 1960-62; engr DuPont Co., Waynesboro, Va., 1962-64; instrument engr. DuPont Co., Newburgh, N.Y., 1964-68, Newark, 1966-78; project engr. DuPont Co., 1978-91; dir. Tetra Tech Richardson, Christiana, Del., 1992—; mem. Del. Ho. of Reps., 1978-80; mem. Del. Senate, 1980—. Patentee in field. Councilman City of Newark, 1973-78. With U.S. Army, 1954-56. Mem. IEEE (sr.), Del. Soc. Profl. Engrs. (Engr. of Yr. 1989), Instrument Soc. Am., Am. Legis. Exchange Coun. (nat. sec., Outstanding Leader, 1989). Republican. Presbyterian. Home: 50 Bridlebrook Ln Newark DE 19711-2061 Office: Tetra Tech Richardson 56 W Main St Christiana DE 19702 also: Del State Senate Legis Hall Dover DE 19901

NEAL, JUDITH ANN, management educator; b. Long Beach, Calif., Jan. 3, 1947; d. Richard Leon and Mildren Ellen (Payne) Robinson; m. David F. Neal, Nov. 26, 1966 (div.); children: David Shaun, Richard Carroll. BSBA, Quinnipiac Coll., 1977; PhD in Adminstrv. Sci., Yale U., 1985. Mem. orgn. devel. staff Honeywell, Phoenix, 1981-83; mgr. orgn. devel. and tng. Circuit-Wise, North Haven, Conn., 1983-85, Honeywell, Joliet, Ill., 1985-87; pres. Judith A. Neal & Assocs., East Haven, Conn., 1987—; assoc. prof. mgmt. U. New Haven, West Haven, 1988—. Mem. Internat. Assn. Orgn. Devel., Bus. and Profl. Women's Assn. (bd. dirs. 1985-87), Acad. of Mgmt. Home: 36 Sylvan Hills Rd New Haven CT 06513-1949 Office: U New Haven 300 Orange Ave West Haven CT 06516

NEAL, RICHARD EDMUND, congressman, former mayor; b. Worcester, Mass., Feb. 14, 1949; s. Edmund J. and Mary H. (Garvey) N.; m. Maureen Conway, Dec. 20, 1975; children—Rory, Brendan, Maura, Sean. B.S., Am. Internat. Coll., Springfield, Mass., 1972; M.P.A., U. Hartford, Conn., 1976; postgrad., U. Mass., Amherst, 1982. Adminstrv. aide to Mayor City of Springfield, Mass., 1973-78, mem. city council, 1978-83, mayor, 1984-88; mem. 101st-102nd Congresses from 2nd. Mass. dist., Washington, DC, 1989—; lectr. history and politics Springfield Tech. Community Coll., Mass., 1973-83; lectr. bus. and govt. Western New Eng. Coll., Springfield, 1979-82; project dir. Springfield Tech. Community Coll., 1979-82. Trustee ARC, YMCA, Springfield. Named to Outstanding Young Men in Am., U.S. Jr. C. of C., Springfield. Mem. Am. Internat. Coll. Alumni Assn. (pres. 1980, Alumni Achievement award 1985). Springfield Library and Mus. Assn. (trustee). Democrat. Roman Catholic. Clubs: Valley Press. John Boyle O'Reilly (Springfield). Office: US Ho of Reps Office of House Mems Washington DC 20510*

NEALE, JOHN HAMILTON, JR., consultant; b. N.Y.C., Nov. 3, 1946; s. John H. and Marjorie (Rose) N.; m. Susan G. Lipinski, Aug. 17, 1973; children: Elizabeth, John III, Charles. AB, U. Mich., 1967; MBA, Columbia U., 1973. Sr. auditor Touche Ross & Co., N.Y.C., 1973-75; fin. analyst Freeport Minerals Co., N.Y.C., 1975-79; mgr. fin. analysts Freeport McMoran Inc., N.Y.C., 1979-82; mgr. cons. svc. Evaluations & Planning Systems, N.Y.C., 1982-85; v.p. cons. svc. Thorn EMI Computer Software Inc., Chelmsford, Mass., 1985-86; v.p. corp. programs Thorn EMI Computer Software Inc., Chelmsford, 1986-87; mktg. mgr. Digital Equipment Corp., Nashua, N.H., 1987-91; pres. Sextant Systems, Newburyport, Mass., 1991—. Mem. City of Rye, N.Y. Human Rights Commn., 1979-83, I.C. Sch. Bd., Newburyport, Mass., 1987-89. Lt. (j.g.) USN, 1968-71. Mem. Am. Inst. CPAs (cert. N.Y.). Republican. Presbyterian. Office: 39 Toppans Ln Newburyport MA 01950-3842

NEALE, TIMOTHY ARTHUR, hospital administrator; b. Abington, Pa., Feb. 26, 1948; s. Edwin A. and Helene R. (Rehbaum) N.; m. Cathleen S. Fitzpatrick; children: Adam, Nathan. BA, Amherst (Mass.) Coll., 1970; MA in Teaching, Brown U., 1971; M in Health Svc. Adminstrn., U. Mich., 1980. Asst. dir. admissions Middlebury (Vt.) Coll., 1971-78; assoc. v.p. Meriden-Wallingford (Conn.) Hosp., 1980-83; v.p. Med. Ctr. Hosp. Vt., Burlington, 1983-89, Mt. Auburn Hosp., Cambridge, Mass., 1989—; bd. dirs. Belmont-Watertown (Mass.) VNA. Fellow Am. Coll. Healthcare Execs., Am. Hosp. Assn. Office: Mt Auburn Hosp 330 Mt Auburn St Cambridge MA 02138-5502

NEALON, WILLIAM JOSEPH, JR., federal judge; b. Scranton, Pa., July 31, 1923; s. William Joseph and Ann Cannon (McNally) N.; m. Jean Sullivan, Nov. 15, 1947; children: Ann, Robert, William, John, Jean, Patricia, Kathleen, Terrence, Thomas, Timothy. Student, U. Miami, Fla., 1942-43; B.S. in Econs, Villanova U., 1947; LL.B., Cath. U. Am., 1950; LL.D. (hon.), U. Scranton, 1975. Bar: Pa. 1951. With firm Kennedy, O'Brien & O'Brien (and predecessor), Scranton, 1951-60; mem. Lackawanna County Ct. Common Pleas, 1960-62; U.S. dist. judge Middle Dist. Pa., 1962—, chief judge, 1976-88; sr. status, 1989—; mem. com. on adminstrn. of criminal law Jud. Conf. U.S., 1979—; lectr. bus. law and labor law U. Scranton, 1951-59; mem. jud. council 3d Cir. Ct. Appeals, 1984—; dist. judge rep. from 3d Cir. Jud. Conf. of U.S., 1987—. Mem. Scranton Registration Commn., 1953-55; hearing examiner Pa. Liquor Control Bd., 1955-59; campaign dir. Lackawanna County chpt. Nat. Found., 1961-63; mem. Scranton-Lackawanna Health and Welfare Authority, 1963—; assoc. bd. Marywood Coll., Scranton; pres. bd. dirs. Cath. Youth Center; pres. Father's Club Scranton Prep. Sch., 1966; chmn. bd. dirs. Mercy Hosp., 1991—; chmn. bd. trustees U. Scranton; vice chmn. bd. trustees Lackawanna Jr. Coll., Scranton; bd. dirs. St. Joseph's Children's and Maternity Hosp., 1963-66, Lackawanna County unit Am. Cancer Soc., Lackawanna County Heart Assn., Lackawanna County chpt. Pa. Assn. Retarded Children, Scranton chpt. ARC, Lackawanna United Fund, Mercy Hosp., Scranton, 1975—; trustee St. Michael's Sch. Boys, Hoban Heights; adv. com. Hosp. Service Assn. Northeastern Pa. Served to 1st lt. USMCR, 1942-45. Recipient Americanism award Amos Lodge B'nai B'rith, 1975; Cyrano award U. Scranton Grad. Sch., 1977; Disting. Service award Pa. Trial Lawyers Assn., 1979; named one of 50 Disting. Pennsylvanians Greater Phila. C. of C., 1980, Outstanding Fed. Trial Judge Assn. Trial Lawyers Am., 1983. Mem. Pa., Lackawanna County bar assn. (Chief Justice Michael J. Eagen award 1987), Friendly Sons St. Patrick (pres. Lackawanna County 1963-64), Pi Sigma Alpha. Club: Scranton Country (Clarks Summit, Pa.) (bd. dirs.). Lodge: K.C. Office: US Courthouse PO Box 1146 Scranton PA 18501-1146

NEBEL, BERNARD JAMES, biology educator; b. Geneva, N.Y., June 5, 1934; s. Bernard Rudolf and Mabel (Ruttle) Nebel; m. Jean Elizabeth Inglis, Sept. 9, 1961 (div. 1987); children: Tamra, Christopher; m. Janet Rose Lowenstein, Aug. 4, 1990. BA, Earlham Coll., 1960; PhD, Duke U., 1965. Postdoctoral fellow Smithsonian Instn., Washington, 1965-68; asst. prof. U. Md., Balt., 1968-70; prof. Catonsville (Md.) County Community Coll., 1970—. Author: (textbook) Environmental Science, 1980, 2d edit., 1987, 3d edit., 1990. Mem. AAAS, Am. Inst. Biol. Sci., Wilderness Soc., Sierra. Democrat. Office: Catonsville CC 800 S Rolling Rd Baltimore MD 21228-5317

NECHES, RICHARD BROOKS, cardiologist, educator; b. Long Branch, N.J., Nov. 22, 1955; s. Jacob and Evelyn (Brooks) N. BS summa cum laude, Wofford Coll., 1976; MD, Med. U. S.C., Charleston, 1979. Diplomate Am. Bd. Internal Medicine, cardiovascular diseases; lic. physician, N.Y., N.J. Resident internal medicine Brookdale Hosp. Med. Ctr., Bklyn., 1979-82; fellow cardiovascular diseases Beth Israel Med. Ctr., N.Y.C., 1982-84, chief fellow cardiology, 1984; pvt. practice cardiology N.Y.C., 1984—; co-chief div. cardiology dept. medicine St. John's Episcopal Hosp., Far Rockaway, N.Y., 1990—; clin. instr. medicine SUNY, Stony Brook, 1987-88; clin. asst. prof. medicine U. Medicine and Dentistry N.J., Robert Wood Johnson Med. Sch., New Brunswick, 1989-91, SUNY Health Sci. Ctr., Bklyn., 1991—; participant internat. cardiology studies. Contbr. articles to profl. jours. Mem. Am. Heart Assn. Fellow Am. Coll. Cardiology, Am. Coll. Angiology, N.Y. Cardiological Soc.; mem. Phi Beta Kappa. Office: St John's Episcopal Hosp Dept Medicine 327 Beach 19 St Far Rockaway NY 11691

NECULA, NICHOLAS, electrical engineering educator, researcher; b. Campulung, Arges, Romania, July 1, 1940; came to U.S., 1985; s. Nicolae and Svetlana (Stepanov) N.; m. Maria-Ana Parau, July 1, 1964; 1 child, Maria-Cristina. MSEE, Poly. Inst., Bucharest, Romania, 1961, PhD in Elec. Engring., 1968. Asst. prof. Sch. Electronics, Poly. Inst., 1961-72, assoc. prof., 1972-85; dean asst. Sch. Electronics Poly. Inst., 1972-76, head dept. telecommunications, 1981-85; prin. systems engr. Contel I.P.C., Stamford, Conn., 1986-91; reviewer Zentralblatt fur Mathematik, Heidelberg, Fed. Republic Germany, 1970-90. Author: Logic Circuits: Automatic Synthesis, 1972, also 3 textbooks; mem. editorial bd. Internat. Jour. on Digital Processes, 1971-77; contbr. numerous articles to profl. jours.; inventor in field. Recipient award Romanian Acad. Scis., 1964, 72. Mem. IEEE (sr.), Internat. Neural Network Soc., N.Y. Acad. Scis. (assoc.).

NEDERLANDER, JAMES LAURENCE, theater owner, producer; b. Detroit, Jan. 23, 1960; s. James Morton and Barbara (Smith) N. Student, Cranbrook Prep, Boston U. Asst. mgr. Pinchnob, Clarkston, Mich.; producer Pineknob, N.Y.C.; v.p. Nederlander, N.Y.C. Assoc. producer plays including The Tragedy of Carmen, 1984 (Tony award 1984), Starlight Express, 1989, Cafe Crown, 1989; assoc. producer musicals On Your Toes, 1987, Legs Diamond, 1988, Barry Manilow on Broadway, 1989; producer show Mort Sahl on Broadway, 1988, Kenny Loggins on Broadway, 1988; co-producer Billy Joel at Yankee Stadium, 1990, Harry Connick Jr. on Broadway, 1990. Mem. Com. Am. Cadelight Vigil, 1990, Nat. Hypterten-sion Benefit, N.Y.C., 1988; bd. trustees Entrepid Museum, 1990. Mem. League N.Y. Theatres, Roundabout Theatre Group, City Athletic Club, LaCosta Country Club.

NEDERLANDER, JAMES MORTON, theater executive; b. Detroit, Mar. 31, 1922; s. David T. and Sarah L. (Applebaum) N.; m. Charlene Saunders, Feb. 12, 1969; children: James Laurence, Sharon, Kristina. Student, Detroit Inst. Tech. Chmn., former pres. Nederlander Orgn., Inc. (formerly Nederlander Producing Co. Am., Inc., N.Y.C., 1966—. Owner numerous theaters including Palace Theatre, Lunt-Fontanne Theatre, Nederlander Theatre, Brooks Atkinson Theatre, Gershwin Theatre, Neil Simon Theatre, Marquis Theatre, Minskoff Theatre, Richard Rodgers Theatre, New Amsterdam Theatre, N.Y.C., Greek Theatre, Pantages Theatre, Henry Fonda Theatre, L.A., Pacific Amphitheatre, Costa Mesa, Calif., Curran Theatre, Golden Gate Theatre, Orpheum, San Francisco, Shubert Theatre, Chgo., Fisher Theatre, Masonic Temple, Detroit, Poplar Creek, Hoffman Estates, Ill., Merriweather Post Pavilion, Columbia, Md., Aldwych Theatre, London, Dominion Theatre, London, Adelphi Theatre, London; producer numerous shows for Broadway including Nick & Nora, Will Rogers Follies, Me and My Girl, Orpheus Descending, Les Liaisons Dangereuses, Legs Diamond, Cafe Crown, Nicholas Nickleby, Annie, La Cage aux Folles, Nine, Applause, Not Now Darling, See Saw, Oliver, Abelard and Heloise, Sherlock Holmes, Treemonisha, Habeus Corpus, Otherwise Engaged, Whose Life is it Anyway?, Betrayal, Woman of the Year, Lena Horne: The Lady and Her Music, The Dresser, Noises Off, Merlin, Night and Day, My Fat Friend, Shirley MacLaine on Broadway, Sweet Charity, Benefactors, Breaking the Code; numerous road show prodns.; touring revivals: Peter Pan, Hello Dolly, Porgy and Bess, The Music Man, I Do! I Do!, Oklahoma, On a Clear Day You Can See Forever, Fiddler on the Roof. Office: Nederlander Orgn Inc 810 7th Ave New York NY 10019-5818

NEDERLANDER, ROBERT E., entertainment and television executive, lawyer; b. Detroit, Apr. 10, 1933; s. David T. and Sarah (Applebaum) N.; m. Caren Berman (div.); children: Robert E. Jr., Eric; Gladys Rackmil, Jan. 1, 1988. BA in Econs., U. Mich., 1955, JD, 1958, LLD (hon.), 1991. Ptnr. Nederlander, Dodge & Rollins, Detroit, 1960-90; pres. Nederlander Orgn., Inc., N.Y.C., 1981—, Nederlander TV & Film Prodns., N.Y.C., 1985—; mng. gen. ptnr. N.Y. Yankees, 1990-91. Regent U. Mich., Ann Arbor, 1969-84; trustee Am. Health Found., 1989—; chmn. Gateway Am., 1991—. Recipient Disting. Alumni Svc. award U. Mich., 1985, Presdl. Soc. Svc. citation, 1988; named Man of Yr. by Gov's. Com. on Scholastic Achievement, N.Y.C., 1991. Fellow ABA, Mich. Bar Assn. Office: Nederlander Orgn 810 7th Ave New York NY 10019-5818

NEEMAR, CAROL LEE, nursing educator; b. Charlottesville, Va., Apr. 14, 1941; d. Howard Lee and Lena Josephine (Loving) Harris; m. Tyrone Francis Neemar, Feb. 21, 1970; 1 child, Natasha Belinda. RN, AAS, N.Y.C. Tech. Coll., Bklyn., 1970; BS, N.Y. Inst. Tech., 1976; MPA, C.W. Post U., 1990. RN; cert. tchr., N.Y. Pvt. duty N.Y. Registry, N.Y.C., 1964-68; LPN-RN Physician's Hosp., Jackson Heights, N.Y., 1968-69; RN, tchr. Nassau Tech. Ctr. BOCES, Westbury, N.Y., 1970—. Mem. Am. Fedn. Tchrs., United Fedn. Tchrs., NAACP, Nostrand Garden Civic Assn., Uniondale Community Coun. Home: 675 Winthrop Dr Uniondale NY 11553-3024

NEFF, MARY ELLEN ANDRE, educator; b. Indiana, Pa., July 6, 1943; d. Frank Vincent and Marie Isabel (Elrick) Andre; children: Gary V. Jr., Traci Dawn. BS, Indiana U. Pa., 1965, MEd, 1971. Tchr. Blairsville (Pa.)-Saltsburg Sch. Dist., Derry (Pa.) Area Sch. Dist. Mem. NEA, PTA, Pa. State Edn. Assn., Blairsville-Saltsburg Edn. Assn. (sec.), Keystone Reading Assn., Nat. Soc. DAR (past vice regent Wm. Kenly chpt., regent), Delta Kappa Gamma (pres. 1986-90, treas. 1990—). Home: 17 Carriage Rd Greensburg PA 15601-9014

NEFF, ROBERT WILBUR, church official, educator; b. Lancaster, Pa., June 16, 1936; s. Wilbur Hildebr and Hazel Margaret (Martin) N.; m. Dorothy Rosewarne, Aug. 16, 1959; children: Charles Scott, Heather Lynn. B.S., Pa. State U., 1958; B.D., Yale Div. Sch., 1961, M.A., 1963, Ph.D., 1969; D.D., Juniata Coll., 1978, Manchester Coll., 1979; D.H.L., Bridgewater Coll., 1979. Asst. prof. Bridgewater Coll., 1964-65; mem. faculty dept. Bibl. studies Bethany Theol. Sem., 1965-77, prof., 1973-77; gen. sec. Ch. of the Brethren, Elgin, Ill., 1978-86; pres. Juniata Coll., 1986—; mem. faculty North Park Sem., No. Baptist Sem., Theol. Coll. No. Nigeria. Author works in field. Mem. governing bd. Nat. Council Chs. of Christ, 1976-86, mem. exec. com., 1979-86; mem. Mid-East panel, 1980, 2d v.p., 1985-86; cen. com. World Council of Chs., 1983-92; rep. Assembly of World Council of Chs., 1983; exec. Com. on Interchurch Relations, 1980-84, mem. del. to China, 1981, chmn. presdl. panel, 1982-84; bd. dirs. Bethany Theol. Sem., 1978-86; bd. dirs. Mellon Bank (Cen.) Nat. Assn., 1987—, exec. com., 1989—; bd. dirs. Huntingdon County and IndustryInc., 1987—; campaign chmn. United Way, Huntingdon County, 1989. Danforth fellow, 1958-69. Mem. Soc. Bibl. Lit., Soc. Old Testament Study, Chgo. Soc. Bibl. Rsch., Soc. Values in Higher Edn., Coun. of Ind. Colls. (nat. bd. dirs. 1991), Pa. Coun. Ind. Colls. and Univs. (exec. com. 1988-90). Democrat. Home: RR 4 Box 37 Huntingdon PA 16652-9709 Office: Juniata Coll 1700 Moore St Huntingdon PA 16652-2119

NEFT, DAVID SAMUEL, marketing professional; b. N.Y.C., Jan. 9, 1937; s. Louis and Sue (Horowitz) N.; m. Naomi Silver, May 31, 1964; children: Michael Louis, Deborah Isabel. BA, Columbia U., 1957, MBA, 1959, PhD, 1962. Dir. info. pub. Info. Concepts, Inc., N.Y.C., 1965-68, treas., chief exec. officer, 1968-70; gen. mgr. Sports Illustrated Enterprises, N.Y.C., 1970-73; pres. Sports Products Inc., Ridgefield, Conn., 1973-76; chief statistician Louis Harris and Assocs., N.Y.C., 1963-65, sr. v.p., 1977-78, exec. v.p., chief exec. officer, 1978-85; dir. research Gannett Co., Inc., N.Y.C., 1985-90, v.p. rsch., 1990—; cons. Fed. Energy Adminstrn., Washington, 1973-75; bd. dirs. Sports Products Inc., Ridgefield, Conn. Author: Statistical Analysis for Areal Distributions, 1966; editor: The Baseball Encyclopedia, 1969; author (with others) The World Book of Odds, 1978, The Sports Encyclopedia: Baseball, 1974, 76-77, 81-82, 85, 87-89, 90-92, The Sports Encyclopedia: Pro Football, 1974, 76, 78, 83, 87, 88-89, 90-91, Pro Football: The Early Years, 1978, 83, 87, The World Series, 1976, 79, 86, The Sports Encyclopedia: Pro Basketball, 1975, 89, 90-91, All-Sports World Record Book, 1974, 75, 76, The Scrapbook History of Pro Football, 1976, 77, 79, The Scrapbook History of Baseball, 1975, The Notre Dame Football Scrapbook, 1977, The Ohio State Football Scrapbook, 1977, The University of Michigan Football Scrapbook, 1978, The Football Encyclopedia, 1991; contbr. articles to profl. and acad. jours. Served with U.S. Army, 1961-63. Mem. Am. Assn. Pub. Opinion Rsch., Profl. Football Rsch. Assn. (v.p. 1985-87), Soc. for Am. Baseball Rsch. Jewish. Home: 525 E 86th St New York NY 10028-7512

NEGELE, JOHN WILLIAM, physics educator, consultant; b. Cleve., Apr. 18, 1944; s. Charles Frederick and Virgil Lea (Wettich) N.; m. Rose Anne Meeks, June 18, 1967; Janette Andrea, Julia Elizabeth. B.S., Purdue U., 1965; Ph.D., Cornell U., 1969. Research fellow Niels Bohr Inst., Copenhagen, 1969-70; vis. asst. prof. MIT, Cambridge, 1970-71, faculty mem., 1971—, prof. physics, 1979—, William A. Coolidge prof., 1991—, assoc. dir. Ctr. for Theoretical Physics, 1988-89, dir. Ctr. for Theoretical Physics, 1989—; cons. Los Alamos Sci. Lab., Brookhaven Nat. Lab., Lawrence Livermore Nat. Lab., Oak Ridge Nat. Lab.; mem. physics div. rev. com. Argonne Nat. Lab., (ILL.), 1977-83; mem. nuclear sci. div. rev. com. Lawrence Berkeley Lab., (Calif.), 1982—; mem. adv. bd., steering com. Inst. for Theoretical Physics, U. Calif.-Santa Barbara, 1982-86; mem. adv. bd. inst. for Nuclear Theory U. Washington, 1990—; program adv. com. Tandem Van de Graaff Accelerator, Brookhaven Nat. Lab., 1977-78, Bates Linear Accelerator, 1977-80, Los Alamos Meson Prodn. Facility, 1986-89, Brookhaven Alternating Gradient Synchraton, 1987—. Author: Quantum Many Particle Systems, 1987; contbr. articles to profl. jours.; editor: Advances in Nuclear Physics, 1977—. Grantee NSF, 1965-69; grantee Danforth Found., 1965-69, Woodrow Wilson Found., 1965, Alfred P. Sloan Found., 1979, Japan Soc. for Promotion Sci., 1981, John Simon Guggenheim Found., 1982. Fellow Am. Phys. Soc. (exec. com. 1982-84, program com. 1980-82, editorial bd. Phys. Rev. 1980-82, exec. com. topical group on computational physics 1990—, chair div. computational physics 1992—, Bonner prize Com. 1984-85), AAAS (nominating com. 1987-91, mem. physics sect. com. 1991—), Fedn. Am. Scientists. Home: 70 Buckman Dr Lexington MA 02173-6000 Office: MIT Dept Physics 6-308 77 Massachusetts Ave Cambridge MA 02139-4307

NEGRI, ROCCO ANTONIO, artist, illustrator; b. Italy, June 26, 1932; came to U.S., 1959; s. Salvarore and Adele (Plattaroti) N.; m. Joan Becky Stewart, May 25, 1958; children: Ronald Edgar, Gene Darius. Student, Art Students League, N.Y.C., 1959-60, Sch. Visual Arts, N.Y.C., 1960-64, Pratt Graphic Ctr., N.Y.C., 1974-75. Illustrator children's books including Renfroe's Christmas, 1968, Journey Outside, 1969, Trouble River, 1969, Casa Means Home, 1970, Tales from Count Lucanor, 1970, Heracles The Strong, 1970, Bantu Tales, 1970, The Legs of the Moon, 1971, Charlie Dick, 1972, Coplas, 1972, The Great Fire, 1973, The Son of the Leopard, 1974, Pampalche of the Silver Teeth, 1976. Home: 77-47 79th St Glendale NY 11385

NEGRI, STEVEN JOSEPH, municipal government official; b. Jersey City, Jan. 30, 1952; s. J. Joseph Negri and Eleanor (McCourt) Negri Yaschak; m. Janis Ann Waldow, May 19, 1984; 1 child, Philip F.W. BA in Pub. Adminstrn., Fairleigh Dickinson U., 1974. Lic. bldg. inspector, N.J. Constrn. supr. Palam Corp., Union City, N.J., 1974-77; asst. chief bldg. inspector City of Union City, N.J., 1977-83; constrn. ofcl. City of Union City, 1983, Borough of Westwood, N.J., 1983-90, Borough of Hillsdale, N.J., 1987—, Borough of Ft. Lee, N.J., 1990—; mem. Union City Planning Bd., 1978-83, Westwood Planning Bd., 1984-90; code ofcl. adviser N.J. State Barrier Free Com., Trenton, 1987—. With U.S. Army, 1969-70, Vietnam. Mem. Bldg. Ofcls. Code Adminstrs. Internat., N.J. Bldg. Ofcls. Assn., Bergen-Passaic Mcpl. Inspectors Assn., N.J. Fedn. Planners. Evangelical Christian. Home: Borough of Ft Lee 309 Main St 47 Roosevelt Ave Fort Lee NJ 07024 Office: Borough of Ft Lee 309 Main St Fort Lee NJ 07024-2294

NEGRIN, HOWARD ELIAS, educational administrator; b. Bronx, N.Y., Jan. 4, 1935; s. Leo Haim and Anna (Goldstein) N.; m. Barbara Kay Orloff Taub, June 4, 1967. BA, NYU, 1956, MA, 1966, PhD, 1977. Grants assoc. Bronx Community Coll./CUNY, 1981; asst. dir. grants Baruch Coll./ CUNY, N.Y.C., 1981-82, coord. grants, 1982-85, dir. grants, 1985-91; assoc. provost for grants and rsch. adminstrn. Hofstra U., Hempstead, N.Y., 1991—. Author manuals: Unfinished Journey, 1971, Western Civilization: A Concise History, 1991; contbr. articles to profl. publs. Bd. dirs. Inst. for Rsch. in History, N.Y.C., 1978-83, 86-88, grants officer, 1979-80, editor newsletter, 1981-83. French Govt. scholar, 1971. Mem. Nat. Coun. Univ. Rsch. Adminstrs., Soc. Rsch. Adminstrs. Jewish. Home: 14 Washington Pl New York NY 10003 Office: 1000 Fulton Ave Hempstead NY 11550

NEGRON, JAIME, business services director; b. San Juan, P.R., Dec. 23, 1939; came to U.S., 1952; s. Rito and Tomasa (Otero) N.; m. Barbara Charlotte Stovall, Nov. 5, 1959; children: Jeannette Michelle, Victoria Frances. BA in Econs., Howard U., 1987. Lic. realtor. Chief receiving & shipping Am. Univ., Washington, 1960-62; book dept. mgr. Am. U., Washington, 1968-71; bookstore mgr. Follett Corp., Chgo., 1962-68, Cath. U., Washington, 1971-74; dir. Howard U. stores Howard Univ., Washington, 1974—; dir. aux. enterprises Howard U., Washington, 1987—; real estate agt. Shannon & Luchs, Vienna, Va., 1988-92; asst. dir. aux. enterprises DeKalb Coll., Atlanta, 1992—; cons. U. Del., Newark, 1988, Wesley Sem., Washington, 1984, R.R. Moton Meml. Inst., N.Y.C., 1974-79. Active Vienna Jaycees, 1970-80. With USN, 1958-60. Mem. Middle Atlantic Coll. Stores (pres. 1984), Nat. Assn. Coll. Stores, Nat. Bd. Realtors, Va. Bd. Realtors. Episcopalian. Office: DeKalb Coll Bldg S 555 N Indian Creek Dr Clarkston GA 30021-2396

NEHRLING, ARNO HERBERT, JR., chemical company executive, retired; b. Richmond, Ind., Mar. 5, 1928; s. Arno Herbert and Irene Thelma (Dahlberg) N.; m. Mary Helen Mudd, Jan. 11, 1958; children: Amy Irene Nehrling Belz, Dorothy Louise Nehrling Murphy. BA, Cornell U., 1950; MBA, Harvard U., 1955. Various supervisory and mgmt. positions E.I. DuPont de Nemours & Co., Wilmington, Del., 1955-64; dir. fin. E.I. DuPont de Nemours & Co., Dusseldorf, Fed. Republic Germany and Mexico City, 1965-71; asst. mgr. credit div., asst. mgr. treasury div., asst. mgr. fgn. and banking div. E.I. DuPont de Nemours & Co., Wilmington, Del., 1972-76, asst. treas., dir. employee compensation and benefits, 1977—. Bd. dir. Geriatric Svcs. of Del. and Peninsula United Meth. Homes. Mem. Fin. Execs. Inst. (past chmn. employee benefits com., past chmn. com. on other post employment benefits), Investment Com. Del. Home: 25 Shipcarpenter Sq Lewes DE 19958-2204

NEIBAUER, RODNEY DEAN, aviator; b. Billings, Mont., Aug. 8, 1937; s. Alexander and Gladys Wren (Mainwaring) N.; m. Marion Helen Taylor, Sept. 5, 1964 (dec. Dec. 1973); m. Eva Jane Cheshire, May 29, 1976; children: Elizabeth, Jennifer, Devon, Haley. Assoc. in Econs., Ea. Mont. U., 1958. Cert. air transport pilot. Capt. US Air, Washington, 1970—. Ensign USN, 1958-62; capt. USNR, squadron commdr. 1976-78. Decorated Navy Commendation medal. Mem. Air Lines Pilots Assn., Old Lyme Country Club (bd. govs. 1985-87). Republican. Home: 2 Duck River Ln Old Lyme CT 06371-1607

NEIDHARDT, WALTER JIM, religion editor, physics educator; b. Paterson, N.J., June 19, 1934; s. Walter Henry N.; m. Janet Williams; children: John, Jerome. ME, Stevens Inst. Tech., 1956, MS in Physics, 1958, PhD, 1962. Assoc. prof. physics N.J. Inst. Tech., Newark, 1968—. Author: (with others) The Christian Frame of Mind, 1989; contbr. articles to profl. jours. Fellow Am. Sci. Affiliation (cons. editor Perspectives on Sci. and Christian Faith 1968—, chairperson publs. com., 1982—, pres. met. sect. 1974-76, 80-82, 81-88); mem. Ctr. for Theology of Natural Sci., Inst. for

Encounter with Sci. and Theology, Assn. Christians in the Math. Scis., Interdisciplinary Bibl. Rsch. Inst., Inst. for Religion in an Age of Sci., Michael Polanyi Soc. N. Am., Karl Barth Soc. N.Am. Mem. Presbyn., Free Meth. Ch. Home: 146 Park Ave Randolph NJ 07869-3413 Office: NJ Inst for Tech Newark NJ 07102

NEIHEISEL, JAMES, geologist, consultant; b. Cin., June 3, 1927; s. Jacob P. and Eleanor (Schwab) N.; m. Betty Hilton, Apr. 4, 1953 (div. Dec. 1981); children: William James, Linda Karen. BS, Ohio State U., 1950; MS, U. S.C., 1958; PhD, Ga. Inst. Tech., 1973. Lic. geologist, Ga. Chemist Va. Carolina Chem. Corp., Charleston, S.C., 1955-57; engrng. petrographer U.S. Army C.E., Marietta, Ga., 1958-77; geologist EPA, Washington, 1977—. Contbr. articles to profl. jours. Lt. (j.g.) USN, 1951-54. Fellow Geol. Soc. Am.; mem. ASCE (assoc., chmn. task com. 1977-79), Geol. Soc. Ga. (sec. 1969-71), Sigma Gamma Epsilon. Home: 6269 Alforth Ave Alexandria VA 22310-3202 Office: EPA ANR 461 401 M St SW Washington DC 20460-0002

NEIL, FRED APPLESTEIN, public relations executive; b. Balt., Nov. 26, 1933; s. Frank and Mollie (Schapiro) Applestein; m. Sheila Tilles, Aug. 30, 1959 (div. May 1980); children: Jay Alan, Brian Mark Applestein, Gail Renee Applestein; m. Dawn Francis Fisher, July 6, 1986. BA, U. Md., 1959. News and sports editor Sta. WITH, Balt., 1959-60; dir. news and sports Sta. WCBM, Metromedia, Balt., 1960-69; press officer Mayor William Donald Schaefer, Balt., 1970-71; gen. mgr. Balt. Banners World Team Tennis League, 1971-72; pres. Fred Neil Assocs., Pub. Rels., Balt., 1972—; staff specialist pub. info. Md. Rehab. Ctr., Balt., 1980-91; owner Cruising for Mems., Ellicott City, 1987—, Dir. Office of Communications and Community Rels., Div. Vocat. Rehab., Balt., 1980—. Contbr. articles to mags., newspapers, newsletters; editor, contbr. Lafayette Sq. newsletter, 1974-82, Fed. Hill Newsletter, 1974-82, Greater Penn Ave. Newsletter, 1974-82, MPCA News Letter, 1982—, Md. Rehab. Assn. News Letter, 1985—, Front & Ctr. newsletter, 1980—. With U.S. Army, 1956-58. Recipient award for spot reporting Chesapeake AP, 1967, award for in-depth sports reporting, 1967, 69, Media Appreciation award U.S. Intercollegiate Lacrosse Assn., 1970, Humanitarian award Md. Rehab. Assn., 1982, Appreciation award 1986, Profl. Svc. award Md. Rehab. Counseling Assn., 1985, Ams. with Disabilities Act award The Task Force on the Rights and Empowerment of Ams. with Disabilities, 1991. Mem. Md. Rehab. Assn. (pres. 1985, 87), Md. Press Club (pres. 1988-89, bd. dirs. 1990-91), Balt. Sports Reporters Assn. (pres. 1964), Balt. Press Reporters Assn. (pres. 1965), Mid-Atlantic Rehab. Adminstrs. Assn. (pres. 1990). Home: 4608 Learned Sage Ct Ellicott City MD 21042-5932

NEIL, SANDI SMITH, communications company professional; b. Plainfield, N.J., Jan. 2, 1962; d. Marcellus Drummond, Jr. and Zenobia Rosmond (DeVore) Smith; m. William Henry Neil, Jr., Apr. 9, 1988; 1 child, Beatrice Evangeline. BA, Glassboro State Coll., 1985. Co-mgr. The Ltd., Sizes Unltd. Div., Upper Darby, Pa., 1987-88; svc. rep. Bell Atlantic, Bell of Pa. div., Phila., 1990—. Author: Reflections of a Black Life, 1991, Bee-Bee Bunny's Great Big Suprise, 1991, I Can Make That Sound, 1991. Mem. Young Adult Usher Bd. African Methodist Episcopal. Office: Bell of Pa 2000 S Broad St Philadelphia PA 19145

NEILL, BEN EARL, artist; b. Quincy, Mass., Dec. 11, 1914; m. Marion E. Kirby, May 21, 1939; children: Robert K., Arthur W., Alan B. Comml. artist, Boston, 1935-42; editorial artist Boston Herald-Traveler, 1946-73; marine artist, Sandwich, Mass., 1973—. Solo exhbns. include Annapolis (Md.) Marine Gallery, 1984, Trees Pl. Gallery, Mass., 1988; group shows include Mystic (Conn.) Ann. Internat., 1978-91, Grand Cen., N.Y.C., 1980, Peabody Mus., Salem, Mass., 1981, Mariners' Mus., Newport News, Va., 1985, Md. Hist. Soc., Balt., 1989; represented in permanent collections: Sandwich (Mass.) Glass Mus., St. Clements Island-Potomac River Mus., Md., pvt. and corp. collections. Recipient Disting. Svc. award Sch. Practical Art, Boston, 1964, award of excellence Mystic Maritime Gallery, 1989. Mem. Internat. Soc. Marine Painters, Am. Soc. Marine Artists (New Eng. regional rep. 1988—, bd. dirs. 1989—). Home and Studio: 88 Wood Ave RD 1 Sandwich MA 02563

NEILL, DENIS MICHAEL, government relations consulting executive; b. Grand Rapids, Mich., Apr. 27, 1943; s. Thomas Patrick and Agnes Josephine (Weber) N.; m. Mary Kathleen Golden, June 11, 1966; children: Mark, Erin. AB cum laude, St. Louis U., 1964, JD cum laude, 1967. Bar: Mo. 1967, D.C. 1969. Gen. atty. Office of Asst. Regional Counsel IRS, Newark, 1967-68; assoc. Arent, Fox, Kintner, Plotkin & Kahn, Washington, 1969-71, Morgan, Lewis & Bockius, Washington, 1971-72; atty. advisor office gen. counsel AID, Washington, 1972-73, asst. gen. counsel legis. and policy coordination, 1973-75, asst. adminstr. legis. affairs, 1975-77; sr. v.p., gen. counsel Aeromaritime Internat. Corp., Washington, 1977-80; counsel Surrey & Morse, Washington, 1980-81; sr. ptnr. Neill & Shaw, Washington, 1981-92, Dalley, Neill, Assevero, Carroll & Nealer, Washington, 1192—; pres. Neill & Co., Inc., Washington, 1981—. Bd. dirs. Barker Found., 1981-86, Fed. City Nat. Bank, Washington, 1981. Lt. USCG, 1968-71. Recipient Superior Unit Citation AID, 1976, Disting. Honor award, 1977. Mem. ABA, Fed. Bar Assn., D.C. Bar Assn., Mo. Bar Assn., Nat. Security Indsl. Assn. (bd. dirs. 1982-90), Capitol Hill Club, Columbia Country Club (Chevy Chase, Md.), Jefferson Islands Club (Washington). Democrat. Home: 5945 Searl Ter Bethesda MD 20816-2022 Office: Neill & Co 815 Connecticut Ave NW Ste 800 Washington DC 20006-4004

NEILSON, ARTHUR, industrial hygienist; b. Oakland, Calif., June 17, 1936; s. Arthur and Gertrude (Lanzer) N.; m. Sandra M. Newcome, Sept. 9, 1961; children: Brenda Ann, Arthur Jr. BS in Chemistry, U. Calif., Berkeley, 1959. Chemist Lawrence Radiation Lab., Livermore, 1956-60; systems specialist Stanford (Calif.) Linear Accelerator Ctr., 1960-61; indsl. hygienist Hartford (Conn.) Ins. Group, 1961-73; dir. ea. region. Fireman's Fund, Newark, 1973-74; prin. researcher Tulane U., New Orleans, 1974-76; sr. indsl. hygienist Stewart-Todd Assocs., Wayne, Pa., 1976-78; pres. Neilson Assocs., Inc., Chadds Ford, Pa., 1978—; assoc. prof. preventative medicine Jefferson Med. Sch., Phila., 1982-84; cons. Dept. Labor, 1980—. Mem. World Safety Orgn. (cert. safety exec.), Bd. Cert. Safety Profls., Am. Indsl. Hygiene Assn., Health Physics Soc. Home: 42 Blue Stone Dr Chadds Ford PA 19317-9311 Office: Neilson Assocs Inc 100 Dickenson Dr Stes 109-110 Chadds Ford PA 19317-9669

NEILSON, ERIC GRANT, physician, educator, health facility administrator; b. Bklyn., Sept. 14, 1949; s. Jack Drew and Lynette Elsie (Lundquist) N.; m. Linda Rae Apolzon, May 27, 1972; children: Tinsley, Sigrid. BS magna cum laude, Denison U., 1971; MD magna cum laude, U. Ala., 1975; MD (hon.), U. Pa., 1987. Asst. prof. U. Pa., Phila., 1980-87, assoc. prof., 1987-91, prof., 1991—, chief renal-electrolyte sect. dept. medicine, 1988—; attending physician Hosp. of U. Pa., 1980—; cons. in field. Med. editorial bds. on sci. jours.; contbr. numerous articles to profl. jours. Chairman med. adv. bd. Lupus Found. of Phila., 1985—; chmn. pathology A study sect. NIH, Bethesda, Md., 1990—; chmn. grant rev. com. Nat. Kidney Found. of Delaware Valley. Recipient Clin. Scientist award Am. Heart Assn., 1980, Young Investigator award Am. Heart Assn., 1985, Established Investigator award Am. Soc. Nephrology/Am. Heart Assn., 1987. Fellow ACP; mem. Am. Soc. Clin. Investigation, Assn. Am. Physicians, Am. Soc. Nephrology, Am. Assn. Immunologists, Am. Fedn. Clin. Rsch. Mem. Soc. of Friends. Office: U Pa 700 Clin Rsch Bldg Renal Electrolyte Sect 422 Curie Blvd Philadelphia PA 19104-6140

NEIMAN, LEROY, artist; b. St. Paul, June 8, 1927; s. Charles and Lydia (Serline) Runquist; m. Janet Byrne, June 22, 1957. Student, Sch. Art Inst. Chgo., 1946-50, U. Ill., 1951, DePaul U., 1951; LittD (hon.), Franklin Pierce Coll., 1976; hon. doctorate, St. John's U., 1980; hon. Doctorate, Iona Coll., 1985. Instr. Sch. Art Inst. Chgo., 1950-60, Saugatuck (Mich.) Summer Sch. Painting, 1957-58, 63, Sch. Arts and Crafts, Winston-Salem, N.C., 1963; instr. painting Atlanta Youth Council, 1968-69; printmaker-graphics, 1971—; artist Olympics, ABC-TV, Munich, 1972; ofcl. artist Olympics, ABC-TV, Montreal, 1976, U.S. Olympics, 1980, 84; computer artist CBS-TV (Superbowl), New Orleans, 1978; ofcl. artist Goodwill Games CNN-TV, Moscow, USSR, 1986. Exhibited one-man shows, Oehlshlaeger Gallery, Chgo., 1959, 61, O'Hana Gallery, London, Gallerie O. Bosc, Paris, 1962, Hammer Gallery, N.Y.C., 1963, 65, 67, 70, 72, 76, 78, 79, 81-83, 85-87, 89, 92, Huntington-Hartford Gallery Modern Art, N.Y.C., 1967, Heath Gallery, Atlanta, 1969, Abbey Theatre, Dublin, Ireland, 1970, Museo de Bellas Artes, Caracas, Indpls. Inst. Arts, 1972, Hermitage Mus., Leningrad, Tobu Gallery, Tokyo, 1974, Springfield (Mass.) Mus. Fine Arts, 1974, 84, Knoedler Gallery, London, 1976, Casa gratica, Helsinki, 1977, Renée Victor, Stockholm, 1977, Okla. Art Ctr., Oklahoma City, 1981, Harrod's, London, 1982; retrospective show, Minn. Mus. Art, St. Paul, 1975, Meredith Long Galleries, Houston, 1978, Hanae Mori Gallery, Tokyo, 1988, New State Tretyakov Mus., 1988, Butler Inst., Youngstown, Ohio, 1990; two-man show, Neiman-Warhol, Los Angeles Inst. Contemporary Art, 1981; exhibited in group shows, Art Inst. Chgo., 1954-60, Carnegie Internat., 1956, Corcoran Gallery Am., Washington, Walker Art Center, Mpls., 1957, Ringling Mus., Sarasota, Fla., 1959, Salon d'Art Mus., Paris, 1961, Nat. Gallery Portraiture, Smithsonian Instn., Washington, Minn. Mus. Art, 1969, Rotunda Della Basana, Milan, Italy, 1971, Royal Coll. Art, London, 1971, Minn. Mus. Art Nat. Tour, 1976-77, Whitney Mus., 1985 ; Master Prints of 19th and 20th Centuries, Hammer Galls., N.Y., 1987; represented in permanent collections, Mpls. Inst. Arts, Ill. State Mus., Springfield, Joslyn Mus., Omaha, Wodham Coll., Oxford, Eng., Nat. Art Mus. Sport, N.Y.C., Museo De Bellas Artes Caracas, Hermitage Mus., Indpls. Inst. Arts, U. Ill., Balt. Mus. Fine Art, The Armand Hammer Collection, Los Angeles; executed murals at, Merc. Nat. Bank, Hammond, Ind., Continental Hotel, Chgo., Swedish Lloyd Ship S.S. Patricia, Stockholm, ceramic tile mural, Sportsmans Park, Chgo.; sculptor 3-piece horse racing motif, 1977; Harlequin, 1983; Defiant Stallone, 1987, Vigilant Panther, 1987; Author: LeRoy Neiman—Art and Life Style, 1974, Horses, 1979, LeRoy Neiman. Posters, 1980, LeRoy Neiman. Catalogue Raisonné, 1980, Carnaval, 1981, LeRoy Neiman: Winners, 1983, Japanese translation, 1985, LeRoy Neiman, Monte Carlo Chase, 1988, The Prints of LeRoy Neiman, 1980-90, Big Time Golf, 1992; illustrator: 12 paintings deluxe edit. Moby Dick, 1975. Served with AUS, 1942-46. Recipient 1st prize Twin City Show, 1953, 2d prize Minn. State Show, 1954, Clark Meml. prize Chgo. Show, 1957, Hamilton-Graham prize Ball State Coll., 1958, Municipal prize Chgo. Show, 1958, Purchase prize Miss. Valley Show, 1959, Gold medal Salon d'Art Modern Paris, 1961; award of merit as nation's outstanding sports artist AAU, 1976; Olympic Artist of Century award, 1979, Gold Medal award St. John's U., 1985. Address: 1 W 67th St New York NY 10023

NEIMARK, EDITH DEBORAH, psychologist, educator; b. Long Branch, N.J., May 24, 1928; d. Solomon J. and Regina (Stein) N. BA, Skidmore Coll., 1949; MA, Ind. U., 1952, PhD, 1953. Instr. Tulane U., New Orleans, La., 1953-55; asst. prof. Goucher Coll., Towson, Md., 1955-56; rsch. psychologist AFP & TRC, USAF, Lackland AFB, Tex., 1956-58; from asst. to assoc. prof. NYU, 1958-64; from assoc. prof. to prof. Rutgers U., New Bruswick, N.J., 1964-91; vis. prof. dept. psychology U. N.Mex., Albuquerque, 1992—. Author: Adventures in Thinking, 1987; editor: Stimulus Sampling Theory, 1967, Moderators of Competence, 1985. Fellow AAAS, Am. Psychol Assn., Am. Psychol. Soc., N.Y. Acad. Scis. Home: 310 Crowells Rd Apt C Highland Park NJ 08904-3368 Office: Rutgers U New Brunswick NJ 08903

NEIS, ARNOLD HAYWARD, pharmaceutical company executive; b. N.Y.C., Feb. 13, 1938; s. Harry H. and Mary Ruth (Bishop) N.; m. Lucy de Puig, Dec. 8, 1989; children by previous marriage: Nancy R., Robert C. B.S. cum laude, Columbia U., 1959; M.B.A., N.Y.U., 1967. With Scott Chem. Co., 1959-64; v.p. mktg., then v.p. Odell, Inc., N.Y.C., 1964-71, pres. Knomark div., 1969-71; pres., chief exec. officer E.T. Browne Drug Co., Inc., Englewood Cliffs, N.J., 1971—; dir. Esquire A.B. Stockholm, Knomark Can. Ltd., E.T. Browne Internat. Fellow Royal Soc. Chemists, Royal Geog. Soc., Am. Inst. Chemists, N.Y. Acad. Scis.; mem. AAAS, Am. Chem. Soc., Am. Pharm. Assn., New Eng. Soc., Explorers Club (v.p., bd. dirs.), Chemists Club, Lotos Club, Soldiers, Sailors and Airmans Club (bd. dirs.). Episcopalian. Home: 898 Park Ave New York NY 10021-0234 Office: PO Box 1613 140 Sylvan Ave Englewood NJ 07632

NEIZVESTNY, ERNST JOSEPH, sculptor; b. Sverdlovsk, Russia, Apr. 9, 1925; came to U.S., 1976; s. Joseph M. and Bella (Abraham) Dejour; married; 1 child, Olga. AA, Acad. Art, Moscow, 1954; BA in Philosophy, Moscow State U., 1954; student, N.Y. Acad. Scis., French Acad. prof. Columbia U., N.Y.; guest prof. art and scis. NYU, N.Y.C., Harvard U., Boston, Yale U., New Haven, Conn., U. Calif., Berkeley, Am. Assn. for Advancement Slavic Studies. Author: On Synthesis in Art, 1983, Neizvestny Speaks, 1984; exhibited in group shows at Magna Gallery, San Francisco, 1985, Cathedral St. John the Divine, N.Y., 1985, Uhlrich Mus. Art, Wichita State U., 1987, Nakhamkin Fine Arts Gallery, N.Y., 1987, Eduard Nakhamkin Fine Arts and Magna Gallery, San Francsico, 1989, Ergane Gallery, N.Y., 1991; represented in permanent collections Mus. Modern Art, N.Y., Musee d'Art Moderne, Paris, Moderna Museet, Stockholm, Vasteras (Sweden) Mus., others. Lt. USSR Army, 1942-45. Decorated Red Star medal, Exceptional Bravery medal; recipient 5 World Competition Art award Aswan Damn Egypt, 1965. Mem. European Acad. Arts, Scis. and Humanities, N.Y. Acad. Scis., Royal Swedish Acad. Arts, Internat. Soc. Human Rights, Inc. Home and Office: 81 Grand St New York NY 10013

NEJELSKI, MARILYN M., civil rights advocate; b. Horton, Kans., July 12, 1934; d. Ray Leonard Mills and Bonnie Marie (Davis) Westberg; m. Paul Arthur Nejelski, Oct. 2, 1965; children: Nicole Rena, Stephen Downing. BA, George Wash. U., 1957; MA, NYU, 1974. Libr. asst. Washington Post, Washington, 1957-58; adminstrv. asst. White House Congl. Rels., Washington, 1961-64; intelligence rsch. analyst Dept. State, Washington, 1964-68; rsch. analyst Fed. Trade Commn., Washington, 1979-80; appointments sec. Nat. Women's Polit. Caucus, Washington, 1980-85; rsch. and project devel. Ind. Cons., Bethesda, Md., 1985-87; exec. dir. Women Judges' Fund for Justice, Washington, 1987—. Contbr. articles to profl. jours. Mem. Washington Bar Study Com. on Gender Bias in Cts., 1987-89. Recipient award Women's Action Orgn., State/ICA/AID, 1981, Superior Hon. award Dept. State, 1966, Florence K. Murray award Nat. Assn. Women Judges, 1991. Mem. Asia Soc. Roman Catholic. Office: Women Judges' Fund Justice 733 15th St NW # 700 Washington DC 20005-2182

NELL, EDWARD JOHN, economist, educator; b. Chgo., July 16, 1935; s. Edward John and Marcella (Roach) N.; m. Onora O'Neill, Jan. 19, 1963 (div. 1975); children: Adam, Jacob; divorced; children: Miranda, Guinevere; m. Marsha Karen Lasker, Nov. 25, 1989. BA, Princeton U., 1957; BA, MA, BLitt, Oxford (England) U., 1957-62. Tutor Nuffield Coll., Oxford, 1959-62; asst. prof. Wesleyan U., Middletown, Conn., 1962-67; lectr., sr. lectr. U. East Anglia, Norwich, United Kingdom, 1967-69; prof. econs. New Sch. for Social Rsch., N.Y.C., 1969—, dept. chair grad. faculty, 1974-75, 84-90; prof. Bennington (Vt.) Coll., 1978-79; vis. prof. U. Rome, McGill U., Montreal, U. Nice, France, U. Orleans, France, U. Bremen, Germany. Author: Prosperity and Public Spending, 1988, Transformational Growth and Effective Demand, 1992, Hard Drugs and Easy Money, 1992, Demanda Efectiva Precios y Salarios, 1982, Historia y Economia Politica, 1980; editor, author: Free Market Conservatism, 1984, Beyond the Steady State, 1992, Nicholas Kaldor and Mainstream Economics, 1991, Growth Profits and Property, 1980, Economics As Worldly Philosophy, 1992; author: (with M. Hollis) Rational Economic Man, 1975; contbr. articles to profl. jours. Vice chmn. Ams. for Dem. Action, Conn., 1965-68; dir. Class Struggle, Inc., N.Y.C., 1980-85; active dir. various peace, civil rights and environ. groups, N.Y.C., 1970—. Rhodes scholar, 1957-60; Bard Ctr. fellow, 1984; Jerome Levy grantee, 1988, 90. Fellow Centro di Studi Economici Avanzati (bd. dirs. 1986-88); mem. Am. Econ. Assn., Assn. Post-Keynesian Econs. (bd. editors 1980—), Eastern Econ. Assn., U.S. Rhodes Scholar Assn., Princeton Club, Phi Beta Kappa. Home: PO Box 1058 Woodstock NY 12498-0961 Office: New Sch for Social Rsch 65 5th Ave New York NY 10003-3003

NELLI, D. JAMES, business school executive, accountant; b. Seneca Falls, N.Y., Feb. 19, 1917; s. Thomas and Vita N.; m. Victoria Margaret Serino, Aug. 31, 1941 (dec. May 1980); children: Thomas, Diane, Joseph, John; m. 2d, Carmel L. Dowd, Sept. 19, 1981; BS, Syracuse U., 1948. CPA, N.Y. Staff acct. Seidman & Seidman, N.Y.C., 1948-49, Stover, Butler & Murphy, Syracuse, N.Y., 1949-55; instr. Syracuse U., 1953; instr. acctg. Central City Bus. Inst., Syracuse, 1955-58, pres., 1958—, also pvt. practice acctg., Syracuse. Served with USNR, 1943-46. CPA, N.Y. Mem. Am. Inst. CPAs, N.Y. State Soc. CPAs, Am. Acctg. Assn., AAUP. Roman Catholic. Clubs: Lakeshore Yacht and Country (Clay, N.Y.), Italian Am. Athletic (Syracuse). Home: 7929 Boxford Rd Clay NY 13041-8606 Office: Cen City Bus Inst 953 James St Syracuse NY 13203-2596

NELSON, ANDREW GEORGE, JR., educator; b. New Haven, Feb. 19, 1926; s. Andrew George Sr. and Viola Mary (Wells) N.; m. Carol Ann Nelson, Apr. 10, 1971; children: Karen, Kristen. BS, U. Md., 1958, MBA, 1964; EdD, Cath. U. Am., 1984. Commd. Lt. (j.g.) USNR, 1960; advanced through grades to comdr. USN, 1972, ret., 1978; with U.S. Govt., 1959-71; asst. prof. U. D.C., Washington, 1971-81; dean Southeastern U., Washington, 1981-82; prof., dean Montgomery Coll., Germantown, Md., 1982—. Branch chief USCG Aux., Washington, 1987-91; accident prevention counselor FAA, Balt., 1991—. Decorated Bronze Star. Mem. Am. Soc. Mil. Comptrollers, Univ. Aviation Assn., Ret. Officers Assn., Aircraft Owners and Pilots Assn., Germantown C. of C. (bd. dirs. 1990—), Germantown Kiwanis. Home: 6760 Kenwood Forest Ln Bethesda MD 20815-6502

NELSON, ARTHUR HUNT, corporate executive; b. Kansas City, Mo., May 21, 1923; s. Carl Ferdinand and Hearty (Brown) N.; m. Eleanor Thomas, Dec. 27, 1954; children: Carl F., Frances, Pamela. AB, U. Kans., 1943; JD, Harvard U., 1949. Bar: Mass. 1949. Staff radiation lab. MIT, 1943-44; sr. engr., cons. Raytheon Mfg. Co., Boston, 1948-52; pvt. practice Boston, 1949; v.p., treas., dir. Gen. Electronic Labs., Inc., Cambridge, Mass., 1951-64, chmn. bd., 1959-63; treas., dir. Sci. Electronics, Inc., Cambridge, 1955-64; treas., dir. Assocs. for Internat. Rsch., Inc., Cambridge, 1954—, pres., 1968—; treas., dir. Victor Realty Devel., Inc., Cambridge, 1959-76, pres., 1972-76, gen. ptnr., 1976—; gen. ptnr. Prospect Hill Exec. Office Park, Waltham, Mass., 1977—; chmn. Nelson Cos., 1990—; bd. dirs. Internat. Data Group, Inc. Pres., trustee Tech. Edn. Rsch. Ctrs., Inc., 1965—; trustee Winsor Sch., Boston, 1978-88, treas., 1978-82; bd. dirs. Charles River Mus. Industry, Waltham, 1986—. Lt. USNR, 1944-46. Mem. ABA, Mass. Bar Assn., Boston Bar Assn., Boston Computer Soc. (bd. dirs. 1985—), Greater Boston C. of C., Harvard Club (Boston), Beta Theta Pi, Phi Beta Kappa, Sigma Xi. Home: 75 Robin Rd Weston MA 02193-2436 Office: 200 5th Ave Waltham MA 02154-8704

NELSON, CAREY BOONE, sculptor; b. Lexington, Mass.; d. William M. and Carey (Butler) Boone; m. Kenneth Warwick Nelson; children: Caren, Kenneth Warwick II, Kimberly, Keith, Kyle, Craig. Student, U. Mo.; BA, Wellesley Coll.; MS in Edn., Wagner Coll. Cert. tchr., N.Y.C., N.Y. State. Tchr. N.Y.C. Pub. Schs.; instr. sculpture Snug Harbor Cultural Ctr., N.Y.C., 1982-84; per diem col., artist USAF, 1974-90. One-women shows Pietrantonio Galleries, N.Y.C., St. Bartholomew's, N.Y.C., Salmagundi Club, N.Y.C., Poly. Prep. Country Day Sch., Bklyn., Epiphany Libr., N.Y.C.; exhibited in group shows Internat. Art Exchange, Monte Carlo, Paris, Cannes, Athens, Victoria Mus. Libr., Melbourne, Australia, numerous others; represented in permanent collections Victoria Libr. Mus., Australia, Sheldon Swope Mus., Esperanza, Antartica, 1988, Durban (Republic South Africa) Mus., also others; sculptures commd. for Am.-Israel Friendship House, Mildred McAffee Horton, Wellesley Coll., Chuck Yeager for USAF, Jimmie Doolittle for USAF, Franklin (N.J.) Mineral Mus., 1980, Munro Monument USCG, 1989, Zinc Miner Monument, Col. Vaughn, Coll. Aeronautics, LaGuardia Airport, N.Y.C., 1991, Nat. League Am. Pen Women, James Madison Monument, Montpelier, Va., 1992. Bd. dirs. Cerebral Palsy Assn., S.I., N.Y., Vis. Nurse Assn., S.I. Named Woman of Achievement Wagner Coll., 1978, Hon. Life Artist Catharine Lorillard Wolfe Art Club, 1990; recipient Philip Eisenberg award Salmagundi, Anna Hyatt Huntington award. Fellow Am. Artists Profl. League, Royal Soc. Arts (London); mem. Composers, Authors and Artists Am. (nat. bd. dirs. 1981-90, 1st pl. award 1982, 84, 86), Soc. Illustrators, Burr Artists (bd. dirs. 1978—), Catharine Lorillard Wolfe Art Club (pres. 1978-81, bd. dirs. 1981—, chmn. 1978-81, Creative Hands award 1987, Artist of Yr. 1985), Nat. League Am. Pen Women (pres. N.Y.C. br. 1981-84, Manhattan N.Y.C. br. 1990-92, pres. 1990—, Woman of Achievement award 1988), Wellesley Coll. Club (pres. S.I.), Kappa Kappa Gamma (Woman of Achievement award 1978). Episcopalian. Home: 282 Douglas Rd Staten Island NY 10304-1526

NELSON, CARL EDWARD, management consultant; b. Bklyn., June 24, 1931; s. Karl Herman and Karin (Rehm) N.; m. Doris Porret Elliot, Nov. 10, 1956; children: Lucille, Bruce, Warren. BCE, Coopers Union, 1954; M Indsl. Engring., NYU, 1959. Dir. ASCE, N.Y.C., 1972-82; v.p. TPM Internat., Darien, Conn., 1982-84, H&M Group, Melville, N.Y., 1984-86; pres. Nelson Enterprises, Huntington Station, N.Y., 1986—; adj. prof. L.I. U., Brookville, N.Y., 1959—, The Cooper Union, N.Y., 1986-90. Contbr. articles to profl. jours. Pres. Haldale Civic Assn., Huntington Station, 1988. With U.S. Army, 1954-56. Mem. Nat. soc. of Profl. Engrs., Phi Delta Kappa, Tau Beta Pi, Chi Epsilon. Republican. Presbyterian. Home: 8 Evans Ct Huntington Station NY 11746-2819

NELSON, CURTIS NORMAN, neurosurgeon; b. Rochester, N.Y., Jan. 31, 1941; s. Clarence N. and Gladys (Weeks) N.; m. Nancy Janes Nelson; children: Kimberly, Christopher, Robert. BSEE, Princeton U., 1963; PhD in Physiology, U. Rochester, 1970, MD, 1972. Diplomate Am. Bd. Neurol. Surgeons. Elec. engr. Bausch & Lomb, Rochester, N.Y., 1963-64; surg. intern Mary Hitchcock Meml. Hosp., Hanover, N.H., 1972-73; resident in neurosurgery Mass. Gen. Hosp., Boston, 1973-78; asst. in neurosurgery Mass. Gen. Hosp., 1978; asst. prof. surgery U. Rochester Med. Ctr., 1978-84, assoc. prof. surgery, 1984—. Mem. Am. Assn. Neurol. Surgeons, Congress of Neurol. Surgeons, Alpha Omega Alpha. Office: 300 White Spruce Blvd Rochester NY 14623-1606

NELSON, DONALD EARL, wood scientist; b. Sturgeon Bay, Wis., July 15, 1934; s. Olaf and Hartha Adeline (Lenius) N.; m. Phyllis Ann Harper, July 27, 1963; children: Julie Lynne, Clara Ann. BS in Forest Products, U. Mich., 1959, MS in Wood Tech., 1961, PhD in Natural Resources, 1983. Instr. wood sci. W.Va. U., Morgantown, 1961-64; rsch. assoc. W.Va. Agriculture Experiment Sta., Morgantown, 1961-64; asst. prof. Cornell U. Coll. Agriculture, Ithaca, N.Y., 1966-68; nat. program leader Extension Svc., USDA, Washington, 1968-86, acting dep. adminstr., 1984-85, nat. program leader, 1987—; head engring. lab. U.S. Army Corps of Engrs., Greenham Common, England, 1954-57; adj. asst. prof. SUNY Coll. Forestry, Syracuse, 1966-68; chair extension svc. awards com. Extension Svc., USDA, Washington, 1978-80; natural resources program coord. Sci. and Edn. Adminstrn., USDA, Beltsville, Md., 1980-81; agy. rep. new farm and forest products task force USDA, Washington, 1985-86. Author: Wood Products Newsletter, 1968—; contbr. articles to profl. jours. Mem. various coms. Oxon Hill (Md.) Meth. Ch., 1985—. With U.S. Army, 1964-67. Recipient George Gevorkiantz Meml. award Lake States Forestry Schs., 1962, Dirs. award Sci. and Edn. Adminstrn., USDA, 1982; Schoen-Rene fellow Sch. Natural Resources, U. Mich., 1962-64. Mem. Am. Forestry Assn., Soc. Am. Foresters (Continuing Edn. cert. 1986), Soc. Wood Sci. and Tech. (bd. dirs. 1982-84, newsletter editor 1978-81, 87—, editorial writer 1980—), Forest Products Rsch. Soc. (chair tech. com. 1986), Epsilon Sigma Phi (pres. Mu chpt. 1990-91), Phi Kappa Phi. Home: 2720 Hidden Valley Ln Accokeek MD 20607 Office: Extension Svc USDA 14th and Independence Ave Washington DC 20250

NELSON, DONALD JOHN, chemistry educator, researcher; b. Perth Amboy, N.J., July 24, 1945; s. Norman A. and Elizabeth (Arva) N. BS in Agrl. Rsch., Rutgers U., 1967; PhD in Biochemistry, U. N.C., 1972. Postdoctoral fellow dept. pharmacology Stanford (Calif.) U., 1972-74; postdoctoral fellow dept. chemistry U. Va., Charlottesville, 1974-75; asst. prof. chemistry Clark U., Worcester, Mass., 1975-79, assoc. prof., 1979-87, prof., 1987—; adj. prof. pharmacology Grad. Sch. Biomed. Scis., U. Mass., Worcester, 1987—. Contbr. numerous articles to profl. jours. 1st lt. U.S. Army, 1972-74. Mem. Am. Chem. Soc. Office: Clark U Chemistry Dept 950 Main St Worcester MA 01610-1473

NELSON, FRANK RAPHAEL, secondary education educator, diving coach, scuba instructor; b. Pitts., Dec. 26, 1948; s. Frank R. and Frances Eileen (Casey) N.; divorced; children: Frank, Melissa, Christopher. BA, St. Vincent Coll., 1970; MS in Edn., Duquesne U., 1973. Cert. tchr. Lifeguard supr. Parks & Recreation Pool Divsn., Pitts., 1966-80; tchr., negotiator Woodland Hills Sch. Dist., Pitts., 1970—, diving coach, 1981—; pvt. practice in home remodeling Pitts., 1977—; scuba instr. Community Coll. Allegheny County Boyce Campus, Pitts., 1973—. Author: (manual) Lifeguard Training, 1971. Pres. Gen. Braddick Edn. Assn., Pitts., 1973-77; grievance

chair Gen. Braddock Sch. Dist., 1971-78; parish coun. St. Mary of the Mt. Ch., Pitts., 1974-77; vol. Red Cross, Pitts., 1966—. Recipient awards marking every 5 yrs. of svc., Red Cross, 1971, 76, 81, 86, 91. Mem. Pa. State Edn. Assn. (negotiator 1970—), Internat. Reading Assn., Keystone State Reading Assn., Gateway Scuba Club (safety officer 1973—). Democrat. Roman Catholic. Home: 344 Grace St Pittsburgh PA 15211 Office: Woodland Hills Sch Dist 531 Jones Ave Braddock PA 15104

NELSON, GREGORY VICTOR, chemicals executive; b. Mpls., Nov. 16, 1943; s. Lowell Albert and Florence Christine (Hove) N.; m. Karen Lynn Johnson, June 17, 1967; children: Erik Jonathan, Elizabeth Ann. BA, St. Olaf Coll., 1965; PhD, U. Calif., Berkeley, 1968. Asst. prof. chemistry Drew U., Madison, N.J., 1968-72, assoc. prof., 1972-79; supr. math. and computational svcs. Celanese Corp., Summit, N.J., 1979-81, mgr. info. and computational svcs., 1981-84, sr. staff assoc., 1984-87; sr. rsch. assoc. Hoechst Celanese Corp., Summit, 1987—; vis. prof. U. Fribourg, Switzerland, 1974-75; ind. adv. bd. dept. chem. engring. Rutgers U., New Brunswick, N.J., 1990—, mem. bd., sec. Ctr. for Computer Aids for Indsl. Productivity, 1988—. Contbr. articles to profl. jours. Mem. Am. Chem. Soc. (sec., chmn. Lackawanna subsect. 1986-89), Biosym Polymer Modeling Consortium (founder 1987). Office: Hoechst Celanese Rsch Div 86 Morris Ave Summit NJ 07901-3900

NELSON, HAROLD FREDERICK, metal company executive; b. Syracuse, N.Y., May 25, 1928; s. Harold F. and Josephine (Smitten) N.; m. Teresa Somerville, Dec. 10, 1955; children: Elizabeth Ann, Harold III, Mary Jo, Norine. BS in Mech. Engring., Cornell U., 1952. Engr. Phelps Dodge Copper Products, Bayway, N.J., 1956-64; gen. supt. Phelps Dodge Copper Products, Bayway, 1964-65, works mgr., 1965-68, v.p., 1968-75, v.p. ops., 1975-81; v.p. western sales & ops. Phelps Dodge Sales Co., Inc., Fort Wayne, Ind., 1981-87; sr. v.p. Phelps Dodge Sales Co., Inc., Fort Wayne, 1987-89, N.Y.C., 1989-91, Bd. dirs. Mountainside, N.J. Recreation Com., Chmn., 1968-78, Jr. Achievement, , v.p., 1965, '75, N.J. Tax Assn., 1965, '75. With U.S. Army, 1953-55. Mem. Copper Devel. Assn., Copper Club, Internat. Copper Devel. Assn. Home: 34 Alwin Ter Little Silver NJ 07739-1725

NELSON, JAMES HAROLD, health sciences administrator; b. Gosnell, Ark., Apr. 26, 1936; s. J.D. and Louise (Gann) N.; m. Betty Sue Leonard, Sept. 21, 1974; children: Amelia Rebecca, Rachel Louise. BS, Ark. State U., 1961, MS, 1969; PhD, Okla. State U., 1972. Registered profl. entomologist. Br. chief U.S. Army Environ. Hygiene Agy., Edgewood, Md., 1972-76; from rsch. area mgr. to div. chief U.S. Army Biomed. R & D Lab., Frederick, Md., 1976-92; project mgr. applied med. systems U.S. Army Med. Materiel Devel. Activity, Ft. Detrick, Md., 1992—; mem. Fed. Work Group Pest Mgmt., Washington, 1977-81; chmn. equipment com. Armed Forces Pest Mgmt. Bd., Washington, 1979-83; cons. dir. engrs. Ft. Detrick, Frederick, 1976—; guest lectr. Acad. Health Scis., U.S. Army, Ft. Sam Houston, Tex., 1986-88. Contbr. articles to profl. jours.; assoc. editor: Jour. Am. Mosquito Control Assn., 1982-88; chmn. editorial bd.: Equipment & Insecticides-Mosquito Control, 1989. With USN, 1954-58. Recipient numerous commendations U.S. Army, Ft. Detrick, 1981-92, R&D Achievement award Asst. Sec. of the Army, 1988, Order of Mil. Med. Merit, 1992. Mem. AAAS, Am. Pub. Health Assn., Entomol. Soc. Am., Assn. Mil. Surgeons U.S., N.Y. Acad. Scis., AMVETS, Am. Legion, Sigma Xi (pres. 1987-88). Republican. Episcopalian. Home: 2419 Tabor Dr Middletown MD 21769-9006 Office: US Army Med Material Devel Activity Fort Detrick MD 21702-5009

NELSON, JANICE EILEEN, paralegal; b. Worcester, Mass., Oct. 1, 1943; d. Joseph and Sally (Kosakowski) Rubler; m. Henry T. Knittel, Jr., Oct. 16, 1965 (div. 1979); children: Christie, Robin, Marcelle, Gary; m. David Nelson, Apr. 11, 1980 (div.). Grad., North High Sch., Worcester, Mass., 1961; student, Lyme Acad. Fine Art, 1985-86. Respiratory therapist St. Vincent Hosp., Worcester, 1963-65, Nassau Community Hosp., Mineola, N.Y., 1966-67, Good Samaritan Hosp., West Islip, N.Y., 1968-69; campaign mgr. Former Selectman Thomas Collimore, Fairfield, Conn., 1975, Former State Senator Myron Ballen, Fairfield, 1976; respiratory therapist VA Med. Ctr., West Haven, Conn., 1980-82; med. asst. Reproductive Med. Assocs., New London, Conn., 1983-86; paralegal O'Brien & Shafner, Groton, Conn., 1986—. Author poetry in Am. Poetry Anthology, 1986-87; artist of pastels, oils, charcoal and watercolor; photographer of landscapes, portraits (amateur); exhibited artwork Mystic (Conn.) Art Assn. Members Show, 1987-89, Mayflower Hotel Washington, 1991; back stage properties American Musical Theatre, 1986. Mem. Rep. Town Mtg., Dems., Groton, 1987-89, Dem. Town Com., 1987-89, Ctr. for Study of the Presidency, Rep. Presdl. Task Force, 1989—, Acad. Polit. Sci., 1988-89; founding sponsor Challenger Ctr., 1990; mem. Environ. Def. Fund; mem. Ox-Fam Am., 1989; founding mem. Am. Air Mus. in Britain; hospitality hostess Rep. Women's Club; elected mem. rep. Town Com., 1976, dist. leader; usher Eugene O'Neill Playwright's Conf., 1988—. John F. Kennedy Libr. hon. fellow, 1989. Mem. NAFE, Nat. Mus. of Women in the Arts, Natural Resources Def. Coun., Am. Acad. Polit. and Social Sci., Wilderness Soc., Internat. Sculpture Ctr., Sotheby's (charter), Nat. Trust, Folio Soc., Internat. Platform Assn., Friends of the Hartford Ballet, UNA-USA, Lyman Allyn Art Mus., Earth Watch, The Newcomer Soc., Nat. Space Soc., others. Roman Catholic. Home: 103 Branford Ave Groton CT 06340-5223 Office: OBrien Shafner 475 Bridge St Groton CT 06340-3700

NELSON, JIMMIE JACK, environmental engineer, consultant, retired military officer; b. McLoud, Okla., Feb. 1, 1928; s. Clifton Edward and Thyra Irene (Miller) N.; B.S. in Chem. Engring., U. Okla., 1949; B.S. in Aero. Engring., Air Force Inst. Tech., 1957, M.S. in Aero. Engring., 1962; m. Beth C. Carlsson, July 14, 1956; children—Paul C., Amy E. Commd. 2d lt. U.S. Air Force, 1949, advanced through grades to lt. col., 1971; sta. in Korea, 1953-54; with SAC, Biggs AFB, 1954-56, Air Force Inst. Tech., 1956-57, 60-62, 5th Air Force, Tokyo, 1957-60, Hdqrs. Systems Command, 1962-66, Pentagon, 1966-70, Da Nang, S. Vietnam, 1970-71; ret., 1971; engr. Fairfax County (Va.), 1972-79, developer, designer Air Monitoring Network, 1979; engr., mgr. research and devel. Am. Petroleum Inst., Washington, 1979-83, environ. cons., 1983—; staff engr. Eagle Tech., Inc., 1984-85; project mgr., 1985-89; sr. engr. Vitro Corp., 1989—; cons. U.S. State Dept., 1973-74. Decorated D.F.C. Mem. AIAA, Am. Chem. Soc., Air Pollution Control Assn. Republican. Baptist. Club: Masons. Contbr. articles to profl. publs. Home: 4308 Adrienne Dr Alexandria VA 22309-2803 Office: Vitro Corp Ste 800 400 Virginia Ave SE Washington DC 20024

NELSON, JOHN HARVEY, museum curator; b. McConnellsburg, Pa., Dec. 30, 1955; s. Watson Holmes and Esther Mary (Mellott) N.; m. Cynthia Ann Hough, June 14, 1991; 1 child, David Sheaffer (stepson). BA, Shippensburg U., 1977. Program dir., disc jockey Sta. WVFC, McConnellsburg, 1977-87; museum curator Jonathan Hager House, Hagerstown, Md., 1987—; sec. Washington County Historical Trust, Hagerstown, Md., 1988-91. Author: McConnellsburg, Pa.-Moments in History, 1986, Joseph Powell 1734-1804, 1987, Zook's Boy, 1988, Down the Pike, 1989, Frontier Forts of Fulton County, Pa, 1992. Mem. Washington County Network and mem. editorial bd. Mem. Fulton County Historical Soc. (pres. 1982-85, dir. 1985-88, historian of the year 1986). Republican. Presbyterian. Home: 541 Guilford Ave Hagerstown MD 21740-6215 Office: City of Hagerstown 1 E Franklin St Hagerstown MD 21740-4978

NELSON, KEITH ADAM, chemistry educator; b. N.Y.C., Dec. 8, 1953; s. Sidney and Doris Nelson; m. Martha Leticia Cortes, Oct. 5, 1981; children: Hannah, Dylan. BS in Chemistry, Stanford U., 1976, PhD in Phys. Chemistry, 1981. Postdoctoral scholar UCLA, 1981-82; asst. prof. chemistry MIT, Cambridge, 1982-87, assoc. prof., 1987-92, prof., 1992—. Contbr. over 80 articles to profl. jours. Recipient Presdl. Young Investigator award NSF, 1985-90, Coblentz prize Coblentz Soc., 1988; fellow Alfred P. Sloan Found., 1987-89. Fellow Am. Phys. Soc.; mem. Am. Chem. Soc., Opitcal Soc. Am., Materials Rsch. Soc., Inter-Am. Photochem. Soc. Office: MIT Dept Chemistry 77 Massachusetts Ave Cambridge MA 02139-4307

NELSON, KEVIN AUSTIN, telecommunication industry supervisor; b. Bklyn., Aug. 6, 1963; s. Hamel James Nelson and Sandra Louis (Lewis) Nelson Bazemore; m. Juanita Rose Hicks, Dec. 19, 1987; 1 child, Alexandria Rae Hicks-Nelson. Telex operator Banque Nationle De Paris, N.Y.C., 1986-88; telex/swift operator Banco Nacional De Mex., N.Y.C., 1988-89, telecommunicaitons supr., 1989—. Editor and pub. mag. When Suddenly..., 1990. With USAF, 1982-86. Democrat. Roman Catholic. Office: Banco Nat De Mex 375 Park 11th Ave New York NY 10152-0002

NELSON, KURT HERBERT, chemist; b. Sweden, Dec. 8, 1924; s. Harry A. and Anna C. (Borggren) N.; m. Sylvia R. Levalley, Sept. 4, 1949; children: Donald, Ann, Debra. BA, Reed Coll., 1949; PhD, U. Wash., 1953. Analytical rsch. chemist Phillips Petroleum Co., Bartlesville, Okla., 1953-60; chemist Tektronix, Portland, Oreg., 1960-62; mem. tech. staff N.Am. Rockwell, Canoga Park, Calif., 1962-70; sr. rsch. chemist Burlington Industries, Greensboro, N.C., 1970-72; supr. Internat. Paper Co., Tuxedo Park, N.Y., 1972—. Contbr. articles to sci. jours.; patentee in field. Cpl. U.S. Army, 1943-46, ETO. Fellow Am. Inst. Chemists; mem. Am. Chem. Soc. Home: 14 Virginia Ave Monroe NY 10950-2216 Office: Internat Paper Longmeadow Rd Tuxedo Park NY 10987

NELSON, LEONARD EARL, retired investment executive; b. Duluth, Minn., Mar. 6, 1944; s. Bernard Julius and Anne Mae (Brozic) N. Student, U. Minn., 1963-67, Acad. Vocal Arts, Phila., 1969-72, NYU, 1975. V.p. Jagerson Assocs., N.Y.C., 1974-81; stockbroker WH Newbold's Son & Co. Inc., Phila., 1981-83; asst. v.p. Butcher & Singer, Phila., 1983-86; v.p. 1st of Phila. Investment Group, 1986—. Soloist 1st Presbyn. Ch., Germantown, Pa., 1981-88; mem. 1st Presbyn. Ch. Phila.; team bd. dirs. Fight Against Drugs. Mem. Phila. Securities Assn., Pine Crest Assn., Stone Harbor Country Club, Northland Country Club, Old York Rd. Country Club, Lulu Country Club, Pensacola Country Club. Republican. Home: Charmant 403A Bayshore Dr Pensacola FL 32507 Office: First Phila Investment Group 2009 Chestnut St Philadelphia PA 19103-3307 also: Charmont 403 A Bay Shore Dr Pensacola FL 32507

NELSON, LINDA BEATRICE D'ANDREA, volunteer worker; b. Waterbury, Conn., Apr. 27, 1926; d. Consalvo August and Margaret Donata (Santoro) D'Andrea; m. Robert Andrew Nelson, June 20, 1949; children: Eric Robert, Forrest Andrew. Grad. high sch., Terryville, Conn. Mem. staff Am. Bd. Anesthesiology, Hartford, Conn., 1958-82. Author: (poetry) Satan's Beat, 1975, Rhyme Remembrances, 1990. Member Greenpeace; charter mem. Burlington (Conn.) Land Trust, 1989; founder Burlington Concerned Citizens, 1987. Mem. Farmington (Conn.) Watershed Assn. Home: 472 Jerome Ave Burlington CT 06013-2314

NELSON, MARIETTA LOU, librarian; b. Benzonia, Mich., Mar. 16, 1928; d. Leonard L. and Florence (Martindale) Case; m. Sherman E. Nelson, Feb. 28, 1953; children: Karen M., Kirsten A. BA, Smith Coll., 1949; MA in Libr. Sci., U. Mich., 1967. Reference libr. Mich. State U., East Lansing, 1968-69; libr. Nat. Inst. Standards & Tech., Gaithersburg, Md., 1970—. Mem. Am. Libr. Assn. Home: 19149 Stedwick Dr Gaithersburg MD 20879-2937

NELSON, MARK H., law association administrator; b. Fargo, N.D., May 29, 1950; s. Harold L. and Joan (Shefstad) N.; m. Connie Gayle George, Nov. 11, 1976; 1 child, Carly Nicole. BSBA, U. N.D., 1981; MBA, Vanderbilt U., 1983. V.p., gen. mgr. Clark Industries, Nashville; chief fin. officer Am. Standard Coal Co., Nashville; prin. Mgmt. Systems of Am., Nashville and Palm Beach, Fla., 1987-90; bus. mgr. Mae Volen Sr. Ctr., Boca Raton, Fla., 1988-90; practice adminstr. Arcaro & Reilly, Providence, 1990—. Mem. Friends of TUVA. Home: 20D Tamarac Dr Greenville RI 02828-2533 Office: Arcaro & Reilly 1500 Turkshead Bldg Providence RI 02903

NELSON, SISTER MARY RENÉE, educator, registrar; b. Bronx, May 8, 1915; d. Clarence Joseph and Mary Agnes (Davey) N. BS in English, Seton Hall U., 1942; MA in French, Case Western Res. U., 1947; postgrad., Cath. U. Am., 1952-53, Fordham U., 1954-60; postgrad, Laval U., Quebec, Que., Can., 1965. Joined Sisters of Christian Charity; cert. English and French tchr., N.J., Pa. Tchr. St. Nicholas Elem. Sch., Jersey City, 1934-41; tchr. bus. and religion West Phila. Cath. Girls High Sch., 1941-42; tchr. English, French and Latin Cen. Cath. High Sch., Reading, Pa., 1942-57; prin. Immaculate Conception Br. Cathedral Girls' High Sch., Bronx, 1957-61; tchr. English, French and journalism Morris Cath. High Sch., Denville, N.J., 1961-69; dean, prin. Bishop Neumann High Sch., Williamsport, Pa., 1969-71; tchr. Immaculata High Sch., Mendham, N.J., 1971-79; tchr. Assumption Coll. for Sisters, Mendham, N.J., 1971—, registrar, 1981—; pub. rels. Assumption Coll. for Sisters; rep. Sisters of Christian Charity on the Interch. Com. of the Mendhams, 1982—, chmn., 1984-85. Author poetry and mag. articles. Recipient Gold Key award Columbia Scholastic Press Assn., 1981. Home: Mallinckrodt Convent Hilltop Rd Mendham NJ 07945

NELSON, RICHARD HENRY, manufacturing company executive; b. Norfolk, Va., May 24, 1939; s. Irvin Joseph and Ethel Blair (Levy) N.; m. Carole Ellen Rosen, Mar. 12, 1966; children: Christopher, Karin. BA, Princeton U., 1961; postgrad., Georgetown U., 1962-63. Spl. asst. to dir. Peace Corps, Washington, 1961-62; mil. aide to v.p. Office of U.S. V.p., Washington, 1962-63; asst. to U.S. Pres. White House, Washington, 1963-66; spl. asst. to sec. HUD, Washington, 1966-68; v.p. Am. Internat. Bank, N.Y.C., 1968-70, Studebaker-Worthington, N.Y.C., 1970-73; pres. Sartex Corp., N.Y.C., 1973-80; pres., chief exec. officer Cogenic, Inc., N.Y.C., 1980-90; chmn. bd. Utility Systems Corp., N.Y.C., 1983—; chmn., chief exec. officer Utility Systems Corp., Southampton, N.Y., 1990-92; chief exec. officer U.S. Envirosystems, Inc., Southampton, 1992—; bd. dirs. Nelco Corp., Laurel, Md.; chmn. bd. Powersave Inc., N.Y.C., 1984—; chmn. bd., chief exec. officer Utility System Fla., Inc. Bd. dirs. Nat. Hypertension Assn., N.Y.C., 1982-90; exec. com. Southampton Assn., N.Y., 1983—; advisor to mayor Historic Preservation Com., Southampton, 1986—; prin. Ctr. Excellence in Govt., Washington, 1987—. 1st lt. U.S. Army, 1962-64. Recipient Presdl. Medal Office of Pres. of U.S., 1965. Mem. Internat. Cogeneration Assn., Am. Gas Assn., Am. Cogeneration Coalition, Ind. Power Producers, Princeton Club, Doubles Club, Southampton Hunt and Polo Club (chmn. bd.), Palm Beach Polo and Country Club, U.S. Polo Assn. Democrat. Home: First Neck Ln Box 1530 Southampton NY 11969 Office: US Envirosystems Inc 12012 Longwood Green West Palm Beach FL 33413

NELSON, RONALD ROY, federal official; b. Sioux Falls, S.D., Nov. 11, 1941; s. Roy John and Edna Olive (Parry) N. BA, U. S.D., 1963; MA, Duke U., 1965, PhD, 1967. Asst. prof. history Western Carolina U., Cullowhee, N.C., 1969-73; mem. profl. staff Senate Fgn. Rels. Com., Washington, 1981-82; dep. rep. to mut. and balanced force reduction talks State Dept., Vienna, Austria, 1982-83; pvt. practice cons. Washington, 1983-85; rep. of Sec. Def. to Conf. on Disarmament Dept. of Def., Geneva, 1985-89, 90—; exec. dir. Am. Fgn. Policy Coun., Great Falls, Va., 1989-90. Author: The Home Office, 1782-1801, 1969; (with others) Soviet Concepts of Peace, Peaceful Coexistence and Detente, 1988; contbr. articles to profl. jours. Capt. U.S. Army, 1967-69, Vietnam, maj., 1973-81; col. USAR, 1988—. Decorated Bronze Star; Woodrow Wilson Found. fellow, 1963, 65. Republican. Lutheran. Home: 4500 S Four Mile Run Dr Arlington VA 22204-3558 Office: OSD/ISP-MN 2D453 Pentagon Washington DC 20301

NELSON, RUTH BASHA, artist; b. Bronx, N.Y., July 1, 1939; d. Louis and Anne Helen (Margolies) Shribnik; m. Jack Roberts; children: Douglas G., Robin A.; m. William Rudd, Nelson, Mar. 9, 1979. BA, CUNY, 1960; MA, NYU, 1976. Instr. Met. Mus. Art, N.Y.C., 1974-76, Coll. of Bahamas, Nassau, 1978-80; adj. instr. Marist Coll., Poughkeepsie, N.Y., 1984-89; arts coord. Ulster County Bd. Coop. Ednl. Svcs., New Paltz, N.Y., 1985-91. One-woman shows Flemington (N.J.) Studio of Arts, 1975, 60, Washington Square East Gallery, N.Y.C., 1976, Flemington Gallery Arts, 1977, Am. Embassy, Nassau, 1978, Green County Coun. on Arts, Catskill, N.Y., 1987, Noho Gallery, N.Y.C., 1988, 90, Manhattanville Coll., Purchase, N.Y., 1989; exhibited in group shows, Fla., N.Y., Bahamas, Denmark, 1978-92; represented in permanent collections Am. Embassy, Nassau, Bahamas, Woodstock (N.Y.) Hist. Soc. Recipient Welfred McGibbon award Mus. Palm Beaches, Palm Beach, Fla., 1980, hon. mention Green County Coun. on Arts, 1986. Mem. Artists Equity, Woodstock Artists Assn. Studio: Rt 212 PO Box 86 Lake Hill NY 12448

NELSON, STANLEY, author; b. Bklyn., June 9, 1933; s. Charles and Celia (Prager) N.; B.A., U. Vt., 1957; m. Betty Jean Minton, June 26, 1966; children—Celia, Lycette. Reporter, Burlington (Vt.) Daily News, 1957-62; sr. writer Medica Materia, N.Y.C., 1962-63; asst. news editor Med. World News, N.Y.C., 1963-65; sr. writer Image, N.Y.C., 1965-66; sr. editor Hosp. Practice, N.Y.C., 1966-69; free-lance med. writer/editor for Consultant, Drug Therapy, Pack Med. Inst., others, 1969-77; internat. editor Pain Topics, 1977—; editor Oncology News, 1977—. Recipient Thomas Wolfe Poetry award N.Y. U. Faculty, 1955. Mem. Nat. Assn. Sci. Writers, Poets and Writers, Inc., Dramatists' Guild, PEN, N.Y. Drama Concept (co-chmn. 1972-74). Author: The Passion of Tammuz, 1959; Idlewild, 1970, revised edit., 1971; The Brooklyn Book of the Dead, 1972; Chirico Eyes, 1976; Travels of Ben Sira, 1977; 101 Fragments of a Prayer, 1980; The Unknowable Light of the Alien (short stories), 1981; Nightriffer (poetry), 1983, Driftin' on a Nightriff, 1988; also numerous plays produced U.S. and Eng. Editor: (with Harry Smith) The Scene/1 (drama anthology), 1973; The Scene/2, 1974; The Scene/3, 1976; The Scene/4, 1977. Editor Gnosis, 1968-72; co-editor Proscenium, 1973-74. Contbr. poetry to profl. jours. Home: 454 37th St Brooklyn NY 11232-2510

NELSON, VITA JOY, editor, publisher; b. N.Y.C., Dec. 9, 1937; d. Leon Abraham and Bertha (Sher) Reiner; m. Lester Nelson, Aug. 27, 1961; children: Lee Reiner, Clifford Samuel, Cara Ritchie. BA, Boston U., 1959. Promotion copywriter Street & Smith, N.Y.C., 1958-59; asst. to mng. editor Mademoiselle Mag., N.Y.C., 1959-60; mcpl. bond trader Granger & Co., N.Y.C., 1960-63; founder, editor, pub. Westchester Mag., Mamaroneck, N.Y., 1968-80, L.I. Mag., 1973-78; found., editor, pub., pres. Moneypaper, Mamaroneck, N.Y., 1981—. Bd. dirs. Westchester Tourism Council, Westchester County, N.Y., 1974-75, Sackerpath Council Girl Scouts U.S.A., White Plains, N.Y., 1976-79; bd. govs. v.p. Am. Jewish Com., Westchester, N.Y., 1979-89. Recipient citation Council Arts, 1972; Media award Pub. Rels. Soc. Am., 1974. Mem. Women in Communications (Outstanding Communicator award 1983), Sigma Delta Chi. Democrat. Home: Pleasant Ridge Rd Harrison NY 10528-1004 Office: Temper of the Times Communications 1010 Mamaroneck Ave Mamaroneck NY 10543-1660

NEMAZEE, REZA, psychologist; b. Teheran, Iran, Sept. 22, 1949; came to U.S., 1966, naturalized, 1949; s. Mohammad Hossein and Luz Belen (Maldanado) N.; BA, Hobart Coll., 1971; MS, SUNY, Oswego, 1977, CAS, 1977; PhD, Syracuse U., 1978; m. Noushin Shams-Molkara, June 30, 1979; children: Shahin, Ali. Instr. rehab. Syracuse U., 1976, clin. supr., 1975-77; clin. asso. W.O. Ward, M.D., PC, Richmond, Va., 1978; asst. prof. rehab. psychology Imperial Med. Ctr. of Iran, Teheran, 1978; rehab. psychologist Iran Rehab. Assocs., Teheran, 1978-79; asst. prof. Coll. St. Joseph the Provider, Rutland, Vt., 1980-81; rehab. psychologist Rehab. Assocs., Rutland, 1981-84; adj. instr. Antioch/New Eng. Grad. Sch., 1982-83; rehab. cons. Rutland Mental Health, 1981, cons. psychologist, 1980-83; cons. psychologist Vt. Div. Vocat. Rehab., 1981—; mem. adv. coun. Vt. Community Mental Health Ctrs., 1982-83; adj. asst. prof. Coll. St. Joseph the Provider, 1981-83; rehab. psychologist, Essex Junction, Vt., 1983—; mem. sci. staff Fanny Allen Hosp., 1984—; dir. Champlain Industries. Lic. psychologist, Vt.; cert. sch. psychologist, Vt., N.Y. Mem. Am. Psychol. Assn., Am. Pers. and Guidance Assn., Am. Rehab. Counseling Assn., Vt. Psychol. Assn. (sec./treas.1987-88, pres. 1989-90), Am. Soc. Clin. Hypnosis, Rotary. Office: 25 Pinecrest Dr Essex Junction VT 05452-2912

NEMEC, VERNITA ELLEN MCCLISH, mixed-media artist, educator; b. Painesville, Ohio, Nov. 30, 1942; d. Vernon William and Ellen (Ludway) McClish; m. David Joseph Nemec, Apr. 18, 1964 (div. 1970). B.F.A. cum laude, Ohio U., 1964; postgrad. Cleve. Inst. Art, 1964-65; M.A., NYU, 1966; postgrad. Bklyn. Mus. Sch. Art, 1967-68, Fashion Inst. Tech., 1969-70, Sch. Visual Arts, 1970-71, Naropa Inst., 1978-79. Student adviser Bklyn. Coll., 1966-67; art specialist pub. schs., N.Y.C., 1967-68; prof. fine arts Rockland Community Coll., Suffern, N.Y., 1970-71, CUNY, 1973-79, Jersey City State Coll., 1976-77, Sch. Visual Arts, N.Y.C., 1977-78; ednl. cons. Middlesex Arts and Edn. Coun., Highland Park, N.J., 1988—; curator, organizer exhibit, Mus. Project for Living Artists, N.Y.C., 1970; co-dir. Whitney Counterweight, N.Y.C., 1977, 81, 83; asst. dir. Susan Caldwell Gallery, 1982; design asst. John Haines Design, N.Y.C., 1983; bd. dirs. Found. New Ideas, 1985; vis. artist Lake Erie Coll., Painesville, 1975, Jersey City State Coll., 1976, U. Calif.-Santa Barbara, 1983; artist-in-residence Millay Colony for Arts, Austerlitz, N.Y., 1981; exec. dir. Artists Talk on Art, 1989—; slide curator art dept. Baruch Coll., N.Y.C., 1990-92; v.p. Heresies Collective, 1992—. Solo exhbns. include: Soho 20 Gallery, N.Y.C., 1975, 77, Jersey City State Coll., 1976, Jersey City Mus., 1977, Fiatal Muveszek Klubia, Budapest, Hungary, 1980, 10 on 8 Gallery, N.Y.C., 1984, Los Angeles Women's Bldg., 1985; group exhibits include: Landmark Gallery, N.Y.C., 1976, Bronx Mus. Art, 1976, David & Long Gallery, N.Y.C., 1977, Hudson Ctr. Gallery, N.Y.C., 1985, Willoughby Fine Arts Ctr., Ohio, 1974, Joseloff Gallery, Hartford, Conn., 1980, exhibits in Europe, Denmark, Hungary, Yugoslavia and Italy; pvt. and pub. collections include Franklin Furnace, Inc., Grupa Junij Belgrade, Asian Art Ctr, N.Y.C., Queensboro Coll. Author: Unmaled, 1978; playwright: Private Places, 1985, The Last Confession, 1982, The Autumn of Her Descent, 1984; founder, artistic dir. The Floating Performance, 1985—. NDEA fellow, 1965-66, Cultural Council Found. fellow, 1978, 79, 84; Jerome Found. grantee, 1988. Mem. Nat. Abortion Rights Action League, NOW, Women's Caucus for Art, Lower Manhattan Loft Tenants Assn., Orgn. Ind. Artists, Dance Theater Workshop Assn. Address: 361 Canal St New York NY 10013

NEMEROFF, MICHAEL ALAN, lawyer; b. Feb. 16, 1946; s. Bernard Gregor and Frances (Gotleib) N.; m. Sharon Lynn Leininger, Sept. 22, 1974; children: Theodore, Patrick, James. BA, U. Chgo., 1968; JD, Columbia U., 1971. Asst. counsel Subcom. on Juvenile Delinquincy of Senate Jud. Com., Washington, 1971-73; assoc. Sidley & Austin, Washington, 1973-78, ptnr., 1978—. Treas. Friends of Jim Sasser, 1978—, Andy Ireland Campaign Com., 1984—. Office: Sidley & Austin 1722 I St NW Washington DC 20006-3705

NÉMETHY, GEORGE, chemistry educator; b. Budapest, Hungary, Oct. 11, 1934; came to U.S., 1954; s. Imre and Mária (Mikó) N.; m. Judith Kesserü, Apr. 26, 1975; children: Kinga, Mária. BA, Lincoln U., 1956; PhD, Cornell U., 1962. Rsch. chemist GE Rsch. Lab., Schenectady, N.Y., 1962-63; asst. prof. of phys. chemistry Rockefeller U., N.Y.C., 1963-72; vis. prof. of biochemistry U. Paris XI, Orsay, France, 1972-74; vis. assoc. prof. of chemistry SUNY, Binghamton, 1974-75; sr. rsch. assoc. of chemistry Cornell U., Ithaca, N.Y., 1975-89; prof. of biomath. sci. Mt. Sinai Sch. Medicine, N.Y.C., 1989—; vis. prof. chemistry U. Federico II, Naples, Italy, 1984, 86; vis. lectr. Inst. Superiore di Sanità, Rome, 1970; lectr. NYU Med. Ctr., N.Y.C., 1971-72. Contbr. over 150 sci. articles to profl. publs. Recipient Pius XI Gold medal Pontifical Acad. Sci., 1972; European Molecular Biology Orgn. sr. fellow, 1973-74. Mem. Am. Chem. Soc., N.Y. Acad. Scis., Am. Soc. Biochemistry, Molecular Biology, Hungarian Scouts Assn. in Exteris (pres. 1973—). Mem. Reformed Ch. Office: Mt Sinai Sch Medicine Dept Biomath Sci 1 Gustave L Levy Pl # 1023 New York NY 10029-6504

NEMIROW, BRUCE IRVING, sales and marketing executive; b. Jersey City, Aug. 4, 1948; s. Charles and Sylvia N.; m. Joan Ruth Klapp, Dec. 21, 1969; children: Kim, Carly, Lindsay. BA, Rutgers U., 1969; postgrad., NYU, 1969-71. V.p. Smith Barney Harris Upham, N.Y.C., 1973-76, Thomson McKinnon Securities, N.Y.C., 1976-80, Moseley Securities, N.Y.C., 1980-86; sr. v.p. Shearson Lehman Bros., N.Y.C., 1986-90, John W. Henry & Co., Westport, Conn., 1990—; arbitrator Am. Stock Exchange, N.Y.C., 1985-91, Nat. Assn. securities Dealers, 1985-91; dir. Westport Capital Mgmt.; treas. Global Capital Mgmt. Editor: Options as a Strategic Investment, 1978, Wall St. Journal Guide to Investment, 1989. With USAR, 1969-75. Home: 16 Woodcock Ln Westport CT 06880-1037 Office: John W Henry & Co Inc 1 Glendinning Pl Westport CT 06880-1242

NEMOTO, TAKUMA, physician; b. Japan, Apr. 10, 1930; came to U.S., 1955; m. Susan M. Mackey, June 18, 1960; children: Carol Ann, Patricia Lynn, david Takuma, Peter Allen. MD, Keiou Sch. Medicine, Tokyo, 1954. Physician Roswell Pk. Cancer Inst., Buffalo, N.Y., 1962-88, Breast Care Ctr., Buffalo, N.Y., 1988—. Fellow ACS, Soc. Surgical Oncology. Office: Breast Care Center 2121 Main Buffalo NY 14214

NEMOY, LEON, retired librarian, research scholar; b. Balta, Ukraine, USSR, Dec. 29, 1901; came to U.S., 1923; s. Abraham and Binah (Halperin)

N.; m. Elizabeth Hackney McGinley, Oct. 20, 1930(dec. 1988). Student, State U., Odessa, USSR, 1918; MA, Yale U., 1926, PhD, 1929; DHL (hon.), Hebrw Union Coll., N.Y.C., 1976. Cataloguer Jewish Acad. Libr., Odessa, 1919-21, Univ. Libr., Lemberg, Poland, 1922; Hebrew and Arabic lit. curator Yale Univ. Libr., New Haven, 1923-66; rsch. assoc. Dropsie Coll., Phila., 1967-87, Annenberg Rsch. Inst., Phila., 1987—. Editor: (book in 5 vols.) Al-Qirqisānī, Kitāb al-anwār, 1939-45; compiler and translator (book) Karaite Anthology, 1952; contbr. numerous articles to scholarly jours. Home: 2200 W Franklin Pky Apt 304E Philadelphia PA 19130-2107 Office: Annenberg Rsch Inst 420 Walnut St Philadelphia PA 19106-3703

NENNEMAN, RICHARD ARTHUR, publishing executive; b. Chgo., Oct. 13, 1929; s. William T. and Fannie (Peterson) N.; m. Katherine Ann LaBrunerie, June 29, 1954; children: Ann Walker, Mary Lisa, Katherine Conley. A.B. magna cum laude, Harvard U., 1951, M.A. in Internat. Affairs, 1953. With No. Trust Co., Chgo., 1957-58; v.p., treas., dir. First Fed. Savs. & Loan Assn., St. Joseph, Mo., 1958-60; with Valley Nat. Bank. Phoenix, 1960-65; asst. v.p., 1963-65; bus. and financial editor Christian Sci. Monitor, Boston, 1965-74; v.p., dir. investment research Girard Bank, Phila., 1974-77; sr. v.p., chmn. trust investment policy com. Girard Bank, 1977-82; editor, exec. producer, TV broadcasting Christian Sci. Pub. Soc., Boston, 1987; mng. editor Christian Sci. Monitor, Boston, 1983-86; editor-in-chief Christian Science Monitor, 1988—; mem. investment com. Gen. Accident Ins. Group., until 1982. Contbr. to Understanding Our Century, 1984; editor: (with Earl Foell) How Peace Came to the World, 1986, The New Birth of Christianity, 1992. Trustee Barnes Found., until 1982; selectman Town of Weston, Mass., 1973-74; chmn. Boston Com. on Fgn. Rels. Served with AUS, 1954-57. Mem. Coun. on Fgn. Rels. Home: PO Box 641 Lincoln MA 01773-0006 Office: Christian Sci Monitor 1 Norway St Boston MA 02115-3122

NENNER, RODNEY ANDREW, international reciprocal-countertrade executive; b. Queens, N.Y., Oct. 11, 1961; s. Robert R. and N. Dona (Samuels) N. BS, Cornell U., 1983; MBA, London Sch. Econs.-Polit. Sci., 1985. Founder, exec. v.p. Artificial Intelligence Applications Corp., Great Neck, N.Y., 1985-87; pres. Artificial Intelligence Applications Corp., 1987-89; mgr. product remktg. and trading Atwood Richards, Inc.; internat. countertrade exec. specializing innn Eastern Europe and former Soviet republics; key rep. Assn. Data Processing Svc. Orgns., Washington, 1986—; speaker in field. Mem. Hazardous Material Rsch. Coun., Cornell Club. Home: 201 W 70th St Apt 8F New York NY 10023-4332 Office: 99 Park Ave New York NY 10016-1503

NEPHEW, ARTHUR WALLACE, financial analyst, educator, researcher; b. Buffalo, Oct. 29, 1953; s. Arthur W. and Edith M. (Arpe) N.; m. Zenna L. Oldshield, Oct. 23, 1982; children: Allison, Cassandra, Samantha, Shelby. BS in Bus., Medaille Coll., 1985. Outreach worker Buffalo N. Am. Indian Culture Ctr., Inc., Buffalo, 1980-83, bookkeeper, 1983-84; fin. analyst ARC, Buffalo, 1985—; instr. Bryant & Stratton Bus. Inst., Buffalo, 1988—. Contbr.: (newsletter) The Perspective, 1982-85. Mem. advisor Cayuga Nation of Indians, Gowanda, N.Y., 1953—; mem. Native Am. Task Force on Higher Edn., Buffalo, 1982-87. Recipient Ambassador award Medaille Coll., 1989. Mem. Am. Mgmt. Assn., Buffalo IBM PC Users Group, U.S. Golf Assn. American Baptist. Home: 135 Goemble Ave Buffalo NY 14211-2403

NERDRUM, ODD, artist; b. Halsingborg, Sweden, Apr. 8, 1944. Student of, Joseph Beuys, Dusseldorf, Fed. Republic of Germany. One-man shows include Gallery Tanum, Norway, 1977, 83, Delaware Art Mus., Wilmington, 1985, Martina Hamilton Gallery, N.Y.C., 1984, 85, 86, 87, U. Art Mus., Long Beach, Calif., 1988, Mus. Contemporary Art, Chgo., 1988, Madison Art Ctr., Wis., 1988, Nelson-Atkins Mus., Kansas City, Mo., 1988, 89; represented in permanent collections Walker Art Ctr., Mpls., La Jolla Mus. Art, Hessisches Landes Mus., Riksgalleriet, Norway, Norsk Kulturrad. Office: Martina Hamilton & Assoc Inc 1623 3d Ave New York NY 10128

NERO, PETER, pianist, conductor, composer, arranger; b. N.Y.C., May 22, 1934; s. Julius and Mary (Menasche) N.; m. Marcia Dunner, June 19, 1956; children—Beverly, Jedd; m. Peggy Altman, Aug. 31, 1977. Student, Juilliard Sch., N.Y.C. Nat. tour with Paul Whiteman on TV and in concert, 1953-57, appearances concert halls, theatres, colls., TV and supper clubs throughout U.S., Eng., France, Holland, Italy, Scandinavia, 1962—; appeared at Grand Gala du Disque, Amsterdam, The Netherlands, 1964, five TV specials on BBC-TV; arranged, appeared and recorded with Boston Pops Orch.; music dir., Philly Pops Orch., 1979—; recording artist for Pro Arte Records, RCA Victor, Arista Records, Crystal Clear Records, Columbia; albums include Peter Nero Now, The Sounds of Love, 1987; appeared in film Sunday in New York; composer: condr. more than 150 symphony orchs., 1971—; pops music advisor Tulsa Philharm., 1987; pops music dir. Columbus Symphony, 1990. Honored by Internat. Soc. Performing Arts Adminstrs., 1986; recipient 8 Grammy nominations, 2 Grammy awards; named #1 Instrumentalist Cashbox Mag. Office: Gurtman & Murtha Assocs 162 W 56th St # 505 New York NY 10019-3876

NERO, WILLIAM THOMAS, SR., academic administrator; b. Providence, Feb. 1, 1935; s. Joseph John Sr. and Henrietta (Petorella) N.; m. Ann Marie Campbell, May 23, 1959; children: Nancy Panciocco, William T. Jr., Joseph A., Daniel T., Patrick F., Christopher P. AB, Providence Coll., 1955, BS, 1976, MBA, 1977; postgrad., Wharton Sch., 1976-77. Cert. fund raising executive. Employment supr. R.I. Dept Employment Security, Providence, 1958-61; regional dir. MDAA, Inc., N.Y., R.I., Southeast Mass., 1961-63; devel. cons. Community Counselling Service, N.Y.C., 1963-67; from dir. annual giving to assoc. v.p. devel. Providence Coll., 1967-82, v.p. devel., 1983-87, v.p. bus. affairs, 1988—; cons. in field. Contbr. articles to profl. jours. Trustee John E. Fogarty Found., Providence, 1987; bd. dirs. Youth Vision, Inc., Providence, 1981-87, bd. dirs. CURE, Inc., Providence, 1971-75; pres. Crestwood Assn., East Providence, R.I., 1968-69; chmn. Johnston Bd. Canvassers, 1990—. Lt. U.S. Army, 1955-57, capt. USAR, 1960. Recipient Disting. Alumnus award LaSalle Acad., 1971, Disting. Faculty/Staff award Greater Providence Coll. Alumni chpt., 1978, Disting. Faculty/Staff award Providence Coll. Nat. Alumni Assn., 1982, United Italian Ams. Disting. Achievement award 1989. Mem. Coun. for Advancement and Support of Edn., Bishop's Capital Funding Study Com., Nat. Assn. Fund Raising Execs., Greater Providence C. of C., Providence Coll. Pres. Coun., Nat. Assn. of Coll. and Univ. Bus. Officers, Eastern Assn. of Coll. and Univ. Bus. Officers, Univ. Club, Landings Country Club, Elks, K.C. Democrat. Roman Catholic. Home: Atwood Ave Cranston RI 02920-3932 Office: Providence Coll River Ave Providence RI 02918-0001

NES, DAVID GULICK, retired diplomat; b. York, Pa., Feb. 17, 1917; s. Charles Motier and Ethel (Billmeyer) N.; m. Elizabeth Taylor Houghton, Dec. 7, 1946; children: Victoria, Nancy, Margaret, Audrey, Wendy. AB in History with hons., Princeton U., 1939; postgrad., Harvard U., 1939-40. With Balt. Sun, 1940-41; div. asst. Dept. State, Washington, 1941-42; fgn. svc. officer Dept. State, 1946-68, assigned to Washington, 1952-54, 56-59; vice consul Am. Consulate, Glasgow, Scotland, 1946-49; 2d sec. Am. Embassy, Paris, 1949-52; dep. chief mission, counselor Tripoli, 1954-56, Rabat, 1959-62; dep. chief mission min. Saigon, Vietnam, 1963-64, Cairo, 1965-67; ret., 1968; columnist, lectr. in field, 1968—. Capt. AUS, 1942-46, CBI. Decorated Bronze Star. Mem. Chevy Chase Golf Club, Green Spring Valley Hunt Club, West River Sailing Club, N.Y. Yacht Club. Home: 15 Crestline Ct Owings Mills MD 21117-4336

NESBIT, DOUGLAS CHARLES, educator; b. London, Eng., Oct. 4, 1926; s. Charles Henry Fletcher and Constance Elspeth (Bruce) N.; B.A., U. Toronto, 1949, Ont. Coll. Edn., 1950; postgrad. U. Western Ont., 1962, 64, 67. Tchr., Bruce Mines (Ont., Can.) Continuation Sch., 1950-51; tchr., later head geography dept. Banting Meml. High Sch., Alliston, Ont., 1951-84; pres. bd. dirs. Brit. Israel World Fedn., 1984—. Past pres., Alliston br. Canadian Bible Soc. With RCAF, 1943-44. Fellow Am. Geog. Soc., Nat. Council Geog. Edn.; mem. Ont. Assn. Geog. and Environmental Edn., Canadian Assn. Geographers, Assn. Am. Geographers, AAAS, Brit. Israel World Fedn. (pres.), Scottish Tartans Soc. (life), Royal Can. Legion, Royal Commonwealth Soc., Monarchist League Can., Can. Inst. Internat. Affairs, Empire Club of Can., South Simcoe Palette Club (past pres.). Home: Box 89, Alliston, ON Canada L0M 1A0

NESBIT, LARRY LEONARD, library administrator; b. Indiana, Pa., Dec. 31, 1944; s. Joseph Franklin and Hazel (Deafenderfer) N.; m. Sandra Walter, June 22, 1969. BS, Indiana U. of Pa., 1966, MEd, 1967; MLS, U. Pitts., 1970; EdD, Pa. State U., 1979. Edn. libr. Mansfield (Pa.) State Coll., 1970-81; libr. dir. Mansfield U., 1981—; cons. Access Pa., Pa. Dept. Edn., Harrisburg, 1987—; bd. dirs. CCSI, Mansfield, Mansfield U. Found., Interlibr. Delivery Svc., Harrisburg; chmn. bd. dirs. Susquehanna Libr. Coop., Williamsport, Pa., State System Higher Edn. Libr. Coun., Harrisburg. Contbr. articles to profl. publs. 1st lt. U.S. Army, 1967-69, Vietnam. Grantee Pa. State Libr., Harrisburg, 1991. Mem. ALA, Assn. for Edn. Communication and Tech., Pa. Assn. Edn. Communication and Tech. Home: 327 Austin Dr Mansfield PA 16933-9749 Office: Mansfield U Mansfield PA 16933

NESBITT, ILSE BUCHERT, artist; b. Frankfurt, Hesse, Fed. Republic Germany, Sept. 6, 1932; came to U.S., 1960; d. Rudolf Oskar Sebastian and Emmi Katharina (Krefter) Buchert; m. Alexander John Nesbitt, Oct. 15, 1966; children: Alexander Hugh, Rupert Sebastian. Student, Art Acad., Hamburg, Fed. Republic Germany, 1954-55, 57-58, Art Acad., Berlin, 1956-57. Co-owner, operator Third & Elm Press, Newport, R.I., 1965—. Author, designer, illustrator: The Best Tailor in the World, 1983, My Garden, 1988; co-author, designer: Weathercocks and Weathercreatures, 1970 (Bronze medal 1971); one-woman shows include Rutgers U. Libr., State U. Libr., Hamburg, Gallery Wolf-Bütow, Frankfurt. Mem. Newport Art Mus. Mem. Soc. Printers. Home and Office: 29 Elm St Newport RI 02840-2404

NESBITT, LLOYD IVAN, podiatrist; b. Toronto, Ont., Can., Sept. 24, 1951; s. Allan Jay and Rose (Shuster) N.; m. Marlene Cindy Wegler, May 13, 1984; children: Hilary Liza, Andrea Eve, Jeffrey Ryan. D in Podiatric Medicine, Calif. Coll. Podiatric Medicine, San Francisco, 1975. Diplomate Internat. Soc. Podiatric Laser Surgery. Residency program Vancouver (B.C.) Gen. Hosp., Can., 1975-76; pvt. practice podiatric medicine Toronto; cons. podiatry Alan Eagleson Sports Medicine Clinic, Toronto, 1979—; lectr. numerous colls., fitness ctrs. and sports medicine confs., Ont., 1979—. Contbr. numerous articles to sports medicine books and jours; editor Canadian Podiatrist Jour., 1979-88. Fellow Can. Podiatric Sports Medicine Acad. (pres. 1979-89, editor newsletter 1977-89); mem. Internat. Soc. Podiatric Laser Surgery (diplomate), Am. Podiatric Med. Assn., Sierra Club. Home: 122 Argonne Crescent, Willowdale, ON Canada M2K 2K1 Office: Madison Ctr Office Tower, 4950 Yonge St Ste 2414, Toronto, ON Canada

NESNICK, VICTORIA GILVARY, educator, writer, lecturer; b. Corona, N.Y., June 15, 1945; d. Victor Carmen and Italia (Signorile) Bonavita; m. Thomas John Gilvary, (div. 1980); 1 child, Amy Victoria; m. Robert John Nesnick. BS, State U., New Paltz, N.Y., 1966; MS, Queens Coll., 1974. permanent cert. sch. dist. adminstr., supr., advance studies, tchr. nursery, kindergarten, grades 1-6, N.Y. Children's supr. St. Dominics Home for Children, Blauvelt, N.Y., 1966-67; tchr. Nanuet (N.Y.) Schs., 1966-67, Bethpage (N.Y.) Schs., 1967—; work with staff devel. and rsch. grants Bethpage Schs., 1986-88; mentor L.I. U., 1990; lectr., workshop leader, insvc. instr., seminar presenter in field. Author: Princess Diana: A Book of Questions and Answers, 1988; editor: Newsletters for Abused Women, 1981; newspaper columnist, 1986-87; contbg. author Reflections mag.; contbr. articles to mags. Exec. bd. dirs., Coalition for Abused Women, Nassau County, N.Y., 1979-80; spkr.for media and universities for abused women, L.I., N.Y., 1979-82; nat. television interviewee on Princess Diana, 1989. Named Woman of the Yr., L.I. U. and Coalition for Abused Women, 1979, No. 1 author, Cen. Blvd. Sch., Bethpage, 1988; recipient Jenkins Meml. award, 1989. Mem. Bethpage Fedn. Tchrs., Am. Fedn. Tchrs., NOW, Women's Nat. Book Assn. N.Y.C., Soc. Children's Book Writers, Phi Delta Kappa. Home: Three Ibsen Ct Dix Hills NY 11746 Office: Ctrl Blvd Sch Central Blvd Bethpage NY 11714-4636

NESSEL, EDWARD HARRY, pharmacist; b. Roselle, N.J., 1945; s. Irving Meyer Nessel and Ruth Eliott; m. Eileen Robin Berstein, 1973; children: Lee Allyson, Jason Eric, Matthew Scott (dec.). BS in Chemistry, Rutgers U., 1967, degree in pharmacy chemistry, 1968, postgrad., 1971; postgrad., Jersey City State, 1970; MS in Bacteriology, Wagner Coll., 1978, MPH, 1978. Registered pharmacist, Calif., N.J., Fla. Researcher, product developer Mennen Cos., Morrisplains, N.J., 1967; pharmacist supr. Pathmark Pharmacies, N.J., 1968-79; pharmacist, mgr. Roxy Drug Co., Inc., Irvington, N.J., 1979-90; diet and nutrition cons. Fanwood Scotch Plaines YMCA, 1985—, masters swim coach, 1984—, swimming and racing cons., head age group coach, asst. sr. coach, 1989-91; head swim coach Jewish Community Ctr. Met. N.J., Orange, 1991—, head swim coach Maccabi, 1990-91; coach N.J. Masters Swimming, 1985—; physiology and sports medicine cons. Nat. Masters Swimming; pres. Jersey Masters Swimming Inc.; sports chair age group and masters swimming Garden State Games Inc., 1991. Contbr. articles on swimming, self def. and physiology to profl. jours. Athletic and swimming cons. N.J. Spl. Olympics, 1986; cons. Essex County Narcotic Strike Force, Garden State Games ofcl.; chairperson govs. coun. phys. fitness for swimming events Garden State Games, 1989, 90. Recipient Presdl. Series award 1986; named N.J. State Pentathlon champion Masters Swimming, 1986, 87, YMCA Masters Nat. Swim champion, 1988. Mem. N.J. Guild Pharmacists, Am. Assn. Microbiologists, N.J. Pharm. Assn., Nat. Rifle Assn., Internat. Practical Shooters Confedn. (N.J. State champion 1982, 83), Am. Swimming Coaches Assn. (master level), U.S. Swimming Coaches Assn. (cert.), Master Swim coaches Assn. Am., Rutgers Coll. Alumni Assn., Willow Grove Swim Club (bd. dirs. 1986—), South River Pistol Club. Home: 10 Irene Ct Edison NJ 08820-1024 Office: JCC Metrowest 760 Northfield Ave West Orange NJ 07052

NESSELROADE, JOHN RICHARD, psychology educator; b. Silverton, W.Va., Mar. 13, 1936; s. John S. and Emma E. (Suck) N.; m. Carolyn S. Boyles, July 12, 1959; children: Cynthia Anne, Jennifer Sue. BS, Marietta Coll., 1961; MA, Univ. Ill., 1965, PhD, 1967. Asst. prof. W. Va. U., Morgantown, 1967-70, assoc. prof., 1970-72; assoc. prof. human devel. Pa. State U., University Park, 1972-75, prof., 1975-83, rsch. prof., 1983-90, disting. rsch. prof., 1990—, dir. Ctr. for Devel. and Health Rsch. Methodology, 1989-91; Hamilton prof. psychology U. Va., Charlottesville, 1991—; cons. rsch. network on successful aging MacArthur Found., Chgo., 1985—. Editor: Handbook of Multivariate Exptl. Psychology, 1988. Sgt. USMC, 1954-57, Japan. Recipient Cattell award Soc. of Multivariate Exptl. Psychology, 1972. Fellow AAAS, APA, Am. Psychol. Soc. (charter). Home: 116 Chestnut Ridge Rd Charlottesville VA 22901-8544

NESSEN, WARD HENRY, typographer, lawyer; b. Empire, Mich., Nov. 29, 1909; s. Henry L. and Louise (Stecher) N.; m. Jane Randall, Apr. 4, 1959. AB, U. Mich., 1931; JD, John Marshall Law Sch., Chgo., 1937; course in acctg. Northwestern U. Grad. Sch., 1946. Bar: Ill. 1937. With trust dept. No. Trust Co., Chgo., 1934-41; sales planning Am. Home Products, 1946-51; sales exec. Permacel Tape Corp., 1951-55; pres. The Highton Co., Newark, 1955-75; sr. v.p. Arrow Typographers, Newark, 1975-84; chmn. Coll. Communications Seminar, 1973. Mem. Civic Clubs Council Greater Newark Area, 1957-59, Bd. Comml. Arbitration N.Y.C., 1982-86; chmn. selection com. Advt. Hall of Fame of N.J., 1983, inductee, 1990. Lt. col. AUS, 1941-46, ETO, assigned SOS. Decorated Bronze Star with oak leaf cluster, Army Commendation medal; recipient Elmer G. Voigt award, 1975; named to Advt. Hall of Fame N.J., 1990. Mem. Typographers Internat. Assn. (pres. 1970-71), N.J. Typographers Assn. (pres. 1957-59), Print/N.J. (pres. 1967-69), Assn. pf Graphic Arts N.Y. (bd. govs. 1967-69), John Monteith Soc., Pres.'s Club of U. Mich., Order of John Marshall, Sigma Phi. Republican. Episcopalian. Clubs: Type Dirs.; Advt. N.J. (bd. govs 1972-84). Home: 11 Euclid Ave Summit NJ 07901-2114

NESTERUK, JULIA ANN, marriage and family counselor; b. Hartford, Conn., Aug. 3, 1955; d. Jacob and Maria (Laszczuk) N. AA, Becker Jr. Coll., Worcester, Mass., 1975; BA magna cum laude, Cen. Conn. State U., 1985, MS, 1991. Ct. recording monitor judicial dept. State of Conn., Hartford, 1975-88; clin. therapist Children's Ctr., 1992—; workshop lectr. Mem. Am. Assn. Counseling and Devel., Internat. Assn. Marriage & Family Counselors. Ukrainian Catholic.

NESTOR, MARILYN FERGUSON, journalist, public relations counselor; b. McKeesport, Pa., Jan. 31, 1932; d. William Gardner and Mildred Alma (Goode) Ferguson; m. Lee Thomas Nestor, Apr. 22, 1966; children: David Lee, Rebecca Nestor Boivin. Student, Chatham Coll., 1949-51; BS, Mich. State U., 1953. Reporter Pitts. Sun-Telegraph, 1955-60; news editor, reporter WTAE-TV, Pitts., 1962-64; ptnr. Lee Nestor Assocs., Pitts., Somerset, 1965-72; chief press rels. Pa. Dept. Edn., Harrisburg, 1972-75; dir. pub. rels., advt. Pa. Lottery, Pa. Dept. Revenue, Harrisburg, 1976-79; playwright N.Y.C., 1982-85; speech writer N.J. Dept. Health, Trenton, 1986-89; smoke free hosp. program dir. N.J. Hosp. Assn., Princeton, 1989; free lance writer Tinton Falls, N.J., 1989—. Co-author: (plays) Even in Laughter, 1981, A Different Harp, 1983. Recipient First Prize news, Pitts. Women's Press Club, 1957, '58, '59, First Prize poetry Tri-County Arts Coun., Johnstown, Pa., 1971, First Prize, playwrighting, Friends of Caldwell Playhouse, Boca Raton, Fla., 1982. Mem. The Dramatists Guild. Home and Office: 2 Jodphur Ct Tinton Falls NJ 07753

NESWALD, BARBARA ANNE, advertising executive; b. N.Y.C., Jan. 14, 1935; d. Edward and Veronica (Presby) Lutz; m. Ronald Neswald, Nov. 15, 1952 (div. Jan. 1957); children: Kurt Thomas, Linda Neswald Hunt, Elizabeth Neswald Williams. Student Hunter Coll. Media dir. R.M. Klosterman Inc., Los Angeles, 1960-64, copy writer, Los Angeles, 1964-73; copy chief Broadway Dept. Stores, Los Angeles, 1973-76; creative dir. Lucky Stores, Inc., Buena Park, Calif., 1976-79; v.p. advt. and communications Top Value Enterprises Co., Dayton, Ohio, 1979-82; sales promotion dir. Strawbridge & Clothier Clover div., Phila., 1982—; mem. adv. bd. Los Angeles Trade Tech. Coll., 1976-77. Bd. dirs. Pa. chpt. UNICEF, 1985-89, Am. Poetry Ctr., 1985-92, Women in Transition, Inc.; bus. and profl. funding com. Acad. Vocal Arts; alumna Community Leadership Seminars, Phila. Recipient various advt. awards; N.Y. Regents scholar, 1952-53. Mem. Am. Mktg. Assn., Women in Communications, Inc., Internat. Mass Retailing Assn. (named Retail Advertiser of Yr. 1990), Soroptomists (bd. dirs. Phila. chpt. 1989-91). Office: 801 Market St Philadelphia PA 19103

NETTER, CORNELIA ANN, real estate broker; b. N.Y.C., July 11, 1933; d. Frank H. and Mary (MacFadyen) N.; divorced; 1 child, Cornelia Jr. Student, U. Denver, 1951-53, C.W. Post Coll., 1958-60; BS, N.Y. State Regents, 1972. Adminstrv. asst. to U.S. Senator J. K. Javits N.Y., 1961-66; spl. asst. to Gov. Nelson A. Rockefeller Office of Gov., N.Y.C., 1966-69; pub. affairs dir. N.Y. State Health Planning Commn., 1969-72; dir. human resource planning and programs N.Y. State Office Planning Svcs., Albany and N.Y.C., 1972-76; pres. Netter Communications, N.Y.C., 1976-83, Netter Real Estate, N.Y.C., 1983—, Independent Brokers Network, 1988—. Founding mem. N.Y. State Women's Polit. Caucus, Albany, 1971; mem. Rep. Family Com., 1986—; mem. steering com. Breakthru Found., N.Y.C., 1983-85; bd. dirs. N.Y. Citiworks, 1987-90; dep campaign mgr. Rockefeller Gubernatorial Campaign, N.Y.C., 1966, dir. spl. groups, 1970; co-campaign mgr. for N.Y., Nixon Presdl. Campaign, 1968, dir. ethnic and spl. groups, 1972; candidate for N.Y. State Assembly, 1974; mem. Rep. County Com. Recipient 1st ann. Residential Deal of Yr. award Real Estate Bd. N.Y., 1989. Mem. Nat. Assn. Realtors, Real Estate Bd. N.Y. (legis. and residential brokers coms.), Downtown Brokers Assn. (chmn. polit. affairs and membership coms.), Greenwich Village C. of C. (bd. dirs. 1988—). Office: Netter Real Estate Ste 1710 853 Broadway New York NY 10003-4703

NETTER, KURT FRED, building products company executive; b. Mannheim, Fed. Republic Germany, Dec. 3, 1919; came to U.S., 1941, naturalized, 1944; s. Arthur and Kate (Gruenfeld) N.; m. Alice Dreyfus, May 26, 1942; children: Nadine, Ronald, Alfred. Student, Swiss Inst. Tech., 1938-39, U. Toronto, 1939-41; BS, Columbia U., 1942. Ptnr. Interstate Engring. and Machinery Co., N.Y.C., 1942-44; officer, dir. Supradur Cos., Inc., 1946—, pres., chief exec. officer, 1953—, bd. dirs.; chief exec. officer subs. Supradur Mfg. Corp., Wind Gap, Pa., Suprawall Corp., Rye, N.Y., Precision Fabricators, Inc., Garden City Park, N.Y., Triton Co., Inc., Rye, Twin City Tool Inc., Olathe, Kans., Supradur Investments Inc., Montreal, Que., Can. Bd. dirs. Selfhelp Community Svcs., Inc., treas., 1970-85, pres., 1985-90, chmn., 1990—. With AUS, 1944-46. Home: 203 Griffen Ave Scarsdale NY 18580-0908 Office: Supradur Cos Inc 411 Theodore Fremd Ave Rye NY 10580-1410

NETTESHEIM, CHRISTINE COOK, federal judge; b. Oakland, Calif., Aug. 25, 1944; d. Leo Marshall and Carolyn Grant (Odell) Cook. BA, Stanford U., 1966; JD, U. Utah, 1969. Bar: Utah 1969, D.C. 1972, Calif. 1982. Clk. to chief judge U.S. Ct. Appeals (10th cir.), 1969-70; trial atty. U.S. Dept. Justice, Washington, 1970-72, Fed. Trade Commn., Washington, 1972-74; litigation Hogan & Hartson, Washington, 1974-76; spl. counsel Pension Benefit Guaranty Corp., Washington, 1976-78; asst. gen. counsel U.S. Ry. Assn., Washington, 1978-80; litigation Shack & Kimball P.C., Washington, 1980-83; judge U.S. Claims Ct., Washington, 1983—. Mem. State Bar Assn. Calif., D.C. Bar Assn., Order of Coif. Republican. Presbyterian. Clubs: Cosmos, University. Office: US Claims Ct 717 Madison Pl NW Washington DC 20005-1011

NEUBAUER, ANTHONY CHARLES, polyolefin processing professional; b. Chgo., May 14, 1953; s. John Peter and Rosemary (Kadolph) N.; m. Mary Elizabeth Hoyer, July 2, 1983; children: Thomas Michael, Elizabeth Anne. BSME cum laude, Cath. U., 1975. Registered profl. engr., W.Va. Equipment engr. Union Carbide Corp., South Charleston, W.Va., 1975-85, polymer processing engr., 1985-90; polymer processing scientist Union Carbide Corp., Bound Brook, N.J., 1990—. Mem. ASME, Soc. Plastic Engrs. Office: Union Carbide PO Box 670 Bound Brook NJ 08805-0670

NEUBAUER, JOSEPH, business executive; b. Oct. 19, 1941; s. Max and Herta (Kahn) N.; children: Lawrence, Melissa. B.S. in Chem. Engring, Tufts U., 1963; M.B.A. in Fin, U. Chgo., 1965. Asst. treas. Chase Manhattan Bank, 1965-68, asst. v.p., 1968-70, v.p., 1970-71; asst. treas. Pepsico Inc., Purchase, N.Y., 1971-72; treas. Pepsico Inc., 1972-73, v.p., 1973-76; v.p. fin. and control Wilson Sporting Goods Co., River Grove, Ill., 1976-77, sr. v.p., gen. mgr. team sports div., 1977-79; exec. v.p. fin. and devel., chief fin. officer, dir. ARA Svcs., Inc., Phila., 1979-81; pres., chief operating officer, dir. ARA Services, Inc., Phila., 1981-83, pres., chief exec. officer, 1983-84; chmn., ceo, pres. ARA Svcs., Inc., Phila., 1984—; bd. dirs. First Fidelity Bancorp, VS Svcs., Ltd., Bell of Pa.; trustee Penn Mut. Life Ins. Co. Chmn., CEO Phila. Orch. Assn., Mann Music Ctr., Inroads/Phila., Inc.; trustee Hahnemann U., Tufts U., Mus. Am. Jewish History, Greater Phila. First Corp., Com. for Econ. Devel., U. Chgo.; bd. govs. Joseph H. Lauder Inst. Mgmt. and Internat. Studies, U. Pa. Mem. Phila. C. of C., Union League, Locust Club, Phila. Club, Bus. Roundtable. Clubs: Union League, Locust, Philadelphia. Office: ARA Svcs Inc ARA Tower 1101 Market St Philadelphia PA 19107-2934

NEUBERG, HANS W., physician; b. Hanover, Germany, Mar. 26, 1921; s. George and Gertrude (Dux) N.; came to U.S., 1937, naturalized, 1943; B.S., Wagner Coll., 1941; M.D., Columbia, 1950; m. Birgit Aron, Apr. 8, 1949; children—Peter G., Gerald W. Intern Presbyn. Hosp., N.Y.C., 1950-51, asst. resident, 1951-53, NRC fellow in medicine, 1953-54, asst. attending physician, 1966-80, assoc. attending physician, 1980-91, attending physician, 1992—; instr. medicine Columbia Coll. Phys. and Surg., 1954-63, assoc. in medicine, 1963-67, asst. prof. clin. medicine, 1967-80, assoc. clin. prof. medicine, 1980-91, clin. prof. medicine, 1992—. Served with AUS, 1943-46. Fellow A.C.P.; mem. Am. Diabetes Assn., Alpha Omega Alpha. Home: 85 Erledon Rd Tenafly NJ 07670-2503 Office: 620 W 168th St New York NY 10032

NEUFELD, RONA, elementary educator; b. Bklyn., June 24, 1949; m. Don Payne. BS, Hunter Coll., 1971; MS, SUNY, Albany, 1973. Tchr. first grade N.Y.C. Pub. Schs., Flushing, N.Y., 1977—; pres. Jazz Line, Jazz Interactions. Editor: JazzLine. Office: Jazz Interactions PO Box 268 Glen Oaks NY 11004

NEUGROSCHL, JILL PAULETTE, financial planning company executive; b. N.Y.C., Mar. 25, 1949; d. Irving and Lillian (Berkowitz) Satler, m. Edward Neugroschl, May 28, 1972; 1 child, Dara Satler. BA in Elem. Edn., Farleigh Dickinson U., 1970; MS in Spl. Edn., Coll. New Rochelle (N.Y.), 1974. Cert. fin. planner; registered securities and investment advisor. Tchr. elem. schs. Yonkers, N.Y., 1970-77; v.p. fin. planning Finesco Assocs., Inc., Lincolndale, N.Y., 1978—; tchr. Brewster (N.Y.) Adult Edn., 1986. Chairperson Conn. Pub. TV Auction Co., New Milford, 1986-89; chairperson Temple Sholom Sch. Bd., New Milford, 1987-89, treas., exec. bd., 1989-90, v.p., 1990-91, pres., 1991—. Mem. Internat. Assn. Fin. Plan-

ning, Inst. Cert. Fin. Planners. Democrat. Jewish. Home: 25 Dean Rd New Milford CT 06776-3824 Office: Finesco Assocs Inc PO Box 700 Lincolndale NY 10540-0700

NEUHAUS, PETER CHARLES, elementary educator; b. Paris, Jan. 12, 1939; s. Max and Catherine (Weszely) N.; m. Carmen marie Maysonet, Apr. 25, 1969; children: Charlotte, Charles. BA in History, CCNY, 1965; postgrad., Universidad Nacional Autonoma, Mexico City, 1966, Columbia U., 1972; Grad. in Edn., CCNY, 1973. Mech. draftsman Marcato Elevator Co., L.I.C., 1958-59; prodn. engr. Fedders Corp., Maspeth, N.Y., 1959-67; elem. sch. tchr. N.Y.C. Bd. Edn. PS19K, Bklyn., 1967-74; tchr. homebound children N.Y.C. Bd. Edn., PS30M, Manhattan, 1974—; group home tutor Queensborough Soc. for Prevention of Cruelty to Children, 1976—. With U.S. Army, 1957-58. Roman Catholic. Home: 48-50 37th St #6M Long Island City NY 11101

NEUHAUSER, MARY HELEN, artist, writer; b. San Antonio, Feb. 17, 1943; d. Gotthelf Friedrich and Edna Earl (Walling) N.; m. Federico Andrea Canuto, Jan. 6, 1972 (div. June 1981). Student, Carnegie-Mellon U., 1962-64, Studio Nera Simi, Florence, Italy, 1964-65. Official portraits in FBI Bldg., Rayburn House Reps. Office Bldg., Trinity Coll., Sidwell Friends Sch., Washington; one-person shows include Potters House Gallery, Washington, AAUW, Bethesda, Md., Martha Washington Library, Alexandria, Va., Thirty-Year Retrospective, Friendship Gallery, Chevy Chase, 1989; exhibited at Nat. Mus. Fine Arts, Smithsonian Instn., Nat. Cathedral, Lincoln Meml., Corcoran Gallery of Art, Monroe House, Arena Stage, Nat. Dem. Club, Veerhoff Galleries, Washington, Curl Gallery, Washington, Capricorn Galleries, Bethesda, Md., Lorenz Gallery, Bethesda, Gallery Orlov, Alexandria, Seloff Gallery of Fine Art, Brownsville, Tex.; work reproduced in newspapers The Washington Post (1st place 1961, 64), The Washington Daily News, The Evening Star, Capitol Hill Roll Call; represented in numerous pvt. collections; contbr. op-ed articles to Washington Post, Bethesda Almanac, Heritage Found. mag. Active St. Joseph's Home for Boys, Washington, 1965-66, Lincolnia (Va.) Day Care Ctr., 1966-67, Meriwether Home for Children, Washington, 1969-70, congl. campaign of Stewart Bainum; county exec. campaign of David Lee Scull, 1986; active supporter, writer Dem. Presdl. campaign, 1988, 92; vol. with Vietnam casualties, Nat. Naval Med. Ctr., Bethesda ARC, 1970-71; active supporter and writer on homeless, 1984—; health care advocate writer, U.S. Senate, 1986—; donator art works to Fed. City Shelter, Washington; vol. 3 shelters for homeless, Washington and Md., 1984—; health care advocate, writer U.S. Senate; writer campaign for Nat. Health Ins. Act, 1989—. Recipient Best-in-Show award, first profl. competition, 1961, 11 awards for abstracts, numerous others; ofcl. portraits in FBI Bldg., Rayburn Ho. of Rep. Office Bldg., Trinity Coll., Sidwell Friends Sch. Mem. DAR. Democrat. Mem. Ecumenical Ch. Home and Studio: 4602 Chevy Chase Blvd Chevy Chase MD 20815

NEUKAM, RANDALL MAURICE, educational consultant; b. Detroit, Mar. 28, 1951; s. Joseph Karl Neukam and Winona (Walsh) Cogan; m. Arja Tellervo Jokinen, Aug. 18, 1972; children: Aria-Ilona, Suvi-Theresa. BA, Eastern Mich. U., 1973; EdS, Ind. U., 1981, postgrad., 1987. Cert. secondary tchr., Mich. Project dir. Ind. U., Bloomington, 1983-85; project mgr. Bibliogem, Inc., Bloomington, 1985-87; instructional designer Newman, Howey & Assocs., Ltd., Indpls., 1987-88, Digital Equipment Corp., Hudson, N.H., 1989—; cons. edn. task force White River Park Devel. Commn., Indpls., 1985, Audubon/Ind. Dept. Nat. Resources, Bloomington, 1985; co-evaluator Faculty Devel. Study, Dean of Faculties, Bloomington, 1985. Designer software Macmillan Spelling Series, 1986, Macmillan Composition-Elementary, 1987, Macmillan Map Skills, 1985. Mem. Nat. Soc. for Performance Instrn., Am. Edn. Research Assn., Pi Lambda Theta. Home: 5 Pavillion Rd Amherst NH 03031-1803 Office: Digital Equipment Corp Digital Dr Merrimack NH 03054

NEUMAN, CHARLES P., electrical and computer engineering educator, consultant; b. Pitts., July 26, 1940; s. Daniel and Frances G. Neuman; m. Susan G. Neuman, Sept. 4, 1967. B.S. in Elec. Engring. with honors, Carnegie Inst. Tech., 1962; S.M., Harvard U., 1963, Ph.D. in Applied Math., 1968. Teaching fellow Harvard U., Cambridge, Mass., 1962-64, research asst., 1964-67; mem. tech. staff Bell Telephone Labs., Whippany, N.J., 1967-69; asst. prof. elec. engring. Carnegie-Mellon U., Pitts., 1969-71, assoc. prof., 1971-78, prof. elec. engring., 1978-83, prof. elec. and computer engring., 1983—. Mem. editorial bd. Internat. Jour. Modelling and Simulation, Control and Computers; contbr. numerous articles to profl. jours. Mem. IEEE (sr., assoc. editor Trans. on Systems, Man and Cybernetics), Inst. Mgmt. Scis., AAAS, Instrument Soc. Am. (sr.), Soc. Harvard Engrs. and Scientists, Soc. Indsl. and Applied Math., Sigma Xi, Phi Kappa Phi, Tau Beta Pi, Eta Kappa Nu. Office: Carnegie-Mellon U Dept Elec and Computer Engring Pittsburgh PA 15213

NEUMAN, ROBERT BALLIN, geologist; b. Washington, Feb. 28, 1920; s. Lester and Janet (Nusbaum) N.; m. Arline Bette Ross, Oct. 23, 1949; children: Elizabeth B., Martha R. BS, U. N.C., 1941; PhD, Johns Hopkins U., 1949. Geologist U.S. Geol. Surveyy, Washington, 1949-80; lectr. Johns Hopkins U., Balt., 1956, 57, U. Oslo, Norway, 1970; rsch. assoc., paleobiology Nat. Mus. Natural History, Washington, 1980—; vis. prof. Va. Poly. Inst. & State U., Blacksburg, Va., 1980; disting. vis. prof. U. Del., Newark, 1982; vis. prof. U. Mich., Ann Arbor, 1988; guest rsch. worker U. Bergen, Norway, 1984, 85; leader U.S. project working group, Caledonide Orogen Project, Internat. Geol. Correlation Program, 1976-86. Author: (govt. report) Geology of the Western Great Smoky Mountains, Tennessee, 1965, Bedrock Geology of the Shin Pond and Stacyville Quadrangles, Maine, 1967, Ordovician brachiopods, Virgin Arm, Newfoundland, 1976; contbr. articles profl. jours. Lt. USN, 1942-46, ETO, PTO. Fellow AAAS, Geol. Soc. Am.; mem. Paleontological Soc., Geol. Assn. Can., Soc. for Sedimentary Geology. Home: 5027 Klingle St NW Washington DC 20016-2653 Office: Nat Mus Nat History E-308 Smithsonian Inst Washington DC 20560

NEUMAN, SANDRA FAYE, communal worker, nurse; b. St. Paul, Apr. 18, 1946; d. Joseph and Dorothy (Rifkin) Lipschultz; m. Richard Neuman, Apr. 7, 1941 (div. Aug. 1988); children: Jennifer, Marc. AS, St. Mary's Coll., Mpls., 1967; student, U. Minn., 1967—. RN, Minn. Operating rm. nurse U. Minn. Hosps., Mpls., 1967-68; staff nurse Twin Cities Airport Med. Clinic, Mpls., 1968; mem. fin. staff Durenberger for Senate, Mpls., 1987-88; asst. dir. maj. gifts United Jewish Appeal, Fedn. of Jewish Philanthropies of Greater N.Y., N.Y.C., 1988-89; dir. east coast region The Jerusalem Found., N.Y.C., 1989-91; Ea. regional dir. Israel Tennis Ctrs., N.Y.C., 1991—; nat. officer, chair women's young leadership cabinet United Jewish Appeal, N.Y.C., 1985-86. Mem. exec. coun. Am. Israel Pub. Affairs Com., Washington, 1985-86; mem. nat. com. Joint Action Com. for Polit. Affairs, Chgo. Recipient Outstanding Young Leadership award Coun. Jewish Fedns., 1981. Mem. Nat. Soc. Fund Raising Execs., Nat. Coun. Jewish Women, Women in Fin. Devel. Home: 401 E 34th St # 15C New York NY 10016-4914 Office: Israel Tennis Ctrs Ste 900 928 Broadway New York NY 10010

NEUMEYER, JOHN LEOPOLD, research company administrator, chemistry educator; b. Munich, Germany, July 19, 1930; came to U.S., 1945, naturalized, 1950; s. Albert and Martha (Stern) N.; m. Evelyn Friedman, June 24, 1956; children: Ann Martha, David Alexander, Elizabeth Jean. BS, Columbia U., 1952; PhD, U. Wis., 1961. Rsch. chemist Ethicon Inc., New Brunswick, N.J., 1952-57, FMC Corp., Princeton, N.J., 1961-63; sr. staff chemist Arthur D. Little Inc., Cambridge, Mass., 1963-69; prof. medicinal chemistry, chemistry Northeastern U., Boston, 1969-91, dir. grad. sch., 1978-85, disting. emeritus prof., 1992—; chmn. bd., co-founder Rsch. Biochem. Inc., Natick, Mass., 1981—; cons. in field. Patentee in field. Contbr. articles to profl. jours., also chpts. to books in field. Mem. Bd. Health, Wayland, Mass., 1968-75, Pesticide Bd., Mass., 1972-75. Served to cpl. U.S. Army, 1953-55. Recipient Lunsford Richardson award, 1961; Sr. Hayes Fulbright fellow, 1975-76. Fellow AAAS (mem. at large 1983-87, chmn. pharm. sci. sect. 1992—), Am. Assn. Pharm. Scis., Acad. Pharm Scis. (rsch. achievement award in medicinal chemistry 1982, Northeastern U. faculty lectr. award 1978, U. disting. prof. 1982-92); mem. Am. Soc. Neurosci., Am. Soc. Exptl. Pharm. & Exptl. Therapeutics, Am. Chem. Soc. (councilor 1985—, trustee 1989—, bd. editors Jour. Medicinal Chemistry 1974-88, chmn. div. med. chem. 1982). Office: Rsch Biochems Inc 1 Strathmore Rd Natick MA 01760

NEUMYER, TERRY R., science educator; b. Harrisburg, Pa., May 13, 1941; s. Clayton L. and Mary E. (Stagemyer) N.; m. Marsha J. Myers, Dec. 18, 1965; children: Todd Michael, Troy Mathew. BS, Shippensburg State U., 1963; postgrad., Messiah Coll., Pa. State U., U. Wis. Tchr. sci. Susquehanna Twp. Sch. Dist., Harrisburg, 1963—; summer staff mem. Pa. Dept. Health, 1965-70, Pa. Dept. Environ. Resources, 1970-75, Polyclinic Med. Ctr., Harrisburg, 1975-83; software reviewer Nat. Sci. Tchrs. Assn., 1989—. Asst. leader Colonial Park (Pa.) Boy Scouts Am., 1975-85; mem. Lower Paxton Twp. (Pa.) Environ. Protection Bd., 1978-79. Named one of Top Ten Tchrs., Pa. Dept. Edn., 1976; grantee U. Wis., 1991. Home: 4832 Springtop Dr Harrisburg PA 17111 Office: Susquehanna Middle Sch 801 Wood St Harrisburg PA 17109

NEUWIRTH, ALLAN CHARLES, designer, director; b. N.Y.C., Jan. 21, 1956; s. David Osias and Bella Jenta (Gajzt) N. BFA, Pratt Inst., 1977. Designer, dir. Studios of Diamond & Diaferia, N.Y.C., 1979-84; producer Klassy Prodns., N.Y.C., 1984—; freelance comedy writer N.Y.C., 1984—; poster designer, The Phoenix Theater, N.Y.C., 1983-84; dir. various stage prodns., N.Y.C., 1985. TV logo and title designer World Series, 1979, ABC News Nightline, 1980, ABC News This Week, 1982, ABC News Closeup, 1983; art dir. (TV shows) Mother's Day, 1983-88, Mother's Minutes, 1984-89; animator (home video) Your Newborn Baby, 1985; dir. (Off-Broadway play) The Butter & Egg Man, 1986; effects animator (films) Sgt. Kabukiman, NYPD, 1990, King's Ransom, 1991; illustrator (book) Where in America is Carmen Sandiego, 1992.

NEVANS, ROY NORMAN, food products executive, producer; b. N.Y.C., July 1, 1931; s. Al Nevans and Lillian (Schiff) Margolis; m. Virginia Place, Dec. 31, 1961; children: Lisa Ann, Laurel Sue, Judith Lynn. BS, U. Pa., 1953; MBA, Columbia U., 1957. Mgmt. trainee Henningsen Foods, Inc., N.Y.C., 1958-60, mgr. export sales div., 1960-65, mgr. nat. sales div., 1965-70, v.p. mktg. Henningsen Foods, Inc., White Plains, N.Y., 1970-90; mng. dir. Henningsen Van Den Burg, Waalyk, Holland, 1979-90, Henningsen Nederland B.V., Waalyk, 1984-90, Henningsen Foods, Ltd., London, 1977-90; pres. Royco Internat. Inc., Greenwich, Conn., 1991—; dir. Global Edn. Mgmt., 1991—, The Wall St. Inst., 1991—; pres. Royal Prodns., Ltd., N.Y.C., 1968-73, Internat. TV Prodns., Ltd., London, 1978—; exec. producer NCM Entertainment, Inc., N.Y.C., 1982—. Producer Broadway shows Gandhi, 1969, Solitaire Double Solitaire, 1972; producer TV series Juke box, 1978-79; exec. producer TV mini-series Roots of Rock and Roll, 1981. Lt. comdr. USN, 1953-56. Mem. NATAS, River Club, Jaguar Touring Club. Home: 19 Roberta Ln Greenwich CT 06830-3953 Office: Royco Internat Inc 19 Roberta Ln Greenwich CT 06830-3953

NEVANS-PALMER, LAUREL SUZANNE, rehabilitation counselor; b. N.Y.C., Aug. 1, 1964; d. Roy N. and Virginia (Place) Nevans; m. Russell Baird Palmer III, Oct. 12, 1991. BA in English, Secondary Edn. cum laude, U. Richmond, 1986, postgrad., 1989—; MA in Edn. & Human Devel., George Washington U., 1991. Group leader S.E. Consortium for Spl. Svcs., Larchmont, N.Y., 1980-85; vocat. instr. Assn. for Retarded Citizens Montgomery County, Rockville, Md., 1986-89; edn. specialist George Washington U. Out of Sch. Work Experience Program, Washington, 1989-90; rsch. asst. George Washington U. Dept. Tchr. Prep. & Spl. Edn., Washington, 1989-91; employability skills tchr., rsch. intern Nat. Rehab. Hosp. Rehab. Engring. Dept., Washington, 1991—; teaching asst. Rehab. Counseling Program, George Washington U., 1991; vocat./ind. living skills specialist The Independence Ctr., 1991—. Recipient traineeship GWU Counseling Dept., 1990, 91. Mem. Nat. Rehab. Assn., Nat. Rehab Counselors Assn., Nat. Career Devel. Assn., Nat. Career Devel. Assn., Am. Assn. Counseling and Devel., Am. Rehab. Counseling Assn. Democrat. Home: 611 Woodside Pky Silver Spring MD 20910-4247 Office: The Independence Ctr 5705 Arundel Ave Rockville MD 20852

NEVELSON, MIKE, sculptor; b. N.Y.C., Feb. 23, 1922; s. Charles and Louise (Berliawsky) N.; m. Marianne Wierenga. Sculptor Sculptotek Inc, New Fairfield, Conn. Studio: Sculptotek Inc 3 Milltown PO Box N New Fairfield CT 06812

NEVERETT, DANIEL JOSEPH, college dean; b. Plattsburgh, N.Y., Jan. 14, 1949; s. Perry J. and Evelyn V. (Miller) N. BS, SUNY, Geneseo, 1970; MS in Counseling and Student Pers. Svcs., SUNY, Albany, 1971. Residence hall dir. SUNY, Alfred, 1971-74, asst. dir. residential life, 1974-77, dean students, 1977-78, dean student life, 1978-80; dir. student svcs. Sch. Vocat. Studies, SUNY Coll. Tech. at Alfred, Wellsville, N.Y., 1980-88, assoc. dean students, 1988-91, acting dean, exec. dir., 1991—. Sec. Alfred Town Planning and Zoning Bd., 1978-92; bd. dirs., sec. Aux. Campus Enterprises 2d Svcs. Mem. Nat. Assn. Student Pers. Adminstrs., N.Y. State Coll. and Student Pers. Assn., N.Y. State Assn. Two-Yr. Colls., Alfred 21st Century Group. Home: Box 554 5344 Elm Valley Rd Alfred NY 14802 Office: SUNY Coll of Tech Sch Vocat Techs Alfred NY 14895

NEVILLE, CHARLES WILLIAM, mathematical consulting firm executive; b. Washington, Apr. 2, 1941. BS in Math. and Physics, Yale U., 1962; PhD in Math., U. Ill., 1972. Inst. math. Washington U., 1967-69; asst. prof. math. U. Tex., El Paso, 1969-72; prof. computer sci. Cen. Conn. State U., 1973-89; pres. CWN Rsch., Berlin, Conn., 1989—; vis. prof. Conn. State Wesleyan U., 1988; vis. asst. prof. of math. U. N.H., 1972-73. Author: Invariant Subspaces of Hardy Classes on Infinitely Connected Open Surfaces, 1975; contbr. articles to profl. jours. Mem. Am. Math. Soc., Math. Assn. of Am., Conn. Acad. of Arts and Scis. Office: CWN Rsch 54 Fawn Dr Kensington CT 06037-3036

NEVILLE, JAMES BRIAN, lawyer; b. Chgo., Aug. 24, 1955; s. James B. and Genevieve (Daley) N.; m. Clare Buckbee Killeen, Aug. 9, 1980; children: John Barrett, William Killeen. BA, Loyola U., 1977; JD, John Marshall Law Sch., 1986. Bar: Ill. 1986, U.S. Dist. Ct. (no. dist.) Ill. 1986, Md. 1987, D.C. 1989. Mng. editor Coconut Grove Clarim, Miami, Fla., 1977-80; copywriter Woodward & Lothrop, Washington, 1980-83; freelance writer Chgo., 1983-87; assoc. Doub, Muntzing & Glasgow, Washington, 1987-91, Newman & Holtzinger, Washington, 1991—. Contbr. articles to various periodicals. Mem. Federalist Soc., Washington, 1991. Mem. ABA (pub. utility subsect.), Fed. Energy Bar Assn., Am. Gas Assn. Republican. Office: Newman & Holtzinger Ste 1000 1615 L St NW Washington DC 20036

NEVISION, JOHN METCALFE, management consultant; b. Phila., July 17, 1943; s. John Adelbert and Dorothy Ada (Metcalfe) N.; m. Nancy Ross McJennett, Oct. 11, 1975; children: Laura Antoinette, Susannah Metcalfe. BA in Math., Dartmouth Coll., 1967. Project mgr. NSF Dartmouth Coll., Kiewit Computation Ctr., Hanover, n.H., 1967-75; ptnr. Formum Nevision, Concord, Mass., 1976-85; prin. engr. Raytheon Corp., Sudbury, Mass., 1985-88; sr. cons. Innovation Assocs., Framington, Mass., 1988-90; chmn. Oak Assocs., Concord, 1990—. Author: The Little Book of Basic Style, 1978, Executive Computing, 1980, The Elements of Spread Sheet Style, 1987, 1-2-3- Spreadsheet Design, 1989, Microsoft Excel Spreadsheet Design, 1990. Mem. Assn. for Computing Machinery, Project Mgmt. Inst., Math. Assn. of Am., Am. Soc. Tng. and Devel. Office: Oak Assocs 500 Thoreau St Concord MA 01742

NEWBOLD, HERBERT LEON, JR., psychiatrist, writer; b. High Point, N.C., Nov. 3, 1921; s. Herbert Leon and Mary Temperance (Sherrod) N.; children: Lucile, Susan. Student, U. Chgo., 1941, Coll. William and Mary, 1941; B.S., Duke U., 1945, M.D., 1945; postgrad., Northwestern U., 1951, New Sch. Social Research, 1960-61. Intern U. Chgo. Clinics, 1945-46, U. Minn., 1949-50; resident Woodlawn Hosp., Chgo., 1946; resident in internal medicine Vanderbilt U. and associated VA Hosp., Nashville, 1946-47; resident in psychiatry U. Ill. and associated VA Hosp., Hines, Ill., 1955-58; practice medicine specializing in internal medicine Newton, N.C., 1947-48; practice medicine specializing in psychiatry Chgo., 1950-55, 1958-60; Asheville, N.C., 1961-70; N.Y.C., 1970—, pvt. practice specializing in psychiatry and neurology, 1976—; instr. neurology and psychiatry Sch. Medicine, Northwestern U., Chgo., 1958-61. Freelance writer, 1950—; novels include 1/3 of an Inch of French Bread, 1961, Long John, 1979, Dr. Cox's Couch, 1979; others under pseudonym, 1950-60; sci. books include text Psychiatric Programming of People, 1972, Mega-Nutrients for Your Nerves, 1975, Doctor Newbold's Revolutionary New Discoveries about Weight Loss, How to master hidden allergies that make you fat, 1977, Physicians Handbook on Orthomolecular Medicine, 1977, Vitamin C Against Cancer, 1979, Mega-Nutrients, 1987, Dr. Newbold's Type A/Type B Weight Loss Book, 1991, Dr. Newbold's Nutrition for Your Nerves, 1992; author: (with others) The New Chemotherapy in Mental Illness, 1958; contbr. articles to profl. jours.; numerous appearances radio and TV. Served with U.S. Army, 1943-45, 46-47. Mem. AMA. Address: 151 E 31st St New York NY 10016

NEWBOLD, JENNIFER, real estate company executive; b. Norfolk, Va., July 21, 1960; d. John Lowe and Judith (Bourne) N. BA, U. Vt., 1982. Office mgr. Data Acquisition Systems, Boston, 1983-85; mgr. Exec. Exchange, Wilmington, Mass., 1985-86; paralegal Mariano & Wolman, N.Y.C., 1987; from property mgr. to asst. v.p. Merchants' Fund, Inc., Silver Spring, Md., 1987-89, v.p., 1989—; dir. Juno Capital Corp., Silver Spring, 1989—. Mem. Property Mgmt. Assn. Office: Mchts Fund Inc Ste 1507 9727 Mt Pisgah Rd Silver Spring MD 20903

NEWBURG, CHARLENE O., career counselor; b. Sioux Falls, S.D., Sept. 18, 1927; d. Abraham I. and Sarah (Agrant) Obstfeld; Mortimer Newburg, April 16, 1950; children: Janet N. Reeds, Patricia N. Stiffman. BA, Bard Coll., 1949; student, Columbia U., 1949-51; MA, NYU, 1966. Cert. counselor; nat. cert. career counselor; N.Y. state cert. guidance counselor. Counselor, coord. Manpower Devel. and Tng., White Plains, N.Y., 1966-70; career advisor White Plains Adult Edn., N.Y.C., 1971-72; psychology instr. Westchester Community Coll., Valhalla, N.Y., 1971-72, interviewer, 1986-87; guidance counselor Fox Lane Middle Sch., Bedford, N.Y., 1972-75; project dir. Catlayst, N.Y.C., 1976-78; program specialist Westchester County Office for Women, White Plains, 1987—; Cons., trainer Nat. Ctr. for Vocat. Edn., Columbus, Ohio, 1980. Trustee Bard Coll., 1962-65, trustee assoc., 1962—; dir./v.p. Pelham Art Ctr., N.Y., 1980-87. Named John Bard scholar Bard Coll., 1948; recipient Wm. Lockwood prize, 1949. Mem. AACD, Nat. Career Devel. Assn., League Women Voters, Westchester Assn. Continuing Edn., Sr. Community Svc. Employment Com., Office for Aging. Office: Westchester County Office for Women 112 E Post Rd White Plains NY 10601-5113

NEWCOMB, ELIZABETH WORMWOOD, geneticist; b. Springfield, Mass., July 26, 1944; d. Paul Nelson and Ruth Helen (Johnson) Wormwood; m. Danforth Newcomb, Nov. 25, 1966; children: Alexander Reynolds, Thomas Munroe. BS in Microbiology/Biochemistry, U. Mass., 1966; MS in Molecular Biology/Biochemistry, Kansas State U., 1971; PhD in Genetics and Immunology, Cornell U., 1982. Rsch. asst. Columbia U., N.Y.C., 1966-69; faculty rsch. asst. Kansas State U. Coll. Vet. Medicine, Manhattan, 1969-71; sr. rsch. asst. Cornell U. Med. Coll., N.Y.C., 1971-76; predoctoral fellow Cornell U. Grad. Sch. of Med. Sci., N.Y.C., 1976-82; assoc. researcher Sloan-Kettering Inst., N.Y.C., 1982-84; rsch. assoc. NYU Med. Ctr., N.Y.C., 1984-85, rsch. asst. prof., 1985-88, asst. prof., 1988—; dir. transgenic mouse rsch. facility NYU, N.Y.C., 1989—. Contbr. over 24 papers to profl. publs. Mem. AAAS, Am. Soc. Microbiology, N.Y. Acad. Scis., Am. Assn. Cancer Rsch. Office: NYU Med Ctr MSB531 550 1st Ave New York NY 10016

NEWCOMBE, DAVID SUGDEN, preventive and internal medicine educator; b. Boston; s. Walter White and Catherine N. (Sugden) N.; m. Sissel Margrethe Newcombe, June 26, 1965; children: Catherine Lee, Kirsten Margrethe, Sarah White. AB, Amherst (Mass.) Coll., 1952; MD, CM, McGill U., Montreal, Que., Can., 1956. Diplomate Am. Bd. Rheumatology, Am. Bd. Toxicology, Am. Bd. Occupational Medicine. Intern Boston City Hosp., 1956-57, fellow, 1960-63; resident Duke U. Med. Ctr., Durham, N.C., 1959-60, Harvard Med. Sch., Boston, 1963-65; asst. prof. medicine U. Va., Charlottesville, 1965-67; assoc. prof. medicine U. Vt., Burlington, 1967-77, Johns Hopkins U., Balt., 1977-82; prof. environ. health scis. Sch. Hygiene and Pub. Health Sch. of Hygiene and Pub. Health, Johns Hopkins U., Balt., 1982—; prof. medicine Johns Hopkins U., Balt., 1982—, dir. div. exptl. pathology-toxicology dept. environ. scis., 1983-87; cons., mgr. health, safety and environ. GE Plastics, 1984, cons., med. dir., 1984—; cons. Roy F. Weston, Inc., 1991—; reviewer Am. Rev. Respiratory Disease, Arthritis and Rheumatism, Jour. Immunology, Annals Rheumatic Diseases, Biochem. Pharmacology, Jour. Rheumatology, Lab. Investigation, Medicine, Toxicology and Applied Pharmacology. Author: Inherited Biochemical Disorders and Uric Acid Metabolism, 1979, Principles and Practice of Medicine, 1979, 22d edit., 1988, Clinical Immunotoxicology, 1992; also numerous articles, chpts. to books. With U.S. Army, 1957-59. Spl. fellow NIH; rsch. fellow Am. Cancer Soc. Fellow Am. Coll. Clin. Pharmacology, New Eng. Rheumatism Soc., Am. Coll. Rheumatology (founding), New Eng. Rheumatism Soc.; mem. Am. Rheumatism Assn., Am. Fedn. for Clin. Rsch., Am. Soc. for Biochemistry and Molecular Biology, Soc. Toxicology, Sigma Xi. Home: 1115 Bellemore Rd Baltimore MD 21210-1210 Office: Johns Hopkins U Sch Hygiene & Pub Health 615 N Wolfe St Baltimore MD 21205-2103

NEWELL, CAM MCGILLICUDDY, sculptor, art dealer; b. Providence, Jan. 27, 1947; s. Raymond J. and Ruth A. (Green) McGillicuddy. BFA, State U., N.Y., 1975; MA, Bennington Coll., 1978. Art dealer M. Knoedler & Co., N.Y.C., 1979-89, Henry & Co., N.Y.C., 1989—; cons. Art Librs. Soc., N.Y.C., 1981-83, Arts Cable T.V., N.Y.C., 1982, City of N.Y., 1985-86; vis. lectr. Princeton U., 1981-83. Author: Catalogue Raissone, 1983. Democrat. Roman Catholic. Office: 40 Central Park S New York NY 10019-1633

NEWHALL, PATRICIA, actress, director, producer; b. Detroit, Feb. 20, 1927; d. Elbridge Gerry and Florence (LeMont) N.; m. Joseph Siegel (dec.). Student, UCLA, 1945-47, U. Calif., Berkeley, 1951, U. Mich, 1951. With various university theaters, 1950-53; actress Bklyn. Acad. of Music, 1953; producer/dir. No Exit, Manhattan, N.Y., 1956, John Millington Synge Trilogy, Manhattan, N.Y., 1957, Blood Wedding, Manhattan, N.Y., 1958; producer/dir./actress La Ronde, Manhattan, N.Y., 1959; producer Shakuntata, Manhattan, N.Y., 1960; co-producer King of the Dark Chamber, Manhattan, N.Y., 1961; producer/dir. New Repertory Theater, Manhattan, N.Y., 1962, GOA, Manhattan, 1968. Translator: La Ronde in Masters of the Modern Drama, 1962; producer, dir. Goa, Manhattan, 1968. Named Most Promising Producer/Dir., 1958. Home: 360 E 55th St New York NY 10022-4118

NEWHOUSE, QUENTIN, JR., social psychologist, educator, researcher; b. Washington, Oct. 20, 1949; s. Quentin Sr. and Berlene Delois (Byrd) N.; m. Brenda Joice Washington, Feb. 17, 1973 (div. Mar. 1984); m. Debra Ann Carter, July 7, 1984; 1 child, Alyse Elizabeth Belinda. BA in Psychology, Marietta (Ohio) Coll., 1971; MS in Psychology, Howard U., 1974, PhD in Psychology, 1980. Asst. prof. Antioch U., Balt., 1976-79; pres. Quentin Newhouse Jr. and Assocs., Inc., Washington, 1981-84; computer systems analyst U.S. Army, Washington, 1984, 85, Alexandria, Va., 1987-88; asst. prof. Howard U., Washington, 1982-88; adj. prof. U. D.C., 1984, 91—, Bowie State U., 1982-86, 91—; mentor Prince George's Community Coll., Largo, Md., 1986-89; statistician Bur. of the Census, Ctr. for Survey Methods Rsch., Suitland, Md., 1991—; computer specialist Bur. of the Census, Ctr. for Survey Methods Rsch., 1988-91; v.p. Bureautots, Inc., Largo, 1989-91. Commr. Prince George's County Children and Youth, Upper Marlboro, Md., 1991—; bd. dirs. Prepare Our Youth, Inc., Tacoma Park, Md., 1990—, Shiloh Bapt. Ch. Nursery, Washington, 1988-90; mem. State of Md. Adv. Com. for Children, Youth and Families, 1992—. Recipient Community Svc. award U. D.C., 1982, 84; named Outstanding Young Man of Am., 1982, 86. Mem. Am. Psychol. Assn., Am. Statis. Assn., Social Sci. Computing Assn., N.E. SAS User's Group (co-chair 1991—), Tau Epsilon Phi (life). Democrat. Office: Bur of the Census Washington Pla Rm 433 Washington DC 20233

NEWICK, CRAIG DAVID, architect; b. Orange, N.J., Feb. 14, 1960; s. Russel Forester and Helen (Welch) N.; m. Linda Hammer Lindroth, June 6, 1987; 1 child, Zachary Eran. BA in Architecture, Lehigh U., 1982; MArch, Yale U., 1987. Registered architect, Conn. Ptnr. Lindroth & Newick, New Haven, 1991—; architect, cons. Riverfront Recapture Inc. Design, Hartford, Conn., 1991. Grantee New Eng. Found. for the Arts, 1992, grantee Rockefeller Found., 1989-90, NEA, 1989-90, Real Art Ways, 1989-90, Found. for Contemporary Performance Art, 1989, 90; recipient 1st place award Am. Visionary Set Design Competition, 1989, 3d place award Astronauts Meml. Design Competition, 1988. Mem. Architecture League N.Y. (mem. young architects forum 1991). Office: Lindroth & Newick 219 Livingston St New Haven CT 06511-2209

NEWLER, JEROME MARC, accountant; b. Irvington, N.J., Dec. 3, 1947; s. Leon and Lola Lee (Warner) N.; m. Holly Ann Ogust, Mar. 13, 1977; children: Jonathan Lane, Andrea Meryl. BBA, Marquette U., 1969; postgrad. in bus. adminstrn., NYU, 1970-74. CPA, N.J. Fgn. tax specialist, supr. ops. Bankers Trust Co., N.Y.C., 1970-74; pub. acct. Howard Kuperman, Newler & Tracy Co., East Orange, N.J., 1974-77; ptnr. Newler & Co., CPAs, Union, N.J., 1977-84; owner J.M. Newler & Co., CPAs, Springfield, N.J., 1984—. Ind. trustee First Fidelity Bank Collective Investment Trust, 1987-90; lectr. N.J. Jud. Coll., N.J. Bar Assn., N.J. Inst. for Continuing Legal Edn., N.J. chpt. Am. Acad. Matrimonial Lawyers, Assn. Probation Officers, Am. Soc. Women Accts.; cons. N.Y. Minority Enterprises. Served with Army N.G., 1969-75. Mem. AICPA, N.J. Soc. CPAs (com. to confer with bench and bar, chmn. com. matrimonial acctg., profession conduct com., chmn. Union County chpt. com. to confer with bench and bar), Nat. Soc. Pub. Accts., Inst. Bus. Appraisers, Marquette U. Alumni Assn. (alumni admissions asst., class agt.), Alpha Epsilon Pi. Lodge: B'nai B'rith. Avocation: 1st degree black belt Chung Do Kwon Tae Kwan Do (awarded 1989). Home: 14 W Mcclellan Ave Livingston NJ 07039-1243 Office: 454 Morris Ave Springfield NJ 07081-1150

NEWLIN, PATRICIA ELLEN, public relations executive; b. Phila., Jan. 1, 1950; d. Dale Allen and Dorothy Lavile (Hanson) N. BA, Ind. U., 1972. Pub. relations specialist Mut. N.Y., N.Y.C., 1975-77; account exec. Richard Weiner Inc., N.Y.C., 1977-79; v.p. Robert Marston & Assocs., N.Y.C., 1979-81; exec. v.p., creative dir. Manning, Selvage and Lee, N.Y.C., 1981-86; pres. The Newlin Co., N.Y.C., 1986—. Inventor PREvaluation, 1985. 1st lt. U.S. Army, 1972-75. Mem. Am. Mktg. Assn., Overseas Press Club, Pub. Rels. Soc. Am. (accredited pub. rels.). Home: PO Box 963 East Hampton NY 11937-0801 Office: Newlin Co 124 E 36th St New York NY 10016-3402

NEWMAN, ANDREW MICHAEL, graphic designer; b. N.Y.C., Dec. 4, 1947; s. George Joseph and Frances (Besner) N.; m. Sue Goble, Jan. 31, 1970; children: Anne Elizabeth, Katherine Goble. BA, Ind. U., 1970; cert. in media arts, Sch. of Visual Arts, N.Y.C., 1975. Sci. and chemistry tchr. Horace Greeley High Sch., Chappaqua, N.Y., 1970-71; sci. tchr. Scarsdale (N.Y.) Jr. High Sch., 1971-72; designer Sterling Mags., N.Y.C., 1975, art editor, 1977-78; assoc. art dir. Edward G. Coyne Advt., N.Y.C., 1976-77; sr. designer Dell Pub. Co., N.Y.C., 1978-80; prin. Andrew M. Newman Graphic Design, Inc., N.Y.C., 1980—; instr. Fashion Inst. Tech., N.Y.C., 1991—. Contbg. author: Humor 87, 1987 (Funny Bone Cert. of Merit 1987), Graphic Design U.S.A. (Desi award 1987, 88, 90), American Corporate Identity, 1990, The Big Book of New American Humor, 1991. Recipient Cert. of Merit, Printing Industries Am., 1988, Creativity Cert. of Distinction, Art Direction Mag., 1987, 88, 90. Mem. Am. Inst. Graphic Arts, Am. Fedn. Musicians, Graphic Artists Guild (rep. to N.Y. Bd. 1988, chmn. computer arts discipline, 1989), Art Dirs. Club.

NEWMAN, BERNARD H., accounting educator; b. N.Y.C., Aug. 25, 1932; s. Harry and Teresa (Brewer) N.; m. Mary Ellen Oliverio, Dec. 26, 1964. BBA, CUNY, 1954; MA, Columbia U., 1957; PhD, NYU, 1966. CPA, N.Y. Sr. pub. auditor Stern, Porter, Kingston & Coleman, N.Y.C., 1954-61; divsnl. contr. Hotel Corp. of Am., Boston, 1961-63; prof. acctg. SUNY, Farmingdale, 1964-68; bus. divsn. dir. Essex County Coll., Newark, 1968-73; mgr. Deloitte, Haskins & Sells (currently Deloitte & Touche), Milan, Italy, 1974-75; chmn. dept. acctg. and fin. Pace U., N.Y.C., 1978-90, prof. acctg., 1975—; cons. various lawyers throughout U.S., 1985—, N.Y.C. Contrs. Office, 1985-90. Co-author: Business Communications, 1976, International Business Communications, 1974; contbr. articles to profl. jours. Auditing advisor N.Y.C., 1985-90; bd dirs., chmn. fin. com. St. Margaret's House, N.Y.C., 1985-90. Recipient Founder's Day award NYU, 1966. Mem. AICPA, Am. Acctg. Assn. (v.p. 1984-85), N.Y. State Soc. CPAs, Inst. Internal Auditors. Home: 106 Morningside Dr New York NY 10027 Office: Pace U Pace Pla New York NY 10038

NEWMAN, BRUCE MURRAY, antiques dealer; b. N.Y.C., Jan. 27, 1930; s. Meyer and Evelyn (Kantor) N.; m. Judith S. Brandus, June 26, 1965; 1 child, Emily Rachel. BA, Pratt Inst., 1953. Pres. Newel Art Galleries Inc., N.Y.C., 1975—. Author: Fantasy Furniture, 1989. Bd. dirs. N.Y.C. Ctr., 1988-90; assoc. mem. Mt. Sinai Med. Ctr., 1981—; trustee Pratt Inst., Bklyn., 1983—. Recipient Designer award Art Dirs. Club, 1984. Mem. Am. Soc. Interior Designers (bd. dirs. 1989—), Victorian Soc. Am. Office: Newel Art Galleries Inc 425 E 53rd St New York NY 10022-5122

NEWMAN, DORIS JEAN, field training manager, trainer; b. Chambersburg, Pa., Feb. 4, 1943; d. Omar Ray and Ida Alice (Reath) Shaffer; m. Roy Fredrick Newman, Mar. 27, 1965; children: Brian A., Rhonda R., Deena D., Darla D. High sch. diploma, Chambersburg Area High Sch., Pa., 1961. Cashier, office personnel Giant Food Store, Chambersburg, Pa., 1961-66; independent rep. Avon Sales, 1971-78; dist. sales mgr. Avon Products, 1978-87; training specialist Avon Products, Newark, 1987-91, dist. sales mgr., 1991—. Republican. Home: 6118 Chambersburg Rd Orrtanna PA 17353-9732

NEWMAN, EDWIN STANLEY, lawyer, publishing company executive; b. N.Y.C., Apr. 26, 1922; s. Gordon H. and Rosalind (Zieph) N.; m. Evaline Ada Lipp, Sept. 2, 1945; children: Scott D., Linda S. Newman Perl. BA summa cum laude, CCNY, 1940; LLB, Columbia U., 1943. Admitted to N.Y. State bar, 1943, U.S. Ct. Internat. Trade. Asst. to pres. Am. Jewish Com., 1946-60; ins. co. exec., 1960-69; v.p., gen. counsel Oceana Publs., Inc., Dobbs Ferry, N.Y., 1969—, also dir.; past lectr. New Sch. Social Research. Author: Freedom Reader, 1963, Hate Reader, 1964, Law of Philanthropy, 1955, Fundraising Made Easy, 1954, Law of Civil Liberty and Civil Rights, 7th edit., 1987; editor: U.S. Internat. Trade Reports, 1981—. Chmn. bd. Elmont Jewish Ctr., 1953-57. Served with U.S. Army, 1943-46, 51-52. Named James Kent scholar, 1943. Internat. Bar Assn., Columbia Law Sch. Alumni Assn., Internat. Assn. Jurists (Italian-Am. sect.), Am. Corp. Counsel Assn., Dobbs Ferry Rotary, Phi Beta Kappa. Home and Office: 75 Main St Dobbs Ferry NY 10522-1632

NEWMAN, GERALDINE ANNE, advertising executive; b. Boston, Apr. 1; d. Joseph M. and Clara (Bistry) N. BS, UCLA; postgrad., Alliance Francaise, Paris, Los Angeles Sch. Fine Arts, NYU. Writer Tinker Dodge and Delano, N.Y.C., 1970-72, Ketchum Advt., N.Y.C., 1972-75, Advt. to Women, N.Y.C., 1975-78; v.p., creative supr. Young and Rubicam, N.Y.C., 1978-83; v.p., assoc. creative dir. Backer Spielvogel Bates Worldwide Internat. Div., N.Y.C., 1983-90; pres. Geraldine Newmand Communications, Inc., N.Y.C., 1990—. County committeewoman Dem. Party, N.Y.C., 1972; advt. adviser Youth at Risk, Breakthrough Found., Food Bank, Food for All, Gifts that Give Back. Featured in Adweek mag., 1986; winner Andy award 1975, 78, 82, 84, Clio award 1982, numerous others. Mem. Ad-net (bd. dirs. 1984-89, creative dir. 1986-89, Pres.'s award 1988). Home: 315 E 72d St New York NY 10021 Office: G Newman Communications Inc 315 E 72nd St New York NY 10021-4625

NEWMAN, HARRY DANIEL, writer; b. Bklyn., Aug. 16, 1961; s. William Newman and Margot (Shapiro) Jackson; m. Ninotchka V. Rosca, Mar. 20, 1990. BS, MIT, 1983. Mem. artistic staff Circle Repertory Co., N.Y.C., 1984-86; exec. dir. Non-Traditional Casting Project, N.Y.C., 1986-89; resident playwright Cin. Playhouse, 1989-90; freelance writer N.Y.C., 1991—; on-site evaluator theatre program Nat. Endowment Arts, Washington, 1988—, theatre program panelist, 1991-92; cons. arts program Rockefeller Found., N.Y.C., 1990-91; panelist Ohio Arts Coun., Columbus, 1990-91. Editor: Uncommon Sense, 1984, Discrete Thoughts, 1987, The Anthropic Principle, 1991; author poetry; plays (produced) Cleaners, 1982, Recess, 1985, The Good Mud, 1989, Suspicious Counterpoint, 1990, The Dark, 1992; contbr. articles to profl. jours. Mem. N.Y. Acad. Scis., Dramatists Guild. Home: 25-11 31st Ave # 1 Astoria NY 11106

NEWMAN, IRA BERNARD, securities company executive, accountant; b. N.Y.C., Apr. 12, 1950; s. Ralph and Rose (Moshcovitz) N.; m. Beth Deborah Offner, July 20, 1975; 1 child, Scott. BA, NYU, 1971, M in Acctg., 1973. CPA, N.Y. Sr. asst. acct. Deloitte Haskins & Sells, N.Y.C., 1973-76; supr. gen. acctg. div. F&M Schaefer Brewing Co., N.Y.C., 1976-80; mgr. fin. reporting and taxation Drake Am. Corp., N.Y.C., 1980-83; controller Quadrex Securities Corp., N.Y.C., 1983-87; v.p., controller, treas. Robert Fleming, Inc., N.Y.C., 1987-89; asst. treas. A B D Securities Corp., N.Y.C., 1989-90; chief fin. officer First Hanover Securities Inc., N.Y.C., 1990—. Mem. AICPA, N.Y. State Soc. CPAs. Home: 8 Woodford Ln Englishtown NJ 07726-2927

NEWMAN, JAMES MICHAEL, lawyer; b. Bklyn., Apr. 3, 1946; s. Sheldon and Ethel (Silverman) N.; m. Lee Galen; children: Danielle Cari, Matthew Evan, Merrie Lee, Cindy Joy, Bradley Curtis. BA, Queens Coll., 1966; JD, NYU, 1969, LLM, 1975. Bar: N.Y. 1970, N.J. 1977. Assoc. Kramer, Marx, Greenlee & Backus, N.Y.C., 1970-73, Forsyth, Decker, Murray & Broderick, N.Y.C., 1973-74; ptnr. Tommaney & Newman, N.Y.C., 1975-82, Goldzweig, Reilly, Grossman & Newman, Marlboro, N.J., 1978-79, Canarick & Newman, Freehold, N.J., 1982-84; pub. defender Marlboro Twp. (N.J.), 1984-86; judge Marlboro Twp., 1986—, Englishtown Boro, 1990—, Farmingdale Boro, 1991—. Dep. mayor Marlboro Twp., 1975-79, dir. econ. devel., 1975-79, dir. commuter affairs, 1974; interim commr. Western Monmouth Utilities Authority, 1977; pres. Marlboro Dem. Club, 1978, trustee, 1979-81; pres. Marlboro Dem. Orgn., 1982; mem. Central N.J. Transp. Bd., 1974-76. Mem. Monmouth County Bar Assn., N.J. Bar Assn., Monmouth County Judges Assn. (sec.), Am. Judges Assn., Masons. Jewish. Office: 64 W Main St Freehold NJ 07751

NEWMAN, JOHN BULLEN, mechanical engineer, researcher; b. Okmulgee, Okla., Sept. 27, 1938; s. William Campbell Jr. and Jean (Bullen) N.; m. Patricia Armstrong Newton, Mar. 30, 1961 (div. July 1972); children: William Harold, Robert David, James Thomas, Steven Michael; m. Sandra Marlene Zeiler, May 18, 1973; 1 child, Scott Alexander. BSME, Stanford U., 1961, MSME, 1962, PhD in Engring. Mechanics, 1965. Registered profl. engr., Pa. Engr. Lockheed Missiles & Space Co., Sunnyvale, Calif., 1962-63; rsch. asst. Stanford (Calif.) U., 1963-65; sr. engr. Bettis Atomic Power Lab., West Mifflin, Pa., 1965-73, fellow engr., 1973-80, adv. engr., 1980—. Contbr. articles to profl. jours. Sec. Bldg. Rehab. Investment Corp., Pitts., 1968-72. Mem. ASME. Office: Bettis Atomic Power Lab PO Box 79 West Mifflin PA 15122-0079

NEWMAN, JON O., federal judge; b. N.Y.C., May 2, 1932; s. Harold W. Jr. and Estelle L. (Ormond) N.; m. Martha G. Silberman, June 19, 1953; children: Leigh, Scott, David. Postgrad., Hotchkiss Sch., 1949; AB magna cum laude, Princeton U., 1953; LLB, Yale U., 1956; LLD (hon.), U. Hartford, 1975, U. Bridgeport, 1980. Bar: Conn. 1956, D.C. 1956. Law clk. to Hon. Earl Warren U.S. Ct. Appeals, 1956-57; sr. law clk. to chief justice U.S. Supreme Ct., 1957-58; ptnr. Ritter, Satter & Newman, Hartford, Conn., 1958-60; counsel to majority Conn. Gen. Assembly, 1959; spl. counsel to gov. Conn., 1959-61; asst. to sec. HEW, 1961-62; adminstrv. asst. to U.S. senator, 1963-64; U.S. atty. Dist. of Conn., 1964-69; pvt. practice law, 1969-71; U.S. dist. judge Dist. of Conn., 1972-79; U.S. cir. judge 2d Cir. Ct. of Appeals, 1979—. Co-author: Politics: The American Way. Mem. bd. dirs. Hartford Inst. Criminal and Social Justice. With USAR, 1954-62. Recipient Learned Hand medal Fed. Bar Coun., 1987. Fellow Am. Bar Found.; mem. ABA, Am. Law Inst., Conn. Bar Assn., Am. Judicature Soc. Democrat. Office: US Ct Appeals 450 Main St Hartford CT 06103-3001*

NEWMAN, LEONARD, chemistry researcher; b. N.Y.C., Jan. 15, 1931; s. Louis and Sarah (Pitlock) N.; m. Jacqueline Muller, June 14, 1953; children: Michael, Beverly. BS, Poly. Inst. Bklyn., 1952; PhD, MIT, 1956. Chemist Nat. Lead, Winchester, Mass., 1956-58, Brookhaven Nat. Lab., Upton, N.Y., 1958—; cons. Antimony Oxide Inst. Am., Washington, 1984-89, U.S. Army, Aberdeen, Md., 1985-87; adj. prof. NYU, N.Y.C., 1985—, Ga. Inst. Tech., 1991—. Mem. editorial adv. bd. Envion. Sci. Tech., Washington, 1982-84. Mem. Am. Chem. Soc., Am. Geophys. Union, Air and Waste Mgmt. Assn. Jewish. Home: 23 Trent Ln Smithtown NY 11787-1262 Office: Brookhaven Nat Lab Dept Applied Scis Upton NY 11973

NEWMAN, LINDA, retired construction company executive; b. Bklyn., July 10, 1937; d. Max and Mae (Goldlust) Lukin; m. Morton Newman, Dec. 29, 1956; children: Jeffrey H., Karen M., Susan L. Student, Hunter Coll., 1955-57. Adminstrv. asst. Princeton Park, Shoreham, N.Y., 1971-73; asst. to pres. Imperial Gardens, South Setauket, N.Y., 1973-76; ops. mgr. Princeton Park, Dix Hills, N.Y., 1976-80, v.p. ops., 1980-83; dir. sales, mktg. and advt. DiCanio, Smithtown, N.Y., 1983-89; v.p. Cons., Inc., Dix Hills, N.Y., 1990-91, ret., 1992. Recipient Best Newspaper Advertisement award Profl. Builder Mag., 1987. Mem. Nat. Assn. Home Builders, Women's Am. Orgn. for Rehab. and Tng. (charter, Imperial Woods chpt. pres. 1981-82), L.I. Builders Inst. (cert.).

NEWMAN, MARK D., agricultural economist; b. Dec. 27, 1950; s. Charles L and Marjorie Newman; m. Carol Kramer; children: Amanda, Peter, Vanessa. BA in Polit. Sci., Pa. State U., 1972; MS in Agrl. Econs., Mich. State U., 1977, MA in Econs. and Bus., 1978, PhD in Agrl. Econs., 1980. Agrl. extension Peace Corps, Benin, West Africa, 1972-75; researcher, instr. Mich. State U., East Lansing, 1975-80; asst. prof. Kans. State U., Manhattan, 1980-83; from asst. prof. to assoc. prof. Mich. State U., 1983-85; coord. mktg. rsch. Macro Analytic Bur., Dakar, Senegal, 1983-85; head Western Europe Econ. Rsch. Svc. USDA, Washington, 1985-88; dir. agribus. and internat. trade rsch. cons. Abt Assocs., Washington and Cambridge, Mass., 1988—; mem. agribus. working group Asia near East and Ea. Europe USAID, 1989-91; mem. Team 92 Commn. of European Communities, 1991—. Mem. editorial bd. North Cen. Jour. Agrl. Econs., 1983-85; contbr. articles to profl. jours. and popular publs., also book chpts. Recipient Excellence in Rsch. award Nat. Coop. Bus. Assn. Mem. Am. Agrl. Econ. Assn., So. Agrl. Econ. Assn., Am. Mktg. Assn., Internat. Assn. Agrl. Economists, European Assn. Agrl. Economy, Internat. Agribus. Assn., French Am. C. of C. Episcopalian. Office: Abt Assocs Inc 4800 Montgomery Ln Ste 600 Bethesda MD 20814-5341

NEWMAN, MARTHA SILBERMAN, foundation consultant; b. Kansas City, Aug. 21, 1930; d. J.D. and Irene (Golling) Silberman; m. Jon O. Newman, June 19, 1953; children: Leigh Anne, Scott Allan, David Blair. BA, Mount Holyoke Coll., So. Hadley, Mass., 1952. Exec. dir. Hartford Courant Found., Hartford, Conn., 1980-87, Fisher Found., W. Hartford, Conn., 1988—; bd. mem. United Way Capitol Region, Hartford, 1987—; coord. Coun. for Found., 1991—; trustee Hartford Courant Found., 1989—. Office: Fisher Found 36 Brookside Blvd Hartford CT 06107

NEWMAN, PAULINE, federal judge; b. N.Y.C., June 20, 1927; d. Maxwell Henry and Rosella N. B.A., Vassar Coll., 1947; M.A., Columbia U., 1948; Ph.D., Yale U., 1952; LL.B., NYU, 1958. Bar: N.Y. 1958, U.S. Supreme Ct. 1972, U.S. Ct. Customs and Patent Appeals 1978, Pa. 1979, U.S. Ct. Appeals (3d cir.) 1981, U.S. Ct. Appeals (fed. cir.) 1982. Research chemist Am. Cyanamid Co., Bound Brook, N.J., 1951-54; mem. patent staff FMC Corp., N.Y.C., 1954-75; mem. patent staff FMC Corp., Phila., 1975-84, dir. dept. patent and licensing, 1969-84; judge U.S. Ct. Appeals (fed. cir.), Washington, 1984—; bd. dir. Research Corp., 1982-84; program specialist Dept. Natural Scis. UNESCO, Paris, 1961-62; mem. State Dept. Adv. Com. on Internat. Indsl. Property, 1974-84; lectr. in field. Contbr. articles to profl. jours. Bd. dirs. Med. Coll. Pa., 1975-84, Midgard Found., 1973-84; trustee Phila. Coll. Pharmacy and Sci., 1983-84. Mem. ABA (council sect. patent trademark and copyright 1983-84), Am. Patent Law Assn. (bd. dirs. 1981-84), U.S. Trademark Assn. (bd. dirs. 1975-79, v.p. 1978-79), Am. Chem. Soc. (bd. dirs. 1972-81), Am. Inst. Chemists (bd. dirs. 1960-66, 70-76), Pacific Indsl. Property Assn. (pres. 1979-80). Clubs: Vassar, Yale. Office: US Ct Appeals 717 Madison Pl NW Washington DC 20439-0002

NEWMAN, ROBERT P., engineering executive; b. El Paso, Tex., July 14, 1953; s. John Taylor and Regina Gertrude (Smith) N.; m. Janet Stevenson N.; m. Michael, Jacqueline. BS in Environ. Sci., Va. Tech., Blacksburg, 1975, MS in Environ. Engring., 1976. Registered profl. engr., Pa., Del., N.J., N.Y., N.C., Va. Environ. engr. Commonwealth Va., Newport News, Va., 1976-79; project mgr. TRW, Inc., Research Triangle Park, N.C., 1979-82; dist. sales engr. Nalco Chem., Raleigh, N.C., 1982-84; v.p. Scott Environ. Tech., Inc., Phila., 1984-91; corp. mgr. air programs EA Engring., Sci. & Tech., Balt., 1991—. Contbr. articles to profl. jours. Polit. advisor to Rep. Candidate for U.S. Congress, Doylestown, Pa., 1990; pres. Civic Assn., New Britain, Pa., 1987-89; advisor Md. Dept. of Environ., Balt., 1992. Recipient Cert. of Disting. Svc., Commonwealth of Va., Newport News, 1979, Excellence in Environ. Publishing award, 1992. Fellow Air and Waste Mgmt. Assn.; mem. Am. Acad. Environ. Engrs. (hon. diplomate), Ill. Hazardous Waste and Rsch. Ctr. Republican. Roman Catholic. Home: 9 Hunt Manor Ct Baldwin MD 21013 Office: EA Engring Sci & Tech 11019 McCormick Rd Hunt Valley MD 21031

NEWMAN, SCOTT DAVID, lawyer; b. N.Y.C., Nov. 5, 1947; s. Edwin Stanley and Evaline Ada (Lipp) N.; m. Judy Lynn Monchik, June 24, 1972; 1 child, Eric. B.A. magna cum laude, Yale U., 1969; J.D., Harvard U., 1973, M.B.A., 1973; LL.M. in Taxation, NYU, 1977. Bar: N.Y. 1974, U.S. Dist. Ct. (so. and ea. dists.) N.Y. 1975, U.S. Ct. Appeals (2d cir.) 1975, U.S. Ct. Claims 1976, U.S. Tax Ct. 1979. Assoc. Dewey, Ballantine, Bushby, Palmer & Wood, N.Y.C., 1973-76, Stroock & Stroock & Lavan, N.Y.C., 1976-78; assoc., ptnr. Zimet, Haines, Moss & Friedman, N.Y.C., 1978-81; tax counsel Phibro-Salomon Inc., N.Y.C., 1981-84; ptnr. Baer, Marks & Upham, N.Y.C., 1984-87; ptnr. Wiener, Zuckerbrot, Weiss & Newman, N.Y.C., 1987-90; ptnr. Whitman & Ransom, N.Y.C., 1990—. Co-author tape casse tes: New Tax Reform Act of 1976, Tax Reform' '78, 1978. Tax Reform Act of 1984, 1986, Tax Reform Act of 1986, 1986; contbr. article to profl. jour. Mem. Phi Beta Kappa. Home: 21 Kipp St Chappaqua NY 10514-2518 Office: Whitman & Ransom 200 Park Ave New York NY 10166-0005

NEWMAN, SHELDON OSCAR, computer company executive; b. N.Y.C., June 25, 1923; s. Morris and Anna (Schlanger) N.; m. Miriam Jasphy, July 30, 1950; children: Barry Marc, Amy Stacy, Andrew Eric. BS in Elec. Engring., CUNY, 1944. Project engr. NASA, Sunnyvale, Calif., 1946-47; gen. mgr. info. and communications div. Sperry Corp., Gt. Neck, N.Y., 1947-67; chmn. bd., chief exec. officer Algorex Corp., Hauppauge, N.Y., 1968—. Chmn. bd. trustees Hosp. for Joint Diseases, Orthopaedic Inst., N.Y.C.; bd. dirs. HJD Rsch. and Devel. Found., Sjogrens Syndrome Found.; pres. Pine Lake Park Coop. Assn., Peekskill, N.Y. Patentee in field. Lt. (j.g.), USN, 1944-46. Mem. IEEE, Archaeol. Inst. Am. (pres.), L.I. Soc., Masons, Tau Beta Pi, Eta Kappa Nu.

NEWMAN, STANLEY, publishing executive; b. Bklyn., July 19, 1952; s. Jerry and Claire (Spital) N.; m. Marlene Rebecca Solomon, Aug. 4, 1974; children: Amanda Barbara, Marc William Howard, Robert Isaac. BS, Bklyn. Coll., 1973; MS, Rutgers U., 1975. Asst. v.p. Merrill Lynch, N.Y.C., 1983-86; v.p. E.F. Hutton, N.Y.C., 1986-87; pres. Crossword Concepts, Massapequa Pk., N.Y., 1987—; editor, publisher Tough Cryptics Mag., Massapequa Pk., N.Y., 1992—, Tough Puzzles Mag., Massapequa Pk., N.Y., 1983—; editor Newsday Crossword, Melville, N.Y., 1988—; pres., founder Am. Crossword Fedn., Massapequa Park, N.Y., 1983—; founding mem. Crossword Hall of Fame, Mil., 1988—. Editor: Bull's Eye Crosswords, 1985-87, Experts Book of Crosswords, 1991—, Crossworder's Own Puzzle Books, 1987-88; author: Inspector Cross Mysteries, 1991—. Winner "The Challengers Tournament of Champions" TV Game Show, 1990; U.S. Open Crossword Champion, 1982, Winning Team mem. World Crossword Championship, 1990. Mem. Newspaper Features Coun., MENSA, Nat. Puzzlers League. Office: Am Crossword Fedn PO Box 69 Massapequa Park NY 11762

NEWMAN, STEPHEN ALEXANDER, chemical engineer, thermodynamicist; b. Auburn, N.Y., Apr. 12, 1938; s. Solomon and Anna (Reich) N.; m. Mary Ellen Lassow, July 26, 1964; children: Sharon Rose, Lori Suzanne. BSChemE, Rensselaer Poly. Inst., 1960; MSChemE, MIT, 1962; PhD, Rutgers U., 1976. Registered profl. engr., N.J. Rsch. engr. M.W. Kellogg Co., Piscataway, N.J., 1962-67; tech. mgr. Foster Wheeler Energy Corp., Clinton, N.J., 1967—; frequent speaker nat. and internat. sci. meetings; organizer, conf./symposium chmn. Nat. Thermodynamics Conf., 1978, World Congress Chem. Engring., Montreal, 1981, Co-Data Congress, Jerusalem, 1984; panel NAS, 1980-82; cons. Nat. Bur. Standards, Washington, 1979; chmn. various project coms. U.S. Dept. Energy, 1977-84. Editor: Thermodynamics of Aqueous Systems with Industrial Applications, 1980, Chemical Engineering Thermodynamics, 1983, Shale Oil Upgrading and Refining, 1983, Acid and Sour Gas Treating Processes, 1985; book and article reviewer Chem. Engring. mag., Gulf Publs., 1980—; contbr. numerous articles to profl. jours. Pres. Mens' Club Temple Israel, Union, N.J., 1980-81. AEC fellow, 1961-62; grantee NSF, 1978, 84. Mem. Am. Inst. Chem. Engrs. (chmn. nat. rsch. com. 1984-85, co-founder Design Inst. Phys. Property Data 1977, vice-chmn. 1979-85, award 1989), Am. Petroleum Inst. (chmn. contractors com. on tech. data 1978—), Gas Processors Assn. (project monitor 1976-85, tech. com.). Jewish. Home: 941 Douglas Ter Union NJ 07083-6523 Office: Foster Wheeler Energy Corp Perryville Corp Park Clinton NJ 08809

NEWMAN, WILLIAM, real estate executive; b. N.Y.C., July 6, 1926; s. Morris B. and Ida (Singer) N.; m. Anita Eagle, Dec. 12, 1948; children: Steven (dec.), Debra Newman Bernstein. BBA, CCNY, 1947. CPA, N.Y. Ptnr. Morris B. Newman & Co., N.Y.C., 1947-61; pres. New Plan Realty Corp., N.Y.C., 1961-72; chief exec. officer New Plan Realty Trust, N.Y.C., 1972—. Lt. USNR, 1944-46. Recipient Gold award Wall St. Transcript, 1986, Bronze award, 1989, Silver, 1990. Mem. Nat. Assn. Real Estate Investment Trusts (chmn. 1990-92), Chief Execs. Orgn., Met. Pres.'s Orgn., Aspinal-Curzon Club (London), Brae Burn Country Club, Boca Rio Golf Club, Sky Club. Office: New Plan Realty Trust 1120 Ave Of The Americas New York NY 10036-6700

NEWMAN, WILLIAM, librarian; b. Czechoslovakia, Feb. 18, 1937; came to the U.S., 1948; s. Leo and Rose (Mendlowitz) N.; m. Vivian Dowling, July, 1964; children: Alexander Lewis, Theodore Reuel. BA, Bklyn. Coll., 1959; MLS, Columbia U., 1960. Adult svcs. libr. Bklyn. Pub. Libr., 1959-63; cataloger Cornell U., Ithaca, N.Y., 1963-65; head reference dept. U. Mont., Missoula, 1965-67; libr., faculty adminstrv. studies York U., Toronto, 1967-69; asst. dir. York U. Librs., Toronto, 1969-71, assoc. dir., 1971-78; univ. libr. Tulane U., New Orleans, 1978-83; dir. Langsdale Libr. U. Balt., 1983—. With U.S. Army, 1960-62. Democrat. Jewish. Office: U Balt 1420 Maryland Ave Baltimore MD 21201-5782

NEWMAN, WILLIAM BERNARD, JR., railroad executive; b. Providence, Nov. 16, 1950; s. William Bernard and Virginia (Crosby) N.; m. Karen O'Connor, Jan. 11, 1951. B.A., Ohio Wesleyan U., 1972; J.D., George Mason U., Arlington, Va., 1977; attended advanced mgmt. program, Harvard U., 1987. Bar: Va. 1977, D.C. 1978. Atty. com. energy Ho. of Reps., Washington, 1978-81; v.p., Washington counsel Consol. Rail Corp. Dept. Govt. Affairs, Washington, 1981—. Mem. ABA, Va. Bar Assn., D.C. Bar Assn. Home: 1009 Priory Pl Mc Lean VA 22101-2134 Office: Consol Rail Corp 990 L'Enfant Pla Washington DC 20024 also: Consol Rail Corp 6 Penn Center Pla Philadelphia PA 19103

NEWMAN, WILLIAM GUY, production manager, writer; b. Neptune, N.J., May 2, 1952; s. Oscar Newman and Gwen Ruth (Hall) Evans; m. Sally Ann Aurnhammer, Sept. 20, 1991; 1 child, William Duncan. Student, Brookdale Coll., 1970-72, New Sch., 1974-76. Co-owner Creative Film Co., Spring Lake, N.J., 1974-79; prodn. coord. MSW Studios, N.Y.C., 1979-82; dir. photography, asst. dir. New Venture Media, Neptune, 1983-85; prodn. mgr., writer Bill Quinn Prodns., Asbury Park, N.J., 1985—; comedy writer Smittee (MTV's mascot), Asbury Park, 1986—, road mgr. Co-author: (TV pilot) The Future of TV, 1985; author: (radio comedy series) SPACE: 1888, 1987; writer and editor promotional trailer for Time Out; writer, filmed and editor numerous indsl. and comml. videos. Fundraiser Greenpeace, Washington, 1985—; mem. Citizens Against Unjust & Severe Enforcement, Environ. Def. Fund. Recipient Telly awards, 1990, 91. Mem. Am. Film Inst., Soc. Associated Performers (v.p. 1990—), Internat. Platform Assn. Democrat. Episcopalian. Club: MBCBS (Manasquan) (v.p. 1977-82, author, editor newsletter, 1975-82). Office: Bill Quinn Prodns 710 Cookman Ave Asbury Park NJ 07712-7008

NEWMARK, HAROLD LEON, biochemist; b. N.Y.C., July 21, 1918; s. Abraham and Mollie W. (Wolf) N.; m. Helen Rosenberg, Mar. 13, 1949 (dec. Aug. 1985); children: Jonathan, Robin L.; m. Phyllis Klein, Sept. 6, 1987. BS, CCNY, 1939; MS, Poly. U., 1950. Chemist Chem. Spec. of N.J.-Syntex, Newark, 1939-41, Intramed Co., N.Y.C., 1946-49, Chase Chem. Co., Newark, 1949-50, Vitarine Co., N.Y.C., 1950-59; chemist Hoffmann LaRoche, Inc., Nutley, N.J., 1966-81, dir. food, agrl. products, 1959-81; chemist Ludwig Inst. for Cancer Rsch., Toronto, Ont., Can., 1981-84; biochem. researcher Sloan-Kettering Inst., N.Y.C., 1984—; adj. prof. Coll. Pharmacy, Rutgers U., Pisacataway, N.J., 1987—. Author, editor: Calcium,

Vitamin D and Colon Cancer, 1991; contbr. over 70 articles to profl. publs. Cpl. USAAF, 1942-46. Mem. AAAS, Am. Chem. Soc., Am. Assn. Cancer Rsch., N.Y. Acad. Scis. Home: 11 Claremont Dr Maplewood NJ 07040-2119

NEWMARK, MARILYN, sculptor; b. N.Y.C., July 20, 1928; d. Edward Ellis and Mabel (Davies) Newmark; student Adelphi Coll., 1945-47, Alfred U., 1949; m. Leonard J. Meiselman, Mar. 15, 1952. Sculptor, specializing in horses, equestrian figures, dogs in sporting scenes; exhibited in group shows: sculpture exhbn. Ky. Derby Mus., Calif. Acad. Sci., NAD, Nat. Arts Club, Nat. Art Mus. of Sport (all N.Y.C.), James Ford Bell Mus., Wis., Smithsonian Instn., Mus. of the Horse, Ky., Washington, Pa. Acad. Natural Scis., Calif. Acad. Scis., Port of History Mus., Pa.; represented in permanent collections Nat. Mus. Racing, Saratoga, N.Y., Internat. Mus. of Horse, Ky. Horse Park, Nat. Art Museum of Sport, also pvt. collections of Harvey Firestone, Whitney Stone, Ogden Phipps, A.B. Hancock Jr., Peggy Agustus, Morgan Firestone, A. Werk Cook. Recipient Anna Hyatt Huntington award, 1970, 71, 72, 75, 78, 80, 81, 82, 83, 86, 88, gold medal, 1973; award Council Am. Artists Socs., 1972, 73, 79, 80; Hudson Valley John Newington award, 1973, 77, gold medal, 1979. Fellow Nat. Sculpture Soc. (council 1973-75, rec. sec. 1976, sec. 1977-79, council 1981-83, 92—, Bronze medal 1986), Am. Artists Profl. League (Gold medal 1974, 77, Medal of Honor 1987); mem. NAD (Ellin P. Speyer award 1974, Artist Fund award 1982), Allied Artists Am. (Gold medal 1981), Pen and Brush Club (gold medal 1977, Salmagundi Club award 1982, 83, 91), Soc. Animal Artists (jury of admissions 1972-75, 1990—, bd. dirs. 1991—), Am. Acad. Equine Art (founding mem., dir. sculpture 1980—), Nassau Suffolk Horsemans Ass. (dir. 1968-82), Catherine Lorillard Wolfe Art Club, Smithtown Hunt Club, Meadowbrook Hunt Club. Address: 22 Woodhollow Rd East Hills NY 11577

NEWSOM, CAROLYN CARDALL, management consultant; b. South Weymouth, Mass., Feb. 27, 1941; d. Alfred James and Bertha Virginia (Roy) Cardall; m. John Harlan Newsom, Feb. 4, 1967; children: John Cardall, James Harlan. AB, Brown U., 1962; MBA, Wharton Sch., 1978; PhD, U. Pa., 1985. Systems engr. IBM, Seattle, 1964-70, Newsom S.E. Services, Seattle, 1970-76; instr. U. Pa. Wharton Sch., Phila., 1978-81; v.p., prin. sr. cons. PA Cons. Group, Princeton, N.J., 1981-88; pres. Newsom Assocs., Yardley, Pa., 1988; ptnr. Bus. Strategy Implementation, Princeton, N.J., 1989-90; pres. Strategy Implementation Solutions, Yardley, Pa., 1990—. Trustee St. Mary Hosp., Langhorne, Pa., 1986—; bd. dirs. Chandler Hall. Mem. Acad. Mgmt., Am. Mgmt. Assn., Am. Soc. for Quality Control, Am. Bus. Women's Assn., Planning Forum, AAUW. Home: Cardalls Corner PO Box F Yardley PA 19067-0403 Office: Strategy Implementation Solutions 1588 Woodside Rd Yardley PA 19067-2611

NEWSOME, FREDERICK VASS, medical educator; b. Charleston, W.Va., July 7, 1946; s. Moses and Ruth (Bass) N.; m. Osila Chindo, Mar. 23, 1974; children: Akasemi, Imhotep, Nubia, Hatshepsut. BA in Chemistry, Harvard U., 1968; MD, W.Va. U., 1972; MSc in Tropical Medicine, London Sch. Hygiene & Tropical Medicine, 1981. Diplomate Am. Bd. Internal Medicine. Instr. in medicine Coll. of Physicians and Surgeons Columbia U., N.Y.C., 1975-76; instr. in medicine Albert Einstein Med. Sch. Albert Einstein Med. Sch., Bronx, 1979-80; sr. lectr. in medicine U. Jos, Nigeria, 1981-88; clin. prof., head dept. of medicine Coll. of Health Scis. Usmanu Danfodio U., Sokoto, Nigeria, 1988-90; chief ambulatory medicine The Meth. Hosp., Bklyn., 1991-92; med. educator Harlem Hosp. Ctr., N.Y.C., 1992—. Contbr. articles to profl. jours. Fellow ACP, West African Coll. of Physicians, Royal Soc. Tropical Medicine and Hygiene; mem. AAAS, Am. Soc. Tropical Medicine & Hygiene, Assn. for Study of Afro-Am. Life and History (life, Washington chpt.). Home: 17 Argyll Ave New Rochelle NY 10804 Office: Harlem Hosp Ctr Dept Med 500 6th St 135th and Malcolm X Ave New York NY 10037

NEWTON, JOHN EDWARD, JR., lawyer; b. Chestnut Hill, Jan. 19, 1954; s. John Edward Sr. and Corinne (Vahlstrom) N. BA, Wheaton Coll., 1975; MBA, Temple U., 1979, JD, 1982. Bar: Pa. 1982, U.S. Ct. Appeals (4th and 3d cirs.) 1984, U.S. Dist. Ct. (ea. dist.) Pa. 1984. Asst. regional counsel HHS, Phila., 1981-86; asst. gen. counsel, asst. sec. Franciscan Health System, Aston, Pa., 1986—, asst. sec., 1988—; asst. sec. Neumann Ins. Co., Englewood, Colo., 1988—. Editorial bd. jour. Neumann Report, 1989; contbr. articles to mags. Vice pres., treas. AIDS Task Force of Phila., 1991-92; bd. dirs. Phila. Community Health Alternatives, Phila., 1991. Mem. Pa. Bar Assn., Beta Gamma Sigma. Home: PO Box 2355 Aston PA 19014

NEWTON, ROBERT RYAN, university administrator, educator; b. Scranton, Pa., Sept. 8, 1935. AB summa cum laude, U. Scranton, 1957; PhL, Fordham U., 1961; STB, Woodstock (Md.) Coll., 1967; STM, Yale U., 1968; EdM, Harvard U., 1968, EdD, 1971. Mem. faculty Loyola-Blakefield, Towson, Md., 1961-64; exec. sec. Jesuit Ednl. Assn. Md., Balt., 1970-71; from asst. prof. to assoc. prof. U. San Francisco, 1978-80; asst. to the acad. v.p. Boston Coll., Chestnut Hill, Mass., 1980, assoc. dean of faculties, 1980-91, assoc. acad. v.p., 1991—. Contbr. articles to profl. jours. Mem. Am. Assn. Higher Edn., Am. Coun. on Edn., Assn. Jesuit Colls. and Univs., Soc. for Coll. and Univ. Planning, Assn. for Gen. and Liberal Edn., Am. Assn. Acad. Deans, Phi Delta Kappa. Roman Catholic. Office: Boston Coll Chestnut Hill MA 02167

NEWTON, V. MILLER, medical psychotherapist, writer; b. Tampa, Fla., Sept. 6, 1938; s. Virgil M. Jr. and Louisa (Verri) N.; m. Ruth Ann Klink, Nov. 9, 1957; children: Johanna, Miller, Mark. BA, U. Fla., 1960; MDiv, Princeton Theol. Sem., 1963; postgrad., U. Geneva, Switzerland, 1962; PhD, The Union Inst., 1981. Min. dir. Flectcher Pl. Urban Social Ministry, Indpls., 1963-65; coord. staff tng. and community rels. Breckinridge Job Corps Ctr., Ky., 1965-66; asst. prof., program dir. social scis. Webster Coll., St. Louis, 1966-69; assoc. prof., program dir. edn. U. South Fla., Tampa, 1969-73; clk. of the cir. ct. Pasco County, Fla., 1973-76; exec. dir. Fla. Alcohol Coalition, Inc., 1979-80; program and nat. clin. dir. Straight, inc., St. Petersburg, Fla., 1980-83; dir. KIDS of Northern Jersey Inc., 1983—; mem. Sec. Task Force Confidentiality and Client Info. System, Fla. Dept. of Health and Rehab. Svcs., 1979-80; chmn. pres.'s adv. Coun. Webster Coll., 1968-69; guest lectr. at the Grad. Inst. of Community Devel. So. Ill. U., 1968-69; cons. Tampa Model Cities Program, 1969-70; chmn. planning com. Tchr. Corps. Nat. Conf.; faculty mem. Internat. U. for Pres., Munich; co-chmn. Mayor's com. on Pre-sch. Edn., Indpls., 1964-65; speaker in field. Author: Gone Way Down: Teenage Drug-Use is A Disease, 1981, Kids, Drugs, and Sex, 1986; co-author: Not My Kid: A Parent's Guide to Kids and Drugs, 1984; appeared on TV programs NBC Mag., 1982, 1986 NBC, 1986, Drugs: A Plague upon America with Peter Jennings ABC, 1988; contbr. articles to profl. jours. Member drug abuse adv. coun. State of N.J., 1985-91; chmn., bd. dirs. Adjustment Madeira Beach, Fla., 1981—, Alcohol Community Treatment Svcs., Inc., Tampa, 1979; pres. Pasco County Coun. on Aging, 1977-79; chmn. bd. San Antonio Boys Village, 1975-76; chmn. Pasco County Data Ctr. Bd., 1973-75, Cen. Pasco Urban Planning Commn., 1972-73; adult del. White House Conf. on Youth, 1971; chmn. Nat. Tchr. Corps Field Coun., 1970-71; pres. Christian Inner City Assn., Indpls., 1964-65; mem. Gov. Ashew's Adv. Com., Pasco County, 1974-76. Aldersgate fellow, 1962; recipient Honor award Nat. LWV, 1963, Cert. Appreciation Pinellas County Bd. of County Commrs., 1982; named Outstanding Young Man of Yr., Indpls. Jaycees, 1965, Outstanding Govt. Leader, Dade City Jaycees, Fla., 1973-74. Mem. Am. Anthrop. Assn., Soc. Med. Anthropology, Psychol. Anthropology, AACD, APHA, Soc. Behavioral Medicine, Phi Delta Theta, Rotary Internat., Order of DeMolay (state master counselor 1957). Democrat. Methodist. Home: 185 Prospect Ave A17H Hackensack NJ 07601-2210 Office: KIDS of North Jersey PO Box 2455 Secaucus NJ 07096-2455

NEWTON, VICTOR JOSEPH, physics educator; b. Boston, Apr. 9, 1937; s. Victor Joseph and Anne Blanche (Grenda) N.; m. Lisa Tyler Haenlein, June 3, 1972; children—Theresa, Catherine. B.S., Spring Hill Coll., 1961, M.A., 1962; Ph.D., MIT, 1966. Assoc. prof. physics Fairfield U., Conn., 1969—, chmn. dept. physics, 1976-85. Contbr. articles to profl. jours. Mem. Fairfield Democratic Town Com., 1981. NSF fellow, 1962-66. Mem. Am. Phys. Soc., AAAS, U.S. Power Squadron, Sigma Xi. Roman Catholic. Club: Fayerweather Yacht (Bridgeport, Conn.). Avocation: sailing. Home: 4042 Congress St Fairfield CT 06430-2041 Office: Fairfield U Fairfield CT 06430

NEY, CHARLES, urologist; b. Harrisburg, Va., June 20, 1912; s. Henry Ney and Julia Salamon; m. Doris Unger, Jan. 28, 1943; children: Alvin Henry, Steven Roger. BA, Johns Hopkins U., 1933, MD, 1937. Diplomate Am. Bd. Urology. Intern surgery Sinai Hosp., Balt., 1937-39; resident surgery Montefiore Hosp., N.Y.C., 1939-40, intern pathology, 1940-41; resident urology Morrisania City Hosp., N.Y.C., 1941-42; cons. urologist Einstein Sch. Medicine, N.Y.C., 1986—, Montefiore Hosp. and Med. Ctr., N.Y.C., 1986—, Bronx Lebanon Hosp. Ctr., N.Y.C., 1986—. Author: Radiographic Atlas G.U. System, 1966, 2d edit., 1981; contbr. articles to profl. jours. Town health officer Town of Easton (N.H.), 1991. Lt. comdr. USN, 1942-46. Home: 340 Sugar Hill Rd Easton NH 03580

NEY, JOANNA MARIA, public relations professional; b. Warsaw, Poland, Dec. 16, 1936; came to U.S., 1946; d. Joseph Fryd and Nora Ney; m. John Oettinger, 1964 (div. 1971). Student, Moravian Sem., Bethlehem, Pa., 1950-55, Dramatic Workshop, N.Y.C., 1955-57, Columbia U., 1961-63, Fordham U., 1987-89. Photo researcher Look mag., N.Y.C., 1955-60; art researcher Am. Heritage, N.Y.C., 1960-61; jr. publicist 20th Century Fox, N.Y.C., 1961-62; freelance publicist various films and cos., N.Y.C. and Paris, 1964-67; staff publicist MGM, N.Y.C., 1968-73; film coord. Warner Bros., N.Y.C., 1975-81; dir. pub. rels. Film Soc. of Lincoln Ctr., N.Y.C., 1982—. Author dance guide, travel guides, articles on dance and film. Mem. Acad. Motion Picture Arts and Scis. (mem. screening com. East Coast). Democrat. Home: 41 W 72d St New York NY 10023

NEYLON, TERRANCE BERNARD, college administrator; b. Peabody, Mass., Sept. 29, 1945; s. James Terrance and Evelyn (Neylon) Kallelis; m. Judith Canty, Aug. 7, 1971; children: Kathryn, Suzanne, Michael, Kevin. BS in Math., U. Mass., 1971; EdM, Salem (Mass.) State U., 1974, Harvard U., 1988; EdD, Harvard U., 1991. Tchr. math. Peabody High Sch., 1972-78; asst. to pres. North Shore Community Coll., Beverly, Mass., 1978-89; dir. administrn. and planning New Eng. Coll. Optometry, Boston, 1990—. Cpl. USMC, 1963-66, Vietnam. Home: 10 Gardner St Salem MA 01970-4854 Office: New Eng Coll Optometry 424 Beacon St Boston MA 02115-1100

NEZIROGLU, FUGEN, psychologist; b. Istanbul, Turkey, Jan. 6, 1953; came to U.S. 1959; s. Cevat and Nezahat (Sehmen) N.; m. Jose Anibal Yaryura-Tobias, Oct. 21, 1978. BA in Psychology magna cum laude, Hofstra U., 1974, PhD, 1977; postgrad., Temple U., Phila., 1978, 79. Diplomate in clin. psychology Am. Bd. Profl. Psychology, in behavioral psychology Am. Bd. Behavioral Psychology; lic., psychologist N.Y. Counselor Nassau County Children's Shelter, 1970-72; sch. psychology intern Farmingdale (N.Y.) Sch. Dist., 1975-76; intake examiner, counselor N. Nassau Mental health Ctr., Manhasset, N.Y., 1972-76; counselor Nassau County Jail, E. Meadow, N.Y., 1976-77; asst. psychologist N. Nassau Mental Health Ctr., 1972-79, asst. rsch. psychologist, 1971-79, chief dept. exptl. psychology, 1977-79; rsch. assoc. NIMH, Hofstra U., Hempstead, N.Y., 1985-86; clin. dir., rsch. assoc., supr. clin. interns Bio-Behavior Psychiatry, Great Neck, N.Y., 1979—; staff psychologist Brunswick Psychait. Hosp., Amityville, N.Y., 1986—; adj. courtesty staff Winthrop U. Hosp., Mineola, N.Y., 1983—; assoc. prof. psychology Hofstra U., 1991, adj. asst. prof. psychology, 1979—; lectr. in field. Editor The Jour. Urban Psychiatry, 1980; contbr. articles to profl. jours. Grantee, Pfizer Co., Wyeth-Ayerst, Ciba-Geigy Corp., Eli Lilly Corp., others. Mem. Am. Psychol. Assn., N.Y. State Psychol. Assn., Nassau County Psychol. Assn. Assn. for Advancement of Behavior Therapy, Nat. Register of Health Svc. Providers in Psychology, Internat. Soc. Rsch. on Aggression, Phobia Soc. Am., Obsessive-Compulsive Found. (sci. adv. bd.), Phi Beta Kappa, Psi Chi. Office: Bio-Behavioral Psychiatry 935 Northern Blvd Great Neck NY 11021-5309

NG, MING TAK, school psychologist; came to U.S., 1967; BA, Mt. Holyoke Coll., 1985; Profl. diploma, Fordham U., 1989. Cert. psychologist, N.Y. Sch. psychologist Bellmore (N.Y.) Pub. Schs., 1989—. Mem. APA (assoc.), NASP, Nassau County Psychol. Assn. Home: 715 Allwyn St Baldwin Harbor NY 11510 Office: Bellmore Pub Schs Bellmore NY 11710

NGUYEN, KIM LOAN THI, electrical engineer; b. Cantho, Vietnam, Nov. 10, 1953; came to U.S., 1972; d. Tang Nhu Truong and Hoa Thi N.; m. Kenneth P. Lee, Sept. 16, 1978; children: Alicia, Tanya, Adrian. B in Math and Sci., Regina Mundi, Saigon, Vietnam, 1972; BSEE, U. Pitts., 1975; MSEE, U. Syracuse, 1978. Analog/circuit design, communications prodn. div. IBM, Kingston, Md., 1975-78; communications, architect IBM, Gaithersburg, Md., 1978-85; systems architect IBM, Rockville, Md., 1985-89; platform mgr. ImagePlus System Support, 1989—.

NGUYEN, NGHI VAN, anesthesiologist; b. Vinh Nghe An, Vietnam, Jan. 2, 1939; came to U.S., 1975; s. Huong Van and Dai Thi (Phan) N.; m. Hanh My Ngo, Jan. 27, 1972; children: Diem, Giao, Don, Dan. MD, Faculty Medicine, Saigon, Vietnam, 1964. Diplomate Am. Bd. Anesthesiology, Am. Acad. Pain Mgmt. Chief surgeon Thu Khoa Nghia Med. Ctr., Cantho, Vietnam, 1973-75; resident anesthesia Dartmouth-Hitchcock Meml. Hosp., Hanover, N.H., 1976-79; staff anesthesiologist, dir. Allegheny Pain Clinic Allegheny Valley Hosp., Natrona Heights, Pa., 1979—. Pres. Vietnamese Cath. Community of Pitts., 1979-86, Vietnamese Assn. Pitts., 1986-90; commr. Pa. Heritage Affairs Commn., Commonwealth Pa., 1991—. Maj., M.C., Army of Rep. of Vietnam, 1964-75. Mem. AMA, Am. Soc. Anesthesiologists, Am. Soc. Regional Anesthesia. Roman Catholic. Home: 1 Custer Ln RD 2 Box 326B Tarentum PA 15084-9634 Office: Allegheny Valley Hosp 1301 Carlisle St Natrona Heights PA 15065

NGUYEN-DINH, THANH, internist, geriatrician; b. Saigon, Vietnam, Nov. 7, 1950; s. Bam and Chanh Thi (Duong) Nguyen-Dinh; m. Kim-Chi Nguyen-Dinh, Oct. 28, 1950; children: Trung, Kim-Trang, Kim-Trinh, Trong. MD, Free U. Brussels, 1974; Tropical MD, Antwerp Tropical Med. Inst., 1975. Diplomate Am. Bd. Internal Medicine, Am. Bd. Geriatric Medicine. Asst. prof. medicine Howard Med. Svc., Washington, 1981—; physician dir. St. Elizabeth Unit, D.C. Gen. Hosp., Washington, 1983—; co-dir. Howard U. Md. Clinics, D.C. Gen. Hosp., 1990—. Contbr. articles to profl. jours. Fellow ACP. Office: 611 S Carlin Springs Rd Ste 211 Arlington VA 22204-1071

NIBLOCK, PHILL, intermedia artist; b. Ind., 1933. With Exptl. Intermedia Found., N.Y.C., 1968—, producer music and intermedia presentations, 1973—, dir., 1985—; prof. video and film prodn. and photography Dept. Performing and Creative Arts CUNY, S.I., 1971—. Films include Morning, Magic Sun, Dog Track, Annie, Max, Raoul, Sur Una and Dos, Trabajando Una and Dos, Tres Familias (Essex, La Purificacion, and Alpatlahua), Four Libras, James Bay, Arctic, Hong Kong, South Africa, Lesotho, Portugal, Brasil 83, parts 1 and 2, Brasil 84, parts one and two, Hungary, China 86, part 3, China 87, part 1 and 2, China 88, parts 1, 2 and 3, Japan, parts 1 and 2; music compositions include Trombone Piece, Winterbloom Too, Fall and Winterblum, Twelve Tones, PK, SLS, PK and SLS, 261.63 + and -, Cello & Bassoon, Second 2 Octaves & a Fifth, First Performance, Held Tones, Unmentionable Pieve for Trombone and Sousaphone, Weld Tuned and Early Winter; videos include (with A. Russell) Terrace of Unintelligibility; recs. include Nothing to Look at, Just a Record, Niblock for Celli, Celli Plays Niblock, Four Full Flutes; performances includeCalif. Inst. Arts, Valencia, 1981, Whitney Mus. at Fed. Hall, N.Y., 1981, Ind. Composers Alliance, L.A., 1982, Het Apollohuis, Eindhoven, The Netherlands, 1983, New Music Am., Hartford, Conn., 1984, Loops Music Ctr., Ghent, Belgium, 1985, Snug Harbor Cultural Ctr., N.Y., 1986, L.A. Film Forum, 1987, Exptl. Intermedia Found., N.Y., 1988, Kunstmus. Bern, Switzerland, 1989, Merkin Concert Hall, N.Y., 1991, Ecole de Arch., Paris, 1991, Angle Intermedia at Dia Art Found, N.Y., 1991; represented in permanent collections including 55 Mercer Gallery, N.Y., Cen. Mich. U. Gallery, Mt. Pleasant, Sub-Tropics Music Festival, Miami, Fla., Carpenter Ctr. Visual Arts Harvard U., Cambridge, Mass., Inst. Contemporary Arts, London. CAPS fellow, Guggenheim fellow; recipients numerous grants/awards including N.Y. State Coun. Arts, 1981, 82, 86, 87, 88, 89, NEA, 1982, 83, 84, 85, 88, N.Y Found. Arts., 1987, Mass. Coun. Arts, 1987, CUNY Rsch. Found., 1984, 85, 89, Found. Contemporary Performance Arts, 1990. Home: 224 Centre St New York NY 10013

NICASTRO-DOHERTY, CYNTHIA MARIE, systems manager; b. Quincy, Mass., Mar. 8, 1958; d. John Joseph and Gina (Roffo) Nicastro; m. Michael Francis Doherty, July 21, 1989; 1 child, Rebecca. BS with honors, Am. Internat. Coll., 1980. Programmer Evans Corp., Braintree, Mass., 1982-83; programmer, analyst Comml. Union Ins., Boston, 1983-84; programmer, analyst John Hancock Property & Casualty, Boston, 1984-85, project leader, 1985-87, systems mgr., 1987—. Vol. Boston Marathon, 1986-91; co. rep. United Way, Boston, 1990. Mem. High Performance Profls., Franklin Country Club. Office: John Hancock Property & Casualty PO Box 854-3 Copley Pl Boston MA 02117

NICCOLINI, DIANORA, photographer, artist; b. Florence, Italy, Oct. 3, 1936; came to U.S., 1946, naturalized, 1960; d. George and Elaine (Augsbury) N. Student Hunter Coll., 1955-62, Art Students League, 1960, Germain Sch. Photography, 1962. Med. photographer Manhattan Eye, Ear and Throat Hosp., 1963-65; organizer med. photography dept., 1st chief med. photographer Lenox Hill Hosp., 1965-67; organizer, head dept. med. and audio visual edn. St. Clare's Hosp., N.Y.C., 1967-76; mem. Third Eye Gallery, N.Y.C., 1974-76; owner Dianora Niccolini Creations, 1976—; instr. photography Camera Club N.Y., 1978-79, Germain Sch. Photography, 1978-79, N.Y. Inst. Photography, 1981-83; one woman shows 209 Photo Gallery, Top of the Stairs Gallery, Third Eye Gallery, 1974, 75, 77, West Broadway Gallery, N.Y.C., 1981, Camera Club N.Y., 1982, Photographics Unltd. Gallery, N.Y.C., 1981, Overseas Press Club, N.Y.C., 1983, Impulse Gallery, Provincetown, Mass., 1983; project dir. Photography over 65, N.Y.C., 1978; pub. portfolios; author: Women of Vision, 1982, Men in Focus, 1983; editor: P.W.P. Times, 1981-82; contbr. to photog. books, 1979, 80; designer greeting cards Flashcards, Inc., 1988-90; contbg. editor Functional Photography, 1979-80, N.Y. Photo Dist. News, 1980; listed in numerous anthologies. Mem. Women Photographers N.Y. (founder 1974), Biol. Photog. Assn., Internat. Ctr. Photography, Am. Soc. Mag. Photographers, Am. Soc. Picture Profls., Profl. Women Photographers (coord. 1980-84), Unity Ctr. Practical Christianity. 1982. Home: 356 E 78th St New York NY 10021-2239

NICCOLINI, DREW GEORGE, gastroenterologist; b. Rockville Center, N.Y., July 27, 1945; s. George D. and Elaine A. (Augsbury) N.; m. Martha Dodge, Jan. 3, 1971; children: Alyssa, Rachael, Lesley, Matthew, Adam. BA, Johns Hopkins U., 1967; MD, Tufts U., 1971. Diplomate Am. Bd. Internal Medicine, Am. Bd. Gastroenterology. Intern St. Elizabeth Hosp., Boston, 1971-72, resident, 1972-74, gastrointestinal fellow, 1974-75; gastrointestinal fellow Faulkner Hosp., Boston, 1975-76; clinician Pentucket Med. Assocs., Haverhill, Mass., 1976—; staff physician Hale Hosp., Haverhill, 1976—, Lawrence (Mass.) Gen. Hosp., 1976—; cons. Holy Family Hosp., Methuen, Mass., 1976—; chief medicine Hale Hosp., haverhill, Mass., 1987-88. Capt. U.S. Army, 1971-77. Fellow Am. Coll. Gastroenterology; mem. ACP, AMA, New Eng. Endoscogy Soc., Am. Soc. Gastroent. Endoscopy, Alpha Omega Alpha. Office: Pentucket Med Assocs 1 Parkway Haverhill MA 01830

NICE, LAWRENCE WILLIAM, institutional parole officer; b. Hanover, N.H., Nov. 17, 1950; s. Philip Oliver and Karen Katrina (Hansen) N.; m. Donna Joyce Cushing, May 5, 1977; children: Joel Benjamin, Rachel Lauren. BA, Tufts U., 1973; MDiv, Oral Roberts U., 1982. Ordained to ministry Bapt. Ch., 1987. Chemistry instr. New Hampton (N.H.) Prep Sch., 1974-76; sec. sch. instr. Christian Fellowship Sch., Laconia, N.H., 1976-80; home improvement/energy savs. sales Newpro, Woburn, Mass., 1983-85; account exec. Wang Labs., Burlington, Mass., 1985; asst. pastor First Bapt. Ch., N. Reading, Mass., 1985—; corrections counselor/case mgr. N.H. State Prison, Concord, 1988-91, institutional parole officer, 1991—; advisor Women's Aglow Internat., 1987-88. Sun. sch. tchr. First Bapt. Ch., Salem, 1991—; bd. dirs. Community Action Belknap-Merrimac Counties, 1976-78, Tulsa, 1980-81.

NICHOLAS, MILLICENT BELLE, sociologist, radiographer, health educator; b. Newark, N.J., Nov. 27, 1938; d. Milton George and Pansie V. Marie (Fields) N. Cert. in radiography, Paterson (N.J.) Gen. Hosp., 1959; BS in Radiol. Sci., Manhattan Coll., 1977; MSW, Rutgers U., 1979. Radiographer Dr. James Koch, Newark, 1959-68; supr. x-ray Cen. Flushing (N.Y.) Med. Group, 1968-69; radiation therapist Med. Group East Side, N.Y.C., 1969; sr. tech. Roosevelt Hosp., N.Y.C., 1969-73; grad. intern U. Medicine and Dentistry N.J., Newark, 1977-79; counselor Am. Cancer Soc., East Orange, N.J., 1981; substitute tchr. Newark Sch. System, 1982-83; asst. prof. Middlesex County Coll., Edison, N.J., 1983, 85—; mem. Middlesex County Coll. Adv. Bd. Instnl. Master Plan, Adv. Bd. Radiology, Presdl. Scholars; Grad. Ceremony Com.; Minority Retention and Recruitment; chmn. Curriculum Revision Subcom., 1991-92; others. Reviewer F.A. Davis Pub. Co., WCB Brown & Benchmark Pub. Co., Delmar Pubs. Inc., Simon & Schuster Pubs., Blackwell Sci. Pub. Inc., Shepherd Inc. Active Scotch Plains (N.J.) Adv. Bd. Sr. Citizens/Residential, 1989—, U. Medicine and Dentistry N.J. Radiography Adv. Bd.; bd. dirs. Essex County Health Systems Agy., Newark. Mem. AAUW (reviewer fellowship program 1992), Am. Soc. Radiol. Techs., N.J. Soc. Radiol. Techs., Rutgers Alumni Assn., NASW, Am. Univ. Radiol. Educators. Home: 22 Country Club Blvd Scotch Plains NJ 07076-2950

NICHOLAS, WENDY PRISCILLA, historic preservation specialist; b. N.J., July 12, 1953; d. Harry K. and Adelaide (Amundsen) N. BA, Duke U., 1975. Asst. dir. Preservation Alliance Louisville-Jefferson County, 1975-81; exec. dir. Providence Preservation Soc., 1981—; bd. dirs. Perservation Action!, Washington, 1983—, Heritage Trust R.I., Providence, 1986—, Nat. Coun. Preservation Execs., 1990—. Columnist Providence Bus. News, 1989—; editor: Walking Thru Louisville, 1976, Treasure Houses of Providence, 1987. Bd. dirs. Smith Hill Ctr., Providence, 1987—. Mem. Providence Art Club.

NICHOLLS, ROBERT LEE, civil engineer, educator; b. Lincoln, Nebr., June 11, 1929; s. Carrol C. and Claire (McDermet) N.; m. Ruth Ann Allen, Aug. 30, 1958; children: David, Jonathan, Carol. BSCE with high honors, U. Colo., 1951; MSCE, Iowa State U., 1952, PhD, 1957. Registered profl. engr., Del., Pa., Iowa, Md. Design engr., constrn. supr. U.S. Army Corps Engrs., Japan, Korea, 1953-55; chief materials engr. and hwy. design engr. Gannett & Fleming, Harrisburg, Pa., 1957-59; prof. civil enginrg. U. Del., Newark, 1959—; geotech. engring. and constrn. materials cons. DuPont, Hercules, Thiokol, others. Author: Composite Construction Materials, 1976; co-author: Civil Engineering Systems, 1972 (also Polish and Spanish edits.); author, editor: ASCE Structural Plastics Selection Manual, 1984; also articles; 7 patents in field. Dist. advance chmn. Boy Scouts Am. Fellow ASCE (pres. Del. sect. 1974-75, recipient nat. citation for sect. activities 1975), Ops. Rsch. Soc. Am., Internat. Soc. Soil Mechanics, Transp. Rsch. Bd., Am. Concrete Inst. Office: Univ Del Civil Engring Dept Newark DE 19716

NICHOLS, ANNE C., controller; b. Bklyn., Nov. 29, 1938; d. Felice and Lucille (Carucci) Graziano; m. Kenneth P. Carrick, Sept. 1958 (div.); m. John Grayson Nichols, Mar. 10, 1967. Grad., Bethpage (N.Y.) High Sch., 1956. Sec. Hirestra Labs., Bethpage, 1956-57; exec. sec. Kiddielane Corp., Westbury, N.Y., 1957-62, Burnham & Co., N.Y.C., 1962-66; asst. to pres. Kensington Orgn., N.Y.C., 1966-71; restauranteur Chumley's Restaurant, N.Y.C., 1971-78; mgr. Merban Corp., N.Y.C., 1974-82; controller First City Capital Corp., N.Y.C., 1982-90, Great Pacific Capital Inc., N.Y.C., 1990—. Mem. Acad Women Achievers (mem. devel. com. 1990-91, auction com. 1991, co-chmn. reunion com. 1991). Office: Great Pacific Capital Inc 767 5th Ave Fl 48 New York NY 10153-4897

NICHOLS, C. WALTER, III, trust company executive; b. N.Y.C., Aug. 25, 1937; s. Charles Walter and Marjorie (Jones) N.; B.A., U. Va., 1959; m. Anne Sharp, Aug. 8, 1959; children—Blair, Sandra, Walter, Hope. Vice pres. Citibank, N.Y.C., 1962-78, Morgan Guaranty Trust Co. N.Y., N.Y.C., 1979—. Bd. dirs. Nichols Found., Inc., 1969—, pres. 1988-90; Choate Rosemary Hall, 1972-77, 82-89, Greenwich House, 1972—, pres., 1984-90, Lower Hudson (N.Y.) chpt. Nature Conservancy, 1978-87, hon. trustee, 1988—, John Jay Homestead, 1980—, Nat. Audubon Soc., 1983-87; mem. adv. bd. N.Y. Zool. Soc. (Bronx Zoo), 1987—. Served to 1st lt. U.S. Army, 1960-62. Decorated Army Commendation medal. Mem. Am. Sunbathing Assn., Naturist Soc. Clubs: Bedford (N.Y.) Golf and Tennis, Pilgrims of U.S. Office: Morgan Guaranty Trust Co NY 9 W 57th St New York NY 10019-2600

NICHOLS, CALEB LEROY, lawyer, educator; b. Sedley, Va., Oct. 19, 1947; s. Alfred Manry and Sylvia Lee (Young) N.; B.A., Norfolk State U., 1970; J.D., U. Conn., West Hartford, 1973; LL.M., Georgetown U., 1977. Bar: Pa. 1974, U.S. Ct. Customs and Patent Appeals 1974, U.S. Ct. Mil. Appeals, 1974, U.S. Ct. Claims 1974, U.S. Customs Ct. 1974, U.S. Tax Ct. 1974, U.S. Supreme Ct., 1977, U.S. Dist. Ct. (ea. dist.) Pa. 1977, U.S. Ct. Appeals (9th cir.) 1977, U.S. Ct. Appeals (4th cir.), 1978, U.S. Ct. Internat. Trade 1981. Legal asst. First Nat. Bank, Portland, Oreg., 1977-78; securities examiner Corp. Commn., Salem, Oreg., 1978-79; examiner atty. Nat. Assn. Securities Dealers, Chgo., 1979-80; legal asst. Legal Svc. Corp. Iowa, Des Moines, 1980; asst. counsel Pa. Dept. Revenue, Harrisburg, 1981-83; dir. Conn. Dept. Banking, Hartford, 1983-87; prof. Western Conn. State Coll., Danbury, 1987—, Ancell Sch. Bus. Western Conn. State U., 1987—; adj. prof. Pace U. Law Sch., 1989; mem. task force Bd. Accountancy Conn. Sec. of State; mem. World Affairs Ctr., Hartford, 1987. Mem. bd. adv. inst. fin. planning Quinnipiac Coll., 1987. Lt. USCG, 1973-77. Mem. N.Am. Securities Adminstrs. Assn. (chmn. disclosure com. 1983-85), Nat. Assn. Securities Dealers, Inc. (arbitrator 1982—), Westchester-Fairfield Corp. Counsel Assn., Practising Law Inst., Inst. Fin. Planning (bd. advisers), Fed. Bar Assn. Democrat. Home and Office: 67 Rowan St Apt 3 Danbury CT 06810-5615

NICHOLS, DAVID ANTHONY, research institute executive; b. Jersey City, Sept. 30, 1940; s. Anthony and Ruth (McKenna) N.; m. Carol Ann Esoldi, Nov. 15, 1966 (div. 1981); children: Karen Naomi, Justin David; m. Linda Walz, May 25, 1984; 1 stepson, Christian Hawkins. AB, Clark U., 1961; PhD, MIT, 1968. Asst. prof. U. Mass., 1966-69, Case Western Res. U., Cleve., 1969-72, Rensselaer Poly. Inst., Troy, N.Y., 1973-74; assoc. prof. SUNY, Albany, 1974-78; v.p. Tellus Inst., Boston, 1976—; bd. dirs. Tellus Inst. for Resource and Environ. Strategies, Boston; cons. numerous orgns. Author: Financing Elections, 1974; contbr. numerous articles to profl. jours. Mem. Am. Polit. Sci. Assn. Home: 1080 Beacon St 3C Brookline MA 02146 Office: Tellus Inst 89 Broad St Boston MA 02110-3509

NICHOLS, DAVID ARTHUR, mediator, retired state justice; b. Lincolnville, Maine, Aug. 6, 1917; s. George E. and Flora E. (Pillsbury) N. A.B. magna cum laude, Bates Coll., 1942; J.D., U. Mich., 1949. Bar: Maine bar 1949, Mass. bar 1949, U.S. Supreme Ct 1954. Pvt. practice Camden, Maine, 1949-75; justice Maine Superior Ct., 1975-77, Maine Supreme Jud. Ct., 1977-88; mediator, 1988—; Mem. Maine Exec. Council, 1955-57; moderator Lincolnville Town Meeting, 1950-74. Mem. editorial bd. Picton Press, 1989—; contbr. to legal and geneal. publs. Chmn. Maine Republican Com., 1960-64; mem. Rep. Nat. Com., 1960-68; chmn. Maine council Young Reps., 1950-54; New Eng. council Young Reps., 1952-54; trustee, past pres. Penobscot Bay Med. Center. Served with USAAF, 1942-45. Fellow Am. Bar Found., Am. Coll. Trial Lawyers; mem. Am. Law Inst., Camden-Rockport C. of C. (past pres.), Maine Hist. Soc., Camden Hist. Soc. (past pres.), Camden Bus. Men's Assn. (past pres.), ABA (bd. govs. 1960-63, ho. dels. 1957-78), Maine Bar Assn., Am. Judicature Soc. (dir. 1960-64), New Eng. Historic Geneal. Soc. (trustee), Bates Coll. Alumni Assn. (past pres.), Maine Trial Lawyers Assn. (past pres.), Phi Beta Kappa, Delta Sigma Rho. Clubs: Odd Fellow, Rotary (past pres.). Home: PO Box 76 Lincolnville ME 04849-0076

NICHOLS, DOUGLAS RICHARD, education educator; b. Lockport, N.Y., Sept. 6, 1946; s. Richard G. and Virginia (Vickers) N.; m. Janet L. Proper, June 6, 1969; children: Meg K., Christine A. BS, SUNY, Geneseo, 1968, postgrad., 1970-72; MS, SUNY, Albany, 1969. Assoc. career devel., asst. dean of students SUNY, Geneseo, 1969-73; asst. prof., dir. career devel. Shippensburg (Pa.) U., 1973—. Pres., v.p. Community Water Assn., Shippensburg, 1985—; chmn. stewardship/fin. ch. coms., Shippensburg, 1987—; leader Cumberland County 4-H Horse Club, Carlisle, Pa., 1991—. Mem. Nat. Career Devel. Assn., Coll. Placement Coun., Mid. Atlantic Placement Assn. (chmn. visitation com. 1976-80, rsch. com. 1981-86), Pa. State System Higher Edn. Career Assn. (pres. 1981-82, v.p. 1985-86). Office: Shippensburg Univ Career Devel Shippensburg PA 17257

NICHOLS, GEORGE CALLOWAY, educational administrator; b. Dallas, Aug. 8, 1943; s. Clarence Williamson and Theda Clark (Wayson) N. AB, Haverford Coll., 1965. Tchr. Collegiate Schs., Richmond, Va., 1965-67, McBurney Sch., N.Y.C., 1967-70; editor Petersen Pub. Co., N.Y.C., 1971-73, Times Mirror Mags., N.Y.C., 1973-75; adminstr. N.Y. Zool. Soc., N.Y.C., 1975-78, Ballet Theatre Found., N.Y.C., 1978-79, Dept. Cultural Affairs, N.Y.C., 1980-81, Internat. Mus. Photography George Eastman House, 1983-85; adminstr., Cooper-Hewitt Mus. Smithsonian Instn., N.Y.C., 1986-89; adminstr. New Sch. for Social Rsch., 1990—. Mem. Nat. Soc. Fund Raising Execs., Art Mus. Devel. Assn. Home: 58 E 80th St New York NY 10021-0249 Office: The Mannes Coll Music 150 W 85th St New York NY 10024-4499

NICHOLS, JAMES HENRY, aerospace engineer; b. Cheverly, Md., Nov. 4, 1962; s. James Henry Jr. and Nelsa Lee (Evans) N. BS, U. Md., 1984. Rsch. analyst Univ. Rsch. Found., College Park, Md., 1980-84; aerospace engr. Naval Air Test Ctr., Patuxent River, Md., 1984—. G.L. Martin Found. scholar, 1980-84. Mem. AIAA (simulation tech. com. 1991—). Home: RR 3 Box 176 Hollywood MD 20636-9504 Office: Naval Air Test Ctr SA 100 Patuxent River MD 20670

NICHOLS, JAMES PHILLIP, insurance agency executive; b. Kenosha, Wis., Jan. 14, 1944; s. Oswald R. and Emily B. (Kowski) N.; student public schs., Kenosha; m. Linda Bedlyon, May 19, 1973; 1 child, Jeremy James. Sales agt. Phoenix Mut. Life, Chgo., 1968-69, office mgr., Phila., 1969-79, sales mgr., 1979—, v.p. corp. fin. svcs., 1979—. With U.S. Army, 1965-67. Mem. Am. Soc. CLU's, Phila. Assn. Life Underwriters, Phila. Gen. Agts. and Mgrs. Assn., Assn. Health Ins. Agts., Nat. Assn. Securities Dealers (registered rep.), Am. Legion. Home: 109 Round Hill Rd Voorhees NJ 08043-1206 Office: Phoenix Mut Life The Bellevue 4th Fl Philadelphia PA 19102

NICHOLS, JOHN DAVID, insurance executive; b. Walton/Oneonta, N.Y., Mar. 18, 1948; s. Sidney Newton and Emily Matilda (Clark) N.; m. Annemarie Margaret Meinke, June 24, 1978; children: David Sean, Christine Marie, James Edmund. BA, Muskingum Coll., 1971. Lic. ins. broker. Underwriter trainee U.S. Fidelity & Guaranty, Scranton, Pa., 1972-73; underwriter U.S. Fidelity & Guaranty, Balt., 1973-76; supervising underwriter U.S. Fidelity & Guaranty, Toledo, Ohio, 1976-77; sr. casualty underwriter The Hartford Ins. Group, Mt. Kisco, N.Y., 1977-81; assoc. account exec. Murray, Schoen & Homer, Inc., Bronxville, N.Y., 1981-84; sr. casualty underwriter Am. Internat. Group, N.Y.C., 1984-85; assoc. account exec. A. Matarasso & Co., Inc., White Plains, N.Y., 1985-88; account exec. Walter Kaye Assocs., Inc., N.Y.C., 1988-90; analyst Interstate Risk Mgmt. Corp., Bedford, N.Y., 1990—; mgr. dirs. and officers liability insurance dept. Interstate Risk Placements, Inc., Interstate Coverage Corp., Bedford, N.Y., 1990—. Asst. scoutmaster Boy Scouts Am., Balt., 1974-75, Yorktown, 1990—, asst. cubmaster, 1990—, Webelos den leader, 1991—, mem. com., 1990—; advisor Jr. Achievement, Balt., 1975-76; bd. mem. Coachlight Condominium Assn., Montrose, N.Y., 1982-84; mem. parish vestry, 1989, 90, 91; ch. del. Inter-Parish Coun., 1990—, N.Y. Diocese Conv., 1990, 91; chmn. Parish Outreach, 1991. Republican. Episcopalian. Office: Interstate Cos PO Box 581 Bedford NY 10506-0700

NICHOLS, KYRA, ballerina; b. Berkeley, Calif., 1959. Studies with, Alan Howard, Pacific Ballet, Sch. Am. Ballet, N.Y.C. With N.Y.C. Ballet, 1974—, now prin. dancer.; created role in: Jerome Robbins' Four Seasons, 1975, John Taras' Concerto for Piano and Wind Instruments, Stravinsky Centennial Celebration, 1982, Jacques d'Amboise's Celebration, 1983. Ford Found. scholar. Office: Peter S Diggins Assocs 133 W 71st St New York NY 10023-3834 also: NYC Ballet Inc NY State Theater Lincoln Ctr Pla New York NY 10023

NICHOLS, RAYMOND STANLEY, actuary, consultant; b. Bridgeport, Conn., May 26, 1946; m. Ellen Lee Van Horne, Nov. 17, 1973; children: Sara Elizabeth, Emily Randall. BA, Bridgeport U., 1970; MS, Ohio State U., 1973. Actuarial asst. Traveler's, Hartford, Conn., 1973-80; 2d v.p., actuary Traveler's, Hartford, 1985-88, Covenant Ins., Hartford, 1980-85; sr. v.p., chief actuary N.H. Group, Manchester, 1988-89; cons. actuary Milliman & Robertson, Bloomfield, Conn., 1989-91; ind. cons., 1991—. Fellow Casualty Actuarial Soc.; mem. Am. Acad. Actuaries. Office: Milliman & Robertson 3 Corporate Pl Bloomfield CT 06002-2413

NICHOLS, ROBERT SHERMAN, JR., hotel executive; b. N.Y.C., Nov. 16, 1945; s. Robert S. and Helen (Brown) N.; m. Nancy Irene Schloman, June 11, 1972; children: Tiffani, Robert III. BS in Bus., U. N.H., 1967; cert. of completion, Stanford U., 1988. Asst. mgr. trainee Marriott Hotels, Washington, 1967, dept. head hotel, 1968-70, exec. com. hotel, 1970-72, gen. mgr. hotel, 1980-81, v.p. human resource devel., 1982-84, v.p. Marriott Inn franchise group, 1972-80, regional v.p. v.p. mid-Atlantic region, 1984-91; sr. v.p. total quality mgmt. Marriott Hotels, Resorts, Stes., 1991—; bd. dirs. Marriott Employees Fed. Credit Union, Bethesda, Md.; mem. curriculum adv. com. No. Va. Community Coll. Hotel, Restaurant, Inst. Mgmt. Curriculum, Annandale, 1985—. Bd. dirs. Washington D.C. Visitors and Conv. Assn., 1988-89, Children's Miracle Network Fund Raising Com., Washington, 1990-91; mem. coun. Operation Enterprise, AMA, Hamilton, N.Y., 1990—. Mem. Va. Hotel Motel Assn. (bd. dirs. 1980-81), Washington Area Bd. Trade. Home: 20125 Darlington Dr Gaithersburg MD 20879-1007

NICHOLSON, WILLIAM GEORGE, director, educator; b. Greenfield, Mass., Sept. 18, 1935; s. William George and Sophia (Stasinopoulos) N.; m. Cornelia Downes, Aug. 30, 1958; children: Alexandra, Christopher, Hugh. AB, Brown U., 1958; MA, Ohio State U., 1963. Tchr. Columbus (Ohio) Acad., 1958-63, Cate Sch., Carpinteria, Calif., 1963-65; tchr., dean of faculty Charlotte (N.C.) Country Day Sch., 1965-68; headmaster Birmingham (Ala.) U. Sch., 1968-69; tchr., dir. coll. placement dept. Taft Sch., Watertown, Conn., 1969—, Independence Found. chair, 1981; assoc. dir. admission Brown U., Providence, 1983-84. Author: (biography) Pete Gray: One Armed Major Leaguer, 1976, The Taft-Thatcher Letters, 1985, Those Who Served, 1990; contbr. articles to profl. jours. Elected mem. Bd. of Edn., Watertown, 1991—. Mem. Soc. for Am. Baseball Rsch. Democrat. Home: 123 North St Watertown CT 06795

NICI, RICHARD JAMES, telecommunications engineering executive; b. N.Y.C., Aug. 29, 1955; s. Salvatore and Christine Nici; m. Janet Testaverde, Aug. 3, 1986; children: James, Karen. B in Engring., Cooper Union, 1977; MS, Columbia U., 1978. Supr. AT&T Bell Labs., Holmdel, N.J., 1978-90; mem. tech. staff Bell Communications Rsch., Red Bank, N.J., 1990—; pres. Advanced Elevator Components, N.Y.C., 1984—. Patentee in field. Home: 1 Tracy Pl Eatontown NJ 07724-3173

NICKARD, GARY LAURENCE, artist; b. Toronto, Can., June 14, 1954; s. Metro and Margot Viola (Walker) N.; m. Patricia Ann Wallace. BA, SUNY, Buffalo, 1978, MA, 1982, MFA, 1986. Individual artist, 1981—; dir., chief curator Ctr. for Exploratory and Perceptual Art, Buffalo, 1981-88; lectr. dept. fine art SUNY, Buffalo, 1987-88; assoc. curator Alternative Mus., N.Y.C., 1988-90; ind. curator, cons., 1988—; dir., chief curator Burden Gallery Aperture Found., N.Y.C., 1990-91. Contbr. articles to profl. jours. Home: 501 Hicks St Apt 401 Brooklyn NY 11231-2925

NICKEL, ALBERT GEORGE, advertising agency executive; b. Pitts., July 12, 1943; s. Frank George and Dorothy (Wiefling) N.; m. Margery Flanders, May 31, 1968; children: Melissa, Mark. AB, Washington and Jefferson Coll., 1965; MBA, Ind. U., 1967. Mktg. rsch. analyst Pfizer, Inc., N.Y.C., 1967, profl. svc. rep., 1967-68, mktg. rsch. mgr., 1968-69, product mgr., 1969-70; product mgr. USV Internat., Tuckahoe, N.Y., 1970-71; account exec. J. Walter Thompson (Deltakos), N.Y.C., 1971-72, account supr., 1972-73; account supr. Sudler & Hennessey, N.Y.C., 1973-77; sr. v.p. mgmt. group supr. Young and Rubicam, N.Y.C., 1977-79; pres., chief oper. officer Dorritie Lyons & Nickel, Inc., N.Y.C., 1979—. Trustee Wilton YMCA, Five Town Found.; bd. dirs., exec. com. Wilton LaCrosse Assn., Healthcare Businesswoman's Assn., Wilton High Sch. Long Range Planning Team. Capt. USAF, 1969. Mem. Am. Coun. on Sci. and Health (bd. dirs.), Pharm. Advt. Coun., Midwest Pharm. Adv. Coun., Wilton Riding Club (pres.), Shore and Country Club, Silver Spring Country Club. Home: 97 Keelers Ridge Rd Wilton CT 06897-1608

NICKEL-MILSTONE, SHERRI J., college official; b. Spring Valley, Sask., Can., Nov. 1, 1961; d. David Martin and Joyce Marlene (Halverson) Nickel; m. David Milstone, Oct. 25, 1987. BS in Psychology, Cen. Mich. U., 1984; MA in Student Pers., Indiana U. Pa., 1986. Sexuality peer educator Cen. Mich. U., Mt. Pleasant, 1981-84; grad. dir. Indiana U. Pa., 1984-86; residence dir. U. N.H., Durham, 1986-87, coord. sexuality edn., rape crisis counselor, 1986-87; coord., student life programs Fitchburg (Mass.) State Coll., 1987-89, asst. dir. residence life, 1988-91, dir. residence life, 1991—. Mem. NOW, Greenpeace. Democrat. Unitarian.

NICKERSON, EUGENE H., federal judge; b. Orange, N.J., Aug. 2, 1918; m. Marie-Louise Steiner; children—Marie-Louise, Lawrie H., Stephanie W., Susan A. A.B., Harvard U., 1941; LL.B. (Kent scholar), Columbia U., 1943; LL.D. (hon.), Hofstra U., 1970, Bklyn. Law Sch., 1991. Bar: N.Y. 1944, U.S. Supreme Ct. 1948. Law clk. to Judge Augustus N. Hand, 2d circuit U.S. Ct. Appeals, 1943-44; to Chief Justice Harlan F. Stone U.S. Supreme Ct., 1944-46; county exec. Nassau County, N.Y., 1962-70; practice law N.Y.C., 1946-61, 71-77; judge U.S. Dist. Ct., Bklyn., 1977—; Counsel N.Y. Gov.'s Com. Pub. Employee Procedures, 1956-58; mem. N.Y. State Law Revision Commn., 1958-59, 77; mem. Met. Regional Council, 1962-70, chmn., 1969-70; mem. adv. council pub. welfare HEW, 1963-65; mem. pub. ofcls. adv. council OEO, 1968. Mem. ABA, Nassau County Bar Assn., Assn. Bar City N.Y. (com. fed. legislation 1971-74, com. on communications 1971-77, com. on judiciary 1974-77), Am. Law Inst., Phi Delta Phi. Office: US Dist Ct 225 Cadman Pla E Brooklyn NY 11201

NICKERSON, GARY ALLAN, lawyer; b. Taunton, Mass., Feb. 12, 1951; s. William Clayton and Dorothy Ellen (Gallipeau) N.; m. Karen Marie Gibeau, June 20, 1987; children: Heather Anne, Seth Allan, Adam George, Chelsea Marie. BS magna cum laude, U. Mass., 1972; JD, Northeastern U., 1975. Bar: Mass. 1975, U.S. Supreme Ct. 1977. Postdoctoral fellow in marine policy Woods Hole Oceanographic Inst., 1975; asst. dist. atty. Cape and Islands Dist. Atty.'s Dist. Office, Barnstable, Mass., 1976-82; spl. asst. U.S. atty. Mass. U.S. Atty.'s Office, Boston, 1982; pvt. practice Barnstable, 1983—; bd. dirs. Sandwich (Mass.) Coop. Bank; mem. Jud. Nominating Commn., Boston, 1991—. Trustee Barnstable County Coop. Extension Svc., 1990—; town meeting moderator, Sandwich, 1979-86; commr. Sandwich Conservation Commn., 1974-78. Mem. Mass. Bar Assn., Barnstable County Bar Assn., Mass. Assn. Trial Lawyers. Office: 3166 Main St Barnstable MA 02630-1107

NICKERSON, PETER AYERS, pathology educator; b. Hyannis, Mass., Feb. 19, 1941; s. Norman O. and Ruth (Ayers) N. AB, Brown U., 1963; MA, Clark U., 1965, PhD, 1968. Teaching asst. Clark U., Worcester, Mass., 1963-66, NASA predoctoral fellow, 1966, USPHS predoctoral fellow, 1966-67; rsch. instr. SUNY, Buffalo, 1967-69, asst. prof., then assoc. prof., 1969-80, prof. dept. pathology, 1980—, dir. grad. studies, 1974—; corp. mem. Marine Biol. Lab., Woods Hole, Mass., 1990. Contbr. over 100 articles to refereed jours. Bd. dirs. Alzheimer's Assn., Buffalo, 1986—. Mem. Am. Assn. Anatomists, Endocrine Soc., Am. Soc. Pathologists, Am. Soc. Cell Biology, Am. Soc. Zoologists, Sigma Xi, Omicron Kappa Epsilon. Office: SUNY Buffalo Dept Pathology Buffalo NY 14214

NICKERSON, RICHARD GORHAM, research company executive; b. Harwich, Mass., Nov. 20, 1927; s. Ephriam Gorham and Elizabeth (Wardle) N.; m. Eileen Florence Tressler, June 7, 1957; children: Holly Anne, Wendy Elyse, Susan Denise. BS cum laude, U. Mass., 1950; PhD, Northwestern U., 1955; postgrad., Poly. Inst. Bklyn., 1955-57; MBA cum laude, Boston U., 1983. Rsch. chemist DuPont, Cellophane Tech. Sect., Richmond, Va., 1954-55, W.R. Grace, Dewey & Almy Div., Cambridge, Mass., 1957-60; v.p. rsch. and devel. Electronautics Corp., Maynard, Mass., 1960-61; pres. Electronautics Corp., Maynard, 1961-63; project leader Polyco Borden Chem. div. Borden, Inc., Leominister, Mass., 1963-65, group leader, 1965-67, devel. mgr., 1967-81, lab. mgr., 1981-87; pres., mng. dir. Boston Profls. Internat., Inc., Hopkinton, Mass., 1987—. Patentee in field. With Chem. Corps, U.S. Army, 1955-57. Mem. Am. Chem. Soc., Soc. Plastics Engrs., Sigma Xi, Phi Lambda Upsilon. Home: 16 Valleywood Rd Hopkinton MA 01748-1635

NICKERSON, WILLIAM MILNOR, district court judge; b. Balt., Dec. 6, 1933; s. Palmer Rice and Eleanor (Renshaw) N.; m. Virginia Arlen Bourne, Apr. 25, 1954; children: Carol Lee, Deborah, Susan, Wendy, Laura. BA, U. Va., 1955; LLB, U. Md., Balt., 1962. Ptnr. Whiteford, Taylor & Preston, Balt., 1962-85; assoc. judge Cir. Ct. Baltimore County, Towson, Md., 1985-90; judge U.S. Dist. Ct. Md., Balt., 1990—. Served to lt. USCGR, 1955-59. Office: US Dist Ct 101 W Lombard St Baltimore MD 21201

NICKSA, GARY WILLIAM, financial executive; b. Hartford, Conn., Aug. 20, 1957; s. Walter Charles and Aurore (Labbe) N.; m. Kimberlee Watts, Oct. 29, 1983; children: Sarah, Jeffrey. BSBA, U. Vt., 1980; MS in Taxation, Bentley Coll., 1985. CPA, Mass. Tax mgr. Coopers & Lybrand, Boston, 1980-86; v.p., chief fin. officer Keith Properties, Inc. and Affiliates, Stoughton, Mass., 1986—. Author: Subchapter S Taxation, 1986. Mem. AICPA, Mass. Soc. CPA. Home: 11 Shirley Rd Wellesley MA 02181-2307

NICKSE, RUTH SPEIRS, psychologist; b. Yonkers, N.Y., June 30, 1931; d. John Yates and Ina (Weeks) Speirs; m. Robert Nickse, 1953 (div. 1964); children: Stephen, Robert, Gail; m. Robert Weieter Balluffi, June 1, 1974; children: Andrew, Barbara, Frank. BS, Cornell U., 1968, MA, 1970, PhD, 1972. Asst. prof. SUNY, Cortland, 1971-74; project dir. Syracuse (N.Y.) Rsch. Corp., 1973-76; fellow Nat. Inst. Edn., Washington, 1976-77; assoc. prof. U. Mass., Boston, 1979-81; pres. Nickse Assocs., Ithaca, N.Y., 1978-79, Brookline, Mass., 1989—; instr. Havard Univ. Extension, Cambridge, Mass., 1981-83; rsch. dir. Adult Svcs./Mass. State Edn. Dept., Quincy, 1979-83; assoc. prof. Boston U., 1983-89; sr. cons. ABT Assocs., Inc., Cambridge, 1990—. Author: (book) Assessing Life Skills Competence, 1980, (monograph) Family and Intergenerational Literacy Practice, 1990; editor: Beyond Competency Testing: Competency Based Education, 1981; contbr. articles to profl. jours. Named Outstanding Adult Educator, Mass. Assn. Adult and Continuing Edn., 1989. Mem. Am. Psychol. Assn., Am. Edn. Rsch. Assn., Mass. Coalition for Adult Literacy (founding mem.), Internat. Reading Assn., Am. Assn. Adult and Continuing Edn. (prog. devel. award 1985), Internat. League for Social Commitment in Adult Edn. Office: Nickse Assocs 58 Monmouth St Brookline MA 02146-5607

NICOL, DOMINIK, writer, photographer; b. nr. Oltenia, Romania, Sept. 25, 1930; came to U.S., 1969, naturalized, 1976; s. Dumitru and Valentina (Sandulescu) Nicolaescu. Diploma in Chemistry and Tech. of Antibiotics, The Tech. Sch., Bucharest, Romania, 1954. Photo-reporter Agerpress, Bucharest, 1950-51; med. photographer Cantacuzino Hosp., Bucharest, 1955-68. Author, editor: Self Encounter, 1979, Ten Oneiric Sketches, 1980, Rendes-Vous sau Intalnire cu mine insumi, 1987; (play) Vacuum (Colocviu de abis), 1979, Vacuum-Void, 1988, Pe portativul vietii, 1992. Home: 320 W 49th St Apt 3 New York NY 10019-7318

NICOL, MARJORIE CARMICHAEL, research psychologist; b. Orange, N.J., Jan. 6, 1929; d. Norman Carmichael and Ethel Sarah (Siviter) N. BA, Upsala Coll., MS, 1978; MPh, PhD, CUNY, 1988. Mgr. advt. prodn. RCA, Harrison, N.J., 1950-58; advt. mgr., writer NPS Advt., East Orange, N.J., 1960-67; pres. measurement and eval., chief exec. officer, psychol. evaluator Nicol Evaluation System, Millburn, N.J., 1967—; chief exec. officer., dir. Rafiki, Essex County, N.J., 1965—. Author: Nicol Index, Nicol Evaluation System, 1991. Officer Montclair Rehab. Orgn., 1981—; founder Met. Opera at Lincoln Ctr. Republican. Presbyterian. Home: 85 Linden St Millburn NJ 07041-2160 Office: PO Box 111 Millburn NJ 07041-0111

NICOL, ROBERT RANSOM, JR., English educator; b. Niagara Falls, N.Y., July 5, 1932; s. Robert Ransom and Mae Victorine (Slaughter) N.; m. Blanche Alice Gough, Aug. 21, 1954; children: Susan Elaine Nicol Greene, James Robert, Sherilynn Gough Nicol Taylor. BA, Niagara U., 1954, MA, 1961; PhD, SUNY, Buffalo, 1966. Supr. employee svcs. ea. div. Moore Bus. Forms, Niagara Falls, 1956-61; instr. Niagara U., Niagara University, N.Y., 1961-66, asst. prof., 1966-74, assoc. prof., 1974-83, prof. English, 1983—; lectr. SUNY, Buffalo, 1974-77; participant Mattelalter Rezeption, Kaprun, Austria, 1990; cons. Rainbow Security Systems, Niagara Falls, 1974, Carbonundum Co., Niagara Falls, 1965, 68; del. People to People Internat., Spokane, 1991. Contbr. articles to profl. publs. Pres. Niagara Frontier Linguistics Soc., Buffalo, 1965-68. 1st lt. U.S. Army, 1954-56, with USAR, 1956-62. Mem. MLA, Medieval Assn. Pacific, Medieval Assn. Am., Southeastern Medieval Assn., Linguistic Assn. Am., Southeastern Medieval and Renaissance Soc., Studies in Medievalism. Home: 746 Van Rensselaer Ave Niagara Falls NY 14305-1848 Office: Niagara U Dept English Niagara University NY 14109

NICOLA-GROSSMILLER, KENNETH N., writer; b. Phila., Oct. 18, 1955; s. Henry and Theresa (Paolini) Grossmiller; m. Michele E. Di-Raddo, Oct. 26, 1991. Student, D.C.C.C., 1991-92, West Chester U., 1992—. Actor Flute Midsummer Nights Dream A.B.C./Capitol City Spl., Phila., N.Y.C., 1976; actor Bobby "Rats" Direct Theatre, N.Y.C., 1976; actor Bo Alexander Love of Life, CBS, N.Y.C., 1978; actor Carmine Fornaro Prizzi's Honor, ABC motion picture, N.Y.C., 1984; asst. to assoc. producer All My Children, ABC, N.Y.C., 1983; asst. prodr. to Nelle Nugent, Foxboro Prodns., N.Y.C., 1987; asst. dir. Everything the Traffic Will Allow, SJS Prodns., N.Y.C., 1989; actor Guildenstern, Marovitz's "Hamlet" Riverside Shakespeare Co., N.Y.C., 1989. Author screenplay: Voice of Heaven, 1989; author teleplay: Only In Your Dreams, 1991, Little Girl Eater, 1991. Mem. Actor's Equity, Screen Actors Guild, Affiliation for TV and Radio Artists. Home and Office: 33 Chester Pike B14 Ridley Park PA 19078

NICOLARDI, DONALD MARC, gastroenterologist; b. Manhattan, N.Y., Mar. 13, 1954; s. Peter James and Rose (Epstein) N.; m. Rena Shectman, June 16, 1984; 1 child, Peter James. BS magna cum laude, CUNY, Bklyn., 1977; MD cum laude, SUNY, Bklyn., 1983. Attending physician LaGuardia Hosp., Forest Hills, N.Y., 1989—, Beth Israel Hosp. North, N.Y.C., 1990—; ptnr. Queens-L.I. Med. Group, Forest Hills, 1992—. Fellow ACP, Am. Bd. Internal Medicine, Am. Coll. Gastroenterology; mem. Am. Soc. for Gastrointestinal Endoscopy, Am. Gastroent. Assn., AMA (Physician's Recognition award 1987, 90), Med. Soc. of the State of N.Y., N.Y. County Med. Soc., Alpha Omega Alpha. Home: 1641 3d Ave Ste 24A East New York NY 10128-3631 Office: Queens LI Med Group 66-07 102d St Forest Hills NY 11374

NICOTRA, JOSEPH CHARLES, artist; b. Corona, N.Y., Aug. 9, 1931; s. Charles C. and Constanta (Maglienti) N.; m. Mary C. LoSquardo, Sept. 9, 1951; children: Therese, Nanette, Marie. Student, Art Students League, N.Y.C., 1955-59, Art Students League, Woodstock, N.Y., 1959-60, Am. Art Sch., N.Y.C., 1960-61; diploma of merit, U. Art, Italy, 1982. Registered artist, N.Y.C. Freelance easel painter N.Y.C., 1962—. One-man shows include Armstrong Gallery, Flushing, N.Y., 1968, La Galerie Mouffe, Paris, 1976, Long Beach Artists Assn. Gallery, N.Y.C., 1978, 79, Long Beach Libr. Art Gallery, 1979, Cam Art Ctr., Bayshore, N.Y., 1982, Pricilla Redford Roe Gallery, Suffork, N.Y., 1982, Queens Mus., 1982, 84, Pla. Del Malfestazione, Italy, 1983, 6th Internat. Biennale, Garbo, Bulgaria, 1983, Flushing Coun. on Culture & Arts, 1986, Atlanta Gallery Generve, 1987, St. Paul's Ch., Beth Page, N.Y., 1992; group shows include 57th St. Gallery, N.Y., 1957, Woodstock, N.Y., 1961, Long Beach (N.Y.) Mus., 1976, Flushing Coun. on Culture & Arts, 1986; represented in permanent collections Nat. Archives, Washington, Queens Mus. Art; prin. works include mural for Queens Mus. Title Wall for Nat. Travel Show. Vol. Artist, tchr., docent, lectr. Queens Mus. Art, Flushing, N.Y., 1972—. With U.S. Army, 1952-54; mem. Queens Coun. Arts, Flushing Coun. Culture and Arts. Recipient Outstanding Svc. award Queens Mus. Art, 1972-91, 1st prize for Oil, Long Beach Mus., 1976; Bernsay scholar, 1958, scholar VA, 1959, 1st prize Long Beach Artists Assn., 1980, Accademia delle Art Gold medal, Italy, 1980, Gold medal for Safety, Peace & Artist Merit, Internat. Parliament, U.S.A., 1983, Accademia D'Europa award, 1983, Statue of Victory, Com. for World Culture, 1984, European Banner of Arts award 1985, Gold Plaque award Italian Accademia, 1987. Mem. Art Students League (life), Orgn. Ind. Artists, Internat. Confedn. Order of Artists (hon.), Queens Mus. Art (hon.), DAV (life). Home and Studio: 59-32 156th St Flushing NY 11355

NIEB, CYNTHIA DELL, educator; b. Niles, Mich., Apr. 2, 1958; d. Charles Stewart and Betty Josephine (Crumb) N. BA, Kalamazoo Coll., 1980; student, So. Meth. U., 1981-84, Cornell U., 1984—; MA in History, Cornell U., 1990. Intern Boston Children's Mus., 1978, Denver Art Mus.,

1980; curator Polk Pub. Mus., Lakeland, Fla., 1981; grad. asst. So. Meth. U., Dallas, 1981-84; teaching asst. Cornell U., Ithaca, N.Y., 1985—; educator, vol. Ithaca Rape Crisis, 1990-91. Mem. Nat. Women's Studies Assn., Orgn. Am. Hist., Soc. Am. City and Regional Planning History, Com. Lesbian and Gay History. Office: Cornell U History Dept 450 McGraw Hall Ithaca NY 14853

NIEBUHR, FRED J(OHN), real estate consultant; b. N.Y.C., Mar. 7, 1926; s. Fred and Helen (Albers) N.; m. Evelyn Daigle, Feb. 14, 1949 (div. Oct. 1979); children: Ronald, Donald, Linda; m. Jean E. Snell, Dec. 1, 1979; 1 child, Richard Lyons. Student, Columbia U., 1948, Adelphi U., 1952. Exec. v.p. Island Realty, Westbury, N.Y., 1953-79; pres. Exec. Realty, Westbury, N.Y., 1979-84, Leonard, Call Taylor Assoc., Hilton Head, S.C., 1984-88; cons. Exec. Realty, Westbury, 1988-89, Island Realty, Melville, N.Y., 1989—; vice-chmn., lectr. Real Inst., C.W. Post U., 1984; mem. panel Am. Arbitration Assn., N.Y.C., 1991—; mem. L.I. Loves Bus., Hauppauge, N.Y., 1971; speaker N.Y. State Assn. Indsl. Agys., Hempstead, N.Y., 1972Bellmore Merrick Cen. High Sch., 1975; chmn. L.I. Home Builders Inst. Comml. Commerce Com., Hempstead, 1970. Mem. Nassau Suffolk Post Vietnam Planning Com., 1970; mem. dinner com. Nat. Leukemia Assn., 1982; chmn. Suffolk County Coun., Boy Scouts Am., 1976. With USN, 1943-46, PTO, 51-52. Mem. Soc. Indsl. Realtors (pres. 1972), Indsl. and Comml. Brokers Soc. (pres. 1970-72). Office: Island Realty 1121 Walt Whitman Rd Melville NY 11747-3005

NIEDERMEIER, CHRISTINE MARIE, lawyer, former state legislator; b. Bridgeport, Conn., Oct. 21, 1951; d. Jerome J. and Marie Perkins N. B.A. in Govt., Georgetown U., 1973, J.D., 1977, LLD (hon.) Sacred Heart U. Legis. analyst in housing and urban affairs Libr. of Congress, Congl. Rsch. Svc., Washington, 1973-74; staff aide to late Gov. Ella T. Grasso of Conn., State Capitol, Hartford, 1975; legis. aide Congressman Christopher J. Dodd of Conn., Washington, 1975-77; assoc. Day, Berry and Howard, Hartford, Conn., summer 1976; schedule and advance aide Nat. Presdl. Campaign of Gov. Edmund G. Brown, Jr., 1976; admitted to Conn. bar, 1977, U.S. Dist. Ct. bar, 1977, D.C. bar, 1979; assoc. firm Trager and Trager, Fairfield, Conn., 1977-81, Winthrop, Stimson, Putnam and Roberts, Stamford, Conn., 1982-87; ptnr. Pullman & Comley, 1987—; Dem. nominee for U.S. Congress 4th dist., 1986, 87; mem. Conn. Ho. of Reps., 1979-87, former mem. govt. adminstrn. and elections com., energy and pub. utilities com., task force on program budgeting and appropriations process, ad hoc legis. com. on arts, past chmn., ranking mem. transp. com., past chmn. appropriations com. subcoms. on jud. collective bargaining and regulation and protection, past chmn., mem. transp. and communications com. Nat. Conf. State Legislators, 1983-84. Lawyers com. rep. United Way Campaign, 1977-79; rep. Dist. 13 Fairfield Rep. Town Meeting, 1977-79; mem. Dem. Town Com., Fairfield; former mem., bd. dirs. Conn. Audubon Soc., Conn. Heart Assn., YWCA Greater Bridgeport; former mem. Oversoght Collaborative, Bridgeport Futures Initiative, U. Bridgeport Bd. Assocs., Fairfield Parking Authority Adv. Com., Parents and Friends of Retarded Citizens, Inc., Fairfield County 2000's Transp. and Housing Coms.; former vice chmn. president's coun. Sacred Heart U.; former mem. Fairfield County Heart Assn.; past bd. dirs. Urban League Greater Bridgeport, Music Found. for Handicapped; bd. dirs. Family Svcs., Woodfield, Greater Bridgeport Regional Bus.-Industry Coun.; former mem. pub. affairs com., YWCA Greater Bridgeport Inc.; former trustee Mus. Art, Sci. and Industry; co-chair, dir. event fundraising Music and Arts Ctr. for Handicapped, 1989; mem. Southwestern Conn. Conf. Exhbn. Authority; mem. legis. adv. com. Sacred Heart Univ.'s Ctr. for Policy Issues; mem. young women's caucus adv. bd. Nat. Women's Caucus; mem. exec. fin. com. Conn. Dem. State Ctrl. Com.; mem. Fairfield county econ. devel. project steering com. Southwestern Area Commerce and Industry Assn. Conn.; mem. coordinating com. and exec. com. Greater Bridgeport United Way's Regional Youth/Adult Substance Abuse Project; grand marshal Barnum Festival Parade, 1992; vice-chmn. Fairfield Sr. Ctr. Building Com.; mem., sec. Lower Fairfield County Conf. Recipient Disting. Service award Georgetown U., 1973. Mem. ABA, Conn. Bar Assn., D.C. Bar Assn., Greater Bridgeport Bar Assn., Delta Kappa Gamma (hon.), Rotary (bd. dirs., community svc. dir. Bridgeport club 1990-91).

NIEDZIELSKA, MARIE-SUZANNE, education consultant, computer scientist; b. N.Y.C., Aug. 4, 1947; d. Edmund L. and R. Isabelle (Paradis) N. BS in Physics, Fordham U., 1969, PhD in Philosophy, 1979. Cert. systems profl. Asst. prof. philosophy U. Hartford (Conn.), 1972-80; mgr. info. systems Travelers Ins. Cos., Hartford, 1981—. Mem. Data Processing Assn., Assn. Systems Mgmt., Computer Profls. Social Responsibility. Home: 49 Brewster Rd Glastonbury CT 06033-1051 Office: 1 Tower Sq Hartford CT 06183-0001

NIEHAUS, ROBERT HENRY, banker; b. Fort Monmouth, N.J., Aug. 18, 1955; s. Robert Frederick and Joanne Cecil (Fath) N.; m. Kate Southworth, June 19, 1982; children: John, Peter, Ann. BA, Princeton U., 1977; MBA, Harvard U., 1982. Assoc. Am. Computer Sales and Leasing, N.Y.C., 1978-79, v.p., 1979-80; assoc. Morgan Stanley and Co., N.Y.C., 1982-86, v.p., 1986-87, prin., 1988-89; mng. dir., 1990—; bd. dirs. Fort Howard Corp., Green Bay Wis., Silgan Corp., Stamford, Conn., Sweetheart Cup Co., Chgo., Waterford Wedgwood plc, Dublin, Ireland, Cargo Van GmbH, Kirchheimbolanden, Germany. Contbg. author: Arthur Young Management Guide to Mergers and Acquisitions, 1989. Nat. com. Student Sponsor Partnership, N.Y.C., 1987—; donor Covenant House, N.Y.C., 1987—. Baker scholar, 1982, David Lawrence scholar, 1976. Mem. Apawamis Club, Cottage Club. Republican. Roman Catholic. Office: Morgan Stanley & Co 1251 Ave Of The Americas New York NY 10020-1104

NIEHOFF, K. RICHARD B., financial executive; b. Cin., May 11, 1943; s. Karl George and Jean (Besuden) N.; children—K. Richard B. Jr., Kelly B. B.A., U. Cin., 1967. Corp. trust officer 5th-3d Union Trust, Cin., 1968-74; v.p., gen. mgr. Sabina (Ohio) Water Co., 1974-76; v.p., sec. Weil, Roth and Irving, Inc., 1974-76; co-mgr., mcpl. fin. dept. Thomson McKinnon Securities, Cin., 1976-79; trustee Cin. Stock Exch., 1974-80, 87-90, chmn. bd. trustees, 1978-79, pres., chief oper. officer, 1979-90; exch. rep. Consol. Quote, Consol. Tape Oper. Coms. and Quote, 1979-90; pres. Fin. Instruments Svcs. Corp., Cin., 1985-90; v.p. Trading Svcs. NASDAQ, 1991—; v.p., sec. Weil Roth & Irving, Inc., 1974-76; past mem. Inter-Market Trading Com., 1980-90, Stock Exch. Chief Execs. Com., 1988-90. Trustee, sec. Contemporary Arts Ctr., 1975-83; mem. devel. com. Tangeman Gallery of Art, 1981-82. Mem. Cin. Stock and Bond Club (past 1st v.p.), Queen City Mcpl. Bond Club (trustee 1974-79), Cleve. Security Traders Assn., Cin. Area C. of C. (devel. and small bus. fin. coms. 1975-78), Univ. Club (Cin.), Miami Club (Cin.), Keeneland Assn. (Lexington, Ky.), N.Y. Stock Exch. Luncheon Club, N.Y. Athletic Club, Phi Alpha Theta. Office: The NASDAQ Stock Market 33 Whitehall St New York NY 10004-2112

NIEHOUSE, OLIVER LESLIE, management consultant; b. St. Louis, July 25, 1920; s. Oliver Lewis and Edythe Mae (Burch) N.; m. Ellen Verdell Sims, Apr. 1, 1945; 1 child, Daniel Lee (dec.). BS, Sir George Williams U., Montreal, 1957; MBA, U. Chgo., 1963; postgrad. NYU, 1968-78; MS, Calif. Am. U., 1979. With Olin Industries Inc., East Alton, Ill., 1941-51, rsch. and devel. supr., 1947-51, mgr. tech. sales, N.Y.C., 1951-55; mgr. advt. and sales devel. TCF of Can., Ltd., Montreal, P.Q., 1955-58; dir. sales Yardley of London Ltd., Toronto, Ont., 1958-60; gen. mgr. Sunbeam Corp., Chgo., 1960-65; v.p., dir. Sunbeam A.G., Zug, Switzerland, 1965-67; mng. dir. Sunbeam Electric Ltd., East Kilbride, Scotland, and London, 1965-67; v.p., gen. mgr. Pantasote Co. of N.Y., N.Y.C., 1967-70; pres. subsidiaries, exec. v.p. Polypump Ltd., Toronto, Ont., 1970-71; asst. prof. Hofstra U., Hempstead, N.Y., 1971-78; pres. Niehouse & Assocs. Inc., Forest Hills, N.Y., 1971—; vis. assoc. prof. grad. div. Mktg. NYU, 1988—; dir. ctr. for mgmt. devel., disting. lectr. in mgmt. Coll. of Bus., Rochester Inst. Tech., 1986-87. Patentee in field. Author 2 books; mem. editorial bd. Management Solutions jour.; contbr. articles to profl. jours. Recipient Disting. Teaching award Hofstra U., 1975. Mem. Nat. Speakers Assn., Acad. of Mgmt., Am. Mktg. Assn., Am. Soc. for Tng. and Devel., Am. Chem. Soc. Home: 175 Kellogg Dr Wilton CT 06897-1414

NIELSEN, DAVID ANDREW, molecular biologist; b. West Bend, Wis., Oct. 27, 1953; s. William Arthur and Margaret Helen (Prehn) N.; m. Susan Mary Saunders, May 5, 1990. BS, U. Wis., 1976; PhD, U. Chgo., 1984. Postdoctoral fellow U. Ill., Urbana-Champaign, 1984-90; sr. staff fellow Nat. Inst. on Alcohol Abuse and Alcoholism, Bethesda, Md., 1990—. Contbr. articles to profl. jours. Postdoctoral fellowship Am. Cancer Soc., 1984-87; predoctoral genetics and regulation tng. grant Pub. Health Svc., 1979-82; recipient Marc Perry Gullen Prize, U. Chgo., 1985. Mem. AAAS, N.Y. Acad. Sics., Am. Soc. Microbiologists, Sigma Xi. Office: Nat Inst Alcohol Abuse & Alcoholism 10/3/c102 9000 Rockville Pike Bethesda MD 20892

NIELSEN, KENNETH LEONARD, academic administrator; b. Staten Island, N.Y., Oct. 4, 1931; s. Leonard and Dagny (Hermansen) N.; m. Doris J. Garrett, Sept. 10, 1955; children: Marla, Dorislee, Timothy. BA, King's Coll., 1954; MDiv, Faith Theol. Sem., 1958. Bus. mgr. Morning Cheer Camps, North East, Md., 1957-77, Buffalo (N.Y.) Christian Ctr., 1958-61; dir. Camp Sandy Hill, North East, 1961-67; food svc. mgr. Houghton (N.Y.) Coll., 1961-65, asst. bus. mgr., 1965-71, bus. mgr., 1971, treas., bus. mgr., 1972—; mem., chmn. Allegany County Indsl. Devel. Agy., Wellsville, N.Y., 1972—; chmn. ins. liaison commn. AABC, Chgo., 1980—; mem., pres. Allegany County Area Found., Wellsville, 1985—; mem. Allegany County Pvt. Industry Coun., Belmont, N.Y., 1984-90; bd. dirs. So. Tier Enterprises Devel. Orgn., Blue Shield Western N.Y., Buffalo, Morning Cheer, North East, Md. Trustee Cuba (N.Y.) Meml. Hosp., 1983-86, 88—; elected rep. Allegany County Legislature, 1990. Mem. Assn. Bus. Adminstrs. Christian Colls. (bd. dirs. 1985—). Republican. Home: 33C Centerville Rd Houghton NY 14744 Office: Houghton Coll Houghton NY 14744

NIELSEN, NIELS HOEG, management consultant; b. Montreal, Que., Can., Nov. 30, 1930; came to U.S., 1969; s. Niels Christian and Anna (Hoeg) N.; m. Joan Shirley Anderson, May 18, 1957; children: Karen Shirley, Niels Eric, Christine Ellen. BA, McGill U., Montreal, 1951, MA, 1954. Market rsch. asst., fin. control analyst, sr. economist Du Pont of Can., Montreal, 1953-60; human resources specialist, employee benefits mgr., sr. computer systems analyst/Massey Ferguson, Toronto, Ont., Can., 1961-67; mgr. spl. projects, employee and pub. rels., dir. compensation and benefits/Domtar, Montreal, 1967-68; dir. corp. benefits Allis-Chalmers, Milw., 1969-71; dir. corp. compensation and benefits Johnson & Johnson, New Brunswick, N.J., 1971-74; dir. compensation and benefits J. C. Penney, N.Y.C., 1974-78; staff v.p. pers. svcs. ARA Svcs., Phila., 1978-80; pres. Princeton (N.J.) Mgmt. Cons., Inc., 1980—. Author: Human Resources Forms and Reports, 1989; developer computer software Salary Survey Manager, 1991. Vice chmn. Coalition for Nuclear Disarmament, Princeton, 1981—; trustee Westminster Choir Coll., Princeton, 1984—; bd. dirs. Rider Coll. Sch. Bus., Lawrenceville, N.J., 1987-90, Family Svc. Agy., Princeton, 1990—. Mem. Am. Compensation Assn. (Outstanding Article award), Soc. Human Resource Mgmt., Assn. Human Resources Systems Profls. Episcopalian. Office: Princeton Mgmt Cons Inc 99 Moore St Princeton NJ 08540-3305

NIELSEN, ROBERT CHARLES, police administrator; b. Putnam, Conn., Nov. 11, 1939; s. Charles Erik and Mary Ann (Wojcik) N.; m. Jean Kempshall, June 6, 1965 (div. Aug. 1984); 1 child, Astrid. BA, U. Conn., 1964, MA, 1967. Cert. FBI Acad., 1981. Resident advisor U. Conn., Storrs, 1964-65; tchr., adminstr., coach Rectory Sch., Pomfret, Conn., 1965-67; supr. ind. residence halls for men, dept. men's affairs U. Conn., Storrs, 1967-69, dir. men's residence halls, dept. men's affairs, 1969-70, asst. dean of men, dept. men's affairs, 1970-71, asst. dean of students, 1971-72, asst. dir. pub. safety div., 1972-74; dir. pub. safety U. Md. Balt. County, Balt., 1974-86, dir. (chief) univ. police, 1986—; lectr. dept. English, U. Conn., 1968-74, U. Md. Balt. County, 1974-77; adj. faculty criminal justice program Catonsville Community Coll., 1977—; assoc. instr. Md. Police Tng. Commn., 1976-78; lectr. campus law enforcement Smith & Wesson Acad., Mass., 1973, crime prevention on the campus Holyoke Community Coll., Mass., 1974; mem. Ea. Conn. Criminal Justice Planning Supervisory Bd., 1973-74; cons. Balt. County Police Dept., 1979-80; presenter in field. Contbr. articles and book revs. to profl. jours. 1st lt. U.S. Army, 1957-59, with USAR, 1959-65. Fellow Acad. Police Sci., Nat. Law Enforcement Acad., 1977; recipient Outstanding Svc. award Commuting Students Assn., 1980, Cert. of Svc., State of Md., 1980, 86, 89, Merit award Student Govt. Assn., 1983, Award for Outstanding Contbns. and Dedication, U. Md. Police, 1984, Award for Outstanding Community Svc., Student Govt. Assn., 1988, Cert. of Appreciation, Bur. Bus. Practice Nat. Foremen's Inst., 1985, Internat. Assn. Bomb Technicians and Investigators, 1986. Mem. Internat. Assn. Campus Law Enforcement Adminstrs., Md. Chiefs Police Assn., Am. Assn. Sch. Adminstrs., Assn. Campus Law Enforcement Adminstrs. for Md., Del., Washington D.C., No. Va., Internat. Assn. Chiefs Police (Cert. of Appreciation 1980, 81), Md. Acad. Criminal Justice Profs., Nat. FBI Acad. Assocs., Internat. Police Mgmt. Assn., Fraternal Order of Police. Office: U Md Police 5401 Wilkens Ave Baltimore MD 21228-5329

NIELSEN, WALDEMAR AUGUST, corporate social policy consultant, writer; b. Greensburg, Pa., Mar. 27, 1917; s. Malta August and Mary Pauline (Shaffer) N.; m. Marcia K. Nielsen, Apr. 22, 1943; 1 child, Signe Barbara. AB in Econ., U. Mo., 1939, BS in Bus., 1939, MA in Polit. Sci., 1940; DPhil (hon.), U. Lagos (Nigeria), 1972. Economist U.S. Govt., Washington, 1940-42, U.S. State Dept., Washington, 1945-46; spl. asst. sec. commerce for Marshall Plan Dept. Commerce, Washington, 1947-48; chief of labor Marshall Plan Hqrs., Paris, 1948-52; officer behavioral scis. program Ford Found., N.Y.C., 1953-54, exec. asst. to pres., 1955-57; officer internat. affairs program, exec. dir. White House Commn. Internat. Affairs, Washington, 1959-60; pres. African Am. Inst., N.Y.C., 1961-68, Waldemar A. Nielsen, Inc., N.Y.C., 1969—; bd. dirs. Home Life Ins., N.Y.C., The Observer, London, Hispanic Policy Devel. Project, N.Y.C.; trustee Nat. Mus. Am. Indians, Washington. Author: Africa, 1965, African Battleline, 1966, The Big Foundations, 1972, The Endangered Sector, 1980, The Golden Donors, 1985; contbr. to nat. publs. Chmn. Internat. Arts Assn., N.Y.C. Lt. USN, 1943-46, PTO. Rhodes scholar, 1939-40; decorated Bronze Star (U.S.), comdr. Legion of Merit (Italy), comdr. Royal Order Phoenix (Greece), Chevalier de l'Ordre de la Valeur Camerounaise, commandeur de l'Ordre National de la Republique du Senegal, officer de l'Ordre National Ivoirien. Sr. fellow Aspen Inst. Humanistic Studies (bd. dirs.); mem. Century Assn., Coun. Fgn. Rels. Democrat. Home: 15 E 91st St New York NY 10128-0648 Office: W A Nielsen Inc 250 Park Ave S New York NY 10003-1402

NIEMEYER, PAUL VICTOR, federal judge; b. Princeton, N.J., Apr. 5, 1941; s. Gerhart and Lucie (Lenzner) N.; m. Susan Kinley, Aug. 24, 1963; children Jonathan K., Peter E., Christopher J. AB, Kenyon Coll., 1962; student, U. Munich, Federal Republic of Germany, 1962-63; JD, U. Notre Dame, 1966. Bars: Md. 1966, U.S. Dist. Ct. Md. 1967, U.S. Ct. Appeals (4th cir.) 1968, U.S. Supreme Ct. 1970, U.S. Dist Ct. (so. dist.) Tex. 1977, U.S. Ct. Appeals (5th cir.) 1978, U.S. Ct. Appeals (3d cir.) 1980. Assoc. Piper & Marbury, Balt., 1966-74, ptnr., 1974-88; U.S. dist. judge U.S. Dist. Ct. Md., Balt., 1988-90; fed. judge U.S. Ct. Appeals (4th cir.), Balt., 1990—; lectr. advanced bus. law Johns Hopkins U., Balt., 1971-75; lectr. Md. Jud. Conf., Md. Ct. Clks. Assn.; mem. standing com. on rules of practice and procedure cts. appeals, 1973-88, atty. grievance com.-hearing panel, 1978-81, select com.-profl. conduct, 1983-85. Co-author: Md. Rules Commentary, 1984, supplement, 1988; contbr. articles to profl. jours. Recipient Spl. Merit citation Am. Judicature Soc., 1987. Fellow Am. Coll. Trial Lawyers, Am. Bar Found., Md. Bar Found., Md. Bar Assn. (Disting. Svc. award litigation sect. 1981), Am. Law Inst.; mem. Wednesday Law Club, Lawyers' Round Table. Republican. Episcopalian. Office: US Cir Ct Md 101 W Lombard St Rm 910 Baltimore MD 21201-2664

NIEMI, RICHARD GENE, political science educator; b. Green Bay, Wis., Jan. 10, 1941; s. Eugene H. and Dorothy M. (Stevens) N.; m. Shirley A. Gill, Aug. 4, 1962; children: Nancy, Patricia, Jennifer, Julie. B.A., Lawrence Coll., 1962; Ph.D., U. Mich., 1967. Asst. prof. U. Rochester, N.Y., 1967-71, assoc. prof., 1971-75, prof. polit. sci., 1975—, disting. grad. teaching prof., 1983-86, chmn. dept., 1979-83, assoc. dean, 1986-89, sr. assoc. dean, 1989-91; vis. prof. U. Lund, Sweden, 1974, 81, U. Iowa, 1985; vis. researcher Kobe U., Japan, 1991. Author: (with M. Kent Jennings) The Political Character of Adolescence, 1974, Generations and Politics, 1981, How Family Members Perceive Each Other, 1974; editor: (with Herbert Weisberg) Controversies in Voting Behavior, 1976, 3d edit., 1992, (with Harold Stanley) Vital Statistics in American Politics, 1988, 3d edit., 1992, (with John Mueller and Tom Smith) Trends in Public Opinion, 1989. Rsch. grantee NIMH, 1969-70, NSF, 1975-77, 80-86, Ford Found., 1972-73; fellow Guggenheim Found., 1983-84., Ctr. for Advanced Study in Behavioral Sci., 1989. Mem. Am. Polit. Sci. Assn., Phi Beta Kappa. Lutheran. Home: 45 Boniface Dr Rochester NY 14620-3333 Office: U Rochester Dept Polit Sci Rochester NY 14627

NIEMIRA, MICHAEL PAUL, economist; b. Newark, Apr. 22, 1955; s. Henry Gerald and Anne (Colamedici) N; m. Nancy Parish, May 28, 1982; 1 child, Andrew. BA, Seton Hall U., 1975; MA, Rutgers U., 1977. Instr. Passaic County Community Coll., Paterson, N.J., 1978; assoc. economist Merrill Lynch, N.Y.C., 1978-82; economist Chem. Bank, N.Y.C., 1982-84; economist, asst. v.p. Paine Webber, N.Y.C., 1984-87; economist, v.p. Mitsubishi Bank, N.Y.C., 1988—; program dir. for econs. Found. for the Study of Cycles, Irvine, Calif., 1988—; cons. Paine Webber, N.Y.C., 1989. Contbg. author: Analyzing Modern Business Cycles, 1990. Mem. Am. Econ. Assn., Nat. Assn. Bus. Economists (Abramson award 1982).

NIENBURG, GEORGE FRANK, home health aide, photographer, scholarship consultant; b. N.Y.C., Feb. 14, 1938; s. Carl George and Louise Elizabeth (Baum) N. Grad., Germain Sch. Photography, 1989. Veterinarian asst. Stamen Animal Hosp., New Rochelle, N.Y., 1966-70; trainer guard dogs Paradise Guard Dog Service, N.Y.C., 1970-71; animal care technician Am. Soc. for Prevention Cruelty to Animals, N.Y.C., 1971-82; security guard Cen. Nat. Investigation agy., New Rochelle, 1983-88; mem. rsch. bd. advisors Am. Biographical Inst., 1989—. Mem. Nat. Rep. Com., Washington, 1986—; mem. nat. leadership coalition Campaign Am., Washington, 1987—; mem. Nat. Rep. Sen. Com., 1989—; sustaining sponsor Ronald Reagan Found., 1987—; chartered founder Presdl. Trust Fund, 1992; charter mem., supporter Battle Normandy Mus., 1988—; sponsor Nat. Rep. Congl. Com., 1983; life mem. Rep. Presdl. Task Force, 1988; charter founder Ronald Reagan Ctr., 1988—; mem. Pres.'s Congl. Task Force, 1990, Rep. Campaign Com., 1991; supporter USN Meml. Owner Navy Plank, 1991. Named in inscription in U.S. Pres. Bush's Spl. Honor Roll, Honor Roll Commemorating the Reagan-Bush Adminstrn., 1991; included in the "Life Member Wall of Honor" at Ronald Reagan Rep. Ctr. Mem. Washington Legal Found. (patron), U.S. Sen. Club, Internat. Freelance Photographer Orgn. (life), Westchester Photographic Soc., Nat. Fedn. Rep. Women, English First, Nat. Wildlife Fedn. (assoc.), Am. Mus. Natural History, Nat. Trust for Hist. Preservation, Am. Space Frontier Com. (sustaining mem.), Nat. Flag Found. (std. bearer 1987—), Internat. Platform Assn., Masons (master 1986—, royal arch and knight templer 1992). Home: 22 Edgewood Park PO Box 511 New Rochelle NY 10802-0511

NIES, HELEN WILSON, federal judge; b. Birmingham, Ala., Aug. 7, 1925; d. George Earl and Lida Blanche (Erckert) Wilson; m. John Dirk Nies ; children: Dirk, Nancy, Eric. BA, U. Mich., 1946, JD, 1948. Bar: D.C. 1961, U.S. Supreme Ct. 1962. Atty. Dept. Justice, Washington, 1948-51, Office Price Stblzn., Washington, 1951-52; assoc. Pattishall, McAuliffe and Hofstetter, Washington, 1960-66, resident ptnr., 1966-77; ptnr. Howrey & Simon, Washington, 1978-80; cir. judge U.S. Ct. Customs and Patent Appeals, 1980-82; judge U.S. Ct. Appeals Fed. Cir., 1982-90, chief judge, 1990—; mem. jud. conf. U.S. Com. on Bicentennial of Constitution; mem. public adv. com. trademark affairs Dept. Commerce, 1976-80; mem. adv. bd. BNA's Patent Trademark and Copyright Jour., 1976-78; bd. visitors U. Mich. Law Sch., 1975-78; adv. for restatement of law of unfair competition Am. Law Isnt., 1986—; speaker World Intellectual Property Orgn., Forum of Judges, Calcutta, 1987. Recipient Athena Outstanding Alumna award U. Mich., 1987, Jefferson medal N.J. Patent Law Assn., 1991. Mem. ABA (chmn. com. 203, 1972-74, com. 504, 1975-76), Bar Assn. D.C. (chmn. patent trademark copyright sect. 1975-76, dir. 1976-78), U.S. Trademark Assn. (chmn. lawyers adv. com. 1974-76, bd. dirs. 1976-78), Am. Patent Law Assn., Fed. Bar Assn., Nat. Assn. Women Lawyers (Woman Lawyer of the Yr. 1980), Order of Coif, Phi Beta Kappa, Phi Kappa Phi. Office: US Ct Appeals 717 Madison Pl NW Washington DC 20439

NIETO, SONIA MARY, educator; b. N.Y.C., Sept. 25, 1943; d. Federico and Esther (Mercado) Cortes; m. Angel Nieto, Jan. 4, 1967; children: Alicia, Marisa. BS, St. Johns U., 1965; MA, NYU, 1966; EdD, U. Mass., 1979. Cert. elem. tchr. Assoc. prof. edn. U. Mass., Amherst, 1980—, dir. cultural diversity and curriculum reform prog., 1980—; instr. Bklyn. Coll., CUNY, 1972-75; speaker, author on multicultural and bilingual edn. and curriculum renewal, workshop leader. Author: Affirming Diversity: The Sociopolitical Context of Multicultural Education, 1992. Mem. Nat. Assn. Bilingual Edn., Mass. Assn. Bilingual Edn., Am. Edn. Rsch. Assn., Phi Delta Kappa. Office: U Mass Sch Edn Furcolo Hall Amherst MA 01003

NIGHTENGALE, ROBERT WEBSTER, JR., advertising executive; b. Hampton, Va., Oct. 29, 1936; s. Robert Webster and Alice Virginia (Burleson) N.; m. Sally Ellen Wagener, June 14, 1958; children: Scott Webster, Jennifer Lyn. Student, William and Mary Coll., 1954-56. Pub. relations rep. DuPont de Nemours Co., Wilmington, Del., 1960-64, advt. asst., 1964-68, advt. div. dir., 1981-85, dir. communications, 1985-91; advt. coord. Hercules, Inc., Wilmington, 1968-69; pres. Communications Cons., Inc., Wilmington, 1969-78, MMI Courier, Wilmington, 1969-78; advt. mgr. Du-Pont Japan, Ltd., Tokyo, 1978-80; pres. Nightengale Assocs., Wilmington, 1990-91, Home Furnishings Coun., 1992—; co-chmn. Home Furnishings Coun., 1990—. Trustee Del. Found. for Retarded Children, Wilmington, 1983-87; trustee Sanford Sch., Wilmington, 1983—, chmn. bd. trustees, 1990—; bd. dirs. Mary Campbell Ctr., Wilmington, 1981—, Wilmington Zool. Soc., 1991—, Del. chpt. ARC, 1991—. 1st lt. USAF, 1956-60. Republican. Baptist. Home: 6 Raintree Rd Chadds Ford PA 19317-9332 Office: Nightengale Assocs Wilmington DE 19810

NIGHTINGALE, ELENA OTTOLENGHI, physician, geneticist, administrator; b. Livorno, Italy, Nov. 1, 1932; came to U.S., 1939; d. Mario Lazzaro and Elisa Vittoria (Levi) Ottolenghi; m. Stuart L. Nightingale, July 1, 1965; children—Elizabeth, Marisa. A.B. summa cum laude, Barnard Coll., 1954; Ph.D., Rockefeller U., 1961; M.D., NYU, 1964. Asst. prof. Cornell U. Med. Coll., N.Y.C., 1965-70, Johns Hopkins U., Balt., 1970-73; fellow in clin. genetics and pediatrics Georgetown U. Hosp., Washington, 1973-74; sr. staff officer NAS, Washington, 1975-79, sr. program officer Inst. Medicine, 1979-82, sr. scholar in residence, 1982-83; spl. advisor to pres. Carnegie Corp. of N.Y., N.Y.C., 1983—, sr. program officer, 1989—; vis. assoc. prof. Harvard U. Med. Sch., Boston, 1980-84, vis. lectr., 1984—; mem. recombinant DNA adv. com. NIH, Bethesda, Md., 1979-83. Editor: The Breaking of Bodies and Minds: Torture, Psychiatric Abuse and the Health Professions, 1985, Prenatal Screening, Policies and Values: The Example of Neural Tube Defects, 1987, Before Birth: Prenatal Screening for Genetic Disease, 1990; contbr. numerous sci. articles to profl. publs. Bd. dirs. Ctr. for Youth Svcs., Washington, 1980-84, Sci. Svc. Inc., Washington, 1985, Amnesty Internat., U.S.A., 1989-91. Sloan Found. fellow, 1974-75. Fellow AAAS (chmn. com. on sci. freedom and responsibility 1985-88), N.Y. Acad. Scis., Royal Soc. Medicine; mem. Harvey Soc., Am. Soc. Microbiology, Am. Soc. Human Genetics (social issues com. 1982-85), Genetics Soc. Am., Inst. Medicine of NAS (chmn. com. on health and human rights 1987-90), Phi Beta Kappa, Sigma Xi. Office: Carnegie Corp NY 437 Madison Ave New York NY 10022-7001

NIHART, FRANKLIN BROOKE, museum director; b. Los Angeles, Mar. 16, 1919; s. Claude Eugene and Vera Howard (Brooke) N.; m. Mary Helen Brosius, Feb. 11, 1945; children: Mary Catherine, Virginia Brooke Nihart-Martinez. BA, Occidental Coll., 1940. Commd. 2d lt. USMC, 1940, advanced through grades to col., 1957; dep. dir. Marine Corps History and Museums, USMC, Washington, 1973—; fellow, past gov., pres. Co. Mil. Historians, 1967-71; founder Marine Corps Hist. Found., 1979; chmn. Com. Mil. Museums Am., 1983—. Decorated Navy Cross, Bronze Star with one gold star. Mem. Am. Assn. Mus., Internat. Coun. Mus., Nat. Firearms Mus. (bd. dirs.), Nat. Hist. Intelligence Mus. (bd. dirs.), Internat. Assn. Mus. Arms and Mil. History (exec. com.), Washington Naval Cors. Circle, Army and Navy Club, Ends of the Earth Club, Masons. Republican. Presbyterian. Office: Marine Corps Mus Navy Yard Washington DC 20374

NIKISCHER, FRANK WILLIAM, SR., restaurant owner and operator; b. Fullerton, Pa., Sept. 26, 1931; s. Frank and Theresa (Steiner) N.; m. Ruth Reese, Aug. 27, 1955 (dec. July 1983); children: Frank Jr., David, Wendy Hann; m. Judith Savitz Mohr, Jan. 1, 1986. BS in Hotel Adminstrn., Pa. State U., 1953. Commd. ensign USN, 1953; advanced through grades to lt. comdr. USNR, ret., 1976; gen. mgr. Walp's Restaurant, Allentown, Pa.,

1956-86; owner, operator Walp's Restaurant, Allentown, 1986—; pres., chief exec. officer Double N., Inc., Allentown, 1986—. Recipient Allentown/Lehigh County C. of C. Small Bus. Coun. Excellence in Bus. award, 1991. Mem. Retired Officers Assn., Naval Res. Assn., Navy League of U.S., Nat. Restaurant Assn., Jr. Hotelmen Am., Pa. State U. Alumni Assn., VFW, Am. Legion, Quarter Deck Soc., Consistory Valley of Allentown (32 degree), Brookside Country Club, Masons, Shriners, Alpha Phi Omega, Sigma Eta Alpha. Republican. Home: 2505 Houghton Lean Macungie PA 18062-9502 Office: Walp's Restaurant and Guesthouse Union Blvd and Airport Rd Allentown PA 18103

NIKKAL, NANCY EGOL, artist, gallery curator; b. N.Y.C., Sept. 23, 1944; d. Arthur N. and Sylvia (Aronson) Schwebel; m. Morton Egol, June 1964; children: Jonathan, Matthew. BA in Art magna cum laude, CUNY, 1973. Tchr., owner Artspace for Children, Tenafly, N.J., 1975-80; pres. Art Appreciation Ltd., Tenafly, 1980-85; gallery curator Williams Ctr. for the Arts, Rutherford, N.J., 1991—. One man shows include Nabisco Brands Ctr., Paramus, N.J., 1988, Williams Ctr. for the Arts, Rutherford, N.J., 1989, Ward-Nasse Gallery, N.Y.C., 1990, Wartuck Gallery, Tenafly, N.J., 1991; exhibited in group exhibitions at City Without Walls Gallery, Newark, 1986, N.J. Ctr. for the Visual Arts, Summit, N.J., 1987, Bergen Mus. of Arts and Sci., Paramus, 1988 and also in Eng., India, Japan; represented in permanent collections at Kawamura Mus. Modern Art, Tokyo, various corps. Mem. Am. Soc. Contemporary Arts, Nat. Assn. Women Artists (exec. bd. 1988—), Salute to Women in the Arts (pres. 1990-92). Home: 22 Dogwood Ln Tenafly NJ 07670

NIKKEL, MICHAEL KENNETH, researcher, consultant, educator; b. L.A., Sept. 7, 1959; s. John Leslie Jr. and Dorothy (MisKimins) N. BBA, So. Meth. U., 1981, BA in Sociology, 1982; BS in Polit. Sci., Stephen F. Austin State U., 1986, MS in Interdisciplinary Studies, 1987; MA in Internat. Rels., Sam Houston State U., 1990. Asst. mgr. Nikkel Family Ranch, San Augustine, 1976-87; rsch. asst. John Nikkel, Petroleum Engring. Cons. Firm, San Augustine, Tex., 1982-83; sales assoc. Britches of Georgetown, Tysons Corner, McLean, Va., 1989-90; adj. instr. U. Md., College Park, 1990; program coord. Atlantic & Pacific Exch. Program, Washington, 1991; researcher, intern Carnegie Endowment for Internat. Peace, Washington, 1991; teaching assoc. Washington Ctr., 1990-92, adj. prof., 1991-92; ind. contractor-cons. various orgns. Rockville, Md., 1989—; profl. developer, Washington, 1989-92; curriculum developer, Rockville, 1990-92. Editor, author: Course Guides for Courses That Teach, 1991-92, Research Guide in International Transactions, 1990-91. Intern for U.S. congressman, Washington, 1988; vol., fundraiser, mem. Kappa Alpha Order, Nacogdahes, Tex., Huntsville, Tex., 1979-85. Go Tex. scholar Houston Livestock Show, 1977. Mem. World Affairs Coun. Washington, Acad. Polit. Sci., Ctr. for the Study of the Presidency, AMBA Execs., U.S. Strategic Inst., Coun. on European Studies, European Community Studies Assn., Japan Soc., Mid. East Inst., UN Student Assn., Am.-Scandinavian Foun., Amnesty Internat., Soc. for Internat. Devel., World Future Soc., Alpha Kappa Delta, Pi Gamma Mu, Pi Sigma Alpha, Psy Chi. Home and office: 257 Congressional Ln # 120 Rockville MD 20852

NILGES, EDWARD GEORGE, software engineer; b. Boston, Nov. 9, 1949; s. Richard G. and Jean E. (Matheson) N.; m. Darlene E. Hitchcock, June 5, 1975 (div. Feb. 1983); children: Edward Arthur, Peter Hitchcock. BA, Roosevelt U., 1972. Programmer, analyst Roosevelt U., Chgo., 1971-74; systems analyst Northwestern U., Evanston, Ill., 1974-75; programmer, analyst Encyclopaedia Britannica, Chgo., 1975-76; mem. sci. staff Bell-No. Rsch., Mountain View, Calif., 1981-86; rsch. programmer analyst Rainier Bank, Seattle, 1986; programmer, cons Princeton (N.J.) U., 1987—; cons. various orgns., 1976—. Asst. scoutmaster Cub Scouts Am., N.Y.C., 1990; vol. Holiday Project, San Jose, 9181, Homeless Christmas Dinner, Berkeley, Calif., 1982, others. Mem. Assn. Computing Machinery. Home: 11A Euclid PO Box # 16 Kingston NJ 08528 Office: Princeton U 87 Prospect Ave Princeton NJ 08544-2007

NILSEN, ANDREW, psychology educator, psychotherapist; b. Jamaica, N.Y., June 11, 1936; s. Olaf and Olive Grace (Reid) N.; m. Dec. 14, 1957 (dec. 1988); 1 child, Robin. BS in Edn., Wagner Coll., 1966, MS in Edn. and Psychology, 1968; MS in Supervision and Adminstrn., CUNY, 1972; PhD, Columbia U., 1985. Cert. tchr., guidance counselor, prin., supt. schs., dir. pupil pers. svcs., N.Y. Asst. chemist Wallerstein Labs., S.I., N.Y., 1956-58; clk. Durabla Mfg. Co., N.Y.C., 1958-60; dir. edn. Eltingville Luth. Sch., S.I., 1962-64; tchr. N.Y.C. Pub. Schs., S.I., 1962-80; ret., 1980; prof. psychology N.J. Univ. System, 1984—; pvt. practice psychotherapy H.E.L.P. Inc., RiverVale, N.J., 1970—, Wayne, N.J., 1970—; cons. to chs. and schs., N.Y., N.J., 1970—; copy editor Letendre Press, Conn., 1990—; copy editor, writer Empathy jour., 1990—. Gay-friendly counselor for referrals Gay Activists Alliance of N.J. Hotline, Teaneck, N.J., 1992—. With Chem. Corps., U.S. Army, 1960-62. Mem. Am. Assn. Sex Educators, Counselors, and Therapists, Internat. Assn. Counselors and Therapists, Soc. for Sci. Study Sex. Office: 184 Rivervale Rd River Vale NJ 07675

NILSEN, KENNETH LOUIS, university program administrator; b. Boston, June 12, 1966; s. Kenneth Louis and Dorothy Kathleen (Chaffers) N. BA, Wagner Coll., 1988; MA, NYU, 1990. Residence dir. Am. U., Washington, 1990—. Mem. Am. Coll. Pers. Assn. (directorate body III 1992). Lutheran. Home and Office: 200 MGC The American U Washington DC 20016

NILVA, SHEILA COLE, travel writer; b. Beloit, Wis., July 24, 1930; d. Joseph M. and Sadie (Abrams) Kohlenberg; m. Daniel Nilva, Apr. 1, 1964; children: Daniella Jo, Stephanie Mara. Student, U. Wis., 1947-50, NYU, 1951-53, New Sch. for Social Rsch., 1951-53. Freelance travel writer, 1948—; owner The Place off Second Ave for Antiques, Inc., N.Y.C., 1958-88; pres. A Tisket A Tasket, N.Y.C., 1981—, ATAT, Inc., N.Y.C., 1990—; pres. 222-11 Apt. Owners Corp., N.Y.C., 1984—. Contbr. numerous articles to major internat. newspapers and mags., 1948—; columnist London Daily Telegraph, 1954-56. Mem. Concerned Citizens of Montauk, L.I., 1985—. Mem. Nat. Acad. TV Arts and Scis. Office: A Tisket A Tasket 475 10th Ave Fl 11 New York NY 10018-1120

NIMAN, JOHN, mathematics educator, consultant; b. Latakia, Syria, June 10, 1938. BS in Physics, Poly. Inst. N.Y., 1965; MS in Physics, U. Wis., 1968; PhD in Math., Columbia U., 1969. Tchr. math. and physics Friends Sch., N.Y.C., 1966-68; asst. prof. math. Hunter Coll., CUNY, N.Y.C., 1968-72, assoc. prof., 1973-77, prof., 1978—; mem. adv. bd. and energy policy studies group Energy Bur.; mem. adv. panel NSF; trustee Pocono Environ. Edn. Ctr., Dingman's Ferry, Pa., 1989—. Author: (with Heath) A Teacher's Companion to Microcomputers, 1985, (with Postman) Mathematics on the Geoboard, An Introduction to Mathematical Patterns; guest editor Sch. Sch. and Math.; contbr. numerous articles to math. and sci. edn. jours. Grantee NSF; fellow NSF, German Govt., Munich, Gottingen, Fulbright fellow, George Schuster faculty fellow. Mem. Explorers Club. Office: Hunter Coll CUNY 695 Park Ave New York NY 10021-5085

NIMOITYN, PHILIP, cardiologist; b. Phila., Mar. 6, 1951; s. Benjamin Solomon and Edith (Ornstein) N.; m. Hillary Rachel Saul, June 11, 1989. BS in Biology with distinction, Phila. Coll. Pharmacy and Sci., 1972; MD, Thomas Jefferson U., 1976. Cert. Nat. Bd. Med. Examiners, Am. Bd. Internal Medicine. Intern Hahnemann U. Hosp., Phila., 1976-77; resident in internal medicine Thomas Jefferson U. Hosp., Phila., 1977-79, cardiovascular disease fellow, 1979-81, instr. medicine, 1981-90, clin. asst. prof., 1990—, attending physician, 1981—; cons. physician Wills Eye Hosp., Phila., 1981—. Author: (with others) Artificial Cardiac Pacing, 1984, Quick Reference to Cardiovascular Disease, 1987, Cardiac Emergency Care, 1991; contbr. articles to profl. jours. Recipient Cert. of Merit for Sci. Exhibits AMA, 1974, 2d prize for sci. exhibits Ind. State Med. Assn., 1974. Fellow Am. Coll. Cardiology; mem. AMA, Pa. Med. Soc., Phila. County Med. Soc. Office: Thomas Jefferson U Hosp 111 S 11th St Ste 6250 Philadelphia PA 19107

NIPPES, ERNEST FREDERICK, metallurgist, educator; b. N.Y.C., Feb. 1, 1918; s. Ernest Frederick and Louise (Kueckes) N.; m. Margaret Louise Hutchens, Sept. 1939 (div.); children: Raymond Allan, Robert Ernest; m. Marilyn Lenore Schue, 1969; children: Deborah Lynne, Stephen Edward, Stuart Joseph. B in Chem. Engring., Rensselaer Poly. Inst., 1938, M in Metall. Engring., 1940, PhD, 1942. Registered profl. engr., N.Y. Mem. faculty Rensselaer Poly. Inst., Troy, N.Y., 1938—, prof. metallurgy, 1954—, chmn. dept. materials engring., 1961-65, dir. rsch. div., 1965-71, dir. office rsch. and sponsored programs (duPont Year in Industry Program), 1962-63, 71-74; pres. Rensselaer Rsch. Corp., Troy, 1965-69; cons. in field, 1939—; Mem. Poestenkill (N.Y.) Zoning Commn., 1955-56. Contbr. numerous articles to profl. jours. Recipient prize Resistance Welding Mfrs. Assn., 1950, 51, 52, 53. Fellow Am. Soc. Metals Internat. (chmn. Eastern N.Y. chpt. 1947, Albert Easton White Disting. Tchr. award 1983), Am. Welding Soc. (hon. mem., bd. nat. dirs. 1960-63, nat. v.p. 1965-68, nat. pres. 1968-69, Ednl. Lecture series 1955, Adams lectr. 1958, Samuel Wylie Miller Meml. medal 1959, Adams Meml. membership award 1965);l mem. AIME, ASTM, Am. Soc. Engring. Edn., Sigma Xi, Tau Beta Pi, Phi Kappa Tau (nat. councilor 1947-53), Phi Lambda Upsilon. Club: Kiwanian (pres. Poestenkill 1953-54). Office: Rensselaer Polytech Inst Troy NY 12181

NIPPO, MURN MARCUS, animal science educator; b. N.Y.C., Feb. 8, 1944. BS, U. Maine, 1965, MS, 1968; PhD, U. R.I., 1976. Asst. prof. Univ. R.I., Kingston, 1976-82; assoc. prof. Univ. R.I., 1982, dept. chair, 1988—. Mem. Am. Soc. Animal Sci. Office: Animal Sci Dept Univ RI Woodward Hall Kingston RI 02881

NISBETT, EDWARD GEORGE, metallurgist; b. Glasgow, Scotland, Feb. 24, 1929; came to the U.S., 1967; s. James and Edith (Cooke) N.; m. Doris Banks, June 13, 1953 (div. 1969); children: Simon F., Andrew J.; m. Zdzislawa Barbara Chojnatska, Nov. 17, 1972. BS in Metallurgy with honors, Glasgow U., 1950; ARTC in Metallurgy, Royal Tech. Coll., Glasgow, 1950. Registered profl. engr., Pa.; chartered engr., U.K. Asst. metallurg. works Bristol (Eng.) Aero Engines Co., 1952-53, English Electric Co., Preston, England, 1953-55; devel. metallurgist Murex Welding Processes Ltd., Waltham Cross, England, 1955-58; chief metallurgist Nat. Vulcan Engring. Ins. Co., Manchester, England, 1958-67; mgr. product metallurgy Nat. Force Co., Irvine, Pa., 1967-87; project cons. Nat. Forge Co., Irvine, Pa., 1990—; cons. Warren, Pa., 1987-89, Metallurg. Svcs. Inc., Louisville, 1989-90; com. mem. Nat. Materials Adv. Bd., Washington, 1982. Co-editor: Steel Forgings, 1984, Residual and Unspecified Elements in Steel, 1989. With RAF, 1950-52. Fellow Inst. Metals, Am. Soc. Metals, ASTM (vice chmn. com. A1 on steel 1985-91). Home: 1262 Conewango Ave Warren PA 16365-4162 Office: Nat Forge Co Front St Irvine PA 16329

NISENHOLTZ, FREDERICK, pharmacist; b. Phila., Oct. 20, 1929; s. Samuel and Sophie (Kaprow) N.; m. Rhoda Annette Altus, Apr. 20, 1958; children: Tina F., Hollie S. BS in Pharmacy, Temple U., 1953. Lic. pharmacist, Pa. Pharmacist Sun Ray Drug, Phila., 1955-56, Davis Pharmacy, Elkins Park, Pa., 1956-57, Levin Pharmacy, Phila., 1957-59; pharmacist, owner Nisenholtz Pharmacy, Phila., 1959—. With U.S. Army, 1953-55, Korea. Mem. Steuben Lodge 113. Office: Nisenholtz Pharmacy 7624 Castor Ave Philadelphia PA 19152-3684

NISSELBAUM, JEROME S., chemist, researcher; b. Hartford, Conn., Dec. 21, 1925; s. Elliot George and Miriam (Steinberg) N.; m. Elaine Block, Aug. 28, 1949; children: Paula Ellen, Harry G., Nancy J. BA, U. Conn., 1949; PhD, Tufts Coll., 1953. Instr. Tufts Coll., Medford, Mass., 1955-57; asst. prof. to assoc. prof. Grad. Sch. Med. Scis. Cornell U., N.Y.C., 1957-68; asst. attending chemist Meml. Hosp. Cancer Rsch., N.Y.C., 1972-81, assoc. attending clin. chemist, 1981-89, attending clin. chemist, 1989—; clin. mem. Meml. Sloan-Kettering Cancer Ctr., N.Y.C., 1989—. Contbr. articles to Ann. Clin. Lab. Sci., Clin. Chemistry, Endocrinology, Jour. Biol. Chemistry. With USAAF, 1944-45. USPHS fellow, 1953-55. Mem. Am. Soc. Biochemistry and Molecular Biology, Am. Chem. Soc., Am. Assn. Clin. Chemistry, N.Y. Acad. Sci. Office: Meml Sloan Kettering 1275 York Ave New York NY 10021-6094

NITCHIE, GEORGE WILSON, retired English educator; b. Chgo., May 19, 1921; m. Laura Margaret Woodard, 1947; children: Katherine, Rebecca, Judith. BA, Middlebury Coll., 1943; MA, Columbia U., 1947, PhD, 1958. From instr. to prof. English Simmons Coll., Boston, 1947-86, chmn. dept., 1972-79, prof. emeritus, 1986—; tchr. Bklyn. Polytech. Inst., 1946-47, NYU, 1947, Northeastern U., 1951, Bridgewater State Coll., 1961-65, Harvard U. Extension, 1953-58. Author: Human Values in the Poetry of Robert Frost, 1960, Marianne Moore: An Introduction to the Poetry, 1969; contbr. articles, poems, revs. to profl. jours. Staff sgt. USAAF, 1943-45, PTO. Mem. AAUP, ACLU. Home: 50 Pleasantview Ave Weymouth MA 02188-3135

NITKO, ANTHONY JOSEPH, educational measurement educator, consultant; b. New Brunswick, N.J., June 9, 1941; s. Anthony John and Veronica (Wawrzusiszyn) N.; m. Veronica (Vail) Nitko, July 25, 1964; children: Anthony Joseph Jr., Marya, Robert Huynh, Meghan. BA, Seton Hall U., 1962; MEd, Rutgers U., 1964; PhD, U. Iowa, Iowa City, 1968. Instr., counselor N.J. State Prison System, Leesburg, 1962-63; rsch. assoc. Learning Research and Development Ctr., Pittsburgh, Pa., 1968-74; asst. prof. U. Pittsburgh, 1968-74, assoc. prof., 1974-78, prof., 1978--; prof. U. Malawi, Zomba, Malawi, 1984-85; cons. Battelle Columbus Labs., Research Triangle Park, N.C., 1970—, USAID/Jr. Secondary Sch. Improvement Project, Gabarone, Botswana, 1988-91; cons. ministry, edn. and culture, Indonesia, 1991, Namibian Primary Edn. Reform Project, Windhoek, Namibia, 1992. Author: Educational Tests and Measurement, 1983; co-author: Measuring Pupil Achievement and Aptitude, 1979; editor Educational Measurements: Issues and Practice jour., 1989-91. Fellow Am. Psychological Assn.; mem. Am. Educational Research Assn., Nat. Coun. on Measurement in Education (bd. dirs. 1984-86, v.p. 1992—), Psychometric Soc., Comparative and Internat. Edn. Soc. Democrat. Roman Catholic. Office: U Pitts 5B26 Forbes Quadrangle Pittsburgh PA 15260

NITZE, WILLIAM ALBERT, lawyer, association executive; b. N.Y.C., Sept. 27, 1942; s. Paul Henry and Phyllis (Pratt) N.; m. Ann Kendall Richards, June 5, 1971; children: Paul Kendall, Charles Richards. BA, Harvard U., 1964, JD, 1969; BA, Oxford U., 1966. Bar: N.Y. 1970, U.S. Supreme Ct. 1987. Assoc. Sullivan and Cromwell, N.Y.C., 1970-72; v.p. London Arts, Inc., N.Y.C., 1972-73; counsel Mobil South, Inc., N.Y.C., 1974-76; gen. counsel Mobil Oil Japan, Tokyo, 1976-80; asst. gen. counsel exploration and producing div. Mobil Oil Corp., N.Y.C., 1980-87; dep asst. sec. for environment, health and natural resources U.S. Dept. State, Washington, 1987-90; pres. Alliance to Save Energy, Washington, 1990—; adv. com. Sch. Advanced Internat. Studies, Washington, 1982—; vis. scholar Environ. Law Inst., Washington, 1990; dir. Charles A. Lindbergh Fund, Mpls., 1990—, Nat. Symphony Orch. Assn., Washington, 1990—. Trustee Aspen Inst., Queenstown, Md., 1988—. Mem. Assn. of Bar of City of N.Y., Coun. on Fgn. Rels., Met. Club, Links Club. Republican. Episcopalian. Home: 1336 30th St NW Washington DC 20007-3349 Office: Alliance to Save Energy 1725 K St NW Washington DC 20006-1401

NITZSCHKE, DALE FREDERICK, university president; b. Remsen, Iowa, Sept. 16, 1937; m. Linda Hutchinson, June 24, 1971; children: Mary Beth, Stephen, Lori, Eric, David. BA in Edn. cum laude, Lora Coll., 1959; MEd in Guidance and Counseling, Ohio U., 1960, PhD in Guidance and Counseling, 1964. Instr. edn. Loras Coll., Dubuque, Iowa, 1964-65, chmn. dept. edn., 1964-65; asst. prof., dir. ednl. placement bur. Ohio U., Athens, 1967-72; assoc. dean profl. and gen. studies, dean edn. State U. Coll. Arts and Sci., Plattsburgh, N.Y., 1972-76; prof. edn., dean Coll. Edn. U. No. Iowa, 1976-80; prof. edn., v.p. acad. affairs U. Nev., Las Vegas, 1980-84; pres. Marshall U., Huntington, W.Va., 1984-90, U. N.H., Durham, 1990—; workshop dir. Evaluation Elem. Schs.; dir. Martha Holden Jennings Founds. Lectureship Series; cons. Athens non-graded high sch.; cons. on personnel mgmt. U. Nev. Reno Med. Sch. Contbr. articles to profl. jours. Bd. dirs., blood chmn. Athens County Red Cross; v.p. Kootoga council Boy Scouts Am.; mem. N.Y. State Policy Bd. in Spl. Edn., 1975-76; nat. adv. com. Personalized Adult Counseling Experience (PACE); coordinator Coll. Drug Edn. Program, Ohio U.; dir. Student Tutors for Ednl. Progress (STEP); coordinator Preparation Program for Inner City and Appalachian Tchrs.; sec. State of Ohio Edn. Deans; bd. dirs. Elvis Presley Mus. and Entertainment Inst., Las Vegas; bd. acad. advisors Am. Inst. for Fgn. Study; chmn. bd. regents State Adv. Com. for Iowa Sch. for Deaf, Iowa Braille and Sight Saving Sch.; mem. State-wide Inter-Instl. Gerontology Com.; bd. dirs. W.Va. Council on Econ. Devel., W.Va. Roundtable, Cabell-Wayne United Way, River Cities Cultural Devel. Council, Community Players, W.Va. Edn. Fund, Inc., Boys Club Huntington, Ronald McDonald House, Huntington, W.Va. Com. on Employment Opportunities and Econ. Devel.; mem. com. on self regulation initiatives Am. Council on Edn.; mem. selection com. Harry S. Truman Scholarship Program; incorporator Trust for N.H. Lands, 1992—; bd. dirs. New Eng. Coun. Recipient Community Leader of Am. award, 1969; Disting. Service award Rotary, 1969; Alexander Meiklejohn award for acad. freedom AAUP, 1984. Mem. Assn. Higher Edn., Am. Personnel Guidance Assn., Nat. Vocat. Guidance Assn., Am. Counselor Edn. Assn., Student Personnel Assn. for Tchr. Edn., Nat. Assn. State Univs. and Land Grant Colls. (chmn. commn. on outreach and tech. transfer 1991—), Huntington C. of C. (bd. dirs.), Athens Jaycees (past pres., chmn. bd., Young Man of Yr. award 1969), Nature Conservancy (trustee N.H. chpt. 1992—). Home: 2 Garrison Ave Durham NH 03824-2315 Office: U NH Office of Pres Main St Durham NH 03824-2521

NIXON, JOYCE ELAINE, chiropractor, educator, consultant; b. Corning, N.Y., Feb. 17, 1925; d. Douglas Lewis and Mina Phiolana (Barnes) Williams; m. Lewis Earl Nixon, June 21, 1946 (div. Nov. 1958); 1 child, Deborah Joy. BA, Webster U., 1945; postgrad., SUNY, Geneseo, 1952-53; student, PBTS Bible Inst., 1946. Adminstr., chiropractic technician Dr. DeLue, Nunda, N.Y., 1958-85, cons., 1986—; instr. Sacro Occipital Research Soc. Internat., Inc., Omaha, 1966-79. Active Genessee Valley Council on Arts, Geneseo, 1967—; pres., bd. dirs. Nunda Community Home, Inc., 1983—. Mem. Internat. Platform Assn., N.Y. State Chiropractic Women's Aux., Nat. Assn. for Female Execs. (N.Y. State chpt.), Sacro Occipital Research Soc. (internat. sec. 1965-70, officer 1976, Disting. Profl. Service Founder's award 1976, Pres.' award 1980), N.Y. State Bus. and Profl. Women's Assn. (bd. dirs. 1963-71), Internat. Fedn. Bus. and Profl. Women, Geneva Bus. and Profl. Womens Clubs Inc. Republican. Home: 3 Meadowbrook Dansville NY 14437-9592

NIXON, PATRICIA RYAN (THELMA CATHERINE NIXON), wife of former President of U.S.; b. Ely, Nev., Mar. 16, 1912; m. Richard Milhous Nixon, June 21, 1940; children: Patricia (Mrs. Edward Finch Cox), Julie (Mrs. Dwight David Eisenhower II). Grad. cum laude, U. So. Calif., 1937, L.H.D., 1961. X-ray technician N.Y.C., 1931-33; tchr. high schs. Cal., 1937-41; govt. economist, 1942-45. Promoter of world wide humanitarian service, volunteerism in U.S. Decorated grand cross Order of Sun for relief work at time of massive earthquake, 1971; Peru; grand cordon Most Venerable Order Knighthood Pioneers Liberia, 1972; named among most admired women George Gallup polls, 1957, 68, 69, 70, 71.

NOAR, MARK DAVID, gastroenterologist, therapeutic endoscopist, internist, consultant, inventor; b. Boston, Sept. 10, 1953; s. Myron Theodore and Phyllis (Krinsky) N.; m. Martine Denise Motard, May 15, 1982; children: Emmanuelle, Ariane. BS in Biology, Ursinus Coll., Collegeville, Pa., 1975; MPH in Internat. Health, Tulane U., 1977; MD, U. Cen. del Este, Dominican Republic, 1980. Intern 5th Pathway program Coll. Medicine and Dentistry N.J.-Newark Beth Israel Hosp., 1980-81; resident in internal medicine U. Nebr. Med. Ctr., Omaha, 1981-84; fellow in gastroenterology SUNY Downstate Med. Ctr., Bklyn., 1984-86; fellow in therapeutic and surg. endoscopy, vis. staff Univ. Hosp. Hamburg, Germany, 1986-87; pvt. practice, Balt., 1988—; clin. cons. in therapeutic endoscopy Bklyn. VA Med. Ctr., 1987; dir. project devel., v.p. med. devel. Ixion, Inc., Seattle, 1987—; staff physician dept. gastroenterology St. Joseph Hosp., Balt., Franklin Square Hosp., Balt.; bd. dirs., dir. ops. Disaster Support Network, Balt., 1990—; session co-chmn. World Congress Gastroenterology Sydney, Australia, 1990, IX European Workshop on Therapeutic Digestive Endoscopy, Brussels, 1991; owner, med. dir. EMA-ASC, Inc., Balt., 1991—. Author: (with N. Soehendra and H. Grimm) A Compendium of Therapeutic Endoscopy for the General Practitioner, 1991; editor-in-chief Internat. Video Jour. Therapeutic and Diagnostic Endoscopy; assoc. editor Endoscopy Rev.; contbr. articles and abstracts to med. jours., chpts. to books; inventor robotic interactive endoscopy simulation. Pub. lectr. Am. Cancer Soc., Balt., 1988—; physician educator Doctor and Lawyer Coalition Against Drugs, Balt., 1991-92. Fellow Royal Soc. Tropical Medicine and Hygiene; mem. ACP, AMA, Am. Coll. Gastroenterologist, Am. Soc. for Gastrointestinal Endoscopy (recipient award for achievement and edn. in diagnostic/therapeutic biliary and pancreatic endoscopy, 1992), Md. Soc. for Gastrointestinal Endoscopy, Baltimore County Med. Soc., Sigma Xi. Office: Endoscopic Microsurgery Assocs 7402 York Rd Ste 100 Baltimore MD 21204-7519

NOBEL, JOEL J., physician; b. Phila., Dec. 8, 1934; s. Bernard D. and Golda R. (Nobel) Judovich; m. Bonnie Sue Goldberg, June 19, 1960 (div.); children—Erika, Joshua; m. Loretta Schwartz, Oct. 28, 1979; 1 child, Adam. A.B., Haverford Coll., 1956; M.A., U. Pa., 1958; M.D., Thomas Jefferson Med. Coll., Phila., 1963. Intern Presbyn. Hosp., Phila., 1963-64; resident in surgery Pa. Hosp., Phila., 1964-65; resident in neurosurgery U. Pa. Hosp., 1965-66; practice medicine specializing in biomed. engring. research Phila., 1968—; dir. research Emergency Care Research Inst., Plymouth Meeting, Pa., 1968-71; dir., pres. Emergency Care Research Inst., 1971—; pres. Plymouth Inst., 1979—; cons. in field; bd. dirs. Consumers Union, 1976-79, 80—, chmn. tech. policy com., exec. bd. Publisher Health Devices, 1971—, Health Devices Alerts, 1977—. Contbr. articles to profl. jours. Served with USNR, 1966-68. Smith, Kline & French fgn. fellow, 1962; grantee HEW, 1968-72; grantee Am. Heart Assn., 1965-66. Mem. Assn. Advancement Med. Instrumentation, Critical Care Med. Soc., Am. Public Health Assn., AMA, Pa. Med. Assn., Am. Def. Preparedness Assn. Clubs: Union League, Sunday Breakfast. Home: 1434 Monk Rd Gladwyne PA 19035-1315 Office: ECRI 5200 Butler Pike Plymouth Meeting PA 19462-1241

NOBILE, JOHN FRANK, food flavor company executive; b. N.Y.C., Dec. 20, 1940; s. Frank and Josephine (Russo) N.; m. Geraldine Claire Fanelli, May 9, 1987; children: Jennifer Lori, Liana Marie, Raquel Lynne. BS in Chemistry, NYU, 1961; MBA, Fordham U., 1971. New products mgr. Fisher Sci. Co., Fairlawn, N.Y., 1961-68; bus. devel. mgr. Union Carbide Corp., N.Y.C., 1968-78; dir. mktg. ITT Corp., Stamford, Conn., 1978-87; v.p., gen. mgr. Flavor Key 2000, Inc., Fairfield, N.J., 1987—. Author: Single Cell Proteins, 1982; patentee in field. Staff sgt. USAF, 1961-63. Recipient Energy Mgmt. award Am. Paper Inst./Nat. Fibrous Pulp Assn. Roman Catholic. Home: 2 Van Fleet Rd Neshanic Station NJ 08853 Office: Flavor Key 2000 Inc 24 Spielman Rd Fairfield NJ 07004-3412

NOBLE, AMANDA STEVENS, computer programmer, analyst; b. Schenectady, N.Y., Nov. 7, 1960; d. Garry Albretsen and Dorothy Rita (Brodie) Stevens; m. Richard Lee Noble, Sept. 25, 1982 (div. June 1992); children: Jenna Lee, Michael Patrick. AAS, SUNY, Morrisville, 1980; student, SUNY, Oswego, 1990—. Cert. data processor. Analyst, programmer Carrier Corp., Syracuse, N.Y., 1980-84, Bristol Labs., Syracuse, 1984-85, Amanda Noble Cons., Sherrill, N.Y., 1985-91, Mincom Cons., Syracuse, 1991—. Swimming ofcl. N.Y. State Cert. Swimming Ofcls., Syracuse, 1984-90. Republican. Presbyterian. Office: Mincom Bus Systems 25 Water St Baldwinsville NY 13027

NOBLE, JAMES KENDRICK, JR., media industry consultant; b. N.Y.C., Oct. 6, 1928; s. James Kendrick and Orrel Tennant (Baldwin) N.; m. Norma Jean Rowell, June 16, 1951; children: Anne Rowell, James Kendrick III. Student, Princeton U., 1945-46; BS, U.S. Naval Acad., 1950; postgrad., USN Gen. Line Sch., 1955-56; MBA, NYU, 1961; postgrad., Sch. Edn., 1962-68. Chartered fin. analyst. Commd. ensign USN, 1950; transferred to USNR, 1957; advanced through grades to capt. USNR, 1973; asst. gunnery officer in U.S.S. Thomas E. Fraser, 1950-51; student naval aviator USNR, 1951-52, pilot asst. ops. officer, 1952-55; instr. U.S. Naval Acad., 1956-57, Officer Candidate Sch., Newport, R.I., 1958; asst. to pres. Noble & Noble, Pub., Inc., N.Y.C., 1957-60; dir. spl. projects Noble & Noble, Pub., Inc., 1960-62, v.p., 1962-65, exec. v.p., 1965-66, dir., 1957-65; dir., v.p. Transl. Pub. Co., N.Y.C., 1958-65; cons. Transl. Pub. Co., 1965-66; v.p., dir. Elbon Realty Corp., Bronxville, N.Y., 1960-65; cons. Elbon Realty Corp., 1965-66; comdg. officer NAIRU R2, 1968-70; staff NARS W2, 1970-71, NRID 3-1, 1971-74; comdg. officer NRCSG 302, 1974-76; sr. analyst F. Eberstadt & Co., 1966-69; sr. analyst Auerbach, Pollak & Richardson, 1969-75, v.p., 1972-75, mgr. spl. rsch. projects, 1973-75, dir., 1975; v.p. rsch. Paine, Webber, Jackson & Curtis, Inc., 1975-77, assoc. dir. rsch., 1976-77; v.p. Paine Webber, N.Y.C., 1977-79; 1st v.p. Paine Webber, 1979-91; pres. Noble Cons. Inc., 1991—; bd. dirs. Curriculum Info. Center, Inc., Denver, 1972-78; instl. investor All Am. Rsch. Team, 1972-90. Author: Ploob, 1949, rev.,

1956; editor pub.: The Years Between, 1966; also articles in various publs. V.p. Bolton Gardens Assn., 1959-61; mem. Bronxville Bd. Edn., 1968-74, pres., 1970-72; Republican co-leader 21st Dist., Eastchester, N.Y., 1961-65; dir. Merit; cons., dir. Space and Sci. Train, 1962-63; trustee St. John's Hosp., Yonkers, N.Y., 1972-92, com. chmn., 1980-92. Fellow AAAS; mem. Info. Industry Assn. (disting. profl. mem.), Nat. Inst. Social Scis., N.Y. Soc. Security Analysts (mem. com. 1971-91, dir. 1975-84, v.p. 1977-81, exec. v.p. 1981-82, pres. 1982-83), Am. Textbook Pub. Inst. (com. chmn. 1964-66), AIAA (mem. com. 1957-61), Media and Entertainment Analysts Assn. (pres. 1969-71), Fin. Analysts Fedn. (dir. 1984-87), Naval Res. Assn. (v.p. N.Y. Navy chpt. 1968-76), Wings Club, Siwanoy Country Club. Mem. Reformed Ch. Home: 45 Edgewood Ln Bronxville NY 10708-1946 Office: Noble Cons Inc 45 Edgewood Ln Bronxville NY 10708-1946

NOBLE, ROBERT WARREN, medicine and biochemistry educator; b. Washington, Feb. 14, 1937; s. Robert Warren Sr. and Alice Merion (Dibble) N.; m. Bernice Katz, Dec. 20, 1962; children: Peter Charles, Benjamin David, Aaron Andrew. BA in Biology, MIT, 1959, PhD in Biophysics, 1964. Postdoctoral fellow Regina Elena Cancer Inst., Rome, 1964-66; rsch. assoc. Cornell U., Ithaca, N.Y., 1967-68; asst. prof. SUNY, Buffalo, 1968-72, assoc. prof., 1972-76; prof. Buffalo, 1976—; chief lab. protein chemistry VA Med. Ctr., Buffalo, 1971—; vis. scientist MRC Lab. of Molecular Biology, Cambridge, Eng., 1975-76; vis. prof. U. Trento, Italy, 1979, 84, 90-91. Co-author: Introductory Biophysics, 1986. Established investigator Am. Heart Assn., 1973-78. NIH grantee, 1968—. Mem. Am. Soc. Biochemistry and Molecular Biology, Biophys. Soc., The Protein Soc. Home: 166 Mona Dr Buffalo NY 14226-4117 Office: SUNY Buffalo Dept Medicine Biochemistry VA Med Ctr Buffalo NY 14215

NOCK, ROBERT WAYNE, insurance company executive; b. Salisbury, Md., Aug. 17, 1949; s. Ernest Jenkins and Florence Anna (Haigh) N.; m. Elizabeth Anne Woodward, Nov. 25, 1975; children: Robert Wayne, Emily Florence. Student, Bridgewater (Va.) Coll., 1967-69. CLU, ChFC, registered rep. Ins. agt. Bankers Life & Casualty, Annapolis, Md., 1973-74; dist. mgr. Bankers Life & Casualty, Wilmington, Del., 1974-75; pres. Nock Ins. Agy., Salisbury, 1975—; owner Nock Apts., Ocean City, Md., 1982—; v.p. Atlantic States United Brokerage, Wilmington, 1989—. Mem. HALT, Washington; mem. Am. Family Assn., Tupelo, Miss. Mem. Delmarva Assn. Life Underwriters (bd. dir. 1985), Nat. Assn. Life Underwriters, Nat. Assn. Health Underwriters (pres. 1990-91), Ind. Ins. Agts. Am., Nat. Assn. Securities Dealers, Health Underwriters of Delmarva (pres., dir. 1990-91), Masons. Republican. Christian. Home: 602 Baltimore Ave Ocean City MD 21842-3829 Office: Nock Ins Agy 1625 N Division St Salisbury MD 21801-3805

NOCKS, JAMES JAY, psychiatrist; b. Bklyn., Apr. 17, 1943; s. Henry and Pearl (Klein) N.; m. Ellen Jane Leblang, June 21, 1964; children: Randy, Jason. BA in English Lit., U. Pa., 1964, MD, 1968. Diplomate Nat. Bd. Med. Examiners, Am. Bd. Psychiatry and Neurology; Cert. in adminstrv. psychiatry Am. Psychiatric Assn. Rotating intern Chgo. Wesley Meml. Hosp., Northwestern U., 1968-69; resident psychiatry U. Pa., Phila., 1969-73; chief alcoholism program VA Med. Ctr., West Haven, Conn., 1975-87; asst. chief psychiatry svc. VA Med. Ctr., 1978-87; chief staff VA Med. Ctr., Coatesville, Pa., 1987—; sr. resident psychiatry U. Pa., 1971-72, chief resident psychiatry, 1972-73, asst. instr. psychiatry, 1971-73; clin. asst. prof. psychiatry Health Sci. Ctr. U. Tex., San Antonio, 1973-75; asst. clin. prof. psychiatry Yale U. Sch. Medicine, New Haven, 1975-80, assoc. clin. prof. psychiatry, 1980-87, clin. prof. psychiatry and human behavior Jefferson Med. Coll., Phila., 1987-91; prof. psychiatry Temple U. Sch. Medicine, Phila., 1991—. Co-author: Psychiatry: Pre-Test, Self-Assessment and Review, 2nd edit., 1982, 3rd edit., 1984; Alcoholic Liver Disease, 1985; contbr. articles to profl. jours. Mem. exec. com. Med. Alumni Soc., U. Pa., 1989—. Major Med. Corps, USAF, 1973-75. Fellow Am. Psychiat. Assn.; mem. Pa. Psychiat. Soc., Phila. Psychiat. Soc., Am. Soc. of Addiction Medicine (cert.), Assn. for Med. Edn. & Rsch. in Substance Abuse, Am. Assn. for Social Psychiatry, Am. Acad. Psychiatrists in Alcoholism & Addictions. Jewish. Office: VA Med Ctr Blackhorse Hill Rd Coatesville PA 19320-3313

NOGAKI, K(EN) RODGER, loss control consultant; b. Seattle, Jan. 3, 1940; s. Takeo and Florence (Matsumoto) N.; m. Jane Ann Wilber, Aug. 16, 1964; children: Jennifer, Geraldine. Student, Newark Coll. Engring., 1966, 68; BS, Fairleigh Dickinson U., 1967. Rsch. technician Allied Chem. Corp., Edgewater, N.J., 1959-67; loss control rep. Sentry Ins. Co., Morristown, N.J., 1967-71, Reliance Ins. Co., Garden City, N.J., 1971-73; regional mgr. loss control Reliance Ins. Co., Phila., 1973-79, v.p. loss control, 1979-85; pres. Controlled Risk Svcs. Inc., Thorofare, N.J., 1985-89, Creative Risk Svcs. Inc., Berlin, N.J., 1989—. Mem. Evesham Twp. (N.J.) Bd. Fire Commrs., 1976-79; fire chief Kettlerun Fire Co., Evesham Twp., 1979-85; chmn. Ellis task force subcom. Evesham Twp. Environ. Commn., 1986—; pres. Phila. chpt. JACL, 1987-88. Mem. Nat. Fire Protection Assn., Am. Soc. Safety Engrs. (profl.), Coalition Against Toxics, Burlington County Fire Chiefs Assn., Marlton Lakes Civic Assn. (Laker of Yr. award 1979). Home: 223 Park Ave Atco NJ 08004-2749 Office: Creative Risk Svcs Inc 272 S White Horse Pike Berlin NJ 08009-1956

NOGEE, JEFFREY LAURENCE, lawyer; b. Schenectady, N.Y., Oct. 31, 1952; s. Rodney and Shirley Ruth (Mannes) N.; m. Freda Carolyn Wartel, Aug. 31, 1980; children: Rori Caitlen, Amara Sonia. BA cum laude, Bucknell U., 1974; JD, Boston U., 1977. Bar: N.Y. 1978, U.S. Dist. Ct. (so. and ea. dists.) N.Y. 1978. Assoc. Hale Russell & Gray, N.Y.C., 1977-83; sr. atty. Ebasco Services Inc., N.Y.C., 1984-88, dir. Countertrade unit, 1985-88; sr. ptnr. Fogh & Nogee Assocs., 1988; ptnr. Brauner, Baron, Rosenzweig, Bauman & Klein, N.Y.C., 1988-90; sr. ptnr. Nogee & Wartel, 1990—; pvt. counsellor for internat. bus. firms, 1987—. Mem. ABA, Assn. of Bar of City of N.Y., Nassau County Bar Assn., Ind. Power Producers N.Y., Phi Beta Kappa, Pi Sigma Alpha. Office: 1065 Old Country Rd Ste 201 Westbury NY 11590-5628

NOLAN, HOWARD CHARLES, JR., state senator, lawyer; b. Albany, N.Y., Aug. 24, 1932; s. Howard Charles and Helen A. (Burke) N.; m. Geraldine Leonard, 1959 (div.); children: Anne, Kathleen, Deborah, Robert, Donna, Lynn, Karen; m. Shannon Logan, 1988. BS, Holy Cross Coll., 1954; JD, Albany Law Sch., 1957. Practice law, Albany, 1961—; sr. ptnr. Nolan & Heller, 1965-87; sr. ptnr. Cooper, Erving, Savage, Nolan & Heller, 1987—; mem. N.Y. State Senate, mem. codes, agrl., mental hygiene and addiction control, rules, fin., bank, Senate Select Com on the Disabled; dir. First Am. Bank; lectr. Mem. adv. bd. Govt. Law Ctr., Albany Law Sch.; v.p. N.Y. State assn. United Cerebral Palsy; chmn. Cerebral Palsy Ctr., Disabled Found.; bd. dirs. Thoroughbred Retirement Found., Albany Area chpt. ARC, St. Peter's Hosp. Found., Crenshaw Community Ctr., Albany Area Urban League; mem. adv. bd. Next Step, Inc., Albany. Served to capt. USMC, 1957-60. Recipient Legis. Service award United Cerebral Palsy; Legislator of Yr. award Nat. Rehab. Assn.; Friend of Law Enforcement award N.Y. State Sheriffs Assn.; Am. Heritage award Italian-Am. Dem. Orgn. N.Y. State; Humanitarian of Yr., Cerebral Palsy Ctr. for Disabled, 1984; award Centro Civico Hispano Americano Orgn., Nat. Assn. Accts., Irish Legislators Soc. Mem. Albany County Bar Assn., Irish Legislators Soc. (treas.), Internat. Narcotics Enforcement Officers Assn., N.Y. State Ct. Officers Assn., Med. Soc. N.Y. State (bd. dirs.), Marine Corps League, Albany C. of C. (pres.). Democrat. Roman Catholic. Lodges: KC, Ancient Order of Hibernians, Kiwanis (Albany). Home: 488 Broadway Albany NY 12207-2906 Office: NY State Senate Rm 809 LOB Albany NY 12224

NOLAN, JOHN THOMAS, JR., oil industry administrator; b. Boston, Apr. 15, 1930; s. John T. Sr. and Margaret M. (Craig) N.; m. Mary Sharkey, May 7, 1955; children: Anne, Margaret, John T. III, Stephen, Michael. AB, Cath. U. Am., 1951; PhD, MIT, 1955. Chemist Texaco, Inc., Beacon, N.Y., 1955-59; group leader Texaco, Inc., Beacon, 1959-69, supr., 1969-79, asst. mgr., 1979-82, assoc. dir., 1982-87, dir. strategic rsch., 1987—; mem. adv. bd. Dutchess County Sci. Fair, Poughkeepsie, N.Y., 1990—. Contbr. over 5 articles to profl. jours. Mem. blue ribbon panel Beacon Sch. Dist., 1987—; chmn. bd. Dutchess Community Coll. Found., Poughkeepsie, 1989—. Mem. AAAS, Am. Chem. Soc., N.Y. Acad. Scis., Assn. Rsch. Dirs., Greater Southern Dutchess C. of C. (bd. dirs. Wappingers Falls, N.Y. chpt. 1989—), Sigma Xi. Home: 18 Relyea Ter Wappingers Falls NY 12590-5824

NOLAN, KAREN LYNN, management training manager; b. Utica, N.Y., Apr. 20, 1963; d. John Brooks and Gladys (Bateson) Haberl. BS in Hotel and Restaurant Mgmt., U. Mass., 1985. Night mgr. Borel Restaurant Corp., Providence, 1985-86; asst. mgr. Uno Restaurants, Framingham, Mass., 1986; gen. mgr. New Eng. Chowder House, Pittsfield, Mass., 1986-87; mgr. Uno Restaurants, Boston, 1987-90; mgr. corp. tng. Uno Restaurants, West Roxbury, Mass., 1990—. Mem. ASTD. Office: Uno Restaurant Corp 100 Charles Park Rd West Roxbury MA 02132-4900

NOLAN, LOUISE MARY, school system administrator, author; b. Boston, Sept. 28, 1947; d. John Joseph and Helen (Spiers) N. BA, Regis Coll., 1969; MEd, Boston U., 1971 postgrad., 1981-82; postgrad Fitchburg State Coll., 1972-74, Salem State Coll., 1977-79; PhD, Boston Coll., 1986, MIT, 1992. Counselor Camp Thoreau, Inc., Concord, Mass., 1964-68; tchr., chmn. sci. dept. John F. Kennedy Meml. Jr. High Sch., Woburn, Mass., 1969-86; asst. supt. schs. for curriculum and instrn. Woburn Pub. Schs., 1986—; instr. Boston Coll., 1992—; initiator Woburn-Sci. Specialist Program, Let's Take Sci. Home Program; co-owner Ruth and Louise Silkscreening, Lexington, Mass., Fancypants, Carlisle, Mass.; bd. dirs. ecology program Curry Coll., Milton, Mass., 1977, Mass. Mid. Sch. Sci. Olympics, North Shore Math and Sci. Collaborative, Newspaper in Edn. Boston Globe; mem. MIT High/ Middle Sch. Math Sci. Tchr. Program. Author: Y.E.S.-A Comprehensive Guide to Students Education Youth in Environmental Sciences; Bioluminscence-An Experimental Guide; Marine Plankton; Health Physical Science, 1983, 87. Active New Eng. League Mid. Schs., Nat. League Mid. Schs. Past vice chmn. Mass. Sci. Fair Com.; bd. dirs. North Shore Sci. and Math. Collaborative, Newspaper in Edn. program The Boston Globe. Sci. & engring. fellow MIT Inst. for Mid. and High Sch., 1992; NSF grantee, 1972-73, 77-79, 81-82; chemistry fellow Boston U., 1983-84, edn. fellow MIT, 1992; For a Cleaner Environ. grantee, 1984-86. Mem. NEA, AAAS, Mass. Tchrs. Assn., Nat. Assn. Sci. Tchrs., Mass. Assn. Sci. Tchrs., Nat. Assn. Biology Tchrs., Nat. Assn. Rsch. in Sci. Teaching, Middlesex County Tchrs. Assn., Biology Roundtable, Woburn Tchrs. Assn., Mass. Supts. Assn., Beta Beta Beta, Pi Lambda Theta, Mus. Fine Arts Club, Concord Art Assn. Club, Mus. of Sci. Club. Democrat. Roman Catholic. Home: 9 Stevens Rd Lexington MA 02173-4126 Office: Joyce Middle Sch High Sch Adminstrn Offices 33 Locust St Woburn MA 01801-4033

NOLAN, RICHARD THOMAS, clergyman, educator; b. Waltham, Mass., May 30, 1937; s. Thomas Michael and Elizabeth Louise (Leishman) N. BA, Trinity Coll., 1960; cert. in clin. pastoral edn., Conn. Valley Hosp., 1962; diploma, Berkeley Divinity Sch., 1962; MDiv., Hartford Sem. Found., 1963; postgrad., Union Theol. Sem., N.Y.C., 1963; MA in Religion, Yale U., 1967; PhD, NYU, 1973; post doctoral, Harvard U., 1991. Ordained deacon Episcopal Ch., 1963, priest, 1965. Instr. Latin and English Watkinson (Conn.) Sch., 1961-62; instr. math. Choir Sch. of Cathedral of St. John the Divine, N.Y.C., 1962-64; instr. math. and religion, assoc. chaplain Cheshire (Conn.) Acad., 1965-67; instr. Hartford (Conn.) Sem. Found., 1967-68, asst. acad. dean, lectr. philosophy and edn., 1968-70; instr. Mattatuck Community Coll., Waterbury, Conn., 1969-70; asst. prof. philosophy and history Mattatuck Community Coll., Waterbury, 1970-74, assoc. prof., 1974-78, prof. philosophy and social sci., 1978-92, prof. emeritus, 1992—; rsch. fellow in med. ethics Yale U., 1978, rsch. fellow in profl. and bus. ethics, 1987; vicar St. Paul's Parish, Bantam, Conn., 1974-88; pastor emeritus St. Paul's Parish, Bantam, 1988—; pres. Litchfield Inst., Inc., Conn. and Fla., 1984—; mem. ethics com. Waterbury Hosp. Health Ctr., 1984-88; vis. and adj. prof. philosophy, theology and religious studies Trinity Coll., Conn., L.I. U., U. Miami, St. Joseph Coll., Conn., Pace U., Teikyo Post U., U. Conn., Hartford Grad. Ctr., Cen. Conn. State U., Barry U., Fla., Broward Community Coll., Fla., 1964—; adj. assoc. in continuing edn. Berkeley Div. Sch. Yale U., 1987-89; Rabbi Harry Halpern Meml. lectr., Southbury, Conn., 1987; guest speaker various chs. and orgns. including Cathedral of St. John the Divine, N.Y. and Trinity Cathedral, Miami; mem. faculty of consulting examiners Charter Oak State Coll., Conn., 1990—; fellow Associated Fellows for Counseling and Psychotherapy, Inc., 1990—; assoc. for edn. Christ Ch. Cathedral, Hartford Conn., 1988—, hon. canon, 1991—; cons. Dept. Def. Activity Non-Traditional Ednl. Support, Ednl. Testing Svcs., Princeton, 1990. Author: (with H. Titus and M. Smith) Living Issues in Philosophy, 7th edit., 1979, 8th edit., 1986, 9th edit., 1993, (with F. Kirkpatrick) Living Issues in Ethics, 1982; editor, contbr. Diaconate Now, 1968; host Conversations With..., 1987-89. Mem. Am. Acad. Religion, Am. Philos. Assn., Authors Guild, Inst. Soc., Ethics and Life Scis., Boston Latin Sch. Alumni Assn., Tabor Acad. Alumni Assn., Phi Delta Kappa. Address: PO Box 483 Bristol CT 06011-0483 also: 2121 W Oakland Park Blvd # 333 Fort Lauderdale FL 33311-1507

NOLIN, CHRISTINE LEA, association executive; b. Auburn, N.Y., Apr. 3, 1952; d. Robert J. and Betty Lou (O'Hora) N.; m. Joseph Tinkelman, Oct. 13, 1991. BA, SUNY, Albany, 1973; MA, SUNY, 1987; Cert. of Assn. Mgmt., U. Md., 1990. Program assoc. N.Y. State Office Lt. Gov., Albany, 1975-78; counsel N.Y. State Assembly Energy Com., Albany, 1979-85; exec. dir. Ind. Power Producers of N.Y., Albany, 1986-89, Cogeneration & Ind. Power Coalition of Am., Washington, 1989—. Contbr. articles to profl. jours. Mem. Am. Soc. Assn. Execs., Greater Washington Soc. Assn. Execs. (com. mem. 1990-91). Office: Electric Generation Assn 2 Wisconsin Cir Bethesda MD 20815-7003

NOLL, CHARLES GORDON, physicist; b. Sunbury, Pa., Dec. 2, 1948; s. J. Herman and Helen Elisabeth (Gelnett) N.; m. Alice Marie Walters, Dec. 20, 1971; children: Carlton Leigh, Benjamin Douglass, Jennifer Nicole. BA, Bloomsburg State Coll., 1970; MS, Ohio State U., 1974, PhD, 1975. Lectr. physics Ohio State U., Columbus, 1975-76; researcher R & D United McGill Corp., Columbus, 1976-78, corp. physicist, Groveport, Ohio, 1978-83, mgr. corp. R & D, 1983-87, dir. tech., 1987-88; engring. group specialist Gen. Dynamics, Ft. Worth, 1989-90; dir. product devel. The Simco Co., Hatfield, Pa., 1990-91, v.p. product devel., 1991—; bd. dirs. Simco Japan; cons. environ. problems. Author: Ensemble Theory for Electrostatic Precipitation, 1980, Computer-Aided Research Tools for Pilot Testing of Pollution Control Equipment, 1981, Industrial Gas Cleaning and Air Pollution Control, 1991. Mem. ASHRAE, IEEE, Am. Phys. Soc., Electrostatics Soc. Am., Am. Ceramics Soc., Air and Waste Mgmt. Assn. (mem. editorial rev. bd.), Sigma Xi, Sigma Pi Sigma. Home: PO Box 396 Sellersville PA 18960-0396 Office: 2257 N Penn Rd Hatfield PA 19440-1998

NOLL, CHERYL KIRK, freelance illustrator; b. Reading, Pa., Dec. 15, 1950; d. George V. and Shirley M. (Rowe) Kirk; m. David H. Noll, Sept. 18, 1982; 1 child, Philip Kirk. BS in Edn., Lebanon Valley Coll., 1972; BFA in Design, RISD, 1977. Tchr. Smyrna (Del.) Sch. Dist., 1972-73; freelance illustrator children's books and textbooks Providence, 1977—; tchr. workshop R.I. State Coun. for the Arts/Artists in Edn., Providence, 1987—. Illustrator (children's books) Kerry's Christmas, 1986, The Snow Kept Falling, 1987, The Wave, 1990, Morgan's Whistle, 1992, The Girl Who Wouldn't See, 1992, That's Not the Way Mommy Does It, 1992. Mem. Parents for Providence Pub. Schs., 1991. Mem. Soc. Children's Book Writers, Graphic Artists Guild. Home: 19 Hooker St Providence RI 02908-1811

NOLL, FRANCIS CHARLES, JR., marketing executive; b. N.Y.C., Feb. 23, 1952; s. Francis C. and Mary C. (DePiano) N.; m. Theresa I. Zotto, Oct. 20, 1973. BBA, Baruch Coll., N.Y.C., 1973. Mktg. mgr. Saks Fifth Ave., N.Y.C., 1973-80; mgr. Citicorp, N.Y.C., 1980-83; v.p. Chase Manhattan Bank, N.Y.C., 1983—. Tchr./mentor Jr. Achievement of N.Y., 1985-88; treas. Lincoln Apts. Corp., 1987-89. Mem. Direct Mktg. Assn., Direct Mktg. Club of N.Y. Roman Catholic. Home: 225 Lincoln Pl Brooklyn NY 11217-3719 Office: Chase Manhattan Bank 2 Chase Pla New York NY 10081

NOLL, MICHAEL WILLIAM, federal agency executive; b. Reading, Pa., June 29, 1944; s. Charles Edward and Esther Catherine (Weinhold) N.; m. Sarah Jane Anson, June 23, 1973; children: Jeffrey David, Gregory Michael. BA, U. Md., 1967; postgrad., Armed Forces Staff Coll., 1985. Packaging specialist U.S. Army Packaging Storage Ctr., Tobyhanna, Pa., 1973-80; program dir. Def. Logmars Program Office, Tobyhanna, 1980-82; supr. systems analyst Def. Depot Ops. Support Office, Richmond, Va., 1982-86; supr. systems analyst Office of Asst. Sec. Def., Washington, 1986-89, acting dir., 1989—. Webelos leader Boy Scouts Am., Fairfax, Va., 1989. With U.S. Army, 1968-71. Recipient Meritorious Civilian Svc. award U.S. Army, Tobyhanna, 1982, Bar Code Industry Achievement award Automatic Identification Mfrs., Pitts., 1982, Nat. Logistics award Nat. Inst. Packaging, Handling and Logistics Engrs., Washington, 1986. Mem. Am. Logistics Assn. (cert. phys. distbn. mgmt.), Soc. Logistics Engrs. (sr.), Am. Nat. Standards Inst. (com. chair 1981-83, author bar code symbols 1983). Presbyterian. Office: OASO C3I 1225 Jefferson Davis Hwy Arlington VA 22202-4301

NOLLAU, LEE GORDON, lawyer; b. Balt., Feb. 6, 1950; s. E. Wilson and Carolyn G. (Blass) N.; m. Carol A. Haughney, Aug. 12, 1978; children: Ann G., Catherine E., Margaret C. BA, Juniata Coll., 1972; MAS, Johns Hopkins U., 1975; JD, Dickinson Sch. Law, 1976. Bar: Pa. 1976, U.S. Dist. Ct. (mid. dist.) 1982, U.S. Dist. Ct. (we. dist.) 1988, U.S. Ct. Appeals (3d cir.) 1980, U.S. Supreme Ct. 1982. Instr. Juniata Coll., Huntingdon, Pa., 1976-78; asst. dist. atty. Centre County, Bellefonte, Pa., 1978-80, dist. atty., 1981; assoc. Litke, Lee, Martin, Grine & Green, Bellefonte, 1981-83, Jubelirer & Assocs., State College, Pa., 1983-87; ptnr. Jubelirer, Nollau, Young & Blanarik, Inc., State College, 1988-89, Jubelirer, Rayback, Nollau, Walsh, Young & Blanarik, Inc., State College, 1989—; mental health rev. officer Centre County, Bellefonte, 1982—. Mem. ABA, Pa. Bar Assn., Pa. Trial Lawyers Assn., Centre Bar Assn. Presbyterian. Office: Jubelirer Rayback Nollau Walsh Young & Blanarik Inc 102 E College Ave State College PA 16801-4708

NOLLEN, STANLEY DALE, business educator; b. Pella, Iowa, Nov. 18, 1940; s. Elmer James and Marie (Wanders) N.; m. Nancy Wilson, July 11, 1965; children: Timothy, Christine. BS, Iowa State U., 1963; MS, Cornell U., 1966; MBA, U. Chgo., 1970, PhD, 1974. Instr. Georgetown U., Washington, 1973-74, from asst. prof. to assoc. prof., 1974-90, prof., 1990—, assoc. dean, 1981-82; market analyst Dow Chem. Co., 1965-67; lectr. U. Ill., 1972; rsch. assoc. Spencer Found., 1972-73; academic vis. London Sch. of Economics, 1982-83; cons. to various orgns., 1975—. Author: (with Brenda Eddy and Virginia Martin) Permanent Part Time Employment: The Manager's Perspective, 1979, New Work Schedules in Practice: Managing Time in Changing Society, 1982; contbr. articles to profl. jours. Grantee U.S. Dept. Labor, 1975-76, Spencer Found., 1977, Carnegie Corp., 1980-81, Atlantic Richfield Found., 1982-83, Nat. Assn. Manufacturers, 1986-87, Pepsico, Inc, 1989, Westinghouse Electric Corp., 1989, NCR Corp., 1990, Georgetown U., 1990. Office: Georgetown U Sch Bus Adminstr Washington DC 20057

NOLTIE, DAVID MAYO, entrepreneur; b. Buffalo, Jan. 21, 1924; s. William Alonzo and Margaret Winifred (Mayo) N.; m. Doris Ann Bartolet, Sept. 11, 1948; children: Ann, Gary. BS in Econs., U. Pa., 1949. Co-founder, v.p. Alpha-Molykote div. Dow Corning, Stamford, Conn., 1951-64; pres. Greenwich (Conn.) Hardware, 1964-65; co-founder, pres. Interrad Corp., Greenwich, 1967-69; founder, chmn. Chronogram Corp., Greenwich, 1970-73, also bd. dirs.; pvt. practice cons., 1973-92; founder, chmn. DMN Internat., Inc., Spring Lake, N.J., 1992—, also bd. dirs. Bd. dirs. Greenwich Health Orgn., 1963-65. 1st lt. USAAF, 1942-45, Prisoner of War, Germany. Republican. Office: DMN Internat Inc PO Box 21 Spring Lake NJ 07762

NOONAN, MICHAEL DENNIS, lawyer; b. Rochester, N.Y., Mar. 23, 1941; s. John Francis Noonan and Catherine Teresa (Hock) Cartwright; m. Patricia Quinn, Sept. 30, 1967; children: Michael Jeffrey, Daniel Quinn, Mark Patrick. BSBA, Georgetown U., 1963; JD, Syracuse U., 1966. Bar: N.Y. 1966, Fla. 1974, D.C. 1978. Ptnr.-in-charge real estate sect. Mousaw, Vigdor, Reeves, Heilbronner & Kroll, Rochester, 1966-77; v.p., dep. gen. counsel, asst. sec. Nat. Corp. for Housing Partnerships, Washington, 1977-89; with HUD, Washington, 1989—; justice Town of Mendon (N.Y.) Ct., 1971-74. Mem. bd. Town of Mendon, 1971-74; bd. dirs. Day Care Tng. Ctr. for Handicapped Children, Rochester, 1969-77. Mem. ABA, N.Y. State Bar Assn., Fla. Bar Assn., D.C. Bar Assn., Washington Met. Area Corp. Counsel Assn. Republican. Roman Catholic. Home: 6710 Norview Ct Springfield VA 22152-3055 Office: HUD 451 7th St SW Washington DC 20410-0002

NOONAN, NORINE ELIZABETH, government science and space programs executive; b. Phila., Oct. 5, 1948; d. Alaric Edwin and Norine (Radford) Freeman . BA, summa cum laude, U. Vt., 1970; MA, Princeton U., 1972, PhD, 1976. Asst. prof. Coll. Vet. Medicine, U. Fla., Gainesville, 1976-81, assoc. prof., 1981; research assoc. prof. Georgetown U., Washington, 1981-82; Am. Chem. Soc. sci. fellow U.S. Senate Commerce Com., Washington, 1982-83; program and budget analyst Office Mgmt. and Budget, Washington, 1983-87, acting br. chief sci. and space programs, 1987-88, br. chief, 1988—; bd. advisors U.S. Found. for the Internat. Space U., 1989-90; lectr. program in sci. and tech. policy George Washington U.; disting. lectr. MITRE Corp. Inst., 1991. Contbr. articles to sci. jours. Vol. Balt. City Fair, 1982—. Soloist Roland Ave. Evergreen Ch. Choir. Bd. dirs. Wolf Trap Farm Pk. Assocs., Wolf Trap Farm Pk. for the Performing Arts, 1988—, exec. com. 1990—, exec. vice chmn., 1991-92, treas., 1992—; mem. adv. coun. Brookings Instn. Ctr. for Pub. Policy Edn., 1989—; treas. White House Athletic Ctr., Potomac Basset Hound Club. Recipient Spl. Performance award Office Mgmt. and Budget, 1987, 88; grantee Fla. div. Am. Cancer Soc., 1977, NIH, 1979, NSF, 1979. Mem. Am. Soc. Cell Biology, AAAS, Assn. Women in Sci. (membership chairperson 1981-82), Phi Beta Kappa (pres. Fla. chpt. 1980-81). Mem. United Ch. of Christ. Avocations: running, purebred dogs, gardening, cooking. Home: 2608 N Calvert St Baltimore MD 21218-4616 Office: Office Mgmt and Budget 725 17th St NW Washington DC 20503-0001

NOONAN, WILLIAM FRANCIS, public relations company executive; b. Irvington, N.J., Sept. 29, 1932; s. Thomas Leo and Rose Anna (O'Reilly) N.; m. Alyce K. Normoyle; 1 child, Jessica L.; children by previous marriage: William J., Thomas M., Robert P., Carol J. B.A. in Journalism, U. Notre Dame, 1954. Asst. promotion mgr. plastics div. Union Carbide Corp., N.Y.C., 1956-62; with Burson-Marsteller, N.Y.C., 1962—; account exec., account supr., group mgr. Burson-Marsteller, 1962-72, exec. v.p., gen. mgr. N.Y.C. office, 1972-83, pres./Americas, 1983-84, vice chmn., pres. internat., 1985-90; pres., chief operating officer N.Y. office Burston-Marsteller, from 1990, now vice chmn.; also bd. dirs. Burson-Marsteller. Served with U.S. Army, 1954-56. Roman Catholic. Office: Burson-Marsteller 230 Park Ave S New York NY 10003-1513

NOONE, BRIAN W., vocational rehabilitation counselor; b. Worcester, Mass., Sept. 26, 1948; s. John Francis Sr. and Ruth Elanor (Reidy) N. BS Edn., Fitchburg State Coll., 1970; MA, Anna Maria Coll., 1977. Cert. social studies, geography, history, distributive edn. tchr., cert. sch. psychologist; lic. cert. social worker. Social studies tchr. Worcester (Mass.) Pub. Schs., 1970-73; distributive edn. tchr.-coord. Bay Path Vocat. High Sch., Charlton, Mass., 1973-76; vocat. rehab. counselor Worcester Area Occupational Tng. Ctr., 1977-88, rehab. supr., 1988—; clinician Quinebaugh Valley Youth and Family Svcs., North Grosvenordale, Conn., 1986—. Bd. dirs. Youville House, Worcester, 1983-86, Spencer (Mass.) Pers. Bd., 1972, Stonegate Condominium Trust, Dudley, Mass., 1987-91. Mem. Nat. Rehab. Assn., AACD. Democrat. Roman Catholic.

NOONE, ROBERT BARRETT, plastic surgeon; b. Scranton, Pa., Oct. 30, 1939; s. Robert Patrick and Margaret Ann (Barrett) N.; m. Barbara Ellen Atkins, May 29, 1965; children: Robert B. Jr., Megan J., Genevieve C., Rebecca B., Theresa Ann. BS, U. Scranton, 1961; MD, U. Pa., 1965. Diplomate Am. Bd. Surgery, Am. Bd. Plastic Surgery. Rotating intern Hosp. of U. Pa., Phila., 1965-66, resident in surgery, 1966-71, resident in plastic surgery, 1971-73; asst. prof. surgery Sch. Medicine, U. Pa., Phila., 1974-83, clin. assoc. prof. surgery, 1983-89; clin. prof. surgery Sch. Medicine, U. Pa., 1989—; head sect. on plastic surgery Pa. Hosp., Phila., 1974-80; chief svc. plastic surgery Bryn Mawr Hosp., Bryn Mawr, Pa., 1977—, Lankenau Hosp., Phila., 1980-91; chmn. dept. surgery Bryn Mawr (Pa.) Hosp., 1991—; bd. dirs. Am. Bd. Plastic Surgery, Phila., 1987—, Plastic Surgery Ednl. Found., Chgo., 1981—, pres., 1989-90. Contbr. articles to profl. jours. Bd. dirs., trustee Rosemont (Pa.) Sch. of the Holy Child, 1983-87. Capt. USAF, 1967-69. Recipient Frank J. O'Hara Disting. Alumnus award U. Scranton, 1986. Fellow Am. Coll. Surgeons; mem. Am. Soc. Plastic and Reconstructive Surgery (bd. dirs. 1989-90), Northeastern Soc. Plastic Surgeons (pres. 1985-86), Robert H. Ivy Soc. (pres. 1982-83), AMA (del. plastic surgery 1986-88), Merion Cricket Club, Phila. Country Club. Republican. Roman

Catholic. Home: 234 Cheswold Hill Rd Haverford PA 19041-1814 Office: Plastic & Reconstructive Surg Assocs 888 Glenbrook Ave Bryn Mawr PA 19010-2506

NOONE, THOMAS MARK, business development consultant; b. New Inn, County Galway, Ireland, Apr. 25, 1927; came to U.S., 1968; s. Thomas and Celia (Martin) N.; m. Ruth Rosemary Angerbauer, Oct. 6, 1972. BSc in Chemistry with honors, U. Manchester, Eng., 1948, PhD, 1954, postgrad., 1950-54; MBA in Mktg., Northwestern U., 1972. Tech. officer I.C.I. Pharm. Div. Ltd., Manchester, 1948-50; rsch. officer The Shirley Inst., Manchester, 1954-58; head product devel. Colgate-Palmolive Ltd., Manchester, 1958-63; tech. dir. Mellowhide Products Ltd., Rochdale, Eng., 1963-68; rsch. assoc. The Richardson Co., Melrose Park, Ill., 1968-72; tech. mgr. Tenneco Chems., Rutherford, N.J., 1972-74; licensing assoc. Rsch. Corp., N.Y.C., 1975-84; pres. Noone Assocs., Teaneck, N.J., 1984—; pres. Chem. Mktg. and Econs. Group, N.Y.C., 1986-87; chmn. Commercial Devel. Assn., Inc., N.Y.C., 1987-90; mem. med. tech. adv. bd. New Life Health Products Corp., Morris Plains, N.J., 1986—. Fellow Royal Soc. Chemistry; mem. Am. Chem. Soc., Tech. Transfer Soc., Licensing Execs. Soc., Am. Inst. Chemists (chmn. 1982-84), Brit. Schs. and Univ. Club (pres. 1990-92), Assn. Cons. Chemists and Chem. Engrs. (pres. 1989-90). Roman Catholic. Office: Noone Assocs 813 Columbus Dr Teaneck NJ 07666-6612

NOORDERGRAAF, ABRAHAM, biophysics educator; b. Utrecht, Netherlands, Aug. 7, 1929; s. Leendert and Johanna (Kool) N.; m. Geertruida Alida Van Nee, Sept. 6, 1956; children: Annemiek,(Mrs. James A. Young), Gerrit Jan, Jeske Inette, Alexander Abraham. B.Sc., U. Utrecht, 1953, M.S., 1955, Ph.D., 1956; M.A. (hon.), U. Pa., 1971. Teaching asst. U. Utrecht, 1949-50, asst. dept. physics, 1951-53, research asst. dept. med. physics, 1953-55, research fellow dept. med. physics, 1956-58, sr. research fellow dept. med. physics, 1959-65; tchr. math. and physics Vereniging Nijverheidsonderwijs, Utrecht, 1951; research asst. U. Amsterdam, Netherlands, 1952; vis. fellow dept. therapeutic research U. Pa., Phila., 1957-58; assoc. prof. biomed. engring. Moore Sch. Elec. Engring., 1964-70, acting head electromed. div., 1968-69, prof. biomed. engring., 1970—; prof. physiology Sch. Vet. Medicine, 1976—, prof. Dutch culture Sch. Arts and Scis., 1983—; prof. medicine Med. Sch. U. Pa., 1990—; assoc. dir. biomed. engring. tng. program Moore Sch. Elec. Engring., 1971-76, asso. dir. sch., 1972-74, chmn. grad. group in biomed. electronic engring., 1973-75, chmn. dept. bioengring., 1973-76, chmn. grad. group bioengring., 1975-76, dir. systems and integrative biology tng. program, 1979-84; vis. prof. biomed. engring. U. Miami, 1970-79, Erasmus U. Med. Sch., Rotterdam, Netherlands, 1970-71, Tech. U., Delft, 1970-71, Polish Acad. Scis., Warsaw, 1975; mem. spl. study sect. NIH, 1966-68, mem. cardiovascular study sect., 1985-89; cons. sci. affairs div. NATO, 1973—; participant numerous internat. confs. in field. Author: (with I. Starr) Ballistocardiography in Cardiovascular Research, 1967, Circulatory System Dynamics, 1978; contbg. author: Biological Engineering, 1969; Editor: (with G.N. Jager and N. Westerhof) Circulatory Analog Computers, 1963, (with G.H. Pollack) Ballistocardiography and Cardiac Performance, 1967, (with E. Kresch) The Venous System: Characteristics and Function, 1969, (with J. Baan and J. Raines) Cardiovascular System Dynamics, 1978, (with Reichenbach-Consten) Two Hundred Years of Netherlands-American Interaction; sci. editor Biophysics and Bioengring. Series, 1976—; contbr. numerous articles to profl. jours.; Referee: Biophys. Jour., 1968—, Physics in Medicine and Biology, 1969—, Bull. Math. Biophysics, 1972-84, Circulation Research, 1973—; mem. editorial adv. bd.: Jour. Biomechanics, 1969-84; assoc. editor: Bull. Math. Biology, 1973-84. Vice pres. Haverford Friends Sch. PTA, 1968-70. Recipient S. Reid Warren Jr. award U. Pa. Sch. Engring. and Applied Sci., 1986, Christian and Mary Lindback award U. Pa., 1988. Fellow IEEE (mem. adminstrv. com. engring. in medicine and biology group 1967-70, mem. edn. com. group biomed. engring. 1968-70, sec. Phila. chpt. 1974-75, mem. regional council profl. group engring. in medicine and biology 1974-77), N.Y. Acad. Scis., AAAS, Explorers Club, Coll. Physicians Phila., Am. Coll. Cardiology, Royal Soc. Medicine London; mem. Nederlandse Natuurkundige Vereniging, Ballistocardiograph Research Soc. U.S.A. (sec.-treas. 1965-67, pres. 1968-70), Biophys. Soc. (charter), European Soc. for Noninvasive Cardiovascular Research (co-founder 1960, sec.-treas. 1960-61, mem. com. on nomenclature 1960-61, officer 1961-62, Herman C. Burger award 1978), Cardiovascular System Dynamics Soc. (co-founder 1976, pres. 1976-80, hon. life 1986), Franklin Inst., John Morgan Soc., Biomed. Engring. Soc. (founding mem., chmn. membership com. 1978-79, dir. 1972-75), Am. Heart Assn., Instrument Soc. Am. (sr. mem.), Soc. Math. Biology (charter mem.), Am. Physiol. Soc., Microcirculatory Soc., Am. Assn. Med. Systems and Informatics, Pa. Acad. Sci., Sigma Xi, Phi Zeta. Presbyterian. Home: 620 Haydock Ln Haverford PA 19041-1208 Office: U Pa 101 Hayden Hall Philadelphia PA 19104-6392

NOPPENBERGER, LOUIS JOHN, commercial banker; b. Balt., Oct. 6, 1963; s. John Louis and Mary Mildred (Murphy) N. BBA, Loyola Coll., Balt., 1985. Cert. cash mgr. Clk. Md. Nat. Bank, Balt., 1984-85, lending trainee, 1985-86, lending officer, 1986-90, sr. lending officer, credit officer, 1990—. Sec. Rainflower Condominium Assn. Named to Dean's List. Mem. Nat. Eagle Scout Assn., Treasury Mgmt. Assn., Balt. Econ. Soc. Republican. Roman Catholic. Home: 10 Rainflower Path Sparks Glencoe MD 21152-8713 Office: Md Nat Bank MS 250515 PO box 17271 Baltimore MD 21203

NORBACK, CRAIG THOMAS, author; b. Pitts., Nov. 14, 1943; s. Howard George and Maybelle Veronica Montaigne (Cosse) N.; m. Judith Carol Shaul, Oct. 12, 1976. BS, Washington U., St. Louis, 1967; postgrad., Drew U., 1986—. Author, co-author, compiler, producer over 150 books, including: The Misspeller's Dictionary, 1972, Everything You Can Get from the Government for Free or Almost for Free, 1975, The Dream Machine: The Golden Age of American Automobiles 1946-65, 1976, Great Songs of Madison Avenue, 1976, Great North American Indians, 1977, The Health Care Directory, 1977, The Older American's Handbook, 1977, The Educational Marketplace, 1978, Famous American Admirals, 1978, Newsweek Travel Guide to the U.S., 1978, The Dow Jones-Irwin Guide to Franchising, 1979, The Horseman's Catalog, 1979, The Must Words, 1979, The Practical Inventor's Handbook, 1979, ABC Complete Book of Sports Facts, 1980, ABC Monday Night Football, 1980-81, 1980, The Bible Almanac, 1980, Check Yourself Out, 1980, The Signet Book of World Winners, 1980, The TV Guide Almanac, 1980, The World's Great News Photos (1840-1980), 1980, The Allergy Encyclopedia, 1981, American Expressions, 1981, The Computer Invasion, 1981, The Consumer's Energy Handbook, 1981, 500 Questions New Parents Ask, 1982, Business Week Almanac, 1982, The International Yellow Pages, 1982, The Puzzle King's Bafflers, 1982, The Associated Press Sunday Crossword Puzzle Book, 1983, Chilton's Job Textbook Series: Advertising Management, 1983, Office Management, 1983, It's a Fact, 1983, National Education Association Parent and Child Success Library: Helping Your Child Read, 1983, How Letters Make Words, 1983, How to Prepare Your Child for School, 1983, Learning the Alphabet, 1983, Learning to Add, 1983, The Ultimate Toy Catalog, 1983, U.S. Publicity Directory, various years, Advertising and Promotion Management, 1983, America Wants to Know, 1983, Certified Professional Secretary modules I through VI, 1984, East Coast Publicity Directory, 1984, Human Resources Yearbook, 1987, 88, 89, 90, Princeton Area Job Finder, 1986-87, Career Encyclopedia, 1987, Travel Publicity Directory, 1987, 88, 89, 90, Arthur Young Guide to Venture Capital, 1987, Hazardous Chemicals on File, 1988, Joint Ventures, 1992, 250 Ways to Make Money, 1992, How to Get a Government Job, 1992, How to Get a Job Abroad, 1992, Outplacement Handbook, 1992, IBM Report, Toys R Us Report, United Nations Report, New York Times Report, 1992, others. Home: 814 Sturwood Way Trenton NJ 08648-1524

NORBECK, TIMOTHY BURNS, medical association executive; b. Buffalo, N.Y., June 29, 1938; s. Carl Francis N. and Helene Smith (Comstock) Browne; children: Carl, Kim, Karin; m. Michèle R. Mathieu, Mar. 24, 1990. BA, Hamilton Coll., 1960. Sales rep. Nat. Steel Corp., Detroit, Milw., Chgo., 1960-67; regional dir. AMA, Chgo., St. Louis, Chgo., 1967-73; exec. dir. R.I. Med. Soc., Providence, 1973-77, Conn. State Med. Soc., New Haven, 1977-; bd. dirs., treas. Conn. Med. Mgmt., Inc., Wallingford, 1984-; asst. treas. Conn. Med. Ins. Co., Wallingford, 1984--; cons. Vt. State Med. Soc., Montpelier, 1987; cons. R.I. Med. Soc., Providence, 1986. Contbr. articles profl. jours. chmn. bd. dirs. Am. Cancer Soc. Conn. Div., Wallingford, 1985-87, mem. nat. com. on field svcs., 1989—, bd. dirs. Conn. div.; bd. dirs. St. Louis County Narcotics Commn., 1967-70; bd. dirs. New Haven Regional Mental Health Assn., 1980-83; pres. Conn. Physicians Guild. Recipient nat. bronze medal, Am. Cancer Soc., 1987. Mem. Am. Soc. Assn. Execs., Am. Assn. Med. Soc. Execs. (bd. dirs.), Rotary. Democrat. Presbyterian. Home: 1400 Hartford Tpke Apt 16 North Haven CT 06473-2167 Office: Conn State Med Soc 160 St Ronan St New Haven CT 06511-2390

NORCINI, JOHN J., JR., medical association administrator; b. Apr. 30, 1952. BA in Psychology, LaSalle U., 1974; PhD in Child Devel., Bryn Mawr Coll., 1981. Rsch. interviewer, asst. Eagleville Hosp., 1975-77; data analyst Am. Bd. Internal Medicine, Phila., 1977-78, assoc. in psychometrics, 1978-81, asst. dir., head psychometric sect., 1981-85, dir. psychometrics, 1985-88, exec. v.p. for evaluation and rsch., dir. psychometrics, 1988—. Contbr. articles, revs. to profl. jours., chpts. to books; mem. editoral bd. Evaluation and the Health Professions. Mem. Am. Assn. Med. Colls., Am. Ednl. Rsch. Assn., Am. Psychol. Assn., Nat. Coun. on Measurement in Edn. Home: 2607 W Darby Rd Havertown PA 19083-1407 Office: Am Bd Internal Medicine University City Sci Ctr 3624 Market St Philadelphia PA 19104-2611

NORCROSS, JOHN CONNER, psychologist, educator; b. Camden, N.J., Aug. 13, 1957; s. George E. and Carol C.; m. Nancy A. Caldwell, June 25, 1981; children: Rebecca, Jonathan. BA, Rutgers U., 1980; MA, U. R.I., 1981, PhD, 1984. Lic. psychologist, Pa. Staff clinician U. R.I. Psychol. Cons. Ctr., 1980-84; clin. psychology intern Brown U. Sch. Medicine Consortium, 1984-85; rsch. fellow Self-Change Lab. U. R.I., 1982-86; pvt. practice clin. psychologist, 1986—; prof. psychology U. Scranton, Pa., 1985—; chmn. dept. U. Scranton, 1987—; vis. prof. U. Guadalajara, 1990; vis. fellow U. London, 1990. Author: Toward Integration: John Norcross in a Dialogue with Windy Dryden, 1991; co-author: Insider's Guide to Graduate Programs in Clinical Psychology, 1992; editor: Brunner/Mazel Integrative Psychotherapy Series, 1986—, Therapy Wars, 1990; co-editor: Handbook of Psychotherapy Integration, 1992; assoc. editor Jour. Psychotherapy Integration, 1990—; mem. editorial bd. 8 jours.; also over 100 articles. Recipient Faculty Equity award U. Scranton, 1989, 91. Fellow Internat. Acad. Eclectic Psychotherapists, Pa. Psychol. Assn.; mem. APA (Jack Krasner award 1992), Assn. for Advancement Psychology, Ea. Psychol. Assn., Soc. for Psychotherapy Rsch., Soc. for Clin. and Preventive Psychology, Am. Evaluation Assn. (charter), Soc. for Exploration Psychotherapy Integration (charter), Sigma Xi, Psi Chi. Home: PO Box 463F Lake Ariel PA 18436-0463 Office: U Scranton Dept Psychology Scranton PA 18510-4596

NORDEN, PETER CHRISTOPHER, title insurance company official; b. Oceanside, N.Y., Apr. 21, 1949; s. Jack Jr. and Ellinor (Goldstein) N.; m. Roberta E. Feiden, Dec. 25, 1971 (div. 1973); m. Rhonda D. Phillips, Sept. 25, 1983. BA, Southampton Coll., 1970; MBA, Suffolk U., 1983. Asst. to pres. Mass. Title Ins. Co., Boston, 1972-75; mgr. Am. Title Ins. Co., Boston, 1975-78; regional v.p. 1st Am. Title Ins Co., Boston, 1978—. Contbr. articles to profl. jours. Mem. Am. Land Title Assn. (edn. com. 1987—), New Eng. Land Title Assn. (pres. 1985), Mass. Mortgage Bankers Assn., Mass. Conveyancers Assn., Nat. Assn. Indsl. and Office Parks, Nat. Assn. Corp. Real Estate Execs. Republican. Jewish. Home: 6 Wentworth Dr Southborough MA 01772-4008 Office: 1st Am Title Ins Co 10 Post Office Sq Boston MA 02109

NORDENBERG, MARK ALAN, legal educator, college dean; b. Duluth, Minn., July 12, 1948; s. John Clemens and Shirley Mae (Tappen) N.; m. Nikki Patricia Pirillo, Dec. 26, 1970; children: Erin, Carl, Michael. BA, Thiel Coll., 1970; JD, U. Wis., 1973. Bar: Wis. 1973, Minn. 1974, U.S. Supreme Ct. 1976, Pa. 1985. Atty. Gray, Plant, Mooty & Anderson, Mpls., 1973-75; prof. law Capital U. Law Ctr., Columbus, Ohio, 1975-77; prof. law U. Pitts., 1977—, acting dean Sch. Law, 1985-87, dean Sch. Law, 1987—; mem. U.S. Supreme Ct.'s Adv. Com. on Civil Rules, Washington, 1988—, Pa. Supreme Ct.'s Civil Procedure Rules Com., Phila., 1986—; reporter civil justice adv. group U.S. Dist. Ct., Pitts. Author: Modern Pennsylvania Civil Practice, 1985. Trustee Thiel Coll., Greenville, Pa., 1987—; bd. dirs. Lawyers Concerned for Lawyers of Pa., Harrisburg. Mem. ABA, Pa. Bar Assn., Allegheny County Bar Assn., Acad. Trial Lawyers Allegheny County, Univ. Club. Office: U Pitts Law Sch 3900 Forbes Ave Pittsburgh PA 15260-0001

NORDENSON, GUY JÉRÔME PIERRE, structural engineer, educator; b. Neuilly/Seine, France, May 15, 1955; came to U.S., 1959; s. Lars Harald and Charlotte Auguste (Weil) N. BSc, MIT, 1977; MSc, U. Calif., Berkeley, 1978. Registered structural engr., Calif., registered profl. engr., Calif. Draftsman Fuller/Sadao and Noguchi Fountains Inc., Long Island City, N.Y., 1975-76; engr. Forell/Elsesser Engrs., San Francisco, 1978-82; assoc. Weidlinger Assocs., N.Y.C., 1982-87; prin. Ove Arup & Ptnrs., N.Y.C., 1987—; lectr. Parsons Sch. Design, N.Y.C., 1983-87; adj. prof. Columbia U. Grad. Sch. Architecture, N.Y.C., 1985—. Mem. ASCE, Earthquake Engring. Rsch. Inst., Archtl. League N.Y. (bd. dirs. 1989—), N.Y. Acad. Scis., Reform Club (London), Racing Club de France (Paris), Eagle Club (Gstaad, Switzerland, life). Home: 299 W 12th St New York NY 10014-1801 Office: Ove Arup & Ptnrs 155 6th Ave New York NY 10013-1507

NORDQUIST, MYRON HARRY, lawyer; b. Kalispell, Mont., Oct. 22, 1940; s. Harry and Guida (Sorenson) N.; m. Barbara Kay Altpeter, Dec. 28, 1967; children: Nels, Silvy, Ingrid. BS, Oreg. State U., 1966; JD, Calif. Western U., San Diego, 1969; SJD, U. Va., 1977. Bar: Calif. 1970, D.C. 1975, Mass. 1983. Atty. Office of Legal Adviser, U.S. Dept. State, Washington, 1970-77; ptnr. Nossaman, Krueger & Marsh, Washington, 1978-82, Duncan, Allen & Mitchell, Washington, 1982-83, Herrick & Smith, Washington, 1984-85, Kelley, Drye & Warren, Washington, 1985-89; pres. Core Corp., Washington, 1989-90; dep. gen. counsel Dept. Air Force, Washington, 1990—. Editor: (books) New Directions in Law of the Sea, 1970-78, Commentary: 1982 Convention on Law of the Sea, 1985—; editor-in-chief Annual Proc. Mem. Ctr. for Oceans Law and Policy, U. Va., Charlottesville, 1978—. Capt. USMC, 1966-69, Vietnam. Office: Dept Air Force 4E856 The Pentagon Washington DC 20330

NORDQUIST, STEPHEN GLOS, lawyer; b. Mpls., May 13, 1936; s. Oscar Alvin Nordquist and Georgiana (Glos) Ruplin; m. Cynthia Alexandra Turner, Aug. 16, 1958 (div. Aug. 1967); children: Darcy Alden, Timothy Turner; m. Regina Frances Stanton, Nov. 1, 1969; 1 child, Nicholas Alden. BA cum laude, U. Minn., 1958, LL.B cum laude, 1961. Bar: Minn. 1961, N.Y. 1962. Assoc. Dewey, Ballantine, Bushby, Palmer & Wood, N.Y.C., 1961-69, ptnr., 1969-85; sr. v.p. W.P. Carey & Co., Inc., N.Y.C., 1985-86, exec. v.p., sec., 1986-87; ptnr. Cole & Deitz (now Winston & Strawn), N.Y.C., 1988-89; of counsel Dreyer and Traub, N.Y.C., 1990-91; pres., bd. dirs. Carey Corp. Property, Inc., Carey-Longmont Inc., Carey-Longmont Real Property, Inc., N.Y.C., 1985-87, 520 East 86th Street, Inc. Mem. Knickerbocker Club (house com.), World Trade Ctr. Club, Club 101. Republican. Congregationalist. Home and Office: 211 E 53rd St Apt 3K New York NY 10022

NOREIKA, SOFIA, real estate broker, owner; b. Naples, Italy, Aug. 20, 1945; d. Antonio and Anna (Gambardella) DeFelice; m. Peter Charles Noreika, Apr. 29, 1972; children: Timothy J., Steven P. Student, Greater Hartford Community Coll., 1970-71; real estate sales lic., U. Conn., 1980, diploma in real estate appraisal, 1985; diploma in real estate finance, 1988. Hostess Holiday Season Restaurant, Waterbury, Conn., 1974-79; owner Sofia Tops Plus, Woodbury, Conn., 1979-84; realtor RE/MAX Properties Unltd., Southbury, Conn., 1984-88; owner Action Realty, Watertown, Conn., 1988—; land developer, Watertown, 1987; dir. Multiple Listing Svc. Greater Waterbury, Inc., 1990—. Den mother Boy Scouts Am., Bethlehem, Conn., 1980-83; vol. Bethlehem Elem. Sch., 1980-85; fund raiser Little League Baseball, Bethlehem, 1983-85, United Way, 1989; sponsor Greater Watertown, 1989; dir. Multiple Listing Svc. of Greater Waterbury, Inc., 1990—. Mem. Waterbury Bd. Realtors, Nat. Assn. Realtors, Conn. Assn. Realtors, Multiple Listing Svc., RE/MAX Hundred Percent Club, RE/MAX Internat. Referral Network. Republican. Roman Catholic. Home: 132 Carriage Dr Middlebury CT 06762-1928 Office: Action Realty 671 Main St Watertown CT 06795-2625

NORFLEET, BRUCE GERARD, journalist, associate producer; b. San Antonio, May 11, 1959; s. Robert G. and Barbara J. (Cunningham) N.; m. Cynthia I. Van Cleef, June 6, 1987. BS in Wildlife Ecology, U. Wis., 1984. Asst. editor Nat. Wildlife Fedn., Washington, 1984-85; researcher, writer, cons. office of elem. and secondary edn. Smithsonian Instn., Washington, 1985, spl. events coor. Nat. Zool. Park, 1985, 86; ind. researcher Norwegian Marshall FUnd, Trondheim, Norway, 1985-86; researcher World Mag. Nat. Geographic Soc., Washington, 1986-89, asst. researcher TV, 1989-92, assoc. prodr., 1992—. Recipient Disting. Achievement award Edn. Press Assn. Am., 1988, 89, Gold award Houston Internat. Film Festival, 1990, Emmy award NATAS, 1989. Office: Nat Geographic TV 1615 M St NW Washington DC 20036-3209

NORIN, ALLEN J., scientist; b. Chgo., July 30, 1944; s. Nathan and Ada (Axelrod) N.; m. Harriett R. Wolf, Aug. 10, 1969; children: Lary, Andy. Student, Wright Jr. Coll., 1963-65; BS, Roosevelt U., 1965-67; MS, U. Houston, 1967-69, PhD, 1969-72. Rsch. assoc. microbiology dept. U. Chgo., 1972-75; asst. prof. Montefiore Med. Ctr. Albert Einstein Coll. Medicine, Bronx, N.Y., 1976-84, assoc. prof., 1985-88; assoc. prof. SUNY Health Sci. Ctr., Bklyn., 1988-90; prof. medicine, anatomy and cell biology Health Sci. Ctr. SUNY, Bklyn., 1990—, dir. transplantation immunology and immunogenetics, 1990—; mem. histocompatibility com. N.Y. Regional Transplant Program, N.Y.C., 1990—, standards com., 1990—. Contbr. numerous articles to profl. jours. NIH grantee, 1977-92. Mem. AAAS, Am. Assn. Immunologists, Am. Soc. Microbiology, N.Y. Acad. Sci., Am. Soc. Histocompatibility and Immunogenetics. Office: SUNY Health Sci Ctr 450 Clarkson Ave # 1197 Brooklyn NY 11203-2098

NORKO, MICHAEL ALBERT, psychiatrist; b. Perth Amboy, N.J., Jan. 26, 1957; s. Albert John and Anne (Yanik) N.; m. Debra Ann Brown, May 19, 1985; children: John Michael, Joanna Elizabeth. BA in Natural Sci., Johns Hopkins U., 1979; MD, SUNY Upstate Med. Ctr., Syracuse, 1983; cert. mental health adminstrn., New Sch. Social Rsch., 1987. Diplomate, Am. Bd. Psychiatry and Neurology. Intern St. Vincent's Hosp. and Med. Ctr., N.Y.C., 1983-84; resident in psychiatry St. Vincent's Hosp. and Med. Ctr., 1984-87; postdoctoral fellow in forensic psychiatry Yale U., New Haven, 1987-88, clin. instr. dept. psychiatry, 1988-90, asst. clin. prof. psychiatry, 1990—; unit chief Whiting Forensic Inst., Middletown, Conn., 1988-92, assoc. dir., 1992—; pvt. practice forensic psychiatry, 1988-92; assoc. dir. Whiting Forensic Inst., Middletown, Conn., 1992—. Contbr. articles to med. jours. Mem. Am. Psychiat. Assn., Conn. Psychiat. Soc., Am. Acad. Psychiatry and Law (Rappeport fellow 1986), Am. Fedn. Musicians, Physicians for Social Responsibility (co-founder, media contact Broome County chpt. 1982-83). Roman Catholic. Office: Whiting Forensic Inst PO Box 70 Middletown CT 06457-0070

NORLIST See LUST, ELENORE

NORMAN, MARSHA, playwright; b. Louisville, Sept. 21, 1947; d. Billie Lee and Bertha Mae (Conley) Williams. B.A., Agnes Scott Coll., 1969; M.A.T., U. Louisville, 1971. Author: (plays) Getting Out, 1977 (John Gassner New Playwrights Medallion, Outer Critics Circle), Third and Oak, 1978, Circus Valentine, 1979, The Holdup, 1980, 'Night, Mother, 1982 (Pulitzer prize 1983, Blackburg prize 1982), Traveler in the Dark, 1984; author book of musical, also lyricist The Secret Garden, 1991 (Tony award 1991); author book of musical The Fortune Teller, 1987; (collection) Four Plays by Marsha Norman, 1988, Sarah and Abraham, 1987, D. Boone, 1992. Nat. Endowment for Arts grantee, 1978-79; Rockefeller playwright-in-residence grantee, 1979-80; Am. Acad. and Inst. for Arts and Letters grantee. Office: Jack Tantleff 375 Greenwich St Ste 700 New York NY 10013-2338

NORQUIST, GROVER GLENN, economist; b. Sharon, Pa., Oct. 19, 1956; s. Warren Elliott and Carol (Lutz) N. BA, Harvard Coll., 1978; MBA, Harvard U., 1981. Exec. dir. Nat. Taxpayers Union, Washington, 1978-79, Coll. Rep. Nat. Com., Washington, 1981-82, Ams. for Reagan Agenda, Washington, 1982-83; chief speechwriter U.S. C. of C., Washington, 1983-85; field dir. Citizens for Am., Washington, 1985; founder, pres. Ams. for Tax Reform, Washington, 1985—; econ. adviser UNITA, Angola, 1985-88; cons. Right to Work Com., Washington, 1990, 91, Citizens Against Govt. Waste, Washington, 1988—, Baltic Am. Freedom League, Washington, 1991. Speechwriter DuPont for Pres. Campaign, Washington, 1987; issues mgr. Bush for Pres. Campaign, Washington, 1988; lectr. Krieble Found., Albania, Romania, 1992; advisor Tory Party Scotland, 1989. Home: 718 North Carolina Ave SE Washington DC 20003 Office: Ams for Tax Reform 1301 Connecticut Ave NW Ste 444 Washington DC 20036

NORRGARD, LEE EDWARD, investigative analyst, consumer affairs advocate; b. Mpls., Mar. 31, 1945; s. Elmer Theodore and Hazel (Johnson) N.; m. Sandra Marie Fallin, July 20, 1974; children: Elayne, Jacob. Student, Tuskegee U., 1965; BA, St. Olaf Coll., 1967. Asst. to pres. Ill. Union Social Svc. Employees, Chgo., 1972-75; exec. dir. Common Cause-Ill., Chgo., 1975-78; chief investigator Better Govt. Assn., Chgo. and Washington, 1978-84; sr. editor Common Cause Mag., Washington, 1984-85; investigative analyst Am. Assn. Ret. Persons, Washington, 1985—; chmn. adv. com. Nat. Assn. Ins. Commrs., Kansas City, Mo., 1987. Co-author: Final Choices: Making End-of-Life Decisions, 1992; author consumer brochures (recipient Ten Best award FDA 1990); contbr. articles to profl. jours. Democrat. Mem. Unitarian Ch. Office: AARP 601 E St NW Washington DC 20049-0002

NORRIS, CHARLES HEAD, JR., lawyer, financial executive; b. Boston, Sept. 14, 1940; s. Charles Head and Martha Marie N.; B.A., U. Pa., 1963, J.D., 1968; M.A., U. Wash., 1965; m. Diana D. Strawbridge, July 27, 1974; 1 dau., Margaret Dorrance. Bar: Pa. 1968. Mem. firm Morgan, Lewis & Bockius, Phila., 1968-77; pres., chief exec. Artemis Corp., 1978-79; chmn. bd., chief exec., 1979-91; chmn. exec. com., vice chmn. bd. Remington Rand Corp., 1979-81; ptnr. Artemis Energy Co., 1980—; trustee maj. stockholders' voting trust Campbell Soup Co., 1987-90; bd. dirs. SBSF Funds, Inc., 1988-91, del. trust, 1987-91. Bd. dirs. Meridian Bancorp Inc., Asprey & Co. Ltd., Margaret Dorrance Strawbridge Found. Pa. II, Soc. Four Arts; mem. Harvard U. Bd. Overseas Com. to Visit the Libr., 1989—; mem. Pa. Commn. Crime and Delinquency, 1980-84; mem. Thouron Award Selection Com., 1985-90; mem. Pa. Electoral Coll., 1980; mem. West Pikeland Twp. Suprs., 1969-72; mem. bd. visitors Carnegie Mellon U. Sch. Urban and Pub. Affairs, 1988-90; corp. mem. Belmont Hill Sch., 1990—. Officer USAF, 1959. Mem. ABA, Pa. Bar Assn., Am. Econ. Assn. Clubs: Phila., Seminole Golf, Knickerbocker, Bath and Tennis (bd. dirs., officer 1982-91), Union League, Vicmead Hunt, Everglades (bd. dirs. 1986-91), Wilmington Country; Sunningdale Golf (Eng.); The Country (Brookline). Office: PO Box 120 Wayne PA 19087-0120

NORRIS, CURTIS BIRD, writer, journalist; b. Quincy, Mass., July 14, 1927; s. Lowell Ames and Helen (Curtis) N.; m. Eileen Patricia Schindler, Mar. 23, 1959; children: Katharine Eileen, Helen Carolyn, Suzanne Elizabeth. AB, Middlebury Coll., 1951; postgrad., Bridgewater (Mass.) State Coll., 1986—. Free-lance writer, 1945—; writer Sikorsky Aircraft Co., Stratford, Conn., 1957-59, N.Am. Aviation, Downey, Calif., 1959-61; editor Hughes Aircraft Co., Fullerton, Calif., 1961-62, Whitman (Mass.) News, 1962-65; sci. writer U. Vt., 1965-66; editor Wareham (Mass.) Courier, 1966-69; med. sci. editor Brown U., Providence, 1969-77; dir. pub. affairs Stonehill Coll., North Easton, Mass., 1977-83; staff columnist Quincy (Mass.) Patriot Ledger, 1982—; dir. Bridgewater State Coll., 1985-87; indsl. rels. dir. Morgan Meml. Goodwill Industries, Boston, 1987-89; instr. Stonehill Coll., North Easton, 1991—; lectr., feature writer Boston Sunday Herald-Traveler, 1963-76, Yankee mag., 1963—; staff investigative reporter Globe Communications, Montreal, Can., 1973—; bd. dirs. pub. rels. programs Composite Tech. Alloys Co., Attleboro, Mass., 1975—; coord. Ea. Writers Conf., Salem, Mass., 1982; cons. pub. rels., 1983—; instr. Stonehill Coll., 1991. Author: Seldom Heard Tales of New England, 1964, Little Known Mysteries of New England, 1992; assoc. editor: Stonehill Alumni News, 1977-81; editor: Stonehill Rev., 1977-83; originator: (TV programs) Health Call, Science Call, Providence; producer: (cable TV program) Seldom Heard Tales of New Eng., 1986-88; represented in anthologies including Yankees Under Steam, 1970, Mysterious New England, 1971, Danger, Disaster and Horrid Deeds, 1974, Best Detective Cases, 1975-77, True Police Yearbook, 1975, 77, Startling Detective Yearbook, 1975-77, The World Wars Remembered, 1979, Best of Old Farmers Almanac, 1991; author manuscripts in Norris Collection, Brown U.; contbr. numerous stories to mags., TV Unsolved Mysteries, 1989. Chmn. publicity Wareham chpt. Am. Cancer Soc., 1966, community chmn.,

1967-69; assoc. mem. Federated Ea. Indian League; bd. dirs. Opera New Eng. of Greater Brockton. With USAAF, 1945-47; capt. Mass. N.G. Recipient Grand award Coun. Advancement and Support of Edn., 1976-77. Mem. New Eng. Press Assn., Am. Defenders of Bataan and Corregidor, Am. Med. Writers Assn., Assn. Am. Med. Colls., Mystery Writers Am., State Def. Force Assn. of the U.S., Kappa Delta Rho. Unitarian. Home: 166 E Main St Norton MA 02766-2310 Office: Morgan Meml Goodwill Industries 1010 Harrison Ave Roxbury MA 02119-2500

NORRIS, FLOYD HAMILTON, financial journalist; b. L.A., Sept. 6, 1947; s. Floyd H. and Martha Leota (Buntin) N.; m. Mary Christine Bockelmann, Oct. 5, 1984. Student, U. Calif., Irvine, 1965-68; MBA, Columbia U., 1982. Reporter Coll. Press Svc., Washington, 1969-70, Manchester (N.H.) Am., 1970-72, Concord (N.H.) Monitor, 1972-74, UPI, Vt. and Ala., 1974-77; press sec. Sen. John Durkin, Washington, 1977-78; fin. writer AP, N.Y.C., 1978-81; columnist Barron's, N.Y.C., 1982-88; fin. columnist N.Y. Times, N.Y.C., 1988—. Office: N Y Times 229 W 43rd St New York NY 10036

NORRIS, JOHN ANTHONY, business executive, federal official, lawyer, editor, educator; b. Buffalo, Dec. 27, 1946; s. Joseph D. and Maria L. (Suite) N.; m. Kathleen E. Mullen, July 13, 1969; children: Patricia Marie, John Anthony II, Joseph Mullen, Mary Kathleen, Elizabeth Mary. BA, U. Rochester, 1968; JD, MBA with honors, Cornell U., 1973; cert., Harvard U. Sch. Govt., 1986. Bar: Mass. 1973. Assoc. Peabody, Brown, Boston, 1973-75; assoc. Powers Hall, Boston, 1975-76, ptnr., mem. exec. com., 1976-80, v.p., dir., 1979-80, chmn. adminstrv. com., 1976-79, chmn. hiring com., 1979-80; chmn. bd., pres., chief exec. officer, founder Norris & Norris, Boston, 1980-85; dep. commr. and chief operating officer FDA, Washington, 1985-88, chmn. action planning and cap coms., 1985-88, chmn. reye syndrome com., 1985-87, chmn. trade legis. com., 1987-88; corporate exec. v.p. Hill & Knowlton, Inc., N.Y.C., 1988—; worldwide dir. Health Scis. Cons. Group., 1988—, chmn. health scis. policy coun., 1989—; mem. faculty Tufts Dental Sch., 1974-79, Boston Coll. Law Sch., 1976-80, Boston U. Law Sch., 1979-83, Harvard U. Public Health Sch., 1988—; mem. bd. editors FDA Drug Bulletin and FDA Consumer Report, 1985-88. Founder, faculty editor-in-chief Am. Jour. Law and Medicine, 1973-81, emeritus 1981—; editor-in-chief Cornell Internat. Law Jour., 1971-73; reviewer New Eng. Jour. Medicine Law-Medicine Notes, 1980-81; assoc. editor Medicolegal News, 1973-75. Mem. U.S. Del. to Japan (chmn.), Austria, Saudi Arabia, 1987, mem., chmn. Finland, Denmark, Italy, 1986; chmn. Mass. Statuatory Adv. Com. on Regulation of Clin. Labs., 1977-83; chmn. Boston Alumni and Scholarship Com., U. Rochester, 1979-85; mem. trustees council U. Rochester, 1979-85; mem. exec. com. Cornell Law Sch. Assn., 1982-85; mem. Mass. Gov.'s Blue Ribbon Task Force on DON, 1979-80, bd. trustees Jordan Hosp., 1978-80, mem. exec. com., 1979-80, chmn., chief exec. officer search com., 1980; chmn. Joseph D. Norris Health, Law and Pub. Policy Fund, 1979—; chmn. bd. Boston Holiday Project, 1981-83; mem. U.S. Pres. Chernobyl Task Force, 1986, vice-chmn. health affects sub-com.; mem. U.S. Intra-Govtl. AIDS Task Force, 1987; mem. IOM Drug Devel. Forum, 1986—, co-chmn. end points sub-com., 1987-88, Fed. Pain Commn., 1984-85. With U.S. Army, 1972-73, with res. Fed. Comprehensive Health Planning fellow, 1970-73; recipient Kansas City Hon. Key award, 1988, Nat. Health Fraud Conf. award, 1988, TOYL award, 1982, FDA Award of Merit, 1987, 88, PHS award, 1987, HHS Sec. award, 1988. Mem. ABA (vice chmn. medicine and law com. 1977-80), Mass. Bar Assn., Am. Soc. Hosp. Attys., Nat. Health Lawyers, Am. Soc. Law and Medicine (1st v.p. 1975-80, chmn. bd. 1981-84, life mem. award 1981), Soc. Computer Applications to Med. Care (mem. bd. 1984-85), Phi Kappa Phi. Home: 531 W Washington St Hanson MA 02341-1020

NORRIS, SUSAN BEATRICE PRIESS, priest; b. Jefferson City, Mo., Mar. 23, 1943; d. Harold Edwin Oswald and Alice Elizabeth (Anderson) Priess; m. Kenneth Scott Norris, Aug. 20, 1966; children: Anne-Elizabeth Mary, John Christopher Philip. BSM, DePauw U., 1965; SMM, Union Theol. Sem., 1968; MDiv, Drew U., 1981; postgrad., Gen. Theol. Sem., 1983-86. Seminarian Ascension Parish, Jersey City, N.J., 1979-81, Ch. of the Redeemer, Morristown, N.J., 1981-83, St. Paul's Episcopal Ch., Westfield, N.J., 1983-86; asst. min. St. John's Episcopal Ch., Elizabeth, N.J., 1986-87; pastoral assoc. Grace Episcopal Ch., Plainfield, N.J., 1987—; chaplain oncology Overlook Hosp., Summit, N.J., 1979-83; chair com. on lang and liturgy Episcopal Diocese of N.J., 1989-90, mem. com. on constitution and canons, 1988—; mem. com. on unified budget, supr. of field work Gen. Theol. Sem., N.Y.C., 1990—. Mem. Sierra Club, Conservation Internat., Nature Conservancy (N.J. chpt.), Planned Parenthhod, Nat. Abortion Rights League. Mem. Episcopal Women's Caucus (pres. 1988-90), Alpha Gamma Delta (rec. sec. 1964-65). Democrat. Home: 1027 Myrtle Ave Plainfield NJ 07063-1119 Office: Grace Episcopal Church 600 Cleveland Ave Plainfield NJ 07060-1727

NORROD, JAMES DOUGLAS, computer subsystems company executive; b. Detroit, Feb. 18, 1948; s. Charles Douglas and Bonnie Gene (Phillips) N.; m. Vickie Carolyn Newsom, Aug. 23, 1969; children: Heather Victoria, April Elizabeth. BS cum laude, Oakland U., Rochester, Mich., 1970; MBA, U. Detroit, 1975. Sales rep. IBM Corp., Detroit, 1970-77, mktg. mgr., 1977-80; v.p. Auto-trol Tech. Corp., Denver, 1980-86; pres., chief exec. officer CGX Corp., Acton, Mass., 1986-87, Adage, Inc., Billerica, Mass., 1987—. Republican. Home: 161 Ember Ln Carlisle MA 01741-1309 Office: Emerald Systems Corp 12230 World Trade Dr San Diego CA 92128 also: Octocom Systems Inc 1 Executive Dr Chelmsford MA 01824

NORTH, HALSEY M., arts management consultant; b. Buffalo, Feb. 15, 1947; s. William Miller and Carolyn (Brown) N.; m. Alice Henderson, Dec. 31, 1971. BA in Econs., Earlham Coll., 1970; MBA, Rollins Coll., 1971; postgrad., Harvard U., 1973. Mng. producer Little Theatre WInston-Salem, N.C., 1971-74; exec. dir. N.C. Arts Coun., Raleigh, 1974-76, Arts and Sci. Coun., Charlotte, N.C., 1976-79; mgr. corp. contbns. Philip Morris Co., N.Y.C., 1979-80; v.p., mgmt. and fundraising cons. C.W. Shaver & Co., N.Y.C., 1980-83; exec. dir. Cultural Coun. Found., N.Y.C., 1983-87; chmn. The North Group Inc., N.Y.C., 1987—; bd. dirs. theatre arts sect. N.C. Dept. Cultural Resources, 1973-74, So. Fedn. State Arts Agys., 1974-76, N.C. Shakespeare Festival, 1977-79, Nat. Assembly Local Arts Agys., 1978-81; treas. N.C. Assn. Arts Couns., 1976-78, Empire State Crafts Alliance, 1984-88; exec. com. Assn. Performing Arts Presenters, 1976-78, bd. dirs., 1976-81, treas., 1979-81; steering com. N.Y.C. Arts Coalition, 1985-87; panelist N.Y. State Coun. on Arts, 1986-88, Nat. Endowment Arts, 1988-89, 92, N.J. State Coun. on Arts, 1990-91. Contbr. to profl. pubis.

NORTH, LEX, marketing and communications administrator; b. Alstonville, Australia, Nov. 17, 1931; came to U.S., 1961; s. Alec and Mary Elizabeth (Mackney) N. BA, Pasadena Playhouse, 1962; AA, Monterey, 1966. Design asst. Abraham, Straus, Bklyn., 1967-73, Montgomery Ward, Kingston, N.Y., 1973-79, Gimbels, N.Y.C., 1979-84; design publicity, advt. Eastman Chem. Co., N.Y.C., 1984-92, supr. mktg. and corp. communications, 1992—. Mem. Pub. Relations Soc. Am. Republican. Presbyterian. Home: PO Box 162 Mount Marion NY 12456-0162 Office: Eastman Chem Co 1133 Ave Of The Americas New York NY 10036-6710

NORTHROP, EDWARD SKOTTOWE, federal judge; b. Chevy Chase, Md., June 12, 1911; s. Claudian Bellinger and Eleanor Smythe (Grimke) N.; m. Barbara Middleton Burdette, Apr. 22, 1939; children: Edward M., St. Julien (Mrs. Kevin Butler), Peter. LL.B., George Washington U., 1937. Bar: Md. 1937. Village mgr. Chevy Chase, Md., 1934-41; pvt. practice Rockville, Md., Washington, D.C., 1937-61; mem. Md. Senate, 1954-61, chmn. fin. com., majority leader, 1959-61; judge U.S. Dist. Ct. Md., Balt., 1961—; chief judge U.S. Dist. Ct. of Md., Balt., 1970-81; mem. Met. Chief Judges Conf., 1970-81; mem. Jud. Conf. Com. on Adminstrn. of Probation System, 1973-79, Adv. Corrections Council U.S., 1976—, Jud. Panel on Multidist. Litigation, 1979—; judge U.S. Fgn. Intelligence Surveillance Ct. of Rev., 1985—. Trustee Woodberry Forest Sch.; founder Washington Met. Area Coun. Govts. & Mass Transp. Agy. Served to comdr. USNR, 1941-45. Recipient Profl. Achievement award George Washington U., 1975, Disting. Citizen award State of Md., 1981, Spl. Merit citation Am. Judicature Soc., 1982. Mem. ABA, Md. Bar Assn. (Disting. Svc. award 1982), D.C. Bar Assn., Montgomery County Bar Assn., Barristers, Washington Ctr. Met. Studies. Democrat. Episcopalian. Club: Chevy Chase (Md.). Lodge: Rotary. Office: US Dist Ct 101 W Lombard St Baltimore MD 21201-2626

NORTHRUP, HERBERT ROOF, economist, business executive; b. Irvington, N.J., Mar. 6, 1918; m. Eleanor Pearson, June 3, 1944; children: James Pearson, Nancy Warren, Jonathan Peter, David Oliver, Philip Wilson. A.B., Duke U., 1939; A.M., Harvard U., 1941, Ph.D., 1942. Instr. econs. Cornell U., 1942-43; sr. hearing officer Nat. War Labor Bd., 1943-45; asst. prof. econs. Columbia U., 1945-49; labor economist Nat. Indsl. Conf. Bd., 1949-52; indsl. relations cons. Ebasco Services, 1952-55; v.p. indsl. relations Penn-Texas Corp., N.Y.C., 1955-58; employee relations mgr. Gen. Electric Co., 1958-61; prof. industry Wharton Sch., U. Pa., Phila., 1961-88; prof. emeritus Wharton Sch. U. Pa., Phila., 1988—; chmn. dept. industry Wharton Sch., U. Pa., 1964-69, dir. indsl. research unit, 1964-88, chmn. Labor Relations Council, 1968-85; cons. and expert witness on manpower, pers. and labor rels. problems for many cos.; arbitrator in labor rels. disputes. Author: Organized Labor and the Negro, 1944, Unionization of Professional Engineers and Chemists, 1946, Economics of Labor Relations, 1950, 9th edit., 1981, Government and Labor, 1963, Readings in Labor Economics, 1963, Boulwarism: Labor Policies of General Electric Company, 1964, Negro and Employment Opportunity, 1965, Hours of Labor, 1965, Compulsory Arbitration and Government Intervention in Labor Disputes, 1966, Restrictive Labor Practices in Supermarket Industry, 1967, Negro in the Automobile Industry, 1968, Negro in the Aerospace Industry, 1968, Negro in the Rubber Tire Industry, 1969, Negro in Paper Industry, 1969, Negro in the Tobacco Industry, 1970, Negro Employment in Basic Industry, 1970, Negro Employment in Southern Industry, 1970, Negro Employment in Land and Air Transport, 1971, Impact of Government Manpower Programs, 1975, Open Shop Construction, 1975, The Impact of OSHA, 1978, Objective Selection of Supervisors, 1978, Black and Other Minority Participation in the All-Volunteer Navy and Marine Corps, 1979, Manpower in the Retail Pharmacy Industry, 1979, The Impact of the ATT-EEO Consent Decree, 1979, Multinational Collective Bargaining Attempts, 1979, Multinational Union Organizations in the Manufacturing Industries, 1980, Employee Relations and Regulations in the 80s, 1982, Internat. Transport Workers' Federation and Flag of Convenience Shipping, 1983, Open Shop Construction Revisited, 1984, Personnel Policies for Engineers and Scientists, 1985, Doublebreasted Operations and Pre-Hire Agreements in Construction: The Facts and the Law, 1987, The Federal Government as Employer: The Federal Labor Relations Authority and the PATCO Challenge, 1988, Government Protection of Employees in Mergers and Acquisitions, 1989, The Railway Labor Act, 1990, also over 275 articles in field. Mem. Am. Econ. Assn., Indsl. Relations Research Assn., Am. Arbitration Assn., Phi Beta Kappa. Clubs: Harvard (N.Y.C.); Harvard-Radcliffe (Phila.); University (Washington), Faculty (U. Pa.). Home and Office: 205 Avon Rd Haverford PA 19041-1612

NORTON, DAVID ASHLEY, health facility administrator; b. Granville, N.Y., Sept. 1, 1941; s. Paul Ashley and Theda Coleen (Licence) N.; m. Diane Clifford, Nov. 7, 1946 (div. Dec. 1988); children: Lisa Marie, Kyle Rena. Orderly Glens Falls (N.Y.) Hosp., 1963-64, from phys. therapy asst. to dir. cardiopulmonary svcs., 1964-85, dir. primary life systems dept., 1985—. With USN, 1959-63. Mem. Am. Lung Assn. (bd. dirs. Adirondack br. 1975-90). Home: 1 Towpath Ln Glens Falls NY 12801 Office: Glens Falls Hosp 100 Park St Glens Falls NY 12801

NORTON, EDGAR ALBERT, JR., finance educator, researcher; b. LaGrange, Ill., Aug. 1, 1957; s. Edgar Albert Sr. and Margaret Louise (Caldwell) N.; m. Rebecca Mae King, Jan. 8, 1983; children: Matthew Stevens, Amy Louise. BS in Computer Sci., Rensselaer Poly. Inst., 1979, BS in Econs., 1979; MS in Fin., U. Ill., 1980, PhD in Econs., 1984. Chartered fin. analyst. Asst. prof. fin. N.W. Mo. State U., Maryville, 1984-86; assoc. prof. Liberty U., Lynchburg, Va., 1986-88; asst. prof. Fairleigh Dickinson U., Madison, N.J., 1988-91, assoc. prof., 1992—; dir. Ctr. for Entrepreneurial Fin. Fairleigh Dickinson U., Inst. for Entrepreneurial Studies, 1992—. Editor: Economic Justice in Perspective: A Book of Readings, 1990; contbr. articles to profl. jours./publs. Recipient Award of Excellence for rsch. paper 36th World Conf. of Internat. Coun. Sml. Bus., 1991; u. Ill. fellow, 1980, 84; NYU grantee, 1988, Fairleigh Dickinson U. grantee, 1989, 90, 91, 92. Mem. Inst. Chartered Fin. Analysts, Fin. Analysts Fedn., N.Y. Soc. Security Analysts, Am. Fin. Assn., Fin. Mgmt. Assn., Acad. of Mgt. Office: Fairleigh Dickinson U Dept Econs and Fin 285 Madison Ave Madison NJ 07940-1099

NORTON, ELEANOR HOLMES, lawyer, educator; b. Washington, June 13, 1937; d. Coleman and Vela (Lynch) Holmes; m. Edward W. Norton, 1965; children: Katherine, John H. BA, Antioch Coll., 1960, MA in Am. Studies, 1963; LLB, Yale U., 1964; LLD (hon.), Cedar Crest Coll., Allentown, Pa., 1969, Bard Coll., Annandale-on-Hudson, N.Y., 1971, Princeton U., 1973, Marymount Coll., 1974, CCNY, 1975, NYU, 1978, Howard U., 1978, Brown U., 1978, Wilberforce U., 1978, Wayne State U., 1980, Syracuse U., 1981, Yeshiva U., 1981, Lawrence U., 1981, Emanuel Coll., 1981, Spelman Coll., 1982, U. Mass., 1983, Smith Coll., 1983, Med. Coll. Pa., 1983, Tufts U., 1984, Bowdoin Coll., 1985. Bar: Pa., 1965, U.S. Supreme Ct., 1968. Law clk. presiding justice Fed. Dist. Ct., 1964-65; asst. legal dir. ACLU, 1965-70; exec. asst. to mayor N.Y.C., 1971-74, chmn. commn. humanities, 1970-77; chmn. commn. humanities EEOC, 1977-81; sr. fellow Urban Inst., 1981-82; prof. law Georgetown U., 1982—; chmn. nat. adv. coun. ACLU; elected del. from D.C. to U.S. Congress, 1990. Author: (with others) Sex Discrimination and the Law: Causes and Remedies, 1975; contbr. articles to profl. jours. Trustee Community Found. Greater Washington, Rockefeller Found., Yale Corp.; bd. dirs. A. Philip Randolph Inst., Bethune Mus. and Archives Nat. Historic Site; catalyst Ctr. Nat. Policy, Manpower Demonstration Research Corp., Martin Luther King, Jr. Ctr. Social Change, Nat. Black Leadership Roundtable, Nat. Polit. Congress Black Women, Nat. Urban Coalition, Pitney Bowes Corp., So. Christian Leadership Conf.; adv. bd. Nat. Women's Polit. Caucus, Women's Law and Policy Fellowship, Workplace Health Fund; chmn. Commn. Future of Women in Workplace, Nat. Adv. Council ACLU; mem. Am. Council Edn., Council Minority Edn., Council Fgn. Relations, U.S. Citizens Com. Monitor Helsinki Accords, exec. panel Ford Found. Project Future of Welfare State, Nat. Acad. Scis. Com. Effects Tech. Change Employment and Working Environment. Recipient Young Woman of Year award Jr. C. of C., 1965; One of 25 Most Influential Women in Am. award Newspaper Enterprise Assn., 1977; Louise Waterman Wise award Am. Jewish Congress, 1971; Harper fellow Yale Law Sch., 1976; vis. Phi Beta Kappa scholar, 1985. Mem. Nat. Acad. Scis. (numerous coms.). Office: 1631 Longworth Washington DC 20515 also: Georgetown U Law Ctr 600 New Jersey Ave NW Washington DC 20001*

NORTON, JEFFREY, publisher; b. Jamaica, N.Y., Aug. 18, 1925; s. Ralph D. and Mabel (Jeffrey) N.; m. Ruth Eldredge, June 25, 1949; children: Bruce Sidney, Christopher Jeffrey, Jeffrey Mathew, Ralph Douglas, Laurie Eldredge; m. Janis Moore Yates, Oct. 20, 1981. BA, Wesleyan U., 1945. Researcher Life mag., Time Inc., N.Y.C., 1945-46; editorial dir. coll. div. McGraw-Hill Book Co., N.Y.C., 1947-64, v.p. editorial div., 1964-67; pres. Macmillan Info. Svcs., N.Y.C., 1967-70; pub. Holt Info. Systems, N.Y.C., 1970-72; pres. Jeffrey Norton Pubs. Inc., Guilford, Conn., 1972—; bd. dirs. Audio Forum Pty., U.K., London, Audio Forum Pty., Australia, Sydney. Mem. Info. Industry Assn. (founder, past pres. 1972). Home: 433 State St Guilford CT 06437-2033 Office: Jeffrey Norton Pubs 96 Broad St Guilford CT 06437-2612

NORTON, LOUIS ARTHUR, dental educator; b. Gloucester, Mass., Jan. 12, 1937; s. Morris Harry and Mamie (Pett) N.; m. Elinor Sue Glaser, July 7, 1963; children: Mark Douglas, Lauren Elyse. AB, Bowdoin Coll., 1958; DMD, Harvard U., 1962, Cert. orthodontist, 1964. Prof. U. Ky., Lexington, 1966-74; prof. dental medicine U. Conn. Health Ctr., Farmington, 1974—; vis. prof. Hadassah Sch. Dental Medicine, Hebrew U., Jerusalem, 1972-73, Royal Dental Coll., U. Aarhus, Denmark, 1988-89; vis scientist Strangeways Rsch. Lab., Cambridge U., Eng., 1980-81; cons. NIMH, 1970-74, Nat. Inst. Dental Rsch., 1974—. Co-author: Education for Orthodontics, 1967; author: Biology of Tooth Movement, 1989. Capt. U.S. Army, 1964-66. Fulbright rsch. fellow Internat. Exchange of Scholars, 1972-73; Fogarty fellow NIH, 1980-81; NATO Sr Guest fellow, 1988-89. Fellow AAAS; mem. Biologic Repair and Growth Soc. (pres. 1987-88, Kappa Delta Rsch. award 1989), Conn. State Orthodontic Soc. (pres. 1987-89), Northeastern Soc. of Orthodontists (dir. 1987). Office: Univ Conn Health Ctr 263 Farmington Ave Farmington CT 06030-0001

NORTON, NANCY SHERRY, podiatrist; b. Balt., Apr. 24, 1961; d. Gerald Lewis and Leona Norton; m. Eli Eisenberg, May 17, 1991; 1 child, Nicole Paige. BA, U. Md., 1983; DPM, Pa. Coll. Podiatric Medicine, 1987. Podiatrist Drs. Cohen & Norton P.A., Bel Air, Md., 1991—, Drs. Stroh & Butler, P.A., Frederick, Md., 1988—. Contbr. articles to profl. jours. Mem. Am. Podiatric Med. Assn., Phi Sigma Sigma (philanthropy chmn. 1985-87), Pi Delta, Phi Kappa Phi, Omicron Delta Kappa. Home: 12254 Bonmot Pl Reisterstown MD 21136-1739 Office: Drs Cohen & North PA 2208 Emmorton Rd # 101 Bel Air MD 21015-6189

NORTON, ROBERT H., financial planning and insurance consultant; b. Newton, Mass., Dec. 26, 1929; s. Hermon and Doris Margaret (Berry) N.; m. Virginia Florence Murray, June 30, 1951; children: Michael, Kathleen, Robert Jr., Edward, Karyn, Kevin, Christa, Collin. Cert. in mech. engring., MIT, 1953, cert. in elec. engring., 1956; MS in Fin. Svcs., Am. Coll. CLU, 1984, MS in Mgmt., 1986. Chartered life underwriter, chartered fin. cons.; registered investment advisor, notary pub. Design engr. various orgns., 1953-58; exec. v.p. T.A.D., Inc., Cambridge, Mass., 1958-66; sales mgr. Aborn Labs., Waltham, Mass., 1966-68; ins. agt. John Hancock Life Ins., Chestnut Hill, Mass., 1968—; fin. planning cons. Norton Fin. Cons., Holliston, Mass., 1973—. Merit badge counselor Boy Scouts Am., Holliston, 1970-72; lectr. St. Mary's Roman Cath. Ch., Holliston, 1970-76; mem., clk. fin. com. Town of Holliston, 1988—. Sgt. USAR, 1949-64. Mem. Million Dollar Round Table (life mem., asst. dir. 1970—). Republican. Roman Catholic. Home and Office: Norton Fin Cons 11 Ashland St Holliston MA 01746-1223

NORTON, THOMAS EDWARD, art and marketing consultant, writer; b. Portland, Maine, Oct. 1, 1934; s. Edward Thomas and Mary Elizabeth (Callan) N.; m. Mary Louise Mullin, 1981; 1 child, Andrew. BS, Fordham U., 1956. Mem. Parke Bernet Galleries, N.Y.C., 1956-63, asst. v.p., 1963-64; v.p. Sotheby Parke Bernet, N.Y.C., 1964-72, sr. v.p., 1972-81; dir. Sotheby's, London and N.Y.C., 1970-81; art and mktg. cons. various galleries N.Y.C., 1981—. Author: 100 Years of Collecting in America, 1985; co-author: Living It Up, 1985. Sgt. U.S. Army, 1957-59. Mem. Century Assn., Appraisers Assn. Am. Roman Catholic. Home: 1035 5th Ave New York NY 10028-0135

NORTON, WILLIAM T., neurochemist; b. Damariscotta, Maine, Jan. 27, 1929; s. Carroll P. and Josephine G. (Eales) N.; m. Lila Mazur, Sept. 13, 1957; children: Hamish W., Adam E. AB, Bowdoin Coll., 1950; PhD, Princeton U., 1954. Rsch. chemist E.I. du Pont de Nemours & Co., Wilmington, Del., 1953-57, instr. neurology, 1957-59, asst. prof., 1959-64, assoc. prof., 1964-71, prof., 1974—; prof. Albert Einstein Coll. Med., N.Y.C., 1971—; mem. NIH Study sect., Bethesda Md., 1971-75; chmn. NIH, Bethesda, 1979-84; cons. Nat. Multiple Sclerosis Soc., N.Y., 1969-80. Contbr. articles to scientific jours., editor: Oligodendroglia, 1984. Office: Albert Einstein Coll Medicine 1300 Morris Park Ave Bronx NY 10461-1924

NORWITZ, STEVEN BARRY, plastic and reconstructive surgeon, health facility administrator; b. Camden, N.J., July 26, 1941; s. Bernard Benjamin and Ruth Norwitz; m. Anita Rochelle Shrager, Aug. 19, 1967; children: Lisa, Nicole, Suzanne. BA, Rutgers U., 1963; MD, Hahnemann Med. Coll., 1967. Diplomate Am. Bd. Plastic Surgery. Resident Kings County Med. Ctr., N.Y., 1967-73; attending physician Monmouth Med. Ctr., Long Branch, N.J., 1973—, Bayshore Community Hosp., Holdmel, N.J., 1973—; chief plastic surgery Riverview Med. Ctr. Hosp., Red Bank, N.J., 1985—; dir. The Plastic Surgery Ctr., Shrewsbury, N.J., 1986—; clin. instr. Hahnemann Med. Coll., Phila. Fellow ACS; mem. AMA, Am. Soc. Plastic and Reconstructive Surgeons, Aesthetic Plastic Surgery Soc., N.J. State Med. Soc., N.J. State Soc. Plastic and Reconstructive Surgeons, Masons (32 degree). Office: Plastic Surgery Ctr 535 Sycamore Ave Shrewsbury NJ 07702

NORWOOD, PAULA KING, medical biostatistics professional; b. Coco Solo, Panama, Aug. 28, 1946; came to U.S., 1946; d. Paul Alfred and Laura Merle (Smith) King; m. Thomas Edward Norwood, Mar. 18, 1972 (div. Aug. 1990); 1 child, David Thomas. BA in Math., Hendrix Coll., 1968; MS in Biometrics, U. Ark., 1970; PhD in Stats., Va. Polytechnic Inst./State U., 1974. Instr. Va. Polytechnic Inst./State U., 1973-74; sr. biometrician Norwich (N.Y.) Pharm. Corp., 1974-77; sr. biometrician Ortho Pharm. Corp., Raritan, N.J., 1977-78, mgr., med. biostats., 1978-81, dir., med. biostats. and data ops., 1981-88, exec. dir., med. biostats. and data ops., 1988-90; v.p., med. biostats. and data ops. worldwide RWJ Pharm. Rsch. Inst., Raritan, 1990—. Mem. Am. Statis. Assn., Biometric Soc., Internat. Biometric Soc. (coun. mem.), Pharm. Mfg. Assn., Drug Info. Assn., Caucus for Women in Stats., Sigma Xi. Office: RWJ Pharm Rsch Inst RR 2 Box 300 Raritan NJ 08869

NOSANOW, BARBARA SHISSLER, museum director; b. Roanoke, Va.; d. Willis M. and Kathryne (Bradford) Johnson; m. Lewis H. Nosanow, Oct. 15, 1973; m. John Lewis Shissler, July 1957 (dec. 1971); children: John Lewis III, Ada Holland. BA, Smith Coll., 1957; MA, Case Western Res. U., 1959. Mng. editor Jour. Aesthetics and Art Criticism, 1959-62; dir. publs. Mpls. Inst. Art, 1964-72; dir. Univ. Gallery, U. Minn., Mpls., 1972-76; spl. project dir. The Art of Russia, 1800-1850, Washington, 1976-79; dir. edn. and exhibits Nat. Archives, Washington, 1976-79; curator edn. Smithsonian Instn., Nat. Mus. Am. Art, 1979-82, asst. dir., 1982-87; dir. Portland (Maine) Mus. Art, 1988—. Office: Portland Mus Art 7 Congress Sq Portland ME 04101-1119

NOSTIN, JOHN M., management information systems specialist; b. New Britain, Conn., Aug. 7, 1947; s. Michael A. and Gloria D. (Murphy) N.; m. Ann Mary Watroba, Aug. 7, 1976; 1 child, William John. AS in Acctg., Draughon's Jr. Coll., Nashville, 1970. Programmer, analyst Security Conn. Life Ins. Co., Avon, Conn., 1970-73; sr. programmer, analyst Aetna Life & Casualty Ins. Co., Hartford, Conn., 1973-74; cons., project mgr. Am. Optical Corp., Southbridge, Mass., 1974-78; cons., project mgr. Digital Equipment Corp., Maynard, Mass., 1978-81, Northboro, Mass., 1982-87; cons. Digital Equipment Corp., Maynard, 1987-89; MIS mgr., program mgr. Digital Equipment Corp., Landover, Md., 1989—. Staff sgt. USAF, 1966-70. Republican. Home: 9890 Washingtonian Blvd Gaithersburg MD 20878-5329 Office: Digital Equipment Corp 8400 Corporate Dr Hyattsville MD 20785-2238

NOTKIN, JEROME JOHANNES, education educator; b. N.Y.C., June 10, 1926; s. Murry and Evelyn (Mofshatz) N.; m. Janice Cohen, Feb. 11, 1951; children: Michael, Susan. BA, NYU, 1949; MA, Columbia U., 1950, EdD, 1956. Tchr. N.Y.C. Pub. Schs., 1950-58; sci. supr. Bd. of Coop. Ednl. Svcs., Deer Park, N.Y., 1958-62; prof. U. Hawaii, Honolulu, 1964-65, No. Mich. U., Marquette, summers 1961-67, Hofstra U., Hempstead, N.Y., 1962—; cons. various L.I. sch. dists., 1962—. Author more than 30 books, 1960—. With U.S. Army, 1944-46, PTO. Recipient several NSF grants, 1962—. Life mem. Nat. Sci. Tchrs. Assn.; mem. Nat. Coun. Tchrs. of Math., Nat. Congress of Aerospace. Home: 15 Oak St Woodmere NY 11598-2647 Office: Hofstra U Hempstead NY 11550

NOTO, PATRICIA HOFFMAN, health, fitness, and recreational facility director; b. Buffalo, Feb. 2, 1954; d. Norman Richards and Evelyne (Ghnassia) H.; m. Anthony John, May 12, 1984. BS, Canisius Coll., 1976; MA, Adelphi U., 1978; postgrad., SUNY, Buffalo, 1978-79. Pool supr. Town of Tonawanda Recreation Dept., Kenmore, N.Y., 1973-77; grad. asst. Adelphi U., 1977-78, SUNY, Buffalo, 1978-79; health and phys. edn. asst. Jewish Ctr. of Greater Buffalo, 1979-80, supr., 1980-81, asst. dir. health and phys. edn., 1981-83, assoc. dir. health and phys. edn., 1983-86, dir. health, fitness and recreation, 1986—; cons. Computer Task Group, Buffalo, 1984—; lectr. on fitness. Contbr. articles to profl. jours. Grantee JM Found., N.Y.C., 1978. Mem. Internat. Dance Exercise Assn., Am. Coll. Sports Medicine, N.Y. State Assn. for Health Phys. Edn. Recreation and Dance (pres. recreation/leisure sect. 1988—), Am. Alliance for Health Phys. Edn. Recreation and Dance, Assn. Jewish Ctr. Workers (chair ea. states chpt. 1981-83), Canisius Coll. Phys. Edn. Alumni Assn. (pres. 1975-76). Republican. Jewish. Home: 114 Swanson Ter Buffalo NY 14221-1342

NOTZON, FRANCIS C., statistician; b. Laredo, Tex., June 28, 1948; s. Claude A. and Elizabeth (Hickey) N.; m. Wanda J. Sampley, Apr. 24, 1971;

children: Charles C., Daniel P. BA in Econs. and History, U. Tex., 1970; MS in Sociology/Demography, U. Wis., 1973, MA in Econs., 1974; PhD in Population Dynamics, Johns Hopkins U., 1989. Demographer Population Labs., Rabat, Morocco, 1973-75; demographer/statistician Nat. Ctr. for Health Statistics, Hyattsville, Md., 1976-78; resident advisor World Fertility Survey, Rabat, Morocco, 1979-80; statistician Nat. Ctr. for Health Statistics, Hyattsville, 1981—. Mem. Am. Pub. Health Assn. Home: 5017 Strathmore Ave Kensington MD 20895-1210 Office: Nat Ctr for Health Stats 6525 Belcrest Rd Rm 1100 Hyattsville MD 20782-2003

NOURI-MOGHADAM, MOHAMAD REZA, mathematics and physics educator; b. Tehran, Iran, July 1, 1949; s. Gholam Reza and Zahra (Razeghian) Nouri-Moghadam; m. Vida Nouri-Moghadam, May 18, 1968; children: Yasaman, Ardavan. BS, U. London, 1972, PhD, 1975. Postdoctoral research fellow U. London, King's Coll., 1975-76; Fulbright sr. research fellow and vis. asst. prof. Princeton U., 1979-80; prof. Sharif U. Tech., Tehran, 1976-87; rsch. fellow Kyoto U., Japan, 1986-87; vis. prof. U. Toledo, Ohio, 1987-88; prof. math. Pa. State U., Lehman, 1991—; assoc. rschr. Internat. Ctr. for Theoretical and Math. Physics, Trieste, Italy, 1988-93. Editor-in-chief Iranian Math. Soc. Bull.; author: Vector and Tensor Analysis. Mem. SIAM, Am. Math. Soc., Internat. Neural Network Soc., London Math. Soc. Office: Pa State U PO Box PSU Lehman PA 18627

NOVACK, JOSEPH, chemical engineer; b. Bklyn., Mar. 31, 1928; s. Isadore and Mollie (Rosenblut) N.; m. Naomi S. Kaplan, Aug. 30, 1953; children: Devorah H., Sandy A. B in Chem. Engring., CCNY, 1949; postgrad., Poly. Inst. Bklyn., 1949-51; MBA, Am. Internat. U., 1960. Engr. Nat. Rsch. Labs., Oakdale, N.Y., 1949-51; engr. Monsanto Co., Indian Orchard, Mass., 1954-64, specialist, 1964-69, sr. specialist, 1969-70, group supr., 1970-77, sr. group supr., 1977-83, prin. investigator, 1983—. Co-patentee in field. 1st lt. U.S. Army, 1951-53. Mem. Am. Inst. Chem. Engrs. Office: Mansanto Chem Co 730 Worcester St Springfield MA 01151-1089

NOVACK, SHELDON, insurance company executive; b. Phila., Apr. 11, 1938; s. Ike and Jeannette (Garber) N.; B.S., Temple U., 1959, M.B.A., 1966; Ph.D., N.Y. U., 1973; m. Goldie Stein, Dec. 17, 1960; children: Seth, Lauren Anne; m. 2d, Barbara Gross, 1982. V.p. Communications Fin. Corp., Phila., 1966-71; prof. Coll. of Ins., N.Y.C., 1971-72; asso. prof., chmn. dept. fin., public policy and bus. econs. L.I. U., Bklyn., 1973-76; faculty Seton Hall U., South Orange, N.J., 1976-79, Widener U., 1979, St. Joseph U., 1982; cons. in field; mng. ptnr. Matrix Leasing, Jenkintown, Pa., 1987, prin. 1984—; dir. Congl. Life Ins. Co., Zim Computer Corp. Bd. dirs. Am. Jewish Cultural Found. Served with AUS, 1960-62. Marcus Nadler fellow, 1966-68. Mem. Am. Fin. Assns., Eastern Fin. Assns., Am., Eastern econ. assns., The Money Marketeers, Econ., Pa. hist. assns., Eastern Assn. Equipment Lessors, Western Econs. and Fin. Assn., Omicron Delta Epsilon, Beta Gamma Sigma. Asso. editor The American Economist Jour., 1976—. Home: 1523 Woodland Rd Jenkintown PA 19046-1235

NOVAK, GREGORY, marketing professional; b. Johnstown, Pa., Oct. 19, 1949; s. Eugene F. and Joan (Tross) N.; m. Naomi Sosia Wall; children: Rebecca, Jeffrey, Jacqueline. BA, U. Vt., 1971. Project dir. Dun & Bradstreet, N.Y.C., 1973-74; sr. analyst Colgate Palmolive, N.Y.C., 1974-76; mgr. brand research R.J. Reynolds, Winston-Salem, N.C., 1976-77, mgr. group new brand rsch., 1977-80, dir. new bus., 1980-81, dir. group mktg., 1981-84; nat. dir. mktg. Deloitte Haskins & Sells, N.Y.C., 1984-90; pres. Novak Mktg. Inc., 1990—. Office: Novak Mktg Inc 237 Park Ave 21st Fl New York NY 10017-3148

NOVAK, JOAN TROSS, writer, artist; b. Johnstown, Pa., Apr. 12, 1927; d. Ludwig Conrad and Margaret Ramsey (Rose) Tross; m. Eugene Francis Novak, (div. Nov. 1976); children: Gregory, Mark. Solo art exhbns. include Nat. Art Ctr., N.Y.C., 1979; group shows include Hanson Galleries, N.Y.C., 1975; author: J-Walking the Universe, 1990, J-Walking the Fascists Reagan and Bush, 1990, Theories of a Patriot, 1990. Democrat. Presbyterian. Home: 303 E 57th St New York NY 10022-2947

NOVAK, JOSEPH DONALD, biological sciences educator; b. Mpls., Dec. 2, 1930; s. Joseph Daniel and Anna (Podany) N.; m. Joan Owen, July 18, 1953; children: Joseph Mark, Barbara Joan, William John. BS, U. Minn., 1952, MA, 1954, PhD, 1958. Teaching asst. U. Minn., Mpls., 1952-56, instr., 1956-57; asst. prof. Kans. State Tchrs. Coll., 1957-59; asst. prof. Purdue U., West Lafayette, Ind., 1959-62, assoc. prof., 1962-67; prof. Cornell U., Ithaca, N.Y., 1967—; cons. to schs., colls. and univs., 1957—; disting. vis. prof. U. N.C., Wilmington, 1980, U. W. Fla., 1987-88. Author: Learning How to Learn, 1984; Educational Psychology: A Cognitive View, 1978; A Theory of Education, 1977; others; contbr. articles to profl. jours. Fellow Tozer Found., Lydia Anderson, 1955-56; research assoc. Harvard U., 1965-66; Fulbright-Hayes Sr. Scholar, Australia, 1980. Fellow AAAS (sec. sect. Q); mem. APA, Am. Inst. Biol. Scis., Nat. Sci. Tchrs. Assn., Nat. Assn. Rsch. in Sci. Teaching (Outstanding Contbns. Sci. Teaching Through Rsch. award 1990), Nat. Assn. Biology Tchrs., Assn. for Edn. of Tchrs. of Sci., Am. Ednl. Rsch. Assn., Sigma Xi. Home: 1403 Slaterville Rd Ithaca NY 14850-6207 Office: Cornell U Dept Edn Kennedy Hall Ithaca NY 14853

NOVAK, RICHARD JOSEPH, education administrator; b. N.Y.C., Mar. 15, 1954; s. Joseph and Martha (Wyrwas) N.; m. Margaret Ann Curry, Aug. 14, 1977; children: Megan, Lucas. BA, Rutgers U., 1976, postgrad.; MA, Princeton (N.J.) Theol. Sem., 1978, Maryknoll (N.Y.) Sem., 1981; EdD, Rutgers U., 1992. Exec. dir. Office of Religious Edn. Diocese of Passaic, Rahway, N.J., 1978-91; asst. dean Rutgers U. Grad. Sch., New Brunswick, 1991—. Contbr. articles to profl. jours. Bd. dirs. Bd. Edn., North Brunswick, 1990—. Mem. Eastern Cath. Conf. of Diocesan Dirs. of Religious Edn. (chairperson 1985-91), Religious Edn. Assn. (bd. dirs. 1990—). Office: Rutgers U Grad Sch 25 Bishop Pl New Brunswick NJ 08903

NOVICK, HAROLD, social services administrator; b. N.Y.C., May 6, 1922; s. Max and Anna (Goldfarb) N.; m. Gladys Schortz, June 10, 1956; children: Michele, David. BS in Social Sci., CCNY, 1947; MS in Social Work, Columbia U., 1949. Caseworker Bklyn. Bur. of Social Svcs., N.Y.C., 1949-52; caseworker, group home supr. Riverdale Children's Assn., N.Y.C., 1952-54; head, supr. Jewish Children's Bur.-Baron DeHirsch Inst., Montreal, 1954-57; dir. social svcs. Glen Mills (Pa.) Sch., 1957-64, program dir., 1964-67, asst. supt., 1967-68, supt., 1968-74; exec. dir. Childrens Ctr., Hamden, Conn., 1975-77, Berkshire Farm Ctr. and Svcs. for Youth, Canaan, N.J., 1977—; mem., cons. Ea. area svc. coun. Coun. on Accreditation, N.Y.C., 1990—. Contbr. articles to profl. jours. V.p. Jewish Fedn. Berkshire County, Pittsfield, 1982—, chmn. Russian Resettlement, 1989—, chmn. community rels. com., 1991—; pres., mem. exec. com., bd. dirs. Knesset Israel Synagogue, Pittsfield, 1984-88, 88—. With Army Med. Corps, 1942-46. Mem. NASW, Internat. Assn. Social Work, N.Y. State Coun. Family and Child Care Agys. (bd. dirs., planning, legis. and devel. com.), Child Welfare League Am. (bd. dirs.), Nat. Assn. Juvenile Corrections Agys. (bd. dirs., exec. com., Donald G. Blackburn award 1991), Childrens Def. Fund, Internat. Assn. Adminstrs. Child Caring Agys., People to People Internat., Rotary Club (Pittsfield). Democrat. Home: Rt 49 Pittsfield MA 01201 Office: Berkshire Farm Ctr & Svcs for Youth Rt 20 Canaan NJ 12029

NOVICK, NELSON LEE, dermatologist, internist, writer; b. Bklyn., June 27, 1949; s. Benjamin and Vivian (Meltzer) N.; m. Meryl Sohnis, June 20, 1971; children: Yonatan, Yoel, Ariel, Daniel, Avraham. BA in Biology magna cum laude, Bklyn. Coll., 1971; MD, Mt. Sinai Sch. Medicine, 1975. Diplomate Am. Bd. Internal Medicine, Am. Bd. Dermatology, Am. Bd. Med. Examiners (bd. dirs. election). Resident in internal medicine Mt. Sinai Med. Ctr., N.Y.C., 1975-78, assoc. attending, 1980—, postgrad. preceptee, 1980-83, clinic chief, dermatology svc., 1983; resident in internal medicine skin and cancer unit NYU Med. Ctr., N.Y.C., 1978-80; assoc. clin. prof. Mt. Sinai Sch. Medicine, N.Y.C., 1980—; cons. Westwood-Squibb Skin Care Info. Ctr., Vaseline Intensive Care Rsch. Author: Saving Face, Skin Care for Teens, Super Skin, Baby Skin, Diseases of the Mucus Membrane, (novel) In the Path of the Wolf; co-author: The External Ear; reviewerAnnals Internal Medicine, Jour. Am. Acad. Dermatology, Internat. Jour. Dermatology; editorial advisor Exec. Health's Good Health Report, Westwood-Squibb Skin Care Info. Ctr., Synder Comm., Your Baby, wallbd. program; former med. editor Current Podiatric Medicine, Jour. Am. Analgesia Soc.; also articles, chpts. to books. Regent's Coll. scholar, 1971, Max and Leah Strauss Fund scholar, 1971, Grand St. Found. scholar, 1971. Fellow ACP (direct election), Am. Acad. Dermatology, Am. Soc. Dermatol. Surgery, Skin Cancer Found. (hon.); mem. AMA, AAAS, Soc. Investigative Dermatology, Skin Phototrauma Found., Internat. Soc. for Androgenic Disorders, Skin Cancer Found. (charter), N.Y. Acad. Scis., N.Y. County Med. Soc., Am. Soc. Dermatologic Surgery, Am. Analgesia Soc. (past bd. dirs.), Nature Conservancy, Audubon Soc., Nat. Geog. Found., N.Y. Zool. Soc., Am. Mus. Natural History, Smithsonian Instn., Nat. Wildlife Fedn., The Wilderness Soc., Author's Guild, Author's League Am., Phi Beta Kappa. Jewish. Office: 328 E 75th St New York NY 10021-3305

NOVOGROD, NANCY ELLEN, editor; b. N.Y.C., Jan. 30, 1949; d. Max and Hilda (Kirschbaum) Gerstein; m. John Campner Novogrod, Nov. 7, 1976; children: James Campner, Caroline Anne. AB, Mt. Holyoke Coll., 1971. Sec. fiction dept. The New Yorker, N.Y.C., 1971-73, reader, 1973-76; asst. editor Clarkson N. Potter, Inc., N.Y.C., 1977-78, assoc. editor, 1978-80, editor, 1980-83, sr. editor, 1984-86, exec. editor, 1987; editor HG (formerly House and Garden mag.), N.Y.C., 1987-88, editor-in-chief, 1988—. Bd. dirs. N.Y. Bot. Garden, 1991, Decorative Arts Trust, 1991; bd. trustees Isabel O'Neil Found. for the Art of the Painted Finish, 1991. Bd. dirs. N.Y. Bot. Garden, The Decorative Arts Trust, 1991—; trustee Isabel O'Neil Found. for the Art of the Painted Finish, 1991. Office: HG 350 Madison Ave New York NY 10017-3704

NOVOTNY, JIRI, biophysicist; b. Kladno, Czechoslovakia, Dec. 15, 1943; came to U.S., 1979; s. Jaroslav and Eva (Foustkova) N.; m. Jarmila Novotny, Feb. 26, 1967; 1 child, Paula. RNDr, Charles U., Prague, Czechoslovakia, 1970, PhD, 1970. Scientist Inst. Organic Chemistry & Biochemistry, Prague, 1970-77; sr. scientist Inst. Molecular Genetics, Prague, 1971-79; from asst. to assoc. prof. Harvard Med. Sch., Boston, 1980-88; dir. dept. Bristol-Myers Squibb Rsch. Inst., Princeton, N.J., 1988—; vis. scientist Oxford U., Eng., 1979; dir. rsch. Pasteur Inst., Paris, 1987; adj. prof. U. Pa., Phila., 1989—; cons. Creative Biomolecules Inc., Hopkinton, Mass., 1984-88, Immulogic, Inc., Cambridge, Mass., 1987-88; mem. sci. adv. bd. Procept, Inc., Cambridge, 1989—. Contbr. articles to jours. Procs. NAS, Nature, Biochemistry. Recipient prize of the Czechoslovak Acad. of Scis., 1979. Mem. Am. Phys. Soc., Am. Soc. Biol. Chemists, Am. Biophys. Soc., Princeton Chess Club, Belle Meade Friends of Music. Home: 101 Red Hill Rd Princeton NJ 08540-1307 Office: Bristol-Myers Squibb Rsch Inst Princeton NJ 08543-4000

NOWACK, GEORGE PAUL, educator; b. Pitts., July 18, 1948; s. George C. Nowack and Eleanor (Finster) Pazzula; m. Carolyn Rose Vogel. BS in Edn., Duquesne U., 1970; postgrad. in English, Trenton State U., 1971-73; postgrad. in Reading, Duquesne U., 1974-76. Cert. Secondary Educator in English. Tchr. drama South River (N.J.) Bd. of Edn., 1970-74; tchr. English Pitts Bd. of Edn., 1974—; co-founder G/C 'Nterprises, Pitts., 1988—; participant summer sci. tng. program, Va. Union U., 1965; acad. team leader Pitts. Pub. Schs., 1976-87, dept. chairperson lang. arts, 1983-86, mem. monitoring achievement com., 1979-87; coord. commonwealth classroom, Allegheny Mid. Sch., 1987-90; participant New Futures Extended Sch. Day Program, 1988—. Author: Grounds Fee, 1987; editor: Voices, 1989, Invader News (Award of Excellence 1987-88), Allegheny Star, 1990-91. Bd. dirs. South River (N.J.) Jaycees, 1971-74; assoc. dir. W.P. ARC, Pitts., 1975-79; dir. Allegheny Players, 1990-91; coord. Pitts. Pub. Schs. One-Act Play Festival, 1991. Grantee NSF, 1965, Allegheny Conf. on Community Devel., 1978-80; named Dir. of Yr. Image Players, 1973-74; recipient Award of Excellence Penspra, 1987-89, Outstanding One-Act Dramatic Presentation award, Garden State Arts Festival, 1974. Mem. ASCD, Nat. Ednl. Forum, Pitts. Fedn. Tchrs., Brockway Landings Yacht Assn. (pres. 1987-89), Sunset Cove Yacht Club (v.p. 1990), Kappa Phi Kappa (sec. 1969 Duquesne U. 1968-69, pres. 1969-70). Home: 123 Hillvue Dr Mars PA 16046-7808

NOWACK, WAYNE KENYON, artist; b. Des Moines, May 7, 1923; s. Bernard F. and Bertha A. (Meeker) N.; m. Jean Ann Curtis, Sept. 19, 1952. Student, Drake U., 1943-45; BA summa cum laude, State U. Iowa, 1947, MA, 1948, MFA, 1950. Art therapist Mental Health Inst., Independence, Iowa, 1951-53, Hall-Brooke Sanitarium, Westport, Conn., 1953-56; assoc. prof. art Union Coll., Schenectady, N.Y., 1957-65; freelance artist, 1965—. Solo exhbns. include Des Moines Art Ctr., 1950, 57, Union Coll., 1957, Albany (N.Y.) Inst. History and Art, 1960, Allan Stone Gallery, N.Y.C., 1967, 70, 74; group shows include Gallery Modern Art, Washington, 1963, Whitney Mus. Am. Art, 1969, Minn. Mus. Art, St. Paul, 1977; represented in pvt. and pub. collections including Ft. Worth Mus., Des Moines Art Ctr., Yale Art Mus., New Haven, Conn., others. Grantee Danforth Found., 1963, Nat. Endowment for Arts, 1973. Home: RR 1 Box 346 Spencer NY 14883-9644

NOWACZEK, FRANK HUXLEY, cable television executive; b. Bklyn., July 6, 1930; s. Frank Huxley and Louise (Blake) N.; m. Alice Elaine Novak, May 21, 1955; children: Richard Alan, Elaine. Student St. Lawrence U., 1948-50; BS in Hotel Adminstrn., Cornell U., 1952; postgrad. in polit. sci. and pub. rels. George Washington U., 1954-58, Am. U., 1954-57. Spl. agt. spl. ops. br. security div. Nat. Security Agy., Def. Dept., 1954-59; asst. to pres., dir. rsch. Nat. Cable TV Assn., Washington, 1959-64; asst. to pres. TeleSystems Corp., Glenside, Pa., 1964-66; v.p., part-owner Newport Cablevision, Vt., 1966-68; v.p. Blackburn & Co., Inc., Washington, 1968-76; v.p. Mid Atlantic region Warner Amex Cable Communications, N.Y.C., 1976-80, sr. v.p. eastern div., Ft. Washington, Pa., 1980-82, sr. v.p. nat. div., Columbus, Ohio, 1982-83; owner Cable Media Co., Worthington, Ohio, 1983-86; pres. Newcable TV Corp., 1985-86; chief oper. officer Bachow & Elkin, Inc. Phila., 1986—; speaker various orgns. Served with CIC, U.S. Army, 1952-54. Mem. IEEE, Soc. Relay Engrs. (Gt. Britain), Cable TV Adminstrn. and Mktg. Assn., Nat. Cable TV Pioneers Assn., Nat. Acad. Cable Programmers, Pa. Cable TV Assn. (pres., dir.), Pa. Cable TV Pioneers Assn., Phila. Cable TV Club (founder), Cornell Soc. Hotelmen, Am. Mgmt. Assn., Nat. Cable TV Assn. (sec. tech. standards com. 1961 chmn. membership com. 1965-66), Cornell U. Alumni Club (life), Phi Delta Theta. Republican. Mem. Dutch Reformed Ch.

NOWAK, HENRY JAMES, congressman; b. Buffalo, Feb. 21, 1935; s. Joseph Jacob and Helen (Batkiewicz) N.; m. Rose Santa Lucia, Nov. 27, 1965; children: Diane, Henry Joseph. BBA, Canisius Coll., 1957; JD, SUNY, Buffalo, 1961; LHD (hon.), Medaille Coll., 1976, Daemen Coll., 1983. Bar: N.Y. 1962. Atty., asst. dist. atty. State of N.Y., Buffalo, 1964-65; asst. dist. atty. Erie County, N.Y., Buffalo, 1965-66; confidential sec. Supreme Ct. Justice Arthur Cosgrove, Buffalo, 1965-66; comptroller Erie County, 1966-74; Mem. 94th-97th Congresses from 37th N.Y. Dist., 98th-102nd Congresses from 33d N.Y. Dist.; chmn. pub. works subcom. on water resources. Served with AUS, 1957-58, 61-62. Named Outstanding Citizen Buffalo Eve. News, 1976, Am-Pol Eagle Citizen of Yr., 1976, Citizen of Yr. Canisius Coll. Bd. Regents, 1983, Man of Yr., Nat. Utility Contrs. Assn., 1981, We. N.Y. Transp. Coun., 1981, Profl. and Businessmen's Assn. Buffalo, Erie County, 1982, N.Y. State Assn. Transp. Engrs., 1983, Congressman of Yr., Nat. Columbus Day Com., 1983; recipient Rockefeller award N.Y. Water Pollution Control Assn., 1984; Niagara Group of Sierra Environ., Protection award, 1988, Citizen of Yr. award Buffalo News, 1991, Quality Integrated Edn. award Buffalo Pub. Schs., 1991. Mem. N.Y. State Bar Assn., Erie County Bar Assn. Office: US Ho of Reps 2240 Rayburn House Office Bldg Washington DC 20515

NOWAK, LAURA STONE, finance educator, consultant; b. N.Y.C.; d. Jesse Nowak and Rosalind Stone; m. William Borenstein; children: Lea, Lou. BA in Econs., CCNY; PhD in Econs., CUNY, 1978. Instr. Bklyn. Coll., N.Y.C., 1974-76; grad. fellow Baruch Coll., N.Y.C., 1976-77; asst. prof. Hunter Coll., N.Y.C., 1977-79, Fordham U., N.Y.C., 1979-86; assoc. prof. Coll. Staten Island, 1986—. Contbr. articles to Jour. Forensic Econs., Rev. of Bus., Jour. Bus. Issues, Trial Lawyers Guide, Am. Economist, Bankers Mag., Handbook of Fixed Income Securities, N.E. Regional Sci. Rev., Quar. Jour. Bus. and Econs. Named Outstanding Young Woman of Yr. Nat. Assn. of Profl. Women, 1982. Mem. N.Y. Women Economists (program dir.), Nat. Assn. Forensic Economists, Am. Econs. Assn. (com. on status of women in econs. profession), Met. Econ. Assn. (treas. 1985-87). Home: 143 W 13th St New York NY 10011-7801

NOWAK, MILTON, chemical company executive; b. N.Y.C., Nov. 2, 1914; s. Robert and Alice (Smigel) N.; m. Dorothy Berkman, May 25, 1940; children: Judith, Edward, Kenneth. BS, Bklyn. Coll., 1934; MS, U. Mich., 1937. Asst. rsch. chemist N.Y. Quinine & Chem. Works, Bklyn., 1934-36; chemist Whiting Filterlite Corp., N.Y.C., 1938-40; chief chemist Nuodex Products Corp., Elizabeth, N.J., 1941-56; v.p. Troy Chemical Corp., Newark, N.J., 1956—. Patentee in field. Mem. Am. Chem. Soc., AAAS, N.Y. Acad. Sci., Soc. Plastic Engrs. Home: 492 Mayhew Ct South Orange NJ 07079-1327 Office: Troy Chem Corp One Ave L Newark NJ 07105

NOWETNER, PATRICIA MARY, mental health specialist; b. Camden, N.J., Oct. 28, 1952; d. George Albert and Jean Gertrude (Cronce) Andrews; m. Thomas robert Nowetner, Mar. 7, 1970; children: David, James. AAS, Burlington County Coll., 1985; BSN, Alfred U., 1987, MSc Edn., 1990. RN, N.Y., N.J. Dental hygienist Dr. Stanley Gold, Willingboro, N.J., 1974-76; EKG technician Rancocas Valley Hosp., Willingboro, 1976-80; staff nurse St. James Hosp., Hornell, N.Y., 1985-86; nurse educator LPN Program BOCES, Hornell, 1986-90; coord. crisis svcs. Counseling Ctr., Wellsville, N.Y., 1986-90; mental health specialist United Health Svcs. Hosp., Binghamton, N.Y., 1990—; nurse educator LPN Program BOCES, Binghamton, 1991—; geropsychiat. cons. Ideal Sr. Living Ctr., Endicot N.Y., 1990; coord. geropsychiat. program United Health Svcs., Binghamto 1990, AIDS cert. counselor, 1992. Mem. Counseling and Devel. Assn. N.Y. State, So. Tier Psychiat. Nurses. Office: United Health Svcs Ho Mitchell Ave Binghamton NY 13903

NOXON, MARGARET WALTERS, community volunteer; b. Detroit, Dec. 16, 1903; d. George Alexander and Ethelwyn (Taylor) Walters; grad., Liggett Sch. for Girls, Det., 1922; life teaching certificate Wayne State U., 1925; student Columbia Tchrs. Coll., 1939-40; m. Herbert Richards Noxon, July 15, 1926 (dec. Aug. 4, 1971). Bd. dirs. Coll. Club, Detroit, 1925-30; mem. Salvation Army Aux., Detroit, 1926—; mem. Coll. Club, Summit N.J., 1941-—; historian D.A.R., N.Y.C., 1943-46, vice regent, 1946-49; dir. New Eng., Women, 1961-64; dir. Woodycrest-Five Points Child Care, 1961-77; bd. dirs. ARC, Summit, N.J., service com. chmn. uniforms and insignias, 1943-45; v.p. N.Y. Infirmary Aux., N.Y.C., 1948-58, bd. dirs., 1959-80. Recipient award for meritorious personal service ARC, 1945. Mem. Nat. Inst. Social Scis., Grand Jury Assn. N.Y. County, D.A.R. (dir. 1950-70), St. David's Soc. State N.Y., English-Speaking Union, Daus. Am. Colonists, AAUW, Southampton Colonial Soc., Nat. Woman's Farm and Garden Assn. (dir. met. br. 1975—, dir. N.Y. State div. 1978-80, mem. nat. council 1978-80), Ch. Women's League for Patriotic Service, Women's Bible Soc. N.Y., Alpha Sigma Tau. Republican. Presbyterian. Clubs: Southampton (N.Y.) Bath and Tennis, City Gardens (dir. 1963-68, mem. adv. com. 1968-74, dir. 1974-80, adv. bd. 1980-83), York (bd. govs. 1965-66, 73-77), Barnard (trustee 1979-81), Sorosis (v.p. 1979-81), Regency (N.Y.C.). Home: PO Box 86 1100 Madison Ave Apt 10C New York NY 10028-0332

NOYE, FRED C., state legislator; b. Harrisburg, Pa., May 13, 1946; s. Charles Arthur and Marie Carolyn (Heckert) N.; m. Debra Kay Noye, July 13, 1973; children: Jeremy Wade, Andrew Charles. AA, Harrisburg Area Community Coll., 1966; BS, Mansfield State Coll., 1968; MEd, Shippensburg State Coll., 1970. Tchr. Cumberland Valley Sch. Dist., Mechanicsburg, Pa., 1968-72; mem. Pa. Ho. of Reps., Harrisburg, 1972-92, caucus chmn., 1978-92. Mem. exec. com. Perry County Rep. Com., 1972—; nat. chmn. Am. Legis. Exch. Coun. Recipient David L. Lawrence Pub. Svc. award, 1984, Outstanding Legislator award Pa. Rifle and Pistol Assn., 1987, Shippensburg U. Disting. Svc. award, 1987, Elsie E. Burk Svc. award for Disting. Svc. to Alumni Mansfield U., 1988, Harrisburg Area Community Coll. Outstanding Alumni award, 1989; named Statesman of Yr. Pa. for Right to Work, 1990. Mem. Perry County Hist. Soc., Perry Historians, Masons, K.P. Lutheran. Home: 15 High St New Bloomfield PA 17068

NOYES, ANDROUS DUANE, product package and display designer, consultant; b. Jackson, Mich., Feb. 8, 1936; s. Francis Duane and Carlene A. (Androus) N.; m. L. Pauline Van Schoick, Apr. 28, 1936; children: Markham Androus, Christopher Charles. BS in Indsl. Design, Pratt Inst., 1960. Jr. designer Paul McCobb Design Assocs., N.Y.C., 1960-62; designer Monte Levin Design, N.Y.C., 1962-63; dir., designer Demartin, Marona, Cranstown & Downes, N.Y.C., 1963-79; prin. designer, sec.-treas. Macey Noyes Assocs., Inc., Wilton, Conn., 1980—. Patentee in field. Dir. Ossining (N.Y.) Jaycees Soapbox Derby, 1972, 74; dist. leader Ossining Dems., 1970-75. Recipient Clio award, 1984. Mem. Package Design Council (Best of the Best award 1985). Republican. Lutheran. Clubs: Westchester Ice Sailing (N.Y.) (commodore 1978-80); Cedar Point Yacht (Westport, Conn.). Office: Macey Noyes Assocs Inc 232 Danbury Rd Wilton CT 06897-4008

NOYES, CHARLES ROBERT, JR., corporate executive; b. Washington, Sept. 29, 1953; s. Charles Robert and Ruby (Parks) N.; m. Linda Sue Knowlton, Apr. 19, 1980; children: Robert E., Jessica A. Journeyman diploma, VA Trade Sch., Lanham, Md., 1976. Steamfitter R.E. Donovan Co., Rockville, Md., 1973-80; v.p. TAC-Communications, Inc., Rockville, 1980-83; chief exec. officer, pres. Noyes Air Conditioning, Rockville, 1983—; v.p. Total Mech. Contractors, 1984—; bd. dirs. Hvac Concepts, Inc., Rockville, Water Treatment Specialists. Mem. Property Mgmt. Assn., Mech. Contractors Assn. Republican. Methodist. Office: Noyes Air Conditioning 5451 Randolph Rd Rockville MD 20852-2615

NOYES, ELISABETH J., university system administrator; b. Hilversum, The Netherlands, Oct. 15, 1940; came to U.S., 1951, naturalized, 1966; d. Louis Jan and Wilhelmina Louise (Bollee) van Epen; m. Arnold Eugene Noyes, Sept. 2, 1961; children: James Louis, Edwin Willard. Postgrad., Middlebury Coll., 1961; MA, U. Mass., 1962; MEd, Salem (Mass.) State Coll., 1966; EdD, Nova U., 1976, postgrad. Instr. German and English North Shore Community Coll., Beverly, Mass., 1965-68, assoc. prof., 1970-76, div. chairperson, 1972-74; dept. chairperson White Pines Coll., Chester, N.H., 1968-70; prof. Mt. Wachusett Community Coll., Gardner, Mass., 1974-75; div. chairperson Bunker Hill Community Coll., Boston, 1976-78, asst. dean, 1978-83; acad. program officer Mass. Bd. Regents of Higher Edn., Boston, 1983-87; dir. acad. planning and program devel. Univ. System N.H., Durham, 1987—; mem. N.H. Post Secondary Edn. Commn., 1987—; cons. N.J. Dept. Higher, Trenton, 1986-89. Trustee White Pines Coll., Chester, 1974-85, vice chmn., 1983-85; trustee Notre Dame Prep. Sch., Fitchburg, Mass., 1980-85, Nashoba Community Hosp., Ayer, Mass., 1983—, chmn. nursing home com., 1985—; chairperson Shirley (Mass.), Sch. Com., 1974-80; moderator Town of Shirley, 1983—; bd. dirs. Mass. Moderators' Assn., 1988—, 2d v.p., 1991-92, sr. v.p., 1992—. Grantee Internat. Edn. Consortium, 1978, Am. Assn. Women Community & Jr. Colls., 1981—; recipient N.H. Phi Delta Kappa award, 1989. Mem. Nat. Coun. Tchrs. English, Conf. on Coll. Composition and Communication, Mass. Women in Pub. Higher Edn. (exec. com. 1982-86, treas. 1983-86), N.H. Women in Higher Edn. Assn., N.E. Regional Conf. on English in two-yr. colls. (exec. com. 1981-84, treas. 1982-84), Greater Boston Regional Edn. Coun. (vice chmn., chair 1978-86), Nat. Coun. State Dirs. Community and Jr. Colls. (system rep.), Modern Lang. Assn., N.E. Regional Conf. on Teaching Fgn. Langs., Chi Omega, Altrurian. Unitarian. Home: 45 Lancaster Rd Shirley MA 01464-2416 also: 37 Clearwater Dr Dover NH 03820 Office: Univ System New Hampshire Dunlap Ctr Durham NH 03824

NOYES, JUDITH GIBSON, library director; b. N.Y.C., Apr. 19, 1941; d. Charles II and Alice (Klauss) Gibson; m. Paul V. Noyes, June 1, 1991; children from previous marriage: Andrea Elizabeth Green, Michael Charles Green. BA, Carleton Coll., 1962; MLS, U. Western Ont., London, Can., 1972. Librarian edn. U. New Brunswick, 1972-74; cataloger Can. Inst. Sci. and Tech. Info., Ottawa, Ont., Can., 1975; sect. head Can. inst. Sci. and Tech. Info., 1976-78, systems devel. librarian, 1979-80, head cataloging, 1980-86; univ. librarian Colgate U., Hamilton, N.Y., 1986—; mem. OCLC Adv. Com. on Coll. and Univ. Librs., 1991—; libr. cons. Noyes & Assocs., Chgo., 1990—. Mem. ALA, Can. Libr. Assn., Am. Coll. and Rsch. Librs. (nominating com. 1988-89, 92-93, legis. com. coll. libr. sect. liaison 1989-91), Internat. Stds. Orgn. (tech. com. 46). Office: Colgate U Everett Needham Case Libr 13 Oak Dr Hamilton NY 13346

NOYES, WALTER OMAR, tree surgeon; b. Brookton, Maine, Aug. 4, 1929; s. Vinal Lloyd and Gladys May (Craig) N.; m. Anne Elizabeth Prout; children: Andrew W., Cynthia A.; m. Lorraine Pearle Gay, June 18,

1983. Grad. high sch., Lee, Maine. Tree climber Bartlett Tree Expert Co., Washington, 1949-50, R.E. Tillgren Tree Co., Brockton, Mass., 1953-55, Hartney Tree Co., Dedham, Mass., 1963-64, Town of Bridgewater, Mass., 1964-69; tree climber, foreman Davey Tree Expert Co., Las Vegas, 1969-70, Maltby Tree Co., Stoughton, Mass., 1970-79; tree lift operator Asplundh Tree Expert Co., Brockton, 1979—; devel. tng. and safety manual for entry-level jobs in field. Contbr. articles to profl. jours. Cpl. U.S. Army, 1951-53. Home: 71 Maplewood Ave Holbrook MA 02343

NUCCI, ANNAMARIA, psychiatrist; b. Nicastro, Catanzaro, Italy, June 4, 1945; d. Thomas and Tina (Pagnotta) N. BA, Montclair (N.J.) State Coll., 1961; MusM, Rosary Coll., 1962; MD, Universita Cattolica, Rome, 1971; PhD, NYU, 1976. Intern Policlinico Gemelli, Rome, 1970-71; resident in psychiatry, fellow in child psychiatry Payne Whitney Clin. Cornell U., N.Y.C., 1971-78; practice medicine specializing in psychiatry N.Y.C. and Cedar Grove, N.J, 1976—; asst. clin. prof. psychiatry N.Y. Med. Coll., N.Y.C., 1982—, 1981—; adj. prof. music NYU, 1976-79; attending psychiatrist Gracie Sq. Hosp., N.Y.C., 1977-79, Mountainside Hosp., Montclair, 1978—, N.Y. Hosp., N.Y.C., 1978—; instr. child psychology Cornell U. Med. Sch., N.Y.C., 1978—; cons. Kateri Residence, N.Y.C., 1985—. Author: Music and Medicine, 1976; (booklet) Layman's Guide to Psychiatry, 1975; poetry. Dir. Italian-Am. Concert Artists Auditions, N.Y.C., 1980-84; bd. dirs. Symphony for the UN, N.Y.C., 1980-84, N.Y.C. Yr. 2000 Com., 1985—. Recipient Anabel Mack Taylor award Pius XII Inst., 1972, Schmidt award J. Schmidt Found., 1979; named Doctor of Yr., Columbia Found., 1978. Mem. Am. Med. Women's Assn. (dir. pub. relations 1981-83), Arts Medicine Assn., N.Y. County Med. Soc., Morgagni Med. Soc., Congress Italian-Am. Orgns. (bd. dirs. 1984—), Ctr. Italian Culture (pres. 1964-68). Republican. Roman Catholic. Home: 5 Westview Ct Cedar Grove NJ 07009-1937 Office: 80 Central Park W New York NY 10023-5204

NUGENT, MAYNARD CHARLES, construction executive; b. Cleve., May 9, 1934; s. Osborne Lionel and Gertrude (Lowenthal) N.; m. Ann Taber, Nov. 20, 1961; children: Brian Taber, Glenn Webber, Lisanne. BS in Engring., Davis & Elkins Coll., 1957; postgrad., U. Pa., 1960-62, Temple U., 1969-70. Registered profl. engr., N.J., Pa. Adminstrv. engr. City of Phila., 1965-68, chief bridge constrn. engr., 1968-73; dir. engr. Constrn. Industry Advancement Fund of N.J., Pennington, 1973-77; mng. dir. Constrn. Industry Advancement Program of N.J., Cranbury, 1977—. Contbr. articles to profl. jours. Mayor Twp. of Ewing (N.J.), 1980, mem. town coun., 1977-80, mem. econ. devel. commn., 1975-91. Recipient Town Coun. Svc. award Twp. Mayors Coun., 1987; named Employee of Yr. Bur. of Surveys and Design, Phila., 1970. Fellow ASCE (dir. Phila. chpt. 1972-73, com. contract adminstrn. 1970—, com. specifications 1977-82); mem. NSPE, Profl. Engrs. in Constrn. of N.J. (treas. 1986—). Unitarian. Office: Constrn Industry Advancement NJ 101 Interchange Plz Cranbury NJ 08512-9581

NUHN, CHARLES KELSEY, advertising executive; b. Ivoryton, Conn., Aug. 6, 1925; s. George Leonard and Marian (Kelsey) N.; m. Ruth Irene Maynard (div. 1979); children: Peter W., Catherine A., James K, John M. Student, Yale U., 1946-47, NYU, 1969. Owner/pres. Nuhn Printing Co., Old Saybrook, Conn., 1953-62; pres. Nuhn Advt., Inc., Old Saybrook and Madison, Conn., 1963-89, Charles Kelsey Nuhn Advt., Madison, 1990; with Retired Advt. Execs. Recruiting Vols., Old Saybrook, Conn., 1991—; artist Old Lyme and Madison, 1987—. Mem. Lyme Acad. of Fine Arts, 1992—; assoc. mem. Lyme Art Assn., 1991—. With U.S. Army, 1945. Mem. Old Saybrook Art Assn. (v.p. 1988-89). Republican. Episcopalian. Home: 81 Lyme St # 512 Old Lyme CT 06371-2336

NUKI, KLAUS, dental educator, researcher; b. Vienna, May 5, 1931; came to U.S., 1957; s. Walter and Regina (Heiber) N.; m. Elizabeth Jill Hollis, Feb. 2, 1963; children: Guy, Keith, Max. BDS, U. London, 1955; MS in Pathology, U. Ill., Chgo., 1960; PhD, U. London, 1967. Lic. dental surgeon, Conn., U.K. House surgeon Queen Victoria Hosp., Esat Grinstead, Surrey, Eng., 1954-56; rsch. asst. dept. oral pathology U. Ill., Chgo., 1957-60, Royal Dental Coll., Aarhus, Denmark, 1963-64; practice gen. dentistry London, 1956-57; lectr. in pathology and periodontics U. London, 1961-67; head dept. oral biology U. Iowa Coll. Dentistry, 1967-75; prof., assoc. dean U. Conn. Health Ctr., Farmington, 1975-88; prof. oral diagnosis U. Conn. Sch. Dental Medicine, Farmington, 1988—. Assoc. editor Jour. Periodontal Rsch., 1975-91; contbr. numerous articles to sci. publs. Office: U Conn Health Ctr Farmington Ave Farmington CT 06032-1709

NULMAN, PHILIP ROY, advertising executive; b. Newark, Sept. 17, 1951; s. Samuel Leo and Sylvia Betty (Krasner) N.; m. Joan Gurian; children: Barrie Sylvia, Samuel Alexander. BA in Liberal Arts, Rutgers U., 1973; postgrad. fellow, George Washington, 1973-74. Copywriter, producer Boy Scouts Am., North Brunswick, N.J., 1976-78; promotions writer McCall Pub. Co., N.Y.C., 1978-79; writer/producer Creative Concepts, Plainfield, N.J., 1979-81; creative dir. FDN&P Advt., Whitehouse Station, N.J., 1981—; adjunct prof. Raritan Valley Community Coll., 1992—; adj. faculty Raritan Valley Community Coll.; lectr. Brookdale Community Coll.; seminar leader in mktg. communications, sales promotion, advt. and pub. rels. Contbr. advertisements to profl. jours. Bd. trustees Leukemia Soc., East Brunswick, N.J., 1985-87. Recipient Jasper awafdrfor Outstanding Radio Campaign, 1988, Gold Link award for pharm. advt., 1988, Silver Microphone award, 1989, Gold Link award for pharm. advt. Mem. Exec. Exch., Alliance for Clean Oceans, Greenpeace, Bus. and Industry Assocs. N.J., Ad Club N.J., Am. Assn. Advt. Agys., Direct Mktg. Assn. Democrat. Jewish. Office: FDN&P Advt 7 Old Hwy 28 White House Station NJ 08889

NULMAN, ROBERT ALAN, mayor, systems engineer; b. Fall River, Mass., Feb. 28, 1942; s. Abraham and Marie Moquin N.; m. Louise Ann Gamage (div. 1982); children: Daniel Edward (dec. 1987), Kimberly Suzanne. BS in Indsl. Mgmt., U. Mass.-Dartmouth, 1963; MBA in Indsl. Mgmt., Ariz. State U., 1968. Registered profl. mgmt. engr. Councilman Clinton (N.J.) Town Coun., 1975-85, coun. pres., 1979-85; mayor Town of Clinton, N.J., 1986—. Active in Clinton Explorer Post (Boy Scouts of Am.) 1986—, Reform Temple of Hunterdon County, bd. dirs., 1987—; commr. Clinton Fire Co. 1980-84; mem. Clinton Hist. Mus. 1974—, Hunterdon Art Ctr. 1974—, Hunterdon County Dem. Com., pres. exec. com. 1987—. Capt. USAF, 1964-71. Recipient Pres.'s Environ. Leadership award U.S. EPA 1987, Man of the Yr. award U.S. Jaycees, Tulsa, 1966, citation of Merit N.J. Mayors Assn., 1988. Mem. U.S. Army Mgmt. Engring. Tng. Agy. (fed. cert.), N.J. Conf. of Mayors (bd. dirs. 1987—), Hunterdon County Conf. of Mayors (pres. 1986—), Hunterdon County Mcpl. Officers Assn. (v.p. 1988, pres. 1989—), N.J. State Water Policy Coun., 1978-82, N.J. Mayors Assn., N.J. League of Municipalities (bd. dirs. 1990—), Assn. for Computing Machinery, Am. Legion. Democrat. Jewish. Home: 21 Union Rd Clinton NJ 08809-1229 Office: Town of Clinton 43 Leigh St Clinton NJ 08809-1398

NULTON, JOHN DAVID, federal official; b. Phila., Aug. 25, 1945; s. John Henry and Thelma Elizabeth (Sterrett) N.; m. Lynn Janet Porter, Oct. 5, 1968; children: Jason David, Jennifer Lynn, Julia Anne. BSME, Drexel Inst. Tech., 1968; MSME, Stanford U., 1970. Reactor program intern U.S. AEC, Washington, 1968-71; dep. dir. Office of Advanced Reactor Programs U.S. Dept. of Energy, Washington, 1986—, 1986-88; dir. new prodn. gas reactor program U.S. Dept. Energy, Washington, 1988—. Bd.dirs. Darnestown Swim and Racquet Club, 1975-77, vice chmn., 1978; mem. adminstrv. bd. Meth. Ch. Gaithersburg, Md., 1978—, chmn. new ch. bldg. com., 1981-82, stewardship coord., 1986—, v.p. Men sect., 1983-84, pres., 1985, chmn. adminstrv. bd., 1985-88, chmn. stewardship com., 1988-91; coach Montgomery County Soccer League, 1983-84. Methodist. Office: US Dept of Energy 1000 Independence Ave SW Washington DC 20585

NUMATA, NOBUO, software company executive, consultant, engineer; b. Ashiya, Hyogo, Japan, Mar. 5, 1954; came to U.S., 1964; s. Jack Tetsuya and Tomoko (Noguchi) N. BEE, Princeton U., 1976; M in Computer Sci., Columbia U., 1979. Registered profl. engr., Japan. Analyst Impex (Japan) Ltd., Tokyo, 1976-78, mgr., 1978-80, v.p., 1980-82, pres., 1982—; pres. Tecnopac Inc., N.Y.C., 1988—; v.p. Am. Tech. Group, Palo Alto, Calif., 1984-86. Contbr. articles to profl. jours. Trustee Princeton-in-Asia, 1979—. Mem. Tokyo Am. Club, Fgn. Corrs. Club Japan, Tokyo Lawn and Tennis Club, Internat. House Japan, Princeton Club of Tokyo, The Tokyo Club, Univ. Club of N.Y.C. Home: 870 United Nations Plz Apt 15B New York NY 10017 Office: Tecnopac Inc 666 Fifth Ave 14th Fl New York NY 10103

NUNAN, FRANCIS A., obstetrician-gynecologist; b. Bryn Mawr, Pa., Feb. 6, 1932; s. Francis Anthony and Mary Kathryn (McCallion) N.; m. Shirley Anne Slater, June 21, 1958; children: Francis A. III, Michael C., James P., Nancy E., Barbara J., Joseph P., Kathryn M. BA, Harvard U., 1954; MD, Temple U., 1958. Diplomate Am. Bd. Ob-gyn. Intern Butterworth Hosp., Grand Rapids, 1958-59; resident Albany (N.Y.C.) Med. Ctr., 1962-65; asst. prof. medicine Albany Med. Coll., 1965—; pvt. practice Albany, 1965—; med. bd. dirs. Cerebral Palsy Soc., Albany, 1970—. Sec. Boys Baseball, Albany, 1960-75; cubmaster Boy Scouts Am., Albany, 1969-74, scoutmaster, 1970-80, bd. dirs., 1974—. Capt. USAF, 1959-62. Mem. Welferts Roost Country Club. Republican. Roman Catholic. Home: 23 De Lucia Ter Albany NY 12211-2005 Office: 317 S Manning Blvd Albany NY 12208-1738

NUNES, ANTHONY CHARLES, physics educator; b. New Bedford, Mass., Nov. 1, 1942; s. Arthur Caetano and Pauline Francis (Boomer) N.; m. Meredith Farrah Holden, Dec. 19, 1967 (div. 1969); 1 child, Helen; m. Simone Edith Duby, Oct. 27, 1972; children: Christopher, Benjamin. BSc in Physics, MIT, 1964, PhD in Physics, 1969. Rsch. assoc. physics dept. Brookhaven Nat. Lab., Upton, N.Y., 1969-71, rsch. assoc. biology dept., 1971-74; physicist Inst. Lane-Langevin, Grenoble, Isere, France, 1974-76; assoc. prof. physics dept. U. R.I., Kingston, 1976-82, prof. physics dept., 1982—; cons. Ferrofluidics Corp., Nashua, N.H., 1987—, Advanced Magnetics, Inc., Cambridge, Mass., 1989—. Mem. Chorus of Westerly, R.I., 1977—. Grantee Rsch. Corp., 1977, NSF, 1978, 81, 84, 89. Mem. AAAS, Am. Phys. Soc., Sigma Xi, Sigma Pi Sigma. Office: U RI Dept Physics Kingston RI 02881

NUNEZ, PATRICIA, rehabilitation counselor; b. Elizabeth, N.J., July 23, 1959. BA in Psychology, Rutgers U., 1980; MA in Rehab. Counseling, Seton Hall U., 1982. Rehab. counselor, program coord. RWJ Rehab. Inst., Edison, N.J., 1983-90; rehab. supr. Continental Rehab. Resources, Inc., Piscataway, N.J., 1990—. Commr. Middlesex County (N.J.) Commn. on Handicapped, 1983-90, Cmmn. on Rehabilitation Counselor Certification, 1992-1997. Switzer scholar, 1990. Mem. Nat. Rehab. Counseling Assn. (pres. 1991), N.E. Rehab. Counseling Assn. (pres. 1986-89). Home: 40 Netherwood Cir Edison NJ 08820 Office: Continental Rehab Resources 1 Corporate Pl S Piscataway NJ 08854-6146

NUNEZ-LAWTON, MIGUEL G., international finance specialist; b. Havana, Cuba, Feb. 8, 1949; came to U.S., 1964; s. Miguel Nunez-Portuondo and Silvia Lawton-Alfonso. BBA, Georgetown U., 1971, postgrad. in Econs., 1973. Asst. treas. Deltec Securities Corp., N.Y.C., 1971; debt specialist internat. econs. dept. World Bank, Washington, 1973—; UNCTAD chief tech. adviser Bureau of the Treasury, Manila, Philippines, 1989-90. Bd. dirs., treas. Friends of Art Mus. of the Americas, OAS, Washington, 1988-90; bd. dirs. Friends of Peru., 1991—. Roman Catholic. Home: 2844 Wisconsin Ave NW Apt 510 Washington DC 20007-4720 Office: World Bank 1818 H St NW Washington DC 20433-0002

NUNN, ROBERT ERIC, engineering educator, consultant; b. Luton, England, Mar. 1, 1947; came to U.S., 1975; s. Robert John Ernest and Constance Mary (Large) N.; m. Edith Ficker, Mar. 20, 1971; children: Elanor Louise, Caroline Marie, Stephanie Fiona. ACGI, Imperial Coll., London, 1969; DIC, Imperial Coll., 1975; BSc in Engring., London U., 1969, PhD, 1975. Registered profl. engr., Ohio; chartered engr., U.K. Engring. apprentice Vauxhall Div., GM Corp., Luton, U.K., 1965-70, purchase engr., 1970-72; devel. engr. USS Chem., Ironton, Ohio, 1975-77; dir. R&D HPM Corp., Mt. Gilead, Ohio, 1977-84, tech. dir., 1984-85; assoc. prof. U. Mass., Lowell, 1985-90, prof., 1990—, chmn. and dept. head, 1992—; engring. cons. 1985—; trustee Plastics Inst. Am., Hoboken, N.J., 1986-90; dir. Plastics Edn. Found., Brookfield, Conn., 1985-88. Contbr. articles to profl. jours.; patentee in field. Fellow Soc. Plastics Engrs. (Injection Molding div. Best Paper award 1981, 89, Leadership award 1982, Chmn.'s award 1985, Engr. of the Yr. award 1989), Plastics and Rubber Inst.; mem. Inst. Mech. Engrs., Am. Soc. Mech. Engrs., Am. Inst. Chem. Engrs., Am. Soc. for Engring. Edn. Home: 19 Windsor Blvd Londonderry NH 03053-3695 Office: Univ Mass Plastics Engring Dept Lowell MA 01854

NUNNELLLEY, ROBERT BERRY, art educator; b. Birmingham, Ala., Sept. 5, 1929; s. Arthur Johnston and Zelah Elizabeth (Hall) N. BA, U. Ark., 1951, MFA, 1956. Grad. asst. U. Ark., Fayetteville, 1954-55; painter N.Y.C., 1956-71; mus. asst. to the dir. Mus. of Contemporary Crafts, 1962-65; prof. art Fairleigh Dickinson U., Rutherford, N.J., 1966—; dir. Maples Gallery Fairleigh Dickinson U., Teaneck, N.J., 1984-89. One-man show Hudson River Mus., Yonkers, N.Y., 1967, So. Vt. Art Ctr., Manchester, 1979, Schenectady Mus., 1979; exhibited in numerous group shows. Recipient purchase award Rockhill Nelson Gallery, Kansas City, Mo., 1955; fellow Boston Mus. Sch., 1952-53, Colorado Springs Fine Arts Ctr., 1954; rsch. grantee Fairleigh Dickinson U., Teaneck, 1967. Democrat. Office: Fairleigh Dickinson U Art Dept Rutherford NJ 07070

NUSBAUM, MARLENE ACKERMAN, marketing professional; b. Portsmouth, Va., June 13, 1949; d. Martin and Betsy Freda (Katz) Ackerman; m. Robert Collier Nusbaum Jr., June 27, 1971; 1 child, Jessica Lynn. Deuxième Degré, Université d'Orléans Tours, 1970; BA magna cum laude, Rutgers U., 1971; MA, Brown U., 1973, PhD with distinction, 1980. Tchr. French Dana Hall Sch., Wellesley, Mass., 1974-75; master French and German Groton (Mass.) Sch., 1975-80; French instr. dept. humanities MIT, Cambridge, 1981; assoc., product mgr. Digital Equipment Corp., Maynard, Mass., 1981-83; mktg. mgr. interactive video Digital Equipment Corp., Bedford, Mass., 1983-85; pvt. practice mktg. cons. Newton, Mass., 1985-91; program mgr. BIS Strategic Decisions, Norwell, Mass., 1991—; mem. mktg. adv. com. Global-Sports Ltd., Boston, 1989-90; cons. editor Heinle & Heinle Pub., Boston, 1981. Author: (with Verdier) Parlez Sans Peur!, 1983, (with Holden-Avard and Verdier) Le Français Sans Peur, 1991, (with Beyer) Beth Israel Hosp. Children's Doctor's Kit for Good Health, 1990. Organizer class size PTA Com., Newton, 1986-88, chairperson roundtable exec. com., 1987-88. Chairperson roundtable, exec. com. Newton PTA Coun., 1987-88. Mem. N.E. Conf. Tchrs. of Fgn. Langs., Am. Coun. Tchrs. Fng. Langs., Mass. Fgn. Lang. Assn.

NUSIM, STANLEY HERBERT, chemical engineer; b. N.Y.C., Oct. 2, 1935; s. Seymour and Ranna T. (Weiner) N.; m. Marcia Anne Borsig, Feb. 21, 1960; children: David Mark, Jill Wendi. BSChemE, CCNY, 1957; MSChemE, N.Y. U., 1960, PhD, 1967. Rsch. engr. Battelle Meml. Inst., Columbus, Ohio, 1956; researcher, chem. engring. Merck & Co. Rsch. Labs. Div., Rahway, N.J., 1957-68; sect. mgr., chem. engring R & D Merck Rsch. Labs. Div., Rahway, 1968-70; tech. svcs. mgr. Merck Chem. Mfg. Div., Rahway, 1970-73, mfg. mgr., 1973-80; dir. subsidiary projects Merck Internat. Div., Rahway, 1981-82, exec. dir. Latin Am., Far East, Near East ops., 1982-88; exec. dir. licensee, Latin Am., Far East, Asia ops. Merck Pham. Mfg. Div., Rahway, 1989—; adv. bd. CCNY Sch. Engring., 1982—. Author: Kinetic Studies on C4 Hydrocarbon Systems, 1967. V.p. men's club Temple Beth Shalom, Livingston, N.J., 1975-78; rep. to bd. edn. Livingston Home and Sch. Assn., 1982-83. Mem. Am. Inst. Chem. Engrs. (bd. dir. N. Jersey sect. 1968-71, scholarship award 1955), Am. Chem. Soc., Tau Beta Pi, Garden State Yacht Club (bd. govs. 1987-88). Jewish. Home: 454165 Prospect Ave West Orange NJ 07052-3214 Office: Merck & Co Inc 126 E Lincoln Ave Rahway NJ 07065-4687

NUTAITIS, CHARLES FRANK, chemistry educator, researcher; b. Wilkes Barre, Pa., Mar. 5, 1958; s. Charles Joseph and Loretta Ann (Galicki) N.; m. Judith Ann Obaza, Sept. 4, 1982. BS in Chemistry, King's Coll., 1980; PhD in Chemistry, Dartmouth Coll., 1985. Rsch. assoc. Dartmouth Coll., Hanover, N.H., 1985, U. Va., Charlottesville, 1986-87; asst. prof. Lafayette Coll., Easton, Pa., 1987—. Contbr. 15 articles to profl. jours. Keck fellow, Keck Found., Easton, Pa., 1987; Pew Found. grantee, Easton, 1990. Mem. Am. Chem. Soc. (sr. chemistry award, 1980), Coun. on Undergrad. Rsch., Middle Atlantic Assn. Liberal Arts Chemistry Tchrs. Roman Catholic. Office: Lafayette Coll Olin Hall Easton PA 18042

NYBERG, DAVID ALAN, educator; b. Ft. William, Ont., Can., Mar. 3, 1943; came to U.S., 1949; s. Carl Albert and Evelyn (Austin) N.; m. Nancy O. Tomkinson, Feb. 20, 1974; children: Jonathan, Noah. AB, Stanford U., 1965, PhD, 1972. Asst. prof. U. Ill. Coll. Edn., Urbana, 1971-73; asst. prof. SUNY Grad. Sch. Edn., Buffalo, 1973-76, assoc. prof., 1976-81, chmn. dept. edn. founds., 1976-77, assoc. dean, 1978-82, prof., 1981—; vis. prof. Simon Fraser U., Vancouver, B.C., 1980; acad. vis. Dept. Ednl. Studies Mansfield Coll.; rch. assoc. Oxford U., England, 1986-87; assoc. editor Ednl. Theory, U. Ill., 1981—; cons. in field. Author: Tough and Tender Learning, 1971, Power Over Power, 1981, (with others) The Erosion of Education, 1981; editor: The Philosophy of Open Education; contbr. articles to profl. jours. Mem. bd. trustees The Park Sch., Buffalo, 1989—. Rsch. grantee Ctr. Dewey Studies. Mem. Philosophy of Edn. Soc. (pres. 1986-87), Philosophy Edn. Soc. Great Britain. Office: SUNY 468 Baldy Hall Buffalo NY 14260

NYDICK, DAVID, superintendent of schools; b. N.Y.C., Feb. 10, 1929; s. Irving and Minnie (Bilibom) N.; m. Gilda Pivnick, June 14, 1953; children: Leslie Ruth, Jay Scott. BA, NYU, 1950, MA, 1952, profl. Diploma, 1960, postgrad., 1960—. Tchr. pub. schs., Great Neck, N.Y., 1954-60; prin. asst. supt. Princeton Pub. Schs., N.J., 1961-65; asst. supt. Jericho Pub. Schs., N.Y., 1965-68, supt., 1968-84; exec. dir. Guide Dog Found., Smithtown, N.Y., 1984-89; supt. Syosset (N.Y.) Pub. Schs., 1989-90, Bethpage (N.Y.) Pub. Schs., 1991—; assoc. prof. L.I. U., 1975—, Hofstra U., 1976—, Pace U., 1978—; asst. prof. Bklyn. Coll., 1979—; arbitrator Am. Arbitration Assn., Better Bus. Bur. Syndicated columnist UPI, Copley News, DANY News, 1962—. Pres., East Plains Mental Health Ctr., 1964—. Served with U.S. Army, 1952-54. Recipient Edn. Achievement award NCCJ, 1975. Mem. N.Y.U. Alumni Assn. (pres. 1971-72), Am. Assn. Sch. Adminstrs., Ednl. Writers Assn., Overseas Press Club, Nat. Press Club, Masons. Home and Office: 22 Lesley Dr Syosset NY 11791-5298

NYE, JUDITH LIN, psychologist, educator; b. Madison, Wis., Nov. 23, 1958; d. William J. and Jeanne F. (Peters) N. BS in Sociology and Anthropology, Va. Commonwealth U., 1982, BS in Psychology, 1982, MS in Psychology, 1985, PhD in Psychology, 1988. Asst. prof. dept. psychology Monmouth Coll., West Long Branch, N.J., 1987--. Contbr. articles to profl. jours. Mem. Am. Psychol. Assn., Am. Psychol. Soc., Southeastern Psychol. Assn., Soc. Advancement Social Psychology, Phi Kappa Phi. Office: Monmouth Coll Dept Psychology West Long Branch NJ 07764

NYE, WILLIAM ROGER, psychologist; b. Haverhill, Mass., Oct. 23, 1940; s. Kenneth Enoch and Virginia Pauline (Cook) N.; m. Marian Barbara Abowitz, June 30, 1970 (div. 1983); children: Michael Shepherd Abowitz Nye; 1 stepson, Christopher J. Wells. BA, Yale U., 1962; MDiv, Union Theol. Sem., N.Y.C., 1965; PhD, Adelphi U., Garden City, N.Y., 1981. Lic. psychologist, N.Y. Pastor Ch. of the Evangel, Bklyn., 1965-77; asst. minister Plymouth Ch. of the Pilgrims, Bklyn., 1977-82; pastor All Souls Universalist Ch., Bklyn., 1983—; exec. dir. Blanton-Peale Counseling Ctrs., Forest Hills, N.Y., 1983—; pres. bd. Met. Assn. of N.Y. Conf. of United Ch. of Christ, 1969-73, moderator, 1982-83. Del. Dem. Nat. Conv., Miami, 1972; pres. Pastoral and Ednl. Svcs., Brklyn., 1983-87, The Vinmont Found., N.Y.C., 1988—; sec. N.Y. Congl. Home for Aged, Bklyn., 1980-88. Mem. Am. Psychol. Assn. Democrat. United Ch. of Christ. Home: 888 E 19th St Brooklyn NY 11230-3108

NYERGES, JOHN ELEK, musician; b. Rochester, N.Y., June 26, 1958; s. Sandor Elek and Lena (Angeline) N.; m. Kathleen Grace Darroch, Apr. 25, 1981; children: Joshua Michael, Elissa Christina, Carina Ann. MusB, U. Rochester, 1980. Pianist, tchr. Rochester City Schs., 1980-85; pianist Jazz Winds Jazz Fest, Westfield, N.Y., 1987; mem. faculty, jazz instr. Hochstein Sch. Music, Rochester, 1988-90; pianist, arranger various artists, record cos., 1988—; pianist, composer Syracuse (N.Y.) Jazz Festival, 1991, 92; pianist, arranger Syracuse Symphony/Miller Beer Urban League, 1990, Urban League/Miller Beer, Syracuse, 1991; pianist Prophecy Records/Jeff Tyzik Studio, Rochester, 1989—; pianist, composer, producer NBR Records/Step Into the Lite Music, Rochester, 1991—; pianist concerts with Rochester Symphony, Buffalo Symphony and Chautauqua Symphony; pianist with Paquito D'Rivera Hochstein Sch., Rochester, 1990; pianist with R.P.O. Vets. Outreach Ctr., Rochester, 1991; featured artist WGMC Radio, Rochester; featured artist WGMC Radio, Rochester, 1992, WBFO Radio, Buffalo, 1992, TV 24/Nat. Pub. TV, 1988-92. Asst. coach Charlotte Youth Athletic Assn., Rochester, 1991. Artist's grantee N.Y. State Coun. Arts, 1989. Mem. Am. Fedn. Musicians. Home and Office: NBR Records/Step Into the Lite Music 40 Tiernan St Rochester NY 14612

NYGAARD, RICHARD LOWELL, judge; b. 1940. BS cum laude, U. So. Calif., 1969; JD, U. Mich. Mem. Orton, Nygaard & Dunlevy, 1972-81; judge Ct. Common Pleas, 6th Dist. Pa., Erie, 1981-88, U.S. Ct. Appeals (3d cir.) Pa., Erie, 1988—. Councilman erie County, 1977. With USNR, 1958-64. Mem. Pa. Bar Assn., Erie County Bar Assn. Office: US Ct Appeals 3rd Ct 500 First Nat Bank Bldg 717 State St Erie PA 16501-1341*

NYLANDER, RICHARD CONRAD, museum curator; b. Boston, May 17, 1944; s. Donald Oliver and Barbara (Gould) N.; m. Jane Louise Cayford, Jan. 27, 1938; 1 child, Timothy Frost. BA, Coll. William and Mary, 1966; MA, SUNY, Oneonta, 1972. Curatorial asst. Soc. for the Preservation of New England Antiquities, Boston, 1967-70, curator of collections, 1970—; mem. Com. for Preservation of the White House, Washington, 1990—. Author: Wallpaper for Historic Buildings, 1983, rev. and enlarged, 1992. Mem. Hist. Dist. Commn., Portsmouth, N.H., 1989—. Mem. Decorative Arts Soc., Cooperstown Grad. Assn., Soc. for Preservation New Eng. Antiquities (life), Warner House Assn. (trustee 1986—). Home: 17 Franklin St Portsmouth NH 03801-4501 Office: Soc for the Preservation New England Antiquities 141 Cambridge St Boston MA 02114-2799

NYMAN, GEORGIANNA BEATRICE, painter; b. Arlington, Mass., June 11, 1930; d. Daniel Eugene Nyman and Irene Krans (Müller) Lombardi; m. David Aronson, June 10, 1956; children: Judith, Benjamin, Abigail. Diploma, Boston Mus. Sch. Art., 1952, student, 1952-54; postgrad., Longy Sch. Music, Cambridge, Mass., 1965-73. interviewer in field. Portraits displayed in Brookline (Mass.) Hosp., Inst. Critical Care Medicine, U. Pitts., McClosky Inst. Voice Therapy, Boston, U.S. Supreme Ct., Washington, New Eng. Sch. of Law, Boston, 1991, Milton (Mass.) Acad.; group exhbns. include Shore Studio Gallery, Boston, 1960, 61, Lee Nordness Gallery, N.Y.C., 1963, Copley Soc. Boston, 1980, Nat. Acad. Design, N.Y.C., 1990; solo exhbns. include Nancy Lincoln Gallery, Brookline, 1990; represented in permanent collections Rose Art Mus., Brandeis U., U. Pitts. Sch. Medicine; commd. portraits include Justice Sandra Day O'Connor, Mr. and Mrs. Pieh-headmaster of Milton Acad., 1992. Jurist Art and Mental Illness--An Itinerary Boston U., 1989; active in LeMoyne Found., Fla., 1989. Recipient Boit prize, 1951, cert. of merit NAD, 1992; Kate Morse fellow Boston Mus. Fine Arts, 1953. Mem. Women's Indsl. Inst. (life mem.), Mass. Soc. Mayflower Descendants. Home and Studio: 137 Brimstone Ln Sudbury MA 01776 also: RR 2, Cornwall, PE Canada C0A 1HO

NYMAN, ROBERT JAY, service company executive; b. Jersey City, July 30, 1948; s. David Nyman and Pearl (Kinsler) N.; m. Judith Ellen Warshaw; children: Corey Todd, Craig Asher. BS, NYU, 1971; D of Bus. Adminstrn. (hon.), Johnson and Wales U. Asst. dir. restaurant assn. Newark (N.Y.) Airport, 1966-71; instr. Ind. U. of Pa., 1971-72; dir. restaurant assn. Allentown (Pa.) Airport, 1972; ops. analyst Marriott Corp., N.Y.C., 1973; hotel food and beverage mgr. Loew's Hotel-Regency Hotel, N.Y.C., 1974-75; dir. food and beverage Hyatt Hotel, Chgo., 1976-77; v.p. Playboys Clubs Internat., Chgo., 1977-80; pres. Food Service Assn., Chgo., 1980-83, The George Lang Corp., N.Y.C., 1983—, The Nyman Group Ltd., 1992—; bd. overseas Ctr. for Food and Hotel Mgmt., N.Y.U., 1984—. Active adv. council Johnson & Wales U., Providence, 1977—, alumni council NYU, 1986—. Recipient Hon. Doctorate of Bus. Adminstrn., Johnson & Walsh U. Mem. Chaine Des Rottisseurs, Nat. Restaurant Assn., Culinary Inst. Am. (amb.). Office: The Nyman Group Ltd 19 Driftwood Dr Livingston NJ 07039

NYQUIST, THOMAS EUGENE, academic administrator; b. Froid, Mont., June 20, 1931; s. Richard Theodore and Lydia (Baker) N.; m. Corinne Elaine Johnson, Dec. 22, 1956; children: Jonathan Eugene, Lynn Marie Nyquist Bergstrausser. BA, Macalester Coll., 1956; MA, U. Mont., 1958; PhD, Northwestern U., 1966. Prof. SUNY, New Paltz, 1968-76; adminstr. cen. div. SUNY, Albany, 1976-90; pres. Nyquist Assocs., New Paltz, N.Y., 1991—; mem. adv. bd. George Washington's Hdqrs., Newburgh, N.Y., 1980—; acad. dir. N.Y. Edn. Dept., Kenya, 1982. Author: (monograph) Urban Africans in South Africa, 1977, (book) African Middle Class Elite,

1983. County legislator Ulster County Legislature, 1976-79; dep. mayor Village of New Paltz, 1983-87, mayor, 1987—; chmn. Centennial Com., New Paltz, 1986-87; bd. dirs. Ulster Region Credit Union, Kingston, N.Y., 1976-87, Partnership in Svc. Learning, 1985—, Ulster Performing Arts Ctr., 1978-82; treas. Lower Hudson Conf., 1988, 89-90, 91—. With U.S. Army, 1952-54, Japan. Fellow SUNY, South Africa, 1975; Ford Found. grantee, 1986. Mem. African Studies Assn., N.Y. African Studies Assn. (exec. bd. dirs. 1973—, co-editor newsletter 1974—), Am. Polit. Sci. Assn. Democrat. Home: 62 S Chestnut St New Paltz NY 12561-1936 Office: Office of Mayor Village Hall 25 Plattekill Ave New Paltz NY 12561-1918

OAKES, JAMES L., federal judge; b. Springfield, Ill., Feb. 21, 1924; m. Evelena S. Kenworthy, Dec. 29, 1973; one son, two daus. by previous marriage. A.B., Harvard U., 1945, LL.B., 1947; LL.D. (hon.), New Eng. Coll., 1976, Suffolk U., 1980. Bar: Calif. 1949, Vt. 1950. Pvt. practice Brattleboro, Vt.; spl. counsel Vt. Pub. Service Commn., 1959-60; counsel Vt. Statutory Revision Commn., 1957-60; mem. Vt. Senate, 1961-65; atty. gen. Vt., 1967-69, U.S. dist. judge, 1970-71; U.S. circuit judge 2d Circuit Ct. Appeals, 1971-89, 92—, chief judge, 1989-92. Address: US Ct Appeals Box 696 Brattleboro VT 05302-0696

OAKES, JOHN GEORGE HARTMAN, publishing company executive; b. N.Y.C., July 15, 1961; s. John Bertram and Margery (Hartman) O.; m. Carin Kuoni, Sept. 23, 1989. BA cum laude, Princeton U., 1983. Freelancer Internat. Herald Tribune, Le Monde, AP, Paris, 1983-85; editor Grove Press, N.Y.C., 1985-87; co-pub. Four Walls Eight Windows, N.Y.C., 1987—; editorial cons. Barricade Books, N.Y.C., 1991—. Editor: In the Realms of the Unreal: Insane Writings, 1991. Bertelsmann scholar, 1992. Home: 130 W 24th St Apt 5A New York NY 10011-1938 Office: Four Walls Eight Windows Inc 39 W 14th St Ste 503 New York NY 10011

OAKLEY, DONALD LILLY, chemistry educator, consultant; b. Port Washington, N.Y., July 16, 1939; s. Alan C. and Malba (Lilly) O.; m. Jane L. Shellenberger, June 10, 1961; children: Judith, Daniel. AB in Chemistry, Gettysburg Coll., 1961; MST in Sci. Edn., Cornell U., 1968, PhD, 1971. Tchr. chemistry and physics North Penn High Sch., Lansdale, Pa., 1965-68; asst. dir. Acad. Year Inst. Cornell U., Ithaca, N.y., 1969-71; prof. sci. Lock Haven (Pa.) U., 1971—; workshop leader, sci. edn. cons. various sch. dists. in cen. Pa., 1975—. Contbr. articles to profl. jours. Bd. dirs. Am. Cancer Soc., Lock Haven, 1981—. Capt. U.S. Army, 1961-65, Germany. Am. Chem. Soc. grantee, 1986-87, 81-91. Mem. Nat. Sci. Tchrs. Assn. (life), Am. Chem. Soc. (chmn. local sect. 1987, bd. dirs. 1981-91), Pa. Sci. Tchrs. Assn. (life), Assn. for Edn. of Tchrs. of Sci., Phi Delta Kappa, Phi Kappa Phi. Republican. Lutheran. Home: Box 234 247 Park Ave Woolrich PA 17779 Office: Lock Haven U 205 Ulmer Hall Lock Haven PA 17745

OAKLEY, JAMES FRANKLIN, III, risk management executive; b. Orange, N.J., Mar. 22, 1947; s. James Franklin and Ruth (Alley) O.; m. Susan Mindnich (div. 1989); 1 child: Kate. Student, Fairleigh Dickenson U., 1966-68. Pres. Merit Agy. of Pa., Inc., Bala Cynwyd, 1971-80, Harbor Hill Excess, Balt., 1980-92, Wilson-Oakley Nat., 1981-82, Nat. Risk Mgmt., Inc., Valley Forge, 1983—. Co-author: The Cooperative Self-Funded Worker's Compensation Trust Method (pat. 1982); contbr. articles to profl. jours. Bd. dirs. Cabrini Coll., Radnor, Pa., 1991. With U.S. Army. Mem. Pinehurst (N.C.) Country Club, Phoenixville (Pa.) C. of C. Office: Nat Risk Mgmt Inc 1288 Valley Forge Rd PO Box 1127 Valley Forge PA 19481

OAKS, MAURICE DAVID, pharmaceutical company executive; b. Everett, Pa., Jan. 22, 1934; s. Jacob Garvin and Hannah Alma (Young) O.; m. Judith Ann Rayne; 1 child, Kimberly. BS in Biology, Franklin and Marshall Coll., 1956. Div. sales mgr. Squibb Pharm., Columbus, Ohio, 1969-71; product mgr. Topical Steriods Squibb Pharm., Princeton, N.J., 1971-74, product mgr. Velosef, 1974-76, group product dir. antibiotics, cardiovasculars, and insulin, 1976-78, dir. product planning, U.S., 1979-80, v.p. world wide mktg. devel., 1980-82, v.p. mktg. svcs., 1982-85, pres. Princeton Pharm. Products, 1985-89; exec. v.p. Squibb Pharm. Group U.S., Princeton, N.J., 1989-90; v.p. worldwide ops. planning Bristol-Myers Squibb Pharms. Ops., Princeton, 1990—; bd. dirs. Nat. Pharm. Coun., McLean, Va., 1985-90, exec. com., 1988-90. Coun. mem. Franklin & Marshall Coll. Commn. on Found. and Corp. Support, Lancaster, Pa., 1987-90, ann. fund class capt., 1991-92; mem. YMCA, Doylestown, Pa. With U.S. Army, 1956-58. Mem. Pharm. Advt. Club, Am. Mgmt. Assn., Squibb Mgmt. Assn. (pres. 1981-82), Bucks County Hist. Soc., Doylestown Country Club. Republican. Methodist. Office: Bristol-Myers Squibb PO Box 4000 Princeton NJ 08543-4000

OATES, JOHNNY, professional baseball team manager; b. Sylva, N.C., Jan. 21, 1946. BS in Health and Phys. Edn., Va. Tech. U. Player minor league team Chgo. White Sox, 1967; player minor league team Balt. Orioles, 1967-71, player, 1970, 72, mgr. minor league team, 1988, coach, 1989-91, mgr., 1991—; player Atlanta Braves, 1973-75, Phila. Phillies, 1975-76, L.A. Dodgers, 1977-79; player N.Y. Yankees, 1980, minor league coach, 1981-83; coach Chgo. Cubs, 1984-87. Named Internat. League Mgr. of Yr., 1988. Office: Balt Orioles Meml Stadium Baltimore MD 21218*

OATES, PETER JOSEPH, medical researcher; b. N.Y.C., July 26, 1947; s. Peter Francis and Helen Cecilia (Delaney) O.; m. Nancy Jean Deffaa, Aug. 21, 1971; children: Peter Michael, Nancy Katherine. BS, Boston Coll., 1969; PhD, Vanderbilt U., 1975, postgrad., 1975-79. Rsch. scientist cen. rsch. div. Pfizer, Inc., Groton, Conn., 1979-81, sr. rsch. scientist, 1981, project leader, 1982-85, sr. rsch. investigator, 1986—; adj. prof. molecular and cell biology U. Conn., Storrs, 1988-92. Contbr. articles to profl. jours. and chpts. to books. Dr. Chaim Weizmann postdoctoral fellow Calif. Inst. Tech., 1976-77, 77-78, 78-79. Mem. Am. Diabetes Assn., European Assn. for Study Diabetes, Am. Soc. for Cell Biology, Am. Physiol. Soc. Roman Catholic. Home: 16 Ferry View Dr Gales Ferry CT 06335-1510 Office: Pfizer Inc Cen Rsch Div Dept Metabolic Diseases Groton CT 06340

OATES, RICHARD PATRICK, biostatistician; b. Gary, Ind., Mar. 17, 1937; s. Francis Henry and Abbie Isabel (Johnson) O.; m. Christina Melnyk, Sept. 8, 1968. BS, Purdue U., 1958; MS, Iowa State U., 1960, PhD, 1964. Rsch. asst. Iowa State U., Ames, 1958-64; postdoctoral fellow NIH, 1964-65; asst. prof. SUNY Upstate Med. Ctr., Syracuse, 1965-75, assoc. prof., 1975-87, prof., 1987—; acting chmn. dept. preventive medicine, 1985-90, chmn., 1990—; cons. Devel. and Evaluation Assn., Syracuse, 1978-79, Eye Rsch. Inst., Syracuse, 1978—, Onon Community Coll., Syracuse, 1982-90; project dir. Cen. N.Y. Occupational Health Clin. Ctr., 1987—. Contbr. articles to profl. jours. Cons. Performing Arts Com., Syracuse, 1966-67. Mem. N.Y. Acad. Scis., Am. Pub. Health Assn., Sigma Xi. Avocations: tennis; cycling; music. Office: SUNY Health Sci Ctr 750 E Adams St Syracuse NY 13210

OATES DOMENICK, KATHRYN, association executive; b. Washington, June 21, 1959; m. Ralph Domenick Jr., May 2, 1987. BBA, George Washington U., 1982. Exec. asst. to pres. Nat. Ctr. Legis. Rsch., Washington, 1982-83; rsch. dir. Am. Bus. Media Coun., Washington, 1983-84; coord. mem. svcs., dir. membership-Edn. Found., dir. ops. Adhesive and Sealant Coun., Inc., Washington, 1984—. Pres. Clermont Tenants Assn., Washington, 1983-84, v.p., pres. Potomac Park Apts. Tenants Assn., Washington, 1985-87; arch. and engring. com. Ft. Ellensworth Condominium Assn., 1991. Mem. Am. Soc. Assn. Execs., Assn. Found. Group. Republican. Methodist. Office: Adhesive/Sealant Coun Inc 1627 K St NW Ste 1000 Washington DC 20006-1702

O'BEIRNE, ANDREW JON, virologist; b. Phila., Oct. 26, 1944; s. Carl Ellis and Gloria M. (Teti) O'B.; m. Patricia Ann O'Neill, June 22, 1968; children: Jonathan, Elizabeth. MPH, U. Mich., 1972, DrPH, 1973. Co-head virus prodn. Whittaker Bioproducts Inc., Walkersville, Md., 1973-74, dir. R & D, 1974-78, v.p. R & D, 1978-80, v.p. ops. and R & D, 1980-83, sr. v.p., 1983—, gen. mgr. diagnostics div., 1984—; lectr., mem. sci. adv. coun. Hood Coll., Frederick, Md., 1983—. With USAF, 1970-71. Mem. Am. Soc. Microbiology, Am. Pub. Health Assn., Am. Assn. Pathologists, N.Y. Acad. Scis., Sigma Xi. Home: 5501 Fernwood Ct Frederick MD 21702-2307 Office: Whittaker Bioproducts Inc 8830 Biggs Ford Rd Walkersville MD 21793-8415

OBER, ERIC W., broadcasting executive. BA, Yale U.; Woodrow Wilson Fellow, Columbia U. With CBS, 1966—; newswriter, producer, exec. producer, asst. news dir., WCBS-TV N.Y.C.; news dir., WCAU-TV, Phila.; news dir. WBBM-TV, Chgo.; v.p. news CBS TV stations, 1981-82; v.p., station mgr. WCBS-TV; v.p., gen. mgr. WBBM-TV Chgo., 1983-84; v.p. pub. affairs broadcasts CBS News, 1984-87; pres. CBS TV Stations, from 1987; now pres. CBS News Div. Served with U.S. Army. Office: CBS Inc 51 W 52nd St New York NY 10019-6101*

OBER, RUSSELL JOHN, JR., lawyer; b. Pitts., June 26, 1948; s. Russell J. and Marion C. (Hampson) O.; m. Kathleen A. Stein, Apr. 8, 1972; children: Lauren Elizabeth, Russell John III. BA, U. Pitts., 1970, JD, 1973. Bar: Pa. 1973, U.S. Dist. Ct. (we. dist.) Pa. 1973, U.S. Tax Ct. 1982, U.S. Ct. Appeals (4th cir.) 1976, U.S. Ct. Appeals (3d cir.) 1979, U.S. Ct. Appeals (D.C. cir.) 1985, U.S. Ct. Appeals (2d cir.), 1990, U.S. Supreme Ct. 1976. Asst. dist. atty. Allegheny County, Pitts., 1973-75; ptnr. Wallace Chapas & Ober, Pitts., 1975-80, Rose, Schmidt, Hasley & DiSalle, Pitts., 1980-92, Meyer, Unkovic & Scott, Pitts., 1992—. Bd. dirs. Parent and Child Guidance Ctr., Pitts., 1983-90, treas., 1985-86, pres., 1986-88; bd. mgmt. South Hills Area YMCA, 1989-91; mem. Mt. Lebanon Traffic Commn., 1976-81; bd. dirs. Whale's Tale Youth Family Counseling Ctr., 1990—. Mem. ABA (discovery com. litigation sect. 1982-88, ho. of dels. young lawyers div. 1982-83), Pa. Bar Assn. (ho. of dels. 1983), Allegheny County Bar Assn. (chmn. young lawyers sect. 1983, bd. govs. 1984, fin. com. 1984-88, mem. coun. civil litigation sect. 1991—), Nat. Bd. Trial Advocacy (diplomate), Acad. Trial Lawyers Allegheny County (fellow 1983—, bd. govs. 1988-90), U. Pitts. Law Alumni Assn. (bd. govs. 1984-89, v.p. 1985-86, pres. 1987-88), Rivers Club, Chartiers Country Club. Home: 393 Parker Dr Pittsburgh PA 15216-1323 Office: Meyer Unkovic & Scott 1300 Oliver Bldg Pittsburgh PA 15222

OBERDORFER, LOUIS F., federal judge; b. Birmingham, Ala., Feb. 21, 1919; s. A. Leo and Stella Maud (Falk) O.; m. Elizabeth Weil, July 31, 1941; children: John Louis, Kathryn Lee, Thomas Lee, William L. A.B., Dartmouth, 1939; LL.B., Yale, 1946. Bar: Ala. bar 1946, D.C. bar 1949. Law clk. to Justice Hugo L. Black, 1946-47; pvt. practice, 1947-51; mem. firm Wilmer, Cutler, & Pickering (and predecessors), 1951-61, 65-77; asst. atty. gen. tax div. Dept. of Justice, 1961-65; judge U.S. Dist. Ct. (D.C. dist.), 1977—; vis. lectr. Yale Law Sch., 1966, 71; adv. com. Fed. Rules Civil Procedure, 1962-84; co-chmn. lawyers com. Civil Rights Under Law, 1967-69. Editor-in-chief Yale Law Jour., 1941. Served to capt. AUS, 1941-46. Mem. ABA, D.C. Bar Assn. (bd. govs. 1972-77, pres. 1977), Ala. Bar Assns., Am. Law Inst., Yale Law Sch. Assn. (pres. 1971-73). Office: US Dist Ct US Courthouse 3D Constitution Ave NE Washington DC 20002-5618

OBERLE, FRANK, Canadian government official; b. Forchheim, Germany, Mar. 24, 1932; came to Can., 1951; m. Joan Kistner, May 31, 1953; children: Ursula, Isabell, Frank, Peter. Pres. Chetwynd Motors Ltd.; ptnr. Chetwynd Forest Industries Ltd.; owner, operator Oberle Ranch; alderman Village of Chetwynd, B.C., Can., 1963-64, mayor, 1968-72; M.P. from Prince George-Peace River dist. Ho. of Commons, Ottawa, Ont., Can., 1972—, opposition critic for forestry, opposition critic for mines, parliamentary sec. to Minister of State (Mines), from 1984, commr. Treaty 8 renovation, 1985, minister of state for sci. and tech., 1985-89, minister of forestry, 1989—, chmn. Indian Affairs and No. Devel. standing com., 1979, mem. Nat. Resources and Pub. Works standing com., mem. Forestry and Fisheries standing com., mem. No. Pipeline standing com., mem. task force on Indian Self-Government, 1982. Author: The Green Ghetto, Equity and Fairness, Towards Solving Canada's Human Resources Paradox, The MacDonald-Cartier Foundation, What's Wrong With Labour Relations in Canada, Reviving the Canadian Dream: A New Approach to Financing Homeownership. Charter pres. Chetwynd C. of C., 1959-60; chmn. Chetwynd and Dist. Hosp. Soc., 1966-72. Mem. Progressive Conservative Assn. of B.C. (pres. 1977). Office: Ho of Commons, Confederation Bldg Rm 576, Ottawa, ON Canada K1A 0A6

OBERLE, GERARD CHARLES JOSEPH, software engineer, tax advisor, lawyer; b. Balt., Feb. 4, 1956; s. Cornelius F. and Rosalie (Gonce) O. AS in Acctg., Norwalk Community Coll., 1977; B Elective Studies, U. Bridgeport, 1979, MBA in Acctg., 1981; JD, N.Y. Law Sch., 1981. Bar: Conn. 1984. Programmer, analyst air correction div. UOP, Inc., Norwalk, Conn., 1982; mgr. fin. data processing systems Gen. Signal Corp., Stamford, Conn., 1982-88; software mgr. Survey Sampling, Inc., Fairfield, Conn., 1988-90; software cons. Digital Equipment Corp., N.Y.C., 1990—; cons. Trirex, Inc., Westport, Conn., 1989. Contbr. articles to profl. jours. Mem. Digital Equipment Computer Users Soc., Stamford Local Users Group (chmn. Stamford 1987-90, vice chmn. 1986-87). Home: 7365 Main St Unit 101 Stratford CT 06497-1300 Office: Digital Equipment Corp 2 Penn PlzNYO-8/Q New York NY 10121-0001

OBERLY, CHARLES MONROE, III, state attorney general; b. Wilmington, Del., Nov. 9, 1946; s. Charles M. and Prudence Elizabeth (Curry) O.; children: Kimberly, Michael and Kristy-Lyn (twins). AA, Wesley Coll., 1966; BAA, Pa. State U., 1968; JD, U. Va., 1971. Bar: Del. Clk. U.S. Dist. Ct., 1971-72; assoc. Morris James Hitchens & Williams, Wilmington, Del., 1972-75; dep. atty. gen. Del. Dept. Justice, 1974-82, state prosecutor, 1976-78; atty. gen. State of Del., Wilmington, 1982—; instr. U. Del. Contbr. articles to law jours. Mem. Phi Beta Kappa, Phi Kappa Phi. Democrat. Lutheran. Office: Office of Atty Gen 820 N French St Wilmington DE 19801-3552*

OBERMANN, RICHARD MICHAEL, governmental technology and policy analyst; b. May 21, 1949; s. Baird J. and Phyllis L. (Weber) O. BS of Engring. in Aerospace and Mech. Scis. cum laude, Princeton U., 1971, PhD in Engring., Aerospace and Mech. Scis., 1977; MS of Engring. in Astronautics and Aeros., Stanford U., 1972; postgrad., Va. Poly. Inst. and State U., Am. U. With MITRE Corp., McLean, Va., 1977-88, engr. transp. systems analysis, transp. energy analysis, telecommunications, project leader, mem. tech. staff in communications and system design; sr. staff officer aeros. and space engring. bd. NRC, Washington, 1988-90, study dir. and analyst technol. and policy issues; mem. profl. staff for space subcom. U.S. Ho. of Reps. Com. on Sci., Space and Tech., Washington, 1990—. Author tech. papers and presentations. Fellow AIAA (assoc.), Brit. Interplanetary Soc.; mem. N.Y. Acad. Scis., IEEE, Internat. Inst. Communications, Japan-Am. Soc., Asia Soc., Am. Astronaut. Soc. (v.p.), Nat. Space Club, Pacific Telecommunications Coun.

OBERST, ROBERT JOHN, financial analyst; b. Hackensack, N.J., Aug. 20, 1929; s. Bernard and Elsie (Schneider) O.; m. Ingrid Heilbut, Oct. 6, 1956; children: Jeanne, Robert John, Carl Edward. PhD in Fin. Mgmt., Columbia Pacific U., 1984. Cert. fin. planner, registered health underwriter. Spl. agt., mgr. Prudential Ins. Co. Am., Asbury Park, N.J., 1958-68; pres. Robert J. Oberst, Sr. & Assocs., Red Bank, N.J., 1969—; chmn. bd. regents Coll. Fin. Planning, Denver, 1978-82. Author newspaper column Fin. Planning, 1986-87; producer, host TV show Fin. Planning Today, 1983—; contbr. articles to profl. jours. Pres. Monmouth/Ocean Devel. Council, Manasquan, N.J., 1981-83; bd. dirs. Monmouth County Council Boy Scouts Am., Ocean, N.J., 1986—; trustee Brookdale Coll. Found., Middletown, N.J., 1986—. Served with USN, 1946-50. Recipient Silver Gull Service award Monmouth/Ocean Devel. Council, 1984. Mem. Inst. Cert. Fin. Planners (cert., Fin. Planner of Yr. award 1979), Internat. Assn. Fin. Planning (bd. dirs. 1986—, pres. 1991-92), Estate Planning Coun. (pres. 1971-72), Million Dollar Round Table (life), Nat. Assn. Life Underwriters, Red Bank C. of C. (bd. dirs.), Registry Fin. Planning Practitioners (chmn. 1987-88), N.J. Assn. Life Underwriters (state pres. 1969-70). Republican. Home: 15 Mulberry Ln PO Box 218 Colts Neck NJ 07722 Office: Robert J Oberst Sr & Assocs 218 Broad St Red Bank NJ 07701-2002

OBERSTEIN, LEONARD HAROLD, rabbi, college official; b. Montgomery, Ala., Mar. 9, 1946; s. Meyer and Pauline (Weinstock) O.; m. Feiga Siegel, Aug. 18, 1969; children: Chaya, Esther, Shmuel, Paul, Abraham, Penina, Yisroel, Jonathan, Joseph, Shoshana, Shira. Grad., Ner Israel Rabbinical Coll., Balt., 1969; MEd, Loyola Coll., Balt., 1969. Ordained rabbi, 1969. Prin. Jewish Community High Sch., Vancouver, B.C., Can., 1970-75, Birmingham (Ala.) Jewish Day Sch., 1975-76; dir. Tchrs. Inst. Ner Israel Rabbinical Coll., Balt., 1977—; rabbi Randallstown Synagogue, Md., 1988—, Shacrei Tfiloh Congregation, Balt., 1983-88; sec. Rabbinical Coun. Balt., 1987—. Bd. dirs. Balt. Jewish Council, 1988—, Shearith Israel Congregation, Balt., 1986—. Democrat. Office: Ner Israel Rabbinical Coll 400 Mt Wilson Ln Baltimore MD 21208-1198

OBLATH, STEVEN BARTLEY, research chemist; b. Los Angeles, Dec. 6, 1954; s. Leo Iszo and Phyllis (Nesburn) O.; m. Deborah Toby Halpern, Sept. 9, 1979; children: Rachel Catherine, Emily Anna. BS in Chemistry, MIT, 1977; MS in Chemistry, U. Calif., Berkeley, 1979, PhD in Chemistry, 1981. Research asst. Lawrence Berkeley (Calif.) Lab., 1978-81; research chemist E.I. Du Pont de Nemours and Co., Aiken, S.C, 1981-86, staff chemist, 1986-89; rsch. assoc., 1989—. Contbr. articles to profl. jours. Mem. ednl. coun. MIT. Mem. Am. Chem. Soc. (sec.-treas. Savannah River chpt. 1987-88), Sigma Xi. Office: EI Du Pont de Nemours & Co Jackson Labs Wilmington DE 19898

OBOLENSKY, IVAN, investment banker, foundation consultant, writer, publisher; b. London, May 15, 1925; s. Serge and Alice (Astor) O. (parents Am. citizens); m. Claire McGinnis, 1949 (div. 1956); children—Marina Ava, Ivan Serge, David; m. Mary Elizabeth Morris, 1959; 1 child, Serge. A.B., Yale U., 1947. Pres. Hotel Investments, Inc., N.Y.C., 1950-58; v.p., treas. Serge Obolensky Assocs., 1952-75; dir., chmn., pres. Ivan Obolensky Inc., pubs., 1956-65; dir. Silver Bear Inc., Atlanta; ptnr. A.T. Brod & Co., investment bankers, Dominick & Dominick Inc., investment bankers, 1965-70, Middendorf Colgate, investment bankers, 1970-73; v.p. C.B. Richard, Ellis/Moseley Hallgarten, investment bankers, 1974-81, Sterling Grace & Co., investment bankers, N.Y.C., 1982-87; sr. v.p. Jesup, Josephthal & Co., investment bankers, N.Y.C., 1987-90; gen. ptnr. Astor Capital Mgmt. Assocs., 1980—; v.p. Capital Mgmt. Assocs., N.Y.C., 1990—; v.p. Shields & Co., N.Y.C., 1990—; cons. and lectr. in field. Author: Rogues' March, 1956; contbr. to Nihon Keizai Shimbun, Tokyo, on precious metals, 1985—, program com. N.Y. Soc. of Security Analysts for pub., oil and gas; contbr. articles to profl. publs. Bd. dirs. Children's Blood Found., N.Y. Hosp., 1952—, pres., 1981; bd. dirs., pres. Josephine Lawrence Hopkins Found., 1971—; bd. dirs. Whitemarsh Found., 1980-90, Marines Emergency Fund, 1980—, U.S.O., 1987—, Audubon Canyon Ranch, Calif., 1989—; bd. dirs. Soldiers, Sailors and Airmen's Club, 1976—, pres., 1987—; bd. dirs. Russian Nobility Assn. in Am., 1990—, treas., 1991—. Lt. (j.g.) USNR, 1943-45, ret., 1980. Mem. Am. Legion, Mil. Order Loyal Legion U.S. (sr. vice comdr. 1955, comdr. 1967-70), St. Elmo Soc., Met. Mus. Art (life mem.), Knickerbocker Club, N.Y. Yacht Club, New Eng. Soc. of N.Y., Army and Navy Club, Explorers Club, Masons (Holland #8 master 1981, dist. dep. grand master 1st Manhattan 1983-84). Office: Shields & Co 71 Broadway New York NY 10006-2601

O'BRIAIN, NIALL P., wood products company executive. Formerly sr. v.p. Fraser Inc., Edmundston, N. B., Canada, pres., 1988—; sr. v.p. Noranda Forest Inc., Toronto, Ont., 1988—. Office: Fraser Inc, 27 Rice St, Edmundston, NB Canada E3V 1S9

O'BRIEN, CHARLES FRANCIS, historian, educator; b. Danbury, Conn., Mar. 21, 1939; s. Francis Joseph and Edith Rose (McLaughlin) O'B.; children: Terence Charles, Marc Charles, Kristin Marie. AB, St. Michael's Coll., 1960; MA, U. Wyo., 1963; PhD, Brown U., 1967. Instr. English U. Wyo., Laramie, 1963-64; asst. prof. history St. Michael's Coll., Winooski Park, Vt., 1964-68; assoc. prof. history Clarkson U., Potsdam, N.Y., 1968—, chiar dept. social scis., 1976-81; cons. Ctr. for Can.-Am. Bus. Rels., Potsdam, 1988-92. Author: Sir William Dawson: A Life in Science and Religion, 1971; contbr. articles to profl. jours. Fulbright lectr. Coun. for Internat. Exch. of Scholars, Tunisia 1979, Morocco 1989. Fellow Ctr. for Rsch. on Vt.; mem. Norwood Lake Assn., Cinema 10 Film Soc. (bd. dirs. 1990—). Democrat. Roman Catholic. Home: 41 S Main St Norwood NY 13668 Office: Clarkson Univ Liberal Studies Potsdam NY 13699

O'BRIEN, CHERYL LYNN, psychotherapist; b. Bklyn., Aug. 26, 1958; d. Stanley Fleischer and Renee (Gerber) Kahn; m. Thomas Maurice O'Brien, July 11, 1987; 1 child, David Barrett. BA in Psychology, Drew U., 1982; MA in Counseling, Montclair State Coll., 1988. Residence counselor VIP House, Orangeburg, N.Y., 1987-88; educator, counselor QUEST, Spring Valley, N.Y., 1988-89; community counselor EurAuPair, Laguna Beach, Calif., 1989—; pvt. practice Spring Valley, 1988—. Mem. Am. Assn. for Counseling and Devel., Assn. Humanistic Edn. and Devel. Jewish. Office: 16 Wolfe Dr Spring Valley NY 10977-5371

O'BRIEN, COLLEEN ANN, editor; b. Manhasset, N.Y., Sept. 8, 1967; d. Donald F. and Eileen T. (Trotter) O'B. BA, Adelphi U., 1989. Intern Adams Unlimited, N.Y.C., 1986-88; editor N.Y. State Med. Soc., Lake Success, 1989—; pub. rels. Delta Gamma Sorority, Garden City, N.Y., 1987-88; feature writer Bonaventure, St. Bonaventure, N.Y., 1985-86. Republican. Roman Catholic. Office: Med Soc State of NY 420 Lakeville Rd New Hyde Park NY 11042-1121

O'BRIEN, EUGENE JAMES, priest; b. N.Y.C., Apr. 12, 1926. AB, Woodstock Coll., 1949, PhL, 1950, MA, 1951, STB, 1955, STL, 1957; MS, Fordham U., 1959. Joined Soc. of Jesus, 1943, ordained priest Roman Cath. Ch., 1956; lic. tchr., sch. adminstr. and supr. Dir. summer session Bklyn. Prep. Sch., N.Y.C., 1958; headmaster, pres. Fordham Prep. Sch., N.Y.C., 1960-79; asst. to pres. Jesuit Secondary Edn. Assn., Washington, 1980-83; headmaster Fairfield (Conn.) Prep. Sch., 1983-85; asst. to pres. Fordham U., Bronx, N.Y., 1986-87, v.p. univ. rels., 1987-91, univ. chaplain, 1992—. Mem. Country Day Sch. Headmasters Assn., N.Y. Acad. Pub. Edn., Lotos Club, Phi Delta Kappa. Home and Office: Fordham U Loyola Hall Bronx NY 10458

O'BRIEN, GEORGE ALOYSIUS, JR., paper company executive; b. Port Arthur, Tex., Dec. 13, 1948; s. George Aloysius and Avril Colleen (Adkins) O'B.; m. Cynthia Jean McCaa, Aug. 16, 1973; children: Erin Colleen, Meghan Anne, Caitlin Jean. BS in Petroleum Engring., U. Tex., 1971, MBA, 1975. Engr. Tesoro Petroleum Corp., San Antonio, 1972-73; exec. asst. Mesa Petroleum Co., Amarillo, Tex., 1975-79; v.p., treas. Transco Energy Co., Houston, 1979-82; sr. v.p., chief fin. officer Spectrum Energy Co., Houston, 1982-83; v.p. Smith Barney Harris Upham & Co., Houston, 1984-86; 1st v.p. E.F. Hutton & Co., N.Y.C., 1986-88; v.p., dir. corp. devel. Internat. Paper Co., Purchase, N.Y., 1988—. Mem. Middlesex Club. Republican. Roman Catholic. Home: 9 Sylvan Rd Darien CT 06820 Office: Internat Paper Co 2 Manhattanville Rd Purchase NY 10577

O'BRIEN, GEORGE DENNIS, university president; b. Chgo., Feb. 21, 1931; s. George Francis and Helen (Fehlandt) O'B.; m. Judith Alyce Johnson, June 21, 1958; children: Elizabeth Belle, Juliana Helen, Victoria Alyce. A.B. in English, Yale, 1952; Carnegie research fellow, U. Chgo., 1956-57, Ph.D. in Philosophy, 1961. Tchr. humanities U. Chgo., 1956-57; successively instr., asst. prof., asst. dean coll. Princeton, 1958-65; on leave in Athens, Greece, 1963-64; spl. honors seminars LaSalle Coll., spring 1963, fall 1964, spring 1965; assoc. prof. philosophy Middlebury Coll., 1965-71, prof., 1971-76, dean of men, 1965-67, dean of coll., 1967-74, dean faculty, 1975-76; pres. Bucknell U., 1976-84, U. Rochester, N.Y., 1984—; Fellow Am. Council Learned Socs., London, Eng., 1971-72. Author: Hegel on Reason in History, 1975, God and the New Haven Railway, 1986, What to Expect from College, 1991; contbr. articles to profl. jours. Trustee LaSalle Coll., Phila., 1965—; bd. dirs. Union Theol. Sem., 1985-90. Mem. Am. Philos. Assn., Phi Beta Kappa. Home: 630 Mt Hope Ave Rochester NY 14620-2731 Office: U Rochester Wilson Blvd # 240 Rochester NY 14620-2241

O'BRIEN, GREGORY FRANCIS, newspaper publisher; b. New Rochelle, N.Y., Mar. 22, 1950; s. Francis Xavier and Virginia (Brown) O'B.; m. Mary Catherine McGeorge, Apr. 19, 1977; children: Brendan, Colleen, Conor. BA, U. Ariz., 1972. Reporter The Ariz. Republic, Phoenix, 1976-79; staff writer Boston Herald Am., 1979-82; sr. writer Boston Mag., 1982-84; reporter The Cape Codder, Inc., Orleans, Mass., 1973-76, editor, pres., 1985—, also bd. dirs.; editor The Cape Codder Press, Orleans, 1988—; pres. The Cape Codder Printery, Inc., Orleans, 1989—, also bd. dirs.; editor-in-chief Cape Cod Bus. Jour., Orleans, 1988-89; editor, pres. The Register, Yarmouth Port, Mass., 1990—; pres., pub. Cape Cod Pub. Co., Orleans, 1990—, also bd. dirs.; bd. dirs. Community Newspaper, Inc., North Shore Weeklies, Inc., Norfolk Newspapers, Inc.; editor, pub. Cape Cod Newspapers, Osterville, Mass., 1992—. Author, editor: An Insider's Guide to

Cape Cod and the Islands, Viking Penquin, 1988, The Sea, The Land, The Life, The Cape Codder Press, 1988, A Guide to Nature on Cape Cod and the Islands, Viking Penquin, 1990; contbr. numerous articles to newspapers and mags. Trustee, vice chmn. Cape Cod Mus. Natural History, Brewster, Mass.; past bd. trustees Trinity Sch. of Cape Cod, Yarmouth, Mass. Award recipient The Ariz. Press Club, Hearst Newspapers, New England Newspaper Assn. Mem. New Eng. Newspaper Assn., New Eng. Press Assn. Roman Catholic. Home: 25 Stoney Hill Rd Brewster MA 02631-1612 Office: Cape Cod Pub Co 5 Namskaket Rd Orleans MA 02653-3202

O'BRIEN, JAMES CHARLES, engineering educator; b. Darby, Pa., July 31, 1949; s. James Charles and Eileen Agnes (Dougherty) O'B.; m. Nancy Kellet Johnson, Feb. 18, 1982; children: Sean, Seamus, Kelly, Molly, Bridget. BECE, Villanova U., 1971; MA, Temple U., 1972; MECE, Villanova U., 1978. Tchr. Phila. Sch. Dist., 1971-82, High Sch. for Engring. and Sci., Phila., 1979-82; prof. engring. Villanova (Pa.) U., 1982—; dir. PRIME, Villanova U., 1982—, dir. Computer Aided Engring. Ctr., 1985—, engring rep. to Faculty Coun., 1989—; cons. in field. Ward leader Dem. Party, Havertown, Pa., 1978-90; chmn. Haverford Twp. Environ. Adv. Com., 1980—; bd. dirs. Haverford Little League, 1985-91. Mem. Am. Soc. Engring. Educators. Roman Catholic. Office: Villanova U Dept Mech Engring Villanova PA 19085

O'BRIEN, JOHN STEININGER, clinical psychologist; b. Lewisburg, Pa., June 3, 1936; s. Peck Zanders and Esther (Steininger) O'B.; m. Joan Irene Romanos, Oct. 1, 1976; children: Peck David, Timothy. AB, Pa. State U., 1967; MA, So. Ill. U., 1969; PhD, Boston U., 1980. Diplomate Internat. Acad. Profl. Psychotherapists, Internat. Acad. Behavioral Medicine/Psychotherapy. Asst. tchr. educable retarded children Selin's Grove (Pa.) State Sch., 1964-66; clin. rsch. asst. Pa. State U., State Coll., 1966-67; rsch. technician Anna (Ill.) State Hosp., 1968; intern Boston City Hosp., 1968-69, from coord. alcohol study unit to psychologist, 1969-73; clin. instr. psychiatryi Sch. Medicine Tufts U., St. Elizabeth's Hosp., Brighton, Mass., 1973-87; dir. psychol. svcs. Baldpate Hosp., Georgetown, Mass., 1981—, dir. outpatient substance abuse rehab. program, 1991—; bio-behavioral cons. Bhavioral Medicine Inst., Quincy, Mass., 1985-88; clin. dir. Social Learning Ctr., Quincy, 1971—; behavioral therapist, clin. coord. TAP Boston Childrens Svc., 1973-76. Author: Moments with Peck, 1982; contbr. articles to profl. jours. Mem. Am. Psychol. Assn., Nat. Register Health Svcs. in Psychology, Soc. Study of Addiction, Assn. Advancement Behavioral Therapy, Am. Assn. Clin. Counselors, Biofeedback Soc. Am., Internat. Acad. Profl. Counselors and Psychotherapists. Home: 72 Kenneth Rd Scituate MA 02066-2950 Office: Baldpate Psychiat Assocs Baldpate Rd Georgetown MA 01833-2301

O'BRIEN, KEITH THOMAS, engineering educator; b. Woking, England, Feb. 7, 1949; came to U.S., 1979; s. Thomas F. and Emily W. (Crabbe) O'B.; children: Siobhan K., Meghan M. BS in Engring., London U., 1971; MS, Leeds U., 1972, PhD, 1974. Enseigant Algerian Inst., Boumerdas, 1976-79; prof. Stevens Inst., Hoboken, N.J., 1979-81; sr. rsch. engr. Celanese, Summit, N.J., 1979-81, 1981-83, staff engr., 1983-85; staff engr. Celanese, Chatham, N.J., 1985-87; devel. assoc. Hoechst Celanese, Chatham, N.J., 1987-88; prof. N.J. Inst. Tech., Newark, 1988—. Patentee in field; editor: Computer Modeling, 1992; contbr. over 200 articles to profl. jours. Rsch. fellow Bradford U., 1974-76. Fellow Inst. Mechanical Engrs., Soc. Plastics Engrs. Episcopalian. Home: 65 Stratford Circle Edison NJ 08820 Office: NJ Inst Tech University Heights Newark NJ 07102

O'BRIEN, MARY DEVON, communications executive, consultant; b. Buenos Aires, Argentina, Feb. 13, 1944; came to U.S., 1949, naturalized, 1962; d. George Earle and Margaret Frances (Richards) Owen; m. Gordon Covert O'Brien, Feb. 16, 1962 (div. Aug. 1982); children: Christopher Covert, Devon Elizabeth; m. Christopher Gerard Smith, May 28, 1983. BS, Rutgers U., 1975, MBA, 1976. Controller manpower Def. Communications div. ITT, Nutley, N.J., 1977-80, adminstr. program, 1977-78, mgr. cost, schedule control, 1978-79, voice processing project, 1979-80; mgr. project Avionics div. ITT, Nutley, 1980-81, sr. mgr. projects, 1981—; cons. strategic planning, N.J., 1983—; bd. trustees South Mountain Counseling Ctr., 1987—; bd. dirs. N.J. Eye Inst.; lectr. in field. Author: Pace: System Manual, 1979, Voices, 1982; contbr. articles to profl. jours. and Maplewood Community calendar. Chmn. Citizens Budget Adv. Com., Maplewood, N.J., 1984-87, chmn. recreation, libr., pub. svcs., 1982-83, chmn. pub. safety, emergency svcs., 1983-84, chmn. schs. and edn., 1984-85; bd. dirs., officer Civic Assn., Maplewood, 1984—; bd. trustees United Way Essex and West Hudson Community Svc. Coun., 1988—; first v.p. Maplewood Civic Assn., 1987-89, pres., 1989-91; chmn. Maple Leaf Svc. award Com., 1987-89, Community Svc. Coun. of Oranges and Maplewood Homelessness, Affordable Housing, Shelter Com., 1988—; chmn. speaker's bur. United Way, 1989—; v.p. mktg. United Way Community Svc. Coun. of Orange and Maplewood, 1990—; mem. Maplewood Zoning Bd., 1983—, Maplewood Bd. Adjustment, 1983—; officer, mem. exec. bd. N.J. Project Mgmt. Inst., 1985—, pres., 1987-88; bd. dirs. Performance Mgmt. Assn.; chmn. Charter Com.; chmn. Internat. Project Mgmt. Inst. Jour. and Membership survey, 1986-87, mktg. com., 1986-89, long range planning and steering com., 1987—; bd. dirs., vice chmn. Coun. Chpt. Pres. Interaction Com., 1986-90, chmn., 1991—, pres. Internat. Project Mgmt. Inst., 1991, chmn., 1992, v.p. Region II, 1989-90; adv. bd. Project Mgmt. Jour., 1987-90, N.J. PMI Ednl., 1987—; liaison officer Internat. Project Mgmt. Inst. and Performance Mgmt. Assocs.; mem. MCA/N.J. Blood Bank Drive; chmn. Maplewood Community Calendar, 1990—; trustee community svc. coun. and edn. program United Way Essex and West Hudson, 1988—, also, chmn. leadership div., chmn. speakers bur., 1991— and mem. communications com., v.p. mktg. community svc. coun., Oranges and Maplewood, 1991—. Recipient spl. commendation for community svc. Twp. Maplewood, 1987; First Place award Anti-Shoplifting Program for Distributive Edn. Club Am., 1981, N.J. Fedn. of Women's Clubs, 1981, 82, Retail Mchts. Assn., 1981, 82; Commendation and Merit awards Air Force Inst. Tech., 1981; Pres.'s Safety award ITT, 1983; State award 1st Pl. N.J. Fedn. of Women's Clubs Garden Show, 1982, Outstanding Pres. award Internat. Project Mgmt. Inst., 1988, Outstanding Svc. and Contbrn. award 1986-87; Cert. Spl. Merit award N.J. Fedn. of Women's Clubs, 1982, Disting. Contbn. award United Way, 1990, Pursuit of Exellence Cost Savings Achievement award ITT Avionics, 1990, Meritorious Svc. Recognition award Internat. Project Mgmt. Inst., 1989-90, Maple Leaf award for outstanding community svc., 1992, Phoebe and Benjamin Shackelford for community leadership and svc. award United Way, 1992, U.S. Ho. Reps. citation, 1992, N.H. Gen. Assembly Senate Resolution for community leadership and svc., 1992, Resolution of Appreciation Township of Maplewood. Mem. Internat. Platform Speakers Assn., Grand Jury Assn., Telecommunications Group and Aerospace Industries Assn., Women's Career Network Assn., Nat. Security Indsl. Assn., Assn. for Info. and Image Mgmt., Internat. Project Mgmt. Inst. (liaison officerpres. 1991—), Performance Mgmt. Assn, ITT Mgmt. Assn., NAFE, Rutger's Grad. Sch. Bus. Mgmt. Alumni Assn., LWV, Maplewood Women's Evening Membership Div. (pres. 1980-82), Lions (Maplewood dir. 1992—, program chmn. 1991-92, N.J. dist. 16E zone chmn. 1992—). Homewood NJ 07040-2616 Office: ITT Avionics 100 Kingsland Rd Clifton NJ 07014-1915

O'BRIEN, MICHAEL JOHN, computer executive; b. Queens, N.Y., Nov. 14, 1960; s. John Michael and Kathleen Mary (Faber) O'B.; m. Cynthia Lee Nadasky, Oct. 6, 1990. BA in Econs., Harvard U., 1983. From assoc. mktg. rep. to account rep. Wang Labs. Inc., N.Y.C., 1983-89, sales exec., 1990—. Mem. IEEE, Harvard Club of N.Y.C. Roman Catholic. Office: Wang Labs Inc 780 Third Ave New York NY 10017

O'BRIEN, MURROUGH HALL, lawyer; b. Portland, Maine, July 23, 1945; s. Francis Massey and Constanze Kathryn (McDonnell) O'B. m. Johannah M. Hart, June 11, 1968; children: John David, Ellen Hart. BA magna cum laude, Harvard U., 1969; JD, U. Maine, 1975. Bar: Maine 1975. Reporter, asst. city editor Evening Express, Portland, Maine, 1970-71; ptnr. firm Dunlap, Wood & O'Brien, Portland, Maine, 1975-80, Dunlap & O'Brien, Portland, Maine, 1980-85, Murrough H. O'Brien, Esquire, Portland, Maine, 1985—; exec. sec. Maine Jud. Coun., Portland, Maine, 1981—. Mem. Keep Maine Scenic Com., 1974-79, So. Coastal Family Planning, Inc., Portland, 1975-79; mem. steering com. Study of the Future of Maine Legal Profession, 1983-89; mem. steering com. Gov.'s Commn. on Land Use Violation, 1983-84; treas. Coalition for Cruise Missile Referendum, 1989; trustee Portland Ministry at Large, 1990—. Served with USNR, 1969-70. Mem. ACLU, Cumberland County Bar Assn. Democrat. Office: 38 High St Portland ME 04101

O'BRIEN, RICHARD DESMOND, university administrator, neurobiologist; b. Sydenham, Eng., May 29, 1929; came to U.S., 1960, naturalized, 1966; s. Joseph Andrew and Louise (Stevens) O'B.; m. Ann Margaret Thom, Mar. 16, 1961; 1 child, Ian Richard; m. Susan Krauss Whitbourne, Sept. 19, 1981, 1 child, Jennifer Louise. B.Sc., Reading (Eng.) U., 1950; Ph.D. in Chemistry, U. Western Ont., Can., 1954, B.A. in Arts, 1956. Soil specialist Ont. Agrl. Coll., Guelph, 1950-51; chemist Pesticide Research Inst., London, Can., 1954-60; faculty Cornell U., 1960-78, prof. entomology, 1964-78, prof. neurobiology, 1965-78, chmn. dept. biochemistry, 1964-65, chmn. sect. neurobiology and behavior, 1965-70, dir. div. biol. scis., 1970-78, Richard J. Schwartz prof. biology and soc., 1977-78; provost U. Rochester (N.Y.), 1978-84; exec. vice chancellor, provost U. Mass., Amherst, 1984-91, chancellor, 1991—; NRC fellow Babraham, Cambridge, Eng., 1956-57; vis. assoc. prof. U. Wis., 1958-59; cons. Melpar Inc., 1960-65, Am. Cyanamid Co., 1960-69; dir. Lincoln First Bank, 1978-84. Author: Toxic Phosphorus Esters, 1960, (with L.S. Wolfe) Radiation, Radioactivity and Insects, 1964, Insecticides, Action and Metabolism, 1967, (with I. Yamamoto) Biochemical Toxicology of Insecticides, 1970, (with E.O. Wilson, others) Life on Earth, 1973, The Receptors, A Comprehensive Treatise, vol. I, 1979; also articles.; Founding editor: Pesticide Biochemistry and Physiology, 1971. Trustee Center for Govtl. Research, 1979-84, vice-chmn., 1980-84; trustee Rochester Mus. and Sci. Center, 1979-84, Donald Guthrie Found. Med. Research, Sayre, Pa., 1977-84; pres. Rochester Area Colls., 1982-84; bd. dirs. Five Colls. Inc., 1990—. Guggenheim fellow Naples, Italy, 1967-68. Fellow AAAS; mem. Am. Chem. Soc. (Internat. award pesticide chemistry 1971), Internat. Brain Rsch. Orgn., Phi Beta Kappa, Sigma Xi. Office: U Mass Office of Chancellor Amherst MA 01003

O'BRIEN, ROBERT BROWNELL, JR., banker; b. N.Y.C., Sept. 6, 1934; s. Robert Brownell and Eloise (Boles) O'B.; m. Sarah Lager, Nov. 28, 1958; children: Robert Brownell III, William Stuart, Jennifer. BA, Lehigh U., 1957; postgrad., NYU, Am. Inst. Banking. Asst. treas., credit officer, br. locations officer Bankers Trust Co., N.Y.C., 1957-63; with George A. Murray Co., gen. contractors, N.Y.C., 1964; also v.p. Bowery Savs. Bank, 1964-69; dir., chief exec. officer Fed. Savs. & Loan Ins. Corp., Washington, 1969-71; chmn. exec. com. Fed. Home Loan Bank Bd., 1969-71; v.p. Bowery Savs. Bank, N.Y.C., 1972; exec. v.p. First Fed. Savs. & Loan Assn., N.Y.C., 1973-75; chmn., chief exec. officer Carteret Savs. Bank, Morristown, 1975-91, also bd. dirs.; mng. dir. Printon Kane Group Inc., Short Hills, N.J., 1991—; dir., chief exec. officer Govs. Bank Corp., West Palm Beach, 1992—; bd. dirs. Centennial Industries, Fed. Home Loan Bank of N.Y., Govs. Bank Corp., Palm Beach, Fla.; vice-chmn., bd. dir. U.S. League of Savs. Instns., Washington, O'Brien Yacht Sales. Contbr. articles to trade mags. Trustee Trinity Pawling Sch., Palm Beach County Housing Partnership, Lehigh U.; chmn. Housing Opportunities Found.; trustee, past chmn. Community Found. of N.J., 1987—; mem. Nat. Commn. on Neighborhoods; vice chmn., bd. dirs. Dalt Found. Mem. Nat. Coun. Savs. Instns. (past chmn.), Essex County Savs. and Loan League (past chmn.), N.J. Savs. League (past chmn.), N.J. Hist. Soc. (past chmn.), Greater Newark C. of C. (bd. dirs.), N.J. C. of C. (bd. dirs.), Union League Club, Delray Beach Yacht Club, Ocean Reef Club, Morris County Golf Club, Somerset Hills Golf Club, Palm Beach Yacht Club. Republican. Episcopalian. Home: 12 Banyan Rd Box 1180 Delray Beach FL 33447-1180 Office: Printon Kane Group Inc PO Box 910 Short Hills NJ 07078

O'BRIEN, ROBERT E., policy analyst; b. Flint, Mich.; s. Robert J. and Molly M. O'B.; m. Ruth N. O'Brien, Aug. 26, 1961; children: Robert, Jane, Jason, Margaret. BS, Georgetown U., 1956; MA, Cath. U., 1966. Budget analyst GM, Milw., 1960; fin. analyst Getty Oil Co., L.A., 1961; economist U.S. Dept. Energy, Washington, 1962, U.S. EPA, Washington, 1963-85; policy analyst USDA, APHIS, Washington, 1985—; v.p. Shakespeare Oxford Soc., Clarksville, Md., 1972—; pres. Leverage Corp., Columbia, Md., 1981—. Author: Chemical Corps in WWII, 1959, Gobrecht Jour., 1982. Republican. Roman Catholic. Home: 6051 Misty Arch Run Columbia MD 21044 Office: US Govt Hyattsville MD 20872

O'BRIEN, ROBERT EMMET, insurance company executive; b. St. Louis, Sept. 13, 1923; s. Algernon Francis Adams and Adeline (von Weisert) O'B.; m. Mary Lou Gallagher, July 20, 1946 (div. 1978); children: Robert Jr., Gardnar, Scott, Derek, Mary Berkeley; m. Marian Achilles, June 30, 1983. BBA, St. Louis U., 1946, MBA, 1947. Prin., ptnr. R. Newman & R. O'Brien, St. Louis, 1946-52; mem. Lloyd's of London, 1952—; pres. North Atlantic Assurance Co. Ltd., London, 1962-75. Apptd. to Bd. Life Govs. Royal Hosp. Putney, West Hill, London, 1969; councillor The Athletic Coun. of U.S., Atlantic Coun. of U.S., Carnegie Found.; mem. U.S. Olympics (Ice) Speed Skating Team, 1939; trustee Errol Flynn Estate, Jamaica and London, 1959-64. Served with AC U.S. Army, 1942-45, ETO, NATOUSA. Decorated DFC (Eng.). Mem. Zurich Internat. Insurers (apptd.), Life Underwriters, Million Dollar Round Table (life), Mid-Atlantic Club, Royal Yacht Club Hobart Tasmania, Royal Yacht Club Tasmania, Army and Navy Club Washington (hon.). Clubs: Devonshire, Irish Nat. Liberal (London). Home: 4829 Bending Ln NW Washington DC 20007-1527

O'BRIEN, ROBERT FRANCIS, lawyer; b. Phila., June 17, 1942; s. Francis X. and Marie (Jandersitz) O'B.; m. Linda A. Reichard, Oct. 26, 1968; children: Jennifer M., Daniel F. BA, LaSalle Coll., Phila., 1964; JD, Rutgers U., 1967. Bar: Pa. 1967, D.C. 1967, N.J. 1969, U.S. Supreme Ct. 1973, U.S. Ct. Appeals (1st and 10th cirs.), U.S. Ct. Appeals (3d cir.) 1967, U.S. Ct. Appeals (5th cir.) 1973, U.S. Ct. Appeals (4th cir.) 1980, U.S. Ct. Appeals (11th cir.) 1983. Commr. N.J. Turnpike Authority, 1979-83. Democrat. Roman Catholic. Office: Tomar Simonoff Law Office 41 S Haddon Ave Haddonfield NJ 08033-1891

O'BRIEN, ROBERT LEONARD, aerospace consultant; b. New Bedford, Mass., July 29, 1936; s. Leonard Louis and Grace (Couto) O'B.; m. Diane Webster, Dec. 19, 1956 (div. May 1980); children: Patricia Anne, Carol Elizabeth, Martha Jean, Robert Leonard Jr., Erin Louise; m. Mary E. Clark, Jan. 2, 1982. BSME, Carnegie Inst. of Tech., 1957, MSME, 1957; postgrad., Rensselaer Poly. Inst., 1957-66. Jr. engr. Lockheed Aircraft Corp., Burbank, Calif., 1956; rsch. asst. Carnegie Inst. of Tech., Pitts., 1956-57; rsch. engr. United Technologies Rsch. Ctr., East Hartford, Conn., 1957-65, supr. air breathing propulsion, 1965-67, chief air breathing propulsion, 1967-72, mgr. propulsion labs., 1972-77, mgr. engring. rsch., 1977-81, mgr. div. coord., 1981-91; ind. cons. Manchester, Conn., 1992—; mem. U.S. gas turbine delegation to China, 1978. Patentee in field. Dist. commdr. U.S. Power Squadrons, Dist. 1, Conn., 1978-80; squadron commdr. Hartford Power Squadron, Hartford, 1971-73. Fellow AIAA (assoc., SEI Architecture Working Group 1990); mem. ASME, Soc. of Automotive Engrs., Bloomfield Fish and Game Club, Internat. Soc. for Air Beathing Engines, Tau Beta Pi, Pi Tau Sigma. Republican. Home & Office: 21 Sharon Dr Manchester CT 06040-6844

O'BRIEN, ROBERT THOMAS, investment company executive; b. Phila., Oct. 7, 1941; s. James Francis Sr. and Mildred Anita (Gomez); m. Aurora Carol Forsthoffer, Nov. 7, 1964; 1 child, Michael Joseph. Cert., N.Y. Inst. Fin., 1963; BS, St. Joseph's U., 1971. Securities trader Brown Bros. Harriman, Phila., 1964-69, portfolio mgr., 1969-77, investment officer, 1977-80, asst. mgr., investment adv., 1980-83; v.p. Newbold's Asset Mgmt., Phila., 1983-85, sr. v.p., 1985—, also bd. dirs., 1990—. Bd. dirs. Cath. Philopatrian Literary Inst., 1973-76, Mary J. Drexel Home, 1992—; mem. fin. and investment com. Neumann Coll., 1990—. Served with USAF and Pa. Air N.G., 1960-67. Mem. Phila. Securities Assn., Air Force Assn. (life), Confederate Air Force (life, wing fin. officer). Republican. Roman Catholic. Clubs: Racquet of Phila., Sailing Assn. (commodore 1980-82); Lewes Yacht, Miles River Yacht, Avalon Yacht, Aronimink Golf, Idle Hour Tennis. Home: 665 Dodds Ln Gladwyne PA 19035-1514 Office: Newbolds Asset Mgmt Inc 937 Haverford Rd Bryn Mawr PA 19010-1523

O'BRIEN, ROGER JOSEPH, management consultant; b. Portland, Maine, Nov. 23, 1947; s. William Andrew and Mary Evelyn (McCarthy) O'B.; m. Irene Marmo, Sept. 6, 1969; children: Jonathan, Cynthia-Marie. BA in Econs., Fordham Coll., 1970; M in Urban Planning, NYU, 1973, PhD, 1985. Tchr. N.Y.C. Bd. Edn., 1970-74; prin. planner Regional Planning Agy. of S. Cen. Conn., New Haven, 1974-76; dir. employment and tng. div. Regional Council of Elected Officials of S. Cen. Conn., New Haven, 1976-78; community devel. adminstr. City of New Britain (Conn.), 1979; devel. adminstr. Town of Hamden (Conn.), 1980-82; pres. cons. firm O'Brien & Marmo Assocs., Hamden, 1982—; trustee United Labor Agy., West Hartford, Conn., 1984—; pres. Hamden Land Conservation Trust Inc., Hamden, 1986—; chmn. Pvt. Industry Council Labor Market Adv. Com., New Haven, 1986—. Author: (with others) Job Training for Women: The Promise and Limits of Public Policy, 1989. Chmn. Community Devel. Adv. Com., Hamden, 1979; cubmaster Cub Scout Pack 610, Hamden, 1985-87; active Hamden Dem. Town Com., 1987—. Grantee NYU, 1972. Mem. Am. Inst. Cert. Planners, Am. Planning Assn., Assn. Pub. Data Users. Democrat. Roman Catholic. Home: 86 Birchwood Dr Hamden CT 06518-1140 Office: O'Brien & Marmo Assocs 3190 Whitney Ave Hamden CT 06518-2340

O'BRIEN, THOMAS HERBERT, small business owner, consultant; b. Altoona, Pa., May 8, 1921; s. Charles Joseph and Ellen Mary (Herbert) O'B.; m. Paulette Mabereau, May 25, 1946 (div. 1978); children: Patrick T., Robert P., Ann M., John J., Kathleen S., Daniel C.; m. Annabelle Goad, May 17, 1980. Student, Pa. State U., 1949, 50; BA in Polit. Sci., Am. U., 1970. Pers. technician U.S. Army, Europe, 1945-48; employment mgr. State of Pa., Clearfield, 1950-56; mgmt. analyst State of Pa., Harrisburg, 1956-65; mgmt. cons. U.S. HEW, Washington, 1965-67, U.S. Dept. Labor, Washington, 1967-84; pvt. practice employment involvement cons. Rockville, Md., 1980—; work and careers chmn. First Global Conf. on Future, Toronto, Ont., Can., 1980. Contbr. articles to profl. jours. Mem. adv. com. Aspen Hill Libr., Rockville, 1990—; vol. arbitrator Better Bus. Bur., Washington, 1987—; vol. mediator D.C. Mediation Svc., Washington, 1990—; officer, bd. dirs. Property Owners of Shenandoah Farms, Front Royal, Va., 1986-88. Cpl. U.S. Army, 1942-45, ETO. Named Arbitrator of Yr., Better Bus. Bur., Washington, 1990. Mem. Assn. for Quality and Participation (chpt. officer 1987-88), World Future Soc. (conf. ofcl. 1979-84), Indsl. Rels. Rsch. Assn., Soc. Profl. in Dispute Resolution. Democrat. Roman Catholic. Home and Office: 4605 W Frankfort Dr Rockville MD 20853-2722

O'BRIEN, THOMAS IGNATIUS, lawyer; b. Troy, N.Y., Dec. 24, 1925; s. Timothy F. and Catherine M. (McCarthy) O'B.; m. Barbara Lasher; children: Kathleen, Stephanie, Alicia. BAE, Rensselaer Poly. Inst., 1946; LLB, JD, Georgetown U., 1951. Bar: N.Y. 1951, U.S. Ct. Appeals (3d cir.) 1968, U.S. Dist. Ct. N.Y. (so. dist.) 1973, U.S. Ct. Appeals (9th cir.) 1973, U.S. Ct. Appeals (2d cir.) 1975, U.S. Ct. Appeals (fed. cir.) 1982, Conn. 1988. Patent examiner U.S. Patent Office, Washington, 1946-51; patent atty. North Am. Phillips, Irvington, N.Y., 1951, Pollard, Johnston, Smythe & Robertson, N.Y.C., 1952-54; patent atty. Union Carbide Corp., Danbury, Conn., 1954-90, chief patents counsel, 1969-90; counsel Morgan & Finnegan, N.Y.C., 1991—. Mem. ABA (chmn. coms.), Am. Intellectual Property Law Assn. (bd. dirs. 1986-89), Pacific Indsl. Property Assn. (pres.), Assn. Corp. Patent Counsel (pres.), Chem. Mfrs. Assn., Internat. Patent and Trademark Assn., Intellectual Property Orgn. (bd. dirs.), Assn. Bar City N.Y. Home: 58 Stonehenge Dr New Canaan CT 06840-3524 Office: Morgan & Finnegan 345 Park Ave New York NY 10154

O'BRIEN, WILLIAM EDWARD, health facility administrator; b. Osceola Mills, Pa., Dec. 25, 1936; s. Raymond Vincent and Lois Minerva (Weston) O'B.; m. Eloise Joanne Mattern, June 5, 1958; children: Jennifer Lynne Horrocks, Kathleen Ruth Meyer, Elizabeth Ann, William Thomas. BSc in Pharmacy, Duquesne U., Pitts., 1962; MSc in Hosp. Pharmacy, Ohio State U., 1965. Registered pharmacist, Pa. Resident in hosp. pharmacy Ohio State U. Hosps., Columbus, 1964; supr. Mercy Hosp., Pitts., 1964-66; asst. dir. pharmacy Jefferson Med. Coll. & Hosp., Phila., 1966-69; mgr. pharmacy and cen. services Milton S. Hershey Med. Ctr., Hershey, 1969-74, mgr. pharmacy, 1974-79, dir. materials mgmt., 1979—; mem. Hosp. Pharmacy Adv. Bd. of E. R. Scquibb & Son, Princeton, N.J., 1971-73, Pharmacy Adv. Coun. of Smith, Kline & French Labs, Phila., 1973-75. Author: (with others) Prevention and Control of Nosocomial Infections, 1987. Bd. dirs. Rotary Internat., Hershey, 1990-91; active Environ. Waste Mgmt. Bd., Hershey, 1991—. With USN, 1954-57. Grantee NSF, 1991. Mem. Am. Soc. Hosp. Materials Mgmt. (cent. Pa. chpt.), Rotary (bd. dirs. 1990-91), KC, Rho Chi Soc. (Alpha Beta chpt., Freshman award, 1959). Republican. Roman Catholic. Office: The Milton S Hershey Med Ctr 500 University Dr Hershey PA 17033

OBRINSKI, VIRGINIA WALLIN, retired school psychologist; b. Stanton, Iowa, Sept. 4, 1915; d. John Edward Wallace and Frances Geraldine (Tinsley) Wallin; m. Peter James Obrinski, May 2, 1981 (dec. Mar. 26, 1989). BA, U. Del., 1936; MEd, Duke U., 1941. Lic. psychologist, Del. Sch. psychologist Del. Dept. Pub. Instrn., Dover, 1936-64, various suburban sch. dists., Wilmington, Del., 1964-67, Mt. Pleasant (Del.) Sch. Dist., 1967-68, Stanton (Del.) Sch. Dist., 1968-69, Conrad (Del.) Area Sch. Dist., 1969-78; ret., 1978. Recipient plaque Del. Coun. for Exceptional Children Fedn., 1985. Mem. APA, Del. Psychol. Assn., Coun. for Exceptional Children, AAUW. Baptist. Home: 311 Highland Ave Lyndalia Wilmington DE 19804

OBRZUT, JAN M., engineer; b. K. Gora, Poland, Aug. 13, 1951; came to U.S., 1985; s. Marian and Marcjanna (Mytnik) O.; m. Maria W. Jedlinska, Oct. 6, 1972; children: Sebastian, Michael, Tomasz. MS in Chemistry, Cracov Poly., 1975, PhD in Tech. Scis., 1981. Postdoctoral rsch. assoc. polymer sci. U. Mass., Amherst, 1985-89; rsch. engr. IBM Corp., Endicott, N.Y., 1989—; adj. instr. Cracov Polytech, Poland, 1981-85. Contbr. articles to profl. jours. Mem. Am. Physical Soc.

O'BYRNE, ELIZABETH MILIKIN, pharmacologist, researcher, endocrinologist; b. Miami, Fla., May 19, 1944; d. Richard Mershon and Anne (Smith) Milikin; m. Brian Kenneth O'Byrne, July 1, 1972; children: Lucy Milikin, Kenneth Daniel. AB, Emory U., 1965, MS in Chemistry, 1968; PhD in Biochemistry, N.Y. Med. Coll., 1985. Assoc. scientist Eli Lilly Rsch. Labs., Indpls., 1968-70; sr. rsch. scientist CIBA-GEIGY Pharms., Summit, N.J., 1970—. Contbr. articles to profl. jours. Mem. AAAS, N.Y. Acad. Sci., Inflammation Rsch. Assn. Home: 234 Sagamore Rd Millburn NJ 07041-2136 Office: CIBA-GEIGY Morris Ave Summit NJ 07901-3920

OCCHIOGROSSO, MARILYN, educator; b. N.Y.C., Oct. 10, 1937; d. William and Estelle (Gelman) Hamburger; m. 1959 (div. 1968); children: Paul, Roy. BA in Math., Bklyn. Coll., 1957, MA in Math., 1961. Cert. secondary sch. adminstr., tchr., N.Y. Asst. prin., tchr. math. Erasmus Hall High Sch., Bklyn., 1957-82; dir. math. AMSCO Sch. Publs., N.Y.C., 1982—; speaker state couns. math. tchr., Fla., La., Maine, N.Y., N.C., Ohio, Tenn., Tex; attended Woodrow Wilson Math. Insts., 1988-90. Author: (textbook series) Reviewing Sequential Mathematics Courses I, II, 1985-86, Reviewing Integrated Mathematics Courses I, II, 1990-91. Grantee NSF, 1969-70, 71. Mem. ASCD, Nat. Coun. Suprs. Math. (task force 1989-92), Nat. Coun. Tchrs. Math., N.Y. State Assn. Math. Suprs., Assn. Math. Tchrs. N.Y. State. Democrat. Jewish. Home: 60 Remsen St Brooklyn NY 11201-3453 Office: AMSCO Sch Publs 315 Hudson St New York NY 10013-1009

OCH, MOHAMAD RACHID, psychiatrist, consultant; b. Damascus, Syria, Apr. 1, 1956; came to U.S., 1981; s. Seifeddine and Souad (Oubari) O.; m. Marianne Noonan, July 24, 1960; children: Seifeddine, Adam. MD, Aleppo (Syria) U., 1980. Psychiat. cons. Human Resource Inst., Brookline, Mass., 1985; med. dir. Spectrum House, Westboro, Mass., 1986-87; assoc. med. dir. Boston Rd. Clinic, Shrewsbury, Mass., 1985—, v.p., 1989—; med. dir. mental health unit Holden (Mass.) Hosp., 1988-90; med. dir. Basic Health Mgmt., Worcester, Mass., 1988-90; asst. med. dir. Boston Rd. Clinic, Shrewsbury, 1986—, Holden Hosp., 1988—, Basic Health Mgmt., Worcester, 1988—; attending psychiatrist, asst. prof. U. Mass. Med. Ctr., Worcester; dir. mental health unit Milford Whitinsville Hosp., 1990—, chmn. dept. psychiatry, 1991—; med. dir. Seven Hills Intensive Residential Treatment Program, 1990—. Mem. Am. Psychiat. Assn., AMA. Moslem. Office: Boston Road Clinic 108 Belmont St Worcester MA 01605-2937

OCHIAI, EI-ICHIRO, chemistry educator; b. Tokyo, Japan, Sept. 15, 1936; came to U.S., 1981; s. Shokichi and Fukue (Fujii) O.; m. Katsuko Abe, Oct. 14, 1965; children: Tomoyuki, Naoyuki. BS, U. Tokyo, 1959, MS, 1961,

PhD, 1964. Instr. U. Tokyo, Japan, 1964-69; postdoctoral U. B.C., Vancouver, Canada, 1969-71; instr. U. B.C., Vancouver, 1971-80; vis. scholar U. Md., College Pk., 1980-81; assoc. prof. Juniata Coll., Huntingdon, Pa., 1981-86; prof. chemistry Juniata Coll., Huntingdon, 1986—. Author: Bioinorganic Chemistry, 1977, Laboratory Introduction to Bioinorganic Chemistry, 1979, General Principles of Biochemistry of the Elements, 1987; contbr. over 80 papers and articles to profl. jours. Mem. Am. Chem. Soc., AAAS. Office: Juniata Coll Chemistry Dept Huntingdon PA 16652

OCHOA, ELIZABETH SUZANNE, psychologist; b. Madrid; came to U.S., 1959; AB, Columbia U., 1982; MA, CUNY, 1984; PhD, Vanderbilt U., 1990. Lic. psychologist, N.Y. Fellow in neuropsychology Beth Israel Med. Ctr., N.Y.C., 1990-91, supervising psychologist in clin. neuropsychology, 1991—. Mem. APA, Soc. for Personality Assessment, Internat. Neuropsychol. Soc. Office: Beth Israel Med Ctr 9 Fierman Dept Psychiatry 317 E 17th St New York NY 10003-3804

OCHS, ROBERT HANSON, industrial consultant, market researcher; b. Quincy, Mass., Aug. 31, 1926; s. Harold Frederick and Mary Brown (Hanson) O.; m. Karen Astrid Scruton, Feb. 1, 1985; 1 child from previous marriage, Priscilla Jeanne. BSEE, Lehigh U., 1947; grad. dipl. in indsl. engring., U. Witwatersrand, Johannesburg, South Africa, 1986. Design and test engr. GE, 1947-51; engring. mgr. Manufacturera Gesa, Mexico City, 1951-54; sr. product engr. Internat. GE, N.Y.C., 1954-61; product mgr. GE, Phila., 1967-72; asst. dir. overseas mfg. Ingersoll-Rand, N.Y.C., 1961-67; mgmt. cons. Wendell Walker Assocs., N.Y.C., 1972-80, Whitehead Morris Ltd. Cons., Randburg, South Africa, 1980-86, Bus. Cons. Ltd., Valley Stream, N.Y., 1987; market analyst Automatic Switch Co. subs. Emerson Electric, Florham Park, N.J., 1987—. Contbr. articles to profl. jours. and papers to tech. socs. Active, lector Joshua Religious Discussion Group, Ch. of the Assumption, Morristown, N.J. Mem. IEEE (sr.), Inst. Indsl. Engrs. (sr.), Am. Prodn. and Inventory Control Soc., Small Bus. Network. Roman Catholic. Home: 20 Stonehenge Rd Morristown NJ 07960-2651 Office: Automatic Switch Co Hanover Rd Florham Park NJ 07932-1819

OCKMAN, NATHAN, physicist; b. N.Y.C., Dec. 29, 1926; s. Louis and Sarah (Levine) O. BS, Purdue, 1949; MS, U. Calif., Berkeley, 1950; PhD, U. Mich., 1957. Postdoctoral fellow Harvard U., Cambridge, Mass., 1957-59; tech. staff RCA Labs., Princeton, N.J., 1959-65, GTE, N.Y.C., 1965-67; rsch. assoc. Einstein Coll. Medicine, Bronx, N.Y., 1970-80; rsch. assoc. dept. physics CCNY, 1981—. Contbr. articles to profl. jours,. Mem. ACLU, N.Y., 1975—, Nat. Resources Def. Coun., N.Y., 1980—, Union Concerned Scientists, 1985, Sierra Club, N.Y., 1990—. With USN, 1945-46. Mem. AAAS, Am. Phys. Soc. Democrat. Home: 137 Riverside Dr New York NY 10024-3702 Office: City College 138th Convent Ave New York NY 10031-9127

OCOCK, RAYMOND HENRY, musician, educator; b. Cumberland, Md., July 22, 1928; s. Arthur Raymond and Lulu Grace (Henry) O.; m. Geraldine Margaret Schlundt, Aug. 1, 1953; children: Brian, Kevin, Alison. BMus, Westminster Coll., 1950; M in Sacred Music, Union Theol. Sem., 1952; postgrad., Case Western Reserve U., 1959-62, U. Mo., Kansas City, 1968-71. Minister of music First Presbybn. Ch., Evansville, Ind., 1952-56; prof. music Westminster Coll., New Wilmington, Pa., 1956—; organist, dir. Westminster Presbyn. Ch., Youngstown, Ohio, 1967-79; official organist Chataqua (N.Y.) Instn., 1970, '71, '89; organist, dir. First Presbyn. Ch., Sharon, Pa., 1979—; organist, choral dir., dean of faculty Sessione Senese Del Musica & Arte, Siena, Italy (summers), 1979—; organ cons., numerous chs.; organ recitalist varous locations in U.S., Italy. Recipient Keystone Salute, Pa. Fedn. Music Clubs, 1991. Mem. Am. Guild Organists (dean Youngstown, Ohio 1969, Pitts. 1984-86), Hymn Soc. Am., Presbyn. Assn. Musicians. (conf. dir. 1988). Democrat. Home: RR 3 Box 426 New Wilmington PA 16142-9729 Office: Westminster Coll PO Box 164 New Wilmington PA 16172-0001

O'CONNELL, ANTOINETTE KATHLEEN, training executive, consultant; b. Phila., July 15, 1944; d. John Joseph and Genevieve Catherine (Moore) O'C. AB, Immaculata Coll., 1966; MA, Villanova U., 1967. Training specialist Towers, Perrin, Foster & Crosby Inc., Phila., 1969-72; asst. personnel mgr. Foremost Ins. Co., Grand Rapids, Mich., 1972-74; mgr. mgmt. devel. and training credit J.C. Penney Co., Inc., N.Y.C., 1974-80; asst. v.p. Am. Express Internat. Banking Corp., N.Y.C., 1980-81; v.p. Marine Midland Bank, N.A., N.Y.C., 1981-87; chmn. Training Profls., Inc., Phila., 1988—; with Am. Inst. Banking, N.Y., 1981-87, pres., 1987. Contbr. articles to profl. jours. Speaker N.Y. State Bankers' Assn., 1986. Me. ASTD (bd. dirs. Phila. and Delaware Valley chpts. 1989—, pres. elect 1992—), Phila. Human Resources Group (rsch. com. 1991—, community svc. com. 1992—). Office: Training Profls Inc 9130 Ayrdale Cres Philadelphia PA 19128-1049

O'CONNELL, BRIAN JAMES, priest, university administrator; b. Hartford, Conn., Aug. 21, 1940; s. Jerry and Mary (Moloney) O'C. AB, Mary Immaculate Sem., 1964, MDiv, 1968; MA, St. John's U., Jamaica, N.Y., 1970; PhD, Ohio State U., 1974. Ordained priest Roman Cath. Ch., 1968. Social studies tchr. St. John's Prep. Sch., Bklyn., 1968-70; lectr. sociology St. John's U., Jamaica, 1970-71, asst. prof. sociology, 1974-79, assoc. prof., 1979-87, assoc. dean arts and scis., 1987-88, also bd. dirs., 1989—; exec. v.p. Niagara U., N.Y., 1988-89, pres., 1989—; bd. dirs. Buffalo Diocesan Schs., 1989—, Vincentian Fathers, Ea. Province, Phila., 1985-91, St. John's U., 1989—, Niagara Catholic High Sch., 1991—, Niagara Falls C. of C., 1989—. Author: Blacks in White Collar Jobs, 1979; also articles. Cons. Bklyn. Ecumenical Coops., 1981-88; mem. Low Income Housing Coalition, Washington, 1986-89. Mem. Niagara Falls C. of C. (bd. dirs. 1989—). Office: Niagara U Office of Pres Niagara University NY 14109

O'CONNELL, CARMELA DIGRISTINA, executive, consultant; b. Johnstown, Pa., Nov. 8, 1925; d. Salvatore and Josephine (Riggio) Digristina; m. Maurice F. O'Connell, Sept. 21, 1974 (dec. Feb. 1984); children: Geraldine, John, Bernard. Diploma, Eastern Secretarial Sch., N.Y.C., Sch. Interior Design, N.Y.C. From typist to sec.-treas. Philip P. Masterson Co., N.Y.C., 1942-72; exec. v.p., bd. dirs. Masterson & O'Connell Inc., N.Y.C., 1972-80, cons., 1981—; founder, pres. N.Y. Appraisal Corp., N.Y.C., 1971-80; cofounder, pres. Park Ave. Appraisal, N.Y.C., 1981—. Mem. N.Y. Rep. Com., 1974—, Met. Opera Guild, N.Y.C., 1986; chmn. Ch. of Our Saviour, N.Y.C., 1986. Recipient Amita award for Bus. Woman of Yr., 1977, Lena Madesin Phillips award N.Y. League/Fortune 500 Bus. and Profl. Women, 1989. Mem. Nat. Fedn. Bus. and Profl. Women's Clubs Inc. (2d v.p. 1964, 1st v.p. 1966). Roman Catholic. Home: 80 Park Ave New York NY 10016-2541

O'CONNELL, CATHERINE ANN, library director; b. Balt., Apr. 8, 1946; d. Timothy Edward and Claire Cecilia (Mewshaw) O'C.; m. C. Michael Helmer, May 28, 1977 (div. June 1980). BA, U. Md., 1968; MS in LS, U. Ill., 1971. Cert. permanent profl. libr., Mich., N.J. Reference asst. Pub. Libr. Annapolis (Md.) and Anne Arundel County, 1968-70, br. libr., 1971-72; head adult svcs. Washington County Free Libr., Hagerstown, Md., 1972-76, asst. dir., 1976-84; dir. Pub. Librs. Saginaw (Mich.), 1984-91, Free Libr. of Woodbridge, N.J., 1991—; cons. Hagerstown Bus. Coll., 1976-79, Woodbridge Cultural Arts Com., 1992—, Woodbridge Cable Com., 1992—. Bd. dirs. Pride, Inc., Saginaw, 1987-91. Recipient Sam Shapiro award U. Ill. Libr. Sch., 1972; Md. Libr. Assn. scholar, 1971. Mem. ALA, Pub. Libr. Assn. (bd. dirs. 1988-91), Mich. Libr. Assn., White Pine Libr. Coop. (bd. dirs. 1984-91), Valley Libr. Consortium (bd. dirs. 1984-91), Mgmt. and Adminstrv. Caucus (bd. dirs. 1988-90), Zonta, Rotary, Beta Phi Mu. Office: Free Pub Libr Woodbridge George Frederick Pla Woodbridge NJ 07095

O'CONNELL, CHARLES FRANCIS, lawyer; b. Boston, Jan. 31, 1955; s. Thomas Patrick and Florence E. (McCarthy) O'C. BS, Boston Coll., 1976; JD, Suffolk U., 1980; LLB, Cambridge U., 1982. Bar: Mass. 1980, U.S. Dist. Ct. Mass. 1981, U.S. Ct. Appeals (1st cir.) 1988, U.S. Tax Ct. 1986, U.S. Supreme Ct. 1988. Tax cons. Touche Ross & Co., Boston, 1980-81; pvt. practice Boston, 1982; assoc. Taylor, Ganson & Perrin, Boston, 1983-87, ptnr., 1988—; adj. prof. law Suffolk U., 1989—; bd. arbitrators Nat. Assn. Securities Dealers; mem. panel of arbitrators N.Y. Stock Exch. Author: Compensating United States Employees Abroad, Vol. 4 of International Business Portfolios, 1988; contbr. author: Bender's Federal Tax Service, 1989. Mem. adv. bd. History of South Boston Project, 1984—. Mem. ABA, Am. Soc. Internat. Law, Mass. Bar Assn., Boston Bar Assn., Nat. Panel Arbitrators, Am. Arbitration Assn., United Oxford-Cambridge U. Club, Beta Gamma Sigma, Phi Delta Phi. Office: Taylor Ganson & Perrin 160 Federal St 16th Fl Boston MA 02110

O'CONNELL, DANIEL CRAIG, psychology educator; b. Sand Springs, Okla., May 20, 1928; s. John Albert and Letitia Rutherford (McGinnis) O'C. B.A., St. Louis U., 1951, Ph.L., 1952, M.A., 1953, S.T.L., 1960; Ph.D., U. Ill., 1963. Joined Soc. of Jesus, 1945; asst. prof. psychology St. Louis U., 1964-66, asso. prof., 1966-72, prof., 1972-80, trustee, 1973-78, pres., 1974-78; prof. psychology Loyola U., Chgo., 1980-89; prof. psychology Georgetown U., Washington, 1990—, chmn., 1991—; vis. prof. U. Melbourne, Australia, 1972, U. Kans., 1978-79, Georgetown U., 1986; Humboldt fellow Psychol. Inst. Free U. Berlin, 1968; sr. Fulbright lectr. Kassel U., W. Ger., 1979-80. Author: Critical Essays on Language Use and Psychology, 1988; contbr. articles to profl. jours. Recipient Nancy McNeir Ring award for outstanding teaching St. Louis U., 1969; NSF fellow, 1961, 63, 65, 68; Humboldt Found. grantee, 1973; Humboldt fellow Tech. U. of Berlin, 1987. Fellow Am., Mo. psychol. assns., Am. Psychol. Soc.; mem. Midwestern, Southwestern, Eastern psychol. assns., Psychologists Interested in Religious Issues, Psychonomic Soc., Soc. for Scientific Study of Religion, N.Y., Mo. acads. sci., AAUP, AAAS, Phi Beta Kappa. Home and Office: Georgetown U Dept Psychology 37th & 0 Sts NW Washington DC 20057

O'CONNELL, DANIEL MOYLAN, artist, municipal official; b. Springfield, Mass., Aug. 24, 1949; s. Daniel Morgan and Anna Mildred (Moylan) O'C. BFA, U. Iowa, 1972, MA, 1975. Founder, artistic dir. Berkshire Artisans, Pittsfield, Mass., 1975—; cultural commr. City of Pittsfield, 1983—; founder, adminstr. Berkshire Writer's Guild, 1991—; cons. in field; commr., gen. mgr. pub. radio Sta. WTBR-FM, Pittsfield Schs., 1990—; founder, developer Black Cultural Ctr., Pittsfield, 1992. Muralist photo realistic murals include A Painted Palace, Under the Elms, The Northend Remembers, Illusion of Grandeur, Vietnam Meml. Lest We Forget, 1961-75, Pittsfield Portrait. Commissioner Pub. Cable TV Commn., Pittsfield, 1989; mem. Mass. Govs. Task Force Community Edn., 1987; mem. exec. bd. Mass. Cultural Coun./Mass. Arts Lottery Coun., 1991; bd. dirs. Pittsfield Arts Lottery Coun., 1990-91; mem. Mayors First Night Commn., 1992. Recipient Design award State of Mass., 1986; Nat. Endowment for Arts grantee, 1985; HUD uban devel. grantee for art, 1992. Mem. Consortium Local Arts Agys. Mass. (bd. dirs. 1987-90), Assoc. Bus. and Community Devel. Edn. Found. (bd. dirs. 1989), Friends of Berkshire Artisans (pres., bd. dirs.), Boys Club Alumni, Eagles, Beta Rho, Kappa Sigma. Democratic. Roman Catholic. Home: 1450 North St Apt 108 Pittsfield MA 01201-1545 Office: Berkshire Artisans Community Arts Ctr 28 Renne Pittsfield MA 01201

O'CONNELL, EDWARD WILLIAM, accountant; b. Jersey City, Nov. 16, 1943; s. Edward David and Gloria (Hahn) O'C.; m. Diana Sages, May 31, 1969; children: Edward, Shawn, Kevin. BS in Acctg., St. Peter's Coll., Jersey City, 1965; M in Liberal Arts, Johns Hopkins U., 1967; MBA, Rutgers U., 1970; A.P.C. in Taxation, NYU, 1974. CPA, N.Y., N.J., Pa. Sr. acct. Price Waterhouse, Newark, 1967-71; ptnr., now mng. ptnr. Wiss & Co., Livingston, N.J., 1971—, chmn. acctg. and auditing com., 1977—, mem. exec. com., 1983—. 1st lt. U.S. Army, 1965-67. Mem. AICPA (auditing standards adv. coun., SEC regulations com., SEC practice sect. exec. com.), N.J. State Soc. CPAs (practice rev. com., acctg. and auditing com., coop. with bankers and other credit grantors com.), N.Y. State Soc. CPAs (fin. and leasing cos. and SEC practice assistance coms., investment bankers and stock exchs. com.), Fin. Acctg. Standards Bd. (small bus. adv. group 1985—). Roman Catholic. Office: Wiss & Co 354 Eisenhower Pky Livingston NJ 07039-1023

O'CONNELL, FRANCIS JOSEPH, lawyer, arbitrator; b. Ft. Edward, N.Y., Mar. 19, 1913; s. Daniel Patrick and Mary (Bowe) O'C.; m. Adelaide M. Nagro, Sept. 27, 1938; children: Chris, Mary Gaynor Lavonas. AB, Columbia U., 1934; JD, Fordham U., 1938; SJD summa cum laude, Bklyn. Law Sch., 1945. Bar: N.Y. 1938, U.S. Dist. Ct. (so. dist.) N.Y. 1942, U.S. Tax Ct. 1941. Counsel and asst. to chmn. exec. com. for labor law and litigation Allied Chem. Corp., N.Y.C., 1942-70; ptnr. Bill & O'Connell and predecessor, Garden City, N.Y., 1970-76; pvt. practice Garden City, N.Y., 1976-85, Cutchogue, N.Y., 1985—; arbitrator, fact-finder, mediator Fed. Mediation and Conciliation Svc., 1970—, N.Y. State Mediation Bd., Am. Arbitration Assn., N.Y. State, Nassau and Suffolk County pub. employment rels. bds., 1970—; adminstrv. law judge N.Y. State Dept. Health, 1979—; instr. labor law and labor rels. Cornell U.; U.S. del. ILO, Geneva, 1948, 59, 69, 72. Author: Labor Law and the First Line Supervisor, 1945, Restrictive Work Practices, 1967, National Emergency Strikes, 1968. Trustee Village of Garden City, 1948-50; mem. bd. edn. Diocese of Rockville Centre (N.Y.), 1972-80; pres. various civic orgns., 1942—. Mem. ABA (labor and internat. law sects.), N.Y. State Bar Assn. (labor com.), Bar Assn. Nassau County (labor and arbitration coms., former chmn. arbitration andlabor law coms.), Mfg. Chemists Assn. (chmn. indsl. rels. com.), U.S. C. of C. (indsl. rels. com.), Southold Indian Mus. (bd. dirs.). Republican. Roman Catholic. Office: PO Box 819 Cutchogue NY 11935-0819

O'CONNELL, GEORGE DANTHINE, artist; b. Madison, Wis., Oct. 16, 1926; s. George and Amelia (Danthine) O'C.; m. Marilyn Winkler, July 12, 1947; 1 child, Timothy. B.S., U. Wis., 1950, M.S., 1951; postgrad., Ohio State U., 1952-53, Rijksakademie Van Beeldende Kunsten, Amsterdam, Netherlands, 1959-60. Instr. painting and printmaking Calif. Coll. Arts and Crafts, Oakland, 1953-54; asst. prof. State U. Coll., Buffalo, 1954-61; asso. prof. U. Md., 1961-68; mus. technician Smithsonian Instn., Washington, summers 1962, 64; prof. State U. Coll., Oswego, N.Y., 1968—; chmn. dept. State U. Coll., 1971-73; participant Art In Embassies program Dept. State, 1966, Vol. Artist Program, U.S. Army, summer 1971; project dir. Nat. Endowment Fine Arts, 1973-74; dir., master printer Grey Heron Press; vis. artist Kent St. U., 1987. One-man shows include State U. Coll., Fredonia, N.Y., 1956, Smithsonian Instn., 1962, Balt. Mus. Art, 1963, U. Md., 1968, Franz Bader Gallery, Washington, 1973, Everson Mus., Syracuse, N.Y., 1977, SUNY at Oneonta, 1980, SUNY at Buffalo, 1980, Miriam Perlman Gallery, Chgo., 1981, 85, Oxford Gallery, Rochester, N.Y., 1981, Munson-Williams Proctor Inst. Sch. Art, 1986, Oswego Art Guild, N.Y., 1988, Luncheon Gallery, Everson Mus., Syracuse, 1989, Forum Restaurant Gallery, SUNY-Oswego, 1989, retrospective 1954-1992, Tyler Art Gallery, SUNY, Oswego, 1992; group shows throughout U.S. including, Butler Inst. Am. Art, 1955, 57, Albright-Knox Gallery, Buffalo, 1961, Bklyn. Mus., 1964, 66, U. Miami, Fla., 1967, No. Ill. U., DeKalb, 1970, Davidson (N.C.) Coll., 1974, Southeastern Printmakers' Conf., 1981, Elvehjem Mus. Art, Madison, Wis., 1980, Oxford Gallery, Rochester, N.Y., 1981, Miriam Perlman Gallery, 1983, 84, Oxford Gallery, Rochester, N.Y., 1986, 87, 88, 89, Boston Printmakers Members Show, 1986-92, Soc. Am. Graphic Artists, 1990-92; represented in over 50 pub. collections including, Library of Congress, Washington, Nat. Collection Fine Arts, Washington, Phila. Mus. Fine Art, Gemeentemuseum Van Schone Kunsten, The Hague, Netherlands, Smithsonian Instn., Balt. Mus. Art, U.S. Embassy, Singapore and Dublin, N.Y. Pub. Library, Brit. Mus., London, Cleve. Mus. Art, SUNY at Buffalo, Portland Mus. Art, Quaker Oats Collection, McDonald Corp. Collection, and others. Recipient Pres.'s award for creative works SUNY-Oswego, 1986, SUNY Chancellor's award for excellence in teaching, 1989, Purchase award Soc. Am. Graphic Artists Exhbn., 1989. Address: 39 Baylis St Oswego NY 13126

O'CONNELL, HENRY FRANCIS, lawyer; b. Boston, Jan. 4, 1922; s. Henry F. and Anna (Cunning) O'C. BA, Boston Coll., 1943, JD, 1948. Bar: Mass. 1948, U.S. Supreme Ct. 1956. House counsel electronics div. Am. Machine & Foundry Co., Boston, 1951-54; sole practice Boston, 1954-60; assoc. Glynn & Dempsey, Boston, 1960-70, Avery, Dooley, Post & Avery, Boston, 1970-88; asst. atty. gen. mcpl. affairs State of Mass., Boston, 1969-88; mcpl. cons. State of Mass., Winthrop, 1989—. Mem. Winthrop Bd. Selectmen, 1958-64, 68-72, chmn. 1960-61, 68-69, 71-72. Lt. USCGR, World War II. Mem. Mass. Bar Assn., Nat. Boating Fedn. (past pres.), Mass. Selectmen's Assn., Mass. Bay Yachts Clubs Assn. (past commodore). Home and Office: 20 Belcher St Winthrop MA 02152-3014

O'CONNELL, JAMES THOMAS, accountant; b. Camden, N.J., Apr. 12, 1963; s. James Andrew and Elizabeth Ann (Perri) O'C.; m. Cheryl Lynn Nielson, Mar. 28, 1987; 1 child, Lauren Christine. BA in Acctg., Rutgers U., 1986. Jr. acct. Meml. Health Alliance, Mt. Holly, N.J., 1987-88; staff acct. Meml. Health Alliance, Mt. Holly, 1989-90, sr. acct., 1990—. Office: Meml Health Alliance 175 Madison Ave Mount Holly NJ 08060-2038

O'CONNELL, JEANNE, financial planner, insurance broker; b. Stoneham, Mass., Dec. 9, 1951; d. Kenneth Edward and Frances Evelyn (Matulewicz) O'C.; 1 child, Ryan Sulloway. Student U. Oreg., 1971-72; BFA cum laude, U. Mass.-Amherst, 1974; U. Calif.-Sacramento, summer 1973; postgrad. Northeastern U., 1975; Suffolk U., MBA, 1984. CPCU, CLU; chartered fin. cons.; assoc. in underwriting; enrolled agt. designation. Ins. clk. S.B. Swaim & Co., Boston, 1969-72, Hollis Perrin & Co., Boston, 1972; underwriting asst. Pub. Service Mut. Ins. Co., Newton, Mass., 1974-77; personal lines analyst Comml. Union Ins. Co., Boston, 1977-80, sr. personal lines analyst, 1980-83, tech. specialist, 1983-88; pvt. practice fin. cons., brokerage Boston, 1988—; instr. ins. and fin. planning Ins. Libr. Boston, 1988—; speaker in field; ind. tax preparer; founder, dir. Red Dragon Arts Coop., Boston, 1983; potter, artist Radcliffe Pottery Studio, Boston, 1980-85. Mem. exec. student adv. bd. Suffolk U., 1982-83, student liason mem. between Exec. MBA Program and regular MBA Program and dean's adv. bd., coordinator Exec. MBA Program Policy Seminar Weekend, 1983. Mem. Internat. Assn. Fin. Planners, NAFE, Soc. CPCUs (bd. dirs. Boston chpt., joint adv. bd. Mass. Ins. Commr.), Soc. Chartered Fin. Cons., Nat. Soc. of Enrolled Agts., Nat. Assn. of Tax Preparers, Delta Mu Delta. Avocations: reading science fiction, photography. Home and Office: 41 Atkins St Brighton MA 02135-1626 Studio: 36 Thayer St Boston MA 02118

O'CONNELL, KEVIN GEORGE, college president, priest; b. Boston, May 22, 1938; s. George Lawrence and Mary Margaret (Cohan) O'C. BA, Boston Coll., 1962, MA, 1963; PhD, Harvard U., 1968; MDiv, Weston Sch. Theology, Cambridge, Mass., 1969. Joined S.J., 1956; ordained priest Roman Cath. Ch., 1969. Vis. prof. Old Testament Woodstock Coll., Balt., Md., 1969-70; vis. prof. theology U. San Francisco, summer 1970; asst. prof. Old Testament Weston Sch. Theology, Cambridge, 1971-77, dir. field edn., 1972-75, assoc. prof. Old Testament, 1977-80; assoc. prof., chmn. dept. religious studies John Carroll U., Cleve., 1981-87; William K. Warren Disting. vis. prof. Roman Catholic studies U. Tulsa, 1987; pres. Le Moyne Coll., Syracuse, N.Y., 1988—; chmn. bd. Joint Archeol. Expedition to Tell el-Hesi, Israel, 1982—. Author: The Theodotionic Revision of the Book of Exodus, 1972; editor: The Tell el-Hesi Field Manual, 1980, Tell el-Hesi: Modern Military Trenching and Muslim Cemetery, 1985, Tell el-Hesi: The Persian Period (Stratum V), 1989, Tell el-Hesi: The Site and the Expedition, 1989; mem. editorial adv. bd. Bible Rev., 1987—. Bd. dirs. Hiawatha Coun., Boy Scouts Am., 1988—; trustee Albright Inst. Archeol. Rsch., Jerusalem, Israel, 1982—, Am. Schs. Oriental Rsch., Balt., 1983—, Boston Coll., 1988—, N.Y. State Commn. on Ind. Colls. and Univs., 1989—, Loyola U., Chgo., 1990—. Kent fellow Danforth Found., 1965-67; Am. Coun. Learned Socs. study fellow, 1970-71, grantee, 1980-81; Grauel Faculty fellow John Carroll U., 1986-87. Mem. Cath. Bibl. Assn., Soc. of Biblical Lit., Internat. Fedn. Cath. Univs. (v.p., mem. coun., 1988—), Syracuse C. of C. (bd. dirs. 1989-91). Office: Le Moyne Coll Office of Pres Syracuse NY 13214-1399

O'CONNELL, MICHAEL LEONARD, psychologist; b. Waco, Tex., July 25, 1935; s. Harvey Leonard and Frances Pauline (Voelkle) O'C.; m. Mildred Thelma Bartlett, Nov. 10, 1956 (div. 1965); children: Stephen, Timothy, Colleen. Student, Rice U., 1952-53; EdM, Harvard U., 1983, EdD, 1992; DD (hon.), Ch. of Modern Apostles, Miami, Fla., 1982. Ordained minister, Ch. of Modern Apostles. Data ctr. mgr. U.S. Steel, L.A., 1956-62; systems programmer U.S. Steel, San Francisco, 1962-68; systems mgr. Sanders Assocs., Nashua, N.H., 1968-72; programming mgr. Rockwell Internat., L.A., 1972-73; engring. mgr. Digital Equipment Corp., Maynard, Mass., 1973-75, product planning mgr., 1975-82, organizational cons., 1982-84, career counselor, 1984-92; prin. Excalibur Cons. & Counseling, Cambridge, Mass., 1991—; mem. Codasyl Exec. Com., Washington, 1975—; chmn. Codasyl Data Description Com., Washington, 1979-82; cons. in field. Author: Data Bases: What's It All About, 1975, Toward An Understanding of The Psychology of Careers, 1991; editorial advisor jour. Info. Systems, London, 1983—. Counselor So. N.H. Crisis Hot Line, Nashua, 1980-82. Cpl. USMC, 1953-56. Tex. Dow Inst. scholar, 1952. Mem. APA, Collaboration in Social Architecture, Marine Corps Assn., Mensa (N.H. proctor 1981-84). Home: 8 Newport Rd Cambridge MA 02140

O'CONNELL, NEIL JAMES, priest, academic administrator; b. Buffalo, May 21, 1937; s. Cornelius James and Marie Katherine (Schneider) O'C. BA, St. Bonaventure U., 1960; STB, Cath. U., Washington, 1964; MA, Siena Coll., 1967; PhD, U. Ga., 1970. Ordained priest Roman Cath. Ch., 1964. Instr. history and sociology St. Francis Coll., Rye Beach, N.H., 1965-67; asst. prof. history Prairie View (Tex.) A&M Coll., 1970-71; asst. assoc. prof. history Fisk U., Nashville, 1971-80, chmn. history, 1975-80, dir. div. fine arts and humanities, 1976-79; acad. dean Erie Community Coll., City Campus, Buffalo, 1980-86; dean faculty and instrn. Elizabeth Seton Coll., Yonkers, N.Y., 1986-89; dean Elizabeth Seton Sch. Assoc. Degree Studies of Iona Coll., Yonkers, N.Y., 1989-90; pres. St. Bonaventure U., St. Bonaventure, N.Y., 1990—. Contbr. articles to jours. in field. Trustee Archbishop Walsh High Sch., Olean, N.Y., 1990—, Bishop Timon High Sch., Buffalo, Trocaire Coll., Buffalo; bd. dirs. Econ. Devel. Zone, Olean, YMCA, Olean, 1990—, Industry, Bus., Commerce, Edn. Coalition, Olean, 1990—; vice chair, bd. dirs. Coll. Consortium for Internat. Studies. Mem. Olean C. of C. (bd. dirs. 1990—), Rotary, Phi Beta Kappa, Phi Kappa Phi, Phi Delta Kappa, Phi Beta Sigma. Democrat. Home: St Bonaventure U Saint Bonaventure NY 14778 Office: St Bonaventure U Office of President Saint Bonaventure NY 14778

O'CONNELL, PETER KINNEY, video and film production company executive; b. Buffalo, Feb. 9, 1964; s. Joseph Michael and Mary Elizabeth (Kinney) O'C. BA, U. Dayton, 1986. Producer WVUD-FM, Dayton, Ohio, 1983-86; field producer Empire State Games Network, Syracuse, N.Y., 1986; pres., chief exec. officer 4-6-8 Prodns., Inc., Buffalo, 1987—; bd. dirs., v.p. Buffalo/Niagara Sales and Mktg. Execs., 1991—. Bd. dirs. Epilepsy Assn. Western N.Y., 1991-92. Recipient Disting. Sales and Mktg. award Sales and Mktg. Execs. Internat., 1992. Mem. Am. Mktg. Assn., Crescent Beach Assn. (v.p. 1989-91, pres. 1992—). Office: 4-6-8 Prodns Inc 1552 Hertel Ave Ste 225 Buffalo NY 14216

O'CONNELL, RICHARD (JAMES), English educator, poet; b. N.Y.C., Oct. 25, 1928; s. Richard James and Mary Ellen (Fallon) O'C.; m. Beryl Evelyn Reeves, Nov. 14, 1978. BS, Temple U., 1956; MA, Johns Hopkins, 1957. Instr. English Temple U., Phila., 1957-61, asst. prof., 1961-69, asso. prof., 1969-86; sr. assoc. prof., 1986—; guest lectr. poetry dept. writing seminars Johns Hopkins U., 1961-74; participant Poetry in Schs. Program, Pa. Council Arts, 1971-73; Fulbright lectr. Am. lit. U. Brazil, Rio de Janeiro, 1960, U. Navarre, Pamplona, Spain, 1962-63. Served with USN, 1948-52. Recipient prize Contemporary Poetry Press, 1972. Mem. PEN, MLA, Asso. Writing Programs, Walt Whitman Poetry Center (dir. 1975-84), Lit. Fellowship Phila. Author: From an Interior Silence, 1961, Cries of Flesh and Stone, 1962, New Poems and Translations, 1963; Brazilian Happenings, 1966, Terrane, 1967, Thirty Epigrams, 1971, Irish Monastic Poems (transl.), 1975, The Word in Time (selected transl. of Antonio Machado), 1975, Sappho (selected transl.), 1975, Lorca (selected transl.), 1976, Middle English Poems (transl.), 1976, More Irish Poems (transl.), 1976, Epigrams from Martial (transl.), 1976, One Hundred Epigrams from the Greek Anthology (trans.), 1977, Hudson's Fourth Voyage, 1978, The Epigrams of Luxorius (transl.), 1984, Temple Poems, 1985, Hanging Tough, 1986, Battle Poems, 1987, Selected Epigrams, 1990, Lives of The Poets, 1990, New Epigrams From Martial (transl.), 1991, The Caliban Poems, 1992; editor: Apollo's Day, 17th Century Songs, 1969; Atlantis Edits., 1962—, Poetry Newsletter, 1971—. Home: 1150 Hillsboro Mile Apt 815 Pompano Beach FL 33062-1701

O'CONNOR, CHRISTOPHER BRYAN, stockbroker; b. Ann Arbor, Mich., May 20, 1969; s. William Edward and Jean Barbara (Parrott) O'C. BA, Gettysburg Coll., 1991. Account exec. Hibbard Brown & Co., Inc., Woodbridge, N.J., 1991—. Mem. Phi Alpha Theta, Pi Lambda Sigma, Pi Sigma Alpha, Phi Gamma Delta (chpt. rec. sec. 1990, Golden Owl 1991). Republican. Presbyterian. Home: 103 Plaza Dr Woodbridge NJ 07095

O'CONNOR, EDWARD THOMAS, JR., lawyer, state senator; b. Jersey City, Oct. 6, 1942; A.B., St. Peter's Coll., 1964; J.D., Fordham U., 1967; LL.M., N.Y.U., 1975; m. Ellen Reuter, 1967; 1 dau., Kerry Ellen. Admitted

to N.J. bar, 1967; ptnr. Shaljian, Cammarata & O'Connor , Jersey City, 1972—; mem. N.J. Senate, 1982—; asst. prosecutor Hudson County, N.J., 1970-72. Bd. dirs. Hudson County Council Social Agys., 1974-76; chmn. N.J. Vietnam Vets. Meml. Commn., 1986—. Served to capt. U.S. Army, 1968-70. Mem. St. Peter's Coll. Alumni Assn. (trustee 1976-81, chmn. ann. fund drive, 1977). Office: 1662 Kennedy Blvd Jersey City NJ 07305 Other: NJ State Senate State Capitol Trenton NJ 08625

O'CONNOR, EDWARD VINCENT, JR., lawyer; b. Yokosuka, Japan, Nov. 9, 1952. BA, Duke U., 1975; JD, N.Y. Law Sch., 1981. Bar: Va. 1982, D.C. 1983. Assoc. Lewis, Kinsey, Dack & Good, Washington, 1982-87; ptnr. Lewis, Dack, Paradiso & Good, Washington, 1988-89, Lewis, Dack, Paradiso, O'Connor & Good, Washington, 1989—; arbitrator D.C. Superior Ct. Mem. Va. State Bar, D.C. Bar, Fairfax County Bar Assn.

O'CONNOR, EILEEN MAE, psychiatrist; b. N.Y.C., Feb. 21, 1944; d. John Thomas and Katherine Eleanor (Mullee) O'C. MD, N.J. Med. Sch., 1977. Diplomate Am. Bd. Psychiatry and Neurology. Instr. Albert Einstein Coll. Medicine, 1981-82; med. dir. Community Mental Health Orgn., Englewood, N.J., 1982-84; pvt. practice psychiatry Fair Lawn, N.J., 1984—. Mem. Am. Psychiat. Assn., N.J. Med. Assn. Office: 4-14 Saddle River Rd Fair Lawn NJ 07410

O'CONNOR, GEOFFREY J., tax lawyer; b. N.Y.C., Jan. 27, 1947; s. A. Richard and Sonya (Ruescher) O'C.; m. Virginia M. Lowe, Oct. 19, 1969; chidlren: Kathryn, Andrew. AB, Georgetown U., 1968, LLM in Taxation, 1976; JD, Cath. U., 1973. Bar: N.Y., D.C. Atty. advisor Office of Chief Counsel of IRS, Washington, 1973-74; atty. advisor to judge U.S. Tax Ct., Washington, 1974-76; assoc. Burke & Burke, N.Y.C., 1976-82; tax counsel Slade & Pellman, N.Y.C., 1982-85, Meltzer Lippe Goldstein & Wolf, Mineola, N.Y., 1985-87; sole practice Garden City, N.Y., 1987—. Trustee Old Westbury (N.Y.) Sch. of the Holy Child, 1984-86, Port Washington (N.Y.) Community Chest, 1980-84, Farrington Close Condominium, Southampton, N.Y., 1988—. With U.S. Army, 1968-70. Mem. Nassau County Bar Assn. Republican. Roman Catholic. Home: 12 Farrington Close Southampton NY 11968-3020

O'CONNOR, JOHN JOSEPH, JR., academic administrator; b. Augusta, Maine, Sept. 5, 1954; s. John Joseph and Elizabeth (Devine) O'C.; m. Michelle K. Sonn, Nov. 15, 1980; 1 child, Carolyn Elizabeth. BA, U. Notre Dame, 1976; MS, NYU, 1987. Press sec. U.S. House Reps., Washington, 1976-80; assoc. v.p. for external affairs NYU, N.Y.C., 1980-87, exec. asst. to the pres., 1987-91, v.p. for univ. rels., 1988—; bd. dirs. Little Red Sch. House, N.Y.C., Greenwich Village Local Devel. Corp., N.Y.C.; chairperson Washington Sq. Pk. Coalition, N.Y.C., 1989—; dir. Wall St. Sem. Found., Washington, 1988-91. Contbr. articles to news publs. Justice of the Peace, State of Maine, Augusta, 1972-86; dir. NYU-N.Y. Police Dept. Watch Team, N.Y.C., 1991—. Recipient Edn. award Am. Legion, Augusta, 1972. Mem. Coun. for Advancement and Support of Edn., NYU Alumni Assn., Greenwich Village C. of C., Lincoln Harbor Yacht Club. Roman Catholic. Office: NYU 70 Washington Sq S New York NY 10012-1091

O'CONNOR, JOHN JOSEPH CARDINAL, archbishop, former naval officer; b. Phila., Jan. 15, 1920; s. Thomas Joseph and Dorothy Magdalene (Gomple) O'C. M.A., St. Charles Coll., 1949, Catholic U. Am., 1954; Ph.D., Georgetown U., 1970; D.R.E., Villanova (Pa.) U., 1976. Ordained priest Roman Cath. Ch., 1945, elevated to monsignor, 1966, consecrated bishop, 1979, created cardinal, 1985; served in Chaplain Corps U.S. Navy, 1952, advanced through grades to rear adm.; assigned to Atlantic and Pacific fleets U.S. Navy, Okinawa and Vietnam; sr. chaplain U.S. Naval Acad.; chief of chaplains U.S. Navy, Washington; aux. bishop, vicar gen. Mil. Vicariate, 1979-83; apptd. bishop of Scranton Pa., 1983-84; archbishop Archdiocese of N.Y., 1984—; Exec. bd. Nat. USO, Georgetown Center Strategic and International Studies, Marine Corps Found. Author: Principles and Problems of Naval Leadership, 1958, A Chaplain Looks at Vietnam, 1969, In Defense of Life, 1981, (with Edward I. Koch) His Eminence and Hizzoner: A Candid Exchange, 1989, (with Elie Wiesel) A Journey of Faith, 1990. Decorated DMS, Legion of Merit (3), Meritorious Service medal. Mem. Am. Polit. Sci. Assn. Office: Archdiocese NY 452 Madison Ave New York NY 10022-6864

O'CONNOR, KEVIN WASHBURN, lawyer; b. Wilmington, Del., Apr. 9, 1955; s. Timothy Edmond and Eilzabeth (Clifford) O'C.; m. Ellen Marie Muldoon, Sept. 1, 1984; children: Katherine, Margaret. Student, Emerson Coll., 1973-75; BA summa cum laude, Macalester Coll., 1977; JD, Am. U., 1984. Bar: Md. 1985. Mem. govtl. affairs staff Am. Speech-Lang.-Hearing Assn., Rockville, Md., 1977-82; assoc. dir. pub. affairs Fedn. Am. Soc. Exptl. Biology, Bethesda, Md., 1982-86; sr. legal analyst, project dir. Office Tech. Assessment, U.S. Congress, Washington, 1986—. Bd. dirs. Cedar Lane Stage, Bethesda, 1986-88. Mem. ABA, Md. Bar Assn. Roman Catholic. Home: 403 Gilmoure Dr Silver Spring MD 20901-2302 Office: US Congress Tech Assessment Washington DC 20510

O'CONNOR, MARTHA SUSAN, educator; b. Manitowoc, Wis., Dec. 16, 1941; d. Kenneth Meredith and Lillian Margaret (Schneider) O'C.; m. Richard Lawrence Allen, Oct. 7, 1961 (div. 1977); children: Richard Phillip, Gregory Scott; m. Stephen Michael Serebin, May 21, 1988. BS, U. Wis., 1973, MS, 1981; PhD, George State U., 1990. Cons., coord. Health Svc. Mgmt., Milw., 1975-76; sr. therapist Mt. Sinai Med. Ctr., Milw., 1976-82; instr. Milw. Area Tech. Coll., 1982-83; assoc. prof. Med. Coll. of Ga., Augusta, 1983-91; program mgr. edn. divsn. Am. Occupational Therapy Assn., Inc., Rockville, Md., 1991-92, dir. accreditation dept., 1992—; cons. Friendship Community Ctr., Augusta, Ga., 1983-91, Edgefield Mental Health Ctr., 1988, Alexander's Corner, 1984-85, Augusta Correctional Inst., 1984-85, N.Y. State Bd. of Edn., 1990. Bd. dirs. Viacom Pub. Access, Shorewood, Wis., 1980-83, LWV, 1984-88, Mental Health Assn. of Greater Augusta, 1983-89, pres., 1990-91. Mem. Am. Occupational Therapy Assn. (sec. 1985), Ga. Occupational Therapy Assn. (job placement chairperson 1990-91). Home: 15937 Yukon Ln Rockville MD 20855-2632 Office: Am Occupational Therapy Assn Inc 1383 Piccard Dr Rockville MD 20850-4316

O'CONNOR, NOREEN CARR, state official; b. Bklyn., July 8, 1939; d. Edward A. and Margaret (Boyle) Carr; m. Michael John O'Connor, June 27, 1959; children: Brian, Terence, Deirdre, Sean. Student, St. John's U., Bklyn., 1957-59; BA, Goddard Coll., Plainfield, Vt., 1977; MEd, U. Vt., 1981. Tchr. Diocese of N.Y., Roman Cath. Ch., Bklyn., 1957-59; substitute tchr. Bd. Coop. Edn. II, Patchogue, N.Y., 1964-73; exec. dir. Youth Employment, Washington County Youth Svc., Montpelier, Vt., 1974-77; spl. edn. tchr. Danville (Vt.) Pub. Schs., 1978; sex equity coord. Vt. Dept. Edn., Montpelier, 1978-81; chief spl. employment Vt. Dept. Personnel, Montpelier, 1981-85; chief voc-tech edn. Vt. Dept. Edn., Montpelier, 1985-87; tchr. spl. needs Barre (Vt.) Area Voc. Ctr., 1987-89; exec. dir. Vt. State Coun. on Voc-Tech. Edn., Montpelier, 1989—; cons. in field; dir. Conf. on Full Employment, Vt. Coun. on Humanities and Pub. Issues, 1978. Bd. dirs. Vt. Girl Scouts U.S.A., 1986-89; mem. Judicial Conduct Bd., Vt., 1991—; commr. Gov.'s Commn. on Status of Women, 1982-89. Recipient Career Woman of the Yr., Bus. Profl. Women, 1982, Leadership award, Voc. Equity Edn. Coun., 1985. Mem. Am. Vocat. Assn., Vt. Vocat. Assn., Assn. for Supervision and Curriculum Devel., Vt. Soc. for Exec. Dirs. Home: RR 1 Marshfield VT 05658-9801 Office: Vt Coun Vocat Edn 2 Prospect St Montpelier VT 05602-3555

O'CONNOR, PAUL JOSEPH, controller; b. Boston, Mar. 4, 1944; s. Joseph M. and Catherine T. (Leary) O'C.; separated; children: Kenneth, Lori, Tara. A in Bus. Adminstrn., Mass. Bay Community Coll., Boston, 1963; BS, Bently Coll., 1970. CPA. Acctg. clk. Magnesium Casting, Hyde Park, Mass., 1964-66; staff acct. Wolf and Co., Boston, 1969-77; acct. Hanover, Mass., 1977-87; contr. James G. Grant Co., Inc., Readville, Mass., 1987—. With U.S. Army, 1966-69, Thailand. Roman Catholic. Office: James C Grant Co Inc R28 Wolcott St PO Box 54 Readville MA 02137

O'CONNOR, PAUL SIMON RORY, market analyst; b. London, Oct. 6, 1966; s. Michael Neville and Pauline Ruth (Teare) O'C. Student, Kent Sch., 1981-83, Am. Sch., Switzerland, 1983-85, U. Paris, 1985-87; BA in French and English Lit., Skidmore Coll., 1987-89. Market analyst H.J. Heinz Co., Pitts., 1989—. Anglican. Home: 6 Burton Mews, London SW1 W9BG, England

O'CONNOR, PETER JOSEPH, fire chief; b. Balt., May 1, 1932; s. Peter Joseph and Elizabeth Veronica (McGovern) O'C.; m. Eileen Doris Strachan, Feb. 7, 1959; children: Karen, Kevin. Lt. Balt. City Fire Dept., 1960-64, capt., 1964-70, bn. chief, 1970-77, bn. comdr., 1977-79, dep. chief, 1979-80, chief fire dept., 1980—. Cpl. U.S. Army, 1950-53. Chmn. Mayor's Arson Task Force, 1981—; mem. Gov.'s Anti-Arson Adv. Com., 1982—. Recipient Citizen's award Balt. City Police Dept., 1973. Mem. Internat. Assn. Fire Chiefs, Balt. City Fire Officers (pres. 1970-79), Ancient Order of Hibernians. Democrat. Roman Catholic. Home: 9 W Lee St Baltimore MD 21201-2455 Office: Office of Fire Chief Balt City Fire Dept 410 E Lexington St Baltimore MD 21202-3557

O'CONNOR, RICHARD, banker, inventor; b. Bklyn., July 22, 1962; s. James Patrick and Frances Rebecca O'Connor. Student, Poly. Inst., Bklyn., 1980-81. With internat. banking dept. Barclays Banks PLC, N.Y.C. Inventor safety candle. Republican. Roman Catholic. Home: 328 Lincoln Ave Brooklyn NY 11208 Office: Barclays Bank PLC 75 Wall St New York NY 10265

O'CONNOR, ROBERT EMMETT, political scientist, educator; b. N.Y.C., July 9, 1945; s. Charles Thomas and Anna Mona (Chisholm) O'C.; m. Linda Wambaugh, June 16, 1974 (div. 1977); m. Janice Joanna Hensyl, July 1, 1978. BA, Johns Hopkins U., 1967; cert., Sorbonne U., Paris, 1969; PhD, U. N.C., 1971. Asst. prof. Pa. State U., University Park, 1971-76, assoc. prof., 1977—; sr. assoc. ICF Inc., Washington, 1985-87; cons. Accion Democratica, Caracas, Venezuela, 1978-84; reviewer NSF, Washington, 1982—. Author: Politics and Structure, 1989; contbr. articles to profl. jours. and chpts. to books; editorial bd. mem. Polity, 1982—; book reviewer: Choice, 1986—. Del. Dem. Nat. Conv., N.Y.C., 1976, 80; chair Liberal Arts Coun. Senators Pa. State U., 1984-85; active Mental Health/Mental Retardation Bd., Centre County, Pa., 1978-83; bd. dirs. Women's Resource Ctr., State College, Pa., 1984-85. U.S. EPA grantee, 1990, 87, Nat. Geographic Soc. grantee, 1992, grantee N.J. Dept. Environ. Protection, 1989, Risk Inst., 1987. Mem. Soc. for Risk Analysis, Am. Assn. for Pub. Opinion Rsch., Pub. Policy Rsch. Assn., Am. Polit. Sci. Assn., Midwest Polit. Sci. Assn., N.E. Polit. Sci. Assn., So. Polit. Sci. Assn. Home: 312 Bailey Ln Boalsburg PA 16827-1313 Office: Pa State U Dept Polit Sci University Park PA 16802

O'CONNOR, SANDRA DAY, U.S. Supreme Court justice; b. El Paso, Tex., Mar. 26, 1930; d. Harry A. and Ada Mae (Wilkey) Day; m. John Jay O'Connor, III, Dec. 1952; children: Scott, Brian, Jay. AB in Econs. with great distinction, Stanford U., 1950, LLB, 1952. Bar: Calif. Dep. county atty. San Mateo, Calif., 1952-53; civil atty. Q.M. Market Ctr., Frankfurt am Main, Fed. Republic of Germany, 1954-57; sole practice Phoenix, 1959-65; asst. atty. gen. State of Ariz., 1965-69; Ariz. state senator, 1969-75, chmn. com. on state, county and mcpl. affairs, 1972-73, majority leader, 1973-74; judge Maricopa County Superior Ct., 1975-79, Ariz. Ct. Appeals, 1979-81; assoc. justice Supreme Ct. U.S., 1981—; referee juvenile ct., 1962-64; chmn. vis. bd. Maricopa County Juvenile Detention Home, 1963-64; mem. Maricopa County Bd. Adjustments and Appeals, 1963-64, Anglo-Am. Legal Exchange, 1980, Maricopa County Superior Ct. Judges Tng. and Edn. Com., Maricopa Ct. Study Com.; chmn. com. to reorganize lower cts. Ariz. Supreme Ct., 1974-75; faculty Robert A. Taft Inst. Govt.; vice chmn. Select Law Enforcement Rev. Commn., 1979-80. Mem. bd. editors Stanford (Calif.) U. Law Rev. Mem. Ariz. Personnel Commn., 1968-69, Nat. Def. Adv. Com. on Women in Services, 1974-76; trustee Heard Mus., Phoenix, 1968-74, 76-81, pres., 1980-81; mem. adv. bd. Phoenix Salvation Army, 1975-81; trustee Stanford U., 1976-80, Phoenix County Day Sch.; mem. citizens adv. bd. Blood Services, 1975-77; nat. bd. dirs. Smithsonian Assocs., 1981—; past Rep. dist. chmn.; bd. dirs. Phoenix Community Council, Ariz. Acad., 1970-75, Jr. Achievement Ariz., 1975-79, Blue Cross/Blue Shield Ariz., 1975-79, Channel 8, 1975-79, Phoenix Hist. Soc., 1974-77, Maricopa County YMCA, 1978-81, Golden Gate Settlement. Recipient Ann. award NCCJ, 1975, Disting. Achievement award Ariz. State U., 1980; named Woman of Yr., Phoenix Advt. Club, 1972. Lodge: Soroptimists. Address: US Supreme Ct 1 First St NE Washington DC 20543

O'CONNOR, STANLEY JAMES, Asian studies educator; b. Des Moines, July 1, 1926; s. Stanley James and Marion (Stout) O'C.; m. Janet Raleigh, Sept. 4, 1952; children: Stanley James, Janet, Cynthia. B.A., Cornell U., 1951, Ph.D., 1964; M.A., U. Va., 1954. Sr. analyst U.S. Govt., Washington, 1952-60; fgn. area tng. fellow Cornell U., 1961-63, prof., 1964—, chmn. dept. Asian studies, 1966-69, chmn. dept. art history, 1970-76, dir. S.E. Asia program, 1979-84; cons. Ford Found.; adv. bd. Andrew D. White Mus., Ithaca, 1969-73, Herbert F. Johnson Mus., 1974-76. Author: Hindu Gods of Peninsular Siam, 1972, (with T. Harrisson) Excavation of the Prehistoric Iron Industry in West Borneo, 1969, Gold and Megalithic Activity in Prehistoric and Recent West Borneo, 1970; mem. editorial bd. Indonesia, Studies on Southeast Asia. Bd. dirs. Historic Ithaca, 1981-82; bd. dirs. Am. Com. for South Asian Art, 1982-85, 89—; adv. bd. Asia Soc. Gallery, 1989—. Served with AUS, 1946-47. JDR 3d Found. fellow, 1966; NEH sr. fellow, 1973-74; vis. fellow Inst. for Southeast Asian Studies, Singapore, 1973-74. Fellow Explorers Club; mem. Assn. Asian Studies (S.E. Asia coun. 1978-81), Royal Asiatic Soc. (Malaysian br.), Siam Soc. Home: 617 Highland Rd Ithaca NY 14850-1411

O'CONNOR, THOMAS PATRICK, college official; b. Erie, Pa., May 27, 1941; s. William Richard and Dorothy Cecile (Benton) O'C.; m. Nadine Schaffer, Aug. 1, 1964; children: Timothy Patrick, Michael Brian. BS, Slippery Rock (Pa.) State U., 1963, MEd, 1967. Elem. tchr. North Hills Sch. Dist., Pitts., 1963-66; asst. dir. admissions Washington (Pa.) and Jefferson Coll., 1966-68, dir. admissions, 1968—. Elder Faith United Presbyn. Ch., Washington, 1976—; v.p. Washington Youth Baseball, 1986—; regional dir. Pony Baseball Internat., Inc., Washington, 1989—; vice chmn. World Series Tournaments, Inc., Washington, 1991. Mem. The Coll. Bd., Nat. Assn. Coll. Admission Counselors, Pa. Assn. Coll. Admission Counselors. Republican. Home: 94 Royal Oak Dr Washington PA 15301-5774

O'CONNOR, TOM, corporate executive, management consultant; b. Boston, June 11, 1942; s. Thomas Henry and Blanche (Cosgrove) O'C.; m. Mary Alice Kelly; 1 child, Michael Kelly O'Connor. BA in econs., U. Mass., 1971; postgrad., U. Wis., Milw., 1971-73, U. Del., 1978, Am. U., 1980. Economist Interstate Commerce Commn., Washington, 1973-74; mgr. planning U.S. Railway Assn., Washington, 1974-75; cons. transp. R.L. Banks & Assocs., Washington, 1975-77; asst. dir. Conrail, Phila., 1977-79; asst. v.p. econs. Assn. Am. R.R.'s, Washington, 1979-82; v.p. DNS Assocs., Inc., Washington, Lexington (Mass.), 1982-88; v.p., ptnr. Snavely, King & Assoc., Washington, 1988—; pres. TRF Cost Analysis chpt., Washington, 1987-89; mem. Transp. Rsch. Bd., Transp. Rsch. Forum. Pres. Green Briar Civic Assn., Fairfax, Va., 1985, Greenbriar Dem. Club, Fairfax, 1984-89, Greenbriar Community Ctr., Fairfax, 1984; v.p. Greenbriar West PTA, Fairfax, 1986-88. Sgt. U.S. Army, 1963-66. Mem. Am. Econs. Assn., Council of Logistics Mgmt., Nat. Def. Assn., Air Force Assn., Phi Beta Kappa, Phi Kappa Phi. Democrat. Roman Catholic. Home: 13222 Point Pleasant Dr Fairfax VA 22033-3515 Office: Snavely King & Assoc 1220 L St NW Washington DC 20005-4018

O'CONNOR, WILLIAM MATTHEW, lawyer; b. Pensacola, Fla., Apr. 5, 1955; s. William Francis and Rosalind (Shea) O'C.; m. Mary Patricia Keepnews, Oct. 13, 1984; children: William Lawrence, Thomas Patrick. BS in Psychology, Fordham U., 1977, JD, 1980. Bar: N.Y. 1981, N.J. 1987, U.S. Dist. Ct. N.J. 1987, U.S. Dist. Conn. 1988, U.S. Dist. Ct. (so., ea., no. and we. dists.) N.Y., 1981, U.S. Ct. Appeals (2nd cir.) 1983. Intern N.Y. Atty. Gen., N.Y.C., 1978-79; legis. intern Am. Lung Assn., N.Y.C., 1979; assoc. Keane & Butler, N.Y.C., 1979-81, Keane & Beane, White Plains, N.Y., 1981-83, Cooperman, Levitt & Winikoff, P.C., N.Y.C., 1983-86; sr. assoc. Sullivan, Donovan, Hanrahan & Silliere, N.Y.C., 1986-87; ptnr. O'Connor Reddy & Jensen, N.Y.C., 1987—. Author: Lobbying Guidebook Am. Lung Assn., 1979. Contbr. articles to profl. jours. Mem. legis. com. pub. schs., White Plains, 1981-82; Dem. committeeman Village of Pelham Manor, N.Y., 1985—. Mem. Assn. Trial Lawyers Am., Fed. Bar Coun., N.Y. State Bar Assn. (mem. comml. and fed. litigation sect., creditor's rights com. 1989—), Westchester Bar Assn. (editor in chief Jour. 1983-89, mem. labor law com. 1981—, com. on profl. ethics 1989—), Fordham ILJ Alumni Assn. (bd. dirs. 1984—), New Rochelle Bar Assn. Democrat. Roman Catholic. Home: 933 Washington Ave Pelham NY 10803-3122 Office: O'Connor Reddy & Jensen 250 Park Ave New York NY 10177

O'DANIEL, GREGORY RICHARD, manufacturing executive; b. Akron, Ohio, Sept. 28, 1948; s. William Jacob O'Daniel and Frances Ann (Esker) Wessel; m. Maxine Marilyn Mansfield, Jan. 20, 1973; children: Tracy, Derrick, Ryan. AA, Sierra Coll., 1971. Br. mgr. Fireside Thrift, Ukiah, Calif., 1973-79; ter. mgr. Neutrogena Corp., Sacramento, Calif., 1979-83; nat. sales mgr. U.S. Cotton, Inc., Saratoga, Calif., 1983-85; v.p. sales and mktg. Laclede Profl. Products, Gardena, Calif., 1985-86; nat. sales mgr. Tempo Sanys, Inc., Somerset, N.J., 1986-89; exec. v.p., gen. mgr. Tempo Sanys, Inc., Northampton, Pa., 1989-90; pres. Hoco Holding Co., Northampton, 1990—; pres., chief exec. officer Temco USA, Inc. subs. of Hoco Holding Co., Northampton, 1990—; dir. Scotts Valley (Calif.) Ednl. Found., 1983-85, Exclusively Health and Beauty Aids, Chgo., 1989—. Dir. Calif. Blind Assn., Sacramento, 1974; asst. treas. Calif. Rep. Party, Newcastle, Calif., 1983; pres. Hightstown (N.J.) Pop Warner Football, 1987-88; football coach Pleasant Valley Mid. Sch., Brodheadsville, Pa., 1989-90. Mem. Nat. Assn. Chain Drug Stores, Gen. Mdse. Distbrs. Coun., Food Mktg. Inst. Home: HC 1 Box 451 Brodheadsville PA 18322-9626 Office: Temco USA Inc 777 Savage Rd # 460 Northampton PA 18067-9089

O'DAY, PAUL THOMAS, trade association executive; b. May 2, 1935; s. James Thomas and Jeannette Irene (Deschenes) O'D.; m. Nancy Frances Eitler, June 16, 1962; children—Kathleen, Maureen, Michael, Ellen. B.A., Am. Internat. Coll., Springfield, Mass., 1958; J.D., Georgetown U., 1963; MPA, Am. U., 1967. Bar: D.C. 1964, U.S. Supreme Ct. 1974. Asst. trade rep. Exec. Office of the Pres., Washington, 1975-77; dep. asst. sec. Dept. Commerce, Washington, 1978-84; pres. Am. Fiber Mfrs. Assn., Washington, 1984—; chmn. Fiber Econs. Bur., 1984—. Corporator Am. Internat. Coll., 1974—; mem. governing coun. Shakespeare Theater Guild, 1989—; prin. Coun. for Excellence in Govt., 1988—; active Washington World Affairs Coun.; bd. dirs. Eisenhower World Affairs Inst., 1992—. Recipient Constl. Law award Georgetown U. Law Ctr., 1962; Alumni award Am. Internat. Coll., 1970; Pres.'s Meritorious Exec. award., 1984; Nat. Inst. Pub. Affairs fellow Princeton U., 1964. Mem. AAAS, Am. Chem. Soc. Club: Cosmos. Home: 8019 Langbrook Rd Springfield VA 22152-1223 Office: Am Fiber Mfrs Assn 1150 17th St NW Washington DC 20036-4603

ODDY, JOHN GEORGE, innkeeper; b. Methuen, Mass., Apr. 14, 1934; s. John George and Dorothy Lucy (Flagg) O.; m. Joan Coughlin, Nov. 12, 1933 (div. 1974); children: John, Diane, Jeffrey. BA, Norwich U., Northfield, Vt., 1957; MEd, Bridgewater U., Mass., 1961; postgrad., Salem State Coll., Mass., 1966-72. Tchr. Abington (Mass.) Schs., 1957-58, Rockport (Mass.) Schs., 1959-61, Maynard (Mass.) Schs., 1961-62; tchr./prin. Newburyport (Mass.) Schs., 1963-73; innkeeper, investor Biddeford Pool (Maine) The Lodge, 1974—; notary pub.; justice of the peace, 1978—. Contbr. articles to profl. jours. With Vt. N.G., 1956-57. Fellow Maine Innkeepers Assn., Nat. Hist. Soc.; mem. Nat. Geog. Assn., Mass. Tchrs. Assn., Nat. Tchrs. Assn. Christian Ch. Home: 19 Yates Biddeford Pool ME 04006

O'DELL, ELIZABETH ANN, controller; b. Jersey City, Apr. 27, 1960; d. William P. and Madeline M. (Conheeney) O'D.; m. Dennis Polizzi, Sept. 7, 1985. BBA, MBA, Pace U., 1982. CPA, N.J. Sr. auditor Touche Ross & Co., Newark, 1982-85; supr. Coopers & Lybrand, Newark, 1985-87; controller/dir. internal ops. Kratos Analytical Inc., Ramsey, N.J., 1987-91; controller Radiodetection Corp., Mahwah, N.J., 1991—. Mem. AICPA, N.J. State Soc. CPA's, NAFE, Am. Woman's Soc. CPA's. Office: Radiodetection Corp 35 Whitney Rd Mahwah NJ 07430-3129

O'DELL, MICHAEL JAMES, social sciences specialist; b. Rhinebeck, N.Y., June 30, 1949; s. Stanley Patrick and Dorothy Marie (Traver) O'D. AA, Dutchess Community Coll., Poughkeepsie, N.Y., 1969; BA, SUNY, Albany, 1971; MA, Cath. U. Am., 1987. Mgr. Brenner's Co., Poughkeepsie, 1972-73; v.p. Brennco, Poughkeepsie, 1973; statistician U.S. Bur. Census, Washington, 1974-80; social scientist program evaluation and methodology div. U.S. GAO, Washington, 1980-84, sr. social scientist human resources div., 1984—; prin. investigator, testifying witness U.S. Senate Spl. Com. on Aging, Washington, 1988. Treas. Fairfax Village, Washington, 1977-86; bd. dirs. Harbour Sq. Owners Inc., Washington, 1989—, asst. treas., 1989-90, treas., 1990—; pres. Washington Coop. Housing Coalition, 1991—, asst. treas., 1990, treas., 1991. Recipient Outstanding Community Svc. award S.E. Neighbors Assn., Washington, 1982. Mem. Am. Assn. for Pub. Opinion Rsch. Democrat. Home: 520 N St SW Washington DC 20024-4574

ODERMATT, BRUNO GEORGE, insurance company executive; b. Horw, Luzern, Switzerland, Oct. 23, 1956; came to U.S., 1989; s. Helchior and Margaritha (Thalman) O.; m. Gabriele H. Maag, Dec. 24, 1987. Student, Peg Bus. Sch., London, Alliance Francaise, Paris; BBA, Grad. Sch. Bus. & Adminstrn., Zurich, Switzerland; postgrad., Bus. & Adminstrn. Sch., Luzern, Switzerland, Grad. Sch., Luzern. Mgmt. cons. Swarovski Mgmt. and Cons., Zurich, 1980-84; acct. exec. Olivetti Switzerland, Zurich, 1984-86; gen. mgr. Bear Frames Ltd., Wetzikon, Switzerland, 1986-87; mgmt. cons. Zurich Ins. Group, 1987-89, Universal Underwriters, Kansas City, 1989-91; v.p. Md. Ins. Group, Balt., 1991—. Contbr. articles to profl. jours. Mem. Swiss-Am. C. of C. Home: 4 Goucher Woods Ct Towson MD 21204 Office: The Md Group 3910 Keswick Rd Baltimore MD 21211

ODHNER, CARROLL GAY, library director, language professional; b. Ovid, Mich., Feb. 21, 1945; d. Kenneth Raymond Chamberlain and Virginia May (Carroll) Schrader; m. John Durban Odhner, Aug. 23, 1972; children: Astrid, Nils, Mark, Ariane. BA, U. Mich., 1966, MA, 1967; postgrad., Rutgers U., 1970. Cert. secondary tchr., Mich. Tchr. remedial English and math. Ovid-Elsie Area Schs., Mich., summers 1966-67; head librarian Am. Internat. Schs., The Hague, Netherlands, 1967-69; acquisitions librarian Rutgers U. Law Sch. Library, Newark, 1969-71, U. Nat. du Zaire, Kisangani, Zaire, 1970-71; instr. library sci., dir. tech. services U. Nat., Lumbumbashi, Zaire, 1971-73; bibliographer, research asst. U. Zambia, Lusaka, 1974-75; librarian Acad. of New Ch., Bryn Athyn, Pa., 1976-82, tech. services supr., 1982-87, dir. library, 1987—. Grad. scholar U. Mich., 1966-67; Carpenter grantee Acad. of New Ch., 1986. Mem. ALA, Pa. Libr. Assn., Tri-State Coll. Libr. Coop. (bd. dirs. 1987—, treas., exec. com. 1988-92, chmn. continuing edn. coun. 1989-92). Home: 493 Newell Dr Huntingdon Valley PA 19006-4035 Office: Acad New Ch 2875 Clg Dr Bryn Athyn PA 19009-9999

ODOJEWSKI, STEPHEN STANLEY, environmental services executive, consultant; b. Buffalo, May 7, 1945; s. Stephen John and Felicia Elizabeth (Sarnowski) O.; m. Carol Ann Myszka, July 20, 1968; children: Michael Jay, Kathryn Marie. BS in Chemistry, Canisius Coll., 1967, MS in Organic Chemistry, 1970. Rsch. chemist Chem-Trol Pollution Svcs., Model City, N.Y., 1972-74; lab. supr. Chem-Trol Pollution Svcs., Model City, 1974-77; lab. mgr. SCA Chem. Waste Svcs., Model City, 1977-79; v.p. tech. svcs. Waste Resource Assocs. Inc., Niagara Falls, N.Y., 1979-83; pres. Waste Resource Assocs. Inc., Niagara Falls, 1983—. Author: RCRA Guidance Manual, 1980, Management of Laboratory Wastes, 1986; writer RCRA Update subscription svc., 1980-86, writer, editor, 1986—. Capt. USAR, 1970-78. Mem. Am. Chem. Soc. Roman Catholic. Office: Waste Resource Assocs Inc 2576 Seneca Ave Niagara Falls NY 14305

ODOM, SUSAN ANN, program analyst; b. Jacksonville, Ill., May 10, 1957; d. Richard Arlington Jr. and Virginia Lea (Quinlan) Osborne; m. David Lee Odom, Aug. 29, 1979; 1 child, Hope Leigh. Student, U. Ill., 1976-80, Trinity Coll., Washington, 1984-87. Prin. investigator U.S. Army Corps of Engrs., Champaign, Ill., 1979-84; mgmt. analyst U.S. Army Corps of Engrs., Washington, 1984-87, with Office of Strategic Initiatives, 1988-89, strategic mgmt. analyst Resource Mgmt. Directorate, 1989-91, career program mgr. Directorate of Resource Mgmt., 1991—; career program mgr. U.S. Army Corps of Engrs., Washington, Va., 1987-88; v.p. DSH Enterprises, Springfield, Va., 1986—; Army C.E. rep. Tri-svcs. Com., WAshington, 1986—; program mgr. Leadership Conf., 1989, 90, 91; project mgr. Mid. and Sr. Mgmt. Conf.; project mgr. Focus 89, 90, 91. Mem. Automated Data Processing Profls., Nat. Assn. Female Execs. Roman Catholic.

O'DONNELL, EDWARD, geologist; b. N.Y.C., Oct. 13, 1938; s. Edward Flannigan and Regina Marie (Walker) O'D.; m. Duck Nee Lee, Aug. 31, 1968; children: Edward, Helen, Nancy. Student, U. Ill., 1960; BS, Queens Coll., 1961; MS, U. Cin., 1963, PhD, 1967. Hydrologist U.S. Geol. Survey, Cin., 1961-62; zooplankton ecologist Lamont Geol. Observatory, Palisades, N.Y., 1963; lectr. Queens Coll., Flushing, N.Y., 1963-65; exploration geologist Amoco, Houston, 1967-68; asst. prof. U. S. Fla., Tampa, 1968-76; geologist U.S. Nuclear Regulatory Commn., Washington, 1976—. Mem. Geol. Soc. Am., Am. Geophysical Union, Am. Assn. Petroleum Geologists, Soc. Econ. Paleontologists and Mineralogists (best paper 1972), Geol. Soc. Wash., Sigma Xi. Office: US Nuclear Regulatory Commn Mail Stop NLS 260 Washington DC 20555

O'DONNELL, MICHAEL PATRICK, education educator; b. Newton, Mass., Mar. 17, 1936; s. Charles Edmond and Mary Ann (O'Donnell) O'D.; m. Lucille Ann Bouchard, Dec. 31, 1962 (div. Aug. 1977); children: Lori Ann, Michelle Maureen, Mark Stephen. BS, U. ME, Orono, 1958, MS, 1959; EdD, Syracuse U., N.Y., 1968. High sch. tchr. Caribou High, Caribou, ME, 1960-62; TV tchr. Ford Foundation Project, Augusta, ME, 1962-63; state dir. edn. TV State Dept. Edn., Augusta, ME, 1963-65, state dir. lang. arts, 1965-68, state dir. edn. rsch., 1968-69; assoc. prof. Westfield State Coll., Westfield, Mass., 1969-70; vis. prof. Bowden Coll., Brunswick, ME, 1974; prof. edn. U. So. ME, Portland, ME, 1970—; scholar in residence U.S. Dept. Edn., Washington, 1975-77; project dir. Community Based Right to Read, USM, Portland, 1972-75, Basic Skills, Right to Read, USM,Portland, 1979-83, Refugee Resettlement Program, USM, Portland, 1982-84, ESL/BE Project, USM, Gorham, Maine, 1990—. Author: Teaching the Untaught, 1974, Teaching the Stages of Reading, 1979, (w. Wood) In the Know, 1985, (w. Wood) Becoming a Reader, 1992. Chmn. Hamlet Tenants Assn., Westbrook, Maine, 1989—. Recipient Disting. Svc. award, State Adult Edn. Assn., Augusta, ME, 1975, U. So. ME, Portland, 1983, U.S. Dept. Edn., Washington, 1977, ME State Reading Assn., Augusta, ME, 1987, New England Reading Assn., Hartford, Conn., 1988. Mem. Internat. Reading Assn., New England Reading Assn., ME Reading Assn., New England Guidance Study, New England Right to Read Task Force. Home: 665 Saco St # 7 Westbrook ME 04092-2021 Office: University of So Maine Rm 218 Bailey Gorham ME 04038

O'DONNELL, PATRICK E., lawyer; b. N.Y.C., Mar. 17, 1937; s. Emmett and Lorraine Antoinette (Muller) O'D.; m. Janet Eve Mottershead, Sept. 21, 1968; children: Patrick Justin, Hollace Tobin, Darcy Tanner. Student, Georgetown U., 1955-58; LLB, Am. Univ., 1962. Asst. corp. counsel City of Washington, 1962-69; spl. asst. to the pres. The White House, Washington, 1971-76; legal counsel to chmn. FCC, Washington, 1969-71; Washington counsel Gen. Electric Co., Washington, 1976-78, J.C. Penney Co., Inc., Washington, 1978-80; regional polit. dir. Howard Baker for Pres., Washington, 1980; asst. dir. legis. affairs Ronald Reagan for Pres., Washington, 1980-81; ptnr. O'Connor & Hannan, Washington, 1981—. Vice chmn. fin. George Bush Com., Washington, 1988; economic affairs counsel Rep. Nat. Com., Washington, 1976-80; bd. dirs. Radio Marti (Presdl. Commn.), Washington, 1981-84. Mem. USO (bd. dirs. 1978-91). Republican. Roman Catholic. Office: O'Connor & Hannan 1919 Pennsylvania Ave NW Ste 800 Washington DC 20006

O'DONNELL, ROBERT JOHN, lawyer, mediator, educator; b. Worcester, Mass., Aug. 3, 1943; s. Joseph C. and Nellie (Baltrukaitis) O'D.; m. Joyce I. Thomas, June 30, 1969 (div. Feb. 1984); children: Gary T., Shaun K. BS in Bus. Adminstrn., U. Calif., Berkeley, 1965; JD, Boston Coll. Law, 1969; cert., Coro Found., San Francisco, 1966. Bar: Vt. 1970, U.S. Dist. Ct. Vt. 1970. Pvt. practice, Woodstock, Vt., 1970—; sr. mediator Pvt. Peace Mediation Svcs., Woodstock, 1984—; dir., sr. instr. Woodstock (Vt.) Inst. for Negotiation, 1989—; adj. faculty mem. Coll. Edn. and Social Svcs., U. Vt., Burlington, 1986—, Woodbury Coll., Montpelier, Vt., 1986—; mem. comml. panel Am. Arbitration Assn., 1990—. Intern San Francisco Neighborhood Legal Assistance Found., 1967; assoc. Harvard Legal Aid Bur., 1967-68; founding dir., pres. Boston Coll. Legal Assistance Bur., 1968-69; justice of peace, Windsor County, 1989—; mem. Pomfret (Vt.) Planning Commn., 1980-90; grand juror, Pomfret, 1985—; mem. coun. Episcopal Diocese of Vt., 1982-86; mem. Woodstock Union High Sch. Bd., 1983-90; bd. dirs. Cen. Vt. chpt. ARC, 1983-89; lay reader, vestryman St. James Episcopal Ch., Woodstock, 1985—; assoc. Nat. Ctr. Assocs. Inc., 1984—. Mem. Vt. Bar Assn. (fee arbitration com. 1974-80, alternative dispute resolution com. 1987—, asst. chmn., 1989—), Windsor County Bar Assn. (pres. 1971-72), Vt. Mediators Assn. (steering com. 1986-87, pres. 1987-89, bd. dirs. 1987—), N.H. Mediators Assn., Soc. for Profls. in Dispute Resolution, Acad. Family Mediators, Assn. Family and Conciliation Ctrs. Republican. Home: Donegal On The Stage Rd South Pomfret VT 05067 Office: 5 The Green Woodstock VT 05091-1261

O'DONOGHUE, JOHN LIPOMI, toxicologist; b. Lowell, Mass., Apr. 12, 1947; s. James Gregory and Sarafina Frances (LiPomi) O'D.; m. Sandra Gail Piekos, June 24, 1967; children: Shawn Michael, Bevin Ruth. Student, U. Mass., 1964-66; VMD, U. Pa., 1970, PhD, 1979. Diplomate Am. Bd. Toxicology. Pathologist Eastman Kodak Co., Rochester, N.Y., 1974-79, pathology group leader, 1979-86, dir. toxicology, 1986-91, dir. health and environment labs., 1991—; adj. assoc. prof. lab. animal medicine and toxicology U. Rochester, 1988—; ad hoc neurotoxicology advisor Scientific USEPA, Washington, 1987-89. Author: Neurotoxicology of Industrial and Commercial Chemicals, 1985; contbr. articles to profl. jours. and others. Recipient Sigma Xi award, 1980; USPHS postdoctoral fellow, 1970. Mem. AVMA, Am. Indsl. Health Coun. (chmn. neurotoxicology subcom. 1986-89), Soc. Toxi cology (exec. com. neurotoxicology specialty 1990). Democrat. Roman Catholic. Home: 3915 Clover St Honeoye Falls NY 14472-9319 Office: Eastman Kodak Co 320B Kodak Park Rochester NY 14652-0001

ODOR, EDWIN MERLE, veterinarian; b. Mason, Ky., Sept. 1, 1940; s. Hubert Berchel and Ruth (Rucker) O.; m. Peggy Elane Hubbard, Sept. 1, 1960 (div. 1986); children: Glen Raymond, Diane Marie, Andrew Todd. BS, Ea. Ky. U., 1962; DVM, Auburn U., 1967; M of Avian Medicine, U. Ga., 1982. Pvt. practice Richmond, Ky., 1967-79; sr. scientist, poultry pathologist U. Del., Georgetown, 1982—; cons. poultry disease, poultry health mgmt., worldwide. Presenter multiple industry/sci. meetings; contbr. articles to profl. jours. Mem. AVMA, Am. Assn. Avian Pathologists, Am. Coll. Poultry Veterinarians. Office: U Del Rt 2 Box 47 Georgetown DE 19947

O'DWYER, BRIAN, lawyer, educator; b. N.Y.C., Oct. 10, 1945; s. Paul and Kathleen (Rohan) O.; m. Marianna Page, Sept. 7, 1968; children: Brendan, Kathleen. AB, George Washington U., 1967, LLM, 1976; MA, Middlebury Coll., 1968, JD, Georgetown U., 1971. Bar: N.Y. 1972, U.S. Dist Ct. (so. ea. and no. dists.) N.Y. 1973, U.S. Ct. Appeals (2d cir.) 1975, U.S. Supreme Ct. 1983. Atty. NLRB, Newark, 1972-73, N.Y. State Labor Bd., 1973-74; mng. ptnr. O'Dwyer & Bernstein, N.Y.C., 1974—; dir. Queens Outreach, Queens, N.Y., 1983—; dir. Malcom King Coll., 1980-88; pres. Bohola Enterprises Inc.; trustee Clara Miller Found., Mayo Found. for the Handicapped. Mem. ABA, Nat. Assn. Coll. and Univ. Attys., Brehon Law Soc., Kappa Sigma (supreme exec. com., citizens adv. com. Quincenntial commn., chmn. Emerald Isle Immigrant Ctr.). Democrat. Roman Catholic. Home: 350 Central Park W New York NY 10025-6504 Office: O'Dwyer & Bernstein 52 Duane St 5th Fl New York NY 10007-1207

OECHSLI, KELLY, author, illustrator; b. Butte, Mont., Feb. 23, 1918; s. Clarence Ernest and Florence Hollis (McDonald) O.; m. Helen Elizabeth Meagher, Dec. 26, 1946; children: Matthew, Eileen, Katherine, Paul. Student, Cornish Sch. Art, Seattle, 1939. Illustrator: Peter Bull, 1971, Walter the Wolf, 1975, In Your Garden, 1985, Herbie's Troubles, 1983 (Ga. U. Children's Book award 1983), Fly Away, 1988, Scruffy, 1988; author, artist: Mice At Bat, 1986; author, illustrator: Mice At Bat, 1986. Sgt. U.S. Army, 1941-45. Democrat. Roman Catholic. Home and Office: 115 Sherman Ave Hawthorne NY 10532-2507

OERTEL, GOETZ K. H., physicist, professional association administrator; b. Stuhm, Germany, Aug. 24, 1934; came to U.S., 1957; s. Egon F.K. and Margarete W. (Wittek) O.; m. Brigitte Beckmann, June 17, 1960; children: Ines M.H. Oertel Weber, Carsten K.R. Abitur, Robert Mayer, Heilbronn, Fed. Republic Germany, 1953; vordiplom, U. Kiel, Fed. Republic Germany, 1956; PhD, U. Md., 1963. Aerospace engr. Langley Ctr. NASA, Hampton, Va., 1963-68; chief solar physics NASA, Washington, 1968-75; analyst Office of Mgmt. and Budget, Washington, 1974-75; head astronomy div. NSF, Washington, 1975; dir. def. and civilian nuclear waste programs U.S. Dept. Energy, Washington, 1975-83; acting mgr. sav. river ops. office, Aiken, S.C., 1983-84; dep. mgr. ops. office, Albuquerque, 1984-85; dep. asst. sec. EH, Washington, 1985-86; pres. Assn. Univs. for Rsch. in Astronomy, Inc. (AURA, Inc.), Washington, 1986—; cons. Los Alamos Lab., N.Mex., 1987—, Westinghouse Electric, 1988—; bd. dirs. AURA, Inc., Inst. for Sci. and Soc., Ellensburg, Wash., IUE Corp. Patentee in field. Fulbright grantee, 1957. Fellow AAAS; mem. Am. Assn. for Advancement of Tech. (bd. dirs.), Am. Phys. Soc., Am. Astron. Soc., Internat. Astron. Union, N.Y. Acad. Scis., Internat. Univ. Exch., Inc. (bd. dirs.), Cosmos Club, Sigma Xi. Lutheran. Home: 9609 Windcroft Way Rockville MD 20854-2864 Office: Assn Univs for Rsch in Astronomy 1625 Massachusetts Ave NW Ste 701 Washington DC 20036-2212

OETTING, MILDRED KATHERINE See SQUAZZO, MILDRED KATHERINE

OFENGAND, EDWARD JAMES, research biochemist, consultant; b. Taunton, Mass., Aug. 15, 1932; s. Samuel J. and Sarah Evelyn (Tornansky) O.; m. Sigrud Friederike Seumel, June 22, 1963; children: Karen Petra, Gunda Stephanie, Erik Arnim. BS, MS, MIT, 1955; PhD, Washington U., 1959. Postdoctoral fellow Med. Rsch. Coun., Cambridge, England, 1959-61, Rockefeller U., N.Y.C., 1961-62; lectr. U. Calif., San Francisco, 1962-66, asst. prof., 1967-68; assoc. mem. Roche Inst. Molecular Biology, Nutley, N.J., 1969-77; full mem. Roche Inst. of Molecular Biology, Nutley, 1978—; adj. prof. Univ. Med. & Dentistry, Newark, 1983—. Author: (chpt.) Ribosome: Structure, Function and Evolution, 1990; editorial adv. bd. Biochemistry, 1985—; editorial bd. Analytical Biochemistry, 1989—; contbr. 108 articles to Biochemistry, Jour. Biol. Chemistry, Proc. Nat. Acad. Sci. U.S.A., others. Pre and postdoctoral fellowships NSF, 1954-61, postdoctoral fellowship NIH, 1962. Mem. Am. Soc. for Biochemistry and Molecular Biology, Sociedad de Biologia de Chile (hon. 1968). Democrat. Jewish. Office: Roche Inst Molecular Biol 340 Kingsland St Nutley NJ 07110-1199

OFFENHARTZ, EDWARD, aerospace executive; b. Bklyn., Mar. 1, 1928; s. Hyman and Anna (Konecky) O.; m. Edith Enevoldsen, Nov. 4, 1951; children: Debra, Marc, Beth, Kay, David. BSME, Poly. Inst. Bklyn., 1948; postgrad., U. Va., 1949-50; student Program for Mgmt. Devel., Harvard U., 1970. Registered profl. engr., Mass. Aero. research scientist NACA, Langley, Va., 1948-56; with Avco Corp., Wilmington and Lowell, Mass., 1956-67, successively research engr., group leader, project engr., sr. project engr., project mgr., project dir., 1956-67; project dir., asst. gen. mgr. ops. Perkin-Elmer Corp., 1967-70; program dir. spl. projects Grumman Aerospace Corp., Bethpage, N.Y., 1970-73, program dir. Earth Limb Measurements Satellite program, 1973-75, mem. def. sci. bd. shuttle task force, 1974-75, program dir. internat. offset mgmt., 1975-82, program dir. mktg. planning, 1982-84; dir. strategic planning Grumman Data Systems Div., Woodbury, N.Y., 1984-90; pres. E.O. Assocs., 1991—; lectr. UCLA, 1965—. Contbr. articles to profl. jours. Mem. AIAA, Sci. Research Soc. Am., Am. Mgmt. Assn. Home: 4 Glen Ln Weston CT 06883-2308 Office: EO Assocs 4 Glen Ln Weston CT 06883

OFFIT, MORRIS WOLF, investment management executive; b. Balt., Jan. 22, 1937; s. Michael and Rhea (Wolf) O.; m. Nancy Silverman, Nov. 26, 1959; children: Ned S., Daniel W. BA in History, Johns Hopkins U., 1957; MBA in Fin., U. Pa., 1959. V.p. investment dept. Mercantile Safe Deposit and Trust, Balt., 1960-68; gen. ptnr. Salomon Bros. Inc., N.Y.C., 1970-80; pres. Julius Baer Securities, N.Y.C., 1980-82, Offit Assocs. Inc., N.Y.C., 1983—; bd. dirs. Preston Corp., Easton, Md., Aegon, USA, Inc., Balt., Merc. Bancshares Corp., Balt., Duty Free Internat., Balt. Chmn. bd. trustees Johns Hopkins U.; mem. adv. coun. Sch. Advanced Internat. Studies, Washington; pres. Jewish Mus.; trustee Union Theol. Sem., Jewish Theol. Sem. Mem. Coun. Fgn. Rels. Office: Offitbank 101 E 52d St New York NY 10022

OFFNER, CARL DAVID, software engineer; b. Bklyn., July 28, 1943; s. Abe and Lillian (Bachman) O.; m. Susan Neiman, Feb. 3, 1973; children: David Ellis, Amy Carol. BA, Harvard U., 1964, PhD, 1978. Cert. sec. sch. math. tchr., Mass. Tchr. Silver Lake Regional Sch. Dist., Pembroke, Mass., 1969-85; software engr. Compass Inc., Wakefield, Mass., 1985-91; staff software engr. Intel, Inc., Hillsboro, Oreg., 1991—. Contbr. articles to profl. jours. Pres. Silver Lake Regional Tchrs. Assn., 1979-85; mem. Dem. Town Com., Pembroke, 1983-85; town coord. U.S. Rep. Studds Re-election, Pembroke, 1984; v.p. Congregation Beth El, Sudbury, Mass., 1988-90; mem. Harvard Strike Reunion Com., Cambridge, Mass., 1989. Mem. Am. Math. Soc., Math. Assn. Am., Assn. Computing Machinery. Democrat. Jewish. Home: 46 Sunset Path Sudbury MA 01776-1369 Office: Digital Equipment Corp ML01-5/U46 146 Main St Maynard MA 01754

OGAKI, MASAO, economics educator; b. Osaka, Japan, Apr. 16, 1958; came to U.S. 1984; s. Masahiro and Teruko O.; m. Rieko Yoshida, Mar. 28, 1982; children: Remu, Reine. BA in Econs., Osaka U., 1982, MA in Econs., 1984; PhD in Econs., U. Chgo., 1988. Asst. prof. econs. U. Rochester, 1988—. Contbr. articles to profl. jours. Ford Motor Co. fellow, 1988, Japanese Studies fellow, 1987-88, Sloan Found. dissertation fellow, 1986-87, Ishizaka Found. fellow, 1984-86. Mem. Am. Econ. Assn., The Econometric Soc. Office: U Rochester Dept Econs Rochester NY 14627-0156

OGDEN, CHRISTOPHER BENNETT, journalist; b. Providence, R.I., Feb. 9, 1945; s. Michael Joseph and Agnes (Bennett) O.; m. Diana Wynne May, Aug. 12, 1967; children: Michael, Margaret. BA, Yale U., 1966. News corrs. UPI, London, 1970-72, Time Mag./UPI, Moscow, 1972-74, Time, L.A., 1975; sr. state dept. corrs. Time, Washington, 1976-78, sr. White House corrs., 1978-81; midwest bur. chief Time, Chgo., 1981-85; London bur. chief Time, London, 1985-89; chief diplomatic corrs. Time, Washington, 1989—. Author: Maggie: An Intimate Portrait of a Woman in Power, 1990. 1st. lt. U.S. Army, 1966-69, Bangkok. Mem. Yale Club of N.Y.C., RAC Club/London, Potomac Boat Club, Annabels. Office: Time Inc 1050 Connecticut Ave NW Ste 850 Washington DC 20036-5334

OGNIBENE, FREDERICK PETER, internist; b. Jamestown, N.Y., Aug. 30, 1953; s. Vincent Larry and Alma Linda (Martinelli) O. BA, U. Rochester, 1975; MD, Cornell U., 1979. Diplomate Am. Bd. Internal Medicine, Am. Bd. Internal Medicine-Critical Care. From intern to resident N.Y. Hosp./Cornell Med. Ctr., 1979-82; from med. to sr. staff fellow Critical Care Medicine Dept. NIH, Bethesda, Md., 1982-87; sr. investigator NIH, Bethesda, 1987—; asst. clin. prof. George Washington U., Washington, 1990—. Manuscript reviewer; contbr. articles and chpts. Mem. Washington Project of the Arts. comdr. Pub. Health Svcs., 1985—. Fellow ACP, Am. Coll. Critical Care Medicine (chair credentials com. 1992—); mem. Cornell U. Med. Coll. Alumni Assn. (bd. dirs.), Am. Fedn. for Clin. Rsch. (sec.-treas. eastern sect. 1987-91, chair-elect 1991—), Am. Fedn. for Clin. Rsch. Found. (trustee), Alpha Omega Alpha. Democrat. Roman Catholic. Home: 2227 20th St NW Washington DC 20009-5075 Office: NIH 9000 Rockville Pike Bldg 10 Bethesda MD 20892-0001

OGORZALEK, LISA LATTAL, health administrator, lawyer; b. Perth Amboy, N.J., July 22, 1956; d. Frank and Ann Theresa (Kaczmarek) Lattal; m. Matthew Joseph Ogorzalek, June 16, 1990. BA, Bucknell U., 1978; M of Health Adminstrn., Duke U., 1980; JD with honors, U. Md., Balt., 1989. Bar: Md. 1989, D.C. 1992. Adminstrv. fellow Albert Einstein Med. Ctr., Phila., 1980-82; adminstr. community medicine Sinai Hosp. of Balt., 1982-85; practice adminstr. physician's office, Glen Burnie, Md., 1985-86; ambulatory svcs. mgr. Johns Hopkins Oncology Ctr., Balt., 1986—. Contbr. chpts. to books, articles to profl. jours. Mem. Md. Bar Assn., Med. Group Mgmt. Assn., Am. Coll. Health Care Execs., Soc. for Ambulatory Care Profls. (bd. dirs. 1990—, chmn. quality com. 1991—), Assn. Health Care Execs. of Nat. Capital Area, Md. Assn. Health Care Execs., Nat. Health Lawyers Assn. Office: Johns Hopkins Oncology Ctr 600 N Wolfe St Baltimore MD 21205

O'GRADY, MARY J., editor, foundation administrator; b. Chgo., Sept. 25, 1951; d. Valentine Michael and Lillian Mary (Quinlan) O'G. Student, St. Mary's Coll., Rome, Italy, 1970-71; BFA, Manhattanville Coll., 1973. Assoc. editor Magnum Photos, N.Y.C., 1973-76; asst. picture editor Modern Photography Mag., N.Y.C., 1976-78; freelance photographer N.Y.C., 1978-80; sr. producer Trans-Atlantic Enterprises, N.Y.C., L.A., 1981-82; dir. pub. info. World Wildlife Fund, Washington, 1983-84; sr. analyst Mead Data Cen., Washington, 1985-87; editor photos U.S. News and World Report, Washington, 1987-90; program dir. Sacharuna Found., 1990—; adminstr. Roland Films, 1991—; cons. Time, Inc., N.Y.C., 1981, Exxon Corp., N.Y.C., 1981-82, U.S. News and World Report, Washington, 1987. Asst. editor: The Family of Woman, 1978; producer (TV shows) A Conversation With..., 1982, The Helen Gurley Brown Show, 1982, Outrageous Opinions, 1982; photo editor America's Best Colleges, 1989, 90, Great Vacation Drives, 1989. Recipient Editorial Excellence award Natural Resources Coun. Am., 1984. Mem. World Affairs Coun., Environ. Grantmakers Assn., Consultative Group on Biol. Diversity.

OGRODNIK, EUGENE C., academic administrator; b. Pitts., June 6, 1948; s. Eugene and Mary Dorothy (Trzcialkowski) O.; m. Karen Jo Shields, Oct. 23, 1974; children: Evan Christopher, Ryann Alisse. BS in Pharmacy, U. Pitts., 1971; MS in Bus., Robert Morris Coll., 1986. Registered pharmacist; lic. funeral dir., embalmer, Pa.; cert. bus. appraiser. Funeral dir. Morasco Funeral Home, Pitts., 1975-77; staff pharmacist Presbyn. U. Hosp., Pitts., 1977-86; dir. Pitts. Inst. Mortuary Sci., 1981—, mem. faculty, 1977—, dean adminstrn., 1982—, pres., chief exec. officer, 1990—; staff pharmacist Magee Woman's Hosp., Pitts., 1986—; cons., prin. Advantage Assocs., Inc., Pitts., 1987—. Contbr. articles to profl. publs. Mem. adv. coun. Point Park Coll., Pitts., 1981—. With U.S. Army, 1972-77. Mem. Nat. Assn. Colls. Mortuary Sci. (pres. 1989-90), Nat. Funeral Dirs. Assn., Inst. Bus. Appraisers, Allegheny County Funeral Dirs. Assn., Pa. Funeral Dirs. Assn. Republican. Roman Catholic. Office: Pitts Inst Mortuary Sci 5808 Baum Blvd Pittsburgh PA 15206-3706

O'HAGEN, PATRICIA, educator; b. Bklyn.; d. Frank and Joan (Minardi) Guarasci; m. George O'Hagen, June 25, 1966 (div. Feb. 1985); children: Brendan, Brian. BS, Fordham U., N.Y.C., 1961; MS, Hofstra U., 1971. Cert. tchr., N.Y. Tchr. Howitt Jr. High Sch., Farmingdale, N.Y., 1961-65, Lawrence (N.Y.) Jr. High Sch., Lawrence, 1965-67, Oceanside (N.Y.) Jr. High Sch., Oceanside, 1968-84, Oceanside Sr. High Sch., Oceanside, 1984—; mem. Curriculum Com., Oceanside, 1987; mem. exec. bd. Oceanside Fedn. Tchrs./Vot-Cope chmn. for polit. action. Author: (biography) Michael Flannery: An Irish Life, 1983, (poetry) Rebirth, 1983, Congressional Report Northern Ireland, 1984, (biography) Alex Minsky Profiled, 1987. Chmn. Irish Nat. Caucus, Nassau County, N.Y., 1982-83; dir. 1983-85, sec. 938-84, pres. 1985-89 of Speakers Bur., Irish Am. Unit Conf. N.Y.; mem. Dem. Com. Woman, Rockville Centre. Recipient Woman of the Year award Nassau County Ancient Order of Hibernians, 1984, Educator of the Year award, Assn. Tchrs. N.Y., 1984. Mem. N.Y. United Tchrs., P.T.A., Irish Am. Unity Conf. , Albany. Roman Catholic. Office: Oceanside Sr High Sch Skillman and Brower Aves Oceanside NY 11572

O'HALLORAN, WILLIAM JOHN, priest, university administrator; b. Springfield, Mass., Nov. 26, 1927; s. F. Thomas and Dorothy M. (Keegan) O'H. AB, Boston Coll., 1951, MA, 1952; PhL, Weston Coll., 1952; MA, Fordham U., 1955, PhD, 1964; STL, Facultés St. Louis, Chantilly, France, 1964. Tchr. Boston Coll. High Sch., 1952-54; prof. Coll. of the Holy Cross, Worcester, Mass., 1964-75; pres. LeMoyne Coll., Syracuse, N.Y., 1976-81; devel. officer Coll. of the Holy Cross, Worcester, 1981-84, v.p., 1984—; bd. dirs. Jesuits of Holy Cross Coll., Inc., Worcester, 1989—, Unity Mutual Life Ins. Co., Syracuse, 1983—. Mem. Jesuits, APA, Eastern Psychol. Assn., Mass. Psychol. Assn., Sigma Xi, Alpha Sigma Nu. Office: Coll of Holy Cross Worcester MA 01610

O'HANDLEY, DOUGLAS ALEXANDER, astronomer; b. Detroit, May 7, 1937; s. Malcolm Joseph and Georgie Roberta (MacPherson) O'H.; m. Christine Jeannette Stube, July 20, 1991; 1 child, Douglas Alexander, Jr. AB, U. Mich., 1960; MS, Yale U., 1964, PhD, 1967. Astronomer U.S. Naval Obs., Washington, 1960-67; scientist Jet Propulsion Lab., Pasadena, Calif., 1967-85; dir. space station Ames Rsch. Ctr., Moffett Field, Calif., 1985-86; mgr. TRW Space Tech. Group, Redondo Beach, Calif., 1986-88; dep. asst. adminstr. office exploration NASA, Washington, 1988—; chmn. com. for protection of human subjects in med. rsch., 1982-85; lectr. grad. sch. Georgetown U., Washington, 1964-67; speaker at med. soc. meetings. Contbr. articles to profl. jours. Bd. dirs. Cath. Big Bros.; extraordinary minister St. Bede's Roman Cath. Ch. Recipient NASA Group Achievement award Planetary Ephemeris Devel. Team, 1982. Fellow Royal Soc. Medicine, Internat. Astronomical Union, Aerospace Med. Assn., AIAA (assoc.). Republican. Home: 1160 Silver Beech Rd Herndon VA 22070-2328 Office: NASA-Office of Explorations coder Z Washington DC 20546

OHANESIAN, GEORGE VAUGHN, financial executive; b. New Britain, Conn., Sept. 11, 1949; s. Vaughn H. and Ethel (Alverde) O.; m. Susan Marie Yanosy, Apr. 28, 1973. BA in Econs., U. Conn., 1971; MBA with distinction, NYU, 1980. Dir. rate and bus. analysis Westinghouse Broadcasting & Cable, Inc., N.Y.C., 1973-85; dir. fin. Prodigy Svcs. Co., White Plains, N.Y., 1985—. Dir. Evelyn Estates Condominium Assn., 1990—. Mem. Zeta Psi, Bta Gamma Sigma. Congregationalist. Home: 8200A Bulls Ferry Rd Apt 3A North Bergen NJ 07047-7011 Office: Prodigy Svcs Co 445 Hamilton Ave White Plains NY 10601-1814

OHANIAN, LEE EDWARD, economist, consultant; b. L.A., Feb. 24, 1957; s. Edward and Martha Loraine (Taylor) O.; m. Nancy Frances Kane, May 28, 1988. BA, U. Calif., Santa Barbara, 1979, MA, 1982; postgrad., U. Rochester, 1988—. Sr. analyst Continental Airlines, L.A., 1981-82; v.p. Security Pacific Bank, L.A., 1982-88; lectr. U. Rochester, N.Y., 1988-92; pvt. practice Rochester, 1990—; asst. prof. econs. U. Pa., Phila., 1992—. Contbr. articles to profl. jours. W. Allen Wallis fellow U. Rochester, 1988—; fellow Nat. Inst. on Aging, 1983-84; recipient Kaplan Prize, 1991. Office: U Pa Dept Econs Philadelphia PA 19104

O'HANLON, JOHN MORE, podiatrist; b. New Rochelle, N.Y., July 7, 1963; s. John Richard and Nancy Catherine (Muller) O'H. BS, SUNY, Albany, 1985; D Podiatric Medicine, Pa. Coll. Podiatric Medicine, 1989. Resident in podiatric surgery Sheehan Meml. Hosp., Buffalo, 1989-90; pvt. practice Armonmk, N.Y., 1991—; staff physician No. Westchester Hosp. Ctr. Emergency med. technician Armonk Fire Dept., 1991. Mem. Am. Coll. Foot Surgeons, N.Y. State Podiatric Med. Soc., Tappan Zee Podiatry Div., Armonk Lions Club. Roman Catholic. Office: 20 Maple Ave Armonk NY 10504-1824

O'HANLON, RICHARD THOMAS, counselor educator, treasurer; b. Chichester, Eng., Dec. 16, 1956; came to U.S., 1957; s. Thomas Joseph and Agnes Cecilia (Mahoney) O'H. BA in Philosophy, St. Hyacinth Coll., 1974; MS in Pastoral Counseling, Loyola Coll., 1987, cert. in advanced studies, 1988. Tchr. St. Francis High Sch., Athol Springs, N.Y., 1974-82, Archbishop Curley High Sch., Balt., 1982-84; editor Franciscan Press, Balt., 1984-90; counselor Lighthouse, Catonsville, Md., 1986-87, County of Balt., 1987-88, Human Life Internat., Gaithersburg, Md., 1990-91; prof. Washington Theol. Union, 1990—; dir. Franciscan Bros., Balt., 1985-88; treas. Cupertino Franciscans, Ellicott City, Md., 1988—; pres. Continuing Edn. Commn., Balt., 1991—. Named Citizen of the Yr., Union League, 1969. Fellow AACD, Md. Assn. Counseling and Devel., Md. Assn. for Religious and Value Issues in Counseling, Assn. for Religious and Value Issues in Counseling. Home: 12290 Folly Quarter Rd Ellicott City MD 21042-1418 Office: Franciscan Friars 12300 Folly Quarter Rd Ellicott City MD 21042-1419

O'HARA, DAVID OAKES, software developer; b. Stamford, Conn., Nov. 12, 1950; s. Charles Edward and Theodora (Oakes) O'H.; m. Janet Livingston McIlvain, May 15, 1976; children: Elizabeth, Caroline. BS, Brown U., 1973; MBA, Babson Coll., 1983. Asst. dir. steel services Data Resources Inc., Lexington, Mass., 1973-82, dir. development personal computers, 1983-85; prod. mgr. EPS McGraw-Hill, Inc., Lexington, Mass., 1986—. Mem. Nat. Assn. Bus. Economists, Tau Beta Pi. Club: Myopia Hunt (Hamilton, Mass.). Office: Data Resources 24 Hartwell Ave Lexington MA 02173-3144

O'HARA, JOHN PATRICK, lawyer, accountant; b. N.Y.C., Jan. 11, 1930; s. Thomas James and Anne (Henry) O'H.; m. Mary Ann Leavey, Oct. 15, 1955; children: Ann O'Hara Carroll, Kathleen O'Hara Geary, Maureen Elizabeth. BBA, St. John's U., N.Y.C., 1952; JD, U. Balt., 1960. Bar: Md. 1960. Spl. agt. FBI, 1955-62; chief counsel, staff dir. subcom. on investigations and oversight Com. on Pub. Works and Transp., Ho. of Reps., Washington, 1962-86; dir. corp. security Flying Tiger Ln., L.A., 1986-89; ptnr. Burgess & O'Hara, Upper Marlboro, Md., 1990-91; cons. Legal Svcs. Corp., Washington, 1990-91, pres., 1991—. 1st lt. USMC, 1952-54. Decorated Nat. Def. Svc. medal, UN medal, Koreaan Svc. medal. Mem. Md. Bar Assn., Bolling AFB Assn., Marines Meml. Assn., Am. Legion. Home: Apt 518 5904 Mt Eagle Dr Alexandria VA 22303

O'HARE, CARRIE JANE, audio engineer, musician; b. N.Y.C., May 17, 1959; d. Alan Joseph and Phyllis Marie (Hannett) O'H.; m. Thomas K. Hogan, May 6, 1990. MusB in Audio Rec., Guitar Performance, Berklee Coll. Music, 1981. Audio engr. Saturday Night Live, NBC, N.Y.C., 1982—; audio cons. Easton Union Ch., Hainesport, N.J., 1985—. Composer: Spare Change, 1978, Never Got Away From Love, 1980. Acitve Greenpeace, Amnesty Internat., Earthwatch. Mem. Audio Engring. Soc., NARAS, Soc. Motion Picture TV Engrs., Nat. Acad. TV Arts and Scis. Democrat. Office: NBC 30 Rockefeller Pla New York NY 10112

O'HARE, DEAN RAYMOND, insurance company executive; b. Jersey City, June 21, 1942; s. Francis and Ann O'H.; m. Kathleen T. Walliser, Dec. 2, 1967; Dean, Jason. BS, NYU, 1963; MBA, Pace U., 1968. Trainee Chubb Corp., N.Y.C., 1963-64, tax advisor, 1964-67, asst. v.p., mgr. corp. fin. devel., 1968-72, sr. v.p., mgr. corp. fin. devel. dept., from 1979, chief fin. officer, from 1979, pres., 1986-88, chmn., chief exec. officer, 1988—; chmn. Chubb Life Ins. Co. N.H., 1981—; chmn., pres. Fed. Ins. Co., 1988—, Vigilant Ins. Co., 1988—; chmn., dir. Bellemead Devel. Corp., 1973—; chmn. Colonial Life Ins. Co. Am., 1980—, Chubb Life Ins. Co. Am., 1980—; bd. dirs. Chubb Ins. Co. Can., Fed. Ins. Co., Vigilant Ins. Co. Dir. Coalition Svc. Industries, The N.J. Partnership; trustee com. for econ. devel., WDC. Mem. Am. Ins. Assn. (chmn. bd. dirs. 1991), ,Urban Land Inst. Clubs: India House, Hanover Square; Halifax (Daytona Beach, Fla.). Home: Lake Rd Far Hills NJ 07931 Office: Chubb Corp 15 Mountain View Rd PO Box 1615 Warren NJ 07061-1615

O'HARE, JOSEPH ALOYSIUS, university president, priest; b. N.Y.C., Feb. 12, 1931; s. Joseph Aloysius and Marie Angela (Enright) O'H. AB, Berchmans Coll, Cebu City, Philippines, 1954, MA, 1955; STL, Woodstock Coll., Md., 1962; PhD, Fordham U., 1968; DHL (hon.), Fairfield U., 1980, Rockhurst Coll., Kansas City, Mo., 1984, Ateneo de Manila U., 1990, CUNY, 1991; DLitt (hon.), Coll. New Rochelle, 1984. Joined Soc. Jesus, 1948; ordained priest Roman Catholic Ch., 1961. Instr. Ateneo de Manila U., 1955-58, prof. philosophy, 1968-72; assoc. editor Am. Mag., N.Y.C., 1972-75, editor-in-chief, 1975-84; pres. Fordham U., Bronx, N.Y., 1984—. Author weekly column Of Many Things (Best Original Column award Cath. Press Assn. 1976, 78, 81, 84). Bd. dirs. Union Theol. Sem., The Asia Soc.; chmn. N.Y.C. Campaign Fin. Bd. Office: Fordham U Office of Pres New York NY 10458

O'HARE-VANMEERBEKE, ANNE MARIE, dietitian; b. S.I., N.Y., Jan. 5, 1960; d. Robert and Ellen O'Hare. BS in Human Ecology, Marywood Coll., Scranton, Pa., 1982. Registered dietitian. Clin. dietitian Custom Mgmt. Corp., Somerset, N.J., 1982-84; food svc. dir. Custom Mgmt. Corp., Westfield, N.J., 1984-86; cons. Anne O'Hare Cons. Svcs. (Cen. N.J.), 1986; asst. food svc. Marriott Corp., Nyack, N.Y., 1986-87; food svc. dir. Marriott Corp., Secaucus, N.J., 1987—; dist. dietitian Marriott Corp., N.J. and N.Y. area, 1988-90; dir. food svc. Marriott Corp., Camden, N.J., 1990—. Mem. Am. Cancer Soc., Am. Heart Assn. Mem. Am. Dietetic Assn. Roman Catholic. Office: West Jersey Health System 100 Atlantic Ave Camden NJ 08104

O'HERN, JANE SUSAN, psychologist, educator; b. Winthrop, Mass., Mar. 21, 1933; d. Joseph Francis and Mona (Garvey) O'H. BS, Boston U., 1954, EdD, 1962; MA, Mich. State U., 1956. Instr. Mercyhurst Coll., 1954-55, Hofstra Coll., 1956-57, State Coll., Salem and Boston, 1957-60; asst. prof. Boston U., 1962-67, assoc. prof., 1967-75, prof. edn. and psychology, 1975—, chmn. dept. counseling psychology, 1972-75, 88-89, dir. mental health edn. program, 1975-81, dir. internat. continuing edn., 1978-81, asst. v.p. internat. edn., 1981; adv. bd. Aquinas Jr. Coll.; pres. ASSIST Internat., Inc., 1989—. Contbr. articles to profl. jours. Trustee Boston Ctr. Modern Psychoanalytic Studies, 1980—. Recipient grants U.S. Office Edn., NIMH, Dept. of Def. Mem. Assn. Counselor Edn. and Suprs., Am. Assn. for Counseling and Devel., North Atlantic Assn. Counselor Edn. and Supervision (past pres.), Mass. Psychol. Assn., Am. Psychol. Assn., Mortar Bd., Pi Lamda Theta, Sigma Kappa, Phi Delta Kappa, Phi Beta Delta. Home: 111 Perkins St Apt 287 Boston MA 02130 Office: Boston U 605 Commonwealth Ave Boston MA 02215-1605

OHNISHI, STANLEY TSUYOSHI, biomedical director, biophysicist; b. Ohtsu City, Japan, Dec. 17, 1931; came to U.S., 1966; s. Teruhiko and Miyoko (Tomoda) O.; m. Tomoko Kirita, Mar. 25, 1958; children: Hiroshi, Noriko. MS in Chemistry, Kyoto (Japan) U., 1956; PhD in Biophysics, Nagoya (Japan) U., 1959. Rsch. prof. dept. hemtology Hahnemann U., Phila., 1984, rsch. prof. dept. biochemistry, 1984; dir. Membrane Rsch. Inst., Phila., 1989—; dir. developing chomotherapeutic drugs Phila. Biomed Rsch. Inst., King of Prussia, Pa., 1989—. Editor: Experimental Techniques in Biomembranes, 1967, Mechanisms Gated Calcium Transport, 1981, Membrane-Linked Diseases, 1992; contbr. 150 articles to Biochem. Biophys. Pharmacology; editor 3 books. Buddhist. Office: Phila Biomed Rsch Inst 502 King Of Prussia Rd Radnor PA 19087

OJALVO, MORRIS SOLOMON, retired mechanical engineer; b. N.Y.C., July 6, 1923; s. Solomon Y. and Boulissa (Barlia) O.; m. Neysa Goldis, June 6, 1949; children: Steven I., Philip K., Beth J. B of Mech. Engring., Cooper Union, 1944; MME, U. Del., 1949; PhD in Mech. Engring., Purdue U., 1962. Registered profl. engr., Md. Rsch. asst. Pa. State U., State College, 1946-47; instr. U. Ill., Chgo., 1947-48; instr., rsch. asst. U. Del., Newark, 1948-50; asst., assoc. prof. U. Md., College Park, 1950-55, evaluator, cons., 1990—; assoc. prof. U. Del., Newark, 1955-56; instr., rsch. asst. Purdue U., West Lafayette, 1956-60; assoc. prof. to prof. George Washington U., Washington, 1960-65; program dir. NSF, Washington, 1965-90; mech. engr. U.S. Naval Ordnance Lab., Silver Spring, Md., summers 1951, 52, 54, Boeing Airplane Co., Seattle, summer 1953, N.Am. Aviation, Inc., L.A., summer 1955, NASA Goddard Space Flight Ctr., Greenbelt, Md., summer 1963, UNESCO, Mexico City, 1967-69. Author: Notes on Fluid Mechanics, 1970; co-author: Quieting: A Home Owner's Guide to Noise Control, 1976. With USN, 1944-46. Recipient Cooper medal, Cooper Union, 1944, NSF fellowship, 1961. Fellow ASME (life); mem. Soc. Automotive Engrs., Am. Soc. Engring. Edn., Fine Particle Soc. (pres. 1978-79, First Hausner award, 1980), Tau Beta Pi. Home: 6006 Broad Branch Rd NW Washington DC 20015-2504

OJIAKU, ALAMEZIE ENWEREAKU, insurance, real estate investment consultant; b. Umundugba, Imo, Nigeria, Sept. 29, 1947; s. Chief Oke and Nwache (Onurah) O.; m. Rubye Joseph, May 10, 1977 (div.); 1 child, Alamezie Jr.; m. Ngozi Caroline Obi, June 6, 1980; children: Chimezie, Nnamezie, Alamezie III, Nnamdi. BA in Econ., Calif. State U., 1978; MSc, Oreg. State U., 1980; PhD, Howard U., 1985. Assoc. prof. U. D.C., Washington, 1981; exec. dir. Ojiaku & Assocs. Fin. Svcs., Silver Spring, Md., 1986; exec. pres. Nigerian Internat. Bus., Washington, 1989; pres. Washington Nat. Properties & Mortgage Corp., Silver Spring, 1990; pres. coun. Wis. Nat. Ins. Co., 1987—; exec. mem. Dave Delto Enterprises, 1990. Contbr. articles to profl. jours. Bus. advisor Nigerian Profl. Orgn., Washington, 1987; bd. dirs. African Cultural Orgn., Washington, 1990. Roman Catholic. Office: Ojiaku & Assocs Fin Svcs 10014 Colesville Rd Ste B Silver Spring MD 20901-2306

O'KANE, FRANCIS ALOYSIUS, sales executive; b. Phila., May 27, 1953; s. Francis Jospeh and Aileene Theresa (Flannery) O'K.; m. Teresa Marie Bertolino, Mar. 21, 1981; children: Francis Christopher, Elizabeth Ann. BA, LaSalle Coll., 1975; postgrad., U. Pa., 1983-84. Salesman Goodall Rubber Co., Balt., 1976-79, BTR, Dorsey, Md., 1979-80; salesman Goodall Rubber Co., Phila., 1980-85, sales mgr., 1986-88; corp. sales mgr. The Briggs Co., Wilmington, Del., 1989—; cons. Stanton Supply, Newark, Delaware, 1986—. Officer O'Mahoney Assn., Phila., 1980-87, pres. 1988-89 (recipient Pres.' plaque 1987); fund raiser Rep. Party, Delaware County, Pa., 1990—. Mem. Vesper Club (Phila.), KC. Republican. Roman Catholic. Office: The Briggs Co 3 Bellecor Dr New Castle DE 19720-1799

O'KEEFE, MELLEN PATRICIA, television producer; b. Everett, Mass., Oct. 5, 1954; d. Christopher Thomas and Mary Rebecca (Cole) O'K. Student, St. Mary of the Woods Coll., Terre Haute, Ind., 1972; BA in Hisotry/Philosophy cum laude, Boston Coll., 1976. TV adminstrv. asst. Varitel Video, San Francisco, 1979; TV prodn. asst. Hillier Prodns., Mill Valley, Calif., 1979; TV prodn. mgr., assoc. producer PM Mag. Westinghouse Broadcasting System, San Francisco, 1980-83; assoc. producer Good Morning America ABC-TV/Capitol Cities, N.Y.C., 1983-87; assoc. producer Rodman Downs Prodns., N.Y.C., 1987-88; field/coordinating producer Sta. WWOR-TV, Secaucus, N.J., 1988; freelance field producer TWA-NYC/The Travel Channel, Italy and Kenya, 1988-89, Kenya and Australia, 1991; field producer Inside Edition King World Prodns., Inc., N.Y.C., 1989-90; judge Internat. Monitor Awards, N.Y.C., L.A., 1989. Active Amnesty Internat., 1987—. Mem. Am. Film Inst. Democrat. Roman Catholic. Home and Office: 126 2nd Pl Brooklyn NY 11231-4102

OKULICZ, WILLIAM CHARLES, molecular endocrinology scientist; b. New Britain, Conn., Nov. 16, 1946; s. William Stanley and Veronica (Wasielewski) O. BS, Rensselaer Polytechnic, 1968; MPH, Yale U., 1971; PhD, U. Conn., 1980. Postdoctoral fellow Worcester Found. for Exptl. Biology, Shrewsburg, Mass., 1980-82, rsch. assoc., 1982-84, sr. rsch. assoc., 1984-87; asst. prof. ob-gyn. U. Mass. Med. Sch., Worcester, 1987—. Contbr. articles to profl. jours. Pres. U. Mass. Golf Assn., Worcester, 1991—; chmn. Yookie Children's Benefit Golf Tournament, Worcester, 1988—. U. Conn. fellow, 1979-80, NIH fellow, 1982-84. Mem. AAAS, Soc. for Exptl. Biology and Medicine, The Endocrine Soc., Am. Soc. for Cell Biology, N.Y. Acad. Scis., Soc. for the Study of Reproduction. Office: U Mass Med Sch Dept Ob-Gyn 55 Lake Ave Worcester MA 01655-0001

OKULSKI, JOHN ALLEN, principal; b. Mineola, N.Y., July 28, 1944; s. John Joseph and Rose (Zebrowski) O.; m. Martina Carol Schoneboom, July 16, 1966; children: Richard, Peter, John. BS, Rutgers U., 1966; MS, C.W. Post Coll., 1972; postgrad., Hofstra U., 1975-76, Queens Coll., 1973. Social studies tchr. Long Beach (N.Y.) Jr. High Sch., 1966-67, Lynbrook (N.Y.) High Sch., 1967-69, Herricks High Sch., New Hyde Park, N.Y., 1969-72; guidance counselor Herricks Jr. High Sch., 1972-75; dept. chmn. sec. sch. guidance Herricks pub. schs., 1975-78; asst. prin. Herricks High Sch., 1978-87; prin. Bay Shore (N.Y.)High Sch., 1987-92, Garden City (N.Y.) High Sch., 1992—. Cubmaster Boy Scouts Am., New Hyde Park, 1975-83; v.p. New Hyde Park Little League, 1978-83. Mem. L.I. Pers. and Guidance Assn. (officer), Mid. States Accreditation Assn. (adv. com. N.Y. chpt.). Presbyterian. Home: 1505 Washington Ave New Hyde Park NY 11040-4332 Office: Bay Shore High Sch 155 3rd Ave Bay Shore NY 11706-6695

OLAND, MARK, lawyer; b. Bklyn., Oct. 25, 1947; s. Jack Oland and Dorothy (Lambert) Kantin; m. Ellen Frances Green, June 28, 1970; children: Jordan Robb, Lauren Faith. BA, U. Vt., 1969; JD, Columbia U., 1972. Bar: Conn. 1972, U.S. Dist. Ct. Conn. 1972. Assoc. Schatz & Schatz, Ribicoff & Kotkin, Hartford, Conn., 1972-76, ptnr., 1976—. Author: (with others) Connecticut Common Interest Ownership Manual, 1985. Bd. dirs. Avon (Conn.) Youth Employment Project, 1986—; bd. dirs. bldg. com. Farmington Valley Jewish Congregation, Sunbury, Conn., 1987—; mem. fundraising com. Hartford Hosp. Juvenile Ctr., 1987—. Mem. Am. Coll. Real Estate Lawyers, Conn. Bar Assn. (chmn. real property sect. 1989—), ABA, Community Assns. Inst. Home: 5 Cadbury Tpke Avon CT 06001-4009 Office: Schatz & Schatz Ribicoff & Kotkin 90 State House Sq Hartford CT 06103-3902

OLCOTT, JOHN WHITING, publishing company executive; b. Orange, N.J., Oct. 20, 1936; s. Egbert Whiting and Marion Richmond (Braillard) O.; m. Hope Bennett Phillips, May 14, 1966 (div. Feb. 1987); children: David Whiting, Bradley Phillips, Carter Howell; m. Isobel Waxman, Nov. 11, 1989. BS in Aero. Engring., Princeton U., 1960, MS in Aero. Engring., 1964; MBA in Gen. Mgmt., Rutgers U., 1970. V.p. Linden (N.J.) Flight Svc., 1960-66; flight rsch. specialist Princeton (N.J.) U., 1966-68; v.p. corp. devel., sr. cons. Aero. Rsch. Assocs. Princeton, Inc., 1968-74; v.p., group pub., editorial dir. McGraw-Hill Aviation Week Group, Rye Brook, N.Y., 1973—. Crew chief, mem. New Vernon (N.J.) Vol. First Aid Squad, 1974—; bd. dirs. Aviation Rsch. and Edn. Found., Washington, 1988—; bd. visitors Aircraft Owner and Pilots Assn. Air Safety Found., Frederick, Md., 1988—; trustee Embry-Riddle Aero. U., Daytona Beach, Fla., 1988—; chmn. panel gen. aviation and commuter tech. NASA, Washington, 1974-86; chmn. panel gen. aviation safety FAA, Washington, 1983-88. Recipient Meritorious Svc. award Flight Safety Found., 1983, Dir.'s award FAA Ctral Region, 1984, Commendation cert. FAA, 1984, Gill Robb Wilson award Embry-Riddle Aero. U., 1986, Journalism award Helicopter Assn. Internat., 1990. Republican. Presbyterian. Office: McGraw-Hill Inc Aviation Week Group 4 International Dr Rye Brook NY 10573

OLCOTT, WILLIAM ALFRED, magazine editor; b. Bklyn., June 29, 1931; s. W. Alfred and Margaret Mary (Carr) O.; m. Anne Maria Gorman, Sept. 7, 1963; children: Christopher, James, Katharine, William, Terence. B.A. in Philosophy, Mary Immaculate Sem. and Coll., Northampton, Pa., 1957; postgrad., Columbia U. Reporter, writer AP, 1960-66; with McGraw-Hill Publs. Co., 1966-80, 81-84, chmn. editorial bd., 1976-77, editor in chief 26 Plus mag., 1973-77, editor in chief Nat. Petroleum News mag., 1977-81, editor in chief Office Adminstrn. and Automation mag., 1984; editor in chief Fund Raising Mgmt. mag., Garden City, N.Y., 1985—; publs. exec. editor Hoke Communications, Garden City, 1989—. Mem. adv. com. Garden City Bd. Edn., N.Y., 1976—; prin. religious edn. home program St. Joseph's Roman Cath. Ch., Garden City, 1976—, mem. pastoral coun., 1990. Recipient Jesse H. Neal Editorial Achievement award Am. Bus. Press, 1974, 80, Golden Mike award Nat. Religious Broadcasters, 1989. Home: 108 Roxbury Rd Garden City NY 11530-2624 Office: 224 7th St Garden City NY 11530-5747

OLCZAK, PAUL VINCENT, psychologist; b. Buffalo, N.Y., May 25, 1943; s. Vincent Henry and Helen (Babula) O.; m. Marie Rose Oliveri, Oct. 20, 1973; children: Paul V. II, Patrick J., Drew M. MA, No. Ill. U., 1969, PhD, 1972. Clin. psychologist Family Ct. Psychiat. Clinic, Buffalo, 1975-77, cons. supervisory psychologist, 1977—; supr. psychol. svcs. Hopevale, Inc., Hamburg, N.Y., 1977-89; clin. psychologist Amherst (N.Y.) Police Dept., 1989—; asst. prof. psychology SUNY, Geneseo, 1977-83, assoc. prof. psychology, 1983-90, prof. psychology, 1990—. Co-editor: Community Mediation, 1991; contbg. author: The POI in Clinical Situations: A Review, 1991, Self-actualization-Polemics Surrounding Its Use, 1991; contbr. articles to profl. jours./publs. Mem. Am. Psychol. Assn., Ea. Psychol. Assn., Midwestern Psychol. Assn., Psychonomic Soc., Soc. Exptl. Social Psychology, Psi Chi, Sigma Xi. Home: 185 N Long St Buffalo NY 14221-5313 Office: SUNY Dept Psychology Geneseo NY 14454

OLD, HUGHES OLIPHANT, research theologian, clergyman; b. Redondo Beach, Calif., Apr. 13, 1933; s. Shadburne Edward and Emma Coulter (Oliphant) O.; m. Mary Chase McCaw, June 12, 1982; children: Hannah Chase, Isaac Houghton Chambers. BA, Centre Coll., 1955; BD, Princeton Theol. Sem., 1958; postgrad., U. Tubingen, 1964-66; ThD, U. Neuchatel, 1971. Ordained to ministry Presbyn. Ch., 1959. Minister Presbyn. Ch., Atglen, Pa., 1959-64, Faith Presbyn. Ch., West Lafayette, Ind., 1972-85; mem. Ctr. for Theol. Inquiry, Princeton, N.J., 1985—. Author: Patristic Roots of Reformed Worship, 1975, Worship, 1984, Reformed Baptismal Rite in the Sixteenth Century, 1989; contbr. numerous articles to scholarly jours. Fellow N.Am. Acad. Liturgy; mem. Union League Phila. Republican. Office: 50 Stockton St Princeton NJ 08540-6813

OLDALE, ROBERT NICHOLAS, geologist; b. North Attleboro, Mass., Aug. 9, 1929; s. Albert Edward and Elsie (Nicholas) O.; m. Gail Carpenter; children: Matthew, Daniel. BS, St. Lawrence U., 1953; postgrad., Cornell U., 1953-55. Geologist U.S. Geol. Survey, Boston, 1955-67, Woods Hole, Mass., 1967—. Contbr. articles to profl. jours.; author of maps. Judge U.S. Yacht Racing Union, New Eng., 1980-91. Fellow Geol. Soc. Am.; mem. Am. Quaternary Assn., Sigma Xi. Home: PO Box 361 53 Oceanview Ave North Falmouth MA 02556-2539 Office: US Geol Survey Quissett Campus Woods Hole MA 02543

OLDANI, NORBERT LOUIS, mathematician, educator; b. Detroit, Nov. 16, 1936; s. Louis and Lillian Oldani. BA, U. Detroit, 1958, MA, 1960. Teaching fellow U. Detroit, 1958-59; analyst AC Spark Plug, Milw., 1961-62; tchr. St. John's U., N.Y.C., 1962-66, Mohawk Valley Community Coll., Utica, N.Y., 1967—. Contbr. several articles to profl. jours. NSf grantee, 1968, 70. Mem. Am. Math. Soc., Math. Assn. Am., N.Y. State Math. Assn. Two-Yr. Colls. (chair curriculum com. 1977-79), Computer Music Soc. Roman Catholic. Office: Mohawk Valley Community 1101 Sherman Dr Utica NY 13501-5308

OLDENBURG, RICHARD ERIK, museum director; b. Stockholm, Sept. 21, 1933; came to U.S., 1936, naturalized, 1959; s. Gösta and Sigrid Elisabeth (Lindforss) O.; m. Harriet Lisa Turnure, Dec. 17, 1960. A.B., Harvard U., 1954. Mgr. design dept. Doubleday & Co., Inc., N.Y.C., 1958-61; mng. editor trade div. Macmillan Co., Inc., N.Y.C., 1961-69; dir. publs. Mus. Modern Art, N.Y.C., 1969-72, dir., 1972—. Served with AUS, 1956-58. Mem. Assn. Art Mus. Dirs. Home: 447 E 57th St New York NY 10022-3064 Office: Mus Modern Art 11 W 53rd St New York NY 10019-5498

OLDHAM, JOHN PHILIP, television marketing executive; b. Portchester, N.Y., Oct. 3, 1943; s. George Peter and Wilma Isabelle (Kelley) O.; m. Mary Elizabeth Morrin, Nov. 15, 1969; children: Siobhan, Chandler, Caitlin. Student, U. Conn., 1964, 65; BS, Syracuse U., 1966. Mgr. Jacks Fabrics, Portchester, 1963-64; media buyer Morton, Stanton Advt., Portland, Oreg., 1965, Compton Advt., N.Y.C., 1966-67, Ogilvy & Mather Advt., N.Y.C., 1967-68; media planner Cunningham & Walsh Advt., N.Y.C., 1969; media dir. D.J. Mendleson Advt., N.Y.C., 1970-73; v.p. Katz Communications, N.Y.C., 1973-86; pres. Oldham Mktg. Corp., Maplewood, N.J., 1986—; cons. Genesis Entertainment, L.A., 1986—, Sandy Frank Film Sales, N.Y.C., 1986—, Pappas Broadcasting, Fresno, Calif., 1988—. Mem. Coalition of Program Distbrs., Nat. Assn. TV Program Execs. Home and Office: Oldham Mktg Corp 450 Ridgewood Rd Maplewood NJ 07040-1127

O'LEARY, COLLEEN ENWRIGHT, anesthesiologist; b. Oswego, N.Y., June 22, 1953; d. Alfred Francis and Shirley (Danaher) Enwright; m. Michael Robert O'Leary, May 6, 1978. BA, State U. Coll. Oswego, 1974; MD, SUNY, 1978. Diplomate Am. Bd. Anesthesiology. Resident in internal medicine Henry Ford Hosp., Detroit, 1978-79; resident in anesthesiology St. Joseph's Hosp. Health Ctr., Syracuse, N.Y., 1979-81, chief resident, fellow, 1981-82; staff anesthesiologist Crouse Irving Meml. Hosp., Syracuse, N.Y., 1982-90; asst. prof. anesthesiology SUNY Health Sci. Ctr., Syracuse, N.Y., 1991—. Mem. Roman Cath., Diocesian Commn. on Women, Syracuse, 1984-88, chairperson, 1985-86; mem. Syracuse Symphony Orch. Physicians Com., 1988-90, co-chairperson, 1990. Fellow Am. Coll. Anesthesiologists; mem. AMA, Med. Soc. State N.Y., Onondaga County Med. Soc., Am. Soc. Anesthesiologists, N.Y. State Soc. Anesthesiologists. Office: SUNY Health Sci Ctr Dept Anesthesiology 750 E Adams St Syracuse NY 13210

O'LEARY, DANIEL FRANCIS, university dean; b. Boston, Apr. 17, 1923; s. Dennis Joseph and Catherine Mary (O'Connell) O'L. BA, Oblate Coll., 1950; EdM, U. Buffalo, 1953, EdD, 1956. Tchr. gen. sci., biology Bishop Fallon High Sch., Buffalo, 1951-62, asst. prin., 1962-65; dir. edn. Oblate Fathers, Washington, 1963-68; prin. Bishop Fallon High Sch., Buffalo, 1968-74; dir. spl. programs Niagara U. (N.Y.), 1974-77, dean spl. programs, 1977-81, dean edn. and continuing studies, 1982-88, dean coll. of edn., 1988—; adj. prof. Mt. St. Joseph's Tchrs. Coll., Buffalo, 1956-64, edn. evaluator reading clinic, 1956-64. Asst. dir. family life dept. Diocese of Buffalo, 1953-64. Mem. AAUP, ASCD, Am. Assn. Sch. Adminstrs, Nat. Coun. for Accreditation Tech. Edn., N.Y. State assn. Tchr. Educators, Am. Assn. of Colls. for Tchr. Edn., Phi Delta Kappa. Roman Catholic. Office: Niagara U Hyde Park Rd Niagara University NY 14109-9999

O'LEARY, DANIEL J., academic administrator; b. Manhasset, N.Y., Apr. 27, 1939; s. Daniel and Catherine B. (Carroll) O'L.; m. K. Michol Bestoso, July 8, 1967; children: Daniel J., Robert L., Kathryn M., Joanna E. AB, St. John's U., Jamaica, N.Y., 1961; MBA, Fairleigh Dickinson U., 1976. Assoc. mgr. ops. Met. Mus. of Art, N.Y.C., 1972-79; asst. dir. Smithsonian Inst., N.Y.C., 1979-80; v.p. Hamilton Coll., Clinton, N.Y., 1980—, acting pres., 1985. Mem. exec. com. Boy Scouts Am., Utica, N.Y.; chair fin. com. Kirkland Art Ctr., Clinton; pres. bd. trustees House of Good Shepherd, Utica. Lt. USN, 1962-66. Mem. Am. Arbitration Assn. (cert.), Newport Yacht Club, Univ. Club. Roman Catholic. Office: Hamilton Coll Clinton NY 13323

O'LEARY, JAMES PATRICK, science museum administrator; b. Fitchburg, Mass., Aug. 31, 1951; s. Richard Joseph and Annie (Keaveny) O.; m. Rose Ann Eggert, July 1, 1978; children: Colin, Brendan, Bridget. BA in Bio., Catholic U., 1973. Planetarium asst. Alice G. Wallace Planetarium, Fitchburg, Mass., 1971; park naturalist Rock Creek Nature Ctr., Washington, 1973; mus. intern Strasenburgh Planetarium, Rochester, N.Y., 1973-74; planetarium specialist Franklin Inst., Phila., 1974-75, Davis Planetarium of Md., Balt., 1975; assoc. producer Davis Planetarium, Balt., 1976; sr. producer Sci. Ctr. Davis Planetarium, Balt., 1986; dir. Davis Planetarium & IMAX Theater, Md. Sci. Ctr., Balt., 1987—; planning cons., Scottish Devel. Agy. Glasgow, Scotland, 1984-85. Author: articles, 1973, 1975, 1978. Area coord. Children's Friendship Project for No. Ireland, Inc., Balt., 1988—. Mem. Internat. Planetarium Soc., Mid. Atlantic Planetarium Soc., Planetarium Assn. of Canada, Internat. Space Theater Consortium. Roman Catholic.

O'LEARY, KATHLEEN A., financial advisor, administrative assistant; b. Washington, Dec. 17, 1946; d. Patrick Christopher and Hilda Elizabeth (Gobrecht) O'Leary; children—Kara Ann, Scott Patrick, Ryan Arthur Thompson, Kelly Marie. Student Montgomery Jr. Coll., 1964-66; Colo. State U., 1974; B.S. in Bus. Adminstrn., U. Md., 1975. Account exec. Sta. WSBT-AM-FM-TV, South Bend, Ind., 1972-74; mgr. advt. and promotion Sta. WGHP-TV, High Point, N.C., 1978-83; account exec. Wheat, First Securities, Greensboro, N.C., 1983-85; investment broker Legg Mason Wood Walker, Greensboro, 1985-88; investment exec. Ferris, Baker Watts, Inc., Bethesda, Md., 1988—; legal sec. Jones, Day, Reavis & Pogue, Washington, 1988-90; legal asst. Santarelli, Smith & Carroccio, Washington, 1991—; lectr. in field. Exec. producer TV show Classic Memories, 1985. Founder, 1st pres., bd. dirs. Big Bros./Big Sisters of High Point, 1981-85; founder, sec.-treas. Furniture City Classic, Inc., High Point, 1981-88 ; founder, bd. dirs. Henredon Classic LPGA Golf Tournament, High Point, 1981-88 ; mem. Leadership High Point, 1987-89; Challenge: High Point grad. and steering com. mem. High Point C. of C., 1984-85; bd. dirs. met. bd. YMCA of High Point, 1981, 82, Adams Meml. YWCA, High Point, 1985-87, Salvation Army Boys Club, 1980-81, Vols. to Ct., Guilford County, 1980-81; Sunday sch. tchr. Immaculate Heart of Mary Ch., High Point, 1980-87; exec. bd. mem. Greater Washington Open LPGA Golf Tournament, 1989-90. Democrat. Roman Catholic. Avocations: creative writing; classical piano.

O'LEARY, PAUL MARTIN, retired economics educator; b. Lawrence, Kans., Nov. 29, 1901; s. Raphael Dorman and Mathilde (Henrichs) O'L. BA, U. Kans., 1922; MA, Harvard U., 1924; PhD, Cornell U., 1929. Instr. Cornell U., Ithaca, N.Y., 1924-29, asst. prof., 1929-36, prof., 1936-67, prof. emeritus, 1967—; dean sch. bus. Cornell U., 1946-52, dean arts and scis., 1952-57; dep. adminstr. Office Price Adminstrn., Washington, 1941-44; mem. commn. Dodge Mission to Occupied Japan, 1949. Author: Corporate Enterprise in Modern Economic Life, 1935, (with others) An Introduction to Money, Banking, and Corporations, 1936.

OLEN, STEPHANIE ROSE, anthropologist; b. Butler, Pa., Jan. 1, 1955; d. Steve X. and Olga Dorothy (Kellar) Olen; m. Paul Robert Kleindorfer, Feb. 9, 1989; stepchildren: Sonia Kleindorfer, Geoffrey Kleindorfer, Erin Kleindorfer. BFA, Moore Coll. of Art, Phila., 1976; MS, U. Pa., 1988, postgrad., 1990—. Rsch. asst. and cons. The Aga Khan Award for Arch.,

Phila., 1978-80; dir. internat. programs and protocol City of Phila., 1986-87, cons., 1987—; pres., chief exec. officer Olen Internat., Ltd., Butler, Pa., 1990—; cons. Ctr. for Risk & Decision processes, The Wharton Sch., Phila., 1990—, Internat. Forum, Wharton Sch., 1990, City of Phila., 1987-88. Mem. Center City Residents Assn., Phila. Rotary Internat. fellow, 1971-72. Mem. Am. Anthropol. Assn., Assn. for Applied Anthropology, Tanzanian Conservation Soc., Internat. Soc. for the Study of Multiple Personality and Disassociation.

OLER, HOWARD WARREN, steel company executive, consultant; b. Balt., Nov. 9, 1929; s. Samuel Howard Jr. and Esther Viola (Thompson) O.; m. Charlotte Lee Heberle, May 23, 1953; children: John Laird, Paul Marden. B of Engring., Johns Hopkins U., 1953. Design engr. State of Md., Balt., 1949-50; sr. hwy. engr. Baltimore County, Towson, Md., 1951-52; mgmt. trainee Bethlehem Steel Corp., Sparrows Point, Md., 1953-54, constrn. engr., 1955-58, area constrn. supr., 1959-61, ops. gen. foreman, 1962-68, asst. area supr., 1969-72, area supr., 1973-81, div. engr., 1982-92, ret., 1992; consulting engr., Phoenix, Md., 1959—. contbr. articles to Antique Scale Soc. of Am. mag. Chmn. indsl. fund drive Boy Scouts Am., Balt., Chesapeake, 1975-82; mem. bd. deacons Upper Cross Bapt. Ch., Harford County region, 1990—; bd. dirs. Green Glade Improvement Assn., Nothern Baltimore County, 1969-72; chmn., trustee Perry Hall Bapt. Ch., Baltimore County, 1970-74; bd. dirs. Baltimore County Hist. Soc., 1987-90. Capt. U.S. Army, 1954-56. Mem. Am. Iron and Steel Inst. (sec. tech. com. on tin mill practice 1988-91, pub. tech. papers), Am. Electro-Plating Soc., Am. Iron and Steel Engrs., Soc. Am. Mil. Engrs., Am. Soc. Civil Engrs., Engrs. Club Md. Republican. Baptist. Home: 4204 Green Glade Rd Phoenix MD 21131-1706

OLESEN, DONALD LOUIS, safety engineer, industrial hygienist, author; b. Chgo., Sept. 26, 1952; s. Burton Walter and Louise Elizabeth (Hersheway) O.; m. Regina Marie Clausen, Sept. 4, 1971; children: Angela Marie, Amy Michelle, Andrea Melissa. BS, Ill. State U., 1983; MBA, N.H. Coll., 1987. Cert. safety profl. Assoc. safety adminstr. Wang Labs., Lowell, Mass., 1983-84; safety adminstr. Wang Labs., Lawrence, Mass., 1984-85; safety and environ. mgr. Avco Rsch. Lab., Everett, Mass., 1985-86; corp. safety engr. Apollo Computer, Inc., Chelmsford, Mass., 1986-90; assoc. Marsh & McLennan Protection Cons., Boston, 1990-91; mgr. risk control svcs. Hobbs Group, Inc., Lexington, Mass., 1991—. Contbr. articles to profl. jours. Mem. Am. Soc. Safety Engrs. (pub. rels. dir. 1988, treas. 1989-90, 2d v.p. 1990-91, 1st v.p. 1992-93, Pres.'s award 1989), Am. Indsl. Hygiene Assn. Roman Catholic.

OLINGER, JOHN PETER, federal trade expert; b. Syracuse, N.Y., July 18, 1947; s. Joseph Martin and Elizabeth (Coughlan) O. BA, Assumption Coll., 1969; MA, SUNY, Binghamton, 1972, PhD, 1973. Lectr. Bayero U., Kano, Nigeria, 1974-78; free-lance writer London and N.Y.C., 1979-81; policy analyst Bread for the World, Washington, 1981-84; adminstrv. asst. Congressman Thomas J. Downey, Washington, 1985-87, legis. asst. for trade, 1986—; assoc. staff mem. Com. on the Budget, Washington, 1985-86, Subcom. on Pub. Assistance and Unemployment Compensation, Com. on Ways and Means, Washington, 1987-88; staff dir. Subcom. on Human Svcs., Select Com. on Aging, U.S. Ho. Reps., Washington, 1989—; mem. adv. bd. Nat. Family Friends Ctr., Washington, 1990—; mem. adv. com. NCOA Pediatric AIDS Project, Washington, 1989—. Contbr. articles to profl. jours. Mem. Washington Project for the Arts, Nat. Dem. Club. Office: Subcom Human Svcs 715 O'Neill US Ho Reps Washington DC 20515

OLITSKI, JULES, artist; b. Snovsk, USSR, Mar. 27, 1922; came to U.S., 1923, naturalized, 1943; s. Jevel and Anna (Zarnitsky) Demikovsky; m. Gladys Katz, 1944 (div. 1951); 1 dau., Eve; m. Andrea Hill Pearce, Jan. 21, 1956 (div. 1974); 1 dau., Lauren; m. Kristina Gorby, Feb. 29, 1980. Student, Academie de la Grande Chaumiere, Paris, 1949-50; BA, NYU, 1952, MA, 1954; postgrad., Beaux Arts Inst., N.Y.C., 1940-42, Nat. Acad. Design, N.Y.C., 1940-42, Ednl. Alliance, N.Y.C., 1947, Zadkine Sch. Sculpture, Paris, 1949. Assoc. prof. art SUNY, New Paltz, N.Y., 1954-55; curator Art Edn. Gallery, NYU, 1955-56; chmn. fine arts div. C.W. Post Coll. L.I. U., Greenvale, N.Y., 1956-63; tchr. Bennington Coll., 1963-67. Exhibited in many one-man shows including Galerie Huit, Paris, 1951, Iolas Gallery, N.Y.C., 1958, French & Co., N.Y.C., 1959-61, Poindexter Gallery, N.Y.C., 1961-68, Bennington (Vt.) Coll., 1962, Kasmin, Ltd., London, 1964-75, 89, Galerie Lawrence, Paris, 1964, David Mirvish Gallery, Toronto, Ont., Can., 1964-78, Nicholas Wilder, L.A., 1966, Corcoran Gallery, Washington, 1967, 74, Am. Pavillion, Venice Biennale Art Exhbn., 1966, 88, Andre Emmerich Gallery, N.Y.C., 1966-89, Zurich, Switzerland, 1973-78, Met. Mus. Art, N.Y.C., 1969, Inst. Contemporary Art, U. Pa., 1968, 86, Lawrence Rubin Gallery, N.Y.C., 1969, 71, 72, 73, Knoedler Contemporary Art, 1973-77, 79, 81, 83, 85, 87, Dart Gallery, Chgo., 1975, FIAL, Paris, 1976, Berlinische Galerie, 1977, Downstairs Gallery, Edmonton, Can., 1980, 82, Janus Gallery, L.A., 1981, Gallery One, Toronto, 1980-90, Yares Gallery, Scottsdale, Ariz., 1986-89, Galerie Wentzel, Hamburg and Cologne, Fed. Republic Germany, 1975, 77, 81, 89, Mus. Fine Arts, Boston, 1973, 77, Whitney Mus. Am. Art, 1973, Galleria Dell'Ariete, Italy, 1974, Corcoran Gallery Art, 1974-76, Waddington Gallery, London, 1975, Galerie Templon, Paris, 1984-85, Hirshhorn Mus., Washington, 1977, Edmonton (Alta., Can.) Art Gallery, 1979, Martha White Gallery, Louisville, 1982, Harcus/Krakow Gallery, Boston, 1978, 81, 82, Harcus Gallery, Boston, 1984, 86, Meredith Long, Houston, 1981, 82, 87, 90, (retrospective) Fondation du Chateau de Jau, Perpignon, France, 1984, La Musee de Valence, France, 1985, Hokin Gallery, Palm Beach, Fla., 1988, Associated Am. Artists, N.Y.C., 1989, (retrospective) Buschlen/Mowatt Gallery, Vancouver, B.C., Can., 1990, Salander-O'Reilly Galleries, N.Y.C., 1990, 92, Gallery Camino Real, Boca Raton, Fla., 1987, 88, 90, 92; exhibited in many group shows including Carnegie Internat., Pitts., 1961, 1965, Washington Gallery Modern Art, 1963, Los Angeles County Mus., 1964, Fogg Art Mus. Harvard, 1965, Pasadena Art Mus., 1965, Mus. Basel, Switzerland, 1965, 74, Whitney Mus. Am. Art, 1972, 73, Musée d'Art Contemporain, Montreal, 1973, Hirshhorn Mus., 1974, Corcoran Gallery Art, 1975, Everson Mus. Art, Syracuse, N.Y., 1976, Bass Mus., Miami, Am. Embassy, Madrid, 1984, Ft. Worth Art Mus., Mus. Art, Ft. Lauderdale, 1986; represented in permanent collections including Mus. Modern Art, N.Y.C., Art Inst. Chgo., Whitney Mus., Corcoran Art Gallery, Nat. Gallery Can., Met. Mus. Art, N.Y.C., Bklyn. Mus., Hirshhorn Mus., Washington, Everson Mus. Art, Syracuse, N.Y., Mus. Fine Arts, Boston, Norman MacKensie Art Gallery, Regina, Can., also pvt. collections; subject book Jules Olitski by Kenworth Moffett, 1981. Recipient 2d prize Carnegie Internat., 1961, 1st prize Corcoran Biennial, Washington, 1967, award for distinction in the arts Univ. Union, U.S.C., 1975, the Milton and Sally Avery Disting. Professorship, Bard Coll., Annandale-on-Hudson, N.Y., 1987. Office: PO Box 440 207 5th Ave Marlboro VT 05344 also: care Salander-O'Reilly Galleries 20 E 79th St New York NY 10021

OLIVA, LAWRENCE JAY, university official, history educator; b. Walden, N.Y., Sept. 23, 1933; s. Lawrence Joseph and Catherine (Mooney) O.; m. Mary Ellen Nolan, June 3, 1961; children: Lawrence Jay, Edward Nolan. BA, Manhattan Coll., 1955; MA, Syracuse U., 1957, PhD, 1960; postgrad., U. Paris, 1959; DHL (hon.), Manhattan Coll., 1987; LLD (hon.), St. Thomas Aquinas Coll., 1988. Prof. history NYU, N.Y.C., 1969—, vice-chancellor acad. planning and services, 1973-75, v.p. acad. planning and services, 1975-77, v.p. acad. affairs, 1977-80, provost, exec. v.p. acad. affairs, 1980-83, chancellor, exec. v.p., 1983-90, pres., 1991—. Author: Misalliance: A Study of French Policy in Russia during the Seven Years' War, 1964, Russia in the Era of Peter the Great, 1969; editor: Russia and the West from Peter to Kruschev, 1965, Peter the Great, 1970, Catherine the Great, 1971; contbr. article and revs. to profl. lit. Trustee Inst. Internat. Edn., NYU. Fribourg fellow, 1959. Mem. Irish-Am. Cultural Inst., Soc. Fellows NYU, Phi Beta Kappa, Phi Gamma Delta. Lodge: Order of Hibernians. Home: 33 Washington Sq W New York NY 10011-9154 Office: NYU New York NY 10012

OLIVA, STAN, singer, composer; b. Newark, Dec. 4, 1952; s. John and Marion (Gibbs) O.; m. Charlotte Jeannette Vandenberg, July 1, 1978; children: Jonathan Hendrik, Alexandra Charlotte. Grad. high sch., Woodbridge, N.J. Instr. Hungry Trout, Wilmington, N.Y., 1981-85; guide, owner Streamside Guide Svc., Spruce Hill, N.Y., 1985—; advisor Hungry Trout Catch & Release Dream Mile, Wilmington, 1981-85; dir. Skinney Legs, Montreal, Que., Can., 1990—; performer Feed the Hungry, Bear Mt. Pk., N.Y., 1986, We Are the World benefit, Lake Placid, N.Y., 1987, Melissa LaRosa Benefit Concert, Keene, N.Y., 1991, Adirondack Songwriters Live, 1992. Composer: Debergerac 2000, 1970; guest appearance TV show Woods and Waters, 1987; performer, dir. Skinney Legs, 1991; guide, advisor TV show Rod & Reel, 1984. Chmn. com. Boy Scouts Am., Keene, 1990; demonstrator Field, Forest & Stream, Essex County Arts Coun., Elizabethtown, N.Y., 1991. Home and Office: HCR1 Box 13 Keene NY 12942

OLIVARES, RENE EUGENIO, translator; b. Santiago, Chile, Feb. 20, 1941; came to U.S. 1979; s. Luis Armando and Amelia del Carmen (Leiva) O. MS, U. Chile, 1971. Engr. Soquimich (Chile), Antofagasta, 1969-71, Codelco (Chile), Santiago, 1971-75; terminologist Entel (Chile), Santiago, 1975-79; translator UN, N.Y.C., 1979—. Editor: Tesauro de la Industria Extractiva del Cobre, 1974, Tesauro de Telecomunicaciones, 1978. Mem. AAAS, Am. Math. Soc., Math. Assn. Am., Blue Army of Fatima. Roman Catholic. Home: 32 W 40th St Apt 3J New York NY 10018-3910 Office: UN 1 United Nations Pla New York NY 10017

OLIVER, BRUCE LAWRENCE, information systems specialist, educator; b. Westfield, Mass., Nov. 20, 1951; s. Ernest Lawrence and Elizabeth (Welchek) O. AS, Greater Hartford Commmunity, 1972; BS, U. Mass., 1974; MBA, U. Hartford, 1989. Cert. tchr. sec. and vocat. edn., Mass., Conn. Comml. sales Gordon Realty, Enfield, Conn., 1972-75; forestry tech. research Dept. Environ. Protection, State of Conn., Hartford, 1973, 1974; res. sales Forsman Realty, Enfield, 1975-77; substitute sec. tchr. Enfield Sch. Systems, 1975-78; collections mgr. New Eng. Bank & Trust, Enfield, 1978-79; ops. CCEC/McCullahg Leasing, Inc., S. Windsor, Conn., 1979-81; pres. Ollie & Ike's, Inc., Enfield, 1985-86; MBA Adj. U. Hartford, W. Hartford, Conn., 1988-89; workstation engr. Travelers, Hartford, 1982-89; v.p. 1st Class Expert Systems, Inc., Wayland, Mass., 1989-90, Microsoft Corp., Boston, 1991—; cons. and pres. Bros. Assocs., Enfield; del. leader Comparative Studies Assn.; Internat. Cultural Exch. with China, Washington; pub. speaker, Speakers Bus., U. Hartford; vis. mem. faculty mgmt. info. sci. U. Hartford, Conn., 1989-91. Author: A Novice's Guide to Personal Computer Buying. Gubernatorial appointee Conn. bd. trustees Reg. Community Colls., 1985-89; vice chmn. Student Affairs and Acad. Policies Com. Hartford, 1987; chmn. and trustee Conn. Data Processing Curriculum Com., Hartford, 1989; elected com. mem. Enfield Democratic Com., 1975; notary pub., Conn., 1972-92; gubernatorial appointee Conn. bd. trustees Community Tech. Colls., 1990-93. Recipient CTM Degree, Toastmasters Internat., Hartford, 1987, State Farmer Degree Conn. Future Farmers Am., DeKalb Agrl. Accomplishment award, cert. of recognition, Bicentennial (USA) Commn., Enfield, 1976, Vigil Hon. BSA: Order of the Arrow, Hartford, 1972, Eagle Sc. Boy Sc. of Am., Hartford, 1967. Mem. World Affairs Coun. of Hartford, Computer Soc. of IEEE, Am. Assn. for Artificial Intelligence, Assn. Community Coll. Trustees, Am. Assn. Community & Tech. Colls., Internat. Platform Assn., Oldefield Farms Homeowners' Assn. (residence com. sec. 1990-91), Hartford County Soil and Water Conservation Dist., Nat. Press Club Found., Robert Schueller's Eagles Club, Masons. Democrat. Roman Catholic. Home: 71 Oldefield Farms Enfield CT 06082-4565

OLIVER, GENE L(EECH), chemist, retired; b. Rockford, Ill., June 7, 1929; s. James and Helen C.E. (Leech) O.; m. Carol Elizabeth Kaiser, June 18, 1955 (div. 1978); children: Fred K., James A., Catherine E.; m. Nancy Williams Warren, Oct. 25, 1980. BS, Beloit Coll., 1950; PhD in Organic Chemistry, Northwestern Univ., 1955. Rsch. chemist Eastman Kodak Rsch. Labs., Rochester, N.Y., 1954-65, rsch. assoc., 1965-71, tech. staff assoc., patent liaison cons., 1971-89. Patentee in field; contbr. articles to profl. jours. Active sister-city orgn. (Rochester-Novgorod, Russia). Mem. Am. Chem. Soc. (councilor Rochester sect. 1974-88, various offices 1962-91), Phi Beta Kappa, Sigma Xi. Unitarian-Universalist. Home: 24 Pine Cone Dr Pittsford NY 14534-3534

OLIVER, LEONARD PAUL, public policy and continuing education consultant; b. Phila., Nov. 3, 1933; s. James Vernon and Annabelle (Hibner) O.; m. Eleanor Ruth Wahlbrinck, Jan. 27, 1962; children: Erika, Britt-Karin. BS, Temple U., 1955; MA, U. Md., 1966; PhD, U. Chgo., 1970. Rumanian interpreter U.S. Army Security Agy., Monterey, Calif., 1956-59; underwriter Allstate Ins. Co., Phila., 1959-60; program officer CIA, Washington, 1960-61; sr. conf. coord. U. Md., College Park, 1963-66; dir. state programs NEH, Washington, 1971-74, dir. bicentennial, 1974-76, spl. asst. to chair, 1976-83; dir. Oliver Assocs., Washington, 1983—; staff assoc. Kettering Found., Dayton, Ohio, 1983—; exec. dir. Labor/Higher Edn. Coun., Washington, 1988—; cons. Study Circle Resource Ctr., Pomfret, Conn., 1989—, AFL-CIO, Washington, 1990—. Author: The Art of Citizenship, 1983, Study Circles, 1987, (chpt.) Study Circles and Collaborative Learning, 1991; mem. editorial bd. Adult Edn. Quarterly, 1987—; contbr. articles to profl. jours. Coord. Neighborhood Watch, Cleve. Park, Washington, 1985—; bd. dirs. Hyde Park Neighborhood Conf., Chgo., 1970, Stoddert Soccer League, Washington, 1986—, dir. coaching, 1986—; dir. Robert Mann for State Del. Campaign, Chgo., 1969. Ford Found. grantee, 1987-90, Exxon Ednl. Found. grantee, 1985-87; named to All-Am. Soccer team NCAA, 1951, 53, 55, U.S. Olympic Soccer team, 1964, U.S. Pan-Am. Soccer team, 1963. Mem. Am. Assn. Adult Continuing Edn., U.S. Soccer Fedn. Coaching ('A' lic. coach, cert. referee), Phi Delta Kappa. Democrat. Unitarian. Home and Office: Oliver Assocs 3429 34th Pl NW Washington DC 20016-3135

OLIVER, PHILIP MANUS, management consultant, president; b. Hartford, Conn., July 25, 1920; s. Bernard John and Elizabeth (Schtiff) O.; m. Elaine Frances Peterson, June 13, 1942 (div. Aug. 1972); children: Tracie Joy, Janice Eva; m. Jean Dorothy Bovard, Mar. 29, 1975; children: Sandra, Deborah, Guy. BA in Personnel & Bus. Mgmt., George Washington U., 1942. Personnel specialist Dept. Army, Chgo., 1940-43; personnel mgr. Dept. Army, Washington, 1946-50; personnel officer U.S. High Commr. for Austria, Vienna, 1950-54; personnel mgr. Creole Petroleum, Caracas, Venezuela, 1954-56; mgr. compensation Tidewater Oil Co., San Francisco, 1956-58; personnel mgr. Lockheed Missiles and Space, Sunnyvale, Calif., 1959-64; personnel dir. Philco-Ford, Palo Alto, Calif., 1964-69; spl. asst., dir. mgmt. systems Dept. Labor, Washington, 1969-70, 72-80; dir. Job Evaluation and Pay Task Force, Washington, 1970-72; cons., pres. The Oliver System, Orrington, Maine, 1980—. Author: The Oliver System, a Job Evaluation and Pay Technology Widely Used in Federal and State Governments. Bd. dirs. Santa Clara United Fund., Sunnyvale, 1969, Hope for Retarded Children, San Jose, Calif., 1968. Recipient Disting. Career Svc. award Dept. of Labor, 1980. Mem. Bangor Art Soc. (treas. 1990—). Baptist. Home and Office: PO Box 81 Orrington ME 04474-0081

OLIVER, SANDRA, art dealer; b. Bronxville, N.Y., Apr. 2, 1941; d. Clarence Charles and Mary Bell E. (McTeique) Simoni; m. Paul Alan Williams, May 2, 1982; children: John Mortimer Wilson, Melissa Anne Wilson, PHilip Keith Wilson. BA, BFA, Marymount Coll., 1963. Art and art history tchr. N.Y.C. Sch. System, 1963-65; art tchr. Diocese Cath. Sch., Westchester, N.Y., 1963-65; comml. artist rep. Weston, Conn., 1979-84; pres. Sandi Oliver, Weston, 1984—. Author catalog: American Impressionist Paul Williams: His Garden and His Oil Paintings, 1961. Recipient 1st prize Christmas Show, Pelham (N.Y.) C. of C., 1960's, Bravo award Revlon Corp., 1980's. Mem. New Eng. Appraisers Assn., Allied Arts Am. Inc., Am. Fedn. Artists, Nat. Mus. Women in Arts (charter mem.). Home: 11 Tubbs Spring Dr Weston CT 06883-1413 Office: Sandi Oliver Fine Art PO Box 1203 Weston CT 06883-0203

OLIVERI, ANN LENORE, marketing executive; b. Chgo., Oct. 19, 1951; d. John Patrick and Katherine Jane (Burdick) Murphy; m. Patrick Aloysious Parenteau, 1974 (div. 1984); m. William Benjamin Oliveri, July 2, 1988. BA, Creighton U., 1973; MBA, George Washington U., 1985. Copywriter The Nebraska, 1973-74; promotion supr. State Dept. Fed. Credit Union, Washington, 1974-75; tech. writer Skidmore Owings & Merrill, Portland, Oreg., 1975-76; dir. mktg. Nat. Assn. Fed. Credit Unions, Arlington, Va., 1976-81; sales mgr. CLB Pubs., Kensington, Md., 1982-85; sr. mgr. mktg. AIA, Washington, 1985-90; asst. staff v.p. Nat. Assn. Home Builders, Washington, 1991—; mng. ptnr. Market Alliances, Chevy Chase, Md., 1991. Author: Chapter Relations Handbook, 1991; editor: The Federal Credit Union, 1986; author: Am. Soc. Assn. Execs. Proc., 1991; pub. AIA Press, 1985. Mem. Am. Mktg. Assn. (v.p. non profit div. 1992), Am. Soc. Assn. Founds. (task force), Greater Washington Soc. Assn. Execs. (com. mem. 1992). Office: Nat Assn Home Builders 15th and M Sts Washington DC 20005

OLIVERI, ROBERT PETER, social worker; b. Patchogue, N.Y., Oct. 1, 1942; s. Ben and Lena (La Valle) O.; B.A., Adelphi U., 1965; M.S.W., SUNY, Albany, 1970; m. Anne Dullberg, June 23, 1973; children: Christopher Robert, Kenneth Mathew. Cert. social worker, N.Y. Community orgn. specialist Suffolk County Dept. Social Service, Hauppauge, N.Y., 1966—; dir. Dataflo Computer Services, Inc., Enfield, N.H., 1987, 88, also bd. dirs.; div. dir. Fgn. Lang. Ednl. Software Div., 1986—; mem. adv. bd. on Decentralization of Social Services in Suffolk County, 1973-74; co-designer award winning programs for Nat. Assn. Counties, 1984, 89; co-author research study on social service delivery. Co-founder Foster Parents Adv. Council of Suffolk, 1972, Ind. Study Group, 1972. With U.S. Army, 1965. Recipient Ednl. Leave award Suffolk County Dept. Social Services, 1969, 70. Mem. Nat. Assn. Social Workers (v.p., dir. Suffolk County chpt. 1972-74, field rep.), Acad. Cert. Social Workers. Home: PO Box 642 Eastport NY 11941-0642 Office: Box 2000 Hauppauge NY 11788

OLIVETO, EUGENE PAUL, organic chemist, consultant; b. N.Y.C., Mar. 15, 1924; s. Joseph and Filomena (Grasso) O.; m. Alma Joyce Bruzza, Nov. 7, 1948; children: Paul, Robert. BS, CCNY, 1943; PhD, Purdue U., 1948. Chemist Schenley Rsch. Inst., Lawrenceburg, Ind., 1943-44; mgr. natural products rsch. Schering-Plough, Bloomfield, N.J., 1948-64; dir. fine chems. rsch. Hoffmann-La Roche, Nutley, N.J., 1964-85; dir. tech. affairs SST Corp., Clifton, N.J., 1985-90; cons., 1985—. Author: (with others) Pyridine & Derivatives, 1962, Organic Reactions in Steroid Chemistry, 1972. Du Pont fellow Purdue U., 1947. Fellow N.Y. Acad. Scis.; mem. ACS, AAAS. Home: 284 Forest Ave Glen Ridge NJ 07028-1808

OLMES, DONALD MARINUS, financial and management consultant; b. Maracaibo, Venezuela, Sept. 8, 1950; came to U.S., 1953; s. Edward Biery and Johanna (Hessels) O.; m. Janet Lynn McMaster; 1 child, Lindsey Jordan McMaster. BA, Grove City (Pa.) Coll., 1972. V.p. Louis M. McMaster, Inc., Eighty Four, Pa., 1973-82; comptroller Weiss Bros. Constrn., McKeesport, Pa., 1982; prin. Olmes & Assocs., Canonsburg, Pa., 1982—; bd. dirs. Somtek, Inc., Winchester Contractors, Inc. Active Falk Sch. PTA. Mem. Inst. Mgmt. Cons., Grove City Alumni Assn., Rivers Club. Home and Office: Olmes & Assocs RR 1 Box 112 Canonsburg PA 15317-9605

OLMSTED, ROBERT WALSH (RICHARD S. DANBURY, III), publisher, editor; b. Washington, Mar. 15, 1936; s. Frances Nicholas (Walsh) O.; m. Elaine B. Olmsted, May 6, 1958; children: Lori Lane Bowman, Suzanne Marie Boas, Julie Elizabeth Lambert, James R. Mason. BA, Mansfield (Pa.) Inst., 1969; BS, Bemidji (Minn.) State Coll., 1974; MA, U. Maine, 1970; PhD, U. Mass., 1977. Ind. ins. salesperson Va. & Pa., 1958-65; tchr. various schs. Maine, N.H., Minn. and, Va., 1970-80; editor, pub. Northwoods Press Inc., 1970-82; pub., editor Conservatory of Am. Letters, Thomaston, Maine, 1982—; Author: Wild Strawberries at 3,000 Feet, 1986, and others. With USAF, 1958. Office: The Olde Rowley Inn Rte 35 North Waterford ME 04267

OLNESS, JOHN WILLIAM, nuclear physicist; b. Broderick, Sask., Can., Sept. 4, 1929; came to U.S., 1932; s. Fredrick Fraas and Esther Victoria (Johnson) O.; m. Margaret Ann Lerro, Aug. 23, 1958; children: Fredrick Iver, Robert Charles, Richard Martin, Christopher Michael, Margaret Kristin. BA, St. Olaf Coll., 1951; PhD, Duke U., 1957. Rsch. assoc. Duke U., Durham, N.C., 1956-58; physicist Aero. Rsch. Labs., Wright-Patterson AFB, Ohio, 1958-63; assoc. physicist Brookhaven Nat. Lab., Upton, N.Y., 1963-68, physicist, 1968—. Author book chpts.; contbr. over 150 articles to sci. jours. V.p. bd. edn. Three Village Schs., L.I., N.Y., 1973-80; chmn. edn. of gifted and talented, 1976-77. Mem. AAAS, Am. Phys. Soc., Sigma Pi Sigma, Sigma Xi. Home: 31 William Penn Dr Stony Brook NY 11790-1325 Office: Brookhaven Nat Lab Physics Bldg 901 A Upton NY 11973

OLSCHWANG, ALAN PAUL, lawyer; b. Chgo., Jan. 30, 1942; s. Morton James and Ida (Ginsberg) O.; m. Barbara Claire Miller, Aug. 22, 1965; children: Elliot, Deborah, Jeffrey. B.S., U. Ill., 1963, J.D., 1966. Bar: Ill. 1966, N.Y. 1984. Law clk. Ill. Supreme Ct., Bloomington, 1966-67; assoc. Sidley & Austin, and predecessor, Chgo., 1967-73; with Montgomery Ward & Co., Inc., Chgo., 1973-81, assoc. gen. counsel, asst. sec., 1979-81; ptnr. Seki, Jarvis & Lynch, Chgo., 1981-84; v.p., gen. counsel, sec. Mitsubishi Electric Am., Inc., N.Y.C., 1983-91, Cypress, Calif., 1991—. Mem. Am. Corp. Counsel Assn., ABA, Ill. Bar Assn., Chgo. Bar Assn., N.Y. State Bar Assn., Bar of Assn. of City of N.Y., Am. Arbitration Assn. (panel arbitrators). Office: Mitsubishi Electric Am 5665 Plaza Dr Cypress CA 90630-5023

OLSEN, DAVID GEORGE, executive search consultant; b. San Francisco, May 3, 1941; s. George Otto and Patricia Marjorie (O'Neill) O.; m. Sandra Jean Amos; children: Cheryl, Kathleen, Janet. BA, U. Calif., Santa Barbara, 1963; MBA, U. So. Calif., 1972. Mktg. rep. IBM Corp., L.A., 1968-76; mktg. support adminstr. IBM Corp., Chgo., 1976-79; mktg. mgr. IBM Corp., Lubbock, Tex., 1979-82; sr. market analyst IBM Corp., White Plains, N.Y., 1982-86; sr. product mktg. adminstr. IBM Corp., Milford, Conn., 1986-89; exec. recruiter Sanford Rose Assocs. of Westchester, Elmsford, N.Y., 1990; pres. Olsen Assocs., Westport, Conn., 1990-91; v.p. Handy HRM, N.Y.C., 1991—. Bd. dirs. Goodwill Industries Lubbock, 1981-82, United Way of Westport-Weston (Conn.), 1982-85; fin. com. Belaga for Gov. Conn., Westport, 1986; mem. Nat. Eagle Scout Assn., 1992—; elected mem. Rep. Town Com., Westport, 1992—. Capt. U.S. Army, 1963-68. Methodist. Home: 3 Spicer Ct Westport CT 06880-4527 Office: Handy HRM 250 Park Ave New York NY 10177-0001

OLSEN, DOUGLAS MARC, personnel manager, artist; b. Levittown, Pa., Apr. 28, 1957; s. Allan Street and Emmajane (Tuttle) O. BA in Studio Art, Principia Coll., Elsah, Ill., 1980. Typesetter, designer Wren Assocs., Princeton, N.J, 1980-85; designer The Speaker Support Group, Princeton, N.J, 1985-86; personnel mgr. Tenacre Found., Princeton, N.J, 1986—; free-lance artist, Trenton, N.J., 1979—. Exhibited in group shows at Lambertville, Trenton, Skillman, N.J., New Hope, Pa., St. Louis; one man shows include St. Louis, Lambertville, New Hope. Lay reader 1st Ch. Christ Scientist, Trenton, 1984-87. Mem. Trenton Artists Workshop Assn. (sec. 1980-81). Home and Office: PO Box 632 Princeton NJ 08542-0632

OLSEN, JOHN WILLIAM, labor union administrator; b. Greenwich, Conn., Mar. 27, 1950; s. William and Helen (Coombs) O.; m. Rose Smeriglio, Apr. 18, 1971; children: Amy, Elizabeth, Christopher. Student, Wright Tech. Sch., 1973. Apprentice Greenwich Plumbing and Heating, 1969-79; journeyman Stockenboyjer Plumbing and Heating, Greenwich, 1979-81; bus. mgr. U.A. Local 133, Greenwich, 1981-87, pres., 1978-79; sec., treas. Conn. State AFL-CIO, West Hartford, 1987-88, pres., 1988—; truste Fairfield-New Haven Apprenticeship Sch., Bridgeport, 1983—, Conn. Plumbers and Pipefitters Pension Fund, Wallingford, 1979—; mem., subchair Conn. Employment and Tng. Com., Wethersfield, 1989—; mem. Conn. Innovations, Inc., Rocky Hill, 1989—. Mem. Dem. State Cen. Com., Hartford, 1986—, Greenwich Dem. Town Exec. Com., 1980—, Gov.'s Bldg. and Constrn. Adv. Com., Hartford, 1987-90, Gov.'s Mgmt. Study Commn., Hartford, 1989-91. Mem. Greenwich Bldg. and Constrn. Trades (pres. 1983-87), Kiwanis (2d v.p. Greenwich chpt. 1987-88). Democrat. Roman Catholic. Office: Conn State AFL-CIO 30 Sherman St West Hartford CT 06110-1997

OLSEN, KENNETH HARRY, manufacturing company executive; b. Bridgeport, Conn., Feb. 20, 1926; s. Oswald and Svea (Nordling) O.; m. Eeva-Liisa Aulikki Valve, Dec. 12, 1950. B.S. in Elec. Engring, MIT, 1950, M.S., 1952. Elec. engr. Lincoln Lab., MIT, 1950-57; founder Digital Equipment Corp., Maynard, Mass., 1957, now pres., chief exec. officer; bd. dirs. Polaroid Corp., Ford Motor Co. Patentee magnetic devices. Mem. Pres.'s Sci. Adv. Com., 1971-73; trustee, v.p. Joslin Diabetes Found.; mem. corp. Wentworth Inst., Boston, MIT, Cambridge; trustee Gordon Coll., Wenham, Mass. Served with USNR, 1944-46. Named Young Elec. Engr. of Year Eta Kappa Nu, 1960. Mem. Nat. Acad. Engring. Office: Digital Equipment Corp 146 Main St Maynard MA 01754-2504*

OLSEN, KEVIN HARRY, cardiologist; b. N.Y.C., Dec. 19, 1956; s. Wilbur and Edith (Reitz) O.; m. Monica Fick. BA, Columbia U., 1978; MD, U. Conn., 1982. Intern internal medicine Lenox Hill Hosp., N.Y.C., 1982-83, resident internal medicine, 1983-85; rsch. fellow cardiology Hartford (Conn.) Hosp., 1985-87, lectr. recovery room nursing and surg. staff, 1985-87; instr. clin. cardiology U. Conn. Sch. Medicine, 1985-87; asst. prof. medicine UMDNJ-Robert Wood Johnson Med. Sch., New Brunswick, N.J., 1987-88; clin. asst. prof. medicine Hahnemann U., Phila., 1989—; dir. invasive cardiology Lackawanna Med. Group, Scranton, Pa., 1988-91; attending physician Community Med. Ctr., Scranton, Mercy Hosp., Scranton, Carbondale (Pa.) Gen. Hosp., Moses Taylor Hosp., Scranton, Robert Wood Johnson Univ. Hosp., New Brunswick, N.J., 1987-88; attending physician, courtesy staff St. Joseph Hosp., Carbondale, Allied Health Svcs., Scranton; attending physician courtesy med. staff sect. cardiology St. Peter's Med. Ctr., New Brunswick, 1987-88; lectr., pseaker in field. Fellow Am. Coll. Cardiology; mem. AMA, Am. Coll. Physicians, Pa. Med. Soc., Lackawanna County Med. Soc. Home: 906 Violet Ter Waverly PA 18471-9999 Office: Cardiovascular Cons Ltd 201 Franklin Ave Scranton PA 18503-1911

OLSEN, LEIF OLE, psychologist, consultant; b. Copenhagen, Mar. 22, 1921; s. Frederick Christian and Helen (Hansen) O.; m. Mary Jane Deletto, Aug. 9, 1979. BA, NYU, 1949, MA, 1950, PhD, 1960. Dir. personnel Am. Cyanamid, N.Y.C., 1949-52, cons., 1952-55; dir. personnel Am. Cancer Soc., N.Y.C., 1955-57, v.p. personnel, 1964-79; dir. mgmt. devel. Allied Chem. Corp., N.Y.C., 1957-61; pres. Percom, Point Pleasant Beach, N.J., 1979—; pvt. practice psychology, N.Y.C., 1961-64. Mem. Am. Psychol. Assn., Eastern Psychol. Assn., Mgmt. Devel. Forum (v.p., pres. 1958-60), Am. Tentative Soc. (trustee 1989—). Home and Office: 5194 Siesta Woods Dr Sarasota FL 34242-1457

OLSEN, ROBERT JOHN, savings and loan association executive; b. N.Y.C., July 8, 1928; s. Christian Marinius and Agnes Geraldine (Jensen) O.; m. Eleanor Marion Peters, June 19, 1981; 1 child, Philip John. BS, Strayer Coll., 1956. Supervisory agt. Fed. Home Loan Bank Bd., N.Y.C., 1956-65; pres., dir. Keystone Savs. & Loan Assn., Asbury Park, N.J., 1965-82; chmn. bd., pres. Rapid Money Svcs., Inc., Deal, N.J., 1977-82, Elmora Savs. and Loan Assn., Elizabeth, N.J., 1982-88; pres. Ramsey (N.J.) Savs. and Loan Assn., 1988-90; pres., mng. agt. Resolution Trust Corp., 1990—; also bd. dirs. Ramsey (N.J.) Savs. and Loan Assn.; pres. 2d Century Corp., Asbury Park, 1980-82; dir. Central Corp. of Savs. & Loans, Newark, 1976-82, Fed. Home Loan Bank N.Y., 1974-77. Councilman, Borough of Oceanport, N.J., 1971-73, 77-80, pres., 1979; police commr. Oceanport, N.J., 1972-80; v.p. Econ. Devel. Corp., Asbury Park, N.J., 1972-81, Oceanport, N.J., 1974-77; mem. Zoning Bd. of Adjustment, Oceanport, 1969-70; mem. Citizens Adv. Coun., Oceanport, 1975-76; dir. Monmouth and Ocean Devel. Coun., Eatontown, N.J., 1974-82; trustee Savs. and Loan Found. of Washington, 1978-82; chmn. N.J. Electronic Funds Transfer Com., 1971-82; mem. Monmouth County Fair Housing Task Force, 1980-82, Monmouth County Vocat. Sch. Bd., 1981-83; pres. Paulinskill Lake Assn., 1987-90, chpt. 56 Heart Assn., Morristown, N.J., 1989. Served with USMC, 1946-48, 1950-56. Mem. N.J. Savs. League (pres. chpt. 1966-67), U.S. Savs. League (vice chmn. com. on internal ops., chmn. remote svc. unit com.), Nat. Assn. Review Appraisers and Mortgage Underwriters, Fin. Mgrs. Soc. (adv. coun.), Nat. Assn. Savs. and Loan Suprs., Nat. Soc. Fin. Examiners, Monmouth County, Eastern Union County Realtors Assn., Sussex County Realtors Assn., Internat. Union Bldg. Socs. and Savs. Assns., Navy League, Assn. U.S. Army., World Trade Club (N.Y.C.), Channel Club (Monmouth Beach, N.J.), Provost Marshals Guild Club (Ft. Monmouth, N.J.), Wheelman's Club (Asbury Park). Home: RR 6 Box 508 Newton NJ 07860-9256 Office: Ramsey Savs & Loan Assn 300 Davidson Ave Somerset NJ 08873

OLSEN, ROLF ARTHUR, JR., sales executive; b. Albany, N.Y., Oct. 1, 1956; s. Rolf A. and Marcelle (More) O.; m. Brenda J. McLellan, Oct. 6, 1984. BBA, U. Maine, 1982. Shop mgr. Naples (Maine) Marina, 1976-79; assembly leadman Dielectric Communications, Raymond, ME, 1979-82, sales adminstr., 1982-84, dir. RF sales, 1984—. Office: Dielectric Communications Tower Hill Rd Raymond ME 04071

OLSHANSKY, PHYLLIS MACKLIN, psychologist; b. N.Y.C., July 19, 1929; d. Joseph and Dorothy (Chasnoff) Macklin; m. Murray Olshansky, Mar. 26, 1950; children: Brian, Emily Macklin, Nicolas Ivan. BA, NYU, 1950, MA, 1961, 64; PhD, Yeshiva U., 1971. Psychologist trainee Jewish Family Services, Bronx and Mt. Vernon, N.Y., 1965-70; lectr. Iona Coll., New Rochelle, N.Y., 1968-69; psychologist Guidance Ctr., New Rochelle, 1969-84, dir. clin. services, 1984—. Mem. Am. Psychol. Assn., N.Y. State Psychol. Assn., Westchester County Psychol. Assn. Democrat. Home: 60 Lakeview Rd New Rochelle NY 10804-2506 Office: Guidance Ctr 875 Mamaroneck Rd Mamaroneck NY 10543-1900

OLSHEN, PAUL ROBERT, insurance broker, consultant; b. N.Y.C., June 4, 1938; s. Henry and Ethel H. (Horowitz) O.; m. Vivian Ina Cohen, July 21, 1940; children: Lisa, Andrew. BA, NYU, Heights, 1960. Prin. Henry B. Olshen & Assocs., N.Y.C., 1960-67; v.p. BRI Coverage Corp., N.Y.C., 1967—; pres. PRO Consultants, Inc., N.Y.C., 1987—. Pres. Livingston (N.J.) Jaycees, 1973; bd. dirs. Temple Beth Shalom, Livingston, 1985—, v.p., 1989; past chmn. Livingston Planning Bd.; Livingston Reclamation. Named Citizen of Month, Livingston Town Council, 1987. Mem. Coun. Ins. Brokers Greater N.Y., Profl. Ins. Agts. N.Y., Independent Ins. Agts. Assn. of N.Y., Livingston Democrat Club. Jewish. Home: 3 Highland Dr Livingston NJ 07039-2808 Office: PRO Consultants Inc 156 William St New York NY 10038-2609

OLSINSKI, PETER KEVIN, international outplacement executive; b. N.Y.C., Aug. 27, 1942; s. Peter Andrew and Mary Lucinda (O'Connor) O.; m. Joan Mary Mahon; children: Marybeth, Peter John. BA, Cathedral Coll., 1964; MS, St. John's U., Jamaica, N.Y., 1971; PhD, St. John's U., 1979. Dir. pers. Bklyn. Diocese, 1968-84; dir. Mainstream Access, N.Y.C., 1984-85; v.p. Fuchs Cuthrell & Co., N.Y.C., 1985-88; sr. v.p. Fuchs Cuthrell & Co., 1988, exec. v.p., 1989-91, sr. exec. v.p., 1991—. Mem. Somerset Hills Hist. Soc., N.J. Mem. Am. Psychol. Assn., Soc. for Indsl. & Orgnizational Psychology, Am. Soc. for Tng. and Devel., Soc. Human Resource Mgmt. Roman Catholic. Office: Fuchs Cuthrell & Co Inc 555 Madison Ave New York NY 10022-3301

OLSON, BONNIE WAGGONER-BRETERNITZ (MRS. O. DONALD OLSON), civic worker; b. North Platte, Nebr.; d. Floyd Emil and Edith (Waggoner) Breternitz; AB, U. Chgo., 1947; m. O. Donald Olson, May 17, 1944; children: Pamela Lynne, Douglas Donald. Dep. clk. Dist. Ct., Lincoln County, Nebr., 1940-42; advt. researcher Burke & Assocs., Chgo., 1942; contbg. newspaper columnist Chgo. Herald-Am., 1943; social worker A.R.C., Chgo., 1942-44, Sacramento, Calif., 1944, Amarillo, Tex., 1945; exec. sec. Econometrica, Cowles Commn. for Rsch. in Econs., Chgo., 1945-47; interior designer, antique dealer. Col.; participant Chgo. Maternity Ctr. Fund Drive, 1953, Chgo. Coun. on Fgn. Rels., 1948-54; mem. Colo. Springs Community Council, 1956-58, chmn. children's div., 1956-58, mem. exec. bd., 1956-58, mem. budget com., 1957-58; mem. Colorado Springs Charter Assn., 1956-60, mem. exec. bd., 1957-59, sec., 1958; chmn. El Paso County PTA, Protective Svcs. for Children, 1959-61; chmn. women's div. fund drive ARC, 1961; mem. League Women Voters, 1957—, mem. state children's law com., 1961-63; chmn. ad hoc com. El Paso County Citizens' Com. for Nat. Probation and Parole Survey, Juvenile Ct. Procedures and Detention, 1957-61; mem. children's adv. com. Colo. Child Welfare Dept., 1959-63, chmn., 1961; del. White House Conf. on Children and Youth, 1960, 70; sec. Citizens Ad Hoc Com. for Comprehensive Mental Health Clinic for Pikes Peak Region, 1966—; mem. Colorado Springs Human Rels. Commn., 1968-71; sustaining mem. Symphony Guild, 1970-72, Fine Arts Ctr., 1957—; mem. Pikes Peak Mental Health Ctr., 1964-67 (bd. dirs.); Colo. observer White House Conf. on Aging, 1981, Colo. Gov.'s Conf. on Aging, 1981, Dist. Atty.'s Child Abuse Task Force, 1986; participant Not Just a Job career planning documentary film Not Just a Job, Radcliffe Coll. Career Svcs., 1990. Recipient Lane Bryant Ann. Nat. Awards citation, 1971; alumni citation for pub. service U. Chgo., 1961. Mem. Am. Acad. Polit. and Social Sci., Nat. Trust Historic Preservation, Women's Ednl. Soc. Colo. Coll. (life), Council on Religion and Internat. Affairs. Episcopalian. Clubs: Quadranglar, University (Chgo.). Home: 86 Buckboard Rd Duxbury MA 02332-4701

OLSON, CARL ERIC, lawyer; b. Center Moriches, N.Y., May 19, 1914; s. August William and Sophie (Maiwald) O.; m. Ila Dudley Yeatts, May 31, 1945; children: Carl Eric, William Yeatts, Nancy Dudley. AB, Union Coll., 1936; JD, Yale, 1940. Bar: Conn. 1941, N.Y. 1947. Assoc. Clark, Hall & Peck, New Haven, 1940-41; assoc. Reid & Priest, N.Y.C., 1946-56, ptnr. 1956-80; pvt. practice, Palm Beach Gardens, Fla., 1981—. Maj. U.S. Army, 1941-45. Mem. ABA, Assn. of Bar of City of N.Y., Am. Arbitration Assn., Inter-Am. Bar Assn., Internat. Bar Assn., Yale Club, PGA Nat. Club. Republican. Congregationalist. Home and Office: 6 Surrey Rd West Palm Beach FL 33418-7088

OLSON, CARL L., educator; b. Newark, N.J., Nov. 12, 1941; s. Carl L. and Rose (Haspel) O.; m. Margaret Eisenhower, June 29, 1968; children: Holly Olson, Kelly Olson. BA, Pa. State U., 1967; MDiv magna cum laude, Drew Theol. Sch., 1970; PhD, Drew U., 1977. Instr. Trenton (N.J.) State Coll., 1976-78; asst. prof. So. Ill. U., Carbondale, Ill., 1978-79, U. N.D., Grand Forks, 1979-80; assoc. prof. Allegheny Coll., Meadville, Pa., 1981—. Author: The Theology and Philosophy of Eliade: A Search for the Centre, 1982, The Mysterious Play of Kali: An Interpretive Study of Ramakrishna, 1990; editor: The Book of the Goddess, 1983; contbr. articles to profl. jours. Mem. Am. Asian Soc., Am. Oriental Soc., Am. Acad. Religion, Soc. for Asian and Comparative Philosophy. Office: Allegheny Coll PO Box 122 Meadville PA 16335-0122

OLSON, CHARLES ERIC, economist; b. Wausau, Wis., June 2, 1942; s. Roland Anthony and Lois (Erickson) O.; student U. Wis., Marathon County, 1960-62; B.B.A. with honors, U. Wis., Madison, 1964, M.S., 1966, Ph.D. (Vilias fellow), 1968; m. Pamela Ann Templin, July 1, 1967 (div. Oct. 1973), children—Sonja Anne, Erika Christine; m. 2d, Carole Emily Collesian, Dec. 1, 1973 (div. Oct. 1990); children—Cora Elizabeth, Sarah Emily; m. 3d, Jeanne Esther Katz, Apr. 14, 1991. Instr., U. Wis., Madison, 1966-68; asst. prof. U. Md., College Park, 1968-71, assoc. prof. bus. adminstrn., 1971-76; sr. economist H. Zinder & Assos., Washington, 1976—, v.p., 1977-79, sr. v.p., 1979—; pres. Olson & Co., Inc., 1980-86, pres. H. Zinder and Assocs., 1986—; cons. Devel. Adv. Service, atty. gens. N.C., Minn., Ky., Mass., Va. U.S. Postal Rate Commn., Dept. Def., numerous electric and gas utilities in U.S. and Can. Testified numerous pub. utility rate cases, before Senate Subcom. on Inter-govtl. Relations; mem. advisory com. research and devel. and energy conservation Fed. Power Commn., 1973-74, vice chmn. rate design task force, 1976—. Mem. Prince Georges County (Md.) Citizens Airpark Advisory Com., 1970-71. Inst. Pub. Utilities grantee, 1967-68; U. Md. grantee, 1970, 76. Mem. Am. Econ. Assn., Transp. and Pub. Utilities Group, Beta Gamma Sigma, Delta Sigma Pi. Author: Cost Considerations for Efficient Electricity Supply, 1970. Contbr. chpts. to books, articles to profl. jours. Home: 10822 Alloway Dr Rockville MD 20854-1503 Office: 1828 L St NW Washington DC 20036

OLSON, DAVID CHALMERS, investment banker; b. N.Y.C., June 11, 1952; s. James C. and Jean (Stewart) O.; m. Tara Ann Nicholson, Sept. 29, 1979; children: Morgan Katherine, Meredith Christina. AB cum laude, Harvard U., 1974, MBA, 1978. Credit analyst U.S. Trust Co., N.Y.C., 1974-76; assoc. Smith Barney Harris Upham, N.Y.C., 1978-81; 2d v.p. Smith Barney Harris Upham, London, 1981-82; dir. investment banking Credit Suisse First Boston Ltd., London, 1982-88, N.Y.C., 1988-90; mng. dir. Nordberg Capital Inc., N.Y.C., 1990-91; exec. dir. Chartered West LB Ltd., N.Y.C., 1991—; bd. dirs. Chartered West LB Ltd., London, 1991—. Spl. gifts chmn. Harvard Coll. Fund, Cambridge, 1974, head class agt., 1975-80; agt. Harvard Bus. Sch. Fund, Cambridge, 1980-84; mem. Deerfield (Mass.) Acad. Alumni Exec. Com., 1990—. Mem. Deerfield Acad. Alumni Assn. (pres. 1992—, trustee 1992—), Univ. Club, Apawamis Club, Mansuring Island Club, Valderrama Swim Club (Spain), Royal Mid Surrey Golf Club (Eng.). Presbyterian. Home: 431 Grace Church St Rye NY 10580-4203

OLSON, FRANK ALBERT, car rental company executive; b. San Francisco, July 19, 1932; s. Alfred and Edith Mary (Hazeldine) O.; m. Sarah Jean Blakely, Oct. 19, 1957; children—Kimberly, Blake, Christopher. AA, City Coll. San Francisco, 1961. V.p. and gen. mgr. Barrett Transp. Inc., San Francisco, 1950-64; v.p., gen. mgr. Valcar Co. subs. Hertz Corp., San Francisco, 1964-68; mgr. N.Y. zone Hertz Corp., N.Y.C., 1968-69, v.p., mgr. eastern region, v.p., gen. mgr. rent-a-car div., exec. v.p. rent-a-car div., gen. mgr., also bd. dirs., 1973-77, pres., chief exec. officer, 1977-80, chmn. bd., 1980, also dir., chief exec. officer, from 1982; chmn., chief exec. officer Allegis Corp., 1987; pres., chief exec. officer United Airlines, 1987; chmn., chief exec. officer Hertz Corp., Park Ridge, N.J., 1987—; bd. dirs. UAL, Becton Dickinson & Co., Cooper Industries. Trustee Nat. Commn. Against Drunk Driving; bd. dirs. Nat. Multiple Sclerosis Soc., World Travel & Tourism Coun., Ethics Resource Ctr., Inc., Swedish-Am. C. of C., Inc.; bd. visitors Berry Coll., Duke U., Fuqua Sch. of Bus. Mem. Olympic Club (Calif.), Pine Valley Golf Club (N.J.), Royal and Ancient St. Andrews (Scotland), Arcola Country Club (Paramus, N.J.), Metropolitan (N.Y.C.). Republican. Roman Catholic. Office: Hertz Corp 225 Brae Blvd Park Ridge NJ 07656-1870

OLSON, HAROLD ROY, computer company executive; b. Escanaba, Mich., Apr. 8, 1928; s. Roy A. and Sara Calla Margarita (Carlson) O.; B.A. in Journalism and Advt., Mich. State U., 1950; m. Angela Davis Hennessy, Sept. 26, 1959. Mail clk. McCann Erickson Co., N.Y.C., 1950, 52-53; book promotion specialist, mgr. mag. promotion McGraw-Hill, N.Y.C., 1953-56; mgr. mag. promotion Reinhold Publishing Co., N.Y.C., 1956-58; space salesman McCall Corp., N.Y.C., 1959-60; pres. Visual Identity, Inc., N.Y.C., 1960-68; mktg. rep. Honeywell Info. Systems, Inc., N. N.Y.C., 1969-86; pres. Hal Olson's EDGE-BUY Express, Inc., 1986—. Served with U.S. Army, 1950-52. Republican. Episcopalian. Home: 12 Stone Dr Westport CT 06880-1225 Office: 26 Quirk Rd Milford CT 06460-3745

OLSON, JEFFREY WILLIAM, editor, writer; b. Evanston, Ill., Jan. 18, 1958; s. William Bernhard and Jeanne (Caldwell) O.; m. Christina Higginson Wadsworth, June 11, 1983; 1 child, Louisa Wadsworth. BA, U. Colo., 1980; AM, U. Chgo., 1983. Salesman/editor New Eng. Press, Shelburne, Vt., 1983-86, mng. editor, 1986-90; sr. editor Soundview Exec. Book Summaries, Bristol, Vt., 1990—; pres., pub. Regional Facts, Inc., Middlebury, Vt., 1986—. Editor: The Vermont Almanac, 1989, 91; contbr. articles, rev. to profl. jours. Home: RR 1 Box 164 Middlebury VT 05753-9620 Office: Soundview Exec Book Summaries 5 Main St Bristol VT 05443-1398

OLSON, LEROY CALVIN, educational administration educator; b. Kane, Pa., Mar. 7, 1926; s. Vernon Reinhold and Gertrude Viola (Hutchins) O.; m. Miriam Marie Vogler, June 19, 1954; children—David Lee, Thomas Edward, Steven Andrew. B.S., Clarion State Coll., 1949; M.Ed., Pa. State Coll., 1950; Ed.D., Pa. State U., 1962; postgrad., U. Del., 1964-65. Tchr.-counselor Boiling Springs (Pa.) High Sch., 1950-52, Gordon Jr. High Sch., Coatesville, Pa., 1952-54; guidance dir. Cen. Dauphin Sch. Dist., Harrisburg, Pa., 1954-57; coordinator pupil personnel services, asst. supt. for instrn. and personnel, acting supt. Alfred I. duPont Sch. Dist., Wilmington, Del., 1957-65; prof. ednl. adminstrn. Temple U., Phila., 1965—; cons. to schs. bds. and dists., also Nat., Wis., Pa. sch. bds. assns. Contbr. articles to profl. jours. Trustee Luth. Ch., 1963-66, chmn. bd., 1976-78, chmn. various coms., discussion groups. Served with USNR, 1944-46, PTO. Recipient Disting. Alumni award Clarion State Coll., 1972. Mem. Am. Personnel and Guidance Assn., AAUP, Am. Assn. Sch. Personnel Adminstrs., Assn. Supervision and Curriculum Devel., Council Profs. Instrn. Supervision, Nat. Staff Devel. Council, Am. Legion, Phi Delta Kappa, Phi Kappa Phi. Republican. Home: 231 Prospect Dr Wilmington DE 19803-5331 Office: Temple U 242 Ritter Hall Philadelphia PA 19122

OLSON, MARK WILLIAM, magazine editor, magazine publisher; b. Chgo., July 3, 1946; s. David Cornelius and Dorothy Ilene (Pomeroy) O.; m. Joan Lea Toms, Aug. 17, 1969. BA, Wheaton Coll., 1968; MDiv, Bethel Theol. Sem., 1971; MS in Journalism, Northwestern U., 1972. Sr. high editor David C. Cook Pub. Co., Elgin, Ill., 1972-74; mng. editor The Other Side mag., Phila., 1974-77, co-editor, 1977-84, editor, 1984-89, editor, pub., 1989—. Baptist. Office: The Other Side 300 W Apsley Philadelphia PA 19144

OLSON, OSCAR JULIUS, international economist; b. Corpus Christi, Tex., Mar. 31, 1933; s. Oscar Julius and Kate (Arnold) O.; m. Patricia Kay Whipple, Nov. 12, 1955; children: Michael Alan, Kirsten Anne Olson Pruski, Kathleen Kay. BA, U. Tex., 1954; MA, Yale U., 1957; postgrad., Fletcher Sch. Law & Diplomacy, Medford, Mass., 1966-67. Fgn. svc. officer Dept. of State, Washington, 1957-84; exec. dir. U.S. Man & the Biosphere Program, Washington, 1976-80; counselor of embassy Am. Embassy, Quito, Ecuador, 1982-84; dir. Latin Am. BERI S.A., Washington, 1985—; cons. internat. office Smithsonian Instn., Washington, 1984-85, Dept. of State, Washington, 1985—. Vice pres. Civitan Club of Arlington, Va., 1991—. Mem. Am. Fgn. Svc. Assn., Diplomatic and Consular Officers, Retired, Sons of Norway, Phi Beta Kappa. Methodist. Home: Rt 70 Box 39A Lignum VA 22726 Office: Beri SA 1808 Swann St NW Washington DC 20009

OLSON, PETER WESLEY, international business educator; b. Amityville, N.Y., June 13, 1950; s. Wesley Harry and Mildred Constance (Petersen) O.; m. Donna Marie Marmorale, July 13, 1974; children: Jessica Marie, Jacqueline Nicole, Stephanie Anne. BA, L.I. Univ., 1972, MBA, 1977. Svc/sales rep. Otis Elevator Co., L.I. City, N.Y., 1973-75; internat. sales rep. Otis Elevator Co., N.Y.C., 1975-79; exec. asst. to v.p. NAO United Techs., Inc., Farmington, Conn., 1979-81; internat. sales mgr. Allied Bronze Corp., L.I. City, 1981-83; pres. Internat. Techs., Inc., Windsor, Conn., 1983-88; prof., curriculum chair, internat. mgmt. Hartford Grad. Ctr., Hartford, Conn., 1988—; exec. dir. internat. devel. Conn. World Trade Inst. (subs. Conn. World Trade Assn., Hartford, 1989—; bd.dirs. China Investment Group, N.Y.C.; mem. adv. bd. dirs. Conn. World Trade Assn., Hartford, 1988—, mem. edn. com., 1988—. Chmn. Spl. Olympics, Windsor, 1983-84; bd. dirs. Earthside Found., Ocala, Fla., 1984-86; elder, mem. edn. com. Trinity Luth. Ch.; lt. Locust Valley Vol. Fire Dept., 1987—. Mem. Am. Mgmt. Assn., Entrepreneurs Assn., Fireman's Exempt Assn., Masons, Kiwanis (v.p. Windsor club 1984), Delta Mu Delta (Nu chpt. pres. 1977-78). Republican. Lutheran. Home: 6 Cedar Ave Locust Valley NY 11560-2341 Office: Hartford Grad Ctr 275 Windsor St Hartford CT 06120-2910

OLSON, RONALD KENNETH, computer consultant; b. Everett, Mass., May 28, 1943; s. Harry Augustine and Mildred Elizabeth (Peterson) O.; m. Joanne Elena Angrisano, Sept. 6, 1965; children: Kristopher Robert, Scott Ronald. Student, Tufts U., 1961-63, U. Md., Wiesbaden, Fed. Republic Germany, 1964-67, Fla. State U., 1967-68; BS in Computer Sci., Boston U., 1971. Sr. programmer Jordan Marsh, Boston, 1968-69; cons. Mgmt. Techniques, Newton, Mass., 1969-71; with Wayside Road Distbn. Ctr. Houghton-Mifflin Co., Burlington, Mass., 1971-73; sr. cons. Interactive Data Corp., Waltham, Mass., 1973-77; project leader Digital Equipment Corp., Maynard, Mass., 1977-80; project mgr., prin. engr. Prime Computer, Inc., Framingham, Mass., 1980-86; pres., sr. systems cons. RKO Systems, Salem, Mass., 1986-91; sr. product support rep. Intersolv, Inc., Cambridge, Mass., 1991—; cons. micro-computer selection com. Salem Pub. Schs., 1984, mentor mid. sch. talented and gifted program, 1985; staff writer Drum Corps Digest, 1970-72, Drum Corps News, 1972-74; instr. evening div. Northeastern U., Boston, 1982—. Pub. rels. dir. 27th Lancers Drum and Bugle Corps, Revere, Mass., 1970-76; coach Salem Youth Soccer, 1980-87; campaign worker O'Donnell for Mayor, Salem, 1980, 82; precinct capt. Centorino for Mayor, Salem, 1986, Gauthier for Mayor, Salem, 1988, Johnson for Mayor, 1989; v.p. St. John's Prep. Father's Club, 1987-88, pres., 1988-90. With USAF, 1964-68. Fellow Boston Computer Soc., Vasa Order Am. (rec. sec. Wenham, Mass. 1988-89). Home and Office: 22 Puritan Rd Salem MA 01970-1250

OLSTEIN, STEPHEN JEFFREY, real estate portfolio manager; b. Huntington, N.Y., Aug. 11, 1952; s. Alan Herbert and Eunice (Townsend) O.; m. Claire McIlwaine, Oct. 17, 1987; children: William R., Elizabeth M. BS, NYU, 1978. Mgmt. analyst TIAA, N.Y.C., 1978-81; v.p. acquisitions Pan Am. Properties Inc., N.Y.C., 1981-82; mng. dir. CIGNA Real Estate Investors, Hartford, Conn., 1983—. With USMC, 1970-73. Office: CIGNA Real Estate Investors S-318 Hartford CT 06152-0002

OLTROGGE, CAL G., human resources executive, psychologist; b. Vallejo, Calif., Dec. 11, 1945; s. George Henry and Eula Maxine (White) O.; m. Gayle Ellen Osborne, June 5, 1965 (div. Dec. 1976); 1 child, David; m. Margaret Marie Bersano, Dec. 27, 1985. AA, Foothill Coll., Los Altos Hills, Calif., 1966; BA, U. Calif., L.A., 1968; MA, Stanford U., 1969; PhD, NYU, 1982. Organizational cons. N.Y.C., 1977-82; personnel rsch. assoc. IBM Corp., Boca Raton, Fla., 1982-83, staff instr. mgmt. devel., 1983-85; sr. personnel rsch. assoc. IBM Corp., Armonk, N.Y., 1985-87; mgr. compensation, benefits IBM Corp., N.Y.C., 1987-89, mgr. exec. resource programs, 1989—; assoc. prof. Fla. Atlantic U., Boca Raton, 1985; prof. Polytech. U., Bklyn., 1989—; prof. Pace U., N.Y.C., 1990—. Capt. U.S. Army, 1970-81. Decorated Commendation medal with one oak leaf cluster; Warburg fellow, 1973. Mem. Soc. for Indsl. and Organization Psychology, Am. Psychol. Assn., Phi Beta Kappa, N.Y. Pipe Club. Democrat. Home: 37 W 72d St Apt 10A New York NY 10023 Office: IBM Corp 590 Madison Ave New York NY 10022-2505

OLVER, JOHN WALTER, congressman; b. Honesdale, Pa., Sept. 3, 1936; s. Helen Fulleborn Olver; m. Rose Alice Richardson, Sept. 12, 1959; children—Martha, Jane. B.S., Rensselaer Poly. Inst., 1955; M.S., Tufts U., 1956; Ph.D., MIT, 1961. Asst. prof. chemistry, U. Mass., Amherst, 1962-68; mem. Mass. Ho. of Reps., Boston, 1969-72, Mass. Senate, 1973-91; mem. U.S. House of Reps. from 1st dist. Mass., Washington, 1991—. Contbr. articles to profl. jours. Democrat. Avocations: hiking; gardening; tennis. Address: US House of Reps Offices of House Members Washington DC 20515*

O'MALLEY, EDWARD PATRICK, accountant, educator; b. N.Y.C., July 31, 1947; s. Edward Patrick and Patricia Mary (Haley) O'M.; m. Rosemary Ann Dowling, Apr. 21, 1973; children: Timothy, Kelly, Maura. BS in Acctg., Fordham U., 1969; MBA in Fin., U. Conn., 1978. CPA, Conn. Sr. acct. Arthur Young & Co., N.Y.C., 1969-72; mgr. treasury Citizens Utilities Co., Stamford, Conn., 1972-76; asst. treas. Internat. Housing Ltd., Wesport, Conn., 1976-80; contr. KEW Photo Labs., Norwalk, Conn., 1980, Fin. Acctg. Found., Norwalk, 1980-86; ptnr. Ruzek O'Malley Burns, Newtown, Conn., 1986—; asst. prof. Teikyo Post U., Waterbury, Conn., 1986-91. Mem. AICPA, Conn. Soc. CPAs, Nat. Assn. Accts. Home: 7 Marc Rd Danbury CT 06810-8262 Office: Ruzek O'Malley Burns 52 Church St Newtown CT 06470

O'MALLEY, EUGENE FRANCIS, investment banker; b. Boston, Mar. 27, 1950; s. Charles Desloge and Mary Louise (Drew) O'M.; m. Kathleen Marie Sullivan, July 10, 1982; children: Charles, Allison, Ryan. BS in Fin., Boston Coll., 1972; MBA, Fordham U., 1979. Cons. Theodore Barry & Assocs., N.Y.C., 1979-82; sr. cons. Touche Ross & Co., Boston, 1982-83; pres. Commerx., Ltd., Boston, 1983-85, Faneuil Hall Capital Group, Boston, 1985-87, Mercant, Inc., Boston, 1988—; ind. cons. Arthur D. Little, Cambridge, Mass., 1988—; Blackstone Ventures, 1989—; incorporator, bd. dirs. Wainwright Bank & Trust, Boston, Seveon Trent Internat. Mem. N.Y. Athletic Club. Roman Catholic. Home: 16 Ravine Rd Wellesley MA 02181-1425 Office: One Boston Pl Boston MA 02108

O'MALLEY, HONOR, hearing educator; b. N.Y.C., Oct. 11; d. Thomas and Josephine (Navoni) O'M.; m. Roger N. Anderson; children: Roger, Jon, Forrest. BA, Marymount Manhattan Coll., 1971; MS, Purdue U., 1973, PhD, 1977. NSF postdoctoral research fellow Northwestern U., Evanston, Ill., 1978; assoc. prof., coord. audiology programs and hearing rsch. lab. Tchrs. Coll., Columbia U., N.Y.C., 1978—. Contbr. articles to profl. jours. Postdoctoral Research fellow NIH, 1977. Mem. Acoustical Soc. Am. (tech. com. 1985-88), Am. Speech, Lang. and Hearing Assn. (audiologic standards com. 1988—), Assn. for Research on Otolaryngology, Am. Geophys. Union. Home: 106 Morningside Dr Apt 51 New York NY 10027-6011 Office: Tchrs Coll Columbia U 525 W 120th St New York NY 10027-6625

O'MALLEY, JOHN EDWARD, medical association administrator, physician; b. Detroit, Oct. 27, 1942; s. Jack Patrick and Anne C. (Jones) O'M.; m. Carol Ann Dellicolli, Aug. 22, 1963; children: Dawn, April. BS, U. Mich., 1963, MD, 1967. Diplomate Am. Bd. Psychiatry and Neurology, diplomate Am. Bd. Med. Mgmt. Pediatric intern Johns Hopkins Hosp., Balt., 1967-68; resident child psychiatry I Hawthorn Ctr., Northville, Mich., 1968-69; resident adult psychiatry II, III Mass. Gen. Hosp., Boston, 1969-71, resident child psychiatry IV, 1971-72; sr. assoc. Children's Hosp., Boston, 1974-85; asst. prof. Harvard Med. Sch., 1974-85; psychiatrist Sidney Farber

Cancer Inst., Boston, 1975-81; attending psychiatrist McLean Hosp., Belmont, Mass., 1985-86; med. dir. Greenville (S.C.) Hosp. System, 1985-87, Meml. Hosp. South Bend, Ind., 1987-88; v.p. clin. affairs The Devereux Found., Devon, Pa., 1988—; clin. assoc. prof. Jefferson Med. Coll., 1990—, U. Pa. Sch. of Med., 1990—; mem. com. Psychiat. Hosp. of Children/Adolescents, Washington, 1988—; panelist Nat. Assn. Pvt. and Psychiat. Hosps., Washington, 1989; chief investigator Psychosocial Sequelae of Surviving Childhood Cancer, Sidney Farber Cancer Inst., Boston, 1975-81; clin. assoc. prof. Jefferson Med. Coll., 1990—, U. of Pa. Sch. of Med., 1990—. Author: Massachusetts General Hospital Handbook of Psychiatric Consultation, 1979, The Damocles Syndrome, 1981; contbr. articles to profl. jours. Bd. dirs. Thom Clinic, Boston, 1977-84, Concord (Mass.) Assabett Sch., 1979-85. Maj. U.S. Army, 1972-74. Fellow Am. Psychiat. Assn., Am. Acad. Child and Adolescent Psychiatry (com. on hospitalization), Am. Orthopsychiat. Assn., Regional Coun. of Child/Adolescent Psychiatry; mem. Am. Coll. Physician Execs. Office: The Devereux Found 19 S Waterloo Rd Devon PA 19333-1533

O'MALLEY, MICHAEL JOHN, judge; b. Pitts., Aug. 7, 1923; s. Michael and Mary Ann (Coyne) O'M.; m. Mary Alice Dempsey, Sept. 6, 1947; children: J. Michael, Susan, Maureen, Joy. BS, U. Pitts., 1948; JD, 1954. Bar: Pa.; U.S. Dist. Ct. (we. dist.) Pa., 1954; U.S. Supreme Ct., 1968. Supr. H.J. Heinz Co., Pitts., 1948-51; pvt. practice in law Pitts.; spl. asst. atty. gen. Commonwealth of Pa., Pitts., 1960-63; chmn. bd. of viewers Allegheny County, Pitts., 1967-71; judge Ct. of Common Pleas, Pitts., 1972-77, pres. judge, 1977-89; adminstrv. judge Orphans' Ct., Pitts., 1989—. 2d lt. USAF, 1942-46. Recipient Tom C. Clarke award Nat. Conf. of Met. Cts., 1981. Mem. ABA, Pa. Bar Assn., Pa. Conf. of State Trial Judges (bd. dirs. 1979-89), Pa. Statewide Rules Com., Nat. Coll. of Probate Judges. Roman Catholic. Home: 1515 Grandin Ave Pittsburgh PA 15216-1837 Office: Orphans Ct Allegheny County 1700 Frick Bldg Pittsburgh PA 15219

O'MALLEY, SHAUN F., accounting firm executive; m. Julie O'Malley; 3 children. BS in Econ., U. Pa. Mem. staff Price Waterhouse, Phila., 1959, Tokyo, Osaka, 1966; mem. nat. office rsch. dept. Price Waterhouse, N.Y.C., 1968-70, mem. nat. office acctg. and auditing svc. dept., 1979; ptnr. Price Waterhouse, Phila., 1970-80, ptnr. in charge, 1980-88; elected to World Firm Coun. of Ptnrs. Price Waterhouse, 1982, elected to Policy Bd., 1984; chmn., sr. ptnr. Price Waterhouse, N.Y.C., 1988—; co-chief exec. officer Price Waterhouse World Firm, N.Y.C., 1990—; mem. emerging markets adv. com. SEC; pres. Fin. Acctg. Found. Editorial bd.: CPA Spokesman; contbr. articles to profl. jours. Mem. exec. com. N.Y.C. Mayor's Pvt. Sector Survey; ptnr. N.Y.C. Ptnrship.; co-chmn. N.Y.C. Alliance for Internat. Bus., Ltd.; adv. bd. Nat. Ctr. on Quality of The Workforce; bd. dirs. Curtis Inst. Music; former chmn. bd. Young Audiences of Ea. Pa.; bd. govs. Pa. Economy League; ea. div. bd. dirs. Greater Philadelphia Internat. Network, chmn. Com. of Seventy; chmn. Phila. Inst. of CPAs com. on acctg. and auditing; bd. dirs. SEI Ctr. Advanced Studies in Mgmt., Wharton Sch. Econ., others. Mem. AICPA. Office: Price Waterhouse 1251 Ave Of The Americas New York NY 10020-1104

O'MALLEY, SUZANNE MARIE, writer; b. Cedar Rapids, Iowa; d. Donald Leo and Irma B. (Waechter) O'Malley; m. Daniel Greenburg, June 28, 1980; 1 child, Zack O'Malley. BA with honors, U. Tex., 1974. Account supr. Dorf/Muller Jordan Herrick Pub. Relations, N.Y.C., 1973-75; editorial asst. Esquire Mag., N.Y.C., 1975, asst. editor, 1976, assoc. editor, 1977, sr. editor, 1977-78, columnist, 1978-80; freelance writer N.Y.C., 1978—. Author: (with Dan Greenburg) How to Avoid Love and Marriage, 1983, (screenplay) Private School, 1983; columnist, editor: Houston City Magazine, 1979-80, D Magazine, 1980; contbr. articles and reviews to newspapers and mags. Mem. Writers Guild Am., Dramatists Guild, Screen Actors Guild, Phi Beta Kappa. Roman Catholic.

O'MALLEY, THOMAS D., diversified company executive; b. N.Y.C., 1941. Grad., Manhattan Coll., 1963. Vice chmn., dir. Salomon, Inc. (formerly Phibro-Salomon, Inc.), N.Y.C.; former chmn., chief exec. officer, pres. Phibro Energy Inc., Greenwich, Conn.; chmn. Argus Investments (formerly Argus Resources), Stamford, Conn., from 1987; now chmn., chief exec. officer Tosco Corp., Conn. Office: Tosco Corp Hdqrs 72 Cummings Point Rd Stamford CT 06902-7912*

OMAN, CHARLES MCMASTER, aerospace engineer; b. N.Y.C., Feb. 22, 1944; s. William Morse and Janet Lyle (McMaster) O.; m. Cherryl Lester Huested, Oct. 26, 1974; children: Katherine, Peter. BSE, Princeton U., 1966; SM, MIT, 1968, PhD, 1972. Asst. prof. aero. and astron. MIT, Cambridge, 1972-77; assoc. prof. div. health sci. and tech. MIT, 1977-79, prin. rsch. scientist dept. aero. and astron., 1979-80, sr. rsch. engr., 1981—, assoc. dir. Man Vehicle Lab., 1981-91; dir. Man Vehicle Lab., Cambridge, Mass., 1992—; cons. NASA, 1979, USN, 1989, U. Space Rsch. Assn., 1981—. Editorial bd. Jour. Vestibular Rsch., 1990—; contbr. over 100 sci. articles to profl. jours.; patentee in field. NASA grantee. Mem. IEEE (sr.), Aero. Med. Assn. (sci. and tech. com.), Soc. for Neurosci., Winchester Boat Club (bd. dirs.). Episcopalian. Home: 5 Highland Ter Winchester MA 01890-1318 Office: Man Vehicle Lab MIT Rm 37-219 Cambridge MA 02139

O'MARA, ETHEL ROSE, writer, former educator; b. N.Y.C., May 31, 1920; d. Adolf and Rose Marie (Kurtz) Leitner; m. William Patrick O'Mara, July 27, 1974; stepchildren—Patricia, Maureen, Susan, William, Michael. A.B., Hunter Coll., 1941; M.S., Fordham U., 1952. Cert. tchr., N.Y. Lab. asst. Bd. Edn., N.Y.C., 1945-56; sci. tchr. Jr. High Sch., Mamaroneck, N.Y., 1956-57, U.S. Army, Berlin, Fed. Republic Germany, 1957-58, Munich, Fed. Republic Germany, 1958-59; sci. tchr., dept. head Edgemont High Sch., Scarsdale, N.Y., 1959-75; freelance writer, 1980-90; floutist, pianist. Composer: America Belongs to God. Author: Calamity Cruise With Bright Spots, 1985. Contbr. articles to mags. Com. chmn. to monitor devel. in Lake Lincolndale area; mem. Natural Resources Def. Coun., Nature Conservancy, Friends of Earth. Recipient Bronze medal N.Y.C. Jr. High Sch. Competition; NSF grantee Am. U., 1961, 64, 67, CCNY, 1964, Coll. at Middleburg, 1967. Mem. Environ. Def. Fund, Common Cause. Union of Concerned Scientists. Lincolndale Property Owners Assn. Roman Catholic. Avocations: travel, music, sailing, skiing, dancing.

O'MARA, JOSEPH JAMES, clinical psychologist; b. Meadville, Pa., Jan. 29, 1938; s. Thomas Joseph O'Mara and Ada Rosanna (Riordan) O'Mara Shiffer. BA, Allegheny Coll., 1959; MA, Kent State U., 1964; PhD, Duquesne U., 1973. Lic. clin. psychologist, Pa. Clin. psychologist Polk (Pa.) State Sch. and Hosp., 1962-66; asst. dir. psychology Western State Sch. and Hosp., Cannonsburg, Pa., 1966-69; clin. psychologist Hamot Community Mental Health Ctr., Erie, Pa., 1970-77; pvt. practice Erie, Pa., 1970-79; asst. dir. dept. psychology Warren (Pa.) State Hosp., 1977-90, ret., 1991—; rsch. dir. Pa. Bar Inst. Socio-Legal Subcom. Pa. Supreme Ct. Com Proposed Standard Jury Instn., Harrisburg, 1969—. Contbr. articles to profl. jours. Bd. dirs. Pa. Mental Health Inc., Phila., 1971-75; treas. N.W. Cleft Palate Inst., Hamot Med. Ctr., Erie, 1971-77. Pa. profl. edn. grantee Duquesne U., 1962-64. Mem. APA, Am. Assn. Mental Retardation, Aviation Country Club of Erie. Home: Springhill 2323 Edinboro Rd Erie PA 16509-3498

OMBERG, ARTHUR CHALMERS, JR., human resource manager; b. Nashville, May 26, 1939; s. Arthur Chalmers and Helen (Philips) O.; m. Susan Heitman, Oct. 26, 1962 (div. 1975); children: Mary Omberg Quaglino, Arthur Chalmers III; m. Mari McMinn, Dec. 6, 1980. BS, John Carroll U., 1962; MA in Indsl. Psychology, Loyola U., Chgo., 1965. Labor relations cons. Honeywell Inc., Mpls., 1965-67; personnel mgr. Gen. Cable Corp., Rome, N.Y., 1967-68; sr. salary analyst Merrill Lynch, N.Y.C., 1968-70; salary adminstrn. mgr. Olivetti Corp. of Am., N.Y.C., 1970-76; compensation officer Citibank, N.Y.C., 1976-80, asst. v.p., 1984-86; dir. personnel programs Comsat, Washington, 1980-84; pres. Omberg Mgmt. Cons., N.Y.C., 1986-88; corp. compensation mgr. Ebasco Svcs., Inc., N.Y.C., 1988—. Mem. Am. Compensation Assn., Soc. of Cin., Mil. Order Stars & Bars. Office: Ebasco Svcs Inc 2 World Trade Ctr New York NY 10048

OMIROS, GEORGE JAMES, medical foundation executive; b. Uniontown, Pa., Oct. 26, 1956; s. Chris George and Alice (Zervoudi) O.; m. Sophia Florent, June 28, 1980; children: Christopher George, Alicia Helene. BS in Polit. and Philosophy, U. Pitts., 1978; M, Cen. Mich. U., 1982. Campaign coordinator, program assoc. SW Pa. chpt. Am. Heart Assn., Greensburg, 1979, fundraising dir., 1979-80, dir. devel., 1980-84; v.p. devel., ops. Western Pa. chpt. Am. Heart Assn., Pitts., 1984-85, dep. exec. v.p., 1985-87, exec. v.p., 1987-88, exec. dir., 1988—, nat. mktg. rep., 1988—, asst. v.p. nat. office, 1991—. Cons. devel. Greek Orthodox Archdiocese, Pitts., 1982—, v.p. 1987—; mem. council, rev. com. Health Systems Agy. Southwest Pa., Pitts., 1983-87; mem. Parish Council, St. Spyridon Greek Orthodox Ch., Monessen, Pa., 1982—. Mem. Nat. Soc. Fundraising Execs. (cert., founder 1980, pres. 1985-87, Outstanding Fundraising Exec. 1990), Pitts. Planned Giving Coun. (founding com. 1983—), Friends of George C. Marshall (steering com.), Uniontown Country Club, Uniontown Rotary (local treas. 1985, sec. 1986, v.p. 1987, pres. 1988), Pitts. Rotary, Masons. Republican. Greek Orthodox. Office: Leukemia Soc Am 13 North 2 Gateway Ctr Pittsburgh PA 15222

OMOHUNDRO, JOSEPH ROGER, historian; b. Beaumont, Tex., Nov. 23, 1910; s. Philip Grymes and Jessie (Sherburn) O. Violin studies with Leon Sametini, Max Bendix, Amy Neill, 1925-36; student, Chgo. Mus. Coll., 1926-28, U. Chgo., 1933-35, Columbia U., 1945-48. Historian The N.Y. Geneal. and Biog. Soc., N.Y.C.; dir. founder Tex. Gulf Hist. Soc., Beaumont, 1964; editor Tex. Gulf Hist. and Biog. Record, Beaumont, 1971-73. Mem. Citizens for Taft com., N.Y.C., 1951-52. Democrat. Office: The NY Geneal and Biog Soc 122 E 58th St New York NY 10022-1909

ONEAL, GLEN, JR., retired physicist; b. Gt. Falls, Mont., Feb. 2, 1917; s. Glen and Marion (Sherrard) O.; B.S., Mont. State Coll., 1940; M.S., U. Pa., 1947; m. Lois Fay, May 23, 1941 (div. Aug. 1968); 1 dau., Fay (Mrs. W. James Redwine); m. 2d, Evelyn Spies Hessenbruch, May 5, 1975. Jr. engr. physicist Public Rds. Adminstrn. Washington, 1941; asso. physicist Naval Ordnance Lab., Washington, 1941-45; physicist Sun Oil Co., Newtown Square, Pa., 1947-55; research physicist Am. Viscose Corp., Marcus Hook, Pa., 1955-63; research physicist Am. Viscose div. FMC Corp., 1963-70, chem. group research, 1970-81, sr. physicist corp. engrng. and constrn., 1981-82. Research asso. Nat. Bur. Standards, 1968-70. Prodn. chmn. Rose Valley Chorus, Media, Pa., 1950-67; bd. dirs. Media (Pa.) Fellowship House, 1971-77. Mem. Am. Phys. Soc., ASTM, IEEE, Sigma Xi. Mem. Soc. of Friends. Home: 128 Yale Ave Swarthmore PA 19081-2021

O'NEIL, CLEORA TANNER, personnel specialist; b. Roosevelt, Utah, Sept. 1, 1946; d. Frank and Pearl (Mecham) Tanner; divorced; 1 child, Sylvia Boroughs. AA, Drury Coll., 1983; BA, Westminster U., 1985. Sec. USAF, Hill AFB, Utah, 1966-74; employee rels. specialist USAF, McClellan AFB, Calif., 1986-90; pers. specialist Pentagon USAF, Washington, 1990—; sec. U.S. Army, Ft. Leonard Wood, Mo., 1981-83, VA Hosp., Salt Lake City, 1983-86.; resident in upper managerial tng. Civilian Air Staff Tng., USAF, Washington, 1990—. Recipient Outstanding USAF Civilian Pers. Program Specialist award, 1989. Mem. Toastmasters (v.p. Aerospace chpt. 1989-90, Toastmaster of Yr. 1989, pres. Am. River chpt. 1989-90, Pres.' award 1990, internat. gov. 1989-90). Office: Pentagon Washington DC

O'NEIL, JAMES EDWARD, state attorney general; b. Mt. Vernon, N.Y., Feb. 28, 1939; s. John James and Miriam (Dillon) O'N.; m. Anne Worrell, May 4, 1985; children: Katherine Reed, Kelsey Ann. BS, Providence Coll., 1963; JD, New Eng. Sch. Law, 1967. Bar: Mass. 1972, R.I. 1978, U.S. Ct. Appeals (1st cir.), U.S. Supreme Ct. Advisor law enforcement assistance adminstrn. U.S. Dept. Justice, Boston, 1972-74; asst. U.S. atty. Boston, 1974-78, dep. chief U.S. atty. Internat. Narcotics Unit Mass., 1975-78; asst. U.S. atty., R.I., 1978-86; head R.I. Drug Task Force, 1981-83; atty. gen. State of R.I., Providence, 1987—. Trial Advocacy adv. Harvard U., Suffolk U., New Eng. Law Sch.; mem., counsel Save the Bay, Providence, 1972; bd. dirs. Conservation Law Found. Mem. R.I. Bar Assn., Mass. Bar Assn. Democrat. Office: Office of Atty Gen 72 Pine St Providence RI 02903-2836*

O'NEIL, LEO E., bishop; b. Holyoke, Mass., Jan. 31, 1928. Ed. Mary-knoll Sem., St. Anselm's Coll., Manchester, N.H., Grand Sem., Montreal, Que., Can. Ordained Roman Cath. priest, 1955; ordained titular bishop of Bencenna and aux. bishop of Springfield (Mass.), 1980-89, co-adjutor bishop Manchester, N.H., 1989-90, bishop, 1990—. Office: Diocese of Manchester St Joseph Cathedral 145 Lowell St Manchester NH 03104-6135*

O'NEILL, BRIAN COLLINS, electronic instrumentation company executive; b. Butte, Mont., May 10, 1934; s. Daniel John and Mary Josephine (Dolence) O'N.; m. Ellen Marie Jones, July 13, 1957; children: Patrice, Erin, Colleen, Kara. BSME, U. Notre Dame, 1956. Engrng. mgr. IBM, Hopewell Junction, N.Y., 1956-91; pres. Neilco Tech. Inc., Millbrook, N.Y., 1976—. Home: RR 2 Box 60 Millbrook NY 12545-9613 Office: Neilco Tech Inc PO Box 833 Millbrook NY 12545-0833

O'NEILL, HARRY WILLIAM, survey research company executive; b. Atlantic City, Jan. 30, 1929; s. Harry William and Marian Elizabeth (Kuhl) O'N.; m. Carmel Gullo, Sept. 21, 1952; children: Sharon Ruth, Randal Bruce. B.A., Colgate U., 1950; M.S., Pa. State U., 1951. Lic. practicing psychologist, N.J. Research analyst Prudential Ins. Co., Newark, 1957-62; with Opinion Research Corp., Princeton, N.J., 1962-87; sr. v.p. Opinion Research Corp., 1970-73, exec. v.p., 1973-80, pres., 1980-85, vice chmn., 1985-87; vice chmn. The Roper Orgn., N.Y.C., 1988—; mem. coadj. faculty Rutgers U., 1959-64; vis. lectr. Woodrow Wilson Sch., Princeton U., 1980-82;. Editor Marketing Research: A Magazine of Management & Applications, 1988—. pres. Nat. Council Public Polls; bd. dirs. Roper Ctr. for Pub. Opinion Research, 1984—, Council. Am. Survey Research Orgns., 1981-83, chmn., 1982-83; mem. Highland Park (N.J.) Human Rights Commn., 1973-77; bd. dirs. Delaware-Raritan Lung Assn., 1974-88, v.p., 1977-82, chmn., 1982-84; fin. chmn. Highland Park Republican Orgn., 1977-89. Served with USAF, 1951-54. Recipient Maroon citation Colgate U., 1975. Mem. Am. Psychol. Assn., Ea. Psychol. Assn., Am. Assn. Pub. Opinion Rsch., Assn. Consumer Rsch., Am. Mktg. Assn., Market Rsch. Coun., Highland Park Rep. Club, Masons, Elks. Presbyterian. Office: The Roper Orgn 205 E 42d St New York NY 10017

O'NEILL, JAMES PAUL, psychiatrist; b. Elizabeth, N.J., Sept. 3, 1958; s. Paul James and Dorothy (Semansky) O'N.; m. Patricia Anne Scott, Aug. 1989. BS in Biology, Niagara U., 1980; MD, U. N.E., Mexico, 1984; MD Fifth Pathway, U Medicine & Dentistry, N.J., 1985. Intern Jersey Shore Med. Ctr., Neptune, N.J., 1985-86; resident in psychiatry U. Medicine & Dentistry, Robert Wood Johnson Med. Sch., Piscataway, N.J., 1986-89, chief resident in psychiatry, 1988-89; attending psychiatrist Monmouth Med. Ctr., Long Branch, N.J.; cons., lectr. in field. Contbr. articles to profl. jours. NIMH fellow, 1988. Mem. AMA (N.J. del. to resident physician sect. 1987-89, Physician Recognition award 1991), Am. Psychiat. Assn., N.J. Psychiat. Assn. (founding pres. resident physician sect. 1987-88, co-chmn. addictive disorders treatment com.), Am. Soc. Internal Medicine, U.S. Life Saving Assn., N.Y. Acad. Sci., Med. Soc. N.J. (del. Monmouth County 1990—), Med. Soc. of N.J. Residents Assn. (chmn. 1987-89). Republican. Home: 107 Lincoln Ave Avon By The Sea NJ 07717 Office: 813 Main St Avon By The Sea NJ 07717 also: 170 Morris Ave Long Beach NJ 07740

O'NEILL, JOHN FRANCIS, chemist; b. Rochester, N.Y., Oct. 18, 1947; s. John Edward and Catherine Alice (Carmody) O'N.; m. Carol Ann Forbes, Aug. 2, 1969; 1 child, Matthew Paul. BS in Chemistry, SUNY, Brockport, 1969. Process chemist E.I. DuPont deNemours, Rochester, 1969-71, shift supr., 1971-73; sr. supr. E.I. DuPont deNemours, Wilmington, Del., 1973, facilities engr., 1974; process engr. GAF Corp., Binghamton, N.Y., 1975-77, coating supr., 1977-78, raw material quality control mgr., 1979-80; area supr. Photoproducts, Glen Cove and L.I., N.Y., 1980-82; product mgr. Peter Cooper Corp., Charlotte, N.C., 1983-87; sr. product mgr., tech. coord. specialties div. SanoFi Bio Industries, Trevrose, Pa., 1987—. With USAR, 1970-79. Mem. Am. Soc. Quality Control, Soc. Imaging Sci. and Tech. Republican. Roman Catholic. Office: SanoFi Bio Industries 8 Nehaminy Interplex Trevose PA 19053

O'NEILL, JOHN T., toy company executive; b. N.Y.C., Oct. 25, 1944; s. John and Rhoda (Dillon) O'N; m. Lois E. McGarry, Oct. 8, 1966; children: John, Margaret, Gregory, Brian. BS in Acctg., Providence Coll., 1962-66. Acct. Arthur Andersen & Co., Providence, 1966-67; ptnr. Peat Marwick, KPMG, Providence, 1970-84; mng. ptnr. Peat Marwick KPMG, 1984-87; sr. v.p. fin. Hasbro, Inc., Pawtucket, R.I., 1987-88; sr. v.p., chief fin. officer Hasbro, Inc., 1988-89, exec. v.p., chief fin. officer, 1990—; mem. pres. coun. Providence Coll.; bd. dirs., past pres. Jr. Achievement R.I.; bd. dirs. Eastland Fin. Corp.; pres., bd. dirs. Galaxy Funds. Trustee Women and Infants Hosp. R.I., Providence; treas., bd. dirs. R.I. Philharmonic Orch., Providence; mem. exec. com. Catholic Charity Fund, Providence. Capt. Med. Service Corps., U.S. Army, 1967-70. Decorated Bronze Star. Mem. AICPA, R.I. CPA Soc., Inst. Mgmt. Accts., Fin. Execs. Inst., Warwick Country Club, Hope Club, Dunes Club, Univ. Club. Office: Hasbro Inc 200 Narragansett Park Dr Pawtucket RI 02861-4342

O'NEILL, MARCIA TAGGART, vocational school administrator; b. Rutland, Vt., Sept. 28, 1947; d. George Luke and Patricia Jean (Smith) Taggart; m. Edward Charles O'Neill, Aug. 16, 1969; children: Timothy Michael, Patrick Edward (dec.), Megan Elaine. Diploma, Vt. Beauty Acad., 1966, Acad. de Montreal, Burlington, Vt., 1990. Lic. mgr. instr., Vt. Stylist Mr. Rays, Concord, N.H., 1966-67, Grants, Rutland, 1967-68, Jean's Beauty Salon, Rutland, 1969-72; mgr. Marcia's Beauty Salon, Castleton, Vt., 1972-77, County Coiffures, Bomoseen, Vt., 1978-85; tchr. aide Underhill I.D. Sch., Jericho, Vt., 1985-87; isntr. O'Briens Tng. Ctr., Burlington, 1987-88, dir. edn., 1988-89, dir., 1989—; demonstrator Beauty for All Seasons, Burlington, 1985-90; libr. cons. Jr. Great Books Found., Jericho, 1986. Room mother Castleton Village Sch., 1975-83; den mother Cub Scouts Am., Castleton, 1977-8; fundraiser Castleton Vol. Fire Dept., 1982-83; vol. Am. Cancer Soc., Underhill, 1985-86. Recipient Achievement award Beauty for All Seasons, 1985, Citizenship award Lions Club, 1984. Mem. Nat. Vocat. Edn. Assn., Vt. Vocat. Edn. Assn., Vt. Assn. Cosmetology, Nat. Assn. Cosmetology, Lakes Region C. of C., Am. Legion Aux. (past pres.), Lioness (past v.p. Castleton Area chpt.), Ladies Oriental Shrine. Roman Catholic. Office: OBriens Tng Ctr Coll 1475 Shelburne Rd South Burlington VT 05403

O'NEILL, MARY JANE, health agency executive; b. Detroit, Feb. 24, 1923; d. Frank Roger and Kathryn (Rice) Kilcoyne; Ph.B. summa cum laude, U. Detroit, 1944; postgrad. U. Wis., 1949-50; m. Michael James O'Neill, May 31, 1948; children: Michael, Maureen, Kevin, John (dec.), Kathryn. Editor, East Side Shopper, Detroit, 1939-45; club editor Detroit Free Press, 1945-48; reporter UP, Milw. and Madison, Wis., 1949; dir. public relations Fairfax-Falls Church (Va.) Community Chest, 1955-60; copy editor Falls Ch. Sun-Echo, 1958-60; free-lance writer, Washington, 1960-63; assoc. editor Med. World News, Washington, 1963-66; dir. public relations Westchester Lighthouse, N.Y. Assn. for Blind, 1967-71; dir. public edn. The Lighthouse, N.Y.C., 1971-73, dir. public relations, 1973-80; exec. dir. Eye-Bank for Sight Restoration, Inc., 1980—. Apptd. by Gov. Cuomo N.Y. State Transplant Coun., 1991—; bd. dirs. N.Y. Regional Transplant Program, 1987-91. Mem. Women in Communications (pres. N.Y. chpt. 1980-81), Eye-Bank Assn. Am. (lay adv. bd. 1981-83, dir. 1983-86), Public Relations Soc. Am., Women Execs. in Pub. Relations (dir. 1982-88, pres. 1986-87), N.Y. Acad. Scis., Cosmopolitan Club. Office: Eye Bank for Sight Restoration 210 E 64th St New York NY 10021-7498

O'NEILL, PATRICIA ANN, writer, linguist; b. Albany, N.Y., Feb. 17, 1964; d. Brian Edward and Joanne (Kosinski) O'N. BA in English, SUNY, Potsdam, 1986; MS in Computational Linguistics, Georgetown U., 1990, postgrad., 1990—. Tchr. English Hiroshima U., Japan, 1986-87; editor, indexer Scan C2C, Washington, summer 1990; program asst. Fulbright Summer Program, Georgetown U., Washington, summer 1991; mo. columnist World Press Internat., Visio Mono mag., Alexandria, Va., 1990—; software reviewer for computer-assisted lang. learning/machine translation programs for the Japanese lang.; contbr. articles to profl. jours. SUNY-Potsdam English scholar, 1986; Latin scholar Mercy High Sch., 1982; Georgetown U. fellow, 1989—. Mem. Japan Am. Soc. of Washington, Pi Sigma Alpha, Sigma Tau Delta. Home: 3726 Connecticut Ave NW Apt 308 Washington DC 20008

O'NEILL, THOMAS NEWMAN, JR., federal judge; b. Hanover, Pa., July 6, 1928; s. Thomas Newman and Emma (Cornpropst) O'N.; m. Jeanne M. Corr., Feb. 4, 1961; children: Caroline Jeanne, Thomas Newman, III, Ellen Gitt. A.B. magna cum laude, Catholic U. Am., 1950; LL.B. magna cum laude, U. Pa., 1953; postgrad. (Fulbright grantee), London Sch. Econs., 1955-56. Bar: Pa. 1954, U.S. Supreme Ct. 1959. Law clk. to Judge Herbert F. Goodrich U.S. Ct. Appeals (3d cir.), 1953-54; to Justice Harold H. Burton U.S. Supreme Ct., 1954-55; assoc. firm Montgomery, McCracken, Walker & Rhoads, Phila., 1956-63; ptnr. Montgomery, McCracken, Walker & Rhoads, 1963-83; judge U.S. Dist. Ct. (ea. dist.) Pa., 1983—; counsel 1st and 2d Pa. Legis. Reapportionment Commns., 1971, 81; lectr. U. Pa. Law Sch., 1973. Articles editor: U. Pa. Law Rev, 1952-53. Former trustee Lawyers Com. for Civil Rights Under Law; former mem. Gov.'s Trial Ct. Nominating Commn. for Phila. County; former mem. bd. overseers U. Pa. Mus. Fellow Am. Coll. Trial Lawyers; mem. Am. Law Inst. (life), Phila. Bar Assn. (chancellor 1976), Pa. Bar Assn. (gov. 1978-81), U. Pa. Law Alumni Soc. (pres. 1976-77), Pa. Conf. County Bar Officers (pres. 1981-82), Order of Coif (pres. U. Pa. chpt. 1971-73), Merion Cricket Club, Edgemere Club, Broadacres Trouting Assn., Phi Beta Kappa, Phi Eta Sigma. Office: US Dist Ct 14613 US Courthouse 601 Market St Philadelphia PA 19106-1510

O'NEILL, WILLIAM EDWARD, writer, activist; b. Hyannis, Mass., June 6, 1960; s. Edward E. and Lorraine M. (Connelly) O'N. BA, Harvard U., 1982. Reporter Nat. Enquirer, Lantana, Fla., 1982-85; freelance journalist Barnstable, Mass., 1986—; publs. mgr. New Alchemy Inst., Falmouth, Mass., 1988-91; bd. dirs. Cape & Islands Self Reliance Inc. Media dir. Great Peace March, Santa Monica, Calif., 1986, Old Jail Ln. Preservation com., Barnstable, Mass., 1987; bd. dirs. Resource Ctr. for Peace and Justice, 1987—. Home and Office: PO Box 222 West Barnstable MA 02668-0222

O'NEILL, WILLIAM GEORGE, philosophy educator, educational administrator; b. Evergreen Park, Ill., July 3, 1943; s. Edwin J. and Myrtle J. (Hutchinson) O'N.; m. Christine M. Rosco, Dec. 26, 1972; children: Maura J., Edwin J. II. BA, Iona Coll., New Rochelle, N.Y., 1964; MA, Boston Coll., 1967, PhD, 1970. Asst. prof. philosophy Iona Coll., 1972-78, assoc. prof., 1978—, chmn. dept. philosophy, 1983-88, dir. institutional planning, 1988—, asst. to pres., 1989—; non-resident faculty in philosophy N.Y. Archdiocese-Neumann Residence, Bronx, N.Y., 1986—. Woodrow Wilson fellow, 1964; Carnegie summer grantee, 1970. Mem. Am. Philos. Assn., Am. Cath. Philos. Assn., Philosophy of Sci. Assn., Metaphys. Soc. Am., Soc. Coll. and Univ. Planners, Am. Assn. Higher Edn., Nat. Cath. Edn. Assn. Democrat. Roman Catholic. Home: 56 Curtis Ln Yonkers NY 10710-4406 Office: Iona Coll New Rochelle NY 10801-1890

ONO, RICHARD DANA, biotechnology executive; b. Bridgeton, N.J., Jan. 16, 1953; s. Frank Hitoshi and Fumi (Yokoyama) O.; m. Anne Wagner, Oct. 10, 1981; children: Alison Celia, Maxwell Wagner. AB, Johns Hopkins U., 1975; AM, Harvard U., 1978, PhD, 1981. Rsch. assoc. U. Mass. Med. Sch., Worcester, 1981-83; dir. bus. devel. Damon Biotech, Inc., Needham Heights, Mass., 1983-86; gen. mgr. Regis McKenna, Inc., Cambridge, Mass., 1986-87; dir. bus. devel. Integrated Genetics, Inc., Framingham, Mass., 1987-89; v.p. bus. devel. Enzytech, Inc., Cambridge, Mass., 1989-91; chief exec. officer, pres. Arcturus Pharm. Corp., Cambridge, Mass., 1991—; co-founder, bd. dirs. Mass. Biotechnology Coun., Inc., Cambridge, 1984-86. Author: Vanishing Fishes of North America, 1983; editor: The Business of Biotechnology from the Bench to the Street, 1991. Affiliate Dunster Ho., Cambridge, Mass., 1990. Recipient Raney award Soc. Ichthyologists and Herpetologists, Washington, 1979. Home: 80 Woodside Ln Arlington MA 02174-2143

ONUFROCK, RICHARD SHADE, pharmacist, researcher; b. Colorado Springs, Colo., July 5, 1934; s. Frank and Mildred Joy (Overstreet) O.; m. Karen Faye Larson, June 15, 1958 (div. 1980); children: Richard Alan (dec.), Amy Mildred. BS in Pharmacy, U. Colo., 1961; diploma, Famous Artists Schs., 1963. Registered pharmacist, Colo., Ariz., South Africa. Pharmacist Aley Drug Co., Colorado Springs, 1961-75, St. Joseph Hosp., Denver, 1976-77, Navajo Nation Health Found., Ganado, Ariz., 1977-81, Kearny (Ariz.) Kenecot-Samarital Hosp., 1984-85, NIH, Warren G. Magnuson Clin. Ctr., Bethesda, Md., 1988—; dir. pharmacy, chief pharmacist Tintswalo Hosp., South Africa, 1981-84; pharmacist, chief pharmacist Miami (Ariz.)-Inspiration Hosp., 1985-88; instr. Coll. of Ganado, 1979-80; asst. in textbook revision and illustration U. Colo., 1961; cons. Heritage Health Care Ctr., Globe, Ariz., 1988. Illustrator Pharmacy for Nurses, 1961, Colo. Jour. of Pharmacy, 1962-64; illustrations exhibited Colo. Springs Fine Art Ctr., 1964-66, Gilpin County Art Assn., Central City, Colo., 1968-74, 1st Nat. Space

Art Show, Denver, 1969. dem. precinct committeeman, 1974-76; den leader Boy Scouts Am., com. mem., 1975-76; fireman, lt. Ganado Vol. Fire Dept., 1977-81; compassionate med. missionary Nazarene Ch., Tintswalo Hosp. Gazankulu, South Africa, 1981-84;bd. dirs. Friends of Libr., Kearny, 1985-87; active Grace Episcopal Ch. Mem. Am. Pharm. Assn., Am. Soc. Hosp. Pharmacists, D.C. Soc. Hosp. Pharmacists, Phi Delta Chi, Delta Sigma Phi. Home: 4831 36th St NW 202 Washington DC 20008 Office: NIH Clin Ctr Pharmacy Dept Bldg 10 Rm 1N257 9000 Rockville Pike Bethesda MD 20892

ONUOHA, EVEREST, English educator; b. Lagos, Nigeria, July 12, 1953; s. Benjamin and Cordelia (Okoro) O.; m. Esther Onuoha, July 1979; children: Vivian, Franklin, William, Stanley, Christian. Student, Alvan Ikoku Coll. Edn., Owerri, Nigeria, 1974; BA, U. Mass., Boston, 1980; MS, Boston State Coll., 1981, PhD, 1988. Cert. in supervision and curriculum devel., tchr., Mass.; nat. cert. tchr. Prof. polit. sci. Wheelock Coll., Boston; assoc. prof. English, Roxbury (Mass.) Community Coll., dir. honors program; chmn. English dept. div. extended edn. Author: Fundamental English Handbook and Rhetoric; contbr. articles to profl. publs. 2d lt. C.E., Biafran Army, 1969-70. Recipient award and citation Mass. Gov.'s Pride in Performance, 1986; fellow Boston U., 1984. Mem. ASCD, Nat. Coun. Tchrs. English, Am. Polit. Sci. Assn., Rotary, Alpha Pi Sigma, Phi Theta Kappa, Pi Gamma Mu.

OOI, BOON S., pension fund administrator; b. Georgetown, Penang, Malaysia, June 2, 1957; came to U.S., 1976; s. Kar S. and Siew E. (Lee) O.; m. Elizabeth Hefferman. BS in Physics, Bates Coll., 1980; MBA in Fin., U. Chgo., 1984. Cert. employee benefits specialist. Sr. valuation technician Cigna, Hartford, Conn., 1980-81; various compensation and benefits positions Towers, Perrin, Forster & Crosby, Chgo., 1981-84; benefist planner Montgomery Ward, Chgo., 1984-86; exec. dir. Coop. Banks Employees Retirement Assn., Boston, 1986—; instr. Boston U., 1990—. Mem. Internat. Soc. Cert. Employee Benefits Specialist (pres. Boston chpt. 1992), Jaycees. Office: Coop Banks Employees Retirement Assn 50 Federal St Boston MA 02110

OOLIE, SAM, investment company executive; b. N.Y.C., Aug. 11, 1936; s. Bernadt S. and Rose (Moyel) O.; m. Marjorie R. Oolie, Dec. 3, 1961; children: Janis, Caroline, Tara. BS in Metallurgy, MIT, 1958; MBA, Harvard U., 1961. Chmn. Food Concepts, Inc., Rutherford, N.J., 1962-85; pres. CFC Venture Capital Corp., Fairfield, N.J., 1984-90; chmn. Oolie Enterprises, Fairfield, 1985—; vice chmn. Am. Mobile, Inc., Secaucus, N.J., 1986-89; chmn. The Nostalgia Network, N.Y.C., 1987-90, New Thermal Corp., Keasbey, N.J., 1991—; bd. dirs. Avesis, Inc., Phoenix, Comverse Techs., N.Y.C., Noise Cancellation Tech., Stamford, Conn., First N.Y. Bank for Bus., N.Y.C. Member exec. com. State of N.J.-Israel Commn., 1989—; commr. Essex County Improvement Authority, 1987-88; trustee Coun. Jewish Fedns., 1986—, Haifa U., 1986—, Garden State Cancer Ctr., 1989—, Beth Israel Med. Ctr., 1990—, Assn. Reform Zionists Am., 1990—, Am. Jewish Joint Distbn. Com., 1990—; pres. United Jewish Fedn. Met. West N.J., 1988-90; vice chmn. United Jewish Appeal, 1986—. Recipient Gates of Jerusalem award Boys Town of Jerusalem, 1990, Israel 40th Ann. medal State of Israel Bonds, 1988. Mem. World Bus. Coun., Harvard Club of N.Y., Greenbrook Country Club. Office: 253 Passaic Ave Fairfield NJ 07004-2524

OOSTDAM, BERNARD LODEWIJK, oceanography educator; b. Amsterdam, The Netherlands, Aug. 13, 1932; came to U.S., 1960; s. Bernardus Laurentius and Catharina Geertruida (Boelsma) O.; m. Rose Adele Petersen, 1963 (div. 1964); 1 child, Daniel Allen; m. Maria Mercia Louw, Aug. 29, 1964; children: Bernard Louw, Erika Patricia. BS with honors, McGill U., Montreal, Que., Can., 1960; MS, Scripps Inst. Oceanography, La Jolla, Calif., 1964; PhD, U. Del., 1971. Supervising staff geologist Ocean Sci. Engring.-DeBeers, Capetown, South Africa, 1963-65; sr. researcher Kuwait Inst. Sci. Rsch., Kuwait, 1976-78; expert marine geologist and coastal engr. UN, Trinida and Tobago, Trinidad and Tobago, 1980-82; prof. Millersville (Pa.) U., 1966—. Recipient Excellence Acad. Svcs. award Pa. Dept. Edn., Harrisburg, 1975. Mem. Island Resources Found., N.J. Marine Educators Assn., Am. Arbitration Assn., The Oceanography Soc. Office: Millersville U Millersville PA 17551

OOSTDYK, ARLENE ROSA, natural health educator, nurse; b. Oxford, N.J., Oct. 28, 1926; d. Ray William and Helen Anna (Renner) Frey; m. Marinus Joseph Oostdyk, Mar. 20, 1948; children: Darlene B. Oostdyk Haberer, Ray Marinus, James Marinus. Grad., Jersey City Hosp. Sch. Nursing, 1947. RN. Sch. nurse Bur. Maternal and Child Health, Alpha and Harmony, N.J., 1947-48, Hawthorne, N.J., 1948-49; nurse Hunterdam Med. Ctr., Fleming, N.J., 1953-60, Warren Hosp., Philipsany, N.J., 1953-60; sch. nurse Hampton Sch. Bd., 1960, Glen Gardner Sch. Bd., 1960; counselor in nutrition Asbury, N.J., 1981—; regional mgr. Natures Sunshine, Spanish Fork, Utah, 1986, divisional mgr., 1989-91, nat. mgr., 1991—; speaker in field. Clk., judge Election Bd., Asbury, N.J., 1967-87. Recipient Didication of Classroom award Internat. Gospel League, 1984. Mem. Am. Inst. Preventive Medicine (Cert. 1986), Jersey City Med. Ctr. Alumni Assn., Sch. Natural Healing (Cert. 1986), Nat. Health Fedn. (life, million dollar club). Republican. Baptist. Home and Office: 752 Mountain View Rd Asbury NJ 08802-1026

O'PAKE, MICHAEL A., state legislator; b. Reading, Pa., Feb. 2, 1940; s. Michael and Anna (Maslar) O'P. AB, St. Joseph's U., 1961; JD, U. Pa., 1964. Atty. O'Pake, Malsnee and Orwig, Reading, 1964—; state rep. Pa. Ho. of Reps., Harrisburg, Pa., 1968-72; state senator Pa. Senate, Harrisburg, 1972—; sec. Senate Dem. Leadership Team; chmn. Senate Com. Intergovernmental Affairs; mem. Senate com. on Agr. and Rural Affairs, Banking and Ins., Rules and Exec. Nominations, State Govt. Mem. Pa. Heritage Affairs Commn., Ben Franklin Partnership Bd.; bd. dirs. Pa. State Police Camp Cadet, 1988, Parents Anonymous Pa.; adv. bd. Pa. State U./ Berks Campus; mem., pres. adv. coun. St. Joseph's U. Recipient numerous civic awards including Nat. award for Meritorious Svc. to Crime Victims Nat. Orgn. for Victims Assistance, 1984, Criminal Justice Alumni award St. Joseph's U., 1988, Pa. Coun. Children's Svc. award. Mem. Slovak League Am. (life.). Democrat. Roman Catholic. Home: 1527 Schuylkill Ave Reading PA 19601-1312 Office: Pa State Senate State Capitol Harrisburg PA 17120

OPALSKI, DOUGLAS VICTOR, state official; b. Trenton, N.J., Feb. 27, 1942; s. Victor Zigmund and Margaret (Szabo) O.; m. Helene Marie Walsh, Sept. 7, 1968; children: Mark, Michael, John. BA in Polit. Sci., Rutgers U., 1963, M in City and Regional Planning, 1971. Planner Middlesex County Planning Bd., New Brunswick, N.J., 1963-75, asst. planning dir., 1975-80, dir. planning and econ. devel., 1980-86; exec. dir. N.J. Council on Affordable Housing, Trenton, 1986—. Mem. Fresh Air Fund, N.Y.C., 1975—, Friends of Fgn. Students, Princeton, N.J., 1982—; mem. team Marriage Encounter (worldwide), Calif., 1982—; trustee Queenship of Mary Ch., Plainsboro, N.J., 1982—. Recipient Outstanding Service award Middlesex County Pvt. Industry Council, 1983, Oustanding Service award Raritan Valley C. of C., 1986. Mem. Am. Inst. of Cert. Planners, Am. Planning Assn. Roman Catholic. Office: NJ Coun on Affordable Housing Care NJ Dept Community Affairs CN 813 Trenton NJ 08625-0813

OPITZ, BERNARD FRANCIS, JR., postal service administrator; b. Springfield, Mass., Dec. 9, 1947; s. Bernard Francis and Bertha Margaret (Diamond) O.; m. Elena Louise Cotti, Oct. 10, 1970 (div. 1979); children: Bernard Francis III, Douglas Richard; m. Patricia Ann Menzer, Feb. 29, 1980; 1 stepchild, Karyn Renee Beaty. AAS, Springfield Tech. Inst., 1968. Sr. detail draftsman Combustion Enging., Windsor, Conn., 1968-71; distbn. clk. U.S. Post Office, 1966-68; with U.S. Postal Svc., Springfield, 1971-89, supr. prodn. planning, 1978-80, customer requirements specialist, 1980-89; dir. city ops. U.S. Postal Svc., Stamford, Conn., 1989-92; sr. ops. performance analyst U.S. Postal Svc. Hdqrs., Washington, 1992—. Mem. Am. Mgmt. Assn., Sacred Heart Alumni Assn., Springfield Tech. Alumni Assn. Roman Catholic. Office: US Postal Svc 475 L'Enfant Plz Rm 7301 Washington DC 20260-7224

OPOTZNER, PAUL MICHAEL, financial executive; b. New Haven, Feb. 2, 1953; s. Samuel and Beatrice (Gordon) O.; m. Jill Barrett, Oct. 12, 1983; children: Joshua, Krysha. Pres. Exec. Foods, Inc., New Haven, 1985—, Fairfield Fin., Inc., Bridgeport, Conn., 1988—; exec. v.p. Synergistic Systems, Inc., West Haven, Conn., 1991—; pres. Fin. Franchises, Inc., Bridgeport, 1990—, Cash-a-Check, Inc., Bridgeport, 1988—. Mem. Nat. Assn. Rev. Appraisers, Nat. Assn. Mktg. Underwriters. Office: Synergistic Systems Inc PO Box 1264 Orange CT 06477-7264

OPPENHEIM, HENRY, psychologist; b. Nuremberg, Bavaria, Germany, Sept. 19, 1926; came to U.S., 1938; s. Willi and Betty (Weissmann) O.; m. Adele S., June 25, 1950; children: Lisa Gail Berzins, Jody O. Gastfriend, Keith B. BS, CCNY, 1949; MA, U. N.C., 1951; PhD, U. Ky., 1955. Clin. psychologist VA Regional Office, Cin., 1955-56, VA Med. Ctr., Northampton, Mass., 1956-89; dir. psychology Northampton State Hosp., 1989-91; cons. Mass. Rehab. Commn., Boston, 1964-89, 92—; rsch. adviser Smith Coll. Sch. Social Work, Northampton, 1966—; cons. Health Pro, 1992—; designated forensic psychologist U. Mass. Med. Sch. Forensic Tng. Program, Worcester, 1991—; psychologist Ctr. for Adults and Families, Westfield, Mass. Contbr. articles to profl. jours. Pres. Congregation B'nai Israel, Northampton, 1976-78, bd. dirs., 1968—. Pvt. U.S. Army, 1946-47. Democrat. Jewish. Home: 104 Jackson St Northampton MA 01060-1660

OPPENHEIM, IRWIN, chemical physicist, educator; b. Boston, June 30, 1929; s. James L. and Rose (Rosenberg) O.; m. Bernice Buresh, May 18, 1974; 1 child, Joshua Buresh. A.B. summa cum laude, Harvard U., 1949; postgrad., Calif. Inst. Tech., 1949-51; Ph.D., Yale, 1956. Physicist Nat. Bur. Standards, Washington, 1953-60; chief theoretical physics Gen. Dynamics/ Convair, San Diego, 1960-61; asso. prof. chemistry MIT, Cambridge, 1961-65; prof. MIT, 1965—; lectr. physics U. Md., 1953-60; vis. assoc. prof. physics U. Leiden, 1955-56, Lorentz prof., 1983; vis. prof. Weizmann Inst. Sci., 1958-59, U. Calif., San Diego, 1966-67; Van der Waals prof. U. Amsterdam, 1966-67. Author: (with J.G. Kirkwood) Chemical Thermodynamics, 1961. Fellow Am. Phys. Soc., Am. Acad. Arts and Scis., Washington Acad. Sci.; mem. Phi Beta Kappa, Sigma Xi. Home: 140 Upland Rd Cambridge MA 02140-3623

OPPENHEIM, ROBERT, beauty industry executive; b. N.Y.C., May 21, 1925; s. Hyman and Hannah (Lieberman) O.; m. Ruth Wigler, Feb. 7, 1954; children: Nancy Ellen, David Paul, Howard P. BS cum laude, Syracuse U., 1950. Product sales specialist McKesson & Robbins, Yonkers, N.Y., 1950-55; asst. sales mgr. Clairol, Inc., N.Y.C., 1955-60, pres. Salon div., 1976-83, chmn. Profl. Products div., 1983-87; dir. mktg. Haircolor div. Revlon, Inc., N.Y.C., 1960-68, dir. mktg. and sales Salon div., 1968-70; exec. v.p. Milton R. Barrie Co., Inc., 1970-71; pres. Oppenheim Communications, N.Y.C., 1987—; pub. Beauty Salon Newletter, N.Y.C., 1971-83, Salon Update, 1988—, The Oppenheim Letter, 1988—; mgmt. cons., 1988—. With AUS, 1942-44, ETO. Mem. Nat. Beauty and Barber Assn. (pres. 1984-85), Am. Beauty Assn. (pres. 1985-86), Masons. Home: 241 Sickletown Rd West Nyack NY 10994-2999 Office: Oppenheim Communications 153 E 57th St New York NY 10022-2119

OPPENHEIMER, BERTRAM JAY, hospital administrator; b. N.Y.C., Mar. 10, 1922; s. Leopold and Kate Blanche (Rosenwasser) O.; married. BA, Cornell U., 1943; BS, NYU, 1944; MD, Washington U., 1950. Diplomate Am. Bd. Med. Examiners, Am. Bd. Internal Medicine. Pvt. practice Yonkers, N.Y., 1954-76; adminstr., chief exec. officer Yonkers Gen. Hosp., 1976—. Capt. U.S. Army, 1943-46. Mem. Rotary. Office: Yonkers Gen Hosp Two Park Ave Yonkers NY 10703

OPPENHEIMER, JAMES WALTER, JR., industrial real estate broker; b. Buffalo, Oct. 8, 1955; s. James W. and Betty L. (Lehman) O. BA in English, Trinity Coll., 1978. Broker Saperston Real Estate Corp., Buffalo, 1978—. Author (song) Emily, 1991. Pres. bd. Meals on Wheels of Buffalo and Erie County, 1988. Republican. Jewish. Home: 45 St James Pl Buffalo NY 14222 Office: Saperston Real Estate Corp 584 Delaware Ave Buffalo NY 14202

OPPENHEIMER, MARTIN FOOTE, securities firm executive, lawyer; b. Washington, Aug. 24, 1948; s. Franz Martin and Margaret Spencer (Foote) O.; m. Annilee Flynn, Aug. 30, 1980; children: Caroline Ward, William Spencer. BA, Yale U., 1972; JD, Georgetown U., 1975. Bar: D.C. 1975, U.S. Supreme Ct. 1980. Pvt. practice law Washington, 1975-80, 82-85; ptnr. Opus Capital, Washington, 1980-82; v.p. Koonce Securities, Inc., Rockville, Md., 1985—; bd. dirs. N.W. Lumber Inc., Cornwall Bridge, Conn., 1989—. Vol. Bush presdl. campaign, Washington, 1988. Mem. Sabre Found. (asst. treas. 1986—), Creamhill Lake Assn. (chmn. table tennis com. 1981—), Met. Club, Aurelian Honor Soc. Republican. Episcopalian. Office: Koonce Securities Inc 6229 Executive Blvd Rockville MD 20852

OPPENHEIMER, SUZI, state senator; b. N.Y.C., Dec. 13, 1934; d. Alfred Elihu Rosenhirsch and Blanche (Schoen) O.; m. Martin J. Oppenheimer, July 3, 1960; children: Marcy, Evan, Josh, Alexandra. BA in Econs., Conn. Coll. for Women, 1956; MBA, Columbia U., 1958. Security analyst McDonnel & Co., N.Y.C., 1958-60, L.F. Rothschild Co., N.Y.C., 1960-63; mayor Village of Mamaroneck, N.Y., 1977-85; mem. N.Y. State Senate, Albany, 1985—; ranking mem. commerce, econ. devel. and small bus., mem. edn., child care, consumer protection, transp., drugs coms., chmn. Senate Minority Task Force on Women's Issues. Former pres. Mamaroneck LWV, Westchester County Village Ofcls. Assn., Westchester Mcpl. Planning Fedn. Recipient Humanitarian Svc. award Am. Jewish Com., 1988, Legis. Leadership award Young Adult Inst., 1988, Legis. award Westchester Irish Com., 1988, Hon. Svc. award Vis. Nurses Svcs., 1989, Humanitarion Svc. award Project Family, 1990, Meritorious Svc. award N.Y. State Assn. Counties, 1990, Friend of Edn. award N.Y. State United Tchrs., 1991; honoree Windward Sch. Ann. Dinner, 1992. Democrat. Jewish.

OPSAHL, RICHARD BERNHARD, aerospace company executive; b. N.Y.C., Apr. 2, 1932; s. Einar Sverre and Clara (Hurm) O.; m. Judith Easton, Nov. 22, 1966; children: Hans Burnet, Kurt Bradford. B Mech. Engring., Rensselaer Poly. Inst., 1953; MEng, Yale U., 1954; MBA, Harvard U., 1963. Dir. tech. liaison Grumman Corp., Bethpage, N.Y., 1976—. Vice chmn. Huntington (N.Y.) Conservation Bd., 1980-90; v.p. L.I. (N.Y.) Forum for Tech., 1985-88; exec. dir. Huntington Super Striders, 1986—, U.S.-Soviet Running Cultural Exch., 1990-92; trustee Sagamore Rowing Assn. Fellow AIAA (assoc., chmn. mgmt. com. 1988-90). Home: 6 Heather Ln Huntington NY 11743-1012 Office: Grumman Corp MS B36-35 Bethpage NY 11714

OPSATA, JAMES BALL, federal government foreign service officer; b. St. Joseph, Mich., May 26, 1908; s. Theodore Ollie and Jennie (Johannson) O.; m. Helen Shoup, June 15, 1937; 1 child, Margaret Ann. BS, Western Mich. U., 1931; MA, Am. U., 1949. Carpenter Theo Opsata Builder, St. Joseph, 1922-29, 35; high sch. tchr. Royal Oak Mich. Schs., 1928-35; writer, exhibition attendant Dept. of Labor, Washington, 1936-39; analyst Fed. Sec. Agy., Washington, 1939-41; personnel dir. Office of Strategic Svcs., Washington, 1941-43; exec. officer Dept. of State, Washington, 1946-51, Office of Price Adminstrn., Washington, 1951-54; foreign svc. officer USIA, Washington, 1954-68. Editorial asst. and writer: Dictionary of Occupational Titles, 1937, Dept. of Labor-U.S. Employment Svc. Lt. USN, Brazil, 1943-46. Mem. Diplomatic and Consular Officers Retired (sec. 1985—, sec. Bacon House Found. 1985—), Am. Foreign Svc. Assn. Home: 1529 Eton Way Crofton MD 21114-1524

O'QUINN, KERRY, writer; b. Austin, Tex., Aug. 19, 1938; s. Trueman Edgar and Hazel (Hedick) O'Q. Student, U. Tex., 1956-62. Art editor Ideal Publ., N.Y.C., 1964-66, Sterling Publ., N.Y.C., 1966-68; radio/TV producer Gray Advt., N.Y.C., 1969-71; co-owner, producer, publ. (with Norman Jacobs) O'Quinn Studios, N.Y.C., 1972-90, Starlog Publ., N.Y.C., 1972-90, O'Quinn Prodns., N.Y.C., 1972-90; adv. coun. U. Tex. Coll. Fine Arts, Austin, 1988-92. Publsher, creator: (magazine) Starlog, 1977. Exec. Coun. Austin Fest. Dance, 1992. Recipient Starry-Eyed Gnomme award Omnicon, Fla., 1983. Mem. Gamma Mu, Delta Upsilon (v.p. Tex. chpt., life), Sigma Delta Chi. Republican. Home: 2300 Windsor Rd E Austin TX 78703 Office: 10 Waterside Pla 35-A New York NY 10010

ORAVITZ, JOSEPH VINCENT, educational association administrator; b. Shamokin, Pa., Dec. 31, 1937; s. Joseph G. and Amelia (Dargavich) O.; m. Roberta Louise Allen, Oct. 21, 1961; children: Suzanne, Beth, JoLene. BS in Edn., Bloomsburg U., 1963. Cert. bus. edn. tchr., Pa. Tchr. bus. Hanover (Pa.) Pub. Schs., 1963-67, chmn. dept. bus., 1966-67, adminstrv. asst. for bus., 1967-70; dir. rsch. and mgmt. svcs. Pa. Sch. Bds. Assn., Harrisburg, 1970-82, exec. dir., 1982—; chmn. budget and audit com. Pa. Pub. Sch. Employees' Retirement Bd.; treas. Pa. Sch. Dist. LKiquid Asset Fund; sec., trustee Pa. Sch. Bds. Ins. Trust; trustee Pa. Sch. Bds. Assn. Legal Assistance Fund; bd. dirs. Pa. Coun. on Econ. Edn.; mem. edn. adv. bd. 19th Congl. Dist.; lectr., panelist at profl. confs. and workshops. With USN, 1955-59. Mem. Nat. Sch. Bds. Assn. (chmn. liaison com., bd. dirs.). Office: Pa Sch Bds Assn 774 Limekiln Rd New Cumberland PA 17070-2398

ORBEN, ROBERT, editor, writer; b. N.Y.C., Mar. 4, 1927; s. Walter August and Marie (Neweceral) O.; m. Jean Louise Connelly, July 25, 1945. Humor and speech writer for entertainment personalities, bus. execs., politicians, 1946—; writer Jack Paar Show, N.Y.C., 1962-63, Red Skelton Hour, Hollywood, Calif., 1964-70; editor Orben's Current Comedy, Wilmington, Del., 1971-89; cons. to Vice Pres. Gerald R. Ford, Washington, 1974; speechwriter Pres. Gerald R. Ford, Washington, 1974-75; spl. asst. to pres., dir. White House speechwriting dept., Washington, 1976-77; speaker on uses of humor in communication, 1977—. Author: 2500 Jokes to Start 'Em Laughing, 1979, 2100 Laughs for All Occasions, 1983, 2400 Jokes to Brighten Your Speeches, 1984, 2000 Sure-Fire Jokes for Speakers, 1986; numerous other books of humor for performers and public speakers. Mem. Writers Guild Am. Unitarian. Club: Nat. Press (Washington). Home: 1200 N Nash St Arlington VA 22209-3644

ORBISON, DAVID VAILLANT, clinical psychologist, consultant; b. Hartford, Conn., Apr. 2, 1952; s. Theodore Tucker and Edith Vaillant (Julier) O.; m. Beth Lynne Fruendt, June 19, 1981; children: Henry Douglas, Charles Vaillant, Samuel Tucker. BA, Yale U., 1974; MA in Psychology, Duquesne U., 1976, PhD in Clin. Psychology, 1986. Psychologist Harmarville Rehab. Ctr., Pitts., 1975-84; pvt. practice Pitts., 1981—; mem. adj. profl. staff Shadyside Hosp., Pitts., 1981—. Fellow Pa. Psychol. Assn. (chmn. program and edn. bd. 1988—); mem. Greater Pitts. Psychol. Assn. (treas. 1984-86, chmn. bd. dirs. 1986-88). Office: 401 Shady Ave Ste 102C Pittsburgh PA 15206-4409

O'REAGAN, KEVIN PATRICK, management consultant; b. Washington, Feb. 12, 1960; s. Robert Thomas and Mary Patricia (Sugrue) O'R.; m. Debra Ann Leahy, Nov. 7, 1987. BSin Info. Systems, U. Md., 1982; MAS in Info. Tech., Johns Hopkins U., 1988, MAS in Mgmt., 1988. Mgr. MCI Telecommunication, Washington, 1984-86; mgmt. cons. Arthur Andersen & Co., Washington, 1982-84, Ernst & Whinney, Washington, 1986-87, Reznick, Fedder & Silverman, Washington, 1987-89, Perot Systems, Washington, 1989-90; pres. First Georgetown Cons. Group, Ltd., Washington, 1990—; instr. Johns Hopkins U., 1991. Mem. Am. Mgmt. Assn. Office: First Georgetown Cons Group Ltd Internat Sq 1825 I St NW Ste 400 Washington DC 20006

O'REILLY, ANTHONY JOHN FRANCIS, food company executive; b. Dublin, Ireland, May 7, 1936; s. John Patrick and Aileen (O'Connor) O'R.; m. Susan Cameron, May 5, 1962 (div.); children: Susan, Cameron, Justine, Gavin, Caroline, Tony; m. Chryss Coulandris, Sept. 14, 1991. Student, Belvedere Coll., Dublin, Univ. Coll., Dublin, Wharton Bus. Sch. Overseas, 1965; B.C.L.; D.C.L. (hon.), Ind. State U.; Ph.D. in Agrl. Mktg, U. Bradford, Eng.; LL.D. (hon.), Wheeling Coll., 1974, Trinity Coll., Dublin, 1978, Allegheny Coll., 1983, De Paul U., Chgo., 1988; D in Bus. Studies (hon.), Rollins Coll., 1978; D in Civil Law honoris causa, Ind. State U., 1980; DBA (hon.), Boston Coll., 1985; D in Econ. Sci. (hon.), Nat. U. Ireland, 1989. Indsl. cons. Weston Evans, 1958-62; personal asst. to chmn. Suttons Ltd., Cork, Ireland, 1960-62; lectr. dept. applied psychology Univ. Coll., Cork, 1960-62; dir. Robert McCowen & Sons Ltd., Tralee, Ireland, 1961-62; mng. dir. An Bord Bainne/Irish Dairy Bd., 1962-66; dir. Agrl. Credit Corp. Ltd., 1965-66, Nitrigin Eireann Teoranta, 1965-66; mng. dir., chief exec. officer Comhlucht Siuicre Eireann Teo. (Irish Sugar Co.) and Erin Foods Ltd., Dublin, 1966-69; joint mng. dir. Heinz-Erin Ltd., 1967-70; mng. dir. H.J. Heinz Co. Ltd., Eng., 1969-71; sr. v.p. N.Am. and Pacific H.J. Heinz Co., 1971-72; exec. v.p., chief operating officer H.J. Heinz Co., Pitts., 1972-73, pres., chief operating officer, 1973-79, pres., chief exec. officer, 1979—, also chmn., 1978—, also bd. dirs.; chmn. Fitzwilton Plc.,Independent Newspapers Plc., Atlantic Resources, Dublin, Am. Ireland Fund.; ptnr. Cawley Sheerin Wynne and Co., solicitors, Dublin; bd. dirs. Bankers Trust N.Y. Corp., Bankers Trust N.Y. Corp., Washington Post Co., London Tablet Found. Inc., Starkist Foods Inc., Ore-Ida Foods Inc. Author: Prospect, 1962, Developing Creative Management, 1970, The Conservative Consumer, 1971, Food for Thought, 1972. Bd. govs. Hugh O'Brian Found., L.A.; mem. counc. Rockefeller U., N.Y.C.; bd. dirs. Assocs. Grad. Sch. Bus. Adminstrn. of Harvard U., Cambridge, Mass.; sr. bd. dirs. The Conf. Bd.; trustee U. Pitts., Com. for Econ. Devel.; mem. Nat. Com. Whitney Mus. Am. Art. Named Hon. Officer Order of Australia, 1988. Fellow Brit. Inst. Mgmt., Royal Soc. Arts; mem. Inst. Dirs., Inc., Law Soc. Ireland (treas.), Grocery Mfrs. Am. (sec., bd. dirs.), Am. Irish Found., Internat. Life Scis. Inst. Nutrition Found. (chmn., chief exec. officer council), Irish Mgmt. Inst. (council), Exec. Council Fgn. Diplomats (bd. dirs.). Clubs: St. Stephens Green, Kildare St., University (Dublin); Annabels, Les Ambassadeurs, Marks (London); Union League, The Links, The Bd. Room (N.Y.C.); Duquesne, Allegheny, Pitts. Golf, Fox Chapel Golf, Pitts. Press, Pitts. Golf (Pitts.); Rolling Rock (Ligonier) (bd. govs.); Lyford Cay (Bahamas). Office: H J Heinz Co 600 Grant St PO Box 57 Pittsburgh PA 15219 also: Mobil Corp 150 E 42nd St New York NY 10017

O'REILLY, DENIS, aluminum company executive, lawyer; b. Pointe Gatineau, Que., Can., Feb. 9, 1950; s. Florian D. and Marielle O'R.; B.A. with honors, Three Rivers U., 1969; L.L.L., Montreal U., 1973; postgrad. Ecole des Hautes Etudes Commerciales, Montreal, 1976; m. Jocelyne Ryter, Aug. 16, 1980; children: Marianne, Patrick. Called to Que. bar, 1975; research worker Sec. of State, Ottawa, Ont., Can., 1971; analyst Datum Sedoj, Montreal, Que., Can., 1972; assoc. firm Lette & Assocs., Montreal, 1973-76; legal officer Aluminum Co. of Can., Ltd., Montreal, 1977-80; chief legal officer, sec. Alcan Smelters and Chems. Ltd., Montreal, 1981-82, also dir. adminstrn.; pres., gen. mgr. Vic Metal Corp., Victoriaville, Que., 1982—; pres., Vic West Steel, Oakville, Ont., 1986—. Mem. Bd. Trade (Que.), Quebec Bar Assn., Can. Bar Assn., Can. Constrn. Assn. (dir.). Office: 1296 So Svc Rd W, Oakville, ON Canada L6L 5M7

O'REILLY, JAMES MICHAEL, chemist; b. Dayton, Ohio, Nov. 25, 1934; s. Michael W. and Viola (Requarth) O'R.; m. Marlene Ann Loy, Feb. 27, 1954; children: James M., Jr., Patrick R., Christopher D., Kevin V., Megan A. BS, U. Dayton, 1956; PhD, Notre Dame U., 1960. Mfg. chemist Nat. Cash Register, Dayton, 1954-56; rsch. chemist Gen. Elec. Rsch. Ctr., Schnectady, N.Y., 1960-67; rsch. mgr. Xerox Corp., Webster, N.Y., 1967-80; rsch. assoc. Eastman Kodak Co., Rochester, N.Y., 1980—. Editor: Physical Aging of Polymers, 1990, Structure and Motion in Polymers, 1980. Fellow Am. Phys. Soc. (chmn. 1975-76). Roman Catholic.

OREM, NICHOLAS RADCLIFFE, computer company executive; b. Bethesda, Md., July 26, 1945; s. Sidney Radcliffe and Margaret Ellen (Davies) O.; m. Phyllis Merian Eddy, June 24, 1967; children: Nicholas R. Jr., Margaret E. BA, Trinity Coll., 1967; MBA with distinction, Dartmouth Coll., 1971. Cop. planner Boise (Idaho) Cascade Corp., 1971-72, controller corp. div., 1972-73; v.p. Logic Assocs., Inc., White River Junction, Vt., 1973—. Staff sgt. U.S. Army, 1968-70, Vietnam. Decorated Bronze Star medal, U.S. Army, Vietnam, 1970. Mem. Lotos Club. Home: RR 1 Box 514 Norwich VT 05055-9524 Office: Logic Assocs Inc PO Box 765 White River Junction VT 05001-0765

ORENDUFF, J. MICHAEL, academic administrator; b. Houston, Apr. 12, 1944; s. Jess J. and Billie L. (Grisham) O.; m. Lai Kent Chew, Sept 13, 1965; children: Jay, Claire. BA, Tex., Austin, 1967; M.A., U. N.Mex., Albuquerque, 1969; PhD, Tulane U., 1972. Instr. Newcomb Coll., New Orleans, 1969-70; faculty mem. S.W. Tex. State U., San Marcos, 1970-82; dean Weber State Coll., Ogden, Utah, 1982-85; v.p. West Tex. State U., Canyon, 1985-88; pres. U. Maine, Farmington, 1988; pres. Southwestern Philos. Soc., 1984-85;

vice chmn. Utah Endowment for the Humnities, 1983-85. Author numerous articles on philos. topics; editor Jour. S.W. Philos. Studies, 1986. Bd. dirs. St. Anthony's Hospice, Amarillo, 1986, Jr. Achievement, Ogden, 1985; trustee Amarillo Art Cen., 1987. Recipient NDEA fellowship U.S. Govt., Pedagogue award, S.W.Tex. Alumni Assn. Mem. Phi Eta Sigma. Home: 100 Main St Farmington ME 04938-1995 Office: U Maine 86 Main St Farmington ME 04938-1990*

ORENSTEIN-BELLIA, JESSICA, publishing company manager; b. Levittown, N.Y., July 8, 1959; d. Martin and Lorraine (Peffer) Orenstein; m. Leonard Mitchell Bellia, Apr. 26, 1987. BS cum laude, C.W. Post Coll., Greenvale, N.Y., 1981, MBA, 1991. Mgr. customer svc. Channel Home Ctrs., Jericho, N.Y., 1978-81; credit collections analyst, then corp. billing mgr. Superior Care Inc., Great Neck, N.Y., 1981-84; supr., now dept. mgr. CMP Pubs., Inc., Manhasset, N.Y., 1984—. Mem. Delta Mu Delta. Home: 17 Chase Ln Levittown NY 11756-1046 Office: CMP Publs Inc 600 Community Dr Manhasset NY 11030-3847

ORESICK, PETER MICHAEL, publisher, writer; b. Ford City, Pa., Sept. 8, 1955; s. Peter and Mary (Gernat) O.; m. Stephanie Lane Flom, Nov. 26, 1977; children: William Gregory, Jacob Stefan, David Max. BA, U. Pitts., 1977, MFA, 1981. Tchr. Pitts. Pub. Schs., 1977-80; writer-in-residence Pa. Coun. on the Arts, Harrisburg, 1977-84, mem. lit. panel, 1986-88, 92—; pub. U. Pitts. Press, 1985—; bd. dirs. Pa. Ctr. for the Book. Author: Definitions, 1990; editor: Working Classics, 1990. Home: 6342 Jackson St Pittsburgh PA 15206-2232 Office: U Pitts Press 127 N Bellefield Ave Pittsburgh PA 15260-0001

ORGANISAK, PAUL JOHN, dance festival association executive; b. Pitts., June 25, 1962; s. Joseph and Elizabeth (McKay) O. Student, U. Mich., 1984. Asst. devel. dir. Pitts. Civic Light Opera, 1986-88; assoc. dir. Pitts. Dance Coun., 1988-91; exec. dir. Am. Coll. Dance Festival Assn., Pitts., 1991—; mem. art adv. bd. Bates Dance Festival, Lewiston, Maine, 1991—; instr. Point Park Coll., Pitts., 1991. Office: Am Coll Dance Festival Assn 201 Wood St 609B Pittsburgh PA 15222

ORING, STUART AUGUST, visual information specialist; b. Bronx, N.Y., Aug. 28, 1932; s. Irving and Helen Flora (Greenhut) O.; m. Mary Carolyn Barth, Aug. 22, 1957; children: Carlene Marie Oring, Sheri Alyce Oring. AAS, Rochester Inst. Tech., 1957; BFA, R.I. Tech., 1959; MA, Am. U., 1970. Photo lab asst. Nat. Geographic, Washington, summer 1957; photography asst. Nepo-Nuss, I.J. Becker Studio Assocs., N.Y.C., 1959-61; freelance photographer pvt. practice, Washington, 1961; indsl. photographer Vitro Corp., Rockville, Md., 1962-64; health photographer Nat. Ctr. Radiol. Health, Rockville, Md., 1964-67; visual inro. specialist ARS Info. div. USDA, Washington, 1967-69; audio visual specialist Nat. AV Ctr., Washington, 1969-71; photojournalist Office of Econ. Opportunity, Washington, 1971-74; visual info. specialist ASCS, U.S. Dept. Agr., Washington, 1974—; photography tchr. Prince George's Community Coll., Largo, Md., 1975—; guest lectr. U. Md. Balto. County, Towson, Md. Author, editor: Understanding Pictures, 1990; contbr. numerous articles to profl. jours.; photos published in books, mags., brochures. Pub. rels. Calvert County Humane Soc., 1990. With U.S. Army, 1952-55, Korea. Recipient Cert. Recognition award Eastman Kodak Co., 1973, Nat. Ctr. Radiol. Halth, Rockville, Md., 1965. Mem. Soc. Photographic Edn. Home: 2570 Redbud Ln Owings MD 20736 Office: ASCS Info Div USDA 14th & Independence Ave SW Washington DC 20250

ORINGER, MAURICE JULES, oral surgeon; b. N.Y.C., June 18, 1905; s. Louis and Gerturde Cynthia (Trommer) O.; m. Helen Jane Ornstein, Apr. 11, 1953. DDS, NYU Coll. Dentistry, 1928. Diplomate Am. Bd. Oral Electrosurgery. Guest instr. Dept. Continuing Edn. 31 U.S. and Fgn. Dental Schs., 1951; profl. lectr. St. Louis U. Dental Sch., 1953-58; pres. Midtown Dental Soc., N.Y.C., 1953; prof. honoraire Ctr. de Perfectionnement en Odonto Stomatologie Cote d'Azur, France, 1966; founder Am. Acad. Dental Electrosurgery, N.Y.C., 1962; cons. ADA Coun. Dental Materials and Devices, Chgo., 1970—; chmn. ADA/ANSI Subcommittee for Electrosurgery Device, Chgo., 1976—; co-founder Am. Bd. Oral Electrosurgery, 1976; adjunct prof. Dept. Biomedical Engrng. U. Miami, 1976-88; cons. Coles Electronic Corp., Phila., 1958-72, Ritter Co., Rochester, N.Y., 1973-75, Cavitron Corp., N.Y.C., 1970-72, Siemens, Bensheim, Germany, 1979-81. Author: Electrosurgery In Dentistry, 1962, 2d ed. 1975, Color Atlas or Oral Electrosurgery, 1984; co-editor: Dental Clinics North America, 1969; contbr. articles to profl. jours. Capt. Acting Theatre Oral Surgeon, 1942-46. Oringer award named in his honor Acad. Dental Electrosurgery. Mem. Am. Dental Assn., Am. Coll. Dentists, Am. Acad. Dental Electrosurgery, Royal Soc. Health. Jewish. Home: 15 W 81st St New York NY 10024

ORISEK, IVAN, business executive, consultant; b. Prague, Czechoslovakia, May 29, 1945; s. Frantisek and Bozena O.; came to U.S., 1976, naturalized, 1981; M.Sc., Czech Tech. U., Prague, 1967; m. Olga Dedina, Sept. 28, 1977; children: Philip, Vena. Sr. research analyst Research Inst. Fuel and Energy Econs., Prague, 1970-75; head ops. research sect. Am. Electric Power Service Corp., N.Y.C., 1976-81; prin. engr. Ebasco Services, Inc., N.Y.C., 1981-86; pres. I&O Assocs. Mortgage Corp., White Plains, N.Y., 1986—. Mem. Nat. Assn. Mortgage Brokers, N.Y. Assn. Mortgage Brokers, Ops. Research Soc. Am. Home: The Tudor Old Orchard St White Plains NY 10604-1010

ORLANDO, DANIELLE, opera company administrator. Artistic adminstr. Opera Co. of Phila. Office: Opera Co Phila The Graham Bldg 20th Fl 1 Penn Sq W Philadelphia PA 19102*

ORLANS, F(LORA) BARBARA, bioethics associate; b. Birmingham, Eng., Jan. 14, 1928; came to U.S., 1956; d. Christopher and Flora Christine (Brookes) Hughes; m. Herbert C. Morton, June 19, 1982; children: Andrew Brookes Orlans, Nicholas Motcomb Orlans. BSc in Physiology/Anatomy, Birmingham (Eng.) U., 1949; MS in Physiology, London U., 1954, PhD in Physiology, 1956. Physiology instr. dept. medicine Johns Hopkins Hosp., Balt., 1956; rsch. pharmacologist Nat. Heart Inst., NIH, Bethesda, Md., 1956-60; freelance writer, 1967-73; sr. staff scientist Med. Ctr. George Washington U., Washington, 1973-74; health sci. adminstr. Nat. Heart, Lung & Blood Inst. NIH, Bethesda, 1974-77; exec. dir., adv. coun. Heart Inst. NIH, Bethesda, 1977-80; staff scientist cardiac diseases NIH, Bethesda, 1979-84; dir. Scientists Ctr. Animal Welfare, Bethesda, 1984-88; rsch. assoc. Kennedy Inst. Ethics Georgetown U., Washington, 1989—; founding pres. Scientists Ctr. Animal Welfare, Bethesda, 1978-84; chair Parks Found. for Animal Welfare, Portland, Maine, 1987-90. Author: Animal Care: From Protozoa to Small Mammals, 1977; editor: Scientific Perspectives on Animal Welfare, 1982, Effective Animal Care & Use Committees, 1987; contbr. articles to refereed jours. Grantee Geraldine R. Dodge Found., Morristown, N.J., 1980-90, ethical values program NSF, 1987-88; Rockefeller Found. scholar, Bellagio, Italy, 1989. Mem. Am. Soc. Pharmacology, Nat. Sci. Tchrs. Assn., N.Y. Acad. Scis., Nat. Assn. Biology Tchrs. Office: Georgetown U Kennedy Inst Ethics 37th and P St NW Washington DC 20057

ORLIDGE, LESLIE ARTHUR, electrical engineer; b. Johnstown, Pa., Nov. 11, 1953; s. Arthur Eugene and Mary Kail (Huffman) O.; m. Kimber Leigh Volkmar, Mar. 26, 1988; children: Jessica Leigh, Julia Leigh. BSEE, BA, Pa. State U., 1977; M.Adminstrv. Sci., Johns Hopkins U., Balt., 1984. Systems engr. AAI Corp., Hunt Valley, Md., 1977-78, lead systems engr., 1979-82, engring. mgr., 1983-85, IR&D program mgr., 1985-87, IR&D tech. dir., 1988-90, prin. devel. engr., 1990-91, mgr. new bus. devel. electronics div., 1991—. Contbr. articles to profl. jours. Mem. IEEE (vice chmn. SCC-20 AI subcom. 1990—), Assn. Computing Machinery, AIAA, Computer Soc. of IEEE, IEEE Instrument and Measurement Soc., Masons (past master 1988), Shriner. Methodist. Home: 1613 Walker Rd Freeland MD 21053-9541 Office: AAI Corp PO Box 126 Cockeysville Hunt Valley MD 21030-0126

ORLOV, DARLENE, management consultant; b. Elizabeth, N.J., July 13, 1949; d. Sol and Evelyn (Perlman) O. BA in English, Secondary Edn., Fairleigh Dickinson U., 1971, MA in English Lit., 1982; MBA in Mgmt. with distinction, N.Y. Inst. of Tech., 1981. Pers. dir. Kayser-Roth Corp., N.Y.C., 1975-76; pers. mgr. Corometrics Med. Systems, Wallingford, Conn., 1976-78; mgr. EEO and communications Internat. Playtex, N.Y.C., 1978-79; pres. Orlov Resources for Bus., Inc., N.Y.C., 1979—; adj. asst. prof. NYU, 1980-88; adj. prof. Marymount Manhattan Coll., N.Y.C., 1981—, adv. bd. Dance Co., 1992—; trustee Fairleigh Dickinson U., Madison, N.J., 1989—. Bd. dirs. The Assoc. Blind, Inc., 1991—. Mem. Cornell Club of N.Y.

ORLOWSKI, KAREL ANN, educator; b. Fremont, Ohio, Dec. 22, 1949; d. Karl and Angeline Marie (Oudersluys) Kooistra; m. Paul Joseph Orlowski, Apr. 28, 1973; 1 child, Jennifer Frann. BA in Music Edn., U. Mich., 1971; MS in Elem. Edn., Dowling Coll., Oakdale, N.Y., 1978. Cert. tchr., N.Y. Tchr. vocal music Patchogue (N.Y.)-Medford Schs., 1971—, lead tchr. music dept., 1986-88, 91—; dir. of musicals Eagle Elem. Sch., 1990—; dir. drama dept. River Elem. Sch., Patchogue, 1974-90, Chosen Few show choir South Ocean Mid. Sch., Patchogue, 1984-90, Notation! show choir Eagle Elem. Sch., 1990—; vocal dir. Friends of Arts, Patchogue, 1986—. Mem. N.Y. State Sch. Music Assn., Suffolk County Music Educators Assn. Republican. Episcopalian. Home: 37 Detmer Rd East Setauket NY 11733-1912 Office: Patchogue-Medford Schs 241 S Ocean Ave Patchogue NY 11772-3787

ORME-JOHNSON, NANETTE ROBERTS, biochemistry educator; b. San Antonio, Apr. 11, 1937; d. Clarence Olin and Rachel Horton Roberts. BS, U. Tex., 1959; PhD, U. Wis., 1973. Rsch. assoc. dept. biochemistry U. Wis., Madison, 1974-79; prin. rsch. scientist dept. chemistry MIT, Cambridge, 1980-82; asst. prof. dept. biochemistry Tufts U Med. Sch., Boston, 1982-87, assoc. prof., 1987—. Contbr. articles to profl. jours. Mem. Beacon Hill Civic Assn. Mem. Am. Soc. Biol. Chemists, Endocrine Soc., Phi Beta Kappa, Delta Phi Alpha, Phi Lambda Upsilon, Sigma Xi. Democrat. Episcopalian. Office: Tufts U Med Sch Dept Biochemistry 136 Harrison Ave Boston MA 02111-1800

ORME-JOHNSON, WILLIAM HENRY, III, chemist, educator; b. Phoenix, Apr. 23, 1938; s. William Henry and Jean Mary (McGhee) O.; m. Nanette Roberts, May 27, 1957 (div. 1982); m. Carol Chamberlain, Aug. 23, 1983; children: Doris Helen, Ruth David, McGhee Charles. Student, Rice U., 1955-57; BS, U. Tex., 1959, PhD, 1964. Postdoctoral fellow U. Wis., Enzyme Inst., Madison, 1965-67, asst. prof., 1967-70; asst. prof. U. Wis., Dept. Biochemistry, Madison, 1970-71, assoc. prof., 1971-73, 1973-79, prof., 1973-79; prof. MIT, Dept. Chemistry, Cambridge, Mass., 1979—; sci. cons. BioTechnica Ltd., Cambridge, 1983—. Contbr. over 150 articles to sci. jours. V.p. The Lyric Stage, Boston, 1990-92. Grantee NIH, 1967—. Fellow AAAS; mem. Am. Chem. Soc., Am. Soc. Biol. Chemists. Episcopalian. Home: 48 Massachusetts Ave Cambridge MA 02139-4322 Office: MIT 77 Massachusetts Ave Cambridge MA 02139-4307

ORMES, JONATHAN FAIRFIELD, astrophysicist, science administrator, researcher; b. Colorado Springs, Colo., July 18, 1939; s. Robert Manly and Suzanne (Viertel) O.; m. Karen Lee Minnick, Dec. 26, 1960 (div.); 1 child, Laurie Kylee; m. Janet Carolyn Dahl, Sept. 12, 1964; children: Marina, Nicholas. BS, Stanford U., 1961; PhD, U. Minn., 1967. NRC assoc. Goddard Space Flight Ctr., NASA, Greenbelt, Md., 1967-69, astrophysicist, 1969, head cosmic radiations br., 1981-82, head nuclear astrophysics br., 1983-87, assoc. chief lab. for high energy astrophysics, 1987-90, chief lab. for high energy astrophysics, 1990—; acting head high energy physics NASA hdqrs., Washington, 1982-83, mem. high energy astrophysics mgmt. ops. working group, 1975-83, mem. cosmic ray program working group, 1984-91; mem. com. on space and solar physics Nat. Acad. Sci., Washington, 1991—. Editor: Essays in Space Science, 1987; assoc. editor astrophysics Phys. Rev. Letters, 1991; contbr. Astrophysics Jour., Phys. Rev. Letters, Astronomy and Astrophysics. Trustee Paint Br. Unitarian Universalist Ch., Adelphi, Md., 1987-88, chair bd. trustees, 1989, numerous positions, 1972-91. Fellow Am. Phys. Soc. (various div. offices); mem. Internat. Astron. Union, Am. Astron. Soc. (sec.-treas. High Energy Astrophysics div. 1985-87), Am. Geophys. Union. Office: NASA Code 660 Goddard Space Flight Ctr Greenbelt MD 20771

ORNA, MARY VIRGINIA, chemistry educator; b. Newark, July 4, 1934; d. Edward Joseph and Julia Eleanor (Lebert) O. BS, Chestnut Hill Coll., 1955; MS, Fordham U., 1958, PhD, 1962; MA, Cath. U., 1967. Prof. chemistry Coll. of New Rochelle, N.Y., 1966—; rsch. assoc. Nat. Inst. Environ., Health Sci., Research Triangle Park, N.C., 1987-88; extramural assoc. NIH, Bethesda, Md., 1984. Author: Cybernetics, Society and Church, 1968, Chemistry and Artists Colors, 1990; editor: History and Preservation of Chemical Instrumentation, 1986, Electrochemistry Past and Present, 1989; contbr. articles to profl. jours.; constructor crossword puzzles N.Y. Sunday Times and various sci. mags. Recipient Nat. Catalyst award Chem. Mfg. Assn., 1984, Innovation award Merck & Co., 1989, Prof. of Yr. award Coun. for Advancement and Support of Edn., 1989; NSF grantee, 1967—. Mem. Am. Chem. Soc. (councilor 1991—, treas. chem. edn. div. 1985—, award 1986, chair history of chemistry div. 1983), Internat. Inst. for Conservation of Hist. and Artistic Works, New Eng. Assn. Chemistry Tchrs., Nat. Sci. Tchrs. Assn. Democrat. Roman Catholic. Home: 16 Hemlock Pl New Rochelle NY 10805-2302 Office: Coll of New Rochelle Dept Chemistry 29 Castle Pl New Rochelle NY 10805-2308

OROMANER, MARK, college dean, sociologist; b. N.Y.C., Mar. 14, 1941; s. Theodore and Faye (Wohlmuth) O.; m. Marilynn Krause, Sept. 3, 1972. BA, NYU, 1963, MA, 1966. Asst. rsch. scientist sociology dept. NYU, N.Y.C., 1966-67; lectr. sociology Hunter Coll. CUNY, N.Y.C., 1966-71; instr. sociology Jersey City State Coll., 1972-77; chair pub. and human svcs. Hudson County Community Coll., Jersey City, 1977-78, asst. to pres. for planning and rsch., 1978-79, dean for acad. affairs, 1979-82, dean, v.p. for planning rsch. and evaluation, 1982-87, exec. v.p., 1987-88, acting/interim pres., 1988-89, dean for planning, 1989—; Mem. editorial bd. History of Sociology, 1978—, Rsch. in Higher Edn., 1985-88; contbr. articles to profl. jours. Mem. Am. Sociol. Assn., Soc. for the Social Studies of Sci., Am. Ednl. Rsch. Assn., Am. Evaluation Assn. Office: Hudson County Community Coll 901 Bergen Ave Jersey City NJ 07306-4301

O'ROURKE, ANDREW PATRICK, lawyer, county official; b. Plainfield, N.J., Oct. 26, 1933; s. Andrew Patrick and Helene (Anderson) O'R.; children: Alice T., Andrew Patrick, Alleen B. BS, Fordham Coll., 1954, LLD, 1962; LLM, NYU, 1965; LLD, Mercy Coll., 1988, Pace U., 1987, Manhattanville Coll., 1986, Marymount Coll., 1986. Bar: N.Y. 1962, U.S. Dist. Ct. (so. and ea. dists.) N.Y., U.S. Ct. Appeals (2d cir.) 1964, U.S. Supreme Ct. 1970. Assoc. Kreindler & Kreindler, N.Y.C., 1963-68; sole practice, Westchester County, N.Y., 1968-82; county exec. Westchester County, White Plains, N.Y., 1983—. Author: Red Banner Mutiny, 1985, Hawkwood, 1989; contbr. articles to profl. jours. Mem. Yonkers (N.Y.) City Coun., 1966-73; mem. Westchester County Bd. Legislators, 1973-82, chmn., 1978-82; del. Rep. Nat. Convention, New Orleans, 1988. Served to capt. USNR. Recipient Seth Lowe award L.I. U., 1984, Tree of Life award Jewish Nat. Fund, 1984, Coun. for Arts award Westchester County Council Arts, 1984, Hispanic Coun. Westchester award, 1985, Disting. Svc. award Putnam Affirmative Action Program Inc., Westchester, 1991. Office: County Office Bldg 148 Martine Ave White Plains NY 10601-3311

O'ROURKE, JAMES, physician, educator; b. Trenton, N.J., Mar. 2, 1925; s. James Joseph and Mary Francis (Fitzgerald) O'R.; m. Marita Florence Howard, June 12, 1954; children: James, Mary Carol, Elizabeth, Margaret. MD, Georgetown U., 1949; MS, U. Pa., 1954. Diplomate Am. Bd. Ophthalmology. Intern St. Francis Hosp., Trenton, 1949-50; postdoctoral fellow U. Pa., Phila., 1950-52; resident in surgery Wills Eye Hosp., Phila., 1952-54; clin. assoc. NIH, Bethesda, Md., 1954-57; asst. prof. surgery Georgetown U., Washington, 1957-60, assoc. prof., 1960-65, prof. surgery, 1965-69; prof. surgery U. Conn. Health Ctr., Farmington, 1969-83, prof. pathology, 1984—; dir. U. Conn. Vision-Immunology Ctr., Farmington, 1985—; bd. dirs. Fidelco Found., Bloomfield, Conn., Conn. Eye Bank, New Britain, Conn. Author: Nuclear Ophthalmology, 1976; contbr. articles to profl. jours. With USNR, 1943-46. NIH grantee, 1957-69, 69-90, 87-92. Mem. Am. Acad. Ophthalmology, Soc. Vascular Medicine and Biology, Cosmos Club, Rotary (Paul Harris fellow 1990). Episcopalian. Home: 113 Main St Farmington CT 06032-2237 Office: U Conn Health Ctr 263 Farmington Ave Farmington CT 06030-0001

ORPHANIDES, GUS GEORGE, chemical company official; b. N.Y.C., Jan. 27, 1947; s. Gus G. and Savesta (Agapetus) O.; m. Jeanne Wood, Feb. 3, 1968; children: Alyson, Paul, Lindsay. BS, Hobart Coll., 1967; PhD, Ohio State U., 1972. Chemist E.I. Du Pont de Nemours & Co., Wilmington, Del., 1974-79, Beaumont, Tex., 1979-81; chemist Air Products, Allentown, Pa., 1981-84, applications mgr., 1984-85, comml. mgr., 1985-88, rsch. mgr., 1988-91, mgr. comml. devel., 1991—. Patentee in field. 1st lt. U.S. Army, 1972-74. Mem. TAPPI, Am. Chem. Soc. Republican. Presbyterian. Home: 3460 W Highland St Allentown PA 18104-2673 Office: Air Products 7201 Hamilton Blvd Allentown PA 18195-9642

ORPHANIDES, NORA CHARLOTTE, ballet educator; b. Bklyn., June 4, 1951; d. M.T. and Mary Elsie (Tilly) Feffer; m. James Mark Orphanides, July 1, 1972; children: Mark, Elaine, Jennine. BA, CUNY, 1973; student, Joffrey Ballet Sch., N.Y.C., 1970-75; postgrad., Princeton Ballet Sch., 1976-86. Cert. speech and hearing handicapped tchr. Sr. sales assoc. Met. Mus. Art, N.Y.C., 1970-86; membership asst. Patrons Lounge, M.M.A., N.Y.C., 1987—; mem. faculty Princeton (N.J.) Ballet Sch., 1983—, trustee emeritus, 1992—. Mem. cast Princeton Ballet ann. Nutcracker, 1985-90. Fundraising gala chmn. Princeton Ballet, 1985, 86, 91-92, chmn. spl. events, 1987—, trustee, 1986—, chmn. Nutcracker benefit, 1990—, Dracula benefit, 1991; vol. libr. Plainsboro (N.J.) Free Libr., 1985; program solicitation chmn. to benefit Princeton Med. Ctr., 1988, T-shirt chmn. benefit, 1990, 91, publicity chmn. ann. June Fete, 1992; mem. worship and arts commn. Nassau Presbyn. Ch., 1989, 90, dinner chmn. Bach Music Festival, 1989, Cambridge Singers, 1990; vol. Nat. Hdqrs. Recording for the Blind, 1991—; trustee Princeton Youth Fund, 1991-92; dinner chmn. Nassau Ch. Music Festival, 1992. Mem. Princeton Med. Ctr. Aux. Democrat. Home: 35 Brearly Rd Princeton NJ 08540-6767 Office: Sch of Princeton Ballet 262 Alexander St Princeton NJ 08540

ORR, DINAH TOTTENHAM, non-profit foundation administrator; b. W. Brighton, England, July 1, 1930; came to U.S., 1958; d. Edmund Loftus and Margaret (Vines) T.; m. Benjamin Allen Groves, Feb. 21, 1953 (div. Feb. 1964); children: Philippa Caroline Johnston, Amanda Frances Tottenham Outerbridge; m. John D.E. Orr, Apr. 10, 1978. Asst. to pres. Internat. Coll. Beirut, Lebanon, 1975-78; exec. dir. Parkinson's Disease Found., N.Y.C., 1978—; bd. dirs. Nat. Orgn. for Rare Disorders, Fairfield, Conn., v.p., 1989; bd. dirs. Nat. Coalition for Rsch., Washington; treas. Health, Safety and Rsch. Alliance N.Y. State. Editor newsletter Parkinson's Disease Found.; mem. editorial adv. bd. Rxemedy. Home: 179 E 79th St New York NY 10021-0431 Office: Parkinsons Disease Found 650 W 168th St New York NY 10032-3702

ORR, LEIGHTON E., glass consultant; b. Pitts., Feb. 11, 1907; s. James A. and May M. (McEwen) O.; m. Mary N. Orr, Oct. 1, 1932 (dec. June 1982); children: Thomas L., Betsy Ann; m. Margaret W. Orr, Oct. 16, 1982. BS in Mech. Engrng., U. Pitts., 1928. Phys. tester Pitts. Testing Lab., 1930-36; head phys. testing Pitts. Plate Glass, 1936-72; pvt. practice glass cons. Tarentum, Pa., 1972—; Patentee in glass fabrication. Dir. Allegheny Hist. Soc., Tarentum, 1986-91. Fellow ASME. Republican. Presbyterian. Home and Office: RR 4 Box 291 Tarentum PA 15084-9517

ORR, SHIRLEY ANN, nurse; b. Oil City, Pa., Mar. 15, 1935; d. John Clair and Orpha Jane Ella (Newell) O. AAS, Rockland Community Coll., 1968. Staff nurse Oil City Area Health Ctr., 1974-85, Charity Hosp., New Orleans, 1985-87, New Orleans Adolescent Hosp., 1987-89, Grandview Health Care, Oil City, 1989-91. Democrat. Home: 214 Lincoln St Oil City PA 16301

ORRINGER, NELSON ROBERT, Spanish literature educator; b. Pitts., Nov. 9, 1940; s. Harry Baer and Alta Ruth (Moses) O.; m. Stephanie Ruth Limberg, June 12, 1965; children: Elise, David, Neal. AB, Dartmouth Coll., 1962; MA, Brown U., 1965, PhD, 1969. Lectr. in Spanish Williams Coll., Williamstown, Mass., 1968-70; asst. prof. Spanish Williams Coll., Williamstown, Mass., 1970-74; assoc. prof. Spanish U. Conn., Storrs, 1974-80, prof. Spanish and Comparative Lit., 1981—, chair comparative lit., 1991—. Author: Ortega and His German Sources, 1979, New German Sources of Ortega's Philosophy, 1984, Unamuno and Liberal Protestants, 1985; mem. editorial bd. Letras Peninsulares, East Lansing, 1968, Ometeca, N. Mex., 1989. Postdoctoral rsch. grantee Fulbright, 1981, 89; named Disting. Vis. Alumni Scholar, Brown U., 1981. Mem. AAUP, Sem. on History of Spanish Philosophy, Soc. of Spanish Phenomenology, Twentieth-Century Spanish Soc., Internat. Assn. of Hispanists (organizing com. 1982-83), Soc. of Sci. and Lit. Home: 42 Ellise Rd Storrs Mansfield CT 06268-1424 Office: Dept Modern and Classical Langs U Conn PO Box 57U Storrs Mansfield CT 06268-0057

ORSATTI, ERNEST BENJAMIN, lawyer; b. Pitts., Nov. 14, 1949; s. Ernest Ubaldo and Dorothy Minerva (Pfeiffer) O.; m. Ingrid Zalman, May 3, 1975; 1 child, Benjamin E. BA, Marquette U., 1971; JD, Duquesne U., 1974; postgrad., Army Command and Gen. Staff Coll., 1984. Bar: Pa. 1974, U.S. Dist. Ct. (we. dist.) Pa. 1974, U.S. Ct. Appeals (3d cir.) 1977, U.S. Supreme Ct. 1978. Assoc. Jubelirer, Pass & Intrieri, Pitts., 1974-81, ptnr., 1981—. Contbg. editor: The Developing Labor Law, 2d edit., 1983. Served to capt. U.S. Army, 1975, lt. col., dep. staff judge adv. 99th ARCOM. Mem. ABA, ACLU, Am. Arbitration Assn., Pa. Bar Assn., Indsl. Relations Rsch. Assn. Democrat. Roman Catholic. Home: 9343 N Florence Rd Pittsburgh PA 15237-4815 Office: Jubelirer Pass & Intrieri 219 Ft Pitt Blvd Pittsburgh PA 15222-1576

ORSKI, C. KENNETH, consulting company executive, lawyer; b. Warsaw, Poland, Mar. 7, 1932; came to U.S., 1946; naturalized, 1953; s. Thaddeus and Irene Orski; m. Jocelyne Schule, Aug. 27, 1968; children—Karine N., Monica J.; m. Barbara K. Klema, Apr. 28, 1978; 1 child, Christopher P. A.B., Harvard U., 1953, LL.B., J.D., 1956. Asst. to pres. Gen. Dynamics Corp., Washington, 1961-66; dir. OECD, Paris, 1966-73; assoc. adminstr. U.S. Dept. Transp., Washington, 1974-78; pres. Urban Mobility Corp., Washington, 1982—. Contbg. author books in field, 1982, 85; contbr. articles to profl. jours. Recipient Outstanding Pub. Service award U.S. Dept. Transp., 1985, Disting. Service award, 1977, Meritorious Service award, 1975. Republican. Home: 4504 Dalton Rd Bethesda MD 20815-3733 Office: Urban Mobility Corp 1133 15th St NW Bldg 1200 Washington DC 20005-2710

ORSOMARSO, DON FRANK, school system administrator; b. Queens, N.Y., Oct. 23, 1925; s. Frank and Angela (Aliano) O.; m. Marguerite Angela Rocco, July 2, 1955; children: Donald Frank, Gail Marie. BA, NYU, 1949, MA, 1953, 55, MBA, 1959; EdD, Nova U., 1975. Tchr. Shaw Ave Sch. Dist. #30, Valley Stream, N.Y., 1955-61; asst. supt. Maple Shade (N.J.) Pub. Schs., 1961-64, Valley Cen. Schs., Montgomery, N.Y., 1964-65, Union Free Sch. Dist. #17, Franklin Sq., N.Y., 1965-70, Newington (Conn.) Sch. System, 1970-78, East Islip Schs., Islip Terr., N.Y., 1978—. Mem. Am. Assn. Sch. Bus. Officials, Conn. Assn. for Advancement Sch. Adminstrs. (v.p. 1976-77, pres. 1977-78), Am. Assn. Sch. Adminstrs., East Islip C. of C., Phi Delta Kappa. Lodge: Lions. Home: 32 Adelhaide Ln East Islip NY 11730-2202 Office: East Islip Schs Craig B Gariepy St Islip Terrace NY 11752-2802

ORT, THOMAS WILLIAM, investment company executive; b. Morristown, N.J., Aug. 21, 1945; s. Paul Lanning and Mildred Henrietta (Vey) O.; m. Susan Vera Danks, June 17, 1967; children: Scott Thomas, Craig Thomas. BS in Commerce, Rider Coll., Trenton, N.J., 1968; postgrad., Lehigh U. Real estate broker Paul L. Ort Real Estate, Hackettstown, N.J., 1968-70; ins. agt. Thomas W. Ort Ins., Hackettstown, 1968-70; br. mgr. Nat. Union Bank, Hackettstown, 1970-83; asst. v.p. Nat. Community Bank, Rutherford, N.J., 1983-85; regional v.p. The Money Store Investment Corp., Union, N.J., 1985—. Capt. Allamuchy-Green First Aid Squad, Allamuchy, N.J., 1983-85; emergency med. technician Dover Hosp. Mobile ICU, 1985. With U.S. Army, 1968-69, Germany. Home: 5 Hawthorne Pl Basking Ridge NJ 07920 Office: Money Store Investment Corp 2840 Morris Ave Union NJ 07083

ORTENBERG, ELISABETH CLAIBORNE See CLAIBORNE, LIZ

ORTENBERG, NEIL DAVID, publishing executive; b. Milw., Aug. 27, 1951; s. Arthur and Muriel (Kotchever) O. BA, Columbia Coll., Chgo., 1977. Customer svc. rep. Liz Claiborne, N.Y.C., 1980-83; pub. Thunder's Mouth Press, N.Y.C., 1981—. Recipient Editor's award N.Y. State Coun. on the Arts, 1985, Carey Thomas award Publisher's Weekly, 1988. Mem.

Coun. of Lit. Mags. & Presses (bd. dirs. 1990—). Democrat. Office: Thnder's Mouth Press 54 Greene St New York NY 10013-2603

ORTENZI, REGINA (GINA RAE ORTENZI), home fashion products designer, educator; b. Cin., Oct. 23, 1949; d. Anthony Henry and Esther (Ciener) O.; m. Robert George Button, May 28, 1978. Student fashion design, U. Cin., 1967-69; B Design, U. Fla., 1972; MFA, U. Ga., 1975. Design dir. Tempo Advt. Agy., Winter Park, Fla., 1972-73, Gloria Vanderbilt, Gloria Concepts, Inc., N.Y.C., 1975-82; pres., co-owner Ortenzi/Button Designs, Jersey City, 1983—; dir. design Beacon Looms, Inc., Teaneck, N.J., 1990; instr. U. Ga., Athens, 1974-75, Rollins Coll., Winter Park, 1975, Parsons Sch. Design, N.Y.C., 1982—; vis. instr. Pratt-Phoenix Sch. Art and Design, N.Y.C., 1980-83. Recipient 1st place award S.E. div. Ford Motor Co. Pinto Competition, 1972, 2d place award Cen. Fla. ADDY Competition, 1973. Mem. Graphic Artists Guild (nat. pres. 1985-87), Internat. Furnishings and Design Assn., Fashion Group, Am. Crafts Coun., Surface Design Assn. Jewish. Office: 3348 Kennedy Blvd Jersey City NJ 07307

ORTH, WILLIAM ALBERT, college president, retired air force officer; b. Coatesville, Pa., Sept. 28, 1931; s. William Frederick and Mary Olive (Wilson) O.; m. Doris Arlene Myers, Sept. 20, 1958; children: Victoria Lynn, Sandra Lee. BS, U.S. Mil. Acad., 1954; MSME, Purdue U., 1961; PhD, Brown U., 1970. Registered profl. engr., Nebr. Commd. 2d lt. USAF, 1954; advanced through grades to brig. gen. U.S. Army, 1978; comdr. 8th SOS USAF, Bien Hoa Air Base, Vietnam, 1970-71; dir. engring.-constrn., asst. dep. chief staff civil engring. Hdqrs. SAC, Offutt AFB, Nebr., 1971-74; prof. physics, head dept. USAF Acad., Colo., 1974-78, dean faculty, 1978-83; ret., 1983; pres. Trident Tech. Coll., Charleston, S.C., 1983-85, Spartan Sch. Aeros., Tulsa, 1985-87, Atlantic Community Coll., Mays Landing, N.J., 1987—. Bd. dirs. United Way, Charleston, 1984, Atlantic City, 1990. Fellow AIAA (assoc.); mem. Am. Assn. Physics Tchrs., Math. Assn. Am. Presbyterian. Office: Atlantic Community Coll Mays Landing NJ 08330

ORTIZ, RAFAEL MONTAÑEZ, computer, laser, video performance/object artist; b. Bklyn., Jan. 30, 1934; s. Joseph H. and Eusabia (Velazquez) O. BS, Pratt Inst., 1964, MFA, 1964; MEd, Columbia U., 1974, EdD, 1982. Instr. grad. art faculty Tchr. Coll. Columbia U., N.Y.C., 1967; instr. art NYU, N.Y.C., 1968; adj. prof. art Fordham U., N.Y.C., 1971, C. W. Post Coll., L.I., N.Y., 1971; adj. prof. art Livingston Coll. Rutgers U., New Brunswick, N.J., 1971, assoc. prof. art Livingston Coll., 1972; assoc. prof. grad. and undergrad. faculty Mason Gross Sch. of Arts, Rutgers U., 1972; prof. I Mason Gross Sch. Arts, 1991—; lectr. panelist Sch. of Visual Arts 4th Ann. Nat. Conf. on Edn. of Artist, 1990; panelist, moderator The Artist in Multiculturalism and Art History, Alternative Mus., Soho, N.Y.C., 1992; speaker, presenter in field. Numerous one-man performances including Piano Destruction Concert, BBC, London, 1966, Mother Father, Mercury Theater, London, 1966, Paper Bag and Piano Destruction Concert, Fordham U., N.Y.C., 1967, Ecce Homo Gallery, N.Y.C., 1967, Theater Ritual, Middle Atlantic States Regional Meeting Am. Theater Assn., Temple U., Phila., 1970, Crossing, Mime Theater, N.Y.C., 1976; physio-psycho-alchemy San Francisco Art Inst., 1982, UCLA, 1985, Twin Palms Gallery, San Francisco, 1985, Museo Del Barrio, N.Y.C., 1988; piano destruction duet Homage to Huelsenback, Museo del Barrio, N.Y.C., 1988; co-exec. dir. and participant in Art and the Invisible Reality Internat. Symposium, Munich, 1988; organizer, participant Internat. Symposium of Art and the Invisible-Reality, U.S.A., Computer-Laser-Video Barcelona Biennale, Spain, 1989, Beograd, Yugoslavia, 1989, Kriens Videodrom, Switzerland, 1989, Franklin-Furnace Mus., N.Y.C., Rutgers U., New Brunswick, N.J., 1989; Vision Quest Gallery Rem, Vienna, Austria, 1988, Vision Quest II Bloomfield Coll., N.J., 1989, Piano Destruction Concert, Hommage to Huelsenback, Soul Release project Alternative Mus., N.Y.C., 1989, Exhbn. Kölnischer Kunstverein, Köln, Computer-Laser-Video, Köln, Fed. Republic Germany, Soul Release-Ritual Kunst Müller Köln, 1989, Soul Release project, Piano Sacrifice concert, Atelier Eva Ohlaw Bildskulpturenaktionmusik, Köln, 1990, Computer-Laser-Video presentations Medienwerkstatt, Vienna, 1991, Berlin Video Festival, 1991, Internat. Video-Art Festival, Rassegna, Italy, 1992; Decade Show Dance Theater Workshop, N.Y.C. performance-ritual sponsored by the New Mus., N.Y.C., The Mus. of Contemporary Hispanic Art, N.Y.C., The Harlem Mus. of Contemporary Art, N.Y.C., 1990; one person sculpture exhbn. Fordham U., N.Y.C., 1967, Alternative Mus., Soho, N.Y.C., 1992, Mus. Modernerkunst, Stiftung Ludwig, Vienna, 1992; group shows include Whitney Mus. Am. Art, N.Y.C.,1965, The Object Transformed, sculpture, Mus. Modern Art, N.Y.C., 1966, Franklin Furnace Mus., N.Y.C.; participated in Internat. Destruction in Art Symposium, London, 1966, Finch Coll. Mus. Art Destruction in Art Symposium Sculpture, 1968, sculpture Everson Mus. Art, Syracuse, N.Y., 1973, sculpture Chgo. Mus. Contemporary Art, 1979, Ancient Roots New Visions, sculpture, Palacio de Mineria Mus., Mexico City, 1980, Rutgers Computer Art Group, Walters Gallery, Rutgers U., 1982, computer animation, Paul Robeson Gallery, Rutgers U., 1983, Computer Art, The Salem Syndrome, Tamasulo Gallery, N.J., 1985, Computer Graphics and Sound, Computer-Laser-Video, Bonnefanten Mus., Maastricht, Holland, 1986, Computer-Laser-Video, De-Haag, Fed. Republic Germany, 1986, Computer-Laser-Video Bridge Game, Mülheim Mus., Fed. Republic Germany, 1986, Computer-Laser-Video Berlin Internat. Video and Film Festival, Coll. of Art, Gwent, Wales, Eng., 1986, 87, Computer-Laser-Video The Kitchen, Techno-Bop 87, N.Y.C.; numerous one-man exhbns. including Rene Gallery Video Installation, Music Reconstruction, Amsterdam, Holland, 1988, Retrospective, sculpture, performance, Computer-Laser-Video, Museo del Barrio, N.Y.C, 1988, Infermental 9, Internat., Video Mag., Dance No. 6, 1989, Computer-Laser-Video, Vienna, Austria, 1990, Computer-Laser-Video, The Internat. Berlin Video and Film Festival, Berlin, 1990, Computer-Laser-Video, Leningrad, Riga-Cine Fantom, USSR, 1990; drawings, Columbia U., N.Y.C., 1975; represented in mus. collections Video Presentation Series I and II Median Werk Statt, Vienna, 1991, Computer-Laser-Video, Stadtisches Kunstmus., Bonn, 1990, Centre Georges Pompidou, Paris, 1990, Ludwig Mus., Cologne, Fed. Republic Germany, 1988, Piano Destruction Fragments, Museo del Barrio, N.Y.C., 1988, Computer-Laser-Video, Mus. Modern Art, Brussels, 1987, Computer-Laser-Video, Friedricheshof Mus., Zurndorf, Austria, 1986, Computer-Laser Video, Everson Mus., Syracuse, N.Y., 1985, Computer-Laser-Video, Museo Del Barrio, 1985; sculpture, Feather Pyramids, Museo del Barrio, 1982, sculpture, Disassembled Sofa, Everson Mus., Syracuse, N.Y.,1972, sculpture, Disassembled Upholstered Chair, Chrysler Mus., Va., 1965, sculpture, Shoe Construct-Destruct, Menil Mus., Houston, 1965, sculpture, Disassembled Sofa, Whitney Mus. Am. Ar, 1964, sculpture, Destroyed Mattress, Mus. Modern Art, 1963. Mem. Mus. Computer Art (founder, pres. 1984), Hispanic Assn. Higher Edn., N.J., Art Educators N.J., Coll. Art Assn., Assn. Rsch. and Enlightenment. Office: Rutgers U Dept Visual Arts 125 New St New Brunswick NJ 08901-1905

ORTIZ RUIZ, AIDA M., university administrator; b. Barranquitas, P.R., Oct. 3, 1940; d. Higinio and Joaquina (Ortiz) O.; m. William Ruiz; 1 child, Philip. BA, U. P.R., 1971; MA, NYU, 1973; MEd, Columbia U., 1988. Tchr. N.Y.C. Bd. Edn., 1972-74; instr. English Queens Coll., N.Y.C., 1974-78; lectr. English Hostos Community Coll., Bronx, N.Y., 1978-83; asst. dean of faculty Hostos Community Coll., Bronx, 1984-86, assoc. dean of academic affairs, 1988-91; coord. freshman yr. programs CUNY, 1991—; coll. bd. mem. Test of Standard Written English Com., 1985-90; mem. CUNY Coun. Internat. Edn., 1989—, Campaign Fund Dr., 1990—, Chancellors Task Force on Writing, 1984-88, chair univ. adv. com. on transfer and articulation; grants adminstr. Title III, VEA, Ford UCCTOP, diamond found. grant Minority Project for Teaching Professions. Contbr. articles to profl. jours. Charter mem. Congress for P.R. Rights, N.Y.C., 1980—; mem. Inst. for P.R. Policy, N.Y.C., 1986—, CUNY Women's Coalition, 1984—. Fellow Ford Found., 1971-73. Fellow ASCD, Academic Affairs Adminstrs., Coll. Composition & Communication, Nat. Assn. Bilingual Educators, Assn. Tchrs. English, Acad. for Humanities & Scis. Office: Hostos Community Coll 500 Grand Concourse Bronx NY 10451-5323

ORTLOFF, GEORGE CHRISTIAN, SR. (CHRIS ORTLOFF), journalist, state legislator; b. Lake Placid, N.Y., Sept. 20, 1947; s. Carl Jacob and Lillian Grace (Travis) O.; m. Ruth Mary Hart, Jan. 28, 1978; children: George Christian Jr., Jonathan Hart. BS, Rensselaer Poly. Inst., 1969; MA, U. Mich., 1975. Reporter, producer Sta. WUOM-FM, Ann Arbor, Mich., 1973-75; report Nat. Pub. Radio, 1973-75; reporter Adirondack Daily Enterprise, Saranac Lake, N.Y., 1976-77, Sta. WNBZ-Am, Saranac Lake, 1975-77; pub. rels. dir. Ctr. for Music, Drama and Art, Lake Placid, 1975-76; pres. Macromedia, Inc., Lake Placid, 1976-82; anchor, mng. editor Sta. WPTZ-TV, Plattsburgh, N.Y., 1981-85; mem. N.Y. State Assembly 110th Assembly Dist., Albany, 1986—; ranking minority mem. Assembly Conservation Com., Albany, 1991—; bd. dirs. Champlain Valley Physicians Hosp. Med. Cen., Plattsburgh; Olympic Games cons. Pageantry World, Inc., Pasadena, Calif., 1988. Author: Lake Placid, The Olympic Years: 1932-80, 1976, A Lady in the Lake, 1985; report, producer (TV news series) "Special Segment", 1981-85 (N.Y. State Broadcasters Best Series award 1982, 83, 84, 85), (TV documentary) A Time to Choose, 1985 (N.Y. State Broadcasters Best award 1986). Chief of ceremonies 1980 Olympic Winter Games, Lake placid, 1978-80; field asst. U.S. Rep. David O'B Martin, Plattsburgh, 1981; county committeeman Essex County Rep. Com., 1980-891; village trustee Lake Placid Village, 1977-81; lay reader Episc. Ch., Lake Placid and Plattsburgh, 1976—. Served with USAF, 1970-73, Vietnam. Recipient Disting. Eagle award Adirondack coun. Boy Scouts Am., 1991. Mem. VFW (post 1466), Elks, Am. Legion (post 326), North Country Vietnam Vets. Assn., Kiwanis (pres. Lake Placid chpt. 1980-81). Home: 23 Morrison Ave Plattsburgh NY 12901 Office: NY State Assembly 722 Legislative Office Bldg Albany NY 12248

ORTMANN, DOROTHEA, music educator; b. Balt., Jan. 12, 1912; d. Otto Rudolph and Margaret May (Donoho) Ortmann; m. Constantine Seletzky, Feb. 14, 1942 (dec.). Cert. in Piano, Peabody Inst., Balt., 1930, cert. in Harmony, 1934, artists diploma, 1935. Tchr. music Peabody Inst., Balt., 1931-41, Miami (Fla.) Conservatory of Music, 1942-45, Dorothea Ortmann-Seletzky Studio, Balt., 1946—; lectr. in field; judge Md. Fedn. of Music. Author: The Music of Otto Ortmann, 1984; composer of works for piano, violin and songs; concert pianist, 1925-61. Mem. Charles Village Civic Assn., Balt., 1976, Balt. Opera Guild. Recipient of Harold Randolph Meml. prize Peabody Inst., 1930. Mem. Charles Village Civic Assn. Republican. Episcopalian.

ORTOLANI, MINOT HENRY, zoo director; b. Buffalo, Aug. 7, 1929; s. Joseph and Sylvia (Jacobi) O.; m. H. Anne Sweeney, June 30, 1956; children—Timothy, John, Terrence. B.S., Canisius Coll., 1951; postgrad., Stonier Grad. Sch. Banking Rutgers U., 1962. With M&T Trust Co., Buffalo, 1957-79; v.p. corp. banking M&T Trust Co., 1969-79; exec. dir. Buffalo Zool. Gardens, 1979—; bd. dirs. Carton Craft Corp. Bd. dirs. Arboretum Soc.; chmn. gen. bus. div. United Fund; bd. dirs., pres. Psychiat. Clinic for Children; v.p., treas. United Negro Coll. Fund; bd. dirs. St. Ritas Home for Children, Nottingham Sch. Sacred Heart, Niagara Frontier Rehab. Center, United Health Found.; chmn. corp. gift div. Catholic Charities. Served with USN, 1951-56; lt. comdr. USNR, 1951-89, ret. Recipient Pres.'s award Daemen Coll., 1989, Disting. Alumnus award Canisius Coll., 1990. Fellow Am. Assn. Zool. Parks and Aquariums; mem. Buffalo C. of C. (chmn. Boost Buffalo com., Small Bus. Com.), U.S. Navy League (v.p., dir.), Buffalo Exec. Assn. (past pres.). Clubs: Park Country, Rotary (dir.). Home: 81 Huntington Ct Buffalo NY 14221-5309 Office: Buffalo Zoo Delaware Park Buffalo NY 14214-1999

ORTOLANI, VINCENT, vocational business educator; b. Rochester, N.Y., July 19, 1941; s. Vincent and Fanny (Micciche) O.; m. Mary Margaret Appel, May 26, 1974; children: Elizabeth, Philip. BS, Niagara U., 1964; MA, The Cath. U. Am., 1968. Tchr. St. John's Middle Sch., Bronx, N.Y., 1967-71, vice prin., 1970-71, prin., 1971-72; instr. Stratford Sch., Rochester, N.Y., 1977-78; adjunct instr. Rochester Inst. of Tech., Nat. Tech. Inst. for Deaf, Rochester, N.Y., 1981-88, asst. prof., 1988—; parent educator Dreikurs Family Edn. Assn. of Rochester (N.Y.), 1980—; cons. pvt. practice, Rochester, 1990—. treas. Dreikurs Family Edn. Assn. of Rochester (N.Y.), 1989-91. Mem. Nat. Edn. Asn., Nat. Edn. Bus. Assn., Ea. Bus. Edn. Assn. Office: Rochester Inst Tech Nat Inst Deaf Carey Bldg PO box 9887 Rochester NY 14623-0887

ORTON, GERALDINE LEITL, psychology and mental health educator, mental health services professional; b. Pitts., May 16, 1939; d. Meinrad M. and Virginia (Traska) L.; m. Guy M. Orton, June 16, 1962; children: Alisa, Guy Christopher. BS, Ind. U. Pa., 1961; postgrad., Scandinavian Sem. for Cultural Study, Valla Folkhogskola, Linkoping, Sweden, 1961-62; MS, Edinboro U. Pa., 1970; PhD, U. Buffalo, 1978. Cert. in counseling psychology and ednl. adminstrn. Elem. sch. tchr. Ripley (N.Y.) Cen. Sch., 1962-70, elem. sch. counselor, 1970-74; program dir. SUNY, Fredonia, 1974-76; asst. prof. Gannon U., Erie, Pa., 1977-81, assoc. prof., 1981—, mem. grad. faculty, 1990—, dir. mental health counseling, 1991—, dir. gen. studies program, 1991—; pvt. practice, 1984—; bd. dirs. mental health counseling program Warren State Hosp., 1984-88, supr. of placements in Warren County, 1984-88; bd. dirs. Home Instrn. Tutorial Program Rsch. Found. SUNY, Fredonia, 1975-76, Learn, Experience and Develop Program, 1974-75; cons. Bur. of Guidance N.Y. State Dept. Edn., Albany, 1983, mental health program Chautauqua County BOCES, Fredonia, 1974, career edn. program Westfield (N.Y.) Acad. and Cen. Sch., 1974; therapist Parents Supporting Other Parents in Sorrow, Erie, 1978; mem. numerous Gannon U. coms. and task forces; presenter in field. Contbr. articles to profl. jours. Mem. adv. bd. Perspective on Women Series: Pub. Com. on the Humanities in Pa.; mem. Primary Prevention Task Force-Youth Svcs. Coordination Coun. Erie County; numerous presentations Pa. schs. Mem. Gamma Mu, Lambda Sigma. Office: Gannon U Dept Mental Health Counseling University Square Erie PA 16541

ORVIS, HAROLD HEACOCK, physician; b. Phila., Jan. 13, 1924; s. Harold Heacock and Leora Alice (Chappell) O.; m. Anna Ruth Schlaanstine, June 4, 1955; children: Stephen, Lynda, John. BS in Biology, Guilford Coll., 1948; MD, Columbia U., 1952. Diplomate Am. Bd. Internal Medicine. Intern D.C. Gen. Hosp., 1952-53; resident George Washington Univ., Washington, 1958, asst. prof. medicine, 1958-63; assoc. prof. preventive medicine Univ. Ill., Chgo., 1963-66; assoc. clin. prof. medicine Hahnemann Univ., Phila., 1972-80; chief internal medicine The Chester County Hosp., West Chester, Pa., 1984—; pvt. practice in internal medicine West Chester, 1971—; cons. cardiology VA Ctr., Martinsburg, W.Va., 1963-65; dir. rehab. ctr. Univ. Ill. Rsch. and Edn. Hosp., Chgo., 1963-66; med. bd. Easter Seal Soc., Chgo., 1965-66; dir. clin. investigations Atlas Chem. Industry, Wilmington, Del., 1966-71. Author: (manual) Diet Manual Univ. Ill., 1966. Pres. Civitan Club, Chgo., 1965-66; scoutmaster Boy Scouts Am., Chester County, Pa., 1967-79. 1st lt. USAF, 1942-46. Named fellow in cardiology Washington (D.C.) Heart Assn., 1955-56, rsch. fellow NIH, Washington, 1956-57. Fellow Am. Coll. Cardiology, Am. Coll. Chest Physicians; mem. Am. Soc. Internal Medicine, Inst. Medicine Chgo., Am. Soc. Nephrology, Am. Soc. Clin. Pharmacists and Therapeutics, Sigma Xi, West Goshen (Pa.) Lions Club. Home and Office: 401 W Pleasant Grove Rd West Chester PA 19382-7117

ORWOLL, EDWARD FRANCIS, chemist; b. Granite Falls, Minn., July 24, 1919; s. Melvin S. and Anna Elizabeth (Hustvedt) O.; m. Joanne C. Smith, July 5, 1947; children: Eric S., Lucinda J., Ann K. BS, Mich. State U., 1940; PhD, U. Mo., 1945. Sr. chemist Sharples Chems., Inc., Wyandotte, Mich., 1943-50; sr. rsch. chemist Niagara Chem. div. FMC Corp., Middleport, N.Y., 1950-52; sr. rsch. chemist Westvaco Chloralkali div. FMC Corp., South Charleston, W.Va., 1952-54; rsch. supr. Niagara Chem. div. FMC Corp., Middleport, 1954-58; rsch. mgr. chems. and plastics div. FMC Corp., Balt., 1958-72; mgr. process devel. organic and agr. div. FMC Corp., Princeton, N.J., 1972-79. Contbr. articles to profl. jours.; 20 patents in field. Vestryman Episcopal Ch., Medina, N.Y., 1956-58; bd. dem. Green Valley Civic Assn., Langhorne, Pa., 1978-79; mem. bd., pres. Fulton County Libr., McConnellsburg, Pa., 1989-91. Mem. Am. Chem. Soc. Home: HC 75 Box 305 Fort Littleton PA 17223-9701

ORZECHOWSKI, ROBERT DAVID, healthcare administrator; b. Reading, Pa., Oct. 29, 1949; s. Robert Leonard and Agnes Eugenia (Leszczynski) O.; m. Christine Lavonne Lehman, Aug. 19, 1972; children: Keegan Derek, Kevin Drew, Kerri Beth. BS, Pa. State U., 1974; MBA, Fairleigh Dickinson U., 1985. Personnel dir. Centre County Govt., Bellefonte, Pa., 1975-76; wage and salary adminstr. HRB-Singer, Inc., State College, Pa., 1976-81; mgr. compensation Kearfott div. Singer Co., Little Falls, N.J., 1981-86; salary and benfits mgr. St. Joseph Hosp., Reading, Pa., 1986-89; bus. mgr. St. Joseph Hosp., 1989—; instr. Pa. State U., Reading, 1987-89, Alvernia Coll.; instr. Reading Area Community Coll., 1986-92, mem. mgmt. adv. com., 1989. Author poetry in literary mag. Bd. dirs. Berks County Vietnam Meml. Commn., Inc., Reading, 1988; vice chmn. Berks County Armed Forces Adv. Com. Mem. Reading C. of C. (mem. com. small bus. 1988-89), Soc. for Human Resource Mgmt. (treas. 1988-89, sec. 1989-90), Vietnam Vets. Am. Home: 2406 Lindale Dr Reading PA 19609-1228 Office: West Reading Ophthalmic 206 N 6th Ave Reading PA 19611-1498

OSAWA, YOSHIO, endocrinologist; b. Tokyo, Japan, May 28, 1930; came to U.S., 1969; s. Rihei and Natsu (Morita) O.; m. Michiko Morita, Mar. 26, 1955; children: Yoichi, George. BS in Chemistry, Tokyo Met. U., 1953; MS in Organic Chemistry, U. Tokyo, 1955, PhD in Organic Chemistry, 1959. Rsch. scientist Teikoku Hormone Mfg. Co. Ltd., Tokyo, 1956-58, chief of div. total synthesis of steroids, 1958-64, prin. rsch. scientist, 1964-67; assoc. rsch. scientist Med. Found. Buffalo (N.Y.), 1969-70, prin. rsch. scientist, 1970-71, 75—, assoc. dir., postdoctoral tng. program in endocrine rsch., 1970-78, program dir., 1978-80, head endocrine biochem. dept., 1975—, assoc. rsch. dir., 1988—; cons. Roswell Park Cancer Inst., Buffalo, 1973—; assoc. rsch. prof. RPCI Div. SUNY, Buffalo, 1981—. Author: (with others) Microsomes, Drug Oxidations, and Chemical Carcinogenesis, 1980, Tissue Culture in Medical Research, 1980, Thyroid Research VIII, 1980; contbr. over 150 articles to profl. jours.; patentee in field. Grantee NIH-Nat. Inst. Child Health and Human Devel., 1970—, Faculty Rsch. award Am. Cancer Soc., 1969-74. Mem. Am. Soc. for Biochemistry and Molecular Biology, Am. Chem. Soc., Japan-Ob/Gyn Soc., Japan Chem. Soc., Endocrine Soc. Office: Med Found Buffalo 73 High St Buffalo NY 14203

OSBERG, GREGORY JOHN, publishing company executive; b. Jamestown, N.Y., June 12, 1957; s. John Raymond and Nancy (Jones) O.; m. Linda Burton, Aug. 22, 1981; children: Eric Burton, Alexander Gregory. BS in Mktg., Colo. State U., 1979. Regional mgr. Chilton Pub., Radnor, Pa., 1979-81; account mgr. U.S. News & World Report, N.Y.C., 1981-84, Fortune, N.Y.C., 1984-85; v.p. advt. sales U.S. News & World Report, N.Y.C., 1985-90; strategic planning dir. Newsweek, N.Y.C., 1990—; chmn. Careers in Communications, Pitts., 1980-81. Mem. Advt. Club N.Y., Lincoln Ctr. Ctr. Circle (exec. com.), Bedens Brook Club. Office: Newsweek 444 Madison Ave New York NY 10022

OSBERG, TIMOTHY M., psychology educator; b. Buffalo, Aug. 11, 1955; s. John Carlton and Adeline Rose (Weichsel) O.; m. Debra A. Morreale, July 14, 1990. BA, SUNY, Buffalo, 1977, MA, 1980, PhD, 1982. Lic. psychologist, N.Y. Intern VA Med. Ctr., Buffalo, 1981-82; from asst. prof. to prof. Niagara (N.Y.) U., 1982—; pvt. practice Niagara Falls, N.Y., 1985—; psychologist Optifast Weight Loss Program, Niagara Falls, 1989-92; editorial bd. Jour. Personality and Social Psychology, 1988-92, Teaching of Psychology, 1991—; presenter in field. Contbr. articles to profl. jours. Vol. group leader pre-release program Attica (N.Y.) Correctional Facility, 1984-90, vol. group leader support group for desert storm families Niagara Falls Air Base, 1991; exec. com. Psychol. Assn. Western N.Y., Buffalo, 1982-87. Recipient Feldman-Cohen Meml. award SUNY, Buffalo, 1977. Mem. Am. Psychol. Assn., Eastern Psychol. Assn., Soc. for Personality Assessment, Assn. Advancement Behavior Therapy, Phi Beta Kappa. Democrat. Roman Catholic. Home: 2652 David Dr Niagara Falls NY 14304-4619 Office: Niagara U Dept Psychology Niagara University NY 14109

OSBORN, DAVID CHILCOAT, accreditation specialist; b. Balt., Aug. 8, 1921; s. Daniel Leonard and Alice Benson (Chilcoat) Osborn; m. Chesta Mae Bair, Aug. 14, 1948; children: Glenn Alan, Keith David, Blaine Daniel. BA, Western Md. Coll., 1942; MA, Pa. State U., 1952; postgrad., U. Md., 1955-65. Advanced profl. teaching cert. English, French, history. History tchr. Bd. Edn. Baltimore County, Towson, Md., 1942-66; accreditation specialist Md. State Dept. Edn., Balt., 1966-91. Fund raiser drive to rebuild U.S. Constallation State of Md., 1958. Fellow Md. Classified Employees Assn.; mem. Phi Delta Kappa. Democrat. Methodist. Home: 15124 Dover Rd Reisterstown MD 21136

OSBORN, DAVID DUDLEY, investment banker; b. N.Y.C., June 15, 1958; s. Donald Robert and Marcia (Lontz) O.; m. Diane Werner, June 29, 1985; 1 child, Emma Mallory. AB summa cum laude, Dartmouth Coll., 1980; postgrad., Princeton U., 1982-83; MBA, Harvard U., 1987. Tchr. St. Mark's Sch., Southborough, Mass., 1980-82; bus. analyst McKinsey & Co., Inc., N.Y.C., 1984-85; assoc. Merrill Lynch Capital Markets, N.Y.C., 1986, McKinsey & Co. Inc., N.Y.C., 1987-89, Kidder, Peabody & Co., Inc., N.Y.C., 1989—. Mem. Am. Printing History Assn., Ephemera Soc. Am., Dartmouth Coll. Club N.Y. (alumni fund raiser 1989—), Harvard Bus. Sch. Club N.Y., Scarsdale Golf Club (Hartsdale, N.Y.), Phi Beta Kappa. Democrat. Home: 201 E 87th St Apt 29B New York NY 10128-3208 Office: Kidder Peabody & Co 10 Hanover Sq Fl 9 New York NY 10005-3516

OSBORN, ELODIE COURTER, arts administrator; b. Bklyn., Dec. 6, 1911; d. Harry Wallace and Besse Johanna Cornelia (Visser) Courter; m. Robert Chesley Osborn, Mar. 18, 1944; children: Nicolas Courter, Eliot Wyckoff. BA, Wellesley Coll., 1933; postgrad., NYU Sch. Fine Arts, 1934-36; cert., Inst. d'art et d'archéologie, Sorbonne, Paris, 1935. Dir. traveling exhbns. Mus. Modern Art, N.Y.C., 1933-48; mem. adv. com. Am. Fedn. Arts, N.Y.C., 1944-56, mem. adv. com., vice chmn. Internat. Com., 1945-53; founder, dir. Salisbury Film Soc., Conn., 1951-80; mem. adv. com. on exhbns. Katonah Art Gallery, N.Y.C., 1977—; bd. dirs. Internat. Film Seminars, N.Y.C., 1968-80, Friends of Art, Wellesley Coll., Mass., Macdowell Colony, Peterborough, N.H., 1970—, sec., 1971, v.p., 1972, hon. trustee, 1977-86, dir. emeritus, 1989. Author: Manual of Traveling Exhibitions, UNESCO, 1953; contbr. articles to profl. jours. Bd. dirs. Salisbury Cen. Sch., Lakeville, Conn., 1952-55, sec. bldg. com., 1949-52; mem. Dem. Town Com., Salisbury, 1951-70; bd. dirs. Marvelwood Sch., Cornwall, Conn., 1963-67, Housatonic Psychiat. Ctr. Mem. Am. Fedn. Arts (adv. com. on film 1983-89). Democrat. Club: Cosmopolitan (N.Y.C.). Home: 392 Taconic Rd Salisbury CT 06068-1209

OSBORN, ROBERT CHESLEY, artist, writer; b. Oshkosh, Wis., Oct. 26, 1904; s. Albert LeRoy and Alice Lydia (Wyckoff) O.; m. Elodie Courter, Mar. 18, 1944; children: Nicolas Courter, Eliot Wyckoff. PhB, Yale U., 1928; student, Brit Acad., Rome, 1928, Acad. Scandinav, Paris, 1929. Tchr. Hotchkiss Sch., 1930-35; free-lance artist, 1945—; flight safety artist U.S. Navy, 1942-85; civilian flight safety artist FAA, 1959-85; mem. Pres.'s Com. on Art Edn. in Pub. Schs., 1964; chmn. art and architecture com. Yale Council, 1953-59. Author: War is No Damn Good, 1946, Low and Inside, 1953, Osborn on Leisure, 1957, The Vulgarians, 1960, Dying to Smoke, 1964, Mankind May Never Make It, 1968, Missile Madness, 1969, An Osborn Festival of Phobias, 1971, Osborn on Osborn, 1984; author, illustrator: Osborn on Conflict, 1984; illustrator books, including: Sense Books, 1941-45; also illustrator for popular mags.; exhibited Downtown Gallery, N.Y.C., 1959, 64, 67, USIA graphic arts show, USSR, 1963, Carpenter Art Ctr., Cambridge, Mass., 1986, Naval Aviation Mus., Washington, 1990; represented by E.L. Stark Gallery, N.Y.C., 1987—; retrospective exhbn. Beinecke Libr., Yale U., 1992. Mem. cen. sch. bd., Salisbury, Conn.; pres. Sharon-Salisbury chpt. United World Federealists. Lt. comdr. USNR, World War II. Decorated Legion of Merit; named hon. naval aviator #11 U.S. Navy, 1976; recipient Disting. Pub. Svc. medal sec. U.S. Navy, 1959; assoc. fellow Berkeley Coll., Yale U., 1958-90. Mem. ACLU, Scroll and Key, Sierra Club, Nat. Trust Hist. Preservation, Elizabethan Club (New Haven).

OSBORNE, ELIZABETH, artist, educator; b. Phila., June 5, 1936; d. Charles Francis and Virginia (Kerns) O.; m. Robert Cooper, Jan. 1964 (div. 1989); 1 child, Audrey O. Cooper. Grad., Pa. Acad. Fine Arts, 1958; BFA with honors, U. Pa., 1959. Prof. art, head of critics Pa. Acad. Fine Arts, Phila., 1965—. One-woman shows include Marian Locks Gallery, Phila., 1978, 88, 92, Fischbach Gallery, N.Y.C., 1980, 82, 84, 87, numerous others; exhibited in group shows at Pa. Acad. Fine Arts, Phila., 1986, Jane Haslem Gallery, Washington, 1989, Pa. State Mus., Harrisburg, 1989, Tatistcheff Gallery, N.Y.C., 1989, Marian Locks Gallery, 1989, numerous others. Recipient travelling fellowships, Pa. Acad. Fine Arts, 1955, 57, 58, Fulbright award, Paris, 1963, Ford Found. purchase prize, 1964, Rosenthal Found. award, Am. Acad. Arts and Letters, 1976; grantee, MacDowell Colony, 1983; artist-in-residence, La Napoule, France, 1989. Studio: 36 N Front St Philadelphia PA 19106-2295

OSBORNE, GEORGE DELANO, arts director; b. Ft. Worth, Aug. 25, 1938; s. Hugh and Eula Catherine (Trent) O.; children from previous marriage: David Warren, Hugh Philip, George Douglas. B in Mus, Oklahoma City U., 1960; M in Mus, Ind. U., 1964; postgrad. in Arts Mgmt., Hartford Grad. Ctr., 1978. Mem. faculty Tex. Tech. U., Lubbock, 1962-64, S.W. Mo. State U., Springfield, 1964-66, Memphis State U., 1966-76, W.Va. U., Morgantown, 1976-78; gen. dir. Memphis Opera, Morgantown, 1971-76, Hartford (Conn.) Chamber Orch., Morgantown, 1978-79, Conn. Opera, Hartford, 1979—, Hartford Chamber Orch., 1979-88, Hartford Ballet, 1982-88. Mem. Hartford Cultural Affairs Commn., 1980. Fulbright scholar, Rome, 1960; Am. Leadership Forum fellow, 1986-87. Mem. Cen. Opera Svc. (regional dir.), Nat. Opera Assn. Home: 26 Riverview Avon CT 06001-2057 Office: Conn Opera Assn 226 Farmington Ave Hartford CT 06105-3501

OSBORNE, PETER, historical society administrator; b. Paterson, N.J., Apr. 17, 1957; s. Peter Jr. and Barbara (Thompson) O.; divorced; 1 child, Ryan Matthew; m. Janis L. McCann, July, 1992. BA in Am. History, Rutgers U., 1983. Registrar Neversink Valley Area Mus., Cuddebachville, N.Y., 1980-81; exec. dir. Minisink Valley Hist. Soc., Port Jervis, N.Y., 1981—; instr. Orange County Community Coll., Middletown, N.Y., 1990—; cons., writer Hist. Resource Svcs., Port Jervis, 1984—; rec. sec. Orange County Hist. Soc., Arden, N.Y., 1988—; corr. sec. Minisink Valley Hist. Soc., Port Jervis, 1981—. Contbr. articles to profl. jours. Bd. dirs. Depot Preservation Soc., Port Jervis, 1984-88; camp inspector NE region Boy Scouts Am., N.J., 1982-88, camping com. mem. Passaic Valley coun., Wayne, N.J., 1983-85. Mem. Am. Ass. State & Local History, Nat. Trust for Hist. Preservation. Unitarian. Office: Minisink Valley Hist Soc 138 Pike St PO Box 659 Port Jervis NY 12771

OSBORNE, RAYMOND LESTER, JR., radiologist; b. N.Y.C., Nov. 23, 1939; s. Raymond Lester and Margaret Forbes (Unangst) O.; m. Elizabeth Ann Parise, May 13, 1972; children: Alexandra Forbes, Raymond Lester III. AB with hons. in English, U. Pa., 1961; postgrad., U. Edinburgh, Scotland, 1959-60, U. Glasgow, Scotland, 1961-62; MD, CM, McGill U., Montreal, 1966. Diplomate Am. Bd. Radiology. Intern in surgery Royal Victoria Hosp., Montreal, 1966-67; resident in surgery Duke U. Med. Ctr., Durham, N.C., 1967-68; resident in diagnostic radiology Yale-New Haven Hosp., 1970-73; assoc. in radiology Duke U. Med. Ctr., Durham, 1973-74; asst. prof. Duke U. Med. Ctr., 1974-75; asst. roentenologist Meml. Sloan Kettering Cancer Ctr., N.Y.C., 1975-78; asst. prof. N.Y. Hosp./Cornell U. Med. Ctr., N.Y.C., 1975-78; clin. asst. prof. Yale U., New Haven, 1979—; sr. attending radiologist Middlesex Meml. Hosp., Middletown, Conn., 1978—. Author: The Radiology of Vertebral Trauma, 1980. Mem. Rep. Town Com., Durham, 1984—. Lt. comdr. USNR, 1969-70. Decorated Navy Commendation medal, Vietnamese Medal of Honor, 1st class. Mem. Radiologic Soc. N. Am., Am. Coll. Radiology, Soc. Thoracic Radiology, Am. Roentgen Ray Soc., AMA, Conn. Radiologic Soc., Conn. Med. Soc., Soc. Med. Radiology, Interam. Coll. Radiology (designated B-reader for respiratory diseases), Nat. Inst. Occupational Safety and Health, Alpha Omega Alpha. Repubican. Home: 65 Wildwood Ln Durham CT 06422-2608 Office: Radologic Assocs PO Box 290 Middletown CT 06457-0290

OSBORNE, RICHARD DE JONGH, mining and metals company executive; b. Bronxville, N.Y., Mar. 19, 1934; s. Stanley de Jongh and M. Elizabeth (Ide) O.; m. Cheryl Anne Archibald, Dec. 14, 1957; children: Leslie Anne, Lindsay Ide, Nicholas de J., Stanley de J. A.B. in Econs., Princeton U., 1956. With Cuno Engrng. Corp., Meriden, Conn., 1956-60; fin., planning and mktg. exec. IBM Corp., Armonk, N.Y., 1960-69; investment adviser Sherman M. Fairchild, N.Y.C., 1969-70; exec. v.p. fin. and bus. devel., dir. Fairchild Camera & Instrument Corp., Mountain View, Calif., 1970-74; v.p. fin. ASARCO Inc. (formerly Am. Smelting & Refining Co.), N.Y.C., 1975-77, exec. v.p., 1977-81, pres., 1981-85, chmn., pres., chief exec. officer, 1985—, also bd. dirs.; bd. dirs. Schering-Plough Corp., Mex. Desarrollo Indsl. Minero (S.A.), E.T. & H.K. Ide, Inc., So. Peru Copper Corp., Copper Devel. Assn., Am. Mining Congress. Trustee Com. Econ. Devel. Mem. AIME, Conf. Bd., U.S. C. of C. (bd. dirs.), Coun. on Fgn. Rels., Coun. of Ams. (bd. dirs.), Am. Australian Assn. (pres., bd. dirs.), Internat. Copper Assn. (bd. dirs.). Clubs: Down Town Assn., Economic, River, Brook, City Midday; Bedens Brook; Sakonnet Golf. Home: 40 E 94th St Apt 32B New York NY 10128-0709 Office: Asarco Inc 180 Maiden Ln New York NY 10038-4925

OSBORNE, SEWARD RUSSELL, writer; b. Catskill, N.Y., June 28, 1946; s. Seward Russell and Doris Virginia (Tompkins) O.; m. Jean Marie Shaver, June 22, 1968; children: Dean, Sarah. Historic site technician Senate House State Historic Site, Kingston, N.Y., 1976-77; contbg. editor Mil. Images, 1980; contbg. author Mil. Collector & Historian, 1984. Author: Holding the Left, The 20th New York State Militia at Gettysburg, July 1, 1863, 1990; editor: The Civil War Diaries of Col. Theodore B. Gates, 20th New York State Militia; contbr. articles to North South Trader's Civil War, 1970s, 1980s, Ulster County Gazette, 1970s, 1980s. With U.S. Army, 1964-65. Cited for erection of monument to 20th N.Y. State Militia on the Gettysburg Battlefield, 1981, 20th N.Y. State Militia on the Battlefield of 2nd Bull Run (Manassas), 1986; selected for inclusion in the Book of Buffs, Masters, Mavens and Uncommon Experts, 1980. Fellow The Co. of Mil. Historians; mem. Ulster County Com. to Save the Grant Cottage (founder, chmn. 1990), Ulster County Genealogical Soc. Born-Again Christian, Zadock Pratt Mus (hon. life mem.). Born-Again Christian. Home: 1329 County Rd 2 Olivebridge NY 12461

OSBORNE-POPP, GLENNA JEAN, principal; b. East Rainelle, W.Va., Jan. 5, 1945; d. B.J. and Jean Ann (Haranac) Osborne; m. Thomas Joseph Ferrante Jr., June 11, 1966 (div. Nov. 1987); 1 child, Thomas Joseph Osborne; m. Brian Mark Popp, Aug. 13, 1988. BA cum laude, U. Tampa, 1966; MA, Fairleigh Dickinson U., 1982; cert., Kean Coll., 1983. Cert. English, speech, dramatic arts tchr., prin./surp. Tchr. Raritan High Sch., Hazlet, N.J., 1966; tchr. Keyport (N.J.) Pub. Schs., 1968-86, coord. elem. reading and lang. arts, 1980-84, supr. curriculum and instrn., 1984-86; prin. Weston Sch., Manville, N.J., 1986-88, The Bartle Sch., Highland Park, N.J., 1988-91, Orange Ave. Sch., Cranford, N.J., 1991—; regional trainer Individualized Lang. Arts, Weehawken, N.J., 1976-86; cons. McDougal/Little Pubs., Evanston, Ill., 1982-83. Contbr. chpt. to: A Resource Guide of Differentiated Learning Experiences for Gifted Elementary Students, 1981. Sunday sch. tchr. Reformed Ch., Keyport, 1975-80, supt. Sunday sch., 1982-84. Mem. ASCD, N.J. Prins. and Suprs. Assn., Union County Elem. Prins. Assn., Order Eastern Star (Tampa, Fla.), Phi Delta Kappa. Republican. Methodist. Office: Orange Ave Sch Orange Ave Cranford NJ 07016-2137

OSEI, EDWARD KOFI, financial analyst, educator, strategic planner; b. Bibiani, Ghana, Jan. 3, 1959; came to U.S., 1975; s. Yaa Agnes (Bosuo) Osei. Student, U. Ghana, 1981; M in Internat. Mgmt., Baylor U., 1984; MA in Internat. Rels., Yale U., 1988; MBA, Stanford U., 1988. Gen. mgr. Express Messengers Ltd., Lagos, Nigeria, 1981-84; sr. fin. analyst Eastman Kodak Co., Rochester, N.Y., 1989-91, strategic planner, 1991—; owner, pres. Ashanti Properties & Mgmt., Rochester, 1990—; adj. prof. strategic mgmt. SUNY, Brockport, 1990—; advisor Boy Scouts Am., Rochester, 1989—; dir. fin. Baiden Settlement Home, Rochester; bd. dirs. C.O.N.E.A., Rochester Nat. Treasures. Yale U. fellow, 1985, Stanford U. fellow, 1986; Baylor U. scholar, 1984. Mem. Nat. Black MBA Assn., AIESEC (project coord., Excellence award 1981), Stanford U. Alumni Assn., Yale U. Alumni Assn., Baylor U. Alumni Assn., Eastman Kodak Black Employees Assn., Toastmasters Internat. Home: 184 Gillette St Rochester NY 14619-2227 Office: Eastman Kodak Co 343 State St Rochester NY 14650-0001

OSER, BERNARD LEVUSSOVE, food and drug consultant; b. Phila., Feb. 2, 1899; s. Harris E. and Frances (Levussove) O.; m. Clara de Hirsch Kotkin, May 27, 1923; children: Zelda Oser Zelinsky, Alan Stuart. BS, U. Pa., 1920, MS, 1925; PhD, Fordham U., 1927. Diplomate Am. Bd. Indsl. Hygiene, Am. Bd. Nutrition, Am. Bd. Clin. Chemists. Asst. physiol. chemistry Jefferson Med. Coll., 1920-21; biochemist Phila. Gen. Hosp., 1922-26; from asst. dir. to dir., v.p. Food Rsch. Labs. Inc. (predecessor FDRL), 1926-57, from dir. to pres., chmn. bd., 1957-74; cons. Bernard L. Oser Assocs., Bayside, N.Y., 1974—; adj. prof. Columbia U. Inst. Nutrition Scis., 1959-71. Co-author, collaborator: Practical Physiological Chemistry, 9th, 10th, 11th edits, 1926-31, 1937; co-author and editor: Practical Physiological Chemistry, 12th, 13th edits., 1947, 54, Hawk's Physiological Chemistry, 14th edit., 1965; editorial bd. Analytical Chemistry, 1946-49, Food Tech., 1947-51; Jour. Agr. and Food Chemistry, 1955-58,; sci. editor Food Drug Cosmetic Law Jour., 1957—, Nutrition Reports Internat., 1974-81; author or co-author over 400 papers and speeches on methods of biological and chemical assay of vitamins, proteins and other nutrients, on the fortification, stabilization and physiological availability of vitamins in pharm. products and fortified foods, on toxicology and safety evaluation of food additives, drugs, pesticides and related chemicals, and on the sci. aspects of food laws and regulations. Trustee Gordon Rsch. Confs., 1954-57; chmn. food sect. Internat. Union Pure and Applied Chemistry, 1961-68; mem. food sci. mission Dept. Agr., 1963, food protection com. NAS-NRC, 1964-71, joint expert com. on food additives FAO-WHO. Recipient Ambassador of Toxicology award Mid-Atlantic chpt. Soc. of Toxicology, 1982. Fellow AAAS, Am. Inst. Chemists, Inst. Food Technologists (pres. 1968-69, Babcock Hart award 1958), N.Y. Acad. Scis., Toxicology Forum, Am. Inst. Nutrition; mem. Am. Chem. Soc. (chmn. div. agrl. and food chemistry 1946-47), Am. Coll. of Toxicology, Am. Coun. on Sci. and Health, Am. Indsl. Hygiene Assn., Am. Inst. of Chemists, Am. Inst. of Nutrition, Am. Soc. of Pharmacology and Exptl. Therapeutics, Assn. of Vitamin Chemists, Nat. Rsch. Coun. (food and nutrition bd.), N.Y. Acad. Medicine (assoc.), N.Y. Inst. Food Technologists (pres. 1968-69), Acad. Toxicological Scis., Soc. of Tech., Teratology Soc., Internat. Soc. Regulatory Toxicology and Pharmacology, Flavor and Extract Mfrs. Assn. (hon.), The Chemists Club (N.Y.), Alpha Epsilon Pi, Sigma Xi (hon.), Phi Tau Sigma (hon.). Home: 655 Pomander Walk Teaneck NJ 07666

OSER, HANS JOERG, research administrator; b. Konstanz, Germany, Dec. 7, 1929; came to U.S., 1957; s. Wilhelm Ernst and Anna Maria (Zipse) O.; m. Hildegard Kaiser, June 14, 1958; children: Patricia, Susanne, Bertram. MS, U. Freiburg, 1954, PhD, 1957. Postdoctoral fellow U. Md., College Park, 1957-58; sr. mathematician Nat. Bur. Standards, Gaithersburg, Md., 1958-64, chief, math. analysis sect., 1964-78, sr. sci. adviser Nat. Measure Lab., 1978-86; exec. dir., commerce tech. adv. bd. Dept. of Commerce, Washington, 1966-67; dir. commerce sci. and tech. fellowship program Nat. Bur. Standards/Dept. of Commerce, Gaithersburg, 1981-86; tech. dir. Soc. Ind. and Applied Math, Phila., 1986-88; sr. assoc Joint Policy Bd. Math., Washington, 1988-90; staff officer bd. math. scis. NRC, Washington, 1990—; adj. prof. U. Coll., U. Md., 1958-63; lectr. Cath. U., Washington, 1964-67. Editor, translator: Functional Equations, 1966, Numerical Analysis, 1971, Boundary Layers of Flow and Temperature, 1973. Chmn. environ. com. Potomac (Md.) Civic Assn., 1970-75; asst. scoutmaster Boy Scouts Am., Potomac, Md., 1972-85, expdn. leader high BSA adventure program, 1977-92. Fellow Washington Acad. Scis., 1968. Mem. Sigma Xi. Home: 8810 Quiet Stream Ct Potomac MD 20854 Office: Nat Rsch Coun NAS-312 2101 Constitution Ave NW Washington DC 20418-0001

OSGOOD, DAVID ALDRICH, psychologist; b. Burlington, Vt., June 30, 1944; s. Edward F. Osgood and Muriel (Aldrich) Lane; m. Carla Newman, June 15, 1968; 1 child, Adam. BA, U. Vt., 1966; MPH, Yale U., 1972; EdD, U. Mass., 1991. Lic. psychologist, Vt. Sci. tchr. U.S. Peace Corps, Guyana, 1966-69; trainer U.S. Peace Corps, Trinidad, W.I., 1968; rsch. asst. U. W.I., Mona, Jamaica, 1970-71; dep. dir. Vt. State Office Child Devel., Montpelier, 1971-72; asst. dir. Ctr. for Svc.-Learning U. Vt., Burlington, 1972-85, psychologist Counseling Ctr., 1985—; psychologist The Growth Ctr, Essex Junction, Vt., 1980—. Editor: The Home Health Handbook, 1971. Mem. Am. Psychol. Assn., Vt. Psychol. Assn., Assn. for Humanistic Psychology, Am. Assn. for Counseling and Devel. Home: PO Box 81 Underhill Center VT 05490-0081 Office: U Vt Counseling Ctr 146 S Williams St Burlington VT 05401-3492

O'SHAUGHNESSY, MARK P., experimental psychologist; b. N.Y.C., Mar. 16, 1959; s. Denis J. and Lucy E. (Dudevior) O'S.; m. Teresa M. Coniglio, Oct. 10, 1987; 1 child, Olivia G. BA in Psychology, Iona Coll., 1981; MA in Psychology, New Sch. Social Rsch., 1984. Human factors engr. Ergo Design, Ft. Lee, N.J., 1984-86; rsch. engr. Covidea, Jericho, N.Y., 1986-88; pres. Consumer Products Rsch., Riverdale, N.Y., 1988—; presenter at profl. confs. Contbr. rsch. papers to profl. publs. Mem. Human Factors Soc. Office: 5800 Arlington Ave Bronx NY 10471-1402

O'SHEA, ARTHUR JOSEPH, psychologist, educator; b. Boston, Sept. 23, 1928; s. Arthur and Delia Marie (Kelly) O'S.; m. Janet Margaret Scully, May 21, 1967; children: Jennifer Marie, Daniel Arthur, Elizabeth Marie. AB, Weston (Mass.) Coll., 1952, MA, 1953; MEd, Boston Coll., 1963, PhD, 1967. Lic. psychologist, Mass.; diplomate Am. Bd. Vocat. Experts. Counselor, asst. prof. Northeastern U., Boston, 1966-68; assoc. dean Boston State Coll., 1968-73, prof., chair dept. psychology, 1973-82; prof., dir. grad. counseling psychology program U. Mass., Boston, 1982—; chmn. bd. Career Planning Assocs., Inc., Dedham, Mass.; pvt. practice as vocat. cons., Needham, Mass., 1974—. Editor: Guide for Occupational Exploration, 1984; author: (test) Career Decision-Making System, 1976; contbr. articles to profl. jours. Mem. APA, ACA (senator 1973-75), Mass. Assn. for Counseling and Devel. (pres. 1972-73), Am. Career Devel. Assn. Democrat. Roman Catholic. Home: 289 Hillcrest Rd Needham MA 02192-4026 Office: U Mass Boston Harbor Campus Boston MA 02125

OSHEOWITZ, MICHAEL WILLIAM, foundation executive; b. N.Y.C., June 3, 1937; s. Frank and Harriet (Lipton) O.; m. Maria Teresa Martinez, June 23, 1965; children: Tania, Manuela. BA, Middlebury Coll., 1959. Security analyst Golkin & Co., N.Y.C., 1959-60, corp. fin. analyst, 1961-62; fin. analyst Arthur Schmidt & Assoc., N.Y.C., 1962-64, v.p., 1965-70, exec. v.p., 1970-80, pres., 1980-89; pres. and trustee Gould Found. for Children, N.Y.C., 1989—; founder, chmn. Sponsors for Ednl. Opportunity, N.Y.C., 1963—; trustee Edwin Gould Acad., Spring Valley, N.Y.,1989—; dir. Raymond B. Carey Found., N.Y.C., 1987—; bd. dirs. Clearpool, Inc., Teach for Am. Dir. Crystal Run Environ. Ctr., Spring Valley, 1989, Frank Lloyd Wright Conservancy, Chgo., 1990. Recipient Eleanor Roosevelt award, 1988, Weber award, United Way, 1989. Mem. N.Y. Soc. Securities Analysts, Fin. Analysts Fed., The Players, Nat. Arts Club.

OSHER, HAROLD LOUIS, cardiologist, educator; b. Portland, Maine, Jan. 11, 1924; s. Samuel and Leah (Lazarovich) O.; m. Peggy Ann Liberman, June 18, 1950; children: Susan, Nancy, Judith, Samuel. BS summa cum laude, Bowdoin Coll., 1943; MD magna cum laude, Boston U., 1947. Diplomate Am. Bd. Internal Medicine, Am. Bd. Cardiovascular Disease. Internship internal medicine Boston City Hosp., 1947-48, residency, 1948-50; fellowship Beth Israel Hosp., 1950; staff mem. heart disease epidemiology study Nat. Heart Inst., Framingham, Mass., 1950-53; pvt. practice cardiology Portland, Maine, 1953—; dir. Cardiac Catheterization Lab. Maine Med. Ctr., Portland, 1955-74; asst. chief medicine Miane Med. Ctr., Portland, 1979-84, dir. div. cardiology, 1972-88, dir. emeritus, 1989—; asst. clin. prof. medicine Tufts U. Sch. Medicine, Portland, 1970-74, assoc. clin. prof., 1974-80; assoc. prof. medicine U. Vt., Portland, 1981—; heart disease cons. Maine's Regional Med. Program, Augusta, 1967-75, dir. coronary care project, 1968-72; dir. Med. Care Devel., Inc., Augusta, 1967-77, pres., 1971-75. Contbr. articles on cardiology to profl. jours. Recipient Brotherhood award Temple Beth El, Portland, 1968, Outstanding Svc. award New Eng. Regional Heart Com., Boston, 1976. Fellow ACP, Am. Coll. Cardiology (gov. 1971-74); mem. Am. Heart Assn. (v.p. 1970-71, pres. Maine affiliate 1966-68, outstanding svc. award 1974), Maine Med. Assn., Cumberland County Med. Soc. Phi Beta Kappa. Jewish. Home: 66 Chadwick St Portland ME 04102-3511 Office: Maine Med Ctr 22 Bramhall St Portland ME 04102

OSHEROFF, MARJORIE HELEN, consultation service executive; b. Wilkes-Barre, Pa., Jan. 17, 1948; d. Solomon and Eleanor (Shlissel) O.; divorced 1986. AS in Nursing, Northeastern U., 1968; BS in Nursing, Boston U., 1970; MS in Mgmt., Lesley Coll., 1987. RN, Mass. Staff nurse Arlington (Mass.) Visiting Nurses, 1970-71, North Miami Gen. Hosp., 1972, Alanticare Med. Ctr., Lynn, Mass., 1972-77; nursing supr. Alanticare Med. Ctr., Lynn, 1977-79, nursing administr., 1979-86; pres. Corp. Eldercare Solutions, Saugus, Mass., 1988-90; dir. Long Term Planning Assocs., Saugus, Mass., 1986—; lectr. on elder care, ednl. and civic orgns., 1986—. Contbr. articles to profl. jours. Mem. Nat. Assn. Pvt. Geriatric Care MGrs. (bd. dirs. 1991—, pres. New Eng. chpt. 1990—), Nurse Entrepreneurs Coun., Mass. Nurses Assn., Sigma Theta Tau. Home: 146 Moulton Dr Lynnfield MA 01940-1439 Office: Long Term Planning Assocs 5 Sweetwater St Saugus MA 01906

OSHIMA, MICHAEL W., lawyer; b. Big Rapids, Mich., Apr. 4, 1957; s. Walter W. and Mitsue (Marutani) O. AB, Brown U., 1979; MA, Harvard U., 1984; JD, NYU, 1987. Bar: N.Y. 1988, D.C. 1989. Sr. rsch. asst. John F. Kennedy Sch. Govt., Cambridge, Mass., 1981-84; assoc. Davis Polk & Wardwell, N.Y.C., 1987-90, Arnold & Porter, N.Y.C., 1990—. Contbr. articles, reports to profl. publs. Counsel, Asian Am. Arts Alliance, Inc., N.Y.C. Mem. Am. Sociol. Assn., Law and Soc. Assn., N.Y. State Bar Assn., Assn. of Bar of City of N.Y. Office: Arnold & Porter 399 Park Ave New York NY 10022-4614

OSHINSKY, JAMES STEVEN, psychologist; b. N.Y.C., Oct. 29, 1951; s. Myron H. and Marilyn (Robinson) O.; m. Candace H. Pinquist, Aug. 19, 1972 (div. 1985); 1 child, Joshua Adam; m. Emily Jane Metcalf, May 27, 1990; 1 child, Breanna Bell. BA, U. Pa., 1972; PhD, U. Tenn., 1977; postgrad., Adelphi U., 1981; Profl. Cert., Derner Inst. Lic. psychologist, N.Y.; cert. sch. psychologist, N.Y. Vis. asst. prof. psychology Ind. U., Bloomington, 1977-78; asst. prof. Adelphi U., Garden City, N.Y., 1978-81; assoc. psychologist Cen. Islip Psychiat. Ctr., N.Y., 1981-84; sch. psychologist Vision Impaired Program, Nassau BOCES, Wantagh, N.Y., 1984-89, Farmingdale (N.Y.) Pub. Schs., 1989—; pvt. practice Baldwin, N.Y., 1982—. Author: Discovery Journal, 1991; feature writer newsletter Free Spirit News and View on Growing Up, 1991-92, War and Young People, 1991; contbr. articles to profl. jours. Bd. dirs. Music for People, Keene, N.H., 1990-91. Mem. APA, Nassau County Psychol. Assn., Pi Kappa Phi.

OSINSKI, MARGARET JEAN, occupational health nurse; b. Buffalo, June 20, 1939; d. Stanley Joseph and Rita (Milbrand) Sowa; m. Joseph George Osinski, Oct. 3, 1964; children: Joseph A. II, Susan M., Matthew S. Student, Canisius Coll., 1957-58; nursing diploma, Mercy Hosp. Sch. Nursing, Buffalo, 1960. RN; cert. occupational health nurse. Staff nurse med. Kenmore Mercy Hosp., Kenmore, N.Y., 1960-61; staff nurse ob-gyn. Yonkers Gen. Hosp., Yonkers, N.Y., 1961; occupational health nurse Chevrolet div. Gen. Motors, Buffalo, 1961-66; staff nurse emergency Kenmore Mercy Hosp., 1974-80; occupational health nurse, safety coord. Nabisco Brands, Inc., Buffalo, 1980-87; occupational health nurse, employee assistance program coord Bell Aerospace Textron, Buffalo, 1987-91. Mem. Western N.Y. Assn. Occupational Health Nurses (pres. 1987-89), Am. & N.Y. State Assns. Occupational Health Nurses, Am. Bd. Occupational Health Nurses, Am. Soc. Safety Engrs., Employee Assistance Profls. Assn., Grand Island (N.Y.) Jr. Football. Republican. Roman Catholic. Home: 3098 Baseline Rd Grand Island NY 14072-1313

OSMAN, MOHAMMED, real estate executive, consultant; b. Ajmair, India, Jan. 2, 1944; came to U.S., 1978; s. Allauddin and Chand (Bibi) Shaikh; m. Amina Sami, Mar. 18, 1983. B in Commerce, U. Karachi, Pakistan, 1964, BA, 1971. Cert. real estate mgmt. Sr. exec. Mohammadi Tobacco Co., Karachi, 1965-74, Falcon Trading Co., Doha, Qatar, 1975-77; real estate sr. exec. Crescent Assocs., N.Y.C., 1984-89; real estate exec. mng. agt. BKL Mgmt. Corp., N.Y.C., 1990—; pres. Tajmahal Constrn. Co., Inc., N.Y.C., 1987—; v.p. Jackson Manor Inc., N.Y.C., 1990—, Sunnyside Owners Corp., N.Y.C., 1990—, 41-15 46th St Owners Corp., N.Y.C., 1990—. Home: 150-51 59th Ave Flushing NY 11355-5426 Office: BKL Mgmt Corp 82 Wall St New York NY 10268-1140

OSMOND, GORDON CONDIE, lawyer, playwright; b. Washington, Nov. 9, 1934; s. Harvard Reginald and Melba (Condie) O. A.B., Columbia U., 1956, J.D., 1959. Bar: N.Y. 1959. Assoc. firm Donovan Leisure Newton & Irvine, N.Y.C., 1959-69, ptnr., 1969—. Author: (plays) A Matter of Tone, Fertile Deception, Full House. Mem. ABA. Office: Donovan Leisure Newton & Irvine 30 Rockefeller Pla New York NY 10112

OSOFF, JEFFREY ARLIN, media executive; b. Everett, Mass., June 5, 1936; s. Meyer and Minerva (Cogan) O.; m. Arlene Shuman, Sept. 23, 1962 (div. Jan. 1988); children: Judith Robin (dec.), David Eric. BA, Bowling Green State U., 1958; MS, Columbia U., 1959. Reporter Boston Globe, 1954-55; reporter Boston Post, 1955-62, rewriteman, 1962-63, acting asst. city editor, 1963-64; dir. News Bur. Brandeis U., Waltham, Mass., 1964-67; asst. dir. pub. affairs Brandeis U., 1967-69, dir. pub. affairs, 1967-76; chmn. bd. Jansson, Inc., Waltham, 1976-87; pres., chief exec. officer JAO Enterprises, Ltd., Lexington, Mass., 1987—; lectr. in journalism and pub. rels. cons. First v.p. Dysuatonomia Found., 1965-66, 74—, bd. dirs., 1965—, pres., 1973-74; bd. dirs. New Eng. region Anti-Defamation League. Served with USAF, 1961-62. Recipient citation for outstanding journalistic reporting Mass. N.G., 1961; several awards for high achievement in graphics. Mem. New Eng. Press Assn., Internat. Thermographic Assn., Printing Industries Am., Printing Industries New Eng., Am. Coll. Pub. Rels. Assn., Jewish Pub. Relations Soc. Am., Pub. Rels. Soc. Am., Publicity Club Boston, Sigma Delta Chi, Zeta Beta Tau. Jewish. Home and Office: 67 Sherburne Rd S Lexington MA 02173-7000

OSOFSKY, ROBERT HARRIS, otolaryngologist; b. Syracuse, N.Y., Sept. 18, 1945. BA, Syracuse U., 1965; MD, SUNY, 1969. Diplomate Am. Bd. Otolaryngology. Intern Parkland Meml. Hosp., 1969-70; surg. resident U. Calif. Med. Ctr., 1970-71, otolaryngology resident, 1971-74; surgeon Baystate Med. Ctr., 1976-85, Mercy Hosp., 1976—; pvt. practice otolaryngology Springfield, Mass., 1976—; otolaryngology cons. Oro-Facial Plastics Clinic We. Mass., 1975-81; mem. teaching house staff Baystate Med. Ctr., 1975-83; sr. clin. instr. Tufts U., 1980-83. Bd. trustees Willie Ross Sch. for Deaf, 1979-80. Fellow Am. Acad. Otolaryngology and Head and Neck Surgery, Mass. Med. Soc., Hampden County Med. Soc. Office: 299 Carew St Springfield MA 01104

OSSEIRAN-HANNA, KHATMEH AZIZ, advocate; b. Sidon, Lebanon, Jan. 28, 1961; came to the U.S., 1972; d. Aziz Aziz and Souhaila Adib (Al-Taqi) Osseiran; m. Ibrahim Aziz Hanna, Apr. 13, 1991. BA in Internat. Affairs, George Washington U., 1982; postgrad., McGill U., 1982-86. Student aid officer Save Lebanon, Inc., Washington, 1982, nat. coord., 1985, exec. dir., 1987—; organizer, researcher Am.-Arab Anti-Discrimination Com., Washington, 1984; assr. dir. Nat. Coun. on Canada Arab Rels., Ottawa, Canada, 1986-87; founder, co-chmn. Am.-Lebanese Pub. Affairs Com., Washington, 1989-91; coord. InterFuture, Washington, 1981-82. Editor, author: (newsletter) Our Hope For Children and Peace, 1989—. Del. Va. Dem. Cen. Com., Arlington, 1988, 89; pres. W&L Beautification Com., Arlington, 1977-78. Scholar InterFuture, 1981. Fellow Inst. Islamic Studies; mem. Pi Delta Phi. Home: 1900 S Eads St # 918 Arlington VA 22202 Office: Save Lebanon Inc 918 16th St NW # 901 Washington DC 20006

OSSERMAN, RICHARD A., lawyer; b. N.Y.C., May 21, 1930; s. Harold A. and Henrietta Letitia (Tonkonogy) O.; m. Gwen Stalberg, July 6, 1954 (dec. 1974); children: Eric Kenneth, Joel Edward; m. Linda Adler, Apr. 15, 1974 (div. Mar. 1986); 1 child, Justin Louis; m. Malka Rimland, Sept. 21, 1986; 1 child, Jordan Harold. AB, Hobart Coll., 1951; JD, Columbia U., 1954; LLM in Taxation, NYU, 1961. Assoc. Weisman, Celler, Allan, Spett & Sheinberg, N.Y.C., 1956-61; ptnr. Weisman, Celler, Allan & Spett, N.Y.C., 1961-73, Pryor, Cashman, Sherman & Flynn, N.Y.C., 1973-78; assoc. Kahr Spitzer & Howard, N.Y.C., 1978-79, Pollner, Mezan & Stolzberg, N.Y.C., 1979-82; ptnr. Robson, Miller & Osserman, N.Y.C., 1982-85; owner, operator Lido Beach Inn, Sarasota, Fla., 1982-90; sr. ptnr. Osserman & Assocs., N.Y.C., 1985—; lectr. to profl. assns. Author: Halfway to Tax Reform, 1972; contbr. articles to profl. jours. With U.S. Army, 1954-56. Republican. Jewish. Office: 708 Third Ave 11th Fl New York NY 10017

OSSIAS, A. LAWRENCE, physician, educator; b. N.Y.C., Mar. 24, 1940; s. David and Dora Ossias; m. Linda Machaelson; children: Geoffrey, Brian. BA, U. Rochester, 1961; MD, Yale U., 1965. Diplomate Am. Bd. Internal Medicine, Am. Bd. Hematology, Am. Bd. Med. Oncology. Asst. clin. prof. medicine Mt. Sinai Sch. Medicine, N.Y.C., 1974—; intern Univ. Rochester; residency Bronx Mcpl. Hosp. Ctr; fellowship Mt. Sinai Hosp, N.Y.C.; asst. attending physician Mt. Sinai Med. Ctr., N.Y.C., 1974—. Surgeon USPHS, 1966-68. Mem. Am. Coll. Physicians, Am. Soc. Hematology, Am. Soc. Clin. Oncology, Phi Beta Kappa. Office: 1112 Park Ave New York NY 10128

OST, WARREN WILLIAM, minister; b. Mankato, Minn., June 24, 1926; s. William Frederick and Margaret Avery (Denison) O.; m. Nancy Nesbitt, May 15, 1954; 1 child, Laura Margaret. BA, U. Minn., 1948; MDiv, Princeton U., 1951; DD (hon.), Moravian Theol. Sem., Bethlehem, Pa., 1971. Ordained to ministry Presbyn. Ch. (U.S.A.), 1951. Min. parishes, Phila., Scranton, Pa., N.J., 1948-51; resident min. Yellowstone Nat. Park, Wyo., 1950-52; dir. A Christian Ministry in Nat. Parks, N.Y.C., 1951—; bd. dirs. Ring Lake Ranch, Dubois, Wyo., 1964—; charter mem. Tourisme-Oecumenique, Geneva, 1967—; cons. Pontifical Commn. on Migration and Tourism, The Vatican, Rome, 1967—. Editor: Gospel, Freedom and Leisure, 1965. Bd. dirs. Prescott Neighborhood House, N.Y.C., 1961—; pres. East 49th Street Assn., N.Y.C., 1961-62. Recipient Pub. Svc. award U.S. Dept. Interior, 1977; named hon. park ranger Nat. Park Svc., 1977. Mem. Assn. Theol. Field Educators, Nat. Park Svc. Employees and Alumni Assn. (life), Conf. Nat. Park Concessioners (life), Denison Soc., Amis du Chemin St. Jacques, Union League Club, Princeton Club, Phi Mu Alpha. Home: 224 E 49th St New York NY 10017-1554 Office: A Christian Ministry in Nat Pks 222 1/2 E 49th St New York NY 10017-1553

OSTAR, ALLAN WILLIAM, higher education consultant; b. East Orange, N.J., Sept. 4, 1924; s. William and Rose (Mirmow) O.; m. Roberta Hutchison, Sept. 10, 1949; children: Karen, Rebecca, John. Cert. engring., U. Denver, 1943; B.A., Pa. State U., 1948; postgrad., U. Wis., 1949-55; LL.D., U. No. Colo., 1968, Eastern Ky. U., 1972, Whittier Coll., 1973; L.H.D., U. Maine, 1975; D.Letters, Central Mich. U., 1975; D.P.S., Bowling Green State U., 1975, R.I. Coll., 1983; D.Higher Edn., Morehead State U., 1977; L.H.D., Appalachian State U., 1977, No. Mich. U., 1978, Dickinson State Coll., N.D., 1979, Towson State U., 1980, Salem State Coll., 1980, Mont. Coll. Mineral Sci. and Tech., 1983, Ball State U., 1984; LL.D., U. Alaska, 1978, Ill. State U., 1983, Western Mich. U., 1984; D. Polit. Sci., Kyung Hee U., Korea, 1984; L.H.D., Fitchburg State Coll., 1986, Bridgwater State Coll., 1988, No. State Coll., 1988, Harris-Stowe State Coll., 1986; LLD, Edinboro U. Pa., 1987, Loch Haven U., Pa., 1989; LHD, No. Ariz. U., 1990, Shepherd (W.Va.) Coll., 1992. Dir. nat. pub. relations U.S. Nat. Student Assn., 1948-49; exec. asst. Commonwealth Fund, N.Y.C., 1952-53; asst. to dean extension div. U. Wis., 1949-52, dir. office communications services, 1954-58; dir. Joint Office Instnl. Research, Nat. Assn. State Univs. and Land Grant Colls., Washington, 1958-65; pres. Am. Assn. State Colls. and Univs., Washington, 1965-91; pres. emeritus Am. Assn. State Colls. and Univs., 1991—; sr. cons. Acad. Search Consultation Svc., 1991—, Penson-Strawbridge, 1991—; adj. prof. edn. Pa. State U., 1990—; mem. nat. adv. bd. Inst. for Mgmt. of Lifelong Edn., Harvard U.; mem. adv. coun. U. Md. Inst. for Rsch. in Higher and Adult Edn.; exec. commr. High Commn. for Peace. Co-author: Colleges and Universities for Change, 1987; contbr. chpts. in books. Bd. dirs. Com. for Improvement of Higher Edn. in the Ams., 1980; life mem. Md. PTA; bd. visitors Air U. With U.S. Army, 1943-46. Decorated Bronze Star; recipient Centennial award for disting. svcs. to edn. U. Akron, 1970, Fogelsanger award Shippensburg (Pa.) State Coll., 1974, World Peace Through Edn. medal Internat. Assn. U. Pres., 1975, Disting. Achievement award, U. So. Colo., 1979, Chancellor's award U. Wis., 1985, Chancellor's medal CUNY, 1986, Disting. Alumnus award Pa. State U., 1989, svc. award Coun. on Internat. Ednl. Exch., 1990, Chancellor's medal Internat. Svc. U. Ark., Little Rock, 1990, Disting. Pub. Svc. medal Dept. of Def., 1991; Alumni fellow Pa. State U., 1975. Mem. Internat. Assn. Univ. Pres. (mem. exec. com.), Sigma Delta Chi. Unitarian-Universalist. Home: 5500 Friendship Blvd Chevy Chase MD 20815 Office: Acad Search Cons Svc 1818 R St NW Washington DC 20009

OSTENDORFF, WILLIAM CHARLES, military officer; b. Shreveport, La., Oct. 22, 1954; s. Thomas Julian and Emilie Anne (Connell) O.; m. Christina Lee Miller, July 16, 1977; children: Rebecca, Chuck, Jeff. BS in Systems Engring., U.S. Naval Acad., 1976; JD with honors, U. Tex., 1984; LLM with distinction, Georgetown U., 1992. Bar: Tex. 1984. Commd. USN, 1976, advanced through grades to comdr., 1991, nuclear submarine officer; nuclear power prog. mgr. Office of Chief Naval Ops., Washington, 1984. Mem. ABA, State Bar Assn. Tex., U.S. Naval Acad. Alumni Assn., Order of the Coif. Episcopalian. Home: 2726 N Edison St Arlington VA 22207-1704

OSTENSO, NED ALLEN, oceanographer, government official; b. Fargo, N.D., June 22, 1930; s. Nels Andres and Estella (Temple) O.; m. Grace Elaine Laudon, June 29, 1963. BS, U. Wis., 1952, MS, 1953, PhD, 1962; postgrad., Johns Hopkins U., 1975. Scientist Arctic Inst. N.Am., Washington, 1956-66; asst. prof. geology and geophysics U. Wis., Madison, 1962-66; dir. marine geol. and geophys. programs Office Naval Rsch., Washington, 1966-69, sr. oceanographer, 1970-77; asst. Presdl. sci. advisor White House, Washington, 1969-70; dir. nat. sea grant coll. program NOAA, Washington, 1977-83, dir. Office Oceanic Rsch., 1983-89, chief scientist, 1989-90, asst. adminstr. for rsch., 1990—; founder Joy/Mac Petroleum, Madison, 1959-65; fellow Fed. Execs. Inst., Charlottesville, Va., 1974, Am. Polit. Sci. Assn., Washington, 1975-76. Cotnbr. over 60 articles on polar regions, oceanography and geophysics to sci. jours., chpts. to books. 1st lt. Signal Corps, U.S. Army, 1953-56. Recipient Antarctic Svc. medal Dept. of Def., 1958, Meritorius Svc. citation NAS, 1959, Superior Accomplishment award USN, 1968; Mt. Ostenso named in his honor, 1963, Ostenso Seamount (Arctic Ocean) named in his honor, 1978. Fellow Geol. Soc. Am., Arctic Inst. N.Am., Marine Tech. Soc., Explorers Club; mem. Acad. Polit. Sci., Am. Geophys. Union, UN Assn. U.S.A., Cosmos Club. Republican. Home: 2871 Audubon Ter NW Washington DC 20008-2309 Office: NOAA/Dept Commerce 1335 East-West Hwy Silver Spring MD 20910

OSTER, FREDERICK W., musical instrument shop owner; b. Phila., June 22, 1952; s. Irwin Louis and Bernice Patricia (Biren) O. BA in History, Fairleigh Dickenson U., 1974. Owner, founder Vintage Instruments, Phila., 1974—; cons. Phillips Auctioneers, N.Y.C., 1979; booking dir. The Main Point, Bryn Mawr, Pa., 1980-81; head musical instrument dept. Christies, N.Y.C., 1981-87; cons. Christies, N.Y.C., London, 1987—; owner Frederick W. Oster Fine Violins, Phila.; ptnr. Rudig & Oster, Inc. and The Violin Shop at Carnegie Hall. Vol. Cherry Tree Music Co-op, Phila., 1978—; founding mem., bd. dirs. Phila. (Pa.) Chamber Orch., 1983-88; organizer Pine St. Civic Assn., Phila., 1988—. Recipient Bucheri scholarship Fairleigh Dickinson U., 1971. Mem. Appraisers Assn. Am., Violin Soc. Am., Am. Musical Instrument Soc., Sporting Club Phila., Delaware Valley Jaguar Club. Home and Office: 1529 Pine St Philadelphia PA 19102

OSTER, KIM, company executive; b. Providence, Jan. 27, 1951; s. Irwin and Jacqueline (Grasser) O.; m. Diane Cherie Crooker, Aug. 14, 1976; children: Stephanie, Allison. BA in Econs., SUNY, Oneonta, 1972; JD, Albany Law Sch., 1976. Bar: N.Y. 1976. With Ayco Corp., Albany, N.Y., 1976—, now sr. v.p. Office: Ayco Corp 1 Wall St Albany NY 12205-3894

OSTER, MARTIN WILLIAM, oncologist; b. N.Y.C., Apr. 9, 1947; s. Joseph A. and Bella O.; B.A. summa cum laude, Columbia U., 1967, M.D., 1971; m. Karen A. Strauss, May 18, 1975; children—Bonnie Felice, Michelle Rae, Nancy Meredith. Intern, resident in medicine Mass. Gen. Hosp., Boston, 1971-73; clin. assoc. div. of cancer treatment Nat. Cancer Inst., Bethesda, Md., 1973-76; asst. prof. medicine Columbia Coll. Physicians and Surgeons, 1976-86, assoc. prof. clin. medicine, 1986—, asst. prof. medicine Cancer Rsch. Ctr., Columbia U., 1976-86, assoc. prof. medicine, 1986—; asst. attending physician Columbia-Presbyn. Med. Center, N.Y.C., 1976-86, assoc. attending physician, 1986—. Served with USPHS, 1973-76. Am. Cancer Soc. jr. faculty clin. fellow, 1976-79; diplomate Am. Bd. Internal Medicine and subsplty. med. oncology. Fellow ACP; mem. AMA (Physician Recognition awards 1976-78, 79-81, 82-84), Am. Assn. Cancer Rsch., N.Y. Cancer Soc., Am. Soc. Clin. Oncology, N.Y. Met. Breast Cancer Group, Phi Beta Kappa, Alpha Omega Alpha. Home: 6 Arrowhead Ln Armonk NY 10504 Office: 161 Fort Washington Ave New York NY 10032

OSTER, ROSE MARIE GUNHILD, language professional, educator; b. Stockholm, Feb. 26, 1934; came to U.S., 1958; d. Herbert Jonas and Emma Wilhelmina (Johnson) Hagetorn; m. Ludwig F. Oster, May 17, 1956; children: Ulrika, Mattias. Fil. mag., U. Stockholm, 1956; D. Phil., Kiel (Germany) U., 1958. Postdoctoral research fellow linguistics Yale U., 1958-60, research fellow Germanic langs., 1960-64, lectr. Swedish, 1964-66; mem. faculty U. Colo., Boulder, 1966-80; assoc. prof. Germanic langs. and lits. U. Colo., 1970-77, prof., 1977-80, chmn. dept., 1972-75; assoc. dean U. Colo. (Grad. Sch.), 1975-79, assoc. vice chancellor for grad. affairs, 1979-80; dean for grad. studies and research U. Md., College Park, 1980-83; prof. Germanic langs. and lits. U. Md., 1980—; me. Fulbright Nat. Screening Com. Scandinavia, 1973, 83-86; mem. selection com. Scandinavia Internat. Exch. of Scholars, 1983; cons. panelist Nat. Endowment for Humanities, 1975—, mem. bd. cons., 1980—; state coord. Am. Coun. on Edn., Colo., 1978-80, Md., 1981-83, dir. dept. leadership program, 1986—; mem. exec. com. Assn. Grad. Schs., 1980-83; mem. dean's exec. com. African-Am. Inst., 1981-85; cons. in field. Contbr. articles and revs. to profl. publs. Carnegie fellow, 1974; grantee Swedish Govt., Am. Scandinavian Found.; grantee German Acad. Exchange Service. Mem. Soc. Advancement Scandinavian Studies (pres. 1979-80), Am. Scandinavian Assn. of Nat. Capital Area (pres. 1983-86), MLA, Am.-Scandinavian Found., Am. Assn. Higher Edn., AAUP, NOW. Home: 4977 Battery Ln Bethesda MD 20814-4931 Office: U Md Jimenez Hall College Park MD 20742

OSTERHOUDT, HANS WALTER, physical chemist; b. Houston, Feb. 29, 1936; s. Walter Jabez and Gretchen Marie (Zierath) O.; m. Marjorie Scott, May 26, 1962; children: David Scott, Thomas Frederick. BS, Colo. State U., 1958; PhD, U. Wis., 1964. Rsch. chemist Armstrong World Industries, Lancaster, Pa., 1964-68; rsch. chemist Eastman Kodak Co., Rochester, N.Y., 1968-70, sr. rsch. chemist, 1970-72, lab. head, 1973-78, rsch. assoc., 1978—. Contbr. articles to Jour. Phys. Chemistry, Jour. Applied Polymer Sci. Mem. Soc. Plastics Engrs. (bd. dirs. Rochester sect. 1988-91), Am. Chem. Soc. Episcopalian. Home: 213 Milton Ave Apt A Syracuse NY 13204-1925 Office: Eastman Kodak Co 1999 Lake Ave Rochester NY 14650-0001

OSTERMAN, KENNETH GEORGE, landscape designer; b. Plainfield, N.J., Apr. 9, 1947; s. George J. and Emily (Poliacik) O.; m. Jennifer Jane Fankhauser, July 17, 1973. Student, U. Wis., 1965-67. Design mgr. Osterman Nursery, Inc., Middlesex, N.J., 1973-90; v.p. Osterman Nursery, Inc., Neshanic, N.J., 1980—; bd. dirs. N.J. Farm Bur., Trenton. Pres. Somerset County Adv. Bd., Bridgewater, N.J., 1991—; charter panel mem. Operation Cooperation, Bridgewater Police Dept. Cpl. USMC, 1969-71. Mem. N.J. Assn. Nurserymen (exec. com. 1972-83), Somerset County Bd. Agriculture (pres. 1990—), 3rd Marine Div. Assn. (N.J. chpt.), Jaycees (middlesex chpt., v.p. 1973-74). Office: Osterman Nursery Inc PO Box 370 Wertsville Rd Neshanic NJ 08853

OSTERMANN, ARTHUR CHRISTOPHER, broadcast executive, producer, reporter; b. N.Y.C., Oct. 12, 1956; s. Anthony Lawrence and Anne Theresa Giardina; m. Mary Carmela Paladino, Sept. 2, 1984. Assoc. in Applied Humanities degree, Brookdale Community Coll., Lincroft, N.J., 1992; postgrad., Rutgers U. On-air personality, newscaster Sta. WADB-FM, South Belmar, N.J., 1985-86; on-air personality, news dir. Sta. WVRM-FM, Hazlet, N.J., 1986-87; on-air personality Sta. WSRR-AM, Washington, N.J., 1987; traffic announcer Shadow Traffic Network, Union, N.J., 1987-89; sr. traffic producer, reporter Metro Traffic Control, N.Y.C., 1989-91. Mem. Freehold Township Rep. Club. Mem. AFTRA. Address: 4010 Bristol Ct Freehold NJ 07728

OSTERNDORF, LOGAN CARL, educator; b. Chgo., Oct. 3, 1917; s. Charles Ernst and Minna Alvina (Alpers) O.; m. Mary Vernon Morgan, July 30, 1955; children: Dana Sue, Dale Morgan. BS in Fgn. Svc. cum laude, Georgetown U., Washington, 1951; MS, U. Wis., 1952. Asst. prof. Va. Poly. Inst. and State U., Blacksburg, 1953-59; dir. progs. and ops. Div. Ednl. Travel, NEA, Washington, 1959-64; UNESCO prog. specialist Inst. Internat. Studies, U.S. Office Edn., Washington, 1965-74; specialist internat. edn. Nat. Ctr. for Edn. Statistics, U.S. Office Edn., Washington, 1974-80; cons. in edn. Silver Spring, Md., 1980—; Angus cattle farmer Dublin, Va., 1980—; bd. dirs. Coun. on Internat. Ednl. Exchange, N.Y.C., 1962-64; founder Scandinavian-Am. Summer U., Aalborg, Denmark, 1961; founder German-Am. Seminar, Tutzing, Bavaria, 1961; project officer Transition From Sch. to Work: An Intercountry Study, Georgetown U., 1979, Adult Learning Opportunities in Nine Industrialized Countries, Ednl. Testing Svc., Princeton, N.J., 1980. Author: Course Offerings, Enrollments and Curriculum Practices in Public Secondary Schools, 1972-73, 74; editor: First Call newsletter, 1977—, Jour. of Coun. on Am. Mil. Past, 1992—. Mem. Va. Farm Bur., Nat. Trust for Historic Preservation, Amnesty Internat. 1st lt. U.S. Army, 1941-47; PTO; ETO. Decorated Bronze Star. Ford Found. grantee, 1957. Mem. Ret. Officers Assn., Coun. Am's. Mil. Past, China Round Table, Alpha Kappa Psi. Democrat. Lutheran. Address: 10206 Lariston Ln Silver Spring MD 20903

OSTFELD, ALEXANDER MARION, advertising agency executive; b. St. Louis, Feb. 13, 1932; s. Simon and Margaret (Fishmann) O.; B.S., Washington U., St. Louis, 1953; postgrad. St. Louis U., 1953-56. Mktg. mgr. lighting div. Emerson Electric Co., St. Louis, 1955-59; dir. research and media Frank Block Assos., St. Louis, 1959-61; research and media supr. Compton Advt., Chgo., 1961-65; media and mktg. supr. Leo Burnett Advt., Chgo., 1965-68; dir. mktg. and account planning, v.p. McCann-Erickson, Chgo., 1968-72, Kenyon & Eckhardt, Chgo., 1972; dir. Canadian and internat. ops. A. Eicoff & Co., Chgo.; owner Alex Ostfeld Co. Advt. and Mktg., Woodbridge, Conn. and Can. Cons. Am. Assn. Advt. Agys., Yale/New Haven Sci. Park. Mem. Am. Mktg. Assn. (sec. St. Louis 1956-57), Internat. Platform Assn., Broadcast Advt. Club, Am. Research Found. Clubs: Chgo. Exec., Woodbridge Hunt (Conn.). Home: 4 Ledge Rd Woodbridge CT 06525-1802 Office: 6 Ledge Rd Woodbridge CT 06525-1802

OSTLING, PAUL JAMES, lawyer; b. Jamaica, N.Y., Sept. 22, 1948; s. John Carl and Margaret Ruth (Reilly) O.; m. Jane B. Mahler, June 1, 1974 (div. 1980); m. Julie Eileen Boyum, Feb. 20, 1982 (div. 1988); m. Danita Kay Hoover, May 3, 1991. BS in Math. and Philosophy, Fordham U., 1969, JD, 1973. Bar: N.Y. 1974, U.S. Dist. Ct. (so. and ea. dists.) N.Y. 1974, U.S. Ct. Appeals (2d cir.) 1974, U.S. Ct. Appeals (4th, 5th, 9th, 10th, 11th cirs.) 1978. Assoc. Chadbourne Parke, N.Y.C., 1973-77; asst. gen. counsel Authur Young & Co., N.Y.C., 1977-79, assoc. gen. counsel, 1979-82, ptnr., assoc. gen. counsel, 1982, nat. dir. human resources, 1985-90; vice chmn. Ernst & Young, N.Y.C., 1990—. Office: Ernst & Young 787 7th Ave New York NY 10019-6018

OSTRANDER, ROBERT EDWIN, United Nations interregional advisor, petroleum company executive; b. Pitts., June 30, 1931; s. Robert Jesse and Elizabeth Raymond (Comstock) O.; m. Margaret Valentina Servello, Dec. 21, 1958; children—Robert Glen, Roseanne. B.A., Cornell U., 1952. Cert. petroleum geologist; registered geol. scientist. Area reservoir engr. Mene Grande Oil Co., San Tome, Venezuela, 1956-61; dist. engr. Oasis Oil Co. of Libya, Tripoli, 1962-67; chief engr. Occidental Oil of Libya, Tripoli, 1967-71; div. head Iranian Oil Consortium, Ahwaz, Iran, 1972-75; mgr. ops. Ultramar Co. Ltd., Mt. Kisco, N.Y., 1975-81; v.p. engring. Weeks Petroleum Ltd., Westport, Conn., 1982-85; mng. dir. Reomag Inc., South Salem, N.Y., 1980—; tech. expert World Bank, Washington, 1981—; cons. UN Secretariat, 1985—; advisor to govts. of China, India, others in Asia, Africa, Middle East; guest lectr. Asian univs., internat. seminars. Contbr. articles to profl. jours. Sec. Rep. Com. Town of Lewisboro ; mem. Rep. Com. Westchester County; pres., dir. Oakridge Condominium Assn., Vista, N.Y. Served to 1st lt. U.S. Army, 1953-55. Mem. Am. Assn. Petroleum Geologists, Assn. Profl. Geol. Scientists, Soc. Petroleum Engrs., Petroleum Exploration Soc. N.Y. Home: 159 Stonemeadow Rd South Salem NY 10590-9547 Office: UN Dept Tech Cooperation for Devel Natural Resources & Energy Rm DC1-894 44th St & 1st Ave New York NY 10017

OSTROFF, JONATHAN BRUCE, paper merchant executive; b. Newark, Apr. 30, 1956; s. William Lazar Ostroff and Joan Ruth (Birinbaum) Zimmer; m. Lisa Jean Maguire, Sept. 9, 1978; 1 child, Kirsten Maguire. BA, Eckerd Coll., 1978. Mgr. Hi-Fi-Fo-Fum Stereo, Venice, Fla., 1978-79; salesman Lewmar Paper Co., Kenilworth, N.J., 1979-87; v.p. Lewmar Paper Co., Kenilworth, 1987—. Mem. Affordable Housing Task Force, Tewksbury Twp., N.J., 1990—; trustee Reform Temple of Hunterdon County, 1990—; 1st v.p. Temple Of Chadash, 1992—. Mem. Nat. Paper Trade Assn. (young exec. forum). Jewish. Office: Lewmar Paper Co 251 S 31st St Kenilworth NJ 07033-1305

OSTROV, JEROME, lawyer; b. Boston, Dec. 2, 1942; s. Harold S. and Etta (Resnick) O.; m. Roberta S. Baruch, Sept. 3, 1978; children: Rebecca Ann, Max Abraham, Julia Grace. BSBA cum laude, Boston U., 1964; JD, Union U., 1967; LLM in Taxation, NYU, 1968; MPA, Harvard U., 1980. Bar: N.Y. 1968, D.C. 1971, Md. 1991. Ptnr. Friedlander Misler et al, 1985—, N.Y.C., 1968-69; law clk. to presiding judge U.S. Tax Ct., Washington, 1969-71; pvt. practice Washington, 1971-73; dep. assoc. gen. counsel U.S. EPA, Washington, 1973-79; fellow John F. Kennedy Sch. Govt., Harvard U., 1979-80; staff counsel U.S. Ho. of Reps., Washington, 1982-83; pvt. practice Washington, 1983—; counsel Inst. Mental Health, Washington, 1984—; bd. dirs. Am. Assocs. Ben Gurion U. of Negev, N.Y.C.; mem. Adas Israel Congregation, Washington, 1987—. Contbr. articles to profl. jours. Mem. ABA. Democrat. Office: Friedlander Misler et al 1101 17th St NW Ste 700 Washington DC 20036

OSTROW, STEPHEN EDWARD, library administrator, art historian; b. N.Y.C., May 7, 1932; s. Herman and Anne (Epstein) O.; m. Claudine Zelnick, Mar. 25, 1962; children: Alan (dec.), Anne-Michele. BA, Oberlin (Ohio) Coll., 1954; MA, NYU, 1959, PhD, 1966. Asst. prof. U.Mo., Columbia, 1962-66; coll. curator Indpls. Mus. of Art, 1966-67; chief curator Mus. of Art Mus. of Art R.I. Sch. of Design, Providence, 1967-71; dir. Mus. of Art R.I. Sch. Dist., Providence, 1971-78; dean, prof. U. So. Calif., L.A., 1978-81; exec. dir. Portland (Oreg.) Art Assn., 1981-84; chief prints and photographs div. Libr. of Congress, Washington, 1984—; cons. U.Miami, Fla., 1977, U. Tex., San Antonio, 1979, Reed Coll., Portland, 1986-89; mem. vis. com. Wheaton Coll., Norton, Mass., 1974-76; vis. lectr. Brown U., Providence, 1970-77. Member R.I. Hist. Preservation Commn., Providence, 1974-76; mem. exec. com. Alliance for Arts Edn., Providence, 1974-76; bd. dirs. Arts in Edn. Com., Providence, 1971-73, Oreg. Advs. for the Arts, Portland, 1981-82. With U.S. Army, 1984-86, ETO. Oberlin Coll. Haskell fellow, 1960; NYU scholar, 1966. Mem. Print Coun. of Am. (trustee 1985—), Phi Beta Kappa. Office: Libr of Congress Washington DC 20540

OSTRY, JONATHAN DAVID, economist, researcher; b. Ottawa, Ont., July 29, 1962; s. Bernard and Sylvia (Knelman) O. BA with distinction, Queen's Univ., 1981; BA with honors, Oxford U., 1983; MSc, London Sch. of Econs., 1984; PhD, U. Chgo., 1988. Economist Internat. Monetary Fund, Washington, 1988—. Contbr. articles to profl. jours. Named Commonwealth scholar Oxford Univ. and London Sch. of Econs., 1981-84, Mackenzie King fellow Mackenzie King Found., 1984-85, Social Sci. Rsch. Coun. fellow, 1984-88, Univ. Chgo. fellow, Chgo., 1984-88, Pew fellow Univ. Chgo., 1986-88. Jewish.

O'SULLIVAN, GERARD ((GERRY)), author; b. N.Y.C., May 22, 1959; s. Thomas and Margaret O'Sullivan. BA summa cum laude, Fordham U., 1981; MA, Vanderbilt U., 1985; postgrad., U. Pa., 1985—. Grad. fellow, instr. U. Pa., Phila., 1985—; book rev. editor Z Magazine, Boston, 1990—; columnist The Humanist Mag., Amherst, N.Y., 1990—, sr. editor, 1991—. Co-author: (book) The Terrorism Industry, 1990, Satanism In America: How the Devil Got Much More Than His Due, 1989; contbg. author: Western State Terrorism, 1991. Mem. Christian Assn. of the U. Pa. (bd. dirs. 1989-91), Phi Beta Kappa. Office: U Pa Ctr for Cultural Studies Williams Hall 420 Philadelphia PA 19104

O'SULLIVAN, JUDITH ROBERTA, museum director; b. Pitts., Jan. 6, 1942; d. Robert Howard and Mary Olive (O'Donnell) Gallick; m. James Paul O'Sullivan, Feb. 1, 1964; children: Kathryn, James. BA, Carlow Coll., 1963; MA, U. Md., 1969, PhD, 1976. Assoc. program coord. Smithsonian Resident Assocs., Washington, 1977-78; dir. instl. devel. Nat. Archives, Washington, 1978-79; exec. dir. Md. State Humanities Coun., Balt., 1979-81, 82-84, Ctr. for the Book, Libr. of Congress, Washington, 1981-82; dep. asst. dir. Nat. Mus. Am. Art, Washington, 1984-87, acting asst. dir., 1987-89; pres., chief exec. officer The Museums at Stony Brook,, N.Y., 1989—; mem. scholarly adv. bd. Am. Film Inst., Washington, 1979—. Author: The Art of the Comic Strip, 1971 (gen. excellence award Printing Industry Am.), Workers and Allies, 1975, The Complete Prints of Leonard Baskin, 1984, The Great American Comic Strip, 1990; editor Am. Film Inst. Catalogue: Feature Films, 1961-70, 1974-77. Trustee Child Life Ctr., U. Md., College Pk., 1971-74; chair Smithsonian Women's Coun., 1988-89. Univ. fellow U. Md., 1967-70, Mus. fellow, 1970-71; Smithsonian fellow Nat. Collection Fine Arts, Washington, 1972-73. Mem. Assn. Assn. Art Mus. Dirs., Am. Assn. Mus., Mid-Atlantic Mus. Conf., AAUW. Home: 50 Main St Stony Brook NY 11790-1913 Office: The Mus 1208 Rt 25A Stony Brook NY 11790-1992

OSWALT, ROBERT MCNEILL, psychology educator; b. Danville, Ill., Sept. 3, 1938; s. Robert Jhn and Katherine (McNeill) O.; m. Dorothy Jane Stein, July 11, 1970; children: Sarah, Michael, Mark. BA, DePauw U., Greencastle, Ind., 1960; MA, La. State U., Baton Rouge, 1962; PhD, La. State U., 1965. Lic. psychologist, N.Y. Staff psychologist The McMurray Co., Chgo., 1964-65; cons. Booz Allen & Hamilton, Chgo., 1965-67; prof. psychology Skidmore Coll., Saratoga, N.Y., 1967—. Contbr. articles to profl. jurs. Home: 8 Bryan St Saratoga Springs NY 12866-1706 Office: Skidmore Coll Saratoga NY 12866

OTANI, MIKE, optical company executive; b. Atsumi, Aichi, Japan, July 25, 1945; s. Yuichi and Miyako (Suzuki) O.; m. Jane Ashley Campbell, Aug. 25, 1976; 1 child, Michael Taro. Degree in Internat. Fin. and Econs., Shiga U., Japan, 1967. Office mgr. Kumagai-Gumi Ltd, Osaka, Japan, 1968-73; dude rancher Tumbling River Ranch, Grant, Colo., 1974-77; merchandiser Nobel, Inc., Denver, 1978-82; v.p. Charmant Eyewear, Inc., Morris Plains, N.J., 1983-88, pres., chief exec. officer, 1988—; bd. dirs. Charmant Optical Co., Ltd., Fukui, Japan, Charmant Optical GMRH Europe, Munich, Optical Manufacturers Assn., Falls Church, Va. Donator Project Literacy U.S., Pitts., 1990, Pa. Coll. Optometry, Phila., 1990; organizer N.J. Fukui Sister State Activity, 1990. Recipient Vendor of Yr. award Walmart, Inc., 1991. Mem. Optical Mfgrs. Assn., Fukui/New York Club (v.p. 1992). Home: 9 October Hill Rd Oak Ridge NJ 07438-9194 Office: Charmant Eyewear Inc 400 American Rd Morris Plains NJ 07950-2451

OTHMER, DAVID ARTMAN, television and radio station executive; b. West Medford, Mass., Mar. 18, 1941; s. Murray Eade and Mary (Artman) O.; m. Nancy Trumbull, Sept. 12, 1965 (div. Dec. 1982); 1 child, Rachel; m. Maureen Barden, June 4, 1983; 1 child, Matthew. BA, Harvard Coll., 1963; MBA, Harvard U., 1966. Asst. to pres. Sta. WNET, N.Y.C., 1974-75, dir. broadcasting, 1975-82, dir. telecommunications, 1982-83; v.p., sta. mgr. Sta. WHYY, Phila., 1983—. Exec. producer (TV show) Science Spots, 1985 (Ohio State award 1985); producer (TV show) Who is Red Grooms?, 1986 (Emmy 1986), various other TV shows, 1980— (Emmy nominations). Home: 4220 Spruce St Philadelphia PA 19104-4040 Office: Sta WHYY 150 N 6th St Philadelphia PA 19106-1589

OTHMER, DONALD FREDERICK, chemical engineer, educator; b. Omaha, May 11, 1904; s. Frederick George and Fredericka Darling (Snyder) O.; m. Mildred Jane Topp, Nov. 18, 1950. Student, Ill. Inst. Tech., Chgo., 1921-23; B.S., U. Nebr., 1924, D.Eng. (hon.), 1962; M.S., U. Mich., 1925, Ph.D., 1927; D.Eng. (hon.), Poly. U., Bklyn., 1977, N.J. Inst. Tech., 1978. Registered profl. engr., N.Y., N.J., Ohio, Pa. Devel. engr. Eastman Kodak Co. and Tenn. Eastman Corp., 1927-31; prof. Poly. U., Bklyn., 1933; disting. prof. Poly. U., 1961—, sec. grad. faculty, 1948-58; head dept. chem. engring., 1937-61; hon. prof. U. Conception, Chile, 1951; cons. chem. engr., licensor of process patents to numerous cos., govtl. depts., and countries, 1931—; developer program for chem. industry of Burma, 1951-54; cons. UN, UNIDO, WHO, Dept. Energy, Office Saline Water of U.S. Dept. Interior, Chem. Corps. and Ordnance Dept. U.S. Army, USN, WPB, Dept. State, HEW, Nat. Materials Advisory Bd., NRC Sci. Adv. Bd., U.S. Army Munitions Command; mem. Panel Energy Advisers to Congress, also other U.S. and fgn. govt. depts.; sr. gas officer Bklyn. Citizens Def. Corps.; lectr. Am. Swiss Found. Sci. Relations, 1950, Chem. Inst. Can., 1944-52, Am. Chem. Soc., U.S. Army War Coll., 1964, Shri RAM Inst., India, 1980, Royal Mil. Coll. Can., 1981; plenary lectr. Peoples Republic of China; hon. del. Engring. Congresses, Japan, 1983; plenary lectr., hon. del. Fed. Republic of Germany, Greece, Mex., Czechoslovakia, Yugoslavia, Poland, P.R., France, Can., Argentina, India, Turkey, Spain, Rumania, Kuwait, Iran, Iraq, Algeria, China, United Arab Emirates; designer chem. plants and processes for numerous corps., U.S., fgn. countries. Holder over 150 U.S. and fgn. patents on methods, processes and engring. equipment in mfg. of pharms., sugar, salt, acetic acid, acetylene, fuel-methanol, synthetic rubber, petro-chems., pigments, zinc, aluminum, titanium, also wood pulping, refrigeration, solar and other energy conversion, water desalination, sewage treatment, peat

utilization, coal desulfurization, pipeline heating, etc.; contbr. over 350 articles on chem. engring., chem. mfg., synthetic fuels and thermodynamics to tech. jours.; co-founder/co-editor: Kirk-Othmer Ency. Chem. Tech., 17 vols., 1947-60, 24 vols., 2d edit., 1963-71, 26 vols., 3d edit., 1976-84, 4th edit., 25 vols., 1992, Spanish edit., 16 vols., 1960-66; editor: Fluidization, 1956; co-author: Fluidization and Fluid Particle Systems, 1960; mem. adv. bd.: Perry's Chem. Engr.'s Handbook; tech. editor: UN Report, Technology of Water Desalination, 1964. Bd. regents L.I. Coll. Hosp., bd. dirs. numerous ednl. and philanthropic instns., engring. and indsl. corps. Recipient Golden Jubilee award Ill. Inst. Tech., 1975, Profl. Achievement award Ill. Inst. Tech., 1978, Award of Honor for Sci. and Tech. Mayor of N.Y.C., 1987, Outstanding Alumnus award U. Nebr., 1989, Citation for Improvement of Quality of Life, Pres. Borough Bklyn., 1989, award for significant contbns. to life Polytechnic U., 1989; named to Hall of Fame, Ill. Inst. Tech., 1981. Fellow AAAS, Am. Inst. Cons. Engrs., Am. Inst. Chemists (Honor Scroll 1970, Chem. Pioneer award 1977), ASME (hon. life, chmn. chem. processes div. 1948-49), N.Y. Acad. Scis. (hon. life, chmn. engring. sect. 1972-73), Instn. Chem. Engrs. (London) (hon. life), Am. Inst. Chem. Engrs. (Tyler award 1958, chmn. N.Y. sect. 1944, dir. 1956-59, Founders award 1991); mem. Am. Chem. Soc. (council 1945-47, E.V. Murphree-Exxon award 1978, hon. life mem.), Soc. Chem. Industry (Perkin medal 1978), Am. Soc. Engring. Edn. (Barber Coleman award 1958), Engrs. Joint Council (dir. 1957-59), Societe de Chimie Industrielle (pres. 1973-74), Chemurgic Council (dir.), Japan Soc. Chem. Engrs., Assn. Cons. Chemists and Chem. Engrs. (award of Merit 1975), Newcomen Soc., Am. Arbitration Assn. (panel mem. or sole arbitrator numerous cases), Deutsche Gesellscaft für Cheme. Apparatewesen (hon. life), Norwegian Club Bklyn., Chemists Club N.Y.C. (pres. 1974-75), Rembrandt Club Bklyn., Sigma Xi (citation disting. research 1983), Tau Beta Pi, Phi Lambda Upsilon, Iota Alpha, Alpha Chi Sigma, Lambda Chi Alpha. Home: 140 Columbia Hts Brooklyn NY 11201-1631 Office: Poly U 333 Jay St Brooklyn NY 11201-2990

OTIS, RICHARD DICKINSON, pathologist; b. Meriden, Conn., Dec. 26, 1924; s. Fessenden Newport and Anna (Gerstenmaier) O.; m. Mary Tourtellot Hamlen, June10, 1949; children: James H., Richard D., Jr., Christopher N., John B. Student premed. tng. program, Trinity Coll., 1945; MD, Yale U., 1949. Diplomate Am. Bd. Pathology, Internat. Bd. Cytopathology. Pathologist Sch. Medicine Yale U., New Haven, Conn., 1952-55; sr. pathologist, dir. anatomic pathology Hartford (Conn.) Hosp., Md., 1955-86; cons. pathologist Hartford (Conn.) Hosp., 1986—. Contbr. articles to profl. jours. Lt. USN, 1950-52. T. Stewart Hamilton grantee TSH Found.; Harvard U. fellow, 1979. Mem. AMA, Internat. Acad. pathologists, Internat. Acad. Cytology, New Eng. Cancer Soc., Coll. Am. Pathologists. Republican. Home and Office: 181 Meadow Neck Rd East Falmouth MA 02536-7712

OTREMBA, BERNARD OTTO, marketing executive; b. Munich, Feb. 3, 1944; came to U.S, 1985; s. Louis E. and Burgl (Koppel) O.; m. Roswitha J. Pietrzyk, Dec. 27, 1984; children: Gabriele Yvonne, Sonya Charlotte. MBA in Econs., Munich Coll., 1970; PhD in Bus. Adminstrn., Pacific Western U., 1987. Pres. Import Export Ltd., Tehran, Iran, 1976-81; dir. bus. devel. Intergraph Europe, Inc., London and Amsterdam, The Netherlands, 1981-84; exec. v.p., gen. mgr. SSI Schaefer Systems Internat. Inc., Eatontown, N.J., 1985-88; pres. Gardner Internat. Ops. Ltd., Tampa, Fla., 1989—. Author: Industrial Psychology and Physiology in Contemporary Management, 1970, Can Computers Draw? CAD in Architecture, 1984, The Interdependence in the Economic Relations Between Industrial and Developing Countries, 1987. Mem. Direct Mktg. Assn., Direct Mktg. Club of N.Y., Am. Mgmt. Assn., Doctoral Assn. N.Y.C. Home: 46 Steeplechase Ct Oceanport NJ 07757-1182

OTT, GILBERT RUSSELL, JR., lawyer; b. Bklyn., Apr. 15, 1943; s. Gilbert Russell Sr. and Bettina Rose (Ferrel) O.; m. Lisa S. Weatherford, Apr. 12, 1986; children: Gilbert R. III, Laura Elisabeth. BA, Yale U., 1965; JD, Columbia U., 1969, MBA, 1969. Bar: N.Y. 1970. Assoc. Chadbourne, Parke, Whiteside & Wolff, N.Y.C., 1969-72, LeBoeuf, Lamb, Leiby & MacRae, N.Y.C., 1972-78; asst. v.p. Kidder, Peabody & Co., Inc., N.Y.C., 1978-79, assoc. gen. counsel, asst. sec., 1978—, v.p., 1979-86, mng. dir., 1986—; asst. sec. Kidder, Peabody Group Inc., N.Y.C., 1986—, v.p., 1989—; v.p. Webster Cash Res. Fund, Inc., N.Y.C., 1980—, sec., 1982-89, gen. counsel, 1982—, also bd. dirs.; sec. Kidder, Peabody Premium Account Fund, 1982-89, v.p., gen. counsel, 1982—, trustee, 1985—; sec. Kidder, Peabody Govt. Money Fund, Inc., 1983-89, v.p., gen. counsel, 1983—. Mem. Assn. of Bar of City of N.Y., Piping Rock Club, Down Town Assn., Univ. Club. Home: 260 Highwood Cir Oyster Bay NY 11771-3205 Office: Kidder Peabody & Co Inc 10 Hanover Sq New York NY 10005-3516

OTT, KEVIN DOWD, association executive; b. Washington, Jan. 21, 1953; s. Jerome B. and Mary Ruth (Dowd) O. BA, U. Va., 1975. Mktg. rep. Honeywell, Inc., Washington, 1978-81; asst. v.p. Nat. Assn. Mfrs., Washington, 1981-87; exec. dir. Coun. on Superconductivity, Washington, 1987—. Editor Superconductor Industry, 1988—. Office: Coun on Superconductivity 1050 Thomas Jefferson St NW #600 Washington DC 20007-3837

OTT, ROBERT LOUIS, electronics executive; b. Wilkes-Barre, Pa., Oct. 8, 1954; s. Bernard George and Louise Aurora (Trainor) O.; m. Donna Marie Smith, Nov. 8, 1980; children: Christopher Bernard, Thomas Stephen, Brian Gerard. Student, King's Coll., 1976. Producer WNEP-TV, Avoca, Pa., 1974-76; regional sales mgr. SHURE, Evanston, Ill., 1976-80; applications mgr. SHURE, 1980-84, internat. sales mgr., 1984-88; nat. sales mgr. Sony, Teaneck, N.J., 1988-90; nat. mgr. distribution Sony, Montvale, N.J., 1990—; mem. CAAG, Chgo., 1980-85. Producer Ghosts of Chicago, 1988. Cable adminstrn. Skokie Cable Television, Ill., 1985. Mem. St. Conrad's Soc. Roman Catholic.

OTTE, DANIEL, entomologist, curator; b. Durban, Republic of South Africa, Mar. 14, 1939; came to U.S., 1959; s. Carl Nils Heinrich and Lillian (Young) O.; m. Laurel Ann Benn, June 7, 1963; children: Jennifer Leslie, Jessica Allison. BS, U. Mich., 1963, PhD, 1968. Asst. prof. zoology U. Tex., Austin, 1969-75; assoc. curator entomology Acad. Natural Sci., Phila., 1975-78, curator, chmn. entomology, 1979—, dir. sci. publs., 1987-88. Author: Communicative Behavior in Grasshoppers, 1970; author, illustrator: The North American Grasshoppers, Vol. 1, 1981, Vol. 2, 1984, The Australian Crickets: Gryllidae, 1983; editor, contbr.: Speciation and Its Consequences, 1989. Mem. Am. Entomol. Soc. (editor Trans. 1977—), Orthopterists Soc. (pres. 1989—). Office: Acad Natural Sci 19th and The Parkway Philadelphia PA 19103

OTTENHOFF, ROBERT GEORGE, television executive; b. Chgo., Apr. 8, 1948; s. Herman and Cornelia (Cevaal) O.; m. Faith Ann Hoogstrate, Aug. 14, 1971; children: Patrick, J. Elliott. M in City and Regional Planning, Rutgers U., 1971. Asst. prof. Rutgers U., New Brunswick, N.J., 1972-78; gen. mgr. Sta. WBGO, Newark, 1978-86; exec. dir. N.J. Network, Trenton, 1987-91; exec. v.p., chief oper. officer PBS, Alexandria, Va., 1991—, also bd. dirs.; mem. Pub. TV Long Range Planning and Programming Task Force, PBS Avd. Panel on Assessment Policy; mem. adv. bd. Internat. Telecommunications Ctr., Ramapo Coll.; exec. com., bd. trustees Ea. Ednl. Network, vice chmn., 1991— ; vice chmn. Orgn. State Broadcasting Execs., chmn. govt. rels. com., 1991. Bd. dirs. N.J. Com. for the Humanities, 1988; mem. sup. ct. com. rels. with media, 1988, Chief Justice appt. Comml. Filming in Ct. Facilities, 1990. Office: Pub Broadcasting Svc 1320 Braddock Pl Alexandria VA 22314

OTTER, MARK WILLIAM, orthopaedic research scientist; b. Urbana, Ill., Apr. 10, 1959; s. Fred August and Kathleen (McKinney) O. BS, U. Conn., 1981; MS, U. Ill., 1983, PhD, 1987. Postdoctoral fellow Helen Hayes Hosp., West Haverstraw, N.Y., 1987-89, chief biomed. rsch. unit, 1989—. Contbr. articles to profl. jours. Grantee Orthopaedic Rsch. and Edn. Found., 1988-90, Aircast Inc., 1990-91. Mem. Bioelectrical Repair and Growth Soc. (coun. mem. 1991—), Am. Soc. for Gravitational and Space Biology, Orthopaedic Rsch. Soc., Am. Phys. Soc., Materials Rsch. Soc., Phi Beta Kappa, Sigma Pi Sigma, Alpha Lambda Delta. Office: Helen Hayes Hosp OERC Rte 9W West Haverstraw NY 10993

OTTERMAN, KENNETH JAMES, real estate investor, author, consultant; b. McKeesport, Pa., Jan. 21, 1949; s. Glenn Ewing Sr. and Beatrice May (Hill) O.; m. Deborah Jean Brown, Aug. 14, 1973; children: Kenneth J. Jr., Forrest G. BS in Bus., Pa. State U., 1973. Prin., real estate investor Ken Otterman & Assocs., Reading, Pa., 1976; bd. advisors D.I.G., Phila., R.E.I.A., Reading; org. mem, investor Berks County Bank, Reading, 1987—. Author: Real Estate Investing for Cash Flow, 1986, Home Ownership Bargains From Your Government, 1986, Rules of the Game, 1984, (course) Become a Real Estate Investor, 1984. Club: R.E.I.A. (Reading) (pres. 1982-85). Office: 2022 E Main St Douglasville PA 19518

OTTO, CHARLES EDWARD, health care administrator; b. Somerville, N.J., Nov. 12, 1946; s. Hans and Virginia (Hegeman) O.; m. Wendy Ann Halsey; June 26, 1971; children: Eric, C. Halsey, Robert. BA, Hobart Coll., Geneva, N.Y., 1968; MBA, U. Pa., 1973. Adminstrv. asst. Mass. Gen. Hosp., Boston, 1970-71; adminstrv. resident Hosp. of U. of Pa., Phila., 1973; adminstrv. asst. Norwalk (Conn.) Hosp., 1974-76; exec. dir. Waveny Care Ctr., New Canaan, Conn., 1977—; bd. chmn. Conn. Assn. of Non-Profit Facilities for the Aged, Wallingford, 1984-86; chmn. regional adv. group Conn. Community Care, Inc., Norwalk, 1983-85. Bd. chmn. S.W. Fairfield Am. Cancer Soc., Norwalk, 1985-87. Served to lt. (j.g.) USNR, 1968-70. Mem. Wharton Healthcare Alumni Assn., Wharton Club N.Y.C., Rocky Point Club. Episcopalian. Home: 12 Lake Dr S Riverside CT 06878-2016 Office: Waveny Care Ctr 3 Farm Rd New Canaan CT 06840-6698

OTTO, GILBERT FRED, zoologist, educator; b. Chgo., Dec. 16, 1901; s. Martin and Fredericka Christina (Rose) O.; m. Loudale Simmons, Dec. 20, 1932; children: Sandra Otto Abbott, Frederick Simmons. AB, Kalamazoo Coll., 1926; MS, Kans. State U., 1927; ScD, Johns Hopkins U., 1929. Instr. Johns Hopkins U., Balt., 1929-31, asst. prof., 1931-42, assoc. prof., 1942-53, asst. dean Sch. of Pub. Health, 1940-47, dir. Parasitology Lab. of Med. Clinics, 1946-53; mgr. Parasitology Rsch. Div. Abbott Labs., North Chicago, Ill., 1953-61; dir. of agrl. and vet. rsch. Abbott Labs., North Chicago, 1961-66; prof. zoology U. Md., College Park, 1966-72, adj. prof., lectr., 1972-80, sr. rsch. assoc., 1980—; lectr. med. entomology Sch. of Hygiene and Pub. Health Johns Hopkins U., 1980-89; cons. Naval Med. Rsch. Inst., 1948-54; mem. sci. adv. bd. biology dept. U. Notre Dame, 1958-67; vis. prof. U. Mich. Biol. Sta., 1946-53; cons. NIH, 1945-50, WHO, 1952-75, FDA, 1941, 77-81; cons. mosquito-borne disease Nat. Acad. Sci., 1983-86; sec. gen. 2d Internat. Congress Parasitology, 1970. Contbr. numerous articles on parasitology to sci. jours; contbr. chpts. to med. and vet. texts. Developer treatment for heartworm in dogs. Chief judge High Sch. Sci. Fairs, Prince Georges County (Md.), 1967-70; trustee B.H. Ransom Meml. Trustee Fund, 1936—, chmn. bd., 1956-73. Named Disting. Alumnus Kalamazoo Coll., 1951, 89, Johns Hopkins U., 1991, Disting. Editor of Yr. Coun. Biology Editors, 1986; recipient Alumni award Johns Hopkins U., 1991, Disting. Vet. Parasitologist, 1992; dedication symposium in his honor Am. Heartworm Soc., 1992. Fellow AAAS, Royal Soc. Tropical Medicine and Hygiene; mem. AVMA (hon. life), Ill. Mosquito Control Assn. (pres. 1960-61; hon. life), Am. Soc. Tropical Medicine, World Assn. Advancement Vet. Parasitology, Am. Soc. Parasitologists (treas. 1937-41, 44, v.p. 1955, pres. 1957; hon. life), Helminthological Soc. Washington (pres. 1936, editor 1952-66; hon. life), Am. Micros. Soc., Am. Heartworm Soc. (hon. life mem.; sec.-treas. 1974-77, asst. editor 1974-77, editor 1977-89, pres. 1977-80), Coun. Biol. Editors (Meritorious award 1986), Johns Hopkins U. Alumni Assn. (Disting. Alumnus award 1991). Home: 10506 Greenacres Dr Silver Spring MD 20903-1211

OTTO, JOHN FRANCIS, diversified financial services company executive; b. St. Louis, May 9, 1919; s. Frank Henry and Laura (DeLargy) O.; m. Carolyn Josephine Feldmann, Feb. 8, 1947; children: John Francis, Carolyn S. Carter, Diane B., Karen L. Student, U. Detroit, 1937-39. Purchasing Timken Detroit Axle Co., Detroit, 1939-40; ops. Am. Airlines Inc., Washington, 1940-43; navigator Air Transport Command, worldwide, 1943-46, Am. Overseas Airline, U.S.-Europe, 1946-48; fin. cons. Merrill Lynch Fenner Beane, N.Y.C., 1948-53; v.p. Strong Carlisle Hammond, Cleve., 1953-54, also bd. dirs.; v.p. Henney Motor Co., Freeport, Ill., 1953-54; also bd. dirs. Henney Motor Co., Freeport; v.p., fin. cons. Merrill Lynch Pierce Fenner Smith, N.Y.C., 1954-82; chmn. profit sharing com. Merrill Lynch Pierce Fenner Smith, 1962-66. Decorated 5 War Meml. medal (Republic of China). Republican. Roman Catholic. Home: Field Point Cir Greenwich CT 06830-7011

OTTO, TAMMY, writer; b. Kenmore, N.Y., Oct. 16, 1960; d. Raymond John and Bette Mae (Symthe) O. LPN, Eric Boces PN II, Cheektowaga, N.Y., 1979; BA summa cum laude, SUNY, Buffalo. Free-lance fiction and poetry writer Buffalo, 1983—; instr. Literacy Vols., Buffalo, 1992—. Author (short story) Catch Can, (play) Sleep, Carlin; collaborator film project with dir. Jay Ruof, 1992. Poetry reader spring award ceremony SUNY, 1987, 89; contbg. mem. Greenpeace, 1987; asst. Buffalo Hist. Soc., 1992—. Recipient Arthur Axelrod Meml. award, 1989, Scribbler's Club of Buffalo prize, 1989, Gregory Capasso Creative Writing award, 1990; Sarah Helen Kish Meml. Found. grantee, 1988. Mem. Golden Key (life). Home: 36 Wren Ave Lancaster NY 14086

OTUGEN, M(EHMET) VOLKAN, aerospace engineer educator; b. Istanbul, Turkey, May 1, 1956; came to U.S., 1979; s. Burhanettin and Kutluay (Tola) O. BS, Tech. U. Istanbul, 1978; MS, Drexel U., 1982, PhD, 1986. Design engr. Halic Shipyard, Istanbul, 1978-79; teaching asst. Drexel Univ., Phila., 1980-82, rsch. asst., 1982-86; rsch. analyst Ariz. State Univ., Tempe, 1986-88; rsch. fellow NASA Lewis Rsch. Ctr., Cleve., summer 1990, 91; asst. prof. aerospace engring. dept. Poly. Univ., Bklyn., 1988—; cons. David Taylor Naval Rsch. Ctr., Annapolis, Md., 1987, Underground Systems, Inc., Armonk, N.Y., 1989, NASA Lewis Rsch. Ctr., Cleve., 1991. Contbr. articles to profl. jours. Mem. AIAA, ASME (exec. com. L.I. sect. 1991), Am. Physiol. Soc., Soc. Naval Architects and Marine Engrs. Office: Poly U RR 00 Farmingdale NY 11735

OU, LO-CHANG, physiology educator; b. Shanghai, China, Oct. 16, 1930; came to U.S., 1964; m. Cynthia Ou, July 10, 1962; children: Winnie, Edward, Emily, Joseph. BS, Peking U., Beijing, 1954; PhD, Dartmouth Coll., 1971. Teaching asst., dept. biochemistry Peking U., Beijing, 1954-60, lectr., dept. biochemistry, 1960-62; demonstrator, dept. physiology Hong Kong U., 1962-64; asst. prof., dept. physiology Dartmouth Med. Sch., Hanover, N.H., 1977-80, assoc. prof., dept. physiology, 1980-85, rsch. prof., dept. physiology, 1985—. NIH rsch. grantee, 1977—. Mem. Am. Physiol. Soc. Office: Dartmouth Med Sch Dept Physiology Lebanon NH 03756

OUNJIAN, MARILYN J., employment and training company executive; b. Harrisburg, Pa., Oct. 24, 1947; d. Stanley Wolf and Rebecca (Darrow) Freeman; m. Irving Henry Schwartz, Aug. 24, 1974 (dec. May 1975); 1 child, Jennifer; m. George Edward Ounjian, July 31, 1982; children: Jonathan, Kori. Student, U. Md. Pres. Today's People, Phila., 1973-81; chmn., founder, chief exec. officer Careers USA, Phila., 1981—; pres., chief exec. officer The Career Inst., Phila., 1981—. Mem. Rep. Senatorial Inner Circle; bd. dirs. Phila. Econ. Devel. Coalition. Named Entrepreneur of Yr. Venture Mag, 1988, Woman Bus. Owner of Yr. Arthur Young and Assoc., 1989; Inc. 500 Corp. Careers USA, 1988. Mem. NAFE, Nat. Assn. Women Bus. Owners, Inst. Am. Entrepreneurs, Greater Phila. C. of C., Pa. C. of C. Office: Careers USA 1825 JF Kennedy Blvd Philadelphia PA 19103

OUSLEY, DAVID ALAN, priest; b. Stow, Mass., Apr. 3, 1951; s. Jack Marston and Nancy Ann (Lambert) O.; m. Jean Elizabeth Baker, May 1, 1982; children: Elizabeth Anne, James Michael Ephraim. BA, Yale Coll., 1973; MA, U. Chgo., 1976, PhD, 1979; postgrad., Nashotah (Wis.) House, 1976-77. Ordained deacon 1979, priest 1979. Asst. instr. Nashotah (Wis.) House Theol. Sem., 1977-78; curate Ch. of St. Mary the Virgin, N.Y.C., 1979-81; tutor The Gen. Theol. Sem., N.Y.C., 1980; curate Trinity-St. Michael's Ch., Fairfield, Conn., 1982-83; pub. Pilgrimage: A Newsletter of Christian Spirituality, Phila., 1982—; rector Ch. of St. James the Less, Phila., 1983—; trustee Frank Gavin Liturgical Found., N.Y.C., 1983—; pres. Phila. (Pa.) Cath. Clerical Union, 1984-89; warden Anglican Priest's Eucharistic League, 1987—; legislator Episcopal Synod of Am., Ft. Worth, 1990—; priest assoc. All Saints Sisters of the Poor, Confraternity of the Blessed Sacrament; priest mem. Ea. Pa. Convocation-Episcopal Synod Am. Contbr. articles to profl. jours. Mem., host Ridge-Allegheny-Hunting Park Civic Assn., Phila., 1983—; mem. 39th Police Dist. Adv. Coun., Phila., 1988-91, Nat. Trust for Hist. Preservation, Phila.; bd. mem. Laurel Hill Cemetery Friends, Phila., 1991—. Mem. Soc. of the Holy Cross (synod chaplain 1991). Office: Church St James the Less 3227 W Clearfield St Philadelphia PA 19132-1822

OUSSANI, JAMES JOHN, stapling company executive; b. Bklyn., Jan. 3, 1920; s. John Thomas and Clara (Tager) O.; m. Lorraine G. Tutundgy, Apr. 25, 1954; children: James J., Gregory P., Rita C. B.M.E., Pratt Inst., 1938-42; J.D. (hon.), Coll. Boca Raton, LLD. Dir. research, mfg. Supertronic Co., N.Y.C., 1943-46; sr. partner Perl-Oussani Machine Mfg. Co., N.Y.C., 1946-49; founder The Staplex Co., Bklyn., 1949, pres., 1949—; exec. dir. Lourdes Realty Corp.; dir. Junios Corp., Gregrita Realty Corp.; producer air sampling equipment for radioactive fallout AEC, 1951—. Mem. Bur. Research Air Pollution Control, Pres.'s Council on Youth Opportunity, Cardinal's Com. for Edn.; trustee Ch. of Virgin Mary; bd. dirs. St. Joan Arc Found., Boca Raton; founding mem. Lumen Christi-Palm Beach Diocese; founder, bd. dirs. Oussani Found.; founder James J. & Lorraine G. Oussani Scholarship Fund, Coll. Boca Raton; mem. cardinal's com. of laity, bishop's com. of laity; mem. council St. John's U.; mem. Lumen Christi Found.; chmn. bd. overseers Lynn U., Boca Raton. Recipient Blue Ribbon Mining award, Sch. Mgmt. award, Aerospace Pride Achievement award. Mem. Adminstrv. Mgmt. Soc., Office Adminstrn. Assn., Nat. Stationery and Office Equipment AssOffice Equipment Assn., Office Execs. Assn., Nat. Office Machine Mfg. Assn., Nat. Office Machine Dealers Assn., Nat. Office Products Assn., Bus. Equipment Mfrs. Assn., Our Lady Perpetual Help Holy Name Soc., Knights of Holy Sepulchre, Knights of St. Gregory, Knights of Malta, Rotary, Salaam Club, Mahopac Golf Club (Lake Mahopac, N.Y.), Internat. Club of Boca Raton, Boca Raton Hotel and Resort Club. Inventor automatic electric stapling machine. Patentee in field. Office: 777 5th Ave Brooklyn NY 11232-1695

OUYANG, LIN MIN, surgeon, educator; b. Ouzou, China, May 17, 1921; children: Lucille, Jeanette, Elizabeth, William, David, Benjamin. Student, Talmage Coll., 1933-41; MD, Fujian Med. Coll., 1947; MS, Temple U., 1957. Diplomate Am. Bd. Colon and Rectal Surgery. Intern Holy Cross Hosp., Salt Lake City, 1952-53, resident, 1953-55; resident Temple U. Med. Ctr., Phila., 1955-57; surgeon Highland Hosp., Rochester, N.Y.; pvt. practice Rochester; retired, 1990; clin. asst. prof. surgery U. Rochester Sch. Medicine. With Chinese Air Force Med. Corp, 1947-51. Mem. AMA, Am. Coll. Surgeons, Am. Colon and Rectal Surgeons, Soc. Internat. Univ. Colon & Rectal Surgery, N.Y. Med. Assn. Home: 6 Standish Way Pittsford NY 14534-2120

OVENS, RICHARD EDMUND, state agency administrator, consultant, educator; b. Middletown, N.Y., Nov. 15, 1942; s. Ritchard E. and Mary (Seeley) O.; m. Rita Lavonne Lorenzen, Feb. 23, 1964; 1 child, David E. AS, Orange County Community Coll., 1976; BA, SUNY, Albany, 1979; cert., Boston U., 1980; MS, L.I. U., 1987. Cert. counselor, N.Y. Trooper N.Y. State Police Dept., Albany, 1965-70, investigator, 1970-79, lt., 1979-86, capt., 1986-87, dir. employee assistance program, 1987—; cons. Nat. Tng. Ctr. of Polygraph Sci., N.Y.C., 1979—; instr. N.Y. State Police Acad., Albany, 1979—; adj. prof. L.I. U. Grad. Sch. Edn., Bethpage, 1989—; bd. dirs. REO Assocs./Edn. Cons., New Paltz, N.Y. Editor: (manual) Law Enforcement Employee Assistance Programs, 1989. Mem. com. Drug Free Schs. & Community Act Consortium, Orange-Ulster BOCES, Goshen, N.Y., 1989-91; coach Little League, Middletown, 1979; asst. scoutmaster First Presbyn. Ch., Middletown, 1970; pres., mem. ch. coun. St. John's Luth. Ch., Middletown, 1976. Fellow Nat. Acad. Cert. Polygraphists (disting.); mem. AACD, Am. Assn. Police Polygraphists, Am. Mental Health Counselor's Assn., N.Y. State Polygraphists Assn., Employee Assistance Profls. Assn. Home: 122 Rt # 208 New Paltz NY 12561 Office: NY State Police Dept Employee Assistance Program Executive Park North Bldg Albany NY 12203

OVER, J. ROBERT, mechanical engineer; b. Chgo., Oct. 11, 1937; s. Robert L. and Lorraine (Mofatt) O.; m. Rita Ann Duggan, June 25, 1960; children: Lance, Tom, Bob, Mike, Heidi. BSME, U. Wis., 1960; MBA, U. Wis., Oshkosh, 1976. Registered profl. engr., Wis. Mfg. mgr. Giddings & Lewis Machine Tool Co., Fond du Lac, Wis., 1962-73; design engr. Harbridge Hva/c Co., Fond du Lac, Wis., 1973-76; mfg. mgr. Moog, Inc., Buffalo, 1976-81; gen. mgr. Moog, Inc., Clearwater, Fla., 1981-88; mfg. mgr. Moog Controls, Inc., Buffalo, 1988—. Lt. U.S. Army, 1960-62. Mem. Soc. Mfg. Engrs., Am. Prodn. and Inventory Control Soc. Republican. Episcopalian. Office: Moog Controls Inc 300 Jamison Rd East Aurora NY 14052

OVERBY, DONALD WESLEY, minister; b. Portland, Oreg., Apr. 18, 1938; s. Swain Erling and Bessie Marie (Scotten) O.; m. Barbara Grace Pischel; children: Kevin Russell, Thomas Warren. BA, Ea. Nazarene Coll., 1973. Ordained elder Ch. of Nazarene, 1975. Salesperson Wanke Panel Co., Portland, Oreg., 1966-70; minister Ch. of the Nazarene, Dennisport, Mass., 1973-76, Kenneth City, Fla., 1976-78, Leesburg, Fla., 1978-88, Jacksonville, Fla., 1988-90, Trenton, N.J., 1990—; dist. sec. Ch. of the Nazarene, North Fla. 1987-90; dist. youth pres. Ch. of the Nazarene, New England 1971-74. Mem. citizens adv. bd. Leesburg (Fla.) Police Dept.1984-88; chaplain Kenneth City (Fla.) Police Dept. 1976-78; sex edn. curriculum com. Lake County (Fla.) Pub. Schs. 1980-84. Mem. North Jacksonville Rotary Club, Leesburg Rotary Club (pres. 1984-85). Republican. Home: 101 Bull Run Rd Trenton NJ 08638-1303

OVEREND, JAMES SCOTT, advertising agency executive; b. Rockville Ctr., N.Y., Nov. 22, 1958; s. William Cob and Patricia (Kosher) O. BA, St. Anselm's Coll., 1980. Account exec. Backer, Spielvogel, Bates, N.Y.C., 1980-88, v.p., account supr., 1988—. Office: Backer Spielvogel Bates 405 Lexington Ave New York NY 10174-0002

OVERLY, HELEN IRENE, company executive, motivational speaker; b. Wyano, Pa., July 17, 1931; d. Edgar Charles and Clara (Bash) O. BS, Glassboro (N.J.) U., 1970. Mgr. catalog office Montgomery Ward, Newark, Del., 1954-57; asst. pers. dir. Wilmington (Del.) Trust Co., 1957-65; dir. women's activities Penns Grove (N.J.) YMCA, 1965-66; tchr. jr. high sch. Upper Penns Neck Sch. Dist., Penns Grove, 1966-72; ptnr. Overly-Raker, McConnellsburg, Pa., 1972-81; pres., chief exec. officer Overly-Raker, Inc., McConnellsburg, 1981—; pres. Chgo. Gift Show, 1990—; bd. assocs. 1st Nat. Bank, McConnellsburg, 1988—. Bd. dirs., past pres. Fulton County Tourist Profl. Agy., McConnellsburg, 1974—, Fulton County Med. Ctr., 1978—; bd. dirs. Assn. for Retarded Citizens, Chambersburg, Pa., 1986, MANTEC, York, Pa., 1990—; bd. dirs. Fulton County Indsl. Devel. Corp. Recipient Employer of Yr. award Pa. Bus. and Profl. Women, 1984, Fulton County Jaycees, 1987, Dedicated Community Svc. award Modern Woodmen Am., 1990. Mem. Fulton County C. of C. (Person of Yr. award 1974), Franklin County Women's Network, Fulton County Med. Ctr. Aux. Republican. Baptist. Office: HC 75 Box 45 Mc Connellsburg PA 17233-9402

OVERMAN, ERIC MARIO, international trade and finance consultant; b. The Hague, The Netherlands, Apr. 21, 1969; came to U.S., 1985; s. John W.J. and Theodora (Wilders) O. BA in Econs., Internat. Polit. Studies, Pepperdine U., 1990; postgrad., Georgetown U., 1991—. Student asst. Pepperdine U., Malibu, Calif., 1988-89, resident asst., 1989-90; internat. bus. mgr. Montage (Soviet-Am. Student Jour.), Malibu, Calif., 1989-90; export mgr. Bijan Fragrances, Inc., Beverly Hills, Calif., 1991; internat. trade and fin. cons. Washington, 1991—; rsch. asst. Georgetown Sch. Fgn. Svc., Washington, 1991—; economist, fin. cons. Menatep Fin. Group, Moscow, summer 1992; mem. working group Calif. Seminar on Internat. Security and Fgn. Policy, Santa Monica, Calif., 1988-90; student amb. to Berlin, Schiller Inst., 1988. D.C. lobbyist Student Govt. Assn., Washington, 1989; vol., mem. Campus Outreach Opportunity League, N.Y.C., 1988; co-founder Pepperdine Vol. Ctr., Malibu, 1989. George C. Page Endowed scholar Pepperdine U., 1988-89, 89-90; recipient Rosemary Lokey award Pepperdine U., 1988-89. Mem. Pepperdine Alumni Assn., Alpha Chi, Phi Eta Sigma. Home and Office: 3945 Connecticut Ave NW 510 Washington DC 20008

OVERTON, DONALD ALBERT, psychologist; b. Troy, N.Y., Dec. 9, 1935; s. Ernest Clark and Evangeline (Smith) O. BSEE, Rensselaer Poly. Inst., Troy, N.Y., 1958; MA, Harvard U., 1960; PhD, McGill U., Montreal, 1962. NSF postdoctoral fellow Ctr. for Brain Rsch., U. Rochester, 1962-64; NIMH postdoctoral fellow neurophysiology Albert Einstein Coll. Medicine,

Bronx, 1964-65, NIMH postdoctoral fellow in clin. psychiatry, 1965-66; asst. prof. psychiatry Temple Med. Sch., Phila., 1966-69, assoc. prof., 1969-88, prof. psychiatry, 1977—; adj. prof. dept. psychology Temple Med. Sch., Phila., 1981-91, prof., 1991—; vis. lectr. psychology CUNY, 1964-66; lectr. psychology U. Rochester, 1962-64; instr. elec. engring. Lafayette Coll., Easton, Pa., 1958-59. Mem. adv. bd. Psychopharmacology Jour., 1968-88; contbr. numerous articles to profl. jours. Recipient Disting. Sci. Contbn. award, Soc. for Stimulus Properties of Drugs, 1986; NIDA grantee. Fellow APA, AAAS; mem. Am. Coll. Neuropsychopharmacology (mem. com. on pub. concern 1980-84), Assn. for Behavioral Sci. and Med. Edn., Behavioral Pharmacology Soc., Ea. Psychol. Assn., Neurosci. Soc., Pavlovian Soc., Psychomic Soc., Soc. of Biol. Psychiatry (membership com. 1979-81), Sigma Xi. Office: Temple U Psychology Dept 13th St & CB Moore Ave Philadelphia PA 19122

OVERTON, MICHELE MARIE, public relations director; b. Buffalo, Nov. 4, 1968; d. John Phillip and Margaret Mary (Kolb) Curtin. BS, Towson State U., 1989; postgrad., Coll. of Notre Dame Md., 1992—. Pub. rels. asst. dir. March of Dimes Birth Defects Found., Balt., 1990-91; pub. rels. dir. Nat. Kidney Found. of Md., Balt., 1991—. Mem. Pub. Rels. Soc. Am., Balt. Pub. Rels. Coun. Roman Catholic. Office: Nat Kidney Found of Md 2526 N Charles St Baltimore MD 21218

OVERWEG, NORBERT IDO ALBERT, physician; b. Enschede, The Netherlands; s. Ido and Bella Theresa (Lievenboom) O.; MD, U. Amsterdam, 1957; m. Angelique de Gorter; children: Eleonore, Elizabeth, Harold. Intern, Univ. Amsterdam Hosp., 1958-60; resident Rochester (N.Y.) Gen. Hosp., 1961-62; postdoctoral fellow dept. pharmacology Columbia U. Coll. Physicians and Surgeons, 1962-65; instr. dept. public health Columbia U., 1965-66; rsch. assoc. dept. surgery Columbia U., 1967-71; rsch. collaborator, asst. attending physician Brookhaven Nat. Lab., 1966-67; asst. prof. dept. physiology and pharmacology N.Y. U., 1971-78; cons. Lung Rsch. Ctr., Yale U. Sch. Medicine, 1972-73; pvt. practice medicine specializing in internal medicine, N.Y.C., 1967—; attending staff St. Clare's Hosp. and Health Center, Cabrini Med. Ctr., Med. Arts Center Hosp.; clin. investigator antihypertension, anti-depressant, anti-anxiety and gastro-intestinal drugs. NIH fellow, 1964-65. Mem. Am. Soc. Pharmcology and Exptl. Therapeutics, Am. Physiol. Soc., Am. Soc. Hypertension, Am. Coll. Clin. Pharmacology, N.Y. Acad. Scis., AAAS, AAUP, Royal Dutch Soc. Advancement of Medicine, Harvey Soc., Netherlands Am. Med. Soc., Eastern Hypertension Soc., N.Y. County Med. Soc., Med. Soc. of N.Y., Sigma Xi. Club: Netherlands of N.Y., Inc. Contbr. articles to profl. jour. Office: 133 E 73d St New York NY 10021

OWEN, BRIAN DENNIS, computer software executive; b. Syracuse, N.Y., July 29, 1955; s. William Dennis and Eleanor Theresa (Sullivan) O.; m. Krystyna Anna Kulczycki, May 30, 1981; children: Christo, Meggie, Molly. BS in Math., Boston Coll., 1978; MBA, U. Pa., 1982. Software cons. Computer Partners, Wellesley Hills, Mass., 1978-85; from mktg. mgr. Unix to mktg. mgr. Networks Digital Equipment Corp., Maynard, Mass., 1985-88; v.p. product div. Oracle Corp., Redwood Shores, Calif., 1988-90; v.p. and gen. mgr. Legent Corp., Westborough, Mass., 1990—. Office: Legent Corp 114 Turnpike Rd Westborough MA 01581-2800

OWEN, DAVID I., history and archeology educator; b. Boston, Oct. 28, 1940; s. Myer Isaac and Ann (Millman) O., m. Susan Kadiff, May 24, 1964; children: Joshua, Ethan. AB, Boston U., 1962; MA, Brandeis U., 1963, PhD, 1969. Rsch. assoc. U. Pa., Phila., 1970-71; asst. curator U. Pa. Mus., 1969-71; asst. ancient near eastern and archeology prof. Dropsie U., Phila., 1971-74; asst. prof. Cornell U., Ithaca, N.Y., 1974-77, assoc.prof., 1977-83, prof., 1984—; trustee Cyprus Am. Archeol. Rsch. Inst., Nicosia, 1981-84, Am. Schs. of Oriental Sch., Balt., 1989—; assoc. editor Jour. Am. Oriental Soc., Ann Arbor, Mich., 1982-84. Author: Neo-Sumerian Texts, 1991; co-author: (with others) Adoption at Old Babylonian Nippur, 1991; editor profl. pubs. Fulbright scholar Fulbright Program, 1966-68; Am. Philos. Soc. grantee, 83-84, Kyosaikai Internat. Cultural Exchange grantee, 1988; Inst. Sackler fellow Tel Aviv U., 1988-89, Sr. Fellowship NEH, 1988-89. Mem. Am. Oriental Soc. (bd. dirs. 1982-84, life), Israel Exploration Soc., Found. Assyriologique Dossin. Home: 1326 E State St Ithaca NY 14850-6206 Office: Cornell U NES Rockefeller Hall 360 Ithaca NY 14853-2502

OWEN, H. MARTYN, lawyer; b. Decatur, Ill., Oct. 23, 1929; s. Honore Martyn and Virginia (Hunt) O.; m. Candace Catlin Benjamin, June 21, 1952; children—Leslie W., Peter H., Douglas P. A.B., Princeton U., 1951; LL.B., Harvard U., 1954. Bar: Conn. 1954. Assoc. Shipman & Goodwin, Hartford, Conn., 1958-61, ptnr., 1961—. Mem. Simsbury (Conn.) Zoning Bd. Appeals, 1961-67, Simsbury Zoning Commn., 1967-79; sec. Capitol Region Planning Agy., 1965-66; bd. dirs. Symphony Soc. Greater Hartford, 1967-73; trustee Renbrook Sch., West Hartford, Conn., 1963-72, treas., 1964-68, pres., 1968-72, hon. life trustee, 1972—; trustee Simsbury Free Library, 1970-84; pres. Hartford Grammar Sch., 1987—, trustee; corporator Hartford Hosp., Inst. Living, Hartford. Lt. USNR, 1954-57. Mem. ABA, Conn. Bar Assn., Hartford County Bar Assn., Am. Law Inst. Republican. Episcopalian. Clubs: Hartford; Princeton (N.Y.C.); Ivy (Princeton, N.J.); Dauntless (Essex, Conn.). Home: 44 Pinnacle Mountain Rd Simsbury CT 06070-1809 Office: One American Row Hartford CT 06103-2819

OWEN, JOHN LAVERTY, human resources executive, consultant; b. Mayfield, Ky., May 28, 1923; s. John Clarence and Lydia (Laverty) O.; m. Marjory Clara Wallace, June 29, 1946; children: John Wallace, David William, Jeffrey Daniel. BA magna cum laude, Westminster (Mo.) Coll., 1944; postgrad., Purdue U., 1945; MS in Psychology, Pa. State U., 1951. Lic. psychologist, Pa. With Hamilton Watch Co., Lancaster, Pa., 1946-70, staff pers. svcs. dir., 1963-70; dir. corp. employee rels. HMW Industries, Inc., Lancaster, Pa., 1970-77; dir. human resources Hamilton Tech., Inc., Lancaster, Pa., v.p. human resources and public rels., 1977-80, 1980-84, sec., v.p. human resources and pub. rels., 1984-85; v.p. human resources Gen. Def. Corp., York, Pa., 1985-88; pres. Performance Systems Internat., 1984—, cons., 1984—; v.p., cons. Greenfield Assocs., Lancaster, 1988-91. Bd. dirs. Lancaster County United Way, 1972-78, 84-86, Lancaster chpt. Nat. Urban League, 1972-81, Assocs. in Downtown Lancaster, 1981-86, Lancaster YMCA, 1984-86, Lancaster Area Arts Coun., 1987-89; bd. dirs. Lancaster Guidance Clinic, 1959-63, pres., 1961-63. Mem. Am. Psychol. Assn., Pa. Psychol. Assn., Ea. Psychol. Assn., Am. Mgmt. Assn., Soc. Human Resource Mgmt. (cert. sr. profl. human resources), Am. Soc. Tng. and Devel., Lancaster Chamber Commerce and Industry, Omicron Delta Kappa, Psi Chi, Phi Kappa Phi, Delta Tau Delta. Republican. Presbyterian.

OWEN, RICHARD, federal judge; b. N.Y.C., Dec. 11, 1922; s. Carl Maynard and Shirley (Barnes) O.; m. Lynn Rasmussen, June 6, 1960; children: Carl R., David R., Richard. AB, Dartmouth Coll., 1947; LLB, Harvard U., 1950; MusD (hon.), Manhattan Sch. Music, 1989. Bar: N.Y. 1950. Practiced in N.Y.C., 1950-74; assoc. Willkie Owen Farr Gallagher & Walton, 1950-53, Willkie Farr Gallagher Walton & Fitzgibbon, 1958-60; pvt. practice, 1960-65; ptnr. Owen & Aarons, 1965-66, Owen & Turchin, 1966-74; asst. U.S. atty. So. Dist. N.Y., 1953-55; trial atty. antitrust div. U.S. Dept. Justice, 1955-58; U.S. dist. judge So. Dist. N.Y., 1974—; asst. prof. N.Y. Law Sch., 1951-53; assoc. counsel N.Y. State Moreland Com. on Alcoholic Beverage Control Laws, 1963-64. Composer, librettist operas A Moment of War, 1958, A Fisherman Called Peter, 1965, Mary Dyer, 1976, The Death of the Virgin, 1980, Abigail Adams, 1987, Tom Sawyer, 1989. Trustee Manhattan Sch. Music, N.Y.C.; founder, bd. dirs. Maine Opera Assn., 1975-85; pres., bd. dirs. N.Y. Lyric Opera Co. 1st lt. USAAF, 1942-45. Decorated D.F.C. with oak leaf cluster, Air medal with 3 oak leaf clusters. Mem. ASCAP, Century Assn., Metropolitan Opera Club, Pine Pond Yacht Club (commodore 1967-70), Chelsea Yacht Club. Republican. Mem. Soc. of Friends. Office: US Dist Ct US Courthouse Foley Sq New York NY 10007-1501

OWEN, ROBERT DEWIT, lawyer; b. St. Louis, Nov. 15, 1948; s. Kenneth Campbell Owen and Mary Elenor (Fish) Luebbers; m. Rebecca Roberts Baxter, June 4, 1977; children: Abigail Mary, James Roy, Charlotte Grace. BA, Northwestern U., 1970; JD cum laude, U. Pa., 1973. Assoc. Sullivan & Cromwell, N.Y.C., 1973-81; ptnr. Towne, Dolgin, Furlaud, Sawyier & Owen, N.Y.C., 1981-83, Owen & Fennell, N.Y.C., 1983-87, Owen & Davis, N.Y.C., 1987—; instr. Nat. Inst. Trial Advocacy, Boulder, Colo., 1988—. Bd. dirs. St. Christopher's-Jennie Clarkson Child Care Svcs., Dobbs Ferry, N.Y.,1991—. Mem. ABA, N.Y. State Bar Assn., Assn. of the Bar/City of N.Y., Nat. Assn. Securities Dealers (bd. arbitrators 1985—), Dobbs Ferry Bd. Archtl. Rev., Colonial Springs Club (pres. 1986—), India House. Episcopalian. Office: Owen & Davis 605 Third Ave New York NY 10158

OWEN, THOMAS LLEWELLYN, investment executive; b. Patchogue, N.Y., June 24, 1928; s. Griffith Robert and Jeanette Roberts (Hatfield) O.; A.B. in Econs., Coll. William and Mary, 1951; postgrad. Columbia U., 1952, N.Y. Inst. Fin., 1960-62; M.B.A., N.Y. U., 1966. Exec. trainee Shell Oil Co., N.Y.C. and Indpls., 1951-59, supr., 1958-59; petroleum and chem. investment analyst Paine, Webber, Jackson & Curtis, N.Y.C., 1959-62; sr. oil investment analyst DuPont Investment Interests, Wilmington, Del., N.Y.C., 1962-66, dir. research, 1964-66; v.p., sr. investment officer, mem. policy, investment coms. Nat. Securities and Research Corp., N.Y.C., 1966-75; sr. investment exec., v.p., portfolio mgr. F. Eberstadt & Co. and Eberstadt Asset Mgmt., Inc., N.Y.C., 1975-85, mem. policy com., 1979-85, also dir. portfolio rev. com.; sr. investment exec., portfolio mgr. Brown Brothers Harriman, N.Y.C., 1985-89; pres., CEO Owen Capital Mgmt., N.Y.C., 1989—. Mem. N.Y. Soc. Security Analysts, Assn. of Investment Mgmt. and Rsch., Oil Analysts Group N.Y., Am. Econ. Assn., Investment Assn. N.Y., Am. Petroleum Inst., Nat. Assn. Petroleum Investment Analysts, Internat. Assn. Energy Economists. Contbr. chpt. "Oil and Gas Industries" to Financial Analysts Handbook, 1975. Home and Office: 251 E 32d St New York NY 10016

OWENS, CAROLE EHRLICH, therapist; b. Mpls., Dec. 7, 1942; d. Jerome D. and Amy Ann (Scott) Schein; B.A., U. Md., 1970; M.A., Cath. U. Am., 1977; D of Social Work Yeshiva U., 1987; children: Todd Frederick, Joseph Eric. Cert. Mental Health Clinician, Mass. Youth advocate, leader Montgomery (Md.) County Recreation Dept., 1970-72, counselor, supr. preadjudication diversion program, Crisis Home Program, Family Service, 1972-74, adminstr. Karma House (residential drug treatment), 1974-75; program devel. dir. Jewish Social Service Agy., Montgomery County, 1975-77, United Jewish Appeal Fedn. of Montgomery County, 1977-79; therapist, educator, writer, cons. in field, Englewood, N.J., 1979—; instr. Cath. U. Cons. to Montgomery County Exec. candidate, 1974; appointee Gov.'s Task Force, Md., 1978; bd. dirs. Jewish Community Center, 1981—, Temple Sinai Sisterhood, Bergen County, N.J., 1981—; pres. chpt. LWV, 1983. Mem. Internat. Platform Assn., AAUW, Am. Personnel & Guidance Assn. (cert.), Am. Assn. Marriage and Family Therapy (clin.), Am. Assn. Jewish Communal Workers, Nat. Assn. Social Workers, LWV (pres. 1983-84), N.Y. Acad. Scis. Author: The Berkshire Cottages: A Vanishing Era, 1984, Clinical Vs. Psychometric Judgement of Alcohol Use, 1987, Bellefontaine, 1989; Stockbridge, 1989; author, editor: The Stockbridge Story; editor: Fund-Raising (Elton J. Kernes); reviewer Kirkus Revs.; contbr. articles in field to profl. jours. Home: PO Box 1207 Stockbridge MA 01262-1207

OWENS, CAROLINE MULFORD, newsletter editor and consultant, public relations consultant; b. Bridgeton, N.J., Apr. 19, 1932; d. Jonathan Elmer and Alice (Westbrook) Mulford; m. James Rigueur Owens, Jr., 1956; children: Cecile Rigueur, Elizabeth Westbrook, Jonathan James. BA, Cornell U., 1953. With advt. dept. DuPont Co., Wilmington, Del., 1953-57; editor and pub. Internat. Boutique Directory, Westport, Conn., 1972-84; pres. Newsletters Plus, Westport, 1983—. Contbr. to numerous publs. in field. Recipient 1991 Entrepreneur of Yr. award for So. New Eng., Matrix award Women in Comm., 1991. Mem. Internat. Assn. Bus. Communicators (exec. officer Westfair chpt. 1983-86), Nat. Fedn. of Press Women (recipient 1st prize 1991), Inst. Am. Entrepreneurs, Women in Mgmt. (dir. 1989-92), Conn. Press Club (pres. 1990-92, recipient various awards 1989-91), Greater Norwalk (Conn.) C. of C. (Sml. Bus. Advocate award 1990), Entrepreneurial Women's Network of S.W. Conn. (pres. 1986-87, v.p. 1984-86, Entrepreneurial Outreach award 1990), Fairfield County Pub. Rels. Assn. (officer 1989-91), others. Episcopalian.

OWENS, GARY MITCHELL, family physician; b. Salisbury, Md., July 31, 1949; s. Avery Donovan and Elizabeth (Mitchell) O.; B.A., U. Pa., 1971; M.D., Thomas Jefferson U., 1975; children: Aaron David, Scott Christopher, Stefanie Erin. Resident in family medicine Wilmington (Del.) Med. Center, 1975-78, chief resident, 1978, teaching assoc. dept. family medicine, 1978-91; practice medicine specializing in family practice, Wilmington, 1978-91; teaching assoc. dept. family medicine St. Francis Hosp., Wilmington, 1978-91; med. dir. Phoenix Steel Co., 1980-87; med. dir. HMO of Delaware Valley, Delaware Plan, 1985-91, Delaware Valley HMO, 1991, assoc. med. dir. Quality Assurance, 1987-91, also chmn. credentials com.; med. dir. Keystone Health Plan East, Phila., 1991—; staff, coun. mem., chmn. reappointment com. Med. Ctr. Del.; cons. NorAm. Chem. Co., 1984-91. Diplomate Am. Bd. Family Practice. Fellow Am. Acad. Family Physicians; mem. AMA, Am. Coll. Physician Execs., Med. Soc. Del. (congress of del. 1986-90), New Castle County Med. Soc., Phila. Acad. Family Physicians , Am. Occupational Med. Assn., Alpha Omega Alpha. Roman Catholic. Home: 19 Circle Dr West Grove PA 19390 Office: PO Box 7516 1901 Market St Philadelphia PA 19104-7516

OWENS, GREGORY RANDOLPH, physician, medical educator; b. Glendale, W. Va., Oct. 3, 1948; s. Elmer Herman and Anne Elizabeth (Kroggel) O.; m. Jane Marie Fleming, June 1, 1974; children: Gregory R. Jr., Allison Fleming. AB cum laude, Princeton U., 1970; MD, U. Pa., 1974. Diplomate Am. Bd. Internal Medicine, Am. Bd. Pulmonary Medicine, Am. Bd. Critical Care Medicine. Intern in internal medicine Hosp. U. Pa., Phila., 1974-75, residency in internal medicine, 1975-77, fellowship pulmonary disease, 1977-78, chief med. resident, 1978-79, fellowship pulmonary disease, 1979-80; asst. prof. medicine U. Pitts., 1980-86, assoc. prof. medicine, 1986—, assoc. chief div. pulmonary medicine, 1984—; chief Montefiore U. Hosp., Pitts, 1991—; dir. Pulmonary Exercise Physiology Lab., Presbyn.-Univ. Hosp., Pitts, 1980—, co-dir. Pulmonary Function Lab., 1980—; co-dir. Occupational Lung Clinic, Falk Clinic, Pitts., 1983—. Contbr. articles to New Eng. Jour. Medicine, Am. Jour. Medicine, Jour. Lab. Clin. Medicine and others, presenter at profl. confs. Coach Oakmont (Pa.) Athletic Assn., 1988—, bd. dirs. Am. Lung Assn. Named awardee Future Leaders of Pulmonary Medicine, Chgo., 1984, Preventive Pulmonary Acad. award NIH, 1988—; grantee, Health Rsch. and Svc. Found., 1980-82, 83-85, NIH Lung Health Study P.I., 1984-89, 1987—. Mem. ACP, Am. Coll. Chest Physicians, Am. Thoracic Soc., Am. Fedn. for Clin. Rsch., Pa. Thoracic Soc. (pres. 1991). Office: U Pitts Sch Medicine 1117 Kaufman Bldg 3471 Fifth Ave Pittsburgh PA 15213

OWENS, JOSEPH HERRON, law educator, professional association executive; b. Winnsboro, S.C., Sept. 30, 1937; s. Joseph Herron and Eva (Nicholson) O. B.A., Univ. S.C., 1960, J.D., 1963; postgrad. Georgetown U. Law Ctr., 1965. Bar: S.C. Trust atty. C&S Nat. Bank, Atlanta, 1964-65; atty. U.S. Dept. Labor, Washington, 1965-66; asst. to U.S. Senator R.C. Byrd, Washington, 1966-73; exec. dir. Council State Rehab. Adminstrs., Washington, 1973—; mem. adj. faculty U. San Francisco, 1975—. Bd. dirs. Nat. Industries for Severely Disabled, 1974-77, St. John's Sch. for Spl. Children, Washington, 1980, Met. YMCA, Washington, 1971; exec. com. Pres.'s Com. on Employment of Handicapped, Washington, 1973—. Served with USAF, 1963-64. Mem. Nat. Rehab. Assn. (President's award 1980), Council for Exceptional Children, Nat. Rehab. Adminstrn. Assn., Assn. U.S. Senate Adminstrv. Assts. and Exec. Secs.

OWENS, MAJOR ROBERT ODELL, congressman; b. Memphis, June 28, 1936; children: Christopher, Geoffrey, Millard. Grad. with high honors, Morehouse Coll., 1956; M.S., Atlanta U., 1957. Mem. Internat. Commn. on Ways of Implementing Social Policy to Ensure Maximum Pub. Participation and Social Justice for Minorities, The Hague, Netherlands, 1972; mem. 98th-102nd Congresses from 12th Dist. N.Y.C., 1983—; chmn. Select Edn. Subcom. House Edn. and Labor Com., Washington, 1987; authority in community devel.; mem. 98th-100th Congresses from 12th Dist. N.Y.; featured speaker White House Conf. on Librs., 1979. Pub. author and lectr. on library sci. Chmn. Bklyn. Congress Racial Equality; v.p. Met. Coun. on Housing, 1964; community coord. Bklyn. Pub. Library, 1964-66; exec. dir. Brownsville Community Coun., 1966-68; commr. N.Y.C. Community Devel. Agy., 1968-73; bd. dirs. community media program Columbia U., N.Y.C., 1973-75; mem. N.Y. State Senate, 1975-82, chmn. Dem. Ops. Com. Major R. Owens Day, named in his honor, City Bklyn., 1971. Office: US Ho of Reps 114 Cannon House Office Bldg Washington DC 20515*

OXMAN, MICHAEL ALLAN, health science administrator; b. Milw., Nov. 7, 1935; s. Hyman Jack and Gertrude (Podell) O.; m. Barbara Jean Cohen, June 29, 1958; children: Mark Joel, Steven Bruce, Linda Beth. BS in Pharmacy, U. Wis., 1958, MS in Pharm. Chemistry, 1960; postgrad., U. Kans., 1960-63; PhD of Medicinal Chemistry, U. Wis., 1963. Registered pharmacist. Rsch. chemist Nat. Arthritis Inst. NIH, Bethesda, Md., 1963-65; rsch. chemist Sterling-Winthrop Rsch. Inst., Rensselaer, N.Y., 1965-68; health scientist adminstr. div. rsch. resources NIH, Bethesda, 1968-74; health scientist adminstr. Nat. Libr. Medicine, Bethesda, 1974-76; health scientist adminstr. Nat. Heart, Lung & Blood Inst. NIH, Bethesda, 1976-78, health scientist adminstr. div. rsch. resources, 1978-90, health scientist adminstr. Nat. Inst. on Aging, 1990—. Contbr. articles to profl. jours. Capt. USPHS, 1963—. Mem. Am. Chem. Soc. Office: NIH 7201 Wisconsin Ave Ste 2C212 Bethesda MD 20892-0001

OZAG, DAVID, savings and loan executive; b. Connellsville, Pa., Apr. 16, 1962; s. Joseph and Barbara Lee (Brady) O. BS, U. Md., 1984, postgrad., 1985; MBA, Mt. St. Mary's Coll., Md., 1987. CPA. Acct. Aronson Greene Fisher and Co., Bethesda, Md., 1984-86, Keller, Zanger and Co., Frederick, 1986-87; controller Grove Hill Enterprises Inc., Frederick, Md., 1985-88; v.p. Standard Fed. Savs. Bank, Gaithersburg, Md., 1988—; owner JD Liquors, Frederick, Md., 1991—; basketball coach Gov. Thomas Johnson High Sch., Frederick, 1987—; instr. Frederick Community Coll., 1988—, Carroll Community Coll., 1990—. Mem. AICPA, Md. Assn. CPA, U. Md. Alumni Assn. Republican. Roman Catholic. Home: 402 Birmingham Dr Frederick MD 21701-6361 Office: Standard Fed Savs Bank 5280 Corporate Dr Frederick MD 21701-8385

OZAWA, SEIJI, conductor, musical director; b. Shenyang, People's Republic of China, Sept. 1, 1935; s. Kaisaku and Sakura Ozawa; m. Vera Motoki-Ilyin; children: Seira, Yukiyoshi. Student, Toho Sch. Music, Tokyo, Japan, 1953-59; studies with, Hideo Saito, Eugene Bigot, Herbert Von Karajan, Leonard Bernstein; student at the invitation of Charles Munch, Tanglewood, 1959. Music dir. Boston Symphony Orch., 1973—. One of three asst. condrs., N.Y. Philharm., 1961-62 season, music dir. Ravinia Festival, 1964-68, music dir. Toronto Symphony Orch., 1965-69, San Francisco Symphony Orch., 1970-76, appointed artistic advisor Tanglewood Festival, 1970, condr. Boston Symphony Orch. Evening at Symphony (Emmy award); music advisor Boston Symphony Orch., 1972-73; guest condr. major orchs. Recipient 1st prize Internat. Competion Orch. Condrs., 1959, Koussevitzky prize Tanglewood Music Ctr., 1960; conducting fellow Tanglewood Music Ctr., summer 1959. Home: via Giardini 941, Saliceta, 41040 Modena Italy Office: Boston Symphony Orch Symphony Hall 301 Massachusetts Ave Boston MA 02115-4511*

OZELLI, TUNCH, economics educator, consultant; b. Ankara, Turkey, May 18, 1938; came to U.S., 1962; s. Sufyan and Saziye (Ozmorali) O.; m. Lale A. Baymur, Dec. 30, 1960 (div. Mar. 1972); children: Selva, Kerem; m. Nancy Ann Goldschlager, Feb. 3, 1974 (div. Dec. 1987); m. Meral Ozdemir, May 9, 1992. MBA, Fla. State U., 1963; PhD, Columbia U., 1968. Rsch. fellow Harvard U., Cambridge, Mass., 1969-70; econ. advisor Office Prime Minister, Ankara, 1970-72; assoc. prof. mgmt. N.Y. Inst. Tech., N.Y.C., 1972—; spl. advisor State Planning Orgn., Ankara, 1989—. Contbr. articles to profl. jour. Ford Found. scholar, 1963-64, Found. for Econ. Edn. fellow, 1986. Mem. Am. Econ. Assn., Middle East Studies Assn., Turkish Mgmt. Assn., Delta Mu Delta. Office: NY Inst Tech Old Westbury NY 11568

OZER, HARVEY LEON, biomedical researcher; b. Boston, July 6, 1938; s. Samuel Louis and Naomi (Smith) O.; m. Joy Hochstadt, Feb. 3, 1960; 1 child, Juliane Hochstadt-Ozer. AB, Harvard U., 1960; MD, Stanford U., 1965. Intern Childrens Hosp., Boston, 1965-66; sr. staff fellow NCI/NIH, Bethesda, Md., 1969-72; sr. scientist Worcester Found. Exptl. Biology, Shrewsbury, Mass., 1972-77; prof. Hunter Coll., CUNY, 1977-88; prof. grad. ctr. CUNY, 1977—; prof., chmn. N.J. Med. Sch., Newark, 1988—; prof. Grad. Sch. Biomed. Scis., N.J. Med. Sch., Newark, 1988—; mem. adv. panels NIH, 1972—, virology study sect., 1978-82; mem. adv. com. Wistar Inst., U. Pa., Phila., 1983-90; mem. basic sci. adv. panel, N.J. Commn. on Cancer Rsch., Trenton, 1989-92. Mem. editorial bd. Molecular Cell Biology, 1980—; co-author: Experiments with Normal and Transformed Cells, 1979; contbr. articles to profl. jours. With USPHS, 1966-68. Rsch. grantee, NIH, Nat. Cancer Inst., Nat. Inst. Aging, 1973—; Damon Runyon Cancer Fund fellow, Karolinska Inst., 1964; Am. Cancer Soc. scholar, 1983-84. Mem. AAAS, Am. Assn. Med. Sch. Microbiology, Am. Soc. Genetics, Am. Soc. Microbiology, Am. Soc. Virology, Tissue Culture Soc., Harvey Soc., N.Y. Acad. Sci., Am. Soc. for Biochemistry and Molecular Biology, Am. Chem. Soc., Sigma Xi. Office: NJ Med Sch 185 S Orange Ave Newark NJ 07103-2714

OZER, JEROME STANLEY, publisher; b. N.Y.C., July 18, 1927; s. Isidore Meyer and Lena (Brusensky) O.; m. Harriet Leibow, Oct. 31, 1953; children: Joseph David, Ira Matthew. BSS, CCNY, 1948; MA, Cornell U., 1949, PhD, 1952. Sr. editor Collier Books, N.Y.C., 1961-62; v.p., editorial dir. Pitman Pub. Corp., N.Y.C., 1962-68; exec. v.p. Arno Press/The N.Y. Times, N.Y.C., 1968-71; pres. Jerome S. Ozer, Pub., Inc., Englewood, N.J., 1971—; adj. prof. social sci. Pace U., N.Y.C., 1956-72; mem. faculty Bergen Community Coll. Author: American Mosaic: Immigrants in American Life, 1975; (with others) Coming to America: Immigrants from the British Isles, 1980; editor: (books) Film Review Annual, 1981—, Opera Annual, 1984—. Mem. Englewood Bd. Edn., 1974-77, pres., 1975-76; trustee Englewood Pub. Libr., 1977—, pres., 1992—. With AUS, 1945-46. Mem. Am. Hist. Assn., Orgn. Am. Historians, Immigration History Soc. Jewish.

OZERO, BRIAN JOHN, chemical engineer; b. Winnipeg, Manitoba, Can., Dec. 14, 1932; came to U.S., 1963; s. Daniel and Mary (Karpiuk) O.; m. Ila Atlas, Dec. 14, 1985. BS in Chem. Engring., Queens U., Kingston, Ontario, Can., 1954; MS in Chem. Engring., NYU, 1968. Technologist Shell Oil Co., Montreal, Quebec, Can., 1954-60; design engr. Chem. Constrn. Co., London, 1960-63; sr. process engr. Sci. Design Co., N.Y.C., 1963-65, process mgr., 1965-75; tech. dir. Halcon SD Group Inc., N.Y.C., 1976-85; sr. process mgr. Tech. Evaluation and Devel. Assocs., Hoboken, N.J., 1986; pres. Scientech Assocs. Inc., N.Y.C., 1986—. Recognized expert in ethylene oxide/ethylene glycol; contbr. articles and chpts. to tech. jours. and encyclopedias in field; patentee in field. Pres. Barrier Beach Preservation Assn., Westhampton, N.Y., 1985-88. Mem. Am. Inst. Chem. Engrs., Rotary. Republican. Roman Catholic. Home: PO Box 1524 Westhampton Beach NY 11978-7524 Office: Scientech Assocs Inc 225 E 36th St Ste 19A New York NY 10016-3628

OZORAK, ELIZABETH WEISS, psychology educator; b. Tacoma Park, Md., June 12, 1957; d. Alfred David and Anne (Kelly) Weiss; m. Etienne Weiss Ozorak, June 14, 1986; 1 child, Nicholas. BA, Wesleyan U., 1978; MA, Harvard U., 1983, PhD, 1987. Asst. prof. dept. psychology Earlham Coll., Richmond, Ind., 1985-89, Allegheny Coll., Meadville, Pa., 1989—. Contbr. articles to profl. jours. Vol. Habitat for Humanity, Meadville, 1990. Thomas Watson Found. fellow, 1978-79; named one of Outstanding Young Women Am., 1988. Mem. Am. Psychol. Assn., Canadian Psychol. Assn., Soc. for Scientific Study Religion. Office: Allegheny Coll Dept Psychology Meadville PA 16335

PACE, RONALD ANTHONY, materials technology company executive; b. New Haven, July 7, 1947; s. Michael N. and Rose (Brillante) P.; m. Teresa A. Giannino, Aug. 12, 1972; children: Robert, Sara, Caroline. BS, U. Conn., 1969, MBA, 1972. Controller plastics B.P. Am., Niagara Falls, N.Y., 1978-79; gen. mgr. chem. equip. B.P. Am., Avondale, Pa., 1979-82; v.p. worldwide mktg. Pfaudler B.P. Am., Rochester, N.Y., 1982-85, v.p. ops. Pfaudler U.S., 1986, v.p., gen. mgr. Pfaudler U.S., 1986-88; gen. mgr. coatings Dainippon Ink & Chems., Pensacola, Fla., 1988-89; dir. planning Johnson Matthey PLC, West Chester, Pa., 1989-90; gen. mgr. Alfa/Aesar Johnson Matthey PLC, Danvers, Mass., 1990—; dir. planning and new bus. devel. Johnson Matthey PLC, West Chester, 1990—; cons. in field. Com. chmn. Athletic Boosters, Pensacola, 1987. Mem. C. of C., Planning Execs. Assn. Office: Johnson Matthey 1401 King Rd West Chester PA 19380-1497

PACHNER, WILLIAM, artist; b. Moravia, Czechoslovakia, Apr. 7, 1915; m. Lorraine Koolman, Oct. 11, 1940; children: Ann, Charles Edward. Student, Acad. of Arts and Crafts, Vienna, 1931-33; DFA (hon.), U. Tampa, 1981. Exhibitions include 50 Year Retrospective: William Pachner Affirmations, 1936-86, Tampa (Fla.) Mus., 1987, Mus. of Fine Arts, St. Petersburg, Fla., 1983; represented in permanent collections Whitney Mus., Rose Gallery of Brandeis Univ., Butler Inst., Ohio, Fort Worth (Tex.) Mus., Iowa State Coll., Hirshorn Mus., Washington, Walter P. Chrysler and others. Recipient Ford Found. awards, 1959, 64; named Guggenheim fellow, 1960. Home: 201 Ohayo Mountain Rd Woodstock NY 12498-2518

PACIE, RON, theatrical producer, director; b. Dearborn, Mich., Apr. 26, 1952; m. Joni Nicole Emanuele, June 13, 1980. Student, U. Mich., Carl Jung U., Zurich, Switzerland. Producer, dir. Murder Mystery, Inc., Huntington, N.Y., 1988—; drama coach, stunt coord., action-scene choreographer, N.Y.C., 1988—; dir. murder mysteries for Queen Elizabeth II and Delta Steamboat Co. cruises, 1990, 91, prodr. 4 shows, 1992; corp. event planner. Dir. dinner theater murder mysteries, 1988-89; producer, dir. off-Broadway play Murder at Midnight, 1990—, in U.S. and Italy; prodr. off-Broadway play Family Reunion, 1992—. Fundraiser United Cerebral Palsy, N.Y.C. Recipient cert. for outstanding achievement in fund raising and support United Cerebral Palsy. Mem. Suffolk County Supporting Arts, Creative Playhouse. Home: 18 Hollywood Pl Huntington NY 11743-4201 Office: Murder Mystery Inc PO Box 1531 Huntington NY 11743-0659

PACK, ROY SANGHUN, financial analyst; b. Corvallis, Oreg., Oct. 22, 1964; s. Moo Young and Haesun (Shin) P. BS, Boston U., 1986; MBA, Pa. State U., 1990. Registered rep. First Investors Corp., Boston, 1986-87; customer svc. rep. Cambridge (Mass.) Trust Co., 1987-88; fin. analyst Air Products and Chems., Inc., Allentown, Pa., 1990—. Mem. Korean Ch. of Lehigh Valley, Whitehall, Pa., 1990—. Home: 980 Barnside Ct Allentown PA 18103 Office: Air Products and Chems Inc 7201 Hamilton Blvd Allentown PA 18195

PADDACK, STEPHEN JOSEPH, aerospace engineering executive; b. Cin., Dec. 26, 1934; s. George Murray and Concha (Gandia) P. B in Aero. Engring., Cath. U. Amer., 1959, M. Aerospace Engring., 1964, PhD, 1973; postgrad., U. Wash., 1959-61, Seattle U., 1960, UCLA, 1962, Cath. U. Am., 1962-73, Georgetown U., 1965. Aero. engr. Boeing Co., Wash., 1959-61; aerospace engr. Goddard Space Flight Ctr. Theoretical Div. NASA, Greenbelt, Md., 1961-67, aerospace engr. spaceflight projects Goddard Space Flight Ctr., 1967-81, chief advanced missions analysis office Goddard Space Flight Ctr., 1981—; vis. prof. U.S. Naval Acad., Annapolis, Md., 1986. Contbr. articles to Jour. Geophysical Rsch., Jour. Geophysical Rsch. Letters, and others. With USCG, 1953-55. Recipient Nat. Def. Edn. Act fellowship, 1966; recipient Disting. Svc. award Cath. U. Am., 1990. Mem. AIAA (mem. space systems tech. com. 1984-87), Am. Geophysical Union. Office: NASA Goddard Space Flight Ctr Greenbelt MD 20771

PADEN, ROBERTA L., corporate administrator; b. Colby, Kans., Feb. 15, 1938; d. Homer Ernest and Harriet (McCafferty) P.; m. Gregory Grosbard, Aug. 20, 1963 (div. Feb. 1984); children: Guy Grosbard, Gayle Grosbard; m. Nigel Casserly, June 7, 1987 (dec. Sept. 1989). BA, Wichita State U., 1966; postgrad., U. Tex., El Paso, 1966-69. English lang. educator Santillana Pub. Co., N.Y.C., 1976-79; project editor Curriculum Concepts, N.Y.C., 1979-80; project control adminstr. Drexel Burnham Lambert, N.Y.C., 1980-90; prin. Legin Am. Corp., N.Y.C., 1990—; project mgmt. cons. DDH&R Consulting, N.Y.C., 1990-91. English lang. editor various text-books, 1977-79; translator: (tchrs. guide) Otras Culturas Series, 1979, (polit. study) Power & Dictatorship, 1981. Democrat. Home & Office: 333 W 86th St Ste 910 New York NY 10024-3112

PADIKAL, THOMAS N., physicist; b. July 9, 1947. BSc, Kerala U., 1967, MSc in Electronics, 1969; MS in Physics, Cleve. State U., 1971; MS in Physcics, U. Cin., 1973, PhD in Physics, 1975. Cert. Am. Bd. of Radiology. Grad. asst. U. Cin., 1971-73, fellow radiol. physics, 1973-75; asst. prof. George Washington U. Hosp., Washington, 1975-77; sr. scientist Nat. Cancer Inst., Washington, 1977-90; dir. med. physics Divine Providence Hosp., Williamsport, Pa., 1981-90, Applied Physics Svcs., Williamsport, 1985—. Author: (with others) Radiation Therapy Planning, 1983, Physics Vade Me Cum, 1983; editor: Medical Physics Data Book, 1982, A Physicist's Desk Reference, 1989. Bd. dirs. N.Am. Communications PA Co. Fellow Atomic Energy Commn., 1967-69. Mem. Am. Assn. Physicists in Medicine (radiation therapy com. sci. coun. 1979-83, tng. radiologist com. ednl. coun. 1979-83, mem. profl. info. and clin. rels. com. 1986-88), Am. Coll. Med. Physics, Am. Coll. Radiology, Am. Phys. Soc., Am. Soc. Therapeutic Radiology and Oncology, Am. Coll. Cardiology. Office: 1791 Ravine Rd Williamsport PA 17701-1752

PADILLA, JAMES EARL, lawyer; b. Miami, Fla., Dec. 28, 1953; s. Earl George and Patricia (Bauer) P. BA, Northwestern U., 1975; JD, Duke U., 1978. Bar: Ill. 1978, U.S. Ct. Appeals (5th and 7th cir.) 1978, U.S. Supreme Ct. 1981, Colo. 1982, U.S. Ct. Appeals (10th cir.) 1982, D.C. 1985, N.Y. 1989. Assoc. Mayer, Brown & Platt, Chgo. and Denver, 1978-84; ptnr. Mayer, Brown & Platt, Denver, 1985-87, N.Y.C., 1988—. Contbg. author: Mineral Financing, 1982, Illinois Continuing Legal Education, 1992. Mem. ABA, Ill. Bar Assn., D.C. Bar Assn., Colo. Bar Assn., N.Y. Bar Assn., Denver Bar Assn., Denver Club. Office: Mayer Brown & Platt 787 7th Ave New York NY 10019-6018

PADILLA, MARIO ALFONSO, telecommunications executive; b. Hamburg, Germany, Aug. 1, 1936; came to U.S., 1956; s. Ramiro and Ursula (Wenneker) P.; m. Arlene Wood, June 19, 1962; children: Christopher, Leslie. BS in Engring., U. Mo., Rolla, 1960; student, U. Ariz., 1960; MS in Indsl. Mgmt., U. Mo., 1962. Factory engr. in semiconductors AT&T, Kansas City, Mo., 1962-71; mgr. patent licensing AT&T, N.Y.C., 1971-75; product mgr. AT&T, Morristown, N.J., 1975-80; product mgmt. dir. AT&T, Morristown, 1980-87, mktg. v.p., 1987-88, product mgmt. v.p., 1988-90, switching systems v.p., 1990—. Home: 39 Brier Ct New Providence NJ 07974-1201

PADNOS, NORMAN, chemist; b. Bklyn., Oct. 23, 1937; s. Herman and Rose (Namowitz) P.; m. Barbara Noble, Feb. 17, 1963 (div. June 1970); children: Rebecca Mae, Celia Rochelle, Elisa Ruth, Stephen Nathaniel; m. Evelyn Angela Patsakos, July 8, 1972; 1 child, Stella Joan. BS, Bklyn. Coll., 1957; PhD, U. Rochester, 1963. Registered profl. engr., N.Y. Asst. prof. N.C. Cen. U., Durham, 1963-68; chemist N.Y.C. Dept. Air Resources, 1968-73; adminstrv. staff analyst N.Y.C. Dept. Environ. Protection, 1973—; adj. prof. Cooper Union 1976, 86, 90. Mem. Am. Chem. Soc., Internat. Solar Energy Soc., N.Y. Acad. Scis., Sigma Xi. Jewish. Home: 2931 Brighton First St Brooklyn NY 11235-8006 Office: NYC Dept Environ Protection 59-17 Junction Blvd Elmhurst NY 11373-5107

PADOVANO, ROSE MARIE, education and religion educator; b. Harrison, N.J., Feb. 5, 1937; d. Thomas Henry and Mary Rose (Cierzo) P. BS, Coll. St. Elizabeth, 1961; MEd, Boston Coll., 1972; EdS, Rutgers U., 1982; DMin, Drew U., 1984. Joined Sisters of Charity, Roman Cath. Ch. Tchr. elem. schs., Bergen/Hudson Counties, N.J., 1956-68; dir. religious edn. Clark, N.J., 1968-71; coord. Outreach Program for Elderly, Parsippany, N.J., 1978; asst. dir. Edn. Improvement Ctr., Morris Plains, N.J., 1978-82; dir. religious edn. St. Anne Parish, Fair Lawn, N.J., 1971-78; cons. Silver Bundett and Ginn, Morristown, N.J., 1987—; assoc. prof. coll. St. Elizabeth, Convent Station, N.J., 1982—; cons. Silver Bundett and Ginn Co.; mem. steering com. Fedn. Sisters of Charity. Author: The Influence of Eliz. Seton Reflected in Dimensions of Her Charism and Educational Ministry, 1984, Growth in Faith, 1982. Mem. Am. Assn. Coll. Tchrs. Edn., N.J. Assn. Tchr. Edn. (bd. dirs. 1988—), Assn. Supervision and Curriculum Devel., Soc. Edn. and Scholars, Teaching Thinking, Sigma Phi Omega. Home: 23 Glendale Rd Flanders NJ 07836-9407 Office: Coll St Elizabeth Convent Station NJ 07961

PAFFRATH, STEPHEN GERARD, financial executive; b. Butler, Pa., Mar. 19, 1953; s. Edward Joseph and Helen Sybil (Graham) P. BS in Bus., Indiana U. Pa., 1975. Purchasing-inventory control agt. Harsco Corp., Butler, 1976-77; mem. compliance monitor staff Tri-County Pvt. Industry Coun., Butler, 1977-79, dir. monitoring unit, 1979-83, asst. dir., chief fin. officer, 1983—. Mem. Pa. Svc. Delivery Area Assn. Home: 810 Herman Rd Butler PA 16001-9244 Office: Tri-County Pvt Industry Coun 121 Sunnyview Cir Butler PA 16001-3550

PAGANO, GEORGE ANTHONY, lawyer; b. Phila., Jan. 22, 1952; s. George Albert and Dorothy Corley (Harman) P.; m. Mary Emily Benn, July 9, 1988. BS in Econs., U. Pa., 1973; JD, U. Mich., 1975; LLM in Taxation, Temple U., 1983. Bar: Pa. 1976, N.J. 1984. Assoc. Butler, Beatty, Greer & Johnson, Media, Pa., 1976-81; pvt. practice Media, 1981-85; ptnr. Arney, Pagano & Friedman, Media, 1985-89, Clouse, Arney, Pagano & Friedman, Media, 1989-91, Pagano, Wills & Friedman, Media, 1992—; bd. dirs. Delaware County Legal Assistance, Media, 1985—. Twp. commr., Springfield (Pa.) Twp., 1984-91, v.p. twp. commn., 1989-90, pres., 1991; solicitor Colwyn Boro, 1991—, Springfield Twp., 1992—; bd. dirs. Family Support Line of Delaware County, 1989—; bd. dirs. Delco Blind/Sight Ctr., 1990—. Mem. Delaware County County Bar Assn. (bd. dirs. 1992—). Republican. Roman Catholic. Home: 39 Old State Rd Springfield PA 19064-1738 Office: Pagano Wills & Friedman 321 W Front St Media PA 19063-2397

PAGANO, JO ANNE, education educator; b. Rochester, N.Y., Dec. 30, 1946; d. John Richard and Marlyn Margaret (Mull) P.; m. William Arnold Gietz, Sept. 30, 1977 (div. May 1983); m. Bruce Peter Berlind, Jan. 17, 1985. BA, U. Rochester, 1973, MS, 1980, PhD, 1982. Assoc. prof. edn. Colgate U., Hamilton, N.Y., 1981—. Co-author: Preparing Teachers as Professionals, 1989; author: Exiles and Communities, 1990; mem. editorial rev. bd. Ednl. Theory, 1988—; editor-in-chief JCT: Interdisciplinary Jour. Curriculum Studies, 1990—; contbr. articles to ednl. jours., chpts. to books. Grantee Ford Found., 1986. Mem. Am. Ednl. Rsch. Assn., Philosophy of Edn. Soc., Am. Ednl. Studies Assn., Nat. Women's Studies Assn. Home: PO Box 237 Hamilton NY 13346-0237 Office: Colgate U Edn Dept 13 Oak Dr Hamilton NY 13346-1338

PAGE, ARTHUR HALLETT, IV, conservator; b. Washington, Feb. 12, 1955; s. Arthur Hallett III and Katherine Ludlow (Kayser) P.; m. Deborah Maria Stephens, Oct. 9, 1982; children: Arthur Hallett V, Katherine Wallace Stephens Page. BA in Art History, U. N.C., 1977; MA in Fine Art Conservation, Cooperstown, 1982. Project dir. Nat. Park Svc., Richmond, Va., 1981 summer; intern Walters Art Gallery, Balt., 1981-82; project mgr. Libr. of Congress Mural Restoration, Washington, 1989-90; chief conservator Page Conservation, Inc., Washington, 1983—; dir. Restoration of Pa. Capitol Murals by Violette Oakley, Harrisburg, 1991—. Mem. Am. Inst. for Conservation (profl. assoc.), Internat. Inst. of Conservation (assoc.), Washington Conservation Guild (pres. 1991-93, bd. dirs. 1986-88). Democrat. Episcopalian. Home: 2921 34th St NW Washington DC 20008-3510 Office: Page Conservation Inc 1300 7th St NW Washington DC 20001-3504

PAGE, B(ENJAMIN) B(AKEWELL), philosophy educator; b. Pitts., June 16, 1939; s. Benjamin and Elizabeth Breese (Curtin) P.; m. Bedriska Schonweitzova, Sept. 7, 1965; children: Vitezslav, Mirko, Nikos, Natasha. BA cum laude, Harvard U., 1962; postgrad., Charles U., Prague, Czechoslovakia, 1965-67; MS, Fla. State U., 1972, PhD, 1970. Tchr. English, Coll. St. Pierre, Port-au-Prince, Haiti, 1960-61; community organizer Mass PAX, Mass. Freedom Movement, Boston, 1962-64; apprentice cabinetmaker J.H. Jones, N.Y.C., 1964; asst. prof. Meharry Med. Coll., Nashville, 1971-72; asst. prof. to prof. Quinnipiac Coll., Hamden, Conn., 1972—. Author: The Czechoslovak Reform Movement, 1963-68; editor: Marxism and Spirituality: An International Anthology; also articles. Ted Ribie scholar Choate Sch., 1954-57; rsch. fellow Internat. Rsch. and Exch. Bd., Czechoslovakia, 1975-76. Mem. Am. Philosophy Assn., World Future Soc., World Fedn. of Future Studies, Czechoslovakia History Conf., Phi Kappa Phi. Office: Quinnipiac College PO Box 163 New Haven CT 06513-0240

PAGE, CHRISTOPHER KENNETH, commercial photographer; b. Phila., Sept. 22, 1966; s. G. Thomas and Susan A. (Anderson) P.; m. Amy Patricia Kaiser, July 7, 1990. Student, E. Stroudsburg (Pa.) U., Grove City (Pa.) Coll., Ithaca Coll. Owner/photographer/visual imagineer Innovative Photography, Suffield, Conn., 1989—. Photographs include: Smith Cove, 1990, Bread and Butter, 1991, litograph, The Swell, 1991. Mem. Profl. Photographers of Am., Sierra Club. Republican.

PAGE, JAMES BENJAMIN, communications executive; b. Fernandina Beach, Fla., Jan. 14, 1952; s. James. P. and Wilma (Melton) P.; m. Patricia June Pierce, Feb. 25, 1975; children: Colleen Elizabeth, Aaron Peyton. Student, Fla. Atlantic U., 1970-71. Dept. mgr., merchandiser various supermarkets, Naples and Tampa, Fla., 1969-82; various editing positions various mags., Tampa, 1980-83; pres. James Page & Assocs. Pub. Rels., Tampa, 1982-84; mgr. spl. projects Martel Labs. Inc., St. Petersburg, Fla., 1984-87; dir. graphic arts Greenhorne & O'Mara Inc, Greenbelt, Md., 1987-91; mgr. graphics div. Visual Communication Svcs. Inc., Temple Hills, Md., 1991—. Patentee Computer Color Separation Process, 1990; contbr. articles to mags. and newspapers. Mem. Washington Apple Pl Users Group. Democrat. Episcopalian. Home: 13108 Oriole Dr Beltsville MD 20705 Office: Visual Communication Svcs 4574 Beech Rd Temple Hills MD 20748

PAGÉ, PIERRE, professional hockey executive; m. Donna Pagá; 1 child, Lauren. Former phys. edn. tchr. Dalhousie U., Can.; asst. to coach Calgary Flames, 1980-82, gen. mgr. and coach various minor league teams, 1982-85, asst. coach, 1985-88; head coach Minn. Northstars, 1989-90; gen. mgr. Que. Nordiques, 1990-92, head coach, 1992—. Office: Quebec Nordiques, 2205 Ave du Colisee, Quebec, PQ Canada G1L 4W7

PAGLIARO, HAROLD EMIL, English language educator; b. N.Y.C., June 19, 1925; s. Harry E. and Linda (Ricci) P.; m. Judith Marie Egan, Sept. 16, 1966; children: Blake, Robert, Susanna, John. AB, Columbia U., 1947, MA, 1948, PhD, 1961. Instr. English, Columbia U., N.Y.C., 1956-60; asst. prof. Columbia U., 1961-63, faculty fellow, 1962, dir. honors sch. gen. studies, 1962-64; asst. prof. Swarthmore (Pa.) Coll., 1964-65, assoc. prof., 1966-69, prof., 1970—, Alexander Griswold Cummins prof. English lit., 1982—, chmn. dept. English lit., 1970-74, 86-91, provost, 1974-79; mem. sr. common room St. Edmund Hall, Oxford (Eng.) U., 1973-74, 79-80; assoc. Columbia U. Seminar 18th Century European Culture, 1982—. Author: Selfhood and Redemption in Blakes's "Songs", 1987; editor: Fielding's Journal of a Voyage to Lisbon, 1963, Major English Writers of the Eighteenth Century, 1969, Studies In Eighteenth Century Culture, Vol. 2, 1972, Vol. 3, 1973, Vol. 4, 1974; contbr. articles to profl. jours. Mem. coll. evaluation bd. Middle States Assn., 1966—. Served with AUS, 1943-45. Decorated Purple Heart; NEH sr. fellow, 1983-84; George Becker fellow, 1988-89. Mem. MLA, Am. Soc. for Eighteenth-Century Studies (editor Proc. 1971-75), Am. Soc. Eighteenth-Century Studies (mem. publs. com. 1974-76). Home: 536 Ogden Ave Swarthmore PA 19081-1129

PAI, SHIH I., aeronautical engineer, educator; b. Tatung, Anhwei, China, Sept. 30, 1913; s. Hsi Chuan and Swe Lin (Cha) P.; B.S. in Elec. Engring., Nat. Central U. China, 1935; M.S., MIT, 1938; Ph.D., Calif. Inst. Tech., 1940; Dr. Tech. h.c., Tech. U. Vienna, 1968; m. Alice Jen-Lan Wang, July 2, 1960; children—Stephen Ming, Sue Yang, Robert Yang, Lou Lung. Prof. aerodynamics Nat. Central U., China, 1940-47; vis. prof. Cornell U., 1947-49; research prof. Inst. Phys. Sci. and Tech., U. Md., College Park, 1949-83, prof. emeritus, 1983—; vis. prof. Tokyo U., 1966, Tech. U. Vienna, 1967, Tech. U. Denmark, 1974, U. Karlsruhe (Germany), 1980-81, U. Paris, 1981; hon. prof. Northwestern Poly. U., Peoples Republic China, 1980—, Zhejiang U., Peoples Republic China, 1985—; cons. Gen. Electric Co., N. Am. Aviation, Boeing Co., Martin Co. Served with Chinese Air Force, 1937-40. Guggenheim fellow, 1957-58; recipient Alexander von Humboldt award, 1980. Fellow Academia Sinica; mem. AIAA, Am. Phys. Soc., German Soc. Applied Math. and Mechanics, Internat. Acad. Astronautics (corr.). Author: 13 tech. books in fluid dynamics, latest being Two-Phase Flows, 1977; Modern Fluid Mechanics, 1981, (with Shijin Lu) The Theroetical and Computational Dynamics of a Compressible Flow, 1991; contbr. numerous articles to profl. jours.; first to experimentally show the importance of coherent structure in turbulent flow, the authority of jet flow from low speed aerodynamics to hyperionic flow; contbr. modern fluid mechanics including magnetic fluid dynamics, radiation gas dynamics and two phase flows. Home: 4301 Sarasota Pl Beltsville MD 20705-2755 Office: U Md Inst Phys Sci Tech College Park MD 20742

PAICOPOLOS, ERNEST MICHAEL, public opinion research company executive; b. Boston, July 11, 1951; s. Michael Frank and Irene Anne (Bosia) P.; m. Gail Miriam Bloom, Feb. 15, 1976. BS, Northeastern U., 1974, postgrad., 1974-75; postgrad., U. Mass., 1976-77. Field researcher Nat. Opinion Rsch. Ctr., Chgo., 1976-77; rsch. asst. Mass. Dept. Mental Health, Boston, 1977-78; v.p. Cambridge (Mass.) Reports, Inc., 1978-88; prin. Opinion Dynamics Corp., Cambridge, 1988—; pres. Am. Insight, 1989—. Author, editor Dextra, polit. newsletter, 1971. Researcher Carter-Mondale Reelection Com., Dem. Nat. Conv., 1980; mem. fin. com. Paleologos for Lt. Gov., Boston, 1990. Mem. Am. Assn. for Pub. Opinion Rsch., Am. Assn. Polit. Cons. Home: 38 High St Stoneham MA 02180-1170 Office: Opinion Dynamics Corp 1 Kendall Sq Bldg 200 Cambridge MA 02139

PAIGE, ALVIN, artist; b. LaGrange, Ga., July 13, 1934; s. Edward and Dora Jane (McGee) P.; m. Susan Lee; children: Monica L., Gaila R., Alvin, Jr., Shanean Paige Foster. Student, Ind. U., 1953-54, Art Inst., Chgo., 1954-55, Munson Proctor Inst., Utica, N.Y., 1962-63, U. Tex., 1980, MIT, 1980, Harvard U., 1980-81; BA in Polit. Sci., Am. Internat. Coll., 1980; MA in Adminstrn., Antioch U., 1981. Enlisted USAF, 1955; dir. spl. events The Beeches Resort, Rome, N.Y., 1962-65; sr. designer Display Workshop, Inc., Hartford, Conn., 1965-68; pres. Art & Design Ctr., Hartford, 1968-69, P.I.E., Inc. Art & Design Agy., 1970-75; sculptor-in-residence, designer, asst. to pres. Am. Internat. Coll., Springfield, 1980—; bd. dirs. Stage West Theatre, Springfield, 1984—; panelist Mass. Coun. for the Arts, Boston, 1984-86, 92. Author: Public Art, Part I, 1980; exhibited UN, N.Y.C., 1982, Mus. Fine Arts, Boston, 1988, People's Republic China, 1989, Boston Govt. Ctr., 1989, Manchester, Vt., 1990, Chesterwood, Nat. Hist. Preservation Mus., Stockbridge, Mass., 1990, St. Maarten, Netherlands Antilles, 1991; commd. Martin Luther King Meml., Springfield, 1988. Mem. Mass. Art Advocacy, Worcester; mem. com. Gateway Pub. Art, Springfield, 1986-87; chmn. Springfield Symphony Renovation; mem. Springfield Bd. Design, 1986-87; bd. dirs. Springfield Mayor's Office Cultural Affairs, 1981—, Berkshire Ballet, Pittsfield, 1985—, Springfield Neighborhood Housing Assn., 1980—, Community Music Sch., 1989—. Recipient Gov.'s award State of Tex., 1958, C.A.S.E. award U.S. Steel Corp., 1982, award Mass. Dept. Discrimination, 1988, Bronze medal Mass. Horticultural Soc., 1992; Alvin Paige Day proclaimed by City of La Grange, 1983; named Artist of Yr., So. Vt. Art Ctr., 1990. Fellow Internat. Soc. Sculptors; mem. Am. Coun. for Arts, Inst. Urban Design, Advt. Club Western Mass., Shanghai Sculptors Soc., Sculpture Soc. Can. Home: 3 East St North Grafton MA 01536-1815 Office: Am Internat Coll 1000 State St Springfield MA 01109-3189

PAIGE, ANITA PARKER, retired English educator; b. Valparaiso, Ind., Feb. 5, 1908; d. Eugene Mark and Grace Agnes (Noon) Parker; m. Robert Myron Paige, Aug. 12, 1933 (dec. 1965); children: Susan Marlowe Paige Morrison, Amy Woods Paige Dunker, Caroline Parker Paige McClennan. AB, Vassar Coll., 1929; MA, U. Chgo., 1930, postgrad., 1931-32. Instr. English Hillsdale (Mich.) Coll., 1930-31, asst. prof., 1931-33; with bd. edn. Anglo-Am. Schs., Athens, 1948-51; tchr. secondary schs. Am. Sch., Teheran, Iran, 1957-58; instr. English Republic of China Mil. Cartographic Sec. group, Taipei, Taiwan, 1960-61; instr. dept. English Nat. Taiwan U., Tapei, 1961-62; intermittent lectr., 1988—; bd. dirs. Ginling Girls Mid. Sch., Taipei, 1960-62. bd. dirs. Community (Presbyn.) Ch., Teheran, Iran, 1957-58. Mem. LWV (chmn. Cook County, Ill. child welfare dept. 1933-36, mem. bd. overseas edn. fund 1966-68), Diplomatic and Consular Officers Ret., Am. Women's Group of Paris, Assn. Am. Fgn. Svc. Women, Asian Am. Forum, Friends of Soochow U., Phi Beta Kappa. Democrat. Congregationalist. Address: 56A G St SW Washington DC 20024

PAIGE, RANDOLPH EUGENE (RANDY PAIGE), television news reporter; b. Petaluma, Calif., Apr. 8, 1952; s. Philip Clark and Barbara Jean (Montgomery) P.; m. Patricia Ann Rohde, Aug. 7, 1976; children: Ryan Michael, Timothy Kyle. BA in Sociology, U. Calif., Santa Barbara, 1975; MS in Mass Communication, San Jose State U., 1984. News anchor/reporter Sta. KSBY-TV, San Luis Obispo, Calif., 1983-85; news reporter Sta. KGUN-TV, Tucson, 1985-87, Sta. WMAR-TV, Balt., 1987—. Recipient Emmy award Investigative Reporting NATAS Southwest Region, 1987, Best Spot News award Md. chpt. Soc. Profl. Journalists, 1988, Best In-Depth News Report award Md. chpt. AP, 1988, Best News Report award Md. chpt. Soc. Profl. Journalists, 1990. Mem. Investigative Reporters and Editors. Office: Sta WMAR-TV 6400 York Rd Baltimore MD 21212

PAIGEN, KENNETH, geneticist, educator; b. N.Y.C., Nov. 14, 1927; s. Alexander and Ida (Kantor) P.; m. Beverly Vandermolen, June 14, 1970; children—Susan, Gina, Mark, David, Jennifer. A.B., Johns Hopkins U., Balt., 1946; Ph.D., Calif. Inst. Tech., Pasadena, 1950. Staff mem. Roswell Park Meml. Inst., Buffalo, 1955-72, dept. head, 1972-82; prof. dept. genetics U. Calif., Berkeley, 1982-89; dir., sr. staff scientist Jackson Lab., Bar Harbor, Maine, 1989—. Mem. AAAS, Am. Assn. for Cancer Rsch., Internat. Mammalian Genome Soc., Human Genome Orgn., Genetics Soc. Am., Am. Soc. for Biochemistry and Molecular Biology, Biophys. Soc., Sigma Xi, Phi Beta Kappa. Democrat. Jewish. Home: Old Farm Rd Bar Harbor ME 04609-0800 Office: Jackson Lab 600 Main St Bar Harbor ME 04609-1500

PAIK, JAMES S., food science educator; b. Seoul, Korea, July 5, 1950; came to U.S., 1980; s. David and Inez (Chung) P.; m. Young Hyum Kim, May 5, 1980; 1 child, Susan. BS in Food Engring., YonSei U., Seoul, 1974; MS in Biochem. Engring., Korea Inst. Advanced Sci. and, Engring., Seoul, 1976; PhD in Food Sci., Rutgers U., 1985. Process engr. Dong-A Corp., Seoul, 1976-80; rsch. assoc. Rutgers U., New Brunswick, N.J., 1985-87; asst. prof. food science U. Del., Newark, 1987—; cons. Celentano, Inc., Verona, N.J., 1985-87, NongShim Corp., Seoul, 1990—. Grantee Westvaco, 1988, CCT Inc., 1989, ICI, 1990. Mem. Am. Chem. Soc., Inst. Packaging Profls. Office: Dept Food Sci U Del Newark DE 19716

PAIKOWSKY, SANDRA ROSLYN, art historian; b. St. John, N.B., Can., Dec. 29, 1945; d. Morton Ernest and Bessie Frances (Rabkin) P.; m. John Richard Fox, Dec. 11, 1982. B.A., Sir. George Williams U., Montreal, Que., Can., 1967; M.A., U. Toronto, 1969. Curatorial asst. Royal Ont. Mus., Toronto, 1967-68; prof. art history Concordia U., Montreal, 1969—; curator Concordia Art Gallery, Montreal, 1981—. Co-pub., co-editor: Jour. Can. Art History, 1972—; author exhbn. catalogues. Mem. Can. Mus. Assn., Univ. Art Assn. Can., Can. Art Mus. Dirs. Orgn. Office: Concordia U Art Gallery, 1455 de Maisonneuve Blvd W, Montreal, PQ Canada H3G 1M8

PAINE, BRUCE EDWIN, financial consultant; b. Amsterdam, N.Y., Dec. 4, 1933; s. Richard Candee and Gladys (Van Vranken) P.; m. Fredericka Ione Zimpel, Feb. 19, 1959 (div. 1968); children: Kevin Bruce, Richard Stephen; m. Charlotte Flanagan, June 15, 1971 (div. 1978); m. Natalie Thompson, May 28, 1983. MusB, Yale U., 1955; student, NYU, 1959-63, U. Pa., 1979-80. Corp. trust adminstr. Morgan Guaranty Trust Co., N.Y.C., 1958-60; asst. to pres., editor Prentice Hall, Inc., Englewood Cliffs, N.J., 1960-62; asst. dir. fl. dept. N.Y. Stock Exch., N.Y.C., 1962-66; corp. v.p. Paine Webber, Inc., N.Y.C., 1966-88; pres. Bruce E. Paine Retirement Planning Assocs., Inc., 1988—; arbitrator N.Y. Stock Exch. Author numerous articles in field. Mem. Internat. Assn. Fin. Planners, Internat. Soc. Pre-Retirement Planners, Found. for Acctg. Edn., N.Y. Inst. Fin., Yale Club N.Y.C., Columbia County Golf Club. Episcopalian. Home: Box 909 Stevers Crossing Rd Philmont NY 12565 also: PO Box 751 Philmont NY 12565

PAINE, DWIGHT MILTON, mathematician, educator; b. Albion, N.Y., Oct. 11, 1931; s. Cuyler Emory and Mabel Lucile (Gray) P.; children: Rachel, Naomi, Graham, Joel. BA, McGill U., 1956; MDiv, Fuller Theol. Seminary, Pasadena, Calif., 1959; MS, U. Wis., 1961, PhD, 1963. Asst. prof. math. Wells Coll., Aurora, N.Y., 1963-67, assoc. prof. math., 1967-72; assoc. prof. math. Messiah Coll., Grantham, Pa., 1972-79, prof. math., 1979—. Author: Biblical Hebrew Introduction, 1986; contbr. articles to profl. jours. Mem. Math. Assn. Am. Mem. Brethren in Christ Ch. Home: 620 Clg Ave Grantham PA 17027-9999 Office: Messiah Coll Grantham PA 17027

PAISNER, CLAIRE VIVIAN, public relations executive; b. Boston, Apr. 10, 1933; d. Philip and Hilda Paisner; children: Renee, Catherine. BA with

Honors, Cornell U., 1955; MA, Harvard U., 1958; postgrad., U. Paris, 1966. Editor-in-chief N.Y. Voice newspaper, N.Y.C., 1969-76; asst. press sec. Manhattan Borough Pres. Percy Sutton, N.Y.C., 1977; pub. rels. coord. Consol. Edison, N.Y.C., 1978-80; pub. info. dir. York Coll., CUNY, Queens, 1981—. Mem. adv. coun. Queens Pub. TV, 1989—, Black Am. Heritage Found., N.Y.C., 1983—. Recipient Journalism award Nat. Newspaper Pubs. Assn., 1970, 71, 74, Reporting award Lincoln U., 1975, 76, 77. Mem. Nat. Honor Soc., Phi Beta Kappa. Office: CUNY York Coll Guy R Brewer Blvd Jamaica NY 11451

PAISNER, MARTIN JAY, plastics engineer; b. N.Y.C., Aug. 7, 1956; s. Abraham and Fannie (Schuinsky) P.; m. Hana Hazout, Jan. 3, 1991. BS in Chemistry, SUNY, Albany, 1977; MS in Metall. Engring., U. Ill., 1981; MBA, U. Del., 1987. Product engr. Hercules, Inc., Wilmington, Del., 1981-89; plastics engr. SCM Chems., Balt., 1989—. Mem. Soc. Plastics Engrs. Office: SCM Chems 3901 Ft Armstead Rd Baltimore MD 21226

PAISS, DORIS BELL, educational and psychological consultant, lecturer, educator; b. Phila., Nov. 19, 1929; d. Simon and Sarah (Freedman) Cohen; m. Lee Paiss, July 26, 1953; children: Jana, Michael. BFA, Barnard Coll., 1954; postgrad. L.A. City Coll., 1962-63; MA, Columbia U., 1963, PhD in Philosophy of Ancient Civilizations, 1976, degree in Geriatrics in Abnormal Psychology, 1978. Active Jewish education, 1963-86; ednl. dir. M.D. Hoffman Regional Hebrew High Sch., Phila., 1973-83; coord. Daroff Campus of Sr. Adult Studies, Raymond and Miriam Klein br. Jewish Community Ctr., Phila., 1982-85, mem. faculty Daroff Campus Adult Studies, 1978-85; cons. Life Care and Retirement, 1985-92; designing support and ednl. programs for stress related memory loss; lectr. on stress, memory, time mgmt., devel. human potential, Phila., 1976-92, guest lectr. Columbia U., U. Wis., U. Calif.-Santa Barbara, Oberlin Coll., Rochester Inst. Tech., Rutgers U., U. Tampa, Coalition for Jewish Edn., writers' confs., community svc. orgns., indsl. seminars; mem. faculty Inst. Awareness, 1980-83, Satinsky Inst. for Blind, 1980-85; free-lance writer and producer comml., indsl. and ednl. films, 1950-70. Recipient numerous awards. Mem. NAFE, Am. Film Inst. Democrat. Jewish. Avocations: research on memory, show music.

PAIVA, JOSEPH MOURA, biotechnology company executive; b. Rahway, N.J., Aug. 18, 1955; s. Joseph A. and Lucille S. (Moura) P.; m. Madeline A. Makoski, Sept. 9, 1978. BS in Acctg., Fairleigh Dickinson U., 1977; MBA, Rutgers U., 1982. CPA, N.J. Sr. acct. Peat, Marwick, Mitchell & Co., Hacksensack, N.J., 1977-80; contr. T.J. McGlone & Co., Inc., Edison, N.J., 1980-83; dir. fin., asst. sec. Cytogen Corp., Princeton, N.J., 1983—; chief fin. officer Cytorad Inc., Princeton, N.J., 1991—; bd. dirs., first v.p. So. N.J. Venture Capital Group, Mt. Holly, N.J., 1985-87; fin. cons., Howell, N.J., 1984-89; pres. Assn. Bioscience Fin. Officers Phila./Princeton chpt. 1992—. Mem. AICPA, N.J. Soc. CPAs, Mensa, Phi Zeta Kappa, Phi Omega Epsilon. Roman Catholic. Home: 15 Obispo Dr Brick NJ 08723-7612 Office: Cytogen Corp 600 College Rd E Princeton NJ 08540-6698

PAJAK, DAVID JOSEPH, lawyer, consultant; b. Buffalo, N.Y., June 19, 1956; s. William H. and Theresa A. (Granato) P.; m. Peggy J. Fisher, Aug. 1, 1981; 1 child, Andrew J. BA, State Coll. Buffalo, 1978; JD, U. Buffalo, 1982. Bar: N.Y. 1983, U.S. Dist. Ct. (we. dist.) N.Y., 1991. Social svcs. counsel Genesee County Dept. Social Svcs., Batavia, N.Y., 1984—; pvt. practice Corfu, N.Y., 1983—; mem. legis. com. N.Y. Fed. on Child Abuse and Neglect, Albany, 1986—, bd. dirs., 1987-89; cons. N.Y. Pub. Welfare Assn., Inc., Albany, 1987-92; pres. Social Svcs. Attys. Assn. N.Y. State, 1990-91; instr. Klassic Karate Studios, Buffalo. Contbr. articles to profl. jours. Mem. Assn. Trial Lawyers Am., N.Y. State Bar Assn., Erie County Bar Assn., Genesee County Bar Assn., Corfu Area Bus. Assn. Republican. Home: 17 E Main St Corfu NY 14036-9665 Office: Genesee Dept Social Svcs 420 E Main St Batavia NY 14020-2599

PAKALNS, GAIL PARSHALL, university administrator; b. Urbana, Ill., Apr. 26, 1945; d. Richard Palmer Parshall and Barbara (Littleton) Combs; m. Alan Rodolfo Pakalns, June 9, 1973; 1 child, Andris Miguel. BA, U. Wis., 1967; MEd, Boston U., 1969; PhD, NYU, 1987. Lic. psychologist, N.Y. Rsch. analyst Wis. Dept. Health and Social Svc., Madison, 1968-69; asst. dir. Barnard Coll. Career Devel., N.Y.C., 1969-71; rsch. asst. Col. Univ. Dept. Com'ty Psych., N.Y.C., 1971-73; psychologist South Beach Psychology Ctr., Bklyn., 1973-81, supr. psychologist, 1981-90; dir. counseling SUNY, Purchase, 1990—. Mem. N.Y. State Psychol. Assn. (pres. div. women's issues 1991—), N.Y.C. Coalition for Women's Mental Health (bd. dirs. 1988-91, editor 1988-90), Manhattan Psychol. Assn. (bd. dirs. 1990-91), Assn. of U. and Coll. Counseling Ctr. Dirs., Phi Beta Kappa. Home: 603 W 111th St Apt 7W New York NY 10025-1806 Office: SUNY 735 Anderson Hill Rd Purchase NY 10577-1402

PAKAN, PATRICIA MARIE, education educator; b. Duquesne, Pa., May 15, 1931; d. Anthony J. and Barbara M. (Chunko) Zewe; m. William A. Pakan, Sept. 4, 1952; children: William A., Kurt P., Dwight A., Barbara M. RN, Mercy Hosp. Sch. Nursing, 1952; BS in Edn. summa cum laude, Kent State U., 1973, MA, 1975; MEd, California U. of Pa., 1981; ABD, U. Rochester, 1992. RN, N.Y. Prof. nursing Uniontown (Pa.) Hosp. Sch. Nursing, 1975-82; dir. of tng. Wesley-on-East, Rochester, N.Y., 1983-85; prof. Monroe Community Coll., Rochester, 1985-88, Community Coll. of Finger Lakes, Canandaigua, 1988-91; mentor Empire State Coll. SUNY, Rochester, 1991—; co-owner, dir. tng. Quest Cons. Ltd., Rochester, 1986—. Contbr. articles to profl. jours. Levy campaign chair Tallmadge (Ohio) City Schs., 1968-75; vol. tchr. ARC, 1970-75; leader Girl Scouts U.S., 1968-70;. Mem. ASTD (organizer community connection), Genessee Valley Nurses Assn., Myasthenia Gravis Assn. Republican. Lutheran. Home: 316 Taylor Rd Mendon NY 14506 Office: SUNY Empire State Coll 9 Prince St Rochester NY 14607-1405

PAKMAN, LEONARD MARVIN, microbiologist; b. Phila., Apr. 8, 1933; s. Abraham and Reba (Dubinsky) P.; m. Alice Perlstein, Mar. 1, 1964; children: David B., James H. BA, U. Pa., 1956, PhD, 1964. Rsch. technician Johnson Found. for Med. Physics of U. Pa., Phila., 1951-56; asst. instr. U. Pa., Phila., 1960-63; asst. prof. Jefferson Univ. Med. Coll., Phila., 1964-70; prof. Temple U. Med. Sch., Phila., 1970—; cons. Franklin Inst. Rsch. Labs, Phila., 1968-70, Tech. Adv. Svc. for Attys., Blue Bell, Pa., 1975—; invited lectr. Beijing Med. U., China, 1987. Contbr. articles to profl. jours. Bd. dirs. Town Watch, Abington, Pa., 1982—, Pub. Health Planning Group, Montgomery County, Pa., 1989-90, Lyme Project, Montgomery County, 1989-90; judge Pa. Jr. Acad. of Sci. Rsch. Competition, Montgomery County, 1983-88. Mem. AAAS, Am. Soc. Microbiology (invited lectr. conf. 1976), Am. Assn. Dental Rsch., Phi Beta Kappa, Sigma Xi. Home: 1034 Beverly Rd Jenkintown PA 19046-3334 Office: Dept Microbiology/Immunol Temple U Med Sch 3400 N Broad St Philadelphia PA 19140-5196

PAKSOY, H. B., history educator; b. 1948. BS, Trinity U., Tex., 1970; MA, U. Tex., Dallas, 1976; DPhil, Oxford (Eng.) U., 1987. Faculty assoc. Ctr. for Middle Eastern Studies Harvard U., Cambridge, Mass., 1986—; instr. dept. history Conn. State U., New Britain, 1987-90, U. Mass., Amherst, 1990-91; cons. NBC News, Moscow, Radio Free Europe-Radio Liberty, Paris, Munich, The Economist, London, Voice of Am., Washington, Woodrow Wilson Ctr. for Internat. Scholars, Smithsonian Instn., Washington. Author: Alpamysh: Central Asian Identity under Russian Rule, 1989; editor: Central Asian Monuments, 1992; also articles. Co-founder telecommunications project Tex. Scottish Rite Crippled Children's Hosp., Dallas, 1980; chmn. youth svc. com. Park Cities Rotary Club, Dallas, 1980-81, chmn. world community svc. com., 1981-82. Grantee Japanese Ministry of Edn., 1991, Fondation Nationale des Scis. Politiques, Centre D'Etudes et de Recherches Internationales, Paris, 1991, Com. of Vice Chancellors and Prins. of Univs. of U.K., 1983-86, Soc. for Cen. Asian Studies, Oxford, 1984, NSF, 1976-77, travel grantee Internat. Rsch. and Exchs. Bd., 1992. Mem. Assn. for Advancement of Cen. Asian Rsch., Inc. (founding editor AACAR Bull., founding pres. 1988-90, mem. exec. coun. 1990—), Am. Assn. Advancement of Slavic Studies, Am. Hist. Assn., Assn. for Asian Studies, Assn. for Study of Nationalities of USSR, Mid. Ea. Studies Assn., Permanent Internat. Altaistic Conf., Oxford Soc. (founder Conn. br. 1987, hon. sec. 1987-90). Home: PO Box 2321 Amherst MA 01004-2321

PALADINO, RAYMOND ANTHONY, county official, counselor; b. Jamestown, N.Y., Sept. 27, 1949; s. Samuel and Doris Mae (Arkielpane) P.; m. Rosemary Edwards Paladino, Mar. 16, 1976; children: Lauren, Ryan. BA, DePauw U., 1971; MS in Edn., St. Bonaventure U., 1975, cert. in guidance and counseling, 1977. Cert. sch. guidance counselor, N.Y. Youth cons. Chautauqua County Drug Edn. Consortium, Ashville, N.Y., 1972-73; sch. guidance counselor Cattaraugus County Bd. of Coop. Ednl. Svcs., Olean, N.Y., 1974-77; employment training counselor Cattaraugus County Employment Training Programs, Olean, N.Y., 1977-79, sr. employment training coord., counselor, 1979—; career counselor Cattaraugus-Allegany County Bd. Coop. Ednl. Svcs., Olean, N.Y., 1986-89. Mem. Am. Assn. Counseling & Devel., Am. Assn. Employment Counseling. Office: Cattaraugus County Employment Tng 1701 Lincoln Ave Ste 6212 Olean NY 14760

PALAGONIA, PETER WALTER, illustrator; b. Bklyn., Sept. 9, 1961; s. Benjamin Anthony and Barbara Elizabeth (Orlowsky) P. Student, Paier Coll., 1987-90, Sch. of Worcester Art Mus., 1979-80, Wooster Art Ctr., 1982-85. Mural artist HUD Apt. Complex, Newark, 1980; contbg. illustrator Mechanix Illustrated Mag., N.Y.C., 1980-83, Benjamin Palagonia & Assoc., Sherman, Conn., 1985; illustrator Trans-Lux Theater Corp., N.Y.C., 1987, Brandt Corp., N.Y.C., 1987; freelance illustrator children's book Sherman, 1988—; lectr. Paier Coll., 1991. Illustrator The Magic House, 1991, The Singing Shepard, 1991, Flit, Flutter, Fly, 1991, The Christmas Cowboy, 1992. Roman Catholic. Home: Cedar Ln Sherman CT 06784-1537

PALAMAR, DAVE, musician; b. Phoenixville, Pa., July 23, 1953; s. John and Mary (Popovich) P.; m. Sharon Denise Garland, Aug. 22, 1988; 1 child, Jordan. Grad. high sch., Phoenixville, Pa. Drummer Airmen of Note/USAF Jazz Ensemble, Washington, 1971-76; leading session musician radio, TV commls., records Washington, 1976-85; house musician Resorts Internat., Atlantic City, N.J., 1985-89; drummer Clint Holmes, 1976—, N.Y. at Night (Prime Time TV), N.Y.C., 1991—; faculty music Glassboro (N.J.) State Coll., 1988-89. Co-author: 4's Complete Guide to Syncopation, 1991. Mem. Percussive Arts Soc. Roman Catholic.

PALAMAR, MARY COYLE, education educator; b. Bklyn., Mar. 23, 1940; d. Timothy and Mary (Rooney) Coyle; m. Peter Palamer, Aug. 26, 1961; children: James, Timothy, Mark. BA, Rutgers U., 1962; MS, SUNY, Brockport, 1971; EdD, U. Rochester, 1978. Tchr. spl. edn. BOCES # 1, Fairport, N.Y., 1971-77; adminstr. BOCES # 2, Spencerport, N.Y., 1978-82; prof., dir. spl. edn. Nazareth Coll. Rochester, N.Y., 1982—. Mem. Coun. Exceptional Children, Assn. Learning Disabled, AAUW, Internat. Assn. Spl. Educators, Assn. Supervision and Curriculum Devel., Nat. Assn. Adults with Spl. Learning Needsn (bd. dirs. 1990—). Roman Catholic. Office: Nazareth Coll PO Box 18950 Rochester NY 14618-0950

PALEK, JIRI, medical educator, researcher, academic administrator; b. Prague, Czechoslovakia, Aug. 6, 1934; came to U.S., 1968; s. Frant and Marie Palek; m. Marie Palek, Oct. 9, 1967; children: Michael, Nicole. MD, Charles U. Sch. Medicine, Prague, 1958. Clin. asst. prof. Med. Sch. Harvard U., Boston, 1973-74; assoc. prof. Med. Sch. U. Mass., Worcester, 1974-78; assoc. dir. div. hematology/oncology St. Vincent Hosp., Worcester, 1974-78; prof. Sch. of Medicine Tufts U., Boston, 1978—; chmn. dept. biomed. rsch., chief div. hematology/oncology St. Elizabeth's Hosp., Boston, 1978—; cons. physician N.E. Deaconess Hosp., Boston, 1976-78; physician U. Mass. Med. Ctr., Worcester, 1976-78; mem. sci. adv. bd. Boston Sickle Cell Ctr., 1988—; reviewer hematology subsplty. panel residency rev. com. Accreditation Coun. for Grad. Med. Edn., 1989—; mem. hematology study sect. NIH, 1978-84; mem. editorial bd., guest editor various hematology jours. Contbr. numerous articles to profl. jours. NIH grantee, 1974—. Fellow ACP; mem. Am. Fedn. Clin. Rsch., Am. Physiology Soc., Am. Soc. Cell Biology, Internat. Soc. Hematology (counillor 1989-90, v.p. 1990—), N.Y. Acad. Scis., Mass. Soc. Med. Rsch. (bd. dirs. 1987—), Leukemia Soc. Am., Red Cell Club, Boston Blood Club. Office: St Elizabeths Hosp Boston 736 Cambridge St Brighton MA 02135-2997

PALERMO, DAVID STUART, retired psychology educator and administrator. BS in Psychology and Edn., Lynchburg Coll., 1951; MS in Psychology, U. Mass., 1953; PhD, U. Iowa, 1955. Rsch. assoc. Iowa Child Welfare Rsch. Sta. U. Iowa, 1955; asst. prof. psychology So. Ill. U., Carbondale, 1955-58; asst. prof. Inst. Child Devel. U. Minn., Mpls., 1958-63; vis. prof. dept. psychology U. Edinburgh, Scotland, 1969-70; sr. Fulbright scholar dept. psychology U. Sydney, Australia, 1975; prof. Inst. Advanced Psychol. Studies Adelphi U., Garden City, L.I., N.Y., 1978-79; assoc. prof. Pa. State U., University Park, 1963-66, prof., 1966—, assoc. dir. Ctr. for the Study of Child, Adolescent Devel., 1984-88, assoc. dean for rsch. and grad. studies, Coll. Liberal Arts, 1988-92; assoc. The Behavioral and Brain Scis., 1982—. Editor Child Development Abstracts and Bibliography, 1971-74; editor Jour. Exptl. Child Psychology, 1973-83, mem. editorial bd., 1966—; mem. editorial bd. Jour. Verbal Learning and Verbal Behavior, 1964-77, Metaphor and Symbolic Activity, 1983—, Cognitive Devel., 1990—; contbr. numerous articles to profl. jours. Recipient Career Devel. award Nat. Inst. of Child Health and Human Devel. award, 1965-70. Fellow APA, AAAS; mem. Soc. for Rsch. in Child Devel., Psychonomic Soc., Ea. Psychol. Assn., Jean Piaget Soc., Am. Psychol. Soc.,1976-79, Internat. Soc. for the Study of Behavioral Devel., Sigma Xi.

PALERMO, NICHOLAS JOSEPH, osteopathic physician; b. Geneva, N.Y., Nov. 7, 1946; s. Nicholas Dominic and Theresa Marie (Bruno) P.; m. Wendy Jean Billings, Aug. 10, 1968 (div. Sept. 1988); children: Tania Anne, Nicholas Joseph Jr. BS in Biology, Norwich U., 1968; MS in Biology, Georgetown U., 1970; DO, Coll. Osteo. Medicine-Surgery, Des Moines, 1976. Cert. lab. dir. Intern Youngstown (Ohio) Osteo. Hosp., 1976-77; pvt. practice Youngstown, 1977-78, Manchester, Conn., 1978—; lab. dir. Manchester Profl. Lab. Inc., 1980—, Metpath Clin. Lab., Manchester, 1990—; chmn. Conn. Bd. Osteo. Med. Examiners, Hartford, 1984—. Umpire Manchester Little League, 1981—; bd. dirs. March of Dimes, 1985; treas. Manchester Health Svcs., 1987-89. Capt. Med. Svc. Corps, U.S. Army, 1971-73. Mem. Am. Coll. Gen. Practice (cert.), New Eng. Osteo. Assembly (bd. dirs.), Am. Osteo. Assn., New Eng. Coll. Osteo. Medicine (clin.), U.N.E. Coll. Osteo. Medicine (clin.), Conn. Osteo. Med. Soc. (v.p. 1980-85, pres. 1986—), Hartford County Med. Assn., Manchester Med. Soc., Am. Legion, Student Osteo. Med. Assn. (life), UNICO, Sigma Sigma Phi (life). Office: 225 Main St Manchester CT 06040-3596

PALERMO, ROBERT JAMES, architect, consultant; b. N.Y.C., Mar. 25, 1949; s. Vitorio and Simone (DiFlorio) P.; m. Lore Bernadette Bilbao, July 22, 1972 (dec. Feb. 1977); m. Patricia Dolores Ward, June 14, 1981; children: Jaime, Justin, Kristen Leigh. BS, CCNY, 1971, BArch, 1972; MBA, Baruch Grad. Ctr., 1974; postgrad., Nat. Asbestos Tng. Inst., 1987. Lic. asbestos investigator; registered architect, N.Y., N.J. Architect Rongved, Wilcox, Erickson, N.Y.C., 1972-73, Welton Becket Assocs., N.Y.C., 1973-75; architect, prin. Jaime Lore Design, Bklyn., 1976—; bd. dir. Nat. Meddlex Med. Constrn. Corp., Hicksville, N.Y., 1981-85; pres. Corp. Design of Am., P.C., 1989—. Mem. Am. Inst. Architects, Soc. Am. Registered Architects, Phi Sigma Kappa. Republican. Roman Catholic. Home: 160 Pelican Rd Middletown NJ 07748-3042 Office: Corp Design of Am PC 461 Park Ave S New York NY 10016-6822

PALEY, STANLEY R., social work professional, psychotherapist; b. N.Y.C., Sept. 18, 1940; s. Harry and Anna (Meyerowitz) P.; (div. 1990); children: Lawrence, Andrew, Robyn. MSW, Adelphi U., 1969. From social worker to social work supr. Queens Children's Psychiat. Ctr., Bellerose, N.Y., 1966-86; dir. of social work Cen. Islip (N.Y.) Psychiat. Ctr., 1986—; sole practice psychotherapy Bohemia, 1969—; instr. Stony Brook (N.Y.) Sch. of Social Welfare, 1988; dir. Epilepsy Assn. of Suffolk, 1986-88; mem. Queensboro Pres. Child Abuse Task Force, 1982-86. Program dir. AIDS Found. of L.I., Bayshore, N.Y., 1990—. With U.S. Army, 1964-70. Mem. NASW, Acad. of Cert. Social Workers, Am. Hosp. Assn. Republican. Jewish. Office: Stanley R Paley RCSW ASCW 70 Middleton Rd #8 Bohemia NY 11716

PALI, ROBERT GEORGE, manufacturing executive; b. Bethlehem, Pa., Mar. 21, 1946; s. George W. and Mildred Louise (Latham) P.; m. Carol Scott Soose, July 15, 1967 (div. July 1989); children: Margaret Louise, Latham George; m. Nina L.S. Burnaford, Sept. 8, 1990. AB in Econs., Lafayette Coll., 1978; MBA, U. Pa., 1979. Chemist Bethlehem (Pa.) Steel Corp., 1967-77; ops. mgr. J.P. Nissen Co., Glenside, Pa., 1979-86, gen. mgr., 1986—. Contbr. articles to profl. jours. Mem. Welding Equipment Mfrs. Assn., Nat. Welding Supply Assn., Am. Supply and Machinery Mfrs. Assn., Theta Delta Chi (pres. bd. trustees 1986-91). Republican. Episcopalian. Home: 2302 Ash Grv Ambler PA 19002-5036 Office: JP Nissen Co 614 N Easton Rd Glenside PA 19038-4301

PALIS, MICHAEL ABUEG, computer science educator; b. Manila, Mar. 24, 1957; came to U.S., 1980; s. Francisco Talavera and Fe (Abueg) P.; m. Emilia Arevalo Jovellana, June 26, 1983; children: Kristen, Courteney. BSEE, U. Philippines, 1979, BS in Physics, 1980; PhD in Computer Sci., U. Minn., 1985. Instr. dept. physics U. Philippines, Quezon City, 1979-80; research and teaching fellow dept. computer sci. U. Minn., Mpls., 1980-85; asst. prof. dept. computer and info. sci. U. Pa., Phila., 1985—; cons. GE Advanced Tech. Labs., Moorestown, N.J., 1989; vis. fellow Army High Performance Computing Rsch. Ctr., Mpls., 1991. Contbr. articles to profl. jours. Grantee NSF, 1991-92. Mem. IEEE, Assn. for Computing Machinery, Math. Assn. Am., Phi Kappa Phi. Office: U Pa Dept Computer-Info Sci 200 S 33d St Philadelphia PA 19104

PALIYENKO, ADRIANNA MARIA, foreign language educator; b. Kingston, Ont., Can., Feb. 28, 1956; came to U.S., 1958; d. Paul and Alexandra (Sawka) P.; m. Levering B. Sherman Jr., Mar. 14, 1986. AB in French Edn., U. N.C., 1977, PhD in French Lit., 1988; MA in French Lit., Boston U., 1983. Tchr. French, dept. head Northwood High Sch., Pittsboro, N.C., 1977-80; asst. d'anglais Lycée Honoré de Balzac, Paris, 1982-83; vis. instr. N.C. State U., Raleigh, 1987-88; lectr. in French U. N.C., Chapel Hill, 1988-89; asst. prof. Colby Coll., Waterville, Maine, 1989—; lectr. and researcher in field. Boston U. fellow, 1980-82; Fulbright-Hays scholar, 1982-83. Mem. MLA, New Eng. MLA, South Atlantic MLA, Am. Assn. Tchrs. of French, Phi Beta Kappa. Office: Colby Coll Dept Romance Langs Waterville ME 04901

PALKOVITZ, ROBIN JOSEPH, family studies educator; b. Hagerstown, Md., Jan. 24, 1954; d. I. Joseph and Caroline (Russell) P.; m. Judy McClanahan, July 17, 1976; children: Nathan, Collin, Ian, Shane. BA in Psychology, U. Va., 1976; MS in Psychology, Rutgers U., 1979, PhD in Psychology, 1980. Instr. psychology Rutgers U., New Brunswick, N.J., 1980; asst. prof. Sterling (Kans.) Coll., 1980-83; asst. prof. U. Del., Newark, 1983-89, assoc. prof., 1989—; mem. adv. bd. Focus on the First 60 Months, Del., 1986-88; expert cons. family ct., Wilmington, 1985-87. Editor: Transitions to Parenthood, 1988; editorial bd. Marriage and Family Rev., 1987—; contbr. articles to profl. jours. Deacon Newark Christian Fellowship, Landenberg, Pa., 1985-89, elder, 1989—. Grantee U. Del., 1984, 85. Mem. Soc. for Rsch. in Child Devel., Christian Assn. for Psychol. Studies, Nat. Coun. on Family Rels., Soc. for Psychophysiol. Rsch., Family Resource Coalition, Sigma Xi (sec. U. Del. chpt. 1986-89). Home: 1040 Newark Rd Lincoln University PA 19352-9801 Office: U Del Individual & Family Studies Newark DE 19716

PALL, ELLEN JANE, writer; b. N.Y.C., Mar. 28, 1952; d. David B. and Josephine H. (Blatt) P.; m. Richard Holmes Dicker, July 12, 1986. BA, U. Calif., Santa Barbara, 1973. Freelance writer for several jours., 1987—; staff assoc. Bread Loaf Writers Conf., Middlebury, Vt., 1986; instr. UCLA-Extension, 1980-83; adj. asst. prof. Fordham U./Coll. at Lincoln Ctr., N.Y.C., 1990-92. Author: (under pen name Fiona Hill) The Trellised Lane, The Wedding Portrait, The Practical Heart, Love in a Major Key, Sweet's Folly, The Autumn Rose, The Love Child, The Stanbroke Girls, 1984, The Country Gentleman, 1987, (as Ellen Pall) Back East, 1983; contbr. articles to N.Y. Times Arts & Leisure, Chicago Tribune, Washington Post; book reviewer. Shane Stevens fellow Bread Loaf Writer's Conf., Vt., 1983. Mem. Am. PEN (freedom to write com., bd. dirs.). Office: care Clyde Taylor Curtis Brown Ltd 10 Astor Pl New York NY 10003-6935

PALLADINO, GRACE, editor; b. Bklyn., Apr. 25, 1953; d. Anthony Michael and Frances Margaret (Festa) P. BA, Mt. Holyoke Coll., 1975; MA, U. Rochester, 1977; PhD, U. Pitts., 1983. Historian Svc. Employees Internat. Union, Washington, 1983, Internat. Brotherhood Elec. Workers, Washington, 1989-91; assoc. editor Samuel Gompers Papers U. Md., College Park, 1984-89, editor Samuel Gompers Papers, 1990—. Author: Another Civil War, 1990 (Avery Craven award 1990), Dreams of Dignity, Workers of Vision, 1991. Mem. coord. com. Women in the Hist. Profession. Predoctoral fellow Mellon Found., 1981-83, Postdoctoral fellow Smithsonian Inst., 1985-86, Skinner fellow Mt. Holyoke Coll., 1981-83. Mem. Assn. Am. Historians, Orgn. Am. Historians. Office: U Md Dept History College Park MD 20742

PALLAI, DAVID FRANCIS, publishing executive; b. N.Y.C., Nov. 7, 1950; s. Alfiero and Clara Aurora (Dignani) P.; m. Jean Therese Leary, June 25, 1977; children: Matthew Gian, Jeremy Michael. BA, Boston Coll., 1972, MA, 1974; MA, Yale U., 1981. Sales rep. Prentice Hall, Inc., Englewood Cliffs, N.J., 1976-77, field editor, 1977-78; acquisitions editor Allyn & Bacon, Inc., Boston, 1978-80; sr. editor PWS Pubs., Boston, 1980-87; sr. editor Addison-Wesley Pub. Co., Reading, Mass., 1987-88, exec. editor, 1988-90; v.p., pub. Acad. Press, Cambridge, Mass., 1990—. Com. mem. Duxbury (Mass.) Hist. Commn., 1984-87. With USNG, 1972-78. Mem. Math. Assn. Am., Mensa, KC, Harvard Club, Yale Club of Boston. Republican. Roman Catholic. Home: 65 Bay View Rd Duxbury MA 02332-5015 Office: Acad Press 955 Mass Ave Cambridge MA 02139

PALLEY, MARIAN LIEF, political science educator; b. N.Y.C., June 28, 1939; d. Samuel and Frances Rose (Levy) Lief; m. Howard A. Palley, Apr. 21, 1961; children: Stephen, Elizabeth. BA, Syracuse U., 1961, MA, 1963; PhD, NYU, 1966. Acting instr. U. Wis., Milw., 1966; asst. prof. Rutgers U., Newark, 1967-70; asst. prof., assoc. prof., prof. polit. sci. U. Del., Newark, 1970—, chairperson polit. sci. dept., 1979-84, dir. women's studies dept., 1989-90; vis. prof. polit. sci. Hebrew U., 1985, U. Adelaide, Australia, 1985; vis. scholar women's studies Ewha U., Korea, 1990; cons. Agy. for Instrnl. Tech., Bloomington, Ind., 1985-87. Co-author: Women and Public Policies, 1982, 87, Urban America and Public Policies, 1977, 81, Politics of Federal Grants, 1981, Tradition and Change in American Party Politics, 1975; contbr. articles to profl. jours. Am. Coun. Edn. fellow, Washington, 1974-75, Fulbright Found. fellow, 1988; Women's Rsch. and Edn. Inst. grantee, 1986. Mem. Am. Polit. Sci. Assn. (sec. 1980-81), Am. Soc. Pub. Adminstrn. (nat. coun. mem. 1990-93), Women's Caucus for Polit. Sci. (pres. 1983-84), So. Polit. Sci. Assn. (v.p. 1992). Democrat. Office: U Del Dept Polit Sci Newark DE 19716

PALLONE, FRANK, JR., congressman; b. Long Branch, N.J., Oct. 30, 1951. Grad. cum. laude, Middlebury Coll., 1973; MA, Tufts U., 1974; JD, Rutgers U., 1978. Councilman City of Long Branch, 1982-88; mem. N.J. Senate, 1984-88, 101st-102nd Congresses from 3d N.J. dist., 1988—. Democrat. Roman Catholic. Office: US Ho of Reps 213 Cannon Washington DC 20515 Address: 540 Broadway Ste 119 Long Branch NJ 07740*

PALLOZZI, DENNIS PETER, school system administrator; b. Paterson, N.J., Nov. 2, 1947; s. Harold Nicholas and Viola (Spacciapoli) P.; m. Patricia C. Cryor, Aug. 12, 1973; children: Regina, Michael, Alexis, Douglas. BS in Edn., Seton Hall U., 1968; MA in Am. History, Montclair State Coll., 1972, MA in Edn. Adminstrn., 1976; EdD in Edn. Adminstrn., Rutgers U., 1981. Tchr. Pub. Sch. # 5, Paterson, 1968-70, Cen. Mid. Sch., Montville, N.J., 1970-76; sch. adminstr. Hopatong (N.J.) Borough Schs., 1976-88; prin. Florence M. Burd Mid. Sch., Andover, N.J., 1988-90; supt. Andover Regional Sch. Dist., 1990—; cons. U. Cons. on Edn., Jamesburg, N.J., 1981—; adj. prof. Sussex County Community Coll., Newton, N.J., 1982-90, Centenary Coll., Hackettstown, N.J., 1985—. Contbr. articles to profl. jours. Coach Byram (N.J.) Little League, 1990. N.J. Coun. on Edn. grantee, 1980. Mem. ASCD, Nat. Soc. for Study of Edn., Phi Delta Kappa. Office: Andover Regional Sch Dist 707 Limecrest Rd Newton NJ 07860-8801

PALM, FRANK RAYMOND, data processing executive; b. Palermo, N.J., Aug. 31, 1937; s. Cecil A. and Eleanor (Wolff) P.; m. Bevery J. Trowbridge, Oct. 4, 1956; children: Susan, Stephen, Gary, Ellen, Frances. MS in Bus. Policy, Columbia U., 1981. Profl. staff IBM, Owego, N.Y., 1956-62; mgr.

IBM, Huntsville, Ala., 1962-68; corp. staff mem. IBM, Armonk, N.Y., 1969-81; dir. info. systems IBM, White Plains, N.Y., 1982-84; dir. Sterling Forest (N.Y.) IBM, 1984-88; project exec. Eastman Kodak IBM, Rochester, N.Y., 1989-91; gen. mgr. systems solutions ctr. Integrated Systems Solutions Corp., Rochester, 1991—. Bd. mem. Orange County Mental Health, Goshen, N.Y., 1987, 88; campaign chair United Way, Orange County, Middletown, N.Y., 1988; bd. mem. Compeer, Rochester, 1991. Recipient Silver Bell award Orange County Mental Health, Goshen, 1990. Home: 4 Vineyard Hl Fairport NY 14450-4602 Office: IBM 1630 Long Pond Rd Rochester NY 14626-4196

PALM, WILLIAM JOHN, mechanical engineering educator; b. Balt., Mar. 1, 1944; s. William John Jr. and Lillian Mary (Hartmann) P.; m. Mary Louise Palm, Aug. 17, 1968; children: Aileen, William IV, Andrew. BS in Engring. Physics, Loyola Coll., Balt., 1966; PhD in Mech. Engring. and Astron. Sci., Northwestern U., 1971. Engr. Ballistic Rsch. Labs., Aberdeen, Md., 1966-67; prof. mech. engring. U. R.I., Kingston, 1971—, dir. Robotics Rsch. Ctr., 1985—; cons. Analysis and Tech. Inc., North Stonington, Conn., 1977—, Vitro Inc., Silver Spring, Md., 1989—. Author: Modeling, Analysis and Control of Dynamic Systems, 1983, Control Systems Engineering, 1986; patentee in field. Asst. cubmaster Boy Scouts Am., Kingston, 1986-89, asst. scoutmaster, 1989—. Mem. ASME, IEEE, AIAA, Tau Beta Pi, Pi Tau Sigma. Office: U RI Wales Hall Kingston RI 02881

PALMAS, ANGELO, clergyman; b. Villanova Monteleone, Italy, Dec. 21, 1914. Student, Pontifical Sem., Cuglieri, Italy; Doctorate in Theology, Pontifical Sem., Cuglieri, 1939; License in Philosophy, Gregorian U., Rome, 1942; Doctorate in Civil and Canon Law, Latran Pontifical U., Rome, 1946. Ordained priest Roman Cath. Ch., 1938, archbishop, 1964. Sec. Apostolic Nunciature, Belgium, 1947-52; auditor Apostolic Nunciature, Switzerland, 1952-54; auditor, counsellor Apostolic Nunciature, Lebanon, 1954-60; mem. Secretariat of State, Vatican, 1960-64; apostolic del. to Vietnam and Cambodia, 1964-69; apostolic Nuncio Colombia, 1969-75; apostolic Pro-Nuncio Ottawa, Can., 1975-90. Address: Via Accursio 8, 00165 Rome Italy

PALMER, ARNOLD DANIEL, professional golfer; b. Youngstown, Pa., Sept. 10, 1929; s. Milfred Jerome and Doris M. Palmer; m. Winnie Walzer, Dec. 20, 1954; children: Peggy Palmer Wears, Amy Palmer Saunders. Student, Wake Forest Coll., LLD, 1970. Profl. golfer, 1954—, businessman, entrepreneur, 1960—; pres. Arnold Palmer Enterprises; nat. spokesman Pennzoil Petroleum Products, Lanier Worldwide, Sears Roebuck, Rolex, Lofts Seed, Cadillac Motor Car, PaineWebber, GTE, Golf mag., Stouffer/Nestle; designer numerous golf courses. Author: Arnold Palmer's Golf Book, 1961, Portrait of a Professional Golfer, 1964, My Game and Yours, 1965, rev. edit., 1983, Situation Golf, 1970, Go for Broke, 1973, Arnold Palmer's Best 54 Holes of Golf, 1977, Arnold Palmer's Complete Book of Putting, 1986, Play Great Golf, 1987. With USCGR, 1951-54. Winner over 90 major golf tournaments, 1955— including Masters Championship, 1958, 60, 62, 64; recipient numerous golf awards including Bob Jones award U.S. Golf Assn., William D. Richardson award Golf Writers Assn. Am., Herb Graffis award Nat. Golf Found.; named Athlete of Decade AP, 1969, Sportsman of Yr. Sports Illustrated mag., 1960, Player of Yr. Profl. Golfers Assn., 1960, 62; Profl. Golfers Assn. Tour Money Leader, 1958, 60, 62, 63; elected to World Golf Hall of Fame, Profl. Golfers Assn. Hall of Fame. Clubs: Latrobe (Pa.) Country; Laurel Valley Golf, Rolling Rock (Ligonier, Pa.); Bay Hill, Isleworth (Orlando, Fla.); Duquesne (Pitts.). Home and Office: PO Box 52 Youngstown PA 15696-0052

PALMER, BARBARA HESLAN, university registrar, director institutional research; b. Utica, N.Y., Feb. 21, 1945; d. Theodore Lewis and Rosemary (Callahan) P.; m. Peter Colin Jordan, Oct. 13, 1979. BA, Elmira Coll., 1967; MA, Syracuse U., 1969; PhD, Boston Coll., 1980. Asst. dean of women Oberlin (Ohio) Coll., 1969-72; asst. dean of students Brandeis U., Waltham, Mass., 1972-73, asst. dean of coll., 1973-76, assoc. dean of coll., 1976-85, dir. instnl. rsch., registrar, 1985—. Am. Coun. Edn. grantee, 1984—. Mem. Am. Assn. Higher Edn., History of Edn. Soc., Assn. Instnl. Rsch., Am. Assn. Collegiate Registrars and Admissions Officers, Pi Lambda Theta. Office: Brandeis U PO Box 9110 Waltham MA 02254-9110

PALMER, DAVID RANDOLPH, securities trader; b. Wheeling, W.Va., May 7, 1961; s. Randolph Edwards and Carolyn (Denton) P.; m. Debra Ann Ehrlich, May 11, 1991. Student, Stern Sch. Bus., N.Y.C., 1988-92. Securities specialist Spear Leeds & Kellogg, N.Y.C., 1989-91; securities trader GBI Securities, N.Y.C., 1991—. Bd. dirs. Adult Returning Students, NYU, 1989-91. Recipient Chancellor's award NYU, 1990. Mem. Am. Stock Exch. Republican. Baptist. Home: 619 Coleman Pl Westfield NJ 07090

PALMER, DOUGLAS H., mayor; b. Trenton, N.J., Oct. 19, 1951; s. George H. and Dorothy (Vaughn) P. BS, Hampton U., 1973. With C.V. Hill Co., Trenton; civil svc. worker N.J. Dept. Motor Vehicles, Trenton; dir. Community Schs. Trenton; asst. dir. Trenton Bd. Edn., dir. purchasing; small bus. owner Trenton; mayor City of Trenton. Bd. dirs. ARC, Urban League Met. Trenton, Forum Project, Rider Coll. Ednl. Opportunity Fund Program, We, Inc., Carver Ctr., NAACP, treas.; freeholder Dem. Party Mercer County, 1981-91; mgr. West End Little League, Trenton, 1965-75, treas., 1975—. Named Outstanding Young Man Am., Del. Valley United Way Bd.; recipient Fai Ho Cha award Omega Psi Phi. Baptist. Home: 284 Spring St Trenton NJ 08618 Office: 319 E State St Trenton NJ 08608

PALMER, JOHN ANTHONY, III, modern language and music educator; b. Worcester, Mass., May 18, 1955; s. John Jr. and Barbara (Dufresne) P. BA in Spanish, Worcester State Coll., 1977, MEd in Ednl. Adminstrn., 1988. Cert. Spanish, French, German and music tchr., Mass. Tchr., head dept. fgn. langs. Mahar Regional Sch., Orange, Mass., 1979-88; adj. prof. Spanish, Worcester State Coll., 1988-90, Fla. Atlantic U., 1991—; instr. voice Worcester Poly. Inst., 1979-81; cantor Ch. of St. Peter, 1977-81, Worcester Eglise Notre Dame des Canadiens, Worcester, 1981-83; adjudicator vocal auditions All-State Music Educators Conf., 1988. Tenor soloist Regis Coll., Boston, Worcester Poly. Inst., Worcester Chorus, Salisbury Singers, Simmons Coll., Boston, Ft. Lauderdale Opera Co. Mem. ASCD, Am. Coun. Tchrs. Fgn. Langs., Nat. Assn. Secondary Sch. Prins., Mass. Assn. Sch. Supts., Mass. Fgn. Lang. Assn., Sigma Delta Pi. Democrat. Roman Catholic. Home: 121 Bailey St Worcester MA 01602

PALMER, KAREN FEDER, psychotherapist; b. N.Y.C., Sept. 12, 1946; d. Sidney and Miriam (Mendeloff) Feder; m. William C. Palmer, June 3, 1978. MSW, Fordham U., 1977. Cert. social worker, N.Y., hypnotherapist. Social worker Bur. Child Welfare, N.Y.C. Dept. Social Svcs., 1968-78; psychotherapist, hypnotherapist Associated Consultation Ctr., N.Y.C., 1978-80; pvt. practice psychotherapy, hypnotherapy N.Y.C., 1980—; tchr. workshops in field; pres. Bogie's Mystery Tours, 1983—. Co-author: Martial Art Movies, 1985, Caribbean Blues, 1988; contbr. articles and columns to profl. publs. Tchr. YMCA, N.Y.C., 1983. Mem. NASW, Mystery Writers Am., Pvt. Eye Writers Am., Am. Crime Writers League.

PALMER, KRISTINE MARGARET, elementary school counselor; b. Wilmington, Del., Apr. 19, 1963; d. Robert Lewis and Rosemary Ann (Piazza) Phillips; m. G. Gregory Palmer, Nov. 2, 1991. BS, Elizabethtown Coll., 1985; MEd, West Chester U., 1990. Cert. sch. counselor, Pa. Psychiat. technician Rockford Ctr., Wilmington, Del., 1985-87; mental health assoc. Meadowwood Hosp., New Castle, Del., 1987-88; sch. counselor Avon Grove Elem. Sch., West Grove, Pa., 1991—. Mem. AACD, Am. Sch. Counselor's Assn., Assn. Specialists in Group Work, Pa. Sch. Counselors Assn., Phi Delta Kappa, Kappa Delta Phi. Office: Avon Grove Elem 110 State Rd West Grove PA 19390-8944

PALMER, LAURENCE CLIVE, electrical engineer; b. Washington, Dec. 25, 1932; s. Clive W. and Mary Virginia (Vanderau) P.; m. Diane Doris Henderson, Feb. 13, 1956; children: Steve C., Valerie. BS, Washington & Lee U., 1955; BEE, Rensselaer Poly. Inst., 1955; MS, U. Md., 1963, PhD, 1970. Dept. dir. Radcom-Emertron div. Litton Systems, Silver Spring, Md., 1957-63; sr. scientist Computer Scis. Corp., Falls Church, Va., 1963-74; prin. scientist Comsat Labs., Communications Satellite Corp., Clarksburg, Md., 1974-90; adv. engr. Hughes Network Systems, Germantown, Md., 1990—. 1st lt. U.S. Army, 1955-57. Mem. IEEE (sr.). Home: 17 River Falls Ct Potomac MD 20854

PALMER, LUCIE MACKAY, artist, lecturer; b. St. Louis, May 23, 1913; d. George Castleman and Suzanne Benton (Cable) Mackay; m. Vincent Palmer, Sept. 2, 1939; 1 child, Lucie. Student, Washington U., St. Louis, 1934-35, Sch. of Mus. of Fine Arts, Boston, 1936-37, Art Students League, N.Y.C., 1938-39. Staff artist ichthyological and anthrop. expdns. to Sulu Sea, South Philippines, Caribbean, Pacific Coast Mex. Exhibited in spl. group show for Pres. of Mex. Recipient Gov.'s award for best landscape Morelos State Art Exhibit, Mex. Mem. Nat. Assn. Women Artists and Sculptors (Cooper prize), St. Louis Artists' Guild, Soc. Women Geographers, N.H. Art Assn. Home: 31 Atlantic Ave North Hampton NH 03862

PALMER, PAUL RICHARD, librarian, archivist; b. Cin., Jan. 21, 1917; s. Gardiner O. and Sarah Ellen (Christy) P. BA, U. Cin., 1949; MS, Columbia U., 1950, MA, 1955. Asst. br. libr. Bklyn. Pub. Library, 1950-51; libr. Columbia U., N.Y.C., 1951-67, libr. sch. libr. svc., 1968, libr. and curator Brander Matthews Dramatic Mus., 1969-73, bibliographer Avery Archtl. Libr., 1974, curator Columbiana Collection, 1974—; cons. Am. Libr. Assn., Chgo. and N.Y.C., 1954-59. Contbr. articles to profl. jurs. With U.S. Army, 1942-45, ETO and NATOUSA. Mem. Theatre Libr. Assn. (exec. coun. 1970-74), Am. Mus. Britain, French Inst., Soc. Hist Preservation, Lincoln Ctr. Film Soc., Manuscript Soc., Church Club of N.Y., Phi Beta Kappa. Episcopalian. Home: 560 Riverside Dr New York NY 10027-3202

PALMER, RONALD EUGENE, military officer; b. Elkins, W.Va., Mar. 29, 1952; s. Smith and Eva Pauline (Ogas) P.; m. Sue Ann Carpenter, June 24, 1972; children: Brian, Brandon, Brent, Brett. AA, Brigham Young U., 1975, BS, 1976; M Health Svc., George Washington U., 1983; MEd, U. So. Miss., 1988. Commd. 2d lt. USAF, 1982, advanced through grades to capt., 1986, dir. patient affairs various hosps., 1983-87; comdr. med. squadron USAF, Kessler AFB, Miss., 1987-88; quality assurance program mgr. Office of Surgeon Gen., Bolling AFB, D.C., 1988—. Rep. precinct mgr., Alexandria, Va., 1978; Sunday sch. pres. Ch. of Jesus Christ of Latter-day Saints, Bowie, Md., 1988, exec. sec., 1989—; cub master Bowie area Boy Scouts Am., 1990—. Home: 12105 Wilmont Turn Bowie MD 20715-1231 Office: USAF Office Surgeon Gen Bolling AFB DC 20332

PALMER, STEVEN WILLIAM, marketing executive; b. Worcester, Mass., Aug. 28, 1950; s. William R. and Eleanor E. (Sivula) P.; m. Judith Elizabeth Burke, June 24, 1972; children: Michael, Kevin. BA in Econs., Va. Mil. Inst., 1972; MBA, Harvard U., 1978. Fin. analyst Norton Co., Worcester, 1978-80; nat. sales mgr. Wood-Tek of Gardner, Mass., 1980-81; product mgr. Webster Industries, Peabody, Mass., 1982; dir. mtkg. info. EG&G Sealol, Cranston, R.I., 1983-87; v.p. mktg. div. Cumberland Engring., South Attleboro, Mass., 1988—. Mem. Fin. Com., Littleton, Mass., 1988—. 1st lt. U.S. Army, 1972-76. Republican. Office: Comberland Engr PO Box 6065 Providence RI 02940-6065

PALMER, STUART HUNTER, educational administrator, sociology educator; b. N.Y.C., Apr. 29, 1924; s. Herman G. and Beatrice (Hunter) P.; m. Anne Barbara Scarborough, June 22, 1946; 1 dau., Catherine. B.A., Yale U., 1949, M.A., 1951, Ph.D., 1955. Asst. to dean Yale Coll., New Haven, 1949-51; instr. sociology New Haven Coll., 1949-51, 53-55; faculty U. N.H., Durham, 1955—; prof. U. N.H., 1964—, chmn. dept. sociology and anthropology, 1964-69, 79-82, dean Coll. Liberal Arts, 1982—; disting. vis. prof. SUNY, Albany, 1970-71; vis. behavioral scientist N.H. Div. Mental Health; vis. prof. U. Sussex, Eng., 1976, U. Ga., 1977; cons. U.S. Office Edn., USPHS, U.S. Office Delinquency and Youth Devel., Dept. Justice; mem. adv. com. for sociology Com. on Internat. Exchange of Persons; mem. exec. com. N.H. Gov.'s Commn. on Crime and Delinquency; co-chmn. Internat. Symposium on Univs. in Twenty-First Century; co-chmn. Internat. Confs. on Stress Rsch., Nat. Commn. Arts and Scis. Author: Understanding Other People, 1955, A Study of Murder, 1960, (with Brian R. Kay) The Challenge of Supervision, 1961, Deviance and Conformity, 1970, (with Arnold S. Linsky) Rebellion and Retreat, 1972, The Violent Society, 1972, The Prevention of Crime, 1973, (with John A. Humphrey) Deviant Behavior, 1980, Role Stress, 1981, Deviant Behavior: Patterns, Sources, and Controls, 1990; also articles. Chmn. bd. trustees Daniel Webster Coll., New Eng. Aero. Inst. Served to lt. AC AUS, 1942-45; Served to lt. AC USAF, 1951-53. Decorated Air medal with 3 oak leaf clusters; Henry Page fellow, 1953-55. Mem. Am. Sociol. Assn., Eastern Sociol. Soc., Internat. Sociol. Soc., Internat. Soc. Criminology, Internat. Soc. Forecasters, Am. Assn. Colls., Council for Liberal Learning, Am. Assn. Higher Edn., Council Colls. Arts and Scis., Nat. Assn. State Univs. and Land-Grant Colls., AAAS, Am. Acad. Polit. and Social Scis., N.Y. Acad. Scis., Am. Assn. Suicidology, Soc. Cross-Cultural Research, Am. Soc. Criminology, Assn. Gov. Bds. Univs. and Colls., Phi Beta Kappa (hon.), Sigma Xi, Alpha Kappa Delta. Home: Riverview Dr Durham NH 03824-3304 Office: U NH Coll Liberal Arts Murkland Hall Durham NH 03824

PALMER, THOMAS HOWARD, JR., retired surgeon; b. Cambridge, Mass., Apr. 19, 1924; s. Thomas Howard and Elizabeth Agnes (Higgins) P.; m. Mary Ellen Herlihy, Feb. 20, 1954; children: Thomas H. III, Edward H., Anne M., David A., James L. Student, Harvard U., 1942-44; MD, Tufts U., 1948. Cert. Am. Bd. Surgery. Intern City Hosp., Boston, 1948-49; resident surgery New Eng. Med. Ctr., Boston, 1949-50, 52-55; staff surgeon Ea. Maine Med. Ctr., Bangor, 1955-89; staff surgeon St. Joseph Hosp., Bangor, 1955-89, chief of surgery, 1967-74, 80-85; med. staff pres. Ea. Maine Med. Ctr., Bangor, 1973-75; dir. Ea. Maint Healthcare, Bangor, 1982—; bd. mem. Maine Peer Rev. Bd. (Med.), Bangor, 1988-89. Contbr. articles to med. jours. Trustee Ea. Maine Med. Ctr., Bangor, 1982-89. Lt. USN, 1943-45, 50-52, Korea. Henry B. Humphrey scholar Harvard U., 1942; Charlton Rsch. fellow Tufts U. Med. Sch., 1950; recipient Disting. Svc. award Ea. Maine Healthcare, 1957. Fellow ACS (pres. Maine chpt. 1969-70); mem. New Eng. Surg. Soc., Maine Med. Assn., Penobscot Med. Soc., AMA. Roman Catholic. Home: 332 Garland St Bangor ME 04401

PALMER, WAYNE LEWIS, television director; b. Camden, N.J., Jan. 24, 1949; s. Paul John and Edna L. (Mitten) P.; m. Nicola E. Williams; 1 child, Shawn Mireille. BS cum laude, Ithaca Coll., 1971. Engr. Sta. WFIL-TV, Phila., 1968-71, Sta. WHYY-TV, Phila., 1971-72, ABC-TV, N.Y.C., 1972-73; engr. Sta. WNET-TV, N.Y.C., 1973-79, assoc. dir., 1979—; assoc. dir. Dick Cavett Show, Bill Moyer's Journal, 1979-82; dir. MacNeil/Lehrer Newshour, N.Y.C., 1990—. Photography exhbns. Trenton (N.J.) City Mus., 1989, Abington Art Ctr., Phila., 1989, The Armory, Phila., 1990, Oakland (Calif.) Mus., 1990; permanent collection Mus. of City of N.Y. Judge ACE Cable Awards, N.Y.C., 1986. Recipient Graphic and Design award Nat. Assn. Ednl. Broadcasters, 1980. Mem. Dirs. Guild Am. Home: 23 W 73d St New York NY 10023 Office: Sta WNET-TV 356 W 58th St New York NY 10019-1804

PALMIERI, ALAIN JOHN VERRON, real estate developer, environmental products manufacturer, consultant; b. N.Y.C., Oct. 27, 1941; s. Edmund Louis and Claude Cecile (Verron) P.; m. Ragnhild Rolfe Schmidt, July 30, 1965 (div. Dec. 1982); children: Alexis, Serena; m. Georgia Wood McEwan, June 5, 1983; 1 child, Stafford. BSLL, Georgetown U., 1965; diploma, cert., U. Grenoble, 1959; diploma, U. Sacro Cuore, Rome, 1964; postgrad. in bus., NYU, 1967-68. Area mgr. for Latin Am., Nabisco, Inc., Internat., N.Y.C., 1969-70; dir. exports Nabisco, Inc. Europe, Brussels, 1970-74; dir. market devel. Nabisco Protein Foods Internat., Brussels, 1974-76, dir. for Europe, 1976-78; mng. dir. Partridge Farms, Ltd., London, 1977-78; mng. ptnr. Devpro Internat. N.V., Burssels, The Hague and, London, 1978-84; gen. ptnr. 114-153 Assocs., Brooklyn Heights, N.Y., 1984—, GPA Indsl. Properties, N.Y.C., 1985—; mng. dir. Montague-Henry Corp., Brooklyn Heights, 1985—; cons., bd. dirs. Reynolds, Cooper-Smith & Co. Ltd., Brighton, Eng., 1982-84; cons. Thermaljet Ltd. div. Grow Group, Louisville, 1983-84; sec., treas. Primary Residence Investigations, Inc., N.Y.C., 1986—; founder, chief exec. officer Environ. Venture Products, 1991, Mr. Filter, Inc., 1991; co-founder fusion adv. coun. Giuliani, adv. coun. New ERA Dems., adv. coun. Cong. Italian-Am. Orgns. Inventor co-extrusion of red meat. Adv. me. U.S.-Yugoslav Econ. Coun., 1977-78; advisor common agrl. policy European Econ. Community, Brussels, Chocolate, Biscuit and Confectionary Coun. of European Community, Brussels, 1973-76; treas. 114-153 Owners Corp., 1986-. Mem. Bklyn. C. of C. (legis. com., chmn. internat. trade com.), Knickerbocker Club. Republican. Episcopalian. Home: 160 E 84th St Apt 20-21D New York NY 10028 also: 9 Robin Brae Dr Warwick NY 10990 Office: MR Filter Environ Products PO Box 22 Gracie Sta New York NY 10028-0022

PALMOSINA, MICHAEL FRANCIS, II, technical service representative; b. Pitts., Nov. 3, 1957; s. Michael Francis and Constance Marie (Perry) P.; m. Mary Beth Pisarski, Oct. 13, 1979; children: Sara Hlynn, Erin Michaliny, Michael Francis III. Cert. completion, Parkway West Area Vocat. Tech., Pitts., 1975; BS in Adminstrn. & Mgmt. magna cum laude, LaRoche Coll., 1992. Quality assurance tech. Calgon Copr., Pitts., 1976-86; application devel. tech. Miles, Inc., Pitts., 1986-92, tech. svc. rep., 1992—. Roman Catholic. Home: 1616 Foote St Conway PA 15027-1242 Office: Miles Inc Mobay Rd Pittsburgh PA 15205-9741

PALTOS, ROBERT N., sales executive; b. Bklyn.; s. Stephen and Olga (St. John) P.; m. Mary Katherine Brigleb, May, 1971; 1 child, Scott Christopher. BA, St. John's U., 1966; MA, NYU, 1968. Market rsch. mgr. Simmons-Boardman, N.Y.C., 1966-70; with nat. sales div. N.Y. Times, N.Y.C., 1970-76; with U.S. sales div. The IHT, N.Y.C. and Paris, 1976-77; account exec. Doremus & Co., N.Y.C., 1977-79; nat. account mgr. AT&T, N.Y.C., 1979-84; regional v.p. sales div. WU Corp., N.Y.C., 1984-88; nat. sales mgr. Prodigy, N.Y.C., 1988—. Bd. dirs. Ramsey (N.J.) Bd. of Edn., 1987—. Mem. Am. Mktg. Assn., Am. Mgmt. Assn. Episcopalian.

PALTROWITZ, STUART MARSHALL, writer; b. Bklyn., Jan. 31, 1946; s. Maurice and Alice (Faden) P.; m. Donna Milman, Aug. 29, 1971; children: Adam, Darren. BA, Hofstra U., 1967; MS, L.I. U., 1976. Author: Animal Soup, 1980, Do You Know Your Boss?, 1983, Robotics, 1983, Time, Strings and Pizzas, 1984, The Springboard Series, 1987, The Bargain Hunter's Guide to Investing in Real Estate, 1991; (book series) The I Hate to Read Series, 1975; (software) Mystery and Adventure Computer Storybook, 1983, Science Fiction Computer Storybook, 1983, The Key Phonics Series, 1985, Mystery Mazes, 1984-86, Computer Crossroads, 1987, Whole Control Express, 1992; (video series) Work World, 1978-89. Recipient Hon. Mention for Song Music City News Song Festival, Nashville, 1984, Mystery Mazes award Portfolio Winner Media and Methods Mag., 1986. Office: 2971 Lee Pl Bellmore NY 11710-5033

PALUMBO, BENJAMIN LEWIS, public affairs consulting company executive; b. Boston, Mar. 4, 1937; s. Guido Americo and Stella Marie (Lombardo) P.; m. Magdalene Julia Palinczar, Nov. 18, 1961; children: Matthew, Jason, Guy. BA, Rutgers U., 1959, MA, 1961. Adminstrv. asst. to Gov. Richard J. Hughes, N.J., 1963-65; dir. rsch. N.J. Dem. Com., Trenton, 1965-66; asst. to commr. N.J. Dept. Transp., Trenton, 1966-70; asst. dean Woodrow Wilsonn Sch., Princeton (N.J.) U., 1970-71; adminstrv. asst. to Senator Harrison Williams, U.S. Senate, Washington, 1971-73, staff dir. Dem. caucus, 1975-77, subcom. on govt. activities and transp., 1977-78; nat. campaign dir. Bentsen for Pres., Washington, 1973-75; dir. fed. govt. rels. Phillip Morris, Inc., Washington, 1978-83; pres. Palumbo & Cerrell, Inc., Washington, 1983—; mem. adv. coun. Inst. Politics, U. So. Calif., L.A., 1978—, Sch. Advanced Internat. Studies, Johns Hopkins U., Bologna, Italy, 1986—. Bd. dirs. Samaritans Washington, 1986—. Mem. Nat. Press Club, Rutgers Club Washington (chmn. bd. dirs. 1990—), Nat. Dem. Club. Democrat. Roman Catholic. Office: Palumbo & Cerrell Inc 1000 Connecticut Ave NW Ste 706 Washington DC 20036-5302

PALUMBO, DOMINIC JOSEPH, aerospace engineer, educator, consultant; b. N.Y.C., Mar. 24, 1945; s. Dominic Patrick and Marie (Tifuri) P.; m. Mary Ann Valenzano, June 3, 1967; children: Christopher, Paul, Dominic. BS in Aerospace Engring., Poly. Inst. Bklyn., 1966, MS in Astronautics, 1967, PhD Aeros.-Astronautics, 1970. Rsch. engr. Fairchild Republic Co., Farmingdale, N.Y., 1974-85, group leader, 1974-75; program mgr. aircraft systems div. Grumman Corp., Bethpage, N.Y., 1985-88, dep. dir., 1988-89; prin. design engr. AAI Corp., Hunt Valley, Md., 1989-91, sect. head systems engring., 1991—; adj. prof. N.Y. Inst. Tech., Westbury, N.Y., 1974—; cons. various aerospace cos., 1983—. Mem. AIAA, Assn. for Unmanned Vehicle Systems, Aeromasters club (pres. 1975-76). Home: 1103 Dulaney Gate Cir Cockeysville Hunt Valley MD 21030-3027 Office: AAI Corp Hunt Valley MD 20000

PALUMBO, DONALD EMANUEL, English educator, department head; b. Pitts., Jan. 17, 1949; s. Emanuel John and Florence Marie (Orlando) P.; m. Joan Reisman, Apr. 30, 1972 (div. 1976); m. Julie Marie Bell, Dec. 30, 1978 (div. 1990); children: anthony D., David Vincent; m. Susan Elizabeth Conshue, May 9, 1992. AB, U. Chgo., 1970; MA, U. Mich., 1971, PhD, 1976. Teaching fellow U. Mich., Ann Arbor, 1971-75; instr. Lamar U., Beaumont, Tex., 1976-78; assoc. prof. No. Mich. U., Marquette, 1978-83; div. head Lorain County Community Coll., Elyria, Ohio, 1983-87; dept. chair Shippensburg (Pa.) U., 1987-92, East Carolina U., N.C., 1992—. Editor: Spectrum of the Fantastic, 1988, Eros in the Mind's Eye, 1986, Erotic Universe, 1986. Mem. Internat. Assn. for Fantastic in Arts (pres. 1989—, treas. 1983-89), Popular Culture Assn. (film area chair 1991—, comics area chair 1980-91). Office: Shippensburg U Shippensburg PA 17257

PALUMBO, JAMES FREDRICK, insurance company executive; b. Everett, Mass., Nov. 30, 1950; s. Bruno James and Lillian Elizabeth (Picardi) P.; m. Nancy Laurie Richards, July 24, 1976; children: Elizabeth Richards, Andrew Reid, Alexander Thomas. BA, Lake Forest Coll., 1973; MBA, Washington U., 1975. Market surveillance analyst Nat. Assn. of Securities Dealers, Washington, 1975-76, asst. treas., 1976-78; regional rep. Student Loan Mktg. Assn., Washington, 1978-79, mgr., 1979-81, dir., 1981-82, asst. v.p., 1982-83, v.p., 1983-87; sr. v.p. Sallie Mae Mgmt. Svcs. Corp., Coll. Constrn. Loan Ins. Assn., Washington, 1987—; participant Govt.-Univ.-Industry Rsch. Roundtable, Washington, 1986. Actor popular and children's theater, 1973-76. Chmn. sports announcers com., D.C. Spl. Olympics, Washington, 1986, 87, D.C. Regional Counsel, Lake Forest Coll., Washington, 1976-80; mem. Elliott Soc. mem. com. Washington U., 1986—, Great Falls (Va.) Hist. Soc.; bd. govs. Lake Forest Coll., 1978-82. Mem. Soc. Coll. and Univ. Planners, Great Falls Swim and Tennis Club (bd. dirs. 1988-91), Alpha Psi Omega. Office: Coll Constrn Loan Ins Assn 2445 M NW Ste 450 Washington DC 20036

PAMPEL, JOSEPH PHILIP STEVENSON, investment executive; b. Findlay, Ohio, Feb. 11, 1932; s. William Sumner and Helen (Stevenson) P.; m. Georgia Anne Hertzman, June 23, 1963; children: Joseph P.S. Jr., Martha Anne. BS in Chem. Engring., Case Inst. Tech., 1954; MBA in Prodn., Fin., Harvard U., 1960. Various banking and investment positions, 1961-79; group controller Charterhouse Group Internat., Inc., N.Y.C., 1979-81; v.p. fin. Charterhouse Group Internat., Inc., 1981-82, v.p., treas. to v.p. banking and investment mgmt., 1982-87; owner, chief exec. J.P. Pampel & Co., N.Y.C., 1987-89; founder, dir. Carpenter Enterprises Ltd., Fenton, Mich., 1987-89; treas. Charterhouse Automotive, N.Y.C., 1987—, Tex. Tech Industries Inc., N. Monmouth, Maine, 1988—; ptnr. Wier & Pampel, Inc., N.Y.C., 1989—; bd. dirs. Charterhouse Automotive, N.Y.C., Carpenter Enterprises, Ltd., Fenton.; tchr. cost acct. grad. bus. sch. Stevens Inst. Tech.; chmn. bd., treas. Blair Industries, Inc., Scott City, Mo., 1987—. Pres., alumni adminstr. Case Inst. Tech., N.Y.C.; past pres. Case Western Res. Alumni in Greater Metro Area, N.Y.C. Lt. (j.g.) USNR, 1954-58. Mem. Harvard Club, Queeche Country Club. Office: Wier & Pampel Inc 780 3rd Ave New York NY 10017-2024

PAN, HENRY YUE-MING, clinical pharmacologist; b. Shanghai, China, Dec. 27, 1946; came to U.S. 1969; s. Chia-Liu and Siu-Ging (Sung) P.; m. Mary Agnes Tse; children: Lincoln Jonathan, Gregory Kingsley. BSc (hon.), McGill U., Montreal, 1969; MS in Toxicology, U. Hawaii, 1973, PhD in Pharmacology, 1974; MD, U. Hong Kong, 1979. Rsch. asst. U. Hawaii, Honolulu, 1969-74, teaching asst., 1970-74; med. officer Queen Mary Hosp., Hong Kong, 1979-81; asst. prof. medicine U. Hong Kong, 1981-85; vis. asst. prof. Stanford (Calif.) U., 1983-85; asst. clin. pharmacology dir. Squibb Inst. Med. Rsch., Princeton, N.J., 1985-87, assoc. clin. pharmacology dir., 1987-88, clin. pharmacology dir., 1988-89, exec. dir. clin. rsch., 1989-91; v.p. clin. rsch. Bristol-Myers Squibb Pharm. Rsch. Inst., Princeton, 1991-92, Du Pont Merck Pharm. Co., Wilmington, Del., 1992—. Contbr. articles to profl. jours. Stanford Asian Med. Fund grantee, 1983-85. Fellow Am. Coll. Clin. Pharmacology, Am. Heart Assn. Coun.; mem. AAAS, Am. Soc. Clin.

Pharmacology and Therapeutics, Am. Soc. for Pharmacology and Exptl. Therapeutics, Am. Fedn. Clin. Rsch., Am. Heart Assn. Roman Catholic. Office: Du Pont Merck Pharm Co PO Box 80026 Wilmington DE 19880-0026

PAN, MARIA WEIYEI, company executive; b. Beijing, China, June 19, 1943; came to U.S., 1965; d. Po Han Liu and Lillian Shufen Lee; m. Ko-chang Casey Pan, Sept. 21, 1968; 1 child, Julie Marie. BSBA, Nat. Taiwan U., Tapei, Taiwan, Republic of China, 1965; MS in Math. Stats., U. Iowa, 1967. Biostatician U. Iowa, Iowa City, 1967-69; mathematician Modern Woodmen of Am., Rock Island, Ill., 1969-73; real esate agent Nelson Realty, Davenport, Iowa, 1974-77; math. U.S. Army, Picatinny Arsenal, N.J., 1978-83; dir. Bus. Plus Corp., N.Y.C., 1989—; real estate agent New Century Assocs.,, East Hanover, N.J., 1983—; dir. LPC Corp., Alhambra, Calif., 1987—; v.p. Handsome Enterprises of N.Y., N.Y.C., 1980—; pres. BusinessPlus Corp. of N.J., Pine Brook, 1990—. Mem. NAFE, Am. Def. Preparedness Assn., Nat. Shoe Travelers Assn., N.J. Assn. Women Bus. Owners, Nat. Contract Mgmt. Assn. Republican. Office: BusinessPlus Corp NJ PO Box 398 Pine Brook NJ 07058-0398

PANAGARIYA, ARVIND, economics educator; b. Jaipur, Rajasthan, India, Sept. 30, 1952; s. Baloo Lal and Mohan (Golecha) P.; m. Amita Somani, Jan. 17, 1981; children: Ananth, Ajay. BA, Rajasthau Coll., India, 1971; MA, U. Rajasthan, 1973; PhD, Princeton U., 1978. Asst. prof. econs. U. Md., College Park, 1978-83, assoc. prof. econs., 1983-89, prof. econs., 1989—; sr. economist World Bank, Washington, 1989—. Contbr. articles to profl. jours. Mem. Am. Econ. Assn. Jain Religion. Home: 309 Eisner St Silver Spring MD 20901-1740 Office: U Md Dept Econs College Park MD 20742

PANAGOULIS, ELIZABETH DOROTHY, psychotherapist, consultant; b. Winthrop, Mass., Aug. 14, 1948; d. Stephen Kenneth and Gilda Ann (Cirace) Piccolo; m. K. Thomas Panagoulis, May 2, 1971; children: Nietra, Kadin. BA, Rivier Coll., 1970, MEd, 1982. Cert. clin. mental health counselor; nat. cert. counselor. Social worker Whidden Meml. Hosp., Everett, Mass., 1970-71; psychotherapist Cath. Charities, Nashua, N.H., 1982-86, Hitchcock Clinic, Nashua, 1986-90, The Counseling Ctr. Nashua, 1990—; exec. bd. mem. Network, Nashua, 1987—; group facilitator oncology-palliative care unit St. Joseph's Hosp., Nashua, 1990—. Mem. AACD, Am. Mental Health Counselors Assn., Am. Orthopsychiat. Assn., N.H. Mental Health Counselors Assn. (sec. 1989), N.H. Assn. Counseling and Devel. Network (exec. bd.). Home: 21 Winchester Dr Hollis NH 03049-5914 Office: The Counseling Ctr Nashua Nashua NH 03060

PANDICK, THOMAS O'DONNELL, state official, lawyer; b. Delhi, N.Y., Jan. 27, 1947; s. Andrew Lawrence and Margaret Catherine (Leal) P.; m. Deborah Pegg, Oct. 22, 1983; children: Kristin Erin, Katherine Margaret. BS, Ithaca Coll., 1969; JD, Union U., 1972. Bar: N.Y. 1973. Atty. Employee Retirement System State of N.Y., Albany, 1973-76, asst. counsel, 1976-79, counsel, 1979-85, dir. investor affairs Ofice State Compt., 1985--. Mem. Nat. Assn. Pub. Pension Attys. (chmn. shareholder rights com.), Boot Group. Presbyterian.

PANDIT, VINAY YESHWANT, business educator; b. Bombay, Dec. 28, 1943; came to U.S., 1969; s. Yeshwant Sakharam and Kusum (Barave) P.; m. Rajashree A. Agharkar, Aug. 16, 1980; children: Ungira, Meghana. BTech, Indian Inst. Technology, Bombay, 1967; MSc, King's Coll., London, 1969; MBA, Columbia U., 1971, M in Philosophy, 1975, PhD, 1978. Cert. Mgmt. Acct. Reader Columbia U., N.Y.C., 1975; asst. prof. SUNY, Fredonia, 1976-77, assoc. prof., 1981-83; asst. prof. SUNY, Buffalo, 1977-81; assoc. prof. St. Bonaventure (N.Y.) U., 1983-89, chmn. faculty senate, 1988-91; prof., chmn. of mktg. and mgmt. sci. St. Bonaventure U., N.Y.C., 1989—; cons. in field. Contbr. articles to profl. jours. Recipient Merck Sharp and Dome award, 1968, 69, Dorab Tata Travel Grant, 1967, British Ministry Technology Fellow, 1969, Columbia U. doctoral scholar, 1971-75, Kennecott Copper Fellow, 1970-71. Fellow Acad. Mktg. Sci. (award for paper 1984); mem. Decision Scis. Inst., Inst. Mgmt. Acctg., Inst. Mgmt. Sci. Office: St Bonaventure U Sch Bus Saint Bonaventure NY 14778

PANDOLFE, WILLIAM DAVID, physical chemist; b. Hartford, Conn., Nov. 5, 1945; s. John and Helen (Bell) P.; m. Elaine Ruth Dyson, Sept. 11, 1976; children: Elizabeth, Lauren. BS in Chemistry, Coll. of the Holy Cross, 1967; MS In Phys. Chemistry, Rutgers U., 1971, PhD in Phys. Chemistry, 1974. Rsch. mgr. APV Gaulin Inc., Wilmington, Mass., 1974—. Contbr. articles to sci. jours. Sgt. U.S. Army, 1968-70. Mem. Am. Chem. Soc., Inst. Food Tech. (profl.). Roman Catholic. Office: APV Gaulin Inc 500 Research Dr Wilmington MA 01887-4400

PANDOLFINI, THOMAS JOSEPH, JR., mathematics and history educator; b. Providence, Dec. 9, 1961; s. Thomas Joseph Sr. and Carolyn Rose (Borkowski) P. BA in Math. and History with honors, R.I. Coll., 1983, MA in History, 1985, MA in Math., 1986. Instr. math. and history R.I. Coll., Providence, 1983—, New Eng. Inst. Tech., Warwick, R.I., 1988-90. Mem. Am. Hist. Assn., New Eng. Hist. Assn., Pi Mu Epsilon, Phi Alpha Theta. Office: RI Coll Mt Pleasant Ave Providence RI 02908-5121

PANES, PAUL BENJAMIN, educational psychologist; b. N.Y.C., June 18, 1928; s. Max and Sophie (Levine) P.; m. Hannah Gross, Oct. 29, 1955; children: Jonathan, Susan. BA, Bklyn. Coll., 1950, MA, 1951; EdD, NYU, 1968. Instr. Reading Inst., NYU, N.Y.C., 1957-61, dir., 1961-68; chmn. dept. basic skills Queensborough Community Coll., N.Y.C., 1968—. Author: Reading the Textbook, 1972, Reading Well in College, 1986; contbr. articles to ednl. jours. With M.I., U.S. Army, 1951-54, Korea. Office: Queensborough Community Coll Bayside NY 11364

PANETH, DONALD J., editor, writer; b. N.Y.C., Feb. 28, 1927; s. Irving and Maud (Kramer) P.; m. Elma Olans, Apr. 10, 1949 (dec. 1987); children: Thea, Ira. BBA, CCNY, 1948; postgrad., Columbia U., 1949-50. Reporter N.Y. Times, 1947-49; free-lance journalist N.Y.C., 1950-56, 73-75, 77-83; rewriteman Daily Mirror, N.Y.C., 1956-63; copy editor The Morning Telegraph, N.Y.C., 1964-65; staff writer Med. Tribune, N.Y.C., 1966-72; copy editor L.I. Press, Queens, N.Y., 1975-77; editor, writer Yearbook of the UN, N.Y.C., 1986—; adj. lectr. English York Coll., CUNY, 1983-86. Author: William Baziotes: A Literary Portrait, 1962, Current Affairs Atlas, 1979, The Ency. of American Journalism, 1983; contbr. articles to Commentary mag., The Nation, Village Voice, Peacework, World Paper, others; editor in chief News Dictionary: People, Places and Events, 1977-80. Mem. The Authors Guild, Willa Cather Pioneer Meml. Democrat. Home: 140 Cabrini Blvd New York NY 10033-3437 Office: UN Office Yearbook of UN 1 United Nations Plz New York NY 10017

PANFILE, PATRICIA MCCLOSKEY, psychologist; b. Nanticoke, Pa., May 27, 1952; d. Sylvester John and Albina Patricia (Gorka) McC.; m. Thomas Patrick Panfile, Nov. 25, 1976; children: Joshua McCloskey, Rebecca McCloskey. BA, King's Coll., Wilkes-Barre, Pa., 1974; MS, Pa. State U., 1976. Cert. sch. psychologist, Pa.; lic. psychologist, Pa. Sch. psychologist Berks County Ind. Unit, Reading, Pa., 1976-80; psychologist in pvt. practice Shillington, Pa., 1981-85, Allentown, Pa., 1985—; psychologist Parkland Sch. Dist., Orefield, Pa., 1989—, Wt. Mgmt. Ctr., Allentown, Pa., 1989-90, Cedar Park Psychology Assoc., Allentown, Pa., 1988-89, Child Guidance Ctr., Allentown, 1987-89. Contbr. articles to profl. convs. Mem. spl. edn. adv. com. Parkland Sch. Dist., 1989—; adv. bd. Lehigh Valley chpt. of CHADD (Children with Attention Deficit Disorders), Allentown, 1989; v.p. Oakland Park Homeowners Assn., 1991-92. Mem. APA, Pa. Psychol. Assn., Lehigh Valley Psychol. Assn. (v.p. 1990-91, newsletter editor 1990-92), Berks Area Psychol. Soc. (pres. 1983-84), Mid-East Pa. Sch. Psychologists Assn., Psi Chi, Delta Epsilon Sigma, St. Thomas Aquinas Soc. Roman Catholic. Home: 12 Bastian Ln Allentown PA 18104-9404 Office: 1251 S Cedar Crest Blvd Allentown PA 18103-6205

PANHORST, DONALD LEE, educator, consultant, speaker; b. Saint Clair, Mo., Mar. 11, 1932; s. Herbert Henry and Cora Helen (Kramme) Kellogg P.; m. Dorothy May Carmichael, June 13, 1953; children: Lynda May Panhorst Lawrence, David Wayne. MusB, Central Methodist Coll., 1953; MusM, Eastman Sch. Music, 1959, MusD, 1968. Dir. music Columbia (Mo.) Pub. Schs., 1953, Crystal City (Mo.) Pub. Schs., 1959-62; dir. instrumental music Rochester (N.Y.) City Sch. Dist., 1962-66; prof. music Edinboro (Pa.) State Coll., 1966-82, chmn. music and drama dept., 1973-82, dean continuing edn., 1982-83, assoc. v.p. acad. affairs, 1983-87, prof. speech and communication studies, 1987-91; cons., speaker Dr. Don. Panhorst Assocs., Edinboro, 1992—. Contbr. articles to profl. jours. Comdr. U.S. Navy, 1953-58. Recipient Coll. Mgmt. Program scholarship Carnegie Mellon U., Pitts., 1980. Mem. Nat. Speakers Assn., Pa. Bandmasters Assn.(pres. 1972-73), Toastmasters Internat. (dist. gov. 1983-84), Ohio Speakers Forum (sec. 1991-92), Erie Tri-State Chpt. Am. Soc. Tng. and Devel. (sec. 1992-93). Home and Office: 100 Harrison Dr Edinboro PA 16412

PANIAGUA, JOHN CHARLES, aerospace engineer, researcher; b. N.Y.C., Mar. 2, 1962; s. Jose Manual and Crescencia (Gay) P. AAS, Coll. Aeros., 1984; BSME, N.Y. Inst. Tech., 1988; MSME, Columbia U., 1991, postgrad., 1991—. Master's fellow, sr. engr. Grumman Aerospace Corp., Bethpage, N.Y., 1984—. Mem. AIAA. Home: 98 05 63d Rd Rego Park NY 11374-1744

PANICCIA, MARIO DOMENIC, architect; b. Torrice, Italy, May 13, 1948; s. Sebastiano and Clara (Mancini) P.; B.Arch., Cooper Union, 1972. With William F. Griffin & Assocs., Milford, Conn., summers 1968-72; designer Raffone, Elovitz & Fischer, Architects & Engrs., Bridgeport, Conn., 1972-75; prin. Paniccia Assocs., Architects & Planners, Bridgeport, 1975-86, Paniccia Architects and Engrs. Inc., 1987—. Nat. Council Archtl. Registration Bds.; registered architect, Conn., N.Y., Tex., Minn., N.J., R.I., Idaho, S.C., Ala., W.Va., Ga., Tenn., Ind., Mich., Mo., Fla., La., Md., Ma., N.C., Ohio, Pa., Iowa, Va., Calif. Commr. Monroe Conservation & Water Resources and Inland Wetland Commn., 1986-90, reapptd., 1990—. Mem. Conn. Soc. Architects (dir. 1979-80, commr. chpt. affairs 1979, commr. community affairs 1980, commr. profl. practice, 1985-86), Bridgeport Assn. Architects (dir. 1979, v.p. 1980, 83, pres. 1981), AIA (nat. housing com. 1988-89, commr. conservation com. 1980—), Nat. Trust Hist. Preservation, Inst. Urban Design, Bridgeport C. of C. Roman Catholic. Clubs: Elks (Fairfield, Conn.); K.C. (3d degree); Exchange (Monroe, Conn.). Home: 25 Easton Rd Monroe CT 06468-1502 Office: Paniccia Architects & Engrs Inc 4270 Main St Bridgeport CT 06606-2306

PANITZ, LAWRENCE, physician; b. Bklyn., Apr. 30, 1928; s. Max and Gussie (Gorenstein) P.; B.A., NYU, 1962, M.D., 1966; m. Adrienne Ruth Luke, June 20, 1965; children—Jennifer, Michael. Intern, St. Joseph's Hosp., Syracuse, N.Y., 1966-67; practice gen. medicine, Elmsford, N.Y., 1967—, Hawthorne, N.Y., 1968—; mem. staff St. Agnes Hosp., White Plains, Phelps Meml. Hosp., North Tarrytown, N.Y., Westchester County Med. Ctr., Valhalla, N.Y., Dobbs Ferry Hosp.; dep. dir. dept. family practice Phelps Meml. Hosp.; dir. Elmsford Med. Ctr.; police surgeon Tarrytown and North Tarrytown, Elmsford, Town of Greenburgh; med. dir. Margaret Chapman Sch. for Exceptional Child, Hawthorne; physician Westchester County Correctional Health Dept., Valhalla; sch. physician Elmsford, N.Y. Served with U.S. Army, 1946-48; lt. col. M.C. USAR (ret.). Diplomate Am. Bd. Family Practice. Fellow Am. Acad. of Family Physicians, AMA, Med. Soc. of the State of N.Y., Westchester County Med. Soc., Westchester Acad. of Medicine. Jewish. Clubs: Shriners, Masons. Home: 49 Roundabend Rd Tarrytown NY 10591 Office: 132 S Central Ave Elmsford NY 10523-3522 Other: 5 Bradhurst Ave Hawthorne NY 10532

PANKEY, HOMER RICHWELL, college president; b. Martinsburg, W.Va., Nov. 3, 1936; s. Homer Nimrod and Jane Beverly (Staples) P.; m. Patricia Ruth Griffith, June 22, 1962; children: Mark Griffith, David Allen. BA, Shepherd Coll., 1958; MA, W.Va. U., 1960, EdD, 1967. Cert. tchr., Md., W.Va. Prin., tchr. Mt. Garfield Elem. Sch., Morgan County, W.Va., 1958-59; tchr. Urbana Elem. Sch., Frederick County, Md., 1960-61; instr. grad. sch. Potomac State Coll. and Wheeling Campus Ctr. extensions W.Va. U., Morgantown, 1961-70, asst. ednl. research, 1964-65; asst. prof. elem. edn. Frostburg (Md.) State Coll., 1961-64; assoc. prof. Calif. U. of Pa., 1965-67, prof., asst. chair elem. edn. dept., 1967-69, prof., chair elem. edn. dept., 1969-73, assoc. dean Coll. Edn., 1973-80, dean grad. studies, 1980-83, v.p. for devel. and external rels., 1983-92; pres. Thomas Coll., Thomasville, Ga., 1992—; pres. Found. for California U. of Pa., 1986-90; mem. chancellor's devel. com. State System Higher Edn.; mem. adv. bd. Equibank, Inc., Pitts.; advisor, cons. curriculum and instrn. Pa. Dept. Edn.; bd. dirs. Interstate Service Corp. of Va.; vis. prof. U. Paris VIII and Ecole Nationale De Commerce; speaker in field. Contbr. articles to profl. jours. Bd. dirs. Better Bus. Bur., Pitts.; pres. Mid-Mon Valley Indsl. Devel. Assn.; treas., bd. dirs. Fayette County Health Ctr.; mem. World Affairs Council, Pitts.; committeeman-at-large Old Trails council Boy Scouts Am., Uniontown, Pa.; dist. rep. Uniontown United Way, 1989—. Recipient Outstanding Prof. Teaching award California U. of Pa. Mem. Pa. State System Higher Edn. Grants Assn. (co-founder, v.p. 1981-82), Coun. for Advancement and Support Edn., Nat. Assn. Trade and Tech. Schs. (mem. accreditation rev. bd.), Internat. Reading Assn. (pres. Calif. state coll. coun. 1966-67), Coun. Grad. Schs., Coll. Reading Assn., Calif. U. of Pa. Alumni Assn. (mem. exec. bd.), Rotary, Phi Delta Kappa (founder Calif. U. of Pa. chpt.). Presbyterian. Home: 21 Hunters Glen Rd Thomasville GA 31792 Office: Thomas Coll 1501 Millpond Rd Thomasville GA 31792

PANSCHAR, RUTH MARY, advertising executive; b. Chgo., July 11, 1964; d. Edward George and Kathleen Mary (Maguire) P. BA in Journalism, U. Wis., 1986. Asst. art dir. Bentley, Barnes & Lynn, Inc., Chgo., 1985; mktg. asst. British Vogue, London, 1986; media buyer Leo Burnett, Ltd., London, 1986-87; account mgr. Van Christo Advt., Boston, 1988—. Office: Van Christo Advt 91 Newbury St Boston MA 02116-3007

PANSON, GILBERT STEPHEN, chemistry educator; b. Paterson, N.J., Apr. 11, 1920; s. Louis Justin and Rose Lucille (Freedman) P.; m. Patricia Devens, June 11, 1944; children: Richard, Leslie. B.S., Brown U., 1941; M.A., Columbia U., 1951, Ph.D., 1953. Asst. prof. Hobart Coll., Geneva, N.Y., 1941-44; research chemist Manhattan Project, Oak Ridge, 1944-46; faculty Rutgers U., Newark, 1946-85, chmn. dept. chemistry, 1964-71; acting undergrad. dean Rutgers U., 1971-73, grad. dean, 1976-83, emeritus, 1985—; vis. prof. U. Calif., Berkeley, 1973-74, U. London, 1980-81; indsl. cons. Contbr. articles to profl. jours. Grantee NSF, NIH. Fellow Am. Inst. Chemists; mem. Am. Chem. Soc. (councilor), Sigma Xi. Home: 8A Yorkshire Dr Cranbury NJ 08512-4724 Office: Rutgers U Dept Chemistry Newark NJ 07102

PANTEL, GLENN STEVEN, lawyer; b. Plainfield, N.J., Sept. 25, 1953; s. Donald and Sarah Libby (Pearlman) P.; m. Lisa Pamela Krop, June 28, 1981; 1 child, Adam Scott. AB, Johns Hopkins U., 1975; JD, U. Pa., 1978. Bar: N.J. 1978, U.S. Dist. Ct. N.J. 1978, Pa. 1978, Fla. 1980, U.S. Ct. Appeals (3d cir.) 1982. Law clk. to presiding judge U.S. Dist. Ct. (so. dist.), Miami, Fla., 1978-79; from assoc. to ptnr. Shanley & Fisher P.C., Morristown, N.J., 1979—, also bd. dirs. Trustee Friday Evening Club Cultural Presenters, Morristown, 1984—, Integrity, Inc., Drug and Alcohol Abuse Program, Newark. Mem. ABA, Fla. Bar Assn., N.J. Bar Assn., Morris County Bar Assn., Phi Beta Kappa. Home: 3 Cross Way Mendham NJ 07945-3120 Office: Shanley & Fisher PC 131 Madison Ave Morristown NJ 07960-6097

PANZER, HANS PETER, chemist; b. Ratingen, Rhineland, Germany, July 26, 1922; came to the U.S., 1957; s. Peter Franz and Margarete Ernestine (Schwellenbach) P.; m. Ursula Hedwig Stratmann, Oct. 22, 1956; children: Peter Hermann, Maria Margaret. MS in Chemistry, U. Muenster, Germany, 1954, PhD, 1957. Postdoctoral fellow Purdue U., Lafayette, Ind., 1957-58; sr. rsch. chemist Am. Machine and Foundry Co., Springdale, Conn., 1959-63; rsch. specialist Gen. Foods Corp., Tarrytown, N.Y., 1963-65; from various supervisory positions to assoc. rsch. fellow Am. Cyanamid Co., Stamford, Conn., 1965—; cons. in field, Stamford, 1991—. Contbr. chpts. to Encyclopedia of Chemical Technology, 3d edition, 1980, Encyclopedia of Polymer Science and Engineering, 2d edition, 1987; contbr. articles to profl. jours.; patentee in field. Mem. Am. Chem. Soc. (div. polymer chemistry, div. polymeric materials, sci. and engring. 1957—), German Chem. Soc. Roman Catholic. Home: 150 Old North Stamford Rd Stamford CT 06905-3963 Office: Am Cyanamid Co 1937 W Main St Stamford CT 06902-4580

PAOLICELLI, LUCIA MARIE, psychologist; b. N.Y.C., Aug. 17, 1961; d. Emanuel Nicholas and Dorothy (Saccente) P. BA, Conn. Coll., New London, 1983; MA, SUNY, Stony Brook, 1985, PhD, 1989. Lic. pscyhologist, R.I. Psychology intern Suffolk Child Devel. Ctr., Smithtown, N.Y., 1985-87; psychology intern Office of Disabled SUNY, 1986-88, testing coord. Psychology Ctr., 1987-88; psychology intern Brown U., Providence, R.I., 1988-89; neuropsychology postdoctoral fellow Braintree (Mass.) Hosp., 1989-90; staff neuropsychologist Neuropsychology Specialists, Providence, 1990; staff psychologist, clin. asst. prof. Child Devel. Ctr. R.I. Hosp., Providence, 1991—. Contbr. articles to profl. jours. Winthrop scholar, 1982, Phi Beta Kappa, 1983; SUNY faculty fellow 1983; Sigma Xi grantee, 1984. Mem. APA, Phi Beta Kappa, Sigma Xi (assoc.).

PAOLINO, MICHAEL ANTHONY, engineering educator, dean; b. Albany, N.Y., Mar. 8, 1939; s. Anthony and Bessie (Malatesta) P.; m. Carole Montgomery, Dec. 2, 1961; children: Patrick, Kevin, John. BS, Siena Coll., 1960; MS, U. Ariz., 1967, PhD, 1972. Registered profl. engr., Va. Commd. officer U.S. Army, 1960, advanced through grades to col., 1982; served as prof. U.S. Mil. Acad., West Point, N.Y., 1973-86; ret. U.S. Army, 1986; prof., dean engring. Lafayette Coll., Easton, Pa., 1986—. Recipient Ralph R. Teetor award Soc. Automotive Engrs., Detroit, 1978. Mem. ASME, Am. Soc. Engring. Edn., Tau Beta Pi, Phi Kappa Phi, Pi Tau Sigma. Roman Catholic. Office: Lafayette Coll Easton PA 18042

PAOLINO, RONALD MARIO, clinical psychologist, consultant, psychopharmacologist, pharmacist; b. Providence, Mar. 15, 1938; s. Lawrence and Mary Corinne (Guglielmi) P.; m. Eileen Frances Quimby, June 18, 1960; children: Lisa Katherine, David Lawrence. Student, Providence Coll., 1955-56; BS in Pharmacy, U. R.I., 1959; MS in Pharmacology, Purdue U., 1961, PhD in Psychopharmacology, 1963, postdoctoral studies in clin. psychology, 1972-74; postdoctoral studies in existential analytic psychotherapy, Okla. Inst. Existential Analysis and Psychotherapy, 1974-75; MA (hon.), Brown U., 1977. Lic. psychologist, R.I., pharmacist, R.I.; nat. registered health svc. provider in psychology; cert. arbitrator. Intern dept. psychiatry and behavioral scis. U. Okla. Health Scis. Ctr., 1974-75; David Ross predoctoral fellow dept. pharmacology/toxicology Purdue U., 1961-63; NIMH postdoctoral fellow in psychology dept. psychology Yale U., 1963-65; asst. prof. pharmacology U. Conn. Sch. Pharmacy, 1965-67; assoc. prof. psychopharmacology Purdue U., 1967-74; NIMH fellow in clin. psychology U. Okla. Health Scis. Ctr., 1974-75; coord. group psychotherapy tng. program Brown U. Program in Medicine, 1983-85, assoc. prof. psychiatry and human behavior, 1976-90, clin. assoc. prof. psychiatry and human behavior, 1990—; pvt. practice; chief drug dependency treatment program VA Med. Ctr., Providence, 1975-87, dir. biofeedback clinic, 1977-87; primary hostage negotiator; mem. Pharmacology and Therapeutic Agts. Com., 1979-87, VA Med. Ctr., coord. VA Contracted Half-Way Project for Substance Dependent Vets., 1981-85, chmn. Pain Mgmt. Task Force, 1984-85, mem. Supervisory Level Pharmacy Profl. Standards Bd., 1990—, mem. Mgmt. Suicidal and Violent Patient Task Force, 1990—, chmn. Outpatient Psychiatry Svcs. Reorganization Task Force, 1991, mem. VA-Dept. Def. Desert Storm Emergency Plan Com., 1991; mem. substance abuse and prevention grant application rev. com. R.I. Adv. Coun. on Substance Abuse, 1982—, prevention, edn. and tng. com. on substance abuse, 1981—, chmn. 1981-82; adj. assoc. prof. psychology, U. R.I., 1982—; mem. planning com. State Conf. on Substance Abuse in the Hispanic Community, 1986; mem. alcohol awareness commn. Episc. Diocese of R.I., 1983-85; gubernatorial appointee Gov.'s Permanent Coun. on Drug Abuse Control, 1978-82; mem. rev. com. for funding of state drug abuse programs R.I. Single State Agy. on Drug Abuse, R.I. Dept. Mental Health Retardation and Hosps., 1978-82; cons. Nurses Renewal Com., 1980-81, substance abuse prevention edn. for elem. sch. children R.I. chpt. ARC, 1977, mem. suicide prevention steering com., 1977; mem.Interagy. Drug Abuse Steering Com., Lafayette, Ind. 1969-72; bd. dirs. Providence VA Med. Ctr. Credit Union; mem. bd. cert. for alcoholism counselors R.I. Assn. Alcohol Counselors, 1979-81; mem. Gov.'s Task Force on Substance Abuse at Adult Correctional Instn., 1977-78, Gov.'s Task Force on Mental Health Svcs. at Adult Correctional Instn., 1977-78, chmn. reclassification of inmates com., 1977-78; chmn. com. on edn. and cert. biofeedback practioners Conn. Biofeedback Soc., 1977-78; summer faculty fellow U. Conn., 1967; vis. scientist lectr. Assn. Am. Colls. Pharmacy, 1972-73; cons. to bus., unions, law enforcement. Author: (2 chpts.) Drug Testing: Issues and Options, 1991; contbr. 37 articles to profl. jours. Bd. dirs. R.I. chpt. Samaritans Internat. Suicide Prevention Orgn., 1978-84; v.p. Experience Jesus Inc.; mem. community adv. bd. Spina Bifida Assn. R.I., 1980-83. Recipient Citation award for svc. and contbns. to formulation of state policy for treatment and prevention of drug abuse Gov. R.I., 1983, Letter of Commendation, Gov.'s R.I. Adv. Coun. on Substance Abuse, 1986, vc. Recognition award DAV, 1990, Spl. Contbn. award Providence VA Med Ctr., 1990. Mem. APA, Am. Group Psychotherapy Assn., Am. Soc. for Pharmacology and Exptl. Therapeutics, Internat. Brain Rsch. Orgn., Internat. Narcotic Enforcement Officers Assn., R.I. Group Psychay Soc. (pres. elect 1991, continuing edn. dir. for psychologists 1990—, exec. bd. 1986—, tng. faculty 1985—, co-dir. tng. 1986-87, tng. adv. bd. 1985-86), R.I. Psychol. Assn. (chmn. substance abuse ins. subcom. 1986-87, rep. Gov.'s Coun. on Mental Health State Plan Com. 1982-84), Rho Chi Hon. Pharm. Soc., Sigma Xi. Office: PO Box 159 Barrington RI 02806-0159

PAONESSA, PHILIP JOHN, corporate professional; b. Niagara Falls, N.Y., Aug. 25, 1951; s. Philip Joseph and Florence Susan (Presti) P.; m. Catherine A. Paonessa, Aug. 26, 1990; 1 child, Sean C. BA in Edn., Niagara U., 1973. Mgmt. trainee Continental Restaurant Systems, San Diego, 1975-76; gen. mgr. R. Turgeon Restaurants, Buffalo, 1976-79, Naegele Restaurants, Mpls., 1980-81; dist. mgr. Monsieur Henri Wines, Ltd., White Plains, N.Y., 1981-83, v.p. ctr. states, 1983-91, v.p. spl. markets, 1991—; v.p. internat. sales Monsieur Henry Wines, Ltd., White Plains, N.Y., 1991—. Mem. Nat. Alcohol Beverage Control Assn., KC. Republican. Roman Catholic. Home: 190 Middle River Rd Danbury CT 06811-2713 Office: Monsieur Henri Wines Ltd 707 Westchester Ave Ste 1L White Plains NY 10604-3102

PAPADIMITRIOU, DIMITRI BASIL, economist, college administrator; b. Salonica, Greece, June 9, 1946; came to U.S., 1965, naturalized, 1974; s. Basil John and Ellen (Tacas) P.; m. Viki Fokas, Aug. 26, 1967; children: Jennifer E., Elizabeth R. BA, Columbia U., 1970; PhD, New Sch. Social Rsch., 1986. V.p., asst. sec. ITT Life Ins. Co. N.Y., N.Y.C., 1970-73; exec. v.p., sec., treas. William Penn Life Ins. Co. N.Y., N.Y.C., 1973-78, also dir.; exec. v.p., provost Bard Coll., 1978—, exec. dir. Bard Ctr., 1980—, Jerome Levy Econs. Inst., 1988—; adj. lectr. econs. New Sch. Social Rsch., 1975-76; prof. Bard Coll., 1978—; fellow Ctr. for Advanced Econ. Studies, 1983; dir. William Penn Life Ins. Co. N.Y.; bd. dirs. Catskill Ballet Theatre, Hudsonia, Inc., mem. adv. com.; bd. govs. Jerome Levy Econs. Inst., 1986—. Trustee ACHAEA Found. Mem. Am. Econ. Assn., Am. Symphony Orch., Am.-Hellenic Banker Assn., Royal Econ. Soc., Am. Fin. Assn., European Econ. Assn., Eastern Economic Assn., Econ. Sci. Chamber of Greece. Home and Office: Bard Coll Annandale on Hudson NY 12504

PAPADOPOULOS, (DENNIS) KONSTANTINOS, physics educator; b. Larissa, Greece, Dec. 29, 1937; m. Susan Barbara Tepper, June 6, 1969; children: Alexander C., Melina. BS in Physics, U. Athens, Greece, 1960; MS in Nuclear Engring., MIT, 1965; PhD in Physics, U. Md., 1968. Rsch. assoc. U. Md., College Park, 1968-69; sr. rsch. physicist Naval Rsch. Lab., Washington, 1969-79; science advisor Office of Fusion Energy, Washington, 1978-79; prof. U. Md., College Park, 1979—; cons. Naval Rsch. Lab., Sci. Applications Inter C., McLean, Va., Atlantic Richfield Co., Washington. Recipient E.O. Hulbert Sci. award Washington Acad. Sci., 1977, Sci. Achievement in Physics award, 1978, Cert. of Commendation, NASA, 1986. Office: U Md Dept of Physics College Park MD 20742

PAPAGEORGIOU, JOHN CONSTANTINE, management science educator; b. Kallithea, Greece, Nov. 22, 1935; came to U.S., 1969, naturalized, 1975; m. Thalia Christidou, 1969; children: Constantine, Elena, Demetrios, Antigone. B.Sc., Athens (Greece) Sch. Econs. and Bus. Scis., 1957; diploma tech. sci., U. Manchester, Eng., 1963, Ph.D. in Mgmt. Scis, 1965. Lectr. Athens Sch. Econs. and Bus. Scis.; also postgrad. Inst. Bus. Adminstrn., Athens, 1966-68; asst. prof. Faculty Adminstrv. Studies, York U., Toronto, Ont., Can., 1968-69; asst. prof. mgmt. Wayne State U., 1969-71; assoc. prof. mgmt. scis. St. Louis U., 1971-72; vis. prof. ops. rsch. Athens Sch. Econs.

and Bus. Scis., 1972-73; assoc. prof. ops. analysis U. Toledo, 1974-76; assoc. prof. mgmt. sci. and coord. Coll. Profl. Studies, U. Mass., Boston, 1976-78; prof., coord. Coll. Profl. Studies, U. Mass., 1978-80; prof. mgmt. scis. dept. Coll. Mgmt. U. Mass., 1980—, chmn. mgmt. scis. dept., 1980-85; head dept. econ. research Agrl. Bank Greece, 1966-67; ops. analyst Esso-Pappas Indsl. Co., Greece, 1967-68; spl. adv. Center Planning and Econ. Research, Greece, 1972-73; cons. in field; condr. seminars. Author: Introduction to Operations Research (in Greek), 1973, Fundamentals of Operations Research, 1973, Management Science and Environmental Problems, 1980; co-author: Data on the Greek Economy, 1966; assoc. editor technos: Ops. Mgmt. Newsletter; editor-at-large: Interfaces; mem. editorial bd. Jour. Managerial Issues, Southwestern Bus. Rev.; editor TIMS COLIME Newsletter; contbr. articles to profl. jours. Served to 2d lt. Greek Army, 1958-60. Greek Govt. scholar, 1962-65; NATO postdoctoral fellow, 1965; Air Force Office Sci. Research fellow, summer 1980. Fellow AAAS; mem. Ops. Rsch. Soc. Am. (1985 nat. meeting program com.), Inst. Mgmt. Scis. (nat. meeting com., 1985, faculty-in-residence com., coll. officer, chpt. officer, activities com.), Am. Inst. Decision Scis. (nat. innovative edn. com. 1981, programs and meetings com. 1983), Hellenic Ops. Rsch. Soc., Sigma Xi. Address: 14 Putney Rd Wellesley MA 02181

PAPAIOANNOU, EVANGELIA-LILLY, psychologist researcher; b. Thessaloniki, Greece, Mar. 22, 1963; came to U.S. 1984; d. Nicholas and Ekaterini (Goulias) P. Bus. studies certificate with high honors, Anatolia Coll., Thessaloniki, Greece, 1983; BA in Psychology magna cum laude, Smith Coll., 1986; postgrad., Am. Univ., Washington, 1989. Guest researcher NIH, Bethesda, Md., 1986—. Author articles in press and profl. jours. Active in Hellenic Soc. for the Health Scis., Bethesda, 1987—. Recipient: scholarships Smith Coll. and Anatolia Coll. Mem. Jean Piaget Soc., Am. Psychol. Assn., Internat. Platform Assn., Alliance Francaise, Smith Coll. Alumnae Assn., Anatolia Coll. Alumni Assn., Nat. Mus. of Women in the Arts, Brazilian-Am. Cultural Inst., Phi Beta Kappa, Psi Chi, Smith Coll. First Group Scholars. Greek Orthodox. Home: Promenade Towers 5225 Pooks Hill Rd Apt 1711N Bethesda MD 20814-2052 Office: NIH 9000 Rockville Pike Bethesda MD 20892-0001

PAPALIAN, GEORGE KEVORK, marketing consultant; b. Providence, June 21, 1922; s. Malkon and Lemonia (Hajinian) P.; m. Catherine Bebirian, Dec. 16, 1951; children: Richard Hovsep, Michael Malkon. BS, NYU, 1949, MBA, 1950. Sales exec. Dan River Inc., N.Y.C., 1953-87; salesman Gabsom Co., N.Y.C., 1949-53; converter, salesman Cohn-Hall Marx Co., N.Y.C., 1941-49; instr., adj. assoc. prof. St. John's U., Jamaica, N.Y., 1951-87, prof. mktg., 1987-89; pres. Mktg. Communications Group, Inc., Westbury, N.Y., 1982-87; cons. Diocese of the Armenian Ch., N.Y.C., 1987—; bd. dirs. The Promotion Agy., Greenwich, Conn., Armenian Ctr. at Columbia U., N.Y.C. Pvt. U.S. Army, 1943-45. Recipient Sales Exec. of Yr. award Dan River Inc., 1984. Mem. Sales & Mktg. Club of N.Y., AAUP, Knights of Vartan (comdr. 1974-75, Man of Yr. 1986). Armenian. Home: 25 Woodoak Dr Westbury NY 11590-1031

PAPAS, IRENE KALANDROS, English educator; b. Balt., Mar. 16, 1931; d. Louis and Kounia (Stamatakis) Kalandros; m. Steve S. Papas, Sept. 10, 1952; children: Fotene Stephenie Tina, Barbara Counia. BA magna cum laude, Goucher Coll., 1968; MA in English Lang. and Lit., U. Md., 1974, postgrad., 1980—. Lic. theology profl.; cert. ESL tchr./tutor; cert. TV prodr. Tchr./tutor various schs., Balt., 1965—; tchr. theology U. Md. Free Univ., College Park, 1979—; author/pub. Ledger Publs., Silver Spring, Md., 1982—; TV producer Arts and Humanities Prodns., Silver Spring, 1991—; lectr. in English, philosophy, Montgomery Coll., Goucher Coll.; instr. English Composition, World Literature, U. Md., College Park, 1968—; adj. faculty various colls. Author: Irene's Ledger Songs of Deliverance, 1982, Irene's Ledger Song at Sabbatyon, 1986; producer/dir. tv. progs. Vol. prog. coord. Storyhour, All Saints Sch. Libr., Balt., 1960s, broadcasting/radio reading for the blind, Washington Ear, Silver Spring, 1970s; tutorial literary; election judge, Montgomery County Suprs. Bd., 1980's, 90's; mem. Byzantine Ch. Choir. Mem. AAUP, Phi Beta Kappa. Democrat. Greek Orthodox. Office: PO Box 10303 Silver Spring MD 20914-0303

PAPASTRAT, HELEN P(ANAYOTA), psychiatrist; b. Binghamton, N.Y., June 13, 1958; d. Peter H. and Mary A. (Angelopoulos) P. AB, Cornell U., 1980; MD, N.Y. Med. Coll., 1985. Postdoctoral fellow dept. psychiatry Sch. Medicine Yale U., New Haven, 1985-89. Mem. AMA, Am. Psychiat. Assn., Alpha Omega Alpha. Greek Orthodox.

PAPATHOMAS, THOMAS VIRGIL, human and machine vision researcher, educator, designer; b. Macedonia, Greece, Feb. 10, 1949; s. Virgil Alexander and Galatia Anastasia (Kotopoulou) P.; m. Georgia Nikolakopoulou, Sept. 11, 1950; children: Lia, Alexander. BS, Columbia U., 1971, MS, 1972, PhD, 1977. Mem. tech. staff AT&T Bell Labs., Whippany, N.J., 1977-82, supr., 1982-83; mem. rsch. staff AT&T Bell Labs., Murray Hill, N.J., 1983-89; assoc. prof. dept. biomed. engring., assoc. dir. Lab. of Vision Rsch. Rutgers U., New Brunswick, N.J., 1989—; Author: Solution Manual for Microelectronics, 1979; contbr. articles to profl. jours.; patentee in field. Author: Solution Manual for Microelectronics, 1979; patentee in field; contbr. to mus. exhibits. Pres. Krikos, A Cultural and Sci. Orgn. Greek-Am. Profls., 1985-86. Columbia U. fellow, N.Y.C., 1971-72. Mem. IEEE, Assn. Computer Machinery, Optical Soc. Am., Sigma Xi, Tau Beta Pi, Eta Kappa Nu. Greek Orthodox. Office: Rutgers U Dept Biomed Engrs PO Box 909 Piscataway NJ 08855-0909

PAPAYANIS, NICHOLAS, educator; b. N.Y.C., Mar. 9, 1940; s. Christopher and Minnie (Strikis) P.; m. Marilyn Lee Adler, Dec. 27, 1987. BA, NYU, 1961; MA, Harvard U., 1963; PhD, U. Wis., 1969. Prof. European and French history Bklyn. (N.Y.) Coll., CUNY, 1968—. Author: Alphonse Merrheim: The Emergence of Reformism in Revolutionary Syndicalism 1871-1925, 1985; contbr. articles to profl. jours. Recipient Fulbright fellowship U.S. Govt., Paris, 1965-66, fellowship Nat. Endowment for the Humanities, 1991-92. Mem. Am. Hist. Assn., French Hist. Assn., Western Soc. for French History, Pi Delta Phi, Phi Beta Kappa. Office: Hist Dept/Bklyn Coll Bedford Ave # H Brooklyn NY 11222-3102

PAPE, EUGENE THOMAS, securities trader; b. N.Y.C., Sept. 22, 1947; s. Joseph Thomas and Ruby (Gillespie) P.; m. Rosalie Jerolemon Armocida, May 8, 1948; children: Pamela, Joseph, Deborah. Page boy N.Y. Stock Exch., N.Y.C., 1965-66, mem., 1978—; telephone clk. Baker, Weeks & Co. Inc., N.Y.C., 1966-75; mem. Am. Stock Exch., N.Y.C., 1975-76; telephone clk. Donaldson, Lufkin & Jenrette, N.Y.C., 1976-78; sr. v.p. Donaldson, Lufkin & Jenrette Securities Corp., Broadway, N.Y.; floor ofcl. N.Y. Stock Exchange, N.Y.C., 1985-91; hearing panel, 1989—. With U.S. ARmy, 1967-69. Mem. NRA, Am. Legion, Elks. Republican. Roman Catholic. Home: 2527 Mahogany Trl Manasquan NJ 08736-2109 Office: Donaldson Lufkin & Jenrette 140 Broadway New York NY 10005-1101

PAPE, WILLIAM JAMES, II, newspaper publisher; b. Waterbury, Conn., Aug. 14, 1931; s. William B. and Helen (Cronan) P.; m. Patricia Moran, Oct. 15, 1959; children: William B. II, Andrew J. BS, U.S. Naval Acad., 1953; MBA, Harvard U., 1959; LHD (hon.), Teikyo Post U., 1991. Commd. ensign USN, 1953, advanced through grades to lt., 1955, resigned, 1957; asst. treas. Ea. Color Printing Co., Waterbury, 1959-63; pres., treas. Ea. Color Printing Co., Avon, Conn., 1977-87; v.p., asst. treas. Am.-Republican Inc., Waterbury, 1963-64, v.p., treas., 1964-72, pres., treas., 1972—; also bd. dirs.; pub. Waterbury Republican-Am., 1972—; bd. dirs. Paper Delivery Inc., Waterbury, Platt Bros., Waterbury, Bank of Boston Conn., 1973-91. bd. dirs. Conn. Coun. Freedom of Info., 1968-88, Conn. Bus. and Industry Assn., 1980-83, Naugatuck Valley Devel. Corp.,Regional Action Coun., Waterbury, 1991, Waterbury YMCA, 1970-78, trustee, 1972—, chmn. trustees, 1976-85; bd. dirs. Conn. Citizens for Jud. Modernization, pres., 1973, 75; trustee Northeast Utilities, 1974—, Conn. Pub. Expenditure Coun. Inc., 1974-77, Teikyo Post U., 1976—; grants com. Waterbury Found., 1980-87; pub. affairs com. Waterbury Hosp., 1984-90, past trustee; incorporator Conn. Found. for Open Govt. Inc.; active Conn. Legislature Commn. to Study Modernization and Unification of Cts., 1973-75, Citizens for Better Govt. Through Reorganization, 1977. Mem. Am. Judicature Soc. (assoc. dir. 1975-76), New England Newspaper Assn. (Conn. bd. govs. 1983-87), Conn. Bar Assn. (task force conflict of interest 1979—), Conn. Daily Newspaper Assn. (pres. 1970, exec. com. 1971-91), Waterbury C. of C. (exec. com., v.p. 1975, chmn. 1977-79, dir. 1980-83, vice-chmn. transp. 1981—), Navy League U.S. (communications bd. 1982), Waterbury Club, Madison Beach Club, Highfield. Republican. Roman Catholic. Home: 55 South St Middlebury CT 06762 Office: Waterbury Rep-Am PO Box 2090 389 Meadow St Waterbury CT 06722

PAPELINO, JEANNINE MARIE, graphic designer; b. Utica, N.Y., Apr. 17, 1968; d. Charles and Annette (Abriola) P. AAS, Mohawk Valley Community Coll., 1988; BFA, Rochester Inst. Tech., 1990. Graphic designer Mohawk Valley Community Coll., Utica, N.Y., 1989, ESH Graphics Inc., Rochester, N.Y., 1990—. Home: 487 Trenton Rd Utica NY 13502

PAPKIN, ROBERT DAVID, lawyer; b. New Bedford, Mass., Feb. 26, 1933; s. Barney and Rose (Shuster) P.; m. Rachel Friedberg, Aug. 29, 1965; children: Steven C., Daniel M. AB, Harvard U., 1954, LLB, 1957. Bar: Mass. 1957, D.C. 1964. Legal asst. NRLB, Washington, 1958-61; assoc. Cox, Langford & Brown, Washington, 1963-66, ptnr., 1966-73; ptnr. Squire, Sanders & Dempsey, Washington, 1973—. Trustee Art Svcs. Internat., 1990—, Am. Friends of the Venezuelan Indians, 1991—. Served with U.S. Army, 1957-58, 61-62. Mem. ABA, D.C. Bar Assn., Fed. Bar Assn., Internat. Bar Assn., Met. Club Washington D.C., Cosmos Club. Democrat. Jewish. Home: 8200 Lilly Stone Dr Bethesda MD 20817-4506 Office: Squire Sanders & Dempsey 1201 Pennsylvania Ave NW PO Box 407 Washington DC 20004

PAPLAUSKAS, LEONARD PAUL, academic administrator, health science educator; b. Wiesbaden, Germany, June 22, 1949; came to U.S., 1950; s. Leonardas and Emilija (Sadauskas) P.; m. Lynn Ellen Verhoeven, Nov. 24, 1972 (div. Jan. 1988); 1 child, Grant Peter; m. Judith Ann Jones, June 30, 1990. BS, Loyola U., 1970; masters equivalent, So. Ill. U., 1972, postgrad. Asst. sec. U.S. adopted names coun. AMA, Chgo., 1974-75; rsch. adminstr. Health & Hosp. Governing Commn., Chgo., 1975-76; asst. dir. Office Rsch. & Sponsored Programs Northwestern U., Evanston, Ill., 1976-84; dir. Office Rsch. & Sponsored Programs, Med. Sch. Northwestern U., Chgo., 1977-84; instr. div. biol. sci. Northwestern U., Evanston, 1983-84; instr. dept. natural sci. Loyola U., Chgo., 1982-84; asst. v.p. rsch. U. Conn. Health Ctr., Farmington, 1984—; cons. NIH, Bethesda, Md., 1977—. Contbr. articles to profl. jours. Bd. dirs. Currier Woods Assoc./Currier Woods Tax Dist., Cheshire, Conn., 1991—; bd. dirs., exec. com. Conn. United for Rsch. Excellence, 1990—. NIH grantee, 1987—. Mem. AAAS, Nat. Coun. Univ. Rsch. Adminstrs., Soc. Rsch. Adminstrs., Mus. of Natural History, Smithsonian Instn. Office: U Conn Health Ctr 263 Farmington Ave Farmington CT 06030-0001

PAPOULIAS, SOTIRI ARIS, chemical executive, engineer; b. Athens, Greece, Aug. 7, 1953; came to U.S., 1974; s. Aristos S. and Olga (Kinnas) P.; m. N. Manolis, Sept. 9, 1981 (div. Feb. 1989). BS magna cum laude, U. Mass., 1977; MS in Engring., U. Fla., 1978; PhD in Engring., Carnegie Mellon U., 1982; MBA, NYU, 1988. Instr. Carnegie Mellon U., Pitts., 1978-82; group head Exxon Rsch. and Engring. Co., Florham Park, N.J., 1982-87; bus. mgr. Internat. Specialty Products, Wayne, N.J., 1987—. Inventor optimized multilayer absorber; contbr. articles to profl. jours. Mem. YMCA, Madison, N.J., 1988-91. Mem. Am. Mgmt. Assn., Am. Filtration Soc., Am. Inst. Chem. Engrs., Metal Powder Industry Fedn. Christian Orthodox. Office: Internat Specialty Products 1361 Alps Rd Wayne NJ 07470-3700

PAPP, JAMES MICHAEL, human resources administrator, director; b. Sommerville, N.J., May 12, 1953; s. James W. and Anna L. (Bodnar) P.; m. Susan P. Papp, Nov. 23, 1985; children: Jonathan L., Jennifer L. BA, St. Vincent Coll., 1975; MA, St. Francis Coll., 1977. Asst. pers. dir. Mercy Hosp., Altoona, Pa., 1979-85, safety coord., 1981-85; dir. human resources Clearfield (Pa.) Hosp., 1985-86, v.p. human resources adminstrn., 1986—, dir. profl. svcs., 1989-90; bd. dirs. Horizon Health Group, Meadville, Pa. Contbg. author: (pamphlet) The Strike Preparedness Handbook, 1990. Mem. employer adv. coun. Clearfield Office of State Job Svc., 1985—; mem. adv. coun. Clearfield County Vocat. Tech. LPN Program, 1986—; v.p. Am. Cancer Soc., Clearfield, 1988-89, pres., 1989-90. St. Francis Coll. scholar, 1976-77. Mem. Am. Soc. Health Care Human Resources Adminstrn., Soc. Human Resource Profls. of HAP BOD, 1989-90, Healthcare Human Resource Assn. Cen. Pa. (v.p. 1987-88, pres. 1989-90), N.W. Chpt. Human Resource Soc., Clearfield/Curwensville (Pa.) Country Club, Kiwanis (bd. dirs. Clearfield chpt. 1986—). Home: 619 Indian Rd Clearfield PA 16830-1002 Office: Clearfield Hosp PO Box 992 Clearfield PA 16830-0992

PAPP, LASZLO GEORGE, architect; b. Debrecen, Hungary, Apr. 28, 1929; came to U.S., 1956; m. Judith Liptak, Apr. 12, 1952; children: Andrea, Laszlo-Mark (dec. 1978). Archtl. Engr., Poly. U. Budapest, 1955; MArch, Pratt Inst., 1960. Designer Harrison & Abramovitz, Architects, N.Y.C., 1958-63; ptnr. Whiteside & Papp, Architects, White Plains, N.Y., 1963-67; pres. Papp Architects, P.C., White Plains, N.Y., 1967—. Mem. Pres.'s Adv. Com. on Pvt. Sector Initiatives; mem. adv. com. Westchester Comunity Coll., 1971—, Iona Coll., New Rochelle, N.Y., 1982—, Norwalk State Tech. Coll., 1983—; v.p. Clearview Sch., 1985-89, pres., 1990—. Fellow AIA (reg. dir. 1983-85); mem. Internat. Union Architects (rep. habitat com. 1986-90), N.Y. State Assn. Architects (v.p. 1977-80, pres. 1981), Am.-Hungarian Engrs. Assn. (bd. dirs. 1978-90), Hungarian Univ. Assn. (pres. 1958-60), Weschester County C. of C. (bd. dirs. 1968-71, vice chmn. bd. for area devel. 1983-89, chmn. bd. dirs. 1989-90), Am.-Hungarian C. of C. (charter 1989—). Home: 1197 Valley Rd New Canaan CT 06840-2428 Office: Papp Architects PC 7-11 S Broadway White Plains NY 10601

PAPPALARDO, ROSA GLORIA, educator; b. Bklyn., Mar. 10, 1932; d. Angelo Charles and Rose (Paternostro) Borgia; m. Leonard Thomas Pappalardo, Apr. 16, 1955; children: Marianne, Leonard, Charles, Roseanne. BS, NYU, 1952, MA, 1953; postgrad., Seton Hall U., 1980-81, Rutgers U., 1984. Art edn. tchr. Islip (N.Y.) Bd. Edn., 1953-54, Herricks (N.Y.) Bd. Edn., 1954-57, 61-62; tchr. spl. edn. Passaic Assn. for Mentally Retarded, Passaic, N.J., 1958-60; supr. art/home edn. Randolph (N.J.) Twp. Schs., 1962—; adj. prof. Jersey City State Coll., 1971—; art cons. Recipient numerout svc. awards. Mem. Arts Coun. of Morris Area, Phi Delta Kappa, Delta Zeta (pres.), and others. Republican. Roman Catholic. Home: 312 Mt Way Morris Plains NJ 07950 Office: Randolph Twp Schs 6 Emery Ave Ste 4 Randolph NJ 07869

PAPPAS, CHARLES ENGELOS, plastic surgeon; b. Phila., May 20, 1946; s. Engelos George and Angelina (Biniaris) P.; m. Marilyn Ann Eisemann, May 19, 1973; children: Evan, Angela, Chrysten. BA, BS, U. Pa., 1968; MD, Temple U., 1972. Intern, then resident in gen. surgery Johns Hopkins Hosp., Balt., 1972-75; resident in gen. surgery Temple U. Hosp., Phila., 1975-76, resident in plastic surgery, 1976-78, chmn. dept. plastic surgery, 1978-81, clin. assoc. prof. surgery, 1981—; chief dept. plastic surgery Meml. Hosp., Phila., 1986—; clin. assoc. plastic surgery Chestnut Hill Hosp., Phila., 1979—; dir. Inst. for Aesthetic Plastic Surgery, Ft. Washington, Pa., 1985—. Contbr. articles to profl. jours. Trustee Germantown Acad., Ft. Washington, 1986—, Commonwealth Nat. Country Club, Horsham, 1988—, Patrons' Charity Found. Fellow ACS, Royal Coll. Surgeons; mem. Am. Soc. Plastic Reconstructive Surgeons (diplomate), Am. Soc. Aesthetic Plastic Surgeons (diplomate). Orthodox. Office: Inst Aesthetic Plastic Surgery Ste 202 467 Pennsylvania Ave Fort Washington PA 19034

PAPPAS, MICHAEL, financial company executive; b. N.Y.C., Sept. 10, 1940; s. Michael Alexander Papadopoulos and Despina (Vrioni) Kokindo; m. Eileen McGovern, Jan. 25, 1969. BBA in Acctg. and Data Processing, Pace U., N.Y.C., 1973. Mgr. acctg. E.F. Hutton, N.Y.C., 1972-75, bus. unit mgr., 1976-77; mgr. payroll and commn. acctg. Drexel Burnham Lambert, N.Y.C., 1977-81, v.p., project mgr., 1981-83, v.p., mgr. gen. acctg., 1983-85, v.p., mgr. fin. info. systems, 1985-86, v.p., govt. reporting coord., 1986-89; dir. compensation Gruntal & Co., Inc., N.Y.C., 1989—. Sgt. U.S. Army, 1963-65. Mem. Securities Industry Assn. (mem. tech. tax com. 1986-88), Hellenic Am. Bankers Assn. (dir. 1991—0. Greek Orthodox. Office: Gruntal & Co Inc 14 Wall St New York NY 10005-2101

PARADIS, JAMES GARDINER, historian; b. Walker, Minn., Oct. 3, 1942; s. Louis Adelard and Rosalie Jane (Gardiner) P.; m. Judith Ellen Schmuckler, July 3, 1970; children: Emily, Rosalind. BS in Natural Sci., St. John's U., 1964; AM in English, NYU, 1971; PhD in English, U. Wash., 1976. Chemistry instr. Harar Tchr. Tng. Inst., Harar, Ethiopia, 1964-66; sci. tchr. Pub. Sch. 143, N.Y.C., 1966-71; English instr. Univ. Wash., Seattle, 1974-76; asst. prof. sci. and tech. communication MIT, Cambridge, Mass., 1977-79, assoc. prof., 1980-89, chmn. writing prog., 1982-85, prof., 1990—; communications cons. Exxon Chemicals Corp., Baton Rouge, La., 1982-83, U.S. Dept. of Interior, Anchorage, Alaska, 1983, Brookhaven Nat. Lab., L.I., N.Y., 1978-90. Author: Thomas Henry Huxley, 1978; co-editor: Victorian Science and Values, 1981, Evolution and Ethics, 1989, Textual Dynamics of the Professions, 1991; editorial cons. MIT Press/Harvard U., 1980-89. Adv. com. Driscoll Elem. Sch., Brookline, Mass., 1990-91. Recipient devel. grant Internat. Bus. Machines, 1986-87, rsch. grant NEH, 1979-80, Am. Philos. Soc., 1976-77. Mem. Modern Lang. Assn., History of Sci. Soc., Soc. for Tech. Communications, British Soc. for History of Sci. Home: 26 Salisbury Rd Brookline MA 02146-2105 Office: MIT 77 Massachusetts Ave Cambridge MA 02139-4307

PARADISE, ROBERT RICHARD, publishing executive; b. Bklyn., Nov. 29, 1934; s. Vincent James and Marie (Sangermano) P.; m. Camille Teresa Cosenza, July 11, 1964; children: Christine, Caren M., Robert V., Steven C. BA, St. Bonaventure U., 1956; MBA, NYU, 1972. Advt. sales rep. The Wall Street Jour., N.Y.C., 1961-63, retail advt. sales mgr., 1963-66, fin. advt. sales mgr., 1966-70, assoc. advt. sales mgr., 1970-74, ea. advt. sales mgr., 1974-80, nat. dir. advt. svc., 1980-85; v.p. adminstrn., mag. & internat. group Dow Jones & Co., Inc., N.Y.C., 1985—; bd. dirs. Am. Demographics, Ithaca, N.Y., 1986, Dow Jones So. Holding Co., Inc., 1988; assoc. pub. Barron's Nat. Bus. and Fin. Weekly, V.P. mag. group , 1988, pub., 1989—. Mem. bd. edn. Scarsdale (N.Y.) Schs., 1986. Served to lt. USNR, 1956-61. Mem. Bus. Profl. Advt. Assn., Advt. Club of N.Y., Fin. Com. Soc., Nat. Investors Rels. Inst. Roman Catholic. Club: Coveleigh (Rye, N.Y.) (bd. govs. 1987). Home: 8 Woods Ln Scarsdale NY 10583-6408 Office: Dow Jones & Co Inc 200 Liberty St New York NY 10281-1003*

PARAN, MARK LLOYD, lawyer; b. Cleve., Feb. 1, 1953; s. Edward Walter and Margaret Gertrude (Ebert) P. AB cum laude in Sociology, Harvard U., 1977, JD, 1980. Bar: Ill. 1980, Mass. 1986. Assoc. Wilson & McIlvaine, Chgo., 1980-83, Lurie Sklar & Simon, Ltd., Chgo., 1983-85, Sullivan & Worcester, Boston, 1985-92; pvt. practice, Boston, 1992—. Mem. ABA, Mass. Bar Assn. Avocations: tornado hunting, observation of severe thunderstorms, photography. Home and Office: 84 Gainsborough St #106W Boston MA 02115

PARAS, NICHOLAS ANDREW, banker, financial advisor; b. Ayia Phylaxi, Cyprus, May 1, 1942; arrived in Greece, 1972; s. Andreas and Myrianthi (Antoniou) P.; m. Sofia Dimitria Stoycheff, Dec. 8, 1968; 1 child, Alexandra Nicholas. Teaching cert., Paedogogical Acad., Nicosia, Cyprus, 1962; B.A. in History, B.Mus., Ohio Wesleyan U., Delaware, 1966; J.D., Ohio State U., 1969; M.A. in Law and Diplomacy, Fletcher Sch. Law and Diplomacy, Boston, 1970. Orch. condr. Nicosia Music Conservatory, Cyprus, 1962-63; global credit analyst Chase Manhattan Bank, N.Y.C., Paris, 1970-76, mgr. 2d v.p., Athens, Salonica, Piraeus, Greece, 1970-76; dir. Ippocampos Maritime Ltd., Piraeus, 1976-80; advisor on shipping and gen. advisor Midland Bank, London and Piraeus, 1979-81; dir. Internapa Fin. Services, Athens, 1980-85; first v.p. Republic Nat. Bank N.Y., N.Y.C., 1985—; cons. advisor Banque Francaise du Commerce Exterieur, Paris, Athens, Cyprus, 1981-85; dir. Napa Maritime, Liberia, Paramount Tourist & Devel. Ltd., Cyprus; advisor BHF Bank, Fed. Republic Germany, Trinkaus & Burkhardt Bank, Fed. Republic of Germany, Switzerland, Battelle Meml. Inst., Columbus, Ohio, Agip Internat., Rome. Author: Banking Opportunities in Cyprus, 1990; contbr. numerous articles to profl. jours.; editor: Cyprus Business Shipping and Taxation News, 1978. Treas. fund raising com. Am. Farm Sch., Salonica, Athens, N.Y.C., 1976—; mem. Queens/L.I. Choir Fedn. of Greek Orthodox Ch.; chmn., pres. Corfe, Christian Orthodox Fellowship, Inc. Ohio Wesleyan U. scholar. Mem. Greek Shipowner's Assn., Cyprus Hotel Assn., Cyprus Law Assn., Brit./Hellenic C. of C., Sigma Chi. Greek Orthodox. Clubs: Hellenic Yacht, Propeller of U.S., Port of Piraeus. Lodge: Masons.

PARAS, SOFIA DIMITRIA, counselor, author; b. Delaware, Ohio, Dec. 31, 1943; d. James Peter and Fotini Dimitria (Dellios) Stoycheff; m. Nicholas Andrew Paras, Dec. 8, 1968; 1 child, Alexandra Nicholas. BA, Ohio Wesleyan U., 1965; cert., Adelphi U., 1987. Tchr. Upper Arlington Schs., Columbus, Ohio, 1966-68; asst. tng. coord. personnel dept. Ohio State U. Hosps., Columbus, 1968-69, art fair coord., 1969; asst. tng. coord. personnel dept. New Eng. Deaconess Hosp., Boston, 1969-70; tng. coord. nursing dept. Meml. Hosp. of Sloan Kettering, N.Y.C., 1970-71; real estate salesperson Gen. Devel. Corp., 1971-72; adminstrv. asst. Ippocampos Maritime and Internship Fin. and Investments, Piraeus, Greece, 1976-81; office mgr. Internapa Fin. Svcs., Athens, Greece, 1981-86; adminstrv. dir. lawyer's asst. program Adelphi U., West Hempstead, N.Y., 1987-88, admissions counselor lawyer's asst. program, 1988—; cons. interior decorator hotel complex Paramount Tourist and Devel. Ltd., Paralimni, Cyprus, 1981-84; nat. nursing conf. coord. Meml. Hosp. Sloan Kettering, St. Louis, 1971. Editor Women's Internat. Club, Athens, 1978-84; author: (poetry book) Observations, 1990, (screenplays) Contract, 1990, Contract II, 1991. Theatre dir. Am. Farm Sch., Salonica, Greece, 1974; program coord. choir recitals St. Nicholas Greek Orthodox, Babylon, N.Y., 1989—; v.p. Internat. Women's Orgn. of Greece, Salonica, 1973-74; sec. Christian Orthodox Fellowship, Inc. Mem. NAFE, Nassau/Suffolk Neighborhood Network, L.I. Ctr. for Bus. and Profl. Women, Kappa Kappa Gamma, Theta Alpha Phi. Office: Adelphi U 165 Pidgeon Hill Rd Huntington Station NY 11746

PARASCOS, EDWARD THEMISTOCLES, utilities executive; b. N.Y.C., Oct. 20, 1931; s. Christos and Nina (Demitrovich) P.; BSME, CCNY, 1956, MSME, 1958; postgrad. ops. rsch. N.Y.U., 1964; m. Jenny Morris, July 14, 1978; children: Jennifer Melissa, Edward Themistocles. Design engr. Ford Instrument, 1957-61; reliability engring. supr. Kearfott div. Gen. Precision Inc., 1961-63; staff cons. Am. Power Jet, 1963-64; reliability mgr. Perkin Elmer Corp., 1964-66; dir. system effectiveness CBS Labs., Stamford, Conn., 1966-72; pres. Dipar Cons. Svcs. Ltd., East Elmhurst, N.Y., Lapa Trading Corp.; gen. mgr. power generation svcs. Consol. Edison Co., N.Y.C., 1972—; pres., chmn. bd. RAM Cons. Assocs.; pres. , 1978-80; chmn. 1st Reliability Engring. Conf. Electric Power Industry, 1974, also 4th conf.; vice-chmn. bd. ann. conf. for electric power industry Inter-Ram; lectr. in field. Registered profl. engr., Calif. Fellow Am. Soc. Quality Control (vice chmn. Reliability div. 1968-70, sr. mem.); mem. Am. Mgmt. Assn., ASME, Am. Statis. Assn., Inst. Environ. Scis., Soc. Reliabilty Engrs., Edison Engring. Soc. Home: 30-02 83d St Jackson Heights NY 11370 Office: 4 Irving Pl New York NY 10003-3502

PARCELLS, BILL (DUANE CHARLES PARCELLS), professional football coach; b. Englewood, N.J., Aug. 22, 1941; m. Judith Parcells; children: Suzy, Jill, Dallas. B.A., Wichita State U., 1964. Asst. coach Hastings Coll. (Nebr.), 1964, Wichita State U. (Kans.), 1969, U.S. Mil. Acad., 1966-69, Fla. State U., Tallahassee, 1970-72, Vanderbilt U., Nashville, 1973-74, Tex. Tech U., Lubbock, 1975-77; head coach U.S. Air Force Acad., Colorado Springs, Colo., 1978; asst. coach New Eng. Patriots, NFL, 1980; asst. coach N.Y. Giants, NFL, 1981-82, head coach, 1983-91; NFL studio analyst NBC Sports, 1991—. Coach NFL championship team N.Y. Giants, 1986. Address: care NBC Sports 30 Rockefeller Pla New York NY 10112*

PARDUSKI, FRANK N., manufacturing executive; b. Wilkes-Barre, Pa., Dec. 13, 1954; s. Frank N. Sr. and Verna M. (Fitz) P.; m. Janis L. Kennedy, Aug. 13, 1977; children: Craig A., Alison G. BS, Pa. State U., 1976. Engring. coord. De Walt Divsn. of B&D, Lancaster, Pa., 1980-82; set up coord. K-D Mfg., Lancaster, Pa., 1982-83; engring. coord. New Standard Corp., Mount Joy, Pa., 1983-85, prodn. and inventory control mgr., 1985—. Mem. parish coun. Assumption Ch., Mount Joy, 1984-91; scout leader Cub Scouts, Boy Scouts Am., Mount Joy, 1980-82. Mem. ASTM, Am. Prodn. and Inventory Control Soc., Inst. Indsl. Engrs., Pa. State Alumni Assn., Bass Angler Sportsman Soc., Am. Legion, N.Am. Fish Club. Democrat. Roman Catholic. Home: 1686 Marietta Pike Mount Joy PA 17552-9735 Office: New Standard Corp 125 Pinkerton Rd Mount Joy PA 17552

PARINI, JAY, English educator, writer; b. 1948, Scranton, Pa.; s. Leo Joseph and Verna Ruth (Clifford) P.; m. Devon Stacey Jersild, June 21, 1981. A.B., Lafayette Coll., 1970; B.Phil., Ph.D., U. St. Andrews-Scotland, 1972, 75. Faculty, Dartmouth Coll., Hanover, N.H., 1975-82; prof. English, Middlebury Coll., Vt., 1982—. Editorial com. mem. Juniper Prize for Poetry, U. Mass. Press, 1984—; founding editor New Eng. Rev. Author: (novel) Singing in Time (poetry), 1972; The Love Run (novel), 1980; Anthracite Country (poetry), 1982; The Patch Boys (novel), 1986; An Invitation to Poetry (textbook), 1986, Town Life (poetry), 1988; Theodore Roethke: An American Romantic, 1979. Author: The Last Station, 1990, Bay of Arrows, 1992; co-editor: Bread Loaf Book of Contemporary Poetry, 1985. Council mem. Vt. Council on the Arts, 1980-82; asst. dir. Bread Loaf Writers Conf., 1982—; mem. Vt. Council on Humanities and Social Scis., 1975—. Am. Council Learned Socs. fellow, 1985-86, Guggenheim fellow, 1992; recipient George Washington Kidd award, 1991. Macknight Black Poetry prize, Lafayette Coll., 1970. Democrat. Episcopalian. Avocations: skiing; tennis; karate. Home: RR 1 Box 195 Middlebury VT 05753-9626 Office: Middlebury Coll Middlebury VT 05753

PARIS, MARGARET LUCY, educator; b. Roxboro, N.C., Sept. 13, 1937; d. Neal I. and Margaret (Hammond) P.; m. Octave S. Stevenson, Apr. 14, 1965 (div. 1980); 1 child, Simone Paris Marthers. BFA, U. N.C., Greensboro, 1961, MFA, 1962; MA, Georgetown U., 1984. Tchr. pub. schs. N.Y. State, 1962-65, Washington, 1965-74; tchr. Duke Ellington Sch. of Arts, Washington, 1974—; lectr. Georgetown U., Washington, 1985—; pres. Studio Gallery, Washington, 1985-86, treas., 1986-88; mem. adv. bd. Md. Coll. Art and Design, Silver Spring, 1986—; mem. exec. bd. Washington Ctr. Photography, 1987-89. Editor, Cityscape, 1974-81; contbr. articles, photography to various publs.; photographs displayed in numerous group exhbns. including Torpedo Factory Art Ctr., Alexandria, Va., 1989, Rockland Art Ctr., 1989, Kohler Arts Ctr., Sheboygan, Wis., 1989, Rutgers U., Camden, N.J., 1990, Nat. Copier Art Exhbn., 1990. Mem. Soc. Photographic Edn., Washington Coalition of Artists. Democrat. Home: 12307 Braxfield Ct Rockville MD 20852-2022 Office: Duke Ellington Sch Arts 35th and R Streets Washington DC 20007

PARIS, STEVEN MARK, software engineer; b. Boston, May 26, 1956; s. Julius Louis and Frances (Keleishik) P. BS, Rensselaer Poly. Inst., 1978; MS, Boston U., 1980, postgrad., 1980-84. Sr. software engr. Prime Computer Inc., Framingham, Mass., 1978-82; sr. analyst Computervision Corp., Bedford, Mass., 1982-84; prin. engr. Lotus Devel., Inc., Cambridge, Mass., 1984-88; pres. Tri-Millennium Corp., 1988-91; sr. researcher Tech. Edn. Rsch. Ctr., Cambridge, Mass., 1991—. Lt. Mass. Civil Def. Recipient Boston Sci. Fair 1st prize, 1973, 74, State of Mass. Sci. Fair 3d prize, 1973, 2d prize, 1974. Mem. Assn. for Computing Machinery, IEEE, Boston Computer Soc., Planetary Soc. Jewish. Office: 2067 Massachusetts Ave Cambridge MA 02140-1338

PARISO, JEAN BRUNNER, real estate professional; b. Reinholds, Pa., Dec. 26, 1925; d. Emory Lutz and Rachel Ebling (Keith) Brunner; m. Jesse Francis Pariso, Aug. 11, 1956; 1 child, Penelope Ann. BA, Cedar Crest Coll., Allentown, Pa., 1947; postgrad., Columbia U., 1948-50. Social caseworker Edwin Gould Found., Inc., N.Y.C., 1947-50; asst. dir. pub. rels. Toy Guidance Coun., N.Y.C., 1950-51; sec. to pres. Charles Schlaifer & Co., N.Y.C., 1951-52; legal sec., asst. prod. ABC, N.Y.C., 1952-54; dir. pub. rels. Cushman & Wakefield, Inc., N.Y.C., 1954-62; asst. dir. Coun. Community Svcs., Princeton, N.J., 1970-72; dir. pub. rels. The Princeton (N.J.) Ballet Soc., 1972-81; sales assoc. Richard A. Weidel Corp. Realtors, Hopewell, N.J., 1987—; pub. info. cons. Community Guidance Ctr., Mercer County, 1988-89. Mem. Montgomery Twp. Bd. Edn., Skillman, N.J., 1962-65; mem. Somerset County Bd. Elections, Somerville, N.J., 1987—; co-chmn. Citizens Com. to elect Kennedy-Johnson, Montgomery Twp., 1960. Democrat. Lutheran. Home: 404 Skillman Rd Skillman NJ 08558-1523 Office: Richard A Weidel Corp 45 W Broad St Hopewell NJ 08525-1891

PARITHIVEL, VELLORE SUNDARARAJAN, surgeon; b. Vellore, Tamilnadu, India, June 19, 1951; s. Vellore Kirshnasamy and Padmavathi Sundararajan; m. Banumathi, Aug. 29, 1974; children: Rajalakshmi, Kavitha, Karthika. MB, BS, Stanley Med. Coll., Madras, Tamilnadu, India, 1973. Diplomate Am. Bd. Surgery, Am. Bd. Surg. Critical Care. Rotating house surgeon Govt. Stanley Hosp., Madras, 1973-74; med. officer Swami Vivekananda Med. Mission, Madras, 1974-75; straight surg. team Misericordia Hosp., Bronx, N.Y., 1975-76; surg. resident Bronx-Lebanon Hosp., 1976-80, chief resident surgery, 1980-81, adj. dept. surgery, 1981-83, assoc. dept. surgery, 1983-89, attending surgeon, 1989—. Author: Complication of Central Venous Line, 1989, Colonoscopy in Cancer, 1990. Fellow ACS; mem. AMA, Soc. Am. Gastro-Intestinal Endoscopic Surgeons, Soc. Critical Care Medicine. Home: 6 Old Forge Ln Tarrytown NY 10591 Office: Bronx Lebanon Hosp Ctr 1650 Selwyn Ave Ste 4-H Bronx NY 10457

PARK, JON KEITH, dentist, educator; b. Wichita, Kans., May 26, 1938; s. William Ray and Eleanor Jeanette (Cunningham) P.; D.D.S., U. Mo., 1964; B.A., Wichita State U., 1969; M.S. in Dental Hygiene Edn., U. Mo., 1971; M.S. in Oral Pathology, U. Md., 1982; cert. in dental radiology U. Pa. Sch. Dental Medicine, 1982. Diplomate Am. Bd. Oral and Maxillo-facial Radiology. Pvt. practice dentistry, Wichita, 1964-67; chmn. dept. dental hygiene Wichita State U., 1967-72; assoc. prof. oral diagnosis, dir. oral radiology Balt. Coll. Dental Surgery, U. Md., 1972—; program dir. U. Md. dental externship, 1974-77; lectr. Essex Community Coll., Harford County Community Coll.; cons. in radiology VA Hosp.; mem. Md. State Radiation Control Adv. Bd., 1981—; mem. Ute Pass Hist. Soc.; bd. dirs. Univ. One Residents' Assn., 1975—; chmn. devel. com. Introduction to Basic Concepts in Dental Radiography, Dental Assisting Nat. Bd., Inc., Am. Dental Assts. Assn., 1991. Recipient U. Md. Media Achievement award, 1977, 78. Fellow Am. Acad. Dental Radiology; mem. ADA, Md. State Dental Assn., Balt. City Dental Soc. (ad hoc com. radiation safety), Am. Acad. Oral Pathology, Orgn. Tchrs. Oral Diagnosis, Am. Theater Organ Soc., Kans. Dental Hygienists Assn. (hon.), Balt. Music Club, Am. Acad. Dental Radiology (ednl. standards com.), Am. Assn. Dental Schs., Internat. Assn. Dental and Maxillofacial Radiology, Balt. Opera Guild, Engring. Soc. Balt., Met. Opera Guild, Balt. Symphony Orch. Assn., Ute Pass Community Assn., Univ. Club, Omicron Kappa Upsilon, Psi Omega. Episcopalian. Patentee pivotal design dental chair.

PARK, LAWRENCE KISONG, safety engineer; b. Balt.; s. Zin Uoo and Seado (Kim) P.; m. Darlene Lynn Stoms, Dec. 30, 1989. BS, Hanpden-Sydney Coll.; MS in Pub. Health, U. Mass. Air quality technician The Charles T. Main, Inc., Boston, 1985-86; indsl. hygienist W.R. Grace & Co., Lexington, Mass., 1986-87, sr. indsl. hygienist, 1987-88; mgr. Nat. Med. Care, Inc., Waltham, Mass., 1988-90, dir., 1990—. Usher Emmanuel Ch., Norwood, Mass., 1990—. Recipient Cert. of Commendation, CNA Ins. Co., 1990. Mem. APHA, Am. Indsl. Hygiene Assn., Am. Soc. Safety Engrs., Nat. Safety Coun., Air Pollution Control. Assn. Home: 24 Benjamin Landing Ln Franklin MA 02038-3216 Office: Nat Med Care Inc PO Box 1653 Lowell MA 01853-1653

PARK, LEE CRANDALL, psychiatrist; b. Washington, July 15, 1926; s. Lee I. and Alice (Crandall) P.; m. Barbara Anne Merrick, July 1, 1953; children: Thomas Joseph, Jeffrey Rawson; m. Mary Woodfill Banerjee, Apr. 27, 1985; stepchildren: Stephen Kumar, Scott Kumar. Grad., Putney Prep. Sch., Vt.; B.S. in Zoology, Yale, 1948; M.D., Johns Hopkins, 1952. Diplomate Nat. Bd. Med. Examiners, Am. Bd. Psychiatry and Neurology. Intern medicine Johns Hopkins Hosp., Osler Clinic, Balt., 1952-53; resident psychiatry USN Hosp., Oakland, Calif., 1954; resident psychiatry Henry Phipps Psychiat. Clinic Johns Hopkins Hosp., 1955-59, asst. psychiatrist, 1955-59, staff psychiatrist, 1959—, staff dept. medicine, 1970—, dir. psychiat. outpatient svcs. and community psychiatry program, 1972-74, asst. dir. clin. svcs. dept. psychiatry, 1973-74, mem. departmental coun., 1974-76; fellow psychiatry Johns Hopkins U., 1955-59, faculty in psychiatry, 1959—, assoc. prof., 1971—, physician charge psychiat. svcs. student health svc., 1961-73; vis. psychiatrist Balt. City Hosp., 1960-61; co-prin., prin. investigator NIMH Psychopharmacology Rsch. Br. Outpatient Study of Drug-Set Interaction, 1960-68, co-dir. (with Eugene Meyer) Time-Limited Psychotherapy Rsch. Grant, 1969-73; pvt. practice psychiatry, 1964—; cons. Met. Balt. Assn. Mental Health, 1961-63, Bur. Disability Ins., Social Security Adminstrn., 1964-81; attending staff Seton Psychiat. Inst., 1966-73, exec. bd., 1970-73; staff Sheppard and Enoch Pratt Hosp., 1974—; conductor rsch. including borderline and narcissistic conditions, long-term effects of childhood emotional abuse, interrelationships of psychotherapy and pharmacotherapy, time ltd. psychotherapy, ethical considerations in clin. rsch. Contbr. articles and chpts. to profl. jours. and books. Served to lt. M.C., USNR, 1953-55, div. psychiatrist 1st Marine Div., Korea, staff psychiatrist USN Hosp., Camp Pendelton, Calif., 1954-55. Fellow Am. Psychiat. Assn. (life, mem. assembly 1983—), AAAS; mem. AMA, AAUP, Am. Psychosomatic Soc., Am. Soc. Adolescent Psychiatry, Am. Coll. Neuropsychopharmacology, Am. Assn. Pvt. Practicing Psychiatrists, Md. Soc. Adolescent Psychiatry, Md. Psychiat. Soc. (pres. 1978-79), Soc. Psychotherapy Rsch., N.Am. Soc. Psychotheraphy Rsch., N.Y. Acad. Scis., Group Therapy Network, Md. Interdisciplinary Coun. Children and Adolescents (treas. 1980-87), Med. and Chirurg. Faculty Md., Balt. City, Baltimore County Med. Socs., Johns Hopkins Med. and Surg. Assn., Md. Assn. Pvt. Practicing Psychiatrists, SAR, Johns Hopkins Club (Balt.), Met. Club (Washington), Farmington Country Club (Charlottesville, Va.), Chevy Chase (Md.) Country Club, Phi Beta Pi. Home: 308 Tunbridge Rd Baltimore MD 21212-3803 Office: 1205 York Rd Ste 35 Lutherville Timonium MD 21093-6268

PARK, MARIAN PATRICIA FORD, financial consultant, accountant; b. Milw., May 12, 1918; d. Charles Eaton and Gladys Harriet (Richardson) Ford; m. Glen Waulters, Mar. 16, 1943 (div. 1946); 1 child, Gary Daniel; m. James Delmar Park, Oct. 9, 1956. Student, Pa. State U. Cashier/bookkeeper Warner Theatres, Milw., 1937-43; tac acct. Capital Acctg. Svc., Harrisburg, Pa., 1955-61; fin. cons. Belco Fed. Credit Union, Harrisburg, Pa., 1961-72; self-employed writer Harrisburg, Pa., 1983—; contest judge for poetry States of Ala., Ky., numerous poetry jours. Author poetry book: Reflections, 1991; author (fiction): Tales of Robin's Wood, 1990, 2d edit. 1991; author numerous poetry chapbooks; guest editor Ala. Newsletter, Birmingham, 1991, Poetic Page, 1991. Named Most Disting. Poet, Jessee Poet, 1986, Poet of the Yr., Editor's Desk, Ocala, Fla., 1986. Fellow Pa. Poetry Soc., Ky. Poetry Soc., Nat. Poetry Soc.; mem. Nat. Shut In Soc. (contbg. mem.). Home: 130 S 3d St #PH17 Harrisburg PA 17101

PARK, MARY WOODFILL, information consultant; b. Nevada, Mo., Nov. 20, 1944; d. John Prosser and Elizabeth (Devine) Woodfill; m. Salil Kumar Banerjee, Dec. 29, 1967 (div. 1983); children: Stephen Kumar, Scott Kumar; m. Lee Crandall Park, Apr. 27, 1985; stepchildren: Thomas Joseph, Jeffrey Rawson. BA, Marywood Coll., 1966; postgrad., Johns Hopkins U., 1983, Goucher Coll., 1986. Asst. to dir. U. Pa. Librs., Phila., 1968-69; investment libr. Del. Funds, Phila., 1969-71; investment officer Investment Counselors Md., Balt., 1980-84, 1st Nat. Bank Md., Balt., 1984-85; pres., founder Info. Consultancy, Balt., 1985—; lectr. Towson State U., Villa Julie Coll., Balt., 1989, Loyola Coll., Balt., 1991-92. Editor, contbr. to profl. publs. Vol. Internat. Visitors' Ctr., Balt., 1979-80, 91; del. White House Conf. on Librs.; mem. Balt. Coun. Fgn. Affairs, 1990, 91, 92; v.p. bd. dirs. Friends of Goucher Libr., 1988-90; mem. Friends of Johns Hopkins Libr., 1988—. Mem. Spl. Librs. Assn. (pres. Balt. chpt. 1991-92), Am. Soc. Info. Sci. Assn. Ind. Info. Profls., Md. Libr. Assn., Am. Psychiat. Assn. Aux. (assembly rep. 1989-90), Assn. Info. and Dissemination Ctrs., Hamilton St. Club (bd. dirs. 1989-92). Office: Info Consultancy 308 Tunbridge Rd Baltimore MD 21212-3803

PARK, MIN-YONG, human factors and safety engineer, educator; b. Kimcheon, South Korea, Feb. 21, 1955; came to the U.S., 1981; s. Heechang and JeongBoon (Park) P.; m. Mihwan Kim, June 28, 1981; children: Stephen, Veronica, John, Caroline. MS, Hayang U., Seoul, 1981, Okla. State U., 1986, Va. Poly. Inst., 1989; PhD, Va. Poly. Inst., 1991. Grad. rsch. and teaching assoc. Okla. State U., Stillwater, 1983-86, Va. Poly. Inst., Blacksburg, 1987-91; asst. prof. N.J. Inst. Tech., Newark, 1991—; assoc. dir. occupational safety and health program N.J. Inst. Tech., 1991—. Contbr. articles to profl. jours. Mem. Acoustical Soc. Am., Am. Soc. for Quality Control, Am. Soc. for Safety Engrs., Nat. Hearing Conservation Assn., Human Factors Soc., Inst. Indsl. Engrs. (Rsch. award 1990), Alpha Pi Mu, Phi Kappa Phi. Roman Catholic. Home: 7 Boynton Dr Livingston NJ 07039 Office: NJ Inst Tech Dept Indsl Engring Newark NJ 07102

PARK, WILLIAM WYNNEWOOD, law educator; b. Phila., July 2, 1947; s. Oliver William and Christine (Lindes) P. BA, Yale U., 1969; JD, Columbia U., 1972; MA, Cambridge U., 1975. Bar: Mass. 1972, D.C. 1980. Assoc. Coudert Frères, Paris, 1972-75; fellow Selwyn Coll., U. Cambridge, Eng., 1975-77; assoc. Hughes, Hubbard & Reed, Paris, 1977-79; prof. law Boston U., 1979—; dir. Morin Ctr. for Banking Law Studies; counsel Ropes & Gray, Boston; legal counsel Trade Devel. Bank, Geneva, Switzerland, 1983-84; adj. prof. Fletcher Sch. Tufts U., Medford, Mass., 1980-86; vis. prof. U. Dijon, France, 1983-84, Inst. Univ. de Hautes Etudes Internationales, Geneva, 1983. Author: International Chamber of Commerce Arbitration, 1984, 2d edit. 1990; contbr. articles and book revs. to profl. jours. Fellow Chartered Inst. Arbitrators; mem. Am. Soc. Internat. Law, Internat. Fiscal Assn., Internat. Law Assn., Union Internat. Avocats. Republican. Unitarian. Clubs: Oxford-Cambridge (London), Yale of N.Y., Harvard of Boston. Office: Boston U Law Sch 765 Commonwealth Ave Boston MA 02215-1401 also: Ropes and Gray 1 International Pl Boston MA 02110

PARKE, CAROL SANTEL, educator; b. Canonsburg, Pa., Dec. 9, 1965; d. Martin Joseph and Ann (Malli) S. BS in Edn., Ind. U. Pa., 1987; MA in Math., U. Pitts., 1989, postgrad., 1991—. Cert. tchr., Pa. Substitute math. tchr. Upper St. Clair (Pa.) Schs., 1987-89, Bethel Park (Pa.) Schs., 1987-89, Mt. Lebanon Schs., Pitts., 1987-89; temp. full-time math. instr. Community Coll. Allegheny County, Pa.; rsch. specialist in math. edn. on Quasar Project Learning Rsch. and Devel. Ctr. U. Pitts., 1990—. Mem. Am. Math. Soc., Nat. Coun. Tchrs. Math. Home: 472 E 7th Ave Tarentum PA 15084-1655

PARKE, ISOBEL, public relations executive; b. Dorset, Eng., Sept. 23, 1926; came to U.S., 1963; d. Charles and Jean Hamilton Gordon (Gardiner) P. MA, Oxford U., 1963. Asst. prin. Ministry of Edn., London, 1947-49; course dir. Moor Park Coll. for Adult Edn., Farnham Surrey, Eng., 1950-63; assoc. counsel Jackson, Jackson & Wagner, Boston, 1964-70; counsel Jackson, Jackson & Wagner, Exeter, N.H., 1970-80, pres., sr. counsel, 1980—. Pres. N.H. Timberland Owners Assn., 1987. Fellow Pub. Rels. Soc. Am. (accredited 1970, counselor's acad. 1974—, bd. dirs. 1985, 86, sec. 1988, nat. coms. 1991, Presdl. Citation 1986, 87, 88); mem. Internat. Pub. Rels. Assn. Office: Jackson Jackson & Wagner 14 Front St Exeter NH 03833-2747

PARKE, JO ANNE MARK, publishing company executive; b. Rochester, Pa., Mar. 8, 1941; d. Robert Kleckner and Alice (Dowling) Mark; m. William Ernst Parke III, May 6, 1963 (div. 1988); children: Alicia Ann, William Ernst IV; m. Robert Arnott Gerhardt, Oct. 19, 1991. Student, U. Strasbourg, France, 1962; BA, Pa. State U., 1963. Reporter Beaver County (Pa.) Times, summers 1959-61, Washington (D.C.) Star, 1963-64; writer Pa. State Dept. Pub. Info., Univ. Park, 1964-65; reporter Centre Daily Times, State College, Pa., 1965-67; editor Spenley Newspapers, Pitts., 1971-72, St. Petersburg (Fla.) Times, 1972-73; freelance writer Phila. Inquirer, 1974-77; editor, assoc. publisher Bus. Digest, Phila., 1978-81; editor Phila. Bus. Jour., 1981-84; v.p. editorial dir. N.Am. Pub. Co., Phila., 1984—; bd. dirs. Graphic Arts Assn. Neographics, Phila., 1984—. Author: All Gods' Children, 1977. Bd. dirs. Mayor's Small Bus. Coun., Phila, 1980-83, C. of C. Small Bus. Coun., Phila., 1980-83. Mem. Women in Communications, Soc. Profl. Journalists (bd. dirs. Phila. chpt. 1990—), Am. Soc. Bus. Press Editors, N.Y. Bus. Press Editors, French-Am. C. of C., Alliance Francaise. Office: N Am Pub Co 401 N Broad St Philadelphia PA 19108-1013

PARKE, JOHN SHEPARD, marketing consultant; b. N.Y.C., Nov. 11, 1933; s. John S. and Dorothy (Simpson) P.; m. Mary Lundy, Aug. 20, 1955; children: John Shepard III, Suzanne Lundy. AB, Dartmouth Coll., 1956; MBA, Amos Tuck Sch., 1957. Sales mgr. Procter & Gamble Co., Cin., 1960, advt. mgr., 1961-69; mktg. dir. Ralston Purina Co., St. Louis, 1969-74; v.p. mktg. Ralson Purina Co., St. Louis, 1974-79; v.p. mktg. and sales Bausch & Lomb, Rochester, N.Y., 1979-81; pres. PPI Mktg. Group, Rochester, 1982—. Mem. trustees coun. Rochester Inst. Tech.; trustee Episcopal House. Capt. USAF, 1957-60. Mem. Genesse Valley Club (Rochester), U.S. Tennis Assn. (chair umpire). Republican. Episcopalian. Home: 215 Ambassador Dr Rochester NY 14610-3404 Office: PPI Mktg Group 110 Allens Creek Rd Rochester NY 14618-3392

PARKER, ALICE CONSTANCE, English educator; b. N.Y.C.; d. Victor G. and Mary (Sutter) Cocoros; children: Raymond A. II, J. Grant, G. Andrew. MA, U. R.I., 1978, PhD, 1983. Acting dir. Arts R.I., Providence, 1973-74; researcher, docent R.I. Sch. Design Mus. of Art, Providence, 1963-73; instr. R.I. Adult Correctional Instn., Cranston, 1978-79; teaching asst. U. R.I., Kingston, 1977-82; adj. lectr. Brown U., Providence, 1987-88; instr. in English U. R.I., Providence, 1982—; cons. in field. Author: The Exploration of the Secret Smile, 1989; editor: Worst Hotel in Town, 1979; contbr. articles to profl. jours. Chair maj. fund raising project R.I. Philharm. Orch., Providence, 1976. Recipient Univ. fellowship U. R.I., 1982, Summer Writers Conf. fellowship, 1980. Mem. Modern Greek Studies Assn., MLA, Assn. for Studies of Am. Indian Lit. Office: U R I 199 Promenade St Providence RI 02908-5006

PARKER, BARBARA L., educator; b. Phila., Dec. 8, 1933; d. Benjamin and Nettie Vivian (Rademan) Parker. BA, UCLA, 1957; MA, CCNY, 1970; PhD, NYU, 1982. Adj. asst. prof. English Baruch Coll. CUNY, N.Y.C., 1982-89; asst. prof. English The William Paterson Coll. N.J., Wayne, N.J., 1989—. Editor: Ecology of Endemic Diseases in the Dez Irrigation Pilot Area: A Report to the Govt. of Iran, 1962; author: A Precious Seeing: Love and Reason in Shakespeare's Plays, 1987; contbr. articles to profl. jours. Active Friends of N.Y. Pub. Library, 1983—, Friends of Bobst Library, 1982—, Bklyn. Hts. Assn., 1975—, Village Ind. Democrats, N.Y.C., 1960-64. Mem. MLA, N.Y. Shakespeare Assn., Renaissance Soc. Am., Shakespeare Assn. Am., Columbia U. Seminars, Nat. Coun. Tchrs. English. Home: 145 Hicks St # 26B Brooklyn NY 11201-2325

PARKER, CLYDE H., personnel executive; b. Phila., July 12, 1943; s. Clyde H. and Josephine (Barefoot) P; divorced; 1 child, Kelly Jo. BS, N.C. State U., 1971. Profl. safety engr. Production mgr. Deering-Miliken, Inc., Williamstown, S.C., 1971-73; industrial rels. mgr. Chicopee Div. Johnson & Johnson, Athens, Ga., 1973-78; human resources mgr. CertainTeed Corp., Athens, 1978-83; dir. mfg. pers. Mannington Mills, Inc., Salem, N.J., 1983—; adj. prof. Camden County Coll., Clementon, N.J., 1983—. Bd. dirs. Am. Cancer Soc.-Crusade Div., New Brunswick, N.J., 1985; placement com. N.J. Epilepsy Found., Trenton, 1986—; mem. gov.'s appt. Uncomp Health Care Com., Trenton, 1987—; mem. human resource coun. Nat. Assn. Mfgs., Washington, 1988; mem. employer consortiumtor Guard & Reserve, Trenton, 1985. Republican. Episcopalian. Home: 502 Curtis Dr. Pennsville NJ 08070 Office: Mannington Mills Inc PO Box 30 Salem NJ 08079

PARKER, ELLIS JACKSON, III, lawyer, broadcaster; b. Haleyville, Ala., Oct. 2, 1932; s. Ellis J. and Elizabeth (Funderburg) P.; m. Nancy Elizabeth Bealer; children: Francis Hill, Ellis Stuart. Student, U.S. Mil. Acad., West Point, N.Y., 1953-57; AB, U. Ala., 1958, LLB, 1960, JD, 1961; diplome de droit, U. Compare, Luxembourg, 1959; cert., Acad. Internat. Law, Hague, The Netherlands, 1960. Bar: Ala. 1960, U.S. Tax Ct. 1960, D.C. 1962, D.C. Ct. Appeals 1972, U.S. Supreme Ct. 1966, U.S. Ct. Appeals D.C. 1972, U.S. Ct. Appeals Md. 1973, U.S. Ct. Claims, 1977. Legis. atty. IRS, Washington, 1961-62; adminstrv. asst. to U.S. Congressman Grant Ala., 1963-64; pvt. practice Birmingham, Ala., 1964—; spl. asst. to Pres. Richard Nixon White House, Washington, 1968-69; v.p., counsel Birmingham Broadcasting Co., 1964-83; ptnr. Taylor, Smith & Parker Law Office, Washington, 1970—; v.p., sec. C.C.C. Devel. Corp., Upper Marlboro, Md., 1968-72; pres. Washington-Ala. News Reports, Washington, 1980—; pres. Sta. WNPT-AM-FM, Tuscaloosa, Ala.; v.p. Sta. WLPH, Birmingham, Ala., Parker Real Estate, Birmingham, N. Haase Real Estate, Washington; ptnr. Linden (Ala.) Radio; founder Women's Nat. Bank, Washington. Mem. Presdl. Inaugural Com., inaugural protocol officer V.p. Agnew, 1968; mem. steering com. Rep. Party, Balt., 1972; chmn. bd. trustees Prince George's Hist. and Cultural Trust, Upper Marlboro, 1974; chmn. bd. advisors Prince George's Equestrian Ctr., Upper Marlboro, 1980; founder, pres. bd. dirs. Hospice of Prince George's County, Upper Marlboro, 1982; mem. Upper Marlboro Devel. Com. Mem. IEEE, ABA, Fed. Communications Bar Assn., Fed. Bar Assn., Inter-Am. Bar Assn., Nat. Assn. Broadcasters Assn., Ala. Broadcasters Assn., Balt. Coun. Fgn. Affairs, Chevy Chase Club, The Maryland Club, St. Andrews Soc., Met. Club (Washington), Assn. Grad. U.S.M.A., The Summit Club (Birmingham), Scabbard and Blade, Pi Kappa Alpha (Gamma Alpha chpt.), Sigma Delta Kappa. Home: 11133 Stephalee Ln Rockville MD 20852-3655 also: 1633 S 15th Ave Birmingham AL 35205 also: 15227 Old Marlboro Pike Upper Marlboro MD 20772

PARKER, FLORA L., educator; b. Jacksonville, Fla., Apr. 24, 1941; d. Handy and Georgia (Hoover) McClendon; m. Donald Parker, June 25, 1975; children: Felicia, Torrence, Calvin, Clarese, Sean. BA in Elem. Edn., Glassboro State U., 1975, MA in Elem. Sch. Teaching, 1991. Tchr. Head-Start program Atlantic Human Resources, Atlantic City, 1966-69; social svc. Model Cities--City of Atlantic City, 1969-71; state day worker N.J. State Day Care Ctr., Atlantic City, 1971-73; tchr. South Main St. Sch., Pleasantville, N.J., 1975-77, Dr. Martin Luther King Sch., Atlantic City, 1977—; part time tchr. Altantic County Jins Shelter, Northfield, N.J., 1975-77. Contbr. poetry to publs. Mem. NCCJ, Atlantic City, 1991, Nat. Coun. Negro Women, Atlantic County, 1991, Nat. Polit. Congress Women, Atlantic County, 1991. Recipient letter of Praise Pres. George Bush, 1990. Mem. Bus. & Profl. Women's Club (Silver Achievement award 1991), Delta Sigma Theta, Inc. (treas. 1981-83), Phi Delta Kappa (cert. Recognition Delta Lambda chpt. 1991). Democrat. Baptist. Home: 708 Second St Northfield NJ 08225

PARKER, FRANK J(OSEPH), real estate educator, consultant, lawyer, priest; b. N.Y.C., Oct. 10, 1940. BS, Holy Cross Coll., 1962; JD, Fordham U., 1965; MTh, Louvain (Belgium) U., 1974. Bar: Mass. 1967. Prof. real estate Boston Coll., Chestnut Hill, Mass., 1969—; pvt. practice real estate cons. Chestnut Hill, 1969—; vis. scholar Urban Land Inst., Washington, 1986-87; cons. Soc. of Jesus of New Eng., Boston, 1981-86, Archdiocese of San Francisco, 1989—, Nat. Soc. for Hist. Preservation, Chgo., 1988-89; trustee Regis Coll., Denver, 1988—. Editor-in-chief Jour. RTC Real Estate, 1991—; mem. editorial bd. The Counsellor. U.S. del. UN Human Rights Comm., Geneva, 1984, UNESCO, Paris, 1983; mem. Mass. Govt. Land Bank, Boston, 1983-88, Gov.'s Adv. Commn. on Legal Svcs., Boston, 1976-80; trustee Regis Coll. Mem. Am. Soc. Real Estate Counselors, Soc. Real Estate Appraisers, Urban Land Inst. Roman Catholic. Office: Boston Coll Sch Mgmt Fulton Hall 403 Chestnut Hill MA 02167-3808

PARKER, FRANK SOLOMON, biochemistry educator, researcher; b. Boston, Jan. 25, 1921; s. Louis J. and Jennie G. Parker; m. Gladys Baker, Sept. 1, 1946; children: Judith Ann, George Edward (dec.). BS in Chemistry, Tufts U., 1942, MS in Chemistry, 1944; PhD in Chemistry, Johns Hopkins U., 1950. Jr. instr. Johns Hopkins U., Balt., 1946-50; asst. prof. Bryn Mawr (Pa.) Coll., 1950-54; from asst. to assoc. prof. SUNY Med. Ctr., Bklyn., 1954-63; from assoc. to full prof. N.Y. Med. Coll., Valhalla, 1963-70, prof., 1970—; spectroscopy trainee MIT, Cambridge, Mass., 1957, vis. scientist, 1982-87; lectr. Infrared Inst. Canisius Coll., Buffalo, summers 1965-67; cons. NSF. Author: Applications of IR Spectroscopy in Biochemistry, Biology and Medicine, 1971, Applications of IR, Raman and Resonance Raman Spectroscopy in Biochemistry, 1983; mem. editorial bd. Jour. Applied Spectroscopy, Can. Jour. Spectroscopy; referee over 10 jours. Office: NY Med Coll Dept Biochemistry Molecular Biology Basic Science Bldg Valhalla NY 10595

PARKER, GENE, author, artist, photographer; b. Fitchburg, Mass., July 31, 1923; s. Aarne J. and Sarah (Kankunen) P.; m. Nancy Stupak (div. 1988); children: Laura, Amy, Rebecca. Student engring ASTP program, U. Maine, 1943-44; BFA, Mass. Coll. Art, 1949. Mgr., co-owner Parker & Eames, Inc., Fitchburg, Mass., 1949-53; art dir. GE Advanced Tech. Lab., Schenectady, N.Y., 1955-64; sr. engring. writer Westinghouse, Annapolis, Md., 1964-66; mem. profl. staff Sanders Assocs. Nuclear Lab., Nashua, N.H., 1966-69; art. dir. U.S. EPA Region 1, Boston, 1979-82; author, artist, pvt. practice Nashua, N.H., 1982-87, Colebrook, N.H., 1988—. Author: Civil Defense Diver Manual, 1956, Gene Parker's Complete Handbook of Skindiving, 1964 (3 revisions), Parker's Illustrated Fishing Lore, 1983; No. N.H. editor New Eng. Out-of-Doors mag.; contbr. articles, photos, art to outdoor mags., jours. oceanographic pubs. Mem. New Eng. Outdoor Writers Assn., Out-

door Writers of Am. Assn., North Country Sportmans Club, Abenaki Chpt. Trout Unlimited, Bungy Beavers Snowmobile Club (pres.). Home and Office: RR 1 Box 328B Colebrook NH 03576

PARKER, JOHN OSMYN, management consultant; b. Denver, May 31, 1919; s. George Lindsey and Marie (Bloedorn) P.; m. Judith Fehr, July 20, 1942; children: Craig Steven, John Fehr, Diane, Newton Lindsey. BS in Bus., U. Colo., 1942. Jr. indsl. engr. U.S. Steel Corp., Gary, Ind., 1942-43; mgr. pers. rsch. Trans World Airlines, Kansas City, Mo., 1945-55; mgmt. cons. Douglas Williams Assocs., N.Y.C., 1955-56; dir. pers. Cen. Hudson Gas & Electric Corp., Poughkeepsie, N.Y., 1956-69, United Hosp., Port Chester, N.Y., 1969-78; v.p. human resources Mountainside Hosp., Montclair, N.J., 1978-83; mgmt. cons.; instr. mgmt. Rutgers U., Ocean County Coll. Chmn. budget div., bd. dirs. United Way, Dutchess County, N.Y., 1963-69; adv. bd. Montclair Salvation Army; pres. Fellowship Club, Presbyn. Ch., 1985, elder, trustee, deacon ; mem. Garden State Philharmonic Chorus. With U.S. Army, 1943-45, ETO. Mem. DAV (comdr. 1988-90, trustee 1990—), Soc. for Human Resourse Mgmt. (rsch. awards com. 1958—, accredited exec. in pers., SPHR), Am. Soc. Tng. Dirs., Am. Mgmt. Assn., Rotary (bd. dir. Rye, N.Y. 1975-78, pres. 1977-78, bd. dirs. Montclair 1978-83, bd. dirs. Central Ocean, Toms River, N.J. 1985-88), Am. Legion (trustee 1990—), Phi Kappa Psi. Republican. Home: 10 Morningside Dr Toms River NJ 08755-5108

PARKER, JOHN SHELDON, internist; b. Altoona, Pa., Apr. 18, 1928; s. John Lawrence and Helen Shea (Crawford) P.; m. Dorris McKean, Dec. 22, 1951; children: Linda, Larry, Pamela, Margaret, Douglas. BA, Washington & Jefferson U., 1952; MD, U. Buffalo, 1957. Diplomate Nat. Bd. Med. Examiners, Am. Bd. Internal Medicine. Internship Edward J. Myer Hosp., Buffalo, 1957-58; pvt. practice Diagnostic Assocs., Latrobe, Pa., 1961—; mem. staff Latrobe Area Hosp., 1961—; residency in internal medicine Edward J. Myer Hosp., Buffalo, 1958-61; clin. asst. prof. medicine Thomas Jefferson Med. Sch., Phila., 1975—. Deacon, elder Latrobe Presbyn. Ch., 1961-91; mem. alumni bd. trustees Washington and Jefferson Coll., Washington, Pa., 1985-90; organizer Latrobe Swim Club, 1975. With USN, 1946-48. Fellow Am. Coll. Medicine, Am. Geriatric Soc., Coll. Physicians of Phila.; mem. Am. Med. Soc. (del., alt. del. 1981-91), Pa. Med. Soc. (del. 1961-91), Westmoreland County Med. Soc., C. of C. (com. on drug edn.). Republican. Presbyterian. Office: Diagnostic Assocs 1100 Ligonier St Latrobe PA 15650-1917

PARKER, KENNETH FRANCIS, JR., communications executive; b. Newburgh, N.Y., Feb. 28, 1964; s. Kenneth Francis and Rosalie (Pellicciotti) P. BA, Marist Coll., 1986. Pub. rels. asst. St. Francis Hosp., Poughkeepsie, N.Y., 1986; graphics proofreader Corp. Graphics Group, Fishkill, N.Y., 1986; dir. corp. communications Vassar Bros. Hosp., Poughkeepsie, 1987—. Mem. Am. Heart Assn. (communications com. 1990—), Profl. Communicators Hudson Valley. Roman Catholic. Home: 11 Valewood Dr New Windsor NY 12553-7438

PARKER, LEROY ALBERT, JR., dental surgery educator; b. Newark, Feb. 12, 1930; s. Leroy Alston and Julia Elizabeth (Klena) P.; m. Ruth Elaine Wecht, June 19, 1954; children: Robert L., William L. DDS, Georgetown U., 1954; BA, Seton Hall U., 1962. Pvt. practice dentistry Union, N.J., 1956-61; dental educator U. Medicine and Dentistry, Newark, 1957—; interim dean U. Medicine and Dentistry of N.J., Newark, 1986-87; assoc. dir. clin. dental rsch. Johnson and Johnson, New Brunswick, N.J., 1965-66. Author: (handbook) Handbook of Dental Asepis, 1965, (chpt.) Clinical Oral Diagnosis, 1965, Peridontal Prosthesis, 1968. Lt. USN, 1954-56. Fellow Am. Coll. Dentists, Internat. Coll. Dentists; mem. ADA, Am. Assn. Dental Schs., Internat. Assn. Dental Rsch., N.J. Dental Assn., Essex County Dental Soc. Roman Catholic. Office: U Medicine & Dentistry NJ 110 Bergen St Newark NJ 07103-2400

PARKER, MAYNARD MICHAEL, journalist, magazine executive; b. L.A., July 28, 1940; s. Clarence Newton and Virginia Esther (Boyce) P.; m. Judith Karen Seaborg, Dec. 11, 1965 (div.); 1 child, Francesca Lynn; m. Susan Fraker, Sept. 15, 1985; children: Nicholas Maynard, Hugh Fraker. B.A., Stanford U., 1962; M.A., Columbia U., 1963. Reporter Life mag., 1963-64, corr. Hong Kong Bur., 1966-67; corr. Hong Kong Bur. Newsweek, 1967-69; Saigon bur. chief Newsweek, Vietnam, 1969-70; chief Hong Kong Bur. Newsweek, 1969-73, sr. nat. affairs editor, 1975-77, asst. mng. editor, 1977-80, exec. editor, 1980-82, editor, 1982—; mng. editor Newsweek Internat. Newsweek, N.Y.C., 1973-75. Contbr. articles to Fgn. Affairs, Fgn. Policy, Reporter, Atlantic. Served to 1st lt. inf. U.S. Army, 1964-66. Mem. Am. Soc. Mag. Editors, Coun. on Fgn. Rels., Overseas Press Club. Episcopalian. Office: Newsweek Mag 444 Madison Ave New York NY 10022-6903

PARKER, NANCY KNOWLES (MRS. CORTLANDT PARKER), publishing executive; b. Buffalo, Aug. 30, 1929; d. Ward Emerson and Barbara Louise (Bull) Knowles; student Chevy Chase Jr. Coll., 1949; m. Cortlandt Parker, Sept. 8, 1951; children: Elizabeth, Cortlandt, Stephen, Nancy Gray. Copy girl Washington Evening Star, 1947-49; reporter Newark Evening News, 1949-51; asst. pub. relations dir. Newark Community Chest, 1951-52; writer Suburban Life mag., Summit, N.J., 1952-55; co-founder, assoc. editor Observor Tribune, Mendham, N.J., 1955-59; woman's editor, Recorder Pub. Co., Bernardsville, N.J., 1959-84, v.p., 1960—; editor New Eng. Wine Gazette (a Recorder Publ.). Former trustee Somerset Hills Community Chest, North Jersey Tng. Sch., Totowa, Morris-Somerset chpt. UN Assn., Bonnie Brae Ednl. Ctr., Millington, N.J. Vis. Homemaker Svc. of Somerset County (N.J.); now trustee, mem. bd. dirs. Camp Brett-Endeavor, Clinton, N.J., N.J. Hist. Soc., Newark, Morristown (N.J.) Meml. Hosp. Mem. Glen Manor House Com., Portsmouth, R.I. Mem. Bus. and Profl. Women, Nat. Soc. Arts and Letters, Southeastern New Eng. Grape Growers Assn., Jr. League, Pen and Brush N.Y.C., New Eng. Wine Coun. (sec.), Friends of Whitehall Colonial Dames Am. (bd. dirs. R.I. chpt.), Colonial Dames of Am. (R.I. chpt.), Newport (R.I.) Garden Club (bd. dirs.), English Speaking Union (bd. dirs. Newport chpt.). Episcopalian. Home: PO Box 962 Far Hills NJ 07931-0962 also: Greenvale Farm & Vineyard 582 Wapping Rd Portsmouth RI 02871 Office: 17 Morristown Rd Bernardsville NJ 07924

PARKER, PATRICIA HOLMES, communications educator; b. Astabula, Ohio, Dec. 31, 1936; d. Don Vern and Katherine (Timlin) P. BS in Edn., U. Dayton, 1965; MA, U. No. Colo., 1974, Loyola U., New Orleans, 1980; postgrad., Ohio U., 1984-87. Tchr. parochial schs., Ohio, Mo., 1957-65, Falls Church, Va., 1965-68, Denver, 1968-71; exec. coord. Archdiocesan Sisters' Coun., Denver, 1971-74; writer, producer Sta. WWL-TV, New Orleans, 1975-76; tchr. E.D. White High Sch., Thibodaux, La., 1981-82; instr. Loyola U., New Orleans, 1976-81; asst. prof. Cen. Mo. State U., Warrensburg, 1982-84; grad. asst. Ohio U., Athens, 1984-87; instr. dept. communication SUNY, Geneseo, 1987-92; talk show host Sta. KMOS-TV, Warrensburg, 1982-83; mem. faculty Inst. for Religious Communication, New Orleans, 1976-79, Elderhostel, Athens, 1987. Writer, producer TV pub. svc. announcements and documentaries. Pres. Denver Sisters' Coun., 1969-70. Mem. Speech Communication Assn., Popular Culture Assn., Women in Communication, Religious Speech Communication Assn., N.Y. State Speech Communication Assn. Democrat. Roman Catholic.

PARKER, PAUL EDMUND, JR., insurance sales professional; b. Brighton, Mass., Oct. 29, 1960; s. Paul Edmund and Mary (Landry) P. BBA, U. Notre Dame, 1982. With Travelers Ins. Co., Balt., 1982-86, account exec., 1985-86; group sales rep. Phoenix Mut. Life Ins. Co., Bethesda, Md., 1986—, field adv. bd., dental ins. proposal adviser, 1989—. Campaign worker Bob Schaeffer for U.S. Congress, Farmingham, Mass., 1980; tchr. St. Isaac Jogues Ch., Balt., 1984-85; coach Parkville Recreation Boys Baseball, Balt., 1985. Mem. Cert. Employee Benefit Specialists, K.C. Roman Catholic. Home: 1 Shawnee Ct Baltimore MD 21234-8601 Office: Phoenix Mut Life Ins Co 4550 Montgomery Ave Bethesda MD 20814-3304

PARKER, ROBERT ANDREW, psychologist, computer consultant; b. Jacksonville, Fla., Mar. 21, 1946; s. Farrand Drake and Laurel (Cook) P. BA with distinction in Psychology, Ohio State U., 1969; MA, U. Regina, Sask., Can., 1976, PhD, 1983. Lic. psychologist, N.Y. Psychologist Weyburn (Can.) Psychiat. Ctr., 1981-85; psychologist No. Westchester Guidance Clinic, Mt. Kisco, N.Y., 1985-87, cons., 1988—; sr. psychologist Abbott House, Irvington, N.Y., 1988-89, cons., 1989—; pvt. practice, White Plains, N.Y., 1988—; assoc. psychologist Rockland Children's Psychiat. Ctr., Orangeburg, N.Y., 1989—; cons. Westchester Mental Health Assn., White Plains, 1990. Author: Waiting for Cargo, 1991; also articles; author computer programs Klopfer I, 1983, Exner I, 1986. Bd. dirs. A Different Start, Yonkers, N.Y., 1990—; mem. client svcs. com. So. N.Y. chpt. Nat. Multiple Sclerosis Soc., White Plains, 1990—. Mem. APA, Can. Psychol. Assn. Home: 16 Newcomb Pl White Plains NY 10606-2004 Office: 499 N Broadway White Plains NY 10603-3242

PARKER, ROBERT LOUIS, physicist; b. Fort Dodge, Iowa, July 4, 1929; s. Oliver Wendell and Louise (Nemecek) P.; m. Vivian Stark, July 27, 1963; children: Susan, David. BS in Physics, MIT, 1951; PhD in Physics, U. Md., 1960. Physicist, solid state rsch. Nat. Inst. Standards and Tech. (formerly Nat. Bur. Standard), Gaithersburg, Md., 1954-86; cons. Washington, 1986—. Author publs. about crystal growth. Home and Office: 3503 1/2 Livingston St NW Washington DC 20015-1757

PARKER, ROBERT ORION, chemical engineer; b. Big Pool, Md., Dec. 24, 1915; s. Orion Horace and Frances Lenore (Furry) P.; m. Helene Marie O'Hara, July 4, 1939 (dec. Oct. 1975); m. Elizabeth Porter Simonelli, Nov. 13, 1976 (dec. Nov. 1990); 1 stepchild, Lynn Paustenbach. BSChemE, Carnegie Inst. Tech., 1936; MS, Columbia U., 1943; D Engring. Sci., NYU, 1959. With Griscom-Russell Co., N.Y.C., 1937-55; pvt. practice cons. N.Y.C., 1955-57, 72-80; instr. Hillyer Coll., Hartford, Conn., 1957; from instr. to assoc. prof. chem. engring. NYU, N.Y.C., 1957-69, prof. chem. and nuclear engring., 1969-73; prof., chmn. dept. gas engring. Inst. Algerien du Petrole, Boumerdes, Algeria, 1980-82; tech. advisor Hyundai Heavy Industries, Co., Ltd., Ulsan, Republic of Korea, 1982-85; pres. Parker, Internat. Cons., Inc., Ulsan, Pitts., 1982-87; corp. dir. Stat-IS, Murrysville, Pa., 1987—. Republican candidate, Plum Borough, Pa., 1991. Mem. Am. Inst. Chem. Engrs., Sci. Rsch. Soc. Am., Sigma Xi, Tau Beta Pi, Theta Tau, Phi Lambda Upsilon. Roman Catholic. Home: 417 Vale Dr Pittsburgh PA 15239-1715 Office: Stat-IS Inc 4093 Old William Penn Hwy Murrysville PA 15668-1824

PARKER, SUSAN BEAUCHAMP, communication executive; b. Salisbury, Md., May 11, 1961; d. Roy Vernon and Ruth (Payne) Beauchamp; m. Bradford Haile Parker, Aug. 17, 1985. BA in Biology, Wake Forest U., Winston-Salem, 1983; MA in Exercise Physiology, U. Md., 1986. Grad. teaching asst. U. Md., College Park, 1984-85; exercise specialist Comsat Corp. Fitness Ctr., Washington, 1985-86; asst. mgr. Xerox Health Mgmt. Ctr., Arlington, Va., 1986-87; mgr. fitness ctr. Manor Care, Inc., Silver Spring, Md., 1987-90, mgr. employee communications and svcs., 1990—; corp. fitness cons. Bob Hall, Inc., Upper Marlboro, Md., 1987. Mem. Am. Coll. Sports Medicine (presenter at nat. meeting 1987), Assn. for Fitness in Bus., Internat. Assn. Bus. Communicators, Beta Beta Beta, Phi Alpha Epsilon, Phi Kappa Phi. Office: Manor Care Inc 10750 Columbia Pike Silver Spring MD 20901-4427

PARKER, THOMAS FRANCIS, artist manager, consultant; b. Springfield, Mass., Aug. 10, 1949; s. Maurice Richard and Frances Louise (Young) P. BA in Speech, U. Mass., 1972. Spl. producer WTIC-FM, Hartford, Conn., 1972-74; artists' rep. Colbert Artists Mgmt., Inc., N.Y.C., 1974-76, Sheldon Soffer Artists Mgmt., Inc., N.Y.C., 1976-84; v.p. Shaw Concerts, Inc., N.Y.C., 1984-90; owner Parker Artists, N.Y.C., 1990—; workshop leader New Eng. Conservatory, Concert Artists Guild, New Eng. Found. for the Arts, Conn. Commn. on the Arts; panelist Chamber Music Am., First Am. Classical Guitar Congress; jury mem. Third Arturo Toscanini Internat. Competition for Conductors, Parma, Italy. Named Disting. Alumnus in the Arts, U. Mass., Dept. Music and Dance, 1987; recipient 125 Alumni to Watch award U. Mass., 1988, Edwin H. Armstrong award Columbia U., 1974. Office: Parker Artists 382 Central Park W Apt 9G New York NY 10025-6032

PARKER, TRACEY KORHERR, counselor; b. Wilmington, Del., June 10, 1968; d. John Vinnege and Nancy Gay (Whitmore) P. BS, U. Del., 1990; MS, Western Md. Coll., 1991. Lifeguard/swim instr. Artesian Water Co., Inc., Wilmington, 1984-88; camp counselor YMCA Camp Tockwogh, Wilmington, summer 1986; light bd. operator Weber-Prianti Prodn., Wilmington, 1984—; freelance interpreter Newark and Wilmington, 1992—; libr. aide Western Md. Coll., Westminster, 1991. Vol. M.S. Sterck Sch. for the Deaf, Newark, 1989-90, tchr.'s aide deaf/blind program, summers 1989, 90; tchr. basic sign lang. course Am. Soc. for Deaf Children, Newark, 1992—; recorder Family Edn. Ctr. of Del., Wilmington, 1992—; vol. Parent Info. Ctr. of Del., Newark, 1992—; mem.-advocate Del. Assn. for the Deaf/Blind, Newark, 1992. Md. State Grange scholar, 1991. Mem. AACD, Nat. Assn. of the Deaf. Christian Scientist.

PARKER, WILLIAM COVINGTON, public relations executive; b. Marshville, N.C., Nov. 5, 1927; s. Lester Leonidas and Willie Covington (Blakeney) P.; m. Rose Field (div. 1974); children: Nancy Durkin Green, David C., Leslie Parker Maidlow, Dan F.; m. Nancy Claire Meyers, June 5, 1979; stepchildren: Christin, Kenneth. BA, U. N.C., 1949. Mgr. N.Y. pub. rels. Westinghouse Electric Corp., N.Y.C., 1952-61; dir. pub. rels. Campbell Soup Co., Camden, N.J., 1961-73, FMC Corp., Chgo., 1973-76; corp. dir. pub. rels. CPC Internat. Inc., Englewood Cliffs, N.J., 1977-92; pres. FMC Found., Chgo., 1973-76. Trustee, Inst. Pub. Relations Rsch. Edn., N.Y.C., 1988, 89. With USN Air Corps, 1945-46. Mem. Pub. Rels. Soc. Am. (chmn. govt. affairs com. 1970, recognition com. 1968, internat. com. 1982, del. nat. assembly 1963-66, 83). Republican. Presbyterian. Home: 528 Fairfax Way Williamsburg VA 23185

PARKER, WILLIAM JAMES, fire research scientist, consultant; b. Sutherlin, Oreg., Dec. 11, 1926; s. Raymond H. and Elizabeth Charlotte (Swift) P.; children: Mark Emery, Loreen. BS in Physics, U. Oreg., 1952, MS in Physics, 1954; DSc in Mech. Engring., George Washington U., 1988. Physicist, thermal radiation br. U.S. Naval Radiol. Def. Lab., San Francisco, 1953-69, head high temperature physics sect., 1959-65, head fire rsch. sect., 1966-69; physicist, fire rsch. sect. Nat. Bur. Standards, Gaithersburg, Md., 1969-90, head fire in constrn. group, 1976-80; head fire dynamics group Nat. Inst. Standards and Tech., Gaithersburg, 1988-90; fire tech. cons. Germantown, Md., 1990—; Heritage vis. scientist U.S. Forest Products Lab., 1985. Contbr. articles to profl. jours.; patent for flash method of measuring thermal diffusivity. With USN, 1945-49, San Diego and China. USN fellow U. Calif., 1965-66; recipient Japan Rsch. award, 1989. Mem. ASTM, Internat. Assn. Fire Safety Sci., Sigma Xi. Home and Office: 13135 Dairymaid Dr # 2T Germantown MD 20874-2316

PARKHOUSE, GERALD CLIVE, business educator; b. Chillaton, Devon, Eng., May 15, 1931; came to U.S. 1958; s. Francis Richard Brace and Olive Beauford (Bickle) P.; m. Valerie B. Hall, Aug. 26, 1976; children: Christopher Philip, Kirsten Ann. BA, Oxford U., Eng., 1953; MA, Oxford U., 1957; MS, Boston U., 1980. With Mobil Oil Corp., various locations, 1953-77; gen. mgr. retail Mobil Oil Co. Ltd., London, 1977-81; mng. dir. Mobil Marine Sales Ltd., London, 1981-85; chmn. Mobil Aviation and Marine Sales Ltd., London, 1985; Corning Glass prof. internat. bus. Elmira (N.Y.) Coll., 1985—. Lt. U.K. Army, 1953-55. Recipient Pres.'s "E" award for export svc., U.S. Dept. Commerce, 1991. Fellow Inst. of Petroleum; mem. Royal Auto. Club U.K., Leander Club U.K., Royal Danish Yacht Club, Elmira City Club, Cheming County C. of C. (internat. trade com.), Southern Tier World Commerce Assn. Episcopalian. Office: Elmira Coll Elmira NY 14901

PARKINSON, THOMAS IGNATIUS, JR., lawyer; b. N.Y.C., Jan. 27, 1914; s. Thomas I. and Georgia (Weed) P.; A.B., Harvard U., 1934; LL.B., U. Pa., 1937; m. Geralda E. Moore, Sept. 23, 1937; children—Thomas Ignatius III, Geoffrey Moore, Cynthia Moore. Admitted to N.Y. bar, 1938, since practiced in N.Y.C.; assoc. Milbank, Tweed, Hope & Hadley, 1937-47, partner, 1947-56; pres. Mar Ltd., 1951—; pres. Breecom Corp., 1972-80, chmn. bd., 1980—; dir., exec. com. Pine St. Fund, Inc., N.Y.C., 1949-83, Trustee State Communities Aid Assn., 1949-83; dir. Fgn. Policy Assn., 1949-53; bd. dirs., exec. com. Milbank Meml. Fund, 1948-84. Mem. Am. Bar Assn., Assn. Bar City N.Y., Pilgrims U.S.A., Brit. War Relief Soc. (officer), Met. Unit Found., Phi Beta Kappa. Clubs: Down Town Assn., Knickerbocker, Union. Office: Breecom Corp 780 Third Ave 25th Fl New York NY 10017

PARKS, BRUCE EDWARD, mechanical engineer, marketing executive; b. N.Y.C., Jan. 23, 1951; s. Charles and Rosalyn (Friedman) P.; m. Mary Ellen Wargo, July 20, 1986; children: Kyle, Leah. BA in English, CCNY, 1973, BSME, 1981. Project engr. United Technologies Corp. and Sikorsky Aircraft, Stratford, Conn., 1981-87; mgr. engring. W.R. Grace & Co. and Emerson & Cuming, Inc., Canton, Mass., 1987-90; mgr. product applications Textron Specialty Materials, Lowell, Mass., 1990—. Recipient Robert L. Lichtin award N.E. region Am. Helicopter Soc., Stratford, Conn., 1983. Office: Textron Specialty Materials 2 Industrial Ave Lowell MA 01851-5199

PARKS, GRACE SUSAN, bank official; b. N.Y.C., Oct. 14, 1948; d. Marco A. and Gloria (Alvino) Vale; m. Louis Parks, Feb. 14, 1988. BS, Pa. State U., 1970; MA, New Sch. for Social Research, 1974; cert. in mgmt. Adelphi U., 1979, MBA, 1980. Bus. office rep. N.Y. Tel. Co., Rockville Centre, 1971-74; social worker Children's Aid Soc., N.Y.C., 1974-75; EEO officer Edwin Gould Svcs., N.Y.C., 1976-79; v.p. fin. instns. and global markets Bankers Trust Co., N.Y.C., 1979—; instr. mgmt. Adelphi U. Grad. Sch. Bus. Adminstrn., 1981—; notary pub. State N.Y., 1978—. Mem. Human Resource Planning Soc., Assn. MBA Execs., Am. Compensation Assn., Wall St. Compensation and Benefits Assn., N.Y. Compensation Assn., Adelphi U. Businesswomen's Alumni Assn. (pres. 1980-82). Office: One Bankers Trust Pla New York NY 10017

PARKS, JOE BENJAMIN, state legislator; b. McAlester, Okla., Dec. 17, 1915; s. James Allen and Mary Florence (Youngblood) P.; m. Florence M. Evans, Oct. 25, 1941; children: Anne, Kathryn. BS in Pub. Adminstrn., Okla. State U., 1939. Div. dir. U.S. VA, Washington, 1946-56; spl. asst., cons. U.S. GSA, Washington, 1957-58; mgr. dist. EDP div. RCA Corp., Washington, 1959-65; mgr. Ea. region Dashew Bus. Machines, Arlington, Va., 1966-68; assoc. adminstr. social and rehab. svc. U.S. Dept. Health, Edn. & Welfare, Washington, 1969-73; dir. mktg. govt. systems div. Booz, Allen & Hamilton, Washington, 1974-75; ptnr. Forbes & Parks, Dover, N.H., 1976—; mem. N.H. State Legislature, Concord, 1985—, chmn. joint com. on elderly affairs, 1987—; mem. com. on health, human svcs. and elderly N.H. State Legislature, 1987-90; chmn. subcom. mileage and electronic roll call, 1989-90, vice chmn. legis. adminstrn. com., 1990—, mem. appropriations com., 1991—; proprietor Portsmouth (N.H.) Athenaenum, 1992—; corporator Wentworth Douglas Hosp., Dover, 1980-89. Columnist Nat. Antiques Rev., 1975-77, Boston Globe N.H. Weekly 1987-88, Foster's Daily Democrat (Dover, N.H.), 1988-90; freelance writer, 1990—. Vice chmn. N.H. State Rep. Com., 1987-88; chmn. Strafford County Reps., 1988. Decorated Bronze Star. Congregationalist. Home and Office: 195 Long Hill Rd Dover NH 03820-6108

PARKS, LOUIS, financial consultant; b. Syracuse, N.Y., Feb. 18, 1955; s. Lloyd C. and Genevieve (Poughon) P.; m. Grace S. Valenzio, Feb. 14, 1988. BA in French, Yale U., 1977; MBA in Fin., Columbia U., 1983. Sales rep. Kobrand Corp., N.Y.C., 1977-81; sr. fin. cons. Merrill Lynch, N.Y.C., 1983—. Home: 377 Rector Pl # 10M New York NY 10280

PARKS, MATTHEW WILLIAM, judge, lawyer; b. Audubon, N.J., July 23, 1925; s. Matthew Alcorn Parks and Elizabeth (Johnson) Undercoffler; m. Grace Elizabeth Wilson, June 19, 1948; children: Gary, Marilyn Parks Kristiniak. BA, Temple U., 1950, JD, 1953. Bar: N.J. 1954, D.C. 1957. Assoc. Albert K. Plone, Camden, N.J., 1954-60; ptnr. Plone, Tomar, Parks & Seliger, Camden, 1960-72; mng. ptnr. Tomar, Parks, Seliger, Simonoff and Adourian, Haddonfield, N.J., 1972-86; judge compensation State of N.J., Trenton, 1987—. Pres., trustee St. George Meth. Ch., Camden, 1957-65; pres. Lions Eye Bank Delaware Valley, Phila., 1988-89. With AUS, 1943-45, prisoner of war, ETO. Decorated Bronze Star. Mem. ABA, N.J. Bar Assn. (chmn. compensation sect. 1962-63), Camden County Bar Assn. (trustee 1984-87, past chmn. compensation sect.), D.C. Bar Assn., Assn. Trial Lawyers Am. (pres. N.J. 1961-62), Lions (pres. Camden 1964-65, N.J. parliamentarian 1979-85, Camden Lion of Yr. award 1970). Republican. Home: 13 E Centennial Dr Medford NJ 08055 Office: NJ Judge Compensation 28 Yard Ave Trenton NJ 08625

PARKS, ROBERT ALLAN, utility company executive; b. Newport, R.I., Jan. 29, 1946; s. Robert John and Marion A. (Fink) P.; children: Karen, Ellen, Lauren. BSBA, U. N.H., 1968; MBA, Babson Coll., 1975. CPA, N.H. Internal auditor Pub. Svc. Co. of N.H., Manchester, 1968-69, cost acct., 1969-70, systems analyst, 1970-76, mgr. of systems, 1976-80, dir., info. systems, 1980-82, v.p., info systems, 1983, v.p., info. systems & div. ops., 1984-85, v.p., info. systems & material mgmt., 1986-92; dir. Office of Info. Tech. Mgmt., State of N.H., Concord, 1992—. Mem. Boston Soc. for Info. Mgmt. Office: State of NH 4 Hazen Dr Concord NH 03301

PARKS, SUSAN JOHNSON, small business owner; b. San Diego, Dec. 9, 1951; d. Charles Robert and Merlene Mae (Yount) J. Grad., Nat. Sch. Dress Design, Evanston, Ill., 1976; diploma, Internat. Pastry Arts Ctr. Owner, prin. Chrysalis, Otd., Albuquerque, 1976-85; mgr. Pride of the Past Shoppe, Albuquerque, 1982-84; owner, prin. We Do Windows, Albuquerque and Santa Fe, N.Mex., 1984-85; asst. mgr., designer sportswear Bonwit Teller, Boston, 1985-87; visual merchandise asst. Bloomingdales, Boston, 1987-89; freelance visual merchandiser, 1990—; fashion educator Newbury Coll., Boston, 1987-89; pastry chef East Meets West, Boston, 1989-92, Mama Maria, 1992—; cons., lectr. in field. Producer radio program, 1982-85. Consumer trainer Family Planning Coun., N.Mex., 1978-85; treas. exec. com. Union Park Assn., Boston, 1988; co-chair design com., inst. fundraiser AIDS Heartstrings, DIFFA. Mem. NAFE, Women in Arts, LWV. Home: 28 Upton St # 3 Boston MA 02118-1610

PARKS, THOMAS KEITH, logistics engineer; b. La Jolla, Calif., May 21, 1951; s. Jack and Katherine Margaret (Hertzel) P.; m. Pamela Anne Tarne, Jan. 26, 1974; children: Thomas Keith Jr., Christopher Scott, David Michael. BS in Gen. Engring., U.S. Naval Acad., Annapolis, 1973. Commd. ensign USN, 1973, advanced through grades to lt.; instr. Naval Submarine Sch., Groton, Conn., 1977-79; resigned USN, 1979; mgmt. cons. Booz, Allen & Hamilton Inc., Arlington, Va., 1979-87; rsch. fellow Logistics Mgmt. Inst., Bethesda, Md., 1987—. Co-author: (tng. courses) Navy Integrated Logistic Support Training Program: Maintenance Planning, 1984, Logistics Engineering Applications, 1986. Mem. Am. Soc. Naval Engrs., AIAA. Republican. Lutheran. Office: Logistics Mgmt Inst 6400 Goldsboro Rd Bethesda MD 20817-5826

PARKS, VINCENT JOSEPH, civil engineering educator; b. Chgo., May 5, 1928; s. Joseph and Nora (Carr) P.; m. Julia Catherine Pyles, Feb. 12, 1955; children: Sean, Michael, David, Nora, Joseph, Gregory, Laurence. AS, Lewis Coll. Sci., 1948; BSME, Ill. Inst. Tech., 1953; MCE, Cath. U. Am., 1963, PhD, 1968. Engr. Andrew Corp., Orland Park, Ill., 1953-55; rsch. engr. Armour Rsch. Found., Chgo., 1955-61; rsch. assoc. Cath. Univ. Am., Washington, 1961-65, asst. prof., 1965-68, assoc. prof., 1968-73, prof., 1973—; rsch. cons. U.S. Naval Rsch. Lab., Washington, 1973-90, Sandia Nat. Lab., Albuquerque, 1980—. Co-author: Moire Analysis of Strain, 1970; editor: Progress in Experimental Mechanics, 1975. Recipient Resident Rsch. Associateship, Nat. Rsch. Coun., Washington, 1971-72, Faculty Rsch. grant Am. Soc. for Engring. Edn., Washington, 1983-89. Fellow ASME, Soc. Experimental Mechanics (Hetenyi 1974, Frocht 1981); mem. Am. Acad. Mechanics, Sigma Xi. Democrat. Roman Catholic. Office: The Cath U Am Dept Civil Engring Washington DC 20064

PARLAKIAN, NISHAN, drama educator; b. N.Y.C., July 11, 1925; s. Raphael and Rose (Ohanian) P.; m. Florence Barbara Mechtel, Dec. 27, 1952; children: Nishan Payel, Elizabeth Rose. BA, Syracuse U., 1948; MA, Columbia U., 1950, Columbia U., 1952; PhD, Columbia U., 1967. Instr. Bronx Community Coll., CUNY, 1961-63; assoc. prof. Pace U., N.Y.C., 1963-70; prof. John Jay Coll. of Criminal Justice, CUNY, N.Y.C., 1970—; artistic dir. Players of the Diocese of Armenian Ch. of Am., N.Y.C., 1972—. Author: (play) Grandma, Pray For Me, 1988; translator: For the Sake of Honor, 1976, Evil Spirit, 1980, Be Nice, I'm Dead, 1990; contbr. articles, plays, poetry to various periodicals. Sgt. Infantry, 1944-46. Recipient Internat. Arts award Columbus: Countdown 1992, 1988; named Fulbright lectr. to Soviet Union, 1991. Mem. Pirandello Soc. of Am. (v.p. 1978—). Mem. Armenian Ch./Episcopalian. Home: PO Box 250204 New York NY 10025-1533 Office: John Jay Coll 899 10th Ave New York NY 10019-1029

PARLAMIS, MICHAEL FRANK, civil engineer, construction company executive; b. Bklyn., May 29, 1940; s. Frank Michael and Phyllis (Burnago) P.; m. Marguerite Koskinas, Aug. 21, 1966; children: Franklin, Christine, Alexander. BSCE, MIT, 1962, BS in Indsl. Mgmt., 1962; MSCE, Stanford U., 1963. Registered profl. engr., N.Y. Engr. Port Authority of N.Y. and N.J., 1963-64; asst. to chief engr. George A. Fuller Co., N.Y.C., 1964-67; pres. Frank Parlamis Inc., Bklyn., 1968—, Parlamis Bros. Inc., Bklyn., 1968—, Hermes Constrn. Corp., Bklyn., 1968—. Author: CPU/PERT As Basis for Management Information Systems in Building Construction, 1966, Regulation of Building Construction in the City of New York, 1967, Greece and the Panama Canal, 1988. Chmn. expansion program Greek Orthodox Cathedral St. John the Theologian, Tenafly, N.J., 1978—; mem. ednl. coun. MIT. Mem. NSPE, MIT Alumni Ctr. N.Y., Am. Inst. Wine and Food, Am. Hellenic Progressive Assn., Tau Beta Pi, Chi Epsilon. Republican. Home: 128 Downey Dr Tenafly NJ 07670-3006 Office: 328 Atlantic Ave Brooklyn NY 11201-5855

PARLATO, ANTHONY CHARLES, lawyer; b. Warsaw, N.Y., May 30, 1962; s. Thomas A. and Carolyn M. (Brown) P.; m. Cynthia Vitale, Oct. 6, 1990. BS in Acctg., Canisius Coll., 1984; JD, SUNY, Buffalo, 1989. Bar: N.Y. 1989; CPA N.Y. Acct. Seidman & Seidman, Buffalo, 1984-87, Lucy Ciancone PC, Buffalo, 1983-90; tax intern Arthur Andersen & Co., Rochester, N.Y., 1988; tax atty. Ernst & Young, Buffalo, 1989—; dir. Buffalo Ballet Theatre, 1989-90. Fundraising com. mem. Camp GoodDays and Spl. Times, Buffalo, 1990—. Mem. AICPA, N.Y. State Bar Assn., N.Y. State Soc. CPAs, Erie County Bar Assn. Home: 28 Glenside Ave Buffalo NY 14223-2532 Office: Ernst & Young 1400 Key Tower 50 Fountain Pla Buffalo NY 14202

PARMER, EDGAR ALAN, radiologist, musician; b. N.Y.C., Sept. 14, 1928; s. Nathan and Selma (Benett) P.; m. Nina Ash (div. 1964); children: Vicki, Robert; m. Judith Rae Parmer, Nov. 22, 1969. AA in Music, UCLA, 1950, BA, 1951, MA; MD, N.Y. Med. Coll., 1958. Lic. physician, N.Y., Calif., Conn. Intern Grasslands Hosp., Valhalla, N.Y., 1958-59; resident Vets. Hosp., Bronx, N.Y., 1959-62; assoc. radiologist, dir. nuclear medicine Mt. Vernon (N.Y.) Hosp., 1962-64; assoc. radiologist Francis Delafield Hosp. Columbia Presbyn. Med. Ctr., 1964-82; pvt. practice New Rochelle, N.Y., 1982—; instr. radiology Columbia U.; vis. fellow dept. radiology Columbia-Presbyn. Med. Ctr.; cons. tech. affairs HEW; mem. staff Radiologic Technicians Program Westchester Community Coll., chmn. adv. com.; cons., staff mem. St. Barnabas Radiology, 1987—; med. dir. Ultrasound Diagnostic Sch., 1985-87; assoc. dir. radiology, dir. ultrasound Strang Clinic; lectr. in field. Contbr. articles to profl. jours.; soloist, recordings include N.Y.C. Symphony Orch., 1940, Burbank (Calif.) Orch., Glendale (Calif.) Orch., MGM Symphony, Westchester Symphony Orch., Westchester Philharm. Orch. Mem., past pres. Doctor's Symphony Orch. N.Y.; sec. bd. dirs., pres. Westchester Philharm. Orch.; past dir., mem. Am. Cancer Soc.; pres. bd. dirs. Premium Point Pk. With U.S. Army. Am. Cancer Soc. grantee. Fellow Am. Coll. Angiology, Am. Inst. Ultrasound Medicine (sr.), Royal Soc. Health, ; mem. AMA, AAAS, Am. Assn. Advancement Boxing (bd. dirs.), Am. Coll. Radiology (past pres. Westchester div.), Am. Coll. Nuclear Medicine, Am. Coll. Med. Imaging, Soc. Nuclear Medicine, N.Y. State Med. Soc., Westchester County Med. Soc., Westchester Radiol. Soc. (past pres.), N.Y. Acad. Sci. Home: 7 Shore Dr New Rochelle NY 10801-5331

PARMET, HERBERT SAMUEL, historian, educator; b. N.Y.C., Sept. 28, 1929; s. Isaac and Fanny (Scharf) P.; m. Joan Kronish, Sept. 12, 1948; 1 child, Wendy. BS, SUNY, Oswego, 1951; MA, Queens Coll., 1957; postgrad., Columbia U., 1958-62. Prof. history Grad. Sch. CUNY, 1968—, disting. prof. history, 1983—; cons. ABC-TV, N.Y.C., 1983, KERA-TV, Dallas, 1986-91, WGBH-TV, Boston, 1988-91. Author: Aaron Burr: Portrait of an Ambitious Man, 1967, Never Again: A President Runs for a Third Term, 1968, Eisenhower and the American Crusades, 1972, The Democrats, 1976, Jack: The Struggles of John F. Kennedy, 1980, JFK: The Presidency of John F. Kennedy, 1983, Richard Nixon and His America, 1990. Cpl. U.S. Army, 1952-54. Grantee, NEH, 1987. Fellow Soc. Am. Historians; mem. Am. Hist. Assn., Orgn. Am. Historians, Authors Guild. Home: 36 Marsten Ln Hillsdale NY 12529-9801 Office: Queensborough Community Coll Dept History 56th Ave at Springfield Blv Bayside NY 11364

PARNES, ROBERT MARK, architect; b. Bronx, N.Y., Nov. 15, 1946; s. Leon and Susan (Farkas) P.; m. Gwenn Pamela Mussman, Mar. 21, 1982; children: Matthew Haskel, Samantha Michele. BArch, Pratt Inst., 1969. Registered architect, N.Y., N.J. Dir. design Kraus Enterprises Inc., N.Y.C., 1974-81, chief architect, 1981-84; pres. RMP Constrn. Cons., Inc., N.Y.C., 1984—; ptnr. Tobin/Parnes Design Enterprises, N.Y.C., 1984—; asst. design instr. Pratt Inst., N.Y.C., 1969; cons. Community Service Soc., N.Y.C., 1974-75. Prin. work include lobbies and pub. spaces for Schack & Schack Real Estate Co., Sidney J. Bernstein Inc., F.M. Ring Assocs., offices and studios for Paul Taylor Dance Co., also various Park Ave. and Fifth Ave apts., stores, corp. hdqrs. including Internat. Thomson Retail Press, Tor Books, HWH Enterprises, fast food establishments, restaurants, and night clubs. Recipient Merit award Signs of the Times mag., 1977. Mem. AIA, N.Y. State Assn. Architects, N.Y. Soc. Architects. Office: Tobin Parnes Design Enterprise RMP Constrn Cons Inc 270 Lafayette St Ste 302 New York NY 10012-3327

PARNHAM, GARY PETER, regional manager; b. Portsmouth, N.H., Apr. 17, 1950; s. Richard Valentine and Rose (Duffy) P.; m. Susan Brand, Dec. 21. B of Edn., U. N.H., 1973. Educator Portsmouth (N.H.) Sch. Dept., 1973-91; regional mgr. Northeast Regional Ctr., Sayville, N.Y., 1991—; cons. in field. Co-author: IMPACT Teaching, 1991. Mem. N.H. task force Substance Abuse Prevention, Concord, 1986; mem. Conservation Commn., Portsmouth, 1977-78. Mem. NEA, Beta Beta Beta (pres. 1971-72), Phi Mu Delta (v.p. 1971-72). Office: Northeast Regional Ctr 15 Pleasant St Concord NH 03301

PAROCHETTI, JAMES VICTOR, weed scientist; b. Spring Valley, Ill., Apr. 24, 1940; s. Marcel and Gladys (Dalzot) P.; m. JoAnn Stephens, Aug. 1, 1964 (div.); children: Catherine, Andrew; m. Joan Loraine Warner, Apr. 2, 1980; children: James II, Amy. BS, U. Ill., 1962; MS, Purdue U., 1964, PhD, 1967. Asst. prof. U. Md., College Park, 1966-70, assoc. prof., 1970-78; nat. program leader extension svc. USDA, Washington, 1978-87; prin. weed scientist Coop. State Rsch. Svc., USDA, Washington, 1987—. Mem. Northeastern Weed Sci. Soc. (Disting. Mem. award 1977, pres. 1979-80), North Ctrl. Weed Sci. Soc., So. Weed Sci. Soc., Western Soc. Weed Sci., Weed Sci. Soc. Am. (Outstanding Ext. Worker award 1980, fellow Weed Sci. Soc. of Am. 1992). Office: CSRS-USDA Washington DC 20250

PAROISSIEN, DAVID HARRY, English educator; b. Middlesbrough, Yorkshire, Eng., Oct. 24, 1939; came to U.S., 1964; s. Reginald Albert and Norah Gertrude (Mitchell) P.; m. Miriam Shinkle, Dec. 19, 1963; children: Catherine, Edwin, Margery. BA in English with honors, U. Hull, Yorkshire, 1961; MA in English, Highlands U., 1965; PhD in English, U. Calif., L.A., 1968. Asst. prof. Dept. English, U. Mass., Amherst, 1968-74, assoc. prof., 1974-84, prof., 1985—; exch. lectr. U. Kent, Canterbury, Eng., 1973-74. Book rev. editor Dickens Studies Newsletter, 1979-82; gen. editor Dickens Quar., 1983—; editor: Charles Dickens Pictures from Italy, 1973, Charles Dickens Selected Letters, 1985; author: Oliver Twist: An Annoted Bibliography, 1986, Companion to Oliver Twist, 1992. Home: 19 Tyler Ct Northampton MA 01060-2107 Office: U Mass Dept English Amherst MA 01003

PARONT, GEORGE JOHN, bishop, institute administrator; b. Flushing, N.Y., Feb. 28, 1953; s. George Henry and Harriet Ann (Warner) P. BA in Scholastic Philosophy, Sacred Theology, St. Mary's U., 1967, MA in Sacred Theology, 1968; postgrad., St. John's U., 1971; cert. human resources devel., Cornell U., 1985. Ordained priest Roman Cath. Ch., 1977; awarded canonical mission Archdiocese San Antonio, 1967; consecrated bishop Roman Cath. Ch., 1990. Chmn. dept. sci. Cath. Youth Orgn. Diocese Bklyn., Cresthaven, N.Y., 1959-71; instr. theology Incarnate Word Acad., San Antonio, 1967-68; tchr. Holy Cross High Sch., San Antonio, 1968-69; asst. pastor St. Gregory's Ch., Ronkonkoma, N.Y., 1977-78; pastor St. John the Evangelist Ch., Brookhaven, N.Y., 1978—; bd. dir. Inst. Roman Cath. Studies, Brookhaven, 1978—; mem. nat. adv. bd. Am. Christian Coll., Tulsa, 1973. Author: Experiments in Electricity, 1962, Experiments in Lights, 1962, The Invalidity of the ThucConsecrations, 1988; editor: The Armorer, 1972-74, The Guardsman, 1972-74; contbr. articles to profl. jours. Sustaining mem. Rep. Nat. Com., 1974—; treas. local 253 AFL-CIO AFSCME, 1971-75, pres. CSEA local 1000-253, 1980-89; mem. labor mgmt. coms. N.Y. State Gov.'s Office Employee Rels., 1987-88. With N.Y.N.G., 1971-83. Author: Experiments in Electricity, 1962, Experiments in Light, 1962, The Invalidity of the Thuc Consecrations, 1988; editor: The Armorer, 1972-74, The Guardsman, 1972-74; contbr. articles to profl. jours. Mem. Found. for Christian Theology, Queens Inst. Anthropology, Archaeol. Inst. Am., Am. Bible Soc., Epsilon Delta Chi, KC. Republican.

PARR, MARY YOHANNAN, library administrator, educator; b. Cleve., June 21, 1927; d. Shlemon and Jemima (Blackford) Yohannan; m. Wendell R. Parr, Oct. 1, 1949. AB, Coll. of Wooster, 1948; MLS, Western Res. U., 1949; postgrad., Tchrs. Coll. N.Y.C., 1961-69. Dir. Willard (Ohio) Meml. Libr., 1950-51; extention libr. San Antonio Pub. Libr., 1953-54; asst. prof. libr. and info. sci. Newark State Coll., Union, N.J., 1955-62; asst. prof. Villanova (Pa.) U., 1962-63; assoc. prof. Pratt Inst., Bklyn., 1963-69; assoc. prof. St. John's U., Jamaica, N.Y., 1969-73, asst. dean tech. svcs., 1984—; head program devel. D.C. Pub. Libr., Washington, 1974; assoc. prof. Hofstra U., Hempstead, N.Y., 1975-83. Contbr. articles to profl. publs. Mem. AAUP, ALA, Assn. Libr. and Info. Sci. Educators, N.Y. Libr. Assn., Cath. Libr. Assn. Office: St John's U Grand Central & Utopia Pkwy Jamaica NY 11439

PARRA, ROBERT JOSEPH, investment banker; b. Calexico, Calif., May 3, 1940; s. Robert Joseph and Josephine Elizabeth (Young) P.; m. M. Germaine Thier, July 29, 1986; children: Christina, Sophia. BS, USAF Acad., 1963; MA, Georgetown U., 1964. Commd. 2nd lt. USAF, 1963, promoted to capt., 1966, resigned, 1967; v.p., gen. mgr. Citicorp, New York, San Francisco, and overseas, 1969-82; dir. Bur. Pvt. Enterprise (AID), Washington, 1982-84; pres. Washington Capital Markets Group, 1984—; bd. dirs. AgriSystems I (Indonesia), Agrolife S.A. (U.S.), Internat. Energy Fin. Ltd. (U.S.), Nat. Agr. Ctrs. (United Kingdom). Republican. Roman Catholic. Office: Robert A Weaver & Assocs 915 15th St NW Ste 400 Washington DC 20005-2305

PARRAVANO, AMELIA ELIZABETH, recording industry executive; b. Providence, Apr. 5, 1951; d. Olindo Luigi and Violet Carmella (Russo) Izzo; m. Grimaldo Antonio Parravano, July 4, 1979; children: Peter Paul, Paula Elizabeth. AA, Roger Williams Coll., 1972; postgrad., R.I. Coll., 1972-73. Owner, operator Aura Arts & Crafts, Cranston, R.I., 1985-88; pres. Peridot Music, Cranston, 1990—; freelance artist Artist Letters League, Cranston, 1992—; singer, songwriter, musician. Active PTA, Cranston, 1991-92; artist mem. R.I. State Coun. on Arts, Providence, 1986-92; active Pawtucket (R.I.) Arts Coun., 1986-92. Mem. Am. Soc. Composers, Authors and Pubs., Songwriters Guild Am., Gospel Music Assn. Home: 17 Woodbine St Cranston RI 02910

PARRIS, CHERYL ANN ELIZABETH, rehabilitation counselor; b. Jan. 8, 1968. BS, Iona Coll., 1988; postgrad., NYU. Program dir. Exxon Corp./RSVP, N.Y.C.; pers. asst. New Rochelle (N.Y.) City Hall; vocational counselor Montifore Hosp., N.Y.; vocat. counselor Ednl. Alliance; vocat./edn. coord. LUCHA, Inc., N.Y.C. Episcopal rep. Nat. Coun. Chs. Mem. NAFE, Union Black Episcopalians, Nat. Episc. Coalition on Alcohol and Drugs, Nat. Coun. Negro Women, Assn. Vocat. Rehab., Assn. Substance Abusers (treas.), Psi Chi, Delta Sigma Theta. Address: 3351 Corsa Ave Bronx NY 10469

PARRISH, EDGAR LEE, financial services executive; b. Washington, Apr. 11, 1948; s. Frank Jennings Parrish and Lorene (Lomax) Parrish.; m. Katherine Ellen MacLachlan, Sept. 12, 1987; children: Robert Alexander Wilson, Stephen Edgar MacLachlan. BS in Commerce, U. Va., 1970. Sr. v.p. Wheat, First Securities, Inc., Washington, 1971-79; v.p. Merrill Lynch, Pierce, Fenner & Smith, Inc., Washington, 1979-82, Phila., 1982-85; sr. v.p., fin. cons. Shearson Lehman Bros., Inc., Phila., 1985-87; sr. v.p., fin. cons. Shearson Lehman Bros., Inc., Washington, 1987—, mem. dirs. coun., 1986, mem. chmn.'s coun., 1987—; Pres. HESCO Corp., Manassas, Va., 1989—, dir., 1988—. Capt. USAFR, 1970-76. Mem. U. Va. Club (Washington), U. Va. Alumni Assn. Democrat. Episcopalian. Home: 4502 Wetherill Rd Bethesda MD 20816-1813 Office: 1050 Connecticut Ave NW Ste 225 Washington DC 20036-5305

PARROT, KENT KANE, producer, writer; b. L.A., June 4, 1911; s. Kent Kane and Mary (Alsop) P.; m. Deirdre Barbara Elland Lumley-Savile, Oct. 21, 1948; children: Jonathan Kent, Richard Halifax, Barbara Elland. BS, U.S. Mil. Acad., 1935; postgrad., Air War Coll., 1955-56; MA in Internat. Affairs, George Washington U., 1967, M of Philosophy, 1975, PhD, 1978. Commd. 2d lt. U.S. Army, 1935; advanced through grades to col. USAF, 1955, ret., 1965; fgn. svc. res. officer Arms Control and Disarmament Agy., 1965-70; owner, producer Markane Co., Inc., Chevy Chase, Md., 1960—. Producer radio mus. The Catch Colt, 1986—; contbr. articles to profl. jours. Mem. U.S./Soviet rels. com. Commn. on Peace Episcopal Diocese of Washington, 1984—. Mem. ASCAP, Am. Fgn. Svc. Assn., Internat. Soc. Polit. Psychology, Fedn. Am. Scientists, Ctr. for Def. Info. (adv. coun. 1987—), Chevy Chase Club, Met. Club of Washington. Democrat. Home and Office: Markane Co Inc 5506 Grove St Bethesda MD 20815-3410

PARRY, CHRISTINE M., vocational rehabilitation counselor; b. Allentown, Pa., Oct. 6, 1964; d. John A. and Joyce J. (Leister) Butera; m. Samuel I. Parry, June 2, 1990. BS in Spl. Edn., Coll. Misericordia, Dallas, Pa., 1986; MS in Rehab. Counseling, U. Scranton, 1990. Cert. rehab. counselor. Spl. edn. tchr. Pittsgrove Twp. Bd. Edn., Elmer, N.J., 1986-89; substitute tchr. Luzerne Intermediate Unit, Kingston, Pa., 1989-90; vocat. rehab. counselor DRS and Assocs., Buffalo, N.Y., 1990—. Mem. AACD, Nat. Rehab. Assn., Assn. Retarded Citizens, Ctr. for Women in Mgmt. Office: DRS And Assocs 300 Delaware Ave Buffalo NY 14202-1807

PARSHALL, GEORGE WILLIAM, research chemist; b. Hackensack, Minn., Sept. 19, 1929; s. George Clarence and Frances (Virnig) P.; m. Naomi B. Simpson, Oct. 9, 1954; children: William, Jonathan, David. B.S., U. Minn., 1951; Ph.D., U. Ill., 1954. Research chemist E.I. duPont de Nemours & Co., Wilmington, Del., 1954-65; research supr. E.I. duPont de Nemours & Co., 1965-79, dir. chem. sci., 1979—; bd. chem. sci. NRC, Washington, 1983-86; Reilly lectr. Notre Dame U., 1980—. Author: Homogeneous Catalysis, 1980; editor: Inorganic Syntheses, 1974, Jour. Molecular Catalysis, 1977-80. Recipient Bailar medal in inorgnaic chemistry U. Ill., 1976. Mem. Am. Chem. Soc. (award in inorganic chemistry 1983, award for leadership in chem. research mgmt. 1989), Nat. Acad. Sci., Am. Acad. Arts Scis., Catalysis Soc. (Phila Catalyst Club award 1978). Episcopalian. Home: 2504 Delaware Ave Wilmington DE 19806-1220 Office: E I du Pont de Nemours & Co Exptl Sta Wilmington DE 19880-0328

PARSON, CHRISTINE JENNIFER N., artist; b. Washington, Nov. 8, 1943; d. John Spies and Cora Maribah (Patterson) Nicoll; m. Andrew M. Egeland Jr., Sept. 12, 1964 (div. 1968); m. James Thomas Parson, Feb. 14, 1969; children: Larissa Nicole, Nathaniel James. BS, U. Va., 1967, MA, 1970. Tchr. of handicapped Montgomery County (Md.) Pub. Schs., 1968-69, Charlottesville (Va.) Pub. Schs., 1967-68, Nat. Children's Ctr., Washington, 1969-73; tchr. art Art League, Alexandria, Va., 1982—; ind. portrait artist Washington, 1974—. One-woman shows include Va. Mus. Art, 1966, Art League, Washington, 1976, Montpelier Cultural Art Ctr., 1981, D.C. Pub. Library, 1982, Capitol Hill Arts Workshop, 1986, City of Alexandria City Hall, 1987, Art League, 1989, Capitol Hill Art League, 1991; represented in pvt. collections. Founder, pres. Friends of S.E. Libr., Washington, 1983; founder Washington Swim Team Booster Club, pres. 1984-85, 88; mem. vestry St. Monica's Ch. Grantee Washington Commn. Arts and Humanities, 1988, 92. Mem. Art League, Capitol Hill Art League, So. Water Color Soc. Episcopalian. Studio: 105 N Union St Alexandria VA 22314-3277

PARSONS, ALVIN LEWIS, public affairs executive; b. Hays, Kans., May 3, 1949; s. Bernard Eugene and Ellen Alma (Steele) P.; m. Elizabeth Luke Nern (div. Feb. 1985); 1 child, Elizabeth; m. Jean Evan Hungiville, June 24, 1989; 1 child, Gregory. BA in Journalism, La. State U., 1971. Reporter St. Petersburg (Fla.) Times, summer 1970; dir. info. Am. Sugar Cane League, New Orleans, 1971-72; pers. rep. La. Power & Light Co., New Orleans, 1972-74; pubs. editor Ga. Power Co., Atlanta, 1974-76; supt. pub. and employee info. Wis. Electric Power, Milw., 1976-81; 2d v.p. corp. communications Lincoln Nat. Corp., Ft. Wayne, Ind., 1981-87; v.p. pub. affairs Am. Ins. Assn., Washington, 1987—; guest lectr. U. Wis., Milw., 1979-81, Ind. U.-Purdue U., Ft. Wayne, 1986-87. Columnist Sugar Bowl newspaper, 1971. Vice chair Community Arts Coun., Ft. Wayne, 1985-86; pres. bd. trustees Pub. Broadcasting of N.E. Ind., Ft. Wayne, 1983-87. Poynter scholar St. Petersburg Times, 1970, Robert Ewing scholar La. State U., 1970. Mem. Internat. Assn. Bus. Communicators (bd. dirs. 1974-76), Nat. Press Club, Soc. Profl. Journalists, Pub. Affairs Coun., Pub. Rels. Soc. Am., Phi Kappa Phi. Presbyterian. Home: 709 Braxton Pl Alexandria VA 22301-2705 Office: Am Ins Assn 1130 Connecticut Ave NW Washington DC 20036-3904

PARSONS, EDMUND MORRIS, diplomat; b. Houston, Oct. 19, 1936; s. Alfred Morris and Virgina (Hanna) P.; m. Elvia Catalina Carrillo, Dec. 10, 1989. AB, Harvard U., 1958; MBA, U. Pa., 1961; MS, MIT, 1970. Fgn. service officer U.S. Dept. State, Washington, 1965-90; 1st sec. Am. Embassy, Mexico City, 1973-76; economist Fed. Res. Bank N.Y., N.Y.C., 1976-77; chief food aid div. U.S. Dept. State, Washington, 1977-80, dir. office devel., 1981-82, dir. office econ. policy, 1983-84; dep. chief mission U.S. Mission to FAO, Rome, 1985-86; dir. Office Ecology and Natural Resources U.S. Dept. State, Washington, 1986-88; dir. Office of Internat. Narcotics Control Programs, 1988-89; min.-counselor for econ. affairs Am. Embassy, Mexico City, 1989-90; pres. Fredonia Enterprises, Inc., Houston, 1990—; co-chmn. Tropical Forest Task Force, Washington, 1986-88; dep. U.S. rep. UN FAO, Rome, 1985-86; alt. U.S. rep. to environ. program U.S. Del. Nairobi, Kenya, 1987. Served to capt. USAF, 1962-72. Mem. Am. Fgn. Svc. Assn., Am. C. of C. of Mex. (bd. dirs. 1989-90), The Univ. Club (Houston). Republican. Methodist.

PARSONS, ESTELLE, actress; b. Lynn, Mass., Nov. 20, 1927; d. Eben and Elinor (Mattson) P.; m. Richard Gehman, Dec. 19, 1953 (div. Aug. 1958); children: Martha and Abbie (twins); m. Peter L. Zimroth, Jan. 2, 1983; 1 child, Abraham. B.A. in Polit. Sci., Conn. Coll. Women, 1949; student, Boston U. Law Sch., 1949-50. Stage appearances include: Happy Hunting, 1957, Whoop Up, 1958, Beg, Borrow or Steal, 1960, Threepenny Opera, 1960, Mrs. Dally Has a Lover, 1962, Ready When You Are C.B, 1964, Malcolm, 1965, Seven Descents of Myrtle, 1968, And Miss Reardon Drinks a Little, 1971, Mert and Phil, 1974, The Norman Conquests, 1975-76, Ladies of the Alamo, 1977, Miss Margarida's Way, 1977-78, The Pirates of Penzance, 1981; adapted, dir., performer Orgasmo Adulto Escapes from the Zoo, 1983, The Unguided Missile, Baba Goya, 1989, Shimada, 1992; film appearances include: Bonnie and Clyde, 1966; Rachel, Rachel, 1967, I Never Sang for My Father, 1969, Dick Tracy, 1990; artistic dir. N.Y. Shakespeare Festival Players, 1986. Recipient Theatre World award, 1962-63, Obie award, 1964; recipient award Motion Picture Acad. Arts and Scis., 1967; Recipient Medal of Honor, Conn. Coll., 1969. Home: 505 W End Ave New York NY 10024-4305

PARSONS, JOHN MORFORD, surgeon; b. Red Bank, N.J., Apr. 14, 1938; s. TheodoreDwight and Margaret (Morfordú P.; m. Dorothy Vietor, July 2, 1969; Timothy Vietor, Jessica Dwight. AB, Lafayette Coll., 1960; MD, Jefferson Med. Coll., 1964. Diplomate Am. Bd. Surgery. Intern N.Y. Hosp. Cornell U. Med. Ctr., N.Y.C., 1964-65, resident in surgery, 1965-69, chief resident surgery, 1969-70; staff surgeon Cooley Dickinson Hosp., Northampton, Mass., 1972—, chief surgery, 1986-92; pvt. practice; councillor Am. Coll. Surgeons, 1986-89; trustee Cooley Dickinson Hosp., 1984-92. Contbr. articles to profl. jours. Bd. dirs. Hampshire Regional YMCA, 1974-80, pres., 1977-79. Lt. Comdr. USNR, 1970-72. Home: 324 Audubon Dr Leeds MA 01053 Office: 190 Nonotuck St Northampton MA 01060

PARSONS, PETER HAROLD, marketing and advertising consultant; b. Bournemouth, Hampshire, Eng., Dec. 8, 1938; came to U.S., 1965; s. Harold Norman and Helen Margaret (Ramsbottom) P.; m. Timi Hall Garritt, June 17, 1967; children: Charles, David, Jason. BA, Trinity Coll., Oxford, Eng., 1962, MA, 1964. Brand mgr. J. Lyons (now named Allied Lyons), London, 1962-63; from account exec. to exec. v.p. internat., dir. Compton Advt. Inc. (now named Saatchi & Saatchi), N.Y.C., 1963-85; pres. Peter Parsons Assocs. Ltd., South Salem, N.Y., 1986—. Lt. Royal Artillery, 1957-59. Mem. Tory Party. Anglican. Home: 89A Elmwood Rd South Salem NY 10590-9359 Office: Peter Parsons Assocs Ltd 89A Elmwood Rd South Salem NY 10590-9359

PARU, MARDEN DAVID, fund raising executive; b. Belmar, N.J., Nov. 18, 1941; s. Isaac and Edith (Rubin) P.; m. Joan Ellen Kemeny, June 5, 1966; children: Victor Milan, Elana Fay. BA, U. Tulsa, 1963; MA, U. Chgo., 1965; postgrad., Syracuse U., 1968-69, Brandeis U., 1970-73. Dir. spl. svcs. Young Men's Jewish Coun., Chgo., 1965-67; asst. dir. Jewish Community Ctr., Syracuse, N.Y., 1967-68; exec. dir. Onondaga County Assn. for Retarded Citizens, Syracuse, 1968-70; lectr., dir. admissions Hornstein program Brandeis U., Waltham, Mass., 1972-74; exec. dir. Jewish Edn. Coun., Montreal, Que., Can., 1974-76, Jewish Fedns. Poughkeepsie-Kingston (N.Y.), 1976-79; exec. v.p. Jewish Fedn. Greater Clifton (N.J.)-Passaic, 1979-82, Cin. Jewish Fedn., 1982-85; dir. N.Y. met. region Am. Technion Soc., N.Y.C., 1985-87; nat. campaign dir. Am. ORT Fedn., N.Y.C., 1987-92; dir. devel. Global Hunger Project, N.Y.C., 1992—; cantor synagogues, Boston, Cin., N.Y. State, Okla., 1960—; cons. on aging pvt. nursing homes, Mass., 1970-74; cons. pvt. Havurot groups, Framingham, Mass., 1970-74. Mem. NASW, Assn. Jewish Community Orgn. Pers. (v.p. 1984-89), Conf. Jewish Communal Svc., Nat. Soc. Fundraising Execs., Acad. Cert. Social Workers. Democrat. Home: 395 S End Ave Apt 29N New York NY 10280-1052 Office: The Hunger Project/Global Office 1 Madison Ave New York NY 10010

PASCARELLA-CANTU, TINA-MARIE, health facility administrator; b. Bradford, Pa., Jan. 2, 1956; d. James John and Virginia Ann (Sopko) Pascarella. AAS in Nursing, Jamestown (N.Y.) Community, 1977; BS in Mgmt., Lesley Coll., 1989; MBA, Northeastern U., 1991. RN. Unit clk. Bradford (Pa.) Hosp., 1971-72, nurses aide, 1972-73, operating room tech., 1973-77, staff nurse, 1977-78; staff nurse, instr. Emerson Hosp., Concord, Mass., 1978-83, nurse mgr., 1983—; chmn. nursing exec. group, Emerson Hosp., 1988-89. Mem. Am. Nurses Assn., Assn. Operating Room Nurses, Mass. Orgn. Nurse Execs., Am. Coll. Sports Medicine, Mass. Middle Mgrs. Assn. Roman Catholic. Office: Emerson Hosp Old Bridge Rd # 9 Concord MA 01742-3011

PASCH, STEVEN JULIAN, produce company executive; b. N.Y.C., Nov. 6, 1952; s. Hans Pasch and Dita Edith (Loewenstein) Rosenbaum; m. Gail Ruth Einhorn; children: David Howard, Melanie Holly. Student in bus., U. Charleston, 1970-71; student, CUNY, 1972-75. From pier laborer to head pier ops. to sales mgr. Jac. Vandenberg, Inc., Bronx, 1975-82; gen. mgr. Fisher Bros. Sales, Inc., Ft. Lee, N.J., and Montreal, Que., Can., 1982-84; pres. Pro-Fruit Mktg., Inc., Allendale, N.J., 1984—. Chmn. Israel Bonds-Allied Industries for Econ. Devel., N.Y., N.J., 1981-89; mem. Bergen County (N.J.) Rep. Orgn., 1988—. Recipient Merit badge of Honor Produce Reporter Co., 1987, Bus. Character award The Red Book, 1988, Prime Ministers Club award Israeli Bonds-Econ. Devel. Coun., 1988, Israel Freedom award Knesset, 1988; grantee trading mem. status Produce Reporter Co., 1988. Mem. Produce Mktg. Assn., United Fresh Fruit & Produce Assn., Ea. Produce Coun. Office: Pro-Fruit Mktg Inc PO Box 258 Allendale NJ 07401

PASCHALL, JEANETTE, scientist, writer, researcher, language counselor; b. Marlin, Tex., Oct. 4, 1921; d. Fred Lynn and Irene (Cable) P. BA in Chemistry, U. Tex., 1943; postgrad., So. Meth. U., 1946-47, New Sch. for Social Research, 1964, 90, Middlebury (Vt.) Coll., 1986, Harvard U., U. Pa., 1980. Research chemist EXXON, Houston, 1943-45; asst. chemist Dr. Pepper Co., Dallas, 1945-49; chief chemist Parade Extract Co., Dallas, 1949-52; owner The Flavor Hall, Dallas, 1952-55; chem. engr. LTV Corp., Dallas, 1955-56; mgr. mktg. research McGraw-Hill Inc., N.Y.C., 1956-72; owner 4M Indsl. Research Co., N.Y.C., 1972—; tech. dir. ITT Corp., N.Y.C., 1974-85; freelance writer N.Y.C., 1986—; owner The Lang. Hall, 1990—. Author: Market for Liquid Gas & Air Handling Equipment, 1962; author initial study Recognit, Rankings of Suppliers to Process Industry, 1962; contbr.

articles to profl. jours. Named Woman Achiever in Industry YWCA, 1983. Mem. Am. Chem. Soc., Am. Inst. Chem. Engrs. Republican. Home: 215 E 68th St New York NY 10021-5718 Office: Lenox Ave # 470 New York NY 10026-3817

PASCHALL, SAMUEL JAMES, army officer; b. Henderson, N.C., Jan. 4, 1929; s. William and Sallie Elenor (Henderson) P.; m. Bettie Pettaway Paschall, Sept. 23, 1961 (div. 1980); children: Michael, Carlyn Maria. BS in Anthropology and Sociology, Bowie State U., 1972, MEd in Spl. Edn., 1973; postgrad., Am. U., Washington, 1974-75; PhD in Ednl. Adminstrn., Calif. Coast U., 1978. Commd. U.S. Army, advanced through grades to sgt. maj., assignments in Europe, 1948-54; with materiel command U.S. Army, Alexandria, Va., 1986-89; substitute instr. spl. edn. Bowie State Coll., 1972-73; program designer, lectr. Am. U., Washington, 1974-79. Pres. Friendly Neighborhood Civic Orgn., Washington. Recipient Outstanding Svc. award, Meritorious Svc. medal, Army Commendation medal, Meritorious Community Svc. award Capitol Press Club. Mem. APHA, Coun. Exceptional Children (mental retardation div., learning disabilities div.), Nat. Assn. Supervision and Curriculum, Am. Mgmt. Assn., Delta Kappa Pi.

PASCRELL, WILLIAM J., JR., mayor, assemblyman; b. Paterson, N.J., Jan. 25, 1937; s. William J. Sr. and Roffie (Loffredo) P., m. Elsie Marie Botto; children: William III, David, Glenn. BS, Fordham U., 1959; MA, Montclair State Coll., 1961; postgrad., Fairleigh Dickinson U. Tchr. Jr. High Sch., Clifton, N.J., 1962, Paramus (N.J.) High Sch., 1962-74; adult sch. tchr. Dwight Morrow High Sch., Englewood, N.J., 1969-70; prof. Fairleigh Dickinson U., Madison, N.J., 1963-68; dir. Dept. Pub. Works City of Paterson, 1974-77, dir. Dept. Policy Planning and Mgmt., 1977-87; mem. N.J. Gen. Assembly, 1988—, chmn. higher edn. com., 1988—, vice chmn. edn. com., 1988—, mem. appropriations com., 1988—; mayor City of Paterson, 1990—. Pres. Paterson Bd. Edn., 1979-82; campaign coord. Robert A. Roe for Gov., N.J., 1977; regional coord. James Florio for Gov., Hudson County, N.J., 1981; active County Chairmen for Sen. Frank Lautenberg, N.J., 1982—; chmn. Passaic County Democrats, N.J., 1982—. With U.S. Army, 1961-67. Named Man of Yr., Mother Cabrini Soc., 1978, Am. Legion (John Road Post), 1983, St. Gerard's Parish, 1988, Assn. Retarded Citizens, 1991. Mem. N.J. Math. Coalition (bd. govs. 1991—), UNICO (Paterson chpt. Man of Yr., 1981), Italian Sport Club. Roman Catholic. Office: Office of Mayor 155 Market St Paterson NJ 07505

PASERMAN, HYMAN JUDAH-MAIER, medical sales executive; b. Munich, Sept. 8, 1949; s. Abraham Adam and Bella (Kestenberg) P.; m. Cheryl Hope Tishelman, Oct. 21, 1971; 1 child, Matthew. BS in Psychology, CCNY, 1972. Sales rep. Reed and Carnrick Pharmaceuticals, Kenilworth, N.J., 1973-76, Mallinckrodt Diagnostics, St. Louis, 1976-78, Narco-Pilling, Ft. Washington, Pa., 1978-80; sales rep., mgr. Vertronix, Larchmont, N.Y., 1980-82; territory mgr. MADA Med. Corp., Carlstadt, N.J., 1983—. Author: Song of the Ancient Suns, 1987. Scoutmaster Edison coun. Boy Scouts Am., 1987. Democrat. Jewish.

PASFIELD, CHARLES JAMES, election company executive; b. Mineola, N.Y., July 21, 1954; s. Robert George and Ruth (Harmon) P.; m. Susan Joy Case, Aug. 7, 1982; children: Krista, Justin. BS, Southwestern Coll., Winfield, Kans., 1975. Paramedic Norwalk (Conn.) Hosp., 1977-80; v.p. The Ind. Election Corp. of Am., Lake Success, N.Y., 1980—. Mem. Stock Transfer Assn., Security Ind. Assn. Corporate Transfer Agt. Assn., Ultra Fitness Health Club. Home: 10 Barrett Ct Nesconset NY 11767-1543 Office: IECA 2335 New Hyde Park Rd New Hyde Park NY 11042-1212

PASHO, PHILIP B., company executive; b. Boston, Dec. 13, 1941; s. William I. and Willa F. Pasho; m. Glenda J. Crane, Sept. 1, 1962; children: Scott Philip, Lisa Ann. EE, Northeastern U., Boston, 1963. Gen. mgr. Fairchild, Mountain View, Calif., 1971-80; prs. Atavar Corp., Scarborough, Maine, 1980-82, Vortech Corp., Gorham, Maine, 1983-87; sr. v.p. Flextronics Inc., Fremont, Calif., 1987-88; v.p. mktg. and sales Automated Assemblies Corp., Clinton, Mass., 1988—; cons. Menlo Bus. Systems, Los Altos, Calif. Mem. SBA-503 Loan Com., Augusta, Maine, 1983-84; mem. Maine Sci. and Tech. Bd., Augusta, 1983-87. Mem. Am. Newcomen, Masons. Republican. Home: 19 Ridge St Winchester MA 01890-3623 Office: Automated Assemblies Corp 25 School St Clinton MA 01510

PASIKOV, IAN DAVID, minister, therapist; b. Detroit, Oct. 6, 1948; s. Charles Herbert and Ann (Gordner) P.; m. Dianne Brancato; 1 child, Michael Jonathon Pasikov. BA, Wayne State U., Detroit, 1969, MAT, 1974. Teaching cert. Tchr. Detroit Pub. Schs., Detroit, 1969-72; asst. dir., dir. student svcs., prin., tchr. Twin Valleys Sch., Wardsville, Ont., Can., 1972-79, exec. dir., 1979-82; administr. 12 Internat. Human Unity Conf., Boston, 1983-84; therapist Life Transformation Program, Dover, N.H., 1990—; min., coord. Green Pastures Estate, Epping, N.H., 1984—; pres. Green Pastures Enterprises, Epping, N.H., 1986—; New England coord., Emissary Found. Internat., Spring, N.H., 1986—. Contbr. article in Convergence Mag., Link Up Mag. Recipient Four Chapels Legion of Honor Mem., The Chapel of Four Chaplains, Phila., 1986. Mem. Am. Assn. Counseling and Devel., Assn. for Humanistic Edn. and Devel., Am. Mental Health Counselors Assn., Renmissance Edn. Assocs., Whole Health Inst. Mem. Emissaries of Divine Light. Home: 38 Ladds Ln Epping NH 03042-2311

PASINSKI, EDMOND, programmer, analyst; b. Jersey City, N.J., Dec. 6, 1955; s. Chester and Ann (Sobolewski) P. BS in Acctg./Bus. Mgmt., St. Peter's Coll., 1978, MS in Sch. Supervision, 1989. Sr. programmer, analyst, coord. data processing Hudson County Vocat./Tech. Sch., North Bergen, N.J., 1979—. Democrat. Roman Catholic. Home: 770 3d St Secaucus NJ 07094 Office: Hudson County Vocat/Tech 8511 Tonnelle Ave North Bergen NJ 07047

PASKAUSKY, DAVID FRANK, oceanographer; b. Waukegan, Ill., Mar. 1, 1938; s. Frank Paul and Blanche Mary (Sorenson) P.; m. Dee Ann Smith, Aug. 13, 1967; children: Blanche Estelle, Anna Louise, Daeva Smitha. SB in Physics, U. Chgo., 1960; MS in Physics, DePaul U., 1964; PhD in Oceanography, Tex. A&M U., 1969. Assoc. prof. U. Conn., Storrs, 1969-75; sci. officer Office of Naval Rsch., Arlington, Va., 1975-78; br. chief U.S. Coast Guard R & D Ctr., Groton, Conn., 1978—; cons. Stone & Webster, Boston, 1971-72, Gilbert Assocs., Reading, Pa., 1972-73. Mem. Geophys. Union, Am. Meteorol. Soc., Explorers Club. Republican. Roman Catholic. Office: US Coast Guard R & D Ctr 1082 Shennecossett Rd Groton CT 06340-6048

PASKOWITZ, HOWARD, accountant; b. Bklyn., Dec. 9, 1932; s. Irving and Fay (Kirschenbaum) P.; m. Saundra Zaretsky, Apr. 11, 1954; children: Karen Elyse, Robin Beth. BS, L.I. U., 1956. CPA, N.Y. Ptnr. H. Paskowitz & Co., CPAs, P.C., N.Y.C., 1957—; pres. bd. dirs. Westover Oil Exploration Corp., N.Y.C., Howda Enterprises, Inc., N.Y.C. Mem. N.Y. State Soc. CPAs, Nat. Conf. CPA Practitioners. Office: H Paskowitz & Co CPA PC 234 Silverlake Blvd Carle Place NY 11514-1603

PASQUALE, FRANK ANTHONY, engineering administrator; b. Jersey City, Oct. 27, 1954; s. Frank F. and Josephine (Marano) P.; m. Elaine J. Rinaldi; children: Frank A. II, Phillip, Marielle. BSME, Fairleigh Dickinson U., 1976; postgrad., U. Mich., 1977. Registered profl. engr., N.J. Supr. chassis engr. Ford Co., Dearborn, Mich., 1976-80; engr. mgr. Bavarian Motor Works of N.Am., Montvale, N.J., 1980-82; enging. mgr. Purolator Products Inc, Rahway, N.J., 1982-85; dir. ops. Inverness Inc., Fairlawn, N.J., 1985-87; v.p. engring. Transworld Inc., East Rutherford, N.J., 1987-91; sr. v.p. engring. Henschel-Steinau, Inc., Englewood, N.J., 1991-92; pres. FPM Devel. Corp., Towaco, N.J., 1992—; cons. Marine-Tech. Corp., Wood-Ridge, N.J., 1985—; bd. dirs. Spin-Tech. Corp., Hoboken, N.J., Internat. Offshore Tackle, Inc., Montville, N.J. Patentee in field. Mem. ASME, Soc. Plastic Engrs., Soc. Automotive Engrs., Soc. Mfg. Enging. Home: 9 Mulbrook Ln Towaco NJ 07082

PASQUARELLI, JOSEPH J., real estate, engineering and construction executive; b. N.Y.C., Mar. 5, 1927; s. Joseph and Helen (Casabona) P.; B.C.E. cum laude, Manhattan Coll., 1949; m. JoAnne Brienza, June 20, 1964; children: Ronald, Richard, June, Joy. Engr., Madigan-Hyland, N.Y.C. and Burns & Roe Inc., N.Y.C., 1949-56; sr. engr., asst. to exec. dir. Office of Sch. Bldgs., N.Y.C. Bd. Edn., 1956-67; dir. design and constrn. mgmt. City U. N.Y., 1967-72; dir. constrn. mgmt. Morse/Diesel Inc., N.Y.C., 1972-76; dir. projects and proposals Burns & Roe Indsl. Svcs. Corp., Oradell, N.J., 1976-80, dir. facilities and infrastructure, 1980-86; dir. design engring, constrn., devel. mgmt. Xerox Realty Corp., Stamford, Ct., 1986-89; exec. v.p. The Galvin Group N.Y.C., 1989-90; assoc. prin. Pei/Galvin Holdings, Ltd., N.Y.C., 1990—; instr. Mechs. Inst., N.Y.C. Community Coll. Applied Arts, Sci., 1955-58. Chmn. United Fund R. for Morse/Diesel Inc., 1973-75; mem. Cardinal's Com. of Laity for Roman Catholic Charities of N.Y.C., 1967-77; mem. North Caldwell (N.J.) Skating Pond Com. Served with U.S. Army, 1944-46. Licensed profl. engr., N.Y., N.J. Fellow ASCE; mem. N.Y. Bldg. Congress (past gov., chmn. legis. com.), NSPE, Mcpl. Engrs., Am. Arbitration Assn. (panel of arbitrators), Chi Epsilon. Club: Essex Fells Country. Contbr. articles to profl. jours. Home: 38 Oak Pl North Caldwell NJ 07006-4554 Office: Pei/Galvin Holdings Ltd 444 Madison Ave New York NY 10022-6903

PASS, CAROLYN JOAN, dermatologist; b. Balt., May 14, 1941; d. Isidore Earl and Rhea (Koplowitz) P.; B.S., U. Md., 1962, M.D., 1966; m. Richard Malcolm Susel, June 23, 1963; children—Steven, Gary. Rotating intern USPHS Hosp., Balt., 1966-67; med. resident St. Agnes Hosp., Balt., 1967-68; dermatology resident and fellow U. Md. Sch. Medicine Hosps., 1968-71; pvt. practice specializing in dermatology, Balt. and Ellicott City, Md., 1971—; mem. staff James Lawrence Kernan, St. Agnes; vol. dermatology clinics U. Md., St. Agnes hosps.; asst. clin. prof. dermatology U. Md. Sch. Medicine, 1978—; mem. exec. com. adv. bd. Nat. Program in Dermatology, 1975. Diplomate Am. Bd. Dermatology. Mem. AMA, Med. and Chirurgical Faculty Md., Balt. City Med. Soc. (del. 1974), Am. Women's Med. Assn., Am. Acad. Dermatology (award exhibit 1970), Soc. Investigative Dermatology, Md. Dermatology Soc. (sec.-treas. 1974-76, pres. 1976-77), Soc. Contemporary Medicine and Surgery, U. Md. Sch. Medicine Alumnae Assn. (bd. dirs. 1987—). Jewish. Clubs: Suburban Country (Balt.); Country Garden. Gourmet. Home: Timberlane 8410 Park Heights Ave Baltimore MD 21208-1716 Office: Pine Heights Med Ctr 1001 Pine Heights Ave Ste 301 Baltimore MD 21229-5291

PASSANTINO, GEORGE CHRISTOPHER, artist, educator; b. Bronx, N.Y.; s. Matthew Michael and Eva Ninfa (Presti) P.; m. Roberta Attias, Oct. 24, 1959; children: Nina, Donna. Student, Art Students League, N.Y.C., 1947-52. Former illustrator Fredman Chaite, N.Y.C.; book designer Reinhart Pubs., N.Y.C.; freelance illustrator Brown & Biglow-Kudner, also others, N.Y.C.; represented by The Little Studio, N.Y.C., Conn., 1952-62; instr., supr. The Famous Artists Sch., Westport, Conn., 1957-72; instr. art U. Bridgeport, Conn., Art Students League, 1978—; portrait painter Portraits Inc., N.Y.C., 1975—, Potrait Brokers of Am., Birmingham, Ala., 1989—; judge, mem. jury, lectr. workshops, Conn., N.J., N.Y., Fla., Pa., Ga. Coauthor: Six Artists Paint a Portrait, 1974, The Portrait and Figure Painting Book, 1979; exhibits include Nat. Acad. of Design, N.Y.C., Wadsworth Antheneum, Hartford, Conn., Stanford (Conn.) Mus. With USMC, 1942-45, PTO. Decorated Purple Heart. Mem. Art Students League (life), Allied Artists Am. Home and Studio: 30 Rising Ridge Rd Ridgefield CT 06877

PASSERO, MICHAEL ANTHONY, internal medicine physician, educator; b. Newark, Mar. 28, 1945; s. Anthony John and Connie (Blasi) P.; m. Mary Ann Cecere, June 14, 1969; children: Michael A. Jr., Christopher John. BA, Dartmouth Coll., 1966, MB, 1967; MD, Harvard U., 1969. Diplomate Am. Bd. Internal Medicine, Am. Bd. Pulmonary Diseases. Med. resident Duke U., Durham, N.C., 1969-72, pulmonary fellow, 1972-74; asst. prof. medicine Brown U., Providence, 1976-83, assoc. prof. medicine, 1984—; dir. pulmonary and critical care medicine Roger Williams Gen. Hosp., Providence, 1976—, assoc. chief medicine, 1984—. Maj. M.C. U.S. Army, 1974-76. Named to Honorable Order of Ky. Cols. Mem. Am. Coll. Chest Physicians (gov. R.I. 1985-91), Am. Thoracic Soc. (sec. eastern sect. 1984—). Office: Roger Williams Med Ctr 825 Chalkstone Ave Providence RI 02908

PASSOW, AARON HARRY, educator; b. Liberty, N.Y., Dec. 9, 1920; s. Morris and Ida (Wiener) P.; m. Shirley Siegel, July 2, 1944; children: Michael Joel, Deborah Miriam, Ruth Gertrude. B.A. cum laude, SUNY-Albany, 1942, M.A., 1947; Ed.D. (Romiett Stevens scholar), Columbia U., 1951. Tchr. sci., math. Stony Point High Sch., N.Y., 1942-43; sci. tchr. Eden Central Sch., N.Y., 1946-48; instr. edn., supr. math. SUNY, Albany, 1948-51; mem. faculty Columbia U. Tchrs. Coll., 1951—, prof. edn., 1952-91, Jacob H. Schiff prof. edn., 1972-91, prof. emeritus, 1991—, chmn. dept. curriculum and teaching, 1968-77, chmn. com. urban edn., 1965-77, dir. div. ednl. instns. and programs, 1975-80; research assoc. Horace Mann-Lincoln Inst. Sch. Experimentation, 1952-65; Fulbright lectr., vis. prof. edn. U. Stockholm, 1967—68; vis. prof. Bar-Ilan (Israel) U., 1973, 81, Tel Aviv U., 1981; dir. Study Washington Pub. Schs., 1966-67; ednl. cons., lectr. edn. disadvantaged, edn. gifted and curriculum devel. Co-author: Organizing for Curriculum Development, 1953, Planning for Talented Youth, 1955, Developing a Curriculum for Modern Living, 1957, Improving the Quality of Public School Programs, 1960; author: Secondary Education for All: The English Approach, 1961; also articles.; editor: Curricular Crossroads, 1962, Education in Depressed Areas, 1963, Education of Disadvantaged: A Book of Readings, 1967, Developing Programs for the Disadvantaged, 1968, Deprivation and Disadvantage: Nature and Manifestations, 1970, Reaching the Disadvantaged Learner, 1970, Urban Education in the 1970s, 1971, Opening Opportunities for Disadvantaged Learners, 1972, The National Case Study: An Empirical Study of 21 National Educational Systems, 1976, Secondary Education Reform: Retrospect and Prospect, 1976, American Secondary Education: The Conant Influence, 1977, The Gifted and the Talented: Their Education and Development, 1979, Education for Gifted Children and Youth, 1980, Reforming the Schools in the 1980s, 1984, Gifted Young in Science: Potential through Performance, 1989. Mem. Englewood Bd. Edn., N.J., 1969-72, pres., 1971. Served to 1st lt. USAAF, 1943-46. Recipient Disting. Alumnus award SUNY-Albany, 1969; Kappa Delta Pi fellow, 1958-59. Mem. NEA (life), Assn. Supervision and Curriculum Devel. (bd. dirs. 1959-62, chmn. rsch. commn. 1961-63, co-chmn. task force edn. culturally disadvantaged 1964-66), Nat. Soc. Study Edn. (bd. dirs. 1975—), Met. Assn. Study Gifted (pres. 1957-58), World Coun. for Gifted and Talented Childen (hon. bd. dirs. 1979-85, pres. 1985-90), Am. Ednl. Rsch. Assn., Comparative and Internat. Edn. Assn. (bd. dirs. 1971-74), Kappa Delta Pi (Laureate chpt., hon.). Jewish (pres. temple 1966-67). Home: 394 Eton St Englewood NJ 07631-4719 Office: Columbia U Tchrs Coll New York NY 10027

PASSWATER, RICHARD ALBERT, biochemist, author; b. Wilmington, Del., Oct. 13, 1937; s. Stanley Leroy and Mabel Rosetta (King) P. BS, U. Del., 1959; PhD, Bernadean U., 1976. Cert. firefighter; m. Barbara Sarah Gayhart, June 2, 1964; children: Richard Alan, Michael Eric. Supr. instrumental analysis lab. Allied Chem. Corp., Marcus Hook, Pa., 1959-64; tech. svcs. rep. F&M Sci. Corp., Avondale, Pa., 1965; dir. applications lab. Am. Instrument Co., Silver Spring, Md., 1965-77; dir. Am. Gen. Enterprises, Minn.; former daily broadcaster Sta. WMCA, N.Y.C., 1980-88; former daily broadcaster Sta. WRNG, Atlanta, 1982-85, Sta. WMCA; rsch. dir. Solgar Nutritional Rsch. Ctr., 1979—, corp. v.p. Solgar Co., Inc.; chmn. Worcester County Emergency Planning Com.; bd. dirs. Worcester Meml. Hosp., Atlantic Gen. Hosp., River Run Assn; pres. Subaqueous Exploration and Archeology Ltd. Author: Guide to Fluorescence Literature, vol. 3, 1974, Supernutrition, 1976, Supernutrition For Healthy Hearts, 1978, Super Calorie, Carbohydrate Counter, 1978, Cancer and Its Nutritional Therapies, 1983, The Easy No-Flab Diet, 1979, Selenium As Food and Medicine, 1980, The Slendernow Diet, 1982, (with Dr. E. Cranton) Trace Elements, Hair Analysis and Nutrition, 1983, The New Supernutrition, 1991. bd. dirs. Sci. Documentation Ctr., Dunfermline, Eng.; Am. Found. Firefighter Health and Safety; chief Ocean Pines Vol. Fire Dept., 1984—; active Emergency Med. Tech.; adviser Nat. Inst. Nutrition Edn.; past adv. bd. Stephen Decatur High Sch., Worcester County Dept. Edn. Cubmaster, 1975-79. Recipient Citizen of Yr. award Ocean Pines, Md., 1987, 5th Ann. Achievement award, 1989, VFW Cert. of Commendation, 1988, Industry award Nat. Inst. Nutritional Edn., 1991. Fellow Internat. Acad. Preventive Medicine, Am. Inst. Chemists; mem. Am. Chem. Soc., Gerontology Soc., Am. Geriatric Soc., Am. Aging Assn., Soc. Applied Spectroscopy, Internat. Found. Preventive Medicine (v.p.), Internat. Union Pure and Applied Chemistry, Royal Soc. Chemistry (London), Internat. Acad. Holistic Health and Medicine, ASTM, Capital Chem. Soc., AAAS, Nutrition Today Soc., Am. Acad. Applied Health Scis. (pres., bd. dir.), Internat. Found. Preventive Medicine (v.p., dir.), Inst. Nutritional Rsch., Internat. Platform Assn., N.Y. Acad. Scis., Nat. Fire Protection Assn. (cert. firefighter level III, com. on properties of hazardous chemicals), Pi Kappa Alpha. Author: Guide to Fluorescense Literature, vol. 1., 1967, vol. 2, 1970, vol. 3, 1974; Supernutrition: Megavitamin Revolution, 1975, paperback edit., 1976; Cancer: Nutritional Therapies, 1978; Super Calorie and Carbohydrate Counter, 1978; Supernutrition for Healthy Hearts, 1977, paperback, 1978; The Easy No-Flab Diet, 1979; Selenium as Food and Medicine, 1980; The Slendernow Diet, 1982; (with E. Cranton) Trace Elements, Hair Analysis and Your Health, 1983; The New Supernutrition, 1991; contbg. author: Fire Protection Guide to Hazardous Materials, 1991; editor Fluorescence News, 1966-77, Jour. Applied Health Scis., 1982-83; mem. editorial bd. Nutritional Perspectives, 1978-86, The Body Forum, 1979-80, Jour. Holistic Medicine, 1981-88, VIM Newsletter, 1979—; contbg. editor Firehouse Mag., 1988—, Jour. Applied Nutrition; contbr. over 250 health articles to mags.; co-editor booklet series Your Good Health; sci. adv. and columnist Whole Foods mag.; patentee in field. Office: 11017 Manklin Meadows Ln Berlin MD 21811-9342

PASTERNAC, ANDRÉ, cardiologist; b. Toulouse, France, July 22, 1937; s. Jacques and Règine P.; came to Can., 1971, naturalized, 1978; adv. math. Lycée Henri IV, Paris, 1956; B.A. in Polit. Sci., Toulouse U., 1963, M.D., Med. Sch., 1968. Intern, Toulouse Univ. Hosp., 1962-63, resident, 1963-64, 66-68; resident Edouard-Herriot Hosp., Lyon, France, 1965-66; Fulbright scholar in cardiology Harvard U., 1968-71; research fellow Peter Bent Brigham Hosp., Boston, 1968-69; Milton fellow Children's Hosp., Boston, 1969-71; fellow in cardiology Toronto (Ont., Can.) U., 1971-72; staff cardiologist Montreal (Que., Can.) Heart Inst., 1972—; asst. prof. medicine U. Montreal, 1972-78, clin. assoc. prof., 1978—; vis. assoc. prof. McGill U., Montreal, 1975-76; vis. lectr. U. Liège (Belgium), 1977, U. Madrid, 1977, U. Warsaw, 1979, 83. Bd. dirs. Heart-Brain Research Found. Inc., N.Y.C. Am. Field Service grantee, Oreg., 1954-55; specialist in cardiology, Paris, Montreal. Mem. French Cardiac Soc., Canadian Cardiovascular Soc., Am. Coll. Cardiology, Am. Heart Assn., Internat. Soc. Heart Rsch., Am. Fedn. Clin. Rsch., N.Y. Acad. Scis. Contbr. articles to profl. jours. Research in stress-related myocardial ischemia and dysfunction, mitral valve prolapse, cardiovascular drugs, cardiomyopathies, catecholamines, neuroendocrine control of the heart, stress and the heart. Home: 3465 Redpath St Apt 406, Montreal, PQ Canada H3G 2G8 Office: Montreal Heart Inst, 5000 Belanger E, Montreal, PQ Canada H1T 1C8

PASTORE, STEVEN LOUIS, consumer organization administrator; b. N.Y.C., Nov. 6, 1948; s. Armond Diaz and Janet (Midkiff) P. BA, Hunter Coll., 1972; MA in U.S. History, No. Ill. U., 1976. Canvass dir. Milw. Alliance Concerned Citizens, 1975-76; investigative reporter Bankers Mag., N.Y.C., 1977-81; editor Human Resources Network, 1979-80; exec. dir. Forum for Forecasting, N.Y.C., 1981-89, Tele-Consumer Hotline, Washington, 1991—. Mem. Nat. Soc. Fund Raising Execs., Progressive Fund Raising Round Table, Alliance Against Fraud in Telemktg., Md. Info. Referral Providers Coun. Home: PO Box 8193 Silver Spring MD 20907-8193

PASTOREK, NORMAN JOSEPH, facial plastic surgeon; b. Moline, Ill., Feb. 8, 1939; s. Joseph Andrew and Rose (Faurone) P.; m. Janice Marie Gloss, Apr. 27, 1986; children: Kate Haviland, Kelly Taylor. AB, Augustana Coll., 1960; MD, U. Ill., Chgo., 1964. Diplomate Am. Bd. Otolaryngology. Intern San Francisco Gen. Hosp., 1964-65; resident U. Ill. Hosps., Chgo., 1965-69; pvt. practice medicine specializing in facial plastic surgery N.Y.C; clin. asst. prof. N.Y. Hosp. Cornell Med. Coll., 1971-83, dir. div. facial plastic surgery dept. otolaryngology, 1977—, clin. assoc. prof., 1983-91, clin. prof., 1991—. Author: Blepharoplasty, 1983, 2d edit., 1988; editor: Aesthetic Facial Surgery, 1990. Lt. comdr. USN, 1969-71. Fellow Am. Acad. Otolaryngology, Am. Acad. Facial Plastic and Reconstructive Surgery (v.p. eastern region 1982-86, pres.-elect 1989-90, pres. 1990-91), ACS; mem. Westchester Country Club, Alpha Omega Alpha. Republican. Mem. Unitarian Ch. also: 110 Lockwood Ave New Rochelle NY 10801

PATANELLI, DOLORES JEAN, physiologist; b. Elkhart, Ind., July 20, 1932; d. Michael and Concetta (Robina) P. BA, NYU, 1955, MS, 1958, PhD, 1962. Asst. to med. dir. population coun. Rockefeller U., N.Y.C., 1956-62; rsch. fellow Merck Inst. Therapeutic Rsch., Rahway, N.J., 1963-72; reproductive physiologist Ctr. Population Rsch., Contraceptive Devel. Br. Nat. Inst. Child Health, Bethesda, Md., 1972—; mem. regional health adv. commn. Health, Edn. and Welfare, N.Y.C., 1970-72;membership com. Soc. Study Reproduction, 1973-75, nominating com., 1980-81; mem. organizing com. testes workshop, 1973—. Editor: (book) Hormonal Control of Male Fertility, 1978; inventor (with others) Spiroxenone, 1972. Recipient Dir.'s award NIH, 1991. Mem. N.Y. Acad. Scis., Endocrine Soc., Am. Assn. Anatomists, Am. Soc. Andrology, Am. Fertility Soc., Sigma Xi. Office: Nat Inst Child Health Ctr Population Rsch 6130 Executive Blvd Rm 600F Bethesda MD 20892

PATCHIS, PAULINE, handwriting expert, consultant; b. Pawtucket, R.I., Apr. 17, 1940; d. Alexander P. Patchis and Rose E. (Acquaviva) Jankowski. Grad., Warwick Police Acad., 1967. Cert. document examiner, U.S., Can. and Europe. Exec. sec. to pers. dir. Ciba-Geigy Pharm. Co., Cranston, R.I., 1963-65; adminstrv. detective Warwick (R.I.) Police Dept., 1967-71; cons. jury selection, graphoanalyst Patchis and Wayne, Warwick, 1971—; lectr., instr. various orgns., 1971—. Contbr. articles to profl. jours. Mem. NAFE, Nat. Forensic Ctr., Mass. Police Fraudulent Check Assn., Study Group of R.I. (co-founder). Home and Office: 67 S Fair St Warwick RI 02888-1651

PATE, JAMES LITTLETON, newspaper publisher; b. Madill, Okla., Nov. 23, 1932; s. Herbert J. and Mary Elizabeth (Gardner) P.; m. Mary Elizabeth Ford, June 10, 1954; children: Martha Jean Gallardo, Herbert J. (dec.), Laura Jane, William Clay. BA in Journalism, U. Okla., 1954. Advt. mgr. The Madill Record, 1956-62, gen. mgr., 1962-68, pubr., 1968—; co-owner Johnston County Capital Democrat, Tishomingo, Okla., 1975—, Hillsboro (Kans.) Star Jour., 1981—; pres sec. to Congressman Bill Brewster, Washington, 1991—. Mem., chmn. Okla. Tourism and Recreation Com., Oklahoma City, 1972-82. 2nd lt. USAR, 1956-60. Mem. Okla. Press Assn. (dir., sec.-treas., 1968-75, pres. 1985, Milt Phillips Leadership award 1986), Nat. Newspaper Assn. (dir. 1976-81, sec.-treas. 1981-84, v.p. 1984-85, pres. 1985-86). Democrat. Presbyterian. Home: 1201 S Eads St Apt 914 Arlington VA 22202-2840 Office: Okla Ho of Reps 1404 Longworth HOB Washington DC 22202

PATEL, ATUL CHIMANLAL, computer company executive, mechanical engineer; b. Bangalore, Karnataka, India, Aug. 8, 1943; came to U.S., 1969; s. Chimanlal Fakirbhai and Sushilaben Chimanlal (Rambhai) P.; m. Bharti Chhotalal, Jan. 23, 1969; children: Deepa Atul, Alpa Atul, Rupa Atul. B. Engring. in Mech. Engring., U. Mysore, India, 1965; M. Engring. in Mech. Engring., U. Baroda, Gujarat, India, 1968; MS in Mech. Design, U. So. Calif., L.A., 1971. Registered profl. engr., N.Y., N.J. Engr. Elecon Engring. Co., Vidyanagar, Gujarat, India, 1965-66; R&D engr. Jyoti Ltd., Baroda, 1969; instr. Roberts Tech. Sch., N.Y.C., 1971-72; exec. engr. DieComp, Inc., Plainfield, N.J., 1972-75; engring. analyst Olivetti Corp. of Am., N.Y.C., 1975-78; mgr. spl. projects Fairchild Rep. Co., Farmingdale, N.Y., 1978-86; pres. Systech, Inc., Dix Hills, N.Y., 1984—; sr. engr. Grumman Corp., Bethpage, N.Y., 1986-88; systems engr. Symbol Techs., Inc., Bohemia, N.Y., 1989-90; chmn. Systech, Inc., 1984—, Patel Systech Pvt. Ltd., Bangalore, 1986—. Author (computer software) SYSTECH Product Definition System, 1987. Member Vols. for India's Progress Club, L.I., 1975, India Assn. L.I., Dix Hills, 1980, Dem. Party, U.S., 1985. Mem. ASME, AIAA, Am. Electronics Assn. (corp.), Assn. for Computing Machinery, Soc. Mfg. Engrs., L.I. Assn. (corp.). Hindu. Office: SYSTECH Inc 61 Scott St Dix Hills NY 11746-6753

PATEL, MAHENDRA RAMBHAI, electronics executive; b. Ndeje, Uganda, Nov. 5, 1939; came to U.S., 1980; s. Rambhai Chaturbhai and Savita G. Patel; m. Kapila M. Patel, Oct. 30, 1965; children: Manisha, Naimish. BSEE with honors, U. Manchester, 1961; PhD, U. Cambridge, 1964. Lectr. elec. engring. U. East Africa, Nairobi, Kenya, 1964-66; researcher Nelson Rsch. Labs., Stafford, Eng., 1966-67; sr. engr. English Electric Computers, Kidsgrove, Eng., 1967-68, Internat. Computers Ltd., West Gorton, Eng., 1969-70; prin. engr. Internat. Computers Ltd., Newcastle-under-Lyme, Eng., 1971-74; chief engr. Internat. Computers Ltd.,

Bracknell, Eng., 1974-80; corp. cons. A.B. Dick Co., Niles, Ill., 1980-82; tech. dir. Digital Equipment Corp., Nashua, N.H., 1982-84, Littleton, Mass., 1984—. Mem. IEEE, Assn. Computing Machinery. Home: 32 Monteiro Way North Andover MA 01845-5327 Office: Digital Equipment Corp 550 King St Littleton MA 01460-1289

PATEL, RAFIQ KASSAMALI, surgeon; b. Bombay, Feb. 20, 1938; came to U.S., 1974; s. Kassamali and Rahembano Patel; m. Yasmina Patel, July 7, 1967; children: Maheen, Samia, Riaz. BS, Xavier Coll., Bombay, 1955; MD, Dow Med. Coll., Karachi, Pakistan, 1960. Cert. diplomate of Brit. Bd. of Surgeons. Assoc. prof. surgery Dow Med. Coll. and Civil Hosp., Karachi, 1965-69; sr. surgeon S.I.T.E. Hosp., Mangopir, Karachi, 1970-72; med. staff pres., chief of staff Fallston Gen. Hosp., Md., 1979; med. dir. Fallston Gen. Hosp., 1980-88, attending surgeon, 1975-92; attending surgeon Hartford Meml. Hosp., Havre de Grace, 1975-92; mem. Aga Khan Found., 1966-73; bd. dirs. Aga Khan Univ. Hosp., Karachi, 1985-92. Fellow Royal Coll. Surgeons, Am. Coll. Surgeons; mem. MED-CHI, Harford Med. Counties Soc. Republic. Republic. Muslim. Office: Walk-In Medical Ctr 1952 Pulaski Hwy Edgewood MD 21040-1617

PATEL, SHIRIS RANCHHODBHAI, anesthesiologist; b. Nikora, Gujarat, India, Nov. 1, 1957; came to U.S., 1987; s. Ranchhodbhai Lallubhai and Sushilaben-Ranchhodbhai Patel; m. Shila Shiris, Apr. 8, 1985; children: Amish, Alpesh. M.B.B.S., U. Ibadan (Nigeria), 1979, diploma in anesthesia, 1981. Cert.. Am. Bd. Anesthesiologists. H.O. registrar, SNR registrar Univ. Coll. Hosp., Ibadan, 1979-85; registrar Royal Surrey County Hosp., Guildford, Eng., 1985-87, Lister Hosp., Stevenage, Eng., 1987; resident, fellow Montefiore Med. Ctr., Bronx, N.Y., 1988-89; attending, asst. prof. Albert Einstein Coll. of Medicine, Bronx, 1989-90; pvt. practice anesthesiology Carson, Newsome & Patel, MD, PA, Laurel, Md., 1990—; chmn. quality assurance anesthesiology dept. Carson, Newsome & Patel, MD, PA, Laurel, 1991—. Fellow Royal Coll. Surgeons Eng., Am. Soc. Anesthesiology. Hindu. Home: 8201 Darting Minnow Laurel MD 20723

PATEREK, TINA MARIE, artist, author, songwriter, inventor; b. Bridgewater, N.J., Sept. 1, 1922; d. Julius Caesar and Mary Anna (DeNicola) Monari; m. Peter Edward Paterek, June 16, 1946. Grad. high sch., Somerville, N.J. Designer Pajama Factory, Manville, N.J., 1947-52; parade chairperson, costume and set designer, composer Sweet Adelines, Plainfield, N.J., 1958-61; sales rep. Avon Products, Inc., Somerville, N.J., 1955-70. Artist, founder Presdl. Portraits' Relay exhibit, Somerville, Presdl. Portraits' touring exhibit, Cen. Jersey; commd. Ann Cook collection; exhibited in group show at Parke-Bernet Galleries, N.Y.C.; pub. songs, poems, paintings; patentee Petorama Pet Exerciser, Jug Handle Hat. Artist, founder Patriotic Pals of Am. Club, 1964. Recipient Nat. Art News award, Songwriters mag. award, Somerset County Christmas Seal Competition award. Mem. Cen. Jersey Deltiological Soc., Inc., Artists and Writers Group Flemington (charter). Roman Catholic. Home: 170 Union Ave Somerville NJ 08876-2620 Office: Art By Tina PO Box 6294 Bridgewater NJ 08807

PATERNOSTRO, PATRICK JOSEPH, accountant; b. Waterbury, Conn., Feb. 10, 1967; s. Pasquale and Kathy (Parker) P. BS in Acctg. cum laude, Quianipiac Coll., 1990. Staff acct. Albert Ruscilowicz CPA, Colchester, Conn. Vol. Conn. Spl. Olympics, Waterbury, Conn., 1985-91, Am. Cancer Soc., 1990. Recipient scholarship Watertown High Sch., 1985, Nat. Assn. Accts., 1989, Conn. Soc. CPAs, 1989. Mem. Waterbury Sportsmen's Club (treas. 1990-91). Roman Catholic. Home: 81 Bunker Hill Rd Watertown CT 06795-3304 Office: Albert J Ruscilowicz CPA 94 Pine St Torrington CT 06790-3230

PATERSON, JAMES JOSEPH, insurance agent; b. Bklyn., July 4, 1937; s. John Bruce and Margaret (Early) P.; m. Patricia Termini, Apr. 18, 1959; children: Bonnie Paterson Okula, Laurie Paterson Anderson, Nina Paterson Becker. Student, Hofstra U., 1955-58. Investigator Retail Credit Co., Garden City, N.Y., 1959-62; claims adjuster Allstate Ins. Co., Hicksville, N.Y., 1962-65; ins. agt. State Farm Ins., Mineola, N.Y., 1965—; sportscaster Sta. WGLI-Radio, Babylon, N.Y., 1976-80; sports dir. Sta. WLIW-TV, Garden City, 1978-81; pub. address announcer N.Y. Jets, Flushing, 1980-83, N.Y. Islanders, Uniondale, 1979-87; back-up announcer N.Y. Mets, Flushing, 1981-86. Vice chmn. N.Y. State Conservative Com., North Hempstead, 1967-70. Cpl. U.S. Army, 1958-62. Office: State Farm Ins 483 Jericho Turnpike Mineola NY 11501-0483

PATERSON, JOHN ALAN, equipment manufacturing company executive; b. Pt. Pleasant, N.J., Oct. 7, 1958; s. Walter Charles and Valerie Lambert (Weddel) P. BA in Fine Arts, Rutgers U., 1981. Carpenter Pt. Pleasant, N.J., 1971-81; tchr. spl. edn. Coastal Learning Ctr., Morganville, N.J., 1981-82; customer svc. mgr. People Express Airlines, Newark, 1982-86; gen. mgr. Hockmeyer Equipment Corp., Harrison, N.J., 1986—. Contbg. artist Women Artists, 1981 (NEA grantee 1981). Home: 1314 Cottage Pl Point Pleasant Beach NJ 08742-4036

PATERSON, ROBERT WILLIAM, mechanical engineer; b. Newark, Jan. 19, 1939; s. Archie and Lila Mae (Stoeckel) P.; m. Joyce Mae Pero, Aug. 12, 1967; 1 child, Robert William. BSE, Princeton U., 1960; MA, Harvard U., 1965, PhD, 1969. Nuclear engr. AEC, Washington, 1960-64; rsch. engr. United Techs. Rsch. Ctr., East Hartford, Conn., 1969-73, mgr. aeroacoustics and exptl. gas dynamics, 1973-87, mgr. gas dynamics and thermophysics, 1987-90, mgr. aerodynamics and environ. scis., 1990—. Contbr. articles to profl. jours.; patentee in field. Lt. USN, 1960-64. Fellow AIAA (assoc.); mem. ASME, Phi Beta Kappa, Sigma Xi. Home: 4 Pinecrest Dr Simsbury CT 06070-2907 Office: United Techs Rsch Ctr Silver Ln East Hartford CT 06118-1010

PATINKIN, MANDY, actor; b. Chgo., Nov. 30, 1952; s. Lester and Doris (Sinton) P.; m. Kathryn Grody, June 15, 1980. Student, U. Kans., 1970-72, Juilliard Sch. Drama, 1972-74. Actor N.Y. Shakespeare Festival, 1975-81; plays include Hotspur in Henry IV, Part 1, Hudson Guild, N.Y.C., Rebel Women, Hamlet, Leave it to Beaver is Dead, Savages; films include Ragtime, 1981, The Big Fix, 1979, Yentl, 1983, Daniel, 1983, French Postcards, 1979, The Last Embrace, 1979, Night of the Juggler, Maxie, 1985, The Princess Bride, 1987, The House on Carroll Street, Alien Nation, Dick Tracy, 1990, The Doctor, 1991, True Colors, 1991; actor Broadway prodns. including Evita (Recipient Tony award 1980), Shadow Box, Sunday In The Park With George, 1984, The Knife, 1987, The Winter's Tale, 1989, Mandy Patinkin In Concert: Dress Casual, 1989, The Secret Garden, 1991; TV appearances include That Thing on ABC, That Second Thing on ABC, Taxi, Midnight Special; albums: Mandy Patinkin, 1989, Mr. Arthur's Place. Recipient Music Achievement award Drama League, 1989. Mem. AFTRA, Screen Actors Guild, Actors Equity Assn. *

PATINKIN, MARK ALAN, newspaper columnist; b. Chgo., Jan. 12, 1953; s. Harold Samson and June (Marks) P.; m. Heidi James, May 10, 1986; children: Ariel Janes, Alex Janes. BA, Middlebury Coll., 1974; PhD in Journalism (hon.), Johnson and Wales Coll., 1985, R.I. Coll., 1989. Reporter Utica (N.Y.) Daily Press, 1974-76, Providence Jour.-Bulletin, 1976-79; syndicated columnist Providence Jour. and Scripps Howard News, 1979—. Author: An African Journey, 1985, The Silent War, 1989. Finalist Pultizer prize, 1987; recipient Presdl. End Hunger award, 1991. Jewish. Office: Providence Jour Bull 75 Fountain St Providence RI 02902-0050

PATMORE, LESTER CLAUDIUS, III, entrepreneur; b. Erie, Pa., Nov. 3, 1946; s. Lester C. Patmore Jr. and Gloria (Royall) Cook; m. Donna L. Parmenter, June 3, 1967; children: Michael, Mark, Meghan. Grad. high sch., Harbor Creek, Pa. Laborer General Electric, Erie, 1964-67; sales rep. L.A. Water Conditioning, City of Industry, Calif., 1967-69; mgr. Bankers Life & Casualty Co., Youngstown, Ohio, 1969-74; owner Patmore Mktg. Cons., Erie, 1974—, Val-Pak of Youngstown, 1977—, Val-Pak of Erie, 1978—; ptnr. Val Pak of Northwestern, Pa., 1984—; cons. Pregnancy Aid Ctr., Erie, 1984—, bd. dirs. Chmn. adminstrn. bd. Wesley United Meth. Ch., Erie, 1982-86; treas. Boy Scouts Am., Erie, 1988-91; commr. Harborcreek Little League; mem. Rep. Presdl. Task Force. Mem. Val-Pak Dealers Assn., Harborcreek Area C. of C. (pres. 1991—).

PATRICK, CRAIG, hockey executive; b. Detroit, May 20, 1946; s. Lynn P.; m. Sue Patrick; children—Erin, Cory, Ryan. M.B.A., U. Denver. Hockey player Calif. Golden Seals, 1971-74; hockey player St. Louis Blues, 1974-75, Kansas City, 1975-76, World Hockey Assn., Minn., 1976-77, Washington Capitals, 1977-79; v.p., gen. mgr. N.Y. Rangers, N.Y.C., 1981-86; dir. athletics and recreation Univ. Denver, 1987-89; gen. mgr. Pitts. Penguins, 1989—. Office: Pitts Penguins Civic Arena Pittsburgh PA 15219*

PATRICK, JOHN FRANKLIN, educator; b. Washington, Nov. 17, 1933; s. Clifford Walker and Dorothy (Knoblauch) P.; m. Barbara Florence Sanders, Apr. 3, 1965; children: Susan Lynn, Robert Franklin. BS, U. Va., 1955; MA, George Washington U., 1961; PhD, U. Md., 1977. Commd. 2nd lt. USAF, 1957, advanced to col., 1981; med. forces advisor Office of Surgeon Gen. USAF, Bolling AFB, Washington, 1981-85; mgmt. trainer Dept. Def., Ft. Meade, Md., 1969; chief, mgr. level program Dept. Def., Ft. Meade, 1969-71, exec. Jr. Officer Career Program, 1971-74, instr. course dir., 1974-77, chief Gen. Edn. Div., 1977-81, sr. edn. and tng. officer, 1985-88, sr. ops. staff officer, 1988-90; adj. assoc. prof. George Washington U., Washington, 1990—; asst. profl. lectr. George Washington U., 1981-85, assoc. profl. lectr., 1985-90. Contbr. articles and reports to profl. jours. and mags. Mem. Am. Soc. Pub. Adminstrn., ASTD, Assn. Mil. Surgeons of U.S., Howard County Alumni Club U. Md. (1st v.p. 1983-87). Methodist. Office: George Washington U Washington DC 20052

PATRICK, MICHAEL JAMES, fire chief; b. Corning, N.Y., Mar. 14, 1960; s. James Edward Patrick and Pricillia (Bonicave) Price. Grad. high sch., Elkland, Pa., 1978. With Nelson (Pa.) Fire Co. Inc., 1978-84, truck capt., 1984-88, 2d asst. chief, 1988, 1st asst. chief, 1989, fire chief, 1990—; asst. fire marshall Pa. State Police, Nelson, 1992. Mem. Nelson Vol. Fire Co., 1978—, Nelson Fireworks Com., 1990—; local coord. Pema, Nelson, 1990—. With USN, 1978-84. Named Fireman of Yr., Neslon Vol. Fire Co., 1990, 91; decorated Expert Rifelman, Good Conduct award. Mem. Tioga County Firemen's Assn. (del. 1990—), Tioga County EMS Coun. (del. 1990—), Beechers Town Club, Moose. Democrat. Roman Catholic. Home: PO Box 164 Nelson PA 16940 Office: Nelson Vol Fire Co Inc PO Box 56 Nelson PA 16940

PATRICK, MICHELE MARY, government official; b. Phila., Apr. 18, 1963; d. George Robert and Mary Elizabeth (Pristic) P. BA in Econs., La Salle U., 1985; M in Govt. Adminstrn., U. Pa., 1990. Intern Phila. Water Dept., 1987; intern, asst. to exec. dir. Global Interdependence Ctr., Phila., 1988-89; intern, asst. to dep. dir. Phila. Fin. Dept., 1989, asst. to fin. dir., 1990; asst. mng. dir. City of Phila., 1990—; speaker, Fulbright Speaker's Bur., London, 1985-86. Recipient Fulbright fellowship, U.K., Bd. Fgn. Scholarships, Washington, 1985, Nat. Resource fellowship, Pacific-Asian Mgmt. Inst., U. Hawaii, 1984, Lindback award, La Salle U., Phila., 1985, Pa. Forensic Assn., State Championships, 1982, 83, 85, Nat. Forensic Assn. Nat. championship, 1985, Meyerson fellowship, U. Pa., Phila., 1987, Pres. Classroom scholarship, Pres. Classroom for Young Ams., Washington, 1982, James and Helen Hovorka scholarship, Coun. Higher Edn., Brookfield, Ill., 1982, 83, 84. dem. Amnesty Internat., Czechoslovak Nat. Coun. Am., Internat. Platform Assn., Omicron Delta Epsilon. Democrat. Roman Catholic. Home: 13049 Stevens Rd Philadelphia PA 19116-1334

PATRICK, STUART KAVANAUGH, investment company executive; b. N.Y.C., May 1, 1939; s. Joseph Alfred and Phoebe (Armstrong) P.; m. Nancy Patricia Richard, Aug. 4, 1962 (div. May 1990); children: Jill Christine, Scott Richard. BA, Princeton (N.J.) U., 1961; MBA in Fin., Northwestern U., 1964. Brand contr. Colgate-Palmolive Co., N.Y.C., 1964-67; fin. analyst Westvaco, N.Y.C., 1967-68; asst. to the comptr. Kraftco Corp., N.Y.C., 1968-69; ptnr. Baird, Patrick & Co., N.Y.C., 1969-75; pres. Baird, Patrick & Co., Inc., N.Y.C., 1976—. Trustee Outward Bound, Inc., Greenwich, Conn., 1984-90, mem. adv. bd., 1990—. Mem. Downtown Assn., Sales Mgrs. Assn. N.Y.C., Montclair Golf Club. Home: 454-334 Prospect Ave West Orange NJ 07052 Office: Baird Patrick & Co Inc 20 Exchange Pl New York NY 10005

PATRICK, THOMAS DONALD, communications and marketing executive; b. Carroll, Iowa, July 22, 1942; s. Donald Harrison and Linette (Cretsinger) P.; m. Patricia Ann Williams, Nov. 18, 1967 (div. 1980); m. Georgia Laykatis O'Brien, Oct. 23, 1981. BA, Drake U., Des Moines, 1970. Photographer AP, UPI, Des Moines, 1961-64; staff photographer, staff writer Des Moines Register, 1964-69; mng. editor Market Communications, Inc., Milw., 1969-71, Big Farmer Mag., Frankfort, Ill., 1971-72; dir. communications and edn. Am. Iron and Steel Inst., Washington, 1972-80; chief exec. officer, pres. The Communicators, Inc., Rockville, Md., 1980-92; pres., chief exec. officer Windstar Enterprises, Inc., Jefferson, Md., 1991—. Photographer various mags. and newspapers. Mem. Direct Mktg. Assn. Washington, Am. Soc. Assn. Execs., Nat. Assn. Industry Edn. Coop. (treas. 1979-80, ednl. sponsorship award 1980), Pub. Rels. Soc. Am. (counselors acad.), Nat. Assn. Exposition Mgrs., Blue Ridge Mountain Country Club (pres. 1987). Democrat. Office: Windstar Enterprises Inc 3603 Fry Rd Jefferson MD 21755-7408

PATTEE, GORDON BURLEIGH, financial executive; b. San Francisco, Apr. 13, 1948; s. William Burleigh and Dorothy Elizabeth (Evans) P.; m. Dailey Jones, Dec. 1, 1972; children: Mary Dailey, Ashleigh Lupton, Gordon Burleigh Paxton. BA in Econs., Stanford U., 1970; MBA, Harvard U., 1975. Loan officer Bank of Calif., San Francisco, 1971-73; assoc. White Weld & Co., N.Y.C., 1974, Lehman Bros. Kuhn Loeb, N.Y.C., 1975-81; mng. dir. A.G. Becker, N.Y.C., 1981-84, Merrill Lynch Capital Mkts., N.Y.C., 1984-87; pres. Map Capital Corp., N.Y.C., 1987—; bd. dirs. ISF, Amsterdam, Holland, Pasqua, Inc., San Francisco, Sesame St. Retail Stores, Inc., Cross Border Enterprises Inc. Bd. dirs. N.Y.C. Ballet, 1989—, Citizens Com. for N.Y.C., 1990—; trustee Presbyn. Hosp., N.Y.C., 1988—; vice chmn. N.Y. Hist. Soc., 1987—, Nat. Victim Ctr., 1990—, The Chapin Sch., 1991—. Republican. Episcopalian. Office: Map Capital Corp 9 W 57th St # 4605 New York NY 10019-2600

PATTEN, EILEEN DUNLEVY, fundraising and public relations executive; b. Paterson, N.J.; d. Robert P. and Julia (Hennessy) Dunlevy; m. Grant A. Patten Jr., Sept. 30, 1950; children: Kathleen Burke, Margaret Alexandra. AB, Coll. of New Rochelle, N.Y., 1944; postgrad., Harvard U., 1954, Rutgers U., 1963. Dir. community rels. Valley Hosp., Ridgewood, N.J., 1959-79; pub. rels. and fundraising cons. Rep. Nat. Com., 1979-80; dir. spl. projects Am. Heart Assn. N.J. Affiliate, 1980-84; dir. pub. affairs and fundraising Hosp. Ctr. at Orange, N.J., 1984—. Founder Ridgewood Sch. System Field Trip Enrichment Program, 1979-82; co-chair Roukema for Congress campaign, N.J., 1978; vol. Am. Heart Assn., ARC, United Way. Mem. N.J. Advt. Club (bd. dirs.), N.J. Press Women, Nat. Fedn. Press Women, Am. Soc. for Hosp. Pub. Rels. and Mktg., N.J. Hosp. Pub. Rels. and Mktg. Assn. Home: 2-115 N Franklin Turnpike Ramsey NJ 07446

PATTENAUDE, RICHARD LOUIS, university administrator; b. Seattle, Feb. 22, 1946; s. Joseph Arthur and Alice June (Vrooman) P.; m. Michele Arlen Stevenson, May 31, 1975; 1 child, Lauren. BA with honors in Econs., Calif. State U.-San Jose, 1968; PhD in Polit. Sci., U. Colo., 1974. Assoc. prof. Drake U., Des Moines, 1974-80, assoc. dean liberal arts, 1976-80; asst. v.p. acad. affairs SUNY-Binghamton, 1980-82, assoc. v.p., 1982-86; v.p. acad. affairs, assoc. prof. polit. sci. Cen. Conn. State U., New Britain, 1986-91; pres. U. So. Maine, Portland, 1991—; cons. in field; panelist, presenter various nat. higher edn. meetings. Contbr. numerous articles to profl. jours., also chpts. to books in field. Commnr. Occupational and Licensing Commn., Iowa, 1978-80; mem. Gov's Com. Efficiency, 1979; mem. adv. council planning dept. City of Binghamton, 1984—; bd. dirs. Broome County United Way, 1985, Greater Hartford Red Cross. Served with U.S. Army, 1969-71, Vietnam. Fanny W. Ames scholar, 1965; Title II fellow, 1970. Mem. Assn. Instl. Research and Planning Officers (v.p. 1983-84, pres. 1984-85), Am. Soc. Public Adminstrn., AAUP, Am. Polit. Sci. Assn., Soc. Coll. and U. Planners. Office: Cen Conn State U New Britain CT 06050

PATTERSON, EDWARD, investment banker; b. N.Y.C., Oct. 16, 1920; s. Arthur C. and Evelyn (Crimmins) P.; m. Joan Metzger, Jan. 10, 1947 (div. 1972); children: Patricia Kean, Lucinda Fleischer, Elizabeth, Christina P. Fay. B.A., Yale U., 1943. Mem. N.Y. Stock Exch., N.Y.C., 1950-56; exec. v.p. Allen & Co., N.Y.C., 1956—, also bd. dirs.; dir. Teleprompter, 1980-82. Guest writer News Leader, Richmond, W.Va.; contbr. articles to N.Y. Times. Trustee Citizens Budget Commn., N.Y.C., 1957-80; trustee Garvan Collection, Yale U., 1968; mem. Fordham U. Council, N.Y.C., 1975; mem. Cardinal's Com. of the Laity. Lt. USNR, 1942-46, ETO. Roman Catholic. Clubs: Deepdale (Manhasset, N.Y.) (pres. 1970-75); Piping Rock (Locust Valley, N.Y.); Friendly Sons of St. Patrick. Office: Allen & Co 711 5th Ave New York NY 10022-3109

PATTERSON, ELIZABETH KNIGHT, biochemist, editor; b. Pitts., Sept. 11, 1909; d. Richard Warren and Elizabeth Starr (Parvin) Knight; m. Arthur Lindo Patterson, Sept. 14, 1935 (div. Nov. 1966). BA, Wellesley Coll., 1930; MS, PhD, Bryn Mawr Coll., 1940; postgrad., Cornell Med. Coll., N.Y.C., 1934-35. Technician Rockefeller Inst., N.Y.C., 1930-34; demonstrator Bryn Mawr (Pa.) Coll., 1942-43; rsch. assoc. dept. genetics and cytochemistry Inst. Cancer Rsch., Phila., 1944-50, assoc. mem., 1950-77, mem., 1977—, editor sci. report Foxchase Cancer Ctr., 1972-83, assoc. editor, 1984—. Contbr. articles to sci. jours. Mem. Am. Soc. Biol. Chemistry and Molecular Biology, Am. Chem. Soc., Am. Assn. Cancer Rsch., N.Y. Acad. Sci., Soc. Growth and Devel., Sigma Xi, Phi Beta Kappa. Democrat. Office: Fox Chase Cancer Ctr 7701 Burholme Ave Philadelphia PA 19111-2497

PATTERSON, JAMES BRENDAN, advertising agency executive; b. Newburgh, N.Y., Mar. 22, 1947; s. Charles H. and Isabelle (Morris) P. B.A., Manhattan Coll., 1969; M.A., Vanderbilt U., 1970. With J. Walter Thompson Co., N.Y.C., 1971—; chmn. J. Walter Thompson U.S., 1987—. Author: novels including The Thomas Berryman Number, 1976 (Edgar Allen Poe award Mystery Writers Am.), The Jericho Commandment, 1979, Virgin, 1980, Legends, 1983, Black Market, 1986. Recipient 6 Clio awards, 1983; recipient Effie awards, 1983. Mem. Phi Beta Kappa. Home: 760 W End Ave New York NY 10025-5523 Office: J Walter Thompson Co 466 Lexington Ave New York NY 10017-3140*

PATTERSON, LELAND FRANCIS, neurologist; b. Wooster, Ohio, Sept. 9, 1937; s. Gordon Miles Patterson and Edith Marie (Angert) Wepler; m. Vincentina Costabile, Apr. 13, 1964 (div. Feb. 1985); children: Katherine, Jennifer, Leland Francis Jr. BS, Ohio U., 1959; MD, Ohio State U., 1963. Diplomate Am. Bd. Neurology. Rotating intern Harrisburg Hosp., 1963-64; resident Washington U. Sch. Medicine, St. Louis, 1964-67; fellow in pediatric neurology George Washington U., Washington, 1969-70; pvt. practice Harrisburg, Pa., 1970—; med. dir. Children's Diagnostic Ctr., Harrisburg, Pa., 1970-80; clin. prof. Hershey Coll. Medicine, Pa. State U., 1975—; cons. RAND Corp., 1987. Div. chmn. team leader United Way, Harrisburg, 1986-91; expert witness com. on licensure and consumer protection Pa. Senate, 1988. Lt. comdr. M.C., USNR, 1967-69. Mem. AMA (alt. del. 1992), Mass. Med. Soc., Pa. Med. Soc. (del. 1985-91, chmn. coun. govt. rels.), Dauphin County Med. Soc. (pres. 1987), Am. Acad. Neurology, Am. Acad. Pain Mgmt., Am. Acad. Thermology. Republican. Office: 1820 Linglestown Rd Harrisburg PA 17110

PATTERSON, MAURICE LEE, mathematics educator, retired; b. Wurtsboro, N.Y., Oct. 28, 1910; s. Horace Lee and Laura Augusta (Reed) P.; m. Ferne Elizabeth Kitson, June 29, 1940; children: Muriel, Janet, Reed. BS in Sci., Alfred U., 1934; MS in Edn., Cornell U., 1939. Cost acct. GE, Schenectady, N.Y., 1928-30; sci. tchr. Alfred (N.Y.) High Sch., 1934-36; sci. tchr. Interlaken (N.Y.) Cen. Sch., 1936-60, dist. prin., 1960-68; supt. of sch. South Seneca Cen. Sch., Interlaken, 1968-70; dir. computer ctr. Bd. of Coop. Edn. Svc., Ithaca, N.Y., 1970-72. Author: (local history) Between the Lakes, 1976, (genealogy) Pioneers of Quarry Hill, 1983; editor: (ch. history) Interlaken Reformed, 1980, Interlaken Hist. Soc. Newsletter, 1945-91; co-editor: (genealogy & history) The Covert Family, 1989. Sec. Interlaken (N.Y.) Firemen's Assn., 1939-44; master Farmerville Masonic Lodge, Interlaken, 1946, sec., 1960-75; pres. Interlaken (N.Y.) Pub. Libr., 1960-83, Interlaken (N.Y.) Hist. Soc., 1972-91, Masonic Hall Assn., 1987-91; exec. com. Regional Conf. Hist. Agy., 1980-82; sec. Finger Lakes Libr. System, Ithaca, 1989-91. Republican. Home: 3605 West Ave Interlaken NY 14847

PATTERSON, POLLY REILLY (MRS. W. RAY PATTERSON), retired communications company executive, civic worker; b. Wilkinsburg, Pa., 1906; d. Thomas L. and Margaret (Coughey) Reilly; m. W. Ray Patterson, Sept. 2, 1943. Student, U. Pitts. With Bell Telephone Co. of Pa., Pitts., 1925-71, clk., mgmt. positions, 1935-64, assoc. pub. rels. staff, 1965-71. Asst. treas. Allegheny County (Pa.) Soc. for Crippled Children, 1962-66, v.p., 1966-70; bd. dirs. Jr. Achievement, Inc., SW Pa., 1950-71, Pa. Soc. Crippled Children and Adults, 1960-68, Pitts. YWCA, 1964-72, Chatham Village Homes, Inc., 1973-76; mem. Allegheny County United Way, 1972—, nat. ho. of dels. Nat. Soc. for Crippled Children and Adults, 1965-67. Named Pitts. Advt. Woman of Yr., 1958, one of Pitts.'s Ten Outstanding Women, Pitts. Sun Telegraph, 1959; recipient Crystal Prism award Am. Advt. Fedn., 1972, 75. Mem. Assn. Pitts. Clubs (bd. dirs. 1946-81, pres. 1952-53), Altrusa Internat. (pres. Pitts. club 1950-51), Pitts. Advt. Club (v.p., sec. 1929-69), Pitts. Bus. and Profl. Women's Club, Telephone Pioneers Am. Home: 402 Olympia Rd Pittsburgh PA 15211-1308

PATTERSON, ROBERT PORTER, JR., judge; b. N.Y.C., July 11, 1923; s. Robert Porter and Margaret (Winchester) P.; m. Bevin C. Daly, Sept. 15, 1956; children: Anne, Robert, Margaret, Paul, Katherine. AB, Harvard U., 1947; LLB, Columbia U., 1950. Bar: N.Y. 1951, D.C. 1966. Law clk. Donovan, Leisure, Newton & Lumbard, N.Y.C., 1950-51; asst. counsel N.Y. State Crime Commn. Waterfront Investigation, 1952-53; asst. U.S. atty. Chief of Narcotics Prosecutions and Investigations, 1953-56; asst. counsel Senate Banking and Currency Com., 1954; assoc. Patterson, Belknap, Webb & Tyler, N.Y.C., 1956-60, ptnr., 1960-88; judge U.S. Dist. Ct. (so. dist.) N.Y., 1988—; counsel to minority select com. pursuant to house resolution no. 1, Washington, 1967; mem. Senator's Jud. Screening Panel, 1974-88, Gov.'s Jud. Screening Panel, 1975-82, Gov.'s Sentencing Com., 1978-79. Contbr. articles to profl. jours. Chmn. Wm. T. Grant Found., 1974—, Prisoners' Legal Services N.Y., 1976-88; dir. Legal Aid Soc., 1961-88, pres., 1967-71; chmn. Nat. Citizens for Eisenhower, 1959-60, Scranton for Pres., N.Y. State, 1964; trustee Millbrook Sch., 1966-78, Vera Inst. Justice, 1981—, New Sch. for Social Research, 1986—, George C. Marshall Found., 1987; mem. exec. com. Lawyers Com. for Civil Rights Under Law, 1968-88; mem. Goldman Panel for Attica Disturbance, 1972, Temporary Commn. on State Ct. System, 1971-73, Rockefeller U. Council, 1986-88, exec. com. N.Y. Vietnam Vets. Meml. Commn., 1982-85, Mayor's Police Adv. Com., 1985-87. Served to capt. USAAF, 1942-46. Decorated D.F.C. with cluster, Air medal with clusters. Mem. ABA (ho. of dels. 1976-80), N.Y. State Bar Assn. (pres. 1978-79), Assn. Bar City N.Y. (v.p. 1974-75), N.Y. County Lawyers Assn., Am. Law Inst., Am. Judicature Soc. (bd. dirs. 1979), Council Fgn. Relations. Republican. Episcopalian. Home: Fair Oaks Farm Cold Spring NY 10516 Office: US Court House Foley Sq New York NY 10007-1501

PATTERSON, THOMAS C., JR., publishing executive; b. Albany, N.Y., Aug. 12, 1949; s. Thomas C. and Mary Sally (Dywer) P.; m. Carol H. Patterson, Oct. 24, 1976; children: Marc David, Lindsay Jaye. BA, SUNY, Albany, 1971, MA, 1973. Cert. tchr. N.Y. Sales mgr. Coca Cola Bottling Co., Albany, 1973-85; branch mgr. Entertainment Pubs., Albany, 1985—. Mem. adv. bd. SUNY, Cobleskill, N.Y., 1991—. Mem. N.Y. State Restaurant Assn. (bd. dirs. 1990—). Roman Catholic. Home: 81 Southbury Rd Clifton Park NY 12065 Office: Entertainment Pubs 12 Century Hill Dr Latham NY 12110

PATTERSON, WILLIAM REMINGTON, JR., computer software engineer, consultant; b. Bryn Mawr, Pa., Feb. 1, 1948; s. William Remington Sr. and Doris (Turner) P.; m. Judith Ann Koehler, Sept. 5, 1970; children: Margaret, Karen. BA, Cleve. State U., 1972, MBA, 1973. Cert. in data processing, computer programming. Programmer, analyst Kranzley & Co., Cherry Hill, N.J., 1978-83; systems cons. and mgr. Penn Mut. Life Ins., Phila., 1983-87; owner, cons. Stratford Techs. Inc., Somerdale, N.J., 1987—. Contbr. articles to profl. jours. Active Bd. of Edn., Somerdale, 1989—. Fellow Life Mgmt. Inst.; mem. IEEE, Data Processing Mgmt. Assn., (pres. Phila. chpt. 1985, Silver Performance award 1986) Assn. Computing Machinery, Ind. Computer Cons. Assn. (officer Phila. chpt. 1991). Democrat. Mem. Soc. of Friends. Home: 8 Poplar Terr Somerdale NJ 08083-2017 Office: Stratford Techs PO Box 123 Stratford NJ 08084-0123

PATTI, LISA MARIE, management consultant; b. Phila., Aug. 14, 1967; d. Frederick Stephen and Theresa (Spina) P. BA in Math., Franklin & Marshall Coll., 1989. Chemistry researcher Franklin & Marshall Coll., Lancaster, Pa., 1986-88; computer systems cons. Andersen Cons., Phila., 1989—. Contbr. articles to profl. jours. Activist Sierra Club, Phila., 1989-91; mem. World Affairs Coun., Phila., 1991. Truman scholar, 1988, Kershner scholar, 1987, Leopold Schepp scholar, 1988-89. Mem. Network Women Computer Tech., Phi Beta Kappa. Office: Andersen Cons 5 Penn Ctr Philadelphia PA

PATTIE, PRESTON STUART, economic consultant; b. Amarillo, Tex., Mar. 19, 1944; s. Hugh L. and Lucille (Watkins) P.; m. Victoria F. Justiniano, FEb. 18, 1970; children: Liliana, Sandra L. BS, Oreg. State U., 1966; MS, Mich. State U., 1976, PhD, 1981. Vol. U.S. Peace Corps, Bolivia, 1966-70; extension agt. Oreg. State U. Extension, Salem, 1970-73; grad. rsch. asst. Mich. State U., East Lansing, 1973-76; econ. policy cons. Robert Nathan Assocs., Managua, Nicaragua, 1976-78; econs. cons. Chemonics Industries, La Paz, Bolivia, 1979-86; dir. for Latin Am., Chemonics Internat., Washington, 1986-90; econ. analyst Devel. Alternatives Inc., Kandy, Sri Lanka, 1990—; econs. cons. Chemonics Internat., Peru, Ecuador, Bolivia, Costa Rica, the Caribbean, 1986-90. Author: Non Conventional Approaches to Seed Development, 1988. Recipient gold medal for contbn. to agr. Bolivian Ministry Agr., 1986, Farm Gate award Santa Cruz (Bolivia) Chamber Agr., 1986. Mem. Internat. Agrl. Econs. Assn. (cert.), Sri Lanka Agr. Econs. Assn. (founding), Alpha Zeta, Phi Kappa Phi. Office: Devel Alternatives Inc 7250 Woodmont Ave Ste 200 Bethesda MD 20814-2951

PATTON, JAMES RICHARD, JR., lawyer; b. Durham, N.C., Oct. 27, 1928; s. James Ralph and Bertha (Moye) P.; m. Mary Margot Maughan, Dec. 29, 1950; children: James Macon, Lindsay Fairfield. A.B. cum laude, U. N.C., 1948; postgrad., Yale U., 1948; J.D., Harvard U., 1951. Bar: D.C. bar 1951, U.S. Supreme Ct. 1963. Attache of Embassy; spl. asst. to Am. ambassador to, Indochina, 1952-54; with Office Nat. Estimates, Washington, 1954-55; atty. Covington & Burling, Washington, 1956-61; sr. partner firm Patton, Boggs & Blow, Washington, 1962—; Lectr. internat. law Cornell Law Sch., 1963-64, U.S. Army Command and Gen. Staff Coll., 1967-68; Mem. Nat. Security Forum, U.S. Air War Coll., 1965, Nat. Strategy Seminar, U.S. Army War Coll., 1967-70, Global Strategy Discussions, U.S. Naval War Coll., 1968, Def. Orientation Conf., 1972; mem. Com. of 100 on Fed. City, Washington; mem. adv. council on nat. security and internat. affairs Nat. Republican Com., 1977-81; bd. dirs. Madeira Sch., Greenway, Va., 1975-81, Lawyers Com. for Civil Rights Under Law, Washington, Legal Aid Soc. Washington; mem. Industry Policy Adv. Com. for Trade Policy Matters, 1984-87; councillor of Atlantic Council of U.S., 1987-90; mem. visiting com. Ackland Art Mus. U. N.C., 1987—. Mem. adv. coun. Johns Hopkins U. Sch. of Advanced Internat. Studies; nat. bd. dirs. Aspen Mus., 1987-90. With U.S. Army, 1954-55. Mem. ABA (past com. chmn.), Inter-Am. Bar Assn. (past del.), Internat. Law Assn., Am. Soc. Internat. Law (treas., exec. council), Washington Inst. Fgn. Affairs, Nat. Gallery (collectors com. 1988-91), Phi Beta Kappa Assocs., Alpha Epsilon Delta. Clubs: Metropolitan (Washington); Brook (N.Y.C.).

PATTON, JOHN MICHAEL, lawyer; b. Washington, Sept. 3, 1947; s. Earl Richard and Frances Anne (Basar) P. BA in History, George Washington U., 1969, JD, 1974; BS in Acctg., U. Md., 1982. Bar: D.C. 1974. Atty. IRS, 1972—. With USAR, 1969-75. Mem. AICPA. Roman Catholic. Home: 3725 Macomb St NW Apt 112 Washington DC 20016-3841

PATTON, KIRK M(ICHAEL), church administrator, accountant; b. Detroit, Aug. 4, 1959; s. DeLane D. and H. Joan (Flynn) P.; m. Amy K. Oliver, Nov. 25, 1988; children: Grace Eliza, Kirk Michael Jr. BA, Ohio State U., 1981; MBA, Ohio U., 1984. CPA, Md., D.C. Mgr. svc. dept. Le Sport Ltd., Worthington, Ohio, 1975-78; machine operator Funk Fine Cast, Columbus, Ohio, 1978-80; salesman Cord Camera Ctrs., Columbus, 1980-82; state examiner Ohio Auditor's Office, Columbus, Athens, 1982-83; grad. teaching asst. Ohio U., Athens, 1983-84; computer cons. Snyder, Young & Co., P.A., Silver Spring, Md., 1984-87; sr. fin. analyst Contel ASC (now GTE Spacenet), Rockville, Md., 1987-90; contr., treas., asst. sec. Gt. Commn. Ministries, Columbia, Md., 1990-91; dir. promotion and hospitality Cedar Brook Community Ch., Gaithersburg, Md., 1989—, bus. adminstr., 1991—. Small group leader New Life Christian Fellowship, Athens, 1983-84; hospitality dir. Valley Brook Community Ch., Silver Spring, 1986. Mem. AICPA, Md. Assn. CPA's, D.C. Inst. CPA's, Washington Area Network (co-founder). Office: Cedar Brook Community Ch 915B Russell Ave Gaithersburg MD 20879-3266

PATTON, PETER CLYDE, data processing executive; b. Wichita, June 11, 1935; s. Claude Patton and Beryl Inez (Jones) Barney; m. Naomi Julia Lawson; children: Peter Jr., Claudia, Theresa, Richard, Phillip. AB in Engring. and Applied Physics, Harvard U., 1957; MA in Math., U. Kans., 1959; PhD in Aerospace Engring., U. Stuttgart, Ger., 1966. Sci. cons. Sperry Rand Internat. Corp., Lausanne, Switzerland, 1961-64; mgr. computer group U. Stuttgart, 1964-66; mgr. UNIVAC System Design, St. Paul, 1966-68; mng. dir. Analysts Internat. Corp., Mpls., 1968-71; dir. computer ctr. U. Minn., Mpls., 1971-83; dir. MCC Parallel Processing Rsch. Program, Austin, Tex., 1983-85, Minn. Supercomputer Inst., Mpls., 1985-87; chmn., chief exec. officer Consortium for Supercomputer Rsch., Mpls., 1986-88; chmn. Spl. Cons. Services, Inc., Mpls., 1988-91; v.p. info. systems and computing U. Pa., Phila., 1991—. Author numerous books and articles; patentee in field. Fellow Inst. for Math. and Application; mem. IEEE (sr.), Assn. for Computing Machinery, Soc. for Indsl. and Applied Math. Home: 6908 Clearview St Philadelphia PA 19119-1927 Office: Univ Pa 3401 Walnut St Ste 230A Philadelphia PA 19104-6228

PATTON, STEPHEN CURRIE, computer consultant; b. Boston, Apr. 7, 1963; s. John Ellis and Nancy Haddleton (Janes) P. BS, BA, Brown U., 1986. Cons. Aamphora Systems Cons., Inc., Lincoln, R.I., 1990—. Mem. Boston Computer Soc., Assn. Computing Machinery, Am. Assn. Individual Investors, Alpha Delta Phi. Republican. Evangelical. Home: 83 Capron Farm Dr Warwick RI 02886-7701

PATZELT, ANTHONY CHARLES, computer systems executive; b. N.Y.C., Sept. 28, 1955; s. Charles Alois and Joan (Davide) P.; m. Heidi Marie Markowitz, Aug. 5, 1978 (div. Sept. 1989); children: Andrea Christine, Daniel John; m. Vivienne Linda McKay, Feb. 24, 1990. BS, Columbia U., 1977, postgrad., 1977-78. Systems programmer Columbia U., N.Y.C., 1976-77, mgr. systems, 1977-78; sr. dir. Dun & Bradstreet, Wilton, Conn., 1978-91; v.p. profl. svcs. Wellington Systems, Inc., Norwalk, Conn., 1991—; cons. in field. Mem. Nat. MS Soc., Rep. Club, Stamford, Conn., 1978-82, Darien, Conn., 1982—. Mem. IEEE, Assn. Computing Machinery, Mensa. Republican. Roman Catholic. Home: 15 Coachlamp Ln Darien CT 06820-5220 Office: Wellington Systems Inc 1 Norwalk W 40 Richards Ave Norwalk CT 06854

PAUGH, PATRICIA LOU, legal administrator; b. Pitts., Oct. 30, 1948; d. Marshall Franklin and Helen Jeanne (Graham) P. BA in English, Columbia U., 1982. Adminstrv. asst. Katz, Robinson, Brog & Seymour, N.Y.C., 1972-75; office mgr. Michael D. Martocci, N.Y.C., 1975-80; adminstrv. mgr. O'Melveny & Myers, N.Y.C., 1982-85, Latham & Watkins, N.Y.C., 1985-88; mgr. Nationwide Legal Svcs., N.Y.C., 1988-89; mgr. legal adminstrn. Aluminum Co. Am., Pitts., 1990—. Mem. Assn. Legal Adminstrs., Am. Mgmt. Assn., Pitts. Legal Adminstrs. Assn., Pitts. C. of C. Republican. Episcopalian. Office: Aluminum Co Am 1501 Alcoa Bldg Pittsburgh PA 15219

PAUL, CAROL ANN, academic administrator; b. Brockton, Mass., Dec. 17, 1936; d. Joseph W. and Mary M. (DeMeulenaer) Bjork; m. Robert D. Paul, Dec. 21, 1957; children: Christine, Dana, Stephanie, Robert. BS, U. Mass., 1958; MAT, R.I. Coll., 1968, Brown U., 1970; EdD, Boston U., 1978. Tchr. biology Attleboro (Mass.) High Sch., 1965-68; asst. dean., mem. faculty biology North Shore Community Coll., Beverly, Mass., 1969-78; master planner N.J. Dept. for Higher Edn., Trenton, 1978-80; assoc. v.p. Fairleigh Dickinson U., Rutherford, N.J., 1980-86; v.p. acad. affairs Suffolk Community Coll., Selden, N.Y., 1986—; faculty devel. cons. various colls., 1979—, title III evaluator, 1985—. Author: (lab. manual and workbook) Minicourses and Labs for Biological Science, 1972 (rev. edit., 1975); (with others) Strategies and Attitudes, 1986; book reviewer, 1973-77. V.p. League of Women Voters, Beverly, 1970-74, Cranford, N.J., 1982-83; alumni rep. Brown U., Cranford, 1972—. Commonwealth Mass. scholar, 1958; recipient Acad. Yr. award NSF, 1968-69, Proclamation for Leadership award Suffolk County Exec., 1989. Mem. AAHE, AAWCJC, POD (planning com. 1977-79), Nat. Coun. for Staff, Profls. and Orgn. Developers (nat. exec. bd. 1979-80), Phi Theta Kappa, Pi Lambda Theta. Roman Catholic. Home: 75 Fairview Cir Middle Island NY 11953-2340 Office: Suffolk Community Coll 533 College Rd Selden NY 11784-2851

PAUL, GERALD, computer company executive; b. Ocean Port, N.J., Jan. 27, 1945; s. Charles and Gertrude (Weiss) P.; m. Robin Beth Werker, Feb. 2, 1969; children: Matthew, Michael, David, Andrew. BA, Rutgers U., 1967; PhD, MIT, 1972. Systems analyst PHI Computer Svcs., Arlington, Mass., 1971-73; sr. cons. Arthur D. Little, Cambridge, Mass., 1973-79; v.p. R & D, Wang Labs., Lowell, Mass., 1979-91, Data Gen. Corp., Westborough, Mass., 1991—. Mem. IEEE Computer Soc., Assn. for Computing Machinery, Am. Phys. Soc. Home: 381 Lincoln St Lexington MA 02173 Office: Data Gen Corp 4400 Computer Dr Westborough MA 01580

PAUL, HERBERT MORTON, lawyer, accountant, taxation educator; b. N.Y.C.; s. Julius and Gussie Paul; married; children: Leslie Beth, Andrea Lynn. BBA, Baruch Coll.; MBA, NYU, LLM; JD, Harvard U. Ptnr. Touche Ross & Co., N.Y.C., 1957-82; assoc. dir.-tax Touche Ross & Co., dir. fin counseling; mng. ptnr. Herbert Paul, P.C., N.Y.C., 1983—; dir. N.Y. Estate Planning Coun.; prof. taxation, trustee NYU. Author: Ordinary and Necessary Expenses; editor: Taxation of Banks; adv. tax editor The Practical Accountant; mem. adv. bd. Financial and Estate Planning, Tax Shelter Insider, Financial Planning Strategist, Tax Shelter Litigation Report; bd. dirs. Partnership Strategist, The Business Strategist; cons. Professional Practice Management Mag.; mem. panel The Hot Line; advisor The Partnership Letter, The Wealth Formula; cons. The Insider's Report for Physicians; mem. tax bd. Business Profit Digest; cons. editor physician's Tax Advisor; bd. fin. cons. Tax Strategies for Physicians; tax and bus. advisor Prentice Hall; contbg. editor. Jour. of Accountancy. Mem. bd. overseers Grad. Sch. Bus., NYU; mem. com. on trusts and estates Rockefeller U.; trustee Alvin Ailey Am. Dance Theatre, Associated Y's of N.Y.; bd. dirs. Alumni Fedn. of NYU; co-chmn. accts. div. Fedn. Philantropies. Served with U.S. Army. Mem. Inst. Fed. Taxation (adv. com. chmn.), Internat. Inst. on Tax and Bus. Planning (adv. bd.), Assn. of Bar of City of N.Y., NYU Tax Soc. (pres., chmn. com. on tax shelters), Bur. Nat. Affairs-Tax Mgmt. (adv. com. on exec. compensation), Am. Inst. CPAs (com. on corp. taxation), Tax Study Group, ABA (tax sect.), N.Y. County Lawyers Assn., N.Y. State Soc. CPAs Dir. (chmn. tax div. com. on fed. taxation, gen. tax com., furtherance com., com. on relations with IRS, bd. dirs.), Nat. Assn. Accts., Assn. of Bar of City of N.Y., Accts. Club of Am., Pension Club, Nat. Assn. Estate Planners (bd. dirs.), N.Y. C. of C. (tax com.), Grad. Soc. Bus. of NYU Alumni Assn. (pres.), Pres. Council (NYU). Clubs: Wall St., City Athletic (N.Y.C.), Inwood Country.

PAUL, IGOR, mechanical engineering educator; b. Kharkov, Ukraine, Oct. 28, 1936; came to U.S., 1952; s. Leo and Lilly (Paul) Polozoff; m. Natalie G. Gruzinov, Aug. 10, 1963; children: Victor, Tanya, Tahisa. BSME, MIT, 1960, MSME, 1961, mech. engr., 1962, ScD in Mech. Engring., 1964. Registered profl. engr., Mass. Prof. mech. engring. MIT, Cambridge, 1964—. Co-author: Practical Biomechanics for the Orthopedic Surgeon, 1978. Recipient Ralph R. Teetor Edn. award SAE, 1966, Kappa Delta award for outstanding orthopedic rsch. Am. Acad. orthopedic Surgeons, 1973. Mem. ASME, Am. Soc. for Engring. Edn., Biomechanics Soc. Am., Biomedical Engring. Soc., Orthopedic Rsch. Soc., Pi Tau Sigma, Sigma Xi (treas. MIT 1980—). Home: 36 Hidden Rd Andover MA 01810 Office: MIT 77 Massachusetts Ave Cambridge MA 02139

PAUL, JAMES DONALD, computer consultant; b. Pitts., June 27, 1956; s. Donald Francis and Theresa (Lepkowski) P.; m. Mary Beth Hartman, June 4, 1984; children: Virginia, Stewart, Elizabeth. BS, Indiana U. Pa., 1978. Tech. writer Med. Data Systems, Dallas, 1982-83; data processing staff British Broadcasting Co., London, 1982; pres. Northtec Design, Pitts., 1983—; cons. No. Health Systems, Pitts., 1986—, Bearing Svc. Co., Pitts., 1987—, Family Health Coun., Pitts., 1988—. Author computer programs; contbr. articles to profl. jours. Treas. Big Bros./Big Sisters Indiana, 1980. Recipient Exceptional Svc. award Open Door, 1980, 81. Mem. Toastmasters Internat. Office: Northtec Design 224 Park Entrance Dr Pittsburgh PA 15228-1825

PAUL, MARTIN GREGORY, surgeon; b. Milan, Dec. 14, 1959; s. Edward D. and Irmgard M. (Reinhardt) P.; m. Ellen Louise Taylor, June 21, 1986; children: Christina Louise, Eric Douglas. B Med. Sci., Northwestern U., Evanston, Ill., 1981; MD, Northwestern U., Chgo., 1983. Diplomate Am. Bd. Surgery. Commd. U.S. Army, 1986, advanced through grades to maj., 1989; asst. chief surgery Bremerhaven (Germany) Army Hosp., 1988-89; chief gen. surgery Nurnberg (Germany) Army Hosp., 1989-92. Fellow ACS (course dir. advanced trauma life support 1991); mem. World Assn. Hepats-Pancreato-Biliary Surgery, Soc. Am. Gastrointestinal Endoscopic Surgeons, Alpha Omega Alpha. Republican. Home: Meierei 10, Stein 6, 8504 Nurnberg Germany Office: 98th Gen Hosp Nuernberg Unit 27401 Box B APO AE 09105

PAUL, ROBERT ARTHUR, steel company executive; b. N.Y.C., Oct. 28, 1937; s. Isadore and Ruth (Goldstein) P.; m. Donna Rae Berkman, July 29, 1962; children: Laurence Edward, Stephen Eric, Karen Rachel. AB, Cornell U., 1959; JD, Harvard U., 1962, MBA, 1964. With Ampco-Pitts. Corp. (formerly Screw & Bolt Corp. Am.), 1964—, v.p., 1969-71, exec. v.p., 1972-79, pres., 1979—, treas., 1973-79, dir., 1969—; v.p., asst. sec., asst. treas., bd. dirs. Parkersburg Steel Corp., Louis Berkman Co., Follansbee Steel Corp., Louis Berkman Realty Co.; bd. dirs. Northwestern Steel and Wire Co., Integra Fin. Corp., U.S. Biochem. Corp.; gen. ptnr. Romar Trading Co.; instr. Grad. Sch. Indsl. Adminstrn., Carnegie Mellon U., 1966-69; trustee Cornell U. Trustee H.L. and Louis Berkman Found., Presbyn. Univ. Hosp.; trustee, treas. Ampco-Pitts. Found., Jewish Healthcare Found. Pitts. Mem. ABA, Mass. Bar Assn., Soc. Security Analysts, Harvard Club, Concordia Club, Harvard-Yale-Princeton Club, Pitts. Athletic Club, Duquesne Club. Republican. Jewish. Office: Ampco-Pitts Corp 600 Grant St Pittsburgh PA 15219-2701

PAUL, SANDRA KOODIN, management consultant; b. N.Y.C., June 6, 1938; d. Benjamin and Eleanor (Epstein) Koodin; divorced. BA, Hunter Coll., 1962; MA, CUNY, 1965, ABD in Indsl. Psychology, 1970. Cert. systems profl. Mgmt. cons. J.K. Lasser and Co., N.Y.C., 1960-64, Shatzkin and Co., N.Y.C., 1965-67; research asst. Hunter Coll., N.Y.C., 1964-65, Random House, Inc., 1967-78; pres. SKP Assocs., N.Y.C., 1978—; adj. assoc. prof., NYU, 1982—; co-chmn. Met. Info. Processing Conf., 1974-88; chmn. adv. com. Book Industry Systems, 1979-80, com. chmn.; mem. network adv. com. Library of Congress. Chmn. info. systems standards bd. Am. Nat. Standards Inst., 1990—. Fellow Nat. Info. Standards Orgn. (chmn. 1985-87), Women's Nat. Book Assn. (v.p.to pres. 1982-86, Book Woman award 1987), Assn. Systems Mgmt. (cert. 1985, pres. 1975-77 Met. chpt. recipient Systems Profl. of Yr. award 1977), Spl. Librs. Assn. (chmn. pub. div. 1978-79), Am. Libr. Assn. (com. mem. 1981-84), Am. Soc. for Info. Scis. Office: SKP Assocs 160 5th Ave New York NY 10010-7000

PAUL, THOMAS WAYNE, psychotherapist; b. Vallejo, Calif., Mar. 25, 1950; s. Thomas Birdsall and Shirley Mae (Osterheld) P.; m. Jean Marie Stout, Sept. 22, 1985. BA, Goddard Coll., 1980, Ma, 1989. Cert. alcohol, drugs counselor, employee assistance profl.; nationally cert. addictions counselor. Civilian program coord., dir. community counseling ctr. Seneca Army Depot, Romulus, N.Y., 1981-85; svcs. mgr. Finger Lakes Alcoholism Counseling and Referral Agy., Seneca Falls, N.Y., 1985-86; dir. outpatient svc. dept., FLACRA, Clifton Springs, N.Y., 1985; dir. employee assistance program Maxwell Hall, Clifton Springs, 1985-86; regional svcs. coord. MEDIPLEX Group, Rochester, N.Y., 1986-87; co-owner Human Progress Enterprises, Newark, N.Y., 1986—; chem. dependency program coord. Hobart & William Smith Colls., Newark, 1985-88; pvt. practice in psychotherapy Geneva and Rochester, N.Y., 1985-88; dir., founder Adult Child & Co-dependency Ctr., Rochester, 1988—; pres. Finger Lakes Alcoholism Counseling & Referral Agy., Clifton Springs, 1983-84, Coun. on Alcoholism of Finger Lakes, Geneva, 1986—; treas. N.Y. State Coalition for Children of Addictions, 1987—, chmn. Rochester chpt., 1986—. Chmn. Combined Fed. Campaign United Way, Romulus, N.Y., 1983-84. Mem. Nat. Assn. Alcohol & Drugs Counselor, Nat. Assn. Children of Alcoholics, N.Y. Fedn. Alcoholism Counselors, Am. Counseling & Devel., N.Y. State Coalition for Children of Addictions. Home: 246 Grace Ave Newark NY 14513-2151 Office: 365 S Main St Geneva NY 14456-2601 also: 11 N Goodman St Rochester NY 14607

PAUL, WILLIAM, physicist, educator; b. Deskford, Scotland, Mar. 31, 1926; came to U.S., 1952; s. William and Jean (Watson) P.; m. Barbara Anderson Forbes, Mar. 28, 1952; children—David, Fiona. M.A., Aberdeen U., Scotland, 1946; Ph.D., Aberdeen U., 1951; A.M. (hon.), Harvard U., 1960. Asst. lectr., then lectr. Aberdeen U., 1946-52; mem. faculty Harvard U., 1953—, Gordon McKay prof. applied physics, 1963-91, Mallinckrodt prof. applied physics, 1991—, prof. physics, 1980—; professeur associé U. Paris, 1966-67; cons. solid state physics, 1954—; Ripon prof., Calcutta, 1984. Author: Handbook on Semiconductors: Band Theory and Transport Properties, 1982; co-editor: Solids Under Pressure, 1963, Amorphous and Liquid Semiconductors, 1980. Carnegie fellow, 1952-53; Guggenheim fellow, 1959-60; Humboldt awardee, 1990; fellow Clare Hall Cambridge U., 1974-75. Fellow Am. Phys. Soc., Brit. Inst. Physics, N.Y. Acad. Scis., Royal Soc. Edinburgh; mem. AAAS, Sigma Xi. Home: 2 Eustis St Lexington MA 02173-5612 Office: Harvard U Pierce Hall Cambridge MA 02138

PAUL, WILLIAM GERALD, educational psychologist; b. Phila., Nov. 27, 1948; s. Walter Michael and Sylvia (Schultz) P. BA in Psychology, Temple U., 1971, MEd in Ednl. Psychology, 1972, PhD in Ednl. Psychology, 1978; postgrad., NYU, 1972-73. Rsch. assoc., statistician Family Ct., 1972; teaching asst. Temple U., Phila., 1976-78; testing and evaluation specialist Sch. Dist. Hamilton Twp., Hamilton Square, N.J., 1979—; part-time rsch. evaluator Child Psychiatry Ctr. St. Christopher's Hosp. for Children, Phila., 1979-82. Mem. Am. Psychol. Assn., Am. Ednl. Rsch. Assn., N.J. Assn. Sch. Adminstrs. (assoc.). Home: 1448 Windsor Park Ln Havertown PA 19083-2706 Office: Hamilton Twp Sch Dist 90 Park Ave Hamilton Square NJ 08690-2024

PAUL, WILLIAM PATRICK, numismatist; b. Phila., Mar. 17, 1950; s. Bernard and Rita (Brotman) P.; m. Rosine Orenbuch, Apr. 7, 1984; children: Thomas Matthew, James Michael. BA, Boston Coll., 1973. Mgr. Am. Heritage Minting, Phila., 1973-76; pres., owner Am. Heritage Minting, Inc., Jenkintown, Pa., 1976—. Author: (with others) A Guide Book of United States Coins, 1982—, Handbook of United States Coins, 1982—; editor: A Guide Book of English Coins, 1982. Mem. Am. Numismatic Assn. (life), New Eng. Numismatic Assn., Numismatic Assn. So. Calif., Cen. States Numismatic Assn., Great Ea. Numismatic Assn. Office: Am Heritage Minting Inc Benjamin Fox Pavilion PO Box 1008 Ste 510 Jenkintown PA 19046

PAULEN, JUDITH ANN, small business owner; b. N.Y.C., Jan. 30, 1947; d. David and Madeline (Freeman) Brenman; m. Robert Martin Paulen, Aug. 27, 1967; children: Craig Daniel, Adam Jonathan, Jessica Leigh. BA, Fairleigh Dickinson U., 1969. Tchr. Ft. Lee (N.J.) Pub. Schs., 1969-71; event planner Fancy That, N.Y.C., 1977-84; owner, mgr.social event planner Judy Paulen Designs, Tenafly, N.J., 1984—; owner, mgr., corp. event planner Paulen Cleary Prodns., Tenafly, 1990—. Trustee Temple Sinai, Tenafly, 1988-92. Mem. NAFE, Internat. Spl. Events Soc., Tenafly C. of C., Am. Women's Econ. Devel. Assn. Office: 29 Washington St Tenafly NJ 07670

PAULHUS, NORMAN GERARD, JR., aerospace engineer; b. Washington, May 19, 1950; s. Norman Gerard and Kathryn Frances (Schwartz) P. BS in Aerospace Engring. with high honors, U. Md., 1970. Transp. intern U.S. Dept. Transp., Washington, 1970-71, aerospace engr. Office of Sec., 1971-72, gen. engr., 1972-82, dep. dir. Office Tech. and Planning Assistance, 1982-87, program devel. officer, Rsch. and Tech., 1987-91; sr. tech. advisor Office of Rsch. Policy and Tech. Transfer, 1991—; mem. com. planning/programming Transp. Rsch. Bd., mem. com. on local transp. financing, com. on rural pub. transp. Editor: (with D. McKelvey and D. Ewing) Proceedings of 4th Nat. Conf. Rural Pub. Transp., 1979, Technology Sharing, 1979; contbr. articles to profl. jours. Recipient U.S. Dept. Transp. Sec.'s award, 1974, Meritorious Achievement award, 1979; Spl. Achievement award, 1984, Superior Achievement award, 1989, Cert. Appreciation Coun. State Govts. 1990, Way to Go award Dept. Transp., 1991, Cert. Appreciation USCG Commandant, 1991. Mem. AIAA, AAAS, Nat. Space Inst., U.S. Naval Inst., Navy League U.S., Planetary Soc., Inst. Noetic Scis., Tau Beta Pi, Sigma Gamma Tau, Phi Kappa Phi. Roman Catholic. Home: 18816 Muncaster Rd Rockville MD 20855-1430 Office: 400 7th St SW Washington DC 20590-0002

PAULSON, LORETTA NANCY, psychoanalyst; b. Los Angeles, Nov. 5, 1943; d. Frank Morris and Rose (Kaufman) Fargo; m. Glenn Lewis Paulson, Dec. 27, 1970 (div. 1984). BA, U. So. Calif., 1966; MS in Social Work, Columbia U., 1969; cert. psychoanalyst, C.G. Jung Inst., N.Y.C. Cert. clin. social worker, N.Y., Conn. Pvt. practice psychoanalysis N.Y.C. and Wilton, Conn., 1976—; faculty, supr., past vice chmn. Inst. Tng. Bd. Mem. NASW (diplomate in clin. social work), Internat. Assn. for Analytical Psychology, Nat. Assn. for Accreditation of Psychoanalysis (bd. dirs., chmn. by-laws com.), N.Y. Assn. for Analytic Psychology (pres., program com.), Conn. Soc. Clin. Social Work (com. on psychoanalysis). Democrat. Office: 6 Turtleback Rd Wilton CT 06897-1223 Office: 334 W 86th St #1A New York NY 10024

PAUSTIAN, JOHN EARLE, chemist; b. Grand Island, Nebr., Mar. 19, 1928; s. Frank Julius and Gertrude (Lindquist) P.; m. Gretchen Jean Brannian, June 6, 1951; children: Deborah, Ann, Robert. BSc, U. Nebr., 1950; MSc, Stevens Inst. Tech., 1957. Chemist U.S. Naval Ordnance Test Sta., Pasadena, Calif., 1951-53; group leader Thiokol Chem. Co., Denville, N.J., 1953-67; prin. rsch. chemist ABB Lummus Crest, Inc., Bloomfield, N.J., 1967—. Contbr. articles to profl. jours.; patentee in field. Mem. Hanover Twp. N.J. Bd. Edn., Whippany, 1967-70; officer Hanover Twp. Landmarks Com., Whippany, 1981—. Mem. Am. Chem. Soc., Catalysis Soc., Morris County Hist. Soc. (treas. 1990—). Office: ABB Lummus Crest Inc 1515 Broad St Bloomfield NJ 07003-3002

PAVLIV, MARK ALEXANDER, architect, urban planner; b. Lakewood, N.J., Aug. 20, 1951; s. Serhij Pavliv; m. Patricia Marie Pape, Nov. 11, 1972; 1 child, Gregory. BArch, Pratt Inst., 1973. Registered architect, N.J., N.Y., Fla.; cert. Nat. Coun. Archtl. Registration Bds. Architect Abcon Industries, N.Y.C., 1972-73; planner, project coord. Beyer Blinder Belle, N.Y.C., 1973-76, dir. energy conservation rsch. and planning, 1977-79, dir. planning and community redevel., 1979-85, sr. assoc., dir. planning and community redevel., 1986-88, dir. project devel. and mktg., 1988-90; exec. v.p., chief exec. officer Roe Design Group, N.Y.C., 1990—; mem. Main Street Program USA. Consulant facilities mgmt. adv. panel United Cerebral Palsy, N.Y.C., 1978-82; mem. Shore Hist. Re-enactment Assn., Ocean Grove, N.J., 1982—; pres., dir. bd. trustees Ocean County Ctr. Performing Arts, Lakewood, 1985—; mem. Main Street Program, 1983—. em. AIA (nat. design honor award 1989), N.J. Soc. Architects (design achievement award Shore chpt. 1989), Am. Planning Assn., Assn. Energy Engrs. (assoc.), Nat. Trust for Hist. Preservation, 12th Regt. Va. Cav., Jaguar Club N.Am. . Mem. AIA (Design Honor award 1988), N.J. Soc. Architects (Shore chpt. design achievement award 1989), Am. Planning Assn., Assn. Energy Engrs. (assoc.), Nat. Trust for Hist. Preservation, Space Coast Devel. Commn. (chmn. comprehensive devel. planning task force), 12th Regt. Va. Cavalry, Jaguar Club N.Am. Ukrainian Catholic. Home: 1105 N Lake Dr Lakewood NJ 08701-1663 Office: Roe Design Group 1500 Broadway New York NY 10036-4015

PAWELEC, WILLIAM JOHN, retired electronics company executive; b. Hammond, Ind., Feb. 15, 1917; s. John and Julia (Durnas) P.; B.S. in Acctg., Ind. U., 1939; m. Alice E. Brown, May 30, 1941 (dec. Dec. 1970); children—William John, Betty Jane Pawelec Conover; m. 2d, June A. Shepard, Nov. 27, 1976 (div. June 1980). Statistician, Ind. State Bd. Accounts, 1939-41; with RCA, 1941—, mgr. acctg. and budgets internat. div., 1957-61, controller internat. div., 1961-68, corp. mgr. internat. fin. ops. and controls, 1968-75, mgr. corp. acctg., 1975-77, dir. internat. acctg., 1977-81, ret., 1981; controller RCA Internat., Ltd., Electron Ins. Co., 1977, RCA Credit Corp., 1979; ret., 1981. Active, Westfield United Fund, 1967—. Mem. Nat. Assn. Accts. (past nat. v.p.), Watchung Power Squadron, N.J. State C. of C.,

Commerce and Industry Assn. N.Y., Stuart Cameron McLeod Soc., Ind. U. Alumni Assn. (pres. N.J. chpt.), Beta Gamma Sigma, Sigma Epsilon Theta. Club: Echo Lake Country. Home: 86 New England Ave Summit NJ 07901-1828

PAWLAK, MARK JOSEPH, editor, poet, educator; b. Buffalo, N.Y., May 29, 1948; s. Joseph Andrew and Eleanor (Prorok) P.; 1 child, Andrai Pawlak Whitted; m. Mary F. Bonina, Aug. 21, 1982; 1 child, Gian Bonina-Pawlak. BS in Physics, MIT, 1970. Poet-in-residence Worcester (Mass.) Pub. Sch. System, 74-75, 75-76; assoc. editor West End Press, Cambridge, Mass., 1977-79; workshop leader Boston (Mass.) Worker Writers, 1978-79; assoc. editor Hanging Loose Press, Bklyn., 1981-82, co-editor, 1982—. Author: (poetry book) The Buffalo Sequence, 1978, All the News, 1985; co-editor: (poetry anthology) Smart Like Me, 1989; poet/performer: Young Artists Circle, Havana, Cuba, 1978, New Eng. Artist Festival, Amherst, Mass., 1981, Polish Am. Community Actr., Buffalo, 1985, 87, 89, Boston (Mass.) First Night, 1988. Recipient fellowship Mass. Artist Found., Boston, 1986. Mem. Lepidopterist's Soc., Boston Mycological Club. Office: PO Box 509 Somerville MA 02144

PAWLICZKO, GEORGE IHOR, academic administrator; b. Rochester, N.Y., Oct. 26, 1950; s. Roman and Irene Olha (Zubryckyj) P.; m. Ann Maria Lencyk, June 10, 1978. BA, St. John Fisher Coll., 1972; MA, Fordham U., 1974, MBA, 1986, PhD, 1989. Admissions counselor Fordham U., Bronx, N.Y., 1977-78; asst. dean Grad. Sch. of Bus. Fordham U., N.Y.C., 1978-81; asst. to pres., dir. mgmt. info. systems Marymount Coll., Tarrytown, N.Y., 1981-82; exec. dir. N.Y. Inst. Credit, N.Y.C., 1982—. Trustee St. Andrew's Ch., Hamptonburgh, N.Y., 1986—. Mem. Shevchenko Scientific Soc., Beta Gamma Sigma, Phi Alpha Theta. Office: New York Inst Credit 71 W 23rd St Rm 506 New York NY 10010-4102

PAWLOWSKI, WALTER CHESTER, management consultant; b. Linden, N.J., Oct. 17, 1947; s. Walter and Claire (Sieczkowski) P.; children: Melissa, Nicole. AAS, Orange County Community Coll., Middletown, N.Y., 1967; BS, SUNY, New Paltz, 1972. Plant mgr. Mech. Rubber Products Co., Warwick, N.Y., 1966-81; v.p. indsl. ops. Occupations, Inc., Middletown, 1981—; cons. Community Devel. Svc., Rochester, N.Y., 1990. Capt. USNG, 1966-72. Mem. Assn. Info Mgmt., Profl. Packaging Assn., Rehab. Workshop Mktg. Assn. Office: Occupations Inc 70 Fortune Rd W Middletown NY 10940-1697

PAWSON, DAVID LEO, marine biologist, educator; b. Napier, New Zealand, Oct. 5, 1938; came to U.S., 1964; s. Leslie Albert and Mary Alice (Wildermoth) P.; m. Mary Tobin, Dec. 8, 1962; children: David Leslie, Erin Katherine. BSc, Victoria U., Wellington, New Zealand, 1959, MSc with honors, 1961, PhD, 1964. Lectr. in zoology Victoria U., 1964; assoc. curator Nat. Mus. Natural History, Smithsonian Instn., Washington, 1964-70, curator, 1970—, chmn. dept., 1970-75, curator/rsch. scientist, 1975—; mem. adj. faculty arts and scis. Harvard U., Cambridge, Mass., 1975—; rsch. assoc. Nat. Mus. New Zealand, Wellington, 1986—; pres. Biomar Assocs., McLean, Va., 1985—; chmn. bd. assoc. editors Antarctic Rsch. Series, Washington, 1975-76. Contbr. articles to profl. publs., chpts. to books. Victoria U. teaching fellow, 1962-63, Smithsonian Instn. regents fellow, 1989. Mem. Am. Assn. Zool. Nomenclature (pres. 1989), Biol. Soc. Washington (pres. 1982), Australian Marine Sci. Assn. Home: 1434 Waggaman Cir Mc Lean VA 22101-4004 Office: Smithsonian Instn Rm W32NHB Washington DC 20560

PAXON, BILL, congressman; b. Buffalo, Apr. 29, 1954; s. Leon W. and Mary P. (Sellers) P. BA, Canisius Coll., 1977. Mem. Erie County Legis., N.Y., 1978-82; N.Y. State assemblyman from 147th Dist., 1983-89; mem. 101st-102nd Congresses from 31st N.Y. dist., 1989—; mem. House coms. on banking, fin., and urban affairs; vets. affairs; select narcotics abuse and control; freshman whip. Mem. Newstead Hist. Soc., N.Y. State Conservation Coun., Erie County Farm Bur., Erie County Judges and Police Execs. Conf. Youngest mem. in history Erie County Legislature. Mem. Buffalo C. of C., Lions. Roman Catholic. Office: US Ho of Reps 1711 Longworth Bldg Washington DC 20515 also: 5500 Main St Williamsville NY 14221*

PAXTON, ALICE ADAMS, artist, architect and interior designer; b. Hagerstown, Md., May 19, 1914; d. William Albert and Josephine (Adams) Rosenberger; m. James Love Paxton Jr., June 26, 1942 (div.); 1 child, William Allen III (dec.). Student, Peabody Inst. Music, Balt., 1937-38; grad., Parson's Sch. Design, N.Y., 1940; studies with J. Laurie Wallace, 1944-46; studies with Augustus Dunbier, 1947-48, Sylvia Curtis, 1949, Milton Wolsky, 1950, Frank Sapousek, 1951. Freelance work archtl. renderings and interior design, N.Y., 1937-40; interior designer, designer spl. furnishings, muralist Orchard and Wilhelm, Omaha, 1940-42; tchr. art classes Alice Paxton Studio, Omaha, 1957-64; tchr. mech. drawing, archtl. rendering and mech. perspective Parson's Sch. Design, N.Y., 1937-40. Designer (interior) Chapel Boys' Town, Nebr., 1942; one-woman show of archtl. renderings Washington County Mus. Fine Arts, Hagerstown, 1944; exhibited group shows at Joslyn Mus., Omaha, 1943-44, Ann. Exhbn. Cumberland Valley Artists, Hagerstown, 1945; represented in permanent collections at No. Natural Gas Co. Bldg., Omaha, Swanson Found., Omaha; also pvt. collections; vol. designer, decorator: recreation room Omaha Blood Bank, ARC, 1943, recreation room Creighton U., 1943, lounge psychiat. ward Lincoln (Nebr.) Army Hosp., 1944; planner, color coordinator Children's Hosp., Omaha, 1947, painted murals, 1948, decorated dental room, 1950; designed Candy Stripers' uniforms; painted and decorated straw elephant bag presented to Mrs. Richard Nixon, 1960; contbr. articles and photographs to Popular Home mag., 1958. Co-chair camp and hosp. coms. ARC, 1943-45, mem. county com. to select and send gifts to servicemen, 1943-46; mem. Ak-Sar-Ben Ball Com., Omaha, 1946-48, Nat. Mus. Women in the Arts, The Md. Hist. Soc.; judge select Easter Seal design, Joslyn Mus., 1946; mem. council Girl Scouts U.S., Omaha, 1943-47; spl. drs. chmn. Jr. League, Omaha, 1947-48, chair Jr. League Red Cross fund dr., 1947-48; bd. dirs., vol. worker Creche, Omaha, 1954-56; mem. Omaha Jr. League; chmn. Jr. League Community Chest Fund Dr., 1948-50; co-chair Infantile Paralysis Appeal, 1944; numerous vol. profl. activities for civic orgns., hosps., clubs, chs., community playhouse, and for establishing wildlife sanctuary. Recipient three teaching scholarships Parson's Sch. Design, 1937-40, presdl. citation ARC activities, 1946, 1st prize Ann. Midwest Show Joslyn Mus., 1943. Mem. Associated Artists Omaha (charter), Internat. Platform Assn., U.S. Hist. Soc., Nat. Mus. Women in Arts (charter), Md. Hist. Soc., Fountain Head Country Club. Republican. Episcopalian. Home: 19614 Meadowbrook Rd Hagerstown MD 21742

PAXTON, R(ALPH) ROBERT, chemical engineer; b. Zion, Ill., Mar. 4, 1920; s. James Robert and Hazel Marie (Lawrence) P.; widowed; children: Nancy, Anne. BSChemE, U. Ill., 1943; ScD, MIT, 1949. Jr. engr. Amoco Corp. (formerly Standard Oil Co. of Ind.), Whiting, 1943-45; instr. chem. engring. U. Colo., Boulder, 1945-47; teaching asst. MIT, Cambridge, 1947-49; asst. prof. chem. engring. Stanford (Calif.) U., 1949-56; sr. engr. chem. engring. GE Co., Pittsfield, Mass., 1956-58; v.p. engring. and planning Pure Carbon Co., St. Mary, Pa., 1958-85; cons. Paxton Cons., St. Mary, 1986—. Author: Mechanical Carbon, 1979. Mem. St. Mary Area Sch. Bd., 1983-85. Fellow Am. Inst. Chemists, Soc. Tribologists and Lubrication Engrs.; mem. ASTM (sec. C-5 com. 1979-81), Am. Inst. Chem. Engrs. (assoc. editor Lubrication Engring. 1970—), Kiwanis (pres. 1980), St. Mary Country Club (sec. 1979-81). Office: Pure Carbon Co 441 Hall Ave Saint Marys PA 15857-1497

PAYNE, BRUCE, management consultant; b. Bakersfield, Calif., Feb. 6, 1911; s. James Bruce and Erma Frances (Deacon) P.; m. Edna Winifred Jessop, June 5, 1935; children: John Bruce, Christopher, Geoffrey Stephens; m. Maria Apparacida DeMello, May 19, 1982. B.S., U. Calif., 1933; M.B.A., Harvard U., 1935. Indsl. engr. Republic Steel Corp., 1935-38; cons. Nat. City Bank of Cleve., 1938-40; v.p., dir. Dyer Engrs., Inc., Cleve., 1940-46; pres., dir. Bruce Payne Consultants Inc., 1946—, Bruce Payne & Assos. Internat., Inc., 1952—, Payne Computer Services, Inc., 1969-77; also Bruce Payne & Assos. de Sud Am., Argentina, Bruce Payne y Associados S.A., Mexico, Bruce Payne Associados, Brazil. Author: Planning for Company Growth, 1963, (with D.D. Swett) Office Operations Improvement, 1967. Trustee Fairfield (Conn.) Country Day Sch., 1951-61. Mem. Inst. Mgmt. Cons. (dir., v.p. 1972-75, founding mem.), Council Internat. Progress in Mgmt. (dir. 1951-55, v.p. 1955-58, v.p. found. 1958—), Soc. Advancement Mgmt. (dir. 1946-50, dir.-at-large 1955, nat. treas. 1950-52, exec. v.p. 1952-53, past nat. pres., nat. adv. council), Harvard Bus. Sch. Assn. (pres. 1950-51, chmn. fund com. 1952-53, mem. fund council 1953-56), Am. Mgmt. Assn., Chief Execs. Forum, Newcomen Soc., English-Speaking Union, Alpha Sigma Phi. Clubs: Economic (N.Y.C.); Harvard (Boston, N.Y.C.). Office: Bruce Payne Cons Inc 140 W End Ave New York NY 10023-6131

PAYNE, DANIEL G., lawyer; b. Bay Shore, N.Y., Apr. 8, 1958; s. Herbert Daniel and Helen Joan (Lofting) P.; m. Anne Marie Browy, Oct. 25, 1986. BA, Union Coll., 1980; JD, Union U., 1984; MA, SUNY, Buffalo, 1991. Counsel N.Y. State Senate Transp. Ctr., Albany, 1985-87; assoc. counsel Legis. Bill Drafting Commn., Albany, 1987; prin. Daniel G. Payne, Atty., Buffalo, 1987—. Candidate Bay Shore Sch. Bd., 1976. Mem. Modern Lang. Assn., Sierra, Audubon Soc. Democrat. Office: PO Box 623 Buffalo NY 14231-0623

PAYNE, DEBORAH ANNE, medical company officer; b. Norristown, Pa., Sept. 22, 1952; d. Kenneth Nathan Moser and Joan (Reese) Dewhurst; m. Randall Barry Payne, Mar. 8, 1975. AA, Northeastern Christian Jr. Coll., 1972; B in Music Edn., Va. Commonwealth U., 1979. Driver, social asst. Children's Aid Soc., Norristown, Pa., 1972-73; mgr. Boddie-Noell Enterprises, Richmond, Va., 1974-79; retail food saleswoman Hardee's Food Systems, Inc., Phila., 1979-81; supr., with tech. tng. and testing and computer depts. Cardiac Datacorp., Phila., 1981—. Mem. bd. advisers Am. Biog. Inst., 1989. Mem. NAFE, Delta Omicron (pres. Alpha Xi chpt. 1978-79, pres. Epsilon province 1980-85, chmn. Eastern Pa. alumni 1986-88, Star award 1979), Am. Soc. Profl. and Exec. Women. Republican. Office: Cardiac Datacorp 1429 Walnut St Fl 2D Philadelphia PA 19102-3201

PAYNE, DONALD, congressman; b. Newark, July 16, 1934. BA, Seton Hall U. Freeholder Essex County, 1973-78; ins. co. exec., prior to 1989, former v.p. computer forms mfr.; mem. Newark Mcpl. Coun., 1982-89, 101st-102nd Congresses from 10th N.J. dist., 1989—. Chmn. World YMCA Refugee and Rehab. Com., 1973-81; pres YMCA's of USA. Democrat. Office: US Ho of Reps Office House Mems Washington DC 20510 also: 970 Broad St Rm 1435-B Newark NJ 07102*

PAYNE, DOUGLAS WILTON, Latin American and Caribbean affairs specialist, writer; b. Neptune, N.J., Jan. 12, 1951; s. Douglas Wilton and Helen (Brophy) P.; m. Nancy Lea Ashley, Sept. 7, 1985. BA in English, Williams Coll., 1972. Freelance writer N.Y.C., 1972-82; mem. staff Freedom House, N.Y.C., 1983-87, dir. hemispheric studies, 1987—. Author: The Democratic Mask: The Consolidation of the Sandinista Revolution, 1985; co-author: (with Mark Falcoff and Susan Kaufman Purcell) Latin America: U.S. Policy after the Cold War, 1991; contbr. articles to profl. jours. Mem. Social Dems., Washington, 1985-91, mem. nat. com., 1991—. Office: Freedom House 48 E 21st St New York NY 10010-7223

PAYNE, RHODA, alumni affairs and financial aid director; b. N.Y.C., June 14, 1934; d. Abraham and Ida (Ulano) Wasserman; m. Donald Ian Payne, June 24, 1956 (div. Oct. 1982); 1 child, Ellen. BS, Juilliard Sch., 1955; MA, Case Western Res. U., 1965, MFA, 1969, PhD, 1971. Dir. drama dept. Cleve. Jewish Community Ctr., 1965-77; dean, dir. admissions and fin. aid Cleve. Inst. of Music, 1977-81; dir. edn. Hebrew Arts Sch., N.Y.C., 1981-85; dir. alumni affairs and fin. aid Juilliard Sch., N.Y.C., 1985—. cons. fin. aid depts. in colls. and univs. Mem. Nat. Assn. Student Fin. Aid Adminstrs., Compassionate Friends (treas.). Office: Juilliard Sch 60 Lincoln Center Plz New York NY 10023-6588

PAYSON, DARRELL ERLON, guidance counselor; b. Waterville, Maine, Dec. 24, 1932; s. Erlon James and Louise Inez (Cates) P.; m. Ann Louise Crosby, Aug. 4, 1956; children: Lorna Jean, Brian Darrell, Raelynn, Amy Louise. BS in Edn., Gorham State U., 1955; MS in Edn., U. Maine, 1958. Cert. in edn., Maine; cert. social studies and history tchr.; cert. counselor, Mass. Social studies tchr. Town of South Portland, Maine, 1958-61, Town of Littleton, Mass., 1961-64; social studies tchr. Town of Concord, Mass., 1964-91, guidance counselor, 1991—; head guidance dept. Concord Mid. Sch., 1980-83, athletic dir., 1975—. Mem. Littleton Recreation, 1962-68; trustee, treas. Littleton Scholarship Trust, 1965-91; treas. Youth Adv., Littleton, 1982-91. With U.S. Army, 1955-57. Recipient 25 Yrs. of Svc. to Littleton Youth award The Commonwealth Bank, 1985. Mem. N.E. Assn. Counseling and Devel., Mass. Tchrs. Assn. (exec. bd. 1991), Mass. Sch. Counselors Assn. (exec. bd. 1991, Counselor of Yr. 1988), Mass. Assn. Counseling and Devel. (Counselor of Yr. 1991). Republican. Episcopalian. Home: 8 Hartwell Ave Littleton MA 01460-1206 Office: Concord Mid Sch Old Marlboro Rd Concord MA 01742-4131

PAYSON, PARKER LAURENCE, journalist; b. N.Y.C., July 21, 1965; s. Phillips Howes Payson and Sheila Whitney (Bullock) Tucker. BA, U. of the South, Sewayee, Tenn.; MBA, U. Chgo. Sports editor Cables News Network, Atlanta, 1984; asst. English editor The Jordan Times, Amman, 1986; fundraiser St. Jude Children's Rsch. Hosp., Arlington, Va., 1988; reporter The Times of the Americas, Washington, 1988; venturer Operation Raleigh, Nairobi, Kenya, 1988; news editor The Washington Report on Middle East Affairs, Washington, 1989—. Co-author: Stealth Pacs, 1989; contbr. articles to profl. jours. Vol. Washington Literacy Coun., 1989—, George Bush Inaugural Com., Washington, 1989. Recipient Queen Noor fellowship Jordarlar Govt. award Duke U., Amman, Jordan, 1986. Mem. Royal British Scientific and Exploration Soc., Cato Inst., Phi Gamma Delta (historian 1984-85). Episcopalian. Home: 4139 36th St S Arlington VA 22206-1805 Office: The Washington Report on Middle East Affairs PO Box 53062 Washington DC 20009-9062

PAZDERA, JOHN PAUL, technical documentalist; b. Jersey City, June 9, 1948; s. Albert Frederick and Helen Katherine (Momat) P.; m. Yolanda Lourdes Lopez, May 26, 1973. BS, Stevens Inst. Tech., 1970; MBA, Fairleigh Dickinson U., 1979. Cert. quality engr. Sales engr. Westinghouse Electric Co., Bloomfield, N.J., 1970-71; tech. dir. Ungerer & Co., N.Y.C., 1972-75; group leader quality control Airwick Industries, Carlstadt, N.J., 1975-78, regulatory affairs specialist, 1979-80; tech. documentalist Am. Home Products, N.Y.C., 1981-91; mgr. regulatory svcs. Lonza Inc., Fair Lawn, N.J., 1991—; adj. prof. advt. Fairleigh Dickinson U., 1982, Rutherford, N.J.; polt. writer Herald-News, Passaic, N.J., 1982-85. Mem. Am. Chem. Soc., Regulatory Affairs Profls. Soc., Am. Soc. for Quality Control. Republican. Roman Catholic.

PAZERA, D. DANIELLE, mental health services professional; b. Derby, Conn., Aug. 19, 1963; d. John Allan and Marie Francis (D'onofrio) Barry; m. Richard Bernard Pazera, Aug. 19, 1990; stepchildren: Keith, Kevin, Kaity. BA, Albertus Magnus Coll., 1986; MS, So. Conn. State U., 1991. Warehouse mgr. Rege, Inc., Mt. Kisco, N.Y., 1984-86; office mgr. Act II Theatre Co., New Haven, 1983-86; recreation/residential instr. CHC Inc., North Adams, Mass., 1986-87; behavior modification counselor Easter Seal Rehab. Ctr. Waterbury, Watertown, Conn., 1987-89; behavior modification specialist Dept. Mental Retardation Southbury (Conn.) Tng. Sch., 1989—. Exec. bd. dirs. The Naugatuck Valley Youth Coun., 1991. Mem. AACD, Am. Mental Health Counselors Assn. Roman Catholic. Home: 25 Nancy Mae Ave Prospect CT 06712-1720

PAZ-PUJALT, GUSTAVO ROBERTO, physical chemist; b. Arequipa, Peru, Aug. 9, 1954; came to U.S. 1973; s. Manuel Eduardo and Raquel Maria (Pujalt) Paz-Bishop; m. Ellen Frances Coey, Nov. 27, 1985; 1 child, Martin. BS in Chemistry, U. Wis., Eau Claire, 1977; PhD in Phys. Chemistry, U. Wis., Milw., 1985. Rsch. scientist Eastman Kodak Co., Rochester, N.Y., 1986-89, sr. scientist, 1989—; vis. scientist MIT, 1988, Kodak-Pathe, Chalon-sur-Saone, France, 1991. Contbr. articles to profl. jours.; patentee in field. Vice pres. Spanish Action Coalition, Rochester, 1990—. Mem. Am. Chem. Soc., Matls. Rsch. Soc. Roman Catholic. Home: 114 Shepard St Rochester NY 14620-1818 Office: Eastman Kodak Co 343 State St Rochester NY 14650-2011

PAZZAGLINI, MARIO PETER, JR., psychologist; b. Endicott, N.Y., Mar. 9, 1940; s. Mario and Dina Julia (Albertini) P.; BA, SUNY, Binghamton, 1961; MA, George Washington U., 1965; PhD, U. Del., 1969. Staff psychologist Del. State Hosp., 1968-72, co-dir. adolescent program, 1972-77; with Bur. of Alcoholism and Drug Abuse State of Del., 1970-83; pvt. practice psychotherapy, Newark, Del., 1973—; mem. staff St. Francis Hosp., Wilmington, Del., 1977—; adj. asst. prof. psychology U. Del., 1972—; clin. instr. Jefferson Med. Sch.; cons. street drug rsch. HEW grantee, 1971, 1972. Author: The Book of Numbers, 1990; contbr. articles to profl. jours. Mem. AAAS, Am. Psychol. Assn., N.Y. Inst. Gestalt Therapy, N.Y. Acad Scis., Sigma Xi. Democrat. Roman Catholic. Research in imagery and ancient use of symbols; also pioneer in-residence adolescent psychiat. treatment, drug treatment for State of Del. (11), street drug use patterns rsch. (11). Office: 523 Capitol Trl Newark DE 19711-3859

PEABODY, DAVID CALDWELL, insurance executive; b. Boston, Jan. 25, 1962; s. George Barry and Nancy Caldwell (Jacobs) P.; m. Elizabeth Sprague Fisk, Nov. 7, 1987. BA in Bus. Adminstrn., 1986. Ops. asst. Merrill Lynch Capital Markets, Boston, 1985-87; partner, sales Wiswall & Kellogg, Inc., Wellesley, Mass., 1987—. Mem. Rotary Club (community svc. chmn. 1990-91, sec. 1991-92). Republican. Office: Wiswall & Kellogg Inc 40 Grove St Wellesley MA 02181-7702

PEABODY, SAMUEL S., III, career officer; b. Washington, Apr. 4, 1953; s. Samuel S. III P.; m. Mary Jane Ducote, Jan. 5, 1980; children: Samantha, Natalie, Rachael, Samuel IV. BS in Animal Sci., Kans. State U., 1984, DVM, 1986. Commd. capt. U.S. Army, 1986; base veterinarian Nellis AFB, Las Vegas, Nev., 1986-89, Incirlick AFB, Adana, Turkey, 1989-90; lab. animal veterinarian U.S. Army Med. Rsch. Inst., Frederick, Md., 1990-91, Naval Med. Rsch. Inst., Bethesda, Md., 1991, Armed Forces Inst. Pathology, Washington, 1992—. Office: Armed Forces Inst Pathology Washington DC 20306

PEACHEY, DENNIS WILLIAM, educational administrator; b. Parry Sount, Ont., Can., Mar. 3, 1943; came to U.S., 1969; s. William H. and Bertha (McEwan) P.; m. Lynn McConachy, July 17, 1971; children: Derek, Meghan. BA, U. Denver, 1966; postgrad., Lehigh U. Assoc. sec. Blair Acad., Blairstown, N.J., 1969-71, sec., 1971-76, asst. headmaster for fin. and devel., 1976—, treas., 1985—; sec., treas. Blair Acad. Corp., Blairstown, N.J., 1985—; pres. N.J. Assn. Ind. Schs. Bus. Adminstrn. Trustee, treas. Catherine Dickson Hofman Libr., Blairstown, 1981-90; trustee Karen Ann Quinlan Ctr. of Hope, Newton, N.J., 1991. Mem. Mid. States Assn. Colls. and Schs. (treas. 1981-89), Assn. Bus. Officers of Prep. Schs. (v.p. 1991, pres. 1992). Home and Office: Blair Acad PO Box 600 Blairstown NJ 07825-0600

PEACOCK, PAUL FREDERICK, electronic publishing company executive; b. Crawley, Sussex, Eng., Aug. 15, 1962; came to U.S., 1985; s. Peter Melville and Adriana (Zeevart) P. BS, Brunel U. of W. London, Middlesex, 1984. Program analyst EPG Computer Svcs., London, 1984-85; project mgr. EPG Am., N.Y.C., 1985-87; mgr. tech. svcs. EPG Am. Inc., N.Y.C., 1987-88; mgr. bus. devel. Tower Hill Svcs. Inc., N.Y.C., 1988-89; dir. mktg. Group Internat. Assocs., N.Y.C., 1989-90; chief exec. officer Conversion Svcs. Internat. Inc., N.Y.C., 1990-91; pres. Floppyback Pub. Internat., Hoboken, N.J., 1991—. Author: Love, War & the Movies, 1991. Fellow British Interplanetary Soc. of London, Hoboken Harriers Club (pres. R.C.). Home: 128 Garden St Hoboken NJ 07030-3702

PEACOCK, ROBERT EDWARD, controller; b. Malone, N.Y., Dec. 30, 1957; s. Richard Joseph Peacock and Madora (Labarre) Cheyne; m. Pamela Sue Poindexter, Sept. 1, 1984; children: Benjamin, Valerie. 3ieme degree, Faculté des Lettres, Rouen, France, 1978; BA in French Lit. cum laude, St. Lawrence U., 1980, BS in Econs. cum laude, 1980; MBA summa cum laude, Suffolk U., 1984. Restaurant mgr. various orgns., 1980-82; fin. analyst Cooley, Inc., Pawtucket, R.I., 1984-87; bus. mgr. components group Sprague Electric, Nashua, N.H., 1987-90; controller Sprague Electric Co., Hudson, N.H., 1990—. Suffolk U. fellow, 1982; St. Lawrence U. scholar, 1976. Mem. Profl. Accts. Office: Sprague Electric Co 267 Lowell Rd Hudson NH 03051-4900

PEACOCK, SHAWN BRIAN, advertising executive; b. Buffalo, Sept. 10, 1960; s. Raymond Warren and Helen Mary (Kennedy) P. AA, Fashion Inst., 1980; BA, State U. Buffalo, 1981. Editor Interview mag., N.Y.C., 1981-83; v.p. Evins/Weintraub Assocs., N.Y.C., 1983-86; supr. copy Bloomingdale's In-House Advt., N.Y.C., 1986-91, Grey Advt., N.Y.C., 1991—; advt. cons. Bklyn Acad. Music, 1986—. Contbr. articles to N.Y. Times, Interview mag., N.Y. Post; editor articles Esquire mag. Mem. adv. com. Mus. Modern Art, N.Y.C, 1984—. Mem. Men's Fashion Assn., Retail Advt. Conf., Fashion Group, Art Dirs. Club. Home: 142 W 19th St New York NY 10011-4103 Office: Grey Advertising 777 Third Ave 14th Fl New York NY 10017

PEAK, DAVID, physicist, educator, researcher; b. Bklyn., Nov. 28, 1941; s. William Henry and Blanche Ethel (Seckendorff) P.; m. Terry L. Handwerger, June 3, 1983. BS, SUNY, New Paltz, 1965; PhD, SUNY, Albany, 1969. Physics instr. SUNY, Albany, 1971-75; asst. prof. physics Union Coll., Schenectady, N.Y., 1975-78; assoc. prof. physics Union Coll., Schenectady, 1978-85, prof. physics, 1985-87, Frank & Marie Bailey prof. physics, 1987—; vis. fellow Princeton (N.J.) U., 1978-79; vis. scientist Argonne (Ill.) Nat. Lab., 1983-84; mem. Union Coll. Bd. Trustees, Schenectady, 1985-88, Nat. Confs. on Undergrad. Rsch. Governing Bd., 1988—. Author: Order and Chaos: Art and Magic, 1991; contbr. 40 articles to profl. jours. Recipient Profl. Devel. award NSF, Washington, 1978, Meritorious Svc. award, Alumni Coun. Union Coll., Schenectady, 1990, New Liberal Arts Spl. Leave award, Sloan Found., 1990-91. Mem. Coun. on Undergrad. Rsch. (founding mem., sec. 1985-87), Am. Physical Soc. (mem. exec. com. N.Y. state), Am. Astron. Soc., Am. Assn. Physics Tchrs., Sigma Xi (com. on sci. edn.). Office: Union Coll Physics Dept Schenectady NY 12308

PEAL, STANLEY, psychiatrist; b. Cin., June 6, 1913; s. Louis and Fannie (Sandler) P.; m. Ethel Doris Solway, Oct. 25, 1945; children: Amy, Frederick, David. BA, U. Cin., 1935, MD, 1937. Diplomate Am. Bd. Psychiatry and Neurology. Gen. internship Cin. Gen. Hosp., 1937-38; resident in neurology Bellevue Hosp., N.Y.C., 1938-39; resident in psychiatry Boston Psychopathic Hosp., Boston, 1939-40, Worcester (Mass.) State Hosp., 1940-41, Sheppard-Pratt Hosp., Towson, Md., 1946-48; assoc. prof. psychiatry Western Psychiat. Inst. Clinic, Pitts., 1951-77; staff psychiatrist Mayview State Hosp., Bridgeville, Pa., 1978-85. Contbr. several articles to profl. jours. Lt. Col. AUS, 1941-45. Fellow Am. Psychiat. Assn. Jewish.

PEALE, NORMAN VINCENT, minister; b. Bowersville, Ohio, May 31, 1898; s. Charles Clifford and Anna (DeLaney) P.; m. Ruth Stafford, June 20, 1930; children: Margaret (Mrs. Paul F. Everett), John, Elizabeth (Mrs. John M. Allen). AB, Ohio Wesleyan U., 1920, DD, 1936; STB, Boston U., 1924, AM, 1924, DD (hon.), 1986; DD, Syracuse U., 1931, Duke U., 1938, Cen. Coll., 1964; LHD (hon.), Lafayette Coll., 1952, U. Cin., 1968, Wm. Jewell Coll., 1952; LLD (hon.), Hope Coll., 1962, Brigham Young U., 1967, Pepperdine U., 1979; STD, Millikin U., 1958; LittD, Iowa Wesleyan U., 1958, Ea. Ky. State Coll., 1964, Jefferson Med. Coll., 1955; LHD (hon.), Northwestern U., 1984, Pace U., 1984, Milw. Sch. Engring., 1985, St. John's U., 1985, Marymount Manhattan, 1985; DD (hon.), Boston U., 1986, Mt. Union Coll., 1988; LHD (hon.), Judson Coll., 1988. Ordained to ministry M.E. Ch., 1922; pastor Berkeley, R.I., 1922-24, Kings Hwy. Ch., Bklyn., 1924-27, Univ. Ch., Syracuse, N.Y., 1927-32, Marble Collegiate Ref. Ch., N.Y.C., 1932-84; founder, pub. (with Mrs. Peale) Guideposts mag. Author: A Guide to Confident Living, 1948, The Power of Positive Thinking, 1952, The Coming of the King, 1956, Stay Alive All Your Life, 1957, The Amazing Results of Positive Thinking, 1959, The Tough-Minded Optimist, 1962, Adventures in the Holy Land, 1963, Sin, Sex and Self-control, 1965, Jesus of Nazareth, 1966, The Healing of Sorrow, 1966, Enthusiasm Makes the Difference, 1967, Bible Stories, 1973, You Can If You Think You Can, 1974, The Positive Principle Today, 1976, The Positive Power of Jesus Christ, 1980, Treasury of Joy and Enthusiasm, 1981, Positive Imaging, 1981, The True Joy of Positive Living, 1984; Have a Great Day, 1985; Why Some Positive Thinkers Get Powerful Results, 1986; Power of the Plus Factor, 1987, The American Character, 1988; co-author: (with Ken Blanchard) The Power of Ethical Management, 1988, The Power of Positive Living, 1990, My Favorite Quotations, 1990, This Incredible Century, 1991, My Christmas Treasury, 1991, My Inspirational Favorites, 1992; co-author: chpt. in Am's. 12 Master Salesmen; writer for various secular and religious periodicals;

Tech. adviser representing Protestant Ch. in filming of motion picture: motion picture One Man's Way, based on biography, 1963; film What It Takes To Be A Real Salesman. Trustee Ohio Wesleyan U., Central Coll.; mem. exec. com. Presbyn. Ministers Fund for Life Ins.; mem. Mid-Century White House Conf. on Children and Youth, Pres.'s Commn. for Observance 25th Anniversary UN; pres. Protestant Council City N.Y., 1965-69, Ref. Church in Am., 1969-70; lectr. pub. affairs, personal effectiveness; chaplain Am. Legion, Kings County, N.Y., 1925-27. Recipient numerous awards including: Freedom Found. award, 1952, 55, 59, 73, 74; Horatio Alger award, 1952; Am. Edn. award, 1955; Gov. Service award for Ohio, 1955; Nat. Salvation Army award, 1956; Disting. Salesman's award N.Y. Sales Execs., 1957; Salvation Army award, 1957; Internat. Human Relations award Dale Carnegie Club Internat., 1958; Clergyman of Year award Religious Heritage Am., 1964; Paul Harris Fellow award Rotary Internat., 1972; Disting. Patriot award Sons of Revolution, N.Y. State, 1973; Order of Aaron and Hur Chaplains Corps U.S. Army, 1975; Christopher Columbus award, 1976; All-Time Gt. Ohioan award, 1976; Soc. for Family of Man award, 1981; Disting. Achievement award Ohio Wesleyan U., 1983; Religion in Media Gold Angel award, 1984; Presdl. Medal of Freedom, 1984; 2d Ann. Family Weekly Nat. Treasure award, 1984; Disting. Am. award Sales and Mktg. Execs. Internat., 1985; Theodore Roosevelt Disting. Service award, 1985; World Freedom award Shanghai Tiffin Club, 1985; Napolean Hill Fedn. Gold medal for Literary Achievement, 1985; St. George Assn. Golden Rule award, 1985, Old Hero award NFL, 1987, Adele Rogers St. John Round Table award, 1987, Communicator of the Yr. award Sales and Mktg. Exec. Internat., Little Rock, 1987, Disting. Achievement award Am. Aging, 1987, Grand Cross award Supreme Council, Mother Council of World of 33d and last degree Masons, 1987, Magellan award Circumnavigators Club, 1987, Van Rensselaer Gold medal Masonic Temple Cin., Silver Buffalo award Boy Scouts Am., 1988, Outstanding Alumnus award Ohio Found. of Ind. Coll., 1989, Merit award in Humanities N.Y. Acad, Dentistry, 1989, Pope John XIII award Viterbo Coll., 1989, George M. and Mary Jane Leader Healthcare award, 1989, John Y. Brown award, 1989, Humanitarian of Yr. award Women's Nat. Rep. Club, 1990, Hance award St. Barnabas Health System, 1990, The Samaritan Inst. award, 1990, Caring Inst. award, 1990, Eleanor Roosevelt Val-Kill medal, 1991, Soaring Eagle award Brethren Home Fedn., 1991. Mem. SAR, Blanton-Peale Inst. (founder), Ohio Soc. N.Y. (pres. 1952-55), Episcopal Actors Guild, Am. Authors Guild, Alpha Delta, Phi Gamma Delta. Republican. Clubs: Metropolitan, Union League, Lotos. Lodges: Rotary, Masons (past grand prelate), Shriners, K.T. Office: 1025 5th Ave New York NY 10028-0134

PEARCE, WILLIAM JOSEPH, public broadcasting executive; b. Ponca City, Okla., Jan. 15, 1925; s. William Thomas and Mary Madeline (Fitzgerald) P.; m. Mary Simmen, June 6, 1964 (div. Mar. 31, 1982); children: Margaret Wickens, Daniel Ethan.; m. Noel Knille, Sept. 1, 1983; children—Ryder Fitzgerald and Tyler Lightsinger (twins); stepchildren: Laura Rutherford Stone, Alexandra Garret Stone. B.A., U. Miami, 1950; postgrad., U. Conn., 1952-53; M.S., Syracuse U., 1959; grad. Advanced Mgmt. Program, Harvard U., 1976, Wharton Sch., U. Pa. Tchr. public schs. East Lyme, Conn., 1953-56; tchr. Dept. Air Force, Japan, 1956-58; exec. producer TV N.Y. State Edn. Dept., Albany, 1959-60; dir. radio-TV Brown U., 1960-65; cons. ETV, Rochester (N.Y.) City Sch. Dist., 1966-68; gen. mgr. Sta. WLIW-TV, Plainview, N.Y., 1968-69; pres., gen. mgr. Sta. WXXI-TV-AM-FM, Rochester, 1969—; bd. dirs. Native Am. Pub. Broadcasting Consortium, N.Y. State Gov.'s TV-Film Adv. Bd.; chmn. N.Y. State Pub. Broadcasting Stas., Brookings Inst. Ctr. Advanced Study, Rochester. Mem. bd. mgmt. Rochester YMCA Camps; v.p. fin. Urbanarium, Rochester Devel. Community. With Signal Corps, USN, 1943-46, PTO. Recipient George Foster Peabody award, numerous other spl. radio and TV programming and prodn. awards for public affairs and performance programs. Mem. Nat. Assn. Pub. TV Stas., Nat. Pub. Radio, Nat. Assn. Broadcasters, N.Y. State Broadcasters Assn. (bd. dirs.), Rochester Radio Reading Svc., Eastern Edn. TV Network, Rochester C. of C., VFW, Univ. Club of Rochester (bd. dirs.), Tennis Club of Rochester, Rotary. Roman Catholic. Office: 280 State St Rochester NY 14614-1033

PEARINCOTT, JOSEPH VERGHESE, educator, physiologist; b. Travancore, India, May 26, 1929; s. George F. and Elizabeth (Kottakaram) P.; B.Sc., Travancore U., 1949; M.Sc., Aligarh U., 1951; Ph.D., Fordham U., 1959; m. Michaeleen Ferrara, May 1, 1958; 1 son, George Joseph. Came to U.S., 1952, naturalized, 1959. Instr. biology Fordham U., N.Y.C., 1952-56; postdoctoral fellow Columbia Coll. Physicians and Surgeons, N.Y.C., 1959-61; research asso., dept. physiology and pharmacology N.Y. Med. Coll., N.Y.C., 1961-62; asst. prof. biology Northeastern U., Boston, 1962-68, asso. prof. biology, 1968—. Mem. N.Y. Acad. Scis., AAAS, Am. Soc. Zoologists, Entomol. Soc. Am., AAUP, Sigma Xi. Home: 61 Webb St Lexington MA 02173-2245 Office: 360 Huntington Ave Boston MA 02115

PEARL, DAVID EUGENE, pianist, composer; b. Denver, Dec. 30, 1960; s. Arden Leonard Pearl and Toni K. Beldock; m. Rubi Miyachi, Aug. 16, 1986. MusB, U. Denver, 1983. pianist performing in N.Y., San Francisco, Santa Fe, N.Mex., Japan. Composer: Winter Scenes, 1982, Tune and Variations, 1991, No Illusion, 1991, Exploration Polar, 1991. Grantee NYSCA, Manhattan, 1989, 90, 91.

PEARL, RICHARD ALAN, neurologist, educator; b. N.Y.C., Feb. 2, 1943; s. Sam and Edith (Friedman) P.; m. Barbara Goldstein, Mar. 28, 1971; children: Laurie, Caroline, Jennifer. BA, U. Pa., 1964; MD, Georgetown U., 1968. Diplomate Am. Bd. Psychiatry and Neurology. Intern Mt. Sinai Hosp., N.Y.C., 1968-69, resident in neurology, 1969-70, 72-74; pvt. practice Smithtown, N.Y., 1974—; chief neurology St. John's Hosp., Smithtown, 1980—, Community Hosp. West Suffolk, Smithtown, 1980-90; asst. clin. prof. neurology Stony Brook (N.Y.) U. Hosp., 1980—. Lt. comdr. M.C., USN, 1972-74. Fellow Am. Acad. Neurology; mem. Assn. for Rsch. in Nervous and Mental Diseases, Alpha Omega Alpha. Office: 307 Middle Country Rd Smithtown NY 11787-2829

PEARLMAN, LOUIS JAY, aviation and advertising company executive; b. Flushing, N.Y., June 19, 1954; s. Herman and Reenie (Nevler) P. BA, Queens Coll., 1976; MBA, Century U., 1980; Degree in Sales Mgmt., SUNY, Buffalo, 1980; PhD in Bus. Adminstrn., Century U., 1983. Pres. Commuter Helicopter Corp., N.Y.C., 1974-75; pres., chief operating officer Trans Continental Airlines, Inc., N.Y.C., 1975—; gen. mgr. U.S. Westdeutsche Luftwerbung GmbH, N.Y.C., 1976-85; chmn., pres., chief exec. officer Airship Internat. Ltd., N.Y.C., 1982—, bd. dirs., 1985—; cons. Queens Coll., CUNY, 1977—; bd. dirs. Fed. Airlines Corp., N.Y.C. Author: Survey and Analysis of the Airline Industry, 1983; song writer. Active Mitchell-Linden Civic Assn., Flushing, 1980-82, Kissimmee (Fla.) Mcpl. Airport, 1985—. Mem. U.S. Power Squadron, Wings Club (disting., recipient Lighter-than-Air award 1987), Lighter-than-Air Soc. (hon.), Young Entrepreneurs Am., Young Millionaires Club, Internat. Air Transport Assn., Blimp Port U.S.A. (pres. 1987—), Friar's Club (N.Y.C.). Home: 1 Bay Club Dr PH-V Bayside NY 11360 Office: Airship Internat Ltd Trans Continental Airlines 7380 Sand Lake Rd Ste 200 Orlando FL 32819-5256

PEARLMAN, MARTIN N., psychologist, educator; b. Bklyn., Apr. 28, 1938; s. Nathan and Mollie (Goldstein) P.; 1 child, Daniel. BA, Bklyn. Coll., 1958; MA, U. Mich., 1960; PhD, Rutgers U., 1975. Lic. psychologist, N.J. Sr. clin. psychologist Cen. Islip State Hosp., N.Y. Dept. Mental Health, 1963-67; clin. sch. psychologist Granite Sch. Dist., Salt Lake City, 1967-69; from instr. to full prof. Middlesex County Coll., Edison, N.J., 1969—, dir. mental health progam, 1972-78; pvt. practice East Brunswick, N.J., 1978—; mem. Nat. Com. for Community Coll. Mental Health Programs, 1972-74. U.S. Pub. Health fellow, 1969-72. Mem. Am. Psychol. Assn. Home: 338 N 4th Ave Highland Park NJ 08904-2742 Office: Middlesex Coll Dept of Psychology Mill Rd Edison NJ 02819

PEARLMAN, PETER STEVEN, lawyer; b. Orange, N.J., June 11, 1946; s. Jack Kitchener and Tiela Josephine (Fine) P.; m. Joan Perlmutter, June 19, 1969; children: Heather, Christopher, Megan. BA, U. Ill., 1967; JD, Seton Hall U., 1970. Bar: N.J. 1970, U.S. Dist. Ct. N.J. 1970, U.S. Tax Ct. 1973, U.S. Supreme Ct. 1974, U.S. Ct. Appeals (2d cir.) 1981, U.S. Ct. Appeals (3d cir.) 1983, U.S. Ct. Appeals (7th cir.) 1985; cert. civil trial atty., 1982. Assoc. Cohn & Lifland, Esquires, Saddle Brook, N.J., 1970-72, ptnr., 1972—; lectr. Nat. Inst. Trial Advocacy, Hempstead, N.Y., 1988—; mem. panel arbitrators Am. Arbitration Assn.; lectr. for Inst. Continuing Legal Edn. for State of N.J.; panel mem. for med. malpractice panel hearing N.J. Supreme Ct. Trustee, Temple B'Nai Or, 1981-82. Mem. ABA, N.J. Bar Assn., Assn. Trial Lawyers Am. Home: 9 Harvey Dr Short Hills NJ 07078-1122 Office: Cohn Lifland Pealman Herrman & Knopf Park 80 Plz W 1 Saddle Brook NJ 07662

PEARLSTINE, NORMAN, newspaper editor; b. Phila., Oct. 4, 1942; s. Raymond and Gladys (Cohen) P.; m. Nancy Colbert Friday, 1988. A.B., Haverford Coll., 1964; LL.B., U. Pa., 1967. Staff reporter Wall Street Jour., Dallas, Detroit, L.A., 1968-73; Tokyo bur. chief Wall Street Jour., 1973-76; mng. editor Asian Wall Street Jour., Hong Kong, 1976-78; exec. editor Forbes Mag., Los Angeles, 1978-80; nat. news editor Wall Street Jour., N.Y.C., 1980-82; editor, pub. Wall Street Jour./Europe, Brussels, 1982-83; mng. editor, v.p. Wall Street Jour., N.Y.C., 1983-91, exec. editor, 1991—; bd. dirs. Am. com. Internat. Press Inst. Bd. dirs. Am. Women's Econ. Devel., Yosemite Nat. Insts. Recipient Editor of Yr. award Nat. Press Found., 1989. Mem. ABA, D.C. Bar Assn., N.Y. Hist. Soc. (chmn., trustee), Coun. Fgn. Rels., Am. Soc. Newspaper Editors. Office: Dow Jones & Co World Fin Ctr 200 Liberty St New York NY 10281-1003

PEARMAN, REGINALD JAMES, educational administrator; b. N.Y.C., May 23, 1923; s. William H. Astoria Arabell (Webb) P.; children—Jeanita, Lydia, Reginald. B.S., NYU, 1950; Ed.D., U. Mass., 1974. Cert. tchr., N.Y. Tchr., N.Y.C. Pub. Schs., 1951-55, supr., 1955-62; with Fgn. Service, State Dept., Caracas, Venezuela, 1962-65, Peace Corps, Washington, 1965-67, AID, Washington, 1967-69; dir. job devel. N.Y.C. Human Resources Adminstrn., 1969-71; ednl. program specialist U.S. Dept. Edn., Washington, 1971-74; mem. adv. com. women's equity U.S. Office of Edn., 1974, task force arts and humanities, 1975-76, task force edn. of gifted, 1976-77, basic edn., 1977, urban edn., 1978, pub. sch. adminstrn., 1979; mem. adv. bd. internship program Am. Pub. Transit Assn., 1977-79; mem. White House Initiative for Historically Black Colls. and Univs., 1982-83; tchr. Calif. State Coll.-Los Angeles, 1966, Cornell U./N.Y. State Sch. Labor and Indsl. Relations, 1968, 70, U. Md., College Park, 1974-76; with Md. Dept. Employment and Tng., Wheaton, 1985-86; counseling coord. Montgomery Coll., 1987—; mem. scholarship selection com. Creative Edn. Found., 1991-92; discussion leader Creative Problem Solving Inst., SUNY, Buffalo, 1991-92; grad. adviser U. Mass./D.C. Publ. Sch. project; also cons. Served with U.S. Army, 1944-47; PTO. Bd. dirs. D.C. Striders youth sports club; mem. Pres.'s Coun. Youth Opportunity, 1968; mem. D.C. ofcls. com. Nat. Youth Games, 1983; ofcl. Potomac Valey Track and Field Assn.; mem. platform com. N.Y. State Liberal Ind. party, 1968. Mem. NCAA All Am. Track Team, 1949; NCCJ fellow, 1953; U. Havana scholar, 1955; U. Pitts. fellow, 1967; named to NYU Hall of Fame, 1974, recipient Disting. Alumni award, 1977; recipient Brotherhood in Sports award B'nai B'rith, 1954; mem. U.S. Olympic Team, Helsinki, 1952. Mem. Nat. Alliance Black Sch. Educators (higher edn. commn.), Phi Delta Kappa. Lutheran. Established 4 Am. records and 3 world records in running events in middle distances. Home: 9118 September Ln Silver Spring MD 20901-3705

PEARSALL, WILLIAM WRIGHT, business executive; b. Geneva, Ill., July 1, 1929; s. Harold W. and Miriam (Wright) P.; m. Margaret Reinert, Sept. 13, 1952; children: Brian W., Susan Lyn, Kathy Lee, Steven W. BS in Bus., Northwestern U., 1951. Sr. applications engr. GM Overseas, N.Y.C., 1951-60; v.p. Euclid Equipment Inc., Freeport, N.Y., 1960-66; gen. mgr. Euclid Equipment Inc., Farmingdale, N.Y., 1966-75; pres. Euclid Equipment Inc., Wheatley Heights, N.Y., 1975-87, pres., chmn. bd., 1987—; pres., chmn. bd. Assoc. Engines Inc., Atlanta. Scoutmaster Boy Scouts Am., Greenlawn, N.Y., 1968-71; mem. Rep. Nat. Com., Washington. Mem. Engine Generator Set Assn. Roman Catholic. Office: Euclid Equipment Inc 2 Washington Ave Wyandanch NY 11798-2411

PEARSE, JOHN MELVILLE, musician, music string innovator, composer, recorder, author; b. Hook, Yorkshire, Eng., Sept. 12, 1939; came to U.S., 1978; s. Ernest Melville and Mabel Irene (Edwards) P. Reporter Rhyl Jour.; columnist Reuters, Thompson Newspapers, Pergamon Press, Frets; reviewer Melody Maker, English Dance and Song, Guitar; actor Rhyl Theater Co.; owner, mgr. Breezy Ridge Instruments Ltd. and John Pearse Music Strings, Center Valley, Pa., 1980—. Author: (music instruction books) The Dulcimer Book, 1965, Teach Yourself Folk Guitar, 1959, John Pearse Balalaika Method, 1967, Stringalong, 1986, others; (children's books): Floppy the Jujiburra, 1967, The Prune and the Pretzel, 1967, Happy Day, 1968, others; sci. fiction stories; composer: over 200 musical compositions including Harasho, 1967, Stop, Now Don't You Come Looking, 1968, Cold Winds of Winter, 1965, Virginia's Fair Shore, 1965, Bow Belles, 1966, McGee's Rag, 1965, Music Room, 1967, Guitar Train, 1965; patentee: holder of three U.S. patents, with four patents pending; records include The Dulcimer Record, 1967, John Pearse, 1967, John Pearse at Baden, 1968, John Pearse, Live!, 1969, Blues, Rags and Raga, 1968, Travelling Man, 1968, Alive and Well...and Living in America, 1978, (with F. Purslow) Rap-a-tap-tap, 1959, Bottoms Up!, 1960, (with D. Poons) One More City, 1967, (with M.F. Rhoads) Together, 1980; TV and film appearances include The Knife of Beria, 1968, The Private Lives of Sherlock Holmes, 1970, The Pre-Raphaelites, 1969, The Homecoming, 1971, The Lady Vanishes, 1975, D-Day, 1974, others. Mem. Guild Am. Luthiers, Assn. Stringed Instrument Artisans. Office: Breezy Ridge Instruments PO Box 295 Center Valley PA 18034-0295

PEARSE, ROBERT FRANCIS, psychologist, educator; b. Detroit, Nov. 15, 1916; s. Forrest F. and Sarah (Roberts) P.; m. Shirley Daniels, Dec. 22, 1947; children: Donald, Richard, Mary Jean. AM, U. Chgo., 1947, PhD, 1950. Diplomate Am. Bd. Profl. Psychology; cert. psychologist, N.Y. Dir. human resources Stop & Shop, Inc., Boston, 1959-64; prof. organizational behavior Boston U., 1964-81; disting. lectr., chmn. mgmt. and mktg., Coll. Bus. Rochester (N.Y.) Inst. Tech., 1981—; cons., Weldon-Harwood Corp., N.Y.C., 1964-72; sr. cons. on exec. effectiveness, improving leadership, Am. Mgmt. Assn., 1961-86. Author: Self Directed Change for the Mid Career Manager, 1976, The High Performance Nonprofit Organization, 1992. 1st lt. USAFR, 1948-53. Fellow APA. Home: 564 Surrey Hill Way Rochester NY 14623-3056 Office: Coll Bus Rochester Inst Tech 1 Lomb Dr Rochester NY 14623

PEARSON, G(EORGE) BURTON, JR., retired trust company executive; b. Middletown, Del., Aug. 8, 1905; s. George Burton and Mary Estelle (Cochran) P.; m. Mary Isbella Turner, June 27, 1941 (dec. Nov. 1962); children: Isabella Turner Pearson Ryan, Margaret Cochran Pearson; m. Edith duPont Riegel, Jan. 4, 1968. AB magna cum laude, Princeton U., 1927; JD, U. Pa., 1931; LLD (hon.), U. Del., 1988. Bar: Del., 1931, U.S. Supreme Ct. 1936. Law clk. Hon. Victor B. Woolley U.S. Ct. Appeals (3d cir.), 1930-31; assoc. atty. Law Office Hugh M. Morris, Wilmington, Del., 1931-39; vice chancellor State of Del., 1939-46; assoc. judge Del. Supreme Ct., 1946-50; sr. v.p., dir., chmn. trust com. Wilmington Trust Co., 1950-70, assoc. dir., mem. trust com., 1970—; mem. adv. bd. Del. Bank, 1959-69. Trustee U. Del., Newark, 1951—, Tower Hill Sch., Wilmington, 1962-73; mem. Newark Spl. Sch. Dist., 1933-41; trustee, now pres. Unidel Found., Inc., Wilmington. Mem. ABA, SAR, Del. Bar Assn. (pres. 1950-52), Am. Law Inst., Soc. Colonial Wars, Soc. of Cin., Chevalier du Tastevin, Alliance Francaise, Wilmington Club (past bd. dirs.), Wilmington Country Club, Greenville Country Club, Fishers Island Country Club, Fishers Island Yacht Club, Mill Reef Club. Home: PO Box 68 Montchanin DE 19710-0068

PEARSON, NATHAN WILLIAMS, broadcasting executive; b. Sewickley, Pa., Aug. 1, 1951; s. Nathan Williams Sr. and Kathleen Patricia (McMurtry) P.; m. Jane Ruth Wallace, Oct. 12, 1985; children: Nathan McMurtry, Howe Quinn. BA and MA in Music, Conn. Wesleyan U., 1974; MBA, Columbia U., 1982. Pvt. practice cons. N.Y.C. and Washington, 1974-82; with McKinsey & Co., N.Y.C. and L.A., 1982-88; chief fin. officer, mng. prin., sec., treas. Broadcasting Ptnrs., Inc., N.Y.C., 1988—. Author: "Goin' to Kansas City", 1987; producer LP records; contbr. articles to profl. jours. Chmn., bd. dirs. Citylore, Inc., N.Y.C., 1986—; treas. Young Audiences, N.Y.C., 1987—. Mem. Soc. for Ethnomusicology, Audio Enging. Soc., Am. Folklore Soc., Wadawanuck Club, Beta Gamma Sigma, Nat. Assn. Broadcasting, Broadcast Fin. Mgmt. Home: 41 Holly Ln Rye NY 10580 Office: Broadcasting Ptnrs Inc 150 W Fifty Fifth St New York NY 10019

PEARSON, NORMAN, academic, planning consultant, writer; b. Stanley, County Durham, Eng., Oct. 24, 1928; arrived in Can., 1954; s. Joseph and Mary (Pearson) P., m. Gerda Maria Josefine Reidl, July 25, 1972. BA in Fine Arts with honors in Town and Country Planning, U. Durham (Eng.), 1951; PhD in Land Economy, Internat. Inst. Advanced Studies, 1979; MBA, Pacific Western U., Colo., 1980, DBA, 1982; PhD In Mgmt., Calif. U. for Advanced Studies, 1986—. Cons. Stanley Urban Dist. Council, U.K., 1946-47; planning asst. Accrington Town Plan and Bedford County Planning Survey, U. Durham Planning Team, U.K., 1947-49, Allen and Mattocks, cons. planners and landscape designers, Newcastle upon Tyne, U.K., 1949-51; adminstrv. asst. Scottish Div., Nat. Coal Bd., Edinburgh, Scotland, 1951-52; planning asst. London Community Coun., Westminster, U.K., 1953-54; planner Central Mortgage and Housing Corp., Ottawa, Ont., Can., 1954-55; planning analyst City of Toronto (Ont., Can.) Planning Bd., 1955-56; dir. planning Hamilton Wentworth Planning Area Bd., Hamilton, Ont., 1956-59; dir. planning for Burlington (Ont.) and Suburban Area Planning Bd. Hamilton, Ont., Can., 1959-62; commr. planning City of Toronto Planning Bd., Burlington, Ont., 1959-62; pres. Tanfield Enterprises Ltd., London, Ont., Can., 1962—, Norman Pearson & Assocs. Ltd., London, Ont., Can., 1962—, Internat. Planning Mgmt. Cons., London, Ont., Can., 1962—; cons. in urban, rural and regional planning, 1962—; life mem. U.S. Com. for Monetary Research and Edn., 1976—; spl. lectr. in planning McMaster U., Hamilton, 1956-64, Waterloo (Ont.) Luth. U., 1961-63; asst. prof. geography and planning U. Waterloo (Ont.), 1963-67; assoc. prof. geography U. Guelph (Ont.), 1967-72, chmn., dir. Ctr. for Resource Devel.; prof. polit. sci. U. Western Ont., London, 1972-78; chmn. bd. dirs. Alma Coll., St. Thomas, Ont., 1990—; adj. prof. of ecological planning and land econs. Internat. Inst. for Advanced Studies, Clayton, Mo., 1980-89; core faculty Doctoral Program in Adminstrn/Mgmt. Walden U., Mpls., 1986—, chair adminstrn.-mgmt., 1989—; mem. acad. policy bd. Walden U.; mem. bd. regents Calif. U. for Advanced Studies, Petaluma, 1987—; mem. Social Scis., Econ. and Legal Aspects Com. of Rsch. Adv. Bd. Internat. Joint Commn., 1972-76; cons. to City of Waterloo, 1973-76, Province of Ont., 1969-70; adviser to Georgian Bay Regional Devel. Coun., 1968-72; real estate appraiser, province of Ont., 1976—; pres., chmn. bd. govs. Pacific Western U., Canada, 1983-84. Author: (with others) An Inventory of Joint Programmes and Agreements Affecting Canada's Renewable Resources, 1964. Editor, co-author (with others) Regional and Resource Planning in Canada, 1963, rev. edit., 1970; editor (with others) The Pollution Reader, 1968. Contbr. numerous articles on town planning to profl. jours. and chpts. in field to books. Pres. Unitarian Ch. of Hamilton, 1960-61. With RAF, 1951-53, res., 1953-60. Decorated Knight of Grace, Sovereign Order St. John of Jerusalem, 1979, Knight of the Order St. Lazarus of Jerusalem, 1991, Internat. Order of Merit, 1991. Fellow Royal Town Planning Inst. (Bronze medal award 1957), Lambda Alpha Internat., Royal Econ. Soc.; mem. Internat. Soc. City and Regional Planners, Am., Canadian insts. planners, Canadian Polit. Sci. Assn. L'Association Internationale des Ingenieurs et des Docteurs ès Sciences Appliquées à l'Industrie. Clubs: Empire; Ontario; University (London), Baconian. Office: PO Box 5362, Station A, London, ON Canada N6A 4L6

PEARSON, RONALD HAYES, designer, metalsmith; b. N.Y.C., Sept. 22, 1924; s. Ralph Mosher and Louise (Hayes) P.; m. Kathleen Harris, 1955 (div. 1971); children: Christopher, Bettina, Nadya, Arn; m. Carolyn Ann Hecker, Mar. 27, 1982. Student, U. Wis., 1942-43, Sch. Am. Craftsmen, Alfred U., 1947-48; LLD (hon.), Portland (Maine) Sch. Art, 1987. Jewelry instr. Sch. for Am. Craftsmen Rochester (N.Y.) Inst. Tech., 1959-61; jewelry instr. Penland (N.C.) Sch. of Crafts, 1968-70, Haystack Mountain Sch. of Crafts, Deer Isle, Maine, 1971, 78, 82; owner, pres. Ronald Hayes Pearson Inc., Deer Isle, Maine, 1948—; vis. artist Haystack Mountain Sch. of Crafts, Deer Isle, 1980, Portland Sch. Art, 1990; design cons. Hickok Jewelry Mfg. Co., Rochester, 1954-56; cons. NEA, Washington, 1974, 76; jewelry designer Kirk-Stieff Co., Balt., 1982-88; commr. Maine Arts Commn., Augusta, 1988—. Designer Vision flatware, 1960 (Prodn. award), Smithsonian flatware, 1978. Trustee Haystack Mountain Sch. Crafts, 1977-90, chmn., 1980-85, Louis Comfort Tiffany Found., 1979-84; bd. vis. Program in Artisanry, Boston U., 1977-84; bd. dirs. James Renwick Alliance, 1990—. With U.S. Merchant Marine, 1943-47. Grantee Louis Comfort Tiffany Found., 1969, NEA, 1973, 78. Fellow Am. Crafts Coun.; mem. Soc. N.Am. Goldsmiths (founding mem.), Maine Crafts Assn. (founding mem., dir.; pres. 1983-84). Democrat. Home and Office: RR 1 Box 158 Deer Isle ME 04627-9709

PEARSON, RONALD W., management consultant; b. Pawtucket, R.I., Apr. 19, 1946; s. Per W. and Florence L. (Forbes) P.; m. Patricia Ann Clark, June 15, 1968; children: Kathryn C., Ronald C. BA, Valparaiso U., 1968; MA, U. Notre Dame, 1970; postgrad., Brown U., 1970-72. Cert. mgmt. cons. Exec. dir. WYCF Inc., Madison, Wis., 1972-73; fgn policy analyst House Rep. Study Com., Washington, 1973; chief of staff Congressman John Ashbrook, Washington, 1973-78, Congressman William Dannemere, Washington, 1979; v.p. Phillips Pub. Inc., Potomac, Md., 1979-81; prin. Pearson & Co., Washington, 1981—; pres. Pearson & Pipkin, Inc., Washington, 1984—. Contbr. articles to profl. jours. Treas. Edn. and Rsch. Inst., Washington, 1975—; v.p. Young America's Found., Herndon, Va., 1974—; bd. dirs. Consumers Rsch., Inc., Washington, 1979—; exec. dir. Conservative Victory Fund, Washington, 1984—. Richard Weaver fellow Intercollegiate Studies Inst., 1971-72; H.B. Earhart Found. fellow, 1970-71. Mem. St. Andrew Soc. Washington, Va. Scottish Games Assn. (bd. dirs.), Inst. Mgmt. Cons. (pres. Washington chpt. 1988-91). Office: Pearson & Pipkin Inc 422 First St SE Ste 208 Washington DC 20003

PEARSON, WILLIAM ROWLAND, nuclear engineer; b. New Bedford, Mass., Sept. 30, 1923; s. Rowland and Nellie (Hilton) P.; BS, Northeastern U., 1953; postgrad. U. Ohio, 1960; m. Arlene Cole Loveys, June 14, 1953; children: Denise, Robert, Rowland, Nancy. Engr., Goodyear Atomic Corp., Portsmouth, Ohio, 1953-63, Cabot Titania Corp., Ashtabula, Ohio, 1963-64; supr. United Nuclear, Wood River, R.I., 1964-72; sr. engr. Nuclear Materials and Equipment Co., Apollo, Pa., 1972-74; engr. U.S. Nuclear Regulatory Commn., Rockville, Md., 1974-90, ret., 1990. Served with USNR, 1942-45. Decorated Air medal. Mem. AAAS, Am. Nuclear Soc., Am. Inst. Chem. Engrs. (chmn. 1966-67). Republican. Baptist. Clubs: Masons, Elks. Home: 14 Meeting Hill Rd Hillsborough NH 03244-4854

PEARTON, STEPHEN JOHN, physicist; b. Hobart, Tasmania, Australia, Jan. 15, 1957; came to U.S., 1982; s. Dennis Gregory and Margaret Faye (Godfrey) P. BS with honors, U. Tasmania, Australia, 1979, PhD, 1983. Exptl. officer Australian Atomic Energy Commn., Sydney, 1981-82; postdoctoral fellow U. Calif., Berkeley, 1982-83; mem. tech. staff AT&T Bell Labs., Murray Hill, N.J., 1984—. Author: Hydrogen in Crystalline Semiconductors, 1991; editor: (conf. proceedings) O, C, H & N in Crystalline Silicon, 1986, Defects in Electronic Materials, 1988, Ion Implanatation for Compound Semiconductors, 1990, Degradation Mechanisms in Compound Semiconductor Devices and Structures, 1990. Mem. Hobart First Aid/Search and Rescue Squad, 1975-77. Recipient scholarship Australian Inst. Nuclear Sci. and Enging., 1979-81. Mem. Am. Physical Soc. (life), Materials Rsch. Soc. Republican. Home: 19 Euclid Ave Summit NJ 07901-2114 Office: AT&T Bell Labs 600 Mountain Ave New Providence NJ 07974-2010

PEASLEE, RICHARD CUTTS, composer; b. N.Y.C., June 13, 1930; s. Amos Jenkins and Dorothy (Quimby) P.; m. Mary Dixon Palmer; Children: Jessica Dixon, Richard Cutts Jr. BA, Yale U., 1952; Diploma, Juilliard, 1956, MS, 1958. teaching artist Lincoln Ctr. Inst., N.Y.C., 1978-81. Composer The Marat/Sade, 1964, Animal Farm, 1984, The Garden of Earthly Delights 1984 (Obie award 1984), Vienna Lusthaus, 1986, Miracolo d'Amore, 1988. Vol. Boys Club of N.Y.C., 1955-60; vol. Jobs for Youth, N.Y.C., 1985-86, bd. dirs., 1985—. Grantee NEA, Washington, 1982, Meet the Composer, N.Y.C.; recipient Villager award, 1979, Marc Blitzstein award Nat. Acad., Inst. of Arts and Letters. Mem. Boadcast Music Inc., Am. Fedn. of Music, Theatre Communication Group (bd. dirs.). Democrat. Mem. Soc. of Friends. Home and Office: 90 Riverside Dr Apt 15A New York NY 10024-5322

PEATMAN, JOHN GRAY, statistician, psychologist; b. Centerville, Iowa, Mar. 16, 1904; s. Clarence Albert and Binney Oriel (Gray) P.; student U. Colo., 1923-25; AB, Columbia U., 1927, MA, 1928, PhD, 1931; m. Lillie Burling, 1927; children: Alice Peatman Dettmers (dec.), John, William; m. 2d, Madeline Martin, 1948 (dec. 1984); 1 dau., Mary Peatman Fitzpatrick.

Mem. faculty CCNY, 1929-70, prof. psychology, 1946-70, emeritus prof., 1970—, chmn. dept., 1953-62, assoc. dean, 1943-53; pres., dir. Office of Research N.Y., 1941-58; vis. prof. stats. Columbia U., 1948; ednl. cons. U.S. Air Force, 1949-50; pres., dir. Res. Cons., Inc., Norwalk, Conn., 1950—. Cons., chmn. arbitration panels ASCAP, 1954-56; bd. dirs. Silvermine, Conn. Community Assn., 1962-63. Fellow AAUP, Am. Psychol. Assn. (chmn. policy and planning bd. 1949-50, past chmn. various coms.), N.Y. State Psychol. Assn. (pres. 1949-50), Psychonomic Soc. (charter), Univ. Club, Phi Beta Kappa, Sigma Xi (pres. CCNY chpt. 1961-62). Unitarian. Author: Descriptive and Sampling Statistics, 1947; Introduction to Applied Statistics, 1963; contbr. monographs, articles in field to profl. lit. Office: Rsch Cons Inc 83 East Ave Norwalk CT 06851-4902

PEBLY, HARRY EUGENE, plastics engineering consultant; b. Sharpsville, Pa., Feb. 1, 1923; s. Harry E. and Esther (Roth) P.; m. Geraldine Katilus, Sept. 3, 1949; 1 child, Amelia Jane. BSChemE, Pa. State U., 1944; MS in Indsl. Engring., Stevens Inst. Tech., 1957. Dir. Plastics Tech. Evaluation Ctr., Dover, N.J., 1960-86; chief organic materials br. Picatinny Arsenal, Dover, 1986-89; cons., Randolph, N.J., 1989—; instr. N.J. Inst. Tech., Hoboken, 1958-67. Compiler: (index) Delaware Composites Design Ency., 1990; developed glossary for Am. Soc. Metals Engring. Materials Handbook, Vol. 1, Composites, 1987. Recipient Meritorious Svc. award Plastics Inst. Am., 1977, Comdr.'s award Picatinny Arsenal, 1989. Mem. Am. Def. Preparedness Assn., Soc. Plastics Engrs., Soc. Plastics Industry (editor ann. conf. proc. The Composites Inst. 1985—, recipient Outstanding Svc. award reinforced plastics div. 1965), Soc. Advanced Material and Process Engrs. Lutheran. Home and Office: 198 Center Grove Rd Randolph NJ 07869-2007

PECHT, MICHAEL GERARD, electronic packaging research director, educator; b. Milw., Feb. 13, 1952; s. George Andrew and Dorothy Ann (Jaworski) P.; m. Judy Mei-Zu Shih, Sept. 7, 1988; children: Joann, Jefferson. BS in Acoustics, U. Wis., 1976, MSEE, 1978, MS in Engring. Mechanics, 1979, PhD in Engring. Mechanics, 1982. Registered profl. engr., Wis., Md. Electronics technician dept. high energy physics U. Wis., Madison, 1971-74, engring. technician dept. natural resources, 1977, teaching asst. dept. electrical engring., 1977-79, rsch. asst., 1979-83; profl. cons. Instrumentations System Ctr., Madison, 1983; asst. prof. dept. mech. engring. U. Md., College Park, 1983-88, assoc. prof., 1988—; founder, dir. CALCE Electronics Packaging Rsch. Ctr., U. Md., 1987—; v.p. Ramsearch Inc., College Park, 1988-92; mem. adv. bd. Cetar Ltd. subs. Philips, 1990—; cons. USAF, 1991—. Mem. editorial bd. Jour. Electronics Mfg., 1990—; book rev. Jour. Quarty Tech., 1989—). Named Outstanding Young Man Am., 1986; recipient Vis. Scholar award Air Force Inst. Tech., Ohio, 1989, Best Paper award Power Conversion Conf., Long Beach, Calif., 1989. Fellow IEEE (sr., editor Trans. on Reliability 1988—), Soc. Mfg. Engrs. (sr., adv. bd. SME Electronics 1990—), SAE (automotive reliability standard com. 1990—), CALS (concurrent electronics engring. task group 1989—). Office: CALCE Electroncs Packaging U Md Rsch Ctr College Park MD 20742

PECK, CHARLES EDWARD, retired construction and mortgage executive; b. Newark, Dec. 1, 1925; s. Hubert Raymond and Helen (White) P.; m. Delphine Murphy, Oct. 15, 1949; children: Margaret, Charles Edward, Katherine, Perry Anne. Grad., Phillips Acad., 1943; student, MIT, 1944; BS, U. Pa., 1949. With Owens-Corning Fiberglas Corp., various locations, 1949-61; sales mgr. home bldg. products Owens-Corning Fiberglas Corp., Toledo, 1961-66; v.p. home bldg. products mktg. div. Owens-Corning Fiberglas Corp., 1966-68, v.p. constrn. group, 1968-75, v.p. bldg. materials group, 1976-78, exec. v.p., 1978-81, bd. dir.; co-chmn. The Ryland Group, Columbia, Md., 1981-82; chmn., chief exec. officer The Ryland Group, Columbia, 1982-90; dir. The Delaware Group of Funds, 1991—; mem. statutory vis. com. U.S. nat. Bur. Standards, 1972-77; mem. adv. com. Fed. Nat. Mortgage Assn., 1977-78, 85-86; vis. com. Mass. Inst. Tech.-Harvard Joint Ctr. for Urban Studies; chmn. Producers Adv. Forum, 1977-81. Mem. vis. com. Harvard U. Grad. Sch. Design, 1981-86; chmn. Howard County United Way Campaign, Md., 1987, co-chmn. community partnerships, 1991—; bd. dirs. Nat. Inst. for Urban Wildlife, 1986-90, United Way Cen. Md., 1987-91, Howard County Gen. Hosp., 1988—, Columbia Festival, Inc., 1988-91, NAHB Rsch. Found., 1989-92, Alliance to End Childhood Lead Poisoning, 1990—; mem. adv. bd. U. Md. Engring. Sch.; adv. bd. continuing edn. Johns Hopkins U., 1988-91; chmn. chancellor's adv. coun. U. Md. System, 1988—; chmn. Univ. Md. Found., 1990—; exec. fellow Kennedy Sch., Harvard U., 1990—; chmn. Affordable Housing Initiative, Columbia, Md., 1990-92. 2d lt. USAAF, 1944-46. Mem. U.S. C. of C. (bd. dirs. 1975-81), Ohio C. of C. (bd. dirs. 1975-81), Depression and Related Affective Disorders Assn. (pres. 1986-89, bd. dirs. 1986—), Rotary of Columbia, Belmont Country Club (Perrysburg, Ohio), Capitol Hill Club (Washington), Talbot Country Club (Md.), City Club (Washington), Ctr. Club (Balt.), Caves Valley Golf Club (Md.), Phi Gamma Delta. Home: 7649 Woodstream Way Laurel MD 20723-1163 Office: PO Box 1102 Columbia MD 21044-0102

PECK, FRED NEIL, economist, educator; b. Bklyn., Oct. 17, 1945; s. Abraham Lincoln and Beatrice (Pikholtz) P.; m. Jean Claire Ginsberg, Aug. 14, 1971; children: Ron Evan, Jordan Shefer, Ethan David. BA, SUNY, Binghamton, 1966; MA, SUNY, Albany, 1969; PhM, NYU, 1984; PhD, Pacific Western U., 1984. Lectr. SUNY, Albany, 1969-70; research asst. N.Y. State Legislature, Albany, 1970; sales and research staff Pan Am. Trade Devel. Corp., N.Y.C., 1971; v.p., economist The First Boston Corp., N.Y.C., 1971-88; mng. dir. Sharpe's Capital Mkt. Assocs. Inc., N.Y.C., 1988-89; pres., chief economist Hillcrest Econs. Group, N.Y.C., 1989—; adj. prof. Hofstra U., Hempstead, N.Y., 1975; lectr. NYU, 1982; mem. faculty New Sch. for Social Rsch., N.Y.C., 1974—; tchr. computer aided edn. N.Y.C. Bd. of Edn., 1990—. Author, editor: (biennial publ.) Handbook of Securities of U.S. Government, 1972-86. Mem. Am. Econ. Assn., Ea. Econ. Assn., Econometric Soc., Nat. Assn. Bus. Economists, Am. Statis. Assn., Beta Gamma Sigma (hon. soc.). Democrat. Jewish. Lodges: Knights Pythias, Knights Khorassan. Office: Credit Lyonnais Securities Hillcrest Econs Group Div 95 Wall St New York NY 10005-4201

PECK, H. DANIEL, literature educator; b. Milw., July 15, 1940; s. Henry Edward and Carmen (Barbulesco) P.; m. Patricia B. Wallace, Apr. 3, 1982; 1 child, Jennifer Peck. BA, Ohio Wesleyan U., 1962; MA, U. Iowa, 1971, PhD, 1974. Asst. prof. to assoc. prof. U. Calif., Santa Barbara, 1972-80; assoc. prof. Vassar Coll., Poughkeepsie, N.Y., 1980-83, prof. lit., 1983—, dir. Am. Culture program, 1989—. Author: Thoreau's Morning Work, 1990, A World by Itself: The Pastoral Moment in Cooper's Fiction, 1977; editor: The Green American Tradition, 1989, New Essays on the Last of the Mohicans, 1992. Am. Coun. Learned Socs. fellow, 1977-78, NEH fellow, 1984. Mem. MLA (chmn. div. 19th Century Am. lit. 1986), Am. Studies Assn. New Eng. Am. Studies Assn. (coun. 1991—), Am. Lit. Assn. Home: 139 College Ave Poughkeepsie NY 12603-2804 Office: Vassar Coll PO Box 226 Poughkeepsie NY 12602-0226

PECK, R. NICHOLAS, insurance company executive; b. Des Moines, Sept. 29, 1939; s. Wayne Scott and Alta Matilda (Carter) P. m. Jennie Christian Lister, Nov. 1, 1968; 1 child, Carter Lister. BA, U. of Mo., Columbia, 1966. Cert. casualty claim law assoc. Adjuster Travelers Ins. Cos. (C-P Claim), Kansas City, Mo., 1966-69; supr. Travelers Ins. Cos. (C-P Claim), N.Y.C., 1969-71; examiner Travelers Ins. Cos. (C-P Claim), Hartford, Conn., 1971-72; assoc. mgr. Travelers Ins. Cos. (C-P Claim), Newark, 1972-75; mgr. Travelers Ins. Cos. (C-P Claim), Balt., 1975-77; dir.-product liability Travelers Ins. Cos. (C-P Claim), Hartford, 1977-86, dir.-spl. liability (Law), 1986—. Co-author: Handling Casualty-Property Claims, 1984. With U.S. Army, 1960-63, Germany. Mem. Rotary (Paul Harris fellow 1990). Republican. Methodist. Home: 171 Wright Rd RFD Collinsville CT 06022 Office: Travelers Ins Co 1 Tower Sq-6PB Hartford CT 06183

PECKER, DAVID J., magazine publishing company president; b. N.Y.C., Sept. 24, 1951; m. Karen Balan, Oct. 31, 1987. BBA, Pace U., postgrad. CPA, N.Y. Sr. auditor Price Waterhouse & Co.; mgr. fin. reporting Diamandis Communications, Inc., N.Y.C., 1979; dir. fin. reporting Diamandis Communications, Inc., dir. acctg., asst. controller; chief oper. officer, chief fin. officer, exec. v.p. pub. Hachette Mags., Inc., N.Y.C., pres., chief oper. officer. Bd. dirs. Pace U., N.Y.C. Mem. Am. Mgmt. Assn., Mag. Pubs. Am. (exec. com.). Office: Hachette Mags Inc 1633 Broadway New York NY 10019-6708

PECORA, MARIA ANTONIA, income tax specialist, accountant; b. Bronxvillie, N.Y., May 30, 1956; d. Herbert Robert and Mary Catherine (Medico) P. BSBA in Acctg. and Fin., Fordham U., 1978; MBA in MIS, Iona Coll., 1982; cert. advanced corp. taxation, Pace U., 1987. Corp. auditor Gimbel Bros. Dept. Store, N.Y.C., 1978; tax auditor N.Y. State Dept. Revenue, White Plains, 1978-80; sales tax analyst Pitney Bowes Inc., Stamford, Conn., 1980-82; tax specialist Pitney Bowes Credit Corp., Norwalk, Conn., 1987-88, sr. tax specialist, 1988-89, supr. fed. income tax dept., 1989—, supr. sale/use of state income taxes, 1983-85, sr. tax analyst, 1985-87. Lions scholar, 1974. Mem. Assn. Women Accts. (bd. dirs. Westchester/Fairfield, Conn. chpts. 1985-87).

PEDALINO, MICHAEL DONALD, executive search consultant; b. East Orange, N.J., Jan. 10, 1931; s. Michael Joseph and Mary (Martino) P.; divorced; children: Cathy, Barbara, Michael, Cynthia. BS in Bus. Adminstrn., U. Ala., 1957. Div. personnel mgr. ITT Corp., N.Y.C., 1958-65; v.p. Kiernan & Co., N.Y.C., 1965-71, Battalia Lotz, N.Y.C., 1971-75; ptnr. Ernst & Whinney, N.Y.C., 1975-86; owner Michael D. Pedalino Assocs., Inc., N.Y.C., 1986-88; appointed ptnr. Internat. Mgmt. Advisors, Inc., N.Y.C., 1989—; cons. White House Task Force on Exec. Manpower, Washington, 1981. Bd. dirs. Veteran's Ensemble Theater Co., N.Y.C., 1981-82. Served to 1st lt. U.S. Army, 1951-55. Mem. Newcomen Soc., British Am. C. of C. Roman Catholic. Club: Union League (N.Y.C.). Home: 308 E 79th St Apt 7E New York NY 10021-0904 Office: Internat Mgmt Advisors 516 5th Ave New York NY 10036-7501

PEDDER, DOUGLAS MICHAEL, procurement manufacturing company director; b. Fall River, Mass., July 3, 1948; s. William F. and Josephine (Hanna) P.; m. Marie T. Beirola, Jan. 20, 1973; 1 child Jason D. Student, Bristol Community Coll., Bryant Coll. Dist. mgr. New Eng. dist. Lexington Textiles, N.Y.C., 1968-73; buyer. Lightolier, Inc., Fall River, Mass., 1974-76; purchasing mgr. Lightolier, Inc., Fall River, 1976-78, corp. dir. procurement, 1984—, new product devel. dir., 1990—; pres. Dynamic Mfg. & Procurement Assocs., Tiverton, R.I., 1989—; cons., writer Simon & Shuster, Conn., 1990-91. Contbr. articles to profl. jours. Supporter Annaugaral, Washington, 1985, Rep. Com., Washington, 1986. Recipient Value Analysis award, Purchasing Mag., Boston, 1979, 1986. Mem. Am. Purchasing Soc. (cert. purchasing profl. exec. 1985, exec. com., cert. com.), Nat. Assn. Purchasing Mgmt., Am. Prodn. Inventory Control Soc., S.E. Mass. Purchasing Mgrs. Assn. (sec. 1976-77, v.p., 1978-79, pres., 1979-80). Roman Catholic. Home: 183 Shove St Tiverton RI 02878-1232 Office: Lightolier Inc 631 Airport Rd Fall River MA 02720-4722

PEDERSEN, B(JARNE) MARTIN, graphic designer; b. Bklyn., Apr. 17, 1937; s. Bernt Olav and Clara (Larsen) P.; m. Arna T. Skaarva, Feb. 15, 1964; children: Ford Eric, Bjorn Christian, Christopher Alexander. Corp. design dir. Am. Airlines, 1966-68; owner Pedersen Design Inc., 1968-76; with Vance Johnson, Kit & Linda Hinrichs, N.Y.C., 1976-78; owner Jonson Pedersen Hinrichs & Shakery, Inc., N.Y.C., 1978-86; Graphis Press, 1986—; lect. and tchr. in field. Work exhibited in Whitney Mus., N.Y., William Paterson Coll., Wayne, N.J. Recipient over 300 major awards for creative work including Col. U. Nat. Mag. award, Herb Lubalin Meml. Mem. Am. Inst. Graphic Arts (former bd. dirs.), N.Y. Art Dirs. Club (former bd. dirs., 7 gold and 3 silver awards), Soc. Illustrators, Soc. Publ. Designers, Type Dirs. Club, Alliance Graphique Internat. Office: Pedersen Design Inc 141 Lexington Ave New York NY 10016-8191

PEDERSEN, CAROLYN HANFORD, artist; b. Syracuse, N.Y., Dec. 12, 1942; d. George Warner and Kathryn (Fox) Hanford; m. Thomas Keith Pedersen, Aug. 15, 1964; children: Thomas Scott, Kirsten Heidi. BS in Edn., Syracuse U., 1964, BS in Audiology and Speech Pathology, 1964. Tchr. watercolor Rockland Ctr. for Arts, West Nyack, N.Y., 1987—; adj. prof. watercolor Coll. of New Rochelle, N.Y., 1990—; represented by Fireside Gallery, Carmel, Calif., White Gallery, N.J., Tillet Gallery, St. Thomas, V.I. Exhibited in group shows at Springfield (Mo.) Mus., Allied Artist, N.Y.C., Audobon Artists, Mus. Fine Arts, Springfield, Mass., Neville Mus., Green Bay, Wis., Patterson (N.J.) Mus., Watercolor West Riverside (Calif.) Mus., Bergen Mus., N.J., others; represented in permanent collections at Mus. Galleries of Hebrew Home for Aged, Riverdale, N.Y.C., Rockland County, New City, N.Y., G.C. Hanford Mfg. Co., Syracuse, N.Y., Minigrip Corp., Community Savs. Bank, Mt. Holyoke, Mass., others; included in "Splash" best contemporary watercolorists, 1991. Juror for local and regional art orgns.; demonstrator watercolors to various orgns.; pres., bd. dirs. Art & Craft Assn. of Rockland, 1975-85; mem. exhbn. com. Rockland Ctr. for Arts, West Nyack, 1988-91. Recipient Traveling Exhbn. award Am. Watercolor Soc., 1984, Dimauro Com. award Acad. Artists Assn., 1985, William Kowalsky Meml. award Adirondack Nat. Exhbn., 1985. Fellow Am. Artist Profl. League; mem. Nat. Watercolor Soc., Nat. Assn. Women Artists, N.E. Watercolor Soc. (membership chmn. 1989-91, Pres.'s award 1990), Artists Equity, Audubon Artist (Alice Melrose Meml. award 1989), Catherine Lorillard Wolfe Art Club (asst. treas. 1990—, Katherine Lovell award 1985, 90).

PEDERSEN, CHRISTINE FRANCES, accountant; b. Camden, N.J., Oct. 25, 1947; d. Walter Edward and Frances B. (Mittleman) P. BA, Rutgers U., 1969. CPA, N.J. Account Liebman & Sandrow CPAs, Cherry Hill, N.J., 1968-76; pvt. practice CPA Haddonfield, N.J., 1976-90; CPA, ptnr. Pedersen & Pedersen CPAs PC, Haddonfield, 1990—. Mem. N.J. Soc. CPA's (pres. 1983-84), AICPA. Office: Pedersen & Pedersen CPA PC 211 Kings Hwy E PO Box 2005 Haddonfield NJ 08033

PEDERSEN, KAREN SUE, electrical engineer; b. Indianola, Iowa, Apr. 27, 1942; d. Donald Cecil and Dorothy Darlene (Frazier) Kading; m. Wendell Dean Pedersen, May 6, 1961; children: Debra Ann Pedersen Schwickerath, Michael Dean. AA, Grand View Coll., Des Moines, 1975; BSEE, Iowa State U., 1977; MBA, Bentley Coll., Waltham, Mass., 1988. Registered profl. engr., Mass. Engr. Iowa Power & Light Co., Des Moines, 1978-80, rate engr., 1980-84; sr. rsch. engr. Boston Edison Co., Boston, 1984-87, sr. engr., 1987—. Ops. chmn. Old South Ch., Boston, 1989-92. Mem. IEEE (Iowa cen. chpt. chmn. 1983-89), Mass. Soc. of Profl. Engrs. (pres.-elect 1991-92), Nat. Soc. Profl. Engrs., Eta Kappa Nu. Republican. Congregationalist. Office: Boston Edison Co 800 Boylston P283A Boston MA 02199

PEDERSEN, WESLEY NIELS, public relations and public affairs executive; b. South Sioux City, Nebr., July 10, 1922; s. Peder Westergaard and Marie Gertrude (Sorensen) P.; m. Angela Kathryn Vavra, Oct. 17, 1948; 1 son, Eric Wesley. Student, Tri-State Coll., Sioux City, Iowa, 1940-41; BA summa cum laude, Upper Iowa U.; postgrad., George Washington U., 1958-59. Editor, writer Sioux City Jour., 1941-50; corr. N.Y. Times, Life, Time, Fortune, 1948-50; editor Dept. State, 1950-53; fgn. svc. officer Dept. State, Hong Kong, 1960-63; fgn. affairs columnist, roving corr., counselor summit meetings and fgn. ministers confs. USIA, 1953-60, chief, worldwide spl. publs. and graphics programs, 1963-69; chief Office Spl. Projects, Washington, 1969-78, Office Spl. Projects, Internat. Communication Agy., 1978-79; v.p. Fraser Assocs., pub. rels., Washington, 1979-80; dir. communications and pub. rels. Pub. Affairs Coun., Washington, 1980—; lectr. creative communications Upper Iowa U., 1975; chmn., Europe, Ambassadorial Internat. Affairs Seminar, Fgn. Svc. Inst., 1975; lectr. internat. pub. rels. Pub. Rels. Inst., Am. U., 1976; lectr. bus. and mgmt. div. NYU, 1976, 77, 78; cons. pub. rels., editorial and design; del. founding sessions 1st Amendment Congress, Phila. and Williamsburg, Va., 1980, exec. com., 1980. Columnist: Pub. Rels. Jour., 1980-85; author: Legacy of a President, 1964, American Heroes of Asian Wars, 1969; co-author: Effective Government Public Affairs, 1981; editor: Escape At Midnight and Other Stories (Pearl S. Buck), 1962, Exodus From China (Harry Redl), 1962, China's Men of Letters (K. E. Priestley), 1963, Children of China (Pearl S. Buck and Margaret Wylie), 1963, The Americans and the Arts (Howard Taubman), 1969, The Dance in America (Agnes de Mille), 1969, Getting the Most from Grassroots Public Affairs Programs, 1980, Cost-Effective Management for Today's Public Affairs, 1987, Making Community Relations Pay Off: Tools and Strategies, 1988, Winning at the Grassroots: How to Succeed in the Legislative Arena by Mobilizing Employees and Other Allies, 1989, Leveraging State Government Relations, 1990, Managing the Business-Employee PAC, 1992, Pub. Affairs Rev. mag., 1980-86, Impact newsletter on nat. and internat. pub. affairs, 1980—; contbr. to The Commissar, 1972, Informing the People: A Public Affairs Handbook, 1981, The Practice of Public Relations, 1984; mem. editorial bd. Pub. Rels. Quar., 1975—, Fgn. Svc. Jour., 1975-81; mem. adv. bd. Pub. Rels. News, 1991—; contbr. articles to profl. jours. Founding chmn. bd. dirs. Nat. Inst. for Govt. Pub. Info. Rsch., Am. U., 1977-80. Served with USAAF, 1943-46. Recipient 2 awards A.P. Mng. Editors Assn., Iowa, 1949, Meritorious Svc. award USIA, 1963, Presdl. Commendation, 1964, 1st prizes Fed. Editors Assn., 1970, 74-75, 1st prizes Soc. Tech. Communication, 1974, 75-76, Gold award Internat. Newsletter Conf., 1982, Silver award, 1985, Eddi award for design excellence Editor's Workshop, 1983, Gold Circle award for outstanding communications Am. Soc. Assn. Execs., 1988-89, Editors' Forum award, 1988-90, Assn. Trends award, 1989-92, Grand prize Nat. Ann. Report Conf., 1989, Communications Concepts awards, 1989-92, MerComm awards, 1990-91, Nat. Media Conf. award, 1989, 90; named Most Outstanding Info. Officer in Exec. Br., Govt. Info. Orgn., 1975, Ky. Col. and Adm. Nebr. Navy, 1984. Mem. Am. Fgn. Svc. Assn., Internat. Assn. Bus. Communicators (Communicator of Yr. Washington chpt. 1978, various awards 1973, 76-78, 84, 90), Nat. Assn. Govt. Communicators (pres. 1978-79, Communicator of Yr. 1977, Disting. Svc. award 1978), Pub. Rels. Soc. Am. (mem. Counselor's Acad. 1980—, chmn. 1st Amendment task force 1980-81, co-recipient Thoth award 1980, 81), Fgn. Svc. Club, Nat. Press Club, Overseas Press Club. Episcopalian. Home: 5214 Sangamore Rd Bethesda MD 20816-2322 Office: Pub Affairs Coun 1019 19th St NW Ste 200 Washington DC 20036-5105

PEDITTO, STEPHANIE M., law clerk; b. Drexel Hill, Pa., Mar. 25, 1950; d. Philip and Martha (Provenzano) P. BA, Wilmington Coll., 1972; JD, No. Va. Law Sch., 1982. Scheduler Fitzpatrick/Klenk Campaigns, Phila., 1973; asst. Indsl. Valley Bank, Phila., 1975-76; scheduler Green for U.S. Senate, Phila., 1976; ct. crier U.S. Ct. Appeals (3d cir.), Phila., 1979-80; law clk. Elias B. Landau, Phila., 1985-87, ind. contractor, Wynnewood, Pa., 1987—. Campaign aide Thomas J. Stapleton for State Rep., Drexel Hill, 1974. Democrat. Roman Catholic.

PEDOWICZ, LEE RICHARD, electrical engineer; b. Bklyn., Sept. 19, 1952; s. Jack Max and Beatrice Belle (Rencoff) P.; 1 child, Jaclyn Michelle. BSEE, Washington Univ., St. Louis, 1974; MS, Ohio State U., 1975. Registered profl. engr., N.Y. Asst. engr. Sargent & Lundy, Engrs., Chgo., 1975-78; assoc. engr. Am. Electric Power Svc. Corp., N.Y.C., 1978; field engr. L.I. Lighting Co., Hicksville, N.Y., 1978-85; sr. system operator Consol. Edison, N.Y.C., 1985-88, gen. supervising engr., 1989-91; subsection mgr., 1991-92; mgr. Consol. Edison, N.Y.C., 1992—. Capt. Dix Hills Fire Dept., 1984; firefighter New Hyde Park Fire Dept., 1989; mem. New Hyde Park Parks and Recreation Commn. Named Man of Yr., Dix Hills Fire Dept., 1982. Mem. IEEE, Power Engring. Soc., Nat. Fire Protection Assn., State Assn. Fire Chiefs, Ohio State U. Alumni Assn., Wasington U. William Greenleaf Eliot Soc., Kappa Sigma. Jewish. Office: Consolidated Edison Co 98 40 Christie Ave Corona NY 11368

PEEBLES, J(OHN) LEONARD, psychologist, consultant; b. Oil City, Pa., Nov. 17, 1949; s. John Cornell Peebles and Harriet Jean (Swartzlander) Mason; m. Barbara F. O'Keeffe, July 27, 1985; 1 child, Alyson Taylor. BA, U. Fla., 1971; MA, Western Mich. U., 1974; postgrad., Boston Coll. Psychologist III Wrentham (Mass.) St. Sch., 1976-88; staff psychologist Bridgewater (Mass.) St. Hosp.; pres. Strategies of Limiting Violent Episodes, Inc., Mansfield, Mass., 1991—. Contbr. chpt. to book. Mem. APA, Assn. for Advancement of Behavioral Therapy, Am. Assn. for Mental Retardation, Assn. for Behavioral Analysis. Home: 5 Pine St Mansfield MA 02048-1721 Office: SOLVE Inc PO Box 237 Mansfield MA 02048-0002

PEELER, MARIE DONA, direct mail company executive; b. Havre de Grace, Md., Sept. 14, 1960; d. Grady Lee and Thelma Marie (Hales) P. Student, Va. Commonwealth U., 1978-80; BS, Towson State U., 1982. Sales mgr., asst. buyer, group mgr. N.J. div. Macy's, Newark, 1981-87; dir. warehouse ops. Bruce McGaw Graphics, Inc., N.Y.C., 1987-88; gen. mgr. Asbury Park Press div. Addresses Unltd., Neptune, N.J., 1988-92; mgr. list svcs. Mailing Svcs., Inc., Hillside, N.J., 1992—; co-chmn. Monmouth County Postal Customer Coun., Red Bank, N.J., 1990—, mem., 1988—; vice-chmn. Postal Customer Coun. Mid N.J., Trenton, 1990-92, mem., 1989—; mem. Kilmer Postal Customer Coun., New Brunswick, N.J., 1990—. Mem. bus. adv. bd. United Cerebral Palsy Lehmann Tech. Edn. Ctr., Neptune, 1991—; neighborhood vol. Am. Cancer Soc., Monmouth County, N.J., 1991. Mem. Mail Advt. Svc. Assn. Internat. (com. mem. 1991-92, editorial adv. bd.). Office: Mailing Svcs Inc 1319 N Broad St Hillside NJ 07205

PEENEY, JAMES DOYLE, executive search consultant; b. Trenton, N.J., Feb. 28, 1933; s. William C. and Emily (Courtney) P.; m. Dorothy Shestko, Aug. 3, 1957; children: Timothy J., Jennifer L., Thomas D. BA, U. Pa., 1955; postgrad., Temple U., 1955-56, U. Mich., 1962-65; MBA, Seton Hall, 1968. Trainee Ford Motor Co., Dearborn, Mich., 1962-65; recruiting mgr. Merck & Co., Rahway, N.J., 1965-68; assoc. Boyden Assocs., N.Y.C., 1968-72; v.p. pers. Mfrs. Hanover Trust, N.Y.C., 1973-74; v.p. Drake Beam Morin, N.Y.C., 1974-78, Goodrich & Sherwood, N.Y.C., 1978-80; pres. Peeney Assocs. Inc., Fanwood, N.J., 1980—. Dist. chmn. Watchung area coun. Boy Scouts Am., Mountainside, N.J., 1976—. Named one of Fifty Leading Retainer Search Films U.S. Exec. Recruiter News, Fitzwilliam, N.H., 1986-88. Mem. Internat. Assn. Corp. and Profl. Recruiters, Princeton Club (N.Y.C.), Renaissance Club (Detroit). Office: Peeney Assoc Inc 141 South Ave Fanwood NJ 07023-1224

PEEPLES, EDWIN AUGUSTUS, advertising executive, author; b. Atlanta, Mar. 2, 1915; s. Edwin Augustus and Robyn Latham (Young) P.; BS, Ga. Inst. Tech., 1936; m. Malvine Lewis Ogle, Mar. 17, 1945; children: Edwin Augustus III, Charles Lewis, Christopher. Copywriter, James A. Greene, Advt., Atlanta, 1936-38; pres. Sudite Chem. Corp., Atlanta, 1938-42, Ordnance Dept., U.S. Army, Phila., 1942-45; mem. editorial staff Fortune mag., 1945; cons. editor Lab. for Reseach & Devel., Franklin Inst., 1946-50; Phila. contracting officer C.E. Phila., 1950-54; sr. v.p., pub. relations dir. Gray & Rogers, Inc., Phila., 1955-72; self-employed advt. agt., Phoenixville, Pa., 1972—; lectr. in field. Bd. dirs. Valley Forge Hist. Soc., 1973-84. Mem. Authors Guild, Phila. Children's Reading Roundtable. Club: Countrymen's (pres. 1976-87). Author: Swing Low, 1945, English edit., 1946; A Professional Story Writer's Handbook, 1960; Blue Boy, 1964; A Hole in the Hill, 1969; Summary for 150th Anniversary History of the Pennsylvania Horticultural Society, 1977, An Inquisitive Eye, 1992; contbr., cons. editor County Lines, 1979—; columnist Country Jour., 1989—; contbr. stories and articles to gen. mags. and profl. jours. Address: Vixen Hill 1611 Kimbeitin Rd Phoenixville PA 19460

PEERS, MICHAEL GEOFFREY, archbishop; b. Vancouver, B.C., Can., July 31, 1934; s. Geoffrey Hugh and Dorothy Enid (Mantle) P.; m. Dorothy Elizabeth Bradley, June 29, 1963; children: Valerie Anne Leslie, Richard Christopher Andre, Geoffrey Stephen Arthur. Zert.dolm., U. Heidelberg, Fed. Republic Germany, 1955; BA, U. B.C., Vancouver, 1956; Licentiate in Theology, Trinity Coll., Toronto, Ont., 1959, DD (hon.), 1977; DD (hon.), St. John's Coll., Winnipeg, Man., 1981, Wycliffe Coll., Toronto, 1987, Kent U., Canterbury, Eng., 1988, Montreal Diocesan Coll., Que., Can., 1989, Coll. of Emmanual and St. Chad, Sask., Can., 1990, Vancouver Sch. Theology, 1991, Thorneloe U., 1991. Ordained to ministry Anglican Ch. as deacon, 1959, as priest, 1960, consecrated bishop, 1977. Asst. curate St. Thomas Ch., Ottawa, 1959-61; chaplain U. Ottawa, 1961-66; rector St. Bede's Ch., Winnipeg, 1966-72, St. Martin's Ch., Winnipeg, 1972-74; dean of Qu'Appelle, Regina, Sask., 1974-77; bishop Qu'Appelle, 1977-82, archbishop, 1982-86; primate The Anglican Ch. Can., 1986—; instr. Ottawa Tchrs. Coll., 1962-66, St. Paul's High Sch., Winnipeg, 1967-69. Office: Anglican Ch Can, Church House 600 Jarvis St, Toronto, ON Canada M4Y 2J6

PEIRCE, GEORGIA WILSON, public relations executive; b. Newton, Mass., Jan. 6, 1960; d. Norris Ridgeway and Anne (McCusker) P. BA, Duke U., 1982. Intern to Speaker of Ho. of Reps., Washington, 1981; prin. PR, etc., Quincy, Mass., 1987—; cons. Mass. Group Insur. Commn., 1985. Contbr. articles to profl. jours. Mem. community rels. com. Vis. Nurse Assn./Hospice of South Shore; mem. com. to elect Mondale-Ferraro, Mass., coord. speakers bur., 1984; mem. charitable trust com. Maj. John F. Regan; com. mem. City of Quincy Recycling Com.; del. Mass. Dem. Conv., 1982, 83; v.p. South Shore Ad Club, 1990-91, mem.-at-large, 1991-92. Recipient Ninth Wave awards, 1989, 1st pla. in Pub. Rels. award, 1989, merit awards,

1992. Mem. NAFE, South Shore C. of C., Small Bus Assn. New Eng., Women's Golf Assn. Mass., Publicity Club New Eng. (Merit Bell Ringer award), Eastward Ho! Country Club Chatham (club champion 1977-81, '83, '91), Wollaston Golf Club. Democrat. Roman Catholic. Home: 71 Bayfield Rd N Quincy MA 02171-2005 Office: PR etc PO Box 172 Quincy MA 02170-0001

PEISER, HERBERT STEFFEN, chemist, consultant; b. Berlin, Aug. 19, 1917; came to U.S., 1957; s. Herbert and Nelly Berta (Tarlau) P.; m. Primrose Elizabeth Elliot, May 7, 1949; children: Primrose Clare Goodman, Georgina Jane Dreibelbis, Alison Jeannie Kretser. BA, Cambridge (Eng.) U., 1939, MA, 1943; DSc, Chungnam Nat. U., Taejon, Korea, 1979. Rsch. crystallographer ICI Ltd., Winnington Cheshire, Eng., 1941-47; sr. lectr. London U., 1947-48; researcher in metallurgy Hadfields Ltd., Sheffield, Eng., 1948-57; rsch. chemist U.S. Nat. Bur. of Standards, Washington, 1957-79; cons. Nat. Inst. Standards and Tech., Gaithersburg, Md., 1979—; cons. Joint Rsch. Centre Commn. of the European Communities, 1984—; cons. U.K. Atomic Energy Rsch. Establishment, Harwell, 1942-45; rsch. fellow Harvard U., Cambridge, 1965-66; vis. scholar Physikalisch-Technische Bundesanstalt, Brunswick, Germany, 1992; head Nat. Bur. Standards Office Internat. Rels., 1969-79; co-sec. panel 5 U.S./Japan Coop. Sci. and Tech. Program, 1962-68; cons. State Dept., AID, USIA, World Bank, Asian Devel. Bank, various UN agys., 1979-91; devel. advisor various govts., 1961-91; U.S. nat. rep. Commn. for Atomic Weights and Isotopic Abondances, Internat. Union Pure and Applied Chemistry, 1987-91. Author, editor: Crystallography, Crystal Growth, 1942-90; contbr. articles to profl. jours. Mem. AAAS, Am. Chem. Soc., Am. Phys. Soc., Cosmos Club. Episcopalian. Home: 638 Blossom Dr Rockville MD 20850-2041 Office: Nat Inst Standards and Tech Adminstrn Bldg 101 Rm 505 Gaithersburg MD 20899

PEIXOTTO, HELEN ESTHER, clinical psychologist, consultant; b. N.Y.C., Apr. 7, 1913. BA, Coll. Mt. St. Vincent, 1934; MA, Columbia U., 1937; PhD, Fordham U., 1940. Lic. psychologist, D.C., Md. Instr. Wheaton Coll., Norton, Mass., 1943-46; asst. psychologist Psychol. Clinic, Honolulu, 1946-49; assoc. prof. Cath. U., Washington, 1949-78; ind. cons. Washington, 1978—. Home and Office: 6451 31st St NW Washington DC 20015-2341

PEIZER, MAURICE SAMUEL, retired medical advertising consultant; b. Hartford, Conn., Aug. 21, 1912; s. David I. and Mary (Pomerantz) P.; BA in Premed. Scis., U. Pa., 1933; tchr.'s cert. in English, Latin and Sci., 1937; postgrad. in journalism Columbia U., 1945, 49, 50; m. Marjorie Knowlton, Aug. 25, 1951; children: Joy P. Gorson, Miriam P. Michalski, Jessica Cathleen (dec.). Asst. to acting chief POW dept. U.S. Office of Censorship, N.Y.C., 1943-45; med. advt. writer Paul Klemtner & Co., Inc., Newark., 1946-52, asst. copy chief, 1952-53, tech. dir. of copy, 1953-57, tech. dir., 1957-58, copy chief, 1958-62; sr. writer, pharm. copy chief, Hutchins Advt. Co., Rochester (N.Y.), 1962-67; group copy supr. William Douglas McAdams Inc., N.Y.C., 1967-78, assoc. creative dir./copy, 1978-79, copy dir., 1979-80; founder Health Care Communications, Cedar Grove, N.J., 1980-90; med. proofreader, editor Metro Transcription Svc., Bloomfield, N.J., 1990—. Pres. Nutley (N.J.) Little Theatre, 1957-59; co-founder Penfield (N.Y.) Players, pres., 1967; mem. publicity com. Nutley (N.J.) Citizens for Kennedy, 1960; mem. ofcl. bd. Meth. Ch., Penfield, N.Y., 1963-67; chmn. missions com. Community Ch., Cedar Grove, N.J., 1969-71, long-range planning com., 1972-74, deacon, 1985-87, pres. Couples Club, 1988, trustee, 1991—; trustee, publicity writer Family and Children's Svcs. of North Essex, 1984-89, Phone Alert Adv. Coun., 1990-91; trustee, pub. rels. dir. Cedar Grove Hist. Soc., 1990—. Fellow Am. Med. Writers Assn. (pres. Met. N.Y. chpt. 1975-76, mem. nat. bd. dirs. 1973-82, chmn. fellowships awards com. 1976-77, mem. exec. com. 1977-80, dir. dept. membership affairs 1977-80, Met. N.Y. chpt. Disting. Service award 1978, Nat. Pres.'s award 1981); mem. AAAS, Pharm. Advt. Council of N.Y. (Med. Copywriting Faculty 1987). Editor CGHS Newsletter (Cert. of Excellence), 1991. Home: 135 Sunrise Ter Cedar Grove NJ 07009-1424 Office: Metro Transcription Svc 1455 Broad St Bloomfield NJ 07003

PEKICH, ELIZABETH KRAMS, lawyer; b. Cheverly, Md., Oct. 14, 1948; d. Harry Francis and Jeanne Elizabeth (Edwards) Krams; children: Stephen Christopher, Elizabeth Juliet, Alexander Eli. BS magna cum laude, U. Md., 1977; JD, George Washington U., 1982. Bar: D.C. 1983. Adminstr. Raleigh Stores Corp., Washington, 1973-83; atty. Lansfam Mgmt. Corp., Balt., 1983—, corp. sec., 1986—. V.p., dir. Sidney Lansburgh III Found., 1989—; bd. dirs. Debel Foods Corp., Elizabeth, N.J., 1986. Mem. ABA, D.C. Bar Assn., Alpha Sigma Lambda, Phi Kappa Phi. Roman Catholic. Home: 10210 Riggs Rd Hyattsville MD 20783-1213 Office: Lansfam Mgmt Corp 300 E Lombard St Ste 15 Baltimore MD 21202-3226

PELADEAU, PIERRE, publishing company executive; b. Montreal, Que., Can., Apr. 11, 1925; s. Henri and Elmire (Fortier) P.; m. Raymonde Chopin, May 26, 1954; children: Eric, Isabelle, Pierre-Karl, Anne-Marie; m. Line Parisien, May 24, 1979; children: Esther, Pierre Jr., Jean. L.Ph., U. Montreal, 1945, M.A., 1947; B.C.L., McGill U., Montreal, 1950. With Quebecor Inc.; pub., printing and forest products holding co. exec. Quebecor Inc., Montreal, 1965—; editor, pres., chief exec. officer Quebecor Inc., 1965—; bd. dirs. Donohue Inc., Sodarcan Inc. Decorated Order of Can., Order of Que. Club: Saint-Denis. Office: Quebecor Inc, 612 St Jacques St, Montreal, PQ Canada H3C 4M8

PELAVIN, DIANE CHRISTINE, small business owner; b. Pensacola, Fla., Nov. 13, 1943; d. Raymond Thomas and LaVerne Norma (Rousch) Blakemore; m. Sol H. Pelavin, Aug. 14, 1966; children: Shayna, Adam. BA, So. Ill. U., 1965; MS, San Jose (Calif.) State U., 1979. Tchr. English Chgo. Pub. Schs., 1965-66; tchr. English and social studies East Prairie Sch., Skokie, Ill., 1966-68; planning analyst Electric Power Rsch. Inst., Palo Alto, Calif., 1977-78; rsch. analyst NTS Rsch. Corp., Durham, N.C., 1978-82; v.p. Pelavin Assocs., Inc., Washington, 1982—; pres. Chesapeake Inst., Washington, 1991. Contbr. numerous articles to profl. jours. Organizer Recycling Ctr., Carbondale, Ill., 1971; leader Brownie, Girl Scouts U.S., Palo Alto, 1977; vol. Chapel Hill (N.C.) Pub. Schs., 1979, Montgomery County (Md.) Schs., 1985-89. U. Chgo. fellow, 1966, NSF fellow, 1968. Mem. Am. Edn. Rsch. Assn. Office: 2030 M St NW Washington DC 20036-3306

PELCYGER, IRAN, principal; b. Bklyn., Feb. 26, 1937; s. Jacob and Yetta (Nabridge) P.; m. Elaine Morley, June 4, 1956; children: Stuart Lawrence, Gwynne Ellice, Wayne Farrol. BS, CCNY, 1959, MA in Sci. and Edn., 1962; postgrad., Yeshiva U., 1963, Adelphi U. and NYU, 1964-67, 68-74. Cert. tchr., ednl. adminstr., N.Y. Tchr., adminstr. various pub. schs., Bklyn., 1959—; tchr., acting chmn. sci. dept., chmn. program dept. Jr. High Sch. 265, Bklyn., 1959-66; tchr. aerospace and gen. sci., chmn. sci. dept. Jr. High Sch. 111, Bklyn., 1966-71, asst. prin., 1971-74; prin. Frances E. Carter Sch., Bklyn., 1974—; adj. instr. Sch. Edn., CCNY, 1988—; mem. ad-hoc com. elem. edn., N.Y. Dept. Edn., 1987, mem. organizing com., moderator edn. conf., 1986—. Contbg. editor: A Guide for Elementary Sch. Prins., 1985, Proceedings of the Mainstream Conf.: Opening Doors to a Brighter Future, 1988; co-writer: Mainstreaming Handbook: A Guide to Implementing. Mem. N.Y.C. Elem. Sch. Prins. Assn. (past pres.), Coun. Suprs. and Adminstrs. (past v.p., exec. bd. 1983—, trustee Welfare Fudn 1986—), N.Y. Acad. Pub. Edn., Nat. Assn. Elem. Sch. Prins., Network for Effective Schs., ASCD, Phi Delta Kappa. Home: 79 Sheryl Cres Smithtown NY 11787-1321 Office: Frances E Carter Sch 242 Cooper St Brooklyn NY 11207-1395

PELL, CLAIBORNE, senator; b. N.Y.C., Nov. 22, 1918; s. Herbert Claiborne and Matilda (Bigelow) P.; m. Nuala O'Donnell, Dec. 1944; children: Herbert Claiborne III, Christopher T. Hartford, Nuala Dallas Yates, Julia L.W. Student, St. George's Sch., Newport, R.I.; A.B. cum laude, Princeton U., 1940; A.M., Columbia U., 1946; 39 hon. degrees. Enlisted USCGR, 1941; served as seaman, ensign North Atlantic sea duty, Africa, Italy; hospitalized to U.S., 1944; instr. Navy Sch. Mil. Govt., Princeton, 1944-45; capt. USCGR; ret.; on loan to State Dept. at San Francisco Conf., 1945, State Dept., 1945-46, U.S. embassy, Czechoslovakia, 1946-47; established consulate gen. Bratislava, Czechoslovakia, 1947-48; vice consul Genoa, Italy, 1949; assigned State Dept., 1950-52; v.p., dir. Internat. Rescue Com.; senator from R.I., 1961—; U.S. del. Internat. Maritime Consultative Orgn., London, 1959, 25th Gen. Assembly, 1970. Author: Megalopolis Unbound, 1966, (with Harold L. Goodwin) Challenge of the Seven Seas, 1966, Power and Policy, 1972. Hon. bd. dirs. World Affairs Council R.I.; trustee St. George's Sch.; trustee emeritus Brown U.; Cons. Democratic Nat. Com., 1953-60; exec. asst. to chmn. R.I. State Dem. Com., 1952-54; chmn. R.I. Dem. Fund drive, 1952, Dem. nat. registration, chmn., 1956, co-chmn., 1962; chief delegation tally clk. Dem. Nat. Conv., 1956, 60, 64, 68. Decorated knight Crown of Italy, Grand Cross Order of Merit Italy, Red Cross of Merit Portugal, Legion of Honor France, comdr. Order of Phoenix Greece, Grand Cross Order of Merit Liechtenstein, Grand Cross Order of Christ Portugal, Order of Henry the Navigator, Portugal, Grand Cross Order of N. Star Sweden, Grand Cross of Merit Knights of Malta, Grand Officer of Merit Luxembourg, Grand Comdr. Lebanon; recipient Caritas Elizabeth medal Cardinal Franz Koenig, Grand decoration of honor in silver with sash Austria, Gold medal of St. Barnabas (Cyprus), recipient Pres.'s Fellow award R.I. Sch. Design, medal Nat. Order of Cedar, Hugo Grotius Commemorative medal The Netherlands. Mem. Soc. Cin. Episcopalian. Clubs: Hope (Providence); Knickerbocker (N.Y.C.); Racquet and Tennis (N.Y.C.), Brook (N.Y.C.); Metropolitan (Washington); Travellers (Paris); Reading Room (Newport); White's (London). Office: US Senate 335 Russell Senate Bldg Washington DC 20510*

PELL, EDWARD SERGEI, author, editor; b. Balt., Apr. 5, 1950; s. Sergei Feodorovich and Dorothy (Prendergast) P. Student, CUNY, 1977; postgrad., Columbia U., 1977-78. Editor Kitchen & Bath Bus., N.Y.C., 1978—. Author: To the Martian Opera, 1991, (screenplay) The Big Lizard, 1990, Fighting Freddie, 1991, (with Leslie Anderson) More Up, 1988. Henry James fellow Columbia U. Sch. Fine Arts, 1977-78. Mem. Mensa. Democrat. Home: 1023 47th St Brooklyn NY 11219 Office: Miller Freeman 1515 Broadway New York NY 10036

PELL, SIDNEY, epidemiologist; b. N.Y.C., Dec. 13, 1922; m. Lola May, July 2, 1950. MBA, CCNY, 1952; PhD, U. Pitts., 1956. Biostatistician E.I. Du Pont de Nemours and Co., Wilmington, Del., 1955-76, mgr. epidemiology sect., 1976-82, sr. cons., 1982-85; epidemiology cons. Wilmington, 1985—; epidemiology cons. Del. Div. Pub. Health, Dover, 1986—. Contbr. articles to New Eng. Jour. Medicine, Jour. Occupational Medicine, Jour. AMA. With U.S. Army, 1943-45, ETO. Recipient Merit in Authorship Hon. Mention, Inds. Med. Assn., 1959. Fellow Am. Coll. Epidemiology, Am. Heart Assn., Am. Pub. Health Assn. Home: 1416 Emory Rd Wilmington DE 19803-5120

PELLAND, PAUL JOSEPH, advertising executive, educator; b. Lowell, Mass., Jan. 24, 1954; s. Norman Joseph and Doris May (LeClair) P.; m. Denise Ann Desrochers, Oct. 8, 1977; children: Allison, Jonathan. AA in Liberal Arts, North Essex Community Coll., Haverhill, Mass., 1973; BA in History and Edn., U. Lowell, 1977. Tchr. jr. high sch. Litchfield (N.H.) Sch. System, 1977-79; dist. mgr. Lowell Sun Pub. Co., 1979-81, mgr. coop. advt., 1981-87; mgr. retail advt. Telegraph Pub. Co., Nashua, N.H., 1987-91, Harte-Hanks Community Newspaper, Framingham, Mass., 1991—; instr. advt. and mktg. Newbury Jr. Coll., Brookline, Mass., 1986—; discussion leader Am. Press Inst., Reston, Va., 1988, 89. Mem. Internat. Newspaper Advt. Mktg. Execs., New Eng. Newspaper Assn., New Eng. Newspaper Advt. Execs. Assn. (bd. dirs. 1990—), Co-op New Eng. (bd. dirs. 1990—). Home: 21 Virginia Rd Tyngsboro MA 01879-2350 Office: Harte-Hanks Community 33 New York Ave Framingham MA 01701-5401

PELLEGRINO, FRANCESCO, physicist; b. Naples, Italy, Jan. 10, 1950; came to U.S., 1960; s. Vincenzo and Antonietta (Cirillo) P.; m. Linda Chester, July 25, 1986; children: Francesco, John, Maria. BS, CCNY, 1972; M, CUNY, 1979, PhD, 1981. Rsch. assoc. Picosecond Laser and Spectroscopy Lab., N.Y.C., 1973-81; sr. engr. Sperry Systems Mgmt. Co., Great Neck, N.Y., 1982—; asst. prof. CCNY, 1980-82; assoc. prof. Queensborough Coll., N.Y.C., 1982-83. Inventor Tanning Aid, 1984; contbr. chpts. in books, articles to profl. jour. Recipient Generoso Pope Meml. award Il Progresso 1968, award Mechanix Illustrated 1968. Mem. Am. Phys. Soc., Soc. Photoinstrumentation Engrs. Office: Paramax 365 Lakeville Rd Great Neck NY 11020

PELLEGRINO, PETER, surgeon; b. Camden, N.J., July 7, 1934; s. Peter and Alice (Alchin) P.; m. Barbara Ann Holdon, June 18, 1960; children—Peter Scott, Kathleen Ann, Lisa Marie. A.B. in Psychology, Franklin-Marshall Sch., 1956; M.D., Hahnemann Med. Coll., 1960. Diplomate Am. Bd. Surgery. Intern, Hahnemann Hosp., Phila., 1960-61, surg. resident, 1961-62, surg. resident, 1965-67, 68, attending surgeon, 1969—; chief dept. surgery Kessler Hosp., Hammonton, N.J., 1969—. Served to capt., U.S. Army, 1962-65. Fellow ACS; mem. Am. Acad. Proctology, Soc. Abdominal Surgeons, AMA, N.J. Med. Soc., Hahnemann Alumni Assn. (1st v.p. 1984). Republican. Home: 3 Stafford Ct Berlin NJ 08009-2209 Office: 777 Profl Ctr Hammonton NJ 08037

PELLER, ALLAN WAYNE, publisher; b. Paterson, N.J., Feb. 3, 1942; s. Nathan L. and Dorothy (Sauer) P.; m. Barbara M. Feit, June 15, 1966; children: Melissa H., Neil L. BA, Upsala Coll., 1970. V.p. Troll Assocs., Mahwah, N.J., 1963-72; pres. A. W. Peller & Assocs., Hawthorne, N.J., 1972—; pres., pub. January Prodns., Inc., Hawthorne, 1973—, Ednl. Impressions, Inc., Hawthorne, 1983—. Mem. Nat. Sch. Supply & Equipment Assn., Ednl. Distbrs. Supply Assn., ALA. Office: January Prodns Inc 210 6th Ave Hawthorne NJ 07506-1556

PELLER, BARBARA M., educational products company executive, author; b. Paterson, N.J., Mar. 13, 1945; d. Nathan H. and Evelyn (Stark) Feit; m. Allan W. Peller, June 15, 1966; children: Melissa, Neil. BA, Douglas Coll., Rutgers U., 1966. Tchr. Glen Rock (N.J.) High Sch., 1966-69; editor January Prodns., Inc., Hawthorne, N.J., 1973-83, creative dir., 1983—; catalog coord., product selection A.W. Peller & Assocs., Hawthorne, 1975—. Author, editor Ednl. Impressions, Inc., Hawthorne, 1985—; author workbooks, study units, audiovisual scripts. Mem. Nat. Assn. for Gifted Children. Office: January Prodns Inc 210 6th Ave Hawthorne NJ 07507

PELLETIER, CLAUDE HENRI, biomedical engineer; b. Riviere-Ouelle, Can., Que., Dec. 15, 1941; s. Lucien Pelletier and Ernestine Michaud. Immatriculation sr., Coll. Universitaire U. Sherbrooke, 1961; B.Sc.A., U. Sherbrooke, 1966; M.Sc.A., Ecole Polytechnique, U. Montreal, 1972. Project engr. Alcan, Alma, Can., 1966-69; mgr. computer ctr. in physiology dept. faculty medicine U. Montreal, 1972-73; biomed. engr. Sacre-Coeur Hosp., Montreal, 1973-75; chief engr. biomed. engring. dept. Montreal Heart Inst., 1975—; lectr. faculty of medicine U. Montreal, 1972-74, research asst. faculty of medicine, 1973-75; cons. Montreal Heart Inst., 1975—. Contbr. articles to profl. jours. Mem. Order of Engrs. Que., IEEE, Assn. Advancement Med. Instrumentation, Assn. Des Physiciens Et Ingenieurs Biomedicaux Du Que. Roman Catholic. Avocations: swimming; tennis. Home: 5732 Plantagenet, Montreal, PQ Canada H3S 2K3

PELLETIER, JEAN, mayor; b. Chicoutimi, Que., Can., Feb. 21, 1935; s. Burroughs and Marie (Desautels) P.; m. Hélène Bhérer, June 3, 1961; children: Jean, Marie. Ed., Laval U., Quebec. Journalist, Sta. CFCM-TV, Quebec, 1957; corr. Radio Can., Qué., 1958-59; press sec. Premier's Office, 1959; exec. sec. Commn. des monuments historiques Qué., 1960-62; stock broker Levesque & Beaubien, 1964-70; v.p. Dumont Express, Québec, 1970-73, L'Action Sociale Ltée, Québec, 1973-77; mcpl. councillor City of Quebec, 1976-77, mayor, 1977-89; chief of staff Leader of the Opposition, 1991—; mem. exec. com. Quebec Urban Community; pres. Expert Group on Old Age People Policies, 1990-91. Past pres. Assn. des scouts du Can., 1969-72; pres. Carnaval de Quebec, 1973; ex-dir. gen. Centraide, 1973-77; v.p. Festival d'art dramatique du Can., 1961-65; mem. Quebec-Ont. Task Force on the Rapid Train Project for Quebec-Windsor Corridor; officer of Ordre de la Pleiade of the Internat. Assembly of French Parliamentarians. Decorated Order of Can., officier Legion of Honor (France). Mem. Fedn. Can. Municipalities (past pres.), Union Municipalities Québec (past pres.); Assn. Mayors French-Speaking Capitals of the World (v.p.). Roman Catholic.

PELLEY, MARVIN HUGH, mining executive; b. St. Anthony, Nfld., Can., Nov. 24, 1947; s. Hugh Albert Pelley and Alma Josie (Harnett) Roberts; m. Velma Delilah Gillard, Nov. 5, 1965; 1 child, Rhonda Mary-Jane. Diploma in engring., Meml. U. Nfld., St. John's, 1969, BSc, 1969; B in Engring. with distinction, Tech. U. N.S., Halifax, 1973. Registered profl. engr. Contract miner Whissel Mining Ltd., Nfld., 1969-71; planning engr. Kaiser, N.S., 1972; gen. foreman opers. Iron Ore Co. Can, Nfld., 1973-74, chief engr., 1975-78; exec. v.p./ptnr. Baumgartl & Assoc., Nfld., 1978-81; mgr. tech. svcs. Denison Mines Ltd. Quintette, B.C., 1981-86; v.p. engring./transp. Curragh Resources Inc., Y.T., 1986-87; exec. v.p. mining Curragh Resources Inc., Ont., 1987-91, pres. projects and coal, 1991, also bd. dirs.; bd. dirs. Stronsay Corp., Ont., Pelly River Mines Ltd., Vancouver, B.C., S-R Internat. Inc., Colo.; presenter in field. Mem. Am. Inst. Mining Engring., Canadian Inst. Mining and Metallurgy, Assn. Profl. Engrs Nfld., Assn. Profl. Engrs. B.C., Assn. Profl. Engrs. Yukon, B.C. Mining Assn. (bd. dirs. 1989). Office: Curragh Inc, 95 Wellington St W Ste 1900, Toronto, ON Canada M5J 2N7

PELLICCIA, DENNIS SALVATORE, musician, songwriter, artist, inventor; b. Bronx, N.Y., Jan. 31, 1944; s. Santo and Concetta (Danzi) P.; m. Robin Rescigno, Aug. 18, 1986. Grad. high sch., Sachem, N.Y. Musician The Buddy Sandy Quintet, N.Y.C., 1960-70; proprietor Quest Gallery, Farmingville, N.Y., 1970-80; propr. Osprey Prodns., Shelter Island, N.Y., 1984—. Songwriter/producer: (album) Diary...Shelter Island, Summer of '85, 1985; artist various paintings and stone reliefs; exhbns. include Royal Ont. Mus., Toronto, Vanderbilt Mus., Centerport, N.Y., Parrish Art Mus., Southampton, N.Y., Guild Hall, East Hampton, N.Y., Wading River (N.Y.) Gallery; inventor Scent and Sound Barrier Deer Control Device, 1990; contbr. articles to profl. jours. Active Shelter Island Hist. Soc., 1988—, Parrish Art Mus., 1990—, Guild Hall, East Hampton, 1990—, Nature Conservancy, 1989—. With U.S. Army, 1967-70. Decorated Vietnam Cross of Gallantry, Air medal with V device and oak leaf cluster. Mem. Am. Soc. Composers Authors and Pubs., Vietnam Helicopter Crew Members Assn. Republican. Office: Osprey Prodns PO Box 1012 Shelter Island NY 11964

PELLICCIONE, FRANK, bank executive; b. Bklyn., Nov. 28, 1942; s. Mario and Alfonscia (Abrozzo) P.; m. Margaret Byne, May 15, 1965 (div. July 1981); children: Frank, Michael, Donna; m. Lucile Pastore, July 1, 1984; children: Gina Marie, Linda. Student, Adelphi U., 1978-86. Bookkeepr 1st Nat. City Bank (Citibank), N.Y.C., 1960-62, teller, 1963-69; ops. supr. Citibank, L.I., N.Y., 1970-74, ops. officer, 1975-77; bank comptroller Citibank, N.Y.C., 1978-80; br. mgr. Citibank, L.I., 1980-84, lending officer, 1984-85, asst. v.p. outside sales, 1985-88, v.p. community/pub. affairs, 1989—; Regional and nat. bd. dirs. Am. Kidney Fund, Washington, L.I., 1989—, Nat. Grand Opera, L.I., 1990—, Advancement for Commerce and Industry, L.I., 1990—; bd. dirs.; bd. dirs. L.I. Coalition for Fair Broadcasting, 1988; mem. com. Suffolk County Vietnam Vets. Meml., L.I., 1988—, L.I. Housing Partnership, 1989—; mem. fundraising com. L.I. AIDS, 1988-89. Recipient Community Svc. award Nassau Boy Scouts, L.I., 1984, Torchbearer award Am. Kidney Fund, L.I., 1990, Community Svc. award Ops. Get Ahead, Roosevelt, N.Y., 1986, March of Dimes, Nassau, N.Y., 1990. Mem. Freeport C. of C. (bd. dirs., pres., Svc. award 1987), Freeport Hi Hello Day Care (bd. dirs. 1984-86, Svc. award 1985), Freeport Sons of Italy (v.p. 1983-85). Republican. Roman Catholic. Home: 331 S Bay Dr # A Massapequa NY 11758-8416 Office: Citibank NA 180 W Merrick Rd Freeport NY 11520-3775

PELLICER, ANGEL, molecular biologist, educator; b. Tarragona, Spain, Aug. 5, 1948; came to the U.S., 1976; s. Francisco and Angeles (Garrido) P.; m. Caridad Aguirre, Aug. 9, 1980. MD, Med. Sch., Valencia, Spain, 1971; PhD, U. Complut, Madrid, 1976; postgrad., Columbia U., 1976-80. Asst. prof. pathology NYU Med. Ctr., 1980-86, assoc. prof., 1986-91, prof., 1991—; mem. pathology study sect. NIH, Bethesda, Md., 1986-90; mem. adv. com. Ctr. for Environ. Health Sci. MIT, Cambridge, 1989—; mem. scientific counsel Ministry of Health, Madrid, 1983—. Contbr. articles to profl. jours. and chpts. to books; assoc. editor: Cancer Rsch., 1988—. Rsch. grantee NIH, 1981—, Am. Cancer Soc., 1984-85, 90—, March of Dimes, 1981-84; scholar Leukemia Soc. Am., 1986-91. Mem. AAAS, Am. Assn. Microbiology, Am. Assn. Cancer Rsch., Am. Assn. Pathologists, N.Y. Acad. Scis., Spanish Inst., Assn. Spanish Profls. (bd. trustees 1988-91). Home: 110 Bleecker St Apt 13C New York NY 10012-2101 Office: NYU Med Ctr Dept Pathology 550 1st Ave New York NY 10016-6402

PELLOW, RITA BOLL, psychologist; b. Pitts., Nov. 15, 1925; d. Raymond A. and Stella (Henson) B.; m. James A. Pellow, Jan. 30, 1948; children—James A., Michael R., David G., Lisa M. B.S., U. Pitts., 1964, M.S., 1966, Ph.D., 1970. Lic. clin. psychologist, cert. sch. psychologist, Pa. Staff psychologist Pitts. Child Guidance, 1968-69, Allegheny Intermediate Unit, 1970-80; pvt. practice clin. and sch. psychology, Pitts., 1977—. Mem. Am. Psychol. Assn., Pa. Psychol. Assn., Greater Pitts. Psychol. Assn., Am. Soc. Clin. Hypnosis, Western Pa. Soc. Clin. Hypnosis, Phi Beta Kappa, Sigma Xi, Mensa. Lodge: Zonta Internat. Home: 105 Oak Park Pl Pittsburgh PA 15243-1145 Office: St Clair Bldg 1725 Washington Rd Ste 404C Pittsburgh PA 15241-1207

PELLS, LOUIS HAMILTON, information specialist; b. Poughkeepsie, N.Y., May 2, 1924; s. Willis John and Marian (Hamilton) Pells; m. Ann Duncan, June 24, 1951; children: Gail, Leah, John Mark. Assoc. in Bus., Green Mt. Coll., Poultney, Vt., 1943; BS in Psychology, St. Lawrence U., 1948; postgrad., Boston U., 1949—. Copywriter, clk., announcer, newsman Sta. WEOK, Poughkeepsie, 1949-51, salesman, local sales mgr., gen. sales mgr., 1951-62, pres., gen. mgr., 1962-76, gen. mgr. Accent Mus. div., 1986-79; mgr. Campbell Mus. Svc., Plymouth, Mass., 1980-82; dir. informational svcs. Cape Cod Community Coll., West Barnstable, Mass., 1982—. With U.S. Army, 1943-46, ETO. Republican. Episcopalian. Office: Cape Cod Community Coll West Barnstable MA 02668

PELOQUIN, LORI JEANNE, clinical psychologist; b. Milw., Sept. 21, 1957; d. Wayne Joseph Peloquin and Jeanne Audrey (Ehlers) Driessen; m. Allen Theodore Retzlaff Jr., May 5, 1990; 1 child, Austin Miles Retzlaff. Student, U. Wis., Eau Claire, 1975-76; BA summa cum laude, U. Minn., 1978; MA, U. Rochester, 1982, PhD, 1985. Lic. psychologist, N.Y. Teaching asst. U. Rochester, N.Y., 1981-83, instr. psychology, 1984; instr., co-dir. early intervention specialist tng. program Strong Ctr. for Devel. Disabilities Rochester Sch. Medicine, 1992—; instr. depts. pediatrics and psychiatry (psychology) U. Rochester Sch. Medicine and Dentistry, N.Y., 1984-92; pvt. practice Rochester, 1985—; sr. instr. Strong Ctr. for Devel. Disabilities U. Rochester Sch. Medicine and Dentistry, 1992—; cons. Rochester Children's Nursery and Bd. Coop. Ednl. Svcs., 1986-90, Hillside Children's Ctr., Rochester, 1985-87; planning coord. Crisis Intervention Program, Rochester, 1985-86; mem. steering com. Early Childhood Intervention Coun. Monroe County, 1989-90; mem. profl. adv. bd. Greater Rochester Attention Deficit Disorder Assn. Contbr. chpts. to books, articles to profl. publs. Mem. APA, Psychologist for Social Responsibility, Rochester Area Assn. Clin. Psychologists (v.p. 1987-89, pres. 1989-90, exec. com. 1990-91, ann. banquet com. chair 1991), Genesee Valley Psychol. Assn. (program com. 1991—), Coalition for Svcs. to Parents with Devel. Disabilities (com. chmn. 1985-90, coord. 1988-90), N.Y. State Psychol. Assn., Assn. for Advancement of Psychology, Mental Health Assn., Phi Beta Kappa. Presbyterian. Office: 247 Park Ave Rochester NY 14607-2723

PELOSI, OLIMPIA ANGELA IPPOLITA, language educator; b. Serino, Avellino, Italy, Aug. 27, 1957; came to U.S., 1988; d. Carmine and Filomena (Verderame) P. Degree in Italian Lit., U. Salerno, Italy, 1978; Degree in Fgn. Langs., U. Salerno, 1981; PhD in Romance Langs. and Lit., U. N.C., 1990. Researcher U. Salerno, Italy, 1978-88; asst. prof. SUNY, Albany, 1990—. Author: Nadja: Frammenti Di Un Ritorno, 1981, Il Sogno Di Polifilo, 1988, Satira Barocca, 1991; editor: Il Re Superbo, 1987, Il Finto Incanto, 1988. Recipient Fellowship Fondazione Giorgio Cini, 1986, Dept. Romance Langs. U. N.C., 1988, 89. Mem. MLA, Am. Assn. Tchrs. Italian, Am. Assn. Italian Studies, Associazione Internazionale Di Studi Di Lingua E Letteratura Italiana. Roman Catholic. Office: SUNY-Albany 1400 Washington Ave Albany NY 12222-0001

PELTZ, MARSHA WACHSMAN, public relations executive; b. Bristol, Pa., Oct. 13, 1957; d. Harold M. and Leona M. (Schatz) Wachsman; m. David Peltz, June 12, 1988. Bachelors, Goucher Coll., 1978. Copygirl Camden (N.J.) Courier Post Newspaper, summer 1977, 78; freelance writer Phila., 1979-80; pub. rels. mgr. Playboy Casino Hotel, Atlantic City, N.J., 1981-83; dir. pub. rels. Claridge Casino Hotel, Atlantic City, 1983-87, Valley Forge Music Fair, Devon, Pa., 1988—; producer Variety Club Telethon/WPVI-TV 6, Phila., 1988—. Named 1984 People to Watch, Atlantic City

(N.J.) Mag., 1984. Mem. Pub. Rels. Soc. Am. (Pepperpot award 1991). Democrat. Jewish. Office: Valley Forge Music Fair 176 Swedesford Rd Devon PA 19333-1199

PELUSO, FRANK ROBERT, photographer; b. Summit, N.J., Nov. 26, 1944; s. Serge Edmond and Filmena (Renzi) P.; m. Lillie Chen, Oct. 17, 1980; children: Christine Chen, Catherine Chen. Student, N.Y. Inst. Photography, 1968. Staff photographer RCA Corp., Somerville, N.J., 1968-72; photographer Frank Peluso Photography, Whitehouse Station, N.J., 1972—; pres. Indsl. Photographers of N.J., Cranford, 1978-80. Fireman Readington (N.J.) Vol. Fire Co., 1972-80. Recipient Award of Excellence Indsl. Photographers of N.J., 1977-86, Law Enforcement mag., 1980, Advt. Photographers of N.J., 1987; named Photographer of Yr., Indsl. Photographers of N.J., 1978. Mem. Art Dirs. Club of N.J. (1st v.p. 1986, numerous awards of Excellence 1979-92), Hunterdon County C. of C. (bd. dirs. 1991—), Somerset County C. of C. Republican. Roman Catholic.

PELUSO, SAMUEL L., lawyer, writer; b. Neptune, N.J., Apr. 29, 1958; s. Andrew and Helen (Williams) P.; m. Jody A. Petroski, Aug. 18, 1979; 1 child, Lena Ann. BA, Bates Coll., 1980; JD, Franklin Pierce Law Ctr., 1983. Bar: N.J. 1985, U.S. Dist. Ct. N.J. 1987. Asst. prof. Prosecutors Office County of Monmuth, Freehold, N.J., 1984-86; prin. Law Office of Samuel L. Peluso, Long Branch, N.J., 1986—. Author: To Live and Die With Dignity, A Guide to Living Wills; contbr. articles to profl. jours. Mem. Monmouth County Bar Assn. Home: 45 Neiman Rd Lakewood NJ 08701-4027 Office: 473 Broadway Long Branch NJ 07740-5901

PELZ, HERMAN H., physician; b. N.Y.C., May 28, 1931; s. Elias and Sima (Mansterman) P.; m. Janice G. nee Gersten, Mar. 1, 1958; children: Ellen, Daniel. BS, L.I. U., 1952; MD, SUNY, Bklyn., 1956. Diplomate Am. Bd. Allergy and Immunology. Pvt. practice specializing in internal medicine/allergies Elmhurst, N.Y., 1961—; chief allergy VA Hosp., Bklyn., 1962—, Wyckoff Hts. Hosp., Bklyn., 1963—; intern Mt. Sinai Hosp. of N.J., 1956-57; medicine residency VA Hosp., Bronx, 1957-58; fellowship in allergy Bklyn. Jewsih Hosp., 1960-61, chief resident in medicine, 1961-62. Author: Primer in Allergy, 1978. Lt. USN 1958-60. Fellow Am. Acad. Allergy, Internat. Acad. Allergology, Am. Genetics Soc. Republican. Jewish. Office: 92-31 57th St Elmhurst NY 11373

PEMBERTON, MELISSIE COLLINS, elementary educator; b. Pembroke, Va., Dec. 25, 1907; d. Walter Wingo and Grace Moore (Musselman) Collins; m. Oakland Herbert Pemberton, May 17, 1930; children: Oakland Herbert Jr., Walter Scott, William Durwood. BA in Edn., George Washington U., 1962; MA equivalency, Md. Bd. Edn., 1968. Tchr. Giles County Bd. Edn., Newport, Va., 1925-30, D.C. Pub. Schs., Washington, 1945-47, Montgomery County Pub. Schs., Rockville, MD, 1955-59, 63-75; tchr. rep. Curriculum Materials Rev., Rockville, Md., 1967-68, Elem. Spl. Edn. Rev. and EvaluationCom. for Textbooks, Rockville, 1970; del. Montgomery Edn. Assn., Rockville, 1967. Leader Montgomery County Govt., Rockville, 1988; sponsor Rep. Nat. Com., Washington, 1988; radio operator U.S.A. FCC, Washington, 1942. Named Civitan Internat. scholar, 1964. Mem. Bon Air Heights Civic Assn., Montgomery County Edn. Assn. (emeritus life mem. 1975), NEA, Md. State Tchrs. Assn., Pi Lamba Theta. Republican. Methodist. Home: 6208 Macarthur Blvd Bethesda MD 20816-3212

PENA, ANTHONY, educator, artist; b. Bklyn., June 13, 1953; s. Vincent and Mercedes (Gonzales) P.; m. Patricia Halpin, June 18, 1974, (div. May 1978); m. Vicki Lynn Verhey, June 29, 1986; 1 child, Vincent Larrea. BFA cum laude, Hunter Coll., 1976; MFA, Bklyn. Coll., 1980, MS, 1980. Special educator Bd. Edn., N.Y.C., 1976-91; coord. The Adaptive Tech. Ctr. of Manhattan, 1991—; dir. The Art Group, Bklyn., 1978-79; artist Latest Wrinkle Gallery, N.Y.C., 1983, Emerging Collector Gallery, N.Y.C., 1986, The Palm Gallery, Bklyn., 1987, Salle Polyvante Ouverte-Sur-Oise, France, 1987, Helio Gallery, N.Y.C., 1989—; coord. Adaptive Tech. Ctr., N.Y.C., 1991—; bd. dirs. Park Slope Artists Council, Bklyn.; mem. Profl. Issues Com., 1987-89. Author poems, 1979; performer: N.Y. Avante-Garde Festival, The Penny Ready Made Corp., 1980; video dir. 1982 (best tech. award); printmaker, 1981, exhibited in Bklyn. Mus. Lending Gallery. Recording sec. Com. to Preserve the Wyckoff House, Bklyn., 1969-71; v.p. Save The Flatbush Town Hall Com., Bklyn., 1972-75. Recipient Outstanding Achievement award Internat. Art Competition, N.Y.C., 1988. Mem. United Fedn. Tchrs. (chpt. leader 1976—). Democrat. Roman Catholic. Home: 477 17th St # 6 Brooklyn NY 11215-6221

PENCE, HARRY EDMOND, chemistry educator; b. Martins Ferry, Ohio, Feb. 4, 1937; s. Harry and Mary (Bell) P.; m. Virginia Waliser, Sept. 5, 1959; children: Lynn, Laura, Heather. BS, Bethany (W.Va.) Coll., 1958; MS, W.Va. U., 1962; PhD, La. State U., 1968. Instr. Washington & Jefferson Coll., Washington, Pa., 1961-65, asst. prof., 1965-66; assoc. prof. SUNY, Oneonta, 1967-69, prof., 1969—; pres. faculty senate SUNY, 1975-77. Author: Study Guide to Accompany Kotz and Purcell's General Chemistry, 2d edit., 1991, (with John Kotz and William Vining) Test Bank to Accompany Kotz and Purcell's General Chemistry, 1991. Mem. AAAS, Am. Chem. Soc., History Sci. Soc., Soc. for Lit. and Sci. Office: SUNY Oneonta Dept Chemistry Oneonta NY 13820

PENDLETON, GAIL RUTH, newspaper editor, writer; b. Franklin, N.J., May 8, 1937; d. Waldo A. and Ruby (Bonnett) Rousset; m. John E. Tyler, Mar. 10, 1956 (div. 1978); children: Gwenneth, Victoria, Christine; m. Jeffrey P. Pendleton, Oct. 1, 1978 (dec. 1992). BA, Montclair (N.J.) State Coll., 1959; M in Div., Princeton (N.J.) Theol. Sem., 1973. Ordained minister Presbyn. Ch., 1974. Tchr. Epiphany Day Sch., Kaimuki, Oahu, Hawaii, 1956-58; editor Women's Sect. Daily Record, Morristown, N.J., 1959-62, reporter, 1963-65; tchr. Hardystown Twp. Sch., Franklin, 1968-69; asst. pastor First Presbyn. Ch., Sparta, N.J., 1973-74; reporter N.J. Herald, Newton, 1976-78, editor lifestyle sect., 1978—. Recipient Ruth Cheney Streeter award Planned Parenthood N.W. N.J., 1985. Mem. N.J. Press Assn. (family sect. layout award 1985, 87, 88, 89, 91, 2nd feature columns award 1986), Zonta. Office: NJ Herald 2 Spring St Newton NJ 07860-2057

PENDLETON, HUGH NELSON, physicist, educator; b. Gallipolis, Ohio, Aug. 14, 1935; s. Hugh Nelson and Helen French (Ware) P.; m. Sylvia Lynn Fasick, Jan. 28, 1958; children: Gail Lynn, Geoffrey Nelson. BS, Carnegie Mellon U., 1956, MS, 1958, PhD, 1961. From instr. to prof. Brandeis U., Waltham, Mass., 1960—. Capt. U.S. Army, 1962-63. Mem. AAAS, Am. Phys. Soc., Math. Assn. Am., Internat. Assn. Math. Physicists. Home: 287 Florence Rd Waltham MA 02154-7628 Office: Brandeis U Physics Dept 415 South St Waltham MA 02254-9110

PENDLETON, WILLIAM JOSEPH, specialty steel company executive; b. Washington, Nov. 8, 1939; m. Annette Pendleton, June 1965; 1 child, Carolyn. BEE, Cath. U., Washington, 1961, JD, 1964. Bar: D.C. 1964. Govt. exec. NASA, Washington, 1964-72; mgr. adminstrv. svcs. Carpenter Tech. Corp., Reading, Pa., 1972-77, dir. gen. svcs., 1977-81, dir. corp. affairs, 1981-89, corp. sec. and dir. corp. affairs, 1989—. Bd. chmn. Caron Found. Weaversville, Pa., 1984-88; vice chmn. Community Gen. Hosp., Reading. Capt. USAF, 1964-67. Mem. Specialty Steel Industry U.S. (chmn. 1980-90), Berks C. of C. Home: 4 Bluejay Dr Reading PA 19610-2804 Office: Carpenter Tech Corp 101 Bern St Reading PA 19601-1203

PENDLEY, DONALD LEE, public relations executive; b. Jersey City, Nov. 5, 1950; s. Donald L. and Loretta M. (Purcell) P.; m. Donna Lynn Meade, Oct. 14, 1984; 1 child, Katelyn. BA, Montclair State Coll., 1972; MA, Syracuse U., 1974. Reporter/rewriter The Herald-News, Passaic, N.J., 1969-72; reporter The Dispatch, Union City, N.J., 1973; writer Keep America Beautiful, Inc., N.Y.C., 1974-75, communications dir., 1976-78, v.p. communications program devel., 1979-84; sr. v.p. communications Greater Newark C. of C., 1985-86; dir. pub. rels. Internat. Coun. Shopping Ctrs., N.Y.C., 1987—. Creator, dir. theatre composer series William Carlos Williams Ctr., 1987-91; creator, dir. SRO Cabaret Series, 1991—. Pres. State Repertory Opera, South Orange, N.J., 1981-85, Ars Musica Chorale, Englewood, N.J., 1979-81. Recipient Award of Excellence Am. C. of C. Execs. 1986, Gold Key awards, Pub. Rels. News, 1982, 86. Mem. Am. Soc. Assn. Execs. (Gold Circle award 1988), Pub. Rels. Soc. Am. (accredited; sec.-treas. assn. sect. 1989-90, vice chmn. assn sect. 1990-91, chmn. 1991-92), Internat. Assn. Bus. Communicators, Am. Mensa, Ltd., (nat. devel. officer 1985-89, regional tng. officer 1989—), Intertel. Home: 32 Hamilton Rd Glen Ridge NJ 07028-1109

PENMAN, PAUL DUANE, nuclear power laboratory executive; b. Williston, N.D., Sept. 25, 1937; s. Robert Roy and Kathryn Erica (Hagstrom) P.; m. Cornelia Dennis, Jan. 9, 1960 (div. June 1986); children: Anne, Robert, Jill; m. Carrie S. Silverblatt, July 14, 1986. BS in Engring. Physics, U. Colo., 1959; MS in Physics, U. Louisville, 1965. Asst. prof. U. Louisville, 1962-65; engr. Bettis Atomic Power Lab., West Mifflin, Pa., 1965-71, mgr., 1971-77, in charge lab. ops., 1977-82, in charge nuclear core mfg., 1982—. Leader Boy Scouts Am., Pitts., 1977-80. Lt. USN, 1959-64. Mem. U.S. Naval Inst., Gyro Internat. (bd. dirs., pres. 1988-90), U. Colo. Alumni Assn. (pres. Pitts. 1971-8o). Republican. Home: 105 Urick Ct Monroeville PA 15146-4919

PENN, JOHN GARRETT, federal judge; b. Pittsfield, Mass., Mar. 19, 1932; s. John and Eugenie Gwendolyn (Heyliger) P.; m. Ann Elizabeth Rollison, May 7, 1966; children: John Garrett, Karen Renee, David Brandon. BA, U. Mass., 1954; LLB, Boston U., 1957; postgrad. pub. and internat. affairs, Princeton U., 1967-68. Bar: Mass 1957, D.C. 1970. Trial atty. Dept. Justice, Washington, 1961-65, atty. tax div., 1961-70; then reviewer, asst. chief gen. litigation sect., assoc. judge Superior Ct. of D.C., Washington, 1970-79; judge U.S. Dist. Ct. D.C., Washington, 1979—. Ex-officio dir. day care program D.C. Dept. Recreation, 1978—. Served with JAGC U.S. Army, 1958-61. Nat. Inst. Pub. Affairs fellow, 1967. Mem. Nat. Bar Assn., Mass. Bar Assn., Washington Bar Assn., D.C. Bar Assn., Am. Judicature Soc., Boston U. Law Sch. Alumni Assn. Episcopalian. Clubs: Nat. Lawyers (hon.). Office: US Dist Ct US Courthouse 3rd & Constitution Ave NW Washington DC 20001*

PENNER, EUNICE B., religious, educational organization administrator; b. Utica, N.Y., Aug. 27, 1925; d. Leonard Charles and May (Cummings) Bowles; m. Lloyd Matteson Penner, Jan. 15, 1955; 1 child, Leland M. BBA, Excelsior Sch., 1944. Sec. County Oneida, Utica, 1944-45; sec. to pres. Oneida Nat. Bank & Trust Co., Utica, 1945-55; office mgr. Oneida County Boiler Works Inc., Utica, 1965-88, cons., 1988—; pres. Internat. Order King's Daughters & Sons, Chautauqua, N.Y., 1990—. Contbr. articles to profl. jours. Republican. Presbyterian. Home: 9292 Sessions Rd PO Box 16 Washington Mills NY 13479 Office: Internat Order King's Daughters & Sons 34 Vincent Ave # 1017 Chautauqua NY 14722-9999

PENNER, RUDOLPH GERHARD, economist, educator; b. Windsor, Ont., Can., July 15, 1936; s. Jacob Gerhard P. and Agnes (Dyck) Bremsteller; m. Alice Braeker, June 27, 1959; children: Eric, Brian. Vis. asst. prof. Princeton U., 1965-66; sr. staff economist Council Econ. Advisers, Washington, 1970-71; prof. U. Rochester, N.Y., 1970-75; asst. dir. econ. Office Mgmt. and Budget, Washington, 1975-77; resident scholar Am. Enterprise Inst., Washington, 1977-83; dir. Congl. Budget Office, Washington, 1983-87; dep. asst. sec. econ. HUD, Washington, 1973-75; sr. fellow Urban Inst., Washington, 1987—. Washington editor BCA Pubs., Montreal, 1987; author: (with Alan Abramson) Broken Purse Strings. Mem. Nat. Economist Club (chmn. 1980-81, pres.), Am. Econ. Assn., Nat. Tax Assn., Nat. Assn. Bus. Economists (bd. dirs.), Manpower Demonstration Rsch. Corp. (bd. dirs.). Republican. Mennonite. Office: Urban Inst 2100 M St NW Washington DC 20037-1207

PENNEY, CHARLES RAND, lawyer, civic worker; b. Buffalo, July 26, 1923; s. Charles Patterson and Gretchen (R) P. B.A., Yale U., 1945; J.D., U. Va., 1951. Bar: Md. 1952, N.Y. 1958, U.S. Supreme Ct. 1958. Law sec. to U.S. Dist. Ct. Judge W.C. Coleman, Balt., 1951-52; dir. devel. office Children's Hosp., Buffalo, 1952-54; sales mgr. Amherst Mfg. Corp., Williamsville, N.Y., 1954-56, also; Delevan Electronics Corp., East Aurora, N.Y.; mem. firm Penney & Penney, Buffalo, 1958-61; pvt. practice, Niagara County, N.Y., 1961—. Mem. Everson Mus. Art, Burchfield Art Ctr., Textile Mus., Mus. N.Mex. Found. 2d lt. U.S. Army, k1943-46. Recipient disting. svc. to culture award Coll. Arts and Scis., SUNY, Potsdam, 1983, Pres.' Disting. Svc. award Buffalo State Coll., 1991. Fellow The Explorers Club; mem. Albright-Knox Art Gallery Buffalo (life), Buffalo Mus. Sci. (life), Buffalo and Erie County Hist. Soc. (life), Niagara County Hist. Soc. (life), Old Ft. Niagara (life), Buffalo Soc. Artists (hon. trustee), Hist. Lockport (life), Landmark Soc. of Western N.Y. (life), Nat. Trust Hist. Preservation, Am. Ceramic Circle, Rochester Mus. and Sci. Center, Historic Lewiston (life), Friends of U. Rochester Libraries (life), Meml. Art Gallery U. Rochester (hon. bd. mgrs., hon. life), Smithsonian Instn., Rochester Hist. Soc. (life); Mus. Am. Folk Art, Am. Hist. Print Collectors Soc., Whitney Mus. Am. Art, Am. Craft Coun., Archives Am. Art, Margaret Woodbury Strong Mus. (charter), Met. Mus. Art, Mus. Modern Art, Mark Twain Soc. (hon.), U. Rochester's Pres.'s Soc. (hon. life), U. Iowa's Pres.'s Club (hon. life), Internat. Mus. Photography, George Eastman House, Va. Law Found., Western Pa. Conservancy, Roland Gibson Art Gallery, SUNY Coll. of Arts and Sci., Genesee Country Mus., Nat. Mus. of Women in the Arts (charter), Am. Assn. Ret. Persons, Ctr. African Studies, Castellani Art Mus. Niagara U., Nat. Geog. Soc. (life), Internat. Sculpture Ctr., Nat. Acad. of Design, Hist. Soc. of the Tonawandas (life), Winslow Homer Soc. (hon. life), Dir.'s Circle (hon. life), Pres.'s Circle Bufallo State Coll. (hon. life), Craftsman Homeowners Club, Peanut Pals, Chi Psi, Phi Alpha Delta. Clubs: Automobile (Lockport); Zwicker Aquatic, Niagara County Antiques (hon.); Rochester Art (hon. life), Plaza Athletic (Rochester). Office: 538 Bewley Lockport NY 14094-2504

PENNEY, DAVID PAUL, pathologist; b. Waltham, Mass., Dec. 11, 1933; s. R.A. and C.I. (Schofield) P.; m. Nancy Ellen Sanford, June 2, 1956; children: D. Jeffrey, Lauri Kay Penney Salvarda. AB, Ea. Nazarene Coll., 1956; AM, Boston U., 1957, PhD, 1962. Instr. anatomy Yale U. Sch. Medicine, New Haven, Conn., 1962-64; asst. prof. anatomy U. Rochester (N.Y.) Sch. Medicine and Dentistry, 1964-69, assoc. prof. anatomy, 1969-78, assoc. prof. oncology, 1978-82, prof. oncology in anatomy, 1982-85, instr. oncology in pathology and lab. medicine, 1985—. Assoc. editor The Anatomical Record Jour., 1985—, Stain Tech. Jour., 1988-90, Biotechnic and Histochemistry Jour., 1991—; contbr. articles to profl. jours. Trustee The Harley Sch., Brighton, N.Y., 1980-83. Fellow The Royal Microscopial Soc.; mem. AAAS, Biol. Stain Commn. (trustee, treas. 1988, chmn. fin. com. 1989—) Am. Assn. Anatomists, Electron Microscope Soc. Am., N.Y. Acad. Sci., Am. Thoracic Soc. : 154 Harwood Circle Rochester NY 14625 Office: Univ Rochester Med Ctr Cancer Ctr Box 704 Rochester NY 14642-0001

PENNEY, ROBERT ANDREW, public affairs and public relations professional; b. Toronto, Ont., Can., Oct. 26, 1955; came to U.S., 1979; s. Robert H. and Joan (Campbell) P.; m. Linda Susan Friedberg, July 29, 1986; children: George, Andrew. BA in Political Sci. and Journalism, Carleton U., 1978. Account supr. Burson Marsteller, Toronto, 1985-87; sr. v.p. Ketchum Pub. Rels., Phila., 1987—. Mem. Pub. Rels. Soc. Am. (exec. com. high tech. sect. 1989-91). Office: Ketchum Pub Rels 1717 Arch St Ste 3300 Philadelphia PA 19103-2786

PENNEY, SHERRY HOOD, university chancellor, educator; b. Marlette, Mich., Sept. 4, 1937; d. Terrance and B. Jean (Stoutenburg) Hood; m. Carl Murray Penney, July 8, 1961 (div. 1978); children: Michael Murray, Jeffrey Hood; m. James Duane Livingston, Mar. 30, 1985. BA, Albion Coll., 1959, LLD (hon.), 1989; MA, U. Mich., 1961; PhD, SUNY, Albany, 1972. Vis. asst. prof. Union Coll., Schenectady, N.Y., 1972-73; assoc. higher edn. N.Y. State Edn. Dept., Albany, 1973-76; assoc. provost Yale U., New Haven, Conn., 1976-82; vice chancellor acad. programs, policy and planning SUNY System, Albany, 1982-88; acting pres. SUNY, Plattsburgh, 1986-87; chancellor U. Mass., Boston, 1988—; chmn. bd. dirs. Nat. Higher Edn. Mgmt. Systems, Boulder, Colo., 1985-87; mem. commn. on higher edn. New Eng. Assn. Schs. and Colls., Boston, 1979-82, Middle States Assn. Schs. and Colls., Phila., 1986-88; mem. commn. on women Am. Coun. Edn., Washington, 1979-81, commn. on govt. rels., 1990—; bd. dirs. Boston Edison Co. Author: Patrician in Politics, 1974; editor: Women in Management in Higher Education, 1975; cons. editor Change mag. and Jour. Higher Edn. Mgmt.; contbr. articles to profl. jours. Trustee Berkeley Div. Sch., Yale U., 1978-82, John F. Kennedy Libr. Found.; bd. dirs. Albany Symphony Orch., 1982-88, U. Mass. Found., Amherst, 1988—, Mcpl. Rsch. Bur., Boston, 1990—, New England Coun., New England Aquarium, Boston Plan for Excellence; corp. mem. United Way, 1990—. Recipient Disting. Alumna award Albion Coll., 1978. Mem. Am. Assn. Higher Edn., Orgn. Am. Historians, Internat. Assn. U. Pres., Greater Boston C. of C. (bd. dirs.), Yale Club (N.Y.C.), Boston Club, St. Botolph Club, Comml. Club. (Boston). Unitarian. Office: U of Mass Office of the Chancellor 100 Morrissey Blvd Boston MA 02125-3393

PENNING, TREVOR MARTIN, biochemist, researcher; b. London, Jan. 1, 1951; s. William D. Penning and Barbara (Cross) Brockwell; m. Christina M.A. Sikora, Aug. 19, 1972; children: Stephen, Sarah-Ann, Adam. BSc in Physiology and Biochemistry, Southampton (Eng.) U., 1972, PhD in Biochemistry, 1976; MA, U. Pa., 1988. Pre-doctoral fellow Southampton U., 1972-76; postdoctoral fellow Sch. Medicine Johns Hopkin's U., Balt., 1976-79, rsch. assoc. Sch. Medicine, 1979-82; asst. prof. Sch. Medicine U. Pa., Phila., 1982-88, assoc. prof. Sch. Medicine, 1988—; corr. Trends in Pharm. Sci., Cambridge, 1983-85; cons. Internat. Cancer Rsch. Data Bank, Phila., 1987-90. Mem. adv. bd. Biochem. Jour., London, 1991—; contbr. articles to Jour. Biol. Chemistry, Proceedings Nat. Acad. Sci. Mem. AAAS, Am. Assn. for Cancer Rsch., N.Y. Acad. Scis., Biochem. Soc. London, John Morgan Soc. Home: 500 Sylvan Way Clifton Heights PA 19018-3734 Office: U Pa Sch Medicine 37th Hamilton Cir Philadelphia PA 19130-3821

PENNINGTON, DOLORES CATHERINE, education director, nurse; b. Dixonville, Pa.; d. Charles Clinton and Vera Evadna (McCullough) Little; m. Clarence Allison Pennington, July 23, 1966 (dec. July 1991); children: Craig Allen, Beverly Lynn. BS, Indiana U. of Pa., 1973, MA, 1983. RN, Pa. Staff nurse Indiana Hosp., 1961-62, head nurse med.-surg. unit, 1962-67, dir. in-svc. edn. and nursing, 1967-74, edn. coord., 1974-75, dir. staff devel., 1975-81, dir. edn., 1981—; mem. adv. com. Indiana County LPN Program, 1982—; bd. dirs. Laurel Highlands Libr. Consortium, Johnstown, Pa., 1975—. Member Am. Heart Assn., Greensberg, Pa., 1980—. Mem. Am. Soc. Health Care Educators, Soc. for Health Care Leaders (bd. dirs. 1975—, pres. Harrisburg, Pa. chpt. 1990-91), Am. Soc. for Healthcare Edn. and Tng., Soc. for Healthcare Edn. Leaders. Office: Indiana Hosp PO Box 788 Indiana PA 15701-0788

PENNINGTON, ELIBERTO ESCAMILLA (BURT PENNINGTON), political aide; b. Corpus Christi, Tex., Oct. 25, 1958; s. Eliberto A. Escamilla and Teresa Molina Vela. Student, Del Mar Coll., Corpus Christi, 1977, St. Edward's U., Austin, Tex., 1977-79, U. Madrid, 1982; BA in fgn. langs., Worcester (Mass.) State Coll., 1983; postgrad., Harvard U., 1984-85. Polit. aide to Mass. Rep. Mark Roosevelt Boston, 1983, 86—; spl. asst. to Rep. Joseph P. Kennedy 2d, 8th dist. Mass. U.S. Ho. Reps., Washington, 1986—; asst. to Sheila Rauch Kennedy, 1987-92; polit. aide Citizens for Joe Kennedy, Boston, 1986—. Spl. asst. to chmn. Citizens Energy Corp., Boston, 1987-88; elected mem. ward 5 Dem. com., Boston, 1987-92; del. Dem. conv. Commonwealth of Mass., 1988, 90; mem. task force on Hispanic dropouts Boston Sch. com., 1990; active Latino Profl. Network, Boston, 1989—, internat. ball com. of Internat. Inst., Boston, 1990, Inquilinos Boricuas en Accion, 1990, Japan Soc. of Boston, 1987, Friends of the Kennedy Libr., Boston, 1986—, Beacon Hill Civic Assn., Boston, 1985. Roman Catholic. Home: 336 8th St SE Washington DC 20003 Office: c/o Joseph P Kennedy 2nd US Ho of Reps Washington DC 20515

PENNINGTON, JEAN ANN THOMPSON, nutritionist; b. L.A., Sept. 24, 1946; d. Thomas Hilbert and Jean Cora (Watson) Thompson; 1 child, Carmella Pennington. BA, U. Calif., Berkeley, 1967, PhD, 1973. Registered dietitian. Rsch./teaching asst. dept. nutrition U. Calif., Berkeley, 1967-72, nutrition instr., extension classes, 1971-72; nutrition instr. San Francisco State U., 1977; instr. nutrition and physiology City Coll. of San Francisco, 1972-79; asst. to the dir. Div. of Nutrition U.S. FDA, Washington, 1979-88, assoc. dir. for dietary surveillance Div. of Nutrition, 1988—. Author 5 books; editor 3 sci. jours.; contbr. articles to profl. jours. Capt. USPHS, 1980—. Recipient Oustanding Svc. medal USPHS Washington, 1991, citation, 1989, others. Mem. Am. Inst. Nutrition, Am. Soc. Clin. Nutrition, Am. Dietetic Assn., Soc. Nutrition Edn., Commd. Officers Assn. Office: FDA 200 C St SW Washington DC 20204-0002

PENNINGTON, RODNEY LEE, engineer; b. Bloomsburg, Pa., Oct. 17, 1946; s. Ernest Eli and Ellen M. (Albertson) P.; m. Patricia Ann Bond, Sept. 4, 1965 (div. 1983); 1 child, Denise Rene; m. Linda Rae Petruna, Aug. 8, 1984. Engring. Tech. Cert., Williamsport Tech. Inst., Pa., 1965; AS in Engring., Williamsport Area Coll., 1972; BS in Engring. Sci., Pa. State U., 1974. Registered profl. engr. N.J. Design engr. Piper Aircraft, Lock Haven, Pa., 1965-66; staff engr. Armstrong World Ind., Lancaster, Pa., 1974-75; project mgr. REECO, Morris Plains, N.J., 1975-78, sales mgr., 1978-80, sales adminstr., 1980-81, engring. mgr., 1981-82, mktg. devel. mgr., 1982-84, v.p. engring. and R&D, 1982—; dir ARTCO, Inc., Morristown. Patentee in field; contbr. articles to profl. jours. With USAF, 1966-70. Recipient Alcan Engring. Sci. award, 1972. Mem. Nat. Coil Coaters Assn. (bd. dirs. 1991-94, chmn. environ. com. 1989-91). Office: REECO 520 Speedwell Ave Morris Plains NJ 07950-2132

PENNISTEN, JOHN WILLIAM, actuary, computer scientist; b. Buffalo, Jan. 25, 1939; s. George William and Lucy Josephine (Gates) P. AB in Math. and Chemistry with honors, Hamilton Coll., 1960; postgrad., Harvard U., 1960-61, U.S. Army Lang. Sch., 1962-63; MS in Computer Sci. with honors, N.Y. Inst. Tech., 1987; cert. in taxation, NYU, 1982; cert. in profl. banking, Am. Inst. of Banking of Am. Bankers Assn., 1988. Actuarial asst. New Eng. Mut. Life Ins. Co., Boston, 1965-66; asst. actuary Mass. Gen. Life Ins. Co., Boston, 1966-68; actuarial assoc. John Hancock Mut. Life Ins. Co., Boston, 1968-71; asst. actuary George B. Buck Cons. Actuaries, Inc., N.Y.C., 1971-75, Martin E. Segal Co., N.Y.C., 1975-80; actuary Laiken Siegel & Co., N.Y.C., 1980; cons. Bklyn., 1981—; timesharing and database analyst banklink corp. cash mgmt. div. Chem. Bank N.Y.C., 1983-85; programmer analyst Empire Blue Cross and Blue Shield, N.Y.C., 1986-88, Mt. Sinai Med. Ctr., N.Y.C., 1988-89, French Am. Banking Corp. (subs. Banque National de Paris), N.Y.C., 1989; sr. programmer analyst Dean Witter Reynolds, Inc., N.Y.C., 1989—; enrolled actuary U.S. Fed. Pension Legis. Bklyn., 1976—. Contbr. articles to profl. jours. With U.S. Army, 1961-64. Mem. AAAS, Soc. Actuaries (fellow), Am. Acad. Actuaries, Practising Law Inst., Am. Mgmt. Assn., Assn. Computing Machinery, IEEE Computer Soc., Am. Assn. Artificial Intelligence, Linguistic Soc. Am., Assn. Computational Linguistics, Am. Math. Soc., Math. Assn. Am., Nat. Model R.R. Assn. (life), Nat. Ry. Hist. Soc., Ry. and Locomotive Hist. Soc. (life), N.Y.C. Opera Guild, Met. Opera Guild, Am. Friends of Covent Garden, Harvard Gra. Soc., Am. Legion, Phi Beta Kappa, others. Home: 135 Willow St Brooklyn NY 11201-2255

PENNOCK, DONALD WILLIAM, mechanical engineer; b. Ludlow, Ky., Aug. 8, 1915; s. Donald and Melvin (Evans) P.; B.S. in M.E., U. Ky., 1940, M.E., 1948; m. Vivian C. Kern, Aug. 11, 1951; 1 son, Douglas. Stationary engring., constrn. and maintenance Schenley Corp., 1935-39; mech. equipment design engr. mech. lab. U. of Ky., 1939; exptl. test engr. Wright Aero. Corp., Paterson, N.J., 1940, 1941, investigative and adv. engr. to personnel div., 1941-43; indsl. engr. Eastern Aircraft, div. Gen. Motors, Linden, N.J., 1943-45; factory engr. Carrier Corp., Syracuse, N.Y., 1945-58, sr. facilities engr., 1958-60, corporate material handling engr., 1960-63, mgr. facilities engring. dept., 1963-66, mgr. archtl. engring., 1966-68, mgr. facilities engring. dept., 1968-78. Staff, Indsl. Mgmt. Center, 1962, midwest work course U. Kan., 1959-67. Mem. munitions bd. SHIAC, 1950-52; trustee Primitive Hall Found., 1985—. Elected to Exec. and Profl. Hall of Fame, 1966. Registered profl. engr., Ky., N.J., D.C. Fellow Soc. Advancement Mgmt. (life mem., nat. v.p. material handling div. 1953-54); mem. ASME, NSPE, Am. Material Handling Soc. (dir. 1950-57, chmn. bd., pres. 1950-52), Am. Soc. Mil. Engrs., Am. Mgmt. Assn. (men. packaging council 1950-55, life mem. planning council), Nat. Material Handling Conf. (exec. com. 1951), Found. N.Am. Wild Sheep (life), Internat. Platform Assn., Tau Beta Pi. Protestant. Mng. editor Materials Handling Engring. (mag. sect.), 1949-50; mem. editorial adv. bd. Modern Materials Handling (mag.), 1949-52. Contbr. articles to tech. jours. Contbg., cons. editor: Materials Handling Handbook, 1958. Home: 24 Pebble Hill Rd Syracuse NY 13214-2406

PENNY, DONALD GORDON, photographer; b. Pasadena, Calif., Feb. 24, 1955; s. Gordon Arthur and Patricia (Keller) P.; m. Mary Paige Siempelkamp. BS in Photographic Arts, Brooks Inst., Santa Barbara, Calif., 1979. Owner, pres., photographer Donald Penny Photography, N.Y.C., 1982—. Contbg. photographer Cosmopolitan USA, 1982-83, Elle USA,

1985, 88, 89, Glamour, 1984-87, Vogue Belleza, 1986, Woman's Journal (U.K.), 1989-92, Cosmopolitan En Espanole, 1990-91, Harpers Bazaar En Espanole, 1990-91, Art in Am., 1989-90. Mem. Vintage Thunderbird Club, Amnesty Internat. Democrat.

PENTCHEFF, NICOLAS, retired freelance broadcaster; b. Lovetch, Bulgaria, Mar. 13, 1911; came to U.S., 1956; s. Pentcho Ivanov and Velitchka (Karadenchev) P.; m. Mary Dean, Sept. 20, 1928; 1 child, Dean. Student, Sch. Commerce, Svishtov, Bulgaria, 1930, Bulgarian Free U., 1933-35; BS, London Sch. Econs., 1942; MA, Columbia U., 1965. Account mgr. Bros. Kehlibaroff, Sofia, Bulgaria, 1930; sec. gen. Bulgarian Temperance Union, Sofia, 1931-33; journalist Zora Newspaper, Sofia, 1933-39; press attache Bulgarian Legation, London, 1940-41, sec., 1947-48; freelance broadcaster Guildford, Eng., 1948-55; broadcaster, chief Bulgarian desk Radio Free Europe, N.Y.C., 1956-86, freelance broadcaster, 1986-91; lectr., adj. prof. Fairfield (Conn.) U., 1970-82; cons. Freedom of Info. Ctr. U. Mo.; speaker in field. Bd. dirs. Rsch. Ctr. for Religion and Human Rights in Closed Socs., N.Y.C., 1985—. Eastern Orthodox. Home: 1000 Dobbs Ferry Rd White Plains NY 10607-2204

PENTELOVITCH, ROBERT ALAN, artist, small business owner; b. Mpls., Oct. 13, 1955; s. Norman Oscar and Esther (Meisel) P.; m. Janet Susan Pattison, Mar. 25, 1984. BFA, Mpls. Coll. Art & Design, 1978; MFA, San Francisco Art Inst., 1980. Artist, proprietor Robert Alan Pentelovitch Studio Fine Arts, N.Y.C., 1980—. J.S. Guggenheim Meml. Found. fellow, 1991—. Home and Office: 340 W 55th St Apt 2D New York NY 10019-3745

PENTLETON, CAROL JUNE, graphic designer; b. New Bedford, Mass., June 8, 1952; d. Stanley Ivan and Bertha Caroline (Best) P.; m. Eric Neil Robinson, Aug. 24, 1980; 1 child, Brett Ivan. BFA, R.I. Sch. of Design, 1974; MFA, Syracuse U., 1982. Art dir. Maxfield Advt., Providence, 1974-75, R. J. LaChance Advt., Providence, 1975-76; creative dir. Carol Pentleton & Others, Design, Providence, 1976-80; art dir. R. I. Mag., Newport, 1980; creative dir. Pentleton Advt./Design, Glocester, R.I., 1980—; adj. assoc. prof. Sacred Heart Univ., Fairfield, Conn., 1980. Mem. Clocester Planning Bd., 1986-91, chairwoman, 1991-92; mem. Glocester Comprehensive Community Plan Commn., 1990—; bd. dirs. No. R.I. Community Child Care Assn., Glocester, 1989-91, Puppet Workshop, Providence, 1979-81. Mem. N.W. Art Assn. R.I., Warwick Arts Foun. (bd. dirs.), Women's Advt. Club R.I. (founding dir. of Supershow), NAt. Gardening Assn., Citizens for Glocester. Unitarian. Office: 685 Chestnut Hill Rd Chepachet RI 02814-1833

PENUGODA, HARAGOPAL KUSUMA, surgeon, urologist; b. Rajahmundry, Andhra Pradesh, India, Feb. 15, 1940; came to U.S., 1967; s. Veeranna and Veera Raju (Ambati) P.; m. Dwaraki Bai Yadama, May 1, 1966; children: Sarita, Namita. AS, Govt. Arts Coll., Rajahmundry, 1957; MD, Andhra Med. Coll., India, 1961, MS in Gen. Surgery, 1970. Resident in gen. surgery Guntur Med. Coll., India, 1963-65, asst. prof. anatomy, 1965-67; postdoctoral fellow St. Luke's, Nazareth, Temple U., St. Christopher's, Phila., 1967-73; resident in urology Temple U., Phila., 1968-72; pvt. practice urology, 1973—; pres. Urologic Assocs. Wilkes Barre, 1980—; chief dept. urology Wilkes Barre Gen. Hosp., 1991—. Contbr. Jour. Investigative Urology. Fellow ACS; mem. AMA, Am. Urologists Assn., Pa. Med. Soc., N.E. Pa. Urol. Soc., Luzerne County Med. Soc. Democrat. Hindu. Office: 35 W Linden St Wilkes Barre PA 18702

PENWELL, RICHARD CARLTON, document company executive; b. Columbus, Ohio, Apr. 2, 1942; m. Patricia Ann Dowell, July 18, 1964; children: Melissa Lee, Amy Elizabeth. BSME, U. Toledo, 1964; MSChemE, Princeton U., 1965; MS in Poly. Sci. and Engring., U. Mass., 1969, PhD in Poly. Sci. and Engring., 1970. Registered profl. engr., Ohio. Project engr. Owens Ill., Toledo, 1965-67; postdoctoral fellow NSF, Strasbourg, France, 1970-71, Northwestern U., Evanston, Ill., 1971-72; scientist, sr. scientist Xerox Corp., Webster, N.Y., 1972-79, mgr. spl. materials, 1979-82, mgr. future products and materials engring., 1982-91, mgr. product assurance, 1991-92, product mgr., 1992—. Mem. adv. bd. exec. edn. Bus. Sch., Ind. U., Bloomington, 1987-91; mem. bd. edn. Penfield (N.Y.) Cen. Sch. Dist., 1981-87, pres., 1984-87; elder, deacon Penfield Presbyn Ch., 1977-82, youth advisor, 1990-92. Mem. Am. Chem. Soc., Sigma Xi, Tau Beta Pi. Republican. Office: Xerox Corp 800 Phillips Rd Webster NY 14580-9791

PENZIAS, ARNO ALLAN, astrophysicist, research scientist, information systems specialist; b. Munich, Germany, Apr. 26, 1933; came to U.S., 1940, naturalized, 1946; s. Karl and Justine (Eisenreich) P.; m. Anne Pearl Barras, Nov. 25, 1954; children: David Simon, Mindy Gail, Laurie Ruth. BS in Physics, CCNY, 1954; MA in Physics, Columbia U., 1958, PhD in Physics, 1962; Dr. honoris causa, Observatoire de Paris, 1976; ScD (hon.), Rutgers U., 1979, Wilkes Coll., 1979, CCNY, 1979, Yeshiva U., 1979, Bar Ilan U., 1983, Monmouth Coll., 1984, Technion-Israel Inst. Tech., 1986, George Washington U., 1992, Rensselaer, 1992, U. Pa., 1992, Ohio State U., 1988, Iona Coll., 1988; Drew U., 1989; ScD (hon.), Lafayette Coll., 1990, Columbia U., 1990, George Washington U., 1992, Rensselaer Univ., 1992, U. Pa., 1992. Mem. tech. staff Bell Labs., Holmdel, N.J., 1961-72, head radiophysics rsch. dept., 1972-76; dir. radio research lab. Bell Labs., 1976-79, exec. dir. rsch., communications scis. div., 1979-81, v.p. rsch., 1981—; adj. prof. earth and scis. SUNY, Stony Brook, 1974-84, Univ. Disting. lectr., 1990; lectr. dept. astrophys. scis. Princeton U., 1967-72, vis. prof., 1972-85; rsch. assoc. Harvard Coll. Obs., 1968-80; Edison lectr. U.S. Naval Rsch. Lab., 1979; Kompfner lectr. Stanford U., 1979; Gamow lectr. U. Colo., 1980; Jansky lectr. Nat. Radio Astronomy Obs., 1983; Michelson Meml. lectr., 1985; Grace Adams Tanner lectr., 1987; Klopsteg lectr. Northwestern U., 1987; Regents' lectr. U. Calif., Berkeley, 1990; Disting. lectr. SUNY, 1990; Lee Kuan Yew Disting. visitor Nat. U. Singapore, 1991; mem. astronomy adv. panel NSF, 1978-79, mem. indsl. panel on sci. and tech., 1982—, disting. lectr., 1987, affiliate Max-Planck Inst. für Radioastronomie, 1978-85, chmn. Fachbeirat, 1981-83; researcher in astrophysics, info. tech., its applications and impacts. Author: Ideas and Information Managing in a High-Tech World, 1989 (pub. in 10 langs.); mem. editorial bd. Ann. Rev. Astronomy and Astrophysics, 1974-78; mem. editorial bd. AT&T Bell Labs. Tech. Jour., 1978-84, chmn. 1981-84; assoc. editor Astrophys. Jour., 1978-82; contbr. over 80 articles to tech. jours.; patentee in field. Trustee Trenton (N.J.) State Coll., 1977-79; mem. bd. overseers U. Pa. Sch. Engring. and Applied Sci., 1983-86; mem. vis. com. Calif. Inst. Tech., 1977-79; mem. Com. Concerned Scientists, 1975—, vice chmn., 1976—; mem. adv. bd. Union of Couns. for Soviet Jews, 1983—; bd. dirs. IMNET, 1986-91, Coun. on Competitiveness, 1989—. Served to lt. Signal Corps, U.S. Army, 1954-56. Recipient Pender award U. Pa., 1992. Mem. NAE, NAS (Henry Draper medal 1977), AAAS, Am. Astron. Soc., Am. Phys. Soc. (Pake prize 1990), Internat. Astron. Union, World Acad. Arts and Sci.

PEOPLES, JOHN CLIFFORD ALEXANDER, health industry manager; b. Aldershot, Hampshire, Eng., Mar. 19, 1942; s. Alexander and Lottie Clara (Webb) P.; m. Judith Lilian Maxted, Mar. 30, 1963 (div. Apr. 1987); children: Nicola Janette, Jillian Andrea; m. Barbara Anne Gundry, May 29, 1987. AIMLS, Inst. Med. Lab. Sci., London, 1963. Rsch. tech. Technicon Instruments Inc., Chertsey, Eng., 1963-65; rsch. group leader Technicon Instruments Inc., Tarrytown, N.Y., 1965-73; tech. dir. ARC, Washington, 1973-82; bus. mgr. hemoanalysis Kontron Instruments Inc., Everett, Mass., 1982-89; v.p. IBG Systems, Inc., Laytonsville, Md., 1990—. Inventor: Autotyper, 1970. Hist. commr. Prince William County, Va., 1980. Mem. Am. Assn. Blood Banks, Mid-Atlantic Assn. Blood Banks (pres. 1976-78). Democrat. Presbyterian. Home: 23510 Pocahontas Dr Gaithersburg MD 20882-3216

PEPIN, JOHN NELSON, materials research and design engineer; b. Lowell, Mass., June 5, 1946; s. Nelson Andre and Leanne Florine (Boucher) P. BS in Mech. Engring., Northeastern U., 1968; MS in Aerospace Engring., MIT, 1970. Aero. engr. Bradway STOL Amphibian Ltd., Raymond, Maine, 1979; staff engr. Fiber Materials, Inc., Biddeford, Maine, 1979-84; pres. Pepin Assocs., Inc., Scarborough, Maine, 1984—; cons. Foster-Miller Engrs., Waltham, Mass., 1985—, Johnson & Johnson Orthopedic Div., Braintree, Mass., 1984-86, Allied Signal Aerospace, South Bend, Ind., 1985—, B.F. Goodrich, Akron, Ohio and Marlboro, Mass., 1986-87. Patentee in field. Capt. USAF, 1974-78. NSF grantee, 1982-84, U.S. Dept. Transp. grantee, 1989—, U.S. Dept. of Energy grantee, 1990—. Mem. Soc. for Advancement of Materials and Process Engring., Seaplane Pilots Assn., MIT Club of Maine (bd. dirs. Portland chpt. 1988). Democrat. Roman Catholic. Home: RR 1 Box 109N Alfred ME 04002-9801

PEPITONE, NATAL M., post office driver; b. Bklyn., Nov. 5, 1944; s. Natal Martin and Rose (Vaccarella) P.; m. Carole Ann Pepitone, Nov. 15, 1969; children: Teresa, Nat, Caroline. Student, Franklyn K. Frome, Bklyn., 1963-66, QBI, Queens, 1967-68. Driver Brinks Inc., N.Y.C., 1969—, U.S. Post Office, N.Y.C., 1985—. Patentee, inventor, and designer. Pres. Our Planet Environ. Non-Profit, N.Y.C., 1985—. Roman Catholic. Home: 97-23 84 St Queens NY 11416

PEPPER, GEORGE BONAVENTURE, philosophy educator; b. Jersey City, N.J., June 17, 1926. BS, St. Peter's Coll., 1948; MA, Fordham U., 1950, PhD, 1958; postgrad., Harvard U., 1961-62. Vis. prof. Talladega (Ala.) Coll., 1968-69; prof. Iona Coll., New Rochelle, N.Y., 1950—. With USN, 1944-46. Rudin fellow Iona Coll., 1989-90. Mem. AAUP, Am. Philos. Assn., Karl Jaspers Soc. N.Am. (founder 1980, chairperson 1986-88). Office: Iona Coll 715 North Ave New Rochelle NY 10801-1890

PEPPIN, RICHARD JOSEPH, engineer; b. Bklyn., Feb. 18, 1943; s. Harry Edmund and Betty H. Peppin; m. Cynthia E. Harrison, July 9, 1970 (div.); Melanie, Scarlett, Ashley. BS in Engring., CCNY, 1965; MSME, Rensselaer Poly., 1969; MS in Theoretical Mechanics, W.Va. U., 1966. Registered profl. engr., N.Y., N.J., Md., Ont. Sr. engr. Sci. Applications, McLean, Va., 1975-77; county noise control engr. Montgomery County Md., Rockville, 1977-79; sr. engr. Jack Faucett Assocs., Chevy Chase, Md., 1979-81; sr. scientist OSHA, Washington, 1981-85; acting chief, safety mgmt. Nat. Park Svc., Washington, 1983-85; head acoustics group Bruel & Kjaer Instruments, Marlboro, Mass., 1983-85; pres. Scantek, Inc., Silver Spring, Md., 1985—; cons. Battelle Meml. Labs., NIST, IAC, Fairfax County, State of Md. Editor: Noise Control, 1979, Community Noise, 1980. Treas. Nat. Women's Symphony, Washington, 1989—; trustee Washington Ethical Soc., 1990-91. Mem. ASHRAE, ASTM (chair subcom. 1982—), ASME (chair safety div. 1979-80, Centenial medal 1980, Dedicated Svc. award 1990), Inst. Environ. Sci. (sr.), Inst. Noise Control Engring. (bd. dirs. 1980—, v.p. 1984—), Acoustical Soc. Am. (working group chair 1988—), Soc. Automotive Engrs. Office: Scantek Inc 916 Gist Ave Silver Spring MD 20910-4943

PERDUE, FRANKLIN P., poultry products company executive; m. Mitzi Henderson Ayala, July 1988. Chmn., exec. com. Perdue Farms Inc., Salisbury, Md., Perdue Inc. subs. Perdue Farms Inc., Salisbury. Office: Perdue Farms Inc PO Box 1537 Salisbury MD 21802-1537

PERDUE, GEORGIA PERSINOS, editor, publisher; b. Salem, Mass., Dec. 13, 1938; d. John Lucas and Katherine (Papageorgiou) P.; m. Roger H. Bergstrom, Sept. 26, 1970 (dec. 1972); children: Roger, John, Mark, Nels; m. Robert E. Perdue Jr., Jan. 6, 1976. BS, Mass. Coll. Pharmacy, 1960, MS, 1962, PhD, 1966. Dir. div. phytochemistry Natural Products Rsch. Labs., Rockville, Md., 1966-69, exec. dir., 1969-71; asst. dir. Bergstrom Toxicology Lab., Rockville, 1972, dir., 1973-77; ptnr. Natural Products Advocates, Rockville, 1978-88; editor, pub. Washington Insight, North Bethesda, Md., 1988—; cons. Amazon Natural Drug Co., Washington, Va., 1972-75. Contbr. articles to profl. jours.; patentee in field. Sec. Wickford Citizens Assn., Rockville, 1978-89, pres., 1979-81; chmn. medicines for missionaries task force 4th Presbyt. Ch., Bethesda, 1981—. Mem. Soc. for Econ. Botany, Am. Soc. Pharmacognosy. Home and Office: Washington Insight 11000 Waycroft Way North Bethesda MD 20852

PEREIRA, KENNETH JOHN, healthcare software executive; b. Providence, Oct. 15, 1957; s. Edmund Sipriano and Jean Francis (McAdams) P.; m. Dianna Lynn Branca, Aug. 31, 1959; children: Nicole Lynn, Kayleigh Jean. BA, Bryant Coll., 1979; postgrad., Babson Coll., 1985—. Computer operator Collyer Wire Co., G&W, Lincoln, R.I., 1974-78, Malina Co., Providence, 1978-79; data processing auditor Gulf & Western, Inc., N.Y.C., 1979-81; sr. systems analyst Acushnet Co., New Bedford, Mass., 1981-82; mgr. systems Nat. Med. Care, Inc., Waltham, Mass., 1982-87; dir. info. svcs. Protocare, Inc., Waltham, 1987-89; pres. Healthcare Automation, Inc., Cranston, R.I., 1989—; cons. in field. Author: Medical Claims Clearinghouse, 1987 (Douglas award 1989). Mem. Data Processing Mgmt. Assn., Tau Epsilon Phi (pres. 1979). Republican. Office: Healthcare Automation Inc 300 Centerville Rd Warwick RI 02886-4321

PEREL, JAMES MAURICE, pharmacology and psychiatry educator, researcher; b. Buenos Aires, Mar. 30, 1933; came to U.S., 1947, naturalized, 1954; s. Aria and Bella (Silverberg) P.; m. Noami Hookman, July 18, 1959 (div. 1971); 1 child, Allan B.; m. Audrey Feldman, Apr. 9, 1972; children: Alissa A., Stephen M. BS, CUNY, 1956; MS, NYU, 1961, PhD, 1964. Nuclear chemist N.Y. Naval Shipyard Lab., Bklyn., 1956-58; assoc. rsch. scientist NYU, Goldwater Meml. Hosp., N.Y.C., 1964-67; asst. prof. medicine and chemistry Emory U., Atlanta, 1967-70; asst. prof. psychiatry Columbia U. Coll. Physicians and Surgeons, N.Y.C., 1970-76; assoc. prof. clin. pharmacology, chief psychiat. rsch. N.Y. State Psychiat. Inst., N.Y.C., 1976-80; chief clin. pharmacology VA Med. Ctr. Highland Drive, Pitts., 1979-83; prof. psychiatry and pharmacology U. Pitts. Sch. Medicine, 1980—, acting chmn. dept. pharmacology, 1985-88; dir. clin. pharmacology Western Psychiat. Inst. and Clinic, Pitts., 1980—; prof. grad. neurosci., 1988—; postdoctoral fellow in clin. pharmacology NIH and NYU, 1964-67; lectr. chemistry CUNY, 1963-67; assoc. rsch. scientist N.Y. State Psychiat. Inst., 1970-76; cons., mem. grant-awarding study sects. NIH, NIMH. Mem. editorial bd. Psychopharmacology, Neuropsychobiology, Therapeutic Drug Monitoring; contbr. over 275 articles to sci. jours., chpts. to books. Recipient Founders Day award NYU, 1974, Julius Koch Meml. award Rho Chi, 1983; numerous rsch. grants, including NIH, NIMH, Founds. Fund for Rsch. in Psychiatry, pharm. cos., pvt. founds. Fellow Am. Inst. Chemists; mem. Am. Soc. Clin. Pharmacology and Therapeutics, Am. Soc. Pharmacology and Exptl. Therapeutics, Soc. for Biol. Psychiatry, Sigma Xi. Jewish. Office: U Pitts Sch Medicine 3811 Ohara St Pittsburgh PA 15213-2593

PERELMAN, LEON JOSEPH, paper manufacturing executive, university president; b. Phila., Aug. 28, 1911; s. Morris and Jennie (Davis) P.; m. Beverly Waxman, Jan. 27, 1945 (div. Apr. 1960); children: Cynthia, David. B.A., LaSalle Coll., 1933, LL.D., 1978; postgrad., U. Pa. Law Sch., 1933-35; L.H.D. (hon.), Dropsie U., 1976. Ptnr. Am. Paper Products Co. (later Am. Paper Products Inc.), Phila., 1935-42, pres., 1943—; pres. Am. Cone & Tube Co. Inc., Phila., 1953—, United Ammunition Container Inc., Phila., 1961—, Ajax Paper Tube Co., Phila., 1962—; vice chmn. bd. Belmont Industries, Phila., 1963—; pres. Dropsie U., Phila., 1978—. Author: Perelman Antique Toy Mus., 1972. Fin. chmn. Valley Forge council Boy Scouts Am., 1968; founder, bd. dirs. Perelman Antique Toy Mus., Phila., 1969; pres. West Park Hosp., 1975-78, 81—; trustee La Salle U., Balch Inst. Ethnic Studies. Served to 1st lt. USAAF, 1942-45. Recipient citation Jewish Theol. Sem., 1965; Beth Jacob award, 1966; award Pop Warner Little Scholars Inc., 1972; Cyrus Adler award Jewish Theol. Sem., 1976. Mem. AAUP, Jewish Publ. Soc. Am. (treas. 1983, v.p. 1991), Franklin Inst., Am. Assn. Mus. Republican. Jewish. Clubs: Union League (Phila.); Masons, Shriners.

PERERA, THOMAS B., psychologist, educator; b. N.Y.C., Nov. 20, 1938; s. Lionel C. and Dorothy B. Perera; m. Gretchen G. Perera, Aug. 28, 1960; children: Daniel G., Thomas B. Jr. AB, Columbia Coll., 1961, MA, 1963, PhD, 1968. Cert. psychologist, N.Y., Vt. Asst. prof. psychology Barnard Coll., N.Y.C., 1966-74, vis. prof., 1975—; assoc. prof. Montclair State Coll., Upper Montclair, N.J., 1974-80, prof., 1980—; vis. prof.; cons. Columbia U., 1960—, Omni Systems Assn., 1978—, sr. rsch. scientist N.Y. State Psychiat. Inst., 1964-71. Contbr. computer programs, articles to profl. jours. Mem. AAAS, Am. Psychol. Assn., Eastern Psychol. Assn., Biofeedback Soc., Southeastern Psychol. Assn. Office: Montclair State Coll Valley and Normal Ave Upper Montclair NJ 07043

PEREZ, LOUIS ANTHONY, radiologist; b. N.Y.C., June 11, 1939; s. Salvatore Lawrence and Valvadina Rose (Ruscillo) P.; divorced, 1988; children: Lisa, Gregg, Nicole; m. Patricia Ann McVey, May 19, 1990. BEE, Manhattan Coll., 1962; MD, SUNY, Bklyn., 1966. Diplomate Am. Bd. Radiology, Am. Bd. Nuclear Medicine. Chief nuclear medicine Misericordia Hosp., Bronx, 1973-75; cons. Manhattan Coll., Radiology Inst., Riverdale, N.Y., 1974-81; chief nuclear medicine Norwalk (Conn.) Hosp., 1975-82; dir. radiology Lawrence Hosp., Bronxville, N.Y., 1982—. Contbr. articles to profl. jours., chpts. to books. Lt. comdr. USN, 1963-77. Grantee, Am. Cancer Soc., 1968-70, USPHS, 1974-75. Mem. Soc. Nuclear Medicine (trustee 1985-89, 92—, chmn. sci. subcom. 1988—, chpt. pres. 1982), Am. Coll. Radiology, N.Y. State Med. Soc., Explorers Club, Alpine Club. Republican. Roman Catholic. Office: Lawrence Radiology Svcs 45 Parkview Ave Bronxville NY 10708-2901

PEREZ, PAUL BONADA, marketing executive; b. N.Y.C., Sept. 21, 1946; s. Joseph Raul and America (Bonada) P.; m. Mary Anne George, June 23, 1973; children: Anna-Maria, Paul Daniel. BA in Econs., St. John's U., 1967; MBA in Mktg., Cornell U., 1969. Asst. product mgr. Lever Bros. Co. Inc., N.Y.C., 1972-74; product mgr. Internat. Playtex, N.Y.C., 1974-76; mktg. mgr. Revlon, N.Y.C., 1976-77; sr. product mgr. Block Drug Co. Inc., Jersey City, 1977-79; group product mgr. Am. Home Foods, N.Y.C., 1979-84; v.p. mktg. Corning (N.Y.) Inc., 1984-91; sr. v.p. mktg. Action Industries, Cheswick, Pa., 1991—. Mem. mktg. com. United Way of Steuben County, Corning, 1988; dir. mktg. achievements awards com., rep. Corning Inc., 1984-90. With U.S. Army, 1969-71. Mem. Conf. Bd. (assoc.), Cookware Mfrs. Assn. (bd. dirs. 1988-90), Cornell Club of N.Y. Roman Catholic. Home: 2691 Timberglen Dr Wexford PA 15090-7562 Office: Action Industries Action Industrial Park Cheswick PA 15024

PERGOLIZZI, ROBERT GEORGE, molecular biologist, educator; b. Bklyn., Feb. 21, 1950; s. Santo Joseph and Marian (Scianna) P.; m. Camille Roxanne Kotowski, Apr. 8, 1972; children: Christopher Dylan, Alexander Joseph. BS in Chemistry, Hofstra U., 1971, MA in Biology, 1974; MA, Columbia U., 1976, MPhil, 1978, PhD in Biochemistry, 1979. Rsch. asst. Waldemar Med. Rsch. Found., Plainview, N.Y., 1971-73, North Shore U. Hosp., N.Y.C., 1973-75; grad. rsch. asst. Columbia U., N.Y.C., 1975-79, post-doctoral fellow, 1980-82; dir. mfg. Enzo Biochem, N.Y.C., 1982-86; dir. recombinant DNA lab. Enzo Biochem, Inc., N.Y.C., 1982-86; dir. molecular genetics North Shore U. Hosp./Cornell U. Med. Coll., N.Y.C., 1986—; asst. prof. pathology Cornell U. Med. Coll., N.Y.C., 1990—; adj. prof. L.I. U., Brookville, N.Y., 1988—; co-dir. transgenic animal facility North Shore U. Hosp./Cornell U. Med. Coll., Manhasset, N.Y., 1990—; inst. liaison N.Y. State Ctr. for Biotech., 1990—; dir. rsch. apprentice program for minority students NIH, 1987—; pres. Starship Enterprises rec. studio, 1989—. Editor: Genetic Engineering, 1982; patentee in field; contbr. articles to profl. jours. Recipient Waldemar Found. award Waldemar Med. Rsch. Found., 1972, Brookdale Found. award, 1978; fellow Columbia U., 1975-79, NIH, 1979-82. Fellow Harvey Soc.; mem. Am. Assn. Cancer Rsch., Am. Soc. Hematology, N.Y. Acad. Scis., N.Y. Biotech. Assn., Am. Soc. Human Genetics. Republican. Roman Catholic. Office: North Shore U Hosp Cornell Med Coll 350 Community Dr Manhasset NY 11030

PERHACH, JAMES LAWRENCE, pharmaceutical company executive; b. Pitts., Oct. 26, 1943; s. James Lawrence and Elizabeth Louise (Hoffman) P.; m. Judith Irene Selter, Apr. 15, 1967; children: Laura Anne, Amy Elizabeth. BS, U. Dayton, 1966; MS, U. Pitts., 1969, PhD, 1971. Sr. scientist dept. pharmacology Mead Johnson Rsch. Ctr., 1971-74, sr. investigator dept. biol. rsch., 1974-76, sr. rsch. assoc. dept. biol. rsch., 1976-77, sr. rsch. assoc. dept. pathology and toxicology, 1977-78, prin. rsch. assoc. dept. pathology and toxicology, 1978-80; dir. pharmacology Wallace Biol. Rsch., Wallace Labs. div. Carter-Wallace Inc., Cranbury, N.J., 1980, exec. dir. biol. rsch., 1980-84, assoc. dir. clin. rsch., 1984-85, dir. clin. investigation, 1985-87, v.p. clin. pharmacology and pharmacokinetics, 1987—; adj. prof. toxicology Phila. Coll. Pharmacy and Sci., 1981—; assoc. faculty Evansville Ctr. Med. Edn., Ind. U., 1973-80; lectr. grad. physiology U. Evansville, 1973-79; grad. teaching asst. U. Pitts., 1967-69, instr. pharmacology and exptl. therapeutics, 1968-69; mem. substance abuse com. Tri-State Area Health Planning Council, Evansville, 1972-75; mem. addictions med. edn. program Evansville Ctr. for Med. Edn-Ind. Sch. Med., 1972-78, Drug Utilization Rev. Council of State of N.J., 1983—, apptd. med. pharmacologist, 1983, sec., 1984, chmn., 1985-86. Contbr. numerous articles and abstracts to profl. jours.; patentee in field. Mem. AAAS, Am. Soc. Clin. Pharmacology and Therapeutics, Am. Soc. Pharmacology and Exptl. Therapeutics, Am. Coll. Clin. Pharmacology, Am. Coll. Toxicology, European Soc. Toxicology, Soc. Exptl. Biology and Medicine, Soc. Neurosci., N.Y. Acad. Sci., Physiol. Soc. Phila., Drug Info. Assn., Sigma Xi. Republican. Roman Catholic. Home: 6 Highfield Ct Lawrenceville NJ 08648-1077 Office: Wallace Labs 301B College Rd E Princeton NJ 08540-6604

PERHACS, MARYLOUISE HELEN, musician, educator; b. Teaneck, N.J., June 15, 1944; d. John Andrew and Helen Audrey (Hosage) P.; m. Robert Theodore Sirinek, Jan. 27, 1968 (div. Jan. 1975). Student, Ithaca (N.Y.) Coll., 1962-64; BS, Juilliard Sch., 1967, MS, 1968; postgrad., Hunter Coll., 1976, St. Peter's Coll., Jersey City, N.J., 1977. Cert. music tchr., N.Y., N.J. Instr. Carnegie Hall, N.Y.C., 1966-69; program developer, coord., instr. urban edn. program Newburgh (N.Y.) Pub. Sch. System, 1968-69; adj. prof. dept. edn. St. Peter's Coll., Jersey City, 1976—; tchr. brass instruments Indian Hills High Sch., Oakland, N.J., 1976; tchr. Jersey City Pub. Schs., 1976-77, N.Y.C. Pub. Sch., Bronx, 1980-84; pvt. tchr. Cliffside Park, N.J., 1976—; vocal music tchr. East Rutherford, N.J., 1990; tchr. music Bergen County Spl. Svcs. Sch. Dist., 1990-91; tchr. gen. music Little Ferry (N.J.) Pub. Schs., 1991-92; lectr. in edn. and entertainment areas, 1992—; singer, trumpeter Norwegian Caribbean Lines, 1981-82, Jimmy Dorsey Band, Paris and London, 1974; music and edn. lecture cir., 1992—. Singer with Original PDQ Bach Okay Chorale, N.Y.C., 1966, Ed Sullivan Show, N.Y.C., 1970, St. Louis Mcpl. Opera, 1970; singer, dancer, actress (Broadway shows) Promises, Promises, 1969-71, Sugar, 1971-72, Lysistrata, 1972; trumpeter (Broadway shows) Jesus Christ Superstar, 1973, Debbie!, N.Y.C., 1976, Sarava!, 1979, Sophisticated Ladies, 1982, Fiddler on the Roof, Lincoln Ctr., 1981; writer, host series on women in music Columbia Cable/United Artists, 1984. Cons. to cadette troop Girl Scouts U.S., Jersey City, 1967-68. Mem. NEA, AFTRA, Actors Equity Assn., Am. Fedn. Musicians (mem. theater com. 1972—, chmn. 1973), Music Educators Nat. Conf., N.J. Music Educators Assn., N.J. Sch. Music Assn., N.J. Edn. Assn., Internat. Women's Brass Conf. (charter), Internat. Trumpet Guild, Mu Phi Epsilon. Democrat. Episcopalian. Home and Office: 23 Crescent Ave Cliffside Park NJ 07010-3003

PERHAM, ROY GATES, artist; b. Paterson, N.J., Apr. 18, 1916; s. Roy Gates and Alice Jeannette (Parsons) P.; m. Titania Joan Robbitts, Mar. 10, 1956; 1 child, Roy Gates 3d. Student, Grand Central Art Sch., N.Y.C., 1936-37. instr. portrait painting Englewood Adult Sch.; lectr. in field. Work represented Diocesan Coll., McGill U., Montreal, Can., South Jersey Coll., Rutgers U., The Conf. Bd, N.Y.C., Peninsula Gen. Hosp., Salisbury, Md., Plimoth Plantation, Plymouth, Mass., Central Coll., Pella, Iowa, Felician Coll., Lodi, N.J., Americana Collection, U. S.C.; portrait of former U.S. Sec. of State Edmund S. Muskie, 1986, portrait of Franklin Delano Roosevelt Jr., 1989. Sec., chmn. Hasbrouck Heights (N.J.) Juvenile Conf. Com., 1967-85; mem. Rent Leveling Bd., Hasbrouck Heights, 1980—. Lodge: Lions (pres. 1966-67, zone chmn. 1974-75, Hasbrouck Heights club). Home and Office: 269 Raymond St Hasbrouck Heights NJ 07604 Studio and Gallery: 248 Boulevard Hasbrouck Heights NJ 07604

PERI, JOHN BAYARD, surface chemistry consultant; b. Stockton, Calif., May 5, 1923; s. John Joseph and Alta Josephine (Scheffer) P.; m. Barbara Anne Miller, July 21, 1946; children: Pamela Elizabeth, Phyllis Irene, Janet Ellen. BS in Chemistry, U. Calif., Berkeley, 1943; MS in Phys. Chemistry, U. Wis., 1948, PhD in Phys. Chemistry, 1949. Rsch. asst. chemistry dept. Univ. Wis., Madison, 1946-49; rsch. chemist Calif. Rsch. Corp., Richmond, Calif., 1949-57; project chemist Standard Oil Co., Whiting, Ind., 1957-58; sr. project chemist Standard Oil Co., Whiting, 1958-60, sr. rsch. scientist, 1960-62; rsch. assoc. R & D dept. Amoco, Whiting, 1962-79; sr. rsch. assoc. R & D dept. Amoco, Naperville, Ill., 1979-86; ind. cons., 1986—; adj. prof. chem. engring. dept. Northeastern Univ., Boston, 1987—. Editorial bd.: Jour. Phys. Chemistry, 1978-82, Jour. Catalysis, 1987—; contbr. articles to profl. jours.; patentee in field. Lt. (j.g.) USNR, 1943-46. Mem. Am. Chem. Soc., Catalysis Soc. N.Am. (bd. dirs. 1980-83, Burwell lectureship 1987-88), Catalysis Soc. New Eng., New Eng. Hist. Geneal. Soc. Home: 2 Tortoise Ln Falmouth MA 02540-1639

PERICH, WESLEY RAYMOND, budget analyst; b. McKeesport, Pa., Dec. 24, 1951; s. Ernest Michael and Joan Audrey (Ellis) P.; m. Cecile Marie Kelley, June 30, 1979; children: John, Kevin. BA, Ind. U. of Pa., 1973; postgrad., U. Pitts., 1977-78. Claims rep. Social Security Adminstrn., Pitts., 1976-81; ops. supr. Social Security Adminstrn., Balt., 1981-88, sr. budget analyst, 1988—. Named Outstanding Sr., Am. Legion, 1965. Mem. KC. Roman Catholic. Home: 10510 Longbranch Rd Cockeysville Hunt Valley MD 21030-3104 Office: Social Security Adminstrn 6401 Security Blvd Baltimore MD 21235

PERIN, ROBERT JEAN, physician; b. Draguignan, France, Nov. 12, 1947; came to U.S., 1949; s. Charles R. and Jeanne C. (Chabert) P.; m. Barbara Marie Gramiak. BS in Biology, Mt. St. Mary's Coll., Emmitsburg, Md., 1969; MD, U. Guadalajara, Mex., 1974. Resident in pediatrics Thomas Jefferson U. Hosp., Phila., 1976-79; chief allergy and pediatrics dept. Underwood Meml. Hosp., Woodbury, N.J., 1985-87. Allergy and Immunology fellow Thomas Jefferson U. Hosp., 1979-81. Fellow Am. Coll. Allergy, Am. Acad. Allergy and Immunology. Office: 630 Salem Ave Woodbury NJ 08096-3192

PERINI, DAVID B., construction company executive; b. Framingham, Mass., May 19, 1937; s. Louis R. and Florence R. P.; m. Eileen Callahan, July 14, 1962; children: Jennifer, David, Kristin, Timothy, Andrea. BS, Coll. of Holy Cross, 1959; JD, Boston Coll., 1962. Asst. to gen. counsel Perini Corp., Framingham, 1962-65; div. counsel Midwest and S.W. divs. Perini Corp., Evansville, Ind., 1965-67, div. counsel Western div., 1968; asst. gen. counsel Framingham, Evansville, Ind., 1968-69, v.p., gen. counsel, 1969-71, vice chmn. bd., 1971-72, pres., chmn., 1972—; bd. dirs. Framingham; chmn. Perini Investment Properties, Inc., State St. Boston Corp., New England Telephone Co., Dennison Mfg. Co. Mem. exec. bd. Boston council Boy Scouts Am., 1976; mem. Pres.' Council Holy Cross Coll., trustee, 1977—. Decorated knight Order of Malta, 1979; recipient Merit citation NCCJ, 1980; named 1 of 10 Outstanding Young Leaders, Boston Jr. C. of C., 1973; medalist Italian Am. Charitable Soc., 1979. Mem. ABA, Mass. Bar Assn., World Assn. Lawyers, Moles (pres. 1980), Soc. Am. Mil. Engrs., Associated Gen. Contractors Am. (chmn. internat. constrn. com. 1980—), Associated Gen. Contractors Mass. (dir. 1973-75). Office: Perini Corp 73 Mt Wayte Ave Framingham MA 01701-5800*

PERKINS, ARTHUR BURKE, industrial engineer, media consultant; b. Meriden, Conn., Mar. 19, 1954; s. Wilson Mix and Patricia Anne (Burke) P.; m. Debra Jayne Wilson, Aug. 19, 1989 (div. Feb. 1991). Maintenance mechanic Wall's Transp. Co., Wallingford, Conn., 1973-75; buyer Anthony Russo Wholesale Vegetable Co., Hamden, Conn., 1976-77; indsl. technician Power Supplies Inc., Middlefield, Conn., 1978-82; engring. assembler Teleco Oilfield Svcs. Inc., Meriden, Conn., 1982-83; test cons. Telephone Utilities Co., Wallingford, 1983-84; layout cord. Madrigal Audio Labs., Inc., Middletown, 1985—; artist commn. work, Wallingford, 1977-78, 1984-85; lectr. modern art Cheshire Acad., 1984. Author poems, essays; actor Sin on the Road, 1972, The Gun, 1978; exhibitor Rose Farm Gallery, East Haddam, Conn., 1983, Wallingford Libr., 1984. Mem. Conn. Citizen Action Group, New Haven, 1982, Four Seasons Art Coun., Wallingford, co-founder 1983, bd. dirs. 1983-85. Recipient Regional Art award Hartford (Conn.) Courant, 1971; recipient Pistol Marksmanship award NRA, Wallingford, 1982; commendation Conn. Bar Assn., New Haven, 1982. Mem. Masons (lodge steward 1983-84, Raised 1982). Libertarian. Home: 135 Union St Deep River CT 06417-1736 Office: Madrigal Audio Labs Inc 2081 S Main St Middletown CT 06457-6133

PERKINS, BILL J., public relations executive; b. Houston, Mar. 3, 1943; s. Jack and Helen Lou (Diggs) P.; m. Barbara Ann Gunn, Sept. 4, 1965; 1 child, Robert Christopher. BA, North Tex. State U., 1965; MSJ, Columbia U., 1966. Mgmt. intern U.S. Atomic Energy Commn., Washington, 1966-68, asst. to chmn., 1968-69; communications mgr. Atomic Indsl. Forum, N.Y.C., 1969-79; exec. dir. Com. for Energy Awareness, Washington, 1980; ptnr. Potomac Communications Group, Washington, 1981—; pres. Nat. Brain Rsch. Assn., 1985-86. Author of free-lance articles and book reviews. Mem. Pub. Rels. Soc. Am., Am. Nuclear Soc. Office: Potomac Communications Group 1720 I St NW # 600 Washington DC 20006-3789

PERKINS, JAMES WINSLOW, builder, contractor; b. Southington, Conn., Sept. 15, 1955; s. Robert Winslow and Florence Corinne (Angelone) P. Student, Tunxis Community Coll., Farmington, Conn., 1973-75. Owner Town & Country Club, Smithfield, R.I., 1975-80, Ad Mark of Mass, Inc., Ludlow, Mass., 1980-84, Car Stereo Distbrs., Inc., West Palm Beach, Fla., 1983-85, Internat. Imports, Lauderdale Lakes, Fla., 1985-88, Modern Sectional Homes, Inc., Southington, Conn., 1989—. Mem. Nat. Assn. Realtors, Cen. Conn. Bd. Realtors, New Eng. Mfrd. Housing Assn., 100 Club of Conn. Republican. Home: 2587 Meriden-wtby Rd Marion CT 06444-9999 Office: Modern Sectional Homes PO Box 153 Marion CT 06444-0153

PERKINS, ROGER ALLAN, lawyer; b. Port Chester, N.Y., Mar. 4, 1943; s. Francis Newton and Winifred Marcella (Smith) P.; m. Katherine Louise Howard, Nov. 10, 1984; children: Marshall, Morgan, Matthew, Justin, Ashley. BA, Pa. State U., 1965; postgrad., U. Ill., 1965-66; JD with honors, George Washington U., 1969. Bar: Md. 1969, Mass. 1975. Trial atty. Nationwide Ins. Co., Annapolis, Md., 1969-72; assoc. Arnold, Beauchemin & Huber, P.A., Balt., 1973; assoc., then ptnr. Goodman & Bloom, P.A., Annapolis, 1973-76; ptnr. Luff and Perkins, Annapolis, 1976-78; sole practice Anapolis, 1978—; temp. adminstrv. hearing officer Anne Arundel County, 1984—; asst. city atty. Annapolis, 1980-82; atty. Bd. Appeals of City of Annapolis, 1986—. Coach youth sports. Mem. ABA, Md. State Bar Assn. (pres.-elect 1991-92, treas. 1988-91, bd. gov. 1985-87, exec. com. 1986-87, sect. delivery local svcs., chmn. judicare com. 1981-83, family and juvenile law sect. coun. 1983-89, chmn. 1987-88), Anne Arundel County Bar Assn. (treas. 1981-83, pres. 1984-85), Gov.'s Task Force on Family Law, 1991—, adv. coun. on family legal needs of low income persons MLSC, 1991. Republican. Methodist. Home: 503 Bay Hills Dr Arnold MD 21012-2001 Office: The Courtyards 133 Defense Hwy Ste 202 Annapolis MD 21401-7015

PERKINS, THOMAS COLE, mortgage and real estate investment officer; b. Oklahoma City, July 3, 1933; s. Leon Blair and Ruth (Cole) P.; m. Priscilla A. Cole, May 1, 1976; 1 child, Laura Catherine. BBA, Okla. U., 1956. CREA. Ptnr. Perkins Bros., Oklahoma City, 1959-62; regional mgr. Northwestern Mut. Life Ins. Co., N.Y.C., 1962-69; v.p. Tchrs. Ins. and Annuity Assn., N.Y.C., 1969, Sonnenblick-Goldman Corp., N.Y.C., 1969-73; pres. Security Mortgage Investors, N.Y.C., 1973-78; mng. ptnr. T.C. Perkins Assn., N.Y.C., 1978-80; v.p. Salomon Bros., Inc., N.Y.C., 1980-81, Coronet Properties, N.Y.C., 1981-90, Union Labor Life Ins. Co., Washington, 1990—; Cert. real estate appraiser. Comdr. USNR, 1956-70. Mem. Nat. Assn. Realtors (cert.), Mortgage Bankers Assn., Urban Land Inst., Kenwood Country Club, Kappa Sigma. Presbyterian.

PERKINSON, HENRY, education educator, author; b. Phila., Nov. 27, 1930; m. Mar. 28, 1953; 5 children. Grad. U. Pa., 1952; postgrad. Harvard U., 1954-59. Mem. faculty Kent State U., Ohio, 1959-63; mem. faculty NYU, N.Y.C., 1963—, now prof. history of edn. Author: The Imperfect Panacea 1968, 2nd edit., 1976, 3rd edit. 1990; The Possibilities of Error, 1971; Two Hundred Years of American Educational Thought, 1976; Since Socrates, 1980; Learning From Our Mistakes, 1984; Getting Better: The Moral Effects of Television, 1991. Served with U.S. Army, 1952-54, Korea. Office: NYU 737 East Bldg New York NY 10003

PERKO, KENNETH ALBERT, JR., real estate executive, mathematics researcher; b. Iron Mountain, Mich., Feb. 9, 1943; s. Kenneth Albert and Alice Ellen (Hamad) P.; m. Susan Jane Roodenburg, Oct. 5, 1968; children: Kathryn Ann, Kenneth Albert. AB, Princeton U., 1964; JD, Harvard U., 1967. Bar: Ohio, N.Y.; cert. real estate broker, N.Y. Assoc. Milbank, Tweed, Hadley & McCloy, N.Y.C., 1967-79; asst. sec. The Rockefeller Group, N.Y.C., 1979—; v.p., gen. counsel Radio City Music Hall, N.Y.C., 1985—; sec. Rockefeller Ctr., Inc., 1990—; lectr. Cambridge U., London, 1979, U. Paris, 1979. Contbr. numerous papers to scholarly jours., 1974—; reviewer Mathematical Reviews, 1980—. Trustee The Princeton Libr., N.Y.C., 1968—, The Rockette Alumnae Found., 1992—. Grantee NSF, Blacksburgh, Va., 1982. Mem. Am. Math. Soc., The Rockefeller Ctr. Club, The Hemisphere Club (counsel 1979-92). Democrat. Roman Catholic. Home: 325 Old Army Rd Scarsdale NY 10583-2643 Office: The Rockefeller Group 1230 Ave of The Americas New York NY 10020-1513

PERLEMAN, LESLIE COOPER, English educator, researcher; b. L.A., Mar. 3, 1948; s. Noe Selig and Florence (Cooper) P.; m. Elizabeth Jane Gerrels, Jan. 3, 1981; 1 child, David Noah. BA, U. Calif., Berkeley, 1970; MA, U. Mass., 1973, PhD, 1980. Post doctoral fellow U. So. Calif., L.A., 1980-83; asst. prof., dir. freshman English Tulane U., New Orleans, 1983-87; asst. dean MIT, Cambridge, Mass., 1987—; cons. writing programs to various Univs. , 1985—. Co-editor: Middle English Letter of Alexander to Aristotle, 1978; contbr. articles to profl. jours. Mem. Nat. Coun. Tchrs. of English (com. on pub. doublespeak). Jewish. Office: MIT 77 Massachusetts Ave Cambridge MA 02139-4307

PERLESS, ROBERT L., sculptor; b. N.Y.C., Apr. 23, 1938; s. Meyer and Ethel (Glassman) P.; m. Ellen R. Kaplan, July 2, 1965. Student, U. Miami, Fla., 1955-59. One-man exhbns. include Bodley Gallery, N.Y.C., 1968, 70, Galerie Simonne Stern, New Orleans, 1969, Bernard Danenberg Gallery, N.Y.C., 1970-72, Bonino Gallery, N.Y.C., 1976; group exhbns. include Bodley Gallery, 1970, Whitney Mus., 1970, Forum Gallery, N.Y.C., 1975, Bonino Gallery, 1975, Houston Gallery, 1976, Aldrich Mus., Ridgefield, Conn., 1978, Taft Mus., Cin., 1980, Aldrich Mus., 1987, Stamford (Conn.) Mus., 1989, Bruce Mus., Greenwich, Conn., 1989, Andre Emmerich's Top Gallant Farm, 1992; rep. permanent collections, Whitney Mus., Aldrich Mus., Chrysler Mus., Norfolk, Va., Everson Mus., Syracuse, N.Y., Okla. Art Center, Oklahoma City, Phoenix Art Mus., Stamford (Conn.) Mus. Address: 37 Langhorne Ln Greenwich CT 06831

PERLIN, MICHAEL LOUIS, law educator; b. Perth Amboy, N.J., Mar. 30, 1946; s. Jacob W. and Sophie L. (Rosenthal) P.; m. Linda Mason, Nov. 1, 1970; children: Julie, Alexander. AB, Rutgers U., 1966; JD, Columbia U., 1969. Bar: N.J., N.Y., U.S. Supreme Ct., U.S. Ct. Appeals (2d cir. and 5th cir.). Law clk. hon. Ralph L. Fusco Superior Ct. N.J., Newark, 1969-70; law clk. hon. Sidney Goldmann Appellate Div. N.J., Trenton, 1970-71; deputy pub. defender N.J. Office of Pub. Defender, Trenton, 1971-74; dir. div. mental health advocacy N.J. Dept. Pub. Advocate, Trenton, 1974-82, spl. counsel to commn., 1982-84; assoc. prof. N.Y. Law Sch., N.Y.C., 1984-90, prof., 1990—; chmn. sect. on law and mental disability Am. Assn. Law Schs., Washington, 1991-92; nat. adv. bd. Inst. Mental Disability and Law, Williamsburg, Va., 1989—; cons. Nat. Inst. Mental Health, Washington, 1979-82. Contbr. articles to profl. jours. Mem. Pres. Carter's Commn. Mental Health, Washington, 1977-78, N.J. Supreme Ct. Commn. Rels., Trenton, 1977-80, N.J. Supreme Ct. Commn. Civil Commitments, Trenton, 1976-84. Mem. Am. Acad., Psychologyh and Law (Amicus award 1988), Am. Soc. Law Medicine, Internat. Acad. Psychiatry and Law (bd. dirs. 1990—). Democrat. Jewish. Office: NY Law Sch 57 Worth St New York NY 10013

PERLIN, RUTH RUDOLPH, museum official, art historian, educator; b. Washington, Apr. 21, 1936; d. Robert Irving and Sadie Lillian (Brown) Rudolph; m. Seymour Perlin, Aug. 21, 1958; children: Jonathan B., Steven M., Jeremy F. BA, Wellesley Coll., 1957; MA, NYU, 1964. Instr. art history Towson (Md.) State U., 1967-69; chief edn. Balt. Mus. Art, 1969-72; curator Nat. Gallery Art, Washington, 1974-80, head dept. extension programs, curator-in-charge, 1980-90, head edn. resources, 1990—; editorial advisor Art and Man, Scholastic mags., N.Y.C., 1980—; reviewer, panelist interagy. com. on audiovisual prodns. USIA, Washington, 1982—. Mem. editorial bd. Studies in History Art, 1976-82, chmn. 1978-82; producer films on art; author texts and ednl. programs on Am. furniture, pottery and textiles, 1978-80; project dir. 1st videodisc on a mus. Nat. Gallery of Art, 1979-82; producer videodisc American Art, 1991-92. Panel mem. youth programs Md. Arts Coun., Balt., 1970-72; former grant reviewer media and youth programs, panel mem. NEH, Washington. Recipient Golden Eagle award for films J.F. Peto and the Idea of Still Life Painting, Coun. on Internat. Nontheatrical Events, 1984, Winslow Homer, 1985, The Nature of the Artist, 1986, John James Audubon: The Birds of America, 1988, William Merritt Chase at Shinnecock, 1990, F.E. Church Landscapes, 1990. Mem. Am. Assn. Mus. (edn. com., surveyor mus. assessment program III 1991—), Mus. Edn. Roundtable (bd. dirs. 1978-82), Nat. Art Edn. Assn. (chmn. subcom. on non-print materials, mem. com. on profl. materials), Coll. Art Assn. Office: Nat Gallery Art Dept Edn Resources Washington DC 20565

PERLISH, HARVEY NEIL (NEIL HARVEY), early education educator, academic administrator, author; b. Phila., Apr. 5, 1921; s. Herman Leonard and Dora (Polay) P.; m. Florence Helen Powell, Mar. 14, 1943 (dec. Apr. 1987); children: Joel, Lillian. BA, U. Pa., 1949, MA, 1965, PhD, 1968. With ednl. projects staff Triangle Broadcasting Corp., Phila., 1945-71; dean Insts. Achievement Human Potential, Phila., 1963—; pres. World Orgn. Human Potential, Phila., 1988-92. Author: Kids Who Start Ahead, Stay Ahead, 1992. Served with USAF, 1943-45, ETO. Fellow Internat. Acad. Child Brain Devel. (sec. 1986—, award 1979). Office: Insts Achievement Human Potential 8801 Stenton Ave Philadelphia PA 19118

PERLMAN, ITZHAK, violinist; b. Tel Aviv, Aug. 31, 1945; s. Chaim and Shoshana P.; m. Toby Lynn Friedlander, 1967; 5 children. Student, Tel Aviv Acad. Music, Juilliard Sch., Meadowmount Sch. Music.; hon. degree in music, Tufts U., 1986. Appeared with N.Y. Philharm., Cleve. Orch., Phila. Orch., Nat. Symphony Orch., most orchs. in U.S., with Berlin Philharm., English Chamber Orch., London Symphony, London Philharm., Royal Philharm., BBC Orch., Vienna Philharm, Concertgebouw; participant numerous music festivals, including Ravinia Festival, Berkshire Music Festival, Aspen Music Festival, Israel Festival, Wolf Trap Summer Festival, recital tours, U.S., Can., S.Am., Europe, Israel, Australia, Far East; recorded for Angel, London, RCA Victor, DG, CBS records. Recipient Leventritt prize 1964. Recipient Leventritt prize, 1964, Grammy awards, 1977, 78, 80-82, 87, Award - Medal of Liberty, 1986; hon. doctorates from Harvard U., Yale U, Brandeis U., Hebrew U.-Jerusalem. *

PERLMAN, MARK, educator, economist; b. Madison, Wis., Dec. 23, 1923; s. Selig and Eva (Shaber) P.; m. Naomi Gertrude Waxman, June 7, 1953; 1 child, Abigail Ruth. B.A., M.A., U. Wis., 1947; Ph.D., Columbia, 1950. Asst. prof. U. Hawaii, 1951-52, Cornell U., 1952-55; asst. prof., then assoc. prof. Johns Hopkins U., 1955-63; prof. econs., history and pub. health U. Pitts., 1963—, univ. prof., 1969—, chmn. dept., 1965-70; vis. fellow Clare Hall, U. Cambridge, 1977, ofcl. visitor univ. faculty econs. and politics, 1976-77; mem. Princeton Inst. Advanced Study, 1981-82; co-chmn. Internat. Econ. Assn. Conf. on Econs. of Health in Industrialized Nations, Tokyo, Japan, 1973, Conf. on Orgn. and Retrieval Econs. Data, Kiel, West Germany, 1975; co-chmn., co-editor Internat. Congress on Health Econs., Leyden, Netherlands, 1980; adj. scholar Am. Enterprise Inst., 1981—; Österreichischer Länderbank Joseph Schumpeter prof. Technische Universität, Vienna, 1982; disting. vis. scholar Beijing Chinese Nat. Acad. Social Scis., 1983; Rockefeller Found. resident scholar Villa Serbelloni, Bellagio, Como, Italy, 1983; vis. prof. Inst. für Weltwirtschaft U. Kiel, 1987, U. Augsburg, 1992; mem. Internat. Com. for Documentation in the Social Scis., UNESCO, 1987—. Author: Judges in Industry: A Study of Labor Arbitration in Australia, 1954, Labor Union Theories in America, 1958, 2d edit., 1976, The Machinists: A New Study in American Trade Unionism, 1962, (with T.D. Baker) Health Manpower in a Developing Economy, 1967; editor: The Economics of Health and Medical Care, 1974, The Organization and Retrieval of Economic Knowledge, 1977, (with G.K. MacLeod) Health Care Capital: Competition and Control, 1978, (with K. Weiermair) Studies in Economic Rationality: X-Efficiency Examined and Extolled, 1990, (with A. Heertje) Evolving Technology and Market Structure: Studies in Schumpeterian Economics, 1990, (with N.H. Ornstein) Political Power and Social Change: The United States Faces a United Europe, 1991; (with C.E. Barfield) Capital Markets and Trade: The United States Faces a United Europe, 1991, Industry, Services, and Agriculture: The U.S. Faces a United Europe, 1991; Political Power and Social Change: The United States Faces a United Europe, 1991; (with F.M. Scherer), Entrepreneurship, Technological Innovation, and Economic Growth: Studies in Schumpeterian Economics, 1992; also articles, essays on health, population change, econ. devel., orgn. econ. knowledge and methodology, econ. productivity, history of econ. discipline; Festschrifts (Sir John Barry, Edgar M. Hoover), 1972; editor: series Cambridge Surveys of Contemporary Economics, Cambridge Surveys of Economic Institutions and Policies, 1991—; cons. editor, later editorial cons. USIA publ., Portfolio on Internat. Econ. Perspectives, 1972-83; cons. editor Economics, 1990—; mng. co-editor Jour. Evolutionary Econs., 1989—; corr. Am. editor Revue d'Economie Politique, 1990—; series editor Great Economists of the World, 1990—. With U.S. Army, 1943-46. Social Sci. Research Council fellow, 1949-50; Ford Found. fellow, 1962-63; Fulbright lectr. Melbourne U., 1968. Mem. Am. Econ. Assn. (founding and mng. editor Jour. Econ. Lit. 1968-81), Royal Econ. Soc., Internat. Union Sci. Study Population, History Econs. Soc. (v.p. 1979-80, pres. elect 1983-84, pres. 1984-85), J.A. Schumpeter Intellectuale Gesellschaft (editor 1986—). Jewish. Club: Athenaeum (London). Home: 5622 Bartlett St Pittsburgh PA 15217-1514

PERLMUTTER, ARTHUR, chemical engineer, process design; b. Lodz, Poland, Feb. 26, 1930; came to U.S., 1960; s. Jacob and Regina (Friedmann) P.; m. Esther Farber, June 9, 1957; children: Ruben George, Janet Regina. BSChemE, U. Havana, 1955; MSChemE, Columbia U., 1965. From jr. chem. engr. to chem. engr. Rayon Fibers Mfrs., Matanzas, Cuba, 1956-59; chem. engr. Goodyear Tire Co. of Cuba, Havana, 1959-60; chem. engr., pilot plant supr. Rheingold Breweries, Bklyn., 1961-67; rsch. chem. engr. rsch. div. Am. Cyanamid Co., Stamford, Conn., 1968-75; sr. process engr. engring div. Am. Cyanamid Co., Wayne, N.J., 1975-80; sr. tech. assoc. chem. div. GAF Corp., Wayne, 1980-83, plant design mgr. chem. div., 1983-86; project mgr. GAF Chems. Corp., Wayne, 1986-90, mgr. plant design, 1990—. Co-author tech. publs.; co-invenotr thermoplastic disposal method. Pres. Queens (N.Y.) Valley Home Owners Civic Assn., 1972-75. Mem. Am. Chem. Soc., Am. Inst. Chem. Engrs. Home: 10-05 Elaine Terr Fair Lawn NJ 07410 Office: GAF Chems Corp Inc 1361 Alps Rd Wayne NJ 07470-3700

PERLMUTTER, BARBARA S., public relations executive; b. Hartford, Conn., Oct. 7, 1941; d. Leon and Ethel (Zinman) Sondik; m. Louis Perlmutter, Dec. 11, 1966; children: Kermit, Eric. BA, Smith Coll., 1963; MA in History, Columbia U., 1965; MBA, NYU, 1979. Analyst Celanese Internat. Co., N.Y.C., 1965-69; sr. econ. analyst Nat. Econ. Rsch. Assoc., White Plains, N.Y., 1979-85; dir. pub. affairs Marsh & McLennan Companies, Inc., N.Y.C., 1985-88, v.p. pub. affairs, 1988—. Office: Marsh & McLennan Companies 1166 Ave of The Americas New York NY 10036-2708

PERLMUTTER, DIANE F., communications executive; b. N.Y.C., Aug. 31, 1945; d. Bert H. and Frances (Smith) P. Student, NYU Grad. Sch. of Bus., 1969-70; AB in English, Miami U., Oxford, Ohio, 1967. Writer sales promotion Equitable Life Assurance, N.Y.C., 1967-68; adminstrv. asst. de Garmo, Inc., N.Y.C., 1968-69, asst. account exec., 1969-70, account exec., 1970-74, v.p., account supr., 1974-76; mgr. corp. advt. Avon Products, Inc., N.Y.C., 1976-79, dir. communications Latin Am., Spain, Can., 1979-80, dir. brochures, 1980-81, dir. category merchandising, 1981-82, group dir. motivational communications, 1982-83, group dir. sales promotion, 1983-84, v.p. sales promotion, 1984, v.p. internat. bus. devel., 1984-85, area v.p. Latin Am., 1985, v.p. advtg. and campaign mktg., 1985-87, v.p. U.S. operational planning, 1987; cons. N.Y.C., 1987-88; sr. v.p. Burson-Marsteller, N.Y.C., 1988—, exec. v.p., mng. dir. consumer products, 1991—; chairperson ann. meeting Direct Selling Assn., Washington, 1982; v.p. Nat. Home Fashions League, N.Y.C., 1975-76; bd. dirs. Double L.P. Industries, Inc., 1988—. Founding bd. mem. Am. Red Magen David for Israel, N.Y.C., 1970-75; mem. adv. coun. Miami Sch. Bus., 1986—, Miami Sch. Applied Scis., 1978-81. Mem. Advt. Woemn of N.Y., Women in Communications, Miami U. Alumni Assn. (pres., chair 1986), Beta Gamma Sigma. Office: Burson-Marsteller 230 Park Ave S New York NY 10003-1513

PERLMUTTER, JACK, artist, lithographer; b. N.Y.C., Jan. 23, 1920; s. Morris and Rebecca (Schiffman) P.; m. Norma Mazo, Dec. 24, 1942; children: Judith Faye, Ellen. Staff Dickey Gallery, D.C. Tchrs. Coll., 1951-68, dir., 1962-68, now prof. art; chmn. printmaking dept. Corcoran Gallery Sch. Art, 1960-82, now prof. art; Fulbright research prof. painting and printmaking Tokyo U. Arts, 1959-60; art cons. Pres.'s Com. to Hire Handicapped. Artist-in-residence, Gibbs Art Gallery, Charleston, S.C., 1974—, NASA artist for, 1st Saturn V moon rocket, Apollo 6, Apollo 16, Orbiter Columbia (space shuttle), Voyager II; Contbg. editor: Art Voices South, 1979-80, Art Voices, 1980-82; numerous one-man shows, U.S. and Tokyo, including, Nat. Acad. Scis., 1981, Arts Club Washington, 1981, Annapolis, Md., 1982; exhibited nat. shows, U.S., Switzerland, Yugoslavia, traveling exhibits, Europe, S.Am., Can., works in, permanent collections, Bklyn. Mus., Cin. Mus. Art, Carnegie Inst. Art, Corcoran Gallery Art, Library Congress, Met. Mus. Art, N.Y.C., Nat. Gallery Art, Washington, Phila. Mus. Art, Walker Gallery, Mpls., Nat. Mus. Modern Art, Tokyo, others. Fellow Internat. Inst. Arts and Letters; mem. Soc. Am. Graphic Artists. Club: Cosmos (Washington). Studio: 2511 Cliffbourne Pl NW Washington DC 20009

PERLMUTTER, NATHAN MARTIN, insurance executive; b. Bklyn., Aug. 14, 1947; s. Joseph Meyer and Molly (Alderoty) P.; m. Rosalyn Taffet, Oct. 31, 1970; children: Jacqueline, Andrea, David. BBA, Pace U., 1971; diploma ChFC, Am. Coll., 1985. CLU, 1978; chartered fin. cons. Sales rep. Met. Life Ins. Co., N.Y.C., 1972-80; gen. agt. Guardian Life Ins. Co., Elmhurst, N.Y., 1980—; pres. NMP Planning, Elmhurst, 1980—, Forest Hills Fin. Group, N.Y.C., 1985—, Holly View Devel. Corp., Monroeville, N.J., 1986—, Perl Brokerage, Forest Hills., 1988—; vice chmn. Parker Brokerage Co., Inc., N.Y.; cons. Nyles Teicher Assocs., Great Neck, N.Y., 1985—, Sutton & Edwards, Inc., Lake Success, 1986—. Contbr. articles to profl. jours. Bd. dirs. Temple Beth Am Brotherhood, Merrick, 1985-87. With USNR, 1974-79. Mem. Pace U. Alumni Assn. (pres. 1987-89), N.Y.C. Assn. Health Underwriters (co-founder, v.p. 1984—), Atlantic Agy. Mgrs. Assn. (pres. 1982-83), Gen. Agts. Mgrs. Assn. (br. pres. 1979-80, Nat. Mgmt. award 1983-88), Million Dollar Round Table (life, mem. of ct. 1988), N.Y.C. Life Underwriters Assn. (pres. 1988-89). Home: 1951 Helen Ct Merrick NY 11566-4931 Office: Forest Hills Fin Group Inc 108-14 72d Ave Forest Hills NY 11375

PERLOV, ALEXANDER KEEVER, music educator; b. Bklyn., Apr. 30, 1933; s. Alexander Perel Perlov and Marion (Markowitz) Saphire; m. Marion Jean Resinol, Sept. 3, 1960; children: Alyssa Jean, Mark Alexander. AB, Duke U., 1954; student, Juilliard Sch., 1961-62. Composer, pianist; music dir., cantor Ch. of the Assumption, Tuckahoe, N.Y., 1982—; music coord. Girls & Boys Club of New Rochelle, 1984—; organist, cantor Ch. of the Nativity, Bronx, 1990-91; gen. mgr. New Rochelle Opera, Inc., 1990—; organist Our Lady of the Rosary Ch., Portchester, N.Y., 1992—; artistic coord. New Rochelle Opera, Inc., 1985-90. Composer: Colours, 1968. Recipient contbn. to comml. TV music scoring award. Mem. Broadcast Music, Inc., Music Educators League Westchester, Archdiocesan Ch. Musicians.

PERMISON, WILLIAM STEPHEN, human resources specialist; b. Shreveport, La.; s. Milford Leonard and Ruth Lillian (Vedlitz) P.; m. Jane Ellen Zabar, Oct. 18, 1986; 1 child, Matthew Ross. BA, Am. U., MEd in Human Resources Mgmt.-Counseling. Cert. profl. counselor, Md.; nat. cert. counselor; cert. sr. profl. in human resources. Prin. Hay Career Cons. div. Hay Assocs., Washington, 1981-82; cons. Rockville, Md., 1982-83; mng. dir. human resources cons. div. Nat. Resources Inc., Rockville, Md., 1983; pres. Human Resource Cons. Inc., Washington, 1984-85; ops. mgr. M.L. Palmer & Assocs., Ltd., Bethesda, Md., 1986-88; profl. recruiter Telecommunications Techniques Corp., Germantown, Md., 1988-89, employment mgr., 1989—. Mem. AACD, Soc. for Human Resource Mgmt., Nat. Vocat. Guidance Assn., Washington Tech. Pers. Forum, Psi Chi. Home: 5209 Continental Dr Rockville MD 20853-1119 Office: Telecommunications Techniques Corp 20400 Observation Dr Germantown MD 20876-4092

PERNAL, MICHAEL EDWARD, academic administrator; b. Hartford, Conn., Aug. 17, 1943; s. Edward F. and Wanda (Zackowski) P.; m. Maureen Lynn Sullivan, June 17, 1967; children: Shaileen, David. BS, Cen. Conn. State Coll., 1965; MA, U. Conn., 1969, PhD, 1975. Tchr. English Talcott Jr. High Sch., West Hartford, Conn., 1965-66, asst. dir. fin. aid, 1969-72; dir. fin. aid Ea. Conn. State U., Willimantic, 1972-77, dean pers. adminstrn., 1977-88, acting v.p. for adminstrn. affairs, 1984-85, exec. dean, 1988—, acting v.p. fin. and adminstrn., 1992—; con. City of Willimantic, 1981. Contbr. articles to profl. jours. Umpire, coach Windham (Conn.) Youth

Orgn., 1972-88; mem. region adv. coun. Manchester (Conn.) Community Coll., 1988; coach Sr. League Baseball, Willimantic, 1991. With USNR, 1966-68, Naples, Italy. Mem. Am. Mgmt. Assn., Ea. Coll. and Univ. Pers. Assn., Wellfleet (Mass.) C. of C., Greater Willimantic C. of C. (bd. dirs. 1992—). Office: Ea Conn State U 82 Windham St Willimantic CT 06226-2212

PERNETTI, ROBYN MARIE, financial analyst; b. Jersey City, Oct. 25, 1964; d. Joseph Edward and Marie Ann (Fusco) P. AA, NYU, 1984, BA, 1985; MBA, Northeastern U., Boston, 1987. Fin. analyst Horn's Inc., Bergenfield, N.J., 1987—; promotions dir. Horn's Inc., 1988—. Author: A Passion Aflame, 1990. Recipient Nat. Honor-Piano award Nat. Fedn. Music Clubs, 1974-77, Superior Rating-Piano award Nat. Fedn. Festivals, 1974-77, Nat. Mem. award Nat. Piano Playing Auditions, 1974-77, Presdl. Physical Fitness award U.S. Govt., 1975-77, Cert. of Merit, Concours Nat. De Français, 1981, Flight award Windrock Aviation, 1989. Mem. AFTRA, Overpeck Riding Ctr., Montclair Riding Acad., Hawaii Diamond Head Climbers Hui, 4-H. Republican. Roman Catholic.

PEROS, VASILIOS, engineering executive; b. Balt., Dec. 29, 1961; s. Michael and Fotini (Frangos) P. BS in Aerospace Engring., Va. Poly. Inst., 1983; MSME, U. Del., 1987. Co-op student Martin Marietta Aero & Naval Systems, Balt., 1980-82; assoc. engr. Martin Marietta Aero & Naval Systems, 1983-84; engr., 1984-85; sr. engr. Martin Marietta Aero & Naval Systems, Balt., 1985-87, group engr., 1987-91, sr. group engr., 1991—. Contbr. articles to profl. jours. Mem. AIAA. Home: 3102 Hamilton Ave Baltimore MD 21214-2637 Office: Martin Marietta Aero 103 Chesapeake Park Pl Baltimore MD 21220

PERPICH, JOSEPH GEORGE, health facility administrator; b. Hibbing, Minn., July 22, 1941; s. Anton R. and Mary Perpich; m. Cathy Sulzberger, Dec. 14, 1974; children: David, Sarah, Abigail. BA (with honors), U. Minn., 1963, MD, 1966; JD, Georgetown U., 1974. Diplomate Am. Bd. Psychiatry and Neurology; bar: U.S. Ct. Appeals D.C. 1975. Intern U. Minn. Hosps., Mpls., 1966-67; resident in psychiatry Mass. Gen. Hosp., 1968-69; psychiat. fellow St. Elizabeths Hosp., Washington; with U.S. Pub. Health Svc., Nat. Inst. Mental Health; sr. profl. assoc. Inst. Med./Nat. Acad. Sci., Washington, 1974-76; assoc. dir. planning & evaluation NIH, Bethesda, Md., 1976-81; v.p. planning & devel. Genex Corp., Rockville, Md., 1981-83, Meloy Labs, Inc., Springfield, Va., 1984-87; v.p. grants & spl. programs Howard Hughes Med. Inst., Bethesda, 1987—; task force mem. Carnegie Commn. on Sci. Technology & Govt., N.Y.C., 1990-92; bd. dirs. Am. Bd. on Internal Medicine, Boston, 1989-92. Author: A Revolution in Biotechnology, 1989, Biotechnology in Society: Private Init, 1986; contbr. articles to profl. jours.; editorial adv. bd. Courts, Health Science & the Law, 1989-92. Mayor Village of Drummond, Chevy Chase, Md., 1990-91, treas., 1988-90. Recipient SES Performance award U.S. Govt., 1980, NIH Dir.'s award, 1979, NIMH Career Devel. award USPHS, 1971-74. Fellow Am. Psychiat. Assn.; mem. ABA, Bar of D.C. Ct. Appeals, Am. Intellectual Property Law Assn., Alpha Omega Alpha. Office: Howard Hughes Med Inst 6701 Rockledge Dr Bethesda MD 20817-1813

PERRIN, CARL RICHARD, English language educator, writer; b. Medford, Mass., Oct. 11, 1930; s. Carl Henry and Jeanette (Babcock) P.; m. Della Marie Smock, Nov. 8, 1952 (div. Dec. 1984); children: Jeanette, Lisa, Philip, Daniel, Edward. BA, U. N.H., 1956; MEd, Rivier Coll., Nashua, N.H., 1959; PhD, Ohio State U., 1973. Tchr. English Hollis (N.H.) High Sch., 1956-58, S.W. High Sch., St. Louis, 1959-65, Gorham (Maine) High Sch., 1974-76; asst. prof. English Defiance (Ohio) Coll., 1965-74; counselor, house mgr. Goodwill of Maine, Portland, 1976-81; instr., head dept. English Casco Bay Coll., Portland, Maine, 1978—. Author: Subject Meets Verb, 1983, Getting Your Point Across, 1990; author articles, short stories and poetry. Sgt. U.S. Army, 1951-54. Mem. Nat. Coun. Tchrs. English, Maine Writers and Pubs. Alliance, Maine Coun. English Lang. Arts, Nat. Writers Club. Office: Casco Bay Coll 477 Congress St Portland ME 04101-3406

PERRIN, CHARLES ROBERT, artist; b. Medford, Mass., July 13, 1915; s. Arthur A. Perrin and Edna (May) Loomis. Student, Sch. Practical Art, Boston, 1935-37. Comml. artist Boston, 1938-42, 46-77; with fine art gallery of watercolors Nantucket, Mass., 1977; owner C. Robert Perrin Gallery, Nantucket, 1966—. Exhibited works in retrospective show, Nantucket, 1990; featured on TV shows; contbr. articles to profl. jours. Sgt. U.S. Army, 1942-45, ETO. Recipient Purchase prize Boston Soc. Independent Artists, 1952, William Pulicover award North Shore Arts Assn., 1954, Ross award Boston Soc. Watercolor Painters, 1955, N.H.R.R. Autumn in New Eng. award, 1958, Richard Mitton Meml. award 32nd Annual Exhbn. Painting by Contemporary New Eng. Artists, 1961, 1st Jury award at Patrons Show, Artist Assn. Nantucket, 1963, 1st Jury award Copley Soc. Boston Crafts, 1965, Critics award Art Dirs. Club Boston, Paul H. Allen Meml. award Copley Soc. Mem. Am. Watercolor Soc., Guild Boston Artists, Artist Assn. Nantucket (George Walling award 1981, Jurors' Choice award, others), New Eng. Watercolor Soc. Home and Office: PO Box 1335 Nantucket MA 02554-1335

PERRIN, JANE FRANCES, insurance company executive; b. Winthrop, Mass., Dec. 19, 1940; d. William Francis and Isabelle Frances (Mythen) Moran; m. James Joseph McDonald, Aug. 21, 1965 (div. 1976); children: Maureen Lynn, Susan Jill, Kevin James; m. Clive Earl Perrin, Nov. 30, 1991. BS in Edn., Salem State Coll., Mass., 1962; Assoc. in Underwriting, Ins. Inst., Malvern, Pa., 1983. Tchr., East Hartford Sch. System, Conn., 1962-66; accountant Watkin Bros. Piano & Organ, Hartford, 1975-76; policy analyst Hartford Steam Boiler Insp. & Ins., 1976-80; supervising underwriter Am. Nuclear Insurers, Farmington, 1981-88, acct. exec., 1988—. Mem. Nat. Assn. Ins. Women (cert.), Am. Nuclear Soc., Nat. Assn. Female Execs., N.Y. Acad. Scis., Hartford Assn. Ins. Women (by-laws chmn. 1984-85), Amnesty Internat., Wadsworth Atheneum. Democrat. Roman Catholic. Avocations: reading, handwriting analysis, travel, crewel embroidery. Home: 84 Ashworth St Manchester CT 06040 Office: Am Nuclear Insurers 29 town Ctr West Hartford CT 06107-2445

PERRIN, KENNETH LYNN, educational council administrator; b. L.A., July 29, 1937; s. Freeman Whitaker and Lois Eileen (Bowen) P.; m. Shirley Anne Cupp, Apr. 2, 1960; children: Steven, Lynne. BA, Occidental Coll., 1959; MA, Calif. State U., Long Beach, 1964; PhD, Stanford U., 1969. Lic. in speech pathology, Calif. Chmn. dept. communicative disorders U. Pacific, Stockton, Calif., 1969-77; dir. edn. and sci. programs Am. Speech-Lang.-Hearing Assn., Rockville, Md., 1977-80; dean Faculty Profl. Studies West Chester U., Pa., 1980-82; acting acad. v.p. West Chester U., 1982, pres., 1983-91; pres. Coun. on Postsecondary Edn., Washington, 1991—; cons. in field, 1969-76; pres. north region Calif. Speech Hearing Assn., 1975-76. Co-author: monograph Prevalence of Communicative Disorders, 1981; contbr. articles to profl. jours.; editor: Guide to Graduate Education Speech Pathology and Audiology, 1980. Chmn. Southeastern chpt. Greater Brandywine Br. ARC; trainee Vocat. Rehab. Adminstrn., 1965-69. Named Disting. Alumnus Sch. Humanities Calif. State U., Long Beach, 1988. Fellow Am. Speech-Lang.-Hearing Assn. (vice chmn. edn. tng. bd. 1975-77 cert. clin. competence in speech pathology); mem. West Chester C. of C. (pres. 1988). Home: 1562A Westmoreland St Mc Lean VA 22101-4327 Office: Coun on Postsecondary Edn One Dupont Cir NW Ste 305 Washington DC 20036

PERRONE, RONALD DAVID, physician, researcher, medical educator; b. Newark, Mar. 24, 1949. BS, Pa. State U., 1971, MD, 1975. Med. researcher Emory U., Atlanta, 1975-78; fellow in nephrology Boston U. Med. Ctr., 1979-82; asst. prof. U. Rochester, N.Y., 1982-83; asst. prof. Tufts U. Sch. Medicine, Boston, 1983-90, assoc. prof., 1990—. Contbr. articles to profl. jours. Mem. ACP, Internat. Soc. Nephrology, Am. Physiol. Soc., Am. Fedn. Clin. Rsch., Am. Soc. Nephrology, N.Y. Acad. Sci. Office: Tufts U New Eng Med Ctr 750 Washington St Boston MA 02111-1533

PERROTTA, FIORAVANTE GERALD, lawyer; b. Lynbrook, N.Y., July 26, 1931; s. Ercole John and Frances (Raimondi) P. B.A., St. John's Coll., 1952, J.D., 1955. Bar: N.Y. 1955, U.S. Supreme Ct. 1971. Asst. U.S. atty. So. Dist. N.Y., 1955-57; assoc. Jackson Nash Brophy Barringer & Brooks, 1957-58; asst. counsel Gov. Rockefeller, N.Y. State, 1959-60, spl. asst., 1961-62; assoc. Simpson Thacher & Bartlett, 1960-61; dep. supt., gen. counsel N.Y. State Ins. Dept., 1963, 1st dep. supt., 1964-66; v.p. USLIFE Holding Corp., 1966-67; exec. asst. to Mayor Lindsay N.Y.C., 1968, fin. adminstr., 1969-70; ptnr. Rogers & Wells, N.Y.C., 1970—; bd. dirs. Sun Life Ins. & Annuity Co. N.Y., USLICO Corp., State of N.Y. Mortgage Agy., Northstar Life Ins. Co. Commr. State Ins. Fund, 1971-77; mem. N.Y. State Fin. Control Bd.; pres. bd. trustees N.Y. Foundling Hosp. Named Young Ins. Man of Yr. N.Y. Ins. Fedn., 1966. Mem. ABA, N.Y. State Bar Assn., Assn. Bar City N.Y., Am. Arbitration Assn. (panel arbitrators), Phi Delta Phi. Republican. Roman Catholic. Home: 20 Sutton Pl S New York NY 10022-4165 also: Clark Ln Essex CT 06426 Office: Rogers & Wells Pan Am Bldg 200 Park Ave New York NY 10166-0005

PERROTTET, CHARLES MICHAEL, company executive; b. Summit, N.J., July 31, 1944; s. Louis John and Bernice (Ryerson) P.; m. Catharine Jacobs, Sept. 6, 1989 (div. 1973); m. Margaret Anne Waldron, Nov. 26, 1976; children: Michael, Jacqueline. BS cum laude, Lehigh U., 1969; MBA, U. Chgo., 1970; MSc, London Sch. Econs., 1971. Economist W.R. Grace Co., N.Y.C., 1971-74, mgr. spl. projects, 1974-76; controller Pfipharmecs, N.Y.C., 1976-78; asst. dir. planning Pfizer Pharms., N.Y.C., 1978-79; dir. corp. planning & devel. The Toro Co., Bloomington, Minn., 1979-81, dir. internat. mktg., 1980-81; v.p. corp. devel. Hasbro/Milton Bradley, Pawtucket, R.I., 1981-87; v.p. corp. studies, chief fin. officer The Futures Group, Glastonbury, Conn., 1987—; dir. TFG Internat., Wilmington, Del., Bliss House, Springfield, Mass. Bd. dirs. Stage West, Springfield, 1985-87. With U.S. Army, 1964-67. Home: 61 Edgewood Ln Glastonbury CT 06033-3849 Office: The Futures Group 80 Glastonbury Blvd Glastonbury CT 06033-4410

PERRY, AMY, environmental advocate; b. N.Y.C., Mar. 16, 1965; d. Roger F. and Isobel Perry; m. Joshua Basseches, June 10, 1990. BA, Harvard U., 1986. Citizen organizer MASSPIRG, Boston, 1986-88, solid waste program dir., 1988—; bd. dirs. Mass Recycle, Worcester, Mass., 1989—; adv. bd. mem. State Solid Waste Adv. Com., Boston, 1988—. Mem. Squantum Community Assn., Quincy, Mass., 1991—; career resource Havard/Radcliffe Career Svcs., Cambridge, Mass. Named as Face to Watch in 92, Boston Mag., 1992. Mem. Environ. Fedn. New Eng. (bd. dirs. 1992—). Office: MASSPIRG 29 Temple Pl Boston MA 02111

PERRY, BRADFORD KENT, academic administrator; b. Boston, Oct. 26, 1942; s. Robert Woodward and Louise (Kent) P.; m. Marilyn Ann Scott, June 13, 1964; children: Katherine, Susan. BA, Harvard U., 1964; MBA, Stanford U., 1970. Commd. ensign USN, 1964, advanced through grades to lt., 1967, served in various locations, 1964-71, resigned, 1971; with Stanford (Calif.) U., 1971-88, asoc. contr., 1981-88; vice chancellor Univ. System N.H., Durham, 1988—; exec. dir. Bus. Mgmt. Inst., Stanford, 1981-86; adv. bd., New Eng. Ctr., Durham, 1988—; bd. govs. N.H. Pub. TV, Durham, 1988—. Office: Univ System NH Meyers Ctr Durham NH 03824

PERRY, CHARLES NORVIN, editor; b. Balt., Mar. 3, 1928; s. William Henry and Hazel Leona (Schmidt) P. Student pub. schs., Balt. With P.P.G. Industries, Inc., Balt., 1944-90; chmn. exec. com., fin. officer, local chpt. United Steelworkers Am., Balt., 1969-82; editor Emergency Svc. Publ., Balt., 1962—. Editor Md. Rescue Jour., 1972—; author emergency med. svc. publs. Chief emergency rescue svc. Office Disaster Control, CD, Balt.; spl. advisor emergency svcs. Gov. State Md.; chief emeritus Balt. Vol. Rescue Squad; spl. asst. emergency med. svcs. Balt. Mayor and City Coun.; mem. Regional Planning Commn. Emergency Med. Svc., 1975—; rescue instr. Fed. CD; bd. dirs. Md. Fire/Rescue Inst., U. Md.; pres. local Dem. orgn.; mem. Dem. Nat. Com. With USN, World War II. Selected Outstanding Citizen P.P.G., 1968-69, 72, Presdl. citation, 1975; commendation Mayor of Balt., 1956, 62, 75, 76, 77, 80, Can. Govt., 1981; named Balt.'s Best, 1977. Mem. Md. Ambulance and Rescue Assn. (life mem., outstanding achievement award 1977, pres. 1986—, chmn. bd. dirs), Nat. Assn. Emergency Med. Technicians (charter), Md. State Ambulance and Rescue Assn. (pres. 1986-87), Internat. Rescue and Emergency Care Assn. (Max L. Spray Meml. award 1980), Chesapeake Soc. Fire and Rescue Instrs., Am. Legion. Lutheran. Home: 2405 Tionesta Rd Baltimore MD 21227-1945 Office: 2405 Tionesta Rd Baltimore MD 21227-1945

PERRY, CHARLES OWEN, sculptor; b. Helena, Mont., Oct. 18, 1929; s. Owen Hindmarch and Margaret Carroll (Bache) P.; m. Sheila Alicia Henry, June 22, 1962; children—Paul, Carlo, Daniela, Patrick, Marco. Student, Columbia U., 1953; M.Arch., Yale U., 1958. Architect Skidmore Owings & Merrill, San Francisco, 1958-64, Prix de Rome Architecture, 1964-66; sculptor-in-residence Dartmouth Coll., 1973. One-man shows include Hansen Gallery, San Francisco, 1964, Waddell Gallery, N.Y.C., 1967, 70, Dartmouth Coll., 1973, Arts Club, Chgo., 1973; group shows include Whitney Mus., 1964, 66, Spoleto Festival, 1967, Venice Biennale, 1970, Quadrienalle di Arte de Roma, 1977, Katonah Gallery, N.Y.; represented in permanent collections, Mus. Modern Art, N.Y.C., Art Inst. Chgo., San Francisco Mus. Art, Dartmouth Coll., U. Mich., Nat. Air and Space Mus., IBM, Charlotte, N.C., Hyatt Regency, San Francisco, Fed. Res. Bank, Mpls., Barnett Plaza, Tampa, Fla., Lincoln Ctr., Dallas, Shell Oil Bldg., Melbourne, Australia, Gen. Electric Hdqrs., Fairfield, Ct., Bushnell Park, Hartford, Ct., Crystal City, Arlington, Va.; patentee in furniture design field. Served with U.S. Army, 1951-53. Decorated Bronze star. Fellow Am. Acad. Rome, Nat. Acad. Design; mem. Sculptors Guild, Nat. Acad. Design Silvermine Guild. Roman Catholic. Club: Century Assn. (N.Y.C.). Home: 20 Shorehaven Rd Norwalk CT 06855-2807 Studio: 3 Raymond St Norwalk CT 06854

PERRY, EDWARD SAMUEL (TED PERRY), film and video educator; b. New Orleans, June 4, 1937; s. Edward Severa and Gertrude (Stevens) P.; m. Miriam Moody, July 9, 1961; children: Melissa K., Megan S., John M., Edward Thad. BA, Baylor U., 1961; MA, U. Iowa, 1966, PhD, 1968. Prof., dir. grad. study Sch. Communication U. Tex., Austin, 1969-71; prof., chair cinema sect. NYU, N.Y.C., 1971-75; dir. dept. film Mus. Modern Art, N.Y.C., 1975-78; prof., chair, dean Middlebury (Vt.) Coll., 1978—; prof. film U. Iowa, Iowa City, 1967-69, SUNY-Purchase, 1974; Luce prof. film Harvard U., Cambridge, Mass., 1977-78; vis. prof. Ctr. Advanced Film Study, Am. Film Inst., L.A., 1982-87. Author: New Film Index, 1975, Fellini's 8-1/2, 1978, Michaelangelo Antonioni, 1986, others; editor: Performing Arts Resources, Vols. 1-3; author plays, including Fausta, 1990; contbr. articles and revs. to theatrical and film jours. Recipient numerous grants. Mem. Univ. Film Assn. (past bd. dirs.), Soc. Cinema Studies, Speech Communication Assn., Inst. Contemporary Art (bd. advisers), Am. Film Inst. (trustee 1980-89, chair exhbn. com.), Anthology Film Archives (bd. dirs. 1983-89), Harvard Film Archives (bd. advisers). Home: 49 South St Middlebury VT 05753-1339 Office: Middlebury Coll Wright Theatre Middlebury VT 05753

PERRY, EDWARD STANLEY, information systems specialist, consultant; b. N.Y.C., Feb. 19, 1942; s. Stanley and Sophie (Ogozaly) P.; m. Rosemarie W. Kuessner, Sept. 4, 1977. BA, Hofstra U., 1963; MBA in Econs., NYU, 1984, Advanced Profl. Cert. in Corp. Fin., 1987, Advanced Profl. Cert. in Internat. Fin., 1989, cert. in data base tech., 1990, cert. in software engring., 1991, cert. in data communications, 1992. Cert. data processor. Programmer Honeywell Corp., N.Y.C., 1967-68; cons. EPG Copmputer Systems, N.Y.C., 1969-71, Computer Horizons, N.Y.C., 1972-74, 76-77; systems officer Bankers Trust, N.Y.C., 1974-76; pres. Comparand Inc., Bayside, N.Y., 1978—. Mem. IEEE, Data Processing Mgmt. Assn., Assn. for Computing Machinery, Ind. Computer Cons. Assn. Office: Comparand Inc PO Box 4442 Flushing NY 11360-4442

PERRY, J. WARREN, health sciences educator; b. Richmond, Ind., Oct. 25, 1921; s. Charles Thomas and Zona M. (Ohler) P. BA, DePauw U., 1944; postgrad., Harvard U., 1948-49; MA, Northwestern U., 1952, PhD, 1955; DSc (hon.), D'Youville Coll., 1990. Instr. St. John's Mil. Acad., Delafield, Wis., 1944-47; counselor, asst. prof. psychology U. Ill.-Chgo., 1953-56; dir. prosthetic-orthotic edn., asst. prof. orthopaedic surgery Northwestern U. Med. Sch., 1957-61; lectr. psychology U. Chgo., 1957-61; asst. chief div. tng. Vocat. Rehab. Adminstrn., HEW, 1961-64, dep. asst. commr. research and tng., 1964-66; prof. health scis. adminstrn. SUNY-Buffalo, 1966-85, dean Sch. Health Related Professions, 1966-77, dean and prof. emeritus, 1985—; Mary E. Switzer Meml. lectr. Dallas, 1977, Lexington, 1991; mem. Task Force for Legis. for Allied Health Professions; mem. com. edn. allied health professions and services, council med. edn. AMA, 1968-73; mem. nat. adv. com. Am. Dietetic Assn., 1970-75, chmn., 1972-75; mem. nat. rev. com., regional med. programs HEW, 1969-72; mem. Inst. Medicine, Nat. Acad. Scis., 1973—, mem. steering com. on manpower policy for primary care, mem. Bd. Health Promotion and Disease Prevention, 1981-83, sr. advisor, com. to study the role of allied health, com. to study med. manpower in VA, 1988-91; mem. spl. med. adv. com. VA, 1974-77; mem. task force on manpower for prevention Fogarty Internat. Inst., NIH, 1975-76; mem. acad. planning com. Mass. Gen. Hosp., 1978-80. Founding editor: Jour. Allied Health, 1972-78, editor emeritus, 1985—; contbr. articles to profl. jours. Bd. dirs. Lyric Opera Guild, Chgo., 1957-61, dir. com. opera edn., 1957-61; chmn. acad. div. drive, council of trustees Buffalo Philharm., 1970-86; bd. overseers Buffalo Philharm. Orch., 1987—; bd. dirs. Goodwill Industries Buffalo, 1969-76; trustee Community Music Sch. Buffalo, 1977-80; mem. adv. bd., v.p. Sisters of Charity Hosp., Buffalo, 1969-87, pres., 1986-88; bd. visitors U. Pitts., 1977-80; mem. council trustees D'Youville Coll., Buffalo, 1978-88, trustee emeritus, 1989—; bd. dirs. Am. Lung Assn. of Western N.Y., 1975-92, pres., 1983; bd. dirs. Am. Lung Assn. of N.Y. State, 1981-85, exec. com., 1989-92; bd. dirs. ARC of Greater Buffalo, Artpark State Performing Arts Ctr., Lewiston, N.Y., 1987—; chmn. N.Y. State Coalition of Smoking or Health, 1987-91; trustee Theodore Roosevelt Inaugural Site Found., 1987, pres., 1991—; bd. advisors Buffalo Council on World Affairs, 1987-88; trustee Buffalo Opera Co., 1989—. Recipient Sustained Superior Service award HEW, 1965; Disting. Service award Am. Orthotics-Prosthetics Assn., 1966; Chancellor's award for adminstrv. service SUNY, 1977; Disting. Author award Jour. Allied Health, 1978; cert. of merit AMA, 1979; 1st Allied Health Leadership award SUNY Stony Brook, 1988; named Ky. Col., 1969, Nebr. adm., 1964. Fellow Am. Soc. Allied Health Professions (pres. 1969-70, cert. of merit 1977, Pres.'s award 1978, Honors of Society 1984); mem. Am. Dietetics Assn. (hon.); Mem. Am. Psychol. Assn., Am. Personnel and Guidance Assn., Nat. Rehab. Assn., Phi Beta Kappa, Phi Delta Kappa (pres. 1955), Delta Tau Delta.

PERRY, JAMES DEWOLF, management consultant; b. Providence, June 24, 1941; s. James DeWolf and Adela (Daingerfield) P.; m. Velura Flora Fifield, Dec. 10, 1966 (div. 1975); children: James DeWolf VI, Robert Scott, Leigh Daingerfield; m. Shirley M. Dunn, May 17, 1986; 1 stepchild, Andre David Simon Bernier. AB, Harvard U., 1963. Fgn. service officer State Dept., Washington, 1964-70; spl. asst. to chancellor U. Mass., Amherst, 1970-75; dir. devel. New Eng. Home for Little Wanderers, Boston, 1975-76, Wheelock Coll., Boston, 1976-78; mktg. dir. Boston Zool. Soc., 1978-81; exec. dir. Big Bro. Assn., Boston, 1981-85, South Shore Day Care, Weymouth, Mass., 1985-87; mgmt. cons. to non-profit orgns. Lenox, Mass., 1978—. Mem. Soc. of Cin. Home and Office: PO Box 1718 Lenox MA 01240-1718

PERRY, JAMES MICHAEL, museum administrator, historian; b. Washington, Jan. 30, 1960; s. Gillmore Milton and Pauline Downer (Hagood) P.; m. Mary Claire Fellows, May 26, 1982; 1 child, Elizabeth Anne. BA in History, Roanoke Coll., 1982; cert. in mus. studies, Coll. of William and Mary, 1984, MA in History, 1984. Hist. area svcs. coord. Colonial Williamsburg (Va.) Found., 1984-90; park ranger Nat. Park Svc. (White House, Clara Barton Nat. Hist. Site), Washington and Glen Echo, Md., 1990-91; vis. programs coord. Supreme Ct. of U.S., Washington, 1991—. Author: Colonial Williamsburg: A Guide for the Handicapped, 1983, Colonial Williamsburg: A Guide for Deaf and Hearing Impaired Visitors, 1984; editor: The Visitor's Companion, 1986; contbr. articles to profl. jours. Vol. disaster svcs. ARC, Washington, 1987—; v.p. Williamsburg Vol. Fire Dept., 1988-90; EMT Bethesda (Md.) Chevy Chase Rescue Squad, 1990—. Mem. Am. Assn. for State and Local History, Am. Assn. Mus., Hist. Soc. Washington, Manuscript Soc., Md. Hist. Soc., Blue Key Soc., Phi Alpha Theta, Pi Gamma Mu. Office: Supreme Ct US One 1st St NE Washington DC 20543

PERRY, JANET ESTELLE, economist; b. Carlsbad, N.Mex., Dec. 15, 1953; d. Vernon Dwain and Margaret Elizabeth (Liston) P.; m. Steve Paul Watson, Aug. 17, 1973 (div. 1975); 1 child, Jenifer Jeanne (dec.); m. Terry Don Mayfield, July 4, 1978; 1 child, Sheena Nicole. BA in Anthropology, N.Mex. State U., 1978, MS in Agrl. Econs., 1981; PhD in Agrl. Econs., Okla. State U., 1990. Anthropologist Cultural Resources Management Div., Las Cruces, N.Mex., 1977-78; econ. Pub. Svc. Co. N.Mex., Albuquerque, 1980-82, Halliburton Svcs., Duncan, Okla., 1984-86; rsch. asst. Okla. State U., Stillwater, 1986-90; agrl. econ. Econ. Rsch. Svc. USDA, Washington, 1990—. Contbr. articles to profl. jours. Del. Okla. Dem. Caucus, Oklahoma City, 1984. Mem. Am. Agrl. Econs. Assn., AAUW, Omicron Delta Epsilon. Methodist. Home: 5120 Thackery Ct Fairfax VA 22032 Office: Farm Firm and Household Well-Being Rsch 1301 New York Ave NW Washington DC 20005-4708

PERRY, JOHN BALDWIN, podiatrist, consultant; b. Stoneham, Mass., Apr. 7, 1961; s. Frederick Richard and Margaret Louise (Wise) P.; m. Maureen Vincenza Kerrigan, July 31, 1988. BA, Merrimack Coll., 1984; D Podiatric Medicine, Scholl Coll. Podiatric Medicine, 1990. Chief resident Cambridge (Mass.) Hosp., Seattle, 1991—, 1991-92. Trustee Wilmington (Mass.) Family Counseling Svc., 1985. With USN, 1981-87. Cardinal Cushing scholar, 1979-84, acad. scholar Ill. Podiatric Med. Aux., 1987. Mem. Am. Podiatric Med. Assn., Am. Podiatric Med. Residents Asssn. (dir. corp. resources 1990-92, trustee 1990-92, regional coord. 1990-92, Meritorious Svc. award 1991). Home: 12 Elm Sq Wakefield MA 01880-1535 Office: Cambridge Hosp 1493 Cambridge St Cambridge MA 02139-1099

PERRY, JOHN CURTIS, history educator; b. Orange, N.J., July 18, 1930; s. Gerald Eugene and Dorothy Lyman (Burt) P.; m. Sarah Hollis French, Sept. 14, 1957; children: Elizabeth, Margaret, Rachel, J. Lyman, Sarah Maria. BA, Yale U., 1953; MA, Harvard U., 1957, PhD, 1960. Instr., then asst. prof. Conn. Coll., New London, 1962-66; from asst. prof. to prof. Carleton Coll., Northfield, Minn., 1966-80; Henry Willard Denison prof. Fletcher Sch. Law and Diplomacy, Tufts U., Medford, Mass., 1980—, dir. North Pacific program, 1984—. Author: Beneath the Eagle's Wings: Americans in Occupied Japan, 1980, Sentimental Imperialists, 1981. Mem. Assn. Asian Studies, Am. Hist. Assn., Tavern Club. Episcopalian. Home: PO Box 63 Lincoln MA 01773-0010 Office: Tufts U Fletcher Sch Medford MA 02115

PERRY, JOSEPH QUENTON, JR., accountant; b. Greenwich, Conn., Aug. 12, 1942; s. Joseph and Kathryn (Reider) P.; B. Acctg., U. Conn., 1964; M. Econs., Pace Coll., 1966; m. Lucille Stafanelli, Aug. 13, 1966; 1 dau., Heather Lynn. Trust officer Morgan Guaranty Trust Co., N.Y.C., 1966-71; sr. acct. Whitman & Ransom, 1971-76; pres. Fiduciary Services, Old Greenwich, Conn., 1976—; dir. Wharton Gord Orch., Inc., Rogers Bus. Service, Claude Heroux Prodns. Inc., Whitaker Prodns. Inc., Tri-Media Inc. Mem. N.Y. State Tax Com., 1967-71. Mem. Am. Inst. C.P.A.s. Republican. Roman Catholic. Club: Burning Tree Country. Home: 64 Circle Dr Greenwich CT 06830-6742 Office: Fiduciary Svcs 79 E Putnam Ave Greenwich CT 06830-5644

PERRY, JOY SUTTON, medical editor; b. South Bend, Ind., July 26, 1941; d. Robert Winfield and Anna Marion (Wagner) Sutton; m. Tomas M. Russell, June 15, 1963 (div. 1983); children: Heather Joy Russell Marvin, Hilary Joy; m. Matthew C. Perry, Aug. 3, 1985. Student, Wilson Coll., 1959-61; BS, U. Wis., 1963. Rsch. asst. U. Wis. Med. Sch., Madison, 1963-67; mem. spl. projects staff Chgo. Heart Assn., 1973-74, 79-85; freelance med. editor various pubs., 1969—; pres., sec.-treas. Soc. Heart Assn. Profl. Staff, Chgo., 1981-85. Editor: (newsletter) The Auxilian, 1987—. Vestry mem. Trinity Episcopal Ch., Elmira, N.Y., 1988—; bd. dirs. Elmira Symphony and Choral Soc., 1991—, performer, 1985—; pres. Thursday Morning Musicales, Elmira, 1988-90; bd. dirs. Arnot-Ogden Med. Ctr. Aux., Elmira, 1987—. Mem. APHA, AAAS, Am. Med. Writers Assn., Am. Soc. Law and Medicine, Am. Heart Assn. Met. Chgo., Coun. Biology Editors, N.Y. Acad. Scis. Republican. Home and Office: 974 Upland Dr Elmira NY 14905-1437

PERRY, KATHRYN ANN HARVEY, human resources director; b. Massena, N.Y., Jan. 26, 1953; d. John Robert and Shirley Mae (Dodge) Harvey; m. Robert Marlin Perry, Feb. 4, 1984. BA, SUNY, Potsdam, 1975; MBA, Clarkson U., 1984. Clerical asst. SUNY, Potsdam, 1973-75, bus. office asst., 1975-76, pers. asst., 1976-83, pers. assoc., 1983-84, acting dir. human resources, 1984-85, dir. human resources, 1985—. Bd. dirs., chair pers. com. potsdam Child Care Ctr., 1990—; mem. audit com. Meth. Ch., Massena,

1988—. Mem. Coll. & Univ. Pers. Assn., SUNY Pers. Com., Potsdam Health & Safety Com., Potsdam Classif Rev. Com., Potsdam Environ. Health & Safety Com., Mid. State Evaluation Com. Potsdam (chair adminstrv. subcom.), Potsdam Planning Com., Potsdam Labor/Mgmt. Coms. (chair). Office: SUNY Potsdam Potsdam NY 13676

PERRY, LESLIE BLAIR, educator, consultant; b. Bluefield, W.Va., May 26, 1942; s. Lonnie and Beatrice Gazelle (Brown) P.; m. Carol Ruth Jones, June 20, 1975; 1 child, Stephen Francis. BS, N.C. A&T State U., 1969; student, Atlanta Law Sch., 1974-75; postgrad., Rutgers U., 1990; student, NYU, 1991—. Cert. tchr. N.Y., Ga., N.C. Tchr. Syracuse (N.Y.) Sch. Dist., 1969-71, Atlanta Pub Schs., 1971-73; draftsman City of Atlanta, 1973-75; tech. asst. SUNY, Farmingdale, 1975-80; jr. acct. 1st N.Y. Bank Bus., N.Y.C., 1980-88; tchr. N.Y.C. Pub. Schs., 1988—; dean students Drafting Com. N.Y.C. Pub. Schs., 1989; faculty advisor Curriculum Devel. Commn. mem. Syracuse Sch. Dist., 1970-71. Mem. legis. adv. com. 10 Senatorial Dist., Laurelton, N.Y., 1983-84; trustee, treas. Religious Orgn., Bklyn., 1979-82; researcher Atlanta Community Rels. Commn., 1974-75; urban assoc. Urban Life Ctr. Ga. State U., Atlanta, 1975. With U.S. Army, 1961-64. Recipient Letter of Appreciation, Atlanta Housing Authority, 1975; Cert. of Achievement Fedn. Laurelton, 1987. Mem. Am. Assn. Sch. Adminstrs., Am. Vocat. Assn., Am. Vocat. Edn. Rsch. Assn., N.Y. State Occupational Edn. Assn. Home: 74 Beverly Pky Freeport NY 11520-2026

PERRY, LINCOLN FREDERICK, artist, educator; b. N.Y.C., May 28, 1949; s. Burton and Dorothy (Burwell) P.; m. Ann Beattie, July 22, 1988. BA in magna cum laude, Columbia U., 1971; MFA, Queens Coll., 1975. Tchr. Univ. N.H., Durham, 1975-80, Univ. Ark., Fayetteville, 1983-84; vis. artist The Univ. Va., Charlottesville, 1985. One-man shows include Northampton Coll. Gallery, Allentown, Pa., 1979, Hildreth Gallery, Nasson Coll., Springvale, Maine, 1980, Walker Art Ctr., Bowdoin Coll., Brunswick, Maine, 1981, Tatistcheff & Co., N.Y.C., 1982, 84, 86, 88, 90-91; exhbns. Simms Fine Art, New Orleans, 1988, Gibbes Mus. Art, Charleston, S.c., 1990-91, N.Y. Acad. Art, N.Y.C., 1990-91, and others; represented in collections Bayly Mus., Charlottesville, Va., Becton Dickinson & Co., Paramus, N.J., Chem. Bank, N.Y.C., and others. Mem. Phi Beta Kappa. Office: c/o Tatistcheff Gallery E 57th St New York NY 10019-3903

PERRY, NANCY TROTTER, former telecommunications company executive; b. Cleve., Jan. 1, 1935; d. Charles Hanley and Mable Dora (Lowry) Trotter; m. Robert Anthony Perry, Apr. 27, 1957. Student, Dunbarton Coll., 1952-53, W.Va. U., 1953-55. Svc. rep. C&P Telephone Co., Balt., 1956-60, adminstrv. asst., 1960-67, staff supr., 1967-69, mgr. consumer affairs, 1979-92. Bd. dirs. Balt. Mus. Industry, 1979—, Tele-Consumer Hotline, 1986-92, Hearing and Speech Agy., 1989—, Md. Info. and Referral Providers Coun., 1990—, Learning Independence Through Computers, Inc., 1991—, Md. Consumer Coun., 1991—, Md. Gerontol. Assn., 1991—. Mem. Soc. Consumer Affairs Profls. in Bus., Md. Ctr. for Ind. Living, Nat. Fedn. of Blind, Alliance for Pub. Technology. Home: 3701 Chatham Rd Ellicott City MD 21042-5105

PERRY, RICHARD ALLAN, pension consultant; b. Worcester, Mass., Mar. 30, 1948; s. Raymond Lawrence and Kathleen Gloria (Corbett) P.; m. Dorothy Ann Stooke, Aug. 30, 1985; children: Monica Lee Perry, Michelle Ann Perry, Becky Lyn Williams, Glenn Paul Williams. BS in Psychology, Georgetown U., 1970; MA in Psychology, Catholic U., 1972. CLU; Chartered fin. cons. Ins. agt. Prudential Ins. Co., Shrewsbury, Mass., 1974-79; sr. ptnr. Fin. Planning Assocs., Worcester, 1979-85; mng. ptnr. Tyler Assocs., Inc., Worcester, 1985-90; exec. v.p. CIPI Systems, Inc., Worcester, 1990—. Researcher, author: Modification of Eating Disorder in Childhood, 1973. Pres. Community Health Mgmt., Inc. Webster, Mass., 1986—; v.p. Samaritan Community Health Svc., Inc., 1982—; vice chmn., Mass. Ins. Commrs. Continuing Edn. Task Force, 1982—. Mem. Worcester Life Underwriters Assn. (pres. 1985, bd. dirs. 1975—); Mass. Assn. Life Underwriters (bd. dirs. 1982—), Am. Soc. Pension Actuaries, Nat. Assn. Estate and Bus. Planning Coun., Am. Soc. CLUs, Nat. Assn. Life Underwriters, Lions, Georgetown U. Alumni Club. Republican. Baptist. Home: 195 Chester St Worcester MA 01605-1062 Office: CIPC Systems Inc 20 Washington Sq Worcester MA 01604-4013

PERRY, SAMUEL CASSIUS, animal science researcher; b. Aniwa, Wis., Sept. 25, 1937; s. Cassius R. and Elsie E. (Oesterreich) P.; m. Beverly S. Morrison, July 12, 1964; children: Pamela, Kimberly, Deborah, Stephen, Barbara, Michael. BS, U. Wis., River Falls, 1959; MS, S.D. State U., 1963; PhD, U. Tenn., 1967. Sr. rsch. bacteriologist Norwich (N.Y.) Pharmacal Co., 1967-70, sr. rsch. II nutritionist, 1970-72, rsch. leader, 1972-73, sect. chief, 1973-77; tech. svcs. nutritionist Hoffmann La-Roche Inc., Nutley, N.J., 1977-81, mktg. mgr., 1981-84, assoc. dir. poultry bus. unit, 1984-85, dir. mktg., 1985-87, dir. animal si. rsch., 1987-89, dir. animal sci. rsch., asst. v.p., 1989—. Mem. Am. Assn. Animal Sci., Poultry Sci., N.Y. Acad. Scis., Am. Rsch. Coun., Am. Dairy Sci. Assn. Republican. Lutheran.

PERRY, WILLIAM ANTHONY, electronics executive; b. Newport, R.I.; s. Lewis P. and Mary M. Perry; m. Myrna B. Perry, Apr. 1970; children: Stephen W., Jonathan L. BSBA, Bryant Coll., 1970. Mktg. specialist Automotive div. Belden Corp., Oak Brook, Ill., 1970-76; dir. catalog sales Datalog div. Chilton Co., Radnor, Pa., 1976-78; field underwriter Mutual Life Ins. N.Y., Providence, 1978-80; sales mgr. Northeastern ins. Assoc.s, Rumford, R.I., 1980-81; applications engr. Submarine Signal div. Raytheon Co., Portsmouth, R.I., 1981-83, sr. sales engr., 1983-85, internat. sales mgr., 1988—; pres. Bahn Enterprises, Inc., Porsmouth, R.I., 1988—; v.p. sales and mktg. Ocean Data Equipment Corp., Fall River, Mass., 1987-92. Sec., treas. Toastmasters Internat., Nashua, N.H., 1972; advisor Neuman Hosp., Thorndale, Pa., 1978. Dollars for Scholars character scholar, 1966. Office: Bahn Enterprises Inc PO Box 656 Portsmouth RI 02871

PERSCH, WILLIAM JOSEPH, JR., public relations executive; b. Montclair, N.J., Jan. 25, 1944; s. William J. and Florence B. (Baierle) P.; BA, Syracuse U., 1966; postgrad. Columbia U., 1967-68, U. N.H., 1970-71; m. Lynda Marie Ingram, Nov. 30, 1979; 1 son by previous marriage, Jonathan Michael; 1 dau., Elizabeth Marie. Asst. dir. creative services United Artists Records Corp., N.Y.C., 1966-68; news editor U. N.H., Durham, 1969-73; asst. dir. public affairs Mass. Mut. Life Ins. Co., Springfield, 1973-82, assoc. dir. pub. relations, 1982-84, dir. pub. relations, 1985-91, dir. community rels., 1992—. Active Pioneer Valley United Way, Hampden County Pvt. Industry Coun. Served with USAR, 1966-72. Mem. Public Relations Soc. Am., Am. Coll. Life Underwriters, Pioneer Valley Press Club, Sigma Delta Chi. Home: 40 Butternut Rd Westfield MA 01085-4116

PERSEK, STEPHEN CHARLES, management educator, mathematician; b. N.Y.C., May 4, 1945; s. Stephen George and Zora Jane (Duzbaba) P. B.S. in Math., MIT, 1967; M.S. in Math., Courant Inst., NYU, 1968, Ph.D. in Math., 1976. Instr. bus. stats. N.Y. Inst. Tech., Old Westbury, N.Y., 1968-77; asst. prof. math. Marist Coll., Poughkeepsie, N.Y., 1977-79; assoc. prof. mgmt. sci. St. John's U., Jamaica, N.Y., 1979—; cons. Purchasing Mgmt. Assocs. N.Y., N.Y.C., 1982—, GSP Cons., Inc., N.Y.C., 1983—. Contbr. articles to profl. jours. Mem. Soc. Indsl. and Applied Math., Am. Math. Soc., Math. Assn. Am., Inst. Mgmt. Sci. Roman Catholic. Home: 160 Banbury Rd Mineola NY 11501-1517 Office: Saint John's U Grand Central and Utopia Pkwys Jamaica NY 11439

PERSHAN, PETER SILAS, physicist, educator; b. Bklyn., Nov. 9, 1934; s. Max J. and Rosa (Bernekow) P.; m. Patricia S. Birke, Aug. 31, 1957; children: Marc, Jill. BS, Poly. Inst. Bklyn., 1956; AM, Harvard U., 1957, PhD, 1960. Rsch. fellow Harvard U., Cambridge, Mass., 1960, asst. prof., 1961-64, assoc. prof., 1964-68, prof., 1968—; mem. lab. tech. staff Bell Telephone, Murray Hill, N.J., 1963-64; dir. Materials Rsch. Lab., Cambridge, 1974-78; vis. prof. MIT, Cambridge, 1978-79; vis. scientist Brookhaven Nat. Lab., Upton, N.Y., 1985-86, guest scientist, 1986—; cons. Sperry Gyroscope Co., Great Neck, N.Y., 1961-63, RCA Corp., Princeton, N.J., 1966-73, Battelle Meml. Inst. Naval Ordnance Lab., Silver Springs, Md., 1969-71; mem. proposal rev. panel Stanford Synchrotron Radiation Lab., 1989—; mem. adv. bd. Advanced Liquid Crystalline Optical Materials Consortium, 1991—. Author: Structure of Liquid Crystal Phases, 1988; co-editor: Resonances, 1990; contbr. articles to profl. jours. Fellow Am. Phys. Soc. (com. internat. freedom scientists 1984-86). Home: 218 Follen Rd Lexington MA 02173 Office: Harvard U Div Applied Scis 29 Oxford St Cambridge MA 02138-2901

PERSOW, MEYER JOSEPH, program analyst; b. St. Louis, July 22, 1958; s. Harold S. and Harriet Lee (Persow) Kadovitz. BA in Polit. Sci., U. Denver, 1980, BA in Secondary Edn., 1980; postgrad., El Paso Community Coll., 1985. Legis. aide Office of the Gov., Denver, 1975; tchr. Sebastian High Sch., Denver, 1977-79; press sec. Barragan for Congress Com., Thornton, Colo., 1980; pvt. practice tutor Denver, 1981-83; adminstrv. asst. Tracks, Internat., Inc., Denver, 1986-87; customer svc. mgr. Continental Airlines, Denver, Washington, 1987-88; program analyst U.S. Office Pers. Mgmt., Washington, 1988—. News editor: The Denver Clarion, 1978-79, author polit. commentary, 1978-80. Vice chmn. North High Campus Concept. Com., Denver, 1976-77; committeeman Dem. Party Cen. Com., Denver, 1976-83; candidate Denver (Colo.) Bd. Edn., 1977, 79; mem. Dem. Party Exec. Com., Denver, 1978-81. Sgt. U.S. Army, 1983-86. Decorated Army Achievement medal U.S. Army, El Paso, 1985. Mem. Internat. Platform Assn., Mortar Bd., Zeta Beta Tau. Office: US Office Pers Mgmt 1900 E St NW Washington DC 20415

PERSSON, CAROL VONA, physical education educator; b. Neptune, N.J., July 3, 1951; d. Salvatore John and Patricia Ann (Haley) Vona. BS, Slippery Rock U., 1973; MA, Montclair State Coll., 1984; D of Phys. Edn., Springfield (Mass.) Coll., 1987. Tchr. Neptune (N.J.) Jr. High Sch., 1973-78, Neptune Sr. High Sch., 1978-85; asst. prof. Keene (N.H.) State Coll., 1987; assoc. prof. Westfield (Mass.) State Coll., 1988—. Vol. Mass. Spl. Olympics Summer Games, Springfield, Mass., 1990; coord. WSC Aerobathon, Westfield, Mass., 1989, Health Fair/Fit Stop, Westfield, 1989. Recipient William A Cuff Meml. award Sch. Profl. Studies, Montclair State Coll., 1990. Mem. AAHPERD (v.p. ea. dist. 1983-85, pres. 1989-90, dist. rep. 1991—, Presdl. medal 1983, 91, merit award 1984, Profl. Honor award 1988, Past Pres. award 1989, nat. bd. govs. 1991—), Mass. Assn. Health, Phys. Edn., Recreation and Dance (v.p. 1987-89, Honor award 1992), N.J. Assn. Health, Phys. Edn., Recreation and Dance (v.p. 1982-84, Outstanding Teaching award 1985). Democrat. Roman Catholic. Office: Westfield State Coll Western Ave Westfield MA 01085-2502

PERSSON, GELORMA ELIZABETH, business consulting company executive; b. Morristown, N.J., Aug. 1, 1931; d. Joseph and Mary Louise (Soranno) Carriero; m. Richard L. Persson, July 29, 1951; children: Synda Lou, Richard L., Sharyce Lee, Joede Marei. Student, Rutgers U., Newark, 1949-50. Cert. in real estate sales, floral design, outdoor gasoline engine. With Millburn N.J.) Florist and Soranno Florist, Morristown, 1940-60; owner Little Silver (N.J.) Repair Ctr., 1965-91, Persson Outdoor Power Equipment, Farmingdale, N.J., 1985—; pres. Bus. Dynamics Assocs., Farmingdale, 1991—; bd. dirs. Jersey Cen. Power & Light, Morristown, 1985—. Producer cable TV show Persson to People, Trenton, N.J., 1982—; contbg. writer Monmouth Bus. Talk, 1987-91. Pres. (sr. citizen devel.) Luftman Towers, Lincroft, N.J., 1983-91; apptd. mem. Nat. Small Bus. Adv. Coun., Washington, 1981—. Small Bus. Com. and Anti-Discrimination Bd., Trenton, 1991—; mem. White House Conf. on Small Bus., 1980, chair, 1986; bd. dirs. N.J. Mental Health Assn., 1988—; chair fundraising N.J. Inst. Tech. Inventors Hall of Fame, 1990-91; mem. bd. advisors Georgian Ct. Coll., 1991—; mem. found. bd. advisors Brookdale Coll., 1988—. Named Woman of Leadership, Girl Scouts U.S., 1988, Woman of Yr., N.J. Bus. and Profl. Women, 1984; featured in articles in Minorities and Women Bus. Mag., 1988, N.J. Bus. Mag., 1986. Mem. N.J. Fedn. Ind. Bus. (guardian 1986—), Eastern Monmouth Area C. of C. (treas., vice chair, pres. 1984-92). Republican. Roman Catholic. Home: 56 S Lake Dr Red Bank NJ 07701 Office: Bus Dynamics Assocs 5106 State Hwy 34 Farmingdale NJ 07727

PERUGINI, JOHN N., television film producer; b. Waterbury, Conn., June 29, 1959; s. Joseph and Lina (Rinaldi) P. BS, Syracuse U., 1981. Electronic journalism editor Sta. WFSB TV Post-Newsweek Stas., Inc., Hartford, Conn., 1981-89; producer, owner Perugini Film & TV, Watertown, Conn., 1989—; dir. GOL, Inc., N.Y.C., 1989—; cons. Techniart, Inc., Unionville, Conn., 1990—, Farmington, Conn., 1989—; cons. Walt Disney World, Orlando, Fla., 1991. Mem. Statue of Liberty-Ellis Island Found., 1984—, Mus. TV & Radio, 1991—. Recipient Boston-New England Emmy NATAS, 1983. Internat. RAdio & TV Soc., Nat. Trust Hist. Preservation, Am. Film Inst. Roman Catholic.

PERUN, JOHN JOSEPH, JR., information systems professional, consultant; b. Danbury, Conn., July 3, 1963; s. John Joseph Sr. and Georgina Diack (Lawler) P. BS in Mgmt., Rensselaer Poly. Inst., 1985; MBA/IS, Pace U., 1992. Profl. cons. Info. Builders, Inc., N.Y.C., 1990—. Mem. Rep. Nat. Com., Washington, 1985—, Citizens Against Govt. Waste, Amnesty Internat. Mem. NRA, Fairfield County Football Ofcls. Assn., Western Conn. Baseball Umpires Assn., ASA Softball Umpires Assn. (Greater Danbury chpt.), Elks, Sigma Phi Epsilon (alumni bd dirs. 1986-90). Roman Catholic. Home: 3 Apple Blossom Ln New Fairfield CT 06812 Office: Info Builders Inc 1250 Broadway New York NY 10001-3701

PERUO, MARSHA HOPE, artist; b. Bklyn., Mar. 21, 1951; d. Teddy and Adele (Tamber) Reinhardt; m. Bruce Peruo, Aug. 25, 1970 (dec. Feb. 19, 1991); 1 child, Derek Bruce. BA, CUNY, Queens Coll., 1971; MFA, Pratt Inst., 1980. Awards chairperson Am. Soc. Contemporary Artists, N.Y.C., 1980-81, corresponding sec., 1981-83, dir., 1983-85, 1st v.p., 1985-87; artist Marsha Peruo, N.Y.C., 1980—. Exhibited nationally in many exhibitions. Vol. tchr. Community Ch. of N.Y., 1989-91. Recipient Dorothy Feigen Meml. award for Graphics, Am. Soc. Contemporary Artists, 1980. Mem. Am. Soc. Contemporary Artists, Colored Pencil Soc. Am., N.Y. Artists Equity Assn., Miniature Artists of Am. Democrat. Unitarian. Office: Marsha Peruo Artist 55 W 14th St # 9B New York NY 10011-7435

PERVIN, LAWRENCE AARON, psychologist, educator, psychotherapist; b. Bklyn., Aug. 3, 1936; s. Murray and Mary (Ruthen) P.; m. Barbara Susan Zucker, June 21, 1958; children: David Joshua, Levi Jonathan. BA, CUNY, 1957; PhD, Harvard U., 1962. Asst. prof., clin. psychologist Princeton (N.J.) U., 1962-68; assoc. dean, assoc. prof. Rutgers U., New Brunswick, N.J., 1968-70; prof. Rutgers U., New Brunswick, 1970—. Author: Personality Theory Research, 5th edit., 1989; editor Psychol. Inquiry, 1990—. Fellow Am. Psychol. Assn., Am. Psychol. Soc. Office: Rutgers U Psychology Dept New Brunswick NJ 08903

PESARESI, BEVERLY JOY, banker; b. Norristown, Pa., Aug. 31, 1961; d. William J. Walizer and Catherine V. (Mench) Attardo; m. Reno J. Pesaresi, Feb. 18, 1984; 1 child, Ashley R. Diploma, Am. Inst. Banking, 1983. Asst. cashier Phillipsburg (N.J.) Nat. Bank, 1986-87, asst. v.p., 1989—; br. mgr. N.J. Savs. Bank, Somerville, 1987-89. Mem. Clinton (N.J.) Guild, 1989—. Mem. Am. Inst. Banking (bd. dirs. 1989—). Home: 1096 W Lafayette St Easton PA 18042-1414 Office: Phillipsburg Nat Bank 39 Laneco Plz Clinton NJ 08809-1263

PESARESI, MASSIMO MANDOLINI, Italian educator; b. Ancona, Marche, Italy, Aug. 23, 1950; s. Leandro and Bruna (Mandolini) P. Laurea in Lettere, U. Rome, 1974, Laurea in Filosofia, 1980; PhD in Italian, Yale U., 1990. Tchr. Liceo Classico, Ancona, Italy, 1977-78; rsch. assoc. Ind. U., Bloomington, 1979-80; teaching asst. dept. Italian Yale U., New Haven, 1984-87, part-time acting instr., 1987-88; vis. instr. Italian Emory U., Atlanta, 1988-89, vis. asst. in Italian, 1989-90; vis. asst. in Italian Georgetown U., Washington, 1990-91; vis. asst. in Italian Columbia U., N.Y.C., 1991-92, asst. prof, 1992. Contbr. articles to profl. jours.; author: Grecian Vistas, 1992; translator books. Dept. of Edn. of Italy scholar, 1975, Ctr. for Semiotic Studies scholar, Urbino, Italy, 1978, NYU scholar, 1980-82, Yale U. scholar, 1985. Mem. MLA. Home: 560 Riverside Dr #19E New York NY 10027 Office: Columbia U Dept Italian New York NY 10027

PESAVENTO, JOSEPH AMEDEO, utilities executive, electrical engineer; b. Iron Mountain, Mich., Jan. 12, 1936; s. Amedeo Frederick and Ann (Judish) P.; m. Sandra Lea Heath, July 9, 1966. BSEE, Marquette U., 1957; MSEE, U. Wis., 1959. Instr. Marquette U., Milw., 1957, U. Wis., Madison, 1957-59; engring. trainee Westinghouse Electric Corp., Pitts., 1959-60, engr., 1960-72, engring. mgr., 1972-75, product assurance mgr., 1975-84, product assurance and facilities mgr., 1984-87, mgr. environ. and facility control, 1988, mgr. div. support svcs., 1990-91; mgr. environ. compliance and facilities planning Westinghouse Electric Corp., Coraopolis, Pa., 1991—; chmn. bus. unit quality control, Westinghouse Electric Co., 1978-82, mem. corp. quality adv. bd., 1982-83, mem. C. of C. Drive, 1984. Contbr. articles to profl. jours.; patentee in field. Bd. dirs. Fox Chapel Mews Assn., 1981—, Pressley Ridge Schs., 1989—; vol. Pitts. Symphony Orch., 1982-87; state recruiter Marquette U. Mem. IEEE, Am. Soc. Quality Control, Pitts. C. of C. (Leadership Pitts. Program 1987), Pitts. Symphony Soc. Club: Longue Vue (Pitts.) (bd. dirs. 1985—). Home: 300 Fox Chapel Rd Pittsburgh PA 15238-2327 Office: Westinghouse Electric Co 400 Fairway Dr Cherrington Corp Ctr Coraopolis PA 15108

PESCI, THOMAS ALBERT, development director, education educator; b. Phila., Sept. 22, 1949; s. Thomas Albert and Doris (Meyfohrt) P. BA magna cum laude, Fordham U., Bronx, N.Y., 1973; MA, U. N.C., Chapel Hill, 1974; MDiv, Weston Sch. Theology, Cambridge, Mass., 1979. Tchr. St. Joseph's Preparatory Sch., Phila., 1974-76; dir. campus min. Loyola High Sch., Towson, Md., 1980-84; dir. vocations Md. Province Jesuits, Balt., 1984-87; dir. devel. & alumni Scranton Preparatory Sch., Scranton, Pa., 1988—; cons. Lilly Endowment Programs, Indpls., 1984-86. Author: Influence of St. John of the Cross on the Late Poetry of T.S. Eliot, 1974. Mem. Coun. for Advancement and Support of Edn., Jesuit Secondary Assn. Edn., Phi Beta Kappa. Roman Catholic. Home: 1000 Wyoming Ave Scranton PA 18509-2993 Office: Scranton Preparatory School 1000 Wyoming Ave Scranton PA 18509-2993

PESNER, CAROLE MANISHIN, art gallery director; b. Boston, Aug. 5, 1937; m. Robert Pesner (dec. 1983); children: Ben, Jonah. BA, Smith Coll., 1959. Asst. dir. Kraushaar Galleries, Inc., N.Y.C., 1959-86, dir., 1986-90, pres., 1991—. Author, editor publs., catalogues in field. Mem. Art Dealers Assn. Am., Internat. Fine Print Dealers Assn. Office: Kraushaar Galleries Inc 724 5th Ave New York NY 10019-4106

PESOLA, ROBERT, stage director, writer; b. Marquette, Mich., Aug. 29, 1949; s. Ernest Ensio and Janice Mary (LeDuc) P.; m. T. Eagan, July 4, 1976; children: Oscar, Jeffrey. BA with high honors, No. Mich. U., 1971. Freelance dir., producer, writer, 1974—; dir. Performance Ensemble at Lincoln Ctr., N.Y.C., 1979; dramaturg Vivian Beaumont Theatre, N.Y.C., 1979-80; literary mgr. Circle in the Sq. Theatre, N.Y.C., 1983-86; script cons. Am. Nat. Theatre and Acad., N.Y.C., 1978-80; editor newsletter Circle in the Sq., N.Y.C., 1984-86; directing cons. Nat. Tech. Inst. for Deaf, Rochester, N.Y., 1985; cons. story devel. United Artists, 1987-88, HBO, N.Y.C., 1987. Playwright: King of Troy, 1977, Incident'ly, 1984: writer, dir. presdl. performance Evening at the White House, 1980; librettist opera: Arms Akimbo, 1988; assoc. producer (Broadway play) Passion, 1983, (off-Broadway play) Danny and the Deep Blue Sea, 1984 (Obie award); dir. play: Rhinoceros, 1979, Errand of Mercy, 1984, Josephine, 1980; contbr. articles to European Travel & Life, Melbourne (Austrlia) Sunday Herald Mag., South China Morning Post, Hong Kong, Endless Vacation mag. mem. policy com. English Speaking Union, N.Y.C., 1986; mem. task force pres.'s commn. Future of No. Mich. U., Marquette, 1988. Mem. Soc. Stage Dirs. and Choreographers. Office: PO Box 950 New York NY 10021-0003

PESS, GARY MARTIN, hand and microsurgeon; b. Bklyn., June 13, 1956; s. Arthur H. and Thelma (Hoffman) P.; m. Lois Nyberg, May 31, 1981; children: Matthew, Rachel, Rebecca. BS with honors, SUNY, Stony Brook, 1977; MD cum laude, Downstate Med. Ctr., 1981. Diplomate Am. Bd. Orthopedic Surgery, added qualification in hand surgery. Gen. surgery intern Beth Israel Hosp., N.Y.C., 1981-82; orthopedic surgery resident NYU Med. Ctr. Bellevue Hosp., N.Y.C., 1982-86; hand and microsurgery fellow Mass. Gen. Hosp. and Harvard U., Boston, 1986-87; partner Cen. Jersey Hand Surgery, Eatontown, N.J., 1987—; gross anatomy instr. NYU Med. Sch., N.Y.C., 1984-85; teaching asst., 1985-86; clin. instr. Harvard U. Med. Sch., Boston, 1986-87; clin. sr. instr. Hohnemann U., Phila., 1988—. Contbr. articles to profl. jours. Baseball coach Ocean (N.J.) Twp. Recreation, 1991—. Recipient Golden Apple Teaching award Mommouth Med. Ctr., Long Beach, N.J., 1990; Rsch. Pub. award Jersey Shore Med. Ctr., Neptune, 1989, 91. Fellow Am. Coll. Surgeons, Am. Acad. Orthopedic Surgeons, Am. Soc. for Surgery of Hand (active); mem. Eastern Orthopedic Assn. (active), N.Y. Hand Soc. (2d place presentation award 1984), Phila. Hand Soc., N.J. Orthopedic Soc. Jewish. Home: 24 Seward Dr Wayside NJ 07712 Office: Cen Jersey Hand Surgery 2 Industrial Way Meridian 1 Eatontown NJ 07724

PESSEN, HELMUT, physical biochemist, researcher; b. Berlin, Germany, Sept. 6, 1921; came to U.S., 1940; s. Eugen and Charlotte (Bieber) P.; m. Norma Cooper Glasner, Mar. 12, 1966. BS in Chem. Engring., Drexel Inst. Tech., 1949; PhD, Temple U., 1961. Cert. agt. U.S. Patent Office. Control chemist Fred Whitaker Wool Co., Phila., 1943-46; rsch. assoc. Am. Viscose Corp., Marcus Hook, Pa., 1947-48; inspector FDA, Phila., 1950; rsch. chemist U.S. Army Q. M. Pioneering Rsch. Lab., Phila., 1950-57; free-lance tech. translator Phila., 1961-63; rsch. scientist, sr. scientist Eastern Regional Rsch. Ctr. USDA, Wyndmoor, Pa., 1963—. Author: Methods in Enzymology, 1973, 85, NMR Applications, 1990; co-editor: New Techniques and Applications of Physical Chemistry to Food Systems, 1991; contbr. numerous articles to profl. jours.; presenter at nat. and internat. confs. With U.S. Army, 1943-45, ETO. Mem. AAAS, Am. Chem. Soc., Am. Crystallographic Assn., Pa. Acad. Sci., Biophys. Soc., Phi Kappa Phi, Sigma Xi, Tau Beta Pi. Office: USDA Ea Regional Rsch Ctr 600 E Mermaid Ln Philadelphia PA 19118-2598

PESSOA, MICHELLE MARIE, graphic designer; b. Bklyn., Feb. 25, 1966; d. Cyril I. and Barbara C. (Shaw) P. BS, MIT, 1988; MS in Package Design, Pratt Inst., 1991. Engring. intern DuPont, Wilmington, Del., 1985; intern Gen. Electric Corp., Burlington, Vt., 1986; graphic designer Electronic Pub. Ctr., N.Y.C., 1989-90; computer graphic designer Goody Products, Inc., Kearny, N.J., 1990—. Callendar scholar Nat. Soc. Black Engrs., 1984, G. Solenti Trust scholar Gov.'s Com. on Scholastic Achievement, 1984. Mem. Packaging Inst. Internat., Am. Inst. Graphic Arts, Nat. Soc. Black Engrs. (treas. 1985-88), Sophomore Coun. (councilwoman 1985-86), Mensa. Democrat. Roman Catholic. Home: 1445 Bedford Ave # 2D Brooklyn NY 11216-3840

PESSONI, PHILIP ANDREW, real estate professional; b. Middletown, Conn., Apr. 6, 1938; s. Joseph Andrew and Helen Marie (Kidney) P.; m. Patricia Kaye Madigan, Jan. 27, 1973; children: Anne Louise, Clare Ellen. BA in Psychology, Wesleyan U., 1959. Credit analyst Hartford (Conn.) Nat. Bank, 1960-63, Irving Trust Co., N.Y.C., 1963-65; pres. Lexington Labs. Inc., N.Y.C., 1965-81; ind. property mgmt. Pound Ridge, N.Y., 1981-88; pres. R.A.M. Group Inc., Greenwich, Conn., 1988—. Mem. Landmarks and Historic Dist. Commn., Pound Ridge, 1977—. Lt. U.S. Army, 1959-63. Mem. Pound Ridge Hist. Soc. (treas. 1980-87). Republican. Home: 323 Salem Rd Pound Ridge NY 10576

PESTEL, MICHAEL CHRISTIAN, sculptor, educator; b. Hildesheim, Fed. Republic Germany, July 8, 1950; came to U.S., 1956; s. Eduard Christian Pestel and Mary Jaqueline Evans; m. Sabine Hake, Dec. 19, 1985. BA, Hartwick Coll., 1972; MFA, Otis Art Inst., 1978. Lectr. in art history Otis Art Inst., L.A., 1980-84; vis. artist, sculpture Crossroads Sch., L.A., 1985-88; asst. prof. in sculpture Chatham Coll., Pitts., 1988—. Prin. works include Sighting Wheel, 1985-86, Sine Wave, 1986, Ohio Gauntlet, 1990, Agrognome, 1990. Named Disting. Tchr. White Ho. Commn. on Presdl. Scholar, 1990; fellowship grant Nat. Endowment for the Arts, 1988. Mem. Coll. Art Assn. Office: Chatham Coll Woodland Rd Pittsburgh PA 15232-2814

PESTKA, SIDNEY, molecular geneticist, microbiologist, educator; b. Drobin, Poland, May 29, 1936; s. Harry and Bernice P.; m. Joan Sparacin, June 19, 1960; children: Robert, Sharon, Steven. BA summa cum laude, Princeton U., 1957; MD, U. Pa., 1961; DSc (hon.), Rider Coll., 1987. Intern in pediatrics and medicine Balt. City Hosps., 1961-62; researcher in biochem. genetics lab. of Dr. Marshall W. Nirenberg NIH, 1962-66, researcher in protein synthesis Nat. Cancer Inst., 1966-69; sect. chief, assoc. mem. dept. biochemistry Roche Inst. Molecular Biology, 1969-74, sect. chief, full mem. dept. biochemistry, 1975-79, full mem., head lab. molecular genetics, 1980-86; prof., chmn. dept. molecular genetics & microbiology Robert Wood

Johnson Med. Sch. U. Medicine & Dentistry of N.J., 1986—, prof. medicine, 1990—; adj. prof. pathology Columbia U., 1972—; Mayer lectr. life scis. MIT, 1986; Found. for Microbiology lectr., 1986-87; mem. editorial bd. Pharmacology and Therapeutics, 1975—, Jour. Interferon Rsch., 1981—, Anticancer Rsch., 1981—, Cancer Communications, 1988—, Jour. Nat. Cancer Inst., 1988-92; assoc. editor Cancer Rsch., 1986—, Jour. Biol. Regulators and Homeostatic Agts., 1986—, Virology, 1989—; column editor Pharm. Tech., 1988—; mem. scientific adv. com. Chimica oggi, 1986—; invited speaker, lectr., chmn., organizer numerous confs., symposiums and workshops. Author: Molecular Mechanisms and Protein Biosynthesis, 1977, Interferons Methods in Enzymology, vol. 78, 1981, vol. 79, 1981, vol. 119, 1986; author, co-author over 385 scientific papers. Apppointed to North Caldwell Bd. Health, 1973—, v.p, 1975-77, pres., 1977-79, 85-90; appointed to Breast Cancer Task Force Com. Nat. Cancer Inst., 1983-84, Breast Cancer Working Group Nat. Cancer Inst., 1984-87, Columbia U. Comprehensive Cancer Ctr., 1985—, NAS Com. on Scholarly Communication with the People's Republic of China, 1986—, Basic Pharmacology Adv. Com. Pharms. Mfrs. Assn. Found., Inc., 1986—, N.J. Cancer Com., Cancer Ctr. Task Force, UMDNJ-Robert Wood Johnson Med. Sch./Johnson & Johnson Task Force, 1988-89, Com. to Rev. Chairmanship of Dept. Environ. and Community Medicine, 1990-91, Basic Rsch. Rev. Com. Am. Found. AIDS Rsch., 1990-92; mem. search com. for dean of Robert Wood Johnson Med. Sch., 1988, for chair of dept. medicine, 1988-89, chmn. search com. for chair physiology/biophysics, 1988-89, mem. appointments & promotions com., 1990—, mem. search com. for dir. Cancer Ctr.; mem. exec. com. Oncology Task Force New Brunswick Affiliated Hosps., 1988-89; mem. sci. adv. bd. Rider Coll., 1990—; dir. grad. program Dept. Molecular Genetics & Microbiology, 1986—; chmn. Univ.-wide Cancer Com., 1986-92. Recipient Selman A. Waksman Award in Microbiology, 1977. Mem. AAAS, Am. Soc. for Biochemistry and Molecular Biology, Am. Soc. for Microbiology, N.Y. Acad. Scis., Internat. Soc. for Interferon Rsch. (councillor 1986-88, sec. 1989—, pres.-elect 1992—), Am. Soc. for Cancer Rsch., Inc., Assn. Med. Sch. Microbiology Chmn., Harvey Soc., Phi Beta Kappa, Sigma Xi. Office: Univ of Med & Dentistry of NJ Dept Molecular Genetics/Microbio 675 Hoes Ln Piscataway NJ 08854-5635

PESZKE, MICHAEL ALFRED, psychiatrist, educator; b. Deblin, Poland, Dec. 19, 1932; s. Alfred Bartlomiej and Eugenia Halina (Grebocka) P.; m. Alice Margaret Sherman, Sept. 20, 1958; children: Michele Halina Olender, Michael Alexander. BA, Trinity Coll., Dublin, Ireland, 1956; MB, BCh, BAO, Dublin U., 1956. Bd. cert. psychiatrist. Staff psychiatrist Yale Student Health Svc., New Haven, 1961-64; asst. prof. sch. medicine U. Chgo., 1964-68; cons. psychiatrist Wesleyan U., Middletown, Conn., 1968-70; asst. prof. Sch. Medicine U. Conn., Farmington, 1970-73, assoc. prof., 1973-80, prof. psychiatry, 1980-90; clin. prof. U. Md. Sch. Medicine, Balt., 1991—; chief psychiatry Perry Point (Md.) VA Med. Ctr., 1991—; dir. psychiat. clin. svcs. John Dempsey Hosp., U. Conn. Health Ctr., Farmington, 1983-87; chief VA Med. Ctr., Newington, Conn., 1987-90. Author: Involuntary Treatment of the Mentally Ill: The Problem of Autonomy, 1975; co-author: (edited by L.A. Pervin, L.R. Reik, W. Dalrymple) The College Drop-out and the Utilization of Talent, 1966, (edited by J. Zusman, E. Bertsch) The Future of Psychiatric State Hospitals, 1975; contbr. articles to profl. jours.; book reviewer Univ. Chgo. Law Rev., 1968, Conn. Law Rev., 1976, Am. Jour. Psychiatry, 1976. Mem. Conn.'s Jud. Law Revision Com., 1982-86, Whiting Forensic Adv. Bd., 1987—; co-chair Commr. Mental Health's Com. to Re-write Conn. Civil Commitment Statutes, 1976-77. WHO travel fellow, United Kingdom, Denmark, Poland, 1977; U. Conn. Research grantee, 1972-87. Fellow APA; mem. Am. Coll. Psychiatrists, Soc. for Mil. History. Home: PO Box 165 Perry Point MD 21902-0165

PETER, PHILLIPS SMITH, lawyer; b. Washington, Jan. 24, 1932; s. Edward Compston and Anita Phillips (Smith) P.; m. Jania Jayne Hutchins, Apr. 8, 1961; children: Phillips Smith Peter Jr., Jania Jayne Hutchins. BA, U. Va., 1954, JD, 1959. Bar: Calif. 1959. Assoc. McCutchen, Doyle, Brown, Enerson, San Francisco, 1959-63; with GE (and subs.), various locations, 1963—; v.p. corp. bus. devel. GE (and subs.), 1973-76; v.p. GE (and subs.), Washington, 1976-79, v.p. corp. govtl. rels., 1980—; bd. dirs. Inst. for Rsch. on Econs. of Taxation; chmn. bd. govs. Bryce Harlow Found., 1990-92. Mem. editorial bd. Va. Law Rev., 1957-59. Trustee Howard U., 1981-89; v.p. Fed. City Coun., Washington, 1979-85; bd. dirs. Carlton. With Transp. Corps, U.S. Army, 1954-56. Mem. Calif. Bar Assn., Order of Colf, Wee Burn Club, Ea. Yacht Club, Farmington Country Club, Ponte Vedra Club, Lago Mar Club, Landmark Club, Congl. Country Club, Georgetown Club, Chevy Chase Club, Pisces Club, F Street Club, Coral Beach and Tennis Club, John's Island Club, Omicron Delta Kappa. Episcopalian. Home: 10805 Tara Rd Potomac MD 20854 also: 1000 Beach Rd Johns Island Vero Beach FL 32963 Office: 690 Ocean Rd Johns Island Vero Beach FL 32963

PETERKA, CYNTHIA JOANNE, college counselor; b. Balt., May 7, 1950; d. James Stephen and Theresa Angela (Fiorenza) P. BA, Fla. State U., 1972; MS, U. Utah, 1977; MLA, Johns Hopkins U., 1988; postgrad., U. Md., 1989—. Sch. psychologist Granite Sch. Dist., Salt Lake City, 1977-81; dir. counseling Westminister Coll. of Salt Lake City, 1981-83, assoc. dean of students, 1982-83; coord. gen. studies Dundalk (Md.) Community Coll., 1983-85, dir. counseling, 1985—; cons. Mountain Bell Telephone Co., Salt Lake City, 1982-83, Bus and Van div. GM, Balt., 1982—; mem. peer rev. team U.S. Dept. Edn., Washington, 1990-92. Sec. bd. govs. Sparrows Point C. of C., Balt., 1985; mem. Balt. County Coll. AIDS Task Force, Balt., 1990-92. Recipient cert. of achievement Nat. Assn. Coll. Activities, 1985; U.S. Dept. Edn. grantee, 1988. Mem. AACD, Am. Coll. Pers. Assn., Am. Coll. Counselor's Assn., Am. Assn. Higher Edn., Nat. Coun. Instr. Adminstrs., Md. Assn. Higher Edn. (instnl. rep.), Am. Coun. Edn. Nat. Indetification Program (instnl. rep.), Southeastern Provider's Assn. Network (chair 1990-91). Office: Dundalk Community Coll 7200 Sollers Point Rd Baltimore MD 21222-4649

PETERS, ALAN, anatomy educator; b. Nottingham, Eng., Dec. 6, 1929; came to U.S., 1966; s. Robert and Mabel (Woplington) P.; m. Verona Muriel Shipman, Sept. 30, 1955; children: Ann Verona, Sally Elizabeth, Susan Clare. BSc, Bristol (Eng.) U., 1951, PhD, 1954. Lectr. anatomy Edinburgh (Scotland) U., 1958-66; vis. lectr. Harvard, 1963-64; prof., chmn. dept. anatomy and neurobiology Boston U., 1966—; Mem. anatomy com. Nat. Bd. Med. Examiners, 1971-75; mem. neurology B study sect. NIH, 1975-79, chmn., 1978-79. Author: (with S.L. Palay and H. deF Webster) The Fine Structure of the Nervous System, 1970, 2d edit., 1976, 3rd edit., 1990, Myelination, 1970; contbr. (with A.N. Davison) articles profl. jours.; mem. editorial bd. Anat. Record, 1972-81, Jour. Comparative Neurology, Jour. Neurocytology, 1972-89, Studies of Brain Function, Cajal Jour. Neuroscis., Anat. and Embryology, Cerebral Cortex; editor: (with E.G. Jones) Cerebral Cortex, 1984—. Served to 2d lt. Royal Army Med. Corps, 1955-57. Mem. Anat. Soc. Gt. Britain and Ireland (Symington prize anatomy 1962, overseas mem. coun. 1969), Assn. Anatomy Chmn. (pres. 1976-77), Am. Anat. Assn. (exec. com. 1986-90, pres. 1992-93), Am. Soc. Cell Biology, Soc. Neuroscis., Internat. Primatological Soc., Cajal Club (Harman lectr. 1990, Cortical Discoverer award 1991). Home: 16 High Rock Cir Waltham MA 02154-2207 Office: Boston U Sch Medicine Dept Anatomy and Neurobiology 80 E Concord St Roxbury MA 02118-2394

PETERS, ALICE, clinical psychologist, psychotherapist; b. Vienna, Austria, Dec. 2, 1915; came to U.S., 1940; d. Robert and Ilona (Gerstl) Petereslka; m. Leo Gottsman, Aug. 16, 1936 (dec. Aug. 1984). BA, New Sch., 1946; MA, CCNY, 1950; PhD, NYU, 1959. Intern in psychology Jewish Hosp., N.Y.C., 1947; psychologist PCA Guidance Ctr., N.Y.C., 1948-50, Remedial Reading Clinic, CCNY, 1950-52; psychologist, supr., mem. faculty Orphanage, Alcoholic Clinic, Knickerbocker Hosp., N.Y.C., 1952-60; supr. psychologist Albert Einstein Med. Sch., N.Y.C., 1960-62, supr. faculty Postgrad. Ctr. for Mental Health, 1962-66; supr. N.Y. Clinic for Mental Health, 1962-64; pvt. practice N.Y.C., 1962—; mem. faculty, cons. Westchester Inst. for Tng. in Pastoral Counseling and Psychotherapy, Yonkers, N.Y., 1966-72. Author: (with others) TAT and CAT, 1954; co-author: (projective test) CAT, 1949; contbr. articles to profl. jours. Recipient Founders Day award NYU, 1961. Mem. APA, Am. Group Psychotherapy Assn., Internat. Psychol. Assn., N.Y. State Psychol. Assn., Ea. Psychol. Assn., World Fedn. for Mental Health. Home: 235 E 57th St New York NY 10022-2842

PETERS, BRYAN PAUL, personnel executive; b. East Chicago, Ind., May 10, 1954; s. Paul Bert and Doris (Ludwick) P.; m. Kathleen Ann Kadrmas, Oct. 1, 1976. BA, U. N.D., 1976; MPA, Golden Gate U., 1979. Personnel rep. Cen. Intelligence Agy., Washington, 1981—; chief of recruitment CIA, Boston, 1989—. Capt. USAF, 1976-81. Office: CIA PO Box 1920 Boston MA 02205-1920

PETERS, DONALD JOSEPH, portfolio manager; b. Balt., July 3, 1959; s. Donald Joseph and Mary Margaret (Creaghan) P.; m. Lora Webster Jaffin, July 8, 1989. BA summa cum laude, Tulane U., 1981; MBA, U. Pa., 1988. Portfolio mgr. Geewax, Terker & Co., Phoenixville, Pa., 1987—. Lt. USN, 1981-87. Mem. Phi Beta Kappa.

PETERS, EDWARD MICHAEL, JR., technology management executive; b. Bethelehem, Pa., Apr. 13, 1954; s. Edward Michael Sr. and Anna Marie (Zermeno) P.; m. Rosemary Ernst Peters, Aug. 3, 1953. BA, Lehigh U., 1976, MS, 1989. Supr. Pa. Bur. State Lotteries, Middletown, Pa., 1978-80; methods analyst Pa. Blue Shield, Camphill, Pa., 1980-82, data analyst, 1982-84; mgr. data adminstrn. Hershey (Pa.) Chocolate Co., 1984-87; v.p. rsch. and strategic tech. Mfrs. Hanover Trust, N.Y.C., 1987-91; v.p. info. tech. Hay Group, Washington, 1991—; adj. instr. Lebanon Valley Coll., Annville, Pa., 1985-86; vis. lectr. Katholike U., Leuven, Belgium, 1989-91. Co-author: Re-Engineering The Application, 1992; contbr. articles to profl. jours. Coord. Dem. Pres. Election Com., Atlanta, 1976; sec. Kiwanis, Hershey, 1986. Recipient Pres.'s award Guide Internat., Chgo., 1989. Democrat. Mem. United Ch. of Christ. Office: Hay Group 1500 K St NW # 1000 Washington DC 20005

PETERS, FRANK ALBERT, chemical engineer; b. Washington, June 3, 1931; s. Charles Albert and Dorothy Lynette (Paine) P.; m. Carol Beattie Taylor, Feb. 25, 1955; children: Thomas, June, Erick, Victor. BSChemE, U. Md., 1955. Devel. engr. Celanese Corp. Am., Cumberland, Md., 1955-58; chem. Engr. U.S. Bur. Mines, College Park, Md., 1958-66; project leader U.S. Bur. Mines, College Park, 1966-70, rsch. supr., 1970-77; chief process evaluation U.S. Bur. Mines, Washington, 1977—. Contbr. over 20 articles to profl. jours. Mem. Am. Inst. Chem. Engrs., Am. Assn. Cost Engrs. Home: 12311 Glen Mill Rd Rockville MD 20854-1928 Office: US Bur of Mines 810 7th St NW # 6202 Washington DC 20241

PETERS, GERALD JOSEPH, physicist; b. Balt., Sept. 29, 1941; s. Harold Raymond and Mary Elizabeth (Schoonmaker) P.; m. Helena Catherine Madrzykowski, Aug. 25, 1967; children: Gregory Joseph, Tamara Catherine. BS in Physics, Loyola Coll., Balt., 1963; MS in Physics, U. Toledo, 1965; postgrad., U. Md., 1969-71, 73-74. Elec. engr., physicist U.S. Naval Ordnance Lab., Silver Spring, Md., 1965-66; rsch. physicist U.S. Naval Surface Weapons Ctr., Silver Spring, 1968-80; physicist, program mgr. U.S. Dept. Energy, Washington, 1980—. Inventor alpha counter timer. Mem. IEEE, Am. Phys. Soc. Home: 16121 Chester Mill Ter Silver Spring MD 20906-1127 Office: US Dept Energy Div High Energy Physics ER 224 GTN Washington DC 20585

PETERS, JOHN OTTO, III, controller; b. Cherry Point, N.C., Oct. 14, 1956; s. John Otto Jr. and Agnes Marie (Solem) P.; m. Rebeca Isreal (div.); m. Diane Ponder, Sept. 26, 1982; children: Mark Otto, Jason Virgel. BBA magna cum laude, Loyola U., Chgo., 1985. CPA, Ill. Buyer, credit mgr. Design Craft Fabric Co., Chgo., 1980-81; auditor Arthur Young, Chgo., 1984-86; supervising auditor Baeshen & Banaga, Arthur Young, Jeddah, Saudi Arabia, 1986-88, Arthur Young, Chgo., 1988-89; sr. fin. acct. FMC Corp., Chgo., 1989-90; plant contr. FMC Corp., Rockland, Maine, 1990—. With U.S. Army, 1975-78. Mem. AICPA, Ill. CPA Soc., Beta Gamma Sigma, Beta Alpha Psi. Republican. Office: FMC Marine Colloids Box 308 Rockland ME 04841

PETERS, MERCEDES, psychoanalyst; b. N.Y.C. Student Columbia U., 1944-45; BS, L.I. U., 1945; MS, U. Conn., 1953; tng. in psychotherapy Am. Inst. Psychotherapy and Psychoanalysis, 1960-70; cert. in Psychoanalysis Postgrad. Ctr. For Mental Health, 1976; PhD in Psychoanalysis, Union Inst., 1989. Cert. psychoanalyst Am. Examining Bd. Psychoanalysis; cert. mental health cons. Social worker various agys., pub. instns., 1945-63; sr. psychotherapist Community Guidance Svc., 1960-75; staff affiliate Postgrad. Ctr. for Mental Health, 1974-76; pvt. practice psychotherapy, Bklyn., 1961—. Contbr. articles to profl. jours. Bd. dirs. Brookwood Child Care Assn., Bklyn Music Sch., chmn. long range planning com. Fellow Am. Orthopsychiat. Assn.; mem. LWV, NAACP, NASW, Brooklyn Heights Mus. Soc., Postgrad. Ctr. Psychoanalytic Soc., Assn. For Psychoanalytic Self Psychology (program com.), N.Y. State Clin. Social Workers. Office: 142 Joralemon St Brooklyn NY 11201-4709

PETERS, RALPH EDGAR, business executive; b. Harrisburg, Pa., Feb. 20, 1923; s. George Edward and Rebecca Flavia (Michener) P.; m. Roberta Jane Shaffer, June 12, 1948; children: Sheila Jane, Gail Marie, Ralph Jr., Bret Edward. Student, U. Pa., 1942; BA in Bus. Adminstrn., Pa. State U., 1948. From payroll supr. to asst. budget supr. Pa. State U., 1948-52; chief acct., pers. officer Haller, Raymond & Brown, State College, Pa., 1952-54; from contr. to chief exec. officer and chmn. bd. Benatec Assocs., Inc. (formerly Berger Assocs., Inc.), Camp Hill, Pa., 1954—; bd. dirs. CCNB Bank, New Cumberland, Pa., 1972—. Chmn. bd. advisors Pa. State U., Harrisburg, 1979-89; chmn. bd. dirs. Holy Spirit Hosp., Camp Hill, 1982-89; past pres. Tri-County United Way, Harrisburg, from 1978; chmn. Pvt. Industry Coun., Harrisburg, 1982-87. With U.S. Army, 1943-45, ETO, 1952-53, Korea. Recipient Community Svc. award Salvation Army, 1980, Disting. Alumnus award Pa. State U., 1980, Disting. Pennsylvanian award Greater Phila. C. of C., 1981. Mem. Pa. C. of C. (bd. dir., transp. com. chmn. 1972-90), Harrisburg Area C. of C. (pres., chmn. 1979-83), Ams. for Competitive Enterprise System (pres. 1981-83), Lions, Masons, Pa. Jaycees (pres. 1955-56, nat. v.p. 1956-57), Delta Sigma Pi. Lutheran. Office: Benatec Assocs Inc 101 Erford Rd Camp Hill PA 17011-1899

PETERS, RICHARD JOSEPH, retired hairstylist, cosmotologist; b. Fairfield, Maine, July 16, 1937; s. Andrew Joseph Peters and Hilda Elizabeth (Wing) Schwartz; m. Concetta Dolly Caramanica, Nov. 16, 1957; 1 child, Michele Lynn Peters. Student, Housatonic Community Coll., 1968-70; DDiv (hon.), Ch. of Universal Brotherhood, Hollywood, Calif., 1974. Owner Fashionette Beauty Salon, Devon, Conn., 1959-63, Hi Fashion Couffures, Stratford, Conn., 1961-63; founder, cons. D&D Wholesale Distbrs., Milford, Conn., 1974—; chmn. sales com. Stoney Brook Coop. Assn., Stratford, 1966-67. Author: Walden House, 1986, Comton House, 1987, Cromwell House, 1988; inventor board game. With U.S. Army, 1954-57. Mem. Italian Am. War Vets, K.C. Republican. Roman Catholic. Home: 15 Ormond St Milford CT 06460-3912

PETERS, RONALD GEORGE, investment banker; b. N.Y.C., May 28, 1944; s. William J. and Evelyn M. (Nahlikova) P.; m. Susan S. Leigh, Aug. 19, 1972; children: Gregory, William, Timothy. BSE, Princeton U., 1966; MBA, Columbia U., 1971. Dept. mgr. Procter & Gamble Co., Balt., 1966-67; v.p. Citibank, N.A., N.Y.C., 1971-80; mng. dir. Oppenheimer & Co., Inc., N.Y.C., 1980—; bd. dirs. Koret, Inc., San Francisco. 1st lt. U.S. Army, 1967-69. Mem. Twilight Cottagers (bd. dirs. 1989—, treas. 1989—). Home: 25 North Dr Carmel NY 10512-1113 Office: Oppenheimer & Co Inc 200 Liberty St New York NY 10281-1003

PETERS, THEODORE, JR., research biochemist, consultant; b. Chambersburg, Pa., May 12, 1922; s. Theodore and Miriam (Lenhardt) P.; m. Margaret Campbell, June 9, 1945; children: Theodore D., James C., Melissa Peters Barry, William L. BS in Chem. Engring., Lehigh U., 1943; PhD in Biol. Chemistry, Harvard U., 1950. Diplomate Am. Bd. Clin. Chemistry. Grad. asst. MIT, Cambridge, 1943-44; rsch. fellow Harvard Med. Sch., Boston, 1948-50; instr. U. Pa. Sch. Medicine, Phila., 1950-51; biochemist U.S. VA Hosp., Boston, 1953-55; rsch. biochemist Mary Imogene Bassett Hosp., Cooperstown, N.Y., 1955-88, rsch. scientist emeritus, 1988—; vis. scientist Carlsberg Laboratorium, Copenhagen, Denmark, 1958-59; guest worker NIH, Bethesda, Md., 1971-72; vis. rsch. prof. U. Western Australia, Perth, 1982; chmn. classification panel FDA, Washington, 1976-79; bd. dirs. Nat. Com. for Clin. Lab. Standards, Villanova, Pa., 1986-87. Editor: Plasma Protein Secretion by the Liver, 1983; chmn. bd. editors Clin. Chemistry, 1979-84; contbr. articles to profl. jours. Chmn. Sewer Bd., Cooperstown, 1975—; mem. Water Bd., Cooperstown, 1973—; chmn. lake com. Otsego County Conservation Assn., Cooperstown, 1972-78. Comdr. USNR, 1944-47, 51-53. Recipient Gold medal Biol. div. Electron Microscope Soc. Am., 1966. Fellow Am. Assn. Clin. Chemistry (pres. 1988, awards 1976, 77, 91); mem. Am. Chem. Soc., Am. Soc. Biol. Chemists (emeritus), Am. Soc. for Cell Biology (emeritus), Protein Soc., Nat. Acad. for Clin. Biochemistry (diplomate), Acad. Clin. Lab. Physicians and Scientists, Phi Beta Kappa. Home: 30 River St Cooperstown NY 13326-1317 Office: Mary Imogene Bassett Hosp Atwell Rd Cooperstown NY 13326-1302

PETERS, THOMAS JOSEPH, computer scientist, mathematician; b. Washington; s. Raymond Joseph and Mary Theresa (O'Neill) P.; m. Kathleen Lillian Faulds, Dec. 20, 1985; children: Amy Theresa, Sean Raymond. BA in Math., New Coll., 1973; MS in Math., U. R.I., 1978; PhD in Math., Conn. Wesleyan U., 1982. Environ. analyst Conn. Dept. Environ. Protection, Hartford, 1973-75; asst. prof. U. Hartford, 1982-83; mem. sr. tech. staff Prime/Computervision, Inc., Bedford, Mass., 1984-88; mem. rsch. staff C.S. Draper Lab., Cambridge, Mass., 1988-89; vis. assoc. prof. U. Conn., Storrs, 1989-90, asst. prof., 1990—; cons. No. Rsch. and Engring. Corp., Woburn, Mass., 1989, Prime/Computervision, Inc., Bedford, 1990. Author: (with others) Innovative Applications of Artificial Intelligence, 1991; contbr. articles to profl. jours. Mem. adv. bd. Conn. Lung Assn., East Hartford, 1982-84; advisor Community Child Guidance Clinic, Manchester, Conn., 1991. Conn. State scholar, 1968-73. Mem. Am. Math. Soc., Assn. for Computing Machinery, Soc. for Indsl. and Applied Math. Office: U Conn Dept Computer Sci & Engring U 155 Storrs CT 06269-3155

PETERSEN, BARRY REX, news correspondent; b. Norfolk, Va., Jan. 14, 1949; s. Kermit and Mavis Lucille (Sutton) P.; m. Sandra H. Petersen, June 7, 1971 (div. Dec. 1984); children: Emily Jensine, Juliette Rose; m. Jan Chorlton, Feb. 14, 1985. BS in Journalism, Northwestern U., 1970, MS in Journalism, 1972. Sports columnist Sidney (Mont.) Herald, 1964-66; city hall reporter Arlington Heights (Ill.) Day, 1968-69; columnist, copy editor Chgo. Today, 1970-71; pub. Daily Northwestern, Evanston, Ill., 1970-71; reporter Milw. (Wis.) Jour., 1971-72; investigative reporter Sta. WITI-TV, Milw., 1972-74; reporter, anchor Sta. WCCO-TV, Mpls., 1974-78; corr. CBS News, L.A., 1978-81, San Francisco, 1981-85, Tokyo, 1986-88, Moscow, 1988-90, London, 1991—; pres. AFRTA, Milw., 1973-74; Josephine B. and Newton N. Minow vis. prof. in communications Northwestern U., Evanston, Ill., 1991. Recipient Investigative Reporting award Wis. Press Assn., 1973. Mem. Assn. Am. Corrs. in London. Lutheran. Home: 146 Walton St, London SW 3, England Office: CBS News/London 524 W 57th St New York NY 10019

PETERSEN, BRUCE LAWRENCE, personnel executive; b. Chgo., Nov. 13, 1941; s. Lawrence A. and Ruth J. (Ervin) P.; m. Arnhild Petersen, June 22, 1963; children: Jan-Erik, Sven. BA in Russian Lang. and Lit., Northwestern U., 1963. Cert. CPCU. Tng. mgr. Neckura Ins. Co., Frankfurt, Germany, 1969-78; mgr. Nationwide Ins. Co., Columbus, Ohio, 1978-86; regional pers./pub. rels. dir. Nationwide Ins. Co., Annapolis, Md., 1986—. Bd. dirs. Md. Seafood Festival, Annapolis, 1986—, Friends of St. John's Coll., Annapolis, 1991—; adv. coun. mem. Hist. Annapolis Found., 1991—. Comdr. USN, 1963-69. Mem. Greater Annapolis C. of C. (bd. dirs. 1989—). Home: 1111 Chesapeake Dr Stevensville MD 21666-2717 Office: Nationwide Ins Co 2500 Riva Rd Annapolis MD 21401-7430

PETERSEN, DAVID JOHN, filmmaker, writer; b. Mpls., June 14, 1958; s. Robert Carl and Anne Katherine (Oriel) P. BA in English with honors, U. Md., 1984. Dir., producer Fax Productions, Inc., Bethesda, Md., 1981-84; dir., editor, composer film Awakening, 1982; dir., writer Bell Atlantic, Washington, 1984-85; producer, dir. Film "Fine Food Fine Pastries, 1985-88; editor Film Roger and Me, 1989, 1989, Smithsonian World Quantum Universe, 1989, 1989-90; dir., producer Smithsonian audio, visual, Washington, 1982; editor Smithsonian Folklife Program, Washington, 1982-83. Dir., producer: (film) Fine Food, Fine Pastries, 1989 (Acad. award nominee); editor, composer: (film) Fine Food, Fine Pastries Open 6 to 9, 1988 (Crystal Apple award, Blue Ribbon award, Gold award, Emmy award, CINE award); dir., co-producer, writer: (film) I Run and Feel Rain: Scenes, 1992. Recipient Disting. Pub. Svc. award, D.C., 1988, Writing fellowship Cafritz Found., 1991, 92, The Corp. of Yaddo, 1991, The Ragdale Found., 1990, The Va. Ctr. for Creative Arts, 1988, 89; grantee D.C. Commn. on Arts, 1989, 90, D.C. Community Humanities Coun., 1986, 88; writing fellow Commington Community of Arts, 1980, 90; named Guest Lectr., Am. U., 1990, St. Lawrence U., 1991, Guest Lectr. and Instr. Carnegie Mellon U. Mem. Nat. Assn. TV Arts and Scis., Assn. Internat. Video and Filmmakers, Nat. Assn. Broadcast Employees and Technicians. Democrat. Home and Office: David Petersen 617 8th St NE Washington DC 20002-5237

PETERSEN, DEAN MITCHELL, waste management professional; b. Waterloo, Iowa, Nov. 13, 1950; s. Guy Albert and Valeria Catherine (Mitchell) P.; m. Maria Rosario Artuz, Mar. 1972 (div. Feb. 1978); m. Sandra Jean Asselin, Aug. 15, 1980; children: Marc Edward Asselin, Liesa Jan, Michael Charles. Student, Ill. Cen. Coll., 1978-79, Rhodes Coll., 1988; A in Bus. Adminstrn. magna cum laude, Shelby State Community Coll., Memphis, 1988. Enlisted USN, 1969, hull maintenance technician, 1969-77; lab mgr. Peoria Color Lab, Peoria Heights, Ill., 1977-79; owner Mitchell-Petersen Photography, Peoria, Ill., 1978-79; purchasing agt., parts mgr., office mgr. Weissman Industries, Waterloo, 1980-84; fleet maintenance mgr. Ben Mogy & Sons, Memphis, 1985-86; program developer Nesretep Bus. Svcs., Lewiston, Maine, 1988—. Author: Vietnam Veteran's Lament, 1986, Book of Dean (A Study of the Sacred Lost Valley Scrolls), 1989, Book of Dean--With Annotation, 1991, Collection, 1991, Dancing Girl, 1991, Lyrics, 1991, Recycling as a Component of Economic Development, 1992; composer: Life of Love, 1988; contbr. articles, photographs to profl. publs.; inventor, designer in field. Recipient Presdl. citation Pres. Ferdinand Marcos, Manila, 1973, Achievement cert. Kodak, 1978. Office: Nesretep Bus Svcs PO Box 1961 Lewiston ME 04241

PETERSEN, GLENN THOMAS, anthropology educator; b. Oakland, Calif., Apr. 13, 1947; s. Roy Albert and Clare Theresa (Ruggle) P. BA, Calif. State Coll., Hayward, 1970; PhD, Columbia U., 1977. Prof. anthropology Baruch Coll., CUNY, 1977—, prof. Grad. Sch. and Univ. Ctr., 1986—, chmn. dept. sociology and anthropology, 1984-90; sr. rsch. fellow Rsch. Sch. Pacific Studies,Australian Nat. U., 1989; vis. prof. internat. rels. U. P.R., 1992-93. Author: One Man Cannot Rule a Thousand, 1982, Decentralization and Micronesian Federation, 1986, Lost in the Weeds, 1990. With USN, 1964-68, Vietnam. Fellow NSF, 1970, Nat. Inst. Gen. Med. Studies, 1970-73, NEH, 1983-84; grantee NIMH, 1973-75. Fellow Am. Anthrop. Assn., Assn. for Social Anthropology in Oceania (bd. dirs. 1992—), N.Y. Acad. Scis. (adv. bd. 1979-81); mem. AAAS, Pacific History Assn., Pacific Sci. Assn. Home: 3G Shirley Ln Trenton NJ 08648-1403 Office: CUNY Baruch Coll 17 Lexington Ave New York NY 10010-5526

PETERSEN, NORMAN RICHARD, JR., religious studies educator; b. Chgo., Aug. 25, 1933; s. Norman Richard and Mildred May (Wilson) P.; m. Antoinette DeRosa, Jan. 28, 1956; children: Kristen, Mark, Joanna. B.F.A., Pratt Inst., 1957; S.T.B., Harvard U., 1961, Ph.D., 1967. Instr., asst. prof. Wellesley Coll., Mass., 1963-69; asst. prof., then assoc. prof. religion Williams Coll., Williamstown, Mass., 1969-77; prof. Williams Coll., 1978-79, Washington Gladden prof. religion, 1980—. Author: Literary Criticism for New Testament Critics, 1978, Rediscovering Paul. The Sociology of Paul's Narrative World, 1985 (Bibl. Archeology Soc. book award 1986, Am. Acad. Religion book award 1987); assoc. editor: Semeia, 1974-82. Mem. Mt. Greylock Regional High Sch. Com., Williamstown, 1980-85. Served with AUS, 1952-54. Mem. Soc. Bibl. Lit., Studiorim Novi Testamenti Societas. Office: Williams Coll Dept Religion Williamstown MA 01267

PETERSEN, RODNEY LAWRENCE, religious institute executive, educator; b. Chgo., Jan. 17, 1949; s. Donald Lawrence and Eileen Lucille (Unruh) P.; m. Priscilla Brooks Cushman, June 12, 1976 (div. 1988); 1 child, Eliot Brooks. BA, Harvard U., 1971, MDiv, 1974, ThM, 1976; PhD, Princeton Sem., 1985. Ordained min. Presbyn. Ch., 1980. Asst. prof. Trinity Evang. Div. Sch., Deerfield, Ill., 1981-86; asst. to pastor Crossroads Ch., Ferney-Voltaire, France, 1987-90; exec. dir. Boston Theol. Inst., Newton, Mass., 1990—; adj. prof. Webster U. in Geneva, Switzerland, 1987—,

Andover Newton (Mass.) Theol. Sch., 1991—; tchr. Biblical Edn. by Extension, Vienna, Austria, 1987-90; cons. non-govtl. orgns., Geneva, 1991—. Author: Introduction to Church History, 1991, Preaching in the Last Days, 1992. Min. Presbyn. Ch., 1985—; bd. dirs. Mass. Coun. Chs., 1990—, Mass. Commn. on Christian Unity, 1991—. Recipient Issue Rsch. grant Assn. Theol. Schs. in the USA and Can., 1986. Mem. Am. Hist. Assn., Am. Acad. Religion, Am. Soc. Ch. History, Assn. for the Sociology Religion, European Bus. Ethics Network, Sixteenth Century Studies Conf. Office: Boston Theol Inst 210 Herrick Rd Newton MA 02159

PETERSON, CATHY HARASTY, artist; b. Johnstown, Pa., June 26, 1957; d. Michael and Stella Mae (Misner) Harasty Sr.; m. Jay Allen Peterson, Nov. 27, 1980. Diploma, Bible Truth Inst., Sunbury, Pa., 1974-76; postgrad., Bible Trust Inst., Sunbury, Pa., 1977; A in Fine Arts, Ivy Sch. of Profl. Art, Pitts., 1980. Instr. North Hills Christian Sch., Pitts., 1982-88; commns. artist specializing in portraiture Sewickley, Pa., 1987—. Republican. Home: 614 Lincoln Pl Sewickley PA 15143-1733

PETERSON, CHESTER GIBE, advertising consultant; b. Bridgeton, N.J., Apr. 27, 1922; s. Daniel Smith and Leanore (Gibe) P.; m. Kathryn Ann Morris, May 19, 1945; children: Donald Morris, Susan Dee. Cert. in Advt. Design, Phila. Mus. Sch. of Art, 1945. Printer, screen operator COWAN Printing & Advt., Bridgeton, N.J., 1940-45; exec. art dir. COWAN Printing & Advt., Bridgeton, 1945-62, Wyble Advt., Millville, N.J., 1962-68, The Franklin Mint, Franklin Center, Pa., 1968-72; sr. v.p. The Franklin Mint, Franklin Center, 1972-86; dir. Franklin Advt. Services, London, 1975-85; prin. C.G. Peterson, Advt. Cons., Bridgeton, N.J., 1986—. Planning bd. mem. City of Bridgeton, N.J.; v.p. Bridgeton Sch. Bd., 1958-62. Lodge: Rotary. Home and Office: 12 Linden St Bridgeton NJ 08302-2115

PETERSON, DENIS J., computer company executive and founder; b. Bklyn.; s. Peter P. and Adrienne (Gregor) P.; m. Janet Euster; children: Leah, Elisha, Raffi, Samara, Peter, Nadia. BA, Hofstra U.; MFA, Pratt Inst.; JD, Va. Law Sch. Prof. L.I. U., C.W. Post Campus, North Merrick, N.Y.; legal counsel U.S. Ho. of Reps., Washington; mem. adv. coun. N.Y.C. Bd. Edn., Bklyn.; mem. commerce com., mem. environ. com. N.Y. State Bus. Coun., Albany, N.Y. Republican. Office: 1500 Jerusalem Ave Merrick NY 11566-1306

PETERSON, ERIC ROBERT, state official; b. Rochester, N.Y., Feb. 9, 1944; s. Alton Robert and Edna Rita (Group) P.; m. Harriet Smith, Aug. 11, 1985. AS, Regents Coll., 1982, BS, 1987; MPA, Harvard U., 1988. Elec. tech. Beech-Nut, Inc., Rochester, 1965-71; complaint clk City Ct. Rochester, 1972-79; legislator Monroe County Legislature, Rochester, 1977-81; sr. rsch. analyst Commn. on State-Local Rels., Albany, 1981-83, dep. dir., 1983—; cons. in field. Author: New York's Revenue Sharing Program: At The Crossroads, 1985; co-author: New Yor's Police Service: Perspectives on the Issues, 1985; co-author on computer case studies. First v.p. North East Area Devel., Rochester, 1975; treas. and bd. dirs. Action For A Better Community, Rochester, 1978-81. Mem. Am. Soc. Pub. Administrn., Am. Acad. Polit. and Social Sci., Rochester Area C. of C. (Disting. Svc. award Jr. C. of C. 1977), Sect. on Intergovtl. Adminstrn. and Mgmt. (regional coord. region 2 1988—), Acad. Polit. Sci., Albany-Colonie Regional C. of C. (capital leadership class 1992). Democrat. Roman Catholic. Home: 17 Roosevelt St Albany NY 12206-1407 Office: Commn on State-Local Rels Agy Bldg 4 14th Fl Albany NY 12248

PETERSON, GARY WILLIAM, concert promoter, producer; b. Faribault, Minn., Sept. 22, 1946; s. Roland Oscar and Betty Lou (Lenzmeier) P.; m. Sharon Marie Neifert, Aug. 31, 1980 (div. May 1989); children: Buffy Jo, Heather, Rachel Peterson Benson. Student, San Diego City Coll., 1968. Owner Gary W. Peterson Prodns., Wilmington, Del., 1969-84; pres. Peterson Prodns., Wilmington, 1984-87; chief exec. officer Centurion Ventures, Wilmington, 1987-89; chief exec. officer Viking Prodns., Inc., Wilmington, 1989—, also chmn. bd.; chief exec. officer Bison Entertainment Corp., Wilmington, 1991—; chmn. Bison Entertainment Corp.; producer Circus Galaxy, San Antonio, 1972; talent mgr. LP Attractions, Wilmington, 1983-84; producer comedy acts 50 Shrine circuses, 1969-74. Feature film appearances include: Godfather III, 1990, Rocky V, 1990, The Fisher King, 1990, 3 Men and a Little Lady, 1990, White Tower, 1990, Teenage Mutant Ninja Turtles II, 1990, also with Del. Theatre Co. To Kill a Mockingbird, 1990. Dir. fund raising VFW, Wilmington, 1977—, Del. Paralyzed Vets., Wilmington, 1988—. With USAF, 1964-67. Mem. Country Music Assn. (orgnl. mem.), Del. Assn. Police (dir. fundraising 1977—, social mem.). Republican. Roman Catholic. Home: I 14 Pot Nets N Millsboro DE 19966 Office: Bison Entertainment Corp Viking Prodns Inc 3526 Silverside Rd Ste 36 Wilmington DE 19810

PETERSON, H. WILLIAM, chemical executive, consultant; b. Yokohama, Honshu Island, Japan, Mar. 9, 1922; came to U.S., 1924; s. Harry William and Alice (Mateer) P.; m. Doris Jane Howe, Apr. 27, 1946; children: Robert, Christine Fitzpatrick, Janet McMillan. BA in Chemistry and Botany, Colgate U., 1946; postgrad., Princeton U., 1949-50, U. Del., 1982-83. Lic. capt. U.S. inland waters U.S. Coast Guard. Researcher, developer ESSO Standard Oil Co., Bayway, N.J., 1946-51; various positions Enjay Chem. Co., N.Y.C., 1951-65; coord. world-wide chem. Gulf Oil Corp., Pitts., 1965-67; gen. mktg. mgr. Gulf Oil-Eastern Hemisphere, London, 1967-71; corp. v.p. chem. mktg., corp. v.p. mktg. Gulf Oil Can. Ltd., Montreal, Que., Can., 1971-77; chief operating officer Corpus Christi Chem. Co., Wilmington, Del., 1977-78; mng. dir. Food Machinery & Chem. Corp. Internat. Chems., Phila., 1979-80; internat. cons. Bozman, Md., 1980—. Patentee in field. Leader Young Christians Assn., 1st Bapt. Ch., Somerville, N.J., 1948-53; lay speaker, mem. adminstrn. bd. Riverview Charge, United Meth. Ch.; chaplain Mil. Order Purple Heart. With USMC, 1942-46, PTO. Decorated Purple Heart, two battle stars. Fellow Am. Inst. Chemists; mem. Am. Chem. Soc. (emeritus). Home and Office: Quakerneck Rd Mulberry Point Bozman MD 21612

PETERSON, IRVIN LESLIE, agricultural organization administrator; b. Earlimart, Calif., Feb. 25, 1926; s. Frank Marcus and Jenny Mabel (Shaulis) P.; m. Patricia Ruth Abbott, May 13, 1951; children: Frank William, Donald Abbott, Alan Frederick. Student, Coll. of Pacific, U. Wash., 1943-45, Columbia U., 1945; BS, U. Calif., Davis, 1951, DVM, 1963. Farm adviser Agrl. Extension Svc. U. Calif., Merced, 1954-59; vet. poultry pathologist Kimber Farms, Inc., Fremont, Calif., 1963-68; mgr. poultry svc. Western Farmers Assn., Seattle, 1968-71; vet. coord. Nat. Poultry Improvement Plan Agrl. Rsch. Svc./USDA, Beltsville, Md., 1971-77; chief staff veterinarian poultry diseases Vet. Svcs./USDA, Hyattsville, Md., 1977-82, sr. coord. Nat. Poultry Improvement Plan, 1982-91; sr. staff vet. poultry diseases U.S. APHIS, 1991—. Lt. (j.g.) USNR, 1943-46, PTO. Mem. World's Poultry Sci. Assn. (sec.-treas. U.S. br. 1982—, bd. dirs. 1988—), D.C. Vet. Med. Assn. (pres. 1984), Beltsville Rotary Club (sec. 1991—). Republican. Methodist. Home: 4214 Taunton Dr Beltsville MD 20705-2858 Office: Vet Svcs USDA Federal Center Bldg Hyattsville MD 20782

PETERSON, JAMES ALLAN, counselor educator, counseling psychologist; b. Redfield, S.D., Oct. 11, 1932; s. Paul Waldemar Peterson and Ruby Viola (Collins) Bergman; m. Neysa Marion McCall, Mar. 23, 1957; children: Sheryl, Kathleen, Susan. BS, Dakota State Coll., 1958; MEd, S.D. State U., 1962; EdD, Boston U., 1968. Lic. psychologist, Vt. Music tchr. Arlington (S.D.) High Sch., 1958-62, counselor, 1960-62; instr., music Dakota State Coll., Madison, S.D., summer 1962; counseling supr. Boston U., 1962-66; prof. counselor edn. U. Vt., Burlington, 1966—; vis. lectr. Fla. State U., Tallahassee, summer 1963, U. R.I., Kingston, summer 1965, 66. Author: Counseling and Values, 1970, 2d edit., 1990. With U.S. Navy, 1953-57. Home: 35 White Birch Ln Williston VT 05495-9536 Office: Univ of Vermont 411 Waterman Burlington VT 05405

PETERSON, JEAN MARGARET, small business company exeucutive, consultant; b. Moretown, Vt., July 15, 1916; d. Philetus Henry and Gertrude (Thompson) Teachout; m. Arthur Camille Cloutier, 1944 (div. 1955); children: Michael Arthur, David Lester, Thomas Camille; m. Frederick Raymond Peterson Sr., Jan. 11, 1977 (dec. Jan. 1983). Grad., St. Johnsbury (Vt.) Acad., 1933; postgrad., Quinsigamond Community Coll., 1981, Worcester State Coll., 1983-84. Entertainer various cities, 1933-77; home-owner data input Hanover Ins. Co., Worcester, Mass., 1978-82; aide, coord. Region II Area Agy. on Aging, Holden, Mass., 1983-85; info. and reference specialist Cen. Mass. Agy. on Aging, West Boylston, Mass., 1985-91; pres. Joint Ventures, Millbury, Mass., 1992—; elder adv. exec. office Elder Affairs, Cen. Mass., 1983—; elder adv. com. Fallon Health Plan, Worcester, 1987-89. Author: Senior Fitness, 1992. Mem. Coun. on Aging, Millbury, 1985-88, exec. bd. Mass. Local Arts Coun., 1989-90; mem. Millbury Arts Coun., 1988-89, chairperson, 1989. Named Silver-Haired Legislator, Commonwealth of Mass., 1983-85; recipient Elder Achievement award U. Mass., 1986. Democrat. Home: 509 Colonial Dr Millbury MA 01527

PETERSON, LARRY WAYNE, music educator; b. Wichita, Kans., Dec. 10, 1941; s. Forrest W. and Hazel G. (Vaught) P.; m. Lucinda D. Minnix, June 26, 1965; children: John W., Martha L. MusB, Tex. Christian U., 1964, MusM, 1969; PhD, U. N.C., 1973. Instr. Jersey City State Coll., 1973-75; asst. prof. George Peabody Coll., Nashville, 1975-77, dir. Sch. Music, 1977-80; chmn. dept. music U. Del., Newark, 1980-85, assoc. prof., 1985—; trustee, chair program com. Del. Inst. for the Arts in Edn., Newark, 1981—; trustee, chair edn. com. Del. Symphony Orch., Wilmington, 1981-89; music cons. IBM, Raleigh, N.C., 1990—; designer, developer hypermedia lessons in field. Author: Complete Organ Works of Simon Lohet, 1975, UD Opera Index Series, 1989; team mem. UD Videodisc Series, 1986 (CINDY award 1986). Chmn. West Newark Civ Assn., 1987-91; pres. Oaklands Pool Assn., Newark, 1988. Capt. USAF, 1964-69. Recipient Alliance for Arts Edn. cert. J. F. Kennedy Ctr., 1984, Nat. Endowment Humanities Sem. award Dartmouth Coll., 1987, Joe Wyatt Challenge award EDUCOM, 1991, 2d prize Masters Innovation award Zenith Corp., 1991; fellow Woodrow Wilson Found., 1971. Mem. Am. Musicological Soc. (regional chair 1979-80), Coll. Music Soc., Comp. Mus. Assn., Internat. Soc. for Tech. in Edn. Democrat. United Ch. of Christ. Home: 243 W Main St Newark DE 19711-3237 Office: U Del Music Dept Newark DE 19716

PETERSON, MARY KAY, academic administrator; b. Irvington, N.J., Sept. 25, 1955; d. Gus Andrew and Lillie Mae (Jones) P.; m. Brett D. Larson, Jan. 1, 1978. Student, Glassboro (N.J.) State Coll., 1973-74, U. Maine, 1974-76; BA, Goddard Coll., 1981. Coord. S.P.E.D.Y. Community Action Agy., Wilton, Maine, 1976-77; vol. dir. women's svcs. Coatesville (Pa.) YWCA, 1980-81, dir. women's svcs., 1981-82; coord. literacy program City of Elwyn, Pa., 1987-88; dir. adult edn. City of Elwyn, Inc., 1988—. Board dirs. Coatesville Day Care Ctr., 1989-90; pres. Coatesville YWCA, 1991—. Mem. Pa. Assn. Adult Continuing Edn. (rep. to bd. Harrisburg, Pa. chpt. 1991—), Pa. Assn. Volunteerism (rep. southeastern chpt. 1990—). Home: PO Box 98A Honey Brook PA 19344-0098 Office: City of Elwyn Inc 111 Elwyn Rd Media PA 19063-4699

PETERSON, QUINTIN, police officer, media liaison officer, writer; b. Washington, Mar. 24, 1956; s. Noah and Grace Pearl (Kelson) P.; m. Janette Latonia Williams, Oct. 27, 1988; children: Destiny Dejahnese, Quintin Noah. Grad., Oshkosh (Wis.) North High Sch., 1975; diploma, Met. Police Dept Tng. Acad., Washington, 1982. Police officer Metro. Police Dept., Washington, 1981—; news media liaison Metro. Police Dept., Washingtin, 1985—, motion picture liaison, 1986—, MPD tng. film writer, 1987—. Assoc. editor Met. Police Dept. Metro-Intercom newsletter, 1989—; author (play) Daylight, 1977 (Nat. Endowment for the Arts award 1978); author: (poetry) Nativity, 1988; co-author: Dealing with the Media, 1992. Recipient Creative Writing award NCTE, 1974, Sci. Fiction Writing award U. Wis., 1974, Acad. Achievement award ABC Program, 1974, Creative Writing fellowship Nat. Endowment for Arts, 1978, Creative Writing grant Commn. on Arts and Humanities, 1979. Mem. Fraternal Order of Police. Home: 162 Darrington St SW Washington DC 20032 Office: Metro Police Dept PIO 300 Indiana Ave NW Rm 2052 Washington DC 20001

PETERSON, RICHARD BURNETT, biochemist; b. Omaha, Apr. 12, 1949; s. John Warren and Elizabeth Irene (Vickers) P.; m. Ann Rosamund Skopek, Oct. 10, 1981; children: Adam Richard, Kathryn Elizabeth. BA, U. Nebr., Omaha, 1971; PhD, U. Wis., Madison, 1976. Rsch. assoc. U.S. Dept. Energy Plant Rsch. Lab. Mich. State U., East Lansing, 1976-78; rsch. assoc. C.F. Kettering Rsch. Lab., Yellow Springs, Ohio, 1978-79; asst. scientist Conn. Agrl. Experiment Sta., New Haven, 1979-82, assoc. scientist, 1982—; vis. scientist Rsch. Inst. for Photosynthesis, Sheffield, Eng., 1987, Estonian Acad. Sci., Tartu, Estonia, 1991. Contbr. articles to profl. jours. USDA grantee, 1990. Mem. AAAS, Am. Soc. Plant Physiologists (editorial bd. 1991—). Office: Conn Agrl Experiment Sta 123 Huntington St New Haven CT 06504

PETERSON, RICHARD SCOT, renaissance scholar, literature educator; b. Ayr, Scotland, July 14, 1938; (parents Am. citizens); s. R. Stanley and Willa Marie (Snyder) P.; m. Lin Kelsey, Aug. 28, 1965; 1 child, Timothy Scot. BA, Princeton U., 1960; MA, U. Calif., Berkeley, 1963, PhD, 1968. Instr. English Princeton (N.J.) U., 1966-69, asst. prof. English, 1969-72; lectr. English U. Va., Charlottesville, 1972-75; asst. prof. English Yale U., New Haven, Conn., 1976-80; assoc. prof. English U. Conn., Storrs, 1980-85, prof. English, 1986—. Author: Imitation and Praise in the Poems of Ben Jonson, 1981; editor: Essays in Literature and Art (runner-up CELS award), 1986; editorial bd. John Donne Jour., 1981—. Fulbright scholar, Oxford U., 1960-61; NEH-Newberry Library fellow, 1976, British Acad.-Newberry fellow, 1984. Fellow Am. Philos. Soc., ACLS, Bibliog. Soc. Am., Spenser Soc. Am. (chair McCaffrey Award Com., 1988-89). Home: 1693 Main St Glastonbury CT 06033-2961 Office: Univ of Connecticut U-25 Storrs CT 06269

PETERSON, RONALD ARTHUR, business executive; b. N.Y.C., July 13, 1938; s. Arthur A. and Muriel (Riesner) P.; children: Alix, Tamara. Student, Art Ctr. Coll. of Design, Pasadena, Calif., 1957-61. Designer Raymond Loewy/William Snaith, 1962-64; prin. Design Plus, 1965-67, Peterson & Blyth Assocs., N.Y.C., 1967—. Bd. dirs. William Reedy Lectr. in Photography, 1988-89. With U.S. Army, 1962-64. Recipient numerous awards from Am. Inst. Graphic Arts, Indsl. Designers Soc. Am., Clios, Package Designers Coun. and others. Mem. Package Design Coun. (ea. chmn. 1989, bd. dirs.), Assns. Profl. Design Firms (bd. dirs. exec. com., sec.), Indsl. Designers Soc. Am., Am. Inst. Graphic Arts, U. Club N.Y. Office: Peterson & Blyth Assocs 216 E 45th St New York NY 10017-3304

PETERSON, SCOTT LEE, music retailer; b. Neresheim, Germany, July 18, 1959; came to U.S., 1962; s. Raymond Bertram and Betty Myra (Holburn) P. BS in Econs., George Mason U., 1984. Dir. edn. Jordan Kitt's Music, College Park, Md., 1984-86, asst. mdse. mgr., 1986-87, msde. mgr., 1987-89, dir. mktg., 1989-91, asst. mgr., 1991-92, mgr., 1992—. Mem. Dumflies (Va.) Magisterial Civic Assn., 1991—. Mem. Nat. Eagle Scout Assn., Masons (master). Home: 8766 Old Colony Way Alexandria VA 22309-1545

PETERSON, VINCENT MICHAEL, SR., security executive; b. Trenton, N.J., June 3, 1932; s. Joseph J. and Margaret I. (Cantwell) P.; m. Mary Ann Zaniewski; children: Barbara, Kathleen, Margaret, Vincent Jr. Student, Mt. St. Mary Coll., 1951-52, San Diego Jr. Coll., 1953, Rider Coll., 1977; N.J. State Police Acad., 1954. Cert. protection profl. Capt. N.J. State Police, Trenton, 1954-82; dir. security Squibb Corp., Princeton, N.J., 1982-90, Metromedia Co., East Rutherford, N.J., 1990—. Mem. N.J. Jaycees, Trenton, 1965. With USN, 1952-54. Mem. Am. Soc. for Indsl. Security, Am. Soc. Crime Lab. Dirs., Harvard Assocs. in Police Sci. (bd. dirs. 1965-82). Home: 8 Forrest Central Dr Titusville NJ 08560-1311

PETERSON, W(ALTER) SCOTT, ophthalmic surgeon; b. Newton, Kans., Sept. 5, 1944; s. Walter F. and Elizabeth (Wiebe) P.; m. Jean Louise Murray, Dec. 16, 1967; children: James Scott, Hilary Jean. BA summa cum laude, Yale U., 1966, MD, 1971. Diplomate Am. Bd. Ophthalmology. Ophthalmic surgeon Eye Assocs. Waterbury (Conn.) PC, 1974—; teaching faculty Yale U. Med. Sch., New Haven, 1975—; cons. West Haven (Conn.) VA Hosp., 1975—. Author: An Approach to Paterson, 1967. Bd. dirs. Waterbury Found., 1985—, sec., 1991—; bd. dirs. Middlebury (Conn.) Land Trust, 1987—, Mattatich Mus., 1990—. Recipient Med. Sci. award Am. Diabetes Assn., 1980. Fellow ACS, Am. Acad. Ophthalmology; mem. New Eng. Ophthal. Soc., MLA, William Carlos Williams Soc., Phi Beta Kappa Assocs. Office: Eye Assocs Waterbury PC 87 Grandview Ave Waterbury CT 06708-2514

PETERSON, WILLIAM DWIGHT, psychiatrist; b. Detroit, July 17, 1954; s. Ervin Ole and Frances Eda (Vanderberg) P.; m. Diane Karen Barnes, July 7, 1984; children: Leif Michael, Neil Christian. AB, U. Mich., 1976; M.D., C.M., McGill U., Montreal, Can., 1981. Lic. physician, Ill., Wis. Resident psychiatry Evanston Hosp. Northwestern U., Evanston, Ill., 1981-85; fellow in child psychiatry U. Wis., Madison, 1985-87; med. officer psychiatry, child & adolescent psychiatry svc. 97th Gen. Hosp., U.S. Dept. of the Army, Frankfurt, Fed. Republic of Germany, 1987—. Nat. Merit scholar Chrysler Corp. Fund, 1972-76. Mem. Am. Psychiat. Assn., Am. Acad. Child & Adolescent Psychiatry, Phi Beta Kappa. Democrat. Office: 97th Gen Hosp Unit 25717 Box 4 APO AE 09242

PETERSON, WILLIAM FRANK, physician, administrator; b. Newark, Sept. 28, 1922; s. Edgar Charles and Margaret Benedict (Heyn) P.; m. Margaret Henderson Lee, June 28, 1946 (div. 1978); children: Margaret Lee, Edward Charles; m. 2d, Mary Ann Estelle McGrath, Nov. 29, 1980. Student, Cornell U., 1940-43; MD, N.Y. Med. Coll., 1946. Commd. lt. U.S. Air Force, 1946, advanced through grades to col., 1963; med. officer U.S. Air Force, 1946-70; chmn. dept. ob-gyn Washington Hosp. Ctr. 1970—; dir. Women's Clinic. Washington, 1971—, Ob-Gyn Ultrasound Lab., Washington, 1974—. Contbr. articles to profl. jours. Chmn., Maternal Mortality Com., 1981—. Decorated Legion of Merit, 1960, 70; Cert. Achievement, Office Surgeon Gen., USAF, 1967. Fellow Am. Coll. Ob-Gyn, ACS, Nat. Bd. Med. Examiners (diplomate), Washington Gynecol. Soc. (exec. council 1980-85). Republican. Episcopalian. Home: 50 Stonegate Dr Silver Spring MD 20905-5701 Office: Washington Hosp Ctr 110 Irving St NW Washington DC 20010

PETERSON, WILLIAM PAUL, mathematics educator, researcher; b. Somerville, N.J., July 2, 1957; s. John Leonard and Geraldine Julia (Golomb) P.; m. Doreen Annettte Bald, Aug. 14, 1982; children: Jeremy Nathan, Nathaniel James. AB, Dartmouth Coll., 1979; MS, Stanford (Calif.) U., 1981, PhD, 1985. Asst. prof. U. So. Maine, Portland, 1985; sr. scientist Palladian Software, Inc., Cambridge, Mass., 1986-88; asst. prof. Middlebury (Vt.) Coll., 1989—. Contbr. article to Jour. Maths. of Ops. Rsch., 1991. New Eng. Consortium for Undergrad. Sci. Edn. grantee, 1990, 91. Mem. Am. Maths. Soc., Math. Assn. Am., Inst. Mgmt. Scis., Ops. Rsch. Soc. Am. Office: Middlebury Coll Dept of Mathematics Middlebury VT 05753

PETRARO, VINCENT L., lawyer; b. Bklyn., Jan. 1, 1956; s. Onofrio John and Antoinette Josephine (Dallara) P.; m. Christine Marie Filippi, Sept. 20, 1980; children: Nina, Peter, Marjorie. BA, St. John's Coll., 1977; JD, St. John's Law Sch., 1980. Bar: N.Y. 1981. Assoc. Sheldon Lobel & Assocs., N.Y.C., N.Y., 1981—; counsel Mem. of Assembly Gregory Becker, Lynbrook, N.Y., 1983-85, State Sen. Dean Skelos, Rockville Centre, N.Y., 1986—. Committeeman East Rockaway (N.Y.) Rep. Com., 1977-91; mem. com. St. Raymond's Roman Cath. Ch., East Rockaway, 1986—, sec. parish sch. bd., 1989—, pres., 1991—. Mem. N.Y. State Bar Assn., Judge Frank A. Gulotta Lodge (pres. 1984-86), State Lodge (chmn. gen. laws and resolutions com. 1989—), Order Sons of Italy in Am. (bd. dirs. N.Y. State Grand Lodge Found., 1989—). Republican. Roman Catholic. Home: 21 Hewlett Point Ave East Rockaway NY 11518-2307 Office: Sheldon Lobel & Assocs 101 Park Ave New York NY 10178-0002

PETRELLO, GEORGE JAMES, college dean, business management consultant; b. Newark, N.J., Apr. 30, 1938; s. John and Rose (Lapore) P.; m. Barbara A. Ledden, Aug. 29, 1964. BA, Montclair State Coll., 1958; MBA, Seton Hall U., 1964; PhD, NYU, 1969. Prof. bus. and econs. Wagner Coll., N.Y.C., 1969-78; dean bus. St. Mary's U., San Antonio, 1978-83; v.p. acad. affairs, provost Bryant Coll., Smithfield, R.I., 1983-86; dean Andreas Sch. Bus. Barry U., Miami Shores, Fla., 1986-90; dean bus. and pub. info., info. sci. L.I. U., Bklyn., 1990—; cons. N.Y.C. Bd. Edn., 1978-79, Mgrs. Union of USSR, 1991—. Author: History of the Association of Independent Colleges & Schools, 1987; co-author: (textbook) Introduction to Business, 1977, Personal Finance, 1978. Trustee Ruth Forman Theater, Miami, Fla., 1987-90, Gold Coast C. of C., Bay Harbor, Fla., 1987-90; active Metro Tech Com., Bklyn., 1990-91. Recipient Founders Day award NYU, 1969, Man of the Month, Bay Harbor Island, Fla., 1987. Mem. Nat. Bus. Edn. Assn., Assn. Ind. Colls. and Schs. (bd. dirs. 1982-88, evaluation cons. 1975—), Bklyn. C. of C., Phi Delta Kappa (fellow 1969-79), Alpha Mu Alpha, Delta Mu Delta. Office: LI U University Pla Brooklyn NY 11201

PETRESS, KENNETH CHARLES, education educator; b. Chgo., Nov. 1, 1939; s. Charles William and Margaret Leona (French) P. BS in Edn., No. Ill. U., 1977, MA, 1979, CAS, 1980; PhD, La. State U., 1988. Cert. secondary educator. Instr. No. Ill. U., DeKalb, 1980-83; lectr. Emporia (Kans.) State U., 1984-86; asst. prof. Univ. Maine, Presque Isle, 1988—; vis. prof. Xi Dian Univ., Xian, China, 1983-84, 85, 90. Contbr. articles to profl. jours.; art exhibitor Presque Isle Pub. Libr., 1989, Univ. of Maine Libr., Presque Isle, 1988, 90. Speaker Rotary, various communities, 1988—, Maine Extension groups, 1988—. Recipient faculty devel. grants C-Span in the Classroom, Washington, 1991, vis. scholar award Xi Dian U., 1990. Mem. Speech Communication Assn., So. States Communication Assn., Internat. Communication Assn., Yale-China Assn. Home: 407 Main St # 3 Presque Isle ME 04769-2811 Office: U Maine/Dept Communications 181 Main St Presque Isle ME 04769-2888

PETRIE, FERDINAND RALPH, illustrator, artist; b. Hackensack, N.J., Sept. 17, 1925; s. Archibald John and Bessie (Rutherford) P.; m. Phyllis C. Haddow, Oct. 19, 1951; children: Beth, David. Advt. cert., Parson's Sch. Design, N.Y.C., 1949; student, Art Students League, 1947-49, Famous Artists Course in Illustration, 1958-59. Illustrator J. Gans Assos., N.Y.C., 1950-69. Free lance illustrator, artist, 1969—, owner, Petrie Gallery, Rockport, Mass., 1971—; represented in permanent collections, U.S. Supreme Ct., Smithsonian Instn., Washington, Indpls. Mus. Art; designer U.S. commemorative stamp design, 2 Zaire commemorative stamps, 1980; Author: Drawing Landscapes in Pencil, 1979; illustrator: The Drawing Book, 1980, The Color Book, 1981, The Alkyd Book, 1982, The Watercolorists Guide to Painting Trees, 1983, The Watercolorists Guide to Painting Skies, 1984; The Watercolorists Guide to Painting Water, 1985, Painting Nature in Watercolor, 1990. Served with U.S. Maritime Service, 1943-46. Mem. Am. Watercolor Soc., Artists Fellowship, Rockport Art Assn., Am. Artists Profl. League, Grand Central Gallery, N.J. Watercolor Soc. Presbyterian. Address: 51 Vreeland Ave Rutherford NJ 07070

PETRIE, HUGH GILBERT, university dean, philosophy of education educator; b. Lamar, Colo., Sept. 21, 1937; s. Charles Albert and Mary Madeleine (Ocsay) P.; m. Patricia Donahoe Bradasich, June 3, 1959 (div. 1978); children: Trent Anthony, Ragan Andrea, Brock Asher; m. Carol Ann Hodges, Aug. 26, 1978; stepchildren: Lara Wardrop, Amy Wardrop. BS in Bus., BS in Applied Math., U. Colo., 1960; Phd in Philosophy, Stanford U., 1965. Asst. prof. Northwestern U., Evanston, Ill., 1965-71; assoc. prof. U. Ill., Champaign/Urbana, 1971-75, prof., 1975-81, assoc. vice chancellor for academic affairs, 1977-80; dean grad. Sch. Edn. SUNY, Buffalo, 1981—; coord. N.E. region Holmes Group, 1986-90, bd. dirs., 1986—; mem. bd. overseers N.E. Regional Lab., 1986-92, chmn., 1986-87; co-chair N.Y. State Task Force on Preparation and Licensure of Sch. Adminstrs.; bd. dirs. Orgn. Int. Affiliates, Am. Edn. Rsch. Assn., 1991—; pres. Tchr. Edn. Conf. Bd., N.Y., 1991—. Author: The Dilemma of Enquiry and Learning, 1981; editor jour. Ednl. Theory, 1980-81; founding mem. bd. editors jour. Ednl. Policy, 1986—; contbr. numerous articles to profl. jours. Mem. commn. on teaching Nat. Assn. State Univs. and Land Grant Colls., 1988-92. Resident assoc. Ctr. for Advanced Study, U. Ill., 1980-81. Fellow Philosophy of Edn. Soc. (pres. 1984-85, mem. exec. com. 1974-76, 82-83); mem. Am. Ednl. Rsch. Assn., Am. Philos. Assn. Office: SUNY 367 Baldy Hall Buffalo NY 14260

PETRO, JANE A., plastic and reconstructive surgeon; b. Erie, Pa., Dec. 17, 1946; d. William Irwin and Virginia (Douglas) Arbuckle; m. Denis J Petro, Mar. 28, 1969 (div. 1982); 1 child, Noah Edward. BS, Eckard Coll., St. Petersburg, Fla., 1968; MD, Pa. State U., 1972. Diplomate Am. Bd. Surgery, Am. Bd. Plastic and Reconstrv. Surgery. Gen. surg. resident U. Louisville, 1972-74, Harrisburg Hosp., Pa., 1974-76; plastic surgery resident Pa. State U., Hershey, 1977-79; burn/microsurg. fellow Albert Einstein Coll. Medicine, Bronx, 1979-80; asst. prof. surgery N.Y. Med. Coll., Valhalla, 1981-85; assoc. prof. surgery N.Y. Med. Coll., 1985—; assoc. dir. burns

Westchester County Med. Ctr., Valhalla, 1981—. Contbr. articles to profl. jours. Recipient Physicians Recognition award, AMA, 1977; McArthur Alumni award for disting. achievement, Eckerd Coll., 1980. Mem. Am. Assn. med. Colls., Assn. Women Surgeons, Am. Assn. Physicians for Human Rights, AAAS, Am. Burn Assn., Am. Cleft Palate Assn., Am. Med. Womens Assn., Inst. of Soc., Ethics and the Life Scis., Soc. for Health and Human Values, N.Y. Acad. Sci., N.Y. Acad. Medicine, Acad. of Compensation medicine, Am. Assn. for Advancement of the Humanities, Am. Fedn. Clin. Research, Wedstchester County Med. Soc., N.Y. Soc. Plastic and Reconstrv. Surgery, N.Y. Reg. Head and Neck Soc., others. Democrat. Presbyterian. Office: Westchester County Med Ctr Burn Unit Valhalla NY 10595

PETROCHENKOV, MARGARET WISE, humanities educator; b. Denver, Oct. 21, 1954; d. Paul Edward Wise and Dorothy Kathleen (Nicholson) Coble; m. Valery Petrochenkov, Dec. 16, 1977; children: Katherine Elizabeth, Gregory Paul. BA, Colo. U., 1977; MA, Ind. U., 1983, PhD, 1991. Program specialist NRC, Washington, 1988-90, 91—. Mem. AAAS, Assn. for Advancement of Tchrs. of East European Langs., Modern Lang. Assn. Russian Orthodox. Home: 327 Branch Dr Silver Spring MD 20901-2615 Office: NRC 2101 Constitution Ave NW Washington DC 20037-2955

PETRONE, WILLIAM FRANCIS, physician, microbiologist, corporate executive; b. Bklyn., Sept. 12, 1949; s. Arthur Carmen and Helen (Kenny) P.; m. Kathleen Anne Baron, Aug. 25, 1979; children: William Gaetano, Katherine Bridget, Jason Daniel. BA, U. Conn., 1972; MS, U. Mass., 1974; PhD, U. R.I., 1978; MD, U. South Ala., 1984. Diplomate Am. Bd. Pediatrics. Rsch. assoc. Coll. Medicine U. South Ala., Mobile, 1978-80; resident in pediatrics Orlando (Fla.) Regional Med. Ctr., 1984-85, W.Va. Univ. Med. Ctr., 1985-87; emergency rm. physician, dir. pediatric emergency svcs. Mercy Hosp., Springfield, Mass., 1987—; pres. Med. Simulation Software. Contbr. articles on inflamation and white blood cell function to sci. jours. Mem. AAAS, AMA, Am. Acad. Pediatrics, Am. Coll. Emergency Physicians, Am. Med. Student Assn., N.Y. Acad. Scis., Sigma Xi. Roman Catholic. Office: Mercy Hosp Emergency Unit PO Box 9012 Springfield MA 01102

PETROV, NICOLAS, dance educator, choreographer; b. Novia Sad, Serbia, Yugoslavia, Dec. 13, 1933; came to U.S., 1967; s. Sergie Nicolas and Iren Rehorovic (Roboz) P.; m. Marion Freyda Brookes, Apr. 11, 1956. Ed., Govt. Theatrical Acad., Novi Sad, 1945-51; apsolvent, Drzavne Pozorisne Skole Baletski, Otsek, 1951; ed, State Ballet Acad. of Belgrade, Yugoslavia, 1951-54, Belgrade Govt. U. Fgn. Langs., 1951-55, U. de Paris à Sorbonne, 1956-58. Dancer Nat. Popular Theatre Serbi, Belgrade, 1951-54, Ballet de France de Janine Charrat, Paris, 1954-56; prin. dancer Balletto Europeo di Nervi, Genova, Italy, 1960-62; dancer, choreographer Radio TV France, Paris, 1960-67; from asst. prof. to prof. dance Point Park Coll., Pitts., 1968-78, prof., 1978—, dir. fine, applied and performing arts dept. and dance div., 1975—; founder, artistic dir. Ballet Russe de Nicolas Petrov, Paris, 1962—, Pitts. Ballet Theatre, Inc., 1967-77, Am. Dance Ensemble, Pitts., 1977-87; choreographer Pitts. Opera, 1967-73, 77—; guest dancer Leonide Massine Festival, Goteberg, Sweden, 1956-57; guest dancer and actor Theatre de Vervie Belgium, 1956-57; guest star dancer Opera Mcpl. de Marseille, Paris, 1960-62. Appeared in ballets, including Scheherazade, Swan Lake, Romeo and Juliet, Le Carnaval, Nutcracker, many others; choreographer (operas) Aida, Pitts., 1967-68, Carmen, Pitts., 1967-68, 80-81, La Traviata, Pitts., 1977-78; (ballets) Romeo and Juliet, Pitts., 1971-72, Cinderella, Pitts., 1973-74, Fantasia, Pitts., 1976-77, numerous others; director dance films including Alice in Wonderland, 1972, Carmina Catulli, 1973-74, Romeo and Juliet, 1975; author: The Dance Method, 1967. Asst. mayoral elections, Pitts., 1968, 77; vol. Pitts. Ballet Theatre. Recipient choreography award Nat. Steel Corp., 1976. Mem. AAUP, Am. Guild Music Artists, Rotary, French Masons (N.Y.C.). Home: 39 Dilworth St Pittsburgh PA 15211-1913 Office: Point Park Coll 201 Wood St Pittsburgh PA 15222-1984

PETRUCCI, JANE MARGARET, medical technologist, laboratory director; b. Providence, R.I., May 26, 1955; d. James Francis and Dorothy Mary (Markarian) P. BA in Biology, R.I. Coll., 1979. Med. technologist Miriam Hosp., Providence, R.I., 1979-82; med. technologist R.I. Blood Ctr., Providence, 1981-83, lab. supr., 1983-89; lab. dir. R.I. Blood Ctr., 1989—. Mem. Vet's. Meml. Auditorium Preservation Assn., Providence, 1989—. Named to Nat. Honor Soc., 1974. Mem. R.I. Blood Banker's Soc. (bd. dirs. 1989—), Am. Assn. Clin. Pathologists (cert. blood bank technologist), Am. Assn. Blood Banks, Am. Assn. Bioanalysts. Office: Rhode Island Blood Ctr 405 Promenade St Providence RI 02908-4823

PETRUCCI, SERGIO, chemistry educator, researcher; b. Rome, Feb. 7, 1932; came to U.S., 1956; s. Alberto and Bianca (Valenti) P.; m. Angela Longobardi, June 8, 1957; 1 child, Stephanie. D in Chemistry, U. Rome, 1955, libera docenza, 1967. Fulbright fellow Yale U., New Haven, 1956-57; asst. prof. U. Rome, 1957-60; NATO rsch. fellow Tech. U. Norway, Trondheim, 1961; rsch. assoc. Princeton (N.J.) U., 1962-64; rsch. asst. prof. U. Md., College Park, 1964-65; asst. prof. chemistry Poly. U., Bklyn., 1965-67, assoc. prof., 1967-70; prof. Poly. U., Farmingdale, N.Y., 1970—. Editor, author: Ionic Interactions, Vols. I and II, 1971; also over 100 articles, chpt. to book. Grantee Army Rsch. Office, 1982-88, 89-92, NSF, 1981-84, 86-94. Mem. Am. Chem. Soc. Office: Poly U Dept Chemistry RR 10 Farmingdale NY 11735

PETRUS, ROBERT THOMAS, business networks executive; b. Manchester, Conn., 1957; s. John Joseph and Geraldine Petrus; m. Laura Lee Waggoner, Nov. 22, 1986; children: Elizabeth Ashley, Nicholas Kent. BA with honors, Trinity Coll., Hartford, Conn., 1979. Mgmt. intern Aetna Life & Casualty Co., Hartford, 1979-82, sr. adminstr. data processing ops., 1982-85, cons. Tech. Ctr., 1985-90; pres. OMOO Corp., Mansfield, Conn., 1990—. Chmn. Conn. Youth for Pres. Ford, 1976; com. mem. Big Bros.-Big Sisters, Hartford, 1982-83; loaned exec. Greater Hartford United Way-Combined Health Appeals Campaign, 1985. Recipient ofcl. citation Conn. Ho. of Reps., 1985. Mem. Phi Beta Kappa, Pi Gamma Mu, Mu Alpha Theta. Republican. Roman Catholic. Office: Omoo Corp 27 Wormwood Hill Rd Mansfield Center CT 06250-1135

PETRUSKY, JOHN W., banker, consultant; b. Johnstown, Pa., June 15, 1935; s. John and Mary P.; m. Azucena Lily, July 4, 1964; children—John T., Dianna L., James W. B.S. in Acctg., Pa. State U., 1961. Worked for Bank of N.Y., N.Y.C., 1961-64; asst. v.p. Dry Dock Savs. Bank, N.Y.C., 1964-68, Leasco Systems Internat., N.Y.C., 1968-69; sr. v.p. Phoenix Systems Internat., N.Y.C., 1969-70; (with Dollar Dry Dock Savs. Bank, N.Y.C., 1970-87, pres., 1985-87; founder, pres. The Petrusky Group, Inc., 1987—. Chmn. Am. Nat. Standards Inst., 1979-81; chmn. Internat. Standards Orgn. 68, Geneva, 1979-86; trustee, treas. Waldorf Sch., Garden City, N.Y., 1986; bd. dirs. Am. Nat. Standards Inst., 1979-81. Served with USAF, 1955-59. Recipient IBM Point of Sale award, 1976; Electronic Funds Transfer award Mutual Inst. Nat. Transfer System, 1980. Copyright computer software for tele-mktg. system, 1989. Republican. Home and Office: 111 Chester Ave Garden City NY 11530-4124

PETRY, CLINTON BROWNING, publisher, association executive; b. Alexandria, Va., Apr. 28, 1921; s. John William and Bessie May (DeVaughn) P.; m. Dorothy Chapman, Sept. 2, 1940 (div. Dec. 1958); 1 child: Clinton Browning II; m. Dolores Mary Thomas, Aug. 14, 1979. Student, U. Md., 1984-85. Pres., pub. Clover Pub. Co., Washington, N.Y.C., 1949-76; mem. staff Geophys. Lab. Carnegie Instn., Washington, 1966-76; chmn., CEO Nat. Supply Assn., Washington, N.Y.C., 1966-86; CEO, exec. dir. Nat. Advertiser's Soc. Promoting Rational English, Washington, 1984—. Editor in chief, pub.: (poetry) The Clover Collection of Verse, 24 vols., 1969-76. With USAF, 1943. Roman Catholic. Home: 4903 70th Pl Hyattsville MD 20784

PETRYLAK, DANIEL PETER, internist, oncologist; b. N.Y.C., May 12, 1959; s. Mykola and Irene (Prystupa) P. BA, Columbia U., 1981; MD, Case Western Res., 1985. Diplomate Am. Bd. Internal Medicine. Internship Bronx Mcpl. Hosp., N.Y., 1985, residency, 1986-88; fellow Meml. Sloan Kettering Cancer Ctr., N.Y.C., 1988-91; asst. prof. clin. medicine Columbia Presbyn. Med. Ctr., N.Y.C., 1991—. Recipient grant Charlotte Geyer Found., 1992. Mem. N.Y. Acad. Scis., Am. Coll. Physicians, Am. Assn. Cancer Rsch. Home: 200 E 66th St New York NY 10021 Office: Columbia Presbyn Med Ctr 161 Fort New York NY 10021

PETRYSHYN, RAYMOND ALEX, biochemistry and molecular biology educator; b. Toronto, Ont., Can., Jan. 2, 1950; came to U.S., 1978; m. Walter and Anne (Philiip) P.; m. Bernadette M. Dunham, Apr. 26, 1986. BSc, York U., 1973, PhD, 1977. Postdoctoral fellow dept. biology MIT, Cambridge, 1977-79; rsch. assoc. div. health scis. and tech. Harvard-MIT, Cambridge, 1979-85, rsch. scientist, 1985-86; asst. prof. Health Sci. Ctr. SUNY, Syracuse, 1986—; project dir. grant supported biomed. rsch. SUNY, Syracuse, 1986—, dir. summer undergrad. rsch. program, 1988—, cons. program project cell-cell communication, 1988—, course coord. prins. biochem. techniques, 1988—. Contbr. articles and revs. to profl. jours, chpts. to books. Can. Muscular Dystrophy Assn. pre-doctoral fellow, Toronto, 1974-77, NATO post-doctoral fellow, Boston, 1977-79; Franco-Am. vis. scientist fellow, Paris, 1985; Sinsheimer Found. scholar, Syracuse, 1988. Mem. Am. Chem. Soc., Am. Soc. Biochemistry and Molecular Biology. Office: SUNY Health Sci Ctr 766 Irving Ave Syracuse NY 13210-1605

PETSKO, GREGORY ANTHONY, chemistry and biochemistry educator; b. Washington, Aug. 7, 1948; s. John and Mary (Santoro) P.; m. Carol Bannister Chamberlain, July 3, 1971 (div. 1982). BA, Princeton U., 1970; DPhil, Oxford U., 1973. Instr. Wayne State U. Med. Sch., Detroit, 1973-75, asst. prof., 1975-78; assoc. prof. MIT, 1979-85, prof. chemistry, 1985-90; Lucille P. Markey prof. biochemistry and chemistry Brandeis U., Waltham, Mass., 1990—; cons. Polygen Corp., Waltham, 1986—. Editor. Jour. Protein Engring., 1988—. Recipient Max Planck award Max Planck Gesellschaft, 1992; Rhodes scholar Oxford U., 1970, Danforth fellow, 1980; Alfred P. Sloan fellow MIT, 1978. Mem. Am. Crystallographic Assn. (Siddhu award 1981), Am. Chem. Soc. (Pfizer award 1987), Biophys. Soc., Am. Soc. Biochemistry and Molecular Biology. Home: 8 Jason Rd Belmont MA 02178 Office: Rosenstiel Ctr Brandeis U Waltham MA 02254-9110

PETTIBONE, PETER JOHN, lawyer; b. Schenectady, N.Y., Dec. 11, 1939; s. George Howard and Caryl Grey (Ketchum) P.; m. Jean Kellogg, Apr. 23, 1966; children: Stephen, Victoria. AB summa cum laude, Princeton U., 1961; JD, Harvard U., 1964; LLM, NYU, 1971. Bar: Pa. 1965, D.C. 1965, N.Y. 1968, U.S. Supreme Ct. 1974. Lectr. Heidelberg (Fed. Republic Germany) U., 1965-67; assoc. Cravath, Swaine & Moore, N.Y.C., 1967-74, Lord Day & Lord, Barrett Smith, N.Y.C., 1974-76; ptnr. Lord Day & Lord, Barrett Smith, N.Y.C. and Washington, 1976—; pres. 1158 Fifth Ave. Corp., N.Y.C., 1991—; pres. North Ferry Co., Shelter Island, N.Y., 1987-90; bd. dirs., vice-chmn. N.Y. State Facilities Devel. Corp., N.Y.C., 1983-89. Trustee, treas. Hosp. Chaplaincy Inc., N.Y.C., 1980-86, Civitas, N.Y.C., 1984—; mem. N.Y. State Gov.'s World Trade Coun., 1989—; bd. dirs. Am. Com. on U.S.-Soviet Rels., 1992—; trustee Union Chapel, Shelter Island, N.Y., 1990—, Geonomics Inst., Middlebury, Vt., 1991—; mem. vestry Ch. of Heavenly Rest, N.Y.C., 1987—. Capt. U.S. Army, 1965-67. Eagle Scout. Mem. ABA, Assn. Bar City N.Y. (chmn. com. on Soviet affairs 1991—), U.S.-USSR Trade and Econ. Coun. Inc. (U.S. co-chmn. legal com. 1980—), Soc. of Cin., Anglers Club of N.Y.C., Shelter Island Yacht Club, Amateur Ski Club N.Y. (pres. 1980-82), Canterbury Choral Soc. (pres. 1983-84), Phi Beta Kappa. Episcopalian. Home: 1158 5th Ave New York NY 10029-6917 also: 10 Wesley Ave Shelter Island Heights NY 11965 Office: Lord Day & Lord Barrett Smith 1675 Broadway New York NY 10019-5820

PETTIS, MICHAEL ALAN, investment banker; b. Zaragoza, Aragon, Spain, June 16, 1958; s. Charles and Huguette Marguerite (Laffont) P. BA, St. Lawrence U., 1979; M. Internat. Affairs, Columbia U., 1981, MBA, 1984. Credit analyst Nat. Westminster U.S.A., N.Y.C., 1982; officer The Mellon Bank, Pitts., 1985-87; asst. v.p. Mfrs. Hanover Trust, N.Y.C., 1987-89; v.p. MG-First Boston, N.Y.C., 1989-91; dir. First Boston Corp., N.Y.C., 1991—. Columbia U. fellow, 1983. Democrat. Roman Catholic. Home: 201 W 101st St Apt 2A New York NY 10025-5044 Office: First Boston Corp 55 E 52d St New York NY 10055

PETTIT, DAWN ESTELLE, educational association administrator; b. London, Feb. 24, 1962; came to U.S., 1978; d. Edward Peter and Eryl Ada (Seth) P.; m. John Lance Fritz, May 11, 1986. BA in History, Columbia Union Coll., 1984. Office mgr. Columbia Union Coll., Takoma Park, Md., 1984-86; dir. coop. edn. Columbia Union Coll., 1986-88; exec. dir. Coop. Edn. Assn., Inc., Beltsville, Md., 1988—; sec. Capital Assn. for Coop. Edn., Washington, 1987-88. Rep. Montgomery Run Villages Assn., Ellicott City, 1992. Mem. Howard County Geneal. Soc., Am. Soc. for Assn. Execs. Adventist. Office: Coop Edn Assn 11710 Beltsville Dr Ste 20 Beltsville MD 20705

PETTIT, HORACE, allergist, consultant; b. Jan. 28, 1903; s. Horace and Katherine (Howell) P.; B.S., Harvard Coll., 1927; M.D., 1931; m. Millicent Lewis, Nov. 22, 1924 (dec.); children: Emily Connery, Horace (dec.), Deborah Myers, Norman; m. Jane Mann Hiatt, May 13, 1950; 1 adopted child, Barbara Mann Ralph. Intern, Bryn Mawr Hosp., 1933-34; asst. instr., instr., assoc. bacteriology U. Pa. Sch. Medicine, 1932-39, instr. medicine, 1939-53; pvt. practice allergy, 1940-42, 1947-75; cons. in allergy Bryn Mawr Hosp., 1963-79, emeritus staff mem., 1979—; cons. allergist Bryn Mawr Coll., 1963-75. Served from maj. to lt. col. AUS, 1942-46. Fellow Coll. Physicians of Phila.; mem. AMA, Am. Acad. Allergy, Am. Soc. Microbiology, Phila. County, Med. Soc., Pa. Med. Soc., Phila. Allergy Soc. (pres. 1958-59), United World Federalists (mem. nat. exec. coun. 10 years), St. Andrew's Soc. Phila. Unitarian. Clubs: Harvard-Radcliffe (Phila.); Merion Cricket (Haverford, Pa.); Camden (Maine) Yacht. Home and Office: 123 Kennedy Ln Bryn Mawr PA 19010-2808

PETTIT, HUBERT CLEVELAND, safety engineer; b. Alfordsville, N.C., Nov. 16, 1944; s. Hubert and Grace Eva (Harris) P.; m. Diana Moore, Nov. 19, 1977; children: Lisa C., Bryan Daniel. BS, N.C. State U., 1971; MS, U. So. Calif., 1986. Commd. USN, 1971, advanced through grades to lt. comdr., ret. 1987; anit-submarine warfare officer U.S. Atlantic Fleet Hdqrs., Norfolk, Va., 1981-84; aircraft mishap safety investigator U.S. Naval Safety Ctr., Norfolk, 1984-87; sr. airworthiness safety engr. Sikorsky Aircraft, div. U.T.C., Stratford, Conn., 1987—. Editor safety bull. Safety Shorts, 1979-80. Mem. Children's Christian Fund, Richmond, Va., 1979—, fin. com. First United Ch., Clinton, Conn., 1988—. Decorated Navy Commendation medal. Mem. Naval Helicopter Assn. (sec. 1975-76), Assn. of Naval Aviation, U.S. Naval Inst., Am. Soc. Safety Engrs., System Safety Soc., Internat. Soc. Air Safety Investigators. Democrat. United Ch. of Christ. Home: 7 Diamond Rd Clinton CT 06413-1172 Office: Sikorsky Aircraft 600 Main St # 300sa Bridgeport CT 06604-5136

PETTIT, JEANNE MARIE, real estate developer; b. Sandy Spring, Md., Feb. 17, 1964; d. John Howard and Jacquelyn (Runkle) P. Student, Shenandoah Coll., 1981-83; BS, Va. Commonwealth U., 1986. Rsch. asst. Joyner & Co., Richmond, Va., 1986-87; comml. salesperson Century 21, Jacksonville, Fla., 1987-89, Mark Robinson & Assocs., Jacksonville, Fla., 1989-90; property mgr. Corp. Mgmt. Inc., Gaithersburg, Md., 1990-91; acct., salesperson Pettit & Griffin, Inc., Gaithersburg, Md., 1991—; corr. sec. Jacksonville Comml. Investment Coun., 1989-90. Composer, actor: (music video) A Quick Twenty Grand, 1990. Recipient 4th Pl. Pocket Billiards award Assn. Coll. Unions Internat., 1984. Mem. Fla. Bd. Realtors, Jacksonville Bd. Realtors. Democrat. Roman Catholic. Home: 18002 Fertile Meadow Ct Gaithersburg MD 20877-3729 Office: Pettit & Griffin Inc 18205D Flower Hill Way Gaithersburg MD 20879-5331

PETTUS, BARBARA WYPER, bank executive; b. Hartford, Conn., Nov. 9, 1947; d. John Stuurman Wyper and Mary Blair (Goodell) Crolius; m. Charlton Messick Pettus, Apr. 19, 1975 (div., 1985). BA, Smith Coll., 1969; MLS, Simmons Coll., 1972, MBA, 1980. Adminstrv. asst. Perkins & Will Architects, Washington, 1969-71; head reference libr. Memorial Hall Libr., Andover, Mass., 1972-77; asst. dir. Memorial Hall Libr., Andover, 1977-79; asst. treas. Chase Manhattan Bank, N.Y.C., 1981-83, 2nd v.p., 1983-88, v.p. U.S. pvt. banking div., 1988-90; v.p. pvt. banking and investment div., team leader Mfrs. Hanover Trust Co., N.Y.C., 1990—. Editor: (mag.) Bay State Librarian, 1977-79. Bd. dirs. Simmons Coll. Alumni Assn., Boston, 1982-84; mem. N.Y. Jr. League, 1987-90. Congregationalist. Home: 21 E 84th St New York NY 10028-2931 Office: Mfrs Hanover Trust Co 270 Park Ave New York NY 10017

PETTY, RONALD FRANKLIN, public relations executive; b. Trenton, Mar. 17, 1947; s. Warren Herman Lee and Geraldine Frances (Roberts) P.; m. Cynthia Ann Hoover, Sept. 16, 1967 (div. 1987); children: Scott Eric, Christopher Lee. BA in Advt., Syracuse U., 1969, BA in Econs., 1972. Asst. sales promotion mgr. Cambridge Filter Corp., Liverpool, N.Y., 1969-72; advt. mgr. Am. Challenger, Fulton, N.Y., 1972, mgr. communications, 1973; advt./pub. rels. account exec. Barlow/Johnson Advt., Fayetteville and Latham, N.Y., 1973-75; advt./pub. rels. account exec. Nowak-Voss Advt., Syracuse, N.Y., 1975-77, dir. pub. rels., 1976-77; pub. relations dir. U.S Pioneer Electronics Corp., Moonachie, N.J., 1977-81, gen. mgr. communications, 1981-82; dir. communications Pioneer Video, Inc., 1982-84; dir. mktg. services SONY Broadcast Products Co., 1984-86; dir. mktg. broadcast and profl. audio products SONY Communications Products Co., 1986-87; dir. corp. communications SONY Corp. of Am., 1987-89; dir. Sony Conf. Ctr. Walt Disney World, 1989-91, mgmt. cons., 1991—; pub. rels. cons. to artist Peter Max; cons. in field. Mem. com. for redistricting, Liverpool (N.Y.) Sch. Bd., 1976; mem. Rockaway Boro Citizens Adv. Com., 1981-82, mem. planning bd., 1982-85, chmn. planning bd., 1983, councilman, 1983-87, chmn. ordinance com., 1984-85, chmn. personnel com., 1986-87, mem. pub. safety com., 1984, 86, 87, mem. pub. works com., 1985-87; del. N.J. State Dem. Conv., 1983; mem. Rockaway Boro Shade Tree Commn., 1983-84; benefactor, patron Met. Opera Assn., 1981-84; sustaining mem. Republican Nat. Com., 1980-83, 86. Recipient citation for community service United Way of Central N.Y., 1976; dir. Project-of-the-Yr. award, Syracuse Jr. C. of C., 1977. Mem. Assn. of Indsl. Advertisers, Public Relations Soc. Am., Electronic Industry Assn. (chmn. show adv. com. 1982). Contbr. articles to profl. jours. Office: 11737 Peach Grove Ln Orlando FL 32821-7918

PETTY, WILLIAM CALVIN, III, investment counselor; b. Port Chester, N.Y., Nov. 24, 1940; s. William Calvin and Helen L. (Lathrop) P.; B.A., Yale U., 1963; m. Nancy Claire Dowling, Nov. 28, 1970; children—Jonathan Calvin, Timothy Dowling. With Dominick & Dominick, Inc., N.Y.C., 1967-69, Estabrook & Co., Inc., N.Y.C., 1969-72, Drexel Burnham, N.Y.C., 1972-73; v.p., nat. sales mgr. Mfrs. Hanover Investment Corp., N.Y.C., 1973-85; prin. Estabrook Capital Mgmt. Inc., 1985—. Pres. Cedar Knolls Colony, Yonkers, N.Y., 1981-82. Served with U.S. Navy, 1963-66. Mem. Assn. Investment Mgmt. Sales Execs. (pres 1985-86), Kent Sch. (chmn. alumni fund), Fedn. Fin. Analysts. Republican. Episcopalian. Club: Yale of N.Y.C., Lawrence Beach. Office: Estabrook Capital Mgmt Inc 430 Park Ave New York NY 10022-3505

PETUSKEY, THOMAS JAMES, elementary education supervisor; b. Elizabeth, N.J., Aug. 4, 1941; s. William Thomas and Mabel Victoria (Schukis) P., m. Carol Marie Sawicki, Aug. 8, 1965; 1 child, Michelle Ann. BA, Fairleigh Dickinson, Rutherford, N.J., 1963; MA, Kean Coll., 1974. Cert. tchr., prin., supr., and sch. adminstr., N.J. Tchr. Elizabeth (N.J.) Bd. Edn., 1964-76, supr., 1977—; pres. Elizabeth's Adminstrv. and Supervisory Coun., Cen. Adminstrv. Coun; negotiator adminstrv. staff contracts. Contbr. articles about wine to local newspaper, Am. Wine Soc. Jour. Mem. Am. Wine Soc. (v.p. 1992—, over 50 awards for homemade wine 1984—, cert. wine judge 1989—, chmn. amateur wine competition 1990), Soc. Wine Educators, Garden State Wine Growers Assn. Republican. Roman Catholic. Home: 7 Crest Rd East Brunswick NJ 08816-2805 Office: Elizabeth Bd Edn 500 N Broad St Elizabeth NJ 07208-3302

PETZINGER, WILLIAM CHARLES, III, public relations executive; b. Morristown, N.J., Mar. 29, 1960; s. William Charles and Margaret Mary (Yanotta) P.; m. Veronica Lee Fielding, Apr. 23, 1987. BA, Montclair (N.J.) State Coll., 1982. Asst. editor Media Masters Inc., Parsippany, N.J., 1982-83; publicist March of Dimes, Fairfield, N.J., 1983-86; account exec. Poppe Tyson, Morris Plains, N.J., 1986-88; pub. rels. mgr. Ednl. Testing Svc., Princeton, N.J., 1988—; ptnr. Fresh Approach, Hamilton, N.J., 1986—. Contbg. editor feature stories in Parsippany-Troy Hills News and the Experienced Citizen, 1982-83. Recipient Effie award, Am. Mktg. Assn., 1987. Mem. Communication, Advt., Mktg. Assn. N.J., Pub. Rels. Soc. Am. (Pyramid award 1991). Roman Catholic. Office: Ednl Testing Svc Rosedale Rd Princeton NJ 08541-0001

PEUGEOT, PATRICK, insurance executive; b. Paris, Aug. 3, 1937; s. Jacques Louis and Edith (Genoyer) P.; m. Catherine Dupont, 1963; children: Hubert, Thomas, Camille. Degree, Ecole Poly., Paris, 1959, Ecol Nat. D'Adminstrn., Paris, 1965. Ins. auditor Ministry of Fin., Paris, 1962-65; auditor Cour des Comptes, Paris, 1965-83; spl. asst. Bur. Planning, Paris, 1966-70; sr. v.p. EMC, Toulouse, France, 1970-72, Hachette Inc., Paris, 1972-74; exec. v.p. ops. AGF Life, Paris, 1974-78; exec. v.p. AGF Reins., Paris, 1979-82; pres. Caisse Cen. de Reassurance, Paris, 1983-85; chmn., chief exec. officer Scor S.A., Paris, 1984—. Home: 82 rue Notre Dame Champs, 75006 Paris France Office: Scor SA, 1 Ave du President Wilson, Paris la Defense France

PEVERLY, FRANCIS WILLIAM, utility engineer, consultant; b. Syracuse, N.Y., May 18, 1963; s. William John and Mary Ann (Bach) P.; m. Christine Ann Yager, Oct. 15, 1988. BS, Clarkson U., 1985; MBA, Marist Coll., 1992. Jr. engr. Cen. Hudson Gas and Electric, Poughkeepsie, N.Y., 1985-86; asst. engr. Cen. Hudson Gas and Electric, Fishkill, N.Y., 1986-87; assoc. engr. Cen. Hudson Gas and Electric, Beacon, N.Y., 1987-89; distbn. supr. Orange and Rockland Utilities, Monroe, N.Y., 1989-91, div. engr., 1991—; power cons. various orgns., Goshen, N.Y., 1989—. Loaned exec. United Way, Poughkeepsie, 1987, mem. allocations com., 1987-88, mem campaign com., 1988. Mem. Am. Inst. Plant Engrs., Assn. Energy Engrs. Republican. Roman Catholic. Home: 135 Grand St Goshen NY 10924-1833 Office: Orange and Rockland 500 Route 208 Monroe NY 10950-1699

PEVOVAR, EDDY HOWARD, theatrical agency executive; b. Lakewood, N.J., Mar. 24, 1953; s. Leo Pevovar and Freida (Gindoff) Pevovar Traeger; step-son of Canard Traeger; m. Christine Lynn Povovar, 1973; children: Kenneth Leon, Faythe Lynne. Grad., DeVry Tech. Inst., 1976; student, Brookdale Coll., 1979; BS in Elec. Engring. and Physics, Kensington U., 1986; postgrad., N.Y. Inst. Photography, 1987-88. Lic. emergency med. technician, N.J. State Dept. Health. Physicist Molecu Wire Corp., 1981-82; chief engr. Quay Corp., 1982-83; systems engr., mgr. bldgs. and projects Gen. Mills Corp., Eatontown, N.J., 1983-84; pres., chief exec. officer engring. firm Strategic Data Systems Corp., Red Bank, N.J., 1983-86; pres., prin. agent Studio 36 Inc., Red Bank, 1983-87; Eddy Howard Agy., Inc., Red Bank, 1987—; speaker Sta. WJLK radio talk radio show, U.S. Juvenile Diabetes Found.; owner antique ctr. and auction, Red Bank, N.J., 1990. Author: Local Area Networks: A Practical Approach, 1983; contbr. articles to profl. jours.; producer Boca Bay Yacht Club network TV series, 1990. Mem. Jaycees (v.p. Toms Rivers chpt. 1981, Springboard award 1981, Keyman awards 1981, Dist. Dirs. cert. 1981, named Jaycee of Qtr. 1981, Jaycee of Month 1981), Eatontown Environ. Commn., 1987—; aux. police officer Eatontown Borough, 1985-88; firefighter Eatontown Fire Dept., 1987, lic. fire official and insp.; sr. mem., v.p. Tinton Falls First Aid Squad, 1989—; pres., chief exec. officer Disaster Mitigation Cons. With USNR, 1972-74. Named Rookie of the Yr., 1987; recipient Firefighters award, 1987. Mem. Soc. Motion Picture and TV Engrs., Nat. Acad. TV Arts and Scis., N.J. Motion Picture and Film Commn., SAG, AFTRA, AGVA, Writer's Guild Am., Authors Guild, Actor's Equity Assn., Am. Guild Mus. Artists, Am. Fedn. Musicians, Hosp. Fin. Mgmt. Assn., IEEE, Soc. Photo-Optical Instrumentation Engrs., Assn. for Computing Machinery, Am. Inst. Physicists, Nat. Fire Protection Assn., Internat. Soc. Fire Svc. Instrs., C. of C. Jewish. Club: U.S. Ferrari Owners Assn. (pres. 1986-87) (N.J.). Office: Studio 36 Inc 106 Monmouth St Red Bank NJ 07701-1109

PEYRONEL, ANTHONY CHRISTOPHER, college official, journalism educator; b. Pitts., Nov. 1, 1961; s. James Eli and Phyllis Ann (Carroll) P.; m. Laurie Jo Shumaker, Sept. 6, 1986; child: Eli Anthony. BA in Speech Communication, Edinboro U., 1983; MA in Journalism and Public Affairs, American U., Washington, 1984. Staff reporter The Leader-Times, Kittanning, Pa., 1984-86; devel. Writer Pa. State U., 1986-87; writer/editor, 1987-88; adj. prof. communication Thiel Coll., Greenville, Pa., 1990—; dir. communications Westminster Coll., New Wilmington, Pa., 1988—, instr. journalism, 1991—. Mem. Coun. for Advancement and Support Edn., Coll. and Univ. Pub. Rels. Assn. Pa, Greater New Castle C. of C. Democrat. Roman Catholic. Home: 6 Gateway Rd New Wilmington PA 16142-1304 Office: Westminster College Market St New Wilmington PA 16142

PFAFFENROTH, PETER ALBERT, lawyer; b. Mineola, N.Y., Mar. 29, 1941; s. Albert and Genevieve Astrid (Anderson) P.; m. Sara Ann Beekey, June 26, 1966; children: Elizabeth Kilmer, Peter Cyrus, Catherine Genevieve. BS in Engring., program in European Civilization, Princeton U., 1963; JD, U. Mich., 1966; LLM in Taxation, NYU, 1972, LLM in Corp., 1976. Bar: N.J. 1966, U.S. Dist. Ct. (N.J. dist.) 1966. With Daimler-Benz, Stuttgart, Fed. Republic Germany, 1961, B.P. Benzin & Petroleum, Hamburg, Fed. Republic Germany, 1962, Office of Internat. Affairs, U.S. Treasury Dept., Washington, 1963, Office of Export Control, U.S. Commerce Dept., Washington, 1964, Commrs. Office, U.S. Patent Office, Washington, 1965; atty. McCarter & English, Newark, 1966-68, Kentz & Gilson, Esqs., Summit, N.J., 1968-69; corp. counsel Tex. Plastics, Maine Sugar Industries, Robbinsville, N.J., 1969-70; atty. c/o Lewis Stein, Esq., Necong, N.J., 1970-71; pvt. practice Chester, N.J., 1971—. Home: Route 24 At Twin Brooks Trail Chester NJ 07930

PFAFFMAN, WILLIAM SCOTT, sculptor; b. Albany, Ga., July 10, 1954; s. Roy Alton and Corabel (Scales) P.; m. Florence Neal, July 14, 1979. BFA, Auburn U., 1976; postgrad., U. Ala., Huntsville, 1976; MA, CUNY, 1978. curator Bklyn. Waterfront Artists Coalition, 1980—; dir. Kentler Internat. Drawing Space, Bklyn., 1989—; artist-in-residence, 1983; vis. artist Reed Deer (Alta., Can.) Coll., 1985, N.Y. State Coll. Ceramics, Alfred, 1985, Wayne State U., Detroit, 1985, Edinborough (Pa.) Coll., 1987, Erie (Pa.) Art Mus., 1987, John F. Kennedy High Sch., Bronx, N.Y., 1987. One-man show CUNY Grad. Ctr. Mall, 1982; exhibited in group shows, 1976—, including Birmingham (Ala.) Mus. Art, 1976, The Clocktower, N.Y.C., 1984, SUNY, Purchase, 1984, Am. Acad. and Nat. Inst. Arts and Letters, N.Y.C., 1985, Queens Mus., 1985, Sculpture Space, Utica, N.Y., 1986, Erie (Pa.) Art Mus., 1987, Willis Gallery, Detroit, 1988, Sander Gallery, N.Y.C., 1988, München Gladbach, Fed. Republic Germany, 1991; commns. include Artpark Sculpture Commn., 1984, N.Y.C. Dept. Gen. Svcs., 1988. Project developer N.Y.C. Artist Housing Program, Bklyn., 1986—. Recipient award Nat. Studio Program, 1983, ann. award in art AAAL, 1985; resident Sculpture Space, 1986; fellow Pollack Krasner Found., 1987; grantee N.Y. State Coun. on Arts, 1987. Home and Studio: 353 Van Brunt St Brooklyn NY 11231

PFEFFER, CYNTHIA ROBERTA, psychiatrist, educator; b. Newark, May 22, 1943; d. Edward I. and Ann Pfeffer. BA, Douglas Coll., 1964; MD, NYU, 1968. Assoc. dir. child psychiatry inpatient unit Albert Einstein Coll. Medicine, Bronx, N.Y., 1973-79; chief child psychiatry inpatient unit N.Y. Hosp. Cornell Med. Ctr., White Plains, N.Y., 1979—; assoc. prof. clin. psychiatry Cornell U. Med. Coll., N.Y.C., 1984—; prof. psychiatry Cornell U. Med. Coll., 1989—; pres. N.Y. Coun. on Child and Adolescent Psychiatry, N.Y.C., 1989—. Author: The Suicidal Child, 1986, Difficult Moments in Child Psychotherapy, 1988; editor: Youth Suicide: Perspectives on Risk and Prevention, 1989. Recipient Erwin Stengel award Internat. Assn. Suicide Prevention, 1987, Wilford Hulse award N.Y. Coun. on Child & Adolescent Psychiatry, 1989. Fellow Am. Psychiat. Assn., Am. Acad. Child and Adolescent Psychiatry (councillor-at-large 1989—, Norbert Rieger award 1988), Am. Psychopathological Assn.; mem. Am. Assn. Suicidology (pres. 1987, Young Contbrs. award 1981, 82). Office: NY Hosp Westchester Div 21 Bloomingdale Rd White Plains NY 10605-1596 also: 40 E 89 St New York NY 10016

PFEFFER, ROBERT, chemical engineer, academic administrator, educator; b. Vienna, Austria, Nov. 26, 1935; came to U.S., 1938, naturalized, 1944; s. Joseph and Gisela (Aberbach) P.; m. Marcia Borenstein, Dec. 24, 1960; children—Michael, Jacqueline. B.Ch.E., N.Y. U., 1956, M.Ch.E., 1958, D.Eng.Sc., 1962. Mem. faculty CCNY, 1957—, asst. prof. chem. engring., 1962-66, asso. prof., 1966-71, prof., 1971—, chmn. dept. chem. engring., 1973-87, Herbert Kayser prof., 1980—, dean grad. studies and research, dep. provost, 1987-88, provost, v.p. acad. affairs, 1988—; vis. prof. Imperial Coll., London, 1969; Fulbright scholar Technion-Israel Inst. Tech., 1976-77; cons. in field. Contbr. articles to tech. publs. Fulbright Hays awardee, 1976-77; DuPont faculty fellow, 1962; NASA faculty fellow, 1964-65. Mem. Am. Inst. Chem. Engrs., Am. Soc. Engring. Edn., Sigma Xi, Tau Beta Pi, Phi Lambda Upsilon. Jewish. Office: CUNY 140th St & Convent Ave New York NY 10031

PFEIFER, KEITH MACHOLD, school superintendent; b. Bryn Mawr, Pa., Jan. 17, 1949; s. Robert T. Pfeifer and Yvonne (Donnelley) Maxwell; m. Nancy Harriman, Aug. 23, 1975; children: Kiersten Dawn, Justin Thomas. BA, Hiram Coll., 1971; MA, U. No. Colo., 1980; postgrad., Pa. State U., 1986. Spl. edn. tchr. Sch. Union #43, Monmouth, Maine, 1973-77; tchr., spl. edn. coord. Sch. Union #42, Readfield, Maine, 1977-83; tchr. State Coll. High Sch., State College, Pa., 1983-84; curriculum and instl. advisor Tuscarora Intermediate Unit, McVeytown, Pa., 1984-86; dir. of pupil personnel svcs. Maine Sch. Adminstrv. Dist. #11, Gardiner, Maine, 1986-87; asst. supt. Sch. Adminstrv. Unit #23, Lincoln, N.H., 1987—; Ednl. cons. State of Maine, 1983-84. Mem. Maine Dem. Party, Augusta, Maine, 1982-84, Belgrade (Maine) Lions, 1986-87. Mem. Am. Assn. for Curriculum Devel., Coun. for Exceptional Children, N.H. Sch. Adminstrs Assocs., Phi Delta Kappa, Omnicron Delta Kappa. Democrat.

PFEIFER, MARCUSE LUCILE, freelance curator and private dealer; b. Little Rock, Nov. 4, 1936; d. Harry William and Raida (Cohn) P. BA, Sarah Lawrence Coll., 1958. Asst. to dir. New Sch. Art Ctr., N.Y.C., 1966-70; dir. photog. art Robert Schoelkopf Gallery, N.Y.C., 1970-76; owner Marcuse Pfeifer Gallery, N.Y.C., 1976-90; freelance curator, pvt. dealer, N.Y.C., 1990—; guest curator Exhbn. Arles, France, 1986, Exhbn. Biennale of Photography, Turin, Italy, 1987; curator Heinrich Harrer's Seven Years in Tibet, Am. Mus. Natural History, N.Y.C., 1991; participant Colloquium on Photography, Sorbonne, Paris, 1988; moderator symposia Black Listed, Whitewashed and Red Handed, Soho 20, 1990, also symposia for N.Y. Camera Club and Assn. Am. Press Photographers, 1991. Arranged collections Gravure, 1974, American Indians from the 19th and Early 20th Century, 1974, Cyanotype, 1975, Catalogue 1 for Robert Schoelkopf Gallery, 1975, The Male Nude, 1978, Thank Heaven for Little Girls/Lewis Carroll, 1979. Mem. ArtTable, Assn. Internat. Photog. Art Dealers (pres. 1982-83, bd. dirs. 1978—).

PFEIFER, RUTH N., executive assistant; b. Rock Island, Ill., Sept. 24, 1932; d. Melford J. and Gina (Eken) Norby; m. Howard William Pfeifer, Sept. 10, 1955; children: Howard M., Helen R., Mary I. AA, Stephens Coll., 1952; BS, U. Ill., 1954. Sec. U. Conn., Storrs, 1976-84; exec. asst. to pres. Quinebaug Valley Community Coll., Danielson, Conn., 1984—. Mem. Appalachian Trail Conf., Appalachian Mountain Club, Long Distance Hikers Assn. Home: 27 Beech Mountain Rd Mansfield Center CT 06250-1604 Office: Quinebaug Valley Community Coll 742 Upper Maple St Danielson CT 06239-1440

PFEIFFER, DAVID GRAHAM, public management educator; b. Dallas, May 13, 1934; s. David C. and Ruth U. (Downing) P.; m. Barbara Glennon, Apr. 5, 1986. BA, U. Tex., 1956; MDiv, Epsicopal Theol. Sem., 1960, MA, 1963; PhD, U. Rochester, N.Y., 1975. Prof. Suffolk U., Boston, 1975—. Office: Suffolk U 8 Ashburton Pl Boston MA 02108-2770

PFEIFFER, EDWARD WESTON, job training professional; b. Trenton, N.J., Feb. 12, 1939; s. Edward and Roseann (Killilea) P.; m. Fia Corona, Mar. 27, 1969; 1 child, Sean Weston. BA, Trenton State Coll., 1968, MEd, 1973; postgrad., Rutgers U., 1978, Trenton State Coll., 1980-81. Cert. sch. adminstrn., tchr. of skill trade. Estimator Internation Constrn. Co., Tampa, Fla., 1959; engr. Greenland Contractors, Thule, Greenland, 1960-62; designer N.J. Dept. Transp., Trenton, 1962-64; indsl. arts tchr. Ewing Twp. Bd. Edn., Trenton, 1964-70; tchr. coord., indsl. arts tchr. Old Bridge (N.J.) Bd. Edn., 1970-74; coord. cooperative edn., tchr. coord. West Windsor Plainsboro Bd. of Edn., Princeton, 1974-76; supr. cooperative edn. N.J. Dept. Edn., Trenton, 1976-88, dir. apprentice tng., 1989-91, program specialist, 1990-91; job tng. advisor to Saudi Arabian govt. U.S. Dept. Labor/Joint Econ. Commn. on Econ. Cooperation, 1992—. Co-author: (manual) Administrative Manual for Cooperative Education, 1990, (text book) Learning for Earning, 1990; contbr. articles to profl. jours. Mem. adv. com. Nat. Child Labor Com., N.Y.C., 1988; mem. vocat. edn. adv. com. Trenton (N.J.) State Coll., 1987—. Recipient Svc. award N.J. Trade & Industry Assn., 1986, Thomas A. McNulty award N.J. Cooperative Ind. Edn. Assn., 1987. Mem. Am. Vocat. Assn. (life), N.J. Vocat. Assn. (life), Nat. Cooperative Work Experience Edn. Assn. (nat. program chair 1978-79, pres. 1980-83), N.J. Schoolmasters Club. Roman Catholic. Home: 74 Rocktown Rd Lambertville NJ 08530 Office: N J Dept Edn CN 500 Trenton NJ 08625

PFEIFFER, JAMES THOMAS, chemist; b. Buffalo, Apr. 8, 1945; s. James George and Louise (Morlock) P. BS, Canisius Coll., 1967. Chemist Pratt & Lambert Inc., Buffalo, 1967-84, sr. chemist, 1984—. Bd. dirs. Empire State Ballet, Buffalo, 1979—, chmn. bd. dirs., 1992. Mem. Am. Chem. Soc. Roman Catholic. Home: 23 Oehman Blvd Buffalo NY 14225-2117

PFEIFFER, LEONARD, IV, executive recruiter, consultant; s. Leonard Jr. and Felicia Constance Pfeiffer; m. Anna Jona Gunnarsson. BA, Harvard U., MBA. Mktg. mgr. Am. Express, N.Y.C., 1970-72; project dir. S.T.I., N.Y.C. and San Francisco, 1972-74; v.p. R. Olivier & Assocs., N.Y.C., 1974-76, A. Kane & Assoc., N.Y.C., 1976-78; v.p., ptnr. Korn/Ferry Internat., Washington and N.Y.C., 1978—. Founding mem. jr. bd. dirs. Washington Ipera, 1983—; bd. dirs. Community Found., Washington, 1982-84, Nat. Ctr. for Missing Children, 1989—; mem. men's com. Project Hope; devel. com. Nat. Head Injury Found. Lt. U.S. Army, 1968-70. Schepp Found. scholar, 1968-70. Mem. Am. Soc. Assn. Execs., Greater Washington Soc. Assn. Execs., Nat. Club Assn., Harvard Club (activities com., admissions com. N.Y.C. chpt. 1975-81, 1st v.p. bd. dirs. Washington chpt. 1985-87), City Club. Office: Korn Ferry Internat 900 19th St NW Washington DC 20006-2105

PFEIFFER, STEVEN EUGENE, molecular cell biologist, educator; b. Watertown, Wis., Aug. 13, 1940; s. Roy Henry and Doris (Haugen) P.; m. Carol Lee Aldrich, June 24, 1965; children: Julie Kristen, Carin-anna, Shaili Margreta. BA, Carleton Coll., 1962; PhD, Washington U., 1967. Postdoctoral fellow Brandeis U., Waltham, Mass., 1967-69; from asst. prof. to prof. U. Conn. Med. Sch., Farmington, 1969—; vis. scientist Pasteur Inst., Paris, 1976-77, European Molecular Biology Lab., Heidelberg, Germany, 1984-85; mem. adv. com. on rsch. Nat. Multiple Sclerosis Soc., N.Y.C., 1989—. Editorial bd.: Jour. Neurosci. Rsch., 1979—, Devel. Neurosci., 1982—, Internat. Jour. Devel. Neurosci., 1991—; editor: Neuroscience Approach Through Cell Cultures I, 1982, II, 1983. Clarinetist Farmington Valley Symphony Orch., 1981—. Josiah Marcy Jr. Faculty scholar, 1976-77; Fulbright fellow, 1983-84. Mem. Am. Soc. Neurochemistry, Soc. for Neurosci., Am. Assn. for Cell Biology. Unitarian. Office: U Conn Med Sch Farmington Ave Farmington CT 06030-0001

PFEIFFER, STEVEN IRA, psychologist; b. N.Y.C., Nov. 10, 1950; s. Murray Robert and Phyllis Selma (Levine) P.; m. Jan Stephanie Leslie, Aug. 25, 1979; 1 child, Andrea Beth. BA, SUNY, Oneonta, 1972; MA, Fairleigh Dickinson U., 1974; PhD, U. N.C., 1977. Diplomate Am. Bd. Profl. Psychology; lic. psychologist. Prof. Fla. Internat. U., Miami, 1977-78, Fordham U., N.Y.C., 1978-80, No. Ariz. U., Flagstaff, 1980-82; staff psychologist dept. pediatrics Ochsner Clinic, New Orleans, 1982-87; exec. dir. Inst. Clin. Tng. and Rsch., Inc., Devon, Pa., 1987—; adj. prof. dept. psychiatry U. Pa. Sch. Medicine; clin. psychologist Delta Assocs., Wayne, Pa., 1988—. Author: Inpatient Treatment of Children and Adolescents, 1992; editor-in-chief Clin. Child Psychology, 1985; editor Comprehensive Mental Care Jour.; also articles. Lt. USNR, 1986—. Nat. Inst. Edn. grantee, 1979; NIMH fellow, 1974-75. Fellow Am. Psychol. Assn.; mem. Am. Assn. Mental Retardation, Am. Orthopsychiat. Assn., Coun. for Exceptional Children, N.H. Soc. Fund Raising Execs., N.H. Coun. Univ. Rsch. Adminstrs., Am. Assn. Children's Residential Ctrs. Office: Devereux Found PO Box 400 Devon PA 19333-0400

PFEIFFER, WERNER BERNHARD, artist, educator; b. Stuttgart, Germany, Oct. 1, 1937; came to U.S., 1961; s. Jakob and Emilie (Nuper) P.; m. Maletta Sundstrom-Ziegler, Jan. 18, 1969; children—Jan-Stephen, Michaela-Veronica. Diploma, Grafische Fachschule, Stuttgart, Akademie Fine Arts, Stuttgart. Instr. Pratt Inst., Bklyn., 1961-64, prof., 1968-75, adj. prof., 1976—; asst. prof. N.Y. Inst. Tech., Westbury, 1965-67; dir. Pratt Adlib Press, Bklyn., 1968-75. Exhibited in over 35 one-man shows. Mem. Soc. Am. Graphic Artists. Address: Flat Rock Rd Cornwall Bridge CT 06754

PFEIL, RONALD HARMON, fund raising consultant; b. Hastings, Nebr., Oct. 12, 1949; s. Harmon Joseph and Ruth Margaret (Ruhter) P.; m. Mary Elizabeth Creigh, June 26, 1971; children: Mary Elizabeth, Thomas Harmon Otto. AB, Harvard U., 1972. Devel. research asst. Harvard U., Cambridge, 1972-74; adminstr. corp. and found. research U. Pa., Phila., 1974-75; dir. info. and records U. Pa., 1975-80, dir. devel. systems and rsch., 1980-84; dir. devel. Fox Chase Cancer Ctr., Phila., 1984-86; dir. devel. prog. Phila. Orch. Assn., 1986-88; v.p. Van Ness Assocs., Inc., Ardmore, Pa., 1988—. Pres. The Parent-Infant Ctr., Phila., 1982-85; panelist, speaker Council for Advancement & Support Edn., 1976-82; bd. dirs. Univ. City Arts League, Phila., 1982-85. Mem. Nat. Soc. Fund Raising Execs. (chpt. bd. dirs. 1986-91, v.p. progs. 1987-88), Harvard-Radcliffe Club of Phila. Democrat. Lutheran. Home: 401 S 47th St Philadelphia PA 19143-1803 Office: Van Ness Assocs Inc 156 Sutton Rd Ardmore PA 19003-3117

PFISTER, DONALD HENRY, biology educator; b. Kenton, Ohio, Feb. 17, 1945; s. William A. and Dorothy C. (Kurtz) P.; m. Cathleen C. Kennedy, July 1, 1971; children: Meghan, Brigid, Edith. AB, Miami U., Oxford, Ohio, 1967; PhD, Cornell U., 1971; AM (hon.), Harvard U., 1980. Asst. prof. biology U. P.R., Mayaguez, 1971-74; asst. prof. biology, asst. curator Farlow Herbarium Harvard U., Cambridge, Mass., 1974-77, assoc. prof. biology, assoc. curator Farlow Herbarium, 1977-80, prof. biology, curator Farlow Herbarium, 1980—, dir. univ. herbaria, 1983—; vis. mycologist U. Copenhagen, 1978; vis. prof. field station U. Minn., Itasca, 1979; master Kirkland House Harvard U., 1982—. Contbr. over 80 articles to profl. jours. Grantee NSF, 1973-75, 81-85, 85—, Am. Philos. Soc., 1975-76, Whiting Found., 1986. Fellow Linnean Soc. London; mem. Mycol. Soc. Am. (sec. 1988-91), Am. Phytopath. Soc., Am. Microbiol. Soc., New Eng. Bot. Club, Sigma Xi. Office: Harvard U Herbaria 22 Divinity Ave Cambridge MA 02138-2020

PFISTER, WALTER JOHN, JR., broadcast executive; b. Sheboygan, Wis., Apr. 28, 1929; s. Walter J. Sr. and Helen Emelia (Jung) P.; m. Patricia A. Conway, June 8, 1957; children: Jenny, Mary, Walter, Nancy. BS, Northwestern U., 1951; MS in Journalism, Columbia U., 1952. Writer CBS News, Chgo., 1953-55; asst. bur. chief NBC News, Chgo., 1955-60; writer Huntley-Brinkley Report NBC News, N.Y.C., 1961-63; TV producer ABC News, N.Y.C., 1963-64, exec. producer Peter Jennings, 1964-66, exec. producer spl. events, 1966-76, v.p., 1976-78; owner, pres. Exec. TV Workshop, N.Y.C., 1978—. Mem. NATAS (Emmy award for Huntley Brinkly Report 1961, for coverage Pres. Nixon's Trip to China 1972), Writers Guild of Am., TV Acad. Arts and Scis. Office: The Exec TV Workshop 36 W 44th St New York NY 10036-8102

PFLANZE, OTTO PAUL, history educator; b. Maryville, Tenn., Apr. 2, 1918; s. Otto Paul and Katrine (Mills) P.; m. Hertha Maria Haberlander, Feb. 20, 1951; children: Stephen, Charles, Katrine. B.A., Maryville Coll., 1940; M.A., Yale U., 1942, Ph.D., 1950. Historian Dept. State, 1948-49; instr. N.Y. U., 1950-51; asst. prof. U. Mass., 1952-58, U. Ill., 1958-61; prof. history U. Minn., 1961-76, Ind. U., 1977-86; Stevenson Prof. of History Bard Coll., Annandale On Hudson, N.Y., 1987—; chmn. Conf. Group Central European History, 1978; mem. exam. bd., grad. record exam Ednl. Testing Service, 1972-76; mem. Inst. Advanced Study, 1970-71, mem. Historisches Kolleg, Munich, 1980-81. Author: Bismarck and the Development of Germany: Vol. 1.-The Period of Unification, 1815-1871, 1963 (Biennal Book award Phi Alpha Theta), rev. edit., 1990, Vol. 2-The Period of Consolidation, 1871-1880, 1990, Vol. 3-The Period of Fortification, 1880-1898, 1990 (3 vols. collectively named Most Outstanding Book in History, Govt. & Polit. Sci. by Assn. Am. Pubs., 1991); co-author: A History of the Western World: Modern Times, 3d edit, 1975; editor: Innenpolitische Probleme des Bismarck-Reiches, 1983; co-editor: Documents on German Foreign Policy, 1918-1945, Vols. I-III, 1949-50; editor Am. Hist. Rev., 1976-85; mem. editorial bd. Jour. Modern History, 1971-73, Central European History, 1972-74. Served to 1st lt. U.S. Army, 1942-46. Fulbright research fellow, 1955-57; fellow Am. Council Learned Socs., 1951-52; fellow Guggenheim Found., 1966-67; fellow Nat. Endowment Humanities, 1975-76; fellow Internat. Research and Exchanges Bd., 1976; fellow Thyssen Stiftung, Essen, 1986; recipient Humanities award McKnight Found., 1962. Mem. Am. Hist. Assn. Office: Bard Coll 101 Fairbairn Hall Annandale On Hudson NY 12504

PFLUM, WILLIAM JOHN, physician; b. N.Y.C., July 30, 1924; s. Peter Arthur and Caroline (Schmidt) P.; BS, Georgetown U., 1947; MD, Loyola U., Chgo., 1951; m. Roseann Sarah Stubing, Oct. 13, 1956; children: Carol Jean, Jeannine, Suzanne, Denise, Peter. Intern, St. Vincent's Hosp., N.Y.C., 1951-52, resident in internal medicine, 1954-55; resident in internal medicine NYU div. Goldwater Meml. Hosp., N.Y.C., 1952-53; resident in allergy Inst. Allergy, Roosevelt Hosp., N.Y.C., 1956; attending internal medicine (allergy and immunology) Overlook Hosp., Summit, N.J., 1958—; assoc. attending Inst. Allergy, Immunology and Infectious Diseases, Roosevelt Hosp., N.Y.C., 1957-92; pvt. practice medicine, specializing in allergy and immunology, Summit, 1957-92; ret.; cons. in field. Served with USAAF, 1943-45; ETO. Decorated Purple Heart, Air medal with two clusters. Diplomate Am. Bd. Allergy and Immunology. Fellow Am. Acad. Allergy, Am. Coll. Allergists, Am. Assn. Clin. Immunology and Allergy; mem. Summit Med. Soc., Am. Assn. Clin. Immunology and Allergy (pres. Mid-Atlantic region 1975-76), Disabled Am. Vets., Mil. Order Purple Heart, Am. Ex-Prisoners of War, 8th Air Force Hist. Soc., World Marathon Runners Assn., Robert A. Cooke Allergy Alumni Assn. Roman Catholic. Home: PO Box 465 Rumson NJ 07760-0465

PFORDRESHER, JOHN CHARLES, English educator; b. Chgo., Oct. 15, 1943; s. Albert George and Virginia Marie (Rausch) P.; m. Karen Louise Floody, 1968; children: Peter, Rebecca. BA, Georgetown U., 1965; PhD, U. Minn., 1970. Asst. prof. U. N.H., Durham, 1970-73; prof. English, Georgetown U., Washington, 1973—; sr. fellow Coun. for Basic Edn., Washington, 1990—. Author, editor: Variorum Edition of Tennyson's Idylls of the King, 1973; author: (with (W.C. Dawson) Matthew Arnold: Prose Writings, Critical Heritage, 1979; England in Literature, 1989, Classics in World Literature, 1989. Lectr. Smithsonian Residents Assn. Program, Washington, 1987—. Mem. Nat. Coun. Tchrs. English (dir. Commn. on Lit. 1989-91), Victorian Inst. (assoc. editor jour. 1985—), SE 19th Century Studies Assn. (bd. dirs. 1987—). Roman Catholic. Office: Georgetown U English Dept Washington DC 20057

PFORR, MARY MARTHA, public health administrator, consultant; b. Balt., Apr. 26, 1948; d. Karl George and Mary Theresa (Krecz) Smith; m. William John Pforr Jr., Feb. 9, 1983; children by previous marriage: M. Melissa, Patrick W. AA, Anne Arundel Community Coll., 1972; BS in Nursing, U. Md., Balt., 1974; MPH, Johns Hopkins U., 1976. Diplomate in quality assurance; cert. nurse adminstr., master hypnotherapist, health edn. specialist, neuro-linguistics practitioner. Asst. prof. nursing Anne Arundel Community Coll., Arnold, Md., 1976-80; dir. tng. Neighborhood Devel. Collaborative, Washington, 1980-81; supr. pub. health nurse Vis. Nurses Assn., Balt., 1981-82; dir. quality assurance Consumer Health Svcs., Inc., Annapolis, Md., 1982-83; program dir. Balt. County Health Dept., Towson, Md., 1983-84; claims specialist Blue Cross Md., Towson, Md., 1984-85; asst. dir. Staff Builders Inc., Balt., Md., 1985-87; nursing instr. South Balt. Gen. Hosp, 1987-88; chief div. quality control State Md. Mental Hygiene Adminstrn., Balt., 1988—; cons. Earl Delarue, Esquire, Towson, 1987, Mark Shar, Esquire, Balt., 1979; chmn., editor Md. Nursing Assn., Balt., 1974. Co-author Geriatric Nursing Assistant, 1980; contbr. articles to profl. jours. Leader Girl Scouts U.S., Pasadena, Md., 1980; den mother Boy Scouts Am., Pasadena, Md., 1980; coord. ARC Anne Arundel County Health Fairs, Balt., 1981. Recipient Leadership award ARC, 1980; CETA grantee State Md., 1979. Mem. Am. Alliance for Health, Phys. Edn., Recreation and Dance, Md. Quality Assurance Profls., Am. Coll. of Med. Quality, Nat. Assn. Quality Assurance and Utilization Rev., Am. Coll. Utilization Rev. Physicians, Md. Pub. Health Assn. (v.p. 1987-89), Pub. Risk Mgmt. Assn., Am. Coll. Health Care Execs., Nat. Assn. Cert. Hypnotherapists, Soroptimists (sec. 1982-84), Soc. Pub. Health Educators, Women of Moose, Sigma Theta Tau, Sigma Zeta. Roman Catholic. Home: 226 Bar Harbor Rd Pasadena MD 21122-3021 Office: Md Mental Hygiene Adminstrn 201 W Preston St Baltimore MD 21201-2323

PFORR, WILLIAM JOHN, state safety officer; b. Balt., Aug. 11, 1947; s. William John and Lois Ann (Stephenson) P.; m. Mary Martha Smith, Feb. 9, 1983. AA, Anne Arundel Community Coll., 1979. Cert. occupational safety and health pub. sector self-inspector, Md. Firefighter Balt. City Fire Dept., 1971-75; dir. handicapped svcs. Anne Arundel Community Coll., Arnold, Md., 1979-80; mgr. apt. complex Anne Arundel County Housing Authority, Glen Burnie, Md., 1980-81; casework assoc. Balt. County Dept. Social Svcs., Catonsville, Md., 1981-85; dist. safety officer Md. State Hwy. Adminstrn., Annapolis, 1985—; cons. environ. safety, geriatric and handicapped rights Thanatology Neighborhood Devel. Collaborative, Washington, 1981. Author: (directory) Services for Geriatric and Handicapped Citizens, 1981; asst. editor, editorial columnist coll. newspaper, 1981. Coord. health fair Anne Arundel Community Coll., 1981; mem. Md. Gov.'s Commn.-EMployment of the Handicapped, 1979-80, Pres.'s Commn. Employment Handicapped, Washington, 1979-80. With U.S. Army, 1966-70. Mem. Am. Soc. Safety Engrs., Soc. Pub. Health Educators, Md. Pub. Health Assn., Nat. Fire Protection Agy., Moose, Am. Legion. Republican. Roman Catholic. Home: 226 Bar Harbor Rd Pasadena MD 21122-3021 Office: State Hwy Adminstrn 138 Defense Hwy Annapolis MD 21401-7041

PFOUTS, JOHN CHRISTOPHER, writer, editor; b. Pasadena, Calif., Nov. 30, 1951; s. John Oldham and Helen Elizabeth (Babbitt) P.; m. Debra Sue Frierson, 1972 (div. 1974). BA, NYU, 1984. Cons. Urban Homesteading Assistance Bd., N.Y.C., 1983-85; copywriter Plenum Press, N.Y.C., 1984-86; editor Iron Horse mag., N.Y.C., 1986-90; editor-in-chief Classic Cycle Rev., Harrisburg, Pa., 1990—; assoc. editor Art Alternatives mag., N.Y.C., 1991—; co-founder Classic Cycle Rev., 1990—. Author: Lead Poisoning, 1991; contbr. articles to profl. jours. Recipient Brighter Image award Am. Motorcyclist Assn., 1989. Mem. Antique Motorcycle Club of Am., Am. Motorcyclist Assn., Kappa Tau Alpha. Office: Classic Cycle Review 641 Seneca St Harrisburg PA 17110

PFUND, PETER HARRY, lawyer; b. Bryn Mawr, Pa., Oct. 6, 1932; s. Harry William and Marie (Haufe) P.; m. Irina Maria Hasse, July 11, 1959; children: Mara, Nicholas Harry. BA in History cum laude, Amherst Coll., 1954; JD, U. Pa., 1959. Bar: D.C. 1959. Atty. adviser office legal adviser U.S. Dept. State, Washington, 1959-66, 68-73, asst. legal adviser for pvt. internat. law, 1979—; atty. legal div. Internat. Atomic Energy Agy., Vienna, 1966-68; legal adviser U.S. Embassy, Bonn, 1973-78. Contbr. articles to profl. jours. and chpts. to books. With U.S. Army, 1954-56. Mem. German Am. Lawyers Assn. (bd. dirs. 1975-78, acting bd. chmn. 1976-77, bd. advisers 1979—), ABA (Theberge award for pvt. internat. law 1987), Deutsch-Amerikanische Juristen Vereinigung. Office: US Dept State L/PIL Washington DC 20520

PHAM, HUNG GIA, management consultant; b. Vung Tau, Vietnam, July 4, 1960; came to the U.S., 1975; s. Cuong Gia and Huong Lan (Hoang) P.; m. Chi Linh Le, June 22, 1991. BSME, Va. Poly. Inst., 1982; MBA, Georgetown U., 1990. Planning engr. AT&T Technols. Inc., Richmond, Va., 1982-86; sr. cons. Deloitte & Touche, Washington, 1990—. Sec. Nat. Asian Am. Voters League, Washington, 1989-90. Office: Deloitte & Touche 1900 M St NW Washington DC 20036

PHARR, ANN E., social services administrator; b. N.Y.C., July 25, 1946; d. John B. and Pauline Anna (Hawkins) P. BS, Howard U., 1968, MS, 1972; MPIA, U. Pitts., 1979, PhD, 1988. Instr. psychology Morgan State U., Balt., 1972-73; psychology instr., rsch. asst. Peace Corps, 1973-75; unit adminstr. CARE, Inc., 1976-78; adminstr., mgmt. U.S. Agy. for Internat. Devel., Tanzania, Uganda, Mali, 1980-83; spl. asst. to dep. commr. D.C. Commn. of Pub. Health, 1986-88; adj. prof. dept. bus., pub. adminstrn. and econs. Bowie (Md.) State U., 1989; mgmt. cons. Pragma Corp., Falls Church, Va., 1989; internat. devel. cons. Roy Littlejohn Assocs., Inc., Washington, 1989-91; internat. tng. cons. Louis Berger Internat., Washington, 1990; pub. health analyst Office Maternal and Child Health, D.C. Comm. Pub. Health, 1990-91; project leader African Am. HIV/AIDS Edn. Program ARC, Washington, 1991-92; program dir. AIDS tng. for staff

serving African Am. drug abusers ARTI, Alexandria, Va., 1992—; internat. tng. cons. Louis Berger Internat., Washington, 1990. Coun. mem. Ballou Adolescent Health Care Ctr., Washington, 1990-91; staff liaison Infant Mortality Rev. Bd. Work Group, Commn. of Pub. Health, Office of Maternal and Child Health, Washington, 1990-91; coun. mem. Adv. Coun., SEC, D.C. chpt. ARC, 1989—; bd. dirs. Child Enrichment Ctr., Washington, 1986—; mem. Black Women in Sisterhood for Action, 1986-87. U. Pitts. scholar, 1979; Commerce Dept. Econ. Devel. Adminstrn. fellow, 1979; recipient Cert. of Appreciation, Contbn. to Women's Program Adv. Com., 1987, Award of Appreciation, 1987. Mem. Am. Soc. Pub. Adminstrn., Nat. Forum of Black Pub. Adminstrs. (asst. chmn. program devel. com. 1987-88), D.C. Urban Mgmt. Assn. Home: 2409 Irving Pl SE Washington DC 20020 Office: ARTI 6101 Stevenson Ave Alexandria VA 22304

PHELAN, FRANCIS JOSEPH, educator, writer; b. Pitts., May 29, 1925; s. James and Annie (O'Donnell) P.; m. Anne Francis Cavanaugh, June 15, 1975. MA in Polit.Sci., Notre Dame U., 1959, MA in Lit., 1962; PhD, U. Coll., Dublin, Ireland, 1966. Assoc. editor Ava Maria Magazine, South Bend, Ind., 1954-59; chairperson English dept. U. Portland, Oreg., 1962-63; asst. prof Notre Dame U., 1966-72; prof. Stonehill Coll., North Easton, Mass., 1978—; dir. Irish Studies, Stonehill Coll., 1974-82; pres. New England Assoc. of Irish Studies, 1975-78. Author: (short story collection) How to Found Your Own Religion, 1962, (novel) Four Ways of Computing Midnight, 1986. Office: Stonehill College North Easton MA 02357

PHELAN, JOHN MARTIN, educator; b. N.Y.C., May 1, 1932; s. John Alfred and Irene Agnes (Boyhen) P.; A.B., Fordham U., 1954, M.A., 1956; Ph.D., N.Y.U., 1968; Ph.L., Woodstock Coll., 1955, S.T.B., 1962, S.T.M., 1964; m. Jane Balinong, July 10, 1971; children: Mary Jo, Regina. Chmn. communications dept. Fordham U., Bronx, N.Y., 1968-76 prof., dir. Inst. Ethics and Policy in Communications, 1976—; dir. Film Study Inst., Lincoln Center, 1970-73. Mem. ACLU (media com.), Century Assn., Yale U. Inst. for Internat. and Area Studies (research affiliate 1983-86). Author: Communications Control, 1969; Mediaworld: Programming the Public, 1977; Disenchantment: Meaning and Morality in the Media, 1980, Apartheid Media, 1987, Communication and the Citizen, 1991. Home: 202 Altamont Ave Tarrytown NY 10591-4203 Office: Fordham U New York NY 10458

PHELAN, PATRICK JOSEPH, metals and chemicals company executive; b. Jackson Heights, N.Y., Mar. 1, 1950; s. Eugene John and Helen (Kiernan) P.; m. Susan Christine Durecko, Apr. 28, 1979. Profl. pilot cert., Embry-Riddle Aero. U., Daytona Beach, Fla., 1971. Inside sales rep. A.D. MacKay, Inc., Darien, Conn., 1975-78; treas. A.D. MacKay, Inc., Darien, 1978-80, v.p., 1980-85, sr. v. p., 1985-88, asst. pres., 1989—; pres. Phelan Golf, Ltd., Darien, 1990—; owner, tax cons. Profl. Tax Svc., Darien, 1992—. Active selectmen's disaster com. Town of Darien, 1989—; active mem., bd. dirs. Southwestern Fairfield County br. Am. Heart Assn., 1989—. 1st lt. Civil Air Patrol, USAF Aux., 1989—. Mem. Am. Powder Metall. Inst., Am. Soc. Metals Internat. (exec. com. so. Conn. chpt. 1980-85, treas. 1985-86, vice chmn. 1986-87, chmn. 1987-88), 100 Club of Conn., Landmark Club, Downtown Athletic Club (N.Y.C.), Bally Bunion Golf Club (County Kerry, Ireland) (life), KC, Kiwanis Internat., Delta Chi. Republican. Roman Catholic. Home: 10 Bailey Ave Darien CT 06820-4411 Office: AD Mackay Inc PO Box 1612 Darien CT 06820-1612 also: Phelan Golf Ltd PO Box 1222 Darien CT 06820-1222 also: Profl Tax Svc 5 Brook St Ste D2 Darien CT 06820

PHELAN, THOMAS, clergyman, educator; b. Albany, N.Y., Apr. 11, 1925; s. Thomas William and Helen (Rausch) P. A.B. (N.Y. State Regents scholar 1942, President's medal 1945), Coll. Holy Cross, Worcester, Mass., 1945; S.T.L., Catholic U. Am., 1951; postgrad., Oxford (Eng.) U., 1958-59, 69-70. Ordained priest Roman Cath. Ch., 1951; pastor, tchr., adminstr. Diocese of Albany, 1951-58; resident Cath. chaplain Rensselaer Poly. Inst., Troy, N.Y., 1959-72; prof. history, dean Sch. Humanities and Social Scis. Rensselaer Poly. Inst., 1972—; pastor Christ Sun of Justice Univ. Parish, Troy, 1971—; chmn. architecture and bldg. commn. Diocese Albany, 1968—; cons. in field. Author Hudson Mohawk Gateway, 1985; author monographs, articles, revs. in field. Treas. The Rensselaer Newman Found., 1962—; pres. Hudson-Mohawk Indsl. Gateway, 1971-84, bd. dirs., exec. com., 1984—; mem. WMHT Ednl. Telecommunications, 1966-77, 84-90, chmn., 1973-77; chmn. Troy Hist. Dist. and Landmarks Rev. Commn., 1975-86, chmn. hist. adv. com., 1987—; v.p. Preservation League N.Y. State, 1979-82, mem. trustees council, 1982-87; pres. Preservation League N.Y. State, 1987-89; sec. and bd. dirs. Partners for Sacred Places, 1989—; bd. dirs. Hall of History Found., 1983-87; trustee Troy Pub. Libr., 1992—, bd. dir. Served with USN, 1943-46. Recipient Paul J. Hallinan award Nat. Newman Chaplains Assn., 1967; ann. award Albany Arts League, 1977; Disting. Community Service award Rensselaer Poly. Inst., 1979; Edward Fox Demers medal Alumni Assn. Rensselaer Poly. Inst., 1986; Disting. Service award Hudson-Mohawk Consortium of Colls. and Univs., 1988; named Citizen Laureate of the State Univ. N.Y. Found. at Albany, 1988; Danforth Found. fellow, 1969-70; grantee Homeland Found., 1958-59; grantee Dorothy Thomas Found., 1969-70. Fellow Soc. Arts, Religion and Contemporary Culture; mem. Ch. Soc. Coll. Work (dir., exec. com. 1970—), Am. Conf. Acad. Deans, Liturgical Conf., Soc. Indsl. Archaeology, Assn. Internat. pour l'Etudes des Religions Prehistoriques et Ethnologiques, Cath. Campus Ministry Assn., Cath. Art Assn., Assn. for Religion and the Intellectual Life (bd. dirs. 1987—). Clubs: Ft. Orange, Troy Country; Squadron A (N.Y.C.). Home: 5 Whitman Ct Troy NY 12180-4732 Office: Rensselaer Poly Inst Troy NY 12180

PHELAN, WILLIAM THOMAS, education educator; b. Boston, Aug. 15, 1941; s. Francis W. and Mildred C. (Crowley) P.; m. Mary Claire Walsh, Dec. 14, 1968; children: Michelle C., Annemarie K. AB, Boston Coll., 1963; MA, Catholic U., 1967; PhD, U. Chgo., 1976. Asst. prof. U. Manitoba, Winnipeg, Can., 1971-74; asst. prof. U. Mass., Lowell, 1974-82, assoc. prof., 1982—, pres. faculty senate, 1991—; cons. various Mass. pub. schs., 1986—; prin. investigator U.S. Dept. Edn. and Founds. funded rsch., 1980-89. Contbr. numerous articles to profl. jours. Incorporator Cambridgeport Bank, Cambridge, Mass., 1979—. Grantee Annie B. Casey Found., N.Y.C., 1988-89, Commonwealth of Mass. Dropout Prevention, 1986-89, Nat. Inst. Edn., Washington, 1980-83. Mem. Am. Ednl. Rsch. Assn. (presenter 1975—), Eastern Ednl. Rsch. Assn., Am. Sociol. Assn., Am. Evaluation Assn. Office: U Mass 1 University Ave Lowell MA 01854-2881

PHELPS, CHARLOTTE DEMONTE, economics educator; b. East Orange, N.J., Jan. 26, 1933; d. Robert William and Marian Ethel (Page) DeMonte; m. Edmund Strother Phelps, 1957 (div. 1969). B.A. magna cum laude, Radcliffe Coll., 1955; M.A., Yale U., 1956, Ph.D., 1961. Research asst. Cowles Found. for Research in Econs., Yale U., 1960-62; instr. Conn. Coll., New London, 1961; research asst. MIT, Cambridge, 1962-63; research staff economist Cowles Found. and Econ. Growth Ctr., Yale U., 1963-65; researcher Social Sci. Research Council Com. on Econ. Stblzn., 1965-68; research asst. prof. dept. econs. Temple U., 1967-68, assoc. prof. dept. econs. Sch. Bus. Adminstrn., 1969—. Author: Unconscious Motivation and Economic Choice, 1981; mem. editorial bd. Jour. Behavioral Econs., 1987-90; contbr. articles in field to profl. jours. Mem. tech. adv. com. Phila. Community Coordinated Child Care Council, 1970-72; lectr. Cheltenham Twp. Adult Sch., 1971; mem. schs. and scholarships com. Harvard-Radcliffe Clubs Phila., 1977-82. Recipient Middle Atlantic Nat. Scholarship, Radcliffe Coll., 1951-52, Julia L. Richardson Scholarship, 1952-55; Overbrook Univ. fellow Yale U., 1955-56, Louis M. Rabinowitz fellow, 1956-57, Ford Found. mgmt. econs. fellow, 1957-59; Commn. on Money and Credit predoctoral grantee, 1959-60; Social Sci. Research Council, Com. on Econ. Stblzn. postdoctoral fellow, 1965-66, 67-68; Temple U. grantee-in-aid, 1969-70, 72, 76-79, 82, 88. Mem. Am. Econ. Assn., Internat. Assn. Research in Econ. Psychology, Cosmopolitan Club Phila., Franklin Inn Club Phila., Yale Club Phila., Phi Beta Kappa. Office: Dept Econs 879 Ritter Annex Temple U Philadelphia PA 19122

PHELPS, FLORA L(OUISE) LEWIS, editor, anthropologist, photographer; b. San Francisco, July 28, 1917; d. George Chase and Louise (Manning) Lewis; m. C(lement) Russell Phelps, Jan. 15, 1944; children: Andrew Russell, Carol Lewis, Gail Bransford. Student, U. Mich.; AB cum laude, Bryn Mawr Coll., 1938; AM, Columbia U., 1954. Acting dean Cape Cod Inst. Music, East Brewster, Mass., summer 1940; assoc. social sci. analyst U.S. Govt., 1942-44; co-adj. staff instr. anthropology Univ. Coll., Rutgers U., 1954-55; mem. editorial bd. Américas mag. OAS, Washington, 1960-82, sr. editor, 1963-71, editor English edit., 1971-74, mng. editor, 1974-82, contbg. editor, 1982-89; N.J. vice chmn. Ams. Dem. Action, 1950; mem. Dem. County Com. N.J., 1948-49. Author articles in fields of anthropology, art, architecture, edn., travel; contbr. Latin Am. newspapers. Mem. AAAS, Am. Anthrop. Assn., Anthrop. Soc. Washington, Latin Am. Studies Assn., Soc. for Am. Archaeology, Soc. Woman Geographers. Home and Office: 3618 Albemarle St NW Washington DC 20008-4216

PHELPS, L(EE) BARRY, mining engineering educator, researcher; b. Quirigua, Guatemala, May 14, 1938; came to U.S., 1938; s. Myron B. and Florence H. (Selsdorf) P.; m. Catherine Schilke, Dec. 11, 1971; 1 child, Edward A. BS, U. Idaho, 1966; M in Engring., Pa. State U., 1972, PhD, 1981. Mining engr., dredge supr. Internat. Mining. Corp., N.Y.C., 1966-70; rsch. asst. Pa. State U., University Park, 1970-72, from instr. to assoc. prof., 1977—; mine planning engr., mine supr. Aluminum Co. Am., Pitts., 1972-75; project engr. Dow Chem. Co., Freeport, Tex., 1976. Contbr. articles to profl. jours., chpts. to books, encyclopedia. Sgt. U.S. Army, 1958-61. Mme. Nat. Stone Assn. (leader task force 1991-92), Pa. Mining Profls. (bd. dirs. 1985—), Soc. Mining Engrs. (exec. com., unit chmn. 1986-90), Silver Wings, Nittany Country Club. Baptist. Home: PO Box 236 Lemont PA 16851-0236 Office: Pa State U 125 Mineral Science Bldg University Park PA 16802

PHELPS, NORMAN THOMAS, educational administrator; b. Malvern, Pa., Mar. 2, 1913; s. Ralph Howell and Sarah (Hopkins) P.; m. Elizabeth Koenig, Mar. 20, 1940; children: Norman T. Jr., Timothy Ralph. BSBA, U. Alaska, 1939; MS, U. Pa., 1946; D Pedagogy (hon.), Chulalongkorn U., Bangkok, 1975. Pres. Phelps Sch., Malvern, Pa., 1946—. Author: Remedial Procedures in Secondary Education, 1958 (award Pa. Dept. Edn. 1959). Comdr. USNR, 1942-46, PTO. Mem. Boarding Sch. Headmasters Assn. of the Middle States (pres. 1973-75), Union League Club (Phila.), Avalon Yacht Club (N.J.), Whitford Country Club (Exton, Pa.), Phi Delta Kappa (life). Office: Phelps Sch Sugartown Rd Malvern PA 19355-2406

PHELPS, RICHARD STEVENS, educational administrator; b. Holden, Mass., Jan. 20, 1938; s. Harold Shaw and Isabelle Lila (Stevens) P.; m. Judith Ann Miller, Aug. 24, 1963; children: Gwendolyn M., Joscelyn T. AA, Worcester Jr. Coll., 1957; BS, Worcester State Coll., 1960, MEd, 1963; cert. advanced grad.-studies, Boston U., 1980, EdD, 1987. Tchr. English Holden Jr. High Sch., 1960-61, Wachusett Regional High Sch., Holden, 1961-65; dir. adult edn., coord. English Adams (Mass.) Pub. Schs., 1965-69; dir. lang. arts Cambridge (Mass.) Pub. Schs., 1969-79, coord. instructional mgmt., 1979-80, dir. basic skills, 1980-91, dir. student/prog. assessment, 1991—; exec. sec., treas. New England Assn. Tchrs. English, 1979—. Recipient Charles Swain Thomas award New Eng. Assn. Tchrs. English, 1991; grantee Commonwealth Leadership Inst., 1990-93. Mem. Assn. Supervision and Curriculum Devel., Nat. Coun. Tchrs. English, New Eng. Assn. Tchrs. English, Internat. Reading Assn., Nat. Coun. on Measurement in Edn., Am. Ednl. Rsch. Assn., Pi Lambda Theta. Home: 77 Oakland Ave Arlington MA 02174-5950 Office: Cambridge Pub Schs 159 Thorndike St Cambridge MA 02141-1597

PHELPS, STEPHEN FERREL, education educator; b. Deshler, Nebr., Nov. 9, 1944; s. Ferrel Edward and Dorothy Myrtle (Gee) P.; m. Sarah Ann Judd, June 1, 1970; children: Rebekah Clare, Nicholas Ferrel. BA in English, Ind. U., 1970, MAT in Theater and Drama, 1972; PhD in Reading Edn., Syracuse U., 1978. Instr. ednl. methods, English Stockton State Coll., Pomona, N.J., 1972-75; assoc. prof. elem. edn. and reading Buffalo State Coll., 1978—; cons. N.Y. State Regents Coll., 1987-90, numerous sch. dists. Contbr. articles to profl. jours. Sgt. U.S. Army, 1967-69. Mem. Internat. Reading Assn., Coll. Reading Assn., U.K. Reading Assn., Orgn. Tchr Educators in Reading, Niagara Frontier Reading Assn. (pres. 1984-85). Office: Buffalo State Coll Dept Elem Edn/Reading 1300 Elmwood Ave Buffalo NY 14222-1095

PHELPS, TIMOTHY HUNT, illustrator, medical educator; b. Richmond, Ind., Oct. 15, 1953; s. James Michael and Carolyn Jeanne (Hunt) P.; m. Lyn Dorothy Guinter, June 23, 1979; children: Kathleen Anne, Kevin Michael. BFA in Fine Arts, Wittenberg U., 1975; MS, U. Mich., 1981. Graphic artist dept. med. illustration Ind. U., Indpls., 1977-79; med. illustration intern Barbara N. Rankin Assocs., Cleve., 1980; graphic artist Exhibit Mus. U. Mich., Ann Arbor, 1980-81; med. illustrator audiovisual edn. Baylor Coll. Medicine, Houston, 1982-86; assoc. prof. illustration, asst. dir., med. illustrator Johns Hopkins U. Sch. Medicine, Balt., 1986—; instr. Guild of Natural Sci. Illustrators, Phila., 1990; vis. lectr. Med. Coll. Ga., 1991, U. Mich., 1991. One man shows include Ann Miller Gallery, Wittenburg U., 1989, Watson's Crick Galery, Purdue U., 1990, Art Assn. of Richmond Gallery, 1992; exhibited in group shows at Dundalk Community Coll., 1990, Watson's Crick Gallery, Purdue U., 1990. Mem. Johns Hopkins Med. Sch. Coun., 1989—. Recipient 2d pl. award Louise E. Whisenhunt Art Assn., 1971, Johnson Sheet Metal Works Found. award, 1971, Creativity award Wittenberg U., 1974, Swain Robinson Merit award 1978, 10 awards Tex. Sci. Communicators, 1984-86, Merit award Printing Industries of Md. and Southeastern Pa., 1989; Horace H. Rackham scholar, 1980. Fellow Assn. Med. Illustrators (membership and continuing edn. coms. 1988—, bd. govs. 1990—, chmn. internship com., co-chmn. workshops 1991, accreditation rev. com. for the med. illustrator 1992—, 4 awards 1984-88), Guild Natural Sci. Illustrators, Delta Sigma Phi (officer 1972-74). Office: Art As Applied to Medicine 1830 E Monument St Ste 7000 Baltimore MD 21205-2100

PHENICIE, MARK ELIHU, lawyer, lobbyist; b. Chambersburg, Pa., Nov. 23, 1954; s. Frederick Elihu and Jean (Brown) P.; m. Kelly Lee Brown, June 16, 1984; children: Carolyn Brown, Margaret Kelly. BA in Polit. Sci. and Econs., Indiana U. of Pa., 1977; JD, Duquesne U., 1980. Bar: Pa. 1980. Counsel, mem. senate edn. com. Pa. Senate, Harrisburg, 1980-81; counsel, state treas. Pa. Dept. Treasury, Harrisburg, 1981-87; legis. counsel Pa. Trial Lawyers Assn., Harrisburg, 1987—. County chmn. Mifflin County Rep. Com., Lewistown, Pa., 1980-84; treas. Rep. State Com. of Pa., Harrisburg, 1984-86. Mem. Mifflin County Bar Assn. Presbyterian. Home: 353 Martingale Dr Camp Hill PA 17011-8314 Office: Pa Trial Lawyers Assn 800 N 3d St Harrisburg PA 17102

PHILBIN, ANN MARGARET, brokerage house executive; b. Clinton, Mass., June 15, 1941; d. John J. and Angela J. (O'Flynn) P. AB, Trinity Coll., Washington, 1962. With Paine Webber, Boston, 1963—, v.p. adminstrn., 1985—; arbitrator N.Y. Stock Exchange, Boston, 1987—. Mem. Trinity Coll. Alumnae Assn. (1st v.p. 1989-92, pres., trustee 1992—). Office: Paine Webber 265 Franklin St Boston MA 02110

PHILBIN, DANIEL MICHAEL, cardiac anesthesiologist; b. Dunmore, Pa., June 2, 1935; s. Leo Patrick and Josephine Theresa (Barrett) P.; m. Patricia Carol Flynn, Nov. 28, 1964; children: Daniel M. Jr., Patrick Francis. BS, Duquesne U., 1957; MD, St. Louis U., 1961; MA (hon.), Harvard Med. Sch., 1990. Diplomate Am. Bd. Anesthesiology. Intern St. Mary's Group Hosps. St. Louis U., 1961-62; resident in anesthesiology Columbia-Presbyn. Med. Ctr., N.Y.C., 1965-67, chief resident anesthesia svc., 1967-68; asst. prof. Harvard Med. Sch., Boston, 1971-79, assoc. prof., 1980-88, prof. anesthesiology, 1988—; dir. cardiac anesthesiology, anesthetist Mass. Gen. Hosp., Boston, 1983—. Editor jour. Anesthesia and Analgesia, 1980-89; contbr. ovewr 100 articles to profl. jours. Lt., M.C., USNR, 1962-64. Recipient Residents Rsch. award Am. Soc. Anesthesiologists, 1969; vis. fellow Magdalen Coll., Eng., 1982-83; Fogarty Sr. Internat. fellow Oxford U., Eng., 1982-83, 92—. Fellow Am. Coll. Cardiology, Am. Coll. Anesthesiologists; mem. Assn. Cardiac Anesthesiologists (pres. 1978-79), Am. Physiol. Soc. (pub. affairs advisor 1982-88). Roman Catholic. Office: Mass Gen Hosp Dept Anesthesiology 32 Fruit St Boston MA 02114-2698

PHILBRICK, MARGARET ELDER, artist; b. Northampton, Mass., July 4, 1914; d. David and Mildred (Pattison) Elder; m. Otis Philbrick, May 23, 1941 (dec. Apr. 1973); 1 child, Otis. Grad., Mass. Sch. Art, Boston, 1937; student, De Cordova Mus., Lincoln, Mass., 1966-67. Juror art shows; exhibited one woman show, Bare Cove Gallery, Hingham, Mass., 1979, Greenwich Garden Ctr., Cos Cob, Conn., 1981; retrospective exhbn. graphics, Ainsworth Gallery, Boston, 1972; exhibited 40 yr. retrospective, Westenhook Gallery, Sheffield, Mass., 1977, 50 yr. retrospective, 1985; group shows, Boston Printmakers, 1948—, USIA tour to Far East, 1958-59, Boston Watercolor Soc., 1956-82, Pratt Graphic Art Ctr., N.Y.C., 1966, New Eng. Watercolor Soc., 1982—; represented in permanent collections Nat. Mus. Fine Arts, Hanoi, Library of Congress, Washington, Boston Pub. Library, Nat. Bezalel Mus., Jerusalem; artist, designer: Wedgwood Commemorative Plates, Stoke-on-Trent, Eng., 1944-55, Nat. Mus. of Women in the Arts, Washington, Wiggin Collection Boston Pub. Library, The Margaret Philbrick Collection Westwood (Mass.) Pub. Libr.; illustrator books; exhibited "The Book as Art" Nat. Mus. of Women in the Arts, 1987, "The Book as Art II", 1989. Recipient purchase Libr. of Congress, 1948; recipient 1st graphics Acad. Artist, Springfield, Mass., 1957, Multum in Parvo Pratt-2d Internat. Miniature Print Exhbn., 1966, 1st prize in floral Miniature Art Soc. Fla., 1986, Ralph Fabri award. Mem. NAD (Ralph Fabri 1977), Boston Printmakers (exec. bd. 1951—, Presentation Print), Acad. Artists, New Eng. Watercolor Soc., Miniature Painters, Sculptors and Gravers Soc. (Founders award), Miniature Art Soc. of N.J., Miniature Art Soc. of Fla. Home: 6 N Main St Sheffield MA 01257 Office: Westenhook Gallery N Main St Sheffield MA 01257

PHILIP, A. G. DAVIS, astronomer, editor, educator; b. N.Y.C., Jan. 9, 1929; s. Van Ness and Lillian (Davis) P.; m. Kristina Drobavicius, Apr. 25, 1964; 1 dau., Kristina Elizabeth Elanor. B.S., Union Coll., 1951; M.S., N.Mex. State U., 1959; Ph.D., Case Inst. Tech., 1964. Tchr. physics, math. and chemistry Brooks Sch., 1954-59; instr. Case Inst. Tech., 1962-64; asst. prof. astronomy U. N.Mex., 1964-66; asst. prof. astronomy SUNY-Albany, 1966-67, assoc. prof., 1967-76, mem. exec. com. Arts and Scis. Council, 1975-76; prof. astronomy Union Coll., Schenectady, 1976—, astronomer Dudley Obs., 1967-81, Frank L. Fullam chair astronomy, 1980-81, editor Dudley Obs. Reports, 1977-81; astronomer Van Vleck Obs., Weslayan U., 1982—, editor contbns. of VVObs., 1982—; vis. prof. Yale U., 1972, 73, La. State U., 1973, 76, 86, Acad. Scis. Lithuania, USSR, 1973, 76, 79, 86, Stellar Data Ctr., Strasbourg, France, 1978, 79, 80, 82, 85, 86; bd. dirs., sec.-treas. N.Y. Astron. Corp.; pres., treas. L. Davis Press, Inc., 1982—, Inst. Space Observations, 1986—; trustee Fund Astrophys. Rsch., 1985—; bd. dirs. NE N.Y. IBM PC User Group, 1990—. Exhibited: 2d Ann. Photography Regional, Albany, 1980; author: (with M. Cullen and R.E. White) UBV Color-Magnitude Diagrams of Galactic Globular Clusters, 1976; (with A. Robucci, M. Frame, K.W. Philip) Mm, Fractal Series, Vol. 1, Midgets on the Spike, 1991; editor: The Evolution of Population II Stars, 1972, (with D.S. Hayes) Multicolor Photometry and the Theoretical HR Diagram, 1975, (with M.F. Mc Carthy) Galactic Structure in the Direction of the Galactic Polar Caps, 1977, (with D. H. DeVorkin In Memory of Henry Norris Russell, 1977, (with Hayes) The HR Diagram, 1978, Problems in Calibration of Multicolor Systems, 1979, (with M.F. McCarthy and G.V. Coyne) Spectral Classification of the Future, 1979, X-Ray Symposium, 1981, (with Hayes) Astrophysical Parameters for Globular Clusters, 1981, (with A.R. Upgren) The Nearby Stars and the Stellar Luminosity Function, 1983, (with Hayes and L. Pasinetti) Calibration of Fundamental Stellar Quantities, 1985, (with D.W. Latham) Stellar Radial Velocities, Horizontal-Branch and UV-Bright Stars, 1985, Spectroscopic and Photometric Classification of Population II Stars, 1986, (with J. Grindley) IAU Symposium No. 126, Globular Cluster Systems in Galaxies, 1987, (with Hayes and Liebert) IAU Colloquium No. 95, The Second Conference on Faint Blue Stars, (with Hayes and Adelman) New Directions in Spectrophotometry, 1988, Calibration of Stellar Ages, 1988, (with A.R. Upgren) Star Catalogues; A Centennial Tribute to A.N. Vyssotsky, 1989, (with P. Lu) The Gravitational Force Perpendicular to the Galactic Plane, 1989, (with D.S. Hayes and S.J. Adelman) CCDs in Astronomy. II. New Methods and applications of CCD Technology, 1990, (with A.R. Upgren and K.A. Janes) Precision Photometry: Astrophysics of the Galaxy, 1991, (with Rebucci, Frame and Philip K.) Midgets on the Spike, vol. I, 1991, (with A.R. Upgren) Objective-Prism and Other Surveys, 1991; lectr. tours (with K.W. Philip) An Introduction to the Mandelbrot Set, 1988-91; contbr. chpts. to books, articles to profl. jours. Served with AUS, 1951-53. Yale U. vis. fellow, 1976; rsch. grantee Rsch. Corp., NSF, NASA, Nat. Rsch. Lab., NAS, Am. Astron. Soc. Fellow AAAS, Royal Astron. Soc., Am. Phys. Soc.; mem. Am. Astron. Soc. (Harlow Shapley lectr. 1973-92, auditor 1977, 79-85), Am. Math. Soc., Internat. Astron. Union (chmn., sec. various coms. and commns., pres. commn. 30, 1982-85, chmn. working group on spectroscopic and photometric data 1985-91), N.Y. Acad. Scis., Astron. Soc. Pacific, Astron. Soc. N.Y. (sec.-treas. 1969—, editor newsletter 1974—), Sigma Xi. Home: 1125 Oxford Pl Schenectady NY 12308-2913 Office: Union Coll Physics Dept Schenectady NY 12308 also: Van Vleck Obs Middletown CT 06457

PHILIPP, RONALD EMERSON, mechanical engineer; b. Easton, Pa., Sept. 1, 1932; s. Karl Henry and Ida Jane (Hildebrand) P.; m. Barbara Mae Smith, Aug. 6, 1955; children: Barbara Jane, Deborah Ann. BSME, Lafayette Coll., 1954; MSME, Lehigh U., 1956; PhD in Mech. Engring., Columbia U., 1964. Instr. in engring. Lafayette Coll., Easton, 1954-56; commd. 2d lt. U.S. Army, 1956, advanced through grades to col., 1974, ret., 1984; engring. instr. U.S. Mil. Acad., West Point, N.Y.; dir. Army Automotive Labs.; dep. comdr. U.S. Armament R&D Ctr., Picatinny Arsenal, N.J.; mgr. rsch. and testing U.S. Golf Assn., Far Hills, N.J., 1984—. Trustee, treas. Property Owners' Assn., Panther Valley, N.J., 1989—; mem. alumni exec. com. Lafayette Coll., 1990—. Mem. ASME, Assn. of U.S. Army, Am. Def. Preparedness Assn., N.Y. Acad. Scis., Sigma Xi. Home: 40 Mocking Bird Hackettstown NJ 07840-2817 Office: US Golf Assn PO Box 708 Far Hills NJ 07931-0708

PHILIPPI, DIETER RUDOLPH, university administrator; b. Frankfurt, Germany, July 26, 1929; came to U.S., 1956, naturalized, 1961; s. Alfred and Ellen Marguerite (Glatzel) P.; BBA, Johann Wolfgang Goethe U., 1952; postgrad. Sorbonne, summers 1951, 52, U. Omaha, U. Tex.; MBA, Canadian Inst. Banking, 1953-55; children: Bianca Maria, Christopher Thomas; m. 2d, Helga Philippi, May 29, 1982; children: Stephan Andreas, Michael Joachim. With Toronto-Dominion Bank, Calgary, Edmonton, Alta., Can., 1953-56; chief acct. Baylor U. Coll. Medicine, Houston, 1956-63; contr. Wittenberg U., Springfield, Ohio, 1963-68; bus. mgr. Park Coll., Kansas City, Mo., 1968-70; bus. mgr., treas. Lone Mountain Coll., San Francisco, 1970-75; v.p. bus. affairs Findlay (Ohio) Coll., 1975-76; bus. mgr. Bologna (Italy) Ctr., The Johns Hopkins U., 1976-78; dir. bus. and fin. Mt. St. Mary's Coll., Los Angeles, 1978-81; asst. to v.p. overseas programs Boston U., Mannheim, Fed. Republic of Germany, 1981-85, dir. adminstrn. and finance, 1985—; Lectr., Laurence U., Santa Barbara, Calif., 1973—; fin. cons. various charitable orgns. Pres., German Sch. of East Bay, 1970-75; campaign coord. United Appeals Fund, 1968, recipient Disting. Svc. award, 1970; active Boy Scouts, Germany, 1948-52, Can., 1952-56, U.S., 1956—, exec. bd. Tecumseh council, 1967-68, recipient Silver Beaver award, Wood badge, 1968. Bd. dirs. Bellaire Gen. Hosp., Greenland Hills Sch., Chaminade Coll. Prep. Sch. Mem. Am. Acctg. Assn., Am., Eastern Fin. Assns., Am. Mgmt. Assn., Am. Assn. Univ. Adminstrs., Nat. Coll. and Univ. Bus. Officers Assn., Western Coll. and Univ. Bus. Officers Assn., Nat. Assn. Accts., Am. Assn. Higher Edn., Coll. and Univ. Personnel Assn., San Francisco Consortium, Alpha Phi Omega. Clubs: Commonwealth of Calif. (San Francisco); Univ. (Kansas City). Office: Boston U Internat Grad Programs Unit 29217 APO AE 09102

PHILLIPPI, JAMES PAUL, education educator, administrator; b. Rockwood, Pa., May 5, 1949; s. James B. and Edna Mae (Schrader) P.; 1 child, Jeffrey M. Deveney. AB, Fairmont (W.Va.) State Coll., 1971; MA, W.Va. U., 1973, EdD, 1985. Tchr. Monongalia County Schs., Morgantown, W.Va., 1971-73, prin., 1973-76, supervising prin., 1976-82; instr. W.Va. U., Morgantown, 1982-85; prof. Johnson (Vt.) State Coll., 1985-88, Castleton (Vt.) State Coll., 1988-92; chmn. edn. dept., dir. grad. programs Coll. St. Joseph the Provider, Rutland, Vt., 1992—; dir. student teaching, chief cert. officer, coord. curriculum instruction and coord. initial tchr. cert. Castleton State Coll., 1988—. Co-author: (handbook) Special Education Camps, 1990. Clk. sch. bd. Addison-Rutland Supervisory Union, Fair Haven, Vt., 1991; bd. dirs., legis. chmn. Vt. State PTA, Washington, 1990; bd. dirs. Fair Haven Sch. Bd., 1990—. Vt. State Edn. Dept. grantee, 1990; named one of Outstanding Young Men of Am., 1981. Mem. Addison-Rutland Supervisory Union Sch. Dirs., Kappa Delta Pi. Home: 5 West St Fair Haven VT 05743-1201

PHILLIPS, BESSIE GERTRUDE WRIGHT, educator, museum trustee; b. Erie, Pa.; d. Charles Clayton and Mary Gertrude (Allen) Wright; m. Stephen Phillips, Oct. 2, 1942 (dec. Jan. 1971); children: Jane Appleton, Margaret Duncan (Mrs. Robert Cummings), Ann Willard (Mrs. Kevin Waters). AB, Fla. State Coll. Women, Tallahassee, 1930; MA, Mount Holyoke Coll., 1933.

Sec. internat. hdqrs. World YMCA, Geneva, 1933-34; math. tchr. Washington Sem., Pa., 1930-32; acad. head, math tchr. Milw.-Downer Sem., Wis., 1934-37; trustee New Eng. Coll., Henniker, N.H., 1952-61, Orme Sch., Mayer, Ariz., 1962—, Penobscot Marine Mus., Searsport, Maine, 1978—; bd. advisers Coun. for Advancement Small Colls., Washington, 1959-69; trustee Peabody Mus., Salem, Mass., 1971—, vis. com. for edn., 1983—; ednl. cons. in field. Bd. dirs. Salem Female Charitable Soc., 1943—, Mack Indsl. Sch., Salem, 1943—. Mem. Nat. Soc. Colonial Dames, Bostonian Soc., Cum Laude Soc., Union Club, Chilton Club, Eastern Yacht Club. Republican. Presbyterian. Home: 30 Chestnut St Salem MA 01970-3129

PHILLIPS, CAROLE CHERRY, financial advisor, writer; b. Phila., May 22, 1938; d. Joseph and Mary (Mitnick) Cherry; B.A., Temple U., Phila., 1959; M.A. in Internat. Relations, U. Pa., 1968, Ph.D. in Econs., 1974; children: Andrew Tilden Greenberg, Elizabeth Clare Sanchez; m. Almarin Phillips, Dec. 19, 1976. Instr., Wharton Sch., U. Pa., 1971-74; investment officer, then sr. investment officer trust div. Provident Nat. Bank, Phila., 1974-76, asst. v.p., spl. projects dir., 1974-80; pres. C.C. Phillips, Personal Fin. Services, Phila., Pa., 1980-90; v.p. Wescott F.P. Group, 1991—; exec. dir. Women's Fin. Ctr., Phila., 1987-89; seminar instr. Money Workshop for Women, Temple U. Div. Continuing Edn., 1979-84; lectr. Walter Bagehot fellowship program Columbia U., 1980. Bd. dirs. Phila. Co., 1978-81, pres., 1981-83; nat. bd. dirs. Fund for an Open Soc., 1979-82; trustee Cherry Found. 1976-86; bd. dirs. Bus. Execs. for Nuclear Age Concerns, 1987—; bd. dirs Womens Way, 1991—. Mem. Am. Econs. Assn., Nat. Assn. Profl. Fin. Advisors, Social Investment Forum, Forum Exec. Women. Author: The Money Workbook for Women, 1982; Money Talk: The Last Taboo, 1984, The New Money Workbook for Women, 1987. Office: One Liberty Pl Philadelphia PA 19103

PHILLIPS, DAVID GEORGE, financial planner; b. Kingston, Pa., Oct. 22, 1931; s. George Henry and Helen (Margavitch) P.; m. Georgia Tomassetti, July 30, 1955; children: Georgia, David William, Ian George, Morgan Henry, Elizabeth. BA, Wilkes Coll., 1971, MBA, 1984. Reporter, suburban editor, city editor Wilkes-Barre Record Wilkes-Barre (Pa.) Pub. Co., 1961-81; field underwriter Mutual of Omaha Cos., Wilkes-Barre, 1984-87, dist. sales mgr., 1987-89; fin. planner IDS Fin. Svcs. Inc., Wilkes-Barre, 1989--; substitute tchr. West Side Voc-Tech High Sch., Pringle, Pa., 1983-84, 84-85. Author: Partners in Progress section of the history of The Wyoming Valley, 1983; editor Mountaintop Eagle, 1981-82; lectr. in advanced newswriting and editing at Wilkes Coll., 1982. Dir. Dallas Area Fall Fair Assn., 1983-84; mem. athletic com., past pres. Masters Swim club, Greater Wilkes-Barre Family YMCA, 1982-84; mem. Back Mountain Coun. on Drug and Alcohol Abuse, 1983. Mem. Internat. Assn. Fin. Planners. Republican. Presbyterian. Home: 99 S Pioneer Ave Wilkes Barre PA 18708-1329 Office: IDS Fin Svcs Inc 100 N Wilkes Barre Blvd Wilkes Barre PA 18702-5235

PHILLIPS, DAVID LOWELL, hospital administrator, consultant, educator; b. Coalinga, Calif., Sept. 8, 1952; s. W. Ross and Amilee Faith (Long) P.; m. Rena Ellen Counsellor, Aug. 27, 1983; children: Erin Counsellor, Jonathan Kim Counsellor. Student, Wheaton (Ill.) Coll., 1970-72; BA with high honors, U. Calif., Santa Barbara, 1974; MS in Edn., Ind. U., 1976; EdD, U. Pa., 1986. Assoc. dean of students Ea. Coll., St. Davids, Pa., 1976-82; dir. corp. and found. relations Ea. Coll. and Ea. Bapt. Theol. Sem., St. Davids and Phila., 1982-85; dir. corp. and found. rels. Children's Hosp. Phila., 1985-89, dir. devel., 1989—; vis. prof. non-profit mgmt. MBA program Ea. Coll; mem. faculty Bell (Pa.) Inst. for Non-Profit Excellence, 1988—, Templeton Inst. for Non-Profit Excellence, 1989—; program assoc. New Era Philanthropy, Inc., Wynnewood, Pa., 1986—. Bd. dirs. Evang. Assn. Promotion Edn., Radnor, Pa., 1985—, Koinonia Health Svcs., Phila., 1986—, Esperanza Health Ctr., Phila., 1987—, Cornerstone Acad., Phila., 1988—. Mem. Assn. for Healthcare Philanthropy, Nat. Soc. Fundraising Execs., Rotary. Home: 616 Woodcrest Ave Ardmore PA 19003-1920 Office: The Childrens Hosp of Phila 34th St and Civic Center Blvd Philadelphia PA 19104

PHILLIPS, DONALD SMITH, psychologist researcher; b. N.Y.C., Jan. 2, 1949; s. Warren Donald and Madeline (Phillips) P. BS in Psychology, Poly. Inst. N.Y., 1979, MS in Psychology, 1991. Rsch. asst. Columbia U., N.Y.C.; rsch. asst. Poly. Univ., Bklyn., 1979—, instr., 1990—; instr. Hofstra U., Uniondale, N.Y., 1984—. Contbr. articles to profl. jours. Recipient Rsch. grant N.Y. State Power Lines, 1982-86, Tchr. of Excellence award Hofstra U., 1987, Conger-Paterson award Hofstra U., 1988, Tchr. of Yr. award Nassau Assn. for Continuing Edn., 1989. Mem. N.Y. Acad. Scis., N.Y. Paleontol. Soc. (pres. 1982—). Office: Poly Univ 333 Jay St Brooklyn NY 11201-2990

PHILLIPS, FRED RONALD, insurance company executive; b. Lewisburg, Pa., May 5, 1940; s. Fred Oscar and Luella Mae (Herold) P.; m. Dorothy Helen Hayes, Feb. 18, 1961; children: Christopher S., George J., Fred R. Jr. Student, U. Pa., 1962-67. CPCU. Underwriter Employers Mut. Casualty Co., Phila., 1958-60, Gen. Accident Ins. Co., Phila., 1960-62; v.p., sec. Pa. Lumbermens Mut. Ins. Co., Phila., 1962—. Dir. Phila. Fire Dept. Hist. Corp. Mem. Chartered Property and Casualty Underwriters Soc., Train Collectors Assn. Am. Office: Pa Lumbermens Mut Ins Co Curtis Ctr Philadelphia PA 19106

PHILLIPS, GARY WILSON, physicist; b. Golden City, Mo., June 11, 1940; s. Phillip Pemberton and Teresa Colleen (Wilson) P.; m. Virginia Louise, July 20, 1963; children: Carol Tracy, Julie Michelle, Brian Scott. BS, MIT, 1962; PhD, U. Md., 1967. Rsch. assoc. U. Wash., Seattle, 1966-69; rsch. scientist assoc. U. Tex., Austin, 1969-71; scientist Teledyne Isotopes, Westwood, N.J., 1971-73; rsch. physicist U.S. Naval Rsch. Lab., Washington, 1973-84, supr. rsch. physics, 1987—. Contbr. articles to profl. jours. Vol. Springfield (Va.) Youth Club, 1976-88, coach, 1982; vol. West Springfield Little League, 1981-84; leader Webelos Scouts, 1981. Mem. Am. Phys. Soc., Am. Astronautical Soc., Sigma Xi, Sigma Phi Sigma. Office: Naval Rsch Lab 4555 Overlook Ave SW Washington DC 20375-0001

PHILLIPS, GEORGE WYGANT, chemical business executive, trade consultant; b. N.Y.C., Aug. 5, 1929; s. George Wygant and Claire (Daus) P.; m. Marilyn Edith Miller, Sept. 6, 1958; children: Elizabeth Miller, John Wygant. BA, Wesleyan U., 1951; postgrad., Iowa State U., 1951-53; PhD, Harvard U., 1957. Rsch. scientist Union Carbide Plastics Co., Bound Brook, N.J., 1957-61; mgr. tech. acquisitions internat. div. Union Carbide Corp., N.Y.C., 1962-65; mgr. tech. rels. group Europe, S. Am. Union Carbide Corp., Geneva, 1965-68; from acct. rep. chems. and plastics div. to product mgr. chems. and plastics div. Union Carbide Corp., N.Y.C., 1968-75, coord. internat. affairs corp. external affairs dept., 1975-81; mgr. trade and tariff affairs corp. pub. affairs dept. Union Carbide Corp., Danbury, Conn., 1981-85; pres. Export Control Cons., Inc., Ridgefield, Conn., 1986—; pres. Envirogas Vehicle Systems, Inc., N.Y.C., 1991—. Dir. Nat. Emergency Response Svc. Coop., Washington, 1991; trustee U.S. Coun. Internat. Bus., 1983-84; mem. U.S. Govt. Industry Sector Adv. Com., U.S. Commerce Dept. Tech. Adv. Com. Mem. Comml. Devel. Assn., Licensing Execs. Soc., Am. Chem. Soc., Chem. Mfrs. Assn., Synthetic Chem. Mfrs. Assn. Home: 94 Deer Hill Dr Ridgefield CT 06877

PHILLIPS, GRAHAM HOLMES, advertising executive; b. London, Jan. 30, 1939; emigrated to U.S., 1965, naturalized, 1974; s. Leonard George and Mary Marjorie (Holmes) P.; m. Laurel Gilbert; 1 child, Debra Ann. Student, RAF Coll. Cranwell, 1957-58; M.B.A., London U., 1962. Mgmt. trainee Shell Internat. Petroleum, Ltd., London, 1957-59; aviation sales rep., 1960-63; aviation sales mgr. Shell Philippines, 1964; with Ogilvy & Mather (U.S.), N.Y.C., 1965—, account mgr., 1965-73; dep. mgr., account supr. Ogilvy & Mather (U.S.), Houston, 1970, v.p., 1971-72, sr. v.p., mgmt. supr., 1972-73; mng. dir. Ogilvy & Mather Inc., Amsterdam, 1973-75; former pres., then chief exec. officer Ogilvy & Mather (Can.) Ltd., Toronto, from 1975, former chmn., from 1979; dir. Ogilvy & Mather, 1978—; former chief fin. officer Ogilvy & Mather Internat., from 1983; former exec. v.p. Ogilvy & Mather (U.S.), N.Y.C., from 1979, former gen. mgr., from 1980, former mng. dir., chief fin. officer, from 1981; now vice chmn. Ogilvy & Mather Worldwide, N.Y.C.; former chmn. Ogilvy & Mather N.Am. Mem. N.Y. Yacht Club. Episcopalian. Office: Ogilvy & Mather 309 W 49th St Worldwide Pla New York NY 10019-7399*

PHILLIPS, HARRIET ELIZABETH, medical illustrator; b. N.Y.C., Mar. 11, 1930; d. John Wilson and Florence Josephine (Hickson) P.; m. Donald Richard Miller, Nov. 18, 1961 (dec.); children: Russell Scott, Melanie Ann. BA, Hunter Coll., 1951; cert., Frank J. Reilly Sch. Art, 1963. Apprentice to instr. med. illustrating Columbia U./Coll. Physicians and Surgeons, N.Y.C., 1951-59; instr. med. illustration Columbia U./Coll. Physicians and Surgeons; prin. Med. Art Svc., N.Y.C. and Warwick, N.Y., 1959—; instr. Bd. Coop. Ednl. Svcs., Goshen, N.Y., 1990—; owner The HEP Press, Warwick. Designer, printer, pub. hand-made books: The Seasons, 1980, My Dear Lizzie, 1986, Black Dirt, 1991. Town of Warwick Recycle com., 1989, conservation bd., 1991—. Mem. Graphic Artists Guild, Soc. Animal Artists, Art Students League, Ctr. Book Arts, Women's Studio Workshop, Assn. Med. Illustrators (25-Yr. Club). Office: Med Art Svc 52 Feagles Rd Warwick NY 10990-2258

PHILLIPS, JAMES MACILDUFF, material handling company executive, engineering and manufacturing executive; b. Carrick, Pa., June 13, 1916; s. John MacFarlane and Harriet (Duff) P.; m. Majorie Watson, June 1940 (div. 1964); children: James M. Jr., William W.; m. Regina Leininger, Apr. 1964 (dec.); children: Jeffrey M., Molly M. BSME, Carnegie Inst. of Tech., 1938; grad., Pitts. Inst. Aeronautics, 1939; ME refresher, Pa. State U. State Coll., 1960; grad., Internat. Corespondence Sch., Scranton, Pa., 1988. Profl. engr. Pa. Draftsmen, engr. Phillips Mine & Mill Supply Co., Pitts., 1933-40, v.p., 1941-77; v.p. engring. Salem Brosius, Inc., Carnegie, Pa., 1956-64; pres. Phillips Corp., Bridgeview, Pa., 1977-83, Phillips Jet Flight, Bridgeville, Pa., 1977-83, Phillips Mine & Mill Inc., Pitts., 1964—; also chmn. bd. Phillips Mine & Mill Inc. Inventor in field; contbr. articles to profl. mags. Bd. dirs. Brashear Assn., Pitts. Mem. Air Force Assn., Aero Club of Pitts., Pa. Pilots Coun. (pres.), Quiet Birdmen (pres.), Early Bird Pilots, Exptl. Aircraft Assn. Aircraft Owners and Pilots Assn. (founding), OX-5 Pioneer Airmen (pres. 1987), St. Clair County Club. Methodist. Office: Phillips Mine & Mill Inc 1738 N Highland Rd Pittsburgh PA 15241-1200

PHILLIPS, JOHN MICHAEL, industrial sales company executive; b. Wilkes Barre, Pa., Mar. 6, 1935; s. John M. and Rose (Sinavage) Filipowicz; m. Janet Rosky P.; m. Nov. 28, 1959; children: John M. III, Beth Lynn, Scott David. Student, Middlesex City Coll., 1968. Credit mgr. Morrison Steel, New Brunswick, N.J., 1965-71; dir. credit Edgcomb Steel, Hillside, N.J., 1971-73; dir. mktg. & sales David Smith Steel, South Plainfield, N.J., 1973-79; salesman Pallet Sales Corp., Plainview, N.Y., 1980-82; sales mgr. Metro Nat. Handling, Whippany, N.J., 1982-86; pres., owner Indsl. Material Handling Inc, Kendall, N.J., 1986—; tchr. Middlesex (N.J.) County Coll., 1977-79; chmn. Nat. Assn. Credit Mgmt., 1971; pres. N.J. Assn. Credit Execs., 1978. Com. mem. South Brunswick Twp., 1977-78. With U.S. Army, 1958-60. Mem. KC (3d degree knight), Elks (exalted ruler 1978). Roman Catholic. Office: Indsl Material Handling Co Inc PO Box 217 Kendall Park NJ 08824-0217

PHILLIPS, KEVIN G., educator; b. Middletown, N.Y., Apr. 22, 1960; s. Myron Arthur and Esther May (Whorrall) P.; m. Sarah Prescott, May 28, 1983. BA, Wheaton Coll., 1982, MA, 1983; MBA, Syracuse U., 1992; EdD, Columbia U., 1992. Dir. Christian edn. 1st United Meth. Ch., Bradenton, Fla., 1983-84; youth dir. Lakewood United Meth. Ch., North Little Rock, Ark., 1985-86; student govt. coord. Tchrs. Coll., Columbia U., N.Y.C., 1987-89; adj. prof. Nyack (N.Y.) Coll., 1988, asst. prof., 1988—, dept. chmn., 1989—; lectr. King's Coll., Briarcliffe Manor, N.Y., 1987; cons. Met. Missions, Andhra Pradesh, India, 1988—, Oriskany (N.Y.) Elem. Sch., 1991; presenter seminars; treas. Leadership Devel. Consultants, 1988—. Contbr. articles, book revs. to profl. publs. Tng. chmn. N.Y.C. area Boy Scouts Am., 1987—, scoutmaster, 1988—. Recipient Good Shepherd award Boy Scouts Am., 1982, Silver Beaver award, 1990. Mem. Assn. Profs. and Researchers of Religious Edn., Coun. for Adult and Experiential Learning, Nat. Assn. Ch. Bus. Adminstrs., Nat. Assn. Profs. Christian Edn., Religious Researchers Assn., Soc. for Scientific Study of Religion, Kappa Delta Phi. Republican. Mem. Christian and Missionary Alliance Ch. Office: Nyack Coll Nyack NY 10960

PHILLIPS, LAUGHLIN, arts administrator; b. Washington, Oct. 20, 1924; s. Duncan and Marjorie Grant (Acker) P.; m. Elizabeth Hood, Mar. 17, 1956; children: Duncan Vance, Elizabeth Laughlin; m. Jennifer Stats Cafritz, Aug. 13, 1975. Student, Yale U., 1942-43; M.A., U. Chgo., 1949. Fgn. service officer, 1949-64; vice consul Hanoi, Vietnam, 1950-53; 2d sec. Tehran, Iran, 1957-59; co-founder Washingtonian mag., 1965, editor, 1965-74, editor-in-chief, 1974-79; pres. Washington Mag., Inc., 1965-79; dir. Phillips Collection, 1972-92, pres. and bd. chmn., 1967—. Washington trustee Fed. City Council, 1974—; Bd. dirs. MacDowell Colony, 1977-79, Nat. Com. for an Effective Congress, 1966—. Served with AUS, 1943-46, PTO. Decorated Bronze Star; chevalier de l'Ordre de la Couronne (Belgium); knight's cross 1st class Order of Danebrog (Denmark); officier Arts et Lettres (France). Clubs: Cosmos (Washington), Metropolitan (Washington), Rolling Rock (Ligonier, Pa.). Home: 3044 O St NW Washington DC 20007-3107 Office: Phillips Collection 1600 21st St NW Washington DC 20009-1090

PHILLIPS, LAWRENCE S., apparel company executive; b. 1927; s. Seymour J. P.; married. B.A., Princeton U., 1948. With Phillips-Van Heusen Corp., N.Y.C., 1948—, v.p., 1951-59, exec. v.p., 1959-68, pres., 1968-87, also chief exec. officer, dir., chmn., 1987—. Mem. Am. Apparel Mfrs. (dir.). Office: Phillips-Van Heusen Corp 1290 Ave Of The Americas New York NY 10104-0095*

PHILLIPS, LEO HAROLD, JR., lawyer; b. Detroit, Jan. 10, 1945; s. Leo Harold and Martha C. (Oberg) P.; m. Patricia Margaret Halcomb, Sept. 3, 1983. BA summa cum laude, Hillsdale Coll., 1967; MA, U. Mich., 1968; JD cum laude, 1973; LLM magna cum laude, Free Univ. of Brussels, 1974. Bar: Mich. 1974, N.Y. 1975, U.S. Supreme Ct. 1977, D.C. 1979. Fgn. lectr. Pusan Nat. U. (Korea), 1969-70; assoc. Alexander & Green, N.Y.C., 1974-77; counsel Overseas Pvt. Investment Corp., Washington, 1977-80, sr. counsel, 1980-82, asst. gen. counsel, 1982-85; asst. gen. counsel Manor Care, Inc., Silver Spring, Md., 1985-91 asst. sec. 1988—, assoc. gen. counsel, 1991—; vol. Peace Corps, Pusan, 1968-71; mem. program for sr. mgrs. in govt. Harvard U., Cambridge, Mass., 1982. Contbr. articles to legal jours. Chmn. legal affairs com. Essex Condominium Assn., Washington, 1979-81; deacon Chevy Chase Presbyn. Ch., Washington, 1984-87, moderator, 1985-87, supt. ch. sch., elder, trustee, 1987-90, pres., 1988-90. Recipient Alumni Achievement award Hillsdale Coll., 1980; Meritorious Honor award Overseas Pvt. Investment Corp., 1981, Superior Achievement award, 1984. Mem. ABA (internat. fin. transactions com., vice chmn. com. internat. ins. law), Am. Soc. Internat. Law (Jessup Internat. Law moot ct. judge semi-final rounds 1978-83), Internat. Law Assn. (Am. br.; com. sec. 1982), D.C. Bar, N.Y. State Bar Assn., Royal Asiatic Soc. (Korea br.), State Bar Mich., Washington Fgn. Law Soc. (sec.-treas. 1980-81, bd. dirs., program coordinator 1981-82, v.p. 1982-83, pres.-elect 1983-84, pres. 1984-85, chmn. nominating com. 1986, 88), Washington Internat. Trade Assn. (bd. dirs. 1984-87), Assn. Bar City N.Y., Hillsdale Coll. Alumni Assn. (co-chmn. Washington area 1977-90). Club: University (N.Y.C.). Home: 4740 Connecticut Ave NW Apt 702 Washington DC 20008-5632 Office: Manor Care Inc 10750 Columbia Pike Silver Spring MD 20901-4427

PHILLIPS, LEONARD ELLIS, JR., town government official; b. Jan. 14, 1943. AAS, SUNY, 1963; B in Landscape Architecture, U. Ill., 1967, BSc, 1967. Registered landscape architect, Mass., Tenn., Ky., N.C., W.Va., Neb., Kans., Md., Mich. Site planner Donald J. Stephens, Assoc./Architects, Loudonville, N.Y., 1966; field landscape architect Wayne County Rd. Commn., Detroit, 1967-69; land use planner Mass. Dept. Natural Resources, Boston, 1969-71; landscape specialist Mass. Port Authority, Boston, 1972; landscape architect Charles T. Main, Inc., Boston, 1972-75, Metcalf & Eddy, Inc., Boston, 1975-77; consulting landscape architect Bayside Engring. Assoc., Inc., Boston, 1977; town planner Town of North Andover, Mass., 1977-78; supt. park and tree div. Town of Wellesley, Mass., 1978—. Author: Municipal Stree Tree Master Planning, 1981, Vandalism Prevention Handbook, 1981, Urban Trees: A Guide for Selection, Maintenance and Master Planning, 1992; lectr. in field; contbr. articles to profl. jours. Merit award Boston Soc. Landscape Architects 1985; Toro landscape industry advancement award Landscape Architecture Found. 1986. Mem. Am. Soc. Landscape Architects, Am. Forestry Assn., Am. Pub. Works Assn., Soc. Mcpl. Arborists (editor monthly jour. City Trees), The Nature Conservancy. Home: 5 Monson Dr Peabody MA 01960-3548 Office: Wellesley Dept Pub Works Park & Tree Div 56 Woodlawn Ave Wellesley MA 02181-3123

PHILLIPS, MARION GRUMMAN, author, civic worker; b. N.Y.C., Feb. 11, 1922; d. Leroy Randle and Rose Marion (Werther) Grumman; m. Ellis Laurimore Phillips, Jr., June 13, 1942; children: Valerie Rose (Mrs. Adrian Parsegian), Elise Marion (Mrs. Edward E. Watts III), Ellis Laurimore III, Kathryn Noel (Mrs. Philip Zimmermann), Cynthia Louise. Student, Mt. Holyoke Coll., 1940-42, BA, Adelphi U., 1981. Civic vol. Mary C. Wheeler Sch., 1964-68, Historic Ithaca, Inc., 1972-76, Ellis L. Phillips Found., 1960-91; bd. dirs. North Shore Jr. League, 1960-61, 64-65, 68-69, Family Svc. Assn. Nassau County, 1963-69, Homemaker Svc. Assn. Nassau County, 1959-61. Author: (light verse) A Foot in the Door, 1965, The Whale-Going, Going, Gone, 1977, Doctors Make Me Sick (So I Cured Myself of Arthritis), 1979; editor: (with Valerie Phillips Parsegian) Richard and Rhoda, Letters from the Civil War, 1982, Wooden Shoes (F. M. Sisson), 1990, Irish Eyes (McTarsneys and Sissions), 1990; editor Jr. League Shore Lines, 1960-61, The Werthers in America-Four Generations and their Descendants, 1987; A B-Tour of Britain, 1986; contbr. articles on fund raising to mags. Mem. New Eng. Hist. Geneal. Soc. (bd. dirs.), Hanover Garden Club, Creek Club, PEO Sisterhood. Episcopalian. Home: Point of View RR 1 Box 274 Sharon VT 05065-9710

PHILLIPS, MARK DOUGLAS, aerospace company executive; b. N.Y.C., Oct. 23, 1953; s. Herbert and Dorinne (Borenstein) P.; m. Deanne Sue Pace, Dec. 28, 1979; children: Cheri, Brooke, Brittany. BA, SUNY, New Paltz, 1975; MA, Calif. State U., Northridge, 1982. Staff scientist Integrated Scis. Corp., Santa Monica, Calif., 1980-82; sr. engr. Martin Marietta Co., Denver, 1982-83; program mgr. CTA, Inc., Englewood, Colo., 1983-88, regional tech. officer, 1988-89; v.p., dep. dir. air traffic systems div. CTA, Inc., Rockville, Md., 1989—. Contbr. articles to profl. jours.; developer human factors engrng. methods and tools for air traffic control. Mem. Air Traffic Control Assn. (Chmn.'s Citation of Merit 1984), Human Factors Soc. Office: 6116 Executive Blvd Rockville MD 20852-4920

PHILLIPS, MICHAEL CANAVAN, biochemistry educator, department chairman; b. London, Feb. 23, 1940; came to U.S., 1978; s. Frederick A. and Annie W. (Woodard) P.; m. Pauline M. Ratcliffe, June 20, 1964; children: Julie, Neil. BS, Southampton (Eng.) U., 1962, PhD, 1965, DSc, 1976. Postdoctoral fellow SUNY, Buffalo, 1965-67; rsch. scientist Unilever Rsch. Lab., Welwyn, Eng., 1967-69, sr. scientist, 1969-78; assoc. prof. biochemistry Med. Coll. Pa., Phila., 1978-80, prof., 1980—, dir. grad. tng. biochemistry dept., 1984-91, chmn. biochemistry dept., 1991—; mem. Nat. Heart, Lung and Blood Rev. Com., Bethesda, Md., 1988-92. Fellow Am. Heart Assn. (mem. at large exec. com. of coun. on arteriosclerosis 1990-92), Am. Soc. Biochemistry and Molecular Biology; mem. Am. Chem. Soc. Office: Med Coll Pa 3300 Henry Ave Philadelphia PA 19129-1191

PHILLIPS, PAMELA KIM, lawyer; b. San Diego, Feb. 23, 1958; d. John Gerald and Nancy Kimiko (Tabuchi) Phillips; m. R. Richard Zanghetti, Sept. 16, 1989. BA cum laude, The Am. U., 1978; JD, Georgetown U., 1982. Bar: N.Y. 1983, U.S. Dist. Ct. (so. dist.) N.Y. 1983. Assoc. Curtis, Mallet-Prevost, Colt & Mosle, N.Y.C., 1982-84, LeBoeuf, Lamb, Leiby & MacRae, N.Y.C., 1984-90; ptnr. LeBoeuf, Lamb, Leiby, & MacRae, N.Y.C., 1991—. Mng. editor The Tax Lawyer, Georgetown U. Law Sch., Washington, 1980-81. Co-chair Halloween benefit The Fresh Air Fund, N.Y.C., 1992, mem. coun., 1991—. Am. Univ. scholar, Washington, 1976-78. Mem. ABA, Women's Bar Assn., Assn. Bar City N.Y. (sec. young lawyers com. 1987-89, chmn. 1989-91, second century com. 1990—, banking law com. 1991—). Home: 107 E 36th St # 3 New York NY 10016-3448 Office: LeBoeuf Lamb Leiby & MacRae 125 W 55th St New York NY 10019

PHILLIPS, PEARL RAPHELITA, real estate executive; b. Savanna La Mar, Westmoreland, Jamaica, Apr. 17, 1941; came to U.S., 1968; d. Hugh Lawrence Rance and Ada Louise (Mullings) Watson; m. Michael I. Phillips, June 9, 1962 (div. Sept., 1977); children: Karim Irving, Felitia Alssandra; m. Michael John Reardon, May 24, 1980. Student, Howard Community Coll., 1974-77, Am. U., 1984-86. Cert. real estate broker Grad. Real Estate Inst. Sr. sec. Nat. Coun. Cath. Men, Washington, 1968-69; exec. sec. Nat. Acad. Sci, Washington, 1969-71; sr. sec. President's Commn., Washington, 1971-72; exec. sec. Westinghouse Health System, Columbia, Md., 1972-76; adminstrv. group mgr. Price, Williams & Assocs., Silver Spring, Md., 1976-78; assoc. broker Merrill Lynch Realty, Silver Spring, 1977-81; pres. Pearl Properties, Silver Spring, 1982—. Organizer Peoples Nat. Party, Linstead, Jamaica, 1966; founding mem. Jamaica Nat. Assn., Washington, 1969, sec. 1969-73. Mem. Internat. Real Estate Fedn., Nat. Assn. Realtors, Md. Assn. Realtors, Cen. Md. Bd. Realtors, Northern Va. Bd. Realtors, Montgomery Bd. Realtors, Prince George Bd. Realtors, D.C. Bd. Realtors. Office: Pearl Properties 10110 Sutherland Rd Silver Spring MD 20901-2400

PHILLIPS, RICHARD RAYMOND, media consultant; b. N.Y.C., July 26, 1950; s. Anthony and Eleanor Filiberti; m. Wanda DiBenedetto, June 28, 1986. BA, NYU, 1972. Account exec. Ted Bates Advt., N.Y.C., 1972-77; exec. v.p. Brooks & Assocs., Greenwich, Conn., 1977-81; group dir. Newmark, Posner & Mitchell, N.Y.C., 1981-83; pres., chief exec. officer HP Corp. Communications, N.Y.C., 1983—; exec. cons. Deutsche Bank A.G., Frankfurt, Germany, 1984—, Mitsui Bank, Tokyo, 1985—, The Olayan Group, Athens, Greece, 1986—, Nat. Westminster Bank, 1990, CS Holding, Zurich, Switzerland, 1990, UN, N.Y.C., 1990, Nat. Westminster Bank PLC, London, 1990, German Econs. Ministry, 1991. Exec. cons. N.Y. Forum on Internat. Bus., N.Y.C., 1988-91. Republican. Roman Catholic. Office: HP Corp Comms Inc 184 5th Ave New York NY 10010-5908

PHILLIPS, ROBERT CHARLES, JR., music educator; b. Brockton, Mass., June 22, 1962; s. Robert Charles Phillips and Janice Elise (Dutra) Clark. Student, Musician's Inst., Hollywood, Calif. Musician New Eng., 1978—, poet, 1982—, tchr., 1984—. Author: (poetry) Sordid Pasts, Storied Future, 1988, Controlled Feedback, 1990. Home and Office: 165 Summer St Brockton MA 02402-3954

PHILLIPS, SARAH ANNE, association executive; b. Bethesda, Md., Feb. 21, 1965; d. John Stephen and Magdalene Anna (Riegler) P.; m. Jeffrey Robert Pellet, Aug. 5, 1989. AA, Dean Jr. Coll., Franklin, Mass., 1985; BA, Rutgers U., 1987. Intern Coleman & Pellet Inc., Union, N.J., 1987, intern coord., 1988; pub. affairs specialist Alliance of Am. Insurers, N.Y.C., 1988-89, sr. pub. affairs specialist, 1989-91, govt. affairs mgr., 1991—. Mem. Pub. Rels. Soc. Am. Office: Alliance of Am Insurers 305 Broadway New York NY 10007-1109

PHILLIPS, THERESA MARIE, educator, consultant; b. Greenport, N.Y., July 23, 1947; d. Harold David and Helen (Wilkonski) Gilson); m. Gregory Douglas Phillips, July 10, 1971; children: Andrew, Sarah. BS, SUNY, Oneonta, 1969, MS, 1974. Cert. tchr. N.Y.; cert. home economist. Tchr. Ellenville (N.Y.) Cen. Sch., 1969-70, Oneida (N.Y.) City Schs., 1970-71, 73—; cataloguer Peru (Ind.) Pub. Libr., 1971-73; tchr. supr. SUNY, Oneonta, 1974-78, 86; cons. N.Y. Dept. Edn., Albany, 1984—, curriculum writer, 1985-86, peer trainer, 1984-86, study circle facilitator trainer, 1990—; bd. dirs. Oneida Area Day care Ctr.; pilot tchr. N.Y. State Home and Career Skills Curriculum, 1984-86; evaluator and trainer Nutrition for Life Program, Cornell U., 1988-89. Co-author: Choosing a Marriage Partner, 1979; creator (video) Psyching Students, 1986; contbr. articles to profl. jours. Leader 4-H, Madison County, 1983—; vol. Madison County Red Cross, Oneida, 1991—; adivsor Future Homemakers Am., Oneida, 1982—; sponser Plan Internat., 1987—. Recipient Fabric Care Edn. award Clorox Co., 1987, Fire Prevention Edn. award Oneida Fire Dept., 1986, Contbn. to Community award Oneida Police Dept., 1988; named Outstanding Consumer Educator Nat. Coalition Consumer Edn., 1991. Mem. ASCD, Am. Home Econs. Assn. (regional bd. mem. 1987, N.Y. State Tchr. Yr. award 1986), Am. Vocat. Assn., Home Econs. Edn. Assn., N.Y. State Home Econs. tchrs. Assn. (coord. of yr. 1982), N.Y. State Occupational Edn. Assn., Madison County Hist. Soc. Office: Oneida City Schs Markell Dr Wampsville NY 13163-9999

PHILLIPS, WARREN HENRY, publishing company director; b. June 28, 1926; s. Abraham and Juliette (Rosenberg) P.; m. Barbara Anne Thomas, June 16, 1951; children: Lisa, Leslie, Nina. AB, Queens Coll., 1947, LHD

(hon.), 1987; JD (hon.), U. Portland, 1973; LHD (hon.), Pace U., 1982, L.I. U., 1987. Copyreader Wall St. Jour., 1947-48; fgn. corr. Wall St. Jour., Germany, 1949-50; chief London Bur., 1950-51, fgn. editor, 1951-53, news editor, 1953-54, mng. editor Midwest edit., 1954-57, mng. editor, 1957-65; exec. editor Dow Jones & Co., 1965-70, v.p., gen. mgr., 1970-71, exec. v.p., 1972, editorial dir., 1971-88, pres., 1972-79, chief exec. officer, 1975-90, chmn. bd., 1978-91, also bd. dirs., 1972—; pub. Wall Street Journal, 1975-88; bd. dirs. Pub. Broadcasting Svc., 1991—; copyreader Stars & Stripes European edit., 1949; pres. Am. Coun. Edn. for Journalism, 1971-73; mem. Pulitzer Prizes Bd., 1977-87. Author: (with Robert Keatley) China: Behind the Mask, 1973. Trustee Columbia U., 1980—; mem. vis. com. Kennedy Sch. Govt., Harvard U., 1984-90, 92—; mem. corp. adv. bd. Queens Coll., 1986-90, found. bd. dirs., 1990—. Named one of Ten Outstanding Young Men in U.S. U.S. Jaycees, 1958; inducted into the Info. Industry Assn's. Hall of Fame, 1984. Mem. Am. Newspaper Pubs. Assn. (bd. dirs. 1976-84), Am. Soc. Newspaper Editors (pres. 1975-76), Bridgehampton Club, River Club. Office: Dow Jones & Co Inc 200 Liberty St New York NY 10281

PHILLIPS, WILLIAM ROBERT, fluid dynamics educator; b. Adelaide, Australia, Apr. 14, 1948; came to U.S., 1986; s. Robert Ray and Eileen Marjorie (Richter) P. BE with honours, Adelaide U., 1970; MEng, McGill U., Montreal, Que., Can., 1974; PhD, Cambridge (Eng.) U., 1978. Rsch. engr. Mt. Isa Mines Ltd., Queensland, Australia, 1971-73; rsch. assoc. McGill U., 1975; lectr. Nat. U. Singapore, 1979-81, sr. lectr., 1981-84; sr. rsch. fellow U. Melbourne, Australia, 1984-85; vis. scientist Cornell U., Ithaca, N.Y., 1986, assoc. vis. prof., 1987-89; assoc. prof. fluid dynamics Clarkson U., Potsdam, N.Y., 1989—. Contbr. numerous articles to sci. jours. Commonwealth U. scholar Govt. of Australia, 1966-70, scholar Nat. Coun. Can., 1974-75; Rolls Royce rsch. fellow Churchill Coll., Cambridge, 1975-78; grantee NSF, 1990-93. Mem. Soc. for Indsl. and Applied Math., Am. Phys. Soc., Sigma Xi. Home: Riggs Dr Box 133 Hannawa Falls NY 13647 Office: Clarkson U 209W Old Main Potsdam NY 13676

PHILO, ERIC SCOTT, financial analyst; b. West Point, N.Y., Aug. 27, 1957; s. Ora Carlton Philo and Francine (Hoberman) Pennimpede; m. Denise Anne Gleason, June 6, 1987. BBA, George Washington U., 1979; MBA, Columbia U., 1983. Chartered fin. analyst. Security analyst Goldman, Sachs & Co., N.Y.C., 1983-87, v.p., media analyst, 1987—. Mem. Assn. for Investment Mgmt. and Rsch.

PHILPOT, WILLIAM DOUGLAS, remote sensing specialist; b. Seattle, Sept. 25, 1947; s. Ernest Wesley and Carrie Mae (Grobmyer) P.; m. Janette Marie Kelly, June 19, 1982; children: David, Brian, Tonya. BA in Music, NYU, 1969; BS in Physics, SUNY, Stony Brook, 1973; MS in Marine Studies, U. Del., 1978, PhD in Marine Studies, 1981. Rsch. asst. marine studies U. Del., Newark, 1973-77; rsch. assoc. Nat. Acad. Scis. (CORSPERS)ú, Washington, 1977; rsch. asst. Coll. Marine Studies, U. Del., Newark, 1978-81; asst. prof. Remote Sensing Program Cornell U., Ithaca, N.Y., 1981-83, rsch. assoc. III, 1983-84, asst. prof. CEE, 1984-90, assoc. prof., 1990—; cons. U.S. Army C.E., Vicksburg, Miss., 1985—; program leader Cornell Lab. for Environ. Applications of Remote Sensing, Ithaca, 1990—. With U.S. Army, 1969-71. Mem. IEEE Geosci. of Remote Sensing, Am. Soc. Photogrammetry and Remote Sensing (pres. N.Y. chpt. 1987-88), Oceanographic Soc., Sigma Xi. Office: Cornell U CLEARS Hollister Hall Ithaca NY 14853

PHILPS, WILLIAM GEORGE, investment banker; b. Toronto, July 28, 1959; came to U.S., 1990; s. Norman Edward and Blanche Honora Philps; m. Pamela A. Valentine, Nov. 5, 1988. B of Commerce, U. Toronto, 1982; MBA, Harvard U., 1986. Internal auditor Imasco Ltd., Toronto, 1982-84; assoc. Wood Gundy Inc., Toronto, 1986-89, v.p., 1989-90; v.p. State St. Bank and Trust Co., Boston, 1991—.

PHINNEY, JOHN FLAGG, financial analyst, surety executive; b. Boston, Jan. 25, 1956; s. Frederick Warren and Eleanor (Sanburn) P. AB, Grinnell (Iowa) Coll., 1978. Field surety underwriter Seaboard Surety, Chgo., 1979-81; surety underwriter Seaboard Surety, N.Y.C., 1982-86, sr. underwriter, 1986-88; sr. underwriting mgr. Am. Internat. Cos., N.Y.C., 1988-91, divisional v.p., 1991—. Mem. Chgo. Child Care Soc., 1980—. Mem. New Eng. Soc. Bklyn., Casualty and Surety Club. Episcopalian. Home: 10 Schemerhorn St Brooklyn Heights NY 11201 Office: Am Internat Cos Bond Div 70 Pine St Brooklyn NY 11208-1631

PHOCAS, GEORGE JOHN, international lawyer, business executive; b. N.Y.C., Dec. 1, 1927; m. Katrin Gorny, Feb. 26, 1966; 1 child, George Alexander. A.B., U. Chgo., 1950, J.D., 1953. Bar: N.Y. 1955, U.S. Supreme Ct. 1962. Assoc. Sullivan & Cromwell, N.Y.C., 1953-56; counsel Creole Petroleum Corp., Caracas, Venezuela, 1956-60; internat. negotiator Standard Oil Co. N.J. (Exxon), 1960-63; sr. ptnr. Casey, Lane & Mittendorf, London, 1963-72, counsel, 1972-76; exec. v.p. Occidental Petroleumm Corp., Los Angeles, 1972-74; adv., U.S. del. UN, ECAFE, Teheran, 1963. Trustee Assn. Naval Aviation, Washington, Owl's Head Aviation Mus., Maine; mem. vis. bd. U. Chgo. Law Sch.; bd. visitors U. Chgo. Law Sch. Capt. U.S. Army. Mem. Law Soc. London, Brit. Inst. Comparative Law, Am. Soc. Internat. Law, ABA, Assn. Bar City N.Y. Clubs: Boodles (London); Metropolitan (N.Y.C.); Sleepy Hollow. Home: 5020 Goodridge Ave Riverdale NY 10471-2913 also: 28 Aubrey Walk, London W87JG, England

PHOENIX, DAVID WILLIAM, engineer; b. Bridgeport, Conn., Oct. 20, 1945; s. Harold Whitney and Arlene Mary (Chalfa) P.; m. Claudia Lee Swanson, Nov. 1, 1973. Student, U. Bridgeport, 1963-64, Johnson State Coll., 1964-67. Inventor scribe wheel retainer. Republican. Home: 64 Main St Southbridge MA 01550-2521 Office: Contract Resources Corp 118 Forest Ave Hudson MA 01749-2800

PIANTADOSI, SHEILA HELENA, infosystems specialist; b. Pawtucket, R.I., May 24, 1959; d. Edward and Helen Catherine (Skorupa) Jachym; m. Thomas Joseph Piantadosi, Sept. 17, 1983; children: Anthony Edward, Stephanie Lynn. BA, R.I. Coll., 1981. Sr. programmer/analyst Meml. Hosp. R.I., Pawtucket, 1979-89; merchandising rep. The Hoover Co., Framingham, Mass., 1989—. Mem. ASPCA. Home: 9 Castle Gate Rd Cumberland RI 02864-5607 Office: The Hoover Co 211 Cochituate Rd Framingham MA 01701-4635

PIASECKI, RICHARD LEO, software engineer; b. Nanticoke, Pa., Jan. 4, 1954; s. Leo Michael and Celia Marie (Blockus) P.; children: Matthew, Katherine. AS in Elec. Engring., Penn State, 1973; BS in Elec. Engring., Lafayette Coll., 1980; MS in Elec. Engring., Lehigh U., 1984. Tech. staff AT&T Bell Labs., Allentown, Pa., 1973—. Mem. IEEE, Eta Kappa Nu, Tau Beta Pi. Office: AT&T Bell Laboratories 1247 S Cedar Crest Blvd Allentown PA 18103

PIASZCZYK, CHRISTOPHER MARK, engineer; b. Paslek, Poland, June 25, 1953; came to U.S., 1978; s. Edward Piaszczyk and Maria (Ostaszewska) Jorga; m. Anna Grace Gorski, Aug. 28, 1978. MS, BS, Warsaw (Poland) Polytech. Inst, 1976; PhD, N.Y. Polytech. Inst., 1983. Registered profl. engr., N.Y. Engr. Am. Bur. Shipping, N.Y.C., 1981-85; program mgr. Grumman Aerospace Corp., Bethpage, N.Y., 1985—. Contbr. articles to profl. jours. Mem. AIAA, ASME, SNAME.

PICARD, DENNIS J., electronics company executive; b. 1932. BBA, Northeastern Univ., 1962. With RCA, 1954-55; elec. engr. Raytheon Co., 1955-59, design engr., 1959-61, sect. mgr., 1961-69, dir. equipment div., data acquisition systems directorate, 1969-76, asst. gen. mgr. ops., equipment div., 1976-77, asst. gen. mgr. ops., equipment div., also corp. v.p., 1977-81, v.p. equipment div., 1981-1985, sr. v.p., gen. mgr. missile systems div., 1985-89, pres., 1989-90, chmn. bd., CEO, 1990—, also bd. dirs. Served USAF 1951-53. Mem. NAE. Office: Raytheon Co 141 Spring St Lexington MA 02173*

PICARD, RICHARD HENRY, physicist; b. Springfield, Mass., Aug. 26, 1938; s. Edmond John and Helene Marie-Rose (Dupuis) P.; m. Katherine Ann Laucks, Jan. 28, 1967; children: Steven, Nicole. BA, Assumption Coll., 1959; MA, Boston U., 1962, PhD, 1968. Physicist Air Force Cambridge Rsch. Labs., Bedford, Mass., 1964-75, Rome Air Devel. Ctr., Bedford, 1976-81, Air Force Geophysics Lab., Bedford, 1981-90; physicist Geophysics Directorate Phillips Lab., Bedford, 1990—; vis. prof. Tufts U., Medford, Mass., 1985—; advisor postdoctoral fellowship program NRC, Bedford, 1988—. Author: (chpt.) The Aurora, 1985; patentee in field; contbr. articles to profl. jours. Com. chmn., leader Boy Scouts Am., Bedford, 1975-81; pres., mem. com. Patrons of Music Students, Bedford, 1985-88. NSF fellow Boston U., 1961-64, scholar Optical Soc. of Am., 1963-64. Mem. Am. Geophys. Union, European Geophys. Soc., Optical Soc. Am., Am. Phys. Soc., Sigma Xi (chpt. sec. Hanscom AFB, Mass., 1978-80). Home: 11 Sherwood Dr Bedford MA 01730-1318 Office: Phillips Lab Geophysics Directorate PL/GPOS Hanscom AFB Bedford MA 01731

PICARO, GARY W., sales engineer; b. Worcester, Mass., Apr. 20, 1950; s. Alvin G. and Mary E. (Simonds) P. ASEE, Worcester Jr. Coll., 1970. Salesman automotive parts Park Ave Dist., Worcester, 1972-78; sales coord. PDN/Pace, Worcester, 1978-85; sales engr. BiJur Lubricating, Bennington, Vt., 1985-89; sales rep. GP Industries, Spencer, Mass., 1989-90; sales engr. The Hope Group, Northboro, Mass., 1990-91, Staubli Corp., Duncan, S.C., 1991—. Home: 62 Pumpkin Ln Charlton MA 01507

PICCIANO, LANA PATRICIA, artist, abstract oil painter; b. Evanston, Ill., Nov. 5, 1946; d. Louis Francis and Lucille Aida (Del Guercio) Raymond; m. Anthony Joseph Picciano, Sept. 6, 1971 (dec. Jan. 4, 1991); 1 child, Christine Abygail. BA, Bloomfield Coll., 1969; postgrad., Rutgers Grad. Sch. Fine Arts, 1979. Pub. rels. chmn. Artists Equity of N.J., 1979-81; fin. chmn. Nat. Assn. Women Artists, N.Y.C., 1987-89. Named Best in D.C. Slide Registry, 1982; grantee Ford Found., 1974. Mem. Artists Equity of N.Y., Nat. Assn. Women Artists, Artists Equity of N.J., Cambridge Art Assn., Framingham Artist Guild. Roman Catholic. Home: 8 Porpoise Dr Centereach NY 11720-3039

PICCININNO, GREGORY LOUIS, company executive; b. Paterson, N.J., May 11, 1965; s. Louis and Pauline (Singelakis) P. BSBA, Northeastern U., 1988; student, London Bus Sch., 1992—. Dir. mktg. Trans-Natural Rsch. Corp., South Orange, N.J., 1990—; pres. Louis Benjamin Inc., Ringwood, 1988—. Am. Field Svc. scholar, 1982. Mem. Beta Gamma Sigma, Phi Sigma Kappa. Home: 591 Stonetown Rd Ringwood NJ 07456-1324 Office: Trans-Nat Rsch Corp 15 Village Plz South Orange NJ 07079-2813

PICCOLO, JOSEPH ANTHONY, university administrator; b. Phila., Aug. 1, 1953; s. Rudolph and Mary C. (Mellela) P.; m. Elizabeth J. Mullarkey, Mar. 24, 1984; children: Mary E., Sarah C., Theresa N. BA, U. Pa., 1975; MBA, LaSalle U., 1992. Mgr. health sci. store U. Pa., Phila., 1973-76; mgr. univ. store Hahnemann U., Phila., 1976-86, dep. chmn. fin. and adminstrn. dept. pathology/lab. medicine, 1986—; v.p. Hahnemann Found. Pathology, Phila., 1986—. Author: (with others): Health Science Store Manual, 1985. Mem. Med. Group Mgmt. Assn., Am. Mgmt. Assn., Hahnemann Found. Pathology Assocs. Inc. (v.p., treas. 1986—). Republican. Roman Catholic. Office: Hahnemann U Dept Pathology Broad and Vine Sts Philadelphia PA 19102

PICCOLO, PHILIP JOSEPH, school system administrator; b. Bklyn., Mar. 9, 1942; s. Felix J. and Mary (Dale) P.; m. Sally A. Bungay, July 15, 1959; children: Mary, Glorinda, Josephine, Theresa, Philip Jr., Sally, Angela. AA magna cum laude, Middlesex County Coll., 1983; BA in Psychology magna cum laude, Kean Coll., 1988, MA in Ednl. Adminstrn., 1991. Cert. sch. bus. adminstr., N.J. Mgr. Am. Investment Co., St. Louis, 1963-74; owner Angela's Italian Restaurant, Morgan, N.J., 1974-79; foreman Old Bridge (N.J.) Bd. Edn., 1979-81; foreman Marlboro (N.J.) Bd. Edn., 1981-87, supr., 1987—; cons. Univ. Med. and Dentistry N.J., Piscataway, 1989—, N.J. Assn. Sch. Adminstrs., Trenton, N.J., 1990, N.J. Assn. Sch. Bus. Ofcls., Bordentown, 1990, The Mgmt. Inst. Glassboro (N.J.) State Coll., various N.J. sch. dists. Contbr. articles to profl. jours. Pres. Mid Madison Girls Softball League, Laurence Harbor, N.J., 1976-79; mem. exec. bd., mgr. Laurence Harbor Little League, 1977-79. Mem. Am. Soc. Safety Engrs., Nat. Fire Protection Assn., N.J. Assn. Designated Persons (1st v.p., now pres.), Phi Kappa Phi (hon. cert.), Alpha Sigma Lambda (hon. cert.). Roman Catholic. Office: Marlboro Bd Edn 1980 Township Dr Marlboro NJ 07746-2298

PICHARDIE, JACQUES CHRISTIAN MARCEL, management executive, hotel consultant; b. Ménestérol, France, Apr. 18, 1940; came to U.S., 1965; s. Léonce Marcel Pichardie and Élodie (Courcelle) Boutin; m. Jeannine Cardoit, Oct. 10, 1960 (div. 1974); children: Béatrice, Nathalie; m. Youmna Takieddine, July 4, 1977. Student, Coll. Moderne, 1952-56, Ecole Hôteliére, 1956-59. Cert. Hotel Adminstr., Mich., 1984; lic. Real Estate Agent, N.H., 1989. Restaurant mgr. Le Parloir d'Eiffel, San Francisco, 1969-70; asst. food and beverage dir. Fairmont Hotel, New Orleans, 1970-72; gen. mgr. Holidy Inns, Inc., Memphis, 1972-76; dir. gen. Hôtel Méridien, Paris, 1976-77; pres. Emir Hotel Mgmt. Co., United Arab Emirates, 1977-81; v.p. corp. food and beverages Ramada Inns, Inc., Phoenix, 1981-84; v.p. Hospitality Assoc., Manchester, N.H., 1984-86, Great Bay Hotels, Inc., Boston, 1986-87; pres. Euro Mgmt. Co. Ltd., Londonderry, N.H., 1987—; pres. Aries Recruiters, Inc., Londonderry, 1987—, Aries Motor Inn, Inc., Gorham, N.H., 1988—, Granite State Hotel Corp., Londonderry, 1989, Cress Motel, Inc., Rochester, N.H., 1990—. Bicentennial participant French Ministry Tourism, 1989. Sgt. French Air Force, 1959-62. Recipient Appreciation award New Orleans Food Festival, 1971, Food Mgmt. award State of Minn. Dept. Edn., 1974; named Dep. Criminal Sheriff, State of La., 1971. Mem. Am. Hotel and Motel Assn., N.H. hospitality Assn. (bd. dirs. 1991). Office: Euro Mgmt Co Ltd 80 Neshus Rd Bldg A 80 Nashua Rd Bldg A Londonderry NH 03053-3426

PICHER, JOHN WILLIAM, state official; b. Waterville, Maine, Feb. 16, 1944; s. Norman Lionel and Lorette Blanche (Loubier) P.; m. Charlotte Marie Houle, June 19, 1965; children: Michael William, Susan Lynn, Jennifer Jo, William John. Student, U. Maine, 1963-65. Engring. technician Maine Dept. Transp., Augusta, 1965-75; supr. community svcs. Maine Bur. Parks and Recreation, Augusta, 1975-87; mgr. community pks. & recreation, Office Comprehensive Planning, Maine Dept. Econ. and Community Devel., Augusta, 1987-92; supr. fed. aid Maine Bur. Parks and Recreation, Augusta, 1992—; agy. staff Maine Land for Maine's Future Bd., Augusta, 1988—; mem. Cardiovascular Health Coun.-Fitness Task Force, Augusta, 1991—. Author, editor: (state report) Recreation, Parks & Open Space, 1990, (computer application) Recreation Management System, 1990, (handbook and tech. assistance materials) Community Recreation Handbook, 1989. Pres. Parent-Tchr. Orgn.-Farrington, Augusta, 1977-78; mem. Augusta (Maine) Bd. Edn., 1984-86. Mem. Nat. Assn. State Outdoor Recreation Liaison Officers, Nat. Recreation & Parks Assn., Maine Recreation and Parks Assn. (chair scholarship com. 1990—), Capitol City and Rifle Club (pres. 1976), Natanis Golf Club. Roman Catholic. Home: 53 Hutchinson Dr Augusta ME 04330-6622 Office: Maine Bur Parks-Recreation State House Sta 22 Augusta ME 04333

PICHINI, GUIDO MICHAEL, security company executive, mayor; b. Reading, Pa., Oct. 13, 1952; s. Quido and Anna V.J. (Lojec) P.; m. Susan Beth Nunemacher, Aug. 24, 1975. BS, Kutztown U., 1974, postgrad., 1974-77; postgrad., Wilson Coll., Chambersburg, Pa., 1980. Tchr. Wyomissing (Pa.) Sch. Dist., 1974-75; sgt. West Lawn (Pa.) Police Dept., 1974-82; instr. Reading Area Community Coll., 1975; dir. security Pagerly Detective Agy., Wernersville, Pa., 1983, Manpower Inc. Reading, 1984-86; detective Berks County Dist. Atty.'s Office, Reading, 1984-91; v.p., chief operating officer Security Guards, Inc., Wyomissing, 1986—, also bd. dirs. Councilman Borough of Wyomissing Hills, 1978-86, mayor, 1986—; mem. Rep. Nat. Com. Recipient 3 commendations Borough of West Lawn, 1980, Key award Lions Club, 1981, Red Triangle award YMCA, 1980. Mem. Nat. Assn. Police Chiefs, Southeastern Pa. Police Chiefs Assn., Am. Soc. Indusl. Sec. (chmn. Schuylkill Valley chpt. 1992), U.S. Bus. Assn., Berks County Narcotics Info. Ctr., Pa. Mayors assn., Berks County Mayors Assn. (pres. 1988). Roman Catholic. Home: 24 Upland Rd Wyomissing Hills PA 19609 Office: Security Guards Inc 600 Park Rd N Wyomissing PA 19610

PICILLO, BUD JOHN, educational association administrator; b. Newark, Aug. 27, 1931; s. William G. and Mary Rose (Brunello) P.; m. Joan Frances Brady, Aug. 22, 1959; children: Kurt, Natalee, Philip, Mark, Gregg, Ross, Kelli, Budd, Gail. BBA, Upsala Coll., 1954; JD, Rutgers U., 1971. Lectr. Upsala Coll., East Orange, N.J., 1954-57; freelance ins. broker Livingston, N.J., 1957-59; tax asst. Montclair (N.J.) Nat. Bank and Trust Co., 1959-61; edn. adminstr. N.J. Inst. for Continuing Legal Edn., Newark and New Brunswick, N.J., 1961—; bd. dirs. para-legal div. Montclair Coll., 1988—, Fairleigh Dickinson U., Madison, N.J., 1989—. Editor: New Jersey Family Law Practice, 1964, Collection Practice, 1965, Estate Planning and Probate Practice in N.J., 1966. Executive v.p. Madison Unico, 1990-91. Mem. ABA, N.J. Bar Assn., Morris County Bar Assn., Non-Profit Mailers Fedn. (bd. dirs. Washington chpt. 1987—). Roman Catholic. Office: New Jersey Inst Continuing Legal Edn One Constitution Sq New Brunswick NJ 08901

PICK, ROBERT YEHUDA, orthopedic surgeon, consultant; b. Haifa, Israel, Dec. 24, 1945; came to U.S., 1957; s. Andre B. and Hanna (Gross) P.; m. Roni L. Kestenbaum, Sept. 25, 1977; children: Benjamin A., Joseph E., Jennifer L., Abigail I. BA, B in Hebrew Lit., Yeshiva U., 1967; MD, Albert Einstein Coll. Med., 1971; MPH, Harvard U., 1979. Diplomate Nat. Bd. Med. Examiners, Am. Bd. Orthopaedic Surgery. Intern Brookdale Hosp., Bklyn., 1971-72; resident in orthopedic surgery Albert Einstein-Bronx (N.Y.) Mcpl. Hosp. Ctr., 1972-74; resident in orthopedic surgery USPHS Hosp., Staten Island, N.Y., 1974-75, asst. chief orthopedic surgery, 1975-77; asst. chief orthopedic surgery USPHS Hosp., Boston, 1977-78; fellow orthopedic trauma Boston City Hosp., 1979-80, assoc. dir. orthopedic surgery, 1980-84, dir. pediatric orthopedics, 1981-83; practice medicine specializing in orthopedic surgery Newton Ctr., Mass., 1984—; instr. orthopedic surgery Boston U., 1980-82, asst. prof., 1982—; adj. asst. prof. health scis. and orthopedics Touro Coll., N.Y.C., 1976-78; dir. spinal screening program Dept. Health and Hosps., Boston, 1979-82; dist. med. advisor U.S. Dept. Labor, Boston, 1984—; cons. Boston Retirement Bd., 1983-84, New Eng. Telephone, Boston, 1985—, Commonwealth of Mass. Pub. Employee Retirement Adminstrn., Boston, 1985-90. Contbr. articles on med. issues to profl. jours. Trustee Young Israel Jackson Heights, Queens, N.Y., 1969-76, pres., 1976-77; sec. Young Israel Brookline, Mass., 1978-79; trustee Maimonides Sch., Brookline, 1990—. Served to lt. comdr. USPHS, 1975-78. Fellow Am. Acad. Orthopedic Surgeons; mem. Am. Physicians Fellowship for Medicine in Israel (trustee 1975—, exec. com. 1976—, asst. treas. 1987-90, treas. 1990—, Man of Yr. award 1977), Nat. Inst. Occupational Safety and Health (traineeship 1978-79), Mensa.

PICKARD, FRANKLIN GEORGE THOMAS, engineering company executive; b. Sudbury, Ont., Can., Sept. 10, 1933; s. Chester William and Margaret Christine (Downes) P.; m. Audrey Elaine Bull, Apr. 27, 1967; children: Barbara, Beverly. BA, Queen's U., Kingston, Ont., 1958. With Falconbridge Ltd., Toronto, Ont., 1957—, concentrator supt., 1967-75, chief metall. engr., 1975-82, v.p., 1982-89, sr. v.p., 1989-90, pres., chief exec. officer, 1991—; also, bd. dirs.; pres. Lakefield Rsch. Can., Ltd., Toronto, 1982—; bd. dirs. Falconbridge Nikkelwerk S.A. (Norway), Falconbridge Dominicane CporA (Dominican Republic), Falconbridge Corp., Toronto. Mem. AIME, Can. Inst. Mining and Metall. Engrs., Mining Assn. Can. (bd. dirs.), Assn. Profl. Engrs. Ont., Nickel Devel. Inst. (bd. dirs., chmn. 1988-90), Ont. Club, Spring Lakes Golf Club, Keoweekey Golf & Country Club. Office: Falconbridge Ltd, 95 Wellington St W Ste 1200, Toronto, ON Canada M5L 2V4

PICKER, LESTER ALAN, consultant; b. Bklyn., Oct. 24, 1947; s. Martin and Bertha (Javer) P.; m. Lois Ruth Borst, Apr. 21, 1967 (div. 1983); children: Jennifer Lynne, Matthew Alan; m. Judith Ann Cobley, Dec. 29, 1984; stepchildren: Christina, Neil. BA, CCNY, 1969; MEd, U. Maine, 1975, EdD, 1978. Tchr. biology Rockland (Maine) Dist. High Sch., 1969-75; teaching asst. U. Maine, Orono, 1975-77, mem. faculty, 1977-78; mem. faculty U. Del., Newark, 1979-85; dir. Marine Resources Ctr., Manteo, N.C., 1978-79; pres., cons. Pyramid Assocs., Inc., Elkton, Md., 1985—. Author: Winter Environmental Studies, 1989; columnist Non-Profits, Inc., 1991, The Baltimore Sun; conbr. over 200 articles to gen. mags. and profl. jours. Grantee NOAA, 1979, 80, 81, DOE, 79, NSF, 1984. Mem. Nat. Marine Educators Assn. (Award of Pres. 1981, 82). Home: 71 Bathon Cir Elkton MD 21921-3610 Office: Pyramid Assocs Inc 71 Bathon Cir Elkton MD 21921-3610

PICKETT, RUSSELL STOUT, data processing executive; b. Wilmington, Del., Oct. 29, 1951; s. John Ernest Jr. and Emma Virginia (Stout) P.; m. Diane Sue Collison, Nov. 6, 1971 (div.); children: Christopher Scott, Ryan Mark. Grad. high sch. Computer operator State of Del., Dover, 1969-73, programmer, 1973-80, systems programmer, 1980-87, project leader, 1987—. Big bro. Big Bros. of Del., Dover, 1973-75; v.p. Cheswold (Del.) Vol. Fire Co., 1972—, ambulance chief, sec. Democrat. Baptist. Home: RR 8 Box 744 Dover DE 19901-1823 Office: Office of Info Systems 801 Silver Lake Blvd Dover DE 19901-2407

PICKETT, STEWARD T. A., ecologist; b. Louisville, Nov. 30, 1950; s. Steward T.A. and Barbara Lee (Lockett) P. BS with honors, U. Ky., Lexington, 1972; PhD, U. Ill., 1977. Asst. prof. Rutgers U., New Brunswick, N.J., 1977-82, assoc. prof., 1982-86; mem. grad. ecology faculty Rutgers U., 1977—; dir. Hutcheson Meml. Forest Ctr. Rutgers U., New Brunswick, N.J., 1984-86; assoc. scientist Inst. Ecosystem Studies, Millbrook, N.Y., 1987-90; scientist Inst. Ecoystem Studies, Millbrook, N.Y., 1990—; adj. prof. U. Conn., 1989—. Co-editor: Ecology of Natural Disturbance and Patch Dynamics, 1985, Ecological Heterogeneity, 1991. Fellow AAAS; mem. Ecol. Soc. Am. (coun. 1988-91), Internat. Assn. Vegetation Sci. (coun. 1989—), Am. Soc. Naturalists, Am. Inst. Biol. Scis., Brit. Ecol. Soc. Office: Inst Ecosystem Studies Box AB Millbrook NY 12545

PICKHARDT, CARL EMILE, JR., artist; b. Westwood, Mass., May 28, 1908; s. Carl Emile and Louise (Fowler) P.; m. Marjorie Sachs, June 15, 1935 (div. 1952); children: Nancy Louise Arnold, Carl Emile III, Sally Anne Duncan; m. Rosamond Forbes Wyman, Mar. 28, 1953. BA, Harvard U., 1931; studied with Harold Zimmerman, 1931-37. Tchr. Fitchburg Art Mus., 1951-62, Worcester Mus. Sch., 1949-50, Sturbridge Art Sch., 1952-60. Author: Portfolio of Etchings, 1942; one-man shows, Berkshire Art Mus., 1941, Doris Meltzer Gallery, N.Y.C., 1961, 68, 70, 71, 72, Jacques Seligmann Gallery, N.Y.C., 1935, 51, 52, 54, Stuart Gallery, Boston, 1946, Margaret Brown Gallery, Boston, 1951, Fitchburg Art Mus., 1951, 91, Lawrence Gallery, Kansas City, Mo., 1955, Artek Gallery, Helsinki, Finland, 1959, Laguna Gloria Art Mus., Austin, Tex., 1966, Radcliffe Coll., 1983, Providence Art Club, 1986, Fitchburg Art Mus., 1991; exhibited in group shows at Carnegie Internat., 1951, Mus. Modern Art, N.Y.C., 1940, 63, 64, Whitney Mus., 1936, Nat. Acad., 1942, 49, Boston Inst. Contemporary Art, 1941, Internat. Exhbn., Japan., 1952, Exhbn. Am. Drawings, France, 1955, Art Inst. Chgo., Calif. Palace of Legion of Honor, 1953, Boston Arts Festival, 1950, Am. Drawing Biennial, Norfolk, 1964, Pa. Acad. Fine Arts, 1968, Laguna Gloria Art Mus., 1973, Fitchburg Art Mus., 1974, 91; represented in permanent collections, Mus. Modern Art, N.Y.C., Boston Mus. Fine Arts, Bklyn. Art Mus., Worcester Art Mus., Library of Congress, N.Y. Pub. Library, Newark Art Mus., Fogg Art Mus., Addison Gallery, Finch Coll. Art Mus., Pa. Acad. Fine Atrs, Boston Pub. Library, Fitchburg Art Mus., Wadsworth Athenaeum, De Cordova Mus. Served with USNR, 1942-45. Ford Found. and Am. Fedn. Arts artist-in-residence Laguna Gloria Art Mus. 1966; recipient Shope prize Nat. Acad. 1942. Address: 66 Forest St Sherborn MA 01770

PICKRON, CARLTON, academic administrator, director academic advising; b. Phila., July 31, 1957; s. Shirley (Smith) Simmons; m. Lisa Ann Coletta, June 7, 1980; children: Charisse Burgundy, Marita Joy. BS, Springfield (Mass.) Coll., 1979, MEd and cert. of advanced study, 1982; EdD, U. Mass., 1991. Nat. cert. counselor. Assoc. phys. dir. Nat. Capital YMCA, Washington, 1978-79, dir. aquatics and spl. programs, 1979-80; counseling coord. Westfield (Mass.) State Coll., 1983-89, asst. to pres., 1989-90, assoc. dean acad. affairs, dir. acad. advising, 1990—. Pole worker Jackson for Pres., Springfield, 1984, 88; vol. Jordan Team, Springfield, 1986, Rainbow Coalition, Amherst, Mass., 1989. Recipient Adminstrv. Merit award Westfield State Coll., 1986, 88, Citation for Outstanding Performance award Commonwealth of Mass., 1989. Mem. Assn. for Multi-Cultural Counseling and Devel., Coun. Minority Educators, Omega Psi Phi. Baptist. Home: 18 Greenwich Rd Amherst MA 01002-3221 Office: Westfield State Coll Western Ave Westfield MA 01085-2502

PICONE, ANTHONY JOSEPH, building contractor; b. Buffalo, N.Y., Sept. 9, 1944; s. Anthony Frank and Anna Marie (D'Anna) P.; m. Judith

Anne Schultz, Sept. 18, 1965; children: Julie Marie, Anthony Charles, Christopher Michael. AAS, Erie County Technical Inst., Buffalo, 1965. Field supr. Picone Constrn. Corp., Buffalo, 1965-70, estimator, 1970-77, pres., chief exec. officer, 1978-81; v.p., chief exec. officer Clarence Assoc. Inc., Buffalo, 1982—; pres. Towne Edge Devel. Group, Inc., Buffalo, 1990—. Mem. Associated Gen. Contractors Am., Gen. Bldg. Contractors N.Y. State, Constrn. Industries Employees Assn., Builders Exch. Buffalo, Transit Valley Country Club. Office: Clarence Assocs Inc 8680 Main St Buffalo NY 14221

PICONE, FRANCES JEAN, gerontologist; b. Bklyn., Dec. 14, 1940; d. Joseph and Frances (Beneduce) P. BA in Psychology, St. Francis Coll., Bklyn., 1971; MS in Edn., L.I. U., 1974; MA in Gerontology, U. Mich., 1978; postgrad., Hunter Coll., Brookvale, N.Y., 1989. Tchr. Holy Rosary Sch., Bklyn., 1963-73; sci. coord. Office of Cath. Edn., Bklyn., 1973-77; dir. of retirement Sisters of Mercy, Bklyn., 1978-86; dir. of sr. housing Cath. Charities, Bklyn., 1986-88; BORO field specialist in aging Bklyn. Cath. Charities, 1988—; sci. cons. Rand McNally, 1970-80, MacMillan Publ., 1984-86, 90—; adj. instr. St. Joseph Coll., Bklyn., 1978-86, Turo Coll., Bklyn., 1986—; mem. Diocese Bklyn. Commn. on Elderly, 1990—. Co-editor nat. newsletter Berakah, 1979-83. Chairperson Nat. Conf. on Aging, 1984. Grantee U. Colo. 1974; recipient Mendelian award Cath. Sci. Coun. 1976. Mem. Nat. Coun. on Aging, N.Y. State Intergenerations Conv. (regional cochair region II N.Y.C. Intergenerational Program), N.Y. State Intergenerational Network, Phi Kappa Phi. Home: 4914 Avenue M Brooklyn NY 11234-3727 Office: Catholic Charities 191 Joralemon St Brooklyn NY 11201-4353

PIDGEON, JOHN ANDERSON, headmaster; b. Lawrence, Mass., Dec. 20, 1924; s. Alfred H. and Nora (Regan) P.; children: John Anderson, Regan S., Kelly; m. Barbara Hafer, May 1986. Grad., Phillips Acad., 1943; B.A., Bowdoin Coll., 1949; Ed.D., Bethany Coll., 1973; D.Litt., Washington and Jefferson Coll., 1979. Instr. Latin, adminstrv. asst. to headmaster Deerfield Acad., 1949-57; headmaster Kiskiminetas Springs Sch., Saltsburg, Pa., 1957—; dir. Saltsburg Savs. & Trust. Served as ensign USNR, 1943-46. Mem. New Eng. Swimming Coaches Assn. (pres. 1956-57), Cum Laude Soc., Delta Upsilon. Home and Office: Kiskiminetas Springs Sch Saltsburg PA 15681

PIDGEON, WALTER PAUL, JR., organization executive; b. Drexel Hill, Pa., Oct. 23, 1942; s. Walter Paul and Lucille (Robinson) P.; m. Susan Wallace, June 28, 1969; children: Walter Paul III, Spencer. BA, Salem Coll., 1965; postgrad., Union Grad. Sch., 1989. Dist. exec. Boy Scouts Am., Reading, Pa., 1965-66, Long Beach, Calif., 1969-71; dist. exec. Boy Scouts Am., Dover, N.J., 1971-74, field dir., 1974-76; fin. dir. Boy Scouts Am., Valley Forge, Pa., 1977-81; v.p. Am. Humanics, Kansas City, Mo., 1976-77; pres. Combined Health, Phila., 1981-85; nat. pres. Am. Coun. on Alcoholism, Balt., 1985—; pres. Trans-Am. Assocs., Balt., 1985. Contbr. articles to profl. pubs. 1st lt. U.S. Army, 1966-69, Vietnam. Recipient leadership award Balt. C. of C., 1989; Am. Coun. on Alcoholism fellow, 1988. Mem. Am. Soc. Assn. Execs. (cert., grad. studies com.), Nat. Soc. Assn. Execs. (cert. fund raising exec.), Internat. Coun. on Alcohol and Addictions, Md. Soc. Assn. Execs. (pres.-elect 1989), Md. Press Club. Republican. Roman Catholic. Office: Am Coun on Alcoholism 5024 Campbell Blvd Ste H Baltimore MD 21236-6950

PIEHLER, WENDELL HOWARD, organist, choir director, fund-raiser; b. Lyons, Kans., Sept. 21, 1936; s. Oscar Harold and Bessie Matilda (Colberg) P.; m. Nancy J. Nyren, Nov. 2, 1974. B.M. summa cum laude, Southwestern Coll., 1958; Mus.M., Yale U., 1961, M.M.A., 1970; Ph.D., U. Conn., 1985. Organist, asst. Yale U., New Haven, 1969-71; organist-choir dir. Whitneyville Congl. Ch., Hamden, Conn., 1969-72; music dir. United Ch. of Green, New Haven, 1973; choir dir. Salem Lutheran Ch., Bridgeport, Conn., 1974; organist, choir dir. St. Peter's Episcopal Ch., Cheshire, Conn., 1976-86; Temple Mishkan Israel, Hamden, 1971—; mem. music com. Trinity Episcopal Ch. on the Green, New Haven, 1987—; sr. adminstrv. asst. Med. Devel. Yale U., 1980-90, office mgr., 1990—; mem. faculty Colby Sawyer Coll., 1961-70, Conn. Coll., 1976; adminstrv. asst. Gordon Sci. Confs., 1961-72. Rec. artist Lyrichord Disc. Patentee in field. Lectr. Neighborhood Music Sch., New Haven, 1975-85; chmn. Lyons High Sch. Scholarship Fund, 1983—; asst. registrar New Haven Democratic Com., 1984—; mem. pres.'s council Southwestern Coll., 1987—. Recipient Service award Cong. Mishkan Israel, 1985; grantee Conn. Commn. Arts, 1976, U. Conn., 1984. Mem. Am. Guild Organists, Shubert Theatre Gold Club, Long Wharf Theatre, Met. Opera Guild, Coll. Music Soc., Am. Musicological Soc., Mory's Assn. Order of Mound. Democrat. Club: Yale. Lodges: Demolay, Chevalier. Avocations: swimming, skiing, traveling, cultural events. Home: Crown Towers 123 York St Apt 18-G New Haven CT 06511-5614 Office: Yale Devel Med Sch PO Box 7611 New Haven CT 06519-0611

PIEKARSKI, KEVIN, corrections officer; b. Rome, N.Y., Aug. 26, 1954; s. Sabine Stanislaus Piekarski and Mary Ellen (Sykes) Morrison; m. Susan Alice Nasci (div.); m. Donna Marie Vaccaro, Nov. 26, 1988; children: Cheri Lynn, Seth Lewis Volney. Cert. med. asst., Mohawk Valley Community Coll., Utica, N.Y., 1987. Officer N.Y. Dept. Corrections, Albany, 1988—.

PIEPER, GEORGE F(RANCIS), JR., aerospace engineering consultant, educator; b. Boston, Jan. 1, 1926; s. George Francis Sr. and Katherine Gertrude (Cross) P.; m. Barbara Ferguson, Dec. 27, 1950; children: Pamela, Lynell. BA, Williams Coll., 1946; MS in Engring., Cornell U., 1949; PhD, Yale U., 1952. Staff mem. radiation lab. MIT, Cambridge, 1944-45; from instr. to asst. prof. physics Yale U., New Haven, 1952-60; project supr. applied physics lab. Johns Hopkins U., Laurel, Md., 1960-64; dir. scis. NASA/Goddard Space Flight Ctr., Greenbelt, Md., 1965-83, assoc. ctr. dir., 1984-86; prof. aerospace engring. U.S. Naval Acad., Annapolis, Md., 1986-91; pvt. practice cons. Edgewater, Md., 1991—; guest worker Max Planck Inst. for Extraterrestrial Physics, Garching, Fed. Republic of Germany, 1971-72. Contbr., co-contbr. articles to profl. jours. Recipient medal for exceptional sci. achievement NASA, 1969, medal for outstanding leadership, 1977, award of merit Goddard Space Flight Ctr., 1986; fellow Carnegie Inst., 1956-57. Fellow Am. Phys. Soc., Am. Astron. Soc., Wash. Acad. Scis.; mem. AAAS, Am. Geophys. Union, Phi Beta Kappa, Sigma Xi. Home and Office: 3155 Rolling Rd Edgewater MD 21037-2601

PIERCE, ALLAN DALE, engineering educator, researcher; b. Clarinda, Iowa, Dec. 18, 1936; s. Franklin Dale and Ruth Pauline (Wright) P.; m. Penelope Claffey, Oct. 27, 1961; children: Jennifer Irene, Bradford Loren. BS, N.Mex. Coll. Agrl. and Mechanic Arts, 1957; PhD, MIT, 1962. Registered profl. engr., Mass. Staff researcher Rand Corp., Santa Monica, Calif., 1961-63; sr. staff scientist Avco Corp., Wilmington, Mass., 1963-66; asst. prof. MIT, Cambridge, 1966-68, assoc. prof., 1968-73; prof. mech. engring. Ga. Inst. Tech., Atlanta, 1973-76, Regent's prof., 1976-88; Leonhard chair in engring. Pa. State U., University Park, 1988—; vis. prof. Max Planck Inst., Goettingen, Fed. Republic Germany, 1976-77; cons. in field. Author: Acoustics: An Introduction to it Physical Principles and Applications, 1981; editor phys. acoustics monograph series, 1988—; contbr. articles on acoustics, wave propagation, vibrations, solid and fluid mechanics to profl. jours. NSF fellow, 1957-60, Shell oil fellow, 1960-61, U.S Dept. Transp. faculty fellow, 1979-80; recipient Sr. U.S. Scientist award Alexander von Humboldt Found., 1976, Cert. of Recognition Nat. Aeronautics and Space Adminstrn., 1984. Fellow Acoustical Soc. Am. (Silver medal 1991), ASME; mem. IEEE, AIAA. Home: 1135 Shamrock Ave State College PA 16801-6968 Office: Pa State U Grad Program Acoustics 157 Hammond Bldg University Park PA 16802

PIERCE, CHARLES ELIOT, JR., library director, educator; b. Springfield, Mass., Dec. 25, 1941; s. C. Eliot and Dora Mason (Redway) P.; m. Barbara G. Hanson, Oct. 18, 1969; children: Sheila H., Charles Eliot III. B.A., Harvard U., 1964, M.A.T., 1966, Ph.D., 1970. Prof. English Vassar Coll., Poughkeepsie, N.Y., 1970-87; dir. Pierpont Morgan Library, N.Y.C., 1987—. Author: (literary criticism) The Religious Life of Samuel Johnson, 1983. Mem. Am. Soc. 18th Century Studies, Century Assn., Grolier Club, Knickerbocker Club. Episcopalian. Home: Clinton Corners Rd Salt Point NY 12578 Office: Pierpont Morgan Libr 29 E 36th St New York NY 10016-3490

PIERCE, CRYSTAL DENISE, management consultant, public relations executive, journalist; b. Phila., July 2, 1953; d. Wendal Andrew and Marie Ellen (Reeve) P. BA, Niagara U., 1975; postgrad., U. Md., 1992—. Cert. pub. rels. profl., Calif. Field rep. Travellers Ins. Co., Voorhees Twp., N.J., 1975-76; prodn. asst. WNYS-TV, Syracuse, N.Y., 1977; advt. sales staff Cahners Publ. Co., L.A., 1978; freelance writer L.A., 1978-80; pub. rels. Calif. Savings & Loan, L.A., 1980-82; corp. and pub. staff United Indian Devel., L.A., 1982-84; pres. Cris Pierce & Assoc., L.A., 1984-89; regional v.p. Nat. Ctr. for Am., Kent, 1989-91; journalist Indian dept. Hispanic Times, Arcadia, Calif., 1984—; co-host SBA's Regional Tribal Conf., 1991; lectr. in field. Editor: United Indian Devel. Assn. Reporter, 1982-89, Indian Bus. & Mgmt., 1989-91. U.S. Marine Corps. Competitive scholar, 1974, Stepen C. Clark scholar N.Y. State Hist. Assn., 1971; recipient Organizational Video award Ind. Film Prodn., 1985, Maharishi award, 1983. Mem. Native Am. Journalists, Internat. Assn. V.P., Pub. Rels. Soc. Episcopalian.

PIERCE, ELIZABETH GAY, civic worker; b. N.Y.C., Mar. 26, 1907; d. Martin and Julia (Stone) Gay; AB, Barnard Coll., 1929; m. William Curtis Pierce, June 19, 1929; children—Martin Gay, Elizabeth Gay (Mrs. Joseph S. Stout, Jr.), Josiah. Vol. worker Boston City Hosp., 1929-30, Community Service Soc., N.Y.C., 1931-32; mem. dependent children's sect. Welfare Council, N.Y.C., 1939-40; chmn. house com. North Shore Holiday House, Huntington, L.I., 1944, pres., 1945; co-chmn. thrift shop com. Knickerbocker Hosp., N.Y.C., 1957-64; mem. exec. com. of women's com. Legal Aid Soc., N.Y.C., 1958-59; mem. Women's Aux. Knickerbocker Hosp. (exec. com. 1960-64); adv. trustee Maine Citizens for Hist. Preservation, 1983-87; trustee Jones Mus. Ceramics and Glass, 1985-89. Mem. Soc. Colonial Dames in State N.Y. (bd. mgrs., 1962-67, corr. sec. N.Y. 1965-67, pres. 1967-70), Nat. Soc. Colonial Dames Am. (pres. 1972-76, nat. pres.), Soc. for Preservation New Eng. Antiquities (Maine council, former chmn. Marrett House), Mayflower Soc. N.Y. (sec. 1985-88), Daus. Founders and Patriots, Nat. Grange. Episcopalian. Club: Colony, Ch. (N.Y.C.). Home: Box 352 Rte 1 West Baldwin ME 04091

PIERCE, FRANCIS CASIMIR, civil engineer; b. Warren, R.I., May 19, 1924; s. Frank J. and Eva (Soltys) Pierce; student U. Conn., 1943-44; B.S., U. R.I., 1948; M.S., Harvard U., 1950; postgrad. Northeastern U., 1951-52; m. Helen Lynette Steinouer, Apr. 24, 1954; children—Paul F., Kenneth J., Nancy L., Karen H., Charles E. Instr. civil engring. U. R.I., Kingston, 1948-49, U. Conn., Storrs, 1950-51; design engr. Praeger-Maguire & Ole Singstad, Boston, 1951-52; chief found. engr. C.A. Maguire & Assocs., Providence, 1952-59, assoc., 1959-69, v.p., 1969-72; sr. v.p. C.E. Maguire, Inc., 1972-76, officer-in-charge Honolulu office, 1976-78, exec. v.p., corp. dir. ops., 1975-87; dir. The Maguire Group, Inc., 1979—, gen. mgr. East Atlantic Casualty Co., Ltd., 1987-88; also dir.; pres. Magma, Inc., tech. ops. service co., 1986-88; lectr. found. engring. U. R.I., 1968-69, trustee, 1987—; mem. Coll. Engring. adv. council, 1986—, U.S. com. Internat. Commn. on Large Dams. Vice chmn. Planning Bd. East Providence, R.I., 1960-73; bd. dirs. R.I. Civic Chorale and Orch., 1986-90. Served with AUS, 1942-46. Recipient Chester H. Kirk Disting. Engr. award U. R.I. Coll. Engring., 1987. Mem. ASCE (chpt. past pres., dir.), R.I. Soc. Profl. Engrs. (nat. dir., engr. of year award 1973), Am. Soc. Engring. Edn., Soc. Am. Mil. Engrs., ASTM, Soc. Marine Engrs. and Naval Architects, Am. Soc. Planning Ofcls., Harvard Soc. Engrs., Scientists, Providence Engrs. Soc., R.I. Soc. Planning Agys. (past pres.). Contbr. articles to profl. jours. Recipient USCG Meritorious Pub. Service award, 1987. Home: 156 Barney St Rumford RI 02916-1114 Office: 225 Foxborough Blvd Foxboro MA 02035

PIERCE, JOHN HEWETT, environmental botanist; b. Winchendon, Mass., Feb. 28, 1912; s. Robert Milton and Frances Evelyn (Hewett) P.; m. Martha Hinckley Chapman, Sept. 16, 1936 (div.); children: Richard Gregory, Cynthia Joy; m. Alice Marian French, Dec. 31, 1974. BA in Botany, Clark U., Worcester, Mass., 1936; MA in Botany, U. Mich., 1941; postgrad., Columbia U., 1942. Field botanist U.S. Nat. Park Svc., Bar Harbor, Maine, 1937; dir. Trailside Bot. Mus. Am. Mus. Natural History, Bear Mountain, N.Y., 1938-41; staff taxonomist N.Y. Bot. Garden, 1941-43; landscape designer George Stoddard & Sons Architects, Seattle, 1946-48; seed researcher Puget Sound Seed Co., 1954-64; botanist Environ. Profl. N.W., 1964-67; dir. Japanese Sch. Horticulture, 1967-70; teaching master Niagara Coll. Sch. Horticulture, Ont., 1977-80; owner Swanson Pierce Enterprises, Lewiston, N.Y., 1980—; mem. evening faculty Everett Community Coll., 1946-72; lectr. Longwood Gardens, Memphis Bot. Gardens, Swarthmore Coll., Cornell Coop. Extension, others. Author: Greenhouse Grow How, 1977, Home Solar Gardening, 1981, 92, Public Gardens and Parks of Niagara, 1989, Easy Lifelong Gardening, 1992; contbr. articles to mags. and newspapers. Mem. Coordinating Coun. Occupational Edn., State of Wash., 1970. With M.C., U.S. Army, 1943-46. Niagara Parks Sch. Horticulture fellow. Mem. AAAS, Internat. Plant Propagators, Internat. Soc. Hort. Sci., Am. Inst. Landscape Architects, Internat. Solar Energy Soc., Rhododendron Soc. Can., Garden Writers Assn. Am., Niagara Peninsula Field Naturalists, Niagara Frontier Bot. Soc., Am. Assn. Bot. Gardens and Arboreta, The Worldwatch Inst., Woodrow Wilson Internat. Ctr. for Scholars, Phi Sigma, Sigma Xi. Republican. Unitarian. Home: RR1 15008 Niagara Pkwy, Niagara on the Lake, ON Canada L0S 1J0 Office: Swanson Pierce Enterprises PO Box 91 Lewiston NY 14092-0091

PIERCE, JOHN PETER, educator, consultant; b. Long Beach, Calif., Jan. 19, 1944; s. John Joseph and Rose Phyllis (Simone) P.; m. Cheryl Hay, Feb. 12, 1972; children: Lora, Ellen, Andrew. BS, Fitchburg State Coll., 1978; MS, Worcester State Coll., 1984. Dept. chair Blackstone Valley Vocat. Tech. High Sch., Upton, Mass., 1974—; asst. prof. Fitchburg (Mass.) State Coll., 1986—. Commr. Worcester (Mass.) Mcpl. Airport, 1990. Named Outstanding Tchr. of the Yr. VFW, Millbury, Mass., 1986-87. Democrat. Roman Catholic. Home: 34 Bauer St Worcester MA 01603-1113 Office: Blackstone Valley Voc Tech Pleasant St West Upton MA 01568-1426

PIERCE, LAWRENCE WARREN, federal judge; b. Phila., Dec. 31, 1924; s. Harold Ernest and Leora (Bellinger) P.; m. Wilma Taylor (dec.); m. Cynthia Straker, July 8, 1979; children: Warren Wood, Michael Lawrence, Mark Taylor. BS, St. Joseph's U., Phila., 1948, DHL, 1967; JD, Fordham U., 1951, LLD, 1982; LLD, Fairfield U., 1972, Hamilton Coll., 1987, St. John's U., 1990. Bar: N.Y. State 1951, U.S. Supreme Ct. 1968. Civil law practice N.Y.C., 1951-61; asst. dist. atty. Kings County, N.Y., 1954-61; dep. police commr. N.Y.C., 1961-63; dir. N.Y. State Div. for Youth, Albany, 1963-66; chmn. N.Y. State Narcotic Addiction Control Commn., 1966-70; vis. prof. criminal justice SUNY, Albany, 1970-71; U.S. dist. judge So. dist. N.Y., 1971-81; judge U.S. Fgn. Intelligence Surveillance Ct., 1979-81; apptd. U.S. cir. judge for 2d Cir., 1981-89, sr. U.S. cir. judge for 2d Cir., 1990—; trustee Practising Law Inst. Vice pres., bd. mgrs. Lincoln Hall for Boys. With AUS, 1943-46, MTO. Mem. ABA (former alt. observer at U.S. Mission to UN), Nat. Bar Assn., Assn. of Bar of City of N.Y. (com. on 2d Century), Havens Relief Fund Soc. (trustee). Roman Catholic. Office: US Ct Appeals US Courthouse Foley Sq New York NY 10007-1501

PIERCE, LISA MARGARET, product and market development manager; b. Nyack, N.Y., June 2, 1957; d. William Twining and Elizabeth (West) P. BA with honors, Gordon Coll., Wenham, Mass., 1978; MBA, Atkinson Sch., Salem, Oreg., 1982. Absent parent locator Dept. Social Svcs., Nyack, 1977-78; paralegal Beverly, Mass., 1978-79; mgr. Reagan Pharmacy, Rockland County, N.Y., 1980; child welfare specialist Dept. Social Svcs., Pomona, N.Y., 1982-83; market analyst Momentum Techs., Parsippany, N.J., 1983-84; systems analyst Booz Allen & Hamilton, Florham Park, N.J., 1984-85; market researcher, forecaster AT&T, Bedminster, N.J., 1985-87, asst. pvt. line product mgr., 1987-89, Integrated Svcs. Digital Network product mgr., 1989—; panelist, contbr. TeleCommunications Assn., San Diego, 1992, Internat. Comm. Assn., Atlanta, Ea. Comm. Forum, N.Y., Nat. Engring Consortium, Chgo; cons. Sidereal, Portland, Oreg., 1982. Tutor Literacy Vols. Am., Somerville, N.J., 1989-91; mem. Jr. League Am., Morristown, N.J., 1987-90; mgr. 6th Congl. Dist. for Carter/Mondale, Manchester, Mass., 1976; mem. Internat. Oceanographic Found., Washington. Grantee in field. Republican. Office: AT&T Rts 202 and 206 N Bedminster NJ 07921

PIERCE, NAOMI LOUISE, graphic designer, cartoonist; b. Boston, Aug. 6, 1963; d. John Norman and Alice Louise (Martin) P. BA, Harvard U., 1986. Editor, prodn. mgr. OG&H Pubs., Boston, 1986-88; prodn. mgr. Bookmakers, Inc., Wilkes-Barre, Pa., 1988-89; prin. Naomi Pierce Design, Somerville, Mass., 1989—. Artist, writer (calendar) Real Men Don't Drink Hazelnut Decaf, 1992. Tchr. North Boston Re-evaluation Counseling Community, 1991—. Recipient John Harvard scholarship, 1986. Home: 141 Elm St # 2 2 Walker Ter Cambridge MA 02138 Office: Naomi Pierce Design Ste 215 One Davis Square Somerville MA 02144

PIERCE, NORMAN BRAYTON, psychologist; b. Acushnet, Mass., Sept. 11, 1940; s. Norman and Hazel May (Gifford) P.; A.B., Bowdoin Coll., 1962; S.T.B., Boston U., 1966, M.A., 1973, Ph.D., 1980; m. Patricia M. Jobe, June 26, 1965 (div.); children: Christine Ruth, Matthew Jobe. Ordained to ministry, Meth. Ch., 1967; registered marriage and family therapist. Pastor Wareham and Marion United Meth. Chs., 1966-68, East Bridgewater United Meth. Ch., 1968-71; psychotherapist in pvt. practice, Hingham, Mass., 1971-82; assoc. dir. South Shore Pastoral Counseling Center, Hingham, 1982-85, staff psychologist South Shore Counseling Ctr., 1985—; clin. supr. Boston Inst. Psychotherapies, 1981-88, 92—, assoc. dir. postgrad. ctr., 1986-91; treas., fin. mgr. Pierce Galleries, Inc., 1971-77. Recipient Goodwin French prize, 1959; James Bowdoin scholar, 1959-62; Nat. Meth. scholar, 1963; Albert Danielsen pastoral counseling fellow, 1975-77; Paul Johnson teaching fellow, 1977-78. Diplomate Am. Inst. Counseling and Psychotherapy; registered psychologist, Mass. Mem. Am. Assn. Marriage and Family Therapy, Am. Assn. Pastoral Counselors, Am. Psychol. Assn., Mass. Psychol. Assn., Mass. Assn. for Psychoanalytic Psychology, New Eng. Soc. Clin. Hypnosis, Phi Beta Kappa. Office: 738 Main St Hingham MA 02043-3386

PIERCE, PRESTON EUGENE, educator; b. Canandaigua, N.Y., June 14, 1946; s. Everett Preston and Margaret Rebecca (Kunes) P.; m. Mary Christine Kaschak, Dec. 4, 1971; children: Rebecca Judith, Stephen Preston. BA, Westminster Coll., 1968; BS, Regents Coll., 1979; MSEd, SUNY, Brockport, 1974; MAT, U. Vt., 1972; EdD, U. Rochester, 1984; MLS, SUNY, Geneseo, 1985; diploma, U.S. Army Command and Gen. Staff Coll., 1983. Cert. tchr., sch. dist. adminstr., sch. media specialist. Tchr. Lehighton (Pa.) Area Sch. Dist., 1969-70, Byron-Bergen Cen. Sch., Bergen, N.Y., 1970-71; tchr., media specialist Victor (N.Y.) Cen. Sch., 1971—; historian Ontario County, Canandaigua, 1983—; project co-dir. U. Hartford Coll. of Engring., West Hartford, Conn., 1988-89; summer faculty Appalachian State U., Boone, N.C., 1988; curriculum writer, Newberry Libr., Chgo., 1978. Contbr. articles to profl. jours. Mem. Ontario County Rep. Com., Canandaigua, 1972—. Maj. USAR, 1967—. Recipient Fellowship Newberry Libr., Chgo., 1977, NEH and Coun. for Basic Edn., 1989, Dist. Award of Merit, Dist. Commr. award Boy Scouts Am., Geneva, N.Y. Mem. Assn. for Supervision and Curriculum Devel., Assn. for Edn. Communication and Tech., Nat. Council for Social Studies, Orgn. Am. Historians, Oral Historians Assn., Seneca Army Depot, Officer's Club, Sons of Am. Revolution, Am. Legion, Res. Officers Assn. Republican. Episcopalian. Home: 209 Davidson Ave Canandaigua NY 14424-1405 Office: Ontario County Historian 3871 County Rd 46 Canandaigua NY 14424-9505

PIERCE, RUSSELL DALE, physicist; b. Iselin, Pa., July 17, 1938; s. Walter Clyde and Audrey Ruth (Kress) P.; m. Elizabeth Ann McMurtry, Dec. 18, 1965; children: David, Michael, Stephen. BS, Carnegie Inst. Tech., 1960, MS, 1961, PhD, 1966. Instr. Carnegie Inst. Tech., Pitts., 1965-66; mem. tech. staff AT&T Bell Labs., Murray Hill, N.J., 1966-85, Reading, Pa., 1985—. Co-patentee method for determining magnetic anistropy field. Deacon Parsippany (N.J.) Bapt. Ch., 1967-85, Maranatha Bapt. Ch., Sinking Spring, Pa., 1991—. Mem. Sigma Xi. Baptist. Office: AT&T Bell Labs 2525 N 12th St Reading PA 19605-2749

PIERCE, SAMUEL RILEY, JR., lawyer, government official; b. Glen Cove, L.I., N.Y., Sept. 8, 1922; s. Samuel R. and Hettie E. (Armstrong) P.; m. Barbara Penn Wright, Apr. 1, 1948; 1 child, Victoria Wright. AB with honors, Cornell U., 1947, JD, 1949; postgrad. (Ford Found. fellow), Yale U., 1957-58; LLM in Taxation, NYU, 1952, LLD, 1972; various other hon. degrees including LL.D., L.H.D., D.C.L., Litt.D. Bar: N.Y. 1949, Supreme Ct. 1956. Asst. dist. atty. County N.Y., 1949-53; asst. U.S. atty. So. Dist. N.Y., 1953-55; asst. to under sec. Dept. Labor, Washington, 1955-56; assoc. counsel, counsel Jud. Subcom. on Antitrust U.S. Ho. Reps., 1956-57; pvt. practice law, 1957-59, 61-70, 73-81, 89—; sec. HUD, 1981-89; faculty N.Y. U. Sch. Law, 1958-70; guest speaker colls., univs.; judge N.Y. Ct. Gen. Sessions, 1959-61; gen. counsel, head legal div. U.S. Treasury, Washington, 1970-73; cons. Fund Internat. Social and Econ. Edn., 1961-67; chmn. impartial disciplinary rev. bd. N.Y.C. Transit System, 1968-81; chmn. N.Y. State Minimum Wage Bd. Hotel Industry, 1961; mem. N.Y. State Banking Bd., 1961-70, N.Y.C. Bd. Edn., 1961, Adminstrv. Conf. U.S., 1968-70, Battery Park City Corp. Authority, 1968-70, N.Y.C. Spl. Commn. Inquiry into Energy Failures, 1977; mem. nat. adv. com. Comptroller of Currency, 1975-80; adv. group commr. IRS, 1974-76; mem. Nat. Wiretapping Commn., 1973-76; dir. N.Y. 1964-65 World's Fair Corp., Internat. Paper Co., Turner Corp.; former dir. Prudential Ins. Co., GE Corp., U.S. Industries, Inc., Rand Corp., 1st Nat. Boston Corp., 1st Nat. Bank Boston, Pub. Svc. Electric and Gas Co., Internat. Basic Economy Corp; gov. Am. Stock Exchange, 1977-80. Contbr. articles to profl. jours. Trustee Inst. Civil Justice, Mt. Holyoke Coll., 1965-75, Hampton Inst., Inst. Internat. Edn., Cornell U., Howard U., 1976-81; bd. dirs. Tax Found. U.S. del. Conf. on Coops., Georgetown, Brit. Guiana, 1956; mem. panel symposium Mil.-Indsl. Conf. on Atomic Energy, Chgo., 1956; fraternal del. All-African People's Conf., Accra, Ghana, 1958; mem. Nat. Def. Exec. Res., 1957-70; mem. nat. exec. bd. Boy Scouts Am., 1969-75; mem. N.Y.C. U.S.O. Com., 1959-61; mem. panel arbitrators Am. Arbitration Assn. and Fed. Mediation and Conciliation Service, 1957—; Bd. dirs. Louis T. Wright Meml. Fund, Inc., Nat. Parkinson Found., Inc., 1959-61; sec., dir. YMCA Greater N.Y., 1960-70; Mem. N.Y. State Republican Campaign Hdqrs. Staff, 1952, 58; gov. N.Y. Young Rep. Club, 1951-53. With AUS, 1943-46; as 1st lt. J.A.G.C. Res., 1950-52. Recipient N.Y.C. Jr. C. of C. Ann. Distinguished Svc. award, 1958, Alexander Hamilton award Treasury Dept., 1973, Disting. Alumnus award Cornell Law Sch., 1988, Disting. Svc. Medallion Nassau County Bar Assn., 1988, Reagan Revolution Medal of Honor, 1989, Presdl. Citizens medal, 1989, Salute to Greatness award Martin Luther King Jr. Ctr., 1989. Fellow Am. Coll. Trial Lawyers; mem. ABA, Assn. of Bar of City of N.Y., Cornell Assn. Class Secs., Telluride Assn. Alumni, Cornell U. Alumni Assn. N.Y.C. (gov.), C.I.D. Agts. Assn. (gov.), N.Y. County Lawyers Assn., Inst. Jud. Adminstrn., Phi Beta Kappa, Phi Kappa Phi, Alpha Phi Alpha, Alpha Phi Omega. Methodist (former mem. commn. on interjurisdictional relations United Meth. Ch.).

PIERCY, MARGE, poet, novelist, essayist; b. Detroit, Mar. 31, 1936; d. Robert Douglas and Bert Bernice (Bunnin) P.; m. Ira Wood, 1982. AB, U. Mich., 1957; MA, Northwestern U., 1958. Instr. Gary extension Ind. U., 1960-62; poet-in-residence U. Kans., 1971; disting. vis. lectr. Thomas Jefferson Coll., Grand Valley State Colls., fall 1975, 76, 78, 80; vis. faculty Women's Writers Conf., Cazenovia (N.Y.) Coll.; Elliston poetry fellow U. Cin., 1986. Author: Breaking Camp, 1968, Hard Loving, 1969, Going Down Fast, 1969, Dance the Eagle to Sleep, 1970, Small Changes, 1973, To Be of Use, 1973, Living in the Open, 1976, Woman on the Edge of Time, 1976, The High Cost of Living, 1978, Vida, 1980, The Moon is Always Female, 1980, Braided Lives, 1982, Circles on the Water, 1982, Stone, Paper, Knife, 1983, My Mother's Body, 1985, Gone to Soldiers, 1987, Available Light, 1988, Summer People, 1989, He, She and It, 1991, Mars and Her Children, 1992. Active Students for Dem. Soc., 1965-69, N.Am. Congress on Latin-Am., 1966-67, Movement for Dem. Soc., 1968-69, Women's Ctr. N.Y., 1969-71, Lower Cape Women's Ctr., 1973-76, New Jewish Agenda, 1986—, Internat. Bd. Israeli Ctr. for Creative Arts, 1986-88, mem. adv. bd., 1989—; cons. N.Y. State Coun. on Arts, 1971, Mass. Found. for Humanities and Coun. on Arts, 1974; mem. Writer Bd., 1985-86; bd. dirs. Transition House, Mass. Found. Humanities and Pub. Policy, 1978-85, Am. Ha-Yam, 1988—; gov.'s appointee to Mass. Cultural Coun., 1990-91, Mass. Coun. on Arts and Humanities, 1986-89; artistic adv. bd. Am. Poetry Ctr., 1988—; lit. adv. panel poetry NEA, 1989. Recipient Borestone Mountain Poetry award, 1968, 74, Lit. award Gov. Mass. Commn. on Status of Women, 1974, Nat. Endowment Arts award, 1978, Carolyn Kizer Poetry prize, 1986, 90, Sheaffer Eaton-PEN New Eng. award lit. excellence, 1989, Golden Rose Poetry prize, 1990, May Sarton award, 1991, Brit ha-Dorot award, 1992. Mem. PEN, NOW (Cape Cod chpt.), Authors Guild, Authors League, Writers Union, Poetry Soc., Am. Nat. Audubon Soc., Mass. Audubon Soc., New Eng. Poetry Club. Address: PO Box 1473 Wellfleet MA 02667

PIERESON, JAMES EUGENE, foundation administrator; b. Grand Rapids, Mich., Oct. 4, 1946; s. Lloyd Eugene and Katherine Louise (Graham) P.; Patricia Giles Leeds, Aug. 28, 1983; 1 child, James Wil-

liam. BA cum laude Polit. Sci., Mich. State U., 1968, PhD in Polit. Sci., 1973. Vis. faculty polit. sci. Ind. U., Bloomington, 1974-75; asst. prof. polit. sci. U. Pa., Phila., 1976-82; vis. faculty polit. sci. U. Minn., Mpls., 1979; program officer John M. Olin Found., N.Y.C., 1982-85; exec. dir. John M. Olin Found., 1986—; trustee John M. Olin Found., N.Y.C., 1987—; mem. adv. com. Simon Grad. Sch. Bus. Adminstrn., U. Rochester, Rochester, N.Y., 1986—. Co-author: Political Tolerance and American Democracy, 1981; contbr. articles to profl. jours. Trustee Adelphi U., 1991—. Evans scholar Evans Scholars Found., 1964-68; NDEA Grad. fellow, 1968-71, NSF Research fellow, 1978-79, U.S. Govt. Mem. Phila. Soc., Am. Hist. Assn., Union League Club. Republican. Roman Catholic. Office: John M Olin Found 100 Park Ave New York NY 10017-5516

PIEROTTI, THOMAS MONROE, human resources administrator; b. Kane, Pa., Aug. 29, 1947; s. Charles Thomas and Ann Marie (Paup) P.; m. Karen Ruth Krepps, Jan. 17, 1977 (div. Jan. 1987); children: Michael Ralph, Matthew Lewis, Gretchen Elizabeth; m. Lynn Mary Hodas, July 7, 1990; 1 child, Sarah Lynne. BA, Alfred U., 1970; MDiv, Luth. Theol. Sem., 1976; ThM, Pitts. Theol. Sem., 1981. Assoc. pastor Zion Luth. Ch., Greensburg, Pa., 1976-78; pastor Luth. Ch. of Our Savior, North Huntingdon, Pa., 1978-82; dir., developer Luth. Svc. Soc. of Western Pa., Warren, Pa., 1982-86; exec. dir. Pastoral Counseling Svc. of Southwestern N.Y., Jamestown, 1983-91; dir. indsl. psychology Addis Assocs., Bradford, Pa., 1986-88; dir. human resources Betts Industries, Warren, 1988—; instr. vols. Hospice of Warren County, 1984—. Supr. Hamilton Twp., Ludlow, Pa., 1985-91. Republican. Home: Box 166 Ludlow PA 16333 Office: Betts Industries 1800 Pennsylvania Ave W Warren PA 16365

PIERRE, ANDREW J., foundation executive, political scientist; b. Vienna, Austria, June 13, 1934; came to U.S., 1941; s. Leo J. and Nina A. (Hutter) P.; m. Clara Grossman, July 5, 1969 (div. 1982). BA, Amherst Coll., 1955; Certificat d'Etudes Politiques, Inst. Polit. Studies, Paris, 1956; M of Internat. Affairs, Columbia U., 1957, PhD, 1968. Rsch. assoc. Brookings Instn., Washington, 1960-61; fgn. svc. officer Dept. State, Washington and London, 1962-64; cons. Dept. State, Washington, 1967-68; sr. fellow Hudson Inst., Croton-on-Hudson, N.Y., 1966-69; sr. fellow, dir. studies Coun. Fgn. Rels., N.Y.C., 1969-87; dir.-gen. Atlantic Inst. Internat. Affairs, Paris, 1987-89; sr. assoc. Carnegie Endowment for Internat. Peace, Washington, 1990—; adj. prof. Columbia U., 1968-69; prof. Sch. Advanced Internat. Studies, Johns Hopkins U., Washington, 1991—; cons. U.S. Dept. State, Dept. Def., 1971—; bd. dirs. Am. Alpbach Found., N.Y.C. Author: Nuclear Politics, 1972, Nuclear Proliferation: A Strategy for Control, 1976, The Global Politics of Arms Sales, 1982. With U.S. Army, 1957-59. Fulbright fellow, Amherst Meml. fellow, 1955-56, NATO Rsch. fellow, 1976, Rockefeller Found. fellow, 1977-78; named Alumnus of Yr., Columbia U., 1983. Mem. Coun. Fgn. Rels., Internat. Inst. Strategic Studies, Am. Polit. Sci. Assn., Arms Control Assn., Internat. Studies Assn., Am. Coun. on Germany, Mid-Atlantic Club Washington, Alumni Soc. Inst. d'Etudes Politiques (trustee). Home: 3032 O St NW Washington DC 20007-3107 Office: Carnegie Endowment for Internat Peace 2400 N St NW Washington DC 20037-1153

PIERRE, MICHAEL JAMES, SR., construction executive; b. Balt., Aug. 24, 1940; s. Leslie John and Edith Avery (Swan) P.; m. Christine Pierre; children: Michael Jr., Barbara, Catherine, Russell. BSBA, U. Balt., 1964. Asst. estimator Mullan Contracting Co., Balt., 1965-67; project mgr., estimator Lacchi Constrn. Co., Balt., 1967-77; gen. mgr. constrn. M. Nelson Barnes & Sons, Cockeysville, Md., 1977-84; project estimator Glen Constrn. Co., Gaithersburg, Md., 1984-86; sr. project estimator Glen Constrn. Co., Gaithersburg, 1986-87, v.p. estimating, 1987-89; v.p. Mullan Contracting Co., Lutherville, Md., 1989-91, pres., 1992—. Mem. Md. Commn. on Physical Fitness, 1983-84. Mem. Am. Inst. Constructors, Road Runners Club (Montgomery County, Md.). Republican. Roman Catholic. Home: 18244 Fox Chase Cir Olney MD 20832-3004 Office: Mullan Contracting Co 2330 W Joppa Rd Lutherville Timonium MD 21093-4609

PIERSON, ANNE BINGHAM, physician; b. N.Y.C., June 9, 1929; d. Woodbridge and Ursula Wolcott (Griswold) Bingham; m. Richard N. Pierson Jr., Nov. 12, 1956 (div. Aug. 1974); children: Richard N. III, Olivia Tiffany Jacobs, Alexandra deForest, Cordelia Stewart Comfort Smela; m. Richard Taliaferro Wright, Nov. 25, 1978. Student, Katharine Branson Sch., Ross, Calif., 1943-47; BA, Vassar Coll., 1951; MD, Columbia U., 1955, MPH, 1972. Intern Lenox Hill Hosp., N.Y.C., 1955-56; substitute internship AUH, Beruit, Lebanon, 1955; mem. staff 7th Day Adventist Hosp., Taipei, Taiwan, 1957; clinic physician, med. dir. Planned Parenthood of Bergen County, Hackensack, N.J., 1960-74, also bd. dirs.; asst. clin. prof. dept. ob-gyn. Columbia U. Coll. Physicians and Surgeons, Internat. Inst. Study of Human Reproduction, 1972-74; med. dir. Memphis Assn. for Planned Parenthood, Inc., 1974-75; staff physician N.Y. Telephone Co., 1976-87; med. dir. Planned Parenthood Assn. Hudson County, 1976-79; physician Sonalysts, Waterford, Conn., 1988—; mem. nat. med. adv. com. Planned Parenthood-World Population, 1966-69. Member Jr. League, 1964—; artist mem. Clinton Art Soc., 1989—, East Lyme Art League, 1991—. Mem. AMA (Physicians Recognition award 1973—), Am. Occupational Med. Assn. , Occupational Med. Soc. Conn., Am. Assn. Planned Parenthood Physicians (exec. com. 1969-71), Nat. Soc. Colonial Dames (life, pres. Vassar Class 1951, 86-91), Cosmopolitan Club. Home: Griswold Point Old Lyme CT 06731 Office: Sonalysts 215 Parkway N Waterford CT 06385-1209

PIERSON, ELLERY MERWIN, psychometrist; b. Eugene, Oreg., Mar. 31, 1935; s. Russell Alford and Doris Amanda (Howard) P.; m. Barbara Suzannah Weber, Nov. 27, 1958; children: Suzanne Christine, Audrey Elaine. BS, Portland State Coll., 1957; MEd, Rutgers U., 1965; PhD, U. Pa., 1975. Rsch. asst. Columbia Coll. Physicians and Surgeons, N.Y.C., 1957-58; lab. asst. RCA, Somerville, N.J., 1958-60; welfare investigator Middlesex County Welfare Bd., New Brunswick, N.J., 1960-61; rsch. asst. Ednl. Testing Svc., Princeton, N.J., 1961-66; rsch. psychologist Franklin Inst. Rsch. Labs., Phila., 1966-67; rsch. assoc. Sch. Dist. Phila., 1967-75, mgr. in rsch., 1975—; cons. in field, Royersford, Pa., 1975—. Mem. Am. Ednl. Rsch. Assn., Nat. Coun. Measurement in Edn., Lions (sec. local club 1984). Office: Sch Dist Phila 21st and The Parkway Rm 407 Philadelphia PA 19103

PIERSON, KENNETH LANTZ, motor carrier safety consultant; b. Akron, Ohio, May 29, 1932; s. Robert Arch and Grace Greer (Lantz) P.; m. Joy Roberta Burchett, June 8, 1952; children: Lavonne, Melinda, Lorrie, Paul, Mark. BS in Bus., U. Md., 1958. Investigator ICC, Balt., 1958-62; mem. staff ICC, Washington, 1962-67; mem. staff Bur. Motor Carrier Safety, Washington, 1967-70, dep. dir., 1970-80, dir., 1980-86; motor carrier safety cons. Glenn Dale, Md., 1987—; mem. Gov.'s Truck Safety Task Force, Annapolis, Md., 1988—; mem. cert. bd. Profl. Truck Driver Inst. Am., Elk Grove, Calif., 1989—. Mem. com. troop 1002 Boy Scouts Am., 1971-91. Sgt. U.S. Army, 1950-53, Korea and Germany. Recipient Bronze medal Fed. Hwy Adminstrn., 1968, Commendations Nat. Motor Carrier Adv. Com., Washington, 1987, Commercial Vehicle Safety Alliance, Washington, 1987. Mem. Am. Soc. Safety Engrs. (chpt. pres. 1978-79), Transp. Rsch. Bd., Sr. Execs. Assn., Am. Legion. Democrat. Methodist. Home and Office: 3300 Glen Ave Glenn Dale MD 20769-9215

PIERSON, RICHARD NORRIS, JR., medical educator; b. N.Y.C., Sept. 22, 1929; s. Richard Norris and Dorothy (Stewart) P.; m. Alice Roberts, Aug. 26, 1974; children by previous marriage: Richard N., Olivia Tiffany, Alexandra de Forest, Cordelia S.C.; stepchildren: Alice W. Dunn, Eric C.W. Dunn. BA, Princeton U., 1951; MD, Columbia U., 1955. Diplomate Am. Bd. Internal Medicine, Am. Bd. Nuclear Medicine. Resident St. Luke's Roosevelt Hosp., N.Y.C., 1955-61, assoc. dir., 1961-65, dir. div. nuclear medicine, 1965-89, dir. body composition unit, 1965—, attending physician, 1975—; prof. clin. medicine Columbia U., 1980—; dir. medicine Hackensack Hosp., 1973-74; staff assoc. Brookhaven Nat. Lab., 1970—; research scholar Lawrence Radiation Lab., Berkeley, Calif., 1970-71. Editor: Quantitative Radiocardiography, 1975. Contbr. articles to profl. jours. Bd. dirs. Englewood Health Dept., N.J., 1966-74; warden St. Paul's Ch., 1980-82, bd. dirs. Empire Blue Cross/Blue Shield, N.Y., 1978-91. Lt. USNR, 1956-58. NIH grantee, 1973-76, 86—; John A. Hartford Found. grantee, 1967-70. Fellow N.Y. Acad. Medicine, ACP; mem. N.Y. County Med. Soc. (pres. 1978-79), N.Y. County Health Svc. Rev. Orgn. (chmn. 1980-82), Am. Bur. Med. Advancement in China (pres. 1979-87), Am. Med. Rev. Rsch. Ctr. (pres. 1985-89, N.Y. State del. to AMA 1978-90), Alliance for Continuing Med. Edn. (pres. 1985-89), Soc. Nuclear Medicine (greater N.Y. area pres. 1982-83, trustee 1991—), P&S Alumni Assn. (pres. 1989-91), Century Club, Englewood Field Club. Home: 60 Lincoln St Englewood NJ 07631-3117 Office: St Lukes Roosevelt Hosp Ctr 425 W 113th St New York NY 10025-1708

PIES, RONALD WILLIAM, physician, writer; b. Rochester, N.Y., June 12, 1952. AB, Cornell U., 1974; MD, SUNY, Syracuse, 1978. Diplomate Am. Bd. Psychiatry and Neurology. Intern then resident SUNY Upstate Med. Ctr., 1978-82; assoc. clin. prof. psychiatry Sch. Medicine Tufts U., Boston, 1988—; dir. tng. edn. Bay Cove-Tufts Mental Health Ctr., Jamaica Plain, N.Y., 1987-88. Author: Inside Psychotherapy, 1983, Psychotherapy Today, 1991, also poetry. Laughlin fellow Am. Coll. Psychiatry, 1980. Mem. Am. Psychiat. Assn., AMA, Am. Acad. Psychiatry and the Law. Office: Tufts U Sch Medicine 750 Washington St Boston MA 02111-1533

PIETERSEN, ALEX ALFONSE, photographer; b. Den Haag, Holland, Mar. 13, 1946; came to U.S. 1974, naturalized, 1980; s. Francois Alfonse Gustave and Geertje Barendina (Ryneveld) P.; m. Patricia Ann Panzer, July 17, 1975; 1 child, Melissa. One man shows at Deltakos, Div. of J. Walter Thompson, N.Y., 1987, J. Walter Thompson, 1988, Croyden Furniture, N.Y.C., 1988, The Mennen Co., Morristown, N.J., 1989, N.Y.C. Dept. Housing and Devel., 1989, 90; group shows include John Paul Assocs., N.Y.C., 1988, Bellcore, Livingston, N.J., 1989, Lever House, N.Y.C., 1991; works in permanent collections at Vizcaya Mus., Miami, Fla., Walt Disney Corp., Fla., Am. Heart Assn. Recipient Award of Merit Winterpark Sidewalk Art Festival, 1988, 91, Boynton Beach Art Festival, 1991, Las Olas Art Festival, Ft. Lauderdale, Fla., 1984; 1st place awards Fishwack Festival, Chatham, N.J., 1990, Plainfield's (N.J.) 26th Ann. Festival of the Arts, 1989, Millburn-Short Hills (N.J.) Art Fair, 1986, Key Biscayne Art Festival, 1984, 85, Osceola (Fla.) Art Festival, 1983, Arti Grass, 1981, many others. Republican. Home: 67 N The Grn Budd Lake NJ 07828

PIETROVITO, JAMES ANTHONY, college dean; b. Batavia, N.Y., Aug. 28, 1949; s. Anthony Columbus and Rita Mary (Panepento) P.; m. Janet Marie Early, June 2, 1973; children: James Anthony, Jr., Daniel Thomas. BA, Lycoming Coll., 1971; MEd, U. Vt., 1973, cert. advanced grad. study, 1981; EdD, Vanderbilt U., Nashville, 1989. Residence hall dir. U. Vermont, 1971-74; coord. student vet. affairs Nathaniel Hawthorne Coll., Antrim, N.H., 1976-77; dir. youth employment and training program So. N.H. Svcs. Inc., Goffstown, N.H., 1978-79; planning cons. N.H. Dept. Edn., Concord, N.H., 1979-81; dean community edn. N.H. Tech. Coll., Manchester, 1981—; advisor Applied Tech. Ctr., Contoocook Valley Regional High Sch., Peterborough, N.H., 1989—; advisor tech. edn. programm Gt. Brook sch., Antrim, N.H., 1990—. Dir. Sci. Enrichment Encounters, Manchester, 1983-88; pres., bd. dirs. N.H. Monastery, New Boston, N.H., 1990—; advisor Crotched Mountain Rehab. Ctr. Vocat. Edn., Greenfield, N.H., 1991. Recipient svc. award Lycoming Coll., 1971. Mem. Nat. Assn. Student Pers. Adminstrs., Am. Assn. Higher Edn., Coun. Occupational Edn., Greater Manchester C. of C. (amb. 1983-88), Phi Delta Kappa (del. So. N.H. chpt. 1980-82, svc. award 1990), Kappa Delta Rho. Office: NH Tech Coll 1066 Front St Manchester NH 03102-8518

PIETRUCHA, MARTIN THOMAS, civil engineer; b. Jersey City, Nov. 4, 1955; s. Bernard Stanley and Sophie Ann (Gelczis) P.; m. Robyn Jane Bottoni, Sept. 12, 1987; children: Douglas Martin, Ellyn Anne. BSCE, N.J. Inst. Tech., 1977; MSCE, U. Calif., Berkeley, 1978; PhD, U. Md., 1990. Registered profl. engr., N.J., Va. Data technician Richard P. Brown Assocs., S.I., N.Y., 1976-77; rsch. asst. N.J. Inst. Tech., Newark, 1977; teaching asst. U. Calif., Berkeley, 1977-78; prin. engr. N.J. Hackensack Meadowlands Devel. Commn., Lyndhurst, 1978-80; rsch. asst. U. Md., College Park, 1980-83; sr. engr. Edwards and Kelcey, Inc., Livingston, N.J., 1983-84; program engr. BioTech., Inc., Falls Church, Va., 1984-85; prin. engr. Ctr. for Applied Rsch., Inc., Great Falls, Va., 1985-89; program officer Transp. Rsch. Bd., Washington, 1989-90; asst. prof. Pa. State U., University Park, 1990—. Contbr. articles to profl. jours. Mem. NSPE, ASCE, Inst. Transp. Engrs., Sigma Xi, Tau Beta Pi, Chi Epsilon. Office: Pa State U Civil Engr Dept 212 Sackett Bldg University Park PA 16802

PIETRUNIAK, ED STEPHEN, financial executive; b. Syracuse, N.Y., Mar. 1, 1956; s. Edmund S. and Pearl (Davidowski) P.; m. Lori Ann Sauro, May 17, 1986; 1 child, Steven. BBA, Niagara U., 1978. CPA, N.Y. Auditor Blue Cross/Blue Shield, Syracuse, 1978-80, Price Waterhouse, Syracuse, 1980-82; fin. analyst Genigraphics, Syracuse, 1982-83; cost acct. Gene Graphics, Syracuse, 1983-84, acctg. mgr., 1984-88; chief fin. officer Liftech Handling, Inc., Syracuse, 1988—. Roman Catholic.

PIETRZAK, ALFRED ROBERT, lawyer; b. Glen Cove, N.Y., June 26, 1949; s. Alfred S. and Wanda M. (Wapniarski) P.; m. Sharon Esther Chizek, July 9, 1978; children: Eric A., Daniel J. BA, Fordham U., 1971; JD, Columbia U., 1974. Bar: N.Y. 1975, U.S. Dist. Ct. (so., ea., we. and no. dists.) N.Y. 1975, U.S. Dist. Ct. (no. dist.) Calif. 1983, U.S. Ct. Appeals (2d cir.) 1975, U.S. Ct. Appeals (9th cir.) 1983, U.S. Ct. Appeals (11th cir.) 1985, U.S. Supreme Ct. 1985. Assoc. Brown & Wood (formerly Brown, Wood, Ivey, Mitchell & Petty), N.Y.C., 1974-82, ptnr., 1983—; mem. C.L.E. faculty Fordham U. Sch. Law.; Bd. editors Commodities Law Letter; adv. bd. Fordham Internat. Law Jour.; contbr. articles to legal jours. Mem. ABA (litigation sect.), Assn. of Bar of City of N.Y. (securities regulation com., futures regulation com.), Am. Law Inst. (lectr.), Securities Industry Assn., Futures Industry Assn. Roman Catholic. Home: 525 Monterey Ave Pelham NY 10803-2513 Office: Brown & Wood 1 World Trade Ctr 58th Fl New York NY 10048

PIETRZAK, DANIEL M., priest, academic administrator; b. Buffalo, Mar. 12, 1939; s. Thaddeus S. and Stella G. (Cybulski) P. BA, St. Hyacinth Coll., 1961; STL, Seraphicum, Rome, 1965; MS, South Conn. State U., 1968; PhD, Fordham U., 1981. Joined Order Friars Minor (Franciscans) Roman Cath. Ch., ordained priest, 1964. Tchr. Kolbe High Sch., Bridgeport, Conn., 1965-67; prof. philosophy and psychology St. Hyacinth Coll.-Sem., Granby, Mass., 1967-76, registrar, 1968-76, acad. dean, 1973-76, pres., 1991—; sem. rector Seraphicum, Rome, 1977-82; min. provincial Franciscan Order, St. Anthony Province, Balt., 1982-91; asst. gen. Order Friars Minor Conventual, Rome, 1976-82. Fordham U. fellow, 1969. Mem. APA, Nat. Cath. Edn. Assn., So. Sci. Study of Religion. Home and Office: 66 School St Granby MA 01033-9786

PIGG, WILLIE HOWARD, political science educator; b. Clifton, Tenn., Apr. 13, 1948; s. Willie Edward and Myra Catherine (Baker) P. BS, U. Tenn., Martin, 1970; MA, U. Tenn., Knoxville, 1978, PhD, 1991. Tchr. social studies Frank Hughes High Sch., Clifton, 1970-74, 75-79; grad. rsch. asst. U. Tenn., Knoxville, 1974-75, grad. teaching asst., 1979-84; asst. prof. polit. sci. Union U., Jackson, Tenn., 1984-86; asst. prof. California U. Pa., 1986—; cons. City Charter Revision Com., Knoxville, 1975, on preparation state and fed. grant applications, Clifton, 1975-77, Met. Govt. Citizen's Com., Jackson, 1986; chmn. UN study project LWV, Jackson, 1985. Contbr. articles to profl. jours. and encys. Recipient Outstanding Teaching award Rutledge Hist. Soc., Jackson, 1986. Mem. Am. Polit. Sci. Assn., Northeastern Polit. Sci. Assn., Pa. Polit. Sci. Assn., Ctr. for Study Presidency, West Tenn. Hist. Soc. (hon.), Pi Sigma Alpha, Phi Alpha Theta, Pi Gamma Mu. Democrat. Home: 2 Springer Ave Uniontown PA 15401-2740 Office: California U Pa Dept Polit Sci California PA 15419

PIGNATARO, LOUIS JAMES, engineering educator; b. Bklyn., Nov. 30, 1923; s. Joseph and Rose (Capi) P.; m. Edith Hoffmann, Sept. 12, 1954; 1 child, Thea. B.C.E., Poly. Inst. Bklyn., 1951; M.S., Columbia U., 1954; Dr. Tech. Sci., Tech. U. Graz, Austria, 1961. Registered profl. engr., N.Y., Calif., Fla. Faculty Poly. Inst. N.Y., 1951-85, prof. civil engring., 1965—, dir. div. transp. planning, 1967—, head dept. transp. planning and engring., 1970, dir. Transp. Tng. and Research Center, 1975; Kayser prof. transp. engring. City Coll., N.Y.C., 1985-88; assoc. dir. Inst. Transp. Systems City Coll., 1985-88; mem. faculty N.J. Inst. Tech., 1988—, disting. prof. transp. engring., 1988—, dir. ctr. transp. studies and research, 1988—; cons. govtl. agys., pvt. firms. Mem. Gov.'s Task Force Advisers on Transp. Problems, Gov.'s Task Force on Alcohol and Hwy. Safety; commr.'s council advisers N.Y. State Dept. Transp.; mem. adv. bd. freight services improvement conf. Port Authority N.Y. and N.J.; mem. adv. com. N.Y.C. Dept. Transp.; mem. rev. com. N.Y.C. Dept. City Planning; mem. Mayor's Transp. Commn., City of Newark. Sr. author: Traffic Engineering-Theory and Practice, 1973; contbr. over 70 papers to profl. jours. Served with AUS, 1943-46. Recipient Distinguished Tchr. citation Poly. Inst. Bklyn., 1965, Dedicated Alumnus award, 1971, Distinguished Alumnus award, 1972; citation for distinguished research Poly. chpt. Sigma Xi, 1975; named Engr. of Year N.Y. State Soc. Profl. Engrs., 1974. Fellow ASCE (dir.), Inst. Transp. Engrs. (Transp. Engr. of Yr. Met. sect. N.Y. and N.J. 1982); mem. Am. Rd. and Transp. Builders Assn. (div. dir.), Transp. Research Bd. (univ. liaison rep., Outstanding Paper award 1980 ann. meeting), Transp. Research Forum, Nat. Soc. Profl. Engrs., Sigma Xi, Chi Epsilon, Tau Beta Pi. Home: 230 Jay St Brooklyn NY 11201-1948 Office: NJ Inst Tech Ctr Transp Studies Rsch 323 Martin Luther King Blvd Newark NJ 07102

PIGNONE, CHARLES JOSEPH, III, marketing executive; b. Troy, N.Y., May 7, 1966; s. Charles Joseph and Frances Ann (Milano) P. BS in Bus., Siena Coll., 1988. Lic. real estate assoc., N.Y. Realtor Manor Homes, Latham, N.Y., 1988-91; mktg. mgr. Lawnmark Lawncare, Albany, N.Y., 1991—. Author: Sinatra: 1939-89, 1989. Pres. Sinatra Soc. Am., Newtonville, N.Y., 1984—. Mem. Soc. for the Advancement Mgmt., Siena Alumni Assn., Sinatra Soc. Japan. Office: Sinatra Soc of Am PO Box 269 Newtonville NY 12128

PIKE, CARL STEPHEN, biologist, educator; b. N.Y.C., Apr. 13, 1945; s. Seymour and Eleanor (Rudder) P.; m. Ellen Faye Leader, Oct. 12, 1969; children: Jill, William. BS, Yale U., 1966, MPhil, 1967; PhD, Harvard U., 1972. Asst. prof. biology Franklin and Marshall Coll., Lancaster, Pa., 1971-77, assoc. prof., 1977-86, prof., 1986—, chairperson, 1986-90. Contbr. numerous articles to profl. jours. Mem. sch. bd. Sch. Dist. Lancaster, 1989—. Office: Franklin and Marshall Coll Dept Biology PO Box 3003 Lancaster PA 17604-3003

PIKE, CHARLES P., physicist; b. Winthrop, Mass., Feb. 21, 1941; m. Sheila M. Hazel, Oct. 12, 1969; children: Kristen, Stephanie. BS, Boston Coll., 1963; MS, Northeastern U., 1969. Physicist Air Force Cambridge Rsch. Lab., Bedford, Mass., 1963-81; br. chief USAF Phillips Lab., Bedford, 1981—. Author: Space Systems Environmental Interactions, 1980; contbr. articles to profl. jours. Recipient Tech. Transfer award Fed. Lab. Consortium, 1988. Office: Phillips Lab/WSSI Hanscom AFB MA 01731

PIKE, JOHN NAZARIAN, physicist; b. Boston, Feb. 13, 1929; s. Arthur Thorndike and Sarah Lucy (Nazarian) P.; m. Margaretta May Horner, Dec. 28, 1957; children: Sally Katharine, Susan Horner. AB, Princeton U., 1951; PhD in Physics & Optics, U. Rochester, 1958. Staff scientist Parma (Ohio) Rsch. Ctr., Union Carbide Corp., 1956-63; mem. physics faculty Baldwin-Wallace Coll., Berea, Ohio, 1961-63; sr. scientist Tarrytown (N.Y.) Tech. Ctr., Union Carbide Corp., 1963-85; pres. J.J. Pike & Co., Inc. Indsl. Optics Cons., Pleasantville, N.Y., 1986—. Contbr. numerous articles to profl. jours. Bd. dirs. United Way of Westchester (N.Y.), 1979-85, chmn. planning com., 1989—. Recipient Harold J. Marshall Citation for Community Svc. United Way of No. Westchester, 1976, Community Svc. Award Union Carbide Corp., 1982. Mem. Optical Soc. Am., Internat. Soc. for Optical Engring. Republican. Home: 71 Cedar Ave Pleasantville NY 10570-1932 Office: JJ Pike & Co Inc PO Box 186 Pleasantville NY 10570-0186

PIKE, RONALD MARSTON, chemist, educator; b. Calais, Maine, Aug. 16, 1925; s. Roscoe Marston and Eugenia Elmyra (Adams) P.; m. Marilyn Cecilia Waris, June 14, 1952; children: Dana Marston, Gretchen Leigh Pike Mourtges. BS, U. N.H., 1949, MS, 1950; PhD, MIT, 1953. Rsch. chemist Union Carbide Corp., Tonawanda, N.Y., 1953-57; prof. chemistry Lowell (Mass.) Tech. Inst., 1957-65, Merrimack Coll., North Andover, Mass., 1965—; vis. prof. Bowdoin Coll., Brunswick, Maine, 1980-81, 84, U.S. Mil. Acad., West Point, N.Y., 1990-91; cons. Riverside Rsch. Labs., Haverhill, Mass., 1965-79, Canton Lab., Inc., Haverhill, 1977-79, AVCO-RAD Corp., Wilmington, Mass., 1959-62. Co-author: Microscale Organic Laboratory, 1986, 2d edit., 1989, Microscale Inorganic Laboratory, 1990, Microscale Organic Laboratory Techniques, 1991. With U.S. Army, 1943-46, PTO, ETO. Recipient Nat. Catalyst award Chem. Mfrs. Assn., 1990, John A. Timm award New England Assn. Chemsitry Tchrs., 1987, Charles Dana Found. award, 1986. Mem. Am. Chem. Soc. (Chem. Health and Safety award 1987, James Flack Norris award 1988), Sigma Xi, Alpha Xi Sigma. Office: Merrimack Coll North Andover MA 01845

PILBEAM, DAVID ROGER, paleoanthropology educator; b. Brighton, Sussex, Eng., Nov. 21, 1940; came to U.S., 1968; s. Ernest Winton and Edith (Clack) P.; m. Maryellen Ruvolo, Dec. 18, 1982; 1 child, Katharine Alexandra. B.A., Cambridge U., 1962, M.A., 1966; Ph.D., Yale U., 1967; M.A. (hon.), Harvard U., 1982. Demonstrator in anthropology Cambridge U., Eng., 1965-68; asst. prof. anthropology Yale U., 1968-70, assoc. prof., 1970-74, prof., 1974-81, prof. anthropology, geology and geophysics, 1974-81, prof. anthropology, 1981-90; Henry Ford II prof. social sci. Harvard U., Cambridge, Mass., 1990—, assoc. dean faculty arts and scis. for undergrad. edn., 1987-92; dir. Peabody Mus., 1990—. Author: Evolution of Man, 1970, Ascent of Man, 1972; co-author: Human Biology, 3d edit., 1988. Fellow Am. Anthropol. Assn.; mem. Am. Acad. Arts and Scis., Nat. Acad. Scis. (assoc.). Office: Harvard U Peabody Mus 11 Divinity Ave Cambridge MA 02138-2096

PILCHER, RICHARD PAUL, actor, educator; b. St. Louis, Apr. 12, 1946; s. Paul Shirley and Dorothy Belle (Pilcher) P.; m. Natalie Joan Smith, Aug. 3, 1985. BA, U. Mo., Kansas City, 1968. Actor Hartford Stage Co., Syracuse Stage, Folger Theatre, McCarter Theatre, St. Louis Repertory, Meadow Brook Theatre, Circle-in-the-Sq., 1969-80; artistic dir., founder Actors Ensemble, Balt., 1981-85; instr. in acting Balt. Sch. for the Arts, Balt., 1981—; assoc. dir. Utah Shakespearean Festival, Cedar City, 1972-73; mem. mentor program Goucher Coll., Balt., 1990—. Contbr. articles to profl. jours. Home: 8 Whirlwind Ct # E Baltimore MD 21207-1518

PILGRIM, DIANNE HAUSERMAN, art museum director; b. Cleve., July 9, 1941; d. John Martin and Norma Hauserman; divorced. BA, Pa. State U., 1963; MA, Inst. Fine Arts, NYU, 1965; postgrad., CUNY, 1971-74; LHD (hon.), Amherst Coll., 1991. Chester Dale fellow Am. wing. Met. Mus. Art, N.Y.C., 1966-68, researcher, 1971, rsch. cons. Am. paintings and sculpture, 1972-73; asst. to dirs. Pyramid Galleries, Ltd., Washington, 1969-71, Finch Coll. Mus. Art, Washington, 1971; curator dept. decorative arts Bklyn. Mus., 1973-88, chmn. dept., 1988; dir. Cooper-Hewitt Mus., N.Y.C., 1988—; mem. adv. com. Gracie Mansion, N.Y.C., 1980; mem. design adv. com. Art Inst. Chgo., 1988—; mem. Hist. House Trust of N.Y.C., Mayor's Office, 1989—. Co-author, curator: (book and exhbn. catalogue) The American Renaissance 1876-1917, 1979, (book) The Machine Age in America 1918-1941, 1986 (Charles F. Montgomery prize Decorative Arts Soc.). Bd. dirs. Nat. Multiple Sclerosis Soc., 1989. Recipient Disting. Alumni award Pa. State U., 1991. Mem. Art Table, Decorative Arts Soc. (pres. 1977-79). Office: Cooper-Hewitt Mus 2 E 91st St New York NY 10128-0669

PILIERO, CATHERINE ANNE, psychotherapist; b. Phila., Dec. 11, 1962; d. James Vincent and Catherine (Duaime) P. BA, Villanova U., 1985; MS, U. Pa., 1985, postgrad., 1985—. Project dir. Salem (N.J.) County YMCA, 1986-86; instr., intern Sexual Disorders Clinic Johns Hopkins Hosp., Balt., 1986; sexuality cons. Hall-Mercer Pa. Hosp., Phila., 1986—; sex offenders therapist Family Counseling Svc., Camden, N.J., 1988—; coord. AIDS edn. INTERAC Mental Health Agy., Phila., 1990—; teaching assoc. U. Pa., 1992; sexual abuse victims therapist South Jersey Counseling Assocs., Haddonfield, N.J., 1989—. Vol. Phila. State Hosp., 1981-84, SPCA, Carneys Point, Md., 1989—, People for Ethical Treatment Animals, Washington, 1989—. Forensic Psychiatry fellow U. Pa., 1991-92. Mem. AACD. Home: 724 Fitzwater St Philadelphia PA 19147-2815

PILLAGALLI, MICHAEL ANTHONY, educational administrator, antique dealer, editor; b. Bryn Mawr, Pa., May 3, 1949; s. Anthony and Julia (Gingetti) P.; divorced; 1 child, Margaret Anne. BS in Edn., Bloomsburg (Pa.) U., 1971; MS in Counseling, Villanova (Pa.) U., 1975. English chair West Chester (Pa.) Sch. Dist., 1985—; antiques dealer Ivystone Antiques,

West Chester, 1975—. Author: 18th Century Arts and Crafts, 1982; editor: Historic Annapolis, 1990. Chair Park and Recreation Bd., West Goshen, Pa., 1989—, Bd. of Historic Rev., West Chester, 1980-87; nomination chair bd. dirs. ARC, Delaware Valley, Pa., 1986—; founding chair Chester County Hist. Soc. Antique Show, 1982—. Named Outstanding Young Educator, Pa. Jaycees, 1985. Mem. NEA, Nat. Coun. Tchrs. English, Zeta Psi. Home: Fox Hill 924 North Hill Dr West Chester PA 19380

PILLAI, ARRACKAL KESAVA BALAKRISHNA, anthropology educator, psychotherapist; b. Changanacherry, Kerala, India, May 9, 1930; came to U.S., 1966; s. V. Potti and Amma (Narayani) P.; m. Radha Pillai; children: Gita, Prita. MA, Kerala (India) U., 1955, East Carolina U., 1968; MPhil, Columbia U., 1972, PhD, 1975. Cert. Am. Bd. Med. Psychotherapists. Prof., chair dept. English Sri Sankara Coll., Kalady, India, 1955-66; dir. Asian Studies, Hollywood Coll., Fla., 1966-67; prof., chair anthropology Ramapo Coll. of N.J., Mahwah, 1972—; co-chair East Asian studies Ramapo Coll. of N.J., 1988—; pvt. practice psychotherapist Riverdale, N.Y., 1986—; trainer psychotherapists, social workers, 1986—; founder Integral Devel. Therapy, Integral Devel. Social Work, Integral Human Devel.; assoc. univ. seminar Columbia U., N.Y.C., 1972—; co-chair nat. com. Anthropology and Social Work, 1988—; founder, chair N.Y. Inst. Integral Human Devel., Riverdale, 1987—. Author: Human Order, 1985, Transcendental Self, 1987, Culture of Social Stratification and Sexism: The Nayars, 1987. Founder, chairperson Devel. Projects, India, 1955-66. Predoctoral fellowship NIMH, 1972-75. Fellow Am. Anthropol. Assn.; mem. Met. Med. Anthropology Assn. (subcom. chair 1980-83), Am. Assn. Counseling and Human Devel., Assn. Multicultural Counseling and Devel., Assn. Asian Studies, Ramapo Anthropology Soc. (founder, dir.), India Devel. Inst. (chair). Office: Sch Am Internat Studies Ramapo Coll 505 Ramapo Valley Rd Mahwah NJ 07430-1623

PILLAI, GOPAL, engineering company executive; b. Quilon, Kerala, India, Nov. 27, 1937; came to U.S., 1971; s. Shankara Pillai and Lakshmi Kutty (Amma) Ponnamma; m. Madhavikutty Nalina Kumari, Nov. 24, 1962; children: Nanda, Shyama, Shankar. BSCE, Coll. Engring., Trivandrum, Kerala, 1958, MS in Structural Engring., 1960; MS in Transp., George Washington U., 1974, postgrad., 1974-75. Registered profl. engr. Va., Ark. Lectr. Coll. Engring., Quilon and Palghat, Kerala, 1960-62; divisional engr. Ministry of Railways, New Delhi, 1962-70; sr. engr. Nigerian Railway Corp., Lagos, Nigeria, 1970-71; constrn. supt. Mozel Devel. Corp., Arlington, Va., 1972-74; sr. engr., site mgr. Northrop Page Communications Engrs., Vienna, Va., 1974-79; sr. engr. T-CAS, Inc., McLean, Va., 1979-81; dir. projects Kramico Societē Anonymē Egyptiēn, Cairo, Egypt, 1981-83; mng. dir. Al Fairuz Trading and Contracting, Ltd. Liability Co., Muscat, Oman, 1983-85; v.p. Constrn. Environ. Inc., Alexandria, 1985-87; sr. v.p. Sheladia Assocs., Inc., Rockville, Md., 1987-90. Mem. Am. Soc. Civil Engrs., Instn. Structural Engrs. (assoc., London), Instn. Engrs. (Calcutta), Am. Cons. Engrs. Coun., Soc. Am. Mil. Engrs., Kerala Assn. Greater Washington. Hindu. Home: 4713 Willet Dr Annandale VA 22003-3949 Office: Sheladia Assocs Inc 15825 Shady Grove Rd Rockville MD 20850-4008

PILLING, JANET KAVANAUGH, lawyer; b. Akron, Ohio, Sept. 5, 1951; d. Paul and Marjorie (Logue) Kavanaugh; m. Martin Jolles, Mar. 6, 1987; children: Madeleine Sloan Langdon Jolles, Jameson Samuel Rhys Jolles. BA, Ohio Wesleyan U., 1973; JD, U. Mo., 1976; LLM, Villanova U., 1985. Bar: Pa. 1976, U.S. Tax Ct. 1976, U.S. Dist. Ct. (ea. dist.) Pa. 1976. Atty. Schnader, Harrison, Segal & Lewis, Phila., 1976-83; gen. counsel Kistler-Tiffany Cos. Schnader, Harrison, Segal & Lewis, Wayne, Pa., 1983—. Mem. Phila. Estate Planning Coun., Montgomery County Estate Planning Coun., Chester County Estate Planning Coun. Mem. ABA, Phila. Bar Assn. (probate sect., tax sect.), Pa. Bar Assn., Phi Beta Kappa, Phi Delta Phi. Office: Kistler Tiffany Cos 987 Old Eagle School Rd Ste 706 Wayne PA 19087-1755

PILLINGER, JAMES J., lawyer, educator; b. N.Y.C., Sept. 11, 1918; s. David N. and Esther (Adler) P.; m. Evelyn Spitzer, Mar. 31, 1946; children: Marc H., Michael H. LLB, St. John's Law Sch., 1942; LLM, NYU, 1970; BPS, Pace U., 1974. Bar: N.Y. 1942, U.S. Tax Ct. 1944, U.S. Dist. Ct. (so. dist.) N.Y. 1944, U.S. Dist. Ct. (ea. dist.) N.Y. 1952, U.S. Supreme Ct. 1960, U.S. Ct. Appeals (2d cir.) 1973. Assoc. law dept., mgr. legal rsch. div., editor law bull. Nat. Surety Corp., N.Y.C., 1939-42; assoc. Bergerman & Hourwich, N.Y.C., 1942-45; ptnr. Pillinger, Raiskin & Weiser, N.Y.C., 1945-61, Metnick, Pillinger & Sutera, N.Y.C., 1961-66; pvt. practice N.Y.C., 1966—; asst. prof. law Pace U., N.Y.C., 1967-71; assoc. prof. law Baruch Coll., CUNY, 1971-88. Contbr. articles to legal jours. Pres. Boys Brotherhood Rep. of N.Y., Inc., 1943-59, bd. dirs, 1970—; legis. asst. N.Y. Gen. Assembly, Albany, 1973-74; mem. N.Y. State Commn. on Economy, Albany, 1974-75. Office: 64-39 212th St Bayside NY 11364

PILON, A. BARBARA, educator; b. Providence; d. Francis L. and Alice F. (Kelly) Cummings; m. Albert J. Pilon Jr., Feb. 6, 1954. AB, Brown U.; MEd, Rhode Island Coll.; PhD, Ind. U., 1969. Cons., lang. arts dept. Johnston (R.I.) Sch. Dist., 1962-64; instr. Westfield (Mass.) State Coll. 1964-65; asst. prof. Ind. U., Indpls., 1969-71; prof., edn. dept. Worcester (Mass.) State Coll., 1972-87, prof., langs., lit. dept., 1987—. Author: Concrete Is Not Always Hard, Teaching Language Arts Creatively in the Elementary Grades; contbr. articles, tapes, monographs to profl. jours. and chpts. in books. Mem. NAt. Assn. Gifted Children (bd. dirs.), NAGC (sec., rec. sec.), Nat. Coun. Tchrs. English, New England Reading Assn. (bd. dirs.).

PILTZIN, NORMAN MEYER, accountant; b. Bklyn., Jan. 21, 1929; s. Elias and Bessie (Charney) P.; m. Rita Mintzer, Oct. 19, 1952 (dec. June 1988); children: Gayle Hollis, Brenda Sue. BBA cum laude, CCNY, 1950, MBA, 1957. CPA, N.Y.; cert. mgmt. acctg. Staff acct. Eisner & Lubin, CPAs, N.Y.C., 1950-54; lectr., acct. Baruch Coll., N.Y.C., 1963-91; pvt. practice acctg. Bklyn., 1954—. Mem. AICPA, Am. Acctg. Assn., N.Y. State Soc. CPAs, Inst. Mgmt. Acctg. Home and Office: 206 Barlow Dr Brooklyn NY 11234-6937

PILVIN, BARBARA JEANNE, librarian; b. Balt., Mar. 4, 1951; d. Harold and Beatrice (Rich) P. AB cum laude, Smith Coll., 1973; MA, Yale U., 1976; MLS, U. Md., 1981. Editorial asst. Libr. of Congress, Washington, 1974; libr. asst. Jewish Community Ctr. of Greater Washington, Rockville, Md., 1978-79; spl. project cataloger U. Pa., Phila., 1982-84; reference libr. Free Libr. of Phila., 1986—; student intern Archives and Manuscripts Dept, McKeldin Libr., U. Md., College Park, 1981, grad. asst. Coll. of Libr. Info. Svcs., 1982. Co-author: Mental and Developmental Disabilities: Directory of Legal Advocates, 1982; co-author, founder, editor newsletter The Alliance, 1987-89; contbr. articles in A New Day: Voices from Across the Land. Reader Broadcaster Radio Reading and Taping Svcs. Washington Ear, Silver Spring, 1974-75, Recs. for the Blind, New Haven, 1977-78, Radio Info. Ctr. for the Blind, Phila., 1983-86; vol. libr. Stanley Meml. Pub. Libr., Laurel, Md., 1982. Mem. NOW (del. nat. conv. Phila. chpt. 1987), Am. Libr. Assn., Am. Printing History Assn., Modern Lang. Assn., Nat. Alliance for the Mentally Ill, Depression and Related Affective Disorders Assn. Democrat. Jewish. Office: Free Libr of Phila Logan Sq Philadelphia PA 19144-3017

PIMPINELLA, RONALD JOSEPH, surgeon; b. Utica, N.Y., Sept. 27, 1935; s. Joseph and Josephine (Payne) P.; B.A. magna cum laude, Syracuse U., 1956; M.D., U. Rochester, 1960; children: Andrea, Giancarlo. Intern, Albany (N.Y.) Med. Center, 1960-61; resident in ear-nose-throat Columbia Presbyn. Med. Ctr., 1962-65; chief ENT, Martin Army Hosp., Ft. Benning, Ga., 1965-67; practice medicine specializing in otolaryngology and facial plastic surgery, Torrington, Conn., 1967-88; ret.; chief otolaryngology Charlotte Hungerford Hosp. Capt. U.S. Army, 1965-67. Fellow Am. Assn. Ophthalmology and Otolaryngology, Am. Acad. Facial Plastic and Reconstructive Surgery, ACS; mem. AMA, Conn. Med. Soc. (pres. otolaryngology sect. 1978-83). Roman Catholic. Contbr. articles to med. jours. Address: Old Farms Condominiun # 32 319 Thomaston Rd Watertown CT 06798

PIÑA-ROSALES, GERARDO, writer, Spanish language educator; b. Cádiz, Spain, Dec. 3, 1948; came to U.S., 1973; s. Rafael and Josefa (Rosales) P.; m. Laurie Norwin, May 25, 1974; 1 child, Mariel. BA, CUNY, 1977, MPhil in Spanish, 1982, PhD in Spanish, 1985. coord. of info. Fundación Cultural Hispánica, N.Y., 1988—; gen. sec. Circulo de Poetas Y Escritores Iberoamericanos, N.Y., 1989—. Adj. lectr. Queens Coll. CUNY, N.Y.C., 1977-80; dir. of lang. program The Spanish Inst., N.Y.C., 1980-81; assoc. prof. Lehman Coll. CUNY, N.Y.C., 1981—; coord. of info. Fundacion Cultural Hispanica, N.Y., 1988—; pres. Circulo de Poetas Y Escritores Iberoamericanos, N.Y., 1992—. Author: Estudios Sobre Teatro Español, 1984, Narrativa Breve de Manuel Andujar, 1988; contbr. articles to profl. jours. Mem. MLA, Assn. Tchrs. Spanish and Portuguese, North Am. Acad. Spanish Lang. Home: 103 Norben Rd Monsey NY 10952-1430

PINCHUCK, CURT PAUL, psychiatrist; b. Bklyn., Feb. 6, 1960. BA, Columbia Coll., N.Y.C., 1982; MD cum laude, SUNY, Buffalo, 1987. Intern, then resident in psychiatry NYU Med. Ctr., N.Y.C., 1987-91; teaching asst. in psychiatry Tisch Hosp., The Univ. Hosp. of NYU Med. Ctr., 1990—; staff psychiatrist Hillside Hosp. of the L.I. Jewish Med. Ctr., 1991—; instr. in psychiatry Albert Einstein Coll. of Medicine, Yeshiva U. Editor: The First Annual 1991-92 New York City Psychiatric Fellowship and Research Guide, 1990. Recipient Gilbert M. Beck meml. prize in psychiatry for acad. excellence SUNY at Buffalo Sch. Medicine, 1987. Mem. AMA, APA (presenter ann. mtgs. 1985, 86), Mesorah Soc. for Traditional Judaism, Med. Soc. State of N.Y., Assn. Orthodox Jewish Scientists, L.I. Jewish Med. Ctr. Staff Soc., NYU Bellevue Psychiat. Soc., Alpha Omega Alpha, Phi Lambda Kappa. Office: Hillside Hosp Glen Oaks NY 11004

PINCK, JOAN BRAVERMAN, management consultant; b. Lowell, Mass., Feb. 27, 1929; d. Edwin and Esther F. (Goodman) Braverman; m. Dan C. Pinck, Aug. 26, 1951; children: Anthony, Jennifer, Alexandra, Charles. AB, Radcliffe Coll., 1950. Dean Pine Manor Coll., Chestnut Hill, Mass., 1969-72; lectr., asst. dean Harvard Bus. Sch., Boston, 1972-76; asst. sec., higher edn. vice-chancellor Commonwealth of Mass., Boston, 1976-79; dir. rsch. adminstrn. and policy Beth Israel Hosp., Boston, 1979-89; prin. The Chilmark Group, Boston, 1989-90; assoc. cons. The TQM Group, Cambridge, Mass., 1990-91; v.p. Juran Inst. Inc., Wilton, Conn., 1991—; bd. dirs. Harvard Community Health Plan, Brookline, Mass., Mass. Soc. for Med. Rsch., Boston. Bd. dirs. Family Counseling/Guidance Ctr., Boston, 1984—, Pub. Responsibility in Medicine and Rsch., The Cambridge Sch. of Weston, Mass., 1977-81. Bunting Inst. fellow, 1967-69; Milton Fund Rsch. grantee Harvard, 1969. Mem. Assn. Univ. Tech. Mgrs., Soc. Rsch. Adminstrs., Harvard Club, Spl. Forces Club of London. Home and office: 26 Dwight St Boston MA 02118

PINCUS, FLORENCE VOLKMAN, clinical psychologist. BA in Psychology, Bklyn. Coll., 1936; MSS in Psychology, New Sch. Social Rsch., 1938; postgrad., CCNY, 1938-39, NYU, 1939-40. Lic. psychologist, N.Y., Ill. Psychologist WPA Remedial Reading and Arithmetic Project, N.Y.C., 1938-40; personnel technician War Dept., Washington, 1942-43; ct. psychologist Juvenile and Domestic Rels. Ct., Richmond, Va., 1944-46; sch. psychologist Bur. Child Guidance, N.Y.C., 1953-57; staff psychologist Hillside Hosp., N.Y.C., 1959-64; psychologist Speech and Hearing Ctr., Queens Coll., N.Y.C., 1964; chief psychologist community mental health program Ill. State Psychiat. Inst., Chgo., 1967-69; sr. psychologist Health Ins. Plan Mental Health Ctr., Bklyn., 1971-81; pvt. practice individual and group psychotherapy N.Y.C. and Chgo., 1957—; sr. clin. assoc. grad. psychology program CUNY, N.Y.C., 1978—; parent educator United Parents Assn. Profl. Panel, 1955-60; cons. Coll. William ad Mary, Richmond, 1945, Mills Coll., N.Y., 1950-52, Pub. Sch. 165, N.Y.C. Bd. Edn., 1957-64, U. Fla., Gainesville, 1970, Head Start, OEO, Child Devel. Group Miss., Edwards, 1965, Emory U. Med. Sch., Atlanta, 1971; pvt. practice, 1957—. Asst. editor Psychologists' League Jour., 1937-40. Speakers' panel Fedn. Jewish Philanthropies, Queens County Mental Health Soc., 1955-64; nat. bd. dirs. Vietnam Vet. Era Nat. Resource Project, 1975—; mem. N.Y. Health Profls. Group, Amnesty Internat., 1986—; co-founder, nat. coord. Psychologists for Social Action, 1968-77. Fellow Am. Orthopsychiat. Assn. (nuclear issues study group 1984—); mem. APA (com. on gay and lesbian concerns 1981-83), Assn. Women Psychologists, Feminist Therapy Inst., N.Y. Soc. Clin. Psychologists (exec. bd. 1974-75), N.Y. State Psychol. Assn. (com. on gay and lesbian concerns 1983-85), N.Y. Soc. Clin. Psychologists (Ann. Holocaust Meml. award 1982). Office: 31112 W 20th St New York NY 10011-3381

PINDER, ALBERT WILLIAM JOSEPH, II, press secretary; b. Grinnell, Iowa, Jan. 6, 1951; s. Albert William Joseph and Dorothy Jean (Watt) P. Student, Grinnell Coll., 1969; BS in Broadcasting and Film, Boston U., 1972; postgrad., U. Iowa, 1976-77. Sports editor, head photographer Grinnell Herald Register, 1972-76, also bd. dirs.; reporter Worcester (Mass.) Telegram, 1979-88; pres. sec. to Congressman Jim Leach U.S. Ho. of Reps., Washington, 1988—. Recipient Best News Story-State of Iowa award Iowa Press Assn., 1978. Mem. Nat. Press Club. Episcopalian. Home: 4220 37th St NW Washington DC 20008-3147 Office: Office Rep Jim Leach 1514 Longworth Bldg Washington DC 20008

PINE, THOMAS ALLEN, computing and automation industry executive; b. Indpls., Aug. 11, 1940; s. Ira Coleman and Esther Ruth (Schuck) P.; m. Patricia Lou Ann Ley, July 9, 1960; children: Mark Joseph, Lorraine Lynn. BS, Purdue U., 1964. Dir. bus. mgmt. IBM, White Plains, N.Y., 1982-84; v.p. maj. accounts Burroughs Corp., Detroit, 1985; pres. Viewpoint Universal Enterprises, Wilton, Conn., 1986-87; corp. v.p. product line mktg. Prime Computer, Inc., Natick, Mass., 1988-89; pres. Prime Wild G.I.S., Inc., Natick, 1989, Corp. Fin. Assocs. Boston Inc., 1990—. Home: 39 Marlborough St Boston MA 02116-2131

PINES, BURTON YALE, foundation executive; b. Chgo., Apr. 6, 1940; s. Hyman and Mary Pines; m. Helene Brenner, May 21, 1972. B.A., U. Wis., 1961, M.A., 1963. Instr. U. Wis., Madison, 1962-65; corr. Time mag., Bonn, Saigon and Vienna, 1966-73, editor, N.Y.C., 1973-81; sr. v.p. Heritage Found., Washington, 1981-92; chmn. Nat. Ctr. for Pub. Policy Rsch., Washington, 1982—; exec. com. Inst. East-West Dynamics; bd. dirs. Independence Inst., Denver, Media Rsch. Ctr. Author: Back to Basics, 1982. Recipient Page One award N.Y. Newspaper Guild, 1976, 77, 78. Jewish. Office: Nat Ctr for Pub Policy Rsch 300 I St NE Ste 3 Washington DC 20002

PINES, WAYNE LLOYD, public relations counselor; b. Washington, Dec. 31, 1943; s. Jerome Martin and Ethel (Schnall) P.; B.A., Rutgers U., 1965; postgrad. George Washington U., 1969-71; m. Nancy Freitag, Apr. 16, 1966; children—Noah Morris, Jesse Mireth. Reporter, city editor Middletown (N.Y.) Times Herald-Record, 1965-68; copy editor Reuters News, 1968-69; asso. editor FDC Reports, Washington, 1969-72; chief Consumer Edn. and Info., FDA, also editor FDA Consumer, 1972-74; exec. editor Product Safety Letter and Devices and Diagnostics Letter, Washington, 1974-75; dep. asst. commr. for pub. affairs, chief press relations FDA, Rockville, Md., 1975-78, assoc. commr. public affairs, 1978-82; adj. prof. Washington Public Affairs Center, U. So. Calif., 1980-81; instr. N.Y.U. Sch. Continuing Edn., 1982-84; spl. asst. to dir. NIMH, 1982-83; sr. v.p., sr. counselor Burson-Marsteller, 1983-87; exec. v.p., dir. med. issues, 1987—; instr. Profl. Devel. Inst., 1983-85; columnist Med. Advt. News., 1985-90. Author: The Sermons of Jerome Martin Pines, Promotion and Advertising Regulations; contbr. numerous articles in field to profl. jours. Home: 5821 Nevada Ave NW Washington DC 20015-2547 Office: Burson-Marsteller 1850 M St NW Washington DC 20036-5803

PING, DOUGLAS EDWARD, food and beverage company executive; b. Albuquerque, July 13, 1960; s. Roy A. and Vivian R. (Theriault) P. AAS, SUNY, Buffalo, 1989, BS in Mgmt., 1992. V.p. Johnson Park Entertainment Inc., Buffalo, 1988—, Johnson Park Mgmt. Corp., Buffalo, 1991—. Co-chmn. Ann. Thanksgiving for Srs., Buffalo, 1988-91, Summer Festival for AIDS Community Svcs., Buffalo, 1989-91. Sarah Helen Kish Meml. scholar, 1988. Mem. Golden Key, Alpha Sigma Lambda (Lambda chpt.). Office: Johnson Park Entertainment 31 Johnson Park Buffalo NY 14201

PINGRY, JULIE See FRASER, JULIA ANN

PINKERT, DOROTHY MINNA, chemist; b. N.Y.C., June 2, 1921; d. Harry and Frieda Dorothy (Pinkert) Klein. A.B., Bklyn. Coll., 1944; M.S., Bklyn. Poly. U., 1952. Creep lab. technician Am. Brakeshoe Co., Mahwah, N.J., 1942-44; rsch. and quality control chemist Reed and Carnrick, Jersey City, 1944-48; chief quality control chemist Gold Leaf Pharmacal Co., New Rochelle, N.Y., 1948-56; rsch. chemist Internat. Salt Co., Watkins Glen, N.Y. and N.Y.C., 1957-61; sr. assoc. drug regulatory affairs Hoffmann-LaRoche Inc., Nutley, N.J., 1962-83. Mem. AAAS, Am. Chem. Soc., Am. Inst. Chemists, Am. Soc. Quality Control, Poly. U. Alumni Assn. (life dir.), N.Y. Acad. Scis. Republican.

PINKERTON, ROBERT BRUCE, mechanical engineer; b. Detroit, Feb. 10, 1941; s. George Fulwell and Janet Lois (Hedke) P.; m. Barbara Ann Bandfield, Aug. 13, 1966; 1 child, Robert Brent. BSME, Detroit Inst. Tech., 1965; MA in Engring., Chrysler Inst. Engring., 1967; JD, Wayne State U., 1976. From mech. engr. to emissions and fuel economy planning specialist Chrysler Engring. Office Chrysler Corp., Highland Park, Mich., 1967-80; dir. engring. Replacement div. TRW, Inc., Cleve., 1980-83; v.p. engring. TRW Automotive Aftermarket Group, 1983-86; v.p. engring. and rsch. Blackstone Corp., Jamestown, N.Y., 1986-89; pres., chief exec. officer Blackstone Corp., Jamestown, 1989-90, Athena Corp., Beaufort, S.C., 1990—, Cedar Crest Corp., Beaufort, S.C., 1990—. Mem. Fripp Island Club, Rotary. Presbyterian. Home: 573 Remora Dr Saint Helena Island SC 29920-9513

PINKNEY, ALPHONSO, educator; b. Fla., Dec. 15, 1928; s. Graham and Althea Margaret (Pinkston) P.; m. Sacha Grocholewska, July 30, 1982 (div. Jan. 1984). AB, Fla. A&M U., 1951; MA, NYU, 1952; PhD, Cornell U., 1961. Prof. sociology Hunter Coll., CUNY, N.Y.C., 1961-69, 75-90, prof. emeritus, 1990—; prof. U. Chgo., 1969-71, Howard U., Washington, 1971-72, U. Calif., Berkeley, 1973-75. Author: Black Americans, 1969, The American Way of Violence, 1972, Red, Black and Green, 1976, The Myth of Black Progress, 1984, Lest We Forget, 1992. Ford Found. fellow, 1960-61, 71. Home: 505 LaGuardia Pl Apt 27E New York NY 10012 Office: Hunter Coll 695 Park Ave New York NY 10021

PINO, CHRISTOPHER JOSEPH, clinical psychologist; b. Canastota, N.Y., Oct. 12, 1942; s. James and Josephine (Tianello) P.; m. Betsey Nelson, Sept. 2, 1967 (div. Apr. 1977); m. Lynn G. English, June 11, 1977; children: Lucienne, Christoher James, Marisa. BA in Psychology, Alfred U., 1965; MA in Psychology, Miami U., Oxford, Ohio, 1966; PhD, Ill. Inst. Tech., 1969. Lic. psychologist. Intern in psychology H.O. Singer Zone Ctr., Rockford, Ill., 1966-67; clin. psychologist J.J. Madden Zone Ctr., Chgo., 1967-68, H.U. Read Zone Ctr., Chgo., 1968-69; supr. clin. psychologist Orleans County Mental Health Clinic, Albion, N.Y., 1969-70; assoc. prof. psychology D'Youville Coll., Buffalo, 1970-80; exec. dir. Monsignor Carr Inst., Buffalo, 1980—; pvt. practice clin. psychology Buffalo, 1970—; assoc. prof. counselor edn. Canisius Coll., part-time 1983-86. Author: Divorce, Remarriage and Blended Family, 1984, Personalized Marriage Preparation and Enrichment, 1986, Training Consultants, 1985, Imagery in Family Diagnosis and Therapy: CVFES Sourcebook, 1991. Bd. dirs. Crisis Services, Buffalo, Step Family Assn. of W. N.Y. Mem. Am. Psychol. Assn., Psychol. Assn. W. N.Y. (sec. 1975-76), Mental Health Assn. Erie County (bd. dirs. 1980-86). Democrat. Roman Catholic. Home: 4070 Harris Hill Rd Buffalo NY 14221-7403 Office: Monsignor Carr Inst 76 W Humboldt Pky Buffalo NY 14214-2698

PINO, H. EDUARDO, clinical psychologist; b. Santiago, Chile, Sept. 25, 1949; came to U.S., 1968; s. Orozimbo and Sylvia (Garrido) P. BS, St. Joseph's U., Phila., 1973; MS, Hahnemann Med. Coll., 1977; D in Psychology, Hahnemann U. and Hosp., 1985. Psychiat. asst. part-time Hahnemann Hosp. Emergency Rm., Phila., 1975; psychol. examiner Hahnemann Community Mental Health Ctr., Phila., 1975-76; sr. clin. psychol. intern Montgomery County Emergency Svcs., Norristown, Pa., 1982-84, staff psychologist part-time, 1983-84; staff psychotherapist CAMCARE Health Corp., Camden and Pennsauken, N.J., 1984-85; forensic psychologist Lenape Valley Found., Bucks County, Pa., 1985-86; staff psychologist Eagleville (Pa) Hosp., 1985; cons. clin. psychologist Eugenia Hosp., Flourtown, Pa., 1984-86; ct. clin. psychologist Ct. of Common Pleas, Phila., 1986—; cons. in group treatment for sexual offenders and individual victims of sexual abuse Joseph J. Peters Inst., Phila., 1991—. Contbr. articles to profl. jours. Recipient award Rotary Internat.. Mem. APA (com. chairperson psychology law divsn. 1990—), Am. Psychology Law Soc. (chairperson internat. affairs com. 1990—), Pa. Psychol. Assn. (mem. editorial com. 1989—, cons. editor 1989-90, 91—), Am. Orthopsychiat. Assn., Am. Profl. Soc. on Abuse of Children, Internat. Soc. on Family Law, Internat. Soc. for Study of Multiple Personality and Dissociation. Office: PO Box 12903 Philadelphia PA 19108-0903

PINSKER, SANFORD, English educator; b. Washington, Pa., Sept. 28, 1941; s. Morris and Sonia (Moliver) P.; m. Ann Shifra Getson; children: Matt, Beth. BA, Washington & Jefferson Coll., 1963; PhD, U. Wash., 1967. Teaching asst. U. Wash., Seattle, 1963-67; asst. prof. Franklin & Marshall Coll., Lancaster, Pa., 1967-74, assoc. prof., 1974-84, prof., 1984-88, Shadek Humanities prof., 1988—; vis. prof. U. Calif., Riverside, 1973, 75. Author: The Schlemiel as Metaphor: Studies in the Yiddish and American-Jewish Novel, 1971, The Comedy that Hoits: An Essay on the Fiction of Philip Roth, 1975, Still Life and Other Poems, 1975, The Languages of Joseph Conrad, 1978, Between Two Worlds: The American Novel in the 1960s, 1978, Philip Roth: Critical Essays, 1982, Memory Breaks Off and Other Poems, 1984, Whales at Play and Other Poems of Travel, 1986, Three Pacific Northwest Poets: Stafford, Hugo, and Wagoner, 1987, others; co-editor Holocaust Studies Ann., Jewish-American History and Culture: An Encyclopedia, 1991; editorial bd. Studies in Am. Jewish Lit., Critique, Ga., Rev., Conradiana, Jour. of Modern Lit. NEH Younger Humanist, 1970-71; Fulbright sr. lectr., Belgium, 1984-85, Spain, 1990-91; Grad. Inst. Modern Letters fellow, 1968; Pa. Humanist, 1985-87. Office: Franklin & Marshall Coll Dept English Lancaster PA 17604

PINSKER, WALTER, allergist, immunologist; b. Bay Shore, N.Y., Mar. 27, 1933; s. Albert and Irene (Kuchlick) P.; m. Tillene Giller, June 15, 1958; children: Neil, Andrew, Susann. BA, U. Rochester, 1954; MD, U. Chgo., 1958. Diplomate Am. Bd. Allergy and Immunology. Intern L.I. Jewish Hosp., New Hyde Park, N.Y., 1958-59; resident internal medicine Bklyn. VA Hosp., 1959-60; resident internal medicine Long Beach (Calif.) VA Hosp., 1960-61, resident allergy and immunology, 1961-62; chief of allergy Letterman Army Hosp., San Francisco, 1962-64; pres. Bay Shore Allergy Group, 1964—; attending physician Mather Hosp., Port Jefferson, N.Y., St. Charles Hosp., Port Jefferson, 1981, Southside Hosp., Bay Shore, 1964—, chief of allergy, Good Samaritan Hosp., West Islip, N.Y., 1964—, chief of allergy; asst. clin. prof. medicine SUNY, Stony Brook, 1968—. Contbr. articles to profl. jours. Bd. visitors Pilgrim State Hosp., Brentwood, N.Y., 1974-77; pres. Suffolk Assn. Children with Learning Difficulties, N.Y., 1972-74; trustee Leeway Sch., Stony Brook, 1974-75, Bay Shore Jewish Ctr., 1974-84; com. for handicapped West Islip Schs., 1971—. Capt. U.S. Army, 1962-64. Recipient Physician's Recognition award AMA, 1969—. Fellow Am. Acad. Allergy and Immunology, Am. Coll. Allergy and Immunology, Am. Assn. Certified Allergists, Am. Coll. Chest Physicians, Am. Assn.- Study of Headaches, N.Y. Acad. Scis., Suffolk Acad. Medicine, Nassau-Suffolk Allergy Soc. (officer, bd. dirs. 1970—, pres. 1980-82). Office: Bay Shore Allergy Group P C 649 Montauk Hwy Bay Shore NY 11706

PINSTRUP-ANDERSEN, PER, educational administrator; b. Bislev, Denmark, Apr. 7, 1939; came to U.S., 1965; s. Marinus and Alma (Pinstrup) Andersen; m. Birgit Lund, June 19, 1965; children: Charlotte, Tina. BS, Royal Vet. & Agrl. U., Copenhagen, 1965; MS, Okla. State U., 1967, PhD, 1969. Agrl. economist Centro Internacional de Agricultura Tropical, Cali, Colombia, 1969-76; dir. agro.-econ. div. Internat. Fertilizer Devel. Ctr., Florence, Ala., 1976-77; sr. rsch. fellow, assoc. prof. Econ. Inst. Royal Vet. & Agr. U., 1977-80; rsch. fellow, dir. food consumption and nutrition policy program Internat. Food Policy Rsch. Inst., Washington, 1980-87, dir. gen., 1992—; dir. food and nutrition policy program, prof. food econs. Cornell U., Ithaca, N.Y., 1987-92; cons. The World Bank, Washington, 1978—, Can. Internat. Devel. Agy., 1982-83, 86, UNICEF, N.Y.C.; cons. subcom. on nutrition UN, Rome, 1980-87. Contbr. numerous articles to profl. jours. With Danish Army, 1958-59. Mem. Internat. Ctr. for Rsch. on Women (bd. dirs.). Home: 1451 Highwood Dr Mc Lean VA 22101 Office: Internat Food Policy Rsch Inst 1200 17th St NW Washington DC 20041

PINTER, GABRIEL GEORGE, physiology educator; b. Bekes, Hungary, June 23, 1925; came to U.S., 1958; s. Lajos and Regina (Szilagyi-Farkas) P.; m. Berit Helgesen, Dec. 19, 1958 (dec. May 1980); children: Renee Astrid,

Eva Ingelill; m. Vera Lederer, May 23, 1984. M.D., U. Sch. of Medicine, Budapest, Hungary, 1951. Asst. prof. U. Sch. Medicine, Budapest, 1951-56; rsch. assoc. U. Inst. Med. Rsch., Oslo, Norway, 1957-58; asst. prof. U. Tenn., Memphis, 1958-61; from asst. prof. to prof. U. Md., Balt., 1961-92, ret.; vis. prof. King's Coll., London, 1990—. Contbr. articles to profl. jours. Recipient A.V. Humbolt prize Fed. Republic of Germany, 1980; Swedish Royal Med. Soc. fellow, Uppsala, Sweden, 1972. Mem. Am. Physiol. Soc., Physiol. Soc. Great Britain, Scandinavian Physiol. Soc., European Soc. Microcirculation.

PINTO, EMANUEL, actuary; b. N.Y.C., Apr. 18, 1952; s. Morris and Annemarie (Sternfeld) P. BA, BS, St. Lawrence U., 1974. Actuarial trainee Home Ins. Co., N.Y.C., 1974-80; actuary/statistician State Rating Bur. of the Mass. Div. of Ins., Boston, 1980-81; v.p. and actuary Met. Reinsurance Co., N.Y.C., 1981-90; v.p. Skandia Am. Reinsurance Corp., N.Y.C., 1991—. Fellow Casualty Actuarial Soc.; mem. Am. acad. Actuaries (Woodward Fondiller prize 1989). Home: 2 Charlton St Apt 11H New York NY 10014-4919

PINTO, ROSALIND, retired educator, civic volunteer; b. N.Y.C.; d. Barney and Jenny Abrams; m. Jesse E. Pinto (dec.); children: Francine, Jerry, Evelyn. BA in Polit. Sci. cum laude, Hunter Coll.; MA in Polit. Sci., History, Columbia U.; postgrad., Queens Coll., LaGuardia Community Coll. Lic. social studies tchr. jr. high sch., N.Y., per diem lifetime substitute; cert. N.Y. State secondary sch. social studies grades 7-12. Substitute tchr., 1966-69, 90, 91—; tchr. social studies Jr. High Sch. 217 Briarwood, N.Y.C., 1969-89; ret., 1989; part-time cluster tchr. social studies and communication arts Pub. Sch. 140, Bronx, N.Y., 1990-91, 92—; participant numerous personal and profl. devel. seminars and workshops. Author curriculum materials; contbr. chpt. to Study Guide for Regents Competency Test in U.S. History and Government; contbr. poems to anthologies. Enrollment asst. Insight Heart Team, 1989; vol. receptionist Whitney Mus., Manhattan; mem. com. on pub. transp., community rels. and history Community Bd. 6, Queens, 1989—; vol. local polit. campaigns. Mem. NAFE, N.Y. Insight Alumni Assn., Forest Hills Van Ct. Homeowners Assn., Cen. Queens. Hist. Soc., Queens Hist. Soc., Columbia U. Grad. Sch. Arts and Scis. Alumni Assn., Hunter Coll. Alumni Assn.

PINTSOV, LEON ARON, computer scientist, consultant; b. St. Petersburg, Russia, Aug. 5, 1948; came to U.S., 1980; s. Aron Moses and Maya (Ronkin) P.; m. Emily Jane Gurevich, May 31, 1969; 1 child, Anna. MS in Math. magna cum laude, U. St. Petersburg, 1970; PhD in Applied Math., St. Petersburg Inst. Engring., 1979; MS in Mgmt. Sci., Renesslaer Poly. Inst., 1988. Mgr. recognition software project ScanOptics, Inc., East Hartford, Conn., 1981-83; mgr. software devel. Pitney Bowes Inc., Danbury, Conn., 1984-88; sr. mem. tech. staff Pitney Bowes Inc., Shelton, Conn., 1988—; cons. USPS, 1987-92, HGC, 1987-92, World Bank, 1987-92. Author: Modeling of Visual Imaging Systems, 1978; contbr. articles to profl. jours.; inventor imaging systems. Mem. IEEE (sr.), Internat. Soc. Neural Networks. Republican. Jewish. Home: 365 Mountain Rd West Hartford CT 06107 Office: Pitney Bowes 35 Waterview Dr Shelton CT 06484

PIOMBINO, ALFRED ERNEST, law consultant, writer; b. Poughkeepsie, N.Y., Oct. 9, 1962; s. Alfred Raymond and Barbara Jean (Elmendorf) P. AS, Dutchess Community Coll., Poughkeepsie, 1983; BS, Marist Coll., 1986, MPA, 1988. Instr. Ulster Community Coll., Stone Ridge, N.Y., 1986-88; pres. Piombino Corp., Poughkeepsie, 1987—; notary pub., N.J., 1989—, N.Y., 1984—; commr. of deed for Conn. in N.Y., 1991—, for Fla. in N.Y., 1992—; mem. Acad. of Legal Studies in Bus.; adj. faculty L.I. U., 1988—, Pratt Inst., 1989—. Author: Notary Public Handbook: A Guide for New York, 1989, Notary Public Handbook: A Guide for New Jersey, 1991, Notary Public Handbook: A Guide for Maine, 1992, Notary Public Handbook: A Guide for Florida, 1992; contbr. articles to profl. jours. Mem. faculty Am. Heart Assn., Dutchess County, N.Y., 1983-88; bd. dirs. ARC, Dutchess County, 1977-82. Recipient Nat. First Aid award Johnson & Johnson, 1978. Mem. Am. Soc. Pub. Adminstrn. (v.p. Dutchess County chpt. 1979-86), Am. Judicature Soc., Am. Arbitration Assn., Am. Soc. Notaries, N.Y. State Assn. Notaries Pub. (founder, pres.), N.E. Regional Bus. Law Assn., Am. Soc. Journalists and Authors, N.J. State Safe Deposit Assn. Roman Catholic. Home: 14 Lynbrook Rd PO Box 3586 Poughkeepsie NY 12603-4608 Office: 80 Washington St PO Box 3539 Poughkeepsie NY 12603

PIONE, FRANCES ELAINE, biotechnology production manager; b. Haverhill, Mass., Oct. 11, 1952; d. Gerald Leo and Ruth Elizabeth (Goldthwaite) Flanagan; m. Richard Allen Pione, Dec. 29, 1983. BS in Biology, U. Mass., 1982. Lab. technician II Clin. Assays/Baxter Travenol, Cambridge, Mass., 1983-84; lab technician III Clin. Assays/Baxter Travenol, Cambridge, 1984, asst. scientist, 1984-86; scientist Advanced Magnetics, Cambridge, 1986-88, prodn. mgr., 1988--. Recipient Tech. award Clin. Assays, 1984, 85, Discretionary award Clin. Assays, 1986. Roman Catholic. Office: Advanced Magnetics 61 Mooney St Cambridge MA 02138-1038

PIONK, RICHARD CLETUS, artist, educator; b. Minn., Apr. 26, 1936; s. Franz E. Spielmann and Esther (Dufrane) Pionk. Cert. in fine arts painting, Art Students League, 1983. Tchr. Art Students League, N.Y.C., 1991—; mem. bd. control Art Students League, 1983-90. Exhibited in one-man shows Moran Gallery, Tulsa, 1985, Connoisseur Gallery, Rhinebeck, N.Y., 1987, 88, 89, 90, Bklyn. Pub. Libr.; exhibited in group shows Queens Mus., N.Y.C., 1982, Hermitage Found., Norfolk, Va., 1985, Monmouth Mus., Lincroft, N.J., 1985, La Societe des Pastellistes de France, Lille, 1987, Canton (Ohio) Art Inst., 1987, Friends Art Mus., Naples, Fla., 1987, Mel Vin Gallery Southern Coll., Lakeland, Fla., 1987, Wind Borne Gallery, Southport, Conn., 1987, 89, The Food Show at Grand Cen. Art Gallery, N.Y.C., 1989, Quincy (Ill.) Art Club, 1989, 90, Jordane Art Gallery, Ft. Myers, Fla., 1990, Pastel Soc., N.Y.C., 1991, Allied Artists, N.Y.C., 1991, Harman-Meek Gallery, Naples, 1992. Mem. Pastel Soc. Am. (1st v.p. 1978-91, exhbn. chmn. 1978—, master pastellist), Allied Artists Am. (bd. dirs. 1986-91, asst. corr. sec. 1986—), Audubon Artists (juror 1989—), Artists Fellowship Inc. (bd. dirs. 1988-91), Nat. Arts Club, Salmagundi Club (mem. curators com., chmn. art com. 1981—). Roman Catholic. Home: 1349 Lexington Ave New York NY 10128-1511 Office: Studio 611 41 Union Sq New York NY 10003

PIOTROWSKI, JOHN HENRY, golf professional, real estate agent; b. Trenton, N.J., Nov. 24, 1949; s. Henry Edward and Helen Marie (Mazurek) P. BA in English, Edn., Trenton State U., 1971; postgrad., Rider Coll., 1977-79. Profl. tour golfer New Zealand, Australia, 1971-74, Tahiti, U.S., etc., 1971-74; head golf profl., dir. golf Knob Hill Country Club, Englishtown, N.J., 1974—; teaching profl. Concordia Country Club, 1989—; rules com. chmn. N.J. PGA, Jamesburg, N.J., 1987-88; real estate agt. Kovacs Agy., Trenton, 1986—. Leading qualifier Nat. Long Driving Championship, Forsgate Country Club, N.J., 1977, 2nd qualifier, 1978; qualifier Nat. Club Profl. Championship Callway Gardens, Ga., 1979. Mem. PGA (exec. com. N.J. sect. 1987), Nat. Corvette Owners Am. (charter). Roman Catholic.

PIOTROWSKI, LINDA SUSAN, physician; d. Sophia C. (Serba) P. BA, John's Hopkins U., 1976, MD, 1981. Intern U. Pa. Hosp., Phila., 1981-82; resident in psychiatry Yale U., New Haven, 1983-85, 86-87; postdoctoral fellow in geriatric psychiatry U. Pa., Phila., 1987-88; assoc. dir. neuropsychiatry Hampton Hosp., Rancocas, N.J., 1988-91; med. dir. Hampton Counseling Ctr., Marlton, N.J., 1991—.

PIPER, JOYCE EILEEN, pharmaceutical company administrator; b. Bronx, N.Y., Feb. 2, 1946; d. Frank and Gertrude (Mikesch) Re Casino. Colo. brokers lic., Jones Real Estate Sch., Denver, 1984. Comml. paper specialist United Bank of Denver, 1978-82; advt. mgr. Wedgecor Steel, Denver, 1983-85; real estate broker Coldwell Banker, Aurora, Colo., 1984-86; exec. sec. to dir. AT&T, Morristown, N.J., 1986-87; office mgr., asst. to pres. Weichert Relocation, Morris Plains, N.J., 1987-89; office mgr., project adminstr. Sandoz Pharmaceuticals, East Hanover, N.J., 1989—. Author: Newsletters to soldiers in Desert Storm, 1990-91. Fund raiser Operation Desert Shield, Morris County, N.J., 1990-91. Recipient Ky. Col. award Gov. of Ky., 1991, Yellow Ribbon award 8 Batallion USMC, 1991, Commendation 416 Command, Gen. Patton's Div., 1991, U.S. Military Post Office, N.Y. APO, 1991. Home: PO Box 312 Boonton NJ 07005-1710

PIPER, W. STEPHEN, health educator; b. Uniontown, Pa., June 4, 1945; s. Warren S. and Rhoda (Nixon) P.; m. Patricia Lewis, Aug. 16, 1945. BS, Lock Haven (Pa.) U., 1970; MS, SUNY, Brockport, 1978. Lakefront summer supr. Chautauqua (N.Y.) Inst., 1965-84; health tchr. Hornell (N.Y.) High Sch., 1970—. Recipient Leon Millot Red Bronze medal Am. Wine Soc., 1988, Seyual Blanc Gold medal, 1988; in top 5 health tchrs. N.Y. State Fedn. Profl. Health Educators, 1977. Methodist. Office: Hornell High Sch Maple City Park Hornell NY 14843

PIRES-HESTER, LAURA J., foundation administrator; b. Wareham, Mass., May 11, 1939; d. John Marcellino and Adeline (Perieira) Pires; m. Melvyn F. Hester, Feb. 17, 1990. BA in English, Smith Coll., 1961; MSW, Columbia U., 1963, MA in Anthropology, 1980, MPhil in Anthropology, 1980, postgrad., 1992—. Program analyst, dir. employment Harlem Youth Opportunities Unltd., N.Y.C., 1963-66; field dir., v.p., cons. Coll. for Human Svcs., N.Y.C., 1966-82; dir. tng. N.Y.C. Welfare Mgmt. System, N.Y.C., 1982-88; sr. program advisor Edwin Gould Found. for Children, N.Y.C., 1988—; cons. in field, 1972-75. Mem. editorial bd. Commun. Schs., 1990—; contbr. articles to profl. publs. Chair Nat. Friends of Ernestina/Morrissey, 1976-82; bd. dirs. Teach for Am., 1989-92, N.Y. Theol. Sem., 1991; v.p. bd. dirs. Edwin Gould Svcs. for Children, 1990—; mem. ch. growth task force, mem. weekday prayer com. Riverside Ch., 1991—, also mem. youth crisis initiative and employment initiative. Recipient Humanitarian award Cape Verdean Vets of New Bedford, 1982, No Time to Lose award N.Y. State Dept. Social Svcs., 1990, Bicentennial award Town of Wareham, 1989. Mem. Am. Anthrop. Assn., N.Y. Regional Assn. Grantmakers (program com.). Home: 50 W 96th St New York NY 10025-6526 Office: Edwin Gould Found Children 23 Gramercy Park S New York NY 10003-1747

PIRET, MARGUERITE ALICE, investment banker; b. St. Paul, May 10, 1948; d. E.L. and Alice P.; children: Andrew, Anne. AB, Radcliffe Coll., 1969; MBA, Harvard U., 1974. Comml. loan officer Bank New Eng. (now Fleet Bank), Boston, 1974-79; mng. dir. Kridel Securities, N.Y.C., 1979-81; pres., founder, dir. Newbury, Piret & Co., Inc., Boston, 1981—; trustee, mem. audit com. Pioneer Fund, Pioneer II Fund, Pioneer Three Fund, Pioneer Bond Fund, Pioneer Mcpl. Bond Fund, Pioneer Money Market Fund. Mem. visitors' com. Am. decorative arts and sculpture Mus. Fine Arts, Boston, 1982—; mem. overseer candidates nominating com. Harvard U.; bd. dirs. nominating com. Harvard Alumni Assn., 1983-86, adv. com. on shareholder responsibility, 1986-87; trustee, mem. exec. com. Univ. Hosp., Boston, 1979—; trustee Mass. Hosp. Assn., 1983-86, Boston Ballet Ctr., Ctr. Dance Edn., 1989—. Mem. Harvard Club. Office: Newbury Piret & Co Inc 26th Fl One Boston Plz Boston MA 02108

PIRKL, JAMES JOSEPH, industrial designer; b. Nyack, N.Y., Dec. 27, 1930; s. James and Ida Bertha (Gigrich) P.; m. Sarah B. W. Woolsey, June 8, 1974; children: Theo, James, Philip. Cert. Advt. Design, Pratt Inst., 1951, B of Indsl. Design cum laude, 1958. With design staff Gen. Motors Corp., Warren, Mich., 1958-65; sr. designer Gen. Motors Corp., 1961-64, asst. chief designer, 1964-65; instr. indsl. design Center for Creative Studies, Detroit, 1963-65; faculty dept. design Syracuse (N.Y.) U., 1965-92, assoc. prof., 1969-73, prof. indsl. design, 1974-92, prof. emeritus, 1992—, coord. indsl. design program, 1979-84, chmn. dept. design, 1985-91; exec. council chmn. Sch. Art, 1976-78, 80-81; sr. rsch. fellow All-U. Gerontology Ctr., 1990-92; prin. James J. Pirkl/Design, Cazenovia, N.Y., 1965—; cons. Brownlie Design, Inc., 1972—, Prince Corp., 1991, Loretto Geriatric Ctr., Sage Marcom Inc., 1988-90, Hazard Mgmt. Co., 1985, Marcom Switches Inc., 1977-82, Cazenovia Abroad Ltd., 1973-81, Holistic Mgmt. Group, Inc., 1981, Pulos Design Assocs., 1972-80, Beck Assocs., 1976, Fed. Prison Industries, 1974, Gen. Electric Co., 1967-70, Genesee Labs., Inc., 1968, N.Y. State Council on Arts, 1968-69, Stettner-Trush, Inc., 1972-78, Strathmore Chem. Coatings, Inc., 1969, 72, Village of Cazenovia, 1979—, Xerox Corp., 1975; chmn. accreditation council Design Found., 1982-84; interviewed on Nat. Pub. Radio. Co-author: Guidelines and Strategies for Designing Transgenerational Products, 1988; co-editor: State of the Art and Science of Design, 1971; co-designer: Gen. Motors Futurama Exhbn, N.Y. World's Fair, 1964-65; contbr. articles to profl. jours., including Design Mgmt. Jour., Jour. Indsl. Designers Soc. Am., Bus. Adminstrn. Jour., Design News, Design Perspectives, Indsl. Design. Mem. Everson Mus. Art, 1977—; chmn. planning commn. Town of Cazenovia, N.Y, 1988—; mem. senate Syracuse U., 1973-80; mem. adv. bd. SEARS Project, 1989-91; chmn. chancellor's citation com., 1988-92; mem. exhbns. com. Syracuse Cultural Resources Coun., 1992—. With SeaBees USN, 1951-55. Fellow Indsl. Designers Soc. Am. (chmn. transgenerational and disabilities com. 1991—, chmn. NASAD liaison com. 1984-88, mem. archives com. 1988—, nat. bd. dirs. 1977-81, chmn. Central N.Y. chpt. 1977-78, v.p. Mid-East region 1978-80, dir., chmn. edn. com. 1980-81, U.S. rep., del. Internat. Congress Socs. Indsl. Design 1989); mem. AAUP, The Design Found. (chmn. accreditation coun. 1982), Nat. Assn. Schs. Art and Design (accreditation evaluator 1985—), nat. Ctr. for a Barrier Free Environment (adv. task force 1981), Human Factors Soc. (consumer products tech. group 1978, tech. group on aging 1987, forensics tech. group 1988), Internat. Congress Socs. Indsl. Design (edn. com.), Author's Guild. Home: RD 5 Meadow Hill Rd Cazenovia NY 13035-9640

PIRODSKY, DONALD MAX, psychiatrist, educator; b. Freeport, N.Y., Feb. 2, 1945; s. Max and Doris Geilhard (Biedermann) P.; m. Susan Jean Linehan, June 14, 1969; children: Laura Anne, Jason Donald. BA, Hofstra U., 1966; MD, SUNY, Syracuse, 1970. Diplomate Am. Bd. Psychiatry and Neurology, Nat. Bd. Med. Examiners. Med. intern Northwestern U. Med. Ctr., Chgo., 1970-71; resident in psychiatry Strong Meml. Hosp., Rochester, N.Y., 1973-74, U. Ariz. Med. Ctr., Tucson, 1974-76; instr. psychiatry SUNY Health Sci. Ctr., Syracuse, 1976-78, attending psychiatrist, 1976—, asst. prof. psychiatry, 1978-85, mem. exec. com. of med. coll. assembly, 1979-82, clin. assoc. prof., 1985—; pvt. practice Syracuse and Fayetteville, N.Y., 1976—; staff psychiatrist, dir. consultation/liaison svc. Syracuse VA Med. Ctr., 1976-87, chmn. pharmacy rev. and therapeutic agts. com., 1980-86; psychiat. cons. Ariz. Sch. for Deaf and Blind, Tucson, 1975-76, Syracuse Devel. Ctr., 1977—, Rochester Sch. for Deaf, 1978-81; ex-officio mem. Family Counseling Agy., Tucson, 1975-76. Author: Primer of Clinical Psychopharmacology: A Practical Guide, 1981, (with Jerry S. Cohn) Clinical Primer of Psychopharmacology: A Practical Guide, 2d edit., 1992; contbr. articles to profl. jours., chpts. to med. books. Lt. comdr. USPHS, 1971-73. Fellow Am. Psychiat. Assn.; mem. AMA, Am. Psychosomatic Soc., Am. Assn. Mental Retardation, Med. Soc. State of N.Y., Onondaga County Med. Soc. Episcopalian. Office: 7000 E Genesee St Fayetteville NY 13066-1100

PIRZIO-BIROLI, CORRADO, European community official; b. Udine, Friuli, Italy, Nov. 25, 1940; came to U.S., 1988; s. Detalmo and Fey (Von Hassell) P.; m. Cecile Cornet D'Elzius; 1 child, Federico. Postgrad diploma Econ. Planning and Indsl. Devel. Programming, The Hague, The Netherlands, 1967; PhD, U. Rome, Italy, 1968. Asst. lectr., econs. Inst. Social Studies, 1968; economic advisor Govt. of Sudan, Khartoum, 1968-70; adminstr. Devel. European Communities Commn., Brussels, Belgium, 1971-75, prin. adminstr., 1975-78; econ. counselor del. European Communities Commn., U.S.A., 1978-82; econ. advisor to pres. European Communities Commn., Brussels, 1982-85; dep. head of div., European Free Trade Area affairs Devel. European Communities Commn., Brussels, Belgium, 1985-88; dep. head of del. European Communities Commn., Washington, 1988-92; head of del. European Communities Commn., Vienna, Austria, 1992—; bd. mem. Global Interdependence Ctr., Phila., 1981—. Contbr. articles to profl. jours.; numerous speaking engagements. Lt. Italian Air Force, 1964-65. Roman Catholic. Office: European Communities Commn 2100 M St NW Washington DC 10037

PISACICH, KEVIN WALTER, electronic sales executive; b. New London, Conn., Mar. 3, 1966; s. Bernard J. and Judith Ann (Huges) P. Student, U. R.I., 1984-86. Svc. technician Electronica, Peace Dale, R.I., 1986-87; founder, pres. KWP Inc., Kingston, R.I., 1985-87; sales assoc. Shore Stereo, Wakefield, R.I., 1987; founder, owner Electronic Svcs. Unlimited, Narragansett, R.I., 1988-90; mgr. Morrone Video, Westerly, R.I., 1988; founder, pres. Techtronics Inc., East Greenwich, R.I., 1989—, Sights and Sounds, Wakefield, R.I., 1990—. Counselor recreation Trudeau Meml. Handicapped Ctr., 1988—; vol. Insight Radio for Blind Vol., 1989—. Republican. Office: Techtronics 2843 S County Trl East Greenwich RI 02818-1728

PISANI, ANTHONY MICHAEL, architect; b. Watertown, Mass., May 18, 1943; s. Anthony Joseph and Josephine Ann (Tortorella) P.; m. Emilia D'Agostino, Aug. 27, 1967; children—Emilia-Bianca, Giancarlo. Diploma, Mus. Sch., 1966; BFA, Tufts U., 1966; MArch., Harvard U., 1971. Registered architect, Mass., Calif., Maine, Mich., N.Y., N.H., Tex., Vt. Project architect Kallmann & McKinell, Architects, Boston, 1971-73, Charles G. Hilgenhurst & Assocs., Boston, 1973-74, Desmond & Lord, Architects, Boston, 1974-77; pres. Anthony M. Pisani & Assocs., Architects, Boston, 1978—; instr. design Boston Archtl. Center, 1971-74; vice- chmn. Boston Landmarks Commn., 1987—. Major works in Eastern U.S., Ireland, Can., Mex., P.R., Japan; contbr. articles to profl. jours. Mem. AIA, Boston Soc. Architects, Constrn. Specifications Inst., Urban Land Inst., Nat. Council Archtl. Registration Bds., Soc. Archtl. Historians. Home: 95 Robinwood Ave Boston MA 02130 Office: 374 Congress St Boston MA 02210-1807

PISANI, ROBERT LOUIS, television personality, writer; b. N.Y.C., Feb. 24, 1956; s. Ralph Raymond and Elizabeth (Schlontz) P.; m. Suzanne Petruzel, May 18, 1986. Student, U. Calif., Berkeley, 1974-76. Human rights activist 1978-80; exec. dir. Internat. Legal Def. Counsel, Phila., 1980-89; real estate corres. CNBC-TV, 1990—; adj. faculty Wharton Sch., U. Pa. Co-author: The Hassle of Your Life: A Handbook for Families of Americans Jailed Abroad, 1982, Investing in Land: How to be a Successful Developer, 1989; contbr. articles to profl. jours.; contbg. editor Real Estate Finance Jour. Mem. adv. bd. Fellowship Commn. Phila., 1978-82; mem. Queen Village Neighbors Assn., Phila., 1981-82; vol. HELP, Inc., Phila., 1981-86, Hahnemann Med. Coll., Coll. Accelerated Program, 1973-74; bd. dirs. South St. Neighbors Assn., Phila., 1981-87, Washington Sq. West Project Area Com., Phila., 1986-91, Washington Square West Civic Assn., 1987-91. Named one of Outstanding Young Men of Am., U.S. Jaycees, 1983 Mem. ACLU, Amnesty Internat. (urgent action network), Phila. Writer's Orgn. (bd. dirs), Nat. Assn. Real Estate Editors. Author's Guild, World Future Soc. Avocations: reading, research, writing.

PISANKO, HENRY JONATHAN, command and control communications company executive; b. Trenton, N.J., Mar. 14, 1925; s. Isadore Stephen and Victoria (Gula) P.; m. Sophia Emily Zudnak, May 29, 1949; children: Barbara, Henry Jonathan, Jr., Michael. B in Naval Sci., U. Notre Dame, 1945, BA, 1947; cert. in Japanese, U. Colo. and Okla. State U., 1945; postgrad. Woodrow Wilson Sch., Columbia U., 1948-50. Constrn. reporter ea. div. F.W. Dodge div. McGraw-Hill, N.Y.C. and Phila., 1950-52; internat. affairs analyst Dept. Def., Washington, 1953-59; ops. officer Dept. Def., Pacific Rim, Japan and Hong Kong, 1960-63; sr. intelligence officer Internat. Security Affairs, Dept. Def., Washington, 1964-70; overseas adminstr. diplomatic telecommunications Dept. State, Asia, Africa, 1971-73; spl. advisor Def. Intelligence Coll., Washington, 1974-75; ctr. dep. chief, adminstrn. dir. Intelligence Community, Washington, 1976-82; exec. officer USA-EIGO Svcs. Co., Rockville, Md., 1983-87; exec. officer USA-EIGO Svcs. Co., Princeton, N.J., 1983-87, now bd. dirs.; bd. dirs. Asia Mgmt. Internat., Princeton; assoc. Bi-Lingual U.S.A. Corp., Bethesda, Md., 1984, Mgmt. Logistics Internat., Arlington, Va., 1983-86. Editor, translator: Yoshio Kodama, 1952; author: (monographs) Items of Inquiry Far East, 1983, Japanese Technology-Ancient Culture, 1985, (pamphlet) Fiber Optics Across the Pacific, 1989. Sponsor, contbr. Pisanko-Kikan, 1982, Hotel Okura, Japan, 1983, Bungei Shunju, Japan, 1988. Lt. J.G., USN, 1942-46. Trenton Times scholar, 1942; recipient Moe Berg award Pub. Securtiy Investigation Agy.-Japan, Tokyo, 1961, telecommunications award Thai Gen. Staff, Bangkok, 1972. Mem. Asian Rsch. Svc., Bus. Devel. Africa, Internat. Inst. Japan, Bus. Execs. for Internat. Security, Internat. Platform Assn., Info. Processing Soc. Japan, Naval Res. Officers Tng. Corps, Unit Alumni Club, Boulder Boys-Japanese Club, Shek-O Club. Office: P K Co Ltd PO Box 1703 Bethesda MD 20817

PISANO, JOHN FRANCIS, dean; b. Pittston, Pa., June 21, 1948; s. Angelo Frank and Francis (SeSalvo) P.; m. Linda Ann Layo, June 26, 1976; children: Angelo, John, Joseph. BA in Govt., King's Coll., Wilkes-Barre, Pa., 1970; MS in Counseling, U. Scranton, 1974; EdD, Temple U., 1985. Inspector Pa. State Harness Racing Commn., Plains, 1966-70; mgr. Modern Bowling Lanes, Exeter, Pa., 1971-74; instr. Scranton (Pa.) Prep. Sch., 1974-76; assoc. prof. counseling Luzerne County Community Coll., Nanticoke, Pa., 1975-81, prof. psychology, 1977-91, dean continuing edn., 1981—; pres. Cookout's Restaurant, Exeter, 1985-87. Active Hazelton (Pa.) Vocat. Tech. Adv. Bd., Retreat State Prison Ednl. Bd., Hunlocks Creek, Pa., State Corr. Instn. Edn. Bd. at Chase, Dallas, Pa., 1985. With USAR, 1970-76. Mem. Luzerne County Guidance Assn., Pa. Assn. for Adult and Continuing Edn., Nat. Univ. Continuing Edn. Assn., Assn. for Continuing Higher Edn. Democrat. Roman Catholic. Home: 11 Spruce St Wilkes Barre PA 18705-2222 Office: Luzerne County Community Prospect St & Middle Rd Nanticoke PA 18634

PISCOTTA, DOLORES, painter, sculpter, pianist, designer; b. N.Y.C., May 30; d. Robert and Juliet Piscotta. Studied piano with Paul Romeo; student, New Sch. Social Rsch., 1967-71. Freelance textile designer, 1971-75; recreation dir. Tower Nursing Home, N.Y.C., 1971-72; founder, dir. The Friends of the Alphabet Pre-Sch., N.Y.C., 1973-85; tchr. classical piano and guitar, 1973—; pres., designer Piscotta Creations, N.Y.C., 1990—. Author: Friends of the Alphabet, Complete Writing Skills for Children Ages 2-5; creator and designer hand-made limited edition treasure boxes; designer Worried Willy line of toys; represented in permanent collections at the Vatican, Monastero di S. Benedetto, Milan, Monastero di San Giovanni, Sapri, Italy. Roman Catholic. Home and Office: Piscotta Creations 8865-16 Ave Brooklyn NY 11214

PISTNER, STEPHEN LAWRENCE, retail chain executive; b. St. Paul, Mar. 14, 1932; s. Leopold and Prudence Charlette (Selcer) P.; children: Paul David, John Alan, Betsy Ann. BSBA, U. Minn., 1953. Pres., chief exec. officer Target Stores, Inc., Mpls., 1973-76, chmn., chief exec. officer, 1976; exec. v.p. Dayton Hudson Corp., Mpls., 1976-77, pres., chief operating officer, 1977-81, also dir.; pres., chief exec. officer Montgomery Ward & Co., Inc., Chgo., 1981-85; chmn. bd., chief exec. officer McCrory Corp., 1985-88; exec. v.p. Rapid-Am. Corp., N.Y.C., 1985-88; chmn., chief exec. officer Ames Dept Stores, Inc., Rocky Hill, Conn., 1990—. Office: Ames Dept Stores Inc 2418 Main St Rocky Hill CT 06067-2598

PISTOLAKIS, NICHOLAS S., advertising executive; b. Athens, Greece, Feb. 15, 1933; s. Stelios Nicholas and Aspasia (Stephano) P.; m. Susan Elizabeth Sell, Dec. 27, 1968; children: Christina, Nicholas Jr. Cert., U. Pa., 1955. Yellow Page rep. Reuben Donnelly Corp., Phila., 1953-54; gen. mgr. West Phila. Newspapers, Inc., 1954-64; Yellow Page rep. Athens, 1964-66; advt. rep. Internat. Herald Tribune, Paris, 1966-69; sales mgr. Dun and Bradstreet Internat., N.Y.C., 1969-79; owner Eclipse Advt. Assocs., Brick, N.J., 1979—; developer tourism plan for Chania, Greece; mktg. cons., N.J., 1984—; cons. Young Marine Co., Asbury Park, N.J., 1984—, PAHCO Machine, Inc., Trenton, 1985—, Plastiglas Molded Products, Trenton, 1985—. Assoc. pub. U.S. Mktg. Guide, 1978 (achievement award 1980), World Products, 1979 (achievement award 1980). Mem. World Trade Club of N.Y. (bd. dirs. 1979-80), Internat. Advt. Assn., Internat. Indsl. Mktg. Club, Nat. Assn. Pubs. Reps., Sales Exec. Club of N.Y., Am. Hellenic Prog. Assn., Am. Legion, Power Squadron Club, Metedeconk Yacht Club (Brick). Republican. Greek Orthodox. Home: 9 Quail Run Brick NJ 08723-5878 Office: Eclipse Industries Internat Eclipse Advt Assocs PO Box 4210 Brick NJ 08723-1410

PISTOLE, THOMAS GORDON, microbiology educator, researcher; b. Detroit, Sept. 17, 1942; s. Leotis Merton Pistole and Lillian Nell (Bosley) Besser; m. Donna Dulcie Straw, Sept. 11, 1965; children: James Alexander, Jennifer Katharine. PhB, Wayne State U., 1964, MS, 1966; PhD, U. Utah, 1969. Postdoctoral fellow U.S. Army, Frederick, Md., 1969-70; research assoc. U. Minn., Mpls., 1970-71; asst. prof. U. N.H., Durham, 1971-77, assoc. prof., 1977-83, prof., 1983—, chmn., 1983-92; chmn., 1983-92; vis. scientist Wiezmann Inst., Rehovot, Israel, 1979; vis. prof. U. Edinburgh, Scotland, 1986. Co-editor: Biomedical Application of the Horseshoe Crab, 1979; mem. editorial bd. Jour. Invertebrate Pathology, 1988-90. NRC fellow, 1969-70, NIH sr. internat. fellow, 1986; grantee NIH, 1975-77, 89-93, NSF, 1981-84. Mem. Am. Soc. for Microbiology, Am. Assn. Immunologists, Am. Soc. Zoologists, Internat. Soc. Devel. and Comparative Immu-

nology, Sigma Xi (sec. local chpt. 1974-76). Unitarian/Universalist. Office: U NH Dept Microbiology Spaulding Life Sci Bldg Durham NH 03824-3544

PI-SUNYER, F. XAVIER, medical educator, medical investigator; b. Barcelona, Catalonia, Spain, Dec. 3, 1933; came to U.S., 1942; s. James and Mercedes (Diaz) Pi-S.; m. Penelope Wheeler; children: Andrea, Olivia, Joanna. BA, Oberlin (Ohio) Coll., 1955; MD, Columbia U., 1959; MPH, Harvard U., 1963. From instr. to asst. prof. Coll. of Physicians & Surgeons, Columbia U., N.Y.C., 1965-76, assoc. prof., 1976-85, prof. clin. medicine, 1985-91; prof. St. Luke's-Roosevelt Hosp. Ctr., N.Y.C., 1991—; from asst. to assoc. attending physician St. Luke's Hosp., N.Y.C., 1965-75; attending physician St. Luke's-Roosevelt Hosp. Ctr., N.Y.C., 1975—, chief div. endocrinology, diabetes and nutrition, 1988—, dir. Obesity Rsch. Ctr., 1988—; mem. adj. faculty Rockefeller U., N.Y.C., 1984—; vis. physician Rockefeller U. Hosp., N.Y.C., 1984—; attending physician Presbyn. Hosp., N.Y.C., 1985—; sr. investigator N.Y. Heart Assn., 1968-73; Hsien Wu investigator St. Luke's-Rochester Hosp., 1982-90; Sigma Xi lectr. Pa. State U., 1989; Howard Heinz vis. prof. Med. Coll. of Pa., 1987; mem. C study sect. Nat. Inst. Diabetes, Digestive and Kidney Disease, 1988—, mem. task force on obesity, 1990—. Contbr. numerous articles to profl. jours. Fogarty Internat. fellow NIH, 1979-80. Mem. Am. Soc. for Clin. Nutrition (pres. 1989-90), Am. Diabetes Assn. (pres.-elect 1991-92, pres. 1992—), Am. Bd. Nutrition (v.p. 1987-88), N.Y. State Health Rsch. Coun., N.Y. Acad. Medicine (com. on pub. health 1983—). Home: 305 Riverside Dr New York NY 10025-5286 Office: St Lukes Roosevelt Hosp Ctr Dept of Medicine 114th St & Amsterdam Ave New York NY 10025

PITAGORSKY, GEORGE, management consultant; b. N.Y.C., July 3, 1942; s. Israel and Grace (Berres) P.; m. Linda Chaikin, Aug. 16, 1964; children: Eric, David. BA in Econs., CUNY, Queens, 1964. Programmer Equitable Life Assurance Soc., N.Y.C., 1964-67; project leader systems mgmt. div. Sperry, Syossett, N.Y., 1967-68; v.p. Software Design Assocs., N.Y.C., 1968-75, pres., founder learning svcs. div., 1977-78; pres., co-founder People & Solutions, Inc., N.Y.C., 1978-82; private practice N.Y.C., 1982—; cons. Esquire, Inc., N.Y.C., 1979-83, Mfrs. Hanover Trust, N.Y.C., 1982-87, Shearson Lehman, 1989—, Bank of Bermuda, 1990—, Dean Witter, 1990—, Merrill Lynch, 1991—; seminar leader Am. Mgmt. Assn., 1989—. Author: Managing the Software Development Process, 1982, Communication and Consulting Skills, 1990, author seminars in field; contbr. articles to jours. Office: Pitagorsky Cons 153 E 32nd St New York NY 10016-2901

PITARRESI, FRANCES LOUISE, controller; b. N.Y.C., Mar. 8, 1948; d. Frank Stanley and Louise Alexandria (Turowska) Deptula; m. Simone Pitarresi, May 30, 1967; children: Frank, Gregory, Catherine, Christopher. BA, NYU, 1968. Acctg. supr., office mgr. Gen. Composition Service, N.Y.C., 1964-78; acctg. mgr. Mediterranean Importing Co., L.I., N.Y., 1978-85; asst. controller World Brands, Inc., L.I., 1985-88; fin. mgr., purchasing mgr. Redmond, Pollio & Pittoni, PC, L.I., 1988—. Co-pres. Spl. Edn. Parent Tchrs. Assn., Sewanhaka Cen. Sch. Dist., 1988—. Recipient Silver GBPSAL award City of N.Y., 1962, 63, Gold GBPSAL award City of N.Y., 1964. Mem. Mensa, Internat. Platform Assn. Republican. Roman Catholic. Office: Redmond Pollio & Pittoni 128 Front St Mineola NY 11501-4401

PITCHON, DANIEL NATHAN, executive search consultant; b. Bronx, N.Y., July 19, 1947; s. Morris and Alice Pitchon; m. Linda Sharon Schwartz, Jan. 18, 1969; children: Nicole Blair, Jordan Craig. BA, CCNY, 1969; postgrad. in indsl. psychology, Baruch Coll., 1969-75. Pers. adminstr. MAI Basic Four, N.Y.C., 1969-71; mgr., human resource devel. SCM Corp., N.Y.C., 1971-75; dir. employee rels. Proctor Silex div. SCM Corp., Phila., 1975-77; div. dir., pers. Seatrain Lines, Inc., Weekawken, N.J., 1977-79; corp. v.p. human resources Seatrain Lines, Inc., N.Y.C., 1979-81; v.p. Deven Assocs., N.J., 1981-83; mng. dir. J.B. Gilbert Assoc., N.Y.C., 1983-91; pres. DN Pitchon Assocs, Ridgewood, N.J., 1991—. Vol. N.Y. Spl. Olympics, N.Y.C., 1988-89, Edges Minority Bus. Orgn., N.Y.C. With USAFR, 1966-71. Mem. Nat. Assn. Corp. and Profl. Recruiters, Am. Soc. Personnel Adminstrn. Democrat. Jewish. Office: DN Pitchon Assocs 60 W Ridgewood Ave Ridgewood NJ 07450

PITCOCK, ALBERT RICHARD, assistant superintendent; b. Waynesburg, Pa., May 22, 1938; s. Charles E. and Mary E. (Ankrom) P.; m. Jo Ann Hundertmark, Dec. 28, 1961; children: Leslie J., Tricia A. BS in Math., Waynesburg Coll., 1961; MEd, U. Pitts., 1969; EdD, W. Va. U., 1989. Math. tchr. Woodbury (N.J.) Sch. Dist., 1961-66; math. tchr. Mt. Lebanon (Pa.) Sch. Dist., 1966-69, adminstrv. asst. to prin., 1969-72, high sch. house prin., 1972-81, dir. pers., 1981-83, asst. dist. supt., 1983-89, 90-91, acting supt., 1989-90, asst. dist. supt., 1991—. Author: Alternative Uses of Surplus School Space in Pennsylvania, Maryland and New Jersey, 1989. Chmn. Sch. Dist. United Way Campaign, Mt. Lebanon, 1982—; pres., v.p., bd. dirs. Robert Boyd Ward Home for Children, Mt. Lebanon, 1981-89; pres.'s adv. coun. Washington & Jefferson Coll., Washington, Pa., 1987-88. Mem. Am. Assn. Sch. Pers. Adminstrs. (nat. employee rels. com. 1986-89, pres. Pa. chpt. 1992—, exec. bd. Pa. chpt. 1986—, exec. bd. Western Pa. chpt. 1981—), Am. Assn. Sch. Adminstrs., Nat. Congress Parents and Tchrs. (hon. life), Pa. Congress Parents and Tchrs. (hon. life), Pa. Assn. Supervision and Curriculum Devel., Pa. Sch. Bds. Assn., Waynesburg Coll. Alumni Bd., Phi Delta Kappa. Presbyterian. Office: Mt Lebanon Sch Dist 7 Horsman Dr Mount Lebanon PA 15228

PITFIELD, PETER MICHAEL, Canadian senator; b. Montreal, June 18, 1937; s. Ward Chipman and Grace Edith (MacDougall) P.; m. Nancy Snow, 1971; children: Caroline, Thomas, Katie. B.A. in Sci., St. Lawrence U., 1955, D. Litt. hon., 1979; B.C.L., McGill U., 1958; D.E.S.D., U. Ottawa, 1961. Bar: Que. 1962; created Queen's counsel, 1972. Assoc. Mathewson, Lafleur & Brown, Montreal, 1956-59; adminstrv. asst. to Minister Justice and Atty. Gen. Can., Ottawa, 1959-61; sec., exec. dir. Royal Commn. on Publs., Ottawa, 1961-62; attache Gov. Gen. Can., 1962-65; sec., research supr. Royal Commn. on Taxation, 1963-66; joined Privy Council Office and Cabinet Secretarial Govt. of Can., 1965, asst. sec. to cabinet, 1967-69, dep. sec. to cabinet for plans, dep. clk. council, 1969-73, dep. minister consumer and corp. affairs, 1973-74, clk. council, sec. to cabinet, 1975-79, 80-82; fellow Harvard U., Cambridge, Mass., 1974, Mackenzie King prof. Canadian studies, 1979-80; mem. Senate of Can., 1982—; vice chmn. Power Corp., Power Fin. Corp.; dir. Great West Life, Investors Group, La Presse, Journaux Trans Cand. Trustee Twentieth Century Fund, N.Y.C.; mem. exec. com. Internat. Inst. Strategic Studies, London. Served to lt. Royal Can. Navy Res. Mem. Can. Bar Assn., Que. Bar Assn., Montreal Bar Assn., Can. Inst. Pub. Adminstrn., Can. Hist. Assn., Can. Polit. Sci. Assn., Internat. Commn. Jurists., Am. Soc. Polit. and Social Sci., Can. Inst. Advanced Research, Beta Theta Pi. Anglican. Club: University (Montreal). Office: Senate of Canada, Parliament Bldgs, Ottawa, ON Canada K1A 0A4

PITKOW, HOWARD SPENCER, physiologist, educator, researcher; b. Phila., May 21, 1941; s. Jack and Molly (Zelinger) P.; m. Ellice Spector; children: Seth Bradley, Stephanie Alison. BA in Biology, U. Pa., 1962, MS in Zoology, 1963; PhD in Endocrinology and Reprodn., Rutgers U., 1971. Instr. histology and embryology Pa. Coll. Podiatric Medicine, Phila., 1965-66, asst. prof. anatomy, 1967-68, asst. prof. physiol. sci., 1969-71, assoc. prof., 1972-77, prof., 1978—, chmn. dept. physiol. sci., 1974-84; lectr. biology Phila. Community Coll., 1972-76; lectr. sci. Bucks County (Pa.) Community Coll., 1978-81; vis. assoc. prof. Hahnemann Med. Coll., Phila., 1980—; adj. prof. biology Drexel U., Phila., 1980; vis. rsch. prof. Temple Health Sci. Ctr., Phila., 1981-84. Mem. editorial rev. bd. Jour. Podiatric Med. Sci., 1971-84, Growth, 1976, Am. Biology Tchr., 1980; contbr. book revs. to numerous jours. Am. Podiatry Assn. fellow, 1966, 68; travel grantee Internat. Union PHysiol. Sic., Paris, 1977, Argonne Nat. Labs., 1978, 79, Internat. Congress Endocrinology, Quebec City, 1984, Vienna, 1991, 2d Internat. award on amino acids and analogues, 1991. Mem. Am. Physiol. Soc. (edn. com. 1985-88), Fedn. Am. Socs. Exptl. Biology, Pa. Acad. Sci. (chair pub. rels. 1986—, corr. sec. 1984—, chair membership recruitment 1987—, investment and fin. com. 1987-90), Phila. Physiol. Soc., Phila. Endocrine Soc. Home: 1210 Newport Mews Dr Bensalem PA 19020-3951 Office: Pa Coll Podiatric Medicine 8th and Race Sts Philadelphia PA 19107

PITMAN, GROVER ALLEN, music educator; b. Corpus Christi, Tex., Nov. 16, 1943; s. John William and Mae Belle (Reese) P.; m. Jacqueline Kay Dunn, Aug. 29, 1966; children: William Dunn, Karen Joanne. BMus, U. Tex., 1965, MMus, 1967; PhD, Cath. U. Am., 1973. Tchr. Fredericksburg (Tex.) Pub. Schs., 1966-67; instr. Muskingum Coll., New Concord, Ohio, 1967-68; solo hornist U.S. Naval Acad. Band, Annapolis, Md., 1968-72; asst. prof. Winthrop Coll., Rock Hill, S.C., 1972-78; assoc. prof. Westminster Coll., New Wilmington, Pa., 1978—; prin. hornist Austin (Tex.) Symphony Orch., 1961-67, Annapolis (Md.) Symphony Orch., 1968-72; hornist Annapolis Brass Quintet, 1968-72, Youngstown (Ohio) Symphony Orch., 1988—. Grantee Winthrop Found., Rock Hill, 1977. Mem. Pa. Collegiate Bandmasters Assn. (pres. 1983-84), Pa. Music Educators Assn. (pres. dist. 5 1984-85), Rotary (pres. New Wilmington chpt. 1986). Episcopalian. Office: Westminster College New Wilmington PA 16172

PITSILOS, LENORE-STAFFIERI, gift association executive; b. Bethlehem, Pa.; d. Richard Leonard and Joanne (Mriglot) Staffieri; m. A.G. Pitsilos, May 23, 1987. A in Bus. Adminstrn., Northampton Community Coll., 1983; BS in Retail Mktg., York Coll. Pa., 1985. Mgr. Hickory Farms Ohio, Bethlehem, 1985-87; copywriter Hess's Dept. Stores, Allentown, Pa., 1987-91; mng. dir. Gift Assn. Am., Bethlehem, 1991—. Mem. Bethlehem Jaycees (treas. 1988-90). Home: 608 W Broad St Bethlehem PA 18018-5221 Office: Gift Assn Am Inc 612 W Broad St Bethlehem PA 18018-5221

PITTAWAY, DAVID BRUCE, investment banker, lawyer; b. Kansas City, Mo., Oct. 4, 1951; s. Alan Ralph and Joanne (Kenney) P. BA with highest distinction, U. Kans., 1972; JD, Harvard U., 1975, MBA with high distinction, 1982. Bar: Md., D.C., Pa. Assoc. Morgan, Lewis and Bockius, Washington, 1975-80; cons. Bain and Co., Boston, 1982-85; v.p. strategic planning, asst. to pres. Donaldson, Lufkin and Jenrette, N.Y.C., 1985-86; mng. dir. Castle Harlan, Inc., N.Y.C., 1986—; chief fin. officer Branford Chain, Inc., N.Y.C., 1987—; bd. dirs. Revere Nat. Corp., Balt., Quantum Restaurant Group, Inc., Roslyn Heights, N.Y., Long John Silver's Holdings, Inc., N.Y.C.; adj. prof. Columbia U., N.Y.C., 1986—. Summerfield scholar, 1972, Baker scholar, 1982. Mem. Harvard Club N.Y., Harvard Club Boston, Phi Beta Kappa. Office: Castle Harlan Inc 150 E 58th St New York NY 10021

PITTMAN, ROBERT WARREN, entertainment executive; b. Jackson, Miss., Dec. 28, 1953; s. Warren E. and Lanita (Hurdle) P.; m. Sandra Hill, July 27, 1979; 1 son, Robert Thomas. Student, Millsaps Coll., 1971-72, Oakland U., 1972-73, U. Pitts., 1973-74; AMP, Harvard U., 1984-85. Disc. jockey Sta. WJDX-FM, Jackson, Miss., 1970-72, Sta. WRIT, Milw., 1972; research dir. Sta. WDRQ, Detroit, 1972-73; program dir. Sta. WPEZ, Pitts., 1973-74, Stas. WMAQ-WKRZ, NBC Radio, Chgo., 1974-77, Sta. WNBC, N.Y.C., 1977-79; exec. producer Album Tracks, NBC TV, N.Y.C., 1977-78; dir., v.p., then sr. v.p. Warner Amex Satellite Entertainment Co. (now MTV Networks, Inc.), N.Y.C., 1979-82; exec. v.p., chief oper. officer Warner Amex Satellite Entertainment Co., N.Y.C., 1983-85, pres., chief exec. officer, 1985-86; pres., chief exec. officer Quantum Media, Inc., N.Y.C., 1986-89; exec. advisor Warner Communications, Inc., N.Y.C., 1989-90; pres., chief exec. officer Time Warner Enterprises, N.Y.C., 1990—, chmn. Ct. TV, 1991—; chmn., CEO, Six Flags Entertainment, 1992—; cons. to radio, 1974, 79; bd. dirs. Atari Games Corp., Six Flags Corp., SMSG. Bd. dirs. One to One Found., N.J. Performing Arts Ctr., N.Y.C. Ballet; chmn. bd. trustees N.Y. Shakespeare Festival; mem. adv. bd. Nat. Multiple Sclerosis Soc. Recipient Program Mgr. of Yr. Billboard, 1977, Program Dir. of Yr. Hall Radio Report, 1978, Entrepreneur award White House SB Conf., 1986; named Innovator of Yr. Performance Mag., 1981, Humanitarian of Yr., AMC, 1984, Time Mag. Man of Yr. runner-up, 1984, Esquire Mag. Under 40 Leadership, 1985; named one of Pioneers of New Am. Start-Up, Success mag., one of five Original Thinkers of 80s, Life mag. Methodist. Office: Time Warner Enterprises 75 Rockefeller Pla New York NY 10019

PITTORE, CARLO, artist; b. N.Y.C., May 14, 1943. B.A. in English, Tufts U., 1966; postgrad. Bklyn. Mus. Sch., 1978. Founder Union Maine Visual Artists, 1975; founder 1st gallery in East Village, La Galleria dell Occhio, 1980; active Mail Art Network, mem. cultural council CETA Artists Project, N.Y.C., 1978-80. Exhibited Brussels, 1983, Dallas, 1984, Tokyo, 1984, Ponte Nosa, Italy, 1984, one-man shows at Bowdoinham Town Hall, Maine, 1985, N.Y.C., N.A.M.E. Gallery, Chgo., 1986, Lincoln Portraits Galley 127, Portland, 1990, Maine Coast Artists, Rockport, 1992; exhibited in group shows at Lerner-Heller Gallery, N.Y.C., Gracie Mansion, N.Y.C., Danceteria, N.Y.C., Kenkeleba Gallery, N.Y.C., 1985, O'Farrell Gallery, Brunswick, Maine, 1985; represented in permanent collections at Mus. Modern Art, N.Y.C., N.Y.C. Pub. Library, Getty Inst. for Art History & the Humanites, L.A., Internat. Electrographic Mus., Univ. de Castilla, La Mancha Cuenca, Spain, Carlo Pittore Archive of Internat. Mail Art, Sonja Henie Mus., Oslo, Norway. Author: Adventures of Carlo Pittore, 1979; Colleagues, 1979; Yurtyet, 1979; Man with an Egg, 1982. Contbr. articles to profl. jours. Max Beckmann scholar Bklyn. Mus. Art Sch., 1977-78. Office: Acad of Carlo Pittore RR 1 Box 2076 Bowdoinham ME 04008-0182

PITTS, EUGENE, III, magazine editor; b. Louisiana, Mo., Aug. 3, 1940; s. Eugene II and Leora Mae (Shetley) P.; m. Sharon Green, May 5, 1973; children: Eugene IV, Stefan Gregory. BA, Northwestern U., 1962. Editor Labor News, Chgo., 1963-65, Guns and Hunting mag., N.Y.C., 1969; assoc. editor Guns mag., Skokie, Ill., 1965-67; asst. editor Audio mag., Phila., 1970-72; editor Audio mag., Phila. and N.Y.C., 1973—. Mem. Audio Engring. Soc. (assoc.). Office: Hachette Mags 1633 Broadway New York NY 10019-6708

PITTS, SAMUEL RICHARD, technology company executive; b. Sewickley, Pa., Aug. 3, 1937; s. John B. and Victoria I. (Disciscio) P.; divorced; children: John B., Roslyn M. BA, U. Pitts., 1959; JD, Dickinson Sch. Law, 1962; postgrad., Harvard U., 1981. Clk. Eugene Caputo, Beaver, Pa., 1963-66; county solicitor Beaver County, Pa., 1964-68; ptnr. Duplaga, Tocci, Ambridge, Pa., 1966-68; solicitor Borough of Baden, Pa., 1967-68; atty. Westinghouse Electric Corp., Pitts., 1968-70, chief counsel, 1970-74, asst. gen. counsel, 1974-80, assoc. gen. counsel, 1980-86, v.p., 1987—; mem., past chmn. Mfr.'s Alliance for Productivity and Innovation, Inc.-Hazardous Materials Mgmt. Coun., Washington, 1986—. Bd. dirs. Pa. Environ. Coun., PHila., 1987—, Ctr. for Hazardous Materials Rsch., Pitts., 1989—, Vocat. Rehab. Ctr., Pitts., 1990—, Pitts. Opera, 1988—, Three Rivers Young People's Orchs., Pitts., 1989—. Mem. ABA, Allegheny County Bar Assn., Pa. Bar Assn. Republican. Roman Catholic. Office: Westinghouse Electric Corp Westinghouse Bldg Six Gateway Ctr Pittsburgh PA 15222

PITTS, STEPHEN JAMES, accountant; b. Ridley Park, Pa., Aug. 31, 1961; s. James W. and Anna A. (Wolf) P. BS in Acctg., Widener U., Chester, Pa., 1983. CPA, Pa., Del. Sr. acct. Deloitte, Haskins & Sells, Phila., 1983-87; comptroller Kenver Corp., Phila., 1987-89; audit supr. Horty & Horty, P.A., Wilmington, Del., 1989—, continuing profl. edn. instr., 1990—. Mem. AICPA, Pa. Soc. CPAs, Del. Soc. CPAs, Inst. Mgmt. Accts. Office: Horty & Horty PA 29 Hill Rd Wilmington DE 19806-2038

PIVAR, JACK JOSEPH, medical equipment company executive, lawyer; b. N.Y.C., Nov. 8, 1948; s. Sidney and Doris (Spivack) P.; m. Barri Ruth Marks, May 23, 1971; children Allyn Julie, Suzanne Jaime. BA, Boston U., 1970; JD, Fordham U., 1973. Bar: N.Y., 1974. Asst. dist. atty. Office of Dist. Atty. N.Y. County, N.Y.C., 1973-77; spl. asst. atty. gen. Dep. Atty. Gen. for Medicaid Fraud, Albany, N.Y., 1977-79; trial atty. N.Y.S. Commn. on Judicial Conduct, Albany, 1979-81; lawyer pvt. practice, Albany, 1982-91; chmn., counsel EFS Health Care Group, Norwood, N.J., 1982—. Mem. ABA. Democrat. Jewish.

PIVER, M. STEVEN, gynecologic oncologist; b. Washington, Sept. 29, 1934; s. Harry Samuel and Sonia (Bard) P.; m. Susan Myers, June 25, 1958; children: Debra Ellen, Carolyn Jan, Kenneth Stuart. BS, Gettysburg Coll., 1957; MD, Temple U., 1961. Diplomate Am. Bd. Ob-Gyn, Am. Coll. Surgeons. Intern Nazareth Hosp., Phila., 1961-62; resident Johns Hopkins U. Hosp., Balt., 1962; resident ob-gyn. Pa. Hosp., U. Pa., Phila., 1965-68; fellow gynecologic oncology U. Tex., Hosp. and Tumor Inst., Houston, 1968-70; asst. prof. gynecologic oncology U. N.C. Sch. Medicine, 1970-71; assoc. chief gynecologic oncology Roswell Park Cancer Inst., Buffalo, 1972-83, founder, dir. U.S. Familial Ovarian Cancer Registry, 1981—, chief gynecologic oncology, 1984—; clin. prof., dir. div. gynecologic oncology SUNY, Buffalo, 1986—. Cons. editor Year Book of Cancer, 1972-88; assoc. editor Nat. Cancer Inst. PDQ, 1984—; mem. editorial bd. The Female Patient, 1989—; author: Ovarian Malignancies: Clinical Care of Adults of Adolescents, 1983; editor: Ovarian Malignancies: Diagnostic and Therapeutic Advances, 1987, Manual of Gynecologic Oncology/Gynecology, 1989, Conversations About Cancer, 1990; contbr. 241 sci. articles to profl. jours.; mem. editorial bd. Topics in Cancer, 1978, Oncology and Biotech. News, 1989—. Bd. dirs. United Way of Buffalo and Erie County, 1986-91; trustee D'Youville Coll., Buffalo, 1989—; pres. Friends of the Night People (homeless shelter), Buffalo, 1988—. Capt. USAF, 1962-64. Hon. fellow Tex. Assn. Obstetricians and Gynecologists, 1983; named Citizen of Yr., Buffalo News, 1989; recipient YMCA Leadership award Buffalo YMCA, 1990, Brotherhood/Sisterhood Award in Medicine (Western N.Y. Region), NCCJ, 1991. Fellow ACS, Am. Coll. Obstetricians and Gynecologists; mem. Am. Soc. Clin. Oncology, Soc. Gynecologic Oncologists, Soc. Surg. Oncology, Am. Radium Soc. Home: 315 Lincoln Pky Buffalo NY 14216-3127 Office: Roswell Park Cancer Inst Elm and Carlton Sts Buffalo NY 14263

PIZZELLA, ANTHONY NICOLA, accountant, realty executive, catering company executive; b. N.Y.C., Oct. 16, 1957; s. Pete and Josephine (Cinotti) P.; m. Cindy Ann Ocera, Mar. 20, 1982; children: Jaclyn Marie, Jeannie Michelle, Jaime Marisa. BBA, Hofstra U., 1978, MBA, 1979. CPA, N.Y.; notary pub. N.Y.; lic. real estate salesman, N.Y. Pvt. practice acctg. Merrick, N.Y., 1979—; sec.-treas. C.O.F. Realty Corp., Massapequa, N.Y., 1981—; owner, sec.-treas. Manor East Caterers, Massapequa, 1981—; acct., co-owner S.I. (N.Y.) & L.I. Devel. Corp., 1986—; ptnr. Aqualift Enterprises, 1990—; staff tax acct. Arthur Anderson & Co., N.Y.C., 1980-81. Mem. Am. Inst. CPA's, L.I. Bd. Realtors, N.Y., State Assn. Realtors, Advancement for Commerce and Industry Club, Beta Gamma Sigma, Beta Alpha Psi. Republican. Roman Catholic. Office: Manor East Caterers 201 Jerusalem Ave Massapequa NY 11758-3308

PLACE, JOHN BASSETT, JR., consulting group executive; b. N.Y.C., Dec. 10, 1953; s. John B.M. and Katherine (Smart) P. BA in Elem. Edn., Colo. Coll., 1976; MA in Early Childhood, Stanford U., 1981. Head tchr. Neskowin (Oreg.) Valley Sch., 1976-77; div. dir. The Children's Sch., New Castle, Del., 1977-78; community devel. dir. Chase Manhattan Bank, N.Y.C., 1978-80; fundraising dir. The Town Sch., N.Y.C., 1981-83; asst. dir. Merricat's Castle Nursery Sch., N.Y.C., 1983-84; pres. DCC/Dependent Care Connection, Westport, Conn., 1984—; speaker, presenter in field. Author: Work and the Family: Does Employer Involvement Pay Off?; contbr. articles to profl. jours. Vol. Conn. Sr. Olympics, Bridgeport, Conn., 1989; mem. Conn. Employee Assistance Chpt., Westport, 1987—. Mem. Nat. Assn. for Edn. Young Children, Nat. Coun. on Aging, Westport Conn. C. of C. Republican. Episcopalian. Office: DCC PO Box 2783 Westport CT 06880-0783

PLAGER, S. JAY, judge, government official, educator; b. Long Branch, N.J., May 16, 1931; s. A.L. and Clara L. (Matross) P.; m. Ilene H. Nagel; children—Anna Katherine, David Alan, Daniel Tyler. A.B., U. N.C., 1952; J.D., U. Fla., 1958; LL.M., Columbia U., 1961. Bar: Fla. 1958, Ill. 1964. Asst. prof. law U. Fla., 1958-62, assoc. prof., 1962-64; assoc. prof. law U. Ill., Champaign-Urbana, 1964-65, prof., 1965-77; dir. Office Environ. and Planning Studies, 1972-74, 75-77; dean, prof. law Ind. U. Sch. Law, Bloomington, 1977-84; prof. law Ind. U. Sch. Law, 1984-90; counselor to undersec. U.S. Dept. Health and Human Svcs., 1986-87; assoc. dir. Office of Mgmt. and Budget Office of Mgmt. and Budget, 1987-88; adminstr. info. and regulatory affairs Exec. Office of the Pres., 1988-89; cir. judge U.S. Ct. Appeals (fed. cir.), 1989—; vis. research prof. law U. Wis., 1967-68; vis. scholar Stanford U., 1984-85. Author: (with others) Water Law and Administration, 1968, Social Justice Through Law-New Approaches in the Law of Property, 1970, (with others) Florida Water Law, 1980. Chmn. Gainesville (Fla.) Planning Commn., 1962-63; mem. Urbana Plan Commn., 1966-70; mem. nat. air pollution manpower devel. adv. com., 1971-75; cons. Ill. Inst. for Environ. Quality, U.S. EPA; chmn. Ill. Task Force on Noise, 1972-76; vice chmn. Nat. Commn. on Jud. Discipline and Removal, 1991—. With USN, 1952-55. Office: US Ct Appeals for Fed Cir The National Courts Bldg 717 Madison Pl NW Washington DC 20439-0002

PLANCHER, ROBERT LAWRENCE, manufacturing company executive; b. N.Y.C., Feb. 21, 1932; s. Murray Leon and Pearl P.; m. Ellen Roslyn, Feb. 14, 1954; children: Kevin, Daryn. B.B.A., CCNY, 1954. With American Brands, Inc., N.Y.C., 1963—; asst. tax dir. American Brands, Inc., 1967, tax dir., 1971, controller, 1978, dir., v.p., controller, 1981-86, sr. v.p., chief acctg. officer, 1986—; bd. dirs. ACCO World Corp., Acushnet Co., Am. Brands Internat. Corp., Am. Franklin Co., The Am. Tobacco Co., Am. Tobacco Internat. Corp., Jim Beam Brands Co., The Franklin Life Ins. Co., The Franklin United Life Ins. Co., Gallaher Ltd., Golden Belt Mfg. Co., MasterBrand Industries, Inc., Mid Atlantic Metro Region Adv. Bd. Arkwright Mutual Ins. Co., Corp. Officers and Dirs. Assurance, Ltd., chmn. audit com. Served with U.S. Army, 1954-56. Mem. Fin. Execs. Inst., Tax Execs. Inst., Nat. Assn. Accts. Office: Am Brands Inc 1700 E Putnam Ave PO Box 819 Old Greenwich CT 06870-0819

PLANT, MARETTA MOORE, public relations and marketing executive; b. Washington, Sept. 4, 1937; d. Henry Edwards and Lucy (Connell) Moore; m. William Voorhees Plant, June 14, 1959; children: Scott Voorhees, Craig Culver, Suzannah Holliday. BS in Bus. Adminstrn., U. Ark., 1959. Owner, mgr. Handcrafts by Maretta, Westfield, N.J., 1966-73; photographer M-R Pictures, Inc., Allendale, N.J., 1973-77; communications asst. United Way-Union County, Elizabeth, N.J., 1977-79; pub. rels. cons. Creative Arts Workshop, Westfield, 1977-81, Coll. Adv. Cons., 1983-89; community rels. coord. Raritan Bay Health Svcs. Corp., Perth Amboy, N.J., 1979-81; dir. pub. rels. St. Elizabeth Hosp., Elizabeth, N.J., 1981-86; dir. mkgt./communications Somerset Med. Ctr., Somerville, N.J., 1986-90; v.p. mktg. and pub. rels. Somerset Med. Ctr., Somerville, 1990—. Trustee Bridgeway House, Elizabeth, 1982-86, Far Hills Race Meeting Assn., N.J., 1989—, pub. rels. com. N.J. Hosp. Assn., Princeton, 1982-83, 89-92, coun. auxs., 1988-92, pub. rels. com., 1989-92; committeewoman Union County Rep. Com., Westfield, 1983-85; bd. dirs., publ. affairs com. Morris Mus., Morristown. Mem. NAFE, Pub. Rels. Soc. Am., Nat. Fedn. Press Women, N.J. Press Women (chmn. communications contest 1990-92), Am. Soc. Hosp. Mktg. and Pub. Rels. (coun. mem. Region II, membership com.), N.J. Hosp. Mktg. and Pub. Rels. Assn. (corr. sec. 1984-86, pres. 1986-88), Internat. Platform Assn., Somerset County C. of C. (mag. com. 1988—), U. Ark. Alumni Assn., Summit-Westfield Assn., Delta Gamma, Coll. Women's (Westfield) Club, Soroptomists (internat., charter). Home: 118 Effingham Pl Westfield NJ 07090-3926 Office: Somerset Med Ctr Rehill Ave Somerville NJ 08876-2546

PLANT, MARK WILLIAM, federal official; b. Ann Arbor, Mich., May 27, 1955; s. Marcus L. and Geraldine M. (Hefter) P. BA, U. Va., 1977; MA, Princeton U., 1979, PhD, 1982. Vice chairperson undergrad. studies UCLA, 1984-86, asst. prof. dept. econs., 1981-87; vis. asst. prof. Princeton (N.J.) U., 1986-87; sr. economist GM, Detroit, 1987-89; dep undersec. econ. affairs U.S. Dept. Commerce, Washington, 1989—, acting undersec. econ. affairs, 1992. Contbr. articles to acad. publs. NSF fellow, 1977-80. Mem. Am. Econ. Assn., Am. Statis. Assn. Republican. Roman Catholic. Office: US Dept Commerce 14th St & Pennsylvania Ave Rm 4850 Washington DC 20009

PLANT, WILLIAM JOSEPH JESSE, chemist; b. Burlington, Vt., Mar. 29, 1926; s. William Eugene and Anna (Barney) P.; m. Anna Louise McCreight, Sept. 9, 1955; children: Richard, Carol, Catherine, William A., Susan, Marianne, Elizabeth. BS, Trinity Coll., Hartford, Conn., 1948; MS, U. Vt., 1950; PhD, U. Tex., 1955. Sr. chemist Gen. Dynamics, Ft. Worth, 1955; rsch. chemist Celanese, Summit, N.J., 1955-58; sr. fellow Mellon Inst., Pitts., 1959-80; sr. rsch. chemist Hercules, Inc., Jefferson, Pa., 1981-91; ret. Hercules Inc., Jefferson, Pa., 1991. Patentee in field. With U.S. Army, 1944-46. Republican. Roman Catholic. Home: 1702 President Dr Glenshaw PA 15116-2149

PLANTE, WILLIAM MADDEN, news correspondent; b. Chgo., Jan. 14, 1938; s. Regis Louis and Jane Elizabeth (Madden) Plante; m. Barbara A. Barnes Orteig, Jan. 18, 1965 (div. 1975); children—Patrick, Michael, Daniel, Christopher, Brian, David; m. Robin L. Smith, May 23, 1987. B.S., Loyola U., 1959; student Columbia U., 1964. Asst. news dir. WISN-TV, Milw., 1960-63; news correspondent CBS News, N.Y.C., Chgo., Washington, 1964—. CBS fellow, 1963-64; recipient Emmy award for news coverage

Acad. TV Arts and Scis., 1972, 85, 87, Radio News reporting award Overseas Press Club, 70, 75. Mem. Soc. Profl. Journalists, White House Corrs. Assn. (del.). Roman Catholic. Avocations: wine, music, running. Office: CBS News 2020 M St NW Washington DC 20036-3368

PLATA-SALAMÁN, CARLOS RAMON, neuroscientist; b. Guadalajara, Jalisco, Mex., Feb. 7, 1959; came to U.S., 1988; s. Manuel Plata and Eva Maria Salamán; m. Kyoko Matsumoto, Mar. 12, 1987. MD, U. Guadalajara, 1984; D of Med. Sci., Kyushu U., Fukuoka, Japan, 1988. Lectr. in pathophysiology, coord. rsch. sect. Dept. Pathophysiology Faculty of Medicine U. Guadalajara, 1979-82; coord. sci. activities Soc. of Boarding Med. Students, Civil Hosp. of Guadalajara, 1981-82; collaborator exptl. physiology teaching program for med. students Kyushu U., 1984-88; postdoctoral fellow Dept. Psychology U. Del., Newark, 1988-90, lectr. of neurobiology and physiology Sch. Life and Health Scis., 1990—, assoc. prof. Sch. Life and Health Scis., 1990—; referee Physiology and Behavior, Brain, Behavior and Immunity, Brain Rsch. Bull. Contbr. articles to profl. jours. including Jour. Neurophysiology, Brain Rsch., Am. Jour. Physiology, Physiology and Behavior, Peptides, Life Scis., and others. Mem. AAAS, N.Y. Acad. Scis., Soc. for Neurosci., Pavlovian Soc., Soc. for the Study of Ingestive Behavior, Human Anatomy and Physiology Soc. Office: U Del Sch Life and Health Scis Newark DE 19716

PLATNICK, KENNETH B., commnications executive; b. Bluefield, W.Va., Dec. 2, 1943; s. Nathan and Edna (Effron) P.; children: Barry, Stefan. BA, Dartmouth Coll., 1964; MA, Columbia U., 1965. News asst. N.Y. Times, N.Y.C., 1965-67; asst. editor nat. affairs Sat. Evening Post, N.Y.C., 1967-68; dir. info. svcs. Am. Stock Exch., N.Y.C., 1968-72; pubs. dir. RCA, N.Y.C., 1972-76; editor The Option Trader, N.Y.C., 1976-80; mng. dir. The Brownstone Group, N.Y.C., 1980—. Co-author: Financial Futures and Investment Strategy, 1985, The Option Game, 1975, Great Mysteries of History, 1971, Student Guide to New York, 1966; editor The Option Trader newsletter, 1976-80. Dir. N.Y. Concertino Ensemble, 1986-88. Mem. Nat. Options Soc. (sec. 1976-79). Office: The Brownstone Group 119 W 57th St New York NY 10019-2303

PLATT, ALAN ARTHUR, international affairs consultant; b. Jamaica, N.Y., Aug. 14, 1944; s. Philip and Ruth (Robinson) P.; m. Kathleen O'Boyle O'Reilley, June 20, 1982; 1 child, Roger Mark. BA, Princeton U., 1965; MA, Johns Hopkins U., 1967; PhD, Columbia U., 1973. Legis. asst. Office of U.S. Senator Edmund Muskie, Washington, 1972-75; lectr. Stanford U., Palo Alto, Calif., 1975-77; chief arms transfer div. U.S. Arms Control and Disarmament Agy., Washington, 1977-80; fellow The Hoover Instn., Palo Alto, 1980-81; sr. staff mem. The Rand Corp., Santa Monica, Calif., 1981-87; cons. on internat. and security affairs Washington, 1987—; vis. lectr. UCLA, 1982-83, Rand Grad. Sch., L.A., 1983-84, Georgetown U., Washington, 1987—; Am. participant USIA, Washington, 1975—. Author: U.S. Senate and Strategic Arms Policy, 1978; editor: Congress and Arms Control, 1978, Arms Control in the Middle East, 1992. European Econ. Community grantee. Mem. Coun. on Fgn. Rels., Internat. Inst. on Strategic Studies, Calif. Arms Control Seminar. Jewish. Home: 3011 Oliver St NW Washington DC 20015-1111

PLATT, HAROLD KIRBY, lawyer; b. Southampton, N.Y., Nov. 7, 1942; s. William Bangs and Edith (Guldi) P.; m. Joan Pritchard, June 20, 1970; 1 child, Timothy Ross. B.S. in Foreign Service, Georgetown U., 1964; J.D., Fordham U., 1971. Bar: N.Y. 1972, U.S. Supreme Ct. 1976, U.S. Dist. Ct. (ea. dist.) N.Y. 1988. Sole practice, Southampton, 1972-77; ptnr. Platt & Platt, Southampton, 1977-80, Platt, Platt & Platt, Southampton, 1980—. Articles editor Fordham Law Review, N.Y.C., 1970-71. Bd. dirs., sec. Southampton Hosp. Assn., 1979-85. Served with Mil. Police, U.S. Army, 1965-67; Germany. Mem. Suffolk County Bar Assn. (fee disputes com. 1974-82, chmn. 1981-82), N.Y. State Bar Assn., ABA. Home: 9 Dovas Path Southampton NY 11968-2830 Office: Platt Platt & Platt 99 Sanford Pl Southampton NY 11968-3338

PLATT, JEROME JOSEPH, psychologist, educator; b. N.Y.C., May 3, 1941; s. Benjamin and Rose (Weissman) P.; m. Arleen Kay Adair, Jan. 20, 1964; 1 son, Gregory. A.B., U. Mo., 1961; M.S., U. Ga., 1965, PhD, 1967. NASA predoctoral trainee U.Ga., 1967; Clin. research psychologist, sr. instr. in psychiatry Hahnemann Med. Coll. and Hosp., 1968-71, asst. prof. mental health scis., 1971-73, assoc. prof., 1973-77, prof., 1977-86, assoc. dir. grad. edn. in psychology, 1977-82; dir. research Hahnemann mental health services at Phila. prisons, 1978-81; clin. fellow Temple U. Sch. Medicine, Phila., 1978-80; prof. dir. div. rsch. Hahnemann Univ. Dept. Mental Health Scis., 1981-86; prof. psychiatry/dir. Ctr. Excellence in Addiction Treatment Rsch. U. Medicine and Dentistry of N.J., Camden, N.J., 1986-91, asst. dean for clin. rsch., 1987-88, acting assoc. dean for rsch., 1988-90; assoc. dean for rsch. Rsch. U. Medicine and Dentistry of N.J., S.O.M. Camden, 1990-91; adj. prof. psychiatry and human behavior Jefferson Med. Coll., 1984-89; rep. U.S. Dept. State/Fed. Republic Germany workshop on drug abuse treatment, 1985; cons. in field; chmn. organizing prog. coms. Dutch/Am. Conf. on Effectiveness of Drug Abuse Treatment, 1987; mem. peer rev. com. Nat. Inst. Drug Abuse, 1984—; chmn. organizing and prog. coms. German/Am. Conf. on Drug Abuse Systems, 1989; mem. various advisory, blue ribbon, other coms., 1986—; vis. scientist, Inst. Therapieforschung, Munich, 1990. Author or editor several books, including Heroin Addiction: Theory, Research, and Treatment, 1977, 2d edit., 1986 (transl. into German 1982), The Psychological Consultant, 1979, Heroin Addiction: Treatment and AIDS, 2d vol., 1989, The Effectiveness of Drug Abuse Treatment, 1990, Drug Addiction Treatment Research, 1992; contbr. numerous articles to profl. jours., chpts. to books. Bd. dirs. Burlington County chpt. Am. Cancer Soc., 1976-79; mem. Mayor's Commn. on Health in the 80s City of Phila., 1982. Grantee Nat. Inst. Drug Abuse, 1978—; clin. fellow Behavior Therapy and Rsch. Soc. Fellow Pa. Psychol. Assn., Am. Coll. Forensic Psychology, Am. Psychol. Assn.; mem. N.J. Psychol. Assn., Eastern Psychol. Assn., AAAS, So. Soc. Philosophy and Psychology Sigma Xi. Office: Hahnemann U Sch Medicine MS 982 Broad & Vine Sts Philadelphia PA 19102-1192

PLATT, JONATHAN JAMES, lawyer; b. Southampton, N.Y., Aug. 3, 1950; s. William Bangs Jr. and Edith Elizabeth (Guldi) P.; m. Linda Lee Tiska, Sept. 23, 1978. BS in Fgn. Svc., Georgetown U., 1972; JD, Fordham U., 1976. Bar: N.Y. 1977, U.S. Dist. Ct. (ea. dist.) N.Y. 1988, U.S. Ct. Appeals (2d cir.) 1988. Assoc. William B. Platt, Jr., Southampton, 1977-78; ptnr. Platt & Platt, Southampton, 1978-80, Platt, Platt & Platt, Southampton, 1980—; counsel Elks, Southampton, 1983—. Mem. ABA (gen. practice sect., probate and trust sect., real property sect. 1985—), N.Y. State Bar Assn. (real property sect., trusts and estates law, gen. practice sect. 1977—, invited participant statewide conf. solo and small firm practioners, 1991), Suffolk County Bar Assn. (justice ct. com., real property com., surrogate's ct.), Elks (hon., exalted ruler 1982-83, hon. life 1989). Republican. Roman Catholic. Office: Platt Platt & Platt 99 Sanford Pl Southampton NY 11968-3338

PLATT, THOMAS COLLIER, chief judge; b. N.Y.C., May 29, 1925; s. Thomas Collier and Louise Platt; m. Ann Byrd Symington, June 25, 1948; children: Ann Byrd, Charles Collier, Thomas Collier, III, Elizabeth Louise. B.A., Yale U., 1947, LL.B., 1950. Bar: N.Y. 1950. Assoc. Root, Ballantine, Harlan, Bushby & Palmer, N.Y.C., 1950-53; asst. U.S. atty. Bklyn., 1953-56; assoc. Bleakley, Platt, Schmidt, Hart & Fritz, N.Y.C., 1956-60, ptnr., 1960-74; judge U.S. Dist. Ct. (ea. dist.) N.Y., Bklyn., 1974-88, chief judge, 1988—; former dir. Phoenix Mut. Life Ins. Co., RAC Corp., McIntyre Aviation, Inc.; atty. Village of Laurel Hollow, N.Y., 1958-74; acting police justice Village of Lloyd Harbor, N.Y., 1958-63. Alt. del. Republican Nat. Conv., 1964, 68, 72; del. N.Y. State Rep. Conv., 1966; trustee Brooks Sch., North Andover, Mass., 1968-82, pres., 1970-74. Served with USN, 1943-46. Mem. Fed. Judges Assn. (sec., bd. dirs. 1982-91). Episcopalian. Clubs: Phelps Assn. (New Haven) (bd. govs. 1960—); Cold Spring Harbor Beach (N.Y.) (bd. mgrs. 1964-70); Yale of N.Y.C. Office: US Dist Ct Uniondale Ave at Hempstead Tpke Uniondale NY 11553 also: US Dist Ct 225 Cadman Pla E Brooklyn NY 11201

PLAUT, THOMAS FRANZ ALFRED, mental health program administrator; b. N.Y.C., Dec. 29, 1925; s. Alfred and Margaret (Blumenfeld) P.; m. Evelyn Z. McPuroff, Dec. 26, 1950 (div. Sept. 1976); children: Melanie, Tony, Jeffrey, Daphne, Iris, Roger; m. Bonnie Ann Cox, Nov. 29, 1976; stepchildren: Carole, Susan. BA, Swarthmore (Pa.) Coll., 1949; PhD, Harvard U., 1956, MPH, 1967. Lic. psychologist, Md. Asst. chief Ctr. for Prevention and Control of Alcoholism, NIMH, Rockville, Md., 1967-69, dir. div. manpower and tng., 1969-71, assoc. dir. for program coordination, 1971-72, counselor to dir., 1972-74, dep. dir., 1974-79, dir. Office of Prevention, 1979-80, spl. asst. dir., 1980-81, acting dep. dir. div. biol. applied sci., 1981-83, asst. chief behavioral sci. rsch. br. exmural rsch. programs, 1983-85, chief mental health resource policy, 1985-86, acting dep. dir. div. applied sci., 1986-90, assoc. dir. program devel. div. applied & svcs. rsch., 1990—; rsch. assoc. Inst. for Study Human Problems, Stanford (Calif.) U., 1962-67; rsch. fellow, instr. community mental health program Harvard U. Sch. Pub. Health, Mass., 1957-61; clin. psychologist Peter B. Bingham Hosp., Harvard U. Med. Sch., Boston, 1952-57. Mem. editorial bd. Potomac Jour., 1976-79; editor: Alcohol Problems: Report to the Nation, 1967; co-author: Personality in Communal Society, 1956, The Treatment Alcoholism, 1967. Mem. adv. com. Cambridge (Mass.) Civic Assn., 1958-60; del. White House Conf. on Aging, Washington, 1961; trustee North Conway Inst., Boston, 1967-69; bd. dirs. Somerset Elem. Sch. PTA, Bethesda, Md., 1976-79. With U.S. Army, 1944-46. Fellow APA; mem. APHA (life), Am. Sociol. Assn., Phi Beta Kappa, Delta Omega. Home: 6410 W Halbert Rd Bethesda MD 20817-5468 Office: NIMH 5600 Fishers Ln Rm 11C-26 Rockville MD 20857-0001

PLAVOUKOS, SPENCER, advertising executive; b. N.Y.C., May 30, 1936; s. George and Elva (Murzi) P.; m. Harriet Phylis Gladstone, Jan. 9, 1964; children: Stacy, Matthew. B.S., Syracuse U., 1961. Account exec. SSC&B, Inc., N.Y.C., 1961-64; account exec. Grey Advt., 1964-67; exec. v.p., dir. account service Manoff Advt., N.Y.C., 1967-79; exec. v.p. SSC&B, N.Y.C., 1979; chmn., chief exec. officer Lintas: N.Y. (formerly SSC&B), N.Y.C., until 1991; formerly vice chmn. Lintas: USA; pres., Lintas: Worldwide, chmn., Lintas: Americas, 1991—. Clubs: Country of New Canaan, Marco Polo (N.Y.C.), St. James (London). Office: Lintas 1 Dag Hammarskjold Plz New York NY 10017-2201*

PLAYER, THELMA B., librarian; b. Owosso, Mich.; d. Walter B. and Grace (Willoughby) Player; B.A., Western Mich. U., 1954. Reference asst. USAF Aero. Chart & Info. Center, Washington, 1954-57; reference librarian U.S. Navy Hydrographic Office, Suitland, Md., 1957-58; asst. librarian, 1958-59; tech. library br. head U.S. Navy Spl. Project Office, Washington, 1959-68, Strategic Systems Project Office, 1969-76. Mem. Spl. Libraries Assn., D.C. Library Assn., AAUW, Canterbury Cathedral Trust in Am., Nat. Geneal. Soc., Internat. Soc. Brit. Genealogy and Family History, Ohio Geneal. Soc., Royal Oak Found., Daus. of Union Vets. of Civil War, Friends Folger Library. Episcopalian. Home: 730 24th St NW Washington DC 20037-2543

PLAZEK, DONALD JOHN, materials science educator; b. Milw., Jan. 12, 1931; s. Stanley and Marian (Parker) P.; m. Patricia Lenore Filkins, Oct. 29, 1955; children: Mary, Joseph, Caroline, Daniel, John, David, Anne. BS in Chemistry, U. Wis., 1953, PhD in Phys. Chemistry, 1957. Postdoctoral rsch. fellow U. Wis., Madison, 1957-58; fellow Mellon Inst., Pitts., 1958-67; assoc. prof. materials engring. U. Pitts., 1967-74, prof., 1974—; adj. prof. chemistry Carnegie-Mellon U., Pitts., 1987—; mem. adv. bd. Jour. Polymer Sci., 1991—. Contbr. papers to profl. publs., chpts. to books. Brit. Rsch. Coun. sr. vis. fellow U. Glasgow, Scotland, 1976-77, Japan Soc. for Promotion of Sci. fellow, 1987-88. Fellow Am. Phys. Soc.; mem. Am. Chem. Soc., Soc. Rheology, N.Am. Thermal Analysis Soc. Office: U Pitts Materials Sci Engring Dept Pittsburgh PA 15261

PLEAS'ANT, TAMMY JEAN, auditor; b. Gettysburg, Pa., July 26, 1962; d. Raymond Smith and Grace Marie (Petry) Gorsuch; divorced; 1 child, Melissa Norrell. Grad. high sch., Union Bridge, Md. Data entry clk. Black & Decker, Hampstead, Md., 1985-86, London Fog/London Town, Eldersburg, Md., 1986-87; telemktg. mgr. ECI Communications, Owings Mills, Md., 1987-89; exec. sec. Richardson and Assocs., Woodlawn, Md., 1990; sales auditor Saks Fifth Ave., Owing Mills, 1990—; aerobics instr., mem. aerobics demonstration team Sini Fitness, Owings Mills, 1991—. With USN, 1981-85. Home: 45 Pittston Circle Owings Mills MD 21117

PLEASANT, URSULA GLADYS, military officer; b. Bronx, N.Y., June 24, 1943; d. Ursula Mildred (Willins) P. AAS, Mercy Coll., 1985. Enlisted U.S. Army, 1976, advanced through grades to sgt.; recruiter, pers. mgr., planner, technician, instr. U.S. Army, Ft. Hamilton, N.Y. Mem. NAACP, CORE, NAFE, Women in Mil. Svc. for Am., Vietnam Vets. Am., 369th Vets. Assn., Nat. Coun. Negro Women, Mercy Coll. Alumni Assn., Chippewa Dem. Club, Order Eastern Star, Order of Cyrene, Heroines of Jericho, Turtles Club. Democrat. Roman Catholic. Home: PO Box 221 Bronx NY 10462-0221

PLEBANI, THOMAS JOSEPH, guidance counselor; b. Trenton, N.J., July 26, 1951; s. Joseph P. and Julie (Juliano) P.; children: Thomas Jason, Eric James. AA, Bucks County Community Coll., 1971; BA, LaSalle Coll., Phila., 1973; MA in Edn., Trenton State Coll., 1978; MA in Counseling, Rider Coll., 1991. Negotiator Ewing Twp. Edn. Assn., Trenton, N.J., 1982-89; tchr. Ewing Twp. Bd. Edn., Trenton, 1976-89; guidance counselor West Windsor-Plainsboro (N.J.) Sch. Dist., 1989—. Mem. NEA, AACD, N.J. Edn. Assn., Chi Sigma Iota, Kappa Delta Pi. Home: 151 Liberty Dr Langhorne PA 19047-3078 Office: West Windsor-Plainsboro Sch Dist 75 Grovers Mill Rd Plainsboro NJ 08536-3105

PLEPLER, RICHARD L., communications consultant, producer; b. Manchester, Conn., Dec. 17, 1958; s. Sanford Jay and Constance (Federman) P. BA in Govt., Franklin and Marshall Coll., 1981. Spl. asst. for spl. projects Office U.S. Senator Christopher J. Dodd, Washington, 1981-84; pres. RLP Inc., N.Y.C., 1985-92; sr. v.p. corp. communications Home Box Office Inc., N.Y.C., 1992—; adv. on corporate affairs strategy Home Box Office, Inc., div. Time Warner. Co-exec. producer : A Search For Solid Ground: The Intifadah Through Israeli Eyes, 1991, "Wasted", a documentary film on teenagers and drugs. Home: 200 E 72d St Apt 8C New York NY 10021 Office: HBO 1100 Ave of the Americas New York NY 10036

PLESKOW, ERIC ROY, motion picture company executive; b. Vienna, Austria; came to U.S., 1939; Film officer U.S. War Dept., 1946-48; asst. gen. mgr. Motion Picture Export Assn., Germany, 1948-50; continental rep. for Sol Lesser Prodns., 1950-51; with United Artists Corp., Far Eastern sales mgr., 1951-52, South African mgr., 1952-53, German mgr., 1953-58, exec. asst. to continental mgr., 1958-59, asst. continental mgr., 1959-60, continental mgr., 1960-62, v.p. in charge fgn. distbn., 1962, exec. v.p., chief operating officer, 1973, pres., chief exec. officer, 1973-78; pres., chief exec. officer Orion Pictures Co., N.Y.C., 1978-82; pres., chief exec. officer Orion Pictures Corp., N.Y.C., 1982-92, also chmn. bd. dirs., until 1992. Office: Orion Pictures Corp 1325 Ave Of The Americas New York NY 10019-6011*

PLEVY, ARTHUR L., lawyer; b. N.Y.C., May 26, 1936; s. Louis and Sarah (Aronowitz) P.; student Bklyn. Coll., 1953-57; BEE, CCNY, 1959; LLB, JD, Bklyn. Law Sch., 1967; children—Scott Eric, Robert Todd. Design engr. I T & T Labs., Nutley, N.J., 1959-60; project engr. Westrex, N.Y.C., 1960-62; sr. mem. tech. staff RCA N.Y.C., 1962-65, patent counsel, RCA Research Center, Princeton, 1965-70; admitted to N.Y. State bar, 1965, N.J. bar, 1970, Supreme Ct. bar, 1970, Ct. Customs and Patent Appeals bar; pvt. practice patent law, Edison, N.J., 1970-91; sr. ptnr. PLevy & Sellito, 1991—; cons. electronic firms; pres. New Ventures, Edison, N.J., 1970—; arbitrator Am. Arbitration Assn. Mem. ABA, N.J. Patent Law Assn., Fed. Bar Assn., N.Y. Bar Assn., N.J. Bar Assn., IEEE, CCPA, Mason. Contbr. numerous articles on electronics, patent and trademark law to profl. jours.; patentee field of electronics. Home: 5 Marigold Ct Princeton NJ 08540-9414 Office: 146 Rte 1 N Edison NJ 08817

PLIMPTON, GEORGE AMES, writer, editor, television host; b. N.Y.C., Mar. 18, 1927; s. Francis T.P. and Pauline (Ames) P.; m. Freddy Medora Espy, 1968 (div. 1988); children: Medora Ames, Taylor Ames; m. Sarah Whitehead Dudley, 1991. Student, Phillips Exeter Acad., 1944; A.B., Harvard U., 1948; M.A., Cambridge (Eng.) U., 1952; L.H.D. (hon.), Franklin Pierce Coll., 1968; Litt.D. (hon.), Hobart Smith Coll., 1978, Stonehill Coll., 1982, L.I.U., 1984, U. S.C., 1986, Pine Manor Coll., 1988. Editor in chief Paris Rev., 1953—, Paris Rev. Edits. (subs. Doubleday and Co.), 1965-72; editor-in-chief Paris Rev. Edits. (subs. Brit. Am. Publs.), 1987—; instr. Barnard Coll., 1956-58; assoc. editor Horizon mag., 1959-61; dir. Am. Lit. Anthology program, 1967-71; assoc. editor Harper's mag., 1972-81; contbg. editor Food and Wine Mag., 1978; editorial adv. bd. Realities, 1978; TV host Dupont Plimpton Spls., 1967-69, Greatest Sports Legends, 1979-81, The Ultimate High, 1980, Survival Anglia, 1980—, Writers' Workshop, 1982, Mousterpiece Theater, 1983—, Challenge, 1987; spl. contbr. Sports Illustrated, 1968—; bd. dirs. Int. Film Investors, 1979-82, Leisure Dynamics, 1983-85. Author: Rabbit's Umbrella, 1956, Out of My League, 1961, Paper Lion, 1966, The Bogey Man, 1968, Mad Ducks and Bears, 1973, One for the Record, 1974, Shadow-Box, 1976, One More July, 1976, (with Neil Leifer) Sports!, 1978, (with Arnold Roth) A Sports Bestiary, 1982, Fireworks, 1984, Open Net, 1985, The Curious Case of Sidd Finch, 1987, The X-Factor, 1990, The Best of Plimpton, 1990; also numerous articles.; editor; Writers at Work, Vol. 1, 1957, Vol. 11, 1963, Vol. 111, 1967, Vol. IV, 1976, Vol. V, 1981, Vol. VI, 1984, Vol. VII, 1987, Vol. VIII, 1989, Vol. IX, 1992, (with Jean Stein) American Journey: The Times of Robert Kennedy, 1970, Pierre's Book, 1971, The Fancy, 1973, (with Jean Stein) Edie, An American Biography, 1982, (with Christopher Hemphill) D.V., 1984; The Paris Review Anthology, 1989, The Writer's Chapbook, 1989, Women Writers at Work, 1989, Poets at Work, 1989, The Norton Book of Sports, 1992, (with Jean Kennedy Smith) Very Special artists, 19921 contbg. editor Gentlemen's Quar., 1983-85, Smart mag., 1988-90, Esquire mag., 1990. Commr. fireworks, N.Y.C., 1973—; trustee WNET, 1973-81, Nat. Art Mus. Sport, 1967—, Police Athletic League, 1976-90, African Wildlife Leadership Found., 1980—, Guild Hall, East Hampton, 1980—, N.Y. Zool. Soc., 1985—; bd. dirs. Dynamite Mus., Nat. Tennis Found., 1979—, Squaw Valley Center for Written and Dramatic Arts, 1979—, Authors Trust Am., 1979, Friends of the Masai Mara, 1986, Friends of Conservation, 1988—; chmn. Books Across the Sea, English Speaking Union, 1988—; bd. dirs., pres. N.Y. Philomusica; mem. adv. bd. Coordinating Council Lit. Mags., 1979, Yoknapatawpha Press, Am. Chess Found., East Harlem Tutorial. Served to 2d lt. AUS, 1945-48. Asso. fellow Trumbull Coll., Yale, 1967; recipient Distinguished Achievement award U. So. Calif., 1967, Blue Pencil award Columbia Spectator, 1981, Mark Twain award Internat. Platform Assn., 1982, Chancellor's award L.I.U., 1986. Mem. NFL Alumni Assn., Am. Pyrotechnics Assn., Pyrotechnics Guild Internat., Explorers Club., Linnean Soc., PEN, Mayflower Descendants Soc. Clubs: Century Assn, Racquet and Tennis, Brook, Piping Rock, Dutch Treat, River, Coffee House, Devon Yacht; Travellers (Paris). Address: 541 E 72nd St New York NY 10021

PLIMPTON, PAULINE AMES, civic worker, writer; b. N. Easton, Mass., Oct. 22, 1901; d. Oakes and Blanche Ames; B.A., Smith Coll., 1922; m. Francis T.P. Plimpton, June 4, 1926; children: George Ames, Francis T.P., Oakes Ames, Sarah Gay. Pres., House of Industry, 1940-48; bd. dirs. Inst. World Affairs, 1940-74, Pub. Edn. Assn., 1933-44; chmn. United Campaign Fund for Planned Parenthood of Manhattan and Bronx, 1946-49; chmn. Planned Parenthood Fedn. Am. campaign, 1959-60, bd. dirs. 1959-67, 70-73; chmn. United Campaign, 1964; bd. dirs. Planned Parenthood of N.Y.C., 1965-74; rep. Western Hemisphere region Internat. Planned Parenthood Fedn., 1970-73; fund raiser, vol. coun. Philharm. Symphony Soc. N.Y., N.Y. Legal Aid Soc., ARC; mem. adv. coun. Friends of the Columbia Librs., 1986—. Recipient Planned Parenthood award for devoted service, 1969. Republican. Unitarian. Clubs: Cosmopolitan, River (N.Y.C.); Piping Rock Ausable (Adirondacks). Contbg. author, editor, compiler Orchids at Christmas, 1975, The Ancestry of Blanche Butler Ames and Adelbert Ames, 1977, Oakes Ames: Jottings of a Harvard Botanist, 1979, The Plimpton Papers: Law and Diplomacy, 1985, A Window on Our World: More Plimpton Papers, 1989. Home: 131 E 66th St New York NY 10021-6129 also: 168 Chichester Rd Huntington NY 11743

PLIMPTON, PEGGY LUCAS, trustee; b. Burgaw, N.C., Nov. 3, 1931; d. David Nicholson and Margaret (MacMillan) Lucas; m. Hollis Winslow Plimpton, June 11, 1955; children: Victoria P. Babcock, Priscilla P. Morphy, Hollis Winslow Plimpton III. AB, Duke U., 1954. Tchr. Clinton (N.C.) Secondary Schs., 1954-55; trustee Cape Cod Conservatory of Music, 1989—. Bd. trustees Carleton Williard Retirement Home, Bedford, Mass., 1968—, Cape Cod Conservatory Music, 1990—; bd. dirs. Episcopal Ch. Women, 1968-78, Brigham & Women's Hosp., Boston, 1975—; pres. Boston Lying-In Hosp., 1970-72; chmn. Mass. Nat. Cathedral Assn., Boston, 1978-80, 1985-88; pres. bd. trustees Women's Ednl. and Indsl. Assn., Boston, 1980-83. Mem. New England Farm & Garden Club (bd. dirs. 1965—), Chestnut Hill Garden Club(bd. dirs. 1970-74), Jr. League (bd. dirs. 1970-76), Jr. League Garden Club (pres. 1981-83), Colonial Dames (bd. mgrs. 1983-89, Vincent Club, Chilton Club. Republican. Episcopalian.

PLITT, JANE RUTH, consultant; b. Suffern, N.Y., Mar. 19, 1948; d. George and Rose (Wollowitz) Plitt; m. James Terrence Bruen, Sept. 1, 1973; children: Brett Plitt Bruen, Beth Plitt Bruen. B.S., Cornell U., 1969. Staff asst. labor rels. Rochester Telephone Corp., N.Y., 1969-71, mgr. labor rels., 1971-73, mgr. staff devel., 1973; exec. dir. NOW, Chgo., 1973-75; cons. Cresap, McCormick & Paget, Chgo., 1975-76; cons. tng., Rochester, 1977-79; adj. faculty Cornell U. Sch. Indsl. and Labor Rels., Rochester Inst. Tech., 1977—; bus. svc. ombudsman N.Y. State Dept. Commerce, Rochester, 1978-79; pres. JP Assocs., Rochester, 1979—, arbitrator, 1979—; adv. bd. dirs. Community Savs. Bank, Rochester, 1981-83; del. White House Conf. on Small Bus., 1986; pres. Small Bus. Coun., 1987-88; regional coord. N.Y. State Small Business Network. Small bus. columnist Rochester Democrat & Chronicle, 1988—; contbr. articles to profl. jours. Chmn. Rochester Charter Commn., 1981; del. Dem. Nat. Conv., 1971; campaign mgr. city ct. campaign, Rochester, 1983; bd. dirs. Rochester Ednl. TV and Radio, 1983—; pres., bd. dirs. Women's Career Ctr., Rochester Women's Network, 1977—. Named Best Ombudsman, N.Y. State Dept. Commerce, 1979, Small Businessperson of Yr., Rochester Small Bus. Coun., 1986, Outstanding Woman of Rochester, Rochester Women's Network, 1991. Mem. Nat. Assn. Women Bus. Owners (founder, pres. Rochester chpt. 1987-88), Indsl. Rels. Rsch. Assn., Rochester C. of C. Address: JP Assocs 165 West Ave Rochester NY 14611

PLOSS, HANNA KAYA MIRECKA, association executive; b. Bytom, Silesia, Poland, Sept. 12, 1928; came to U.S. 1966; d. Wiktor Jozef and Luiza-Zyta (Von Immisch) Mirecki; m. Sidney Ploss, June 24, 1966 (div. 1988). MS, Jagiellonien U., Krakow, Poland, 1951; PhD, Heidelberg U., 1956; Dipl. in Arts Design, St. Martins Sch. Art, London, 1959. Writer Polish Radio, Katowice, 1948-52, Polish TV, Katowice, 1956-59; dir., designer fashion house Warsaw, 1959-62; exec. dir. Am. Ctr. of Polish Culture, Washington, 1991—. Author: The Road Across the Bridge, 1955, The Ballad of My Street, 1962; author play: Nightingale Allee, 1963; contbr. articles and short stories to publs. Nat. pres. Am. Coun. Polish Culture, Washington, 1988—, pub. rels. program dir..., bd. dirs, 1966-88. Mem. Polish Am. Arts Assn. (pres. 1985-88). Democrat. Roman Catholic. Home: 5205 Sangamore Rd Bethesda MD 20816 Office: Am Ctr Polish Culture 2025 O St NW Washington DC 20036

PLOSSER, CHARLES IRVING, economics educator; b. Birmingham, Ala., Sept. 19, 1948; s. George Gray and Dorothy (Irving) P.; m. Janet Schwert, June 26, 1976; children: Matthew, Kevin, Allison. B.E. cum laude, Vanderbilt U., 1970; MBA, U. Chgo., 1972, PhD, 1976. Cons. Citicorp Realty Cons., N.Y.C., 1972-73; lectr. Grad. Sch. Bus., U. Chgo., 1975-76; asst. prof. Grad. Sch. Bus. Stanford (Calif.) U., 1976-78; asst. prof. econs. W.E. Simon Grad. Sch. Bus., U. Rochester (N.Y.), 1978-82, assoc. prof., 1982-86, prof., 1986-89; Fred H. Gowen prof. econs. U. Rochester, N.Y., 1989-92, John M. Olin Disting. prof. econs. and pub. policy, 1992—, acting dean W.E. Simon Grad. Sch. Bus., 1990-91, 92—. Editor, Jour. Monetary Econs., 1983—, Carnegie-Rochester Conference Series on Public Policy, 1989—; contbr. articles to profl. jours. 1st lt., U.S. Army, 1972-73. NSF research grantee, 1982, 84. Mem. Am. Econs. Assn., Econometrics Soc., Am. Fin. Assn., Am. Statis. Assn., Tau Beta Pi, Beta Gamma Sigma. Home: 95 Ambassador Dr Rochester NY 14610-3402 Office: U Rochester WE Simon Grad Sch Bus Rochester NY 14627

PLOTCH, WALTER, management consultant, fund-raising counselor, educator; b. N.Y.C., July 19, 1932; s. Harry and Belle (Lebowsky) P.; AB, Queens Coll., 1957; MA, Harvard U., 1959, postgrad., 1959-61; m. Yvette

Gabrielle Lambert, Mar. 15, 1956; children: Allison, Jennifer, Adrienne. Instr. history Pine Manor Jr. Coll., Wellesley, Mass., 1960-62; analyst L.F. Rothschild & Co., N.Y.C. and Boston, 1962-64; community cons., 1964-65; edn. dir. for New Eng., Anti-Defamation League of B'nai B'rith, 1965-68, nat. edn. dir., 1968-76; v.p. Brakeley, John Price Jones Inc., N.Y.C., 1976-79, sr. v.p., dir., 1979-90; sr. v.p. The Oram Group, Inc., N.Y.C., 1990—; mem. faculty Grad. Sch. Mgmt. and Urban Affairs, New Sch. Social Rsch.; lectr. Harvard U. Grad. Sch. Edn.; cons. Harcourt, Brace, Plenum Pubs. Bd. dirs. Schizophrenia Found., 1975-90; nat. bd. dirs. NCCJ, 1980-84, Nat. Charitable Info. Bur., mem. exec. com., 1986—. Served with USCGR, 1953-55; Korea. Grantee, U.S. Office Edn., Dept. Labor, N.Y. Council Humanities; teaching fellow Harvard U., 1959-61. Mem. Princeton Club, U. Washington Club, Phi Alpha Theta. Democrat. Jewish. Co-editor: Pluralism in a Democratic Society, 1977; gen. editor: The Job Corps Intergroup Relations Series, 1974; author articles in field, contbg. editor Grants mag., Jour. Sponsored Research 1978-82.

PLOTKIN, CARY HOWARD, English educator; b. N.J., Apr. 18, 1950; s. Roy and Eleanor (M.) P.; m. Marie-Therese Brincard, June 1980. BA, Yale U., 1971; postgrad., Ludwig-Maximillians U., Munich, 1971-72; MPhil, Columbia U., 1974, PhD, 1985. Tchr. French St. Ann's Episcopal Sch., Bklyn., 1976-77; asst. prof. Barnard Coll./Columbia U., N.Y.C., 1985—. Author: The Tenth Muse, 1989, (libretto) My Kinsman, Major Molineux, 1976. Woodrow Wilson Found. fellow, 1971, Deutscher Akademischer Austauschdienst, 1971-72. Mem. Phi Beta Kappa, MLA. Home: 710 W End Ave New York NY 10025-6808

PLOTKIN, MARTIN, mathematics educator, management consultant; b. N.Y.C., June 30, 1945; s. Bernard and Mildred Rose (Ringel) P.; m. Carol Ann Broadbelt, July 15, 1979; children: Zachariah, Candice. Profl. Dipl., Pace U., N.Y.C., 1980, MS in Adminstrn., 1980, MS in Edn., 1970. Tchr. math. N.Y.C. Bd. of Edn., 1965—; curriculum specialist N.Y.C. Bd. Edn., 1985—; pres. Veskin Assocs., N.Y.C., 1984—. Editor newsletter: Figure It, 1990—. Recipient Proclamation from N.Y.C. for contbns. to city, 1984. Mem. United Fedn. Tchrs. (Trachtenberg award 1989, elected ofcl.), Unity Caucas. Jewish. Home: RR 6 Box 610 Elmer NJ 08318

PLOTNICK, GARY DAVID, cardiologist; b. Balt., Nov. 23, 1941; s. Alvin Bernard and Evelyn Ruth (Altschul) P.; m. Leslie Karol Parker, Feb. 11, 1967; children: Michael, Daniel. BA, Johns Hopkins U., 1962; MD, U. Md., 1966. Resident U. Md. Hosp., Balt., 1966-72; gen. med. officer USN, Danang, Vietnam, 1968-69; rsch. fellow Johns Hopkins Hosp., Balt., 1972-74; from asst. prof. to prof. Sch. of Medicine U. Md., Balt., 1974—; assoc. prof. Johns Hopkins Sch. Medicine, 1988—; dir. echocardiography U. Md. Hosp., 1986—, dir. cardiology fellowship, 1987—; editorial bd. Jour. of Am. Coll. of Cardiology, 1987—, Jour. Non-Invasive Cardiology, 1987—. Fellow Am. Coll. Cardiology, Coun. of Clinical Cardiology, Am. Coll. Physicians;mem. Am. Soc. Echocardiography (bd. dirs.). Democrat. Jewish. Home: 7918 Winterset Ave Baltimore MD 21208-3111 Office: Univ Hosp 22 S Greene St Baltimore MD 21201-1544

PLOTZ, CHARLES MINDELL, physician; b. N.Y.C., Dec. 6, 1921; s. Isaac and Rose (Bluestone) P.; m. Lucille Weckstein, Aug. 5, 1945; children: Richard, Thomas, Robert. B.A., Columbia U., 1941, D.Sc., 1951; M.D., L.I. Coll. Medicine, 1944. Diplomate: Am. Bd. Internal Medicine. Intern New Haven Hosp., 1944-45; resident internal medicine Kings County Hosp., 1945-46, Maimonides Hosp., 1948-49; postdoctoral research fellow USPHS, Columbia Coll. Phys. and Surgs., 1949-50; practice medicine, specializing in internal medicine Bklyn., 1950—; chief Arthritis Clinic, attending physician Kings County Hosp. Center, 1950-85; chief L.I. Coll. Hosp. (Arthritis Clinic), 1950-65; asst. attending physician Mt. Sinai Hosp., 1955—; chief Mt. Sinai Hosp. (Arthritis Clinic), 1955-65, Arthritis Clinic, State U., Hosp., 1967-85; asst. physician Columbia-Presbyn. Med. Center, 1949-71; attending physician Bklyn. State Hosp.; dir. ambulatory care Bklyn. Hosp.Ctr., 1991—; cons. physician Peninsula Gen. Hosp., Jamaica Hosp.; cons. on rheumatology VA Hosp., Bklyn., L.I. Coll. Hosp.; cons. family practice Luth. Med. Ctr.; vis. cons. internal medicine Jewish Gen. Hosp., Mont., Que., Can., 1965; cons. internal medicine Avicenna Hosp. and Wazir Akbar Hosp., Kabul, Afganistan, 1965; prof. medicine, dir. continuing edn., chmn. dept. family practice SUNY Downstate Med. Ctr., 1967-91, prof. emeritus medicine and family practice, 1991—; Fulbright lectr. U. Paris, 1984, 91; professorial lectr. Mt. Sinai Sch. Medicine, 1992—. Editorial adv. bd.: Pakistan Med. Forum; editor-in-chief: Clin. Rheumatology in Practice, 1981—; editor-in-chief: Advances in Rheumatology, 1986—. Mem. nat. bd. govs. Arthritis Found., 1964-82, bd. govs. N.Y. chpt., 1965—, v.p., 1971-83, trustee, 1977-82, N.Y. chpt. sr. v.p., 1977-82, vice chmn. bd. trustees, 1983-85, 87—, pres., 1985-87; trustee Leo N. Levi Meml. Nat. Arthritis Hosp., Alumni Fund-Alumni Assn. SUNY Downstate Med. Center, Bklyn. Inst. Arts and Scis., Bklyn. Bot. Garden; mem. adv. bd. MEDICO, corp. mem., 1977—; treas. Internat. League Against Rheumatism, 1981-89; trustee Internat. League Against Rheumatism Trust, 1981-89. Served to capt. AUS, 1946-48. WHO fellow U. Negev, 1974. Fellow ACP, Am. Acad. Family Physicians (Charter), N.Y. Acad. Medicine (chmn. edn. com. 1976-78); mem. AMA, N.Y. State, Kings County med. socs., Am. Fedn. Clin. Research, Harvey Soc., N.Y. State, Bklyn. socs. internal medicine, AAUP, Am. Rheumatism Assn. (past sec.-treas.), N.Y. Rheumatism Assn. (past pres., exec. com.), Soc. Tchrs. Family Medicine, Am., N.Y. State acads. family physicians, Mystery Writers of Am., Internat. Soc. for Rheumatic Therapy (chmn. 1987-89), Soc. Urban Physicians, Sigma Xi, Alpha Omega Alpha; hon. mem. Rheumatology Soc. France, Rheumatology Soc. Japan, Rheumatology Soc. Mexico, Rheumatology Soc. Brazil, Rheumatology Soc. Yugoslavia, Rheumatology Soc. Norway, Med. Soc. Czechoslovakia, Rheumatology Soc. Egypt. Club: Heights Casino. Home: 184 Columbia Hts Brooklyn NY 11201-2186 also: 450 Clarkson Ave Brooklyn NY 11203

PLOTZ, PAUL HUNTER, research physician; b. Bklyn., Oct. 19, 1937; s. Milton B. and Helen (Ratnoff) P.; m. Judith Abrams, Sept. 1, 1963; children: John M.G., David A. AB, Harvard U., 1958, MD, 1963. Intern, resident Beth Israel Hosp., Boston, 1963-65; clin. assoc. NIH, Bethesda, Md., 1965-68; Heleh Hay Whitney fellow Nat. Inst. for Med. Rsch., London, 1968-70; sr. investigator Arthritis and Rheumatism br. NIH, Bethesda, 1970-84, chief connective tissue diseases sect., 1984—; clin. prof. Uniformed Svcs. U. Health Scis., Bethesda, 1983—. Contbr. chpts. to books, articles to profl. jours. Co-chmn. Com. of Concerned Scienetists, N.Y.C., 1985—. Capt. USPHS. Recipient prize Société Francaise de Rhumatologie, Paris, 1981, Philip Hench award Assn. Mil. Surgeons U.S., 1984, Outstanding Svc. medal USPHS, 1991. Fellow ACP (gov. for HHS 1990—); mem. Am. Soc. for Clin. Investigation, Am. Coll. Rheumatology, Am. Assn. Immunologists. Office: Clin Ctr 9N244 NIH Bethesda MD 20892

PLOWCHA, CHARLENE SNYDER, education and home economics educator; b. Indiana, Pa., Nov. 19, 1946; d. Gordon and Blanche (Burba) Snyder; m. Paul G. Plowcha, Oct. 12, 1968; 1 child, P. Adam Plowcha II. BS, Indiana U. Pa., 1968, MEd, 1977; EdD, Pa. State U., 1987. Cert. home economist. Tchr. home econs. Brockton (Mass.) Sr. High Sch., 1970-74; assoc. prof. edn. Mansfield (Pa.) U., 1978—, asst. to v.p. student affairs, 1988-90, chair dept. home econs., 1989-91. Editor (newsletter) Interface, 1986-87. Chair So. Tioga Home Econs. Adv. Bd., Mansfield, 1987—; com. mem., counselor Boy Scouts Am. Troop 106, Mansfield, 1987—. Urban Edn. fellow State System Higher Edn., Harrisburg, Pa., 1988-90, grantee Bur. Vocat. Edn., Pa. State U., 1988-89. Mem. ASCD, Am. Home Econs. Assn., Am. Vocat. Assn., Pa. Home Econs. Assn. (sec. v.p. 1988-89), Phi Delta Kappa, Kappa Omicron Nu (advisor 1986—). Office: Mansfield Univ 203A Retan Ctr Mansfield PA 16933

PLOWMAN, ROBERT JACOB, archivist, educator; b. Hanover, Pa., May 17, 1939; s. Walter Schmucker and Pauline Gertrude (Oyler) P.; m. Maryann Morrissey, Sept. 6, 1969; children: Elizabeth, Amy, Alexander, Emily. BS, Villanova U., 1961, MA, 1962; PhD, Cath. U. of Am., 1971. Asst. prof. Westmoreland County Community Coll., Youngwood, Pa., 1971-73; archivist Nat. Archives, Washington, 1973-75; archivist, dir. Nat. Archives-Mid Atlantic Region, Phila., 1975—; adj. prof. Villanova (Pa.) Univ., 1980—. Pres. Tri-County Girls Soccer League, Delaware County, Pa., 1987—. Mem. Geneal. Soc. Pa. (bd. dirs. 1989—), Delaware County Hist. Soc. (bd. dirs. 1984—), Hist. Soc. for the U.S. Dist. Ct. of Ea. Pa. (bd. dirs. 1985—). Democrat. Roman Catholic. Home: 5 Braeburn Rd Havertown PA 19083-2318 Office: Nat Archives-Mid Atlantic 9th and Market Sts Rm 1350 Philadelphia PA 19107

PLUMMER, E. BRUCE, library director; b. Toledo, Feb. 27, 1938; s. Paul Abel and Bernadine (Wert) P.; m. Mary Louise Girsch, Sept. 9, 1967; children: Andrew, Jonathan. BA, Ohio Wesleyan U., Delaware, Ohio, 1960; MLS, Kent State U., Ohio, 1967. Secondary tchr. Cin., 1960-65; dir. libr Worcester State Coll., Worcester, Mass., 1980—; treas. Mass. Conf. Chief Librs., Worcester, Mass., 1991—; pres. Cen. Western Mass. Resource Sharing, Worcester, 1991—; bd. mem. Worcester Area Coop. Network Librs., 1990—. Contbr. articles to profl. jours. Pres. Friends of Worcester Pub. Libr., Mass., 1990-91; bd. mem. Lit. Vol. Am., Worcester, Mass., 1989—. Mem. Worcester Art Mus., Mechanics Hall, Mass. Libr. Assn., New ENgland Libr. Assn., Assn. Coll. and Rsch. Librs. Mem. Unitarian Ch. Home: 66 Navasota Ave Worcester MA 01602-1119 Office: Worcester State Coll 486 Chandler St Worcester MA 01602-2597

PLUTZER, MARTIN DAVID, psychiatrist, educator; b. N.Y.C., Apr. 27, 1944; s. Jesse and Rose (Schaum) P.; m. Mary Anne Higgins; 1 child, Anne. MD, U. Pitts., 1968. Intern Montefiore Hosp., Phila., 1968-69; resident Downstate Med. Ctr., Bklyn., 1969-71; resident Med. Coll. Pa., Phila., 1973-74, assoc. prof., dir. med. studies edn. in psychiatry, 1980—. Major U.S. Army, 1971-73. Mem. Am. Psychiat. Assn. (teaching award 1991), Am. Psychoanalytic Assn. Home: 724 E Manoa Rd Upper Darby PA 19083-4113

PNIAKOWSKI, ANDREW FRANK, structural engineer; b. Grodno, Poland, Aug. 18, 1930; s. Josef Leon and Janina (Kodzynski) P.; Diploma Engr., Politechnika Warszawska, 1952; m. Margaret M. Czajkowski, Aug. 15, 1957; 1 dau., Mary. Bridge design and field engr. Govt. of Poland, Ministry of R.R., Warsaw, 1952-57; bridge design engr. Dept. Hwys., of Ont. (Can.), Toronto, 1958-66; sr. structural engr. Sverdrup & Parcel Assos. Inc., Boston, 1967-71; chief structural engr. Louis Berger & Assos. Inc., Waltham, Mass., 1972—; cons. engr. in transp., bridges, hwys., railroads, pub. bldgs., others. Registered profl. engr., Ont., Mass., Maine, N.H. Mem. Assn. Profl. Engrs. of Province Ont., NSPE. Roman Catholic.

POBER, ZALMON, physiologist, educator; b. Phila., July 31, 1939; s. Benjamin and Sarah Ann (Marcus) P.; m. Cheryl Ann Goodman, June 4, 1969. BS, Drexel U., 1962; MBA, Western New Eng. Coll., 1984; MS, Thomas Jefferson U., 1965, PhD, 1968. Physiologist R&D Command U.S. Army, Natick, Mass., 1968-76; asst. prof. Mass. Coll. Pharmacy, Springfield, 1976-81, assoc. prof., 1981—; cons. Continuing Profl. Edn. Svcs., Springfield, 1984—. Contbr. articles to profl. jours.; patentee in field. Mem. Am. Physiol. Soc., Phila. Physiol. Soc., N.Y. Acad. Sci., Sigma Xi. Home: 5 Applewood Cir Easthampton MA 01027-1309 Office: Mass Coll Pharmacy 24 Bellamy Rd Springfield MA 01119-2416

POCCIA, DOMINIC LOUIS, biology educator; b. Utica, N.Y., Aug. 8, 1945; s. Louis Joseph and Frances Marie (Surace) P.; m. Alison Gordon, May 18, 1971 (div. 1979); 1 child, Joseph. BS, Union Coll., 1967; AM, Harvard U., 1968, PhD, 1971; AM (hon.), Amherst Coll., 1987. Asst. prof. Wellesley (Mass.) Coll., 1971-72, SUNY, Stony Brook, 1974-78; asst. prof. Amherst (Mass.) Coll., 1978-82, assoc. prof., 1982-87, chair, biology dept., 1983-85, prof., 1987—; vis. scholar U. Calif., Berkeley, 1986-87; vis. prof. Stanford U. Hopkins Marine Sta., Pacific Grove, Calif., 1988; adj. prof. U. Mass., Amherst, 1984—. Contbr. articles to profl. jours. Recipient grants, NIH, 1975-86, 89-91, NSF, 1990—. Mem. Am. Soc. Cell Biology, Phi Beta Kappa, Sigma Xi.

POCH, HERBERT EDWARD, pediatrician, educator; b. Elizabeth, N.J., Sept. 4, 1927; s. William and Min (Herman) P.; m. Leila Kosberg, Aug. 27, 1952; children: Bruce Jeffrey, Andrea Susan, Lesley Grace. AB, Columbia U., 1949, MD, 1953. Diplomate Am. Bd. Pediatrics. Intern Kings County Hosp. Ctr., Bklyn., 1953-54; resident Babies Hosp., Columbia-Presbyn. Med. Ctr., N.Y.C., 1954-56; pvt. practice medicine specializing in pediatrics Elizabeth, 1956-92; chmn. dept. pediatrics, 1973-83; pres. med. staff, 1989, attending pediatrician Elizabeth Gen. Med. Ctr., 1973, sr. attending pediatrician, 1990; attending pediatrician St. Elizabeth Hosp., 1968, chmn. dept. pediatrics, 1971-81, attending pediatrician Monmouth Med. Ctr., 1991—, assoc. program dir. pediatrics; instr. pediatrics Columbia U., 1956-72, asst. clin. prof. pediatrics, 1972-91. With AUS, 1945-46. Fellow Am. Acad. Pediatrics; mem. N.J. Med. Soc. Address: 124 Chilton St Elizabeth NJ 07202

POCHICK, FRANCIS EDWARD, financial consultant; b. Metuchen, N.J., May 28, 1931; s. Frank Stephen and Bertha Barbara P.; student Rutgers U., 1949-50, 54-55; m. Shirley Ann Elliott, Feb. 16, 1957; children—Bonnie Lynn, Keith Francis. Agt., New Eng. Mut. Life Ins. Co., Newark and New Brunswick, N.J., 1958-61; agt. Lambert M. Huppeler Co., Inc., N.Y.C., 1962-64, cons., 1964, sr. cons. employee benefits, 1968—. Active adv. bd. Mercer Fund, Community Found. N.J., 1986—, Rec. for the Blind, Princeton, 1989, charitable devel. officer Nat. Found., Inc., 1992, Nat. Coun. on The Aging. Served with USMC, 1951-54. Mem. Am. Soc. Pension Actuaries, Nat. Assn. Life Underwriters, Internat. Assn. Fin. Planners, Estate Planning Council. Home: 118 Orchard Ave Hightstown NJ 08520-3403 Office: PO Box 804 Hightstown NJ 08520-0804 also: No Jersey Br 30 Two Bridges Rd Fairfield NJ 07004

POCKRISS, LEE JULIEN, composer; b. N.Y.C., Jan. 20, 1927; s. Joseph and Ethel (Price) P.; m. Sonja Meier, Dec. 4, 1977. BA, Bklyn. Coll., 1948; MA, NYU, 1950. Composer TV, songs, film, theatre, 1952-56, producer of records, orchestrator, 1957-88; pres. Emily Music Corp., N.Y.C., 1960—. Recipient 1st prize Young Am. Composers, Am. Fedn. Am. Music Clubs, 1950, two Grammy nominations. Mem. ASCAP (Country Music awards), Songwriters Guild Am., Dramatists Guild.

PODELL, HOWARD IRWIN, inventor, chemical engineer; b. N.Y.C., Apr. 12, 1917; s. Morris and Anna Podell; m. Lillian Gordesky, June 3, 1945; children: Lenore Podell Sempert, Elaine Podell-Blume. BA, Columbia Coll., 1938; BSChemE, Columbia Engring. Sch., 1940. Cert. profl. engr., N.Y., registered patent agt. Aero. engr. U.S. Navy Dept., Long Island, N.Y., 1941-43; sr. project aero. engr. GM, Trenton, N.J., 1943-46; chief engr. Star Fuse Co. Inc., N.Y.C., 1946-60; cons. engr. Howard I. Podell P.E., New Rochelle, N.Y., 1960—; dir. Hydrogelix Inc., New Rochelle, 1982—, Vanguard Rsch. Inc., Mamaroneck, N.Y., 1987—; adj. prof. Bklyn. Poly. Inst., 1957-60. Pres. Larchmont-Mamaroneck Democrat Club, 1960. Mem. Am. Chem. Soc., Nat. Soc. Profl. Engrs. (dir. N.Y. chpt. 1953-60). Home and Office: 28 Beachfront Ln New Rochelle NY 10805-3301

PODET, ALLEN HOWARD, philosophy and religious studies educator, rabbi; b. Cleve., Dec. 18, 1934; s. Irving Mayer and Becky (Podlubnai) P.; m. Caryl Ann Elizabeth Walker, Apr. 4, 1970 (annuled 1980); m. Valerie Jill Postman, Dec. 27, 1981. BA, U. Ill., 1956; MHL, Hebrew Union Coll., Cin., 1962, DHL, 1964; DD (hon.), Hebrew Union Coll.-Jewish Inst. Religion, N.Y.C., 1988; PhD, U. Wash., 1979. Rabbi Temple Israel, Dayton, Ohio, 1962-64, Temple Sinai, Bellevue, Wash., 1964-70; lectr. U. Wash., Seattle, 1970-74, asst. prof., 1974-80, assoc. prof., 1980-84; prof. State U. Coll., Buffalo, 1984—; chaplain USN, Buffalo, 1965—; bd. dirs. Jewish Fedn., Buffalo, 1974-80. Author: Success and Failure, 1988; editor European Judaism jour., 1986—. Capt. USNR, 1965—. Pres. Eastside Conf. Religion and Race, 1968-72; mem. Standing Com. Jews, Christians & Muslims, 1976—; bd. govs. Leo Baeck Coll., London, 1977—. Democrat. Home: 617 Niagara St # 1 Buffalo NY 14201-1044 Office: State U Coll B1-237 1300 Elmwood Ave Buffalo NY 14222-1095

PODHORETZ, HARRIETTE, psychologist, psychoanalyst; b. N.Y.C., Nov. 28, 1932; d. John and Leah (Bressler) Miller; m. Jan. 22, 1958; children: Jane, James. BS in Edn., CCNY, 1953, MA in English Edn., 1966; MA in Psychology, Fordham U., N.Y.C., 1973; PhD, Fordham U., 1974. Lic. psychologist, N.Y. Tchr. N.Y.C. Pub. Schs., 1953-59; psychotherapist Jamaica Ctr. Psychotherapy, N.Y.C., 1968-72; psychotherapist in pvt. practice N.Y.C., 1972-75, pvt. practice psychology, 1975—; pvt. practice psychology Scarsdale, N.Y., 1979—. Author chpts. to books. Mem. Am. Psychol. Assn., NYCAPS, NPAP. Home: 253 Garth Rd Scarsdale NY 10583-4050 Office: 51 E 42nd St New York NY 10017-5404

PODHORETZ, NORMAN, magazine editor, writer; b. Bklyn., Jan. 16, 1930; s. Julius and Helen (Woliner) P.; m. Midge Rosenthal Decter, Oct. 21, 1956; children: Rachel, Naomi, Ruth, John. A.B., Columbia, 1950; B.H.L., Jewish Theol. Sem., 1950, LL.D. (hon.), 1980; B.A. (Kellett fellow), Cambridge (Eng.) U., 1952, M.A., 1957; LHD (hon.), Hamilton Coll., 1969, Yeshiva U., 1991. Assoc. editor Commentary, 1956-58, editor in chief, 1960—; editor in chief Looking Glass Library, 1959-60; Mem. U. Seminar Am. Civilization, Columbia, 1958. Author: Doings and Undoings, The Fifties and After in American Writing, 1964, Making It, 1968, Breaking Ranks, 1979, The Present Danger, 1980, Why We Were in Vietnam, 1982; The Bloody Crossroads, 1986; editor: The Commentary Reader, 1966. Chmn. new directions adv. com. USIA, 1981-87. Served with AUS, 1953-55. Fulbright fellow, 1950-51. Mem. Coun. on Fgn. Rels., Com. on the Present Danger. Office: Commentary 165 E 56th St New York NY 10022-2709

PODSTAWSKI, ROBERT MICHAEL, facilities management executive; b. Little Silver, N.J., Jan. 1, 1946; s. Theodore Charles and Teresa Ann (Kukla) P.; m. Barbara Ann Cigolini, Dec. 1, 1984; children: Alex, Theo. BA in Bus. Adminstrn., Econs., 1974. FAA aircraft mechanic United Air Lines, Jamaica, N.Y., 1970-74; staff acct. United Air Lines, N.Y.C., 1974-79, staff indsl. engr., 1979-80; mgr. terminal maintenance United Air Lines, Jamaica, 1980-82; mgr. bldg. maintenance NBC, N.Y.C., 1982-83, dir. plant ops., 1983-84, dir. facilities planning and constrn., 1984-87, mng. dir. broadcast systems engr., 1987-90; gen. mgr. corp. svcs. Matsushita Electric Corp. Am., Secaucus, N.J., 1990—. Mem. Morris County Planning Bd., Morristown, N.J., 1976-77, Lincoln Park (N.J.) Bd. Adjustment, 1976-78. Mem. Internat. Facilities Mgrs. Assn., Internat. Soc. Facilities Execs., nat. Street Rod Assn., North Jersey Street Rod Assn.

POE, MARTIN, biophysicist; b. St. Louis, Sept. 26, 1942; s. Martin Turner and Rosemary (Raub) Poe; m. Joan Cathie Peterson, June 26, 1965; 1 child, Alison Crystal. BS in Physics, MIT, 1964; PhD in Biophysics, U. Pa., 1968. Postdoctoral fellow E.I. du Pont de Nemours & Co., Wilmington, Del., 1968-70; sr. rsch. biophysicist Merck & Co., Inc., Rahway, N.J., 1970-74, rsch. fellow, 1974-79, sr. rsch. fellow, 1979-84, sr. investigator, 1984—; Byron Reigel lectr. Northwestern U., Evanston, Ill., 1979. Contbr. articles to Proceeding NAS, Biochemistry, Jour. Biol. Chemistry. Mem. Am. Chem. Soc., Am. Soc. for Biochemistry and Molecular Biology, Biophys. Soc. Office: Merck & Co Inc 120 E Lincoln Ave Rahway NJ 07065-4607

POEHLER, THEODORE OTTO, university dean, engineer, researcher; b. Balt., Oct. 20, 1935; s. Theodore O. and Marion E. (Rohde) P.; m. Anne Otter Evans, Dec. 30, 1961; children: Theodore, Jeffrey. BS, Johns Hopkins U., 1956, DEng, 1961. Mem. sr. staff Applied Physics Lab., Laurel, Md., 1963-68, prin. staff physicist, 1969-73, supr. Quantum Electrons Group, 1974-83; dir. Eisenhower Rsch. Ctr. Johns Hopkins U., Laurel, 1983-89; assoc. dean Sch. Engring. Johns Hopkins U., Balt., 1990—; chmn. bd. dirs. Tech. Devel. Ctr., Balt., 1991—. Author: (with others) Detectors in Methods of Experimental Physics, 1990; contbr. more than 130 articles to profl. jours. including Phys. Rev., Applied Physics. Capt. U.S. Army, 1962-63. Recipient Nat. Capital award Coun. Engring. and Archtl. Socs. Mem. AAAS, IEEE, Am. Phys. Soc., Am. Chem. Soc., Materials Rsch. Soc. Office: Johns Hopkins U 34th and Charles Sts Baltimore MD 21218

POERIO, JOSEPH ROSS, educational administrator; b. Pitts., Sept. 22, 1944; s. Joseph Ross Sr. and Micheline R. (Grande) P.; m. Paula Wassel, Aug. 10, 1968; children: Bryan Joseph, Lisa Marie. BS in Bus. Edn. cum laude, Youngstown U., 1967; MS in Bus. Edn., Univ. Pitts., 1970, postgrad., 1971—. Cert. tchr. bus. edn., cooperative edn., data processing; cert. vocat. adminstr. Tchr. bus. edn. Sto-Rox High Sch., McKees Rocks, Pa., 1967-69; various positions to coord. supervisory instrnl. specialist Pitts. Pub. Schs., 1969-87, assoc. dir. applied tech. and career devel., 1987—. Devel. curriculums for Community Coll. of Allegheny County, Pitts. Sch. Dist. Vol. Dormont (Pa.) Libr., 1983—; parent rep. Keystone Oaks Budget Adv. Com., Dormont, 1987, 91; v.p. PFO, Hills Dale Elem. Sch., Keystone Oaks Sch. Dist., Dormont, 1983. Recipient Dedicated Svc. award Pitts. Chpt. Distributive Edn. Clubs of Am., 1988. Mem. Nat. Bus. Edn. Assn., Ea. Bus. Edn. Assn. (chmn. inst. rsch. 1990-91), Am. Vocat. Assn., Pa. Vocat. Assn., Pitts. Adminstrs. Assn., Tri-State Bus. Edn. Assn. (life), Pa. Bus. Edn. Assn. (exhibits chmn., Educator of Yr. award 1990, 91), Nat. Assn. Suprs. Bus. Edn., Delta Pi Epsilon, also others.

POFSKY, NORMA LOUISE, interior designer; b. Bklyn., Mar. 21, 1945; d. Abraham and Bessie (Kammerman) Eiger; m. Leonard Harris Pofsky, Dec. 29, 1968; children: Russell, Jonathan. BS in Edn., SUNY, Buffalo, 1965; MS in Edn., Queens Coll., 1968; cert., N.Y. Sch. Interior Design, 1987. Cert. neuro-linguistic programming practitioner. Tchr. Sachem Cen. Sch. Dist., Holtsville, N.Y., 1965-66, N.Y.C. Schs., 1966-70; asst. designer Quadric, Inc., N.Y.C., 1986-87; pres. Norma Pofsky, Inc., Marlboro, N.J., 1987-. Work appeared in Planning the Perfect Living Room, 1991, also in newspaper, 1992; designer newspaper article Night and Day, 1988, mag. article Contrasting Statements, 1990. Mem. Am. Soc. Interior Designers, N.J. Assn. Women Bus. Owners, Western Monmouth C. of C. (women in bus. com. 1988—), Allied Bd. Trade. Jewish. Home and Office: 21 Geanne Way Marlboro NJ 07746-1266

POGO, GUSTAVE JAVIER, cardiothoracic surgeon; b. Buenos Aires, Feb. 7, 1957; came to U.S., 1964; s. Angel Oscar and Beatriz (Garcia-Tuñon) P.; m. Janis Teitler, Feb. 17, 1983; children: Michael Tyler, Katherine Elizabeth. BA, NYU, 1979, MD, 1983. Gen. surgery resident North Shore Univ. Hosp., Manhasset, N.Y., 1983-88; cardiothoracic surgery resident Mt. Sinai Sch. Medicine, N.Y.C., 1988-91; attending, cardiothoracic surgery North Shore Univ. Hosp., Manhasset, 1991—. Contbr. articles to profl. jours. Fellow Am. Coll. Cardiology (assoc.); mem. Soc. Thoracic Surgery (candidate). Office: North Shore Univ Hosp 300 Community Dr Manhasset NY 11030

POHL, HENRY SIDNEY, internist/gastroenterologist, university dean; b. Monticello, N.Y., Aug. 28, 1946; s. Julius and Yetta (Becker) P.; m. Joni Ann Goldberg, July 31, 1977; children: Troy Goldberg-Pohl, Jessie Goldberg-Pohl. BS, SUNY, Albany, 1968; MD, Chgo. Med. Sch., 1972. Diplomate Am. Bd. Internal Medicine, Am. Bd. Gastroenterology. Intern Albany (N.Y.) Med. Ctr. Hosp., 1972-73, resident in medicine, 1973-75; fellow in gastroenterology Lahey Clinic-New Eng. Deaconess Hosp., Boston, 1975-77; spl. asst. in endoscopy Lahey Clinic Found., Boston, 1977-78; asst. prof. medicine SUNY Upstate Med. Ctr., Syracuse, 1978-83; staff. physician in gastroenterology VA Med. Ctr., Syracuse, 1978-83; assoc. clin. prof. medicine Albany Med. Coll., 1983—, dir. Office of Med. Edn., assoc. dean for med. edn., 1987—. Contbr. articles to profl. jours. Bd. dirs., mem. rev. adv. bd., exec. bd. dirs. Health Systems Agy., 1990—;. Mem. AMA, Med. Soc. State of N.Y., Albany County Med. Soc., Am. Assn. Med. Colls., Am. Gastroenterol. Assn., Beta Beta Beta. Office: Albany Med Coll 47 New Scotland Ave A-34 MS-103 Albany NY 12208

POIAN, EDWARD LICIO, historian; b. Trieste, Friuli, Italy, June 10, 1946; came to U.S., 1954; s. Angelo Del Picollo and Zaira (de Bourbon-Comelli) P.; m. Maria Del Carmen Lopez Cintron, Nov. 22, 1969 (div. Mar. 1980); children: Jeanne Marie, Nicole Anna; m. Nancy FLynn, Sept. 18, 1982. AS, U.S. Govt. Inst., 1965; BS, Mercy Coll., 1988; MS, L.I. U., 1989; PhD, U. N. Mex., 1991. Chief exec. Budget Fin. Inc., Pittsfield, Mass., 1968-70; acting postmaster U.S. Postal Svc., Chappaqua, 1971-80; pres. chief exec. Nat. Assn. Letter Carriers, Cappaqua, N.Y., 1973-78; v.p. Lehman Bros Khun Loeb, N.Y.C., 1980-83; chief exec. officer Cosmopolitan Armaments, N.Y.C., 1983-90; intern The UN Univ., 1989-90; prof. history Mercy Coll., Dobbs Ferry, N.Y., 1991—, prof. history and polit. sci., 1991—; cons. in field; trustee archaeology dept. U. Trieste, 1986—; rector The Internat. Ednl. Rsch. Found. Inc., Yonkers, N.Y., 1991—; intern UN Univ., 1990; dir. history and govt. assn. Mercy Coll., 1988. Author: On the Outside Looking In, 1972, Peace and Regional Security Through Education in Africa, 1992, Problems in Coordination Among Western Donor Governments in Relations to Multilateral and Social Programmes of the United Nations System, 1990; contbr. articles to profl. jours. Active Amnesty Internat. With USCG, 1963-67. Decorated Knight of Malta Cross of Gregory the Great Vatican

City. Recipient UN award, 1988. Fellow World Assn. of Former United Nations Interns and Fellows; mem. VFW, Yonker Hist. Soc., Am. Soc. Polit. Sci., Am. Legion, Freedom Coalition, Phi Alpha Theta, Phi Gamma Mu. Republican. Roman Catholic. Home: 709 Warburton Ave Apt 3E Yonkers NY 10701-1663 Office: Mercy Coll Dept History and Polit Sci. 555 Broadway Dobbs Ferry NY 10522

POIS, JOSEPH, lawyer, educator; b. N.Y.C., Dec. 25, 1905; s. Adolph and Augusta (Lesser) P.; m. Rose Tomarkin, June 24, 1928 (dec. May 1981); children: Richard Adolph (dec.), Robert August, Marc Howard.; m. Ruth Livingston, Nov. 27, 1983 (div. 1984). A.B., U. Wis., 1926; M.A., U. Chgo., 1927, Ph.D., 1929; J.D., Chgo.-Kent Coll. Law, 1934. Bar: Ill. 1934, Pa. 1978. Staff mem. J.L. Jacobs & Co., Chgo., 1929-35; jr. partner J.L. Jacobs & Co., 1946-47; gen. field supr. Pub. Adminstrn. Service, Chgo., 1935-38; chief adminstrv. studies sect. U.S. Bur. Old Age and Survivors Ins., 1938-39; chief adminstrv. and fiscal reorgn. sect. U.S. Bur. Budget Exec. Office of Pres., 1939-42; dir. finance State of Ill., 1951-53; counsel, asst. to pres., v.p., treas., dir. Signode Corp., 1947-61; prof. U. Pitts., 1961-76, emeritus, 1976—, chmn. dept. pub. adminstrn., 1961-71, asso. dean, 1973-75; dir. Vision Service Plan of Pa., 1984-85; cons. ECA, 1948, Dept. State, 1949, 62-65, U.S. Dept. Def., 1954, Brookings Instn., 1962-63, AID, 1965, Indian Inst. Pub. Adminstrn., 1972, Commn. on Operation Senate, 1976, Pitts. Citizens' Task Force on Refuse Disposal, 1976-78; mem. cons. panel Comptroller Gen. of U.S., 1967-75. Author: The School Board Crisis: a Chicago Case Study, 1964, Financial Administration in the Michigan State Government, 1938, Kentucky, Handbook of Financial Administration, 1937, Public Personnel Administration in the City of Cincinnati, 1936, (with Edward M. Martin and Lyman S. Moore) The Merit System in Illinois, 1935, Watchdog on the Potomac: A Study of the Comptroller General of the United States, 1979; contbg. author: The New Political Economy, 1975, State Audit-Developments in Public Accountability, 1979. Mem. Chgo. Bd. Edn., 1956-61; pres. Chgo. Met. Housing and Planning Council, 1956-57, Immigrants Service League, Chgo., 1960-61; dir. Pitts. Council Pub. Edn., 1965-67; mem. citizens bd. U. Chgo., 1958-78; mem. Pitts. Bd. Pub. Edn., 1973-76; bd. dirs. Pitts. Center for Arts, 1977-85, World Federalist Assn. Pitts., 1984—, Pitts. dist. Zionist Orgn. Am., 1979-81, mem. Hunger Action Coalition, Pitts., 1985-86; mem. Allegheny County Bd. Assistance, 1981-90, chmn. 1981-87. Served from comdr. to capt. USCGR, 1942-46. Decorated Navy Commendation medal; recipient alumni citation for pub. service U. Chgo., 1960; award for pub. service U.S. Gen. Accounting Office, 1971. Mem. ABA, Am. Acctg. Assn., Chgo. Bar Assn., Fed. Bar Assn., Allegheny County Bar Assn., Am. Polit. Sci. Assn., Am. Soc. Pub. Adminstrn. (award for pub. svc. Pitts. area chpt. 1985), Ctr. for Study of the Presidency, Govt. Fin. Officers Assn., Fin. Execs. Inst., Inst. Mgmt. Accts., Royal Inst. Pub. Adminstrn. (Britain), U. Chgo. Alumni Club (pres. Pitts. chpt. 1981-84), Army and Navy Club (Washington), Phi Beta Kappa, Pi Lambda Phi, Phi Delta Phi. Home: 825 Morewood Ave Pittsburgh PA 15213-2950

POISSANT, CHARLES-ALBERT, paper manufacturing company executive; b. Montréal, Que., Can., Sept. 13, 1925; s. Adrien and Antoinette (Courchesne) P.; m. Florence Drouin, June 23, 1951; children: Louise, Marc-André Hélène, Isabelle. Chartered acct., U. Montréal, 1953. Chartered acct, Que. Ptnr., pres. Poissant Thibault affiliate Peat Marwick Thorne, Montréal, 1947-87; chmn. exec. com., chmn. bd. Donohue, Inc., Québec City, Que., 1987—, chmn., chief exec. officer, 1988—; bd. dirs. Quebecor, Inc., Montréal, Premier Choix: TVEC, Inc., Montreéal, Hydro-Que., Montréal, Nat. Bank Can., Montréal, Sacred Heart Hosp., Montréal, Parc Technologique Quebec Metro. Author: Taxation in Canada of Non-residents, 1976, Commentary on Canada-Germany Tax Agreement, 1976, How to Think Like a Millionaire, 1985 (transl. into 7 langs.). Mem. Can. Pulp and Paper Assn. (exec. bd. Montréal chpt. 1988—), Pulp and Paper Rsch. Inst. Can. (exec. bd. Montréal chpt. 1989—), Que. Mfrs.' Assn. (exec. bd. Montréal chpt. 1992—), C.D. Howe Inst., Bus. Coun. on Nat. Issues, Club St.-Denis, United Svcs. Club, Laval-sur-le-Lac. Roman Catholic. Home: 333 Somerville, Ahuntsic, PQ Canada H3L 1A4 Office: Donohue Inc, 801 St-Louis Rd, Quebec, PQ Canada G1S 4W3

POISSANT, HERVE JULIEN, university administrator; b. Biddeford, Maine, Jan. 14, 1930; s. Andre Arthur and Beatrice (Angers) P.; m. Madeleine Therese Boucher, June 14, 1958; children: Martine, Daniel, Robert, Rachel, Marie-Therese, Denise, Michelle. BA, St. Francis Coll., Biddeford, 1955; MA, Calvin Coolidge Coll., 1961; MS, U. So. Calif., L.A., 1974. Cert. French tchr., media specialist. French-Latin tchr. St. Francis High Sch., Biddeford, 1954-55; prof. French, Latin St. Francis Coll., Biddeford, 1957-73, dir. French-Can. Inst., 1972-75, dir. audio-visual svcs., 1968-80; dir. bookstore U. New Eng., Biddeford, 1980-87, dir. aux. svcs., 1987—; dir. mail svcs. U. New Eng., Biddeford, 1979—; adv. bd. mem. Franco-Am. TV series U. Maine, Orono, 1977-78; dir. lang. lab. St. Francis Coll., Biddeford, 1965-73. Contbr. articles to profl. jours. Bd. mem. Biddeford Bd. Edn., 1968-72; com. mem. Kennedy Elem. Sch. Bldg., Biddeford, 1972; com. mem. Congl. Election Com., Biddeford. With USN, 1955-57. Recipient honors Soc. St. Jean Baptiste de Bienfaisance, Biddeford 1982, 92, Richelieu Club, Biddeford 1974, 88 (past pres.). Mem. U. So. Calif. Alumni Assn., Soc. St. Jean Baptiste de Bienfaisance (sec.), L'Union St. Jean Baptiste d'Amerique, U. So. Calif. Alumni Assn. (life), U. New Eng. Pres.'s Club, Club Richelieu de Biddeford (past pres.). Home: 45 Western Ave # 104 Biddeford ME 04005-2222 Office: U New Eng 11 Hills Beach Rd Biddeford ME 04005-9526

POLACEK, DEBORAH, nursing consultant; b. N.J., Nov. 18, 1955; d. Richard and Jean (Balderson) P. BSN, Seton Hall U.; postgrad., Montclair State Coll. RN, N.J. Staff nurse pediatric critical care Children's Hosp. N.J., Newark, 1977-79, 80-84; staff nurse pediatrics N.C. Meml. Hosp., Chapel Hill, 1980; case mgr. Essex County Spl. Child Health Svcs., Belleville, N.J., 1984-85; ind. nursing cons., 1985—; me. coord. N.J. Spl. Olympics; cons. Answer Care, 1989. Vol. United Cerebral Palsy North Jersey, Earth Watch, 1990. Mem. ANA, NAFE, N.J. State Nurses Assn., Nat. Nurses in Bus. Assn.

POLACH, JAROSLAV GEORGE (JAY POLACH), international economist and lawyer, government official; b. Ostrava, Czechoslovakia, Apr. 20, 1914; s. Francis and Marie (Pach) P.; came to U.S., 1952, naturalized, 1957; A.B., Tech. Coll., Ostrava, 1933; D. Law, Masaryk U., Brno, Czechoslovakia, 1938; M.A. in Econs., Am. U., Washington, 1958, Ph.D. in Econs., 1962; LL.M., George Washington U., 1959; m. Eva Bozena Mocek, Feb. 8, 1943. Corp. counselor, mem. bd. adminstrn. Czechoslovakian Metall. Works, Ferromet, 1946-48; internat. analyst, editor U.S. Govt., Washington, 1948-60; staff economist, research asso. Resources for Future Inc., Washington, 1961-70; sr. industry economist Econ. Adv. group IRS, Washington, 1970-75; sr. advisor energy, internat. economist Office of Sec. Treasury, Washington, 1975-84; fin. and mgmt. cons. Jay Polach Internat. Assocs., 1984—; sr. research assoc. Ctr. for Internat. Studies U. Pitts., 1984-86; bd. dirs. Cagas Precision & Rsch. Corp., Bound Brook, N.J., 1984—; lectr. econs. and indsl. orgns. U. Md., 1970-78. Bd. dirs. Internat. Research Inst., Inc., 1968-69. With Czechoslovakian Armed Forces, 1939-43, RAF, 1943-45. Recipient cert. of achievement IRS, 1973. Mem. Czechoslovak Soc. Arts and Scis. Am. (chmn., past editor), Am. Sokol (exec. com. 1970-85, chmn., trustees 1987—), Am. Soc. Internat. Law (standing com. nuclear energy world order 1968-73), Internat. Assn. Energy Economists, Internat. Econs. Soc., Oxon Hill Tennis & Swimming Recreation Club (bd. dirs. 1983-85). Contbr. articles and revs. to profl. publs. Home: 225 Panorama Dr Oxon Hill MD 20745-1028

POLACHEK, SOLOMON WILLIAM, economics educator, consultant; b. Washington, Aug. 27, 1945; s. Harry and Blanche (Katz) P.; m. Dora Eisenberg, July 23, 1972; 1 child, Nathaniel. AB, George Washington U., 1967; PhD, Columbia U., 1973. Postdoctoral fellow U. Chgo., 1972-73; from asst. prof. to assoc. prof. U. N.C., Chapel Hill, 1973-83; prof. econs. SUNY-Binghamton, 1983—, acting chair econs., 1987; referee numerous acad. jours., pubs., govt. orgns., 1973—; cons. to govt. agys., law firms, 1975—; expert witness U.S. Civil Rights Commn., Washington, 1984, U.S. Senate Subcom. Hearings, Washington, 1985; vis. research prof. Erasmus U., Netherlands, 1984; vis. prof. Cath. U., Leuven, 1987, Bar Ilan U., 1992, Tel Aviv U., 1992; speaker, presenter in field. Mem. editorial bd. Internat. Studies Quar., 1989—, Conflict Mgmt. and Peace Sci., 1989—; contbr. articles to profl. publs. Presdl. fellow Columbia U., N.Y.C., 1968-72; Ford Found. faculty fellow, 1974-75; nat. fellow Hoover Instn., Stanford U., Palo Alto, Calif., 1979-80; grantee various govt. agys., 1975-85. Mem. Am. Econ. Assn., Econometric Soc., Internat. Peace Sci. Soc. (exec. com. 1983), Ea. Econ. Assn. (program com. 1985), N.Am. Econ. and Fin. Assn. (program com. 1989), Avocations: travel, swimming, cross-country skiing. Office: SUNY Dept Econs Binghamton NY 13901

POLAK, JACQUES JACOBUS, economist, foundation administrator; b. Rotterdam, The Netherlands, Apr. 25, 1914; came to U.S., 1940; s. James and Elisabeth F. Polak; m. Josephine Weening, Dec. 21, 1937; children: H. Joost, Willem L. MA in Econs., U. Amsterdam, 1936, PhD in Econs., 1937; PhD in Econs. (hon.), Erasmus U., Rotterdam, 1972. Economist League of Nations, Geneva, Switzerland and Princeton, N.J., 1937-43, Netherlands Embassy, Washington, 1943-44; advisor UN Relief & Rehab. Adminstrn., Washington, 1943-44; from div. chief, asst. dir. to dir. rsch. dept. IMF, Washington, 1947-80, exec. dir., 1981-86; fin. cons. World Bank, Washington, 1987-89, Orgn. Econ. Coop. and Devel., Paris, 1987-89; pres. Per Jacobsson Found., Washington, 1987—; profl. lectr. Johns Hopkins U., Balt., 1949-50, George Washington U., 1950-55. Author: (with J. Tinbergen) The Dynamics of Business Cycles, 1950; author: An International Economic System, 1953, Financial Policies and Development, 1989; contbr. articles to profl. jours. Fellow Econometric Soc., Royal Netherlands Acad. Sci. (corr.); mem. Cosmos Club (Washington). Home: 3420 Porter St NW Washington DC 20016-3126 Office: care Internat Monetary Fund Washington DC 20431

POLAKOSKI, RAYMOND ROBERT, automotive executive; b. Jersey City, N.J., Nov. 8, 1947; s. Raymond Robert and Anne Marie (Fahey) P.; m. Barbara Jeanne Dawson; children: Lauren Marie, Kathleen Ann. BS, St. Peter's Coll., 1969; MBA, U. Phoenix, 1985. Warranty specialist Volkswagen of Am. Inc., Englewood Cliffs, N.J., 1971-73; mgr. svc. merchandising Volkswagen of Am. Inc., Englewood Cliffs, 1973-79; svc. ops. mgr. Volkswagen of Am. Inc., Columbus, Ohio, 1979-81; region svc. mgr. Volkswagen of Am. Inc., Denver, 1981-86; v.p. svc. Jaguar Cars, Inc., Mahwah, N.J., 1986—. Mem. Soc. Automotive Engrs. (com. mem. maintenance div., Detroit, 1986—). Republican. Home: 1 Audubon Dr Denville NJ 07834-1302 Office: Jaguar Cars Inc 555 Macarthur Blvd Mahwah NJ 07430-2327

POLAKOWSKI, KENNETH MICHAEL JOSEPH, science educator; b. Bayonne, N.J., Mar. 13, 1953; s. Joseph Stanley and Margaret (Sims) P.; m. Erin Maureen Walker, Sept. 25, 1982; children: Sara Koren, Christopher Daniel. BA, Montclair State U., 1975, M, 1985. Tchr., sci. Rutherford (N.J.) Sch. Dist., 1975—. Mme. N.J. Edn. Assn. (negotiation chmn. 1981—, membership chairperson 1981—). Home: 66 Edison Ave Nutley NJ 07110

POLAN, ANNETTE LEWIS, artist; b. Huntington, W.Va., Dec. 8, 1944; d. Lake and Dorothy (Lewis) P.; m. Arthur Lowell Fox Jr., Aug. 31, 1969 (separated); children: Courtney Van Winkle Fox, Arthur Lowell Fox III. 1st degree, Inst. des Profs. de Francaise, Paris, 1965; BA, Hollins Coll., 1967; postgrad., Corcoran Sch. Art, 1968-69. Vis. artist Art Therapy Italia, Vignale, Italy, 1986; dir. summer program La Napoule Art Found., Chateau de la Napoule, France, 1987, 88, 90; guest lectr. China, Japan, 1989; prof. Corcoran Sch. Art, Washington, 1974—; chmn. painting dept. Corcoran Coll. Art, Washington, 1991—. Illustrator: Say What I Am, 1989, Relearning the Dark, 1991. Mem. Corcoran Faculty Assn. (pres. 1988-89). Office: Corcoran Sch Art 1701 New York Ave NW Washington DC 20002-3325

POLANSKY, DAVID SAMUEL, composer, musician; b. Cambridge, Mass., June 24, 1945; s. Hyman Arnold and Beatrice (Radnofsky) P.; m. Elaine Satinover, June 21, 1970; children: Aaron, Lauren. BA, U. Mass., 1967; B of Mus. Edn., Berklee Coll. Music, 1975. Music educator Berklee Coll. of Music, Boston, 1975-78; music tchr. Wellesley (Mass.) Pub. Sch., 1980-81, Medford (Mass.) Pub. Sch., 1981-83; composer, producer Great Am. Music, Natick, Mass., 1983-91; performing artist in cultural enrichment programs for children, 1986-91; guest lectr. in early childhood edn. Author, facilitator (workshop) Self Esteem and The Music Channel, 1988-91; played trumpet with Arthur Fiedler, Sandler and Young, Ray Bolger, The Platters, Henny Youngman, 1965-91; arranged music for Pearl Bailey, Louis Belson, Tommy Dorsey; composer: Animal Alphabet Songs, 1982 (Artists' Found. Fellow 1981), Basics, Blues & Bop, 1980, 3 Hannu7kah Blessings, 1989, I Like Dessert, 1987 (Music City Song Festival finalist). Recipient grand prize Sheet Music Mag., 1979, composition contest winner Jewish Music Commn., 1991. Home: 17 Arlington Rd Natick MA 01760

POLANYI, JOHN CHARLES, chemist, educator; b. Jan. 23, 1929; m. Anne Ferrar Davidson, 1958; 2 children. BSc, Manchester (Eng.) U., 1949, MSc, 1950, PhD, 1952, DSc, 1964; DSc (hon.), U. Waterloo, 1970, Meml. U., 1976, McMaster U., 1977, Carleton U., 1981, Harvard U., 1982, Rensselaer U., Brock U., 1984, Lethbridge U., Sherbrooke U., Laval U., Victoria U., Ottawa U., 1987, Manchester U. and York U., England, 1988, U. Montreal, Acadia U., 1989, Weizmann Inst., Israel, 1989, U. Bari, Italy, 1990, U. B.C., 1990, Concordia U., 1990, McGill U., 1990; LLD (hon.), Trent U., 1977, Dalhousie U., 1983, St. Francis-Xavier U., 1984. Mem. faculty dept. chemistry U. Toronto, Ont., Can., 1956—; prof. U. Toronto, 1962—, Univ. prof., from 1974; William D. Harkins lectr. U. Chgo., 1970; Reilly lectr. U. Notre Dame, 1970; Purves lectr. McGill U., 1971; F.J. Toole lectr. U. N.B., 1974; Philips lectr. Haverford Coll., 1974; Kistiakowsky lectr. Harvard U., 1975; Camille and Henry Dreyfus lectr. U. Kans., 1975; J.W.T. Spinks lectr. U. Sask., Can., 1976; Laird lectr. U. Western Ont., 1976; CIL Disting. lectr. Simon Fraser U., 1977; Gucker lectr. Ind. U., 1977; Jacob Bronowski meml. lectr. U. Toronto, 1978; Hutchinson lectr. U. Rochester, N.Y., 1979; Priestley lectr. Pa. State U., 1980; Barré lectr. U. Montreal, 1982; Sherman Fairchild disting. scholar Calif. Inst. Tech., 1982; Chute lectr. Dalhousie U., 1983; Redman lectr. McMaster U., 1983; Wiegand lectr. U. Toronto, 1984; Edward U. Condon lectr. U. Colo., 1984; John A. Allan lectr. U. Alta., 1984; John E. Willard lectr. U. Wis.; 1984, Owen Holmes lectr. U. Lethbridge, 1985; Walker-Ames prof. U. Wash., 1986, John W. Cowper disting. vis. lectr. U. Buffalo, SUNY, 1986; vis. prof. chemistry Tex. A&M U., 1986; Disting. vis. speaker U. Calgary, 1987; Morino lectr. U. Japan, 1987; J.T. Wilson lectr. Ontario Sci. Ctr., 1987; Welsh lectr. U. Toronto, 1987; Spiers Meml. lectr. Faraday div. Royal Soc. Chemistry, 1987; Polanyi lectr. Internat. Union Pure & Applied Chemistry, 1988; W.N. Leis lectr. Atomic Energy of Can. Ltd., 1988; Consol. Bathurst vis. lectr. Concordia U., 1988; Priestman lectr. U. N.B.; 1988, Killam lectr. U. Windsor, 1988; Herzberg lectr. Carleton U., 1988; Falconbridge lectr. Laurentian U., 1988; DuPont lectr. Ind. U., 1989; C.R. Mueller lectr. Purdue U., 1989; mem. sci. adv. bd. Max Plank Inst. for Quantum Optics, Fed. Republic Germany, 1982; mem. Nat. Adv. Bd. on Sci. and Tech., 1987; hon. cons. Inst. Molecular Sci., Okazaki, Japan, 1989-91; founding mem. Can. Com. on Sci. and Scholars. Co-editor: (with F.G. Griffiths) The Dangers of Nuclear War, 1979; contbr. articles to jours., mags., newspapers; producer: film Concepts in Reaction Dynamics, 1970. Bd. dirs. Can. Ctr. for Arms Control and Environment; founding mem. Can. Pugwash Com., 1960. Decorated officer Order of Can., companion Order of Can.; recipient Marlow medal Faraday Soc., 1962; Centenary medal Chem. Soc. Gt. Brit., 1965; with N. Bartlett Steacie prize, 1965; Noranda award Chem. Inst. Can., 1967; award Brit. Chem. Soc., 1971; Mack award and lectureship Ohio State U., 1969; medal Chem. Inst. Can., 1976; Henry Marshall Tory medal Royal Soc. Can., 1977; Remsen award and lectureship Am. Chem. Soc., 1978, Nobel Prize in chemistry, 1986, Isaac Walton Killam Meml. prize, 1988; co-recipient Wolf Prize in Chemistry, 1982; Sloan Found. fellow, 1959-63; Guggenheim fellow, 1979-80. Fellow Royal Soc. Can. (founding mem. com. on scholarly freedom), Royal Soc. London (Royal medal 1989), Royal Soc. Edinburgh; mem. Nat. Acad. Scis. U.S. (fgn.), Am. Acad. Arts and Sci. (hon. fgn., mem. com. on internat. security studies), Pontifical Acad. Scis., Rome. Office: U Toronto Dept Chemistry, 80 St George St, Toronto, ON Canada M5S 1A1*

POLATNICK, JEROME, biochemist, consultant; b. N.Y.C., Oct. 4, 1922; s. Jack and Gussie (Seiden) P.; m. Selma Amster, Aug. 21, 1948; children: Lois, Judith, Barbara. PhD, Columbia U., 1954. Rsch. chemist Schenley Rsch. Inst., N.Y., 1943-47, N.Y. Bot. Gardens, N.Y.C., 1948-50; biochemist Columbia U., N.Y.C., 1950-54; prin. investigator Manhattan Eye & Ear Hosp., N.Y.C., 1954-57; rsch. chemist Plum Island Animal Disease Ctr. U.S. Dept. Agrl., Greenport, N.Y., 1957-80, acting lab. chief, 1980-85; cons. Southold, N.Y., 1986—. Contbr. articles to profl. jours. Recipient Presdl. citation, 1965. Mem. Am. Chem. Soc., Am. Soc. Microbiology, Sigma Xi. Home: 1230 Crittens Ln Southold NY 11971-1914

POLAYES, IRVING MARVIN, plastic surgeon; b. New Haven, Sept. 2, 1927; s. Abraham Noah and Ida (Stern) P.; m. Marcia Kresel, July 1, 1951 (dec. Apr. 1985); children: Roy Peter, Amy Lynn; m. Marian Fox Wexler, Sept. 28, 1986. BA, Duke U., 1948; DDS, Columbia U., 1953; MD, Albany Med. Coll., 1959. Diplomate Am. Bd. Plastic Surgery. Intern Albany (N.Y.) Med. Ctr., 1959-60, fellow plastic surgery, 1963-65; pvt. practice medicine specializing in plastic and reconstructive surgery Albany (N.Y.) Med. Ctr., New Haven, 1965—; attending plastic surgeon Yale New Haven Med. Ctr., 1965—, assoc. chief plastic surgery, 1969—; attending plastic surgeon St. Raphael's Hosp., New Haven; cons. plastic surgeon West Haven (Conn.) VA Hosp., Gaylord Hosp., Wallingford; clin. prof. plastic and reconstructive surgery Yale Med. Sch., 1977-86. Co-author: Diseases of the Salivary Glands, 1976. Concertmaster, violinist New Haven Civic Symphony Orch., 1970-84—; v.p. New Haven Symphony Orch., 1977—. Lt. comdr. USNR, 1954-56. Fellow ACS; mem. N.E. Soc. Plastic Surgeons (founding mem.), Am. Assn. Plastic Surgeons, Am. Soc. Plastic and Reconstructive Surgeons, Am. Trauma Soc., N.Y. Regional Soc. Plastic and Reconstructive Surgeons (bd. dirs.), New Eng. Soc. Plastic and Reconstructive Surgeons (pres. 1979-80), Am. Soc. Maxillofacial Surgeons (pres. 1979-80, lectr. syllabus-maxillofacial basic course), Soc. Head and Neck Surgeons, Am. Soc. Aesthetic Plastic Surgery, Conn. Med. Soc., New Haven County Med. Soc., Alpha Omega Alpha. Home: 49 N Racebrook Rd Woodbridge CT 06525-1407 Office: 60 Temple St New Haven CT 06510-2716

POLAYES, MAURICE BENJAMIN, electronic and industrial test equipment distributing company executive; b. New Haven, May 9, 1923; s. Abraham N. and Ida (Stern) P.; student Colo. U., 1941-43, Boston U., 1952; spl. degree Harvard U. Grad. Sch. Bus. Adminstrn., 1971; m. Adele Toby Oren, Apr. 22, 1963; children—Andrew, Gregory. Staff engr. Sta. WELI, New Haven, 1943-44, Sta. WSTC, Stamford, Conn., 1944; sr. engr. Sta. WLAW, ABC, Boston, 1944-56; engr. in charge radio Andover Police Dept., 1946-51; sales mgr. N.E. area Philips Indsl. Instrumentation Dealer, 1954-59; pres. Addelco Corp., Needham, Mass., since 1959—; pres. Astro Communications Co.; mgmt. cons., 1955—; adviser on disaster communications, 1954—. Active Boy Scouts Am. Registered profl. engr., Mass. Fellow Am. Soc. for Nondestructive Testing (past chmn. Boston sect.); mem. IEEE (life), Nat. Soc. Profl. Engrs., Am. Inst. Aeros. and Astronautics, Soc. for Exptl. Stress Analysis, Instrument Soc. Am., Harvard Bus. Sch. Assn. Boston. Clubs: Harvard (Boston), Harvard Faculty. Contbr. articles on nondestructive testing, instrumentation and applications, phys. measurement applications, automated electronic testing procedures to profl. publs. Home: 82 Pine Grove St Needham MA 02194-1766 Office: 20 Freeman Pl Needham MA 02192

POLCARI, STEPHEN, art historian; b. Boston, Jan. 22, 1945; s. Roy Polcari and Rose Nunes; m. Beth Alberty, June 15, 1990. BA, Columbia U., 1967, MA, 1971; PhD, U. Calif., Santa Barbara, 1980. Curator De Cordova Mus., Lincoln, Mus., 1976; instr. Bklyn. Coll., CUNY, 1978; asst. prof. U. Ill., Champaign, 1979-82, SUNY, Stony Brook, 1983-90; dir. Archives Am. Art, N.Y.C., 1991—; vis. mem. Inst. for Advanced Study, Princeton, N.J., 1982-83; visitor Nat. Mus. Am. Art, Washington, 1991. Author: Abstract Expressionism and the Modern Experience, 1991; also articles. Rsch. fellow NEH, 1982-83. Mem. Coll. Art Assn., Alumni Mems. Inst. for Advanced Study. Office: Archives Am Art 1285 Ave Of The Americas New York NY 10019-6028

POLEMITOU, OLGA ANDREA, accountant; b. Nicosia, Cyprus, June 28, 1950; d. Takis and Georgia (Nicolaou) Chrysanthou. BA with honors, U. London, 1971; PhD, Ind. U., Bloomington, 1981. CPA, Ind. Asst. productivity officer Internat. Labor Office/Cyprus Productivity Ctr., Nicosia, 1971-74; cons. Arthur Young & Co., N.Y.C., 1981; mgr. Coopers & Lybrand, Newark, 1981-83; dir. Bell Atlantic Network Svcs., Inc., Phila., 1983—; chairperson adv. coun. Extended Day Care Community Edn., West Windsor Plainsboro, 1987-88. Contbr. articles to profl. jours. Bus. cons. project bus. Jr. Achievement, Indpls., 1984-85. Mem. NAFE, AICPAs, Nat. Trust for Hist. Preservation, Ind. CPA Soc., N.J. Soc. CPAs (com. of mems. in industry and commerce), Princeton Network of Profl. Women. Home: PO Box 401 Princeton Junction NJ 08550-0401 Office: Bell Atlantic Network Svcs Inc 1717 Arch St 31st Fl Philadelphia PA 19103

POLENZ, JOANNA MAGDA, psychiatrist; b. Cracow, Poland, Oct. 20, 1936; came to U.S., 1961; d. Mieczyslaw and Nusia (Goldberger) Uberall; m. Daryl Louis Polenz, July 8, 1962 (div. 1991); children: Teresa Ann, Daryl Philip, Elizabeth Sophia. MD, U. Sydney, Australia, 1960; MPH, Columbia U., 1992. Diplomate Am. Bd. Psychiatry and Neurology. Intern Bklyn. Hosp., 1961-62; resident Mt. Sinai Med. Ctr., N.Y.C., 1962-65; ednl. fellow Mt. Sinai Med. Ctr., 1965-66, rsch. assoc., 1966-67; med. dir. Tappan Zee clin. Phelps Meml. Hosp., Tarrytown, N.Y., 1968-71, dir. dept. psychiatry, 1972-77; sr. attending psychiatrist Meml. Hosp. Ctr., 1972—; pvt. practice Briarcliff Manor, N.Y., 1971—; lectr. in field. Author: In Defense of marriage, 1981; (with other) Test Your Marriage IQ, 1984, Test Your Success IQ, 1985; contbr. articles to profl. jours.; numerous TV appearances including Phil Donahue, 1988, Oprah Winfrey 1984. Grant Found. grantee, 1970. Fellow Am. psychiatric Assn., Royal Soc. for Health; mem. AMA, N.Y. Acad. Scis., Pan Am. Med. Assn., Westchester Psychiatric Assn. (sec. 1982-85, chair person fellowship com. 1989). Office: 142 N State Rd Briarcliff Manor NY 10510-1443

POLEVOY, NANCY TALLY, lawyer, social worker, genealogist; b. N.Y.C., May 27, 1944; d. Charles H. and Bernice M. (Gang) Tally; m. Martin D. Polevoy, Mar. 19, 1967; children: Jason Tally, John Gerald. Student, Mt. Holyoke Coll., 1962-64; BA, Barnard Coll., 1966; MS in Social Work, Columbia U., 1968, JD, 1986. Bar: N.Y. 1987. Caseworker unmarried mothers' svc. Louise Wise Svcs., N.Y.C., 1967, caseworker adoption dept., 1969-71; caseworker Youth Consultation Svc., N.Y.C., 1968-69; asst. rsch. scientist, psychiat. social worker dept. child psychiatry NYU Med. Ctr., N.Y.C., 1973-81; adv. ct. apptd. spl. advs. Manhattan Family Ct., N.Y.C., 1981-82; cons. social work, 1981-86; matrimonial assoc. Ballon, Stoll & Itzler, 1987, Herzfeld & Rubin, P.C., 1987-88; pvt. practice, N.Y.C. Contbr. articles on early infantile autism and genealogy to profl. jours. Mem. Parents' Adv. Bd. Riverdale Country Sch., 1988—; mem. program bd. Manhattan div. United Jewish Appeal Fedn., 1990—; mem. archives com. Cen. Synagogue, 1991—; trustee Am. Jewish Hist. Soc., 1992—. Recipient French Govt. prize, 1963. Mem. Bar Assn. of City of N.Y., N.Y. State Bar Assn. (child custody com. of family law sect.), Nat. Assn. Social Workers, Acad. Cert. Social Workers, Am. Jewish Hist. Soc. (trustee), Barnard Coll. Alumni Assn. (v.p. 1966). Home and Office: 1155 Park Ave New York NY 10128

POLGAR, ANTOINE JEAN, association administrator; b. Clermont-Ferrand, France, Oct. 7, 1940; came to U.S., 1942; s. Janos and Monique (Leveque) P.; m. Nickler Gerard, June 29, 1966 (div. 1990); children: Antoine-Robert, Alexis Elizabeth Laura. Student, Lycee Francais N.Y., 1952-57, Hofstra U., 1958-62, New Sch. for Social Rsch., 1963, Bard Coll., 1964; D (hon.), Universite Nat. d'Haiti, Port-au-Prince, 1971. Exec. sec. Am. Festival Negro Arts, N.Y.C., 1963-65; assoc. dir. Panam. Assn., Washington, 1968-70; dir., press attache Haiti Govt. Press and Info. Svc., Washington, 1968; mng. editor The Impartial Citizen Newspaper, Syracuse, N.Y., 1980—; exec. dir. Kahre-Richardes Family Found., Baldwinsville, N.Y., 1972—, Panam./Panafrican Assn., Baldwinsville, 1970—; minority bus. cons., Syracuse, 1978—; multicultural textbook cons. Ednl. Assessment Pub. Co., San Diego, 1991-92; coord. 7th Internat. Panafricanist Congress, Cotonou, Benin, West Africa, 1991; ethnic studies curriculum cons. Mankato (Minn.) State Coll., 1974; coord. publ. diplomacy program, 1970—, coord. activities pub. interest litigation unit, 1984—; crisis mgmt. team cons. Jamaica Progressive League, 1978—; adminstr. UN Gen. Assembly Symphonic/Choral Concert Gala Observance, 1976; media advisor Emperor of Ethiopia in Exile, 1992—. Translator: Poetry of President Leopold Sedar Senghor of Senegal, 1963-65; producer: (recording) Songs of Senegal, 1977; author numerous poems. Democrat. Roman Catholic. Home: 14 Sunset Ter Baldwinsville NY 13027-1112 Office: Impartial Citizen Newspaper PO Box 143 Baldwinsville NY 13027

POLGAR, LESLIE GEORGE, venture executive; b. Budapest, Hungary, July 26, 1943; s. Laszlo Polgar and Antonia (Szilard) Polgar Zala; m. Susan Elisabeth Cook, May 8, 1965; children: DAvid Szilard, Sara Elisabeth. BS in Physics and Math., U. Mich., 1965; PhD in Physics, Carnegie-Mellon U., 1971; MBA, U. Conn., 1977. Mgr. environ. planning, rsch. scientist TRC Environ. Cons., East Hartford, Conn., 1972-77; sr. assoc. Am. Petroleum Inst., Washington, 1977-79; dir., elec. materials mgr., corp. planning Stauffer Chem. Co., Westport, Conn., 1979-86; v.p. Emcore Corp., Somerset, N.J., 1986-88, Bertram Labs., Inc., Somerville, N.J., 1988—; reviewer Conservation Found., Washington, 1979; cons. Photon Kinetics, Beaverton, Oreg., 1988; adj. assoc. prof. George Washington U., Washington, 1978; invited speaker Nat. Petroleum Refiners Assn., 1977, World Congress on Small Bus., 1987; vis. physics scientist Tech. U. of Eindhoven, The Netherlands, 1971-72. Contbr. articles to profl. jours. Trustee First Unitarian Soc. of Plainfield (N.J.), 1991—; fund raiser Carnegie-Mellon U., Pitts., 1975-87, alumni recruiter, 1991—. Mem. IEEE, Am. Phys. Soc., U. Mich. Alumni Assn., U. Conn. Alumni Assn., Sigma Xi, Phi Kappa Phi, Beta Gamma Sigma. Home: 12 Northridge Way Warren NJ 07059-5332 Office: Bertram Labs Inc 72 Readington Rd Somerville NJ 08876-3541

POLIAK, AARON, obstetrics-gynecology educator; b. Buenos Aires, Apr. 30, 1925; came to U.S., 1964; s. Jose Poliak and Aida Cherniausky; m. Sara Schmukler, Jan. 6, 1951; children: Susana, Jorge, Jose. BA, Riuadauia Coll., Buenos Aires, 1937; MD, U. Buenos Aires, 1949, PhD, 1955. Jr. attending resident in gen. surgery T. Alvarez Hosp., Buenos Aires, 1949-51; resident ob-gyn. Campo de Mayo Army Hosp., Buenos Aires, 1951-53; rotating intern Mt. Sinai Hosp. Greater Miami (Fla.), 1964-65; chief resident ob-gyn. Ch. Home & Hosp., Balt., 1965-66; fellow ob-gyn., instr. ob-gyn. Johns Hopkins U., Balt., 1966-68; dir. female endocrinology Lincoln Hosp., Bronx, N.Y., 1968-77, dir. dept. ob-gyn., 1972-77; dir. gynecology Bronx Mcpl. Hosp. Ctr., 1978-79, dir. dept. ob-gyn., 1980-83, chief gynecology, 1983—; prof. ob-gyn. Albert Einstein Coll. Medicine, Yehsiva U. Mem. ACS, Am. Coll. Ob-Gyn., Am. Fertility Soc., N.Y. Obstet. Soc., Bronx Obstet. and Gynecol. Soc. Jewish. Office: Albert Einstein Coll Medicine 1300 Morris Park Ave Bronx NY 10461-1924

POLIAN, BILL, professional football team executive; b. N.Y.C., Dec. 8, 1942; m. Eileen Polian; children: Lynn, Chris, Brian, Dennis. Grad., NYU. Asst. coach Manhattan Coll., 1965-67; asst. coach football U.S. Mcht. Marine Acad., 1968-70, head coach baseball, 1971-75; scout Kansas City Chiefs, 1978-82; dir. player personnel Winnipeg (Can.) Blue Bombers, 1983; dir. personnel Buffalo Bills, 1984-85, gen. mgr., v.p. adminstrn., 1985—; Mem. competition com. NFL, 1989—. Named NFL Exec. of Yr., 1991. Office: Buffalo Bills 1 Bills Dr Orchard Park NY 14127-2296

POLING, WESLEY HENRY, educational administrator; b. Akron, Ohio, May 22, 1945; s. Elmer Francis and Norma May (Flickinger) P.; m. Carol Ann Young, Aug. 17, 1968; children: Jason Alder, Todd Wesley. BA, Ohio Wesleyan U., 1968; MDiv, Yale U., 1971; PhD, U. Conn., 1983. Dir. parents program Yale U., New Haven, 1971-73, dir. alumni records, 1973-86; v.p. for devel. and alumni rels. Goucher Coll., Towson, Md., 1986—; treas. Dist. I CASE, 1985-86, program chair Conf., 1984-85. Chmn. bd. mgrs. Cen. br. YMCA of New Haven, 1976-83; v.p., treas. Balt. Choral Arts Soc., 1989—; bd. dirs. Roland Park Pl., Balt., 1991—. Berkeley Coll., Yale U. fellow. Mem. Williams Club, Phi Delta Kappa. Home: 900 Stone Barn Rd Baltimore MD 21286 Office: Goucher Coll 1021 Dulaney Valley Rd Baltimore MD 21204-2753

POLINSKY, JOSEPH THOMAS, logistics manager; b. Kingston, Pa., Mar. 10, 1947; s. Joseph Patrick and Margaret Ceclia (Matej) P.; m. Donna Lee Miles, Dec. 28, 1968 (div. Nov. 1990); children: Jon Douglas, Jennifer Susan, Jeffrey David. BSBA, King's Coll., 1968; MBA in Mgmt., Fairleigh Dickinson U., 1977. Fin. svcs. specialist Bell Labs., Murray Hill, N.J., 1968-74; adminstrv. asst. Bell Labs., Whippany, N.J., 1974-76, supr. adminstrn. svcs., 1977; tech. employment rep. Bell Labs., Holmdel, N.J., 1977-80; sr. systems analyst Bellcore, Short Hills, N.J., 1981-82; mgr. tech. employment Bell Labs., Piscataway, N.J., 1983-85, mgr. logistics, 1986—. Mem. indsl. com. United Way, Morris County, N.J., 1977, allocation com., Monmouth County, N.J., 1985; cub master Boy Scouts Am., Raritan, N.J., 1983-86; mem. Bd. Adjustment, Raritan, 1988-89. With U.S. Army, 1969-70. Roman Catholic. Home: 14 Normandie Ln Raritan NJ 08869 Office: Bellcore 6 Corp Pl Piscataway NJ 08854

POLISAR, BARRY LOUIS, author, singer, songwriter; b. Bklyn., Nov. 18, 1954; s. Max and Anita Joyce (Buchalter) P.; m. Roni Lynn Prusky, Oct. 31, 1981; children: Evan Nathan, Sarah Hannah. BA magna cum laude, U. Md., 1977. speaker, presenter, fundraiser in field. Author: Snakes and the Boy Who Was Afraid of Them, The Snake Who Was Afraid of People, Don't Do That, The Haunted House Party, Noises From Under the Rug, Dinosaurs I Have Known, The Trouble with Ben; singer, songerwriter Juggling Babies, Family Concert, I Eat Kids, My Brother Thinks He's A Banana, Naughty Songs for Boys and Girls, Songs for Well Behaved Children, others, (video tapes) I'm a 3-Toed, Tripled-Eyed, Double-Jointed Dinosaur (Parents Choice award), My Brother Threw Up on My Stuffed Toy Bunny. Jewish. Home and office: 2121 Fairland Rd Silver Spring MD 20904

POLITAN, NICHOLAS H., judge; b. Newark, Nov. 13, 1935; m. Marian E. Politan; children: Nicholas H. Jr., Vincent J. Bar: N.J. 1961, U.S. Dist. Ct. N.J. 1961, U.S. Ct. Appeals (2d cir.) 1969, U.S. Ct. Appeals (3d cir.) 1971, U.S. Tax Ct. 1972, U.S. Supreme Ct. 1973. Law clk. to Hon. Gerald McLaughlin U.S. Ct. Appeals (3d cir.), Newark, 1960-61; sr. ptnr. Cecchi and Politan, Lyndhurst, N.J., 1961-64, 72-87; litigation ptnr. Krieger, Chodash & Politan, Jersey City, 1964-72; dir., chmn. exec. com. County Trust Co., Lyndhurst, 1980-87; judge U.S. Dist. Ct. N.J., 1987—; instr. legal rsch. and writing Rutgers U. Law Sch., 1963. Mng. editor Rutgers Law Rev., 1959; contbr. articles to rprofl. jours. Office: US Dist Ct PO Box 999 Newark NJ 07101-0999

POLITY, LEDDY SMITH, preschool director; b. Wrightsville, Pa., Nov. 6, 1936; d. Michael Kenneth and Vivian Lentz (Birnstock) Smith; m. Richard Milton Polity, Sept. 15, 1956; children: Karen, Bruce, Jennifer. Student, Gettysburg (Pa.) Coll., 1954-56, Kean Coll., 1966-74. Cert. early childhood edn. Tchr. Little Folks Nursery Sch., Woodbridge, N.J., 1966-67; co-founder, tchr. Presbyn. Nursery Sch., Matawan, 1967; dir. Presbyn. Nursery Sch., 1982—; cons. community services bd. Brookdale Community Coll., 1977-82; workshop presentor, various community groups statewide. Contbr. articles to profl. jours.; appeared as TV panelist on N.Y. and N.J. talk shows. Mem. Sch. Aged Child Care Task Force, N.J. Dept. Human Services, 1983; ad hoc citizens adv. bd., N.J. Bur. of Licensing, 1981, 85, 86-87; Sunday sch. tchr., Cross of Glory Luth. Ch., Aberdeen, 1963-73, Sunday Sch. supt., 1974-76, vacation sch. dir., 1976-78; coordinator, Girl Scouts of U.S., Matawan, 1976-79; apptd. to Gov's. Child Care Adv. Council of N.J., 1984—. Mem. N.J. Shore Chpt. Assn. for Edn. of Young Children (pres. 1976-78), N.J. Assn. for Edn. of Young Children (lit. chmn. 1978-80, 1st v.p. 1980-82, state pres. 1982-84, exec. bd. advisor 1984-86), Assn. for Edn. of Young Children (state conf. planner, 1980, 81, 82). Home: 144 Idlebrook Ln Matawan NJ 07747-1747 Office: Presbyn Nursery Sch 33 Hwy 34 Matawan NJ 07747-1957

POLK, CHARLES, electrical engineer, educator, biophysicist; b. Vienna, Austria, Jan. 15, 1920; came to U.S., 1940, naturalized, 1943; s. Heinrich and Amalie (Canar) P.; m. Dorothy R. Lemp, Apr. 27, 1946; children: Dean F., Gerald W. Student, U. Paris-Sorbonne, 1939; BS, Washington U., 1948; MS, U. Pa., 1953, PhD, 1956. Engr. RCA Victor div., Camden, N.J., 1948-52; rsch. and teaching assoc. U. Pa., 1952-57; prof. elec. engring. Drexel Inst. Tech., Phila., 1957-59; tech. staff RCA Labs., Princeton, N.J., 1957-59; prof. elec. engring. U. R.I., 1959—, chmn. dept., 1959-79; head elec. scis. and analysis sect. engring. div. NSF, Washington, 1975-76; acting dir. engring. div. NSF, 1976-77; vis. prof. elec. engring. Stanford U., 1968-69, U. Wis., Madison, 1983-84. Editor Handbook of Biologial Effects of Electromagnetic Fields; contbr. articles to profl. publs. Mem. R.I. Legis. Commn. on Electricity Rates, 1974-75. With AUS, 1943-46. NSF Superior Accomplishment award, 1977. Fellow IEEE (chmn. Phila. chpt. profl. group antennas and propagation 1954-55, vice chmn. Providence sect. 1963-64, chmn. 1964-65, com. on man and radiation 1987—, mem. adminstrn. com., engring. in med. and biology soc.); mem. Am. Geophys. Union (nat. com. on space electricity 1974-75), AAAS, AAUP, Am. Soc. for Engring. Edn., N.Y. Acad. Scis., Internat. Sci. Radio Union, Bioelectromagnetics Soc. (pres. 1988-89), Bioelec. Repair and Growth Soc. (coun. mem. 1990—), Sigma Xi, Tau Beta Pi. Home: 53 Springhill Rd Kingston RI 02881-1805

POLL, JOAN FRANCES, psychiatrist; b. N.Y.C., Mar. 18, 1950; m. Leonard Stern; 2 children. BA cum laude, Washington U., St. Louis, 1972; MD, N.Y. Med. Coll., 1976. Diplomate Am. Bd. Psychiatry and Neurology. Intern in pediatrics Albert Einstein Coll. of Medicine (BMHC), N.Y.C., 1976-77, resident in psychiatry, 1977-79; fellowship in child psychiatry Child Study Ctr. Yale U., New Haven, 1979-81; pvt. practice child, adolescent and adult psychiatry Westport, Conn., 1981—; asst. clin. prof. psychiatry Yale U., New Haven, 1981—; candidate Western New Eng. Inst. for Psychoanalysis. Mem. Am. Psychiat. Assn., Am. Psychoanalytic Assn. (affiliate), Am. Acad. Child and Adolescent Psychiatry, Conn. Psychiat. Assn. (sec. 1986—), Conn. Coun. Child and Adolescent Psychiatry, Norwalk Med. Soc. Office: 16 Bushy Ridge Rd Westport CT 06880-2105

POLLACK, BRUCE, banker, real estate consultant; b. Bklyn., June 15, 1951; s. Bernard and Grace (Mishanie) P.; children: Gennifer Ellen, Gregory Adam, Erica Dawn. BS, L.I. U., Bklyn., 1973, MBA with honors, 1979. Sr. appraiser Citizens Savs. & Loan Assn., Woodside, N.Y., 1973-77; chief appraiser Walter Oertly Assocs., N.Y.C., 1978, Flushing (N.Y.) Savs. Bank, 1978-81; v.p., real estate specialist Citibank, N.A., N.Y.C., 1981-90; pres. Met. Realty Solutions, Bklyn., 1990—. Contbr. to The Appraisal Jour., Real Estate Rev., Multi-Housing News, other publs. Recipient Pub./Pvt. Partnership award Ocean Pkwy. Community Devel. Corp., 1984, award Consolidated Edison, 1986. Mem. Young Mortgage Bankers Assn., N.Y. State Soc. Real Estate Appraisers, Bklyn. Bd. Realtors (bd. dirs.), Rho Epsilon. Home: 15 Mackay Pl Brooklyn NY 11209-1040 Office: Met Realty Solutions 15 McKay Pla Brooklyn NY 11209

POLLACK, JEFFREY STUART, internal medicine physician; b. Bklyn., July 27, 1956; s. Ephraim Leo Pollack and Sandra Claire (Weisburg) Bosworth; m. Amarilis Altagracia Canelo, Jan. 11, 1979. BA in Chemistry, U. So. Calif., 1977; MD, U. Nordestana, Dominican Republic, 1981. Intern Misericordia Hosp. Med. Ctr., Bronx, N.Y., 1981-82; resident Arlene Fuld Med. Ctr., Trenton, N.J., 1982-84; pvt. practice, Mays Landing, N.J., 1984—; med. dir. Plus-N.J., Absecon, 1992, Ocean Point Health Care Ctr., Somers Point, N.J., 1990—; mem. staff Shore Meml. Hosp., Somers Point, 1984—. Mem. Am. Soc. Internat. Medicine, N.J. Med. Soc., Atlantic County Med. Soc. Democrat. Jewish. Office: Shore Internal Medicine PA Harding Hwy Mays Landing NJ 08330

POLLACK, JORDAN ELLIS, pharmaceutical company executive; b. N.Y.C., June 16, 1934; s. Irving and Ann Pollack; m. Francine Hornstein, Aug. 23, 1959; children: Robert, Randi. BS in Pharmacy, Columbia U., 1956; MBA in Mktg., Iona Coll., 1971. Registered pharmacist, N.Y., N.J., Fla. Salesman/market researcher Geigy Pharm., Ardsley, N.Y., 1959-70; account exec. William Douglas McAdams, N.Y.C., 1970-71; account supr. Grey Advt., N.Y.C., 1971-75; account dir. Carrafiello-Diehl Advt., Irvington, N.Y., 1975-79; sr. product mgr. Knoll Pharms., Whippany, N.J., 1979-85, mgr. new product planning, 1985-88, dir. new bus. devel., 1988—. Chmn. Florham Park (N.J.) Airport Adv. Com., 1989—; apptd. to Florham Park Zoning Bd. of Adjustment. With U.S. Army, 1957-59. Mem. Pham. Advt. Coun., Am. Soc. Hosp. Pharmacists, N.J. Soc. Hosp. Pharmacists, Lic. Exec. Soc. Home: 4 Partridge Ln Florham Park NJ 07932-1753 Office: Knoll Pharm 110 S Jefferson Rd Whippany NJ 07981

POLLACK, LOUIS, telecommunications company executive; b. N.Y.C., Nov. 4, 1920; s. Benjamin and Lena (Woloshen) P.; m. Dorothy Silverman, Feb. 4, 1945; children—Annette Pollack Rachlin, Barbara, Lawrence. B.E.E., CCNY, 1953; postgrad., Stevens Inst. Tech., 1954-55. Registered profl. engr. Dir. transmission system ops. ITT Fed. Labs., Nutley, N.J., 1943-67; exec. dir. Comsat Labs., Clarksburg, Md., 1967-80; v.p. world systems div. Communications Satellite Corp., Washington, 1980-84; cons. Satellite System design, 1984—; del. XVIII Gen. Assembly Nat. Acad. Sci. Contbr. articles to profl. jours.; patentee in field. Fellow IEEE; mem. AIAA (asso. fellow), Nat. Soc. Profl. Engrs., Sigma Xi. Office: 15321 Delphinium Ln Rockville MD 20853-1725

POLLACK, MARK WILLIAM, educational administrator; b. Bedford, Mass., May 10, 1958; s. Maurice and Mary Bridget (Bohan) P. BA in History, NYU, 1979, MA in History, 1982. Student The Gray Line, Inc., Boston, 1979-80; mgr. fgn. commitment dept. European-Am. Bank, N.Y.C., 1980-83; exec. dir. CLN Assocs., Inc., Framingham, Mass., 1984-88; cons. Framingham, 1988; dir. adminstrn. Mass. Sch. Profl. Psychology, Dedham, Mass., 1989—. Mem. Mass. Assn. Adult and Continuing Edn., Boston Computer Soc. Home: 14 Youngs Rd Dedham MA 02026-3418 Office: Mass Sch Profl Psychology 322 Sprague St Dedham MA 02026-5250

POLLACK, MILTON, federal judge; b. N.Y.C., Sept. 29, 1906; s. Julius and Betty (Schwartz) P.; m. Lillian Klein, Dec. 18, 1932 (dec. July 1967); children—Stephanie Pollack Singer, Daniel A.; m. Moselle Baum Erlich, Oct. 24, 1971. A.B., Columbia U., 1927, J.D., 1929. Bar: N.Y. 1930. Assoc. Gilman & Unger, N.Y.C., 1929-38; ptnr. Unger & Pollack, N.Y.C., 1938-44; propr. Milton Pollack, N.Y.C., 1945-67; dist. judge U.S. Dist. Ct. (so. dist.) N.Y., 1967—, sr. status, 1983; mem. com. on ct. adminstrn. Jud. Conf., 1968-87, mem. Jud. Panel on Multi-dist. Litigation, 1983—. Mem. Prospect Park So. Assn., Bklyn., pres., 1948-50, counsel, 1950-60, bd. dirs., 1945-60; mem. local SSS, 1952-60; Chmn. lawyers div. Fedn. Jewish Philanthropies, 1957-61, vice chmn., 1954-57; chmn. lawyers div. Am. Jewish Com., 1964-66, bd. dirs., from 1967; Bd. dirs. Beth Isreal Hosp.; trustee Temple Emanu-El, from 1977, v.p., from 1978. Recipient Learned Hand award Am. Jewish Com., 1967, Proskauer medal lawyers div. Fedn. Jewish Philanthropies, 1968, Disting. Svc. medal N.Y. County Lawyers Assn., 1991; decorated chevalier Legion of Honor (France). Mem. ABA, N.Y. State Bar Assn., Assn. of Bar of City of N.Y. (Disting. Svc. medal 1991), Columbia Law Sch. Alumni Assn. (pres. 1970-72), Harmonie Club (bd. trustees), Quaker Ridge Country Club. Office: US Dist Ct US Courthouse Foley Sq New York NY 10007-1501

POLLAK, DAVID PAUL, computer software developer; b. Chgo., Jan. 2, 1964; s. Fred Hugo and Mae Pollak. BA cum laude, R.I. Coll., 1987; JD cum laude, Boston U., 1991. Pres. System Software Design, Providence, 1978-88; tech. specialist Cubby, Inc., N.Y.C. and Providence, 1986-91; pres. Athena Design, Inc., Boston, 1991—.

POLLAK, LOUIS HEILPRIN, federal judge, educator; b. N.Y.C., Dec. 7, 1922; s. Walter and Marion (Heilprin) P.; m. Katherine Weiss, July 25, 1952; children: Nancy, Elizabeth, Susan, Sarah, Deborah. A.B., Harvard, 1943; LL.B., Yale, 1948. Bar: N.Y. bar 1949, Conn. bar 1956, Pa. bar 1976. Law clk. to U.S. Supreme Ct. Justice Rutledge, 1948-49; with firm Paul, Weiss, Rifkind, Wharton & Garrison, N.Y.C., 1949-51; atty., spl. asst. to Dept. State, 1951-53; asst. counsel Amalgmated Clothing Workers Am., 1954-55; mem. faculty Yale Law Sch., 1955-74, dean, 1965-70; Greenfield prof. U. Pa., 1974-78, dean Law Sch., 1975-78, lectr., 1980—; U.S. dist. judge for Eastern dist. Pa., 1978—; vis. lectr. Howard U. Sch. Law, 1953; vis. prof. U. Mich. Law Sch., 1961, Columbia Law Sch., 1962. Author: The Constitution and the Supreme Court: A Documentary History, 1966. Mem. New Haven Bd. Edn., 1962-68; chmn. Conn. adv. com. U.S. Civil Rights Commn., 1962-63; mem. bd. NAACP Legal Def. Fund, 1960-78, v.p., 1971-78; chmn. New Haven Human Rights Com., 1963-64. Served with AUS, 1943-46. Mem. ABA (chmn. sec. individual rights 1970-71), Assn. Bar City N.Y., Fed. Bar Assn., Phila. Bar Assn., Am. Law Inst. (coun. 1978—). Office: US Dist Ct 16613 US Courthouse 601 Market St Philadelphia PA 19106-1510

POLLAK, TIM, advertising agency executive. Exec. v.p. Young & Rubicam N.Y., 1987; pres., chief exec. officer DYR Worldwide (now HDM Wordwide), from 1987; also corp. chief exec. officer HDM Worldwide; pres., chief exec. officer HDM USA, N.Y.C., 1987-90, Young & Rubicam NY, N.Y.C., 1990; now vice chmn. Wunderman Worldwide; bd. dirs. Young & Rubicam, Inc. Mem. Internat. Advt. Assn. (pres. N.Y. chpt., mem. worldwide bd. dirs.). Office: Young & Rubicam NY 285 Madison Ave New York NY 10017-6401

POLLAN, ANDREA STEFANIE, art gallery director and curator; b. Washington, Mar. 31, 1961; d. Hans Paul and Marie Elisabeth (Perraglio) P. Student, Sorbonne, Paris, 1982; BA in Art History magna cum laude, Yale U., 1984. Intern Internat. Exhibitions Found., Washington, 1980; framing cons. Am. Art Assocs., Bethesda, Md., 1981; asst. to dir. rights and reproductions Yale U. Art Gallery, New Haven, 1983-84; adminstrv. asst. admissions dept. Lesley Coll., Boston, 1984; asst. dir. devel. Trust for Mus. Exhbns., Washington, 1985-87; assoc. dir. Wallace Wentworth Gallery, Washington, 1987-88; dir. City Gallery, Washington, 1988-89; curator The Arthy Orgn. Collection, Bethesda, Md., 1989-91; curator-in-residence, Emerson Gallery, McLean (Va.) Project for the Arts, 1992—; writer, critic in field. Editor art catalogue; dir., choreographer ballet, 1982 (1st prize). Founder, The Kunstraum, 1988. Mem. Washington Project for Arts, Am. Coun. Arts, Nat. Mus. Women in Arts, Yale Club, Kenwood Country Club. Home: 4101 Cathedral Ave NW Washington DC 20016-3585

POLLARD, EDWARD ELLSBERG, publishing executive; b. Plainfield, N.J., Apr. 22, 1945; s. Goldwin Smith and Mary (Ellsberg) P.; m. Marilyn Pfaff, June 27, 1970 (div. Dec. 1976); 1 child, Nicholas Cooke Ellsberg; m. Carolyn Jans, June 14, 1985. BS in Econs., U. Pa., 1968. Salesman Solo Realty, Phila., 1968-71, McClain Securities, Phila., 1971-73; pres. Pa. Indls. Realty, King of Prussia, 1973-78, Old MacDonald's Foods, Lewistown, Pa., 1979-82, Remington Press, Ltd., St. Davids, Pa., 1983—; dir. Montgomery Sch., Chester Springs, Pa., 1987—; chmn. Heirs and Beneficiaries, Inc., Bryn Mawr, Pa., 1991—. Bd. dirs. Radnor Hist. Soc., Wayne, Pa., 1989—; state pres. Fathers' and Children's Equality, Drexel Hill, Pa., 1981-83; commr. Radnor Twp., Pa., 1992—. Democrat. Methodist. Home: 11 Fairview Dr Wayne PA 19087-3618

POLLARD, HARVEY B., physician, neuroscientist; b. San Antonio, May 26, 1943. BA in Biology, Rice U., 1964; MS in Biochemistry, U. Chgo., 1969, MD, 1969, PhD, 1973. Rsch. assoc. NIH-Nat. Inst. Arthritis and Metabolic Diseases, Bethesda, Md., 1969-71, sr. investigator, 1972-74, 1977-79, sect. chief, 1979-81; lab. chief Nat. Inst. Diabetes, Digestive and Kidney Diseases, Bethesda, 1981—. Contbr. over 200 articles to profl. jours. With USPHS, 1969—. Recipient Commendation medal USPHS, 1982, Alumni award for Disting. Svc., U. Chgo. Alumni Assn., 1989, NIH Inventor's award, 1991. Mem. Biophys. Soc., Soc. for Neurosci., Am. Soc. for Pharmacology and Exptl. Therapeutics, Soc. for Cell Biology. Office: NIH Bethesda MD 20892

POLLARD, MICHAEL ROSS, lawyer, health policy researcher and consultant; b. Flint, Mich., Apr. 14, 1947; s. Gail Winton Pollard and Evelyn Georgeanna (LeMire) Goplen; m. Penelope Brigham, Aug. 22, 1970. AB in Polit. Sci., U. Mich., 1969; JD, Harvard U., 1972, MPH, 1974. Bar: Mass. 1972, D.C. 1975. Profl. assoc. for program devel. Nat. Acad. Scis. Inst. Medicine, Washington, 1974-77, dir. law and ethics div., 1977-78; atty. advisor Office of Policy Planning, FTC, Washington, 1978-81, asst. dir. Bur. Consumer Protection, 1981-83; dir. Office of Policy Analysis, Pharm. Mfrs. Assn., Washington, 1983-88; exec. dir. Am. Pharm. Inst., Washington, 1988-89; counsel Michaels & Wishner P.C., Washington, 1988-89, ptnr., 1989—; cons. Nat. Ctr. for Health Services Research, Rockville, Md., 1975-80, Office Tech. Assessment U.S. Congress, 1984—. Contbr. articles to profl. jours. Treasurer Nat. Leadership Coalition on AIDS, 1988—; dir.-at-large Nat. Commn. on Certification of Physician Assts., 1991—, James B. Angell scholar U. Mich., 1967, 68, 69. Mem. ABA, Phi Beta Kappa, Pi Sigma Alpha. Democrat. Club: Harvard (Washington). Home: 7300 Maple Ave Chevy Chase MD 20815-5108 Office: Michaels & Wishner PC 1726 M St NW Ste 500 Washington DC 20036-4502

POLLARO, PAUL PHILIP, artist; b. N.Y.C., Aug. 2, 1921; s. Charles and Maria (Aprile) P.; m. Jo Ann Stover, July 16, 1962 (div. Nov. 1979); children: Lauren, Paul Jr.; m. Laura Clayton, Apr. 2, 1985. Student, Art Students League, Pratt Graphic Ctr. Instr. painting The New Sch. of Social Rsch., N.Y.C., 1964-69; vis. artist Notre Dame U., South Bend, Ind., 1965-67; asst. prof. art, chmn. art dept. Wagner Coll., Staten Island, N.Y., 1970-73; asst. dir. The MacDowell Colony, Peterborough, N.H., 1973-76; pvt. practice Hancock, N.H., 1976—. One-man shows include Jersey City Mus., N.J., 1966 (second prize), S.I. Mus. Art, N.Y., 1973, Manchester Inst. Arts and Scis., Manchester, N.H., 1970-85, Chryser Mus., Norfolk, Va., 1991. Sgt. U.S. Army, 1942-45, PTO. Tiffany Found. grantee, N.Y.C., 1967, N.H. State Coun. Arts grantee, 1985; The MacDowell Colony fellow, 1965-69. Roman Catholic. Home: Norway Hill Hancock NH 03449

POLLEY, DOUGLAS CRAIG, financial consultant; b. N.Y., Aug. 10, 1958; s. Robert Lyle and Betty Lou (Short) P.; m. Paula Jean Wright, Oct. 24, 1987; children: Mark Louis Samaha, Melissa Lynn Samaha. BS summa cum laude, U. Albany, 1981; cert. in microelectronics, Northeastern U., 1985; MBA, Boston U., 1990. Purchasing agt. Data Gen. Corp., Westboro, Mass., 1982-85; sr. buyer and planner Stratus Computer, Marlboro, Mass., 1985-88, purchasing mgr., 1988-90; fin. cons. Merrill Lynch, Worcester, Mass., 1990—. Author, editor: Math-Art or Science, 1980. Mem. Beta Gamma Sigma. Roman Catholic. Office: Merrill Lynch 440-446 Main St 440 Main St Worcester MA 01608

POLLICOVE, HARVEY MYLES, manufacturing executive; b. Utica, N.Y., May 28, 1944; s. Maxwell Hymen and Carolyn (Vogel) P.; m. Catherine Mary Keady, Aug. 3, 1968; children: Carolyn, Sarah. AAS, Monroe Community Coll., 1968; BS, U. Rochester, 1973. Sr. engr. supr. optics Eastman Kodak Co., Rochester, 1978-82; engring. mgr. optics Eastman Kodak Co., 1982-84, mfg. mgr., 1984-86, mgr. tech. mkts. (internat.), 1986-89; dir. Ctr. for Optics Mfg. U. Rochester, 1989—; lectr. in field. Editorial adv. bd. (optics mag. for mfg.) Laser Focus World, 1990—; contbr. articles to profl. jours. Advisor High Tech. of Rochester, 1988-89; advisor tech. applications rev. bd. Strategic Def. Initiative Orgn., 1990—; industry advisor Monroe Community Coll., 1986—. Mem. Am. Precision Optics Mfrs. Assn. (exec. com. 1987—, elected to bd. dirs. 1990-93), Internat. Soc. for Optical Engring., Optical Soc. Am. Home: 177 Georgian Court Rd Rochester NY 14610-3416 Office: U Rochester Inst Optics Ctr for Optics Mfg Rochester NY 14627

POLLOCK, LARRY RICHARD, university student programs and services director; b. Clarion, Pa., Aug. 21, 1937; s. Carl Richard and Grace Mae (Kent) P.; children: Lisa Rae D., Brian Lloyd Richard, Jeaneane Leann. BS, Pa. State U., 1966; MS, Drexel U., 1971; MA, Glassboro State Coll., 1973; MEd, Indiana U. of Pa., 1974, DEd, 1987. Nat. cert. counselor. Asst. mgr. G.C. Murphy Co., McKeesport, Pa., 1955-67; coord. coop. edn. Drexel U., Phila., 1967-72; dir. student programs and svcs. Pa. State U., New Kensington, 1972—. With USMC, 1960-63. Mem. Pa.Coll. Pers. Assn. (exec. bd. 1976—), AACD, Pa. Pers. Guidance Assn., Nat. Bd. Cert. Counselor, Pa. Assn. for Adult Continuing Edn., New Kensington C. of C., Rotary (Lower Burrell). Office: Pa State U 3550 7th Street Rd New Kensington PA 15068-1798

POLLOCK, MARK STEPHEN, financial executive; b. Phila., Jan. 14, 1959; s. Edwin Morgan and Reba (Stein) P.; m. Jodi Lynn Myerowitz, Sept. 12, 1987. BBA, Temple U., 1983. CPA, Pa., Fla. Staff acct. Laventhol and Horwath, Miami, Fla., 1983-85, sr. acct., 1985-86; corp. acctg. mgr. Nuclear Rsch. Corp., Warrington, Pa., 1986-87, contr., 1987-88, chief fin. officer, 1988—. Mem. AICPA, Pa. Inst. CPAs, Fla. Inst. CPAs, Nat. Assn. Accts. Republican. Home: 404 Remington Ct Chalfont PA 18914-2208

POLLOCK, NEAL JAY, electronics executive; b. Phila., Feb. 4, 1947; s. Sol J. and Shirley (Buchsbaum) P. BA in Physics, U. Pa., 1968; MS in Engring. Sci., Pa. State U., 1972; MBA, Temple U., 1975; postdoctoral, George Washington U., 1978-82. Student trainee Naval Air Devel. Ctr., Warminster, Pa., 1964-68, physicist, 1968-69, electronics engr., 1969-75, plans and programs asst., 1975-76; asst. for interface Naval Air Systems Command, Washington, 1976-78, budget and fin. mgr., 1978-79, asst. program mgr. for acoustic sensors, 1979-84; project engr. Naval Sea Systems Command, Washington, 1984-87; br. head, supr. electronics engring. Space and Naval Warfare Systems Command, Washington, 1987-90, div. head, 1990—; EEO counselor Naval Sea Systems Command, Washington, 1986. Co-author: Extended Radiometer Analysis-The Point Target; contr.: Organizations in a Changing Society, 1977. Unit commr. Boy Scouts Am., 1975-76; vol. income tax asst. Ayuda and Spanish Catholico, Washington, 1976-77; active, life

mem. Save the Redwoods League, San Francisco, 1987, Nature Conservancy, Charlottesville, Va., 1988, Archeological Conservancy, Friends of the Arlington Libr., 1989—, Nat. Parks and Conservation Assn., 1990—, suriname termites and Hawaii dolphins expeditions Earthwatch; active mem., patron sponsor Pearl Buck Found., Prevention of Blindness Soc., Internat. Rescue Com., others. USN Student Engring Devel. scholar, 1964, Phila. Mayor's scholar, 1964, Nat. Sci. Found. scholar Stevens Inst. Tech., 1963. Mem. Soc. Naval Architects and Marine Engrs., Assn. Scientists and Engrs. (life, keyman 1987), Alaska Natural History Assn. (life), Pa. State Alumni Assn. (life), Centurion Club, Clipper Club (life), Admirals Club (life), Ionosphere Club (life), Worldclub (life), Amb's. Club (life), Red Carpet Club (life), U.S. Air Club (life), Northeast High Sch. Alumni Assn., Pa. State U. Alumni Assn., Thomas Jefferson Pronaos AMORC (master 1980-82), Atlantis Lodge AMORC (sec. 1984-85, treas. 1985-88, chmn. conv. 1980), Masons (32 degree), Beta Gamma Sigma. Republican. Home: 2500 S Fern St Arlington VA 22202-2538 Office: SPAWARSYSCOM PMW 169-2 Washington DC 20363-5100

POLLOCK, SAMUEL JOSEPH, hydrogeologist; b. Providence, May 1, 1932; s. Hyman Louis and Ida (Cohen) P.; m. Joyce Adamsky, Aug. 16, 1959; children: Jeffrey, Mark, David. BA, Brown U., 1954, MS, 1956; postgrad., U. Colo., 1957, Ohio State U., 1990. Registered profl. geologist and hydrogeologist. Geologist U.S. Geol. Survey, Providence, 1955-56, 58-59, Washington, 1957-58, Arlington, Va., 1959; geologist-hydrologist U.S. Geol. Survey, Boston, 1959-88; hydrogeologist Mass. Hwy. Dept., Wellesley, 1988—; specialist U.S. Geol. Survey, Mass. Dept. Pub. Works, Boston, Wellesley, 1964—; mem. transp. rsch. bd. spl. com. NAS, Washington, 1990-92. Author 23 books, 1960—. Tchr. Lexington (Mass.) Adult Edn., 1972—. Mem. Am. Water Works, Nat. Ground Water Assn., New Eng. Water Works, Am. Inst. of Hydrology. Home: 35 Sherburne Rd Lexington MA 02173 Office: Mass Hwy Dept 99 Worcester St Wellesley MA 02181

POLLOCK, WILLIAM JOHN, high technology secondary school administrator; b. N.Y.C., Nov. 25, 1943; s. Edward and Rose (Favero) P.; m. Jennie Ann Taccetta, Jan. 28, 1967; children: John-Paul, Elizabeth. BSEd, CCNY, 1967; MSEd, Trenton State Coll., 1985. Tchr. N.Y.C. Pub. Schs., 1967-69; tchr. electronics Howell High Sch., Farmingdale, N.J., 1970-85, dept. supr., 1985-89; vice-prin. Monmouth County Vocat. Schs., Middletown, N.J., 1989-90; prin. High Tech. High Sch., Brookdale Community Coll. Campus, Lincroft, N.J., 1990—; pres. suprs.' assn. Freehold (N.J.) Regional High Sch. Dist., 1988-89; pres. exec. bd. Region V Libr. Coop., Freehold, 1989—. Asst. scout master Jackson (N.J.) area Boy Scouts Am., 1987—; pres. exec. bd. St. Mary Acad., Lakewood, N.J., 1987-89; mem. Ocean County Agrl. Devel. Bd., Toms River, N.J., 1989—. 1st lt. U.S. Army, 1969-70, Vietnam. Decorated Bronze Star medal, 1970. Mem. ASCD, Nat. Assn. Secondary Sch. Prins., N.J. Assn. Supervision and Curriculum Devel., Internat. Tech. Edn. Assn., Am. Vocat. Edn. Assn., Prins. and Suprs. Assn., K.C. Office: High Tech High Sch PO Box 119 Lincroft NJ 07738-0119

POLON, MARTIN ISHIAH, science and technology consultant; b. Chgo., May 18, 1942; s. Solomon I. and Bernice V. Polon; m. Janine Petit, Feb. 11, 1984. BA, UCLA, 1964, MA in TV, 1968, postgrad., 1970. Dir. audiovisual services UCLA, 1970-80; founder Computer Merchandising and Software Merchandising Mags., 1980-83; prin. Polon Rsch. Internat., Boston, 1983—; lectr. U. Lowell (Mass.); assoc. prof. U. Colo., Denver, forecaster consumer acceptance of high tech.; speaker various convs. and profl. orgns. Mem. bd. rev. Audio Engring. Soc. Jour.; contbr. over 400 articles to mags. and profl. jours.; occasional contbr. (TV shows) Bus. World. Mem. Audio Engring. Soc. (bd. govs. 1985—, chmn. edn. com. 1986—, v.p., mem. bd. rev. jour., 2d term gov. 1989, Gov.'s award for svc. in edn.), Soc. Motion Picture and TV Engrs. (com. on audio), Soc. Profl. Audio Rec. Studios, Assn. Profl. Rec. Studios (U.K.), Japan Soc. Boston, Sapphire Audio Group, U.S. Naval Inst., Boston Audio Soc.

POLONSKY, ARTHUR, artist, educator; b. Lynn, Mass., June 6, 1925; s. Benjamin and Celia (Hurwitz) P.; children: Eli, D.L., Gabriel. Diploma with highest honors, Sch. of Mus. Fine Arts, Boston, 1948. Instr. art Boston Mus. Sch., 1950-60, Brandeis U., 1954-65; assoc. prof. Sch. Arts, Boston U., 1965-90, prof. emeritus, 1990—. One-man shows, Boris Mirski Gallery, Boston, 1950, 54, 56, 64, 66, Boston Public Library, 1969, 90, Durlacher Gallery, N.Y.C., 1965, Mickelson Gallery, Washington, 1966, 74, Boston Ctr. for Arts, 1983, Starr Gallery, Boston, 1987, Fitchburg Art Mus., 1990; group shows include, Met. Mus., N.Y.C., 1950, Stedelijk Mus., Amsterdam, The Netherlands, 1950, Carnegie Internat. Expn., 1951, Inst. Contemporary Art, Boston, 1960, Mus. Fine Arts, Boston, 1976, Boston Arts Festival, 1985, Expressionism in Boston, Decordova Mus., Lincoln, Mass., 1986, Decordova Mus., Lincoln, 1987; represented in permanent collections, Mus. Fine Arts, Boston, Fogg Mus., Harvard U., Addison Gallery of Am. Art, Andover, Mass., Stedelijk Mus., Walker Art Center, Mpls. Recipient Louis Comfort Tiffany award for painting, 1951, 1st prize Boston Arts Festival, 1954; European travelling fellow Sch. Mus. Fine Art, Boston, 1948-50. Mem. AAUP. Address: 364 Cabot St Newtonville MA 02160

POLOUKHINE, OLGA, artist; b. Paris, Nov. 1, 1934; came to U.S., 1948; d. Nikita and Sophie (Schidlovsky) Koulomzin; m. Nicolas Poloukhine, Nov. 20, 1960; children: Olga, Michael, Elena. BA, Rutgers U., 1956; MA, Columbia U., 1960. Cert. art tchr. K-12, N.Y. Art tchr. Nyack (N.Y.) Schs., 1957-59, White Plains (N.Y.) Sch. System, 1959-60, Locust Valley (N.Y.) Pub. Schs., 1960-62. Exhibited in group shows at Wunchs Art Gallery, Taller Galeria Forte, Barcelona, Spain, Richard Gallery, Northeastern U., Boston Le Chateau Royal de Collioure, France, Hecksher Mus., N.Y., Nassau County Fine Arts Mus., N.Y., Fine Arts Mus. of L.I., Long Beach Mus. of Art and numerous others; represented in permanent collections at IBM, AT&T, N.Y. Telephone Co., NYNEX, O.C.A. and other corp. and pvt. collections. Mem. L.I. Graphic Eye Gallery (founder, pres. 1989-91), Nat. Assn. Women Artists, Internat. Graphic Art Found., Manhattan Graphics Ctr., Nat. Mus. of Women in the Arts (charter). Eastern Orthodox. Home: Westways Littleworth Ln Sea Cliff NY 11579

POLSELLI, ROCCO LOUIS, SR., mathematics educator; b. Phila., Nov. 25, 1943. BS in Math., Widener U., 1967, postgrad., 1986. Instr. Bordentown (N.J.) Mil. Inst., 1967-68, Claymont (Del.) High Sch., 1968-69, Interboro High Sch., Glenolden, Pa., 1969-72, Del. Tech. and Community Coll., Wilmington; sr. lectr. Widener Way Adult Edn. Program, Wilmington, 1986—, Evening div. Widener U., 1987—, Widener U., Chester, Pa., 1980-86; instr. Brandywine Coll. of Widener U., Wilmington; instr. math. LaSalle U., 1986-87. Author: Algebraic Arithmetic, A Developmental Approach to College Algebra, rev. edit., 1990, Algebraic Arithmetic, Solutions Manual, 1991, Elementary Calculus, 1990, Elementary Statistics, 1990, Statistical Analysis, 1990; co-author: Fundamentals of Mathematics, 1990, Business Mathematics, A Practical Approach, 1989. Mem. Math. Assn. Am., Interstate Developmental Edn. Assn.

POLSKY, LOUIS SANFORD, obstetrician/gynecologist; b. Longview, Tex., July 20, 1932; s. Sam and Ruth (Glass) P.; m. Joyce Misthal, Jan. 22, 1961; children: Gary Steven, Jay Howard, Jeffrey Carl. BA, U. Tex., 1954; MD, U. Tex., Galveston, 1958. Intern Phila. Gen. Hosp., 1958-59, resident, 1961-64; pres. Prospect Women's Med. Ctr., P.A., Hackensack, N.J., 1980—. Contbr. articles to profl. jours. Lt. USN, 1959-61. Fellow ACS, Am. Coll. Ob-Gyn., Am. Fertility Soc., Gyn. Laser Soc., Am. Colposcopists, Am. Lararoscopists. Jewish. Office: Prospect Women's Med Ctr 120 Prospect Ave Hackensack NJ 07601

POMERICO, THOMAS MICHAEL, communications company executive; b. Bklyn., Oct. 15, 1954; s. Thomas J. and Catherine (McCaffery) P.; m. Gerarda Pavel, Dec. 27, 1975; children: Thomas, Melanie, Regina. AAS, Brookdale Community Coll., 1986. Enlisted U.S. Army, 1973; sta. chief SATCOM U.S. Army Agy., Ft. Monmouth, N.J., 1973-84; resigned U.S. Army, 1984; asst. mgr. Earth Sta. facility ARGO Communications, Englewood, N.J., 1984-86; field mgr. Eastern Microwave, N.Y.C., 1987-90; dir. ops. CS Communications, Englewood, 1990-91; communications tech. Charter Trading Corp., Kuwait City, Kuwait, 1991; sr. staff specialist MCI Internat., Piscataway, N.J., 1991—.

POMEROY, DAVID WARDELL, clergyman; b. South Bend, Ind., Sept. 29, 1939; s. Wardell Baxter and Martha Catherine (Sindlinger) P.; m. Ann Frances Krick, Sept. 7, 1963; children: Wardell Keith, Kira Lynne, Bruce Darren, Jill Lucienne. BA, DePauw U., 1960; MDiv, Union Theol. Sem., 1964. Pastor The People's Ch., Long Beach, N.Y., 1964-68; minister to youth First Congl. Ch., Chappaqua, N.Y., 1968-72; from assoc. dir. broadcasting to dir. electronic media Dept. Communication, Nat. Coun. Chs., N.Y.C., 1972—; assoc. pastor United Ch. of Spring Valley, N.Y., 1986—; chmn. Interfaith Broadcasting Commn., N.Y.C., 1989—, NABS-WACC, Key Biscayne, Fla., 1991; interim pastor New Hyde Park (N.Y.) Community Ch., 1973-74, Briarcliff (N.Y.) Congl. Ch., 1979-80, Community Ch. of the Pelhams, N.Y., 1982-83. Contbr. articles to profl. jours.; exec. producer TV programs: Someone Is Listening, The Face of All the Earth, Spirit of the Rising Son. Can. Ossining (N.Y.) Village Bd., 1977. Recipient Blue Ribbon for Into the Mouths of Babes, Am. Film Festival, 1978, Angel Award of Excellence for Someone is Listening, 1989, Wilbur award Religious Pub. Rels. Coun., 1989. Mem. Nat. Fedn. of Local Cable Programmers, Nat. Assn. Ednl. Broadcasters, Assn. for Edn. Communications and Tech., ACLU, Nat. Acad. TV Arts and Scis., World Assn. for Christian Communication (mem. exec. com. of the N.Am. Regional Assn. 1990-91). Liberal Party. United Ch. of Christ. Home: 684 Union Rd Spring Valley NY 10977 Office: Nat Coun Chs 475 Riverside Dr #856 New York NY 10115

POMEROY, ROBERT WATSON, III, consultant; b. N.Y.C., May 22, 1935; s. Robert W. and Estelle C. (Bassett) P.; B.A., Stanford U., 1958; postgrad. Am. U. of Beirut, 1958-59; m. Jane Graham Adams Ramsay, Feb. 11, 1960; children: Janet Fraser, Seth Bassett. Sales mgr. Fin. Services, Overseas Brokerage Services, Beirut, 1958-60; exec. asst. to gen. mgr. Internat. Basic Economy Corp., Brazil, 1961-64; dir. Arbor Acres, S.A., Indusquima S.A., Sao Paulo, Brazil, 1961-64; fin. analyst Inter-Am. Devel. Bank, Washington, 1965-73; advisor Inter-Am. Devel. Bank, Washington, 1973-87; chmn. Washington area Bus. Resource Group, Nat. Coordinating Com. for Promotion History, 1977-80; mem. founding steering com., treas., dir. Nat. Council on Public History, 1979-83; cons. Pres.'s Commn. on Fgn. Lang. and Internat. Studies, 1979; founding dir. The Maine Consortium, 1981; adv. bd. dept. history Ariz. State U., 1981—; founding dir. Nat. Ctr. for Study of History, sec.-treas., 1984—; bd. advisors MTSU Ctr. for Hist. Preservation, 1985—; bd. dirs. Limington Hist. Soc., 1989—; cons. to programs in public history and internat. studies. Served with Signal Corps, U.S. Army, 1954-56. Mem. Am. Hist. Assn., Orgn. Am. Historians (com. on public history 1982-83), Newcomen Soc. N.Am. Author: Educating Historians for Business: A Guide for Departments of History, Careers for Graduates in History, Careers in Information Management, Business and History, Insurance and History; co-author: Historic Preservation Family Tree, Value History; mem. nat. bd. editors Public Historian, 1980—; editorial policy bd. Office, Technology and People, 1981—; editor (with David F. Trask) The Craft of Public History. Contbr. articles to profl. jours. Home and Office: RR 1 Box 679 Cornish ME 04020-9726

POMILLA, FRANK ROCCO, physics educator; b. Bklyn., Oct. 1, 1926; s. Anthony and Carmela (Policano) P.; m. Clara Mercurio, June 13, 1953; children: Anthony, Mary Nasso, Francis, Paul. BS, Fordham U., 1948, MS, 1949, PhD, 1963. Assoc. prof. St. John's U., N.Y.C., 1949-64; rsch. scientist Grumman Aerospace Co., Bethpage, N.Y., 1964-67; prof. York Coll., mem. grad. faculty physics CUNY, 1967—, chmn. dept. natural scis., 1970-71; dir. Ctr. for Sci. & Math., York Coll.; project dir. tchr. enhancement and student tng. NSF grants U.S. Dept. Edn., 1969-90. Co-author: Atomic Physics, 1969; contbr. articles to profl. jours. Trustee Elmont (N.Y.) Union Free Sch. Dist., 1968-85, Sewanhaka Cen. High Sch. Dist., Elmont, 1977-84; bd. dirs. Elmont Youth Outreach, 1988—; life mem. Elmont PTA, 1985. Mem. IEEE, Am. Phys. Soc., Am. Assn. Physics Tchrs., Sigma Xi (chpt. pres. 1975). Office: CUNY York Coll 94-20 Guy Brewer Blvd Jamaica NY 11003

POMPAN, JACK MAURICE, management consultant; b. N.Y.C., Jan. 23, 1926; s. Maurice A. and Helen (Schmidt) P. m. Esther Scharaga, July 4, 1958; children: Neil Charles, Lori Beth. BS in Indsl. Mgmt., Ga. Inst. Tech., 1948; MBA with distinction, NYU, 1973, advanced profl. cert., 1978. Trainee to budget mgr. Redmond Co., Owosso, Mich., 1948-55; mgmt. cons. Coopers and Lybrand, N.Y.C., 1955-60; contr. Hazel Bishop Inc., N.Y.C., 1960-61; treas. Floyds Stores Inc., Valley Stream, N.Y., 1961-66; pres. Farmers Pantry Inc., Mamaroneck, N.Y., 1966-68; v.p. pub. div. Intext, Inc., N.Y.C., 1968-74; prin. Baxter, Pompan & Storr, Mgmt. Cons., and predecessors, Greenwich, Conn. and N.Y.C., 1974-83, Jack M. Pompan, Mgmt. Cons., Rockville Centre, N.Y., 1983—; adj. prof. Hofstra U., 1977, Roth Grad. Sch. Bus. Adminstrn., C.W. Post Ctr., L.I. U., 1974-79, NYU, 1982-89. Bus. and econs. editor Info. Please Almanac, 1978-82. Trustee edn. chmn., v.p. Cen. Synogogue, Rockville Centre, N.Y., 1983-86, pres. 1986-88. Lt. USNR, 1943-46, 51-53. Mem. Am. Fin. Assn., NYU Bus. Forum, Inst. Mgmt. Accts. (cert. merit 1953), Regional Planning Assn., Am. Prodn. and Inventory Control Soc., Money Marketeers, Am. Jewish Com., Accts. Club of Am. Office: 389 Raymond St Rockville Centre NY 11570-2735

POMPOSELLO, THOMAS ANTHONY, music and video producer, musician, composer; b. N.Y.C., July 17, 1949; s. Peter Anthony and Rose Rita (DeMattina) P.; m. Christine Hallam, 1969 (div 1979); m. Barbara Shortell, 1981 (div. 1986); m. Patricia Iverson Lawrence, July 17, 1987; 1 child, Travis Peter; stepchildren: Deron, Joshua, Charlie. BA, L.I. Univ., 1980. Ind. music and video producer, 1983—; host blues program Sta. WBAI-FM, N.Y.C.; blues bandleader, music tchr., 1973-83. N.Y. chmn. Grammy in the Schools, 1989-91. Recipient Clio awards, Broadcast Design Assocs. award, Nat. Blues Found. award, SIGGRAPH Computer Animation award. Mem. NARAS (trustee 1990-92), SAG, ASCAP, ASIFA, NATAS, Am. Fedn. Musicians. Office: Pomposello Prodns 150 W 28th St Ste 1702 New York NY 10001

PONCHICK, ROSANNE SUSAN, elementary school educator; b. N.Y.C., Feb. 10, 1944; d. Joseph and Pauline (Kaufman) P. BA, Paterson State Coll., 1965, MA, 1969; MA, NYU, 1974; postgrad., NYU, Fairleigh Dickinson U. Cert. elem. edn. tchr., supr., adminstr., N.J., Calif. Tchr. 1st grade Livermore (Calif.) Sch. Dist., 1965-67; tchr. 2d grade Teaneck (N.J.) Pub. Schs., 1967—. Author, compiler: Words Within Words, 1980. Recipient Innovative Teaching award Bus. Week mag., 1990. Mem. NEA, N.J. Edn. Assn., Bergen County Edn. Assn. Office: Teaneck Bd of Edn Merrison Ave Teaneck NJ 07666

POND, GLORIA DIBBLE, educator; b. Merced, Calif., Mar. 10, 1939; d. Frank Burton and Joyce (Rickabaugh) D.; m. J. Lawrence Pond, Nov. 13, 1959; 1 child, Scott Lawrence. BA, Bennington (Vt.) Coll., 1960; MA, Wesleyan U., Middletown, Conn., 1968; Cert. Adv. Study, Wesleyan U., 1974. Editorial asst. Newsweek mag., N.Y.C., 1956, 58, 59, The Houston Chronicle, 1957; reporter, asst. editor The Rockland Independent, Suffern, N.Y., 1960-62; instr. New Haven U., 1967; from lectr. to prof. Mattatuck Community Coll., Waterbury, Conn., 1968—. Author: Succeed: Write Now, 1978, Write, Simply Write, 1979; contbr. articles to profl. jours. Founding chmn. Comprehensive Health Planning Coun. Cen. Naugatuck Valley, 1958-74; chmn. Conn. Siting Coun., New Britain, 1976-91; mem. Conn. Energy Adv. Bd., Hartford, 1977-91; mem. Adv. Coun. to State Health Commr., 1986—; mem. Dem. Town Com., 1969-88, State Platform Com., 1974-86. Grantee, Wesleyan U., 1964-70. Mem. Conn. Libr. Assn. (scholar for libr. progs. 1988—), Conn. Humanities Coun. (scholar for community progs.), Western Conn. Bird Club (publicist 1985-90). Democrat. Office: Mattatuck Community Coll 750 Chase Pky Waterbury CT 06708-3000

POND, PEGGY ANN, librarian; b. Balt., Sept. 27, 1951; d. William Garland and Charlotte Jane (Zepp) Born; m. William Wright Pond, May 13, 1950; children: Stephany Erin, Averil Paij. BA, U. Md., 1973; MLA, We. Md. Coll., 1988. With Carroll County Gen. Hosp., Westminster, Md., 1969-86; tchr. English Carroll County Bd. Edn., Westminster, 1973-76, 86-89; ptnr., mgr. Classic Lady Clothing, Westminster, 1985-89; info. asst. Carroll County Pub. Library, Westminster, 1989-90; program asst. Carroll County Pub. Libr., Westminster, 1990—; tutor Carroll County Bd. Edn., 1979-84. Fair judge Carroll County 4-H Assn., 1983—; elections judge Carroll County Elections Bd., 1984—. Mem. ALA, NEA, Md. Libr. Assn., Md. Tchrs. Assn., Order of Eastern Star (worthy matron 1982-84). Republican. Methodist.

POND, THOMAS ALEXANDER, physics educator; b. L.A., Dec. 4, 1924; s. Arthur Francis and Florence (Alexander) P.; m. Barbara Eileen Newman, Sept. 6, 1958; children: Arthur Phillip Ward, Florence Alexandra. A.B., Princeton U., 1947, A.M., 1949, Ph.D., 1953. Instr. physics Princeton U., 1951-53; asst. prof., then assoc. prof. physics Washington U., St. Louis, 1953-62; prof. physics SUNY, Stony Brook, 1962-81, chmn. dept., 1962-68, exec. v.p., 1967-79, acting pres., 1970, 75, 78; prof. physics Rutgers U., New Brunswick, N.J., exec. v.p., chief acad. officer, 1982-91, acting pres., 1990, univ. prof., 1991—; Bd. dirs. Action Com. for L.I., 1978-80, Tri-State Regional Planning Commn., 1979-82; trustee Univs. Research Assn., 1985-87; bd. dirs. Fermilab, 1987-89. Served to ensign USNR, 1943-46. Mem. Am. Phys. Soc., Phi Beta Kappa, Sigma Xi. Home: 8 Campbells Brook Rd White House Station NJ 08889-9469 Office: Rutgers Univ New Brunswick NJ 08903

PONG, DAVID BERTRAM PAK-TANG, historian, educator; b. Hong Kong, Sept. 28, 1939; came to the U.S., 1969; s. James Tak-Ming and Lily Yun-Yu (Yeung) P.; m. Barbara Kwok-Hung Mar, Jan. 6, 1973; children: Amanda Wai-Yun, Cynthia Wai-San, Myra Wai-Jing. BA (honors), U. London, 1963, PhD, 1969. Rsch. fellow inst. hist. rsch. U. London, 1965-66, fellow in Far Eastern history, 1966-69; asst. prof. U. Del., Newark, 1969-73, assoc. prof., 1973-89, prof., 1989—; rsch. fellow inst. advanced studies Australian Nat. U., Canberra, 1978-81; vis. assoc. prof. Princeton (N.J.) U., 1988; dir. East Asian studies U. Del., 1990—, chmn. dept. history, 1992—. Editor: T'ai-wan hai-fang ping kai-shan jih-chi, 1972; author: A Critical Guide to the Kwangtung Provincial Archives Deposited at the Public Record Office of London, 1975; co-editor, contbr.: Ideal and Reality: Social and Political Change in Modern China, 1860-1949, 1985. Grantee Am. Coun. Learned Socs., 1973-74. Mem. Assn. for Asian Studies (councillor coun. confs. 1991-94, pres. Mid-Atlantic region 1986-87), Soc. for Qing Studies. Office: U Del Dept History Newark DE 19716

PONTE-CASTAÑEDA, PEDRO, mechanical engineering educator; b. Santa Cruz, Tenerife, Spain, Jan. 5, 1961; came to U.S., 1977; s. Pedro Ponte-Pedreira and Glenda (Castañeda) De Ponte. BS, BA, Lehigh U., 1982; SM, Harvard U., 1983, PhD in Applied Math., 1986. Rsch. officer U. Bath (Eng.), 1986-87; asst. prof. Johns Hopkins U., Balt., 1987-90, U. Pa., Phila., 1990—. Contbr. articles to profl. jours. Recipient Rsch. Initiation award NSF, 1988; grantee NSF, Air Force Office of Sci. Rsch.. Mem. ASME, Soc. for Indsl. Applied Math. Office: U Pa 220 S 33d St Philadelphia PA 19104-6315

PONTECORVO, GIULIO, economist; b. Little Falls, N.J., July 24, 1923; s. Giulio and Dorothy (Scott) P.; AB, Dartmouth Coll., 1946, MCS, 1947; PhD, U. Calif., Berkeley, 1956; m. Margaret M. Thatcher, July 19, 1947; children: Michael, Guy, Anthony, Andrew. Mem. faculty Columbia U., 1963—, prof. econs., 1968—; vis. prof. U. Calif., Berkeley, U. Colo., Bowdoin Coll., U. Wash., Seattle, U. Buenos Aires, U. Bergen; chmn. Found. Internat. Bus. Cycle Rsch. Served with AUS, 1943-46. Contbr. to profl. publs. Office: Columbia U 601 Uris Hall New York NY 10027

PONTIUS, JOHN SAMUELS, federal official; b. Bethesda, Md., May 30, 1945; s. Harry Edgar and Kathryn Samuels P.; m. Jane McAdams, 1972; children: John Samuels Jr., James McAdams. BA magna cum laude, Gettysburg Coll., 1967; MPA, U. So. Calif., 1970, D of Pub. Adminstrn., 1984. Legis. asst. Congressman Wilson, Calif., 1971-74, adminstrv. asst., 1974-80; adminstrv. asst. Congressman Norman Lent, N.Y., 1981-82, U.S. Rep Norman Sisisky, Va., 1983; specialist Am. Govt. Congl. Rsch. Svc. Libr. Congress, 1984—. With USAR, 1969-75. Recipient Commendation award City of L.A., City of Torrance, City of Gardena. Mem. Am. Polit. Sci. Assn., Am. Soc. Pub. Adminstrn., Capitol Hill Toastmasters Club (former pres.). House Adminstrv. Assts. Alumni Assn. (bd. dirs.), Phi Beta Kappa, Pi Lambda Sigma. Home: 127 S Van Buren St Rockville MD 20850-2802 Office: Congressional Rsch Service Library of Congress Washington DC

PONTOPPIDAN, MYANNA, musician; b. Monterrey, Calif., Oct. 30, 1959; d. Henning and Yonna Michaela (Sahmel) P. Student, Berklee Coll. Music, 1974, U. Mass., 1975. Sax player Lilith, Boston, 1976-79; sax/percussion player Bill Bellamy Band, Boston, 1980-83; sax player Girls' Night Out, Boston, 1984-87; song writer, band leader, sax player Myanna, Boston, 1989—; pres. Bridge City Records, Boston, 1991—, Bridge City Music, Boston, 1991—. Song writer, sax player (album) Myanna, 1991 (winner Boston Music Awards Outstanding Local Jazz Act, 1992). Office: Myanna PO Box 258 Boston MA 02130

POOL, PHILIP BEMIS, JR., investment banker; b. N.Y.C., Apr. 11, 1954; s. Philip B. and Virginia Middleton (French) P.; m. Joan H. Barnes, May 19, 1978; children: Elliott Livingston, Victoria Middleton. BS in Commerce, U. Va., 1976; MBA, Columbia U., 1980. Asst. treas. The Bank of N.Y., N.Y.C., 1976-78; v.p. Kidder Peabody & Co., Inc., N.Y.C., 1980-85; mng. dir. Merrill Lynch & Co., N.Y.C., 1985—. Mem. Down Town Assn., Piping Rock Club (gov. 1989—), Lyford Cay Club, Racquet and Tennis Club. Republican. Episcopalian.

POOL, WILLIAM ROBERT, pharmaceutical executive; b. Ft. Lauderdale, Fla., May 14, 1937; s. Robert Arthur and Marjorie (Wylam) P.; m. Mary Ann McClave, Jan. 3, 1958; children: Michael, Robert, Karen, David. BS, Fla. State U., 1960, MS, 1963, PhD, 1966. Sci. tchr. Leon High Sch., Tallahassee, Fla., 1960-63; pharmacologist, toxicologist Hoffmann LaRoche, Nutley, N.J., 1966-76; dir. toxicology G.D. Searle, Skokie, Ill., 1977-84; dir. toxicology ctr. Pfizer, Amboise, France, 1984-88; dir. safety assessment med. rsch. div. Am. Cyanamid, Pearl River, N.Y., 1988—. NIH fellow, 1963-66. Home: 27 Marget Ann Ln Suffern NY 10901-3314 Office: Am Cyanamid Med Rsch Div Pearl River NY 10965

POOLE, EDWARD OTTO, minister; b. Phila., Feb. 17, 1931; s. Robert Jr. and Anna K. (Kolbe) P.; m. Marian Ruby Barr, Aug. 9, 1958; children: Ellen Poole Morgan, Alice Poole Temnick, Leah Poole Greenwood, Sara Barr Poole. AB, Wheaton (Ill.) Coll., 1953; MST, Temple U., 1956; ThM, Princeton (N.J.) Sem., 1959. Ordained to ministry Presbyn. Ch. (U.S.A.), 1956. Asst. pastor Glading Meml. Presbyn. Ch., Phila., 1956-59; pastor 1st Presbyn. Ch., Port Kennedy, Pa., 1959-64, Hillsborough Presbyn. Ch., Belle Mead, N.J., 1964-69, Sherwood Presbyn. Ch., Washington, 1970-76; area counselor Major Mission Fund, Presbyn. Ch. (U.S.A.), Butler, Pa., 1977-79; area min. Beaver-Butler Presbytery, Zelienople, Pa., 1980-89; interim pastor Livingston (N.J.) Presbyn. Ch., 1990-91; supply min. Newark and Phila. Presbyteries, 1991-92; interim pastor 1st Presbyn. Ch., Mineola, N.Y., 1992—; mem. Presbytery of L.I., N.Y. Mem. Presbytery of Newark. Home: 50 Kenilworth Rd Mineola NY 11501-4621 Office: First Presbyn Ch of Mineola 1st and Main Sts Mineola NY 11501-3898

POOR, ALFRED EASTON, computer analyst, consultant; b. Havre De Grace, Md., July 23, 1951; s. Charles L. Poor and Sidney (Lockwood) Tynan; m. Barbara Louise Thode, June 18, 1973; children: Anna Louise, Alexander Edward. BA, Harvard U., 1973; PhD, Union U., 1982. Tchr. Germantown Friends Sch., Phila., 1973-76, Fairfield (Conn.) Pub. Schs., 1977-78; community resource coord. Region 15 Schs., Middlebury, Conn., 1978-82; founder, prin. Soft Industries, Southington, Conn., 1982-88; pvt. practice cons. Perkasie, Pa., 1988—; contbg. editor P.C. mag., N.Y.C., 1989—. Author: The Hewlett-Packard Laser-Jet Printer Handbook, 1988, The Data Exchange, 1989; contbr. articles to profl. jours. Bd. dirs. Washington Montessori Sch., New Preston, Conn., 1986-87.

POPE, ALBERT AUGUSTUS, entrepreneur; b. Panama, July 12, 1944; came to U.S., 1944; s. Ralph Linder Jr. and Thelma Evangelina (de Morales-Brid) P.; m. Renata Maria Sandra Borsetti, Nov. 30, 1985; 1 child, Charles Albert. BA, Harvard U., 1968. V.p. Deltec Securities Corp., N.Y.C., 1970-74; asst. v.p. Morgan Guaraney Trust, N.Y.C., 1974-78; pres. Montenay Energy, N.Y.C., 1978-85; mng. dir. Crysen-Montenay, Ft. Lee, N.J., 1984-85; ptnr. Essex Cement Co., Port Newark, N.J., 1985-88; chmn., pres. A.A. Pope/Terra Nova Investments Inc., Standfordville, N.Y., 1986—; bd. dirs. USA Cartrx Inc., Pope/Petronx Corp., N.Y., InovEnergy, Boston. Mem.

India House, Royal Soc Arts, Mashomac Fish and Game Club (N.Y.). Home: Stone Oaks Farm PO Box 557 Bangall NY 12506

POPE, ANNE ELIZABETH, psychologist; b. N.Y.C., Sept. 2, 1942; d. Vernon K. Pope and Elizabeth (Welt) Frank. BA, Goddard Coll., 1972. Research dept. psychiatry Mass. Gen. Hosp., Boston, 1966-69; program planner, developer Task Oriented Community, Waltham, Mass., 1969-77; program planner Mass. Dept. Mental Health, Medfield, 1977-79, Westboro, Mass., 1979-82; dir. clin. svcs. Mass. Dept. Mental Health, Framingham, Mass., 1982-88; writer Mass. Dept. Mental Health, Southboro, Mass., 1988-89; dir. human svcs. Hubbard Regional Hosp., Webster, Mass., 1989—; cons. N.H. Dept. Mental Health, 1987-88, Faulkner Breast Ctr. Author: The Psychiatric Community, 1972, English Springer Spaniels, 1986; writer for popular, comml. women's mags. on mental health, family dynamics, pet therapy. Mem. Am. Psychol. Assn., NOW. Home: 50 Hayward Rd Acton MA 01720-3004 Office: Mass Dept Mental Health 225 Turnpike Rd Southborough MA 01772-1704

POPE, INGRID BLOOMQUIST, artist, sculptor, lecturer; b. Arvika, Sweden, Apr. 2, 1918; came to U.S., 1928; d. Oscar Emanuel and Gerda (Henningson) Brostrom; m. Howard Richard Bloomquist, Feb. 14, 1941 (dec. Nov. 1982); children: Dennis Howard, Diane Cecile Connelly, Laurel Ann Shields; m. Marvin Hoyle Pope, Mar. 9, 1985. BA cum laude, Manhattanville Coll., 1979, MA in Humanities, 1981; MA in Religion, Yale Div. Sch. Yale U., 1984. lectr. Nat. Assn. Am. Pen Women, Greenwich, Soroptimist Club, Greenwich, Greenwich Travel Club, Ch. Women United Greenwich, 1st Congl. Ch., Scarsdale, N.Y., 2d Congl. Ch., Greenwich, 1st Congl. Ch., Stamford, Conn., 1st Ch. of Round Hill, St. Mary Ch., Greenwich. Exhbns. include Manhattanville Coll. Purchase, N.Y., Yale Div. Sch., Ch. of Swedes in N.Y.C., Greenwich Arts Coun., Greenwich Arts Soc. Past bd. dirs. N.Y.C. Mission Soc., Greenwich YWCA, Greenwich Acad. Mother's Assn.; trustee First Ch. Round Hill, Greenwich, mem.; pres. Ch. Women United, Greenwich, 1989-91; bd. dirs. Greenwich Chaplaincy. Mem. AAUW, Nat. Assn. Pen Women, English Speaking Union, Yale Club N.Y.C. and Greenwich, Stanwich Club, Travel Club. Home: 538 Round Hill Rd Greenwich CT 06831-2641

POPE, MARVIN HOYLE, retired language educator; b. Durham, N.C., June 23, 1916; s. Charles Edgar and Bessie Cleveland Sorrell P.; m. Helen Thompson Bretana, Sept. 4, 1948 (dec. Feb. 5, 1979); m. Ingrid Brostrom Bloomquist, Mar. 9, 1985. AB, Duke U., 1938, AM, 1939; PhD, Yale U., 1949. Instr. dept. religion Duke U., Durham, 1947-49; asst. prof. Hebrew Yale U., New Haven, 1949-55, assoc. prof., 1955-64, prof. Semitic langs. and lit., 1964-86, prof. emeritus, sr. rsch. scholar, 1986—; Haskell lectr. Oberlin Coll., 1971, vis. lectr. Cath. U. Lublin, Poland, 1977, Fulbright lectr. U. Aleppo, Syria, 1980; Wickenden lectures Miami U., Oxford, Ohio, 1982; Fulbright Rsch. scholar Inst. Ugaritforschung U. Muenster, Fed. Republic Germany, 1986, 90; Hooker disting. vis. prof. McMaster U., Hamilton, Ont., Can., 1986; bd. dirs. Am. Sch. of Oriental Rsch., Jerusalem, Hebrew Union Coll. Bibl. and Archeol. Sch., Jerusalem; trustee Albright Inst. Archeol. Rsch., Jerusalem; fellow Pierson Coll. Yale U. Author: El in the Ugaritic Texts, 1955; The Book of Job, 1973, Song of Songs, 1977 (Nat. Religious Book award 1978), Syrien Die Mythologie der Ugariter und Phoenizier, 1962; contbr. articles to scholarly jours. and dictionaries. Mem. rev. standard version Bible com. Nat. Coun. of Chs., 1960—; mem. 1st Ch. Round Hill. With USAAF, 1941-45, PTO. Nat. Endowment for Humanities Rsch. grantee, 1980—. Mem. Am. Oriental Soc., Am. Schs. Oriental Rsch., Soc. Bibl. Lit., Am. Soc. Study Religions, Columbia U. Seminar for Study of Hebrew Bible, Yale Club, Oriental Club New Haven, Mory's Club, Stanwich Country Club, Phi Beta Kappa. Home: 538 Round Hill Rd Greenwich CT 06831-2641

POPECKI, JOSEPH THOMAS, library director, consultant; b. Saginaw, Mich., Nov. 25, 1924; s. Joseph Sebastian and Anna Pearl (Schreiber) P.; m. Jeanne Marie Gillespie, Jan. 29, 1949; children: Judith Marie Holmgren, Matthew Joseph, Mark Andrew, John Michael. BA, Sacred Heart Sem., 1945; MLS, Cath. U. Am., 1949. Various positions Cath. U. Am. Librs., Washington, 1947-58, 50-67, acting dir., 1965-67, lectr. grad. edn., 1950-67; founder, pres. Mid-Atlantic Assoc., Inc., Washington, 1960-67; lectr. libr. sci. Grad. Sch. USDA, Washington, 1950-67; dir. libr. St. Michael's Coll., Colchester, Vt., 1967-90; dir. emeritus, archivist St. Michael's Coll. Libr., Colchester, Vt., 1990—; coord. Elderhostel program St. Michael's Coll., Colchester, Vt., 1990—; commr., chair Chittenden County Transp. Authority, Burlington, Vt., 1973-83; mem. adv. coun. Vt. Local Rds. Program, Colchester, 1982—; mem., chair Vt. Adv. Coun. for Hist. Preservation, Montpelier, Vt., 1969-77; trustee, sec. Burlington Coll., 1980—. Author: Near-Print Duplication, 1954, Union List Serials, Washington, D.C., 1967, Institutional Self-Study of Saint Michael's College, 1990, The Parish of St. Mark, Burlington, Vermont 1941-91, 1991; editor: Thesaurus, Nursing, Biomedical Lit., 1967; contbr. numerous articles to profl. jours. Clk. ward 4 City of Burington, 1987—; chair St. Michael's Coll., United Way Campaign, Colchester, 1982-89; mem. adv. coun. RSVP, Burlington; commr. Fletcher Free Libr. Bd., Burlington. Mem. Vt. Archeol. Soc., Inc. (treas., past pres. 1968—), Vt. Libr. Assn., Vt. New Eng. Libr. Assn., Am. Mgmt. Assn., Vt. Hist. Soc., New Eng. Archivists, Northwestern Vt. Model Railroading Soc. (sec.). Democrat. Roman Catholic. Home: 33 Woodridge Dr Burlington VT 05401-2741 Office: St Michaels Coll Libr Winooski Pk Colchester VT 05439-2525

POPKAVE, MURRAY WARREN, lawyer; b. Pottsville, Pa., Dec. 26, 1941; s. Leopold S. and Helen (Greenfield) P.; m. Carol J. Goldstein, May 20, 1973; children: David, Daniel, Rebecca. BS, Pa. State U., 1963; JD, Dickinson Sch. Law, 1966. Estate tax atty. IRS, Phila., 1966-73; legal counsel Nathan S. Kolbes Assocs., Inc., Bala Cynwyd, Pa., 1973-80; atty. Phoenix Mutual Life Ins. Co., Phila., 1980-85, Neil J. Barsky & Assocs., Phila., 1985-88; corp. counsel Creative Tax Planners, Inc., Phila., 1988—; registered rep. Nat. Assn. Securities Dealers, Phila., 1980—. Bd. dirs. Access, Inc., Conshohocken, Pa., Best Nest, Inc., Abington, Pa., Com. on Christian Approach to Jews, Phila., Access Svcs., Inc., Conshohocken. With U.S. Army, 1966-72. Mem. Am. Soc. Pension Actuaries (assoc.), Nat. Assn. Life Underwriters, Pa. Bar Assn., Schuylkill County Bar Assn., Pottsville Club, Pa. State U. Alumni Assn. (life). Office: Creative Tax Planners Inc 1608 Walnut St Ste 1600 Philadelphia PA 19103

POPKIN, JOEL, economic consulting company executive; b. Trenton, N.J., July 6, 1932; s. Nathaniel Robert and Betty (Finkle) P.; BS in Econs., U. Pa., 1954, PhD, 1965; m. Elizabeth Rose Alk, Oct. 17, 1968; children: Neil Robert, Sara Rachel. Asst. economist Allied Chem. Co., N.Y.C., 1957-59; lectr., researcher U. Pa., Phila., Northwestern U., Evanston, Ill., George Washington, U., Washington, 1960-64; econometrician Dept. Commerce, Washington, 1964-66; div. chief, asst. commr. U.S. Bur. Labor Stats., Washington, 1966-73; sr. staff economist President's Council of Econ. Advs., Washington, 1973-74; dir., mem. rsch. staff Nat. Bur. Econ. Rsch., Washington, 1974-78; pres. Joel Popkin And Co., Washington, 1978—. Served as lt. USAR, 1955-57. Fellow Am. Statis. Assn.; mem. Am. Econ. Assn., Conf. Bus. Economists (chmn. 1989), Nat. Assn. Bus. Economists, Internat. Assn. for Rsch. on Income and Wealth. Clubs: Nat. Economists (chmn. bd., pres. 1978-80); Cosmos. Home: 6706 Loring Ct Bethesda MD 20817-3148 Office: 1101 Vermont Ave NW Washington DC 20005-3521

POPKIN, JOYCE GAIL, psychologist; b. Bklyn., Nov. 18, 1947; d. Gilbert and Fally (Mardex) P.; m. Theodore William Hilgeman, July 19, 1987; 1 child, Alexandra Elaine. BA, Queens Coll., 1968; EdM, Temple U., 1970, PhD, 1984. Licensed psychologist, N.Y.; cert. sch. psychologist, N.Y., N.J., Pa. Sch. psychologist Comsewogue Sch. Dist., Port Jefferson Station, N.Y., 1971—; pvt. practice psychology, 1991—; workshop leader Nat. Ctr. for Study Corporal Punishment, 1979-80; mem. Dropout Prevention Com., Comsewogue Schs., 1986—, attendance policy com., 1986-87; supr. Masters and Doctoral Level Interns, Comsewogue Schs., 1988-89. Bd. dirs. Sylvan Gardens Coop., Miller Place, N.Y., 1984-87, 89—. Mem. APA, Suffolk County Psychol. Assn. (sch. psychology com. 1990—), Nat. Assn. Sch. Psychologists. Home: 22 Paul Revere Ln Centerport NY 11721-1610

POPLAWSKI, PAUL EDWIN, psychotherapist; b. Phila., Aug. 22, 1949; s. Edwin Joseph and Ellen Catherine (Jones) P.; BA in Psychology, U. Del., 1972; M in Human Services, Lincoln U., 1978; PhD in Psychoednl. Processes, Temple U., 1989. Lic. psychologist. Clin. supr., psychotherapist Bur. Alcoholism and Drug Abuse, Newark, Del., 1971-75, dir. Newark Counseling Ctr., 1975-76, dir. tng. and edn., 1979—, coordinating state troubled employees program, 1983—, dir. outpatient care, Wilmington, Del., 1976-79; co-founder Nat. Tng. Network, 1982, Psychology of Music Rsch., 1984; pvt. practice psychotherapy, Newark, Del., 1976—. Composer electronic music. Nat. Inst. Alcohol Abuse and Alcoholism grantee, 1979-82, Nat. Inst. Drug Abuse grantee, 1979-83. Mem. Am. Soc. Tng. and Devel., N.Y. Inst. for Gesalt Therapy. Roman Catholic. Home: 72 Welsh Tract Rd Apt 110 Newark DE 19713-2221 Office: Div Alcoholism Drug Abuse and Mental Health 1901 N Dupont Hwy New Castle DE 19720-1100

POPP, CHARLOTTE LOUISE, health development center administrator, nurse; b. Vineland, N.J., July 26, 1946; d. William Henry and Elfriede Marie (Zickler) P. Diploma in Nursing, Luth. Hosp. of Md., Balt., 1967; BA in Health Edn., Glassboro (N.J.) State Coll., 1972; MA in Human Devel., Fairleigh-Dickinson U., 1981. Cert. Sch. Nurse, N.J., Health Educator, N.J. Charge nurse Newcomb Hosp., Vineland, N.J., 1967-71; supr. Vineland Rehab. Ctr., 1971-72; charge nurse Bridgeton (N.J.) Hosp., 1972-73; dir. insvc. edn. Millville (N.J.) Hosp., 1973-76; dir. hosp. insvc. edn. Vineland Devel. Ctr. State of N.J., 1976-78, program asst. Vineland Devel. Ctr., 1978-87; dir. habilitation planning services State of N.J., Vineland Devel. Ctr., 1987—, lead program coord. Vineland Devel. Ctr., 1981—; exam proctor State of N.J. Bd. Nursing, Newark, 1973—. Editorial rev. bd. (jour.) Nursing Update, 1973-77. Instr. basic life support, Am. Heart Assn., bd. dirs. Tri-county chpt., 1979-83, South Jersey chpt., 1983-90. Mem. ANA, N.J. State Nurses Assn., Am. Assn. Mental Retardation, South Jersey Insvc. Exch. (life), Smithsonian Assn., Luth. Hosp. of Md. Alumni Assn., Glassboro State Coll. Alumni Assn., Fairleigh-Dickinson U. Alumni Assn. Lutheran. Office: Vineland Devel Ctr 1676 E Landis Ave Vineland NJ 08360-2901

POPP, ROBIN RENEE, non profit development professional, consultant; b. Pitts., May 9, 1965; d. Robert Ernest and Evangeline Josephine (Matragas) P. BA, Emerson Coll., Boston, 1986. Communications coord. Friends Program, Concord, N.H., 1986-87; devel. assoc. N.H. Symphony Orchestra, Manchester, N.H., 1987-89; free lance cons. pvt. practice, Manchester, N.H., 1989-90; assoc. dir. devel. N.H. Assn. for Blind, Concord, N.H., 1990—; ind. skin care cons. Mary Kay Cosmetics, Goffstown, N.H., 1990—. Asst. to communications coord., Mass. Democratic State Cm., Boston, 1985; vol. United Way of Merrimack County, Concord, N.H., 1986-87, 91—, Am. Cancer Soc., Bedford, N.H., 1989—; deacon Brookside Congl. Ch., Manchester, N.H., 1990—. Mem. N.H. Coun. Fundraising, N.H. Women's Forum, Success for Women Entrepreneurs, Bus. and Profl. Women's Assn. Democrat. Mem. United Ch. of Christ Congl. Office: NH Association for Blind 25 Walker St Concord NH 03301-4599

POPPEL, SETH RAPHAEL, business executive; b. Bklyn., Mar. 17, 1944; s. Frank M. and Fritzi R. (Axenzow) P.; BS magna cum laude, L.I. U., 1965; MBA, Columbia U., 1967; m. Danine Vokt, Jan. 5, 1974; children: Clarysa, Jared, Stacy. Asst. prof. L.I. U., Greenvale, N.Y., 1967-68; v.p. Synergistic Systems Corp., N.Y.C., 1968-77; v.p., dir. corp. planning Chase Manhattan Corp., N.Y.C., 1977-90; chmn., pres. Am. Vision Ctrs. , N.Y.C., 1990—; owner harness horses Seth Poppel Stables, 1983—; founder, owner, operator Seth Poppel Yearbook Archives, 1986—. E.I. DuPont fellow, 1965-67, Downie Muir fellow, 1965-66; recipient Claire F. Adler award in math., 1964-65. Mem. Am. Statis. Assn., Ops. Research Soc. Am., Inst. Mgmt. Sci., Nat. Assn. Bus. Economy, N.Am. Soc. Corp. Planning, U.S. Trotting Assn., Beta Gamma Sigma, Psi Chi, Omega Epsilon. Home: 38 Range Dr Merrick NY 11566-3233 Office: 90 John St New York NY 10038-3202

POPPER, ROBERT DAVID, computer and management consultant; b. Budapest, Hungary, Dec. 10, 1927; came to U.S., 1950; s. Eugene Andrew and Ilona Angela (Nagy) P.; m. Mary Elizabeth Metzel, June 26, 1956; children: Ilona, Robert, Thomas, Margaret, Emily, John, Edward. BA, George Washington U., 1959, MA, 1961; postgrad., Yale U., 1961-64. Assoc. rsch. scientist Human Scis. Rsch., Inc., Washington, 1959-62; cons. Dunlap and Assocs., Darien, Conn., 1962-65; dir. ops. rsch. and systems devel. Glidden Co., Cleve., 1965-70; dir. corp. MIS Sandoz, Basle, Switzerland, 1970-72; sr. v.p. strategic planning and MIS U.S. Trust Co., N.Y.C., 1972-80; sr. v.p. MIS J. Walter Thompson Co., N.Y.C., 1980-82; pres. info. products group Squibb Corp., Lawrenceville, N.J., 1982-87; chief exec. officer New Dimensions Cons., Princeton, N.J., 1982—. Trustee Buxton Sch., Williamstown, Mass., 1987—. With U.S. Army, 1956-58. Co-author: The Physical Effects of Nuclear Attack, 1961. Mem. Am. Econ. Assn., Am. Statis. Assn., Am. Math. Assn., Data Processing Mgmt. Assn., Am. Arbitration Assn., Yale Club (N.Y.C.). Republican. Roman Catholic. Office: New Dimensions Cons Inc 539 Kingston Rd Princeton NJ 08540-4058

POPPERS, PAUL JULES, anesthesiologist, educator; b. Enschede, Netherlands, June 30, 1929; came to U.S., 1958; naturalized, 1963; s. Meyer and Minca (Ginsburg) P.; m. Ann Feinberg, June 3, 1969; children: David Matthew, Jeremy Samuel. MD, U. Amsterdam, 1955. Diplomate Am. Bd. Anesthesiology. Instr. anesthesiology Columbia U., N.Y.C., 1962-63, assoc., 1963-65, asst. prof. anesthesiology, 1965-71, assoc. prof. anesthesiology, 1971-74; prof., vice chmn. dept. anesthesiology NYU, 1974-79; prof., chmn. dept. anesthesiology SUNY, Stony Brook, 1979—; cons. Brookdale Med. Ctr., Bklyn., 1975—, VA Med. Ctr., Northport, N.Y., 1979—, Booth Meml. Hosp., Flushing, N.Y., 1979—, Am. Hosp. Paris, 1989—; cons., lectr. USN Regional Med. Ctr., Portsmouth, Va., 1975-83. Author: Regional Anesthesia, 1977; editor: Beta Blockade and Anaesthesia, 1979; section editor Jour Clin. Anesthesia, 1990—; mem. editorial bd. Internat. Jour. Clin. Monitoring and Computing, 1990—; internat. bd. editors Anaesthesiology Digest, 1991—; contbr. numerous articles to profl. jours. NIH postdoctoral rsch. fellow, 1961; recipient medal Polish Acad. Scis., Poland, 1987, Univ. medal Jagiellonian U., Krakow, Poland, 1987, 1st Sci. award Post-grad. Assembly in Anesthesiology; named Hon. Prof. Anesthesiology, U. Leiden, The Netherlands, 1977. Fellow Am. Coll. Anesthesiology, Am. Coll. Ob-Gyns., Royal Soc. Medicine, Post-Grad. Assembly in Anesthesiology (hon. chmn. 1989—); mem. Am. Soc. Anesthesiologists, Assn. Univ. Anesthesiologists, Soc. Acad. Anesthesia Chmn., Internat. Anesthesia Rsch. Soc., Soc. Obstetric Anesthesia and Perinatology, Jerusalem Acad. Medicine, Am. Soc. Pharmacology and Exptl. Therapeutics, Fedn. Am. Soc. Exptl. Biology, Sigma Xi. Office: SUNY Sch Medicine Health Scis Ctr Stony Brook NY 11794-8480

POPRAWSKI, TADEUSZ JERZY, research entomologist; b. Fontaine-L'Eveque, Hainaut, Belgium, Oct. 25, 1947; arrived in Can., 1975; s. Johann and Ludmila (Nowak) P.; m. Natalia Krystyna Milej-Poprawski, July 25, 1970; 1 child, Kalinka. BSc in Agr. with honors, McGill U., Montreal, Can., 1979, PhD with honors, 1985. Rsch. entomologist USDA, Paris, 1983-84, 87-90, Ithaca, N.Y., 1990—; rsch. assoc. USDA, Paris, 1985-87, Boyce Thompson Inst., Ithaca, 1984-85. Author: (with others) Safety of Microbial Insecticides, 1990; contbr. articles to profl. jours. Mem. Entomol. Soc. Am., Internat. Orgn. for Biol. Control, N.Y. Acad. Scis., Entomol. Soc. Can., Entomol. Soc. Que., Soc. for Invertebrate Pathology, Indian Soc. for Biocontrol Advancement. Home: 700 Warren Rd 24-1A Ithaca NY 14850 Office: USDA Tower Rd at Cornell Ithaca NY 14853

PORTEOUS, CHARLES ROBERT, JR. (SKIPP PORTEOUS), communications executive, writer; b. Hartford, Conn., Feb. 7, 1944; s. Charles Robert and Marian Berle (Guy) P.; m. Linda Marie Silvernail, Mar. 25, 1965 (div. Feb. 1977) children: Angela Monique, Charles Mark, Marylisa; m. Barbara Ann Simon, May 1, 1983. Student, Life Bible Coll., Los Angeles, 1966-67, East Los Angeles Community Coll., 1969, Columbia Greene Community Coll., 1978. Ordained to ministry Missionary and Evangelistic Ch., 1968; cert. radio mktg. cons. Evangelist Chapel on the Strip, Hollywood, Calif., 1967-68; pastor Pasadena (Calif.) Christian Fellowship, 1968-74, West Copake (N.Y.) Reformed Ch., 1974-76, Agape House Christian Ctr., Hillsdale, N.Y., 1976-77; sales exec., promoter various radio stas. and newspapers, N.Y., Mass., 1977-84; pres. Inst. for First Amendment Studies, Inc., Gt. Barrington, Mass., 1984—; radio and TV talk show guest, nationwide, 1986—; researcher TV news networks, Penthouse, Playboy mags. Pub. newsletters The Freedom Writer, Walk Away, Gt. Barrington, 1984—, Freedom Writer Faxsheet; author: Jesus Doesn't Live Here Anymore-From Fundamentalist to Freedom Writer, 1991; author mag. articles, columns; inventor in field. Elim fellow. Democrat. Unitarian Universalist. Office: The Freedom Writer PO Box 589 Great Barrington MA 01230-0589

PORTER, BARRY M., marketing professional; b. Boston, Nov. 6, 1953; d. Bernard and Thelma (Gerber) P. BS, Springfield Coll., 1971. EMT Stavis Ambulance, Brookline, Mass., 1975-77, Gen. Ambulance, Needham, Mass., 1984-86; mktg. support prof. Gerber Electronics, Norwood, Mass., 1986—. Sec. mgr. ea. Mass., Am. Radio Relay League, Newington, Conn., 1988-91, sect. emergency coord., 1985-91. With USN, 1977-84. Mem. Boston Computer Soc. (chair online svcs. com. 1989—), Boston Computer Soc. Amateur Radio Group (group dir. 1989—), Boston Computer Soc. (mem. svcs. com. 1988—), Masons, Shriners. Home: 47 Erin Rd Stoughton MA 02072 Office: Gerber Electronics 128 Carnegie Row Norwood MA 02062

PORTER, BERNARD HARDEN, consulting physicist, author, publisher; b. Porter Settlement, Maine, Feb. 14, 1911; s. Lewis Harden and Etta Flora (Rogers) P.; m. Helen Elaine Hendron, July 15, 1946 (div. Aug. 1947); m. Margaret Eudine Preston, Aug. 27, 1955 (dec. April 1975); m. Lula Mae Blom, Sept. 9, 1976 (div. Nov. 1986). BS, Colby Coll., 1932; MS, Brown U., 1933; DSc (hon.), Inst. Advanced Thinking, Calais, Maine, 1959. Physicist Acheson Colloids Corp., Port Huron, Mich., 1935-40; rsch. physicist Manhattan Dist. Engrs., Princeton, N.J., Berkeley, Calif. and Oak Ridge, 1940-45; cons. physicist San Francisco and Pasadena, Calif., Waldwick, N.J., Rockland, Belfast, Maine, 1945—; chmn. bd. Bern Porter Inc., Pasadena, Rockland, Belfast, 1945—; pres. Bern Porter Books, Pasadena, Rockland, Belfast, 1929—, Bern Porter Internat., Belfast, 1974—; cons. Internat. Exec. Service Corps, 1968, SBA, 1968-88. Author: The 14th of February, 1971, I've Left, 1971, Founds, 1972, Hand Coated Chocolates, 1972, Contemporary Italian Painters, 1973, Trattoria Due Forni, 1973, The Book of Do's, 1974, The Manhattan Telephone Book, 1975, Run-On, 1975, Where, 1975, Selected Founds, 1975, Gee-Whizzles, 1976, Don't Book, 1981, Last Acts, 1985, My, My, 1985, Left Leg, 1988, Neverends, 1988, Numbers, 1989, Sweetend, 1989; contbr. numerous articles to profl. jours. Rep. candidate for gov. Maine, 1969; bd. dirs. Inst. Advanced Thinking, Belfast, chmn. bd., 1959—. Recipient awards PEN, 1975, 76, 77, Authors League, 1977; Carnegie author, 1975; diploma merit Centro Studi E Scambi Internazionale, Rome, 1976; Nat. Endowment for Arts lit. award, 1979. Fellow Am. Astronautical Soc., Tech. Pub. Soc., Am. Rocket Soc. (assoc.), Soc. Tech. Writers and Pubs. (assoc.), Internat. Acad. Poets (London) (founding); mem. Am. Phys. Soc., Soc. Internat. Devel., Nat. Soc. Programmed Instrn., Phi Beta Kappa, Sigma Xi, Kappa Phi Kappa, Chi Gamma Sigma. Methodist. Clubs: Fenway (Boston); Algonquin, St. Andrews (N.B., Can.). Address: 22 Salmond Rd Belfast ME 04915

PORTER, BURTON FREDERICK, philosophy educator, author; b. N.Y.C., June 22, 1936; s. John and Doris (Neloway) P.; m. Susan Jane Porter, May 10, 1966 (div. 1974); 1 child, Anastasia; m. Barbara Taylor Metcalf, Dec. 31, 1980; 1 child, Mark Graham Bevan. B.A. in Philosophy cum laude with spl. hons. in lit., U. Md., 1959; postgrad., Oxford U., Eng.; Ph.D., St. Andrews U., Scotland, 1968. Asst. prof. philosophy U. Md., London, 1966-69; assoc. prof. philosophy King's Coll., Wilkes-Barre, Pa., 1969-71; prof. philosophy, chmn. dept. Russell Sage Coll., Troy, N.Y., 1971-87; prof. philosophy, head Dept. Humanities-Communications Drexel U., Phila., 1987-91; dean arts and scis. Western New Eng. Coll., Springfield, Mass., 1991—. Author: Deity and Morality, 1968, Philosophy, A Literary and Conceptual Approach, 1974, 80, Personal Philosophy: Perspectives on Living, 1976, The Good Life, Alternatives in Ethics 1980, 91, Reasons for Living: A Basic Ethics, 1988, Religion and Reason, 1992; also articles and book revs. Named Best Educator in History of the Instn., King's Coll., 1971, Outstanding Educator Am., NEA, 1975. Mem. Am. Philos. Assn., MLA. Home: 151 Erdenheim Rd Philadelphia PA 19118-1849 Office: Western New Eng Coll Arts & Scis Dean's Office Springfield MA 01119

PORTER, DARWIN FRED, writer; b. Greensboro, N.C., Sept. 13, 1937; s. Numie Rowan and Hazel Lee (Phillips) P. B.A., U. Miami, 1959. Bur. chief Miami Herald, 1959-60; v.p. Haggart Assocs., N.Y.C., 1961-64; editor, author Arthur Frommer Inc., N.Y.C., 1964-67, Frommer/Pasmantier Pub. Corp., N.Y.C., 1967-86, Prentice Hall Press, N.Y.C., 1987-90, Simon & Schuster, N.Y.C., 1991—. Author: Frommer Travel Guides to Eng., 1964, Frommer Travel Guides to Spain, 1966, Frommer Travel Guides to Scandinavia, 1967, Frommer Travel to Los Angeles, 1969, Frommer Travel Guide to London, 1970, Frommer Travel Guide to Lisbon/Madrid, 1972, Frommer Travel Guide to Paris, 1972, Frommer Travel Guide To Morocco, 1974, Frommer Travel Guide to Rome, 1974, Frommer Travel Guide to Portugal, 1968, Frommer Travel Guide to England, 1969, Frommer Travel Guide to Italy, 1969, Frommer Travel Guide to Germany, 1970, Frommer Travel Guide to France, 1970, Frommer Travel Guide to Caribbean, Bermuda, the Bahamas, 1980, Frommer Travel Guide To Switzerland, 1984, Frommer Travel Guide to Austria and Hungary, 1984, Frommer Travel Guide to Bermuda and the Bahamas, 1985, Frommer Travel Guide to Scotland and Wales, 1985, Frommer Travel Guide to the Virgin Islands, 1991, Frommer Travel Guide to Scotland, 1992, Frommer Travel Guide to Jamaica/Barbados, 1992, Frommer Travel Guide to Puerto Rico, 1992; (novels) Butterflies in Heat, 1976, Marika, 1977, Venus, 1982. Recipient Silver award Internat. Film and TV Festival N.Y., 1977. Mem. Soc. Am. Travel Writers, Smithsonian Assocs., Sigma Delta Chi. Home: 75 St Marks Pl Staten Island NY 10301-1606

PORTER, EDWIN DAVID, artist; b. Chgo., May 18, 1912; s. Harry E. and Anna (Pondel) P.; m. Marion Oettinger, Dec. 3, 1948. Student, Northwestern U., 1932-33, Art Inst. of Chgo., 1938. Economist War Prodn. Bd., Washington, 1942; founder David Porter Gallry, Washington, 1942; ptnr. The G Place Gallery, Washington, 1943; owner David Porter Gallery (formerly The G Place Gallery), Washington, 1944; v.p., pub. Cosmopolitan mag., N.Y.C., 1952-55; nat. sales mgr. Screen Gems, 1955-58; owner Art Lending Gallery, N.Y.C., 1953-59, Mus. of Modern Art, N.Y.C., 1953-59; artist-in-residence Dartmouth Coll., 1964-65; tchr. figure drawing Cooper Union, N.Y.C., 1965; lectr. in demonstrations of acrylic relief sculpture techniques Corcoran Mus. Art Sch., Washington, 1967-68; tchr. painting workshops Guild Hall Mus., fall and winter, 1975-78. Exhibited in group shows at 9th Street Show, N.Y.C., 1951, Arturo Schwarz Galleria d'Arte, Milan, 1962; one man shows include Alexander Iolas Hugo Gallery, N.Y.C., Deerfield (Mass.) Acad., Galerie Hervé, N.Y.C., The New Gallery, N.Y.C., The Obelisk Gallery, Washington, Tirca Karlis Gallery, Provincetown, Galleria L'Incontro, Rome, Southampton Art Gallery, N.Y.C., 1986, 88, Ann Ross Gallery, N.Y.C., Auslander Gallery, N.Y.C., Royal Athena II, N.Y.C., Libr. of Circulating Paintings, N.Y.C., Nassau C. C., 1983, Hampton Sq. Art Gallery, Westhampton Beach, N.Y., Bologna Art Gallery, East Hampton, N.Y., 1992. Subject of article Archives of Am. Art Jour., 1989. Dir. East End Hospice, 1988—. Recipient 1st award Provincetown Arts Festival, 1958, prize Carnegie Internat., 1958. Home and Studio: PO Box 71 Wainscott NY 11975-0071

PORTER, GLENN, museum and library administrator; b. New Boston, Tex., Apr. 2, 1944; s. Pat Paul and Mary Lee (Sanders) P.; m. K.T. Wimberly, June 1, 1968 (div. 1986); m. Barbara H. Butler, Dec. 18, 1987. BA, Rice U., 1966; MA, Johns Hopkins U., 1968, PhD, 1970. Asst. prof. bus. history Harvard Bus. Sch., Boston, 1970-76; dir. regional econ. history research ctr. Hagley Mus. & Library, Wilmington, Del., 1976-83, dir., 1984—. Editor Bus. History Rev., 1970-76; editorial bd. Jour. Am. History, 1977-80, Del. History, 1982—, Bus. History Rev., 1983-92; author: (with Harold C. Livesay) Merchants and Manufacturers, 1971; Rise of Big Business, 1860-1910, 1973, rev. edit., 1992, The Workers World at Hagley, 1981; gen. editor: Ency. of Am. Econ. History, 1980, The Papers of John D. Rockefeller, 1991. Mem. cons. com. Nat. Survey of Historic Sites and Bldgs., Washington, 1976-79; council mem. Del. Humanities Council, 1981-83. Recipient Cultural Achievement award, U.S. Dept. Interior, 1979; NEH grantee, 1977-82, 81-83, 85-92. Mem. Bus. History Conf. (pres.1987), Soc. for History of Tech., Soc. Archtl. Historians, Am. Assn. Mus., Mid-Atlantic Assn. Mus., Phi Beta Kappa. Office: Hagley Mus & Libr PO Box 3630 Wilmington DE 19807-0630

PORTER, IAN HERBERT, pediatric educator, medical center administrator; b. Copenhagen, Denmark, Nov. 14, 1929; s. Reginald and Ingeborg (Grandjean) P.; divorced; children: Julian, Robert. MB BS, St. Thomas's Hosp.-London U., 1956. Resident St. Thomas's Hosp., London, 1956-58,

Royal Postgrad. Med. Sch., London, 1958-59; fellow The Johns Hopkins U. Sch. Medicine, Balt., 1960-62; rsch. fellow Royal Postgrad. Med. Sch., London, 1962-63; chief med. genetics Albany (N.Y.) Med. Coll., 1963-80, chair dept. pediatrics, 1968-79; dir. birth defects inst. N.Y. State Dept. Health, Albany, 1969; med. dir., v.p. med. affairs Albany Med. Ctr., 1986—; mem. N.Y. State Coun. Grad. Med. Edn., 1990—. Mem. editorial bd. Am. Jour. Med. Genetics, 1980—. Bd. dirs. St. Gregory's Sch. for Boys, Albany, 1969-75; v.p. Albany Inst. History and Art, 1979-80, 87-89. Fellow Am. Acad. Pediatrics (trustee 1982-91, bioethics com. 1990—); mem. Am. Soc. Human Genetics (bd. dirs. 1972-75), Soc. Pediatric Rsch., Soc. Health and Human Values, Coll. Physician Execs., Am. Pediatric Soc., Alpha Omega Alpha. Home: 205 Jay St Albany NY 12210-1807 Office: Albany Med Ctr New Scotland Ave Albany NY 12208-3516

PORTER, JACK NUSAN, writer, sociologist, historian, Jewish activist; b. Rovno, Ukraine, USSR, Dec. 2, 1944; came to U.S., 1946; s. Irving Puchtik and Faye (Merin) P.; m. Miriam Almuly, Sept. 18, 1977; children: Gabriel, Danielle. Cert., Machon Inst., Jerusalem, 1963; BAS cum laude, U. Wis., Milw., 1967; MA, PhD, Northwestern U., 1971; postgrad., Harvard U. Extension Course, 1980-81; lic.real estate, Lee Inst., Brookline, Mass., 1982. Rsch. assoc. Harvard U. Ukrainian Rsch. Inst., Cambridge, Mass., 1982-84; pres. The Spencer Group (Real Estate Devel. and Cons.), Newton, Mass., 1984—; exec. dir. The Spencer Sch. Real Estate, Newton, 1986—; dir. The Spencer Inst. for Bus. and Soc., Newton, 1984—; asst. prof. Coll. of Basic Studies Boston U., 1989-90; vis. lectr. Boston U. Met. Coll., 1987, 88, Bryant Coll., Smithfield, R.I., 1991; presenter White House Conf. on the Family, 1980; mem. Gov. Dukakis' Adv. Coun., 1982-84; panelist on Comparative Genocide, the Famous Oxford Conf., 1988. Author or editor 25 books and anthologies including Confronting History and Holocaust, Sexual Politics in Nazi Germany, Kids in Cults, Jews and the Cults, Jewish Partisans, The Jews As Outsider, The Sociology of Business, The Sociology of Jewry, Handbook on Cults & Sects, Curriculum Guides in Business; contbr. over 250 articles and revs. to jours. in field; founder, editor Jour. of the History of Sociology, 1977-85, The Sociology of Bus. Newsletter, 1977-79; co-author: Conflict and Conflict Resolution, 1987, (with Ruth Taplin) New Technology, New Society?; editor: Genocide and Human Rights, 1982. Founder Holocaust Survival Video Project, Newton, Mass., 1992—. John Atherton fellow Breadloaf Writers Conf., Middlebury, Vt., 1976; recipient Spl. award Boston Police Dept., 1986. Mem. PEN (newsletter com. 1992—), Am. Sociol. Assn., B'nai B'rith Realty Club, Harvard Club. Democrat. Jewish. Home and Office: 8 Burnside Rd Newton MA 02161-1401

PORTER, JAMES H., chemical engineering executive; b. Port Chester, N.Y., Nov. 11, 1933; s. George James and Josephine (Hall) P.; m. Sandra Adrienne Knox, Sept. 8, 1958 (div. Dec. 1969); children: Michael Brandon, Adrienne Michelle, Lynn Sharon; m. Jennifer Anne Waterhouse, Feb. 26, 1978. BSChemE, Rensselaer Poly. Inst., 1955; ScD, MIT, 1963. Tech. svc. engr. Exxon, Linden, N.J., 1955-58; rsch. engr. Chevron Rsch. Corp., Richmond, Calif., 1963-67; mgr. process design Abcor Inc., Cambridge, Mass., 1967-71; assoc. prof. MIT, Cambridge, 1971-76; v.p. energy div. Energy Resources Co. Inc., Cambridge, 1976-79; pres. Energy and Environ. Engring. Inc., Somerville, Mass., 1979—; sci. adv. bd. U.S. EPA, Washington, 1976-83. Author: Chemical Equilibria in C.H.O. Systems, 1976; patentee in field. Bd. dirs. Tisbury Waterways Inc., Vineyard Haven, Mass., 1990, Trustees of Reservation, Boston, 1991, Cambridge Adult Edn. Ctr., Cambridge, 1988, sec., 1991. Mem. Am. Inst. Chem. Engrs., Nat. Orgn. Black Chemists and Chem. Engrs. (pres. 1978-79, bd. dirs., Founders award 1983), Sigma Xi, Pi Delta Epsilon. Home: PO Box 1131 Vineyard Haven MA 02568 Office: Energy & Environ Engring Inc 35 Medford St Somerville MA 02143

PORTER, JENNIFER GARNER, human resources professional; b. Ann Arbor, Mich., Aug. 14, 1959; m. Scott Douglas Porter. BA, U. N.H., 1981. Employment interviewer and benefits adminstr. Brooks Bros., N.Y.C., 1981-84; asst. mgr. benefits The Ford Found., N.Y.C., 1984-87, mgr. benefits & compensation, 1987—. Dir., sec. Country Meadows' Homeowners' Assn., Ossining, N.Y., 1991—. Mem. Working in Employee Benefits, N.Y. Soc. Cert. Employee Benefit Specialists, N.Y. Bus. Group on Health, N.Y. Compensation Assn. (asst. treas. 1989-92). Office: The Ford Found 320 E 43rd St New York NY 10017-4816

PORTER, JOHN HILL, public relations executive; b. Kane, Pa., Oct. 22, 1933; s. Hugh Clinton and Louise (Hill) P.; m. Sandra Van Fossen, Aug. 25, 1956 (div. 1981); children—John, Allison, Gardiner; m. Louise Bertels, Aug. 15, 1981; children—Campbell, Colin. B.S. in Econs., U. Pa., 1955; postgrad., U. Minn., 1956-57. Account exec. Benton & Bowles, N.Y.C., 1955, 57-59; sr. v.p. Ogilvy & Mather, N.Y.C. and London, 1959-70; dir. pub. affairs U.S. Peace Corps, Washington, 1970-72; chmn. Porter Novelli, Washington, 1972-86, N.Y.C., 1986—. Bd. overseers Sch. Nursing, U. Pa., Phila., 1982-87; trustee U. Pa., 1980-86, Penn. Med. Ctr., Phila., 1987-89. With U.S. Army, 1955-57. Republican. Office: Porter Novelli 1633 Broadway New York NY 10019-6708

PORTER, JOHN WESTON, guidance counselor, administrator; b. Fostoria, Ohio, Dec. 26, 1939; s. William Thomas and Ida Elizabeth (Carter) P.; student U. Cin., 1958, BA, Heidelberg Coll., 1961; MA in Community Psychology, U. D.C., 1973, MA in Counseling, 1975; postgrad. Antioch Coll., 1974, Frostburg (Md.) State Coll., 1970, George Washington U., 1968; cert. Nat. Bd. Cert. Counselors. Claims rep. Social Security Admnstrn., Cleve. and Akron, Ohio, 1961-62; office mgr. Phoenix Cos., Washington and L.A., 1966-70; researcher, grad. student Frostburg State Coll., U. D.C., 1970-73; edn. and career devel. specialist D.C. Public Schs., 1973-79, career edn. unit, 1979-83, Career Assessment Ctr., 1983-85, asst. dir. guidance and counseling, 1985—; mem. community adv. coun. Washington Hosp. Ctr., 1987—. Vice chmn. adv. council Group Health Assn., Washington 1977-79, 81-83; sec. Md.-D.C. Am. Coll. Testing Coun., 1987-88, vice chair, 1988-90, chair, 1990-91; pres. N.E. Hill Found., 1990-91. Lt. USNR, 1962-66. Recipient awards Ohio Acad. of Sci., 1954-57, Cleve. Plain Dealer Operation Demonstrate, 1956, svc. award Heidleberg Coll. Publs., 1961, recognition certs. D.C. Assn. Career Devel., 1975, 1976, D.C. City Council, 1982, Childrens Edn. Found., 1990; recipient recognition award Outstanding Contbn. to Guidance and Counseling 1987. Mem. D.C. Assn. Counseling and Devel. (sec. 1977-78, treas. 1975-77, 91-92, exec. bd., 1975-80, pres. 1979-80, trustee 1989-92, Mem. of Yr. 1980, Outstanding Leadership award 1980), Assn. Counseling and Devel. (chmn. govt. relations North Atlantic region 1980-81, cert. for outstanding contbn. in govt. relations 1982, Recognition award 1987), Am. Sch. Counselors Assn. (career guidance com., leadership recognition cert. 1987, chair rsch. com. 1990-91), Nat. Assn. Career Devel. (assembly del. 1984), D.C. Sch. Counselors Assn., D.C. Career Devel. Assn. (treas. 1983-86, exec. bd. 1983-90), N.E. Hill Guidance and Counselors Found. (pres. 1990-92), Children's Edn. Found. (adv. com. 1989—, fund raising com. 1989—), Assn. for Counselor Edn. and Supervision, Ret. Officers Assn., Phi Delta Kappa. Episcopalian. Home: 1700 Harvard St NW Washington DC 20009-2918

PORTER, KT, pharmaceutical company information officer; b. Houston, Oct. 10, 1944; d. George Franklin and Agatha (Fredrick) Wimberly; div. BA in Biology, Rice U., 1967. Rsch. technician New Eng. Deaconess Hosp., Boston, 1970-71, sr. rsch. asst. cancer rsch. inst., 1971-76; documentalist Adria Labs., Wilmington, Del., 1976-78; biostats. cons. ICI Pharms. Group, Wilmington, 1978-79, quality assurance analyst, 1979-83, med. info. coord., 1983-90, sr. med. writer, 1990—. Author: (tng. program) Introduction to Cardiovascular Drugs; editor newsletter For Your Med. Info.; contbr. articles to profl. jours. NSF grantee, 1966. Mem. AAAS, N.Y. Acad. Sci., Am. Med. Writers Assn., Drug Info. Assn., Tri-State Bird Rescue, Rsch., Rehab., Sigma Xi. Office: ICI Pharms Group Wilmington DE 19897

PORTER, NORA ROXANNE, freelance graphic designer; b. Waterville, Maine, June 28, 1949; d. Thomas Joseph and Cecilia Anne (Joseph) Belanger; m. Charles Henry Porter II, Nov. 1, 1969; children: Katherine, Elizabeth. BA, Cornell U., 1971. Free-lance graphic artist Poughkeepsie, N.Y., 1978—; art dir. Hudson River Sloop Clearwater, Poughkeepsie, 1989—; graphics coord. Hudson River Revival, Poughkeepsie, 1981—, mem. exec. com., 1985—; design coord. Challenge of the Hudson Regatta, 1990. Prin. works include The Hudson River Series, 1978, Panorama of the Hudson River, 1979, The Hudson River Primer, 1992. Designer, writer, curator Mid-Hudson Arts and Scis. Ctr., 1986-87.

PORTER, RICHARD FRANK, aerospace engineer; b. Cornwall, N.Y., May 17, 1943; s. Richard Alva and Linnea Cleone (White) P.; m. Colleen Marie Stolley; children: Michelle Marie, Lisa Raquel. BS in Aerospace Engring., U. Fla., 1965, MS in Aerospace Engring., 1967. Engr. Westinghouse Electric Corp., Balt., 1967-81, fellow engr., 1981-82, supervisory engr., 1982—; adj. faculty Anne Arundel Community Coll., Arnold, Md., 1976-82; exec. coun. 6th and 7th Digital Avionics Systems Conf., 1984, 85; chmn. industry adv. coun. U. Md. Calce Rsch. Ctr., Coll. Park, Md., 1988-90. Patentee in field; contbr. articles to profl. jours. Bd. dirs. Community Assn., Millersville, Md., 1983-84; chmn. Arch. Control Com., Millersville, 1975—. Mem. AIAA (v.p. 1989—, chmn. 1991-92, 25-yr. award 1989), Inst. Environ. Scis. (nat. mtg. session chmn. 1985-86). Office: Westinghouse Electric Co PO Box 746339ms Baltimore MD 21203-6672

PORTER, RICHARD JAMES, real estate broker, art historian; b. Bellefonte, Pa., Jan. 2, 1950; s. David Louis and Anna Louise (McGary) P.; m. Jeanne Chenault, Apr. 16, 1977; children: Andrew C., Julia M. BA, Pa. State U., 1971, MA, 1973, PhD, 1983. Instr. Middle Tenn. State U., Murfreesboro, 1973-76; registrar, curator Pa. State U. Mus. Art, University Park, 1977-85; chair grad. program in mus. studies Syracuse (N.Y.) U., 1985-86; sales assoc. Villager Realty, State College, Pa., 1986-88; sales assoc. Associated Realty, State College, 1988-91, assoc. broker, 1991—; instr. Polley Real Estate Schs., Greensburg, Pa., 1991—; cons. local not-for-profit orgns., State College, 1986—; dir. Ctr. County, Pa. Bd. Realtors, State College, 1989—, v.p., 1992—. Author exhbn. catalogs in field, 1989—. Dir. Nittany Valley Symphony, State College, 1990—; chmn. Columbus Quincentenary Preservation Com., Ctr. County, 1990-91. Recipient CRS designation Nat. Mktg. Inst., 1991. Mem. Nat. Assn. Realtors, Pa. Assn. Realtors (recipient Grad. Realtors Inst. designation 1989, Pa. Assn. Realtors Excellence Life award, 1991), Ctr. County Hist. Soc. (mem. exhbn. com. 1988-91), State College Choral Soc., State College Community Theatre, Torch Internat. (pres. 1990-91), Am. Assn. Museums (nat. coun. 1982-85), Kiwanis. Episcopalian. Home: PO Box 249 Lemont PA 16851 Office: Associated Realty 1612 N Atherton St State College PA 16803

PORTER, STEVEN BRIAN, insurance company executive; b. St. Petersburg, Fla., Dec. 23, 1961; s. Carlos O'Brien and Nancye Elizabeth (Wilson) P.; m. Jacqueline Carol Stein, May 12, 1984; children: Brian Matthew, Jonathan Mark. AA in Mgmt., St. Petersburg Jr. Coll., 1981; BA in Mgmt., U. South Fla., 1982. Claims adjuster Liberty Mut. Ins. Co., Tampa, 1983-87; claims supr. Liberty Mut. Ins. Co., Norfolk, Va., 1987-89; home office claims examiner Liberty Mut. Ins. Co., Dover, N.H., 1989—; instr. Ins. Tng. Placement, Gray, Maine, 1991. Writer, actor videotape Ethics in Responsible Loss Management, 1991. Contbr. Rep. Nat. Com., Washington, 1991, 92. Home: 3 Woodland Green Rochester NH 03868 Office: Liberty Mut Ins Co 100 Main St Dover NH 03820-3882

PORTER, WILLIAM JOSEPH, arborist, consultant; b. Bklyn., Nov. 21, 1924; s. Thomas John and Estelle Eleanor (Herman) P.; m. Helen Agnes Myers, Jan. 30, 1948 (div. 1974); children: Karen, Michael, Bruce, Thomas. Cert. tree expert, N.J. Tree climber Porter Bros., Rumson, N.J., 1940-43, mgr., 1946-58; owner Porter's Tree Experts, Rumson, N.J., 1958-67; exec. sec. N.J. Shade Tree Fedn., New Brunswick, 1980—; cons. N.J. Natural Gas Co., Wall. Bd. dirs. Community Forestry Com., Trenton, N.J., 1989, N.J. ReLeaf, Trenton, 1990. With USN, 1943-46. Mem. Internat. Soc. Arboriculture (bd. dirs. N.J. chpt.), Am. Soc. Cons. Arborists, N.J. Arborist Assn. (pres. 1963-64, approved arborist, Arborist of Yr. award 1964, Appreciation award 1967), N.J. Soc. Cert. Tree Experts (pres. 1968-70, Appreciation award 1972), N.J. Shade Tree Fedn. (pres. 1970-72, Appreciation award 1989), Bd. Tree Experts (v.p. 1963-80). Home: 27 Brookside Ave Hazlet NJ 07730-2263 Office: NJ Shade Tree Fedn PO Box 231 New Brunswick NJ 08903-0231

PORTER, WILLIAM ROBERT, academic administrator; b. Bklyn., Nov. 3, 1922; s. William E. and Laura E. (Manger) P.; m. Jeanne Merle Sargent, Oct. 7, 1949. BS, U.S. Naval Acad., 1946; BSEE, Mass. Inst. Tech., 1948; Naval Engr., MIT, 1955; MSEE, Mass. Inst. Tech., 1955; PhD, U. Calif., 1960; MA, U. Md., 1968. Enlisted USN, 1940, commd. ensign, 1946, advance through grades to capt., 1967, retired, 1973; dir. edn. C.S. Draper Lab., Cambridge, Mass., 1973-74; v.p. academic affairs SUNY Maritime Coll., Ft. Schuyler, 1974—. Home and Office: SUNY Maritime College Fort Schuyler Bronx NY 10465

PORTERA, ALAN AUGUST, religious educator; b. Buffalo, Jan. 29, 1951; s. Albert Andrew and Adele Beatrice (Pecorella) P.; m. Marcia Jean Urbaniak, May 16, 1975; 1 child, Alanna Jachelene. BS, State U. Coll. N.Y., Buffalo, 1974; MS in Edn., Niagara U., 1981; doctoral candidate, SUNY, Buffalo, 1984. Cert. nursery sch., kindergarten, grades 1-6, and art grades K-12, N.Y. Tchr. St. Gregory's, Williamsville, N.Y., 1974-75, St. Mark's, Buffalo, 1975-76, St. James, Depew, N.Y., 1977-79, St. Teresa's, Niagara Falls, N.Y., 1979-89; dir. religious edn. St. Joseph's, North Tonawanda, N.Y., 1978—, Saint Joseph's, Niagara Falls, 1990—; cons. edn. sales Knowledge Nest, Chgo., 1989-90; religious edn. moderator Region 26, 29, 30, Diocese of Buffalo, 1981-83. Author: Concern for Peace and Justice, 1981, Foundations for Faith Formation, 1989, Fundamental Building Blocks of Faith, 1991. Named Religious Educator of the Year Diocese of Buffalo, 1979. Mem. ASCD, Nat. Cath. Educators Assn., We. N.Y. Assn. Dirs. and Coords. Religious Educators (v.p. 1985-87). Democrat. Roman Catholic. Home: 8420 Troy Ave Niagara Falls NY 14304-4333 Office: St Joseph's Catechetical Ministries 1451 Payne Ave North Tonawanda NY 14120-2596 also: 625 Tronolone Pl Niagara Falls NY 14301

PORTERFIELD, CRAIG ALLEN, psychologist, consultant; b. Geneva, N.Y., May 11, 1955; s. Paul Laverne and Elizabeth Louise (Mearns) P.; m. Alta Marie Herring, Aug. 1977; children: Aleine Michelle, Brian Matthew. Student, Sorbonne U., Paris, 1975-76; BA, St. John Fisher Coll., 1977; MA, U. Tex., Austin, 1982, PhD, 1985. Lic. psychologist, N.Y., Del.; cert. sch. psychologist, N.Y. Program evaluation intern Austin Ind. Sch. Dist., 1980, psychol. intern, 1982-83; program evaluator Austin Child Guidance Ctr., 1981-82; evaluation mgr. Child, Inc., Austin, 1981-82; staff therapist Psychotherapy Inst., Austin, 1984-85; consulting psychologist Albany (N.Y.) Psychol. Assocs., 1987-90; staff psychologist Berkshire Farm Ctr. and Svcs. for Youth, Canaan, N.Y., 1985-87, dir. rsch., 1987-90; psychologist Del. Psychiatry Svcs., Dover, 1990—; adj. asst. prof. SUNY-Albany, 1986-87, 89-91; psychologist privileges dept. psychiatry Kent Gen. hosp., Dover, 1990—; adv. com. life skills curriculum Lake Forest Sch. Dist., Harrington, Del., 1991; co-founder, advisor Children with Attention Deficit Disorders of Kent County, Del. Grantee N.Y State Integrated Task Force on Substance Abuse Programs for Youth, 1988. Mem. APA, Del. Psychol. Assn., Nat. Trust Historic Preservation, Wild Quail Country Club. Office: Del Psychiatry Svcs 1001 S Bradford St Dover DE 19901-4141

PORTS, MICHAEL ALLAN, water resources engineer; b. Balt., July 12, 1948; s. Charles Clayton and Ouida Jenette (Blake) P.; m. Lois Gail Seltzer; children: Kelly, Kimberly, Carver. BSCE, U. Md., 1970, MS, 1974. Registered profl. engr., profl. hydrologist; cert. profl. soil erosion control specialist. Hydrologist State Water Resources Adminstrn., Annapolis, Md., 1970-75, chief watershed permits, 1975-80; project mgr. Fed. Energy Regulatory Commn., Washington, 1980-81; sr. hydraulic engr. Michael Baker, Jr., Inc., Houston, 1981-82; chief hydraulic engr. Daniel, Mann, Johnson & Mendenhall, New Orleans, 1982-89; prin. hydraulic engr. Parsons Brinckerhoff, Balt., 1989—. Editor: Hydraulic Engineering, 1989; contbr. articles to profl. jours. Fellow ASCE (chmn. water resources div. 1991-92); mem. Am. Inst. Hydrology, Am. Water Resources Assn., Engring. Soc. Balt., Irish Channel Corner Club, Md. Hist. Soc., Tex. State Geneal. Soc., Ala. Geneal. Soc., Geneal. Soc. Pa. Republican. Office: Parsons Brinckerhoff 301 N Charles St Ste 200 Baltimore MD 21201

PORUSH, JEROME GERSHON, nephrologist; b. Bklyn., Nov. 15, 1930; s. Solomon and Dora (Morowitz) P.; m. Ruth L. Helman, Mar. 28, 1953; children: Maureen, Daniel, Karen. Student, NYU, 1948-51; MD, SUNY, Bklyn., 1955. Diplomate Am. Bd. Internal Medicine, subspecialty of nephrology. Chief renal div. Maimonides Hosp. of Bklyn., 1962-66; chief Div. Nephrology and Hypertension Brookdale Hosp. Med. Ctr., Bklyn., 1966—; prof. medicine SUNY, Bklyn., 1979—; rep. Nat. Kidney Found./Nat. High Blood Pressure Ednl. Prog., Bethesda, Md., 1989-91. Editor: Hypertension and the Kidney, 1985; Renal Disease in the Aged, 1991; contbr. articles to profl. jours. Capt. U.S. Army Med. Corp, 1956-58. Recipient Honig award Nat. Kidney Found., N.Y.C., 1983, Disting. Svc. award, 1983, Pres.'s award, 1986, Frank L. Babbott award Alumni Assn. SUNY, 1990. Fellow Am. Coll. Physicians, Am. Coll. Clin. Pharmacology; mem. Am. Physiol. Soc., Am. Fedn. Clin. Rsch., Am. Soc. Nephrology, N.Y. Soc. Nephrology (pres. 1978-79). Home: 10 E 70th St # 10C New York NY 10021-4947 Office: Brookdale Hosp MC Brookdale Plz Brooklyn NY 11212-3139

PORZECANSKI, ARTURO CUSIEL, economist; b. Montevideo, Uruguay, Nov. 2, 1949; came to U.S., 1966; s. Bernardo and Stephanie (Kochmann) P.; m. Nina Ramondelli, May 25, 1974; children: Marc Vito, Katia Julia. BA, Whittier Coll., 1971; MA, U. Pitts., 1974, PhD, 1975. Rsch. economist Ctr. for Latin Am. Monetary Studies, Mexico City, 1975-77; sr. economist Morgan Guaranty Trust Co. N.Y., N.Y.C., 1977-89; chief economist Republic Nat. Bank N.Y., N.Y.C., 1989—; mem. econ. adv. com. Am. Bankers Assn., Washington, 1990—. Mem. Am. Econ. Assn., Nat. Assn. Bus. Economists, Coun. on Fgn. Rels. Republican. Home: 144 E 84th St Apt 9D New York NY 10028-2041 Office: Republic Nat Bank NY 452 Fifth Ave 9th Fl New York NY 10018

PORZIO, PATRICK FRANCIS, financial executive, portfolio manager; b. N.Y.C., Nov. 27, 1937; s. Fred D. and Antoinette (Prevete) P.; m. Susan Ruth Burstein, Aug. 17, 1969; 1 child, Denise Ann. BS in Acctg., St. John's U., Bklyn., 1959; MBA in Taxation, Pace U., 1966. Chief acct. The Amsinck Corp., N.Y.C., 1959-65, asst. controller, tax mgr., 1966-69, controller, 1970-71, v.p., treas., 1972-77; controller H.J. Baker & Bro., Inc., N.Y.C., 1977-79, treas., 1979, v.p., treas., 1980-82, v.p., chief fin. officer, 1983—, also bd. dirs., 1980—; bd. dirs. W&T Investing Co., In., N.Y.C., 1980—, A&F Investing Co., Inc., N.Y.C., 1980—. Mem. Nat. Assn. Credit Mgrs. (trustee 1983-85), Huntington Yachting Club, KC. Republican. Roman Catholic. Office: HJ Baker & Bro Inc 100 E 42d St New York NY 10017

POSER, JOAN RAPPS, artists agent; b. Plainfield, N.J., Apr. 10, 1940; d. Mandel Max and Marion Davidson Rapps; m. Jay Sanford Poser, Nov. 15, 1964; children: Lester Philip, Toby Anne. BA, U. Conn., 1962. Self-employed travel cons. Lancaster, Pa., 1976-79; tchr. McDonogh Sch., Balt., 1982-90; artist's agt. Joan E. Poser Assocs. Agts. in the Arts, Balt., 1978—; co-owner, v.p. Poser's Apparel, Inc., Pa., 1990—. Pres. Lancaster Town Fair, 1974, Temple Beth El Sisterhood, 1973-77; pres. and devel. chmn. Md. Assocs. for Dyslexic Adults and Youth, Inc., 1989-91; campaign chair Bus. and Profl. Women, Assoc. Jewish Charities, Balt., 1985; spl. events chair Cultural Arts Inst. Chizuk Amuno Congregation, 1986-90, trustee, 1986-90; bd. dirs. Janus Sch., Lancaster, 1991—, Lancaster Jewish Community Ctr., 1991—, Temple Beth El, 1991—. Mem. Hadassah. Democrat. Home: 119 Greenview Dr Lancaster PA 17601-4988

POSNER, BRUCE FREDERICK, not-for-profit foundation executive, consultant; b. N.Y.C., Dec. 28, 1954; s. Jacob and Sylvia (Wouk) P.; m. Deborah Joan Vowler, Feb. 14, 1989; 1 child, Nathaniel Wouk Adam. BS with honors, Fordham U., 1975. With Fund for the City of N.Y., 1976—, systems analyst, programmer, 1979-82, dep. dir. info. svcs., 1982-85, program dir., 1985-90, v.p., 1990—; classical programming dir. Sta. WFUV, N.Y.C., 1974-75, host Concert Grande, 1977—; treas. Chilmark Rsch. Assocs., N.Y.C., 1979-81; mem. adv. com. Reference Point, Teaneck, N.J., 1988—; cons. Citizen's Com. for Children of N.Y., N.Y.C., 1983; bd. Composers Collaborative; mem. decentralization panel Cultural Coun. Found., N.Y.C., 1989—; mem. Tech. Task Force Coun. Founds.; contbr. Notes, Soc. for Med. Decision-Making Soc. for Pub. Adminstrn. Author: (with others) Assuring Quality Out-Patient Care for Children, 1988. Lectr. Computers for Social Change, N.Y.C., 1986, 87, 88; mem. Tech. Task Force Coun. on Founds. Mem. N.Y. Acad. Scis., AAAS, Wagner Soc. of N.Y. (lectr., pianist 1987—), Am. Mus. Natural History, N.Y. Zool. Soc., Fordham Univ. Glee Club (accompanist 1973-76), Fordham U. Women's Chorale (accompanist 1974-76). Home: 360 Cabrini Blvd Apt 5L New York NY 10040-3645 Office: Fund for the City of NY 121 6th Ave Fl 6 New York NY 10013-1590

POSNER, DAVID MARK, family physician; b. N.Y.C., June 27, 1945; s. Herbert and Anne (Seidman) P.; children: Nicole, Eric, Andrea Kate. Student, Bard Coll., 1958; BA, Hofstra U., 1962; DO, U. Health Scis., Kansas City, Mo., 1972; MBA, Loyola Coll., Balt., 1991. Diplomate Am. Bd. Family Practice. Pvt. practice Balt., 1981—; chief exec. officer Triam Aviation Inc., Balt., 1990—; bd. dirs. Cygne Cons. Inc., Balt. Asst. surgeon gen. Pub. Health Svc., 1972-73. Home: 4348 Wild Filly Ct Ellicott City MD 21042 Office: 1020 Saint Paul St Baltimore MD 21202

POSNER, HENRY J., photographer; b. Bronx, N.Y., Dec. 10, 1951; s. Norman Statsinger and Ruth Lee (Glass) P.; m. Virginia Ann Bucci, Feb. 26, 1984; 1 child, Rachel Bucci. BA, Wash. U., St. Louis, 1973. Caseworker II Mo. Divsn. Family Svcs., St. Louis, 1973-75; dir. photography Delma Studios, N.Y.C., 1975-85; dir. ops. Prestige Portraits, Edison, N.J., 1985-91; account mgr. Lifetouch, Oceanside, N.Y., 1991—. Bd. dirs., v.p. Hudson View Owners' Corp., Yonkers, N.Y., 1992. Mem. Profl. Photographers Am. (cert.), Profl. Photographers N.Y., Nikon Profl. Svcs., Bronica Profl. Svcs., Kodak Pro Passport. Jewish.

POSNER, JEROME BEEBE, neurologist, educator; b. Cin., Mar. 20, 1932; s. Philip and Rose (Goldberg) P.; m. Gerta Grunen, Aug. 29, 1954; children: Roslyn, Joel, P.J. B.S., u. Wash., 1951; M.D., U. Wash., 1955. Intern King County Hosp., Seattle, 1955-56; asst. resident in neurology U. Wash. Affiliated Hosps., Seattle, 1956-59; fellow in neurology U. Wash. Affiliated Hosps., 1958-59; spl. fellow NIH, U. Wash., 1961-63; instr. medicine U. Louisville Sch. Medicine, 1959-61; attending neurologist King County Hosp., 1962-63; asst. prof. neurology Cornell U. Med. Coll., N.Y.C., 1963-67; assoc. prof. Cornell U. Med. Coll., 1967-70, prof., 1970—, vice chmn. dept. neurology, 1978-87; asst. attending neurologist N.Y. Hosp., 1963-67, asso. attending neurologist, 1967-70, attending neurologist, 1970—; asso. Cotzias Lab. of Neuro-Oncology, Sloan Kettering Inst. Cancer Research, N.Y.C., 1967-76; mem. Cotzias Lab. of Neuro-Oncology, Sloan Kettering Inst. Cancer Research, 1976—; chief neuropsychiat. service, attending physician dept. medicine Meml. Hosp. for Cancer and Allied Diseases, 1967-75, attending physician, 1975—, chmn. dept. neurology, 1975-87, 89—, Cotzias chair neuro-oncology, 1986; mem. med. adv. bd. Burke Rehab. Center, White Plains, N.Y., 1973—; adj. prof., vis. physician Rockefeller U. and Hosp., N.Y.C., 1973-75; vis. physician Rockefeller U. Hosp., 1980—; mem. med. adv. bd. Assn. for Brain Tumor Research, 1974—; mem. neurology B study sect. NIH, 1972-76. Author: (with F. Plum) Diagnosis of Stupor and Coma, 3d edit, 1980, (with H. Gilbert, L. Weiss) Brain Metastasis, 1980; Mem. editorial bd.: Archives of Neurology, 1971-76, Annals of Neurology, 1976-80, Am. Jour. Medicine, 1978—, N.Y. Med. Quarterly, 1979—; Contbr. articles to med. jours. Served with M.C. U.S. Army, 1959-61. Mem. Am. Acad. Neurology (Farber Brain Tumor award 1983), AAAS, Am. Assn. Cancer Research, Am. Electroencephalographic Soc., Am. Fedn. Clin. Research, AMA, Am. Neurol. Assn., Am. Physiol. Soc., Harvey Soc., Internat. Assn. Study of Pain, N.Y. Acad. Sci., Inst. of Medicine, Soc. Neuroscis., Can. Neurol. Soc. (hon.), Alpha Omega Alpha. Office: Meml Sloan-Kettering Cancer Ctr 1275 York Ave New York NY 10021-6094

POSNER, LOUIS JOSEPH, lawyer, accountant; b. N.Y.C., May 29, 1956; s. Alex Pozner and Hilda G. (Gottlieb) Weinberg; m. Betty F. Osin, June 21, 1986; 1 child, Daniel. BS in Acctg., Drexel U., 1979; MS in Taxation, Pace U., 1985; JD, NYU, 1989. Bar: N.Y. 1990, N.J. 1990, U.S. Dist. Ct. (so. and ea. dists.) N.Y. 1990, D.C. 1991; CPA, N.Y. Auditor Arthur Andersen & Co., CPAs, Phila., 1979-81; tax sr. Kenneth Leventhal & Co., CPAs, N.Y.C., 1981-82; tax mgr. Mann Judd Landau, CPAs, N.Y.C., 1983-86; tax dir. Integrated Resources, Inc., N.Y.C., 1986-89; pvt. practice N.Y.C., 1989—. Mem. ABA, AICPAs, N.Y. State Bar Assn., Assn. of Bar of City of N.Y., N.Y. State Soc. CPAs (tax com. 1985-90, mem. faculty found. for acctg. edn. N.Y.C. chpt. 1989-90), Mensa (coord. spl. interest group N.Y.C. chpt. 1978-90). Home: 300 E 71st St Apt 11J New York NY 10021-5248 Office: 575 Madison Ave Ste 1006 New York NY 10022

POSSEHL, JERRY ROY, naval architect; b. Buffalo, Oct. 4, 1942; s. Norman Arthur and Janet (Rossiter) P.; m. Dorothy Ann Merry, June 26, 1968; children: Barbara Jean, Steven Alan. BSE in Naval Architecture, U Mich., 1965. Naval architect Bur. Ships, Washington, 1963-67, Mare Island Naval Shipyard, Vallejo, Calif., 1967-68, Naval Sea Systems Command, Washington, 1968—; head surface warship stability br. Naval Sea Systems Command, 1988—. Mem. Soc. Naval Architects and Marine Engrs., U.S. Naval Inst. (silver). Republican. Home: 1771 Crofton Pky Crofton MD 21114-2333 Office: Naval Sea Systems Command Code #55W4 Washington DC 20782

POST, ANNE BRETZFELDER, artist; b. St. Louis; d. Ira Lewis and Belle (Schlesinger) Bretzfelder; m. Joseph Post, Mar. 1, 1942; children: David Louis, Thomas Charles. BA in Fine Arts, Bennington Coll., 1938. Works in sculpture, drawing, painting, collage, constrn., water color; exhibited in U.S., Europe, Japan, Israel. Mem. N.Y. Artists Equity. Home: 29 Washington Sq W New York NY 10011

POST, DAVID ALAN, broadcast executive, producer; b. N.Y.C., Oct. 20, 1941; s. Emil R. and Ruth (Rosen) P.; m. Arline Goldbrum, June 10, 1962 (div. 1981); children: Randee, Lori, Jill; m. Katlean de Monchy, Dec. 13, 1984. Student, CCNY, 1959-61; grad., Fleigenheimer Ins. Inst., 1961, N.Y. Inst. Fin., 1968. Sales rep. Aetna Life Ins. Casualty, Hartford, Conn., 1961-63; sales mgr. Globe Rubber Products, Phila., 1963-67; ptnr. Zuckerman Smith and Co., N.Y.C., 1968-71; dir. corp. fin. Andersen and Co., N.Y.C., 1971-72; exec. v.p., dir. R.K. Pace Post Investment Bankers, N.Y.C., 1973-76; chmn., chief exec. officer, founder Page Am. Group, Inc., Hackensack, N.J., 1976-86, also bd. dirs.; vice chmn., founder Channel Am. LPTV Holdings, Inc., N.Y.C., 1986—; founder, chmn. Producers Showcase TV Inc. Contbr. articles to INC. mag.; creator several TV series. Mem. Nat. Assn. TV Programming Execs., Nat. Greyhound Assn., David A. Post Found. Republican. Jewish. Home: 400 E 57th St New York NY 10022-3019 Office: Channel Am TV Network 19 W 21st St Fl 2 New York NY 10010-6805 also: 10th Fl 115 E 57th St New York NY 10022

POST, FREDERICK, banker; b. N.Y.C., Apr. 29, 1962; s. Hans Joachim and Ersilia Rita (Mancusi) P. BS in Ops. Rsch., Columbia U., 1983; MBA in Fin., NYU, 1988. With Swiss Bank Corp., N.Y.C., 1982—, v.p. mgmt. info. systems, 1989—; v.p. mgmt. info. systems Swiss Bank Corp., Basel, Switzerland, 1989-90; v.p. mcht. banking Swiss Bank Corp., N.Y.C., Switzerland, 1990-91; v.p. strategic planning Swiss Bank Corp., Zürich, Switzerland, 1991—. Home: 314 W 77th St New York NY 10024-6868 Office: Swiss Bank Corp PO Box 395 New York NY 10023-0449

POST, KENNETH W., law enforcement executive; b. Saugerties, N.Y., Apr. 2, 1953; s. Claude Howard and Ada Marie (Stage) P.; m. Cheryl Lynn Wood; children: Kenneth W. II, Ashley Alexandria. AAS in Criminal Justice, Ulster Community Coll., Stone Ridge, N.Y., 1980; cert., FBI Nat. Acad., Quantico, Va. From dep. sheriff to adminstrv. lt. Sheriff's Dept. County of Ulster, Kingston, N.Y., 1975-83, sheriff, 1984-86; owner, pres. Ken Post & Assocs. Law Enforcement/Security Cons.'s, Saugerties, 1987—. Recipient letter of commendation Gov. State of N.Y., Albany, 1986, numerous awards state and fed. law enforcement agys., 1975-86. Office: Ken Post & Assocs PO Box 54 Saugerties NY 12477-0054

POST, NANCY, organizational development executive; b. Bklyn., May 11, 1957; d. Joseph and Betty (Meltzer) P. BA, U. Pa., 1979; MA, Traditional Acupuncture Inst., 1984; cert., Houston Sch. for Psychotherapy, 1978. Diplomate nationally in acupuncture; lic. psychotherapist, Pa., Md. Dir. Health Wellness Project, Phila.; prin. investigator Facilitators, Inc., Las Vegas, Nev.; dir. faculty and rsch. Merriam Hill Ctr., Cambridge, Mass.; prin. Post Enterprises, Phila.; founder Systems Energetics; exec. coach Wharton Advanced Mgmt. Program, 1991—. Grantee in field. Mem. Orgn. Devel. Network, Pa. Acupuncture Soc. Home: 616 W Upsal St Philadelphia PA 19119-3626

POST, ROBERT LICKELY, physiologist; b. Phila., Nov. 4, 1920; s. Levi Arnold and Grace Hutcheson (Lickely) P.; m. Grace Elizabeth Rawlings, Oct. 22, 1947. BS magna cum laude, Harvard U., 1942, MD, 1945. Intern Hartford (Conn.) Hosp., 1945-46; instr. Med. Sch. U. Pa., Phila., 1946-48, vis. prof. Med. Sch., 1991—; from instr. to prof. Med. Sch. Vanderbilt U., Nashville, 1948-91. Recipient Cole award Biophys. Soc., 1983. Home: 3300 Darby Rd Apt 6303 Haverford PA 19041-1074 Office: U Pa Sch of Medicine Dept of Physiology Philadelphia PA 19104-6085

POSTERARO, ANTHONY FRANCIS, periodontist; b. N.Y.C., Dec. 5, 1915; s. Vincent and Connie Dora (Iorio) P.; m. Lygia M. Paganelli, June 23, 1943; children: Anthony Francis Jr., Robert, David. AB, Fordham U., 1939; DDS, St. Louis U., 1943; cert. in periodontia, NYU, 1952. Pvt. practice N.Y.C., 1947—; dental surgeon Boys Club N.Y., N.Y.C., 1947-50; mem. dental staff N.Y. Eye and Ear Infirmary, N.Y.C., 1952-56; instr. periodontics NYU Coll. Dentistry, N.Y.C., 1952-56, asst. prof. periodontics and oral medicine, 1956-68, assoc. prof., 1969-70, assoc. prof. grad. prosthodontics, 1970-72, assoc. prof. periodontics, 1973-75, clin. assoc. prof., 1976-88; sec. William J. Gies Found. for Advancement Dentistry, Bethesda, Md., 1975-89. Assoc. editor Annals Dentistry, 1963-79. Spl. examiner Mcpl. CSC City N.Y., 1955; mem. adv. com. N.Y. State Edn. Dept., 1970. Capt. AUS, 1943-46, PTO. Recipient Instr. of Yr. award NYU Sr. Class and Student Coun., 1961, 63, 64, 66, sv. citation NYU Coll. Dentistry, 1977, Chmn.'s award Am. Cancer Soc., N.Y.C., 1986, 87, 88, Pierre Fauchard award Pierre Fauchard Acad., 1988. Fellow Am. Coll. Dentists (chmn. 1968-69), N.Y. Acad. Dentistry (chmn. exec. com. 1960, 72, 73, pres. 1973); mem. ADA (del. 1964-77), 1st Dist. Dental Soc. (pres. 1963), Delta Sigma Delta, Omicron Kappa Upsilon. Roman Catholic. Home: 19 Byron Ln Larchmont NY 10538 Office: 115 E 61st St New York NY 10021

POSTHUMUS, CAROL LAYTHAM (MRS. JOHN T. MOHAN, JR.), public relations executive; b. Passaic, N.J., Feb. 13, 1944; d. Lawrence and Martha Alice (Laytham) P.; m. Robert L. Wintemberg, (div. Dec. 1980); 1 child, Timothy Del; m. John T. Mohan, Jr., Nov. 1, 1986. BA in English, Pa. State U., 1965. Reporter, theatre critic The Daily Collegian, State Coll., Pa., 1964-65; mng. editor Froth Mag., State Coll., 1964-65; staff writer The Herald-News, Passaic, 1965; editorial copy writer Conde Nast Mags., N.Y.C., 1965-66; editor, reporter, columnist Today Newspapers, Wanye, N.J., 1972-78; pub. information officer, pub. rels. mgr., advt. mgr. Fairleigh Dickinson U., Rutherford, N.J., 1978-85; cons. Rutgers U., Newark, N.J., 1986-87, 92, State of N.J., Div. on Women, Trenton, 1987-88, Fordham U., N.Y.C., 1986-90; cons. Am. Cyanamid, 1986—, Fairleigh Dickinson U., 1987—, Blunt Hann Sersen Inc., 1990—. Editor: Fordham U. President's Report, 1984-85, 85-86 (Silver award 1987), Inside Fordham, 1986-88, The Bride's Reference Book, 1966, newsletter, Parent-Tchr. Orgn., Wayne, 1973-75; contbr. articles to mags. Bd. dirs. Lakeland Valley Family YMCA, Wayne, 1974-76. Recipient News Writing award, Pica Club of North Jersey, 1977, Hist. Feature Writing award, Exxon Corp., 1976, Outstanding Sr. award, Pa. State U., 1965. Mem. N.J. Press Assn. (writing awards 1974-77), Greater Wayne Area C. of C., Packanack Lake Country Club. Republican. Presbyterian. Office: CLP/PR 22 Packanack Lake Rd Wayne NJ 07470-5810

POSTON, JOHN MICHAEL, biochemist; b. Kalispell, Mont., Oct. 16, 1935; s. Howard Joseph and Mabel Lenore (Iverson) P.; m. Annette Marlane Dapp, July 15, 1967; children: Janice Marie, Susanne Marlene, Todd Russell. BS in Chemistry, Mont. State Coll., 1958; MS in Biochemistry, U. N.D., 1960, PhD in Biochemistry, 1970. Chemist Nat. Heart Inst. NIH, Bethesda, Md., 1961-69, rsch. biochemist Nat. Heart, Lung and Blood Inst., 1970—; mem. organizing com. Int Symposium on Cellular Regulation, Bethesda, 1984, Symposium on Cellular Regulation, New Orleans, 1990. Contbr. over 25 articles in biochemistry to profl. jours. Bd. dirs. Glenbrook Found., Bethesda, 1982-85, The Ivymount Sch., Rockville, Md., 1985—. NIH predoctoral fellow NIH, 1969-70; recipient travel grant Int. Symposium on Metabolism, Charleston, S.C., 1980. Mem. Am. Chem. Soc., Am. Soc. Biochemistry and Molecular Biology, Am. Soc. Microbiology, Sigma Xi. Lutheran. Home: 29 Orchard Way S Rockville MD 20854-6129 Office: NHLBI Lab of Biochemistry 3/216 NIH Bethesda MD 20892

POTASEK, MARY JOYCE, physicist, researcher; b. Mpls., Oct. 27, 1945; d. Chester and Millie Potasek. BA in Math., Coll. St. Catherine, 1967; MS in Physics, U. Ill., 1970, PhD, 1974. Research asst. U. Ill., Urbana, 1970-74; research scientist Internat. Bus. Machines, Watson Research Ctr., Yorktown Heights, N.Y., 1974-75; NSF, AAUW postdoctoral fellow Princeton (N.J.) U., 1975-78; NATO postdoctoral fellow Max Planck Inst., Gottingen, West Germany, 1978-80; mem. tech. staff AT&T, Princeton, 1980-86, AT&T Bell Labs., Murray Hill, N.J., 1986-90, Columbia U., N.Y.C., 1990—. Contbr. articles to profl. jours. Mem. AAAS, Optical Soc. of Am., Am. Phys. Soc., Phi Beta Kappa, Pi Mu Epsilon. Home: 197 Dodds Ln Princeton NJ 08540-4105

POTEAT, HARRY TOWSLEY, pathologist; b. Phila., Feb. 23, 1961; s. John and Janis (Towsley) P.; m. Paula Kadison, May 27, 1990. BA, Pomona Coll., 1984; ScD, Harvard Sch. Pub. Health, 1990; MD, Duke U., 1991. Researcher Haseltine Lab./Dana Farber Cancer Inst., Boston, 1987-90; resident Brigham & Women's Hosp., Boston, 1991—; speaker in field. Contbr. articles to Science, Jour. of Virology. Recipient Grad. fellowship NRSA, 1987-89. Mem. AAAS, AMA, Harvard Club of Boston, Sigma Xi. Home: 382 Commonwealth Ave Apt 21 Boston MA 02215-2827

POTOCKI, KENNETH ANTHONY, physicist; b. Chgo., Oct. 8, 1940; s. Stanley Matthew and Sophie (Wazienska) P.; m. Donna Jean Anderson, Aug. 19, 1964; children: John Kyle, Dawn Sophia, Clinton Casimir. BS in Physics, Loyola U., Chgo., 1962; MS in Physics, Ind. U., 1965, PhD in Physics, 1968. Prin. prof. staff mem. Applied Physics Lab. Johns Hopkins U., Laurel, Md., 1970—; edn. cons. Johns Hopkins U., Balt., 1971—; Capt. U.S. Army, 1968-70. Mem. Am. Phys. Soc., Am. Geophys. Union, Assn. Quality and Participation, Am. Def. Preparedness Assn. Home: 15460 Union Chapel Rd Woodbine MD 21797-7716 Office: Johns Hopkins U Applied Physics Lab Johns Hopkins Rd Laurel MD 20723-6099

POTOREIKO, JEAN FRANCES, emergency complaint operator; b. Bklyn., Apr. 4, 1940; d. John Patrick Reeves and Callie Belle (Bales) Reeves-Foster; m. Henry James Potoreiko, Jan. 2, 1958; children: Barbara Ann, Joan Marie, Henry James Jr., Patricia Jean, Lisa Louise, Pamela Ellen, Douglas Bryant, Meredith Rose. Grad. high sch., Bklyn. Telephone co. operator N.Y. Telephone Co., N.Y.C., 1956-57; waitress, hostess Brass Rail, N.Y.C., 1966-68; wire bonder Circuit Tech., Farmingdale, N.Y., 1974-76; inspector Circuit Tech., Farmingdale, 1977-79; custodian, bus driver South Manor Sch. Dist., Manorville, N.Y., 1981-83; interviewer Dept. of Commerce, N.Y.C., 1983-85; emergency complaint operator Suffolk County Police Dept., Yaphank, N.Y., 1985—. Republican. Roman Catholic. Home: 25 Florence Dr Manorville NY 11949-9513

POTTER, EMMA JOSEPHINE HILL, language educator; b. Hackensack, N.J., July 18, 1921; d. James Silas and Martha Loretta (Pyle) Hill; m. James H. Potter, Mar. 26, 1949. AB cum laude with honors in Classics (scholar), Alfred (N.Y.) U., 1943; AM, Johns Hopkins U., 1946. Tchr. Latin, Balt. County Pub. Schs., 1943-44; instr. French, Spanish, Balt. Poly. Inst., 1950-83; instr. Spanish adult edn. classes, 1946-48; treas. Bruno-Potter Inc., acctg. Trustee James Harry Potter Gold Medal, ASME. Mem. Johns Hopkins U., Alfred U. alumni assns., Internat. Platform Assn., N.J. Assn. Women Bus. Owners, Johns Hopkins U. Faculty Club. Democrat. Home: 419 3d Ave Avon By The Sea NJ 07717

POTTER, LEROY MINTEER, podiatrist; b. Chgo., June 13, 1936; s. Leroy Reed and Mary Alice (Minteer) P.; m. Julia Ann Hovey (div. Dec. 1973); children: John Theodore, Julia Elizabeth; m. Jeanne Marie Kaltenbach, Dec. 24, 1975. Student, Allegheny Coll., 1954-56, U. Pitts., 1956-57; DPM, Ohio Coll. Podiatric Medicine, 1962. Diplomate Am. Bd. Podiatric Medicine, Am. Soc. Pain Mgmt. Clinician Youngstown (Ohio) Foot Clinic, 1972-74; pvt. practice Butler, Pa., 1964—; mem. staff Butler County Meml. Hosp., 1991. Bd. mem. Irene Stacey Mental Health, Butler, 1971-73, Butler Symphony, 1968-73, Dept. Pub. Welfare, Butler, 1971-73. Recipient Ernest E. Eaton award Boy Scouts Am., Butler, 1954, Eagle Scout award, New Brunswick, N.J., 1952. Mem. Pa. Podiatric Med. Assn. (bd. mem. 1974-78, pres. N.W. div. 1972-74), Alumni Assn. Ohio Coll Podiatric Medicine (bd. mem. 1987-91). Office: 425 N Main St Butler PA 16001-4361

POTTER, MARK JAMES, secondary education educator; b. Balt., Apr. 11, 1962; s. Donald W. and Patricia (Terzi) P. BS, Towson State U., 1984, MEd, 1991. Cert. secondary tchr., Md. Tchr., dir. devel. Archbishop Curley High Sch., Balt., 1984—; v.p. St. Clement Sch. Bd. Edn., Balt., 1990—. Editor Archbishop Curley High Sch. Alumni Newsletter, 1987—, Archbishop Curley Family Newsletter, 1987—, Archbishop Curley High Sch. Ann. Report, 1987-91. Mem. Cath. Orgn. Devel. Execs., Nat. Cath. Edn. Assn., Nat. Eagle Scout Assn., Towson State U. Alumni Assn. (chairperson admissions com.), Sons of Italy, KC. Republican. Office: Archbishop Curley High Sch 3701 Sinclair Ln Baltimore MD 21213-2079

POTTER, MARSHALL RICHARD, government official; b. Washington, Jan. 16, 1948; s. Charles and Martha (Caplin) P.; m. Sigla Chana Narzisenfeld, Nov. 14, 1976; children: Shaya Joseph, Reena Rachel, Talya Aviva. BEE with high honors, U. Md., 1971, MEE, 1973, MS in Computer Sci., 1979. Electronics engr. David Taylor Naval Ship Research and Devel. Ctr., Bethesda, Md., 1971-73, Def. Communications Agy., Reston, Md., 1973-80; head Software Engring. br. Naval Electronics Systems Command, Washington, 1980-84; asst. for tech. Office of the Asst. Sec. of the Navy, Washington, 1984-87, dir. tech. assessment div., 1987-90, dir. systems engring., 1990—; adj. assoc. prof. U. Md., Coll. Park, 1987-91; dir. Systems Engring. Mgmt. Office of the Asst. Sec. of the Navy, Washington, 1991—. Mem. IEEE, Assn. of Computing Machinery, Tau Beta Pi, Eta Kappa Nu, Omicron Delta Kappa. Jewish. Home: 10910 Oakwood St Silver Spring MD 20901-4419 Office: Office of the Asst Sec Navy Bldg 166 Washington Navy Yard Washington DC 20374

POTTER, PATRICIA ANN, psychiatrist; b. Portsmouth, Va., Sept. 22, 1951; d. Maxwell Gideon and Bernice Vivian (Padget) P. BA, Harvard U., 1973; MD, Tufts U., 1977. Diplomate Am. Bd. Psychiatry and Neurology, Am. Bd. Psychiatry, Am. Bd. Child Psychiatry. Intern in medicine Meml. Hosp., Worcester, Mass., 1977-78; resident in psychiatry Tufts Affiliated Hosps., Boston, 1978-82; fellow in child psychiatry McLean Hosp., Belmont, Mass., 1982-84, asst. child psychiatrist, 1984—; instr. in psychiatry Harvard U. Med. Sch., Boston, 1984—; cons. psychiatrist Thom Clinic, Boston, 1984-88, Brandeis U., Waltham, Mass., 1987—. Mem. Mass. Psychiatric Soc., Mass. Med. Soc., Am. Acad. Child and Adolescent Psychiatry, N.Eng. Coun. Child and Adolescent Psychiatry, Am. Psychiatric Assn., Am. Psychoanalytic Assn. Office: 1280 Massachusetts Ave Cambridge MA 02138-3840

POTTER, PEGGY MARIE, broadcast executive; b. Rochester, N.Y., Jan. 23, 1955; d. Milton Lester and Marie Elizabeth (Howe) P. Student, Adirondack Community Coll., 1983, 85, 87. Office mgr. Zales Jewelers, Greece, N.Y., 1973-74, Lynn, Lynn & Miller, Albany, N.Y., 1974-83; bus. mgr. JAG Communications, Albany, 1983-87; corp. bus. mgr. Radio Terr. Inc., Albany, 1987—; bus. mgr. Hudson House, Inc., Cold Springs, N.Y., 1990—. Mem. Broadcast Cable Fin. Mgmt., Am. Legion Aux. (pub. rels. 1983-84). Office: Radio Terrace Inc 341 Northern Blvd Albany NY 12204

POTTER, RICHARD KEVIN, management company executive; b. Washington, Sept. 7, 1959; s. Lawrence Donovan and Mary Helen (Montgomery) P. BA, St. Mary's Coll., 1983; MBA, Loyola Coll., 1990. Cert. mgmt. cons. Contr. Borg-Warner Corp., Washington, 1983-85; fin. mgr. York (Pa.) Internat., 1985-88, mktg. group mgr., 1988-90; pres. Atlantic Internat. Mgmt. Corp., York, 1990—; bd. dirs. Inst. for Closely Held Cos., York, Pache Corp., Waldorf, Md. Author: Service Excellence for Small Business, 1990; contbr. articles to profl. jours. Pres. Student Govt. Assn., St. Mary City, Md., 1982-83, Coll Reps., 1982-83; pres. Hunters Hill Community Assn., York, 1990. Recipient Outstanding Citizen award Balt., 1985, Outstanding Contbn., Jr. Achievement, 1987. Mem. Inst. Mgmt. Cons., Platonic Soc. (pres. 1988—), York C. of C. Office: York Internat 30 Copperwood Ct York PA 17404-9720

POTTER, ROBERT ARTHUR, foundation administrator, communications consultant; b. New River, Tenn., Nov. 11, 1938; s. Gordon Byrd and Frances Elizabeth (Phillips) P.; m. Blair Burns, 1974; children: Lillian Howard, Gordon Leonard. BA, San Francisco State U., 1965. Newsman Wall St. Jour., San Francisco, 1965, UPI, San Francisco, 1965-66; writer/editor McGraw-Hill Publs., San Francisco/Washington, 1966-69; pub. affairs officer Johns Hopkins Sch. Medicine, Balt., 1969-71; assoc. dir. programs in pub. understanding of sci. AAAS, Washington, 1971-73; dir. info. Oak Ridge (Tenn.) Associated Univs., 1973-80; dir. univ. communications U. Mich., Ann Arbor, 1980-87; dir. communications Howard Hughes Med. Inst., Bethesda, Md., 1987—; cons. Gov's. Commn. on Nursing Homes, Balt., 1972-73, Study on Surg. Svcs. in the U.S., Balt., Chgo., 1973-75, Nat. Cancer Inst., Washington, 1974-75, U. Chgo.Med. Ctr., 1983, Lincoln U., Oxford, Pa. 1987-91. Contbr. articles to profl. jours. Chmn. United Way Campaign U. Mich., Ann Arbor, 1982; mem. pub. affairs commn. Mich. Heart Assn., Lansing, 1980-82. Recipient award of excellence Soc. for Tech. Commnunications, 1976, award of distinction Creativity/Art Direction mag., 1977, 91, citation Coun. for Advancement of Edn., 1982, Grand Gold medal, 1987. Mem. Nat. Press Club, Communications Network in Philanthropy. Office: Howard Hughes Med Inst 6701 Rockledge Dr Bethesda MD 20817

POTTER, TREVOR ALEXANDER MCCLURG, lawyer; b. Chgo., Oct. 24, 1955; s. Charles Steele and Barbara (McClurg) P. AB, Harvard Coll., 1978; JD, U. Va., 1982. Bar: Ill. 1983, D.C. 1988. Spl. asst. to asst. atty. gen. Office Legal Policy U.S. Dept. Justice, Washington, 1982-84; asst. gen. counsel FCC, Washington, 1984-85; assoc. Wiley, Rein & Fielding, Washington, 1985-88, ptnr., 1988-91; commr. Fed. Election Commn., Washington, 1991—. Mem. overseer's vis. com. Meml. Ch., Harvard U., Cambridge, Mass., 1987—. Republican. Episcopalian. Mem. ABA (vice-chmn. com. on election law, adminstrv. law sect. 1991-92). Office: Fed Election Commn 999 E St NW 9th Fl Washington DC 20463

POTTER, VINCENT GEORGE, philosophy educator; b. N.Y.C., Oct. 18, 1928; s. Vincent George and Mary Margaret (Hogan) P. AB, Bellarmine Coll., Plattsburg, N.Y., 1953, PhL, 1954; STL, St. Albert De Louvain, Belgium, 1961; PhD, Yale U., 1965. Instr. philosophy St. Peter's Coll., Jersey City, 1954-57; from asst. prof. to dept. chmn. Fordham U., Bronx, 1965-78, rector, Jesuit Community, 1978-83, v.p. for acad. affairs, 1987-92, prof. philosophy, 1992—. Author: C.S. Peirce on Norms and Ideals, 1969, Readings in Epistemology: Descartes, Locke, Berkeley, Hume, Kant, 1988, Philosophy of Knowledge, 1989; editor: Doctrine and Experience, 1984; editor-in-chief Internat. Philos. Quar., 1985—; contbr. articles to profl. jours. Trustee Fordham U., 1978-83. Mem. Am. Philos. Assn., Am. Cath. Philos. Assn., Soc. for Advancement of Am. Philosophy, C.S. Peirce Soc. (pres.). Roman Catholic. Office: Fordham U Adm 112 Bronx NY 10458

POTTER, WILLIAM BLAKE, language professional, educator; b. Evanston, Ill., Nov. 28, 1955; s. Jack and Jean (Scott) P. BA in Drama, N.Mex. State U., 1979; MA in English, CUNY Grad. Ctr., 1990, postgrad., 1990—. adj. prof. of English, Coll. of Staten Island, N.Y., 1990—; active Friday Forum com., CUNY Grad. Ctr., 1990-91. Actor numerous theatrical prodns.; bd. dirs. No Empty Space Theatre, Staten Island, 1987—. Recipient citation for excellence in acting, Am. Coll. Theatre Festival, Dallas/Ft. Worth, 1978, finalist Irene Ryan scholarship, 1978. Mem. U.S. Chess Fedn., ACLU, People for the American Way, Modern Lang. Assn., Mensa. Democrat.

POTTER, WILLIAM JAMES, investment banker; b. Toronto, Ont., Can., Aug. 11, 1948; s. William Wakely and Ruby Loretta (Skidmore) P.; m. Linda Lee, Nov. 25, 1972; children: Lisa Michelle, Meredith Lee, Andrew David. AB, Colgate U., 1970; MBA, Harvard U., 1974. With White Weld & Co., Inc., N.Y.C., 1974-75, Toronto Dominion Bank, Toronto (Can.) and N.Y., 1975-78; group mgr. Toronto Dominion Bank, Toronto, 1979-82; 1st v.p. Barclays Bank PLC, N.Y.C., 1982-84; mng. dir. Prudential-Bache Securities, Inc., N.Y.C., 1984-89; gen. ptnr. Sphere Capital Ptnrs., N.Y.C., 1989—; pres. Ridgewood Ptnrs. Ltd., N.Y.C., 1989—; advisor Ladenberg Thalman Internat., 1990—; bd. dirs. first Australia Fund Inc., Md., First Australia Prime Income Fund Inc., Md., First Autralia Prime Income Co. Ltd., New Zealand, Heartland Fin. Corp., Impulsora del Fondo Mex., Mexico City, Alexandria Bancorp, Can., First Commonwealth Fund, Md. Author: Finance for the Minerals Industry, 1985. Bd. dirs. Glen Ridge (N.J.) Community Fund, 1985—, fin. Glen Ridge Congl. Ch., 1985—. Mem. Nat. Fgn. Trade Coun. (bd. dirs., chmn. fin. com.), Harvard Club, Williams Club (N.Y.C.), Nat. Club (Toronto), Glen Ridge Country Club (N.J.), Buck Hill Country Club (Pa.), Capitol Hill Club (Washington), Internat. Platform Assn. (Washington). Congregationalist. Office: Ridgewood Ptnrs Ltd 261 Madison Ave New York NY 10016

POTTERFIELD, JOAN ELLEN, software engineer; b. Queens, N.Y., May 19, 1953; d. Joseph Ralph and Eleanor (Chotiner) P.; m. John Glen Myers, June 23, 1984. BA, Brown U., 1975. Software engr. Digital Equipment Co., Maynard, Mass., 1975-79, Computer Scis. Internat. Deutschland, Flensburg, Fed. Republic Germany, 1980-81; sr. software engr. GE, Fort Washington, Pa., 1982—. Age Group award Houston Tenneco Marathon, 1989, 90, Marine Corps Marathon, Washington, 1989, ODS Portland (Oreg.) Marathon, 1990. Mem. IEEE Computer Soc., Mid Atlantic Athletic Congress, Delco Road Runners Club. Democrat. Unitarian. Office: GE PO Box 8048 Philadelphia PA 19101-8048

POTTERS, EDWARD PAUL, computer system professional, painter; b. Glen Ridge, N.J., Dec. 10, 1951; s. Milton and Sally (Wienrauch) P.; m. Jean Marie Sheredos, July 2, 1983; 1 child, David John. Painting and drawing instr. Union County Coll., Cranford, N.J., 1982-87; with system support dept. AT&T, Parsippany, N.J., 1984-85; system adminstr. Mitchell Supreme Fuel Co., Orange, N.J., 1987—. One man exhbns. include Union Coll., Cranford, 1984, Alumni Exhbn., 1986, N.J. Fellowship Exhbn., 1988; represented in permanent collections Kean Coll., Union, N.J.. N.J. State Coun. on Arts fellow, 1983, 87. Home: 11 Brittany Rd Succasunna NJ 07876

POTTIE, DAVID LAREN, magazine publisher; b. Groton, Conn., Aug. 24, 1952; s. Laren Maurice and Eleanor Jean (Makowicki) P. Student, Cen. Conn. State Coll., 1970-73. Fisherman various sailing and comml. boats, 1973-77; owner The Market, New London, Conn., 1977-82; photographer CT Video, Old Saybrook, Conn., 1982-85; photographer, owner Shore News Svc./Photo, Stonington, Conn., 1985—; owner, dir. Shore News Svc./Video, Stonington, 1985—; pub., editor Sound Waves Mag., Stonington, 1990—, Dining Out in Southeastern New Eng. mag. Mem. Holy Ghost Soc. Republican. Roman Catholic. Home and Office: 30 Shawondassee Dr Stonington CT 06378-2424

POTTLE, CHRISTOPHER, electrical engineering educator; b. New Haven, Feb. 14, 1932; s. Frederick Albert and Marion Isabel (Starbird) P.; m. Marcia Lorraine Blanchard Suthon, June 17, 1961; children—Samuel W., Manette B., John F. B.Engring., Yale U., 1953; M.S., U. Ill., 1958, Ph.D., 1962. Asst. prof. Cornell U., Ithaca, N.Y. 1962-66, assoc. prof., 1966-80, prof. elec. engring., 1980—, assoc. dean coll. engring, 1986-90. Contbr. articles to profl. jours. Chmn. Area Congregations Together Tompkins County, Ithaca, 1978-83; nat. treas, Episcopal Peace Fellowship, Washington, 1985—. With U.S. Army, 1954-56. Fulbright scholar, 1966-67. Mem. IEEE (sr.), Assn. Computing Machinery. Democrat. Episcopalian. Home: 107 Irving Pl Ithaca NY 14850-4711 Office: Cornell U Sch Elec Engring 384 Engr and Theory Ctr Ithaca NY 14853

POTTS, BERNARD, lawyer; b. Balt., Aug. 22, 1915; s. Phillip Louis and Anna (Novey) P.; m. Frieda Hochman, 1949; children: Phillip Louis, Neal Allen, Bryan H., Andrea Maria. ABA, Balt. Coll. Commerce, 1936; LLB, Eastern U., Balt., 1949; JD, U. Balt., 1950. Bar: Md. 1950. Tax cons. Balt., 1936-49, since practiced in Balt., 1949—; ptnr., sr. counsel Potts & Potts, Balt., 1975—. Founder, counsel Gamber Community Vol. Fire Co., 1968; founder, pres. Mary Dopkin's Children's Fund, 1950-60; founder, v.p. Boys Town Homes Md., 1965-80; founder, chmn. Accident and Prevention Bur. Md., 1965-75; pres. Safety First Club Md., 1966-68; mem. Md. bd. NCCJ, 1976-80; bd. dirs. NCCJ-Md. Conf. Social Concern, 1976-80; co-founder, co-chmn. Greater Balt. Mental Health Coun., 1980; founder E. Balt. Children's Fund, Coun. Ind. Self-Help, Police Community Rels. Couns.,

Crime Prevention Bur. Md.; co-founder Md. chpt. Boys & Girls Club Am., 1988; pro bono adviser, bd. dirs. Patterson Emergency Food Ctr. & Soup Kitchen, Bea Gaddy Homes for Homeless Women & Children Inc.; pro bono atty. Trancare, Inc., Md. Vernon Youth Ctr. Served with AUS, 1943. Recipient cert. police community rels. Mich. Police Inst., 1961, Disting. Citizens award Office Gov. Md., 1971, Presdl. citation Balt. City Council, 1977, Outstanding Alumnus award Mt. Vernon Law Sch., Eastern U., 1970, Wheel Master's award Metro Civic Assn., 1963; numerous awards B'nai B'rith, Safety First Club Md. Am. Bar Assn., Fed. Bar Assn., Am. Trial Lawyers Assn., Balt. Bar Assn., Met. Civic Assn. Balt. (v.p. 1968-80), Humanitarian Assn. Md. (v.p.), Jewish War Vets. (past post comdr.), Masons, B'nai B'rith (past pres. Balt. 1965, internat. commr. community svcs. 1972—, sec. CVS exec. commn.). Home: 3206 Midfield Rd Baltimore MD 21208-4420 Office: Ste 1207 Court Sq Bldg Baltimore MD 21202

POTTS, HAROLD FRANCIS, JR., elevator company executive; b. Pittsfield, Mass., July 25, 1955; s. Harold Francis and Dorothy (Anderson) P.; m. Annie Laura Towle, May 14, 1977; children: David Francis, Douglas Norman, Joseph Harold. AA, Holyoke (Mass.) Community Coll., 1975; BS in BA, We. New Eng. Coll., Springfield, Mass., 1977; MBA, We. New Eng. Coll., 1989. Sales rep. Bay State Elevator Co., Springfield, Mass., 1977-81; customer svc. mgr. Bay State Elevator Co., 1981-84, v.p., treas., 1984-91; pres., 1991—; bd. dirs. Bay State Elevator Co., 1986—; treas., bd. dirs. Air Flyte, Inc., Westfield, Mass., 1989—. Sec. Sch. Bldg. com. Town of Granville, Mass., 1987-90, mem. fin. bd., 1988-89, moderator, 1990-91. Mem. Assn. Am. Weather Observers (v.p. 1988-89, sec. 1991—), Mt. Washington Observatory (ops. com. 1992—), The Master's Sch. (devel. com. 1991—). Republican. Home: Hartland Hollow Rd Granville MA 01034 Office: Bay State Elevator Co PO Box 1210 Springfield MA 01101-1210

POTTS, TIMOTHY ALAN, executive; b. Middletown, Conn., Oct. 21, 1951; s. Alan Samuel and Rita (Miller) P.; m. Diane Nancy Frate, Apr. 4, 1970; children: Tamera, Timothy Jr., Rebecca. BSME, Northeastern U., 1974, MSME, 1974; MBA, U. COnn., 1979. Application engr. Dorr-Oliver, Stamford, Conn., 1974-78, mktg. engr. internat., 1978-80, sr. mktg. engr. internat., 1980-83, mgr. value engr., 1983-85; dir. mktg. Mott Metallurgical, Farmington, Conn., 1985-86; v.p. sales, mktg. Intec Corp., Trumbull, Conn., 1986-89; pres., chief exec. officer Sira Inc., Darien, Conn., 1989—. Inventor in field; contbr. articles to profl. jours. Dist. rep. Rep. Town Meeting, Darien, 1976-78. Mem. Tech. Assn. Pulp and Paper Industry. Republican. Roman Catholic. Office: Sira Inc 722 Post Rd Darien CT 06820

POTVIN, DOUGLAS LEO, loan specialist; b. Fredericksburg, Va., Oct. 14, 1966; s. Frank Leo and Betty Jane (Martin) P.; m. Sara Ann Stump, Nov. 25, 1989. BSc, Bridgewater Coll., 1989. Computer clk. Nat. Marine Fisheries Svc., Silver Spring, Md., 1986-88, loan asst., 1989-91, loan specialist, 1991—. Active Combined Fed. Campaign, 1989. Home: 38R Enon St # 218 Beverly MA 01915 Office: Nat Marine Fisheries Svc One Blackburn Dr Gloucester MA 01930

POTWIN, CONNIE MARIE, nurse; b. Pittsfield, Mass., Nov. 13, 1962; d. Ronald Arthur and Linda Mae (Neff) P.; m. Mark Jeffrey Kreplin, Sept. 10, 1988; 1 child, Alyssa Marie. Assoc., Morrisville (N.Y.) Coll., 1984. Nurse's aide Chase Meml. Nursing Home, New Berlin, N.Y., lic. practical nurse; nurse's aide Bapt. Retirement Ctr., Scotia, N.Y.; registered profl. nurse Amsterdam (N.Y.) Meml. Hosp., 1984-88, nurse preceptor, 1988-91; nurse Vis. Nurses Svc. Assn., Schenectady, N.Y., 1991—, Community Health Ctr., Johnstown, N.Y., 1991—. Regents Nursing scholar, 1981-84. Mem. People for the Ethical Treatment Animals. Republican. Roman Catholic. Home: RD 5 Pine Meadow Trailer Pk Amsterdam NY 12010

POUCHER, JOHN SCOTT, systems engineer, physicist; b. Evanston, Ill., Apr. 10, 1945; s. George Edward and Marcia Irene (Smith) P.; m. Lois Miriam Gross, Aug. 2, 1969; children: Gregory Evan, Brian Eric. BS, MIT, 1967, PhD, 1971. Instr. in physics MIT, Cambridge, Mass., 1971-74; asst. prof. physics Vanderbilt U., Nashville, 1974-80; mem. tech. staff AT&T Bell Labs., Holmdel, N.J., 1981-86, disting. mem. tech. staff, 1986—; vis. fellow Cornell U., Ithaca, N.Y., 1978-79. Contbr. articles to Phys. Rev. Letters, Phys. Letters, Phys. Rev., other jours. and confs. Mem. IEEE, AIAA, Am. Phys. Soc., Union Concerned Scientists, Fedn. Am. Scientists, Common Cause, Sigma Xi. Office: AT&T Bell Labs 101 Crawfords Corner Rd Holmdel NJ 07733-1948

POULIN, RONALD F., internist; b. Lynn, Mass., Nov. 9, 1948; s. E.J. and Eleanor E. (Palmer) P.; m. Charlotte Ann Kershaw, July 1, 1972; children: Douglas, Amy. BS, McGill U., Montreal, Can., 1970; MD, Tufts U., 1974. Diplomate Am. Bd. Internal Medicine; diplomate Am. Bd. Internal Medicine Oncology. Intern Wis. U. Med. Sch., Madison, 1974-75, resident, 1975-77; fellow Harvard U., Boston, 1977-79; pvt. practice Lexington, Mass., 1979—; bd. dirs. Symmes Care, Arlington, Mass.; corporator Symmes Hosp., Arlington, 1992—. Mem. Rotary. Office: 16 Clarke St Lexington MA 02173-4900

POUNCEY, PETER RICHARD, college president, classics educator; b. Tsingtao, Shantung, China, Oct. 1, 1937; came to U.S., 1964; s. Cecil Alan and Eugenie Marde (Lintilhac) P.; m. Bethanne McNally, June 25, 1966; 1 son, Christian; m. Susan Rieger, Mar. 21, 1973; 1 dau., Margaret; m. Katherine Dalsimer, June 9, 1990. Lic. Phil., Heythrop Coll., Eng., 1960; B.A., Oxford U., Eng., 1964, M.A., 1967; Ph.D., Columbia U., 1969; AM (hon.), Amherst Coll., 1985; LLD (hon.), Williams Coll., 1985; LHD (hon.), Doshisha U., 1987; LLD (hon.), Wesleyan U., Mass., 1989; LHD (hon.), Trinity Coll., 1990. Instr. classics Fordham U., Bronx, N.Y., 1964-67; asst. prof. Columbia U., N.Y.C., 1969-71, dean Columbia Coll., 1972-76, assoc. prof., 1977-83, prof. classics, 1983-84; pres. Amherst Coll., Mass., 1984—; cons. classical lit. Columbia Ency., 1970-73; trustee Columbia Univ. Press, 1972-75. Author: The Necessities of War: A Study of Thucydides' Pessimism, 1980 (Lionel Trilling award 1981). Trustee Brit.-Am. Edn. Found., N.Y.C., 1971-75. Recipient Great Tchr. award Soc. Columbia Grads., 1983. Mem. Am. Philol. Assn., Phi Beta Kappa. Office: Amherst Coll Office of Pres Amherst MA 01002

POUTASSE, EDMUND JOSEPH, health care consultant; b. Boston, June 16, 1931; s. Edmund Joseph and Mae Francis (Vahey) P. AA, Boston U., 1952, BS, 1954, MS, 1969. Sr. pub. health advisor USPHS, Atlanta, 1963-72; ptnr. Laffin, Dodge & Ptnrs., Waltham, Mass., 1972-74; v.p. Health Care Fin. Cons., Newport Beach, Calif., 1974-78; exec. dir. Hi-Desert Med. Found., Joshua Tree, Calif., 1978-81; cons. Hyannis, Mass., 1981—. Columnist op-ed page Cape Cod Times, 1983—. Served as sgt. USAF, 1954-58. Mem. VFW, DAV. Home: 226 Old Bass River Rd Apt 110 South Dennis MA 02660-3806

POVERO, SISTER MARY BORROMEO, nun, educator; b. Geneva, N.Y., Mar. 9, 1920; d. Alfred and Teresa (Pardi) P. BA in Edn., Nazareth Coll., Rochester, N.Y., 1942; MA in Modern Lang., Villanova U., 1962. Tchr. Aquinas Inst., Rochester, 1944-46, Saint Ann High Sch., Hornell, N.Y., 1951-53, Holy Family High Sch., Auburn, N.Y., 1953-56, Notre Dame High Sch., Elmira, N.Y., 1956-65, Our Lady of Mercy High Sch., Rochester, 1942-43, 46-51, 1965—; writer exam questions N.Y. State Regents, Albany, 1970-73. Moderator Alumnae Assn. of Our Lady of Mercy High Sch., 1986—. Recipient Veritas award Mercy High Sch., 1991. Fellow Fgn. Lang. Assn. of Tchrs. of Rochester Area, N.Y. State Assn. Fgn. Lang. Tchrs., Classical Assn. of the Empire State. Roman Catholic. Home: 1437 Blossom Rd Rochester NY 14610-2211 Office: Our Lady of Mercy High 1437 Blossom Rd Rochester NY 14610-2211

POVEY, THOMAS GEORGE, office systems company executive; b. Norristown, Pa., Dec. 27, 1920; s. Thomas and Blanche (Groff) P.; B.S., Temple U., 1948; m. Bettina O. Houghton, June 2, 1945; children—Bettina C., Denise E. With Sperry Remington div. Sperry Rand Corp., Phila., also Newark, N.Y.C., 1948-76, eastern regional gen. sales mgr., 1960-63, nat. gen. sales mgr., N.Y.C., 1966-67, dir. mktg., Marietta, Ohio, 1968-71, v.p. mktg., 1972-73, v.p. fed. govt. mktg., Washington, 1973-76; pres. Remco Bus. Systems, Inc., Washington, 1976—; lectr. Newark High Sch., 1954-56, Belleville (N.J.) High Sch., 1956-58, Fairleigh Dickinson Coll., Paterson, N.J., 1957-58, Pace Coll., N.Y.C., 1965—, Georgetown U., 1974, ednl. TV, N.Y.C., 1965—. Dir. Community Fund, Essex Fells, N.J., 1967. Served as 1st lt. with USAF, 1942-45. Decorated Air medal; named Remington Dartnell Salesman of Yr., 1950. Mem. Smithsonian Assocs., Internat. Systems Dealer Assn. (bd. dirs. 1977-78, Founders award 1991), Office Systems Equipment Coop. (pres. 1978-80), Pi Delta Epsilon (pres. 1948). Republican. Methodist. Home: 227 Cape St John Rd Annapolis MD 21401-7211 Office: 8000 Parston Dr Forestville MD 20747

POVMAN, MORTON, lawyer; b. Bklyn., Jan. 13, 1931; s. Morris and Dora (Lifschitz) M.; m. Sandra Arkow, June 8, 1958; children: Michael, Bruce. BBA, Bernard Baruch Coll., CCNY, 1952; LLB, Bklyn. Law Sch., 1955. Atty. in pvt. practice N.Y.C., 1955—; mem. N.Y. City Coun., 1971—; bd. dirs. First Rehab. Ins. Co., Manhasset, N.Y.; gen. counsel Physician Reciprocal Insurers, Manhasset, 1983—. Dist. leader Democratic Party of Queens, 1970—; tras. Dem. County Com., N.Y.C.-Queens, 1976—; bd. dirs. Jewish Ctr. Kew Gardens Hills, N.Y.C.-Queens, 1980—. Recipient Svc. award United Jewish Appeal, 1980, Svc. award State of Israel Bonds, 1980, Disting. Svc. award Yad Benjamin Edn. Ctr., 1987. Mem. N.Y. State Trial Lwyers Assn. Home: 14704 75th Ave Flushing NY 11367-2932 Office: 10818 Queens Blvd Flushing NY 11375-4789

POWELL, BARBARA, clinical psychologist; b. Dexter, Mo., Apr. 25, 1929; d. Clarence Albert and Ethel (Mohrstadt) P.; m. Richard W. O'Neill, Jan. 3, 1953 (div. 1966); children: Richard W., Susan P., Jennifer A., Julia K.; m. 2d, Charles J. McCarthy, May 13, 1967 (div. 1978); m. 3d, David S. Burt, June 16, 1983. BA, Wellesley Coll., 1950; MA, Columbia U., 1967; PhD, Fordham U., 1975. Copywriter, Parade mag., 1951-52, McCall's, 1952-53; publicity dir. Silvermine Guild Art, New Canaan, Conn., 1964-66; reporter Bridgeport (Conn.) Post, 1964-69; psychologist Dunlap & Assos., Darien, Conn., 1966-67; dir. Guidance Center for Women, U. Conn., 1968-69; intern N.Y. Hosp., Westchester, 1972-73; psychologist St. Mary's in-the-field, Valhalla, N.Y., 1973-77, Behavior Therapy Inst., White Plains, N.Y., 1975-78; pvt. practice clin. psychology, Rowayton, Conn., 1976—; lectr. U. Conn., 1976-77; co-founder, assertive tng. leader Woman's Place, Darien. USPH grantee, 1970-71. Mem. Am. Psychol. Assn., Am. Assn. Marriage and Family Therapists, Am. Assn. Advancement Behavior Therapy, Soc. Clin. and Exptl. Hypnosis, Phi Beta Kappa, Sigma Xi. Author: Careers for Women after Marriage and Children, 1965; How to Raise a Successful Daughter, 1979; Overcoming Shyness, 1979; The Complete Guide to Your Child's Emotional Health, 1984; Alone, Alive and Well, 1985; Good Relationships Are Good Medicine, 1987. Address: 24 Covewood Dr Rowayton CT 06853 also: Mansion Beach PO Box 1036 Block Island RI 02807

POWELL, JACK LAVERNE, psychology educator; b. Tyler, Tex., Sept. 2, 1959; s. Paul Edward and Constance Evelyn (Macgray) P.; m. Lori Lynn Snow, July 20, 1991. BA in Psychology summa cum laude, William Jewell Coll., Liberty, Mo., 1981; MA in Psychology, U. Mo., St. Louis, 1983, PhD in Psychology, 1987. Rsch. analyst Washington U. Sch. Medicine, St. Louis, 1986-88; asst. prof. psychology Mo. Bapt. Coll., St. Louis, 1983-88; asst. prof. psychology U. Hartford, West Hartford, Conn., 1988—, dir. undergrad. psychology, 1988—; cons. Ctr. for Social Rsch., 1989—. Reviewer Jour. Nonverbal Behavior, 1989—, Jour. Social Behavior and Personality, 1990—; contbr. articles to profl. jours. Big bro. Big Bros. and Big Sister, Hartford, 1989—. Mem. Am. Psychol. Assn., Am. Psychol. Soc., Ea. Psychol. Assn., Soc. for Advancement Social Psychology, Soc. for Judgment & Decision Making, Sigma Xi, Phi Kappa Phi. Office: U Hartford 200 Bloomfield Ave West Hartford CT 06117-1500

POWELL, JOSEPH LESTER (JODY POWELL), public relations executive; b. Vienna, Ga., Sept. 30, 1943; s. Joseph Lester and June Marie (Williamson) P.; m. Nan Sue Jared, Apr. 23, 1966; 1 child, Emily Claire. Student, U.S. Air Force Acad., 1961-64; BA in Polit. Sci., Ga. State U., 1966; post grad., Emory U., 1967-70. Press sec. Gov. Jimmy Carter, Atlanta, 1971-74, 75-76, Pres. Jimmy Carter, Washington, 1977-81; columnist Los Angeles Times Syndicate, 1982-87; news analyst ABC News, Washington, 1982-87; prof. Boston Coll., 1985-86; chmn., chief exec. officer Powell Adams & Rinehart, Washington, 1987—. Author: The Other Side of the Story, 1984. Baptist. Office: Powell Adams & Rinehart 1901 L St NW Ste 300 Washington DC 20036-3506

POWELL, LARSON MERRILL, investment advisory service executive; b. Pittsfield, Mass., Mar. 8, 1932; s. Harry LeRoy and Elsie Madeline (Larson) P.; m. Anne C. Millett, Dec. 8, 1956; children: Larson Merrill, Anne Coleman, Miles Sloan. AB Harvard U., 1954; student Columbia U. Law Sch., 1957-59. News editor, reporter Boston Daily Globe, 1954, 56-57; security analyst Moody's Investors Service, N.Y.C., 1959-62, regional mgr., 1964-67, v.p., 1967-68; pres. instl. investment mgmt. div. Anchor Corp., Elizabeth, N.J., 1968-70; pres. Res. Research, Ltd., N.Y.C., 1971—, Powell Publs. Corp., N.Y.C., 1980—. Bd. mgrs. W.Side br. YMCA of Greater N.Y., 1970-79, mem.-at-large citywide bd., 1976-79; chmn. men's com. Am. Mus. Natural History, 1970-72; mem. Boro of Manhattan Community Planning Bd. 7, 1966-69; bd. dirs. Children's Home of Portland, 1986—, Sweetser Children's Home, 1988—, Episcopal Camp and Conf. Center, 1978-80. With AUS, 1954-56. Fellow Fin. Analysts Fedn.; mem. Internat. Soc. Fin. Analysts, N.Y. Soc. Security Analysts, N.Y. Newsletter Pubs. Assn. Episcopalian. Club: Harvard (N.Y.C.); Cumberland (Portland, Maine). Editor, pub. Powell Monetary Analyst, 1971—, Powell Gold Industry Guide and Internat. Mining Anlayst, 1976—, Powell Alert, 1980-88. Home: 196 Flaggy Meadow Rd Gorham ME 04038-2023 Office: PO Box 4135 Portland ME 04101-0335

POWELL, LEWIS FRANKLIN, JR., retired U.S. Supreme Court justice; b. Suffolk, Va., Sept. 19, 1907; s. Lewis Franklin and Mary Lewis (Gwathmey) P.; m. Josephine M. Rucker, May 2, 1936; children: Josephine Powell Smith, Ann Pendleton Powell Carmody, Mary Lewis Gwathmey Powell Sumner, Lewis Franklin, III. B.S., Washington and Lee U., 1929, LL.B., 1931, LL.D., 1960; LL.M., Harvard, 1932. Bar: Va. 1931, U.S. Supreme Ct. 1937. Practiced law in Richmond, 1932-71; mem. firm Hunton, Williams, Gay, Powell and Gibson, 1937-71; assoc. justice U.S. Supreme Ct., 1972-87; chmn. emeritus Colonial Williamsburg Found.; mem. Nat. Commn. on Law Enforcement and Adminstrn. Justice, 1965-67, Blue Ribbon Def. Panel to study Def. Dept., 1969-70. Served to col. USAAF, 1942-46, 32 months overseas. Decorated Legion of Merit, Bronze Star; Croix de Guerre with palms (France); Trustee emeritus Washington and Lee U.; hon. bencher Lincoln's Inn. Fellow Am. Bar Found. (pres. 1969-71), Am. Coll. Trial Lawyers (pres. 1969-70); mem. ABA (gov., pres. 1964-65), Va. Bar Assn., Richmond Bar Assn. (pres. 1947-48), Bar Assn. City N.Y., Nat. Legal Aid and Defender Assn. (v.p. 1964-65), Am. Law Inst., Soc. Cin., Sons Colonial Wars, Commonwealth Club (Richmond), Phi Beta Kappa, Phi Delta Phi, Omicron Delta Kappa, Phi Kappa Sigma. Presbyterian. Office: care US Supreme Ct 1 First St NE Washington DC 20543*

POWELL, LOIS CECILE, nurse; b. Bronx, N.Y., Feb. 7, 1941; d. James Grayson and Rita Louisa (Peters) Harris; m. James Carl Powell, Jan. 21, 1966; children: Lauren Michele, Nicole Denise. AAS, Pace U., 1975; BS, SUNY, White Plains, 1985; MS in Psychiat. Mental Heath Nrusing, Columbia U., 1992. RN, Psychiat. Mental Health Nursing. Staff nurse-alcoholism program St. Vincent's Hosp. Westchester, Harrison, N.Y., 1975-77, coord. adolescent program, 1977-85, clin. specialist, 1986—; cons. and lectr. in field. Mem. Suicide Task Force (co-chair task force on adolescent suicide 1987-89), White Plains, 1985—, Nurses Intervention Team, White Plains, 1984—, Internat. Yr. of Children Task Force, White Plains; pres., bd. dirs. Hudson Valley Singers Corp., Hastings, N.Y., 1985-86. Mem. NAFE, Soc. Adolescent Medicine, Am. Psychiat. Nurses Assn., Am. Nurses Assn. (cert. in psychiat. mental health nursing). Democrat. Roman Catholic. Office: St Vincent's Hosp 240 North St Harrison NY 10528-1524

POWELL, MILES, JR., investment and business broker; b. Mt. Holly, N.J., June 27, 1926; s. Miles and Grace (Taylor) P.; m. M. Jeanne Parker, Aug. 28, 1948; children: Phyllis, Kimberlee, Kristin. B Chem. Enging., U. Del., 1950. From salesman to product mgr. E.I. DuPont & Co., Wilmington, Del., 1950-61; from sales mgr. to exec. v.p., bd. dirs. Chemplast, Inc., Wayne, N.J., 1961-82; v.p. Norton Co., Wayne and Worcester, Mass., 1982-84, Chem. Fabrics, Manchester, N.H., 1984-85; pres., owner Powell Assocs., Medford, N.J., 1985—, Siltef, Inc., Medford, 1985—; bd. dirs. Standard Tool, Lyndhurst, N.J. With USAAF, 1944-45. Mem. Soc. Plastics Engrs. (life, pres. R.I.-S.E. Mass. sect. 1955), Soc. Plastic Industries (life, bd. dirs. 1974-78, pres. fluoropolymer div. 1974-76), Plastic Pioneers (life), Plastics Acad. (life), West Hudson Mfrs. Assn. (various offices), Pine Valley Golf Club (N.J.), Jupiter Hills Golf Club (Fla.). Republican. Baptist. Home: 19351 SE Lakeside Dr Jupiter FL 33469 Office: 3L N Main St # 68 Medford NJ 08055-2411

POWELL, RICHARD CORTLAND, advertising executive; b. Paterson, N.J., June 19, 1953; s. John Charles and Julia (Tomashitus) P.; m. Barbara A. Clark, May 30, 1957 (div. Nov. 1981). Student, Passaic County Community Coll., 1982-84. Artist Westwood Industries, Paterson, 1976-77; mgr. advt. and mktg. svcs. MagneTek Universal Mfg., Paramus, N.J., 1977—. Author: Shark Tooth Basics, 1985; contbr. articles to profl. jours. Mem. Montclair Art Mus., Catskill Flyfishing Ctr. Recipient 1st place drawing award Ea. Fedn. Mineralogy Soc., 1988. Mem. N.J. Paleontology Soc., Soc. Vertebrate Paleontology, NRA, Montclair Art Mus., Am. Mus. Natural History, Catskill Fly Fishing Ctr., Billiard Congress Am., Universal Autograph Collectors Club. Home: 7 White Oak Ln Wayne NJ 07470-3018 Office: MagneTek Universal Mfg 200 Robin Rd Paramus NJ 07652-1414

POWELL, STEPHEN CLARKE, special education educator; b. Washington, June 14, 1950; s. Francis Kirkman and Clara (Madison) P.; m. Glennis Perkins, June 16, 1973 (div. Jan. 1988); children: Stephen Kirkman, Lauran Eunique; m. Ronnelle G. Powell, Oct. 28, 1989. BA, Howard U., 1972. Spl. ed. tchr. D.C. Pub. Schs., Washington, 1972—; cons. D.C. Community Prevention Partnership, Washington, 1991—; advisor Super Leaders/Super Teams, Washington, 19876—; program dir. Substance Abuse Prevention Office, D.C. Pub. Schs., 1990, ARE, Washington, 1984. Chmn. Mayor's Youth Support Task Force, Washington, 1992—; facilitator Turning Points Program, Washington, 1982—; retreat coord. Youth Action Team, Washington, 1991—. Named Most Admired Black Male, Afro Am. Newspaper, 1990; named Coach of Yr., Eastern Bd. of Ofcls., 1972, recipient Pres.'s award, 1991. Mem. D.C. Coaches Assn. Home: 418 Kenyon St NW Washington DC 20010 Office: DC Community Prevention Partnership 1400 K St NW Ste 750 Washington DC 20004

POWERS, BRUCE RAYMOND, writer, academic administrator; b. Bklyn., Dec. 10, 1927; s. George Osborne and Gertrude Joan (Bangs) P.; m. Dolores Anne Dawson, July 25, 1969; children: Christopher, Patricia. Student U. Conn., 1947-49; AB, Brown U., 1951, MA, (tuition scholar 61-62), 1965; postgrad. U. Pa., 1961. Announcer/engr. Sta. WNLC, New London, Conn., 1946-47; tng. officer CIA, Dept. Def., 1951-55; TV sales/service rep. NBC, 1955; TV news writer and reporter Movietone News, United Press Assns., Inc., 1955-56; asst. to pres. Gotham-Vladimir Advt., Inc., 1956-57; asst. account exec. D'Arcy Advt. Co., 1957-58; asst. campaign dir. Community Counselling Services, Inc., 1958-59; fund-raising campaign dir. Tamblyn & Brown, Inc., 1959-60; instr. Brown U., Providence, 1963-65, Ryerson Poly. Inst., Toronto, 1966, Nazareth Coll., Rochester, N.Y., 1966-67; asst. prof. English and communication studies Niagara U., Lewiston, N.Y., 1967-86, assoc. prof., 1986—, chmn. permanent curriculum com. English dept., 1970-71, dir. Film Repertory Center, 1971—, dir. communication studies program, 1973-87; producer-mgn. dir. Exptl. Film retrospective, N.Y. State Coun. of the Arts, Buffalo, 1972; panelist-judge Artists Com. 2d World Festival of Animated Films, Zagreb, Yugoslavia, 1974; lectr., vis. artist ARTPARK, Lewiston, N.Y., 1975; project dir. Bicentennial Symposium, N.Y. State Am. Revolution Bicentennial Commn., Buffalo, N.Y., 1975-76; research assoc. Center Culture and Tech., U. Toronto, 1977-81; keynote speaker Dupont de Nemours & Co. Health and Safety Conf., Buffalo, 1990. Co-author (with Marshall McLuhan): The Global Village, Oxford, 1989; editor The Film and Study Guide, 1973-74. Served with USNR, 1945-46, PTO. Recipient Carpenter prize in elocution, Brown U., 1951. Mem. MLA, Broadcast Edn. Assn., Soc. Cinema Studies, Am. Soc. Journalism Sch. Adminstrs., Assn. for Edn. in Journalism and Mass Communication, Internat. Exptl. Film Soc. (founding pres. 1971-73), Western N.Y. Audio-Visual Assn., N.Y. Coll. English Assn., Phi Beta Kappa. Roman Catholic. Home: 915 Sun Valley St North Tonawanda NY 14120-1952 Office: Niagara U Lewiston NY 14109

POWERS, CHARLES WILLIAM, environmental ethicist; b. Chgo., Sept. 29, 1941; s. Raymond Allen and Elizabeth Browne (Miller) P.; m. Barbara Ley Toffler, Apr. 17, 1982; children: Samuel Bruce Toffler, Anna Laura Elizabeth Powers, Aaron Michael Toffler, Catherine Linnea Powers, Judith Nell Toffler. BA with honors, Haverford (Pa.) Coll., 1963; MDiv with honors, Union Theol. Sem., 1966; diploma, Oxford U., 1965; MPhil, Yale U., 1968, PhD, 1969. Instr. Princeton (N.J.) U., 1968-69; asst. prof. Yale U., New Haven, 1969-72, assoc. prof., 1972-75; dir. pub. responsibility Cummins Engine Co., Columbus, Ind., 1975-76, exec. dir. corp. responsibility, 1976-78, v.p. pub. policy, 1978-80; founding exec. dir. The Health Effects Inst., Cambridge, Mass., 1980-84; founding pres. Clean Sites, Inc., Alexandria, Va., 1984-87; mng. ptnr. Resources for Responsible Mgmt., Boston, 1987—; cons. hazardous waste mgmt. Appropriations Commn. of U.S. Ho. of Reps., Washington, 1987-89; pres. Resources for Responsible Site Mgmt., Boston, 1989—, Inst. for Responsible Mgmt., Boston, 1985—; founding exec. dir. Inst. for Evaluating Health Risks, Irvine, Calif. and Washington, 1989; lectr. ethics Tufts U., 1989—. Co-author: The Ethical Investor, 1972, Can the Market Sustain an Ethic?, 1978, Ethics in the Education of Business Managers, 1980. Mem. adv. coun. The Carnegie Commn. on Sci., Tech. and Govt., 1989—; bd. dirs., chmn. fin. devel. com. The Climate Inst., 1987—; adv. com. Environ. and Occupational Health Scis. Inc., 1988—; bd. dirs. and founding exec. dir. Clean Sites, Inc., 1984—, Health Effects Inst. Asbestos Rsch., 1989—. Recipient Rene Dubos Environ. Award Rene Dubos Ctr. for Human Environments, 1991; Inst. of Politics fellow Kennedy Sch. Govt., 1980; Kent fellow Danforth Found., 1966; Columbia U. Internat. fellow, 1965; recipient The Haverford award Haverford Coll., 1972. Office: Resources for Responsible Mgmt 264 Beacon St Boston MA 02116-1236

POWERS, DONALD MATTHEW, JR., chemist; b. Hagerstown, Md., Feb. 14, 1941; s. Donald Matthew Sr. and Madeline Lorretto (Ullrich) P.; m. Renate Otto, Sept. 3, 1967; children: Michael Ernst, Heidi Madeline. BS, Wheeling Coll., 1963; PhD, Cornell U., 1969. Postdoctoral fellow NIH, Bethesda, Md., 1969-71; staff biochemist NIH, Bethesda, 1971-76; clin. chemist Hahnemann Med. Coll. and Univ., Phila., 1976-78; from clin. chemist to dir. tech. svcs. Eastman Kodak Clin. Products Div., Rochester, N.Y., 1978-91; mgr. tech. and regulatory affairs Eastman Kodak Clin. Products Div., Rochester, 1991—; chairholder area com on evaluation protocols Nat. Com. for Clin. Lab. Standards, Villanova, Pa., 1988—. Editor: Interference Testing Guidelines, 1984. Mem. Am. Soc. Clin. Chemistry (program chmn. Phila. sect. 1977-78), Regulatory Affairs Profls. Soc., Health Industry Mfrs. Assn. (tech. and regulatory adv. com.), Sigma Xi.

POWERS, EDWARD JOHN, JR., bank analyst, consultant; b. Boston, Nov. 23, 1938; s. Edward John and Mary (Joyce) P.; m. Katherine Powers (div. June 1974); 1 child, Michael E. BS in Fin., Boston Coll., 1960; MBA, U. Chgo., 1962. Chartered fin. analyst. Assoc. economist, bank stock analyst Grace Nat. Bank, N.Y.C., 1962-66; economist, bank stock analyst Marine Midland Bank Inc., N.Y.C., 1966-72; v.p., dir. rsch., economist 2d dist. securities M.A. Schapiro & Co. Inc., N.Y.C., 1972-78; v.p., dir. rsch. Coburn & Meredith Inc., N.Y.C., 1978-92; cons. economist William D. Witter, N.Y.C., 1978-92; v.p., dir. rsch. Coburn & Meredith Inc., Hartford, Conn.; pres. Powers Orient Inc., N.Y.C., 1977-91; mng. ptnr. Asia/Pacific Powers Investment Co., N.Y.C., 1977-91. Contbr. articles to publs.; appeared in 4 films. Named Forecast of Yr. Am. Statis. Assn., 1969. Mem. Am. Econ. Assn., Fin. Analyst Fedn.-N.Y. Soc. Democrat. Roman Catholic. Office: CO Burns & Meredith Inc 15 Lewis St Hartford CT 06103

POWERS, EDWIN MALVIN, consulting engineer; b. Denver, July 20, 1915; s. Emmett and Bertha Malvina (Guido) P.; m. Dorothy Lavane Debler, Jan. 18, 1941; children: Dennis M., Kenneth E., James M., Steven R. BS in Chem. Engring., U. Denver, 1939, MS, 1940. Registered profl. engr., N.J., Colo., Fall Out Analysts Engr., U.S. Fed. Emergency Mgmt. Agency, 1975-87. Prodn. supr. Nat. Aniline Div., Buffalo, 1940-45; engr., project supr. Merck & Co., Rahway, N.J., 1945-67, chief project coordinator, 1967-72, purchasing engr., 1972-82; ret., 1982; cons. engr., Conifer, Colo., 1982—. Capt. Air Raid Wardens, River dist., Buffalo, 1942-45. Mem., del. Conifer

Home Owners Assns. Protect Our Single Homes, 1984-86, Regional Environ. Assn. Concerned Home Owners, 1985-86, task force area devel. Hwy. 285/ Conifer Area County Planning Bd. Community, 1986-88. Mem. NSPE, Am. Chem. Soc. (emeritus), Am. Inst. Chem. Engrs. (treas. N.J. 1960, exec. com. 1961-63). Home and Office: 26106 Amy Circle Dr Conifer CO 80433-6102

POWERS, EVA AGOSTON, clinical psychologist; b. Budapest, Hungary, Mar. 30, 1938; came to U.S., 1940, naturalized, 1945; d. Tibor and Jeanne Iseult (Watson) Agoston; A.B., Smith Coll., 1960; M.A., Boston U., 1962; Ph.D., 1969; m. James F. Powers, July 4, 1960; children—Wayne, Glenn. Psychologist, Childrens' Hosp. Med. Center Boston, 1964-69, Newton (Mass.) Sch. System, 1969-71, Conway (N.H.) Sch. System, 1972-78; dir. child and youth services Seacoast Regional Counseling Center, Portsmouth, N.H., 1979-80; pvt. practice psychol. counseling, Portsmouth, 1980—; cons. to Maine Sch. System, 1978, Center of Hope, Conway, N.H., 1971-73; supr. tng. program N.H. Dept. Edn., Concord, 1972-74. NIMH grantee, 1961, 62; S. Burt Wolbach Research Fund grantee, 1968. Mem. Am. Psychol. Assn., Maine Psychol. Assn., N.H. Psychol. Orgn., Mass. Psychol. Assn., Nat. Assn. Psychologists, Sigma Xi, Phi Beta Kappa. Contbr. articles to profl. publs. Office: 127 High St Portsmouth NH 03801-3708

POWERS, JAMES CARTER, theatrical business manager; b. Ft. Wayne, Ind., May 30, 1936; s. Bernard and Irene (Ackerman) Carter. Student, Ind. U., 1956-59. Pres. James Powers Profl. Artists, Inc., N.Y.C., 1968—; bd. dirs. Hollywood (Fla.) Beach Resort, Jane Alexander, Inc., N.Y.C., Zaz-Huff, Inc., N.Y.C., HQB Enterprises, Inc., N.Y.C., Robert Mira Stable, Inc., N.Y.C. Democrat. Episcopalian. Office: James Powers Inc 60 E 42nd St Ste 1158 New York NY 10165

POWERS, JAMES F., psychologist; b. Montague, Mass., Mar. 13, 1938; s. James H. and Helen Alice (Fuller) P.; m. Eva Agoston, July 4, 1970; children: Wayne, Glenn. AB, Amherst Coll., 1959; MA, Harvard U., 1961; EdD, Boston U., 1983. Lic. psychologist, N.H., Maine. Psychologist team leader York (Maine) County Counseling, 1982-83; psychologist Powers Assocs., Portsmouth, N.H., 1983—; cons. York (Maine) Sch. System, 1982—; cons. Eliot (Maine) Sch. System, 1987—, Portsmouth N.H. Kids Program, 1991; profl. adv. bd. Seacoast Chadds, 1990—. N.H. Psychol. Assn. fellow, Woodrow Wilson fellow. Mem. APA, N.H. Psychol. Orgn. (pres.), Maine Psychol Assn., Phi Beta Kappa. Office: Powers Assocs 127 High St Portsmouth NH 03801-3708

POWERS, JOHN KIERAN, lawyer; b. Schenectady, Aug. 2, 1947; s. Paul Joseph and Anne Marie (Leahy) P.; children: Erin Kelly, Megan Kerry. BS, U. Notre Dame, 1969; JD, Union U., Albany, N.Y., 1972. Bar: N.Y. 1973, U.S. Dist. Ct. (no. dist.) N.Y. 1973, U.S. Dist. Ct. (so. and ea. dists.) N.Y. 1982, U.S. Ct. Appeals (2d cir.) 1984, U.S. Supreme Ct. 1985, U.S. Dist. Ct. Vt. 1988. Assoc. Medwin and McMahon, Albany, 1973-77; pvt. practice law, Albany, 1973-80; pres. John K. Powers, P.C., Albany, 1980-87; ptnr. Powers and Santola, 1987—; trustee N.Y. State Lawyers Polit. Action Com., 1983-88, treas., 1989—; co-counsel N.Y. State Head Injury Assn., 1983-85. Contb. articles to publs. Fellow Roscoe Pound Found. Mem. ABA (sustaining, vice-chair, legis. subcom., automobile law com., trial and ins. practice sect., state leader com. on state legis. sect.), Nat. Coll. Adv. (co-founder), Assn. Trial Lawyers Am. (life, state del. 1990, bd. govs. 1990—), Am. Bd. Trial Advocates (advocate), N.Y. State Bar Assn. (sustaining, lectr., chmn. legis. com. trial lawyers sect.), N.Y. State Trial Lawyers Assn. (sustaining, bd. dirs. 1983-88, chmn. key person legis. com., chmn. pubs. com., chmn. atty. referral com., exec. com. 1986—, treas. 1988-89, v.p. 1989-91, 1st v.p. 1990-91, pres.-elect 1991-92, pres. 1992—, award of merit, 1990, award of excellence 1991), N.Y. Trial Lawyers Inst. (lectr. and program chmn. 1981—, treas. 1988-89, pres. 1992—), Capitol Dist. Trial Lawyers Assn. (bd. dir. 1979-81, v.p. 1983-85, pres. 1985-86), Pa. Trial Lawyers Assn., Alban County Bar Assn. (lectr.), Chief Judge's Com. to Improve Availability of Legal Svcs., Chief Judge's Pro-Bono Monitoring Com., Civil Justice Found. (guest lectr. Albany Law Sch., Albany Med. Coll.), Trial Lawyers for Pub. Justice, Lions (pres. Scotia, N.Y. chpt. 1979-80). Democrat. Roman Catholic. Home and Office: 600 Broadway Albany NY 12207-2205

POWERS, KENNETH WILLIAM, chemical engineer; b. Paterson, N.J., Mar. 27, 1930; s. Leslie R. and Maria C. (Pistono) P.; m. Anna M. Selvage, Sept. 12, 1953; children: Matthew R., Clifford A. BChemE, Cornell U., 1953, PhD in Chem. Engring., 1956. Chem. engr. Exxon Chem. Co., U.S.A., Linden, N.J., 1956—. Contbr. articles to profl. jours.; patentee in field. Mem. Phi Kappa Phi, Tau Beta Pi, Sigma Xi. Home: 145 Robbins Ave Berkeley Heights NJ 07922 Office: Exxon Chem Co USA PO Box 45 Linden NJ 07036

POWERS, MICHAEL KEVIN, architectural and engineering executive; b. Boston, Feb. 3, 1948; s. Albert Thomas and Claire Marie (Sullivan) P.; m. Patricia Marie Collins, July 10, 1971; children: Kristin Michelle, Jennifer Anne. BSCE, Northeastern U., 1971. Registered profl. engr., N.Y., Vt., Minn, Maine, Mass., N.H., Ky. Staff engr. Edwards and Kelcey, Boston, 1967-70; project mgr. DeLeuw Cather & Co., Boston, 1971-80; exec. v.p., dir. engring. Symmes Maini & McKee Assocs., Cambridge, Mass., 1980—; guest speaker Tradeline Forum on Bus. and Tech., Boston, 1986, 87, 88, Microcontamination Conf. and Exposition, Santa Clara, Calif., 1987; lectr. facility design MIT, 1989, 92. Contbr. articles to profl. jours. Mem. Inst. Environ. Scis. (sr.), ASCE, Mt. River East Condominium Assn. (trustee). Roman Catholic. Office: Symmes Maini & McKee Assocs Inc 1000 Massachusetts Ave Cambridge MA 02138-5304

POWERS, SCOTT, producer, actor; b. Chgo., Aug. 23, 1948; s. Raymond Alford and Ruby Marilyn (Ivacko) P. BS, Ithaca Coll., 1970; MBA, Fairleigh Dickinson U., 1971. Producer Young & Rubicam, Inc., N.Y.C.; account exec. Kelly, Nason, Inc., N.Y.C.; sr. account exec. Bozell & Jacobs, Inc., N.Y.C.; account supr. Foote, Cone & Belding, Inc., N.Y.C.; actor N.Y.C., L.A., 1982—; pres. Scott Powers Prodns., Inc., N.Y.C., 1988—. Author: Commercial Print: the Actor's Guide to Survival, 1992; contbr. articles to publs.; cartoonist Thankyounext, 1990—. Mem. Better Bus. Bur. N.Y.C., 1991—, Kinckerbocker Rep. Club, N.Y.C., 1971—; bd. dirs. Profl. Comedians Assn., N.Y.C., 1988-91, v.p., 1989-91; judge Internat. Film and TV Festivals, N.Y.C., 1991—. Mem. AFTRA (bd. dirs. 1989-91), SAG, Actor's Equity Assn., NATAS (judge Emmys 1985—), N.Y.C. C. of C., Met. Club, N.Y. Athletic Club, Players Club, Mensa, Intertel. Republican. Congregationalist. Home: 180 Central Park S New York NY 10019 Office: Scott Powers Prodns Inc 150 Fifth Ave Ste 623 New York NY 10011

POWLEDGE, FRED ARLIUS, freelance writer; b. N.C., Feb. 23, 1935; s. Arlius Raymond and Pauline (Stearns) P.; m. Tabitha Morrison, Dec. 21, 1957; 1 child, Pauline Stearns. AB in English, U. N.C., 1957. Writer, editor AP, New Haven, 1958-60; reporter Atlanta Jour., 1960-63, N.Y. Times, N.Y.C., 1963-66; freelance journalist, 1966—; lectr. New Sch., N.Y.C., 1967-69, 80-82; narrator, co-producer, writer WNET-TV/13, N.Y.C., 1972. Author: Black Power/White Resistance: Notes on the New Civil War, 1967, To Change a Child: A Report on the Institute for Developmental Studies, 1967, Model City: A Test of American Liberalism: One Town's Efforts to Rebuild Itself, 1970, Mud Show: A Circus Season, 1976, Born on the Circus, 1976, The Backpacker's Budget Food Book, 1977, Journeys Through the South, 1979, So You're Adopted: A Book About the Experience of Being Adopted, 1982, Water: The Nature, Uses and Future of Our Most Precious and Abused Resource, 1982, A Forgiving Wind: On Becoming a Sailor, 1983, Fat of the Land, 1984, The New Adoption Maze: And How to Get Through It, 1985, You'll Survive, 1986, Free at Last? The Civil Rights Movement and the People Who Made It, 1991. With USAR, 1957. Russell Sage fellow Russell Sage Found., 1966-67; travel and study grantee Ford Found., 1971. Mem. Author's Guild. Office: care F Joseph Spieler 410 W 24th St New York NY 10011-1303

POZZUOLI, JOSEPH ANTHONY, lawyer; b. N.Y.C., Oct. 5, 1953; s. Anthony and Vera (Fierro) P.; m. Louise Elder, Nov. 6, 1988. BA, Fordham U., 1975, JD, 1978. Bar: N.Y. 1979. Pvt. practice, New Rochelle, N.Y., 1979—; arbitrator N.Y.C. Civil Ct., Bronx, N.Y., 1979—; fiduciary N.Y. State Surrogate Ct., N.Y.C., 1991—. Pres. Pelham Bay Little League, Inc., Bronx, 1977; counsel Pelham Bay Mchts. Assn., 1979-83, Pelham Bay Golden Age Ctr. Inc., 1981—, Bronx County Conservative Com., 1987-88,. Mem. N.Y. State Bar Assn., New York County Lawyers Assn. Roman Catholic. Office: 527 Main St New Rochelle NY 10801-6334

PRABHU, CATHERINE DUDLEY, school system administrator; b. Cortland, N.Y., Dec. 5, 1941; d. Arthur Joseph and Catherine Norma (Hilsinger) Dudley; m. Ramesh Chandra Prabhu, Jan. 26, 1974; 1 child, Neil R. BS, SUNY, Oswego, 1964; MEd, U. Rochester, 1969; EdD, SUNY, Buffalo, 1988. Cert. tchr., sch. adminstr., N.Y. Primary sch. tchr. Blue Creek Sch., North Colonie C.S., Latham, N.Y., 1964-66; middle sch. tchr. Brighton Schs., Rochester, N.Y., 1966-69; dir. skills ctr. Brighton Schs., 1970-72, resource tchr., 1972-84, curriculum specialist, 1981; cons. San Diego County Office Edn., San Diego, 1985; dir. Calif. Young World, San Jose, Calif., 1986; prin., asst. supt. Mt. Pleasant Cottage Sch., UFSD, Pleasantville, N.Y., 1986—; adj. instr. Nazareth Coll., Pittsford, N.Y., 1971-72; workshop presenter Pittsford Cen. Schs., Rush Henrietta Pub. Schs., Assn. for Children with Learning Disabilities, Middle Schs. Assn., Jr. League Rochester, Internat. Reading Assn., Brighton Schs. Life mem. PTA, Brighton, 1974—. Mem. ASCD, Am. Assn. Sch. Adminstrs., N.Y. State Coun. Sch. Supts., N.Y. State Mid. Schs. Assn. Office: Mt Pleasant Cottage Sch UFSD Broadway Pleasantville NY 10570

PRAGER, JONAS, economics educator, consultant; b. N.Y.C., Nov. 5, 1938; s. Julius and Bella (Tannenberg)P.; m. Helen May, June 9, 1963; children: Joel B., Sharon. AB magna cum laude, Yeshiva Coll., N.Y.C., 1959; PhD, Columbia U., 1964. Asst. prof. NYU, N.Y.C., 1964-69, assoc. prof. econs., 1969—, dir. grad. studies, 1977-81, 86-89; vis. sr. economist Bank of Israel, Jerusalem, 1965-67; lectr. USIA, India, Yugoslavia, West Germany, 1983, 84, France, Hungary, 1989; Fulbright Hays faculty rsch. fellow U.S. Dept. Edn., Israel, 1971, 1982-83. Author: Fundamentals of Money, Banking, and Financial Institutions, 1982, 2nd edit., 1987; editor: Monetary Economics: Controversies in Theory and Policy, 1971; contbr. articles to profl. jours. Am. Philos. Soc. rsch. grantee, 1974-76. Mem. Am. Econ. Soc., Hagop Kevorkian Ctr. for Near Eastern Studies, C.V. Starr Ctr. for Applied Econs. Office: NYU Dept Econs 269 Mercer St New York NY 10003

PRAH, PAMELA MARIE, journalist; b. Latrobe, Pa., June 22, 1963; d. Lonnie Joseph and Eleanor Ruth (Stefl) P. BS in Journalism, Ohio U., 1985; postgrad., Am. U., 1987. Assoc. editor McGraw-Hill Pub., Washington, 1986-87; editor Internat. Pubs., Washington, 1987—; staff editor Bur. Nat. Affairs, Washington, 1989—; spl. corr. Bur. Nat. Affairs, Heidelberg, Germany, 1991—; intern 13-30 Pub. Co., Knoxville, Tenn., 1985, Tribune Rev., Greensburg, Pa., 1985, McGraw-Hill World News, London, 1985; editor Athens Mags., 1985, mng. editor, 1984, The Awakening, 1985. Scholar Ohio U., Athens, 1981-85. Mem. Soc. Profl. Jounalists (Washington chpt.), Women Communications, Kappa Tau Alpha. Democratic. Roman Catholic. Home: HQ USAREIR CMR 420 Box 2194 APO AE 09063

PRAIRIE, CELIA ESTHER FREDA, biochemistry educator; b. Buenos Aires, Sept. 30, 1940; came to U.S., 1963; d. Rafael Emilio A. and Celia Esther (Seijo) Freda; m. James Roland Prairie, Sept. 19, 1970; children: James Roger, Caryn Elizabeth. BS, U. Buenos Aires, 1961, MS, 1963; PhD, U. Pa., 1967. Fellow Nat. Rsch. Inst., Buenos Aires, 1961-63; rsch. assoc. dept. therapeutic rsch. U. Pa., Phila., 1967-70; postdoctoral rsch. assoc. Lab. Molecular Embryology, Arco Felice, Naples, Italy, 1970; lectr. biology and chemistry depts. Holy Family Coll., Phila., 1974-75, asst. prof. biology dept., 1975-80, assoc. prof., 1980-85, prof. biochemistry, 1985—, chmn. dept. natural scis. and math., 1986-88, acting chmn. biology dept., 1982-86; sr. teaching staff assoc. Marine Biol. Lab., Woods Hole, Mass., 1968-69. Contbr. articles to profl. jours. Bd. dirs. Lower Bucks County Community Ctr., 1970—. Fellow USPHS, 1963-65, U. Pa., 1965-66, Am. Coun. Edn. and Fund for the Improvement of Post Sec. Edn., 1983-84. Mem. AAAS, Am. Inst. Biol. Scis., N.Y. Acad. Scis., Nat. Geog. Soc., Sigma Xi. Democrat. Mem. Religious Soc. of Friends. Home: 31 Fullturn Rd Levittown PA 19056 Office: Holy Family Coll Frankford and Grant Aves Philadelphia PA 19114

PRASAD, VISHWANATH, mechanical engineering educator; b. Muzaffarpur, Bihar, India, Nov. 18, 1949; came to U.S. 1980; s. Kishori Prasad and Ramkumari (Devi) Gupta; m. Sushma Prasad, Dec. 14, 1972; children—Preeti Priya, Gaurav. B.S. in Mech. Engring., Patna U., 1971; M.Tech., Indian Inst. Tech., 1978; Ph.D., U. Del., 1983. Tech. asst. H.S.C.L., Bokaro Steel City, India, 1972-73; research asst. Indian Inst. Tech., Kanpur, 1977-78; lectr. Patna U., India, 1973-76, 78-80; teaching asst. U. Del., Newark, 1980-83; vis. asst. prof. Clemson U., S.C., 1983-84; asst. prof. mech. engring. Columbia U., N.Y.C., 1984-87, assoc. prof., 1987—; cons. various indsl. insts.; presenter articles in field to nat. and internat. confs. Contbr. articles to profl. jours. Mem. ASME, AIAA, Pi Tau Sigma, Sigma Xi. Hindu. Home: 212 Woodland Rd New Milford NJ 07646-2308 Office: Columbia Univ Mech Engring Dept 220 Mudd Bldg New York NY 10027

PRATT, ALICE FORD, small business owner, music educator; b. Fairmont, W.Va., June 15, 1926; d. Dorsey Mackin and Gladys Sabina (Clem) Ford; m. William Spach Pratt, Mar. 28, 1953; children: Nancy, Sallie, Anna Laurie, James. Diploma in nursing, Duke U., 1948; diploma in pub. health, U. Pitts., 1950; diploma in pub. health edn., U. N.C., 1952; postgrad., Montgomery Coll., 1968-70. Pub. health nurse Marion County Health Dept., Fairmont, 1948-51; head nurse out patient Meml. Hosp., Chapel Hill, N.C., 1952-53; pvt. piano instr. Potomac, Md., 1969-91; owner Pratt Market Svc., Potomac, 1984—. Sec. Potomac Area Music Tchr. Assn., 1975-90. Mem. Montgomery County Music Assn. (judge, monitor 1989—). Republican. Lutheran. Home: 8403 Aqueduct Rd Potomac MD 20854-6207

PRATT, BURT CARLTON, foundation executive; b. Lititz, Pa., May 13, 1911; s. William A. and Laura G. (Becker) P.; m. Dorothy M. McCaslin, May 23, 1931; 1 dau., Patricia Pratt Knodel. B.S. in Chem. Engring, Bucknell U., Lewisburg, Pa., 1933; Ph.D. in Organic Chemistry, Cornell U., 1938. With E.I. duPont de Nemours & Co., Wilmington, Del., 1938-73; asso. dir. central research dept. E.I. duPont de Nemours & Co., 1951-64, exec. sec. com. ednl. aid, 1964-73; dir. Crystal Trust, Wilmington, 1973—. Bd. dirs., treas. Wilmington Coll., 1976—, Wilmington Music Sch., 1970—; bd. dirs. Del. Symphony Assn., 1989—. Mem. Am. Chem. Soc., AAAS, Sigma Xi. Address: 1088 Du Pont Bldg Wilmington DE 19898

PRATT, EDMUND TAYLOR, JR., pharmaceutical company executive; b. Savannah, Ga., Feb. 22, 1927; s. Edmund T. and Rose (Miller) P.; m. Jeanette Louise Carneale, Feb. 10, 1951; children: Randolf Ryland, Keith Taylor. BSEE magna cum laude, Duke U., 1947; MBA, U. Pa., 1949; hon. degrees, L.I. U., Marymount Manhattan Coll., Poly. U. of N.Y., St. Francis Coll. With IBM Corp., 1949-51, 54-57, asst. to exec. v.p., 1956-57; with IBM World Trade Corp., 1958-62, contr., 1958-62; asst. sec. fin. mgmt. Dept. Army, 1962-64; contr. Pfizer, Inc., N.Y.C., 1964-67, v.p. ops. internat. subs., 1967-69, chmn. bd., pres. internat. subs., 1969-71, exec. v.p., 1970-71, pres., 1971-72, chmn., chief exec. officer, 1972-90, chmn., 1972-92, also bd. dirs.; bd. dirs. Chase Manhattan Corp., Internat. Paper Co., GMC. Bd. dirs. N.Y.C. Partnership; mem. N.Y. State Bus. Adv. Coun.; mem. Emergency Com. for Am. Trade; mem. adv. com. for trade policy and negotiations; mem. Nat. Indsl. Adv. Coun. for Opportunities Industrialization Ctrs. of Am. Lt. (j.g.) USNR, 1952-54. Mem. Bus. Roundtable (immediate past chmn., mem. policy com.), N.Y. C. of C. and Industry (bd. dirs.), Rus. Coun., Phi Beta Kappa.

PRATT, GEORGE CHENEY, federal judge; b. Corning, N.Y., May 22, 1928; s. George Wollage and Muriel (Cheney) P.; m. Carol June Hoffman, Aug. 16, 1952; children: George W., Lise M., Marcia S., William T. B.A., Yale U., 1950, LL.B., 1953. Bar: N.Y. 1953, U.S. Supreme Ct. 1964, U.S. Ct. Appeals 1974. Law clk. to Charles W. Froessel (Judge of N.Y. Ct. Appeals), 1953-55; assoc. then ptnr. Sprague & Stern, Mineola, N.Y., 1956-60; ptnr. Andromidas, Pratt & Pitcher, Mineola, 1960-65, Pratt, Caemmerer & Cleary, Mineola, 1965-75; partner Farrell, Fritz, Pratt, Caemmerer & Cleary, 1975-76; judge U.S. Dist. Ct. (Eastern Dist. of N.Y.), 1976-82, U.S. Circuit Ct. Appeals for 2d circuit (Uniondale), N.Y., 1982—; disting. vis. prof. Hofstra Law Sch., 1979—; adj. prof. St. John's U. Law Sch., 1978—, Touro Law Sch., 1985—. Mem. N.Y. State Bar Assn., Nassau County Bar Assn. Mem. United Ch. of Christ. Office: US Ct Appeals Uniondale Ave at Hempstead Tpk Uniondale NY 11553

PRATT, JOHN ROLLA, college administrator; b. Barre, Vt., Oct. 30, 1940; s. Elmer Dutton and Olive Ina (Tilton) P.; m. Margaret Ann Mackoul, Sept. 25, 1965; children: Karen Marie Pratt Randall, Christine Marie Pratt Cavagnah. BS in Econs., U. Vt., 1963; M. in Hosp. Adminstrn., U. Mich., 1965. Asst. adminstr. Maine Med. Ctr., Portland, 1965-71; health planner So. Maine Comprehensive Health, Portland, 1971-72; exec. dir. Brattleboro (Vt.) Meml. Hosp., 1972-74; hosp. liaison Bay State P.S.R.O., Inc., Boston, 1974-75; exec. dir. Braintree (Mass.) Hosp., 1975-76; cons. Mass. Dept. Pub. Health, Boston, 1976-77; exec. dir. Lakeville (Mass.) Hosp., 1977-89; dir. program in long-term care adminstrn. St. Joseph's Coll., Windham, Maine, 1989—; chmn. ethics com. Maine Health Policy Adv. Coun., Augusta, 1990—; bd. dirs. Maine Consortium for Health Profl. Edn., Augusta, 1990—. Contbr. articles to profl. jours. Fellow Am. Coll. Healthcare Execs.; mem. Am. Hosp. Assn. Republican. Office: St Josephs Coll Windham ME 04062

PRATT, LINDA, educator; b. Mass., May 28, 1948. BA, U. Mass., 1970, MEd, 1975, EDd, 1978. Cert. elem. edn., reading specialist, reading supr. Prof., dir. grad. reading program Elmira (N.Y.) Coll.; prof. Gonzaga U., Spokane, Wash.; insvc. tchr. U. Mass., Amherst; reading specialist Southwick (Mass.) Pub. Sch. System. Mem. IRA, NCTE, Nat. Reading Conf., Kappa Delta Pi, Phi Delta Kappa, Kappa Delta Gamma. Office: Elmira Coll Elmira NY 14901

PRATT, RICHARD HOUGHTON, physics educator; b. N.Y.C., May 5, 1934; s. Karl Chapman and Gertrude (Gennis) P.; m. Elizabeth Ann Glass, Nov. 1, 1958; children—Jonathan Peter, Kathryn Eileen, Mary Caroline, Paul Chapman. A.B., U. Chgo., 1952, S.M., 1955, Ph.D., 1959. Rsch. assoc. Stanford U., 1959-61, asst. prof., 1961-64; assoc. prof. physics U. Pitts., 1964-69, prof., 1969—, acad. dean semester at sea, fall 1984, adminstrv. dean, spring 1990; program dir. theoretical physics NSF, Washington, 1987-89; cons. Lawrence Livermore Nat. Lab.; prin. investigator Dept. Energy, NSF. Fellow Am. Phys. Soc., AAAS; mem. Sierra Club (chmn. Pa. chpt. 1976-80, v.p. Appalachian region 1982-84), European Phys. Soc., Internat. Radiation Physics Soc. (sec. 1985—), Phi Beta Kappa. Home: 1131 Shady Ave Pittsburgh PA 15232-2809

PRATT, RICHARDSON, JR., retired college president; b. N.Y.C., Mar. 25, 1923; s. Richardson and Laura C. (Parsons) P.; m. Mary Esterbrook Offutt, Aug. 12, 1944; children: Laura Pratt Gregg, Thomas R., David. O. A.B., Williams Coll., 1946, LL.D. (hon.), 1978; M.B.A., Harvard U., 1948; LL.D. (hon.), St Joseph, 1984. Econ. analyst, sec. com. on human relations Exxon Co., 1948-52, dist. mktg. mgr., 1953-63, mktg. planning and evaluation, 1964-71; chmn. Charles Pratt & Co., Inc., 1971—; pres. Pratt Inst., Bklyn., 1972-90; bd. dirs. Dime Savs. Bank N.Y., Bklyn. Union Gas Co.; mayor Village of Lloyd Harbor (N.Y.), 1983—. Trustee Near East Found., Fedn. Protestant Welfare Agys.; mem. governing bd. Bklyn. Mus., Bklyn Bot. Gardens; chmn. bd. dirs. Greenwood Cemetery. Served to ensign USNR, 1943-46. Presbyterian. Home: 30 Dock Hollow Rd Cold Spring Harbor NY 11724-1002 Office: Charles Pratt & Co Inc 355 Lexington Ave New York NY 10017-6603

PRATT, ROBERT LEONARD, company executive; b. East Rockaway, N.Y., Jan. 12, 1947; s. Leonard Charles and Florence (Ranges) P.; m. Victoria Rose Brennan, Aug. 15, 1950. BA, Wesleyan U., Middletown, Conn., 1969; JD, Georgetown U., 1973; MPA, Harvard U., 1974. Bar: D.C. 1974. Legis. asst. Congressman Robert Drinan, U.S. Ho. of Reps., Washington, 1974-77; exec. dir. New Eng. Congl. Caucus, Washington, 1977-81; dir. for internat. trade and govt. relations Thermo Electron Corp., Waltham, Mass., 1981-85; chief exec. officer PRAXIS Inc., Waltham, 1985—; chmn. bd. dirs. Internat. Inst. for Energy Conservation, Washington, 1984—. Mem. D.C. Bar Assn., ABA. Democrat. Home: 9 Brook Trail Rd Wayland MA 01778-3705 Office: PRAXIS Inc 300 Third Ave Waltham MA 02154

PRATT, SHERWOOD LAMBERTSON, industrial equipment executive; b. Kansas City, Mo., June 5, 1932; s. George Oramel and Elizabeth Sherwood (Lambertson) P.; m. Jane Kentnor, Oct. 13, 1956 (div. June 1970); children: Jeffrey, Susan; m. Doris Nelson, Jan. 27, 1979; 1 child, Elizabeth. BA in Econs., Yale U., 1955; MBA in Fin., NYU, 1969; MLA in Art History, Boston U., 1991. Pres. W.S. Rockwell Co., Fairfield, Conn., 1958-68; gen. mgr. Englehard Minerals and Chems., Inc., Carteret, N.J., 1970-72; owner Sherwood Cons., Inc., Boston, 1979-88; exec. v.p., gen. mgr. High Vacuum Equipment Co., Hingham, Mass., 1988-90; pres. Vacuum Solutions, Inc., Hingham, Mass., 1990—; pres. Archtl. Glass Co., Mass., 1986—. Patentee glass works. Pres. Wakemen's Boys Club, Southport, Conn., 1968. With USN, 1956-57. Mem. Rotary (pres. Fairfield chpt. 1968). Republican. Episcopalian. Office: Vacuum Solutions Inc 110 Industrial Park Rd Hingham MA 02043-4394

PRATTE, LOUIS, judge; b. Quebec City, Que., Can., Nov. 29, 1926; s. Garon and Georgine (Rivard) P.; m. Charlotte Tremblay, July 2, 1953; children—Marie, Francois. Grad. Faculte de droit et des scis economiques, Laval U.; diplome d'etudes superieures en droit prive, U. Paris. Bar: Que. 1950. Mem. trial div. Fed. Ct. Can., 1971-73; judge Fed. Ct. Appeal, Ottawa, Ont., 1973—. Office: Fed Ct Appeal, Kent & Wellington Sts, Ottawa, ON Canada K1A OH9

PRAWEL, SHERWOOD P., civil engineer, educator; b. Buffalo, Jan. 17, 1932; s. Sherwood Peter and Janet (Telfair) P.; m. Florence Litrice Diehl, May 1, 1954; children: Sherwood P., David A., Timothy P., Eric J., Jennifer M. BCE, Ga. Inst. Tech., 1953, MCE, 1957; PhD, U. Waterloo, 1971. Field engr. Bethlehem Steel Co., various cities, 1956-58; asst. prof. civil engring. SUNY, Buffalo, 1958-63, assoc. prof., 1963-75, assoc. prof. civil engring. and architecture, 1975-80, assoc. prof. civil engring. and earthquake engring., 1980—; bd. cons. Internat. Ferracement Info. Ctr., Bangkok, 19786; lectr. masonry renovation seminars Internat. Masonry Inst., 1991-92. Author: Modern Methods of Engineering Computations, 1969, Introduction to Structural Engineering, 1979; mem. editorial bd. Jour. Archtl. Planning and Rsch., 1980—; also articles. Capt. USMC, 1953-56. NSF grantee. Mem. ASCE, Am. Concrete Inst. (tech. com.), Earthquake Engring. Rsch. Inst., Masonry Soc. (tech. com.), Rotary (bd. dirs. Grand Island chpt. 1990—), Chi Psi. Office: SUNY Dept Civil Engring Buffalo NY 14260

PREATE, ERNEST D., JR., state attorney general; b. Scranton, Pa., Nov. 22, 1940; s. Ernest D. Sr. and Anne (Janeczek) P.; children: Elizabeth D., Alexandra V. BS in Econs., U. Pa., 1962, JD, 1965. Dist. atty. Lackawana County, 1977-89; atty. gen. State of Pa., Harrisburg, 1989—. Capt. USMC, 1966-69, Vietnam. Recipient Outstanding Svc. to Edn. award Pa. Sch. Bds. Assn., 1990, Law Enforcement Achievement award Nat. Italian Am. Found., 1989, Dist. Svc. to Law Enforcement award Pa. County Detectives and State Investigators Assn., 1985, ADL of B'nai B'rith Americanism award 1991, First Ann. Law and Justice award Sons of Italy, 1989, Gold Medal Man of the Yr. award Pa. State Lodge Sons of Italy, 1991, Dist. Svc. award Marine Corps League, 1991. Mem. nat. Assn. Attys. Gen. (chmn. ea. regional attys. gen., chair criminal law com., rep. to ABA, chmn. Govt. and Public Sector Lawyers div. of ABA), Assn. Govt. Attys. in Capital Litigation (region 5 v.p.), Exec. Working Group of U.S. Dept. Justice, Am. Legion, Marine Corps League, VFW, Kiwanis, Sigma Chi. Republican. Office: Office of Atty Gen Strawberry Sq 16th Fl Harrisburg PA 17120

PREATE, JOSEPH GERARD, financial consultant; b. Scranton, Pa., Sept. 2, 1961. BA in Econs., Villanova U., 1983. Assoc. v.p. Merrill Lynch, Wilkes Barre, Pa., 1983—. Mem. Unico Nat. (pres. Scranton chpt. 1990-92), Lions (pres. 1992—), Old Forge. Republican. Roman Catholic. Home: 115 N Franklin Wilkes Barre PA 18701

PREEDE, NYDIA, artist, retired teacher; b. N.Y.C., Nov. 7, 1926; d. Alexander and Alma Margretha (Andersen) P. BA, Monmouth Coll., 1962, MA, 1973. Fed. civil svc. employee, 1951-78, secondary and adult level educator, 1959-73; juror Nat. Assn. Women Artists; film coord. NEA. Exhbns. include Ark. Wildlife Fedn., Nat. Anti-Vivisect. Soc. (1st pl. award 1991), New Yorker show, Barcelona, 1990, Vergeau Mus. Art, Quebec, Can., 1991, Ariel Gallery, N.Y.C. Art Mine, N.Y.C., Audubon Artists 50th Ann. Show, N.Y.C.; work selected for Am. 500 show in Argentina, Aug., 1992; traveling show Nat. Assn. Women Artists-Butterfly, 1991-92. Mem. Women in the

Arts, Artist Equity, Nat. Assn. Women Artists (C. Horman Meml. award 1988), Am. Artists Profl. League, Nat. Art Club (assoc.). Mem. Women in the Arts, Artist Equity, Nat. Assn. Women Artists, Am. Artists Profl. League, Nat. Art Club (assoc.). Home: PO Box 344 Eatontown NJ 07724

PREGGER, FRED TITUS, retired physics educator, astronomy educator; b. Paterson, N.J., May 14, 1924; s. Herman and Lena Emma (Schwaeble) P.; m. Betty Mayhew, Apr. 18, 1953; children: Brian H., Bruce A. BA, Montclair (N.J.) State Coll., 1948, MA, 1950; EdD, Columbia U., 1956. Cert. 5-12 sci. tchr., N.J. Tchr. sci. Wayne (N.J.) Jr.-Sr. High Sch., 1948-52; tchr. physics West Orange (N.J.) High Sch., 1952-55; asst. prof. sci. Trenton (N.J.) State Coll., 1955-58, assoc. prof., 1958-62, prof. physics, 1962-88, chmn. dept., 1968-80, prof. emeritus, 1989—; lectr. astronomy Georgian Court Coll., Lakewood, N.J., 1988—; mem. edn. com. Pub. Svc. Electric and Gas Co., Newark, 1982—, mem. rsch. adv. coun., 1988-91. Contbr. articles to profl. jours. Radiation coord. Mercer County CD, Trenton, 1957-64. With USAAF, 1943-46. Grantee NSF, 1969-80, Pub. Svc. Electric and Gas Co. and Jersey Cen. Power & Light Co., 1981-89. Mem. NSTA, Am. Assn. Physics Tchrs. (exec. bd. N.J. sect. 1974—, pres. 1975-77), N.J. Sci. Tchrs. Assn. (plaque 1988), Trenton Torch Club, Masons. Presbyterian. Home: 42 Harbourton-wood Rd Pennington NJ 08534 Office: Trenton State Coll Physics Dept Hillwood Lakes CN 4700 Trenton NJ 08650-4700

PREISKEL, BARBARA SCOTT, lawyer, association executive; b. Washington, July 6, 1924; d. James and B. Beatrix Scott; m. Robert H. Preiskel, Oct. 28, 1950; children: John S., Richard A. BA, Wellesley Coll., 1945; LLB, Yale U., 1947. Bar: D.C. 1948, N.Y. 1948, U.S. Supreme Ct. 1960. Law clk. U.S. Dist. Ct., Boston, 1948-49; assoc. Poletti, Diamond, Roosevelt, Freidin & Mackay, N.Y.C., 1949-50; assoc. Dwight, Royall, Harris, Hoegel & Caskey, N.Y.C., 1950-54, cons., 1954-59; cons. Ford Found. Fund for the Republic, N.Y.C., 1954; dep. atty. Motion Picture Assn. Am., Inc., N.Y.C., 1959-71, v.p., legis. counsel, 1971-77, sr. v.p., gen. atty., 1977-83; sole practice N.Y.C., 1983—; bd. dirs. GE, Fairfield, Conn., Mass. Mut. Life Ins. Co., Springfield, Textron, Inc., Providence, Am. Stores Co., Salt Lake City, The Washington (D.C.) Post Co. Mem. Pres.'s Commn. on Obscenity and Pornography, 1968-70, Am. Arbitration Assn., 1971-87, N.Y.C. Bd. Ethics, 1976-89, Inst. Civil Justice, 1984-86, Citizens Com. for Children, N.Y.C., 1966-72, 85-91, Child Adoptive Service of State Charities Aid Assn., N.Y.C., 1961-68, Hillcrest Ctr. for Children, N.Y.C., 1958-61, Fedn. Protestant Welfare Agys., N.Y.C., 1959-61, 64—, N.Y. Philharm. Soc., 1971—, Am. Women's Econ. Devel. Corp., 1981—, Med. Edn. for South African Blacks, Inc., Washington, 1985-89; bd. dirs. Wiltwyck Sch., N.Y.C., 1950—, chmn. bd., 1969-78; successor trustee Yale Corp., New Haven, 1977-89; trustee Ford Found., N.Y.C., 1982—, Am. Mus. of Moving Image, 1986—, Wellesley Coll., 1988—; mem. distbn. com. N.Y. Community Trust, Inc., N.Y.C., 1978—, chmn. dist. com. N.Y. Community Trust, 1990; chmn. council advisors Hunter Coll. Sch. Social Work, 1985-89; mem. Dumpson chair com., Fordham U., N.Y.C., 1981-89; bd. dirs. Tougaloo Coll. Econ. Devel. Corp., 1991—. Recipient Meritorious award Nat. Assn. Theatre Owners, 1970, 72, Alumni Achievement award Wellesley Coll., 1975, Tribute to Women in Internat. Industry award YWCA, 1984, Elizabeth Cutter Morrow award, 1985, Outstanding Contbrs. award Am. Women's Econ. Devel., 1985, Dirs. Choice award Nat. Women's Econ. Alliance Found., 1989, Keystone award Fedn. Protestant Welfare Agys., 1991. Mem. ABA, Assn. of Bar of City of N.Y. (mem. exec. com. 1972-76), ACLU (bd. dirs.), Century Assn., Cosmopolitan Club, Yale Club, Wellesley Club. Episcopalian. Office: 36 W 44th St New York NY 10036-8102

PREISS, BETH, economist; b. N.Y.C., Oct. 4, 1954; d. Alvin and Eileen (Wolfe) P. BA in Econs. with honors, Grinnell Coll., 1976; MA in Econs., Princeton U., 1979. Economist Dept. HUD, Washington, 1980-82; sr. economist Freddie Mac, Washington, 1982-86; editor-in-chief Freddie Mac, McLean, Va., 1990—, editor-in-chief Secondary Mortgage Markets, 1990-92, prin. economist office of chmn., 1992—; v.p. Imperial Corp. of Am., San Diego, 1986-89. Contbr. articles to profl. jours. Mem. Women in Housing and Fin., Am. Econs. Assn., Am. Real Estate and Urban Econs. Assn., Economists Against the Arms Race. Home: 1015 33rd St NW Washington DC 20007-3523 Office: Freddie Mac 8200 Jones Branch Dr Mc Lean VA 22102-3110

PREISS, DAVID C., corporate consultant; b. Pretoria, South Africa, Aug. 22, 1950; came to U.S., 1975; s. Henry J. and Rita R. (Danzig) P.; m. Nancy F. Matlow, Dec. 19, 1976; children: Matthew E., Allison M. BA with honors, U. Johannesburg, Witwatersrand, South Africa, 1976; MA, Princeton U., 1977; MBA, Columbia U., 1982. Rsch. asst. U.S. Ho. Reps., Washington, 1978-80; v.p. fin. Comsat Gen. Corp., Washington, 1982-86; asst. v.p. fin. ERC Internat. Inc., Fairfax, Va., 1986-88; v.p. fin., chief fin. officer Environ Corp., Washington, 1988-89; cons. David Preiss Assocs., 1989—. Democrat. Jewish. Home: 8506 W Howell Rd Bethesda MD 20817-6827

PREISS, IVOR LOUIS, radiochemist educator; b. N.Y.C., Mar. 24, 1933; s. Louis H. and Caroline (Rozum) P.; m. Jean M. Sevor, Jan. 15, 1956 (div. 1969); m. Lorraine M. Dxson, July 27, 1970; children: Susan, Sharon, Sandra, Bradley, Michelle. BS, Rensselaer Poly. Inst., 1955; MS, U. Ark., 1957, PhD, 1960. Design draftsman Tech. Corp., Elmsford, N.Y., 1953-54; rsch. fellow U. Ark., Fayetteville, 1957-60; rsch. assoc. physics dept., lectr. chemistry Yale U., New Haven, Conn., 1961-66; assoc. prof. chemistry Rensselaer Poly. Inst., Troy, N.Y., 1966-71, prof., 1971—, prof. nuclear engring. and engring. physics, 1991—; cons. Canberra Industry, Meriden, Conn., 1960-78, GE Rsch. and Devel. Ctr., Schenectady, N.Y., 1980—, NIH, Bethesda, Md., 1985—, Gould Elec. Inc., GE Corp. Rsch. Ctr.; expert witness on environ. heavy metals; mem. chemistry, physics and math. applications com. on nuclear and radio chemistry NAS/NRC. Contbr. over 80 tech. papers and revs. to profl. publs. V.p. region-dist. PTA, Colonie, N.Y., 1970-75; bd. dirs. N.Y. State PTA, Albany, 1975-78. Mem. AAAS, Am. Chem. Soc. (membership chair 1966), Am. Phys. Soc., Zeta Psi (pres.), Sigma Xi. Home: 6 County View Rd Latham NY 12110-1304 Office: RPI Cogswell Lab Troy NY 12180

PRENTICE, EUGENE MILES, III, lawyer; b. Glen Ridge, N.J., Aug. 27, 1942; s. Eugene Miles and Anna Margaret (Kiernan) P.; m. Katharine Kirby Culbertson, Sept. 18, 1976; children: Eugene Miles IV, Jessie Kirby, John Francis. BA, Washington and Jefferson Coll., 1964; JD, U. Mich., 1967. Bar: N.Y. 1973, U.S. Dist. Ct. (so. dist.) N.Y. 1973, U.S. Dist. Ct. (ea. dist.) N.Y. 1974, U.S. Ct. Appeals (2d cir.) 1974. Mgmt. trainee Morgan Guaranty Trust, N.Y.C., 1967-68, 71-73; assoc. White & Case, N.Y.C., 1973-78; assoc. Windels, Marx et al, N.Y.C., 1978-80, ptnr., 1980-84; ptnr. Brown & Wood, N.Y.C., 1984—; pres. Midland (Tex.) Sports, Inc., 1990—; bd. dirs. Nat. Life Ins. Co., Montpelier, Vt. Trustee Vt. Law Sch., South Royalton, 1984—, Washington and Jefferson Coll., Pa., 1985—. Capt. U.S. Army, 1968-70. Mem. ABA, Assn. of Bar of City of N.Y. Republican. Clubs: Links, Union League, N.Y. Athletic Club (N.Y.C.), Spring Lake Bath & Tennis. Home: 34 W 95th St New York NY 10025-6701 Office: Brown & Wood One World Trade Ctr New York NY 10048

PRESCOTT, JOHN HERNAGE, aquarium executive; b. Corona, Calif., Mar. 16, 1935; s. Arthur James and Henrietta (Hernage) P.; m. Sandra Baker, Sept. 26, 1985; children by previous marriage—Craig C., Blane R. B.A., UCLA, 1957; postgrad., U. So. Calif., Los Angeles, 1958-60; cert. advanced mgmt. program, Harvard U. Curator Marineland of the Pacific, Palos Verdes, Calif., 1957-70, v.p., 1966-70, gen. mgr., 1970-72; exec. dir., v.p. New Eng. Aquarium, Boston, 1972—; corporator Woods Hole Oceanographic Inst., Mass., 1976-90; chmn. mem. com. sci. advisers Marine Mammal Commn., Washington, 1977-80; dir. Mus. Inst. Teaching Sci., Boston, 1984—; chmn. Humpback Whale Recovery Team NOAA, Washington, 1987—; mem. U.S. delegation Internat. Whaling Commn., 1989-91. Author: Aquarium Fishes of the World, 1976. Editor: Georges Bank: Past, Present, Future, 1981, Right Whales: Past and Present Status, 1986. Bd. dirs. Boston Mcpl. Rsch. Bur., 1981—, Boston Am. Heart Assn., 1983-86, Nat. Oceanographic and Atmospheric Adminstrn., Washington, 1987—; mem. Marine Fisheries Adv. Com.; trustee 100 Friends of Mass., 1991—. Recipient commendation for efforts to conserve whales U.S. Ho. of Reps., 1971, Ann. Sci. award for Conservation, Am. Cetacean Soc., 1969. Fellow Am. Assn. Zool. Parks and Aquariums (bd. dirs. 1985-90); mem. AAAS, Soc. Marine Mammalogy, Am. Assn. Mus., Sea Edn. Assn. (trustee 1986—), Explorers Club (chmn. New Eng. sect. 1981-85). Office: New Eng Aquarium Corp Cen Wharf Boston MA 02110

PRESS, ARTHUR I., health services company executive, consultant; b. N.Y.C., July 19, 1934; s. Albert and Edith (Bockon) P.; m. Helen Lynn Press, June 21, 1959; children: Alan, Frederick, Terri, Laurie. BS, L.I. U., 1968, MBA with honors, 1971; postgrad., NYU, 1974—. CPA, N.Y. Acct. various acctg. firms N.Y., 1954-62; auditor-in-charge U.S. Army Audit Agy., N.Y., 1962-65; assoc. adminstr., dep. med. dir. Maimonides Med. Ctr., N.Y., 1965-70, adminstrn., 1977-79; v.p. Bronx Lebanon Med. Ctr., N.Y., 1970-77; chief exec. officer Accredited Care Inc., Alpha Health Svc. Corp., N.J., Fla., White Plains, N.Y., 1979-91; exec. v.p. Mainstream Pers. Group Inc., White Plains, 1992—; cons. Adept Recruiting Corp., N.Y., 1990—, Corps. Under 20,000,000, 1970—; adj. prof. Manhatton Borough of N.Y., 1979-83; preceptor grad. students NYU, 1974-79, Barusch Sch. Bus., 1978, 79. Recipient Adminstr. Meritorious award Internat. Security Assn., N.Y., 1975. Fellow Am. Health Assn. Office: Mainstream Pers Group Inc 13-7 Granada Crescent White Plains NY 10607

PRESS, FRANK, geophysicist, educator; b. Bklyn., Dec. 4, 1924; s. Solomon and Dora (Steinholz) P.; m. Billie Kallick, June 9, 1946; children: William Henry, Paula Evelyn. BS, CCNY, 1944, LLD (hon.), 1972; MA, Columbia U., 1946, PhD, 1949; DSc (hon.), 23 univs. Rsch. assoc. Columbia U., 1946-49, instr. geology, 1949-51, asst. prof. geology, 1951-52, assoc. prof., 1952-55; prof. geophysics Calif. Inst. Tech., 1955-65, dir. seismol. lab., 1957-65; prof. geophysics, chmn. dept. earth and planetary scis. MIT, 1965-77; sci. advisor to pres., dir. Office Sci. and Tech. Policy, Washington, 1977-80; inst. prof. MIT, 1981; pres. Nat. Acad. Scis., 1981—; mem. Pres.'s Sci. Adv. Com., 1961-64; mem. Com. on Anticipated Advances in Sci. and Tech., 1974-76; mem. Nat. Sci. Bd., 1970—; mem. lunar and planetary missions bd. NASA; participant bilateral scis. agreement with Peoples Republic of China and USSR; mem. U.S. delegation to Nuclear Test Ban Negotiations, Geneva and Moscow. Author: (with M. Ewing, W.S. Jardetzky) Propagation of Elastic Waves in Layered Media, 1957, (with R. Siever) Earth, 1986; also over 160 publs.; co-editor: (with R. Siever) Physics and Chemistry of the Earth, 1957—. Recipient Columbia medal for excellence, 1960, pub. service award U.S. Dept. Interior, 1972, gold medal Royal Astron. Soc., 1972, pub. service medal NASA, 1973; named as most influential scientist in Am., U.S. News and World Report, 1982, 84, 85. Mem. Am. Acad. Arts and Scis., Geol. Soc. Am. (councilor), Am. Geophys. Union (pres. 1973), Soc. Exploration Geophysicists, Seismol. Soc. Am. (pres. 1963), AAUP, NAS, Am. Philos. Soc., French Acad. Scis., Royal Soc. (U.K.), Nat. Acad. Pub. Adminstrn., Legion of Hon. (officer 1989), Acad. Scis. of USSR (fgn. mem.). Office: National Acad of Sciences 2101 Constitution Ave NW Washington DC 20418-0001

PRESSER, CARY, research engineer; b. Bklyn., June 20, 1952; s. Harry and Regina Deborah (Lieberman) P.; m. Karen Leslie Antonoff, Feb. 27, 1977; children: Yona Ruth, Aliza Miriam. BSc in Aerospace Engring., Poly. U., 1974, MSc in Aero. Engring., 1975; DSc in Aero. Engring., Technion-Israel Inst. Tech., 1980. Teaching instr., research asst. Technion-Israel Inst. Tech., Haifa, 1975-80; engr. Nat. Inst. Standards and Tech., Gaithersburg, Md., 1980—. Contbr. articles to profl. jours. Recipient Sustained Superior Performance award Nat. Inst. Standards and Tech., 1983-89, Silver medal award U.S. Dept. Commerce, 1991; Lady Davis grad. fellow Technion-Israel Inst. Tech., 1975-76. Fellow AIAA (assoc., terrestrial energy systems tech. com., Best Paper award propellants and combustion tech. com. 1987, 89, 92—, propellants and combustion tech. com. 1987-90); mem. ASTM (com. on particle sixe measurements), N.Y. Acad. Scis., ASME (mem. com. heat transfer in energy systems), Inst. Liquid Atomization and Spray System, Am. Inst. Chem. Engrs., Assn. Orthodox Jewish Scientists, Combustion Inst. (symposium program rev. subcom.), Instrument Soc. Am., Sigma Xi (admissions com. NIST chpt.), Sigma Gamma Tau, Tau Epsilon Phi. Office: Nat Inst Standards & Tech Bldg 221 Rm B 306 Gaithersburg MD 20899

PRESSLER, PHILIP BERNARD, advertising executive, educator; b. Balt., May 3, 1946; s. James William and Jean Callista (Colgan) P.; m. Catherine Mary Dale, Jan. 11, 1973 (div. Feb. 5, 1987); children: Julie, Brian, Elizabeth. BA, Villanova U., 1969; MA, Washington Theol. Coalition, 1972. Sales rep. 3M Co., Wilmington, Del., 1972-76; systems cons. Tab Products Co., Pennsauken, N.J., 1976-78, Compugraphic Corp., Bala Cynwyd, Pa., 1978-80; advanced to pres., chief exec. officer Pro-file Systems, Inc., Conshohocken, Pa., 1980-88; br. mgr. Document Mgmt. Group, Inc., Malvern, Pa., 1988-89; owner Pressler Assocs., Wayne, Pa., 1988—; pres. PNS Assocs., Inc., Wayne, 1990—; prof. Manor Jr. Coll., Jenkintown, Pa., 1985—; bd. dirs. Bus. Systems and Security Mktg. Assn., Kalamazoo, 1986—; chmn. bd. Assn. Records Mgrs. and Adminstrn., Phila. (Pres.'s award, 1986). Author: Equipment Cost Study, 1981; inventor acoustical panel the Baffle, file directory, conversion fileback; patentee Addendex (award 1990). V.p. Glenhardie Condominium Assn., Wayne, Pa., 1987-88, pres., 1988-90. Named to Inc. 500 Inc. Mag., 1985-86. Mem. Office Automation Soc. Internat., Glenhardie Country Club. Roman Catholic. Home and Office: 322 Drummers Ln Wayne PA 19087-1547

PRESSLY, BARBARA, state legislator; b. Chgo., May 13, 1937; d. C. David and Esther (Rustad) Brown; m. George Byrne Pressly, 1960; children: Patricia, George Jr., Robert. BS, U. Ill., 1960. Former mem. N.H. Ho. of Reps.; mem. Hillsborough County Exec. Com.; alderman-at-large Nashua, N.H.; mem. N.H. State Senate. Mem. Nashua Hist. Dist. Commn.; deaconess First Congl. Ch., Nashua, 1980-83. Mem. Kings Daus. Benevolent Soc. Democrat. Address: 80 Concord St Nashua NH 03060

PRESSLY, WILLIAM LAURENS, art history educator; b. Chattanooga, Apr. 1, 1944; s. William Laurens and Alice (McCallie) P.; m. Nancy Lee Dorfman, July 12, 1970; 1 child, David Blake. AB, Princeton U., 1966; PhD, NYU, 1974. Asst. prof. dept. history of art Yale U., New Haven, 1973-79, assoc. prof., 1979-82; sr. lectr. dept. art U. Tex., Austin, 1982-83; assoc. prof. dept. art and art history Duke U., Durham, N.C., 1985-87; assoc. prof. dept. art history and archaeology U. Md., College Park, 1987—. Author: The Life and Art of James Barry, 1981, A Catalogue of the Paintings in the Folger Shakespeare Library, 1992, (exhbn. catalogue) James Barry: The Artist as Hero, 1983; contbr. articles to profl. publs. Guggenheim meml. fellow, 1983-84, Morse fellow, 1975-76. Fellow Royal Soc. Arts; mem. Coll. Art Assn., Am. Soc. for Eighteenth-Century Studies, Walpole Soc., Phi Beta Kappa. Home: 6135 31st St NW Washington DC 20015-1515 Office: U Md Dept Art History Rm 1211-B Art/Sociol Bldg College Park MD 20742

PRESSMAN, EDWARD J., business executive; b. N.Y.C., June 21, 1940; s. David and Anne (Engel) P.; m. Jane Kohn (div. 1981), children: Susan, Mark; m. Arlene Gilbert, Sept. 5, 1982; 1 child, Deborah. BA, Columbia Coll, 1962. Salesman McAliece Paper Corp., N.Y.C., 1962-69, sec., sales mgr., 1969-76, pres., 1976-80; pres. Owen-McAliece Paper Corp., N.Y.C., 1980—. Class correspondent: (mag.) Columbia College Today. Sec. Tri-Village Little League, Huntington, N.Y., 1977-78; pres. Cow Harbor Soccer Club, Huntington, 1980-81. Fellow John Jay Assoc. (Columbia); Mem. Soc. Columbia Graduates (bd. dirs. 1991—), L.I. Baroque Ensemble (pres. 1989—). Office: Owen-McAliece Paper Corp 266 Spring St New York NY 10013-1405

PRESSMAN, STEVEN, economics and finance educator; b. Bklyn., Feb. 23, 1952; s. Jerome and Phyllis Pressman; m. Jane Agar, Jan. 1, 1988. BA in Philosophy, Alfred U., 1973; MA in Philosophy, Syracuse U., 1975; PhD in Econs., New Sch. for Social Rsch., 1983. Asst. prof. econs. and fin. Monmouth Coll., West Long Branch, N.J., 1981-87; assoc. prof. Monmouth Coll., West Long Branch, 1987—. Editorial bd. Rev. of Polit. Economy, 1987—, Ea. Econ. Jour., 1988—, assoc. editor, 1989—. Mem. Am. Econ. Assn., Assn. Evolutionary Econs., Ea. Econ. Assn., History Econs. Soc., Western Econ. Assn. Home: 1803 Willow Dr #a Asbury Park NJ 07712-2841 Office: Monmouth Coll West Long Branch NJ 07764

PRESSMAN, TODD EVAN, psychotherapist; b. Phila., Oct. 9, 1960; s. Maurie David and Rosalie (Shein) P. BA, U. Pa., 1983; MA, U. of South Fla., 1985; PhD, Saybrook Inst., 1992. Psychotherapist Inst. for Psychiat. Wellness, Phila., 1986—, exec. v.p., 1990—; seminar leader in psycho-spiritual growth techniques Inst. for Psychiat. Wellness, 1986—. Composer (ballet) Aladdin, 1988; choreographer (modern dance) Group Motion, 1980—; contbr. articles to profl. jours. Volunteer Phila. Com. for the Homeless, 1988; bd. dirs. Horizon House, Phila., 1989—. Recipient Svc. award Phila. Resource and Networking Assn., 1989. Mem. ACA, Pa. Psychol. Assn. Home: 261 St James Pl Philadelphia PA 19106-3936 Office: Inst Psychiat Wellness 35 Kings Hwy E Haddonfield NJ 08033-2009

PRESTON, ANDREW JOSEPH, pharmacist, drug company executive; b. Bklyn., Apr. 19, 1922; s. Charles A. and Josephine (Rizzutto) Pumo; B.Sc., St. John U., 1943; m. Martha Jeanne Happ, Oct. 10, 1953; children: Andrew Joseph Jr., Charles Richard, Carolyn Louise, Frank Arthur, Joanne Marie, Barbara Jeanne. Cert. bus. intermediary. Mgr. Press Club, Bklyn. Nat. League Baseball Club, 1941-42; purchasing agt. Drug and Pharm. div. Intrassind, Inc., 1947; chief pharmacist Hendershot Pharmacy, Newton, N.J., 1949; agt. Bur. of Narcotics, U.S. Treasury Dept., 1948-49; owner Preston Drug & Surg. Co., Boonton, N.J., 1949-86; chief exec. officer Preston Pharmaceutics, Inc., Butler, N.J., 1970-80, chief exec. officer Preston Bus. Cons., Inc., Kinnelon, N.J., 1987—; commr. N.J. State Bd. Pharmacy, 1970-72, pres., 1973; organizer State of N.J. Drug Abuse Speakers Program, 1970-76; chmn. Morris County Drug Abuse Coun., 1969-70; lectr. drug abuse and narcotic addiction various community orgns., 1968-78; mem. adv. bd. Nat. Community Bank, Boonton, N.J., 1973. Chmn. bldg. fund com. Riverside Hosp., Boonton, 1963; mem. Morris County (N.J.) Rep. Fin. Com., 1972; pres. Ronald Reagan N.J. Re-Election Adv. Bd., 1984; mem. exec. com. Gov. Tom Kean Annual Ball, 1985-86; chmn. Pharmacists of N.J. for election of Pres. Ford, 1976, Pharmacists for Gov. Tom Kean, 1981-84, N.J. Pharmacists for Reagan/Bush '84; mem. exec. com. Morris County Overall Econ. Devel. Com., 1976-82; chmn. Pharmacists for Fenwick, 1982; v.p. Kinnelon Rep. Club, 1980, Rep. Com., Kinnelon, 1990. Served to lt. (j.g.), USNR, 1943-46. Recipient Bowl Hygeia award Robbins Co., 1969, E.R. Squibb President's award, 1968, N.J. Pharm. Square Club award, 1969. Mem. Am. Pharm. Assn., N.J. Pharm. Assn. (mem. econs. com. 1960-65, pres. 1967-68, Oscar Singer Meml. award 1987), Nat. Assn. of Retail Druggists, Internat. Narcotic Enforcement Officers Assn., N.J. Narcotic Enforcement Officers Assn., Nat. Assn. Realtors, N.J. Assn. Realtors, Morris County Bd. Realtors, Internat. Bus. Brokers Assn. (cert. bus. intermediary), Inst. Bus. Appraisers, Pharmacists Guild Am. (pres. N.Y. div. 1946-47), Pharmacists Guild of N.J., N.J. Public Health Assn., Morris County Pharm. Assn., Morris-Sussex Pharmacists Soc., Am. Legion, St. John's Alumni Assn. Roman Catholic. Clubs: Elks, K.C., Smoke Rise. Contbr. editorials to profl. jours. Home and Office: 568A Pepperidge Tree Ln Kinnelon NJ 07405

PRESTON, BETH BROWN, linguist, author; b. Cleve., Mar. 7, 1953; d. James Beaty and Jeannette (Glover) Oliver; m. Otis W. Brown Jr., Sept. 4, 1973 (div. 1980); children: Otis William III, Tonya, David Jr., Andy, Connie, Thomas. AB, Bryn Mawr Coll., 1976; MFA, Goddard Coll., 1981; PhD in Comparative Lit., U. Pa., 1982; EdD, Temple U., 1982. Cert. secondary English tchr. Asst. adminstr. Settlement Music Sch., Phila., 1975-76; sec. Am. Coll. of Physics, Phila., 1976-78; actuarial asst. The Hay Group, Phila., 1978-79; sec. sociology dept. U. Pa., Phila., 1979-80; med. researcher Children's Hosp., Phila., 1980; sec. membership div. Univ. Mus. U. Pa., Phila., 1981; substitute tchr. English Woodrow Wilson High Sch., Camden, N.J., 1985; med. sec. Temple U. Hosp., Phila., 1986; Mellon postdoctoral fellow U. Pa., Phila., 1991—; lectr., fellow Univ. Mus., Phila., 1990—. Author: (poetry) Kaze, 1985, Lightyears, 1973-76, 82, Blue Cyclone, 1982 (CBS Lit. Award), Satin Tunnels (nominated William Carlos Williams award 1990), A Prehistory of Love, 1990, Adam of Ife, 1991. Mem. Phila. Anthrop. Soc., 1980—. Served with USNG, 1981. Recipient Bread Loaf Award Middlebury Coll., Vt., 1979, 80, Pa. Coun. on the Arts award; nominated for Alice Faydi Castagnola prize, Oxygen, 1991. Mem. Poets and Writers, Am. Acad. of Poets, Associated Writing Programs, Poetry Soc. of Am. Democrat. Mem. Nichiren Shoshu of Am. Home: 5943 Belmar Ter # 2 Philadelphia PA 19143-5210 Office: U Pa 33rd and Civic Center Blvd Philadelphia PA 19104

PRESTON, FAITH, college president; b. Boston, Sept. 14, 1921; d. Howard Knowlton and Edith Smith (Wilson) P.; m. Winthrop Wadleigh, Dec. 19, 1970. B.A., Boston U., 1944; M.A., 1945; Ed.D., Columbia U. Tchrs. Coll., 1964. Tchr. Georgetown (Mass.) High Sch., 1945-47; tchr. Stoneham (Mass.) High Sch., 1947-50, Endicott Jr. Coll., Beverly, Mass., 1950-53; dir. research P.R. Jr. Coll., 1953-55; dean adminstrn., 1955-63, v.p., 1963-65; pres. White Pines Coll., 1965-91, pres. emeritus, 1991—, also trustee. Author: David and the Handcar, 1950, Jose's Miracle, 1955, The Silver Box, 1979. Mem. bd. incorporators Cath. Med. Ctr., Manchester, N.H., 1978—; bd. dirs. Caregivers; pres. bd. dirs. N.H. Assn. for Blind; trustee funds Chester Congl. Bapt. Ch., deacon, 1988—. Kellogg fellow, 1964. Mem. Am. Assn. Jr. Colls., Phi Lambda Theta, Kappa Delta Pi, Delta Kappa Gamma. Republican. Clubs: Univ. Women's (London); The College (Boston); Fortnightly. Home: PO Box 25 Chester NH 03036-0025 Office: White Pines Coll Office of the Pres Chester St Chester NH 03036-4305

PRESTON, RICHARD MCCANN, creative company executive, writer; b. Cambridge, Mass., Aug. 5, 1954; s. Jerome and Dorothy (McCann) P.; m. Michelle Parham, May 11, 1985. BA summa cum laude, Pomona Coll., 1977; PhD in English, Princeton U., 1983. Staff writer Princeton (N.J.) U., 1984-85; chmn., chief exec. officer Urania, Inc., Princeton, 1986—. Author: First Light, 1987, American Steel, 1991; regular contbr. articles to The New Yorker mag. Award judge Am. Inst. Physics, N.Y.C., 1989-92. Recipient Sci. Writing award Am. Inst. Physics, 1988.

PRESTON, SEYMOUR STOTLER, III, manufacturing company executive; b. Media, Pa., Sept. 11, 1933; s. Seymour Stotler and Mary Alicia (Harper) P.; m. Jean Ellen Holman, Sept. 8, 1956; children: Courtney J., Katherine E., Alicia D., Shelley S. B.A., Williams Coll., 1956; M.B.A., Harvard U., 1958. With Pennwalt Corp., Phila., 1961-89; exec. v.p. in charge of chems. and equipment ops., worldwide Pennwalt Corp., 1975-77, pres., chief operating officer, 1977-89, also dir.; pres., chief exec. officer Atochem N.Am., West Chester, 1990—; bd. dir. Core States Fin. Corp., Phila. Nat. Bank, The Lawrenceville (N.J.) Sch., 1982—. Trustee Shipley Sch., Bryn Mawr, Pa., 1976-88, Acad. Natural Scis., 1981—; bd. mgrs. Franklin Inst., Phila., 1980— . Served to 1st lt. USAF, 1958-61. Mem. Soc. for Chem. Industry, Greater Phila. C. of C. (dir. 1979—), Union League (Phila.), Radnor Hunt Club (Malvern, Pa.). Office: Elf Atochem N Am Inc 3 Parkway Philadelphia PA 19102

PREUS, ANTHONY, philosophy educator; b. Perth Amboy, N.J., July 5, 1936; 1 son, Christian; m. Meredith Pell; 1 son, Alexander, 1 dau. Caroline. B.A. in Classics summa cum laude, Luther Coll., 1958; B.A. in Literae Humaniores, Oxford U. (Eng.) 1962, M.A., 1966; Ph.D. in Philosophy Johns Hopkins U., 1968. Grad. asst., teaching asst. philosophy Johns Hopkins U., 1962-63; acting asst. prof. philosophy SUNY-Binghamton, 1964-66, asst. prof., 1966-71, assoc. prof., 1971-80, prof., 1980—, spl. admissions instr., 1969, resident dir. Mediterranean Studies, 1973-74, chmn. grad. com., 1974-76, chmn. classical and near eastern studies dept., 1980-83, acting chmn. Philosophy dept., 1991; adj. assoc. prof. dept. preventive medicine SUNY-Upstate Med. Ctr., 1980—; vis. philosopher Tougaloo Coll., 1983; bass violinist Harpur Coll. Orch., 1965-71. Author: Science and Philosophy in Aristotle's Biological Works, 1975; Aristotle and Michael of Ephesus On the Movement and Progression of Animals, 1981; editor: (with John P. Anton) Essays in Ancient Greek Philosophy, Vol. II, 1983, vol. III, 1989, vol. IV, 1991, vol. V, 1992; contbr. book revs. and articles to profl. jours. Mem. Lourdes Hosp. Instl. Rev. Bd., Binghamton, 1978—, chmn., 1982-87, ethics com., 1987—. Fellow Woodrow Wilson Found., 1958-59, Fels, Found., 1963-64, Nat. Humanities Inst., 1978-79; grantee SUNY Found., 1968, 70, 73, 78, Am. Council Learned Socs., 1971-72, NSF, 1977-78, NEH, 1980-81, 82-83; Rhodes scholar, 1959-62. Mem. Soc. Ancient Greek Philosophy (sec. 1980—), Am. Philos. Assn., Am. Philological Assn., Club: Triple Cities Hiking (dir. 1982-86, coord. Finger Lakes Trail Sect. 1983—).

PREVIATO, EMMA, mathematics educator; b. Badia Polesine, Veneto, Italy, Nov. 29, 1952; came to U.S., 1978; d. Pierluigi and Bice (Costato) P. Laurea in Math., U. Padua, Italy, 1974; MA in Math., Harvard U., 1979, PhD in Math., 1983. Assoc. prof. U. Padua, 1974-78; teaching fellow Harvard U., Cambridge, Mass., 1978-83; asst. prof. dept. math. Boston U., 1983—; reviewer Math. Reviews, Ann Arbor, Mich., 1985—, NSF, Washington, 1984—; vol. scientist Boston Mus., 1988—; vis. prof. Math. Scis.

Rsch. Inst., Berkeley, Calif., 1991. Swedish Royal Soc. fellow, Stockholm, 1986-87, English Sci. Engring. Rsch. Ctr. fellow, London, 1987-88; recipient award NSF, Princeton, 1984-85. Mem. Am. Math. Soc., London Math. Soc., Assn. Women in Math. Roman Catholic. Office: Boston U 111 Cummington St Boston MA 02215-2411

PREVIDI, ROBERT, communications executive, retired; b. N.Y.C., Aug. 12, 1935; s. William T. and Lucy (Soldano) R.; m. Taimi Fagerstrom, Jan. 1962; children: Robert, Jr., Jeffrey. BA in Econs., Hunter Coll., 1958; MA in Polit. Sci., CUNY, 1987. V.p., advt. and promotion Citibank, N.Y.C., 1972-75; sr. v.p., mktg., pub. rels. European Am. Bank, N.Y.C., 1975-85; v.p., dir. corp. communications Citibank, N.Y.C., 1985-91. Author: (book) Civilian Control Vs. Military Rule, 1988; contbg. author: Re: Army Chiefs of Staff; contbr. articles to profl. jours. Candidate for Congress, 3rd Congl. Dist., N.Y., 1988, 90; candidate for town supr. North Hempstead, N.Y., 1991. Recipient awards Am. Mktg. Assn., 1988, Fin. Advt. and Mktg. Assn., 1988. Mem. The Downtown Assn., The Naval War Coll. Found., Ctr. for Study of the Presidency (mem. nat. adv. coun.). Republican. Roman Catholic.

PREVILL, ARTHUR ERNEST, retired engineer; b. Rand, W.Va., Oct. 9, 1921; s. Harry Victor and Josephine (Olish) P.; m. Dorothy Martha Beaulieu, Sept. 19, 1952; children: Arthur E. Jr., Victor G., Amanda J., Steven M. BSEE, W.Va. U., 1946. Registered profl. engr., Fla., Md., D.C., Va., N.J., Pa., Del., Ga., Ala. Layout engr. West Pa. Power Co., Pitts., 1946-48; apllications engr. GE, Lynn, Mass., 1948-49; elec. engr. Johns-Manville Corp., Manville, N.J., 1949-51; design engr. Austin Co., Roselle, N.J., 1951-53; field engr. Rust Co., USAF Testing Lab., Tullahoma, Tenn., 1953-54; design engr. So. Co., Birmingham, Ala., 1954-55; head elc. div. E.J. Sullivan & Assocs., N.Y.C., 1955-58; asst. supr. M.W. Kellogg Co., N.Y., Md., 1958-60; prin. A.E. Previll & Assocs., Silver Spring, Md., 1960-71; engring. mgr., v.p. UPI of Westinghouse and DESC, Balt. and, Va., 1971-84. Mem. Am. Legion, Toastmaster.

PRIBRAM, JOHN KARL, physics educator; b. Chgo., Feb. 1, 1941; s. Karl H. and Helen (Finegan) P.; m. Hope Dimock Brown, June 22, 1963; children—Sarah Hope, Margaret Ann. A.B., Middlebury Coll., 1962; M.A., Wesleyan U., 1965; Ph.D., U. Mass., 1973. Instr. physics Bates Coll., Lewiston, Maine, 1970-73, asst. prof., 1973-80, assoc. prof., 1980-89, prof., 1989—, chair dept. physics and astronomy, 1985—; vis. asst. prof. dept. physics U. Ill., 1979-80; vis. assoc. prof. dept. physics and astronomy Dartmouth Coll., 1987-88. Contbr. articles to profl. jours. Corporator Autumn Pub. Library, Maine, 1974—. Danforth assoc., 1981—; Andrew Mellon fellow, 1977-78; NSF grantee, 1978, 81, 87; Research Corp. grantee, 1972-73. Mem. Am. Phys. Soc., Am. Assn. Physics Tchrs., History of Sci. Soc., Sigma Xi. Avocations: hiking; bird watching.

PRICE, BARBARA GRAHAM, guidance counselor; b. Reading, Pa., Jan. 16, 1965; d. Robert Bruce and Florence Mary (Focht) Graham; m. John Robert Price, Dec. 30, 1989. BA in Internat. Rels., Bucknell U., 1987, MS Edn., 1989. Cert. elem. and secondary guidance counselor. Guidance counselor Lewisburg (Pa.) Area High Sch., 1989-90, Mifflinburg (Pa.) Area Mid. Sch., 1990—. CPR, first aid instr. ARC, Union County, 1989—; ambulance lt. William Cameron Engine Co., 1987-88. Mem. AACD, Am. Sch. Counselors Assn., Susquehanna Valley Sch. Counselors Assn., Susquehanna Valley Critical Incident Stress Mgmt. Team (clin. dir. 1990—), Alpha Lambda Delta. Republican. Episcopalian. Home: 93 Fairview Rd Lewisburg PA 17837-8841 Office: Mifflinburg Area Mid Sch E Market St Mifflinburg PA 17844-1412

PRICE, BARBARA NEFF, college administrator; b. York Springs, Pa., May 30, 1938; d. Kenneth Russell Neff and Barbara Beatrice (Baeshore) Cochran; m. William Evan Price, Nov. 25, 1977; children: Barbara Elizabeth Youngman Galli, Charles Ludwig Youngman II, Christopher Karl Landmesser. BA in Psychology, Lycoming Coll., 1960; MS in Counseling, U. Scranton, 1970; PhD in Ednl. Leadership, U. Pa., 1985. Cert. counselor, sch. supt. Tchr. St. Boniface High Sch., Williamsport, Pa., 1963-66, South Williamsport (Pa.) Sch. Dist., 1966-67; counselor Dallas (Pa.) Sch. Dist., 1972-75, dir. counseling, 1975-81; dir. careers/placement Keystone Jr. Coll., La Plume, Pa., 1981-82, Luzerne County Community Coll., Nanticoke, Pa., 1982—; cons. Victims Resource Ctr., Wilkes-Barre, Pa., 1990—, Pa. State U., University Park, 1990—. Mem., editor Jr. League Wilkes-Barre, 1967-89; pres. bd. Victims Resource Ctr., Wilkes-Barre, 1989; exec. bd. Community Counseling Svcs., Wilkes-Barre, 1980—; adminstrv. bd. Shavertown (Pa.) Meth. Ch., 1985—. Named Pa. Counselor of Yr., Pa. Sch. Counselors Assn., Hershey, 1981; recipient Lifetime Membership award Victims Resource Ctr., Wilkes-Barre, 1989, Svc. award Community Counseling Svcs., Wilkes-Barre, 1990. Mem. AACD, World Future Soc., Mid Atlantic Career Counseling Assocs. (pres. 1989-90, coll. rep. award 1989, Ross Narghang award 1990), Luzerne County Counselors Assn. (pres. 1978-80), Phi Kappa Phi, Phi Delta Kappa, Delta Kappa Gamma. Methodist. Home: 980 Huntsville Rd Wilkes Barre PA 18708-9701 Office: Luzerne County Community Coll Prospect St Nanticoke PA 18634

PRICE, DAVID MCCLELLAN, medical ethics educator; b. Detroit, Aug. 8, 1936; s. Alvin E. and Mary (McClellan) P.; m. Kashala Hill, 1958 (div. 1979); children: Cynthia, Jonathan, Benjamin; m. Patricia A. Murphy, Sept. 2, 1979. AB, U. Mich., 1958; MDiv., Yale U., 1962; PhD, Mich. State U., 1974. Ordainted to Prebyterian Ministry, 1962, honorably retired, 1990. Pastor Westminster Presbyn. Ch., Troy, N.Y., 1962-64; dir. Mich. Commn. United Ministries in Higher Edn., Flint, East Lansing, Mich., 1965-72; adminstr. Mich. State U. Coll. of Osteopathic Medicine, E. Lansing, 1972-74; mem. faculty Mich. State U. Coll. Human Medicine, E. Lansing, 1974-78, Univ. of Medicine and Dentistry of N.J., N.J. Med. Sch., Newark, 1979—; ethicist St. Barnabas Med. Ctr., Livingston, N.J., 1991—; trustee Citizens Com. on Biomed. Ethics, Inc., Summit, N.J., 1986—; cons. Bd. Med. Examiners, Trenton, N.J., 1989-90, The Bioethics Commn., Princeton, N.J., 1991—. Contbr. articles to profl. jours. Mem. Plan and Policy Devel. Com., State Health Coord. Coun., N.J., Trenton, 1991. Mem. Hastings Ctr., Soc. for Health and Human Values, Am. Soc. for Law and Medicine, Soc. for Bioethics Consultation. Democrat. Home: 85 White Oak Dr Califon NJ 07830-3411 Office: U Medicine & Dentistry NJ NJ Med Sch 185 S Orange Ave Newark NJ 07103-2714

PRICE, GLENDA DELORES, university dean; b. York, Pa., Oct. 10, 1939; d. William B. Price and Zelma E. Holmes McGeary. BS, Temple U., 1961, MEd, 1969, PhD, 1979. Clin. lab. specialist. Cytotechnologist Temple U. Hosp., Phila., 1961-67; faculty Coll. Allied Health Professions, Temple U., Phila., 1967-79, asst. dean allied health, 1979-86; dean allied health Sch. Allied Health Professions, U. Conn., Storrs, 1986—. Contbr. articles to profl. jours., chpts. to books. Bd. trustees U. New Eng., Biddeford, Maine, 1989—; bd. dirs. Windham Hosp., Willimantic, Conn., 1989—, E. Hartford VNA, 1989—; allied health adv. Pew Health Prof. Commn., Durham, N.C., 1991—. Recipient Leadership Award SUNY-Buffalo, 1982; named Mem. of the Yr., Pa. Soc. for Med. Tech., 1979; decorated Legion of Honor, Chapel of Four Chaplains, 1977. Mem. Am. Soc. Allied Health Professions (sec. 1985-87), Am. Soc. for Med. Tech. (pres. 1979-80), Alpha Kappa Alpha, Alpha Mu Tau, Alpha Eta, Phi Kappa Phi. Democrat. Baptist. Office: U Conn 358 Mansfield Rd Storrs Mansfield CT 06268

PRICE, GLENN ALBERT, retired nuclear physicist; b. Mpls., Feb. 9, 1923; s. Hugh Bruce and Jennie May (Swab) P.; m. Charlotte Louise Jones, June 6, 1950; children: Beverly, Daniel, David, Albert. BS, U. Ky., 1946; MS, U. Ill., 1948, PhD, 1952. Technician Los Alamos (N.Mex.) Sci. Lab., 1944-46; physicist Brookhaven Nat. Lab., Upton, N.Y., 1952-70, head acad. rels., 1970-85; cost-free expert Internat. Atomic Energy Agy., Vienna, Austria, 1987-89; ret., 1990; cons. Oak Ridge (Tenn.) Nat. Lab., 1985-87, Brookhaven Nat. Lab., 1986; advisor Indian AEC, Bombay, 1967. Contbr. articles to profl. publs. With U.S. Army, 1942-46. AEC predoctoral fellow, 1950-52. Mem. Am. Nuclear Soc. Home: 92 Pondview Rd Weare NH 03281

PRICE, JAMES EDWARD, federal government executive; b. Paterson, N.J., Feb. 5, 1941; s. Lawrence A. and Mary (Popp) P.; m. Joanne Ennis, Feb. 10, 1979; children: Rosemary, Donna, James, Robert, John, Elke. AA, U. Md., 1972, BS summa cum laude, 1974; MBA, Cen. Mich. U., 1976; postgrad., George Mason U., 1985—. Command sgt. maj. U.S. Army, 1958-82; dep. dir. evaluation and standards U.S. Army Engr. Sch., Ft. Belvoir, Va., 1982-83; program analyst Hdqrs. Dept. of Army Pentagon, Washington, 1983-86; dep. program and project mgr. Dept. Defense, Falls Church, Va., 1986-88, dep. dir. for strategic planning, 1988-89; prof. systems mgmt. Info. Resource Mgmt. Coll. Nat. Def. U., Washington, 1989-92; prof. systems mgmr. Def. Systems Mgmt. Coll., Ft. Belvoir, 1992—. Mem. Am. Assn. Pub. Adminstrs., Project Mgmt. Inst., Internat. Acad. for Info. Systems, Data Processing Mgmt. Assn., Phi Kappa Phi, Alpha Sigma Lambda. Home: 6856 Heatherway Ct Alexandria VA 22310

PRICE, JOAN WEBSTER, art educator, artist, curator; b. Camden, N.J., Jan. 8, 1931; d. George Mott and May A. (Kyne) W.; m. Herbert Price; children: David Webster, Joel Leigh. BFA, BS in Edn., Temple U., 1954; MA, Columbia U., 1958, EdD, 1971. Cert. tchr., N.Y. Recreation leader Phila. Recreation Ctr., 1953-54; art tchr. Madison (N.J.) Pub. Schs., 1954-57, Clark Jr./Sr. High Sch., East Meadow, N.Y., 1963-65; enameling instr. Great Neck (N.Y.) Adult Edn., 1957-59; instr., asst. prof. art Suffolk C.C., Selden, N.Y., 1965-67; lectr. CUNY, Queens, 1967-68; prof. art dept. The City Coll., CUNY, N.Y.C., 1968—; artist-in-residence, fellow Va. Ctr. Creative Arts, Sweetbriar, 1984; v.p., bd. dirs. Inst. for Study Art in Edn., N.Y.C., 1976-78; guest curator The Bronx (N.Y.) Mus. Art, 1976; curator exhibit and catalog Ageless Perceptions I, 1988, Ageless Perceptions II, 1989. Prin. works include solar sculpture Sun Altar, 1980. Mem. Am. Abstract Artists (exhbn. chair 1991-92, rep. U.S. com. 1979), N.Y. N.J. Nat. Womens Caucus, N.Y. State Art Tchrs. Assn., N.Y.C. Art Tchrs. Assn. (co-pres., cochair 1973, art adv., educator 1984), Univ. Coun. Art Edn., Nature Conservancy, Internat. Soc. for the Arts, Scis. and Tech., Sculpture Internat. Home: 35 Ridgewood Ter Maplewood NJ 07040 Office: CCNY Art Dept 138th St and Convent Ave New York NY 10031

PRICE, LESTER LEE, naval flight officer; b. Eufaula, Ala., Jan. 3, 1955; s. Lester Johnson and Jill (Howell) P.; m. Laurie Poitras, Oct. 6, 1984; children: Elisabet, Lacey, Daniel, Kathryn. BS, U.S. Naval Acad., 1978. Chief engr. USS Fidelity, Panama City, Fla., 1979-81; pers. officer Patrol Squadron 46, Moffett Field, Calif., 1982-85; exec. asst., instr. U.S. Naval Acad., Annapolis, Md., 1985-88; targeting program coord. Chief of Naval Ops., Washington, 1988-90; tactics officer dept. head Patrol Squadron 26, Brunswick, Maine, 1991—. Sub-editor (revision): Knight's Modern Seamanship, 1986, Division Officer's Guide, 1987. Recipient Navy Commendation medal, 1988. Mem. Naval Acad. Alumni Assn., Naval Acad. Athletic Assn., Nat. Eagle Scout Assn. (officer rep. 1985-88). Republican. Methodist. Home: HC33 Box 61U Arrowsic ME 04530 Office: Patrol Squadron 26 VP 26 Brunswick ME 04011

PRICE, MARGARET ANN, business owner; b. Richmond, N.Y., July 7, 1951; d. George Townley III and Claire Adreanne (Savarese) P.; m. Michael Anthony Carver, May 15, 1978; 1 child, Jonathan Pleam Carver. BA, Rutgers U., 1976. Graphic artist Tabloid Pubs., Highland Park, N.J., 1976-77, Hadwen, Inc., Bennington, Vt., 1977-79; artist, printer Action Graphics, Bennington, 1979-81; owner Inkspot Press, Bennington, 1981—. Bd. dirs. Bennington Project Independence, treas., 1991-93; mem. adv. bd. High Sch. Vocat. Program, Bennington, 1988—; chmn. Tourism Group/2010 Com., Bennington, 1986. Mem. AAUW (treas. 1990—), Printing Industries New Eng., Rotary. Home: RR 1 Box 250 Shaftsbury VT 05262-9801 Office: Inkspot Press 736 Main St Bennington VT 05201-2633

PRICE, PAUL MARNELL, lawyer; b. Binghamton, N.Y., July 23, 1959; s. Paul B. and Rita E. (Marnell) P.; m. Teresa Lynn Doll, Sept. 26, 1987; 1 child, Kayla Marie. BS in Chemistry-Bus. cum laude, Scranton (Pa.) U., 1981; JD magna cum laude, Syracuse U., 1984. Bar: N.Y. 1985. Assoc. Levene, Gouldin & Thompson, Binghamton, 1984-87; mem. Hickey, Sheehan & Gates, P.C., Binghamton, 1987—. Mem. Estate Planning Council of So. Tier, Binghamton, 1985—. Mem. N.Y. State Bar Assn., Broom County Bar Assn. Democrat. Roman Catholic. Office: Hickey Sheehan & Gates PC 160162 Hawley St Binghamton NY 13901-4094

PRICE, PETER JACK, physicist; b. London. BA, Oxford (Eng.) U., 1948; PhD in Theoretical Physics, Cambridge (Eng.) U., 1951. Rsch. assoc. Duke U., 1951-52; with Princeton (N.J.) Inst. for Advanced Study, 1952-53; theoretical physicist rsch. div. IBM, 1953—. Assoc. editor Phys. Rev., 1964-66; mem. editorial bd. Jour. Applied Physics, Applied Physics Letters, 1989-91; contbr. articles to profl. jours., chpts. to books. Fellow Am. Phys. Soc. Office: IBM Rsch Div T J Watson Rsch Ctr Yorktown Heights NY 10598

PRICE, PETER MICHAEL, molecular biology researcher, educator; b. Rockville Center, N.Y., Aug. 7, 1946; s. Lewis E. and Emilie G. (Bruderer) P.; m. Addie M. Carter, Aug. 9, 1971; 1 child: Amelia C. BS, Cornell U., 1968; PHD, NYU, 1973. Assoc. Mt. Sinai Sch. Medicine, N.Y.C., 1975-77, sr. instr., 1977-79; vis. scientist U. Calif., San Francisco, 1979; asst. prof. Mt. Sinai Sch. Medicine, N.Y.C., 1979-87, assoc. prof., 1987—; presenter in field. Contbr. over 40 articles to refereed jour. Mem. Murray Hill Com., N.Y.C. Mem. Am. Soc. for Biochemistry & Molecular Biology, AAAS, Union League Club N.Y., Am. Alpine Club. Office: Mt Sinai Sch Medicine Dept Medicine 1 Gustave L Levy Pl New York NY 10029-6504

PRICE, RICHARD TAYLOR, family physician; b. Perkasie, Pa., Apr. 4, 1930; s. Harold Norwood and Florence Mae (Spoerl) P.; m. Kathleen Ann Schnerr, Aug. 9, 1958; children: Steven Taylor, Sally Ann. BA, Lehigh U., 1951, MS, 1952; MD, Jefferson Med. Coll., 1956. Intern/resident Meth. Hosp., Phila., 1956-57; family physician Perkasie, 1957-58; ptnr. Pennridge Med. Assocs., Perkasie, 1960—; med. dir. Pennridge Sch. Dist., Perkasie, 1960—; pres. med.-dental staff Grandview Hosp., 1969; clin. instr. dept. family medicine Thomas Jefferson U., Phila., 1976—. Bd. dirs. Grandview Found., Sellersville, 1990—; trustee Grandview Hosp., 1990-91. Capt. M.C. USAF, 1958-60. Mem. AMA, Am. Acad. Family Practice, Pa. Med. Soc., Bucks County Med. Soc., Pennridge C. of C., St. Stephen's U. C. of C. Republican. Office: Pennridge Med Assocs 1301 N 5th St Perkasie PA 18944-2256

PRICE, ROBERT EDMUNDS, civil engineer; b. Lyndhurst, N.J., Jan. 8, 1926; s. William Evans and Charlotte Ann (Dyson) P.; B.S. in Civil Engring., Dartmouth Coll., 1946; M.S., Princeton U. 1947; m. Margaret Akerman Menard, June 28, 1947; children—Robert Edmunds, Alexander Menard. Mgr., P&S Standard Vacuum Oil Co., N.Y., London and Sumatra, 1947-55; project engr. Metcalf & Eddy, Cons. Engrs., Boston, 1956-59; structural engr. Lummis Co., Cons. Engrs., Newark, 1960-61; mgr. engring. materials Interpace Corp., Wharton, N.J., 1961-78; pres. Openaka Corp., Denville, N.J., 1979—; cons. cement and concrete design and constrn. Mem. Denville Bd. Health, 1963-66, chmn., 1966; mem. Denville Bd. Adjustment, 1966-69. Served with USNR, 1943-46. Registered profl. engr., N.J., Md. Fellow Am. Concrete Inst. (dir. 1981-84); mem. ASTM (chmn. subcom. spl. cements 1976-84, hon. mem. com. C-1), Nat. Assn. Corrosion Engrs. Episcopalian. Home: Lake Openaka Denville NJ 07834 Office: Openaka Corp 565 Openaki Rd Denville NJ 07834-9642

PRICE, STEVEN, lawyer, communications executive; b. N.Y.C., Feb. 14, 1962; s. Robert and Margery (Wiener) P. BA, Brown U., 1984; LLD, Columbia U., 1989. Reporter The Gainesville (Fla.) Sun, 1983; mergers analyst Goldman Sachs and Co., N.Y.C., 1984-86; v.p. PriCellular, Inc., N.Y.C.; v.p. Price Communications Corp., N.Y.C., 1986-89, also bd. dirs.; spl. asst. to chief del. to nuclear and space talks U.S. Dept. State, Washington and Geneva, 1989-90, cons. nuclear space talks del., 1990-91; assoc. Davis, Polk & Wardwell Attys., 1990—; bd. dirs. N.Y. Law Jour. Co. Mem. Phi Beta Kappa. Home: 25 E 86th St New York NY 10028-0553

PRICE, TREVOR ROBERT PRYCE, psychiatrist, educator; b. Concord, N.H., Nov. 29, 1943; s. Trevor Alaric and Beatrice (Dinsmore) Pryce; m. Margaret Ann Bowring, June 8, 1991; children by previous marriage: Trevor Breton, Elizabeth Anne. BA, Yale U., 1965; MD, Columbia U., 1969. Diplomate Am. Bd. Psychiatry and Neurology (examiner 1985—), Am. Bd. Internal Medicine, Nat. Bd. Med. Examiners. Intern in medicine Med. Ctr. U. Calif., San Francisco, 1969-70; resident in internal medicine Med. Ctr. of U. Calif., San Francisco, 1972-74; resident in psychiatry Dartmouth Med. Sch., Hanover, N.H., 1974-77, asst. prof., assoc. prof. psychiatry and medicine, 1977-85; assoc. prof., prof. psychiatry U. Pa. Sch. Medicine, Phila., 1985-88; dir. psychiat. in-patient svcs. Hosp. of U. Pa., 1985-88; prof. psychiatry Med. Coll. Pa., Pitts., 1989-90, prof. psychiatry and medicine, 1991—, chmn. dept., 1989—, pres. Allegheny Neuropsychiat. Inst., 1992—; editorial reviewer 7 psychiat. and med. jours., 1978—; bd. dirs. Coll. Health Consortium, Inc., Phila., 1986—; mem. blue ribbon bd. Alzheimer's Disease Alliance, Western Pa., 1989—; bd. dirs. Allegheny Neuropsychiat. Inst. Mem. editorial bd. Convulsive Therapy, 1984—, Jour. Neuropsychiatry and Clin. Neurosci., 1992—, Allegheny Gen. Hosp. Jour. Neurosci., 1992—; contbr. numerous articles to med. jours., chpts. to books. Mem. N.H. Commn. on Laws Effecting Mental Health, 1974-75; bd. dirs. Advanced Studies Program, Friends of St. Paul's Sch., Concord, N.H., 1983-87. Recipient William C. Menninger award Cen. Neuropsychiat. Assn., 1977, Faculty Teaching award dept. psychiatry Dartmouth Med. Sch., 1984, numerous grants, 1975-88. Fellow Am. Psychiat. Assn.; mem. Pa. Psychiat. Assn., Soc. Biol. Psychiatry, Am. Neuropsychiat. Assn., Assn. for Acad. Psychiatry, Am. Assn. Dirs. Psychiat. Residency Tng., Yale Club Pitts., H-Y-P Club of Pitts. Office: Allegheny Gen Hosp 320 E North Ave Pittsburgh PA 15212-4772

PRICE, VICKI JEAN, pharmacist, business owner; b. Johnstown, Pa., Nov. 23, 1955; d. Victor Samuel and Aline Vivian (Waite) Bantly; m. William Vinton Price Jr., Oct. 10, 1981; children: Susan Elizabeth, William Vinton. BS in Pharmacy, Ohio No. U., 1978. Lic. pharmacist, Ohio, Pa. Intern pharmacy Westmont Drugs, Johnstown, 1974, 76, Mary Rutan Hosp., Bellefontaine, Ohio, 1977-78; pharmacist St. Rita's Med. Ctr., Lima, Ohio, 1978-81, Mercy Hosp., Johnstown, 1981-86; owner, pres. O.P.T.I.O.N. Care, Johnstown, 1986—; cons. nursing home Lima Convalescent Home, 1979-81; speaker St. Rita's Med. Ctr., Lima, 1978-81; mem. Home Nursing Agy. Hospice Bd., 1991-93. Editor, writer Pharmacy newsletter, 1979-81. Asst. chmn. Ladies for Scout Golf Tournament, Roaring Spring, 1985, chmn., 1986; mem. legis. com. Pharmacy Soc., Johnstown, 1986, 88; mem. Pharmacy Polit. Action Com., Johnstown, 1987, 88; pharmacy liaison AIDS Lifeline Program St. WJAC, Johnstown, 1988—; mem. advisory. com. Home Nursing Hospice, 1991—, pres. 1991, chmn. 1992. Mem. Pharm. Soc. (sec. 1985-86, 1st v.p. 1986, pres. elect 1987, pres. 1988—), Cambria Somerset Bedford Soc. (2nd v.p. 1985, sec. 1985-86, pres. elect 1987, 90, pres. 1988), Am. Heart Assn. (instr. CPR 1980-81, 81-86, pres. 1991, chmn. 1992), Womens Golf Assn. Western Pa. Club (Pitts.), Soroptimist. Republican. Lutheran. Home: 1324 Luzerne Street Ext Johnstown PA 15905-2155 Office: OPTION Care 1425 Scalp Ave Johnstown PA 15904-3314

PRICE, WILLIAM JAMES, organization executive; b. Alexandria, Ohio, Dec. 3, 1918; s. Lewis J. and Mary (Wright) P.; m. Betty Kistler, Aug. 22, 1943; children—Mary Barbara, Sarah Margaret, Lewis Charles. A.B., Denison U., 1940, Sc.D., 1969; M.S., Rensselaer Poly. Inst., 1941, Ph.D., 1948; DS of Anatomy, Davidson U., 1969. Research physicist Bendix Aviation Corp., 1942-45, Battelle Meml. Inst., Columbus, Ohio, 1948-50; head dept. physics Air Force Inst. Tech., Dayton, Ohio, 1950-57; chief modern physics br. Aero. Research Lab., Dayton, 1957-59; chief scientist Aero. Research Lab., 1959-63; exec. dir. Air Force Office Sci. Research, 1963-74; mgmt. cons., 1974-78; coordinator World Peacemakers, 1978—; instr. Rensselaer Poly. Inst., 1948; prof. Air Force Inst. Tech., Dayton, Ohio, 1950-57; An organizer Yokefellowship in Nation's Capital, 1964; fed. exec. fellow The Brookings Instn., 1967-68; chmn. Congl. Commn. Govt. Procurement Study Group Research and Devel., 1970-71. Author: Nuclear Radiation Detection, rev. edit, 1964; Co-author: National Security and Christian Faith, 1982, Building Christian Community Pursuing Peace with Justice, 1983, (handbook) World Peacemaker Groups, 1979; Author: also numerous articles. Mem. The Ch. of the Saviour, 1972—; Bd. dirs. Yokefellows Internat., 1967-71, Washington Lift, Inc., 1971-76, World Peacemaker, 1978—. Recipient Alumni citation Denison U., 1965, Outstanding Unit award citation Office Aerospace Research, 1965, Outstanding Unit award citation Air Force Inst. Tech., 1964. Mem. Am. Phys. Soc., A.A.A.S., Phi Beta Kappa, Sigma Xi, Tau Beta Pi (hon.). Home: 11427 Scottsbury Ter Germantown MD 20876-6010

PRICE BODAY, MARY KATHRYN, choreographer, small business owner; b. Fort Bragg, N.C., May 20, 1945; d. Max Edward and Katharine (Jordan) P.; m. Les Boday (div. 1982); children: Shawn Leon Boday, Irmali Ferecho Boday; m. Richard A. Weil, May 1, 1986. BFA, U. Okla., 1968, MFA, 1970; studies with David Howard, 1992—. Soloist dancer Mary Anthony Dance Co., N.Y.C., 1971-74, Larry Richardson Dance Co., N.Y.C., 1971-73; dancer Pearl Lang Dance Co., N.Y.C., 1971-73, Gaku Dance Theater, N.Y.C., 1972-74; ballet mistress and soloist dancer St. Gallen Ballet, Switzerland, 1974-75; dancer, tchr. Zurich Ballet, Switzerland, 1975-76; asst. prof. U. Ill., Champaign-Urbana, 1976-79; artist-in-residence Cornish Inst., Seattle, 1979-80; pres. The Dance Works, Inc., Seattle, 1981-90; dir. Seahurst Ballet, 1982-84; pres. The Dance Works, Inc., Erie, Pa., 1990—; dir. dance dept., asst. prof. Mercyhurst Coll., Erie, Pa., 1990—; tchr. Harkness Ballet N.Y., Mary Anthony Dance Sch., Zurich Ballet, Nat. Acad. Arts Ill., Jefferson High Sch. Performing Arts Portland, also choreographer; tchr. Summer Dance Lab.; choreographer Mary K. Price Dance Co., U. Ill., Nat. Acad. Arts, Cornish Inst., Seahurst Ballet; tchr. Kneeland Workshops, Port Townsend, Wash., 1988; tchr., co-dir. Kneeland Seminars, Las Vegas, Nev., Port Townsend, summers 1989, 90, Oklahoma City U., summer 1990, Am. Coll. Dance Festival, 1991; tchr. Pa. Gov's Sch. of the Arts, 1991, 92, David Howard summer seminar Mercyhurst Coll., summer 1992. Choreographer 3 ballets Ballet Co. St. Gallen, 1988, dance concert Mary & Friends, Seattle, 1990, The Nutcracker for Warner Theatre Erie; co-choreographer The Nutcracker ballet, 1991—; artistic dir. Lake Erie Ballet, 1991—. Outstanding Dancer award U. Okla., 1968; named one of Outstanding Young Women of Am., 1977. Office: The Dance Works Inc 255 W 40th St Erie PA 16508-3066 also: Mercyhurst Coll Dept Dance 501 E 38th St Erie PA 16546

PRICHARD, PETER S., newspaper editor; b. Auburn, Calif., Dec. 18, 1944; s. Jarvis B. and Floris C. (Smith) P.; m. Ann O'Donnell, Nov. 13, 1971; children: Oliver W., Lindsay M. AB, Dartmouth Coll., 1966. Wire editor Greenwich (Conn.) Time, 1970-72; reporter Democrat and Chronicle, Rochester, N.Y., 1972-75; assoc. news dir. WOKR TV, Rochester, N.Y., 1975-76; reporter Times Union, Rochester, 1976-78; asst. to chmn. communications Gannett Co. Inc., Rochester, 1980-82, dir. communications, Office of Chief Exec., 1980-82; columns editor USA Today, Washington, 1982-83, dep. assoc. editorial dir., 1983-84, assoc. editorial dir., 1984-86, mng. editor spl. projects, 1986-87, sr. editor, 1988, editor, sr. v.p., news, 1988—; sr. v.p. News Gannett Co. Inc., Washington, 1988—, chief news exec., 1990—. Author: The Making of McPaper: The Inside Story of USA Today, 1987 (Frank Luther Moh Rsch. award Kappa Tau Alpha 1987). Vice chmn., bd. trustees Washington Journalism Ctr., 1989—. With U.S. Army, 1967-69, Vietnam. Decorated Bronze Star. Mem. Nat. Press Club, Am. Soc. Newspaper Editors (Reston, Va.) (various coms. 1985—). Office: USA Today 1000 Wilson Blvd Arlington VA 22209-3901

PRIDE, DOUGLAS SPENCER, minister; b. Latrobe, Pa., Jan. 13, 1959; s. Spencer MacVeagh and Kathleen (Tidd) P.; m. Elizabeth Armstrong, June 5, 1982; children: Kathryn Elizabeth and Jennifer Suzanne (twins), Pamela Campbell. BA, Westminster Coll., 1980; MDiv, Pitts. Theol. Sem., 1983, postgrad., 1988—. Ordained to ministry Presbyn. Ch., 1983. Asst. pastor Shadyside Presbyn. Ch., Pitts., 1983-85, assoc. pastor, 1985-91; pastor The Presbyn. Ch. of Clearfield, Clearfield, Pa., 1992—; chaplain palliative care program West Penn Hosp., 1983-86; chaplain Clearfield Hospice. Bd. dirs. Pitts. Theol. Sem., 1983-86; mem. alumni coun. Westminster Coll., New Wilmington, Pa., 1986-90, pres., 1989-90; bd. dirs. Bethesda Ctr., Pitts.; 1st v.p. Spina Bifida Assn., Pitts., 1987-89, pres., 1989—, bd. dirs. 1984, sec. bd., 1985-87. Mem. Hundintdon Presbytery, Jewish Community Ctr., Univ. Club, Clearfield Corwensville Country Club. Republican. Home: 2538 Meadow Rd Clearfield PA 16830-1140

PRIDEAUX, JOHN RAYMOND, JR., insurance agency executive; b. Morristown, N.J., June 14, 1931; s. John Raymond and Doris Gertrude (Griffith) P.; m. Dolores May Tett, Aug. 14, 1954; children: John Raymond III, Donna Jean, Nanette Joy, Tracey Lynne. Student, Bucknell U., 1949-50; BBA, Upsala Coll., 1956. Ins. agt. Griffith-Prideaux Inc., Morristown, 1953—, pres., 1964—, chmn. bd., 1980—; bd. dirs., mem. loan com., chmn. audit com. 1st Morris Bank, Morristown; prin. Govt. Ins. Cons., Morristown, 1976—; fund adminstr. Morris County Ins. Fund, Morristown, 1987-90; bd. dirs. PIA Mgmt. Svcs. Inc., Glenmont, N.Y., 1988—, asst. treas.,

1988-89, treas., 1989-92, chmn. bd., 1992—. Trustee, treas. No. N.J. Ann. Conf., United Meth. Ch., 1983-86; mem. govt. affairs task force St. Clare's Hosp., Denville, N.J.; trustee Correctional Instn. for Women, Clinton, N.J., 1973-76, 84-87; trustee, treas. Indian Lake Community Club; mem. exec. com. Morris-Sussex Area coun., asst. scoutmaster Boy Scouts Am.; trustee, chmn. planning and program com. Morris County Soc. Crippled Children and Adults; committeeman Denville Twp., 1962; also others. Sgt. USMC, 1950-52, Korea. Mem. Soc. Cert. Ins. Counselors (cert., trustee N.J. 1979-85, chmn. 1984-85), Profl. Ins. Agts. N.J. (pres. 1990-91), Washington assn. N.J., Morris County C. of c. (bd. dirs. 1974-80), Rotary (pres. Denville 1962, Paul Harris fellow 1983), Tau Kappa Epsilon. Republican. Home: 26 Zeek Rd Morris Plains NJ 07950 Office: 225 Madison Ave PO Box 1917 Morristown NJ 07962

PRIEVE, DENNIS CHARLES, chemical engineering educator; b. Portage, Wis., Sept. 1, 1947. BSChemE, U. Fla., l, 1970; MChemE, U. Del., 1972, PhD in Chem. Engring., 1974. Tech. svc. student-engr. Westvaco Corp., North Charleston, S.C., 1966-70; summer rsch. engr. Westvaco Corp., 1970; rsch. fellow, dept. chem. engring. Univ. Delaware, Newark, 1970-73; teaching assoc., dept. chem. engring. Univ. Delaware, 1973-74; asst. prof., chem. engring. Carnegie Mellon Univ., Pitts., 1975-80, assoc. prof., chem. engring., 1980-83, prof., chem. engring., 1983—, vice chmn. faculty, Coll. of Engring., 1985-86, chmn. faculty, Coll. of Engring., 1986-87; vis. prof. chem. engring. Princeton Univ., 1984-85; chmn. Procter & Gamble fellowship award com., div. of colloid & Surface sci. Am. Chem. Soc., 1983-84. Editorial bd.: Langmuir, 1989—, Butterworth-Heinemann Series on Colloid and Surface Engineering, 1990—; adv. bd. Jour. Colloid Interface Sci., 1982-84; contbr. articles to profl. jours. Mem. Am. Inst. Chem. Engrs. (nat. program com., chmn. group 1 fundamentals 1991—, chmn. area 1c interfacial phenomena 1987-90, vice chmn. 1984-87, mem. 1975—). Office: Carnegie Mellon U Dept Chem Engring Pittsburgh PA 15213

PRIMACK, LEONARD, mortgage company executive; b. Bklyn., Apr. 16, 1936; s. Victor and Jennie (Derechinsky) P.; m. Sandra Lowell, May 19, 1968; children: Jonathan, Adam. BA, CCNY, 1957; MBA, NYU, 1966. Asst. to chmn. T. Rowe Price Assocs., Inc., Balt., 1963-65; fin. analyst SEC, Washington, 1965-67; portfolio mgr. Lazard Freres Co., N.Y.C., 1967-72; v.p. Lionel D. Edie & Co., Inc., N.Y.C., 1972-75; v.p. Steve Grief & Assocs., Inc., Encino, Calif., 1975-77; pres. Leonard Primack Assocs., Ltd., Commack, N.Y., 1977—. Advisor Braintrust pub. Dep. chmn. Town of Smithtown Zoning Bd. Appeals. With U.S. Army, 1958-60. Recipient Real Estate award Real Estate Newsletter, 1983. Mem. L.I. Assn., Mortgage Bankers Assn., Hauppange Indsl. Assn., Rotary. Home and Office: 133 Parkway Dr N Commack NY 11725-4908

PRIMIS, JEFF, sales executive; b. Bklyn., Sept. 14, 1949; s. Nathan and Sylvia (Goldberg) P.; m. Margaret Paula Harrington, Sept. 5, 1970; children: Benjamin Scott, Alex Bradley. B of Liberal Arts, CCNY, 1970. Retail buyer Abraham & Straus Dept. Store, Bklyn., 1971-77; divisional mdse. mgr. Gimbels Dept. Store, Pitts., 1977-85; v.p. sales and mktg. Brookline Fabrics, Pitts., 1985-87; nat. sales mgr. Benthin Systems, Sewickley, Pa., 1987—. Mem. Pitts. Athletic Assn., Lakeview Racquet Club. Home: 3161 Haberlein Rd Gibsonia PA 15044

PRIMIS, LANCE ROY, newspaper executive; b. Bklyn., June 16, 1946; s. David and Sybil (Schiller) P.; m. Ellen Linda Wildman, June 16, 1946; children: Blair S., Ashley K. BA in English, U. Wis., 1968. Sales rep. Scott Paper Co., N.Y.C., 1968-69; with N.Y. Times, 1969—, retail advt. rep., 1969-72, asst. class advt. mgr., 1972-76, retail advt. mgr., 1976-79, dir. advt. promotion and rsch., 1979, advt. dir., 1979-80, v.p. advt., 1981-82, sr. v.p. advt., from 1982, former v.p., gen. mgr., now pres., gen. mgr. Mem. Internat. Newspaper Advt. Execs. (chmn. nat. advertiser rels. com.), Am. Assn. Advt. Agys., Nat. Sales Assn., Proprietary Assn., Cosmetic Toiletry Fragrance Assn., Internat. Newspaper Promotion Assn., N.J. Advt. Club. Office: NY Times Co 229 W 43rd St New York NY 10036-3913*

PRIMMER, GEORGE MELVIN, JR., broadcast executive; b. Beverly, Mass., Jan. 21, 1954; s. George Melvin Sr. and Martha Mary (Westmoreland) P.; m. Ann Marie Parrott, Aug. 24, 1985. BS in Acctg., Northeastern U., 1986. Acctg. mgr. Am. Pacemaker Corp., Woburn, Mass., 1976-81; bus. mgr. Pilgrim Retirement Ctr., Peabody, Mass., 1981-82; contr. Am. Shoe Machinery, Danvers, Mass., 1982-88; bus. mgr. Saga Communications Inc., Sta. WZID-FM and WFEA-AM, Manchester, N.H., 1988—. Sgt. USAF, 1972-76. Home: 555 Canal St Apt 1604 Manchester NH 03101-1523 Office: Sta WZID-FM WFEA-AM 500 N Commercial St Manchester NH 03101-1151

PRIMPS, WILLIAM GUTHRIE, lawyer; b. Ossining, N.Y., Sept. 8, 1949; s. Richard Byrd and Mary Elizabeth (Guthrie) P.; m. Sophia Elizabeth Beutel, Aug. 25, 1973; children: Emily Ann, Elizabeth Armstrong, William Andrew. BA, Yale U., 1971; JD, Harvard U., 1974. Bar: N.Y., 1975. Assoc. LeBoeuf, Lamb, Leiby & MacRae, N.Y.C., 1974-82; ptnr. LeBoeuf, Lamb & MacRae, N.Y.C., 1983—; counsel to Bd. Zoning Appeals, Bronxville, 1988-89, chmn. 1989-91. Me. class coun. Yale U., New Haven, 1986-91; trustee Village of Bronxville, 1991—; deacon Reformed Ch. Bronxville. Mem. ABA, N.Y. State Bar Assn., Assn. Yale Alumni (class rep. 1986-91), Yale Club, Bronxville Field Club. Republican. Home: 71 Summit Ave Bronxville NY 10708-1815 Office: LeBoeuf Lamb Leiby & MacRae 125 W 55th St New York NY 10019

PRINCE, HAROLD, theatrical producer; b. N.Y.C., Jan. 30, 1928; s. Milton A. and Blanche (Stern) P.; m. Judith Chaplin, Oct. 26, 1962; children: Charles, Daisy. AB, U. Pa., 1948, DFA (hon.), 1971; LittD, Emerson Coll., 1971. chmn. Performing Arts Libr., N.Y.C. Co-producer Pajama Game, 1954-56 (Antoinette Perry award), Damn Yankees, 1955-57 (Antoinette Perry award), New Girl in Town, 1957-58, West Side Story, 1957-59, Fiorello, 1959-61 (Antoinette Perry award, Pulitzer prize), Tenderloin, 1960-61, A Call on Kuprin, 1961, They Might Be Giants, London, 1961, Side by Side by Sondheim, 1976; producer Take Her, She's Mine, 1961-62, A Funny Thing Happened on the Way to the Forum, 1962-64 (Antoinette Perry award), Fiddler on the Roof, 1964-72 (Antoinette Perry award), Poor Bitos, 1964, Flora the Red Menace, 1965; dir., producer: She Loves Me, 1963-64 (London 1964), Superman, 1966, Cabaret, 1966-69 (Antoinette Perry award 1968), Zorba, 1968-69, Company, 1970-72 (Antoinette Perry award 1972), A Little Night Music, 1973-74 (Antoinette Perry award 1975), Pacific Overtures, 1976; co-dir., producer Follies, 1971-72, Faust; co-producer, dir. Candide, 1974-75, Merrily We Roll Along, 1981, A Doll's Life, 1982; dir. A Family Affair, 1962, Baker Street, 1965, Great God Brown, 1972-73, The Visit, 1973-74, Love for Love, 1974-75, Ashmedai, 1976, On The Twentieth Century, 1978, Evita (London, 1978, Broadway, 1979, L.A., 1980, Australia, 1980, Chgo., 1980, Detroit, 1982), Sweeney Todd, The Demon Barber of Fleet Street, Broadway, 1979, London, 1980, Silverlake, 1980, Willie Stark, 1981, Candide, 1982, Madama Butterfly, 1982, Turandot, 1983, Play Memory, 1984, End of the World, 1984, Diamonds, 1984, Grind, 1985, Cabaret Revival, 1987, Roza, 1987, Phantom of the Opera, London, 1986, N.Y.C., (Antoinette Perry award) 1988, La Fanciula del West, Don Giovanni, N.Y. City Opera, 1989, Faust, Met. Opera, 1990; adapter, dir. Grandchild of Kings, 1992, Kiss of the Spider Woman, the Musical, 1992; co-producer films The Pajama Game, 1957, Damn Yankees, 1958; dir. films Something for Everyone, 1970, A Little Night Music, 1978. Mem. coun. Nat. Endowment Arts; pres. League N.Y. Theatres, 1964-66; chmn. Performing Arts Libr., N.Y.C. Recipient 16 Antoinette Perry (Tony) Meml. awards, Critics Circle awards, Pulitzer prize, 1961, Best Mus. award London Evening Standard, 1955-58, 72. Office: 10 Rockefeller Plz New York NY 10020

PRINCE, JULIUS S., retired foreign service officer, physician; b. Yonkers, N.Y., July 21, 1911; s. Julius and Clara B. (Rich) P.; m. Eleanora Molloy, July 6, 1943; children: Thomas Marc, Tod Ainslee, Richard M. Johnson. B.A., Yale U., 1932; M.D., Columbia U., 1938, M.P.H., 1948; Dr.P.H., Harvard, 1957. Intern Sinai Hosp., Balt., 1939-40; asst. resident medicine N.Y. U. div. Goldwater Meml. Hosp., 1941-42; dist. state health officer N.Y. State Dept. Health, Jamestown, 1948-58; chief pub. health div. USAID, Ethiopia, 1958-67; prin. investigator demonstration and evaluation project AID, 1959-67; chief Africa div. Population and Humanitarian Affairs, Population Office, AID, Washington, 1967-73; dir. Africa Regional Population Office, Accra, Ghana, 1973-74; chief health, population and nutrition projects U.S. AID/Ghana, Accra, 1974-76; cons. internat. health Am. Pub. Health Assn., 1977-78, Pacific Cons., Inc., 1978-82, RONCO Inc., 1982; pub. health specialist/sr. health advisor One Am., Inc., 1982-87; sr. pub. health and nutrition specialist Internat. Sci. and Tech. Inst. Inc., 1985—; cons. internat. health ref. sustainability of AID supported health population and nutrition programs, Ghana, 1963-85, Ctr. Devel. Info. and Evaluation, U.S. Agy. Internat. Devel. AID, 1988, Annotated History of AID-Supported Health/Nutrition Research: From Outset to Present, 1991-92, Introduction and Background U.S. Office of Health, 1991, Compendium of Abstracts, 1985—, USAID, Univ. Ctr./Rsch. and Univ. Devel. Linkages, 1992. Served from lt. to maj. M.C. Royal Canadian Army, 1942-46. Recipient Letter of Commendation, Adj. Gen. Can. Army, 1946, Superior honor award AID, 1968, Letter of Commendation, 1977. Fellow Am. Pub. Health Assn., Am. Coll. Preventive Medicine, Royal Soc. Health, Soc. Applied Anthropology, Wash. Acad. Scis.; mem. AMA, N.Y. State Pub. Health Assn. (pres. 1957), Pan Am. Med. Assn., Am. Assn. World Health (exec. com.), Internat. Union Sci. Study Population, AAAS, Internat. Health Soc. (pres. 1979), Internat. Soc. on Hypertension in Blacks, Population Assn. Am., Soc. Internat. Devel., Nat. Coun. Internat. Health (award 1992), N.Y. Acad. Scis., World Med. Assn., Soc. Prospective Medicine. Home: 7103 Pinehurst Pky Chevy Chase MD 20815-3144 Office: Internat Sci and Tech Inst Inc 1601 N Kent St Ste 918 Arlington VA 22209-2105

PRINCE, MELVIN, marketing educator; b. Bklyn., Feb. 6, 1932; s. Louis and Florence (Werfel) P.; m. Sheila Pazornik, Dec. 18, 1955; children: Robert, Carole. PhD, Columbia U., 1962. With J.B. Williams, N.Y.C., 1971-80, Marsteller, Inc., N.Y.C., 1980-83, Nat. Grand Scanning, Inc., N.Y.C., 1986-87; prof. Fordham U. Grad. Sch. Bus., N.Y.C., 1987—; pres. Prince Assocs., Darien, Conn., 1985—; cons. Met. Transit Authority, N.Y.C., 1991—. Author: Consumer Research, 1982. Active Darien Community Assn. With U.S. Army, 1953-55. Mem. Am. Mktg. Assn., Am. Statis. Assn. Home: 83 Hoyt St Darien CT 06820-3120 Office: Fordham Univ GBA 113 W 60th St New York NY 10023

PRING, MARTIN JOHN, publisher, writer; b. Bristol, U.K., Feb. 27, 1943; came to U.S., 1978; s. Frederick William and Winifred (Mackay) P.; m. Ann Payne, Sept. 1965; children: Martin John Jr., Laura Catherine. BS in Econ., Southampton U., U.K., 1963. Pres. Internat. Inst. for Econ. Rsch., Conn., 1980—. Author: Technical Analysis, 1st edit., 1980, 2nd edit., 1985, 3rd edit., 1991, How to Forecast Interest Rates, 1981, McGraw Hill Handbook of Future International Investing Made for 1981, 1984; editor The Prime Market Rev. Office: Internat Inst for Econ Rsch 6 Bee Brook Rd Washington Depot CT 06794-1501

PRINGLE, THOMAS WALKER, stockbroker; b. Hartford, Conn., Sept. 19, 1957; s. William George and Polly (Peterson) P.; m. Andrea Rolzhausen, Sept. 14, 1991. BS in Communications, Boston U., 1981. Ptnr., v.p. Mark Securities, Inc., West Hartford, Conn., 1983—, registered rep., 1983—. Mem. Internat. Assn. Fin. Planning, Univ. Club Hartford. Republican. Office: Mark Securities Inc 1007 Farmington Ave West Hartford CT 06107-2107

PRINTZ, PHILIP HALLIE, early childhood educator; b. LaCrosse, Wis., Nov. 11, 1947; s. Warren Henry and Ethel May (Spaulding) P. BA, U. Wis., Eau Claire, 1974; postgrad., Lesley Coll., 1983-86; MEd, Cambridge Coll., 1988. Cert. speech and lang. therapist, early childhood adminstr., Mass. Tchr. spl. needs Boston Pub. Schs., 1975-77, speech and lang. clinician, 1977-81; speech and lang. clinician Coop. Ednl. Svc. Agy., LaCrosse, Wis., 1981-83; master tchr. Lesley Ellis Sch., Cambridge, Mass., 1983-85; headmaster lesley Ellis Sch., Cambridge, Mass., 1985-90; exec. dir. Concord Children's Ctr., Concord, Mass., 1990-92; assoc. dir. New England Resource Access Project, Newton, Mass., 1992—; Mem. Office for Children Spl. Needs Task force, Boston, 1990-92. Staff sgt. USAF, 1967-71. Mem. Nat. Assn. Edn. Young Children, Nat. Orgn. Rural Educators, New Eng. Assn. Edn. Young Children, Boston Assn. Edn. Young Children (bd. dirs. 1991—), Greater Boston Dir. Collaborative, Somerville C. of C. Democrat. Home: 132 W Adams St Somerville MA 02144 Office: Edn Devel Ctr 55 Chapel St Newton MA 02160

PRINZIVALLI, JOSEPH ANTHONY, JR., statistician; b. N.Y.C., May 10, 1955; s. Joseph A. and Concetta L. (DeMarino) P.; m. Laudelina J. Fernandez, Oct. 18, 1981. BA, Queens Coll., 1978; MA, Columbia U., 1985. Adminstrv. asst. Coll. Physicians and Surgeons Columbia U., N.Y.C., 1980-85; staff supr. AT&T, Morristown, N.J., 1985—; adj. instr. math. Raritan Valley Community Coll., Somerville, N.J., 1988, Middlesex County Coll., Edison, N.J., 1990. Mem. Friends of North Brunswick (N.J.) Twp. Libr., 1989. Mem. Am. Econ. Assn., N.J. Jazz Soc., Phi Beta Kappa, Psi Chi. Democrat. Roman Catholic.

PRIOR, KATHERINE FAITH, art appraiser; b. Montreal, Que., Can., Sept. 19, 1949; d. Roger Williams Prior and Faith (Kenyon) Prior Rollins; m. Gregory T. Gaura, Jan. 31, 1970 (div. 1972). BA, Cath. U., 1971; postgrad., Md. U., 1971-72; appraisal studies program, NYU, 1987-89. With Franz Bader Gallery, Washington, 1970-76; arts adminstr., cons. Nat. Endowment for Arts, Washington, 1976-81; pres. EPHEBI: Art for 21st Century, Inc., Washington, 1981—; art history tchr. The Madeira Sch., Greenway, Va., 1983; exec. dir. Am. Ctr. Stanislavski Theatre Art, Inc., N.Y.C., 1987—; commr. D.C. Commn. on Arts, 1983-87, chmn. dance panel, 1984-86, murals program, 1986; pres., bd. dirs. Lettumplay, Inc., Washington, 1976-78. Co-curator Sincerely San Francisco Mus. Temporary Art, 1981; art critic Art Express mag., 1981-82, Washington Rev. of the arts, 1982, Latino Newspaper, 1982, curator PATINA: Exhibition at White Ho. Conf. on Aging, 1981; pres. The Art and Music Exch., 1986-90; dir. Father Hartke Legacy, 1986—. Commr., mem. mayor's blue ribbon com. of arts D.C. Commn. on Arts, Washington, 1985-87; arts coord. Star Island Conf. on Arts, 1981-89; bd. dirs. Library Theatre, 1983-84, Gala Hispanic Theatre, 1984-85, The Am. Ctr. Stanislavski Theatre Arts, 1991, Joan Barrett Scholarship Fund, 1988-91. Recipient Key to the City of Knoxville, City of Tenn., 1979. Mem. Am. Soc. of Appraisers (cert., sr. mem.), Assn. of Am. Appraisers., Phi Beta Kappa. Office: 2122 Massachusetts Ave NW Washington DC 20008-2833 also: 315 W 54th St New York NY 10019

PRISCO, DOROTHY DESTENO, college official and dean; b. Hoboken, N.J., Jan. 27, 1942; d. Dominick and Martha (Balacco) DeSteno; m. Salvatore Prisco, July 15, 1967; 1 child, Lisa Natalie. BA, Bard Coll., 1964; MA, Jersey City Stat Coll., 1968; MS, U. Ala., Tuscaloosa, 1975; EdD, Rutgers U., 1983. Cert. English tchr., N.J. Tchr. English, Sacred Heart Acad., Hoboken, N.J., 1964-65, North Bergen (N.J.) High Sch., 1965-69, Tuscaloosa Acad., 1969-70; editor, copywriter McCall's Needlework and Crafts mag., N.Y.C., 1974-77; mem. faculty, div. chmn. Centenary Coll., Hackettstown, N.J., 1977-84, exec. asst. to pres., 1985-86, v.p. for acad. affairs, dean coll., 1986—; manuscript cons. Prentice Hall and John Wiley Pub., N.Y.C., 1983-86; mem. evaluation team Mid. States Assn., Phila., 1991—; lectr. series in the humanities funded by N.J. Dept. Higher Edn., 1985-86. Co-author: Fashion Merchandise Information, 1986; contbg. author: (Elizabeth Carteret biography) in Past and Promise: Lives of N.J. Women, 1990; mem. editorial bd. Nat. Assn. Women in Edn., 1991—. Coord. community svc. Centenary Coll. and United Meth. Ch., Hackettstown, 1989-91. Recipient Disting. Svc. award Rutgers U., 1989; grantee United Meth. Ch., 1989-90, N.J. Dept. Higher Edn., 1989-90, Ronetco Corp., 1990. Mem. Coun. Ind. Colls. (program participant 1991—), Am. Coun. on Edn. (rep. to nat. identification program for advancement women in higher edn. adminstrn. 1985—), Rutgers U. Grad. Sch. Edn. Alumni Assn. (pres. 1991—). Office: Centenary Coll 400 Jefferson St Hackettstown NJ 07840-2184

PRISCO, DOUGLAS LOUIS, physician; b. N.Y.C., Nov. 30, 1945; s. Frank James and Isabel (Gaetano) P.; AB, Georgetown U., 1967; postgrad. N.Y. U., 1967-68; MD, U. Rome, 1974; m. Marianne Paula Mangano, Jan. 8, 1972; children: Jennifer Leigh, Douglas Louis, Dana Lauren, Andrew Michael. Intern, Mt. Sinai Svcs., Elmhurst, N.Y., 1974-75, resident in medicine, 1975-77, pulmonary medicine fellow, 1977-79; practice medicine specializing in pulmonary medicine, N.Y.C., New Hyde Park, N.Y., 1979-81; clin. asst. in medicine Bklyn. Hosp., 1979-81; pulmonary cons. and admitting physician Booth Meml. Hosp.; chief pulmonary medicine Deepdale Gen. Hosp.; clin. asst. Mt. Sinai Sch. Medicine N.Y.C., 1977-79; physician adviser St. Barnabas Hosp., 1981-82; pres. Met. Pulmonary Assocs., P.C., 1980—, Met. Pulmonary, P.C., 1985—; physician adv. to Elmhurst Gen. Hosp., Queens County Profl. Standards Rev. Orgn., 1979-85; co-chmn. quality assurance com. downstate region Island Peer Rev. Orgn., 1990—, chmn. protem regional quality assurance com.-Downstate, N.Y.C., 1990-91, chmn., 1991—. Bd. dirs. Queens County Profl. Standards Rev. Orgn., 1984-85; mem., cons. Queens div. Island Peer Rev. Orgn., 1985—. Diplomate Am. Bd. Internal Medicine, sub-bd. Pulmonary Diseases. Mem. Rep. Senatorial Inner Cir., 1990. Fellow Am. Coll. Chest Physicians; mem. ACP, Am. Lung Assn. Queens (bd. dirs. 1988—), U.S. Power Squadron, Nat. Assn. of Residents and Interns, N.Y. Acad. Scis., Queens County Med. Soc. Roman Catholic. Club: Port Washington Yacht (former chmn. jr. activities 1987-88, fleet surgeon 1991—), Capitol Hill Club (Washington). Office: 1575 Hillside Ave New Hyde Park NY 11040-2501

PRITCHARD, LUCILLE MARTIN, mental health services professional; b. Acushnet, Mass., Apr. 5, 1945; d. Conrad Carroll and Jennie Anna (Reed) Martin; m. Robert Edward Prichard, July 4, 1968; children: Kelly Kristen, Kristen Carole. BA, SUNY at Albany, 1967, MA, 1968; M in Profl. Studies, SUNY at New Paltz, 1983; postgrad., U. Mass. N.Y. State Permanent Teaching Cert. Grades 7-12. Acad. counselor SUNY, Albany, N.Y., 1966-71; faculty mentor Empire State Coll., New Paltz, N.Y., 1983-85; exec. dir. Mental Health Assn. in N.Y.S., Albany, N.Y., 1985-86; adjunct faculty SUNY, New Paltz, Empire State, New Paltz, N.Y., 1986—; chief exec. officer Mental Health Assn. in Ulster, Kingston, N.Y., 1978—; mem. Gov.'s Coun. on Adolescent Suicide, Albany, 1984-86, N.Y. State Mental Health Svcs., Albany, 1989—; mem. steering com. Gov.:s Conf. on Prevention, Albany, 1983; chair of bd. Am. Soc. Mental Health Assn. Profls., Alexandria, Va., 1986—. Contbr. articles to profl. jours. Recipient Nat. Joseph Brown Staff Excellence award, Nat. Mental Health Assn., Alexandria, Va., 1989. Mem. Jr. League of Kingston, Orthopscyhiatry, YWCA of Ulster County, Ulster C. of C. Home: 105 Fair St Kingston NY 12401-4801 Office: Mental Health Assn 221 Tuytenbridge Rd Kingston NY 12401-7039

PRITCHARD, WILLIAM BAKER, utility company executive; b. Chgo., Apr. 22, 1950; s. Irving and Virginia (Baker) P. Grad., Lincoln Acad., Newcastle, Maine, 1969. Prin. Regional Taxi Co., Newcastle, 1969-72; dir. purchasing Windham Coll., Putney, Vt., 1976-79; with ops. div. Vt. Yankee Nuclear Power Corp., Vernon, 1979-86; policy adminstr. Vt. Yankee Nuclear Power Corp., Battleboro, 1986-87, govt. affairs rep., 1987—. V.p. Epilepsy Assn. Vt., Rutland, 1978-80; mem. Brattleboro (Vt.) Town Charter Revision Commn., 1980-81, Brattleboro Union High Sch. Bd., 1980-83, Brattleboro Bd. Civil Authority, 1980-84, Union High Sch. Charter Commn., 1984-85; Justice O' Peace, State of Vt., 1980-84; treas. Vt. Dem. State Com., Burlington, 1980-85; vice chmn. Brattleboro Bd. Listers, 1986—; grand juror Town of Brattleboro, 1987—. Named one of Outstanding Young Men Am., 1981. Mem. Profl. Reactor Operators Soc. Lodge: Kiwanis (pres. Brattleboro chpt. 1984-85, lt. gov. New Eng. chpt. 1985-86), Elks. Home: PO Box 8122 Brattleboro VT 05304-8122 Office: Vt Yankee Nuclear Power Corp Ferry Rd Rte 5 Box 169 Brattleboro VT 05301

PRITCHETT, JERRY COSTON, trade association executive; b. Union Springs, Ala., May 29, 1940; s. William Edgar and Johnnie (Clyde) P.; m. Claude Michelin, Aug. 30, 1975; children: Loic, Luke. BA, U. Ala., 1962; postgrad., George Washington U., 1963-64. Spl. asst. U.S. House of Reps., Washington, 1962-65; dir. legis. affairs NAPHCC, Washington, 1965-70; dir. govt. affairs Mech. Contractors Assn. Am., Rockville, Md., 1970-75, dir. pub. affairs, 1975-85, dep. v.p., 1985—; exec. dir. Mech. Contracting Found., Rockville, 1991—. Mem. Internat. Assn. Employee Benefit Plans (com. mem.), Associated Specialty Contractors (trustee), Am. Soc. Assn. Execs. Episcopalian. Office: Mech Contractors Assn Am 1385 Piccard Dr Rockville MD 20850-4340

PRITCHETT, THOMAS HENRY, chemist; b. Madisonville, Ky., Oct. 5, 1954; s. David H. and Mary Francis (Lowery) P.; m. Tarea J. Roach, May 24, 1980; m. Sharon Patterson, Sept, 1976 (div. 1978). AB in Sci., Chemistry, Computer Sci., Murray State U., 1978, MB in Chemistry, 1984. Rsch. tech. Albert Einstein Coll. of Med., Bronx, N.Y., 1980-81; gas chromatography tech. Murray State U., 1982-84; mass spectrometry chemist York Rsch. Cons., Denver, 1984-86; mass spectrometry group leader Envirosponse Inc., Edison, N.J., 1986; chemist U.S. EPA Environ. Response Team, Edison, N.J., 1986—; co-chmn. EPA Air Sampling Protocols Workgroup, 1990—, chair Rep. Air Sampling Tech. Guidance Workgroup, 1989—, tech. adv. com. Air/Superfund, 1988. Contbr. articles to profl. jours. Recipient numerous awards EPA. Mem. Air & Waste Mgmt. Assn. (tech. subcommittee, v.chair. 1991—), Am. Chemical Soc. Episcopalian. Office: US EPA ERT MS101 2890 Woodbridge Ave Edison NJ 08837-3679

PRITHAM, HOWARD GEORGE, surgeon; b. Waltham, Mass., Oct. 13, 1940; s. Howard Charles and Dorothy Clark (Thayer) P.; m. Ellen Barbara Davis, Sept. 3, 1965; children: David, Ellen Jean, Gregory. BS, Tufts Coll., 1962; MD, Tufts Med. Coll., 1966. Diplomate Am. Bd. Surgery. Resident in surgery Mary Hitchcock Hosp., Lebanon, N.H., 1970-74; mem. staff in surgery Littleton (N.H.) Regional Hosp., 1974—. Lt. Comdr. USN, 1967-70. Fellow ACS; mem. Northeast Med. Assn., New Eng. Surg. Soc. Office: 105 Cottage St Littleton NH 03574

PRIVITERA, JOHN NATHAN, company executive; b. Buffalo, July 27, 1944; s. James Francis and Marjorie Elaine (Sparks) P.; m. Lorraine Rheta Atherton, Dec. 30, 1977; children: Kristin, Noel. BS, LeMoyne Coll., Syracuse, N.Y., 1966; MS, Niagara (N.Y.) U., 1971; MBA, York (Pa.) Coll., 1981. Mgr. safety, sec. TRW, Jamestown, N.Y., 1966-67; plant personnel mgr. RJR Ind., Cambridge, Md., 1967-72; dist. personnel mgr. Sealtest div. Kraft, Balt., 1972-77; corp. labor rels. mgr. Dentsply Internat., York, Pa., 1977-79; mgr. employee rels. Continental Group, Greenwich, Conn., 1979-81; dir. indsl. rels. Clevepak Corp., White Plains, N.Y., 1981-85; v.p. human resources Union Corp., Pitts., 1985-86; sr. ptnr. J.T. Knowlton Assocs., Red Lion, Pa., 1986—; instr. U. Balt., 1971-73; charter mem. Nat. Task Force for Protective Svcs., Wyncote, Pa., 1988—. Author: Productivity Improvement, 1991; columnist Security Mag.., Bus. Mo. of Cen. Pa., 1987—. Bd. dirs. York Coll. Alumni Bd., 1988-89. Mem. Am. Soc. Tng. and Devel., Indsl. Rels. Rsch. Assn., Am. Soc. Personnel Adminstrn. (pres. 1971-72). Republican. Roman Catholic.

PROAKIS, ANTHONY GEORGE, pharmacologist; b. Chios, Greece, May 26, 1940; came to the U.S., 1946; s. George John and Fotine (Parikakis) P.; m. Nancy Lee Pietranton, Feb. 23, 1963; children: Lisa Ann, Andrea Lynn, Steven Anthony. BS in Pharmacy, W.Va. U., 1962; PhD in Pharmacology, Purdue U., 1972. Pharmacist Medco Pharmacies Inc., L.A., 1962-63, mgr., 1963-66, v.p., 1966-67; gen. mgr. Guardian Pharmacies Inc., L.A., 1967-69; sr. rsch. biologist A.H. Robins Rsch. Labs., Richmond, Va., 1972-77, rsch. assoc., 1977-80, group mgr., 1980-90; pharmacologist U.S. FDA, Rockville, Md., 1990—; adj. asst. prof. Med. Coll. Va., Richmond, 1989—; grant reviewer Am. Heart Assn., Richmond, 1982-86. Contbr. articles to profl. jours.; patentee in field. NIH postdoctoral fellow, 1969-72. Fellow Am. Coll. Clin. Pharmacology; mem. Am. Soc. for Pharmacology and Experimental Therapeutics, Soc. for Experimental Biology and Medicine, Am. Heart Assn., Rho Chi, Phi Kappa Phi, Sigma Xi. Home: 2200 Normandstone Dr Midlothian VA 23113-9652 Office: US FDA HFD-110 5600 Fishers Ln Rockville MD 20852-1750

PROBSTEIN, IAN EMIL, poet-critic, translator, foreign language educator; b. Minsk, Russia, July 12, 1953; came to U.S., 1989; s. Emil Michael and Rebecca (Kritser) P.; m. Tatiana Mamaeva, Nov. 20, 1986. BA in English and Spanish, Minsk U., 1974, MA in English and Translation, 1975; MA in Linguistics, Moscow Acad. Sci., 1986. Poet and translator Moscow (Russia) Publishing Houses, 1980-89; fellow, tutor Soviet Writers Union, Moscow, 1983-87; prof. English as a fgn. lang. Sch. of Adult Edn., Acad. of Scis., Moscow, 1985-88, chmn. fgn. langs., 1989; prof. ESL Touro Coll., N.Y.C., 1990—; adj. prof. of Russian The New Sch. for Social Rsch., N.Y.C., 1990—, NYU, N.Y.C., 1990—. Translator: Venezuelan Poetry, 1986, Mexican Poetry, 1986, Octave, Poetry of Latvia, 1986; translator, author: English 20th Century Poetry in Russian Translation, 1985, Library of Classics & Contemporaries, 1987, Longfellow, Whitman, Library of the U.S. Literature, 1986, Octave, 1987, Mexican Poets, 1987, Poetry of

Venezuela, 1988, Finding a Job in the USA, 1991. Mem. MLA, Am. Comparative Lit. Assn., Am. Assn. Tchrs. of Slavic and Ea. European Langs.

PROCTOR, ROBERT ALEXANDER, diplomat; b. Santa Rosa, Calif., Mar. 8, 1950; s. George Alan and Dorothea (Escherich) P.; m. Lois Ann Jensen, Nov. 22, 1986; 1 child, Kristen Andrea. BA, Stanford U., 1973; CD, Bologna Ctr., Italy, 1974; MA, Columbia U., 1975; MIPP, Johns Hopkins U., 1989. Liaison officer U.S. Sinai Field Mission, Egypt, 1978-79; staff asst. to ambassador U.S. Embassy, Jeddah, Saudi Arabia, 1979-80; country officer for Zambia and Malawi U.S. Dept. State, Washington, 1980-81; chief polit. sect. U.S. Embassy, Dar es Salaam, Tanzania, 1981-83; prin. officer U.S. Info. Office, Tromsoe, Norway, 1983-84; counselor for polit. affairs U.S. Embassy, Oslo, 1984-86; sr. country officer for Nigeria U.S. Dept. State, Washington, 1986-88, dir. policy and coord. staff Office of the Dir. Gen., 1989-91; counselor for polit. affairs U.S. Embassy, Kingston, Jamaica, 1991—. Contbr. articles to profl. jurs. Mem. Am. Fgn. Svc. Assn. Office: Kingston Dept of State Washington DC 20521-3210

PROFFITT, JOHN RICHARD, investment banking executive; b. Grand Junction, Colo., Sept. 12, 1930; s. Hillus D. and Joy Elaine (Lindsay) P.; m. Claire Boyer Miller, May 8, 1965; children: Cameron Lindsay, William Boyer. BA in Edn., U. Ky., 1953, MA in Polit. Sci., 1961; postgrad., U. Mich., 1959-65. Asst. dean of men, instr. polit. sci. dept. U. Ky., Lexington, 1957-59; teaching fellow U. Mich., Ann Arbor, 1961-63, 63-65; asst. dir. Nat. Commn. on Accrediting, Washington, 1966-68; dir. accreditation and eligibility staff U.S. HEW, Washington, 1968-75, dir. div. eligibility and agy. evaluation, 1975-80; dir. div. instnl. and state incentive programs U.S. Dept. Edn., Washington, 1980-82; pres. The Clairion Corp., Bethesda, Md., 1982-84, Nat. Asbestos Removal, Inc., Beltsville, Md., 1985-90; pres. Commonwealth Environ. Svcs., Inc., Alexandria, Va., 1987-91, also chmn. bd. dirs.; chmn. Internat. Environ. Engrs., Inc., Alexandria, Va., 1991—; pres. Canterbury Investment Internat., Vienna, Va., 1992—; cons. Conn. State Commn. Higher Edn., Hartford, 1967, Am. Coun. Edn., Washington, 1970; cons. U.S. HEW, 1967, 68; mem. study steering com. Am. Vocat. Assn., Washington, 1968; exec. sec. Nat. Adv. Com. on Accreditation and Instnl. Eligibility, Washington, 1968-80; mem. gen. com. Nat. Study Sch. Evaluation, Alexandria, 1970-78; mem. task force Edn. Commn. of the States, Denver, 1972; subcom. chmn. Fed. Interagency Com. on Edn., Washington, 1974-76; lectr., presenter profl. confs. Co-author: Accreditation and Certification in Relation to Allied Health Manpower, 1971; contbg. author: Health Manpower: Adapting in the Seventies, 1971, Accreditation in Teacher Education, 1975, Transferring Experiential Credit, 1979; contbr. articles to profl. and govtl. agy. publs., 1968-79. v.p., bd. dirs. Nat. Accreditation Coun. for Agys. Serving the Blind, N.Y.C., 1985; pres., chmn. bd. dirs. Found. for Advancement of Quality Svcs. for the Blind, Alexandria, 1988. 1st lt. USAF, 1953-55, Japan and Korea. Higher edn. fellow Univ. Mich., 1959. Mem. Club Internat. (Chgo.), Island Club (Hope Sound, Fla.), Thoroughbred Club Am. (Lexington, Ky.), Tower Club (Vienna, Va.), Sigma Nu. Democrat. Mem. Christian Ch. Home: 11008 Spring House Ct Potomac MD 20854-1452

PROIETTI, ROSE MARIE, nursing educator; b. Woonsocket, R.I., Jan. 19, 1948; d. Vincent and Filomena (Gesualdi) P.; m. Mark Savory, Feb. 5, 1988. Diploma, R.I. Hosp. Sch. Nursing, 1968; BA in Psychology, U. Hartford, 1979; MBA in Health Care, U. Conn., 1982. With State Exam for RN, Providence, 1968—. Patron The Morris Mus., Morristown, N.J., 1991. Mem. Nurse Cons. Assn., Assn. Operating Room Nursing, Assn. Advancement Med. Instruments. Home: 26 Vom Eigen Dr Convent Station NJ 07961

PROKESCH, CLEMENS ELIAS, physician; b. Dorchester, Mass., Nov. 21, 1918; s. Solomon Zischa and Ray Lillian (Brooks) P.; m. Jeanne Harriet Chase, Apr. 29, 1945 (dec. May 1976); children: Richard Chase, Steven Edward, Linda Dale Prokesch Foster; m. Natalie Gourse, July 27, 1980. BS, Yale U., 1939; MS, MIT, 1945; MD, NYU, 1949, cert. in internal medicine, 1952. Intern Englewood (N.J.) Hosp., 1949-50, resident in internal medicine, 1950-51; pvt. practice, 1954—; sr. active attending physician Lawrence and Meml. Hosp., New London, Conn., 1954—. Capt. USAF, 1952-54. Mem. German Soc. Ea. Conn. (v.p.), Thames Stamp Club (pres. 1959-84, pres. emeritus 1984—). Democrat. Jewish. Home: 30 Admiral Dr New London CT 06320 Office: 435 Montauk Ave New London CT 06320

PROKOPCHAK, STEVE DAVID, pastor, counseling administrator; b. Lancaster, Pa., Oct. 22, 1954; s. Joseph and Georgina (Crowe) P.; m. Mary Elizabeth Mohr, May 24, 1975; children: Joshua Cale, Marc Christopher, Brooke Megan. M. Human Svcs., Lincoln U., Oxford, Pa., 1987. Social worker, dir., houseparent Olson Lodge Fellowship, Crossfork, Pa., 1977-85; social worker The Bair Found., Harrisbur, Pa., 1985-87; dir. counseling Dove Christian Fellowship, Ephrata, Pa., 1987—. Autohr: Called Together (a Premarital Manual), 1989, Helping in the Local Church, A Helper's Notebook, 1991. Tchr. Dove Sch. the Bible, Ephrata, 1988-92. Sgt. USAF, 1971-75. Mem. AACD. Office: Dove Christian Fellowship 1924 W Main St Ephrata PA 17522-1111

PROKOPOVICH, S. RICHARD, nuclear engineer; b. Sewickley, Pa., July 9, 1948; s. Stanley and Julia (Pastelak) P.; m. Phyllis B. Stock, Aug. 30, 1975; children: Cynthia Rebecca, Ryan Edward. BS in Physics, Pa. State U., 1970; postgrad., Carnegie Mellon U., Pitts., 1974-78. Nuclear control operator Duquesne Light Co., Shippingport, Pa., 1974-77; reactor engr. Duquesne Light Co., 1977-80; prin. engr. Westinghouse Electric Corp., Monroeville, Pa., 1980—. Contbr. articles to profl. jours. Mem. Am. Nuclear Soc., Masons, Shriners. Home: 645 Miranda Dr Pittsburgh PA 15241-2041 Office: Westinghouse Elec Co PO Box 355 Pittsburgh PA 15230-0355

PROKOPY, JOHN ALFRED, government official, consultant; b. Phila., May 23, 1926; s. John A. and Mary Genevieve (Frushour) P.; m. L. Maureen St. Pierre, July 10, 1948 (div. 1970); children: Cheryl Holland, Dale O'Neill, Scot Douglas, Kent, Keith; m. Martha A. Cashman, Oct. 23, 1986; stepchildren: Daniel M. Cashman, Elizabeth Huck, Moira Huck, Marta Huck. Diploma, Bentley Coll. (formerly, Bentley Sch. Acctg. and Fin.), Boston, 1950, Lee Inst., Boston, 1971; BBA, Northeastern U., Boston, 1956. Lic. real estate broker and notary pub., Mass. Chief acct. gen. contractors, Boston, 1950-56; contr. Peters & Co., Inc., Boston, 1956-61; purchasing systems analyst Dept. Def., Boston, 1961-90, termination contracting officer, 1990—; bd. dirs., past pres. Fed. Credit Union, Boston, 1971-78; lectr. to profl. assns., 1975—; purchasing cons. in field, 1988—. Contbr. articles to profl. publs. Recipient Spl. Svc. award Dept. Def., 1977, Outstanding Performance award, 1979. Fellow Nat. Contract Mgmt. Assn. (cert. profl. contract mgr.). Home: 538 Brook Rd Milton MA 02186-2823

PRONER, SANFORD CLAY, podiatrist; b. N.Y.C., May 29, 1955; s. William and Mildred P.; m. Rhonda Norman, June 4, 1989. BA in Biology, SUNY, Binghamton, 1977; D of Podiatric Medicine, Ill. Coll. Podiatric Medicine, 1981. Diplomate Am. Bd. Podiatric Orthopedics. Resident Surg. Podiatric Residency, St. Joseph Hosp., Phila., 1981-83; pvt. practice Bronxville, Dobbs Ferry, N.Y., 1983—; chief podiatry Community Hosp., Dobbs Ferry, 1991—. Mem. Dobbs Ferry Lions, 1990—. Fellow Am. Coll. Foot Orthopedics; mem. Am. Coll. Foot Surgeons (assoc.), Am. Podiatric Med. Assn., N.Y. Podiatric Med. Assn. Home and Office: Sanford C Proner 1428 Midland Ave Bronxville NY 10708-6042

PROSPERINO, ROBERT, banker; b. Torino, Italy, Apr. 17, 1966; came to U.S., 1972; s. Domenico and Angela (Zappavigna) P.; m. Anna Marie Difalco, Nov. 3, 1990. BS in Fin., Manhattan Coll., 1988. Staff acct. Eastchester Savs. Bank, White Plains, N.Y., 1988-89; mgr. acctg. Liberty Nat. Bank, Danbury, Conn., 1989-90, supr. ops., 1990—. Mem. Delta Mu Delta. Home: 1102 Farmdale Rd Brewster NY 10509-9225 Office: Liberty Nat Bank 28 Shelter Rock Rd Danbury CT 06810-7050

PROSSER, TERRANCE WALSH, insurance professional; b. Ogdensburg, N.Y., Dec. 14, 1946; s. Donald Douglas Prosser and Dorothy Ann (Walsh) Hartman; m. Dianne Michelle Fronczak, June 29, 1985; 1 child, Colleen Anne. BS in Econs., SUNY, Brockport, 1970; CLU, Am. Coll., 1980, Chartered Fin. Cons., 1982. CLU, Chartered Fin. Cons. Sales agt. Prudential, Rochester, N.Y., 1970-80, sales mgr., 1980-82, devel. sales mgr., 1982-83, sales mgr., 1983-85; dist. mgr. Prudential, Middletown, N.Y., 1985-88, Norwalk, Conn., 1988—. Sgt. U.S. Army, 1969-75. Mem. Tarrytown Boat Club. Roman Catholic. Office: Prudential Ins 535 Connecticut Ave Norwalk CT 06854-1700

PROUT, GERALD ROBERT, chemical company regulatory affairs professional; b. N.Y.C., Sept. 20, 1949; s. Charles Henry and Dorothy (Baldwin) P.; m. Claudia Elizabeth Rand, Feb. 16, 1949; children: Tyler Owen, Drew Aaron, Evan Randall, Colby Reed. BA, Westminster Coll., 1971; MA, Duke U., 1972, Am. U., 1978. Mgr. pub. affairs Whirlpool, Benton Harbor, Mich., 1972-75, mgr. govt. relations, 1975-76; mgr. pub. affairs Burson Marsteller, Washington, 1976-79, v.p., 1979; mgr. external rels. FMC Corp., Phila., 1979-82, dir. pub. affairs, 1982-87, dir. regulatory affairs, 1987—. Contbr. articles to publs. 1st lt. USAR, 1973-82. Office: FMC Corp 1627 K St NW Washington DC 20006-1702

PROVORNY, FREDERICK ALAN, lawyer; b. Bklyn., Sept. 7, 1946; s. Daniel and Anna (Wurm) P.; m. Nancy Ileene Wilkins, Nov. 21, 1971; children: Michelle C., Cheryl A., Lisa T., Robert D. BS summa cum laude, NYU, 1966; JD magna cum laude, Columbia U., 1969. Bar: N.Y. 1970, U.S. Supreme Ct. 1973, D.C. 1975, Mo. 1977, Md. 1987, Calif. 1989; CPA, Md., Mo. Law clk. to Judge Harold R. Medina U.S. Ct. Appeals (2d cir.), N.Y.C., 1969-70; asst. prof. law Syracuse (N.Y.) U., 1970-72; assoc. Debevoise, Plimpton, Lyons & Gates, N.Y.C., 1972-75, Cole & Groner P.C., Washington, 1975-76; with Monsanto Co., St. Louis, 1976-86, asst. co. counsel, 1978-86; pvt. practice Washington, 1986-89; ptnr. Provorny & Jacoby, Washington, 1989-91; counsel Shaw, Pittman, Potts & Trowbridge, Washington, 1991—; lectr. Bklyn Law Sch., 1973-74; pres. Sci. and Tech. Assocs., Inc., 1986-91. Contbr. articles to profl. jours. Trustee Christian Woman's Benevolent Assn. Youth Home, 1979-83. Mem. ABA, Am. Law Inst., Fed. Bar Assn., Assn. of Bar of City of N.Y. (environ. law com. 1985-88), Bar Assn. Met. St. Louis (treas. young lawyers sect. 1980-81), Am. Arbitration Assn. (panel comml. arbitrators), Philo-Mt. Sinai Lodge No. 968, Masons, Beta Gamma Sigma. Jewish. Home: 11803 Kemp Mill Rd Silver Spring MD 20902-1511 Office: Shaw Pittman Potts & Trowbridge 2300 N St NW Washington DC 20037-1122

PROVOST, DONALD MOORE, retail financial executive; b. Washington, July 22, 1941; s. Donald Lozier and Florence (Macaroff) P. BSBA, Lehigh U., 1963; MBA in Fin., Columbia U., 1968. Fin. analyst W.R. Grace & Co., N.Y.C., 1968-73; asst. to pres. W.R. Grace & Co. Confectionery Div., Chgo., 1973-75; mgr. budgets Sewing Products Group-Singer, Stamford, Conn., 1975-80; dir. planning Plessey North Am., White Plains, N.Y., 1980-82; dir. fin. planning Channel Home Ctrs. Inc., Whippany, N.J., 1982-90; founder, CEO retail strategy cons. Proflyers Inc., Kinnelon, N.J., 1990—. Pres. Kinnelon Vol Fire Co., 1990-92. Lt. USNR, 1963-67. Mem. S.R., Smoke Rise Club, Green Pond Club. Republican. Home and Office: 341 Brookvale Rd Kinnelon NJ 07405

PROVOST, LLOYD, insurance trade association executive; b. N.Y.C., June 1, 1931; s. Lloyd and Elizabeth Bucklin (Peet) P.; m. Cherry Ainslie Collins, Jan. 5, 1957; children—Lloyd, Andrew, Alden. B.A., Brown U., 1953. Underwriter, Am. Surety Co., N.Y.C., 1955-59; underwriter Surety Assn. Am., N.Y.C., 1959-68, asst. sec., 1968-78, sec., 1978-81, gen. mgr., 1981-82, pres., 1982—. Troop treas. Essex council Boy Scouts Am., Glen Ridge, N.J., 1970-83; v.p. Glen Ridge Community Fund, 1977; exec. v.p. Family and Children's Services, Montclair, N.J., 1981. Served to cpl. U.S. Army, 1953-55. Congregationalist. Clubs: City Mid-Day (N.Y.C.); Montclair Golf (N.J.). Home: 57 Douglas Rd Glen Ridge NJ 07028-1227 Office: Surety Assn of Am 100 Wood Ave S Iselin NJ 08830-2716

PROWN, JULES DAVID, art historian educator; b. Freehold, N.J., Mar. 14, 1930; s. Max and Matilda (Cassileth) P.; m. Shirley Ann Martin, June 23, 1956; children: Elizabeth Anderson, David Martin, Jonathan, Peter Cassileth, Sarah Peiter. AB, Lafayette Coll., 1951, DFA (hon.), 1979; AM, U. Del., 1956, Harvard U., 1953; PhD, Harvard U., 1961. Dir. Hist. Soc. Old Newbury, Newburyport, Mass., 1957-58, Old Gaol Mus., York, Maine, 1958-59; asst. to dir. Harvard U., Fogg Art Mus., Cambridge, Mass., 1959-61; instr. to prof. history of art Yale U., New Haven, 1961—, curator collections, 1963-68; vis. lectr. Smith Coll., Northampton, Mass., 1966-67; dir. Yale Ctr. for Brit. Art, New Haven, 1968-76; assoc. dir. Nat. Humanities Inst., New Haven, 1977; bd. dirs. Yale U. Press, New Haven; trustee Whitney Mus., N.Y.C., 1975—; mem. editorial adv. bd. Am. Art-Smithsonian, Washington, 1986—; mem. vis. com. dept. architecture and art Princeton U., 1986—; mem. editorial bd. Art Bull., N.Y.C.; bd. dirs. Ctr. for Advanced Study in the Visual Arts. Author: John Singleton Copley, 2 Vols., 1966, American Painting from Its Beginnings to the Armory Show, 1969, The Architecture of the Yale Center for British Art, 1977, (catalogue) American Art from Alumni Collections, 1968. Recipient George Washington Kidd award Lafayette Coll., 1986. Mem. Am. Antiquarian Soc., Coll. Art Assn., Am. Studies Assn., The Walpole Soc., The Royal Soc. Arts. Office: Yale U History of Art Dept 56 High St West Haven CT 06516-2019

PRUDDEN, GEORGE ALAN, health policy analyst; b. Pasadena, Calif., Sept. 12, 1953; s. Terry M. and Margaret (Maule) P. BS in Biology, Am. U., 1975; BS, George Washington U., 1978; MBA, Loyola Coll., Balt., 1988. Cert. flight instr. Physician asst. So. Md. Hosp. Ctr., Clinton, 1978-82, Ch. Hosp., Balt., 1982-85; dir. program mgmt. div. Washington Pain and Rehab. Ctr., 1985-86; physician asst. Dimension Health Corp., Cheverly, Md., 1986-88; program mgr. United Mine Workers Am. Health and Retirement Funds, Washington, 1988-91; assoc. coord. physician assts. Prince George's Med. Ctr., Cheverly, Md., 1991—; clin. preceptor physician asst. program, George Washington U., 1978-88, Hahnemann U., Phila., 1980-88. Contbr. articles to profl. publs. Fellow Am. Acad. Physican Assts. (jour. referee 1988—), Md. Acad. Physician Assts.; mem. Caucus Exec. and Adminstrv. Physician Assts. (steering com.). Home: 10850 Green Mountain Cir Columbia MD 21044-2345 Office: Prince Georges Hosp Ctr 3001 Hospital Dr Cheverly MD 20785

PRUD'HOMME, HECTOR ALEXANDER, freelance writer; b. N.Y.C., Sept. 1, 1961; s. Hector Peart and Erica (Child) P. BA in History, Middlebury (Vt.) Coll., 1984. Researcher, reporter N.Y. Mag., N.Y.C., 1987-89; sr. staff writer Bus. Month Mag., N.Y.C., 1989-90; staff writer Time Mag., N.Y.C., 1991; freelance writer N.Y.C., 1991—. Home: 85 E 10th St Apt # 6-M New York NY 10003

PRUETT, GORDON EARL, religious studies educator; b. Raton, N.Mex., Oct. 16, 1941; s. Ozie D. and Velma Lorraine (Smith) P.; m. Elspeth Grant, July 23, 1966; children: Jenzi, Caroline. BA, Yale U., 1963; MA, Princeton U., 1967, Oxford (Eng.) U., 1981; PhD, Princeton U., 1968. Asst. prof. Lehigh U., Bethlehem, Pa., 1968-69; asst. prof. Northeastern U., Boston, 1969-74, assoc. prof., 1974—; vis. lectr. Westminster Choir Coll., Princeton, N.J., 1967-68; chairperson English dept. Northeastern U., Boston, 1976-80. Author: Meaning and End of Suffering, 1987; contbr. articles to profl. jours. Fellow NEH. Mem. Am. Acad. Religion (sect. head New Eng. 1990-93), Assn. Yale Alumni (del. 1989-92). Office: Northeastern U Dept Philosophy & Religion Boston MA 02115

PRUETT, KYLE DEAN, psychiatrist, educator; b. Raton, N.Mex., Aug. 27, 1943; s. Ozie Douthitt Pruett and Velma Lorraine Smith; m. Leslie Ann Bloom, Aug. 14, 1965; children: Elizabeth Storr, Emily Farrar. BA in History, Yale U., 1965; D of Medicine, Tufts U., 1969. Intern Mt. Auburn Hosp.-Harvard U., 1969-70; resident in psychiat. medicine Tufts-New England Med. Ctr., Boston, 1970-72; child psychiatry fellow Child Study Ctr., Yale U., New Haven, 1972-74, asst. clin. prof. psychiatry, 1975-79, assoc. clin. prof., 1979-87, clin. prof., 1987—; dir. child devel. unit Yale U., 1982—; attending physician dept. child psychiatry Yale-New Haven Hosp., 1972—; cons. psychiatrist Guilford (Conn.) Pub. Schs., 1977—; vis. scholar Sch. Medicine, U. Vt., 1987, Sch. Medicine, U. N.Mex., 1988; mem. editorial bd. Med. Problems of Performing Artists jour., 1983—, Fathers mag., 1987—; bd. dirs. Nat. Ctr. for Clin. Infant Programs, Washington. Author: The Nurturing Father, 1988 (Am. Health Book award 1988); contbr. numerous articles to profl. jours. Mem. med. adv. bd. Conn. Multiple Sclerosis Soc., Hartford, 1985—, Scholastic, Inc., 1988—, Yale U. Program for Humanities in Medicine, 1989—, World Assn. for Infant Psychiatry, 1979—; cons. Neighborhood Music Sch., New Haven, 1986—. Vis. fellow Anna Freud Clinic, London, 1975; recipient Mayoral Citation, City of Indpls., 1987. Mem. Am. Acad. Child and Adolescent Psychiatry, Am. Psychiat. Assn., Soc. for Rsch. in Family Therapy, Physicians for Social Responsibility, Yale U. Glee Club Alumni Assn. (pres. 1985-89). Home: 10 Fernwood Dr Guilford CT 06437-2349 Office: Yale Child Study Ctr 333 Cedar St New Haven CT 06510

PRUNTY, PATRICIA LOUISE, fundraiser; b. Springfield, Mass., Mar. 21, 1962; d. George Sebastian and Beverly Mae (Keene) Dimauro; m. Michael Arthur Prunty, Sept. 20, 1986; 1 child, Peter James. BA, Western New Eng. Coll., 1984. Fundraiser Bard Coll., Annandale, N.Y., 1986—. Democrat. Roman Catholic. Home: RR 1 Box 467 Pine Plains NY 12567-9527 Office: Bard Coll Annandale NY 12504

PRUPAS, MELVERN IRVING, video consultant, studio agent; b. Montreal, Que., Can., Dec. 16, 1926; s. Harry and Esther (Braunstein) P.; student Sir George Williams U., 1943-45, Montreal Tech. Inst., 1946, Mt. Allison U., 1967, N.Y. State Coll. Agr., 1970, Cornell U., 1971, U. Guelph, 1971-72; m. Sheila Ditkofsky, 1948 (div. 1981); children: Michael, Lorne, Norman, David, Dianne. m. Myrtle Levine, Sept. 17, 1981. Salesman, Crescent Cheese Co., 1947-50, sales mgr., 1951-56, dir., v.p., 1956-72, dir., v.p., sec., 1972-77; v.p., dir. Maycrest Co. Ltd., 1960-77; sec.-treas., dir. Les Produits Laitiers Marieville (Que., Can.) Ltee., 1956-72, v.p., sec., dir., 1972-77; founder En Ville newspaper, 1962; pres., dir. Ambassador Food Sales Ltd., 1981-92; sec.-treas., dir. Proops Press Inc., 1967-70 (all Montreal); pres. Dadnaram Ltd. of Montreal, 1972—; dir. planning Internat. Cinema Corp., Montreal and L.A., 1980-81; pres. MPA Video Distbrs., 1981-85, chmn. 1985-86; chmn. MPA Video Inc., 1985-86; chmn. Regional Video Distbrs. Inc., Halifax, Nova Scotia, 1985-86; pres. MPA Investment Properties Inc., 1985—, Mel Prupas Cons., 1986—, Prupas Studio Cons., 1987—, Mel Prupas Assocs., 1989—, MPA Laser Eco., 1991—, MPA Envirolaser, 1991—. Bd. dirs., mem. YM-YWHA of Montreal, 1954-72, gov., 1956-66, gov.-benefactor, 1967—, met. campaign chmn., 1966, founder track and field club, 1954; cubmaster Boy Scouts of Can., Mount Royal, 1960-71; chmn. food div. Combined Jewish Appeal, Montreal, 1961-63, trade coord., 1964-65, vice chmn. trades. 1969-70, vice chmn. spl. names, 1972-73; bd. dirs. Jewish Nat. Fund Montreal, 1970-72; v.p. Algonquin Home and Sch. Assn., 1971-72. Commdg. officer, major Wm. Dawson Can. Army Cadets, W.O.1 Kiwanis Air Cadets, 1940-45. Recipient Scouters Warrant, Boy Scouts of Can. 1963; Chevalier Medal, Chaine des Rotisseurs, 1964; Ida Steinberg Meml. trophy Combined Jewish Appeal, 1969; Golden Gloves Heavyweight Boxing Champion, 1942; mem. Can. Olympic Basketball Team, 1948. Mem. Province of Que. Food Brokers Assn. (dir. 1968-70), Food Service Execs., Assn., Can. Restaurant Assn., Chaine de Rotisseurs in Montreal Baillage, Confrerie Des Vignerons De St. Vincents, Guilde des Fromagers Confrerie de Saint-Uguzon, Montreal Bd. of Trade, Can. C. of C., Comml. Travellers Assn. Can., Food Brokers Assn. Can., Can. Importers Assn., Video Distbrs. Assn. Can. (v.p. 1983), Can-Israel C. of C., Am. Mus. Natural History, Playwrights Workshop, Jewish Theol. Sem. Am., Canadian Council Christians and Jews, Mt. Royal Property Owners Assn. (dir. 1968-70); dir. Congregation Beth El 1960-65, v.p. 1964-65, sec. 1969-70, v.p. 1971-73, pres. 1973-75). Mem. Y.M.-Y.W.H.A., B'nai B'rith., Cedarbrooke Golf and Country Club, Montreal Anglers and Hunters Club, Canadian Club, Amici Club (pres. 1950-51, 65-66), Rotary. Home: 5350 MacDonald Ave, Ste 1706, Montreal, PQ Canada H3X 3V2

PRUSOFF, WILLIAM HERMAN, educator, biochemical pharmacologist; b. N.Y.C., June 25, 1920; s. Samuel and Mary (Metrick) P.; m. Brigitte Auerbach, June 19, 1948 (dec. Apr. 1991); children—Alvin Saul, Laura Ann. B.A., U. Miami, Fla., 1941; M.A., Columbia U., 1947, Ph.D., 1949. Research assoc., instr. pharmacology Western Res. U., 1949-53; mem. faculty Yale Med. Sch., 1953—, prof. pharmacology, 1966-90, prof. emeritus. sr. rsch. scientist, 1990—, acting chmn. dept., 1968; cons. in field, 1965—. Mem. Am. Assn. Cancer Research, Am. Chem. Soc., Am. Soc. Biol. Chemists, Am. Soc. Pharmacology and Exptl. Therapeutics, Am. Soc. Microbiology, Am. Soc. Virology, Soc. Chinese Bioscientists in Am., Sigma Xi. Home: De Forest Dr Branford CT 06471 Office: Yale U Sch Medicine New Haven CT 06510

PRUTZMAN, PRISCILLA ROSE, conflict resolution organization administrator; b. Boston, Dec. 23, 1946; d. William Kuntz and Thelma (Knoll) P. BA, Colo. Women's Coll., Denver, 1969; MA, New Sch. for Social Rsch., 1980. Cert. tchr., N.Y. Dir. Children's Creative Response to Conflict, Nyack, N.Y., 1972—; co-chair Consortium of Peace Rsch. Edn. and Devel., George Mason U., 1991—; pres. Ulster Sullivan Mediation, N.Y., 1988—; facilitator Mayor's Office N.Y.C. Increase the Peace Corps, 1992—. Co-author: The Friendly Classroom for a Small Planet, 1977, Children's Songs for a Friendly Planet, 1987. Bd. dirs. Shadow Box Puppet Theatre, N.Y.C., 1987—; mem. Multicultural Group of Community Bds. of San Francisco, 1991—. Mem. Nat. Assn. for Mediation in Edn. (task force). Office: Children's Creative Response to Conflict Box 271 Nyack NY 10960

PRUZANSKY, JOSHUA MURDOCK, lawyer; b. N.Y.C., Mar. 16, 1940; s. Louis and Rose (Murdock) P.; m. Susan R. Bernstein, Aug. 31, 1980; 1 child, Dina Gabrielle. BA, Columbia Coll., 1960, JD, 1965. Bar: N.Y., 1965, U.S. Dist. Ct. (ea. and so. dists.) N.Y., 1968, U.S. Supreme Ct., 1980. Ptnr. Scheinberg, DePetris & Pruzansky, Riverhead, N.Y., 1965-85, Greshin, Ziegler & Pruzansky, Smithtown, 1985—; mem. exec. coun. N.Y. State Conf. Bar Leaders, 1984—, chmn. 88-89; mem. grievance com. Appellate Div. 10th Judicial Dist., 1992—; mem. adv. bd., Ticor Title Gaurantee Co., 1992—. Trustee Suffolk Acad. Law, Suffolk County, N.Y., 1979-89; mem. secondary sch. adv. com. Columbia U.; mem. Suffolk adv. bd. Fund for Modern Cts. Fellow ABA Found., N.Y. State Bar Found.; mem. ABA (probate and real property sect.), N.Y. State Bar Assn. (ho. dels. 1982—, v.p. 1991-92, mem.-at-large exec. com. 1992—, nominating com. 1986-91, spl. com. women and law 1986-91, task force on adminstrv. adjudication 1986—, task force on small firms 1991—, chair by-laws com. 1991—, trusts and estates sect.), Suffolk County Bar Assn. (bd. dirs. 1979-89, pres. 1985-86), N.Y. County Lawyers Assn., Nassau County Bar Assn., Suffolk Bar Pac (chmn. 1987-88), Columbia U. Law Alumni Assn. Suffolk County (dir. 1989—). Office: Greshin Ziegler & Pruzansky 199 E Main St Smithtown NY 11787-2899

PRYJMAK, PETER GOTHART, industrial engineer; b. Würzburg, Fed. Republic of Germany, Feb. 25, 1949; came to U.S., 1951; s. Peter and Else Freida (Proske) P.; m. Kathleen Ann Hankla, June 7, 1974; children: Peter Michael, Daniel Gregory, Renae Christine. BA in Physics, U. Nebr., 1974. Enlisted USN, 1968, advanced through grades, commd., 1974; served on USS DEG1 Brooke, Vietnam, 1970, USS AD-19 Yosemite, 1975-77, USS DDG-18 Semmes, 1977-79; staff of comdr. Commandant 6th Naval Dist., Charleston Naval Base, 1979; resigned USN, 1979; lt. comdr. USNR, resigned, 1989; sr. field service engr. Westinghouse Electric Corp., Pitts., 1981-83, sr. quality assurance engr., 1983—. Mem. Am. Welding Soc., Am. Assn. Artificial Intelligence, IEEE. Republican. Home: PO Box 42 New Stanton PA 15672-0042 Office: Westinghouse Electric Corp PO Box 355 Pittsburgh PA 15230-0355

PRYLUCK, CALVIN, film and television educator; b. N.Y.C., Jan. 30, 1924; s. Herschel and Sabina (Feldman) P.; m. Naomi Grunin, 1950; children: Judi, Seth. BA, NYU, 1952; MFA, UCLA, 1960; PhD, U. Iowa, 1973. Film producer Purdue U., Lafayette, Ind., 1960-68; instr. U. Iowa, Iowa City, 1969-71; assoc. prof. U. N.C., Chapel Hill, 1971-79; prof. Temple U., Phila., 1979—. Author: Meaning in Motion Pictures, 1976; contbr. numerous articles on documentary film and social contexts to profl. jours. With U.S. Army, 1944-46. Mem. Univ. Film and Video Assn. (editorial v.p. 1981-89). Jewish. Home: 216 E Mt Pleasant Ave Philadelphia PA 19119-1832

PRYOR, FREDERIC L., economist; b. Owosso, Mich., Apr. 23, 1933; s. Millard H. and Mary S. Pryor; B.A., Oberlin (Ohio) Coll., 1955; Ph.D., Yale U., 1962; m. Zora Prochazka, Mar. 26, 1964; 1 child, Daniel. Asst. prof. econs. U. Mich., 1962-64; rsch. economist Yale U., 1964-67; prof. econs. Swarthmore (Pa.) Coll., 1967—; rsch. dir. Pa. Tax Commn., 1979-81; Trustee Tougoloo Coll. Author: The Communist Foreign Trade System, 1963; Public Expenditures in Communist and Capitalist Nations, 1968; Property and

Industrial Organization in Communist and Capitalist Nations, 1973; The Origins of the Economy, 1977; A Guidebook to the Comparison of Economic Systems, 1985, Revolutionary Granada, 1987, The Political Economy of Poverty, Equity and Growth: Malani and Madagascar, 1990, The Red and the Green: The Rise and Fall of Collective Agriculture, 1992. Office: Swarthmore Coll Swarthmore PA 19081

PRYOR, PETER MALACHIA, lawyer, insurance company executive; b. Savannah, Ga., May 18, 1926; s. George Wendell and Mae (Calloway) P.; m. Velma Whitehead, July 21, 1946 (div. Feb. 1967); m. Barbara Jean Singleton, Mar. 31, 1967; children: Cynthia, Guinevere, Peter Jr., Marcus. BA, Siena Coll., 1952; LLB, Union U. Albany Law Sch., 1954, JD, 1968; LLD, Siena Coll., 1988. Bar: N.Y. 1954, U.S. Supreme Ct. 1976. Atty. Gen. Practice Law and Mcpl. Cons., Albany, N.Y., 1954-64; asst. atty. gen. N.Y. State Atty. Gen., Albany, N.Y., 1964-67; gen. counsel Pure Waters Authority and Environ. Facilities Corp., Albany, N.Y., 1967-72; chmn. N.Y. State Consumer Protection Bd., Albany, N.Y., 1972-75; gen. atty. N.Y. State Ins. Fund, Albany, N.Y.C., N.Y., 1976-81; of counsel Cooper, Erving, Savage, Nolan & Heller, Albany, N.Y., 1981-88; pres. Peter M. Pryor Assocs., Inc., Albany, 1984—; prin. Law Offices of Peter M. Pryor, Albany, 1988—; trustee Albany Law Sch. Union U., Albany, 1990—; Siena Coll., Loudonville, N.Y., 1987—, Russell Sage Coll., Troy, N.Y., 1988—; mem. com. on character & fitness N.Y. Supreme Ct. appellate div. Bd. dirs. Albany Inst. History & Art, 1986—, Albany Hist. Found., Capital City Housing Devel. Fund, Albany; pres. Albany Urban League, Albany NAACP. Sgt. U.S. Army, 1941-45, ETO. Recipient Human Rights award City of Albany, 1989, Disting. Svc. award Albany Urban League, 1989. Mem. Fort Orange Club, Univ. Club. Home: 134 Central Ave PO Box 6010 Albany NY 12210 Office: PO Box 6010 Albany NY 12206-0010

PRZYBYLSKI, PAMELA ANN, advertising executive; b. N. Tonawanda, N.Y., Dec. 12, 1959; d. Stanley F. and Alice S. (Hurko) P. BS in Graphic Design, SUNY, Buffalo, 1981. Layout artist Ellis Singer Webb & Assocs., Buffalo, 1981-82; jr. art dir. Ellis Singer Group, Buffalo, 1982-83, mech. dept. mgr., 1983-85; graphic designer Buffalo, 1985-86; art dir. Nemes & Czajkowski, Williamsville, N.Y., 1986, creative dir., 1987-90; creative dir., owner Prism Creative, Tonawanda, N.Y., 1991—. Mem. Art Dirs./Communicators Club Buffalo, Profl. Communicators Western N.Y. (gold award for color illustration 1990, silver award for art direction 1990, silver award for color illustration 1990, 91, 92, bronze award for art direction 1990, 91).

PSAROS-HARTIGAN, DENISE KAY, small business owner; b. Bklyn., May 27, 1960; d. John George and Jeanette (Ruffini) Psaros; m. Daniel Patrick Hartigan, Sept. 22, 1984; children: Daniel John, Chelsea Anne. BS in Air Commerce Flight Tech., Fla. Inst. Tech., 1982. Lic. comml., instrument and multi-engine pilot. Sec., treas. Brook Jewelers, Inc., Saddle Brook, N.J., 1982-87, pres., owner, 1987—. Cons., judge Bergen Tech. Schs., N.J., 1990. Gemological Inst. Am. scholar, 1984. Mem. Jewelers of Am., Nat. Assn. Women Bus. Owners, N.Y. Jewelers Assn., Jewelers Security Alliance, Saddle Brook C. of C., N.J. Women Bus. Owners (v.p. 1988—, Teal Heart award 1992). Republican. Roman Catholic. Office: Brook Jewelers Inc 487 Market St Saddle Brook NJ 07662

PSIHARIS, NICHOLAS See HARRICE, NICHOLAS CY

PSUTY, NORBERT PHILLIP, marine sciences educator; b. Hamtramck, Mich., June 13, 1937; s. Phillip and Jessie (Proszykowski) P.; m. Sylvia Helen Zurinsky, June 13, 1959; children: Eric Anthony, Scott Patrick, Ross Phillip. BS, Wayne State U., 1959; MS, Miami U., Oxford, Ohio, 1960; PhD, La. State U., 1966. Rsch. assoc. Coastal Studies Inst., La. State U., Baton Rouge, 1962-64; instr. dept. geography and dept. geology U. Miami, Coral Gables, Fla., 1964-65; asst. prof. geography U. Wis., Madison, 1965-69; assoc. prof. geography and geol. scis. Rutgers U., New Brunswick, N.J., 1969-73, prof., 1973—, chmn. dept. marine and coastal scis., 1991—, dir. Marine Scis. Ctr., 1972-76, dir. Ctr. for Coastal and Environ. Studies, 1976-90, assoc. dir. Inst. Marine and Coastal Studies, 1990—; mem. sci. com. Thalassas, Vigo, Spain, 1988—. Co-author: Living with the New Jersey Shore, 1986, Coastal Dunes, 1990; mem. editorial bd Coastal Mgmt., 1981—, Jour. Coastal Rsch., 1987—; contbr. numerous articles to scholarly jours., chpts. to books, monographs. Mem. Water Policy Bd., East Brunswick, N.J., 1981-83, N.J. Shoreline Adv. Bd., Trenton, 1984—; chmn. N.J. Gov.'s Sea Level Rise Com., Trenton, 1987-90; referee U.S. Volleyball Assn. Recipient Disting. Pub. Svc. award Pres. of Rutgers U. 1988; numerous grants including NSF, Nat. Park Svc., EPA, Office Naval Rsch., Nat. Sea Grant Program, NOAA, 1961—. Mem. AAAS, Assn. Am. Geographers, Coastal Soc. (pres. 1980-82), Internat. Geog. Union (vice chair commn. on coastal environ. 1988-92, editor newsletter 1984-92), N.J. Acad. Sci. (pres. 1982). Office: Rutgers U Ctr Coastal Environ Studies Busch Campus New Brunswick NJ 08903

PUCCINI, CHRISTOPHER JOHN, research scientist; b. Saranac Lake, N.Y., Dec. 11, 1950; s. Carl Robert and Raphael Joan (Louis) P.; m. Lynn Ann Adornato, Jan. 23, 1975 (div. Aug. 1983); children: Simon Michael, Peter Eliah; m. Deborah Kay Nagle, Mar. 11, 1989. AAS in Lab. Tech., Mohawk Valley Community Coll., 1974; BS in Biotech., SUNY, Rochester, 1984. Rsch. assoc. Masonic Med. Rsch. Lab., Utica, N.Y., 1974-75; rsch., devel., engring. Eastman Kodak Co., Rochester, 1976-86, molecular biologist, 1986-91, membrane processes rsch. scientist, 1991—. Copyrighted artistic and sci. concept of Spectragons; contbr. articles to profl. jours. Recipient fellowship Masonic Found. Med. Rsch. and Human Welfare, 1975. Mem. Phi Theta Kappa. Roman Catholic. Home: 63 Holcroft Rd Rochester NY 14612 Office: Eastman Kodak Co 1990 Lake Ave Rochester NY 14612

PUCCIO, JOSEPH ANTHONY, librarian; b. Phila., Aug. 12, 1955; s. Joseph and Ethel Anna (Renfro) P.; m. Barbara Alan Tapley, Feb. 18, 1978. A.A., Bucks County Community Coll., 1975; B.A., U. South Fla., 1977, M.A. in Library and Info. Sci., 1983. Library technician Univ. South Fla., Tampa, 1980-83; intern Library of Congress, Washington, 1983-84, librarian serial and govt. publs. div., 1983-89, pub. svc. officer collections mgmt. div., 1989—; book reviewer Tampa Tribune, 1981-83. Compiler bibliography computer periodicals Library of Congress, 1985, rev. edit., 1988; author: Serials Reference Work, 1989; co-editor: LCPA Broadside, 1988-89. Mem. Soc. Am. Baseball Research, ALA, Library Congress Profl. Assn. (mem. editorial bd. 1985, co-editor LCPA Broadside 1988-89). Democrat. Avocation: short story writing. Home: 7406 Finns Ln Lanham MD 20706-1216 Office: Collections Mgmt Div Washington DC 20540

PUCIK, VLADIMIR, business educator; b. Prague, Czechoslovakia; came to the U.S., 1975; s. Jozef and Juliana (Grossman) P.; m. Lang-Hoan Thi Pham, May 23, 1978; children: David, Mariana. Sr. profl. fellow Japan Found., 1990-91, 79-80, rsch. fellow Fulbright Commn., 1989-90, Social Sci. Rsch. Coun. fellow, 1980-81. Mem. Acad. Mgmt., Acad. Internat. Bus., Strategic Mgmt. Soc. Office: Cornell U CAHRS ILR Sch 393 Ives Hall Ithaca NY 14853-3901

PUCILOWSKI, JOSEPH JOHN, JR., government senior executive; b. Millville, N.J., Mar. 13, 1942; s. Joseph J. Sr. and Alice Elizabeth (Guinn) P.;m. Linda Joanne Olson, Jan. 25, 1964 (div. Sept. 1984); children: Linda Anne, Joseph J. III, Mary Alice, Kristin, Adam George; m. Maryann Giambalvo, Apr. 5, 1986; 1 child, Francine. BA in Physics, Rutgers U., 1963; MSEE, Fairleigh Dickinson U., 1976. Physicist U.S. Atomic Energy Commn., New Brunswick, N.J., 1963-66, U.S. Army Electronics Command, Ft. Monmouth, N.J., 1966-77; electronics engr. Project Mgr. Army Tactical Data Systems, Ft. Monmouth, 1977-78; chief computer resources and project engring. br. U.S. Army Communications R&D Command, Ft. Monmouth, 1978-81; dep. dir. ctr. for tactical computer systems U.S. Army Communications Electronics Command, Ft. Monmouth, 1981-82, assoc. tech. dir., 1982-89, dir. product assurance and testing, 1989-90, dir. C3 systems, 1990—. Mem. IEEE (sr.), Armed Forces Communications Electronics Assn. (presl. 1988-89, bd. dirs. 1987—, Appreciation plaque 1989), Assn. of U.S. Army (bd. dirs. 1986—). Home: 105 Darien Rd Howell NJ 07731-1807 Office: US Army Communication Electronics Command AMSEL RO C3 D Fort Monmouth NJ 07703

PUDNOS, STANLEY HERBERT, insurance executive; b. N.Y.C., Dec. 4, 1930; s. Lewis R. and Fannie (Cohen) P.; m. Shirley M. Satmary, Sept. 4, 1955; children: Adam, Jay, Eric. BS, CCNY, 1952. Various adminstrv. positions, 1952-55; owner Stanley H. Pudnos Ins., Old Bridge, N.J., 1955-76; officer Pudnos-Borrus Inc., Old Bridge, N.J., 1976—; cons. tech. adv. svc. for attys.; advisor on ins. State Senator John Gallagher; instr. ins. brokers lic. preparation courses; mem. continuing and licensing ednl. adv. com. N.J. Dept. Ins., 1989—. Mem. transp. com. Town of Old Bridge; active Jewish War Vets. With U.S. Army, 1953-55. Recipient cert. State of N.J. Mem. Nat. Assn. Security Dealers, N.J. Soc. Assn. Execs., Ind. Agts. N.J. (county pres.), Ins. Brokers Assn. N.J. (exec. v.p. 1974—), Middlesex Ins. Agts. (pres.), Old Bridge C. of C. (bd. dirs.), KP (pres., chancellor Old Bridge chpt.), Kiwanis (pres. Old Bridge chpt.), B'nai Brith. Lodges: KP (pres., chancellor Old Bridge chpt.), Kiwanis (pres. Old Bridge chpt.). Home: 37 York St Old Bridge NJ 08857-2121 Office: Pudnos-Borrus Inc 333 Us Hwy 9 Old Bridge NJ 08857-2840

PUDZIANOWSKI, ANDREW THADDEUS, chemist; b. Ludwigsburg, Germany, Dec. 2, 1947; came to U.S., 1951; s. Casimir and Zdzislawa Maria (Kapusta) P.; m. Anna Marie Kucharski, Jan. 2, 1982; children: Lydia Anne, Emily Slawa. BS in Chemistry with honors, U. Ill., Chgo., 1970, MS in Chemistry, 1974, PhD in Phys. Chemistry, 1979. Rsch. asst. immunochem. rsch. Evanston (Ill.) Hosp., 1970-71; rsch. asst. genetics dept. Stanford (Calif.) Med. Sch., 1979; postdoctoral fellow SRI Internat., Menlo Park, Calif., 1979-81, staff scientist, 1981-82; rsch. investigator Squibb Inst., New Brunswick, N.J., 1982-85, Squibb/Bristol-Myers Squibb, Princeton, N.J., 1985-91; sr. rsch. investigator CADD Group Bristol-Myers Squibb, Princeton, 1991—. Mem. ACLU, AAAS, Am. Chem. Soc., N.Y. Acad. Scis., Amnesty Internat. Office: Bristol Myers Squibb PO Box 4000 Princeton NJ 08543-4000

PUELLO, CHRISTOPHER ALAN, banker; b. Bklyn.; s. Robert Antonio and Agnes Cecelia (Johnson) P. BA in Polit. Sci. cum laude, Bklyn. Coll. of CUNY, 1980; MBA in Fin. magna cum laude, Columbia U., 1988; postgrad., Yale U., 1970-73. Counselor and recruiter admissions, fin. aid Bklyn. Coll. of CUNY, 1980-82; banking analyst Fed. Res. Bank of N.Y., N.Y.C., 1984-89; credit analyst Chem. Bank, N.Y.C., 1989—. Mobil Oil Corp. Achievement scholar, 1970-73; W.R. Grace fellow, N.Y.C., 1982-84; recipient Yale Club N.Y. Book award, 1970. Office: Chem Bank 633 Third Ave New York NY 10017

PUFF, JEAN ELLINGWOOD, civic worker; b. Evanston, Ill., July 25, 1924; d. Lloyd and Margaret (Brown) Ellingwood; m. Henry b. Puff, June 10, 1950; children: James Raymond, Margaret Elizabeth. BA, Northwestern U., 1945, BS in Nursing, 1947. Nurse, student health svc. Northwestern U., Evanston, Ill., 1947-48; pres. Gov. Wentworth Arts Coun., N.H., 1973-81; bd. dirs. Wolfeboro (N.H.) Playhouse, 1975-82; gov. Wentworth Arts Coun.; vol. Delta Gamma vision screening, Buffalo, 1960-65, Buffalo Philharmonic, 1959-69; mem. Huggins Hosp. Aid (Wolfeboro), Friends of Music of the Smithsonian Instn.; life mem. Ridley Coll. Womans Guild, St. Catherine, Ont., Can. Mem. Northwestern U. Med. Sch. Alumni Assn., Northwestern U. Alumni Assn., Rep. Women's Fedn., Ridley Coll. Woman's Guild (life), Wolfeboro Garden Club, Delta Gamma. Presbyterian. Home: Box 743 Springfield Point Wolfeboro NH 03894

PUFFER, BARBARA WARZECHA, corporate communications and management specialist; b. Phila., June 29, 1951; d. Stanley George and Barbara Jean (Maloney) Warzecha; m. Thomas R. Puffer. BA in Journalism, U. Bridgeport, 1972; MA in Corp. and Polit. Communications, Fairfield U., 1976. Suburban reporter New Haven Register, 1973; advt. asst. Union Trust & Co., New Haven, 1973-76; mgr. pub. rels. Phoenix Mut. Life, Hartford, Conn., 1976-77; mgr. corp. pub. rels. So. New England Tel., New Haven, 1977-84; mgr. advt. Sonecor Systems div. So. New England Tel., New Haven, 1984-85; mgr. corp. communications Barnes Group, Inc., Bristol, Conn., 1985—; freelance writer, 1973—; assoc. producer CBS Network Sports, N.Y.C., 1977, 78. Event dir., coach, trainer Internat. Spl. Olympics, 1979—; vice chmn. exec. bd., pub. edn. chmn. Conn. Spl. Olympics, 1979-81, 88—; bd. corporators, mem. devel. and mktg. com. Am. Sch. for Deaf, 1986-91, bd. dirs., capital campaign steering com., 1991—; exec. bd. Bristol, Plymouth, Burlington United Way, 1986-90, founder and chmn. New Cambridge Soc. United Way, 1990—; exec. bd. Bristol Girls Club Family Ctr., 1987-90, bd. dirs., trustee, 1990—, founder and chair Bristol Plus awards, 1989-91; exec. bd. Exceptional Cancer Patients, 1988; big sister ptnr. Big Bros./Big Sisters, 1992—. Named Communicator of Yr. Conn. chpt. Internat. Assn. Bus. Communicators, 1975, 83, Lou Bachman Meml. Outstanding Vol. United Way, 1991. Mem. New Eng. Assn. for Bus., Industry and Rehab., Conn. Pvt. Industry Coun. (mktg. com. greater New Haven sect. 1980), Nat. Panel Consumer Arbitrators, New Haven Better Bus. Bur., Internat. Assn. Bus. Communicators (accredited, pres. Conn. 1979-80), NAFE, Nat. Assn. Breast Cancer Orgns., Nat. Coalition Cancer Survivorship, Am. Cancer Soc., Conquer, U. Bridgeport Alumni Assn. (v.p. 1985-89, chmn. alumni house 1990—), Sch.-Bus. Partnership (mentor, coord. 1989—), Guilford Boat Owners. Republican. Roman Catholic. Office: Barnes Group Inc Exec Office 123 Main St Bristol CT 06010-6376

PUGH, ANDREW TUCKER, international company executive; b. White Plains, N.Y., Aug. 9, 1959; s. Roger Vaughan and Joanne (Sacco) P.; m. Kristen Jean Mertz, July 3, 1988. MPA, Harvard U., 1991; postgrad., Princeton (N.J.) U., 1988—. Lending officer Citibank, N.A., Istanbul, Turkey, 1982-83; lending officer, asst. mgr. Citibank, N.A., Khartoum, Sudan, 1984-85; dep. adminstr. CARE, Khartoum, Sudan, 1985-86; dep. regional mgr. CARE, N.Y.C., 1988-90; program coord. in Iraq, Russia and Togo CARE, 1991-92. Woodrow Wilson fellow Princeton U., 1987; World Bank scholar, 1987-88. Office: CARE 660 1st Ave New York NY 10016

PUGH, JAMES WHITWORTH, biomedical engineer; b. Jan. 4, 1946. BS in Metallurgy, MIT, 1968, PhD in Biomedical Engring., 1972. Registered profl. engr., N.Y.; USCG Operator's Lic.; lic. pvt. pilot. Postdoctoral fellow in bioengring. MIT, Cambridge, 1972; dir. biomechanics lab. Hosp. for Joint Diseases & Med. Ctr., 1972-79; dir. div. bioengring. Hosp. for Joint Diseases Orthopaedic Inst., 1979-84; rsch. prof. dept. orthpaedics, tech. dir. Gait Lab. SUNY, Stony Brook, 1985-86; dir. biomed. engring., metallurgy, materials sci. Inter-City Testing & Cons. Corp., Mineola, N.Y., 1986—; vis. prof. bioengring. Cooper Union Sch. Engring., N.Y.C., 1986-87, adj. assoc. prof., 1982-85; affiliate prof. bioengring. U. Wash., Seattle, 1989—; rsch prof. dept. orthopaedics SUNY, 1985-86; asst. prof. orthopaedics Mt. Sinai Sch. Medicine, CUNY, 1973-81, assoc. prof., 1981-84; adj. assoc. prof. dept. occupational health and safety NYU, 1981-85; others; lectr. in field. Contbr. numerous articles to profl. jours. Mem. ASME, ASTM, AAAS, NSPE, Am. Soc. Metals, Soc. Automotive Engrs., Orthopaedic Rsch. Soc., N.Y. State Soc. Profl. Engrs., Soc. for Biomaterials, Joint Med. Study Group, Soc. Plastics Engrs., Nat. Assn. Profl. Accident Reconstructionists, Sigma Xi. Home: 620 Broadway # 2F New York NY 10012-2616

PUGH, LAWRENCE R., textile corporation executive; b. 1933; (married). Grad., Colby Coll., 1956. Div. sales mgr. Borden Inc., 1958-66; product mgr., gen. mktg. mgr. Hamilton Beach Co., 1966-70; dir. mktg. Ampex Corp., 1970-72; group pres. Beatrice Foods Co., 1972-80; pres. V.F. Corp., Wyomissing, Pa., 1980-83, chmn., chief exec. officer, 1983—. Office: VF Corp Box 1022 Reading PA 19603

PUGLIESE, ANTHONY PAUL, construction company executive, educator; b. Phila., Oct. 4, 1942; s. Henry and Philomena (Strate) P.; m. Joyce Elaine Daily, Sept. 26, 1970; children: Marc, Alicia. BS in Acctg., Temple U., 1966. Vice pres. constrn. lending People's Bond & Mortgage Co., Phila., 1964-70; pres. J & A Properties, Inc., Mt. Laurel, N.J., 1970-79; constrn. mgr. Ciotti Constrn. Co., Reading, Pa., 1979-83; owner, mgr. Pugliese Homes Inc., $, 1983—; cons. Kardon Investment Co., Phila., 1967-70; prof. constrn. mgmt. Pa. State U., 1989—. Mem. Nat. Home Builders Assn., Pa. Home Builders Assn., Home Builders Assn. Berks County, Nat. Fedn. Ind. Bus., Berks County C. of C., Exeter Golf Club (bd. dirs. 1986-88). Democrat. Roman Catholic. Office: 4228 St Lawrence Ave Reading PA 19606-2818

PUGLIESE, PAUL JOSEPH, real estate broker, developer, architect; b. Falls Church, Va., Jan. 13, 1952; s. Pasquale Joseph Pugliese and Marie Virginia (Lamparelli) Orsini; m. Laura Colburn Ierardi, Aug. 11, 1984; children: Juliana Sterling, Alexander Colburn. BA in Environ. Design summa cum laude, SUNY, Buffalo, 1973; MArch, Yale U., 1977. Lic. architect, Conn. Ptnr. Design Directions, Old Greenwich, Conn., 1977-86; designer I.M. Pei and Ptnrs., Architects, N.Y.C., 1978-81; v.p. Priess Briemeister Architects, Stamford, Conn., 1981-86; dir. consulting Greenwich (Conn.) Land Co., Inc., 1986-89, pres., 1989—; mem. archtl. rev. commn. Greenwich, 1983-90, chmn., 1990—; mem. bd. dirs. Bruce Mus., Greenwich, 1991—. Mem. Greenwich Bd. Realtors, Indian Harbor Yacht Club. Republican. Office: Greenwich Land Co Inc 2 Benedict Pl Greenwich CT 06830-5358

PUGLIESE, ROCCO VINCENT, lobbyist; b. Trenton, N.J., June 16, 1953; s. Joseph and Helen Rose (Bossio) P.; m. Debra Ann Mannino, Oct. 11, 1980; children: Tanza Marie, Anthony Joseph Robert. BA, Gannon U., 1975; MPA, Pa. State U., 1977. Rsch. analyst Pa. State Senate, Harrisburg, 1975-76, Pa. Ho. of Reps., Harrisburg, 1976-78; exec. dir., lobbyist Pa. Food Processors Assn., Harrisburg, 1978—; pub. affairs cons. Pugliese Assocs., Harrisburg, 1983—; pres. Coun. Food Processing Execs., Washington, 1986-87, State Coun. Farm Orgns., Harrisburg, 1989-91. Bd. dirs. Cen. Pa. chpt. Leukemia Soc., 1985-90, pres., 1987-88. Office: Pugliese Assocs 600 N 3d St Harrisburg PA 17101

PUIG, ANGELA RENEE, career and job development professional; b. Bronx, N.Y., Dec. 20, 1966; d. Angelo and Janice Claire (Simms) P. BA in History, Ea. Coll., St. Davids, Pa., 1988. Legal researcher Caitlin Grey, Haddonfield, N.J., 1988; asst. mgr. Am. History Mus. Shop Smithsonian Instn., Washington, 1989-90; career and job devel. profl. Camden County Coll., Blackwood, N.J., 1990-91. Candy striper Garden State Community Hosp., Marlton, N.J., 1980-83. Mem. U.S. Dist. Ct. N.J. Hist. Soc., Smithsonian Assocs., Phila. Art Mus., Kennedy Ctr., South Jersey Ctr. for Arts. Republican. Roman Catholic. Office: Camden County Coll PO Box 200 Blackwood NJ 08012-0200

PUIG, JANICE CLAIRE, psychologist; b. N.Y.C., Feb. 1, 1944; d. James Clarence and Mae (Wesley) Simms; m. Angelo Puig, Dec. 19, 1964; 1 child, Angela Reneé. BA, CUNY, 1971; MEd, Rutgers U., 1975, EdD, 1976. Dir. psychology Archway Schs., Atco, N.J., 1981-82; clin. psychologist Marlboro (N.J.) Psychiat. Hosp., 1982-84, Ancora Psychiat. Hosp., Hammonton, N.J., 1984-87; cons. Puig Assocs., Cherry Hill, N.J., 1987—; cons. Puig Assocs., Cherry Hill, N.J., 1987—; clin. psychologist Drenk Meml. Guidance Ctr., Burlington, N.J., 1979-82; adj. prof. Glassboro (N.J.) State Coll., Trenton (N.J.) State Coll., 1987—; sch. psychologist Camden (N.J.) Pub. Schs., 1978-81, Lawnside (N.J.) Pub. Schs., 1990-91, Moorestown (N.J.) Pub. Schs., 1991—. Contbr. articles to profl. jours. Scholarship Jewish Found. for Edn. of Girls, 1969-71; fellow NIMH 1971-74, Rutgers U. 1975; grantee Rutgers U. 1975. Mem. APA, Am. Assn. Marriage and Family Therapists (chmn. N.J. Ad Hoc Com. for Minority Affairs, chpt. v.p.) Nat. Assn. Sch. Psychologists, N.J. Psychol. Assn., South Jersey Psychol. Assn., CUNY, Alumni Assn., Rutgers U. Alumni Assn. Roman Catholic. Home: 63 Lakeside Dr Marlton NJ 08053-2704 Office: Puig Assocs 1060 Kings Hwy N # 314 Cherry Hill NJ 08034-1910

PULGRAM-ARTHEN, LUCIA DEIRDRE, religious non-profit administrator; b. Atlanta, Nov. 5, 1956; d. William Leopold and Lucia (Fairlie) Pulgram; m. Andras Corban-Arthen, Apr. 9, 1983; children: Donovan Andru, Lucia Isobel. BA in History and Drama, Tufts U., 1978; MA in Counseling Psychology, Lesley Coll., 1986. Dir. The EarthSpirit Community, Medford, Mass., 1983—; program coord. Ctr. for Community Resources, Medford, Mass., 1988—; nat. pub. info. officer Covenant of the Goddess, Berkeley, Calif., 1991-92, nat. second officer, 1990-91, nat. ethics officer, 1985-87. Contbr. articles to profl. jours. Mem. LaLeche League Internat., Co-op America. Office: The EarthSpirit PO Box 365 Medford MA 02155

PULHAMUS, AARON RAE, counselor, educator; b. Paterson, N.J., May 21, 1938; s. Aaron and Maybelle (Snook) P.; m. Marlene L. Weeder, Aug. 20, 1960; children: A. Steven, Thomas E., Nancy L. BA, W.Va. Wesleyan Coll., 1960; MA, NYU, 1962; MPA, Rutgers U., 1977, EdD, 1985. Asst. prof. Fairleigh Dickinson Univ., Teaneck, N.J., 1966-68; asst. dean admstrn. N.J. Inst. of Tech., Newark, 1968-75, exec. asst. to pres., 1975-77; asst. program dir. N.J. Dept. Higher Edn., Trenton, N.J., 1977; v.p. for bus. N.J. Inst. Tech., Newark, 1978-80, exec. dir. employee rels., 1980-88, lectr. mgmt., 1988—; cons. N.J. Dept. Community Affairs, Trenton, 1991. Contbr. articles to profl. jours. Bd. mem. Bessie Green Community, Newark, 1990—; vol. St. Joseph's Hosp., Paterson, N.J., 1990—, N.J. AIDS Interfaith Network, Montclair, N.J., 1991—. Fellow Acad. Coll. and Univ. Pers. Assn.; mem. AACD, ASTD, ASPA, Acad. Mgmt., Indsl. Rels. Assn. Home: 68 Minnisink Rd Totowa NJ 07512-1919 Office: N J Inst Tech University Heights Newark NJ 07102

PULIAFITO, CARMEN ANTHONY, ophthalmologist, laser researcher; b. Buffalo, Jan. 5, 1951; s. Dominic F. and Marie A. (Nigro) P.; m. Janet H. Pine, May 19, 1979. AB cum laude, Harvard Coll., 1973, MD magna cum laude, 1978. Diplomate Am. Bd. Ophthalmology. Resident Mass. Eye and Ear Infirmary, Boston, 1979-82, retina fellow, 1982-83; instr. Harvard Med. Sch., Boston, 1983-85, asst. prof., 1985-89, assoc. prof., 1989-91; dir. div. continuing edn. dept. ophthalmology Harvard Med. Sch., 1989-91; vis. scientist MIT Regional Laser Ctr., Cambridge, 1982, asst. prof. health scis. and tech. program, 1987-89, assoc. prof., 1989—; mem. staff Mass. Eye and Ear Infirmary, Boston, 1983; bd. dirs. Morse Laser Ctr. Mass. Eye and Ear Infirmary, 1986-91; dir. New Eng. Eye Ctr. 1991—; prof., chmn. Dept. Ophalmology, Tufts U. Sch. Medicine, 1991—; prof. Biomedical Engring., Tufts U. 1991—. Author (with D. Albert) Foundations of Ophthalmic Pathology, 1979; (with R. Steinert) Principles and Practice of Ophthalmic YAG Laser Surgery, 1984; editor-in-chief jour. Lasers in Surgery and Medicine, 1987—; contbr. 60 sci. articles to profl. jours. Fellow Am. Acad. Ophthalmology. Roman Catholic. Home: 236 Glen Rd Weston MA 02193-2237 Office: New England Eye Ctr 750 Washington St Boston MA 02111

PULIS, MICHAEL PATRICK, aerospace engineer; b. Portsmouth, Va., Aug. 9, 1966; s. Fred and Perrine (Smith) P. AS in Engring., No. Va. Community Coll., Annandale, 1987; BS in Aerospace Engring., Va. Tech. Inst. & State U., 1989. Aerospace engr. EER Systems, Seabrook, Md., 1989—. Advisor Adopt-a-Sch. Program, Annandale, 1986. Mem. AIAA (Allied Design Competition award 1989). Republican.

PULLEN, DAVID JOHN, physicist and educator; b. Merton, Surrey, Eng., June 28, 1936; came to U.S. 1963; s. Arthur Lester and Alexandra Q. (Griffiths) P.; m. Heather Morgan, Aug. 6, 1960; children: Katrina, Adrian, Lester, Andrew. BSc with first class honors, London U., 1958; DPhil, Oxford U., Eng., 1963. "1851" rsch. fellow Oxford U., 1961-63; instr. MIT, 1963-65; asst. prof. physics U. Pa., Phila., 1965-70; assoc. prof. Lowell (Mass.) Tech. Inst., 1970-73; prof. physics U. Mass./Lowell, 1973—; ptnr. CPS Nuclear, Nashua, N.H., 1990—; cons. Internat. Atomic Energy Agy., Vienna, Austria, 1991—. Contbr. over 70 articles on nuclear physics to profl. jours.; author: Physics Laboratory Experiments, 3 edits., 1975-83. Royal Commn. for Exhbn. of 1851 rsch. fellowship, 1961-63. Mem. Am. Phys. Soc., Am. Assn. Physics Tchrs., Sigma Xi. Home: 2 Reeves Rd Bedford MA 01730-1335 Office: U Mass/Lowell 1 University Ave Lowell MA 01854-2881

PULLEN, RICHARD OWEN, lawyer, communications company executive; b. New Orleans, Nov. 6, 1944; s. Roscoe LeRoy and Gwendolen Sophia Ellen (Williams) P.; m. Frances G. Eisenstein, Jan. 24, 1976 (div. 1986). B.A. in Econs., Whitman Coll., 1967; J.D., Duke U., 1972. Bar: D.C. 1972. Fin. mgmt. trainee Gen. Electric Co., Lynn, Mass., 1967-69; sr. atty. domestic facilities div. Common Carrier Bur., FCC, Washington, 1972-79, atty. advisor Office of Opinions and Rev., 1979-81; chmn. definitions and terminology of joint industry, govt. com. for preparation of U.S. Proposals 1977 Broadcasting Satellite World Adminstrv. Radio Conf.; v.p. Washington office Contemporary Comm. Corp., New Rochelle, N.Y., 1981-91; v.p., gen. counsel Comm. Innovations Corp., New Rochelle, 1991—. With USCGR, 1967-75. Mem. ABA, Fed. Comm. Bar Assn., Fed. Bar Assn., Internat. Platform Assn. Republican. Unitarian.

PULLEY, BRENDA DIANE, association executive; b. Kansas City, Mo., May 9, 1958; d. Joseph Edward and Rose Ann (Hundley) P. BS, Cen. Mo. State U., 1980. Profl. staff mem. U.S. House Reps. Energy Environ. and Safety, Washington, 1983-85, U.S. House Reps. Exports adm Tourism, Samll Bus. Subcom., Washington, 1985-89; exec. dir. Nat. Assn. Chem. Recyclers, Washington, 1989—. Tutor Washington Col. Tchrs., 1990. Democrat. Office: Nat Assn Chem Recyclers 1875 Connecticut Ave NW Ste 1200 Washington DC 20009

PULLIN, JORGE ALFREDO, physics researcher; b. Buenos Aires, Feb. 26, 1963; came to U.S., 1989; s. Archie Ernest and Evangelina (Rostagno) P.; m. Gabriela Ines Gonzalez, Oct. 7, 1989. MSc in Physics, Inst. Balseiro, Bariloche, Argentina, 1986, PhD in Physics, 1988. Asst. prof. U. Cordoba, Argentina, 1988—, mgr. computer systems physics dept., 1988-89; rsch. assoc. Syracuse (N.Y.) U., 1989-91, U. Utah, 1991—; grant reviewer ANEP, Govt. of Spain, 1991—. Reviewer Math. Revs., 1988—, Soc. for Indsl. & Applied Math. Rev., 1991—, Cambridge U. Press, 1991—; referee Physics Letters, 1990—, Phys. Rev., 1990—, Am. Jour. Physics, 1991—, Jour. Math. Physics, 1991—; contbr. articles to profl. jours. Mem. Internat. Soc. Gen. Relativity.

PULLING, REBECCA ANN, academic administrator; b. Union City, Pa., Sept. 23, 1964; d. Donald Delbert Pulling and Joanne Lee (Bryant) Munzert. BA, Allegheny Coll., 1986; MA, Bowling Green State U., 1989. Residence hall mgr. Bowling Green (Ohio) State U., 1986-88, residence hall dir., 1988-89; dir. housing Mt. Ida Coll., Newton Centre, Mass., 1989-90; asst. dir. residence life Simmons Coll., Boston, 1990—; steering com. New Eng. Student Affairs Placement Conf., Boston, 1990-91. Vol. Somerville (Mass.) Homeless Coalition, 1991—. Mem. Mass. Coll. Pers. Assn., Am. Coll. Pers. Assn., Northeast Assn. Coll. and Univ. Housing Officers, Boston Area Coll. Housing Assn. (steering com. 1991—). Office: 305 Brookline Ave Boston MA 02215-4166

PULSIFER, MARGARET BIGWOOD, psychologist; b. Boston, Nov. 16, 1959; d. Harold Smith and Brenda (MacHugh) Bigwood; m. Peter Emery Pusifer, Aug. 2, 1987. BA, Boston Coll., 1981, MA, 1983; PhD, SUNY, Buffalo, 1989. Lic. psychologist, Md. Clin. psychology extern, St. Elizabeths Hosp., Washington, 1987-88, clin. psychology intern, 1988-89; postdoctoral fellow Johns Hopkins U. Sch. Med., Balt., 1989-90; pediatric psychologist Kennedy Inst. for Handicapped Child./ Johns Hopkins, Balt., 1990—. Mem. Jr. League of Washington, 1989—. Mem. Am. Psychol. Assn., Md. Psychol. Assn., Nat. Acad. Neuropsychology. Office: Kennedy Inst for Handicappe 707 N Broadway Baltimore MD 21205-1832

PUMA, SAMUEL GEORGE, JR., public safety director, educator, consultant; b. Buffalo, May 29, 1951; s. Samuel George and Betty Ann (Miller) P.; m. Susan Carol Klubek, July 9, 1977. BS, SUNY, Buffalo, 1975, MS, 1977. Rsch. analyst Buffalo Police Dept., 1973-75; dir. pub. safety Canisius Coll., Buffalo, 1975—, asst. prof. criminal justice, 1980—; instr. Erie County Cen. Police Svcs. Acad., Buffalo, 1981—. Trustee Erie County Cen. Police Svcs., 1987—, chmn., 1988-90. Recipient Cert. Appreciation for Disting. Svc., Erie County Cen. Police Svcs., 1986, Chmn.'s award, 1989; grad. fellow Sch. Social Svcs. SUNY, 1973; named One of Outstanding Young Men of Am., 1990. Mem. Internat. Assn. Campus Law Enforcement Adminstrs., Am. Acad. Prof. Law Enforcemtne, Judge and Police Exec. Conf., United Fedn. Police, N.Y. State Fedn. Police, N.Y. State Mcpl. Police Trainer Assn., Criminal Justice Honor Soc., Sigma Xi, Delta Tau Kappa. Office: Canisius Coll 2001 Main St Buffalo NY 14208-1098

PUMPHREY, JANET KAY, editor; b. Balt., June 18, 1946; d. John Henry and Elsie May (Keefer) P. AA in Secondary Edn., Anne Arundel Community Coll., Arnold, Md., 1967, AA in Bus. and Pub. Adminstrn., 1976. Office mgr. Anne Arundel Community Coll., 1964—; mng. editor Am. Polygraph Assn., Severna Park, Md., 1973—; archives researcher Am. Polygraph Assn., Severna Park, 1973—. Editor: (with Albert D. Snyder) Ten Years of Polygraph, 1984, (with Norman Ansley) Justice and the Polygraph, 1985, A House Full of Love, 1990. Mem. Rep. Nat. Sustaining Com. Mem. NAFE, Am. Polygraph Assn. (hon.), Md. Polygraph Assn. (affiliate), Internat. Platform Assn., Anne Arundel County Hist. Soc., Alumni Assn. Anne Arundel Community Coll. Republican. Methodist. Home: 3 Kimberly Ct Severna Park MD 21146-3703 Office: Am Polygraph Assn PO Box 1061 Severna Park MD 21146-8061

PURCELL, EDWARD MILLS, physics educator; b. Taylorville, Ill., Aug. 30, 1912; s. Edward A. and Mary Elizabeth (Mills) P.; m. Beth C. Busser, Jan. 22, 1937; children: Dennis W., Frank B. B.S. in Elec. Engring, Purdue U., 1933, D. Engring. (hon.), 1953; Internat. Exchange student, Technische Hochschule, Karlsruhe, Germany, 1933-34; A.M., Harvard U., 1935, Ph.D., 1938. Instr. physics Harvard U., 1938-40, asso. prof., 1946-49, prof. physics, 1949-58, Donner prof. sci., 1958-60, Gerhard Gade Univ. prof., 1960-80, emeritus, 1980—; sr. fellow Soc. of Fellows, 1949-71; group leader Radiation Lab., MIT, 1941-45. Contbg. author: Radiation Lab. series, 1949, Berkeley Physics Course, 1965; contbr. sci. papers on nuclear magnetism, radio astronomy, astrophysics, biophysics. Mem. Pres.'s Sci. Advisory Com., 1957-60, 62-65. Co-winner Nobel prize in Physics, 1952; recipient Oersted medal Am. Assn. Physics Tchrs., 1968, Nat. Medal of Sci., 1980, Harvard medal, 1986. Mem. Am. Philos. Soc., NAS, Phys. Soc., Am. Acad. Arts and Scis., Royal Soc. (fgn. mem.). Office: Harvard U Dept Physics Cambridge MA 02138

PURCELL, GEORGE RICHARD, artist, postal employee; b. Clayton, N.Y., May 4, 1921; s. George Thomas and Katherine Eileen (Eagan) P.; m. Mary Sutter, Apr. 3, 1961. BS, Niagara U., 1947; postgrad., Syracuse U., 1952-53, 55-56. With Eagan Real Estate, Syracuse, 1948-49; claims interviewer N.Y. State Div. Unemployment Ins., 1949-50, 52; with U.S. Postal Service, Syracuse, 1957—, cert. classifier of mails, 1975-77, with registry dept., 1977—; tutor philosophy, 1971—. Exhibited in Central N.Y. Art Open, 1981, Drake Gallery, Fayetteville, N.Y., 1982, Assoc. Artists Gallery, Syracuse, 1983, 91, Fayetteville Art Festival, 1984, Recreation Generation Art Exhibit, 1982—, DeWitt (N.Y.) Libr., 1986—, Fayetteville Libr., 1988—, N.Y. State Fair, 1990. Founder, pres. Syracuse chpt. Cath. Med. Mission Bd., 1973-76, rep., 1976—; mem. Cath. Near-East Welfare Assn., Book Mission Prgram, New Mems. Art Show Manlius Libr., 1991; del. Presdl. Trust, 1992; apptd. Inst. des Hautes Etudes, Legion de L'Aigle de mer, Order of Holy Cross of Jerusalem, Order Knight Templars of Jerusalem, Alliance Universelle Pour La Paix. Served with U.S. Army, 1943-46. N.Y. State War Service scholar, 1955. Fellow Internat. Biog. Assn. (life); mem. Am. Cath. Philos. Soc. (assoc.), Am. Biog. Inst. (life assoc., rsch. bd. advisors nat. div.), Internat. Soc. Neoplatonic Studies, Am. Watercolor Soc., Associated Artists, Soc. Ancient Greek Philosophy, Dele Confedn. of Chivalry. Roman Catholic. Home: 1 Gregory Pky Syracuse NY 13214-1601

PURCELL, PHILIP JAMES, financial services company executive; b. Salt Lake City, Sept. 5, 1943; s. Philip James and Shirley (Sorensen) P.; m. Anne Marie Mc Namara, Apr. 2, 1964; children: David, Peter, Mark, Michael, Paul, Philip, Thomas. B.B.A., U. Notre Dame, 1964; M.Sc. in Econs., London Sch. Econs. and Polit. Sci., U. London, 1966; M.B.A., U. Chgo., 1967. Mng. dir., cons. McKinsey & Co., Inc., Chgo., 1967-78; v.p. planning and adminstrn. Sears, Roebuck and Co., Chgo., 1978-82; pres., chief operating officer, then chmn., chief exec. officer Dean Witter Fin. Svcs. Group, N.Y.C., 1982—; also bd. dirs. Dean Witter Fin. Svcs. Inc., N.Y.C.; bd. dirs. Dean Witter Realty Inc., Dean Witter Reynolds Inc., Dean Witter Reynolds Internat., Inc., Sears Consumer Fin. Corp., Securities Industry Assn.; mem. coun. Grad. Sch. Bus., Univ. Chgo.; mem. adv. coun. Univ. Notre Dame Bus. Sch., Ind. Served with USNR. Roman Catholic. Clubs: Economic of Chgo., The Chgo.; Bond of N.Y. (N.Y.C.). Office: Dean Witter Fin Svcs Group 2 World Trade Ctr 66th Fl New York NY 10048

PURCELL, STEVEN RICHARD, international management consultant, engineer, economist; s. Jacob Louis and Bertha P. B of Mech. and Indsl. Engring., NYU, 1950; MS in Indsl. Engring., Columbia U., 1951; EdM, Harvard U., 1968. Registered profl. engr., Can. Lectr. engring. NYU Coll. Engring., N.Y.C., 1948-50; gen. mgr. Dapol Plastics Co., Inc., Boston, 1956-58; gen. div. mgr. Am. Cyanamid Co., Sanford, Maine, 1958-61; sr. prin. Purcell & Assocs., mgmt. cons., N.Y.C., 1961-66; prof., div. chmn. Bristol Coll., Fall River, Mass., 1966-68; assoc. dean grad. faculty adminstrv. studies York U., Toronto, Ont., Can., 1969-71; chief economist Dept. Manpower and Immigration, Ottawa, Ont., Can., 1970-71; cons. Treasury Bd., Ottawa, 1971-72; dir. urban and internat. environ. policy Ministry of State for Urban Affairs Internat. Activities, Ottawa, 1973-74; mem. com. on challenges of modern soc. NATO, Ottawa, 1973-74; mem. sci., econ. policy com. OECD UN, Ottawa, 1973-74; prof. Grad. Sch. Bus. Adminstrn. and Econs. Algonquin Coll., Ottawa, 1974-76; advisor, cons. House of Commons, 1976-77; sr. prin. Purcell & Assocs., Washington, 1977-80, pres., 1981—; exec. dir. nat. coastal zone mgmt. adv. com. NOAA U.S. Dept. Commerce, Washington, 1980-81; profl. lectr. Northeastern U. Grad. Sch. Bus. Adminstrn., Boston, 1953-56, U. Toronto, 1968-69, George Washington U. Grad. Sch. Bus. Adminstrn., Washington, 1979; vis. prof. Rensselaer Poly. Inst. Advanced Mgmt. Program, 1967, U. Ottawa Grad. Sch. Bus. Adminstrn., 1971-74; lectr. Council for Internat. Progress in Mgmt., N.Y.C., 1960, Royal Bank Can. Mgmt. Assn., Toronto, Ont., 1970; corp. appointment cons. Harvard U., Cambridge, Mass., 1967-68; cons. Govt. Venezuela, 1967-68, Can. Inst. Bankers, Toronto, 1969-70; internat. sr. adviser NASA, 1985-86, mem. nat. adv. bd. Ctr. for Nat. Policy; dir. Rental Resource Corp., 1986—. Contbr. articles on indsl. orgn., sci. policy and fin. to profl. jours. Lt. AC, USNR, 1943-46. Mem. UN Assn., Soc. for Advancement of Mgmt. (pres. 1949-50, leadership award 1950), Tau Beta Pi, Alpha Pi Mu (v.p. 1949-50), Columbia Univ. Club (Washington, trustee 1982-84, chmn., sr. trustee 1984-85), Harvard Univ. Club. Home and Office: 12904 Old Chapel Pl Bowie MD 20720-3368

PURDUM, ROBERT L., steel manufacturing company executive; b. Wilmington, Ohio, 1935; married. BS, Purdue U., 1956. With U.S. Navy and Ind. Toll Road Commn., 1956-62; with Armco Inc., Middletown, Ohio, 1962—, dist. engr. metal product div., 1962-66, sales staff, 1966-72; dist. mgr. Columbus, Ohio, 1972-76; gen. mgr. adminstrn. Armco Inc., Columbus, Ohio, 1976-78; v.p. div. subs., pres. Midwestern Steel, Kansas City, Mo., 1978-80; area v.p. Midwestern Steel, Columbus, Ohio, 1980-82; group v.p., chief exec. officer steel svcs. group Middletown, Ohio, 1982-86; exec. v.p., chief operating officer Armco Inc., Middletown, Ohio; pres., chief operating officer Armco Inc., Parsippany, N.J., 1986-90, pres., chief exec. officer, 1990—, also. bd. dirs., chmn. Capt. USNR. Recipient Disting. Engring. Alumnus award Purdue U., 1986. Office: Armco Inc 300 Interpace Pky Parsippany NJ 07054-1100

PURDY, GEORGE DONALD, JR., computer consultant; b. Hackensack, N.J., Aug. 28, 1939; s. George Donald and Ora (Hovsepian) P. Chief operator Distillation Engring. Co., Livingston, N.J., 1961-62; asst. to chief engr. Jersey City (N.J.) Welding and Machine Works, 1962-69; programmer Newark (N.J.) Beth Israel Med. Ctr., 1969-72, Ultimace Systems, Maywood, N.J., 1973-75; programmer analyst Am. Export Lines, N.Y.C., 1975-77; systems analyst Charles P. Young Inc./Redaction System, N.Y.C., 1977-79; sr. mem. tech. staff Delta Resources Inc., N.Y.C., 1979—. Developer computer programs Screen and Outline/Dropshadow in GM1 Compaction Code. Mem. N.Y. Acad. Scis. (life), Assn. Computing Machinery. Home: 136 Chestnut St Rutherford NJ 07070 Office: Delta Resources Inc 1133 Avenue of the Americas New York NY 10036

PURGAVIE, CHARLES SAMUEL, social science educator; b. Rumson, N.J., May 6, 1929; s. James and Catherine Burgess (Armour) P.; m. Greta Cecilia Svelling, Mar. 23, 1957; children: Greta Laurie, Charles Samuel Jr. AS in Pub. Adminstrn., Ocean County Coll., Toms River, N.J., 1971; BA in Polit. Sci., Stockton State Coll., Pomona, N.J., 1973; MS in Pub. Adminstrn., London Sch. Econs., 1976. State trooper, capt. N.J. State Police, W. Trenton, 1953-85; asst. prof. Trenton State Coll., 1985-86; asst. prof., coord. criminal justice program Ocean County Coll., Toms River, N.J., 1987—; cons. Purgavie Assocs., Ship Bottom, N.J., 1985—; conductor seminars in field. Mem. N.J. Football Ofcls. Orgn., N.J. Interscholastic Assn., N.J. Criminal Justice Assn., Am. friends of the London Sch. Econs., Internat. Assn. Chiefs of Police, Internat. Police Assn. Home: 277 W 11th St Ship Bottom NJ 08008-6311 Office: Ocean County Coll College Dr Toms River NJ 08753-2001

PURRINGTON, ROBERT, innkeeper; b. Franklin, N.H., May 22, 1939; s. Carl Hoben and Margaret (Fallon) P.; m. Carolyn Gage, Feb. 6, 1982. BS, U. Mass., 1966. Innkeeper Wayside Inn, Sudbury, Mass., 1989—; founder Barcada Tech. Inc., Eastham, Mass. Designer software for hospitality industry. Bd. dirs. Am. Cancer Soc., 1990-91. With USN, 1958-62. Mem. Mass. Restaurant Assn., Am. Hotel Motel Assn., Assn. Ind. Innkeepers. Republican. Roman Catholic. Home and Office: Wayside Inn Sudbury MA 01776

PURSEL, ROBERT WAYNE, JR., computer programmer-analyst; b. Phillipsburg, N.J., May 30, 1966; s. Robert Wayne Sr. and Elizabeth Ann (Smith) P. AS in Math., Somerset County Coll., North Branch, N.J., 1987; BS in Commerce, Rider Coll., 1989, MBA, 1992. Info. mgr. AT&T, East Brunswick, N.J., 1989—. Mem. Am. Fedn. Musicians. Home: 3910 Quail Ridge Dr Plainsboro NJ 08536 Office: AT&T 100 Naricon Pl East Brunswick NJ 08816

PUSTERLA, THOMAS EDWARD, podiatrist; b. Jersey City, July 21, 1951; s. Charles and Ann (Ayroldi) P.; m. Carolyn Jean Riley, June 15, 1975; 1 child, Elizabeth Riley. BS, Fairleigh Dickenson U., 1977; D of Podiatric Medicine, N.Y. Coll. Podiatric Medicine, 1985. Diplomate Am. Bd. Podiatric Examiners. Chemist Lever Bros. Co., Edgewater, N.J., 1972-78; product engr. G.A.F. Corp., N.Y.C., 1978-80; podiatric surg. resident West Essex Gen. Hosp., Livingston, N.J., 1985-86; staff Summit (N.J.) Podiatry Group, 1986—; pvt. practice Chester, N.J., 1988—; podiatrist Rockaway (N.J.) Podiatry, 1990—. Mem. Am. Podiatric Med. Assn., N.J. Podiatric Med. Soc. (bd. dirs. 1988-89, 90-92, western div. chmn. 1990-92, sec.-treas. 1988-90, edn. chmn. 1987-89), Am. Coll. Foot Surgeons (assoc.), Am. Bd. Podiatric Surgeons, Am. Assn. Podiatric Sports Medicine. Office: Rte 206 & 24 Chester NJ 07930

PUSTILNIK, JEAN TODD, educator; b. Ranger, Tex., Dec. 12, 1932; d. Lonnie Elvin and Frances Elvira (Lee) Todd; m. David Daniel Pustilnik, Aug. 15, 1959; children: Palma Elyse, Leslie Royce, Bradley Todd. BA, U. Okla., 1954; MA, St. Joseph Coll., West Hartford, Conn., 1983. Asst. buyer Foley's, Houston, 1954-58; buyer Kerr's, Oklahoma City, 1958-59; mgr. Woodward & Lothrup, Washington, 1959-61; instr. M. Webster Jr. Coll., Washington, 1961-63; tchr. West Hartford (Conn.) Bd. Edn., 1974—; instr. St. Joseph Coll., 1976—; curriculum creator Conn. Home Econs. Dept., Middletown, 1985-88. Mem. Am. Home Econs. Assn., Hadassh (pres. 1967-71), Hartford Golf. Home: 48 Westwood Rd West Hartford CT 06117-2252

PUTH, ROBERT CHRISTIAN, economist, educator; b. Appleton, Wis., Apr. 27, 1936; s. George J. and Marie Elizabeth (Roemer) P.; m. Sally Burnside Jones, Feb. 13, 1960; children: Nancy Caroline, Linda Margaret. BA, Carleton Coll., 1958; MA, Northwestern U., 1965; PhD, Northwestern, 1967. Mgmt. trainee Equitable Life Assurance Soc., Omaha, 1958; supr. Equitable Life Assurance Soc., Sacramento, 1959-60; asst. prof. econs. Earlham Coll., Richmond, Ind., 1965-67; asst. prof. U. N.H., Durham, 1967-74, assoc. prof., 1974-83, prof., 1983—. Author: Supreme Life, 1975, American Economic History, 1982, 2d edit., 1988; editor Current Issues in the American Economy, 1981. Served with U.S. Army, 1958-59. Mem. Am. Econ. Assn., Econ. History Assn. Home: 41 Cataract Ave Dover NH 03820-4335 Office: U NH McConnell Hall Durham NH 03824

PUTMAN, GEORGE WENDELL, geoscience educator, consultant; b. Schenectady, N.Y., Dec. 11, 1929; s. Joseph Wendell and Marion Frances (Smith) P.; m. Carol Lombard Grupe, Sept. 1, 1957; children: David, Noel. BS in Chemistry, Union Coll., Schenectady, 1951; MS in Geology, Pa. State U., 1958, PhD in Geology, Geochemistry, 1961. Rsch. assoc. Pa. State U., 1959-61; geochemist Calif. div. Mines and geology, San Francisco, 1961-67; assoc. prof. SUNY, Albany, 1967—; rsch. fellow SUNY and NSF, 1969-72; chmn. dept. geol. scis. SUNY, Albany, 1972-73; ind. cons., 1969—; pres. Terran Rsch. Inc., Canastota, N.Y., 1988—; prin. Terran Environ., Inc., Canastota, N.Y., 1990—; mem. U.S. EPA Sci. and Tech. Com., 1991—. Contbr. articles to profl. jours.; patentee in field. With USN, 1953-55. NSF grantee, 1969-72; N.Y. State Energy Rsch. and Devel. Authorty and U.S. Dept. Energy rsch. grantee, 1979-82. Fellow Geol. Soc. Am.; mem. Am. geophys. Union. Home: 1225 Sandra Ln Niskayuna NY 12309-2610 Office: Terran Environ Inc RR 5 Box 610 Canastota NY 13032-9424

PUTNAM, WILLIAM LOWELL, travel bureau director; b. Springfield, Mass., Oct. 25, 1924; s. Roger Lowell and Caroline Piatt (Jenkins) P.; m. Joan Fitzgerald, Sept. 29, 1951; children: Katherine Elizabeth, W. Lowell. Grad., Harvard Coll., 1945. With Springfield C. of C., 1950-52; founder, chmn. Springfield TV Corp., 1952-84; with Carroll Travel Bur., 1984—; vice chmn. Assn. Maximum Svc. Telecasters, 1975-84; sec.-treas. NBC Affiliates, 1980-83. Active Nat. Forest Adv. Bd., Washington, 1961-68; sole trustee Lowell Observatory, Flagstaff, Ariz. 1st lt. U.S. Army, 1943-45. Decorated Siver Star, Bronze Star, Purple Heart. Mem. Assn. Canadian Mountain Guides (hon.), Alpine Club Can. (hon.), Appalachian Mountain Club (hon.), Am. Alpine Club (pres. 1974-76, treas. 1977-91, hon.), Internat. Union Alpine Clubs (Am. del., v.p.). Democrat. Roman Catholic. Home: 406 Longhill St Springfield MA 01144-1407 Office: Carroll Travel 1 Monarch Pl Springfield MA 01144-1003

PUTNEY, JOHN FRASER, II, advertising executive; b. St. Louis, Jan. 23, 1939; s. John Fraser and Elizabeth (O'Brien) P.; m. Nancy Gillespie, Apr. 8, 1967 (div. Apr. 1981); children: John Fraser III, Colin Gillespie; m. Jennifer A. Wherry, Dec. 8, 1984; children: Allen Fraser, Emma Elizabeth, James Terrill. BS, Washington U., 1965. Product mgr. Ralston Purina, St. Louis, 1968-70; gen. mgr. The Clorox Co., Oakland, Calif., 1970-75; dir. of mktg. Basic Am. Foods, San Francisco, 1975-78; v.p., mktg. Ogden Food Products Corp., Rochelle Park, N.J., 1978-84; sr. v.p. Grey Advt., Inc., San Francisco, 1984-86; sr. v.p., mgmt. rep. Tracy-Locke, Inc., Denver, 1986-88; pres. Putney & Assocs., Wilkes-Barre, Pa., 1988—; bd. dirs. Northeastern Pa. Philharmonic, Avoca, Pa. Bd. dirs. San Francisco (Calif.) Chamber Symphony Orch., 1984-86. Mem. Am. Advt. Fedn., N.E. Pa. Advt. Club (dir. 1989—, pres. 1991), Westmoreland Club. Republican. Episcopalian. Home: 1465A Sutton Rd Wilkes Barre PA 18708-9542 Office: Putney & Assocs 1101 N Washington St Wilkes Barre PA 18705-1817

PUTUKIAN, LISA ANN, management consultant; b. Newton, Mass., July 16, 1959; d. John H. and Elissa A. (Bedrosian) P. BA, Yale U., 1981; MBA, Harvard U., 1988. Ops. mgr. Omaha Symphony Orch., 1981-85; spl. projects mgr. ImmunoGen, Cambridge, Mass., 1988-90; mgr. Cambridge office Quintiles, Inc., 1990—; mgr. Conn. Chamber Orch., 1979-81; ind. cons. to healthcare and biotech. cos., Mass., 1988-90. Prin. oboist MIT Symphony, various community chamber orchs., 1988—. Mem. Harvard Club Boston.

PUTZRATH, RESHA MAE, toxicologist; b. Camden, N.J., Sept. 9, 1949; d. Franz Ludwig and Pearl (Robins) P.; m. Lawrence Smedley Olson, May 13, 1978. BA in Physics cum laude, Smith Coll., 1971; MS in Biophysics, U. Rochester, 1974, PhD in Biophysics, 1978. Diplomate Am. Bd. Toxicology. Rsch. fellow Med. Sch. Harvard U., Boston, 1977-79, fellow Sch. Pub. Health, 1979-81; cons. U.S. Environ. Protection Agy., Washington, 1981-82; assoc. scientist Nat. Acad. Scis., Washington, 1982-83; sr. assoc. ENVIRON Corp., Washington, 1983-86, project mgr., 1986-91; mgr. environ. programs Orgn. Resources Counselors Inc., Washington, 1991—; mem. faculty Found. for Advanced Edn. in Scis., NIH, Rockville, Md., 1982-86; exec. dir. Acad. Toxicol. Scis., Washington, 1983-84; mem. FDA Planning Bd., Washington, 1984-86. Author: Elements of Toxicology and Chemical Risk Assessment, 1986. Nat. evaluator NSTA-NASA Space Shuttle Student Involvement Project, Washington, 1982-86. Mem. Am. Coll. Toxicology, Biophys. Soc., ASTM, Environ. Mutagen Soc., Assn. forWomen in Sci. (nat. councilor 1989-92, Washington chpt. v.p. 1982-83, pres. 1985-87), Phi Beta Kappa. Home: 3223 N St NW Washington DC 20007-2830 Office: Orgn Resources Counselors 1910 Sunderland Pl NW Washington DC 20036

PUZZELE, JAMES ALBERT, foreign exchange broker; b. Queens, N.Y., July 18, 1951; s. Rocco James and Edith (Vinciguerra) P.; m. Carol Jean Moscato, Aug. 22, 1970; children: Teresa, James Jr. Student, Am. Inst. Banking, N.Y.C., 1970-71. Internat. banker Marine Midland Bank, N.Y.C., 1968-73; fgn. exch. broker Kirkland, Whittaker & Mallon, N.Y.C., 1973-75, Lasser Bros., Inc., N.Y.C., 1975-76, Savage Lane Ltd., N.Y.C., 1976-77, Garvin Guybutler, N.Y.C., 1977-80; exec. v.p. Moscato & Puzzele, Inc., N.Y.C., 1980-81; v.p. Fulton Prebon (U.S.A.) Inc., N.Y.C., 1981—; mem. Forex Assn. of N.Am., N.Y.C., 1974-80. Home: 885 N William St Baldwin NY 11510-1436

PYE, MORT, newspaper editor; b. Rochester, N.Y., May 28, 1918; s. Arthur and Lillian (Palley) P.; m. Florence M. Newhouse, Oct. 31, 1942; 1 son, Richard. Student, U. Ill., 1936-38; B.S., Coll. City N.Y., 1940; L.H.D., Seton Hall U., 1975, Upsala Coll., 1978, N.J. Inst. Tech., 1986. Various editorial positions L.I. Daily Press, 1941-57; asso. editor Newark Star-Ledger, 1957-63, editor, 1963—. Served with VIII Corps AUS, 1944-45. Decorated Bronze Star; Croix de Guerre France). Office: Newark Morning Ledger Co 1 Star Ledger Plz Newark NJ 07102-1200

PYLE, ALAN JAMES, trust company executive; b. Toronto, Ont., Can., Aug. 27, 1946; s. Donald Graham and Mary Christine (Shaughnessy) P.; m. Mary Lou Pyle, May 9, 1975 (div. Nov. 1989); children: Ryan, Christopher, Andrew, Colin; m. Cora Alexandra Broadhurst. BA in Econs. with honors, U. Toronto, 1968; MBA, Stanford U., 1970. Systems analyst IBM Can., Toronto, 1970-71; fin. analyst Traders Group, Toronto, 1972-73; sr. v.p. Mercantile Bank Can., Toronto, 1973-86; exec. v.p. First City Trust, Toronto, 1986—; bd. dirs. Portland Lakes Devels., Halifax, N.S., Can. Mem. Can. water polo team Pan Am. Games, 1967, 71, Olympic Games, 1972. Home: 91 Walmsley Rd, Toronto, ON Canada M4V 1X7

PYLE, JAMES HARFORD, elementary school educator; b. Manila, May 26, 1947; s. James Harford Jr. and Mary Jeanne (Baker) P.; m. Sheila Joan Moy; 1 child, Catherine. AB in Philosophy, Princeton (N.J.) U., 1970; MusM, Yale U., 1978. Cert. music tchr., N.Y. Teaching fellow Yale U., New Haven, 1976-79, Manhattan (N.Y.) Sch. of Music, 1979-81; pvt. practice, 1982-92; tenured mem. faculty Harrison (N.Y.) Bd. of Edn., 1982—; mem. faculty Ctr. for Creative and Performing Arts, Huntington, N.Y., 1985-91; freelance musician, 1972-82. Reviewer Daily Princetonian, 1968-69, Backstage, 1979-81. Unger scholar, Reed scholar, 1964-69; Kawai Edn. Found. grantee, 1989, Texaco grantee, 1991. Mem. NEA, Am. Fedn. Tchrs. Home: 25 Lake St Apt # 7K White Plains NY 10601 Office: Parsons Meml Sch Harrison NY 10528

PYLES, ROBERT PHILLIP, art director; b. Marlinton, W.Va., June 29, 1931; s. Glen Parker and Mae Verna (Burr) P.; m. Shirley Sue Hamrick, Mar. 29, 1955 (div. Aug. 1972); children: Panda Gail Pyles Harris, Derry Drew, Zon Vern. BA, W.Va. U., 1958. Artist Houze Glass Corp., Point Marion, Pa., 1959-71, designer, 1968-71, asst. art dir., 1972-79, art dir., 1980-87, mgr. art svcs. and training, 1988—. Patentee see-view tumbler. With U.S. Army, 1952-54. Home: 820 Ridgeway Ave Morgantown WV 26505-5748 Office: Houze Glass Corp 5th And Main Sts Point Marion PA 15474

PYLINSKI, ALBERT, JR., insurance company executive; b. New Berlin, N.Y., June 6, 1953; s. Albert and Marian Lucelia (Sprague) P.; m. Danica Camille Adams, June 7, 1980; children: Brenton Thomas, Sarah Adams. BS, Syracuse U., 1985; diploma specialized tng., Coll. Ins., N.Y.C., 1977, 79, Lloyds of London, 1986. Acct. N.Y. Cen. Mut. Fire Ins. Co., Edmeston, 1973-85, asst. treas., 1985-86, treas., 1986—, v.p., 1987—, also bd. dirs.; v.p. fin., treas., bd. dirs. Home Mut. Ins. Co. Binghamton (N.Y.), 1989—. Trustee Edmeston Free Library, 1981-84. Mem. Ins. Acctg. and Systems Assn., Soc. Ins. Accts., Nat. Assn. Mut. Ins. Cos., Cooperstown (N.Y.) Country Club)bd. dirs., treas. 1980—), Albert F. Stager, Inc. (treas., bd. dirs. 1991—), N.E. Otsego County Chpt. Am. Red Cross (bd. govs. 1991). Roman Catholic. Office: NY Cen Mut Fire Ins Co Central Pla E Edmeston NY 13335

PYNN, MARIA ELENA, international development and training consultant; b. Buenos Aires, Oct. 22, 1941; d. Jorge Alberto and Cecile Mary (Dawson) Berghmans; m. Thomas Damon Pynn, Dec. 20, 1966 (div. July 1988). Cert. in ESL, Brit. Lyceum, Buenos Aires, 1959; AA, Manatee Jr. Coll., 1970; BA, U. N.Mex., Albuquerque, 1973, MA, 1974. Instr. in lang. Out of Door Sch., Sarasota, Fla., 1967-70; chief fgn. langs. St. Stephen's Sch.,

Bradenton, Fla., 1970-72; instr. in spl. edn. U. N.Mex., Albuquerque, 1974-77, program specialist, 1977-79; Fulbright lectr. in spl. edn. Ecuador, S.Am., 1976-77; program dir. Miranda Assocs., Inc., Bethesda, Md., 1979-83; exec. dir. ACCESS, Inc., Bethesda, 1979-83; Washington rep. Experiment in Internat. Living, Brattleboro, Vt., 1983-86; tng. dir. and sr. planning program officer U.S. Peace Corps, Washington, 1986—; bd. dirs. Refugee Women in Devel., Inc., Washington. Mem. Fulbright Alumni Assn. Roman Catholic. Home: 3713 S George Mason Dr # 1302 Falls Church VA 22041 Office: US Peace Corps 1990 K St NW Washington DC 20526-1103

QADEER, SHEIKH ABDUL, psychiatrist; b. Delhi, India, Apr. 2, 1940; came to U.S., 1972; s. Sheikh Abdul and Akbari Begum Kareem; m. Moiney Aziz, June 1, 1951; children: Farzana, Omar, Rubina, Usman. M.B., BS, Dow Med. Coll., Karachi, Pakistan, 1964; D.P.M., R.C.P., R.C.S., Royal Colls. Physicians & Surgeons, England, 1969; M.R.C. in Psychiatry, Royal Coll. Psychiatrist-United Kingdom, England, 1972. Cert. psychiatrist, N.Y. Resident in psychiatry various locations in England, 1967-69; intern Jinnah Postgrad. Med. Ctr., Karachi, Pakistan, 1964-67; House officer Goodmayes Hosp., London, 1967-69; registrar Goodmayes Hosp., 1969-72; staff psychiatrist Elmira Psychiat. Ctr., Elmira, N.Y., 1972-75; cons. psychiatrist Elmira, Corning, N.Y., 1975; unit chief Elmira Psychiat. Ctr., 1975—; cons. psychiatrist area hosps., Elmira, 1975—; pres. Med. Staff Orgn., Elmira Psychiat. Ctr., 1982-84. Mem. Am. Psychiat. Assn., Med. Soc. State N.Y., Twin Tier Assn. Psychiatrists N.Y./Pa. (pres. 1986-89). Muslim. Home: 246 Orchard Dr Big Flats NY 14814-9753

QUACKENBUSH, ROBERT MEAD, artist, author, psychoanalyst; b. Hollywood, Calif., July 23, 1929; s. Roy Maynard and Virginia (Arbogast) Q.; m. Margery Clouser, July 3, 1971; 1 child: Piet Robert. Bachelor Profl. Arts, Art Ctr. Coll. of Design, Pasadena, Calif., 1956; grad., Ctr. Modern Psychoanalytic Studies, 1991. Art dir. Scandinavian Airlines System, N.Y.C. and Stockholm, 1956-61; pvt. practice N.Y.C., 1961—; educator Robert Quackenbush Studios, N.Y.C.; lectr. U.S., Europe, Middle East and South Am.; TV performer Ednl. TV; mem. faculty N.J. Ctr. for Modern Psychoanalysis. Author/artist over 150 books for young readers including Detective Mole Mystery Series (winner Edgar Allen Poe Spl. Award 1982), the Miss Mallard Mystery Series and a humorous biography series; producer: TV series Dear Mr. Quackenbush and The Great American Storybook for Educational Television. With U.S. Army 1951-53. Recipient 2 citations for outstanding Troop Info. & Edn. instrn. from commanding gen. 31st Infantry Div. 1953, 3 time winner Am. Flag Inst. award for outstanding contbn. to field of children's lit. 1976, 77, 81. Mem. Mystery Writers of Am., Author's Guild, Author's League of Am., Holland Soc. of N.Y., Nat. Assn. for Advancement of Psychoanalysis, Soc. Modern Psychoanalysts. Home: 460 E 79th St Apt 14E New York NY 10021-1445 Office: Robert Quackenbush Studios 223 E 78th St New York NY 10021-1222

QUAGLIANA, PAUL MICHAEL, aeronautical engineer; b. Buffalo, Oct. 5, 1967; s. Paul Earl and Judith Mildred (Nebrich) Q. BSME, Cornell U., 1989, M of Engring., 1990. Aeronautical engr. Calspan Corp., Buffalo, 1989—. Mem. AIAA (assoc.), ASME (assoc.). Office: Calspan Corp PO Box 400 Buffalo NY 14225-0400

QUANDT, RICHARD EMERIC, economics educator; b. Budapest, Hungary, June 1, 1930; came to U.S., 1949, naturalized, 1954; s. Richard F. and Elisabeth (Toth) Q.; m. Jean H. Briggs, Aug. 6, 1955; 1 son, Stephen. BA, Princeton U., 1952; MA, Harvard U., 1955, PhD, 1957; Dr. Econs. (hon.), Budapest U. Econs. Scis., 1991. Mem. faculty Princeton U., 1956—, prof. econs., 1964—, Hughes-Rogers prof. econs., 1976—, chmn. dept., 1968-71, 85-88; dir. Fin. Rsch. Ctr., 1982—; rsch. prof. Ford Found., 1967-68, dir., 1983—; cons. Alderson Assocs., 1959-61; sr. cons. Mathematica, Inc., 1961-67; cons. Internat. Air Transport Assn., 1974-75, N.Y. Stock Exch., 1976-77, N.Y. State Dept. Edn., 1978; adviser Am.-Hungarian Found., 1977-78; editorial advisor Holt, Rinehart & Winston, 1968-72; fin. adviser Inst. for Rsch. in History, 1986; sr. advisor Andrew W. Mellon Found., 1989—; vis. prof. Birbeck Coll., 1981, U. Leicester, 1989-92; mem. Census Adv. Com., 1983-86. Author: (with J. M. Henderson) Microeconomic Theory: A Mathematical Approach, 1958, 2d edit., 1971, 3d edit., 1980, (with W.L. Thorp) The New Inflation, 1959, (with B.G. Malkiel) Strategies and Rational Decisions in the Securities Option Market, 1969; editor: The Demand for Travel: Theory and Measurement, 1970; (with S.M. Goldfeld) Nonlinear Methods in Econometrics, 1972, Studies in Nonlinear Estimation, 1976; (with P. Asch) Racetrack Betting: The Professor's Guide to Strategies, 1986, (with M. Peston) Prices, Competition and Equilibrium, 1986, The Econometrics of Disequilibrium, 1988, (with H.S. Rosen) The Conflict Between Equilibrium and Disequilibrium Theories, 1988; also numerous articles; editorial bd.: Applied Econs., Econs. of Planning, Rev. Econ. and Stats., 1980-91; assoc. editor: Econometrica, 1976-80, Jour. Am. Statis. Assn, 1974-80, Bell Jour. Econs., Jour. of Comparative Econs., 1988-91, Empirica, 1988—. Recipient merit citation Jagiellonian U., Poland, 1991, gold medal Eötös Lóránd U., Budapest, 1991; Guggenheim fellow, 1958-59; McCosh fellow, 1964; NSF Sr. Postdoctoral fellow, 1971-72. Fellow Am. Statis. Assn., Econometric Soc.; mem. Am. Econ. Assn., Math. Programming Soc., Econometric Soc. (mem. coun. 1985-88), Am. Philos. Soc. Home: 162 Springdale Rd Princeton NJ 08540-4948 Office: Princeton U Fin Rsch Ctr Dept Econs Princeton NJ 08544

QUANN, JOAN LOUISE, language educator, real estate broker; b. Phila., Oct. 14, 1935; d. John Joseph and Pauline Cecelia (Karpink) Q. Diploma, U. Paris, 1963; BA in French, U. Pa., 1976; grad., Temple U. Real Estate Inst., 1988. Lic. real estate broker. Exec. sec. to chief fgn. corr. Newsweek, Inc., Paris, 1964-70; internat. editorial asst. Newsweek, Inc., N.Y.C., 1971-73; exec. sec., adminstrv. asst. Richard I. Rubin & Co., Inc., Phila., 1977-91; tchr. French and English to speakers of other langs. The Sch. Dist. of Phila., Bd. Edn., 1991—. Judge of elections City of Phila., 1977-81. Mem. AAUW (2d v.p. membership 1985-87, bd. dirs., corr. sec. 1987-91, chair awards com. 1991—), Alliance Francaise, La Societe Francophone Arts et Loisirs (bd. dirs. 1988—), Pa. Acad. Fine Arts, MLA of Phila. and Vicinity. Republican. Roman Catholic. Office: Sch Dist of Phila Bd Edn 21st St S of The Pkwy Philadelphia PA 19103-1099

QUATTROCCHI, JOHN ANTHONY, financial services executive; b. Bklyn., Sept. 6, 1962; s. Joseph and Carmela (Cucuzza) Q. BS in Fin., St. John's U., 1984. Unit supr. Crossland Savs. Bank, Bklyn., 1980-84; asst. v.p. Prudential-Bache Securities, N.Y.C., 1984-88; asst. ops. mgr. Deutsche Bank G.S.I., N.Y.C., 1988-89; v.p. software devel. Ambac Indemnity Corp., N.Y.C., 1989—. Home: 1557 78th St Brooklyn NY 11228-2521

QUAYLE, J(AMES) DANFORTH, Vice President of United States; b. Indpls., Feb. 4, 1947; s. James C. and Corinne (Pulliam) Q.; m. Marilyn Tucker, Nov. 18, 1972; children: Tucker Danforth, Benjamin Eugene, Mary Corinne. BS in Polit. Sci., DePauw U., Greencastle, Ind., 1969; JD, Ind. U., 1974. Bar: Ind. 1974. Ct. reporter, pressman Huntington (Ind.) Herald-Press, 1965-69, assoc. pub., gen. mgr., 1974-76; mem. consumer protection div. Office Atty. Gen., State of Ind., 1970-71; adminstrv. asst. to gov. State of Ind., 1971-73; dir. Ind. Inheritance Tax Div., 1973-74; mem. 95th-96th Congresses from 4th Dist. Ind.; U.S. Senator from Ind., 1981-89, V.P. of U.S., 1989—; tchr. bus. law Huntington Coll., 1975. Capt. Ind. Army N.G., 1970-76. Mem. Huntington Bar Assn., Hoosier State Press Assn., Huntington C. of C. Club: Rotary. Office: The White House Office of Vice President 1600 Pennsylvania Ave NW Washington DC 20501-0002*

QUAYLE, MARILYN, wife of Vice President of U.S.; b. 1949; d. Warren and Mary Alice Tucker; m. J. Danforth Quayle, Nov. 18, 1972; children: Tucker, Benjamin, Corinne. BS in Polit. Sci., Purdue U., 1971; JD, Indiana U., 1975. Pvt. practice atty. Huntington, Ind., 1974-76. Author: (with Nancy T. Northcott) Embrace the Serpent, 1992. Office: Old Exec Office Bldg Rm 258 Washington DC 20500*

QUEBEDEAUX, BRUNO, educator; b. Arnandville, La., June 8, 1941; s. Bruno Sr. and Iola (Guidry) Q.; m. Maureen Fahey, Aug. 13, 1966; children: Mark E., Annette M., Michael J., Adele M. BS, La. State U., 1962, MS, 1963; PhD, Cornell U., 1968. Horticulturist Tex. A&M U., College Station, 1963-65; rsch. scientist E.I. du Pont de Nemours & Co., Wilmington, Del., 1968-80; team leader/COP U.S. AID Contract, Mauritania, 1980-83; chmn. dept. horticulture U. Md., College Park, 1983-90, prof., 1983—. Assoc. editor Crop Sci. Soc. Am., Madison, Wis., 1979-82; editor: Horticulture and Human Health, 1988; author: (publ.) Oxygen: New Factor Controlling Reproductive Growth, 1973. Bd. dirs. League of Internat. Food Edn., Washington, 1987-90; sch. bd. chmn. Internat. Sch. Nauakchott, Mauritania, 1980-82; asst. scout master Boy Scouts Am., Wilmington, 1978-80; bd. dirs. Chapelcroft Civic Assn., Wilmington, 1978-80, v.p., 1975-77. Recipient Merit award USDA/ARS Nat. Resources, 1989. Fellow Am. Soc. Hort. Sci. (v.p. internat. merit 1988-89, L. Ware award 1962); mem. Am. Soc. Plant Physiology (pres. 1989-90, pres. Washington sect. 1990-91), Am. Soc. Agronomy (assoc. editor 1979-82), N.Y. Acad. Sci., Alpha Zeta. Home: 2417 Laurelwood Ter Silver Spring MD 20905-6419 Office: U Md Horticulture Dept College Park MD 20742-5611

QUEEN, DANIEL, acoustical engineer, consultant; b. Boston, Feb. 15, 1934; s. Simon and Ida (Droker) Q.; 1 child, Aaron Jacob. Student, U. Chgo., 1951-54. Quality control mgr. Magnacord, Inc., Chgo., 1955-57; project engr. Revere Camera Co., Chgo., 1957-62; dir. engring. for Amplivox products Perma Power Co., Chgo., 1962-70; prin. engr. Daniel Queen Assocs., Chgo., 1970—; pres. Daniel Queen Labs., Inc., Chgo., 1980—; chmn. Am. Nat. Standards Subcom. PH7-6, mem. com. PH-7; mem. standards com. P8-5 Electronic Industries Assn. Contbr. editor Sound and Communications, 1973—; patentee in field; contbr. papers to profl. jours., also articles to trade and popular jours.; editorial bd. Jour. Audio Engring. Soc., 1978—. Fellow Audio Engring. Soc. (standards mgr., chmn. tech. coun.), mem. IEEE (sr.), ASTM, AAAS, Am. Nat. Standards Inst. (sec. com. S4 on audio engring.), Acoustical Soc. Am. (chmn. Chgo. regional chpt. 1976-78, mem. engring. acoustics com.), Midwest Acoustics Conf. (pres. 1971-72), Chgo. Acoustical and Audio Group (pres. 1969-70), Assn. Ednl. Communications and Tech., Soc. Motion Picture and TV Engrs. (audio rec. and reprodn. com.), Am. Pub. Health Assn., Nat. Coun. Acoustical Cons., Catgut Acoustic Soc. Office: 239 W 23d St New York NY 10011

QUELER, EVE, conductor; b. N.Y.C.. Student, Mannes Coll. Music, CCNY. Music staff, N.Y.C. Opera, 1958-70, asso. condr., Ft. Wayne (Ind.) Philharm., 1970-71, founder, music dir., Opera Orch., N.Y., 1968, condr. Lake George Opera Festival, Glen Falls, N.Y., 1971-72, Oberlin (Ohio) Music Festival, 1972, Romantic Festival, Indpls., 1972, Mostly Mozart Festival, Lincoln Center, 1972, New Philharmonia, London, 1974, Teatro Liceu, Barcelona, 1974, 77, San Antonio Symphony, 1975, guest condr., Paris Radio Orch., 1972, P.R. Symphony Orch., 1975, 77, Mich. Chamber Orch., 1975, Phila. Orch., 1976, Montreal Symphony, 1977, Cleve. Orch., 1977 (Recipient Martha Baird Rockefeller Fund for Music award 1968, named Musician of Month, Mus. Am. Mag. 1972), N.Y.C. Opera, 1978, Opera Las Palmas, 1978, Opera de Nice, 1979, Nat. Theatre of Prague, 1980, Opera Caracas, Venezuela, 1981, San Diego Opera, 1984, Australian Opera, Sydney, 1985; recording CBS Masterworks, 1974, 76, Hungaroton Records, 1982-85. Office: Herbert Barrett Mgmt 1776 Boadway Ste 504 New York NY 10019 also: Opera Orch NY 228 W 72nd St Ste 2R New York NY 10023*

QUELLER, FRED, lawyer; b. N.Y.C., July 10, 1932; s. Victor and Helen (Cenzer) Q.; m. Stephanie Tarler, Aug. 29, 1965; children: Jessica, Danielle. BA, CCNY, 1954; JD, NYU, 1956. Bar: N.Y. 1956, U.S. Dist. Ct. (so. and ea. dists.) N.Y. 1958, U.S. Supreme Ct. 1960, U.S. Ct. Appeals (2d cir.) 1967, Fla. 1980; cert. diplomate civil trial advocacy Nat. Bd. Trial Advocacy, cert. adv. Am. Bd. Trial Advs. Sole practice, N.Y.C., 1956-70; ptnr. Queller & Fisher, N.Y.C., 1970—, now sr. ptnr.; lectr. N.Y. County Lawyers Assn., Practicing Law Inst., Med. Soc. State of N.Y., N.Y. Women's Bar Assn., Victims for Victims, Council of N.Y. Law Assocs., Bklyn. Coll. Inst. for Retired Profls. and Execs., Nassau Acad. Law, Mt. Sinai Med. Ctr., 1975-91; panelist Med. Malpractice Panel of Supreme Ct. State of N.Y., County of N.Y. 1973-91; arbitrator Compulsory Arbitration Service of State of N.Y., 1st Jud. Dept., 1975-91; co-chmn. jud. screening com. of lawyers' com., 1979; adminstrv. sec. ad hoc com. for Preservation of an Elected Judiciary, 1977-80; counsel com. for elected judiciary, 1981-84; mem. coordinating council on lawyer competence of Conf. of Chief Justices, 1983-84. Contbr. articles to profl. jours. Chmn. Big Apple Pothole and Sidewalk Protection Corp., 1982-83, pres. 1984-87. Mem. Am. Soc. Legal and Indsl. Medicine, Assn. Bar City of N.Y., Bronx Bar Assn., Am. Bd. Trial Advs. (lectr., pres. N.Y. chpt. 1988-90), N.Y. State Bar Assn. (com. on automobile liability 1981-91, com. on products liability ins. 1986-91, torts reparation com. 1983-91), ABA (trial techniques com. 1984), Fla. Bar Assn., Met. Women's Bar Assn. (bd. dirs. 1975-83, lectr. 1975-87, treas. 1978-80, v.p. 1980-81), N.Y. Criminal and Civil Cts. Bar Assn., Bklyn. and Manhattan Trial Counsel Assn., N.Y. County Lawyers Assn., Bklyn. Bar Assn., N.Y. State Trial Lawyers Inst. (dean 1988-91), N.Y. State Trial Lawyers Assn. (bd. dirs. 1970-91, 86-91, lectr. 1975-87, v.p. 1980-83, pres. 1984-86, chmn. products liability com. 1980-81, chmn. brief bank com. 1982-84, chmn. expert bank com. 1982-84, nominating com. 1986-91, Pres.'s award 1986, Disting. Service award 1986), Assn. Trial Lawyers of City N.Y. (bd. dirs. 1975-91), Assn. Trial Lawyers Am., Nat. Judicature Soc., Nat. Coalition Victims Attys. and Cons., Nat. Adv. Coun., Nat. Com. for Furtherance Jewish Edn. (bd. dirs. 1980-91, Man of Yr. 1984), Inst. Jewish Humanities (bd. dirs. 1985-91, Humanitarian award 1988), Jewish Trial Lawyer's Guild (gov. 1977-91), Lawyers Polit. Action Com. (trustee 1984-86), NYU Law Rev. Alumni Assn. Clubs: Downtown Athletic (N.Y.C.). Assoc. editor NYU Law Rev., 1955-56. Office: Queller & Fisher 110 Wall St New York NY 10005-3801

QUELLMALZ, HENRY, printing company executive; b. Balt., May 18, 1915; s. Frederick and Edith Margaret (Shaw) Q.; m. Marion Agar Lynch, Aug. 2, 1940; children: Lynn Quellmalz Johnson, Susan Quellmalz Mastan, Jane Quellmalz Carey. . BA with high honors, Princeton U., 1937. Pres. Princeton Advt. Agy., 1936-37; dir. pers. Macy's Men's Store, 1938-40; asst. mgr. Fowlers Dept. Store, Glens Falls, N.Y., 1940-41; pers. dir. U.S. Army Post Exchs., Ft. Meade, Md., 1941-44; with Boyd Printing Co., Albany, N.Y., 1944—, pres., 1952-84, chmn. bd., 1984—; v.p. Q Corp. U.S.; agt. for WHO publs., 1965—; adv. bd. First Trust Co., Albany, 1965-66, Bankers Trust Co., Albany, 1967-83, First Am. Bank N.Y., 1984-86. Campaign chmn. ARC, Albany, 1956, 57; bd. govs. Doane Stuart Sch., Albany, 1977-79, treas. bd., 1977-78; vice chmn. Family Svc. Assn. Am. Salute to Families, 1979—, Nat. UN Day com., 1980-82; mem. adv. bd. Ind. Coll. Fund of N.Y., 1971—; bd. dirs. Am. Assn. World Health, 1977-82, Combined Health Appeal of Capitol Dist., Inc., 1984, Camelot Home for Boys, 1975; trustee St. Peter's Hosp. Found., Albany, 1982—, asst. sec., 1987-89, chmn. bd. dirs., 1989—. With AUS, 1943. Recipient Pres.'s award Am. Assn. Mental Deficiency, 1976; 25 Yrs. Svc. award N.Y. State Bar Assn., 1983, 34 Yrs. Svc. Award Am. Sociol. Assn., 1985. Mem. Albany Area C. of C., Printing Industry Am. Assn. of East Cen. N.Y., (pres. 1958), Princeton Club, Ft. Orange Club, Hudson River Club. Democrat. Episcopalian. Home: 1 Park Hill Dr Apt 6 Albany NY 12204-2142 Office: 49 Sheridan Ave Albany NY 12210

QUERALT, MICHAEL, computer company executive, business consultant; b. N.Y.C., Sept. 12, 1962; s. Joseph and Guadalupe (Taveras) Q.; m. Isabel Tomas, Aug. 23, 1981; 1 child, Sonia. Jr. programmer Philips-Teixido, Barcelona, Spain, 1980-81; sr. programmer Hispano Olivetti, Barcelona, 1981-83; gen. mgr. Authorized Computer Dealers, Scarsdale, N.Y., 1983-84, Computer Factory, Yonkers, N.Y., 1984-89, Entre Computer Ctr., Huntington, N.Y., 1989—; owner, mgr. M.I.S. Internat., Dobbs Ferry, N.Y., 1989—; sales mgr. Computerland, Stamford, Conn., 1989—; cons. Paceart, Wayne, N.J., 1988—, Teachware, Greenwich, Conn., 1989—; internat. cons. E.V.M. Systems, Wayne, 1989—. Author: How To Export, 1989. Mem. Am. Mgmt. Assn. Roman Catholic. Home and Office: 62 Main St Dobbs Ferry NY 10522-2112

QUESENBERRY, MICHAEL STEPHEN, biochemist; b. Radford, Va., July 11, 1963; s. Glenn Robert and Barbara Elaine (Marshall) Q. BS, Hampden-Sydney Coll., 1985; MA, Columbia U., 1986, MPhil, 1988, PhD, 1991. Post-doctoral fellow dept. biology Johns Hopkins U., Balt., 1991—. Contbr. articles to profl. jours. Recipient Nat. Rsch. Svc. award NIH, 1991-94. Mem. AAAS, Am. Chem. Soc. Office: Dept of Biology Johns Hopkins U Mudd Hall 34th and Charles Baltimore MD 21218

QUESNEL, DAVID JOHN, materials science edducator; b. Plattsburg, N.Y., Apr. 5, 1950; s. Joseph Rene and Mildred G. (Yerdon) Q.; m. Lisbeth S. Wong, Sept. 1, 1973; 1 child, Alicia M. B in Engring., SUNY, Stony Brook, 1972; M in Materials Sci., Northwestern U., 1974, PhD in Materials Sci. and Engring., 1977. Registered profl. engr., N.Y. Asst. prof. U. Rochester, N.Y., 1977-82, assoc. prof., 1982-89, prof., 1989—. Contbr. numerous articles to profl. jours. Recipient initiation award NSF, 1978, Ralph K. Teetor Ednl. award Soc. Automotive Engrs., 1989; Alexander von Humboldt fellow, 1985-86. Mem. ASME, Metall. Soc., Am. Soc. for Metals, Materials Rsch. Soc. Office: U Rochester Dept Mech Engring Rochester NY 14627

QUICK, JOE AKERS, JR., environmental health executive, consultant; b. Denver, Oct. 27, 1945; s. Joe Akers Sr. and Mary Elizabeth (Hinson) Q.; m. Mary Kathryn Mulkey, Dec. 6, 1964; children: Angela Dawn Quick Hesano, Joe Akers III. BS in Biology and Chemistry, Fla. State U., 1966; MA in Biology and Environment, U. South Fla., 1972; MSChemE, Tex. A&M U., 1977. Cert. indsl. hygienist, environ. trainer, safety profl. Sect. supr. Fla. Dept. Natural Resources, St. Petersburg, 1966-75; project leader The Dow Chem. Co., Freeport, Tex., 1975-77, biorsch. supr., 1977-79; supr. environ. lab. The Dow Chem. Co., Midland, Mich., 1979-84, corp. indsl. health tng. coord., 1984-88, environ. data base mgr., 1988-90; pres. ITS Techs. Corp. subs. Indsl. Tng. Systems Corp., Marlton, N.J., 1990—; sci. cons. Silver Burdett Pubs., Morristown, N.J., 1990-91; tech. cons. Indsl. Tng. Systems Corp., Marlton, 1990—; columnist, cons. Marihe Hobbyist News Publs., Normal, Ill., 1972-83. Author: Marine Disease Primer, 1990; author, editor 3 books and chpts in books; contbr. numerous articles to profl. jours. Bd. dirs. Kiwanis Internat., Midland, 1979-90; mem. edn. com. United Meth. Ch., Moorestown, N.J., 1990—. U.S. Dept. Energy grantee, 1978. Mem. Am. Indsl. Hygiene Assn., Am. Soc. Safety Engrs., Nat. Environ. Tng. Assn. (testing cons. Phoenix, Ariz. 1991—), Air and Waste Control Assn., Water Pollution Control Fedn., Phi Kappa Phi. Republican. Office: ITS Techs Corp 9 E Stow Rd Marlton NJ 08053

QUIGLEY, DIANNE PATRICIA, foundation executive; b. Haverhill, Mass., Aug. 28, 1955; d. Bernard J. and Laura Elizabeth (Cross) Q. BA, U. Mass., 1977. Vocat. counselor Newton (Mass.) Area Ceta, 1978-81; social worker CAPIC Child Devel. Ctr., Chelsea, Mass., 1981-82; founder and adminstr. Child Devel. Ctr., Inc., Chelsea, Mass., 1982-87; adminstr., co-founder Childhood Cancer Rsch. Inst., Arlington, Mass., 1987—. Mem. Women in Devel. Office: Concord Profl Ctr 747 Main St Concord MA 01742

QUIMBY, FRED WILLIAM, pathology educator, veterinarian; b. Providence, Sept. 19, 1945; s. Edward Harold and Isabel (Barber) Q.; m. Cynthia Claire Connelly, Aug. 21, 1965; children—Kelly Ann, Cynthia Jane. V.M.D., U. Pa., 1970, Ph.D., 1974. Diplomate Am. Coll. Lab. Animal Medicine. Hematology fellow Tufts Med. Coll., Boston, 1974-75, instr. pathology, 1975-76, asst. prof., 1976-79; assoc. prof. pathology Cornell Med. Coll., N.Y.C., 1979—, N.Y. State Vet. Coll., Ithaca, 1979—; dir. lab. animal medicine Tufts-New Eng. Med. Ctr., Boston, 1975-79; dir. Ctr. Research Animal Resources, Cornell U., Ithaca, 1979—. Editor: Clinical Chemistry of Laboratory Animals, 1988, Animal Welfare, 1992, Lab. Animal Sci.; chmn. editorial bd. ILAr News, 1988-91; contbr. 100 sci. papers and abstracts. Greenfield Trust scholar, 1966-70; N.H. Rural Rehab. Corp. scholar, 1966-70; U. Pa. scholar, 1969-70. Mem. Am. Assn. Lab. Animal Sci. (pres. Northeast br. 1978-79; B. Trum award 1979), World Vet. Assn. (treas. exec. com. 1990). Episcopalian. Home: 115 Terraceview Dr Ithaca NY 14850 Office: NYSCVM Cornell U 221 VRT Ithaca NY 14853-6401

QUIMBY, WALTER, recreational products executive; b. Balt., Apr. 9, 1946; s. Dudley Thomas and Joyce Sophie (Karlovich) Q.; m. Carole Ann Williams, Nov. 29, 1969 (div. 1989); children: Jonathan Kyle, Julie Elizabeth; m. Nancy Lee Sorrell, July 22, 1990. BS in Mktg., U. Md., 1972. V.p. Am. Original Foods, Bridgeville, Del., 1972-78, Jenkins Foods Corp., Milford, Del., 1978-81, Dover (Del.) Pool & Patio Ctr., Inc., 1981-85; pres. Water World, Inc., Easton, Md., 1985—. With USCG, 1968-72. Mem. NSPI (pres. Rehoboth, Del. chpt. 1988-89, pres., treas. Virginia Beach, Va. chpt. 1990-92). Democrat. Lutheran.

QUINDLEN, ANNA, journalist, author; b. 1953; m. Gerald Krovatin; children: Quin, Christopher. Attended, Barnard Coll. Began career as reporter New York Post; moved to New York Times, wrote About New York column, became dep. met. editor; wrote Life in the 30's column N.Y. Times, and syndicated, 1986-89; now syndicated columnist N.Y. Times. Author: Living Out Loud, 1986, (novel) Object Lessons, 1991. Recipient Pulitzer Prize for Commentary, 1992. Office: care NY Times 229 W 43rd St New York NY 10036-3913*

QUINN, CARROLL THOMAS, law firm management consultant; b. Brunswick, Ga., Nov. 14, 1946; s. Thomas Gregory and Norma (Allen) Q.; children: Todd Michael, Jeffrey Carroll. Student, USAF Acad.; BA, St. Anselm's Coll., 1968; JD, New England Sch. Law, 1974. Bar: Mass. 1974. Area mgr. Parke Davis & Co., Detroit, 1968-76; nat. sales mgr. Whitestone Products, Piscataway, N.J., 1976-79; gen. mgr. USM Weathershield Systems, Stanhope, N.J., 1979-82; prin. Computer Universe, Stanhope, 1982—, Compu-vid, Stanhope, 1986--, Fejot, Inc., Nashua, N.H., 1985--; v.p. mktg. and sales FCS, Inc., Stanhope, N.J., 1984-86; prin. Laserlitho Allamuchy (N.J.) Desktop Publs. and Printing, 1988—. Mem. ABA, Mass. Bar Assn. Home: 56 Goldfinch Dr Hackettstown NJ 07840-3009 Office: Panther Valley Village Sq Allamuchy NJ 17820

QUINN, CHARLES ANDREW, electronics company executive; b. Phila., Oct. 31, 1931; s. Ignatius A. and Mary R. (Suermann) Q.; m. Joan Ann Cahill, June 12, 1954; children: Charles, Michael J., Mark D., Megan Quinn Deless. BEE, Villanova U., 1954; MBA, Duquesne U., 1964. Various positions Westinghouse Elec. Group, Pitts., 1957-65; mgr. materials RCA Corp., Camden, N.J., 1965-74; v.p. ops. RCA Corp., Indpls., 1974-83; v.p., gen. mgr. RCA Corp., Lancaster, Pa., 1983-87; v.p. corp. svcs. Sony Corp., Park Ridge, N.J., 1987—. Mem. Am. Mgmt. Assn. (purchasing coun. 1988—), Hamilton Club (Lancaster), Bent Creek Golf Club (Lancaster), Moss Creek Golf Club (Hilton Head Island, S.C.), KC. Republican. Roman Catholic. Home: 745 Ridge Rd Terr Smoke Rise NJ 07405 Office: Sony Corp Am 1 Sony Dr Park Ridge NJ 07656

QUINN, DOROTHY ANN, bank executive; b. Boston, Aug. 20, 1956; d. Thomas Patrick and Mary Agnes (Panico) Duffy; m. Evan Bruce Quinn, Nov. 2, 1986; 1 child, Juliette Kathleen. BA, U. Maine, 1978. Communications specialist Ohio State U., Columbus, 1980-81; mktg. svcs. coord. Interactive Data Corp., Waltham, Mass., 1982-84; communications specialist Interactive Data Corp., Lexington, Mass., 1984-89; 2nd v.p. Chase Access Svcs. Corp., Lexington, 1989—, second v.p., 1992—. Mem. Boston Computer Soc., Adobe Tech. Exch. Office: Chase Access Svcs Corp 95 Hayden Ave L3 C1 Lexington MA 02173-9144

QUINN, EDWARD FRANCIS, III, orthopedic surgeon; b. Washington, Apr. 28, 1944; s. Edward F. Jr. and Louise Q.; m. Audrey Dickinson; 1 child, Edward Francis IV. BS, U. Md., 1968, MD, 1969. Diplomate Am. Bd. Orthopedic Surgery, Am. Bd. Neurol. and Orthopedic Surgery. Intern Ohio State Univ. Hosp., Columbus, 1969-70; resident USN Hosp., Bethesda, Md., 1971-74; staff Milford (Del.) Meml. Hosp., 1975—, pres. med. staff, 1992—; cons. staff Beebe Hosp., Lewes, Del., 1975—, Nanticoke Meml. Hosp., Seaford, Del., 1975-90, Kent Gen. Hosp., Dover, Del., 1981-90, attending staff, 1990—. Bd. advisors So. Campus of Goldey Beacon Coll., 1987-91. Lt. comdr. USN, 1970-75. Fellow ACS, Am. Acad. Neurol./Orthopaedic Surgery, Internat. Coll. Surgeons; mem. AMA, Med. Soc. Del., Sussex County Med. Soc., Am. Fracture Assn., So. Med. Assn., Del. Soc. Orthopaedic Surgeons, Ea. Orthopaedic Assn., So. Orthopaedic Assn., Acad. Neuro-Muscular Thermography, Chemonucleolysis Adv. Bd., Milford Rotary Club, Rotary Internat. (Paul Harris fellow 1986), Am. Acad. Disability Evaluation Rsch. Physicians, Am. Legion, So. Del. C. of C. (bd. dirs. 1983-90). Republican. Office: Dickinson Med Group 800 N Du Pont Hwy Milford DE 19963-1091

QUINN, GERALD V., video specialist, writing consultant; b. Kingston, Pa., Feb. 24, 1952; s. Alexander A. and Marie (Benesky) Q. BA in Sociology and Edn., Kings Coll., Wilkes-Barre, 1977; postgrad., Trenton (N.J.) State Coll., 1980-82, Mercer County Community Coll., 1983-85. Teaching asst. Children's Day Sch., Trenton, 1977-78; tchr. East Windsor (N.J.) Regional

Schs., 1978-81; media specialist N.J. Dept. Human Svcs., Trenton, 1981—; prin., v.p. mktg. Byteware Inc., Lawrenceville, N.J., 1982—; cons. Jerry Smith Assocs., Phila., 1986-90. Author: getting the Most From Your Video Gear, 1986, The Camcorder Handbook, 1987, The Fax Handbook, 1989; editor newsletter Birds Exotic Inc., Cinaminson, N.J., 1987; creator greeting cards. Mem. People for the Ethical Treatment of Animals, 1986—, Nat. Humane Soc., 1985—, Internat. Fund for Animal Welfare, 1986—, Assn. for the Severely Handicapped, also asst. editor newsletter, 1987. Mem. Authors Guild, Am. Fedn. Musicians, Phila. Avi-Cultural Soc., N.J. Microcomputers Users Group. Republican. Roman Catholic. Home and Office: Byteware Inc 29 Carolina Ave Trenton NJ 08618-1607

QUINN, JAMES DAVID, bearing/seal manufacturing company executive; b. Cleve., Oct. 23, 1929; s. Harold Martin and Marion Elizabeth (White) Q.; m. Jeanne Ann Beidler, July 3, 1952; children: Daniel, Stephen, Peter, Jennifer, Carolyn, Adam. BSChemE, U. W.Va., 1953. Rsch. engr. Dow Chem. Co., Freeport, Tex., 1953-55, plant supr., 1955-57; field salesman Haveg Corp., Houston, 1957; project mgr. Haveg Corp., Wilmington, Del., 1958-59, mgr. aerospace div., 1959-62, mktg. mgr., 1962-64; exec. v.p. Pure Industries, Inc., St. Marys, Pa., 1964-65, pres., 1966-92, chmn., 1966—; bd. dirs. Integra Bank North, Titusville, Pa., Indspec Chem., Pitts.; ptnr. Comml. Realty Co., St. Mary's, 1981—. bd. dirs., v.p. Bucktail coun. Boy Scouts Am., 1965—, Andrew Kaul Meml. Hosp., St. Marys, 1968-78; bd. dirs. Dubois (Pa.) Ednl. Found., 1970—, also past pres.; chmn. St. Mary Area Leadership Club, 1990-91. With U.S. Army, 1947-49. Named grand marshall Meml. Day parade Am. Legion, St. Marys, 1983; recipient Silver Beaver award Boy Scouts Am., 1986. Mem. Nat. Elec. Mfrs. Assn. (chmn. carbon sect. 1971-73), St. Marys Country Club (bd. dirs., pres. 1971-73). Home: 628 Sherry Rd Saint Marys PA 15857-3436 Office: Pure Industries Inc 441 Hall Ave Saint Marys PA 15857-1497

QUINN, JOHN ALBERT, chemical engineering educator; b. Springfield, Ill., Sept. 3, 1932; s. Edward Joseph and Marie (Von De Bur) Q.; m. Frances Wilkie Daly, June 22, 1957; children: Sarah D., Rebecca V., John E. BSChemE, U. Ill., 1954; PhDChemE, Princeton U., 1959. Faculty mem. chem. engring. U. Ill., Urbana, 1958-70; prof. chem. engring. U. Pa., Phila., 1971—, Robert D. Bent prof. chem. engring., 1978—, chmn. dept., 1980-85; vis. prof. chem. engring. Imperial Coll. U. London, 1965-66, 86; vis. scientist MIT, 1980; mem. sci.adv. bds. Sepracor, Inc. Marlborough, Mass., 1984—, The Whitaker Found., Mechanicsburg, Pa., 1987—; Mason lectr. Stanford U, 1981; Katz lectr. U. Mich, 1985; Reilly lectr. U. Notre Dame, 1987. Contbr. articles to profl. publs.; editorial advisor Jour. Membrane Sci., 1975—, Indsl. and Chem. Engring. Rsch., 1987-88, Revs. in Chem. Engring., 1980—; pioneer researcher on mass transfer and interfacial phenomena. Recipient S. Reid Warren Jr. award for disting. teaching U. Pa., 1974; sr. postdoctoral fellow NSF, 1965-66; Sherman Fairchild scholar Calif. Inst. Tech., 1985. Fellow AAAS; mem. NAE, Am. Acad. Arts and Scis., Am. Chem. Soc., Am. Inst. Chem. Engrs. (Allan P. Colburn award 1966, Alpha Chi Sigma award 1978), Internat. Soc. Oxygen Transport to Tissue, Sigma Xi, Phi Lambda Upsilon, Tau Beta Pi. Home: 275 E Wynnewood Rd Merion Station PA 19066-1627 Office: Univ Pa 220 S 33d St Towne Bldg Philadelphia PA 19104-6393

QUINN, KATHERINE B., public relations executive, educator; b. Rochester, NY, May 18, 1951; d. Eugene Vincent and Frances Mildred (Burns) Q. BA in English and Speech, SUNY, Brockport, 1973; postgrad., Monroe Community Coll., Rochester, Syracuse U. Accredited in pub. rels. Traffic/ops. exec. WHFM/WHAM Radio, Rochester, 1973; ops. exec. WHEC-TV, Rochester, 1974-76; creative assoc. Conklin, Labs and Bebee Inc., Syracuse, N.Y., 1978-84; account exec., pub. rels. Rumrill-Hoyt Inc., Rochester, 1984-91; pres. QuinnTessence Pub. Rels., Rochester, 1991—; adj. faculty Rochester Inst. Tech., 1987—, SUNY, Brockport, 1990—. Office: QuinnTessence Pub Rels 2040 Westside Dr Rochester NY 14624-2029

QUINN, ROBERT CHARLES, author; b. Portland, Maine, Oct. 12, 1930; s. Leo Joseph and Mary Pearl (Sawyer) Q.; children: Kathleen, Patrick, G. Dawn, Robert L., Timothy, Elizabeth. Sales mgr. Portland, 1952-70, self-employed designer, 1970-91; pvt. practice protectioneer Richmond, Maine, 1992—. Author: With Cannon Roaring, 1992. With USMC, 1947-52. Mem. Marine Corps League (VAVS rep. 1975-91), SAR, Am. Legion, Masons. Home: 31 N Front St Richmond ME 04357

QUINN, THOMAS JOSEPH, JR., advertising executive; b. Sharon, Pa., Nov. 28, 1951; s. Thomas Joseph Sr. and Mary Ellen (Burns) Q.; 1 child, Thomas J. III. BS in Advt., U. Fla., 1976. Media planner Benton & Bowles, N.Y.C., 1978-79; account exec. Ted Bates, N.Y.C., 1979-82; account supr. Slater, Hanft, Martin, N.Y.C., 1982-83; sr. v.p. mktg. Aloysius Butler & Clark, Wilmington, Del., 1983-85; chief exec. officer, pres. DeDonato, Gladstone & Quinn, Inc., Wilmington, 1985—; adj. prof. Wesley Coll., Dover, Del., 1985-86, chmn. pub. rels. adv. coun., 1986-89, now bd. dirs. Bd. dirs. Com. 100, Wilmington, 1990—, Am. Heart Assn. Del., Wilmington, 1987—, Am. Lung Assn. Del., Wilmington, 1989—. Mem. Am. Mktg. Assn. (pres.-elect Del. chpt. 1987-88, pres. 1988-89), Del. State C. of C. (legis. action com. 1988, 89), Phi Kappa Phi. Roman Catholic. Office: DeDonato Gladstone & Quinn Inc 1225 N King St Ste 500 Wilmington DE 19801-3217

QUINN, TIMOTHY CHARLES, JR., lawyer; b. Caro, Mich., Mar. 3, 1936; s. Timothy Charles and Jessie (Brown) Q.; m. Linda Ricci, June 21, 1958; children: Gina M., Samantha E., Timothy Charles III. BA, U. Mich., 1960; JD, Columbia U., 1963. Bar: N.Y. 1963, U.S. Dist. Ct. (so. and ea. dists.) N.Y. 1965, U.S. Ct. Appeals (2d cir.) 1967. Assoc. Clark, Carr & Ellis, N.Y.C., 1963-69, Casey, Tyre, Wallace & Bannerman, N.Y.C., 1969-71, Arsham & Keenan, N.Y.C., 1971; assoc. Conboy, Hewitt, O'Brien & Boradman, N.Y.C., 1972-74, ptnr., 1975-83, mem. exec. com., 1981-83; ptnr. Quinn, Cohen, Shields & Bock, N.Y.C., 1983-88, Quinn & Suhr, White Plains, N.Y., 1988—; arbitrator N.Y.C. Civil Ct., 1982-88 , Am. Arbitration Assn., N.Y.C., 1966—, 9th Jud. Dist., 1988—. Mem. ABA, N.Y. State Bar Assn., Westchester County Bar Assn., Assn. of Bar of City of N.Y., N.Y. State Trial Lawyers Assn., Nat. Assn. R.R. Trial Counsel, Conf. Freight Loss and Damage Counsel, N.Y. Law Inst., Def. Rsch. Inst., Westchester Country Club. Home: 34 Pinehurst Dr Purchase NY 10577-1307 Office: Quinn & Suhr 170 Hamilton Ave White Plains NY 10601-1715

QUINN-CORDERO, MARY, public relations executive, marketing educator; b. Bklyn., May 28, 1955; d. Raymond Leo and Catherine Mary (Martin) Quinn; m. Reynaldo Cordero, Aug. 23, 1980. BA in Journalism, L.I. U., 1976; MBA in Mktg., Fordham U., 1984; postgrad., U. London, summer 1975. Assoc. editor Modern Floor Coverings Mag., N.Y.C., 1976-77; community rels. asst. Rahway (N.J.) Hosp., 1977-79; asst. dir. pub. rels. Brookdale Hosp. Med. Ctr., Bklyn., Jan. 1979 to May 1979; sales promotion writer Marsh and McLennan Inc., N.Y.C., 1979-81; pub. rels. account exec. Ins. Info. Inst., N.Y.C., 1982-84; 2nd v.p., pub. rels. mgr. Chase Manhattan Bank, L.I., N.Y., 1984-87; pres. Prase Mktg., L.I., N.Y., 1987—; prof. mktg. Concordia Coll., Westchester, N.Y. Bd. dirs. East Yaphank Civic Assn. Recipient award for internat. understanding Rotary Found., Fed. Republic Germany, 1987; scholar L.I. U., 1972-76, N.Y. State Regents, 1972-76. Mem. NAFE, Pub. Rels. Soc. Am. (L.I. chpt.), Nat. Assn. Women Bus. Owners.

QUINONES, WILLIAM BILL, security investigator, musician; b. Bklyn., July 7, 1962; s. Enrique and Carmen (Inrizary) Q. Student, Kingsborough Community Coll., 1982-83, Magnum Sch. Inc., 1990-91. Cert. pistol instr.; cert. securityh officer. Asst. mgr. security Marlows Dept. Store; skip tracer Irving & Newman Bailbonds; security, supr., investigator, bodyguard Robert Bruce Mclane Assocs.; producer Bklyn. Boy Music Prodns.; trumpet player touring Mexico City, Calif., Tex., San Francisco, San Diego, Hollywood, P.R., Los Nietos del Rey, Venezuela, Curacao; freelance writer, composer, music arranger and music tchr.; superior Career Inst. Sch. for Claims Ins. Investigators. TV shows include Siempre En Domingo; performed with Savannah Concert Show Band. Mem. Neighborhood Watch Patrol, N.Y.C., 1990-92; mem. Citizens Com. N.Y.C., 1990-91; vol. Mayor Vol. Action Ctr. Recipient award Citizens Com. Neighborhood Watch Patrol, 1992. Mem. ASCAP. Roman Catholic. Home: 1544 Putnam Ave Brooklyn NY 11237

QUINTANA, JORGE OVIDIO, agronomist, researcher, consultant; b. Managua, Nicaragua, Apr. 6, 1952; came to U.S., 1978; s. Emilio and Silvia (Bonilla) Q.; m. Lorraine Adlin Legall, Mar. 23, 1974 (div. 1979); 1 child, Emilio Quetzalcoatl; m. Elizabeth Anne Angell, July 26, 1980; 1 child, Amanda Nicole. Agronomist engr., Escuela Nacional de Agricultura y Ganaderia, Managua, 1970-74; MS in Soil Scis., Cornell U., 1978-80, PhD in Soil Scis., 1983-87. Extensionist supr. Inbierno, Esteli, Nicaragua, 1975-76; mgr. soil project Inst. Nicaraguense de Tecnicas Agropecuarias, Managua, 1976-78; head dept. argonomy Midinra, Managua, 1980-81; dir. soil program Direccion Gen. de Tecnologia Agricola-Ministerio de Agricultura y Reforma Agraria, Managua, 1982, head dept. soil fertility, 1983; tech. cons. Centro de Pewquisa Agricola do Cerrado-Empresa Brasileira de Pesquisa Agropecuaria, Brasilia, Brazil, 1985-86; tech. coord. Midinra/FAO-UN, Managua, 1987-88; head indigenous argonomist Preservation Networking Ctr., Berkshire, N.Y., 1988—; rsch. assoc. Cornell U., Ithaca, 1989—; bd. dirs. IPNC; vis. prof. U. Nacional, Managua, 1980-83; cons. Plenty-Canada, Ontario, 1988-92; soil survey coord. Osa Golfito, Costa Rico, 1991. Author: Fertilizer Manual, 1988, Soil Survey of Golfito, 1991, 3 poetry books, 1991; contbr. articles to profl. jours. Mem. Com. of Indian People of Nicaragua, 1980-81; adv. Misurasata, Nicaragua, 1981. Scholarship recipient ENAG, 1970-74, Latin Am. Scholarship Program Am. Univs., 1978-80, Tropsoil Aid, 1983-87. Mem. Coun. of Indigenous People Economics. Office: Cornell U 903 Bradfield Hall Ithaca NY 14853

QUINTANILLA, FAUSTINO, artist, art gallery director; b. Leon, Spain, Apr. 9, 1948; s. Nicanor Quintanilla and Petra Santamarta; m. Christine Angelilli, 1974; children: Peter, Christian, Laetitia. PhB, St. Maria de la Vid, Burgos, Spain, 1967; BTh, Lateran U., Rome, 1971; BA in Liberal Arts, Wagner Coll., 1974; MFA in Printmaking, Pratt Inst., 1978. Caseworker Mission of Immaculate Virgin, S.I., N.Y., 1974-76; tchr., gallery dir. St. Peter High Sch., New Brunswick, N.J., 1981-90; dir. Queensborough Community Coll. Art Gallery, Bayside, N.Y., 1990—; adj. asst. prof. printmaking Coll. S.I. SUNY, 1991—; curator exhibits including Women Printmakers, 1991, Ecuador: Arte y Tradicion, 1991, Labyrinth, 1992; N.Y. exhibit coord. Light Pieces Synthesis, N.Y., 1976-86; masterprinter Werner Graphics, 1980-82, Naomi Tiepich & Gail Eckerman, 1980-86; dir. Elizabeth Anne Seton Meml. Gallery, 1988—. One man shows include Springan Gallery, Matawan, N.J., 1991; other exhbns. include Kade Gallery Wagner Coll., S.I., 1972, 74, 76, 77, Second Story Spring St. Soc., N.Y., 1975, Blue Unicorn, S.I., 1975, 76, Met. Mus., N.Y.C., 1975, 77, Avery Fisher Hall Lincoln Ctr., N.Y.C., 1975, Pratt Inst., Bklyn., 1975, 78, Hanson Galleries, N.Y.C., 1977, New House Galleries Snug Harbor Cultural Ctr., S.I., 1979, Upstairs Gallery, S.I., 1983, Salon des Nations Centre Internat. ol'Art Contemporain, Paris, 1983, Robert Wood Johnson U. Hosp., New Brunswick, 1985, St. Peter's High Sch., New Brunswick, 1990, Elizabeth Anne Seton Meml. Gallery, 1990; multi media performances include Modular Running Concepts: Conceptual Syntesis, 1985, Modular Running Concepts: Requiem, 1990; represented in permanent collections including N.Y. Pub. Libr., Augustiniam Gen. Archives-Libr., Rome, also numerous pvt. collections; co-editor, founder Artview mag., 1976-77; contbr. articles to profl. jours. Recipient N.Y. Telephone Co. award S.I. Mus., 1979, Queensborough Pres.'s Arts Recognition award, 1991. Mem. Am. Assn. Mus., Coll. Art Assn. Am., Nat. Acad. Design. Home: 73 Highland Rd Staten Island NY 10308 Office: Queensborough Community Coll Art Gallery-Mus 222-05 56th Ave Bayside NY 11364-1497

QUINTERO, RONALD GARY, management consultant; b. Detroit, Jan. 5, 1954; s. John Urdiales and Jean Lorraine (Morton) Q.; m. Barbara Kay McDaniel, June 15, 1985; children: Jean Marie, Alexandra Lisa. AB, Lafayette Coll., 1975; MS, NYU, 1976, APC, 1978. CPA, N.Y.; cert. fin. analyst, fin. planner, mgmt. acct., fraud examiner, insolvency and reorgn. acct. Sr. mgr. Peat, Marwick, Mitchell & Co., N.Y.C., 1975-85; workout cons. Zolfo, Cooper & Co., N.Y.C., 1985-87; assoc. Bear, Stearns & Co., Inc., N.Y.C., 1987-88; prin. R. G. Quintero & Co., N.Y.C., 1988—; mng. dir. Chartered Capital Advisers, Inc., N.Y.C.; adj. prof. New Sch. for Social Rsch., N.Y.C., 1983-85; adj. prof. N.Y. Inst. Fin., N.Y.C., 1988—; instr. Ctr. for Profl. Edn., Berwyn, Pa., 1991—. Author: (book and cassette) Mergers and Acquisitions, 1990; contbg. author several books; contbr. articles to profl. jours.; creator: Quintero Index of Bankrupt Stocks. Mem. AICPAs, Am. Bankruptcy Inst., N.Y. Soc. CPAs (chmn. com. 1990-91, Max Block Disting. Article award 1990, Outstanding Discussion Leader 1991), Turnaround Mgmt. Assn. (bd. dirs.). Office: R G Quintero & Co 145 4th Ave New York NY 10003

QUIROZ, RODERICK SOTELO, retired research meteorologist; b. Ajo, Ariz., Nov. 6, 1923; s. Francisco Carmelo and Rosa (Sotelo) Q. BA in Meteorology, UCLA, 1950; MS in Meteorology, U. Md., 1970; MS in Spanish, Georgetown U., 1991. Civilian rsch. meteorologist Air Weather Svc. USAF, Washington, 1950-66; rsch. meteorologist NOAA, Washington, 1966-85; mem. U.S. Com. on Standard Atmosphere, Washington, 1968-71; lectr. in field. Editor: Meteorological Investigations of the Upper Atmosphere, 1968; contbr. numerous articles to profl. jours. Tech. sgt. USAF, 1943-48, CBI. Fellow Am. Meteorol. Soc. (chmn. com. on atmospheric problems of aerospace vehicles 1969-70, chmn. com. on the upper atmosphere 1977-78), Washington Acad. Scis.; mem. Am. Geophys. Union, Sigma Delta Pi. Home: 4520 Yuma St NW Washington DC 20016-2044

QUISGARD, LIZ WHITNEY, painter, sculptor; b. Phila., Oct. 23, 1929; d. Kenneth E. and Elizabeth (Warwick) Whitney; children: Kristin, Berit. Grad. night sch., Md. Inst. Coll. Art, 1947, grad. day sch., 1949; student, Johns Hopkins U., evenings 1952-58; pupil of, Morris Louis, 1958-60; BFA in Painting, Md. Inst., 1966, MFA in Sculpture, 1966. Pvt. tchr. painting Balt., 1955-65; tchr. Balt. Hebrew Congregation, 1962-80; mem. faculty Md. Inst. Coll. Art, 1965-76, Goucher Coll., 1966-68, Balt. Jewish Community Ctr., 1974-78, Villa Julie Coll., Stevenson, Md., 1978-80; art critic Balt. Sun, 1969-71, Craft Horizons, 1969-72, The Paper, 1971-72; designer prodns. Center Stage, Goucher Coll., Johns Hopkins U.; lectr. in Md., Va., W.Va., Pa., Ark., Ohio, N.Y., N.J. One-woman exhbns. include Jefferson Pl. Gallery, Washington, 1960, Key Gallery, N.Y.C., 1960, Emmerich Gallery, N.Y.C., 1962, Goucher Coll., Balt., 1966, U. Md., 1969, Gallery, 707, Los Angeles, 1974, Arts and Sci. Center, Nashua, N.H., 1975, Gannon Coll., Erie, Pa., 1978, Mechanic Gallery, Balt., 1978, Marymount Manhatten Coll., N.Y.C., 1983, Tiffany's windows, N.Y.C., 1984, Mussari Arts Ctr., N.Y.C., 1984, Starkman Gallery, N.Y.C., 1984, Fordham U., N.Y.C., 1985, Landmark Tower, Stamford, Conn., 1986; Provident Bank, Phila., 1986; Henri Gallery, Washington, 1987, Artemisia Gallery, Chgo., 1987, Savannah (Ga.) Coll. Art and Design, 1987, Western Md. Coll., Westminster, 1988, Life of Maryland Gallery, Balt., 1988, Franz Bader Gallery, Washington, 1989, Fairleigh Dickinson U., N.J., 1990, Herr-Chambliss Gallery, Hot Springs, Ark., 1990, Huntington (Ind.) Coll., 1991, Bergdorf Goodman Windows, 1991; group exhbns. include, Balt. Mus., 1951-53, 58, Corcoran Gallery Area Show, 1956, 64, Corcoran Biennial Show, 1963, Peale Mus., Balt., 1947, 56, Butler Inst. Am. Art, Youngstown, Ohio, 1957, Provincetown (Mass.) Art Assn., 1955, U. Colo., 1963, Pa. Acad. Am. Art ann., 1964, Chgo. Art Inst., 1965, Gallery 707, 1973, S. Houston St. Gallery, N.Y.C., 1974, Balt. Mus. travelling show, 1978, Mus. of Hudson Highlands, Cornwall, N.Y., 1983, Catskill Gallery (N.Y.), 1983; represented in permanent collections U. Ariz., U. Md., U. Balt., Johns Hopkins U., Lever House, N.Y.C., Center Club, Balt., Libyan Mission to UN, Englewood, N.J., Datalogix Corp., Valhalla, N.Y., Gt. Northern Nekoosa Corp., Norwalk, Conn., Quality Inns, Newark, Can. Imperial Bank of Commerce, N.Y.C., Rosenberg Diamond Co., N.Y.C., Marsh, Inc., Indpls., Kirkpatrick and Lockhart, Pitts., Fordham U., N.Y.C., Atlantic Realty, Atlanta, Miss. Mus. Art, Jackson; also pvt. collections; executed mural William Fell Elem. Sch., Balt., 1980, Urban Wall, Atlanta, 1990, floor painting Vet.'s Stadium, Phila., 1992. Recipient Best in Show award Loyola Coll. Invitational, Balt. 1966; scholar Md. Inst., 1947-49; Rinehart fellow in sculpture, 1964-66. Address: 145 Reade St New York NY 10013

RAAB, HERBERT NORMAN, retail executive; b. N.Y.C., Nov. 7, 1925; s. Jacob and Pauline (Neuwirth) R.; m. Blanche Muriel Levin, Jan. 27, 1952 (dec. Mar. 1981); children: Nancy Renée, James Harris; m. Carmen Sandra Fernandez, Aug. 17, 1986. AB, Harvard U., 1947; postgrad., Harvard U. Bus. Sch., 1947-48, Seton Hall U. Law Sch., 1972-75. V.p. Bamberger Div. R.H. Macy Inc., N.Y.C., 1968-75, v.p., 1975-78; pres. and chief exec. officer W&J Sloane, N.Y.C., 1978-80; pvt. practice cons. N.Y.C., 1980-84; sr. v.p. Wayside Furniture Co., Milford, Conn., 1984-90; adj. prof. U. Bridgeport (Conn.), 1986-91. Jewish.

RAAB, IRA JERRY, lawyer; b. N.Y.C., June 20, 1935; s. Benjamin and Fannie (Kirschner) R.; divorced; children: Michael, Shelley; m. Katie Rachel McKeever, June 30, 1979; children: Julie, Jennifer, Joseph. BBA, CCNY, 1955; JD, Bklyn. Law Sch., 1957; MPA, NYU, 1959, postgrad., 1961; MS in Pub. Adminstrn., L.I. U., 1961; MBA, Adelphi U., 1990. Bar: N.Y. 1958, U.S. Dist. Ct. (so. and ea. dists.) N.Y. 1960, U.S. Supreme Ct. 1967, U.S. Tax Ct. 1976, U.S. Ct. Appeals (2d cir.) 1977. Pvt. practice Woodmere, N.Y., 1958-87, 89—; agt. Westchester County Soc. Prevention of Cruelty to Children, White Plains, N.Y., 1958; counsel Dept. Correction City of N.Y., 1959, trial commr. Dept. Correction, 1976, asst. corp. counsel Tort div., 1963-70; staff counsel SBA, N.Y.C., 1961-63; counsel Investigation Com. on Willowbrook State Sch., Boro Hall, S.I., N.Y., 1970; gen. counsel Richmond County Soc. Prevention of Cruelty to Children, Boro Hall, 1970-81; pro bono counsel N.Y.C. Patrolmen's Benevolent Assn., 1974-81; rep. to UN Internat. Criminal Ct., 1977-78; arbitrator Small Claims Ct., Day Cts., N.Y.C., 1970—, L.I. Better Bus. Bur., 1976—, Nassau County Dist. Ct., 1978—; hearing officer Nassau County Supreme Ct., 1982—; spl. master N.Y. County Supreme Ct., 1977—; lectr. community and ednl. orgns.; instr. paralegal course Lawrence Sch. Dist., N.Y., 1982-84. Chairman Business-men's Luncheon Club, Wall St. Synagogue, 1968-79; sec. Community Mediation Ctr., Suffolk County, 1978-80, exec. v.p., 1980-81; vice chmn. Woodmere Inc. Com., 1980-81; mem. adv. bd. Nassau Expressway Com., 1979-80; bd. dirs. Woodmere Mchts. Assn., 1979-80, v.p., 1979-83, chmn., 1984—; candidate for dist. ct. judge Nassau County, 1987, 88, 89, 91. Recipient Consumer Protection award FTC, 1974, 76, 79, Recognition award Pres. Ronald Reagan, 1986, Man of Yr. award L.I. Coun. of Chambers, 1987. Mem. Am. Judges Assn. (nat. treas. 1978-82, exec. com. 1978—, gov. dist. II 1973-78, 82-83, 89—, chmn. civil ct. ops. com. 1975-76, chmn. ednl. film com. 1974-77, editorial bd. Ct. Rev. mag. 1975-79, 82-86, chmn. speakers' bur. com. 1976-77, chmn. legis. com. 1983—, historian 1988—, William H. Burnett award 1983), Am. Judges Found. (pres. 1977-79, chmn. bd. trustees 1979-83, treas. 1974-75, 76-77, trustee 83—), Assn. Arbitrators of Civil Ct. City N.Y. (past pres.), ABA (chmn. cts. and community com. 1988—, exec. com. jud. adminstrv. div. lawyers conf. 1989—), N.Y. State Bar Assn. (sec. dist., city town and villages cts. com.), Nassau County Lawyers Assn., Nassau County Bar Assn. (mem. criminal cts. com., matrimonial and family ct. com., ct. com., ethics com.), Profl. Group Legal Svc. Assn. (past pres.), Internat. Assn. Jewish Lawyers and Jurists (com. to draft Internat. Bill of Rights of Privacy 1982, coun. 1981—, bd. govs. 1984—), Am. Arbitration Assn. (arbitrator 1975—, adv. bd. community dispute ctr. 1979-81), K.P. (past chancellor comdr.). Democrat. Jewish. Address: 375 Westwood Rd Woodmere NY 11598

RAAB, LAWRENCE EDWARD, English educator; b. Pittsfield, Mass., May 8, 1946; s. Edward Louis and Marjorie (Young) R.; m. Judith Ann Michaels, Dec. 29, 1968; 1 child, Jennifer Caroline. BA, Middlebury Coll., 1968; MA, Syracuse U., 1972. Lectr. Am. U., Washington, 1970-71; jr. fellow U. Mich. Soc. Fellows, Ann Arbor, 1973-76; prof. English Williams Coll., Williamstown, Mass., 1976—. Author: (poems) Mysteries of the Horizon, 1972, The Collector of Cold Weather, 1976, Other Children, 1987. Creative Writing fellow Nat. Endowment Arts, 1972, 84; recipient Bess Hokin prize Poetry mag., 1983; residencies at Yaddo, 1979-80, 82, 84, 86-90. Office: Williams Coll English Dept Stetson Hall Williamstown MA 01267

RAAM, SHANTHI, cancer researcher; b. Madras, India, Nov. 26, 1941; came to U.S. 1964, naturalized 1977; BSc in Zoology, U. Madras, 1960, MS in Parasitology, 1962; PhD in Immunology, Immunochemistry, U. Ga., 1973. Rsch. asst. dept. zoology U. Madras, India, 1962-64, U. Tenn., Knoxville, 1964-65; teaching asst. Med. Coll. Ga., Augusta, 1968-70; teaching asst. then rsch. asst. U. Ga., Athens, 1970-73; postdoctoral rsch. fellow then rsch. assoc. Cancer Rsch. Ctr. Sch. Medicine Tufts U., Boston, 1973-85; dir. oncology lab. Lemuel Shattuck Hosp., Boston, 1976-85; assoc. prof. (rsch.) Sch. Medicine Tufts U., Boston, 1985—; chmn. ad hoc peer rev. com. NIH, 1989-90, adv. com. for clin. trials and cancer interventions, 1990—; mem. program com. Internat. Congress on Breast Diseases, 1990. Editor, pubr.: Immunology of Steroid Hormone Research. Recipient Kenneth Dodgson Meml. Lectr. award U. Ga., Athens, 1991. Office: Tufts Med Cancer Unit Lemuel Shattuck Hosp 170 Morton St Boston MA 02130

RABADEAU, MARY FRANCES, protective services official; b. Elizabeth, N.J., July 13, 1948; d. Russell John and Frances (Hanley) R. Student, Union Coll., 1967-69; MEd, Kean Coll., 1976. Officer City of Elizabeth Police Dept., N.J., 1978-82, detective, 1982-83, sgt., 1983-87, lt., 1987-91, capt., 1991—; instr. Union County Police Acad. Trustee Blessed Sacrament Ch., Elizabeth, N.J., 1989—. Named one of Outstanding Young Women in Am., 1983. Mem. N.E. Assn. Women Police (cert., Merit award), Elizabeth Police Patrolman's Benevolent Assn., Elizabeth Police Superior Officers Assn. (treas. 1983-91, v.p. 1991), Am. Soc. Law Enforcement Trainers, Emerals Soc. Democrat. Roman Catholic. Home: 46C4 Sandra Circle 829 Madison Ave Westfield NJ 07090 Office: Elizabeth Police Dept 1 Police Plz Elizabeth NJ 07201-2397

RABELER, STEVEN WALTER, engineer, musician, songwriter; b. Delhi, N.Y., Jan. 27, 1958; s. Paul Walter and Mathilde (Menke) R. BA, Alfred U., 1981; MS, Rensselaer Poly. Inst., 1982. Engr. Gen. Dynamics, Ft. Worth, 1983-87, GE, Moorestown, N.J., 1988—; ptnr. Resume Designs, Mt. Laurel, N.J., 1991—. Contbr. articles to tech. jours.; composer over 200 songs. Recipient Van Karmen award, 1987. Homew: 409 Evans Ct Mount Laurel NJ 08054

RABEN, JOSEPH, editor, lecturer, consultant; b. N.Y.C., Sept. 3, 1924; s. Abraham and Frances (Goldner) R.; m. Marguerite Bloch, June 8, 1952 (div. Feb. 1987); children: Jeremy Bloch, Elizabeth; m. Estelle Manette, Mar. 17, 1988. BA, U. Wis., 1944; MA, Ind. U., 1949, PhD, 1954. Teaching fellow Ind. U., Bloomington, 1950-52; instr. Princeton (N.J.) U., 1952-54; from instr. to prof. Queens Coll. CUNY, N.Y.C., 1954-84; dir. Paradigm Press, Inc., Sarasota, Fla., 1984-87; editor SCHOLAR, N.Y.C., 1991—. Editor: Computer Assisted Research in the Humanities, 1977; co-editor: Data Bases in the Humanities and Social Sciences, 1980; founding editor Computers in the Humanities, 1966-86; contbr. articles to profl. jours. With AUS, 1945-46. Pub. grantee NSF, 1968, Mellon Found., 1991; rsch. grantee Sloan and Carnegie Founds., 1980-81. Mem. Modern Lang. Assn. (life), Assn. Computers and the Humanities (founding pres. 1979-81). Democrat. Office: PO Box F New York NY 10028-0025

RABER, DOUGLAS JOHN, chemist; b. N.Y.C., Nov. 13, 1942; s. John W. and Harriet (Neuroth) R.; m. Nancy K. Raber, Mar. 13, 1977; children: Wendy, Jessica. AB, Dartmouth Coll., 1964; PhD, U. Mich., 1968. Asst. prof. chemistry U. South Fla., Tampa, 1970-75, assoc. prof., 1975-80, prof., 1980-90; staff dir. Bd. Chem. Scis. and Tech., NRC, Washington, 1991—. Co-author: Organic Chemistry, 1988; contbr. articles to profl. jours. NIH postdoctoral fellow Princeton U., 1968-70; Alexander von Humboldt fellow U. Erlangen-Nurnberg, Germany, 1978-79. Office: NRC 2101 Constitution Ave NW Washington DC 20418

RABIE, MOHAMED, economics educator, writer; b. Yazour, Palestine, June 5, 1940; came to U.S., 1976; s. Abdulaziz Mohamed Rabie and Sabha (Abdullatif) Bayrum; m. Maha Halabi, June 23, 1969; children: Aseel, Haneen, Kareem. BSc in Agrl. Econs., Ain Shams U., Cairo, 1962, MSc in Rural Sociology, 1963; MA in Econs., U. Houston, 1968, PhD in Econs., 1970. Prof. Kuwait U., 1970-76; adj. prof. Georgetown U., Washington, 1976-77, 82-83; pres. Internat. Trade & Investment Inc., Houston, 1977-82; exec. dir. Inst. Palestine Studies, Washington, 1983-84; adj. prof. Johns Hopkins U., Washington, 1984-85, Am. U., Washington, 1985-87; pres. Ctr. for Ednl. Devel., Washington, 1987—; chmn. bd. Arab Economists Corp., Kuwait, 1973-77; mem. bd. Fund for Tech. Assistance for African Countries, Cairo, 1975-77; mem. adv. bd. Internat. Inst. for Ethnic Group Rights, Munich, 1989—, Search for Common Ground, Washington, 1991—. Author: The Other Side of Arab Defeat, 1987, The Politics of Foreign Aid, 1988, A Vision for the Transformation of the Middle East, 1990, The New World Order, 1992, and four other books; contbr. articles to profl. jours. Office: Ctr for Ednl Devel 1000 Potomac St NW Ste 30L Washington DC 20007-3501

RABIL, ALBERT, JR., humanities educator; b. Rocky Mount, N.C., May 8, 1934; s. Albert and Sophie Mae (Safy) R.; m. Janet Spain, Aug. 29, 1956;

children—Albert, III, J. Alison. B.A., Duke U., 1957; M.Div., Union Theol. Sem., 1960; Ph.D., Columbia U., 1964. Instr. religion Trinity Coll., Hartford, Conn., 1964-65, asst. prof., 1965-68; asst. prof. hist. theology Chgo. Theol. Sem., 1969-71; assoc. prof. SUNY-Old Westbury, 1971-74, prof., 1974-77, disting. teaching prof. humanities, 1977—; program dir. NEH Summer Inst., 1992. Author: Merleau-Ponty, 1967 (Ansley award 1964), Erasmus and the New Testament, 1972, Laura Cereta, 1981, (with others) Her Immaculate Hand, 1983, Erasmus' Paraphrases of Romans and Galatians, 1983; editor: Renaissance Humanism (3 vols.), 1988; editor, translator: Knowledge, Goodness, and Power, 1991; co-editor Renaissance Quarterly, 1992—. Travelling fellow Union Theol. Sem., 1960, Soc. for Values in Higher Edn., 1961; grantee. Fulbright Found., 1961, NEH, 1981. Mem. Erasmus Rotterdam Soc. (mem. editorial bd. 1980—), Soc. for Values in Higher Edn. (bd. dirs. 1981-90), Columbia U. Renaissance Seminar (assoc. 1979—), Renaissance Soc. Am. (bd. dirs. 1991—). Democrat. Home: 324 Post Ave # 9H Westbury NY 11590-2225 Office: SUNY PO Box 210 Old Westbury NY 11568-0210

RABIN, MITCHELL JAY, psychotherapist, acupuncturist, educator, writer; b. Forest Hills, N.Y., May 12, 1954; s. Monte and Marilyn Joan (Handman) R. BA with honors, Bard Coll., 1976; MA with honors, Antioch Coll., 1979; cert. in acupuncture with honors, Tri-State Inst. of Traditional Chinese Acupuncture, Stamford, Conn., 1984. Pres. Mitch Prodns., Westport, Conn., 1970-72, Rabin Resources, N.Y.C., 1985—; dir. Ctr. for Creative Well Being, N.Y.C., 1986—; v.p. Spa Blazers Internat., N.Y.C., 1988—; pvt. practice in psychotherapy and acupuncture Westport and N.Y.C., 1980—; dir. A Better World Mind Fitness Ctr., N.Y.C., 1991—; cons., lectr. stress mgmt.; instr. Chinese Martial Art, N.Y.C., 1989—. Translator: The Interior Realization (Hubert Benoit), 1985. Mem. Am. Assn. Acupuncture and Oriental Medicine, Acupuncture Coalition of N.Y. (pres. 1984-85), Am. Orthopsychiatric Assn. Office: A Better World 230 E 15th St Ste 4G New York NY 10003-3940

RABINER, LAWRENCE RICHARD, electrical engineer; b. Bklyn., Sept. 28, 1943; s. Nathan Marcus and Gloria Hannah (Bodinger) R.; m. Suzanne Login, June 23, 1968; children—Sheri Lynn, Wendi Beth, Joni Elizabeth. B.S., MIT, 1964, M.S., 1964, Ph.D., 1967. Mem. tech. staff AT&T Bell Labs., Murray Hill, N.J., 1967-70, supr. human machine voice communications group, 1971-85, head speech rsch. dept., 1985-90, dir. info. principles rsch. lab., 1990—. Author: Theory and Application of Digital Signal Processing, 1975; Digital Speech Processing, 1979; Multirate Digital Signal Processing, 1983. Bd. dirs. Summit Jewish Community Ctr., N.J., 1985-90. Fellow Nat. Acad. Engring., NAS, IEEE (pres. ASSP Soc. 1974-75, Piori award 1980, Soc. award 1980, Centennial award 1984), Acoustical Soc. Am. (Biennial award 1974). Republican. Jewish. Home: 58 Sherbrook Dr Berkeley Heights NJ 07922-2346

RABINOWITCH, DAVID GEORGE, sculptor; b. Toronto, Ont., Can., Mar. 6, 1943; came to U.S., 1972; s. Joseph and Ruthe (Calverley) R.; m. Sheila Martin, June 1966 (div. 1981); m. Catrina Neiman, Mar. 14, 1983. BS, U. Western Ont., London, 1966. Instr. sculpture Yale U., New Haven, 1974-75; prof. sculpture Staatliche Kunstakademie Düsseldorf, Germany, 1984—. Sculptures include Box Troughs, 1963, Fluid Sheet Pieces, 1964, Gravitational Vehicles, 1965, Tubers and Wood Constructions, 1966-67, Phantoms, 1967, Sectioned Mass Constructions, 1968, Metrical Constructions, 1973—, Tyndale Constructions, 1974—, Construction of Vision Drawings, 1969—, Ottonian Drawings, 1977—. Recipient CAPS award N.Y. State Coun., 1974, Lynch-Staunton award of distinction Can. Coun., Ottawa, Ont., 1977; J.S. Guggenheim Meml. Found. fellow, N.Y.C., 1975, Nat. Endowment Arts fellow, Washington, 1986-87. Mem. Royal Can. Acad. Arts and Scis. Home: 49 E 1st St New York NY 10003-9324

RABINOWITZ, HARVEY ALLEN, direct mail company executive, consultant, lecturer; b. Johnstown, Pa., Jan. 2, 1931; s. Jack Harvey and Rosalyn (Berney) R.; m. Geri F. Friedman, Feb. 17, 1968 (dec. Jan. 1991); 1 child, Jack Ross. BA, U. Pitts., 1953. Asst. sales mgr. Berney Bros., Johnstown, 1953-67; mgr. spl. projects Credit Bur., Inc., Pitts., 1968; contr. Jack H. Samuels & Co., Pitts., 1969-70; pres., chief exec. officer W.S. Ponton, Inc., Pitts., 1970—. Contbr. articles to profl. jours. and newspapers. Mem. Direct Mktg. Assn., Smaller Mfrs. Assn., Better Bus. Bur., Direct Mktg. Club N.Y., United Comml. Travelers, Travelers Protection Assn., Pitt Varsity Letter Club, Kiwanis, Rotary, Masons, Shriners, Moose, Elks. Republican. Jewish. Home: 1414 Hawthorne St Pittsburgh PA 15201

RABINOWITZ, JOSEPH LOSHAK, biochemist, educator; b. Odessa, Ukraine, Nov. 4, 1923; came to U.S. 1940, derivative citizen; s. Laib J. and Rachel (Loshak) R.; m. Josephine G. Feldmark, June 23, 1946; children—Malva, Lois, Martin. B.Sc., Poly. Nat. de Mexico, 1939; B.Sc., Phila. Coll. Pharmacy and Sci., 1943; M.Sc., U. Pa., 1948, Ph.D., 1950; hon. doctorate U. Bordeaux, France, 1979. Chief radioisotope research VA Hosp., Phila., 1953—; prof. biochemistry U. Pa., Phila., 1970—, assoc. prof., 1963-70, asst. dean basic scis. Sch. Dental Medicine, 1980-83; cons. in field. Author: (with R. Myerson) Medicinal Chemistry, 1967-71; (with G. Chase), Radioisotope Methodology, 1954. Contbr. articles to profl. jours. Served with U.S. Army, 1943-46. Decorated Silver medal for research, Bordeaux, France, 1973, Brass medal for research, Nancy, France, 1975; Fulbright prof., Copenhagen, 1957. Fellow Am. Inst. Chemists; mem. Am. Soc. Biol. Chemistry. Republican. Jewish. Avocation: collecting books of owls. Office: Radioisotope Research VA Hosp 39th and Woodland Ave Philadelphia PA 19104

RABINOWITZ, MAYER ELYA, educator, librarian; b. N.Y.C., Jan. 31, 1939; s. Simcha Rabinowitz and Dvora (Resnikoff) Masovetsky; m. Renah Lee Levine, June 16, 1965; children: Adi, Dalya, Ayelet. BA, BHL, Yeshiva U., 1960, MA, 1961; MHL, Jewish Theol. Sem., 1965, PhD, 1974. Ordained rabbi, 1967. Instr. Jewish Theol. Sem., N.Y.C., 1970-74, asst. prof., 1974-76, dean students Tchrs. Inst., 1974-76, from assoc. dean to dean Grad. Sch., 1976-88, assoc. prof., 1976—, libr., 1988—; mem. com. on Jewish law and standards Rabbinical Assembly, N.Y.C., 1978—; chair Joint Bet Din Conservative Movement, N.Y.C., 1990—. Author: Sefer Hamordekhai Giftin, 1990; contbr. articles to profl. jours. Mem. Assn. Jewish Studies, Assn. Jewish Librs. Office: Jewish Theol Sem 3080 Broadway New York NY 10027

RABINOWITZ, MICHAEL ABRAHAM, clothing executive; b. Cape Town, Cape, South Africa, Jan. 3, 1940; s. Harry and Rachel (Zeldin) R.; m. Annie Regine Drukier (div.); children: Natalie Raymonde, Stephanie Miriam. Grad. high sch., Cape Town, Rep. South Africa, 1955. Mng. dir. M.A. Rabinowitz & Co. Ltd., Johannesburg, Rep. South Africa, 1966-76; chief exec. officer M.A. Rabinowitz Corp, Bridgewater, Conn., 1976—, Publicis Advt., Inc., N.Y.C., 1978—; importer french lingerie, Lejaby, France, 1976, Le Bourget, France, 1977, Huit, France, 1986, Huber, Austria, 1991. Creator racer back bras, 1984; pub. French Bra catalog, 1987. Republican. Jewish. Club: Vertical (N.Y.C.). Office: Rte 67 PO Box 309 Bridgewater CT 06752

RABON, RONALD RAY, retail jewelry store chain executive; b. Dothan, Ala., Apr. 27, 1955; s. Billy R. and Mary E. (Bruner) R.; m. E. Marie Hall, Oct. 25, 1974 (div. Sept. 1985); 1 child, Courtney Marie; m. Sheri L. Smith, Dec. 28, 1989. AS, Wallace Community Coll., Dothan, 1975. Cert. in diamond grading and evaluation Gemologist Inst. Am. Payroll clk., ironworker Daniels Constrn., Dothan, 1973-75; estate planner R&R Ins. Agy., Dothan, 1975-76; v.p. merchandising Wilbro Co. Inc., Dothan, 1976-84; owner, pres. Courtney's Jewelers Inc., Dothan, 1984-87, Knight Detective Agy., Dothan, 1986-88; sr. merchandiser Reliable Stores Inc., Columbia, Md., 1988-89; dir. merchandising Glennpeter Jewelers, Schenectady, 1989-91, v.p. merchandising, 1991-92, sr. v.p. adminstrn., 1992—. Lt. gov. Ala. dist. Circle K Interntat., 1974-75, gov., 1975-76. Recipient awards U.S. Jaycees, Circle K Internat. Mem. Nat. Assn. Jewelry Appraisers (charter). Republican. Baptist. Home: 1700 Western Ave Apt 512 Albany NY 12203-4327 Office: Glennpeter Jewelers 108 Erie Blvd Schenectady NY 12305-2203

RABOSKY, JOSEPH GEORGE, engineering consulting company executive; b. Sewickley, Pa., May 20, 1944; s. Mary Helen (Mayer) Rabosky; m. Suzanne Lazzelle, Aug. 23, 1969. BS, Pa. State U., 1966; MS in Engring., W.Va. U., 1969, MSCE, 1973; PhD, U. Pitts., 1984. Project engr. Chester Engrs., Coraopolis, Pa., 1969-70; project mgr. Calgon Corp., Pitts., 1970-73, sect. leader, 1979-85, mktg. mgr., 1985-86; sr. environ. specialist Mobay Chem. Corp., Pitts., 1975-79; project engr. Morris Knowles, Inc., Pitts., 1973-74; project mgr. Penn Environ. Cons., 1974-75; engring. mgr. Baker/TSA, Inc., Pitts., 1986-89; mgr. Chester Engrs., Pitts., 1989-92; prin. AquaTerra, Inc., Harmony, Pa., 1992—; adj. prof. U. Pitts., 1985-88, Pa. State U.-Beaver, McKeesport and New Kensington campuses, 1985—. Bd. dirs. Moon Twp. Mcpl. Authority, 1980-89. Mem. NSPA, Pa. Soc. Profl. Engrs. (sec., bd. dirs. 1989-90), Am. Acad. Environ. Engrs. (diplomate), Water Pollution Control Fedn., Water Pollution Control Assn. Pa. (chmn. rsch. com. 1984-89, 91—, mem. program com. 1984-89), Western Pa. Water Pollution Control Assn. (officer), Internat. Water Conf. (mem. exec. bd. 1989—). Home: 104 Wynview Rd Coraopolis PA 15108-1033

RABOY, DAVID GEOFFREY, economist; b. Chgo., Mar. 13, 1952; s. Sol and Marguerite (Marvin) R.; m. Cathay Lee Bomar, Oct. 22, 1987; 1 child, David Geoffrey Jr. BA in Econs., SUNY, Buffalo, 1978; MA in Econs., George Washington U., 1981, PhD in Econs., 1986. Assoc. dir. tax analysis Nat. Assn. Mfrs., Washington, 1979-81; exec. dir. Inst. Rsch. on Econs. of Taxation, Washington, 1981-83; legis. dir. Senator William V. Roth, Washington, 1983-86; chief econ. cons. Patton, Boggs & Blow, Washington, 1986—. Author, editor: Essays in Supply Side Economics, 1982, The Value-Added Tax: Orthodoxy and New Thinking, 1989; contbr. articles on econ. policy to profl. jours. Mem. Am. Econs. Assn., Nat. Tax Assn., Tax Inst. Am., Nat. Assn. Bus. Economists (pres. nat. capital chpt. 1984), Omicron Delta Epsilon. Office: Patton Boggs & Blow 2550 M St NW Washington DC 20037-1301

RABUFFO, JEFFREY VINCENT, urologist; b. Bklyn., June 16, 1939; s. Vincent Michael and Bernadette (Terhune) R.; m. Judith Moore, Aug. 11, 1963 (div. Feb. 1990); children: Paul, Mark, Courtney. B.S., Georgetown U., 1961, MD, 1965. Lic. physician, Va., Conn.; diplomate Am. Bd. Urology. Intern Mercy Hosp., Buffalo, 1968-69; resident gen. surgery Porvidence Hosp., Washington, 1968-69; resident urology Georgetown U., Washington, 1969-73; v.p. Middletown (Conn.) Surg. Group, 1976—; pres. med. staff Middlesex Hosp., Middletown, 1980-82; mng. ptnr. Kaimar Realty, Middletown, 1985—; pres. Conn. Surgicenter Inc., Middletown, 1985—; sr. attending physician sect. urology dept. surgery Middlesex Hosp.; assoc. physician dept. surgery div. urology U. Conn. Health Ctr.; mem. staff Rocky Hill Vets. Hosp., Elmcrest Psychiat. Inst., Student Health Svcs., Wesleyan U.; assoc. mem. dept. surgery U. Conn. Health Ctr.; clin. instr. dept. surgery U. Conn.; mng. ptnr. Middletown Profl. Park Ltd. Partnership I, II; med. bus. cons. Cromwell Imaging Ctr. Regional chmn. Lt. Gov.'s State Com. for U. Conn. for devel. Noether chair in Italian history. Named Physician of Yr., Family Practice Residency Program, Middlesex Hosp., Middletown, 1989. Fellow ACS; mem. AMA, Am. Urol. Assn., Conn. State Med. Soc., Middlesex County Med. Soc. Home: Skunk Misery Rd Higganum CT 06441-4435 Office: Middletown Surg Group 520 Saybrook Rd Middletown CT 06457-4700

RACHLIN, STEPHEN LEONARD, psychiatrist; b. N.Y.C., Mar. 6, 1939; s. Murray and Sophie (Rodnitsky) R.; m. Florence Einsidler, Nov. 22, 1962; children: Michael Ira, Robert Alan. BA, NYU, 1959; MD, Albert Einstein Coll. Medicine, 1963. Diplomate Nat. Bd. Med. Examiners, Am. Bd. Forensic Psychiatry, Am. Bd. Psychiatry and Neurology. Internship UCLA, 1963-64; resident, chief resident in psychiatry Mt. Sinai Hosp., N.Y., 1964-67; staff psychiatrist Bronx Psychiat. Ctr., Bronx, N.Y., 1969-72; asst. chief svc. Bronx Psychiat. Ctr., 1970-72, chief svc., 1972-74; dep. dir. Meyer-Manhattan Psychiat. Ctr., N.Y.C., 1974-76; acting dir. Meyer-Manhattan Psychiat. Ctr., 1976-77; dep. dir. Manhattan Psychiat. Ctr., N.Y.C., 1977; clin. dir. dept. psychiatry & psychology Nassau County Med. Ctr., E. Meadow, N.Y., 1978-80; assoc. chmn. dept. psychiatry & psychology Nassau County Med. Ctr., 1979-80, chmn. dept. psychiatry & psychology, 1980—; assoc. prof. clin. psychiatry sch. medicine SUNY, Stony Brook, 1978-87, prof. clin. psychiatry, 1987—; spl. prof. law sch. law Hofstra U., Hempstead, N.Y., 1983—. Editor in chief Psychiat. Quar., 1990—; contbr. articles to profl. jours. Lt. comdr. USNR, 1967-69. Mem. Am. Psychiat. Assn. (chmn. com. on adminstrv. psychiatry 1987—, assembly rep. 1991—), N.Y. State Psychiat. Assn. (chmn. com. on pub. psychiatry 1986—), Am. Assn. Psychiat. Adminstrs. (pres. 1989-90), Am. Acad. Psychiatry and the Law (pres. tri-state chpt. 1988-90), Am. Assn. Gen. Hosp. Psychiatrists (pres. elect 1991—), Am. Bd. Forensic Psychiatry (dir. 1990—, treas. 1992—), Am. Hosp. Assn. (governing coun. sect. for psychiat. and substance abuse 19910—), Hosp. Assn. of N.Y. State (chmn. com. on mental health svcs. 1992—). Office: Nassau County Med Ctr Dept Psychiatry and Psychology 2201 Hempstead Tpke East Meadow NY 11554-5400

RACHOW, LOUIS A(UGUST), librarian; b. Shickley, Nebr., Jan. 21, 1927; s. John Louis and Mable (Dondlinger) R. B.S., York Coll., 1948; M.S. in L.S., Columbia U., 1959. Librarian York Coll., Nebr., 1949-54; instr. library asst. Queens Coll., N.Y.C., 1956-57; serials acquisition asst. Columbia U. Law Library, N.Y.C., 1957-58; asst. librarian Univ. Club, N.Y.C., 1958-62; librarian Hampden-Booth Theatre Library at the Players, N.Y.C., 1962-86, curator, 1986-88; library dir. Internat. Theatre Inst. U.S., N.Y.C., 1989—; cons. theatre sect. U. Calif., San Diego, new campuses program, 1964, Music Ctr. Operating Archives, Los Angeles, 1985; mem. library adv. bd. Eugene O'Neill Meml. Theatre Center, 1966—. Editor, compiler: Guide to Performing Arts, 1968; assoc. editor Am. Notes and Queries, 1971-74, asst. editor, 1967-71; mem. editorial adv. bd. Nat. Dir. for Performing Arts and Civic Ctrs.; editor Performing Arts series Gale Info. Guide, 1976-83, Theatre and Performing Arts Collections, 1981; contbr. articles and revs. to profl. jours. Mem. adv. bd. Am. Theatre Co., OKC Theatre Prodns. Served with AUS, 1954-56. Mem. Theatre Library Assn. (rec. sec. 1966-67, pres. 1967-72, 81-83, v.p. 1976-80, editor Broadside 1973-81), ALA, Spl. Libraries Assn. (sec.-treas. mus. group N.Y.C. chpt. 1964-66), N.Y. Library Club (pres. 1979-80), Am. Theatre Assn., ANTA, New Drama Forum Assn. (pres. 1983-86), Am. Soc. Theatre Research, N.Y. Tech. Services Librarians (sec. Kelcey Allen award com. 1968), Archons of Colophon (convener 1982-83), Episcopal Actors Guild (bd. dirs. 1976—). Club: Players. Home: 528 W 114th St New York NY 10025-7841 Office: Internat Theatre Inst/US 220 W 42nd St New York NY 10036-7211

RADDER, JOSEPH HENRY, advertising executive; b. Buffalo, May 11, 1920; s. Alvah Humphrey and Mabel Eva (Smith) R.; m. Marguerite Scudder, Oct. 14, 1943 (dec. Mar. 1982); children: Joel A., Jon E. Student, U. Buffalo, 1942; PhD (hon.), Medaille Coll., 1976. Creative dir. Baldwin Bowers & Strachan, Buffalo, 1945-57, The Rumrill Co., Buffalo, 1957-62; exec. v.p., pres. Comstock Advt., Inc., Buffalo, 1975-79; v.p. Healy, Schutte & Comstock, Buffalo, 1980-82; freelance writer Ft. Lauderdale, Fla., 1983-84; pres. Joseph H. Radder Mktg., Williamsville, N.Y., 1984—. Mem. com. Citizens Rapid Transit Com., Buffalo, 1985—. Tech. sgt. U.S. Army, 1942-45. Recipient Silver medal Am. Advt. Fedn., 1976. Mem. Profl. Communicators of N.Y., Niagara Frontier Advt. Assn. (pres. Buffalo chpt. 1976). Republican. Roman Catholic. Office: 8420 Main St Buffalo NY 14221-5894

RADER, DENNIS, strategic technology consultant, educator; b. N.Y.C., Sept. 12, 1940; s. Everett and Rebecca (Kefer) R.; m. Barbara Ann Ray, July 16, 1967; children: Sharon, Michael. BCE, The Cooper Union, 1961; ScM, Brown U., 1963, PhD, 1966. Postdoctoral fellow engring. Brown U., Providence, 1966-67; asst. prof. engring. & applied sci. Yale U., New Haven, 1967-71, assoc. prof., 1971-73; sr. rsch. project engr. Schlumberger Rsch., Ridgefield, Conn., 1973-78; mgr. engring. physics NL Industries, Houston, 1978-80; v.p. rsch., devel. & engring. Teleco, Meriden, Conn., 1980-87; pres. Triad Group, Woodbridge, Conn., 1987—; adj. prof. mech. engring. Yale U., New Haven, 1989—; vice-chmn. Tech. & Mfg. Coun., New Haven, 1989—; bd. dirs. Mfg. Assocs. New Haven County, 1989—. Patentee for Percussion Method & Apparatus for the Investigation of Casing Cement in a Borehole; contbr. chpts. to books. Chmn. spl. awards com. Conn. Sci. Fair Assn., 1987-90; mem. nominating com. Nat. Sci. Scholars Program, Conn., 1991—. Mem. ASME, Am. Mgmt. Assn. Home: 11 Fraser Dr Woodbridge CT 06525-1428 Office: Triad Group 264 Amity Rd # 210 Woodbridge CT 06525-2200

RADER, NANCY LOUISE DE VILLIERS, psychology educator, consultant; b. Danbury, Conn., May 21, 1948; d. Martin Anthony and Elsie Concetta (Lauricella) R.; m. David Strutt de Villiers, Sept. 6, 1975; 1 child, Alyssa Jane. AB magna cum laude, Smith Coll., 1970; PhD, Cornell U., 1976. Asst. prof. psychology UCLA, 1974-82, dir. Infant and Child Lab., 1979-82, scholar Found. for Child Devel., 1982-83, postdoctoral fellow, rsch. psychologist Neuropsychiat. Inst., 1983-84; vis. scholar Cornell U., Ithaca, N.Y., 1979, rsch. assoc., 1984-85; asst. prof. Ithaca Coll., 1985-90, assoc. prof., 1990—. Contbr. articles to profl. jours., chpts. to books. Bd. dirs. Coddington Community Ctr., Ithaca, 1991—. Fellow NDEA, 1968, 71-74, Ford Found., 1970-74; grantee NIMH, 1982. Mem. APA, Am. Psychol. Soc., Soc. for Rsch. in Child Devel., Internat. Soc. for Study Behavioral Devel., Internat. Soc. for Ecol. Psychology, Ea. Psychol. Assn., Sigma Xi (pres. Ithaca Coll. chpt. 1988-89), Phi Kappa Phi. Home: 201 Eastman Hill Rd Willseyville NY 13864-9711 Office: Ithaca Coll Psychology Dept Ithaca NY 14850

RADER, RANDALL RAY, judge; b. 1949. BA magna cum laude, 1974; JD with honors, George Washington U., 1978. Bar: D.C., U.S. Ct. Appeals (fed. cir.) 1990, U.S. Claims Ct., U.S. Supreme Ct. Legis. asst. to Congresswoman Virginia Smith U.S. Ho. of Reps., 1975-78; mem. staff Ways and Means Com. U.S. Ho. Reps., 1978-81; chief counsel subcom. on Constn. U.S. Senate Judiciary Com., chief counsel, staff dir. subcom. on patents, copyrights and trademarks, 1981-87; counsel to Senator Orrin Hatch, 1981-87; judge U.S. Ct. Claims, Washington, 1988-90, U.S. Ct. Appeals (fed. cir.), Washington, 1990—. Contbr. articles to profl. jours.; co-editor: Criminal Justice Reform, 1983. Mem. Fed. Bar Assn. Office: US Ct Appeals Fed Cir 717 Madison Pl NW Ste 913 Washington DC 20439-0002

RADER, RHODA CASWELL, academic program director; b. St. Johnsbury, Vt., July 2, 1945; d. Wilbur Forrest and Aline Emma (Langevin) Caswell; m. William Garrett Rader, May 10, 1969; children: Lorelei May, Peter William, Lisa Anne. Diploma with highest honors, Albany Bus. Coll., 1966; AA with highest distinction, Community Coll. Vt., 1987; BSBA summa cum laude, Trinity Coll., 1987. Asst. comptroller Middlebury (Vt.) Coll., 1980-84, budget dir., 1984—. Mem. Nat. Assn. Accts., Nat. Assn. Coll. and Univ. Bus. Dirs., Nat. Identification Program for Women in Higher Edn. (instl. rep.), Vt. Higher Ednl. Planning Commn. (instl. rep.), Nat. Assn. Female Execs. Office: Middlebury Coll Middlebury VT 05753

RADFORD, GARY PAUL, communication educator; b. Sutton-in-Ashfield, Nottingham, Eng., Dec. 13, 1961; came to U.S., 1986; s. Howard and Elsie May (Ball) R.; m. Marie Louise Hein, June 17, 1989; 1 child, Meg Kathleen. BA, Sheffield (Eng.) Poly., 1983; MS, So. Ill. U., 1984; PhD, Rutgers U., 1991. Lectr. Sheffield City Poly., 1984-86; instr. Rutgers U., New Brunswick, N.J., 1989-90; asst. prof. William Paterson Coll., Wayne, N.J., 1990—. Author: Communication and Human Behavior-Instructors Manual, 1988; editor N.J. Jour. Communication. Mem. Speech Communication Assn., Internat. Communication Assn., Eastern Communication Assn., Fla. Communication Assn. Episcopalian. Office: William Paterson Coll 300 Pompton Rd Wayne NJ 07470-2103

RADFORD, KENNETH CHARLES, ceramic engineer; b. Manchester, England, July 1, 1941; came to the U.S., 1968; s. Frederick Owen and Evelyn Vivien (James) R.; m. Janice Ann Radford; children: Amanda, Joanna, Celia. BS in Metallurgy, Imperial Coll. London U., 1963, PhD in Metallurgy, 1967. Rsch. staff Imperial Coll., 1966-68; sr. engr. Westinghouse R&D, Pitts., 1968-78, fellow engr., 1978-83, adv. engr., 1983-84, mgr., 1984—. Contbr. articles to profl. jours.; patentee in field. Mem. Am. Ceramic Soc., Instn. Metallurgists, Metals Soc. Office: Westinghouse Sci & Tech Ctr 1310 Beulah Rd Pittsburgh PA 15235-5098

RADIGAN, FRANK XAVIER, pharmaceutical company executive; b. Paterson, N.J., Apr. 13, 1933; John Joseph and Susan Clair (Brett) R.; m. Julia Lou Smith, Aug. 27, 1960 (div. Nov. 1988); children: Francis Gregory, Patricia Louise, Brett Frasier. AB in Sociology, Seton Hall U., 1955; MBA Mktg., U. Hartford, 1968. Asst. mgr. Beneficial Fin. Co., Newark, 1955-57; hosp. rep. Becton-Dickinson Co., Rutherford, N.J., 1957-58; dist. mgr. Merck Sharp & Dohme, West Point, Pa., 1958—. Chmn. St. John the Baptist Social Justice, New Freedom, Pa., 1981-85; mem. Passaic County Dem. Com., 1985-86. Capt. USAR, 1956. Mem. Am. Mktg. Assn., Md. Pharmacists Assn. (chmn. indsl. rels. com.), W.Va. Pharm. Soc., Balt. Pharm. Assn. (hon. pres. 1989), Hopewell Fish and Game Assn., Bon Air Country Club, Elk, Lion (pres. Glen Rock 1975-76, 86-88). Roman Catholic. Home and Office: 8130 Loch Raven Blvd Baltimore MD 21204-8305

RADNER, SIDNEY HOLLIS, retired rug company executive; b. Holyoke, Mass., Dec. 8, 1919; s. William I. Radner; m. Helen Jane Cohen, Dec. 12, 1946; children: William Marc, Richard Scott. Student, Yale U., 1941. Ret. pres. Am. Rug Co., Holyoke; lectr., cons., investigator crooked gambling, U.S. Armed Forces, FBI, gov. of Can., various state and mcpl. police vice squads; appearances in BBC film on Houdini as well as various TV shows, incl. "In Search of..."; leading collector and expert on Houdini, incl. nat. pub. TV appearance in "Houdini"; dir. Houdini Magical Hall of Fame, Niagara Falls, Ont., Can.; stockholder Am. Rug Co. Author: Radner on Poker, Radner on Dice, Radner on Roulette and Casino Games, How to Detect Card Sharks; contbr. articles to profl. jours. Past pres. Holyoke C. of C.; co-founder Volleyball Hall of Fame; bd. dirs. Greater Springfield (Mass.) Better Bus. Bur. (past bd. dirs.); hon. curator, dir. Houdini Hist. Ctr., Appleton, Wis. Served with criminal investigation div. U S. Army, 1942-46. Mem. Soc. Am. Magicians (occult investigation com.), Internat. Brotherhood Magicians, Magic Circle (assoc. inner circle London chpt.), Magicians Guild (charter), Magic Collector's Assn. (charter, Honor award 1992), Am. Platform Assn., Houdini Club of Wis. (hon.), Nat. Assn. Bunco Investigators, Rotary, Mason, Shriners. Jewish. Home: 1050 Northampton St Holyoke MA 01040-1321 Office: 1594 Dwight St Holyoke MA 01040-2397

RADOMISLI, MICHEL, psychologist; b. Istanbul, Turkey, Dec. 29, 1931; came to U.S., 1957; s. Hirsch and Sol (Leon) R.; children: Gregory, Timothy. BS, Robert Coll., Istanbul, 1951; AM, Columbia U., 1958; PhD, NYU, 1962. Clin. coord. Lincoln Inst. for Psychotherapy, N.Y.C., 1962-65; pvt. practice N.Y.C., 1964—; asst. clin. prof. Albert Einstein Coll. of Medicine, N.Y.C., 1968-76; assoc. clin. prof. Med. Coll. Cornell U., N.Y.C., 1976—; Lic. psychologist, N.Y. Author chpt. in book; reviewer various jours.; contbr. articles to profl. jours. Eugene Higgins fellow Columbia U., 1957-58, Rockefeller Found. fellow, 1958-62. Fellow Am. Bd. Med. Psychotherapists; mem. APA, N.Y. State Psychol. Assn. Office: 55 E End Ave New York NY 10028

RADWAY, DEBORAH BROOKE, assistant town manager; b. Hanover, N.H., Nov. 5, 1956; d. Laurence Ingram and Patricia Ann (Headland) R. BA in Am. Studies, Smith Coll., 1979. Mng. dir. Mohawk Trail Chamber Music Festival, Greenfield, Mass., 1980-83; adminstrv. asst. Town of Northfield, Mass., 1983-86, Towns of Erving, Warwick, Wendell, Mass., 1984-88; asst. town mgr. Town of Lexington, Mass., 1988—; pres., bd. dirs. Pioneer Valley Folklore Soc., Inc., Northampton, Mass., 1980-84; coord. Circuit Riders Assn. of Mass., Northfield, 1986-87. Editor: (monthly newsletter) Pioneer Valley Folklore Soc., 1980-82, (publs.) Mohawk Trail Chamber Festival, 1980-83; music reviewer: (daily newspaper) Daily Hampshire Gazette, 1981. Chmn. Northampton (Mass.) Coun. for the Arts, 1980-81; exec. com. Franklin County Solid Waste Dist., Greenfield, Mass., 1986-87; commr. Montague (Mass.) Civic Ctr. Commn., 1986-91. Mem. Internat. City Mgmt. Assn. (cert. in mgmt.), Mass. Mcpl. Assn., Mass. Mcpl. Mgmt. Assn. (nominating com. 1990—, legis. com. 1988-90). Democrat. Office: Town of Lexington 1625 Massachusetts Ave Lexington MA 02173-3801

RADYCKI, DIANE JOSEPHINE, art historian, writer; b. Chgo., Dec. 4, 1946; d. Casimir Constantine and Sophie Jeanette (Wilczynski) R. BA, U. Ill., 1969; MA, Hunter Coll., 1975; MA, Harvard U., 1983, now PhD candidate. Research assoc. Met. Mus. Art, N.Y.C., 1980-81; teaching fellow Harvard U., Cambridge, Mass., 1984-85, 87—; intern Busch-Reisinger Mus., Cambridge, 1984-85; guest-curator Fogg Mus., Cambridge, 1983, 87, 88. Transl. editor: Letters and Journals of Paula Modersohn-Becker, 1980. Agnes Mongan fellow, 1982-84, Fulbright fellow, 1989-91. Fellow AAUW; mem. Coll. Art Assn. Office: Harvard U Fine Arts Dept Cambridge MA 02138

RAE, PETER MURDOCH MACPHAIL, molecular biologist, biotechnologist; b. Alexandria, Scotland, Jan. 7, 1944; came to U.S., 1949; s. Peter MacPhail and Helen (Murdoch) R.; m. Margaret Elizabeth Engel, Mar. 28, 1971; 1 child, Andrew Murdoch. AB, U. Calif., Davis, 1965, MA, 1966; PhD, U. Chgo., 1970. Lectr. Harvard U., Cambridge, Mass., 1970-71; postdoctoral fellow Max-Planck Inst., Tübingen, Germany, 1971-73; asst. prof. Yale U., New Haven, 1973-76, assoc. prof., 1976-83; sr. rsch. scientist Molecular Diagnostics, Inc. (name now Miles Rsch. Ctr.), West Haven, Conn., 1983-85; prin. staff scientist (name now Miles Rsch. Ctr.) Molecular Diagnostics, Inc., West Haven, Conn., 1985-90; del. scientist Bayer AG, Wuppertal, Germany, 1990-92; sect. head Inst. for Molecular Biols., Miles Rsch. Ctr., West Haven, Conn., 1992—. Rsch. grantee NSF, NIH. Office: Miles Rsch Ctr 400 Morgan Ln West Haven CT 06516-4175

RAE, ROBERT KEITH, politician; b. Ottawa, Ont., Can., Aug. 2, 1948; s. Saul Forbes and Lois Esther (George) R.; m. Arlene Perly, Feb. 23, 1980; children: Judith Florence, Lisa Ruth, Eleanor Grace. BA, U. Toronto, Ont., 1969, LLB, 1977; BPhil, Oxford U., 1971. Bar: Ont. 1980. M.P. from Broadview-Greenwood dist. Ho. of Commons, 1978-82, fin. spokeman New Dem. Party, 1979-82; mem. for York South, provincial legislature Ont., 1982-90, leader official opposition, 1987-90; premier Province of Ont., Toronto, 1990—; spl. lectr. in indsl. rels. U. Toronto, 1976-77. Contbr. articles on law and politics to profl. jours. Mem. com. on univ. govt. U. Toronto, 1968-69; community worker London, Eng., 1973-74; extensive legal aid and community worker, Toronto, 1974—; asst. to Can. gen. counsel United Steelworkers Am., 1975-77; vice chmn. Can.-U.S. Interparliamentary Group, 1979-82. Rhodes scholar Oxford U., 1971. Office: Parliament Bldgs, Office of Premier, Toronto, ON Canada M7A 1A2

RAFAEL, OTALORA, computer scientist, consultant; b. Bogota, Colombia, June 21, 1955; came to U.S., 1984; s. Jorge and Josefina (Cadavid) O.; m. Maria Teresa Revollo, Aug. 9, 1991. BS in Indsl. Engring., U. Los Andes, Bogota, 1978, MS in Systems Engring., 1979; MS in Computer Sci., Pa. State U., 1987. Programmer U. Los Andes, 1979-80, dir. projects, 1980-84; programmer/analyst Pa. State U., University Park, 1985-87; project engr. Systems Modeling Corp., Pitts., 1988-91, sr. project engr., 1991-92; sr. programmer Cybernetics Systems Internat., Miami, Fla., 1992—. Home: 11853 SW 12th St Pembroke Pines FL 33025 Office: Cybernetics Systems Internat 2600 Douglas Rd Ste 700 Coral Gables FL 33134

RAFALOWSKI, JANICE ANN, psychologist, educator; b. Trenton, N.J., Nov. 5, 1950; d. Walter and Josephine (Juliano) R.; m. Arthur Lincoln Mahony, June 26, 1976; children: Ryan Walter, Colin Raymund. BA magna cum laude, U. Md., 1972; MA, Fairleigh Dickinson, 1974; PhD, New Sch. for Social Rsch., 1982. Student asst. Greystone Park Psychiat. Hosp., Morris Plains, N.J., 1972-74; clin. intern Inst. for Psycho-Integrity, Mount Freedom, N.J., 1984-85; prof. psychology County Coll. Morris, Randolph, N.J., 1976—; clin. cons. Morris County Prosecutor's Office, Morristown, N.J., 1984, Badische Analin Soda Fabriken, Parsippany, N.J., 1984-85. Mem. substance abuse edn. com. County Coll. of Morris, Randolph, 1988-90, alcohol and drug adv. com. Morris County, Morristown, N.J., 1990-91. Recipient Fed. Tuition grant New Sch. for Social Rsch., 1974-82. Mem. APA, NEA, N.J. Edn. Assn., Faculty Assn. County Coll. Morris, Phi Beta Kappa. Home: 5 Philips Manor Towaco NJ 07082 Office: County College of Morris Rt 10 and Center Grove Rd Randolph NJ 07869

RAFETTO, JOHN, podiatrist; b. Phila., Mar. 29, 1950; s. Willard John and Anne (Brumbaugh) R.; m. Eleni Mallas, Dec. 5, 1987; children: Dominic Giovanni, Gianna Maria. BS, Pa. State U., 1974; postgrad., Ceux Sch. Medicine, Cuernavaca, Mex., 1977-79; D Podiatric Medicine, Ohio Coll. Podiatric Medicine, 1984. Diplomate Am. Bd. Podiatric Surgery. Resident Parkview Hosp., Phila., 1984-86; pvt. practice Paoli, Pa., 1986—. Mem. ACD, Am. Podiatric Med. Assn., Am. Diabetic Assn. Office: 1440 Russell Rd Ste 204 Paoli PA 19301-1252

RAFFERTY, JENNIFER LEE, English educator; b. Bridgeport, Conn., Sept. 20, 1960; d. Anthony Colette and Shirley Jean (Sabo) Zaccara; m. John Powell Rafferty, Aug. 8, 1981; children: Bryce John, Keefe Wynn. BA in English, Trinity Coll., 1982, MA in English, 1984; PhD in English, U. Conn., 1991. Tchr. English Sacred Heart, Greenwich, Conn., 1982-84, Rye (N.Y.) Country Day Sch., 1984-86, Avon (Conn.) High Sch., 1987; teaching asst. U. Conn., Storrs, 1990; vis. prof. English Trinity Coll., Hartford, Conn., 1992—. Mem. MLA, Am. Lit. Assn., Mark Twain Cir. Am., Mark Twain Meml. Republican. Mem. Congregational Ch. Home: 18 Pelham Rd West Hartford CT 06107-2718

RAFTERY, WILLIAM A., management consultant; b. N.Y.C., Sept. 11, 1925; s. John J. and Clara A. (Martino) R.; m. Vivian A. Moncton, Aug. 29, 1953; children: Donna Lynn, Linda Leighanne. BA in Econs., Tufts U., 1948; MBA, NYU, 1952. V.p. mktg. Signal-Stat Corp., Bklyn., 1948-62; exec. v.p. Surelock Mgmt. Co., Newark, 1956-62; pres. Technorm Corp., Linden, N.J., 1954-62, Motor and Equipment Mgmt. Assn., Englewood Cliffs, N.J., 1962-91, Raftery Cons., Alpine, N.J., 1991—; dir. Am. Soc. Assn. Execs., Washington, 1982-86, Maval Mgt. Co., Twinsburg, Ohio, 1991. 1st lt. USN, 1943-46.

RAGAZZO, ANTHONY, JR., university administrator; b. Hackensack, N.J., Aug. 20, 1967; s. Anthony Sr. and Lorraine (Fecile) R. BA, Am. U., 1989, MA, 1991. Asst. to dir. student activities The Am. U., Washington, 1988-89, asst. conduct coun. adminstr., 1989-90, acting conduct coun. adminstr., 1990-91; conduct coun. adminstr., 1991—. Mem. Assn. Counseling and Devel., Assn. Student Jud. Affairs, Am. Coll. Personnel Assn., Nat. Assn. Student Personnel Adminstrs. Home: 3040 Idaho Ave NW # 707 Washington DC 20016-5436 Office: Am U Office of Dean of Students Washington DC 20016

RAGGI, REENA, federal judge; b. Jersey City, May 11, 1951. BA, Wellesley Coll., 1973; JD, Harvard U., 1976. Bar: N.Y. 1977. U.S. atty. Dept. Justice, Bklyn., 1986; ptnr. Windels, Marx, Davies & Ives, N.Y.C., 1987; judge U.S. Dist. Ct. (ea. dist.) N.Y., Bklyn., 1987—. Office: US Courthouse 225 Cadman Pla E Brooklyn NY 11201

RAGGIO, WILLIAM GERARD, management consultant; b. Bklyn., July 28, 1956; s. Robert Anthony and Marie Louise (Schaal) R. BA, Wake Forest U., 1978. Head teller L.I. Trust Co., Old Westbury, N.Y., 1978-81; mgr. Edgewood Hotel, Old Westbury, 1981-83; asst. mgr. control dept. Joint Computer Ctr., Mineola, N.Y., 1983-85; assoc. SKP Assocs., N.Y.C., 1985—; asst. mng. agt. Book Industry Study Group, N.Y., 1987—. Contbr. articles to profl. jours. Mem. Book Industry Systems Adv. Com. (rec. sec. 1987-91), Serials Industry Systems Adv. Com., Women's Nat. Book Assn. (asst. mng. agt. 1987-91), Am. Book Producers Assn. (mng. agt.). Office: SKP Assocs 160 5th Ave New York NY 10010-7000

RAGIN, DEBORAH FISH, research psychologist, consultant; b. Cleve., Oct. 16, 1956; d. John and Juanita Marrietta (Brown) Fish; m. Luther M. Ragin Jr., June 8, 1984; 1 child, Renee Michelle. AB, Vassar Coll., 1978; MA, Harvard U., 1984, PhD, 1985. Higher sci. officer Econ. and Social Rsch. Coun., London, 1985; program asst. Bd. Coop. Ednl. Svcs. Nassau County, Carle Place, N.Y., 1986-87; rsch. coord. Rsch. Found. CUNY, N.Y.C., 1987-89; rsch. scientist N.Y. State Psychiat. Inst., N.Y.C., 1989-92; Aaron Diamond postdoctoral fellow Beth Israel Med. Ctr., Chem. Dependency Inst., N.Y.C., 1992—, rsch. fellow, 1992—; cons. in field. Contbr. articles to profl. publs. Bd. dirs. Ft. George Head Start Program, N.Y.C., 1989. Beinecke Found. fellow, 1977. Mem. Am. Psychol. Assn. Home: 160 Cabrini Blvd New York NY 10033-1137 Office: Beth Israel Med Ctr Chem Dependency Inst 55 E 34th St New York NY 10016

RAGIN, DEREK LEE, vocalist; b. New Burgh, N.Y., June 17, 1958; s. Henry R. (stepfather) and Ethen Yvonne (Young) Delaney. BM, Oberlin Conservatory, Ohio, 1980, MMT, 1980. Substitute tchr. Davidson County Pub. Schs., Nashville, 1980-81; counter tenor, 1982—. Counter-tenor with English Baroque Orch. and Monteverdi Choir in Salzburg, London and Stuttgart; debut with Met. Opera in Handel's Julius Caesar, 1988; sang role of David in Handel's Saul in Tel Aviv and Haifa, 1990; N.Y. recital debut at Met. Mus. Art, 1991. Recipient Purcell-Britten prize for Concert Singers, Aldeburgh Found., 1983, 1st prize 35th Internat. Music Competition of Munich, 1986, Spl. prize Jury of the Lyric Vocal Competition of Monte Carlo, Monaco, 1988. Home: 106 1/2 9th Ave Newark NJ 07107

RAGIN, LUTHER MACK, JR., financial executive; b. N.Y.C., Aug. 21, 1955; s. Luther M. Ragin and Jean (Blackwell) Carpenter; m. Deborah Fish, June 8, 1984; 1 child, Renee Michelle. AB, Harvard U., 1977, M in Pub. Policy, 1980. V.p. Chase Manhattan Bank, N.Y.C., 1981-89; chief fin. officer Earl G. Graves Ltd., N.Y.C., 1989—. Bd. dirs. Open Housing Ctr. of N.Y., N.Y.C., 1989—. Office: Earl G Graves Ltd 130 5th Ave New York NY 10011-4306

RAGINS, HERZL, surgeon, educator; b. Tel Aviv, July 27, 1929; came to U.S., 1929; s. Aaron and Ida (Kraus) R.; m. Karen Anderson, Sept. 16, 1979; 1 child, Jonathan Daly. BS, U. Ill., 1949; MS, MD, U. Ill., Chgo., 1951; PhD, U. Chgo., 1956. Intern Cook County Hosp., Chgo., 1951-52; surg. resident U. Chgo. Clinics, 1952-53, 55-60; gastrointestinal endoscopy fellowship Beth Israel Hosp., N.Y.C., 1972-73; clin. prof. surgery A. Einstein Coll. Medicine, Bronx, N.Y., 1973—. Contbr. articles to profl. jours. Capt. USAF, 1953-55, Korea. Mem. Am. Coll. Surgeons, Am. Soc. Gastrointestinal Endoscopy, Am. Gastroent. Assocs., Am. Physiol. Soc., Soc. Alimentary Tract Surgeons. Office: Med Office 1601 Tenbroecn Bronx NY 10401

RAGLE, JOHN LINN, chemistry educator; b. Colorado Springs, Colo., Feb. 4, 1933; s. Richard Charles and Jane Addams (Hulbert) R.; m. Roberta Ann Litzerman, July 26, 1990. BS, U. Calif., Berkeley, 1954; PhD, Wash. State U., 1957. Asst. prof. U. Mass., Amherst, 1957-60, assoc. prof., 1964-67, prof., 1968-75, 1976—; rsch. assoc. Cornell U., Ithaca, N.Y., 1960-62; scientist Northrop Space Labs., Hawthrone, Calif., 1962-64; vis. assoc. prof. U. B.C., Vancouver, Can., 1967-68; vis. prof. Technische Hochschule, Darmstadt, Fed. Republic Germany, 1975-76. Contbr. articles to profl. jours. Recipient Sr. U.S. Scientist award von Humboldt Stiftung, 1975. Mem. Am. Phys. Soc., Am. Chem. Soc. Republican. Office: U Mass Dept Chemistry Amherst MA 01003

RAGO, ROSALINDE TERESA, advertising executive; b. Trenton, N.J., Nov. 27, 1952; d. V. Frank and Rosella Eleanor (Salvate) R.; m. Richard Christian Lyman, Aug., 1974 (div. Sept. 1980). BA, Ithaca (N.Y.) Coll., 1974; PhD, Tulane U., 1981. Rsch. exec. Ogilvy & Mather, N.Y.C., 1981-83, v.p., dir. of rsch., 1987-90, sr. v.p., dir. advt., planning and rsch., 1990—; assoc. rsch. dir. J. Walter Thompson, N.Y.C., 1984-86; assoc. dir. internat. rsch. BBDO, N.Y.C., 1986-87; mem. copy rsch. coun. Advt. Rsch. Found., N.Y.C., 1987—. Mem. Am. Mktg. Assn. (career adv. coun. N.Y.C. chpt. 1987—), N.Y. Acad. Sci. Office: Ogilvy & Mather 309 W 49th St New York NY 10019-7316

RAGSDALE, JAMES MARCUS, editor; b. Turlock, Calif., July 24, 1938; s. George Alexander and Ruby Mabel (Thomas) R.; children: Marc, Meredith, David. BA, San Jose (Calif.) State Coll., 1961. Mng. editor Solano Rep., Fairfield, Calif., 1961-62; gen. assignment rep. Press Courier, Oxnard, Calif., 1962-64; reporter AP, Charleston, W.Va., 1964-67; corr. in charge AP, Spokane, Washington, 1967-68; news editor AP, Seattle, 1968-69; chief of bur. AP, Charleston, 1969-71, Boston, 1971-75; asst. to pub. The Standard-Times, New Bedford, Mass., 1975-76; editor The Standard-Times, New Bedford, 1976—; Pulitzer judge Pulitzer Prize, N.Y., 1986-87. Co-chmn. First Night New Bedford, 1987-88, pres., 1989-90; co-chmn. People's Celebration July 4th, 1986-89. Mem. Soc. Prof. Journalist (past pres. 1983-84), Acad. of New Eng. Journalist (Yankee Quill award 1988), Mass. Bar Assn. (co-chmn. bench bar press com. 1984-85). Office: Standard-Times Pub Co 555 Pleasant St New Bedford MA 02740-6257

RAHL, LESLIE LYNN, consultant, entrepreneur; b. N.Y.C., May 16, 1950; d. Myron and Esther (Botwin) Horwitz; m. Jeffrey Mark Lynn, Dec. 20, 1969 (div. 1981); m. J. Andrew Rahl Jr., Apr. 30, 1989; 1 child, Kevin; stepchildren: Kaitlin, Stephen. SB, MIT, 1971, MBA, 1972. V.p., dept. head Citibank, N.Y.C., 1972-91; pres. Leslie Rahl Assocs., N.Y.C., 1991—; bd. dirs. Internat. Swap Dealers Assn., N.Y.C., 1988-91; mem. task force WEIRD instruments. Contbr. articles to profl. jours. Bd. dirs., treas. 60 East End Ave. Assn., N.Y.C., 1986—. Recipient On the Rise award Fortune. Mem. Internat. Assn. Fin. Engrs. (adv. bd.), Madison Beach Club. Office: Leslie Rahl Assocs 60 East End Ave New York NY 10028

RAHM, DAVID ALAN, lawyer; b. Passaic, N.J., Apr. 18, 1941; s. Hans Emil and Alicia Katherine (Onuf) R.; m. Susan Eileen Berkman, Nov. 23, 1972; children: Katherine Berkman, William David. AB, Princeton U., 1962; JD, Yale U., 1965. Bar: N.Y. 1966, D.C. 1986. Assoc. Paul, Weiss, Rifkind & Wharton, N.Y.C., 1965-66, 1968-69; asst. counsel N.Y. State Urban Devel. Corp., N.Y.C., 1969-72, assoc. counsel, 1972-75; counsel real estate div. Internat. Paper Co., N.Y.C., 1975-80; ptnr. Stroock & Stroock & Lavan, N.Y.C., 1980-83, sr. ptnr., 1984—; mem. legis. com. Real Estate Bd. N.Y., 1988-92; lectr. Old Dominion Coll., Norfolk, Va., 1967-68, NYU, 1986—; mem. editorial bd. Comml. Leasing Law and Strategy, 1988—. Contbr. articles to profl. jours. Fund raiser corp. com. N.Y. Philharm, N.Y.C., 1980-84; trustee Manhattan Sch. Music, 1989—, treas., 1991—. Mem. ABA (comml. leasing com. 1987-88, pub./pvt. devel. com. 1989—, real property sect.), N.Y. State Bar Assn. (real property sect.), Assn. of Bar of City of N.Y. (housing and urban devel. com. 1977-80, 81-84, real property com. 1989-92), Princeton Club. Democrat. Presbyterian. Office: Stroock Stroock & Lavan 7 Hanover Sq New York NY 10004-2594

RAHMAN, ABU TAYEB RAFIQUR, United Nations official; b. Ashrafpur, Feni, Bangladesh, July 1, 1936; came to U.S., 1958; s. Abidur Rahman and Fatima Begum; m. Saleha Choudhury, Sept. 1, 1963; children: Farhana, Tamanna, Nashra. M Polit. Sci., Dacca U., 1956; MPA, Karachi U., 1958; PhD, Duke U., 1969. Expert in pub. adminstrn. Rural Devel. Acad., Comilla, Bangladesh; assoc. prof. polit. sci. Dacca (Bangladesh) U., 1969-71; assoc. dir. Internat. Devel. Rsch. Ctr., Ottawa, Ont., Can., 1971-80; sr. cons. Internat. Devel. Rsch. Ctr., Ottawa, Ont., 1971-72; sr. econ. affairs officer devel. adminstrn. div. UN, N.Y.C., 1981-88, chief div., 1989—. Pres. Bangladesh-Can. Soc., Ottawa, 1976, Deshantari Community Group, Ottawa, 1977. Mem. Bangladesh Polit. Sci. Assn., Bangladesh Devel. Forum, East Pakistan Polit. Sci. Assn. (sec. 1970). Home: 122 Taxter Rd Irvington NY 10533 Office: UN Devel Adminstrn Div DCI 964 New York NY 10017

RAHNER-REIMANN, PATRICIA ANNE, guidance counselor, educational administrator; b. Rockville Centre, N.Y., July 30, 1957; d. William and Patricia (McCormack) Rahner; m. Robert John Reimann, Aug. 20, 1988. BA, Molloy Coll., 1979; MS in Edn., St. John's U., Jamaica, N.Y., 1983, profl. diploma, 1989. Cert. elem. sch. tchr., sch. counselor, adminstr., N.Y.; nat. cert. counselor. Elem. tchr. St. Agnes Cath. Sch., Rockville Centre, N.Y., 1979-82; grad. asst. St. John's U., 1982-83, Fordham U., N.Y.C., 1983-84; guidance counselor Stella Maris High Sch., Rockaway Park, 1983-85; guidance counselor John F. Kennedy High Sch., Bellmore, 1985-91, dept. asst. for guidance, 1991—; dir. alternative edn. program Bellmore-Merrick (N.Y.) Cen. High Sch. Dist., 1989—, asst. prin. summer sch., 1990. Mem. AACD, N.Y. State Counselors Assn., Nassau County Counselors Assn., Mental Health Counselors Assn. Roman Catholic. Home: 1544 James Rd Wantagh NY 11793-3127

RAICHEL, DANIEL RICHTER, physicist, consultant, educator, researcher; b. Paterson, N.J., Aug. 22, 1935; s. Israel and Regina (Richter) R.; m. Geri Wahrman, Mar. 23, 1967; children: Adam Mark, Dina Karen. BME, Rensselaer Poly. Inst., 1957; SM in Nuclear Engring., MIT, 1958; degree in mech. engring., Columbia U., 1962; EngScD, NYU, 1970. Chief scientist Dathar Corp., Ramsey, N.J., 1971-76; pvt. practice cons. engr., 1976—; prin. Raichel Tech. Group, Midland Park, N.J., 1976—; prof. Pratt Inst., Bklyn., 1983-91, Cooper Union, N.Y.C., 1990—; cons. GE Astrospace, Princton, N.J., 1981, 99; prin. cons. Gorca Systems Inc., Cherry Hill, N.J., 1989—; reviewer energy program N.Y.C. Office of Bus. Devel., 1988-92. Co-author: Applied Kinematics, 1967; contbr. over 60 articles to profl. jours. John McMullen fellow Cornell U., 1958-59, NASA fellow Calif. Inst. Tech., 1991-92; N.Y. State Sci. and Tech. Found. grantee, 1991. Mem. ASME, Am. Acoustical Soc., Audio Engring. Soc., Sigma Xi, Tau Beta Pi. Office: Raichel Tech Group PO Box 287 Midland Park NJ 07432-0287

RAI-CHOUDHURY, PROSENJIT, high technology company executive; b. Dhubri, Assam, India, May 1, 1937; came to U.S., 1966; s. Bankim Rai-Choudhury; m. Margaret Niall, Mar. 13, 1959; 1 child, Indira. BS, U. Gauhati, Assam, 1956; diploma in grad. studies, U. Birmingham, Eng., 1957; MASc, U. B.C., Vancouver, Can., 1959; PhD, U. Pitts., 1970. Mem. sci. staff No. Electric R&D, Ottawa, Ont., Can., 1962-66; mgr. device devel. Westinghouse R&D Ctr., Pitts., 1967-89; v.p. tech. Solid State Measurements, Inc., Pitts., 1989—. Contbr. over 70 articles to sci. jours.; patentee in field. Mem. IEEE (sr.), Electrochem. Soc. (past v.p., editor conf. proc.), Minerals, Metals and Materials Soc. (past chmn. electronics materials com.). Office: Solid State Measurements 110 Technology Dr Pittsburgh PA 15275-1026

RAILKAR, SUDHIR BALKRISHNA, mechanical engineer; b. Bombay, Jan. 19, 1956; came to U.S., 1982; s. Balkrishna L. and Suman B. (Suman-Patil) R.; m. Aruna M. Railkar, Apr. 19, 1988. BS in Stats., U. Bombay, 1976, BME, 1981; MSME, La. State U., 1984; PhD in Mech. Engring., U. Minn., 1990. Sr. rsch. assoc. dept. chemistry, chem. engring. Highly Filled Materials Inst./Stevens Inst. Tech., Hoboken, N.J., 1990—. Contbr. rsch. papers to profl. jours. Mem. AIAA, ASME. Home: 566 Mount Prospect Ave Clifton NJ 07012 Office: Highly Filled Materials Inst Stevens Inst Tech Hoboken NJ 07003

RAILSBACK, DAVID PHILLIPS, state official, laywer; b. Newton, Mass., Aug. 21, 1950; s. David and Mary Ann (Phillips) R.; m. Elizabeth Stone, June 7, 1973; 1 child, Meredith. BS summa cum laude, Lehigh U., 1972; JD cum laude, Suffolk U., 1978; LLM, Boston U., 1981. Bar: Mass. 1978, R.I. 1979, U.S. Dist. Ct. R.I. 1979, U.S. Tax Ct. 1979, U.S. Dist. Ct. Mass. 1980. Law clk. R.I. Supreme Ct., 1978-79; assoc. Tillinghast, Collins, and Graham, Providence, 1979-81; exec. v.p., gen. counsel New Eng. Rd. Machinery Co., Fitchburg, Mass., 1981-91; asst. state treas. Commonwealth Mass., 1991—; bd. dirs. Assabet Leasing Corp., Railsback Corp. Chmn. crusade com. R.I. chpt. Am. Cancer Soc., 1979-82. Mem. Mass. Bar Assn., R.I. Bar Assn., Turks Head Club, Capitol Hill Club. Republican. Home: 42 Saw Mill Rd Concord MA 01742-2220 Office: New Eng Rd Machinery Co State House Rm 227 Boston MA 02133

RAIMONDI, PETER JOHN, III, lawyer, financial counselor; b. Winthrop, Mass., July 28, 1955; s. Peter John Jr. and Erma Dorothy (Oliver) R.; m. Christine Mary Welch, Aug. 29, 1976; children: Elizabeth, Jessica. Student, Mass. Coll. of Art, 1977-80; BLS, Boston U., 1980, JD, 1983. Bar: Mass. 1984. Fin. cons. The AYCO Corp., Inc., Albany, N.Y., 1983-84; portfolio mgr., sr. fin. cons. Weston Fin. Group, Wellesley, Mass., 1984-86; co-founder, mng. dir. The Colony Group, Inc., Boston, 1986—; bd. dirs. Arnold, Fortuna & Lane Advt., Boston. Mng. editor Probate Law Jour., Boston U., 1982-83; contbr. articles to mags. and profl. jours. Mem. adv. com. Town of Winthrop, Mass., 1989. Mem. ABA, Mass. Bar Assn., Boston Bar Assn., Internat. Assn. of Fin. Planners. Home: 1 Seal Harbor Rd Apt 208 Winthrop MA 02152-1050 Office: The Colony Group Inc 199 State St Boston MA 02109-2601

RAINES, THERON WADE, literary agent; b. Pine Bluff, Ark., Sept. 26, 1925; s. Thomas Wade and Hallie (Kersh) R.; m. Joan Binder Korman, July 29, 1971; 1 child, Keith B. Korman. Student, U. Ark.; BA, Columbia U., 1948, Oriel Coll., Oxford, Eng., 1950; MA, Columbia U., 1951, Oriel Coll., Oxford, Eng., 1955. Agt./ptnr. Raines & Raines, N.Y.C., 1961. Author: Three Girls and a Woman Named Death, 1984, The Singing, 1988. 2d Lt. navigator USAF, 1943-45. Kellett fellow, 1948-50. Mem. Assn. Author's Reps., Phi Beta Kappa. Home and Office: Raines & Raines 71 Park Ave New York NY 10016

RAINONE, MICHAEL CARMINE, lawyer; b. Phila., Mar. 4, 1918; m. Ledena Tonioni, Apr. 10, 1944; children: Sebastian, Francine. LLB, U. Pa., 1941. Bar: Pa. 1944, U.S. Dist. Ct. Pa. 1944, U.S. Supreme Ct. 1956. Sr. ptnr. Rainone & Rainone, Phila., 1945—. Del. 3d Cir. Jud. Conf., 1984. Bd. dirs. Community Coll. Phila., 1970-85; past pres. Nationalities Svc. Ctr.; commr. Fellowship Commn., 1973-82; bd. dirs., mem. govt. rels. com. Mental Health Assn. Southeastern Pa., 1979-81; pres. Columbus Civic Assn. Pa., Inc., 1984-91; chmn. Lawyers Biog. Com. Hist. Soc., U.S. Dist. Ct.; trustee Balch Inst. for Ethnic Studies, 1989-92; regional v.p. Nat. Italian-Am. Found.; pres. Seaview Harbor Civic Assn., 1990—. Recipient Disting. Svc. award Nationalities Svc. Ctr., 1975, Man of Yr. award Columbus Civic Assn., 1969, Legion of Honor Chapel of Four Chaplains, 1979, Bronze Medallian award, 1982, commendation Senate Pa., 1982. Mem. ABA, Internat. Acad. Law and Sci., Assn. Trial Lawyers Am., Justinian Soc. (bd. govs. 1980-83), Pa. Bar Assn., Pa. Trial Lawyers Assn. (bd. govs. 1982-84), N.Y. Trial Lawyers Assn. (assoc.), Phila. Bar Assn. (bd. dirs. 1980-83, asst. sec. 1983, 84), Lawyers Club Phila. (pres. 1982-84), Phila. Trial Lawyers Assn. (pres. 1982-83), Nat. Italian-Am. Bar Assn. (bd. govs. 1985-90, historian 1987-90, pres. 1991—), Am. Arbitration Assn. (arbitrator 1950—). Home: 2401 Pennsylvania Ave Philadelphia PA 19130-3061 Office: 1528 Walnut St #800 Philadelphia PA 19102-3612

RAISELIS, RICHARD, artist; b. Bridgeport, Conn., July 15, 1951; s. George Andrew and Regina (Trojanowski) R.; m. Susan Enid Warren, June 12, 1983; 1 child, Diana Warren. BA, Yale U., 1973; MFA, Temple U., 1976. Vis. asst. prof. Temple U., Tyler Sch. Art, Phila., 1979-80; lectr. fine arts CUNY, York Coll., Jamaica, 1981-82; asst. prof., adj. Temple U., Dept. Architecture, Phila., 1979-83; instr. Met. Mus. Art, N.Y.C., 1983; asst. prof. Temple U. Abroad, Rome, Italy, 1986-88, U. Mich. Sch. Art, Ann Arbor, 1983-89, Boston U. Sch. Visual Art, 1989—; sec., exec. com. U. Mich. Sch. Art, Ann Arbor, 1985-86. Curator of exhibition of paintings "Pittura Figurativa Americana", 1988. Recipient Mich. Coun. for the Arts grant, 1985, Horace H. Rackham Rsch. grant U. Mich., 1985, John Courtney Murray Travel fellowship Yale U., 1973, Painting Purchase prize Skowhegan Sch. of Painting & Sculpture, 1972, Josef Albers scholarship Skowhegan Sch. of Painting & Sculpture, 1972. Office: Boston U Sch Visual Art 855 Commonwealth Ave Boston MA 02215

RAISNER, JOSEPH CRAIG, school administrator; b. Harrisburg, Pa., Dec. 30, 1952; s. Joseph Harry and Lois Elaine (Laman) R.; m. Jean Elizabeth Stuckey, Aug. 24, 1974; children: Tara Elizabeth, Joseph Justin. BS, Mansfield (Pa.) State Coll., 1974; MEd, Pa. State U., 1984. Music tchr. Camp Hill (Pa.) pub. schs., 1976-79, Susquenita schs., Duncannon, Pa., 1979-86; adminstr. Little Brown Bear's Day Care, Marysville, Pa., 1976—, Childcare Placement Agy., Marysville, 1986-90, Ednl. Mgmt. Svc., Marysville, 1986—; validator Nat. Assn. Edn. Young Children, Washington, 1986—; instr. early childhood edn. Harrisburg Area Community Coll., 1990—; conductor workshops in field; guest lectr. Pa. State U., 1985. Mem. Marysville Fire Dept., 1988—; active Boy Scouts Am. Mem. Nat. Assn. Edn. Young Children, Pa. Assn. Child Care Providers, Capitol Area Assn. Edn. Young Children, Pa. Fedn. Sportsmen (pres. 1988), Marysville Sports Club, Masons, Shriners (mus. dir. Zembo temple chanters 1988—, band dir. concert band 1989-91). Republican. Methodist. Home: 203 Kings Hwy Marysville PA 17053-9401 Office: Ednl Mgmt Svcs PO Box 26 Marysville PA 17053-0026

RAISZ, LAWRENCE GIDEON, medical educator, consultant; b. N.Y.C., Nov. 13, 1925; s. Erwin Joseph and Marie Georgette (Patai) R.; s. Helen Martin, June 5, 1948; children: Stephen, Matthew, Jonathan, Katherine, Nicholas. Student, Harvard U., 1943, MD, 1947; DOdontology (hon.), U. Umea, Sweden, 1990. Diplomate Am. Bd. Internal Medicine, Nat. Bd. Med. Examiners. Intern Harvard Med. Svc., Boston City Hosp., 1947-48; resident in medicine Cushing VA Hosp., 1950, Boston VA Hosp., 1952-54; asst. and instr. in physiology NYU-Bellevue Med. Ctr., 1948-50; asst. and instr. in medicine sch. medicine Boston U., 1953-56; chief renal sect. Boston VA Hosp., 1954-56; asst. chief radioisotope svc. Syracuse VA Hosp., 1956-57; asst. prof. medicine Coll. Medicine SUNY, Syracuse, 1956-61; assoc. prof. pharmacology and medicine Sch. Medicine U. Rochester, 1961-66, assoc. prof. medicine Sch. Medicine, 1966-68, prof. pharmacology, toxicology, and medicine Sch. Medicine, 1966-74, chief div. of clin. pharmacology Sch. Medicine, 1961-74; prof. medicine, head div. of endocrinology and metabolism Sch. Medicine U. Conn., Farmington, 1974—; sr. assoc. physician Strong Meml. Hosp., Rochester, 1961-68, physician, 1968-74; acting chmn. dept. pharmacology Sch. Medicine, U. Rochester, 1962-63, vis. prof. pharmacology, toxicology and medicine Sch. Medicine and Dentistry, 1974-

76; vis. assoc. prof. pharmacology Sch. Medicine Stanford U., 1966; vis. prof. Coll. Medicine U. Lagos, Nigeria, 1973; mem. gen. B study sect. NIH, 1986-88; mem. subspecialty bd. on endocrinology and metabolism Am. Bd. Internal Medicine, 1990—; mem. U.S.-Japan Malnutrition Panel, 1985-91; clin. investigator Syracuse VA Hosp., 1957-60; William N. Creasy Vis. Prof. Clin. Pharmacology Med. Sch. Dartmouth Coll., 1977; chmn. Gordon Conf. on Bones and Teeth, 1980; Edwin B. Astwood lectr. Endocrine Soc., 1983. Mem. numerous editorial bds.; contbr. more than 300 articles to profl. jours. With USNR, 1943-45; capt. AUS, 1950-52. Spl. Rsch. fellow Nat. Inst. Arthritis and Metabolic Disease, Strangeways Rsch. Lab., 1960-61, Nat. Inst. Dental Rsch. NIH, 1971-72; Burroughs-Wellcome scholar in Clin. Pharmacology, 1963-68; recipient Prix Andre Lichtwitz, 1980, Class of 1947 Disting. Prof. award Med. Sch. U. Wis., 1988. Mem. AAAS, Am. Fedn. for Clin. Rsch., Am. Soc. for Clin. Investigation, Am. Soc. for Pharmacology and Exptl. Therapeutics, Endocrine Soc., Assn. Am. Physicians, Conn. Endocrine Soc. (pres. 1976), Am. Soc. for Bone and Mineral Rsch. (pres. 1980-81, William F. Neuman award 1986), Conn. Acad. Sci. and Engring., Sigma Xi. Home: 118 Waterville Rd Farmington CT 06032-1624 Office: U Conn Health Ctr 263 Farmington Ave Farmington CT 06030-0001

RAITEN, DANIEL JAY, scientist; b. N.Y.C., Mar. 16, 1951; s. Allen Leslie and Marjorie (Herfort) R.; children: Aurora Heather, Terra Marisa. BA, SUNY, Oswego, 1973; BS, Kans. State U., 1977; MS, Pa. State U., 1980, PhD in Nutrition Sci. Postdoctoral fellow Child Study Ctr. Yale U., New Haven, 1984-86; rsch. nutritionist Children's Nat. Med. Ctr., Washington, 1986-89; adj. prof. dept. human health and food systems U. Md., College Park, 1986—; sr. staff scientist Life Sci. Rsch. Office Fedn. Am. Soc. Exptl. Biology, Bethesda, Md., 1990—. Mem. Am. Soc. Clin. Nutrition, Am. Inst. Nutrition, N.Y. Acad. Scis. Office: Fedn Am Soc Exptl Biology Life Sci Rsch Office 9650 Rockville Pike Bethesda MD 20814-3998

RAJKOVIC, DRAGOLJUB STEVAN, investment company executive, trade consultant; b. N.Y.C., Feb. 18, 1965; s. Dragoljub and Gordana (Mihailovic) R. BA in Econs., Tufts U., 1986. Mgmt. cons. Peat Marwick Main & Co., N.Y.C., 1986-87; co.-founder, v.p. Chase Investment Cons. Group, Acton, Mass., 1987—, Chase Global Data & Rsch., Acton, 1987—; trade cons. Adminco, Lima, Peru, 1987—, Worknet, Buenos Aires, 1986—. Editor: Chase Global Investment Almanac, 1988—. Mem. Latin Am. Soc. (pres. 1984-86). Office: Chase Investment Cons Group 409 Massachusetts Ave Acton MA 01720-3710

RAKOV, ROBERT WILLIS, surgeon; b. Goshen, N.Y., Nov. 12, 1926; s. Daniel and Helen Ernestine (Buckheit) R.; m. Beatrice Emily, July 8, 1951; children: Kathryn Lynn, Lisa Helen, Robert Daniel. MD, Syracuse (N.Y.) U., 1949. Diplomate Am. Bd. Surgery. Intern Pa. Hosp., Phila., 1949-51, resident, 1951-54, 56-57; ret. chief of surgery Arden Hill Hosp., Goshen, N.Y., 1986. Chmn. Orange County Aviation Bd., Goshen. Lt. USN, 1954-56. Mem. Mid-Hudson Surg. Soc. (former pres.), Goshen Rotary Club. Episcopalian. Home: 711 Homestead Ave Maybrook NY 12543-1307

RALES, STEVEN M., automotive parts company executive; b. Pitts., Mar. 31, 1951; married. BA, DePauw U., 1973; JD, America U., 1978. With Equity Group Holdings, Washington, 1979—; chmn. bd., chief exec. officer Danaher Corp., Washington, 1984—, now chmn. bd. Office: Danaher Corp 1250 24th St NW Washington DC 20037-1124*

RALL, DAVID PLATT, pharmacologist, educator; b. Aurora, Ill., Aug. 3, 1926; s. Edward Everett and Nell (Platt) R.; children: Jonathan D., Catharyn E.; m. Mary Gloria Monteiro, Apr. 22, 1989. B.S., North Central Coll., Naperville, Ill., 1946; M.S., Northwestern U., 1948, M.D., Ph.D., 1951. Intern Bellevue Hosp., N.Y.C., 1952-53; officer USPHS, 1953-90, asst. surgeon gen., 1971-90; sr. investigator Lab. Chem. Pharmacology, Nat. Cancer Inst., NIH, Bethesda, Md., 1953-55, Clin. Pharmacology and Exptl. Therapeutics Service, 1956-58, head service, 1958-63; chief Clin. Pharmacology and Exptl. Therapeutics Service (Lab. Chem. Pharmacology), 1963-69; assoc. sci. dir. for exptl. therapeutics Nat. Cancer Inst., 1966-71; dir. Nat. Inst. Environ. Health Scis., 1971-90, dir. Nat. Toxicology Program, 1978-90; adj. prof. pharmacology U. N.C., Chapel Hill, 1972-90. Mem. AAAS, Am. Assn. Cancer Rsch., Am. Soc. Clin. Investigation, Am. Soc. Pharmacology and Exptl. Therapeutics, Inst. Medicine (bd. on internat. health, trustee emult. def. fund), Soc. Occupational and Environ. Health, Soc. Toxicology. Home: 5302 Reno Rd NW Washington DC 20015-1908

RALL, WILFRID, neuroscientist; b. Los Angeles, Aug. 29, 1922; s. Udo and Doris (Keiser) R.; m.; children from previous marriage—Sara E., Madelyn W. B.S. summa cum laude, Yale U., 1943; M.S., U. Chgo., 1948; Ph.D., U. N.Z., 1953. Jr. physicist Manhattan Project, U. Chgo., 1943-46; biophysics fellow U. Chgo., Woods Hole, Mass., 1946-48; lectr., sr. lectr. physiology, biophysics U. Otago, Dunedin, N.Z., 1949-56; head biophysics div. Naval Med. Research Inst., Bethesda, Md., 1956-57; biophysicist, office math. research. Nat. Inst. Arthritis and Metabolic Diseases, Bethesda, 1957-67, sr. research physicist math. research br. Nat. Inst. Diabetes and Digestive and Kidney Diseases, 1967—; mem. NRC Com. on Brain Scis., 1968-73. Contbr. articles to profl. jours. Rockefeller Found. fellow, 1954-55. Mem. Soc. Neurosci. (nat. council 1970-72, chpt. pres. 1981-82), Internat. Brain Research Orgn. (central council 1968-73, U.S. nat. com. 1972-76), Biophys. Soc., Am. Physiol. Soc., Physiol. Soc. U.K., AAAS, Wilderness Soc. Office: NIH Bldg 31 Room 4B-54 Bethesda MD 20892

RALPH, ANDREW QUENTIN, editor, publisher; b. N.Y.C., Oct. 20, 1946; s. Martin Nathaniel and Evelyn Lorraine (Armstrong) R. Student, New Coll., Sarasota, Fla., 1965-66. Parts clk., machine assembler Bryant Chucking Gridner Corp., Springfield, Vt., 1966-68; front end mgr., grocery mgr. Purity Supreme, West Lebanon, N.H., 1968-69; piper Bryant Chucking Gringer Corp., Springfield, Vt., 1969-70; press helper Dartmouth Printing Co., Hanover, N.H., 1970-73; salesman, installer Dome East Corp., hicksville, N.Y., 1971-74; parts clk. Decato Bros. Sales/Svc., Lebanon, N.H., 1973-74; painter, designer Founded Bannerman signs, White River Junction, Vt., 1975-87; designer, marketer, founder ALC Graphics & Mktg., White River Junciton, Vt., 1988—; editor, pub., founder A Long Cycle Observer, White River Junciton, Vt., 1991—. Author: (with others) Dome Builders Handbook I, 1975, II edit., 1978; designer three registerd svc. marks. With USAFR, 1965-69. Office: A Long Cycle Observer PO Box 4132 White River Junction VT 05001-4132

RALPH, STEVAN BRADLEY GRAEME, management consultant; b. Ottawa, Can., June 27, 1955; s. Bradley Robert and Verne May (Proctor) R.; m. Vivian Ligo, Dec. 26, 1989. BA in Econs., Queen's U., Ont., Can., 1976; MA in Philosphy, Louvain Coll., Belgium, 1987; LLB, Western U., Ont., 1979; LLM, Cambridge U., Eng., 1988; PhD candidate, Georgetown U., 1992. Bar: Ont. 1980. Gen. mgr. Levy & Vallance, Ottawa; lawyer Dominion Bridge, Montreal, Can.; pres. SBR & Co., Toronto and Washington. Mem. Queens Alumni D.C. (founder, dir.). Roman Catholic.

RAMACHANDRAN, KRISHNAN, computer graphics executive; b. Aug. 15, 1946; came to U.S., 1968; s. T. Krishnan and Saraswathi Krishnan; m. Karthia J. Ramachandran, Sept. 7, 1975; children: Radha, Meena. BEE, U. Madras, 1968; MSEE, U. Calif., Davis, 1970, PhD in Elec. Engring., 1975. Mem. tech. staff Bell Labs, Whippany, N.J., 1977-81; M.T.S. Bell Labs, Holmdel, N.J., 1981-83, Bellcore, Red Bank, N.J., 1983—. Patentee in field. Mem. IEEE. Office: Bellcore 331 Newman Springs Rd Red Bank NJ 07701-5699

RAMAKRISHNA, KILAPARTI, environmentalist; b. Rajahmundry, Andhra, Pradesh, India, Oct. 13, 1955; s. Ramadas and Kanakaratnam (Bandaru) K.; m. Anjali D. Malwade, Mar. 31, 1983. B.Law, Coll. Law, Andhra U., India, 1976; PhD, Sch. Internat. Studies, India, 1985. Asst. prof. Indian Soc. of Internat. Law, New Delhi, India, 1980-85; Fulbright vis. scholar Harvard Law Sch., Cambridge, Mass., 1985-87; marine policy fellow Woods Hole Oceanographic Inst., Woods Hole, Mass., 1986-88, sr. assoc. internat. environ. law, dir. sci. in pub. affairs, 1989—; vis. prof. Dept. Internat. Rels., Boston U., 1987-88, 91; cons. in field. Contbr. articles to profl. jours. Bd. dirs. Boston Fulbright Com., 1986-90. Mem. Internat. Coun. Environ. Law, Sigma Xi. Hindu. Home: 60 Gardiner Rd Woods Hole MA 02543-1116 Office: Woods Hole Rsch Ctr 13 Church St # 296 Woods Hole MA 02543-1007

RAMAMURTI, RAVI, business educator, consultant; b. New Delhi, India, Mar. 23, 1952; came to U.S., 1977; s. Balakrishnan and Visalam (Sankara Iyer) R.; m. Meena Ramachandran; children: Bharat, Gita, Arjun. BS in Physics, Delhi (India) U., 1972; MBA, Indian Inst. Mgmt., 1974; D in Bus. Adminstrn., Harvard U., 1982. Cons. Govt. of India Planning Commn., New Delhi, 1974-75; corp. planner BHEL, New Delhi, 1975-77; asst. prof. Northeastern U., Boston, 1981-85, assoc. prof., 1988—; cons. UN, N.Y.C., 1985-86; vis. asst. prof. Bus. Sch. Harvard U., Boston, 1986-88. Author: State-owned Enterprises in High-technology Industries, 1987; editor: Privitization and Control of State-owned Enterprises, 1991. Mem. Strategic Mgmt. Soc., Acad. Mgmt., Boston Area Pub. Enterprise Group, Acad. Internat. Bus. Hindu. Home: 15 Stimson Ave Lexington MA 02173-7516 Office: Northeastern U Hayden 309 Boston MA 02115

RAMANARAYANAN, MADHAVA PRABHU, science administrator, researcher, educator; b. Varapuzha, Kerala, India, Feb. 5, 1945; came to U.S., 1972; s. Srinivasa Madhava and Priyothama (Shenoy) Prabhu; m. Leelavati Murthy, Sept. 2, 1972; children: Malini, Ananth. BS, American Coll., Madurai, India, 1964, MS, 1966; PhD, Indian Inst. Sci., Bangalore, India, 1972. Post-doctoral research worker dept. biochemistry Coll. Physicians and Surgeons of Columbia U., N.Y.C., 1972-75; staff assoc. Inst. Cancer Research, Columbia U., N.Y.C., 1975-81; dir. research & devel. Diagnostic Reagent Tech., Teaneck, N.J., 1981-85; v.p. research & devel. Visual Diagnostics, Inc., Teaneck, 1985-88; pres. Windsor Park Labs., Inc., Teaneck, 1988—; lectr., instr. postgrad. courses Am. Acad. Otolaryngic Allergy. Contbr. sci. articles to profl. jours. Fellow Am. Inst. Chemists, Nat. Acad. Clin. Biochemistry; mem. N.Y. Acad. Scis., Am. Chem. Soc., Internat. Union Pure and Applied Chemistry, Am. Assn. for Clin. Chemistry.

RAMAPRASAD, KACKADASAM RAGHAVACHAR, physical chemist; b. Bangalore, India, Dec. 8, 1938; came to U.S., 1965, permanent resident, 1971; s. Kackadasam Raghavachar and Saroja (Narasimhachar) R.; m. Rukmani Raghavachari, July 14, 1968; children: Saroja, Venkat. BS in Chemistry with honors, U. Mysore, Bangalore, 1958; MS in Phys. Chemistry, NYU, 1971, PhD, 1972. Trainee Bhabha Atomic Rsch. Ctr. Tng. Sch., Bombay, India, 1958-59, rsch. asst., jr. sci. officer chemistry div., 1959-65; teaching fellow N.Y.U., N.Y.C., 1965-71, duPont teaching asst., 1967-68; maitre-assistant dept. de chimie physique, U. Geneva, 1972-73; chemist Ecole Poly-technique Federale de Lausanne, Switzerland, 1974; rsch. assoc. dept. chemistry Princeton (N.J.) U., 1974-77, rsch. assoc., mem. profl. rsch. staff dept. chem. engring., 1977-79; sr. scientist Chronar Corp., Princeton, 1979-89; sr. scientist Electron Transfer Techs., Inc., Princeton, 1990—. Recipient Founder's Day award N.Y. U., 1972. Mem. Am. Chem. Soc., Sigma Xi. Contbr. articles to profl. publs. Office: Electron Transfer Techs Inc PO Box 160 Princeton NJ 08542

RAMBO, SYLVIA H., federal judge; b. Royersford, Pa., Apr. 17, 1936; d. Granville A. and Hilda E. (Leonhardt) R.; m. George F. Douglas, Jr., Aug. 1, 1970. BA, Dickinson Coll., 1958; JD, Dickinson Sch Law, 1962; LLD (hon.), Wilson Coll., 1980. Bar: Pa. 1962. Atty. trust dept. Bank of Del., Wilmington, 1962-63; pvt. practice Carlisle, 1963-76; public defender, then chief public defender Cumberland County, Pa., 1974-76; judge Ct. Common Pleas, Cumberland County, 1976-78, U.S. Dist. Ct. Middle Dist. Pa., Harrisburg, 1979—; asst. adj. prof. law Dickinson Sch. Law, 1973, 76, 77. Mem. Nat. Assn. Women Judges, Pa. Trial Lawyers Assn., Phi Alpha Delta. Democrat. Presbyterian. Office: US Dist Ct PO Box 868 Harrisburg PA 17108-0868

RAMENOFSKY, MAX LANTIN, pediatric surgeon; b. LaSalle, Ill., May 2, 1939; s. Abraham Isidore and Elizabeth (Lantin) R.; m. Melissa Babish, Mar. 11, 1975; children: Alexis Meri, Jamie Ann, Robert Jacob. AB, Dartmouth Coll., 1961; MD, U. Tenn., 1965. Diplomate Am. Bd. Surgery (Gen. & Pediatric Surgery). Asst. prof. surgery Tufts U., Boston, 1976-81; assoc. prof. surgery U. Ala., Mobile, 1981-83, prof. surgery pediatrics, 1983-88; prof. surgery U. Pitts., 1988-90; dir. pediatric trauma Children's Hosp. Pitts., 1988-90; prof. surgery Med. Hosp. Pa., Pitts., 1990—; dir. pediatric trauma Allegheny Gen. Hosp., Pitts., 1990—. Editor: (textbook) Advanced Trauma Life Support, 4th, 5th edits., 1989, '90; contbr. over 200 articles to profl. jours. and chpts. to books. Cmdr. U.S. Navy. Recipient commendation Mayor, Boston, 1978, City Coun. Pitt. 1990, U.S. Navy, 1991. Fellow ACS (chmn. advanced trauma life support com. 1987—, exec. com., com. on trauma 1987—), Soc. Pediatric Emergency Medicine (exec. com. 1988—), Am. Surg. Assn., Am. Pediatric Surg. Assn. (chmn. trauma com. 1978-82), So. Surg. Assn., Am. Assn. Surgery of Trauma, Am. Acad. Pediatrics, Ea. Assn. Surgery of Trauma, Soc. Univ. Surgeons. Office: Allegheny Gen Hosp 320 E North Ave Pittsburgh PA 15212-4772

RAMER, RICHARD C., antiquarian bookseller; b. Bklyn., Aug. 8, 1942; s. Benjamin Ramer and Dorothy (Bellaff) Ramer Issacs; m. Julieta do Carmo Goncalves, Sept. 3, 1983. BA, Bklyn. Coll., 1965; MA in Latin Am. History, Ind. U., 1967. Pres. Richard C. Ramer, Old & Rare Books, N.Y.C., 1969—. N.Y. State Regents fellow, 1965-67, Lehman fellow, 1967-69. Mem. Antiquarian Booksellers' Assn. Am., Antiquarian Booksellers' Assn. (U.K.), Internat. League Antiquarian Booksellers, Am. Portuguese Soc. (bd. dirs. 1991—), Gremio Literario (Lisbon, Portugal), Gremio Internat. Vala Comun (Lisbon), Grolier Club, Old Book Table. Home and Office: 225 E 70th St New York NY 10021-5211

RAMEY, CARL ROBERT, lawyer; b. Binghamton, N.Y., Feb. 15, 1941; s. Clinton W. and Hester May (Wisdom) R.; m. Maryan Sitzenkopf, Aug. 11, 1962 (div. Sept. 1987); children: Mark Alan, Christian David; m. Karen Reichard, Nov. 28, 1987. AB, Marietta Coll., 1962; MA, Mich. State U., 1964; JD, George Washington U., 1967. Bar: D.C. 1968, U.S. Dist. Ct. D.C. 1968, U.S. Ct. Appeals (2d, 3d, 4th, 5th, 7th and 9th cirs.), U.S. Supreme Ct. 1972. Assoc. McKenna, Wilkinson & Kittner, Washington, 1967-71, ptnr., 1971-86; ptnr. Wiley, Rein & Fielding, Washington, 1986—. Contbr. articles to profl. jours., chpt. to Copyright Law Symposium, 1969; editorial staff George Washington Law Rev., 1965-67. Recipient First Prize award Nat. Nathan Burkan Meml. Writing Competition, ASCAP, 1969. Mem. ABA, Fed. Communications Bar Assn. (treas. 1977-78), D.C. Bar Assn. Republican. Episcopalian. Home: Quiet Cove 27023 Rigbylot Rd Easton MD 21601-7667 Office: Wiley Rein & Fielding 1776 K St NW Washington DC 20006-2304

RAMIN, KURT, accounting executive; b. Liebenwalde, Berlin, Germany, Nov. 6, 1942; came to U.S., 1976; s. Erwin and Erna (Lehmann) R.; m. Anglika Brandau, Oct. 4, 1968 (dec. 1971); m. Melissa K. Cochran, Dec. 30, 1972; children: John-Paul, Alexandra. Diploma, Fachhochschule, Cologne, Fed. Republic of Germany, 1968; MBA, Cen. Mich. U., 1971. Cert. employee benefits specialist; CPA, Ohio. Controller Dow Corning, Munich, 1968-76; internat. controller Emery Industries, Cin., 1976-81; v.p. fin. and adminstrn. Beiersdorf Inc., Norwalk, Conn., 1981-86; ptnr. Coopers & Lybrand, N.Y.C., 1987—. Chairman German Sch. of Conn., 1985—. Mem. Fin. Execs. Inst. (pres. Westchester Conn. Chpt. 1991—), CDS Internat. (treas., bd. dirs. N.Y. chpt. 1986—). Home: 17 Ravenwood Dr Weston CT 06883-1410 Office: Coopers & Lybrand 1301 Ave Of The Americas New York NY 10019-6022

RAMIREZ, ARTHUR CHRISTOPHER, bank executive; b. Bklyn., Mar. 22, 1937; s. Arthur C. and Mary A. (Sierchio) R.; m. Frances Angela Laino, Feb. 9, 1958; children: Scott Arthur, Lois Ann Ramirez Carr. BS in Acctg., Rutgers U., 1968; cert. diploma, Stonier Grad. Sch. Banking, 1973. Loan interviewer Mfrs. Hanover Trust Co., N.Y.C., 1956-62; mgr. consumer loan dept. Irvington (N.J.) State Bank, 1962-64; mgr. consumer lending Essex County State Bank, West Orange, N.J., 1964-65; sr. v.p. Hackensack (N.J.) Trust Co. (now Garden State Nat. Bank), 1965-80; 1st sr. v.p. Nat. Community Bank, Maywood, N.J., 1980—. Bd. mem. Hackensack (N.J.) Med. Ctr. Found., Tetecboro (N.J.) Aviation Mus. and Hall of Fame, Bergen County (N.J.) Girl Scouts Am., all present. 1st lt. USAR, 1955-63. Mem. Hudson County Bankers Assn. (past pres.). Home: 19 Weiss Rd Saddle River NJ 07458-1323 Office: Nat Community Bank 113 W Essex St Maywood NJ 07607-1020

RAMIREZ, PAUL MICHAEL, psychology educator, researcher, neuropsychologist; b. N.Y.C., May 15, 1951. BA, CUNY, 1973; MPhil, CCNY, 1987, PhD, 1990; MA, NYU, 1976, CCNY, 1980. Lic. psychologist, N.Y., N.J. Clin. asst. N.Y. Hosp.-Cornell Med. Ctr., N.Y.C., 1978-79; psychology assoc. Downstate Med. Ctr., Bklyn., 1979-81; clin. psychology intern Hutchings Psychiat. Ctr., Syracuse, N.Y., 1981-82; dir. neuropsychology New Medico TBI Program, Milford, Conn., 1983-84; dep. chief of svc. neuropsychiatry svc. Bronx Psychiat. Ctr., 1984-88; sr. clin. neuropsychologist Columbia-Presbyn. Med. Ctr., N.Y.C., 1988—; mem. med. sch. faculty Coll. of Physicians and Surgeons Columbia U., N.Y.C., 1990—; mem. adj. psychology faculty Hunter Coll., CUNY, 1982—; guest reviewer Jour. of Reading, 1987-88, Jour. of Ednl. Psychology, 1991-92; clin. tng. cons. N.Y. State Office Vocat. Rehab., N.Y.C., 1983-84; rsch. cons. SUNY Coll. of Optometry, 1989-90; clin. and rsch. cons. N.Y. State Psychiat. Inst., N.Y.C., 1990-91. Editor Jour. Ednl. Neuropsychology, 1981-88; contbr. articles to profl. jours. NSF fellow CUNY, 1978-81; recipient Recognition award N.Y. State Head-Injury Assn., 1984. Mem. APA, Internat. Neuropsychol. Soc., N.Y. Acad. Sics., Internat. Reading Assn. (chmn. neuropsychol. issues SIG 1980-91), N.Y. Neuropsychology Group (bd. dirs. 1990—).

RAMIREZ, PAUL ROBERT, obstetrician-gynecologist; b. Bronx, N.Y., Nov. 18, 1950; s. Luciano and Maria Emilia (Gonzalez) R.; m. Carolyn Marie Longhi, Nov. 11, 1972; children: Leah Marie, Elyssa Anne, Nathan Paul, Adam Paul. BA in Psychology, Yale U., 1972, MD, 1976. Diplomate Am. Bd. Ob-Gyn. Intern, resident, chief resident in ob-gyn Yale-New Haven Hosp., 1976-80; pvt. practice New Haven, Guilford and Essex, Conn., 1980-84; clin. instr. Ob-gyn Sch. Medicine Yale U., 1981-84; asst. prof. ob-gyn, residency program coord., med. dir. outpatient clinics, chief div. gynecology Case Western Res. U., Cleve., 1984-86; chmn. dept. ob-gyn, attending physician St. Vincent's Med. Ctr., Bridgeport, Conn., 1986-91; chief Dept. Ob-Gyn, attending physician Middlesex (Conn.) Hosp., 1992—; med. dir. families and infants Together Program Cleve. Regional Perinatal Network, 1985-86; pediatric and adolescent gynecologic cons. Rainbow Babies and Children's Hosp., Cleve., 1985-86; cons., mem. plan devel. com. Bridgeport Mayor's Select Com. on Infant Mortality, 1987-91; cons., mem. health profls. adv. com. Fairfield County chpt. March of Dimes Birth Defects Found., Norwalk, Conn., 1988—; mem. bd. dirs. St. Vincent's Physicians IPA, 1988-91; mem. Am. Bd. Ob-Gyn Dist. I Adv. Coun., 1988—; rep. com. on underserved women Am. Coll. Ob-Gyn Dist. I, 1990—; mem. EPSDT program adv. com. State of Conn. Dept. of Income Maintenance, 1989-90; ob-gyn cons. div. Family Reproduction, Dept. of Health Svcs. State of Conn.; asst. prof. clin. ob-gyn U. Conn. Sch. Medecine, 1992—. Sports coach Lakewood-Trumbull (Conn.) YMCA, 1987-88. Co-asst. chmn. Greater Bridgeport Adolescent Pregnancy Task Force, 1990-91; mem. Bridgeport Child Advocacy Coalition Com. on Substance Abuse in Pregnancy, 1990-91; rep. ob-gyn to Mayor's Health Task Force City of Bridgeport, 1991. Fellow Am. Coll. Ob-Gyn (adv. com. dist. 1, 1988—, maternal morality rev. com. 1990—, perinatal/morbidity/mortality com. 1991—); mem. Conn. Med. Soc. (com. on statewide med planning 1988—), Fairfield County Med. Assn. (com. on Legis. 1987—), Conn. Hosp. Assn. (cons., mem. clinician panel for obstetrics 1989—), Yale Club Ea. Fairfield County (sec. 1989-90). Democrat. Roman Catholic. Office: Middlesex Hosp 28 Crescent St Middletown CT 06457

RAM-MOHAN, L. RAMDAS, physics educator; b. Poona, India, July 21, 1944; came to U.S., 1964; s. L. A. and Kalyani (Ramanathan) Ramdas; m. Sita Raman, Sept. 12, 1969; children: Arun, Sumati. BSc in Physics with honors, Delhi U., 1964; MS in Physics, Purdue U., 1967, PhD in Physics, 1971. Rsch. assoc. Inst. Theoretical Physics, Free U. of Berlin, 1971-73; sr. rsch. fellow Nat. Sci. Acad., New Delhi, 1973-75; instr. physics, rsch. assoc. Purdue U., West Lafayette, Ind., 1975-78; asst. prof. dept. physics Worcester (Mass.) Poly. Inst., 1978-80, assoc. prof., 1980-85, prof., 1985—; cons. in field, 1979-85; pres., cons. Quantum Semiconductor Algorithms, Northboro, Mass., 1991—. Contbr. articles to profl. publs. Mem. IEEE, Am. Phys. Soc., Sigma Xi. Office: Worcester Poly Inst Physics Dept 100 Institute Rd Worcester MA 01609-2276

RAMOS, JUAN IGNACIO, mechanical engineering educator; b. Bernardos, Spain, Jan. 28, 1953; came to U.S., 1977; s. Florentino and Maria (Sobrados) R. B in Aero. Engring., Madrid Poly. U., 1975; MA, Princeton U., 1979, PhD, 1980; Dr. Engring., Madrid Poly. U., 1983. Instr. Carnegie-Mellon U., Pitts., 1980, asst. prof., 1980-85, assoc. prof., 1985-89, prof., 1989—; cons. PPG Industries, Pitts., 1982-84, Software Engring. Inst., Pitts., 1986, Life systems, Inc. 1988; mech. engr. Babcock & Wilcox, Santander, Spain, 1975; design engr. aero. constrns. LTD, Madrid, Spain, 1976-77. Author: Internal Combustion Engine Modelling, , 1989; editor: Applied Mathematical Modelling, International Jouranl of Numerical Methods for Heat and Fluid Flow; contbr. articles to profl. jours. Served to 2d lt. Aero. Engring. Co., Spain, 1975-77. NASA Faculty fellow, Cleve., 1982, 88; Van Ness Lothrop fellow, 1979-80; recipient Nat. award Aero. Engring. His Majesty King of Spain, 1977, Aero. Engring. medal 1977; Guggenheim fellow, 1977-80. Mem. Soc. for Indsl. and Applied Math., AIAA (faculty advisor 1980-86), Soc. Automotive Engrs. (Ralph R. Teetor, Warrendale, Pa., 1981), Sigma Xi. Roman Catholic. Avocations: tennis, classical music, reading. Office: Carnegie-Mellon U Dept Mech Engring Frew St Pittsburgh PA 15213-3824

RAMPEN, LEONARDUS EDUARD, broadcasting company executive; b. Surabaya, Indonesia, Mar. 29, 1928; came to Can., 1952; s. Wilhelmus Christiaan and Julie (Ramakers) R.; m. Sybil Salvin Calverley, Apr. 11, 1954; children—William, Edmund Leveson, Christopher, Hugo, Benjamin. B.A. in Art History, U. Toronto, 1953, M.A. in Art History, 1955. Graphic designer CBC, Toronto, Ont., 1953-61; TV producer current affairs CBC, Toronto, 1961-65, exec. producer TV current affairs, 1965-67, exec. producer TV religious program, 1967-80; dir. TV programming CBC, Montreal, Que., 1980-91; cons. Can. Intefaith Network, Toronto, 1983-85, Nat. Inst. on Mental Retardation, Toronto, 1979—; mem. documentary jury Prix Italia, Bologna, Italy, 1975; mem. bilingual jury Nat. Mag. Awards, Toronto, 1981-83; vice chmn. Prix Anik, Montreal, 1984-85. Recipient Gabriel award for Man Alive; grantee Can. Council, 1971, 81, Nat. Inst. for Mental Retardation, 1985. Mem. IATSE (stewart CBC Toronto, pres. 1957), Art Dirs. Club (exec. mem. 1959), Assn. TV Producers (exec. mem. 1967, pres. 1967). Roman Catholic.

RAMPULLA, LEONARD MICHAEL, architect; b. S.I., N.Y., May 5, 1954; s. Philip V. and Libera G. (Pistilli) R.; m. Rita Felice Franzonello, Sept. 28, 1986; 1 child, Leann Elizabeth. BS in Architecture, CCNY, 1978, BArch, 1981. Registered architect, N.Y., N.J. Tech. draftsman Rampulla Assocs. Architects, S.I., 1976-79, Harrison & Abromowitz, N.Y.C., 1979-81; job capt. Rampulla Assocs. Architects, S.I., 1981-87, architect, 1987—; speaker, lectr. Civic Orgns. and Sch. Workshops. Bd. dirs. S.I. Vote Yes; adv. coun. S.I. Tech. High Sch., 1991. Mem. AIA (treas. S.I. chpt. 1991), N.Y. AIA, Soc. Mil. Engrs., Nat. Coun. Architects Registration Bd. Office: 155 3rd St Staten Island NY 10306-2209

RAMSAY, ROLAND THOMAS, psychologist; b. Bellaire, Ohio, Nov. 5, 1936; s. Roland Theodore and Olga (Cattabiani) R.; m. Jodie Price, June 10, 1960; 1 child, Elizabeth Jane. BSc, Ohio State U., 1961, MA, 1966; PhD, U. Pitts., 1971. Diplomate Am. Bd. Profl. Psychology. Supr. tech. svcs. testing sect. Ohio State Employment Svc., Columbus, 1961-65; supr. pers. devel. U.S. Steel, Clarion, Pa., 1966-70; lectr. Grad. Sch. Indsl. Adminstrn. Carnegie-Mellon U., Pitts., 1971-75; human resources psychologist Ramsay Corp., Pitts., 1973—; cons. psychologist to various nat. and internat. cos. Author: Management's Guide to Effective Employment Interviewing, 1979, The Testing Manual, 1984. Pres. bd. Chartiers Mental Health and Mental Retardation, Inc., Pitts., 1984; bd. dirs. Wesley Inst., Pitts., 1985-92. With U.S. Army, 1957-59. Recipient Merit award Pitts. History & Landmarks, 1981. Mem. APA, AACD, Am. Soc. Pers. Adminstrn., Soc. Indsl. and Organizational Psychology (div. counseling psychology), Assn. Measurement and Evaluation in Guidance, Nat. Career Devel. Assn., Soc. for Human Resource Mgmt., Pitts. Pers. Assn. Home: 2105 Hycroft Dr Pittsburgh PA 15241-2213 Office: Ramsay Corp 1050 Boyce Rd Pittsburgh PA 15241-3907

RAMSAY, WILLIAM CHARLES, writer; b. N.Y.C., Nov. 6, 1930; s. Claude Barnett and Myrtle Marie (Scott) R.; m. Charlotte Appleton Kidder, June 10, 1988; children from previous marriages: Alice, John, Carol Ramsay Serrano, David. BA in English Lit., U. Colo., 1952; MA in Physics, UCLA,

1957, PhD in Physics, 1962. NFS postdoctoral fellow U. Calif., San Diego, 1962-64; asst. prof. U. Calif., Santa Barbara, 1964-67; tech. mgr. Systems Assocs., Inc., Long Beach, Calif., 1967-72; sr. environ. economist U.S. AEC, Bethesda, Md., 1972-75; tech. adviser U.S. Nuclear Regulatory Agy., Washington, 1975-76; sr. fellow Resources for the Future, Washington, 1976-83, Ctr. for Strategic and Internat. Studies, Washington, 1983-85; sr. staff officer NAS, Washington, 1985-86; freelance writer, cons. Washington, 1986—; cons. Vols. in Tech. Assistance, Arlington, Va., 1987-90, Internat. Resources Group, Washington, 1991. Author: Unpaid Costs of Electrical Energy, 1979, Bioenergy and Economic Development, 1985; co-author: Managing the Environment, 1972, Energy in America's Future, 1979. Buenos Aires Conventional fellow, 1952, NSF fellow, 1962; NATO scholar, 1960, 62. Mem. Am. Phys. Soc., Am. Astron. Soc., Internat. Assn. Energy Economists, Washington Ind. Writers, Writers' Ctr. (bd. dirs.). Home and Office: 2930 Foxhall Rd NW Washington DC 20016-3429

RAMSAY, WILLIAM MORRILL, military officer, pilot; b. Hyannis, Mass., Mar. 30, 1955; s. William Frederick and Patricia Ann (Morrill) R.; m. Debbie Ramsay. BS in Aero. Engring., USAF Acad., 1977. Commd. 2d lt. USAF, 1977, advanced through grades to maj., 1990; fighter pilot USAF, Hahn Air Base, Fed. Republic Germany, 1979-81, Keflavik, Iceland, Span Gdahlem Air Base, Fed. Republic Germany, 1982-85, Homestead AFB, Fla., 1985-87, Otis ANGB, Mass., 1988—. Mem. Air Force Assn. Republican. Episcopal.

RAMSDEN, KATHARINE LEE, public relations executive; b. Providence, July 16, 1958; d. Richard James and Sallie (McLean) R.; m. Michael Zvi Rabin, Aug. 17, 1986; children: Hannah Barnard, David Aron. BA, Mt. Holyoke Coll., 1980; MS in Journalism with honors, Columbia U., 1984. Sr. rsch. assoc. Greenwich (Conn.) Assocs., 1981-83; rsch. editor Sylvia Porter's Personal Fin., N.Y.C., 1983-85; asst. v.p. corp. communications div. Merrill Lynch & Co., N.Y.C., 1985-87; asst. v.p., dir. pub. rels. Thomson McKinnon, N.Y.C., 1987-88; mgr. communications Am. Brands, Greenwich, 1988-89; dir. external communications Dean Witter Reynolds, N.Y.C., 1989—. Contbr. articles to profl. publs. Alumnat vol., fundraiser Mt. Holyoke Coll., South Hadley, Mass.; commr. social svcs. Town of Darien, Conn.; mem. Darien Dem. Town Com.; coord. CAreer Advisory Network. Democrat. Jewish. Office: Dean Witter Reynolds 2 World Trade Ctr Fl 74 New York NY 10048-0203

RAMSEY, DONALD DAVID, accounting educator; b. Jersey City, Sept. 1, 1935; s. David John and Astrid Florence (Okerlund) R. BA, Columbia Union Coll., 1956; MBA, Am. U., 1969. CPA, cert. data processor. Cashier Columbia Union Coll., Takoma Park, Md., 1956-60; mgr. data processing Columbia Union Coll., Takoma Park, 1960-72; assoc. prof. acctg. U. D.C., Washington, 1972—, chmn. dept. acctg., 1982-90; owner All Books Considered, Takoma Park, 1991—. Arbitrator Montgomery County Office Consumer Affairs, Rockville, Md., 1974—; elected coun. mem. City of Takoma Park, 1980-82; bd. dirs. Takoma Park (Md.) Symphony Orch. Soc., 1990—. With U.S. Army, 1958-60, USAR, 1960-64. Mem. AICPA, Am. Acctg. Assn., Md. Assn. CPA's, D.C. Inst. CPA's, Data Processing Mgmt. Assn., Am. Canal Soc., Mensa. Democrat. Home: 8116 Roanoke Ave Takoma Park MD 20912-6229 Office: Univ D C Dept Acctg MB19 4200 Connecticut Ave NW Washington DC 20008

RAMSEY, DOUGLAS K., television anchor, journalist; b. Norman, Okla., June 15, 1951; s. Edwin P. and Madeline (Willowquet) R.; m. Amm Polya, Dec. 30, 1977 (div. 1985). BA in Polit. Sci., UCLA, 1970; MA in European Studies, Coll. Europe, Brussels, 1971; MA in Internat. Affairs, Johns Hopkins U., 1972. Freelance corr. Washington Post, Brussels, 1973-74; writer The Economist, London, 1975; corr. The Economist, Tokyo, 1976-79, NBC News, N.Y.C., 1985-87; bus. editor Newsweek, N.Y.C., 1979-82; exec. prodr. Bus. Times on ESPN, N.Y.C., 1982-85; mng. editor. Fin. News Network, N.Y.C., 1987-91; anchor CNBC/Fin. News Network, Ft. Lee, N.J., 1991—. Author: (non-fiction) The Corporate Warriors; contbr. columns to N.Y. Times, L.A. Times, Fin. Times. Mem. Authors Guild. Office: CNBC 2200 Fletcher Ave Fort Lee NJ 07024

RAMSEY, GREGORY ARNOLD, federal official; b. Worcester, Mass., Nov. 30, 1948; s. Boyd Wilbur and Irene (Matson) R. AAS in Hotel/Restaurant Mgmt., U. Mass., 1969; BS in Elem. Edn., Framingham State Coll., 1973. Respiratory therapy tech. Hahnemann Hosp., Worcester, 1973-75; with support svcs. dept. New England Deaconess Hosp., Boston, 1975-76, Mount Vernon Hosp., Alexandria, Va., 1976-80; procurement coord. U.S. Ry. Assn., Washington, 1980-83; support svc. supr. United Mine Workers Health & Retirement Funds, Washington, 1983-85; v.p. adminstrv. svc. Meritor Savs. Bank, FA, Arlington, Va., 1985-88; cons. Annandale, Va., 1988-89; supr., mgmt. analyst U.S. Dept. Agriculture, Washington, 1989—.

RAMSEY, HARRY EDGAR, JR., hematologist, oncologist; b. Altoona, Pa., July 22, 1943; s. Harry E. and Ida S. (Scofield) R.; children: Harry III, David M. BS, Juniata Coll., 1964; MD, Jefferson U., 1968. Diplomate Am. Bd. Internal Medicine, Am. Bd. Hematology, Am. Bd. Oncology. Resident in medicine Reading (Pa.) Hosp., 1971-73; fellow in hematology, oncology Hohnemann Hosp., Phila., 1973-75; physician Reading Hosp., 1975—. Cert. diver Profl. Assn. Driving Instrs. Cpt. U.S. Army, 1969-71, Viet Nam. Decorated Bronze Star. Mem. Am. Soc. Hematology, Am. Soc. Clin. Oncologists, Am. Coll. Physicians, Pa. Med. Soc., Berks County Med. Soc., Shriners. Republican. Methodist. Office: Berks Hemato-Oncology Assoc 301 S 7th Ave West Reading PA 19611

RAMSEY, HENRY, JR., retired judge, law school dean, lawyer; b. Florence, S.C., Jan. 22, 1934; s. Charles Arthur and Nellie Tillman; m. Evelyn Yvonne Lewis, June 11, 1961 (div. Sept. 1967); children: Charles, Githaiga, Robert, Ismail; m. Eleanor Mason Ramsey, Sept. 7, 1969; children: Yetunde, Abeni. Student, Howard U.; BA, U. Calif., Riverside, 1960; LLB, U. Calif., 1963. Bar: Calif., 1964, U.S. Supreme Ct., 1967. Dep. dist. atty. Contra Costa County, Calif., 1964-65; pvt. practice Ramsey & Rosenthal, Richmond, Calif., 1965-71; prof. law U. Calif., Berkeley, 1971-80; judge Superior Court County of Alameda State Calif., Oakland, 1980-90; dean Howard U. Sch. Law, Washington, 1990—; vis. prof. law U. Texas., Austin, 1977, U. Colo., Boulder, 1977-78, Am. Indian Law Ctr. U. N.Mex., 1980; mem., pres. Coun. Legal Edn. Opportunity, Washington, 1987—; chair Law Sch. Admission Coun.-Bar Passage Rate Study Group, 1990—. Mem. City Coun. Berkeley, 1973-77, Criminal Justice Planning Bd., County of Alameda, 1973-76; trustee City of Berkeley Libr., 1973-74; bd. dirs. Redevel. Agy., Berkeley, 1971-73. With USAF, 1951-55. Recipient Jefferson Jurist award Calif. Assoc. Black Lawyers, 1986, Disting. Alumnus award U. Calif., 1987, Disting. Svc. award Wiley Manuel Law Found., 1987. Mem. ABA (mem. sect. legal edn. and admissions to bar 1982—, chair 1991-92), Nat. Bar Assn., Nat. Ctr. State Courts (mem. commn. trial court performance stds. 1987—, Dist. Svc. award 1990), Am. Law Inst., Am. Judicature Soc., Calif. Judges Assn., Cosmos Club, Federal City Club, Alpha Phi Alpha. Democrat. Office: Howard U Sch of Law 2900 Van Ness St NW Washington DC 20008

RAMSEY, LYNN ALLISON, public relations executive; b. Phila., July 31, 1944; d. Charles Edward and Edna Berry (Whetstone) R. Student, Inst. European Studies, Vienna, Austria, 1964-65; BA, Boston U., 1967. Copy editor Am. Heritage Pub. Co., N.Y.C., 1969-71; producer, writer Rick Carrier Film Prodns., N.Y.C., 1971-72; mng. editor New Ingenue mag., N.Y.C., 1973-75; freelance writer N.Y.C., 1975-80; v.p., mgr. pub. relations Cunningham and Walsh (acquired by Ayer Pub. Relations 1987), N.Y.C., 1981—; v.p., mgr. Ayer Pub. Rels., N.Y.C., 1988—. Author: Gigolos: The World's Best-Kept Men, 1978; photographer: FLY: The Complete Book of Sky Sailing, 1974; contbr. articles to profl. jours. Mem. Fgn. Policy Assn. 1982-87; sec. U.S.A. Bald Eagle Command, 1975—. Mem. Pub. Rels. Soc. Am. (accredited), The Fashion Group, Women's Jewelry Assn.

RAMSEY, MARY LOU, educator, human resources consultant; b. Somerville, N.J., Jan. 15, 1947; d. John Berkaw and Winnie Atkinson R. BA, Clark U., 1969; MA, Rider Coll., 1971; EdD, Fairleigh Dickinson U., 1977. Registered profl. counselor, N.J. Social worker Clinton (N.J.) Correctional Instn., 1969-72, dir. profl. svcs., 1972-75; dir. spl. programs Northampton County Area Community Coll., Bethlehem, Pa., 1975-76, dir. profl. svcs., 1976-78; asst. prof., chair dept. counseling and pers. svcs. Trenton (N.J.) State Coll., 1978-84, assoc. prof., chair dept. counseling and pers. svcs., 1984-87, prof., chair dept. counseling and pers. svcs., 1987—; cons., Milford, N.J., 1978—. Contbr. articles to profl. jours. Mem. AACD, N.J. Assn. for Counseling and Devel., N.J. Assn. for Counselor Edn. and Supervision, Gerontol. Soc. N.J., North Atlantic Regional Assn. for Counselor Edn. and Supervision, Assn. for Counselor Edn. and Supervision, Kappa Delta Pi, Sigma Phi Omega, Chi Sigma Iota. Home: 161 Miller Park Rd Milford NJ 08848-1964 Office: Trenton State Coll Dept Counseling and Pers Svcs Hillwood Lakes CN4700 Trenton NJ 08650-4700

RAMSEY, NORMAN, physicist, educator; b. Washington, Aug. 27, 1915; s. Norman F. and Minna (Bauer) R.; m. Elinor Jameson, June 3, 1940 (dec. Dec. 1983); children: Margaret, Patricia, Janet, Winifred; m. Ellie Welch, May 11, 1985. AB, Columbia U., 1935; BA, Cambridge (Eng.) U., 1937, MA, 1941, DSc, 1954; PhD, Columbia U., 1940; MA (hon.), Harvard U., 1947; DSc (hon.), Case Western Res. U., 1968, Middlebury Coll., 1969, Oxford (Eng.) U., 1973; DCL (hon.), Oxford (Eng.) U., 1990; DSc (hon.), Rockefeller U., 1986, U. Chgo., 1989, U. Sussex, 1990, U. Houston, 1991, Carleton Coll., 1991, Lake Forest Coll., 1992. Kellett fellow Columbia U., 1935-37, Tyndall fellow, 1938-39; Carnegie fellow Carnegie Inst. Washington, 1939-40; assoc. U. Ill., 1940-42; asst. prof. Columbia U., 1942-46; assoc. MIT Radiation Lab., 1940-43; cons. Nat. Def. Research Com., 1940-45; expert cons. sec. of war, 1942-45; group leader, asso. div. head Los Alamos Lab., 1943-45; assoc. prof. Columbia U., 1945-47; head physics dept. Brookhaven Nat. Lab. of AEC, 1946-47; assoc. prof. physics Harvard U., 1947-50, prof. physics, 1950-66, Higgins prof. physics, 1966—; sr. fellow Harvard Soc. of Fellows, 1970—; Eastman prof. Oxford U., 1973-74; Luce prof. cosmology Mt. Holyoke Coll., 1982-83; prof. U. Va., 1983-84; dir. Harvard Nuclear Lab., 1948-50, 52-53, Varlan Assos., 1963-66; mem. Air Forces Sci. Adv. Com., 1947-54; sci. adviser NATO, 1958-59; mem. Dept. Def. Panel Atomic Energy; exec. com. Cambridge Electron Accelerator and gen. adv. com. AEC. Author: Nuclear Moments and Statistics, 1953, Nuclear Two Body Problems, 1953, Molecular Beams, 1956, 85, Quick Calculus, 1965; contbr.: articles Phys. Rev.; other sci. jours. on nuclear physics, molecular beam experiments, radar, nuclear magnetic moments, radiofrequency spectroscopy, masers, nucleon scattering. Trustee Asso. Univs., Inc., Brookhaven Nat. Lab., Carnegie Endowment Internat. Peace, 1962-85, Rockefeller U., 1977-90; pres. Univs. Research Assocs., Inc., 1966-72, 73-81, pres. emeritus, 1981—. Recipient Presdl. Order of Merit for radar devel. work, 1947, E.O. Lawrence award AEC, 1960, Columbia award for excellence in sci., 1980, medal of honor IEEE, 1983, Rabi prize, 1985, Monie Ferst award, 1985, Compton medal, 1985, Rumford premium, 1985, Oersted medal, 1988, Nat. medal of sci., 1988, Nobel prize for physics, 1989; Guggenheim fellow Oxford U., 1954-55. Fellow Am. Acad. Sci., Am. Phys. Soc. (coun. 1956-60, pres. 1978-79, Davisson-Germer prize 1974); mem. NAS, French Acad. Sci., Am. Philos. Assn., AAAS (chmn. physics sect. 1977), Am. Inst. Physics (chmn. bd. govs. 1980-87), Phi Beta Kappa (senator 1979—, v.p. 1982-85, pres. 1985-88), Sigma Xi. Home: 24 Monmouth Ct Brookline MA 02146-5634 Office: Harvard U Lyman Lab Cambridge MA 02138

RAMSEY, NORMAN PARK, federal judge; b. Fairchance, Pa., Sept. 1, 1922; s. Joseph L. and Florence (Bennett) R.; m. Margaret Quarngesser, Apr. 15, 1944 (dec. 1979); children: Margaret S. Ramsey Newman, Mary S. Ramsey Gilvarg, Christine M. Ramsey North, Ann L. Ramsey Grossman; m. Tucky Patz, July 10, 1982. Student, Loyola Coll., Balt., 1939-41; LL.B., U. Md., 1947. Bar: Md. 1946. Law clk. to judge U.S. Dist. Ct., 1947-48; asst. U.S. atty., 1948-50; assoc. Semmes, Bowen & Semmes, Balt., 1951-54; partner Semmes, Bowen & Semmes, 1957-80; asst. atty. gen. Md., 1955, dep. atty. gen. Md., 1955-57; lectr. U. Md. Law Sch., 1951-71; judge U.S. Dist. Ct. Md., 1980-91; sr. judge U.S. Dist. Ct. Md., 1991—. Pres., Balt. CSC, 1963-70; pres. Bd. Sch. Commrs., 1975. Served to 1st lt. USMCR, 1943-46. Mem. Bar Assn. Balt. City, ABA (ho. of dels. 1961-81, bd. govs. 1975-78), Md. Bar Assn. (bd. govs. 1965-75, pres. 1973), Order of Coif, Phi Kappa Sigma. Home: 304 Wendover Rd Baltimore MD 21218-1127 Office: US Dist Ct 101 W Lombard St Baltimore MD 21201-2626

RAMSEY, PETER CHRISTIE, bank executive; b. N.Y.C., Oct. 1, 1942; s. Norman Carnegie and Rosalie Amelia (Christie) R.; m. Maryalice Ives, Nov. 15, 1969. BA, Brown U., 1964. Mgmt. trainee Irving Trust Co., N.Y.C., 1965-67; account exec. Hayden Stone, N.Y.C., 1967-72; regional sales mgr. Autex, Inc., Chgo., 1972-78; v.p. Chem. Bank, N.Y.C., 1978—. Mem. coun. of chairs YMCA Greater N.Y., N.Y.C., 1987—; chmn. bd. mgrs. McBurney YMCA, N.Y.C., 1980—. Mem. Brown U. Club. Home: 345 E 80th St New York NY 10021-0644

RAMSEY, PRISCILLA R., literature educator; b. Charleston, S.C., Sept. 30, 1940; d. George and Thelma (Lee) Rogers. BA in Psychology, Temple U., 1962; PhD in Literature, The Am. Univ., 1975. Community organizer, 1962-67, secondary sch. educator, 1967-71; asst. prof. English dept. English Dept., Rutgers U., Newark, 1975-79; grad. teaching asst. The Am. U., Washington, 1972-75; assoc. prof. dept. Afro-Am. studies Dept. Afro-Am. Studies, Howard U., Washington, 1979—; lectr. and presenter in field. Contbr. numerous articles and papers to profl. jours. Recipient Rutgers U. Faculty Rsch. award, 1978-79, The U.S. Dept. Labor award, 1986. Mem. MLA, Coll. Lang. Assn., Middle Atlantic Writers Assn., Critical Theory Study Group. Home: 1121 University Blvd W Apt 118 Silver Spring MD 20902-3317

RAMSIER, PAUL, composer, psychotherapist; b. Louisville, Ky., Sept. 23, 1927; s. Paul and Lucie (Hermann) R. PhD., N.Y.U., 1972; MSW, SUNY, Stony Brook, 1976. Composer N.Y.C., 1950—, psychotherapist in pvt. practice, 1977—; adj. prof. music N.Y.U., 1970—. Composer numerous musical compositions, including Divertimento Concertante on a Theme of Couperin, 1965, Eusebius Revisited, 1980. Huntington Hartford Fellow, 1960, McDonell Fellow, 1963, Yaddo Fellow, 1970; recipient NEA Grant, 1975. Mem. ASCAP. Home and Office: 210 Riverside Dr New York NY 10025

RANALD, RALPH ARTHUR, government official, educator; b. N.Y.C., Nov. 25, 1930; s. Josef A. and Pearl R.; AB, UCLA, 1952, MA, 1954; AM, Princeton U., 1958; postgrad. (Carnegie fellow) Law Sch., Harvard U., 1961-62, 76-77, grad. Exec. Program in Nat. and Internat. Security, 1978; PhD, Princeton U., 1962; m. Margaret Florence Loftus, Feb. 26, 1955; 1 dau., Caroline. Teaching asst. UCLA, 1951-53; univ. fellow, rsch. asst. Princeton (N.J.) U., 1956-59; asst. prof. Fordham U. Grad. Sch., N.Y.C., 1959-65; asst. dean acad. affairs, prof. Coll. Arts and Scis., NYU, N.Y.C., 1965-69; prof. CUNY, 1969—; spl. policy asst. HEW, Washington, 1968-69, Office of Mgmt. and Budget, 1976-77; sr. cons. U.S. Dept. Def., 1969-70, 77-78; mem. staffs Dept. Def. and Army Gen. Staff, U.S. Govt. Long Com., 1989; vis. prof. and cons. univs. including U. So. Calif., summers 1968-74, Calif. State U., SUNY-Buffalo, UCLA, summer 1985. Treas. N.Y. State Com. for Public Higher Edn., 1975-78, mem. com., 1970—. 1st lt. U.S. Army, 1953-56, to col., 1977-78, res., 1978—. Recipient U.S. Legion of Merit, 1983. Sr. fellow Am. Soc. Pub. Adminstrn. (selection com. for fellows, 1970-74); mem. Res. Officers Assn. U.S. (life), Harvard U. Law Sch. Assn., Assn. of Princeton U. Grad. Alumni, U.S. Army War Coll. Alumni Assn., John F. Kennedy Sch. of Govt. Alumni Assn., Harvard U. Alumni, Princeton Club of N.Y., Army and Navy Club, Phi Beta Kappa. Author: Management Development in Government, 1979, George Orwell, 1965; contbr. reports, articles to publs. in law, govt. and edn. Home: 700 7th St SW #315 Washington DC 20024

RANAURO, JOHN NICHOLAS, high tech firm executive; b. Hadock, Pa., May 9, 1945; s. Nicholas Frank and Ada Theresa (Marsicola) R.; m. Frances Mary Butz, Oct. 12, 1968; children: John, Matthew. BS, King's Coll., 1987, AS in Bus. Adminstrn., 1987. Artist, self-employed Hazleton, Pa., 1980-84; cons. N.Y.C. and, Pa., 1987-89; pres. Bau, East Petersburg, Pa., 1989—. Inventor Computerized Braille Printer, 1987 (3d place award 1987), LJC-DBMS, 1984 (scholarship award 1984); holder copyrights. Vice-pres. Sacred Heart Parish, Lancaster, Pa., 1990, chmn. fin. com., 1990. With U.S. Army, 1962-65. Recipient scholarship Holy Cross Father's, King's Coll., Wilkes-Barre, Pa., 1986. Roman Catholic. Home: 6550 Hollow Dr East Petersburg PA 17520-1004 Office: Bau 6550 Hollow Dr East Petersburg PA 17520-1004

RANCK, JAMES BYRNE, JR., neuroscience researcher, educator; b. Frederick, Md., Aug. 17, 1930; s. James Byrne and Dorothy Irene (Schwieger) R.; m. Helen Haukeness, June 9, 1961; 1 child, Mary Haukeness. BA, Haverford Coll., 1952; MD, Columbia U., 1955. Intern U. Chgo. Clinics, 1955-56; scientist NIH, Bethesda, Md., 1956-58; postdoctoral fellow Dept. Physiology U. Washington, Seattle, 1959-61, instr., 1961-62; from asst. prof. to prof. U. Mich., Ann Arbor, 1962-75; prof. SUNY Health Sci. Ctr., Bklyn., 1975—. Home: 100 Bank St New York NY 10014-2123 Office: SUNY Dept Physiology 450 Clarkson Ave Brooklyn NY 11203-2098

RANCK, ROBERT DALE, general contractor; b. Elmira, N.Y., Nov. 3, 1934; s. Harry L. and Anna E. (Cotner) R.; m. Susan J. Todd, Mar. 18, 1961; children: Leslie J., Karen E. Grad. Sch. Sales Mgmt. and Mktg., Syracuse U., 1971. Customer engr. Univac, Boston, 1959-63; sales engr. Computer Control Co., Albuquerque, 1963-65; regional sales mgr. Computer Control Co., Chgo., 1965-68; market mgr., then product mgr. Honeywell-Mini Computers, Framingham, Mass., 1968-71; group product mgr. Honeywell-Mini Computers, Welsley, Mass., 1971-73; v.p. sales Datatrol, Hudson, Mass., 1974-80; v.p. credit Associated Dry Goods, N.Y.C., 1980-87; owner, contractor Robert Ranck Builders, Amherst, N.H., 1987—. With U.S. Army, 1955-58. Republican. Methodist. Home and Office: 3 Old Quarry Ln Amherst NH 03031-1720

RAND, ARTHUR GORHAM, JR., food science educator, researcher; b. Boston, Sept. 29, 1935; s. Arthur G. and Mary (Nisbet) R.; m. Cynthia Pollard Rand, Sept. 3, 1960; children: Wesley, Douglas, Karen. BS, U. N.H., 1958; MS, U. Wis., 1961, PhD, 1964. Grad. rsch. asst. U. Wis., Madison, 1958-63; asst. prof. U. R.I., Kingston, 1963-70, assoc. prof., 1970-75, prof., 1975—, chmn. food sci. and nurtition, 1981-90, acting assoc. dean resource devel., 1986; vis. prof. U. NSW, Australia, 1971, Cook Coll., Rutgers U., New Brunswick, N.J., 1990. Author book chpt.; patentee in field; contbr. articles to profl. jours. Mem. Jr. C. of C., S. Kingstown, R.I., 1967-70; coach Youth Soccer, S. Kingstown, 1979, 85-86. Mem. Inst. Food Technologists (program com. 1986-89), Am. Soc. Enology and Viticulture, Am. Inst. Nutrition, Internat. Assn. Milk, Food, Environ. Sanitarians, Phi Kappa Phi, Phi Tau Sigma. Office: U R I Food Sci & Nutrition Rsch C 530 Liberty Ln West Kingston RI 02892-1802

RAND, JOELLA M., nursing educator; b. Akron, Ohio, July 9, 1932; d. Harry S. and Elizabeth May (Miller) Halberg; m. Martin Rand; children: Craig, Debbi Stark. BSN, U. Akron, 1961, MEd in Guidance, 1968; PhD in Higher Edn. Adminstrn., Syracuse U., 1981. Staff nurse Akron Gen. Hosp., 1953-54; staff-head nurse-instr. Summit County Receiving, Cuyahoga Falls, Ohio, 1954-56; head nurse psychiat. unit Akron Gen. Hosp., 1956-57; instr. psychiatric nursing Summit County Receiving, Cuyahoga Falls, 1957-61; head nurse, in-service instr. Willard (N.Y.) State Hosp., 1961-62; asst. prof. Alfred (N.Y.) U., 1962-76, assoc. prof., assoc. dean, 1976-78, acting dean, 1978-79, dean, 1979-90, dean coll. profl. studies, 1990-91, prof. counselor edn., 1991—; cons. N.Y. State Regents Program for Non-Collegiate Sponsored Instrn., 1984, Collegiate Programs for N.Y. State Dept. Edn., 1985; accreditation visitor Nat. League of Nursing, 1984-92. Recipient Teaching Excellence award Alfred U., 1977, Mary E. Gladwin Outstanding Alumni award Akron U. Coll. Nursing, 1983, Alfred Alumni Friends award, 1989. Mem. N.Y. State Coun. of Deans (treas. 1984-88), Genesee Regional Consortium (v.p.), Western N.Y. League Nursing (bd. dirs. 1991—), Genesee Valley Edn. Com. (chair 1984-86), Nat. League Nursing (accreditation vis. 1984-92), Friend of Alfred Alumnae, Sigma Theta Tau (treas. Alfred chpt. 1984-85). Office: Alfred U 343 Myers Hall Alfred NY 14802

RAND, MARTHA ELIZABETH, mental health clinician; b. N.Y.C., Nov. 30, 1950; d. Arthur and Jean (MacNeish) R.; m. David Louis Ryzman, Apr. 20, 1986. BA, CUNY, 1972; cert. in dance and movement therapy, Inst. of Sociotherapy, N.Y.C., 1978; MA, New Sch. for Social Rsch., N.Y.C., 1982; diploma, Swedish Inst., 1985; MSW, Fordham U., 1990. Adj. prof. yoga and dance Queensborough Community Coll., Queens, N.Y., 1978, 80; dep. dir. communications and spl. projects N.Y. State Spl. Prosecutor for Health, Social Svc. and Welfare, N.Y.C., 1978-79; instr. phys. edn. YWCA., N.Y.C., 1981-82, Human Rels. Ctr. New Sch. for Social Rsch., 1982-90; ptnr. Help Yourself Assocs., N.Y.C. and Montclair, N.J., 1981—; recreation dir. Coler Hosp., N.Y.C., 1985-86; ptnr. Lively Earth Yoga Studio, N.Y.C., 1984-85; staff clinician inpatient and intermediate care program eating disorders unit St. Clare's Hosp., Boonton, N.J., 1986—; ptnr. Lively Earth Yoga Studio, N.Y.C., 1984-85; dance therapist Very Spl. Arts N.J., 1989. Mem. Am. Massage Therapy Assn., Internat. Assn. Eating Disorder Profls. (cert. eating disorder therapist), Am. Group Psychotherapy Assn., Nat. Assn. Social Workers.

RANDALL, ALEXANDER, V, entrepreneur; b. Phila., Aug. 12, 1951; s. Alexander IV and Josephina Giovanna (Perlingiero) R.; m. Cameron Hall, Aug. 5, 1978; 1 child, Alexander VI. AB, Princeton U., 1973; MA, Columbia U., 1974, MEd, 1975, EdD, 1978. Lectr. overseas div. U. Md., Heidelberg, Germany, 1978-79, Tokyo, 1979-81; pres., founding ptnr. Boston Computer Exch., 1982—; exec. dir. East West Edn. Devel. Found., Boston, 1990—; keynote speaker meetings and symposia for businesses, govt. groups and svc. orgns. Author: Seat on the Exchange, 1987 (award 1987), Alex Randall's Used Computer Handbook, 1990; corr. Personal Computer TV; writer monthly mag. column The Well-Wired Entrepreneur, Success Mag. Am. participant USIA, 1986-87, Voice of Am. commentator, 1991. Mem. Boston Computer Soc. (sect. founder), Internat. Platform Assn., Smaller Bus. Assn. New Eng. (entrepreneurs award 1990). Quaker. Office: Boston Computer Exch PO Box 1177 Boston MA 02103-1177

RANDALL, PEGGY, fundraising executive; b. Boston, May 18, 1961; d. James E. and Dorothy (Rausch) R.; m. Neamet Elsayed, Oct. 28, 1990. BA in History cum laude, Rutgers U., 1983; MA in Am. Studies, U. Pa., 1984. Program adminstr. Social Sci. Rsch. Coun., N.Y.C., 1984-86; rsch. assoc. Health Svcs. Improvement Fund, N.Y.C., 1986-88; asst. dir. Authors Guild, N.Y.C., 1989-92; dir. Nation assocs. The Nation, N.Y.C., 1992—. Mem. Phi Beta Kappa, Phi Alpha Theta. Office: The Nation 72 5th Ave New York NY 10011

RANDALL, RICHARD STUART, political science educator; b. N.Y.C., Mar. 3, 1935; s. Leslie Van and Dorothy (Ahrens) R.; m. Laurie Wilson. BA, Antioch Coll., 1956; MS, PhD, U. Wis., 1966. Editor Maywood (Ill.) Herald, 1958-60; asst. prof. U. Nebr., Lincoln, 1965-69; assoc. dean Univ. Coll. NYU, N.Y.C., 1971-72, from assoc prof. to prof., 1969—; chair dept. politics NYU, N.Y.C., 1973-79, 89—. Author: Censorship of the Movies, 1968 (Broadcast Preceptor award for excellence Broadcast Industry Conf., 1969), Freedom and Taboo, 1989, Self-Regulation in the American Film Industry, 1970. Mem. Am. Polit. Sci. Assn., Internat. Soc. Polit. Psychology, Law ans Soc. Assn. Home: 321 Hartford Rd South Orange NJ 07079 Office: NYU Dept of Politics Washington Sq New York NY 10003

RANDALL, RICHARD WILLIAM, optometrist; b. Jamestown, N.Y., Nov. 29, 1931; s. Harry William and Claudia (Thompson) R.; m. Diane Nowak; children: David, Deborah, Douglas, Dawne, Allan, Kimberly. OD, Ill. Coll. Optometry, 1963. Optician House of Vision Inc., Chgo., 1960-63; pvt. practice optometry Geneseo, N.Y., 1963—; chief optometry sect. No. Livingston Health Ctr., Geneseo, 1974-77, Red Jacket Med. Ctr., Dansville, N.Y., 1975-77; pres. Lad-Nar Realty, Inc.; pres., gen. mgr. Ladco Internat.; exec. dir. Ladco Rental Property, Geneseo Profl. Bldg. (all Geneseo); clin. investigator Bausch & Lomb; lectr. OptiFair East, N.Y.C., 1982, 86, OptiFair West, Calif., 1985; cons. in field. Contbr. articles to profl. jours. Exec. dir. Livingston County (N.Y.) Traffic Safety Bd., 1976-82; bd. dirs. Rochester, N.Y. Safety Coun., 1982—; mem. Geneseo Ambulance Squad, N.Y. State Emergency Med. Technicians, 1981-88; bd. dirs. Geneseo Fire Dept., 1982-84; dep. coord. STOP-DWI Adv. Com., Livingston County, 1982; dep. sheriff county of Livingston, 1966—. With USAF, 1951-53, Korea. Recipient scholarship award Am. Bd. Opticianry, 1960, Clin. Optometry award Ill. Coll. Optometry, 1963. Fellow Am. Acad. Optometry; mem. Am. Optometric Assn. (practice enhancement adv. task force 1982-83), N.Y. State Optometric Assn. (chmn. master plan com. 1976-78), Optometric Ctr. N.Y., Better Vision Inst., Am. Pub. Health Assn., Coun. Sports Vision. Methodist. Office: 4384 Lakeville Rd PO Box 2020 Geneseo NY 14454

RANDALL, ROBERT L(EE), industrial economist; b. Aberdeen, S.D., Dec. 28, 1936; s. Harry Eugene and Juanita Alice (Barstow) R. MS in Phys. Chemistry, U. Chgo., 1960, MBA, 1963. Market devel. chemist E.I. du Pont

de Nemours & Co., Inc., Wilmington, Del., 1963-65; chem. economist Battelle Meml. Inst., Columbus, Ohio, 1965-68; mgr. market and econ. rsch. Kennecott Copper Corp., N.Y.C., 1968-74, economist, 1974-79, dir. new bus. venture devel., 1979-81; pres., mng. dir. R.L. Randall Assocs., Inc., 1981—; economist U.S. Internat. Trade Commn., Washington, 1983—; pres., exec. dir. The RainForest ReGeneration Inst., 1986—; indsl. panel policy rev. of effect of regulation on innovation and U.S.-internat. competition U.S. Dept. Commerce, 1980-81. Contbr. articles to profl. jours.; contbg. author: Computer Methods for the '80's. Mem. AAAS (organizer ann. meeting Tropical Forest Regeration Symposium), AIME (econs. coun., sec. mineral econ. subsect.), Am. Econ. Assn., Am. Statis. Assn., Am. Chem. Soc., Soc. Mining Engrs., Chemists Club N.Y.C., Metall. Soc., N.Y. Acad. Scis., Nat. Econs. Club Washington (sec., reporter), Assn. Environ. and Resource Economists. Home: 1727 Massachusetts Ave NW Washington DC 20036-2153 Office: US Internat Trade Com 500 E Street SW Washington DC 20436

RANDALL, THOMAS JOSEPH, social worker, writer; b. Bklyn., June 6, 1945; s. Harold James and Muriel Frances (Glass) R.; m. Judi Culbertson, June 22, 1974; 1 son, Andrew. BA, St. Lawrence U., 1967. Caseworker Suffolk County Dept. Social Svcs., Hauppauge, N.Y., 1970-90, sr. caseworker, 1990—. Co-author, photographer Permanent Parisians, 1986, Permanent New Yorkers, 1988 (listed as One of Best Reference Books 1988 N.Y. Pub. Libr.), Permanent Californians, 1989, Permanent Londoners, 1991. Coach little league, Port Jefferson, N.Y., 1976, 77; worker Anti-Shoreham Nuclear Campaign, Nesconsett, N.Y., 1979-80. Served to ensign USN, 1969. Democrat. Mem. Unitarian Ch. Home: 211 Hawthorne St Port Jefferson NY 11777

RANDEL, WILLIAM PEIRCE, English educator; b. N.Y.C., Jan. 7, 1909; s. William Adonijah and Mabel Lucy (Peirce) R.; m. Janet Hosmer Belknap, July 3, 1931; children: William Peirce Jr., Elizabeth Peirce. BS, Columbia U., 1932, PhD, 1945; AM, U. Mich., 1933; BA, Denison U., 1981. Instr. rhetoric U. Minn., St. Paul, 1936-45; asst. prof. English Mo. Sch. Mines, Rolla, 1945-47; assoc. prof., then prof. Fla. State U., Tallahassee, 1947-65; prof. English U. Maine, Orono, 1965-74, Lloyd Elliott chair in English, 1972-74, prof. emeritus, 1974—; summer instr. U. Mo., 1947, U. Minn., 1950, Duke U., 1952; Coe prof. U. Wyo., 1959; Truman Act tchr. U. Helsinki, Finaldn, 1950-51; Fulbright prof. Am. civilization U. Athens, Greece, 1955-56; Smith-Mundt Act prof. Univ. Coll. W.I., 1957-58; Fulbright Act prof. U. Bologna, 1965; mem. coun. of colls U. Maine, Orono, 1968-71, chmn., 1970-71. Author: Orphic Sayings as Originally Written by Bronson Alcott, 1939, Edward Eggleston: Author of The Hoosier Schoolmaster, 1946, reprint edit., 1962, The Ku Klux Klan: A Century of Infamy, 1965, Centennial: American Life in 1876, 1969, American Revolution: Mirror of a People, 1973, The Evolution of American Taste, 1978; contbr. articles to numerous scholarly publs. Recipient alumni citation Denison U., 1971, 350th Anniversary medallion U. Helsinki, 1990. Mem. MLA, AAUP, Am. Dialect Soc., Am. Name Soc., Internat. Assn. Univ. Profs. English, Modern Humanities Rsch. Assn., Am. Studies Assn., New Century Club, Phi Delta Theta. Democrat. Home: RR 1 Box 180 Waterboro ME 04087-9705

RANDELL, JOSEPH DAVID, airline executive; b. Corner Brook, Newfoundland, Can., Feb. 20, 1954; s. Sterling A. and Mercedes O. (Locke) R.; m. Kathryn Janet Oxford, Sept. 3, 1977; children: David, Adam, Leah, Rebecca. B in Indsl. Engring., Tech. U. Nova Scotia, Halifax, 1976; MBA, Meml. U. Newfoundland, St. John's, 1985. Mgr. market devel. Ea. Provincial Airways, Gander, Newfoundland, 1976-77, asst. to v.p. mktg., 1977-78; dir. product planning Ea. Provincial Airways, Halifax, 1978-79; asst. mgr. Locke's Elec. Ltd., Corner Brook, 1979-80; v.p. Atlantis Corp. Ltd., St. John's, 1981-86; trans. cons. Atlantis Cons. Ltd., St. John's, 1980-81; exec. v.p. Air Nova Inc., Halifax, 1986-88, pres., CEO, 1988—; Dir. Air Transp. Assn. Can., Ottawa, 1991, 92. Dir. Bedford (Can.) Econ. Devel. Commn., 1992. Sexton Scholar, Tech. U. Nova Scotia, 1976. Mem. Assn. Profl. Engrs. of Nova Scotia. Anglican. Home: 110 Peregrine Ctr, Bedford, NS Canada b4a-3c1 Office: Air Nova, PO Box 158, Elmsdale, NS Canada B0N 1M0

RANDOLPH, ARTHUR RAYMOND, judge, lawyer; b. Riverside, N.J., Nov. 1, 1943; m. Eileen J. O'Connor, May 18, 1984; children from previous marriage: John Trevor, Cynthia Lee. BS, Drexel U., 1966; JD summa cum laude, U. Pa., 1969. Bar: Calif. 1970, D.C. 1973, U.S. Supreme Ct. 1973. Law clk. to hon. judge Henry J. Friendly U.S. Ct. Appeals, 2d Cir., N.Y.C., 1969-70; asst. to solicitor gen. U.S. Dept. Justice, Washington, 1970-73, dep. solicitor gen., 1975-77; ptnr. Sharp, Randolph & Green, Washington, 1977-83, Randolph & Truitt, Washington, 1983-87, Pepper, Hamilton & Scheetz, Washington, 1987-90; judge U.S. Ct. Appeals (D.C. cir.), Washington, 1990—; spl. asst. atty. gen. State of Mont., 1983-90, State of N.Mex., 1985-90, State of Utah, 1986-90; mem. adv. panel Fed. Cts. Study Com., 1989-90; spl. counsel Com. on Standards of Ofcl. Conduct, U.S. Ho. of Reps., 1979-80; adj. prof. law Georgetown U. Law Ctr., 1974-78; exec. sec. Atty. Gen.'s Com. on Reform of Fed. Jud. System, 1975-77; mem. com. on Fed. Rules of Evidence U.S. Justice Dept., 1972; chmn. Com. on Govtl. Structures, McLean, Va., 1973-74. Recipient Spl. Achievement award U.S. Dept. Justice, 1971. Mem. Am., Calif., D.C. bar assns., Am. Law Inst., Order of Coif. Home: 8708 Fenway Dr Bethesda MD 20817-2712 Office: US Ct Appeals 3rd & Constitution Ave NW Washington DC 20001

RANELLI, JOHN RAYMOND, footwear and apparel company executive; b. New London, Conn., Sept. 25, 1946; s. Frank Robert and Sue Mary (Bongo) R.; m. Paula Jean Contillo, June 8, 1968; children: Carina, Christina, Jennifer. Student, U. Loyola, Rome, 1966-67; A.B. in History, Coll. Holy Cross, 1968; M.B.A., Dartmouth Coll., 1973. Fin. analyst Gen. Motors Corp., N.Y.C., 1973-74; mgr. fin. adminstrn. No. Telecom, Inc., Nashville, 1975-76; asst. treas. No. Telecom. Inc., Nashville, 1976-77; treas. No. Telecom, Inc., Nashville, 1977-78; asst. controller No. Telecom, Ltd., Montreal, Que., Can., 1978-79; treas. ARA Services Inc., Phila., 1980-81, v.p., treas., sec. to fin. com., dir., mem. retirement com., 1981-83, pres. Aero Enterprises div., 1983-85; chief fin. officer, mem. exec. com. Atcor, Inc., Harvey, Ill., 1985-87; v.p., chief fin. officer Cyclops Industries, Mt. Lebanon, Pa., 1987-88; v.p., treas. Ames Dept. Stores, Inc., Rocky Hill, Conn., 1989-90; sr. v.p. fin., adminstrn. and chief fin. officer Timberland Co., Hampton, N.H., 1990—. Co-author: Mutual Savings Banking at the Crossroads: Renaissance or Extinction, 1973. Bd. dirs. Easter Seals Ea. Conn. With submarine force USN, 1968-71. Decorated Nat. Def. medal; Fulbright Scholar, 1968. Mem. Fin. Exec. Inst., Coll. Holy Cross Alumni Assn. Lodge: K.C. Office: The Timberland Co 11 Merrill Indsl Pkwy Hampton NH 03842

RANGANATHAN, BABU GOPAL, retail service associate; b. Madras, Tamil Nadu, India, June 13, 1957; came to U.S., 1964; s. Vasudeva and Vasantha Ranganathan; m. Sheila Victor, Aug. 24, 1989. BA in Theology, minor in Biology, 1982. Author: Origins?, 1988, Korean edition, 1992. Republican. Baptist. Home: 68 Fox Chase Ln West Hartford CT 06117

RANGEL, CHARLES BERNARD, congressman; b. Harlem, N.Y., June 11, 1930; s. Ralph and Blanche (Wharton) R.; m. Alma Carter, July 26, 1964; children: Steven, Alicia. BS, NYU, 1957; JD, St. John's U. Sch. Law, 1960; LLD (hon.), Wagner Coll., 1982, Atlanta U., 1983, St. John's U., Mt. Sinai Sch. Medicine, NYU, Howard U., 1988, Hofstra U., 1989. Bar: N.Y. 1960. Asst. U.S. atty. So. Dist. N.Y., 1961-62; mem. N.Y. State Assembly, 1966-70, 92nd-102nd Congresses from 19th, now 16th N.Y. dist., 1971—; mem. ways and means com., chmn. select com. on narcotics abuse and control. Served with AUS, 1948-52, Korea. Decorated Bronze Star, Purple Heart (U.S.); Korean presdl. citations. Home: 40 W 135th St New York NY 10037-2504 Office: US Ho of Reps 2252 Rayburn House Office Bldg Washington DC 20515

RANIOLO, FRANK JOSEPH, rubber and chemical company executive; b. N.Y.C., Aug. 16, 1934; s. Salvatore and Catherine (Battaglia) R.; m. Ida Capolino, June 16, 1956; 1 child, Robert T. BBA, B.M. Baruch Sch. Bus., 1961. Traffic and ins. clk. Baird Rubber & Tog Co., Inc., N.Y.C., 1951-53, asst. traffic mgr., 1955-61; v.p., gen. mgr. Robert B. Baird & Co., Inc., N.Y.C., 1962-72; v.p. Natural Rubber Inspection Svc., N.Y.C., 1972-73; mem. Alcan Rubber & Chem., Inc., N.Y.C., 1973, pres., chief exec. officer, 1975—. Advisor U.S. Dept. Commerce-USTR, Washington, 1978. Sgt. U.S. Army, 1953-54, Korea. Mem. Am. Chem. Soc. Roman Catholic. Office: Alcan Rubber & Chem Inc 29 Broadway Fl 19 New York NY 10006-3201

RANIS, GUSTAV, economist, educator; b. Darmstadt, Germany, Oct. 24, 1929; s. Max and Bettina (Goldschmidt) R.; m. Ray Lee Finkelstein, June 15, 1958; children: Michael Bruce, Alan Jonathan, Bettina Suzanne. BA summa cum laude, Brandeis U., 1952, hon. degree, 1982; MA, Yale U., 1953, PhD, 1956. Asst. adminstr. program and policy AID, 1965-67; dir. Econ. Growth Ctr. Yale U., New Haven, 1967-75, prof. econs., 1964—, Frank Altschul prof. internat. econs., 1981—; vis. prof. Colombia, 1976-77; cons. World Bank, AID, Ford Found., ILO, FAO, Inter-Am. Devel. Bank; Ford Found. vis. prof. U. de los Andes, Bogota, Ford Found., Colegio de Mex., 1971-72. Author: (with John Fei) Development of the Labor Surplus Economy: Theory and Policy, 1964, (with Fei and Shirley Kuo) Growth with Equity: The Taiwan Case, 1979, (with Keijiro Otsuka and Gary Saxonhouse) Comparative Technology Choice in Development, 1988, (with F. Stewart and E. Angeles-Reyes) Linkages in Developing Economies: A Philippine Study, 1990, (with S.A. Mahmood) Political Economy of Development Policy Change, 1992; editor: Taiwan: From Developing to Mature Economy, 1992; co-editor: The State of Development Economics, 1988, Science and Technology: Lessons for Development Policy, 1990. Trustee Brandeis U., 1967—, chmn. acad. affairs com., 1986—, Ford Found. Faculty fellow Social Sci. Rsch. Coun. fellow, Japan, 1955-56. Mem. Am. Econ. Assn., Coun. Fgn. Rels., Overseas Develop. Coun. (mem. adv. com.). Home: 7 Mulberry Rd Woodbridge CT 06525-1716 Office: Yale U Econ Growth Ctr 27 Hillhouse Ave New Haven CT 06520-1987

RANKEL, LILLIAN ANN, chemist; b. N.Y.C., Mar. 30, 1944; d. Robert Andrew and Lillian Hope (Erbe) R.; m. Andrew Jackson, Jan. 2, 1981; children: Robert, David, Lillian. BS, Molloy Coll., Rockville Center, N.Y., 1966; MS, Fordham U., 1968; PhD, Princeton U., 1977. Assoc. mem. tech. staff Bell Telephone Labs., Murray Hill, N.J., 1968-73; assoc. in chemistry Mobil R&D Corp., Princeton, N.J., 1977—. Patentee in field; contbr. articles to profl. jours. NIH fellow, 1974-77, Atomic Energy Commn. fellow, 1967-68. Mem. Am. Chem. Soc., Catalysis Club Phila. Office: Mobil R&D Corp PO Box 1025 Princeton NJ 08543-1025

RANKIN, CLYDE EVAN, III, lawyer; b. Phila., July 3, 1950; s. Clyde Evan, Jr. and Mary E. (Peluso) R. A.B., Princeton U., 1972; J.D., Columbia U., 1975; postgrad. Hague Acad. Internat. Law, 1975. Bar: N.Y., N.J., D.C., U.S. Supreme Ct. Law clk. to judge U.S. Dist. Ct. So. Dist. N.Y., 1975-77; assoc. Debevoise, Plimpton, Lyons & Gates, N.Y.C., 1977-79; assoc. Coudert Bros., N.Y.C., 1979-83, ptnr., 1984—. Trustee The Rensselaerville (N.Y.) Inst., 1989—. Stone scholar, 1974. Mem. ABA, Assn. of Bar of City of N.Y., N.Y. State Bar Assn., D.C. Bar Assn., N.J. Bar Assn. Roman Catholic. Club: Amateur Comedy (N.Y.C.). Contbr. article to legal jour. Office: Coudert Bros 200 Park Ave New York NY 10166-0005

RANKIN, JUANITA ROSE, accountant; b. Bridgeton, N.J., Nov. 1, 1949; d. Andrew Jackson and Jessie Lee (Bryant) Rankin; m. Ronald Delaneo Smith, Mar. 23, 1968 (div. Nov. 1978); 1 child, LaJuana. BS, Glassboro State Coll., 1982. Operating acct. Communications-Electronics Command U.S. Army, Ft. Monmouth, N.J., 1984—; with Task Force at Strategic Agency U.S. Army, Ft. Belvoir, Va., 1991; part-time instr. Union Tech. Inst., Neptune, N.J., 1989-90; mem. task force at Strategic Logistics Agy., Dept. Army, Ft. Belvoir, Va., 1991. Bd. dirs. Bridgeton Housing Devel. Corp., 1984-85; pres. Bridgeton High Sch. PTA, 1982; trustee Macedonia Bapt. Ch., Neptune, N.J., 1986. Mem. Am. Soc. Mil. Compts., Nat. Assn. Negro Bus. and Profl. Women (fin. sec. Cen. Jersey club 1988-90), Assn. Govt. Accts. (dir. edn. Cen. N.J. chpt.). Democrat. Baptist. Home: 2130 Aldrin Rd Apt 6A Asbury Park NJ 07712-2441 Office: US Army Communications and Electronics Command AMSEL COP FA JD Fort Monmouth NJ 07703-5009

RANKIN, THOMAS ROBERT, advertising and public relations executive; b. Rochester, N.Y., July 2, 1947; s. Robert Thomas and Alice May (Caister) R.; m. Lauren Ann Radtke, June 10, 1978; children: Jason, Carolyn. BA, U. R.I., 1974. Editor, pub. Just Pulp The Magazine of Pop Fiction, R.I., 1975-81; freelance copywriter R.I., 1978-82; v.p., dir. pub. rels. S.B.N., Seekonk, Mass., 1982-87; pres. Martin Thomas, Inc., Providence, 1987—. Mem. PRSA, Am. Diabetes Assn. (mktg./communications counsel, vol. of yr. 1990), Counselors Acad., Soc. Plastics Engrs., Soc. Plastics Industry. Office: Martin Thomas Inc One Smith Hill Providence RI 02903

RANKIN-SMITH, PAMELA, photographer; b. Kansas City, Kans., Jan. 12, 1918; d. Dexter Leon and Ruth Dee (Millard) Rankin; m. George W. Witcher, 1943 (div. 1945); 1 child, Vann Leigh Witcher; m. A. Arthur Smith, 1968 (dec. 1968). Diploma, Dallas Little Theater, 1936; student, U. Tex., 1937-41; lic. in real estate, New Sch., N.Y.C., 1954; cert., Sogetsu Sch. Ikebana, N.Y.C., 1989-91. Real estate agt. N.Y.C., 1954-91; arranger Ikebana flowers Met. Mus. Art, N.Y.C., 1989-91. One-woman photography shows include Soho/Stieglitz Gallery, N.Y.C., 1978, La Galerie, Paris, 1979, Donnell Libr., N.Y.C., 1979, Fed. Hall, N.Y.C., 1978, Nikon House, N.Y.C., 1980, Overseas Press Club, N.Y.C., 1980, Le Gallery, Kent, Conn., 1981, Camera Club N.Y., N.Y.C., 1985. Mem. PEN, Photographic Adminstrs., Inc., Actors' Equity Assn., Am. Soc. Mag. Photographers, Ikebana Internat., Nat. Guild Decoupeurs, Mcpl. Art Soc., Nat. Arts Club, Camera Club N.Y. Home: 150 E 69th St New York NY 10021-5704

RANSIL, BERNARD J(EROME), research physician, methodologist, consultant, educator; b. Pitts., Nov. 15, 1929; s. Raymond Augustine and Louise Mary (Berhalter) R. BS, Duquesne U., 1951; PhD in Phys. Chemistry, Cath. U. Am., 1955; MD, U. Chgo., 1964. NRC-NAS rsch. assoc. Nat. Bur. Standards, Washington, 1955-56, cons. heat div. thermodynamics sect., 1956-62; cons. NASA exobiology project, Washington, 1962-68; rsch. assoc. and dir. diatomic molecule project Lab. Molecular Structure and Spectra, physics dept. U. Chgo., 1956-63; intern Harbor Gen. Hosp., UCLA, Torrance, 1964-65, Guggenheim fellow, 1965-66; from rsch. assoc. in medicine to assoc. prof. in medicine Harvard Med. Sch., Boston, 1966—; asst. physician, dir. Core Lab., Clin. Rsch. Ctr. Beth Israel Hosp., Boston, 1974—; cons. Prophet project NIH, Bethesda, Md., 1971-88, exec. com., 1986—, Howard Hughes Med. Inst., Boston, 1979-80, Coop. Cataract Rsch. Group, Boston, 1981-83; vis. scientist Rockefeller U., 1985, Scripps Rsch. Found., 1986, Calif. State U., 1986, U. Pitts. Med. Sch., 1987. Author: Abortion, 1969, Background to Abortion, 1979; editor: Life of a Scientist: Autobiography of Robert S. Mulliken, 1989, (videocassettes) Elements of Statistics and Data Analysis, 1985, diatomic molecules studies, 1960-80; contbr. numerous articles and book revs. in sci. jours. and non-sci. periodicals. Recipient alumni rsch. award Cath. U. Am., 1969, Duquesne U. centennial award, 1978. Mem. numerous profl. socs. Office: Beth Israel Hosp Dept Medicine Boston MA 02215

RANSOHOFF, PRISCILLA BURNETT, psychologist, educator; b. Pitts., June 16, 1912; d. Levi Herr and Clara Amelia (Brown) Burnett; m. James Hampton Johnston, Aug. 4, 1934; 1 child, Priscilla Burnett; m. Nicholas Sigmund Ransohoff, Nov. 27, 1947. BS, U. Pitts., 1941; MA, Columbia U., 1952, EdD, 1954. Dir. rehab. Monmouth Med. Ctr., Long Branch, N.J., 1944-54; pres. Cons. Assocs., Inc., Long Branch, 1954-64; v.p. Dale-Elliot Mgmt. Cons., N.Y.C., 1958-60; edn. adviser U.S. Army Electronics Command, Ft. Monmouth, N.J., 1964-78; organizational effectiveness staff officer U.S. Army Communications Materiel Readiness Command, Ft. Monmouth, 1978—; co-adj. prof. Ocean County Community Coll., Toms River, N.J.; co-adj. instr. Monmouth Coll., West Long Branch, N.J., Brookdale Community Coll., Lincroft, N.J. Founder, pres., chmn. bd. Monmouth Rehab. Workshop, Red Bank, N.J., 1954-58; vice chmn. N.J. del. Women's Conf., Houston, 1977; chmn. Amelia Earhart Found. Monmouth County chpt., 1987—. Recipient CECOM Comdr.'s Internat., 1982, Woman of Yr. award Zonta, 1984, 90, Pres.'s award AUSA, 1990; cert. practitioner neuro linguistic programming. Mem. Internat. Platform Assn., Federally Employed Women (pres. 1973, 74, chpt. pres. 1984-85, 89—), Assn. U.S. Army (sec., adv. com. to nat. exec. bd., 3 yrs.), Assn. U.S. Army (sec., drug and alcohol com. Ft. Monmouth chpt., suicide prevention and intervention coun., human resource coun., civilian adv. com. to nat. bd. 1986—), Pi Lambda Theta, Kappa Delta Pi, Delta Zeta, Zonta Internat. (bd. dirs. Monmouth County chpt., chmn. Amelia Earhart Found.), Order of Eastern Star. Home: 13 River Ave Monmouth Beach NJ 07750-1336 Office: Aviation Rsch and Devel Activity Fort Monmouth NJ 07703

RANSONE, ROBIN KEY, proposals consultant; b. Ft. Worth, Mar. 28, 1933; d. Reuben Key and Lilyan Paula (Hudzietz) R.; m. Paula Jane McBride, Jan. 30, 1959; children: William Key, Cheryl Elizabeth. BS in Aero. Engring., Tex. A&M U., 1956, postgrad., 1966; postgrad., UCLA, 1963, U. Tex., 1979-82. Flight test program mgr. Air Force Flight Test Ctr., Edwards AFB, Calif., 1963-68; devel. engr. Am. Airlines, Inc., N.Y.C., 1968-72; dir. aero. oper. systems office NASA, Washington, 1972-73; vis. assoc. prof. U. Va., Charlottesville, 1973-76; sr. specialist tech. communicating Vought Corp., Dallas, 1976-82; proposals dir. Fairchild Rep. Co., Farmingdale, N.Y., 1982-84; v.p. systems devel. MJI Assocs., Inc., Centerport, N.Y., 1984-86; pres. R.K. Ransone Assocs., Inc., Smithtown, N.Y., 1986—. Inventor hand held helicopter performance computer. Elder 1st Presbyn. Ch., Smithtown, 1984-87; founder, pres. Huntington Pk. Homeowners Assn., Duncanville, Tex., 1981-82; trustee Trinity United Meth. Ch., Duncanville, 1979-82, chmn. bldg. com., 1981-82. Capt. USAF, 1956-63. Fellow AIAA (assoc.); mem. Am. Soc. Automotive Engrs., Tech. Mktg. Soc. Am., Assn. Proposal Mgmt. Profls., Antelope Valley Photography Assn. (founder, pres. Lancaster, Calif. chpt. 1966-67), Toastmasters (pres. Edwards AFB chpt. 1964-68).

RAO, RAMGOPAL PALAKURTHI, healthcare company executive; b. Hyderabad, India, Aug. 15, 1942; came to U.S., 1965; s. Seshgir P. and Arya (K.) R.; m. Sandhya R. Kulkarni, June 15, 1969; children: Sameer, Sushant, Neeraj. BSEE, Regional Engring. Coll., A-P, India, 1965; MSEE, Okla. State U., 1966; postgrad., MIT, 1966-68; MBA, Northeastern U., 1972. Systems engr. Honeywell, Inc., Waltham, Mass., 1966-69; sr. engr. Digilab Inc., Cambridge, Mass., 1970-71; dir. engring. Digilab Inc., Cambridge, 1971-73, dir. svc., 1974-76, v.p. mfg., 1976-80; div. mgr. Biorad Labs./ Ophthalmic Div., Cambridge, 1980-90; pres., chief exec. officer Tomey Technology, Inc., Cambridge, 1991—; gen. mgr. Tomey Corp., U.S.A., Cambridge, 1991—. Pres. Mass. Soc. to Prevent Blindness, Belmont, 1990—. Mem. IEEE. Home: 31 Stewart Rd Needham MA 02192-1119 Office: Tomey Technology Inc 325 Vassar St Cambridge MA 02139-4893

RAO, SETHURAMIAH LAKSHMINARAYANA, United Nations officer; b. Mysore, Karnataka, India, Apr. 28, 1942; came to U.S., 1967; s. Ramakrishniah Sethuramiah and Bhageerathi; m. Sudha Bagur Viswanath, Jan. 1, 1971; children: Rekha, Kumar. MSc, U. Mysore, 1963; MPH, U. N.C., 1968; cert., U. Mich., 1969; PhD, U. Pa., 1971. Asst. prof. Brown U., Providence, 1971-73; UN adviser Govt. of Sri Lanka, Colombo, 1974-77; chief population and devel. UN Population Fund, N.Y.C., 1978-82, chief policy br., 1982-90; country dir. UN Population Fund, Addis Ababa, Ethiopia, 1991-92; dep. dir. info. & extern rels. UN Population Fund, N.Y.C., 1992—. Author: Socio-Religious Factors in Fertility, 1973; co-author: Population Problems of Sri Lanka, 1977, Population Program Experience, 1991; contbr. articles to profl. jours. V.p. Mysore Self Reliance Assn., Mangalore, 1963-65, Indo-Am. Forum for Polit. Edn., N.Y., 1989-90; founder, pres. New Eng. Kannada Koota, Providence, 1972-73. Mem. Delta Omega. Home: 143 Nelson Rd Scarsdale NY 10583 Office: UN Population Fund 220 E 42d St New York NY 10017

RAO, TUMKUR KRISHNA MURTHY SREEPADA, nephrologist, consultant; b. Kolar, India, June 4, 1944; came to U.S., 1967; s. T.K. Krishna Murthy and Nagamma Rao; m. Pushpa Rao, Mar. 9, 1972; children: Kiran, Sheethal. PUC, Nat. Coll. Bangalore, India, 1960; MBBS, Bangalore Med. Coll., India, 1966. Clin. instr. N.J. Coll. Medicine, Newark, 1970-71; asst. clin. instr. SUNY Health Sci. Ctr., Bklyn., 1971-73, instr. in surgery, 1973, asst. prof. surgery, 1974-75, asst. prof. medicine, 1975-78, assoc. prof. medicine, 1979—, assoc. dir. renal div., 1981—; bd. dirs. hemodialysis unit Kings County Hosp.; cons. Wyckoff Heights Hosp., Bklyn., 1973—, Bklyn. VA Hosp., 1975—. Presenter in field; author over 80 abstracts; contbr. over 80 articles to profl. jours. Pres. Karnataka State Med. and Dental Alumni Assn. Am., 1984-90; exec. v.p Nargis Dutt Meml. Found., 1989—. Recipient N.Y. Asian-Am. Lions award, 1980, fellowship Madras (India) Med. Coll., 1985, Kasturba Med. Coll., India, 1985. Fellow Am. Coll. Physicians; mem. Internat. Soc. Nephrology, Am. Soc. Nephrology, N.Y. Soc. Nephrology, Am. Soc. Artificial Internal Organs, Internat. Soc. Artificial Organs, Internat. Transplantation Soc., Nat. Kidney Found. Hindu. Office: SUNY Health Sci Ctr 450 Clarkson Ave Box 52 Brooklyn NY 11203

RAOUF, RAOUF ALI, engineering educator; b. Jerusalem, Jordan, Nov. 21, 1960; came to U.S., 1984; s. Ali Parviz and Mahasen (Dejani) R.; m. Kathryn Ann Kaechele, Feb. 29, 1988; children: Suzanne Dejani, David Ali. BS in Civil Engring., U. Jordan, 1983; MS in Engring. Mechanics, VA. Poly. Inst. and State U., 1986, PhD in Engring. Mechanics, 1989. Grad. rsch. and teaching asst., dept. engring. sci. & mechs. Va. Poly. Inst. and State Univ., Blacksburg, 1984-89; postdoctoral rsch. assoc. Joint Inst. Advancement Flight Sci George Washington U., NASA Langley Rsch. Ctr., Hampton, Va., 1989-90; asst. prof. U.S. Naval Acad., Annapolis, Md., 1990—; vis. rsch. scientist Air Force Inst. of Tech./Wright-Patterson AFB, Dayton, summers 1989, 90; dir. Dept. Computer Aided Design and Integrated Graphics U.S. NAval Acad., 1992—; cons. engr. Madi and Ptnrs., Amman, Jordan, 1983-84. Contbr. articles to profl. jours. Rsch. grantee Naval Acad. Rsch. Coun. Mem. AIAA, Am. Soc. Mech. Engrs. (assoc. mem.), ASCE (assoc. mem.). Office: US Naval Acad Dept Mech Engring Annapolis MD 21402

RAPAPORT, WILLIAM JOSEPH, computer science educator, cognitive scientist; b. Bklyn., Sept. 30, 1946; s. Frank Henry and Harriet Floret (Flanders) R.; m. Barbara Sirvetz, May 1976 (div. Oct. 1981). BA, U. Rochester, 1968; MA, Ind. U., 1974, PhD, 1976; MS, SUNY, Buffalo, 1984. Tchr. math. Inwood Jr. High Sch., N.Y.C., 1968-69, Walden Sch., N.Y.C., 1969-71; assoc. instr. philosophy Ind. U., Bloomington, 1971-72, asst. to editor Nous, 1972-75, assoc. instr. math., 1975; asst. prof. philosophy SUNY, Fredonia, 1976-83, assoc. prof., 1983-84; asst. prof. computer sci. SUNY, Buffalo, 1984-88, assoc. prof., 1988—, assoc. dir. Semantic Network Processing System rsch. group, 1984—; Steelman vis. scientist Lenoir-Rhyne Coll., 1989. Co-author: Logic: A Computer Approach, 1985; editor spl. issue Nous, 1991; book rev. editor Minds and Machines, 1991—; mem. editorial bd. various jours.; also articles. Recipient Chancellor's award for excellence in teaching SUNY, Fredonia, 1981, Master Scholar award New Eng. Assn. Grad. Schs., 1989, Disting. Alumnus award Ind. U., 1990; grantee NSF, NEH, SUNY Rsch. Found., 1977-90. Mem. Soc. for Machines and Mentality (pres. 1991—), Am. Philos. Assn. (essay prize 1982), Am. Assn. for Artificial Intelligence, Assn. for Computational Linguistics, Cognitive Sci. Soc., also others. Office: SUNY Dept Computer Sci Buffalo NY 14260

RAPHAEL, DANA, health science association director; b. Hartford, Conn.; children: Brett, Seth, Jessa. BS, Columbia U., 1956, PhD, 1966. Asst. dir. United Artists TV, N.Y.C., 1973-74; dir. Human Lactation Ctr., Westport, Conn., 1974—; asst. adj. prof. Anthropology Ctr. for Lifetime Learning, Fairfield, Conn., 1973-76; lectr. Yale Sch., Conn., 1980—; cons. in field. Author: The Tender Gift: Breastfeeding, 1973, Being Female: Reproduction Power and Change, 1975, Breastfeeding: Food Policy in a Hungry World, 1978; (with Flora Davis) Only Mothers Know, 1985; contbr. numerous articles to profl. jours.; appeared on TV shows regarding lactation, weaning and child abuse Geraldo, Sally J. Raphael, Jim Grant; radio stas., Chgo. Cleve., Milw., Rochester, N.Y., India, Japa, Eng. Named Outstanding Woman, Nat. Fedn. Bus. and Profl. Women, 1976; Fulbright grantee, Japan, 1989, 91. Mem. Soc. of Friends. Office: The Human Lactation Ctr Ltd 666 Sturges Hwy Westport CT 06880

RAPHAELSON, ARNOLD HERBERT, economist, educator; b. Worcester, Mass., Oct. 13, 1929; s. Louis and Celia (Ostroff) R.; A.B. in English, Brown U., 1950; M.S. in Journalism, Columbia U., 1951; M.A. in Econs., Clark U., 1956, Ph.D., 1960; m. Ruth Camann, July 4, 1951; children—Marc, Jonathan, Joshua. City staff reporter Worcester Telegram, 1953-55; lectr. part-time Clark U., 1957-58; asst. prof. econs. U. Maine, 1958-60, asso. prof., 1960-66; counsel Subcom. on Intergovtl. Relations, U.S. Senate, 1964-65; asso. prof. econs. Temple U., Phila., 1966-70, prof., 1970—; cons. to govt. agys., 1964—. Mem. Upper Dublin (Pa.) Ednl. Adv. Com., 1972-78. Served with U.S. Army, 1951-53. Mem. Am. Econ. Assn., Health

Econs. Research Orgn. Jewish. Contbr. articles on health econs. to profl. jours. Office: Temple U Speakman Hall Dept Econs Philadelphia PA 19211

RAPKIN, GRACE ZUCKER, marketing consultant; b. Chgo., Aug. 9, 1958; m. Bruce David Rapkin, Aug. 3, 1986. BA in Internat. Affairs, U. Ill., 1980, MBA, 1984. Mgr. mktg. SLM Instruments, Inc., Urbana, Ill., 1984-86, 92d St YM-YWHA, N.Y.C., 1986-88; mktg. cons. Hartsdale, N.Y., 1988—. Mem. Am. Mktg. Assn. (founder, chair Leadership Coun. 1987-90). Office: 45 Harvard Dr Hartsdale NY 10530-2006

RAPKIN, JEROME, def. industry exec.; b. Wilmington, Del., Aug. 1, 1929; s. Harry and Ida (Hermann) R.; B.S. in Marine Engring., U.S. Naval Acad., 1952; M.S. in E.E., U.S. Naval Postgrad. Sch., 1959; postgrad. Armed Forces Staff Coll., 1965, Catholic U. Am., 1978; m. Janet Vansant, Nov. 4, 1954; children—Keith, Leigh, Paige. Commd. ensign U.S. Navy, 1952, advanced through grades to capt., 1979; dir. Surface Warfare Systems Naval Sea Systems Command, Washington, 1974-75; comdr. Destroyer Squadron 26 Surface Force Atlantic, Norfolk, Va., 1975-78; head surface to surface warfare, chief naval ops., Washington, 1978; dir. programs and budget Chief Naval Material, Washington, 1979; v.p. engring. devel. Ocean Systems div. Gould, Inc., Cleve., 1979-83; head combat systems USE Corp., 1983-85; v.p. def. systems Dynamac, 1985-88; sr. v.p., COO CASDE Corp., 1988-91; sr. v.p. Simms Industries, Inc., 1991—. Decorated Navy Meritorious Service medal, Navy Commendation medal with gold star. Mem. Navy League U.S. (nat. treas. 1987—), U.S. Naval Inst., Am. Soc. Naval Engrs., Am. Def. Preparedness Assn., Surface Navy Assn. Home: 3139 Catrina Ln Annapolis MD 21403 Office: Simms Industries 9841 Broken Land Pkwy Ste 300 Columbia MD 21046

RAPOPORT, BENZION JAKOB, psychologist; b. Szczuczyn, Poland, Dec. 11, 1929; came to the U.S., 1946; s. Aaron and Feygva (Jerushalmy) R.; m. Gloria Olenberg, June 2, 1957; children: Aaron, Faye, Lisa. BA, Bklyn. Coll., 1952; MSW, U. Pa., 1955; PhD, Yeshiva U., 1968. Chief social worker Lonf Island Consultation Ctr., 1955-59, Mental Health Inst., N.Y.C., 1960-61; staff psychologist Callagy Hall, N.Y.C., 1961-62; dir. psychol. ctr. Queens Consultation Ctr., N.Y.C., 1963-70; dean tng. inst. Queens Ctr. for Psychotherapy and Rsch., N.Y.C., 1965-70; dir. psychol. ctr. Ctr. for Counseling Svcs., N.Y.C., 1970-89; dean tng. Rapoport Inst., N.Y.C., 1990—; pvt. practice, Canaan, Nyack, N.Y.C., N.Y., 1955—. Contbr. articles to profl. jours. and chpts. to books. Mem. Am. Psychol. Assn., Acad. Cert. Social Workers, Nat. Assn. Social Workers (diplomate). Jewish. Office: 24 5th Ave New York NY 10011-8858

RAPP, ILANA BETH, actress, television production tape editor; b. Bklyn., Oct. 4, 1968; d. Stanley Jonas and Lea (Bayers) R. BA, SUNY, Stony Brook, 1990. Actress N.Y.C., 1969—; editor QUADV sci. fiction mag., Sayreville, N.J., 1985—; pub. rels. counselor The Pub. Eye, Sayreville, 1986-90. Appeared in Broadway play Golda, off Broadway, Traveling, Lady, others; films include Going In Style, Radio Days, Ragtime; TV appearances include 3-2-1 contact, Tex., All My Children, A Dr.'s Story; radio show Eternal Light; mem. prodn. team Working It Out, American Playhouse, Daytime Emmy Awards; contbr. articles to Statesman and profl jours. Flynn Writing scholar Flynn & Sons, 1986. Mem. Screen Actors Guild, Am. Fedn. TV & Radio Artists, Actors Equity Assn. Office: 82 Marsh Ave Sayreville NJ 08872-1342

RAPP, JOHN, accountant; b. Wuppertal, Germany, Feb. 24, 1920; came to U.S. in 1949.; s. Ernest and Anne R.; m. Doris Joy Stern, Mar. 14, 1953; 1 child, Marianne Helene (dec.). BS in Econs., London U., 1945; MS, Columbia Sch. Bus., N.Y.C., 1952. Cert. acct., N.Y., N.J. Sr. acct. Price Waterhouse, N.Y.C., 1949-54; sr. acct. James Barr, N.Y.C., 1954-57, Hurdman and Cranstoun, N.Y.C., 1957-67, Seidman and Seidman, N.Y.C., 1967-68; reviewer and mgr. Sharlach Ress Goldrich, Hackensack, N.J., 1968-70; reviewer Louis Sternbach, N.Y.C, 1970-72, Anchin Block and Anchin, N.Y.C, 1972-74, Harry Goodkin and Co., N.Y.C, 1978-83, Joseph Graf and Co., N.Y.C, 1983-90; chmn. Accts. for the Pub. Interest, N.Y.C., 1978-84, dir. API/Support Ctr., 1984—. Bd. dirs. Vacations and Sr. Ctrs. Assn., N.Y.C., 1976—, treas., 1981-88, v.p., 1988—; bd. dirs. Summit lay com. on Edn., N.J., 1967—, Summit Area Community council, 1973-79. Served as sgt. British Army, 1940-45, ETO. Fellow Inst. of Chartered Accts. (Eng. and Wales); mem. AICPA, N.Y. Soc. CPAs (bd. dirs. 1981-84), N.J. Soc. CPAs. Republican. Jewish.

RAPPAPORT, CAREY MILFORD, electrical engineering educator; b. Tokyo, Jan. 9, 1959; came to U.S., 1964; s. Paul Julian and Evelyn (Hampton) R.; m. Ann Welke Morgenthaler, Nov. 12, 1989. BSEE, BS in Math., MSEE, EngEE, MIT, 1982, PhD, 1987. Asst. prof. elec. and computer engring. Northeastern U., Boston, 1987—; cons. AJ Devaney Assocs., Boston, 1987—; co-founder Berry Rappaport Assocs., Newton, Mass., 1990—. Author: Progress in Electromagnetics Research, Vol. I, 1989; contbr. articles to profl. jours.; patentee in field. Recipient MIT K.T. Compton award, 1985. Mem. IEEE (H.A. Wheeler award 1986), Sigma Xi, Eta Kappa Nu. Home: 53 E Quinobequin Rd Newton MA 02168-1806 Office: Northeastern U 235 Forsyth Boston MA 02115-5024

RAPPAPORT, MARGARET M., psychologist, author, consultant; b. Buffalo, Nov. 16, 1947; d. Leo J. and Marie L. (Fischle) Williams; m. Herbert Rappaport, Oct. 20, 1969; children: Amanda, Alexander. BA, U. Buffalo, 1967; MA, SUNY, 1969; PhD, MD, U. Colo., 1971. Prof., researcher Univ. Dar es Salaam, Tanzania, 1970-74; with Rappaport Assocs., Phila., 1974—; exec. dir. Inst. for Parent/Child Svcs., Phila., 1978—; mem. adj. faculty Temple U., Phila., 1974—; program dir. Frontrunners, 1978—; child care/devel. cons. to media especially TV, 1984—; program dir. First Steps, 1986—. Author books and articles on parenting and family life, monographs on existential psychology. Mem. AAUP, AOPA, NOW, Nat. Assn. for Edn. of Young Children, Del. Valley Assn. for Edn. of Young Children, Inter Seaplane Pilots Assn., Ninety-Nines Internat. Assn. Women Pilots, Soaring Soc. Am., Phila. Cricket Club, Cosmopolitan Club. Republican. Avocation: private pilot of airplanes, seaplanes and sailplanes. Home: 562 Innsbrook Estates Wright City MO 63390

RAPPAPORT, MARK, film and video maker; b. N.Y.C., Jan. 15, 1942; s. Harry and Rose (Halperson) R.; m. Helen Niki Logis, July 28, 1969 (div.). BA, Bklyn. Coll., 1964. Writer, dir., editor (videos) Mark Rappaport-The TV Spinoff, 1980, Postcards, 1990 (1st prize Best Dramatic Short, USA Film Festival, nat. broadcast PBS), Rock Hudson's Home Movies, 1992, (films) Casual Relations, 1973, Mozart In Love, 1975 (Critics prize Toulon Film Festival), Local Color, 1977 (Best Fiction Film award, Best Feature Film award, 1 of 5 prize winners Am. Ind. Features, Sundance Festival), The Scenic Route, 1978 (named Most Original and Innovative Film of Yr., Brit. Film Inst., Best Art Direction of Yr. award Soho News), Impostors, 1980, Chain Letters, 1985; numerous retrospectives include The British Film Inst. at Nat. Theatre, London, 1980, Collective for Living Cinema, 1985, Madrid Film Festival, 1986, Figueira Da Foz Film Festival, 1989. Guggenheim fellow, 1987. Home and Office: 16 Crosby St New York NY 10013

RASHFORD, MERCEDES AVALYN, family therapist, clinical services coordinator; b. Kinston, Jamacia, Feb. 23, 1962; came to U.S., 1977; d. Barrington Augustus and Percess Veronica (Riley) Mattison; m. Robert Anthony Rashford, July 25, 1987. BA in Psychology, Temple U., 1983, MEd in Counseling Psychology, 1986. Mental health counselor Horizon House, Inc., Phila., 1985-87; lead counselor PSI Assocs., Washington, 1987-88; clin. supr. Montgomery House, Gaithersburg, Md., 1988-89; family therapist Montgomery County Govt. Parents and Children Together Program, Rockville, Md., 1989—; cons. Cedar Grove Elem. Sch., Damascus, Md., 1991—. Mem. student govt. Calif. State U., 1979-81, mem. student cabinet, Calif., 1979-81, Black affairs com., 1979-81. Mem. Am. Assn. for Counseling and Devel. Home: 10117 Durango Dr Damascus MD 20872-2360 Office: Parents and Children Together 401 Hungerford Dr Rockville MD 20850-4155

RASKIN, ALLEN, psychologist, researcher; b. Bklyn., Oct. 9, 1926; s. Alexander and Ada (Trombler) R.; m. Theol Shayne, May 31, 1957; children: Lawrence Eliot, Sarah Anne. BA, Syracuse U., 1949; MS, U. Ill., 1951, PhD, 1954. Lic. psychologist, Md., D.C. Staff psychologist VA Hosp., East Orange, N.J., 1955-58; Rsch. psychologist Outpatient Rsch. Lab., Washington, 1958-61; sect. chief NIMH, Rockville, Md., 1961-86; dir. psychology div. Lafayette Clinic, Detroit, 1986-88; rsch. prof. U. Md., Balt., 1988—; mem. ADAMHA AIDS adv. com., Rockville, 1990—; cons. FDA, 1975—; mem. VA Coop. Studies Human Subject Com., Perry Point, Md., 1990—. Editor: Psychopathology and Cognitive Loss in the Elderly, 1979, Age and the Pharmacology of Psychoactive Drugs, 1981. With U.S. Army, 1945-46, PTO. Fellow APA, Am. Coll. Neuropsychopharmacology, Am. Psychopathological Assn., Am. Psychol. Soc. Home: 7658 Water Oak Point Rd Pasadena MD 21122-2358

RASKIN, NOEL MICHAEL, thoracic surgeon; b. Bklyn., May 29, 1947; s. Rubin and Pauline (Sturm) R.; m. Deborah M. Axelrod, Feb. 27, 1987; children: Max, Ben. BA, NYU, 1969; MD, N.Y. Med. Coll., 1977. Intern St. Vincent's Hosp., N.Y.C., 1977-78; resident SUNY, Stony Brook, 1978-82; fellow in cardio-thoracic surgery U. Miami, Fla., 1982-84, fellow in thoracic oncology, 1984-85; attending surgeon Beth Israel Med. Ctr. and Cabrini Med. Ctr., N.Y.C., 1985-89; thoracic surgeon Kriser Lung Cancer Ctr., N.Y.C., 1989; attending surgeon Dover (N.J.) Gen. Hosp., 1989-91; surgeon pvt. practice N.Y.C., 1992—. Fellow ACS, Am. Coll. Chest Physicians; mem. AMA, Soc. Thoracic Surgeons, Gen. Thoracic Surg. Club. Office: 41 5th Ave New York NY 10063

RASMUSSEN, D. SCOTT, environmental scientist, consultant; b. Endicott, N.Y., Dec. 9, 1958; s. Allan Eric and Irene (Hill) R.; m. Alison Lee Eldridge, Aug. 8, 1981 (div. Sept. 1986); m. Lisa Marie Chimento, Apr. 21, 1990. BS in Chemistry, Syracuse (N.Y.) U., 1981; BS in Environ. Chemistry, SUNY, Syracuse, 1981; MS in Environ. Pollution Control, Pa. State U., 1983. Rsch. technician Agway, Inc., Syracuse, 1979-80; rsch. asst. Pa. State U., University Park, 1981-83; environ. specialist GAI Cons., Inc., Pitts., 1984-86; soil chemist Earth Sci. Cons., Export, Pa., 1986-87; sr. environ. scientist Clough, Harbour & Assoc., Albany, N.Y., 1987-91; environ. cons. Civil & Environ. Cons., Pitts., 1991—. Mem. Hazardous Materials Rsch. Inst., Air and Waste Mgmt., N.Y. Bus. Coun., Water Pollution Control Fedn. Home: 1044 Hastie Rd PO Box 2341 Pittsburgh PA 15234 Office: Civil & Environ Cons Foster Plaza XI 790 Holiday 3 Winners Cir Pittsburgh PA 15220

RASMUSSEN, STEPHEN MARK, aerospace engineer; b. Narrowsburg, N.Y., Sept. 4, 1967; s. Ronald Mills and Jane Anne (Drum) R. BS in Aerospace Engring., Syracuse (N.Y.) U., 1989. Aerospace engr. Naval Air War Ctr. Aircraft Div., Lakehurst, N.J., 1989—. Mem. ASME (assoc.), AIAA. Republican. Lutheran.

RASMUSSON, EUGENE MARTIN, research meteorologist; b. Lindsborg, Kans., Feb. 27, 1929; s. Martin Erick and Alma Sophia (Nelson) R.; m. Georgene Ruth Sachtleben, Aug. 7, 1960; children: Mary, Ruth, Elizabeth, Kristin. BS, Kans. State U., 1950; MS, St. Louis U., 1963; PhD, MIT, 1966. Forecaster Nat. Weather Service, St. Louis, 1956-64; rsch. meteorologist Geophysical Fluid Dynamics Lab, Princeton, N.J., 1964-70; chief, rsch. div. Ctr. for Experiment Design, NOAA, Washington, 1970-79; chief, diagnositc br. Climate Analysis Ctr., NOAA, Camp Spring, Md., 1979-86; sr. rsch. scientist U. Md., College Park, 1986—; mem. numerous coms. and panels U.S. Nat. Acad. Sci., World Climate Rsch. Program-UNESCO. Contbr. articles to profl. jours. 1st Lt. USAF, 1951-55. Recipient Silver medal, U.S. Dept. Commerce, Washington, 1973, Adminstr. award, Nat. Oceanic and Atmospheric Adminstrn., Washington, 1983. Fellow Am. Meteorological Soc. (Jule Charney award, 1989); mem. Am. Geophysical Union, AAAS. Lutheran. Office: U Md Dept Meteorology College Park MD 20742

RASO, MARGARET MILDRED, educator; b. Yonkers, N.Y., Aug. 22, 1933; d. Michael and Josephine Rose (Pisco) Trotta; m. Anthony Joseph Raso, Oct. 31, 1964; children: Joanne Marie, Michael Anthony. BS in Elementary Edn., Fordham U., 1955; MA in Edn., Fairfield U., 1961. Cert. elementary tchr., high sch. English, N.Y. Tchr. Yonkers (N.Y.) Pub. Schs., 1955-65; substitute tchr. Rockland County Schs., 1966-68, '75-87; real estate salesperson Trilling, Century 21 Assocs., Suffern, New City, N.Y., 1985-87; juvenile justice chmn. Cen. Hudson PTA Dist., N.Y., 1977-79; family ct. monitor, 1978-79; del. Leadership Conv. NEA, West Point, N.Y., 1968. Inventor: hosiery donning and removing appliance, 1984. Auditor 12th Ward Rep. Club, Yonkers, 1962; mem. legal com. Pine Creek Area Assn., Fairfield Conn., 1974-80. Named Hon. Life Mem. Yonkers (N.Y.) PTA, 1962; recipient Spl. Olympics award, 1985. Mem. Columbiettes (major degree), Cath. Alumni Club (social com. chmn.). Home: 2 Dutch Ct West Nyack NY 10994-1701

RASSAM, GHASSAN NOEL, information scientist; b. Mosul, Iraq, July 11, 1942; came to U.S., 1962; s. Noel Mikhael Rassam and Sophie (Bekhazi) R.; divorced; children: Anne Yasmine, Ziyad Paul-Noel. MS, Miami U., Oxford, Ohio, 1963; PhD, U. Minn., 1967. Asst. prof. info. sci. Wis. State U., River Falls, 1967-68, Youngstown (Ohio) State U., 1968-69; geologist Iraq Nat. Oil Co., Baghdad, 1967-70, ELF/ERAP Oil Co., Paris, 1970-72; editor-in-chief Am. Geol. Inst., Alexandria, Va., 1972-87; group dir. Am. Geophys. Union, Washington, 1989—; commr. Atomic Energy Establishment, Baghdad, 1970; chmn. Cogeodoc, 1985—. Editor: Multilingual Thesaurus of Geoscience, 1988; contbr. articles to profl. jours. Fellow Fulbright Found., Washington, 1963. Mem. AAAS, Am. Geophys. Union, Assn. Info. Sci., Assn. Earth Sci. Editors (pres.1988), Internat. Coun. Sci. and Tech. Info., Geosci. Info. Soc. Office: Am Geophys Union 2000 Florida Ave NW Washington DC 20009-1231

RASTEGAR, FARZAD ALI, investment banker; b. Teheran, Iran, June 25, 1956; came to U.S., 1980; s. Morteza and Rabeeh (Baghai-Kermani) R. BS with honors, Royal Sch. Mines, U. London, 1977; MBA, Columbia U., 1982. Asst. v.p. Phoenix Earth Resources Corp., San Francisco, 1982-83; v.p. Capital Properties Inc., N.Y.C., 1984-85, also bd. dirs.; exec. v.p. Asian Oceanic Real Estate Corp., N.Y.C., 1986-87; spl. cons. Wellsford Group, N.Y.C., 1988—; bd. dirs. RENAFA Inc., Atlanta, Side Hill Farms Inc., London, Filofax Group, plc, London. Lt. Imperial Iranian Army, 1977-79. Mem. Instn. Mining and Metallurgy, Engring. Coun. U.K., Royal Sch. Mines, Nat. Alumni Assn. Columbia Bus. Sch. (bd. dirs. 1984-88). Office: Wellsford Group Inc 375 Park Ave New York NY 10152-0002

RATCHFORD, ROGER LIONEL, secondary school educator; b. Norwalk, Conn., Oct. 18, 1933; s. Francis Thomas and Irene Audrey (Sharkany) R.; m. M. Gail Gruber, Aug. 10, 1963; children: Moira, Michael, Brendan. AB, Coll. of the Holy Cross, 1955; MA, Fairfield U., 1966; EdD, Nova U., 1989. Cert. Latin, French, English, computers. Tchr. Woburn (Mass.) High Sch., 1956-58, Fairfield (Conn.) Prep Sch., 1958—; adj. prof. Fairfield (Conn.) U., 1980—; golf coach, Fairfield Prep, 1965—. Author: Improving Writing in Secondary Schools, 1989. Pres. Soc. to Advance the Retarded, Norwalk, 1975-77, 85-87, bd. dirs., 1969-91. Recipient Conn. Disting. Svc. award in Golf Nat. Fedn. of Intersch. Coaches, 1989, Coaching award Sportsmen of Westport (Conn.), 1986. Mem. ASCD, CALICO, Nat. High Sch. Coaches Assn. (Golf Coach of Yr. 1986, 89), Am. Assn. Tchrs. French, Coun. of Lang. Tchrs., Conn. Assn. for Retarded Citizens (bd. dirs. 1972-89, Vol. of Yr. 1988). Republican. Roman Catholic. Office: Fairfield Prep Sch N Benson Rd Fairfield CT 06430-5152

RATCLIFF, JAMES LEWIS, administrator; b. Indpls., Mar. 3, 1946; s. Perry Albert and Viola Ruth (Hall) R.; m. Carol Rocklin Kay, Dec. 24, 1984 (dec.). Student, Raymond Coll.; B of History, Polit. Sci., Utah State U., 1968; MA in History, Wash. State U., 1972, PhD, 1976. Dir. Ctr. for the Study of Higher Edn.; dir. Nat. Ctr. Postsecondary Teaching/Learning/Assessment Pa. State U., University Park; prof., leader higher edn. section Iowa State U., Ames; assoc. prof. Fla. Atlantic U., Boca Raton; asst. prof. Wash. State U., Pullman. U.S. Dept. Edn. grantee. Mem. Am. Assn. Community Jr. Colls., Assn. Study Higher Edn. (bd. dirs.), Coun. Universities Colls. (past pres., bd. dirs.), European Assn. for Inst. Rsch.,Consortium Higher Edn. Rschs., Phi Delta Kappa, Phi Kappa Phi, Phi Alpha Theta.

RATCLIFFE, RYAN COOPER, airline pilot; b. Long Beach, Calif., Oct. 19, 1959; s. Herbert Cooper and Lois Marie (Hart) R.; m. Anne Marie Fischer, Sept. 5, 1987; children: Lauren Anne, Ryan Cooper Jr. BS in Civil Engring., USAF Acad., 1981; MS in Systems Mgmt., U. So. Calif., 1985. Registered profl. engr... in training, Colo. Commd. 2nd lt. USAF, 1981, advanced through ranks to capt., 1985; standardization/evaluation instr., co-pilot USAF, Mather AFB, Calif., 1982-85; asst. flight commdr., instr. pilot, flight test pilot USAF, Sheppard AFB, Tex., 1985-88; resigned USAF, 1988; first officer USAir, Charlotte, N.C., 1988—; instr. pilot McClellan AFB Aero Club, Sacramento, 1983-85; real estate sales person Dave Rhone Realty, Wichita Falls, Tex., 1986-88. Named One of Outstanding Young Men Am., 1987. Mem. Airline Pilots Assn. Home: 10100 Wedge Ct Charlotte NC 28277-8729 Office: USAir Greater Pitts Internat Airport Pittsburgh PA 15231

RATH, ANTOINETTE PETRILLO, speech and language pathologist; b. Norristown, Pa., Jan. 9, 1959; d. Bruno and Clara Josephine (Fioravanti) Petrillo; m. Jeffrey Todd Rath, Oct. 27, 1985; 1 child, Eliazabeth Claire. BS in Edn., West Chester State U., 198l, MA Communicative Disorder, 1985; cert. prin.-supr., Glassboro State Coll., 1988. Speech-lang. pathologist Delaware County Intermediate Unit, Media, Pa., 1981-82, Don Guanella Sch., Springfield, Pa., 1982-85; speech-lang. pathologist West Deptford (N.J.) Pub. Schs., 1985—, staff devel. trainer, bldg. coord., 1987—; asst. supr. ednl. programming for day tng. eligible students Gloucester County Day Tng. Ctr., Williamstown, N.J., 1990-91; supr. spl. edn. and spl. svcs. Clayton (N.J.) Pub. Schs., 1991—. Mem. Am. Speech-Lang-Hearing Assn. (cert. clin. competency), Assn. for Supervision and Curriculum Devel., NEA. Roman Catholic. Home: care Herma Simmons Sch 300 W Chestnut St Clayton NJ 08312

RATH, WILLIAM COLLINS, police officer; b. Bronx, N.Y., Sept. 28, 1946; s. William J. and Catherine (Culleton) R. Student, SUNY. Police officer N.Y.C. Police Dept., 1967-73, detective, 1973-82, sgt., 1982-89, lt., 1989—. Recipient 155 deptl. awards N.Y.C. Police Dept. Mem. N.Y.C. Police Dept. Honor Legion, Emerald Soc., Anchor Club, Holy Name Soc. Roman Catholic. Home: 3187 Hatting Pl Bronx NY 10465-4066

RATHFURD, MICHAEL, state government executive. Secretary of State State of Del., 1992—. Office: State Dept Townsend Building Dover DE 19901*

RATHNAM, LINCOLN YESU, investment company executive; b. Westfield, Mass., May 5, 1949; s. Punuri Yesu and Virginia Bertha (Libby) R.; m. Deborah Parrish Ford, Sept. 5, 981; children: Lincoln Edward, Sarah Virginia, Hope Alexandra. AB, Dartmouth Coll., 197l; DPhil, Oxford U., 1976. Chartered fin. analyst. Investment analyst CIGNA Corp., Bloomfield, Conn., 1979-84; investment analyst Scudder, Stevens & Clark, Inc., Boston, 1984—, mng. dir. Latin Am. group, 1986—. Mem. Fin. Analysts Fedn., Boston Security Analysts Soc. (bd. dirs.), Pub. Utility Analysts Boston.

RATHNAM, PREMILA, endocrinologist, educator; b. India, 1936; came to U.S., 1959; m. C. S. Narasimhan. BSc, U. Madras, India, 1955; MS, U. Wis., 1962; PhD, Seton Hall U., 1966. Mem. staff Med. Coll. Cornell U., N.Y.C., 1966—, assoc. prof. div. reproductive endocrinology, 1978—. Lalor Found. fellow, 1968; recipient various travel grants. Mem. Am. Chem. Soc., Endocrine Soc., Am. Soc. Exptl. Biology, N.Y. Acad. Scis. Office: Cornell U Med Coll 1300 York Ave New York NY 10021-4896

RATNER, HAROLD, pediatrician, educator; b. Bklyn., June 19, 1927; s. George and Bertha (Silverman) R.; BS, Coll. City N.Y., 1948; MD, Chgo. Med. Sch., 1952; m. Lillian Gross, Feb. 4, 1961; children—Sanford Miles, Marcia Ellen. Intern, Jewish Hosp., Med. Center Bklyn., 1952-53, resident in pediatrics, 1953-55; practice medicine specializing in pediatrics, Bklyn.; clin. instr. pediatrics SUNY Downstate Med. Center, N.Y.C., 1955-67, clin. asst. prof., 1967-69, clin. assoc. prof., 1969-87; lectr. pediatrics, 1987—; chief of pediatrics Greenpoint Hosp., Bklyn., 1967-80, pres. med. staff, 1970-71, 74-80; dir. ambulatory services Woodhull Med. and Mental Health Center, Bklyn., 1980-83; clin. assoc. prof. pediatrics SUNY-Bklyn., 1983-87, lectr., 1987—; clin. assoc. prof. pediatrics, N.Y.U., 1987-90; med. specialist Nathan Kline Inst. for Psychiat. Research, Orangeburg, N.Y., Rockland Psychiat. Ctr., Orangeburg, N.Y., 1986-88, unit chief med. services, 1988-90; assoc. clin. dir. and dir. medicine Manhattan Psychiat. Ctr., N.Y.C., 1990—; mem. adv. council to pres. N.Y.C. Health and Hosp. Corp., 1970-71, 74-80, 81-83, sec., 1975, v.p., 1976-80; mem. med. bd., dir. Camp Sussex, camp for underprivileged children; bd. dirs. Kings County Health Care Rev. Orgn., Bklyn., 1976-84, past co-chmn. hosp. rev. com., continuing med. edn., med. care evaluation com. Trustee Village of Saddle Rock (N.Y.), 1980—. Served with AUS, 1945-47. Diplomate Nat. Bd. Med. Examiners, Am. Bd. Pediatrics. Fellow Am. Pediatric Soc., Am. Soc. Clin. Hypnosis, Bklyn. Pediatric Soc., Kings County Med. Soc., Royal Soc. Health; mem. AMA, Soc. Clin. and Exptl. Hypnosis, Am. Pub. Health Assn., Am. Soc. Clin. Hypnosis, N.Y. State Soc. Clin. Hypnosis, Kings County Med. Soc., Pan-Am. Med. Socs. Democrat. Jewish. Contbr. articles to med. jours. Home: 55 Blue Bird Dr Great Neck NY 11023-1001

RATNER, LILLIAN GROSS, psychiatrist; b. N.Y.C., Aug. 18, 1932; d. Herman and Sarah (Widelitz) Gross. BA, Barnard Coll., 1953; postgrad. U. Lausanne (Switzerland), 1954-56; MD, Duke U., 1959. Diplomate Bd. Pediatrics, Am. Bd. Psychiatry and Neurology, Am. Bd. Child Psychiatry; m. Harold Ratner, Feb. 4, 1961; children: Sanford Miles, Marcia Ellen. Intern Kings County Hosp., Bklyn., 1959-60, resident, 1967-70, fellow in child psychiatry, 1969-70, psychiatrist devel. evaluation clinic, 1970-72; resident Jewish Hosp. Bklyn., 1960-62, fellow in pediatric psychiatry, 1962-63; physician in charge pediatric psychiat. clinic Greenpoint (N.Y.) Hosp., 1964-67; pvt. practice psychiatry, Great Neck, N.Y., 1970—; clin. instr. psychiatry Downstate Med. Ctr., Bklyn., 1970-74, clin. asst. prof., 1974—; lectr. in psychiatry Columbia U., 1974—; psychiat. cons. N.Y.C. Bd. Edn., 1972-75, Queens Children's Hosp., 1975—; mem. med. bd. Camp Sussex (N.J.), 1963—, Saras Ctr., Great Neck, N.Y., 1977—. Fellow Am. Acad. Pediatrics, Am. Acad. Psychiatry, Am. Acad. Child Psychiatry, Am. Soc. Clin. Hypnosis (past pres.); mem. AMA, Am. Psychiat. Assn., Nassau Psychiat. Assn., Bklyn. Psychiat. Assn., Bklyn. Pediatric Soc. (sr. mem.), Nassau Pediatric Socs., Soc. Adolescent Psychiatry, N.Y. Coun. Child Psychiatry, Soc. Clin. and Exptl. Hypnosis, Am. Med. Women's Assn. (past pres. Nassau), N.Y., Kings County med. socs., N.Y. Soc. Clin. Hypnosis (past pres.), Internat. Soc. for Study of Multiple Personality and Dissociation (founder, pres. L.I. component study group). Home and Office: 55 Blue Bird Dr Great Neck NY 11023-1001

RATNER, WAYNE ELLIOT, import company executive; b. Bklyn., Dec. 9, 1950; s. Louis and Ruth Rose (Blau) R.; m. Leslie Steinberg, June 22, 1972 (div. June 1975); m. Jane Iris Eisen, Oct. 5, 1975; children: Richard Farrell, Jeremy Brian. BS in Biology, Fairleigh Dickinson U., 1972. Dialysis technician Eugene Schupak, M.D., Queens, N.Y., 1974-75; salesman Stanfre Industries, N.Y.C., 1975-76; v.p., gen. mgr. Merchant's Importing, Inc., Providence, 1976—. Home: 111 Wood Cove Dr Coventry RI 02816-6525 Office: Merchants Importing Inc 65 Pavilion Ave Providence RI 02905-1523

RATNER-GANTSHAR, BARBARA GRACE, development director; b. Phila.; d. Jules and Samuella (Isadora) Ratner; m. Martin Gantshar, June 1961 (div. 1984); children: Judith Susan Claire, Lois Nichole Merraine, David Joseph. MS, Simmons Coll., 1985. Project dir. Boston Family Inst., Brookline, Mass., 1982-84; exec. dir. Summer's World Ctr. for the Arts, Worcester, Mass., 1985-87; assoc. dir. of devel. Am. U., Washington, 1987-88; dir. devel. Harford Day Sch., Bel Air, Md., 1988-90, Balch Inst. for Ethnic Studies, Phila., 1991—; fair coord. Mass. and R.I. Antiquarian Booksellrs Assn., 1978-79; cons. Alzheimer's Disease Ctr., Falls Ch., Va., 1988, The Galleries, Wellesley, Mass., 1984-85, The Etz Chaim Ctr., Balt., 1990. Author: A Beacon Was Hoisted in Boston, 1975, Philadelphia: The City and the Bell, 1976. Mem. Fedn. Allied Jewish Appeal (bd. dirs. women's div.), Nat. Prospect Rsch. Assn., World Affairs Coun., Nat. Soc. of Fundraising Execs., Ethnic Studies Assn., Antiquarian Booksellers Assn. Am. (emeritus), Planned Giving Study Group, Internat. Visitors Ctr., Met. Opera Nat. Coun., Am. Prospect Rsch. Assn., World Affairs Coun., Mendelsshohn Club Phila. (bd. dirs.), Star Forum Cherry Hill (bd. dirs.). Democrat. Jewish. Home: 409 Society Hill Blvd Cherry Hill NJ 08003-2412 Office: Balch Inst for Ethnic Studies 18 S 7th St Philadelphia PA 19106-2388

RATTAN, ARLENE IVY, neuropsychologist, researcher; b. Smithers, B.C., Can., July 10, 1955; came to U.S., 1985; d. Leland Stewart and Linda Ivy (Strimbold) Bremner; m. Gurmal Rattan, Apr. 3, 1982; children: Ashley Tej, Michael Rajan. BA, U. Victoria, B.C., Can., 1978; cert. in teaching, Simon Fraser U., Burnaby, B.C., Can., 1981; MA, Ball State U., 1985, PhD, 1988. Lic. psychologist, Pa.; cert. sch. psychologist, Ind., Pa. Family support worker Ministry of Human Resources, Houston, B.C., Can., 1978-81; tchr. Prince George (B.C., Can.) Sch. Dist., 1982-85; postdoctoral fellow Western Psychiat. Inst. & Clinic, Pitts., 1988-90, neuropsychologist, 1990—; psychologist Forbes Regional Health System, Monroeville, Pa., 1991—. Author chpts. in books. NIH grantee, 1987-89. Mem. APA, Nat. Assn. Sch. Psychologists, Nat. Acad. Neuropsychology, Internat. Neuropsychol. Soc., Greater Pitts. Psychol. Assn. Office: Western Psychiat Insts Clinic 3811 Ohara St Pittsburgh PA 15213-2593

RATTNER, ROBERT MITCHELL, photographer, journalist; b. N.Y.C., May 26, 1952; s. Harry and Hannah (Sekel) R.; m. Dian Massa, Mar. 23, 1975. BA, NYU, 1974, MA, 1977. Photographer, journalist pvt. practice, N.Y.C., 1979-91; photographer, journalist pvt. practice Stony Creek, Conn., 1991—. Contbr. articles to popular jours. Dir. Wildlife Preservation Trust Internat., Phila., 1988—; advocacy Ind. for Conservation and Environ. Issues. Grantee Marty Forscher, Parsons New Sch. World Image Awards, N.Y.C., 1991. Mem. Am. Soc. Mag. Photographers.

RAU, RALPH RONALD, physicist; b. Tacoma, Sept. 1, 1920; s. Ralph Campbell and Ida (Montgall) R.; m. Maryjane Uhrlaub, June 2, 1944; children: Whitney Leslie, Littie Elise. B.S. in Physics, Coll. Puget Sound, 1941; M.S. in Physics, Calif. Inst. Tech., 1943, Ph.D. in Physics, 1948. Asst. prof. physics Princeton U., 1947-56; Fulbright research prof. physics Ecole Polytechnique, Paris, 1954-55; physicist Brookhaven Nat. Lab., Upton, N.Y., 1956-66; chmn. dept. physics Brookhaven Nat. Lab., 1966-70, assoc. dir. for high energy physics, 1970-81; adj. prof. U. Wyo.; vis. prof. MIT, 1984-88; staff scientist Desy Lab., Hamburg, Fed. Republic Germany, 1984-85. Trustee U. Puget Sound, 1978-84. Named Alumnus Cum Laude U. Puget Sound, 1968; recipient Alexander von Humboldt U.S. Sr. Scientist award 1988. Mem. Am. Phys. Soc., N.Y. Acad. Sci. Office: Brookhaven Nat Lab Upton NY 11973

RAUAM, NAIMA, artist, photographer, writer; b. Hanau, Fed. Republic of Germany, Feb. 26, 1946; d. Walter and Naadi (Tombak) R. Student, Art Students League N.Y., 1964-69. Freelance fine artist N.Y.C., 1964—. Exhibited in solo and group shows, U.S. and abroad; contbr. articles to profl. jours. Recipient Popular prize Artists Assn., 1985. Mem. Nat. Arts Club (Pres.'s award 1990, Grumbacher award 1985, Popular award 1986, House of Heydenryk award 1985), Artists' Fellowship, Art Students League, Artists Equity. Office: Art in the Afternoon 146 Beekman St New York NY 10038

RAUCH, CHARLES FREDERICK, JR., academic official; b. Lancaster, Ohio, Oct. 24, 1925; s. Charles Frederick and Mary Catherine (Getz) R.; m. Diane Matilda Wilcox, Jan. 1, 1951 (div. July 1974); 1 child, Frederick Whitman; m. Esther Eleze Nettles, Apr. 25, 1975. BS, U.S. Naval Acad., 1947; MSME, U.S. Naval Postgrad. Sch., Monterey, Calif., 1957; MBA, Ohio State U., 1980, PhD, 1981. Commd. ensign USN, 1947, advanced through grades to rear adm., 1972; comdg. officer nuclear submarines, New London, Conn., 1962-66; systems analyst, sr. naval advisor, spl. asst. Office Chief Naval Ops., Washington and Saigon, Vietnam, 1967-71; dir. human resource mgmt. programs Office Chief Naval Ops., Washington, 1971-76; ret., 1976; asst. prof. U. Maine, Orono, 1981-84, dir. fin. mgmt., 1984-91, exec. dir. bus. and fin., 1991—; cons. to dep. asst. sec. def., Washington, 1976; cons. Maine Maritime Acad., Castine, 1982-84, dir. Maritime Career Devel. Inst., 1984. Contbg. author: Leaders and Managers: International Perspectives on Managerial Behavior and Leaderships, 1984. Decorated. D.S.M. with gold star. Mem. Acad. Mgmt., Inst. Mgmt. Scis., Greater Bangor C. of C. (chmn. com. on univ.-community rels. 1986-89, bd. dirs. 1988), Navy League, Maine Audubon Soc., Phi Kappa Phi, Beta Gamma Sigma. Episcopalian. Home: 102 Stillwater Ave Orono ME 04473 Office: U Maine 118 Alumni Hall Orono ME 04473

RAUCH, RICHARD ALLAN, marketing consultant, marketing educator, author, researcher; b. N.Y.C., Mar. 16, 1929; s. S.S. and J.S. (Breslau) R.; m. Joan Resnick, June 17, 1951; children: Robert Andrew, Steven Paul, Linda Karen. BS, Ind. U., 1950, MBA, 1952; PhD, NYU, 1979. Various positions Gotham Equipment Corp., N.Y.C., 1954-62, dir. mktg., 1962-64, pres., 1965-71; pres. CPE Industries, Hauppauge, N.Y., 1972-74; dir. bus. div. Southampton (N.Y.) Coll., 1975-81; dean Sch. Bus. Quinnipiac Coll., Hamden, Conn., 1982-83; prof. mktg. L.I. U., Brookville, N.Y., 1984—, chmn. mktg. dept., 1989; pres. Comml. Refrigerator Distbg. Assn., N.Y.C., 1958-59, Ea. Refrigeration Mfg. Assn., 1960-61, Nat. Comml. Refrigerator Sales Assn., Phila., 1962-63; mktg./advt. cons. Costan/Foremost, N.Y., 1986—; mem. Ind. U. Deans Assocs., 1983—; cons. Federated Foods, Inc., 1987—, First Nat. Supermarkets, Inc., Oyster Bay, N.Y., 1987—, Costan Spa, Belluno, Italy, 1986-89; bd. dirs. R.A. Rauch & Assocs., La Jolla, Calif., 1990, The CEO Group, Woodbury, N.Y., 1990—; faculty marshall Southampton Coll., C.W. Post Campus, L.I.U.; mem. faculty various colls. and univs. Contbr. articles to research jours.; patentee airdrive device for conveyor. Mem. Ind. U. Pres.'s Ptnrs., 1989; bd. dirs. Gates/Ridge Civic Assn., Woodbury, N.Y., 1986—. Served to lt. USAF, 1952-53. Food Mktg. Inst. grantee, 1979; named Outstanding Prof. Village Voice, 1981. Mem. L.I. Advt. Club (faculty advisor 1984-84), Am. Mktg. Assn. (faculty advisor 1984-88), Comml. Refrigerator Mfrs. Assn. (tech. com. 1987-89), Ind. U. Varsity Club, Delta Mu Delta (hon.), Phi Delta Kappa, Delta Pi Epsilon. Home: 31 Orchard Dr Woodbury NY 11797-2827 Office: LI U Dept Mktg Greenvale NY 11548

RAUL, ROBIN, aeronautical engineer, researcher; b. Bhilai, India, Mar. 13, 1958; came to U.S., 1982; s. Masih Dan and Florence (Kaushal) Gartia; m. Carmen Tartera, Dec. 22, 1990. B of Tech., Indian Inst. Tech., Kharagpur, India, 1980; MS, Indian Inst. Sci., Bangalore, India, 1982; PhD, U. Md., 1989. Rsch. assoc. Applied Physics Lab., Johns Hopkins U., Luarel, Md., 1989-91. Mem. AIAA. Office: Applied Physics Lab Johns Hopkins Rd Laurel MD 20723-1140

RAUM, BERNARD ANTHONY, lawyer, county court official, educator; b. Washington, June 7, 1944; s. Bernard Raymond and Zelphia Florence (Norton) R.; m. Cynthia Lee Duvall, Feb. 14, 1964 (div. Aug. 1973); 1 child, Anthony Patrick; m. Deborah Ann Lewis, Oct. 28, 1973 (div. Nov. 1986); m. Diane Marie Tonner, July 1, 1989. A.A., U. Balt., 1967, J.D., 1970; M.Forensic Scis., George Washington U., 1983. Bar: Md. 1970, U.S. Ct. Appeals (4th cir.) 1974, U.S. Supreme Ct. 1976. Asst. atty. gen. State of Md., Balt., 1972-77; sr. asst. states atty. chief circuit ct. div. Howard County States Atty., Ellicott City, Md., 1979-81; master in chancery Circuit Ct. for Howard County, Ellicott City, 1981—; lectr. Cantonsville Community Coll., Md., 1980—; asst. professorial lectr. dept. forensic scis. George Washington U., 1984—; asst. prof., Dundalk Community Coll., 1986—; asst. prof. Univ. Md., College Park. Mem. Md. State Bar Assn., Howard County Bar Assn., Nat. Coun. Juvenile and Family Ct. Judges, Md. Inst. for Continuing Profl. Edn. of Lawyers (bd. trustees 1980-81), Am. Acad. Forensic Scis., Md. Coun. Masters, Am. Inn of Ct. #103 (co-founder, pres. 1990—), Aircraft Owners and Pilots Assn., Rotary. Avocations: flying, photography, karate, sailing. Office: Cir Ct for Howard County Courthouse Ellicott City MD 21043

RAUNIYAR, GANESH PRASAD, agricultural economist; b. Kathmandu, Nepal, Nov. 11, 1954; came to U.S., 1985; s. Rameshwar Prasad and Sita (Devi) R.; m. Durga Shakya, June 12, 1984; 1 child, Jyoti Kumari. Intermediate in sci., Amrit Sci. Coll., Kathmandu, 1970; BSc in Agr. and Animal Husbandry (hons.), GB Pant U., Pantnagar, India, 1973; M of Econ., Thammasat U., Bangkok, 1978; PhD, Pa. State U., 1990. Farm mgr. Tobacco Rsch. Sta., Janakpur, Nepal, 1973-78; head planning and rsch. Tobacco Devel. Co., Janakpur, 1978-84; mgmt. adviser Unicef, Kathmandu, 1984-85; grad. asst. Pa. State U., University Park, 1987-89, project assoc., 1990—; cons. Internat. Fund for Agrl. Devel., Rome, 1992, South-East Consortium for Internat. Devel., Washington, 1991—; devel. cons. USAID, Kathmandu, 1984; agro-socioeconomist GITEC GmbH, Dusseldorf, Germany, 1980. Fulbright scholar Pa. State U., 1985-87, USAID scholar, India, 1970-73; Agrl. Devel. Coun. fellow, Bangkok, Thailand, 1976-78; rsch. grantee Agrl. Devel. Coun., Nepal. Mem. Am. Agrl. Econs. Assn., Am. Econ. Assn., Internat. Assn. Agrl. Economists, Soc. for Internat. Devel., Northeastern Agrl. and Resource Econ. Assn., Sigma Xi, Gamma Sigma Delta. Home: 1E Graduate Cir State College PA 16801-5866 Office: Pa State Univ 313 Weaver Bldg University Park PA 16802

RAUSCHENBERG, DALE EUGENE, music educator; b. Youngstown, Ohio, Jan. 13, 1938; s. Marvin Wilson and Colyn May (Wilhide) R.; m. Theresa Mary Neustupa, June 3, 1964; children: David Edward, Daniel Eric, Catherine Marie. B Music Edn., Youngstown State U., 1960; M Music Performance, Ind. U., 1963. Music dir. Mercer (Pa.) County Schs., 1963-64, Cardinal Mooney High Sch., Youngstown, 1965-66; percussion instr. Youngstown State U., 1965-66; assoc. prof. music Towson State U., Balt., 1966—; percussionist Youngstown Philharmonic, 1957-60, John Devol Orch., Culvermore, N.J., 1960; auxiliary percussionist Balt. Symphony Orch., 1967—; free-lance percussionist Md. Ctr. for Pub. Broadcasting, Balt., 1967—, Balt. Ctr. for Performing Arts, 1967—. Composer Discussion, 1963, What?, 1964; arranger Tchaikowsky's Arabian Dance, 1986, Scott Joplin's Solace, 1986, Scott Joplin's Palm Leaf Rag, 1989; contbr. articles to profl. jours. Served to capt. USAR, 1960-69. Recipient 3d prize, 3d Ann. W.Va. U. Composition Symposium, 1960. Mem. Am. Fedn. Musicians, Percussive Arts Soc. (pres. Md. chpt. 1979—), Nat. Assn. Coll. Wind and Percussion Instrs., Am. Soc. Composers, Authors and Pubs., Phi Mu Alpha Sinfonia (pres. Delta Eta chpt. 1959-60). Home: 29 Othoridge Rd Lutherville Timonium MD 21093-5412 Office: Towson State U Dept Music York Rd Baltimore MD 21204-5204

RAUX, DONALD JAMES, accountant, consultant; b. Ilion, N.Y., June 17, 1949; s. John Daniel Raux and Mary Elizabeth (Boulia) Wiley; m. Donna L. Mowers, July 27, 1968 (div. Jan. 1982); children: Donald J. II, Renee Aimee. BS in Pub. Acctg. cum laude, postgrad SUNY, Albany, 1971; MS in Acctg., 1990. CPA, NY. Supr. audit Peat, Marwick, Mitchell, & Co., Albany, N.Y., 1971-78; instr. CPA rev. course Person-Wolinski, Albany, 1977-79; ptnr. Galka and Raux CPA's, Clifton Park, N.Y., 1978-82; pvt. practice acctg., Ballston Lake, N.Y., 1982—; auditor, cons. Saratoga County Infirmary Ballston Spa, N.Y., 1978—, Kingsway Arms Nursing Ctr. Inc., Schenectady, N.Y., 1984-85, Troy Cemetary Assn., Troy, N.Y., 1978-90. Montgomery County Infirmary, 1986-88; auditor Wesley Health Care Ctr. Inc., Saratoga Springs, N.Y., 1978—, asst. prof. acctg. Siena Coll., 1986—. Bd. dirs. Parents Without Ptnrs., Clifton Park, 1983—. Served with U.S. Army, 1971-77. Recipient Reeves award 1985. Mem. Healthcare Fin. Mgrs. Assn. (pres. 1978-79, Fullmer award, 1980), Am. Inst. CPA's, N.Y. State Soc. CPA's. Republican. Roman Catholic. Club: Mc Gregor Country (Saratoga Springs). Home: 151 Wooddale Dr Ballston Lake NY 12019-9367 Office: 151 Wooddale Dr Ballston Lake NY 12019-9367

RAVECHÉ, ELIZABETH SCOTT, immunologist; b. Stuttgart, Fed. Republic of Germany, Nov. 21, 1950; (parents Am. citizens); d. Williard Warren and Justine (Dorney) Scott; m. Harold Joseph Raveché, Jan. 26, 1974; children: John, Justin, Bernice, Beth. BS, Seton Hill Coll., 1972; PhD, George Washington U., 1977. Rsch. scientist NIH, Bethesda, Md., 1972-79, sr. investigator, 1980-85; assoc. prof. immunology Albany (N.Y.) Med. Coll., 1985-89, U. of Medicine and Dentistry, Newark, N.J., 1989—. Contbr. 14 chpts. to books and 50 sci. articles to profl. publs. Sec. PTA, Hoboken, N.J., 1991. Fellow Washington Acad. of Sci. (Outstanding Researcher award, 1983); mem. Am. Assn. Immunologists, Am. Assn. Pathologists. Office: Dept of Pathology U Medicine-Dentistry NJ 185 S Orange Ave Newark NJ 07103-2714

RAVEN, JACQUES ROBERT, investment banker; b. Paris, France, Feb. 4, 1933; came to U.S., 1942; s. Robert F. and Toinette (Meyer-Levy) R.; m. Charlotte Beaumelou, Oct. 8, 1973; children: Robert Courtney, Jeffrey Laurence, Sophie Charlotte. Diploma, Inst. Polit. Sci., Paris, 1953; Dipl. Econs., U. Paris, 1953; BA, U. Calif., Berkeley, 1955; Doctorate with honors, U. Madrid, Spain, 1956. Sr. loan officer U.S. Dept. State, Washington amd New Delhi, 1959-64; dep. dir. UN Devel. Program, Beirut, Lebanon, 1964-66; rep. for Europe Wells Fargo Bank, San Francisco, 1967-69; sr. mgr. Price Waterhouse & Co., Paris, 1969-71; sr. v.p., gen. mgr. Banque Nat. de Paris, San Francisco, Toronto, Manila, 1972-81; internat. v.p. Lazard Freres & Co., N.Y.C., 1981-83; mng. dir., founder Quadreon Capital Corp., N.Y.C., 1984-91; prin. Cedar Grove Captial, Inc., N.Y.C., 1992—; bd. dirs. French Am. Bilingual Sch. Mem. World Affairs Coun. (trustee), San Francisco Com. on Fgn. Rels., Univ. Club.

RAVEN-RIEMANN, CAROLYN SUE, actress, model, small business owner; b. Evergreen Park, Ill., Dec. 7, 1945; d. Eugene Alexander and Eloise Irene (McGhee) Raven; m. Herbert Friedrich Riemann, Aug. 1, 1981. BA, Northwestern U., 1967. Model, actress Mannequin Models, N.Y.C., 1969-86, several talent agts., 1969—; model Les Girls Ltd., N.Y.C., 1986—, Johnston Models, Greenwich, Conn., 1986—; owner, pres. The OrchidPhile, Stamford, Conn.; pres. The OrchidPhile, Stamford, Conn.; sec., treas. GearGrip, Inc., Stamford, 1983—; author, pub., owner OrchidPhile Log. Mem. SAG, AFTRA, Am. Orchid Soc. (edn. com.), Greater N.Y. Orchid Soc., Internat. Phalaenopsis Alliance, Inc. (co-founder, sec. 1990—), Northwestern U. Alumni Assn., Tri Delta Sorority Alumni Soc. Republican. Congregationalist.

RAVINDRA, NUGGEHALLI MUTHANNA, physics educator; b. Hyderabad, India, Oct. 1, 1955; s. Nuggehalli Garudachar and Padma (Srinivasa) Muthanna; m. Pushpa Seetharaman, July 11, 1984; children: Krishna, Pradeep. BS with honors, Bangalore (India) U., 1974; MS, Bangalore (India) U., India, 1976; PhD, Roorkee (India) U., 1982. Rsch. fellow Roorkee U., 1977-81, postdoctoral fellow, 1981-82; scientist Ctr. Nat. Recherche Sci., Montpellier and Paris, 1982-84, Internat. Ctr. Theory Physics, Trieste, Italy, 1984-85, Microelectronics Ctr N.C., Research Triangle Park, 1985-86; rsch. assoc. prof. physics Vanderbilt U., Nashville, 1986—; assoc. prof. N.J. Inst. Tech., Newark, 1987—; investigator SEMATECH, N.J., 1988-90, BELLCORE, Redbank, N.J., 1988-91, N.J. Commn. Sci. and Tech., 1990-92. Mem. IEEE, Electro Chem. Soc. Home: 20 Brantwood Dr Summit NJ 07901-2964 Office: NJ Inst Tech Microelectronics Rsch Ctr Newark NJ 07102

RAVITCH, DIANE SILVERS, historian, educator, author, government official; b. Houston, July 1, 1938; d. Walter Cracker and Ann Celia (Katz) Silvers; m. Richard Ravitch, June 26, 1960 (div. 1986); children: Joseph, Steven (dec.), Michael. BA, Wellesley Coll., 1960; PhD, Columbia U., 1975; LHD (hon.), Williams Coll., 1984, Reed Coll., 1985, Amherst Coll., 1986, SUNY, 1988, Ramapo Coll., 1990, St. Joseph's Coll., N.Y., 1991. Adj. asst. prof. Tchrs. Coll., Columbia U., N.Y.C., 1975-78, assoc. prof., 1978-83, adj. prof., 1983-91; asst. sec. office educational rsch. and improvement U.S. Dept. Edn., Washington, 1991—, counselor to the sec. edn., 1991—. Author: The Great School Wars, 1974, The Revisionists Revised, 1977, The Troubled Crusade, 1983, The Schools We Deserve, 1985, (with others) Educating an Urban People, 1981, The School and the City, 1983, Against Mediocrity, 1984, Challenges to the Humanities, 1985, What Do Our 17 Year Olds Know?, 1987, The American Reader, 1990; co-editor: The Democracy Reader, 1992. Chair Ednl. Excellence Network, 1988-91; trustee N.Y. Pub. Libr., N.Y.C., 1981-87, hon. life trustee, 1988—; bd. dirs. Woodrow Wilson Nat. Fellowship Found., 1987-91, Coun. Basic Edn., 1989-91. Guggenheim fellow, 1977-78; Phi Beta Kappa vis. scholar. Mem. Nat. Acad. Edn., Am. Acad. Arts and Scis., Soc. Am. Historians. Office: US Dept Edn Office Edn Rsch Improvement 555 New Jersey Ave NW Rm 600 Washington DC 20208-5530

RAVITCH, RICHARD, lawyer; b. N.Y.C., July 7, 1933; children: Joseph, Michael. Grad., Columbia U., 1955, Yale U. Law Sch., 1958. Former chmn. HRH Constrn. Corp., N.Y. State Urban Devel. Corp.; former chmn. Bowery Bank, Met. Transp. Authority, N.Y.; gen. ptnr. Blackstone Group, N.Y.C., 1990—; pres., chief exec. officer players rels. com. Major League Baseball, 1991. Candidate N.Y.C. mayoral race Dem. primary, 1989. Office: 350 Park Ave New York NY 10022

RAVITZ, LEONARD J., JR., physician, scientist, consultant; b. Cuyahoga County, Ohio, Apr. 17; s. Leonard Robert and Esther Evelyn (Skerball) R. BS, Case Western Res. U., 1944; MD, Wayne State U., 1946; MS, Yale U., 1950; spl. studies of epistemology, field physics and cybernetics under F.S.C. Northrop, PhD, 1973-80. Diplomate Am. Bd. Psychiatry and Neurology, 1952. Rsch. asst. EEG to A.J. Derbyshire PhD Harper Hosp., Detroit, 1943-46; spl. trainee in hypnosis to Milton H. Erickson MD Wayne County Gen. Hosp., Eloise, Mich., 1945-46; rotating intern St. Elizabeth's Hosp., Washington, 1946-47; jr./sr. asst. resident in psychiatry Yale-New Haven Hosp.; asst. in psychiatry and mental hygiene Yale Med. Sch., 1947-49, rsch. fellow to Harold S. Burr PhD sect. neuro-anatomy, 1949-50; sr. resident in neuropsychiatry Richard S. Lyman svc. Duke Hosp., Durham, N.C., 1950-51; instr. Duke U. Med. Sch., Durham, 1950-51; assoc. to R. Burke Suitt MD Pvt. Diagnostic Clinic, Duke Hosp., Durham, 1951-53; assoc. Duke U. Med. Sch., 1951-53; vis. asst. prof. neuropsychiatry and asst. to vis. prof. Richard S. Lyman, MD Meharry Med. Ctr., Nashville, 1953; asst. dir. profl. edn. in charge tng. U. Wyo. Nursing Sch. affiliates; chief rsch. rehab. bldg. Downey VA Hosp. (now called VA Hosp.), North Chicago, Ill., 1953-54; assoc. psychiatry Sch. Medicine and Hosp., U. Pa., Phila., 1955-58; dep. asst. sec. def. in charge of health and med. Dep. Asst. Sec. Def. in Charge of Health and Med., E.H. Cushing, MD, Pentagon, 1958; dir. tng. and rsch. Ea. State Hosp., Williamsburg, Va., 1958-60; pvt. practice neuropsychiatry specializing in hypnosis Norfolk, Va., 1961—; psychiatrist, cons. Div. Alcohol Studies and Rehab., Va. Dept. Health (later Va. Dept. Mental Health and Mental Retardation), 1961-81; psychiatrist Greenpoint Clinic, Bklyn., 1983-87, 17th St. Clinic, N.Y.C., 1987-92; sec.-treas. Euclid-97th St. Clinic, Inc., Cleve., 1957-63, pres., 1963-69; clin. asst. prof. psychiatry, SUNY Health Sci. Ctr. Med. Sch., 1983—; psychiatrist Downstate Mental Hygiene Assocs., Bklyn., 1983—; pvt. cons., Cleve., 1961-69, Upper Montclair, N.J., 1982—; lectr. sociology Old Dominion U., Norfolk, 1961-62, cons. nutrition rsch. project, Old Dominion U. Research Found., 1978-90; spl. med. cons. Frederick Mil. Acad., Portsmouth, Va., 1963-71; cons. Tidewater Epilepsy Found., Chesapeake, Va., 1962-68, USPH Hosp. Alcohol Unit, Norfolk, 1980-81, Nat. Inst. Rehab. Therapy, Butler, N.J., 1982-83; participant 5th Internat. Congress for Hypnosis and Psychosomatic Medicine, Gutenburg U., Mainz, Fed. Republic Germany, 1970; organizer symposia on hypnosis in psychiatry and medicine, field theory as an integrator of knowledge, hypnosis in office practice, history of certain forensic and psychotherapeutic aspects of the study of man, Williamsburg, Va., 1959-60; founding pres. Va. Soc. Clin. Hypnosis, 1959-60, Found. for Study Electrodynamic Theory of Life, 1989—. Asst. editor Jour. Am. Soc. Psychosomatic Dentistry and Medicine, 1980-83; mem. editorial bd. Internat. Jour. Psychosomatics, 1984—; contbr. sects. to books, articles, book revs., abstracts to profl. publs.; discoverer electromagnetic field correlates of hypnosis, emotions, psychiatric/med. disorders and aging and electrocyclic phenomena in humans which parallel those of other life forms, earth and atmosphere underwriting beginning short- and long-range predictions, such seemingly disparate phenomena united under a single regulating principle defined in terms of measurable field intensity and polarity. Sr. v.p. Willoughby Civic League, 1971-75. 1st lt. AUS, 1943-46. Lyman Rsch. Fund grantee, 1950-53. Fellow AAAS, Am. Psychiat. Assn., N.Y. Acad. Scis., Am. Soc. Clin. Hypnosis (charter), Royal Soc. Health (London); mem. Norfolk Acad. Medicine, Soc. for Investigation of Recurring Events, Va. Med. Soc., Nu Sigma Nu, Sigma Xi. Office: SUNY Health Sci Ctr Med Sch Dept Psychiatry Box 1203, 450 Clarkson St Brooklyn NY 11203-2098 also: PO Box 9409 NorA 23505-0409

RAWICZ, ANDREW PETER, chemical company executive; b. Warsaw, Poland, June 29, 1934; came to U.S., 1948; s. Zych Joseph and Krystyna (Zmijewski) Rawicz-Szabuniewicz; m. M. Patricia Heinzen, Oct. 21, 1960; children: Michelle, Kimberley, Michael, Douglas, David. BS in Indsl. Engring., U. Dayton, 1957; MBA, Xavier U., 1959. Various positions Gen. Tire & Rubber, Marion, Ind., 1957-60; planning mgr. Internat. Playtex, Dover, Del., 1960-68; ops. mgr. Lesney Products, Carlstadt, N.J., 1968-70; gen. mgr. Eckmar Corp., Emigsville, Pa., 1970-71; pres. Quartronics Inc., Syracuse, N.Y., 1971-73, ISCC Chems., Inc., Emigsville, Pa., 1973—; chmn. regulatory panel Pa. Small Bus. Conf., 1990. Dir. York (Pa.) County Ind. Devel. Authority, 1982-89. With USAFR, 1959-67. Recipient Keystone award of merit State of Pa., Harrisburg, 1986. Mem. Nat. Assn. Chem. Mfrs., Nat. Fedn. Ind. Small Bus. (sr. guardian 1987-91), Nat. Assn. Solvent Recyclers (dir. 1983-86), York Area C. of C. (chmn. environ. com. 1980-86), York Area Rotary Club (bd. mem. 1986-89), Pa. Chamber Bus. and Industry.

RAWL, ARTHUR JULIAN, chemical company executive, accountant, consultant, author; b. Boston, July 6, 1942; s. Philip and Evelyn (Rosoff) R.; m. Karen Lee Werby, June 4, 1967; 1 child, Kristen Alexandra. BBA, Boston U., 1967, postgrad, 1972-74. CPA, Mass., N.Y., La. Audit mgr. Touche Ross & Co., Boston, 1967-77; audit mgr. Touche Ross & Co., N.Y.C., 1977-79, ptnr., 1979; ptnr. Touche Ross & Co., Newark, 1980-88, N.Y.C., 1988-89; ptnr. Deloite & Touche, N.Y.C., 1989; exec. v.p., chief fin. officer Hanlin Group, Inc., Linden, N.J., 1990—; bd. dirs. BiakalInterPlast (USSR), Kuperwood Enterprises, Hanlin Group, Inc.; mem. adj. faculty Boston U., 1971-75. Contbr. articles to profl. journals, mags. and trade publs. Mem. Newton Upper Falls (Mass.) Hist. Commn., 1977; bd. dirs. Sherburne Scholarship Fund Boston U., 1977-80; mem. Englewood (N.J.) Planning Bd., 1981-83; trustee Englewood Bd. Edn., 1983-85, 89—, pres., 1991—; trustee, treas. exec. com. Englewood Econ. Devel. Corp., 1986-89; fin. and compensation com. Dwight Englewood Sch., 1985-90; mem. parent devel. com. Mt. Holyoke Coll., 1991—. Served to 2d class petty officer USN, 1960-63. Fellow AICPA, Mass. Soc. CPAs, N.Y. Soc. CPAs; mem. Am. Legion, Navy League U.S., N.J. Hist. Soc. (bd. govs., exec. com., nominating com., treas. 1987—), St. George's Soc. N.Y., Univ. Club, Essex Club, Englewood Club, Sloane Club (London). Home: 72 Booth Ave Englewood NJ 07631-1907 Office: Hanlin Group Inc Foot of S Wood Ave Linden NJ 07036

RAWLINGS, SAMUEL CRAIG, psychologist; b. Wichita, Kans., Sept. 7, 1938; s. Roy Bird and Virginia (Knisley) R.; m. Janet MacPhail, May 22, 1960 (div. 1980); children: Megan Malinda, Chainy Anne; m. Kathy J. Bowers, June 6, 1981; 1 child, Jamison Ryan. BS, Calif. State U., Fullerton, 1964; MS, U. Miami, 1968, PhD, 1970, postgrad., 1971. Rsch. asst./assoc. U. Miami, Coral Gables, Fla., 1966-71; sch. psychologist Dade County Pub. Schs., Miami, 1969-70; asst. prof. U. Houston, 1971-74; program dir. Nat. Eye Inst., NIH, Bethesda, Md., 1975-77; asst. prof. U. Tex. Health Sci. Ctr., San Antonio, 1977-80; sci. review adminstr. NIH, Bethesda, 1980-86, chief behavioral/neuro scis. and dir. of rsch. review sect., 1986—; NIH rep. Fedn. of Behavior, Psychol. and Cognitive Scis., Washington, 1989—. Contbr. articles to profl. jours.; co-editor: Methodological Issues in Aging Research, 1985; editorial bd. NIH Peer Review Notes, 1989—. With U.S. Army, 1960-61. NSF sci. reviewer, 1970-78, Vision Rsch sci. reviewer, 1968-71; Nat. Soc. to Prevent Blindness grantee, 1979-80, Fight for Sight grantee, 1979-80. Home: 6536 Farmingdale Ct Rockville MD 20855-1505 Office: NIH Westwood Bldg Rm 310 Bethesda MD 20892

RAWLINS, WILSON TERRY, chemist; b. Edinburg, Tex., Nov. 8, 1949; s. Ralph Terry and Josephine Ray (Wilson) R.; m. Elizabeth Helen Brown, Mar. 29, 1975; children: Kyle Garrett, Adriana Fay. BS in Chemistry, U. Tex., 1972, BA in Math., 1972; PhD in Chemistry, U. Pitts., 1977. Prin. scientist Phys. Scis. Inc., Woburn, Mass., 1977-86; group leader aeronomy and surface chemistry Phys. Scis. Inc., Andover, Mass., 1986-87, mgr. chem. scis., 1987—. Contbr. articles to profl. jours. Mem. Am. Geophys. Union, Combustion Inst., Soc. Photo-optical Instrumentation Engrs. Office: Phys Scis Inc 20 New England Bus Ctr Andover MA 01810

RAWSON, CLAUDE JULIEN, literature educator; b. Shanghai, China, Feb. 8, 1935; came to U.S., 1985; s. Bernard and Helen (Sapiro) R.; m. Judith Ann Hammond, July 14, 1959; children: Hugh, Tim, Mark, Harriet, Annabel. BA, Oxford (Eng.) U., 1955, MA, BLitt, 1959. English lectr. U. Newcastle, Eng., 1957-65; from lectr. to prof., chmn. dept. U. Warwick, Coventry, Eng., 1965-85, hon. prof., 1986—; George Sherburn prof. English U. Ill., Urbana, 1985-86; George M. Bodman prof. English Yale U., New Haven, Conn., 1986—; vis. prof. U. Pa., Phila., 1973, U. Calif., Berkeley, 1980. Author: Henry Fielding and the Augustan Ideal, 1972, 2d edit., 1991, Gulliver add the Gentle Reader, 1973, 2d edit., 1991, Order from Confusion Sprung, 1985, 2d edit., 1992, Satire and Sentiment 1660-1830, 1992; editor: Modern Lang. Rev. and Yearbook of English Studies, London, 1974-78; gen. editor: Cambridge (Eng.) History of Literary Criticism, 1983—, Unwin Critical Libr., London, 1974—; chmn., gen. editor: Yale Boswell Papers, 1990—. Recipient Cert. of Merit for Disting. Svc. Conf. of Editors of Learned Jours., 1988; Andrew Mellon fellow Clark and Huntington Libr., 1980, 90, Guggenheim fellow, 1991-92, Sr. Faculty fellow Yale U., 1991-92; NEH grantee, 1991. Mem. MLA, Modern Humanities Rsch. Assoc. (life mem., com. mem.

1974-88), Internat. Soc. 18th Century Studies, Am. Soc. for 18th Century Studies, Brit. Soc. for 18th Century Studies (pres. 1973-74). Office: Yale U Dept English Box 3545 Yale Sta New Haven CT 06520

RAY, BONNIE MACDOUGALL, educator; b. Somers Point, N.J., Sept. 15, 1947; d. Willis Clayton and Maude Barbara (Deans) MacDougall; m. Kalyan B. Ray, Aug. 23, 1980; 1 child, Pia Margaret. BA, Cedar Crest Coll., 1969; MA, Columbia U., 1970, PhD, 1982. Tchr. of English The Chapin Sch., N.Y.C., 1975-79; tchr. English The Spence Sch., N.Y.C., 1984-86; asst. prof. Bergen Community Coll., Paramus, N.J., 1986-90, assoc. prof., 1990—; program coord. The Am. Lang. Program Bergen Community Coll., Paramus, 1988—; adj. asst. prof. Queens Coll., Flushing, N.Y., 1983-88. Co-translator: City of Memories, 1991; contbr. articles to profl. jours. V.p. Acad. of Indian Art and Culture, Rockaway, N.J., 1988—. Mem. Tchrs. of English as a Second Lang., The Integration Project. Roman Catholic. Home: 166 Parmelee Ave Hawthorne NJ 07506-2925 Office: Bergen Community Coll 400 Paramus Rd Paramus NJ 07652-1508

RAY, DAN KEITH, association executive; b. Waynesville, N.C., Nov. 28, 1948; s. Jack Ray and Georgia Davis Price. BA, Mars Hill Coll., 1971. Pres. Third Sector Mgmt., Washington, 1975-85; sr. mgr. Peat Marwick, N.Y.C., 1985-89; pres., chief exec. officer Am. Craft Coun., N.Y.C., 1989—. Author: Resource Development System, 1987. Democrat. Baptist. Home: 20 5th Ave Apt 10D New York NY 10011-8860 Office: Am Craft Coun 72 Spring St New York NY 10012-4019

RAY, DAVID GILBERT, psychologist; b. Hazleton, Pa., Oct. 18, 1952; s. Eugene and Martha Lorraine (Gilbert) R.; m. Kathleen Ruth Meachum, Dec. 31, 1973 (div. Apr. 1990); children: David Jr., Jennifer, Anne; m. Virginia Maclay Madden. BS, Pa. State U., 1974, MEd, 1975. Cert. clin. mental health counselor. Counselor Juniata Valley MH/MR Partial Hospitalization Program, Lewistown, Pa., 1975-77; dir. Juniata Valley MH/MR Partial Hospitalization Program, Lewistown, 1977-81, Out-Patient Psychiat. Svc. of Lewistown (Pa.) Hosp., 1981-86; pvt. practice Lewistown, 1986—; cons. Hospice The Bridge Lewistown Hosp., 1981—. Mem. Am. Assn. Counseling Devel., Pa. Psychol. Assn. Republican. Lutheran. Home: 10 Shelly Dr Reedsville PA 17084 Office: 43 Chestnut St Lewistown PA 17044

RAY, DEBASISH, systems analyst; b. Calcutta, India, Nov. 21, 1954; came to U.S., 1981; s. Amarendra Nath and Lila (Sirkar) R.; m. Sanjukta Das, May 15, 1985; 1 child, Rohit Ray. B in Tech., IIT Kharagpur Dept. Naval Arch., 1977; MS in Engrng. in Naval Arch., U. Mich., 1982, MS in Mech. Engring., 1983. Naval architect Garden Reach Shipbuilders and Engrs., Calcutta, India, 1977-80; teaching asst. U. Mich. Dept. Naval Architecture, Ann Arbor, Mich., 1982-83; sr. systems analyst Syscon Corp., Washington, 1983-86; project mgr. The Baham Corp., Columbia, Md., 1986—; editor Dept. Jour. Naval Architecture, Kharagpur, India, 1975-76. Author: Computer Aided Design Optimization of Marine Propellers (3 publs.), 1982. Mem. Soc. Naval Architects and Marine Engrs., Am. Soc. Mech. Engrs., Am. Soc. Naval Engrs., Indian Inst. Naval Architects. Home: 7262 Procopio Circle Columbia MD 21046 Office: The Baham Corp 5501 Twin Knolls Rd # 102 Columbia MD 21045

RAY, EVA KONIG, biomedical consultant; b. Zagreb, Yugoslavia; d. Franjo and Erna (Kohn) K.; m. Edward Ray, Aug. 3, 1952; children: Judith, Diane, David, Jean. BA, Cornell U., 1955; MA, PhD, Bryn Mawr Coll., 1973. Postdoctoral fellow dept. Ophthalmology Med. Sch. of U. Pa., Phila., 1972-74, rsch. assoc. Scheie Eye Inst., 1974-76; asst. prof. dept. biochemistry/physiology Med. Coll. of Pa., Phila., 1976-83, dean of women, 1980-83; technology cons. Steg, Ray and Assocs., Villanova, Pa., 1983—; chairperson Gordon Rsch. Conf., Kingston, R.I., 1988, 90; chair sci. adv. bd. BRT Inc., Troy, N.Y., 1981-83; exec. v.p. Scientists and Engrs. unit B'nai B'rith, 1988-90. Dem. committeewoman, Villanova, 1985-90. Mem. AIAA (space processing com.), Am. Soc. Microbiology, Assn. Women in Sci., Am. Soc. Gravitational and Space Biology, Aerospace Med. Assn., Sigma Xi. Home: 1222 Prospect Hill Rd Villanova PA 19085-2115

RAY, GORDON THOMPSON, communications executive; b. N.Y.C., Jan. 31, 1928; s. John Henry and Hama Thompson (Potter) R. m. Ingrid Ray; children: Stuart, John, Lawrence, Carl. BEE, Rensselaer Poly. Inst., 1954; PhD, Midwest Coll. Engring., 1983. With The Bell System, various locations, 1954-83; successively engr., chief engr. N.Y. Tel., Albany, Utica, Jamaica, White Plains, N.Y., Bklyn., 1983; asst. v.p. long range planning N.Y. Tel., N.Y.C.; former mem. tech. staff Bell Tel. Labs., N.Y.C., Murray Hill and Holmdel, N.J.; engr. AT&T, N.Y.C.; dir. Bell System Computer Seminar; del. CCITT, Body Planning Internat. Direct Distance Dialing; v.p. planning NYNEX Materiel Enterprises Co. subs. NYNEX Corp., 1983-84, sr. v.p. NEC Am. Inc., Melville, N.Y., 1985-91, exec. v.p., 1992—; mem. bus. and industry ctr. SUNY, adv. bd. Marine Scis. Rsch. Ctr., Harriman Coll., Stonybrook; bd. govs. Firestone; bd. dirs. NEC Am. Inc., NEC Rsch. Inst., L.I. Assn.; exec. com. Computer and Communications Industry Assn. Trustee U.S. Coun. for Internat. Bus.; mem. exec. com. Akron Golf Charaties. With U.S. Army, 1946-49. Mem. AAAS, NSPE (sr. mem.), IEEE (sr. mem.), IEEE Communications Soc. (past chmn. quality assurance mgmt. com., internat. communications field award com.), N.Y. Acad. Scis., Am. Mgmt. Assn., Cedarbrook Country Club, Firestone Country Club (bd. govs.). Office: NEC Am Inc 8 Old Sod Farm Rd Melville NY 11747-3148

RAY, MICHAEL JOSEPH, metallurgical engineer; b. Pitts., Feb. 28, 1937; s. August D. and Josephine M. (Lopinto) R.; m. Barbara Jean Schrift, Sept. 24, 1982. BSMetE, U. Pitts., 1965. Hot mill metallurgist Allegheny Ludlum Steel Corp., Brackenridge, Pa., 1965-68; metall. engr. Am. Shear Knife Co., Homestead, Pa., 1968-71; cold mill metallurgist Crucible Steel Co., Midland, Pa., 1971-73; metall. engr. Beryllium Corp., Reading, Pa., 1973-81, Conrail, Altoona, Pa., 1981—. Mem. AIME, Am. Railway Engring. Assn. (chmn. revision rail specification 1987-89, chmn. ad hoc com. 1987-89, Commendation award 1990), Am. Soc. for Metals, Iron and Steel Soc., Nat. Railway Hist. Soc. (solicitor 1988). Democrat. Roman Catholic. Home: 112 Bel Dr Hollidaysburg PA 16648-9662 Office: Conrail 2nd St Juniata Altoona PA 16603

RAY, WILLIAM F., banker; b. Cin., Sept. 17, 1915; s. William F. and Adele (Daller) R.; m. Helen Payne, 1939; children: Katharine Ray Sturgis, Barbara Ray Stevens, Mary Ray Struthers, Margaret Ray Gilbert, Whitney Ray Dawson, William F. III, Susan. A.B., U. Cin., 1935; M.B.A., Harvard, 1937. With Brown Bros. Harriman & Co., 1937—, asst. mgr., 1944-49; mgr. Brown Bros. Harriman & Co., Boston, 1950-67; ptnr. Brown Bros. Harriman & Co., N.Y.C., 1968—; trustee emeritus Atlantic Mut. Ins. Co., N.Y.C.; mem. internat. bd. advisors Australia and New Zealand Banking Group, Ltd., 1987-91; bd. dirs. U.S.-New Zealand Bus. Coun. Bd. dirs. Robert Brunner Found., Downtown-Lower Manhattan Assn., Inc., 1978-89. Mem. Bankers Assn. for Fgn. Trade (pres. 1966-67), Harvard Bus. Sch. Assn. (pres. 1963-64, exec. coun.), Robert Morris Assocs. (pres. N.E. 1962-63), Pilgrims U.S., Am. Australian Assn. (hon. dir.), U.S.-New Zealand Bus. Coun., S.R. (life), Asia Soc. (Ann. award 1988), Skating Club (Boston)(pres. 1956-58), Brookline (Mass.) Country Club, Union Club (N.Y.C.), India House (N.Y.C.), Apawamis Club (Rye, N.Y.), Fishers Island (N.Y.) Club, Ardsley (N.Y.) Curling Club, Mountain Lake Club (Lake Wales, Fla.), Order of Australia (hon., officer), Order of Malta, Phi Beta Kappa Assocs. (hon. bd. dirs.). Republican. Home: 1 E End Ave New York NY 10021-1182 Office: Brown Bros Harriman & Co 59 Wall St New York NY 10005-2818

RAYHER, JOHN (JACK RAYHER), marketing professional; b. N.Y.C., Sept. 22, 1946; s. John and Mildred Frances (Bokor) R.; m. Barbara "Erica" Daly, Oct. 26, 1974. BA, St. Francis, 1969; MBA, CUNY, 1978. Buyer R.H. Macy, N.Y.C., 1969-72; devel. mgr. Interactive Market Systems, N.Y.C., 1972-76; product mgr. Gen. Foods, White Plains, N.Y., 1976-82; v.p. account supr. NW Ayer, N.Y.C., 1982-89; v.p., account dir. Citicorp POS Info. Svcs., Stamford, Conn., 1990—; sec., treas. Hair Regrowth Ctrs. Am. Inc., N.Y.C., 1988-90. Contbg. editor jour. Tamarac Times, 1987-89. Recipient Silver Effie Am. Mktg. Assn., N.Y.C., 1984, Best TV Comml. award Advt. Age, Chgo., 1985, Bronze Lion award Internat. Advt. Film Festival, Cannes, 1986, Town Crier awards Fin. Advt. and Mktg. Assn., N.Y.C., 1987. Home: 29 Squirrel Ln Levittown NY 11756-3612 Office: Citicorp POS Info Svcs 750 Washington Blvd Stamford CT 06901-3725

RAYMOND, ARTHUR JOSEPH, economics educator; b. Putnam, Conn., Feb. 18, 1949; s. Arthur J. Sr. and Rita E. (Tetreault) R.; m. Helene M. Lucas, July 18, 1982; 1 child, Samantha H. BSBA, Bryant Coll., 1971; MA in Econs., Tufts U., 1972, PhD in Econs., 1990. Instr. Washington & Jefferson Coll., Washington, Pa., 1976-81; vis. instr. Wheaton Coll., Norton, Mass., 1982; instr. Harvard U., Boston, 1983; asst. prof. Suffolk U., Boston, 1983-85; lectr. Tufts U., Medford, Mass., 1985-91; lectr. MBA program Babson Coll., Wellesley Hills, Mass., 1985-91; asst. prof. Muhlenberg Coll., Allentown, Pa., 1991—; mem. editorial adv. bd. Dishkin Publ., Conn., 1988—. Contbr. articles to profl. jours. Scholar Tufts U., 1972-76; rsch. grantee Muhlenberg Coll., 1992. Mem. Am. Econ. Assn., Am. Fin., Western Econ. Assn., World Affairs Coun. Office: Muhlenberg Coll Econs Dept 2400 Chew St Allentown PA 18104

RAYMOND, CHARLES WALKER, III, infosystems engineer; b. Cambridge, N.Y., Sept. 1, 1937; s. Charles Walker 2nd and Anita Angelina (Cervi) R.; m. Mary Lucille Calahan, June 24, 1961 (div. Feb. 1975); children: Charles Walker IV, Peter Timothy; m. Lorraine Janet Santerre, June 17, 1976. BA, U. Conn., 1960; MA, U. Del., 1971; Master Mil. Arts & Scis., USA Command-Gen. Staff Coll., Fort Leavenworth, Kans., 1975. F.A. officer 3/4th arty., 2d inf. brigade and 1/29th artillery, 5th infantry div. U.S. Army, Fort Devens, Mass., 1961-63; infantry battalion advisor 3/41st infantry 22d ARVN div., mil. assistance adv. group-Vietnam U.S. Army, Kontum, Republic of Vietnam, 1963-64; co. comdr. co. E, 10th bn., 2d tng. brigade Fort Jackson, S.C., 1965-66; fire support officer 2/19th artillery airborne, lst cavalry div., An Khe, Republic of Vietnam, 1966-67; asst. prof. mil. sci. U. Del., Newark, 1967-71; combat devel. staff officer U.S. Army Tng and Doctrine Command, Aberdeen Proving Ground, Md., 1971-74; instr. joint ops. South Asia U.S. Army Command and Gen. Staff Coll., Ft. Leavenworth, 1977-81; store mgr. Rite Aid Corp., Bennington, Vt., 1982; sr. staff mem. BDM Internat., Inc., McLean and Eatontown, Va., N.J., 1983-87; sr. mem., tech. staff GTE Govt. Systems Corp., Billerica, Mass., 1987-89; dir. N.J. ops. MANDEX Inc., Tinton Falls, N.J., 1990-91; prin. engr. Computer Scis. Corp., Eatontown, N.J., 1991—. Photographic exhibitions. Vice-chmn. City Meml. Day Parade Com., Newark, Del., 1968-73; village clk. Village of Old Bennington, Vt., 1982. Lt. col. U.S. Army 1960-81. Decorated Legion of Merit, Bronze Star with "v" two oak leaf clusters, Meritorious Svc. medal, Combat Infantryman badge, ARCOM with oak leaf cluster, 11 air medals. Mem. Assn. U.S. Army, Armed Forces Communications-Electronics Assn. (editor newsletter 1984-85, Citation 1986), Soc. of Logistics Engrs., Am. Def. Preparedness Assn., MENSA, Retired Officer's Assn., Disabled AMVETS, Phi Kappa Tau. Roman Catholic. Office: Computer Scis Corp 145 Wyckoff Rd Eatontown NJ 07724-1842

RAYMOND, DONALD LAURENCE, public relations executive; b. N.Y.C., Dec. 4, 1931; s. Margaretta (Reed) R.; m. Marcella A. Loftus, Dec. 23, 1932; children: Donald J., Lenore, Joan. BA, St. Francis, Bklyn., 1957; MA, Seton Hall U., 1960. Dir. AIAA, N.Y.C., 1961-66; supr. AT&T Bell Labs., Murray Hill, N.J., 1966-69; dept. head AT&T Bell Labs., 1969-78; dist. supr. AT&T Bell Labs., N.Y.C., 1978-80; mgr. AT&T Bell Labs., Short Hills, N.J., 1980-87; editorial dir. AT&T Bell Labs., 1987—. Contbr. articles to P.R. Jour., 1974, 79, 89. Lt. comdr. USN, 1952-75. Recipient Golden Quill award Internat. Assn. Bus. Communicators, 1985. Mem. Pub. Rels. Soc. Am., Soc. Tech. Communication. Office: AT&T Bell Labs 101 JFK Pky Short Hills NJ 07078

RAYMOND, F. DOUGLAS, III, lawyer; b. Phila., May 12, 1958; s. F. Douglas Jr. and Carolyn Sue (MacReynolds) R.; m. Elizabeth Tuan Partridge, June 28, 1980; children: Peter Randolph, Alexander Partridge, Louisa Woodword. AB cum laude, Harvard U., 1980; JD magna cum laude, U. Pa., 1985. Bar: Pa. 1985, U.S. Ct. Appeals (3d cir.) 1986. Comml. banker Fidelity Bank, Phila., 1980-82; jud. clk. U.S. Ct. Appeals (3d cir.), Phila., 1985-86; assoc. Drinker, Biddle & Reath, Phila., 1986—. Contbr. articles to law jours. Mem. Independence Hall Assn. (bd. dirs., sec. 1984—), Franklin Found. (bd. dirs. 1982—). Home: 8 Briar Rd Strafford PA 19312 Office: Drinker Biddle & Reath 1100 PNB Bldg Broad and Chestnut Sts Philadelphia PA 19107

RAYMOND, MICHAEL WILLIAM, data processing executive; b. Manchester, Conn., Jan. 21, 1957; s. William Thomas and Barbara Ann (Belasky) R.; m. Susan Ellen Bostrom, June 24, 1978; 1 child, Christopher. BEE, U. Hartford, 1980. Engr. KCR Inc., East Hartford, Conn., 1980-84; project engr. Gen. Digital Corp., Manchester, 1984-86; dir. engring. and mfg. KCR Tech. Inc., East Hartford, 1986-91; prin. Scan-Code Internat., East Hartford, 1991—. Patentee in field. Mem. IEEE, Planning Forum, Soc. for Imaging Sci. Home: 56 Stone Hedge Ln Bolton CT 06043-7441 Office: Scan-Code Internat 130 Prestige Park Rd East Hartford CT 06108

RAYMOND, SAMUEL, computer consultant, retired educator; b. Chester, Pa., Feb. 7, 1920; s. Samuel Murdock and Sara Taylor (Griffith) R.; m. Mary Vernon Hanson, Oct. 27, 1951; children: Elizabeth, Griffith. BA, Swarthmore Coll., 1941; MA, U. Pa., 1942, PhD, 1945. Internship Grad. Hosp., Phila.; residency in pathology Hosp. U. of Pa., Phila., 1958-63; asst. prof. Columbia U., N.Y.C., 1951-57; asst. to assoc. prof. U. Pa., Phila., 1958-91, prof. emeritus, 1991—. Inventor in field. Home and Office: 31 Bar Neck Woods Hole MA 02543

RAYNER, ROBERT MARTIN, financial executive; b. London, Sept. 21, 1946; s. Henry John and Kathleen Mary (Edwards) R.; m. Mindy S. Miller, May 28, 1979. BSc with honors in Eng., Bristol (Eng.) U., 1968; MBA, Columbia Bus. Sch., 1976. Sr. engr. Halcrow and Ptnrs., London, 1968-74; fin. dir. Pepsico Inc., Purchase, N.Y., 1976-88; pres. constrn. materials group, chief fin. officer Essroc Corp., Berkeley Heights, N.J., 1988—; bd. dirs. ESSROC Materials Inc., Berkeley Heights, N.J., San Juan Cement Co., Puerto Rico. Mem. Inst. Civil Engrs. Office: ESSROC Corp 2 Oak Way Connell Corp Ctr II Berkeley Heights NJ 07922

RAYNOLDS, HAROLD, JR., retired state education commissioner; b. Chgo., Feb. 7, 1925; s. Harold and Dorothy (Smith) R.; m. Ann Richards Ellis, June 1950 (div. 1968); children—Christopher, Timothy, Madeline, Dorothy, m. Patricia Adele Miller, Jan. 20, 1973. B.S., Cornell U., 1948, M.A., 1953; postgrad., NYU, 1968-69. Cert. supt. schs., N.Y., Maine, Alaska. Supt. schs. Cape Elizabeth Sch. Dist., Maine, 1969-74; supt. schs. Portland Sch. Dist., Maine, 1974-79; commr. edn. State of Maine, Augusta, 1979-83, State of Alaska, Juneau, 1983-86, Commonwealth of Mass., 1986-91; interim supt. Windsor Cen. Supervisory Union Sch. Dist., Woodstock, Vt., 1991—. Contbr. articles to ednl. jours. Mem. Vt. Senate, 1965-66; chmn. Vt. Bd. Edn., Montpelier, 1963-68; trustee U. Maine, Orono, 1979-83; Dem. candidate for U.S. Congress, Vt., 1962. Staff sgt. U.S. Army, 1943-45, ETO. Mem. Am. Assn. Sch. Adminstrs., Chief State Sch. Officers, Phi Delta Kappa. Unitarian-Universalist.

RAYNOR, RICHARD BENJAMIN, neurosurgeon, educator; b. N.Y.C., Aug. 16, 1928; s. Murray and Mildred (Pitt) R.; m. Barbara Golob; children: Geoffrey, Michele. BME, U. Mich., 1950; MD, U. Vt., 1955. Diplomate Am. Bd. Neurol. Surgery. Intern Mt. Sinai, N.Y.C., 1955-56; residency Neurol. Inst. Presbyn. Hosp., N.Y.C., 1956-57, Nat. Hosp., London, 1957; residency neurosurgery Neurol. Inst. Presbyn. Hosp., 1958-62; assoc. in neurosurgery Coll. Physicians and Surgeons Columbia U., N.Y.C., 1965-77; clin. assoc. prof. NYU, N.Y.C., 1977-84, clin. prof., 1984—; pvt. practice neurosurgery, N.Y.C., 1965—. Consulting editor Spine; contbr. over 35 articles to profl. jours., chpts. to books. Served as capt. U.S. Army, 1962-64. Fellow Am. Coll. Surgeons; mem. Cervical Spine Research Soc. (pres. 1986-87), Am. Assn. Neurol. Surgeons, Congress Neurol. Surgeons. Club: University (N.Y.C.). Office: 112 E 74th St New York NY 10021-3562

RAYNSFORD, ROBERT WAYNE, JR., government executive; b. Neptune, N.J., July 13, 1935; s. Robert Wayne and Maud Marshall (Mason) R.; m. Irmela Ellen Reichelt, Apr. 23, 1964. BA, Williams Coll., 1957; MA, Harvard U., 1963, PhD, 1966. Economist Metallgesellschaft AG, Frankfurt, Fed. Republic Germany, 1963-66, U.S. Dept. Commerce, Washington, 1966-68; sr. economist U.S. Office of Mgmt. and Budget, Washington, 1968-71, various exec. positions, 1972-83; chief economist U.S. Army, Washington, 1984—. Capt. USAF, 1957-60. Woodrow Wilson fellow, 1960. Mem. Am. Econ. Assn., Sr. Execs. Assn., Am. Soc. Mil. Compts., Phi Beta Kappa. Episcopalian. Club: City Tavern. Home: 3850 Tunlaw Rd NW Washington DC 20007-4806 Office: HQDA (SAFM RB) Washington DC 20310

RAYOME, MARK FRANCIS, carpenter, military instructor; b. Watertown, N.Y., Aug. 20, 1960; s. Francis Barclay and Rose (Biondillio) R.; m. Marilee Ann Van Vleck, Feb. 14, 1982; children: David Barclay, Katelyn Rachelle. Enlisted USN, 1978; aircraft mechanic Atkron 35 USN, Oceana, Va., 1978-80; aircraft mechanic Helsuppron 6 USN, Norfolk, Va., 1980-83; carpenter 62nd Navmobconstbatt USN, Gulfport, Miss., 1983-85, project supr. 7th Navmobconstbatt, 1985-87, combat instr. 20th Naval Constrn. Regiment, 1987-89; tng. head RNMCB-13 Seabees USN, Rochester, N.Y., 1989—; constrn. mgr. Parker Constrn., Conesus, N.Y., 1989-90; carpenter Spoleta Constrn., Rochester, 1990—; cons. 20th Navconstreg USN, Gulfport, 1989—; instr. NROTC, Rochester, 1991—; combat arms instr. N.E. U.S. Res. Cmmunity, 1989—. Author tactics manuals. Mem. U.S. Naval Inst. Home: Judson Rd Canton NY 13617 Office: Eastman Kodak Co Ridge Rd W Rochester NY 14622

RAYSON, GLENDON ENNES, internist, preventive medicine specialist, writer; b. Oak Park, Ill., Dec. 2, 1915; s. Ennes Charles and Bernice Margaret (Rowland) R. AB, U. Rochester, 1939; MD, U. Ill., Chgo., 1948; MPH, Johns Hopkins U., 1965; MA, Northwestern U., 1965. Diplomate Am. Bd. Internal Medicine, Am. Bd. Preventive Medicine. Resident in internal medicine Presbyn.-St. Luke's Hosp., Chgo., 1953-56; physician-in-charge Contagious Disease Hosp., Chgo., 1956-58, asst. med. supt., 1958-64; rsch. assoc. Sch. Hygiene and Pub. Health Johns Hopkins U., Balt., 1966-71; internist Johns Hopkins Hosp., 1971-82, Columbia Free State Health Plan, Balt., 1984-91; pvt. practice Balt., 1984—; attending internist emergency rm. South Balt. Gen. Hosp., 1982-84; asst. prof. health sci. U. Ill., Chgo., 1958-64; fellow in gastroenterology and endocrinology Presbyn.-St. Luke's Hosp., 1956-58. Contbr. articles to med. jours., chpt. to book. Vol. physician, Vietnam, 1968, 71, 72, 73. Capt. M.C., USAF, 1951-53. Fellow Am. Coll. Preventive Medicine, Am Geriatrics Soc.; mem. AMA, Am. Pub. Health Assn. Home: 337 Poplar Point Rd Perryville MD 21903-1803 Office: 218 N Charles St #1407 Baltimore MD 21201-4021

RAYSOR, FRANK WANNAMAKER, II, management executive; b. Greenville, S.C., Jan. 24, 1943; s. Henry Ayer Raysor and Melba Lucille (Burgess) Gamble. AB, Duke U., 1964; MBA, Harvard U., 1966. Fin. analyst Davenport & Co., Richmond, Va., 1966-70; mgr. cash planning Jos. E. Seagram & Sons, Inc., N.Y.C., 1970-71, bus. mgr. to chmn., 1971—; pres. BME Three Towers, Inc., N.Y.C., 1984—; dir. Office Am., Inc., Richmond, Va., 1987—. Treas., dir. Upward, Inc. (youth ednl. program), N.Y.C., 1977—. Mem. Harvard Club (N.Y.), Phi Beta Kappa. Episcopalian. Home: 136 E 76th St New York NY 10021 Office: Jos E Seagram & Sons Inc 375 Park Ave New York NY 10152

RAZEY, SANDRA LYNN, travel and food services administrative assistant; b. Kingston, N.Y., June 27, 1963; d. Philip Benjamin and Marianne Francis (Harlow) R. Student, Mercy Coll., Loch Sheldrake, N.Y., 1987; postgrad., Mercy Coll., White Plains, N.Y. Front office cashier Sheraton Boston Hotel and Towers, 1987-88; clerical trainee IBM, Kingston, 1988-89; adminstrv. asst. PepsiCo, Inc., Purchase, N.Y., 1989—. Presbyterian. Office: PepsiCo Inc 700 Anderson Hill Rd Purchase NY 10577

RAZZANO, FRANK CHARLES, lawyer; b. Bklyn., Feb. 25, 1948; s. Pasquale Anthony and Agnes Mary (Borgia) R.; m. Stephanie Anne Lucas, Jan. 10, 1970; children: Joseph, Francis, Catherine. BA, St. Louis U., 1969; JD, Georgetown U., 1972. Bar: N.Y. 1973, U.S. Dist. Ct. (so. dist.) N.Y. 1973, U.S. Dist. Ct. (es. dist.) N.Y. 1973, N.J. 1976, D.C. 1981, Va. 1984, U.S. Dist. Ct. N.J. 1976, U.S. Dist. Ct. Md. 1977, U.S. Dist. Ct. (no. dist.) Calif. 1981, U.S. Dist. Ct. D.C. 1982, U.S. Ct. Appeals (2d cir.) 1973, U.S. Ct. Appeals (3d cir.) 1975, U.S. Ct. Appeals (D.C. and 5th cirs.) 1983, U.S. Ct. Appeals (4th cir.) 1984, U.S. Ct. Appeals (6th cir.) 1990, U.S. Supreme Ct. 1976, U.S. Dist. Ct. (ea. dist.) Va., 1989. Assoc. Shea & Gould, N.Y.C., 1972-75; asst. U.S. atty. Dist. of N.J., Newark, 1975-78; asst. chief trial atty. SEC, Washington, 1978-82; ptnr. Shea & Gould, Washington, 1982—; lectr. in field. Civil law editor Rico Law Reporter; mem. adv. bd. Corp. Confidentiality and Disclosure Letter; contbr. articles to legal jours. Scoutmaster Vienna coun. Boy Scouts Am., 1984. Recipient spl. achievement award Justice Dept., 1977, spl. commendation, 1978. Mem. ABA, Va. Bar, D.C. Bar (chmn. litigation sect. 1987-89, vice-chmn. coun. sects. 10988-89), Phi Beta Kappa, Eta Sigma Phi. Roman Catholic. Home: 1713 Paisley Blue Ct Vienna VA 22182-2326

RAZZANO, PASQUALE ANGELO, lawyer; b. Bklyn., Apr. 3, 1943; s. Pasquale Anthony and Agnes Mary (Borgia) R.; m. Maryann Walker, Jan. 29, 1966; children: Elizabeth, Pasquale, Susan, ChristyAnn. BSCE, Poly. Inst. Bklyn., 1964; student law, NYU, 1964-66; JD, Georgetown U., 1969. Bar: Va. 1969, N.Y. 1970, U.S. Ct. Appeals (2d, 3d, 7th, 9th and fed. cirs.), U.S. Supreme Ct., U.S. Dist. Ct. (so., ea. and western dists.) N.Y., U.S. Dist. Ct. (we. dist.) Tex., U.S. Dist. Ct. Hawaii, U.S. Dist. Ct. Conn. Examiner U.S. Patent Office, 1966-69; assoc. Curtis, Morris & Safford, P.C., 1969-71, ptnr., 1971-91; ptnr. Fitzpatrick, Cella, Harper & Scinto, 1991—; guest lectr. U.S. Trademark Assn., Practicing Law Inst., N.Y.U. Law Ctr. Bd. editors: Licensing Jour., 1986—, Trademark Reporter, 1987—; book rev. editor, 1989-91, pub. articles editor, 1991-92; domestic articles editor, 1992—. Rep. committeeman Rockland County. Recipient Robert Ridgeway award, 1964. Mem. ABA (guest lectr.), Fed. Bar Assn., N.Y. Patent Law Assn. (bd. dirs. 1985—, sec. 1988—), Am. Patent Law Assn., N.Y. Bar Assn., Va. Bar Assn., Italian Am. Bar Assn., Bar Assn. City of N.Y., N.Y. Athletic Club, Minute Man Yacht Club. Republican. Roman Catholic. Address: 15 White Woods Ln Westport CT 06880 also: 14 Deerwood Trail Lake Placid NY 12946

RE, EDWARD D., law educator, retired federal judge; b. Santa Marina, Italy, Oct. 14, 1920; s. Anthony and Marina (Maetta) R.; m. Margaret A. Corcoran, June 3, 1950; children: Mary Ann, Anthony John, Marina, Edward, Victor, Margaret, Matthew, Joseph, Mary Elizabeth, Mary Joan, Mary Ellen, Nancy Madeleine. BS cum laude, St. John's U., 1941, LLB summa cum laude, 1943, LLD (hon.), 1968; JSD, NYU, 1950; PhD (hon.), Aquila, Italy, 1960; LL.D. (hon.), St. Mary's Coll., Notre Dame, Ind., 1968, Maryville Coll., St. Louis, 1969, N.Y. Law Sch., 1976, Bklyn. Coll., CCNY, 1978, Nova U., 1980, Roger Williams Coll., 1982, Dickinson Sch. Law, Carlisle, Pa., 1983, Seton Hall U., 1984, Stetson U., 1990; LLD (hon.), William Mitchell Coll. Law, 1992; L.H.D. (hon.), DePaul U., 1980, Coll. S.I., CCNY, 1981, Pace U., 1985; D.C.S. (hon.), U. Verona, Italy, 1987; J.D. (hon.), U. Bologna, Italy, 1988. Bar: N.Y. 1943. Appointed faculty St. John's U., N.Y., 1947, prof. law, 1951-69, adj. prof. law, 1969-80, Disting. prof., from 1980; vis. prof. Georgetown U. Sch. Law, 1962-67; adj. prof. law N.Y. Law Sch., 1972-82, Martin disting. vis. prof., from 1982; spl. hearing officer U.S. Dept. Justice, 1956-61; chmn. Fgn. Claims Settlement Commn. of U.S., 1961-68; asst. sec. ednl. and cultural affairs U.S. Dept. State, 1968-69; judge U.S. Customs Ct. (now U.S. Ct. Internat. Trade), N.Y.C., 1969-91, chief judge, 1977-91, chief judge emeritus, 1991—; Mem. adv. com. on appellate rules Jud. Conf. U.S., 1976-88; mem. Jud. Conf. U.S., 1986-91, exec. com. long range planning, 1990-91; chmn. adv. com. on experimentation in the law Fed. Jud. Ctr., 1978-81; Mem. bd. higher edn. City of N.Y., 1958-69, mem. emeritus, 1969—; Jackson lectr. Nat. Coll. State Trial Judges, U. Nev., 1970. Author: Foreign Confiscations in Anglo-American Law, 1951, (with Lester B. Orfield) Cases and Materials on International Law, rev. edit, 1965, Selected Essays on Equity, 1955, Brief Writing and Oral Argument, 4th rev. edit, 1977, 6th edit., 1987, (with Zechariah Chafee, Jr.) Cases and Materials on Equity, 1967, Cases and Materials on Equity and Equitable Remedies, 1975; (with Joseph R. Re) Law Students' Manual on Legal Writing and Oral Argument, 1991; chpt., freedom in internat. soc. Concept of Freedom (edited Rev. Carl W. Grindel), 1955; Cases and Materials on Remedies, 1982, 2d edit., 1987; contbr. articles to Legal jours. Served with USAAF, 1943-47; col. JAGC, ret. Decorated Grand Cross Order of Merit Italy; recipient Am. Bill of Rights citation; Morgenstern Found. Interfaith award; USAF commendation medal; Distinguished service award Bklyn. Jr. C. of C., 1956. Mem. ABA (ho. of dels. 1976-78, chmn. sect. internat. and comparative law 1965-67), Bklyn. Bar Assn., Assn. of Bar of City of N.Y., Am. Soc. Internat. Law, Am. Fgn. Law Assn. (pres. 1971-73), Am. Law Inst., Fed. Bar Council (pres. 1973-74), Am. Assn. Comparative Study Law (pres.), Am. Justinian Soc. Jurists (pres. 1974-76), Scribes Am. Soc. Writers

on Legal Subjects (pres. 1978). Office: St Johns U Sch Law Jamaica NY 11439 also: US Ct Internat Trade One Federal Pla New York NY 10007

READE, CLAIRE ELIZABETH, lawyer; b. Waltham, Mass., June 2, 1952; d. Kemp Brownell and Suzanne Helen (Dorntge) R.; m. Earl Phillip Steinberg, Nov. 22, 1980; children: Evan Samuel, Emma Miriam. BA, Conn. Wesleyan U., 1973; JD, Harvard U., 1979; MA in Law and Diplomacy, Tufts U., 1979. Bar: Mass. 1980, D.C. 1983. Sheldon fellow Harvard U., Cambridge, Mass. and, Republic of China, 1979-80; assoc. Ropes & Gray, Boston, 1980-82; assoc. Arnold & Porter, Washington, 1982-86, ptnr., 1987—. Exec. editor: International Trade Policy: The Lawyer's Perspective, 1985; contbr. articles to profl. jours. Mem. ABA, D.C. Bar Assn., Fed. Bar Assn., Am. Soc. Internat. Law, Washington Coun. Lawyers, Women in Internat. Trade. Office: Arnold & Porter 1200 New Hampshire Ave NW Washington DC 20036-6802

READER, BARBARA, lawyer; b. Bklyn., Apr. 5, 1955; d. Malcolm and Claire (Weisberg) Reader; m. David Gelernter, Mar. 5, 1955 (div. 1984). BA, Yale U., 1977; JD, St. John's U., Queens, N.Y., 1983. Bar: N.Y. 1983. Research assoc. Nat. Econ. Research Assocs., Antitrust div., N.Y.C., 1977; research analyst Fed. Res. Bank of N.Y., N.Y.C., 1977-80; law clk. Superior Ct. State of Conn., New Haven, 1983-84; assoc. Albert Pastore & Ward, Greenwich, Conn., 1984-85, Block, Graff, Danzig, Jelline & Mandel, N.Y.C., 1985-86; asst. gen. counsel Bank Leumi Trust Co. of N.Y., N.Y.C., 1986-91; pvt. practice N.Y.C., 1991—. Mem. ABA, N.Y. Bar Assn., Conn. Bar Assn., Bar Assn. City N.Y. Independent. Jewish. Home: 275 W 96th St Apt 7A New York NY 10025 Office: 470 Park Ave S 12th Fl S New York NY 10016

READING, GEORGE PAUL, plastic surgeon; b. Washington, May 10, 1929; s. Oliver Scott and Martha Clare (Gothard) R.; m. Miriam Sample, July 18, 1953 (div. Dec. 1980); children: Rebecca, Lindsay; m. Margery Schbrock, Dec. 27, 1984. BS, Northwestern U., 1951, MD, 1954. Asst. to assoc. prof. plastic surgery SUNY, Buffalo; prof. plastic surgery U. Rochester, N.Y., 1992—; chmn. residency rev. com. plastic surgery, U. Rochester, 1990-92. Mem. Am. Soc. Plastic and Reconstructive Surgeons (v.p. to pres. 1988-89). Office: 601 Elmwood Ave Rochester NY 14642

READING, KATHLEEN ADELL, educator; b. Torrington, Conn., Sept. 26, 1944; d. Harry Bertrand Jr. and Esther Adell (White) R. Lic. practical nurse, Bristol Hosp., 1964; student, Calif. State U., Long Beach, 1975. Practical nurse Bristol (Conn.) Hosp., 1963-68, Hoag Meml. Hosp., Newport Beach, Calif., 1968-76, Waterbury (Conn.) Hosp., 1976-77; tchr. 1st grade Regan Elem. Sch., Waterbury Bd. Edn., Waterbury, 1978—. Fund raiser Jump Rope for Heart program Am. Heart Assn., Waterbury, 1981-86. Mem. Conn. Edn. Assn., Waterbury Tchrs.' Assn. Roman Catholic. Home: 248 Hillside Ave Naugatuck CT 06770-2737

REAGIN, NANCY RUTH, history educator; b. Washington, Jan. 6, 1960; d. Ronald William and Ann (Thiel) R.; m. William McEnery Offutt Jr., June 15, 1985. BA, U. Calif., Berkeley, 1982; MA, Johns Hopkins U., 1985, PhD, 1990. Teaching asst. Johns Hopkins U., Balt., 1987; lectr. U. Tex., Austin, 1989-90; asst. prof. Pace U., N.Y.C., 1990—. Activist, organizer McClennan County Dems., Waco, Tex., 1989-90. Deutscher Akademischer grantee, 1985-87, NEH grantee, 1990. Mem. Am. Hist. Assn., Berkshire Conf. of Women's Historians. Office: Pace U Dept Social Scis Pace Pla New York NY 10038

REAGLES, KENNETH W., rehabilitation psychologist, educator; b. Lone Rock, Wis., Nov. 4, 1940; s. Donald and Dora (Webster) R.; m. Susan A. Simonson, Jan. 30, 1964; 1 child, Jennifer. BS, U. Wis., 1962; MS, San Diego State U., 1966; PhD, U. Wis., 1969. Rsch. assoc., rsch. dir. U. Wis., Madison, 1969-75; prin. K.W. Reagles & Assocs., Syracuse, N.Y., 1969—; co-owner, adminstrv. dir. Pelion, Inc., Syracuse, 1981—; prof., chmn. rehab. svcs. Syracuse U., 1982—; vis. rsch. prof. Bar-Ilan U., Ramat Gan, Israel, 1969-70; cons. U.S. Rehab. Svcs. Adminstrn., Washington, 1975—. Author: (with Goldstein and Amman) Refusal Skills: Reducing Adolescent Drug Use, 1990. Recipient cert. of Merit, Nat. Inst. Disability Related Rsch., Washington, cert. of Appreciation, Gov., State of Wis., Madison, 1973, Disting. Profl. Svc. award Cen. N.Y. Nat. Rehab. Assn., Syracuse, 1977. Mem. Nat. Coun. on Rehab. Edn. (pres. 1983-84), Nat. Rehab. Assn., Nat. Rehab. Counseling Assn., Am. Rehab. Counseling Assn. (pres. 1979-80), Wis. Rehab. Assn. (pres. 1978). Office: KW Reagles & Assocs 500 S Salina St Ste 218 Syracuse NY 13202-3302

REARDON, MARY AGNES, painter, muralist, design consultant; b. Quincy, Mass., July 19, 1912; d. Daniel Bartholomew and Mary Agnes (Cashman) R. AB, Harvard U., 1934; BFA, Yale U., 1938; pvt. studies with Jean Charlot, David A. Siqueiros; HHD (hon.), New Eng. Sch. Law, 1974. Instr. workshops Boston Mus. Fine Arts; assoc. prof. Emmanuel Coll., Boston, 1952-72; muralist mosaic murals domes Nat. Shrine Immaculate Conception, Washington, 1970-73, murals in oil Balt. Cathedral, 1973, mosaic murals St. Mary's Cathedral, San Francisco, mosaic mural domes walls St. Louis Cathedral, 1981-88; paintings Ch. St. Martin De Porres, Montserrat Island, B.W.I., 1992; painter many portraits including Cardinals Cushing and Medeiros, Hon. Francis Murphy. Vol. church work, art mus. and socs. Recipient Radcliffe Alumnae Recognition award Radcliffe Alumnae Assn., 1984; Pres.'s medal Internat. Exposition of Sacred Art, Italy, 1966. Mem. Nat. Soc. Mural Painters, North Shore Arts Assn., Cambridge Art Assn., Copley Soc., South Shore Art Ctr., Harvard Club of Boston, Hingham Harvard Club, Old Colony Radcliffe Club (past pres.). Republican. Roman Catholic. Avocations: sailing, swimming, landscape watercolors. Home and Office: 12 Martins Ln Hingham MA 02043-1020

REATEGUI, JULIO ANTONIO, engineering company executive; b. Lima, Peru, July 27, 1956; came to U.S., 1979; s. Julio and Aida (Rodriguez) R.; m. Magiela Roxana Ibarcena, Sept. 26, 1983; children: Julio Alonso, Claudia Maria. BSEE, Universidad Nacional de Ingenieria, Lima, 1978; MSEE, U. Md., 1980; MBA, Loyola Coll., Balt., 1987. Registered profl. engr., Peru. Electronic engr. Bur. Radiological Health, Rockville, Md., 1979-81; sr. engr. Bendix Corp. Environ. and Process Instruments Div., Largo, Fla., 1981-82; sr. engr. Allied/Bendix Environ. Systems Div., Balt., 1983-85, staff engr., 1985-86, project engr., 1986-88; mgr. engring. indsl. products div. Environ. Tech. Group, Balt., 1988—. Patentee in field. Mem. IEEE, Instrument Soc. Am., Sigma Xi. Roman Catholic. Home: 37 Spring Glen Ct Cockeysville Hunt Valley MD 21030-2443

REATH, GEORGE, JR., lawyer; b. Phila., Mar. 14, 1939; s. George and Isabel Duer (West) R.; children from a previous marriage: Eric, Amanda; m. Ann B. Rowland, 1990. BA, Williams Coll., 1961; LLB, Harvard U., 1964. Bar: Pa. 1965, U.S. Dist. Ct. (ea. dist.) Pa. 1965. Assoc. Dechert Price & Rhoads, Phila., 1964-70, Brussels, 1971-74; atty. Pennwalt Corp., Phila., 1974-78, mgr. legal dept., asst. sec., 1978-87, sr. v.p.-law, sec., 1987-89; sr. v.p., gen. counsel, sec. Elf Atochem N.Am., Inc. (formerly Pennwalt Corp.), Phila., 1990—; bd. dirs. Internat. Bus. Forum, Inc., 1978-91. Trustee Children's Hosp., Phila., 1974—, sec., 1980-81, vice chmn., 1984—; bd. mgrs. Phila. City Inst. Libr., 1974—, treas., 1981-89, pres., 1989—; bd. dirs. Phila. Festival Theatre for New Plays, 1983—, Cen. Phila. Devel. Corp., 1987—, Bach Festival Phila., 1990—, v.p., 1992—); bd. dirs. Crime Commn. Del. Valley, fist vice chmn., 1992—. Mem. ABA, Pa. Bar Assn., Phila. Bar Assn., Am. Soc. Corp. Secs., Am. Corp. Counsel Assn., Racquet Club Phila., Penllyn Club, Phila. Aviation Country Club, Winter Harbor Yacht Club, Phi Beta Kappa. Office: Elf Atochem NAm Inc 3 Parkway Philadelphia PA 19102-1322

REAVY, COLLEEN, accountant; b. Trenton, N.J., Nov. 24, 1965; d. George C. and Antoinette (Halas) R. BS in Acctg., Temple U., 1988. CPA, Pa. Sr. acct. J.H. Williams & Co., Kingston, Pa., 1988—.

REBECCHI, JOHN ARNOLD, marketing executive, business consultant; b. N.Y.C., Oct. 17, 1954; s. Robert Joseph and Isabelle (VanDeventer) R.; m. Patricia Ann Rebecchi, July 14, 1980; children: John, James. AAS in Bus., Suffolk Community Coll., Selden, N.Y., 1974; BS in Acctg., St. John's U., Jamaica, N.Y., 1976; MBA, N.Y. Inst. Tech., 1982. Cost analyst Hartman Systems, Huntington, N.Y., 1976-78; cost accountant Keel Mfg. div. of Pickwick Internat., Hauppauge, N.Y., 1978-80, asst. controller, 1980-82; controller Disc Graphics, Inc., Hauppauge, 1983-85, v.p. mktg. and adminstrn., 1988—; v.p. mktg. Am. Diagnostic Ctrs., Commack, N.Y., 1985-86, Digital Diagnostic Systems, Syosset, N.Y., 1986-88; pres. 92-37 Metro Corp., Forest Hills, N.Y. Pres. Serendipity Day Care, Inc., Hauppauge, 1990—. Mem. Hauppauge Indsl. Assn. (v.p., bd. dirs. 1989—), Delta Mu Delta. Republican. Roman Catholic. Office: Disc Graphics Inc 10 Gilpin Ave Hauppauge NY 11788-4770

REBER, RAYMOND ANDREW, chemical engineer; b. Bklyn., Apr. 16, 1942; s. Herbert and Dorothy Agnes (Schmidt) R.; m. Anita Jean Roe, June 22, 1963; children: Laura Jean Bucci, Paul Raymond, Jill Anita. BChemE, NYU, 1963, MChemE, 1966. Design engr. M.W. Kellogg, N.Y.C., 1964-66, process devel. engr., 1967-69; devel. engr., supr. Union Carbide, Tarrytown, N.Y., 1970-74, lic. bus. mgr., 1975-81; new bus. devel. mgr. Union Carbide, Danbury, Conn., 1982-84; tech. mgr. Union Carbide, Tarrytown, 1985-87; dir. of tech. UOP, Tarrytown, 1988—. Patentee in field. Commr. Montrose (N.Y.) Improvement Dist., 1970—; referee West County Approved Soccer Official Assn., N.Y. High Schs., 1977-91. Recipient Kirkpatrick award McGraw-Hill, 1967, award 1987. Mem. Am. Inst. Chem. Engrs., Nat. Soc. Profl. Engrs., Am. Water Works Assn. Episcopalian. Office: UOP 777 Old Saw Mill River Rd Tarrytown NY 10591

REBERT, BRUCE, local government administrator; b. Hanover, Pa., Aug. 26, 1951; s. Michael Bucher and Marian (Gitt) R.; m. Miyo Moriuchi, May 13, 1978; children: Jessica, Trudy. BA, Occidental Coll., 1973. Asst. mgr. Borough of Hanover, Hanover, Pa., 1974-87, mgr., 1988—; v.p. Gitt Moul Hist. Properties, Hanover, 1976—; sec. Hanover Leisure Coun., 1978-82, Borough of Hanover, 1986-89; chmn. York County Employment and Tng. Coun., 1983. Author: History of Borough Affairs, 1976; editor (pamphlet) A Walking Tour of Hanover, 1978; editor, producer (video) Hanover 1938-1942, 1982. Bd. dirs. Hanover Day Nursery, 1974—; v.p. Historic York, 1984; treas. York 2000 Commn., 1988-91. Mem. Soc. of Friends. Home: 216 Broadway Hanover PA 17331 Office: Borough of Hanover 44 Frederick St Hanover PA 17331

REBICEK, VINCENT STASS, interior designer, speciality store executive; b. Scranton, Pa., Sept. 5, 1922; s. Anthony and Catherine (Mikolayczak) R. Student at N.Y. Sch. Design, N.Y.C., 1940. Head interior decoration dept. Cleland-Simpson, Scranton, Pa., 1944-48; owner Vincent S. Rebicek-Distinctive Interiors, Scranton, 1948—; owner Things (specialty store), Scranton, 1967—. Contbr. articles to profl. jours. Mem. St. Stanislaus Polish Nat. Cath. Ch. Mem. Am. Soc. Interior Designers., Scranton C. of C. Republican. Home: 831 Prescott Ave Scranton PA 18510-2298

RECANATI, ELIAS ISAAC, shipping company executive; b. Thessaloniki, Greece, Mar. 30, 1932; came to U.S., 1951; s. Maurice and Lina (Capuano) R.; m. Lily Mordoh, Sept. 18, 1968; 1 child, Maurice. BS, NYU, 1956, MBA, 1958. V.p. Maritime Overseas Corp., N.Y.C., 1956—. Pres. The Am. Friends of the Jewish Mus. of Greece, N.Y.C., 1988—. Mem. N.Y. Athletic Club. Office: 43 W 42d St 12th Fl New York NY 10036

RECHT, MILTON RICHARD, investment banker, consultant, lawyer; b. Bklyn., July 4, 1948; s. Ben and Lillian (Rosenblum) R.; m. Susan Diane Goodman, Mar. 11, 1973; children: Daniel, Allison. BA, Columbia U., N.Y.C., 1971; MBA, Columbia U., 1981; JD, Union U., 1975. Mgr., cons. Deloitte Haskins & Sells, N.Y.C., 1984-85; v.p. Shearson Lehman Bros., N.Y.C., 1985-86, Chase Manhattan Bank, N.Y.C., 1981-84, 86-87; prin. Recht & Co., Mt. Kisco, N.Y., 1987—; adj. prof. fin. grad. sch. bus. Columbia U. Home: RR 5 Mount Kisco NY 10549-9805 Office: Recht & Co 25 Dogwood Rd Mount Kisco NY 10549

RECHTER, LEO E., bank executive; b. Vienna, Austria, Sept. 6, 1927; arrived in U.S., 1957; s. Joseph David and Yetta (Kipel) R.; m. Fortunee Toni Bouba, Oct. 9, 1958; 1 child, Debbie Elizabeth Rechter. BA summa cum laude, Queens Coll., 1973; MBA in Internat. Bus. summa cum laude, Pace U., 1977. V.p. Mfg. Hanover Trust/Chem. Bank, N.Y.C., 1976—. Recipient Letter of Commendation, White House, Washington, 1978. Mem. Delta Mu Delta. Office: 270 Park Ave 6th Fl New York NY 10017

RECK, GREGORY MILTON, aerospace engineer; b. Greenville, Ohio, Dec. 5, 1946; s. Ronald and Marie (Supak) R.; m. Barbara K. Petroff, Apr. 17, 1971; 1 child, Chelsea Marie. BS in Aerospace Engring., U. Cin., 1969; postgrad., Harvard U., 1985. Various positions NASA, 1964-90; dir. for space tech. NASA, Washington, 1990—. Recipient Disting. Alumni award U. Cin., 1992, Meritorious Presdl. Rank award U.S. Office Pers. Mgmt., 1992. Mem. AIAA, Phi Eta Sigma. Republican. Home: 2003 Gervais Dr Falls Church VA 22043 Office: NASA Independence Ave & 7th St SW Washington DC 20546

RECK, NORMA JEAN, organization official; b. Washington, Pa., Nov. 21, 1933; d. Atilio Reck and Edith Lillian (Houskie) Gatscher. BS cum laude, Pa. State U., 1955, MEd Counseling-Guidance, 1958; MS in Bus., Cen. Mich. U., 1980. Cert. tchr., counselor, N.J., Mich., Va. Tchr. pub. schs., Haddon Heights, N.J., 1956-57; counselor, mgr. tech. personnel Aames Bur. Employment, Detroit, 1957-58; pers. specialist Burroughs Corp., Detroit, 1958-59; tchr. fgn. langs. Allen Park (Mich.) Pub. Schs., 1959-66, Fairfax County Pub. Schs., Fairfax, Va., 1966-89; tech. editor Water Pollution Control Fedn., Alexandria, Va., 1987—; former cons. computer and movie cos. Bd. dirs. Greenbelt Coop., Savage, Md., 1973; umpire U.S. Mid. Atlantic Tennis Assn., 1970-73; treas. Linden Square Homes Assn.; active Washington Invitational Tennis. Senatorial scholar. Mem. ASTD (corp. com. McLean, Va. chpt. 1987—), Wash. Ind. Writers, Am. Soc. Assn. Execs., Ski Club Washington (bd. dirs. 1973-75, columnist 1976-79), Capitol Hill Tennis Club. Avocations: travel, tennis, reading, golf, bridge. Home: 9609 Lindenbrook St Fairfax VA 22031-1120 Office: Water Environment Fedn 601 Wythe St Alexandria VA 22314-1937

RECKFORD, THOMAS JOSEPH, political risk analyst, consultant; b. N.Y.C., Mar. 3, 1943; s. Joseph Samuel Reckford and Janet (Sidenberg) Limburg; m. Ruth Bockhorn, Mar. 17, 1974 (div. Jan. 1978); m. Jane Edgerton, Nov. 28, 1981. BA magna cum laude, Harvard U., 1964. Analyst Cen. Intelligence Agy., Langley, Va., 1968-73; sr. internat. analyst Eaton Corp., Washington, 1976-80; v.p. Intermatrix, Inc., Westport, Conn., 1980-81; sr. advisor Govt. Rsch. Corp., Washington, 1985-86; sr. fellow Ctr. for Strategic and Internat. Studies, Washington, 1986-90, sr. assoc., 1990—; sr. cons. The Parvus Co., Silver Spring, Md., 1991—; pvt. practice cons. Washington, 1980—; adj. prof. Georgetown Univ., Washington, 1981-82; bd. dirs. World Affairs Coun. of Washington, D.C., 1989—; adv. coun. Washington (D.C.) Ctr. of Asia Soc., 1979—. Co-author: Building Asean, 1987. Trustee The Arena Stage, Washington, 1980-82. Sgt. U.S. Army, 1964-67. Mem. Coun. for Internat. Bus. Risk Mgmt. (dir. 1980-84), Univ. Club Washington, Kenwood Country Club, Harvard Club N.Y., Harvard Club Washington. Home: 4504 Yuma St NW Washington DC 20016-2044

RECKLIES, ADELE ROGERS, small business owner; b. Cleve., Oct. 29, 1949; d. William Michael and JoAnn Carol (Thomas) Rogers; m. Donald Fred Recklies, Sept. 5, 1970. BA, Kent (Ohio) State U., 1971, MA, 1974; PhD, Ohio State U., 1983. Draper's asst. Barbara Matera, Ltd., N.Y.C., 1982-87; owner Adele Recklies Co., Bklyn., 1987—; guest lectr. various knitting guilds and yarn shops, 1990—. Mem. Assn. of Theatrical Artists and Craftspeople, Am. Craft Coun., Costume Soc. of Am. Home and Office: 420 4th Ave # 1 Brooklyn NY 11215-3216

RECTOR, BRUCE JOHNSON, financial analyst; b. Baton Rouge, Oct. 13, 1953; s. James Wallace and Vinetta Alice (Johnson) R.; m. Terry Ellen Aiple, Jan. 28, 1978; children: Mariel, Eleanor. BSEE, U. Va., 1985; MBA, U. Pa., 1989. Engr. Unisys Corp., Paoli, Pa., 1985-87; sr. fin. anaylst Unisys Corp., Blue Bell, Pa., 1989—; external cons. PNC Fin. Corp., Phila., 1988. Vol. Phila. Com. for Homeless, 1985—. Mem. IEEE, U. Va. Club (treas. 1991-92). Home: 486 Cassatt Ct West Chester PA 19380-1733 Office: M/S CA SE10 PO Box 500 Blue Bell PA 19424

REDD, JOHN GORDON, physical education educator; b. Columbus, Ohio, May 8, 1923; s. William Floyd and Alma Louise (Biederman) R.; children: John Gordon, Jane Ellen. BS, Ohio State U., 1946; MA, U. Mich., 1951, PhD, 1957. Tchr.-coach Gahanna (Ohio) High Sch., 1947-48; tchr.-coach Lincoln High Sch., Ypsilanti, Mich., 1949-57; prof. Montclair (N.J.) State Coll., 1957—. Author: Let's Choose Partners, 1969, Programmed Learning, 1969. Chair Verona (N.J.) Recreation Com., 1959—. Mem. Am. Alliance for Health, N.J. Assn. for Health, Phys. Edn. and Recreation (past pres.'s award 1967), N.J. Edn. Assn. Home: 23 Wayland Dr Verona NJ 07044-2330 Office: Montclair State Coll Health Professions Dept Normal Ave Montclair NJ 07043-1607

REDDEN, CATHERINE MCEACHERN, librarian; b. Exeter, N.H., Apr. 12, 1949; d. John Hugh Jr. and Stella Louise (Shaw) McEachern; m. Donald McIntyre Redden, July 1, 1972. BS, Plymouth State Coll., 1971; MLS, U. R.I., 1984. English instr. Pinkerton Acad., Derry, N.H., 1971-86; libr. dir. Leach Libr., Londonderry, N.H., 1986—; libr. tech. instr. Univ. System of N.H., Durham, 1991. Judge N.H. State Spelling Bee, Manchester, 1976-90; Sun. Sch. tchr. Presbyn. Ch., Londonderry, 1979-85; rep. Plymouth State Coll. Alumni Admissions Info. Com., 1983-85. Grantee Baker and Taylor 1983. Mem. ALA, Nat. Tchrs. English, New Eng. Libr. Assn., N.H. Libr. Assn. (pres. 1991-92, v.p. 1990-91, scholarship chair 1988-90), N.H. Ednl. Media Assn., Merri-Hill-Rock Libr. Coop. (chair 1988-90), Toastmasters Internat. Home: 180 Porpoise Way Portsmouth NH 03801 Office: Londonderry Leach Libr 276 Mammoth Rd Londonderry NH 03053

REDDING, JAMES FRANCIS, psychologist; b. Jersey City, Apr. 19, 1931; s. James F. and Mary E. (McCoy) R.; m. Patricia Ann McCann, Sept. 3, 1956; children: James F. Jr., Elizabeth, Patrick, Robert, Margaret. BA, St. John's Coll., N.Y.C., 1956; MS in Edn., St. John's U., N.Y.C., 1958, PhD, 1970. Cert. psychologist, sch. psychologist, permanent secondary English tchr., N.Y.; cert. permanent secondary English tchr., N.Y.C. Tchr. English, Jr. High Sch. 118, Bronx, N.Y., 1956-59, North Babylon (L.I., N.Y.) High Sch., 1960-61; sch. psychologist Cogiague (N.Y.) Pub. Schs., 1961—; rsch. dir. Huntington (N.Y.) Youth Bd., 1969-79; pvt. practice psychotherapy, Huntington, 1980-81, 84-86; clin. dir. Stress Mgmt. Ctr., Huntington, 1981-84; cons. to staff Indsl. Home for Blind, Hempstead, N.Y., 1982-84; lectr. C.W. Post Coll., L.I. U., 1954-57, Suffolk Community Coll., 1967-69, St. John's U., 1975. With U.S. Army, 1951-53. N.Y. State War Svc. scholar, 1956. Mem. APA, N.Y. State Tchrs. Assn., Copiague Tchrs. Assn. (pres. 1965-66), Phi Delta Kappa. Republican. Roman Catholic. Homee: 1 Jeffery Rd Oakdale NY 11769 Office: Copiague Pub Schs Great Neck Rd Copiague NY 11726-5208

REDDY, KALLURU JAYARAMI, molecular biologist, educator; b. Andhra Pradesh, India, Apr. 15, 1953; came to U.S., 1980; s. Subba and Venkatamma R.; m. Satya Cheekireddy, May 12, 1984; children: Gowtham, Divya. BSc, Sri Venkateswara U., 1972; MSc, S. V. U., 1974; PhD, U. Miami, 1984. Jr. rsch. fellow Indian Inst. Tech., Kharagpur, India, 1974-76; jr. plant physiologist Indian Agrl. Rsch. Inst., New Dehli, 1976-80; grad. rsch. asst. Univ. Miami, Fla., 1980-84; postdoctoral fellow Univ. Mo., Columbia, 1985-89; rsch. scientist Purdue Univ., West Lafayette, Ind., 1989-90; asst. prof. SUNY, Binghamton, N.Y., 1990—. Mem. Am. Soc. for Microbiology. Office: SUNY-Binghamton Dept Biol Scis Binghamton NY 13902

REDDY, SURESH BADDAM, engineering researcher; b. Hyderabad, India, Aug. 11, 1965; came to U.S., 1986; s. Shankar and Indira Devi (Vangeti) R. B. Tech. with honors, Indian Inst. Tech., Kharagpur, India, 1986; MS, Ohio State U., 1988; postgrad., MIT, 1989—. Rsch. assoc. Ohio State U., Columbus, 1987-88, teaching assoc., 1988-89; teaching asst. MIT, Cambridge, 1989, rsch. asst., 1989—. Contbr. articles to profl. jours. Mem. Amnesty Internat. USA, 1991—. Univ. fellow Ohio State Univ., 1986-87. Mem. Sigma Xi (assoc.). Office: MIT Room 35-303 77 Massachusetts Ave Cambridge MA 02139

REDDY, THOMAS BRADLEY, battery company executive; b. Amesbury, Mass., Sept. 11, 1933; s. Anthony William and Loretta Clare (Hanley) R.; m. Josina Maria van der Maas, Dec. 29, 1956 (div. Apr. 1977); children: David P., Peter J., Josina C.; m. Mary Ellen Scarborough, July 9, 1988. BS, Yale U., 1955; PhD, U. Minn., 1960. Rsch. assoc. U. Ill., Urbana, 1959-61; mem. tech. staff Bell Telephone Labs., Murray Hill, N.J., 1961-65; sr. rsch. chemist cen. rsch. div. Am. Cyanamid Co., Stamford, Conn., 1965-68, group leader, 1968-72, prin. rsch. chemist, 1972-79; dir. tech. Power Conversion, Inc., Hawker Siddeley Group, Elmwood Park, N.J., 1980-88; dir. mil. mktg. Power Conversion, Inc., Hawker Siddeley Group, Saddle Brook, N.J., 1988-89, v.p., 1989—; mem. spl. com. for lithium batteries Radio Tech. Commn. for Aeronautics, Washington, 1991—. Contbr. articles to sci. jours., chpts. to books; patentee in field. Bd. dirs. Pound Ridge (N.Y.) Planning Bd., 1982-85; mem. Pound Ridge Water Control Commn., 1977-79, 80-82, chmn., 1981-82, 85-88; mem. Yale Alumni Schs. Com., Westchester County, N.Y., 1977-88. Rice fellow GE Ednl. and Charitable Found., 1958-59. Mem. Am. Chem. Soc., Electrochem. Soc. (bd. dirs. 1969-71, mem. fin. com. 1971-73, mem. ways and means com. 1973-75, mem. tech. com. 1975-77), Bronxville Field Club. Home: 30 Elm Rock Rd Bronxville NY 10708-4203 Office: Power Conversion Inc 495 Boulevard Elmwood Park NJ 07407

REDISH, EDWARD FREDERICK, physicist, educator; b. N.Y.C., Apr. 1, 1942; s. Jules and Sylvia (Coslow) R.; m. Janice Copen, June 18, 1967; children: A. David, Deborah. AB, Princeton U., 1963; PhD, MIT, 1968. CTP fellow U. Md., College Park, 1968-70, asst. prof., 1970-74, assoc. prof., 1974-79, prof., 1979—, chair dept. phys. astronomy, 1982-85; vis. prof. Ind. U., Bloomington, 1985-86; vis. fgn. collaborator CEN, Saclay, France, 1973-74; co-dir. U. Md. Project in Physics and Ednl. Tech., 1983—, Comprehensive Unified Physics Learning Environment, 1989—; mem. Nuclear Sci. Adv. Com., Dept. of Energy/NSF, 1987-90; mem. program adv. com. Ind. U. Cyclotron Facility, 1985-89, chmn., 1986-89. Author: (software) Orbits, 1989; editor: Procs. Conf. on Computers in Physics Instrn., 1990; contbr. over 50 articles to profl. jours. Named Sr. Resident Rsch. Assoc., NAS-NRC, 1977-78; recipient Inst. medal Cen. Rsch. Inst. for Physics, 1979, Leo Schubert award Wash. Acad. Sci., 1988, Educator award Md. Assn. Higher Edn., 1989, Glover award Dickinson U., 1991. Fellow Am. Phys. Soc., AAAS, Wash. Acad. Sci.; mem. Am. Assn. Physics Tchrs. Office: U Md Dept Physics College Park MD 20742-4111

REDKEY, EDWIN STORER, history educator; b. Washington, Sept. 19, 1931; s. William Henry and Lucille (Storer) R.; m. Nancy Lee Jenks, June 22, 1963; children: David Henry, Elizabeth. BA, U. Wash., 1954; BD, Princeton Theol. Sem., 1960; MA, Yale U., 1964, PhD, 1967. Asst. and acting chaplain Middlebury (Vt.) Coll., 1960-62; dean Trumbull Coll. Yale U., New Haven, 1965-68, asst. prof. history, 1967-68; assoc. prof. history U. Tenn., Knoxville, 1968-71; assoc. prof. history SUNY, Purchase, 1971—, dean student affairs, 1971-78; lectr., USIA, Asia, Africa, 1978. Author: Black Exodus, 1969; editor: Respect Black, 1971. Trustee, Whitby Sch.-Am. Montessori Ctr., Greenwich, Conn., 1974-86, pres., 1983-86; bd. dirs. Old Greenwich Riverside Community Ctr., 1974-77. Lt. (j.g.) USN, 1954-57. Rsch. fellow Am. Coun. Learned Socs., 1977-78. Mem. Orgn. Am. Historians, Am. Mil. Inst., Am. Acad. Religion. Democrat. Presbyterian. Office: SUNY Humanities Div Purchase NY 10577

REDLER, SHERRY PRESS, audiologist; b. N.Y.C.; d. Martin M. and Elsie (Opin) Press; BA, Adelphi U., 1954; M.S., So. Conn. State Coll., 1971, postgrad., 1976-79; children—Michael, Steven, Lynda. Speech pathologist Roslyn (N.Y.) Public Schs., 1954-56; tchr. drama Rollins Coll., Winter Park, Fla., 1961-63; personnel counselor Internat. Bus. Assn., Pitts., 1965; speech pathologist Fairfield (Conn.) Public Schs., 1968-75, ednl. audiologist, 1976—; clin. audiologist Rehab. Center, Bridgeport, Conn., 1975-76; sign lang. instr. Bridgeport Rehab. Center, 1976-78, Staples High Sch., Westport, Conn.; instr. So. Conn. State Coll., New Haven, 1976—; lectr., cons. in field; ind. evaluator of programs for hearing impaired; author, project dir. Title IV Fed. Grant, Conn., 1976-80; mem. Conn. State Task Force to assess services provided to mentally retarded, 1981—; author, project dir. sch. audiology program, Conn., 1981. Trustee Congregation B'Nai Israel, 1985-90, chmn. older adult com.; mem. com. to revise hearing screening guidelines, Conn., 1987, State Conn. com. to establish guidelines for services to hearing impaired children, 1988—; mem. commn. on community rels., urban issues com., 1989—; mem. commn. on the elderly. Mem. Am. Acad. Audiology, Conn. Speech and Hearing Assn. (co-chmn. com. on edn. hearing impaired

1976—), NEA, Conn. Edn. Assn., Fairfield Edn. Assn., Am. Speech and Hearing Assn., Am. Ednl. Audiology Assn. (1st v.p. 1986—, pres. 1987-88), Conn. Audiology Assn. (v.p. 1991). Home: 28 Lockwood Cir Fairfield CT 06430-2645 Office: 60 Thompson St Fairfield CT 06430

REDLICH, DONALD HAROLD, choreographer, educator; b. Winona, Minn., Aug. 17, 1929; s. Walter Carl and Kathryn (O'Donnell) R.; B.S., Winona State U., 1950; postgrad. U. Wis., Madison, 1950-53. Tchr. Sarah Lawrence Coll., 1964-81; dir. Don Redlich Dance Co., N.Y.C., 1966—; mem. faculty NYU, 1981—, Rutgers U., 1983—; choreographer: Passin' Through, 1959, Earthling, 1963, Stigmata, 1971, Patina, 1974, Lake of Fire, 1975, Traces, 1975, Disposal, 1981; dir. Woyzeck, Nat. Theatre of Deaf, 1970, Volpone, 1978; Stumble Up to Stand, 1982, Vintage, 1983, Signals/ Alarms, 1984, Pierrot Lunaire, 1986, Set of Five Dances, 1987, L'Histoire du Soldat, 1988, ELECTRIKALEIDOSCOPE, 1990, FACADE, 1991. Panelist Nat. Endowment Arts, 1973-77, grantee, 1968, 75, 81-88; N.Y. State Council on Arts grantee, 1970-84. Mem. AAUP, Actors Equity, Am. Guild Mus. Artists.

REDLICH, MARC, lawyer; b. N.Y.C., Nov. 25, 1946; s. Louis and Mollie R.; m. Janis Redlich, Jan. 16, 1982; children: Alison, Suzanne. BA, Queens Coll., 1967; JD, Harvard U., 1971. Bar: Mass. 1971, U.S. Dist. Ct. 1971, U.S. Ct. Appeals (1st cir.) 1974, U.S. Ct. Appeals (5th cir.) 1984. Assoc. Guterman, Horvitz, Rubin & Rudman, Boston, 1971-75; mem., sr. dir. Widett, Slater & Goldman, Boston, 1975-84; prin. Law Offices of Marc Redlich, Cambridge, Mass., 1984—. Mem. ABA, Mass. Bar Assn. (governing coun. civil litigation sect.), Boston Bar Assn., Assn. Trial Lawyers Am., Nat. Assn. Coll. and Univ. Attys., Harvard Sq. Bus. Assn. (bd. dirs. 1989-92), Cambridge C. of C., Friends of Switzerland Inc. (bd. dirs. 1991—, assoc. pres. 1992—), German Am. Bus. Club of Boston, Phi Beta Kappa. Office: 1000 Massachusetts Ave Cambridge MA 02138-5304

REDLO, ROCHELLE MARCIA, educator; b. Buffalo, Oct. 3, 1949; d. Harry and Belle (Kushner) R. BS, SUNY, Buffalo, 1970, MS in Edn., 1971, postgrad., 1982-84. Educator Buffalo Sch. System, 1971-72, Depew (N.Y.) Pub. Schs., 1973—; computer sales Tek Computer Ctr., Snyder, N.Y., 1984-85; asst. dir. Maryvale Community Edn., Cheektowaga, N.Y., 1987-89. Sunday sch. tchr. Williamsville, N.Y., 1981-84; treas. sch. social orgn. Depew (N.Y.) Elem., 1984-88; robot promoter, Williamsville, 1983; chairperson, United Way, Depew Pub. Schs., 1984. Mem. Nat. Community Edn. Assn., Maryvale Community Edn. Adv. Coun., N.Y. State United Tchrs., Depew Tchrs. Orgn., Assn. for Supervision and Curriculum Devel. Home: 151 Charlesgate Cir East Amherst NY 14051-1275

REDMAN, JOHN ROBERT, hematologist-oncologist; b. Gardiner, Maine, Dec. 19, 1950; s. Robert Gray and Priscilla H. (Shields) R.; m. Joan Marie Doyle, Aug. 10, 1985; children: Allison Marie, Elizabeth Ann. AB, Bowdoin Coll., 1973; MD, U. Vt., 1977. Diplomate Am. Bd. Internal Medicine, Am. Bd. Hematology, Am. Bd. Med. Oncology. Med. resident Cornell Cooperating Hosps., N.Y.C., 1977-80; hematology-oncology fellow Meml. Sloan-Kettering Cancer Ctr., N.Y.C., 1980-85; asst. prof. M.D. Anderson Cancer Ctr., U. Tex., Houston, 1985-90; dir. med. affairs Theradex Systems Inc., Princeton, N.J., 1990-91; dir. clin. R & D Wyeth-Ayerst, Phila., 1991—; legis. task force on cancer in Tex., 1985-86. Co-editor: Hodgkin's Disease: The Consequences of Survival, 1990; contbr. 100 articles to profl. jours. Fellow ACP; mem. Am. Soc. Clin. Oncology, Am. Soc. Hematology, Am. Assn. Cancer Rsch. Office: Wyeth-Ayerst PO Box 8299 Philadelphia PA 19101-8299

REDMAN, ROBERT SHELTON, dentist, pathologist; b. Fargo, N.D., Aug. 1, 1935; s. Kenneth and Elizabeth Francis (McMillan) R.; m. Barbara Darlien Klug, Sept. 14, 1958; 1 child, Melissa Darlien. Student, S.D. State U., 1953-55; BS, DDS, U. Minn., 1959, MSD, 1963; PhD, U. Wash., 1969. Cert. Am. Bd. Oral Pathology. Clin. asst. prof. sch. dentistry U. Minn., Mpls., 1963-64, assoc. prof., 1969-75; assoc. prof. sch. dentistry U. Colo., Denver, 1975-78; staff dentist, chief oral pathology rsch. lab. Dept. Vets. Affairs Med. Ctr., Washington, 1978—; Denver, 1975-78; clin. assoc. prof. Balt. Coll. Dental Surgery U. Md., 1989—; cons. Children's Orthopedic Hosp., Seattle, 1966-69; program specialist in oral biology Dept. Vets. Affairs, Washington, 1982-86. Contbr. 12 chpts. to books and over 60 articles to profl. jours. Capt. U.S. Army, 1959-61. Fellow Am. Acad. Oral Pathology; mem. ADA, Am. Inst. Nutrition, Internat. Assn. Dental Rsch. (program chmn. salivary rsch. group 1982-86), Tissue Culture Assn., Omicron Kappa Upsilon. Presbyterian. Office: Dept Vets Affairs Med Ctr Oral Pathology Rsch Lab 50 Irving St NW Washington DC 20422-0002

REDMOND, DOUGLAS MICHAEL, cosmetics executive; b. Central Islip, N.Y., May 13, 1954; s. Ronald George and Josephine Bernadette (Donelon) R.; m. Millie Vidal, Oct. 13, 1985; children: Douglas Michael Jr., Brandon Richard, Chelsea Lynn. BA in Bus., SUNY, Oneonta, 1976; MS, SUNY, Stony Brook, 1984. Ops. mgr. Whitman Labs Ltd., Petersfield, Eng., 1981-82; line supr. Estee Lauder Inc., Melville, N.Y., 1976-78; materials supr. Estee Lauder Inc., Melville, 1978-79, prodn. control mgr., 1979-81, materials mgr., 1980-81; cons. Estee Lauder Internat., N.Y.C., 1982-83; dir. materials Estee Lauder Internat., Melville, 1983-86, dir. mfg. svcs., 1986-88, exec. dir., 1988—; prin. Redmond Enterprises Inc., East Islip, N.Y., 1987—, Global Decisions, Inc., 1991—. Active in Bush campaign Rep. Com., Babylon, N.Y., 1988. Mem. Am. Prodn. and Inventory Control Soc. Roman Catholic. Office: Estee Lauder Internat 350 S Service Rd Melville NY 11747-3233

REDSTONE, SUMNER MURRAY, entertainment corporation executive, lawyer; b. Boston, May 27, 1923; s. Michael and Belle (Ostrovsky) R.; m. Phyllis Gloria Raphael, July 6, 1947; children: Brent Dale, Shari Ellin. B.A., Harvard U., 1944, LL.B., 1947. Bar: Mass. 1947, U.S. Ct. Appeals (1st cir.) 1948, U.S. Ct. Appeals (8th cir.) 1950, U.S. Ct. Appeals (9th cir.) 1948, D.C. 1951, U.S. Supreme Ct. 1952. Law sec. U.S. Ct. Appeals for 9th Circuit, San Francisco, 1947-48; instr. law and labor mgmt. U. San Francisco, 1947; spl. asst. to U.S. Atty. Gen., Washington, 1948-51; partner firm Ford, Bergson, Adams, Borkland & Redstone, Washington, 1951-54; pres., chief exec. officer Nat. Amusements Inc., Dedham, Mass., 1967—, chmn. bd., 1986—; chmn. bd. Viacom Internat. Inc., Viacom Inc., N.Y.C., 1987—; prof. Boston U. Law Sch., 1982, 85-86. Chmn. met. div. NE Combined Jewish Philanthropies, Boston, 1963; mem. corp. New Eng. Med. Ctr., 1967—, Mass. Gen. Hosp.; trustee Children's Cancer Rsch. Found.; chmn. Am. Cancer Crusade, State of Mass., 1984-86; Art Lending Libr.; sponsor Boston Mus. Sci.; chmn. Jimmy Fund Found., 1960; v.p., mem. exec. com. Will Rogers Meml. Fund; bd. dirs. Boston Arts Festival; bd. overseers Dana Farber Cancer Ctr., Boston Mus. Fine Arts; mem. presdl. adv. com. on arts John F. Kennedy Center for Performing Arts; bd. dirs. John F. Kennedy Libr. Found. Served to 1st lt. AUS, 1943-45. Decorated Army Commendation medal; recipient William J. German Human Rels. award Am. Jewish Com. Entertainmetn and Communication Div., 1977, Silver Shingle award Boston U. Law Sch., 1985, Variety New England Humanitarian award, 1989; named Communicator of Yr., B'nai Brith Communications and Cinema Lodge, 1980, Man of Yr., Entertainment Industries Div. of UJA Fedn., 1988, Pioneer of Yr., Motion Picture Pioneers, 1991. Mem. ABA, Nat. Assn. Theatre Owners (chmn. bd. dirs. 1965-66), Theatre Owners Am. (asst. pres. 1960-63, pres. 1964-65), Motion Picture Pioneers (bd. dirs.), Boston Bar Assn., Mass. Bar Assn., Harvard Law Sch. Assn., Am. Judicature Soc., Masons, Univ. Club, Harvard Club. Home: 98 Baldpate Hill Rd Newton MA 02159-2825 Office: Nat Amusements Inc 200 Elm St Dedham MA 02026-4536

REECE, RICHARD TERRANCE, religious organization administrator; b. Phila., Sept. 5, 1935; s. George and Jennie (Devlin) R. BS in Chemistry, Niagara U., 1961; MS in Chemistry, Cath. U., 1965; MA in Theology, DeSales Sch., 1965. Tchr. chemistry Salesianum High Sch., Wilmington, 1956-58; camp medic Camp DeSales, Bklyn., 1958-61; tchr. chemistry N.E. Cath. High Sch., Phila., 1965-66, vice prin., 1966-77; vice prin. Bishop Ireton, Alexandria, Va., 1977-83; chair Oblates of St. Francis DeSales Inc., Wilmington, Del., 1983—. Chair Data Processing Com., Phila., 1966-77; bd. dirs. Allentown Coll., Center Valley, Pa., 1983—; chmn. bd. DeSales Sch. of Theology, Washington, 1983—, Salesianum High Sch., Wilmington, 1983—. Mem. Assn. Supervison and Curriculum Devel., Coun. Maj. Supt. of Men (bd. dirs.). Roman Catholic. Home: 2200 Kentnene Pkwy Wilmington DE 19806 Office: Oblates St Francis De Sales PO Box 1452 Wilmington DE 19899-1452

REED, BERENICE ANNE, art historian, artist, government official; b. Memphis, Jan. 1, 1934; d. Glenn Andrew and Berenice Marie (Kallaher) R. BFA, St. Mary-of-the-Woods Coll., Ind., 1955; MFA in Painting and Art History, Istituto Pio XII, Villa Schifanoia, Florence, Italy, 1964. Cert. art tchr., Tenn. Comml. artist Memphis Pub. Co., 1955-56; arts adminstr., educator pub. and pvt. instns., Washington, Memphis, 1957-70; arts adminstr. Nat. Park Svc., 1970-73; mem. staff U.S. Dept. of Energy, Washington, 1973-81, U.S. Dept. Commerce, Washington, 1983-84, Exec. Office of the Pres., Office of Mgmt. and Budget, Washington, 1985; with fin. mgmt. svc. U.S. Treasury Dept., Washington, 1985—; cons. on art and architecture in recreation AIA, 1972-73; artist-in-residence St. Mary-of-the-Woods Coll., Ind., 1965; guest lectr. instr. Nat. Sch. Fine Arts, Tegucigalpa, Honduras, 1968; mem. exec. com. Parks, Arts and Leisure Project, Washington, 1972-73; researcher art projects, Washington, 1981-83. Bd. dirs. Am. Irish Bicentennial Com., 1974-76; advisor Royal Oak Found. Recipient various awards for painting. Mem. Soc. Woman Geographers, Nat. Soc. Arts and Letters, Ctr. for Advanced Study in Visual Arts, Art Barn Assn. (bd. dirs. 1973-83). Roman Catholic. Home: PO Box 34253 Bethesda MD 20827-0253 Office: Dept Treasury Fin Mgmt Svc 401 14th St SW Washington DC 20227-0001

REED, EMILY ANN FABRYCKI, criminal justice analyst; b. South Bend, Ind., Sept. 5, 1941; d. Richard Edward and Leona Marie (Kochanowski) Fabrycki; m. Thomas James Reed, Dec. 29, 1962; children: Martin, Valerie. BA, Marquette U., 1963; MPA, U. Hartford, 1978; PhD, U. Mass., 1982. Asst. planner Town of Enfield, Conn., 1979; instr. Western New Eng. Coll., Springfield, Mass., 1979; lectr. St. Joseph Coll., West Hartford, Conn., 1978-81; asst. prof. Ursinus Coll., Collegeville, Pa., 1982-83; mgmt. analyst State of Del., Div. of Corps., Dover, Del., 1983-84; coll. tchr. La Salle U., Brandywine Coll., Phila., 1989; mgmt. analyst State of Del., Criminal Justice Coun., Wilmington, 1985—. Contbr. articles to profl. jours. Mem. Am. Polit. Sci. Assn., Am. Soc. for Pub. Adminstrn., Del. Assn. for Pub. Adminstrn., Justice Rsch. and Statis. Assn. Office: State of Del Criminal Justice Coun 820 N French St 4th Fl Wilmington DE 19801

REED, GAIL SIMON, psychoanalyst; b. N.Y.C., Apr. 21, 1943; d. Jeff B. and Helen L. Simon; m. Thomas Alexander Reed, Oct. 1, 1965; children: William Trowbridge, Danielle Alexandra. AB, Bryn Mawr Coll., 1964; MA, Yale U., 1970, PhD, 1976; Diploma in psychoanalysis, Nat. Psychol. Assn. for Psychoanalysis, 1985. Cert. nat. psychoanalyst. Adj. lectr. dept. English CUNY, 1970-77, U. Conn., Stamford, 1976-78; pvt. practice psychoanalysis and psychotherapy N.Y.C., 1978—; mem. faculty, tng. analyst Nat. Psychol. Assn. for Psychoanalysts, 1985—; faculty extension divsn. N.Y. Psychoanalytic Inst., N.Y.C., 1989—; founder, pres. Group for the Study of Psychoanalytic Process, Inc., Haddonfield, N.J., 1988—; mem. faculty Inst. for Psychoanalytic Tng. and Rsch. Contbr. articles to profl. jours. Woodrow Wilson Found. fellow, 1964; recipient Recent Grad. Jour. Prize, Jour. Am. Psychoanalytic Assn., 1985. Mem. APA, Internat. Psychoanalytical Assn., N.Y. Freudian Soc., Inst. Psychoanalytic Tng. and Rsch., Internat. Assn. for History Psychoanalysis. Office: 1199 Park Ave New York NY 10128-1711

REED, GEORGE ELLIOTT, surgery educator; b. N.Y.C., Aug. 4, 1923; s. Morris and Mary (Swetsby) R.; m. Thelma Bilik (dec. 1968); children: Elizabeth E., George E. Jr. DVM, Cornell U., 1944; MD, NYU, 1951. Diplomate Am. Bd. Surgery, Am. Bd. Thoracic Surgery. Successively intern, resident, chief resident NYU Bellevue Med. Ctr., N.Y.C., 1951-56, Berg fellow, 1956-58; from asst. prof. to assoc. prof. surgery NYU, N.Y.C., 1959-69, prof., 1969-77; prof. N.Y. Med. Coll., Valhalla, 1977—; cons. surgery N.Y. State Dept. Health, Albany, 1963-90, VA, N.Y.C., 1969-77, Lennox Hill Hosp., N.Y.C., 1971-91, Kingston (N.Y.) Hosp., 1971-90; presenter in field. Contbr. articles to profl. jours., chpts. to books. Capt. U.S. Army, 1944-47. Fellow ACS, Am. Coll. Cardiology; mem. Am. Assn. Thoracic Surgery, Soc. Thoracic Surgeons, Alpha Omega Alpha (faculty). Office: Westchester County Med Ctr Macy 203 Valhalla NY 10595

REED, JAMES WILLIAM, JR., law firm administrator, forensic photographer; b. Rome, N.Y., Feb. 7, 1947; s. James William Sr. and Teresa (Soriano) R.; m. Michele Ann Turner, Oct. 11, 1980; children: Danielle, Brittany, Stephanie. BA, CCNY, 1969; postgrad., N.Y. Inst. Fin., 1969-71, N.Y. Law Sch., 1974-75. With Smith, Barney & Co., Inc., N.Y.C., 1969-72; adminstrv. asst. to sr. litigating ptnr., dept. head Simpson Thacher & Bartlett, N.Y.C., 1972—; pres. J&R Visual Prodns., Inc., Freeport, N.Y., 1974—. Meml. chmn. Baldwin-Freeport unit Am. Cancer Soc., 1985-87, pres., 1983-88, chmn. pub. rels., 1983-88; bd. dirs. Arts Coun. at Freeport, 1984, 85; Greater N.Y. area logistics coord. Cystic Fibrosis Found., 1989; mem. Salvation Army Corps, 1985—; planning bd. commr. Village of Freeport, 1984-87. Mem. Kiwanis Internat. (pres. 1984-86, lt. gov. div. 1988-89, rep. to UN, internat. com. on maj. emphasis programs), Holy Name Soc., K.C. (trustee 1989—, grand knight 1986-89), Rep. Club of Freeport, Toastmasters Internat. (pres. 1984-87). Republican. Roman Catholic. Home: 766 Guy Lombardo Ave Freeport NY 11520-6213 Office: Simpson Thacher & Bartlett 425 Lexington Ave New York NY 10017-3903

REED, JEFFREY GARTH, software manager, organizational psychologist; b. Black Creek, Wis., Mar. 28, 1948; s. George Edward and Norma Groeling (Renneisen) R.; m. Sylvia F. Kollasch, Apr. 18, 1981; 1 child, Daniel Benjamin. BA in Polit. Sci., Muskingum Coll., 1970; MLS, U. Md., 1971; MA in Psychology, Towson State U., 1976; PhD in Psychology, Kans. State U., 1979; cert. in bus., NYU, 1983. Lic. psychologist, N.Y. Asst. reference libr. Bucknell U., Lewisberg, Pa., 1971-73; ednl. researcher Kans. State U., 1975-79; asst. prof. indsl. and orgnl. psychology SUNY, Geneseo, 1979-83; organizational cons. Rochester, N.Y., 1983-85; user interface developer Xerox Corp., Webster, N.Y., 1985-89, mgr. user interface software design, 1989-91, electronics and system software program mgr., 1991—; participant Careers in Bus., NYU, 1983. Co-author: Library Use, 1983, 2d edit., 1992; patentee in field; contbr. articles to profl. jours. Bd. sec. Webster Montessori Sch., 1987-90. NIMH summer fellow U. Mass., 1977, ALA fellow, Dallas, 1971. Mem. APA, Am. Psychol. Soc., Soc. for I/O Psychology. Home: 7 Brewster Ln Pittsford NY 14534-2880 Office: Xerox Corp 800 Phillips Rd Webster NY 14580-9791

REED, JOHN FRANCIS (JACK REED), congressman, lawyer; b. Providence, Nov. 12, 1949; s. Joseph Anthony and Mary Louise (Monahan) R. BS, U.S. Mil. Acad., 1971; M in Pub. Policy, Harvard U., 1973, JD cum laude, 1982. Bar: D.C. 1982, R.I. 1983. Commd. 2d. lt. U.S. Army, 1971, served with 82d Airborne Div., 1973-77; asst. prof. U.S. Mil. Acad., West Point, N.Y., 1977-79; resigned U.S. Army, 1979; assoc. Sutherland, Asbill & Brennan, Washington, 1982-83, Edwards & Angell, Providence, 1983-89; mem. R.I. Senate, 1984-90; mem. 102d Congress from 2d R.I. dist., 1990—, mem. edn. and labor com., judiciary com., mcht. marine and fisheries com.; active Arms Control and Fgn. Affairs Caucus, Congl. Caucus on Human Rights, Congl. Caucus on Women's Issues, Congl. Arts Caucus, L.I. Sound Congl. Caucus, N.E.-Midwest Congl. Caucus, Congl. Fire Caucus, Congl. Clearinghouse on the Future, Army Caucus, Travel and Tourism Caucus, elected officials adv. bd. Dems. 2000. Author: (with others) American National Security, 1981. Recipient Disting. Svc. award AARP, 1989, John Fogarty award, 1990, Disting. Legislator award United Way Southeastern New Eng., 1988. Mem. ABA, R.I. Bar Assn., D.C. Bar Assn., Environ. and Energy Study Inst., Phi Kappa Phi. Democrat. Roman Catholic. Office: US Ho of Reps 1229 Longworth HOB Washington DC 20515 also: Dist Office 355 Centerville Rd Bldg 3 Warwick RI 02886

REED, JOSEPH, JR., chemist; b. Bradenton, Fla., Jan. 18, 1944; s. Joseph and Pauline (Martin) R.; m. Beverly Surcy; 1 child, Joseph Surcy. BA, Lincoln U., 1966; MA, Temple U., 1971; PhD, Brown U., 1974. Supr. Du Pont, Gibbstown, N.J., 1966-70; mem. tech. staff Bell Labs., Murray Hill, N.J., 1974-77; staff rsch. chemist Exxon Rsch. and Engring., Annandale, N.J., 1977-86; program dir. NSF, Washington, 1986—. Contbr. articles to profl. jours. Mem. math. task force Prince Georges Pub. Schs., Prince Georges County, Md., 1990-91. Mem. Am. Chem. Soc. Orgn. Black Scientists. Home: 13114 Larkhall Cir Fort Washington MD 20744-6444 Office: NSF 1800 G St NW Washington DC 20550-0002

REED, JOSEPH VERNER, JR., diplomat; b. N.Y.C., Dec. 17, 1937; s. Joseph V. and Permelia (Pryor) R; m. Marie Maude Byers, Dec. 19, 1959; children: Serena, Electra. BA, Yale U., 1961. With office of pres., The World Bank, Washington, 1959-62; asst. to pres. Internat. Bank for Reconstrn. and Devel., 1961-63; asst. to dir. Chase Manhattan Bank, 1963-68, v.p., exec. asst. to chmn., 1969-81; U.S. amb. to Morocco, 1981-85; amb. to ECOSOC of UN, N.Y.C., 1985-87; undersec. gen. UN, 1987-89; U.S. chief of protocol, The White Ho., Washington, 1989-91; U.S. rep. to UN Gen. Assembly, 1992—. Mem. Coun. on Fgn. Rels., Met. Club, Links club, River Club. Republican. Episcopalian. Home: 591 Riverside Rd Greenwich CT 06831 Office: Under-Sec-Gen Spl Rep of Sec Gen Pub Affairs UN Ste 3161A New York NY 10017

REED, LEON SAMUEL, defense analyst; b. Warren, Ohio, July 6, 1949; s. Walter Charles and Lois Avalene (Botroff) R. BA in Econs. and Journalism, Antioch Coll., 1971; m. Margaret Smith, Dec. 27, 1975 (div.); children: Samuel Currier, Stephen Walter, Catherine Lois. Project dir. Council on Econ. Priorities, N.Y.C. and Washington, 1970-75; sr. mem. profl. staff Joint Com. on Def. Prodn., U.S. Congress, Washington, 1975-77; mem. profl. staff Com. on Banking, Housing and Urban Affairs, U.S. Senate, Washington, 1977-81; analyst TASC, 1981-82, mgr. contingency planning, 1982-85, mgr. indsl. resources dept., 1985-91, dir. indsl. and mfg. scis. div., 1991—; bd. dirs. Council on Econ. Priorities, 1971-73; del. White House Conf. on Youth, 1971. Mem. exec. com., Randolph Civic Assn., 1977-83, pres., 1978-80; asst. chair Coalition on Sensible Transp.; v.p. North Bethesda Congress of Citizens Assns., 1983-84, pres., 1984-86, sec., 1986-88; mem. Montgomery County Council of Pres., 1982-88, chmn. 1986-87. Mem. Disciples of Christ Ch. Co-author: Guide to Corporations, 1973, Report of the National Critical Technologies Panel, 1991; author: Military Maneuvers, 1975, Resource Management: A Historical Perspective, 1988; contbr. Strategic Survey, 1981-82, The American Defense Mobilization Intrastructure, 1983; author numerous congressional and exec. br. reports, mag. and jour. articles.

REED, LOWELL A., JR., federal judge; b. Westchester, Pa., June 21, 1930; s. Lowell A. Sr. and Catherine Elizabeth (Pauly) R.; m. Diane Benson, Jan. 23, 1954; children: Jeffrey Barton, Lowell Andrew, Diane S. Marsh, Christopher Benson. BBA, U. Wis., 1952; JD, Temple U., 1958. Bar: Pa. 1959, U.S. Dist. Ct. (ea. dist.) Pa. 1961, U.S. Ct. Appeals (3d cir.) 1962, U.S. Supreme Ct. 1970. Corp. trial counsel PMA Group, Phila., 1958-63; assoc. Rawle & Henderson, Phila., 1963-65, gen. ptnr., 1966-88; judge U.S. Dist Ct., Phila., 1988—; lectr. law Temple U., 1965-81, Pa. Bar Inst., 1972-87. Contbr. articles to profl. jours. Elder Abington (Pa.) Presbyn. Ch.; past mem. Pa. Senate Select Com. Med. Malpractice; past pres., bd. dirs. Rydal Meadowbrook Civic Assn.; bd. dirs. Abington Sch. Bd., 1971, World Affairs Coun. Phila., 1983-88; trustee Abington Meml. Hosp., 1983-88, 90—. Lt. comdr. USNR, 1952-57. Recipient Alumni Achievement award Temple U. 1988. Mem. ABA, Pa. Bar Assn., Phila. Bar Assn. (chmn. medico legal com. 1975, constl. bicentennial com. 1986-87, commn. on jud. selection and retention 1983-87), Temple Inn of Ct. (pres. 1990—), Temple U. Law Alumni Assn. (exec. com. 1987-90), Hist. Soc. U.S. Supreme Ct., Hist. Soc. U.S. Dist. Ct. Ea. Dist. Pa. Republican. Home: 1056 Huntingdon Rd Abington PA 19001-4605 Office: US Dist Ct 11614 US Courthouse Independence Mall W Philadelphia PA 19106

REED, REX, author, critic; b. Ft. Worth, Oct. 2, 1938; s. Jimmy M. and Jewell (Smith) R. BA, La. State U., 1960. Film critic Holiday mag., Women's Wear Daily, 1968-71; music critic Stereo Rev., 1968-75; syndicated columnist Chgo. Tribune-N.Y. Daily News Syndicate, 1971—; film critic N.Y. Daily News, 1971-75; now columnist N.Y. Observer, N.Y.C.; critic At the Movies, public TV series, 1986. Appeared in film Myra Breckenridge, 1970, Superman, 1978; author: Do You Sleep in the Nude?, 1968, Conversations in the Raw, 1969, Big Screen, Little Screen, 1971, People Are Crazy Here, 1974, Valentines and Vitriol, 1977, Travolta to Keaton, 1979; author: (novel) Personal Effects, 1986. Office: NY Observer 54 E 64th St New York NY 10021-7326*

REED, THOMAS JAMES, law educator; b. Joliet, Ill., Jan. 1, 1940; s. Thomas p. and Bernardine M. (Dorsey) R.; m. Emily A. Fabrycki, Dec. 29, 1962; children: Martin, Valerie. BA, Marquette U., 1962; JD, Notre Dame Law Sch., 1969. Bar: Ind. 1969, U.S. Dist. Ct. (so. dist.) Ind. 1969, U.S. Ct. Appeals (7th cir.) 1974, Mass. 1977, U.S. Dist. Ct. Mass. 1979, Pa. 1982, U.S. Ct. Appeals (3rd cir.) 1982. Assoc. Reller, Mendenhall, Kleinknecht & Milligan, Richmond, Ind., 1969-76; asst. prof. law We. New Eng. Coll. Sch. Law, Springfield, Mass., 1976-79, assoc. prof., 1979-81; assoc. prof. Widener U. Del. Law Sch., Wilmington, Del., 1981-84, prof., 1984—, assoc. dean, 1984—; hist. preservation planner City Planning Assn., Mishawaka, Ind., 1969-71, Hist. Centerville (Ind.), Inc., 1970-76, Old Richmond, 1975-76. Contbr. articles to profl. jours. Reporter Del. Appellate Handbook, Wilmington, 1984—. Mem. ABA, Fed. Bar Assn., Ind. Bar Assn., Pa. Bar Assn. Roman Catholic. Office: Widener U Law Sch 4601 Concord Pike PO Box 7474 Wilmington DE 19803-0409

REED, THOMAS LLOYD, JR., English literature educator; b. Oberlin, Ohio, June 13, 1947; s. Thomas Lloyd and Betsy Noyes (Mook) R.; m. Daisy Brooks Foote, June 5, 1982 (div. 1984); m. Dorothy Craigie Grant, May 23, 1987; 1 child, Abigail Stuart. BA in English, Yale U., 1969; MA in English, U. Va., 1970, PhD in English, 1977. Assoc. prof. English Dickinson Coll., Carlisle, Pa., 1977—; assoc. dir. Camp Pemigewasset, Wentworth, N.H., 1973—. Author: Middle English Debate Poetry and the Aesthetics of Irresolution, 1990; contbr. articles to profl. jours. Fulbright fellow, Oxford, U.K., 1975-76. Mem. MLA, AAUP, Medieval Acad. Am. Office: Dept English Dickinson Coll Carlisle PA 17013

REED, WALTER GURNEE DYER, lawyer; b. N.Y.C., July 11, 1952; s. Stanley Forman and Harriet Tailer (Dyer) R.; m. Cynthia Ann Stewart, Sept. 6,1986. BA magna cum laude, Harvard Coll., 1974; JD, Columbia U., 1977. Bar: N.Y. 1978, R.I. 1983. Assoc. Milbank, Tweed, Hadley & McCloy, N.Y.C., 1977-81; assoc. Edwards & Angell, Providence, 1981-83, ptnr., 1983—. Bd. dirs. Children's Mus. R.I., Pawtucket, 1984—, Providence Athenaeum, 1991—. Scholar Kent U., Stone scholar. Mem. ABA, R.I. Bar Assn. (chmn. com. on corp. law 1991—), N.Y.C. Lawyers Assn., Spouting Rock Beach Assn., Hope Club, Agawam Hunt Club. Democrat. Congregationalist. Home: 14 Cooke St Providence RI 02906-2006 Office: Edwards & Angell 2700 Hospital Trust Providence RI 02903-2438

REED, WILLIAM C., information systems professional; b. Phila., July 14, 1951; s. David Winfield Jr. and Mary Palmer (Grace) R.; m. Joan Danielle Rozanski, Nov. 26, 1988; children by previous marriage: Amy, Alison, Andrea, Amber. AA, Bucks County Community Coll., 1971; BA, Drexel U., 1973; AA, Mercer County Community Coll., 1977; MS, Rutgers U., 1981. Programmer analyst Bucks County Community Coll., Newtown, Pa., 1970-73; adv. analyst Keane Assocs., Paoli, Pa., 1973-77; dir. infosystems Thomas Jefferson U., Phila., 1977-86; v.p. ops. and info. systems Geisinger System Svcs., Danville, Pa., 1986—; adj. faculty various univs. and colls., 1974—; cons. Winfield Palmer Assocs., Bloomsburg, Pa., 1976—; instr. Healthcare Mgmt. Inst., Inc., Clear Lake, Iowa, 1990—; presenter at profl. confs. Contbr. articles to profl. pubs. Vol. fireman, chief various fire depts., 1967—; bd. dirs. Handicapped Tng. Adv. Bd., Phila., 1980-83. Recipient Heroism award Bucks County Chiefs Assn., 1981. Mem. Soc. Info. Mgmt., Am. Med. Informatics Assn., Healthcare Fin. Mgmt. Assn., Healthcare Info. Systems Exec. Assn. (chmn. 1991), Healthcare Info. and Mgmt. Systems Soc. (bd. dirs. 1991—), Mensa. Office: Geisinger System Svcs Inc North Academy Ave Danville PA 17822-3011

REEDY, HARRY LEE, insurance company executive; b. Lebanon, Pa., Dec. 25, 1945; s. Harry Lee and Charlotte (Weedmark) R.; m. Linda Bartley, Nov. 7, 1970; children: Jennifer Beth, Sara Emily. BS in Indsl Engring., Pa. State U., 1967; MBA, U. Conn., 1977. Mgmt. asst. Bell Telephone Pa., Phila., 1967-70; field engring. rep. Travelers Cos., Hartford, Conn., 1971-72, ops. analyst, 1972-76, supervising ops. analyst, 1976-79, sr. mgmt. cons., 1979-83, adminstr. consumer affairs, 1983-85, asst. dir. consumer affairs, 1985-90; dir. corp. customer svc. John Hancock Fin. Svcs., Boston, 1990-91, dir. Ctr. for Quality, 1991—; mem. consumer affairs com. Ins. Info. Inst., N.Y.C., 1988-90. Contbr. articles to trade publs. Participant Leadership Greater Hartford, 1985; bd. dirs., treas. Woodland Manor Condominium Assn., Manchester, Conn., 1986-87. With U.S. Army, 1968-70. Fellow Ins. Con-

sumer Affairs Exch. (treas. 1985-87, v.p. 1987-88, pres. 1988-90), Soc. Consumer Affairs Profls. (v.p. New Eng. chpt. 1991-92); mem. Am. Coun. Life Ins. (consumer affairs com. 1987), Am. Soc. Quality Control, Beta Gamma Sigma. Democrat. Home: 205 Homestead St Apt B12 Manchester CT 06040

REELING, GLENN EUGENE, psychology educator, researcher; b. Dover, Pa., Aug. 21, 1930; s. Irvin Roy and Dora lMay (Swartz) R.; m. Patricia ann Glueck, Aug. 18, 1962; children: Craig, Aimée. BS, Pa. State U., 1952; MS, U. N.Mex., 1958; postgrad., U. Cin., 1958-59; EdD, Ind. U., 1962. Tchr. math. and sci. Kennard-Dale Jr. and Sr. High Sch., Fawn Grove, Pa., 1954-55; tchr. 5th grade Newberrytown (Pa.) Elem. Sch., 1955-56; tchr. gen. math. grade 9 Albuquerque Pub. Schs., 1956-59; tchr. math. and sci. jr. and sr. high schs. Cin. Pub. Schs., 1959-60; teaching assoc. Ind. U., Bloomington, 1960-62; test editor Houghton Mifflin Co., Boston, 1962-63; dir. testing and rsch. Montclair (N.J.) Pub. Schs., 1963-66; prof. psychology and edn. Jersey City State Coll., 1966—. Cpl. U.S. Army, 1952-54, Korea. Mem. AACD, Am. Edn. Rsch. Assn., Am. Psychol. Assn., Am. Assn. Higher Edn., New Jersey Edn. Assn. Higher Edn. (bd. dirs. 1978—), Phi Delta Kappa. Lutheran. Home: 4 Cutlass Way Box M Waretown NJ 08758-9621 Office: Jersey City State Coll Kennedy Blvd Jersey City NJ 07305

REENTS, WILLIAM DAVID, chemist; b. Portsmouth, Va., Jan. 18, 1954; s. William David Sr. and Natalie Ann (Botelho) R.; m. Patricia Ann Stabile, June 25, 1977; children: Michael J., Stephen A. BS in Chemistry, Monmouth Coll., 1976; PhD in Chemistry, Purdue U., 1980. Mem. tech. staff AT&T Bell Labs., Murray Hill, N.J., 1980-87, disting. mem. tech. staff, 1987—. Author: (chpt.) Atomic and Molecular Clusters, 1990. Leader Cub Scouts, Middlesex, N.J., 1988-91. Mem. Am. Soc. Mass Spectrometry, Am. Chem. Soc. Office: AT&T Bell Labs Rm 1A-216 600 Mountain Ave PO Box 636 New Providence NJ 07974-0636

REESE, DANIEL WILLIAM, finance company executive, bank executive; b. Abington, Pa., Apr. 5, 1953; s. Joseph Hammond Reese and Patricia (Welsh) Somers; m. Carol Olwert. Student, Georgetown U. Sch. Fgn. Service, 1974-75; BS in Polit. Sci., Trinity Coll., 1975; MS in Bus., Columbia U., 1985. Researcher Fed. Election Commn., Washington, 1975, spl. asst. to chmn., 1975-77; spl. asst. to gov. State of Conn., 1977-81; mgr. Citibank NA, N.Y.C., 1981-83, ops. mgr., 1983-85; v.p., state mgr. Citicorp, Westport, Conn., 1985-88; sr. v.p. Conn. Nat. Bank, Hartford, Conn., 1988—; bd. dirs. Charles Ives Ctr. Arts, Danbury, Conn., 1986—; alumni dir. Trinity Coll., 1977-79. Chmn. New Fairfield (Conn.) Democrat. Town Com., 1987—. Democrat. Episcopalian. Home: 2 Hudson Dr New Fairfield CT 06812-3801 Office: Conn Nat Bank 70 Farmington Ave Hartford CT 06105-3788

REESE, ERROL LYNN, university administrator, dentist; b. Fairmont, W.Va., May 3, 1939; s. Edgar B. and Elizabeth (Carpenter) R.; m. Julia Hinebaugh, June 8, 1963; children: Daniel, Elizabeth. BS, Fairmont State Coll., 1960; DDS, W.Va. U., 1963; cert. of tng., U. Detroit, 1968, MS, 1968. Grad. asst. Sch. Dentistry U. Detroit, 1966-68; asst. prof. Sch. Dentistry U. Md., Balt., 1968-73, assoc. prof. Sch. Dentistry, 1978, prof. Sch. Dentistry, 1978—, from assoc. dean to dean Sch. Dentistry, 1973-90, pres., 1990—. Capt. U.S. Army, 1963-66. Mem. ADA, Am. Assn. Dental Schs. (pres. 1989-90), Am. Acad. History of Dentistry, Nat. Found. Dentistry for Handicapped, Acad. Gen. Dentistry Found. Office: U Md 520 W Lombard St Baltimore MD 21201

REESE, JULES DOUGLAS, engineering executive; b. Bay Shore, N.Y., July 28, 1952; s. Julius H. and Dora Louise (Eisele) R.; m. Emily Gay Williams, Mar. 20, 1976 (div. 1990); 1 child, Joel. BSCE, U. Mass., 1974; M in Engring., U. Fla., 1975. Geotech. engr. Briggs Engring & Testing Co., Norwell, Mass., 1975-78; v.p. Atec Assocs., Inc., Columbia, Md., 1978-85; pres. Ind. Testing Labs., Rockville, Md., 1985-88; sr. v.p. Profl. Svc. Industries, Balt., 1988—. Mem. ASCE, ASTM, NSPE, Am. Concrete Inst., Internat. Soc. Soil Mechanics and Found. Engrs. Lutheran.

REESE, MARCIA MITCHELL, sculptor; b. Cleve., Sept. 27, 1929; d. Nathan and Eve (Freifield) Mitchell; m. Marvin S. Reese, Apr. 3, 1949; children: David S., Nancy E. BA, Case Western Res. U., 1951. One woman shows at Chem. Bank, Great Neck, 1980, CAPA Rotational Arts Exhbns., 1980, Xerox Corp., 1980, Bloomingdale's, N.Y.C., 1981, Chem. Bank, North Shore Towers, 1982, The Port Washington Libr. Gallery, 1982, The Gallery at the Bryant Libr., 1986, Gallery at Lincoln Ctr., 1986, Plandome Gallery, 1991; ; permanent collections at Hofstra Mus., MONY Fin. Svcs. World Hdqrs., N.Y.C., Manhattan Real Estate Conversion Corp., N.Y.C.; also pvt. collections locally, nationally and internationally. Group exhbns. include Broome Street Gallery, N.Y.C., Nat. Acad. Sic., Nat. Arts Club, N.Y.C., NAWA Ann. Exhbn., N.Y.C., Artists Network on GN, Wisser Libr., N.Y. Inst. Technol., Nassau County Mus. of Art, 1991; Stone Sculpture Soc., Lever House, N.Y.C., Artists Network of GN, Bank of Great Neck, Guild Hall, East Hampton, N.Y., Arline McDaniel Galleries, Simsbury, Conn., Stone Sculpture Soc., Crystal Pavilion, 1990; Hutchins Gallery, C.W. Post Coll., Guild Hall, 1989, Phoenix Gallery, others. Recipient Sculpture award Fourth Open Juried Exgbn., So. Nassau Unitarian Ch., 1989, Mamaroneck Artists Guild Helen and Robert Fleder award, 1988, Salmagundi Club Sculpture award, 1984 (2), Suburban Art League Sculpture award (2), 1979, Ind. Art League Excellence in Sculpture award, 1979, Nat. Art League Spl. Award for Sculpture, 1979. Mem. Nat. Assn. Women Artists (Dr. Max Ellenberg Sculpture award 1991, Cleo Hartwig Sculpture award 1989), Artists Network of Great Neck at Chelsea Ctr. (Sculpture award 1990), Stone Sculpture Soc. of N.Y., Inc., Internat. Sculpture Ctr., Sculptors Affiliates, Sculptors Inc. (pres), Artists Network of Great Neck (scholarship chair), Archaeol. Inst. Am. (L.I. soc. grants chair), Am. Rsch. Ctr. in Egypt, Cyprus Am. Archaeol. Rsch. Inst., L.I. Craft Guild. Home and Office: PO Box 1318 Great Neck NY 11023-0318

REESE, RONALD CRAIG, physician; b. Harrisburg, Pa.; s. Earl Joseph and Catherine Elizabeth (Hughes) R.; m. Rebecca Sharon Weis, June 5, 1983; children: Brian Alexander, Daniel Tyler. BA in Physics, Franklin & Marshall Coll., 1979; MD, Pa. State U., 1983. Diplomate Nat. Bd. Med. Examiners. Intern Nassau County Med. Ctr., East Meadow, N.Y., 1983-84; radiology resident NYU Med. Ctr., N.Y.C., 1984-88, chief resident, 1987-88. Inventor fiber optic connector, 1983. Med. advisor Mountainside Hosp. Sch. of Radiography, 1990—. Kershner physics scholar Franklin & Marshall Coll., Lancaster, Pa., 1979; recipient Dr. Aaron B. Chausmer award Nat. Student Research Forum, Galveston, Tex., 1983. Mem. Radiol. Soc. N.Am., Am. Coll. Radiology, Radiol. Soc. of N.J., Radiology Quality Assurance Com. (chmn. 1990—), Med. Records Com. Republican. Home: 17 Fairmount Ave Montclair NJ 07043-2404 Office: Montclair Radiol Assocs PA 116 Park St Montclair NJ 07042-2987

REESE, WILLIAM SHERMAN, antiquarian bookseller; b. Havre de Grace, Md., July 29, 1955; s. William Blain and Katharine (Jackson) R.; m. Margaret D. Hurt, May 21, 1988. BA, Yale U., 1977. Pres. William Reese Co., 1979—; advisor Western Americana Collection, Yale U. Libr., New Haven, 1981—. Author: Six-Score, 1976, rev. edit., 1989, The Printer's First Fruits, 1990; contbr. articles on Am. bibliography to profl. jours. Vice-chair Yale Libr. Assocs., New Haven, 1988—; treas. Friends of Am. Art, Yale, New Haven, 1980—. Fellow Silliman Coll., Yale U., Morgan Libr., N.Y. Mem. Grolier Club, Century Assn., Club of Odd Volumes, Am. Antiquarian Soc., Yale Club, Elizabethan Club. Democrat. Office: William Reese Co 409 Temple St New Haven CT 06511-6821

REESE, WILLIAM WILLIS, banker; b. N.Y.C., July 8, 1940; s. Willis Livingston Meiser and Frances Galletin (Stevens) R.; BA, Trinity Coll., 1963; MBA, JD, Columbia U., 1970. Admitted to N.Y. bar, 1972; rsch. analyst Morgan Guaranty Trust Co., N.Y.C., 1971-73, investment rsch. officer, 1973-77, asst. v.p., 1977-86, v.p., 1986— . Bd. dirs. N.Y.C. Ballet, 1975-87, Counseling and Human Devel. Ctr., 1977-89, 3d St. Music Sch. Settlement, 1976—; trustee Millbrook Sch., 1972-91. Served with USAF, 1963-67. Mem. Am., Inter-Am., N.Y. State (sec. com. on internat. law 1973-76), Dutchess County bar assns., N.Y. Soc. Security Analysts, Certified Fin. Analysts, Assn. Bar City N.Y., Union, Club, Racquet and Tennis Club, Rockaway Hunt Club, Soldiers', Sailors' & Airmen's Club (bd. dirs. 1991—), Mt. Holyoke Lodge. Republican. Episcopalian. Office: 910 Park Ave New York NY 10021 also: Morgan Guaranty Trust Co 9 W 57th St New York NY 10019-2600

REEVE, RICHARD ROBERT, school psychologist; b. Brockton, Mass., Apr. 2, 1948; s. Walter Leroy and Esther May (Richards) R.; m. Elizabeth Gale Kurtz, June 10, 1978; children: Jennifer Anne, Erin Rebecca. Student, Boston U., 1966-68, BA, 1970, EdM, 1971; DEd, Pa. State U., 1981. Lic. psychologist, Pa.; cert. sch. psychologist, Mass., Pa. Psychologist Crotched Mountain Rehab. Ctr., Greenfield, N.H., 1971-73; grad. asst. Pa. State U., University Park, 1973-76; sch. psychologist Appalachia Intermediate Unit 08, Hollidaysburg, Pa., 1976—; pvt. practice Martinsburg, Pa., 1983—. Capt. Civil Air Patrol, 1983—. Mem. Nat. Assn. Sch. Psychologists, Laurel Mountain Psychol. Assn. (nominating chmn. 1988), Nat. Assn. Elem. Sch. Prins., Sierra Club, Benscreek Canoe Club, Phi Delta Kappa. Home: RR 1 Box 9 Martinsburg PA 16662-9602 Office: Appalachia Intermediate 08 227 Bedford St Hollidaysburg PA 16648-1715

REEVES, BARRY LUCAS, research engineer; b. St. Louis, Jan. 11, 1935; s. Raymond O. and Frances M. (Lucas) R.; m. Marilyn Alva Riester, May 8, 1954; children: Katherine, Michael, Janet. BS, Washington U., St. Louis, 1956, MS, 1958, PhD, 1960. Rsch. assoc. McDonnell Aircraft Corp., St. Louis, 1959-60; postdoctoral rsch. fellow Calif. Inst. Tech., Pasadena, 1960-64; staff scientist Avco Corp., Wilmington, Mass., 1964-68, sr. staff scientist, 1968-74, sr. cons. scientist, 1974-86; prin. scientist Textron Corp., Wilmington, 1986—; con. Space Gen. Corp., L.A., 1962-63, Nat. Engring. & Sci. Co., Pasadena, 1963-64, Aerojet Corp., Azusa, Calif., 1964; contr. engring. symposiums; reviewer Jour. Fluid Mechanics, Physics of Fluids, Jour. Applied Mech., AIAA Jour. Contbr. over 30 articles to profl. jours. Mem. Snow Mountain Farms Assn., Vt., 1982—, U.S. Tennis Assn., 1973-85. Fellow Convair Aircraft Corp., 1958, NSF, 1959; postdoctoral fellow Air Force Office Sci. Rsch., 1960, 61, rsch. grantee, 1962, 63. Mem. Am. Inst. Physics, Smithsonian Assocs. (assoc.), Sigma Xi, Tau Beta Pi, Pi Tau Sigma (past v.p., treas.). Home: 10 Hillcrest Pky Winchester MA 01890-1427 Office: Textron Corp 201 Lowell St Wilmington MA 01887-2969

REEVES, EDMUND HOFFMAN, III, specialty food distributor executive; b. Easton, Pa., Sept. 14, 1949; s. Edmund Hoffman Jr. and Constance Irene (Bartholomew) R.; m. Maryclaire Ratican, Aug. 19, 1972; children: Courtney Ann, Edmund Hoffman IV, Brendan Gill. AA, Camden County Coll., Blackwood, N.J., 1970; BA in Econs., Lynchburg Coll., 1972; MBA in Food Mktg., St. Joseph's U., Phila., 1979. Mgmt. trainee Acme Markets, Inc., Phila., 1972-76; store supr. Acme Markets, Inc., 1976-81; regional mgr., zone mgr. Shaffer Clarke & Co., Inc., Old Greenwich, Conn., 1982-83; merchandising mgr. Shaffer Clarke & Co., Inc., 1984-85, nat. sales mgr., 1985, v.p. sales & mktg., 1986-87; exec. v.p. The Next Step, Inc., Englewood Cliffs, N.J., 1988-90, R.W. Frookies, Inc., Englewood Cliffs, 1988-90; v.p. sales Yankee Food Distributors, Ayer, Mass., 1990—; cons. Dirty Potato Chip (Chicasaw Chips), Memphis, 1988-89, Simpson's Salsa, Englewood, N.J.; bd. dirs. R.W. Frookies, Inc., Englewood Cliffs. Alumni bd. dirs. Lynchburg Coll., 1989; asst cubmaster, com. chmn. Boy Scouts Am., Trumbull, Conn., 1987-89, asst. scoutmaster, Haddonfield, N.J., 1968-69. Mem. Nat. Food Distributor Assn., Biscuit & Cracker Distributor Assn. (speaker), Trumbull Men's Club (pres.). Republican. Presbyterian. Home: 181 Lake Ave Trumbull CT 06611-1844

REEVES, JOHN DRUMMOND, English language professional, writer; b. Troy, N.Y., Dec. 8, 1914; s. Robert Brockway and Emma Caroline (Mausert) R.; m. Mary Markwick Moore, Sept. 1, 1951. AB, Williams Coll., Williamstown, Mass., 1937; AM, Columbia U., 1941. Instr. in Eng. Irving Sch., Tarrytown, N.Y., 1937-40, Horace Mann Sch., N.Y.C., 1940-41, 46-47; asst. prof. of classics and Eng. Whitman Coll., Walla Walla, Wash., 1956-62; assoc. prof. English Millikin U., Decatur, Ill., 1962-65; lectr. in Eng. Hofstra U., Hempstead Long Isl., N.Y., 1965-73; now ret. Contbr. articles to profl. jours. Lt. USNR, 1941-45, PTO. Mem. AAUP, Coll. Eng. Assn., Am. Coun. Learned Soc. (reg. assoc. 1957-59), Walla Walla Archaeol. Assn. (pres. 1959-62), SR (N.Y. state chpt.), Masons. Republican. Home: Newey Ln Brookhaven Long Island NY 11719

REEVES, JOSEPH WILLIAM, school system administrator; b. Fairbanks, Alaska, June 14, 1953; s. Joseph William and Ola M. (Sargent) R. m. Suzanne Spencer, Nov. 1, 1980. BA, Salisbury U., 1975; MS, SUNY, Albany, 1982, Cert. of Advanced Study, 1988, postgrad., 1988—. Prin., tchr. Aleutian Region Sch. Dist., Cold Bay, Alaska, 1976-78; asst. edn. insp. Peace Corps, Kabala, Sierra Leone, 1978-80; dir. edn. Albany (N.Y.) Inst., 1980-86; sr. mgr. N.Y. State Sch. Bds. Assn., Albany, 1986-89, dir. bd. devel., 1989—. Author: (workbook) School Board Self Assessment, 1989, Board Planning, 1990. Curator exhibition People of Great Peace, 1982. Recipient People of Great Peace award N.Y. State Coun. on the Arts. Mem. Am. Soc. Assn. Execs., Comparative and Internat. Edn. Soc., Nature Conservancy, Sea Kayak Assn., Sierra Club. Democrat. Office: NY State Sch Bds Assn 119 Washington Ave Albany NY 12210-2204

REEVES, MARYLOU, financial planner; b. Summit, N.J., Dec. 19, 1959; d. Richard Otto and Helen Elizabeth (Drennan) Wellbrock; m. Richard Harold Reeves, Jan. 13, 1985; children: Rachael Elizabeth, Thomas Mack. BS in Commerce, Rider Coll., 1981. Cert. Fin. Planner; Registry of Fin. Planning Practitioners. Asst. v.p. E.F. Hutton, N.Y.C., 1981-86, Summit Bancorp., Summit, N.J., 1986-89; owner Thomas Mack Assocs., Rockaway, N.J., 1989—. Contbr. newspaper column. Councilwoman Rockaway Twp., N.J., 1988—; mem. Civic Affairs Com., White Meadow, N.J., 1987—; vice chmn. Rockaway Twp. Rep. Com., 1987. Mem. Internat. Assn. Fin. Planners. Republican. Roman Catholic. Office: Thomas Mack Assocs 31 Valley View Dr Rockaway NJ 07866

REEVES, PATRICIA RUTH, heavy machinery manufacturing company executive; b. Bklyn., Mar. 26, 1931; d. Maurice G. and Ethel Helen (Kessler) Der Brucke m. Cedric E. Reeves, June 22, 1952. BA, Adelphi U., 1952. Chief of records sect. Hydrocarbon Rsch., Inc., N.Y.C., 1952-65; lead sec. C.F. Braun & Co., Murray Hill, N.J., 1965-69; exec. sec. Wilputte Corp., Murray Hill, N.J., 1969-75, adminstrv. asst., 1975-79, sales coord., 1979-81, pers. adminstr., 1981-82; sales coord. Krupp Wilputte Corp., Murray Hill, N.J., 1982-84; pers. adminstr. Somerset Techs., Inc., N.J., 1984-85, pers. mgr., 1985—. Pres. Mountain Jewish Community Ctr., Warren, N.J., 1976-77, bd. dirs., 1972-81. Mem. NAFE, AAUW, Women's Netsork Cen. N.J. (v.p., editor newsletter 1981-83, coord. career assistance 1984-85, membership chmn. 1986—), Am. Soc. Pers. Adminstrs. (membership chmn. 1986-88, sec. 1986-88), Soc. Human Resources Adminstrn. (sec. Cen. N.J. chpt. 1986-88, v.p. 1988-89, pres. 1989-90), SHRM (sec.-treas. N.J. coun. 1990—). Jewish. Home: 89 Knollwood Dr Watchung NJ 07060-6245 Office: Somerset Tech Inc Weston Canal Rd Somerset NJ 08873-5101

REEVES, ROGER DEFOREST, systems manager, educator; b. Providence, Aug. 8, 1949; s. Curtis DeForest and Dorcas Grace (Smith) R.; m. Emily June Robinson, Mar. 22, 1980; children: Jennifer, Meghan. BA, R.I. Coll., 1971, MAT, 1975. Tchr. Cranston (R.I.) Sch. Dept., 1971-78; systems mgr., asst. v.p. PW Group, Inc., Providence, 1978—; instr. R.I. Coll., Providence, 1983—. Vestryman, jr. and sr. warden Ch. of Transfiguration, Cranston, 1983—. Office: PW Group Inc 20 Washington Pl Providence RI 02903-1328

REFINSKI, JOSEPH ANTHONY, educator; b. Orange, N.J., July 7, 1954; s. Chester Walter and Antoinette (DeCarlo) R. BA in History, Seton Hall U., 1976, MA in Secondary Edn., 1978. Cert. tchr. social studies and history, N.J. Tchr. Columbia High Sch., Maplewood, N.J., 1977-78; tchr. and coach Edison Jr. High Sch., Westfield, N.J., 1978-85, Verona (N.J.) High Sch., 1985-86, Costley Sch., East Orange, N.J., 1986—; photographer and cons. N.J. Bicentennial Commn., Mahwah, 1987—. Coord. nat. competition on Constitution and Bill of Rights, Washington, 1988, Nat. Commn. on U.S. Constitution, Calabasas, Calif., 1989; active in local Constitution Day projects, 1987, 88; tchr. edn. adv. com. Seton Hall U., 1992—. Recipient Bicentennial Leadership award Ctr. for Civic Edn., Calabasas, 1989, Alumni Svc. award Seton Hall U.; Thomas Jefferson fellow, 1991. Mem. ASCD, Nat. Coun. Social Studies, Found. for U.S. Constn. (founding mem.), Athletics Congress, Seton Hall U. Alumni Assn. (pres. 1990-92), Phi Alpha Theta, Kappa Delta Pi. Roman Catholic. Home: 73 Bell St Orange NJ 07050-1508

REGAN, DAVID MICHAEL, health care administrator; b. Phila., Oct. 3, 1955; s. James Rodman and Dorothy Marie (Jones) R.; m. Cathy Jean Aspril, June 13, 1981; children: Bethany Ann, Sarah Kathleen. BA, Franklin and Marshall Coll., 1977; MS in Health Planning and Adminstrn., Pa. State U., 1984. Adminstrv. asst. York (Pa.) Hosp., 1983; asst. dir. office emergency med. services Pa. State U., University Park, 1983-84; adminstrv. asst., research analyst L.I. Jewish Med. Ctr., New Hyde Park, N.Y., 1984-85; asst. adminstr. Geisinger Clinic, Lewistown, Pa., 1985-88, mgr. of revenue, reimbursement, 1987-90, adminstrv. dir. primary care svcs., 1990—; bd. dirs. Geisinger Fed. Credit Union. Mem. Med. Group Mgmt. Assn., Juniata Area C. of C. (bd. dirs. 1987-88), Nat. Health Lawyers Assn., Rotary Club. Office: 100 North Academy Ave Danville PA 17822-3101

REGAN, EDWARD VAN BUREN, state government official, comptroller; b. Buffalo, May 14, 1930; m. Susan G. Regan; children: Jane, Julian, Kate. BA, Hobart Coll., 1952; LLB cum laude, SUNY, Buffalo, 1964. Exec. Erie County Exec. Office, Buffalo, 197-178; compt. State of N.Y., Albany, 1979—. Ex officio mem. bd. overseers Rockefeller Inst. Govt., N.Y.C., 1983—; mem. bd. overseers RPI Sch. Mgmt., N.Y.C., 1985—, NYU Grad. Sch. Bus. Adminstrn., N.Y.C., 1981—. Recipient John LaFarge Meml. award for interracial justice Cath. Interracial Coun. N.Y., 1981, Pub. Svc. award SUNY-Buffalo Sch. Law Alumni Assn., 1981, Disting. Leadership award Assn. Govt. Accts., 1981. Republican. Roman Catholic. Office: NY State Comptrs Office A E Smith State Office Bldg Albany NY 12236

REGAN, FREDERIC DENNIS, cardiologist, internist; b. Newburyport, Mass., Aug. 21, 1921; s. Dennis and Catherine R. (Haley) R.; w. Margaret amary Regan. Student Syracuse U., 1940-42; M.D., U. Buffalo, 1945; children: Denise, Frederic, Michael. Intern, USPHS Hosp., S.I., N.Y., 1945-46, research fellow in cardiology, 1947, resident in medicine, dep. chief medicine, chief cardiac clinic, 1950-52; practice medicine specializing in cardiology and internal medicine; chief of medicine Richmond Meml. Hosp. and Health Ctr. (now S.I. Univ Hosp.), dir. medicine; instr. medicine N.Y. Hosp.; organizer, dir. Gateway State Bank. Diplomate Am. Bd. Internal Medicine. Fellow ACP, Am. Coll. Cardiology, N.Y. Cardiology Soc.; mem. Richmond County Med. Soc. (pres. 1961-62). Office: 347 Edison St Staten Island NY 10306-3034

REGAN, RICHARD JOSEPH, political science educator; b. Morristown, N.J., Oct. 26, 1930; s. Joseph Michael and May Catherine (Cella) R. A.B., St. Peter's Coll., 1952; Ph.L., Woodstock Coll., Md., 1957, S.T.L., 1964; Ph.D., U. Chgo., 1967. Assoc. prof. Fordham U., Bronx, N.Y., 1968-87, prof., 1987—. Author: American Pluralism and the Catholic Conscience, 1963; Conflict and Consensus, 1967; Private Conscience and Public Law, 1972; Moral Dimensions of Politics, 1986; On Laws, Morality and Politics, 1988. Roman Catholic. Office: Fordham U Bronx NY 10458

REGENBAUM, SHELLY HAYA, English educator; b. Jerusalem, Nov. 24, 1941; d. Zorah Shapira and Dinah (Kazarnovsky) Sirotinsky; m. Kenneth Regenbaum, June 23, 1973 (dec. 1978); children: Shir, Livi. BA in English, Hebrew, Hebrew U., 1965; MA in English, Sheffield U., 1969; PhD in English, Bar-Ilan U., 1979. Lectr. English Haifa (Israel) U., 1978-79; tchr. drama Rubin Music Acad., Jerusalem, 1979-80; lectr. Kansas State U., Manhattan, 1983-86; instr. U. Kans., Lawrence, 1986-87, asst. prof., 1987-89; asst. prof. Western New Eng. Coll., Springfield, Mass., 1989—; vis. asst. prof. speech Kansas State U., Manhattan, 1980-83. Nat. judge Margalit Prize for Performing Arts, Jerusalem, 1979-80. Mem. MLA, Tikkun. Jewish. Office: Western New Eng Coll Springfield MA 01119

REGENSBURG, EDWARD ALAN, artist, clinical art psychotherapist, art therapy educator; b. N.Y.C., Oct. 7, 1953; s. Milton and Dorothy (Rose) R.; m. Sharman Lynn Mancher, Oct. 5, 1985; 1 child, Corey Miles. AA in Art, Nassau (N.Y.) Community Coll., 1973; BS in Art Edn., SUNY, New Paltz, 1975; MA in Creative Arts Therapy, Hofstra U., 1980. Registered art therapist. Clin. art psychotherapist Drug Treatment and Edn. Ctr. North Shore U. Hosp./Cornell Med. Coll., Manhasset, N.Y., 1976-82, activities coord./art therapist Day Treatment and Psychiatry, 1982-87; dir. art therapy Sagamore Children's Ctr., Dix Hills, N.Y., 1987-91; program coord./supervising art therapist Pederson Krag Continuing Treatment Ctr., St. James, N.Y., 1991-92; exec. dir. North Shore Creative Rehab. Ctr., Inc., Great Neck, N.Y., 1992—; prof. art therapy L.I. Univ./C.W. Post Coll., Brookville, N.Y., 1985—; pvt. practice Huntington, N.Y., 1982—; book reviewer Jour. Arts in Psychotherapy, 1991. Exhibited in group showings at East Hills (N.Y.) Gallery, 1982, Per La Casa, Huntington, N.Y., 1983, Internat. Art Exposition, N.Y.C., 1984, Shirley Scott Gallery, Southampton, N.Y., 1985, Dyansen Gallery of Soho, N.Y.C., 1986, Peri-Renneth Gallery, Southampton, 1987, Meisner Gallery, Farmingdale, N.Y., 1989, Axis Mundi Gallery, Sag Harbor, N.Y., 1989, Ward-Lawrence Gallery, N.Y.C., 1990, Hutchins Gallery, Brookville, N.Y., 1991, Meisner Soho, 1992.

REGENSTREIF, HERBERT, lawyer; b. N.Y.C., May 13, 1935; s. Max and Jeannette (Hacker) R.; m. Patricia Friedman, Dec. 20, 1967 (div. July 1968); m. Charlotte Lois Levy, Dec. 11, 1980; 1 child, Cara Rachael. BA, Hobart Coll., 1957; JD, N.Y. Law Sch., 1960; MS, Pratt Inst., 1985. Bar: N.Y. 1961, Ky. 1985, U.S. Dist. Ct. (ea. and so. dists.) N.Y. 1962, U.S. Tax Ct. 1967, U.S. Ct. Appeals (2d cir.) 1962, U.S. Supreme Ct. 1967. Ptnr. Fried & Regenstreif, P.C., Mineola, N.Y., 1963—; cons. in field; arbitrator Dist. Ct., Nassau County, N.Y., 1989—, N.Y.C. Civil Ct., 1984-86. Contbr. articles to profl. jours. County committeeman Dem. Com., Queens County, N.Y., 1978-79. Mem. Bar Assn. Nassau County, Ky. Bar Assn., Phi Delta Phi, Beta Phi Mu, Hobart Club of N.Y. (gov. 1968-69). Jewish.

REGNIER, ROLAND JOHN, sales and marketing executive; b. Amsterdam, Netherlands, June 15, 1953; came to U.S., 1956; s. John Peter and Paula M. (Carlier) R.; m. Felicia A. Desmarais, May 14, 1983. BA in Psychology cum laude, Boston U., 1975; MBA with honors, Bryant Coll., 1983. Dept. mgr. Jordan Marsh Dept. Stores, Boston, 1975-77; store mgr. CVS, Div. of Melville, Woonsocket, R.I., 1977-79, buyer, 1979-86; dir. mktg. Martin Roberts Assocs., Natick, Mass., 1986-89, pres., 1989—. Mem. New England Health and Beauty Care Assn. (bd. dirs. 1991—, pres. 1992—), Nat. Assn. Gen. Mdse. Reps. (regional v.p. 1991—). Republican. Baptist. Home: 735 Sherman Farm Rd Harrisville RI 02830-1115 Office: Martin Roberts Assocs 23 Strathmore Rd Natick MA 01760-3658

REHBERGER, GUSTAV, artist; b. Riedlingsdorf, Austria, Oct. 20, 1910; s. Joseph and Elizabeth (Piff) R.; brought to U.S., 1923, naturalized, 1928; student Art Inst. Chgo., 1924-27, Art Instrn. Schs., Mpls., 1926-28. Illustrator dir. Esquire mag., N.Y.C., 1949-60, Coronet mag., 1949-62; prof. art Old Mill Art Ctr. Adirondacks, 1964-66, Am. Art Sch., N.Y.C., 1969-72, Art Students League N.Y., 1972—. Fine arts painter, also former illustrator for nat. mags., motion picture promotion, books; designer, illustrator nat. advt. campaigns; one-man shows: Stevens-Gross Gallery, Chgo., 1950, Soc. Illustrators, N.Y.C., 1957, 65, Old Mill Art Ctr. of Adirondacks, Elizabethtown, N.Y., 1964, 65, 66, Nat. Arts Club, Montreal, 1967, Wyoming Valley Art League, Wilkes-Barre, Pa., 1967, Wickersham Gallery, N.Y.C., 1971, Jacques Seligmann Gallery, N.Y.C., 1977, Snug Harbor Cultural Ctr., S.I., N.Y., 1991; exhibited in group shows: NAD, N.Y.C., Audubon Artists, N.Y.C., Allied Artists Am., N.Y.C., Internat. Water Color Show at The Art Inst. Chgo., 1938, Chgo. and Vicinity Exhbn. The Art Inst. Chgo., 1935-40, Pastel Society Am., Wichita, Kans., Abelle Gallery, Princeton, N.J., 1985, Nat. Galleries, London, Nat. Gallery, Washington, Princeton, N.J., Am. Water Color Soc., N.Y.C., Nat. Drawing Exhbn., Oklahoma City; represented in permanent collections: Lyman Allyn Mus., New London, Conn., St. Johns U., N.Y.C., Sports Hall, Peking, China, also pvt. collections in U.S., Can., Europe, China, Saudi Arabia; commissioned works include: World War II Murals at Union Sta., Chgo., 1942, portrait of "Mama" Kutsher Kutsher's Resort, Monticello, N.Y., 1965, painting of Beethoven for the Beethoven Soc., Fed. Republic Germany, 1979; invited by city of Bonn, Fed. Republic Germany, to present art/music performance tributing Beethoven, 1986 (resulting painting presented to the Beethoven Archives); subject of articles in several mags. including Newsweek, Am. Artist; lectr., painting and drawing demonstrator The Spirit of Form, Movement and Expression; condr. nationwide workshops anatomy and figure drawing. Served with USAAF, 1943-45, ETO. Recipient award for most creative painting Audubon Artists Exhbn., 1949, Art Dirs. Show award, N.Y.C., 1954, 55, Soc. Typographic Arts award, Chgo., 1936, Award

Allied Arrists Am., 1974, Award Pastel Soc. Am., 1976, Dirs. award, 1979, Exceptional Merit award, 1981Lever House award, 1982, elected master pastelist, 1984, assn. award, 1984, Popular Vote award, 1985; Knickerbocker Artists award, 1984; named to Pastel Soc. Am. Hall of Fame, 1988. Mem. Allied Artists Am., (award in oil painting 1974, 81), Pastel Soc. Am. (founding mem., former 1st v.p., mem. adv. bd.), Audubon Artists, Allied Artists, Am. Acad. Taos. Pioneer in use expressionism in Am. illustration and design. Address: Carnegie Hall Studio 1206 New York NY 10019

REHNQUIST, WILLIAM HUBBS, U.S. Supreme Court justice; b. Milw., Oct. 1, 1924; s. William Benjamin and Margery (Peck) R.; m. Natalie Cornell, Aug. 29, 1953; children: James, Janet, Nancy. BA, MA, Stanford U., 1948; MA, Harvard U., 1949; LLB, Stanford U., 1952. Bar: Ariz. Law clk. to former justice Robert H. Jackson, U.S. Supreme Ct., 1952-53; with Evans, Kitchel & Jenckes, Phoenix, 1953-55; mem. Ragan & Rehnquist, Phoenix, 1956-57; ptnr. Cunningham, Carson & Messenger, Phoenix, 1957-60, Powers & Rehnquist, Phoenix, 1960-69; asst. atty.-gen. office of legal counsel Dept. of Justice, Washington, 1969-71; assoc. justice U.S. Supreme Ct., 1971-1986, chief justice, 1986—; mem. Nat. Conf. Commrs. Uniform State Laws, 1963-69. Author: Grand Inquests: The Historic Impeachments of Justice Samuel Chase and President Andrew Johnson, 1992; contbr. articles to law jours., nat. mags. Served with USAAF, 1943-46, NATOUSA. Mem. Fed., Am. Maricopa (Ariz.) County bar assns., State Bar Ariz., Nat. Conf. Lawyers and Realtors, Phi Beta Kappa, Order of Coif, Phi Delta Phi. Lutheran. Office: Supreme Ct US 1 1st St NE Washington DC 20543

REIBMAN, JEANETTE FICHMAN, state senator; b. Ft. Wayne, Ind., Aug. 18, 1915; d. Meir and Pearl (Schwartz) Fichman; m. Nathan L. Reibman, June 20, 1943; children: Joseph M. Edward D., James E. AB, Hunter Coll., 1937; LLB, U. Ind., 1940; LLD, Lafayette Coll., 1969; hon. degree, Lehigh U., 1986, Wilson Coll., 1974, Cedar Crest Coll., 1977, Moravian Coll., 1990. Bar: Ind., 1940, U.S. Supreme Ct. 1944. Pvt. practice law Ft. Wayne, 1940; atty. U.S. War Dept., Washington, 1940-42, U.S. War Prodn. Bd., Washington, 1942-44; mem. Pa. Ho. of Reps., 1956-66, Pa. State Senate, Harrisburg, 1966—; chmn. com. on edn. Pa. State Senate, 1971-81, minority chmn., 1981-90; mem. Edn. Commn. of the States. Trustee emeritus Lafayette Coll.; bd. mem., Pa. Med. Coll., Pa. Higher Edn. Assistance Agy., Pa. Coun. on Arts, Camphill Schs. Recipient Disting. Dau. of Pa. award and medal Gov. Pa., 1968, citation on naming of Jeanette F. Reibman Adminstrn. Bldg., East Stroudsburg State Coll., 1972, Pub. Svc. award Pa. Psychol. Assn., 1977, Jerusalem City of Peace award Govt. Israel, 1977; named to Hunter Coll. Alumni Hall of Fame, 1974. Mem. Hadassah (Myrtle Wreath award 1976), Sigma Delta Tau, Delta Kappa Gamma, Phi Delta Kappa, Order Ea. Star. Democrat. Jewish. Office: 711 Lehigh St Easton PA 18042-4397 also: Pa State Senate State Capitol Harrisburg PA 17120

REICH, BARRY ALAN, psychologist; b. Bklyn., Feb. 22, 1950; s. Isidore Irving and Clarabel (Padwa) R.; m. Nancy Carol Iannucci. BA, Hofstra U., Hempstead, N.Y., 1972, MA, 1974, PhD, 1977. Diplomate Am. Acad. Pain Mgmt. Instr. bio-behavioral sci. Nassau County Sci. Mus., Plandone, N.Y., 1974; adj. prof. psychology Hofstra U., Hempstead, N.Y., 1974-78; researcher Family Svc. Assn., Hempstead, N.Y., 1974-78; dir. youth program Nassau County Youth Bd., Mineola, N.Y., 1976-78; rsch. dir. Vera Inst., N.Y.C., 1978-80; dir. behavioral medicine L.I. Headache Ctr., Mineola, 1984-89; adj. med. staff Winthrop U. Hosp., Mineola, 1984—; dir. comprehensive pain program Nassau Pain & Stress Ctr., Westbury, N.Y., 1979—; mental health cons. Nassau County Police Dept., Mineola, 1980—; clin. instr. CME Winthrop U. Hosp., Mineola, 1984—; rev. cons. Chubb Ins. Co., East Meadow, 1985—, Ednl. Testing Svc., Princeton, N.J., 1980. Contbr. articles to profl. jours., chpts. to books; radio host WGBB Talk Radio, 1989—. Hofstra U. scholar, 1976. Mem. APA, Internat. Assn. for Study of Pain, Am. Assn. for Study of Headache, Nat. Migraine Found., Traditional Acupuncture Found., Soc. of Med. Hypnoanalysts. Office: Nassau Pain & Stress Ctr 355 Post Ave Westbury NY 11590-2265

REICH, FERENC, entertainer, pianist; b. Miskolc, Hungary, June 13, 1930; came to U.S., 1962; s. Arthur and Bella (Benedek) R. PhD, Sch. Economies, Budapest, Hungary, 1952, Sch. Art and Music, Budapest, Hungary, 1954. Dir. mktg. Budapest Theater, 1954-56; pianist, entertainer various hotels, restaurants, clubs, Brussels, 1956-62, Paris, London, Amsterdam, 1958-62, N.Y.C., 1962-70; pianist, entertainer cruise ships, resorts, Caribbean, 1970-80, hotels, restaurants, clubs, Washington, 1980-87, The White House, The Presidential Yacht, Washington, 1983-87; booking agent, owner Do-Re-Mi Agy., Washington, 1985—; cons. Broadway shows, Am. mus. Hungarian State Radio, Budapest, Voice of Am. Radio, Washington, 1988; spl. guest appearance on Votre Choix, Can. Broadcasting Corp.. Republican. Home: 2151 Florida Ave NW Washington DC 20008-1903

REICH, HERB, editor; b. N.Y.C.; s. Herman S. and Hattie (Davis) R.; m. Gerri Toog, Aug. 7, 1960; children: Amanda Suri, Elizabeth Jo. B.A., Bklyn. Coll., 1950; M.A., Bklyn. Coll. and Kings County Hosp., 1951; postgrad., Columbia U., 1951-54. Author sketches and lyrics Tamiment Revues (Pa.), 1951; staff writer NBC-TV, N.Y.C. and Los Angeles, 1955-57; research coordinator Inst. for Motivational Research, Croton-on-Hudson, N.Y., 1958-59; research dir. Scientist and Engr. Technol. Inst., N.Y.C., 1960-64; mng. editor SETI Pubs. Inc., N.Y.C., 1961-64; sr. editor Odyssey Press, N.Y.C., 1964-65; editorial dir. Profl. and Tech. Programs Inc., N.Y.C., 1966-72; dir. Behavioral Sci. Book Service, N.Y.C., 1966-72; dir. behavioral scis. program Basic Books Inc., N.Y.C., 1973-79; editor intersci. div. John Wiley & Sons. Inc., N.Y.C., 1979-87, sr. editor profl. and trade div., 1987—; pres. H&G Reich, rsch., advt. & polit. cons., 1980—; researcher, statistician, rsch. cons. Am. Found. for Blind, Pepsi Cola Co., Nowland and Co., Communications and Media Rsch. Svcs.; freelance TV writer. Mng. editor: Odyssey Sci. Library Encyclopedia of Engineering, Signs and Symbols, 1965, Dictionary of Physics and Mathematics Abbreviations, Signs and Symbols, 1965, Dictionary of Electronics Abbreviations, Signs and Symbols, 1965; contbr.: Random House Dictionary of the English Language, 1967, revised edit., 1987, The Greatest Revue Sketches, 1982; TV writer: Broadway Open House, 1951, Milton Berle Texaco Star Theatre, 1952, All-Star Revue, 1952, Tonight Show, 1956, Red Buttons Show, 1954. Co-founder, vice chmn. Mt. Vernon United for Better Edn., N.Y., 1970-73; mem. Westchester County Democratic Com., 1972-76; exec. com. Mt. Vernon Dem. City Com., 1973-76; mem. supt.'s adv. com. Hastings Schs., Hastings-on-Hudson, N.Y., 1981-82. Recipient Gold award of excellence for radio advt. Advt. Club of Westchester, 1980; recipient Gold and Bronze awards of excellence for radio advt. Advt. Club of Westchester, 1981. Mem. AAAS, Am. Psychol. Assn., N.Y. Acad. Scis., Internat. Platform Assn., Alpha Phi Omega.

REICH, HERBERT J., electrical engineering educator; b. Staten Island, N.Y., Oct. 25, 1900; s. Jacques and Caroline (Bellinger) R.; m. Anne Elizabeth Evans, Apr. 3, 1926 (dec. 1974); children: Robert J., Donald E. Student, Deep Springs Coll., Calif., 1917-20; BS in Mech. Engring., Cornell U., 1924, PhD in Physics, 1928. Instr. Cornell U., Ithaca, N.Y., 1924-29; asst. prof. elec. engring. U. Ill., Urbana, 1929-36, assoc. prof., 1936-39, prof. elec. engring., 1939-46; tech. rsch. assoc. Radio Rsch. Lab. Harvard U., Cambridge, Mass., 1944-46; prof. elec. engring. Yale U., New Haven, 1946-62, prof. engring. and applied sci., 1962-69, prof. emeritus, 1969—; mem. faculty Deep Springs Coll., 1969-70, 76-82; mem. coms. Internat. Electrotech. Commn., 1960-72, chmn. microwave tube subcom., 1965-72. Author: Theory and Applications of Electron Tubes, 1939, 44, Principles of Electron Tubes, 1941, Functional Circuits and Oscillators, 1961; co-author: Ultra-High Frequency Techniques, 1942, Microwave Theory and Techniques, 1953, Microwave Principles, 1957, Theory and Applications of Active Devices, 1966; editor 20 vols. on electronics and communications; contbr. articles to profl. jours. Fellow IEEE (electron tube standards com. 1955-69, chmn. 1964-66), Am. Phys. Soc., Inst. Radio Engrs. (chmn. com. on edn. 1945-53, bd. editors 1943-51, bd. dirs. 1944, 48-57); mem. AAUP, Sigma Xi, Tau Beta Pi, Phi Kappa Phi. Republican. Congregationalist. Home and Office: 8 Park St Groveland MA 01834-1120

REICH, MICHAEL WILLIAM, brokerage house executive; b. Batavia, N.Y., June 7, 1956; s. August William and Lois Atla (Patterson) R.; m. Patricia Dale Duken, July 1, 1978; children: Kelly Rae, Adam Michael. Student, SUNY, Geneseo, 1974-76. Parts mgr. Chrysler Corp., Victor, N.Y., 1978-80; fin. cons. Shearson Lehman Hutton, Inc., Batavia, 1980—; v.p. Shearson Lehman Hutton, Batavia, 1986—, br. mgr., 1989-90; br. mgr. Shearson Lehman Bros. (formerly Shearson Lehman Hutton), Batavia, 1990—. Bd. dirs. Genesee Community Coll. Found., Batavia, 1988—, United Way of Genesee County, Batavia, 1986—, chmn., 1986-87; chmn. exec. dir. search com. YMCA, Batavia, 1988; deacon 1st Presbyn. Ch., Batavia. Recipient Spl. Citation for Exceptional Vol. Service ARC, Batavia, 1986. Mem. Chmn.'s Coun., Founder's Club, Blue Chip Club. Republican. Presbyterian. Office: Shearson Lehman Bros 83 Main St Batavia NY 14020-2101

REICH, MURRAY HERBERT, chemical engineer, consultant, researcher; b. Bklyn., May 29, 1922; s. Israel and Rose (Reiter) R.; m. Naomi A. Pollack, Mar. 26, 1949; children: Michael Robin, Leslie Alan, Pamela Nadine. BAChemE, CCNY, 1943; MS, Akron U., 1954; MEd, Trenton Stat U., 1974; EdD, Columbia U., 1982. Rsch. chemist FMC Corp., Princeton, N.J., 1956-62; devel. chemist Princeton Chem Rsch., 1962-75, tech. dir., 1975-77; dir. Premac Assocs., Princeton, 1977—; counselor Rutgers U., New Brunswick, 1979-82; v.p. Biolan Corp., Princeton, 1989—; cons. Savant Assoc., 1989-90, Tyndale Plains-Hunter, Ltd., 1991—. Patentee epoxy resins, solid molded golf balls, degradabel agril. mulch films and polyolefins, patents pending; contbr. articles to profl. jours. Pres. Princeton Jewish Ctr., 1966-68; fin. chair Princeton Rsch. Forum, 1987-89, Holistic Health Assn. Princeton, 1985-87; mem. adv. coun. Ret. Sr. Vol. Program, 1986—. With USN, 1943-45; PTO. Mem. Am. Chem. Soc., AACD, Soc. Plastics Engrs. Princeton Rsch. Forum. Democrat. Home and Office: Premac Assocs 184 Loomis Ct Princeton NJ 08540-3439

REICH, PAUL SETH, bank officer; b. Bklyn., Nov. 5, 1955; s. Murray and Evelyn (Undank) R. BS in Acctg., Bklyn. Coll., 1978; MBA, Pace U., 1980. CPA; cert. fraud examiner. Audit trainee N.Y. State Controller's Office, N.Y.C., 1978-79; staff auditor Morgan Gauranty Trust, N.Y.C., 1979-81; sr. auditor Israel Discount Bank, N.Y.C., 1981-84, audit officer, 1984-86, asst. mgr., 1987-88, asst. v.p., 1989; asst. v.p. The Bank of N.Y., N.Y.C., 1989—. Mem. N.Y. State Soc. CPAs, AICPA, Nat. Assn. Cert. Fraud Examiners, Inst. Internal Auditors. Office: The Bank of New York 101 Barclay St New York NY 10286-0001

REICH, ROBERT BERNARD, political economics educator; b. Scranton, Pa., June 24, 1946; s. Edwin Saul and Mildred Dorf (Freshman) R.; m. Clare Dalton, July 7, 1973; children: Adam, Samuel. BA, Dartmouth Coll., 1968, MA (hon.), 1988; MA, Oxford (Eng.) U., 1970; JD, Yale U., 1973. Asst. solicitor gen. U.S. Dept. Justice, Washington, 1974-76; dir. policy planning FTC, Washington, 1976-81; mem. faculty John F. Kennedy Sch. Govt. Harvard U., Cambridge, Mass., 1981—; chmn. biotech. sect. U.S. Office Tech. Assessment, Washington, 1990-91; bd. dirs. Econ. Policy Inst., Washington. Author: The Next American Frontier, 1983, Tales of a New America, 1987, The Work of Nations, 1991; co-author: The Power of Public Ideas, 1987; contbg. editor The New Republic, Washington, 1982—; chmn. editorial bd. The Am. Prospect, 1990—. Mem. governing bd. Common Cause, Washington, 1981-85; bd. dirs. Bus. Enterprise Trust, Palo Alto, Calif., 1989—; trustee Dartmouth Coll., Hanover, N.H., 1989—. Rhodes scholar, 1968; recipient Louis Brownlow award ASPA, 1983.

REICH, WALTER, research psychiatrist, educator; b. Rzeszów, Poland, July 6, 1943; came to U.S., 1947; s. Simon and Anna (Nussbaum) R.; m. Tova Rachel Weiss, June 10, 1965; children: Daniel S., David E., Rebecca Z. AB, Columbia U., 1965; MD, NYU, 1970; cert. in psychiatry, Yale U., 1973. Diplomate Am. Bd. Med. Examiners, Am. Bd. Psychiatry and Neurology. Fellow, asst. instr. psychiatry Yale U., New Haven, 1971-73, lectr., 1973—; assoc. rsch. psychiatrist NIMH, Bethesda, Md., 1973-75; psychiatrist The Pres.'s Biomed. Panel, Washington, 1975-76; dir. advanced studies NIMH, Rockville, Md., 1976-86, sr. rsch. psychiatrist, 1976—; rsch. prof. psychiatry Uniformed Svcs. U. Health Scis., Bethesda, 1986-88, prof. psychiatry, 1988—; sr. rsch. assoc., then sr. scholar Woodrow Wilson Internat. Ctr. Scholars, Washington, 1985—; cons. U.S. Holocaust Meml. Coun., Washington, 1981-83; chmn. program in med. and biolog. scis. Washington Sch. Psychiatry, 1975-85; rsch. assoc. Forum on Psychiatry and the Humanities; mem. univ. seminar on polit. psychology George Wahington U. Author: A Stranger in My House: Jews and Arabs in the West Bank, 1984; editor: Origins of Terrorism: Psychologies, Ideologies, Theologies, World Views; contbr. numerous articles to profl. jours. Nat. vice chmn. Com. Concerned Scientists, N.Y.C., 1985—. Capt. USPHS, 1973—; mem. Carnegie Endowment for Internat. Peace. Kennan Inst. Advanced Russian Studies fellow, 1982-83; Lustman fellow Davenport Coll. Yale U., 1984, 91—; recipient Adminstr.'s award for meritorious achievement Alcohol, Drug Abuse, and Mental Health Assn., 1978; David J. Fish meml. lectr. Brown U., 1984; Albert Kahn meml. lectr. Boston U., 1991. Fellow Am. Psychiat. Assn. (com. human rights, task force on terrorism); mem. AMA, AAAS (com. sci. freedom and responsibility). Home: 200 Primrose St Bethesda MD 20815-3323 Office: Woodrow Wilson Internat Ctr Smithsonian Instn Bldg Washington DC 20560

REICH, WILLIAM MICHAEL, advertising executive; b. N.Y.C., July 28, 1943; s. William Adolph and Mildred Joan (Chestaro) R.; m. Carmela Louise Ezzone; children: Concetta M., John M., Russell D. Student, N.Y.C. Community Coll., 1961-62, Sch. Visual Arts, N.Y.C., 1962-65. Tech. illustrator Grumman Aerospace Corp., Bethpage, N.Y., 1965-67; tech. illustrator Dayton T. Brown, Inc., Bohemia, N.Y., 1967-68, art dir., 1968-69, art dir., prodn. mgr., 1969-71, sales and estimating mgr., 1971-74; art dir. Volt Info. Scis., Garden City, N.Y., 1974-75, salesman, 1975-78, directories mgr., 1978-80; corp. publs. mgr. Loral Microwave Group, Hauppauge, N.Y., 1980—. Recipient Bronze award Gold Book, 1980, Cert. of Merit award, Printing Industries of Metro N.Y., 1983. Mem. Bus. Profl. Advt. Assn., L.I. Advt. Club (Cert. of Merit award 1980-82, 85). Republican. Clubs: L.I. Studebaker (Massapequa, N.Y.) (pres.). Office: Loral Microwave Narda 435 Moreland Rd Hauppauge NY 11788-3994

REICHARD, JOHN FRANCIS, association executive; b. Abington, Pa., June 2, 1924; s. Francis Radcliffe and Katharine (Butler) R.; m. Ruth Naomi Nachod, Aug. 5, 1950; children: Scot, John Nicholas. BA, Wesleyan U., 1949, postgrad., 1949-50; postgrad., Glasgow U., Scotland, 1950-51. Instr. English/humanities Wesleyan U., Middletown, Conn., 1951-52, Ohio Wesleyan U., Delaware, 1952-54; internat. campus adminstr. U.S. Nat. Student Assn., Cambridge, Mass., 1954; exec. dir. Internat. Student Assn. Greater Boston, 1955-60; pres. Phila. Coun. for Internat. Visitors, 1960-73; internat. coord. Phila. 76, 1973-75; exec. dir. Global Interdependence Ctr., 1975-79; exec. v.p. NAFSA: Assn. of Internat. Educators, Washington, 1980—. Sec. bd. Internat. Devel. Conf.; mem. internat. program com. USDA Grad. Sch. Counselor Meridian House Internat.; travel adv. com. U.S. Travel Svc., 1963-64; pres. Nat. Coun. Internat. Visitors, 1963-65; organizer, co-chmn. Internat. Yr. of Child, UNICEF, Phila., 1977-78; internat. adv. bd. Bryn Mawr Coll., 1975-79; chmn. schools com. Phila. steering com. on alumni affairs Wesleyan U., 1968-76; adv. bd. Hariri Found.; mem. Nat. Liaison Com. on Fgn. Student Admissions. Contbr. articles to profl. jours. Served with USAAF, 1943-46. Winchester fellow Wesleyan U., 1949; Fulbright scholar Glasgow U., 1950-51; recipient Tribute of Appreciation, U.S. Dept. State, 1973, Svc. award Coun. on Internat. Ednl. Exch., 1991. Mem. Am. Coun. on Internat. Edn. (secretariat, commn. on internat. edn.), Internat. Ednl. Exch. Liaison Group (chmn. 1982-84), Test of English as a Fgn. Lang. (policy coun.), Fulbright Alumni Assn. (v.p. 1978-80), Cosmos Club, Phi Beta Kappa. Democrat. Home: 4974 Sentinel Dr Apt 301 Bethesda MD 20816-3571 Office: NAFSA Assn Internat Educators 1875 Connecticut Ave NW Washington DC 20009-5728

REICHART, STUART RICHARD, lawyer; b. N.Y.C., Nov. 18, 1924; s. Stanley and Rae (Wein) R.; m. Joan Feirtag, Mar. 28, 1981. LLB, Bklyn. Law Sch., 1948; LLM, NYU, 1951. Bar: N.Y. 1949, D.C. 1971, U.S. Supreme Ct. Adminstrv. judge Armed Services Bd. Contract Appeals, Washington, 1966-72; asst. gen. counsel for procurement USAF, Washington, 1972-75, dep. gen. counsel, 1975-78, gen. counsel, 1978-81; of counsel Fried, Frank, Harris, Shriver & Jacobson, Washington, 1982-90; instr. govt. procurement Ohio State U., U. Dayton, U. Md., 1960-70. Contbr. legal articles on govt. procurement to profl. jours. Served with AUS, 1942-45; served to col. USAF, 1951-71. Decorated Legion of Merit, D.F.C., Air medal with silver oak leaf cluster, Purple Heart; recipient Disting. Civilian Service medals Dept. Air Force, 1979, Dept. Def., 1982, Stuart R. Reichart award USAF, 1982. Mem. ABA, Fed. Bar Assn. Lodge: Masons. Home and Office: 8000 Grand Teton Dr Rockville MD 20854-4074

REICHBLUM, AUDREY ROSENTHAL, public relations executive; b. Pitts., June 28, 1935; d. Emanuel Nathan and Willa (Handmacher) Rosenthal; m. M. Charles Reichblum, Jan. 25, 1956; children: Robert Nathan, William Mark. Student, Bennington Coll., 1952-53; BS, Carnegie Mellon U., 1956. Accredited Pub. Rels. Soc. Pitts. Founder, creator, chmn. Pitts. Children's Mus., 1970-73; mag. writer Pitts. Mag., 1978; dir. pub. rels. Pitts. Pub. Theater, 1978-79; pres. arPR audrey reichblum PUB. RELS. inc., Pitts., 1980—; pub. rels. cons., bd. mem. Pitts. Planned Parenthood, 1980—, United Jewish Fedn., Bus. and Profl. Women, Pitts., 1980—, Pitts. City Theater, 1985—. Recipient Gold Cindy award Info. Film Producers Am., 1982, award of excellence Internat. Assn. Bus. Communicators, Pitts., 1986. Mem. Pub. Rels. Soc. Am. (award of merit 1983, G. Victor Barkman award for excellence 1984), Women in Comm. (Matrix-sales promotion award 1987), Nat. Assn. Women Bus. Owners, Exec. Women's Coun., Am. Women in Radio and TV, Am. Mktg. Assn., Rotary. Office: arPR Inc 1 Gateway Ctr Pittsburgh PA 15222-1416

REICHERT, BRUCE ROBERT, business consulting executive; b. Chgo., Dec. 7, 1942; s. Walter Frederick and Helen (Wellman) R.; m. Kathy E. Smith, May 1977 (div. July 1980). BSC in Acctg., DePaul U., 1973; MBA, Roosevelt U., 1976. Fin. dir. Milton Bradley Ltd., London, 1974-76; mgr. cost devel. Rockwell Corp., Pitts., 1976-77; controller, plastics div. ITT Corp., Madison Heights, Mich., 1978-80; mgr. fin. control ITT Corp., N.Y.C., 1980-82, mgr. cost control, 1982-84; controller Summagraphics, Fairfield, Conn., 1984-86; pres. Mgmt. Controls Corp., Fairfield, 1986—; bd. dirs. Malberg Enterprises, Inc., Bus. Connections, Inc., Royal Travel Network, Inc. Author: U.S. Lady, 1966, One-Up Production, 1986, Autofact '87, 1987, Flow Dymanics, 1987; editor Spotlight on Cost newsletter, 1985; columnist Paper Age MAg. Served with U.S. Army, 1966-69. Home: 15C Heritage Sound Milford CT 06460 Office: Mgmt Controls Corp 58 River St Milford CT 06460-3381

REICHERT, LEO EDMUND, JR., biochemist, endocrinologist; b. N.Y.C., Jan. 9, 1932; s. Leo and Anne (Holstein) R.; m. Gerda Sihler, July 20, 1957; children: Leo, Christine, Linda, Andrew. B.S., Manhattan Coll., N.Y.C., 1955; Ph.D., Loyola U., Chgo., 1960. Asst. prof. biochemistry Emory U. Med. Sch., Atlanta, 1960-66; dir. human and animal pituitary hormone isolation program NIH, Emory U. Sch. Medicine, 1960-75; assoc. prof. Emory U. Med. Sch., 1966-72, prof., 1972-79; prof., chmn. dept. biochemistry Albany (N.Y.) Med. Coll., 1979-88, prof. biochemistry, 1988—; dir. human and animal hormone isolation and distbn. program (NIH), Emory U. Med. Sch., 1960-75; mem. adv. bd. Nat. Pituitary Agy., 1971-74; com. on glycoprotein hormones Nat. Hormone and Pituitary Program, 1968-86; mem. reproductive biology study sect. NIH, 1971-75; mem. adv. panel on cellular physiology NSF, 1983-86, div. of integrative and neuro biology, 1992; mem. WHO Expert Adv. Panel on Biol. Standardization, 1984—, Nat. Bd. Med. Examiners, Part I, 1989-91. Mem. editorial bd. Endocrinology, 1967-75, Molecular and Cellular Endocrinology, 1977-83, 90—, Biology of Reproduction, 1968-70, 86-90, Andrology, 1983-86, Molecular Andrology, 1989—; contbr. over 200 articles to profl. jours.; U.S. patentee in field. Served with USMC, 1950-52. List among 75 endocrinologists, 1000 scientists most cited, 1965-78. Mem. Am. Soc. Biol. Chemists, Endocrine Soc. (Ayerst award 1970), AAAS, Androlgy Soc. (council 1983-87), Soc. for Study of Reprodn. Home: 10 Laurel Dr Albany NY 12211-1618 Office: Albany Med Coll Dept Biochemistry Albany NY 12208

REICHGOTT, MICHAEL JOEL, medicine educator, dean, physician; b. Newark, July 26, 1940; s. Leo and Gertrude (Millman) R.; m. Lynn Gay Haar, Dec. 22, 1962; children: Jay Howard, Seth Alan, Douglas Jordan. AB, Gettysburg (Pa.) Coll., 1961; MD, Albert Einstein Coll. Medicine, 1965; PhD, U. Calif., San Francisco, 1973. Diplomate Am. Bd. Internal Medicine. Fellow in clin. pharmacology U. Calif., 1969-72; asst. prof. U. Pa., Phila., 1973-81, assoc. prof., 1981-84; assoc. prof. Albert Einstein Coll. of Medicine, Bronx, 1984—, assoc. dean of students and grad. med. edn., 1989—; med. dir. Bronx Mcpl. Hosp. Ctr., 1984-89; bd. dirs. Holy Cross Care Systems, Inc., South Bend, Iowa; presenter in field. Contbr. articles to profl. jours. V.p. Larchmont (N.Y.) Temple, 1990-92, pres., 1992-94. Maj. M.C., U.S. Army, 1967-69, Vietnam. Fellow ACP (com.); mem. Assn. Am. Med. Colls. (com. 1990—), N.Y. Acad. Medicine, Phila. Acad. Medicine, Soc. for Gen. Internal Medicine (com.). Office: Albert Einstein Coll of Medicine 1300 Morris Park Ave Bronx NY 10461-1924

REICHMAN, ALLEN, psychiatrist; b. N.Y.C., July 10, 1932; s. Morris M. and Gizella (Schwartz) R.; m. Harriet Susan Siegel, June 11, 1968; children: Mark B., Andrew J. AB, NYU, 1953; MD, Georgetown U., 1957. Diplomate Am. Bd. Psychiatry and Neurology, Am. Bd. Forensic Psychiatry. Intern, fellow in medicine Jersey City Med. Ctr., 1957-59; resident in psychiatry Inst. of Living, Hartford, Conn., 1959-61, Georgetown U. Hosp., Washington, 1961-62; chief psychiatrist Inst. for Crippled and Disabled, N.Y.C., 1964-68; attending psychiatrist Mt. Sinai Svc. at Elmhurst, N.Y.C., 1966-68; chief day treatment North Shore U. Hosp., Manhasset, N.Y., 1969-70; med. dir. forensic svcs. Nassau County Dept. Mental Health, East Meadow, N.Y., 1973—; pvt. practice Mineola, N.Y., 1964—. Contbr. articles to profl. jours. Capt. U.S. Army, 1962-64, Korea. Fellow Am. Psychiat. Assn., Nassau Acad. Medicine; mem. Nassau Psychiat. Soc. (pres. 1980-81, chmn. ethics com. 1984—). Jewish. Office: 190 Willis Ave Mineola NY 11501-2639

REID, BARBARA ADDISON, human resources administrator; b. Rendville, Ohio, June 16, 1943; d. Isaac Norman and Mary (Addison) R.; m. Leon Noel Brathwaite, Jan. 20, 1973 (div. May 1987); 1 child, Leon Philip Addison Brathwaite. BS, Northeastern U., 1974, MEd., 1985; DEd, U. Mass., Amherst, 1992. Asst. mgr. staffing Harvard U., Cambridge, Mass., 1969-78; dir. Personnel Tufts U., Medford, Mass., 1978-85; dir. human resources Automatic Data Processing, Waltham, Mass., 1985—; lectr. in bus. adminstrn. Northeastern U., Boston, 1980—; cons. small businesses in Mass., R.I. Town meeting mem. Town of Burlington, Mass., 1992. Martin Luther King scholar Northestern U., 1973-74. Mem. N.E. Human Resources Assn. (bd. dirs. 1989—), Health Club New Eng., Kappa Delta Pi, Sigma Epsilon Rho. Democrat. Episcopalian. Home: Zero Francis Wyman Rd Burlington MA 01803 Office: Automatic Data Processing 225 2nd Ave Waltham MA 02154-1134

REID, BEVERLY ANN, educational administrator; b. Greensburg, Pa., Mar. 3, 1949; d. Frank Leroy and Hilda (Smith) Hogg; m. Robert Murray Reid, June 16, 1979. BS, Ind. U. of Pa., 1971; MA, Washington Coll., 1975; PhD, U. Md., 1983. Tchr. Kent County Pub. Schs., Rock Hall, Md., 1971-77; coord. tchr. edn. ctr. U. Md., College Park, 1982-84, dir. ctr. for community edn. devel., 1983-84; resource tchr. Anne Arundel County Pub. Schs., Annapolis, Md., 1984-85, adminstrv. intern, 1985-87, asst. prin., 1987-90, pers. specialist, 1990—. Fern D. Schneider scholar, 1981. Mem. ASCD, Assn. Sch. Bus. Ofcls., Phi Delta Kappa, Delta Kappa Gamma (chpt. officer). Home: 507 Wilson Rd Crownsville MD 21032-1630 Office: Bd Edn Div Human Resources 2644 Riva Rd Annapolis MD 21401-7305

REID, CHARLES HENRY, musical director; b. Phila., Jan. 16, 1929; s. Clarence Jackson and Helen Gertrude (Reeves) R.; m. Norma Jane Matthews, Apr. 7, 1951; children: Bonnie Louise, Charles Henry Jr., Bruce Edwin, Christopher Jackson. BS in Music, Temple U., 1952; MusM, West Chester U., 1964. Choral dir., tchr. William Penn High Sch., New Castle, Del., 1951-60, P.S. du Pont High Sch., Wilmington, Del., 1960-70, Sanford Sch., Hockessin, Del., 1970-74, Springer Jr. High Sch., Wilmington, 1974-76; coord. music, choral dir. Tatnall Sch., Wilmington, 1976-90; retired, 1990; organist, choirmaster Ch. Farm Sch., Eston, Pa., 1949-51, Redeemer Presbyn. Sch., Phila., 1951-52, Hanover Presbyn. Sch., Wilmington, 1952-64, Trinity Episcopal Ch., Wilmington, 1964-89, Temple Beth Shalom, Wilmington, 1970-80, Limestone Presbyn. Ch., 1990—; guest dir. Sussex Co. Ch., Del., 1966, 72, 74, 81, 84, No. Del. Oratorio Soc., Wilmington, 1973-811 chorus master Opera Del., Wilmington, 1966-71; asst. dir. State Music Camp, Dover, Del., 1952-64. Composer: The Beatitudes, 1953, The Hills/Christ, 1967. Pres. Penn Acres Civic Assn., New Castle, 1959-61; mem. Wilmington Music Commn., 1956-63. Recipient scholarship, Presser

Found., Temple U., 1948-52. Mem. Music Edn. Nat. Conf., Am. Choral Dirs. Assn. Republican. Presbyterian. Home: 614 Loveville Rd Hockessin DE 19707

REID, ELIZABETH SINKIEWICZ, higher education administrator; b. Weymouth, Mass., July 12, 1962; d. Robert John and Betty Flood (Dowd) Sinkiewicz; m. Stephen John Reid, Sept. 9, 1989. BA, Brandeis U., 1984; EdM, Harvard U., 1986; cert. with honors, Goethe Inst., Bremen, Fed. Republic of Germany, 1981. Tour planner, operator Beckham Travel Agy., Canton, Mass., 1984; apprentice Sinkiewicz Electric, Inc., Weymouth, 1984-86; baker Angelo's Supermarket, Weymouth, 1985; receptionist, data entry clk. Hotels of Distinction, Inc., Boston, 1985; spl. asst. to asst. dean grad. admissions and fin. aid Harvard U., Cambridge, Mass., 1985-87; residence dir. Westfield (Mass.) State Coll., 1987-88; asst. dir. residential life Worcester (Mass.) Poly. Inst., 1988—; career counselor Worcester Poly. Inst., 1991—. Coord. Big Brother/Big Sister, Waltham, Mass., 1982-84; Youth Coun. Adv. com. Town of Weymouth, 1985-86. Fed. Republic of Germany scholarship, 1980. Mem. Mass. Assn. Women in Edn. (newletter chair, 1990-92), N.E. Assn. Coll. and Univ. Housing Officers (New Profl. scholarship 1989), Am. Coll. Pers. Assn., Mass. Coll. Pers. Assn., Worcester Residence Life Network (program com. chair, 1989, 90, conf. chair, 1991). Roman Catholic. Home: Worcester Polytechnic Inst 100 Institute Rd Box 2783 Worcester MA 01609

REID, EVERETT COOLIDGE, II (CHIP REID), musician, music educator; b. Torrington, Conn., May 15, 1957; s. Everett Coolidge and Jean Ethel (Wylie) R.; m. Audrey Lynn Keywan, May 29, 1981; children: David Matthew, Emily Elizabeth. Student, Western Conn. Coll., 1975-76, North Tex. State U., 1976-78, Hartford Conservatory, 1978-79. Drummer Hartford, Conn., 1980-86; piano player Landerman Talent Agy., East Hartford, Conn., 1987-89; pvt. music tchr. Torrington, 1986—; pres. Pop-zzical Pub., Torrington, 1991—, Pop-zzical Tapes, Torrington, 1991—; cons. various small musical groups, Litchfield County, 1980—. Composer (instrumental) Lenny's Plan, 1980 (Nat. Assn. Music Merchants contest winner 1983); composer numerous songs including First Time for Edgar, America You've Got a Lucky Face, Reach Out Help the Children; pub. The Music Poster, 1988. Fundraiser Operation Torrington Homefront, 1991, Christmas Village, 1991, St. Jude's Hosp., 1992; percussionist Torrington Civic Symphony, 1971; pres. Young Peoples Fellowship, 1969. Mem. ASCAP. Republican.

REID, GEORGE WAYNE, theologian; b. Oklahoma City, Sept. 19, 1930; s. Earl and Nolene (Alexander) R.; m. Julia Cordwell, Aug. 28, 1955; children: Deborah, George Jr. BA, Union Coll., 1952; MA, Seventh-day Adventist Sem., 1953, MDiv, 1955; ThD, Southwestern Bapt. Theol. Sem., 1976. Ordained to ministry Seventh-day Adventist, 1959. Pastor Okla. Conf. of Seventh-day Adventists, 1956-67; chmn. dept. religion Southwestern Adventist Coll., Keene, Tex., 1967-82; assoc. editor The Adventist Rev., Silver Spring, Md., 1982-84; dir. Bibl. Rsch. Inst., Silver Spring, 1984—. Author: A Sound of Trumpets: Americans, Adventists & Health Reform, 1982; contbr. articles to profl. jours. Mem. Am. Acad. Religion, Am. Soc. Ch. History, Adventist Theol. Soc., Andrews Soc. for Religious Studies. Seventh-day Adventist. Home: 4710 Greencastle Rd Laurel MD 20707-3142 Office: Bibl Rsch Inst 12501 Old Columbia Pike Silver Spring MD 20904-6600

REID, GORDON MACDONALD, coal company executive; b. Glasgow, Scotland, May 19, 1935; came to U.S., 1957; s. William Davis and Jessie May (Halliday) R.; m. Janet Anne Mechan, Nov. 10, 1956 (div. Apr. 1982); children: Kenneth, Thomas, Alan; m. Gail Crawford, June 5, 1982; 1 child, Andrew. BSc in Metallurgy, Glasgow U., 1955. Foundry metallurgist Crouse-Hind Co., Syracuse, N.Y., 1957-60; tech. salesman Debevois Anderson Co., N.Y.C., 1960-63, v.p., 1966-69; foundry mgr. Black Clawson Co., Everett, Wash., 1963-66; sr. v.p. Derby & Co., Pitts., 1969-76; exec. v.p. Crown Coal & Coke Co., Pitts., 1976—; pres. Wellsville Terminals Co., 1979—; v.p. Kenova (W.Va.) Terminal Co., 1976—, The Keystone Co., Wilmington, Del., 1980—, Kenterm, Inc., Wilmington, 1980—. Mem. AIME, Duquesne Club, Erie Yacht Club, Masons, Shriners (noble), Jesters (treas. 1990—). Republican. Presbyterian. Home: 140 Fieldgate Dr Pittsburgh PA 15241-2150 Office: Crown Coal & Coke Co 200 9 Parkway Ctr Pittsburgh PA 15220-3616

REID, HELENA PATRICIA, recruitment administrator; b. Phila., Jan. 21, 1959; d. Frank Edward and Alice (Carson) R. Student, Wilmington Coll., 1976-77; AA, Phila. Sch. Office Tng., 1980. Researcher Chilton Inc., West Chester, Pa., 1982-83; asst. sales coord. Wharton Bus. Sch., Phila., 1982-86; recruitment asst. Univ. Pa. Law Sch., Phila., 1986—. Rec. sec. Mt. Sinai Holiness Ch. of Am., Inc., Phila., 1980-84, site com. mem., 1991—; choir dir. Bethel Holy Temple, Phila., 1991—. Pentecostal. Home: 1920 Mather Way Apt A Philadelphia PA 19117-1023 Office: 3400 Chestnut St Philadelphia PA 19104-6204

REID, INEZ SMITH, lawyer, educator; b. New Orleans, Apr. 7, 1937; d. Sidney Randall Dickerson and Beatrice Virginia (Bundy) Smith. BA, Tufts U., 1959; LLB, Yale U., 1962; MA, UCLA, 1963; PhD, Columbia U., 1968. Bar: Calif. 1963, N.Y. 1972, D.C. 1980. Assoc. prof. Barnard Coll. Columbia U., N.Y.C., 1972-76; gen. counsel youth div. State of N.Y., 1976-77; dep. gen. counsel HEW, Washington, 1977-79; inspector gen. EPA, Washington, 1979-81; chief legis. and opinions, dep. corp. counsel Office of Corp. Counsel, Washington, 1981-83; corp. counsel D.C., 1983-85; counsel Laxalt, Washington, Perito & Dubuc, Washington, 1986-90, ptnr., 1990-91; counsel Graham & James, 1991—; William J. Maier, Jr. vis. prof. law W.Va. U. Coll. Law, Morgantown, 1985-86. Author: Together Black Women, 1972; contbr. articles to profl. jours. and publs. Bd. dirs. Homes and Ministries Bd. United Ch. of Christ, N.Y.C., 1978-83, vice chmn., 1981-83; chmn. bd. govs. Antioch Law Sch., Washington, 1979-81; chmn. bd. trustees Antioch U., Yellow Springs, Ohio, 1981-82; bd. trustees Tufts U., Medford, Mass., 1988—, Lancaster (Pa.) Sem., 1988—; bd. govs. D.C. Sch. Law, 1990—, chmn., 1991—. Recipient Emily Gregory award Barnard Coll., 1976, Arthur Morgan award Antioch U., 1982, Service award United Ch. of Christ, 1983, Disting. Service (Profl. Life) award Tufts U. Alumni Assn., 1988. Office: Graham & James 2000 M St NW Washington DC 20036-3307

REID, LANGHORNE, III, merchant banker; b. Dallas, Apr. 3, 1950; s. Langhorne Jr. and Mary Anne (Beasley) R.; m. Sally Wolf, Dec. 26, 1972 (div. Aug. 1977); m. Eve Catherine Murphy, Sept. 6, 1986. BA in Psychology, U. Tex., Austin, 1972, JD, 1975; MBA, U. Pa., 1977. Bar: Tex. 1975. V.p. Dillon, Read & Co., Inc., N.Y.C., 1977-82; mng. dir. Drexel Burnham Lambert Inc., N.Y.C., 1982-87; co-dir. mergers and acquisitions Paine Webber Group, N.Y.C., 1987-89; ptnr. Gordon Investment Inc., N.Y.C., 1989—; bd. dirs. Animed Inc., N.Y.C., 1982-86, 455 E. 57th Inc., N.Y.C., 1983-87, Windmill Holdings, 1989—, Empire Holding Corp., 1991—; pres. Partnership Svcs., 1992—. Trustee, treas. Animal Med. Ctr., N.Y.C., 1981—. Mem. Tex. Bar Assn., River Club N.Y. Home: 4441 Belfort Pl Dallas TX 75205 Office: Gordon Investment Inc 100 Crescent Ct Ste 250 Dallas TX 75201

REID, MARION L., lieutenant governor, former politician, educator; b. North Rustico, P.E.I., Can., Jan. 4, 1929; d. Michael Doyle and Loretta Whelan; m. Lea P. Reid, June 29, 1949; children: Maureen and Colleen (twins), Kevin, Bethany, Marylea, David, Andrew, Tracy. Tchr.'s lic., Prince Wales Coll., P.E.I., 1947. Tchr. elem. schs. P.E.I., from 1947; prin. St. Ann's Elem. Sch., Hope River, 1964-68; mem., dep. speaker Legis. Assembly of P.E.I., Charlottetown, 1974-84, speaker, 1984-86, opposition house leader; lt. gov. P.E.I., Charlottetown, 1990—; past bd. govs., sec., mem. various coms. P.E.I. Tchrs. Fedn. Pres. Sterling Women's Inst.; charter mem. Queen Elizabeth Hosp. Found. Named Dame of Grace, Order of Hosp. of St. John of Jerusalem, 1990. Mem. Cath. Women's League, Zonta Club. Address: Govt House, PO Box 846, Charlottetown, PE Canada C1A 7L9

REID, OCTAVIUS T(ED), III, securities broker; b. Abington, Pa., Aug. 27, 1964; s. Octavius T. Jr. and Joan Lorretta (Lee) R. BA, Rutgers U., 1986. Stockbroker Dean Witter, Cherry Hill, N.J., 1986—. Vol. Soup Kitchen Sunday Breakfast, Camden, N.J., 1986—; mem. Am. Heart Assn. Mem. So. N.J. Devel. Coun., Nat. Black MBA Assn., Rutgers U. African-Am. Alumni Assn. (treas. New Brunswick N.J. 1989—), Omega Psi Phi. Home: 416 Park Pl Cherry Hill NJ 08002

REID, PHILIP DEAN, biology educator; b. Ypsilanti, Mich., Mar. 6, 1937; s. Bert C. and Inez (Heckathorn) R.; m. Cathy Hofer, Sept. 28, 1984; children: Taylor C., Alana B. BS, Ea. Mich. U., 1962; MA, U. Mo., 1964; PhD, U. Mass., 1970. Biologist UniRoyal Chem. Div., Bethany, Conn., 1964-66; postdoctoral fellow U. Calif., Riverside, 1970-71; mem. faculty Smith Coll., Northampton, Mass., 1971—; dir. grad. study Smith Coll., 1976-79, 91-92, asst. to pres., 1979-85, chair dept. biology, 1986-89. Contbr. Ency. Britannica Yearbook; contbr. over 40 articles to profl. jours. Bd. dirs. Hampshire Regional YMCA, Northampton, 1980-91. With U.S. Army, 1958-60, ETO. Mem. AAAS, Am. Soc. Plant Physiologists, Plant Growth Regulator Soc. Am., Torrey Bot. Club., Sigma Xi. Home: 57 Main St Haydenville MA 01039-9715 Office: Smith Coll Dept Biol Scis Northampton MA 01063

REIDEL, CARL HUBERT, environmental studies educator; b. Chgo., Mar. 5, 1937; s. Jack Hubert and Dolores June (Ciovino) R.; m. Delores J. Baril, July 22, 1961 (div. Mar. 1985); children: Ingrid Eve, Kristin Dee, Jonathan Carl; m. Jean Richardson, July 29, 1990. BA, U. Minn., 1958, PhD, 1969; MPA, Harvard U., 1964. Dist. forest ranger U.S. Forest Svc., Carson City, Nev., 1958-63; staff forester U.S. Forest Svc., Ogden, Utah, 1964-65; instr. U. Minn., Mpls., 1965-69; asst. dir., asst. prof. William Coll., Williamstown, Mass., 1969-71; rsch. fellow Harvard U., Cambridge, Mass., 1971-72; dir., prof. environmental studies U. Vt., Burlington, 1972—; vis. scientist Yale U., New Haven, 1977-79; policy cons. Tenn. Valley Authority, 1976-84; trustee New England Natural Resources Ctr., Boston, 1986—. Author: Yankee Forest, 1978; editor: New England Prospects, 1982; contbr. articles to profl. jours. Justice of the Peace State of Vt., Ferrisburgh, 1988—; rep. No. Forest Coun., 1988-91; chmn. Vt. Natural Resources Coun., Montpelier, 1985-86. 2d lt. U.S. Army, 1960-61. Named Environ. master EPA, 1990; recipient Honor award Soil Conservation Soc. Am., 1985, Svc. award Vt. Natural Resource Coun., 1985. Fellow Vt. Acad. Arts and Scis.; mem. Soc. Am. Foresters, Am. Forestry Assn. (bd. dirs. 1972—, pres. 1976-78), Nat. Wildlife Fedn. (vice-chmn., bd. dirs. 1991—). Democrat. Episcopalian. Office: Univ Vt 153 S Prospect St Burlington VT 05401-3595

REIDY, ROGER PATRICK, production company executive; b. Newton, Mass., Mar. 17, 1925; s. Maurice Alphonse and Mildred (Levi) R.; m. Imelda America Menor, June 30, 1969; children: Dana R., Abby R., James P. AB in Engring., Harvard Coll., 1944; MS in Civil Engring., Harvard U., 1947; AB in Philosophy, St. John's Sem., 1958, AB in Theology, 1962. Pvt. filmmaker, engr. Newton Highlands, Mass., 1947-55; missionary priest Sons of Mary Missionary Soc., Framingham, Mass., 1955-69; exec. v.p. Harvest Films, Inc., N.Y.C., 1969-72; producer, pres., treas. Am. Prodns., Boston, 1972—. Lt. (j.g.) USNR, 1943-46. Roman Catholic. Office: Am Prodns-AMPRO 101 Tremont St Boston MA 02108-5004

REILEY, T. PHILLIP, systems analyst; b. Ft. Lewis, Wash., May 5, 1950; s. Thomas Phillip and Anne Marie (Russick) R. BSc in Biophysics, Pa. State U., 1973; postgrad. in Bus. Adminstrn., Rutgers U.; MBA, NYU, 1991. Inventory supr. Leland Tube Co., South Plainfield, N.J., 1973-76; prodn. inventory control supr. Bomar Crystal Co., Middlesex, N.J., 1976-79; prodn. control mgr. Codi Semicondr. Inc., Linden, N.J., 1979-81; mfg. systems analyst Western Union Info. Systems, Mahwah, N.J., 1981-85; sr. systems analyst Nabisco Brands Biscuit Div., Parsippany, N.J., 1985—. Mem. Am. Prodn. and Inventory Control Soc. (past chmn. ednl. com. Raritan Valley chpt.), N.Y. Acad. Scis., Mensa. Republican. Home: 56 Carlton Club Dr Piscataway NJ 08854-3114 Office: Nabisco Brands 100 Deforest Ave East Hanover NJ 07936-2897

REILLEY, DENNEN, research agency administrator, educator; b. Greenwich, Conn., Mar. 1, 1937; s. Philip Francis and Florence Rita (Junkersfeld) R.; B.S.S., Fairfield U., 1959; M.Ed., U. Hartford, 1965; postgrad. U. Conn., 1965-70; PhD Calif. Coast U., 1989; m. Margaret Randall Dougherty, Dec. 26, 1976; children: Philip F., Christopher J., Diane L., Elizabeth S., Katherine M. Tchr., New Britain (Conn.) Public Schs., 1960-65, West Hartford (Conn.) Public Schs., 1965-69, 72-73; mem. faculty Central Conn. State Collre New Britain, 1969-72; dir. field services Edn. Devel. Center, Newton, Mass., 1973-82; sr. asso., chief exec. officer Applied Research Assocs., Sharon, Mass., 1980—; adj. faculty U. Wyo., U. Minn.; cons. Am. Humane Assn., Edn. Devel. Center. Mem. New Britain Republican town com., 1961-65. Recipient Rosemary Ames award Am. Humane Assn., 1983. Mem. Nat. Council Social Studies (conv. speaker 1963-79, curriculum com. 1974-77, field services bd. 1977-80), Conn. Council Social Studies (pres. 1965-66), NEA (life), Assn. Supervision and Curriculum Devel., Am. Humane Soc. (conv. speaker 1980-91). Author: Training Program for Animal Care and Control Professionals, Sources: A Resource Guide to Funding Assistance for Parenting Programs, Education for Parenthood Conference Report; the Tri-State Parenting Collaborative, (with Jan Mokros) Summary of Exploring Childhood Evaluation Findings, Management Perspectives for Animal Care and Control Professionals, Board Perspectives For Nonprofit Organizations, Long Range Planning For Nonprofit Organizations; contbr. articles to profl. jours. Conducts mgmt. seminars nationally, Not-for-profit orgns., 1982—. Office: 57 Brook Rd Sharon MA 02067

REILLEY, JAMES CLARK, artist/cartoonist; b. Detroit, Nov. 4, 1919; s. James Aloyisus and Lillian May (Cole) R.; m. Beatrice C. Clemente, May 10, 1952; children: James A. (dec.), Anthony Francis, Beatrice Anita. Grad., Art Inst. of Pitts., 1948. Artist Banner Advt., Phila., 1948-49; layout artist Lit Bros. Dept. Store, Phila., 1949; comic book illustrator John Prentice, Long Island, N.Y., 1950; artist DuPont Co., Wilmington, Del., 1950-59; artist/owner Jim Reilley Studio, Wilmington, 1959—. Sgt. USAAF, 1942-45. Roman Catholic. Home: 110 N Broad St Penns Grove NJ 08069-1269 Office: Jim Reilley Studio 200 W 10th St Wilmington DE 19801-1633

REILLY, DANIEL PATRICK, bishop; b. Providence, May 12, 1928; s. Francis E. and Mary (Burns) R. Student, Our Lady of Providence Sem., 1943-48, Grand Seminaire, St. Brieuc, France, 1948-53, Harvard U., 1954-55, Boston Coll., 1955-56; D. (hon.), Providence Coll., St. Michael'sColl., Holy Apostles Coll. and Sem., Salve Regina Coll., Our Lady of Providence Coll., Sacred Heart U. Ordained priest Roman Catholic Ch., 1953; asst. pastor Cathedral Saints Peter and Paul, Providence, 1953-54; asst. chancellor Diocese of Providence, 1954-56, sec. to bishop, 1956-64, chancellor, 1964-72, adminstr., 1971-72, vicar gen., 1972-75; became monsignor, 1965, consecrated bishop, 1975; bishop of Norwich, Conn., 1975—; Conn. state chaplain K.C., 1976—; Episcopal moderator Nat. Cath. Cemetery Corp., 1977-87; mem. ad hoc com. to aid ch. in Ea. Europe NCCB/U.S. Cath. Conf., also mem. adminstrv. com.; mem. pro-life com. NCCB, 1989—; mem. Priestly Life and Ministry com., 1991—; past pres. New Eng. Consultation Ch. Leaders; mem. drafting com. U.S. Cath. Conf. Pastoral Letter, mem. com. on communications; mem. Holy See Pontifical Coun.-Cor Unum, 1984-89. Trustee Cath. Mut. Relief Soc. Omaha, 1979—, St. John's Sem., Brighton, Mass., 1987—; bd. dirs. United Way Southeastern Conn., 1976—, Conn. Drug and Adv. Coun., 1978-80; chmn. bd. Cath. Relief Svcs., 1978-86; mem. fin. and budget com. U.S. Cath. Conf., 1985-87; chancellor Holy Apostles Coll. and Sem., Cromwell, Conn., 1985; mem. Conn. Cath. Conf., Christian Conf. Conn.; pres. Conn. Interfaith Housing. Lodge: Rotary. Home: 274 Broadway Norwich CT 06360-3527 Office: 201 Broadway PO Box 587 Norwich CT 06360-0587

REILLY, EDWARD ARTHUR, lawyer; b. N.Y.C., Dec. 17, 1943; s. Edward Arthur and Anna Marguerite (Sautter) R.; children: M. Teresa, Edward A. A.B., Princeton U., 1965; J.D., Duke U., 1968. Bar: N.Y. 1969, N.C. 1971, Fla. 1979, Conn. 1983. Asst. dean law sch. Duke U., 1970-72; assoc. Shearman & Sterling, N.Y.C., 1972-80, ptnr., 1980-87; ptnr. Harlow, Reilly, Derr & Stark, Research Triangle Park, N.C., 1988-90; counsel Morris & McVeigh, N.Y.C., 1991—. Served to lt. USNR, 1968-70. Fellow Am. Coll. Trust & Estate Counsel; mem. N.Y. State Bar Assn., N.C. Bar Assn., Fla. Bar Assn., Conn. Bar Assn. Episcopalian. Office: Morris & McVeigh 767 3rd Ave New York NY 10017-2023

REILLY, EDWARD JOHN, fire protection consulting company executive; b. Syracuse, N.Y., Apr. 2, 1923; s. John Paul and Margaret (Shamock) R.; m. Marjorie Helen Cook, Jan. 29, 1949; children: Maureen Ann, Patrick Brian, Thomas Kevin, Timothy John, Dennis Edward, Daniel Lawrence. BA, St. Bonaventure U., 1949; postgrad., Fordham U., 1949-51. Dir. info. Nat. Fire Sprinkler Assn., N.Y.C., 1956-70; v.p. Nat. Fire Sprinkler Assn., Mt. Kisco, N.Y., 1970-77; exec. v.p. Nat. Fire Sprinkler Assn., Paterson, N.Y., 1976-77; pres. Nat. Fire Sprinkler Assn., Patterson, N.Y., 1977-85, ret., 1985; pres. Ed Reilly Assocs., Kinderhook, N.Y., 1985—. Editor: Sprinkler Quar., 1956-74, Sprinkling of News, 1968-77; contbr. articles to profl. jours. Capt. Rep. Nat. Com., N.Y.C., 1949-52, leader Rep. Bronx election campaign, 1950-51; mem. 8th Air Force Hist. Soc.; trustee Kinderhook Meml. Libr. With USAAF, 1943-45. Named Fire Protection Engring. Man of Yr., Manhattan Coll., N.Y.C., 1985; recipient Henry Parmalee award for outstanding lifetime achievement to fire protection in Am., 1987. Mem. Full Gospel Businessmen's Fellowship Internat., Am. Legion (chpt. vice comdr. 1950-51). Roman Catholic. Address: 12 Chatham St Kinderhook NY 12106

REILLY, HAROLD V. PAT, museum executive director; b. Hackensack, N.J., July 2, 1924; s. Harold V. and Edith Ellen (Wolter) R.; m. Alice M. Morrissey, Sept. 23, 1947 (div.); children: Michele L., Richard V., Debra A. McNerny. BA, Pace Inst., 1947. Photo journalist The Record Newspaper, Hackensack, N.J., 1948-52; pub. rels. dir. U.S. Steamship Lines, N.Y.C., 1953-69, Pan Am. Airways, N.Y.C., 1969-73; pres. H.V. Pat Reilly Assoc., Oradell, N.J., 1973—; cons. dir. Aviation Hall of Fame of N.J., Teterboro, 1973—; travel journalist various mags., N.J., 1973—; trustee Aviation Hall of Fame of N.J., Teterboro, 1972-92; co-founder Musee Am., Ver-sur-Mer, France, 1987-92. Author: Balloon to the Moon, 1992, New Jersey's Aeronautical Heritage, 1984, Pictorial History Teterboro Airport, 1983; writer: (film) Superliner Writes Headlines, 1964, Memories of an Airfield, 1985; contbr. more than 1,000 travel columns to mags. Advisor Salvation Army, Hackensack, 1973-92; co-founder Vets. for Eisenhower, Bergen County, N.J., 1952. Sgt. Mech Cavalry, 1943-45. Recipient Preservation Leadership award, 1990, Edn. Championship, 1991. Mem. Am. Legion, Rotary, N.J. Mus. Assn., N.J. Hist. Soc., Working Press Assn. of N.J., North Am. Travel Journalist. Home and Office: 285 Genther Ave Oradell NJ 07649-2108

REILLY, JAMES PATRICK, import and distribution company executive; b. Vineland, N.J., July 19, 1940; s. Joseph Patrick and Frances Margaret (Brown) R.; m. Ann Mary Vastano, Sept. 15, 1962; children: James Patrick, Diane, Michael, Christine. BS in Acctg., St. Joseph's U., Phila., 1962. CPA, N.J. Audit mgr. Price Waterhouse, Newark, 1962-68; sr. v.p., chief fin. officer Metrocare Inc., South Amboy, N.J., 1969-74; sr. v.p. Hanson Industries, Iselin, N.J., 1975-81; sr. v.p., chief fin. officer Fasig-Tipton Inc., Elmont, N.Y., 1981-84; pres., chief operating officer N.Am. Watch Co., N.Y.C., 1985-89; pres., chief exec. officer, dir. Cantel Industries, Fairfield, N.J., 1989—. Mem. KC. Roman Catholic. Office: Cantel Industries Inc 180 Passaic Ave Fairfield NJ 07004-3503

REILLY, JOHN HURFORD, French educator; b. Penn Yan, N.Y., Oct. 31, 1934; s. Thomas Angelo and Mildred Ansley (Hurford) R. BA, Syracuse U., 1956; postgrad., U. Montpellier, France, 1956-57; MA, U. Wis., 1958, PhD, 1964. Instr. Bowling Green (Ohio) State U., 1961-63; lectr. Queens Coll. of CUNY, Flushing, 1963-64, instr., 1964-67, asst. prof., 1967-71, assoc. prof., 1971-79, prof. French, 1979—, dean arts and humanities, 1982—. Author: Jean Giraudoux, 1978, Arthur Adamov, 1974, Intermezzo, 1967. Mem. Phi Beta Kappa. Home: 10 Park Ave Apt 19A New York NY 10016-4338 Office: Queens Coll Kissena Blvd Flushing NY 11367

REILLY, JOHN REGIS, transportation executive; b. Pitts., Sept. 27, 1935; s. Matthew P. and Margaret C. (Bohn) R.; m. Margaret A. Conway, June 2, 1962; children: Kevin, Daniel, Megan. BS, Duquesne U., 1961. Sales rep. U.S. Rubber Corp., Pitts., 1961-63; terr. mgr. Hunt-Wesson Industries, Pitts., 1963-66; safety engr. Crum-Forster Ins. Cos., Pitts., 1966-69; div. safety engr. Koppers Co., inc., Pitts., 1969-72; dir. corp. safety Fisher Sci. Group, Inc., Pitts., 1972-89; mgr. health and safety dept. Port Authority of Allegheny County, Pitts., 1989—; lectr., tchr. to various convs. and univs., 1972—. Tech. cons. to film: 28 Grams of Prevention, 1975 (Golden Eagle award CINE); author audio/visual presentation Worker Right-to-Know and Hazard Recognition, 1989; author: Fisher Manual of Lab Safety, 1975; contbr. articles to profl. publs. Instr. ARC, Pitts., 1975-82. Mem. Am. Soc. Safety Engrs. (admissions com. 1970—, Pres. Circle award 1990), Western Pa. Safety Coun. (bd. dirs. 1990), Nat. Safety Coun. Home: 76 Victoria Cir Pittsburgh PA 15220-2707 Office: Port Authority Allegheny Co 2235 Beaver Ave Pittsburgh PA 15233-1080

REILLY, ROBERT KEVIN, sales and marketing official; b. Rahway, N.J., Sept. 13, 1953; s. Robert Richard and Helen (Medvigy) R.; m. Mary Consuela MacDonald, May 19, 1978; children: Kathleen Anne, Colleen Erin. BS, U. Scranton, 1975; postgrad., Rutgers U., Newark, 1977-78; MBA, Bryant Coll., 1983. Prodn. planner Fedders corp., Edison, N.J., 1975-76, C.R. Bard, Inc., Murray Hill, N.J., 1976-78; master planner Dennison Mfg. Co., Inc., Framingham, Mass., 1978-80; sr. project planner The Foxboro (Mass.) Co., 1980-85; gen. mgr. Sandwich (Mass.) Lumber Co., Inc., 1986-91; sales and mktg. product rep. atlantic Building Products, Inc., Lakeville, Mass., 1991—; adj. instr. Newbury Coll., Brookline, Mass., 1984—, Anna Maria Coll., Paxton, Mass., 1988-89; fin. advisor Corpus Christi Ch., Sandwich, Mass., 1991—. Mem. KC (grand knight 1988-89, fin. sec. 1989—, dist. warden, 1990—, Knight of Yr. Sandwich Coun. 1991). Roman Catholic. Home: 19 Oxford Rd East Sandwich MA 02537-1314 Office: Atlantic Bldg Products Inc Rte 18 Lakeville MA 02347

REILLY, WILLIAM KANE, government official, lawyer, conservationist; b. Decatur, Ill., Jan. 26, 1940. B.A. in History, Yale U., 1962; J.D., Harvard U., 1965; M.S. in Urban Planning, Columbia U., 1971. Bar: Ill., Mass. 1965. Atty. firm Ross & Hardies, Chgo., 1965; asso. dir. Urban Policy Center, Urban Am., Inc., also Nat. Urban Coalition, Washington, 1969-70; sr. staff mem. Pres.'s Council Environ. Quality, 1970-72; exec. dir. Task Force Land Use and Urban Growth, 1972-73; pres. Conservation Found., Washington, 1973-89, World Wildlife Fund, Washington, 1985-89; adminstr. U.S. EPA, Washington, 1989—; former dir. Concern, Inc.; bd. dirs. Sol Feinstone Environ. Awards, Piedmont Environ. Council; chmn. bd. Partners for Livable Places, 1980-88; former trustee Am. Farmland Trust; chmn. Natural Resources Council Am., 1982-83; trustee German Marshall Fund U.S.; former trustee Northeast Utilities; del., workshop chmn. White House Conf. Balanced Growth and Econ. Devel., 1978; adv. Garden Club Am.; mem. citizens adv. com. to Habitat, 1976; UN Conf. Human Settlements. Editor: the use of Landm 1974; author articles in field, chpts. in books. Served to capt., CIC U.S. Army, 1966-67. Clubs: University (Washington), Univ. (N.Y.C.), Explorers (N.Y.C.). Office: EPA 401 M St SW Washington DC 20460-0002

REIMAN, DONALD HENRY, English educator; b. Erie, Pa., May 17, 1934; s. Henry Ward and Mildred Abbie (Pearce) R.; m. Mary Warner, 1958 (div. 1974); 1 child, Laurel Elizabeth; m. Hélène Liberman Dworzan, Oct. 3, 1975. A.B., Coll. of Wooster, 1956, Litt.D., 1981; M.A., U. Ill., 1957, Ph.D., 1960. Instr. English, Duke U., Durham, N.C., 1960-62, asst. prof., 1962-64; assoc. prof. U. Wis., Milw., 1964-65; adj. assoc. prof. grad. program in English CUNY, 1967-68; adj. prof. Columbia U., N.Y.C., 1969-70, sr. rsch. assoc. in English, 1970-73; vis. prof. St. John's U., Jamaica, N.Y., 1974-75; editor Shelley and His Circle, Carl H. Pforzheimer Library, N.Y.C., 1965-86, N.Y. Pub. Libr., 1986—; vis. lectr. U. Ill., 1963; vis. prof. U. Wash., Seattle, 1981, NYU, 1992; Lyell reader in bibliography Oxford U., 1988-89; cons. Harvard U. Press, Yale U. Press, Princeton U. Press, John Hopkins U. Press, Garland Pub. Inc., W.W. Norton, Oxford U. Press, others. Author: Shelley's The Triumph of Life, A Critical Study, 1965, 2d edit., 1979, Percy Bysshe Shelley, 1969, 2d edit., 1990, (with D.D. Fischer) Byron on the Continent, 1974; English Romantic Poetry, 1800-1835, 1979, Romantic Texts and Contexts, 1987, Intervals of Inspiration: The Skeptical Tradition and the Psychology of Romanticism, 1988; editor: Shelley and His Circle, Vols. V-VI, 1973, Vols. VII-VIII, 1986, The Romantics Reviewed: Contemporary Reviews of English Romantic Writers, 9 vols., 1972; (with S.B. Powers) Shelley's Poetry and Prose: A Norton Critical Edition, 1977; The Romantic Context: Poetry, 128 vols., 1976-79; (with M.C. Jaye and B.T. Bennett) The Evidence of the Imagination, 1978; gen. editor: Manuscripts of the Younger Romantics; I The Esdaile Notebook: A Facsimile, 1985, II The Mask of Anarchy: Facsimiles, 1985, III Hellas, 1985, V The Harvard Shelley Poetic Manuscripts, 1991; editor in chief: The Bodleian Shelley Manuscripts,

1984—; I Peter Bell The Third and the Triumph of Life, 1986, VII Shelley's Last Notebook and Other MSS, 1990; mem. edit. com. adv. bd. Milton and the Romantics, 1975-80, Studies in Romanticism, 1977—, Romanticism Past and Present, 1980-86, Text, 1981—, Nineteenth-Century Literature, 1986—, Nineteenth-Century Contexts, 1987—; contbr. articles to books and profl. jours. Active Common Cause. Am. Coun. Learned Socs. fellow, 1963-64, Wesleyan Ctr. Advanced Studies fellow, 1963-64, NEH fellow, 1978; grantee Am. Coun. Learned Socs., 1961, NEH, 1983—. Mem. AAUP, MLA (life), Modern Humanities Rsch. Assn. (life), Wordsworth-Coleridge Assn. Am. (founder), Byron Soc. (Am. com. 1973—), Keats-Shelley Assn. Am. (bd. dirs., treas. 1973-91, v.p. 1991—, Disting. Scholar award 1987), Bibliog. Soc. Am., Soc. Textual Scholarship (exec. com. 1981—), Coleridge in Somerset Assn., Charles Lamb Soc., Assn. for Documentary Editing. Democrat. Presbyterian. Home: 6495 Broadway Apt 6M Bronx NY 10471-2700 Office: NY Pub Libr Rm 226 5th Ave # 42D New York NY 10011-8800

REIMER, JEFFREY CHARLES, data processing consultant; b. Pitts., Jan. 26, 1963; s. Charles Duerr and Catherine Irene (Munce) R. AS in Computer Sci., California (Pa.) U., 1983, BS in Mgmt. and Computer Sci., 1985, MS in Bus. Adminstrn., 1990. Lic. stockbroker. Data mgmt. coord. Washington (Pa.)-Greene Community Action, 1985-88; programmer analyst A.C. Coy Co., Canonsburg, Pa., 1988-89; data processing supr. J Wood div. WCI, Milroy, Pa., 1989-91; investment exec. USLICO Securities, Arlington, Va., 1989—; mng. rep. Nat. Telephone & Communications, Charleroi, Pa., 1991—. V.p. mfg. Jr. Achievment Dist., Charleroi, Pa., 1981; treas. Rep. Party, Washington, 1986. Mem. Elks. Home: RR 1 Box 573C Charleroi PA 15022-9109

REIMERS, NAOMI HEADLEY, guidance counselor, educator, retired; b. Johnstown, Pa., Aug. 29, 1920; d. Clarence Roy and Jane Mable (Eakins) Hammel; m. Earl William Headley, Aug. 6, 1940 (dec. Sept. 1981); m. Charles Frederick Reimers, Jan. 1, 1984; 1 child, Sharon Lee. BA, Keuka Coll., 1940; MS, SUNY, Buffalo, 1955, PhD, 1973. Cert. counseling, sec. sch. English, K-8 common br. subjects. Spl. edn. tchr. Sweet Home Cen. Schs., Williamsville, N.Y., 1940-43; high sch. English tchr. Sweet Home Cen. Schs., Williamsville, 1950-58, guidance counselor, 1958-77; bd. dirs. Erie County Mental Health Assn., 1962-68; adminstrv. v.p. internat. bd. Parents Without Ptnrs., 1965-68; nat. trainer social outreach program Widowed Persons Svc., AARP, 1980-90; exec. com. N.Y. State Ret. Tchrs. Assn., 1991—; lectr., workshop leader ednl. and self-help orgns., 1978—. Editor: (bi-monthly newsletter) The Bellringer, 1965-68, (guidance series) Seeing Ourselves, 1970-76; contbr. articles to profl. jours. Recipient Community Svc. award Western N.Y. Pers. and Guidance Assn., 1965, Outstanding Alumni award Keuka Coll., Keuka Park, N.Y., 1975, Ecumenical and Community Svc. award Buffalo and Erie County Coun. of Chs., 1988, Outstanding Svc. and Support award Canine Helpers for the Handicapped Inc., 1990. Mem. Delta Kappa Gamma. Republican. Methodist. Home: 247 Greenwood Dr East Aurora NY 14052-1351

REINA See **COHEN, REINA JOYCE**

REINER, GLADYS AISMAN, art consultant; b. N.Y.C., June 17, 1926; d. Alexander and Lillian (Harrison) Aisman; m. Jules Reiner, Feb. 12, 1948; children: Laura, Wendy. BA, NYU, 1948. Social worker N.Y.C., 1948-50; co-owner Reiner Realty Co., N.Y.C., 1990—. Contbr. articles to profl. jours. Mem. Mus. Modern Art, Whitney Mus., Guggenheim, Met. Mus. Art, Hofstra Mus. Art. Office: Reiner Realty Co PO Box 875 Old Lyme CT 06371-0875

REINERT, CLIFFORD DANIEL, aerospace executive; b. Pottstown, Pa., Nov. 20, 1946; s. Daniel Renninger and Marion Joyce (Nester) R.; m. Sandra Lee Fronheiser Reinert, Apr. 7, 1947; children: Tracy Lynn, Bradley Scott. Degree in Bus. mgmt., Peirce Jr. Coll., 1967; degree in Bus. Adminstrn., Ursinus Coll., 1979. Property adminstrn. Firestone Plastics Co., Pottstown, Pa., 1967-72; fin. analyst Firestone Tire & Rubber Co., Pottstown, Pa., 1972-80; program cost GE Co., Valley Forge, Pa., 1980-85; section adminstrn. GE Space Systems, Phila., 1985-88; adminstr. GE Aerospace, Valley Forge, Pa., 1988—; resource devel. RAC Assoc., Reading, Pa., 1990-91; distbr. Nightingale-Conant, Chgo., 1990-91. Auditor Douglas Twp. Gilbertsville, Pa., 1987—. Recipient Cert. Appreciation AIAA, Phila., 1991. Mem. AIAA (sr. mem., Greater Phila. sect., chmn., vice chmn., pub. policy councilman), CTM Pottstown Toastmasters Club. Home: 15 Estate Rd Boyertown PA 19512-1703 Office: GE Company Mail Stop 11B11 PO Box 8555 Philadelphia PA 19101-8555

REINERT, CRAIG GERARD, sales representative; b. Wilmington, Del., Oct. 17, 1967; s. Gerard E. and Patricia (Moyer) R. BA, Purdue U., 1989. Sales rep. Kibun Products Internat., Raleigh, N.C., 1989-90, Hallmark, Edison, N.J., 1990—. Home and office: 122 Hana Rd Edison NJ 08817-2043

REINERT, KENNETH ALLEN, economist; b. Springfield, Mass., Mar. 13, 1958; s. Robert Henry and Rosemarie (Drada) R.; m. Gelaye Debebe, May 11, 1991. BA, Boston U., 1980, MA, 1982; MA, U. Md., 1985, PhD, 1988. Internat. economist U.S. Internat. Trade Commn., Washington, 1988-91; lectr. U. Md., Catonsville, 1990-91; sr. internat. economist U.S. Internat. Trade Commn., Washington, 1991—; vis. asst. prof. Wellesley Coll., 1992—. Contbr. articles to profl. jours. Recipient Trade and Devel. fellowship U. Md., 1987-88, Award for Excellence in Geography, Boston U., 1980, Prof. Augustus Howe Buck scholarship Boston U., 1978-80. Mem. Am. Econ. Assn., Eastern Econ. Assn., Internat. Trade and Fin. Assn. Office: US Internat Trade Commn 500 E St SW Washington DC 20436

REINGOLD, IRVING, electronic engineer; b. Newark, Nov. 13, 1921; s. Harry and Anna (Naiman) R.; m. Marilyn Louise Cooper, Oct. 30, 1948; children: Lynne Barbara, Robin Gail. BS, Newark Coll. Engring., 1942, Engr., 1949. Lic. profl. engr., N.J. Sect. chief Electronics Tech. Devices Lab., Ft. Monmouth, N.J., 1955-63, deputy br. chief, 1963-67, br. chief, 1967-75, div. dir., 1975-81, deputy lab. dir., 1981-85; pvt. practice cons. Deal, N.J., 1985—; deputy army mem. DOD Adv. Group on Electron Devices. Contbr. articles to profl. jours. Recipient Frances Rice Darne award, 1978, Electronic Engring. Mgmt. award, 1985, Comdr's award U.S. Dept. Army, Meritorious Civilian Svc. award, Beatrice Winner Meml. award Soc. Info. Display, 1988, Profl. Achievement award IEEE, 1990; fellow Soc. Info. Display, 1973, IEEE, 1975. Mem. MIT Elec. Acad., Sigma Xi. Jewish. Home: 409 Runyon Ave Deal NJ 07723-1447

REINGOLD, IVER DAVID, chemistry educator; b. Concord, N.H., Aug. 29, 1949; s. Earle Martin and Irma Ruth (Pearlmutter) R.; m. Kay Suzanne Balmer, Dec. 28, 1974; children: Colin Walter, Alison Elizabeth. AB, Dartmouth Coll., 1971; PhD, U. Oreg., 1976. Asst. prof. Middlebury (Vt.) Coll., 1979-86; assoc. prof. Juniata Coll., Huntingdon, Pa., 1988—; vis. asst. prof. Haverford (Pa.) Coll., 1978-79, U. Chgo., 1983-84; vis. assoc. prof. Lewis & Clark Coll., Portland, Oreg., 1986-88. Grantee Rsch. Corp., NSF, Petroleum Rsch. Fund. Mem. Am. Chem. Soc., Coun. on Undergrad. Rsch., Pa. Assn. Gifted Edn. (pres. Huntingdon chpt. 1991—). Office: Juniata Coll Dept of Chemistry Huntingdon PA 16652

REINHARD, ARTHUR ELLIOT, physician; b. Bklyn., Sept. 3, 1933; s. David and Anne (Sackstein) R. BA, Cornell U., 1954; MD, NYU Med. Sch., 1958. Dep. dir. medicine Kingsbrook Jewish Med. Ctr., Bklyn., 1963-67, 69—; asst. prof. medicine Downstate Med. Ctr., Bklyn., 1963-67, 69—. Lt. col. U.S. Army, 1967-69, Vietnam. Mem. AMA, ACP, Bklyn. Gastroenterology Assn., Kings County Med. Soc., N.Y. State Med. Soc. Jewish. Office: Kingsbrook Jewish Med Ctr 585 Schenectady Ave Brooklyn NY 11203

REINHARD, KEITH LEON, advertising executive; b. Berne, Ind., Jan. 20, 1935; s. Herman L. and Agnes V. R.; m. Rose-Lee Simons, Nov. 7, 1976; children: Rachel, Elizabeth; children by previous marriage: Christopher, Timothy, Matthew, Geoffrey, Jacqueline. Student public schs., Berne. Comml. artist Kling Studios, Chgo., 1954-56; mgr. tech. communications dept. Magnavox Co., Ft. Wayne, Ind., 1957-60; creative/account exec. Biddle Co., Bloomington, Ill., 1961-63; exec. v.p., dir. creative services, pres. Needham, Harper & Steers, Inc., Chgo., from 1964; then chmn., chief exec. officer Needham, Harper & Steers/USA, Chgo.; also dir. Needham, Harper & Steers, Inc.; chmn., chief exec. officer DDB Needham Worldwide Inc., N.Y.C., 1986—, chmn. exec. com., 1989—. Episcopalian. Office: DDB Needham Worldwide Inc 437 Madison Ave New York NY 10022-7001*

REINHARDT, NICHOLAS, electrical technology consultant; b. Cin., Jan. 15, 1932; s. Harry Alfred and Helen Rosemary (Pinney) R.; m. Elizabeth Dixon Wright, Mar. 28, 1953 (div. 1986); children: Zen Clarke, Thomas Logan. BA, Harvard Coll., 1953; MBA, Harvard Sch. Bus., 1956. Instrument rated comml. pilot. Mfg. engr. Westinghouse Elec. Corp., Pitts., 1953-54; R&D engring. mgr. EG&G, Inc., Boston, 1956-70; v.p. and founder Concord Computing Corp., Bedford, Mass., 1970-72, Impulse Engring. Inc., Lexington, Mass., 1981-84; R&D engring. mgr. Electromagnetic Launch Rsch., Cambridge, Mass., 1986-88; R&D mgr. Integrated Applied Physics, Waltham, Mass., 1988—; prin. N. Reinhardt, Cons., Lexington, 1972—; vis. scientist MIT Fusion Power Lab., 1991. Inventor various elec. and mech. instruments and machines (9 U.S. patents), 1962—; designer world's first Megawatt Hydrogen Thyratron, 1975; contbr. articles to profl. jours. Mem. IEEE (sr.), Electrostatic Soc. Am., Cambridge Entomological Club, Associated Pilots, Harvard Mus. Assn., Cambridge Boat Club. Home: 440 Concord Ave Lexington MA 02173 Office: Integrated Applied Physics 50 Thayer Rd Waltham MA 02154

REINHART, RICHARD MERCER, JR., marketing professional; b. Phila., Sept. 16, 1942; s. Richard M. and Mary Platt (Cross) R.; divorced; children: Robert, Stephanie. BA in English, Muhlenberg Coll., 1965. Prodn. controller The Franklin Mint, Yeadon, Pa., 1967-70; asst. v.p. Nat. Liberty Corp., Frazer, Pa., 1971-74; v.p. Cavanagh Mktg. Corp., King of Prussia, Pa., 1974-76; pres. C.A.M.A., Inc., Hightstown, N.J., 1976—. Pres. Internat. Clamshell Pitching Club of Cape May (N.J.), 1976—; staff mem. Sta. WRDV-FM, 1989—. Mem. Phila. Direct Mktg. Assn. (v.p.), Direct Mktg. Assn. List Leaders, Cape May Cottagers' Assn., Aircraft Owners and Pilots Assn., Muhlenberg Coll. Alumni Assn., The No-Tones Acappella Singing Group. Home: 115 Carlton Ave Trenton NJ 08618-1421 Office: CAMA Inc PO Box 930 Hightstown NJ 08520-0930

REINHOLD, WALTER WILLIAM, organist, educator; b. Elizabeth, N.J., July 1, 1939; s. Walter Eric and Frances (Kleitsch) R. MusB, Westminster Choir Coll., Princeton, N.J., 1961; M of Sacred Music, Union Theol. Sem., N.Y.C., 1963; MA, NYU, 1967. Organist, choirmasteer, lectr. religion 1st Presbyn. Ch., Kearny, N.J., 1961—; lectr. music and humanities NYU, N.Y.C., 1968—; pres. Cultural Resources, Inc., Cranford, N.J., 1988—. Author: Computer Software History Western Civilization Culture 1.0, 1989, Culture 2.0, 1992. Mem. Am. Musicological Soc., Am. Guild Organists, Nat. Assn. Scholars, Spode Soc. Presbyterian. Office: 30 Iroquois Rd Cranford NJ 07016-3371

REINHORN, ANDREI M., civil engineering educator, consultant; b. Bucharest, Romania, Oct. 23, 1945; s. Moritz A. and Dina (Rosenfeld) R.; m. Tova A. Waldman, Oct. 15, 1968; children: Michael, Gad. BSc, Technion - Israel Inst. Tech., Haifa, 1968, DSc, 1978. Registered profl. engr., N.Y., Israel. Structural engr. Milstein & Singer, Cons. Engrs., Tel Aviv, 1972-73; structural engr. Haifa, 1973-79, Buffalo, 1980-85; vis. asst. prof. SUNY, Buffalo, 1979-81, asst. prof., 1981-86, assoc. prof., 1986-90, prof., 1990—; cons. Niagara Machine & Tolls, Buffalo, 1982—, WSF Industries, Buffalo, 1983—, Walt Disney World, L. Buenavista, Fla., 1986, Westinghouse, 1987-89, West Valley Nuclear Site, 1989; investigator at Nat. Ctr. Earthquake Engring. Rsch. Inventor, patentee press brake deflection compensation structure, patent disclosure on active bracing system for vibration mitigation; contbr. sci. articles to profl. jours. Pres. W.E.S.T. Age Group Swim Club, Buffalo, 1985. Served to capt. Israel Def. Force, 1968-72. Rsch. grantee NSF, 1983, 86-91, Nalge/Snyder Industries, 1987. Mem. ASCE (faculty advisor 1981-83, bd. dirs. 1986—, v.p. 1991—, Outstanding Service award 1982, 83, N.Y. State Profl. Engring. Educator of Yr. award 1991), Am. Concrete Inst., Earthquake Engring. Research Inst. Home: 12 Troy View Ln Buffalo NY 14221-3522 Office: SUNY Buffalo Dept Civil Engring 231 Ketter Hall Amherst NY 14260

REINIG, JAMES WILLIAM, radiologist; b. Augusta, Ga., May 20, 1954; s. William Charles and Marion (Borgstrom) R.; m. Ellen McGill Tinkler, June 14, 1980; children: Margaret, Ann. AB, Harvard Coll., 1976; MD, Med. U. S.C., 1980. Diplomate Am. Bd. Radiology, Am. Bd. Nuclear Medicine. Intern, resident, fellow in diagnostic radiology & nuclear medicine Med. U. of S.C., Charleston, 1980-84; staff radiologist NIH, Bethesda, Md., 1984-86; med. dir. Anne Arundel MRI, Annapolis, Md., 1986—. Contbr. articles to profl. jours. Recipient Editor's Recognition award Jour. Radiology, 1987, 88, 89, 90, 91. Mem. AMA, Soc. Magnetic Resonance in Medicine, Radiol. Soc. N.Am., Am. Roentgen Ray Soc., Am. Coll. Radiology. Presbyterian. Office: Anne Arundel MRI 235 Jennifer Rd Annapolis MD 21401-3041

REINITZ, JOYCE BARABAN, social worker; b. N.Y.C., Feb. 4, 1945; d. David and Min (Sarch) Baraban; m. Michael Reinitz, Aug. 10, 1975; children: Jed, Paul. BA, U. Conn., 1967; MSW, Columbia U., 1971. Social worker Neurol. Inst. Columbia Presbyn. Hosp., N.Y.C., 1971-73; social worker, therapist Jewish Family Svcs., N.Y.C., 1973-75; social worker, therapist, supr. 5th Ave. Ctr. for Psychotherapy, N.Y.C., 1975-78; pvt. practice N.Y.C., 1978-86; dir. Ctr. for Integrated Recovery, N.Y.C., 1986—; supr. sch. social work NYU, 1976-77; tng. staff Rubenfeld Synergy Tng., N.Y.C., 1984-88. Mem. NASW, N.Y. Soc. Ericksonian Hypnotherapy, Employee Assistance Profls., N.Y. Fedn. Alcohol Counselors, Com. for Physicians Health, Network Allied Profls. Office: Ctr for Integrated Recovery 14 W 17th St New York NY 10011-5716

REINTZEL, WARREN ANDREW, trust company executive; b. Phila., Jan. 4, 1945; s. Warren H. and Lorna (Geibel) R.; m. Susan Rodgers, Dec. 20, 1969; children: Lisa S., Kurt W. BA with high honors, U. Del., 1967; MA in History, Rutgers U., 1968; JD, U. Pa., 1971. Trust adminstrn. trainee First Pa. Bank, Phila., 1971, trust adminstr., 1972-73, trust officer, 1973-79, sr. trust officer, 1979-81; v.p. Provident Nat. Bank, Phila., 1981-86; v.p., head trust adminstrn. dept. Glenmede Trust Co., Phila., 1986—. Bd. trustees Wanamaker Inst., Phila., 1989—, Meml. Fund, Luth. Ch. of our Saviour, Haddonfield, N.J., 1989—. Mem. Phila. Bar Assn., Phila. Fin. Assn. (treas. bd. trustees 1987-89), Phila. Estate Planning Coun. (trustee 1991), Corp. Fiduciaries Assn. Phila. (mem. personal trust com. 1986-89), Phi Beta Kappa. Republican. Office: Glenmede Trust Co 229 S 18th St Philadelphia PA 19103-6144

REIS, ARTHUR HENRY, JR., university administrator; b. Chgo., Nov. 6, 1946; s. Arthur Henry and Ardell Louise (Tholotowsky) R.; m. Karen Wessell, June 17, 1970 (div.); children: Sally Wessell, Rodger Henry. BA, Cornell Coll., Mt. Vernon, Iowa, 1968; MA, Harvard U., 1969, PhD in Chemistry, 1972. Staff chemist Argonne (Ill.) Nat. Lab., 1974-79; adminstr., mem. faculty dept. chemistry Brandeis U., Waltham, Mass., 1979-82, dir. sci. resources and planning, 1982-86, assoc. dean for resources and planning, 1986-89, dir pre-coll. program Initiative Forefront Topics in Sci., 1983-89, project dir. Ctr. for Complex Systems, 1987—, assoc. provost, 1990-91, acting provost, dean of the faculty, 1991-92; assoc. provost Brandeis U., South Saint Waltham, Mass., 1992—. Contbr. chpts. to books, articles and abstracts to profl. jours. Chmn. adminstrv. bd. United Meth. Ch., Wellesley, Mass., 1984-91. 1st lt. USAF, 1970-74. Moore fellow in organic chemistry, 1970. Mem. Am. Chem. Soc., Am. Crystallographic Soc., Nat. Coun. Univ. Rsch. Adminstrs., Coun. for Chem. Rsch., Soc. Rsch. Adminstrs., Coun. on Fed. Rels., Phi Beta Kappa. Home: 28 Williams St Arlington MA 02174-5624 Office: Brandeis U Irving 104 PO Box 9110 415 South St Waltham MA 02254-2700

REIS, DONALD JEFFERY, neurologist, neurobiologist, educator; b. N.Y.C., Sept. 9, 1931; s. Samuel H. and Alice (Kiesler) R.; m. Cornelia Langer Noland, Apr. 13, 1985. A.B., Cornell U., 1953, M.D., 1956. Intern N.Y. Hosp., N.Y.C., 1956; resident in neurology Boston City Hosp.-Harvard Med. Sch., 1957-59; Fulbright fellow, United Cerebral Palsy Found. fellow London and Stockholm, 1959-60; research asso. NIMH, Bethesda, Md., 1960-62; spl. fellow NIH, Nobel Neurophysiology Inst., Stockholm, 1962-63; asst. prof. neurology Cornell U. Med. Sch., N.Y.C., 1963-67; asso. prof. neurology and psychiatry Cornell U. Med. Sch., 1967-71, prof., 1971—, First George C. Cotzias Disting. prof. neurology, 1982—; mem. U.S.-Soviet Exch. Program; mem. adv. coun. NIH; bd. sci. advisers Merck, Sharpe & Dohm, Sterling Rsch. Group; cons. Eli Lilly, Servier Pharms.; bd. dirs. China Seas, Inc., Charles Masterson Burbe Rsch. Found. Contbr. articles to profl. jours.; mem. editorial bd. various profl. jours. Recipient CIBA Prize award Am. Heart Assn. Fellow AAAS, ACP; mem. Am. Physiol. Soc., Am. Neurol. Assn., Am. Pharmacol. Soc., Am. Assn. Physicians, Telluride Assn., Am. Soc. Clin. Investigation, Century Assn., Ellis Island Yacht Club (commadore), Phi Beta Kappa, Sigma Xi, Alpha Omega Alpha. Home: 190 E 72d St New York NY 10021 also: 73 Water St Stonington CT 06378 Office: 1300 York Ave New York NY 10021-4896

REISACHER, CARL RAYMOND, lawyer; b. Pitts., Nov. 20, 1958; s. Raymond Melvin and Mary Louise (Geltz) R. BSBA, Duquesne U., 1979, JD, 1988; MBA, U. Pitts., 1980. Bar: Pa. 1988. Asst. corp. sec. Wean United, Inc., Pitts., 1982-86; corp. sec. Wean United, Inc., 1986-87; assoc. Reed Smith Shaw & McClay, Pitts., 1988—. Office: Reed Smith Shaw & McClay 435 6th Ave Pittsburgh PA 15219-1809

REISCHE, ALAN LAWRENCE, lawyer; b. Laconia, N.H., June 6, 1939; s. G. Merrill and Y. Natalie (Camann) R.; m. Joan B. Lazarus, July 11, 1965; children: James F., Margaret Ann. BA cum laude, Harvard U., 1962; LLB, U. Pa., 1965; LLM in Taxation, Boston U., 1970. Bar: N.H. 1965, U.S. Dist. Ct. N.H. 1968, U.S. Tax Ct. 1973. Ptnr. Sheehan, Phinney, Bass & Green, Manchester, N.H., 1965—; mem. bd. examiners State N.H., 1990-93. Mem. ABA, N.H. Bar Assn. Office: Sheehan Phinney Bass & Green 1000 Elm St Manchester NH 03101-1702

REISER, DAVID RICHARD, financial services company executive; b. Providence, Oct. 9, 1959; s. Milton P. and Hilda L. Reiser; m. Margaret A. Hoffinger, Aug. 11, 1985. BS, Rensselaer Polytech. Inst., 1981, MBA, 1982; MS, Coll. of Fin. Planning, 1991. Cert. fin. planner; lic. life accident and health ins. salesman; registered real estate salesman. Pres. Tech. Mgmt. Ltd., Providence, 1981-82; asst. to pres. Phoenix Data Systems, Albany, N.Y., 1982-84; dir. mktg. CAD/CAM Specialists, Schaumburg, Ill., 1984-85, Silicon Design Labs, Liberty Corner, N.J., 1985-86; v.p. GE Fin. Svcs./Kidder Peabody Retirement and Estate Planning, Providence, 1986—. Author: CAD/CAM Marketing Study, 1981. Mem. adv. bd. Womans and Infants Hosp., Providence, 1989—; adv. R.I. State Sci. Fair, Providence, 1990—; bd. dirs. Southeastern Mass. Region III Sci. Fair, Fall River, Mass., 1989—. Mem. Internat. Bd. Cert. Fin. Planners, Inst. Cert. Fin. Planners, Rensselaer Polytech. Inst. Alumni Club (pres. southeastern New England chpt. 1988—). Office: GE Fin Svcs/Kidder Peabody 1200 Fleet Center Providence RI 02903

REISER, EVELYN ELLIS, technical writer; b. Glen Ridge, N.J., Aug. 9, 1941; d. Theodore Aladar and Rose (Matyas) Ellis; m. Aug. 23, 1967 (div. 1969); 1 child, Frank Theodore. BS in English with honors, Boston State Coll., 1972, MEd in English, 1976. Bus. mktg. asst. New England Telephone, Boston, 1978-82; asst. facilities mgmt. AT&T, Basking Ridge, N.J., 1982-83; tech. writer Bellcore, Livingston, N.J., 1983—; mentor, methods, procedures Bellcore, Livingston, 1987—. Contbr. N.J. Citizens for Action, 1987—; mem. World Wildlife Fund, ASPCA. Recipient Exemplary Voluntary Efforts award U.S. Dept. Labor, 1989. Republican. Baptist. Home: 110 Westville Ave Caldwell NJ 07006-5815 Office: Bellcore 290 W Mt Pleasant Ave Livingston NJ 07039-2747

REISMAN, HAROLD BERNARD, biochemical engineer, consultant; b. Bklyn., Oct. 29, 1935; s. Jacob and Esther (Krystal) R.; m. Miriam Blessing Fish, Sept. 4, 1960; children: Jocelyn, Joseph. BS, Columbia U., 1956, PhD, 1965; MS, Cornell U., 1959. Sect. mgr. Merck & Co., Rahway, N.J., 1961-73; dir. mfg. Stauffer Chem. Co., Westport, Conn., 1973-88; v.p. ops. Organogenesis Inc., Cambridge, Mass., 1989—; mem. indsl. adv. bd. Mich. Biotech. Inst., Lansing, 1988—. Author: Economic Analysis of Fermentation Processes, 1988. Fulbright grantee Istituto Superiore di Sanita.

REISMAN, OTTO IGNAZ, physics educator, nuclear engineer; b. Vienna, Austria, July 29, 1928; came to U.S., 1951; s. Fred and Olga (Rozsa) R.; m. Eva Goliger; children: Edith, Deborah. BS in Physics, CCNY, 1957; MS in Physics, NYU, 1960, ME in Nuclear Engring., 1968, PhD in Nuclear Engring., 1973. Lic. fallout shelter analyst Dept. Def. Jr. engr. Weston Electric Instruments Corp., Newark, 1957-58; project engr. Bendix Corp., Teterboro, N.J., 1958-61; instr. physics St. Peter's Coll., Jersey City, 1961-62; asst. prof. physics N.J. Inst. Tech., Newark, 1962—; Parenter in field to profl. meetings. Contbr. articles to profl. jours. Mem. Am. Nuclear Soc., Am. Assn. Physics Tchrs. Home: 452 Ft Washington Ave New York NY 10033-4600 Office: NJ Inst Tech Dept Physics 323 High St Nutley NJ 07110-1434

REISMAN, RICHARD ROY, information services executive; b. Morristown, N.J., Apr. 12, 1947; s. Julius and Sylvia (Gindes) R.; m. Christine Zubrovich, June 3, 1972 (div. 1978); 1 child, Elizabeth; m. Dana Reed, Aug. 2, 1989. AB in Applied Math., Brown U., 1968; MS in Indsl. Engring., Lehigh U., 1972. Sr. info. systems staff Western Electric, N.Y.C., 1968-74; mgr. computer svcs. planning Mobil Corp., N.Y.C., 1974-84, mgr. hdqrs. ops., 1984-86, mgr. network mgmt., 1986-88; dir. computers and communications Standard & Poors, N.Y.C., 1988-90; dir. product devel. Baseline II, Inc., N.Y.C., 1990—. Mem. Assn. for Computing Machinery (nat. lectr. 1973-75). Office: Baseline 838 Broadway New York NY 10003

REISNER, GERALD SEYMOUR, biology educator; b. Bklyn., Apr. 10, 1926; s. Irving Reisner and Bessie (Shure) Sachs; m. Estelle Siegel, Aug. 21, 1949; children: Susan, Andrew, Bruce, Rebecca. AB, SUNY, Albany, 1949; PhD, Cornell U., 1956. Sci. tchr. Altamont (N.Y.) High Sch., 1949-52; plant physiologist USDA, Ithaca, N.Y., 1952-56; prof. sci. Goddard Coll., Plainfield, Vt., 1956-58; prof. biology Allegheny Coll., Meadville, Pa., 1958—; microbiologist USDA, Beltsville, Md., 1964-65, Bd. of Health, Meadville, Pa., 1958-70; advisor Inst. Rev. Bd. Meadville H.C., 1989—. Contbr. articles to profl. jours. Chmn. United Way, Meadville, 1990. With U.S. Army, 1943-46. Recipient Rsch. fellowship Nat. Acad. Sci., 1964, Ctr. Biology of Natural Systems, 1971. Mem. N.Y. Acad. Sci., Am. Soc. for Microbiology. Democrat. Jewish. Home: 356 Ben Avon St Meadville PA 16335-1220 Office: Allegheny Coll N Main St Meadville PA 16335-1111

REISS, JAMES HENRY, neurosurgical consultant; b. N.Y.C., July 26, 1938; s. Alfred and Homora (Friedmann) R.; m. Luce Lauer, June 10, 1961; children: Thomas, Hugh, Peter, Susan. AB, Harvard U., 1958, MD, 1962. Diplomate Am. Bd. Neurol. Surgery. Student advisor, instr. gen. edn. Harvard Coll., Cambridge, Mass., 1959-61; instr. neuroanatomy Albert Einstein Coll. Medicine, Bronx, N.Y., 1963-65, resident neurosurgery, 1963-68; asst. prof. surgery U. Tex. S.W. Med. Sch., Dallas, 1970-71; pvt. practice neurosurgery Springfield, Mass., 1971-91; neurosurg. cons. Springfield, 1992—. Maj. USAF, 1968-70. Recipient Fiction Prize, Atlantic Monthly, 1957/58. Democrat. Jewish. Home: 110 Overbook Rd Longmeadow MA 01106 Office: 125 Liberty St Springfield MA 01103

REISS, JOHN BARLOW, lawyer; b. London, Aug. 29, 1939; came to U.S., 1963; s. James Martin and Margaret Joan (Ping) R.; m. Mary Jean Maudsley, Aug. 6, 1967 (div. 1978); m. Kathleen Strouse, Aug. 2, 1979; 1 child, Juliette Blanche. BA with honors, Exeter U., Devon, Eng., 1961; AM, Washington U., St. Louis, 1966; PhD, Washington U., 1971; JD, Temple U., 1977. Bar: Pa. 1977, N.J. 1977, D.C. 1980, U.S. Dist. Ct. N.J. 1977, U.S. Supreme Ct. 1981, U.S. Dist. Ct. D.C. 1982. Economist Commonwealth Econ. Com., London, 1962-63; asst. prof. Allegheny Coll., Meadville, Pa., 1967-71; assoc. prof. Stockton State Coll., Pomona, N.J., 1971-75; asst. health commr. State of N.J., Trenton, 1975-79; dir. office of health regulation U.S. Dept. HHS, Washington, 1979-81; assoc. Baker & Hostetler, Washington, 1981-82; assoc. Dechert Price & Rhoads, Phila., 1982-86, ptnr., 1986—, asst. chair health law group, 1983-91; chmn. Health Law Group, 1991—. Mem. editorial bd.: Topics in Hosp. Law, 1985-86, Hosp. Legal Forms Manual, 1985—, Jour. Health Care Tech., 1984-86; contbr. Hosp. Contracts Manual, 1983—; contbr. articles to profl. jours. and chpts. to books. Bd. dirs. Gateway Sch. Little Children, Phila., 1986—. 2d Lt. Brit. Territorial Army, 1962-63. Pub. Health Svc. fellow, 1979-81, English Speaking Union fellow, 1963-66, Econ. Devel. Adminstr. fellow Washington U., 1966-67. Mem. Nat. Health Lawyers Assn., N.J. Soc. Hosp. Attys.,

Phila. Bar Assn., Am. Hosp. Assn., N.J. Hosp. Assn., Brit. Am. C. of C. of Greater Phila. (bd. dirs. 1991). Democrat. Home: 415 Wister Rd Wynnewood PA 19096-1808 Office: Dechert Price & Rhoads 4000 Bell Atlantic Tower 1717 Arch St Philadelphia PA 19103-2713

REISS, MARTIN HAROLD, manufacturing company executive; b. Long Beach, N.Y., Aug. 16, 1935; s. Arthur and Mary (Schreckinger) R.; m. Rhea Cohen, June 24, 1956; children—Mitchell, Randi, Robyn. B.S., MIT, 1956; M.S., Ohio State U., 1959; M.S., MIT, 1961. Staff member MIT Inst. Lab., Cambridge, 1959-61; tech. dir. Raytheon Co., Sudbury, Mass., 1961-65; pres. Alarmtronics Engring., Newton, Mass., 1965-73, Gamewell Corp., Medway, Mass., 1973-83, chmn. bd., 1983-90; dir. Cerberus Techs., Inc., Waltham, Mass., 1990—; sustaining fellow MIT, 1981—; bd. overseers WPI Fire Scis., Worchester, Mass., 1985—, chmn., 1989—; dir. Practicorp, Newton, 1984-88; dir., treas. Nat. Fire Protection Research Found., Quincy, Mass., 1982—; dir. Nat. Fire Protection Assn., Quincy, 1991—. Patentee in field. Trustee Mass. Bay Community Coll., Wellesley, 1980-90, chmn. bd., 1985-86. Served to capt. USAF, 1956-59. Mem. Nat. Elec. Mfg. Assn. (sect. chmn. 1983-85, Man of Yr. award 1985), Automatic Fire Alarm Assn. (pres. 1978-80, Man of Yr. award 1985, bd. dirs. 1980—), Soc. Fire Protection Engrs. (bd. dirs. 1988—). Office: Cerberus Techs Inc 51 Sawyer Rd Waltham MA 02154-3448

REISS, NATHAN M(ORRIS), meteorology educator; b. N.Y.C., Dec. 13, 1940; s. Leonhard and Irma (Goldblum) R.; m. Rose S. Wiesen, Aug. 25, 1968; children: Jeffrey, Laura. BS, CCNY, 1963; MS, Tex. A&M U., 1970; PhD, NYU, 1973. Meteorologist U.S. Weather Bur., Richmond, Va., 1963; rsch. asst. NYU, N.Y.C., 1968-72; instr., asst. prof. meteorology Rutgers U., New Brunswick, N.J., 1972, assoc. prof., 1979, dir. grad. program in meteorology, 1981—, acting chmn. dept., 1988-90, vice chmn. dept., 1990-91, chmn. dept., 1991—. Contbr. over 60 articles to profl. jours. Capt. USAF, 1963-67. Mem. Am. Meteorol. Soc. (pres. N.J. chpt. 1977-78), Air and Waste Mgmt. Assn. (chmn. microcomputer users com. 1983-86, student affairs com. 1989—, higher edn. div. 1990—), N.Y. Acad. Scis. (chmn. atmospheric scis. sect. 1979-80). Home: 308 Wayne St Highland Park NJ 08904-2718 Office: Rutgers U Dept Meteorology Cook Coll PO Box 231 New Brunswick NJ 08903-0231

REISS, ROBERT MARSHALL, orthopaedic surgeon; b. Long Beach, N.Y., Sept. 12, 1929; s. George Samuel and Anne Evelyn (Smith) R.; m. Sandra Jean Barnes, May 25, 1966; children: Michael Barnes, Jody Smith. BA, Columbia U., 1951, MD, 1959. Diplomate Am. Bd. Orthopaedic Surgery. Surg. intern St. Luke's Hosp., N.Y.C., 1959-60, surg. resident, 1960-61; orthopaedic resident Presbyn. Hosp., N.Y.C., 1961-64, chief orthopaedic resident, 1964-65; attending physician Huntington (N.Y.) Hosp., 1965—, chief dept. orthopaedic surgery, 1987—. Lt. (j.g.) USN, 1951-54, Korea. Fellow ACS (membership com. 1981—), Am. Acad. Orthopaedic Surgery (mem. com. 1983-86). Home: 9 Quail Hill Rd Lloyd Harbor NY 11743 Office: East Huntington Orthopedic Group 166 E Main St Huntington NY 11743-2975

REISSMANN, THOMAS LINCOLN, chemist; b. Wilmington, Del., Feb. 12, 1920; s. Ludwig and Margaretha (Schumann) R.; m. Maria Ann Robinson, Sept. 15, 1951; children: Alan, Elizabeth. BS in Chemistry, Pa. State U., 1942, MS in Chemistry, 1947, PhD in Chemistry, 1949. Asst. chief chemist Ky. Ordinance Works, Paducah, 1942-46; chemist Ethicon, Inc. (div. of Johnson and Johnson), New Brunswick, N.J., 1949-51, asst. to assoc. to sr. chemist, 1951-59, mgr. suture rsch., 1959-68, mgr., collagen products, 1968-72, mgr., chem. quality assurance, 1972-80, asst. to corp. dir. quality assurance, 1980-82, retired, 1982; cons. in field, Martinsville, N.J., 1982—. Patentee in field. Councilman, pres., Bound Brook N.J. Borough, 1960-66; bd. dirs. Somerset County, N.J. Mental Health Bd., 1976—, Pa. State U. Coll. of Sci. Alumni Bd., 1986—; adv. com. Somerset Hosp. Rsch., 1988—. Thomas L. Reissmann award established at Pa. State U., State Coll., 1985—. Democrat. Home: 24 Hillcrest Rd Martinsville NJ 08836-9643

REIST, ANDREAS, engineering firm executive; b. Zurich, Switzerland, Aug. 17, 1955; came to U.S., 1986; s. Walter Albert and Charlotte (Gerber) R. BSME, HTL Engring. Sch., Rapperswil, Switzerland, 1982. Mng. dir. Ferag AG, Hinwil, Switzerland, 1982-85; pres. Ferag Inc., Bristol, Pa., 1985-89; chief exec. officer, 1985—, also chmn. bd. dirs. Lt. Swiss army. Office: Ferag Inc Keystone Indsl Park PO Box 137 Tullytown PA 19007-0098

REITER, HENRY H., psychologist, educator; b. N.Y.C., May 13, 1936; s. David and Betty (Teicher) R. BA, NYU, 1957; MA, Hofstra U., 1959; PhD, St. John's U., Jamaica, N.Y., 1963. Diplomate in behavioral medicine. Assoc. prof. psychology C.W. Post Coll. of L.I. U., 1961—; dir. East Hills Cons., Roslyn, N.Y., 1966—, Cancer Hyno-Imagery Ctr., Roslyn, 1980—. Contbr. over 50 articles to profl. jours. Mem. APA, N.Y. State Psychol. Assn., Nassau County Psychol. Assn., Psychol. Law Soc., Am. Soc. Clin. Hypnosis. Office: Internat Acad Health Care 70 Glen Cove Rd Roslyn Heights NY 11577-1722

REITER, HOWARD LEE, political scientist, educator; b. Hanover, Pa., Sept. 29, 1945; s. Harry and Sally (Hayden) R.; m. Laura Rosen, June 28, 1972. BA, Cornell U., 1967; AM, Harvard U., 1969, PhD, 1975. Instr. U. Notre Dame, Ind., 1972-74; prof. U. Conn., Storrs, 1974—; lectr. U.S. Info. Agy., Western Europe; cons. CBS News, N.Y.C., 1980. Author: Selecting the President, 1985 (Choice Mag. award 1986-87), Parties and Elections, 1987; mem. editorial bd. Polity, 1980—. Recipient Pi Sigma Alpha award N.E. Polit. Sci. Assn., 1975; Fulbright scholar, 1987. Mem. Phi Beta Kappa. Office: U Conn PO Box U24 Storrs Mansfield CT 06269-1024

REITTINGER, DONNA LIS, psychology educator; b. Cohoes, N.Y., July 2, 1949; d. John Henry and Loretta Ann (Stalter) Lis; m. William George Reittinger, Nov. 20, 1981. BA, SUNY, Albany, 1971, MS, 1974, PhD, 1978. Adj. instr. Hudson Valley Community Coll., Troy, N.Y., 1973, Schenectady (N.Y.) County Community Coll., 1973, Coll. St. Rose, 1975; instr. Coll. St. Rose, Albany, 1978—; adjunct instr. Russel Sage Coll., Troy, N.Y., 1975-77; prof. Coll. St. Rose, Albany, 1992—; cons., instr. Nat. Tchr. Corps, Albany, 1973-75; cons. Russell Sage Coll., Troy, N.Y., 1975-77. Contbr. articles to profl. jours., 1978—. Vol. instr. St. Peter's Hospice, Albany, N.Y., 1990-91. Mem. Am. Psychol. Assn. Home: 7 Cedarcrest Dr Saratoga Springs NY 12866-5324 Office: Coll St Rose Western Ave Albany NY 12203-1026

REITZ, H(OWARD) WESLEY, construction company executive; b. Bellefonte, Pa., Apr. 17, 1947; s. Myron Wesley and Isabel (Jodon) R.; m. Carol Frances Stamm, Nov. 27, 1965; children: Brian Wesley, Douglas Myron, Karen Lea. BSCE, Pa. State U., 1969. Registered profl. engr., Pa., Va., W.Va. Survey and quality control technician The Lane Constrn. Co., Meriden, Conn., 1966-67, job engr., 1968-72, asst. supt., 1973-74, supt., 1975-78, 1979-83, asst. dist. mgr., 1984, dist. mgr., 1985—. Mem. ASCE, NRA, Am. Concrete Inst., Northumberland County Hist. Soc., Berks County Hist. Soc., Moose. Republican. Methodist. Home: 1828 Walnut Grove Dr State College PA 16801-8440 Office: The Lane Constrn Corp 965 E Main St Meriden CT 06450-6004

RELKIN, PARRIS CRAIG, stage producer; b. Boston, Sept. 18, 1954; s. Jerome J. and Henrietta J. (Hoe) R. BA, Cen. Mich. U., 1980. Prodn. mgr. Limbo Theatre, N.Y.C., 1983-84; promotion mgr. Tony Gonda Design, N.Y.C., 1984-85; bus. rep. Actors Equity Assn., N.Y.C., 1986-90; mng. dir. Home for Contemporary Theatre and Art, N.Y.C., 1990-91; asst. producer, co-author, co-editor BEER NUTS Blazing Blue Prodns., N.Y.C., 1991—. Gen. mgr. Rushmore Arts Festival, 1992. Mem. Actors Equity Assn. Office: Home Contemporary Theatre 61 E 8th St Ste 315 New York NY 10003

RELMAN, ARNOLD SEYMOUR, physician, educator; b. N.Y.C., June 17, 1923; s. Simon and Rose (Mallach) R.; m. Harriet Morse Vitkin, June 26, 1953; children: David Arnold, John Peter, Margaret Rose. A.B., Cornell U., 1943; M.D., Columbia U., 1946; LLD (hon.), U. Pa.; ScD (hon.), Med. Coll. Wis., Union U., Med. Coll. Ohio, CUNY; DMSc (hon.), Brown U.; DLH (hon.), SUNY; LittD (hon.), Temple U. Diplomate Am. Bd. Internal Medicine. House officer New Haven Hosp., Yale, 1946-49; NRC fellow Evans Meml., Mass. Meml. hosps., 1949-50; practice medicine, specializing in internal medicine Boston, 1950-68, Phila., 1968-77; asst. prof., prof. medicine Boston U. Sch. Medicine, 1950-68; dir. Boston U. Med. Services, Boston City Hosp., 1967-68; prof. medicine, chmn. dept. medicine U. Pa.; chief med. services Hosp. of U. Pa., 1968-77; editor New Eng. Jour. Medicine, Boston, 1977-91, editor emeritus, 1991—; sr. physician Brigham and Women's Hosp., Boston, 1977—; prof. medicine Harvard Med. Sch., 1977—; Cons. NIH, USPHS. Editor: Jour. Clin. Investigation, 1962-67, (with F.J. Ingelfinger and M. Finland) Controversy in Internal Medicine, Vol. 1, 1966, Vol. 2, 1974; contbr. articles to profl. jours. Trustee Columbia U., 1990—; bd. dirs. Hastings Ctr. Recipient Columbia Alumni Gold medal, 1980, Disting. Service award Am. Coll. Cardiology, 1987. Fellow Am. Acad. Arts and Scis., ACP (master, John Phillips medal 1985); mem. Assn. Am. Physicians (council, pres. 1983-84), Am. Physiol. Soc., AMA, Mass. Med. Soc., Inst. Medicine of Nat. Acad. Scis. (council 1979-82), Am. Soc. Clin. Investigation (past pres.), Am. Fedn. Clin. Research (past pres.), Phi Beta Kappa (senator 1991—), Alpha Omega Alpha. Office: Brigham and Women's Hosp Dept of Medicine 75 Francis St Boston MA 02115-6195

REMALEY, ALLEN RICHARD, secondary education educator, school system administrator; b. Clearfield, Pa., Apr. 23, 1939; s. John R. and Ruth V. (Sarvey) R.; m. Marilyn E. Baughman, Sept. 15, 1959; children: Brooks Marcel, Janine Michelle. BS in Edn., French, Lock Haven (Pa.) U., 1964; MA in French, Pa. State U., 1969; DA, SUNY, Stony Brook, 1990. Tchr. French Bradford (Pa.) Area High Sch., 1964-68; NDEA non teaching fellow Pa. State U., University Park, 1968-69; head fgn. lang. dept., tchr. French Saratoga Springs (N.Y.) City Schs., 1968-89; head fgn. lang. dept. Saratoga Springs City Schs., 1989—. Contbr. articles to profl. jours. Organizer of the Community's Foreign Language Night, 1974-89. Cpl. USMC, 1957-60, PTO. Mem. Saratoga Springs Tchrs. Assn. (bldg. rep. 1986-89), Am. Assn. Tchrs. French (pres. Hudson Valley chpt. 1975-77), N.Y. State Assn. Foreign Language Tchrs. (bd. dirs. 1988-90, recipient Ruth E. Wasley Disting. Foreign Language Tchr. in the State of N.Y. award, 1984). Republican. Home: 4 W Circular Ct Saratoga Springs NY 12866-6013 Office: Saratoga Springs High Sch West Circular St Saratoga Springs NY 12866

REMALEY, ANDREW JACOB, construction executive; b. Greensburg, Pa., June 24, 1951; s. Robert and Sara (Leslie) R.; divorced; 1 child, Gavin Andrew. Student, Montgomery County C.C. Pres. Emaley Constrn. Co., Inc., Villanova, Pa., 1983—. Musician, percussionist, and drummer, 1965-92; designer houses, 1973-92. Mem. Nat. Assn. Home Builders, Nat. Assn. Remodelers.

REMBAR, JAMES CARLSON, psychologist; b. N.Y.C., May 4, 1949; s. Charles Isaiah and Billie Ann (Olsson) R.; m. Jill Bailin, June 4, 1988. BA, Sarah Lawrence Coll., 1972; MA, U. Mich., 1976, PhD, 1978. Cert. Psychoanalyst, N.Y., psychologist. Clin. psychologist U. Mich. Med. Ctr., Ann Arbor, 1978-80; instr. psychology in psychiatry N.Y. Hosp. Cornell U. Med. Coll., White Plains, 1980-84, clin. asst. prof., 1984—, coord. child and adolescent psychology Westchester div., 1982-87; pvt. practice clin. psychologist Irvington, White Plains, N.Y., 1981—; faculty Westchester Ctr. Study Psychoanalysis and Psychotherapy, 1989—; cons. Andrus Children's Home, Yonkers, N.Y., 1987—. Contbr. articles to profl. jours., chpt. in book. Mem. Am. Psychol. Assn., N.Y. State Psychol. Assn., Westchester County Psychol. Assn., Psychoanalytic Assn. Westchester Ctr. Home and Office: 9 Sunnyside Pl Irvington NY 10533-1300 Office: 499 N Broadway White Plains NY 10603-3242

REMLINGER, FREDERICK ENDRE, graphic designer; b. New Brunswick, N.J., Dec. 30, 1957; s. Frederick Cornelius and Eleanor (Yuhaz) R.; m. Janet Nichols, Sept. 22, 1984; 1 child, Frederick Thomas. Student, Middlesex County Coll., 1975-77; BA, Spectrum Advt. Inst., 1977-80; student, Sch. Visual Arts, 1986-90. Art dir. Greenfield Distbrs., East Brunswick, N.J., 1979-80; illustrator Worrell Publs., Union, N.J., 1980-83; art dir. Timely Advt., Plainfield, N.J., 1983-86; promotional artist Warner-Lambert/Parke Davis, Morris Plains, N.J., 1986—. Barbara Swain Meml. grantee, 1979. Republican. Roman Catholic.

REMMERS, KURT WILLIAM, university administrator; b. Mineola, N.Y., Dec. 13, 1944; s. Herbert Kort and Irene Mary (Kelly) R.; children: Kirsten Norma, Megan Jennifer. BA in History, Westminster Coll., New Wilmington, Pa., 1966, MEd in Guidance and Counseling, 1967; MA in Ednl. Communications, NYU, 1970. Asst. dir. Ctr. for Ednl. Tech. Jersey City State Coll., 1969-70; dir Media Resource Ctr. Drew U., Madison, N.J., 1970—; founder, pres. Phokus, Inc., Madison, 1977—; producer, dir. Vital Link, Ednl. Consortium for Cable, 1978-79; workshop leader No. N.J. Video Symposium, Essex County Coll., Newark, 1977-79; founder, bd. dirs. N.J. Ednl. Media Consortium, 1974-76; ofcl. videographer Caesarea (Israel) Maritima Joint Expedition, 1984, Peace Mission, Masaya, Nicaragua, 1986; producer videotape Madisonian of the Yr., 1990. Producer, dir.; Conversation with Paul Hardin, 1987, Habitats in Balance, 1987, Images in Ice, 1988, Interface, 1988, Hartz Ferry, 1989, Purolator-Courier, 1989, Megamation, 1989, Daycare Today, 1989, Mead Hall Fire, 1989, Toon Kuijpers-Artist, 1989, Thomas Kean, Tenth President of Drew, 1990, USGA-Coming Home to Golf, 1990, others. With USAR, 1966-72. Recipient Cape award CTN, 1989, 90. Mem. Nat. Ednl. Assn. for Broadcasting. Democrat. Home: 56 Greenwood Ave Madison NJ 07940-2123 Office: Phokus Inc PO Box 361 Madison NJ 07940-0361

REMUS, MICHAEL T., accountant; b. Passaic, N.J., Nov. 8, 1957; s. Walter A. and Anna T. (Conway) R.; m. JoAnn McConaghy, June 25, 1985; children: Michael T., Jesse Lee. BA, William Paterson coll., Wayne, N.J., 1979. CPA. Pvt. practice Michael T. Remus, CPA, PA, Hamilton, N.J., 1985—. Treas. Kiwanis Club Hamilton (N.J.) Twp., 1990-91, Princeton (N.J.) Sr. Resource Ctr., 1990-91. Fellow New Soc. CPAs; mem. Am. Inst. CPAs. Office: 108 Robin Dr Trenton NJ 08619-1369

REN, CHUNG-LI, engineer; b. Chefoo, China, June 1, 1931; came to U.S., 1955; s. Shantsai and Fooching (Wang) R.; m. Rosalie Fen Lo, Aug. 4, 1962; children: Eric W., Caroline W. BSEE, Taiwan Coll. Engring., 1953; MSEE, U. Notre Dame, 1957; PhD in Electro Physics, Polytech Inst. Bklyn., 1964. Teaching asst. U. Notre Dame, South Bend, Ind., 1956-57; grad. asst., sr. lectr. Polytech Inst. Bklyn., Microwave Rsch. Inst., 1959-65; disting. mem. tech. staff AT&T Bell Labs., North Andover, Mass., 1965-90; lead engr. Mitre Corp., Advanced Satellite Terminals and Tech., Bedford, Mass., 1990—; speaker and panelist in field. Patentee in field; contbr. articles to profl. jours. Rsch. fellow Polytech Inst. Bklyn., 1957-59. Mem. IEEE (mem. review bd. 1982—, sr.), Sigma Xi. Office: The Mitre Corp Burlington Rd Bedford MA 01730

RENDELL, EDWARD GENE, mayor, lawyer; b. N.Y.C., Jan. 5, 1944; s. Jesse T. and Emma (Sloat) R.; B.A. in Polit. Sci., U. Pa., 1965; J.D., Villanova (Pa.) U., 1968; m. Marjorie Osterlund, July 10, 1971; 1 son, Jesse Thompson. Admitted to Pa. bar, 1968, U.S. Supreme Ct., 1981; asst. dist. atty., chief homicide unit Office Dist. Atty. Phila., 1968-74; dep. spl. prosecutor Phila., 1976; former dist. atty. Phila., from 1977; mayor City of Phila., 1992—. Served as 2d lt. USAR, 1968-74. Recipient Man of Year award VFW, 1980, Am. Cancer League, 1981; Disting. Public Service award Pa. County Detectives Assn., 1981. Mem. Am. Bar Assn., Pa. Dist. Attys. Assn. (legis. chmn. 1979—), Phila. Bar Assn., United Jewish Orgns., Jewish War Vets. Democrat. Club: B'nai B'rith. Home: 3425 Warden Dr Philadelphia PA 19129-1417 Office: City Hall Office of Mayor Room 215 Philadelphia PA 19107

RENDL-MARCUS, MILDRED, artist, economist; b. N.Y.C., May 30, 1928; d. Julius and Agnes (Hokr) Rendl. BS, NYU, 1948, MBA, 1950; PhD (Dean Bernice Brown Cronkhite fellow 1950-51), Radcliffe Coll., 1954; m. Edward Marcus, Aug. 10, 1956. Economist, GE, 1953-56, Bigelow-Sanford Carpet Co., Inc., 1956-58; lectr. econs. evening sessions CCNY, 1953-58; rsch. investment problems in tropical Africa, 1958-59; instr. econs. Hunter Coll. CUNY, 1959-60; lectr. econs. Columbia U., 1960-61; rsch. econ. devel. Nigeria, West Africa, 1961-63; sr. economist Internat. div. Nat. Indsl. Conf. Bd., 1963-66; asst. prof. Grad. Sch. Bus. Adminstrn., Pace Coll., 1964-66; assoc. prof. Borough of Manhattan Community Coll., CUNY, 1966-71, prof., 1972-85; vis. prof. Fla. Internat. U., 1986; prin. MRM Assocs., Rendl Fine Art; corp. art econ. cons.; fine arts appraiser; participant Internat. Economical Meeting, Amsterdam, 1968, Econs. of Fine Arts in Age of Tech., 1984, Internat. Economic Assn. N.Am., Laredo, Tex., 1987-88, Soc. Southwestern Economists, San Antonio, 1988, New Orleans, 1989, Dallas, 1989, Houston, 1991, S.W. Soc. Economists, San Antonio, 1992, San Diego, 1990, 92, Reno, 1991, Western Econ. Assn. Internat., 1990, Ind. U. Pa., 1990, London, 1992. Exhibited New Canaan Art Show, 1982, 83, 84, 85, New Canaan Soc. for Arts Ann., 1983, 85, New Canaan Arts, 1985, Silvermine Galleries, 1986, Stamford Art Assn., 1987, Women in the Arts at Phoenix Gallery, Group Show, N.Y.C., 1988, Parkview Point Gallery, Miami Beach, Fla., 1982-89, Art Complex, New Canaan, 1988-89; group shows include Lever House, N.Y.C., 1990, Cork Gallery, Lincoln Ctr., N.Y.C., 1990, Women's Caucus for Art, San Antonio, 1990, Artist's Equity, Borrome St. Gallery, N.Y.C., 1991, Greater Hartford Architecture Conservancy, 1991; symposium participant Sienna, Italy, 1988, South Fla. Art Ctr., Miami Beach, 1990; contbr. articles to Women in the Arts newsletter, 1986-87, Coalition Womens Art Orgns., 1986-87. Bd. dirs. N.Y.C. Coun. on Econ. Edn., 1970—; mem. program planning com. Women's Econ. Roundtable; participant Eastern Econ. Assn., Boston, 1988, Art and Personal Property Appraisal, NYU, 1986-88. Recipient Disting. Svc. award CUNY, 1985. Fellow Gerontol. Assn.; mem. Internat. Schumpeter Econs. Soc. (founding), Am. (vice chmn. ann. meeting 1973), Met. (sec. 1954-56) econ. assns., Indsl. Rels. Rsch. Assn., Audubon Artists and Nat. Soc. Painters in Casein (assoc. 1987-88) Allied Social Sci. Assn. (vice chmn. conv. 1973), AAUW, N.Y.C. Women in Arts, Women's Econ. Roundtable, Greater Hartford Architecture Conservancy, NYU Grad. Sch. Bus. Adminstrn. Alumni (sec. 1956-58), Radcliffe Club, Women's City Club (art and landmarks com.). Author: (with husband) Investment and Development of Tropical Africa, 1959, International Trade and Finance, 1965, Monetary and Banking Theory, 1965; Economics, 1969; (with husband) Principles of Economics, 1969; Economic Progress and the Developing World, 1970; Economics, 1978; also monographs and articles in field. Econ. and internat. rsch. on industrialization less developed areas, internat. debtor nations and workability of buffer stock schemes, pricing fine art; columnist economics of art, Art As An Investment, Money Substitute, or Consumer Durable Good Art Valuation; Prices and Varied Appraisals, Women in the Arts Found. Newsletter, other profl. publs. Home: PO Box 814 New Canaan CT 06840-0814 Office: Art Complex PO Box 814 New Canaan CT 06840-0814 also: 7441 Wayne Ave Miami Beach FL 33141

RENDON, MARIO IVAN, psychiatrist; b. Medellin, Antioquia, Colombia, May 9, 1938; came to U.S., 1966; s. Jairo and Melania (Cardona) R.; m. Diane Cristine Courchesne, Oct. 4, 1969; children: Adan, Renata. MD, U. Antioquia, 1963. Diplomate Am. Bd. Psychiatry and Neurology, Am. Bd. Child Psychiatry. Intern Hosp. St. Vicente De Paul, Medellin, 1962-63; med. dir. Hosp. Urrao and Andes, 1963-66; resident in psychiatry Fairfield Hills Hosp., Newtown, Conn., 1966-67; resident, fellow in child psychiatry Bellevue Hosp., N.Y.C., 1967-70, mem. faculty, 1970-79; clin. dir. Leake and Watts Children's Home, Yonkers, N.Y., 1979-89; dir. bilingual-bi-cultural Hispanic svc. Bronx Mcpl. Hosp. Ctr., N.Y.C., 1989-90; dir. dept. psychiatry Lincoln Hosp., N.Y.C., 1990; mem. attending faculty Aecom-Montefiore, N.Y.C., 1981-86; clin. assoc. prof. psychiatry NYU Med. Ctr., 1982-89, AECOM, 1989—; prof. clin. psychiatry N.Y. Med. Coll., 1989—. Editor: Am. Jour. of Psychoanalysis, 1984-91. Fellow Am. Acad. Psychoanalysis, Am. Acad. Child and Adolescent Psychiatry; mem. Am. Orthopsychiat. Assn., Am. Psychiat. Assn., Am. Inst. for Psychoanalysis, Assn. for Advancement of Psychoanalysis (pres. 1979-81). Home: 333 E 30th St Apt 8L New York NY 10016-6472 Office: Lincon Hosp 234 E 149th St Bronx NY 10451-5504

RENFRO, PATRICIA ELISE, librarian, university official; b. Nelson, Lancashire, Eng.; d. Henry Lawrence and Maud (Thompson) Candlin; m. Charles Gilliland Renfro, June 21, 1969; children: Rebecca Elise, James Lawrence. BA in English and History with honors, U. York, Eng., 1966; acad. postgrad. diploma, U. London, 1968; MA in History, U. Ky., 1981. Libr. asst. Holborn br. London Borough of Camden Pub. Librs., London, 1966-67, sr. asst. libr., 1968-69; dep. acquisitions libr. Folger Shakespeare Libr., Washington, 1969-70; cataloger Libr. Co. of Phila., 1970-72; reference libr. U. Pa. Librs., 1972-73; reference libr. U. Ky. Librs., 1975-76, head of reference svcs., 1976-78; exec. sec. U. Ky. Libr. Assocs., U. Ky., 1979-80; reference libr. U. Pa., 1982-83, head circulation svcs. Van Pelt Libr., 1983-85, asst. dir. librs. for pub. svcs., 1985-89, assoc. dir. librs., 1989—; mem. info. resource mgmt. com., edn. subcom. 1990-91; mem. programs adv. com. Rsch. Librs. Group, 1991—. Contbr. articles to profl. jours. Mem. ALA, Assn. Coll. and Rsch. Ligrs. (rsch. com. 1992—). Home: 11 E Princeton Rd Bala Cynwyd PA 19004-2242 Office: U Pa Librs Philadelphia PA 19104

RENICK, CHARLES MATHEW, merchant marine academy official; b. Keyser, W.Va., June 17, 1926; s. Charles Phillips and Mary Eloise (Liller) R.; m. Rose Mary Arnos, Apr. 14, 1951; children: Charles Mathew Jr., Peter, Timothy, Christina. BS in Marine Transp., U.S. Mcht. Marine Acad., 1947; postgrad., Georgetown U., 1948-49, Fgn. Svc. Inst., 1949-50; MS in Edn., L.I. U., 1973. Ship's officer Moore McCormick Lines, N.Y.C., 1948; staff officer Fgn. Svc., Dept. State, Washington, 1948-49; marine loss supr. Ins. Co. N.Am., Phila., 1952-60; alumni and placement officer U.S. Mcht. Marine Acad., Kings Point, N.Y., 1961-70, advanced through grades to capt., 1972, dir. external affairs, 1970-79, dep. chief staff, 1989—, bd. dirs. Found., 1961—; founder, exec. dir., trustee Am. Mcht. Marine Mus., 1979—. Officer USN, 1950-52, capt. Res. ret. elder North Shore Presbyn. Ch., Gt. Neck, N.Y., 1961—; chmn. career adv. com. Gt. Neck Bd. Edn., 1979-83. Named Man of Yr., Gt. Neck Bus. Assn., 1991. Mem. Naval Res. Assn. (life), U.S. Mcht. Marine Acad. Alumni Assn. (Meritorious Alumni Svc. award 1962, Outstanding Profl. Achievement award 1977), Propeller Club Port N.Y. Democrat. Office: US Mcht Marine Acad Kings Point NY 11024

RENNER, GERARD WILLIAM, acoustical engineer, consultant; b. Dorchester, Mass., Dec. 23, 1921; s. William Donatus and Mary Agnes (McGue) R.; children: William F., John J. AB, Harvard U., 1943. Registered profl. engr., Mass. Rsch. assoc. Harvard Underwater Sound Lab., Cambridge, Mass., 1943-45, Harvard Systems Rsch. Lab., Cambridge, 1946; dept. mgr. Submarine Signal Co., Boston, 1946-48, Raytheon Corp., Boston, Portsmouth, R.I., 1948-63; rsch. assoc. Lowell (Mass.) Rsch. Inst., 1963-69; dir. devel. Hazeltine Corp., Avon, Mass., 1969-72; pres. Applied Rsch Associates, Dorchester, Mass., 1972—. Recipient Merit award U.S. Bur. Ordnance, Washington, 1945. Mem. IEEE (life mem.), Acoustical Soc. Am. Home and Office: Applied Rsch Assocs 51 Bellevue St Dorchester MA 02125-2454

RENNER, SIMON EDWARD, steel company executive; b. Florence, S.C., Feb. 5, 1934; s. Simon Samson and Ruby (Pickett) R.; m. Katherine May Schneider, May 10, 1958; children: Katherine Leah, J. Eric, Philip E., S. Todd. B.S., Yale U., 1956; diploma, Carnegie Mellon U., 1972. Gen. mgr. specialty steel Jones & Laughlin Steel Corp., Pitts, 1973-74; gen. mgr. basic steel Jones & Laughlin Steel Corp., Pitts., 1974-75, v.p. prodn., 1975-77, pres. eastern div., 1977-79, corp. v.p., 1979-86; pres. LTV R.R.'s, 1986—. Vice pres. Allegheny Trails council, Boy Scouts Am.; pres. Quigley High Sch. Bd. Ed., Baden. Pa., 1982. Capt. USMC, 1956-59. Mem. Am. Iron and Steel Inst. (chmn. mfg. com. 1980-82), Assn. Iron and Steel Engrs., Am. Short Line RR Assn. (bd. dirs.). Republican. Clubs: Duquesne (Pitts.); Allegheny Country (Sewickley, Pa.); Harvard-Yale-Princeton. Home: 104 Willow Rd Sewickley PA 15143 Office: LTV RRs 3600 2d Ave Pittsburgh PA 15219

RENOFF, RONALD HAMILTON, limousine service executive; b. Balt., Sept. 13, 1939; s. Paul Vernon and Margaret Hamilton (Houghton) R. BS, U. Md., 1964. Sales staff Chesapeake Cadillac, Balt., 1970-75; div. mgr. Sears Roebuck & Co., Key West, Fla., 1968-70; sales engr. Renoff Assocs., Balt., 1966-68; pres. Chesapeake Limousine Svc., Inc., Balt., 1975—. With USCGR, 1964-70. Mem. Limousine Assn. Md. (bd. dirs. 1988—, founding pres. 1988-89), The Auto. Funeral Assn. (bd. dirs. 1991-92), Varsity Club of Balt. (pres. 1981-82, 84-85). Home: PO Box 69 Severna Park MD 21146 Office: Chesapeake Limosine Svc Inc 1 Eugenia ave Ferndale MD 21061

RENTSCHLER, CATHY, editor; b. Anniston, Ala., Nov. 2, 1947; d. Robert J. and Christine (McClellan) Rentschler; m. Gary L. Bogart, Oct. 11, 1975. BA, Jacksonville (Ala.) State U., 1969; MLS, Fla. State U., 1971. Tchr. Calhoun County Bd. Edn., Anniston, 1969-70; cataloger The H.W. Wilson Co., Bronx, N.Y., 1971-75, editor, 1975—. Mem. ALA, Spl. Librs.

Assn., Women's Nat. Book Assn. (pres. 1986-88). Episcopalian. Office: The HW Wilson Co 950 University Ave Bronx NY 10452-4297

RENZA, JOHN SEBASTIAN, JR., accountant; b. Providence, June 2, 1948; s. John Sebastian and Marie (Teigue) R.; m. Marianne Emma, Sept. 7, 1970; children: John S. III, Gregory J. BSBA magna cum laude, Bryant Coll., 1970; MBA, Providence Coll., 1979. CPA, R.I. Acct. Peat, Marwick & Co., Providence, 1970-75; pres. Renza & Co., CPAs, Inc., Cranston, R.I., 1975—; prof. acctg., Community Coll. R.I., Lincoln, 1975—. Trustee, Bryant Coll., Smithfield, R.I., 1982—, Moses Brown Sch., Providence, 1989—; treas., Com. to Re-elect Sen. John Chafee, Providence, 1978—; chmn. bd. dirs., R.I. Telecommunications Authority, Providence, 1985-91; pres. PBS-TV Channel 36 Found., Providence, 1988-91. Mem. AICPA, R.I. Soc. CPAs (bd. dirs. 1987-90), Greater Cranston C. of C. (bd. dirs., treas. 1988-90), Lions. Republican. Roman Catholic. Office: 1220 Pontiac Ave Cranston RI 02920-4456

REOHR, JANET RUTH, psychologist, educator; b. Auburn, N.Y., Apr. 25, 1948. BS, SUNY, Cortland, 1970; MEd, Boston U., 1975, EdD, 1978. cert. tchr., N.Y. Elem. sch. tchr. Commack (N.Y.) Sch. Dist., 1970-71; tchr. Newark Jr. High Sch., 1971-73; asst. dir. parks and recreation Camillus (N.Y.) Recreation Dept., 1973-74; adminstrv. asst. humanistic, devel. and organizational studies Boston U., 1976-78; instr. psychology No. Essex Community Coll., Haverhill, Mass., 1978-79, Northeastern U., Boston, 1979-80; cons. Beacon Rsch. Assocs., Boston, 1979; prof. psychology Russell Sage/Jr. Coll. Albany, N.Y., 1980-89, chair social sci. div., 1985-89, interim dir. learning resources ctr., 1989; assoc. dean acad. affairs, dir. grad. studies Castleton (Vt.) State Coll., 1989—; cons. tng. div. N.Y. State Dept. Civil Svc., Albany, 1981-82, New Eng. Assn. Schs. and Coll. Accreditation Team. Author: Friendship: An Exploration of Structure and Process; contbr. articles to profl. jours. Chair Educators for Social Responsibility Albany Chpt., 1981-86. Mem. APA, Internat. Soc. Study Personal Relationships, Eastern Psychology Assn., Am. Assn. Higher Edn., Nat. Assn. Acad. Affairs Adminstrs. (Vt. state commr. 1990—), Vt. Women in Higher Edn. (conf. chair 1991, mem. state bd. 1991—). Roman Catholic. Home: 8 Church St Poultney VT 05764-1005 Office: Castleton State Coll Castleton VT 05735

REPASI, STEPHEN, graphic artist, freelance illustrator, cartoonist; b. Kunmadaras, Hungary, Oct. 19, 1958; came to U.S., 1989; s. Istvan and Ilona (Andrasi) R.; m. Marie Szemeti, Sept. 15, 1984. BA, Juhasz Gyula Coll., Szeged, Hungary, 1982. Graphic artist Kultura Hungarian Fgn. Trading Co., Budapest, Hungary, 1982-87; salesman Futon World, Inc., Warwick, R.I., 1990-91; paste-up/layout artist Trader Pub. Co., Cranston, R.I., 1991; graphic artist Desmark/Tamerlane Corp., Smithfield, R.I., 1991—; sole propr. Aquaprint Enterprises, North Providence, R.I., 1992. Designer displays for book fairs, Frankfurt, Milan, Stockholm, 1982-87; illustrator, cartoon artist Aquarium Fish Mag., 1991—. Home: 520 Smithfield Rd # 301 Providence RI 02904

REPASKE, ROY, molecular biologist; b. Cleve., Mar. 17, 1925; s. Matthew and Irene (Zajatz) R.; m. Anne Christine Colm, July 29, 1950; children: David Roy, William Allen, Carol Anne. B.S., Western Res. U., 1948; M.S., U. Mich., 1950; Ph.D., U. Wis., 1953. Instr. to assoc. prof. Ind. U., Bloomington, 1954-59; biochemist NIH Bethesda, Md., 1959-78, molecular biologist, 1978—, dep. lab. chief LMM, 1991—; cons. Martin-Marietta Co., Balt., 1961, NASA, Washington, 1962-65; mem. com. on Detection of Extra-terrestrial life, USPHS, 1965; asst. program dir. U. Mich. summer program, Interlocken, 1963, 64; vis. rsch. assoc. Naval Med. Rsch. Inst., Bethesda, Md., 1989-90; mem. editorial bd. Jour. of Microbiology, 1962-67; instr. Found. for Advanced Studies in Scis., Bethesda, 1966-73; program dir. NSF Biochemistry, 1973-74. Active Boy Scouts Am., Bethesda, U.S. AEC fellow, 1951-53. Fellow AAAS; mem. Am. Soc. Biol. Chemists, Am. Soc. Microbiology (chmn. gen. div. 1963-64), Am. Soc. Virology, Fedn. of Am. Socs. for Exptl. Biology, Sigma Xi, Beta Theta Pi. Club: Am. Recorder Soc. (pres. 1968, 71-73). Avocations: amateur string quartet and recorder playing, gardening. Office: NIH 9000 Rockville Pike Bethesda MD 20892-0001

REPKO, WILLIAM CLARKE, banker; b. New Haven, June 25, 1949; s. John Edward Jr. and Beatrice Jane (Martin) R.; m. Susan Sillcox, Oct. 29, 1983; children: John Edward III, Meaghan Ann, Andrew Spotswood, Parker Yates, Thomas Strong. Student, Lehigh U., 1973. Rep. Mfrs. Hanover Trust Co., N.Y.C., 1975, asst. sec., 1976-77, v.p., 1980-85, sr. v.p., 1985-89, mng. dir., 1989—; v.p. European Am. Bank, N.Y.C., 1980; mng. dir. Chem. Banking Corp., N.Y.C., 1990—. Mem. Stanwich Club. Republican. Office: Chemical Banking Corp 270 Park Ave New York NY 10017

REPPERT, JOAN GARLAND SMITH, non-profit agency executive; b. Boston; d. James Kelley and Thelma Alverna (Garland) Smith; m. James Donald Reppert; children: Rebecca, James, Matthew, Peter, Rachel, Daniel. BA, Radcliffe Coll./Harvard U., 1952. Social worker Head Start, Berks County, Pa., 1977-78; information edn. program dir. YWCA, Reading, Pa., 1978-80; exec. dir. Reading-Berks Human Rels. Coun., 1980—; gov. Police Athletic League Bd., Reading, 1981—; dir. Berks Community Action Program Bd., Reading/Berks, 1983-86, 88—. Trustee Washington Presbyn. Ch., 1991—; mem. Berks Community TV Bd., 1992. Mem. ASCD, Nat. Assn. Human Rights Workers, Exec. Coun. Human Svcs. Agys. (treas. 1985-87, pres. 1987-89), Am. Assn. for Affirmative Action. Office: Reading-Berks Human Rels Coun 230 N 5th St Reading PA 19601-3309

REPPERT, WILLIAM DOWNING, physician, hospital administrator; b. Bethlehem, Pa., Nov. 12, 1923; s. Levi Jacob and Mildred Adele (Downing) R.; m. Angela Regina Schmid, May 29, 1947; children: Richard, Susan, Cynthia, William Jr. BA, Lehigh U., 1947; MD, Temple U., 1951. Diplomate Am. Bd. Internal Medicine. Intern St. Luke's Hosp., Bethlehem, 1951-52; pvt. practice Bethlehem, 1952-75; chief medicine St. Lukes Hosp., Bethlehem, 1975-90, emeritus chief medicine, 1990—. Chmn. Bd. Health, Fountain Hill, Pa., 1985—; active Bd. Hogar Crea, Bethlehem, 1978-79. With U.S. Army, 1943-46. Fellow ACP; mem. Assn. Program Dirs. in Internal Medicine, Temple Med. Sch. Alumni (bd. dirs. 1989—), Alpha Omega Alpha. Methodist. Home: 626 Norway Pl Bethlehem PA 18015-4438 Office: St Lukes Hospital 801 Ostrum St Bethlehem PA 18015-1065

REPS, DAVID NATHAN, finance educator; b. N.Y.C., July 30, 1926; s. Samuel and Fannie (Ginsberg) R.; m. Helene Shifrin, Aug. 10, 1958; children: Tamara, Aaron, Steven, Jennifer. BSEE, Columbia U., 1948; MSEE, U. Pitts., 1953, PhD, 1966. Elec. utility systems engr. Westinghouse Elec. Corp., Pitts., 1950-63, corp. planner, 1963-67; prin. mgmt. svcs. Ernst & Young, N.Y.C., 1967-75; prof., chmn. bus. econs., fin., pub. policy L.I. Univ., N.Y.C., 1975-78; prof. fin. Pace U., Pleasantville, N.Y., 1978—; v.p. Video Frame Store, Inc., N.Y.C., 1983—, The Photoboard Group, N.Y.C., 1989-92; v.p. and treas. Digital Video Photo Imaging, Inc., N.Y.C., 1992—; bd. dirs. The Storyboard Group, Inc., N.Y.C. Contbr. articles to profl. jours. With USN, 1944-46. Home: 98 Soundview Ave White Plains NY 10606-3617 Office: Pace U Bedford Rd Pleasantville NY 10570-1002

RESCH, CYNTHIA FORTES, educator; b. Providence, Dec. 9, 1951; d. Alfred Antone and Mabel (Duarte) F.; m. Joseph Bernard Resch III, June 26, 1982; children: Jeffrey, Jason, Steven, Kayla. BA, R.I. Coll., 1974; postgrad., U. Sorbonne, Paris, 1975, U. Valencia, Spain, 1979, Providence Coll., 1981. Cert. secondary edn. tchr., R.I. Tchr. French and Spanish North Kingstown (R.I.) High Sch., 1977—. Active Women for a Non-Nuclear Future, Providence, 1982—; advisor N. Kingstown High Sch. Internat. Club. Mem. NEA, R.I. Fgn. Lang. Assn. Office: North Kingstown High Sch 150 Fairway Dr North Kingstown RI 02852-6207

RESCONICH, SAMUEL, chemistry educator; b. Portage, Pa., July 31, 1933; s. Carl and Mary (Patney) R. BS, St. Francis Coll., Loretto, Pa., 1954; PhD, Purdue U., 1960. Teaching asst. Purdue U., Lafayette, Ind., 1954-56, Westinghouse fellow, 1956-59, postdoctoral fellow, 1959-60; prof. chemistry St. Francis Coll., Loretto, 1960—. Sch. bd. dir. Portage Area Sch., 1990. Mem. Am. Chem. Soc., Rotary Club (pres. 1969, 78), Sigma Xi, Alpha Chi Sigma. Democrat. Byzantine Catholic. Home: 1319 Gillespie Ave Portage PA 15946-1529 Office: St Francis Coll Chemistry Dept Loretto PA 15940

RESCORLA, ROBERT ARTHUR, psychology educator; b. Pitts, May 9, 1940; s. Arthur R. and Mildred J. (Jenkins) R.; children: Eric, Michael. BA, Swarthmore Coll., 1962; PhD, U. Pa., 1966; MA, Yale U., 1974. Successively asst. prof., assoc. prof., prof. Yale U., New Haven, 1966-80; prof. psychology U. Pa., Phila., 1981—, James Skinner prof. sci., 1986—. Author: Pavlovian Second-Order Conditioning, 1980. Contbr. articles to profl. jours. William James fellow, 1988. Mem. APA (pres. div. 3 1985, Disting. Sci. Contbn. award 1986), Am. Psychol. Soc.; mem. NAS, AAAS (pres. sect. J, psychology 1988-89), Soc. Exptl. Psychologists (Warren medal 1991), Psychinomic Soc. (mem. governing bd. 1979-85, chmn. publ. bd. 1985-86), Ea. Psychol. Assn. (bd. dirs. 1983-86, pres. 1986-87). Office: U Pa Dept Psychology 3815 Walnut St Philadelphia PA 19104-6196

RESDEN, DEE KRONENBERG, graphic designer; b. Springfield, Mass., Feb. 10, 1948; d. Philip Andrew and Jeannette Laura (Colby) K.; m. Ronald Everett Resden, Apr. 20, 1974; children: Philip Eben, Alison Alysa. BFA, Phila. Coll. Art, 1970. Artist Educators Pub. Co., Inc., Cambridge, Mass., 1970-71; graphics specialist Ginn & Co., Lexington, Mass., 1971-74; tech. illustrator Cahners Pub., Boston, 1974-76; freelance graphic technician Houghton Mifflin Co., Boston, 1976-77; designer Donley Co., North Attleboro, Mass., 1978-81; art dir. Action Mate Toys, North Attleboro, 1986-90; owner, mgr. DKR Graphics, Norton, Mass., 1981—; ptnr., creative dir. Up-Starts Mktg., Franklin, Mass., 1990—. Mem. NAFE, Women's Success Network (exec. dir., memmbership com. 1989-90, chmn. 1990-91), United C. of C. Home: 100 Plain St Norton MA 02766-2908 Office: Up-Starts Mktg 7 Copperfield Ln Franklin MA 02038-2651

RESDEN, RONALD EVERETTE, product development engineer medical devices; b. Littleton, N.H., Oct. 27, 1944; s. Lawerence A. and Rita Mae (Bowen) R.; m. Dee Kronenburg, Apr. 20, 1974; children: Philip, Alison. Cons. Franklin Mfg. Co., Norwood, Mass., 1984—, Boston Sci. Co., Watertown, Mass., 1985—, Via Med, Easton, Mass., 1986—, White Marsh Labs., Balt., 1989—, Spectraphos Malmo Sweden, 1991—, Vision Scis. Inc., Natick, Mass., 1991—. Author: Hologram Control Transfer, 1984; inventor, patentee in field. Home and Office: Resden Rsch 100 Plain St Norton MA 02766-2908

RESLER, EDWIN LOUIS, JR., aerospace engineering educator; b. Pitts., Nov. 20, 1925; s. Edwin Louis and Ruth Elizabeth (Blesh) R.; m. Frances Williams, June 26, 1948; children: Edwin W., Timothy M., Carl L., Daniel P., Suzanne M . BS, U. Notre Dame, 1947; PhD, Cornell U., 1951. Rsch. assoc. Cornell U., Ithaca, N.Y., 1948-51, asst. prof. aero. engring., 1951-52, dir. grad. sch. aerospace engring., 1963-73, dir. Sibley Sch. Mech. and Aerospace Engring., 1972-77, J.N. Pew Jr. prof. engring., 1968—; assoc. rsch. prof. U. Md., 1952-56; cons. Diesel and Gas Engring., Beaver Falls, N.Y.; mem. sci. bd. Sonex Rsch. Inc. Patentee in field; contbr. articles to profl. jours. Lt. (j.g.) USN, 1944-46. Fellow AIAA; mem. Am. Inst. Physics, Am. Phys. Soc., Internat. Sci. Radio Union, Internat. Acad. Astronautics, Sigma Xi, Sigma Pi Sigma. Home: 162 Turkey Hill Rd Ithaca NY 14850-2939 Office: Cornell U Sibley Sch Mech and Aero Engring Ithaca NY 14853

RESNICK, ELAINE BETTE, psychotherapist, clinical social worker; b. Orlando, Fla., Apr. 2, 1944; d. Julius Milton and Annette (Chusid) Bernstein; m. Peter Schuyten (div. 1973); m. Richard B. Resnick, May 21, 1975; children: Demian, Jesse, Nora; 1 stepchild, Deborah. BA with honors, N.Y. Univ., 1966; MSW, Hunter Coll. of Social Work, 1971; postgrad., Columbia Pacific U., 1992—. Cert. psychotherapy, N.Y.; clin. social work, N.Y. Field work supr. NYU, N.Y.C., 1973-82, York Coll., N.Y.C., 1976-77; clin. dir. div. drug abuse N.Y. Med. Coll., N.Y.C., 1977-83, instr., 1978-82, clin. instr., 1982-83; pvt. practice N.Y.C., 1973—; clin. dir. Ctr. Psychiatry & Family Therapy, N.Y.C., 1986—; field work supr., Wurzweiler Sch. of Social Work, Yeshiva U., 1991—; psychiat. social worker N.Y. State Psychiat. Inst., 1970-71; social worker Intensive Family Counseling Unit N.Y.C. Dept. Social Svcs., 1969-70; psychiat. social worker, St. Vincent's Hosp., 1970; adj. asst. prof. NYU Grad. Sch. Social Work, 1977-82. Contbr. articles to profl. jours.; responsible for numerous presentations in field. Parent vol. Bank St. Sch. for Children, N.Y.C., 1990-92. Psychiat. Social Work fellow NIMH, N.Y.C., 1970-71. Fellow Soc. Clin. Social Work Psychotherapists, Am. Orthopsychiat. Assn.; mem. NASW, Nat. Registry of Health Care Providers in Clin. Social Work, Soc. for Advancement of Self Psychology, Assn. Med. Edn. and Rsch. in Substance Abuse, Orton Dyslexia Soc.

RESNICK, HENRY ROY, pharmacist; b. N.Y.C., Dec. 12, 1952; s. Samuel and Miriam (Jacobson) R.; m. Mary Lee Monroe, Sept. 13, 1981; children: Jacob Monroe, Aaron Leo. BS in Pharmacy, L.I. U., 1975, MS in Drug Info. & Communication, 1978. Pharmacist Sagamore Childrens Ctr., Melville, N.Y., 1976-77; staff pharmacist Montefiore Hosp. and Med. Ctr., N.Y.C., 1977-80; mgr. clin. pharmacy svcs. Beth Israel Med. Ctr., N.Y.C., 1980-82, asst. dir. pharmacy, 1982-87, supervising pharmacist methadone maintenance treatment program, 1982-90, sr. assoc. dir., 1987-90; dir. pharmacy New Rochelle (N.Y.) Hosp. Med. Ctr., 1990—; adj. clin. instr. Arnold and Marie Schwartz Coll. Pharmacy Health Scis., N.Y.C., 1980-82. Mem. Am. Soc. Hosp. Pharmacists, N.Y. State Coun. Hosp. Pharmacists (monitoring com. on legis. 1989-90, joint com. with industry 1989-90, govt. and affairs com. 1991—), Westchester Soc. Hosp. Pharmacists (chmn. legis., constitution and bylaws com. 1991-92, exec. com. 1991—, pres.-elect 1992—, del. N.Y. State coun. hosp. pharmacists 1992). Office: New Rochelle Hosp Med Ctr 16 Guion Pl New Rochelle NY 10801-5503

RESNICK, MARCIA AYLENE, photographic artist, educator; b. Bklyn., Nov. 21, 1950; d. Herbert Leonard and Sonia Martha (Panich) R.; m. Wayne Kramer, 1982 (div. 1984). BFA, Cooper Union, 1972; MFA, Calif. Inst. Arts, 1973. Adj. instr. photography Queens Coll., CUNY, 1973-79, NYU, 1974-76, Cooper Union, N.Y.C., 1976, Internat. Ctr. Photography, N.Y.C., 1979-82, Pratt Inst., Manhattanville (N.Y.) Coll., 1987-88, La Guardia Comml. Coll., CUNY, 1988, Staten Island Coll., CUNY, 1988. One-woman shows include Gallery 115, Santa Cruz, Calif., 1974, Galerie Ricke, Cologne, Fed. Republic Germany, 1976, 78, Suzan Penzner, N.Y.C, 1976, Photoworks Gallery, The Fine Arts Bldg., N.Y.C., 1977, Lightworks Gallery, Syracuse, N.Y., 1977, Gotham Book Mart, N.Y.C., 1978, Night Gallery, N.Y.C., 1984, Ideé Gallery, Toronto, Ont., Can., 1985, U. Dallas, 1987; exhibited in group shows at Harvard Fogg Mus., Boston, 1974, Sidney Janis Gallery, N.Y.C., 1975, Tex. Ctr. for Photographic Studies, 1975, Rene Block Gallery, N.Y.C., 1975, Light Gallery, N.Y.C., 1975, San Francisco Mus. Modern Art, 1975, 85, Hallwalls, Buffalo, 1976, Visual Studies Workshop, Rochester, N.Y., 1977, L.A. Inst. Contemporary Art, 1978, Art Inst. Chgo., 1978, George Eastman House, Rochester, 1978, Friends of Photography, Carmel, Calif., 1980, The Kitchen, N.Y.C., 1980, U. Guelph, Ont., 1981, Gray Art Gallery, N.Y.C., 1981, P.S.I., N.Y.C., 1981, Mus. Fine Arts, Houston, 1983, Queens Mus., 1986, Wadsworth Athenaeum, Hartford, Conn., 1991; author: Tahitian Eve, 1975, See, 1975, Landscape, 1975, Re-visions, 1978. Nat. Endowment for Arts grantee, 1975, 78, Creative Artists Pub. Svc. Program grantee, 1977. Mem. Soc. for Photographic Edn., Coll. Art Assn., Nat. Art Edn. Assn., Visual Studies Workshop (Rocherster). Home: 2 Grove St New York NY 10014-5315

RESNICK, STEPHANIE, lawyer; b. N.Y.C., Nov. 12, 1959; d. Ronald and Diane Gross. AB, Kenyon Coll., 1981; JD, Villanova U., 1984. Bar: Pa. 1984, N.J. 1984, N.Y. 1990; U.S. Dist. Ct. (ea. dist.) Pa. 1984, U.S. Dist. Ct. N.J. 1984, N.Y. 1990. Assoc. Cozen and O'Connor, Phila., 1984-87, Fox, Rothschild, O'Brien & Frankel, Phila., 1987—; mem. investigative div. Commn. on Jud. Selection and Retention, Phila., 1988—, mem. subcom. on investigative div. tng. and commn. guidelines, 1992. Active Vols. for the Indigent Program, Phila., 1987—; mem. investigative divsn. Commn. Jud. Selection and Retention, Phila., 1988—, subcom. on investigative divsn. tng. and commn. guidelines, 1992. Mem. ABA, Pa. Bar Assn. (disciplinary bd. study com. 1989-91, profl. liability com. 1992—), Phila. Bar Assn., N.J. Bar Assn., N.Y. Bar Assn. Home: 2 Independence Pl Apt 2306 Philadelphia PA 19106 Office: Fox Rothschild O'Brien & Frankel 2000 Market St Fl 9 Philadelphia PA 19103-3291

RESNIK, DAVID ALAN, manufacturing company executive; b. Providence, R.I., June 9, 1956; s. Sol Leon and Esther (Petersohn) R.; m. Susan Winoker, Aug. 12, 1979; children: Joshua Michael, Alissa Joy. BA, U. Pa., 1978, MS, 1979. Gen. mgr. Emblem & Badge, Inc. (merger with Westcalind Corp. 1988), Providence, 1980—, exec. v.p., 1986-87, pres., 1987—; v.p. Polar Cap Ice, Inc. Contbr. articles to profl. jours. Mem. Soc. Econ. Paleontologists and Mineralogists, Internat. Orgn. Paleobotany, Paleontol. Soc., Bot. Soc. Am., Boston Computer Soc., Profl. Assn. Diving Instrs. (cert. master scuba diver trainer), Rotary. Jewish. Office: Emblem & Badge Inc PO Box 6226 Providence RI 02940-6226

RESSLER, HAROLD KIRKBY, diplomat; b. N.Y.C., Nov. 22, 1944; s. David Blair and Elizabeth (Kirkby) Ressler; m. Gabriella Plimpton, Sept. 12, 1981; children: Christopher Kirkby, Julia Antonia Plimpton. BA, Yale U., 1966; JD, Harvard U., 1969. Bar: U.S. Dist. Ct. N.J. 1970, U.S. Ct. Appeals (3d cir.) 1970, U.S. Dist. Ct. (so. dist.) N.Y. 1972, U.S. Ct. Appeals (2d cir.) 1972. Dep. atty. gen. State of N.J., 1971-72; assoc. atty. White & Case, N.Y.C., 1972-81; diplomat U.S. Dept. of State, Washington, 1981—; advisor Lehman Bros., N.Y.C., 1991-92; founder Ressler Vineyards, Cutchogue, N.Y., 1981—. Campaign mgr. James Shue for Congress, N.J., 1970. Mem. Shelter Island Yacht Club, Yale Club of N.Y.C. Home: 1021 Park Ave New York NY 10028

RESTANI, JANE A., federal judge; b. San Francisco, Feb. 27, 1948; d. Roy J. and Emilia C. Restani. BA, U. Calif., Berkeley, 1969; JD, U. Calif., Davis, 1973. Bar: Calif., 1973. Trial atty. U.S. Dept. Justice, Washington, 1973-76, asst. chief comml. litigation sect., 1976-80, dir. comml. litigation sect., 1980-83; judge U.S. Ct. Internat. Trade, N.Y.C., 1983—. Mem. Order of Coif. Office: US Ct Internat Trade 1 Federal Pla New York NY 10007*

RESTIANO, RICHARD ANGELO, photographer, small business owner; b. S. I., May 9, 1948; s. Angelo and Marge (Giannetti) R.; m. Vincenza Anna Faustini, Aug. 16, 1970; children: Alessandra, Richard Angelo Jr., Claudia, Randall. BS, Fordham U., 1970. Tchr. N.Y.C. Bd. of Edn., 1970-71; photographer Josten's Am. Yearbook Co., 1971-72; pres. N.Y. Photographic, Inc., 1972-78; rep. Westchestesr County BOCES, 1978-87; pres. Nat. Photo Dynamics, Inc., 1979—. Mem. Yonkers (N.Y.) Hist. Soc., Salesian High Sch. Devel. Coun.; advisor Jr. Achievment of Mt. Vernon, N.Y.; appointed mem. Village of Bronxville Lighting Com., 1990; chmn. Bronxville-Eastchester Tuckahoe Community Fund Bus. Donation Drive, chmn. golf outing, 1988, 89, 90, bd. dir.s, 1990; co-chmn. allocations com. Am. Cancer Soc., Bronxville, campaign coord., 1989, 90, 91; sec. Bronxville C. of C.; me. parish coun. St. Joseph's Ch.; past pres. Longvale Homeowner's Assn. Mem. N.Y. State Profl. Photographer's Assn. (pres. 1988-89), Westchester Profl. Photographer's Assn., Bronxville C. of C. Retail Mcht.'s Assn., Profl. Photographers Am., Rotary (pres. elect 1991—), Lions (past pres.), St. Joseph's Men's Club (past pres.). Home: 10 Merriam Pl Bronxville NY 10708-2730

RESTON, MARY JO, newspaper publishing executive; b. Kenosha, Wis., May 16, 1937; d. Edwin Bart and Evelyn Marie (Drinkwater) O'Brien; m. Richard Fulton Reston, Oct. 16, 1965. BS, U. Wis., 1959. Tchr. English, speech Lincoln Jr. High Sch., Beloit, Wis., 1959-61; adminstrv. asst. Rep. Party Hdqrs., Washington, 1961-62; dept. mgr. Blue Cross-Blue Shield, Washington, 1963-66; free-lance journalist Moscow and London, 1966-72; with advt. sales dept. Vineyard Gazette newspaper, Edgartown, Mass., 1975-80, bus. mgr., 1980-85, gen. mgr., 1985—, also bd. dirs.; pub. Vineyard Gazette newspaper, Edgartown, 1988—. Bd. dirs. Martha's Vineyard Hosp., Oak Bluffs, Mass., 1979—, Vineyard Environ. Research Inst., Martha's Vineyard, Mass., 1984—. Office: Vineyard Gazette 34 S Summer St Edgartown MA 02539

RESTREPO, JOSÉ LUIS, international organization administrator; b. Medellin, Colombia, Nov. 24, 1930; came to the U.S., 1962; s. Cipriano and Julia (Velez) R.; m. Maria Rosario Angulo, July 19, 1956; children: Felipe, Patricia Loria, Nicolas, David, Daniel. MBA, U. Pa., 1955; JD, U. Bolivariana, Colombia, 1958. Dean bus. econs. U. Medellin, 1956-60; chief city planning Municipality of Medellin, 1960; dir. nat. budget Govt. Colombia, Bogota, 1960-62; various pos. OAS, Washington, 1962-91, spl. advisor unit for promotion of democracy, 1991—. Author: Colmenar del Monte, 1991; contbr. articles to profl. jours. Roman Catholic. Office: OAS 17th & Constitution Aves NW Washington DC 22101

RETSEMA, JAMES ALLAN, microbiologist; b. Muskegon, Mich., Feb. 27, 1942; s. Jay and Christine Retsema; m. Arija Bets, Oct. 18, 1969; children: Anna Aria, Andrew James. BS, Mich. State U., 1964; MS, U. Iowa, 1967, PhD, 1969. Postdoctoral fellow U. Wis., Madison, 1969; rsch. scientist cen. rsch. div. Pfizer, Inc., Groton, Conn., 1969-75, sr. rsch. scientist, 1975-79, project leader, 1979-83, mgr., 1983-90, rsch. advisor, 1990—. Fellow Am. Acad. Microbiology. Office: Pfizer Inc Cen Rsch Eastern Point Rd Groton CT 06340

RETTEK, S(USAN) ILSA, clinical psychologist; b. N.Y.C., Dec. 24, 1958; d. Seymour Rettek and Marion (Stern) Seidemann; m. Alan Leslie Hochberg, Sept. 15, 1991. BA, SUNY, Purchase, 1980; MA, New Sch. for Social Rsch., 1983, PhD, 1990. Lic. psychologist, N.Y. Resident counselor Westchester Mental Health Assn., N.Y.C., 1978-80, asst. community program dir., 1980-82; psychology extern Downstate Med. Ctr. State U. Hosp., N.Y.C., 1984-85; psychology clk. Fifth Ave Ctr. for Counseling and Psychotherapy, N.Y.C., 1984-85; intake worker Washington Square Inst. for Psychotherapy and Mental Health, N.Y.C., 1987; psychology intern Albert Einstein Coll. Medicine/Bronx Psychiat. Ctr., N.Y.C., 1987-88; psychologist Beth Israel Med. Ctr., N.Y.C., 1989—, Albert Einstein Coll. Medicine, Bronx Psychiat. Ctr., N.Y.C., 1988—; rsch. asst. SUNY Downstate Med. Ctr., Bklyn., 1986-87; lectr. U. Allahabad, India, 1986; preceptor New Sch. for Social Rsch., N.Y.C., 1986-87, co-investigator, 1984-91; pvt. practice Cross-Cultural Psychotherapy and Consultation Svc., 1991—. Grantee NSF, 1985. Mem. APA, Internat. Assn. for Cross-Cultural Psychology, Nat. Register Health Svc. Providers in Psychology, N.Y. State Psychol. Assn. Democrat. Jewish. Home: 427 6th St Apt 2 Brooklyn NY 11215-3606 Office: Bronx Psychiat Ctr Ginsburg OPC Ward 25 1500 Waters Pl Bronx NY 10461-2723

RETTIG, CAROLYN FAITH, educator; b. Tarentum, Pa., June 30, 1951; d. William and Jennie Annetta (Lear) Ambrose; m. Gary Alan Rettig, July 10, 1985. BS in Edn., Ind. U. Pa., 1973; MA in Student Personnel, Slippery Rock U., 1988. Cert. English tchr. jr. high, secondary schs. Jr. high tchr. Saxonburg and Butler, Pa., 1974-75; English tchr. Butler Area High Sch., 1975-76; assessor community needs Butler County Community Coll., Pa., 1977-78; tchr. English Butler Area Sch. Dist., 1978—, speech and debate coach, 1979-84, curriculum writing coord., 1986-87; chmn. English dept. Butler Intermediate High Sch., 1986-88; chmn. English dept. Butler Intermediate High Sch., 1986-88; coord. fin. aid counselor practicum Butler County Community Coll., 1988. Pub. high sch. student art and lit. mag., 1988-91. Mem. Butler Edn. Assn., Pa. State Edn. Assn., NEA. Democrat. Lutheran. Home: 261 Fisher Rd RD 1 Cabot PA 16023 Office: Butler Intermediate High Sch 151 Fairground Hill Rd Butler PA 16001-5627

RETZKY, ALLAN ABRAHAM, trading company executive; b. Bklyn., Oct. 6, 1937; s. Harold and Pauline (Adelman) R.; m. Susan J. Kotlus, Dec. 23, 1962; children: Deborah, Andrea. B.Met.E., Rensselaer Poly. Inst., 1959; MBA, Harvard U., 1962. Cons. S.D. Leidesdorf & Co., N.Y.C., 1962-67; dir. fin. analysis Continental Copper & Steel Industries, N.Y.C., 1967-70; group v.p. Primary Industries Corp., N.Y.C., 1970—; faculty internat. fin. NYU, 1992—. Treas. Altro Health and Rehab. Svcs., N.Y.C., 1980-90. Office: Primary Industries Corp 666 5th Ave New York NY 10103

REUTER, CAROL JOAN, insurance company executive; b. Bklyn., June 1, 1941; d. Michael John and Elizabeth Lucille (Garmer) R. BA, St. John's U., 1962. Exec. dir. N.Y. Life Found., N.Y.C., 1979-89, sec., 1989-90, pres., 1990—, bd. dirs., 1992—; asst. v.p. N.Y. Life Ins. Co., N.Y.C., 1984-89, corp. v.p., 1990—. Mem., former chmn. contbns. coun. Conf. Bd., N.Y. Contbns. Adv. Group; mem. corp. assocs. United Way Am.; vice chmn., mem. corp. adv. com. United Way of Tri-State; mem. nat. corp. adv. com., former chmn. nominating com. Found. Ind. Higher edn. Named Acad. of Women's Achievers, YWCA, 1987. Republican. Roman Catholic. Office: NY Life Ins Co 51 Madison Ave New York NY 10010-1603

REUTTER, EBERHARD EDMUND, JR., educator; b. Balt., May 28, 1924; s. Eberhard Edmund and Irene Louise (Loewer) R.; m. Bettie Marie Lytle, Aug. 16, 1947; 1 son, Mark Douglas. B.A., Johns Hopkins U., 1944;

M.A., Columbia U., 1948, Ph.D., 1950. Dir., Tokyo Army Edn. Program Sch., 1945-47; head math. dept. Barnard Sch., N.Y.C., 1947-49; mem. faculty Tchrs. Coll., Columbia U., 1950—, prof., 1957—; vis. prof. U. Alaska, 1960, 66, U. P.R., 1954, U. So. Calif., 1960; speaker, cons. Coordinator spl. edn. projects NAACP Legal Def. Fund, 1965-68. Author: The School Administrator and Subversive Activities, 1951, Schools and the Law, 5th edit., 1981, (with W.S. Elsbree) Staff Personnel in the Public Schools, 1954, (with R.R. Hamilton) Legal Aspects of School Board Operation, 1958, (with W.S. Elsbree) Principles of Staff Personnel Administration in Public Schools, 1959, (with L.O. Garber) The Yearbook of School Law, 1967, 68, 69, 70, Legal Aspects of Control of Student Activities by Public School Authorities, 1970, The Law of Public Education, 3d edit., 1985, The Courts and Student Conduct, 1975, The Supreme Court's Impact on Public Education, 1982; also articles, chpts. in books. Chmn. citizens adv. com. Emerson (N.J.) Bd. Edn., 1954-57. Served from pvt. to 1st lt. inf. AUS, 1943-46. Recipient Marion A. McGhehey award for outstanding service in field edn. law, 1986. Mem. Nat. Orgn. Legal Problems of Edn. (pres. 1967), AAUP, Am. Assn. Sch. Adminstrs., NEA, Am. Assn. Sch. Personnel Adminstrs., Internat. Personnel Mgmt. Assn., Phi Beta Kappa, Kappa Delta Pi, Phi Delta Kappa. Home: 316 Grand Blvd Emerson NJ 07630-1157 Office: Teachers Coll Columbia Univ New York NY 10027

REVELLE, PENELOPE LOUISE, environmental issues educator, author; b. N.Y.C., Sept. 17, 1941; d. Maximilian A. and Maude L. (Peltier) Rottmann; m. Charles S. ReVelle, June 12, 1962; children: Cynthia, Elizabeth. BS in Biochemistry, Cornell U., 1962, PhD in Biochemistry, 1968. Instr. biology Ithaca (N.Y.) Coll., 1969-70, instr. cellular physiology, 1970-71; instr. biology Essex Community Coll., Balt., 1971-75, lectr. environ. sci., 1975-76, adj. prof. biology and environ. sci., 1989—; lectr. environ. sci. The Johns Hopkins U., 1992—. Author: (with C. ReVelle) Sourcebook on the Environment: The Scientific Perspective, 1972, The Environment: Issues and Choices for Society, 1980, 3rd edit., 1988, The Global Environment: Securing a Sustainable Future, 1992. Predoctoral fellow NIH, 1966-67. Mem. AAAS, Pi Kappa Phi, Sigma Xi. Mem. Unitarian Ch. Office: Essex Community Coll Dept Biology Rossville Blvd Baltimore MD 21237

REVENS, JOHN COSGROVE, JR., state senator, lawyer; b. Providence, Jan. 29, 1947; s. John C. and Rita M. (Williams) R.; AA, C.C. of R.I., 1966; BA, Providence Coll., 1969; JD, Suffolk U., 1973; m. Susan L. Shaw, Aug. 31, 1974; children: Leigh Elizabeth, Marcie Greene, Emily May. Mem. R.I. Ho. of Reps., 1968-74, sec. house steering com., 1971-74, mem. edn. and welfare com., 1968-70; admitted to R.I. bar, 1973; pres. firm Revens, Blanding, Revens & St. Pierre, Warwick, R.I., 1977—; mem. R.I. Senate, 1974-89, 1991—, mem. jud. and labor coms., 1974, chmn. jud. com., 1980-83, majority whip, 1977-80, Senate majority leader, 1983-89; dir. Abington Mut. Fire Ins. Co., Abington Ins. Co., Patrons Fire Ins. Co. R.I., New Eng. Bd. Higher Edn., 1975-83, chmn., 1977-81; past chmn. Children's Code Commn., 1979-83; bd. dirs. C.C. of R.I. Found., Vols. of Warwick Schs., R.I. Acad. Decathalon Assn.; mem. Commn. on Jud. Tenure and Discipline, 1982-84, Family Ct. Bench Bar Com., 1980-82, Women and Infants Hosp. Corp., 1983—; commr. Uniform State Laws, 1982-84. Mem. ABA, R.I. Bar Assn., Kent County Bar Assn., R.I. Trial Lawyers Assn., Am. Arbitration Assn. (panel of arbitrators 1980—), KC. Democrat. Roman Catholic. Office: 946 Centerville Rd Warwick RI 02886-4373

REVERCOMB, GEORGE HUGHES, federal judge; b. Charleston, W.Va., June 3, 1929; s. Chapman and Sara (Hughes) R.; m. Mary McCall Collins Henderson, Oct. 10, 1960. AB, Princeton (N.J.) U., 1950; JD, U. Va., 1955, LLM in Jud. Process, 1982. Bar: Va. 1955, W.Va. 1956, D.C. 1959, U.S. Supreme Ct. 1964. Pvt. practice Washington and, W.Va. and Va., 1955-56, 59-69; atty. corp. law dept. and legal asst. FCC, Washington, 1956-59; assoc. dep. atty. gen. Dept. Justice, Washington, 1969-70; judge D.C. Superior Ct., 1970-85, U.S. Dist. Ct. D.C., 1985—; vis. lectr. U. Va. Law Sch., Charlottesville, 1977-85; vice chmn. U.S. Delegation 4th UN Conf. on Prevention of Crime and Treatment of Offenders, Kyoto, Japan, 1970. Served to 1st lt. USAF, 1951-53. Fellow Am. Bar Found.; mem. ABA (chmn. nat. conf. state trial judges 1984-85), D.C. Bar Assn., Va. Bar Assn., W.Va. Bar Assn. Presbyterian. Office: US Dist Ct US Courthouse 3rd & Constitution Aves NW Washington DC 20001

REVILLE, MICHAEL WILLIAM, lawyer; b. Buffalo, N.Y., Nov. 9, 1959; s. Eugene Thomas and Joan Arlene (Schmelzinger) R. BA, SUNY, Buffalo, 1982, JD, 1985. Bar: Ohio 1987, U.S. Dist. Ct. (no. dist.) Ohio 1987. Assoc. Jones, Day, Reavis & Pogue, Cleve., 1987-91, Nat. Fuel Gas Distbn. Corp., Buffalo, 1991—. Editor Buffalo Law Rev., 1986-87. Bd. dirs. Greater Buffalo Counseling Ctrs., 1992—, United Way of Buffalo, 1992—, United Way of Cleve. Home: 186 Chapin Pkwy Buffalo NY 14209 Office: Nat Fuel Gas Distbn Corp 10 Lafayette Sq Buffalo NY 14202

REYER, ALLAN KENT, principal; b. Natrona Heights, Pa., July 18, 1948; s. Raymond Marcel Sr. and Anne Elizabeth (Smith) R.; m. Karen Marie Blumetti, Apr. 20, 1947; children: Scott Allan, Jeffrey Allan. BS Edn., California U., California, Pa., 1970; MEd, Duquesne U., 1973. Cert. indsl. arts tchr., secondary edn. adminstr. Tchr. N.E. Beaver County Sch. Dist., Elwood City, Pa., 1970-74; tchr. N.ken-Arnold Sch. Dist., New Kensington, Pa., 1974-80; draftsman Tippin's Engring. Co., Etna, Pa., 1980-83; tchr. Highlands Sch. Dist., Natrona Heights, 1983-85; asst. prin. Highlands Sch. Dist., 1985-89, prin., 1989—; cons. graphic arts New Kensington Arnold Sch. Dist., 1980-81; dept. head Highlands Sch. Dist., Natrona Heights, 1988—. Co-chair fin. com. 1st Evang. Luth. Ch., Vandergrift, 1991—. Mem. ACD, Nat. Assn. Secondary Sch. Prins., Pa. Assn. Secondary Sch. Prins., Am. Assn. Sch. Adminstrs., Nat. Middle Schs. Assn., W. County Computer Users Group, Phi Sigma Pi. Republican. Office: Highlands Middle Sch Argonne Dr at Broadview Blvd Natrona Heights PA 15056

REYES, EDUARDO MENDOZA, III, mathematics educator; b. Manila, Oct. 21, 1964; came to U.S., 1985; s. Lius Ramos and Marta (Mendoza) R. BS in Math. summa cum laude, U. the Philippines, Quezon City, 1984; MS in Math., U. Ill., 1985; postgrad., SUNY, Stony Brook. Instr. dept. math. U. the Philippines, Quezon City, 1984-85; T.A. dept. math. U. Ill., Urbana, 1985-87; actuarial assoc. Hartford (Conn.) Life Ins. Co., 1987-88; actuarial analyst Mercer-Meidinger-Hansen Cons. Co., Boston, 1988-90; teaching asst. dept. math. Tufts U., Medford, Mass., 1990; T.A. dept. math. SUNY, Stony Brook, 1990—. Nat. Sci. Devel. Bd. scholar (Philippines), 1981, Integrated Acad. Program for the Scis. scholar (Philippines), 1981. Mem. Soc. Actuaries (assoc.), Phi Kappa Phi (acad. distinction 1985). Roman Catholic. Office: SUNY Stony Brook NY 11794-3651

REYES, FRANCISCO I., reproductive endocrinologist, researcher; b. Mexico City, Jan. 5, 1935; came to U.S., 1980; s. Francisco T. Reyes-Boccaccio and Maria Rodriguez de Reyes; m. Urte Erm, Dec. 21, 1971 (div. 1989); children: Urte, Andrea, Carmen; m. Mary A. Bray, Mar. 21, 1991. B in Biol. Sci., A. von Humboldt Coll., Mexico City, 1952; MD, Univ. Nacional de Mexico, Mexico City, 1959. Diplomate Am. Bd. Obstetrics and Gynecology, sub-bd. Reproductive Endocrinology. Intern Cambridge (Mass.) City Hosp., 1961-62; resident U. Manitoba, Winnipeg, Manitoba, Can., 1967-71; asst. prof. U. Man., Winnipeg, Can., 1972-78; internship Cambridge (Mass.) City Hosp., 1962-63; residency Univ. Manitoba Hosp., Winnipeg, Manitoba, Can., 1967-71; head div. reproductive endocrinology U. Man., Winnipeg, Can., 1972-80, assoc. prof., 1978-80; prof., dir. reproductive endocrinology SUNY, Bklyn., 1980-91; dir. Fertility and Hormone Ctr. of N.Y., Bklyn., 1991—; hosp. staffs: Univ. Manitoba Health Svc. Ctr., Winnipeg, 1972-80, Suny Health Svcs. Ctr., 1980-91, Long Island Coll. Hosp., (vol.), 1991—; vis. scientist Primate Rsch. Ctr., N.Mex. State U., Holloman AFB, 1980—. Contbr. articles to profl. jours. Deutscher Akad. Austauschdienst fellow Govt. of Germany, 1959-61; R.S. McLaughlin Found. traveling fellow, Can., 1971-72. Fellow Royal Coll. Physicians and Surgeons Can.; mem. Soc. Can. Investigators in Reprodn. (caucus 1976-78), Am. Fertility Soc., Endocrine Soc., Am. Coll. Obstetricians and Gynecologists, Soc. Gynecologic Investigation, Soc. Reproductive Endocrinologists (founding). Office: Fertility/Hormone Ctr NY 161 Atlantic Ave Brooklyn NY 11201-5641

REYNOLDS, ANGUS STUART, JR., academic dean; b. Bainbridge, N.Y., Mar. 11, 1936; s. Angus Stuart and Charlotte R. (Plankenhorn) R.; m. Emiko Anne Teruya, Oct. 4, 1967; children: Elizabeth, Mari Ellen, Thomas Charles. BS, Springfield (Mass.) Coll., 1957; BA, U. Md., 1962; MS, Canisius Coll., 1965; MPA, U. Okla., 1979; EdD, George Washington U., 1986. Various managerial positions Govt. of U.S., various locations, 1957-77; pres. Reynolds Internat., Reston, Va., 1977-78; sr. cons. Control Data Edn. Co., Washington, 1978-83; chief cons. Control Data Corp., Rockville, Md., 1983-87; dir. grad. program N.Y. Inst. Tech., Old Westbury, 1987-88, assoc. dean, 1988—; cons. Bd. Edn. of N.Y.C., 1989-90; bd. dirs. Ctr. for Gulf Studies, Washington; sr. assoc. The World Group, N.Y., 1991—; tech. dir. ARCON, 1991—. Editor: Technology Transfer, 1984, Instructional Technology News, 1988—; co-author: Selecting and Developing Media for Instruction, 1992, Globalization: The International HRD Consultant's and Practitioner's Handbook, 1992; series editor: Computer-based Training, 1991—; mem. editorial bd. Tng. and Devel; consulting editor: HRD Software, 1991—. Advisor bus. and industry Bd. Edn., Washington, 1982-86; bd. dirs. United Black Fund Mgmt. Svcs. Corp. United Way, 1986. Recipient Nat. Silver medal Polish Falcons of Am., 1963, Key to the City Govt. of Lackawanna, N.Y., 1963. Mem. Am. Soc. Tng. and Devel. (bd. dirs. internat. div. 1985-86, computer learning group 1983-85, Nat. Torch award 1989, Internat. Tng. Leadership award 1992dir. instructional tech. div., 1988—), Washington Soc. Tng. and Devel. (pres. 1984, Outstanding Mem. award 1985, Outstanding Internat. Trainer of Yr. award 1986), Soc. Applied Learning Tech. (sr.). Home: PO Box 585 Central Islip NY 11722-0585 Office: NY Inst Tech French Chateau Old Westbury NY 11568

REYNOLDS, C(LAUDE) LEWIS, JR., materials scientist, researcher; b. Roanoke, Va., Dec. 16, 1948; s. Claude Lewis and Lois Anne (Warren) R.; m. Sherryl Ann Allbright (div. Apr. 1989); children: Karen, Brian, Kristin; m. Mary Elizabeth Derr, Aug. 29, 1989; 1 child, Jeff. BS in Physics, Va. Mil. Inst., 1970; MS in Materials Sci., U. Va., 1972, PhD in Materials Sci., 1974. Sr. materials scientist U. Va., Charlottesville, 1974-75; rsch. assoc. in physics U. Ill., Urbana, 1975-77; sr. project engr. Union Carbide Corp., Indpls., 1977-80; disting. mem. tech. staff AT&T Bell Labs., Reading, Pa., 1980—. Contbr. over 75 articles to profl. jours.; co-patentee LPE apparatus with improved thermal geometry, self-aligned rib-waveguide high power laser, fabrication of GaAs integrated circuits. Mem. IEEE, AAAS, Am. Phys. Soc., Materials Rsch. Soc., Am. Assn. Physics Tchrs., Sigma Xi. Methodist. Office: AT&T Bell Labs 2525 N 12th St Reading PA 19612-3566

REYNOLDS, EDWIN WILFRED, JR., teacher; b. Englewood, N.J., Mar. 23, 1937; s. Edwin W. and Ellen H. (Hueber) R.; m. Sharon Policastro, Feb. 12, 1983. BA cum laude, Fairleigh Dickinson U, 1961, MAT magna cum laude, 1966; postgrad., NYU, 1964-65, Seton Hall U., 1970-71, Montclair State Coll., 1972-73. Cert. social studies tchr., supr., tchr. psychology, N.J. Supr. installation Western Electric Co., N.Y.C., 1961-65; tchr. social studies Teaneck (N.J.) High Sch., 1965—, chmn. dept. social studies, 1968-71; supr. social studies Teaneck Secondary Schs., 1971-80, supr. grades K-12, 1980—, supr. bus. edn. grades 7-12, 1984—; bd. dir. Global Learning, Inc.; sr. state cons. in Holocaust Edn., N.J.; curriculum coord. Ctr. for Holocaust/Genocide Studies, Ramapo Coll.; guest lectr. Kean Coll.; coord. M.A.T. program Fairleigh Dickinson U., 1969-71; mem. planning com. N.E. Regional Social Studies Conf., mem. steering com. Mid-Atlantic Conf.; mem. N.J. Dept. Edn. Social Studies Adv. Com., N.J. Gov.'s Adv. Coun. for Holocaust Edn. in the Pub. Schs.; cons. world history Scott Foresman Pub. Co. Author curriculum devel. and learning guides, 1973—; co-editor: Holocaust and Genocide: A Search for Conscience. Elder Presbyn. Ch., U.S. With USN, 1955-57. Recipient Human Rights award Temple Beth Tikvah, 1985, Brotherhood award B'nai B'rith No. and Pascack Valleys, 1986, Daniel Roselle Lectr. award Mid. States Coun. for Social Studies, 1988. Mem. Nat. Coun. for Social Studies (former bd. dirs), N.J. Coun. for Social Studies (bd. dirs., past pres.), Greater Bergen County (N.J.) Coun. for Social Studies (bd. dirs., past pres.), Social Studies Suprs. Assn. (past pres.), Assn. Ednl. Suprs. (past pres.), Assn. Supervision and Curriculum Devel., Am. Hist. Assn., Phi Delta Kappa, Phi Omega Epsilon. Home: 231 Thayer St Westwood NJ 07675-6254 Office: Teaneck Pub Schs 1 Merrison St Teaneck NJ 07666-4616

REYNOLDS, GARY KEMP, librarian; b. Phila., June 2, 1944; s. Thomas Clifford and Lillian Olive (Thompson) R.; m. Regina Romano, May 16, 1970; 1 child, Elizabeth Alexandra Marie. BA in History (with honors), Pa. State U., 1973, BA in E. Asian Studies magna cum laude, 1973; MA in E.Asian Studies, U. Mich., 1975, MLS, 1976. Reference librarian George Washington U., Washington, 1977-80; reference specialist congl. rsch. svc. Libr. of Congress, Washington, 1980—. Book reviewer of jours.; contbr. articles to profl. jours. Sgt. USAF, 1962-66. Mem. Phi Beta Kappa, Phi Kappa Phi, Phi Alpha Theta, Mensa. Republican. Episcopalian. Home: 7603 Marian Ct Falls Church VA 22042-3515 Office: Libr of Congress Washington DC 20540

REYNOLDS, HERBERT YOUNG, physician, internist; b. Richmond, Va., Aug. 20, 1939; s. George Audney and Pearle Maupin (Young) R.; m. Anne Browning Leavell, July 11, 1964; children: Nancy, George, William Stuart. BA in English, U. Va., 1961, MD, 1965; MA (hon.), Yale U., 1979. Diplomate Am. Bd. Internal Medicine, Am. Bd. Allergy and Immunology. Intern in medicine The N.Y. Hosp., Cornell Med. Ctr., N.Y.C., 1965-66, asst. physician, fellow in medicine, 1966-67; clin. assoc., lab clin. investigator Nat. Inst. Allergy and Infectious Diseases, NIH, Bethesda, Md., 1967-70, chief clin. assoc. lab. clin. investigation, 1968-69; sr. investigator lab. of clin. investigation Nat. Inst. Allergy and Infectious Diseases, NIH, 1971-76; chief resident, instr. medicine U. Hosp. U. Wash., Seattle, 1970-71; assoc. prof. internal medicine, head pulmonary div. Sch. Medicine Yale U., New Haven, 1976-79, prof., 1979-88; J. Lloyd Huck prof. medicine, chmn. dept. Pa. State U.-Milton S. Hershey Med. Ctr., 1988—; mem. exec. com. Coll. Medicine Pa. State U.-Hershey Med. Ctr., 1988—, mem. exec. bd. U. Hosp., 1988—, mem. fin. bd. acad. enrichment fun, 1988—, mem. dean's adv. com., 1988—, others; cons. in infectious diseases Nat. Naval Med. Ctr. NIH, Bethesda, 1971-76, clin. rsch. com. mem., 1971-76, chmn., 1974, med. bd. mem., 1974-76, pulmonary disease adv. com. div. of lung diseases Nat. Heart, Lung and Blood Inst., 1978-82, mem. sci. counselors bd., 1984-88, mem. data and safety monitoring bd. registry of patients with deficiency of Alpha-1 Antitrypsin, 1989—. Assoc. editor or mem. editorial bd. Lung, 1978—, Am. Jour. Medicine, 1979-86, Jour. Clin. Investigation, 1980-86, Am. Rev. Respiratory Disease, 1980-87, Jour. Applied Physiology, 1981-89, Resident Physician, 1981—; contbr. articles to profl. jours. Mem. parent com. Troop 1 Boy Scouts Am., Madison, 1979-82; bd. dirs. Neighborhood Music Sch., Guilford, Conn. 1978-87; active All Saints Episc. Ch., Hershey; mem. pulmonary infections com. Cystic Fibrosis Found., Bethesda, 1980-86; mem. coun. sci. advisors Parker B. Francis Found., Kansas City, Kan., 1983-87; mem. internat. com. World Orgn. for Sarcoidosis and other Granulomatous Disorders, 1987—; bd. dirs., mem. coun. Am. Lung Assn., 1989—, various com. positions, 1990—; coach Guilford Soccer League, 1985-88. Surgeon, USPHS, 1967-70, 75-76. John Edward Nobel fellow, 1961-65; named Outstanding Med. Specialist in USA, Town and Country Mag., 1989, One of 400 Best Drs. in U.S. Good Housekeeping Mag., 1991. Fellow ACP (coun. subspecialty socs. 1989—), Am. Coll. Chest Physicians (program com. 1978-84), Infectious Disease Soc. Am.; mem. Am. Thoracic Soc. (sec.-treas. 1987-88, bd. dirs. 1989—, v.p. 1988-89, pres.-elect 1990-91, pres. 1991-92, various com. positions 1980—), Am. Soc. Clin. Investigation, Assn. Am. Physicians, Am. Assn. Immunologists, Am. Fed. Clin. Rsch., Am. Clin. and Climatological Soc., Interurban Clin. Club (emeritus 1989), Assn. Profs. of Medicine, Sachem's Head Yacht Club, Farmington Country Club, Raven Soc., Alpha Omega Alpha, Phi Beta Kappa, Omicron Delta Kappa, Sigma Xi. Republican. Home: 226 E Caracas Ave Hershey PA 17033 Office: Pa State U Milton S Hershey Med Ctr 850 University Dr Hershey PA 17033

REYNOLDS, JEAN EDWARDS, publishing executive; b. Saginaw, Mich., Dec. 11, 1941; d. F. Perry and Kathrine (Edwards) R.; m. Cary Wellington, Sept. 10, 1975 (div. 1982); children, Bradley, Abigail, Benjamin. BA, Wells Coll., 1963; postgrad., CCNY, 1965-67. Asst. editor, sr. editor trade book div. Prentice-Hall, Englewood Cliffs, N.J., 1963-66; dir. children's books Prentice-Hall, Englewood Cliffs, 1966-69, McCall Pub. Co., N.Y.C., 1969-71; sr. v.p., editorial dir. Franklin Watts Inc., N.Y.C., 1971-75; pres. Pet Projects Inc., Ridgefield, Conn., 1975-81; editor in chief young people's publs. Grolier Inc., Danbury, Conn., 1981-89; pres. The Millbrook Press, Brookfield, Conn., 1989—; bd. dirs. Kiper Enterprises, Oswego, N.Y. Bd. dirs. Jewish Home for the Elderly, Fairfield, Conn., 1989-90, Book Industry Study Group, 1991—, The Wooster Sch., Danbury, Conn., 1992—; pres. Jewish Fedn. Greater Danbury, 1991—; chair Conn. Ctr. for the Book, 1991—. Mem. ALA, Children's Book Coun., Mensa. Jewish. Home: 33 Corntassle Rd Danbury CT 06811-3208 Office: The Millbrook Press Inc 2 Old New Milford Rd Brookfield CT 06804-2426

REYNOLDS, KEITH LAMAR, artist; b. Seattle, June 20, 1929; s. Lamar Guernsey and Clarice Charlotte (Wirfs) R.; m. Theckla Ann Arthur, 1950 (div. 1967); m. Sandra Joan Ratliff, 1969. BS, U. Oreg., 1952; B Profl. Arts, Art Ctr. Coll. Design, L.A., 1956. Art dir. McCann-Erickson Advt., N.Y.C., 1956-59, art dir., group head, 1959-61; pres., sr. designer Nesbitt Reynolds Inc. Film Co., N.Y.C., 1961-69, SARN, Inc. Advt. & Pub. Rels., N.Y.C., 1966-69; exec. v.p. Wetzel Assoc. Mus. Designers, Boston, 1969-76; pres. Mystic River Studios Inc., Conn., NH, 1976—; gallery artist various U.S./internat. galleries, 1960—. Mem. Soc. Illustrators (artist), Mystic Art Assn. (pres. 1981-82). Home and office: Mystic River Studios RR 2 Box 387 Sanbornville NH 03872-9721

REYNOLDS, NANCY BRADFORD DUPONT (MRS. WILLIAM GLASGOW REYNOLDS), sculptor; b. Greenville, Del., Dec. 28, 1919; d. Eugene Eleuthere and Catherine Dulcinea (Moxham) duPont; m. William Glasgow Reynolds, May 18, 1940; children: Kathrine Glasgow Reynolds, William Bradford, Mary Parminter Reynolds Savage, Cynthia duPont Reynolds Farris. Student, Goldey-Beacom Coll., Wilmington, Del., 1938. One-woman shows include Rehoboth (Del.) Art League, 1963, Del. Art Mus., Wilmington, Caldwell, Inc., 1975, Wilmington Art Mus., 1976; exhibited group shows Corcoran Gallery, Washington, 1943, Soc. Fine Arts, Wilmington, 1937, 38, 40, 41, 48, 50, 62, 65, NAD, N.Y.C., 1964, Pa. Mil. Coll., Chester, 1966, Del. Art Ctr., 1967, Met. Mus. Art, N.Y.C., 1977, Lever House, N.Y.C., 1979; represented in permanent collections Wilmington Trust Co., E.I. duPont de Nemours & Co., Children's Home, Inc., Claymont, Del., Children's Bur., Wilmington, Stephenson Sci. Ctr., Nashville, Lutheran Towers Bldg., Travelers Aid and Family Soc. Bldg., Wilmington, Bronze Fountain Head, Longwood Gardens, Kennett Square, Pa. Guide; contbr. articles to profl. jours. Organizer vol. svc. Del. chpt. ARC, 1938-39; chmn. Com. for Revision Del. Child Adoption Law, 1950-52; pres. bd. dirs. Children Bur. Del.; pres., trustee Children's Home, Inc.; del. regent Gunston Hall Plantation, Lorton, Va.; mem. adv. com. Longwood Gardens, Kennett Sq., Pa.; garden and grounds com. Winterthur (Del.) Mus.; mem. rsch. staff Henry Francis DuPont Winterthur Mus., 1955-63. Recipient Confrerie des Chevaliers du Tastevin Clos de Vougeot-Bourgogne France, 1960; Hort. award Garden Club Am., 1964, medal of Merit, 1976; Dorothy Platt award Garden Club of Phila., 1980; Alumni medal of merit Westover Sch., Middlebury, Conn. Mem. Pa. Hort. Soc., Wilmington Soc. Fine Arts, Mayflower Descs., Del. Hist. Soc., Colonial Dames, League Am. Pen Women, Nat. Trust Hist. Preservation. Garden Club of Wilmington (past pres.), Garden Club of Am. (past asst. zone 4 chmn.), Vicmead Hunt Club, Greenville Country Club, Chevy Chase Club (Washington), Colony Club (N.Y.C.). Episcopalian. Address: PO Box 3919 Greenville DE 19807

REYNOLDS, PATRICIA ELLEN, artist; b. Portchester, N.Y., Apr. 6, 1934; d. Edwin and Anna (Pacewicz) Steeg; student SUNY, Plattsburg, 1951-52, Moon Bus. Sch., N.Y.C., 1953; pupil of Robert Whitney, Mario Cooper; m. Carlyle Reynolds, Oct. 4, 1953 (div. 1991); children: Clifford, Stephanie. Watercolor painter, Willsboro, N.Y., condr. workshops in field, mem. art juries; one-woman exhbns. include Gallerie Camille Renaud, Paris, 1979, Hollsworthy Gallery, London, 1980, Center Modern Design, Riyadh, Saudi Arabia, 1981-83; group exhbns. include Schenectady Mus., SUNY, Plattsburgh, St. Lawrence U., Canton, N.Y., Center for Music, Drama and Arts, Lake Placid, N.Y., 1980, Audubon Artists Ann., 1980, Fleming Mus., Burlington, Vt., Am. Watercolor Soc. travel exhbn., 1982, 87 (Lina Newcastle award) Salmagundi Club 1983, 88, 89, 91, 92 (Gold Medal award), 1983, Nat. Works on Paper, 1982, Nat. Exhbn. Am. Watercolors, 1983, 84, 87 (travel exhbn. award), William Kawalsky Meml. award, 1991; Allied Artist Exhibition, 1987, 91; Watercolor West Exhbn., 1988, Mid-west W.C. Soc. Exhbn., 1983, 89, 92, Nat. Watercolor Soc., 1991, Advandack Park Centennial award, Multi-Focus award, 1992; represented in permanent corp., univ. and pvt. collections. Recipient Best of Show award No. Vt. Artists, 1970, 71, 76, 78, 79, Outstanding Woman Artist award Am. Pen Women, 1975, Benedictine Nat. award, 1975, Adirondack Art Exhbn. award, 1973, North Country award, Allied Artists Am. (assoc.), Cen. N.Y. Watercolor Soc., Adirondack Art Assn., No. Vt. Artists, Copley Soc. Boston. Address: Willsboro Point Rd # 390 Willsboro NY 12996

REYNOLDS, RICHARD KENT, corporate executive; b. Glen Ridge, N.J., Sept. 25, 1956; s. Martin Andre and Diane Mary (Schappert) R.; m. Jane Moore Henry, Oct. 7, 1982; children: Jack, Kate, Patrick. BSBA, U. Denver, 1979. Sales engr. Tiger Equipment and Svc. Corp., Chgo., 1980-82; sales mgr. Monarch Engring. & Svc. Corp., Milford, Conn., 1982-86; exec. v.p. R.H. Crown Co. Inc., Johnstown, N.Y., 1986—; bd. dirs. Nathan Littauer Svc. Corp., Gloversville, N.Y., Nathan Littauer Hosp., Gloversville. Mem. Winged Foot Golf Club, Pine Brook Golf Club (bd. dirs. 1989—). Republican. Home: 600 S William Johnstown NY 12095 Office: RH Crown Co 100 N Market Johnstown NY 12095

REYNOLDS, ROBERT JOEL, economist, consultant; b. Indpls., May 13, 1944; s. Joel Burr and Betty (Schimpf) R.; m. Lucinda Margaret Lewis, May 27, 1979; children: Joel, Sarah. BSBA in Fin., Northwestern U., 1965, PhD in Econs., 1970. Asst. prof. econs. U. Idaho, Moscow, 1969-73, assoc. prof., 1973-75; asst. dir, sr. economist econ. policy office Dept. Justice, Washington, 1973-81; sr. economist, v.p. ICF Inc., Washington, 1981-87, sr. v.p., 1987-91; exec. v.p., prin. Econsult Corp., Washington, 1991—; vis. assoc. prof. U. Calif., Berkeley, 1976-77, Cornell U., Ithaca, N.Y., 1981. Reviewer: NSF, Rand Jour. of Econs., Internat. Econ. Rev., Internat. Jour. Indsl. Orgn., Jour. Indsl. Econs., Am. Econ. Rev.; mem. editorial bd. Managerial and Decision Econs.; contbr. numerous papers to profl. jours. Recipient Dow Jones award Wall St. Jour., 1965; AT&T grantee, 1971-72, Brookings Instl. grantee, 1968-69; NDEA fellow, 1965-69. Mem. AAAS, Am. Econ. Assoc., Econometric Soc., Royal Econ. Soc., Am. Statis. Assn., European Assn. for Rsch. in Indsl. Econs., Soc. for the Promotion of Econ. Theory, Math. Assn. Am. Congregationalist. Home: 9228 Farnsworth Dr Rockville MD 20854-4503 Office: Econsult Corp Ste 370 901 15th St NW Washington DC 20005

REYNOLDS, ROBERT WEBSTER, public relations; b. Ossining, N.Y., Feb. 20, 1941; s. Clifton Elmer and Marie (Webster) R.; m. Mary Tibbetts Gregory, Dec. 20, 1961; children: Robert, Jill. BA, Dartmouth Coll., 1963; MBA, Columbia U., 1964. Traffic mgr. N.J. Bell, Morristown, 1967-69; pub. info. mgr. N.J. Bell, Newark, 1969-71; dist. mgr. residence N.J. Bell, Clifton, 1971-73; dist. mgr. bus., 1973-75; dist. mgr. pub. affairs Newark, 1975-81; consumer affairs mgr. AT&T, Basking Ridge, N.J., 1981-83; pub. rels. mgr. AT&T Communications, Basking Ridge, N.J., 1983-85. Dir. Nat. Coun. on Crime and Delinquency, San Francisco, 1981—, The Alliance N.Y. State Arts Coun., Stewart Airport, 1988-90; pres. N.J. Coun. Econ. Edn., Trenton, 1981-82; state coord. "Take a Bite Out of Crime" Campaign, Newark, 1980-81. Decorated Bronze Star. Mem. Pub. Rels. Soc. Am., Warner Lodge. Republican. Presbyterian. Office: AT&T Bell Labs 101 John F Kennedy Pkwy Short Hills NJ 07078

REYNOLDS, THOMAS P., company executive; b. Anchorage, Mar. 24, 1952; s. William George and Shirley Jane (Cook) R.; m. Susan Marie Badowski, May 1, 1982. B Design, U. Colo., 1975. Mktg. rep. Consumers Mktg. Corp., Boston, 1976-80; sales mgr. A.B. Dick Co., Milford, Conn., 1980-81; regional mgr. A.B. Dick Co., N.Y.C., 1981-83; area nat. account mgr. Harris Corp., N.Y.C., 1983-84, dist.mgr., 1984-89; dist.mgr. Hewlett-Packard Co., Glastonbury, Conn., 1989-90; regional dir. Motorola/Codex, Wallingford, Conn., 1990-92; ea. area dir. mktg. Motorola/Codex, Clifton, N.J., 1992—. Home: 4943 Madison Ave Trumbull CT 06611-1534

REYNOLDS, TOM, communications executive; b. Torrington, Conn., Aug. 20, 1950; s. Theodore Joseph and Lena (Cirillo) Bruttomesso; m. Linda Perlini, May 21, 1977; children: Tricia, Kimberly. Diploma, Leland Powers Sch. Radio, 1970. News and sports dir. Sta. WOWW, Naugatuck, Conn., 1970-72; reporter, anchor Sta. WRCQ, Farmington, Conn., 1972-73; sales rep. Sta. WOWW, Waterbury, Conn., 1973-74; ops. mgr. Sta. WIOF, Waterbury, 1974-77; gen. mgr. Full of Baloney Corp., Waterbury, 1977-81; sports dir. Sta. WPOP, Hartford, Conn., 1981-83, news dir., 1983-86; communications dir. YMCA Met. Hartford, 1986—; voting mem. Conn. Soc. to Prvent Blindness, Middletown, Conn., 1984—; trustee Martin Luther King

Jr. Youth Found., Hartford, 1984-88; trainer YMCA of the U.S.A., Chgo., 1987—. Vol. Boy Scouts Am., Newington, Conn., 1987-88. Mem. Internat. Assn. Bus. Communicators (Bronze Quill 1988), Pub. Rels. Soc. Am. Roman Catholic. Office: Hartford YMCA 160 Jewell St Hartford CT 06103-2006

REYNOLDS, W(YNETKA) ANN, university system administrator, educator; b. Coffeyville, Kans., Nov. 3, 1937; d. John Ethelbert and Glennie (Beanland) King; m. Thomas H. Kirschbaum; children—Rachel Rebecca, Rex King. BS in Biology-Chemistry, Kans. State Tchrs. Coll., Emporia, 1958; MS in Zoology, U. Iowa, Iowa City, 1960, PhD, 1962; DSc (hon.), Ind. State U., Evansville, 1980; LHD (hon.), McKendree Coll., 1984, U. N.C., Charlotte, 1988, U. Judaism, L.A., 1989, U. Nebr., Kearney, 1992; DSc (hon.), Ball State U., Muncie, Ind., 1985, Emporia (Kans.) State U., 1987; PhD (hon.), Fu Jen Cath. U., Republic of China, 1987; LHD (hon.), U. Nebr., Kearney, 1992. Asst. prof. biology Ball State U., Muncie, Ind., 1962-65; asst. prof. anatomy U. Ill. Coll. Medicine, Chgo., 1965-68, assoc. prof. anatomy, 1968-73, research prof. ob-gyn, from 1973, prof. anatomy, from 1973, acting assoc. dean acad. affairs Coll. Medicine, 1977, assoc. vice chancellor, dean grad. coll., 1977-79; provost, v.p. for acad. affairs, prof. ob-gyn. and anatomy Ohio State U., Columbus, 1979-82; chancellor Calif. State Univ. system, Long Beach, 1982-90, prof. biology, 1982-90; cons. and lectr. in field; prof. biology Calif. State U., Dominguez Hills, 1982-90; hon. prof. biol. scis. San Francisco State U., 1982-90; clin. prof. ob/gyn. UCLA, 1985-90; chancellor CUNY, 1990—; co-chair Fed. Task Force on Women, Minorities and Handicapped in Sci. and Tech., 1987-90; adv. bd. Congl. Black Caucus Inst. Sci., Space and Tech., 1987—; bd. dirs. Regional Rsch. Inst. So. Calif., 1984-87; co-chair Humanitas Coun. L.A. Ednl. Partnership, 1986-89; bd. dirs. Maytag Corp., Abbott Labs., Am. Electric Power Co., Humana, Inc. Contbr. chpts. to books, articles to profl. jours; assoc. editor Am. Biology Tchr., 1964-67. Active numerous civic activities involving edn. and the arts; chair Econ. Literacy Coun. Calif., 1983-89; bd. dirs. Am. Council for the Arts, 1986—, Calif. Econ. Devel. Corp., 1984-90; trustee Internat. Life Scis. Inst.-Nutrition Found., 1987—, Southwest Mus., L.A., 1986-90, L.A. County High Sch. For Arts Found., 1985-90. Recipient Disting. Alumni award Kans. State Tchrs. Coll., 1972, Calif. Gov.'s Award for the Arts for an Outstanding Individual in Arts in Edn., 1989, Prize award Cen. Assn. Obstetricians and Gynecologists, 1968; NSF Predoctoral fellow, 1958-62, Woodrow Wilson Hon. fellow, 1958. Fellow Calif. Acad. Scis., Am. Coll. Obstetricians and Gynecologists (assoc.); mem. AAAS, Am. Assn. Anatomists, Am. Diabetes Assn., Am. Soc. Zoologists, Am. Assn. for Higher Edn. (bd. dirs. 1984-86), Endocrine Soc., Perinatal Rsch. Soc., Soc. Exptl. Biology and Medicine, Soc. Gynecologic Investigation (sec./treas. 1980-83, pres. 1992-93), Nat. Assn. Systems Heads (pres. 1987-88), Calif. C. of C. (bd. dirs. 1990), Sigma Xi. Office: CUNY Office of the Chancellor 535 E 80th St New York NY 10021-0767

REZEK, GEOFFREY ROBERT, management consultant; b. Queens, N.Y., Nov. 23, 1941; s. Joseph and Louise (Martin) R.; m. Jacqueline Ann Greenfield, Aug. 23, 1973; children: Christopher Robert, Joseph Paul. BS in Indsl. Mgmt., L.I. U., 1964, MS in Mgmt. Engring., 1966. Cert. purchasing mgr. Indsl. engr. IBM Corp., East Fishkill, N.Y., 1965-67; systems engr. IBM Corp., Garden City, N.Y., 1967-73; mfg. industry specialist IBM Corp., Garden City, 1973-81, N.Y.C., 1981-83; mfg. industry mktg. IBM Corp., Norwalk, Conn., 1983-91; prin. G.R. Rezek & Assocs., Darien, Conn., 1991—. With USNG, 1967-73. Mem. Am. Prodn. and Inventory Control Soc. (cert., v.p. bd. dirs. 1973-76, 91), Nat. Speakers Assn., Inst. Indsl. Engrs. (sr.). Home and Office: GR Rezek & Assocs 110 Raymond St Darien CT 06820-4926

RHEINBOLDT, WERNER CARL, mathematics educator, researcher; b. Berlin, Sept. 18, 1927; came to U.S., 1956; s. Karl L. and Gertrud (Hartwig) R. Dipl Math, U. Heidelberg, Fed. Republic Germany, 1952; Dr rer nat, U. Freiburg, Fed. Republic Germany, 1955. Mathematician Computer Lab., Nat. Bur. Standards, Washington, 1957-59; asst. prof. math., dir. Computer Ctr., Syracuse (N.Y.) U., 1959-62; dir. Computer Sci. Ctr., U. Md., College Park, 1962-65, prof. math. and computer sci., 1965-78, dir. applied math. program, 1974-78; A.W. Mellon prof. math. U. Pitts., 1978—; cons. various orgns., 1965—; cons. editor Acad. Press, Inc., N.Y.C., 1987—; mem. adv. panel NSF, Army Rsch. Office, Office Naval Rsch., NASA. Author: (with J. Ortega) Iterative Solution of Nonlinear Equations in Several Variables, 1970; Methods of Solving Systems of Nonlinear Equations, 1974, Numerical Analysis of Parametrized Equations, 1985; contbr. over 120 articles to sci. jours. With German Army, 1943-45. Recipient Av. Humboldt Disting. Scientist award, Alexander von Humboldt Found., Germany; grantee NSF, 1965—, Office Naval Rsch., 1972—. Fellow AAAS; mem. Am. Math. Soc., Soc. for Indsl. and Applied Math. (editor 1964—, v.p. publs. 1976, pres. 1977-78, coun. 1979-80, trustee, 1982, chmn. bd. trustees 1985-90). Office: U Pitts Dept Math and Stats Pittsburgh PA 15260

RHEINS, CARL JEFFREY, dean, educator, historian; b. Cin., Sept. 17, 1945; s. Joseph Melvin and Gertrude (Mandell) R.; m. Brenda Dale Evertz, July 8, 1979; children: Jason Gabriel, Jaclyn Gail. BS, U. Wis., 1967; MA, SUNY, Albany, 1970; PhD, SUNY, Stony Brook, 1978. Lectr. Judaic studies SUNY, Stony Brook, 1974-78, asst. to provost, 1978-79, 81-86; dir. acad. affairs Nat. Found. Jewish Culture, N.Y.C., 1980-81; asst. dean Adelphi U., Garden City, N.Y., 1986-87, assoc. dean, 1987, exec. asst. to pres., 1987-90, dean student life and devel., 1990—; bd. dirs. Coalition on Higher Edn., Jewish Community Rels. Coun., N.Y.C. Contbr. author: Yearbook of the Leo Baeck Inst., 1978, 80, 81; co-editor: Jewish Almanac, 1980 (dual main selection Jewish Book Club of Am. 1981). Active nat. governing coun. Am. Jewish Congress, N.Y.C., 1986-87; 1st v.p. Am. Jewish Congress, Suffulk County, N.Y., 1985-87; bd. govs. Am. Jewish Com. L.I. Region, N.Y., 1984-85. Summer fellow NEH, 1987. Mem. Phi Kappa Phi, Phi Alpha Theta, Alpha Epsilon Pi. Home: 5 Merrimac Ct Dix Hills NY 11746 Office: Adelphi U Office Dean Student Life & Devel 106 Harley Ctr Garden City NY 11530

RHEINSTEIN, JOHN, phyicist, consultant; b. Gerdelegen, Fed. Republic of Germany, May 23, 1930; came to U.S., 1934; s. Max and Elizabeth J. (Abele) R.; m. Mary Elizabeth Jones, Dec. 15, 1956; children Bruce, Lila Renata, Eric. AB, Dartmouth Coll., 1951; MS, U. Chgo., 1957; PhD, Tech. U., Munich, Fed. Republic of Germany, 1961. Staff mem. MIT Lincoln Lab., Lexington, 1961-66, assoc. group leader, 1966-69; asst. site mgr. MIT Lincoln Lab., Kwajalein, Marshall Islands, 1969-71, assoc. site mgr., 1971-73; group leader MIT Lincoln Lab., Lexington, 1973-90; cons. Carl Blake Assocs., Lexington, 1990—. Lt. (j.g.) USN, 1951-54. Recipient Spl. Recognition award, IEEE, 1969, Best Paper of Yr. award, Jour. of Defense Rsch., 1984. Home and Office: 10 Gould Rd Lexington MA 02173-1012

RHEINSTEIN, PETER HOWARD, government official, physician, lawyer; b. Cleve., Sept. 7, 1943; s. Franz Joseph Rheinstein and Hede Henrietta (Neheimer) Rheinstein Lerner; m. Miriam Ruth Weissman, Feb. 22, 1969; 1 child, Jason Edward. B.A. with high honors, Mich. State U., 1963, M.S., 1964; M.D., Johns Hopkins U., 1967; J.D., U. Md., 1973. Bar: Md., D.C.; diplomate Am. Bd. Family Practice 1977, recert. 1983, 89. Intern USPHS Hosp., San Francisco, 1967-68; resident in internal medicine USPHS Hosp., Balt., 1968-70; practice medicine specializing in internal medicine Balt., 1970—; instr. medicine U. Md., Balt., 1970-73; med. dir. extended care facilities CHC Corp., Balt., 1972-74; dir. drug advt. and labeling div. FDA, Rockville, Md., 1974-82, acting dep. dir. Office Drugs, 1982-83, acting dir. Office Drugs, 1983-84, dir. Office Drug Standards, 1984-90; dir. medicine staff, Office Health Affairs FDA, 1990—; adj. prof. forensic medicine George Washington U., 1974-76; WHO cons. on drug regulation Nat. Inst. for Control Pharm. and Biol. Products, People's Republic of China, 1981—; advisor on essential drugs WHO, 1985—; FDA del. to U.S. Pharmacopeial Conv., 1985-90. Co-author: (with others) Human Organ Transplantation, 1987; spl. editorial advisor Good Housekeeping Guide to Medicine and Drugs, 1977—; mem. editorial bd. Legal Aspects Med. Practice, 1981-89, Drug Info. Jour., 1982-86, 91—; contbr. articles to profl. jours. Recipient Commendable Svc. award FDA, 1981, group award of merit, 1983, 88, group commendable svc. award, 1989. Fellow Am. Coll. Legal Medicine (bd. govs. 1983—, treas., chmn. fin. com. 1985-88, 90-91, chmn. publs. com. 1988—, Pres.'s awards 1985, 86, 89, 90, 91), Am. Acad. Family Physicians; mem. AMA, ABA, Drug Info. Assn. (bd. dirs. 1982-90, pres. 1984-85, 88-89, v.p. 1986-87, chmn. ann. meeting 1991, N.Am. steering com. 1991—, Outstanding Svc. award 1990), Fed. Bar Assn. (chmn. food and drug com. 1976-79, Disting. Svc. award 1977), Med. and Chirurgical Faculty Md., Balt. City Med. Soc., Johns Hopkins Med. and Surg. Assn., Am. Pub. Health Assn., Md. Bar Assn., Math. Assn. Am., Soc. Indsl and Applied Math., Mensa (life), U.S. Power Squadrons, Mich. State U. Alumni Assn. (life), U. Md. Alumni Assn. (life), Johns Hopkins U. Alumni Assn., Chartwell Golf and Country Club, Annapolis Yacht Club, Johns Hopkins Club, Delta Theta Phi. Home: 621 Holly Ridge Rd Severna Park MD 21146-3520 Office: FDA Office of Health Affairs Dir Medicine Staff 5600 Fishers Ln Rockville MD 20857-0001

RHETT, HASKELL EMERY SMITH, foundation administrator, educator; b. Evanston, Ill., Aug. 29, 1936; s. Haskell Smith and Eunice Campbell (Emery) R.; m. Roberta Teel Oliver, Sept. 9, 1961 (div. 1973); children: Kathryn Emery, Cecily Coffin; m. Anita Mary Osper, May 30, 1983; 1 child, Katherine Leone. AB, Hamilton Coll., 1958; MA, Cornell U., 1967, PhD, 1968. Asst. to the pres. Hamilton Coll., Clinton, N.Y., 1961-64; rsch. asst. Cornell U., Ithaca, N.Y., 1964-66; rsch. assoc. U. London, 1966-67; dir. program devel. Ednl. Testing Svc., Princeton, N.J., 1967-73; asst. chancellor N.J. Dept. Higher Edn., Trenton, 1973-85; v.p. The Coll. Bd., N.Y.C., 1985-90; pres. The Woodrow Wilson Nat. Fellowship Found., Princeton, 1990—. Author: Going to College in New Jersey, 1978; contbg. author: Government's Role in Supporting College Savings, 1990. Commr. N.J. Pub. Broadcast Authority, Trenton, 1983-85; mem. Nat. Task Force on Student Aid Problems, Washington, 1974-75; trustee Dominican Coll., San Rafael, Calif., 1990—; del. Dem. Nat. Conv., Miami, 1972; sr. warden Trinity Episcopal Ch., Princeton, 1988—, vestryman, 1979-82, dep. Gen. Conv., Detroit, 1988, Phoenix, 1991. Lt. USNR, 1958-61. Nat. Def. fellow U.S. Govt., 1966-67, Eliot-Winant fellow Brit.-Am. Assocs., 1982, Harvard U. fellow, 1985. Mem. Am. Assn. for Higher Edn., Nat. Assn. State Scholarship and Grant Programs (pres. 1976-78), Nassau Club, Cornell Club, Springdale Golf Club. Home: 43 Van Kirk Rd Princeton NJ 08540-4212 also: PO Box 53 Blue Hill Falls ME 04615 Office: The Woodrow Wilson Nat Fellowship Found PO Box 642 Princeton NJ 08542-0642

RHIEW, FRANCIS CHANGNAM, physician; b. Korea, Dec. 3, 1938; came to U.S., 1967, naturalized, 1977; s. Byung Kyun and In Sil (Lee) R.; m. Kay Kyungja Chang, June 11, 1967; children: Richard C., Elizabeth. BS, Seoul Nat. U., 1960, MD, 1964. Intern, St. Mary's Hosp., Waterbury, Conn., 1967-68; resident in radiology and nuclear medicine L.I.U.-Queens Hosp. Ctr., N.Y., 1968-71; instr. radiology W. Va. U. Sch. Medicine, Morgantown, 1971-73; mem. staff Mercy Hosp. and Moses Taylor Hosp., Scranton, Pa., 1973—, also dir. nuclear medicine; clin. instr., Temple U., 1987—; pres. Radiol. Consultants, Inc., 1984—. Served with M.C., Korean Army, 1964-67. Recipient Minister of Health and Welfare award, 1963; certified Am. Bd. Nuclear Medicine. Mem. AMA, Soc. Nuclear Medicine, Radiol. Soc. N.Am., Am. Coll. Nuclear Medicine, Am. Coll. Radiology, Am. Inst. Ultra Sound, Country Club Scranton, Pres.'s Club U. Scranton, Elks. Home: 14 Lakeside Dr Clarks Summit PA 18411 Office: 746 Jefferson Ave Scranton PA 18501

RHOADES, DENNIS KEITH, legal foundation administrator; b. Burbank, Calif., Aug. 1, 1944; s. Charles Bernis Rhoades and Madeline Fern (Miller) Regan; m. Julie Rae Zukovsky, Nov. 10, 1970 (div. Sept. 1984). BA, UCLA, 1966; postgrad., U. Wyoming, 1970-71. Spl. asst. to gen. counsel VA, Washington, 1978-79; field ops. dir. VA, L.A., 1983-84; exec. dir. White House Vets. Com., Washington, 1980-81, Vietnam Vets. Am., Washington, 1984-85; nat. econs. dir. Am. Legion, Washington, 1985-88; exec. dir. Agt. Orange Class Assistance Program, Washington, 1989—; bd. dirs. Inst. for Vets. Studies Purdue U., 1979-81; mem. vets. com. Office of Sec. Labor, Washington, 1984-88, readjustment adv. com. VA, Washington, 1985-88; exec. com. Pres.'s Com. on Employment of People with Disabilities, Washington, 1987-89. Author: (with others) Viet Vet Survival Guide, 1985. With U.S. Army, 1967-70, S.E. Asia. Recipient Outstanding Young Man in Am. award U.S. Jaycees, 1978, Outstanding Svc. award Nat. Assn. Concerned Vets., 1980, Profl. Svc. award Fed. Exec. Bd., 1985, Leadership award Pres.'s Com. on Employment of People with Disabilities, 1988. Mem. VFW, Vietnam Vets. Am., Am. Legion. Democrat. Office: Agt Orange Class Assistance Program PO Box 27413 Washington DC 20038-7413

RHOADES, LAWRENCE WOODRUFF, retired education educator; b. Newark, May 22, 1922; s. William L. and Viola (Tompkins) R.; m. Amalia Elizabeth Buhlmann, Jan. 5, 1982; children: Laurie Ann, Leslie Elizabeth Rhoades Polson. BS, Glassboro State Coll., 1942; MA, Columbia U., 1948, EdD, 1954. Cert. tchr., prin., sch. adminstr., N.J., Mich. Teaching prin. Stillwater (N.J.) Bd. Edn., 1947-50; prin. Verona Sch., Battle Creek, Mich., 1950-53, Franklin Sch., Summit, N.J., 1954-62; asst. supt. Franklin Twp (N.J.) Bd. Edn., 1962-64; prof. edn. Jersey City State Coll., 1964-91. With USAAF, 1943-46. Mem. Assn. Supervision and Curriculum Devel., NEA, N.J. Edn. Assn., N.J. Profs. Ednl. Adminstrn., Phi Delta Kappa. Home: 5 Berkshire Dr Berkeley Heights NJ 07922-2604

RHOADS, GEORGE GRANT, medical epidemiologist; b. Phila., Feb. 11, 1940; s. Jonathan Evans and Teresa (Folin) R.; m. Frances Ann Secker, June 5, 1965; children: Thomas C., James E. MD, Harvard U., 1965; MPH, U. Hawaii, 1970. Intern Hosp. of U. Pa., Phila., 1965-66, resident in internal medicine, 1966-68; resident in preventive medicine U. Hawaii Sch. Pub. Health, 1968-71; epidemiologist Japan-Hawaii Cancer Study, Honolulu, 1974-75; assoc. prof. U. Hawaii, Honolulu, 1974-79, chair dept. pub. health sci., 1978-81, dir. gen. preventive medicine, 1978-81, prof. pub. health, 1979-82; chief epidemiology br. Nat. Inst. Child Health and Human Devel./NIH, Bethesda, Md., 1982-89; prof., dir. grad program in pub. health U. Medicine and Dentistry N.J.-Robert Wood Johnson Med. Sch., Piscataway, 1989—. Contbr. more than 100 articles on the epidemiology of non-infectious diseases to profl. jours. Recipient Dirs. award NIH, 1987, EEO award NICHD, 1984. Fellow Am. Coll. Physicians; mem. Am. Epidemiol. Soc. Mem. Soc. of Friends. Office: Environ and Occupational Health Scis Inst PO Box 1179 681 Frelinghuysen Rd Piscataway NJ 08855-1179

RHOADS, JONATHAN EVANS, surgeon; b. Phila., May 9, 1907; s. Edward G. and Margaret (Ely Paxson) R.; m. Teresa Folin, July 4, 1936 (dec. 1987); children: Margaret Rhoads Kendon, Jonathon Evans Jr., George Grant, Edward Otto Folin, Philip Garrett, Charles James; m. Katherine Evans Goddard, Oct. 13, 1990. BA, Haverford Coll., 1928, DSc (hon.), 1962; MD, Johns Hopkins U., 1932; D. Med. Sci., U. Pa., 1940, LLD (hon.), 1960; DSc (hon.), Swarthmore Coll., 1969, Hahnemann Med. Coll., 1978, Duke U., 1979, Med. Coll. Ohio, 1985; DSc (Med.) (hon.), Med. Coll. Pa., 1974, Georgetown U., 1981, Yale U., 1990; LittD (hon.), Thomas Jefferson U., 1979. Intern Hosp. of U. Pa., 1932-34, fellow, instr. surgery, 1934-39; asso. surgery, surg. research U. Pa. Med. Sch., Grad. Sch. Medicine, 1939-47, asst. prof. surg. research, 1944-47, asst. prof. surgery, 1946-47, assoc. prof., 1947-49; J. William White prof. surg. research U. Pa., 1949-51; prof. surgery Grad. Sch. Medicine, U. Pa., 1950—; prof. surgery and surg. research U. Pa. Sch. Med., 1951-57, prof. surgery, 1957-59; provost U. Pa., 1956-59, provost emeritus, 1977—, John Rhea Barton prof. surgery, chmn. dept. surgery, 1959-72, prof. surgery, 1972—, asst. dir. Harrison dept. surg. research, 1946-59, dir., 1959-72; chief surgery Hosp. U. Pa., 1959-72, chmn. med. bd., 1959-61; dir. surgery Pa. Hosp., 1972-74; surg. cons. Pa. Hosp., Germantown (Pa.); mem. staff Hosp. of U. Pa.; dir. J. E. Rhoads & Sons, Inc.; mem. bd. pub. edn., City of Phila., 1965-71; co-chmn. Phila. Mayor's Commn. on Health Aspects of Trash to Steam Plant, 1986, chief justice Pa. Com. on Phila. Traffic Ct.; former mem. bd. mgrs. Haverford Coll., chmn., 1963-72, pres. corp., 1963-78, emeritus bd. mgrs. 1989—; bd. mgrs. Friends Hosp. of Phila.; trustee Coriell Inst. Med. Rsch., 1957-90, v.p. sci. affairs, 1964-76, trustee, 1990—; trustee GM Cancer Rsch. Found.; chmn. bd. trustees Measey Found.; trustee emeritus Bryn Mawr Coll.; mem. com. in charge Westtown Sch.; treas. Germantown Friends Sch.; cons. Bur. State Services, VA, 1963; nat. adv. gen. medical scis. council USPHS, 1963; cons. to div. of medical scis. NIH, 1962-63; adv. council Life Ins. Med. Research Fund., 1961-66; Pres. Phila. div., 1955-56; chmn. adv. commn. on research on pathogenesis of cancer Am. Cancer Soc., 1956-57, del., 1956-61, dir. at large, 1965—, pres., 1969-70, past officer dir., 1970-77, hon. life mem., 1977—; chmn. surgery adv. com. Food and Drug Adminstrn., 1972-74; chmn. Nat. Cancer Adv. Bd., 1972-79; Mem. Am. Bd. Surgery, 1963-69, sr. mem., 1969—. Author, co-editor: Surgery: Principles and Practice, 1957, 61, 65, 70; author: (with J.M. Howard) The Chemistry of Trauma; mem. editorial bd. Jour. Surg. Rsch., 1960-71, Oncology Times, 1979—; co-editor: Accomplishments in Cancer Research, 1979-91; editor: Jour. Cancer, 1972-91, editor emeritus, 1991—; mem. editorial bd. Annals of Surgery, 1947-77, emeritus, 1977—, chmn., 1971-73; mem. editorial adv. bd. Guthrie Bull., 1986—; contbr. articles to med. jours., chpts. to books. Trustee John Rhea Barton Surg. Found. Recipient Roswell Park medal, 1973, Papanicolaou award, 1977, Phila. award, 1976, Swanberg award, 1987, Benjamin Franklin medal Am. Philos. Soc., Medal of the Surgeon Gen. of U.S.; hon. Benjamin Franklin fellow Royal Soc. Arts. Fellow Am. Med. Writers Assn., Am. Philos. Soc. (sec. 1963-66, pres. 1977-84), ACS (regent, chmn. bd. regents 1967-69, pres. 1971-72), Royal Coll. Surgeons (Eng.) (hon.), Royal Coll. Surgeons Edinburgh (hon.), Deutsches Gesellschaft für Chirurgie (corr.), Assn. Surgeons India (hon.), Royal Coll. Physicians and Surgeons Can. (hon.), Coll. Medicine South Africa (hon.), Polish Assn. Surgeons (hon.), Royal Coll. Surgeons in Ireland (hon.), AAAS (sec. med. sci. sect. 1980-86); mem. Hollandsche Maatschappij der Wetenschappen (fgn.), Am. Public Health Assn., Assn. Am. Med. Colls. (chmn. council acad. socs. 1968-69, disting. service mem. 1974—), Fedn. Am. Socs. Exptl. Biology, Am. Assn. Surgery Trauma, Am. Soc. Clin. Nutrition, Am. Trauma Soc. (founding mem., v.p., chmn. bd. dirs. 1986[illegible]), AMA (co-recipient Goldberger award 1970, Dr. Rodman and Thomas G. [illegible] award 1980), Pa. Med. Soc. (Disting. service award 1975), Phila. County Med. Soc. (pres. 1970, Strittmater award 1968), Coll. Physicians Phila. (v.p. 1954-57, pres. 1958-60, Disting. Service award 1987), Phila. Acad. Surgery (pres. 1964-66), Phila. Physiol. Soc. (v.p. 1945-46), Am. Surg. Assn. (pres. 1972-73, Disting. Service medal, trustee found.), Pan Pacific Surg. Assn. (v.p. 1975-77), So. Surg. Assn., The Internat. Surg. Group (pres. 1958), Internat. Fedn. Surg. Colls. (v.p. 1972-78, pres. 1978-81, hon. pres. 1987—), Fellows of Am. Studies, Soc. of U. Surgeons, Soc. Clin. Surgery (pres. 1966-68), Am. Assn. for Cancer Research, Am. Chem. Soc., Am. Physiol. Soc., Coun. Biology Editors, Internat. Soc. Surgery (hon.) N.Y. Acad. Scis., Surg. Infection Soc. (pres. 1984-85), Surgeons Travel Club (pres. 1976, hon. mem.), Am. Inst. Nutrition, World Med. Assn., Am. Acad. Arts and Scis., Inst. of Medicine (sr.), Soc. for Surgery Alimentary Tract (pres. 1967-68), Southeastern Surg. Congress, Soc. Surg. Chmn. (pres. 1966-68), Buckingham Mountain Found. (sec., treas.), James IV Soc. (hon.), Phi Beta Kappa, Alpha Omega Alpha, Sigma Xi. Clubs: Rittenhouse, Union League, Philadelphia; Cosmos (D.C.). Office: 3400 Spruce St Philadelphia PA 19104-4220

RHOADS, MICHAEL DENNIS, sales executive; b. Vinton, Iowa, June 25, 1949; s. Lloyd and Marilyn Mae (Appleton) R.; m. Gayle Annette Young, Nov. 21, 1970 (div. Nov. 1990); children: Melissa, Angela, Lori, Alan. BS in Indsl. Edn., Iowa State U., 1973; MBA, York Coll. of Pa., 1984. Order detailer, sales rep. Fisher Controls Inc., Marshalltown, Iowa, 1973-75; inside sales engr. C. B. Ives Co. Inc., King of Prussia, Pa., 1975-79; outside sales engr. C. B. Ives Co. Inc., York, Pa., 1979-85, br. mgr., 1985-87; v.p. process instrumentaion sales C.B. Ives Co. Inc., King of Prussia, 1987-90, v.p., sales mgr., 1990—, sr. v.p., 1992—. Youth group leader Meth. Ch., Center Square, Pa., 1977-79; instr. Continuing Adult Edn., Marshalltown, 1973-75. With USN, 1968-70, Vietnam. Mem. Instrument Soc. Am. (v.p. 1984-86, pres. 1986-87, Best Sect. Pres. award 1987, Old Shoe award 1990), Am. Legion, VFW. Lutheran. Home: 205 Claremont Ln Downingtown PA 19335-1563 Office: CB Ives Co Inc 601 Croton Rd King Of Prussia PA 19406-3197

RHODA, CHRISTOPHER HERBERT, systems analyst; b. Houlton, Maine, Sept. 24, 1966; s. Herbert Ervin and Pamela Ann (Wilson) R.; m. Carol Lynn Ellis, Aug. 6, 1988. BS, Thomas Coll., 1988, MBA, 1989. Systems analyst Thomas Coll., Waterville, Maine, 1988—. Trustee Ch. of the Nazarene, 1990—. Mem. Data Processing Mgmt. Assn., DEC Users Soc. Office: Thomas Coll 180 W River Rd Waterville ME 04901-5097

RHODES, BARRY, management consultant; b. N.Y.C., May 9, 1947; s. George and Blanche (Altman) R.; m. Joanne Veronica Chow, Oct. 23, 1976; children: Megan Erica, Caitlin Carrie. BS in Govt., Boston U., 1969; MEd, U. Mass., 1971. VISTA vol. U.S. Govt., Pitts., 1969; tchr. Boston Pub. Schs., 1970; ptnr. Simon, Radlo, Rhodes, Amherst, Mass., 1972-73; coord. Marathon House, Dublin, N.H., 1974-75; dir. Marathon House, Coventry, R.I., 1976; v.p. The Rhodes Inst., Boston, 1977-78; spl. asst. Office of Gov. N.H., Concord, 1979-82; exec. v.p. Applied Resources Corp., Bridgeport, Conn., 1983-86; pres. Barry Rhodes, Inc., Sharon, N.H., 1986—; bd. dirs. Odyssey House, Inc., Hampton, N.H.; cons. AMA, Chgo., 1983—. Author: Using Information Systems, 1983; contbr. articles to profl. jours. Mem. Gov.'s Halfway House Commn., Concord, 1980-83, Pub. Health Trust, Concord, 1982-83; town chmn. N.H. Dem. party, Sharon, 1987-91, gen. ct. candidate Hillsborough Dist. 8, 1988; mem. Zoning Bd. Adjustment, Town of Sharon, 1987-89, selectman, 1989—; participant White House Conf. for Drug Free Am., 1988; liaison between White House staff and Nat. Assn. State Alcohol and Drug Abuse Dirs., White House Conf. on Prescription Drugs, 1980; bd. dirs. Andy's Playhouse, Inc., Wilton, N.H. Mem. Internat. Narcotic Enforcement Officers Assn., Alcohol and Drug Problems of Am., Informal Steering Com. on Prescription Drug Abuse. Jewish. Office: Barry Rhodes Inc 328B Jarmany Hill Rd Sharon NH 03458

RHODES, FRANK HAROLD TREVOR, university president, geologist; b. Warwickshire, Eng., Oct. 29, 1926; came to U.S., 1968, naturalized, 1976; s. Harold Cecil and Gladys (Ford) R.; m. Rosa Carlson, Aug. 16, 1952; children: Jennifer, Catherine, Penelope, Deborah. B.Sc., U. Birmingham, 1948, Ph.D., 1950, D.Sc. (hon.), 1963; LL.D. (hon.), Coll. Wooster, 1976, Nazareth Coll. Rochester, 1979; L.H.D. (hon.), Colgate U., 1980, John Hopkins U., 1982, Wagner Coll., 1982, Hope Coll., 1982, Rensselaer Poly Inst., 1982, LeMoyne Coll., 1984, Pace U., 1986, Alaska Pacific U., 1987, Hamilton Coll., 1987; D.Sc. (hon.), U. Wales, 1981; D.Sci. (hon.), U. Ill., 1986; DLitt, U. Nev., Las Vegas, 1982. Post-doctoral fellow, Fulbright scholar U. Ill., 1950-51, vis. lectr. geology, summers 1951-52; lectr. geology U. Durham, 1951-54; asst. prof. U. Ill., 1954-55, assoc. prof., 1955-56; dir. U. Ill. Field Sta., Wyo., 1956; prof. geology, head geology dept. U. Wales, Swansea, 1956-68, dean faculty of sci., 1967-68; prof. geology and mineralogy Coll. Lit., Sci. and Arts, U. Mich., 1968-77, dean, 1971-74, v.p. for acad. affairs, 1974-77; pres., prof. geology Cornell U., Ithaca, N.Y., 1977—; Gurley lectr. Cornell U., 1960; Bownocker lectr. Ohio State U., 1966; Case lectr. U. Mich., 1976; dir. NSF, Am. Geol. Inst., summer field inst., 1963; Australian vice-chancellors' visitor to Australian univs., 1964; vis. fellow Clare Hall, Cambridge, Summer 1982; Bye fellow Robinson Coll., Cambridge, Summers, 1986, 87; Am. Fulbright Disting. fellow, Kuwait, 1987. Author: The Evolution of Life, 1962, 2d edit., 1976, Fossils, 1963, Geology, 1972, Evolution, 1974, Language of the Earth, 1981; author numerous articles and monographs on sci. and edn. Trustee Carnegie Found. for Advancement Teaching, 1978-86, vice chmn., 1983-85, chmn. 1985-86; trustee Gannett Found., 1983—; trustee Com. for Econ. Devel., 1984—; bd. trustees Andrew W. Mellon Found., 1984; bd. dirs. KMI Continental, Inc., 1979-86, Tompkins County Trust Co., 1984—, Gen. Electric Co., 1984—, Nat. Broadcasting Corp., 1986—, Am. Council on Edn., 1983—, vice chair, 1985-86, chair, 1986-88; bd. overseers Meml. Sloan-Kettering Cancer Ctr., 1979—; chmn. adv. bd. Gannett Ctr. for Media Studies, 1984—; mem. Nat. Sci. Bd., 1987—, Internat. Exec. Service Corps Council, 1984—. NSF sr. vis. research fellow, 1965-66; mem. Nat. Sci. Bd., 1987—. Fellow Geol. Soc. London (council 1963-66, Bigsby medal 1967); mem. Palaeontol. Assn. (v.p. 1963-68), Brit. Assn. Advancement Sci., Geol. Soc. Am., Am. Assn. Petroleum Geologists, Soc. Econ. Paleontologists and Mineralogists, Phi Beta Kappa (hon.). Office: Cornell U Office of President Ithaca NY 14853*

RHODES, KENNETH ANTHONY, JR., lawyer; b. Scranton, Pa., Aug. 8, 1930; s. Kenneth Anthony Sr. and Martha (Morgan) R.; m. Mary Lammot Belin, Sept. 21, 1958; children: Anthony L.B., Victoria Lammot, William C. AB, Dickinson Coll., 1952; LLD, Harvard U., 1955. Bar: Pa. 1956, U.S. Dist. Ct. (mid. dist.) Pa. 1956. Fgn. service officer U.S. Dept. State, 1958-62; ptnr. Oliver, Price & Rhodes, Scranton, 1962—; lectr. bus. law, Keystone Jr. Coll., 1962-64; bd. dirs. Sauer-France, Melun, Fonderie Musil, Dammerie-les-lys, France. Pres. Mus. Assn. Scranton, 1962-76; pres., bd. dirs. Lackawanna Hist. Soc., Scranton, 1964-89. With U.S. Army, 1956-58. Republican. Episcopalian. Clubs: Waverly (Pa.) Country. Home: Stonewood Waverly PA 18471 Office: Oliver Price & Rhodes 220 Penn Ave Ste 300 Scranton PA 18503-1930

RHODES, ODELLA JEANNE, wellness center executive; b. Emporia, Va., Apr. 6, 1934; d. Robert Alfred and Odella Virginia (Smith) Harrell; m. John

Nathan Rhodes, Sept. 26, 1978; 1 child, Odella Dianne Moats. BA summa cum laude, Shepherd Coll., 1975; MA, W.Va. U., 1982; CPN, Nutritionists Inst. Am., 1986. Cert. profl. nutritionist. Resource tchr. Washington County Bd. Edn., Hagerstown, Md., 1965-82; co-owner J & J Health & Fitness, Hagerstown, 1982—; dir. Jeanne Rhodes Wellness Ctr., Hagerstown, 1982—; nutrition cons., lectr. various orgns., 1984—. Author: Fat to Fit Without Dieting, 1988, (booklet) Peak, 1988, (mag.) Shape, 1982; featured instr.: (video tape) Interval Aerobics Plus, 1989. Dir., participant aerobic marathons Muscular Dystrophy, Am. Heart Assn., Hagerstown, 1985—; lectr. Pub. Health Svc. Seminars, Hagerstown, 1989—. Mem. Hagerstown C. of C. Home: Main St Gapland MD 21736 Office: Jeanne Rhodes Wellness Ctr 363 S Cleveland Ave Hagerstown MD 21740

RHODES, RONDELL HORACE, biology educator; b. Abbeville, S.C., May 25, 1918; s. Leslie Franklin and Pearl Lee (Clinkscales) R.; B.S., Benedict Coll., Columbia, S.C., 1940; M.S., U. Mich., 1950; Ph.D., N.Y.U., 1960. Instr. biology Lincoln U., Jefferson City, Mo., 1947-49; asst. prof. Tuskegee (Ala.) Inst., 1950-55; teaching fellow N.Y.U., 1955-61; mem. faculty Fairleigh Dickinson U., Teaneck, N.Y., 1961—, prof. biol. scis., 1968-88, prof. emeritus, 1988—; chmn. dept., 1966-70, 73-76, 79-82. Served with AUS, 1942-46. Mem. AAAS, Am. Inst. Biol. Scis., Am. Soc. Zoologists, AAUP, Nat. Assn. Biology Tchrs., N.Y. Acad. Scis., Sigma Xi. Democrat. Episcopalian. Home: 122 Ashland Pl Apt 5H Brooklyn NY 11201-3910 Office: Fairleigh Dickinson U Teaneck NJ 07666

RHULE, HOMER ALBERT, insurance association executive, consultant; b. Williamsburg, Pa., Nov. 21, 1921; s. Raymond Albert and Edna Rachael (Greaser) R.; m. Helen Louise Ritchey, Oct. 16, 1950; children: Ann Ritchey, Raymond Albert. BA in Bus. Adminstrn., Am. Univ., 1942; post-grad., Stanford U., 1943; BA in Bus. Adminstrn., Pa. State U., 1947; post-grad., Drexel U., 1968-69. Adjustor, supr. Liberty Mutual Ins. Co., Phila., San Francisco, 1947-51; claims mgr. Transamerica Ins. Co., Harrisburg and Pitts., Pa., 1951-54; owner Rhule Adjustment Co., Altoona, Pa., 1954-55; claims mgr. Crum & Forster Ins. Co.'s, Phila., 1955-69; regional claims mgr. Crum & Forster Ins. Co.'s, N.Y.C., 1969-78; asst. v.p. Crum & Forster Ins. Co.'s, Basking Ridge, N.J., 1978-87; exec. dir. Pa. Ins. Guaranty Assn., Phila., 1987—; pres. Claims Mgrs. Coun., Phila., 1955-62; chmn. Selective Svc. Bd. 107, Bryn Mawr, Pa., 1956-70, Arbitration-Spl., Phila., 1967-69. Commd. Post 355 Am. Legion, Bala Cynwyd, Pa., 1962; dep. commr. 9th Dist. Pa. Am. Legion, Ea. Pa., 1963-64. 2d lt. U.S. Army, 1942-46, ETO. Mem. Masons, F&AM 220, Harrisburg Consistory, Lu Lu Temple. Republican. Presbyterian. Home: 414 Bainbridge St Philadelphia PA 19147-1538 Office: Pa Ins Guaranty Assn 1620 Suburban Sta Bldg Philadelphia PA 19103

RHYNE, CHARLES SYLVANUS, lawyer; b. Charlotte, N.C., June 23, 1912; s. Sydneyham S. and Mary (Wilson) R.; m. Sue Cotton, Sept. 16, 1932 (dec. Mar. 1974); children: Mary Margaret, William Sylvanus; m. Sarah P. Hendon, Oct. 2, 1976; children: Sarah Wilson, Elizabeth Parkhill. BA, Duke U., 1934, LLD, 1958; JD, George Washington U., 1937, DCL, 1958; LLD, Loyola U., Calif., 1958, Dickinson Law Sch., 1959, Ohio No. U., 1966, De Paul U., 1968, Centre, 1969, U. Richmond, 1970, Howard U., 1975, Belmont Abbey, 1982. Bar: D.C. 1937. Pvt. practice Washington; sr. ptnr. Rhyne & Rhyne; gen. counsel Nat. Inst. Mcpl. Law Officers, 1937-88, of counsel; prof. govt. and aviation law George Washington U., 1948-53; prof. govt. Am. U., 1939-44; gen. counsel Fed. Commn. Jud. and Congl. Salaries, 1953-54; spl. cons. Pres. Eisenhower, 1957-60; Dir. Nat. Savs. & Trust Co., 1941-76, ACCIA Life Ins. Co., 1966-84; Mem. Internat Commn. Rules Judicial Procedures, 1959-61, Pres.'s Commn. on UN, 1969-71; spl. ambassador, personal rep. of Pres. U.S. to UN High Commr. for Refugees, 1971-73. Author: Civil Aeronautics Act, Annotated, 1939, Airports and the Courts, 1944, Aviation Accident Law, 1947, Airport Lease and Concession Agreements, 1948, Cases on Aviation Law, 1950, The Law of Municipal Contracts, 1952, Municipal Law, 1957, International Law, 1971, Renowned Law Givers and Great Law Documents of Humankind, 1975, International Refugee Law, 1976, Law and Judicial Systems of Nations, 1978, Law of Local Government Operations, 1980; editor Mcpl. Atty., 1937-88; contbr. articles to various publs. Trustee George Washington U., 1957-67, Duke U., 1951—. Recipient Freedoms Found. award for creation Law Day-U.S.A., 1959; Alumni Achievement award George Washington U., 1960; Nat. Bar Assn. Stradford award, 1962; 1st Whitney M. Young award, 1972; Harris award Rotary, 1974; U.S. Dept. State appreciation award, 1976; Nansen Ring for refugee work, 1976, 1st Peacemaker award Rotary Internat., 1988. Mem. ABA (pres. 1957-58, chmn. ho. dels. 1956-58, chmn. commn. world peace through law 1958-66, chmn. com. aero. law 1946-48, 51-54, chmn. internat. and comparative law sect. 1948-49, chmn. UN com., chmn. commn. on nat. inst. justice 1972-76, nat. chmn. Jr. Bar Conf. 1944-45, Grotius Peace award 1958, Gold medal 1966), D.C. Bar Assn. (pres. 1955-56, Disting. Svc. award 1976), Inter-Am. Bar Assn. (v.p. 1957-59), Am. Bar Found. (pres. 1957-58, chmn. fellows 1958-59), Internat. Bar (founder's patron 1947, v.p. 1957-58), Am. Judicature Soc. (dir. life), Am. Law Inst. (life), Am. Soc. Internat. Law (life), World Peace Through Law Ctr. (pres. 1963-89), World Jurist Assn. (life, pres. 1989-91, hon. pres. for life), Nat. Aero. Assn. (dir. 1945-47), Washington Bd. Trade, Duke U. Alumni Assn. (chmn. nat. coun. 1955-56, pres. 1959-60), Barristers, Met. Club, Nat. Press Club, Congl. Country Club, Nat. Lawyers Club (life), Univ. Club, Delta Theta Phi, Order of Coif (life), Omicron Delta Kappa, Scribes. Home: 1404 Langley Pl Mc Lean VA 22101-3010 Office: Rhyne & Rhyne 1000 Connecticut Ave NW Ste 202 Washington DC 20036-5302

RIBEIRO, LANCE EDWARD, technical specialist; b. Pawtucket, R.I., Aug. 21, 1962; s. Edward Brian and Susan Christine (Potter) R.; m. Caroline Borno, Nov. 10, 1983 (div. Feb. 1990); 1 child, Jeffrey Steven; m. Lisa Dubois, Apr. 6, 1990. BS, Stevens Inst. Tech., 1984. Programmer, analyst Innovative Software Assocs., N.Y.C., 1982-86; pres. Interface Systems Svcs., Somerset, N.J., 1986-87; analyst SIAC, N.Y.C., 1987-88; systems analyst Fed. Res. Bank N.Y., N.Y.C., 1988—. Mem. Mensa. Home: 25 N Pickel Ave Washington NJ 07882-1505 Office: Fed Res Bank NY 59 Maiden Ln New York NY 10038-4502

RICCIARDI, CHRISTINE SECOLA, international trade association administrator; b. New Haven, Apr. 19, 1963; d. Carl Albert and Marie Rose (Pupello) Secola; m. Carmine C. Ricciardi, Nov. 24, 1990. BA, Fairfield (Conn.) U., 1985. Edit. asst. Conn. Woman Mag., Fairfield, 1984-85; corr. internat. money transfer div. Chase Manhattan Bank, N.Y.C., 1985-86; editor employee communications Port Authority of N.Y. & N.J., N.Y.C., 1986-88; bd. adminstr. World Trade Ctrs. Assn., Inc., N.Y.C., 1988—, dir. mem. svcs., 1990—. Editor, contbg. author Corporate Communications, 1986—; contbg. writer newspaper and mag. articles and trade publs., 1988—. Vol. mem. Conn. Spl. Olympics Com., 1981-82; big sister Conn. Big Sister Program, Bridgeport, 1984-85. Recipient Good Citizenship award City of Hamden, Conn., 1981. Mem. Am. Soc. Assn. Execs., Internat. Assn. Bus. Communicators, Alpha Mu Gamma. Office: World Trade Ctrs Assn Inc 1 World Trade Ctr Ste 7701 New York NY 10048

RICCIARDI, FRANK ANTHONY, advertising agency account administrator; b. East Orange, N.J., June 13, 1950; s. Rocco and Mildred (Matilasso) R.; m. Kathleen Susan Coleman, Nov. 24, 1973. BS in Mktg., Fairleigh Dickinson U., 1973. Sales rep. Johnson Scale Co., West Caldwell, N.J., 1972-73, Dista Product div. Eli Lilly, Indpls., 1973-78; mktg. rep. Drug Distbn. Data div. IMS Am., Wayne, N.Y., 1978-81; sales analysis mgr. E.R. Squibb & Sons, Inc., Princeton, N.J., 1981-83; data mgmt. supr. Ciba-Geigy Corp., Summit, N.J., 1983-84, market rsch. analyst, 1984-86, sr. market rsch. analyst, 1986-87; asst. account exec. C&G Advt., Ciba-Geigy Corp., Florham Park, N.J., 1987, account exec., 1987-88, account supr., 1988—. Mem. Verona Lions Club. Republican. Roman Catholic. Office: C&G Advt Ciba-Geigy 556 Morris Ave Summit NJ 07901

RICCIARDI, LOUIS MICHAEL, brokerage house executive; b. Worcester, Mass., Oct. 15, 1959; s. Michael Joseph and Mary Theresa (Searles) R.; m. Cynthia Anne Booth, Mar. 20, 1982. BA, Bridgewater State Coll., 1981. Account exec. Shearson/Am. Express, Brockton, Mass., 1981-83; v.p. Thomson McKinnon, Taunton, Mass., 1983-87, Dean Witter-Reynolds, Taunton, Mass., 1988—; bd. corporators Bristol County Savings Bank, Taunton, Mass., 1985—; mem. Nuveen Adv. Coun., Chgo., 1986—. Contbr. articles to profl. jours. Bd. corporators Morton Hosp., Taunton, Mass., 1987—; pres. Heart of Taunton (Mass.) Revitalization Corp., 1988-89; bd. chmn. Bridgewater State Coll., Bridgewater, Mass., 1990—. Mem. Taunton Area C. of C. (dir. 1988—), Taunton Rotary Club (pres. 1991-92), Bridgewater Coll. Alumni Assn. (treas. 1988—). Republican. Roman Catholic. Home: 3 Cinder Hill Path Lakeville MA 02347

RICCIO, DAVID ANTHONY, chemical process engineer; b. Hartford, Conn., May 6, 1947; s. Anthony and Elva (Pison) R. AS in Engring. Sci., Housatonic Community Coll., Bridgeport, Conn., 1976; BSChemE, Rensselaer Poly. Inst., 1979. Registered profl. engr., N.Y. Process engr. Hess, St. Croix, V.I., 1979-80; sr. process engr. Bechtel, Houston, 1980-86; sr. proposal engr. Pyropower Corp., San Diego, 1986-88; prin. process engr. John Brown Engring. & Constrn., Stamford, Conn., 1988—. Mem. Am. Inst. Chem. Engrs. (liaison 1990—), Phi Lambda Upsilon, Tau Beta Pi. Roman Catholic. Home: 153 Knapps Hwy Fairfield CT 06430

RICE, ALAN HARRISON, architect; b. Carbondale, Ill., Sept. 5, 1963; s. William Ward Sr. and Katherine Campbell (Gray) R.; m. Kimberly K. Wadley, Oct. 14, 1989. B in Sci., Rensselaer Polytech. Inst., 1985, BArch, 1986. Designer Sawmill River Post and Beam, Leverett, Mass., 1985; designer, CAD mgr. Pepin Assocs., Bloomfield, Conn., 1986—; photographer Pepin Assocs., Bloomfield, 1986—. Editor, author: (with others) (book) Back To Main Street, 1986. Mem. AIA (assoc.), Conn. State Architects Assn. (computers in architecture com. 1988-90), Conn. CAD Assn. (chmn. 1989—). Unitarian. Home: 24 Giddings Ave Windsor CT 06095-3702 Office: Pepin Assocs 4 Barnard Ln Bloomfield CT 06002-2414

RICE, ARGYLL PRYOR, Hispanic studies and Spanish educator; b. Va.; d. Theodorick Pryor and Argyll (Campbell) R. BA, Smith Coll., 1952; MA, Yale U., 1956, PhD, 1961. Spanish instr. Yale U., New Haven, 1959-60, 61-63; asst. prof. Spanish, Conn. Coll., New London, 1964-67, assoc. prof., 1967-72, prof., 1972—, chair dept. Hispanic Studies, 1971-74, 77-84. Author: Emilio Ballagas: poeta o poesia, 1967, Emilio Ballagas, Latin American Writers III; editor in chief Carlos A. Sole, Charles Scribner's Sons, 1989. Mem. MLA, Am. Assn. Tchrs. of Spanish and Portuguese, New Eng. Coun. Latin Am. Studies, Phi Beta Kappa. Avocations: music, tennis. Home: 133 Cliffmore Rd West Hartford CT 06107-1123

RICE, BARBARA LYNN, stage manager; b. Hartford, Conn., Nov. 9, 1955; d. Joe Roger and Betty Barbara (Baxter) R. BA in Theatre and French, Ind. U., 1978; MFA in Directing, U. Cin., 1982. free-lance stage mgr., N.Y.C. Dir. The Open Eye: New Stagings, N.Y.C., 1989; stage mgr. 20 Years Ago Today, Cin., 1989, Fourscore & 7 Years Ago, Paramus, N.J., 1989-90, Hanging the President, N.Y.C., 1990; prodn. asst. Kiss of the Spiderwoman, Purchase, N.Y., 1990. Mem. Actors' Equity Assn., Stage Mgrs. Assn. Presbyterian. Home: 412 W 56th St Apt 10 New York NY 10019-3647

RICE, CHARLES DUNCAN, academic dean, history educator, writer; b. Aberdeen, Scotland, Oct. 20, 1942; came to U.S., 1969; s. James Inglis and Jane Meauras (Scroggie) R.; m. Susan Ilene Wunsch, July 5, 1967; children: James Duncan, Samuel Duncan, Jane Emma. MA with 1st class honors, U. Aberdeen, 1966; PhD, U. Edinburgh, Scotland, 1969. Lectr. history U. Aberdeen, 1966-69; asst. prof. history Yale U., New Haven, 1970-76, assoc. prof., 1976-79; prof. history Hamilton Coll., Clinton, N.Y., 1979-85, dean, 1979-85; prof. history, dean faculty of arts and sci. NYU, 1985—, vice chancellor, 1991—. Author: Rise and Fall of Black Slavery, 1975, The Scots Abolitionists, 1982; assoc. editor: Slavery and Abolition, 1979-86; contbr. articles and revs. in field. Trustee The Peddie Sch., Hightstown, N.J., 1973-82, 86—. C. & J. Henry Fund fellow, 1965-66, Am. Coun. Learned Socs. fellow, 1969-70, Morse fellow, 1976-75. Home: 37 Washington Sq W # 15A New York NY 10011-9181 Office: NYU Faculty of Arts & Scis 5 Washington Sq N New York NY 10003-6635

RICE, DAVID EUGENE, JR., trade association administrator, lawyer, consultant; b. Greenwood, S.C., July 1, 1916; s. David Sr. and Mamie Elizabeth (Johnson) R.; m. Virginia E. Dunning, Dec. 24, 1947 (div. 1955); m. Beryl Lena Carter, June 5, 1971. BA, Ohio State U., 1937; JD, Northwestern U., 1941; LLM, Yale U., 1950. Bar: Md., 1946. Assoc. prof. Lincoln U., St. Louis, Mo., 1946-48; Sterling fellow Yale Law Sch., New Haven, 1948-50; dean Tex. So. U. Sch. Law, Houston, 1950-55; savs. officer Ill. Fed. Savs. and Loan Assn., Chgo., 1956-65; assoc. dir. Chgo. Small Bus. Opportunity Corp. (name now CEDCO), Chgo., 1965-67; dir. project outreach Nat. Bus. League, Washington, 1967-68, asst. to pres. and dir. constituency affairs, 1969-83, v.p. constituency affairs, 1984-86, exec. v.p., 1987—; liaison Nat. Student Bus. League, Washington, 1975-92; dean Cert. Insts.: Nat. Bus. League, Washington, 1977-87; resident hist./archivist Nat. Bus. League, Washington, 1981—. Editor: National Bar Journal, 1947-48; contbr. articles to profl. jours. Chmn. rules com. D.C. Black Rep. Coun., Washington, 1985—; active D.C. Black Rep. Scholarship Fund, Inc., 1985—; mem. subcom. trade and commerce D.C.-Dakar Capital Cities Friendship Coun., 1986—; mem. Kool achiever awards screening com. Nabisco Nat. Leadership Visitation Program; trustee Met. African Meth. Episcopal Ch., 1986—, chair leadership retreat, 1990, mem. loan negotiating com. With CIC, AUS, 1943-45, Corps Mil. Police, 1945-46. Mem. Nat. Bar Assn., Nat. Bus. League (Life), Minority Trade Assn. Roundtable of SBA, Coun. of 100, U.S./African Bus. Exch., Yale Law Alumni Assn., Northwestern U. Law Alumni Assn., Ohio State U. Alumni Assn., Pigskin Club, Kappa Alpha Psi. Republican. Office: Nat Bus League 1629 K St NW Ste 605 Washington DC 20006

RICE, DONALD BLESSING, Secretary of Air Force; b. Frederick, Md., June 4, 1939; s. Donald Blessing and Mary Celia (Santangelo) R.; m. Susan Fitzgerald, Aug. 25, 1962; children: Donald Blessing III, Joseph John, Matthew Fitzgerald. BSChemE, U. Notre Dame, 1961, DEng (hon.), 1975; MS in Indsl. Adminstrn., Purdue U., 1962, PhD in Mgmt. and Econs., 1965, D. Mgmt. (hon.), 1985; LLD (hon.), Pepperdine U., 1989. Dir. cost analysis Office Sec. Def., Washington, 1967-69, dep. asst. sec. def. resource analysis, 1969-70; asst. dir. Office Mgmt. and Budget, Exec. Office Pres., 1970-72; pres., chief exec. officer The Rand Corp., Calif., 1972-89; sec. USAF, 1989—; bd. dirs. Vulcan Materials Co., Pacific Enterprises, Wells Fargo Bank, Wells Fargo & Co.; mem. Nat. Sci. Bd., 1974-86; chmn. Nat. Commn. Supplies and Shortages, 1975-77; mem. Nat. Commn. on U.S.-China Relations; mem. nat. adv. com. oceans and atmosphere Dept. Commerce, 1972-75; mem. adv. panel Office Tech. Assessment, 1976-79; adv. council Coll. Engring., U. Notre Dame, 1974-88; mem. Def. Sci. Bd., 1977-83, sr. cons., 1984-88; U.S. mem. Trilateral Commn.; dir. for sec. def. and Pres. Def. Resource Mgmt. Study, 1977-79. Author articles. Served to capt. AUS, 1965-67. Recipient Sec. Def. Meritorious Civilian Service medal, 1970; Ford Found. fellow, 1962-65. Fellow AAAS; mem. Am. Econ. Assn., Council Fgn. Relations, Inst. Mgmt. Scis. (past pres.), Los Angeles Area C. of C. (dir.), Los Angeles World Affairs Council (dir.), Tau Beta Pi. Office: Sec of the Air Force The Pentagon 4E871 Washington DC 20330-1000

RICE, FRANK JOSEPH, biology educator; b. Putnam, Conn., Oct. 10, 1924; s. John Andrew and Lillian (Phillips) R.; m. Kathleen Mary Ryan, Aug. 23, 1952; children: Marilyn, Andrew, Janet, William, Thomas, Catherine, David. BS, Colo. State U., 1950; MS, U. Wyo., 1951; PhD, U. Mo., 1956. Geneticist USDA, Miles City, Mont., 1956-61; asst. prof. biology Fairfield (Conn.) U., 1961-66, assoc. prof., 1966-79, prof., 1979—; lectr. Norwalk (Conn.) Community Coll., 1961-66; cons. Hartford (Conn.) Dept. Pub. Health, 1966-69. Contbr. articles to profl. jours. Mem. Fairfield Rep. Town Meeting, 1963-69, moderator, 1967-69; mem. Greater Bridgeprot Transit Dist., Fairfield, 1972-80, Conn. Pub. Transp. Authority, Hartford, 1975-80. Sgt. AUS, 1943-44. Mem. Fun Luving Square Dance Club. Roman Catholic. Home: 126 Hulls Hwy Southport CT 06490-1136 Office: Fairfield U N Benson Rd Fairfield CT 06430-5152

RICE, JERRY MERCER, research laboratory administrator; b. Washington, Oct. 3, 1940; s. John Earle Rice and Leona (Mercer) Greiner; m. Mary Jane Janocha, Jan. 10, 1978; children: Stacey Lynn, Stephen Mark. BA, Wesleyan U., 1962; PhD, Harvard U., 1966. Commd. officer USPHS; research scientist Nat. Cancer Inst., Bethesda, Md., 1966-81, chief Lab. of Comparative Carcinogenesis, Frederick, Md., 1981—; lectr. univs., profl. groups, med. socs. Editor: Perinatal Carcinogenesis, 1979. Co-editor: Organ and Species Specificity in Chemical Carcinogenesis, 1983, Perinatal and Multigeneration Carcinogenesis, 1989; contbr. rsch. articles and revs. in mechanisms of chem. carcinogenesis to profl. jours. Mem. Am. Soc. Microbiology, Am. Chem. Soc., Am. Assn. Cancer Research, Am. Assn. Pathologists, Teratology Soc., Phi Beta Kappa, Sigma Xi. Avocation: viticulture. Home: 3213 Coquelin Ter Bethesda MD 20815-4840 Office: Nat Cancer Inst Frederick Cancer Rsch & Devel Ctr Frederick MD 21702

RICE, MARGARET MARY, speech and language therapist; b. S.I., N.Y., Aug. 22, 1959; d. John Lawrence and Anna Marie (Mullaney) R. AA, CUNY, 1979; BA, SUNY, Cortland, 1981; MBA, Wagner Coll., 1986. Cert. tchr. speech and hearing impaired, N.Y. Speech and lang. therapist N.Y.C. Bd. Edn., 1981—, speech and lang. evaluator, 1985—. Home: 163 Locust Ave Staten Island NY 10306

RICE, PATRICIA D., business educator; b. Hudson, N.Y., Apr. 11, 1943; d. Anthony and Mary (Rushkoski) DeCrosta; m. Llewellyn S. Rice, Feb. 12, 1966. AAS in Med. Sectl. Sci., Alfred (N.Y.) State Coll., 1963; BS in Bus. & Econs., Nazareth Coll., Rochester, N.Y., 1972, MS in Edn., 1975. Med. sec. Drs. Glazer, Denton, Holden, Otto, Albany, N.Y., 1961-66, Dr. Lawrence Tilis, Rochester, 1966-70; tchr. Nazareth Acad., Rochester, 1971-72, Canandaigua (N.Y.) Acad., 1972-83; assoc. prof. bus. Finger Lakes Community Coll., Canandaigua, 1983—; bd. dirs. Canandaigua Fed. Credit Union, 1991—, chmn. supervisory com., 1985—; mem. scholarship com. CUNY-SUNY Office Tech. & Sectl. Educators, 1991—. Community Coll. of Finger Lake DILE grantee for desktop publishing, 1990. Mem. NEA, N.Y. State Bus. tchrs. Assn., Assn. for Bus. Communication, Granger Homestead Soc., Ontario County Hist. Soc., Clifton Springs Country Club Women's Assn. (pres. 1985-86), Delta Kappa Gamma. Office: Finger Lakes Community Coll 4355 Lakeshore Dr Canandaigua NY 14424-8395

RICE, PAUL JACKSON, lawyer, educator; b. East St. Louis, Ill., July 15, 1938; s. Ray Jackson and Mary Margaret (Campbell) R.; m. Carole Jeanne Valentine, June 6, 1959; children: Rebecca Jeanne Ross, Melissa Ann Hansen, Paul Jackson Jr. BA, U. Mo., 1960, JD, 1962; LLM, Northwestern U., 1970; student, Command and Gen. Staff Coll., 1974-75, Army War Coll., 1982-83. Bar: Mo. 1962, Ill. 1969, U.S. Dist. Ct. (no. dist.) Ill. 1970, U.S. Ct. Appeals (D.C. cir.) 1991, U.S. Supreme Ct. 1972. Commd. 1st lt. U.S. Army, 1962, advanced through grades to col., 1980; asst. judge advocate 4th Armored Div., Goeppingen, Fed. Republc Germany, 1966-69; dep. staff judge advocate 1st Cavalry Div., Republic Vietnam, 1970-71; inst., prof. The Judge Adv. Gen. Sch., Charlottesville, Va., 1971-74, commdt., dean, 1985-88; br. chief Gen. Law Br., Pentagon, 1975-78; chief adminstrv. law div. Office Judge Adv. Gen., Pentagon, Washington, 1978-79; staff judge adv. 1st Inf. Div., Ft. Riley, Kans., 1979-82, V Corps U.S. Army, Frankfurt, Fed. Republic Germany, 1983-85, USACAC, Ft. Leavenworth, Kans., 1989-90; faculty Indsl. Coll. Armed Forces, 1988-89; chief counsel Nat. Hwy. Traffic Safety Adminstrn., Washington, 1990—. Contbr. articles to profl. jours. Granted Legal Svc. award State of Hessen, Weisbaden, Fed. Republic Germany, 1985, Cert. Merit U. Mo. Alumni Assn., 1987. Mem. ABA, Fed. Bar Assn. (pres. local chpt. 1986-88), Mo. Bar Assn., Ctr. For Law and Nat. Security, U. Va. Sch. Law (1985-89), Lion Tamers, Phi Delta Phi. Methodist. Home: 7835 Vervain Ct Springfield VA 22152-3147 Office: Chief Counsels Office NCC01 Nat Hwy Traffic Safety Adm 400 7th St SW Washington DC 20590-0002

RICH, ARTHUR GILBERT, chemist; b. Bklyn., Mar. 21, 1936; s. Harry and Eva (Levine) R.; m. Althea Elaine Brandwein, Nov. 22, 1964; children: Steven Edward, Felice Lauren. BS, Columbia U., 1957; MS, U. Iowa, 1959, PhD, 1962. Lic. pharmacist, N.Y., Ill. Group leader Schmid Labs., N.Y.C., 1962-65; sr. scientist Johnson & Johnson Baby Products Co., New Brunswick, N.Y., 1965-69; group leader Ortho Pharm. Corp., Raritan, N.J., 1969-72; program mgr. Avon Products, Inc., Suffern, N.Y., 1972-88; v.p. sci. De Laire, Inc., N.Y.C., 1988—. Fellow Royal Soc. Health; mem. Soc. of Cosmetic Chemists, Am. Pharm. Assn., N.Y. Acad. Sci., Sigma Xi.

RICH, FRANK HART, critic; b. Washington, June 2, 1949; s. Frank Hart Rich and Helene Bernice (Aaronson) Fisher; m. Alexandra Rachelle Witchel, 1991; children from previous marriage: Nathaniel Howard, Simon Hart. B.A. in Am. History and Lit. magna cum laude, Harvard U., 1971. Co-editor Richmond (Va.) Mercury, 1972-73; sr. editor, film critic New Times mag., N.Y.C., 1973-75; film critic N.Y. Post, N.Y.C., 1975-77; film and TV critic Time mag., N.Y.C., 1977-80; chief drama critic N.Y. Times, N.Y.C., 1980—. Author: (with others) The Theatre Art of Boris Aronson, 1987. Mem. N.Y. Drama Critics Circle. Office: The NY Times 229 W 43rd St New York NY 10036-3913

RICH, HARRY LOUIS, physicist, marine engineering consultant; b. N.Y.C., Apr. 30, 1917; s. Meyer and Annie (Nemser) R.; m. Irene Silverman, July 3, 1941; children: Michelle, Margo. BA, Bklyn. Coll., 1939; postgrad., George Washington U., 1941-50. Physicist David Taylor Model Basin, USN, Carderock, Md., 1941-65; prin. physicist David Taylor Ship R & D Ctr., Carderock, 1965-74; pvt. practice cons., marine engring. Bethesda, Md., 1974—; U.S. rep. Internat. Electro Tech. com., N.Y.C., 1964-74, Internat. Standards Com., N.Y.C., 1964—; sci. advisor USN and Korean Navy, 1971-72. Contbr. articles to Shock and Vibration Symposium, Inst. for Environ. Scis. Recipient Superior Civilian Svc. award USN, Washington, 1966, Civilian Svc. award USN, Seoul, 1972. Fellow Acoustical Soc. Am., Inst. for Environ. Scis.; mem. Cosmos Club (Washington). Home and Office: 6765 Brigadoon Dr Bethesda MD 20817-5418

RICH, HERBERT, medical educator; b. N.Y.C., Nov. 25, 1915; s. Emanuel Gustav and Helen (Friedman) R.; m. Florence Ruth Robins, June 24, 1951; children: Ellen, Heather. BA, Bklyn. Coll., 1938; MA, Columbia U., 1957, MS, 1960. Statistician N.Y.C. Health Dept., 1959-65, chief statis. div., 1965-66; asst. prof. N.Y. Med. Coll., N.Y.C., 1966-68, assoc. prof., 1968-80, clin. assoc. prof., 1980—; assoc. dir. spl. rsch. Am. Heart Assn., N.Y.C., 1957-65; vis. lectr. Columbia U., N.Y.C., 1958-63. Contbr. articles to profl. jours. With Signal Corp., U.S. Army, 1942-43. Mem. Am. Coll. Epidemiology (mem. emeritus), Am. Pub. Health Assn., Soc. Epidemiologic Rsch. Jewish. Home: 38 Park West New Hyde Park NY 11040-3504

RICH, JOHN KRAUSE, public safety professional; b. Carlisle, Pa., Sept. 25, 1957; s. Donald Willard Rich and Mary Ellen (Weiskie) Borges; m. Linda Marie Snyder, Mar. 29, 1980; children: Andrea M., Jaime L., John Paul. AS in Criminal Justice, Harrisburg Area Community Coll, 1978; student, Pa. State Police Acad., 1979; B in Adminstrv. Justice, Shippensburg U., 1982. Emergency dispatcher Cumberland County, Carlisle, Pa., 1977-86; police officer North Middleton Twp., Carlisle, 1978-80, Hampden Twp., Mechanicsburg, Pa., 1980-83; hearing officer Cumberland County Cts., Carlisle, 1983-87; chief driving under influence dept. Cumberland County Dist. Attys. Office, Carlisle, 1986—; pres. Street Gard, Inc., Rolling Springs, Pa., 1987—; mem. adv. bd. Cumberland County, 1987—; sch. dir. South Middleton Sch. Dist., Bowling Springs, Pa., 1989—. Mem. Nat. Rep. Assn., Washington, 1979—. Mem. Pa. Driving Under Influence Assn. Republican. Mem. Evangelical Free Ch. Office: Street Gard Inc 400 Glenn Ave Boiling Springs PA 17007-9527

RICH, KENNETH MALCOLM, management consultant; b. Newark, N.J., Aug. 17, 1946; s. Lucien Ludwell and Grace (Hardy) R.; m. Sandra Ann Arrington; children: Stephen Montgomery, Khristine Nicole. AB in Chemistry, Lafayette Coll., 1967; MBA in Fin., Mktg., U. Chgo., 1969; cert. in acctg., NYU, 1979. Assoc., corp. fin. Kuhn, Loeb & Co., N.Y.C., 1969-73; special asst. to the asst. sec. policy, devel. and rsch. HUD, Washington, 1973-74; mng. dir. fgn. investments The Dornbush Co., Atlanta, 1974; resident v.p. Citibank, N.A., N.Y.C., Athens and Dubai, U.A.E., 1975-78; mng., cons. div. Peat, Marwick, Mitchell & Co., N.Y.C., 1978-80; mng., strategic planning Gen. Elec. Credit Corp., Stamford, Conn., 1981-83; sr. v.p. Paul R. Ray & Co., Inc., N.Y.C., 1983—, mem. mktg. com., 1985-88,

chmn. fin. svcs. practice com., mem. compensation com., 1989—, also bd. dirs., 1989—; trustee Lafayette Coll., Easton, Pa., 1970-75. Chief umpire Ridgefield (Conn.) Little League, 1980-89. Recipient Clifton P. Mayfield Outstanding Young Alumnus award Lafayette Coll., 1980, Standard Oil of N.J. fellow U. Chgo., 1967-69. Presbyterian. Home: 67 St Johns Rd Ridgefield CT 06877-5524 Office: Paul R Ray & Co Inc 101 Park Ave New York NY 10178-0002

RICH, MILTON, public relations executive; b. Bklyn., June 3, 1913; s. David and Sadie (Brenner) R.; m. Adele Pancer, Mar. 19, 1939; 1 child, Meredith Ina. Student, Bklyn. Coll., 1937-40. Sch. sports reporter World-Telegram, N.Y.C., 1939-42; sports writer N.Y. Post, N.Y.C., 1945-49; exec. editor Advt. Daily, N.Y.C., 1949-51; pub. rels. dir. CBS, N.Y.C., 1951-61; prin. Milton Rich Assoc. Inc., N.Y.C., 1961—; pub. rels. dir. Internat. Radio/TV Soc., N.Y.C., 1955-58; pub. rels. assoc. Greater N.Y. Fund, N.Y.C., 1959-60. Home and Office: Milton Rich Assoc Inc 555 W Madison Ave New York NY 10022

RICH, MITCHELL JEFFREY, lawyer, consultant; b. N.Y.C., Sept. 24, 1954; s. Irwin B. Rich and Mickie (Schneider) Schreiber; m. Susan Ann Williams, June 12, 1983. BA, SUNY, Old Westbury, 1982; JD, Touro Sch. Law, 1985. Bar: N.Y. 1986. V.p. Alpha Plaza Employee's Assn., Hicksville, N.Y., 1980-82; assoc. Glassman, Elias & Bernstein, N.Y.C., 1986-87, Rosenberg, Minc, Bryer & Armstrong, N.Y.C., 1987—; founding ptnr., cons. Rich & Kenny, Merrick, N.Y., 1991—; legal cons. Alpha Plaza Employee's Assn., Hicksville, 1982-88. Recipient internship Law Student Civil Rights Rsch. Project, N.Y.C., 1984. Mem. N.Y. State Bar Assn., Delta Theta Phi (chpt. pres. 1984-85). Democrat. Office: Rosenberg Minc Bryer et al 122 E 42nd St New York NY 10168-0002

RICH, PETER HAMILTON, ecology educator, limnologist; b. Wellfleet, Mass., Nov. 7, 1939; s. Earle Glenwood and Florence (Richardson) R.; m. Sept. 21, 1960 (div. 1975); 1 child, Jonathan Carter. BA, CUNY, 1963; MS, Mich. State U., 1966, PhD, 1971. Rsch. assoc. Brookhaven Nat. Lab., L.I., N.Y., 1970-72; asst. prof. ecology U. Conn., Storrs, 1972-80, assoc. prof., 1980—. Office: U Conn 75 S Eagleville Road Ext Storrs Mansfield CT 06269-0001

RICH, PHILIP DEWEY, publishing executive; b. Nashua, N.H., Feb. 1, 1940; s. John Parker and Olive Frances (Hussey) R.; m. Leslie Ann Burke, June 14, 1974 (div. 1982). AB magna cum laude, Harvard U., 1961; MA, NYU, 1962; postgrad., Princeton U., 1962. Editor Houghton Mifflin Co., Boston, 1964-73; asst. mng. editor UpCountry Mag. Berkshire Eagle, Pittsfield, Mass., 1976-77; editor Book Creations Inc., Canaan, N.Y., 1977-80, editor in chief, 1980-91, v.p., executive editor, 1991—. Office: Book Creations Inc Schillings Crossing Rd Canaan NY 12029

RICH, ROBERT PETER, retired mathematician; b. Lowville, N.Y., Aug. 28, 1919; s. Charles William and Agnes Catherine (Keegan) R.; widowed; children: Elaine Alice, David William. AB, Hamilton Coll., 1941; PhD in Math., Johns Hopkins U., 1950. Mathematician Applied Physics Lab. Johns Hopkins U., Laurel, Md., 1950-90. Author: Internal Sorting, 1972. Pres. Md. Acad. Scis., Balt., 1963-72. 1st sgt. AUS, 1941-45, ETO. Republican. Roman Catholic. Home: 1109 Schindler Dr Silver Spring MD 20903-1033

RICH, WALTER GEORGE, railroad transportation executive; b. Oneonta, N.Y., Jan. 9, 1946; s. George C. and Dorretta (Gregg) R.; m. Karine Schmook, July 14, 1990. BA, Syracuse (N.Y.) U., 1968, JD, 1971. Gen. mgr. Delaware Otsego Corp., Oneonta, 1966-68, v.p., gen. mgr., 1968-71; pres. Delaware Otsego Corp., Cooperstown, N.Y., 1971—, N.Y.Susquehanna & Western Rwy., Cooperstown, 1980—; bd. dirs. Delaware Otsego Corp., Cooperstown, Norwich (N.Y.) Aero Producrs. Mem. Friends of Bassett Hosp., Cooperstown, 1988—; mem. Rep. Com., Delaware County, 1990—; commr. of elections Rep., Delaware County, 1971-78; trustee Glimmerglass Opera, Cooperstown, 1986—. Mem. Nat. Rwy. Hist. Soc., Newcomen Soc., Eastern Gen. Mgrs. Assn. (pres. 1985, sec. 1986—), Lexington Group in Transp., N.Y. Athletic Club (N.Y.C.), Ft. Orange Club (Albany), Union League Club (Phila.). Episcopalian. Office: Delaware Otsego Corp 1 Railroad Ave Cooperstown NY 13326-1110

RICHARD, VIRGINIA RYNNE, lawyer; b. Mt. Vernon, N.Y., Aug. 6, 1943; m. Peter L. Richard. BA, Manhattanville Coll., 1965; LLB, NYU, 1969. Bar: N.Y. 1969, Colo. 1973. Assoc. Kane, Dalsimer, Sullivan, N.Y.C., 1970-72, 76-82, ptnr., 1982—; pvt. practice Denver, 1973-75; chmn. trademark appeals com. Fed. Cir. Bar Assn., 1991-92. Contbr. articles to profl. jours. Mem. ABA, U.S. Trademark Assn. (trademark reporter, mem. editorial bd., chmn. subcom. 1982-87), N.Y. Patent, Trademark and Copyright Lawyers Assn. (bd. dirs. 1990—). Office: Kane Dalsimer Sullivan 711 3d Ave 20th Fl New York NY 10017

RICHARDS, BENJAMIN FRANKLIN, JR., civil engineer; b. Woodbury, N.J., July 8, 1941; m. Dolores Ruth Hyndman, July 25, 1964; children: Joy Caroll, Melody Ruth, Benjamin Franklin III. BSCE, Drexel Inst. Tech., 1964; MS, U. N.C., 1966; postgrad., U. R.I., 1968-72. Registered profl. engr., N.Y., N.J., Vt., Mass. Process engr. Permutit Co., Paramus, N.J., 1964-65; sr. engr. N.J. State Dept. Health, Trenton, 1966-68; asst. prof. Stockton State Coll., Pomona, N.J., 1972-76; cons. engr. Mays Landing, N.J., 1976-80, Wells, Vt., 1980—. Mem. ASCE, Chartered Inst. Arbitrators (assoc.), Chi Epsilon. Republican. Home and Office: PO Box 677 Wells VT 05774-0677

RICHARDS, CARL STEVEN, recording industry executive, songwriter, television show host; b. Franklin, N.J., Nov. 2, 1949; s. William C. and Alma E. (Card) R.; m. Lois E. Conklin, Dec. 20, 1969; children: Carl Jr., Tammy, John, Carrie. Drywall specialist Shuback Drywall, Chester, N.Y., 1981-92; owner Tune Tone Records, Bainbridge, N.Y., 1986-92; host "Keeping Country Strong" Cable Access-8, Port Jervis, N.Y., 1992; v.p. Four Tones Pub., N.Y. Composer, recording artist popular songs including "Rollin Faster Down the Line," 1990, "Tips of My Fingers," 1991 (winners Billboard Mag. songwriting contest, Port Jervis, 1990, 91), Tip Doe Dance, Deep Freeze Momma. Named No. 1 country band in Tri-State area Music Machine mag., 1990; recipient In Tune award for originality The Times Herald Record, 1990. Mem. Country Music Assn., Tri-State Country Music Assn. (v.p. 1991, pres. 1992), Broadcast Music Inc. (affiliated writer 1981—, pub. 1990—), Nashville Songwriters Internat., Elks, Moose. Home and Office: 29 Seward Ave Port Jervis NY 12771

RICHARDS, CECILIA DIANNE, mechanical engineer; b. Kennett, Mo., Sept. 19, 1954; d. John Frederick Poole and Mari Louise (Bledsoe) Collins; m. Robert Foster Richards, Sept. 15, 1989. BSc in Math., U. B.C., Can., 1977, BSME, 1982, MSME, 1985; PhD in Engring., U. Calif., Irvine, 1990. Engr. H.A. Simons Internat., Vancouver, Can., 1982-83, ITT Barton Instruments Co., City of Industry, Calif., 1985-86; rsch. engr. N.I.S.T. Bldg. and Fire Rsch. Lab., Gaithersburg, Md., 1990—. Contbr. articles to profl. jours. Fellow Nat. Rsch. Coun. 1990, U. Calif. 1989, 87, 88, 86. Mem. ASME, AIAA (Gordon Oates Air Breathing Propulsion award 1989), Inst. for Liquid Atomization and Spray Systems, Combustion Inst. Office: NIST Bldg & Fire Rsch Lab Bldg 224 B-258 Gaithersburg MD 20899

RICHARDS, GEORGE THOMAS, corporate professional; b. New Castle, Pa., Oct. 3, 1932; s. Barton Erwin and Elizabeth Ann (Weingartner) R.; m. Ann Marie Stiegler, Nov. 29, 1958; children: Thomas Barton, Barbara Ann, Sally Elizabeth, Nancy Marie. BA, Pa. State U., 1954; MBA, Harvard Bus. Sch., Boston, 1958. Salesman Alcoa, Mpls., 1958-61, The Dexter Corp., Windsor Locks, Conn., 1961-62; product mgr. The Dexter Corp., Windsor Lakes, Conn., 1962-67, sales mgr., 1967-76, v.p., sales and mktg., 1976-82, v.p., gen. mgr., 1983-86; pres. Vitex Packaging, Inc., Suffolk, Va., 1987—. pres. TEA Assn. U.S.A., Inc., 1991—. Cpl. U.S. Army, 1954-56. Mem. Hopmeadow Country Club. Republican. Congregational. Home: 11 Buttonwood Dr Simsbury CT 06070-1728 Office: Vitex Packaging Inc PO Box 730 Suffolk VA 23434-0730

RICHARDS, GEORGE WHITFIELD, III, manufacturing company executive; b. Phila., Feb. 1, 1941; s. George W. II and Thelma (Ross) R.; m. Lucy Helena Forster, Dec. 7, 1941; children: George IV, David, Andrew. AB, York Coll., 1963. With sales and purchasing dept. G. Whitfield Richards Co., Phila., 1963-75, exec. v.p., 1975-79, pres., chief exec. officer, 1979—; bd. dirs. New Manayunk Corp., Phila., North Light Inc., Phila. Pres. Radnorshire Civic Assn., Radnor, Pa., 1979-81; chmn. local troop Boy Scouts Am., Radnor, 1978-84. Mem. Wire Assn. Internat. (pres. bd. dirs. 1984-88), Am. Soc. Lubrication Engrs., Am. Soc. Metals, Oil Trades Phila., Phila. C. of C., Yacht Club of Stone Harbor, Georgetown Yacht Club, Corinthian Yacht Club of Phila. Office: G Whitfield Richards Co 420210 Main St Philadelphia PA 19127-2095

RICHARDS, HILDA, university administrator; b. St. Joseph, Mo., Feb. 7, 1936; d. Togar and Rose Avalynne (Williams) Young-Ballard. Diploma nursing St. John's Sch. Nursing, St. Louis, 1956; BS cum laude, CUNY, 1961; MEd, Columbia U., 1965, EdD, 1976; MPA, NYU, 1971. Dep. chief dept. psychiatry Harlem Rehab. Ctr., N.Y.C., 1969-71; prof., dir. nursing Medgar Evers Coll., CUNY, N.Y.C., 1971-76, prof., assoc. dean, 1976-79; dean Coll. Health and Human Service, Ohio U., Athens, 1979-86; provost, v.p. for acad. affairs Indiana U., Pa., 1986—; mem. Gov.'s Council on Disabled Persons, Columbus, Ohio, 1982-84; mem. Gov.'s State Social Service Adv. Com., Columbus, 1982-86; mem. Ohio Planning Com., Am. Council Edn., 1981-86. Author: (with others) Curriculum Development and People of Color: Strategies and Change, 1983; editor Black Conf. on Higher Edn. Jour., 1989—. Mem., chmn. Athens, Hocking, Vinton Community Health Bd., 1980-86; mem. Community Relations Com., Athens, Ohio, 1984-86; mem. Fair Housing Task Force, Athens County, Ohio, 1984-86; mem. exec. com., bd. dirs. Consortium for Health Edn. in Appalachia Ohio, Inc., Athens, 1982-86; mem. Indiana County Community Action, 1986-91, Econ. Devel. Commn., 1986—, Citizens Ambulance Service of Ind. County, 1987—; mem. exec. com. edn. Ind. Chpt. NAACP, 1989—; bd. dirs. Avanta Network, Big Bros./Big Sisters of Ind. County, 1989—; bd. mem. Pa. Acad. for the Profession of Teaching, 1990—; exec. com. Pa. Black Conf. on Higher Edn., 1988—. Recipient Rockefeller Found. award Am. Council Edn., Washington, 1976-77; USPHS trainee, NIMH, Columbia U., N.Y.C., 1963-65, bd. dirs. Big Bros. Big Sisters, Indiana County, 1989—. Martin Luther King grantee NYU, N.Y.C., 1969-70, Gunt Found. grantee Harvard Inst. Ednl. Mgmt., Cambridge, Mass., 1981. Mem. ANA, Assn. Black Nursing Faculty in Higher Edn. (bd. dirs. 1989—), Pa. Nurses Assn., Assn. Black Women in Higher Edn., Inc., Nat. Black Nurses Assn. (bd. dirs., 1st v.p. 1984—, editor jour. 1985—), Nat. Assn. Women in Edn., Am. Soc. Allied Health Professions (chmn. equal representation in allied health), Am. Coun. Edn. (exec. com. coun. fellows), Ohio Nurses Assn. (human rights com. and psychiat. mental health practice assembly 1982-86), Phi Delta Kappa, Sigma Theta Tau, Zonta Club of Ind. County. Democrat. Avocations: needlepoint, travel. Home: 3091 Warren Rd Indiana PA 15701-9747 Office: Ind U Pa Office of Provost 205 Sutton Hall Indiana PA 15705

RICHARDS, JAMES JOHN, college dean; b. Franklin Square, N.Y., June 4, 1941; s. James August and Ann (Drougalis) R.; m. Elizabeth Cluff Lascelle, Dec. 5, 1970; children: Elizabeth Ann, James George. BA in Psychology, Hofstra U., 1964, MS in Counseling, 1969, postgrad., 1990—. Asst. to pres. Hofstra U., Hempstead, N.Y., 1965-69; counselor C.W. Post Coll., Greenvale, N.Y., 1969; counselor Nassau Community Coll., Garden City, N.Y., 1970-75, chmn. dept. student pers. svcs., 1975-79, assoc. dean students, 1979-83, dean students, 1983—. Mem., v.p. Carle Place (N.Y.) Bd. Edn., 1986-89; mem. BOCES Citizens Adv. Coun., Westbury, N.Y., 1990-92; mem. L.I. Forum of Responsible Educators to End Discrimination, 1991-92; v.p. SUNY Coun., 1991-93. Mem. L.I. Coun. Student Pers. Adminstrs. (pres. 1990-92), Westbury-Carle Pl. Rotary (pres. 1991-92). Episcopalian. Home: 142 Webster St Westbury NY 11590-1848 Office: Nassau Community Coll Garden City NY 11530

RICHARDS, JUDITH OLCH, arts administrator; b. Glendale, Calif., Dec. 16, 1947; d. Saul and Thelma (Zarnett) Olch; m. William Arthur Richards, May 2, 1971; children: Nathan Samuel, Sarah Leslie. BA, U. Calif., Berkeley, 1969; MA, U. N.Mex., 1971. Curator project dir. Bronx (N.Y.) Museum of Arts, 1976-78; guest curator Greenburgh Nature Center, Scarsdale, N.Y., 1978; devel. asst. Hudson River Museum, Yonkers, N.Y., 1978-80; assoc. dir. Ind. Curators Inc., N.Y.C., 1980—; special exhibition curator Ind. Curators Inc., 1987. Mem. Am. Assn. Museums, Nat. Assn. Artists Orgn. Office: Independent Curators Inc 799 Broadway Rm 205 New York NY 10003-6836

RICHARDS, LOUISE SUTERMEISTER, social services agency administrator; b. Washington, Apr. 30, 1949; d. Oscar and Betty (Wilson) Sutermeister; m. John William Richards. BA in History of Religion, Bryn Mawr Coll., 1971; MSW, U. Md., 1987. Exec. dir. Md. Salem Children's Trust, Frostburg, 1977—. Named Woman of the Month, Garrett County Br. AAUW, Dec. 1987. Democrat. Presbyterian. Office: Md Salem Childrens Trust Lower New Germany Rd Star Rte Box 60 C Frostburg MD 21532

RICHARDS, PAMELA SPENCE, library and information studies educator; b. N.Y.C., June 2, 1941; d. Guy and Mary Frances (Lavine) R.; m. Jacobus W. Smit, June 6, 1969; children: Guy, Marijke. BA magna cum laude, Harvard U., 1963; MA, Columbia U., 1966, MLS, 1971, DLS, 1979. Adminstrv. asst. German dept. Columbia U., N.Y.C., 1963-69, rsch. assoc. Grad. Sch. Bus., 1972-76; reference libr. Westchester Community Coll., Valhalla, N.Y., 1976, 77; instr. Grad. Sch. Libr. Svc. Rutgers U., New Brunswick, N.J., 1977-79, asst. prof. Grad. Sch. Libr. and Info. Studies, 1979-84, assoc. prof. Sch. Communication, Info. and Libr. Studies, 1984-91, prof., 1991—. Author: Scholars and Gentlemen, 1984, Marketing Books and Journals to Europe and the United Kingdom, 1986; editor-in-chief Jour. of Rutgers U. Librs., 1980—; assoc. editor Libr. Quarterly, 1985—, Internat. Libr. Rev., 1989—. Summer fellow NEH, 1982, Am. Philos. Soc., 1983; Martinus Nijoff Found. grantee, 1990; recipient Acad. Specialist award U.S. Info. Agy., 1987, Libr. Edn. Specialist, USSR Coun. Librs. and Am. Coun. Learned Studies, 1991. Mem. ALA, Am. Soc. Info. Sci. (chmn. internat. rels. com. 1988-91), Assn. for Libr. and Info. Sci. Edn. Home: 90 Morningside Dr New York NY 10027-7124 Office: Rutgers U Sch Info & Libr Studies 4 Huntington St New Brunswick NJ 08901-1071

RICHARDS, PAUL GRANSTON, geophysics educator, seismologist; b. Cirencester, Eng., Mar. 31, 1943; came to U.S., 1965; s. Albert George and Kathleen Margaret (Harding) R.; m. Jody Margaret Porterfield, June 1, 1968; children: Mark, Jessica, Gillian. BA, Cambridge (Eng.) U., 1965; MS, Calif. Inst. Tech., Pasadena, 1966, PhD, 1970. Prof. geol. scis. Columbia U., N.Y.C., 1971—, chmn. dept. geol. scis., 1980-83; Co-author: Quantitative Seismology, 2 vols., 1980. Guggenheim Found. fellow, 1977-78, MacArthur Found. fellow, 1981-86. Fellow Royal Astron. Soc.; mem. Am. Geophys. Union (Macelwane award 1976), Coun. Fgn. Rels. Episcopalian. Office: Lamont-Doherty Geol Obs Palisades NY 10964

RICHARDS, PAUL WILLIAM, mechanical engineer; b. Scranton, Pa., May 20, 1964; s. James Joseph and Angela (Cordaro) R. BSME, Drexel U., 1987; MSME, U. Md., 1991. Mech. technician USN NAVSSES, Phila., 1984-86; mech. engr. U.S. Navy NACSSES, Phila., 1987, NASA/GSFC Verification Office, Greenbelt, Md., 1987-88, Electromech. Br., NASA, Greenbelt, 1988-90, Flight Robotics div. NASA, Greenbelt, 1990-91, Satellite Servicing, NASA, Greenbelt, 1991-92, Hubble Space Telescope Project, NASA, Greenbelt, 1992—. Patentee robotic wrist. Vol. Spl. Olympics, Washington, 1988-91, Doing Something, Washington, 1991. Ens. USNR, 1990—. Recipient Honor award Nat. Hon. Mech. Engring. Soc., 1984. Mem. ASME, AIAA, Nat. Soc. Profl. Engrs., Am. Soc. Naval Engrs., Md. Soc. Profl. Engrs., NASA Aircraft Club, NASA Scuba Club. Republican. Roman Catholic. Home: 639 8th St NE Washington DC 20002-5237 Office: NASA Goddard Space Flt Ctr Code 442 Greenbelt MD 20771

RICHARDS, REUBEN FRANCIS, natural resource company executive; b. Aug. 15, 1929; s. Junius A. and Marie R. (Thayer) R.; m. Elizabeth Brady, Nov. 28, 1953; children: Reuben Francis, Timothy T., Andrew H. AB, Harvard U., 1952. With Citibank, N.A., N.Y.C., 1953-82, exec. v.p., 1970-82; chmn. Inspiration Resources Corp., N.Y.C., 1982-92, Terra Industries Inc. (formerly Inspiration Resources Corp.), N.Y.C., 1992—; bd. dirs. Adobe Resources Corp., N.Y.C., Ecolab, Inc., St. Paul, Potlach Corp., San Francisco, Independence Mining Co., Inc., Elko, Nev., Minorco, Luxembourg; chmn. bd. dirs. Engelhard Corp., Menlo Park, N.J.; chmn. Minorco (U.S.A.) Inc. With USNR, 1948-50. Office: Terra Industries Inc 250 Park Ave New York NY 10177-0001

RICHARDS, RHODA ROOT WAGNER, civic worker; b. Phila., Oct. 2, 1917; d. Edward Stephen and Rhoda Earley (Root) Wagner; student U. Pa., 1937-39; A.A., Wildcliff Jr. Coll., 1938; m. J. Permar Richards, Jr., May 18, 1940; children: Patricia A.V. Richards Cosgrave, J. Permar III. Profl. artist; founder, chmn. Hosp. Corps, Navy League Service, 1941-43; chmn. ARC Nurses Aide Corps, Jacksonville, Fla., 1944-45, Long Beach, Calif., 1945-46; founder, chmn. Fiesta Benefits, Hahnemann Hosp., 1950-57; former chmn. jr. com. Met. Opera; bd. dirs. Phila. Lyric Opera Co.; chmn. Ring for Freedom Republican Campaign of S.E. Pa., 1960; pres. Emergency Aid of Pa., 1961-64; v.p. bd. dirs. Inglis House, Phila., 1977-82; pres. women's bd. Phila. div. Am. Cancer Soc., 1978-81, hon. life mem.; gen. chmn. 1st Ann. Washington Crossing Assembly, 1978; trustee Baldwin Sch.; co-chmn. fundraising com. Ambulatory Service Pavilion, Presbyn.-U. Pa. Med. Center; vice chmn. Women's Commn. for Bicentennial, 1976; bd. dirs., mem. Apleford Commn. Parsons-Banks Arboretum. Vol., chmn. women's bd. Phila. div. Am. Cancer Soc., 1978-86; vol. Phila. chpt. Lupus Found., 1980-81; mem. Delaware Valley women's bd. Freedoms Found. at Valley Forge; past v.p. women's assn., past chmn. fin. com., chmn. centennial spl. event and gen. com. for the celebration Bryn Mawr Presbyn. Ch.; hon. col. corps of cadets Valley Forge Mil. Acad. and Jr. Coll.; founder, chmn. Rittenhouse Preservation Coalition, 1982—; founder, v.p., asst. treas. Preservation Coalition of Greater Phila., 1984—; mem. Hospitality, Phila. Style; chmn. bd. dirs. Emergency Aid of Pa. Found., chmn. 75th anniversary celebration, fin., long range planning, investment coms.; liaison Fairmont Park Waterworks Com. Recipient Crusade award Am. Cancer Soc., 1976; spl. award for community service St. John's Settlement House, 1977; Florence A. Sanson award for patriotism, 1986; named Disting. Dau. of Pa., 1985. Mem. Phila. Mus. Art, Pa. Acad. Fine Arts, Hahnemann Hosp. Women's Assn. (Phila. chpt.), DAR, Daus. of the Cincinnati, Dames of Loyal Legion, Nat. Soc. Colonial Dames of XVII Centuary, Dames Sovereign Mil. Order Temple of Jerusalem, Honolulu Mus. Art, Geneal. Soc. Pa., Am. Hist. Soc., Nat. Trust for Historic Preservation, Smithsonian Instn., Friends of Independence Hall, Friends of Hist. Cliveden, Andalusia Friends. Clubs: Sedgeley, Cosmopolitan, Peale, Bald Peak Colony. Home: 1250 Lafayette Rd PO Box 608 Bryn Mawr PA 19010

RICHARDS, ROGER THOMAS, acoustical scientist; b. Akron, Ohio, June 19, 1942; s. Clyde Irvin and Thelma Josephine (Whitaker) R.; m. Mary Ellen Harris-Warren, Aug. 9, 1986. BS in Physics, Westminster Coll., New Wilmington, Pa., 1964; MS in Physics, Ohio U., 1968; PhD in Acoustics, Pa. State U., 1980. Grad. asst. in physics Ohio U., 1965-67, research asst. in acoustics, 1967-68; asso. engr. transducer lab. Gen. Dynamics/Electronics Co., Rochester, N.Y., 1968-69, engr. acoustics dept., 1969-71; NASA trainee Pa. State U., 1971-74, grad. asst. in acoustics, 1974-80; staff asso. Applied Research Lab., State College, Pa., 1976-80; tech. staff marine systems div. Rockwell Internat., Groton, Conn., 1980-84; sr. scientist Bolt Beranch & Newman, New London, Conn., 1984-87; physicist Nav. Underwater System Ctr., New London, 1987—. Fellow NASA. Mem. Acoustical Soc. Am., AIAA, Nat. Speleological Soc. (life, vice chmn. Nittany Grotto 1975-76), Am. Cryptographic Assn., AAAS, U.S. Chess Fedn. (capt. Pa. State U. team 1973, cert. tournament dir., life), Am. Go Assn., Am. Contract Bridge League (pres. local club 1970-71), U.S. Othello Assn. (corp. dir. 1979-84, Midwestern Othello champion 1979), N.Y. Acad. Scis., Pa. State U. Alumni Assn. (alumni council and exec. bd. 1973-74), Sigma Xi, Kappa Mu Epsilon, Sigma Pi Sigma (nat. del. 1967). Contbg. editor Othello Quar., 1979-84, editorial staff The Cryptogram, 1984—; contbr. articles to profl. jours.; research in acoustic propagation and scattering, sonar transducer and array design. Home: 34 Cove Side Ln Stonington CT 06378-2902 Office: Nav Underwater System Ctr New London CT 06320

RICHARDSON, ALLYN ST. CLAIR, chemical engineer; b. Edmonton, Alberta, Can., Nov. 16, 1918; s. Herbert Victor and Gertrude Claire (Driver) R.; m. Nancy May Marston, Dec. 16, 1940 (div. 1957); children: Gary, Bryan H., Timothy V., Sheldon Blodgett. BSChemE, U. B.C., Vancouver, 1941; MS, Harvard U., 1949, PhD, 1955. Dist. engr. dept. nat. health Govt. of Can., Vancouver, B.C., 1942-45; dist. engr. Govt. of Can., Edmonton, Alberta, Can., 1946-50; rsch. engr. Harvard U., Cambridge, Mass., 1950-55; design group leader radar dept. Raytheon Co., Weston, Mass., 1955-57; asst. prof. Tufts U., Medford, Mass., 1957-60; project engr. Trans-Sonics, Inc., Burlington, Mass., 1960-65; cons., sanitary engr. WHO, Washington, Venezuela, Iran, 1965-67; dir. office R & D U.S. EPA, Boston, 1967-84; owner D/B/A Computility, West Groton, Mass., 1985—; chmn. Bd. Water Commrs., Town of Groton, 1982—; cons. United Rsch., Inc., Cambridge, 1957-60, U.S. Army Mateirals Lab., Natick, Mass., 1957-60. Contbr. articles to profl. jours. Recipient Grad. Study & Travel fellowship The Rockefeller Found., 1948-49. Mem. IEEE, Boston Computer Soc., Am. Water Works Assn., New Eng. Water Works Assn., Mass. Water Works Assn., Nat. Assn. Ret. Fed. Employees (pres. Minuteman chpt. 1991-92), Masons, Duke of Connaught Lodge #64 Brit. Columbia Registry. Home: 81 Pepperell Rd West Groton MA 01472-0257 Office: Computility 81 Pepperell Rd PO Box 257 West Groton MA 01472

RICHARDSON, CHARLES MARSH, electrical engineer; b. Leominster, Mass., May 24, 1925; s. James Putnam and Sarah Belle (Marsh) R.; m. Mildred Ann Crowley, Nov. 19, 1949 (dec.); children: Charles Michael, James Dana. BSEE, Worcester Poly. Inst., 1945; MS in Edn., C.W. Post, Greenvale, N.Y., 1975; postgrad., C.W. Post, 1975-78. Registered profl. engr.; cert. elem. tchr., secondary math., physics, gen. sci., spl. edn. Engr. magnetron devel. Raytheon Mfg. Co., Waltham, Mass., 1945-51; engr., standards Sperry Gyroscope Co., Great Neck, N.Y., 1951-53; sales engr. G. Curtis Engel & Assoc., Ridgewood, N.J., 1953-54; sr. engr. Sperry Corp., Great Neck, N.Y., 1954-70; owner, dir. Learning Foundations, Hauppauge, N.Y., 1970-86; sr. engr. Sperry (Unisys) Corp., Great Neck, N.Y., 1983-89; adj. prof. spl. edn. and reading C.W. Post Coll., 1979-81; pres. Ednl. Engring., Huntington Station, N.Y.; founder, exec. dir. The Literacy Coun. Patentee in field; contbr. articles to profl. jours. Mem. Orton Dyslexia Soc., Balt., Literacy Adv. Com., U.S. Dept. Justice. Mem. IEEE (pre-coll. edn. com.). Home: 133 Lodge Ave Huntington Station NY 11746-2808

RICHARDSON, DAVID BACON, freelance writer; b. Maplewood, N.J., July 13, 1916; s. Percy Bacon and Elizabeth (Jones) R.; m. Ruth Cummings (dec.); children: Hilary C., Julia R. Neilson, Francesca Richardson-Allen. BA, Ind. U., 1940; postgrad. fellow Coun. on Fgn. Rels., Princeton U., 1953-54. Combat corres. Yank, The Army Weekly, 1942-45; corr. Time Mag., India, Fed. Republic Germany, U.K., Mideast, Mexico, 1945-56; assoc. editor U.S. News & World Report, Washington, 1956-59; bur. chief S.Am. U.S. News & World Report, Buenos Aires, 1959-64; chief domestic news burs. U.S. News & World Report, Washington, 1964-73; chief European corr. U.S. News & World Report, Rome, 1974-81; chief nat. corr. U.S. News & World Report, Washington, 1981-82; freelance writer Washington, 1983—; lectr. in field, 1986—. Contbr. to books The Best From Yank, 1945, Yank, the GI Story of the War, 1947. Pres., bd. dirs. Greenbriar Condominium, Washington, 1984-87. Tech. sgt. U.S. Army, 1941-45. Decorated Legion of Merit, Bronze Star; recipient Valor medal of Nat. Headliners Club. Mem. Coun. Fgn. Rels., Washington Inst. Fgn. Affairs, Overseas Writers Assn., Soc. Profl. Journalists, Cosmos Club (Washington). Home and Office: 3900 Watson Pl NW Washington DC 20016-5701

RICHARDSON, DAVID WILLIAM, manufacturing executive; b. Putnam, Conn., May 23, 1948; s. William Joseph and Rita Aurora (Bonosconi) R.; m. Helen Kathleen Murray, July 21, 1972; 1 child, Troy James Gorman. BS in Chem. Engring., U. Conn., 1982. Process engr. Poron div. Rogers (Conn.) Corp., 1974-78, tech. mgr., 1978-82, ops. mgr. Poron and Fiberloys div., 1982-83, tech. mgr. Poron composites, 1983-87, mgr. composite materials div., 1987—. Mme. bus. and industry adv. coun. Quinebaug Valley Community Coll. With U.S. Army, 1966-69. Decorated Purple Heart. Mem. Am. Inst. Chem. Engrs., Am. Mgmt. Assn. Home: PO Box 194 East Woodstock CT 06244-0194 Office: Rogers Corp One Technology Dr Rogers CT 06263

RICHARDSON, F. C., academic administrator; b. Memphis, Sept. 22, 1936; m. Bernice Tanner. AB in Biology, Rust Coll., 1960; MS in Biology, Atlanta U., 1964; PhD in Botany, U. Calif., Santa Barbara, 1967. Asst. prof.

botany Ind. U. N.W., Gary, 1967-71, assoc. prof., 1971-82, prof., 1982-84, chair dept. biology, 1971-72, chair div. arts and scis., 1972-84; prof. Jackson (Miss.) State U., 1984-85, v.p. for acad. affairs, 1984-85; v.p. for acad. affairs Moorhead (Minn.) State U., 1985-89; prof. SUNY, Buffalo, 1989, pres., 1989—; cons., evaluator North Ctrl. Assn., 1987-89; mem. commn. on elem. schs. Mid. States Assn., 1990—; mem. Commn. on Minorities in Higher Edn., Am. Coun. on Edn.; mem. task force on outcomes and accountability Coun. on Postsecondary Edn., 1991—. Mem. editorial bd. Negro Ednl. Rev., 1977—, exec. editor, 1981—; contbr. numerous articles to profl. jours. Mem. fellowship selection com. for Martin Luther King, Jr. Fellowship Program, Woodrow Wilson Nat. Fellowship Found., Chgo., 1969-74; bd. dirs. Lake County Assn. for Retarded Citizens, 1969-75; chair Ind. U. N.W./Community Adv. Bd. for Spl. Svcs., 1970-74; mem. Gary Air Pollution Control Adv. Bd., 1970-84, chair; chair steering com. for creation of Gary Neighborhood Svcs., Inc., 1970-71, bd. dirs., 1971-84; mem. N.W. Ind. Clean Air Coordinating Com., N.W. Ind., 1970-73, Comprehensive Health Planning Coun., 1971-75, Com. on Sci. and Tech. R&D, State of Minn., 1987, Moorhead Chamber Edn. Task Force, 1987-88; mem. Gary Bd. Health, 1972-82, sec., 1976-79, pres., 1979-82; bd. dirs. Meth. Hosps., Gary, 1973-84, Med. Ctr. of Gary, Inc., 1975-81, Greater Buffalo Devel. Found., 1989—, Buffalo Soc. Natural Scis., 1989—, Western N.Y. Tech. Devel. Ctr., Inc., 1991—, Buffalo Fine Arts Acad., 1991—; mem. Lake area planning and allocation com. United Way, 1981-83, chair Lake area campaign exec. group, 1982-83, bd. dirs. United Way Buffalo and Erie County, 1990—; mem. local organizing com. World Univ. Games 1993, 1989—; mem. bd. govs. NCCJ of Western N.Y., 1989—. Univ. scholar Atlanta U., 1962-64; fellow NSF, 1966, U. Calif., 1967-68. Mem. Am. Inst. Biol. Scis., Bot. Soc. Am., Internat. Soc. Plant Morphologists, Am. Assn. State Colls. and Univs. (SCAN team 1986). Home: 152 Lincoln Pky Buffalo NY 14222-1012 Office: SUNY Office of Pres 1300 Elmwood Ave Buffalo NY 14222

RICHARDSON, JEAN, environmental educator; b. Northumberland, U.K., Apr. 29, 1943; came to U.S., 1965; d. Philip and Isabella Curry (Todd) R.; m. Carl H. Reidel, July 29, 1990; children: Sarah, Elizabeth, Gwyneth Rachel. BS, U. Newcastle-on-Tyne, Eng., 1965; MS, U. Wis., 1967, PhD, 1970. Teaching asst., rsch. fellow U. Wis., Madison, 1965-70; field asst. New Zealand, 1971-76; assoc. Tyler and Bruce Law Firm, St. Albans, Vt., 1978-81; assoc. prof., assoc. dir. environ. program U. Vt., Burlington, 1981—; adv. bd. nat. fellowship program W.K. Kellogg Found., Battle Creek, Mich., 1989—. Editorial bd.: Journal of International Environmental Affairs, 1989—. Vice chmn. Vt. Natural Resources Coun., Montpelier, 1984-86; chmn. town planning and zoning bd. Town of Fairfield, Vt., 1984-89; bd. dirs. Nat. Wildlife Fedn., Washington, 1991—; mem. sci. coun. Internat. Ctr. Environ. Protection of Baikal Region, Siberia, USSR, 1991—. W.K. Kellogg fellow, 1985-88. Mem. Environ. Law Inst. Democrat. Episcopalian. Home: PO Box 3055 North Ferrisburg VT 05473-9998 Office: U Vt Environ Program 153 S Prospect St Burlington VT 05401-3595

RICHARDSON, JONATHAN LYNDE, biology educator; b. Phila., May 15, 1935; s. Arthur Hall and Dorothy Lee R.; m. Alice Catherine Elmore, Aug. 5. 1963; children: Catherine Woods, Mary Stavers. BA, Williams Coll., 1957; MA, U. New Zealand, Wellington, 1960; PhD, Duke U., 1965. Post-doctoral fellow Tropical Fish Culture Rsch. Inst., Malacca, Malaysia, 1964-66; from asst. prof. to prof. biology dept. Franklin & Marshall Coll., Lancaster, Pa., 1966-80; prof. biology dept. Franklin & Marshall Coll., Lancaster, 1980-82, Reiff prof. of biology, 1982—, chmn., 1983-87; interim dir. North Mus. Franklin & Marshall Coll., Lancaster, 1990-91; vis. fellow Australian Nat. U., Canberra, Australia, 1980-81; chmn. Sewer & Water adv. Com., Lancaster County Planning Commn., Lancaster, 1976-80. Author: Dimensions of Ecology, 1987; contbr. over 15 articles to profl. jours. Pres. Friends of Brent Sch., Inc., Baguio, Philippines, 1984—; sr. warden St. James Episcopal Ch., Lancaster, 1987-88; bd. dirs. Lancaster County Coun. of Chs., 1989—, Lancaster County Conservancy, 1991—. Recipient Fulbright fellowship, New Zealand, 1958-59, postdoctoral fellowship, Malaysia, NSF, 1964-66, NSF grants, 1969-73, US-Australia Coop. Sci. fellowship, Canberra, Australia, 1980-81. Mem. AAAS, Am. Inst. Biol. Sci., Am. Soc. Limnology and Oceanography, Ecolog. Soc. Am., Soc. Internat. Limnologiae. Home: 1718 N Harvard St Arlington VA 22201-5117 Office: Franklin & Marshall Coll Biology Dept Lancaster PA 17604-3003

RICHARDSON, JOSEPH BLANCET, educational facilities planning consultant; b. Louisville, Nov. 12, 1936; s. Orla Coburn and Alma (Mason) R. m. Mary Irene Murphy, Dec. 27, 1960; children: Pamela, Joseph Blancet Jr., John, Karen. BSCE, The Citadel, 1958; BA with high honors in Zoology, Rutgers U., 1973, PhD in Zoology, 1979; MS in Anatomy, N.Y. Med. Coll., 1975. Design engr. Ky. Hwy. Dept., 1958-59; tech. rep. Shell Oil Co., Balt., 1968-72; asst. prof. biology Ramapo Coll., Mahwah, N.J., 1976-80, program coord. for biology, 1979-80, asst. dir. campus planning, 1980-82, dir. campus planning, 1982-86; pres. Richardson Recreational Svcs., Inc., Kinnelon, N.J., 1981-88, Whitehall Assocs., Inc., Kinnelon, 1986—. Trustee Kinnelon (N.J.) Bd. Edn.; dir. recreational water testing programs Kinnelon Environ. Commn., 1977-82; pres. Morris County Ednl. Svcs. Commn. Served to Capt. U.S. Army, 1959-68; Vietnam. Mem. N.J. Sch. Bds. Assn., Soc. Am. Mil. Engrs. (treas. N.J. post 1988-90), The Citadel Alumni Assn., Rutgers U. Alumni Assn., N.Y. Med. Coll. Alumni Assn., N.Y. Acad. Sci., 3d Bn. 113th Inf. Officers Assn. (pres. 1982-83), 50th Armored Div. Officers Assn. (pres. 1984-85), Sigma Xi. Republican. Roman Catholic. Home and Office: 65 Fayson Lake Rd Butler NJ 07405-3129

RICHARDSON, JOSEPH BLANCET, retail executive; b. Wurtzburg, Germany, Mar. 18, 1963; came to U.S. 1965; s. Joseph and Irene (Murphy) R.; m. Sandra Diane Garland, July 17, 1985; children: Elizabeth Marie, John David. BA, Rutgers U., 1986. First mate Balboa Inc., Brielle, N.J., 1984-87; with R.H. Macys, Eatontown, N.J., 1987-88; dept. mgr. Sears Roebuck & Co., New Brunswick, N.J., 1988-90, Freehold, N.J., 1990—; ptnr. The Assemblers, Franklin Park, N.J., 1991—; cons. Whithall Assoc., Kinnelon, N.J., 1990—. Author: A Manual for Retail, 1991. Republican. Roman Catholic. Home: 31 Lindsey Ct Franklin Park NJ 08823

RICHARDSON, MIDGE TURK, magazine editor; b. Los Angeles, Mar. 26, 1930; d. Charles Aloysius and Marie Theresa (Lindekin) Turk; m. Hamilton Farrar Richardson, Feb. 8, 1974. BA, Immaculate Heart Coll., L.A., 1951, MA, 1956; postgrad., U. Calif., Santa Barbara, Duquesne U., U. Pitts. Mem. Immaculate Heart Community, Roman Catholic Ch., 1948-66; asst. to dean Sch. Arts, NYU, 1966-67; coll. editor Glamour mag., N.Y.C., 1967-74; editor-in-chief Co-Ed mag.; also editorial dir. Forecast and Co-Ed mags., N.Y.C., 1974-75; editor-in-chief Seventeen mag., N.Y.C., 1975—; lectr. Tishman seminars Hunter Coll., N.Y.C., 1975-77. Host, guest TV and radio programs.; Author: The Buried Life: A Nun's Journey, 1971, Gordon Parks: A Biography for Children, 1971; also articles. Bd. dirs. YMCA, N.Y.C., 1972-73, Timothy Dwight Sch., 1979-83, Girl Scout council Greater N.Y., 1979-82; life trustee Internat. House. Recipient award Outstanding Women in Pub., 1982; winner ASME Nat. Mag. award for fiction, 1984. Mem. Am. Soc. Mag. Editors (winner Nat. Mag. award for fiction 1984), Fashion Group. Democrat. Clubs: River, Meadow. Office: Seventeen Mag 850 3rd Ave New York NY 10022-6222

RICHARDSON, RUTH GREENE, social worker; b. Washington, Mar. 30, 1926; d. Arthur Alonzo and Ruth Naomi (Conway) Greene; m. Frederick D. Richardson, June 7, 1968; 1 child, Arthur William Boler. BS, St. Louis U., 1948; MSW, Washington U., St. Louis, 1950. Exec. dir. Anna B. Heldman Community Center, Pitts., 1962-64; assoc. dir. Hillhouse Assn., Pitts., 1964-67; assoc. dir. Dixwell House, also supr. group work services in community schs., New Haven, 1967-69; exec. dir. Three Rivers Youth Inc., Pitts., 1969-91; adv. bd. Sch. Social Work, U. Pitts., 1979-80; pres. Assn. Residential Youth Care Agys., 1973-77; artist, photographer, social work cons. Peoples Art Show Carnegie, 1991; pres., bd. dirs. Pa. Council Vol. Child Care Agys., 1973-78; asst. v.p. Allegheny Children and Youth Services Council, 1974-76. Participated in juried nat. art shows: Westmoreland County Mus., 1992, Three Rivers Art, 1992. Bd. dirs. Children's Council Western Pa.; adv. council Booth Home; bd. dirs. Nat. Assn. Homes for Children, Campfire Boys and Girls, 1988, South Arts, YWCA Greater Pitts. Recipient Social Assistance award Pitts. region Women's Am. ORT, 1975, Internat. Yr. of Child award region III, HEW, 1979; Jurors award, 1991, Images Show, 1991, Pitts. Black Artists William Pitt Union Gallery U. Pitts, 1986, Purchase prize Images III Waterworks, 1st prize in water color South Arts Sr. Citizen Show, Purchase prize Community Coll. Show, Ann. Svc. award Children's Coun. Western Pa., 1990. Mem. Child Welfare League Am., Nat. Assn. Social Workers, Pitts. Watercolor Soc., Pa. Soc. Watercolor Painters, Pitts. Soc. Artist, Black Adminstrs. in Child Welfare, Creative Lens, Visions (v.p.). Presbyterian. Paintings exhbited in Pitts. region. Home and Office: 23 Stratford Ct Carnegie PA 15106-1575

RICHARDSON, SAMUEL DAVID, construction executive, consultant; b. Christiansburg, Va., Apr. 18, 1942; s. Otha Abner and Josephine (Duncan) R.; m. Carol Duncan, Sept. 17, 1966 (div. Mar. 1981); m. Darlene Dare Thomas, June 28, 1983. BS in Civil Engring., VPI, 1970. Registered Profl. Engr. Assoc. engr. Va. Elec. and Power Co., Richmond, 1970-71; chief subdivision and drainage engr. Henrico County, Richmond, Va., 1971-75; constrn. engr. Dept. Pub. Works Henrico County, Richmond, Va., 1975-80; chief of inspection div. Dept. of Pub. Works Anne Arundel County, Annapolis, Md., 1980-87; pres. Richardson Constrn. Mgmt. Corp., Annapolis, Md., 1989—; cons. engr. Land Tech. Corp., Annapolis, Md., 1987—. With USN, 1961-65. Mem. Am. Soc. Civil Engrs., Nat. Soc. Profl. Engrs., Am. Pub. Works Assn., County Engrs. Assn. of Md. Democrat. Baptist. Home: 2831 Seasons Way Annapolis MD 21401

RICHARDSON, WILLIAM CHASE, university administrator; b. Passaic, N.J., May 11, 1940; s. Henry Burtt and Frances (Chase) R.; m. Nancy Freeland, June 18, 1966; children: Elizabeth, Jennifer. B.A., Trinity Coll., 1962; M.B.A., U. Chgo., 1964; Ph.D., 1971. Research assoc., instr. U. Chgo., 1967-70; asst. prof. health services U. Wash., 1971-73, assoc. prof., 1973-76, prof., 1976-84, chmn. dept. health services, 1973-76; assoc. dean U. Wash. Sch. Public Health, 1976-81, acting dean, 1977, 78; dean U. Wash. Grad. Sch., vice provost, 1981-84; exec. v.p., provost, prof. dept. family and community medicine Pa. State U., 1984-90; pres. Johns Hopkins U., Balt., 1990—, prof. dept. health policy, mgmt.; cons. in field. Author: books, including Ambulatory Use of Physicians Services, 1971, Health Program Evaluation, 1978; contbr. articles to profl. jours. Kellogg fellow, 1965-67. Fellow Am. Public Health Assn.; mem. Inst. Medicine, Nat. Acad. Scis. Office: Johns Hopkins U Office of Pres Charles & 34th Sts Baltimore MD 21218*

RICHARDS-WRIGHT, GENEVIEVE MERCEDES, educator, trainer; b. Frederiksted, St. Croix, V.I., Oct. 20; d. Ivan Alexander and Doris Augusta (Griles) Richards; m. Van Curtis Wright, May 7, 1977. BA, CUNY, N.Y.C., 1968; MSc in Elem. Edn., CUNY, Bklyn., 1973; advanced cert. in adminstrn. and supervision, CUNY, 1980. Tchr. N.Y.C. Bd. Edn., Bklyn., 1968-73, 76-80, 84-88, tchr. of libr., 1973-76, tchr. of Spanish as a 2d lang., 1980-84, tchr.-trainer, 1988-90; tchr. specialist N.Y.C. Tchrs. Ctr. Consortium, 1990-91, staff developer, 1991—; mem. Comprehensive Sch. Improvement Program, Bklyn., 1985—; sec. Bklyn. chpt. S.M.O.O.T.H. Club, 1987—. Action team mem. East Bklyn. Congregations, Bklyn., 1984—; teen minister St. Laurence Teen Group, Bklyn., 1989—. Recipient Community Svc. award Jack and Jills of Am. Jr. Teens, 1986. Mem. ASCD, Assn. Black Educators N.Y. (charter life), Bklyn. Reading Coun. Roman Catholic.

RICHART, JOHN DOUGLAS, investment banker; b. Urbana, Ill., Jan. 16, 1947; s. Frank Edwin and Elizabeth Norma (Goldthorp) R.; m. Nan Jackson, June 27, 1970. BS in Engring., U. Mich., 1967, MS in Engring., 1968; MBA, Harvard U., 1973. V.p. Donaldson, Lufkin and Jenrette Securities Corp., N.Y.C., 1973-82; mng. dir. Chase Investment Bank div. Chase Manhattan Bank, N.A., N.Y.C., 1982-89; 1st v.p. mgr. mergers and acquisitions Australia and New Zealand Banking Group, N.Y.C., 1989-91; pres. Richart & Co., Upper Montclair, N.J., 1991—. Lt. (j.g.) USCG, 1968-71. Mem. Harvard Bus. Sch. Club N.Y., Montclair Golf Club, Bradford Bath and Tennis Club, PGA West. Republican. Home: 15 Bradford Way Cedar Grove NJ 07009-1933 Office: Richart & Co 209 Cooper Ave Montclair NJ 07043-1850

RICHETTI, JOHN JOSEPH, English educator, writer, editor; b. N.Y.C., Nov. 14, 1938; s. Miguel and Maria Louisa (Braconi) R.; m. Frances Ellyn Palminteri, Sept. 14, 1960 (div. 1986); children: Dion, Noel; m. Deirdre Ada Whitaker, Aug. 4, 1987. BA, St. Francis Coll., 1960; MA, Columbia U., 1961, PhD, 1968. Instr. St. John's U., Bklyn., 1961-65; asst. prof. Columbia U., N.Y.C., 1967-70; assoc. prof. Rutgers U., New Brunswick, N.J., 1970-74, prof., 1975-87; Sugarman prof. U. Pa., Phila., 1987—, chmn., dept. English, 1991—. Author: Popular Fiction Before Richardson, 1969, Defoe's Narratives, 1975, Philosophical Writing, 1983; editor: Cambridge Univ. Studies in Eighteenth-Century Literature and Thought, Cambridge, Eng., 1967—. Guggenheim Found. fellow, 1971, Am. Coun. Learned Soc. fellow, 1976, NEH sr. fellow, 1990. Office: U Pa 34th and Walnut St Philadelphia PA 19104

RICHEY, CHARLES ROBERT, federal judge; b. Logan County, Ohio, Oct. 16, 1923; s. Paul D. and Miriam (Blaine) R.; m. Agnes Mardelle White, Mar. 25, 1950; children: Charles R. Jr., William Paul. BA, Ohio Wesleyan U., 1945; LLB, Case-Western Res. U., 1948. Bar: Ohio 1949, D.C. 1951, U.S. Supreme Ct. 1952, Md. 1964. Legis. counsel former congresswoman Frances P. Bolton, Ohio, 1948-49; practice in Washington and Chevy Chase, Md., 1950-71; founding partner firm Richey & Clancy, Washington and Chevy Chase, Md., 1964-71; gen. counsel Md. Pub. Service Commn., 1967-71; judge U.S. Dist. Ct. D.C., 1971—; sat by designation as mem. U.S. Ct. Appeals for D.C., 1972-75, 77-85; mem. Temporary Emergency Ct. Appeals, 1983-84, Commn. on Criminal Law and Adminstrn. of Probation System of Jud. Conf. U.S., 1984-88; lectr. speech, debate coach Am. U., 1954-55; adj. prof. trial advocacy-practice Georgetown Law Center, 1976—, mem. adv. bd. CLE Program, 1979—; mem. faculty Nat. Coll. State Judiciary, 1973-75, Fed. Jud. Center, 1976-86, U.S. Atty. Gen.'s Advocacy Inst., Washington, 1974-85; spl. counsel, councilmanic redistricting, Montgomery County Govt., 1965-66; vice chmn. Charter Revision Commn., 1967-68; frequent lectr. ABA and ATLA ann. meetings, CLE programs of Am. Law Inst.-ABA, Practicing Law Inst. and other Bar and civic groups throughout U.S.; mem. Jud. Coun., D.C. Cir., 1991—; co-chair 3d cir. of Sentencing Inst. for D.C., 1984, 3d and 7th cirs., 1992. Author: Manual on Employment Discrimination and Civil Rights Actions in the Federal Courts; contbr. articles to numerous profl. jours. Legal counsel Boys' Clubs Greater Washington, 1966-71; affiliate mem. D.C. Urban Renewal Council and Citizens Housing Commn., 1961-64; chmn. parents assn. Sidwell Friends Sch., Washington, 1968-70; mem. Montgomery County Bd. Appeals, 1965-67, chmn., 1966-67; trustee Immaculata Coll., Washington, 1970-73, Suburban Hosp. Bethesda, Md., 1967-71. Recipient Outstanding and Dedicated Public Service award Montgomery County, Md., 1966, 68; Cert. Disting. Citizenship award Gov. Md., 1971; Annual Award of Merit Adminstrv. Law Judges of U.S., 1979; Outstanding U.S. Fed. Trial Judge, Am. Trial Lawyers Assn., 1979; Humanitarian of Yr. award, Howard U. Law Sch. Alumni Assn., 1979; Justice Harold Hitz Burton Award, Cleveland Club of Washington, 1990; Judge H. Carl Moultrie Award of Jud. Excellence, D.C. Area Trial Lawyers Assn., 1990. Life fellow Am. Bar Found.; mem. ABA (ho. of dels. 1981-85, chmn. com. on alcohol and drug abuse 1973-76, chmn. com. on sentencing probation and parole 1976-77, mem. council criminal justice sect. 1976-80, chmn. nat. adv. com. Project ADVoCATE 1976-80, chmn. nat. conf. fed. trial judges 1980-81, officer and mem. exec. com. 1975-85, mem. council jud. adminstrv. div. 1980-81, co-chair sentencing inst. for 1st, 3d and D.C. cirs. at Otisville, N.Y. 1984, co-chair for sentencing inst. for D.C., 3d and 7th cirs. 1992), D.C. Bar, Bar Assn. of D.C., Md. Bar Assn., Am. Judicature Soc., Assn. Trial Lawyers Am. (faculty Nat. Coll. Advocacy 1975-77), Supreme Ct. Hist. Soc. (founding mem.), Edward Bennett Williams Am. Inn. of Ct. (master, charter), Soc. of Benchers of Case-Western Res. U. Sch. Law, Omicron Delta Kappa, Delta Sigma Rho, Pi Delta Epsilon, Phi Delta Phi, Phi Gamma Delta (gen. counsel 1960-63). Methodist. Club: Nat. Lawyers (Washington). Lodge: Masons (33 degree). Home: 8101 Connecticut Ave Apt 501C Chevy Chase MD 20815-2810 Office: US Dist Ct US Courthouse 3rd & Constitution Ave NW Washington DC 20001

RICHINO, MARTHA ELISABETH, educator; b. Titusville, Pa., Feb. 13, 1942; d. George William and Elizabeth (Shepard) Becker; m. Michael J. Richino, Aug. 15, 1964; children: Beth, Cheryl, Michael. BS, Lock Haven U., 1964; postgrad., Temple U., 1965; MEd, West Chester U., 1981; postgrad., Villanova U., 1991—. Cert. tchr. and sch. counselor, Pa. Helath and phys. edn. tchr. Cameron County Sch. Dist., Emporium, Pa., 1964-68; sch. counselor Middle Bucks Area Vocat. Tech. Sch., Jamison, Pa., 1981-84, 85—, Cen. Bucks Sch. Dist., Doylestown, Pa., 1984-85; mem. Carl Perkins practioners com. Pa. Dept. Edn., 1990—, guidance devel. curriculum com., 1990—. Contbr. articles to profl. jours. Mem. Village Improvement Assn., Doylestown, 1985—. Fellow mem. NEA, Pa. State Edn. Assn., Middle Bucks Edn. Assn. (sec. 1983-84), Pa. Sch. Counselors Assn. (vocat. tech. edn. chair 1986—, exec. bd. mem. 1982—), Pa. Vocat. Assn. (ea. Pa. pres. 1990—), Bucks County Sch. Counselors Assn. (pres. 1984-86). Office: Middle Bucks Sch Dist 2740 Old York Rd Jamison PA 18929

RICHMAN, DAVID MARC, theater educator; b. Phila., Feb. 11, 1951; s. Samuel Joseph and Sylvia (Cohen) Richman-Dickter; m. Susan Fay Lichtman, Mar. 24, 1974; children: Sam, Beatrice. BA, Harvard U., 1972; PhD, Stanford U., Palo Alto, Calif., 1978. From asst prof. to assoc. prof. English U. Rochester, N.Y., 1977-88; asst. prof. to assoc. prof. theater U. N.H., Durham, 1988—. Author: Laughter, Pain & Wonder; Shakespeare's Comedies and the Audience in the Theater, 1990; contbr. articles to profl. jours. Lib. adv. coun. mem. State of N.H., 1991. Grantee Am. Philos. Soc., 1984, Nat. Endowment for Humanities, 1991. Home: 16 Cowell Dr Durham NH 03824-2417 Office: U NH Dept Theater & Dance PCAC College Rd Durham NH 03824

RICHMAN, JEFFREY ELLIOT, science and medical writer, editor; b. N.Y.C., May 2, 1949; s. Michael Joseph and Harriet (Gold) R.; m. Laura Karen Goodman, Nov. 4, 1979; 1 child, Daniel Eric. BS in Chemistry, U. Rochester, 1970, PhD in Chemistry, 1975; diploma in piano, Mannes Coll. Music, N.Y.C., 1987. Postdoctoral fellow Dept. Chemistry U. Rochester, N.Y., 1975-76, Columbia U., N.Y.C., 1976-77; staff writer Med. Tribune, N.Y.C., 1977-78; account exec., sci. writer Manning, Selvage & Lee, N.Y.C., 1978-79; sr. editor Jour. Respiratory Diseases, Greenwich, Conn., 1979-84, mng. editor, 1984-87; sect. head, sr. editor Patient Care/Med. Econs. Montvale, N.J., 1987—. Mem. editorial adv. com. Med. Econs. Pub., 1991—. Mem. environ. adv. com., Ridgewood, N.J., 1986-87; mem. Vol. Admissions Network, U. Rochester, Wyckoff, N.J., 1984—. Recipient cert. of merit Neal Editorial award Bus. Press Am., N.Y.C., 1990. Mem. AAAS, Am. Chem. Soc., Nat. Assn. Sci. Writers, N.Y. Acad. Sci. Democrat. Office: Patient Care/Med Econs Pub Co 5 Paragon Dr Montvale NJ 07645-1742

RICHMAN, LAURA K., learning consultant; b. N.Y.C., Jan. 17, 1948; d. Joseph and Frances (Sturm) Kruger; m. Albert Richman, June 21, 1970; children: Allison, Deborah. BA, George Washington U., 1969; MA, Kean Coll., 1972, postgrad., 1980. Social worker West Orange (N.J.) Community House, 1969-70; supplemental tchr. Bd. of Edn., North Plainfield, N.J., 1972-73; homebound instr. Bd. of Edn., Summit, N.J., 1979; supplemental tchr. Bd. of Edn., Chatham Borough, N.J., 1979-80; learning cons., child study team coord. Ind. Child Study Teams, Jersey City, 1980-84, 88—; learning cons. Bd. of Edn., Livingston, N.J., 1983—; learning cons., owner Resources for Youth, Livingston, N.J., 1984—; lectr. in field. Com. mem. Jewish Community Ctr., West Orange, 1975-90, N.J. YM & YWHA Round Lake Camp for Learning Disabilities, 1989—; treas., mem. adminstrn. for fund raising Nat. Coun. of Jewish Women, Essex County, 1973—. Mem. N.J. Assn. of Learning Cons., Orton Soc., Am. Assn. for Counseling and Devel., Assn. Measurement and Evaluation In Counseling and Devel., Children with Attention Deficit Disorders. Home and Office: 235 W Hobart Gap Rd Livingston NJ 07039

RICHMAN, LILLIAN BEATRICE, lawyer; b. N.Y.C., Oct. 18, 1924; d. Leo and Rose (Aranov) Sorrin; m. George Richman, Mar. 1, 1953 (dec. Apr. 1985); 1 child, David E. RN, Kings County Hosp. Sch Nursing, N.Y.C., 1947; BA magna cum laude, Queens Coll., N.Y.C., 1971; JD, St. John's U., 1974. Bar: N.Y. 1975, U.S. Dist. Ct. (so. dist.) N.Y. 1976, U.S. Dist. Ct. (ea. dist.) N.Y. 1977. RN, various positions various hosps. N.Y.C., 1947-56; office nurse, 1956-67; assoc. Bower & Gardner, N.Y.C., 1974-79, ptnr., 1979-90, of counsel, 1991—; lectr. med. malpractice law; cons. in field. Mem. N.Y. Bar Assn., Phi Beta Kappa. Office: Bower & Gardner 110 E 59th St New York NY 10022-1304

RICHMAN, MARC HERBERT, engineer, educator; b. Boston, Oct. 14, 1936; s. Samuel and Janet (Gordon) R.; m. Ann Raeshel Yoffa, Aug. 31, 1963. B.S., MIT, 1957, Sc.D., 1963; M.A., Brown U., 1967. Registered profl. engr., Mass., R.I. Cons. engr., 1957—; engr. shipbldg. div. Bethlehem Steel Corp., Quincy, Mass., 1957; instr. metallurgy MIT, Cambridge, 1957-60, research asst. dept. metallurgy, 1960-63; instr. metallurgy div. univ. extension Commonwealth of Mass., 1958-62; asst. prof. engring. Brown U., Providence, 1963-67, assoc. prof., 1967-70, prof., 1970—, dir. central electron microscopy facility Materials Research program, 1971-86, dir. undergrad. program, 1991—; pres. Ednl. Aids of Newton Inc., Providence, 1968-71, Marc H. Richman Inc., Providence, 1981—; guest scientist Franklin Inst., Phila., 1959; vis. prof. U. R.I., Kingston, 1970-71; biophysicist dept. medicine Miriam Hosp., Providence, 1974-87; bioengr. dept. orthopaedics R.I. Hosp., 1979—. Author: Introduction to Science of Metals, 1967; also articles; editor Soviet Physics: Crystallography, 1970—; mem. editorial adv. bd. Metallography, 1970—; mem. editorial adv. bd. Jour. Forensic Engring., 1985—. Served to maj. Ordnance Corps, U.S. Army, 1963. Fellow Nat. Acad. Forensic Engrs. (cert.), Am. Inst. Chemists; mem. NAFE (bd. cert. diplomate in forensic engring.), Inst. Metals (U.K.), Am. Soc. Metals (sec.-treas. 1965-68, chmn. R.I. chpt. 1968-69, Albert Sauveur Meml. award 1968, 69), Am. Inst. Metall. Engrs., Nat. Soc. Profl. Engrs., Am. Soc. Engring. Edn. (Outstanding Young Faculty award 1969), Providence Engring. Soc. (pres. 1991-92, Freeman award for engring. achievement 1989), B'nai B'rith, Sigma Xi, Tau Beta Pi. Home: 291 Cole Ave Providence RI 02906-3452 Office: Brown U Div Engring Box D Providence RI 02912 also: One Richmond Sq Providence RI 02906

RICHMAN, PETER, electronics executive; b. N.Y.C., Nov. 7, 1927; s. Emil H. and Janet (Seidler) R.; m. Vivian Hoffman, July 29, 1951; children: Meredith, Jeremy. BS, MIT, 1946; MS, NYU, 1953. Asst. chief engr. Reeves Instrument Corp., Garden City, N.Y., 1948-58; chief engr. Epsco, Inc., Cambridge, Mass., 1959-60; v.p., co-founder Rotek Instrument Corp., Watertown, Mass., 1960-64; v.p. Weston-Rotek, Lexington, Mass., 1964-67; cons. electronics engr. Lexington, 1967—; founder, pres. KeyTek Instrument Corp., 1975—; mem. NRC/Nat. Acad. Scis./Nat. Acad. Engring. Evaluation Panel for electricity div. Nat. Bur. Standards; mem. sci. adv. groups for several indsl. and sci. orgns. Patentee in precision electronic instrumentation; pioneer in precision dc and audio-frequency measurements, surge electrostatic discharge generation and electrostatic discharge measurements; contbr. articles to profl. jours. Mem. bd. overseers Boston Mus. Sci. Fellow IEEE; mem. Electromagnetics Acad., Instrument Soc. Am. (sr.), Sigma Xi, Tau Beta Pi.

RICHMAN, ROBERT MICHAEL, chemistry educator; b. Pasadena, Calif., Apr. 27, 1950; s. Peter and Evelyn (Immerman) R.; m. Linda Dochter, Aug. 14, 1976. AB, Occidental Coll., 1971; MS, U. Ill., 1972, PhD, 1976. Postdoctoral fellow Calif. Inst. Tech., Pasadena, 1976-77; asst. prof. Carnegie Mellon U., Pitts., 1977-84, asst. dept. head, 1984-87; assoc. prof. inorganic chemistry, chair sci. dept. Mt. St. Mary's Coll., Emmitsburg, Md., 1987—; reader Coll. Bd. chemistry exam, Princeton, N.J., 1987—. Contbr. articles to profl. jours. Recipient NSF fellowship, 1976-77, NASA faculty fellowship, 1988. Mem. Am. Chem. Soc., Mid-Atlantic Assn. Liberal Arts Chemistry Tchrs. Office: Mount St Marys Coll Emmitsburg MD 21727

RICHMAN, STEPHEN I., lawyer; b. Washington, Pa., Mar. 26, 1933; m. Audrey May Gefsky. BS, Northwestern U., 1954; JD, U. Pa., 1957. Bar: Pa. 1958, U.S. Dist. Ct. (we. dist.) Pa. Ptnr. Ceisler, Richman, Smith Law Firm, P.A., Washington; bd. dirs. Three Rivers Bank; lectr. U. South Fla. Sch. Medicine, W.Va. U. Med. Ctr. Grand Rounds, Am. Coll. Chest Physicians, Pa. Thoracic Soc., Am. Thoracic Soc., The Energy Bur., Coll. of Am. Pathologists, Allegheny County Health Dept., Am. Pub. Health Assn., Internat. Assn. Ind. Accident Bds. and Commns., Indsl. Health Found., Nat. Coun. Self-Insurers Assn., Am. Iron and Steel Inst., Can. Thoracic Soc., I.L.O./N.I.O.S.H., Univs. Associated for Rsch. and Edn. in Pathology, Am. Cermaics Soc., Nat. Sand Assn.; mem. adv. com. U.S. Dist. Ct. Western Dist. Pa. Author: Meaning of Impairment and Disability, Chest, 1980, Legal Aspects for the Pathologist, in Pathology of Occupational and Environmental Lung Disease, 1988, A Review of the Medical and Legal Definitions of Related Impairment and Disability, Report to the Department of Labor

and the Congress, 1986, Medicolegal Aspects of Asbestos for Pathologists, Arch. Pathology and Laboratory Medicine, 1983, Legal Aspects of Occupational and Environmental Disease, Human Pathology, 1992, other publs. and articles; author House Bill 2103 and 885 amending Pa. Workmen's Compensation Act. Mem. legal com. Indsl. Health Found., Pitts. Mem. ABA (vice chair workers compensation and employers liability law com., toxic and hazardous substance and environ. law com., lectr.), Pa. Bar Assn. (former mem. coun. of worker's compensation sect., lectr., contbg. author bar assn. quarterly 1992), Assn. Trial Lawyers Am., Pa. Chamber Bus. and Industry (workers' compensation com., chmn. subcom. on legis. drafting, lectr.). Home: 820 E Beau St Washington PA 15301-2906 Office: Washington Trust Bldg Ste 200 Washington PA 15301

RICHMOND, HAROLD NICHOLAS, lawyer; b. Elizabeth, N.J., Apr. 5, 1935; s. Benjamin I. and Eleanor (Turbowitz) R.; m. Elaine Zemel, June 16, 1957 (div. Nov. 1972); children: Bonnie J. Ross, Michele Weinfeld; m. Marilyn A. Wenrich, Aug. 26, 1973; children: Eric L., Kacy L. BA, Tulane U., 1957; LLB, NYU, 1961, LLM in Taxation, 1965. Estate tax examiner IRS, Newark, 1963-65; tax mgr. Puder & Puder/Touche Ross & Co., CPAs, Newark, 1965-73; ptnr. Sodowick Richmond & Crecca, Newark, 1973-84; prin. Harold N. Richmond, West Orange, N.J., 1984-86; ptnr. Wallerstein Hauptman & Richmond, West Orange, 1886-91, Hauptman & Richmond, West Orange, 1992—. With U.S. Army, 1959-60. Mem. ABA, N.J. Bar Assn., Essex County Bar Assn. (chmn. tax com. 1989). Office: 200 Executive Dr West Orange NJ 07052-3303

RICHNER, CLIFFORD, newspaper publisher; b. N.Y.C., June 9, 1952; s. Robert and Edith (Murofchick) R. AB with honors, Georgetown U., 1974, JD, 1978. Bar: N.Y. 1979, U.S. Dist. Ct. (so. and ea. dists.) N.Y. 1979. Teaching fellow Georgetown Law Ctr., Washington, 1977-78; assoc. Shea and Gould, N.Y.C., 1978-80, Donovan, Leisure, Newton & Irvine, N.Y.C., 1980-82; assoc. pub. Richner Publs., Inc., Lawrence, N.Y., 1982-87, pub., 1987—; pres. Prime Publs., Inc., Lawrence, 1987—; lectr. Am. Press Inst., Reston, Va., 1988. Editor: Georgetown Univ. Law Journal, 1976-78. Bd. dirs. Five Towns United Way, Woodmere, N.Y., 1988-90, chair bus. div. 1990—. Mem. Nat. Newspaper Assn., Suburban Newspapers Am., Press Club L.I., Soc. Newspaper Design, N.Y. Press Assn. (bd. dirs. 1986-90, 92—). Office: Richner Publs Inc 379 Central Ave Lawrence NY 11559-1616

RICHTER, DOROTHY ANNE, geologist, consultant; b. New Britain, Conn., June 26, 1948; d. Otto Gerhardt and Anne M. (Gaffney) R. BS, Bates Coll., 1970; MS, Boston Coll., 1973; postgrad., Harvard U., 1975-80. Lic. geologist, N.C.; cert. profl. geologist, AIPG. Staff rsch. geologist MIT, Cambridge, 1972-76; chief geologist Rock of Ages Corp., Barre, Vt., 1976-84; prin. Hager-Richter Geosci., Inc., Salem, N.H., 1984—; cons., expert on dimension quarries, failures of bldg. and monumental stone. Contbr. 22 articles and papers to profl. jours. Mem. ASTM (mem. com. C18 on dimension stone, com. D18 on soil and rock), Geol. Soc. Am., N.H. Geol. Soc., Vt. Geol. Soc. (treas. 1981-83), Geol. Soc. Maine, Sigma Xi. Office: Hager-Richter Geosci Inc 8 Industrial Way # 10D Salem NH 03079-2837

RICHTER, HENRY ANDREW, electrical engineer; b. Lancaster, Mass., Dec. 27, 1930; s. Benjamin David and Agnes Ellis (Kilgour) R. Cert., Franklin Tech. Inst., 1953; AEE, Worcester Jr. Coll., 1957. Technician Gen. Electric Co., Lynn, Mass., 1957-58; asst. engr. Raytheon Co., Wayland, Mass., 1958-63; assoc. engr. Raytheon Co., Waltham, Mass., 1963-69, engr., 1969—. Pres. Lancaster Social Svc. Assn., 1977—; chmn. Lancaster Bd. Selectmen, 1984-90; sustaining mem. Rep. Nat. Com., 1987—; trustee Clinton Hosp. Assn., 1986-90; bd. dirs. Clinton Home for Aged People, 1983—. With U.S. Army, 1953-55. Mem. Am. Legion (color guard 1983—). Congregationalist. Home: Neck Rd Lancaster MA 01523-2235 Office: Lancaster Bd Selectmen Town Hall Main St Lancaster MA 01523

RICHTER, KAREN JUNE, solid mechanics engineer, researcher; b. Blue Island, Ill., Feb. 23, 1949; d. Edwin Anton and Joy Shirley (Histed) R.; m. Michael Thomas O'Bannon, Feb. 1, 1969 (div. Dec. 1979); 1 child, Brian Richter. BA, Knox Coll., 1971; MS, U. Wis., 1979, PhD, 1987. Exec. dir. Sunny Day Play Sch., Prairie Du Chien, Wis., 1972-78; teaching asst. U. Wis., Madison, 1978-83, tutor, rsch. asst., 1981-82; asst. prof. Ohio State U., Columbus, 1984-85; cons. Inst. for Def. Analyses, Alexandria, Va., 1987; rsch. staff Inst. for Def. Analysis, Alexandria, 1987—; lectr. U. Md., College Park, 1988-91. Co-author: (textbook) Engineering Mechanics: Statics and Dynamics, 1987. Mem. AIAA, Am. Soc. Engring. Edn., Sigma Xi. Office: SFRD Inst for Def Analysis 1801 N Beauregard St Alexandria VA 22311

RICHTER, ROBERT, film producer; b. N.Y.C., Oct. 23, 1929; 4 children. AA, Telluride Assn. Jr. Coll., 1949; BA, Reed Coll., 1952; postgrad., U. Iowa, 1953; MA, Columbia U., 1964. Scriptwriter U. Iowa, Iowa City, 1953-54; social worker U. Oreg. Med. Sch., Portland, 1955-57; producer, reporter Oreg. Pub. TV/Radio, Portland, 1957-63; reporter N.W. region N.Y. Times, 1962-63; producer, writer CBS News, N.Y.C., 1964-68; ind. documentary producer, pres. Richter Prodns., N.Y.C., 1968—; prodr., dir., writer Nova, Sta. WGBH-TV, Boston, 1976-77, 78-79, 88, 92; prodr. Closeup, ABC, N.Y.C., 1977-78, The Human Animal, NBC, 1986; judge Emmy awards, festivals; cons. pub. TV publs.; lectr. at univs. Producer, writer, reporter over 50 documentaries; contbr. articles to N.Y. Times, Christian Sci. Monitor, also others. Trustee Reed Coll., Portland, 1980-84; bd dirs. CARE, Inc., N.Y.C., 1982—; lectr. U.S. Info. Svc., Yugoslavia, Fed. Republic Germany, 1985. Recipient 4 Am. Film Festival awards, 3 DuPont Columbia awards, Emmy awards, U.A. and Internat. Festival awards, Global 500 award UN Environ. Program; Acad. award nominee for best documentary short, 1982. Mem. Internat. Radio and TV Soc., NATAS, Investigative Reporters and Editors, Assn. Ind. Video and Filmmakers (pres. 1982—), Soc. Profl. Journalists-Sigma Delta Chi. Office: Richter Prodns 330 W 42nd St New York NY 10036-6902

RICHTER, TODD BENJAMIN, investment banker; b. N.Y.C., Apr. 15, 1957; s. Fred William and Patricia Rose (Schwartz) R. BBA, Coll. of William and Mary, 1979; MBA, Ind. U., 1981. Health care analyst Oppenheimer & Co., N.Y.C., 1980; sr. equity rsch. analyst Morgan Stanley & Co., N.Y.C., 1981-88; sr. v.p., dir. health care equity rsch. Dean Witter Reynolds, N.Y.C., 1988—; mem. bd. advisors Health Care Competition Mag., Washington, 1987—. Mem. bd. advisors Ind. U. Sch. of Bus., Bloomington, 1988—. Mem. Am. Hosp. Assn., Fedn. Am. Health Systems, Nat. Ski Patrol, Old Oaks Country Club. Home: 127 E 30th St # Ph New York NY 10016-7302 Office: Dean Witter Reynolds 2 World Trade Ctr Fl 63D New York NY 10048-0203

RICIOPPO, ERIC, public relations professional; b. Rockville Center, N.Y., Mar. 31, 1955; s. Pat and Margaret R.; m. Francine Ciccimarro, Aug. 5, 1990. BA in Sociology, Pembroke State U., 1977; MA in Communication Arts, N.Y. Inst. Tech., 1985. Community rels. rep. L.I. Lighting Co., Mineola, N.Y., 1980-84; on-camera reporter L.I. News Tonight, Old Westbury, N.Y., 1984-85; communications mgr. Norstar Bank, Garden City, N.Y., 1985-87; pub. rels. exec. Howard Blankman, Inc., Westbury, N.Y., 1987-91; dir. L.I. ops. Paul Buiar Assocs., Inc., N.Y.C., 1991—; adj. instr. Hofstra U., Hempstead, N.Y., 1985-90. Committeeman Am. Cancer Soc., 1985—. Mem. Pub. Rels. Profls. L.I. (founding pres. 1990—), Pub. Rels. Soc. Am. (v.p. L.I. chpt. 1988-90), Internat. Assn. Bus. Communicators (communications excellence award 1990).

RICKARDS, DEBRA JEAN, sales executive; b. Burlington, N.J., Oct. 29, 1952; d. Wallace Eugene and Meryl Constance (New) Alligood; m. Donald A. Rickards, Sept. 9, 1978 (div. Dec. 1987); 1 child, Bernard H. Purchasing and material mgr. Omni-Tek, Feasterville, Pa., 1977-82; product mktg. mgr. Almo Electronics, Phila., 1982-86; br. mgr. TTI, Inc., Mt. Laurel, N.J., 1986—. Vol. Spl. Olympics, Bucks County, 1984; pres., founder Women in Electronics, Pa., 1978-81. Mem. NAFE. Lutheran. Office: TTI 100 Century Pkwy Ste 120 Mount Laurel NJ 08054

RICKERSON, STUART EUGENE, lawyer; b. Plainfield, N.J., Jan. 22, 1949; s. Malcolm John and Violet Ellen (North) R. AB in Politics cum laude, Princeton U., 1971; JD, Georgetown U., 1975. Bar: N.J. 1975, U.S. Ct. Appeals (3d crct.) 1979, U.S. Supreme Ct. 1982, N.Y. 1982, Minn. 1988. Assoc. McCarter & English, Newark, 1975-81; asst. counsel Eli Lilly and Co., Indpls., 1981-86; gen. counsel, sec. Cardiac Pacemakers, Inc. (subs. of Eli Lilly and Co.), St. Paul, 1986-89; assoc. gen. counsel Philip Morris, Inc., N.Y.C., 1989-90; prin. Offices of Stuart E. Rickerson, Del mar, Calif., 1990-91; gen. counsel Keene Corp., N.Y.C., 1991—, also sec., 1991—. Contbr. to profl. pubs. Reunion chmn. Princeton U. Class of 1971, 1976-81, 91-96, sec., 1986-91; chmn. athletics com. Alumni Coun. Princeton U., 1979-81. Mem. Internat. Assn. Def. Counsel (vice chmn. corp. coun. 1989-91), Def. Rsch. Inst. (steering com. drug and device law sect. 1985-92), The Tiger Inn (bd. govs. 1978—). Office: Keene Corp 49th Fl 200 Park Ave New York NY 10166

RICKERT, ALFRED E., English educator, playwright; b. N.Y.C., Nov. 1, 1930; s. Alfred and Tillie (Kratz) R.; m. Margaret Krone, Feb. 22, 1957; children: Paul, Susan. BS, NYU, 1952, MA, 1953; PhD, U. Denver, 1967. Tchr. N.Y. Pub. Schs., N.Y.C., 1952-57, Denver Pub. Schs., 1957-59; prof. English Franklin (Ind.) Coll., 1959-62; mem. faculty SUNY, Oswego, 1962-91, prof., 1972-91. Playwright All We Can Hope For, 1984, Rub-A-Dub, 1986, The Working Force, 1988, Wellerton Revisited, 1989, Billy's Play, 1991. Recipient Duthie award N.Y. State Community Theatre Assn., 1981. Fellow Am. Assn. Community Theatre. Office: SUNY Oswego Swetman Hall Oswego NY 13126

RICKERT, EDWIN WEIMER, investment consultant; b. Connersville, Ind., June 17, 1914; s. Edwin and Grace (Weimer) R.; A.B., Columbia U., 1936; m. Ruth Alma Fulcher, July 9, 1942; children—Jean Adelia, Wendy Grace, Allen Edwin. Security analyst, economist Mackubin, Legg & Co., Balt., 1936-40; indsl. analyst Office of Prodn. Mgmt., Washington, 1940-41; supr. commodity econ. research Standard Brnds, Inc., N.Y.C., 1946-53; with Brundage, Story & Rose, N.Y.C., 1953—, partner, 1966-83, sr. investment cons., 1984—. Trustee, Columbia U. Press, 1977—; bd. visitors Columbia Coll., N.Y., 1986—. Served to capt. U.S. Army, 1941-46; ret. lt. col. Res. Mem. Investment Counsel Assn. Am., N.Y. Soc. Security Analysts. Republican. Presbyterian. Clubs: India House (N.Y.C.); Grachur (Balt.). Home: 56 Dogwood Ln Rockville Centre NY 11570-1501 Office: 1 Broadway New York NY 10004-1007

RICKERT, ROBERT RICHARD, pathologist, educator; b. Harrisburg, Pa., Oct. 19, 1936; s. Alton G. and Henrietta (Gey) R.; m. Sonja Murray Hansen, Aug. 26, 1961; children: Kristin, Robin, Anne. AB, U. Mich., 1958; MD, John Hopkins U., 1962. Diplomat Am. Bd. of Pathology. Intern Yale-New Haven (Conn.) Med. Ctr., 1962-63, resident, 1963-64, 66-67; rsch. assoc. Atomic Bomb Casulty Commn., Hiroshima, Japan, 1964-66; asst. prof. of Pathology Yale U. Sch. Med., New Haven, 1968-70; attending Pathologist Yale New Haven Med. Ctr., 1968-70; dir. of Surg. Pathology U. Med. and Dentistry N.J. Med. Sch., Newark, 1970-73, assoc. prof. Pathology, 1974—; adj. assoc. prof. of Pathology Columbia U. Coll. of Physicians & Surgs., N.Y.C., 1974-89; clin. prof. of Pathology U. of Med. and Dentistry of N.J. Med. Sch., Newark, 1985—; co-chmn. Dept. of Pathology St. Barnabas Med. Ctr., Livingston, N.J., 1973—. Author and co-author of more than 60 articles an dhcpts. for profl. pubs. on pathology. Chmn. med. com. Am. Cancer Soc., N.J., 1989-91, v.p. 1991—. Surg. USPHS, 1964-66, Hiroshima. Fellow Coll. Am. Pathologists, Am. Soc. Clin. Pathologists, U.S.-Can. Acad. Pathology; mem. AMA, N.J. Soc. Pathologists (pres. 1980-82), Gastrointestinal Pathology Soc. (pres. 1988-89), Med. Soc. N.J., Acad. Medicine N.J. (trustee 1988—), Am. Soc. Cytology, Short Hills Club, Phi Beta Kappa, Alpha Omega Alpha. Republican. Congregational. Office: St Barnabas Med Ctr Dept Pathology Livingston NJ 07039

RICKETTI, JAMES CARMEN, surgeon, podiatrist; b. Trenton, N.J., July 16, 1955; s. Frank Joseph and Francis Adeline (DeLorenzo) R.; m. Maria Hrabowskyj, July 9, 1983; 1 child, James Peter. BA in Biology, Rider Coll., 1977; D in Podiatric Medicine, Ohio Coll. Podiatric Medicine, 1981. Diplomate Am. Bd. Podiatric Orthopedics. Cons. Cleve. Indians, 1980-81; resident James C. Giuffree Med. Ctr., 1981-82; pvt. practice Mercerville and Hightstown, N.J., 1982—; staff podiatric physician Inst. for Medicine in Sports Hamilton Hosp., 1984-87; cons. Boston Red Sox, 1985-86; cons. N.J. br. Internat. Dance and Exercise Assn., 1986—; keynote speaker Orthopedic Coll. Podiatric Medicine Sports Seminar, Atlantic City, 1988, Ont. Soc. Chiropodists, Toronto, Can., 1989. Expert (films) Podiatric Athletic Taping, 1978, Aerobic Dance Injury, 1984, The Running Shoe Today, 1985, Computerzied Gait Analysis, 1986. Bd. dirs. YMCA, Hamilton, N.J., 1990-93. Fellow Am. Coll. Foot Orthopedics, Am. Acad. Podiatric Sports Medicine (oral examiner 1991), Am. Acad. Clin. Electrodynography and Gait Analysis. Roman Catholic. Home: 11 Red Cedar Dr Trenton NJ 08690-2223 Office: 1799 Klockner Rd Trenton NJ 08619-2794 also: Rte 130 Hightstown NJ 08619

RICKIN, SHEILA ANNE, personnel executive; b. N.Y.C., Oct. 13, 1945; d. Louis and Ethel (Schmukler) Bernstein; BA, CCNY, 1966; postgrad. N.Y.U.; MBA, Pace U., 1988. Research asst. pre-baccalaureate program CCNY, 1966-68; placement counselor Elaine Revell, Inc., N.Y.C., 1968; adminstr. assoc. to chief exec. officer Planned Parenthood Fedn. of Am., N.Y.C., 1969-74; personnel mgr. Family Circle Mag./N.Y. Times Mag. Group, 1974-87; sr. human resources rep., Drexel Burnham Lambert, 1987-88; asst. v.p., dir. pers. and adminstrn. Oppenheimer Mgmt. Corp. div. MassMut. Ins. Co., 1989—. Mem. Am. Compensation Assn., Human Resources Soc., Internat. Found. Benefits, Am. Mgmt. Assn., Am. Soc. Tng. and Devel. (securities industry group), N.Y. Human Resources Planners, N.Y. Pers. Mgrs. Assn. (program com.), Mag. Pubs. Assn. (pers. com. 1978-87). Office: Oppenheimer Mgmt Corp 2 World Trade Ctr New York NY 10048

RICKMAN, RAY, bookseller, television program producer and host; b. Gallatin, Tenn., Nov. 25, 1948; s. James Bailey Rickman and Betty (Richards) Rickett. Student, Wayne State U., 1971. Chief asst. U.S. Congressman John Conyers, Detroit, 1971-74; exec. dir. Jefferson-Chalmers Redevel. Project, Detroit, 1974-77, Harmony Village Redevel. Project, Detroit, 1977-79, Providence Human Rels. Commn., 1980-83; adminstrv. asst. Asst. Sec. Welfare, Mass., 1979-80; asst. equal opportunity officer Mass. Housing Fin. Agy., 1983-86; producer, host Minority Affairs talkshow Sta. WSBE-TV, R.I., 1985—; owner Cornerstone Books, Providence, 1986—; State rep., 1986—; chmn. Dexter Commn., Providence, 1983-87; bd. dirs. Langston Hughes Arts Ctr., 1987-89; commr. Providence Hist. Dist. Commn., 1987—; trustee R.I. Hist. Soc., 1989—. Guest writer Detroit Free Press, Providence Jour., 1978—. State Rep., R.I., 1986—. Recipient R.I. Black Media award R.I. Black Media Coalition, 1989. Mem. ACLU. Democrat. Home: 19 Pratt St Providence RI 02906 Office: The Capitol Providence RI 02903

RICKS, THOMAS EDWIN, journalist; b. Beverly, Mass., Sept. 25, 1955; s. David Frank and Anne (Russell) R.; m. Mary Catherine Giblin, Oct. 10, 1981. BA, Yale U., 1977. Instr. Lingnan Coll., Hong Kong, 1977-79; asst. editor Wilson Quar., Washington, 1979-81; reporter Wall St. Jour., Atlanta, Miami, 1982-86; dep. bur. chief Wall St. Jour., Miami, 1986; reporter Wall St. Jour., Washington, 1987-89, feature editor, 1989-92, Pentagon corres., 1992—. Office: Wall St Jour 1025 Connecticut Ave NW Ste 800 Washington DC 20036-5477

RICKTER, DONALD OSCAR, chemist; b. Rio Dell, Calif., May 5, 1931; s. Oscar and Wealthy May (Murphey) R.; m. Phyllis May Carlson, Aug. 21, 1959; children: David Rickter Rain, Paul Carlson Rickter. AB, U. Calif., Davis, 1952, MS, 1954; PhD, Mich. State U., 1964. Instr. Santa Ana (Calif.) Coll., 1957-59; scientist, info. mgr. Polaroid Corp., Cambridge, Mass., 1964—. Contbr. articles to profl. jours. With USN, 1955-57. Mem. Am. Chem. Soc. (alt. councilor 1985-92), New Eng. Online Users Group. Unitarian Universalist. Office: Polaroid Corp 750 Main St # 1R Cambridge MA 02139-3583

RIDDICK, ANDREA CELESTINE, accountant; b. Bklyn., Jan. 9, 1963; d. Cicero and Shirley Temple (Magee) R. BBA in Acctg., Bernard M. Baruch Coll., 1986. Profl. tax preparer. Acctg. intern Victoreen Inc., Carle Place, N.Y., 1985-86; acct. Pinkerton's Inc., Manhattan, N.Y., 1986-88; tax acct. Fleischman & Co., CPAs, Manhattan, 1988-89; acct. Am. Internat. Group/Fin. Products, Manhattan, 1989, Fed. Aviation Adminstrn./John F. Kennedy Internat. Airport, Queens, N.Y., 1989—. Mem. 145th St. Neighborhood Block Assn., Queens, 1980—, Square Deal Civic Assn., Queens, 1991—. Recipient Bernard M. Baruch Incentive award Bernard M. Baruch Coll., Manhattan, 1981-82. Mem. N.Y. State Assn. CPA Candidates, Baruch Coll. Alumni Assn., Fed. Women's Prog. Democrat. Home: 11457 145th St Jamaica NY 11436-1140

RIDDLE, JAMES DOUGLASS, college administrator; b. Austin, Tex., Oct. 8, 1933; s. Prebble Elmer and Jewel Lee (Nalley) R.; m. Marilyn Brown Moore, Sept. 8, 1956; children: Mary Elizabeth, Margaret Allison, Charles Douglass. BA in History and Govt., Southwestern U., 1958; MDiv in Theology and Social Ethics, Boston U. Sch. Theology, 1962; postgrad., Boston U., 1962-65; D Ministry, San Francisco Theol. Sem., 1991. Ordained to ministry Meth. Ch., 1963, transferred to United Ch. of Christ, 1966. Copastor The First Parish Ch., Lincoln, Mass., 1963-67; sr. pastor The Community Ch., Chapel Hill, N.C., 1967-80, First Ch. of Christ Congl. United Ch. of Christ, Springfield, Mass., 1980-89; v.p. devel. Am. Internat. Coll., Springfield, 1989—; teaching fellow, lectr. in human rels. Boston U. Sch. Bus., 1960-64. Mem. governing bd. Nat. Coun. Chs., 1969-72, commn. on faith and order, 1969-72, com. on future ecumenical structure, 1971-72; chmn. commn. on ecumenical study and svc. United Ch. of Christ, 1969-75, del. gen. synod, mem. exec. coun., 1969-75; pres. N.C. Legal Def. Fund, 1969-80, Orange-Chatham Counties Community Action Agy., 1970-76, Chapel Hill-Carrboro Inter-Ch. Coun. Housing Corp., 1969-77; mem. bd. Community Care Mental Health Ctr., 1980-90, chair, 1985-88; mem. governing bd. Greater Springfield Coun. Chs., 1980-86, Downtown Econ. Devel. Corp., Springfield Cen., 1981—, StageWest Regional Theatre Co., 1982—, Springfield YMCA, 1982-87, City of Springfield 350th Anniversary, 1984-87, Springfield Adult Edn. Coun., 1984—; corporator Zone Arts Ctr., 1986—; chair Downtown Ministry Project, 1981-84. Named Person of Yr. NOW, 1987; recipient 350th Anniversary Medallion, City of Springfield, 1986. Mem. ACLU, Coun. for Advancement and Support of Edn., Nat. Soc. Fund Raising Execs., Estate Planning Coun. Hampden Country, New Eng. Devel. Rsch. Assn., Acad. Religion and Mental Health, Soc. Sci. Study of Religion, Inst. Soc., Ethics and Life Scis., Congl. Christian Hist. Soc. (mem. bd. 1987—), Assn. Humanistic Psychology, Common Cause (nominating com. 1989—), The Reality Club of Springfield, Springfield Rotary. Democrat. Home: 283 Longhill St Springfield MA 01108-1413 Office: Am Internat Coll 1000 State St Springfield MA 01109-3189

RIDDLE, MARK ALAN, child psychiatrist; b. Huntingburg, Ind., Feb. 18, 1948; s. James G. and Louise (Burgdorf) R.; m. Clarine Carol Nardi, Aug. 15, 1971; children: Carl, Julia. BA, Ind. U., 1970, MS, 1973, MD, 1977. Intern in pediatrics Ind. U. Med. Ctr., Indpls., 1977-78; resident in psychiatry Sch. Medicine Yale U., New Haven, 1978-81; fellow in child psychiatry Yale Child Study Ctr., New Haven, 1981-83; asst prof. child psychiatry Sch. Medicine Yale U., New Haven, 1983-89, assoc. prof. child psychiatry, 1989—. Assoc. editor Jour. Child and Adolescent Psychopharmacology; contbr. articles to profl. jours. Bd. dirs. Calvin Day Care Ctr., New Haven, 1988—; mem. med. com. Tourette Syndrome Assn., 1989—. Mem. Am. Acad. Child and Adolescent Psychiatry (editorial bd. Jour.). Home: 240 Yale Ave New Haven CT 06515-2231 Office: Yale Child Study Ctr PO Box 3333 New Haven CT 06510-0333

RIDGE, JOHN CHARLES, geology educator, educator; b. Bethlehem, Pa., Mar. 9, 1955; s. Jack Russell and Laura May (Lynch) R.; m. Mary Jo Healy, May 18, 1985. BS in Geol. Sci., Lehigh U., 1977, MS in Geol. Sci., 1983; PhD in Geology, Syracuse U., 1985. Teaching asst. dept. geology Lehigh U., Bethlehem, Pa., 1977; teaching asst. dept. geology Syracuse (N.Y.) U., 1980-83, lectr., 1983-85; asst. prof. Tufts U., Medford, Mass., 1985-91, assoc. prof., 1991—. Grantee NSF, 1989-91. Mem. Geol. Soc. Am., Am. Geophys. Union, Nat. Assn. Geology Tchrs., Soc. Econ. Paleontologists and Mineralogists (sec.-treas. Ea. sect. 1991—). Democrat. Home: 25 Brooks Park Apt 5 Medford MA 02155-4555 Office: Dept Geology Tufts U Medford MA 02155

RIDGE, THOMAS JOSEPH, congressman; b. Munhall, Pa., Aug. 26, 1945; m. Michele Moore, 1979. B.A., Harvard U., 1967; J.D., Dickinson Coll. Law, Carlisle, Pa., 1972. Bar: Pa. 1972. Sole practice Erie, Pa., 1972-82; mem. 98th-102nd Congresses from Pa. 21st Dist., 1983—; former dist. atty. Erie County, former legal instructor. Mem. Erie County Republican Com.; bd. dirs. St. Mary's Home, Erie, Cathedral Prep Sch. Alumni Assn., Greater Erie Community Action Com., Greater Erie Golf Classic; exec. dir. Erie County Library. Served with inf. U.S. Army, 1968-70, Vietnam. Office: US Ho of Reps 1714 Longworth House Office Bldg Rm 1331 Washington DC 20515*

RIDGWAY, PRISCILLA, association executive; b. Schenectady, N.Y., May 1, 1943; d. Whitman and Priscilla (Hawley) R. BS in Edn., Russell Sage Coll., 1970. Exec. dir. Mystery Writers Am., N.Y.C., 1987—. Mem. crime Writers' Assn., Internat. Assn. Crime Writers. Office: Mystery Writers Am 17 E 47th St Fl 6 New York NY 10017-1920

RIDICK, JOYCE MARIE, nun, psychologist, educator; b. Worcester, Mass., Sept. 20, 1941; d. John Andrew and Anne Elizabeth (Bataitis) R. BS with highest honors, DePaul U., 1969; PhD, U. Chgo., 1972. Joined Sisters of St. Casimir, Roman Cath. Ch., 1959. Tchr. Archdiocese of Chgo., 1962-65, 66-69, Archdiocese of Joliet, Plano, Ill., 1965-66; asst. prof., assoc. prof., then prof. Gregorian U., Rome, 1972-92; assoc. prof. psychology Sacred Heart Maj. Sem., Detroit, 1989-91; formation asst., asst. prof. St. Joseph's Major Sem., Yonkers, 1991—, St. John Neumann Residence, Riverdale, N.Y., 1991—; exec. dir. Ctr. Consultation, Gregorian U., 1974-89. Author: Treasures in Earthen Vessels, 1984; co-author: Entering and Leaving Vocation: Intrapsychic Dynamics, 1976 (internat. Quinquennial prize for sci. study of religion 1976), Anthropology of Christian Vocation, vol. II, 1989, Psychological Structure and Vocation, 1988; contbr. chpts. to books, articles to profl. publs. Grantee NIMH, 1969-70. Mem. Am. Psychol. Assn. (cert.), Lithuanian Cath. Acad. Art and Sci. (v.p. 1987-89). Home: 500 W Hartsdale Ave Hartsdale NY 10530-1008 Office: St Joseph's Sem Dunwoodie Yonkers NY 10704

RIDOUT, THEODORE CORNER, JR., education educator; b. Concord, Mass., Sept. 1, 1942; s. Theodore Corner and Margaret (Pettingell) R.; m. Christine Furstenberg, Dec. 20, 1970; children: Daniel Furstenberg, Matthew Theodore, Timothy A. BA, Wesleyan U., 1964; MEd, Temple U., 1968; EdD, Columbia U., 1971. Vol. U.S. Peace Corps, Las Anod, Somali Republic, 1964-66; tchr. corps intern Temple U., Phila., 1966-68; dir. peace corps tng. Columbia U., 1969; second lang. specialist Min. Edn., Kabul, Afghanistan, 1971-73; prof. communication Bunker Hill Community Coll., Charlestown, Mass., 1973-91, coord. devel. edn., 1990—. Author: Dari Book 4, 1971, Pashto Book 4, 1971. mem. Internat. Reading Assn. Home: 10 Sherman Bridge Rd Wayland MA 01778-1214 Office: Bunker Hill Community Coll Rutherford Ave Charlestown MA 02129-3754

RIEBER, JESSE ALVIN, urban planner; b. N.Y.C., Mar. 18, 1945; s. Jesse Paul and Edith Thyra (Marion) R.; m. Sheryl Virginia Theobald, June 12, 1969 (div. Oct. 1971); m. Marnie Dianne Campbell, Dec. 11, 1971; children: Kahlil Jason, Jennifer Edith. BA, Syracuse U., 1968; MA, U. Man., Winnipeg, Can., 1974, M City Planning, 1981; postgrad., Lesley Coll., 1990—. Researcher Econ. Cons. Corp., Syracuse, 1968; policy analyst II edn. Man. Govt., Winnipeg, 1969-70, policy analyst III environ. dept., 1984-86; pres., prin. J.A. Rieber & Assocs., Winnipeg, 1970-86; prin. planner Town of Barnstable, Hyannis, Mass., 1986; planning assoc. A.M. Wilson & Assocs., Osterville, Mass., 1986-89; pres. J.A. Rieber, Marsons Mills, Mass., 1989-90; community devel. cons., 1990—. Chmn. 10th conf. internat. affairs U. Man., 1972; chmn. Citizens Ad Hoc Com., Winnipeg, 1984, spokesperson, 1985. Fellow U. Man., 1970. Mem. Can. Inst. Planners, Am. Planning Assn. Buddhist. Home and Office: 836 Strawberry Hill Rd Centerville MA 02632-2561

RIEBESEHL, E. ALLAN, lawyer; b. N.Y.C., July 7, 1938; s. Harold J. and Phyllis Riebesehl; m. Suzanne C. Moore, July 28, 1963; children: Gregory, Christopher. BA, CCNY, 1961; JD, Fordham Law Sch., 1966; LLM, NYU, 1972. Bar: N.Y. 1966, U.S. Tax Ct. 1968, U.S. Supreme Ct. 1970, U.S. Ct. Appeals (2d cir.) 1971, U.S. Dist. Ct. (ea. dist.) N.Y. 1973, U.S. Dist. Ct. (so. dist.) N.Y., 1974. Tax atty. Kennecott Copper Corp., N.Y.C., 1966-69, Celanese Corp., 1969-70, Pan Am. World Airways, N.Y.C., 1970-71; sole practice, Garden City, N.Y., 1971—. adj. prof. Touro Law Sch. Past pres. Woodbury-Syosset Republican Club; past v.p. Syosset Hosp. Community

Adv. Bd. With USMC, 1961-66. Fellow Am. Acad. Matrimonial Lawyers. Internat. Acad. of Matrimonial Lawyers; mem. ABA, Am. Judicature Soc., C.W. Post Tax Inst., Am. Arbitration Assn., Cath. Lawyers Guild (past pres.), N.Y. State Bar Assn., Nassau County Bar Assn. (bd. dirs.), Suffolk County Bar Assn., Nassau Lawyers Assn., Lawyers in Mensa. Club: Kiwanis (past pres.) (Mineola, N.Y.). Co-author: New York Practice Guide: Domestic Relations; mem. bd. editors Matrimonial Strategist, The N.Y. Domestic Rel. Reporter; contbr. articles to profl. jours. Office: 666 Old Country Rd Garden City NY 11530-2002

RIEDER, CORINNE JANE, university secretary, educator; b. Inglewood, Calif., Apr. 8, 1939; d. William Byron Holman and Susie Jane (Moore) Stringham; m. Ronald Olrich Rieder, June 25, 1966; children: Alyssa, Corinne, Melanie Anne. AB, UCLA, 1961; EdM, Harvard U., 1965, EdD, 1971. Tchr. L.A. Pub. Schs., 1961-62; vol. and program officer Peace Corps, Dominican Republic, 1962-64; edn. adviser Agy. Internat. Devel., Dominican Republic, 1964; dir. edn. planning N.Y.C. Planning Dept., 1969-71; analyst U.S. Dept. Health, Edn. and Welfare, Washington, 1971-72, assoc. dir. Nat. Inst. Edn., 1972-78; study dir. Office of Mgmt. and Budget, Washington, 1978-79; exec. v.p., dean Bank St. Coll. of Edn., N.Y.C., 1979-82; dir. fed. rels. Columbia U., N.Y.C., 1982-88, sec. of univ., 1988—; dir. Harvard Alumni Assn., Cambridge, Mass., 1977-79; advisory coun. Cornell U. Coll. Human Ecology, Ithaca, N.Y., 1978-81; bd. dirs. Hoff-Barthelson Music Sch., Scarsdale, N.Y., 1989—, 1st v.p., 1987—. Editorial bd. Teachers College Record, 1990—; contbr. articles to profl. publs. Mem. Citizen's Nominating Com., Scarsdale, N.Y., 1991—. Ford Found. fellow, Harvard U., 1964. Mem. Women's Econ. Roundtable, Scarsdale Tennis Club, Phi Delta Kappa, Pi Lambda Theta. Home: 8 Church Ln S Scarsdale NY 10583-5604 Office: Columbia U 308 Low Memorial Libr New York NY 10027

RIEDER, RONALD FREDERIC, hematologist, educator; b. N.Y.C., July 13, 1933; s. Martin Moses and Jeanne (Gerzog) R.; m. Daniele Piette Catelas, June 12, 1962; children: David, Isabelle. BA, Swarthmore Coll., 1954; MD, NYU, 1958. Diplomate Am. Bd. Internal Medicine. Med. intern NYU div. Bellevue Hosp., N.Y.C., 1958-59, asst. resident, 1959-60, 64-65; postdoctoral fellow dept. microbiology NYU, 1960-61; postdoctoral fellow Inst. Pasteur, Paris, 1961-62; postdoctoral fellow, assoc. in medicine Johns Hopkins Hosp., Balt., 1962-64; assoc. in medicine Albert Einstein Coll. Medicine, Bronx, N.Y., 1965-67; rsch. assoc. in hematology Montefiore Hosp., Bronx, 1965-67; asst. prof. medicine Health Sci. Ctr., SUNY, Bklyn., 1967-71, assoc. prof., 1971-76, prof., 1976—; dir. hematology SUNY, Bklyn., 1976-88; mem. med. adv. bd. Cooley's Anemia Found., N.Y.C. Contbr. numerous articles on exptl. hematology to sci. jours. Recipient Career Scientist award N.Y.C. Health Rsch. Coun., 1969-72, Faculty Scholar award Macy Found., 1975, Career Rsch. awards Irma T. Hirschl Charitable Trust, 1973-77; NIH rsch. grantee, 1967—. Mem. ACP, Am. Soc. Hematology, Assn. Am. Physicians, Soc. for Clin. Investigation. Office: SUNY Health Sci Ctr 450 Clarkson Ave Brooklyn NY 11203-2098

RIEDERS, FREDRIC, forensic toxicologist; b. Vienna, Austria, July 9, 1922; came to U.S., 1939; s. Kalman and Ethel Julia (Quastler) Rozsa; m. Betty Jean Stockwell, Apr. 28, 1955; children: Eric F., Michael F., Michel F., Carl W., Julia H. AB, Wash. Sq. Coll., 1948; MS, NYU, 1949; PhD, Thomas Jefferson U., 1952. Diplomate Am. Bd. Forensic Toxicology, Am. Bd. Clin. Chemistry. Jr. toxicologist Office of Chief Med. Examiner, N.Y.C., 1946-49; fellow in indsl. toxicology Jefferson Med. Coll., Thomas Jefferson U., Phila., 1949-52; from instr. to assoc. prof. dept. pharmacol. Jefferson Med. Coll., Phila., 1952-56, prof. pharmacology and toxicology, 1960—; chief toxicologist Dept. of Health, Med. Examiner, Phila., 1956-70, dir. poison info., 1956-70; dir. labs. Universal Med. Svcs. Inc., King of Prussia, Pa., 1969-70; lab. dir. Nat. Med. Svcs. Inc., Willow Grove, Pa., 1970—. Contbr. articles to profl. jours. Cpl. U.S. Army, 1942-46, ETO. Recipient Disting. Alumnus award Thomas Jefferson U. Coll. Grad. Studies, 1992. Fellow Am. Acad. Forensic Scis. (chmn. toxicology sect. 1957—, A.O. Gettler award 1986), Am. Chem. Soc.; mem. Am. Soc. Pharm. Exptl. Therapeutics, Internat. Assn. Forensic Toxicologists (charter). Republican. Lutheran. Office: Nat Med Svcs Inc 2300 Stratford Ave Willow Grove PA 19090-4195

RIEDESEL, CLARK ALAN, educator; b. Davenport, Iowa, July 21, 1930; s. F. Clark and Dorothy H. (Franco) R.; children: Christine, Mark, Claudia, Matthew, Craig. BA, Cornell Coll., 1951; MA, U. Iowa, 1956, PhD, 1962. Tchr. Lisbon (Iowa) Schs.; tchr., elem. prin. Albany (Ill.) Schs., 1953-56; prof. edn. SUNY, Plattsburgh, 1956-61, Kansas State U., Manhattan, 1962-63, Pa. State U., University Park, 1963-69, Ga. State U., Atlanta, 1970-72; prof., edn. dept. dir., software lab. dir. SUNY, Buffalo, 1972—. Author: Teaching Elementary School Math, 1967, 75, 80, 85, 90, Handbook: Elementary School Math, 1975, Mathematics for Elementary Teachers, 1975; software author Sunburst, 1989, 90; contbr. articles to profl. jours. Grantee NSF, 1962, 66, 68, 74. Mem. ASCD, Nat. Coun. Tchrs. Math (editor The Arithemtic Teacher, 1967-72), Nat.Coun. Social Studies Tchrs. Episcopalian. Office: SUNY Buffalo 593 Baldy Hall Buffalo NY 14260

RIEFF, PHILIP, sociologist; b. Chgo., Dec. 15, 1922; s. Gabriel and Ida (Hurwitz) R.; m. Alison Douglas Knox, Dec. 31, 1963; 1 son by previous marriage, David. BA, U. Chgo., 1946, MA, 1947, PhD, 1954. Teaching fellow U. Chgo., 1946, instr., 1947-52; asst. prof. Brandeis U., Waltham, Mass., 1952-57; fellow Ctr. for Advanced Study in Behavior Scis., Palo Alto, Calif., 1957-58; assoc. prof. sociology U. Calif., Berkeley, 1958-61; prof. U. Pa., Phila., 1961—, Univ. prof. sociology, 1965-67, Benjamin Franklin Prof. Sociology, 1967—; chief editorial cons. Beacon Press, Boston, 1952-58; vis. assoc. prof. Harvard U., 1960; vis. fellow Ctr. for Study of Dem. Instns., Santa Barbara, Calif., 1963-64; Gauss lectr. Princeton U., 1975; Terry lectr. Yale U., 1976-77. Author: Freud: The Mind of the Moralist, 1959, rev. edit., 1961, The Triumph of the Therapeutic: Uses of Faith After Freud, 1966, Fellow Teachers, 1973, The Feeling Intellect, 1990; editor The Collected Papers of Sigmund Freud (10 vols.), 1961; assoc. editor Am. Sociol. Rev., 1958-61; founding editor Jour. Am. Acad. Arts and Scis., 1956-59, Daedalus. Chief cons. planning dept. Nat. Coun. Chs., 1961-64. Named Fulbright Prof. U. Munich, 1959-60, Guggenheim fellow, 1970, Sometime fellow All Souls Coll., Oxford. Fellow Royal Soc. Arts London; mem. Libr. Co. Phila., Am. Sociol. Assn., Soc. Sci. Study Religion (mem. coun.), Societe Europeene de Culture, Garrick Club of London. Office: U Pa Dept Sociology Philadelphia PA 19174

RIEFLER, JOHN FRANKLYN, III, pharmaceutical company executive; b. Flushing, N.Y., July 12, 1947; s. John Franklyn Jr. and Mary (Smith) R.; m. Susan Pearson, Jan. 16, 1982; children: John Franklyn IV, Elizabeth Ann. BS in Biology, Bucknell U., 1969; postgrad., Columbia U., 1969-70, 71-72; MS in Microbiology, Med. U. S.C., 1975; MD, St. George's U., 1982. Intern in internal medicine New Britain (Conn.) Gen. Hosp., 1982-83, resident in internal medicine, 1983-84; resident in internal medicine Hahnemann U., Phila., 1984-85, infectious diseases fellowship, 1985-87; pvt. practice, Grafton, Mass., 1987-88; assoc. dir. antiinfectives clin. devel. sect. Lederle Labs., Pearl River, N.Y., 1988—. Contbr. articles to profl. jours. Maj. USAR, 1970-76, 88-91, Saudi Arabia. Fellow Mass. Med. Soc.; mem. ACP, Am. Soc. Microbiology, Infectious Diseases Soc. of Am., Sigma Xi, Phi Sigma. Home: 423 Colwell Ct Ridgewood NJ 07450-1407 Office: Lederle Labs Bldg 190 Rm 401-F 401 N Middletown Rd Pearl River NY 10965-1299

RIEGLER, SUSAN GERMAINE, community services and organizational development professional; b. Hackensack, N.J., Dec. 5, 1960; d. John Joseph and M. A. Riegler. Student, Johannes Gutenberg U., Germany, 1982; BA summa cum laude, Wellesley Coll., 1983; MBA, Boston U., 1990; postgrad., Harvard U., 1991—. Fin. analyst Salomon Bros., N.Y.C., 1982; adminstrv. asst. Stone ctr. Devel. Studies, Wellesley, Mass., 1983; rsch. coord. Boston U. Med. Ctr., 1983-84; cons. Human Svcs./Rsch., Boston, 1984-85; planner Jobs and Community Svcs., Boston, 1985-86, spl. asst., 1986-87, asst. dir., 1987-90; project mgr. Boston Mayor's Office on Policy, 1990-91; mem. staff Freshman Seminar Program Harvard U., Cambridge, 1991—; founder Pub. Mgrs.' Roundtable, Boston, 1990—. Author Retreat on a Shoestring, 1989. Mem. Employee Assistance Soc. N.Am., Virginia-Monadnock Neighborhood Assn. Roman Catholic. Home: 56 Monadnock St Dorchester MA 02125-2306

RIELLY, JAMES SCOTT, treasurer; b. N.Y.C., May 8, 1963; s. Robert John and Eileen (Bohan) R.; m. Maria Sementilli, June 14, 1987; 1 child, Tara Sean. BSBA, Bucknell U., 1985. CPA, Pa. Staff acct. Deloitte Haskins & Sells, N.Y.C., 1985-87, sr. acct., 1987-89; treas. Baring Bros. & Co. Inc., N.Y.C., 1989—. Recipient Pa. CPA award Pa. Soc. CPAs, 1985, Svc. award Phi Gamma Delta, Bucknell U. chpt., 1985. Mem. AIPCA, Securities Industries Assn. Roman Catholic. Home: 112 Cedar Rd East Northport NY 11731-4336 Office: Baring Bros & Co Inc 667 Madison Ave New York NY 10021-8029

RIEMER, AMY ROBIN, public relations executive; b. Bklyn., May 11, 1963; d. Allan Nadel and Joan Linda (Kraut) Frommer; m. Stan Forrest Riemer, Dec. 17, 1988. BA, Glassboro State Coll., 1985. Pub. rels. asst. account exec. KCS & A Pub. Rels., N.Y.C., 1985-87; pub. rels. account exec. Edelman Pub. Rels., N.Y.C., 1987-89; pub. rels. mgr. Reed Exhbns., Stamford, Conn., 1989—. Mem. Pub. Rels. Soc. Am. (profl. devel. chmn. 1990—). Jewish. Office: Reed Exhbns 1100 Summer St Stamford CT 06905-5513

RIENZO, ROBERT JAMES, radiologist; b. Jersey City, N.J., July 27, 1949; s. James Joseph and Marie Nicoletta (Bernardo) R.; m. Janice Meyer, Apr. 8, 1972 (div. Dec. 1991); 1 child, Michael Robert; m. Catherine Elizabeth Rafferty, Jan. 11, 1992; 1 child, Robert Francis. AB, Cornell U., 1971; MD, N.Y. Med. Coll., 1975. Diplomate Am. Bd. Radiology, Am. Bd. Nuclear Medicine. Resident St. Vincent's Hosp., N.Y.C., 1975-80; staff physician Jefferson Hosp., Pitts., 1980-81, Allentown (Pa.) Hosp., 1981—. Contbr. articles to profl. jours. Mem. Exch. Club Western LeHigh, Emmaus, Pa., 1983—. Mem. AMA (Physicians Recognition award 1986—), Soc. Nuclear Medicine, Am. Coll. Nuclear Physicians, Am. Coll. Radiology, Am. Inst. Ultrasound in Medicine. Office: LeHigh Valley Hosp 1200 S Cedar Crest Blvd Allentown PA 18105

RIES, RICHARD RALPH, government science administrator; b. New Ulm, Minn., Nov. 16, 1935; s. Edmund W. and Adelia M. (Gag) R.; m. Erika Loew, July 18, 1964; children: Stefan, Thomas. BS in Physics, St. Edward's U., 1957; MS, U. Minn., 1959, PhD, 1963. Rsch. assoc. Max Planck Inst. for Chemistry, Mainz, Germany, 1963-64; instr. in physics Harvard U., Cambridge, Mass., 1964-65; asst. program dir. NSF, Washington, 1965-66; dep. NSF, Tokyo, 1966-70; regional mgr. Europe NSF, Washington, 1970-75, dep. div. internat. programs, 1975-76; dir. ops. Sci., Tech. and Internat. Affairs, Washington, 1977-85, exec. officer, 1985-90, dir. div. internat. programs, 1990-91; deputy dir. Sci., Tech. and Internat. Affairs, 1991—. Contbr. articles to profl. jours. Named Man of the Yr. St. Edward's U., 1957, Alumni scholar, 1953-57; recipient Disting. Svc. award NSF, 1986. Mem. Am. Phys. Soc., AAAS, Harvard Alumni Club. Home: 2500 Childs Ln Alexandria VA 22308 Office: NSF 1800 G St NW Washington DC 20550

RIESE, BEATRICE, artist, consultant; b. The Hague, The Netherlands, Sept. 22, 1917; came to U.S., 1940; d. Walther and Hertha (Pataky) R. Grad., Ecole d'Art et de Dessin, Paris, 1940; postgrad., Va. Commonwealth U., 1943-45. Mem., artist Pleiades Gallery, N.Y.C., 1982—; pres. Am. Abstract Artists, N.Y.C., 1987—. Mem. adv. coun. Snite Mus. Art, Notre Dame, Ind., 1987—. Home and Office: Am Abstract Artists 470 West End Ave 9-D New York NY 10024

RIESENBERG, MARK ELLIOT, sales trainer, consultant, motivational speaker; b. N.Y.C., Sept. 22, 1947; s. Max and Shirley (Cohen) R.; m. Terry Marsha Weissman, May 20, 1979; children: Kate Meredith Blair, Courtney Alexandra. BA in Econs., C.W. Post Coll., 1969. Ctr. chmn. Internat. Meditation Soc., Edison, N.J., 1972-77; dist. mgr. Southland Corp., Parsippany, N.J., 1978-87; founder, pres. Human Resources Unltd., West Orange, N.J., 1987—; com. chmn. Occupational Ctr., Orange, 1990—. Mem. Toastmasters Internat., Nat. Speakers Assn., Sales & Mktg. Execs. N.Y., Metro Newark C. of C. (profl. svcs. com. 1988-90). Jewish. Home and Office: Human Resources Unltd 29 Gilbert Pl West Orange NJ 07052-3946

RIETHLE, WILLIAM EDWARD, III, utility company executive; b. Bklyn., Nov. 27, 1948; s. William Edward Jr. and Iris (Sullivan) R.; m. Donna Jeanne Souder, Aug. 23, 1973 (div. 1987); children: Erik Marc, Case William. BA in Biology, U. Pa., 1970; MS in Environ. Sci., Drexel U., 1972; MS in Health Physics, Rutgers U., 1974; MBA, Northeastern U., 1990, cert. advanced studies in fin., 1991. Rsch. asst. Albert Einstein Med. Ctr., Phila., 1970-72; head, radioimmundassay lab. Middlesex Gen. Hosp., New Brunswick, N.J., 1972-73; engr. Ebasco Svcs., N.Y.C., 1973-75, Stone & Webster, N.Y.C., 1975-76; environ. mgr. GPU Nuclear Corp., Middletown, Pa., 1976-1982; mgr. tech. svcs. Nuclear Energy Svcs., Danbury, Conn., 1982-83; group mgr. Yankee Atomic Electric Co., Bolton, Mass., 1983--; mem. Mass. Low-Level Radioactive Waste Mgmt. Bd., Boston, 1988—. Pres. Boylston (Mass.) Little League, 1987; mem. Worcester Art Mus., 1989—; sec. Worcester City Rep. Com. USPHS fellow, 1971, 72, 73. Mem. Am. Nuclear Soc., Health Physics Soc., Am. Soc. Testing and Materials. Republican. Home: 3803 Knightsbridge Close Worcester MA 01609-1161 Office: Yankee Atomic Electric Co 580 Main St Bolton MA 01740-1398

RIFELJ, CAROL DE DOBAY, foreign language educator, academic administrator; b. Milw., Dec. 29, 1946; d. Raymond and Gertrude Helene (Niefer) de D.; m. Anton Rifelj, June 28, 1969; 1 child, Claire. BA, U. Wis., 1968, MA, 1969, PhD, 1972. From asst. to assoc. prof. Middlebury (Vt.) Coll., 1972-85, chair French dept., 1977-79, 82-83, 90-91, dean French Sch., 1985-87, dir. Sch. in France, 1984-85, 88-89, prof., 1985—; dean faculty, 1991—. Author: C'est'a'dire, 1980, Word and Figure, 1987; mem. editorial bd. U. Press of New Eng., 1990—; contbr. articles to profl. jours. NEH fellow, 1976-77 Sch. of Criticism and Theory fellow, 1979, Am. Coun. Learned Socs. fellow, 1983-84. Mem. Modern Lang. Assn., Interdisciplinary 19th Century Studies Assn., N.E. Modern Lang. Assn. Office: Middlebury Coll Old Chapel Middlebury VT 05753

RIFFIN, THOMAS KIM, psychologist; b. Boston, Oct. 7, 1952; s. Paul V. and Natalie (Harris) R.; m. Pamela J. Martin, June 10, 1978; children: Timothy Max, Catherine A. BA, Boston U., 1975; MA, Antioch U., Keene, N.H., 1979; PsyD, Mass. Sch. Profl. Psychology, 1989. Lic. psychologist, Mass. Staff clinician Northshore Mental Health Ctr., Salem, Mass., 1979-85; psychologist Cambridge (Mass.) Ct. Clinic, 1985—; psychologist, asst. dir. psychology of tng. Met. State Hosp., Waltham, Mass., 1987—; pvt. practice Milford-Franklin Counseling Svcs., Inc., Milford, Mass., 1991—; clin. instr. psychology Cambridge Hosp., Harvard Med. Sch., 1990—. Mem. APA, Mass. Psychol. Assn., Nat. Register Health Svc. Providers. Home: 4 Legion Rd Weston MA 02193-2153

RIFKIN, LARRY JAY, medical products executive; b. Phila., Dec. 14, 1960; s. Marvin John and Rita Vivian (Shore) R. BS in Psychology, U. Charleston, W.Va., 1982. V.p. Phone Owners Group, Cherry Hill, N.J., 1982-84; dist. mgr. Oxford Med. Corp., Fla., 1984-86; regional mgr. Puritan Bennett Med. Corp., Boston, 1986-89; co-founder, exec. v.p., chief operating officer Action Life Alert Inc., Mt. Laurel, N.J., 1989—. Mem. Masons (master 1991). Republican. Jewish. Home: 107 Kelly Cv # B Mount Laurel NJ 08054-2735 Office: Action Life Alert Inc 139 Gaither Dr Ste F Mount Laurel NJ 08054-1737

RIFKIND, ARLEEN B., physician, researcher; b. N.Y.C., June 29, 1938; d. Michael C. and Regina (Gottlieb) Brenner; m. Robert S. Rifkind, Dec. 24, 1961; children—Amy, Nina. B.A., Bryn Mawr Coll., 1960; M.D., NYU, 1964. Intern Bellevue Hosp., N.Y.C., 1964-65, resident, 1965; clin. assoc. Endocrine br. Nat. Cancer Inst., 1965-68; research assoc., asst. resident physician Rockefeller U., 1968-71; asst. prof. medicine Cornell U. Med. Coll., N.Y.C., 1971-82, assoc. prof. medicine, 1983—, asst. prof. pharmacology, 1973-78, assoc. prof., 1978-82, prof., 1983—; chmn. Gen. Faculty Council Cornell U. Med. Coll., 1984-86, Nat. Inst. Environ. Health Scis. Rev. Com., 1985-86; mem. toxicology study sect. Nat. Inst. Health, 1989-91, chmn. 1991—; bd. sci. counselors U.S. Agy. for Toxic Substances and Disease Registry, 1991—. Contbr. articles to profl. jours. Chmn. Friends of the Library, Jewish Theol. Sem. Am., 1984-86; trustee Dalton Sch., 1986-92; mem. Environ. Health and Safety Coun. Am. Health Found., 1990—. Recipient Andrew W. Mellon Tchr.-Scientist award, 1976-78; USPHS spl. fellow, 1968-70, 71-72. Mem. Endocrine Soc., Am. Soc. Clin. Investigation, Am. Soc. Pharmacology and Exptl. Therapeutics, AAAS, Soc. Toxicology. Office: Cornell U Med Coll Dept Pharmacology 1300 York Ave New York NY 10021-4896

RIGA, KATHLEEN MARIE, elementary school counselor; b. Buffalo, Dec. 23, 1965; d. Francis Joseph and Jane Mary (Burke) R. BA, SUNY, Buffalo, 1987, EdM, 1991. Admissions counselor Daemen Coll., Amherst, N.Y., 1988-90; sch. counselor Balt. City Pub. Schs., 1991—. Vol. coord. Chesapeake Habitat for Humanity, Balt., 1991—. Democrat. Home: 110 W 39th St Apt 709 Baltimore MD 21210 Office: Balt City Pub Schs 200 E North Ave Baltimore MD 21202

RIGAUX, CHRISTOPHER MICHAEL, publications specialist; b. Chgo., Mar. 31, 1960; s. Armand Jules and Katharine Marie (Bird) R.; m. Anne R. Deruyttere, Sept. 2, 1988; 1 child, Valerie. BA, U. Notre Dame, 1982; cert. publs. specialist, George Washington U., 1985. Mgr. Common Concerns Bookstore, Washington, 1984-85; publs. coord. Eric Clearinghouse on Higher Edn., Washington, 1985-87, mng. editor, 1987-90; publs. coord. Nat. Ctr. Edn. in Maternal and Child Health, Washington, 1990-91, dir. publs., 1991—. Vol. tchr. Washington Literacy Coun., 1988—. Mem. Washington Book Pubs., Washington Edpress (steering com. 1988-90). Democrat. Roman Catholic. Office: Nat Ctr Edn Maternal and Child Health 2000 15th St N Ste 701 Arlington VA 22201-2617

RIGAUX-BRICMONT, BENNY PATRICK, marketing educator; b. Ixelles, Brabant, Belgium, June 22, 1943; s. Claude Léonard Rigaux and Louise (Barré) Bricmont; m. Jill Byrne, Aug. 4, 1984. Ingénieur Commercial, Catholic U. Louvain, Belgium, 1967, Ingénieur Commercial et de Gestion, 1969, Docteur en Sciences Economiques Appliquées, 1977; M.A. in Applied Econs., U. Pa., 1971. Research assoc. Ctr. for Socio-Econ. Studies in Advt. and Mktg., Louvain, 1968-79; asst. prof. Laval U., Quebec, 1979-81, assoc. prof., 1981-87, prof., 1987—; vis. scholar Sloan Sch. Mgmt., MIT, Boston, 1984-85, Nankai U., Tianjin, People's Republic of China, 1986, 90, 91; vis. fellow European Inst. for Advanced Studies in Mgmt., Brussels, 1985, 90-91. Author: La Prise de Décisions Economiques Dans la Famille, 1977; also articles; guest editor Rsch. et Applications en Mktg. Bd. dirs. Mt. Desert Festival of Chamber Music. Served as Res. Capt.-Commandant in Belgian Field Art., 1966—. Decorated Officier de l'ordre de la Couronne et Chevalier de l'ordre de Léopold, King of Belgium. Mem. Am. Mktg. Assn. (Que. chpt. pres. 1982-83), Assn. Francaise Mktg., Euro-China Rsch. Assn. Mgmt., Inst. Mil. Québec, Assn. for Consumer Research, European Mktg. Acad., Adminstrv. Sci. Assn. Can. Avocations: photography; tennis; classical music, Mt. Desert Island. Home: 909 Mgr Grandin #302, Ste-Foy, PQ Canada G1V 3X8 Office: Faculté des Sci de L' Adminstrn, Cité Universitaire, Ste-Foy, PQ Canada G1K 7P4

RIGEL, DARRELL SPENCER, dermatologist, educator, skin cancer researcher; b. Montclair, N.J., June 20, 1950; s. Geldon and Gertrude (Kochansky) R.; m. Beth Carol Hollander, Aug. 4, 1974; children: Ethan, Adam, Ashlee. SB, MIT, 1972, SM, 1974; MD, George Washington U., 1978. Diplomate Am. Bd. Dermatology. Intern N.Y. Hosp.-Cornell Med. Ctr., N.Y.C., 1978-79; resident in dermatology NYU Med. Ctr., 1979-82, dermatologic surgery and oncology fellow, 1982; chief resident NYU Hosp., Bellevue Hosp., Manhattan VA Hosp., 1981-82; pvt. practice N.Y.C., 1982—; dir. dermatology PMI Strang Clinic, N.Y.C., 1982-90; attending physician NYU Hosp., N.Y.C., 1983—, Bellevue Hosp. Ctr., N.Y.C., 1983—; clin. instr. dermatology NYU Med. Ctr., 1983-86, clin. asst. prof., 1986-90, clin. assoc. prof., 1991—; sci. cons. to numerous cos. and orgns.; pres., chief exec. officer Iris, Inc., N.Y.C., 1987—. Author, editor: Pigmentated Lesions, 1985, Cancer of the Skin, 1989; contbr. numerous articles to profl. jours. Bd. dirs. Am. Cancer Soc., N.Y.C., 1985—. Recipient nat. citation Am. Cancer Soc., 1987. Fellow Am. Acad. Dermatology (nat. asst. sec.-treas., bd. dirs., chmn. presdl. comm. on melanoma and skin cancer, chmn. on computer tech. 1985-89, Presdl. citation 1985); mem. AMA, Dermatologic Soc. Greater N.Y. (v.p. 1988, pres. 1989), Iris Golf Club (pres. 1987-89). Office: 213 Madison Ave 35 E 35th St 2d Fl New York NY 10016

RIGGIN, LEE PEPPER, retired fraternal organization administrator; b. Clearfield, Pa., Aug. 21, 1924; s. Elmer Edwin Sr. and Zora (Pepper) R.; m. Doris Lee Harrington, Mar. 7, 1945; children: Robert Sidney, Connie R. Chapis. Grad. high sch., Laurel, Del., 1943. Ins. cons. Met. Life Ins. Co., Salisbury, Md., 1948-68; field svc. rep. Kiwanis Internat., Indpls., 1968-89; ret., 1989. Sec. Rep. Club, Laurel, 1950; councilman City of Laurel, 1963-69; mem. Sussex dist. exec. com. Boy Scouts Am., adminstrv. bd. Centenary Meth. Ch., Laurel. Sgt. U.S. Army, 1943-46. Mem. Am. Legion (comdr. 1953), Kiwanis (pres. Laurel chpt. 1963, lt. gov., 1965.). Methodist.

RIGGS, LORRIN ANDREWS, psychologist, educator; b. Harput, Turkey, June 11, 1912; parents Am. citizens; s. Ernest Wilson and Alice (Shepard) R.; m. Doris Robinson, 1937; children—Douglas Rikert, Dwight Alan. A.B., Dartmouth Coll., 1933; M.A., Clark U., 1934, Ph.D., 1936. NRC fellow biol. scis. U. Pa., 1936-37; instr. U. Vt., 1937-38, 39-41; with Brown U., 1938-39, 41—, from asst. to assoc. prof., 1938-51, prof., 1951—, L. Herbert Ballou prof., 1960-68, E.J. Marston Univ. prof., 1968-77, prof. emeritus, 1977—; Guggenheim fellow U. Cambridge, 1971-72. Author sci. articles on vision, physiol. psychology. Recipient Kenneth Craik award Cambridge U., 1979, Prentice medal Am. Acad. Optometry, 1973. Mem. AAAS (chmn., v.p. sect. 1 1964), APA (div. pres. 1962-63, Disting. Sci. Contn. award 1974), Eastern Psychol. Assn. (pres. 1975-76), Optical Soc. Am. (Tillyer medal 1969, Ives medal 1982), Nat. Acad. Scis., Am. Physiol. Soc., Internat. Brain Rsch. Orgn., Soc. for Neurosci., Soc. Exptl. Psychologists (Howard Crosby Warren medal 1957), Assn. Rsch. in Vision and Ophthalmology (pres. 1977, Friedenwald award 1966), Am. Acad. Arts and Scis., Am. Psychol. Soc. (William James fellow 1989), Sigma Xi (chpt. pres. 1962-64). Club: University (Providence). Home: Kendal at Hanover # 1020 80 Lyme Rd Hanover NH 03755-1225

RIGNEY, DAVID ROTH, biophysics educator; b. Carbondale, Ill., Dec. 27, 1950; s. Carl Jennings and Margaret Ruth (Roth) R. BA, U. Tex., Austin, 1972; student in physiology, U. Tex. Med. Sch., San Antonio, 1972-74; student in chem. physics, Université Libre, Brussels, 1976-78; PhD in Physics, U. Tex., 1978. Rsch. fellow Inst. for Cancer Rsch., Phila., 1978-81, biophysicist, 1981-86; asst. prof. Med. Sch. Harvard U., Boston, 1986—; rsch. assoc. MIT, Cambridge, Mass., 1986—; assoc. dir. bioengring. lab. Beth Israel Hosp., Boston, 1986—; cons. NIH, Bethesda, Md., 1985—, NASA, Washington, 1985—. Author computer programs; contbr. articles to profl. jours.; designer scientific instruments. Rsch. grantee Whitaker Found., NIH. Mem. Am. Heart Assn., Biophys. Soc., Cell Kinetics Soc., Soc. Analytical Cytology, Tissue Culture Assn., Internat. Neural Network Soc. Office: Beth Israel Hosp Rm KB26 330 Brookline Ave Boston MA 02215-5491

RIGO-JOSEPH, SANDRA LUISA, English writing specialist, educator; b. Bklyn., Jan. 31, 1962; d. Felipe' Rigo and Verna Agelica Mongerard; 1 child, Tyrone Christen-Adam Joseph Jr. BA, L.I. U., 1989, MA, 1991. Writing specialist, prof. writing L.I. U., Bklyn., 1990—; pvt. adult tutor, Bklyn., 1990—. Author: Voices in A Dream, 1991; editor newsletter For the People, 1991. Mem. PTA Sparks of African Genius Emerging, Bklyn., 1990-92. Mem. Sigma Tau Delta. Democrat. Office: L I U University Pla Brooklyn NY 11201

RIHA, WILLIAM EDWIN, beverage company executive; b. New Brunswick, N.J., Sept. 15, 1943; s. William Edwin and Grace Blue (McDowell) R.; m. Joan Ann Murphy, June 25, 1967; children: William Edwin III, Jennifer Dawn. BS, Rutgers U., 1965, MS, 1969, PhD, 1972. Mgr. product devel. Hunt-Wesson Foods, Inc., Fullerton, Calif., 1972-76; dir. tech. svcs. Cadbury N.Am., Hazleton, Pa., 1976-78; mgr. food tech. Peter Paul Cadbury, Inc., Naugatuck, Conn., 1978-80; group mgr. U.S. product devel. PepsiCo, Valhalla, N.Y., 1980-84, dir. internat. product devel., 1984-89; v.p. R&D J. E. Seagram & Sons, Ltd., White Plains, N.Y., 1989—. Capt. USAR, 1965-73. Mem. Inst. Food Technologists (grad. fellowship Nestle 1968), Indsl. Rsch. Inst. (membership com. 1990-92), Sigma Xi. Home: 231 Mimosa Cir Ridgefield CT 06877-2539 Office: JE Seagram & Sons Ltd 3 S-Corp Park Dr White Plains NY 10604

RILEY, DAVID D., advertising agency executive; b. Meriden, Conn., Jan. 1, 1961; s. David M. and Peggy L. Riley. BFA, Marist Coll., Poughkeepsie, N.Y., 1983. Artist Mason & Madison, Bethany, Conn., 1983; prodn. coord. The Agy., Waterbury, Conn., 1983-86; pres. Graphik Impressions Advt., Meriden, 1986—. Mem. Am. Assn. Advt. Agys., Nat. Assn. Self-Employed, Conn. Art Dirs. Club, Art Dirs. Club Hartford, Conn. Hotel and Motel Assn., Small Bus. Svcs. Bur., Meriden C. of C. Office: Graphik Impressions Advt 445 Colony St Meriden CT 06450-2051

RILEY, DAVID JOSEPH, medical educator; b. N.Y.C., Sept. 6, 1942; s. Edwin Glover and Gertrude (Pfanner) R.; m. Katherine Elizabeth Moran, June 9, 1969; children: Meredith Ann, Gavin Douglas. BA, Johns Hopkins U., 1964; MD, U. Md., 1968. Diplomate Am. Bd. Internal Medicine. Intern Balt. City Hosps., 1968-69, resident, 1969-70; fellow in pulmonary disease U. Pa., 1970-72; resident Johns Hopkins Hosp., Balt., 1972-73; asst. prof. Robert W. Johnson Med. Sch. U. Medicine and Dentistry N.J., New Brunswick, N.J., 1972-76; assoc. prof. Robert Wood Johnson Med. Sch., New Brunswick, N.J., 1976-86, prof. medicine, 1986—; adj. prof. physiology and biophysics Robert W. Johnson Med. Sch., 1990—; mem. grad. faculty Rutgers U., 1986—. Contbr. articles to profl. jours. With U.S. Army N.G., 1966-70. Mem. Am. Thoracic Soc. (chmn. cell molecular biology assembly 1991—, pres. ea. sect. 1987-88), N.J. Thoracic Soc. (pres. 1988-90). Democrat. Episcopalian. Office: Robert Wood Johnson Med Sch 675 Hoes Ln Piscataway NJ 08854-5635

RILEY, JAMES JOSEPH, union executive; b. Cleve., Nov. 12, 1919; s. Frank James and Mary Jane (Connor) R.; m. Ruth Marie Pearce, Apr. 10, 1939; children—Janet M., Nancy C., Catherine A., James F., Thomas M., Dennis J., Ruth E., Mary H., John R. B.S., Western Res. U., 1940. Mem. Cleve. Motion Picture Operators Union, Local 160, 1941—; partner Electric Speed Indicator Co. (weather instrument maker), Cleve., 1965-67; bus. agt. Internat. Alliance of Theatrical Stage Employees and Moving Picture Operators of U.S. and Can., Cleve., 1967-78; internat. gen.-sec. treas. Internat. Alliance of Theatrical Stage Employees and Moving Picture Operators of U.S. and Can., N.Y.C., 1978—, internat. trustee, 1969-78; v.p. Union Label and Service Trades dept. AFL-CIO, 1979—. Editor: Bull., Internat. Alliance Quar, 1978—. Served to lt. USNR, 1943-46, PTO. Roman Catholic. Home: 15801 Edgecliff Ave Cleveland OH 44111-1949 Office: 1515 Broadway Ste 601 New York NY 10036

RILEY, KAREN LEE, dental assistant educator; b. Altoona, Pa., Jan. 19, 1958; d. David Howard and Rose Virginia (Stetter) Hescox; m. Robert John Riley Jr., June 26, 1982. AS in Dental Hygiene, Allegany Community Coll., 1982; BS in Vocat. Edn., Pa. State U., 1989, MEd in Indsl. Edn., 1991. Registered dental hygienist. Surg. asst. Oral Surgery Assocs., Hollidaysburg, Pa., 1976-80; dental hygienist Dr. Robert Sloss, Tyrone, Pa., 1982-83, Dr. Rudy Marcell, Altoona, Pa., 1983-85; dental asst. tchr. Altoona (Pa.) Area Vocat.-Tech. Sch., 1985—; adv. mem. Pa. State U., University Park, 1988—; bd. dirs. Health Occupation Students of Am., Pa., 1989—; lead tchr. Cen. Pa. Lead Tchr. Ctr., Altoona, 1990—; tchr. resource person Pa. State U., State College. Sponsor Home Nursing Agy., Altoona, 1985-91, Blair County Spl. Learning Ctr., Altoona, 1988-91; vol. Red Cross, Altoona, 1989-90, Cancer Soc., Altoona, 1990-91. Recipient Presentation award Am. Vocat. Assn. Health Occupations Educators, L.A., 1991. Mem. Cen. Pa. Dental Hygiene Assn. (sec. 1986-87, membership chairperson 1989-90, pres. 1982-83, 1991-92), Pa. State Alumni Assn., Iota Lamba Sigma (v.p. 1989-90, pres. 1990-91), Golden Key Nat. Honor Soc. Office: Altoona Area Vocat Tech Sch 1500 4th Ave Altoona PA 16601

RILEY, MARILYN GLEDHILL, communications executive; b. Pitts., Pa., July 17, 1954; d. John Edward and Mary Elizabeth (Ogden) Gledhill; m. John F. Riley Jr. AS with high honors, Community Coll. of Allegheny County, 1981; BS in Bus. Adminstrn. cum laude, Robert Morris Coll., 1985. Sec. MODCOM Assocs., Pitts., 1977-79, asst. account exec., 1979-82, account exec., 1982-84; gen. mgr. MODCOM Advt., Pitts., 1984-90, v.p., gen. mgr., 1989-90; dir. communications Allegheny County Med. Soc., Pitts., 1990—; guest speaker Pa. State U., Robert Morris Coll., Allegheny Community Coll., 1987. Mem. editorial bd. Nursing News, 1991. Communications vol. North Hills Art Festival, McCandless, Pa., 1986-87; judge Jefferson (Pa.) Hosp. Poster Contest, 1987; bd. mgrs. YMCA North Boroughs; reading tutor Greater Pitts. Literacy Coun., 1988-89; bd. dirs. Rachel Carson Homestead Assn. Recipient Communications Mgmt. Honors award Robert Morris Coll. Mem. Bus./Profl. Advt. Assn. (bd. dirs., v.p. edn.), North Hills C.of C., SMC Pa. Small Bus. Coun. (ambassador and special events com.), Pitts. Advt. Club, Internat. Tng. in Communications (sec. 1986-87, v.p. 1987-88), Alpha Tau Sigma. Office: Allegheny County Med Soc 713 Ridge Ave Pittsburgh PA 15212-6098

RILEY, PATRICK JAMES, professional basketball coach; b. Rome, N.Y., Mar. 20, 1945; s. Leon R.; m. Chris Riley; children: James Patrick, Elisabeth. Grad., U. Ky., 1967. Guard San Diego Rockets, 1967-70; guard Los Angeles Lakers, 1970-75, asst. coach, 1979-81, head coach, 1981-90; head coach N.Y. Knicks, 1991—; guard Phoenix Suns, 1975-76; broadcaster Los Angeles Lakers games Sta. KLAC and Sta. KHJ-TV, Los Angeles, 1977-79, NBC Sports, 1990-91; player NBA Championship Team, 1972, coach, 1982, 85, 87, 88. Named NBA Coach of Yr., 1990. Office: care NY Knickerbockers 4 Pennsylvania Pla New York NY 10001*

RILEY, ROBERT ANNAN, III, social services administrator, financial consultant; b. Balt., Jan. 2, 1955; s. Robert Jr. and Elfrieda Bertha (Mueller) R.; m. Adama Ly, July 31, 1987. BA in English, Yale U., 1979. Vol. Peace Corps, Gabon, Africa, 1979-83; adminstr. tng. Peace Corps, Gabon, 1983-84, assoc. dir. adminstrn., 1984-86; assoc. dir. adminstrn. Peace Corps, Mali, 1986-88; mgmt. analyst internat. ops. Peace Corps, Washington, 1988-89, chief adminstrv. officer, planning and budget officer for Africa region, 1989-92; regional adminstr. for West Africa Plan Internat., 1992—; mem. Coun. for Excellence in Govt. Fellowship, 1990-91. Author of several computer fin. software programs, 1985—. Fellow Coun. for Excellence in Govt., 1990-91. Democrat. Episcopalian. Home: Villa Diadhou, Quarter Ouakam, Dakar Senegal Office: Plan Internat, Pyrotechnie 14 Mermoz, BP 21121 Dakar-Ponty, Dakar Senegal

RILEY, THOMAS AURALDO, German language educator; b. Bath, Maine, Apr. 29, 1907; s. Thomas Alexander and Elizabeth Ann (Baker) R.; m. Elizabeth Dobler, Mar. 30, 1910; 1 child, Peter Bernard. AB, Bowdoin Coll., 1928; AM, Yale U., 1938; PhD, Harvard U., 1946. Instr. German Smith Coll., Northampton, Mass., 1931-37; asst. prof. Bowdoin Coll., Brunswick, Maine, 1939-73. Editor various books, articles. Recipient Fulbright grant, Austria, 1954-55, Munich, 1987-88, Guggenheim grant, Munich, 1957-58. Republican. Home: 25 Boody St Brunswick ME 04011-3046

RILEY, WILLIAM, corporate executive, writer; b. Indpls., June 30, 1931; s. Leo Michael and Edna (Wilhelm) R.; m. Laura Etz, Apr. 20, 1957. AB, U. Notre Dame, 1952; LLB, Yale U., 1955. V.p., dir., chmn. Ivy Corp., Atlanta, 1960-80; chmn. Moore-Handley, Inc., Birmingham, Ala., 1981—; bd. dirs. Tru-Die, Inc., Franklin Pk., Ill., Fabco-Air, Inc., Gainesville, Fla. Author: (with Laura Riley) Guide to the National Wildlife Refuges, 1979 (Pulitzer prize nominee). Trustee The Raptor Trust, Basking Ridge, N.J., 1980—; bd. dirs. Nat. Wildlife Refuge Assn., Potomac, Md., 1985—, Hawk Mountain Sanctuary Assn., Kempton, Pa., 1989—, Nat. Audubon Soc., N.Y.C., 1990—. With U.S. Army, 1957-58. Mem. Met. Club of N.Y.C. Office: 745 5th Ave Ste 1803 New York NY 10151-1803

RIMA, PHILIP WOODRING, electronics engineer; b. Sago Twp., Minn., Oct. 21, 1921; s. Gile Clinton and Alberta Mary (Woodring) R.; m. Norma Nichols, Apr. 5, 1944 (div. 1953); children: Craig Alan, Larry Philip, Albert Jeffrey (dec.); m. Ingrid H. Rima, June 23, 1956; children: David Woodring Rima, Eric Max Rima. BSEE, Drexel U., 1968, MBA, 1972. Enlisted USMC, 1940, advanced through grades to master sgt., ret., 1960; project engr. Emtech div. Am. Electronics Labs. Industries, Colmar, Pa., 1965-70, program mgr., 1970-75; mktg. engr. Am. Electronics Labs. Industries, Colmar, 1975-80; mgr. bus. devel. Flam & Russell, Horsham, Pa., 1981-83; v.p. mktg. Internat. Micro Industries, Cherry Hill, N.J., 1983-88; cons. Internat. Micro Industries, Smart Card Systems, TTL Techs., Phila., 1988—; chief exec. officer Blue Skies, Inc., Elkins Park, Pa., 1971—. Contbr. articles to profl. jours. Mem. IEEE, IEPS, SPIE. Home and Office: 7402 Mountain Ave Melrose Park PA 19126-1304

RIMILLER, RONALD WAYNE, podiatrist; b. Rome, N.Y., July 21, 1949; s. Harold Henry and Ida (Scherz) R.; m. Janice Ann Bombara, June 30, 1973; children: Joseph Harold, Lori Ann. BA, Colgate U., 1971; D Podiatric Medicine, Pa. Coll. Podiatric Medicine, 1979. Diplomate Am. Bd. Podiatric Orthopedics. Pvt. practice, Elmwood, Conn., 1979—; cons. Hartford (Conn.) Hosp., 1982—. Lt., EMT, Tunxis Hose Co. No. 1, Unionville, Conn., 1990—. Recipient achievement award Tunxis Hose Co. No. 1, 1989. Fellow Am. Coll. Foot Orthopedists; mem. APHA, Internat. Coll. Podiatric Laser Surgery (assoc.), Acad. Ambulatory Foot Surgery (assoc.), Am. Acad. Podiatric Sports Medicine (assoc.), Am. Acad. Sports Medicine, Am. Podiatric Med. Assn. Roman Catholic. Home: 65 Sylvan Ave Unionville CT 06085-1170 Office: 1123A New Britain Ave West Hartford CT 06110-2412

RIMLAND, LISA PHILLIP, writer, composer, lyricist; b. Stamford, Conn., Mar. 27, 1954; d. Maurice Louis and Eva (Kreiz) R. BA, U. Conn., 1978. Composer numerous songs, including Your Heart or Mine, 1990, Drive Me Crazy, 1991, Send Me an Angel, 1992; contbr. articles, essays to profl. jours. Recipient DAR award, 1969; Nat. Merit scholar, 1972. Mem. ASCAP. Home: PO Box 408 Storrs Mansfield CT 06268-0408

RIMPEL, AUGUSTE EUGENE, JR., management and technical consulting executive; b. St. Thomas, V.I., Aug. 25, 1939; s. Auguste Eugene and Leah Eudora (Harris) R. B.A. magna cum laude, Inter-Am. U. P.R., 1957; M.S. in Ch.E., M.I.T., 1961; Ph.D., Carnegie Inst. Tech., 1964; M.B.A., Columbia U., 1964-65; m. Maria Czernetski, Sept. 23, 1966; children—Nicole, Christopher. Research chem. engr. Am. Cyanamid Co., Stamford, Conn., 1961-62; with Arthur D. Little, Inc., Cambridge, Mass., 1965-75, sr. staff mem., 1973-75; commr. of commerce, spl. advisor to gov. for econ. affairs Govt. U.S. V.I., St. Thomas, 1975-78; mem. corp. spl. staff Arthur D. Little, Inc., Cambridge, 1978-81, also v.p. Arthur D. Little Internat., Inc.; v.p. Booz-Allen and Hamilton, Inc., 1981-83; v.p., ptnr., Price Waterhouse 1983—. Bd. dirs. Caribbean/Cen. Am. Action, 1979-91; mem. U.S. del. World Bank Conf. on Caribbean Econ. Devel., 1977-78; mem. subcoms. on internat. econ. devel. U.S. C. of C., 1980-83; V.I. rep. White Ho. Conf. on Balanced Nat. Growth and Econ. Devel., 1978; bd. dirs. travel adv. bd. U.S. Dept. Commerce, 1977-78; pres. Caribbean Tourism Assn., 1977-78; bd. dirs., mem. exec. com. Caribbean Tourism Research Center, 1976-78. Mem. Am. Inst. Chem. Engrs., Am. Chem. Soc., Am. Inst. Chemists, Soc. Internat. Devel., Sigma Xi. Office: 1801 K St NW Washington DC 20006-1394

RINALDI, FRANK THOMAS, podiatrist; b. Bklyn., Oct. 14, 1948; s. Thomas Louis and Marie Louise (Giordano) R. BS, Bklyn. Coll., 1970; DPM, N.Y. Coll. Podiatry, 1974. Diplomate Am. Bd. Podiatric Surgery. Podiatrist in pvt. practice Foot Health Group, Bklyn., 1974—. Author: Atlas of Rear Foot Surgery, 1985. Baseball coach Youth Orgn., N.J., 1986—. Fellow Am. Coll. Foot Surgeons, Am. Coll. Foot Orthopedists; mem. N.Y. Podiatric Soc. (v.p. 1986-90), Am. Assn. Hosp. Podiatry (pres. 1987-88), Kings County Podiatry (pres. 1986-87), Am. Podiatric Med. Assn. (del. 1989). Home and Office: 8508 18th Ave Brooklyn NY 11214-2958

RINALDI, GERARD W., artist, publisher. BFA, MFA, MS. Lectr., artist-in-residence Byram Hills Schs., Armonk, N.Y., 1966—; pub. 9N-2N-8N Newsletter, Stamford, Conn., 1986—. Artist of numerous exhbns. of works with sci. basis. Pres. B.L.A. Recipient numerous grants. Home: PO Box 16732 Stamford CT 06905-8732

RINALDI, KEITH STEPHEN, lawyer, accountant; b. Poughkeepsie, N.Y., Aug. 3, 1952; s. John Kevin and Corinne Frances (McCagg) R.; m. Debra Jean Knapp, Sept. 4, 1983; children: Gabrielle P., Matthew Keith, Alessandra Corinne. BS in Acctg., Fordham U., 1974; JD, N.Y. Law Sch., 1977; LLM in Taxation, NYU, 1978. Bar: N.Y. 1978, U.S. Tax. Ct. 1978, U.S. Dist. Ct. (so. and ea. dists.) N.Y. 1979, U.S. Dist. Ct. (no. dist.) N.Y. 1982. Acct., v.p., tax counsel Rinaldi Tax, Inc., Poughkeepsie, 1975—; prin. Keith S. Rinaldi P.C., Poughkeepsie, 1984—; propr., broker Arlington Assocs. Realty Co., Poughkeepsie, N.Y., 1985—. Counsel Police Athletic League of Poughkeepsie, 1982—, Mid Hudson Italian Am. Cultural Found., Inc., Poughkeepsie, 1983—, Dutchess County War Casualty Com., Poughkeepsie, 1985-87, Town of Poughkeepsie Police Benevolent Assn., 1988—; bd. dirs., counsel Big Bros./Big Sisters of Dutchess County, Inc., 1990—. Mem. ABA, N.Y. Bar Assn., Dutchess County Bar Assn., Fordham U. Alumni Assn., N.Y. Law Sch. Alumni Assn., NYU Alumni Assn. Republican. Roman Catholic. Home: Halls Corners Rd Millbrook NY Office: The Rinaldi Bldg 10 Arlington Ave Poughkeepsie NY 12603-1604

RINALDO, HELEN, interior designer; b. Manville, N.J., July 5, 1922; d. Zigmond and Kate (Szymanski) Ossowski; student summer and evening classes N.Y. Sch. Interior Design, 1964; student N.Y. U., 1964, Somerset County (N.J.) Coll., 1975-76; m. Nicholas Rinaldo, Feb. 7, 1948; children—Linda Ann, Lorraine Ann. Interior designer W. & J. Sloane, Red Bank and Short Hills, N.J., 1981, Lord & Taylor, Paramus, N.J., 1974; owner Rinaldo Interiors, Scotch Plains, N.J., 1959-65; designer local firms; speaker career day local sch. Mem. Hist. Commn. Twp. of Branchburg (N.J.), until 1982. Mem. Allied Bd. Trade (N.Y.C.), Internat. Platform Assn. Home and Office: 69 Partridge Ln Cherry Hill NJ 08003-1945

RINALDO, MATTHEW JOHN, congressman; b. Elizabeth, N.J., Sept. 1, 1931; s. Matthew John and Ann (Papaccio) R. B.S., Rutgers U., 1953; M.B.A., Seton Hall U., Newark, 1959; D. Pub. Adminstrn., NYU, 1979. Pres. Union Twp. Zoning Bd. Adjustment, 1962-63; mem. Union County Bd. Freeholders, 1963-64, N.J. Senate, 1968-73, 93d-102nd Congresses from 12th Dist. N.J., 1972-82, from 7th Dist. N.J., 1984—; instr. Rutgers U. Extension Div., 1961-71. Bd. dirs. Union County Heart Assn., UNICO. Recipient Man of Year award Union, Plainfield and Maplewood chpts. UNICO Nat.; award Rod and Gun Editors Met. N.Y., Health Freedom award; named Outstanding Young Man of Year, Union County Jaycees; Knight of Year, Union council KC; Citizen of Year award B'nai B'rith; also honored by N.J. State Fireman's Mut. Benevolent Assn.; also honored by Cath. War Vets.; also honored by Hadassah; also honored by Union County Heart Assn.; also honored by Policemen's Benevolent Assn.; also honored by VFW; also honored by State Grand Jurors Assn.; also honored by others. Republican. Roman Catholic. Clubs: KC (4 deg.), Lions, Elks. Home: 142 Headley Ter Union NJ 07083-6976 Office: US Ho of Reps 2469 Rayburn House Office Bldg Washington DC 20515

RINDGE, DEBORA ANNE, art historian; b. Santa Monica, Calif., Dec. 5, 1956; d. John Francis and Mary Anne (Alpine) R. BA, U. Calif., Santa Barbara, 1978; MA, Ohio State U., 1980. Instr. art history U. Ala., Birmingham, 1980-82; dir. duPont Gallery, Lexington, Va., 1982-86; art historian Washington, 1986—. Mem. Coll. Art Assn., Archives of Am. Art, Assn. Historians of Am. Art, Am. Studies Assn., History Photography Assn. Home: 7921 Mandan Rd # 103 Greenbelt MD 20770-2831 Office: U Md Dept Art History College Park MD 20742-1335

RINEHART, ROBERT, history educator; b. Washington, Nov. 7, 1938; s. John Paul and Lorraine (Martin) R.; m. Nana Merete Jessen, Jan. 8, 1966; children: Niels Robert, Paul Martin, Benjamin Knud. BA, La Salle Coll., Oxford, 1961; postgrad., Exeter Coll., Oxford U., 1965; PhD, Georgetown U., 1975. Instr. U. Copenhagen (Denmark), 1965-66; asst. prof. history George Mason U., Fairfax, Va., 1967-73; historian Fgn. Area Studies The Am. U., Washington, 1975-86; chmn. Scandinavian Studies Fgn. Svc. Inst., Arlington, Va., 1986—; adj. prof. history George Washington U., Washington, 1988—. cons. Moran Stahl and Boyer Inc., Boulder, Colo., 1990—. Co-author (book series) Country Studies, 1975-89; editor, co-author (books) U.S. Finnish Dipolmatic Relations, 1992, Beneath the Northern Star, 1992. Mem. Soc. Advancement of Scandinavian Studies, Conf. of European Studies, St. Ansgar's League. Roman Catholic. Home: 3051 Porter St NW Washington DC 20008 Office: Fgn Svcs Inst 1400 Key Blvd Arlington VA 22209

RINES, CAROL MARY WILLIAMSON, state and foundation official; b. Boston, Dec. 29, 1943; d. Ralph Woodling and Irene Philomena (Arsenault) Williamson; m. John Hurley, 1964 (div. 1966); m. Robert Harvey Rines, Dec. 29, 1972; 1 child, Justice Christopher. AS in Bus., Burditt Jr. Coll., Boston, 1967; student, Suffolk U., 1968-70; BA in Psychology, Notre Dame Coll., 1990. Trustee Children's Trust Fund for State of N.H., Concord, 1986—, chair, Gov.'s appointee, 1990—; v.p., bd. dirs. Acad. Applied Sci., Boston, Concord, Oxford, Eng., 1975—; pres. N.H. Child and Family Svcs., 1990—, mem. exec. bd., 1986—; pres. Jr. Svc. League of N.H., 1978-79; founding dir. Concord Parents and Children Children's Place, 1980-84; mem. State Task Force Reach to Recovery, Am. Cancer Soc., 1987—. Inventor 2 patents for typewriter automatic margin detector, 1978, 80. Mem. Rep. Trust, Washington, 1987—; grant adminstr. Concord United Way, 1986-87; mem. edn. com. Concord Unitarian Ch., 1980-82, fin. com., 1989-90, music com. Mem. Highland Club, Acad. Applied Sci. Ctr. for Edn. and Devel., Alpha Sigma Lamda. Home: 13 Spaulding St Concord NH 03301-2571 Office: Acad Applied Sci 1 Maple St Concord NH 03301-4314

RINGE, HENRY RALPH (BUZZ RINGE), author, producer; b. Phila., Apr. 30, 1936; s. Thomas B.K. Ringe and Mary (Brick) Rhoads; m. Cynthia A. Smith, Sept. 8, 1962 (div. 1978); children: Jennifer, Alexandra, Benjamin; m. Sarah T. Funk, Apr. 25, 1981. Student, Yale U., 1954-56, U. Pa., 1959-60; AB, Franklin and Marshall Coll., 1962. Tchr. Green Vale Sch., Glen Head, N.Y., 1963-66, Episcopal Acad., Merion, Pa., 1966-67; asst. to dir. market rsch. Aitkin-Kynett Co., Inc., Phila., 1967-68; writer, editor, producer, dir., dir. of the archives NFL Films, Inc., Mt. Laurel, N.J., 1968-87; author Marlton, N.J., 1987—; part-time writer, editor, producer, dir., NFL Films, Inc., 1987—. Author: Score! My 25 Years with the Broad Street Bullies, 1990. With USN, 1956-58. Home and Office: 605 Westerly Dr Marlton NJ 08053-1069

RINGVALD, MIGUEL ANDRÉS, financial administrator, international consultant; b. Uruguay, Aug. 1, 1956; came to U.S., 1985; s. Americo J. and Ana (Malat) R.; m. Vardit Berkovitz, Sept. 28, 1980; children: Ohad, Jonathan. BA in Econs., Hebrew U., Jerusalem, 1979; MBA in Fin., Boston U., 1986. Oficina Hispana, Boston, 1986-87, La Alianza Hispana Inc, Boston, 1987—; internat. cons. Inter-American Devel. Bank, Washington, 1991. Co-author: Guide to A Successful Leveraged Buyout, 1987. Office: La Alianza Hispana 409 Dudley St Roxbury MA 02109

RING-WILSON, KRISTINE, nurse educator; b. Troy, N.Y., Oct. 18, 1948; d. Arthur J. and Joan (Leffler) Ring; m. Clark K. Wilson, May 1978; children: Clark K. III, Catherine Ring. BSN, SUNY, Plattsburgh, 1970; MS in Nursing, Russell Sage Coll., 1974. RN, N.Y. Staff nurse, head nurse, clin. specialist VA Hosp., Albany, N.Y., 1970-73; mem. faculty Russell Sage Coll., Troy, 1974; cons. Regents Coll., Albany, 1977-89, program assoc., 1989—; mem. adj. faculty Maria Coll., Albany, 1980-84, Jr. Coll. Albany, 1985, Hudson Valley Community Coll., Troy, 1989—. Mem. Capital Dist. Nurses Assn. Home: 30 Nott Rd Rexford NY 12148-1310

RINSKY, JUDITH LYNN, foundation administrator, educator consultant; b. Sept. 12, 1941; d. Allen A. Lynn and Sophie (Schwartz) C.H.E.; m. Joel C. Rinsky, Jan. 29, 1963; children: Heidi Mae Schnapp, Heather Star, Jason Wayne. BA in Home Econs., Montclair State Coll., 1963. Notary pub., N.J. Tchr. home econs. Florence Ave. Sch., Irvington, N.J., 1963-66; substitute tchr. Millburn-Short Hills Sch. System, 1978-82, 90—, sr. citizen coord., 1982-87; respite care coord. Essex County Respite Care, East Orange, N.J., 1988-90; pvt. practice educator Short Hills, N.J., 1990—; bd. mem. adv. com. gerontology Seton Hall U., 1984-90; coord. Mayor's Adv. Bd. St. Citizens, Millburn-Short Hills, 1982-87. Pres. Deerfield Sch. PTA, 1979-80, Millburn High Sch. PTA, 1983-85; co-chmn. Charles T. King Student Loan Fund dinner dance, 1981; mem. Handicapped Access Study com. 1983-85; bd. dirs. Coun. on Health and Human Svcs., 1985-90, mem., 1985—. Mem. Lake Naomi Assn. (chmn. sailing com. 1981), N.J. Home Econs. Assn., Am. Home Econs. Assn., Rotary (chairperson Interact Club 1987—, pres. Millburn chpt. 1992—, bd. dirs. 1992—), Notary Pub. N.J. Home: 23 Winthrop Rd Short Hills NJ 07078-1411

RINSLAND, ROLAND DELANO, university official; b. Low Moor, Va., Apr. 11, 1933; s. Charles Henry and Lottie (Parks) R.; A.B. with distinction, Va. State U., 1954; A.M., Tchrs. Coll., Columbia U., 1959, profl. diploma, 1960, Ed.D., 1966. Asst. to dean of men Va. State Coll., Petersburg, 1952-54; asst. purchasing agt. Glyco Products Co., Inc., N.Y.C., 1956-57; asst. office of registrar Tchrs. Coll., Columbia U., N.Y.C., 1957-66, registrar, 1966-72, asst. dean for student affairs, also registrar, dir. office doctoral studies, 1972—; mem. Tchrs. Coll. Devel. Council, 1974-76, 91—; rep., presenter of degrees Tchrs. Coll., Japan, 1989, 91. Served to 1st lt. AUS, 1954-56. Designated Important and Valuable Human Resource of USA Am. Heritage Research Assn. First Am. Bicentenium. Mem. N.Y. State Personnel and Guidance Assn., Am. Coll. Personnel Assn., Nat. Soc. Study Edn., Am. Ednl. Research Assn., Middle States, Am. assns. collegiate registrars and admission officers (inter-assn. rep. to state edn. depts. on tchr. cert. 1973-74, mem. com. on orgn. and adminstrn. registrars activities 1973, 74-76), Assn. Records Execs. and Adminstrs. (charter mem., by-laws and program chmn. 1969), Am. Acad. Polit. and Social Sci., Am. Assn. Higher Edn., Assn. Instl. Research, Internat. Assn. Applied Psychology, Soc. Applied Anthropology, Am. Assn. Counseling and Devel., Assn. Study of Higher Edn., AAAS, N.Y. Acad. Scis., Met. Opera Guild, NEA (Leah B. Sykes award for life mem.), Scabbard and Blade, Kappa Phi Kappa, Phi Delta Kappa, Kappa Delta Pi. Home: 25 W 68th St New York NY 10023-5302 Office: 525 W 120th St New York NY 10027

RIORDAN, JAMES FRANCIS, biochemistry educator; b. New Haven, Feb. 6, 1934; s. Michael J. and Helen M. Riordan; m. Charlotte C. Hart, Sept. 19, 1970; children: Cynthia, Barbara, James, Michelle. BS, Fairfield U., 1955; MS, Fordham U., 1957, PhD, 1961; MA, Harvard U., 1987. Instr. U.S. Mcht. Marine Acad., Kings Point, N.Y., 1957-58, Fordham U., N.Y.C., 1958-61; rsch. assoc. Med. Sch. Harvard U., Boston, 1964-65, assoc. in biochemistry, 1965-68, asst. prof., 1968-71, assoc. prof., 1971-87, prof., 1987—; asst. dir. clin. chemistry Peter Bent Brigham Hosp., Boston 1965-79; med. dir. clin. chemistry Brigham and Women's Hosp., Boston, 1979—. Contbr. articles to profl. jours. Mem. AAAS, Am. Chem. Soc., Am. Soc. Biochemistry and Molecular Biology, Brae Burn Country Club, Harvard Club of Boston. Home: 80 Putnam St Newton MA 02165-2433 Office: Harvard U Sch Medicine 250 Longwood Ave Boston MA 02115-5719

RIORDON, JOHN BERNARD, museum director; b. Bathurst, N.B., Can., Dec. 4, 1947; s. Thomas Francis and Mary Antoinette (Quinn) R.; m. Marie Lilliane Theriault, June 14, 1973; children: Melissa, Thomas, Edward, Jillian. BA, St. thomas U., Fredericton, N.B., 1970; postgrad., St. Mary's U., Halifax, N.S., 1973. Gallery asst. St. Mary's U. Art Gallery, Halifax, 1971-73; curator Centennial Art Gallery, N.S. Mus. Fine Arts, Halifax, 1973-75; dir. Art Gallery N.S., Halifax, 1975—; expert examiner (fine art) Cultural Property Export and Import Rev. Bd., Ottawa, 1986-90. Author: (exhbn. catalogs) Francis Silver, 1982, C. Anthony Law: A Retrospective, 1989, Nova Scotia Folk Art: Canada's Cultural Heritage, 1989. Past chmn. Jr. Achievement Halifax, 1984; past chmn. bldg. com. Children's Aid soc., 1986; mem. Art Allocation Com., Halifax, 1987-89. Recipient art mus. tour of U.S. U.S. Info. Agy., 1986. Mem. Visual Arts Nova Scotia (ad hoc), Internat. Coun. Museums, Can. Museums Assn., Can. Art Mus. Dirs. Assn. (treas. 1986-89), The Smithsonian Instn., Arts atlantic (Charlottetown, adv. bd. 1980-90), Am. Assn. Museums, Halifax Bd. Trade. Home: 25 Crestview Dr, Halifax, NS Canada B3P 1G1 Office: Art Gallery NS, 1741 Hollis St at Cheapside, Halifax, NS Canada B3J 3C8

RIPKA, G. ELIZABETH, management consultant, professor; b. Phila., Apr. 18, 1924; d. Walter and Grace E. (Stevenson) R.; m. Henry A. Homont, Sept. 6, 1949; 1 child, Elizabeth Ann. BS, Temple U., 1946, MEd, 1948, EdD, 1963. Instr., Temple U., Phila., 1948-54; asst. prof. Harcum Coll., Bryn Mawr, Pa., 1954-57, Beaver Coll., Glenside, Pa., 1957-65; assoc. prof., chair dept. Drexel U., Phila., 1965-71; adj. prof. Pa. State U., Media, 1975—; cons. U.S. Office Pers. Mgmt., 1969—. Chair bd. dirs. Phila. House, 1977-89, InHoOh Korea Ctr., Phila., 1966-74; v.p. Valley Forge Coun. Rep. Women, 1978-89. Remington Rand fellow, 1958; recipient Disting. Service award InHoOh Korea Ctr., 1974. Mem. Am. Vocat. Assn., AAUP, Nat. Bus. Edn. Assn., Phi Delta Gamma (sec.-treas. 1951-54), Delta Pi Epsilon,

Phi Gamma Nu. Presbyterian. Home: 2011 White Horse Rd Berwyn PA 19312-2127

RIPKEN, CALVIN EDWIN, JR. (CAL RIPKEN), professional baseball player; b. Havre de Grace, Md., Aug. 24, 1960. Player minor league teams Bluefield, Miami, Charlotte, Rochester, 1978-81; player Balt. Orioles, 1981—. Recipient Rookie of Yr. award Internat. League, 1981, Rookie of Yr. award Baseball Writers Assn., Am. League, 1982; named Am. League Most Valuable Player, 1983, 91; Major League Player of Yr., The Sporting News, 1983: named to Am. League All-Star Team, 1983-87. Office: care Balt Orioles Memorial Stadium Baltimore MD 21218*

RIPLEY, MARY MONCRIEFFE LIVINGSTON, zoological collector; b. N.Y.C.; d. Gerald Moncrieffe and Eleanor Hoffman (Rodewald) Livingston; m. Sidney Dillon Ripley II, Aug. 18, 1949; children: Julie Dillon Ripley Ridgely, Rosemary Livingston Ripley Lanius, Sylvia McNeil Ripley Addison. Student pvt. sch., N.Y.C. With OSS, Washington, Algiers, Italy and People's Republic of China, 1942-45; zool. collector Assam, India, 1950, Indonesia, 1954, New Guinea, 1960, Bhutan and India, 1967, 68, 73, 74, 75, Nepal, 1975, People's Republic of China and Tibet, 1980, Arunachal Pradesh, India, 1981-82, 88; collector entomology, ornithology Peabody Mus., Yale U., New Haven, 1950-64; collector entomology, ornithology Smithsonian Instn., Washington, 1969, 88; dir. women's com. Smithsonian Instn. Resident Assn., 1965—; rsch. affiliate dept. entomology U.S. Nat. Mus., Washington, 1973—; mem. expedition Aldatra Island, Seychelles, 1991. Contbr. photographs to Smithsonian Mag., 1973-75, 81, People Mag., 1975. Bd. dirs. Animal Rescue League, Washingotn, Home for Incurables, Washington. Recipient Henry Medal, 1984; Dedication Mary Livingston Ripley Garden, The Mall, Smithsonian Instn., Washington, 1988. Mem. Soc. Women Geographers, Lords Manor Soc. N.Y., Colonial Dames Am., Colony Club (N.Y.C.), Colonial Lords Manor Club (N.Y.C.), Sulgrave Club (Washington). Episcopalian. Home (winter): 2324 Massachusetts Ave NW Washington DC 20008 Home (summer): PO Box 210 Litchfield CT 06759

RISHER, CAROL ADRIENNE SEEGER, trade association administrator; b. Rockville Centre, N.Y., Nov. 10, 1946; d. Louis and Alicia (Krasilovsky) Seeger; m. John R. Risher Jr., June 9, 1974; children: David, Michael, Mark, Conrad. AB, U. Rochester, 1968. Mgmt. trainee Gt. Western United Corp., N.Y.C., Denver, 1968-70; supr. Western Electric Corp., Omaha, 1970-72; dir. rsch., corp. devel. Am. TV and Communication, Washington, 1972-74; dir. subscription cable Nat. Cable TV Assn., Washington, 1974-75; info. officer Nat. Commn. on New Technol. Uses of Copyrighted Works, Washington, 1975-77; dir. copyright and new tech. Assn. Am. Pubs., Washington, 1977—; exec. dir. Internat. Intellectual Property Alliance, Washington, 1984-92; trustee Copy Right Soc. U.S.A., N.Y.C., 1982-84; mem. steering com. Maret Minority Enrollment Com., 1988—. Bd. dirs. Jewish Community Coun., Washington, 1974-78, Temple Sinai, Washington, 1974-77; bd. dirs., sec. D.C. Jewish Community Ctr., Washington, 1988—. Office: Assn Am Pubs 1718 Connecticut Ave NW Washington DC 20009

RISING, GERALD RICHARD, mathematics educator, nature columnist; b. Rochester, N.Y., Jan. 15, 1927; s. Walter Vernon and Emma Victoria (Peterson) R.; m. Muriel Jean Nixon (div. 1962); children: Gerald Richard, Susan Nixon; m. Doris Ann Copeland, Mar. 28, 1969. BA in English, U. Rochester, 1948, EdM, 1951; MS in Math., U. Notre Dame, 1961; PhD, NYU, 1965. Cert. tchr. secondary sch. math., English, history, sci., N.Y., supervision, Conn. Tchr. math. Warsaw (N.Y.) Cen. Sch., 1949-51, Johnson City (N.Y.) High Sch., 1951-53, Brighton High Sch., Rochester, 1953-58, U. Rochester, NYU, 1957-64; dept. chair math. Greece Olympia High Sch., Rochester, 1958-60; coord. math. Pub. Schs., Norwalk, Conn., 1960-64; dir. math. Minn. Nat. Lab., St. Paul, 1964-66; asst. dir. Minnimath Ctr., U. Minn., Mpls., 1964-66; from assoc. prof. to disting. teaching prof. SUNY, Buffalo, 1966—, dir. gifted math. program, 1980—. Author: The Third "R": Math Classroom Teaching, 1978, Guidelines for Teaching Mathematics, 1966, 72; editor Math in the Secondary School Classroom, 1972; columnist Nature Watch, The Buffalo News; over 100 articles to profl. jours. Ensign USNR, 1944-47. Recipient Disting. Teaching Prof. award SUNY, 1986, Chancellor's award, 1981, Outstanding Faculty award U. at Buffalo Found., 1979, Disting. tchr. award Student Assn., 1980. Mem. Buffalo Ornithol. Soc., Assn. Math. Tchrs. N.Y.State, Math. Assn. Am., AAAS. Democrat. Home: 295 Robin Hill Dr Buffalo NY 14221-1639 Office: U at Buffalo Baldy 580 Buffalo NY 14260

RISLEY, HENRY BRAINARD, protective service official; b. Torrington, Conn., Feb. 12, 1946; s. Henry Brainard and Margery (Utz) R.; m. Suzanne K. Stanton, May 10, 1967, (div. May 1979); m. Peggy M. Madore, July 3, 1981; children: Henry, Matthew, Amy. BS, Mich. State U., 1968, MS, 1970. Vocational counselor RGC, State Prison So. Mich., Jackson, 1970-72, asst. dep. warden, 1974-77; supr. program planning Dept. of Corrections, Lansing, Mich., 1972-74; dep. warden Mich. Tng. Unit, Ionia, 1977-78; reception ctr. administrator Riverside Correction Facility, Ionia, 1978-81; dep. warden Ypsilanti (Mich.) Mens Correction Facility, 1981; warden Montanta State Prison, Deer Lodge, 1981-88; adult bur. chief Del. Dept. of Corrections, Smyrna, 1988—; mem. Del. Criminal Justice Coun., 1988—. Board dirs. Highlands Coop. (low income housing), Lansing, 1973-74; v.p. Powell County Med. Found., Deer Lodge, 1987. Mem. Am. Corrections Assn., N.Am., Assn. of Wardens and Supts., Mont. Corrections Assn. (bd. dirs. 1984-88), Western Corrections Assn. (bd. dirs. 1984-88), Mich. Corrections Assn. (prog. com. 1973-74), Mid. Atlantic States Correctional Assn., Del. Corrections Assn., Deer Lodge C. of C. (pres. 1987), Deer Lodge Rotary (pres. 1987), Dover Capital City Rotary. Home: RR 1 Box 137 Smyrna DE 19977-9755 Office: Del Dept Corrections 80 Monrovia Ave Smyrna DE 19977-1597

RISLEY, JOHN HOLLISTER, sculptor, educator; b. Brookline, Mass., Sept. 20, 1919; s. Edward Hammond and Ada (Simpson) R.; m. Mary Kring, June 2, 1949; children: Kathryn Hanford, John Hollister Jr. BA, Amherst Coll., 1942; BFA, RISD, 1949; MFA, Cranbrook Acad., Bloomfield, Mich., 1951. Cons. Mut. Security Agy., The Philippines, 1951-52; prof. art Wesleyan U., Middletown, Conn., 1954—; cons. U.S. govt., Taipai, Taiwan, 1960, Peace Corps, P.R., 1964. One-man show Full House Gallery, N.Y.C., 1989; represented in permanent collections Henry Hunting Art Gallery, Calif., Fred Olsen Found., Conn., Rose Art Gallery, Brandeis U., Waltham, Mass., Cleve. Garden Ctr., South Kent Sch., Conn., Ea. Conn. State Coll., Hartford (Conn.) Jewish Community Ctr., Gaylord Hosp., Conn., Ford Found., Colby Coll., Maine, Wesleyan U., U. Conn., U. Maine, Taft Sch., Slater Meml. Mus., Conn., Mus. Contemporary Crafts, also others. Mem. examining bd. Charter Oak Coll., Farmington, Conn., 1987—; mem. Commn. on Arts and Culture, Middletown, 1987—. 1st lt. AUS, 1942-46, PTO. Recipient sculpture award Maine Arts Festival, 1961, sculpture prize Silvermine Guild Art, 1964, 1st prize Festival Human and Satire, Bulgaria, 1981, purchase prize Beth El Temple, West Hartford, Conn., 1982. Mem. Soc. Conn. Craftsmen (master craftsman award 1991). Home: 30 Maple Shade Rd Middletown CT 06457-5107 Office: Middletown U Dept Art Middletown CT 06475

RISOM, JENS, furniture designer, manufacturing executive; b. Copenhagen, May 8, 1916; came to U.S., 1938; naturalized, 1944; s. Sven J. and Inger Risom; m. Iben Haderup, Dec. 12, 1939 (dec. Jan. 1977); children: Helen Ann, Peggy Ann, Thomas Christian, Sven Christian; m. Henny Panduro, May 12, 1979. Student, Krebs, Denmark, 1922-27, St. Anne, 1927-32, Niels Brock Bus. Coll., 1932-34, Sch. Fine Arts and Industry, Denmark, 1935-38. Freelance furniture designer, 1939-46; pres. Jens Risom Design, Inc. (became subs. Dictaphone Corp. 1970), N.Y.C., 1946-73; v.p. Dictaphone Corp., 1970-72; pres. Design Control, New Canaan, Conn., 1973—; cons. design, mktg., space planning. Trustee RISD, New Canaan Libr., others. With AUS, 1943-45, ETO. Recipient awards Archtl. League, Am. Inst. Internat. Design, also numerous Danish and Am. design awards. Mem. Indsl. Designers Soc. Am. Home and Office: 103 Chichester Rd New Canaan CT 06840-3913 also: Box 596 Block Island RI 02807

RISS, ERIC, psychologist; b. Vienna, Austria, Oct. 10, 1929; s. David S. and Rebecca (Schneider) R.; came to U.S., 1940, naturalized, 1945; B.A., Bklyn. Coll., 1950; Ph.D., NYU, 1958; diplomate Am. Bd. Psychotherapy; m. Miriam Barbara Schoen, July 22, 1956; children—Arthur, Suzanne, Wendy. Pvt. practice psychotherapy, family therapy, marriage counseling, N.Y.C., 1952—; sr. psychologist N.Y.C. Diagnostic Center, 1954-57; with Marriage and Family Life Inst., N.Y.C., 1956—; cons., 1956-58, dir. pub. edn., 1960-73, chmn. bd. dirs., 1961-73, dir., 1973—; mem. attending staff, supr. psychotherapy and family therapy Payne Whitney Psychiat. Clinic, N.Y. Hosp., N.Y.C., 1971-78; clin. instr. psychology and psychiatry Cornell U. Med. Coll., 1971-72, clin. asst. prof., 1973-78; dir. Inst. for Exploration of Marriage, 1976-84; chief psychologist Artists, Writers and Performers Psychotherapy Center, 1978—; lectr. Bklyn. Coll., 1955-62; cons. Fordham Hosp., 1956-68; psychotherapist N.Y. Neuropsychiat. Center, 1958-60; psychotherapist Community Guidance Service, N.Y.C., 1958-61. Mem. Am. Acad. Psychotherapy, N.Y. State Marriage, Family and Child Counseling Assn. (pres. 1971-72), Acad. Family Psychology, Am., N.Y. State psychol. assns. Contbr. numerous articles to profl. jours. Office: 174 E 73d St New York NY 10021

RISSMEYER, PATRICIA ANN, college dean; b. Queens, N.Y., Jan. 30, 1956; d. Walter Henry and Joan Mary (Reilly) R. BS, U. Hartford, 1978; MEd, U. Mass., 1981; postgrad., SUNY, Buffalo, 1991—. Staff assoc, staff asst., sr. head residence, head residence U. Mass. Housing Svcs., Amherst, 1978-83; dir. residence life and housing St. Mary's Coll., Notre Dame, Ind., 1983-88; dean of students Canisius Coll., Buffalo, 1988—; mediator U. Mass. Mediation Project, Amherst, 1980-83; cons. United Way Youth Svcs., Buffalo, 1988—. Bd. dirs. Sex Offense Svcs., South Bend, Ind., 1987; vol. Runaway Shelter, South Bend, 1985-88. Mem. Nat. Assn. Student Pers. Adminstrs. Office: Canisius Coll 2001 Main St Buffalo NY 14208-1098

RISTAU, EDSEL PAUL, recruiter; b. Warren, Pa., Feb. 26, 1942; s. Paul E. and Mary B. (Tulowitzke) R.; m. Jeanne Alice York, June 20, 1964; children: Matthew Paul, Derek John. BA, Lycoming Coll., 1964. Sales rep. Remington Rand Office Systems, Washington, 1965-69, Farrington Mfg. Co., Springfield, Va., 1969-71, Honeywell Info. Systems, Rochester, N.Y., 1971-73, Sybron Corp., Rochester, 1973-87; pres. Mgmt. Recruiters of the Finger Lakes, Inc., Victor, N.Y., 1987—. Sgt. USAR, 1965-71. Republican. Mem. United Ch. of Christ. Home: 26 Kings Lacey Way Fairport NY 14450-3238 Office: Mgmt Recruiters 10 E Main St Ste 204 Victor NY 14564-1334

RISTICH, MIODRAG, psychiatrist; b. Belgrade, Yugoslavia, July 19, 1938; came to U.S., 1967; s. Teodosije and Gordana (Isailovic) Ristic; m. Yvonne Muriel Cunliffe, May 6, 1967; children: Katharine Alexandra, Elizabeth Victoria. MD, U. Belgrade, 1962. Diplomate Am. Bd. Psychiatry and Neurology. Psychiatric resident Manhattan Psychiatric Ctr., NYU, 1980-83; Med. dir. Cambridge State Hosp., Cambridge, Minn., 1967-72; dir. Willowbrook State Sch., Staten Island, N.Y., 1972-74; med. dir. DeWitt Nursing Home, N.Y.C., 1976—; pvt. practice psychiatry, N.Y.C., 1973—. Treas. St. Bartholomew's Episcopal Ch., Hohokus, N.J. 1987. Mem. AMA, Am. Psychiat. Assn., Am. Assn. for Geriatric Psychiatry, Royal Coll. Psychiatrists. Republican. Home: 37 Sunrise Ln Saddle River NJ 07458-1631 Office: DeWitt Nursing Home 211 E 79th St New York NY 10021-0891

RISTINO, ROBERT J., public relations executive; b. Boston, Dec. 24, 1943; s. Arthur Ristino and Anna (Meneguzzi) Dunn; m. Mary Margaret Cummings, Sept. 21, 1965; children: Laurie Ann, Gaelin Elizabeth. BA, Northeastern U., 1966; MS, Boston U., 1980; PhD, U. Mass., 1991. News bur. editor Bentley Coll., Waltham, Mass., 1970-71; assoc. editor GE, Lynn, Mass., 1971; asst. dir. pub. rels. Salem (Mass.) Hosp., 1972-76; pvt. practice cons. Stoneham, Mass., 1976-78; dir. community rels. Mercy Hosp., Springfield, Mass., 1978-83; v.p. pub. affairs Leonard Morse Hosp., Natick, Mass., 1983-85; v.p. pub. rels. Intercare Health System, Worcester, Mass., 1985-88, The Med. Ctr. Cen. Mass., Worcester, 1988—. Contbr. articles profl. jours., 1985-90. Capt. U.S. Army, 1966-69. Avocations: astronomy, photography, running. Fellow Am. Soc. Hosp. Mktg. and Pub. Rels. (bd. dirs. 1990—); mem. New Eng. Hosp. Pub. Rels. and Mktg. (pres. 1988-90, award of excellence 1982, 1st pl. award ann. reports 1983, Evans Houghton Meml. award 1987, 1st pl. writing award 1990, 1st pl. ext. pubs. 1991), Pub. Rels. Soc. Am. (bd. dirs. Boston chpt. 1984, 91—). Office: The Med Ctr Cen Mass 281 Lincoln St Worcester MA 01605-2192

RISTORI, ALLAN JOHN, editor, author; b. Bklyn., June 1, 1936; s. John William and Catherine (Asaro) R.; m. Vivien Blohm, June 25, 1966 (div. 1967); m. Kathleen Johnson, Nov. 8, 1976; children: Sherilynn, Michael, Cynthia. BA cum laude, Colgate U., 1958. Mgmt. trainee W.T. Grant Co., Levittown, N.Y., 1958; salesman Harry C. Miller Co., N.Y.C., 1963-68; dir. field testing Garcia Corp., Teaneck, N.J., 1968-78; saltwater editor The Star-Ledger, Newark, 1984—; metro. editor Saltwater Sportsman, Boston, 1980—; inshore editor Fishing World, Floral Park, N.Y., 1976—; mem. Mid-Atlantic Fishery Mgmt. Coun., Dover, Del., 1977-80; capt. charter boat Sheri Berri II, Pt. Pleasant, N.J., 1984—. Author: Saltwater Fish Identifier, 1992, North American Saltwater Fishing, 1990, Fishing for Bluefish, 1984, 3d edit. 1990; contbr. numerous mag. and newspaper articles. Exec. dir. Emergency Com. to Save America's Marine Resources, Englewood Cliffs, N.J., 1972-76, Metro Fishing Classic, Manasquan Park, N.J., 1988—, Harbor Festival Fishing Rodeo, N.Y.C. Named Mako Marine Outdoor Writer of the Yr., 1983, Old Salt award N.J. Travel and Tourism Assn., 1978; winner Saltwater Mag. Article, Outdoor Writers Assn. Am., 1989. Mem. Am. Fishing Tackle Mfrs. Assn. (chmn. legis. com. 1976-78), Atlantic Profl. boatmens Assn. (exec. dir. 1980-85), Outdoor Writers Assn. Am., Rod and Gun Editors of Metro. N.Y., Point Pleasant Charter Boat Assn., Fedn. of Sportsmen's Clubs (hon. life mem.), Phi Beta Kappa. Republican. Roman Catholic. Home and Office: 1552 Osprey Ct Manasquan Park NJ 08736

RITCH, HERALD LAVERN, finance company executive; b. Los Angeles, Feb. 13, 1951; s. Herald Lester and Caroline (Lillevold) R.; m. Linda Suzanne Lundberg, June 11, 1972; children: Eleanor Loring, Seth Alden. BA in Econs., Stanford U., 1973; MBA, U. Pa., 1975. Assoc. Dean Witter Reynolds, Inc., N.Y.C., 1975-79, v.p., 1979-82, mng. dir., mgr. merger and acquisition dept., 1982-83; v.p. Kidder, Peabody & Co, Inc., N.Y.C., 1983-86, mng. dir., 1987-88; gen. ptnr. Freeman Spogli & Co., N.Y.C., 1988-90; managing dir. Donaldson Lufkin & Jenrette, N.Y.C., 1991—. Contbr. articles to profl. jours. Bd. dirs. Greenwich Assn. Retarded Citizens. Mem. Stanwich Club, Met. Club. Office: Donaldson Lufkin & Jenrette 140 Broadway New York NY 10005-1285

RITCH, THOMAS ALDEN, engineering executive; b. Freeport, Tex., July 26, 1955; s. Thomas Alden and Peggy Jean (Mullis) R.; m. Julie Jean Kestner, Aug. 15, 1987. BSEE, U. Tex., 1980; MBA, U. Phoenix, 1989-92. Design engr. Motorola, Austin, Tex., 1981-82, field apps. engr., 1982-83, hardware designer, 1983-84, project leader, 1985-87; mktg. mgr. Motorola, Tempe, Ariz., 1988-90, engring. mgr., 1990-91; product marketer Intel, Chandler, Ariz., 1987-88; dir. systems products Ross Tech., Austin, 1991; v.p. engring. Ironics, Inc., Ithaca, N.Y., 1991—. Republican. Episcopalian. Home: 100 Graham Rd #13F Ithaca NY 14850 Office: Ironics Inc 798 Cascadilla St Ithaca NY 14850

RITCHIE, DAVID MALCOLM, pharmacologist; b. Woodbury, N.J., Apr. 13, 1950; s. Malcolm Wood and Ruth Maryland (Stevens) R.; m. Deborah Ann Jones, Jan. 29, 1972; children: Christopher David, Jillian Shannon. AB, Rutgers U., 1972; MSc, Hahnemann U., 1974, PhD, 1976. Rsch. assoc. Med. Coll. Pa., Phila., 1976-78; from scientist to sr. scientist Ortho Pharm., Raritan, N.J., 1978-85; prin. scientist R.W. Johnson Pharm. Rsch. Inst., Raritan, 1985-91; rsch. fellow R.W. Johnson Pharm. Rsch. Inst., Rariton, 1991—. Contbr. articles to profl. jours.; patentee in field. Chmn. West Windsor (N.J.) Recreation Commn., 1988-89; coach West Windsor Soccer Assn., West Windson Little League, 1983—. Mem. Internat. Soc. Immunopharmacology, Am. Soc. Exptl. Therapeutics, N.Y. Acad. Scis., Inflammation Rsch. Assn., Am. Heart Assn. Home: 15 Scott Ave Princeton Junction NJ 08550-1022 Office: R W Johnson Pharm Rsch Inst RR 2 Raritan NJ 08869

RITCHIE, GARRY HARLAN, television broadcast executive; b. Earling, W.Va., Aug. 18, 1938; s. Edgar Harlan and Elsie Pearl (Meador) R.; m. Nancy Lee Gladwell, June 14, 1958; children: Arthur Harlan, Michael Lee. Student, U. Charleston, 1956-60; student, Baldwin-Wallace Coll., 1965; BA, Thomas Edison State Coll., 1979. Engr., reporter Sta. WTIP Radio, Charleston, W.Va., 1956-60; sta. mgr. Sta. WRON Radio, Ronceverte, W.Va., 1960-63; reporter, newscaster Stas. WDOK AM & FM Radio, Cleve., 1963-65, Sta. WHK AM & FM Radio, Cleve., 1965-67; reporter, assignment editor Scripps-Howard Broadcasting Co., Sta. WEWS-TV, Cleve., 1967-69; from news dir. to sta. mgr. Scripps-Howard Broadcasting Co., Sta. WEWS-TV, 1969-82; cable news mgr. corp. office Scripps-Howard Broadcasting Co., Westport, Conn., 1982-83; asst. gen. mgr. Scripps-Howard Broadcasting Co., Sta. WCPO-TV, Cin., 1983-84; v.p., gen. mgr. Diversified Communications, Sta. WCJB-TV, Gainesville, Fla., 1984-86, Diversified Communications, Sta. WYOU-TV, Scranton, Pa., 1986-91; pres. broadcast div. Diversified Communications, Portland, Maine, 1991—. Bd. dirs. Hippodrome Theatre, Gainesville, 1985-86, Vol. Ctr. Alachua County, Gainesville, 1985-86, Crimetrac Gainesville, Fla., 1985-86, Police Adv. Commn., Gainesville, 1985-86, Barnett Bank Alachua County, Gainesville, 1986, Scranton chpt. ARC, 1988-91, Better Bus. Bur. Northeast Pa., Scranton, 1988-91, United Way Lackawanna County, Scranton, 1989-91; bd. dirs., v.p. Girls Club Alachua County, Gainesville, 1985-86; mem. adv. bd. Scranton Area Found., 1989-91; trustee Keystone Jr. Coll. Laplume, Pa., 1991-92. Recipient 5 Emmy awards Cleve. chpt. NATAS, 1973-80. Mem. Nat. Assn. Broadcasters, Nat. Assn. TV Programming Execs., Pa. Assn. Broadcasters (bd. dirs. 1989-91), Greater Scranton C. of C. (bd. dirs. 1987-90), Downtown Scranton Bus. Assn. (bd. dirs. 1989-91), Rotary (bd. dirs. Scranton 1989-91), Rotary Club Portland (Maine). Republican. Methodist. Home: 14 Hemlock Dr Cumberland Center ME 04021-9586 Office: Diversified Communications 5 Milk St Portland ME 04101-4170

RITCHIE, J. MURDOCH, pharmacologist; b. Aberdeen, Scotland, June 10, 1925; came to U.S. 1956; s. Alexander Farquharson and Agnes Jane (Bremner) R.; m. Brenda Rachel Bigland; children: Alasdair J., A. Jocelyn. BSc, Aberdeen (Scotland) U., 1944, U. Coll. London, 1949; PhD, U. Coll. London, 1952, DSc, 1960; MA, Yale U., 1968; DSc, Aberdeen U., 1987. Lectr. physiology U. Coll. London, 1949-51; sci. staff Nat. Inst. Med. Rsch., London, 1951-55; asst. prof. to prof. Albert Einstein Coll. Medicine, N.Y.C., 1954-63, prof. pharmacology, 1963-68; prof. and chmn. pharmacology Yale U., New Haven, 1968-74, dir. biol. scis., 1975-78, prof. pharmacology, 1968—. Contbr. articles to profl. jours.; editor sci. books and jours. Fellow Royal Soc., Univ. Coll. London. Home: 47 Deepwood Dr Hamden CT 06517-3414 Office: Yale Univ Sch Medicine 333 Cedar St New Haven CT 06510-3289

RITCHIE, ROYAL DANIEL, economic development executive; b. Takoma Park, Md., Dec. 28, 1945; s. Thomas Joseph and Dorothy Queen (Royal) R.; m. Karen Louise Turner; children: Matthew, Jessica, Heather. Student Glassboro State U., 1965-66, Columbia Union Coll., 1966-67. V.p., dir. Assoc. Developers Internat., Inc., Washington, 1968-75, Internat. Fin. and Mgmt. Corp., Washington, 1975-77; project mgr. Sheraton Corp., Washington, 1977-78; v.p. East Balt. Developers, Inc., 1979-82, East Balt. Contractors, Inc., 1979-82; dir. econ. devel. East Balt. Community Corp., 1979-82, Stouffer Harbor Place Hotel, Balt., 1986-88, project mgr., 1988—; dir. devel. Somerset House, Inc., 1982-86; mng. gen. ptnr. HFA Homes for Ams.; ltd. ptnr. C & R Contracting Assocs.; pres. RDR Contracting Assn., Inc.; pres. Hanlon Park Condominimum Assn., Inc. , 1st v.p. Prince George's Rep. Club, 1982-85; chmn. Com. for Better Govt., Riverdale, Md., 1984—; mem. 22d legis. dist. Md. State Rep. Cen. Com., 1982-86; 2d v.p. Prince George's County Civic Fedn., Inc., 1984, pres. 1985-86, 88; chmn. Quality Health Care Action Com., Inc. Mem. Am. Concrete Inst. (com. on rehabilitation, repair of concrete com.), Montgomery County C. of C. (econ. devel. com.), Prince George's County Bd. Trade, Balt. Coun. on Fgn. Affairs, Lions (v.p. Riverdale club). Adventist. Home: 4715 Oliver St Riverdale MD 20737-2040 Office: Somerset House Inc 5610 Wisconsin Ave Chevy Chase MD 20815

RITTENBACH, KAREN JOAN, chemical engineer; b. Colorado Springs, Colo., May 20, 1959; d. James Francis and Mary Ann (Roman) McGuire; m. Klaus Hermann Rittenbach, May 2, 1987. BS in Chem. Engring., Rutgers U., 1981. Product engr. E.I. DuPont de Nemours & Co., Parlin, N.J., 1981-83, supr., 1983-84, prodn. supr., 1984-86, product mgr., 1986-89, rsch. engr., 1989-90, with tech. field sales, 1990-91, ops. supr Rsch. Lab., 1991; staff rsch. engr., master scheduler DuPont Imaging Systems, Parlin, 1992—. Vol. speaker career days, local schs. Recipient Corp. Accomplishment awards for CSL-film, 1986, He-Ne laser film, 1987, Color Symposium, 1989, CSF Films, 1990. Mem. NAFE, Soc. Imaging Sci. and Tech., Mensa, Sierra Club. Office: Dupont Imaging Systems Rsch Cheesequake Rd Parlin NJ 08859-1039

RITTER, ANN L., lawyer; b. N.Y.C., May 20, 1933; d. Joseph and Grace (Goodman) R. B.A., Hunter Coll., 1954; J.D., N.Y. Law Sch., 1970; postgrad. Law Sch., NYU, 1971-72. Bar: N.Y. 1971, U.S. Ct. Appeals (2d cir.) 1975, U.S. Supreme Ct. 1975. Writer, 1954-70; editor, 1955-66; tchr., 1966-70; atty. Am. Soc. Composers, Authors and Pubs., N.Y.C., 1971-72, Greater N.Y. Ins. Co., N.Y.C., 1973-74; sr. ptnr. Brenhouse & Ritter, N.Y.C., 1974-78; sole practice, N.Y.C., 1978—. Editor N.Y. Immigration News, 1975-76. Mem. ABA, Am. Immigration Lawyers Assn. (treas. 1983-84, sec. 1984-85, vice chair 1985-86, chair 1986-87, chair program com. 1989-90, chair speakers bur. 1989-90, chair media liaison 1989-90), N.Y. State Bar Assn., N.Y. County Lawyers Assn., Assn. Trial Lawyers Am., N.Y. State Trial Lawyers Assn., N.Y.C. Bar Assn., Watergate East Assn. (v.p., asst. treas. 1990—). Democrat. Jewish. Home: 47 E 87th St New York NY 10128-1005 Office: 420 Madison Ave New York NY 10017

RITTER, CARL ALAN, pharmacology educator; b. Confluence, Pa., Jan. 23, 1932; s. John M. and Louise (Frantz) R.; m. Jeanette; 1 child, Alan. Diploma, The Manlius Sch., N.Y., 1950; AB, Syracuse U., 1955; PhD in Pharmacology, SUNY, 1964. Teaching and rsch. fellow in pharmacology N.Y. State, 1957-60; predoctoral fellow in pharmacology USPHS, 1960-64; postdoctoral fellow in biophysics U. Pa./Johnson Rsch. Found., Phila., 1963-66; asst. prof. of pharmacology Sch. of Vet. Medicine/U. Pa., Phila., 1966-71, head, lab of pharmacology, 1968-71, assoc. prof. pharmacology, 1972—; advanced tng. dept. anatomy U. Pa., 1982-83, advanced tng. dept. pathobiology, 1989-90; Fogarty internat. fellow USPHS/Inst. of Pathology/Karolinska Inst., Stockholm, Sweden, 1967. Patentee in field. Recipient grants Pa. Dept. Agr., 1991—, U. Pa. Rsch. Found., 1991-92. Home: 27 N Elm Ave Clifton Heights PA 19018-4103

RITTER, DONALD LAWRENCE, congressman, engineer; b. N.Y.C., Oct. 21, 1940; s. Frank and Ruth R.; m. Edith Duerksen; children: Jason, Kristina. B.S. in Metall. Engring., Lehigh U., 1961; M.S. in Phys. Metallurgy, MIT, 1963, Sc.D., 1966. Mem. faculty Calif. State Poly. U., also contract cons. Gen. Dynamics Co., 1968-69; mem. faculty dept. metallurgy and materials scis., asst. to v.p. for research Lehigh U., 1969-76; mgr. research program devel., 1976-79; mem. 96th-102d congresses from 15th Pa. dist., 1979—; mem. energy and commerce com. and subcoms. telecommunications and fin.; ranking minority mem. transp. and hazardous materials; mem. sci., space and tech. com. and subcoms. environment and tech. and competitiveness; chmn. house Rep. task force on tech. and policy; co-chair Cngl. High Tech. Caucus; ranking minority mem. house Commn. on Security and Cooperation in Europe (Helsinki Commn.), mem. since 1980—; co-chmn. ad hoc com. on Baltic states and Ukraine; treas. Congl. steel caucus; mem. Congl. textile and apparel caucus; mem. Am. Security Council; mem. environ. and energy study conf.; sci. exchange fellow U.S. Nat. Acad. Scis.-Soviet Acad. Sci., Baikov Inst., Moscow, 1967-68. Contbr. articles to sci. and engring. jours. Bd. dirs. Nat. Metric Council, Baum Art Sch. of Allentown Art Mus., Bach Choir Bethlehem, Pa.; ex officio mem. bd. assocs. Muhlenberg Coll., Allentown; mem. polit. sci vis. com. MIT, Cambridge; mem. adv. com. Combat Pilots Assn. Recipient Taxpayers' Best Friend award Nat. Taxpayers Union, Guardian of Small Bus. awards Nat. Fedn. Independent Bus., 1979—, Award for disting. pub. svc. IEEE, 1990; hon. mem. Fraternal Order Police, Good Shepherd Home for Elderly. Fellow Am. Inst. Chemists (honor scroll award); mem. NSPE, ASM (disting. life), ASME, Pa. Soc. Profl. Engrs., Tri-Boro Sportsmen Assn. , Lehigh County Farmers Assn., Sigma Xi, Tau Beta Pi, Pi Mu Epsilon. Unitarian. Lodges: Elks, Masons. Home: Upper Saucon Township Coopersburg PA 18036 Office: 2202 Rayburn House Office Bldg Washington DC 20515

RITTER, MALCOLM FRANK, science writer; b. St. Paul, Aug. 3, 1954; s. Winfield Arthur and Mary Jean (Thompson) R.; m. Jane Margaret Wilson, Sept. 5, 1982; children: Matthew Wilson, Scott MacArthur. BA summa cum laude, U. Minn., 1976. Reporter, columnist Bismarck (N.D.) Tribune, 1976-

79; reporter Rapid City (S.D.) Jour., 1979-84; sci. writer AP, N.Y.C., 1984—. Chmn. bd. trustees Chelsea Community Ch., N.Y.C., 1986-89. Fellow Knight Ctr. Specialized Journalism, 1989, 91. Mem. Nat. Assn. Sci. Writers, Phi Beta Kappa. Office: AP 50 Rockefeller Pla New York NY 10020

RITTER, ROBERT JOSEPH, lawyer; b. N.Y.C., Aug. 11, 1925; s. Robert Reinhart and Mary (Mandracchia) R.; m. Barbara Willis Foust, Oct. 1, 1955 (div. May 1977); children: Robert Thornton, Jan Willis Ritter Kelly, Nancy Carol Ritter dePoortere. Student, Bklyn. Poly. Inst., 1943; BA cum laude, Queens Coll., 1949; JD, NYU, 1953, LLM in Internat. Law, 1955. Bar: N.Y. 1953. Acct. UN Secretariat, N.Y.C., 1949-54; asst. counsel RCA Corp., N.Y.C., 1955-58; atty. CIBA-GEIGY Corp., Ardsley, N.Y., 1958-60, AT&T Bell Tel. Labs., Inc., Murray Hill, N.J., 1960-70; tax atty. AT&T Techs., Inc., N.Y.C., 1970-85; mgr. fin. AT&T Corp. Hdqrs., Parsippany, N.J., 1985-87; asst. sec. 14 subs. telephone cos. AT&T, 1985-87; v.p. CPPS Tax Cons., N.Y.C., 1987—. Contbr. articles to legal jours. Pres. Harry B. Thayer chpt. Tel. Pioneers Am., N.Y.C., 1983-84; trustee, sec. United Way Cen. N.J., Milltown, 1989—, chmn. community div. govt. rels. coms., 1990—; corp. program dir. Vol. Action Ctr. of Middlesex County, N.J., 1988; mem. adv. bd. Dept. Human Svcs., State of N.J., 1991—; mem. adv. coun. Project Resources, State of N.J., 1987—; bd. dirs. Somerset Hillis YMCA, Bernardsville, N.J., 1971-73, Greater Raritan Pvt. Industry Coun., New Brunswick, N.J., 1989—; Dem. cand. N.Y. State Assembly, Westchester County, N.Y., 1965; chmn. Am. Cancer Soc. Fund Drive, Bronxville, N.Y., 1964. With USAAF, 1943-46. Recipient Crusade award Am. Cancer Soc., 1965, Masonic Svc. award, 1947, Am. Legion Citizenship award, 1943, Vol. of Yr. award United Way, 1991. Mem. ABA (sr. lawyers div. 1990—), Nat. Tax Assn.-Tax Inst. Am. (chmn., advisor state sales and use taxation com. 1984-88, chmn. prodn. exemption subcom. 1978-84), Nat. Eagle Scout Assn., Assn. of Bar of City of N.Y., Internat. Platform Assn., Legal Aid Soc., NYU Law Alumni Assn., Perth Amboy (N.J.) C. of C. (exec. dir. 1988-89), Rossmoor Tennis Club (pres. 1987-88), Church of N.Y. Club, Kiwanis (1st v.p. 1970-71), Sigma Alpha. Democrat. Episcopalian. Home: 3-N Village Mall Jamesburg NJ 08831-1534 Office: CPPS Tax Cons Yorkville Sta PO Box 7022 New York NY 10128-0010

RITTER, WILLIAM FREDERICK, civil and agricultural engineering educator; b. Stratford, Ontario, Canada, Mar. 25, 1942; came to U.S., 1966.; s. John Louis and Norma Willehmine (Foerster) R.; m. Carol-Anne Gertrude Turner, June 25, 1966; children: John WIlliam, Amy Lynn. BSA, U. Guelph (Ontario), 1965; BAS, U. Toronto, 1966; MS, Iowa State U., 1968, PhD, 1971. Rsch. assoc. Iowa State U., Ames, 1966-71; asst. prof. U. Del., Newark, 1971-77, assoc. prof., 1977-82, prof., 1982—; owner Ritter Engring., Elkton, Md., 1984—; sr. engr. Environ. Cons. Internatl, Broadkill Beach, Del., 1991—. Editor: Irrigation and Drainage, 1991; contbr. over 190 articles to profl. jours. and tech. reports. Pres. Newark Day Nursery, 1984-86. Recipient Superior Achievement award U.S. EPA, Phila., 1979; Salzberg fellow U. Del., 1987. Mem. ASCE, Am. Soc. Agrl. Engrs. (Young Engr. of Yr., 1981, Country Side Engring. Award, 1988), Am. Water Works Engrs. Assn., Water Pollution Control Fedn. Lutheran. Home: 63 Papermill Rd Elkton MD 21921-3518 Office: U Del Newark DE 19717

RITTERMAN, JUDITH LYNN, social services administrator, consultant. BA in Elem. Edn., CUNY, 1970; MS in Clin. Mental Health Counseling, L.I. U., 1980; postgrad., SUNY, Stony Brook, 1978-79. Dir., family therapist Community Family Growth Svcs., Holbrook, N.Y., 1980—; adj. faculty mem. dept. counseling L.I. U., 1989—; cons. Brookhaven Hosp., Patchogue, N.Y., 1981-84, Ileitis/Colitis Group, 1983, Marital Crisis Ctr., NOW, Bay Shore, N.Y., 1981-82; supr., instr., lectr. Community Family Growth Svcs., Holbrook, 1983—; cons. clin. supr. Family Cons. Svcs., Bay Shore, 1985-87, Youth Environ. Svcs., Massapequa, N.Y., 1987—, employee assistance prog. Town of Islip, N.Y., 1987—, Luth. Community Svcs., Hauppauge, 1986—; grad. student internship supr. dept. counseling L.I. U., Brookville, N.Y., 1986—; lectr. in field. Contbr. articles to profl. jours. Pres. Open Door Soc. of L.I., 1975-76; mem. youth bd. Town of Islip, 1979-80; chairperson bd. dirs. Holbrook Youth Devel. Corp., 1977-78; mem. ctr. on volunteerism Adelphi U., 1978-82; mem. comprehensive planning com. Suffolk County Youth Bd., 1979-81; mem. mental health planning com. Suffolk County Youth Bur., 1980-81. Recipient C. Eugene Morris Outstanding Alumnus award, L.I. U. Mem. AACD, N.Y. State Mental Health Counselors Assn. (pres.-elect), N.Y. Assn. Counselor Educators and Suprs., Internat. Assn. Marriage and Family Counselors (co-founder N.Y. chpt., ethics com. 1991), Am. Assn. Marriage and Family Therapists (clin. mem./approved supr., edn. and tng. coun.), Am. Mental Health Counselors Assn. (Profl. Svc. award 1992), N.Y. State Assn. for Counseling and Devel. (regional v.p., exec. bd. 1989), Assn. Counselor Educators and Suprs., Western Suffolk Counselor's Assn.

RITTNER, CARL FREDERICK, educational administrator; b. Boston, Feb. 28, 1914; s. Philip and Augusta (Beich) R.; m. Eunice Carin, 1940; 1 child, Stephen. BS in Edn., Boston U., 1936, EdM, 1937. Ednl. cons. Boston, 1940's; founder, dir. Rittners Floral Sch., Boston, 1947—. Coauthor: Flowers for the Modern Bride, 1965, Arrangements for All Occasions, 1966, Flowers for the Modern Bride (In Living Color), 1968, Rittner's Silver Anniversary Book, 1972, Dried Arrangements, 1978, Rittners Guide to Permanent Flower Arranging, 1978, Vase Arrangements for the Professional Florist, 1979, Christmas Designs, 1979, Flowers for Funerals, 1980, Manual of Wedding Design Styles, 1980, Contemporary Floral Designs, 1983, Floral Designs for That Special Occasion, 1985, Inexpensive Bread & Butter Designs, 1986. Mem. Am. Floral Svcs., Soc. Am. Florists, Florist Transworld Delivery Svc., Teleflora, Phi Delta Kappa. Office: 345 Marlborough St Boston MA 02115

RITZER, LONNIE MARK, lawyer; b. N.Y.C., Oct. 13, 1954; s. Aaron and Florence (Miller) R.; m. Allyn Susan Feinstein, Mar. 12, 1983. BS in Acctg., Bklyn. Coll., 1976; JD, Md. Law Sch., 1979. Bar: Md. 1979, U.S. Dist. Ct. Md. 1979, U.S. Tax Ct. 1979. Assoc. Gordon Feinblatt, Balt., 1979-86, ptnr., 1986-87; ptnr. Shapiro and Olander, Balt., 1987—; panelist Md. Sales and Use Tax for Nat. Bus. Inst., Tax Aspects of Partnership Agreements Seminar, 1987-92, Taxation for Md. Corps., 1990, Md. Ltd. Liability Co. for Md. Inst. for Continuing Profl. Edn. of Lawyers. Contbr. articles to profl. jours. Mem. Balt. Assn. of Tax Counsel (pres. 1990-91). Home: 6 Dyson Dan Ct Reisterstown MD 21136-1847 Office: Shapiro and Olander 36 S Charles St Baltimore MD 21201-3020

RITZMAN, THOMAS ALEXANDER, obstetrician-gynecologist; b. Mayaguez, P.R., Feb. 18, 1914; s. Ernest Gregory and Lois (Alexander) R.; m. Jane Montgomery Lucey, Feb. 15, 1941 (div. May 1990); children: Thomas J., Martha J., Paul J.; m. Hannah Criste, Apr. 5, 1991. BA, Yale U., 1936; MD, Harvard U., 1940. Lic. physician, N.H. Obstetrician-gynecologist Concord (N.H.) Hosp., 1946-80; med. hypnoanalyst Am. Acad. Med. Hypnoanalysts, 1973—. Contbr. articles to profl. jours. Republican. Office: 553 Rte 3A Bow NH 03304

RIVARD, PAUL EDMUND, museum director; b. Sanford, Maine, Aug. 21, 1943; s. Joseph Paul and Claire Rachael (Demers) R.; B.A., U. Maine, 1965; postgrad. Clark U., Worcester, Mass., 1965-66; M.A., SUNY, 1967, postgrad. Cooperstown Grad. program, 1966-67; m. Suk Hi Lee, Jan. 14, 1970; children—Sonya Lee, Christopher Lee. Supr. interpepation Mystic (Conn.) Seaport, 1967; dir. Slater Mill Historic Site, Pawtucket, R.I., 1969-74; dir. Rockwell Corning Mus., Corning, N.Y., 1974-77, Maine State Mus., Augusta, 1977-91; dir. Mus. Am. Textile History, North Andover, Mass., 1991—; cons. in field. Served with U.S. Army, 1967-69. Recipient Jaycee Outstanding Young Man award, Pawtucket, 1973. Mem. Am. Assn. Mus., Am. Assn. State and Local History, Soc. Indsl. Archeology. Author: Pawtucket at 300, 1971, Guidebook to the Slater Mill Historic Site, 1972, Samuel Slater, 1973, Weaving Exhibition Catalogue, 1974, The Painter's West, 1976, Made in Maine, 1985, Lion, 1987, Maine Sawmills, 1991. Office: Mus Am Textile History 800 Massachusetts Ave North Andover MA 01845

RIVARD, WILLIAM CHARLES, mechanical engineering educator; b. Detroit, Sept. 2, 1942; s. William John and Ruby Marie (Theel) R.; m. Betty L. Slocum, Nov. 21, 1964; children: Michele, Traci. BS, U. Detroit, 1965, MS, 1966; PhD, Ill. Inst. Tech., 1968. Staff mem. explosive systems div. Los Alamos (N.Mex.) Nat. Lab., 1968-71, assoc. group leader theoretical div., 1971-80; v.p., co-owner Flow Sci., Inc., Los Alamos, 1980-87; Arthur O. Willey prof. mech. engring. U. Maine, Orono, 1987—; pres. Fluid Systems, Inc., East Holden, Maine, 1988—; cons. Exxon Rsch. Ctr., Florham Park, N.J., 1989—, Superconducting Supercollider Lab., Dallas, 1989—, Aerospatiale, Les Mereaux, France, 1989—, Technischer Uberwachungs-Verein, Hanover, Fed. Republic of Germany, 1985-88. Contbr. articles to profl. jours. Grad. fellow NSF, 1967, NASA, 1968. Office: U Maine Mech Engring Dept Orono ME 04469

RIVELLI, WILLIAM RAYMOND ALLAN, photographer; b. Providence, May 10, 1935; s. William and Virginia C. (Capece) R.; m. Margaret A. Cronin, June 2, 1963 (dec. 1973); children: William Dante, Sarah Kerry; m. Cynthia Jean Lepore, Sept. 7, 1974; 1 child, Taylor Elia. BA, Brown U., 1957. Asst. to photographer Life Mag., N.Y.C., 1959-60, 1960-61; photographer Rivelli Photography, N.Y.C., 1963—; instr. Sch. Visual Arts, N.Y.C., 1991—. Subject/photographer profile and portfolio Communications Art, 1982; dir. photography, photographer multi-media slide presentation Naked Chambers, 1987; chosen contbr.: American Photography, 1990; artist, photographer exhbn. Cathedral Portfolio, 1991-92; exhibited in groups shows Art Dirs. Club Exhbns., N.Y., N.J., Mass., Can., 1976-86, Advt. Photographers Awards Ann. Exhbn., 1991; photographer ann. report Meade Corp., N.Y., 1974, Ad Club, Chgo., 1976. Recipient Cert. of Excellence award Art Dirs. Club, 1976-82, Creativity Cert. of Excellence award Art. Dir. Mag., 1976-77. Mem. Am. Soc. Mag. Photographers (nat. bd. dirs. 1987-89, participant Kodak Traveling Exhbn. 1986-87), Am. Inst. Graphic Arts, Advt. Photographers Am. (participant Kodak Exhbn. 1989, Ann. Book award 1991), Indsl. Photographers Assn. (bd. dirs. 1979-80). Office: 303 Park Ave S Apt 508 New York NY 10010

RIVERA, EIDA LUZ, educator; b. Fajardo, P.R., June 5, 1957; d. Angel Luis and Nylda Luz (Roman) Carmona; m. Juan Antonio Rivera, Nov. 12, 1982; 1 child, Juan Antonio Jr. BS, L.I. U., Bklyn., 1979, MS, 1984. Cert. tchr., N.Y. Tchr. Bedford Stuyvesant Early Childhood Ctr., Bklyn., 1978-82, Bklyn. Sch. Dist., 1982—; tutor Faculty Tutoring Svc., N.Y.C., 1988—; home instr. tchr. Mem. NAFE, ASCD, Assn. for Supervision and Curriculum Devel. Home: 1434 E 88th St Brooklyn NY 11236-5120 Office: PS 28 1001 Herkimer St Brooklyn NY 11233-3120

RIVERIN, BRUNO, financial center executive; b. Chicoutimi, Que., Can., Mar. 29, 1941. BSEE, Laval U., Que., 1966; MBA in Fin., U. Sherbrooke, Que., 1970; postgrad., U. Paris, 1971. Sales engr. Esso and Gentec, Toronto and Montreal, 1966-68; analyst Air Can., Montreal, 1968-71; fin. analyst Caisse de dépôt et placement du Québec, Montreal, 1971; account officer, asst. to sr. v.p. Mercantile Bank, Montreal, 1971-77; v.p. fin., adminstrn. Fédération des Caisses Populaires Desjardins de Montréal de l'Ouest-du-Québec (Desjardins Group), Montreal, 1977-80; pres., chief operating officer Caisse centrale Desjardins, Montreal, 1980-87; pres., chief exec. officer The Montreal Exch., 1987—; deputy gov. Can. Investor Protection Fund, 1987—; chmn. Internat. Fin. Ctrs. Orgn. of Montreal (IFCOM), 1988—. Bd. dirs. Ste-Justine Hosp. Found., Montreal, 1988—, Armand-Frappier Found., Montreal, 1988—, Can. Securities Inst., 1991—, Que. Aeronautical Tng. Centre, Chicoutimi, 1991—. Mem. C.D. Howe Inst. (Que. div.), Ordre des ingénieurs du Québec, French C. of C., Laval U. and Sherbrooke U. Alumnae Assn., St. Denis Club, Montreal Amateur Athletic Assn., Richelieu Golf Club. Office: Montreal Exch, 800 Victoria Sq PO Box 61, Montreal, PQ Canada H4Z 1A9

RIVERS, CARYL ANN, journalist, educator; b. Washington, Dec. 19, 1937; d. Hugh Francis and Helen (Huhn) R.; m. Alan Lupo, May 20, 1962; children: Steven, Alyssa. AB in History, Trinity Coll., Washington, 1959; MS in Journalism, Columbia U., 1960. Feature writer L.I. Press, Jamaica, N.Y., 1960-61; feature editor Middletown (N.Y.) Record, 1961-62; corr. Washington El Mundo, San Juan, P.R., 1961-66; free-lance writer Winthrop, Mass., 1966-90; prof. journalism Boston U., 1974—. Author: Virgins, 1984, Girls Forever Brave and True, 1986, Occasional Sins, 1987, Intimate Enemies, 1988, Indecent Behavior, 1990, More Joy Than Rage: Crossing Generations with the New Feminism, 1991; co-author: (with Grace Baruch and Rosalind Barnett) Lifeprints, 1983, Beyond Sugar and Spice, 1979, (with Alan Lupo) For Better, For Worse, 1981; screenwriter: (TV dramas) The Cheats, 1989 (Am. Scene award AFTRA, 1989), A Matter of Principal, 1990 (Gabriel award Nat Assn. Cath. Broadcasters 1990); creative cons. (TV drama) Jenny's Song, 1988; writer-in-residence The Washington Star, 1976; contbr. numerous articles to mags., including N.Y. Times mag., Saturday Review, Ms., Rolling Stone, The Nation, Mother Jones, Mc Calls, Glamour, Working Woman, Ladies Home Jour., Woman's Day, Redbook, and to newspapers, including L.A. Times, Boston Globe, Washington Post, Balt. Sun. Bd. dirs. Ford Hall Forum, Boston. Recipient Yankee Quill award New Eng. chpt. Assn. Profl. Journalists, 1989; named Best Columnist, New Eng. Women's Press Assn., 1979, Best Mag. Writer, 1978. Mem. NOW (bd. dirs. Legal and Ednl. Def. Fund), Writers Guild (screenwriters div.), Internat. Women's Forum. Democrat. Office: Boston U 640 Commonwealth Ave Boston MA 02215-2422

RIVERS, KENNETH JAY, judicial administrator, consultant; b. N.Y.C., Feb. 13, 1938; s. Alexander Maximillian and Albertina Ray (Gay) R.; m. Leah B. Files, Sept. 21, 1957 (div.); children: Londa Denise, Nancy Laura, Terrie Ruth, Kenneth J. Jr. AAS in Criminal Justice, St. Francis Coll., Bklyn., 1978, BS in Criminal Justice, 1978; MPA, L.I. Univ., 1981. Correction officer N.Y.C. Dept. Correction, 1965-69; ct. officer N.Y. State Unified Ct. System, N.Y.C., 1969-71, asst. ct. clk., 1971-73, sr. ct. clk., 1973-85, assoc. ct. clk., 1985-88, prin. ct. clk., 1988-90, dep. chief clk., 1991—; tng. instr. N.Y. State Unified Ct. System, N.Y.C., 1985—, pers. assessor, 1985—; lectr. John Jay Coll. NYU, N.Y.C., 1987. Author: Juvenile Crime Survey, 1982, New York State Jury Selection, 1984. Bd. dirs. Parkway Consumers Med. Coun., Bklyn., 1983—, Cen. Bklyn. Tenant's Rights, 1988—. Recipient Leadership award Tribune Soc., N.Y. State Cts., 1987, Svc. award, 1988, Cert. of Merit award Fedn. Afro-Am. Civil Svc. Orgns., 1987. Mem. ASPA, Internat. Pers. Mgmt. Assn., Acad. Polit. Sci., Conf. Minority Pub. Adminstrs., Masons. Democrat. Methodist. Office: NY State Family Ct 60 Lafayette St New York NY 10013-4048

RIVERS, PAMELA SUSAN, consultant, banker, journalist; b. N.Y.C., Mar. 11, 1966; d. Harry Karl and Susan Ann (Reid) R. BS, St. John's U., 1989. Ptnr. PT Prodns., N.Y.C., 1989—; quality assurance mgr. Chemical, N.Y.C., 1989—; asst. coord. Mark Jackson Celebrity Games (N.Y. Knicks), N.Y.C., 1988—; owner Dimples, Inc., Cambria Heights, N.Y., 1990—; asst. coord., dancer Yo MTV Raps, N.Y.C., 1990. Recipient Outstanding Leadership award St. John's, 1987-88, Am. Poetry award Am. Poetry Anthology. Mem. Delta Sigma Theta (treas. 1986-88, fundraising chairwoman), Phi Chi Theta.

RIVET, DIANA WITTMER, lawyer, developer; b. Auburn, N.Y., Apr. 28, 1931; d. George Wittmer and Anne (Jenkins) Wittmer Hauswirth; m. Paul Henry Rivet, Oct. 24, 1952; children: Gail, Robin, Leslie, Heather, Clayton, Eric. BA, Keuka Coll., 1951; JD, Bklyn. Law Sch., 1956. Bar: N.Y. 1956, U.S. Dist. Ct. (ea. and so. dists.) N.Y. 1975. Sole practice, Orangeburg, N.Y., 1957—; county atty. Rockland County (N.Y.), 1974-77; asst. to legis. chmn. Rockland County, 1978-79; counsel, adminstr. Indsl. Devel. Agy., Rockland County, 1980-91, Rockland Econ. Devel. Corp., 1981-90; counsel, exec. dir. Pvt. Industry Coun. Rockland County, 1980-90; pres., chief exec. officer Environ. Mgmt. Ltd., Orangeburg, 1980—; mem. air mgmt. adv. com. N.Y. State Dept. Environ. Conservation 1984—; pres. Indoor Enviroment Ltd. Pres. Rockland County coun. Girl Scouts U.S., 1981-84; chmn. Rockland County United Way campaign, 1983-84, 88-89, bd. dirs. 1988—, Rockland County Assn., West Nyack, 1981—, Leadership Rockland. Recipient Community Svc. award Keuka Coll., 1965, Disting. Svc. award Town of Orangetown, 1970, Disting. Svc. award Rockland County, 1989, Econ. Devel. award Rockland Econ. Devel. Corp., 1990; named Businessperson of Yr., Jour. News, Rockland County, 1982. Mem. ABA, N.Y. State Bar Assn. (mcpl. law sect. exec. com. 1976-83, environ. law sect. exec. com. 1974-86). Democrat. Mem. Religious Soc. of Friends. Home: 1 Lester Dr Orangeburg NY 10962

RIVIN, DONALD, chemist; b. Bklyn., Oct. 5, 1934; s. Solomon and Anne (Duberstein) R.; m. Marcia Toby Siegel, Aug. 19, 1956; children: Nancy, Alissa, Russell, Rachel. BA, Columbia U., 1955, MA, 1957, PhD, 1960. Researcher Cabot Corp., Billerica, Mass., 1959-74, dir. fine particle tech. dept., 1974-80, corp. rsch. fellow, 1980-88, mgr. environ. health, 1980-88; sect. chief materials U.S. Army Natick (Mass.) Rsch., Devel. and Engring. Ctr., 1988—; chmn. Environ. Health Com., 1978-81; cons. Health Effects Inst., Cambridge, Mass., 1985—; invited lectr. NATO Advanced Study Inst., 1979, Gordon Rsch. Conf. Elastomers, 1982. Contbr. articles to profl. jours. Pres. Lake Watershed Assn., Mass., 1970-76; chmn. Regional Resource Recovery Coun., Mass., 1978-80. Grantee rsch. NSF; recipient Best Paper award rubber div. ACS, 1975. Mem. AAAS, Internat. Union Pure and Applied Chemistry, Am. Carbon Soc. (exec. com. 1985—), Catalyst Soc. New Eng., Am. Chem. Soc., Sigma Xi, Phi Lambda Upsilon. Jewish. Office: US Army Rsch Devel and Engring Ctr Natick MA 01760-5019

RIVINUS, FRANCIS MARKOE, business executive; b. Phila., Aug. 19, 1915; s. Francis and Lillian (Megary) R.; m. Anne Hutchins, June 25, 1938; children: Timothy, Sarah Lowndes, Susanna, Judith, Mark, Mary. Grad., Noble and Greenough Sch., 1933; student, Heidelberg Coll., Germany, 1933; AB, Harvard U., 1938. Clk., agt. Pa. R.R., Penn. Mut. Life Ins. Co., 1938; pres. Smith Kline * French Labs., Phila., 1938-68; v.p., pres. internat. div. Chesbrough-Ponds, 1968-69; pres. Internat. House Phila., 1970, Schuylkill Valley Nature Ctr., Phila., 1983, 78; dir. Girard Co., Girard Trust Bank, Phila., 1973-78; devel. officer Phila. Zool. Soc., 1973, 78. Comdr. USNR. Decorated Legion of Merit, Naval Unit Citation. Mem. Order Brit. Empire, Ind. Hall Assn. (dir.), Harvard Club (Phila.). Home: 201 W Evergreen Ave Apt 604 Philadelphia PA 19118-3829

RIXON, JAMES MICHAEL, bank officer; b. Elizabeth, N.J., Jan. 18, 1945; s. Joseph Samuel Rixon and Maizie Marie (Amidon) Kusky; m. Nancy Lynn Fulton, Oct. 17, 1981; 1 child, Joseph Ryan. BS, Lincoln Meml. U., 1969; local pastors degree, Drew U., Madison, N.J., 1986; postgrad., Wesley Theol. Sem., Washington, 1987—, U. Del., 1989-91, Ea. Theol. Sem., Phila., 1990—. Tchr. Elkton City Schs., Elkton, Md., 1969-70; tchr. Parma City Schs., Parma, Ohio, 1970-71; managerial trainee Suburban Trust Co., Westfield, N.J., 1971-72; various banking positions United Counties Trust Co., Elizabeth, N.J., 1972-77; asst. br. mgr. United Counties Trust Co., 1977-79, First Fidelity Bank/South Jersey, Burlington, N.J., 1979-81; br. adminstr. First Fidelity Bank/South Jersey, 1981-82, asst. credit mgr., 1982-85, head comml. credit dept., 1985-92; br. mgr. 1st Fidelity Bank, Ocean City, N.J., 1992—; pastor Eldora (N.J.), Belleplain and Delmont United Meth. Chs., 1988—; instr. 1st Fidelity Bancorp., 1990-92. Recipient Grand Cross of Colors, N.J. Rainbow for Girls, Linwood, N.J., 1984; named Barbershopper of Yr., Atlantic City Barbershop Chorus, Pleasantville, N.J., 1984, one of Outstanding Young Men of Am. Nat. Jr. C. of C. Mem. Atlantic City Barbershop Chorus (music dir. 1984—), Rainbow for Girls, Masons, Order of Eastern Star. Republican. Home: 5925 Berry Dr Mays Landing NJ 08330-2335

RIZZI, DEBORAH L., public relations executive; b. Jersey City, N.J., Feb. 26, 1955; d. Edwin Joseph and Beulah Marie (Ardoin) R. BA, Rutgers U., 1977. Program dir. Am. Cancer Soc., Jersey City, 1977-79; internat. program asst. Stevens Inst. Tech., Hoboken, N.J., 1980; dir. pub. rels. United Hosps. Med. Ctr., Newark, 1981-90; dir. practice devel. Stryker Tams & Dill, Newark, 1990—; adv. bd. Nat. Boxing Safety Ctr., Newark, 1984-88; sr. producer Children's Miracle Network Telethon, N.J., 1985-90. Contbg. author: (book) Children With HIV Source Book, 1990, (booklet) Guide for Victims of Sexual Assault, 1985, Child With AIDS . . . Guide for the Family, 1986; co-producer: (video) Diagnosing Sexual Assault in Children, 1990. Mem. Am. Hosp. Assn. (Nat. Touch Stone award 1987), Pub. Rels. Soc. Am., Nat. Assn. Law Firm Marketers, N.J. Hosp. Assn. (Percy award 1986, 88, 90). Office: Stryker Tams & Dill Two Penn Plaza East Newark NJ 07105

RIZZIELLO, PATRICIA DERRICKSON, computer company executive, consultant; b. Trenton, N.J., May 28, 1940; d. George Lionel Derrickson and Ethel Knight (Baker) Rarling; m. Jerry R. Rizziello, Sept. 26, 1959; children: Kimberly, Jerry R. Jr. Student, Mercer County Coll., 1966-68, Rider Coll., 1973-75. Mgr. data ctr. McGraw Hill, Highstown, N.J., 1963—; pres., founder TLC Tape Libr. Cons., Yardville, N.J., 1981—; bd. dirs., mem. adv. bd. Help Desk Inst., 1990. Contbr. articles to profl. jours. Recipient Speaker Recognition award Help Desk Inst. Mem. Computer Assocs. UCCEL (nat. adv. bd.), Delaware Valley Data Entry Assn. for Computer Operation Mgrs., Data Processing Mgrs. Assn., Disaster Recovery of Delaware Valley. Republican. Baptist. Home: 3 Rock Royal Rd Yardville NJ 08620-1611

RIZZITELLO, NICHOLAS ANTHONY, chiropractic physician; b. Newark, Jan. 5, 1953; s. Nick and Mary (Napolitano) R.; m. Maria Christina Insalaco; children: Nicholas Anthony III, Angelo Michael. Student, U. Albuquerque, 1970, Rutgers U., 1971-73; D of Chiropractic, Columbia Inst. of Chiropractic, N.Y.C., 1976. Diplomate Nat. Bd. Chiropractic Examiners. Pvt. practice Irvington, N.J., 1977—; v.p. The Back Dr., 1984—. Recipient Essex County Young Rep. of Yr. award. Mem. Am. Chiropractic Assn., Am. Chiropractic Assn. Coun. on Sports Injuries and Physical Fitness, N.J. Chiropractic Soc. (bd. dirs. legis. com., sports coun.),No. N.J. Chiropractic Soc. (legis. com.), Found. for Chiropractic Edn. and Rsch., Am. Coll. Sports Medicine, Am. Athletic Trainers Assn., U.S. Fencing Assn., Irvington C. of C., Masons, Moose, Tau Kappa Epsilon. Roman Catholic. Home: 44 Kinder Dr Bloomfield NJ 07003-5549 Office: 1200 Clinton Ave Irvington NJ 07111-2094

RIZZO, GARY EDWARD, college dean; b. Erie, Pa., Mar. 28, 1944; s. Carl Joseph and Marie Grace (Manuele) R.; m. Patricia Sue Kundtz, Nov. 15, 1969; children: Brian, Gary, Thomas. BS, Gannon U., Erie, Pa., 1967; MS, Case Western Res. U., Cleve., 1969; PhD, U. Pitts., 1974. Nat. cert. counselor. Counselor Cuyahoga Community Coll., Cleve., 1969-71, Westmoreland County Community Coll., Youngwood, Pa., 1972-82; dir. counseling Montgomery Community Coll., Blue Bell, Pa., 1982-84, assoc. dean lifelong learning, 1984-89, assoc. acad. dean, 1989—; cons. in field. Am. Coun. on Edn. fellow, 1984-85; named Outstanding Faculty Mem., Westmoreland Community Coll., Greensburg, Pa., 1974. Fellow Am. Coun. on Edn.; mem. Pa. Coll. Personnel Assn. (bd. dirs. 1984-88, Outstanding Contbr. 1988), Am. Coll. Personnel Assn., Montgomery County Counselors Assn. (cons.), Pa. Counseling Assn. (dir. Outstanding Counseling Ctr. 1982). Home: 2167 Pheasant Hill Way Lansdale PA 19446-5066 Office: Montgomery County Comm Coll 340 Dekalb Pike Blue Bell PA 19422-1412

RIZZO, THOMAS DIGNAN, orthopedic surgeon; b. N.Y.C., May 25, 1931; s. Peter Cyrus and RoseAnn (Dignan) R.; m. Jean Foley; children: Thomas D. Jr., Peter F., James G., Kathryn AnnMarie, William J., Francis V. BS cum laude, Georgetown U., 1958, MD cum laude, 1956. Diplomate Am. Bd. Orthopedic Surgery, Nat. Bd. Med. Examiners. Intern Georgetown U. Med. Ctr., Washington, 1956-57; asst. resident surgeon St. Vincent's Hosp., N.Y.C., 1957-58; resident in orthopedic surgery Hosp. for Spl. Surgery, N.Y.C., 1958-59, fellow in orthopedic surgery, 1961-62; resident fellow in orthopedic surgery Newington Hosp. for Crippled Children, Conn., 1962; pvt. practice Bronxville, N.Y., 1962—; clin. cons. orthopedic surgery N.Y. State Dept. Health, 1965; assoc. dir. orthopedics Lawrence Hosp., Bronxville, 1970-79, attending staff, 1963—; asst. attending St. John's Riverside Hosp., Yonkers, N.Y., 1963-74, sr. attending surgeon, 1974-87, dir. dept. orthopedic surgery, 1975-86, courtesy staff, 1987—; assoc. attending Dobbs Ferry Hosp., 1970-73, cons. staff, 1973—; asst. attending Hosp. for Spl. Surgery, N.Y.C., 1963, Doctors Hosp., 1973-80; asst. attending surgeon N.Y. Hosp., 1981-83. Med. adv. bd. Bapt. Home for Aged; bd. trustees Fordham Prep. Sch., 1987—; mem. Westchester Health Planning Coun., 1983-92, sec., 1988-89; bd. dirs. Hudson Valley Health Systems Agy., 1988—. Fellow ACS, Am. Acad. Orthopedic Surgeons, Am. Acad. Legal and Indsl. Medicine, N.Y. Acad. of Medicine, Westchester Acad. Medicine (bd. trustees 1968—), Am. Orthopedic Foot and Ankle Soc.; mem. AMA, N.Y. State Med. Soc. (county del. 1975-87), Westchester County Med. Soc. (bd. dirs. 1968—, pres. 1975-76), Irish Am. Orthopedic Soc., N.Y. State Soc. Orthopedic Surgeons, Ea. Orthopedic Assn., Georgetown U. Alumni Assn. (bd. govs. 1970-73, chpt. v.p. 1970-72), KC, Knight of Malta, Knight of Holy Sepulchre, Alpha Omega Alpha. Home: 633 California Rd Bronxville NY 10708 Office: 77 Pondfield Rd Bronxville NY 10708

ROA, FRED, financial company executive. BS in Acctg., Fairleigh Dickinson U. CPA, N.J.; enrolled to practice before IRS. Tax ptnr.; pres. Telesis, Franklin Lakes, N.J.; lectr. in field. Contbr. numerous articles to profl. jours.; author chpt. in Handbook of Business Valuations, 1992. Mem. Nat. Assn. Home Care, Nat. Assn. Durable Med. Equip. Suppliers, N.Y. Assn. Health Care Providers, Expert Witness Network, Nat. Assn. Pub. Accts. Office: Telesis 795 Franklin Ave Franklin Lakes NJ 07417

ROACH, RALPH LEE, health science facility administrator; b. Silver Spring, Md., Mar. 27, 1957; s. William A. and Mary B. (Collins) R.; m. Susan Diane Schirmacher, Aug. 17, 1985. BA, Messiah Coll., 1982; MS, Shippensburg U., 1985. Inventory controller Messiah Coll., Grantham, Pa., 1977-85; therapist, crisis interviewer Stevens Mental Health, Carlisle, Pa., 1983-86; psychotherapist Holy Spirit Community Mental Health Inst., Camp Hill, Pa., 1986—; presentor, cons. Lebanon (Pa.) Valley Coll., 1986; vocat. tng. mgr. Ctr. for Indsl. Tng., Mechanicsburg, Pa., 1985-87; program mgr. living unltd. program univ. hosp. rehab. ctr. for children and adults Pa. U. Hosp. Milton S. Hershey Med. Ctr., Hershey, Pa., 1987—; adj. faculty Elizabethtown Coll., 1987—; presenter at profl. confs. Edn. dir. Cumberland Valley Ch., Dillsburg, Pa., 1980-83; presentor Gov.'s Com. on Handicapped, Harrisburg, Pa., 1986; presentor Office of Spl. Edn. and Rehab., Harrisburg, 1987. Mem. NRA, Pa. Specialists in Group Work, Pa. Crisis Intervention Assn., Pa. Assn. Rehab. Facilities, Keystone State Head Injury Found. Presbyterian. Home: 101 Jefferson St Duncannon PA 17020-9602 Office: Pa U Hosp Rehab Ctr Milton S Hershey Med Ctr PO Box 850 Hershey PA 17033-0850 also: Avalon Affiliates RC 101 Jefferson St Duncannon PA 17020

ROBAK, ROSTYSLAW WSEWOLOD, psychologist, educator; b. Passau, Fed. Republic Germany, Nov. 15, 1948; s. Bohdan and Maria (Makhobey) R.; m. Loretta J. Tallon; 1 child, Marika. BA, Seton Hall U., 1970; MA, Fairleigh Dickinson U., 1973; PhD, Hofstra U., 1976. Diplomate and fellow Am. Bd. Med. Psychotherapists; lic. psychologist N.Y., Pa., Mass. Psychologist Rockland Children's Psychiat. Ctr., Orangeburg, N.Y., 1977-79, No. Westchester BOCES, Yorktown Heights, N.Y., 1979-81, Sullivan County Mental Health Svcs., Monticello, N.Y., 1981-85; clin. dir. Daytop Village, Parksville, N.Y., 1986-88; prof. Pace U., Pleasantville, N.Y., 1988—; dir. M.S. program in substance abuse counseling Pace U., 1992—; adj. prof. Orange County Community Coll., Middletown, N.Y. 1985-88; founding faculty advisor Pace U. chpt. Psi Chi Nat. Honor Soc., 1991—. Author: A Primer for Today's Substance Abuse Counselor, 1991. Mem. APA, Nat. Assn. Alcoholism & Drug Abuse Counselors, Nat. Register Health Svc. Providers in Psychology. Office: Pace Univ Pleasantville NY 10570

ROBARTS, JOHN TREMAINE, principal; b. Lynn, Mass., Jan. 24, 1940; s. Tremaine Morris and Ruth Augusta (Sandstrom) R.; m. Nancy Leigh Robarts, July 8, 1961 (div. 1985); children: Kent Richard, Kristin, Lisa Leigh; m. Emily Frances Starr Jacobs-Robarts, Dec. 20, 1985; stepchildren: James Jacobs, Heidi Jacobs, Beth Jacobs. AB, Bowdoin Coll., 1962; EdM, Salem State Coll., 1966. Cert. sch. supt., prin., guidance dir., pupil personnel svcs. dir., guidance counselor, sch. psychologist, Latin and English tchr. Tchr., adj. counselor, dir. pupil personnel svcs. Gloucester (Mass.) Pub. Schs., 1964-71; dir. pupil personnel svcs. Watertown (Mass.) Pub. Schs., 1971-72, Marblehead (Mass.) Pub. Schs., 1972-75; sr. ptnr. R & K Assocs., Beverly, Mass., 1975-77; dir. mktg. G. A. Levow, Inc., Newton, Mass., 1977-87; spl. edn. dir., sch. adjustment counselor Uxbridge (Mass.) Pub. Schs., 1987-90; prin. Uxbridge (Mass.) High Sch., 1990—; assoc. prof. Salem (Mass.) State Coll., 1970-75; dir. Uxbridge (Mass.) Adult Edn. Program, 1987-89; coord. Uxbridge Extension Campus, Quinsigamund Community Coll., 1989. Contbr. articles to profl. jours. Assoc. mem. Uxbridge Dem. Town Com., 1987—; co-chmn. Study Com., Blackstone Valley Higher Edn. Consortium, Uxbridge, 1988—; sec. Blackstone Valley Regional Vocat. Sch. Com., Upton, Mass., 1991—. Recipient Community Participation award Greater Boston Assn. for Retarded Children, 1972, Spl. Edn. Adminstr. of the Yr. award Mass. Assn. for Children with Learning Disabilities, 1974-75, Gov.'s Community Builder award for literacy Commonwealth Literacy Corp., 1989. Mem. Phi Beta Kappa. Democrat. Home: 178 Granite St Uxbridge MA 01569-1231 Office: Uxbridge High Sch 62 Capron St Uxbridge MA 01569-1530

ROBB, JAMES WILLIS, educator; b. Jamaica, N.Y., June 27, 1918; s. Stewart Everts and Clara Johanna (Mohrman) R.; m. Cecilia Uribe-Noguera, 1972. Student, Inst. de Touraine, Sorbonne, 1937-38; B.A. cum laude, Colgate U., 1939; postgrad., U. Nacional de Mex., 1948; M.A., Middlebury Coll., 1950; Ph.D., Catholic U. Am., 1958. Instr. Romance langs. Norwich U., 1946-50; asst. prof. Romance langs. George Washington U., Washington, 1950-58, assoc. prof., 1958-66, prof., 1966-88, prof. emeritus, 1988—. Author: El Estilo de Alfonso Reyes, 1965, 78, Repertorio Bibliográfico de Alfonso Reyes, 1974, Prosa y Poesía de Alfonso Reyes, 1975, 84, Estudios sobre Alfonso Reyes, 1976, Por los Caminos de Alfonso Reyes, 1981, Imágenes de América en Alfonso Reyes y en Germán Arciniegas, 1990; contbr. articles to profl. jours. With USNR, 1942-46. Recipient Alfonso Reyes Internat. Lit. prize, 1978; Lit. Diploma of Merit, State of Nuevo León and City of Monterrey, Mex., 1979; OAS grantee, 1964; Am. Philos. Soc. grantee, 1977. Mem. MLA, Asociación Internacional de Literatura Iberoamericana, Am. Assn. Tchrs. Spanish and Portuguese, Asociación Norteamericana de Colombianistas. Office: George Washington U Romance Langs Dept Washington DC 20052

ROBB, JANETTE CONSUELA, rehabilitation counsellor; b. Bklyn., Oct. 31, 1956; d. John Eugene and Lynn (Smith) White; m. Steven Leroy Robb, Sept. 9, 1984. BA, NYU, 1976; MEd, Hofstra U., 1979. Cert. rehab. counselor; cert. rape crisis counselor. Vocat. evaluator Goodwill Industries of N. Y., Astoria, N.Y., 1970-80; vocat. evaluator, counselor UCP, Queens, N.Y., 1980-84; supr. vocat. svc. Pathways Inc., Long Branch, N.J.; vocat. counselor N.J. Div. Vocat. Rehab., Tom River, N.J., 1985-89; clin. supr. Monmouth Ctr. for Vocat. Rehab., Tinton Falls, N.J., 1989—; pres. J. Robb & Assocs., Lakewood, N.J., 1990—. Recipient U.S. Govt. scholarship, Washington, 1987. Mem. NAACP, Nat. Rehab. Assn., Employee Assistance Profl. Assn., Am. Assn. for Counseling and Devel. Democrat. Baptist. Home: 954 Jessica Ct Lakewood NJ 08701-3653

ROBBIN, TONY, artist; b. Washington, Nov. 24, 1943; s. Barney Morton and Lillian (Kolker) R.; m. Rena Kosensky, July 1, 1975; 1 child, Max. BA, Columbia U., 1965; BFA, MFA, Yale U., 1968. One man shows include Louise Peterson Gallery, Winter Park, 1983, McNay Art Inst., San Antonio, 1983, Davis/McClain Gallery, Houston, 1984, Tibor de Nagy, N.Y.C., 1979, 80, 81, 83, 88, OK South Gallery, Miami, 1987, Broadway Windows, N.Y.C.; exhibited in group shows at Dayton Art Inst., 1987-88, Tibor de Nagy Gallery, N.Y.C., 1988, Chgo. Acad. Sci., 1989, Hungarian Nat. Gallery, Budapest, 1989, Ben Sahn Gallery, 1990, Sangre de Cristo Art Ctr., Pubelo, 1991, Bronx Mus. Arts, 1991.

ROBBINS, AUGUSTUS, III, construction company executive; b. Hickman, Ky., Dec. 26, 1926; s. Augustus and Marie Elizabeth (Hogan) R.; m. Jane Mebley, June 23, 1950; children: Sharon E., Augustus IV, Cynthia L., C. Keith. BS in Civil Engring., Va. Military Inst., 1948. Project engr. Esso Corp., Balt., 1948-50; v.p. Drummond & Co., Balt., 1950-63; exec. v.p. Ratrie, Robbins and Schweizer, Balt., 1963-90; consulting engr. pvt. practice, Balt., 1990—. Chmn. Coun. Boy Scouts Am., Balt. 1991. Recipient Civic Achievment award Bldg. Congress and Exchange, Balt., 1987, Medallion of Honor, Virginians of Md., Balt., 1991. Mem. Constrn. Industry Ednl. Found. (bd. dirs., 1989—, pres. 1989-90), Md. Asphalt Assn. (bd. dirs. 1970—, pres. 1981-82), Engring. Soc. Balt. (v.p. 1983), Am. Arbitration Assn., Va. Military Inst. Alumni Assn. (pres. 1980). Episcopalian. Home: 207 Midhurst Rd Baltimore MD 21212 Office: 803 Gleneagle Ct Towson MD 21204

ROBBINS, CAROLE RITA, freelance medical writer; b. Hartford, Conn., July 2, 1937; d. Irving George and Anne (Zaiman) Robbins; m. Stephen A. Myers, June 20, 1959 (div. Dec. 1975). BA in Math, U. Conn., 1961; postgrad., Radcliffe Inst., 1974; MPH, Yale U., 1991. Computer programmer History Book Club, Stamford, Conn., 1963-66; systems specialist IBM Corp., White Plains, N.Y., 1966-72; instr. computer sci. Bryant and Stratton Coll., Boston, 1974-75; freelance med. writer ESRD mag., Hartford, 1977—. Author: A Primer of Left-Handed Embroidery Scribners, 1974; contbr. numerous articles to popular nephrology mags. Bd. dirs. Am. Assn. Kidney Patients, 1982-86. Am. Kidney Fund scholar, 1981-82. Jewish. Home: 5 Pepperbush Way Windsor CT 06095

ROBBINS, CLARENCE RALPH, chemist; b. Point Marion, Pa., Aug. 25, 1938; s. Delmar C. and Ethel L. (Johnson) R.; m. Marjorie Gene Johnson, June 11, 1961; children: Laura Jane, Mark Joseph. BS, W.Va. Wesleyan Coll., 1960; PhD, Purdue U., 1964. Rsch. scientist Colgate Palmolive Co., Piscataway, N.J., 1964—, disting. fellow, 1990—; editorial adv. bd. Internat. Jour. Cosmetic Sci., 1990-91. Author: Chemical and Physical Behavior of Human Hair, 1st edit., 1979, Japanese edit., 1982, 2d edit., 1988; contbr. more than 40 articles to profl. jours.; patentee in field. Mem. Soc. Cosmetic Chemists (editor jour. 1987-91, Maison G. de Navarre medal 1989, Lit. award 1984, Best Paper awards 1978, 85, 86, 89). Home: 1726 Woodfield Rd Martinsville NJ 08836-9638 Office: Colgate Palmolive Co 909 River Piscataway NJ 08854

ROBBINS, CORNELIUS (VAN VORSE), educational administrator; b. Wilmington, Del., Nov. 2, 1931; s. Cornelius V. and Irene (Tatman) R.; children: Eva Robbins Burke, Susan, Laurel Robbins Truax, Melissa Robbins Beegle. B.A. in Polit. Sci, U. Del., 1953, M.Ed. in Social Scis, 1961; Ed.D. in Ednl. Adminstrn, U. Pa., 1964. Mem. faculty U. Del., 1957-58; tchr. Marshallton (Del.) Sch. Dist., 1958-60, Mt. Pleasant (Del.) Sch. Dist., 1960-62; asst. to dir. sch. study councils U. Pa., 1962-64; dean instrn. Ocean County Coll., 1965-67; dean of coll. Community Coll. of Delaware County, Pa., 1967-69; sr. assoc., coll. div. dir. McManis Assocs., Washington, 1969-70; pres. Genesee Community Coll., 1970-75; assoc. chancellor for community colls. SUNY, 1975-85; acting pres. Potsdam State Coll. (N.Y.), 1982-83; pres. Cobleskill (N.Y.) Coll. Agr. & Tech., 1985-92; prof. edn. adminstrn. SUNY, Albany, N.Y., 1992—; cons. Middle States Assn. Colls.; area liaison officer U.S. Mil. Acad., 1972; chmn. SUNY West Pres.'s Council and mem. Chancellor's Council, 1973, 85, 91. Contbr. articles to profl. publs. Served with U.S. Army, 1954-56. Recipient Outstanding Educator's award N.Y. State Assn. Jr. Colls., 1975, Disting. Svc. award Faculty Coun. Community Colls., 1988. Mem. Am. Assn. Higher Edn., State Dirs. of Community Colls. Assn., Phi Delta Kappa. Office: SUNY 329 Ed Bldg 1400 Washington Ave Albany NY 12222

ROBBINS, DEBORAH THATCHER, composer, pianist; b. Wareham, Mass., Mar. 18, 1953; d. Frederick Ernest and Madeline Eleanor (Guilford) Thatcher; m. David Mervyn Robbins, June 11, 1983; children: Sarah, Joshua, Zachary. Grad. high sch., Wareham; grad., Barbizon Modeling Sch., Boston, 1972; student, Cape Cod Conservatory Music, Barnstable, Mass. Cert. fashion modeling instr. Composer, pianist Nightstar Records, Inc., Yarmouthport, Mass., 1989—; concert pianist Cape Pla. Hotel, Hyannis, Mass., 1991; pres., owner Dact Pub. Co., Yarmouthport, 1989—. Composer, pianist (album) Journey Home, 1990, Silhouettes, 1990, Dancing With the Moon, 1992. Concert pianist The United Way, New Bedford, Mass., 1990, Beautification of New Bedford, 1991, 92, Yarmouthport Playground Fund, 1991; vol. Mass. Soc. for Prevention of Cruelty to Children, Mashpee C. of C., 1991. Recipient 1989 Quarter-Milennial Homecoming award for Songwriting and Modeling. Mem. Mashpee C. of C. (concert pianist 1991). Office: Nightstar Records Inc PO Box 602 Yarmouth Port MA 02675-0602

ROBBINS, GEOFFREY RALPH, veterinarian, toxicologist; b. Swindon, Eng., Dec. 17, 1929; came to U.S., 1964; s. Ralph U. and Kathleen R. (Hunt) R.; m. Betty Bishop; children: Michael R., Keith A., Kenneth G., Alan E. Grad, London U., 1956. Diplomate Am. Coll. Toxicology; mem. Royal Coll. Vet. Surgeons. Dir. toxicology Schering Plough Corp., Bloomfield, N.J., 1964-79; chief exec. officer Cosmopolitan Safety Inc., Lafayette, N.J., 1980—; expert witness Sci. Law Assocs., Lansing, Mich., 1978—. Mem. AAAS, Royal Vet. Surgeons, N.Y. Acad. Scis. Office: Cosmopolitan Safety Inc PO Box 71 Lafayette NJ 07848

ROBBINS, JACOB, biomedical researcher, endocrinologist; b. Yonkers, N.Y., Sept. 1, 1922; s. Samuel and Tillie (Sanoff) R.; m. Jean Adams, Sept. 4, 1949; children: Alice Elizabeth, Susan Lynn, Mark Samuel. AB, Cornell U., Ithaca, N.Y., 1944; MD, Cornell U., N.Y.C., 1947. Intern in medicine N.Y. Hosp., N.Y.C., 1947-48; resident Meml. Hosp., N.Y.C., 1948-50, rsch. fellow, 1949-53, asst. attending physician, 1953-54; commd. sr. asst. surgeon USPHS, 1954, advanced through grades to med. dir., 1963, ret., 1989; rsch. scientist NIH, Bethesda, Md., 1954—; chief clin. endocrinology br. Nat. Inst. Diabetes, Digestive and Kidney Diseaes, NIH, Bethesda, 1963-92; chief endocrinology sect. genetics antibiochemistry br. Nat. Inst. Diabetes, Digestive and Kidney Diseaes, NIH, 1992—; asst. Sloan KEttering Inst., N.Y.C., 1953-54; instr. Cornell U. Med. Coll., 1950-54, George Washngton U. Sch. Medicine, Washington, 1955-61; vis. scientist Carlsberg Lab., Copenhagen, 1959-60; vis. prof. Stellenbosch U., Capetown, Union South Africa, 1967, Gumma U., Maebashi, Japan, 1970. Editor-in-chief Endocrinology, 1968-72; editor rsch. monographs; also numerous articles on thyroid rsch., chpts. on thyroidology. Recipient Meritorious Svc. medal USPHS, 1971. Mem. Am. Thyroid Assn. (pres. 1974-75, Parke Davis award 1980, Disting. Svc. award 1983), Endocrine Soc., Am. Soc. for Clin. Investigation, Assn. Am. Physicians, Am. Physiol. Soc., European Thyroid Assn., Japan Endocrine Soc. (hon.). Home: 7203 Bradley Blvd Bethesda MD 20817-2127 Office: NIH Bldg Bldg 10 Rm 8N315 Bethesda MD 20892

ROBBINS, JEFFREY HOWARD, consultant, research writer, educator; b. N.Y.C., Mar. 29, 1941; s. Stanley Samuel and Miriam (Cooper) R.; m. Marsha Sue Rimler, Nov. 3, 1984; 1 child, Nina Camille. BSME, Carnegie Mellon U., 1962; MS in Physics, U. N.Mex., 1966, ABD in Physics, 1967; postgrad., U. Calif., Berkeley and L.A., 1963-64. Summer rsch. assoc. Linde Co., Tonawanda, N.Y., 1961; rsch. engr. N.Am. Aviation (Rockwell), Downey, Calif., 1962-64; summer rsch. assoc. Los Alamos (N.Mex.) Sci. Lab., 1965; sr. engr. Radio Engring. Labs., L.I., N.Y., 1968-70; engring. cons. PRD Electronics, Syosset, N.Y., 1972-73; sr. applications engr. Bendix Corp., Teterboro, N.J., 1974-76; sr. applications engr. Giordano Assocs., Franklin Lakes, N.J., 1977-81, Racal-Redak, Mahwah, N.J., 1981-83; tech. cons. Allied Signal Corp., Teterboro, 1983—; evening sch. instr. New Sch. for Social Rsch., N.Y.C., 1979-85. Author: On Balance and Higher Education, 1970; contbr. articles to profl. jours. Organizing co-moderator Future Impact of Artificial Intelligence, Robotics Forum, 1984. Recipient first prize for essay The World and I Mag., 1990; NDEA fellow, 1966-67, others. Mem. IEEE, N.Y. Acad. Sci., Sigma Xi, Phi Kappa Phi, Pi Tau Sigma. Jewish. Home: 215 Adams St #10A Brooklyn NY 11201 Office: Cassiopeia Cons Inc Box 335 Long Beach NY 11561

ROBBINS, JEROME, choreographer, director; b. N.Y.C., Oct. 11, 1918; s. Harry and Lena (Rips) R. Student, NYU, 1935-36, hon. degree, 1985; D.F.A. (hon.), Ohio U., 1975; studied ballet, modern, Spanish and Oriental dance.; hon. degree, CUNY, 1980. Mem. panel N.Y. Council on Arts, 1973-77, Nat. Council on Arts, Nat. Endowment for Arts, 1974-80. Debut as dancer Sandor-Sorel Dance Center, 1937; dancer Broadway musicals Great Lady, Stars in Your Eyes, Keep Off the Grass, Straw Hat Review, 1938-40, Ballet Theatre, N.Y.C., 1940-44, soloist, 1941-44; choreographer Ballet Theatre, 1944-48; choreographer N.Y.C. Ballet, 1949-90, assoc. artistic dir., 1949-59, ballet master, 1969-83, co-ballet master in chief, 1983-89, dir., Ballets: U.S.A., 1958-61, Jerome Robbins Chamber Dance Co. tour Peoples' Republic China (sponsored by U.S. Internat. Communications Agy.), 1981; ballets also in repertories of Am. Ballet Theatre, Joffrey Ballet, Royal Swedish Ballet, Batsheva Ballet, Royal Danish Ballet, Boston Ballet, Nat. Ballet Can., Harkness Ballet, Royal Ballet, London, Australian Ballet, San Francisco Ballet, Pa. Ballet, Dance Theatre of Harlem, Paris Opera Ballet, Bayerischen Staatsoper Munich, La Scala, Opernhaus, Zurich, Finnish Ballet, Star Dancers Found.; ballets choreographed include Fancy Free, 1944, Interplay, 1945, Afterthought, 1946, Facsimile, 1946, Summer Day, 1947, Pas de Trois, 1948, The Guests, 1949, (with Balanchine) Jones Beach, 1950, Age of Anxiety, 1950, Pied Piper, 1951, The Cage, 1951, Ballade, 1952, Fanfare, 1953, Afternoon of a Faun, 1953, Quartet, 1954, The Concert, 1956, N.Y. Export: Opus Jazz, 1958, Moves, 1959, Les Noces, 1965, 3X3, 1961, Events, 1961, (with Balanchine) Firebird, 1970, Dances at a Gathering, 1969, In the Night, 1970, The Goldberg Variations, 1971, Requiem Canticles, 1972, (with Balanchine) Dumbarton Oaks, 1972, (with Balanchine) Pulcinella, 1972, Watermill, 1972, Scherzo Fantastique, 1972, Circus Polka, 1972, Beethoven Pas de Deaux, 1973, Dybbuk Variations, 1974, Introduction & Allegro for Harp, 1975, Une Barque Sur L'Ocean, 1975, Concerto in G (later in G Major), 1975, Ma Mere l'oye, 1975, Chansons Madecasses, 1975, Other Dances, 1976, A Sketchbook, 1978, Le Bourgeois Gentilhomme, 1979, The Four Seasons, 1979, Opus 19: The Dreamer, 1979, Rondo, 1981, Andantino, 1981, Piano Pieces, 1981, (with Pulchinella 1972 and Firebird 1970) Allegro con Grazia, 1981, The Gershwin Concerto, 1982, Four Chamber Works, 1982, Glass Pieces, 1983, I'm Old Fashioned, 1983, Antique Epigraphs, 1984, Brahms/Handel (with Twyla Tharp), 1984, Eight Lines, 1985, In Memory Of ..., 1985, Quiet City, 1986, Piccolo Balletto, 1986, Ives, Songs, 1988, N.Y.C. Retrospective of Jerome Robbins' Ballets, 1989; choreographer Broadway musicals On the Town (based on ballet Fancy Free), 1945, Billion Dollar Baby, 1946, High Button Shoes, 1947, Miss Liberty, 1949, Call Me Madam, 1950, The King and I, 1951, Two's Company, 1952; dir. and choreographer stage musicals Peter Pan, 1954, Bells Are Ringing, 1956, West Side Story, 1957 (Donaldson and Antoinette Perry awards), Gypsy, 1959, Fiddler on the Roof, 1964 (Antoinette Perry awards for choreography and direction 1980, 89); TV versions Peter Pan, 1955-60 (Emmy award); nat. tour, 1981; co-dir. (with George Abbott) Pajama Game (stage version), 1952; prodn. supr. Funny Girl (stage version), 1964; choreographer motion pictures The King and I, 1956, West Side Story, 1960 (Academy Awards for choreography and direction, Screen Dirs. Guild award, Laurel award); dir. plays Oh Dad, Poor Dad, Mama's Hung You in the Closet and I'm Feeling So Sad, 1962, Mother Courage and Her Children, 1963, Jerome Robbins' Broadway, 1989 (Antoinette Perry awards direction, best mus. 1989); TV credits include Two Duets, 1980, Live from Studio 8H (An Evening of Jerome Robbins Ballets), 1980. Decorated chevalier Order Arts and Letters (France); recipient numerous awards for prodns. including 5 Donaldson awards, 4 Antoinette Perry awards, 2 Academy Awards, and Sylvania, Emmy, Dance Magazine, Box Office Blue Ribbon, Evening Standard Drama (London), Screen Dirs. Guild, Laurel, Drama Critics, and City of Paris awards, Capezio Dance award, 1976, recipient Handel medallion N.Y.C., 1976, Kennedy Ctr. honors, 1981, Brandeis U. Creative Arts award, 1984, Lifetime Achievement award, Astaire awards, 1985, Nat. medal of Arts, 1988; named best choreographer Theatre des Nations, 1959. Mem. Am. Acad. and Inst. Arts and Letters (hon., Commonwealth award 1990). Office: care NYC Ballet NY State Theater Lincoln Ctr Pla New York NY 10023

ROBBINS, JOHN WILLIAM, foundation administrator; b. Honesdale, Pa., Oct. 21, 1948; s. Seamon Laverne and Edith Mary (Smith) R.; m. Linda Kaye Stephens, Nov. 3, 1973; children: Julie Lynn, Laura Kaye, Mary Ellen. AB, Grove City Coll., 1969; MA, Johns Hopkins U., 1970, PhD, 1973. Legis. asst. U.S. Ho. of Reps., Washington, 1973-75, 79-81, adminstrv. asst., 1981-85; economist Heritage Found., Washington, 1975-77; editor Western Islands, Boston, 1977-79; pres. Trinity Found., Jefferson, Md., 1979—; found. exec. Durell Found., Berryville, Va., 1988-91; cons. in field, 1985-88; tchr. Chesapeake Theol. Sem., Washington, 1981-84; tchr., dir. Sangre de Cristo Sem., Westcliffe, Colo., 1987—; pres. The Inst. for Policy Innovation, 1991—. Author: Answer to Ayn Rand, 1974, Pat Robertson: A Warning, 1988, The Case Against Indexation, 1976, Cornelius Van Til: The Man and the Myth, 1986, Scripture Twisting in the Seminaries, 1985; editor: Essays on Ethics and Politics, 1992, Education, Christianity and the State, 1987, Gordon H. Clark: Personal Recollections, 1990; editor The Freeman mag., 1992—. Mem. Evang. Theol. Soc. Presbyterian. Office: Trinity Found PO Box 700 Jefferson MD 21755-0700

ROBBINS, KENNETH L., advertising agency executive. Exec. v.p. SSC & B (now Lintas Worldwide), N.Y.C.; now chmn., chief exec. officer Lintas Worldwide. Office: Lintas Worldwide 1 Dag Hammarskjold Plz New York NY 10017-2201

ROBBINS, LEE DAVID, bank executive; b. Greenwich, Conn., June 11, 1953; s. Alfred Carl and Frances Barbara (Witewski) R.; m. Helene Ann Astorino, Aug. 13, 1983; 1 child, Lauren Marie. BBA, Nichols Coll., 1975; grad., Conn. Police Acad., 1976; Cert. Completion, Conn. Sch. Fin. and Mgmt., 1987; postgrad., Nat. Sch. Fin. and Mgmt. Mgr. dept. Caldor, Inc., Riverside, Conn., 1975; police officer Town of Bethel, Conn., 1975-78; mgmt. trainee State Nat. Bank Conn., Bridgeport, 1978-79; sr. examiner Union Trust Co., Stamford, Conn., 1979-83; auditing officer City Savs. Bank of Meriden, Conn., 1983-88, asst. v.p. fin. and data processing, 1988—; aux. trooper Conn. State Police Dept., Bethany, 1983—. Mem. Nat. Assn. Accts., Thrift Auditors of Conn. (program devel. com. 1986), Group 1 of Conn., Savs. Bank Forum, Savs. Banks Assn. Conn. (mem. mgmt. and edn. com. 1987, 89), Inst. Internal Auditors, Masons. Home: 34 Hillview Ave Hamden CT 06514-1814 Office: City Savs Bank of Meriden 180 Research Pkwy 14 W Main St Meriden CT 06450

ROBBINS, LILLIAN CUKIER, psychology educator; b. Nancy, France, Sept. 6, 1933; came to U.S., 1943; BA, CCNY, 1954; MA, U. Ill., 1956; PhD, NYU, 1961. Cert. psychologist, N.Y. Research psychologist NYU Med. Ctr., 1962-67; asst. prof. Hunter Coll., N.Y.C., 1967-70, CCNY, 1970-71; assoc. prof. Rutgers U., Newark, 1971-76, prof., 1976—; prin. investigator Citizen's Com. for Children, N.Y.C., 1973-75; dir. coll. honors program Rutgers U., Newark, 1980—. Contbr. articles to profl. jours. Chair women's issues Am. Jewish Com., N.Y.C., 1984-86. Mem. AAAS (life), AAUP (exec. council), Am. Psychol. Assn., Phi Beta Kappa. Democrat. Jewish. Home: 49 E 96th St New York NY 10128-0782 Office: Rutgers U Newark NJ 07102

ROBBINS, ORREN BOURNE, newspaper publisher; b. Hyannis, Mass., July 20, 1932; s. Percy Burton and Sara Hatch (Jones) R.; m. Bonnie Jean Eldredge, Apr. 24, 1952; children: Orren Bourne Jr., David Mervyn, Stephen Wayne. Grad., Barnstable High Sch., Hyannis. Advt. sales rep. Cape Cod Standard-Times, Hyannis, 1958-71; gen. mgr. Press-Rep., Plattsburgh, N.Y., 1971-74; Gen. mgr. Cape Cod Standard-Times, Hyannis, 1974-79; pub. The Traverse City (Mich.) Record-Eagle, 1979-86, The Standard-Times, New Bedford, Mass., 1987—. Bd. dirs. United Way Greater New Bedford, 1987—, Downtown New Bedford, Inc., 1988—. Mem. Am., Newspaper Pubs. Assn., New Eng. Newspapers Assn., Mass. Newspaper Pubs. Assn., New Bedford Area C. of C., Country Club New Bedford, Rotary, Elks. Republican. Office: Standard-Times Pub Co 555 Pleasant St New Bedford MA 02740-6257

ROBBINS, PHILIP, journalist, educator; b. Hickman, Ky., Apr. 7, 1931; s. Augustus Jr. and Marie Elizabeth (Hogan) R.; m. Patricia Forlifer, June 23, 1956; children: Lynn, Elizabeth, Frederick. BA, Washington & Lee U., 1952; MA, Columbia U., 1955. Reporter, city desk asst. Balt. Evening Sun, 1955-57; reporter, city desk editor Hopewell (Va.) Daily News, 1957-62; asst. city editor, metro news editor Washington Evening Star, 1962-71; assoc. prof., prof. journalism George Washington U., Washington, 1971—, chair journalism dept., 1973-90, dir. journalism, 1991—; cons. Ctr. for Fgn. Journalists, Reston, Va., 1986—. Author-editor Port of Baltimore Handbook, 1956. Sgt. maj. U.S. Army, 1952-54, Korea. Mem. Soc. Profl. Journalists (chair Stars & Stripes Freedom of Info. com. 1987—, pres. Washington chpt. 1987-88), Assn. for Edn. in Journalism. Home: 4520 25th Rd N Arlington VA 22207-4102 Office: George Washington U 801 22d St NW Rm T-409 Washington DC 20052

ROBBINS, STANLEY LEONARD, pathologist, educator; b. Portland, Maine, Feb. 27, 1915. BS, MIT, 1936; MD, Tufts U., 1940. Diplomate Am. Bd. Pathology. Intern Mallory Inst. Pathology, Boston, 1940-41, resident, 1941-44, asst. pathologist, 1945-53, assoc. dir., 1953-66; dir. Malory Inst. Pathology, Boston, 1966-72; asst. prof. Sch. Medicine, Boston U., 1947-50, assoc. prof., 1950-57, prof. pathology, 1957-80, chmn. dept. pathology, 1964-80; asst. prof. Med. Sch., Tufts U., Boston, 1947-50; vis. prof. Med. Sch., Harvard U., Boston, 1980—; pathologist Brigham and Women's Hosp., Boston, 1980—; vis. prof. U. Glasgow, Scotland, 1959-60, Hebrew U., Jerusalem, 1976-77; cons. VA Hosp., Boston, 1965-80, Univ. Hosp., Boston, 1970-80. Author: Robbins Pathologic Basis of Disease, 4th edit., 1989, Basic Pathology, 5th edit., 1992, Companion Handbook to Robbins Pathologic Basis of Disease, 1990. Trustee Boston Med. Libr., Combined Jewish Philanthropies; bd. dirs. Jewish Family Children's Svc.; past chmn. rsch. allocation com. Mass. Heart Assn. Fellow Am. Soc. Clin. Pathologists (hon.); mem. AAAS, U.S. and Can. Acad. Pathology (designated Disting. Pathologist 1990), Mass. Med. Soc. (Disting. Leader in Am. Medicine 1980), New Eng. Soc. Pathologists (pres. 1955), Am. Assn. Pathologists, Am. Assn. Med. Mus., Am. Soc. Clin. Investigation, Alpha Omega Alpha. Home: 1010

Memorial Dr Cambridge MA 02138-4859 Office: Brigham and Women's Hosp 75 Francis St Boston MA 02115-6195

ROBBINS, WILLIAM RANDOLPH, minister; b. West Hartford, Conn., May 22, 1912; s. Harry E. and Matilda Sydney (Franklin) R.; m. Sarah Craig Wright, June 6, 1942 (dec. Dec. 25, 1986); children: Henry Craig, Sarah Franklin Robbins Jenks, Thomas Nelson. BA, Princeton U., 1934; MDiv, Yale U., 1941, STD (hon.), 1984; postgrad., Oxford U., Eng., 1946-47, 82. Ordained priest Episcopal Ch., 1942. Asst. min. St. George's Ch., N.Y.C., 1941-43; rector St. Peter's Ch., Cazenovia, N.Y., 1943-49, St. Thomas's Ch., New Haven, 1949-84; founder St. Thomas's Day Sch., 1956, pres. sch. corp., 1956-84, headmaster emeritus, 1984—; chaplain Mil. Order Fgn. Wars U.S., past chaplain gen.; chaplain in chief Mil. Order Loyal Legion U.S.; chaplain le comite francais de Souvenir de laFayette, Civil Def. New Haven area, Old Guard City of N.Y., 2d co. Gov.'s Foot Guard, Conn., New Haven County Sheriff's Assn. Founder Christian Community Action, New Haven; sec. New Haven Archdeaconry; mem. Berkeley Divinity Sch. coun., Yale U.; bd. dirs. Lord's Day Alliance, New Haven Vis. Nurse Assn. 1st lt. U.S. Army, to lt. col. N.Y. N.G., to capt. USCG Aux. Recipient Alumni Disting. Ministry award Berkeley Div. Sch., Disting. Mil. Svc. award N.Y. State Guard, Outstanding Achievement award Princeton U. Class of 1934; assoc. fellow Trumbull Coll., Yale U. Mem. Conn. Acad. Arts and Scis., Soc. Descendants Colonial Govs. (chaplain gen.), Soc. Descendents Colonial Clergy (past chaplain gen.), The Soc. the Cin. (chaplain), Soc. Colonial Wars (chaplain), Soc. Descendents Knights of Garter, The Pilgrims, Dartmouth House English-Speaking Union, Most Venerable Order St. John's Hosp. Jerusalem, Berkeley Divinity Sch. Alumni (past pres.), Order of Knighthood, St. John of Jersulaem (sub-chaplain), Order of Hist. Mil. Commands (chaplain), Union Club of N.Y., Royal Tennis Court (Hampton Court Palace, Eng.), Oxford U. Club (life), Royal Tennis Ct. Club, Hampton Ct. Palace Club, Princeton Club, Union Club (N.Y.C.), Elizabethan of Yale Club, Royal Bermuda Yacht Club, Grad. Club (New Haven). Home: 24 Battis Rd New Haven CT 06514

ROBBINS-WILF, MARCIA, English educator; b. Newark, Mar. 22, 1949; d. Saul and Ruth (Fern) Robbins; m. Leonard A. Wilf, June 21, 1970; 1 child, Orin. Student, Emerson Coll., 1967-69, Seton Hall U., 1969, Fairleigh Dickinson U., 1970; BA, George Washington U., 1971; MA, NYU, 1975; postgrad., St. Peter's Coll., Jersey City, 1979, Fordham U., 1980; MS, Yeshiva U., 1981, EdD, 1986; postgrad., Monmouth Coll., 1986. Cert. elem. tchr., N.Y., N.J., reading specialist, N.J., prin., supr., N.J., adminstr., supr., N.Y. Tchr. Sleepy Hollow Elem. Sch., Falls Church, Va., 1971-72, Yeshiva Konvitz, N.Y.C., 1972-73; intern Wee Folk Nursery Sch., Short Hills, N.J., 1978-81, dir. day camp, 1980-81, tchr., dir., owner, 1980-81; adj. prof. reading Seton Hall U., South Orange, N.J., 1987, Middlesex County Coll., Edison, N.J., 1987-88; asst. adj. prof. L.I. U., Bklyn., 1988, Pace U., N.Y.C., 1988—; ednl. cons. Cranford High Sch., 1988; presenter numerous workshops; founding bd. dirs. Stern Coll. Women Yeshiva U., N.Y.C., 1987; adj. vis. lectr. Rutgers U., New Brunswick, N.J., 1988. Chairperson Jewish Book Festival, YM-YWHA, West Orange, N.J., 1986-87. mem. early childhood com., 1986—, bd. dirs., 1986—; vice chairperson dinner com. Nat. Leadership Conf. Christians and Jews, 1986; mem. Hadassah, Valerie Children's Fund, Women's League Conservative Judaism, City of Hope, assoc. bd. bus. and women's profl. div. United Jewish Appeal, 1979; vol. reader Goddard Riverside Day Care Ctr., N.Y.C., 1973; friend N.Y.C. Pub. Libr., 1980—; life friend Willburn (N.J.) Pub. Libr.; pres. Seton-Essex Reading Coun., 1991-92. Co-recipient Am. Heritage award, Essex County, 1985; recipient Award Appreciation City of Hope, 1984, Profl. Improvement awards Seton-Essex Reading Council, 1984-86, Cert. Attendance award Seton-Essex Reading Counci, 1987. Mem. N.Y. Acad. Scis. (life), N.J. Council Tchrs. English, Nat. Council Tchrs. English, Am. Ednl. Research Assn., Coll. Reading Assn. (life), Assn. Supervision and Curriculun Devel., N.Y. State Reading Assn. (council Manhattan), N.J. Reading Assn. (council Seton-Essex), Internat. Reading Assn., Nat. Assn. for Edn. of Young Children (life N.J. chpt., Kenyon group), Nat. Council Jewish Women (vice chairperson membership com. evening br. N.Y. sect. 1974-75), George Washington U. Alumni Club, Emerson Coll. Alumni Club, NYU Alumni Club, Phi Delta Kappa (life), Kappa Gamma Chi (historian). Club: Greenbrook Country (Caldwell, N.J.); George Washington Univ. Home: 242 Hartshorn Dr Short Hills NJ 07078-1914 also: 820 Morris Turnpike Short Hills NJ 07078

ROBERT, PAUL LEO, lawyer; b. Holyoke, Mass., Aug. 13, 1955; s. Leo Adalbert and Hermanita Raina (Cote) R.; m. Maureen Ann Moore, July 20, 1979; children: Allison Marie, Erin Bridget, Matthew Paul. AB, Coll. of Holy Cross, 1977; JD, Fordham U., 1980. Bar: Mass. 1980, N.Y. 1981, Va. 1982, U.S. Supreme Ct. Asst. counsel strategic systems programs Dept. Navy, Washington, 1980-85, prin. asst. counsel, 1985-87; asst. counsel Hamilton Standard divsn. United Techs. Corp., Windsor Locks, Conn., 1987-90; sr. counsel United Techs. Corp., Hartford, Conn., 1990—. Editor Fordham Urban Law Jour., 1979. Mem. Va. State Bar Assn., K.C. Republican. Roman Catholic. Office: United Tech Corp United Tech Bldg Hartford CT 06101

ROBERTO, ALBERT GENE, safety consultant; b. Providence, Nov. 29, 1943; s. Albert and Ida Marie (Mazza) R.; m. JoAnn Frazier, Oct. 18, 1975; children: Jonathan Albert, Alison Joy. BS in Chemistry, U. R.I., 1965. Cert. safety profl. Office supr. Phoenix Cos. of Hartford, Buffalo, 1968-75; office mgr. State Mutual Life Ins. Co., East Providence, R.I., 1976-78; sr. job developer Nat. Alliance of Bus., Providence, 1978-82; asst. safety cons. Wausau Ins. Cos., Belmont, Mass., 1982-84; safety cons. Wausau Ins. Cos., Burlington, Mass., 1984-89; sr. safety cons. Wausau Ins. Cos., 1989—. Mem. Legis. Adv. Com., Ho. of Reps., Cranston, R.I., 1982-84. 1st lt. U.S. Army, 1965-68. Mem. Am. Soc. Safety Engrs. (profl.), R.I. Safety Assn. (profl.). Home: 40 Seymour Ave Cranston RI 02910-3234 Office: Wausau Ins Cos 25 Burlington Mall Rd Burlington MA 01803-4100

ROBERTS, CELIA ANN, librarian; b. Bangor, Maine, Feb. 6, 1935; d. William Lewis and Ruey Pearl (Logan) R.; A.A., U. Hartford, 1957, B.A., 1961; postgrad. So. Conn. State Coll., 1963—. With catalog, acquistion and circulation depts. U. Hartford Library, 1956-65; librarian Simsbury (Conn.) Free Library, 1965; reference librarian Simsbury Public Library, 1969—. Tchr. ballet classes, 1965-66; ballet mistress Ballet Soc. Conn., Inc., 1968-70; with corps de ballet Conn. Opera Assn., 1963-64; active in prodns. Simsbury Light Opera Assn., 1964, 69. Mem. ALA, Conn. Library Assn., Simsbury Hist. Soc., Ont. Geneal. Soc., New Eng. Historic and Geneal. Soc., AAUW (past pres. Greater Hartford br.), Pro Dance, DAR (Abigail Phelps chpt.), Conn. Soc. Genealogists, Soc. Mayflower Descs. Conn., Dance Masters Am. Universalist. Office: 725 Hopmeadow St Simsbury CT 06070-2243

ROBERTS, COKIE, broadcaster. BA in Polit. Sci. with distinction, Wellesley Coll., 1964. Reporter CBS, Athens; congl. corr. PBS-TV's MacNeil-Lehrer Newshour; spl. corr. This Week with David Brinkley and Nightline ABC News; sr. news analyst newsmag. Morning Edition Nat. Pub. Radio. Co-host weekly pub. TV program on congress The Lawmakers, 1981-84; producer, host pub. affairs program Sta. WRC-TV, Washington; producer Sta. KNBC-TV Serendipity, L.A. (award for excellence in local programming, Emmy nomination for children's programming); contbr. articles to mags. Recipient Everett McKinley Dirksen award for disting. reporting of congress, 1987, Corp. Pub. Broadcasting award, 1988, Edward R. Murrow award, 1990. Office: Nat Pub Radio 2025 M St NW Washington DC 20036*

ROBERTS, DAVID CARON, computer scientist; b. Abilene, Tex., Sept. 13, 1944; s. Robert Henry and Ada Louise (Buckingham) R.; m. Mary Jane Fallis, May 30, 1965; 1 child, Lindsay Ann. BS in Engring. Sci., Johns Hopkins, 1965; MS in Engring., U. Pa., 1968; MS in Computer Sci., U. Md., 1973. Research scientist Pa. Research Assocs., Phila., 1965-69; mgr. data processing systems Informatics Inc., Rockville, Md., 1969-74; tech. dir. Ocean Data Systems, Rockville, 1974-75; project engr. CIA, Washington, 1975-81, info. systems arch., 1985—; v.p. Oracle Systems Corp., Menlo Park, Calif., 1981-85; adj. prof. George Washington U., 1975-87. Contbr. articles to profl. jours. Mem. IEEE, Assn. Computing Machines. Democrat. Club: Potomac Tennis. Home: 8833 Harness Trl Rockville MD 20854-2556 Office: CIA Washington DC 20505

ROBERTS, DONALD ALBERT, cable television executive, marketing, media consultant; b. Boston, Dec. 17, 1935; s. Albert Arthur and Linette Violette (Ouelette) R.; m. Gabrielle Dorothy St. Laurent, Apr. 20, 1957; children: Lynne Dianne, Tammy Denise. Student, U. Maine, 1987-88, Liberty U., 1988-89. Program mgr., dir. sports Sta. WIMA-TV, Lima, Ohio, 1965-68; v.p., gen. mgr. Sta. WABK/WKME, Gardiner, Maine, 1968-74; pres., owner Sta. WRDO, Augusta, Maine, 1974-77; cons. group gen. mgr. Valley Communications, Bangor, Maine, 1977-78; pres., owner Roberts Advt. Agy., Augusta, 1977-78; v.p., gen. mgr. Sta. WLOB AM/FM, Portland, Maine, 1978-80, Sta. WKCG/WFAU, Augusta, 1980-83; pres., owner Roberts & Co., Augusta, 1983—; exec. v.p. mktg., programming and advt. sales State Cable TV Corp., Augusta, 1983—; cons. New Eng. Ziebart Dealers Assn., 1982—. Contbr. articles to profl. jours. Pres. Auburn (Maine) City Coun., 1957-60; chmn. Jefferson-Jackson Dinner, Rockland, Maine, 1959, Preserve Augusta Neighborhood Assn., 1989—; del. Dem. State Conv., Bangor, 1980; city councilor-at-large of Augusta, 1990—. Named Maine Sportscaster of Yr. Nat. Sportscasters Assn., 1962, 63; recipient Tiger award Maine Broadcasting System, 1965. Mem. So. Kennebec Valley Realtors Assn., Cable Advt. Bur., Cable TV Adminstrs. and Marketers, Ohio Sportscasters Assn. (co-founder 1965), Maine Assn. Broadcasters (bd. dirs.), Kennebec Valley C. of C. (bd. dirs.). Home and Office: 44 Longwood Ave Augusta ME 04330-4131

ROBERTS, EDWARD BAER, technology management educator; b. Chelsea, Mass., Nov. 18, 1935; s. Nathan and Edna (Podradchik) R.; m. Nancy Helen Rosenthal, June 14, 1959; children: Valerie Jo Roberts Friedman, Mitchell Jonathan, Andrea Lynne. BS and MS in Elec. Engring., MIT, 1958, MS in Mgmt., 1960, PhD in Econs., 1962. Founding mem. system dynamics program MIT, 1958-84, instr., 1959-61, asst. prof., 1961-65, assoc. prof., 1965-70, prof., 1970—, David Sarnoff prof. mgmt. of tech., 1974—, assoc. dir. research program on mgmt. of sci. and tech., 1963-73, chmn. tech. and health mgmt. group, 1973-88, chmn. mgmt. of tech. and innovation, 1988—; co-founder, pres. Pugh-Roberts Assocs., Inc., Cambridge, Mass., 1963-89, chmn., 1989—; co-founder, dir. Med. Info. Tech., Inc., Westwood, Mass., 1969—; dir. MIT-Boston VA Joint Ctr. on Health Care Mgmt., 1976-80, MIT Mgmt. of Tech. Program, 1980-89, chmn., 1989—; co-founder, gen. ptnr. Zero Stage Capital Group, 1981—; bd. dirs. Advanced Magnetics, Inc., Cambridge, Laser Scis., Inc., Cambridge, Superior Sensors Inc., Cambridge, Digital Products Inc., Waltham, Mass. Author: The Dynamics of Research and Development, 1964, Systems Simulation for Regional Analysis, 1969, The Persistent Poppy, 1975, The Dynamics of Human Service Delivery, 1976, Entrepreneurs in High Technology, 1991; prin. author, editor: Managerial Applications of System Dynamics, 1978; editor (with others) Biomedical Innovation, 1981; editor: Generating Technological Innovation, 1987; mem. editorial bd. IEEE Trans. on Engring. Mgmt., Internat. Jour. Tech. Mgmt., Indsl. Mktg. Mgmt., Jour. Engring. and Tech. Mgmt., Jour. Product Innovation Mgmt., Sloan Mgmt. Rev., Tech. Forecasting and Social Change. Mem. IEEE, Inst. Mgmt. Sci., Sigma Xi, Tau Beta Pi, Eta Kappa Nu, Tau Kappa Alpha. Home: 17 Fellsmere Rd Newton MA 02159-1306 Office: 50 Memorial Dr Cambridge MA 02139

ROBERTS, ELIZABETH ANN, executive; b. Springfield, Mass., Mar. 20, 1943; d. D.F. and Fannie (Dasso) Amedeo; m. William Raymond Roberts, May 18, 1963; children: Dennis Raymond, Mark Francis; m. Catherine Crinella; 1 child, Anthony. Student, Springfield Tech. Community Co, 1983. Asst. credit mgr. Broadlees Dept. Store, West Springfield, Mass.; sec. Safe Deposit Bank & Trust, Springfield, 1961-64; substitute tchr. Springfield Sch. Dept.; treas., office mgr. William Roberts Electric Co., 1987—. Democrat. Roman Catholic. Home and Office: 322 Holcomb Rd Springfield MA 01118-2617

ROBERTS, ETHAN SHAWN, family therapist; b. N.Y.C., July 15, 1954; s. George Robert and Marcia (Shattles) Roberts. BA, Hofstra U., 1982, MA, 1985. Counselor Cath. Charities, South Ozone Park, N.Y., 1982-85; coord. of family svcs. Youth Environ. Svcs., Massapequa, N.Y., 1986—; pvt. practice Amityville, N.Y., 1989—; adj. prof. dept. health and phys. edn. Long Island U., 1989—; workshop presenter in field. Author: (with others) The Role of Fun in Family Therapy, 1991; contbr. articles to profl. jours. Mem. AACD, Internat. Assn. for Marital and Family Therapists. Home: 119 Raymond St Rockville Centre NY 11570-2540 Office: Youth Environ Svcs 30 Broadway Massapequa NY 11758-5034

ROBERTS, GAIL ANN, educator; b. Bronx, N.Y., June 7, 1961; d. Barry Stanley Levey and Estelle Florence (Reisner) Cohen. BS in Spl. Edn., Millersville, U., 1983; M Counselor Edn., Millersville, 1987. Cert. tchr., counselor, Pa. Tchr. Intermediate Unit 13, East Petersburg, Pa., 1983-90, Manheim (Pa.) Cen. Sch. Dist., 1990—; youth care worker Barnes Hall, County of Lancaster, Pa., 1986-88; homebound student instr. Warwick Sch. Dist., Lititz, Pa., 1989. Recipient Gift of Time tribute Am. Family Inst., 1991, 92. Mem. AACD. Home: 43 Winding Way Lititz PA 17543-9345 Office: Manheim Cen Sch Dist 71 N Hazel St Manheim PA 17545-1500

ROBERTS, GLENN ERIC, professional association executive; b. Bayonne, N.J., July 13, 1947; s. Wilfred R. and Dorothy (Schaubam) R.; m. Katharine F. Roberts, June 11, 1983; children: Margaret, Abigail. BA, Oberlin Coll., 1968. Reporter Raleigh Times, 1968-72; legis. dir. Bd. Suprs., San Francisco, 1980-82, Republic of Palau, Micronesia, 1985-87, U.S. Rep. Norman Mineta, Washington, 1981-87, Sen. Barbara Mikulski, Washington, 1987-90, Fragrance Materials Assn., Washington, 1990—. Named Hon. Citizen Republic of Palau, 1987. Office: FMA Ste 925 1620 I St NW Washington DC 20006

ROBERTS, JANINE, family therapist; b. Olympia, Wash., May 5, 1947; d. Fred B. Roberts and Phyllis (Heaton) Pennell; m. Gerald Weinstein; 1 child, Natalya; m. David McGill, Aug. 26, 1990; children: Jesse, Heather. BA, U. Wash., 1970; MEd, Antioch Grad. Sch., Phila., 1971; EdD, U. Mass., 1982. Vol. VISTA, Newark, 1965-66; tchr. Phila. Pub. Schs., 1970-73; head tchr. Univ. City New Sch., Phila., 1973-76; family therapist Northampton Ctr. for Children & Families, Mass., 1979-81; assoc. prof. U. Mass., Amherst, 1982—; cons. to numerous mental health agencies, 1981—. Co-editor, author (with others): Rituals in Families & Family Therapy, 1988; co-author: Rituals for Our Times, 1992; adv. editor Family Process, 1989—; co-editor Jour. of Strategic & Systemic Therapies, 1986—; contbr. articles to profl. jours. and books. Bd. dirs. Friends of the Libr., Leverett, 1990-92. Lilly Endowment Teaching fellow U. Mass., 1988-89,. Jr. fellow Inst. for the Advanced Study of the Humanities, Amherst, 1988. Mem. Am. Family Therapy Therapy Assn. (bd. dirs. 1991-93), Am. Assn. for Marriage and Family Therapy (program and publs. com. 1990-92, governt. rels. com., clin. mem.). Home: 38 Putney Rd Leverett MA 01054 Office: U Mass 460 Hills S Amherst MA 01003

ROBERTS, KATHLEEN JOY DOTY, educator; b. Jamaica, N.Y., Apr. 19, 1951; d. Alfred Arthur and Helen Caroline (Sohl) Doty; m. Robert Louis Roberts, Nov. 24, 1974; children: Robert Louis, Michael Sean, Kathleen Meagan. BA in Edn., Queens Coll., 1972, MS in Spl. Edn., 1974; cert. of advanced study in ednl. adminstrn. Hofstra U., 1982. Cert. N.Y. State Dept. Mental Hygiene; cert. sch. adminstr., math tchr., N.Y.; lic. spl. edn. supr., ednl. adminstr. Health conservation tchr. Woodside Jr. High Sch., Woodside, N.Y., 1973-77; coord. spl. edn. dept., Ridgewood (N.Y.) Jr. High Sch., 1977-81; adminstrv. asst., health coord., compliance coord., resource tchr. mentor Grover Cleveland High Sch., Ridgewood, N.Y., 1981—. Author: Closed Circuit Television and Other Devices for the Partially Sighted, 1971. Legis. chmn. Fairfield Jr./Sr. PTA and Massapequa Coun.; leader (Webelos) Boy Scouts Am., 1992—. Mem. AAUW, DAR, NEA, N.Y. State Tchrs. Assn., Coun. for Exceptional Children, Soc. Mayflower Descendants, Colonial Daus. of 17th Century (pres. 1985-91, registrar historian, 1991—, nat. chmn. hist. activities com. 1988-91, nat. councillor, publicity chmn. 1991—), Pilgrim Edward Doty Soc. Republican. Home: 52 Hicksville Rd Massapequa NY 11758-5843 also: Lake Ariel PA Office: Grover Cleveland High Sch 2127 Himrod St Flushing NY 11385-1299

ROBERTS, KENNETH BARRIS, lawyer; b. N.Y.C., Mar. 21, 1954; s. Howard Bertram and Gloria Betty (Feinstein) R.; m. Karen Ilsa Dietshe, June 28, 1987. BA in Psychology, Duke U., 1976; JD, U. Mich., 1980. Bar: N.Y. 1982. Assoc. Hawkins, Delafield & Wood, N.Y.C., 1980-87, ptnr., 1988—. Mem. Assn. Bar City N.Y., Downtown Athletic Club, City Club Washington. Office: Hawkins Delafield & Wood 67 Wall St New York NY 10005-3101

ROBERTS, KENNETH DOUGLAS, hospital administrator; b. Astoria, N.Y., Oct. 13, 1949; s. George William and Bernardine (Taggart) R.; m. Catherine Mullens, Aug. 14, 1976; children: Ross, Leanne, Remington and Jackson (twins). BS in Econs., SUNY, Oneonta, 1971; MPH in Health Policy Planning and Adminstrn., NYU, 1977; MBA in Fin., Hofstra U., 1981. Sr. staff asst. Group Health Inc., N.Y.C., 1973-76; adminstrv. resident South Nassau Communities Hosp., Oceanside, N.Y., 1976-77, asst. dir., 1977-82; assoc. dir. adminstrn. John T. Mather Meml. Hosp., Port Jefferson, N.Y., 1982-84, sr. v.p., 1985-86, pres., 1986—; pres. Nassau-Suffolk Health Care Assocs., L.I., 1981-82; bd. dirs. Hosp. Underwriters Mut., Albany, N.Y. Mem. agy. execs. coun. United Way L.I.; chmn. Nassau-Suffolk Polit. Activities Com., L.I., 1989, 90, 91. Mem. Am. Coll. Healthcare Execs., N.Y. Acad. Medicine (blood supply and svcs. com.), Nassau-Suffolk Hosp. Coun. (govt. rels. com. L.I. chpt. 1990, 91), Lions (bd. dirs. Port Jefferson chpt.). Roman Catholic. Office: John T Mather Meml Hosp North Country Rd Port Jefferson NY 11777

ROBERTS, KEVIN FRANCES, business manager; b. Portland, Maine, July 20, 1948; s. Ralph C. and Mary (Ridge) R.; m. Claire Ann Beaudoin, May 20, 1989; children: Kristina, Alyson. Student, We. New England, 1980-90. Supr. Tileflex Corp., Springfield, Mass., 1969-75, gen. supr., 1975-78, plant mgr., 1978-81, dir. ops., 1981-89, bus. mgr., 1989—. Bd. dirs. Huntington Disease Soc., Boston, 1988-91, pres., 1985-90. With U.S. Army, 1966-69, Vietnam. Home: 45LaFond Dr Chicopee MA 01020 Office: Tielflex Corp 603 Hendee St Springfield MA 01109

ROBERTS, PETER A., banker; b. N.Y.C., Apr. 11, 1951; s. Louis Aaron and Ida Ann (Sterman) Rottenberg. B.A., Colgate U., 1973; M.B.A., Stanford U., 1976. Vol. VISTA, Louisville, 1973-74; v.p., investment banker Morgan Stanley & Co., N.Y.C., 1976-82; investment banker Lazard Freres, N.Y.C., 1982-86, gen. ptnr., 1985-86; chmn., chief exec. officer College Savs. Bank, Princeton, N.J., 1987—. Mem. N.Y. Athletic Club, Metedeconk Nat. Golf Club (Jackson, N.J.), Omicron Delta Epsilon. Republican. Office: College Savs Bank 5 Vaughn Dr Princeton NJ 08540-6313

ROBERTS, PHILIP GWYNNE, JR., surgeon; b. Pitts., Aug. 26, 1939; s. Philip G. and Mary G. (Richards) R.; m. Judith Lynn Colbeck, May 30, 1964; children: Philip G. III, Susan Lynn. Student, Franklin & Marshall Coll., 1957-59; BA in English, U. Pitts., 1961; MD, Temple U., 1965. Cert. Am. Bd. Orthopaedic Surgery; Diplomate Am. Bd. Orthopedic Surgery. Intern, surgery resident St. Luke's Hosp., Bethlehem, Pa., 1965-67; physician, lt. comdr. USN, 1967-69; orthopaedic surgery resident U. Pa., Phila., 1969-72; orthopaedic surgeon Sevick-Roberts Assocs., Inc., State Coll., Pa., 1972—; chmn. dept. surgery Centre Community Hosp., State Coll., 1978-85, asst. chief ofstaff, 1985-88; team physician State Coll. Area Schs., 1972—. Ruling elder State Coll. Presbyn. Ch., 1977-83, deacon, 1974-77. Recipient Am. Legion award, 1954. Fellow Am. Acad. Orthopaedic Surgeons; mem. Am. Coll. Sports Medicine, Centre County Med. Soc., U. Pa. Orthopaedic Alumni, Masonic Blue Consistory and Jaffa Shrine, Am. Legion Post 245. Republican. Presbyterian. Home: 576 Shadow Ln State College PA 16803 Office: Sevick and Roberts Assocs 911 University Dr State College PA 16801

ROBERTS, RANDOLPH WILSON, science educator; b. Scranton, Pa., Oct. 8, 1946; s. S. Tracy and Alecia Francis (Sullivan) R.; m. Martha Jeanne Burnite, July 12, 1969 (div. Dec. 1985); children: Gwendolyn Suzanne, Ryan Weylin; m. Ava Elaine Brown, June 17, 1989. AB in Biology, Franklin & Marshall Coll., 1968, MA in Earth Scis., 1974; MS in Sci. Teaching, Am. U., 1977; MS in Counseling, Western Md. Coll., 1990; postgrad., U. Md., Towson State U., Union Inst., Cin., Johns Hopkins U. Cert. tchr., counselor, tax cons. Tchr. sci. Woodlawn Jr. High Sch., Balt., 1968-73, Deer Park Jr. High/Mid. Sch., Randallstown, Md., 1973-87, Franklin Mid. Sch., Reisterstown, Md., 1987-89; sci. dept. chmn. and counselor Balt. County Home & Hosp. Sch., 1989—; math. & sci. tchr. Loyola High Sch., Towson, Md., summers 1981-86, Talmudical Acad., Pikesville, Md., 1983-86; ednl. cons. Scott & Fetzer Co., Chgo., 1981-86; founder, owner, pres. Tax Assistance, Ltd., Owings Mills, Md., 1981—; curriculum cons. Balt. County Bd. Edn., Towson, 1977, 78. Author: Earth Sciences Workbook, 1979. Mem. handbell choir Glyndon (Md.) Meth. Ch., 1992—, scholarship and fin. com., 1981-88; treas. Boy Scouts Am. Pack 315, Reis, Md., 1986-90, Webelos Den leader, 1987-90, advancement chmn. Troop 315, 1990—. Mem. NEA, AACD, Balt. Road Runners, World Wildlife Fund, Nature Conservancy, Chesapeake Bay Found., Phi Delta Kappa, Mu Upsilon Sigma, Chi Sigma Iota. Home: 9 Indian Pony Ct Owings Mills MD 21117-1210 Office: Home and Hosp Sch 6229 Falls Rd Baltimore MD 21209-2199

ROBERTS, RICHARD ROBERT, lobbyist; b. Wheeling, W.Va., Aug. 15, 1941; s. Guy Leeton and Stella (Vezzetti) R.; m. Mary Amelia Musar, Dec. 17, 1977. BA in History, U. Ga., 1964. News dir. Sta. WISK-AM Radio, Americus, Ga., 1963-64; dir. spl. programs Sta. WROM AM/FM Radio, Rome, Ga., 1964-66; instr. history Thornwood Acad., Rome, 1964-66; dir. TV woodward Acad., College Park, Ga., 1966-68; prof. communications California (Pa.) State Coll., 1968-77; exec. asst. Congressman Austin J. Murphy, Washington, 1977-80; v.p. Outdoor Advt. Assn. Am., Washington, 1980-85; pres. Am. Coun. Hwy. Advt., Washington, 1985—; mng. ptnr. Roberts and Co., North Beach, Md., 1985—; lectr. U.S. War Coll., Washington, 1981-90, U. Md., College Park, 1985-90. Contbr. to profl. publs. Mem. North Beach Zoning Appeals Bd., Tourism Caucus U.S. Congress, Washington; dir. photography Major Crime Scenes Team, North Beach. Officer U.S. Mcht. Marine. Recipient Adminstrs. award VA, 1982, Wilbur award Religious Pub. Rels. Coun., numerous awards for advt. campaigns. Mem. Chesapeake Area Profl. Chpt. Assn. Office: Roberts and Co PO Box 809 North Beach MD 20714-0809

ROBERTS, SAMUEL SMITH, television news executive; b. Port Chester, N.Y., Feb. 8, 1936; s. Robert M. and Lillian (Smith) R.; children by previous marriage: Nancy, Pamela; m. Harriet Rubin, July 27, 1975; children: Rachel, David. BS, Northwestern U., 1957. Reporter UPI, N.Y.C., 1961; news editor Capital Cities Broadcasting, Providence, 1962; reporter CBS News, N.Y.C., 1962-65, assoc. producer Spl. Reports, 1965-67; assoc. producer CBS Evening News with Walter Cronkite, N.Y.C., 1967-78; producer CBS Evening News, N.Y.C., 1978-81; sr. producer CBS News Spl. Events, N.Y.C., 1981; nat. editor CBS News, 1982-84, fgn. editor, 1984-87, exec. dir. internat. broadcast services, 1987-92, dir. programming, exec. prodducer, 1992—. Served to lt. USN, 1957-61.

ROBERTS, WILLIAM, history educator; b. Weehawken, N.J., July 24, 1945; s. William and Elizabeth Ann (Helble) R. BA, Fairleigh Dickinson U., 1967; MA, Fordham U., 1969; MPhil, CUNY, 1987, PhD, 1988. Assoc. prof. history Fairleigh Dickinson U., Teaneck, N.J., 1970—. Author: Dictionary of Modern Italian History, 1983, Prophet in Exile, 1989, Bibliography of Modern Italian History, 1990, A History of Sicily, 1992. Mem. Cen. Westchester Humane Soc., Elmsford, N.Y., 1990; mem. adv. panel in European history NEH, 1990; adviser Kappa Alpha Psi, 1992. Recipient Outstanding Faculty award Edward Williams Coll., Fairleigh Dickinson U., 1992. Mem. Phi Omega Epsilon. Office: Fairleigh Dickinson U Kotte Pl Hackensack NJ 07601-6112

ROBERTS, WILLIAM ALLAN, engineering company executive; b. N.Y.C., Nov. 16, 1930; s. Israel and Sophie (Steinberg) Rabinovitch; m. Lorrayne Krinsky, July 10, 1954; children: Steven, Susan, Andrea. BChemE, NYU, 1951; MSChemE, Columbia U., 1958; PMD, Harvard U., 1976. Registered profl. engr. N.J., Tex., Mass., Ky., Pa., Mich. Jr. engr. Standard Brands, N.Y.C., 1951-53; project engr. Columbia U., N.Y.C., 1953-56; project mgr. Englehard Industries, Newark, 1956-60; mgr. engring. Chem. Constrn. Corp., N.Y.C., 1960-74; pres. Nichols Engring. and Rsch. Corp., Belle Mead, N.J., 1974-78; mgr. contracts Am. Air Filter, Louisville, 1978-80; project mgr. Lummus Corp., Bloomfield, N.J., 1980-83; pvt. engr. Ramsey, N.J., 1983-88; mgr. contracts Toyo U.S.A., Greenwich, Conn., 1988—. Pres. Parents Assn., The Tng. Sch. at Vineland, N.J., 1987-89; active Assn. for Retarded Citizens. Mem. Am. Chem. Soc., Harvard Bus. Sch. Club. Home: 277 Nottingham Rd Ramsey NJ 07446-2655 Office: Toyo USA Inc 8 Sound Shore Dr Greenwich CT 06830-7242

ROBERTS, WILLIAM HOOTON, IV (), company executive; b. Durango, Colo., Mar. 6, 1953; s. William Hooton and Mary Jane (McKinley) R.; m. Kelly Leone Kendall, Oct. 21, 1961. Student, El Paso Community Coll., Colo., 1972-73, Shippensburg (Pa.) State Coll., 1979-81. Site coord. Ket Svcs., Inc., Chambersburg, Pa., 1978—; owner, mgr. Heirloom Portraits, Chambersburg, Pa., 1990—. Published fine art photographer in Am. References, 1990. With U.S. Army, 1972-78. Recipient award Fine Art Photography Salon, Washinngton County, Md., 1989, 90. Mem. Profl. Photographers Am. Republican. Unitarian. Home: 11651 Tanyard Hill Rd Orrstown PA 17244-9618

ROBERTSON, ALAN GORDON, educational consultant; b. Jackson Heights, N.Y., Aug. 15, 1928; s. William Gordon and C. Olivia (Holst) R.; m. Barbara L. Dexter, Nov. 1, 1952; children: David Alan, Elizabeth Anne. BA, Queens Coll., 1949; AMT, Harvard U., 1950; EdD, NYU, 1960; postdoctoral, SUNY, Albany, 1970-72. Cert. career counselor. Tchr., guidance counselor N.Y.C. Bd. Edn., 1950-55; dir. guidance Plainedge Pub. Schs., Bethpage, N.Y., 1955-63; rsch. assoc. N.Y. State Edn. Dept., Albany, 1963-65, dir., Div. Edn. Program Evaluation, 1967-76, chief, Bur. Occupational Edn. Rsch., 1965-67, 76-84; cons. Delmar, N.Y., 1984—; cons. Joint Com. on Testing, Washington, 1987-92, Nat. Occupational Info. Coord. Com., Bismark, N.D., 1987-88; project mgr. Ctr. Advanced Study in Edn., CUNY, 1985-86. Author: 200 Years of Vocational and Practical Arts Education in New York, 1991; contbg. author: (textbooks) Counselor's Guide to Career Assessment Instruments, 1988, Case Studies in Testing an Interdisciplinary Approach, 1992. Bd. trustees St. Andrew's Soc. Albany, N.Y., 1988-92; bd. trustees, investments chair First United Meth. Ch., Delmar, N.Y., 1989-92. Mem. Am. Vocat. Edn. Rsch. Assn. (pres. 1967-68), Assn. Measurement and Evaluation in Counseling (pres. 1985-86), Clan Donnachaidh Assn. Scotland (del. 1985), U.S. Naval Inst., Mendelssohn Male Chorus (part capt.), Yankee Male Chorus, Steuben Athletic Club Albany, N.Y. Home: 198 Adams St Delmar NY 12054-3214

ROBERTSON, ANDREW, ecologist, research administrator; b. Port Huron, Mich., Sept. 15, 1936; s. Andrew and Agnes M. (Atkins) R.; m. Mary S. Johnson, Dec. 19, 1965; children: Andrew, Ian C. BS, U. Toledo, 1958; MA, U. Mich., 1961, PhD, 1964. Assoc. limnologist Gt. Lakes rsch. U. Mich., Ann Arbor, 1964-68; assoc. prof. dept zoology U. Okla., Norman, 1968-71; fish biologist Internat. Field Yr. for Great Lakes project office NOAA, Rockville, Md., 1971-74; chief biology and chemistry Gt. Lakes Rsch. Lab. NOAA, Ann Arbor, 1974-81; dep. dir. Office of Marine Pollution Assessment NOAA, Rockville, 1981-83, dir. Nat. Marine Pollution Program Office, 1983-86, chief ocean assessment divsn., 1986-91, chief coastal monitoring and bioeffects assesment divsn., 1991—; staff asst. U.S. Ho. Reps., Washington, 1979-80; pres. Internat. Assn. Gt. Lakes Rsch., 1977-78. Author, editor: Lake Ecosystem Modeling, 1979; author: (with others) Ecosystems of the World, 1984, Toxic Contaminants and Ecosystem II, 1988; contbr. articles to Jour. of Great Lakes Rsch., Am. Midland Naturalist, 1975. Mem. Am. Soc. of Limnology and Oceanography, Ecol. Soc. Am., Estuaries Rsch. Fedn. Home: 9336 Orchard Brook Dr Rockville MD 20854-2325

ROBERTSON, ARTHUR KENNETH, JR., entrepreneur, minister, communications specialist; b. Oakland, Calif., May 20, 1937; s. Arthur Kenneth Robertson and Laura Bernice Arnerich; m. Linda Louise Kauffman, June 15, 1963; 1 child, Scott Alan. BA in Econs. and Pre-law, UCLA, 1959; ThM in New Testament, Greek, Dallas Theol. Sem., 1963; STM in Pastoral Psychology, N.Y. Theol. Sem., 1968; PhD in Edn., NYU, 1975. Ordained to ministry Plymmouth Brethren Ch., 1963. Chaplain USAR, Bklyn., 1964-65; pastor, tchr. Bklyn. Believer's Chapel, 1964-72; prof. The King's Coll., Briarcliff Manor, N.Y., 1968-81; pres. Effective Communication and Devel., Inc., Ossining, N.Y., 1981—; pres. book div. E.C. & O Inc., Ossining, 1991—; co-founder, dir. Billing Adjustment Cons., Ossining, 1991—; cons. to various companies, including IBM, AT&T, GM, Gen. Foods, Brystol-Myers, F.B.I. Acad., R.R. Donnelly, BMW, Nestlés Co., N.Y. Life, and Du Pont. Author: The Gospel of Matthew, 1975, Values that Pay: Business Ethics, 1986, The Four Hour Day, 1991, Language of Effective Listening, 1991; contbr. articles to profl. publs. Founder, chmn. Westchester County Leadership Prayer Breakfast, White Plains, N.Y., 1985—; co-chmn. Fernbrook Parents' Orgn., Ossining, 1980; mem. adv. bd. Christian Herald Found., Chappaqua, N.Y., 1988—; mem. adv. coun. Westchester County Prison Fellowship; edler Community Bible Ch., Ossining, 1985—. 1st lt. U.S. Army, 1963-64. Recognition day named in his honor, White Plains, Mar. 21, 1991. Mem. Internat. Listening Assn. (life, founding mem.), Westchester County C. of C.

ROBERTSON, BALDWIN, physicist, chemical engineer; b. L.A., Sept. 26, 1934; s. Ann Dyer, Apr. 7, 1962; children: Rebecca C., Sarah E., Baldwin V. BSEE with distinction, Stanford U., 1956, MSEE, 1957, PhD in Physics, 1965. Predoctoral fellow physics dept. Stanford U., Palo Alto, Calif., 1956-59; instr., rsch. assoc. physics dept. Cornell U., Ithaca, N.Y., 1964-66; postdoctoral rsch. assoc. phys. chem. div. Nat. Bur. Standards, Gaithersburg, Md., 1966-68, heat physicist heat div., 1968-70, gen. physicist Inst. Basic Standards, 1970-72, physicist mechanics div., 1974-83, chem. engr. chem. process metrol. div., 1983-91; chem. engr. biotech. div. Nat. Inst. Standards and Tech., Gaithersburg, Md., 1991—. Patentee in field; contbr. articles to profl. jours. Office: Nat Inst Standards and Tech A353 Chemistry Gaithersburg MD 20899

ROBERTSON, BRENT PARISH, aerospace engineer; b. St. Boniface, Manitoba, Can., Sept. 30, 1961; came to U.S., 1984; s. John Graham and Audrey Carol (Johnson) R.; m. Diane Louise Roach, Sept. 7, 1985; children: Bryan P., Kevin S. B in Engring. Sci., U. Toronto, 1984; MS, U. Va., 1985. Sr. aerospace engr. PRC Kentron, Hampton, Va., 1985-86; project engr. Analytical Mechanics Assocs., Hampton, 1986-89; staff engr. McDonnell Douglas Space Systems, Seabrook, Md., 1989—. Contbr. articles to profl. jours. U. Va. fellowship, 1984. Mem. AIAA, Canadian Aviation and Space Inst. Home: 8508 Moon Glass Ct Columbia MD 21045-5630 Office: MDSSC 7404 Exec Place Seabrook MD 20706

ROBERTSON, CHARLES JAMES, museum director; b. Houston, Sept. 12, 1934; s. Charles James and Felide Corinne (O'Brien) R. BA, U. Va., Charlottseville, 1956; MA, Harvard U., 1958; student, U. London Courtauld Inst., 1960; JD, George Washington U., 1964. Atty. Dow, Lohnes & Albertson, Washington, 1964-69; adminstr. Richard H. Chamberlain, M.D. & Assoc., Phila., 1969-75; assoc. dir. N.C. Mus. Art, Raleigh, 1975-77; deputy dir. Nat. Mus. Am. Art, Smithsonian Inst., Washington, 1977—; treas., exec. com. Am. Assn. Mus., Washington, 1982-84; mem. adv. com. Octagon House Mus., Washington, 1989—; bd. mem. Victorian Soc. Am., Phila., 1990—; mem. Historic Preservation Review Bd. of the Dist. of Columbia, 1992—. Contbr. articles to profl. jours. Pres. Dupont Circle Conservancy, Washington, 1978-92; v.p., bd. mem., Dupont Circle Citizens Assn., Washington, 1980-83, 86; juror, Renchard Prize, Hist. Soc. Washington, 1986. Recipient Z Prixe in English Lit., U. Va., Charlottseville, 1956, Rumrill fellowship Harvard U., Cambridge, Mass., 1956-57. Mem. Soc. Archtl. Historians, Soc. Decorative Arts, Delta Theta Phi Law Frat., Phi Beta Kappa. Office: Nat Mus Am Art Smithsonian Instn Washington DC 20560

ROBERTSON, DAVID ALAN, museum director, educator; b. Jefferson City, Mo., Oct. 10, 1950; s. Roy Victor and Mary Jane (Threlkeld) R. BA in English, U. Mo., 1973, MA in Art History, 1976; PhD in Art History, U. Pa., 1983. Museum asst. U. Mo. Museum, Columbia, 1975-76; tech. asst. Victoria and Albert Museum, London, 1976; curatorial asst. Yale Ctr. for British Art, New Haven, Conn., 1977-78; teaching fellow U. Pa., Phila., 1978-81; staff supr. Rosenbach Museum and Library, Phila., 1980-82; museum dir. Dickinson Coll., Carlisle, Pa., 1982—; Fulbright prof. U. Munich, Germany, 1989-90; mem. selection com. Fulbright Commn., Bonn, Germany, 1989; grant reviewer Inst. Mus. Svcs., Washington, 1989-91. Penfield fellow U. Pa., Vienna, Austria, 1981-82, Kress fellow Kress Found., London, 1976, Vienna, 1980. Mem. Am. Assn. Museums, Coll. Art Assn., Historians of Netherlandish Art, Assn. Coll. and Univ. Museums and Galleries. Office: Dickinson Coll High St Carlisle PA 17013-3015

ROBERTSON, EDWIN DAVID, lawyer; b. Roanoke, Va., July 5, 1946; s. Edwin Traylor and Norma Burns (Bowles) R.; m. Anne Littelle Ferratt, Sept. 7, 1968, 1 child, Thomas Therit. BA with honors, U. Va., 1968, LLB, 1971. Bar: N.Y. 1972, U.S. Ct. Appeals (2d cir.) 1972, U.S. Dist. Ct. (ea. and so. dists.) N.Y. 1973, U.S. Supreme Ct. 1975, U.S. Dist. Ct. (ea. dist.) Mich. 1986. Assoc. Cadwalader, Wickersham & Taft, N.Y.C., 1972-80; ptnr. Cadwalader, Wickershaft & Taft, N.Y.C., 1980—. Bd. dirs. Early Music Found. N.Y.C., 1983—; mem. Oratorio Soc. of N.Y.C., 1988—. Mem. ABA, Fed. Bar Coun., N.Y. County Lawyers Assn. (chmn. bankruptcy com. 1983-87, bd. dirs. 1985-88), Assn. of Bar of City of N.Y. (com. on state cts. of superior jurisdiction 1987-90, fed. legis. com. 1990—), Oratorio Soc. N.Y. (bd. dirs. 1988—), Jefferson Soc., Order of Coif, Soc. Colonial Wars, Phi Beta Kappa, Phi Kappa Psi. Republican. Episcopalian. Club: Down Town (N.Y.C.). Home: 315 E 72d St New York NY 10021 Office: Cadwalader Wickersham & Taft 100 Maiden Ln New York NY 10038-4818

ROBERTSON, JAMES BURROUGH, II, executive assistant; b. Collingswood, N.J., Jan. 10, 1944; s. John B. and Dorothy E. (Taylor) R.; m. Sandra M. Crouse, Dec. 21, 1943; children: David A., Andrew D. BS, Springfield (Mass.) Coll., 1966, MA, 1969, CAS, 1973. Cert. tchr. Dir. phys. edn. Eric Norfeldt Sch., West Hartford, Conn., 1968-72; assoc. prof. Springfield Coll., 1973-91, exec. asst. to the pres., 1991—; cons. St. John's Sch., Houston, 1988, Manchester (Conn.) Pub. Schs., 1991. Co-pres. Suffield (Conn.) Acad. Parent's Assn., 1989-91; corporator Children's Study Home, Springfield, 1980—; mem. Forest Park Civic Assn., Springfield, 1975—. Named Disting. Prof. Humanics, Springfield Coll., 1988-89; inducted to South Jersey Wrestling Hall of Fame, 1982, Collingswood High Sch. Athletic Hall of Fame, 1992. Mem. Am. Alliance for Health, Phys. Edn., Recreation and Dance (PEPI coord. 1987-88). Home: 18 Washington Rd Springfield MA 01108-2541 Office: Marsh Meml Springfield Coll Springfield MA 01109

ROBERTSON, JAMES SYDNOR, retired nuclear medicine physician, government agency official; b. Richmond, Va., Nov. 27, 1920; s. Paul Augustus and Beth O'Ferrall (Whitacre) R.; m. Ruth Elizabeth Henrici, Jan. 15, 1944; children: Kathleen Mary, John Paul, Marion Adelle. BS, U. Minn., 1943, MB, 1944, MD, 1945; PhD in Physiology, U. Calif., Berkeley, 1949. Diplomate Am. Bd. Nuclear Medicine. Head med. physics Brookhaven Nat. Lab., Upton, N.Y., 1950-75; cons. nuclear medicine Mayo Clinic, Rochester, Minn., 1975-84; dir. human health Office Energy Rsch., U.S. Dept. Energy, Washington, D.C., 1984-91. Author, editor: Compartmental Distribution of Radiotracers, 1983; contbr. articles to profl. jours. Served to capt. USN. Fellow AAAS; mem. Am. Physiol. Soc., Health Physics Soc., Radiation Rsch. Soc., Soc. Nuclear Medicine, Math. Assn. Am., Masons. Democrat. Methodist. Home: 18909 Tributary Ln Gaithersburg MD 20879-3409

ROBERTSON, JENNIFER LOUISE, consumer electronics executive; b. Mineola, N.Y., June 11, 1963; d. John Hamilton and Wilma Ann (Hammerle) R. BA in Econs., St. Lawrence U., 1985. Asst. buyer Bloomingdale's, N.Y.C., 1986-88, dept. mgr., 1988-89; customer svc. mgr. Cicena, Inc., N.Y.C., 1989, product mgr., 1989-91, v.p. ops., 1991—.

ROBERTSON, KATHY ANN, real estate developer; b. Balt., Aug. 2, 1959; m. Calvin D. Robertson; children: Courtney, Kelley. BArch, Hampton Inst., 1983; postgrad., Johns Hopkins U., 1990, Catonsville Community Coll., 1991-92. Grad. architect Edmunds & Hyde, Inc., architects, Balt., 1983-87; project architect Bancroft Homes, developers/builders, Owings Mills, Md., 1987-88; project coord. Lapicki-Smith Assocs., P.A., architects, Balt., 1988-90; project architect J.W. Mack Design Ptnrship., Balt., 1990-91; fee inspector HUD, Balt., 1991-92; devel. dir. Sandtown-Winchester Community Devel. Corp., Balt., 1992—. Bd. dirs. Sandtown-Winchester Devel. Corp., Balt., 1990-92; bd. trustees Sharp St. Meml. United Meth. Ch., Balt., 1989—. Recipient Sandtown-Winchester award Sandtown-Winchester Improvement Assn., 1991. Mem. Black Women in Architecture. Office: Sandtown Winchester Community Devel Corp 1343 N Calhoun St Baltimore MD 21217

ROBERTSON, LUCRETIA SPEZIALE, interior designer, author; b. Pitts., Feb. 23, 1944; d. Louis Albert and Irene (Lavenka) Speziale; m. Ronald Paul Parlato, Aug. 21, 1965 (div. Dec. 1967); m. William Sterling Robertson III, Feb. 3., 1973; children: Evan Alexander, Ian Stewart. BFA in Art History, Fine Arts and Archtl. Design, Smith Coll., 1965. Asst. art dept. Condé Nast-Mademoiselle, N.Y.C., 1965-66; dir. fashion M. Lowenstein and Sons, N.Y.C., 1966-67; fashion coordinator Vogue/Butterick Pattern Co., N.Y.C., 1967-70, creative dir. advt./promotions, 1970-73; prin. Lang/Robertson, Ltd., N.Y.C. and Montclair, N.J., 1975—; cons., designer Boussac of France, N.Y.C., 1975—; cons. Burlington Industries, N.Y.C., 1976-79, Levolor/Lorentzen, Parsippany, N.J., 1980—; designer McCalls Patterns, N.Y.C., 1979-81, AABE Fabrieken, Tillburg, Holland, 1983-85. Author: (ghost-writer) Body and Beauty Secrets of the Superbeauties, 1978, Decorating with Fabric, 1986; contbr. to Am. Psychiat. Press, Inc.; presenter paper on vol. work to 5th Nat. Conv. on Pediatric AIDS, L.A., 1989. Vol. St. Luke's Ch. Outreach program, Montclair, 1978—, Whole Theatre Co., Montclair, 1980—, AIDS Resource Found. for Children, Newark; singer N.J. Oratorio Soc.; vol. pediatric AIDS, Albert Einstein Coll. Medicine, Bronx, N.Y.; devel. bd. Hyacinth Found. AIDS Resources, N.J.; mem. Montclair AIDS Task Force; organizing com. St. Luke's Episcopal Ch. AIDS Task Force. Mem. Smith Club. Democrat. Episcopalian. Office: 36 Eagle Rock Way Montclair NJ 07042-2017

ROBERTSON, NAN, journalist, correspondent; b. Chgo., July 11, 1926; d. Frank and Eva (Morrish) R.; m. Allyn Baum, Feb. 24, 1950 (div. 1961); m. Stanley Levey, Aug. 27, 1961 (dec. 1971). B.S. in Journalism, Northwestern U., 1948. Spl. corr. Paris Herald Tribune, Paris, Berlin and London, 1948-55, Milw. Jour., Paris, Berlin and London, 1948-55, Stars and Stripes, Paris, Berlin and London, 1948-55, Am. Daily, Paris, Berlin and London, 1948-55; reporter, corr. N.Y. Times, N.Y.C., Washington and Paris, 1955-83; reporter culture N.Y. Times, N.Y.C., from 1983. Author: The Girls in the Balcony: Women, Men and The New York Times, 1992. Recipient Pulitzer prize for feature writing, 1983; recipient Page One award N.Y. Newspaper Guild, 1983, Front Page award N.Y. Newswomen's Club, 1961, 80, 82, N.Y. Press Club award, 1983; MacDowell Colony fellow, 1981, 83; Woodrow Wilson nat. fellow, 1983. Episcopalian. Address: care Kelly Susa Random House Inc 201 E 50th St New York NY 10022

ROBERTSON, RICHARD BOYD, transportation executive; b. Richmond, Va., Nov. 14, 1936; s. Walter Gray and Annie Bruce (Boyd) R.; m. Patricia Jean Atkinson, Aug. 29, 1959; children: Elizabeth Bruce, Richard Boyd Jr. BSCE, Va. Mil. Inst., 1958; cert. in hwy. traffic, Yale U., 1961; M in Regional Planning, U. N.C., Chapel Hill, 1964. Transp. planning engr. Va. Dept. Hwys., Richmond, 1958-67; exec. dir. Richmond Regional Planning Dist. Commn., 1967-70; dir. state transp. planning Office of the Gov., Richmond, 1971; spl. cons. Office of Sec. Dept. Transp., Washington, 1971-72; dir. transp. Appalachian Regional Commn., Washington, 1972-81; assoc. adminstr. for policy Fed. Hwy. Adminstr. U.S. Dept. Transp., Washington, 1981-89; sr. assoc. Linton, Mields, Reisler, Cottone, Washington, 1989-90; dir. gen. Inter. Road Fedn., Washington, 1990—. Mem. Rep. Party of Va., 1971—, Rep. Party, Washington, 1971—. Fellow Inst. Transp. Engrs.; mem. ASCE, Internat. Bridge, Tunnel and Turnpike Assn., Internat. Pub. Works Fedn., Road Gang. Republican. Presbyterian. Home: 2167 Kings Gardens Way Falls Church VA 22043-2594 Office: Internat Road Fedn 525 School St SW Washington DC 20024-2729

ROBERTSON, SUZANNE MARIE, educator; b. Canton, Ohio, Nov. 21, 1944; d. Jules Michael and Emma Louise (Olmar) Franzen; m. William K. Robertson, June 30, 1973 (dec. 1979). BS in Early Childhood Edn., Kent State U., 1966; M in Early Childhood Edn., Southern Conn. U., 1976; postgrad., Fairfield U. and U. Bridgeport, 1981-82. Kindergarten tchr. Ridgefield (Conn.) Bd. Edn., 1966—; children's gymnastics instr. Ridgefield (Conn.) YMCA, 1982-83, Sherman Parks & Recreation, Conn., 1983-85. Toy designer; mem. nat. adv. bd. Learning Mag. Campaign vol. Cancer Fund of Am., Sherman, 1980-81. Awarded Honorable Mention Learning Mag., 1989; recipient Profl. Best Teaching awards. Mem. NEA, Tchrs. Assn. Supporting Children (chmn. 1986-89, Fairfield County pub. rels. com. 1986-89), Conn. Edn. Assn., Internat. Platform Assn., Sherman Hist. Soc., Phi Delta Kapp (historian 1989-90, rsch. rep. 1990-91). Office: Farmingville Elem Sch Farmingville Rd Ridgefield CT 06877-4227

ROBERTSON, WILLIAM, IV, foundation administrator; b. Glen Ridge, N.J., Sept. 12, 1943; s. William R. III and Shirley (Anderson) Volpe; m. Harriette Alicia Sorenson, May 30, 1970; children: Paige, William V. BS, Parsons Coll., Fairfield, Iowa, 1966; MA, Sam Houston State U., 1969. Staff officer Nat. Acad. Scis., Washington, 1971-79; program dir. Andrew W. Mellon Found., N.Y.C., 1979—. Trustee Rumson (N.J.) Country Day Sch., 1984-91, Ctr. for Plant Conservation, St. Louis, 1985—. Office: Andrew W Mellon Found 140 E 62d St New York NY 10021

ROBIN, MITCHELL WOLFE, psychology educator, psychotherapist; b. Bklyn., Apr. 30, 1944; s. Benjamin and Lee (White) R.; m. Regina Catherine Spires, Mar. 26, 1972; children: Elaine Dara Robin, Abigail Alice. BBA, CCNY, 1965; MA, New Sch. for Social Rsch., 1969; PhD, NYU, 1984. Cert. clin. supr. rational-emotive therapy, N.Y. Assoc. prof. N.Y.C. Tech. Coll., Bklyn., 1968—; faculty New Sch. for Social Rsch., N.Y.C., 1970-89; staff psychotherapist Inst. for Rational-Emotive Therapy, N.Y.C., 1986—; cons. to various groups on performance anxiety, 1970—. Co-author: (psychol. test, with Ray DiGiuseppe) ABSII, 1988; author book chpt.; editor: Jour. of Rational-Emotive and Cognitive Behavior Therapy, 1990. Exec. dir. Sea View Playwright's Children's Theatre, 1984. IRET fellow, 1986. Democrat. Jewish. Office: New York City Tech Coll Social Sci Dept 300 Jay St Brooklyn NY 11201-2902

ROBINSON, ALAN THISTLE, sports writer; b. Parkersburg, W.Va., Apr. 19, 1951; s. Harold B. and Mary L. (Thistle) R. Student, W.Va. U., 1969-70; BBA, Mountain State Coll., 1973. Sports writer Parkersburg News, 1971-72, The Intelligencer, Wheeling, W.Va., 1972-75; sports editor AP, Charleston, W.Va., 1975-82, Pitts., 1982—. Named W.Va. Sportswriter of Yr. Nat. Sportwriters and Sportcasters 1976, 78. Mem. Am. Assn. Baseball Writers (pres. Pitts. chpt. 1985, 90), Am. Assn. Pro Football Writers, Am. Assn. Basketball Writers, N. Am. Pro Hockey Writers, Heisman Trophy Selection Com. Episcopalian. Office: Associated Press 6 Gateway Ctr Ste 222 Pittsburgh PA 15222

ROBINSON, AUBREY EUGENE, JR., federal judge; b. Madison, N.J., Mar. 30, 1922; s. Aubrey Eugene and Mabel (Jackson) R.; m. Sara E. Payne, Dec. 31, 1946 (dec.); children: Paula Elaine Robinson Collins, Sheryl Louise; m. Doris A. Washington, Mar. 17, 1973. B.A., Cornell U., 1943, LL.B., 1947. Bar: N.Y. and D.C. 1948. Practice with law firms Washington, 1948-65; assoc. judge Juvenile Ct. D.C., 1965-66; assoc. judge U.S. Dist. Ct. D.C., 1966—, chief judge, 1982—; gen. counsel Am. Council Human Rights, 1953-55, dir., 1955; mem. D.C. Commrs.'s Com. Child Placement Regulations, 1954-62; adj. prof. Am. U., 1975-84. Mem. D.C. Pub. Welfare Adv. Council, 1963-65; mem. Washington Urban League Adoption Project, 1959; mem. membership steering com. Health and Welfare Council D.C., 1961-66, Jud. Council of USA, 1982—; mem. budget steering com. Health and Welfare Council Nat. Capital Area, 1963-66; mem. exec. com. Interreligious Com. Race Relations, 1966-67; exec. com., bd. dirs. D.C. Citizens for Better Pub. Edn., 1964-66; trustee United Planning Orgn. D.C., 1963-66, Washington Ctr. Met. Studies, 1967-74, Cornell U., 1982—; bd. dirs. Family and Child Services Washington, 1954-63, v.p., 1958-61; bd. dirs. Family Service Assn. Am., 1958-68, Washington Action for Youth, 1962-64, Barney Neighborhood Settlement House, 1962-64, Eugene and Agnes E. Meyer Found., 1969-85, Consortium Univs. Washington Met. Area, 1969-74, Fed. Jud. Ctr., 1978-82; mem. adv. council Cornell Law Sch., 1974-80. Served with AUS, 1943-46. Mem. ABA (mem. com. cts. and community 1972—, mem. adv. com. judges function 1970-72), Nat. Conf. Fed. Trial Judges (chmn. 1973). Office: US Dist Ct US Courthouse 3rd & Constitution Ave NW Washington DC 20001

ROBINSON, BERNARD PAHL, thoracic surgeon, educator; b. N.Y.C., Apr. 12, 1919; s. Nathaniel and Augusta (Strauss) R.; m. Gloria Joyce Rehfuss, Oct. 3, 1943; children: Lawrence, Andrew. BS, NYU, 1938; MD, L.I. Coll. Medicine, 1942. Diplomate Am. Bd. Surgery, Am. Bd. Thoracic Surgery. Assoc. attending surgeon Mt. Sinai Hosp., N.Y.C., 1956—; asst. clin. prof. surgery Mt. Sinai Sch. Medicine, N.Y.C., 1968—. Capt. U.S. Army, 1943-46. Fellow Am. Coll. Surgeons, Am. Coll. Chest Physicians; mem. N.Y. Soc. for Thoracic Surgery. Jewish. Home: 4601 Henry Hudson Pkwy Bronx NY 10471 Office: Mt Sinai Hosp 8 E 83d St New York NY 10028

ROBINSON, BERT GILBERT, dancewear company executive, consultant; b. N.Y.C., May 12, 1942; s. William and Sadie (Sheines) R.; m. Ilene Early, May 18, 1968 (div. 1978); m. Maureen Ryan, Oct. 31, 1981; 1 child, Ryan Gordon. Student, Poly. Inst. N.Y., 1960. Corp. dir. fin. planning Kinney Shoe Corp., N.Y.C., 1960-72; dir. corp. budget F.W. Woolworth Co., 5, 1972-76; chief fin. officer Vida Shoes Internat., 5, 1976-77; pres. R.R.A. Cons. Svcs., Inc., 5, 1977—; sr. v.p. Ballet Makers, Inc., Totowa, N.J., 1989—. Fund raiser Sta. WNET-TV, PBS, N.Y.C., 1975. Mem. Planning Forum, Am. Mgmt. Assn. Democrat. Jewish. Home: 166 E 34th St New York NY 10016 Office: Ballet Makers Inc 1 Campus Rd Totowa NJ 07512

ROBINSON, BINA AITCHISON, publisher, newsletter editor; b. Schenectady, N.Y., Aug. 31, 1923; d. Thomas Cant and Winifred Maud (Binless) Aitchison; m. David Dunlop Robinson, May 14, 1944; children: Challice Binless, Jean Aitchison, Andrew McLeod, Janet Davison. BA, U. Rochester, 1944. Tchr. Phila. Pub. Schs., 1944-45, Brockport (N.Y.) Cen. Sch., 1946-47, Harley Sch., Rochester, N.Y., 1947-52; engring. asst. GE, Pittsfield, Mass., 1945-46; entrepreneur, developer, mgr. Swain (N.Y.) Ski Ctr., 1947-77; founder, coord., editor, prin. writer Coalition to Protect Animals in Parks & Refuges, Swain, 1985—; editor, prin. writer The Civil Abolitionist, 1985—; Am. cons. Drs. in Brit. Against Animal Experiments; vis. lectr. schs. and colls. Contbr. articles to publs. Bd. dirs., past pres. Allegany County Soc. Prevention Cruelty Animals, Wellsville, N.Y., 1978—. Mem. Am. Anti-Vivisection Soc., Nat. Resources Def. Coun., Internat. Primate Protection League, Nat. Alliance for Animals, N.Y. State Coalition for Animals, Action on Smoking and Health, Union Concerned Scientists, Civis/Civitas (exec. dir. 1983-91, bd. dirs. 1983—). Home and Office: 1 Main St Swain NY 14884-0026

ROBINSON, CHARLES EDWARD, English educator; b. Farmington, W.Va., Jan. 14, 1941; s. Charles E. and Amy M. (Flynn) R.; m. Peggy Kemno, Aug. 24, 1963; children: Clare, John. BA, Mt. St. Mary's Coll., Emmitsburg, Md., 1962; PhD, Temple U., 1967. Guest prof. U. Essen, Germany, 1972; prof. English U. Del., Newark, 1965—, dir. grad. studies, 1981—; NEH panelist, Washington, 1979, 81, 83, 88. Editor: Mary Shelley: Collected Tales, 1976, Byron and Contemporaries, 1982, William Hazlitt: Twenty-Seven New Holograph Letters, 1987, Mary Shelley's Proserpine and Midas, 1992; author: Shelley & Byron, 1976; co-editor: Mary Shelley Reader, 1990. Am. Coun. Learned Socs. grantee-in-aid, 1972,79, NEH travel to collections grantee, 1986; recipient Disting. Alumni award Mt. St. Mary's Coll., 1977. Mem. MLA, Byron Soc., Keats-Shelley Assocs., Internat. Byron Soc. (bd. dirs. 1979—), Am. Byron Soc. (bd. dirs. 1976—). Roman Catholic. Office: English Dept U Del Newark DE 19716

ROBINSON, DONALD LOUIS, legislative educator; b. Ottawa, Ill., Dec. 8, 1936; s. Arthur and Louise Ethel (Freebury) R.; m. Sara Katharine Moore, Aug. 4, 1962; children: Marshall Jackson, Margaret Moore. BA, Northwestern U., 1958, MA, 1959; PhD, Am. U., 1963. Adminstrv. asst. to Congressman from Wis., Washington, 1963-73; exec. asst. to chmn. U.S. Ho. of Reps. Banking Com., Washington, 1973-75; dir. Washington Internship program Boston U., 1976—; pres. Robinson Assocs. Inc., Washington, 1975—; founder, chmn. Congl. Internship Program, Washington, 1965-86; prof. polit. sci. George Washington U., Washington, 1965-80, Boston U., Washington, 1976—. Mem. agy. rev. com. United Way, Washington, 1980-85; treas. Met. Washington Arthritis Found., Washington, 1976—. Lt. (j.g.) USN, 1959-62. Mem. Alpha Tau Omega, Alpha Phi Omega, Phi Mu Alpha, Phi Alpha Theta, Pi Gamma Mu, Pi Sigma Alpha, Phi Kappa Phi, Phi Beta Delta. Democrat. Episcopalian. Home: 3717 Harrison St NW Washington DC 20015-1815 Office: Robinson Assocs Inc 3717 Harrison St NW Washington DC 20015-1815

ROBINSON, DONALD WARREN, educator, artist; b. New Bedford, Mass., Sept. 18, 1932; s. Warren Fowler and Mary Irene (Johnson) R.; m. Dolores Carole Lee, July 9, 1955; 1 child, Richard Allen. BFA, U. Ga., 1953; MFA, Columbia U., 1954; EdD, Rutgers State U., 1983. Instr. art

Wagner Coll., summer 1953, Gettysburg (Pa.) Coll., 1954-55; tchr., head dept. art elem. and secondary schs. Edison Twp. (N.J.), 1957-67; vice prin. John Adams Jr. High Sch., Edison, 1967-73; prin. M.L. King Sch., Edison, 1973-86; prin. H. Hoover Mid. Sch., Edison, 1986-90; pvt. cons. in field; workshop leader N.Y.C. Tchrs., S.I. Mus., N.Y., 1961-63. Works exhibited in Va., Md., Pa., N.Y. and Ga. Elder Presbyn. Ch. Served with USN, 1955-57. Mem. John Dewey Soc., Art Students League N.Y. (life), N.J. Prins. and Suprs. Assn., Printmaking Coun. of N.J., Phi Kappa Phi, Kappa Delta Pi, Phi Delta Kappa. Home: 55 Frost Ave W Edison NJ 08820-3157

ROBINSON, (DAVID) DUNCAN, museum administrator, art historian; b. Kidsgrove, Staffordshire, Eng., June 27, 1943; came to U.S., 1981; s. Tom and Ann Elizabeth (Clarke) R.; m. Elizabeth Anne Sutton, Jan. 7, 1967; children: Amanda Jane, Thomas Edward, Charlotte Elizabeth. B.A., Clare Coll., U. Cambridge, Eng., 1965; M.A., Clare Coll., U. Cambridge, 1969, Yale U., 1967. Asst. keeper paintings and drawings Fitzwilliam Mus., Cambridge, 1970-76, keeper paintings and drawings, 1976-80; fellow, lectr. Clare Coll., 1975-81; chief exec. officer Paul Mellon Ctr. for Studies in Brit. Art, London, 1981—; dir. Yale Ctr. for Brit. Art, New Haven, 1981—; adj. prof. Yale U., 1981—; vis. com. dept. painting restoration Met. Mus. Art; mem. council mgmt. William Blake Trust, 1983—; bd. govs. Yale U. Press, 1987—. Author: A Companion Volume to the Kelmscott Chaucer, 1975, Stanley Spencer, 1979, Morris & Co. in Cambridge, 1980, Town, Country, Shore and Sea: British Watercolors from VanDyck to Nash, 1982, Stanley Spencer, 1990. Mem. adv. panel Arts Coun. of Gt. Britain, 1978-81, vice chmn. art adv. panel, 1981, coun. mem., 1981; mem. art and artifacts indemnity adv. panel Fed. Coun. on the Arts and the Humanities, 1991—, chmn., 1992—. Mellon fellow, 1965. Fellow Royal Soc. Arts; mem. Walpole Soc. (coun. 1986-89), Ct. Acad. Arts and Scis., New Haven Colony Hist. Soc. (bd. dirs. 1991—), Friends of the Georgian Group (trustee 1992—), Athenaeum Club (London), Century Club, Yale Club (N.Y.C.), Am. Friends of the Georgian Group (bd. dirs. 1992—). Home: 142 Huntington St New Haven CT 06511-2017 Office: Yale Ctr-British Art 1080 Chapel St New Haven CT 06520

ROBINSON, FLORINE SAMANTHA, marketing professional; b. Massies Mill, Va., Feb. 4, 1935; d. John Daniel and Fannie Belle (Smith) Jackson; m. Frederick Robinson (div. 1973); children: Katherine, Theresa, Freda. BS, Morgan State U., 1976; postgrad., U. Balt., 1977-81, Liberty U., 1987. Writer, reporter Phila. Independent News, 1961-63; freelance writer, editor Balt., 1963-71; asst. mng. editor Williams & Wilkins Pubs. Inc., Balt., 1971-76; mktg. rep., then mktg. mgr. NCR Corp., Balt., 1977—; assoc. minister, trustee Christian Unity Temple, Balt., 1976—; bd. dirs. Armstrong & Bratcher, Inc., Balt. Editor: Stedman's Medical Dictionary, 1972; contbr. articles to profl. jours. Active PTA, Balt., 1963-65; bd. dirs. Howard Pk. Civic Assn., Balt., 1967—, pres. 1991—; leader, cons. Girl Scouts USA, 1970-73. Recipient Excellence in Rsch. award Psi Chi, 1976, Citizen citation Mayor of Balt. Mem. NAFE, Mid-Atlantic Food Dealers Assn., Am. Soc. Notaries, Internat. Platform Assn., Edelweiss Club, Order of Eastern Star. Democrat. Home: 3126 Howard Park Ave Baltimore MD 21207-6715

ROBINSON, FRANK, professional baseball manager; b. Beaumont, Tex., Aug. 31, 1935; s. Frank and Ruth (Shaw) R.; m. Barbara Ann Cole, Oct. 28, 1961; children: Frank Kevin, Nichelle. Student, Xavier U., Cin. Baseball player Cin. Reds, 1956-65, Balt. Orioles, 1966-71, Los Angeles Dodgers, 1972, Calif. Angels, 1973-74; player Cleve. Indians, 1974-76, mgr., 1975-77; coach Calif. Angels, 1977; coach Balt. Orioles, 1978-80, 85-87, mgr., 1988-91, asst. to gen. mgr., 1991—; mgr. San Francisco Giants, 1981-84; batting coach Milw. Brewers, 1984. Author: (with Al Silverman) My Life is Baseball, 1967, (with Barry Steinbach) Extra Innings, 1989, Frank the First Year, 1976. Named Rookie of Yr. Nat. League, 1956, Most Valuable Player, 1961, Am. League, 1966, Am. League Mgr. of Yr., 1982, 89; mem. World Series Championship Team, 1966, 70, Nat. League All-Star Team, 1956-57, 59, 61.62, 65, Am. League All-Star Team, 1966-67, 69-71, 74; inducted into Baseball Hall of Fame, 1982. Office: care Balt Orioles 333 W Camden Baltimore MD 21201

ROBINSON, FRANK BROOKS, SR., architect; b. Pitts., Oct. 5, 1931; s. Alexander Laughlin and Martha (Brooks) R.; m. Jean Ackerman; children: Andrea Robinson Albrittain, Shelley Brooks Robinson, Frank Brooks Jr. BA, Yale U., 1954; BArch, Carnegie Mellon U., 1960. Registered architect, Pa. V.p. Regional Indsl. Devel. Corp., Pitts., 1962-78; dep. sec. commerce Commonwealth of Pa., Harrisburg, 1978-79, dir. econ. devel. and gov.'s office, 1980-81; pres. Regional Indsl. Devel. Corp., Pitts., 1982—; trustee Carnegie Inst., Pitts., 1989—, Sta. WQED, Pitts., 1987, Carnegie Hero Commn., Pitts., 1965. Trustee Magee Women's Hosp., Pitts., 1962—; chmn. Pub. Auditoriam Authority, Pitts., 1980—. Capt. USAF, 1954-57. Orgn. Am. States fellow, 1961, Dalian U. fellow, 1987. Mem. Duquesne Club, Rolling Rock Club, Fishers Island (N.Y.) Club. Republican. Episcopalian. Office: Regional Indsl Devel Corp Frick Bldg Ste 1220 Pittsburgh PA 15219

ROBINSON, FRANKLIN WESTCOTT, museum director; b. Providence, R.I., May 21, 1939; s. Charles Alexander and Celia (Sachs) R.; m. Margaret Dredge; 1 child, John Alexander. B.A., Harvard U., 1961, Ph.D., 1970. Instr. Wellesley Coll., 1968-69; asst. prof. Dartmouth Coll., 1969-75; assoc. prof. Williams Coll., 1975-79; dir. Williams Coll. Mus., 1976-79, Mus. of Art, R.I. Sch. Design, Providence, 1979-92, Herbert F. Johnson Mus. Art, Cornell U., Ithaca, N.Y., 1992—. Author: Gabriel Metsu, 1975, Seventeenth Century Dutch Drawings from American Collections, 1977, Dutch and Flemish Paintings from the Ringling Mus, 1980. Fulbright fellow, 1961-62. Mem. Assn. Art Mus. Dirs., Coll. Art Assn. Clubs: Century, Hope. Office: Herbert F Johnson Mus Art Cornell U Ithaca NY 14853-4001

ROBINSON, GLYNNE, photographer, writer; b. Fredericksburg, Va., Feb. 23, 1934; d. Frederick Hampden and Jessie (Maguire) Robinson; children: Elizabeth, William, Katherine. AB, Wells Coll., 1956; postgrad. in history of art Columbia U., 1957; postgrad. in journalism NYU, 1975; photography student, The New Sch., 1967, 71, of Ansel Adams, Yosemite, Calif., 1968, Paul Caponigro, Bethel, Conn., 1969-71. Cert. media specialist, N.Y.C. Bd. Edn. With news and publicity dept. Riverdale Neighborhood House, 1974-76; staff photographer, The Reporter, publ. Ethical Culture Schs., N.Y.C., 1974-76; condr. photostudy project, N.Y.C. pub. sch., 1974-75; guest lectr. U. Maine, 1979; condr. photog. workshop for jr. high sch. students sponsored by N.Y. Pub. Libr., 1973; pub. The Lakeville (Conn.) Jour., The Millerton (N.Y.) News. Works appeared in publs. including N.Y. Times, Washington Post, N.Y. Daily News, Christian Sci. Monitor, Village Voice, San Francisco Chronicle, L.A. Times, Asia, Am. Heritage; featured in Women At Their Work, 1977; author: Writers in Residence, 1981; one-woman photog. shows Soho Photo Gallery, N.Y.C., 1974, Wells Coll., 1973, N.Y. Pub. Libr., 1973; participant group exhibits: Riverdale Neighborhood House, N.Y.C., 1968, Guild Hall, Easthampton, N.Y., 1970, Soho Photo Gallery, 1973, Wells Coll., 1974-75, Carnegie House, N.Y.C., 1978, Cosmopolitan Club, N.Y.C., 1976, Community Gallery Met. Mus. Art, 1976. Mem. Am. Soc. Mag. Photographers. Club: Cosmopolitan. Home: 15 E 91st St Apt 11C New York NY 10128-0648

ROBINSON, IMOGENE DECROW, museum director; b. Searsport, Maine, Oct. 4, 1901; d. Frank Porter and Grace (Crockett) Decrow; m. Roger William Robinson, Feb. 25, 1938; 1 child, Roger Lee. Grad., Dean Acad., Franklin, Mass., 1921. Dir. Willard House and Clock Mus., Grafton, Mass., 1968—; bd. dirs. Bay State Hist. League, Boston. Chair ladies com. Wayside Inn, Sudbury, Mass.; chair Blind Assn. Worcester County; pres. Grafton Garden Club. Fellow Nat. Assn. Watch and Clock Collectors; mem. Grafton Hist. Soc. (v.p.). Republican. Home: 115 Old Upton Rd Grafton MA 01519-1308

ROBINSON, IRWIN JAY, lawyer; b. Bay City, Mich., Oct. 8, 1928; s. Robert R. and Anne (Kaplan) R.; m. Janet Binder, July 7, 1957; children: Elizabeth Binder Robinson Schubiner, Jonathan Meyer, Eve Kimberly Wiener. AB, U. Mich., 1950; JD, Columbia U., 1953. Bar: N.Y. 1956. Assoc. Breed Abbott & Morgan, N.Y.C., 1955-58; asst. to ptnrs. Dreyfus & Co., N.Y.C., 1958-59; assoc. Greenbaum Wolff & Ernst, N.Y.C., 1959-65; ptnr. Greenbaum Wolff & Ernst, 1966-76; sr. ptnr. Rosenman & Colin, N.Y.C., 1976-90; of counsel Pryor, Cashman, Sherman & Flynn, 1990-92; ptnr. Phillips, Nizer, Benjamin, Krim & Ballon, N.Y.C., 1992—; treas. Saar-steel, Inc., Whitestone, N.Y., 1970—; mem. adv. bd. Mahoney, Cohen & Co., 1980—. Bd. dirs. Henry St. Settlement, N.Y.C., 1960-85, Jewish Community Ctr. Assn. N.Am., N.Y.C., 1967—; bd. dirs. Heart Rsch. Found., 1989—, pres., 1991—. Sgt. U.S. Army, 1953-55. Mem. ABA, N.Y. State Bar Assn., Assn. of Bar of City of N.Y., Internat. Bar Assn., Philippine-Am. C. of C. (bd. dirs. 1970—), Thai-Am. C. of C., Inc. (bd. dirs. 1992—, pres. 1992—), Vietnam-Am. C. of C. (bd. dirs. 1992—). Republican. Jewish. Clubs: Sunningdale Country (Scarsdale, N.Y.); Rockefeller Ctr. (N.Y.C.). Home: 4622 Grosvenor Ave Bronx NY 10471-3305 Office: Phillips Nizer Benjamin Krim & Ballon 31 W 52d St New York NY 10019-6167

ROBINSON, JAMES LEROY, architect; b. Longview, Tex., July 12, 1940; s. Willie LeRoy and Ruby Nell R.; B.Arch., So. U., 1964; M.C.P. (Martin Luther King fellow, 1972), Pratt Inst., 1972; m. Annabell Hilton; children: James LeRoy II, Kerstin Gunilla, Maria Theresa Narvaez, Jasmin Marisol, Ruby Nell, Kenneth Arne. Architect, Port of N.Y. Authority, 1964; architect, store planner W.T. Grant, 1964; with Herbst & Rusciano, AIA, 1965; architect Carson, Lundin & Shaw, N.Y.C., 1966, Kennerly, Slomanson & Smith, N.Y.C., 1967-69, architect-on-bus., 1969; pres. Robinson Architects, P.C., N.Y.C., 1969—; pres. NAROB Devel. Corp.; vis. prof. CUNY; adj. prof. Pratt Inst. Bd. dirs. Boys Club Am. Served with U.S. Army, 1966. Decorated knight Order of St. John, Knights of Malta; recipient AIA design award, 1976. Mem. Am. Arbitration Assn. (arbitrator), N.Y. Council Black Architects. Democrat. Works include: Stuyvesant Heights Christian Church, David Chavis House, Fulton Ct. Houses, Sinclair Houses, Hamilton Heights Terr., Eliot Graham Houses, Sojourner Truth Houses, Nehemiah Plan, Casas Theresa, N.Y.C. Postal Data Ctr., Mt. Carmel Bapt. Ch., Consol. Edison Collection Center, Casas Theresa, Jasmin Houses. Home: 67 Murray St New York NY 10007-2126 Office: 5 Beekman St New York NY 10038

ROBINSON, JANET LEE, auditor; b. Winchester, Va., Feb. 26, 1955; d. Clarence Gail and Martha Gold (Clendening) R.. BA, Wilson Coll., Chambersburg, Pa., 1977; Med. Tech. Cert., Lankenau Hosp., Phila., 1981. Cert. med. technologist. Rsch. asst. Temple U. Sch. Medicine, Phila., 1977-79, Hahnemann Med. Coll. and Hosp., Phila., 1979-80; tech. writer W.B. Sanders Pub. Co., Phila., 1979-81; biologist pharmacology dept. Merck & Co., West Point, Pa., 1981-84, staff biologist pharmacology dept., 1984-87, quality assurance assoc. regulatory affairs dept., 1987-90, sr. quality assurance assoc. regulatory affairs dept., 1990—. Writer for Saunders Dictionary and Ency. of Lab. Medicine and Technology, 1984; contbr. articles to profl. jours. Vol. Hospice of North Pa. V.N.A., Lansdale, 1990-91, Norristown (Pa.) Hosp., 1986-87. Mem. N.Y. Acad. Scis., Am. Soc. Clin. Pathologists, Drug Info. Assn.

ROBINSON, JEROME DAVID, chemical engineer; b. Stamford, Conn., Jan. 30, 1941; s. Harry Benjamin and Beatrice (Aberbach) R.; m. Sheila Lynn Kanitzky, June 21, 1964; children: Steven, Ronald. BChemE, CCNY, 1963; MChemE, U. Del., 1966, PhD, 1968. R & D chem. engr. E.I. duPont de Nemours & Co., Deepwater, N.J., 1963-64; process engr. Am. Cyanamid Co., Wayne, N.J., 1968-75, process supr., 1975-78, mgr. environ. engring., 1978-80, dir. process engring., 1980-85, dir. engring. & tech., 1985—; instr. chem. engring. U. Del., Newark, 1967; adj. prof. chem. engring. N.J. Inst. Tech., Newark, 1969-70. Mem. Am. Inst. Chem. Engrs.

ROBINSON, JOHN BOWERS, JR., bank holding company executive; b. Laconia, N.H., Oct. 9, 1946; s. John Bowers and Lee (Osborn) R.; m. Jane Frances Moore, Aug. 31, 1968; children: John Paul, Claire Frances, David Moore, Leanne Elizabeth, Gregory Joseph, Peter August. BA, Fairfield U., 1968; MBA, Adelphi U., 1977. V.p., asst. to pres. Hempstead Bank, N.Y., 1977-79, exec. v.p., 1979-81, pres., 1981-82; v.p. planning Norstar Bancorp, Inc., Albany, N.Y., 1982-84, exec. v.p., 1984-87, pres., 1987-88; exec. v.p. Fleet Fin. Group (formerly Fleet/Norstar Fin. Group), Albany, 1988—; bd. dirs. Fleet Trust Co., Rochester, N.Y., Fleet Bank-N.H., Nashua, Fleet Bank-Maine, Portland, Fleet Bank N.Y., Albany, Fleet Bank of N.Y., N.A., Buffalo, Fleet Bank, Melville, N.Y.; mem. N.Y. State Banking Bd., 1990—, N.Y. State Bus. Coun., 1990—, Albany Med. Ctr., 1989—, Siena Coll., Loudonville, N.Y., 1989—. Mem. Ft. Orange Club, Schuyler Meadows Club. Home: 208 Graffunder Dr Albany NY 12204-1302 Office: Fleet Fin Group Peter D Kiernan Plz Albany NY 12207

ROBINSON, JOHN JEFFREY, school system administrator, educator; b. Chester, Pa., May 4, 1941; s. Oliver Elwood and Dorothy Elizabeth (Simmons) R.; m. Patricia Ann Elizabeth Kral, Oct. 7, 1966. BS, Millersville U., 1964; MEd, Cheyney U., 1972; postgrad., Pa. State U., 1983, 86, Temple U., 1966, 87. Cert. tchr., Pa., supervisory I, supervisory II. Elem. tchr. Upper Darby (Pa.) Sch. Dist., 1964-66, tchr. indsl. arts, 1966—; owner Gradyville Woodworks Cabinet Shop, 1978—; evaluator Middle States Assn., Phila., 1973, 92. Contbr. articles to profl. jour. Tax collector Edgmont Twp., Gradyville, Pa., 1983—; chairperson Edgmont Twp. Planning Commn., Gradyville, 1976-83, chairperson curriculum Pa. Indsl. Arts Assn., Harrisburg, 1975; bd. dirs. Children and Youth Svcs. of Delaware County, Media, Pa., 1986-89. Mem. Internat. Tech. Edn. Assn., Am. Vocat. Assn., Tech. Edn. Assn. Pa., NEA, Upper Darby Edn. Assn., Pa. State Edn. Assn. Republican. Methodist. Home: 1101 Clover Ln Box 177 Gradyville PA 19039-0177 Office: Upper Darby Sch Dist Lansdowne Ave and School Ln Upper Darby PA 19082

ROBINSON, JOHN NATHANIEL, artist; b. Washington, Feb. 18, 1912; s. William Lorenzo and Blanche (Turner) R.; m. Gladys Ernestine Washington, Sept. 1, 1934; children: John Nathaniel Jr., Robert and Roberta (twins), Ronald, Blanche, Betty, Douglas (dec.). Kitchen helper, cook, supervisory cook St. Elizabeths Hosp., 1926-70; mem. Commn. on Arts and Humanities, Washington, 1975-80; art juror Greater S.E. Hosp., Washington, 1991. Exhibited in group shows at Barnett-Aden Gallery, Washington, Times-Herald Outdoor Art Fair, Washington, Atlanta U., Anacostia Mus., Washington, Corcoran Art Gallery, Washington, Emmanuel Bapt. Ch., Washington, Oxon Hill (Md.) Libr.; represented in permanent collections at Howard U., Washington, Atlanta U., Corcoran Art Gallery, Washington, The Washigton Post, Curtis Properties, Inc., Washington, D.C. Superior Ct., Washington, 10th St Bapt. Ch., Washington, Emmanuel Bapt. Ch., Washington. Recipient Art award-outdoor fair Washington Times Herald, 1941-48, A Tribute to Excellence award S.E. Community Hosp. Found., Washington, 1987, Black History Honors, Blacks in Govt., Washington, 1982, Outstanding Achievement in Art award St. Elizabeth's Hosp., Washington, 1985, Popular Vote Prize, Atlanta U., 1945-51. Home: 2904 Langston Pl SE Washington DC 20020

ROBINSON, JOHN ROWLAND, lawyer; b. N.Y.C., June 11, 1935; s. John Newbold and Sylvia Robinson; m. Barbara Ward Gahan, Jan. 31, 1959; children: Christopher, Abigail, Rowland, John. Student, Harvard U., 1954-57, postgrad., 1973; AB in History, Boston U., 1961, JD, 1964. Bar: N.Y., U.S. Dist. Ct. (so. dist.) N.Y., U.S. Ct. Appeals (2d cir.), U.S. Supreme Ct. Clk. Sullivan & Worcester, Boston; assoc. Simpson, Thacher & bartlett, N.Y.C.; asst. U.S. atty. U.S. Atty.'s Office for So. Dist. N.Y., N.Y.C.; ptnr. Rooney & Robinson, N.Y.C.; sr. exec. v.p., chmn. fin. com. Sperry and Hutchinson Co., N.Y.C.; pres., chmn. Beinecke Found., Rye, N.Y., 1981—; counsel Conn. Bank & Trust Co., Hartford, 1984-86; pvt. practice, Rye, N.Y., 1986—; former cons. Open Space Inst., N.Y.C.; ptnr. Robash, Inc., Wilmington, Del.; lectr. Practising Law Inst.; vis. prof. U. R.I. Sch. Urban Planning, 1974-75. Editor: Farmland Preservation Directory. Past trustee USS Constrn. Mus., Boston, Foxcroft Sch., Va., St. Georges Sch., Newport, R.I., 1976-80, Greenwich (Conn.) County Day Sch., 1979-81, Beinecke Libr., Yale U., New Haven, 1981; founder, trustee, atty. Natural Resources Def. Coun., N.Y.C., 1969—; sec. bd. trustees, mem. exec. com. Boston U., 1978-92; mem. com. to advise arts and scis. Com. to Visit Harvard Coll., Harvard U., 1989—; hon. nat. trustee Ducks Unltd.; bd. dirs. Round Hill Assn., Greenwich. Sgt. U.S. Army, 1956-62. Recipient Young Lawyer's award Boston U. Law Sch., 1975, Silver Shingle award, 1989. Mem. ABA, Assn. Trial Lawyers Am., Fed. Bar Assn., Boston U. Law Sch. Alumni Assn. (past pres.), N.Y. Yacht Club, Harvard Club N.Y., Round Hill Club,, Mill Reef Club (Antigua, bd. dirs., sec.). Episcopalian. Office: 14 Elm Pl Rye NY 10580

ROBINSON, JOSEPH DANIEL, physician, author, educator; b. N.J., July 27, 1943; s. Julius and Clara Robinson; m. Marylin Girard, July 3, 1977; children: David, Joshua, Micah, Noah. BA, Princeton U., 1965; MD, Yale U., 1970. Med. resident N.Y. Hosp.-Meml. Sloan Kettering, 1970-72; clin. assoc. NIH, Bethesda, Md., 1972-74; physician Washington, 1975—; asst. clin. prof. medicine George Washington U. Sch. Medicine, Washington, 1975—. Contbr. articles to profl. jours. Lt. comdr. USPHS, 1972-76. Mem. Mem. AAAS, AMA, Am. Coll. Physicians, Am. Soc. Internal Medicine, Royal Soc. Tropical Medicine & Hygiene. Office: 1056 Thomas Jefferson St NW Washington DC 20007

ROBINSON, MICHAEL FRANCIS, private art dealer and appraiser; b. London, Oct. 6, 1954; came to U.S., 1978; s. Canon Joseph and Anne (Antrobus) R. Student, King's Coll., London, 1968-72; LLB, King's Coll., London U., London, 1976; postgrad., The Coll. Law, London, 1976-77, Centre Study European Law, London & Luxembourg. Head rare books Brentano's, Inc., N.Y.C., 1978-81; head rare books Phillips Auctioneers, N.Y.C., 1981-85, auctioneer fine arts, 1982-85; pres. M.F. Robinson & Assocs., N.Y.C., 1985—; cons. to mus. and pvt. collectors, IRS, 1989—; bd. dirs. N.Y.W. Pub., Inc., N.Y.C., 1987—; Prforzheimer lectr. N.Y. Pub. Libr., N.Y.C., 1989; chmn. writers panel San Francisco Internat. Antique Fair, 1989, 90. Author articles Archtl. Digest, Connoiseur, Art and Auction, Manuscripts and other mags.; contbg. editor The Am. Book Collector, Art and Auction; assoc. editor Jour. Guild of Bookworkers; editor Treasures of Eton College, The Pierpont Morgan Library, 1990; joint editor, co-author: Treasures of the Pierpont Morgan Collections, 1991-92. Chmn. The Bach Ensemble, N.Y., 1984—. Mem. The Hon. Soc. Inner Temple (Duke of Edinburgh Scholar 1974), The Manuscript Soc., The Hardwick Soc. Episcopalian. Club: The Worshipful Co. of Wax Chandlers (London). Lodge: Masons (curator 1984—). Office: 1269 1st Ave New York NY 10021-5611

ROBINSON, MICHAEL HILL, zoological park director, biologist; b. Preston, Eng., Jan. 7, 1929; came to U.S. 1984; s. Samuel and Ethel (Hill) R.; m. Barbara Cragg Robinson, May 19, 1955. B.S., U. Wales, U.K., 1963; D.Phil., U. Oxford, Eng., 1966. Tchr. sci. U.K. Secondary Schs., 1953-60; sr. sci. master Camborne Grammar Sch., 1958-60; biologist Smith. Tropical Research Inst., Panama, 1966-71; vis. lectr. U. Pa., Phila., 1969; reader in biology New U. Ulster, No. Ireland, 1971; biologist Smithsonian Tropical Research Inst., Panama, 1971-84; asst. dir. Smithsonian Tropical Research Inst., 1980, acting dir., 1980-81, dep. dir., 1981-84; adj. prof. U. Miami, Coral Gables, Fla., 1981—; dir. Nat. Zool. Park, Washington, 1984—. Contbr. articles to profl. jours. Sci. fellow Zool. Soc. London, 1956. Fellow Linnean Soc., Royal Entomol. Soc., Inst. Biology; mem. Papua New Guinea Sci. Soc., Brit. Arachnological Soc., Internat. Soc. Tropical Ecologists, Am. Arachnological Soc., Soc. for Study of Animal Behavior. Home: 2729 Ordway St NW Apt 5 Washington DC 20008-5052 Office: Nat Zool Pk 3001 Connecticut Ave NW Washington DC 20008-2598

ROBINSON, PATRICIA SNYDER, lawyer; b. Hoboken, N.J., Dec. 5, 1952; d. Anthony James and Agnes Loretta (Riordan) Snyder; m. Daniel Lewis Robinson, Aug. 27, 1978. BA summa cum laude, Montclair State Coll., 1975; MSc, Rutgers U., 1980; JD, Rutgers U., Newark, N.J., 1986. Bar: N.J. 1986, U.S. Dist. Ct. N.J. 1986, U.S. Ct. Appeals (3d cir.) 1992. Grad. asst. Rutgers U., New Brunswick, N.J., 1975-77; chemist AT&T Bell Labs., Murray Hill, N.J., 1977-80; mgr. AT&T, Bedminster, N.J., 1980-87; atty. Norris, McLaughlin & Marcus, Somerville, N.J., 1987, Collier, Jacob & Mills, Somerset, N.J., 1987—. Contbr. articles to profl. jours. Mem. ABA, N.J. State Bar Assn., Somerset County Bar Assn., N.Y. Acad. Sci., Phi Kappa Phi. Office: Collier Jacob & Mills 580 Howard Ave Somerset NJ 08873

ROBINSON, PETER BULLENE, musician, composer; b. Kansas City, Mo., July 2, 1949; s. David Weaver and Margaret Evelyn (Sherwood) R.; m. Mary Healy Fasenmyer, Dec. 29, 1984; 1 child, Nathan. BA in English, Princeton (N.J.) U., 1972. Staff asst. U.S. Senator Robert Dole, Washington, 1973-74; pianist, band leader Muehlebach Hotel, Kansas City, 1975-79; legis. asst. U.S. Rep. Larry Winn Jr., Washington, 1979-82; freelance pianist and composer Washington, 1982—. Performances include Jefferson Hotel, 1983-84, Ritz-Carlton Hotel, 1984-88, 92—, Georgetown Inn, 1988-89, Old Ebbitt Grill, 1989-90; performer, composer: (rec.) Peter Robinson Live in Washington, 1984, (compact disc) Orginally, 1989. Mem. ASCAP. Home: 4302 Locust Ln Bethesda MD 20816-2522

ROBINSON, RALPH C., horticulturist; b. Tuscaloosa, Ala., Sept. 7, 1957; s. Ralph C. and V. Alice (Olnstead) R. BS, Canisius Coll., Buffalo, 1979; MBA, SUNY, Buffalo, 1982, PhD, 1989. Instr. SUNY, Buffalo, 1981-89; adj. prof. Daemen Coll., Buffalo, 1990—; owner Rob's Mini-o-Lets, Tonawanda, N.Y., 1986—; pres. N.Y. State African Violet Judges Coun., 1991—. Asst. editor Gesneriad Jour. of Photography. Mem. Am. Econ. Assn., African Violet Soc. Am. (Best New African Violet Cultivar award 1989, 90, 91, dir. 1990—), N.Y. State African Violet Soc. (treas. 1987-92), African Violet Soc. Western N.Y. (pres. 1982-84, 1990—), Niagara Frontier Bicycle Club (sec. 1991—), Buffalo Racquet Club. Democrat. Home: 96 Harriet St Tonawanda NY 14150-2310

ROBINSON, RICHARD JAMES, construction executive; b. Port Chester, N.Y., Feb. 26, 1952; s. James Thomas and Alice (Hyler) R.; m. Candace Ann Harnett, Oct. 11, 1975; children: Richard, Franklin, James, Jillian. BA in Mktg., Am. History, Franklin Pierce Coll., 1974. Pres. Woodhaven Lumber & Millwork Inc., Point Pleasant, N.J., 1976—. Sec. Brielle (N.J.) Planning Bd., 1989—. Mem. N.J.Shore Builders Assn. (v.p. 1987-91), N.J. Builders Assn. (trustee 1986—), Manasquan River Golf Club, Manasquan River Yacht Club. Home: 917 Hilltop Pl Brielle NJ 08730 Office: Woodhaven Lumber 1303 Richmond Ave Point Pleasant Beach NJ 08742

ROBINSON, RICK J., advertising executive; b. Knoxville, July 26, 1951; s. Herbert and Lima Raye (McClellan) R.; m. Claudia Diane Payne, Oct. 3, 1970. BBA, U. Tenn., 1976. Entrepeneur Ft. Walter, Fla., 1976-79; mktg. mgr. Elm Hill/Frosty Morn MEats, Nashville, 1979-83; dir. mktg. Liberty-land/City of Memphis, 1983-84; v.p. Swearingen and Conaway Advt., Memphis, 1984-87; pres. So. Creative Communications, Memphis, 1987-88; sr. acct. supr. Gilbert Whitney and Johns, N.Y.C., 1988-90; v.p. Poppe-Tyson/Bozell, Morris Plains, N.J., 1990—. Mem. tourism com. Nashville C. of C., 1981-82; tutor Jr. Achievement, Memphis, 1984-88. Home: 41 Upper Dr Watchung NJ 07060 Office: Poppe Tyson 201 Littleton Rd Morris Plains NJ 07062

ROBINSON, ROBERT ARMSTRONG, pension fund executive; b. Waterbury, Conn., Sept. 11, 1925; s. Robert and Ethel (Armstrong) R.; m. D. Ann Harding, June 7, 1947; 1 child, Gayllis Robinson Ward. A.B. magna cum laude, Brown U., 1950, M.A., 1952; postgrad., U. Ill., 1954-55; Litt. D., Episcopal Theol. Sem. Ky., 1971; D.C.L., U. South, 1972; LL.D., Nashotah House, Oconomowoc, Wis. Instr. English Brown U., 1950-53; instr. English, asst. prof. rhetoric U. Ill., 1953-56; trust officer Colonial Bank & Trust Co., Waterbury, 1956-63; v.p., trust officer Colonial Bank & Trust Co., 1963-65, sr. trust officer, 1965-66; v.p., sec. Ch. Pension Fund and Affiliates, Ch. Life Ins. Corp., Ch. Ins. Co., Ch. Agy. Corp., Ch. Hymnal Corp., 1966-67, exec. v.p., 1967-68, pres., dir., 1968-91; pres. emeritus Ch. Pension Fund and Affiliates, Ch. Life Ins. Corp., et al., 1991—; mgr. East Side House Settlement; bd. dirs. Seabury Press, Inc., Mariners Instl. Funds, Inc., Mariner Tax Free Instl. Fund, UST Master Funds, Morehouse Pub. Co., Inc., Mariner Funds Trust, Mariner Equity Trust, Pigmy Corp., U.S.T. Master Money Funds, Rosiclare Lead and Flourspar Mining Co., others; cons. to exec. dir. Pension Benefit Guaranty Corp. Trustee Hillspeak, Eureka Springs, Ark., Canterbury Cathedral Trust in Am., Hoosac Sch. Washington Nat. Cathedral, Nashotah Theol. Sem., Wis., H.B. and F.K. Bugher Found., Living Ch. Found.; mem. exec. com. N.Y. couns. Boy Scouts Am., Ch. Pensions Conf.; mem. econ. adv. bd. Columbia U. Grad. Sch. Bus. Adminstrn. With inf. AUS, 1943-46. Decorated Bronze Star, Purple Heart with oak leaf cluster, Knights of Malta, Order St. John. Fellow Am. Numis. Soc.; mem. Conn. Bankers Assn. (v.p., head trust div.), Am. Numis Assn., Newsomen Soc., Phi Beta Kappa. Republican. Episcopalian (vestryman). Clubs: St. Andrew's Soc. (N.Y.C.), Brown (N.Y.C.), Union League (N.Y.C.), Church (N.Y.C.), Country of New Canaan, Athenaeum (London), Pilgrims, Union, Met. (Washington), Yeaman's Hall (Charleston, S.C.). Home: 251 Laurel Rd New Canaan CT 06840-2707 Office: 800 2d Ave New York NY 10017

ROBINSON, SHARON BETH, health science association administrator; b. Balt., Sept. 28, 1959; d. Edward and Ruth Ann (Fishman) R.; divorced. BS, Towson State U., 1981; MS, Johns Hopkins U., 1986. Exec. asst. Congress of Neurol. Surgeons, Balt., 1983-86; office adminstr. Md. Inst. Emergency Med. Svcs., Balt., 1986-87; coord. spl. projects U. Md. Med. Systems, Balt., 1986-88; adminstr. Am. Bd. Med. Genetics, Bethesda, Md., 1988—. Mem. Catonsville Community Coll. Alumni Assn. (bd. dirs. 1984-89, sec. 1986, v.p. 1987, pres. 1988). Office: Am Bd Med Genetics 9650 Rockville Pike Bethesda MD 20814-3998

ROBINSON, WALKER LEE, neurological surgeon; b. Balt., Oct. 13, 1941; s. Edward Findol and Wilma Lee (Walker) R.; m. Mae Elizabeth Meads, Apr. 9, 1966; 1 child, Kimberly, Walker Jr. BSChemE, Morgan State Coll., 1962; MD, U. Md., 1970. Bd. cert. neurosurgeon. Capt. U.S. Army, El Paso, Tex., 1962-64; mgr. C & P Telephone Co., Balt., 1964-66; intern surgery Strong Meml. Hosp., Rochester, N.Y., 1970-71; resident neurosurgery U. Md., Univ. Hosp., Balt., 1971-74, 75-76; fellow neurology U. London, Eng., 1974-75; dir. neurotrauma U. Md., Shock Trauma Ctr., Balt., 1989-91; head pediatric neurosurgery U. Md., Balt., 1978, assoc. prof. neurosurgery and pediatrics, 1989—; acting chmn. div. neurosurgery U. Md. Med. Sch., Balt., 1990—; cons. Nat. Cancer Inst., Bethesda, Md., 1985-91, N.I.N.C.D.S., Bethesda, 1983-91; mem. editorial bd. Jour. of the Nat. Med. Assn., Washington, 1985-87; chmn. membership com. Am. Assn. Neurosurgery, Chgo., 1991-93. Contbr. articles to profl. jours. and chpts. to books. Bd.d irs. East Balt. Community Corp., 1978-85, Variety Club of Balt., 1989-90, Urban Cardiology Rsch. Ctr., Balt., 1987-91. Named Disting. alumni Fund for Edn. Excellence, 1991, Honoree, Afram Expo-Urban Svcs., 1989, Pual Harris fellow Rotary Internat., 1990; grantee NIH, 1991. Fellow Am. Coll. of Surgeons; mem. AMA, Am. Soc. Pediatric NeuroSurgery, Balt. Urban Svcs. Found. (pres. 1986-87), Clarence Green NeuroSurg. Soc. (pres. 1984-88), Black Faculty and Staff Assn. (pres. 1989-90), State Med. Assn. (legis. com. 1990-92). Home: 3701 Cedar Dr Baltimore MD 21207 Office: U of Maryland Med Sch 22 S Greene St Baltimore MD 21201

ROBINSON, WILKES COLEMAN, lawyer; b. Anniston, Ala., Sept. 30, 1925; s. Walter Wade and Catherine Elizabeth (Coleman) R.; m. Julia Von Poellnitz Rowan, June 24, 1955; children: Randolph C., Peyton H., Thomas Wilkes Coleman. A.B., U. Ala., 1948; LL.B., U. Va., 1951, J.D., 1970. Bar: Ala. 1951, Va. 1962, Mo. 1966, Kans. 1983. Assoc. Bibb & Hemphill, Anniston, Ala., 1951-54; city recorder City of Anniston, 1953-55; judge Juvenile and Domestic Relations Ct. of Calhoun County, Ala., 1954-56; atty. legal dept. GM&O R.R., Mobile, Ala., 1956-58; commerce counsel, asst. gen. atty. Seaboard Air Line R.R., Richmond, Va., 1958-66; commerce counsel Monsanto Co., St. Louis, 1966-70; gen. counsel, v.p. Marion Labs., Inc., Kansas City, Mo., 1970-79; pres. Gulf and Gt. Plains Legal Found., Kansas City, Mo., 1980-85; atty. Howard, Needles, Tammen & Bergendoff, Kansas City, 1985-86, also bd. dirs.; v.p. S.R. Fin. Group, Inc., Overland Park, Kans., 1986-87; judge U.S. Claims Ct., 1987—. Bd. govs. Kansas City Philharmonic Orch., 1975-77. Served with USNR, 1943-44. Mem. Army Navy Country Club, Skyline Club, Masons, Shriners, Phi Beta Kappa (past treas. Kansas City, Mo. chpt.), Phi Eta Sigma, Phi Alpha Theta, Kappa Alpha. Episcopalian. Home: 2353 S Queen St Arlington VA 22202-1550 Office: US Claims Ct 717 Madison Pl NW Washington DC 20005-1011

ROBINSON, WINDSOR CALVERT, historian, consultant, photographer; b. Gardner, Mass., June 17, 1950; s. Alwynn Glenn and Marguerite Ruth (Allen) R. AS in Gen. Studies, Mt. Wachusett Community Coll., 1973; BA in History, Franklin Pierce Coll., 1977; MEd in History, Worcester State Coll., 1981. Cons. Gardner Heritage State Park Touring Exhibit, 1984-85, Boston Mus. Design Group, Somerville, 1985-86. Photographer (book) Gardner: A Portrait of Its Past, 1978; editor (books) The Diary of Aaron Greenwood, Vol. I, 1983, Vol. II, 1984, Vol. III, IV, 1986, Vol. VI, 1990. Mem. Gardner Hist. Commn., 1975-86, treas., 1978-86; editor index vols. I-V Gardner News Weekly, 1986; mem. Gardner Rep. City Com., 1976—, precinct warden, 1982—; mem. Gardner Mus., Inc., 1977-89, trustee, 1982-89; v.p. South Gardner Hist. Soc., 1991—. Mem. South Gardner Hist. Soc. (v.p. 1991—), Phi Alpha Theta.

ROBISON, JAMES EVERETT, consulting company executive; b. Alfred, N.D., Nov. 22, 1915; s. John J. and Myrtle (Klundt) R.; m. Jeanette Hoffman, June 6, 1942 (dec.); 1 child, Martha Ann Davies. A.B., U. Minn., 1938; M.B.A., Harvard U., 1940; Sc. D. (hon.), Suffolk U., 1968. Salesman Nashua Mfg. Co., N.Y.C., 1940-46, Textron, Inc., N.Y.C., 1947-53; chief textile br. OPS, Washington, 1951; pres., chief exec. officer, dir. Indian Head, Inc., N.Y.C., 1953-67; chmn. bd., chief exec. officer Indian Head, Inc., 1967-72, chmn. fin. com., 1971-75; pres. Lonsdale Enterprises, Inc., 1975—; bd. dirs. Houbigant, Inc. Mem. com. univ. resources Harvard U., 1966-69, mem. vis. com. Grad. Sch. Bus. Adminstrn., 1966-72, 73-79; chmn. bd. Assocs. Harvard Bus. Sch., 1968-70, bd. dirs., 1988-92; trustee Air Force Aid Soc., 1968—, mem. fin. com., 1969—; bd. dirs. Bus. Com. for Arts, 1973-80; trustee Com. Econ. Devel., 1965-74, Calif. Inst. Tech., 1970—; vice chmn. president's coun. U. Vt. Sch. Bus., 1982-89. Maj. USAAF, 1942-46. Decorated D.F.C., Air Medal with three oak leaf clusters; recipient Distinguished Service award Harvard Bus. Sch. Assn., 1969; Outstanding Alumni award U. Minn., 1974. Mem. Conf. Bd., Am. Textile Mfrs. Inst. (bd. dirs. 1961-64), Harvard Bus. Sch. Assn., Soaring Soc. Am., U.S. C. of C., Air Force Res. Assn., Harvard Club, Harvard Bus. Sch. Club Greater N.Y. (past bd. dirs., pres. 1967-68), Stanwich Club (Greenwich, Conn.), Bedford Golf and Tennis Club (N.Y.), Lyford Cay Club (Bahamas), Phi Delta Theta. Home: Windmill Farm 12 Spruce Hill Rd Armonk NY 10504-2605 Office: Lonsdale Enterprises Inc 20 Haarlem Ave White Plains NY 10603-2223

ROBISON, KENNETH GERALD, former naval officer, national security consultant; b. Great Falls, Mont., Sept. 30, 1938; s. Perry Russell and Ruth Elsie Helen (Johnson) R.; m. Mary Margaret Michele Crovitz, Mar. 6, 1964; children: Karin Michele, Mark Charles. Student, U. Wash., 1958; BA, U. Mont., 1960, postgrad., 1965; postgrad., George Mason U., 1991. Commd. ensign USN, 1960, advanced through grades to capt., 1980, intelligence officer, 1960; asst. naval attache U.S. Embassy, Stockholm, 1975-78; asst. chief of staff intelligence U.S. Naval Forces Europe, London, 1980-84; dir. plans, policy and requirements Office Naval Intelligence, Washington, 1984-88; ret., 1988; sr. assoc. Booz, Allen & Hamilton, 1988—. Author: Prisoner of War Debrief--Capt. James Bond Stockdale, 1973; contbr. articles to genealogical jours. Decorated comdr. Order Star (Sweden), Legion of Merit, Meritorious Svc. medal with oak leaf cluster, Navy Commendation medal, Presdl. Unit Commendation medal. Mem. Mont. Hist. Soc., Nat. Geneal. Soc., U.S. Naval Inst., Armed Forces Communications Electronics Assn., Am. Legion, VFW, Army and Navy Club, Phi Alpha Theta, Delta Sigma Phi. Republican. Presbyterian. Home: 8241 Taunton Pl Springfield VA 22152-2428 Office: Booz Allen & Hamilton Inc 1953 Gallows Rd Vienna VA 22182-3934

ROBISON, OLIN CLYDE, educator, former college president; b. Anacoco, La., May 12, 1936; s. Audrey Clyde and Ruby (Cantrell) R.; m. Sylvia Margaret Potter, Apr. 10, 1959; children: Gordon Reece, Blake Elliott, Mark Edward. BA, Baylor U., 1958, LLD, 1979; D.Phil., Oxford (Eng.) U., 1963; LHD (hon.), Ehrenburger-Johannes Gutenberb U., Mainz, Fed. Republic Germany, 1977, Monterey Inst. Internat. Studies, 1982; LLD (hon.), U. Vt., 1989. Dean students San Marcos (Tex.) Acad., 1963-64; regional officer Peace Corps, Washington, 1964-65; dir. univ. affairs Peace Corps, 1965-66; spl. asst. dep. under-sec. for polit. affairs Dept. State, Washington, 1966-68; asso. provost for social scis. Wesleyan U., Middletown, Conn., 1968-70; provost, dean faculty, sr. lectr. govt. and legal studies Bowdoin Coll., Brunswick, Maine, 1970-75; prof. polit. sci. Middlebury (Vt.) Coll., 1975—, pres., 1975-90; pres. Salzburg Seminar, 1991—; cons. State Dept., 1968-72, 77—; bd. dirs. Investment Co. Am.; cons. Paine Webber Mitchell Hutchins Inc., Am. Council Life Ins., 1968-81, Washington Forum, Met. Life Ins. Co. Bd. dirs. Atlantic Info. Center for Tchrs., London, 1970-77; exec. com. New Eng. Colls. Fund; bd. dirs. Am. Com. on U.S.-Soviet Rels., Washington; chmn. Vt. com. Rhodes Scholarship Trust, 1976-77; bd. dirs. Am. Coun. Young Polit. Leaders, 1968-78, 81—, Inst. East-West Security Studies, N.Y.C., Nat. Spinal Cord Injury Assn., Washington, Atlantic Coun. U.S., 1973-78, 81—, U.S. Commn. for United World Coll. Schs.; mem. U.S. Adv. Commn. on Public Diplomacy, 1978-83, chmn., 1978-81; adviser U.S. del. Conf. on Security and Coop. in Europe, Belgrade, 1977-78; U.S. del. Conf. on Security and Coop. in Madrid, 1980, in Vienna, 1986-87; mem. Royal United Svcs. Inst. Def. Studies, London; bd. dirs. Nat. Endowment for Democracy, 1984-92; bd. dirs., chmn. Chatham House Found., 1985-92. Named Ehrenburger Johannes Gutenberg Universität, Mainz, Fed. Republic Germany, 1977; Rockefeller Found./Aspen Inst. fellow, 1978-79; Presdl. fellow Aspen Inst. Humanistic Studies, 1979-80. Mem. Internat. Inst. Strategic Studies (London), Soc. Values in Higher Edn., Council Fgn. Relations, Royal Inst. Internat. Affairs (London) (fgn. asso.), UN Assn. U.S. (panel on approaches to collective security), Atlantic Treaty Assn. (Atlantic edn. com. 1972—). Baptist. Clubs: Federal City (Washington); Century (N.Y.C.); United Oxford and Cambridge (London). Home: Horse Farm Rd Middlebury VT 05753 Office: Middlebury Coll Painter House Middlebury VT 05753

ROBISON, SUSAN MILLER, psychologist, educator, consultant; b. Chgo., Nov. 15, 1945; d. William Louis and Constance Mary (Maloney) Miller; m. Philip Dean Robison, Dec. 27, 1969; 1 child, Christine Alyssa. BS, Loyola U., Chgo., 1967; MS, Ohio U., 1969, PhD, 1971. Lic. psychologist, Md. Asst. prof. psychology Ohio U., Lancaster, 1970-72; prof. psychology Coll. Notre Dame, Balt., 1972—; pvt. practice Ellicott City, Md., 1982—; leadership cons. Nat. Coun. Cath. Women, Washington, 1987—. Author: Sharing Our Gifts, 1987, 2d edit., 1992, Discovering Our Gifts, 1989, Thinking and Writing in College, 1991. Troop leader Girl Scouts U.S.A., Ellicott City, 1982-85, mem. adv. bd. Girl Scouts Central Md., 1987-88; mem. adv. bd. Archdiocese of Balt., 1986. Mem. Am. Psychol. Assn., Am. Assn. Sex Educators, Counselors and Therapists, Assn. for Advancement Behavior Therapy. Home: 3725 Fond Hill Dr Ellicott City MD 21042

ROBOCK, ALAN, meteorology educator; b. Boston, Sept. 7, 1949; s. Stefan Hyman Robock and Shirley Ruth (Bernstein) Fox; m. Sherri Lynne Carpini West, May 12, 1990; children: Brian, Danny. BA, U. Wis., 1970; SM, MIT, 1974, PhD, 1977. Vol. Peace Corps, The Philippines, 1970-72; rsch. scientist Lawrence Livermore (Calif.) Lab., 1973; asst. prof. dept. meteorology U. Md., College Park, 1977-82, assoc. prof., 1982—; snow forecaster Montgomery County (Md.) Pub. Schs., 1980-81; state climatologist State of Md., 1991—. Editor Jour. Climate and Applied Meteorology, 1985-87; contbr. articles to profl. publs., chpts. to books. Mem. AAAS (Congressional sci. fellow 1986-87), Am. Geophys. Union, Am. Meteorol. Soc., Fedn. Am. Scientists. Office: U Md Dept Meteorology College Park MD 20742

ROBOHM, PEGGY ADLER (PEGGY ADLER), researcher, consultant, writer, illustrator; b. N.Y.C., Feb. 10, 1942; d. Irving and Ruth (Relis) Adler; m. Jeremy Abbott Walsh, June 1, 1962 (div. Dec. 1968); children: Tenney Whedon, Avery Denison (Mrs. Adam Lapidus); m. Richard A. Robohm, Dec. 24, 1976; stepchildren: Erick John, Kurt William, Kim Alene (Mrs. John L. Moore). Student, Bennington Coll., 1959-60, Columbia U., 1962. Illustrator, author childrens books, 1958—; agt. Jan J. Agy., Inc., N.Y.C., 1981-82; freelance talent scout Cuzzins Mgmt., N.Y.C., 1982-83; personal mgmt. and pub. rels. cons. Madison, Conn., 1983—; rsch. assoc. SIG Steve Fredericksen, Pvt. Investigator, Conn. and N.Y., 1990—; investigative researcher, writer, lit. cons., 1986—, pub. speaker, 1991—. Author, illustrator: The Adler Book of Puzzles and Riddles, 1962, The 2nd Adler Book of Puzzles and Riddles, 1963, Metric Puzzles, 1977, Math Puzzles, 1978, Geography Puzzles, 1979; author: Hakim's Connection, 1988; co-author: Skull and Bones: The Skeleton in Bush's Closet?, 1988; illustrator numerous books including (Humane Soc. of U.S. pubs.) Pet Care, 1974, Caring for Your Cat, 1974, Hot and Cold, 1959, Numbers New and Old, 1960, Do a Zoomdo, 1975, Reading Fundamentals for Teen-Agers, 1973; graphic designer various book covers, posters, co. logos: PR, Sweetie, Baby, Cookie, Honey (Freddie Gershon), 1986; researcher Passion and Prejudice: A Family Memoir (Sallie Bingham), 1989, The Village Voice, 1992, numerous others; cons. The President's Private Eye: The Journey of Detective Tony U. From N.Y.P.D. to the Nixon White House (Anthony Ulasewicz with Stuart McKeever), 1990; cons., researcher Bush's Boys Club: Skull and Bones, 1990; cons. Spy Saga (Philip H. Melanson), 1990; contbr. Lies of Our Times; licensee/story cons. 60 Minutes, 1991; cons., researcher London Sunday Times, 1991; source Village Voice, 1991, 92; rsch. asst. The Connecticut Cowboy, 1992; rsch. and document retrieval CNN, Kroll Assocs., 1992; contract cons. Ho. of Reps. Fgn. Task Force, 1992. Founder Shoreline Youth Theatre, Inc., 1979, mem. adv. bd., 1981-86; bd. dirs. The Greens Condominium Assn. of Branford, Conn., 1975-78, Arts Coun. of Greater New Haven, 1971-73, Planned Parenthood of Greater New Haven, 1972-73, Assassination Archives and Rsch. Ctr., Washington, 1990—; v.p., bd. dirs. Pub. Info. Rsch., Washington, 1989; hon. mem. Forgotten Families. Mem. Nat. Conf. Personal Mgrs., Dramatists Guild, Authors League Am., Assassination Archives and Rsch. Ctr., Inc. (Washington bd. dirs. 1990—), Conn. Soc. Genealogists, Inc., Yale Club of New Haven, AFIO. Home and Office: Connections 45 Lawson Dr Madison CT 06443-3111

ROBROCK, RICHARD BARKER, II, telecommunications executive; b. Cleve., Dec. 29, 1941; s. Richard Barker and Helen Rita R.; children: Kristin, Karl. BS in Engring. Sci., Case Inst. Tech., Cleve., 1963, MSEE, 1965, PhD in Elec. Engring., 1967. Mem. tech. staff Bell Labs., Holmdel, N.J., 1967-69, supr., 1970-77; supr. Bell Labs., Naperville, Ill., 1977-79, dept. head, 1979-83; dir. Bell Labs., Piscataway, N.J., 1983-84; asst. v.p. Bellcore, Piscataway, N.J., 1984—; participant MIT Sloan Sch. Sr. Exec. Program, Boston, 1988. Contbr. 36 articles to profl. jours.; patentee in field. Fellow IEEE; mem. AAAS, Sigma Xi, Tau Beta Pi. Office: Bellcore 444 Hoes Ln Piscataway NJ 08854-4104

ROBSON, FRED LEE, mechanical engineer, researcher; b. East Liverpool, Ohio, June 8, 1936; s. Howard Clayton and Margaret Mae (Burbick) R.; m. Cynthia Palabay, Sept. 10, 1960; children: Christopher, Mark. BS in Aero. Engring., U. Fla., 1959; MSME, U. Conn., 1962, PhD, 1966. Analytical engr. Pratt & Whitney Aircraft, Middletown, Conn., 1959-61; rsch. asst. U. Conn., Storrs, 1961-65; sr. rsch. engr. United Tech. Rsch. Ctr., East Hartford, Conn., 1965-70, chief utility power systems, 1970-74, mgr. indsl. power systems, 1974-81, mgr. indsl. tech., 1981—. Co-author: Methods of Advanced Power Generation, 1983. Recipient tech. utilization award AIAA, 1970, tech. application award NASA, 1982. Mem. ASME, Sigma Xi, Pi Tau Sigma. Home: 99 Burrows Hill Rd Amston CT 06231-1204 Office: United Techs Rsch Ctr 411 Silver Ln East Hartford CT 06118-1104

ROBY, CHRISTINA YEN, data processing specialist, instructor; b. Shanghai, China; came to U.S., 1980; d. Hai Zhou and Yun Qui (Zhang) Yen; m: Ronald L. Roby; 1 child, Colin H. BS, Jiao-Tung U., Shanghai, 1957; MS, U. Balt., 1986. Lic. engr., Peoples Republic of China. Chief mech. engr. Shenyang Valve Rsch. Inst., China, 1958-1980; computer system operator U. Balt., 1984, rsch. asst., 1984-86; sales assoc. V. F. Assocs., Inc., Balt., 1986-88; system analyst Computer Data Systems, Inc., Rockville, Md., 1988-89; data processing specialist Dept. of Health and Mental Hygiene, Balt., 1989—; instr. Community Coll. of Balt., 1986, 88; cons. Nat. Ins. Agency, Balt., 1988. Author: Guide to Using MS-DOS, 1988; contbr. author Japanese-Chinese Electrical Mechanical Industry Dictionary, 1980; transl., editor Analysis of Gas, Impurities and Carbide in Steel, 1961; contbr. articles to profl. jours. Vol. tutor U. Balt., 1983; vol. tchr. Chinese Lang. Sch., Balt., 1985-86, 90-92; lectr. Internat. Festival Exhbn., 1986. Recipient Cert. of appreciation Chinese Language Sch., Balt., 1986. Mem. NAFE, Sci. and Tech. Assn., Beta Gamma Sigma, Delta Mu Delta.

ROCA, CARLOS MANUEL, sales executive; b. San Juan, P.R., Aug. 24, 1962; s. Gaspar and Geraldine (Barnett) R. BS in Fin., Villanova U., 1984. Pres., chief exec. officer Main Line Foto, Conshohocken, Pa., 1983—. Named Employer of the Yr., Assn. Svcs. for the Blind, 1989. Mem. Latin Am. Mgmt. Assn., Hispanic 500. Republican. Roman Catholic. Home: 848 King Of Prussia Rd Wayne PA 19087-3610 Office: Main Line Foto 1100 E Hector St Conshohocken PA 19428-2374

ROCCA, ROBERT ANGELO, financial analyst; b. Pyrites, N.Y., Jan. 4, 1954; s. Guy Lewis and Ethel (Rogers) R. BS, St. Lawrence U., 1976; MBA, Clarkson U., 1977. Bus. mgr. Wadhams Hall Coll., Ogdensburg, N.Y., 1977-79; asst. dir. mktg. and fin. St. lawrence County office Econ. Devel., Canton, N.Y., 1979-81; cost and credit mgr. Gould Inc., Watertown, N.Y., 1981-84; div. controller Little Rapids Corp., Potsdam, N.Y., 1984-88; cost supr. Aluminum Co. Am., Massena, N.Y., 1988-90, plant acct., 1990-91; fin. analyst Aluminum Co. Am., Pitts., 1991—; cons. in field. V.p. Canton Cen. Sch. Bd. Edn., 1987-88, pres., 1989-90; dir. St. Lawrence County C. of C., 1985, v.p., 1986-87, pres., 1987-88, treas., 1990-91; mem. Canton-Potsdam Hosp. Corp. Bd., 1990-91. Mem. Nat. Assn. Accts., Assn. MBA Execs., Better Bus. Bur. Panel of Consumer (arbitrator), Am. Mensa. Democrat. Home: 1873 Fairhill Rd Allison Park PA 15101 Office: Aluminum Co Am 1501 Alcoa Bldg Pittsburgh PA 15219

ROCCANOVA, LOUIS PATRICK, molecular and cell biologist; b. Bklyn., Mar. 17, 1965. Student, L.A. Coll. Chiropractic, 1987; BA, Hofstra U., 1987; MA, Hunter Coll., 1989. pvt. practice tutor, L.I., N.Y., 1982—. Adj. lectr. Hunter Coll., N.Y.C., 1988-89; grad. asst. Queens Coll., Flushing, N.Y., 1989—; Pres. People Against Chem. Abuse, Massapequa, N.Y., 1988—. Mem. AAAS, Am. Mus. Natural History. Roman Catholic. Home: 315 Banbury Rd Massapequa NY 11758 Office: Queens Coll 65-30 Kissena Blvd Flushing NY 11367

ROCHE, JAMES JOSEPH, minister, columnist; b. Ludlow, Mass., May 17, 1953; s. William Burke and Lorraine (Parent) R.; m. children: Richard, Alexandra, Bjorn; m. D. Grubb, 1989. BA with honors, Clark U., 1976; MA, Vt. Coll., 1983; MDiv, Union Theol. Sem., 1987; postgrad., Columbia U.; PhD, Union Inst., 1991. Lic. prof. counselor, Mass.; lic. marriage and family therapist;lic. rehab. counselor. Program dir. Mountainview Family Svcs., Nev., 1978-84; pastoral life liaison The Riverside Ch., N.Y.C., 1984-86; asst. min. Mid. Collegiate Ch. of N.Y., N.Y.C., 1986-88; min. Unitarian Ch. of Norfolk, Va., 1988-89; nat. syndicated columnist human sexuality, 1988-89; mem. faculty Mercy Coll., N.Y.C., 1990—. Mem. adv. bd. United AIDS Relief Effort, N.Y.C., 1987-89, Youth Out and United, Norfolk, 1988-89. Mem. Am. Assn. Sex Edn., Counselors and Therapists, Am. Assn. for Counseling and Devel., AAAS, Nat. Writers Union, Nat. Press Photographers Assn., Nat. Bd. Cert. Counselors, Am. Assn. for Adult Continuing Edn. Democrat. Home and Office: 747 Union St Brooklyn NY 11215-1247

ROCHE, JOHN EDWARD, human resources management consultant; b. St. Albans, N.Y., Nov. 11, 1946; s. John F. and Carolyn C. (Miller) R.; children: Christopher B., Danielle. BA, Marist Coll., 1968, MBA, 1975; MS in Edn., SUNY, New Paltz, 1974. Tchr. Kingston (N.Y.) City Schs., 1968-76; employment supr. ACLI Internat. Inc., N.Y.C., 1976-78; dir. pers. Balfour MacLaine Internat., N.Y.C., 1978-80; mgr. employee rels. Harcourt Brace Jovanovich, N.Y.C., 1980-82; nat. dir. pers. Hayt, Hayt & Landau, Great Neck, N.Y., 1982-86; pres. Pers. Mgmt. Svcs., Great Neck, N.Y., 1983-86, Martin-Roche Assocs., Inc., Levittown, N.Y., 1986-92; asst. prof. N.Y. Inst. Tech., Old Westbury, 1989—; pres. M-R Franciship Corp., Levittown, 1989-92; pres. Martin-Roche Internat. Ltd., Plainview, 1992—. Exec. dir. Jr. Achievement, Kingston, 1972-76. Mem. Am. Compensation Assn. (cert. compensation profl.), Soc. for Human Resource Mgmt. (cert. sr. profl. in human resources), KC (grand knight 1967-68). Republican. Roman Catholic. Home: 17 Meadow Ln Syosset NY 11791-4126 Office: Martin-Roche Internat Inc 1670 Old Country Rd Plainview NY 11803

ROCHE, LYNN F., educator; b. Bklyn., Dec. 3, 1960; d. David P. Roche III. AS in Early Childhood, SUNY, Farmingdale, 1981; BS in Spl. Edn., St. John's U., Jamaica, N.Y., 1983; MS in Spl. Edn., St. John's U., 1988, PD in Ednl. Adminstrn. and Supervision, 1990. Tchr. asst. Little Village Sch., Garden City, N.Y., 1981-82; tchr. of emotionally disturbed J.H.S. 8, Jamaica, N.Y., 1983-86, Poseidon, Los Angeles, 1986-87; ednl. coord., mainstream coord. P.S. 80, Jamaica, N.Y., 1987-91; rsch. asst. Peabody Coll. Vanderbilt U., Nashville, 1991—; spl. edn. cons. Paul J. Cooper, Bklyn., 1991; mem. project Basics I.H.S. 8, Jamaica, N.Y., 1983-86; sec. Pupil-Pers. Commn., P.S. 80, Jamaica, 1987-91. Cons., instr. How To Use The Apple Computer; co-author: A Study Guide for Foolin' Around with Infinity, 1987, Handbook for the Special Education Paraprofessional, 1990. Mem. Council for Exceptional Children. Republican. Roman Catholic. Home: Apt L-6 2601 Hillsboro Rd Nashville TN 37212 Office: Vanderbilt U Spl Edn George Peabody Coll Nashville TN 37241

ROCHE, WILLIAM JOHN, plastics manufacturing executive, vocational school instructor; b. Erie, Pa., Jan. 15, 1953; s. Paul Conaty and Margaret Mary Roche; children: Jill, Paul, Kevin; m. Jane Katherine Hammond, Mar. 1, 1986. BS/BA, John Carroll U., 1975. Sales clk. Injection Molders Supply, Cleve., 1975-76; from prodn. engr. to asst. mgr. Erie Plastics, Corry, Pa., 1976-83, mgr. engring., 1983-84, v.p., 1984-91; pres. Keystone Recycling, Meadville, Pa., 1991—; instr. Regional Skill Ctr., Erie, 1978—, Job Link, Erie, 1991. Pres. Brokenstraw Players Theatre, Corry, 1976-78. Recipient Spl. Svc. award Vocat. Indsl. Clubs, Corry, 1982. Mem. Soc. Plastics Engrs. (edn. chair 1978-88, spl. achievement award 1988, 89, edn. award 1989, named Man of Yr. 1990, pres. 1991-92), Erie Engring. Soc. (outstanding mem. 1991), Corry Country Club. Republican. Roman Catholic.

ROCHELLE, JAMES MONROE, private investigator; b. N.Y.C., July 1, 1930; s. S. Nathaniel and Doris M. (Glenofsky) R.; m. Irma Jacqueline Rochelle, May 2, 1954; children: Roxanne E., Paul, David N. Student, Coll. Empire State, 1986. Bail bondsman State of N.Y., 1953—, pvt. investigator, 1977—; polygraph examiner Backster Lie Detection, N.Y.C., 1978—; cons. in field. Staff sgt. USAF, 1948-52. Mem. Assn. Lic. Detectives of N.Y. State, Internat. Narcotic Enforcement, Am. Polygraph Assn., World Assn. Detective, Empire State Polygraph Soc. (pres. 1989—), Soc. Profl. Investigators, Fed. Investigators Assn. (assoc.), Aircraft Owners and Pilots Assn., Yonkers Jaycees (pres. 1958). Republican. Office: Rochelle Security Testing 284 New Main St Yonkers NY 10701

ROCHLIN, PHILLIP, retired chemist, association executive, librarian; b. N.Y.C., Mar. 24, 1923; s. Louis and Dora (Rubin) R.; m. Ruth Munt, Dec. 31, 1954 (div. 1987); children: Jennifer Louise, Kevin Louis. BS in Chemistry, CCNY, 1943; MS, NYU, 1949; MLS, Rutgers U., 1960. Chemist various cos., N.J., 1943-63; sci. analyst, engring. specialist Libr. of Congress, Washington, 1963; supervisory chemist, mgr. tech. libr. Naval Propellant Plant, Indian Head, Md., 1963-68; chief accessions and indexing br. Nat. Hwy. Safety Inst., Washington, 1968-69; supervisory chemist, dir. tech. info. div. Naval Ordnance Sta., Indian Head, 1969-78; chemist, tech. info. specialist Naval Ordnance Sta., Indian Head, 1979-84; instr. Charles County (Md.) C.C., 1970-79. Editor Philatelic Lit. Rev., 1956-60; contbr. articles to profl. jours. Mem. Am. Chem. Soc., Assn. for Recorded Sound Collections (exec. dir. 1985—), Am. Philatelic Soc. Home: 11200 Lockwood Dr #1805 Silver Spring MD 20901 Office: Assn Recorded Sound Collections PO Box 10162 Silver Spring MD 20914

ROCK, SANDRA KAYE, store manager; b. Lebanon, Pa., Feb. 4, 1952; d. John Edgar and Anna Elizabeth (Phillippy) Forney; m. Krall K. Hostetter, Jan. 1, 1972 (div. 1978); children: Todd H., Duane Eric; m. Darryl Lynn Rock, Oct. 5, 1985. Student, Lebanon Valley Coll., Annville, Pa., 1978-83, Lebanon Valley Coll., Annville, Pa., 1990. Clk., sewing instr. Singer Co., Lebanon, Pa., 1970-72; asst. mgr. Turkey Hill Minit Markets, Lancaster, Pa., 1977-78, store mgr., 1978-79, area mgr., 1979-84, gasoline mgr., store inventory mgr., 1985, tng. adminstr., 1986-87, dist. mgr., 1988-89, dir. store ops., 1989-92; dist. mgr. Avon, York, Pa., 1987-88. Mem. NAFE. Mem. Brethren Ch. Home: 171 Ridings Way Lancaster PA 17601

ROCKAFELLOW, DEBORAH SUSAN, school system administrator; b. Red Bank, N.J., Dec. 17, 1954; d. Louis S. and Shirley M. (Krapf) Van Zandt; m. Phillip E. Rockafellow. BS, Monmouth Coll., 1976; MEd, Rutgers U., 1983, postgrad., 1988—. Bus. educator high schs., adult schs., community colls., N.J., 1977-89; edn. program specialist N.J. State Dept. Edn., Trenton, 1989-91; teaching asst. Rutgers U., 1987-88. Lt. USCGR, 1973—. Mem. ASTD, AAUW, N.J. Bus. Edn. Assn. (exec. bd. 1986-90), Res. Officers Assn., Phi Delta Kappa. Home: 2310 Bennett Ave Point Pleasant Beach NJ 08742-4318

ROCKART, JOHN FRALICK, information systems reseacher; b. N.Y.C., June 20, 1931; s. John Rachac and Janet (Ross) R.; m. Elise Jean Feldmann, Sept. 16, 1961; children: Elise B. Liesl, Scott F. AB, Princeton U., 1953; MBA, Harvard U., 1958; PhD, MIT, 1968. Sales rep. IBM, 1958-61, dist. med. rep., 1961-62, fellow in Africa, 1962-64; instr. MIT, Cambridge, Mass., 1966-67; asst. prof. IBM, Cambridge, Mass., 1967-70, assoc. prof., 1970-74, sr. lectr., 1974—; dir. MIT, Cambridge, 1976—; bd. dirs. Keane, Inc.,

Boston, Comshare, Inc., Ann Arbor, Mich., Transition Systems, Inc., Boston, Multiplex, St. Louis. Co-author: Computers & Learning Process, 1974, Rise of Managerial Computing, 1986, Executive Support Systems, 1988 (Computer Press Assn. 1989); contbr. articles to profl. jours. Trustee New Eng. Med. Ctr., Boston; mem. Mass. Gov. Adv. Coun. on Info. Tech., Boston. Lt. USN, 1953-56. Mem. Assn. for Computing Machinery, Inst. for Mgmt. Sci., Ops. Rsch. Soc. Am., Soc. for Info. Mgmt. (bd. dirs. mem. at large 1989-93), New Eng. Med. Ctr. Audit Com., Weston (Mass.) Golf Club, Lake Sunapee Country Club (New London, N.H.). Republican. Unitarian. Home: 150 Cherry Brook Rd Weston MA 02193-1308 Office: CISR MIT Sloan Sch Mgmt E40-187 77 Massachusetts Ave Cambridge MA 02139-4307

ROCKAS, LEO, English educator; b. Rochester, N.Y., Oct. 12, 1928; s. John Constantine and Crystal (Tsychlas) R.; m. Virginia Louise Rouvina, June 25, 1960; children: Nia, Anastasia. AB, U. Rochester, AM; PhD, U. Mich. Instr. Wayne State U., Detroit, 1957-60; asst. prof. Rochester Inst. Tech., 1960-61; asst. to full prof. SUNY, Geneseo, 1961-67; prof. English Briarcliff Coll., Briarcliff Manor, N.Y., 1967-71, U. Hartford, West Hartford, Conn., 1971—. Author: Modes of Rhetoric, 1964, Ways In, 1984, A Creative Copybook, 1989, Style in Writing, 1992. With U.S. Army, 1946-48. Home: 89 Highridge Rd West Simsbury CT 06092-2003 Office: U Hartford Dept English Hartford CT 06117

ROCKEFELLER, DAVID, banker; b. N.Y.C., June 12, 1915; s. John Davison Jr. and Abby Greene (Aldrich) R.; m. Margaret McGrath, Sept. 7, 1940; children: David, Abby A., Neva, Margaret D., Richard G., Eileen M. BS, Harvard U., 1936, LLD (hon.), 1969; PhD, U. Chgo., 1940; LLD (hon.), Columbia U., 1954, Bowdoin Coll., 1958, Jewish Theol. Sem., 1958, Williams Coll., 1966, Wagner Coll., 1967, Harvard U., 1969, Pace Coll., 1970, St. John's U., 1971, U. Liberia, 1979, U. Notre Dame, Am. Univ., 1987, U. Miami, 1988. Sec. to Mayor Fiorello H. La Guardia, 1940-41; asst. regional dir. Office Def., Health and Welfare Services, 1941-42; 2d v.p. Chase Nat. Bank, 1948-49, v.p., 1949-51, sr. v.p., 1951-55; sr. v.p. Chase Nat. Bank (merged with); Bank of Manhattan; exec. v.p. Chase Manhattan Bank, 1955-57, vice chmn. bd., 1957-61, chmn. bd., 1961-81, pres., chmn. exec. com., 1961-69, chief exec. officer, 1969-80, chmn. internat. adv. com., 1981—, also dir.; chmn. bd. Rockefeller Group, Inc.; chmn. bd. Rockefeller Ctr. Properties, Inc. Author: Unused Resources and Economic Waste, 1940, Creative Management in Banking, 1964. Mem. exec. com. Downtown Lower Manhattan Assn., 1958—, chmn., 1958-75; trustee, chmn. bd. Rockefeller U., 1950-75, chmn. exec. com., 1975—; chmn. emeritus Rockefeller Bros. Fund; hon. trustee Rockefeller Family Fund; life trustee U. Chgo.; trustee, chmn. bd. Mus. Modern Art, 1987—; bd. overseers Harvard Coll., 1954-60, 62-68, 73-74; chmn. Ams. Soc. Capt. AUS, 1942-46. Decorated Legion of Honor France; Order of Merit, Italy; recipient award of merit N.Y. chpt. AIA, 1965; medal of Honor for City Planning N.Y.C., 1968; Charles Evans Hughes award NCCJ, 1974. Mem. Internat. Exec. Service Corps (dir., chmn. 1964-68), Center Inter-Am. Relations (dir., hon. chmn.), Council Fgn. Relations (dir. 1949—, v.p. 1951-70, chmn.). Clubs: Harvard, Univ., Century, Links, Knickerbocker. Address: 30 Rockefeller Pla New York NY 10112 Office: Rockefeller Group Inc 1230 Ave Of The Americas New York NY 10020-1513*

ROCKENSIES, JOHN WILLIAM, mechanical engineer; b. N.Y.C., May 30, 1932; s. John William and Wilma (Mercz) R.; m. Marion Pauline Peachman, Sept. 16, 1956; children: Kenneth John, Karen Martha Rockensies Steinbeck. B of Mech. Engring., CCNY, 1954, M of Mech. Engring., 1960; postgrad., Bklyn. Polytechnic Inst., 1955, Columbia U., 1956. Registered prof. engr., N.Y. Jet engine performance and compressor devel. Curtiss Wright Corp., Woodridge, N.J., 1954-56; product devel. engr. Sperry Gyroscope Corp., Lake Success, N.Y., 1956-60; sr. test engr. Pratt & Whitney Corp., East Hartford, Conn., 1960-62; project engr. Stratos Corp., Bayshore, N.Y., 1962; prin. propulsion engr. Republic Aviation Corp., Farmingdale, N.Y., 1963-64; power plant design engr., group leader, project engr., engr. mgr. Grumman Aerospace Corp., Bethpage, N.Y., 1964—; mem. SAE E-32 Engine Condition Monitoring com., 1983. Author tech. papers in field. Recipient Apollo Achievement award NASA, Washington, 1970. Assoc. fellow AIAA; mem. NSPE, ASME, U.S. Power Squadrons (sr.). Presbyterian. Home: 65 Parnell Dr Smithtown NY 11787-2428 Office: Grumman Aircraft Systems MS B69-001 Bethpage NY 11713-5820

ROCKFELD, MICHAEL, educational administrator; b. Bronx, N.Y., July 9, 1951; s. Max and Lily (Kasten) R.; m. Antonia Sisca, May 1, 1979. AS, Fashion Inst. Tech., N.Y.C., 1973; BA, CUNY, 1975, MS, 1979, profl. degree, 1981. Lic. wildlife rehabilitator, N.Y. Spl. edn. tchr. Life-Skills Sch., Ltd., Rego Park, N.Y., 1973-81, ednl. supr., 1981-83, ednl. dir., 1983-88; founder, dir. L.I. Infant Devel. Program, Merrick, N.Y., 1984—. Mem. steering com. N.Y. State Coalition for Children with Spl. Needs, Birth to Five, 1987; mem. N.Y. State Regional Planning Group, 1988—. Mem. Coun. for Exceptional Children, Assn. for Persons with Severe Handicaps, Nassau County Direction Ctr. Office: LI Infant Devel Program Inc 2174 N Hewlett Ave Merrick NY 11566-3606

ROCKMORE, DANIEL NAHUM, mathematician; b. Boston, Dec. 5, 1961; s. Ronald Marshall and Miriam (Miller) R. AB in Math., Princeton U., 1984; MA in Math., Harvard U., 1986, PhD in Math., 1989. Asst. prof. math. Columbia U., N.Y.C., 1989—; vis. scientist IBM, 1989. Fellow Fulbright, 1984, NSF, 1985, IBM, 1989. Mem. Am. Math. Soc. Home: 15 Beacon Hill Dr Metuchen NJ 08840-1603 Office: Columbia U Dept Math New York NY 10027

ROCKOFF, S. DAVID, physician, educator; b. Utica, N.Y., July 21, 1931; s. Samuel and Sarah (Rattinger) R.; m. Jacqueline Garsh; children—Lisa E., Todd E., Kevin D. A.B., Syracuse U., 1951; M.D., Albany Med. Coll., 1955; M.Sc. in Medicine, U. Pa., 1961. Diplomate: Am. Bd. Radiology. Intern U.S. Naval Hosp., Bethesda, Md., 1955-56; resident and fellow in radiology, USPHS trainee dept. radiology p. of U. Pa., Phila., 1958-61; staff radiologist NIH, Bethesda, Md., 1961-65; asst. prof. radiology Yale U. Sch. Medicine, New Haven, 1965-68; assoc. prof. Yale U. Sch. Medicine, 1968; asst. attending radiologist Yale-New Haven Med. Center, 1965-68; assoc. prof. radiology Washington U. Sch. Medicine, St. Louis, 1968-71; asst. radiologist Barnes and Allied Hosps., St. Louis, 1969-71; cons. radiologist VA Hosp., St. Louis, 1969-71, Homer G. Phillips Hosp., St. Louis, 1968-71; prof. radiology George Washington U. Sch. Medicine, Washington, 1971—; chmn. dept. radiology George Washington U. Sch. Medicine, 1971-77, head pulmonary radiology, 1978—, interim chmn. dept. radiology, 1989-90; cons. NIH, 1972—; vis. prof. Hadassah U., Beersheba U., Rambam Hosp., Israel, 1977; cons. in radiology VA Hosp., Washington, 1972-77, U.S. Naval Med. Center, Bethesda, 1973-77; mem. diagnostic radiology adv. com. NIH, 1973-76; mem. Cancer Research Manpower Rev. Com., NIH, 1978. Editor-in-chief: Investigative Radiology, 1965-76; editor-in-chief emeritus, 1976—; editor Jour. Thoracic Imaging, 1985; Contbr. numerous articles to med. jours. Served with USN, 1955-58; Served with USPHS, 1961-63. Recipient numerous USPHS grants. Fellow Am. Coll. Radiology (pres.-elect D.C. chpt. 1976), Am. Coll. Chest Physicians; mem. Am. Fedn. Clin. Research, D.C. Med. Soc. (mem. med.-legal com. 1975-78), AMA, Radiol. Soc. N.Am., Assn. Univ. Radiologists, Soc. Thoracic Radiology (pres. 1983-84, exec. dir. 1984-87). Home: 11508 W Hill Dr Rockville MD 20852-3749 Office: George Washington U Sch Medicine 901 23d St NW Washington DC 20037

ROCKWELL, ELIZABETH GOODE, dance company director, consultant, educator; b. Portland, Oreg., Sept. 10, 1920; d. Henry Walton and Elizabeth (Harmon) Goode; m. William Hearne Rockwell, Feb. 3, 1948; children: Enid, Karen, William. BA, Mills Coll., 1941; MA, NYU, 1946. Instr. dance Monticello Jr. Coll., Alton, Ill., 1941-42; dir. masters program in dance Smith Coll., Northampton, Mass., 1946-48; 1st dir. dance dept. High Sch. of Performing Arts, N.Y.C., 1948-51, 53-54; dir. Elizabeth Rockwell Sch. Dance, Bedford, N.Y., 1956-86, Rondo Dance Theater, Bedford, 1971—; dance critic Dance Observer, N.Y.C., 1944-46; dance cons. Nat. Assn. Health, Phys. Edn. & Recreation, Balt., 1947, PAVE, Title III, Com. Va., Richmond, 1968-70; choreographer theater prodns. YMHA, 92nd, N.Y.C., 1952; v.p. Contemporary Dance Prodns., N.Y.C., 1958-63. Choreographer (suite of dances) Jazz Suite, 1966, (50-minute dances) Catch the Wind, 1969, Genesis, 1972 (narrative modern ballet) The Executioner, 1974, Decathalon, 1982; dir. (subscription series) Dance-Art-Poetry-Jazz, 1978-79, (dance/music 1600-1900) Stages in Ages, 1981, (Am. dance revivals) Masterpieces of American Dance, 1982-84, Dances of the Decades, 1985-90, (revival & new choreography) Dances of Our Times, 1991. Bd. dirs. Coun. for Arts in Westchester, White Plains, N.Y., 1978-79, affiliate, 1978—. Recipient Medal for Performance Israeli Army, 1966, Award for Excellence in Arts Edn. Alumnae of High Sch. of Performing Arts, 1990, various grants N.Y. State Coun. on Arts, 1971-92, Coun. Arts in Westchester, 1973-92, dance touring program grant Nat. Endowment for Arts, 1976-79. Mem. Am. Dance Guild, Westchester Dance Coun. (program dir. 1965-69), Assn. Am. Dance Cos. Home: 957D Heritage Hills Dr Somers NY 10589-1913 Office: Rondo Am Dance Theater PO Box 17 Bedford NY 10506-0017

ROCKWELL, NORMAN, security service official; b. Bklyn., July 8, 1927; s. Sidney Z. and Reginia (Morganthau) R.; m. June 30, 1954 (div. 1983); children: Richard, Lori, Heather; m. Karanela Lazarus, Sept. 30, 1987. BBA, Pace U., 1951. Chief exec. officer Metro. Main Co., Nutley, N.J., 1962-85; chief exec. officer, chmn. Profl. Security, Nutley, 1971—. Mem. Alpine C. of C. (pres. 1979-80), Edgewood Country Club, Polo Club. Home: 17160 Hunnington Pkwy Boca Raton FL 33496 also: 45 Long Ridge Rd Montvale NJ 07670 Office: Profl Security 43 River Rd Nutley NJ 07110-3411

ROCKWELL, SARA CAMPBELL, biologist, educator; b. Somerset, Pa., Sept. 8, 1943; d. W. Paul and Rebecca June (Mostoller) C.; m. Charles Rockwell, 1965 (div. 1991); children: Rebecca Jane, Karen Renee. BS, Pa. State U., 1965; PhD, Stanford U., 1971; MA (hon.), Yale U., 1990. Postdoctoral fellow Stanford U., Palo Alto, Calif., 1971-72, 74; attache de recherche Inst. Gustave Roussy, Villejuif, France, 1973; asst. prof. Yale U. Sch. Medicine, New Haven, Conn., 1974-78, assoc. prof., 1978-84, prof. rsch., 1984-89, prof., 1989—; mem. scientific adv. com. Am. Cancer Soc., Atlanta, 1990—; mem. study sect. NIH, Bethesda, Md., 1982-86; mem. vis. com. Brookhaven Nat. Lab., Upton, N.Y., 1987-91; cons. Am. Coll. Radiology, 1991—. Contbr. articles to profl. jours.; assoc. editor: Radiation Rsch., 1989—, Cell & Tissue Kinetics, 1982-91, Cell Proliferation, 1991—. Grantee NIH, 1974—, Am. Cancer Soc., 1979—; Damon Runyon Found. fellow, 1971-72, 74, USPHS fellow, 1966-71. Mem. Radiation Rsch. Soc. (councilor 1985-88), Cell Kinetics Soc. (pres. 1982-83, v.p. 1981-82), AAAS, Bioelectromagnetics Soc., Am. Assn. for Cancer Rsch., Am. Soc. for Therapeutic Radiology and Oncology (assoc.), Women in Cancer Rsch., AAUW, Nature Conservancy, Nat. Wildlife Fedn. Office: Yale U Sch Medicine Dept Therapeutic Radiology PO Box 3333 New Haven CT 06510-0333

RODDA, BRUCE EDWARD, biostatistician; b. Schenectady, N.Y., June 21, 1942; s. Charles Jr. and Eleanor Ruth (Bullock) R.; m. Jeanne M. Viau; 1 child, Matthew. BA, Alfred U., 1965; MS, Tulane U., 1967, PhD, 1969; MBA, Fairleigh Dickinson U., 1982. Assoc. dir. Merck and Co., Rahway, N.J., 1976-78, dir., 1978-82, sr. dir., 1982-87; v.p. Ayerst Labs., N.Y.C., 1987-88; v.p. BDM Bristol-Myers Squibb, Princeton, N.J., 1988—; guest investigator Rockefeller U., 1978; prof. biostats. U. Ill., Rockford, 1979-90; cons. VA and NIH, Washington, 1972—; asst. prof. pharmacology Indiana U., Bloomington, 1972-78. contbr. numerous articles to profl. jours. Fellow Royal Stats. Soc., Am. Stats. Assn., Biometric Soc. (regional adv. bd.); mem. Drug Info. Assn., Am. Soc. for Clin. Pharmacology (chmn. Council III 1986-89), Soc. Clin. Trials, Sigma Xi, Delta Mu Delta. Office: Bristol Myers Squibb Pharm Rsch Inst PO Box 4000 Princeton NJ 08543-4000

RODDEY, ALYCE, educator, consultant; b. Richmond, Va., May 14, 1932; div.; children: Debra Denise Hildreth, Sondra Yvonne Proctor. BA, Va. Union U., 1952; postgrad., George Washington U., 1958, 68, 70, Trinity Coll., 1980, 81, 85, Catholic U., 1984, 85, Am. U., 1979. Cert. tchr., D.C. Tchr. elem. sch. D.C. Pub. Schs., 1955-87, reading specialist, 1966-81, resource ctr. developer, 1986-87; project guide for schoolwide reading programs, ednl. cons. Enterprises, Unlimited, Rockville, Md., 1987—; instr. speed reading Bowie State Coll., Bowie, Md., summer 1970. Author: Reading Systems program, 1971, 90. Vol. reading cons. Sat. tutorial project, parent workshop, PUSH/EXCEL, Washington, 1981. Mem. D.C. Coun. Internat. Reading Assn., NAFE, Alpha Kappa Alpha. Democrat. Roman Catholic. Office: Enterprises Unltd 118 Monroe St Rockville MD 20850-2543

RODEFER, JOANNE MARIE, military officer; b. Abington, Pa., Sept. 9, 1953; d. John Power and Marie Claire (Gorman) Flanigan; m. Karl Douglas Rodefer, June 14, 1980. BA, St. Joseph's Coll., 1975; MS, Air Force Inst. Tech., 1980. Commd. 2d lt. USAF, 1975, advanced through grades to lt. col., 1990, officer in charge F-4E aircraft maintenance unit, 1981; chief mission systems br. Hdqrs. USAFE, Ramstein AB, Germany, 1982-84, chief aircraft avionics br., 1984-85; comdr. Equipment Maintenance Squadron, Shaw AFB, S.C., 1987-88, spl. asst. to dep. comdr. for maintenance, 1988; maintenance supr. 363rd Aircraft Generation Squadron, Shaw AFB, 1986-87, comdr., 1988-90; asst. dep. comdr. for maintenance 363rd Tactical Fighter Wing, Shaw AFB, 1990; maintenance staff officer, dir. maintenance USAF, Washington, 1991—. Mem. com. Shaw/Sumter Community Coun., Sumter, 1987-90. Mem. Soc. Logistics Engrs. (cert. profl. logistician), Air Force Inst. Tech. Alumni Assn., Air Force Assn., Maintenance Officer Assn. (sec.). Republican. Roman Catholic. Home: 1237 Madison St Alexandria VA 22314-1656 Office: Hdqrs USAF/LGMM Washington DC 20330-5130

RODEN, JON-PAUL, computer science educator; b. Vernon, Conn., July 15, 1943; s. Paul James and Evelyn Mary (McCarthy) R. BS, SUNY, Oswego, 1965; MS, Cen. Conn. State U., 1970. Tchr. elem. sch. Vernon Pub. Schs., 1965-68, tchr. anatomy and physiology, 1969-79, tchr. computer sci., 1980-82, dist. chmn. computer sci., 1982—, staff devel. presentor, 1986—; tech. advisor Capitol Region Edn. Coun., 1981—; presenter Inst. for Tchrs. and Learning, Conn. Dept. Edn., 1990—; mem. adv. com. Affiliate Newsletter Svc., 1992—. Assoc. editor: Logo Activities, 1985; writer, editor numerous teaching guides. Pres. U. Conn. Friends of Soccer, 1987-89; corporator Newington (Conn.) Children's Hosp., 1978—, mem. bd. govs., 1988—; mem. Vernon Rep. Town Com., 1978—; celebrant Celebration of Excellence Conn. State Dept. Edn., 1991. Mem. NEA, Conn. Edn. Assn. (editorial bd. 1991—), New Eng. Assn. Tchr. Educators, Conn. Computer Educators, Phi Delta Kappa (exec. bd. 1991—), Delta Kappa Epsilon. Roman Catholic. Lodges: Elks, Masons, Shriners. Home: 12 Mt Vernon Dr Vernon Rockville CT 06066-6512 Office: Vernon Pub Schs 777 Hartford Tpke Vernon Rockville CT 06066-5100

RODGERS, IMOGENE SEVIN, toxicologist; b. Rochester, Pa., Nov. 13, 1945; d. Irvin Edward and Hester Pearl (Barto) Sevin; m. John W. Horm (div. 1974); m. James Earl Rodgers, July 4, 1982; 1 child, Kimberly. BS, U. Pitts., 1967; PhD, Duquesne U., 1975. Rsch. asst. U. Pitts., 1968-71; postdoctoral assoc. Allegheny Gen. Hosp., Pitts., 1975-76; chemist Dept. Health Human Svcs. Nat. Inst. Occupational Safety and Health, Rockville, Md., 1976-80; health scientist U.S. Dept. Labor/OSHA, Washington, 1980-89; sci. coord. EPA, Washington, 1989—; guest lectr. OSHA Tng. Inst., Chgo., 1989. Author: (with others) Handbook of Radiation Measurement and Protection, 1979; contbr. articles to profl. jours. Mem. APHA, Soc. for Risk Analysis, N.Y. Acad. Sci., Soc. for Occupational and Environ. Health, Rho Chi. Home: 2302 Eagle Rock Pl Silver Spring MD 20906-3248 Office: EPA RD-672 401 M St SW Washington DC 20460-0002

RODGERS, KIRK PROCTER, international organization executive, environmentalist; b. Balt., Oct. 15, 1932; s. Samuel Procter and Florence Eugenia (Besley) R.; m. Karen Frances Johnson, Jan. 3, 1959; children: Brian Kirk, Kimberly Paige. BA in Geography, Yale U., 1954, MS in Natural Resource Conservation, 1956. Timber surveyor U.S. Forest Svc., Colo., Calif., 1953-54; land use planner Balt. (Md.) County Planning Commn., 1955; natural resources specialist, dept. econ. affairs Orgn. of Am. States, Washington, 1960-63, chief natural resources unit, dept. econ. affairs, 1963-69, dir. dept. regional devel. and environment, 1970—; permanent sec. Interamerican Travel Congress, Washington, 1986—; pres. Besley and Rodgers Inc., Woolford, Md., 1988—; mem. U.S. com. Sci. Com. on Problems of the Environment, Washington, 1990—; advisor environment program UN, 1986. Author: Physical Resource Investigations for Economic Development, 1969, Integrated Regional Development Planning, 1984; contbr. The Careless Technology-Ecological Consequences of Internat. Development, 1970. Lt. (j.g.) USNR, 1956-58. Recipient Grad. fellowship Conservation Found., Yale U., 1955-56, Population Workshop fellowship Ford Found., Washington, 1956. Mem. Soc. for Internat. Devel., Tidewater Farm Club, Forest Farmers Assn. (bd. dirs. 1990—). Home: 3508 Stoneybrae Dr Falls Church VA 22044 Office: Orgn American States 1889 F St NW Washington DC 20006

RODGERS, MARY COLUMBRO, university chancellor, English educator; b. Aurora, Ohio, Apr. 17, 1925; d. Nicola and Nancy (DeNicola) Columbro; m. Daniel Richard Rodgers, July 24, 1965; children: Robert, Patricia, Kristine. AB, Notre Dame Coll., 1957; MA, Western Res. U., 1962; PhD, Ohio State U., 1964; postgrad., U. Rome, 1964-65; EdD, Calif. Nat. Open U., 1975, DLitt, 1978. Tchr. English Cleve. elem. schs., 1945-52, Cleve. secondary schs., 1952-62; supr. English student tchrs. Ohio State U., 1962-64; asst. prof. English U. Md., 1965-66; assoc. prof. Trinity Coll., 1967-68; prof. English D.C. Tchrs. Coll., 1968—; pres. Md. Nat. U., 1972—; chancellor Am. Open U., 1965—; dean Am. Open U. Acad. Author numerous books and monographs, latest works include: A Short Course in English Composition, 1976, Chapbook of Children's Literature, 1977, Comprehensive Catalogue: The Open University of America System, 1978-80, Open University of America System Source Book, V, VI, VII, 1978, Essays and Poems on Life and Literature, 1979, Modes and Models: Four Lessons for Young Writers, 1981, Open University Structures and Adult Learning, 1982, Papers in Applied English Linguistics, 1982, Twelve Lectures on the American Open University, 1982, English Pedagogy in the American Open University, 1983, Design for Personalized English Graduate Degrees in the Urban University, 1984, Open University English Teaching, 1945-85: Conceptual History and Rationale, 1985, Claims and Counterclaims Regarding Instruction Given in Personalized Degree Residency Programs Completed by Graduates of California National Open University, 1986, The American Open University, 1965 t0 1985: History and Sourcebook, 1986, New Design II: English Pedagogy in the American Open University, 1987, The American Open University, 1965 to 1985: A Research Report, 1987, The American Open University and Other Open Universities: A Comparative Study Report, 1988, Poet and Pedagogue in Moscow and Leningrad: A Travel Report, 1989, Foundations of English Scholarship in the American Open University, 1989, Twelve Lectures in Literary Analysis, 1990, Ten Lectures in Literary Production, 1990, Analyzing Fact and Fiction, 1991, Analyzing Poetry and Drama, 1991, Some Successful Literary Research Papers: An Inventory of Titles and Theses, 1991, A Chapbook of Poetry and Drama Analysis, 1992, others. Fulbright scholar U. Rome, 1964-65. Fellow Cath. Scholars; mem. Poetry Soc. Am., Nat. Coun. Tchrs. English, Am. Ednl. Rsch. Assn., Am. Acad. Peots, Ohioana Libr. Assn., Friends John Henry Newman Assn., Writer's Ctr. Md., Pi Lambda Theta. Home and Office: Coll Heights Estate 3916 Commander Dr Hyattsville MD 20782-1027

RODGERS, RHONDA LEE, health facility administrator; b. Anawalt, W.Va., July 9, 1939; d. Joseph Charlie and Dorothy Lois (Jones) Music; m. Robert Allen Rodgers, June 5, 1960; children: Tammy, Tina, Toni, Terry. Diploma, Laird Meml. Sch. Nursing, Montgomery, W.Va. Nursing supr. W.Va. State Hosp., Spencer, 1960-62; nurse Dr. Robert Smith, Chestertow, Md., 1962-63; nurse supr. Del. State Hosp., New Castle, 1964-66; asst. office mgr., bookkeeper adminstr. Neurology Assocs., Wilmington, Del., 1966—. Home: 29 Dempsey Dr Newark DE 19713-1930 Office: Neurology Assocs 1228 N Scott St Wilmington DE 19806-4060

RODGERS, ROBERT ALLEN, rehabilitation engineer; b. Montgomery, W.Va., Aug. 7, 1939; s. Boyd Benton and Mary Frances (Elliot) R.; m. Rhonda Lee Music, June 5, 1960; children: Tammy Sue, Tina Ann, Toni Lynn, Terry Allen. AB in Secondary Edn., Glenville State Coll., 1962; MS, Va. Commonwealth U., 1974; postgrad., Del Tech, 1989—. Head math dept. Queen Anne County Dept. Edn., Suddlersville, Md., 1962-63; surveyor Nuttel Co., Chestertown, Md., 1963; spl. edn. tchr. Del. State Hosp., Farnhurst, 1963-65; counselor, rehab. counselor, then sr. rehab. counselor Del. Div. Vocat. Rehab., Wilmington, 1965-87, rehab. engr., 1987-91; v.p., gen. mgr. R&T Enterprises, Unltd., Wilmington, 1991—; cons. in living with cancer Wilmington Med. Ctr., Wilmington VA Hosp., 1977-82; rehab. cons. to Del. Curative Workshop, Wilmington, 1982—; honorarium lectr., speaker on epilepsy and cancer Coppin State Coll., Balt., 1978-79; frequent lectr., presenter seminars U. Del. Grad. Nursing Sch., Lincoln U. Grad. Sch. Vocat. Rehab. Counseling. Designer devices for disabled persons. Active Boy Scouts Am., Wilmington. Recipient Award of Merit Lenape Dist. Boy Scouts Am., Newark, Del., 1986, numerous awards for youth svcs.; named Man of the Yr. Am. Biog. Inst., 1991. Mem. NEA, Md. Tchrs. Assn., Nat. Rehab. Assn. (region 3 sec. 1969-71), Del. Rehab. Assn., First State Rehab. Counselors Assn. (co-founder, pres. 1972), Am. Radio Relay League, First State Amateur Radio CLub (past pres.), NRA, Airplane Pilot and Owners Assn. Baptist. Lodges: Kiwanis, Moose. Home and Office: 29 Dempsey Dr Newark DE 19713-1930

RODGERS, SUZANNE HOOKER, ergonomics consultant, physiologist; b. Rochester, N.Y., Dec. 26, 1939; d. John Ashmead and Priscilla May (Bodman) Rodgers. AB, Vassar Coll., 1961; PhD, U. Rochester Med. Ctr., 1967. Postdoctoral fellow USPHS Middlesex Hosp., London, 1966-68; ergonomist Eastman Kodak Co., Rochester, N.Y., 1968-82; cons. Rochester, N.Y., 1982—. Author: Working With Backache, 1985; tech. editor, prin. author Ergonomic Design for People at Work, 1983, 86. Bd. dirs., chmn. com., v.p. Rochester Philharm. Orch. Inc., Rochester, 1969-75; bd. dirs. Opera Theatre Rochester, 1969-75; bd. dirs., chmn. com., pres. Monroe County Bd. Health, Rochester, 1979-88. Mem. Soc. Mfg. Engrs., Human Factors Soc. (pres. Western N.Y. chpt. 1971-72). Home and Office: 169 Huntington Hls Rochester NY 14622-1121

RODGERS, THELMA ELAINE (JUNE RODGERS), communications consultant; b. Pitts.; One child, Walter D. Thomas III. BA in Communication, Chatham Coll., 1979; postgrad., Carnegie Mellon U., 1991—. Broadcast journalist Cox Broadcasting Corp., Atlanta, 1972-78; broadcast journalist Westinghouse Electric Corp., Pitts., 1978-80, mgr. internat. customer svc., 1980-85, mgr. corp. internal communication rsch., 1987—. Contbr. articles to profl. jours. Mem. Mortar Bd.

RODINO, PETER WALLACE, JR., lawyer, former congressman; b. Newark, June 7, 1909; s. Peter and Margaret (Gerard) R.; m. Marianna Stango, Dec. 27, 1941; children: Margaret (Mrs. Charles Stanziale, Jr.), Peter III. LLB, U. Newark (now Rutgers U.), 1937; LLD (hon.), Lehigh U., 1975, Rutgers U., 1975, N.Y. Law Sch., 1975, Princeton U., 1975, Seton Hall U., 1976, Bklyn. Law Sch., 1976, Yeshiva U., 1979, Potomac Sch. Law, 1979, Fairleigh Dickinson U., 1981, Columbus Sch. Law, 1981, Cath. U. Am., 1981, Duquesne U., 1982; LHD (hon.), LeMoyne Coll., 1974, Gov.'s State U., 1977, Jersey City State Coll., 1977, Georgetown U., 1977; DCL (hon.), St. John's U., 1974. Bar: N.J. 1938. Practice gen. law Newark; mem. 81st-100th Congresses from 10th N.J. Dist., 1949-1989; dean N.J. congl. delegation, chmn. House Com. on Judiciary; sr. mem. Select House Com. on Narcotics Abuse; sr. mem. Intergovtl. Com. for European Migration, 1962-72, chmn., 1971-72; ptnr. Rodino and Rodino, East Hanover, N.J., 1989—; mem. Pres.'s Select Commn. Immigration Refugee Policy, Nat. Commn. for Rev. Antitrust Laws and Procedures; del. North Atlantic Assembly, 1962—, chmn. sci. and tech. com., to 1972; chmn. working group control narcotics; congl. observer Disarmament Conf., Geneva, 1958; former vis. prof. law Seton Hall U., South Orange, N.J., other schs. Served with 1st U.S. Armored Div. in North Africa, Italy; with Mil. missions Italian Army; discharged as capt. 1941-46. Decorated Bronze star U.S.; Knight grand cross Order of Merit Republic of Italy; Gold medal Knights of Lithuania; Knight Sovereign Order Malta; Knight comdr. Equestrian Order of St. Agata, Republic of San Marino; others; recipient citation for outstanding service Free Polish Govt.; Guglielmo Marconi award Order Sons of Italy in America, 1967; A. Philip Randolph Inst. award, 1975; Humanitarian award Internat. B'nai B'rith, 1975; Hubert H. Humphrey Civil Rights award Leadership Conf. on Civil Rights, 1978; numerous others. Democrat. *

RODINO, VINCENT LOUIS, insurance company executive; b. N.Y.C., June 25, 1929; s. Vincenzo and Sofia (De Toro) R.; m. Marie Green; children: Peter Vincent, Vincent Douglas. BA, NYU, 1957. CLU. With The Equitable Fin. Cos., N.Y.C., 1946—, chief mktg. services sector, 1983-84, chief traditional products sector, 1984-86, chmn., chief exec. officer Traebco subs., 1984-86, chief sales support sector, 1986-89; dep. pres. northeastern region Equitable Ins. Cos., N.Y.C., 1989—; trustee Life Underwriter Tng. Council, Washington, 1987. Served as sgt. U.S. Army, 1951-53. Mem. Assn. Advanced Life Underwriting, Nat. Assn. Life Underwriters, N.Y.C.

Chpt. CLU's. Office: The Equitable Fin Cos 200 Plaza Dr Secaucus NJ 07094-3607

RODIS, NICHOLAS, education educator; b. Nashua, N.H., Jan. 24, 1924; s. Christos and Eftihia (Harris) R.; m. Eve Karafotis, July 3, 1949; children: Christopher, Peter, Kristine. AB, Harvard U., 1949; MEd, Am. Internat. Coll., 1951. Coach basketball and football Am. Internat. Coll., Springfield, Mass., 1949-54; coach football, basketball, baseball U. Conn., Storrs, 1954-62; spl. asst. for athletic programs U.S. Dept. of State, Washington, 1962-67; dir. athletics Brandeis U., Waltham, Mass., 1967-84, prof. phys. edn., 1984—; exec. dir. U.S. Collegiate Sports Coun., Waltham, Mass., 1987—; sports regulations commn. Internat. Univ. Sports Fedn., Brussels, Belgium, 1987—; bd.d irs. World Univ. Games, Buffalo, 1989—, U.S. Collegiate Sports Coun., Waltham, 1987—. Author: U.S. Collegiate Sports Coun., 1990. Co-chmn. Athletes for Robert F. Kennedy, Washington, 1968, Athletes for Hubert Humphrey, Washington, 1968. Named to Greek Athletic Hall of Fame, 1986. Mem. Nat. Football Found. and Hall of Fame (bd. dirs. 1980—), AHEPA Permanent Olympics in Greece Com. (chmn. 1987—. Democrat. Greek Orthodox. Office: Brandeis U South St Waltham MA 02254

RODITI, CLAUDIO BRAGA, jazz musician; b. Rio de Janeiro, May 28, 1946; came to U.S., 1970; s. Alberto and Deise (Braga) R. Student trumpet, Varginha, M.G., Brazil, 1956; student, Berklee Coll. Music, Boston, 1970-72. Trumpeter Herbie Mann Band, 1978, Dizzy Gillespie's UN Orch., 1988—. Music leader (LP recording) Claudio!, 1985, (compact discs) Gemini Man, 1988, Slow Fire, 1989, Two of Swords, 1991, Milestones, 1992. Democrat. Roman Catholic.

RODMAN, ALAN GEORGE, pharmaceutical researcher; b. Lynn, Mass., May 1, 1933; s. Hyman and Dorothy (Leboff) R.; m. Judith Frances Rosenfield, July 5, 1954 (div. 1987); children: Elizabeth, Leslie, Valerie. BS in Pharmacy, Northeastern U., 1954. Asst. pharmacy mgr. Hosp. Pharmacy, Brighton, Mass., 1954-57; mem. pharm. sales staff Schering Corp., Kenilworth, N.J., 1957-63; pharm. researcher Syntex Labs., Natick, Mass., 1963—. Mem. Natick Town Meeting, 1960; mem. Natick Aux. Police/Civil Def., 1976. Mem. Am. Pharm. Assn., Am. Heart Assn., Natick Kiwanis, Elks (co-chmn. drug awareness com. 1986), Masons. Republican. Jewish. Home and Office: 1323 Worcester Rd Framingham MA 01701-8963

RODMAN, JOHN GRAY, radio news executive; b. Portland, Maine, July 8, 1951; s. Harold Albert and Dorothy (Gray) R.; m. Laurel Gelo, June 30, 1973; children: Colin John, Evan Harold. BS in Journalism, Boston U., 1978; postgrad., Harvard U., 1991. Reporter Sta. WDEW, Westfield, Mass., 1969-70; reporter, producer Sta. WMEX, Boston, 1972-76; ops. mgr. Sta. WEZE, Boston, 1977-79; Kendrick Found. rsch. grantee Boston, 1979-81; reporter, anchorman IMS Radio Network, Washington, 1981-84; ops. mgr. Sta. WXNE-TV, Boston, 1984-85; v.p. news and programming Sta. WEEI Newsradio, Boston, 1985-89; news dir. Sta. WCDJ, Boston, 1989—; lectr. Northeastern U., Boston; contbg. reporter NBC Radio News, CBS (Radio Sta. New Svc.), 1985-89, NBC, 1989—. Contbg. author: The High Cost of Indifference, 1984. Elder 1st Presbyn. Ch., Quincy, Mass., 1975—. Served alt. mil. duty Survival Inc., Quincy, Mass., 1970-72. Co-recipient Nat. Headliner award Press Club Atlantic City, 1986; recipient regional award for reporting AP, 1988. Mem. Radio and TV News Dirs. Assn., Sigma Delta Chi. Office: WCJD 68 Commercial Wharf Boston MA 02110-3894

RODMAN, MICHAEL ALAN, risk management insurance consultant; b. Boston, Feb. 1, 1940; s. Maurice and Charlotte (Dobkin) R.; m. Naida E. Hershfield, Mar. 20, 1965; children: Deborah, Charles. BBA, U. Mass., 1961. CPCU. Insur. broker Strauss-Mann Ins. Assocs., Boston, 1963-69; v.p., cons., prin. J.H. Albert Internat. Ins. Advisors, Needham, Mass., 1969—. Trustee Temple Israel of Natick, Mass., 1978—, pres., 1985-87. Mem. Soc. Risk Mgmt. Cons. (bd. dirs. 1988-90, chmn. membership com. 1989-92). Jewish. Home: 25 Cider Mill Rd Framingham MA 01701-3967 Office: JH Albert Internat 72 River Park St Needham MA 02194-2631

RODNEY, JIM ANTHONY, auditor, accountant, consultant; b. Portsmouth, Dominica, June 18, 1962; came to U.S., 1985; s. Fitz and Helena Rodney. AAS in Bus. Mgmt., CUNY, 1985; BA in Acctg., Clark U., 1987; MBA, N.Y. Inst. Tech., 1990. Ins. examiner N.Y. State Dept. Ins., N.Y.C., 1988-89; acct., cons. Jim Rodney & Assocs., N.Y.C., 1989-90; auditor N.Y.C. Dept. Fin., N.Y.C., 1990—; mgmt. cons. Jim Rodney & Assocs., N.Y.C., 1990—. Mem. La Guardia Community Coll. Alumni Assn., Clark Coll. Alumni Assn., N.Y. Inst. Tech. Alumni Assn., Alpha Kappa Mu. Roman Catholic. Office: NYC Dept Fin 345 Adams St Brooklyn NY 11201-3719

RODOLITZ, GARY MICHAEL, civil engineer, consultant; b. N.Y.C., July 25, 1950; s. Abraham Jonas and Anna (Cohen) R.; m. Barbara Gale Friedman, Jan. 13, 1974; children: Lauren Sara, David Evan. BA, NYU, 1973, BSCE, 1973. Registered profl. engr., N.Y. Mng. ptnr. David Lauren Assocs., Ltd., Westbury, 1983—; mng. ptnr. Rodolitz Orgn., Westbury, 1984—; chief exec. officer Mitchel Field Bldg. and Contracting Corp., Westbury, 1982—. Designer, builder Mitchel Field Corp. Ctr., Garden City Ctr., Nassau County, N.Y. Bd. dirs., sec., treas. Assn. for a Better L.I.; bd. dirs. Hebrew Ednl. Soc.; pres. BOMA, L.I.; bd. dirs., treas. Nassau County Bus. Corridor Transp. Mgmt. Assn. Mem. ASCE, N.Y. Acad. Scis., Nat. Soc. Profl. Engrs., N.Y. State Soc. Profl. Engrs., Nat. Com. Furtherance Jewish Edn. (bd. dirs., Edn. award 1986), Am. Mus. Natural History, Tau Beta Pi. Jewish. Avocations: photography, reading, guitar. Office: Rodolitz Orgn Garden City Ctr 100 Quentin Roosevelt Blvd Garden City NY 11530-4843

RODRIGUES, CAROL MARIA, secondary school educator; b. Manchester, N.H., Dec. 17, 1947; d. Carlos and Anna (Andersen) R. BA, Notre Dame Coll., Manchester, 1970, MEd, 1980, Cert., 1982. Asst. to registrar Notre Dame Coll., Manchester, 1966-70; bus. tchr. West High Sch., Manchester, 1970-76; work experience coord. Meml. High Sch., Manchester, 1976—; instr. Notre Dame Coll., 1987. Mem. NEA, Manchester Edn. Assn., New Eng. Bus. Assn., Nat. Bus. Edn. Assn., Am. Vocat. Assn. Home: 199 Barrett St Manchester NH 03104-2884

RODRIGUES, CLARENCE CONSTANCIO, industrial engineer, educator; b. Bombay, India, Dec. 1, 1958; came to U.S., 1983; s. Natividad Geraldo and Blanche Mabel (Santos) R.; m. Nicola Netto, Sept. 30, 1989. B in Engrng., U. Bombay, 1980; M in Tech., Indian Inst. Tech., Bombay, 1982; MCE, Tex. A&M U., 1985, PhD in Indsl. Engrng., 1988. Cons. engr. Associated Indsl. Cons., Bombay, 1982-83; asst. prof. Trenton (N.J.) State Coll., 1987-89, adj. prof., spring 1990; sr. assoc. Brian P. Little & Assocs., Paoli, Pa., 1989—; mgr. corp. engrng., ergonomics Campbell Soup Co., Camden, N.J., 1990—; adj. prof. U. Pa., Phila., 1991—, tech. expert law firm Wasselbry & Assocs., Pa., 1987; cons. United Parcel Svcs., Syracuse, 1989, Opex Corp., Moorestown, N.J., 1989-90; speaker Internat. Ergonomics and Safety Conf., Ohio, 1989, Internat. Indsl. Engrs. Conf., Toronto, Ont., Can., 1989; guest host Nat. Soc. Black Engrs., 1988-89. Contbr. articles to profl. jours. Mem. Am. Inst. Indsl. Engrs. (guest speaker 1988, editor 1989-90), Am. Inst. Safety Engrs., Tex. Water Utilities Assn., Human Factors Soc. Home: 1124 Chanticleer Cherry Hill NJ 08003-4834 Office: Campbell Soup Co Campbell Pl # 190 Camden NJ 08103-1702

RODRIGUEZ, JOAQUIN, geology educator; b. N.Y.C., Jan. 9, 1934; s. Manuel and Placidina Rodriguez; m. Patricia Anne Wagstaff, Sept. 11, 1966. BA, Hunter Coll., 1955; MS, Ohio State U., 1957; PhD, Ind. U., 1960. Lectr. Hunter Coll, CUNY, N.Y.C., 1959-62, instr., 1962-64, asst. prof., 1964-69, assoc. prof., 1970-78, prof. of geology, 1979—; mem. panel grad. rsch. fellowship program NSF, 1971, 90-91, mem. panel instrumentation and lab. improvement program, 1991; mem. com. of examiners grad. record exam in geology Ednl. Testing Svc., Princeton, N.J., 1986-92. Contbr. articles to Jour. of Paleontology, Jour. of Geol. Edn., Nat. Assn. Geology Tchrs. Mem. Demarest (N.J.) Environ. Commn., 1989-92; pres. Demarest Nature Ctr., 1982. Grantee Petroleum Rsch. Fund, 1983-86, CUNY/PSC, 1978-80, 83-85; Shuster Faculty fellow, 1970. Fellow Geol. Soc. Am.; mem. AAAS, Paleontol. Soc., Computer Oriented Geol. Soc., Soc. for Sedimentary Geology, Internat. Paleontol. Assn., Sigma Xi. Office: Hunter Coll Geol & Geog 695 Park Ave New York NY 10021-5085

RODRIGUEZ, JOEL DE JESUS, electronics company executive; b. Havana, Cuba, July 21, 1957; came to U.S., 1966, naturalized; s. Jose Manuel and Zoila Estrella (De La Concepcion) R.; m. Marie C. Cacciola, Sept. 15, 1984; children: Cali Marie, Kyle Joel, Jared Nicholas. ASMET cum laude, Westworth Inst., Boston, 1977; BSET, Northea. U., 1982. Design engr. electronic switch mfr., 1977-81, corp. tech. sales rep., 1981; tech. regional sales rep. Metal Bellows Corp. div. Parker Hannifin Aerospace, 1981-83; pres., chief exec. officer B.E.A. Inc., Acton, Mass., 1983—; %D. Instr. USCG Aux., Boston, 1986—. Mem. Am. Welding Soc. Republican. Roman Catholic. Home: 153 Concord St Nashua NH 03060 Office: BEA Inc 271 Great Rd Acton MA 01720

RODRIGUEZ, JOSÉ MANUEL, chemical company executive; b. Middlesex, Eng., June 24, 1945; came to U.S., 1980; s. Joaquin and Maria (Marin) R.; m. Christina Jean, July 3, 1970; children: Christiane, Karla, Alejandro Jose. BS in Chem. Engrng., Mexico City Nat. U., 1968. Asst. quality control mgr. Kimberly Clark Mexico, Mexico City, 1966-69; gen. mgr. Tanatex Mexicana SA de CV, Mexico City, 1970-80; v.p. mfg. Sybron Chems., Birmingham, N.J., 1980-83; pres. Europe div. Sybron Chems., Paris, 1983-89; pres. Europe div., group v.p. Sybron Chems., Birmingham, 1989—; bd. dirs. Quimica Aromatica S.A., Mexico City, Tecnologia Ambiental S.A., Mexico City. Mem. Am. Inst. Chem. Engrs., Am. Chem. Soc., Hazardous Materials Rsch. Assn. Roman Catholic. Office: Sybron Chems Inc 100 Birmingham Rd Birmingham NJ 08011-0066

RODRIGUEZ, MARTHA CECILIA, guidance counselor; b. Santa fe de Bogota, Colombia, Dec. 30, 1957; came to U.S., 1975; d. Laurentino and Sofia (Penuela) R. BA, Mercy Coll., Dobbs Ferry, N.Y., 1981; MS Edn., L.I.U., 1985. Cert. sch. counselor. Community liaison specialist Bd. Coop. Ednl. Svcs., Ardsley, N.Y., 1981-84; guidance counselor New Rochelle (N.Y.) Sch. Dist., 1984—. Camp dir. San Gabriel Summer Camp, New Rochelle, summer 1979; v.p. San Gabriel Hispanic Orgn., New Rochelle, 1979-81. Mem. Westchester, Putman, Rockland Assn. Counseling and Devel. (trustee 1990-93), N.Y. State Assn. Counseling, N.Y. State Sch. Counselors Assn., Family Info. Referral Svc. Team, Westchester Hispanic Profls. Roman Catholic. Office: Isaac E Young Mid Sch 270 Centre Ave New Rochelle NY 10805-2401

RODRIGUEZ, RAMON JOSEPH, academic administrator; b. Manhattan, N.Y., June 5, 1938; s. Pedro and Francisca (Ortiz) R.; m. Phyllis Ann Rodriguez, Sept. 5, 1959; children: Ramon, Steven, Stephanie. BS in Edn., NYU, 1961; MEd in Indsl. Tech., CUNY, 1966; MS in Counseling Edn., L.I. U., 1977; EEO Cert., Cornell U., 1982. Statis. chartist Indsl. Conf. Bd., N.Y.C., 1957-61; indsl. arts tchr. Wantagh (N.Y.) High Sch., 1961-69; asst. dean spl. programs SUNY Coll. of Tech., Farmingdale, N.Y., 1969-74, assoc. dean, EOP dir., 1974-78, asst. v.p., dean of students, 1978-85, acting v.p., 1985, assoc. v.p., dean of students, 1986—; participant on numerous faculty coms. and campus bds., 1970—; advisor Phi Theta Kappa, 1976-80, Latinos United, 1971-75, Black Student Union, 1971-75; dir. weekend tutoring Lawence High Sch. and Farmingdale (N.Y.) Coll., 1970-78; dir. emotionally disturbed Cath. Charities, N.Y.C., 1964-67, counselor, emotionally disturbed, 1963-64; dir. spl. svcs. HEW, Washington, 1970-78. Oral examiner N.Y. State Dept. Civil Svc., N.Y.C., 1980; youth leader Sachem Youth Adv. Group, Holbrook, N.Y., 1969-79; leader Boy Scouts Am. Cub Scout Pack 80, Holbrook, 1969-75; v.p. Puerto Rican Heritage House, Brentwood, N.Y., 1978-80; referee Western Suffolk Basketball Assn., 1981—; mem. N.Y. State Faculty Senate Com., 1970-72. Recipient Excellence in Profl. Svc. award Farmingdale Coll Foun., 1990, Cert. of Achievement Town. Bd. Isip, County of Suffolk, 1982, Citation Achievement award Gov. Mario Cuomo, 1985. Mem. L.I. Coun. Student Personnel Adminstrs. (v.p. 1985-89, Outstanding Svc. award 1980), United Univ. Professions (Profl. Excellence award 1991), Coll. Student Personnel Assn. Roman Catholic. Office: SUNY Coll Tech Melville Rd Farmingdale NY 11735-2221

RODRIGUEZ, RAUL, human resources specialist; b. N.Y.C., Feb. 28, 1950; s. Juan and Carmen (Velazquez) R.; m. Maribel Alvarez, Dec. 24, 1977; children: Raul Miguel, Marisol Juliet, Melanie Megan. BA, Stonybrook U., 1972; MA, Hunter Coll., 1976. Lic. real estate broker, N.Y. Dep. exec. dir. Massive Econ. Neighborhood Devel. Inc., N.Y.C., 1975-77, exec. dir., 1977-79; exec. dir. East Harlem Coun. for Community Improvement Inc., N.Y.C., 1979—; chmn. Milbank Frawley Coun., N.Y.C., 1972-74, Lakeview Homes, N.Y.C., 1974-76; vice-chmn. Human Svcs. Consortium E. Harlem, N.Y.C., 1979-84; chmn. housing com. Community Planning Bd. #11, N.Y.C., 1983-85. Elected dist. leader Dem. Party, N.Y.C., 1975-85, elected state committeeman, 1976-84; elected mem. Sch. Dist. #4, N.Y.C., 1980-83 (Edn./Recognition award 1983). Recipient Leadership award Schaefer Brewing Co., 1973, Youth Leadership award Youth Adv. Coun., 1976, Devotion of Svc. award Sr. Citizens of E. Harlem, 1977, Ptnr. in Edn. award N.Y.C. Pub. Schs., 1981, Leadership award Angel Luis Rios Softball League, 1983, Dedication and Commitment award 111th St. Oldtimers, 1985, Support and Assistance award Police Dept. N.Y.C., 1986, Community Svc. award SCAN of N.Y., 1990, cert. Merit Assembly State of N.Y., 1990, cert. Merit N.Y. State Assembly P.R.-Hispanic Task Force, 1991, Commendation award State of N.Y. Office Mental Retardation and Devel. Disabilities, 1991. Roman Catholic. Home: 96 Jasper Ave Teaneck NJ 07666-3817 Office: East Harlem Coun Community Improvement 413 E 120th St New York NY 10035-3602

RODRIGUEZ, RITA MARIA, bank executive; b. La Havana, Cuba, Sept. 6, 1944; came to U.S., 1960; Tomas and Adela (Mederos) R.; m. E. Eugene Carter, Jan. 7, 1972; 1 child, Adela-Marie R. Carter. BBA, U. Puerto Rico, 1964; MBA, NYU, 1968, PhD, 1969. Bus. adminstrn. asst. prof., then assoc. prof. Harvard Bus. Sch., Cambridge, Mass., 1969-74, 74-78; fin. prof. U. Ill., Chgo., 1978-82; dir. Export-Import Bank of U.S., Washington, 1982—; cons. U.S. Internal Revenue Svc., 1982, Polaroid Corp. and Indsl. Devel. Bank in Ecuador (Corporacion Financiera Nacional), 1978-82; bd. dirs. Acad. Fin./Ednl. Devel., Washington, 1989—; bd. advisors Pew Econ. Freedom Fellows, Washington, 1991—. Author: (with E. Eugene Carter) International Financial Management, 1976, secondedit., 1979, 3rd edit., 1984; (with Heinz Riehl) Foreign Exchange and Money Markests, 1983, Japanese, Spanish, Portuguese translations; Foreign Exchange Markets: A Guide to Foreign Currency Operations, 1977; Foreign Exchange Management in U.S. Multinationals, 1980; contbr. numerous fin. articles to profl. publs. Recipient Outstanding Achievement award, Nat. Coun. of Hispanic Women, 1986; Outstanding Hispanic Achievement award, Hispanic Corp. Achievers, 1988; National Leadership award-Government, The Nat. Network of Hispanic Women, 1989. Mem. Coun. Foreign Rels., Am. Econ. Assn. Roman Catholic. Home: 3075 Ordway St Washington DC 20008 Office: Export-Import Bank of U.S. 811 Vermont Ave NW Washington DC 20571

RODRIGUEZ-MUNGUÍA, JUAN CLÍMACO, education educator; b. Perú, Mar. 30, 1938; came to U.S., 1970; s. Florencio and Isabel (Munguia) R.; m. Elizabeth Helena, Mar. 30; children: Bridget, Patricio, Teresa. BA, Cath. U., Lima, Peru, 1961; MEd, Cath. U., 1966; EdD, U. Mass., 1975. Asst. dean admissions Cath. U., Lima, Perú, 1961-70, asst. prof., 1968-70; supr., project dir. bilingual bur. Mass. Dept. Edn., Boston, 1970-78; asst. head master English High Sch., Boston, 1979-84; dir. Bilingual Spl. Edn. Program, Bridgewater (Mass.) State Coll., 1984-87; assoc. prof. coll. of edn. U. Lowell, Mass., 1987—. Contbr. articles to profl. jours. Grantee Mass. Bd. Regents Higher Edn., 1987, U.S. Dept. Edn., 1988, 89. Mem. Nat. Assn. Bilingual Edn., Tchrs. English as Second Lang., Soc. Intercult. Tng. and Rsch. Roman Catholic. Home: 147 Park Ave Arlington MA 02174-5828 Office: U Mass Lowell 1 University Ave Lowell MA 01854-2881

RODRIGUEZ-SAINS, RENE S., physician, educator; b. Santiago, Cuba, July 25, 1952; came to U.S., 1960, naturalized, 1968; s. Emilio Rene Rodriguez and Caridad Sains; m. Juanita Laszlo, Aug. 31, 1974; children: Daniel Rene, Diana. BA cum laude, CUNY, 1973; MD, NYU, 1977. Diplomate Nat. Bd. Med. Examiners, Am. Bd. Ophthalmology. Dermatology rsch. fellow NYU Med. Ctr., N.Y.C., 1973-77, intern dept. medicine, 1977-78; resident in ophthalmology Manhattan Eye, Ear and Throat Hosp., 1978-81, chief resident in ophthalmology, 1980-81, asst. attending surgeon, 1981-85, assoc. attending surgeon Ophthalmic Plastic & Reconstructive Surgery, Ocular Tumor & Orbital Clinic, 1985-89, surgeon dir. Ophthalmic Plastic & Reconstructive Surgery Clinic, 1989—, surgeon dir., chief Ocular Tumor & Orbital Clinic, 1989—; Heed Ophthalmic Found. fellow Manhattan Eye, Ear and Throat Hosp.-N.Y. Hosp., Cornell U. Med. Ctr., 1981-82, resident instr. dept. ophthalmology, 1983-85; adj. asst. prof. dermatology NYU, 1981-88 ; clin. asst. prof. opthalmology, Mt. Sinai Med. Ctr.; attending surgeon Dept. Opthamology, Plastic and Reconstructive Surgery div., Bronx VA Hosp., 1985-88; clin. asst. prof. Dept. Ophthamology, NYU Med. Ctr., 1988—. Mem. med. adv. bd. Skin Cancer Found., 1980—; mem. NYU Malignant Melanoma Clin. Coop. Group, 1981—, mem. Barraquer Inst. Barcelona, Spain, N.Y. Soc for Clin. Ophthalmology. Contbg. editor Jour. Dermatologic Surgery ad Oncology, 1980—; co-author: Malignant Melanoma, 1979; contbr. articles to med. jours. Fellow Am. Coll. Surgeons; mem. AMA, N.Y. State Ophthalmol. Soc., Am. Assn. Ophthalmology, Assn. Rsch. in Vision and Ophthalmology, Contact Lens Assn. Ophthalmologists, N.Y. County Med. Soc., Med. Soc. State N.Y., Am. Acad. Ophthalmology. Office: 178 E 71st St New York NY 10021

RODZIANKO, PAUL, corporate executive; b. Washington, Oct. 22, 1945; s. Paul and Aimee Rodzianko; m. Chauncie McKeever, May 1988; children: Marina, Alexander. BA, Princeton U., 1967; MA, Inst. Critical Langs., 1967. With GE Co., 1967-76; pres. U.S. Geothermal Corp., N.Y.C., 1976-77, Geothermal Energy Corp., N.Y.C., 1977-83, Geothermal Food Processors, Inc., Fernley, Nev., 1979-82; exec. v.p. Grace Geothermal Corp., 1981-83, bd. dirs., 1981-83; pres. Bay Capital Corp., Oyster Bay, N.Y., 1983-85, Data Port Co., 1985-86; bd. dirs. McGill Environ. Systems, Inc.; chmn. bd. dirs. Mt. Hope Hydro, Inc., Halecon, Inc., Component Bldg. Systems, Inc. Vice chmn. Russian Orthodox Theol. Fund, 1978—; chmn. Mt. Hope Waterpower Project, 1989—. Fellow Royal Geog. Soc., Explorers Club, New Eng. Soc.; mem. Geothermal Resouces Coun. (bd. dirs., chmn. audit com. 1980-82), Nat. Inst. Social Scis., Rockaway Area C. of C. (bd. dirs.), Camp Fire Club, Tuxedo Club, Lions (Paul Harris fellow 1988-92). Office: PO Box 896 625 Mt Hope Ave Dover NJ 07802

ROE, DAVID ALLEN, operations research analyst; b. Casper, Wyo., Feb. 19, 1955; s. Richard Allen and Verlie May (Kelly) R.; m. Nancy Dorothy Hack, Feb. 8, 1986. BA in Econs., Lehigh U., 1977; MA in Econs., U. Va., 1990. Mgr. logistics analysis Ketron Div. Bionetics Corps., Warminster, Pa., 1985—. Prin. developer Space Warfare Logistics Optimization Model, 1987; developer ARmy Readiness Prediction, 1990. Small Bus. Innovative Rsch. grantee USN, 1990. Mem. Ops. Rsch. Soc. Am., Soc. Logistics Engrs., Inst. Cost Analysis, CATO Inst. (sponsor). Office: Ketron Div Bionetics Corp Warminster PA 18974

ROE, GEORGEANNE THOMAS, information brokerage executive; b. Washington, Apr. 1, 1945; d. George Albert and Lois Rose (Baker) Haun; m. Frank S. Weidner, Feb. 6, 1966 (div. Apr. 1969); m. John Steadman Roe, Apr. 11, 1969. BA in English, Simmons Coll., 1971, MS in LS, 1972; MBA, Babson Coll., 1980. Dir. Holbrook (Mass.) Pub. Libr., 1972-79; adminstrv. asst. Comprehensive Group Resources, Newton, Mass., 1980-84; bus. svcs. libr. Southeastern Mass. U., Dartmouth, 1984-85; ptnr., cons. Perry, Roe & Assocs., Millis, Mass., 1985—; asst. to dir. New Eng. Wild Flower Soc., Framingham, Mass., 1989—. Trustee Millis Pub. Libr., 1985-91. Mem. ALA, Assn. Ind. Info. Profls., Mass. Libr. Trustees Assn., New Eng. Libr. Assn., Mass. Libr. Assn. (chmn. intellectual freedom com. 1976-78), Women Entrepreneurs Homebased (exec. sec. 1988—), P.E.O. (guard chpt. AM-MA 1990—, corr. sec. 1992—). Home: 111 Acorn St Millis MA 02054-1410 Office: New Eng Wild Flower Soc 180 Hemenway Rd Framingham MA 01701-2636

ROE, ROBERT A., congressman; b. Wayne, N.J., Feb. 28, 1924; s. Robert A. and Lillian (Thornton) R. Student, Oreg. State U., Wash. State U. Former corp. exec.; mayor Wayne Township, 1956-61; mem. gov.'s cabinet, commr. conservation and econ. devel. State of N.J., Trenton, 1963-69; mem. 91st-102nd Congresses from 8th N.J. Dist., 1969—; chmn. Pub. Works and Transp. Com.; mem. Select Com. on Aging.; Committeeman Wayne Twp. Gov. Body, 1955-56; mem. Passaic County Bd. Chosen Freeholders, 1959-63, dir., 1962-63. Mem. exec. bd. Altaha council Boy Scouts Am., mem. nat. council; trustee Chilton Meml. Hosp.; mem. pres.'s adv. bd. Tombrock Coll., West Paterson, N.J.; mem. community adv. council William Paterson Coll. N.J. Served with AUS, World War II, ETO. Named Man of Year N.J. Jr. C. of C., 1959, Water Conservationist of Yr. N.J. State Fedn. Sportsmen's Clubs, 1966, Ann. Golden Medal award Garden Clubs N.J., 1969, State of Israel Bonds Scroll of honor, 1971, D.A.V. citation, 1971, citations Nat. Small Bus. Assn., 1972, citations Pres.'s Com. Employment Handicapped, 1972, Nat. Humanitarian award Joint Handicapped Council Nat. Soc. Handicapped, 1972, Disting. Service award Nat. Council Urban Econ. Devel., 1975, numerous leadership and service awards. Hon. fellow Am. Acad. Med. Adminstrs.; mem. Wayne C. of C. (past pres.), VFW, Am. Legion. Clubs: Optimist, Elk. Office: US Ho of Reps 2243 Rayburn House Office Bldg Washington DC 20515*

ROED, JORGEN, hotel industry executive; b. Aarhus, Denmark, Aug. 11, 1935; came to U.S., 1980; s. Niels Anton Marius and Ellen Margrethe (Pedersen) R.; m. Kirsten Fogh Boulstrup, Aug. 6, 1960; children: Jeanette, Susanne, Charlotte, Bettina. BA, Aarhus Tchrs. U., 1959. Tchr. Aarhus Ednl. System, 1959-60; mng. dir. Skrivrit/Esselte Studium Ltd., Copenhagen, 1961-68; mng. dir., chief exec. officer Scanticon Ltd., Aarhus, 1969-82; pres., chief exec. officer, also bd. dirs. Scanticon Internat., Inc., Princeton, N.J., 1979—; regional chief exec. Inter-Continental Hotels Corp., N.Am., N.Y.C., 1987-88; pres., chief exec. officer, also bd. dirs. Scanticon Corp., Princeton, 1982-91; consul of Sweden, Royal Swedish Consulate, Denmark, 1974-82; chmn. Prudential-Scanticon Joint Venture, Mpls., 1985-91; vice chmn. U.S. West Real Estate-Scanticon Joint Venture, Denver, 1987—. Contbg. author: Management Development and Training Handbook, 1983; contbr. articles to bus. mags. Nat. pres., Round Table Denmark, 1969-71; chmn. High Sch. Foraeldreskolen, Aarhus, 1975-79. Decorated knight 1sat class Royal No. Star (Sweden). Mem. Pres. Assn., Corps Consulaire, Danish Mgmt. Soc. Office: Scanticon Corp 105 College Rd E Princeton NJ 08540-6622

ROEDDER, EDWIN WOODS, geologist; b. Monsey, N.Y., July 30, 1919; s. Hans and Edna (Woods) R.; m. Kathleen Rea; children: Spencer, Lucy. BA, Lehigh U., 1941; MA, Columbia U., 1947, PhD, 1950; DSc (hon.), Lehigh U., 1976. Rsch. engr. Bethlehem Steel Corp., Bethlehem, Pa., 1941-46; predoctoral fellow Geophys. Lab., Carnegie Inst., Washington, 1946-47; asst. in geology Columbia U., N.Y.C., 1946-49; asst. prof., assoc. prof. U. Utah, Salt Lake City, 1950-55; chief solid state group U.S. Geol. Survey, Washington, 1955-60, staff geologist, 1960-62, geologist, 1962-73, rsch. geologist, 1974-87; assoc. Harvard U., 1987—; scientist emeritus U.S. Geol. Survey, Washington, 1987—; mem. or cons. various adv. bds, vis. coms., panels for U.S. govt. and several universities. Author: Composition of Fluid Inclusions, 1972, Fluid Inclusions, 1984; editor: Research on Mineral Forming Solutions, 1965, Fluid Inclusion Research (ann. book), 1968—; patentee in field. Recipient Exceptional Sci. Achievement medal NASA, 1973, Disting. Svc. medal U.S. Dept. Interior, 1978, Abraham Gottlob-Werner medaille Deutschen Min. Gesellschaft, 1985, Cyril Purkyne medal Czech Geol. Survey, 1991; grantee NSF, others. Fellow AAAS, Am. Geophys. Union (pres. V.G. and P. sect. 1978-80), Mineral Soc. Am. (v.p. 1981-82, pres. 1982-83, Washington A. Roebling medal 1986); mem. NAS, Geochem. Soc. (sec. 1967-70, v.p. 1975-76, pres. 1976-77), Soc. Econ. Geologists (R.A.F. Penrose medal 1988). Office: Harvard U Dept Earth & Planetary Scis Cambridge MA 02138

ROEDEL, PAUL ROBERT, steel company executive; b. Millville, N.J., June 15, 1927; s. Charles Howard and Irene (Voorhees) R.; m. June Gilbert Adams, June 25, 1951; children—Beth Anne, Meg Adams. B.S. in Accounting, Rider Coll., 1949. With Carpenter Tech. Corp., Reading, Pa., 1949—; asst. controller Carpenter Tech. Corp., 1957-65, controller, 1965-72, treas., 1972-73, v.p. fin., treas., 1973-75, exec. v.p., 1975-79, pres., 1979—, chief operating officer, 1979-81, chief exec. officer, 1981—, dir., 1973—, chmn., chief exec. officer, 1987—; dir. Meridian Bancorp Inc., 1974—, Gen. Public Utilities Corp., 1979—, P.H. Glatfelter Co., 1992—. Bd. dirs. Hawk Mountain coun. Boy Scouts Am., Children's Home Reading; trustee Gettysburg Coll.; pres. Wyomissing Found.; bd. dirs. Reading Ctr. City Devel. Fund, 1976. With USNR, 1945-46. Mem. Fin. Execs. Inst., Stainless Steel Industry U.S. (chmn. adv. bd. 1984-86), Pa. Bus. Roundtable, Reading-Berks

C. of C., Mfrs. Assn. Berks County. Home: 416 Wheatland Ave Reading PA 19607-1326 Office: Carpenter Tech Corp 101 Bern St Reading PA 19601-1203

ROEDER, EDWARD, III, journalist, publisher; b. N.Y.C., Sept. 1, 1948; s. Edward Jr. and Patricia (Cosgrove) R. Student, Fla. State U., 1966-70. Free lance journalist, 1969-80; counsel Subcom. on Fed. Spending, Efficiency, Open Govt. U.S. Senate, 1975-76; nat. polit./fin. editor UP Internat., Washington, 1990; chmn. Sunshine Press Svcs., Inc., Washington, 1980—. Author: PACs Americana,1982; editor Congress on Disk, 1986-91, Pac-Track, 1989-91; contbr. articles to profl. jours. Home: 1220 G St SE Washington DC 20003-2901 Office: Sunshine Press Svcs 325 Pennsylvania Ave SE Washington DC 20003-1100

ROEHM, EDWARD CHARLES, money market specialist; b. N.Y.C., Nov. 14, 1946; s. Perry R. and Mary Jane (Dignan) R.; m. Mary Ann Wettach, Sept. 15, 1979; children: Rebecca B., Anne W. BBA, Syracuse U., 1969. Mgr. Fairfield County Trust Co., Stamford, Conn., 1969-72; broker-trader J.M. Lummis & Co., New Canaan, Conn., 1974-81; pres., owner, broker-trader The Jesup Group, Inc., Fairfield, Conn., 1981-92; founder, pres., CEO The Woodruff Co., Weston, Conn., 1992—. Episcopalian. Home: Three Slumber Corners Weston CT 06883 also: 11 Vestal St Nantucket MA 02554 Office: The Woodruff Co 3 Slumber Corners Weston CT 06883

ROËL, RAYMOND ALLEN, marketing editor and writer; b. Huntington, N.Y., June 22, 1955; s. Edmund Lawrence and Leslie Adele (Gonzalez) R.; m. Jane Sharp Appleyard, Sept. 6, 1986; children: Christopher Edward, Daniel Allen. AB, Brown U., 1977. Chmn., co-founder NewSource, Inc., Huntington, N.Y., 1979-83; editor Fund Raising Mgmt., Direct Mktg. mag., Garden City, N.Y., 1983-89; dir. worldwide communications Ogilvy & Mather Direct, N.Y.C., 1990—. Co-author: How to Borrow Money, 1983; editor: Business to Business Direct Marketing, 1987, Electronic Marketing Manual, 1992. Pub. rels. chmn. Direct Mktg. Day in N.Y., N.Y.C., 1991—. Recipient Golden Eagle award, 1982. Home: 22 Dickinson Ave East Northport NY 11731 Office: Ogilvy & Mather Direct 309 W 44th St New York NY 10019

ROEMER, MICHAEL, economist, consultant, educator; b. N.Y.C., June 6, 1937; s. David Edwin and Pauline (Herman) R.; m. Linda Cohen, Aug. 27, 1960; children: Margery Roemer McDonald, Brian. BS, Stanford U., 1959, SM in Engring. Sci., 1960; SM in Indsl. Mgmt., MIT, 1962, PhD in Econs., 1968. Fellow in Africa MIT, Nairobi, Kenya, 1962-64; internat. economist, acting chief program and policy divsn. AID, Washington, 1967-70; devel. advisor Harvard Devel. Adv. Svc., Cambridge, Mass., 1971-74; lectr. econs. Harvard U., Cambridge, 1974-84, sr. lectr., 1984—, fellow Inst. for Internat. Devel., 1974—, dep. dir., 1979-80, exec. dir., 1980-84; mem. adv. bd. Internat. Ctr. for Econ. Growth, Inst. for Contemporary Studies, San Francisco, 1985—. Author: Fishing for Growth: Export-led Development in Peru, 1950-1967, 1970, (with Stern) Appraisal of Development Projects: A Practical Guide with Case Studies from Ghana, 1975, (with Kim) Studies in the Modernization of the Republic of Korea, 1945-1975, 1979 ,(with Stern) Cases in Economic Development, 1981, (with others) Economics of Development, 1983, 2d edit. 1987, 3d edit., 1992; co-editor: Parallel Markets in Developing Countries, 1989, Markets in Developing Countries: Parallel, Fragmented and Black, 1991; co-editor Reforming Economic Systems in Developing Countries, 1991; also articles. Exxon Edn. Found. grantee, 1979. Mem. Am. Econ. Assn. (editorial bd. Quar. Jour. Econs. 1981-84). Office: Harvard Inst Internat Devel One Eliot St Cambridge MA 02138

ROEMMELE, BRIAN KARL, electronics, publishing, financial and real estate executive; b. Newark, Oct. 4, 1961; s. Bernard Joseph and Paula M. Roemmele. Grad. high sch., Flemington, N.J. Registered profl. engr., N.J. Design engr. BKR Techs., Flemington, N.J., 1980-81; acoustical engr. Open Reel Studios, Flemington, 1980-82; pres. Ariel Corp., Flemington, 1983-84, Ariel Computer Corp., Flemington, 1984-89; pres., chief exec. officer Ariel Fin. Devel. Corp., N.Y.C., 1987-91, Avalon Am. Corp., Temecula, Calif., 1990—; pres. Coupon Book Ltd., 1987-89, Value Hunter Mags., Ltd., AEON Cons. Group, Beverly Hills, Calif.; bd. dirs. Waterman Internat., Whitehouse Station, N.J., 1st Am. Payment Systems Temecula; electronic design and software cons., L.A., 1980—. Pub., editor-in-chief: Computer Importer News, 1987—. Organizer Internat. Space Week or Day, 1978-83; lectr. Trenton State Mus., N.J., 1983; chmn. Safe Water Internat., Paris. Mem. AAAS, AIAA, IEEE, Boston Computer Soc., Ford/Hill Forum, Am. Soc. Notaries, Planetary Soc. Office: Avalon Am Corp PO Box 1615 Temecula CA 92593-1615

ROEPERS, ALEXANDER JOOST, investment executive, advisor; b. The Hague, The Netherlands, Mar. 3, 1959; came to U.S., 1981; s. Cornelis J. and Agnes Helena (Von Hasselt) R. BBA, Nijenrode Sch. Bus., The Netherlands, 1980; MBA, Harvard U., 1984. Universal Instrument Corp., Binghamton, N.Y., 1981-82; Corp. devel. Dover Corp., N.Y.C., 1983; dir. corp. devel. Thyssen Bornemisza Group, Inc., N.Y.C., 1984-88; founder, pres. Atlantic Investment Mgmt., N.Y.C., 1988—. Office: Atlantic Investment Mgmt 405 Park Ave Ste 500 New York NY 10022-4405

ROFF, BARRY LAURANCE, social services executive; b. Bklyn., Feb. 28, 1947; s. Milton M. and Lillian (Dinney) R.; divorced; children: Jessica, Matthew. BA, Bklyn. Coll., 1967; MA, The New Sch. for Social Rsch., N.Y.C., 1970, PhD, 1977; cert., New Hope Guild Ctr., N.Y.C., 1980; cert. in employee rels. law, Inst. for Applied Mgmt. & Law, N.Y.C., 1985. Tchr., counselor N.Y.C. Bd. Edn./Pace/Bed-Stuy Co-Op, 1967-70; employment counselor N.Y. State Employment Svc., N.Y.C., 1970-72; asst. prof. CUNY, 1972-76; cons., team leader N.Y. State Office Mental Retardation, N.Y.C., 1978; dir. program rev. N.Y.C. Dept. Mental Health, 1978-81; pvt. practice psychotherapy N.Y.C., 1980-84; assoc. exec. dir. Altro Health & Rehab. Svcs., N.Y.C., 1981-88; dep. dir. Manhattan Bowery Corp., N.Y.C., 1988—; cons. Med. & Health Rsch. Assn., N.Y.C., 1985. Bd. dirs. Coalition of Voluntary Mental Health Agys., N.Y.C., 1987-91; mem. adv. com. Einstein Coll. Medicine Rsch. & Tng. Ctr., N.Y.C., 1985-87. Recipient Samuel and Rose Hurewitz award Fedn. Jewish Philanthropists, N.Y.C., 1986. Mem. APA, N.Y. State Psychol. Assn., Am. Orthopsychiat. Assn. Office: Manhattan Bowery Corp 275 7th Ave 5th Fl New York NY 10001

ROGALSKI, LOIS ANN, speech and language pathologist; b. Bklyn.; d. Louis J. and Filomena Evelyn (Maro) Giordano; m. Stephen James Rogalski, Jun e 27, 1970; children: Keri Anne, Stefan Louis, Christopher James, Rebecca Blair, Gregory Alexander. BA, Bklyn. Coll., 1968; MA, U. Mass., 1969; PhD., NYU, 1975. Lic. speech and lang. pathologist, N.Y. Speech, lang. and voice pathologist Rehab. Ctr. of So. Fairfield County, Stamford, Conn., 1969, Sch. Health Program-P.A. 481, Stamford, 1969-72; pvt. practice speech, lang. and voice pathology Sch. Health Program-P.A. 481, Scarsdale, N.Y., 1972—; cons. Bd. Coop. Ednl. Svcs., 1976-79, Handicapped Program for Preschoolers for Alcott Montessori Sch., Ardsley, N.Y., 1978—; rsch. methodologist Burke Rehab. Ctr., 1977. Mem. profl. adv. bd. Found. for Children with Learning Disabilities, 1978—; bd. dirs. United Way of Scarsdale-Edgemont, 1988-89. Fellow Rehab. Svcs. Adminstrn., 1968-69; N.Y. Med. Coll., 1972-75. Mem. N.Y. Speech & Hearing Assn., Westchester Speech & Hearing Assn., Am. Speech, Hearing & Lang. Assn. (cert. clin. competence), Coun. for Exceptional Children, Assn. on Mental Deficiency, Am. Acad. Pvt. Practice in Speech Pathology & Audiology (bd. dirs., treas. 1983-87, pres. 1987-89), Internat. Assn. Logopedics & Phoniatrics, Sigma Alpha Eta. Office: PO Box 1242 Scarsdale NY 10583-9242

ROGDAKIS, CONSTANTINE MICHAEL, manufacturing and retail executive; b. N.Y.C., Feb. 14, 1954; s. Michael Constantine and Aristea Rogdakis; m. Elizabeth Nona Rocca, July 20, 1975; children: Michael, Evan, Christopher. BA, John Jay Coll., 1977. Sales rep. Columbia Dance Frocks, N.Y.C., 1970-89, ptnr., v.p. sales, 1987-89; owner, mgr. Flair Bridal and Formal Shop, Plainfield, N.J., 1978—; pres. Flair Bridal Shop, Totowa, N.J., 1981-90. Home and Office: 35 Princeton Dr Syosset NY 11791-6740

ROGÉ, RONALD WILLIAM, financial planner, investment management executive; b. Bklyn., Mar. 7, 1947; s. Frederick William and Nancy (Rinaldo) R.; m. Patricia Mack, March 29, 1970; 1 child, Steven. AAS, N.Y.C. Community Coll., 1968; BS, L.I. U., 1970; MS, Poly. U., Bklyn., 1975. SEC registered investment advisor; cert. fin. planner. Planning engr. N.Y. Tel. Co., N.Y.C., 1970-78, product mgr., 1978-83; mgr. fin. planning NYNEX Enterprises, N.Y.C., 1983-85, staff dir. employee benefits, 1986-90; pres. R.W. Rogé & Co., Inc., Centereach, N.Y., 1986—. Mem. L.I. Assn. With USN, 1966-72. Mem. Internat. Assn. for Fin. Planning, Nat. Assn. Personal Fin. Advisors (chmn. pub. rels. com., elected dir. N.E./Mid Atlantic region), Am. Mktg. Assn. (exec. mem.), Inst. Cert. Fin. Planners (cert. fin. planner), Am. Assn. Individual Investors. Republican. Roman Catholic. Home and Office: RW Rogé & Co Inc 86 Woodview Ln Centereach NY 11720-4060

ROGERS, BRIAN CHARLES, investment manager; b. Beverly, Mass., June 27, 1955; s. Charles E. and Margaret A. (Sweeney) R.; m. Mary Jo Skayhan, Oct. 7, 1979; children: Hilary, Peter, Sydney. AB, Harvard Coll., 1977; MBA, Harvard Bus. Sch., 1982. Chartered fin. analyst, investment counselor. Asst. treas. Bankers Trust Co., N.Y.C., 1977-80; mng. dir. T. Rowe Price Assocs., Balt., 1982—. Bd. dirs. Balt. County Econ. Devel. Commn., 1988—, Fund for Ednl. Excellence, Batl. 1988-92. Home: 3 Ruxlea Ct Baltimore MD 21204-6401 Office: T Rowe Price Assocs 100 E Pratt St Baltimore MD 21202

ROGERS, DEBORAH LYNN, psychologist; b. Wichita, Dec. 24, 1951; d. Robert Earl and Marion Louise (Jones) Fulton; m. Joseph Dirk Rogers, Feb. 17, 1978; 1 child, Casondra Victoria. BS, U. Wyoming, 1981; MA, U. No. Colo., Greeley, 1981; PhD, U. Texas, 1988. Personnel rsch. psychologist AF Human Resources Lab., San Antonio, 1981-84; manpower policy analyst Office of Sec. of Def. State of D.C., Washington, 1988-92; psychologist Dept. of the Air Force, Malcolm Grow Med. Ctr., Andrews AFB, Md., 1992—; cons. in field. With USAF, 1981—. Fellow Inter-Univ. Seminar on Armed Forces and Soc.; mem. Am. Psychol. Assn., Assn. Human Resources Mgmt. and Organizational Behavior, Acad. of Mgmt., Am. Mgmt. Soc. Office: Malcolm Grow Med Ctr Dept of Air Force SGMS Andrews AFB MD 20331-5300

ROGERS, EDWARD SAMUEL, communications company executive; b. Toronto, Ont., Can., May 27, 1933; s. Edward Samuel and Velma Melissa (Taylor) R.; m. Loretta Anne Robinson, Sept. 25, 1963; children: Lisa Anne, Edward Samuel, Melinda Mary, Martha Loretta. BA, Trinity Coll., U. Toronto, 1956; LLB, Osgood Hall Law Sch., 1961; DSc (hon.), Clarkson U., 1989; LLD (hon.), U. Victoria, 1990. Bar: Ont., 1962. Founder, prin. Rogers Telecommunications Ltd., Toronto, 1960—; pres., chief exec. officer Rogers Communications Inc., 1978—; chmn. Unitel Communications, Inc., 1986—; bd. dirs. The Hull Group, The Toronto Dominion Bank, Can. Pub. Corp.; vice-chmn. Rogers Cantel Inc., Rogers Cable TV Ltd., Rogers Cablesystems Ltd., Rogers Broadcasting Ltd., Rogers Cantel Inc., Rogers Cantel Mobile Inc. Bd. Dirs. Wellesley Hosp., Jr. Achievement Can. Mem. Royal Can. Yacht Club, Albany Club, Granite Club, York Club, Muskoka Golf & Country Club, Rideau Club Ottawa, Can. Club N.Y., Lyford Cay Club (gov.), Balboa Bay Club, Sigma Chi (Beta Omega chpt.). Progressive Conservative. Mem. Anglican Ch. Office: Rogers Communications Inc, Comml Union Tower PO Box 249, Toronto, ON Canada M5K 1J5

ROGERS, FRED MCFEELY, television producer and host; b. Latrobe, Pa., Mar. 20, 1928; s. James Hillis and Nancy (McFeely) Flagg; m. Sara Joanne Byrd, July 9, 1952; children: James Byrd, John Frederick. MusB, Rollins Coll., 1951; MDiv, Pitts. Theol. Sem., 1962; DHL (hon.), Thiel Coll., 1969; HHD (hon.), Eastern Mich. U., 1973; LittD (hon.), St. Vincent Coll., 1973, U. Conn., 1991; DD (hon.), Christian Theol. Sem., 1973, Washington and Jefferson Coll., 1984, Westminster Coll., 1987; LHD (hon.), Yale U., 1974, Lafayette Coll., 1977, Washington and Jefferson Coll., 1984, Linfield Coll., 1982, Duquesne U., 1982, Slippery Rock Coll., 1982, U. S.C., 1985, MacMurray Coll., 1986, Drury Coll., 1986, Bowling Green State U., 1987; DFA (hon.), Carnegie-Mellon U., 1976; MusD (hon.), Waynesburg Coll., 1978, U. Ind., 1988; LLD (hon.), Hobart and William Smith Colls., 1985, U. Conn., 1991, Ind. U., Pa., 1992, Boston U., 1992, Moravian Coll., 1992. Adj. prof. U. Pitts., 1976; pres. Family Communications, Inc., Pitts.; asst. producer NBC, N.Y.C., 1951-53; exec. producer Sta. WQED, Pitts., 1953-62; producer, host CBC, Toronto, Ont., 1962-64; exec. producer, host Mister Rogers' Neighborhood (PBS), Pitts., 1965—. Author: Mister Rogers Talks with Parents, 1983, Mister Rogers' First Experiences Books, 1985, Mister Rogers' Playbook, 1986, Mr. Rogers Talks About Divorce, 1987, Mister Rogers-How Families Grow, 1988; producer five audio cassettes of original songs-Many Ways to Say I Love You; composer: Mr. Rogers' Songbook; host, writer, producer five one hour videocassettes home videos CBS, 1987-88. Chmn. child devel. and mass media forum White House Conf. on Children; mem. Esther Island Preserve Assn.; bd. dirs. McFeely Rogers Found. Recipient Peabody award for finest children's TV program; award for excellence in children's programming Nat. Ednl. TV; Emmy award, 1980; Ohio State award, 1983, ACT award, 1984, The Christopher award, 1984, Ga. Assn. Broadcasters award, 1984; Lamplighter award Ednl. Press. Assn. Am., 1985; Disting. Service award Spina Bifida Assn. Am., 1985; Children's Book Council award, 1985, Emmy award for outstanding writing in children's series, 1985, Assn. Childhood Edn. award, 1986; Director's award-Ohio State award, 1986; Gold medal Internat. Film and TV Festival, 1986, award Nat. Assn. State Dirs. Migrant Edn., 1987, Ollie award Am. Children's TV Festival, 1987, Immaculata (Pa.) Coll. medal, 1988, Bronze medal Internat. Film and TV Festival, 1988, Outstanding Pa. Author award, 1988, Parent's Choice award, 1987, 88, Spl. Recognition award Nat. Assn. Music Mchts., 1989, PBS award in recognition of 35 yrs. in pub. TV, 1989, Hall of Fame aaward Sction for Children's TV, 1988, Man. of Yr. award Pitts. Vectors, 1990. Mem. Luxor Ministerial Assn. Presbyterian. Office: 4802 5th Ave Pittsburgh PA 15213-2956

ROGERS, FREDERICK MACKAY, technical trade association adminsistrator; b. Boston, Nov. 18, 1930; s. Rupert Browning Jr. and Margaret Abigail (Mackay) R.; m. Lois Eugenie Wicken, Dec. 27, 1952; children: Frederick M. Jr., Geoffrey M. BA in Econs., Norwich U., 1952. Nat. sales mgr. DuPont Co., Wilmington, Del., 1954-85; mng. dir. Rsch. and Engring. Coun. of the Graphic Arts Industry, Chaddsford, Pa., 1985—. Bd. dirs. Graphic Arts Literacy Alliance, Pitts., 1988—, Environ. Conservation Bd., 1985-91; bd. dirs. Edn. Coun. of the Graphic Arts, 1989—; scout master Boy Scouts Am., Detroit, Dallas, Wilmington, Del., 1964-72; active community ch. 1st lt. U.S. Army, 1952-54. Named Craftsman of Yr. Nat. Assn. of Photolithographers, 1991. Mem. Kennett Square Golf and Country Club, DuPont Country Club, Graphic Arts Assn. of Phila., Graphic Arts Tech. Found., Lambda Chi Alpha. Republican. Presbyterian. Home: 31 Clifton Dr Kennett Square PA 19348-2737 Office: R&E Coun PO Box 639 Chadds Ford PA 19317-0610

ROGERS, IRENE, librarian; b. Yonkers, N.Y., Oct. 12, 1932; d. Franklyn Harold and Mary Margaret (Nealy) R.; B.S. in Edn., New Paltz State Tchrs. Coll., 1954; M.L.S. (N.Y. State Tng. grantee), Columbia U., 1959. Tchr., West Babylon (N.Y.) Sch. System, 1954-57, Yonkers Sch. System, 1957-58; reference librarian Yonkers Pub. Library, 1959-67, adult services coordinator, 1967-73, asst. library dir., 1973—. Mem. Mayor's Adv. Com. Consumer Edn., Yonkers, 1970—; active United Way of Yonkers; mem. curriculum adv. com., report card revision com. Office Supt. Schs., 1982; mem. Yonkers unit Am. Cancer Soc. West Library System grantee, 1966. Mem. ALA, Westchester, N.Y. library assns., Soroptimists (pres. 1978-79, 80-81, sec. dist. I North Atlantic region), Bus. and Profl. Women's Club (pres. Yonkers chpt. 1989-90). Home: 41 Amackassin Ter Yonkers NY 10703-2213 Office: 7 Main St Yonkers NY 10701

ROGERS, JAMES GARDINER, accountant, educator; b. St. Louis, May 6, 1952; s. Gardiner and Virginia Joy (Goodbar) R.; m. Barbara May Baird, Feb. 14, 1976; children Andrew Baird, Benjamin Baird, Samuel Baird. BA, Washington & Lee U., 1973; MBA, Am. U., 1975. CPA. Credit officer loan workout div. Phila. Nat. Bank, Phila., 1975-78; mgr. cash and banking Gen. Waterworks Corp., Phila., 1978-81, asst. treas., 1981-85; v.p. fin., treas. Phila. Presbyn. Homes, Inc., Phila., 1985-88; dir. devel. Eastern Coll., St. Davids, Pa., 1988—; ptnr., bd. dirs. PC Mgmt. Enterprises, Inc., Bryn Mawr, Pa.. Treas. Lower Merion Bapt. Ch., Bryn Mawr, 1978-85; v.p. Lupus Foundn. of Am., Inc., Washington, 1985-87, asst. v.p., 1982-85, bd. dirs., 1977—; pres., bd. dirs. Pa. Lupus Foundn., Wayne, 1973—, bd. dirs. Mem. Mensa. Republican. Club: Merion Cricket (Haverford, Pa.). Home: 308 Chamounix Rd Wayne PA 19087-3612 Office: Eastern Coll Saint Davids PA 19087

ROGERS, JUDITH W., judge. AB cum laude, Radcliffe Coll., 1961; LLB, Harvard U., 1964; LLM, U. Va., 1988; LLD (hon.), D.C. Sch. Law, 1992. Bar: D.C. 1965. Law clk. Juvenile Ct. D.C., 1964-65; asst. U.S. atty. D.C., 1965-68; trial atty. San Francisco Neighborhood Legal Assistance Found., 1968-69; atty. U.S. Dept. Justice, 1969-71; gen. counsel Congl. Commn. on Organization of D.C. Govt., 1971-72; coordinator legis. program Office of Dep. Mayor D.C., 1972-74, spl. asst. to mayor for legis., 1974-79, corp. counsel, 1979-83; assoc. judge D.C. Ct. Appeals, 1983-88, chief judge, 1988—; mem. D.C. Law Revision Commn., 1979-83, Mayor's Commn. on Crime and Justice, 1982; vis. com. Harvard U. Sch. Law, 1984-90; trustee Radcliffe Coll., 1982-90; mem. grievance com. U.S. Dist. Ct. for D.C., 1982-83. Bd. dirs. Wider Opportunities for Women, 1972-74, Friends of the D.C. Superior Ct., 1972-74. Named Woman Lawyer of Yr., Women's Bar Assn. D.C. Fellow ABA; mem. D.C. Bar Assn., Phi Beta Kappa. Office: DC Ct Appeals 500 Indiana Ave NW 6th Fl Washington DC 20001

ROGERS, JULIETTE MARIE, French language educator; b. Mahopac, N.Y., Sept. 30, 1961; d. Raymond Keith and Mary Lou (Benson) R. BA, Oberlin Coll., 1983; PhD, Duke U., 1990. Staff asst. Harvard U., Cambridge, Mass., 1983-84; instr. English Lycée d'Arsonval, Brive, France, 1984-85; instr. French Duke U., Durham, N.C., 1985-90; asst. acad. dir. Educo program Duke U., Paris, 1988-89; asst. prof. French U. N.H., Durham, 1990—. Named Grad. Tuition scholar Duke U., 1985-90, Dissertation Rsch. grantee Govt. of France, 1988-89, Summer Faculty Rsch. fellow U. N.J., 1991, 92; recipient Fulbright Teaching Assistantship award Govt. of France, 1984-85. Mem. Modern Lang. Assn., Am. Tchrs. French. Office: U NH Dept French & Italian Durham NH 03824

ROGERS, KATHARINE MUNZER, English language educator; b. N.Y.C., June 6, 1932; d. Martin and Jean (Thompson) Munzer; B.A. summa cum laude, Barnard Coll., 1952; Fulbright scholar, Newnham Coll., Cambridge U., 1952-53; Ph.D., Columbia U., 1957; m. Kenneth C. Rogers, Aug. 4, 1956; children: Margaret, Christopher, Thomas. Instr. English, Skidmore Coll., Saratoga Springs, N.Y., 1954-55, Cornell U., 1955-57; lectr. to prof. English, Bklyn. Coll., 1958-88; mem. doctoral faculty CUNY, 1972-88; rsch. prof. literature The Am. U., Washington, 1989—. Mem. MLA. Author: The Troublesome Helpmate: A History of Misogyny in Literature, 1966; William Wycherley, 1972; Feminism in Eighteenth Century England, 1982; Frances Burney: The World of "Female Difficulties", 1990. Editor anthologies: The Signet Classic Book of 18th and 19th Century British Drama; Selected Writings of Samuel Johnson, 1981, The Meridian Anthology of Early American Women Writers, 1991; co-editor: (with William McCarthy) The Meridian Anthology of Early Women Writers: British Literary Women from Aphra Behn to Maria Edgeworth, 1987. Contbr. articles to profl. jours. Home: 6202 Perthshire Ct Bethesda MD 20817-3348 Office: The Am U Dept Literature Washington DC 20016

ROGERS, KENNETH CANNICOTT, physicist, federal agency administrator; b. Teaneck, N.J., Mar. 21, 1929; s. Ralph Waldo and Ruth (Geltner) R.; m. Katharine Munzer, Aug. 4, 1956; children: Margaret, Christopher, Thomas. BS, St. Lawrence U., 1950, DHL (hon.), 1983; MA, Columbia U., 1952, PhD, 1956; M of Engring. (hon.), Stevens Inst. Tech., 1964, D of Engring (hon.), 1987. Research assoc. Lab. Nuclear Studies Cornell U., Ithaca, N.Y., 1955-57; asst. prof. physics Stevens Inst. Tech., Hoboken, N.J., 1957-60, assoc. prof., 1960-64, prof., 1964-87, head physics dept., 1968-72, acting provost, dean of faculty, 1972, pres., 1972-87, pres. emeritus, 1987—; commr. U.S. Nuclear Regulatory Commn., Washington, 1987—; bd. dirs. 1st Jersey Nat. Corp., Pub. Svc. Electric and Gas Co. Trustee Christ Hosp.; mem. N.J. Gov.'s Commn. on Sci. and Tech. Fellow Royal Soc. Arts, AAAS; mem. Am. Phys. Soc., IEEE (sr.), N.Y. Acad. Scis., Am. Assn. Physics Tchrs., Am. Assn. Higher Edn., Regional Plan Assn. (N.J. com.), Newcomen Soc. (chmn. N.J. com.), N.J. C. of C. (state dir. 1974-87), Sigma Xi. Club: Cosmos. Home: 6202 Perthshire Ct Bethesda MD 20817-3348 Office: Nuclear Regulatory Commn 1717 H St NW Washington DC 20555-0002

ROGERS, KENNETH R., advertising executive. Exec. v.p. Backer Spielvogel Bates, N.Y.C., until 1991; pres., chief operating officer Backer Spielvogel Bates, Inc., N.Y.C., 1991—. Office: Backer Spielvogel Bates Inc The Chrysler Bldg 405 Lexington Ave New York NY 10174-0002*

ROGERS, LEE JASPER, lawyer; b. Fort Monmouth, N.J., May 6, 1955; s. Peter and Ethel Mae (Williams) R.; m. Vanessa Walisha Yarbrough, Apr. 18, 1981 (div. Oct. 1988); 1 child, Stephanie Alexandria. Student, Drew U., 1975, Monmouth Coll., 1975; BA in History, Hampton Inst., 1977; JD, Howard U., 1980. Pvt. practice Red Bank, N.J., 1981-91; asst. dep. pub. defender Ocean County region, Toms River, N.J., 1991-92; vol. counsel Pro Bono Legal Svcs., Red Bank, N.J., 1982-91; pres., chmn. bd. Jay-Mar Entertainment Enterprises Inc., 1986—. Author numerous poems. Vocalist singing group Pizazz, and Nu Eara 1991—. Mem. ABA, NAACP (exec. com. Red Bank chpt. 1983-88), Assn. Trial Lawyers Am., Elks (sec. ho. com. Bates club 1988-90, loyal knight 1990-91). Baptist. Home: 298 Shrewsbury Ave Apt 3 Red Bank NJ 07701-1319 Office: 298 Shrewsbury Ave Red Bank NJ 07701-1319

ROGERS, RUTH ANN, small business owner; b. Pawtucket, R.I., Nov. 28, 1946; d. Arthur T. and Evelyn G. (Kenney) Charbonneau; m. Earl William Rogers Jr., Jan. 9, 1983. Degree in real estate, Bristol Coll., 1988. Owner E & R Hobbies & Crafts, Middleboro, Mass., 1991. Home: 22 Mockingbird Way East Taunton MA 02718-1088 Office: E & R Hobbies & Crafts Thatchers Middleboro MA 02346

ROGERS, SHARON J., university official; b. Grantsburg, Wis., Sept. 24, 1941; d. Clifford M. and Dorothy L. (Beckman) Dickau; m. Evan D. Rogers, June 15, 1962 (div. Dec. 1980). BA summa cum laude, Bethel Coll., St. Paul, 1963; MA in Libr. Sci., U. Minn., 1967; PhD in Sociology, Wash. State U., Pullman, 1976. Lectr., instr. Alfred (N.Y.) U., 1972-76; assoc. prof. U. Toledo, 1977-80; assoc. dean Bowling Green (Ohio) State U. Librs., 1980-84; univ. libr. George Washington U., Washington, 1984-92; asst. v.p. acad. affairs George Washington U., Washington, 1989-92, 1989-92; assoc. v.p. George Washington U., Washington, 1992—, assoc. v.p. acad. affairs, 1992—, co-dir. Univ. Teaching Ctr., 1990—; mem. users coun. Online Computer Libr. Ctr., 1985—, pres., 1989-90, mem. rsch. adv. com., 1990-92, trustee, 1992—. Contbr. articles to profl. jours. Bd. dirs. ACLU, Toledo, 1978-84. Jackson fellow U. Minn., 1964-65; NSF trainee Wash. State U., 1969-72. Mem. ALA (coun. 1987-91, pub. com. 1989-93, chmn. 1990-92), Assn. Coll. and Rsch. Librs. (pres. 1984-85), Am. Social. Assn., Washington Rsch. Libr. Consortium (bd. dirs. 1987-90), Universal Serials and Book Exch. (bd. dirs., treas. 1987). Office: George Washington U Rice Hall 2121 I St NW Washington DC 20052

ROGERS, THEODORE COURTNEY, investment company executive; b. Lorain, Ohio, Aug. 25, 1934; s. William Theodore and Leona Ruth (Gerhart) R.; m. Elizabeth B. Barlow, June 28, 1984; children by previous marriage: Pamela Anne Rogers Harmon, Theodore Courtney Jr. BS in Social Sci., Miami U., Oxford, Ohio, 1956; postgrad. Johns Hopkins U., 1957; MBA summa cum laude, Marquette U., 1968. With Armco Inc., 1958-80; pres. Olympic Fastening Systems, 1970-74, with Bathey Mfg. Co. subs., 1970, group v.p. indsl. products, 1971-74, exec. v.p. Nat. Supply Co. subs., Houston, 1974-76, pres., 1976-80, v.p. parent co., 1976-79, group v.p. parent co., 1979-80; pres., chief operating officer NL Industries, Inc., N.Y.C., 1980-82, pres., chief exec. officer, 1982-83, chmn., pres., chief exec. officer, 1983-87; ptnr. Am. Indsl. Ptnrs., N.Y., 1987—; bd. dirs. MCorp. Bd. dirs. United Cerebral Palsy Rsch. and Ednl. Found., Inc., Am. Alliance for Rights and Responsibilities; chmn. bd. Theatre for New Audience, City Ctr., Darby Internat. Corp., McCorp, Easco Corp.; chmn. N.Y.C. Cerebral Palsy Fund Drive, Easco Aluminum, Sunshine Materials; mem. campaign com. United Way Tri State, Lincoln Ctr. for Performing Arts; chmn. bd. N.Y.C. Ballet. Lt. USN, 1956-58. Mem. Petroleum Equipment Suppliers Assn. (bd. dirs.), Young Pres. Orgn., Bus. Roundtable, Poets and Writers Club (bd. dirs.), Achille Track Club (founder, bd. dirs.), Ramada Club, Houston Country Club, Links Club, Sky Club, Econ. Club, Met. Club Washington, The Union Club of Cleve., Beta Gamma Sigma (bd. dirs.' table), Kappa Phi Kappa. Office: Am Indsl Ptnr 200 Park Ave Ste 3122 New York NY 10166-3196

ROGERS, WILLIAM CUSHING, film director, educator; b. Boston, Jan. 14, 1959; s. Mark B. and Susan (Cushing) R. Student, Sundsta Gymnasiet, Karlstad, Sweden, 1978; BA, Amherst Coll., 1982. Tchr. U. N.H., Durham, 1983-89, Keene (N.H.) State Coll., 1991—; assoc. producer Vella Prodns., Waltham, Mass., 1983-85; dir. Coruway Film Inst., Madbury, N.H., 1989—. Actor film Imported Bridegroom, 1988 (award Boston Film Festival 1989); dir., producer documentary My Uncle Joe, 1991 (award New Eng. Film Festival, CINE Golden Eagle, Blue ribbon Am. Film and Video Festival, TASH Disting. Media award); lighting designer Jail Brake, 1990; contbr. articles to profl. jours. Home and Office: Coruway Film Inst 29 2d St # 2 Dover NH 03820-3311

ROGERS, WILLIAM EDWARD, risk management executive, writer; b. Uniontown, Pa., Sept. 30, 1947; s. William Eugene Rogers and Mildred Madge (Friend) Thomas; m. Nancy Louise Ewig, Apr. 6, 1968 (div. 1977); children: David William, Stephen John; m. Maribeth Ann Crum, July 8, 1977. BA, U. Pitts., 1979; MS, Ind. U. of Pa., 1981. Cert. safety prof., assoc. risk mgmt.; CPCU. Electronic technician Radio Corp. Am., Meadow Lands, Pa., 1967-68, J.M. Communications, Johnstown, Pa., 1972-77; dir. risk mgmt. Conemaugh Valley Meml. Hosp., Johnstown, Pa., 1977-87; mgr. risk mgmt. svcs. The Gleason Agy., Inc., Johnstown, Pa., 1987—; ptnr. Country Rd. Publs., Summerhill, Pa., 1991—. Author: How to Cut Workers' Comp Costs: 115 Proven Ways, 1991; mem. editorial adv. bd. Hosp. Risk Mgmt. Mag., 1986—; contbr. articles to profl. jours. Bd. dirs. Am. Cancer Soc., Cambria County, Pa., 1985-88; committeeman Rep. Party, Cambria County, 1991-92. With USN, 1968-72. Named to Risk Mgmt. Hon. Roll Bus. Ins. Mag., 1986. Mem. Am. Soc. for Healthcare Risk Mgmt. (diplomate, pres. 1984, bd. dirs. 1982-85), Pa. Assn. for Healthcare Risk Mgmt. (pres. 1981, bd. dirs. 1981), Western Pa. Safety Coun. Republican. Home: RD 1 Box 226 Sidman PA 15955 Office: The Gleason Agy Inc BT Financial Pla PO Box 8 Johnstown PA 15907

ROGERS, WILLIAM IRVINE, management consultant; b. Bklyn., Dec. 10, 1927; s. Thomas Irvine and Kathryn Gertrude (Erdmann) R.; m. Ruthanne Chadwick, Aug. 28, 1954; children: Geoffrey Chadwick, Christopher Scott. BA, Adelphi U., 1949; MS, U. Vt., 1952; PhD, U. Iowa, 1956. Rsch. asst. U. Vt., Burlington, 1949-53; teaching asst. U. Iowa, Iowa City, 1953-56; assoc. technologist Gen. Foods Corp., 1956-57, project leader, 1957-59; sr. cons. Arthur D. Little, Inc., Cambridge, Mass., 1959-84, chief biochem. pharmacology lab., 1960-70, sr. cons. organizational and managerial devel., 1970-84; pres. Chadwick Rogers Inc., Ipswich, Mass., 1984-90, founder, 1990—; vis. lectr. Brandeis U., 1985—; cons., lectr. Boston U. Corp. Edn. Ctr., 1986—. Co-author: Taking Charge - Personal Effectiveness in Organizations, 1980; author: Working With People, 3d edit., 1991; patentee in field. Mem. Arthur D. Little Alumni Assn. (bd. mem. 1985-90). Home and Office: Chadwick Rogers Inc 53 Turkey Shore Rd Ipswich MA 01938-2333

ROGERWICK, EDWARD ANTHONY, management consultant; b. Teaneck, N.J., May 28, 1938; s. Edward Vincent and Margaret (Hasenflugh) R.; m. Carole Ann Fanning, Oct. 7, 1961; children: Christina, Pamela, Michelle, Theresa, Stephanie. BA in Communication Arts, Seton Hall U., 1960; postgrad., U. Md., Munich, 1961-62. Specialist mktg. communications Gen. Electric Co., Schenectady, N.Y., 1964-66; mgr. mktg. communications Gen. Electric Co., Bala Cynwyd, Pa., 1966-67; mgr. employee communications Gen. Electric Co., N.Y.C., 1967-73; prin. communications cons. Towers, Perrin, Forster & Crosby, N.Y.C., 1973-85; v.p., prin. communications cons. Alexander & Alexander Cons. Group, N.Y.C., 1985—; commr. Freehold Twp. Hist. Preservation Commn. Capt. U.S. Army, 1961-64. Mem. Internat. Assn. of Bus. Communicators, Del. Valley Assn. of Designers and Printers, Am. Soc. of Personnel Adminstrn. Home: 81 Juniper Dr Freehold NJ 07728-2852 Office: Strategies 2000 81 Juniper Dr Freehold NJ 07728

ROGGE, JOEL JAY, minister, lawyer, psychologist; b. N.Y.C., Dec. 15, 1934; s. Leo and Mollie Harrison; m. Virginia Alice Wilson, Dec. 27, 1959; children—Rebekah Leah, Michael Gabriel, Stephen Job; m. Cathy Louise Clark, Feb. 22, 1975; 1 child, Mary Elizabeth; m. Maryellen Gongas, Sept. 10, 1983; children: Sarah Alexandra, Hadrian Solomon. BS NYU, 1955; JD Columbia U., 1958; postgrad. Nashotah House, 1965-67; MDiv Episc. Theol. Sch., 1968; STM Andover Newton Theol. Sch., 1969, DMin, 1975; EdD Harvard U., 1976. Bar: N.Y. 1959, D.C. 1960, Wis. 1967, Mass. 1968, N.H. 1971; lic. psychologist, Mass. Atty. Office Gen. Counsel, HEW, 1959-60; individual practice law, Washington, 1960-61; assoc. firm Dickstein & Shapiro, Washington, 1961-62; atty. U.S. Commn. on Civil Rights, 1962-65; ordained to ministry Episcopal Ch. as deacon, 1968, as priest, 1969; pastor North St. Union Congl. Ch., Medford, Mass., 1968-70; vicar St. Martin's Chapel, Fairlee, Vt., 1971; counselor alcoholism clinic Contra Costa County Health Dept., Martinez, Calif., 1972-73; clin. dir. outpatient service North Shore Council on Alcoholism, Danvers, 1974-78; practice pastoral psychotherapy, 1977—; dir. Danvers Pastoral Counseling Center, 1977-82; clin. dir. Parish Pastoral Counseling Centers, Danvers, 1981-82; assoc. rector Calvary Episcopal Ch., Danvers, 1979-83; assoc. Andover Newton Theol. Sch., Newton Centre, Mass., 1980-82; sole practice law, Mass., 1984—. Episcopal Ch. Found. fellow, 1968-71. Mem. N.H. Bar Assn., Am. Assn. Pastoral Counselors (diplomate, gov., nat. legis. chmn., 1981-84, sec. N.E. region 1980-84),n., Mass. Psychol. Assn., Masons. Address: 74 County Rd Ipswich MA 01938

ROGGENKAMP, KAREN LEE, playwright, director, actress; b. Warren, Pa., Aug. 30, 1956; d. Timothy Edward Nelson and Sandra Lee (Schussler) Broadhurst; children: Heather, Laura, Lisa. Grad. high sch., Titusville, Pa. Dir. Titusville Winter Theatre, 1990, 92, actress, 1992; author: No Time Like the Present, 1991. Bd. dirs. Titusville Winter Theatre, 1991-92. Mem. Dramatist Guild, Author's League Am. Home: 321 N Monroe St Titusville PA 16354

ROGINSKI, RAYMOND STEPHEN, neuroscientist, anesthesiologist; b. Jersey City, Nov. 27, 1955; s. Edward Stanley and Carmella Phyllis (Maiuro) R.; m. Sharon Claire Krieger, June 4, 1988; 1 child, Melissa Rae. BS, MS, Yale U., 1977; MS, Albert Einstein Coll. Medicine, 1981, MD, PhD, 1985. Resident in anesthesiology Albert Einstein Coll. of Medicine, Bronx, N.Y., 1985-89; clin. asst., prof. anesthesiology Univ. of Medicine and Dentistry of N.J., Newark, 1989-91; instr. dept. neurosci. Albert Einstein Coll. of Medicine, Bronx, 1989-91; clin. asst. prof. anesthesiology UMDNJ, New Brunswick, 1991—. Contbr. many sci. papers and articles to sci. and biomed. jours. Recipient Yale Greek prizes, 1973, 74. Mem. Phi Beta Kappa. Office: Anesth RWJ Med Sch One Robert Wood Johnson Pl CN19 New Brunswick NJ 08903-0019

ROGOW, LOUIS MICHAEL, oncologist, educator; b. Jersey City, June 20, 1944; s. Irving and Helen (Grollman) R.; m. Enid Zazeela, Jan. 24, 1982; children from previous marriage: Ilisa, Jay. BS, Trinity Coll., 1965; MD, Hahnemann U., 1969. Diplomate Nat. Bd. of Med. Examiners; cert. radiology, radiation oncology. Instr. radiology Radiation Oncology N.Y. Med. Coll., N.Y.C., 1973-75, asst. prof., 1975-77; dir. radiaton oncology, hyperthernia John F. Kennedy Med. Ctr., Edison, N.J., 1977—; clin. asst. prof. radiology, U. Medicine and Dentistry, Rutgers Med. Sch., New Brunswick, N.J., 1983—; instr. Sch. of Nuclear Medicine Technology, John F. Kennedy Med. Ctr., Edison, N.J., 1984—. Contbr. articles to profl. jours. Bd. trustees Am. Cancer Soc. (N.J. div.). Clin. fellow Am. Cancer Soc., 1971, 73, faculty fellow Am. Cancer Soc., 1975, 76. Mem. Am. Soc. of Theraputic Radiology and Oncology, Am. Endocurie Therapy Soc., Am. Radium Soc., N.Y. Cancer Soc., Oncology Soc. of N.J. Office: John F Kennedy Med Ctr Radiation Oncology-Hyperthermia Edison NJ 08818

ROHAN, VIRGINIA BARTHOLOME, academic official; b. Helena, Mont., Apr. 19, 1939; d. William Franklin and Virginia Marie (Gibson) Bartholome; m. William Patrick Rohan, Dec. 29, 1962; children: Virginia Marion, William Patrick Jr., Christopher James. AB summa cum laude, St. Teresa's Coll., 1960; MA in Am. Lit., Cath. U. Am., 1961; postgrad., Kans. U., 1961-62; PhD in English, U. Mass., 1974. Instr. western civilization program Kans. U., Lawrence, 1961-62; instr. English St. Joseph Coll., Emmitsburg, Md., 1962-63; lectr. English U. Mass., Amherst, 1975-76; research assoc. Smith Coll. Devel. Office, Northampton, Mass., 1976-77, asst. dir. for founds., 1977-80, dir. devel. services, 1980-89; asst. v.p. devel. U. Vt., Burlington, 1989-90, interim v.p. for devel. and alumni rels., 1990—; lectr. English Holyoke (Mass.) Community Coll., 1976-77, Mt. Holyoke Coll., South Hadley, Mass., 1977-78; faculty, mgmt. Inst. for Women in Higher Edn., Wellesley, Mass., 1983; pres. Investments Unltd. Inc., Northampton, 1983-84. Author: (play) The Happy Prince, 1959; contbr. articles to profl. jours. Treas., bd. dirs. Friends WFCR (pub. radio), Amherst, 1983-85. Fellow Woodrow Wilson Found., 1960-61. Mem. Women in Devel. in Western Mass. (co-founder, chair 1983-85), Council for Advancement and Support Edn. (faculty, panelist, roundtable chair, discussant 1979-87), Kappa Gamma Pi, Pi Beta Phi. Address: 165 Twin Oaks N South Burlington VT 05403 Office: U Vt Grasse Mount 411 Main St Burlington VT 05401-3470

ROHDE, BARBARA JO, consultant, public affairs researcher; b. Jamestown, N.D., July 9, 1952; d. Lorenz and Opal Irene (Sandvik) R. BA, U. N.D., 1973; MPA, U. Denver, 1980. Asst. press sec. Office Lt. Gov., St. Paul, 1975-76; program dir. Office of Gov., St. Paul, 1976-78; chief of staff Cong. Byron Dorgan, Washington, 1981-86; dir. State of Minn., Washington, 1987-91; pres. Am. 2000 Coun., Washington, 1991—; rsch. fellow Humphery Inst. Pub. Affiars, U. Minn.; cons. Sagamore Assocs., Washington. Mem. transition team Voluntary Sector, Office of Mayor Sharon Pratt Dixon, Washington, 1991. Mem. Leadership Am., Women Execs. in State Govt. (nat. bd. 1990—), Women in Trnasp., Women in Internat. Trade, Women in Govt. Rels., Orgn. Lic. Women Pilots (chmn. 1984), Jr. League of Washington (bd. dirs. 1987—). Democrat. Lutheran. Home: 2440 Virginia Ave NW Apt 1203D Washington DC 20037-2626

ROHDE, JOHN HANS, operations executive; b. Egeln, Germany, July 4, 1929; s. Wilhelm Friedrich and Louise Adele (Buschner) R.; m. Christel Elizabeth Wehrenberg, Apr. 24, 1954; children: Joan Evelyn, Karen Sylvia, Denise Marion. B in Mech Engring., Aachen U., Fed. Republic Germany, 1954; M in Indsl. Engring., Can. Inst. Sci. and Tech., 1959; PhD in Indsl. Mgmt., Aachen U., 1960; postgrad., Inst. Pour l'Etude des Methodes de Direction de l'Enterprise, Switzerland, 1975; D in Sci., London Inst. Applied Research, 1975. Gen. cons. S.A. Birn & Co., Louisville, 1961-70; dir. indsl. engring. Automotive div. ITT, Brussels, 1971-79; dir. ops. Automotive div. ITT, Southfield, Mich., 1979-80; dir. indsl. engring. REVLON, Inc., Edison, N.J., 1981-85; chmn. CSM Mgmt. Cons. Inc., Sea Bright, N.J., 1986—; cons. A.T. Kearney, N.Y.C., 1986-88, Coopers & Lybrand, N.Y.C., 1988—. Author: Indirect Manpower Productivity, 1985; contbr. articles to profl. jours. Mem. Inst. Indsl. Engrs. (sr.), Soc. Automotive Engrs. (sr.), Methods Time Measurement Assn. for Standards and Research, Am. Mgmt. Assn. Republican. Home and Office: 1540 Ocean Ave Ste 5 Sea Bright NJ 07760

ROHER, MARJORIE MAE, county official; b. Md., July 15, 1963; d. Richard Thomas and Carolyn Joyce (Jarrett) R. Student, Montgomery Coll., Rockville, Md., 1981-89. Sec. I Tracor Jitco, Inc., Rockville, Md., 1980-84; office svcs. mgr. Montgomery County Govt., Rockville, 1984—. Sec. Christian Edn. Commn., Wheaton, Md., 1986-88, 92; pres. Keeneland Homeowners Assn., Gaithersburg, Md., 1989—; tchr. Hughes United Meth. Ch., Wheaton, 1984-89, activities coord., newsletter editor Young Adult Group, 1990—, SALT Group. Recipient Outstanding Svc. award Montgomery County Govt., Rockville, 1985, 86, 88, 89. Republican. Methodist. Home: 14604 Keeneland Cir Gaithersburg MD 20878-3771 Office: Montgomery County Govt 51 Monroe St Ste 905 Rockville MD 20850-2407

ROHLOFF, ALBERT CHRISTIAN, marketing, research company executive; b. Nashville, Feb. 23, 1926; s. Christian Philip and Ida Marie (Wickbolt) R.; m. Lauurice Nadine Pohly, June 17, 1950; children: John Christian, Jean Louise. BS, Antioch Coll., 1950; PhD in Math. Stats., Purdue U., 1955. Sr. rsch. statistician Lever Bros. Co., Edgewater, N.J., 1954-56; sr. ops. analyst Lever Bros. Co., N.Y.C., 1945-64, dir. mktg. analysis, 1964-70; cons., Leonia, N.J., 1970-71; vice chmn. Mgmt. Sci. Assocs., Inc., Pitts., 1971-91; chmn. Market Sci Assocs., N.Y.C., 1991—. Contbg. author: Promotion Decisions Using Mathematical Models, 1967; also articles. Mem. Palisades Park (N.J.) Bd. Edn., 1960-62. With USNR, 1944-46, PTO. Mem. Inst. Mgmt. Sci. Presbyterian. Home: 246 Christie Hts Leonia NJ 07605-1525 Office: Market Sci Assocs 1500 Broadway New York NY 10036-1518

RÖHM, EBERHARD, lawyer; b. Munich, Germany, Nov. 16, 1940; came to U.S., 1970, naturalized, 1977; JD, U. Heidelberg-U. Bonn, Fed. Republic Germany, 1968, Fordham U., 1976. Bar: Fed. Republic Germany 1973, N.Y. 1975, U.S. Dist. Ct. (so. dist.) N.Y. 1975, U.S. Ct. Appeals (2d cir.) 1975, U.S. Tax Ct. 1976, U.S. Supreme Ct. 1982. Prin. Law Offices Röhm Internat., P.C., N.Y.C., 1975-89; ptnr. Fulbright & Jaworski, N.Y., 1989—. Contbr. many articles and lectures on internat. pvt. and Am. corp. law to profl. jours. Founding dir., sec. German Forum, N.Y., German Sch. N.Y. Mem. ABA, N.Y. State Bar Assn., Assn. Bar City N.Y., Internat. Bar Assn., Am. Arbitration Assn. (arbitrator 1976—), N.Y. Fgn. Lawyers Assn. (chmn. 1974-83), German Am. Law Assn. (bd. dirs. 1977-81), Am. Soc. Internat. Law, Am. Fgn. Law Assn., Consular Law Soc., Explorers Club, Deutscher Verein (bd. dirs. N.Y.C. 1981-84). Home: 485 Park Ave New York NY 10022 Office: Fulbright & Jaworski 666 Fifth Ave New York NY 10305

ROHNER, RONALD PRESTON, anthropology educator; b. Calif., Apr. 17, 1935. BS in Psychology, U. Oreg., 1958; MA in Anthropology, Stanford U., 1960, PhD in Anthropology, 1964. Prof. anthropology and family studies U. Conn.; dir. Ctr. for Study Parental Acceptance and Rejection, U. Conn. Author nine books; contbr. numerous articles to profl. jours., chpts. to books. Pres. bd. dirs. Natchaug Psychiat. Hosp.; bd. dirs. Conn. Assn. for Prevention Child Abuse and Neglect. Fellow APA, Am. Psychol. Soc., Am. Anthropol. Assn.; mem. Soc. Cross-Cultural Rsch. (pres. 1983), Internat. Assn. Cross-Cultural Psychology (exec. coun. 1976-78), Soc. Psychol. Anthropology, Child Protection Coun. Northeastern Conn. Home: 255 Codfish Falls Rd Storrs Mansfield CT 06268-1425 Office: U Conn Ctr Study Parental Acceptance and Rejection Storrs CT 06269-2158

ROHOVSKY, MICHAEL WILLIAM, medical products executive; b. Youngstown, Ohio, Feb. 26, 1937; s. Joseph Edward and Mary Theresa (Rakocy) R.; m. Karen Andreas, Mar. 31, 1965; children: Stephanie Ann, Paul Edward. DVM, Ohio State U., 1960, MS, 1965, PhD, 1967. Head pathology sect. Merrell-Nat. Labs., Cin., 1969-72; head pathology lab. Arthur D. Little, Inc., Cambridge, Mass., 1972-77; dir. of rsch. Pitman-Moore, Inc., Washington Crossing, N.J., 1977, v.p. rsch., 1977-79, V.p. rsch. and quality assurance, 1979-81; dir. orthopaedic rsch. Johnson & Johnson Products, New Brunswick, N.J., 1981-82, dir. orthopaedic rsch. and med. affairs, 1982-86, dir. med. affairs, 1986-87; v.p. rsch. Johnson & Johnson Orthopaedics, Raynham, Mass., 1986—; adj. asst. prof. pathology U. Cin., 1969-72. Capt. USAF, 1960-62, ETO. State of Ohio scholar, 1954-60. Fellow Am. Coll. Vet. Pharmacology and Exptl. Therapeutics, AAAS; mem. Am. Vet. Med. Assn., Am. Coll. Vet. Pathologists (diplomate), Assn. for Applied Gnotobiotics, Am. Assn. Lab. Animal Sci., Internat. Acad. Pathology, Alpha Psi (treas., v.p., award 1959), Phi Zeta. Republican. Office: Johnson & Johnson Orthopaedics PO Box 350 Raynham MA 02767-0600

ROHRBACH, LEWIS BUNKER, investment company executive; b. Phila., Oct. 28, 1941; s. Lewis Henry and Ruth Elizabeth (Bunker) R.; m. Suzanne Potts, June 20, 1964 (div. 1974); m. Suzanne Potts, June 20, 1964 (div. 1974); m. Carol Allen Cressman, June 28, 1980; children: Elisabeth Christina Croössmann. BA, Amherst Coll., 1963. Cert. genealogist. Credit analyst Provident Tradesman Bank and Trust Co., Phila., 1963-66; instl. security analyst Butcher & Sherrerd, Phila., 1966-69; asst. v.p. Endowment Mgmt. & Rsch. Corp., Boston, 1969-72; v.p. Arnhold & S. Bleichroeder, N.Y.C., 1972-73; pres. Picton Corp., Rockport, Maine, 1973—; pres. Picton Corp., Rockport, 1972—. Author: Rohrbach Genealogy, 1970, 77, 82 (1st prize Md. Hist. Soc. 1971); editor: Boston Taxpayers in 1821, 1988. Trustee New Eng. Hist. Geneal. Soc., Boston, 1991-93; pres. Rohrbach Found., Rockport, Maine, 1968—. Mem. Camden Yacht Club, Pa. German Soc., Swiss Am. Hist. Soc., Maine Geneal. Soc., Soc. Mayflower Descendants in the State of Maine. Society of Friends. Home: 43 Sea St Rockport ME 04856 Office: Picton Press PO Box 1111 Camden ME 04843-1111

ROHRBACH, W(ILLIAM) THOMAS, financial executive; b. Orange, N.J., Nov. 28, 1947; s. William B. and Marjorie (Bruno) R.; m. Mallory Jahn, Aug. 23, 1975; children: Carl, William, Carrie. BA, Lehigh U., 1970, MBA, 1974. CPA, N.J. Sr. acct. Mobil Oil Corp., N.Y.C., 1971-73; v.p. Sony Corp. Am., Park Ridge, N.J., 1974-85; v.p., chief fin. officer Kline & Co. Inc., Fairfield, N.J., 1986—, also dir. V.p. Bd. Edn., Franklin Lakes, N.J., 1991. Mem. AICPA, N.J. Soc. CPAs. Home: 151 Birch Rd Franklin Lakes NJ 07417-2703 Office: Kline & Co Inc 165 Passaic Ave Fairfield NJ 07004-3502

ROHRLICH, FRITZ, physicist; b. Vienna, Austria, May 12, 1921; came to U.S., 1946; s. Egon and Illy (Schwartz) r.; m. Beulah Friedman, June 24, 1951; children: Emily H., Paul E. ChemE, Israel Inst. Tech., 1943; PhD, Harvard U., 1948. Mem. Inst. for Advanced Study, Princeton, N.J., 1948-49; rsch. assoc. Cornell U., Ithaca, N.Y., 1949-51; lectr. Princeton U., 1951-53; assoc. prof. U. Iowa, Iowa City, 1953-60, prof., 1960-63; prof. Syracuse (N.Y.) U., 1963-91, prof. emeritus, 1991—; Fulbright lectr., 1974. Author: Classical Charged Particles, 1965, From Paradox to Reality, 1987 (with J.M. Jauch) Theory of Photons and Electrons, 1955; assoc. editor Am. Jour. Physics, 1975-77, Jour. Math. Physics, 1980-82; mem. editorial bd. Phys. Rev. D, 1987-89; contbr. more than 120 articles to profl. jours. Named Hon. Prof. U. Graz, Austria, 1974. Fellow Am. Physical Soc.; mem. AAAS, Philosophy Sci. Assn., N.Y. Acad. Sci., Phi Beta Kappa. Office: Syracuse U Syracuse NY 13244-1130

ROHRLICH, GEORGE FRIEDRICH, social economist; b. Vienna, Austria, Jan. 6, 1914; came to the U.S., 1938; s. Egon Ephraim and Rosa (Tenzer) R.; m. Laura Ticho, Feb. 3, 1946; children: Susannah Ticho Feldman, David Ephraim, Daniel Mosheh. D in Legal Scis., U. Vienna, Austria, 1937, Gold Dr.'s Diploma Law, 1987; PhD (univ. refugee scholar), Harvard U., 1943. Diplomate Consular Acad. Vienna, 1938. Social economist sect. public health and welfare Supreme Comdr. Allied Powers, Tokyo, 1947-50; socioecon. program analyst and developer U.S. Govtl. Policies, 1950-59; sr. staff mem. social security div. ILO, Geneva, 1959-64; vis. prof. social econs. and policy U. Chgo., 1964-67; prof. econs. and social policy Temple U., 1967-81, prof. emeritus, 1981—; dir. econs. and bus. programs Temple U. Japan, Tokyo, 1987-88; founder, past bd. dirs. Inst. Social Econs. and Policy Rsch.; sr. lectr. Sch. Social Work, Columbia U., 1968-69; dir. rsch. P.R. Commn. Integral Social Security System, San Juan, 1975-76; cons. in field; lectr. USIA, Brazil, 1984; co-dir., Keynoter Nat. Conf. Community Dimensions of Econ. Enterprise, 1984; ILO cons. Govt. Mauritius, 1985. Author: Social Economics—Concepts and Perspectives, 1974; others; editor books, the most recent being: Checks and Balances in Social Security, 1986, Environmental Management: Economic and Social Dimensions, 1976; contbr. articles to profl. publs.; assoc. editor Rev. of Social Economy; editorial adv. bd. Internat. Jour. Social Econs., U.K. Former mem. bd. dirs. Health and Welfare Coun. Greater Phila. Recipient festschrifts Internat. Jour. Social Econs., vol. 10, no. 6/7, 1983, vol. 11, nos. 1/2 and 3/4, 1984; Brookings rsch. tng. fellow, 1941-42; Ford Found. travel grantee, 1966; Fulbright rsch. scholar N.Z., 1980. Mem. AAAS, Assn. Social Econs. (pres. 1978-79, disting. mem. 1983, disting. scholar-Divine award 1989), Am. Econ. Assn., Indsl. Rels. Rsch. Assn. (charter), Internat. Soc. Labor Law and Social Security, Am. Risk and Ins. Assn., Nat. Acad. Social Ins. (elected), Harvard Club of Phila. Democrat. Jewish. Home: 7913 Jenkintown Rd Cheltenham PA 19012-1106 Office: Temple U Sch of Bus and Mgmt Philadelphia PA 19122

ROHSENOW, WARREN MAX, retired mechanical engineer, educator; b. Chgo., Feb. 12, 1921; s. Fred and Selma (Gorss) R.; m. Katharine Towneley Smith, Sept. 20, 1946; children—John, Brian, Damaris, Sandra, Anne. B.S., Northwestern U., 1941; M.Eng., Yale, 1943, D.Eng., 1944. Teaching asst., instr. mech. engring. Yale, 1941-44; mem. faculty Mass. Inst. Tech., 1946-85, prof. mech. engring., 1955-85, dir. heat transfer lab., 1954-85, prof. emeritus, 1985; Chmn. bd. dirs. Dynatech Corp.; bd. dirs. Thermanl Process System, West Newton Savs. Bank. Author: (with Choi) Heat Mass and Momentum Transfer, 1961; Editor: Developments in Heat Transfer, 1964, (with Hartnett) Handbook of Heat Transfer, 1973, 2d edit., 1985. Served as Lt. (j.g.) USNR, 1944-46; mech. engr. gas turbine div. Engring. Expt. Sta. Annapolis, Md. Recipient Pi Tau Sigma gold medal Am. Soc. M.E., 1951; award for advancement sci. Yale Engring. Assn., 1952; merit award Northwestern Alumni, 1955. Fellow Am. Acad. Arts and Scis., Nat. Acad. Engring., Am. Soc. M.E. (hon. mem., Heat Transfer Meml. award 1967, Max Jakob Meml. award 1970); mem. Sigma Xi, Tau Beta Pi, Pi Tau Sigma. Home: 32 Carroll St Falmouth ME 04105-1908 Office: MIT Cambridge MA 02139

ROITSCH, PAUL ALBERT, pilot; b. Hermosa Beach, Calif., Oct. 15, 1926; s. George Arthur and Margaret (Pattillo) R.; m. Phyllis T.A. McCoy, Aug. 26, 1955; children—Sharon Elise, Alison Carol, Paul Eric. BA, U. So. Calif., 1952; postgrad. U.S. Navy Test Pilot Sch., 1965. Copilot, navigator Pan Am. Airways, San Francisco, 1952-53, pilot, 1955-64, asst. chief pilot tech., Jamaica, N.Y., 1965-69, chief pilot tech., 1969-73, line pilot, 1973-86, pres. Paul Roitsch Assocs., Internat. Aviation Cons., Greenwich, Conn., 1986—, pilot Civil Air Transport, 1954-55. Served with USN, 1944-49, 53-54. Mem. AIAA, Soc. Automotive Engrs. (safety standardization adv. com., airplane handling qualities and flight deck design com., recipient cert. of appreciation 1981), Internat. Soc. Air Safety Investigators. Home: John St Greenwich CT 06831-2609 Office: PO Box 786 Greenwich CT 06836-0786

ROJAS, LOUIS EDWARD, religious brother; b. Bogota, Colombia, Mar. 31, 1947; came to U.S., 1957; s. Rojelio and Elvira Mary (Millan) R. AA, Thomas A. Edison State Coll., 1978, BA in Theology and History, 1982; MS in Pastoral Counseling, Iona Coll., 1990. Asst. mgr. Pallottine Sem., Washington, 1973-75; asst. dir. Pallottine Ctr., Balt., 1977-85; tchr. Cardinal Gibbons High Sch., Balt., 1982-85; dir. Pallottine Apostolic Assn., Washington, 1985-87; counselor Omni House, Glen Burnine, Md., 1987-88; mgr., counselor My Bros. Place, Bklyn., 1988-89; counselor Family Counseling Svc., N.Y.C., 1989-90; superior Pallottines, South Orange, N.J., 1990—; substance abuse counselor EGMC, 1991—; buddy Prince George's (Md.) Community Health Dept., 1986-88, AIDS Ctr. of Queens (N.Y.) County, 1988, 90; counselor Camp Glow, Balt., summer 1979-89; bd. dirs., regional rep. Dignity, Balt., 1986-88, Queens, N.Y., 1991—. With U.S. Army, 1968-70. Mem. ASCD, AACD, Assn. Multicultural Counseling and Devel., Am. Mental Health Counselors Assn., Assn. for Religious and Value Issues in Counseling, Nat. Assembly of Religious Bros., Communication Ministry, Nat. Assn. Alcoholism and Drug Abuse Counselors, N.J. Assn. Counseling and Devel., Soc. Cath. Apostolate. Home: 204 Raymond Ave South Orange NJ 07079-2305

ROJER, OLGA ELAINE, German language educator, translator; b. Curaçao, Netherlands Antilles, Mar. 29, 1953; came to U.S., 1972; BA cum laude, Mt. Holyoke Coll., 1976; MA with distinction, The Am. U., 1978; PhD, U. Md., 1985. Vis. asst. prof. German and Spanish St. Mary's Coll. Md., St. Mary's City, 1986-87; asst. prof. German The Am. U., Washington, 1987—; translator Nat. Geog. Soc., Washington, 1985—. Author: Exile in Argentina 1933-1945, 1990. Mem. MLA, South Atlantic MLA, Am. Assn. Tchrs. German, Soc. for Exile Studies, Women in German, Mid. Atlantic Coun. Latin Am. Studies, Am. Translators Assn. Office: Am U Dept Lang and Fgn Studies 4400 Massachusetts Ave NW Washington DC 20016

ROLEN, STANLEY ROBERT, pharmacist; b. Beaver Dam, Wis., Nov. 24, 1934; s. H. Wallace and Irene M. (Andrews) R.; m. Jane L. Sheehan, Jan. 21, 1961; children: Andrew, Elizabeth, Carolyn. BS in Pharmacy with honors, Union U., 1956. Product devel. pharmacist Norwich (N.Y.) Pharmacal Co., 1959-60, mfg. pharmacist, 1960-63, sr. mfg. pharmacist, 1963-69; prodn. supt. Morton-Norwich, Greenville, S.C., 1969-70; asst. mgr. pharm. ops. Wyeth-Ayerst Internat., Inc. (formerly Wyeth Internat. Ltd.), Radnor, Pa., 1970-72, mfg. products mgr., 1972-77, asst. prodn. dir., 1977-80, dir. prodn., 1980-85, asst. v.p. prodn., 1985—. Served with U.S. Army, 1956-58. Named Dist. Alumnus, Albany Coll. Pharmacy, 1981. Mem. Am. Pharm. Assn., Pharm. Mfrs. Assn. Internat. Tech. (steering com. 1991). Republican. Lodges: Masons, Shriners. Home: 103 Noel Cir Exton PA 19341-1752 Office: Wyeth-Ayerst Internat Inc PO Box 8616 Philadelphia PA 19101-8616

ROLETT, ELLIS LAWRENCE, medical educator, cardiologist; b. N.Y.C., July 10, 1930; s. Daniel Meyer and Mary Elaine (Warshaw) R.; m. Virginia

Ann Vladimir, Mar. 25, 1956; children: Roderic Lawrence, Barry Vladimir, Daniel Alfred. B.S., Yale U., 1952; M.D. cum laude, Harvard U., 1955. Diplomate: Am. Bd. Internal Medicine, Am. Bd. Cardiovascular Disease. Intern, resident in medicine Mass. Gen. Hosp., Boston, 1955-56, 59-61; asst. resident N.Y. Hosp.-Cornell U. Med. Ctr., N.Y.C., 1956-57; Am. Heart Assn. research fellow Peter Bent Brigham Hosp., Boston, 1961-63; mem. faculty U. N.C., Chapel Hill, 1963-74, then prof., 1971-74; prof. UCLA, 1974-77; chief cardiology VA Wadsworth Hosp., Los Angeles, 1974-77; prof. Dartmouth Med. Sch., Hanover, N.H., 1977—; chief cardiology Dartmouth-Hitchcock Med. Ctr., Hanover, N.H., 1977-87; vis. scientist August Krogh Inst., Copenhagen, 1984; mem. merit rev. bd. cardiovascular studies VA, 1976-79, chmn., 1978-79; mem. regional rsch. rev. com. New Eng. Am. Heart Assn., 1978-83; mem. sci. bd. Stanley J. Sarnoff Endowment for Cardiovascular Sci., 1992—. Contbr. articles to profl. jours. Bd. dirs. N.H. affiliate Am. Heart Assn., 1978-85; pres. N.H. affiliate Am. Heart Assn., 1983-85. Served to capt. M.C. USAF, 1957-59. Recipient Lederle Med. Faculty award, 1965-68, USPHS Career Devel. award, 1967-72; grantee USPHS/NIH, 1964-76, VA Merit Rev. Rsch. Program, 1975-77, Mathers Found., 1984-86, Am. Heart Assn., 1989-91. Mem. AAAS, Am. Coll. Cardiology, Am. Fedn. Clin. Research, Am. Heart Assn., Am. Physiol. Soc., Internat. Soc. Heart Research, Phi Beta Kappa, Alpha Omega Alpha. Home: 4 Balch Hill Ln Hanover NH 03755 Office: Dartmouth-Hitchcock Med Ctr Dept Cardiology Lebanon NH 03756

ROLLAND, LUCIEN G., paper company executive; b. St. Jerome, Que., Can., Dec. 21, 1916; s. Olivier and Aline (Dorion) R.; m. Marie de Lorimier, May 30, 1942; children: Nicolas, Natalie, Stanislas, Dominique, Christine, Etienne, David. Student, Coll. Jean de Brebeuf, Montreal; Profl. Engr., Loyola Coll., U. Montreal, B.A., B.A.Sc., C.E., also D.C.Sc. (hon.), 1960. Registered profl. engr. With Rolland Paper Co. Ltd. (name changed to Rolland inc. 1979), 1942—, v.p., gen. mgr., 1952, pres., gen. mgr., 1952-78, pres., chief exec. officer, 1978—, chmn. pres., chief exec. officer, 1984, chmn., chief exec. officer, 1985, chmn., 1991; chmn. bd. dirs. Rolland Paper Corp.; pres. Dessalu Limitee, Tarascon Holdings, Inc.; bd. dirs. PWA Rolland Decor Inc. Bd. govs. Notre-Dame Hosp., Montreal Children's Hosp., Montreal Gen. Hosp., Hôpital Marie Enfant. Decorated knight comdr. Order St. Gregory. Mem. Canadian Mfrs. Assn., Can. Pulp and Paper Assn. (exec. bd.), Corp. Profl. Engrs., Montreal Bd. Trade, Province of Que., C of C, Montreal C. of C., Engring. Inst. Can. Home: 1321 Sherbrooke St W, Apt B-60, Montreal, PQ Canada H3G 1J4 Office: Rolland Inc, 2000 McGill College Ave, Montreal, PQ Canada H3A 3H3

ROLLINS, JUDITH ANN, educator, researcher, writer; b. Boston; d. Edward Bryant and Edith Frances (Wade) R. BA, Howard U., 1970, MA, 1972; PhD, Brandeis U., 1983. Instr. Sociology Fed. City Coll., Washington, 1972-77; asst. prof. Sociology N.E. U., Boston, 1983-84; asst. prof. Sociology Simmons Coll., Boston, 1984-89, assoc. prof. Sociology, 1989—. Author: Between Women, 1985 (Am. Sociol. Assn. award 1987). Office: Simmons Coll 300 The Fenway Boston MA 02115

ROLLINS, THOMAS CHRISTIAN (CHRIS ROLLINS), advertising executive; b. Balt., Aug. 2, 1959; s. Herbert Lester and Betty Lee (Thomas) R. BA, Hood Coll., 1984; MBA, Frostburg (Md.) State U., 1988. Pub. service dir., music dir. Sta. WFMD-AM/WFRE-FM Radio, Frederick, Md., 1980-86; account exec. Sta. WZYQ-FM Radio, Frederick, 1987-88; dir. advt. and pub. rels. Frederick Underwriters, Inc., 1988—; prin. Chris Rollins Media, 1989—. Contbr. articles to profl. jours. Chair community rels. com. Frederick Meml. Hosp., 1988—; appropriations com. United Way Frederick County, 1988—. Recognized for best news operation UPI, 1983. Mem. Pub. Rels. Soc. Am., Frederick County Advt. Fedn. (charter, sec. 1988-89, v.p. 1989-90, pres. 1990-91, Silver medal award 1990, Crystl Prism award 1992, govtl. rels. chair 1991—), Sigma Chi. Republican. Methodist. Home: 19 E 4th St Frederick MD 21701-5256 Office: Frederick Underwriters Inc 1201 East St PO Box 235 Frederick MD 21701-0235

ROLSTON, RICHARD GERARD, industrial welding and heating company executive; b. Bklyn., Apr. 17, 1947; s. Robert Joseph and Meta (Marshall) R.; m. Pamela Ann Mangan, Oct. 23, 1971; children: Sandra Ann, Cathleen Elizabeth. Student, N.Y. Tech. Inst., 1965-71. Dist. svc. mgr. Meenan Oil Co. Inc., Hicksville, N.Y., 1975-81; instr. adult edn. BOCES III, Dix Hills, N.Y., 1975-77; svc. mgr. Secom Equipmemt Sales, East Massapequa, N.Y., 1981-85; gen. mgr. Miller, Proctor, Nickolas Inc., East Massapequa, 1985-86; v.p., gen. mgr. Am. Burner Corp., Commack, N.Y., 1986-88; gen. mgr. A.N.S. Welding & Heating Corp., West Babylon, N.Y., 1988—; pres. Stair Rolston, Inc., mfr.'s rep., Bethpage, N.Y., 1991—; cons. Underwriters Labs, Chgo., 1986—. Inventor diagnostic tester--oil burners; contbr. articles to repair manuals. Mem. ASHRAE, Nat. Assn. Power Engrs., Nassau Suffolk Oil Heat Svc. Mgrs. Home: 180 N 3rd St Bethpage NY 11714-2106

ROMAN, ERNAN, marketing executive; b. Quito, Ecuador, Oct. 5, 1950; came to U.S., 1958; s. Murray Roman and Eva Cseko; m. Sheri Joan Struhl, May 13, 1979; children: Elias Vale, Helaina Mali. BA, Antioch Coll., 1972; MBA, Fairleigh Dickinson U., 1983. Account exec. CCI Telemarketing, N.Y.C., 1971-73, dir. sales, 1973-77, v.p. mktg., 1977-82, sr. v.p. mktg., 1982-83; pres. Ernan Roman Direct Mktg., Douglas Manor, N.Y., 1983—; pioneered methodology of integrated direct marketing. Author: Integrated Direct Marketing: Techniques and Strategies for Success, 1988; contbr. to mktg. books, numerous profl. jours. Cons. Queens (N.Y.) Dem. Party, 1987; advisor Ctr. Def. Info., Washington, 1987. Mem. Direct Mktg. Assn. (Mktg. Leader award 1981, Echo award 1985).

ROMAN, JOHN JOSEPH, cartoonist, illustrator; b. Hartford, Conn., Nov. 23, 1950; s. John J. and Helen (Zigman) R.; m. Irena S. Roomgeller, Aug. 25, 1972. BA, New Eng. Sch. Art & Design, Boston, 1974. Free-lance illustrator various firms, Boston, 1974-80; nationally syndicated cartoonist (Gunther comic strip) The McNaught Syndicate, N.Y.C., 1980-82; free-lance illustrator, cartoonist various firms, Boston, 1982-85; internat. syndicated cartoonist Biography Sunday Comics United Feature Syndicate, N.Y.C., 1985-90; instr. New Eng. Sch. Art and Design, Boston, 1987-90; vis. instr. Syracuse U. MFA Program, N.Y., 1990—. Works in permanent archive collection of Mus. Cartoon Art, San Francisco, 1989. Sgt., U.S. Army, 1969-71. Named for Best Newspaper Feature in Interest of Youth, Am. Legion Aux. Golden Press awards, N.Y.C., 1988; recipient Journalism award for newspaper feature Women's Sports Found., N.Y.C., 1988, Illustration award L.A. Soc. Illustrators, 1990, awards of excellence Illustration, Graphic Design USA, 1990, 91, 92 (2). internat. Illustration award Best Illustration Category, Internat. Advt. Festival, 1991, Illustration award L.A. Soc. Illustrators, 1991. Mem. Nat. Cartoonist Soc. Home and Office: PO Box 571 Scituate MA 02066-0571

ROMAN, STANFORD AUGUSTUS, JR., physician, educator; b. N.Y.C.; s. Stanford Augustus and Ivy L. (White) R.; children: Mawiyah Lythcott, Jane E. Roman-Brown. AB, Dartmouth Coll., 1964; MD, Columbia U., 1968; MPH, U. Mich., 1975. Diplomate Nat. Bd. of Med. Examiners. Assoc. dir. ambulatory care Columbia U. Harlem Hosp., N.Y.C., 1972-73; instr. in medicine Columbia U., N.Y.C., 1972-73; clin. dir. Healthco, Inc., Soul City, N.C., 1973-74; dir. amblatory care, asst. prof. medicine Boston City Hosp., 1974-78; asst. dean Boston U. Sch. Medicine, 1975-78; med. dir. D.C. Gen. Hosp., Washington, 1978-81; assoc. dean acad. affairs Dartmouth Med. Sch., Hanover, N.H., 1981-86, assoc. prof., 1981-87, dep. dean, 1986-87; dean, v.p., prof. medicine Morehouse Sch. Med., Atlanta, 1987-89; sr. v.p., med. and profl. affairs Health and Hosps. Corp., N.Y.C., 1989-90; dean med. sch. CUNY, 1990—; dir. Boston Comprehensive Sickle Cell Ctr., 1975-78; asst. prof. medicine U. N.C., Chapel Hill, 1973-74, Boston U. Sch. Medicine, 1973-74; bd. dirs. Nat. Bd. Med. Examiners, Phila. Mem. AMA, APHA, Nat. Med. Assn., N.Y. State Coun. Grad. Med. Educators, Dartmouth Club of N.Y., 100 Black Men, Inc. Democrat. Episcopalian. Office: CUNY Med Sch Consert Ave and 138th St J 909 New York NY 10031

ROMAN-BARBER, HELEN, corporate executive; b. Dec. 20, 1946. LLB, U. Paris, 1971, M of Internat. Law, 1972. Chmn., chief exec. officer Roman Corp. Ltd., Toronto, Ont., Can. Office: Roman Corp Ltd, 200 King St W Box 82, Toronto, ON Canada M5H 3T4

ROMANESE, GINO, real estate executive; b. Montreal, Que., Can., July 26, 1957; s. Bruno and Angelina (LePore) R.; m. Anna Rossi, May 3, 1980; children: Marisa, Michael. B of Commerce (hon.), Concordia U., 1979. Sales rep. A.E. LePage, Montreal, 1975-79, br. mgr., 1979-81, regional mgr., 1981-86; sr. v.p., div. mgr. Royal LePage, B.C., 1986-87, Que., 1987-88; exec. v.p. Royal LePage, Ont., 1988—; lifetime mem. Montreal Real Estate Bd., pres., 1986. Mem. Can. Real Estate Assn., Real Estate Inst. Can. (FRI 1979, CMR 1979). Office: Royal LePage Real Estate Svcs, 39 Wynford Dr, Don Mills, ON Canada M3C 3K5

ROMANIES, MICHAEL EDWARD, computer systems executive; b. Phila., Nov. 8, 1962; s. Aleck and Ann Devaney, Dec. 27, 1986; children: Jacqueline Ann,, Michael Joseph. AS in Engring. Sci., Camden County Coll., 1982; BSEE, Wilkes U., 1985, postgrad., 1990—. Product mktg. engr. Sprague Solid State, Willow Grove, Pa., 1987; sr. product mktg. engr. Sprague Solid State, Willow Grove, 1987; mktg. mgr. Online Computer Systems, Inc., Germantown, Md., 1987-88; dir. bus. devel. and ops. Online Computer Systems, Inc., Germantown, 1988-90, div. gen. mgr., v.p., 1990—. Office: Online Computer Systems Inc 20251 Century Blvd Germantown MD 20874-1162

ROMANO, JOSEPH ANTHONY, marketing, public relations executive; b. Bklyn., Sept. 5, 1946; s. Anthony Wilbur and Anne (Fusco) R.; m. Linda Rose Giacalone, Sept. 23, 1972; children: Nicholas Joseph, Christine Dianne. Student, Villanova U., 1964-66; BS in Pharm. Scis., Columbia U., 1970, D Pharmacy, 1972. Clin. resident Lenox Hill Hosp., N.Y.C., 1970-72; asst. dean, asst. prof. Columbia U., N.Y.C., 1972-76; asst. dean, prof. SUNY, Buffalo, 1976-78; assoc. dean, assoc. prof. U. Wash., Seattle, 1978-83; assoc. dir. medicine Pfizer Labs., N.Y.C., 1983-85, product mgr., 1985, asst. to exec. v.p., 1985-87; sr. v.p., group dir. Hill & Knowlton, Inc., N.Y.C., 1987-88; exec. dir. external affairs Sandoz Pharm. Corp., N.Y.C., 1988-89; pres. Audio Visual Med. Mktg., N.Y.C., 1989-92; vice chair Nelson Communications, Inc., N.Y.C., 1992—; mem. U.S. Nat. Adv. Com. Health Profls., Washington, 1980-85. Co-author: Clinical Pharmacology, 1980, Pharmacy State Board Reviews, 1976, 78, 85, The Vitamin Book, 1985; cons. editor Med. Intercom, N.Y.C., 1986-89; contbr. articles to profl. jours. Fellow Royal Soc. Health London; mem. Am. Pharm. Assn., Am. Soc. Hosp. Pharmacists, Am. Assn. Colls. Pharmacy, U.S. Golf Assn., Rho Chi. Republican. Office: Nelson Communications Inc 41 Madison Ave New York NY 10010

ROMANO, MARJORIE JEAN, educator; b. Hackensack, N.J., Jan. 30, 1933; d. William Henry and Marjorie (Hughes) Backus; m. Antonio H. Romano, Aug. 22, 1953; children: Stephen, James, Charles. BA, Rutgers U., 1954, U. Cin., 1973; MA, U. Conn., 1979. Cert. elem. sch. tchr., Conn.; intermediate adminstr. Tchr. Windham Pub. Schs., Willimantic, Conn., 1973-84, program dir., 1984—. Mem. Assn. for Supervision and Curriculum Devel., Nat. Assn. Bilingual Edn., Tchrs. English to Speakers of Other Langs., Delta Kappa Gamma, Phi Delta Kappa (sec. Conn. chpt. 1987-89). Office: Windham Pub Schs 322 Prospect St Willimantic CT 06226-2208

ROMANO, SISTER GERALDINE, alcohol/drug counselor; b. Amsterdam, N.Y., July 7, 1937; d. Daniel and Lena Marie (Cerullo) R. AA, Villa Walsh, Morristown, N.J., 1960; BS, Seton Hall U., 1974, MA, 1976. Joined Religious Tchrs. Filipinni, 1955; cert. alcoholism counselor, addictions specialist. Tchr. Newark Archdiocese, 1958-74; prin. Our Lady of Mt. Carmel Sch., Orange, N.J., 1974-80; tchr. Albany Archdiocese, Schenectady, 1980-85; intake specialist St. Peter's Hosp., Albany, N.Y., 1987—; vol. Hospice, Schenectady, 1980—; Eucharistic minister St. Clare's Hosp., Schenectady, 1980-87. Mem. AACD, Am. Mental Health Assn., N.Y. State Counseling and Devel. Assn. Roman Catholic. Home: 1383 Pleasant St Schenectady NY 12303-1934 Office: St Peters Addiction Recovery Ctr 315 S Manning Blvd Albany NY 12208-1789

ROMANOWSKI, RICHARD RONALD, physician, gynecologist, educator; b. Buffalo, N.Y., Apr. 19, 1932; s. Ignatius Marion and Michaelena (Rockna) R.; m. Mary Anne Michalski, June 11, 1958; children: Roslyn, Ronda Lee, Marcus, Richard Michael. BS cum laude, Canisius Coll., 1954; MD, U. Buffalo, 1958. Diplomate Am. Bd. Ob-gyn. Intern San Francisco Gen. Hosp., 1958-59; resident Millard Fillmore Hosp., 1959-62, Roswell Pk. Inst., 1962-63; pres. Med. Assocs. in Gynecology and Obstetrics, Buffalo and Williamsville, N.Y., 1980—; clin. asst. prof. in ob-gyn. SUNY, Buffalo; attending staff dept. ob-gyn. Millard Fillmore Hosp., Sister's Hosp., Children's Hosp. Past bd. mem. Ask Women, Buffalo, Millard Fillmore Hosp. Mem. AMA, Am. Coll. Ob-Gyn., Am. Assn. Gynecol. Laparoscopists, Erie County Med. Soc., Cath. Physicians Guild (exec. com., past pres., nat. del.), Buffalo Ob-Gyn. Soc. (past pres., v.p.), Tri Beta (past pres.). Office: Med Assocs in Ob-Gyn 1000 Youngs Rd Williamsville NY 14221

ROMBERGER, JOHN ALBERT, scientist; b. near Klingerstown, Pa., Dec. 25, 1925; s. Ralph T. and Carrie (Bahner) R.; student Hershey Jr. Coll., 1947-49; B.A., Swarthmore Coll., 1951; M.S., Pa. State U., 1954; Ph.D., U. Mich., 1957; post doctoral, Calif. Inst. Tech., 1957-60; m. Margery Janet Davis, June 17, 1951; children—Ann I., Daniel D. Plant physiologist, Forest Physiology Lab., U.S. Forest Service, U.S. Dept. Agr., Beltsville, Md., 1961-82; vis. scientist Swedish U. Agrl. Scis., Alnarp, 1983, Inst. Agrl. Scis., Zamosc, Poland, 1985, Agrl. U., Warsaw, 1988. Lay leader Unitarian Ch. Served with AUS, 1945-46. Fellow Poland-U.S. Interacad. Exchange Program, U. Silesia, Katowice, 1981, 83. Fellow AAAS; mem. Am. Soc. Plant Physiologists, Bot. Soc. Am., Am. Inst. Biol. Scis., Soc. for History Tech., Sigma Xi. Author: Meristems, Growth, and Development in Woody Plants, 1963, (with Z. Hejnowicz and J.F. Hill) Plant Structure: Function and Development, 1992; editor: Internat. Rev. Forestry Research, 1963-70, Beltsville Symposia in Agrl. Research, 1976-78. Contbr. articles on devel. and theoretical biology to profl. jours. Home: 2005 Forest Hill Dr Silver Spring MD 20903-1533

ROMBOLA, ANTHONY MARIO STEPHEN, construction executive, consultant; b. Abington, Pa., Feb. 14, 1953; s. Pasquale Girolamo and Jennie Celeste (Ruzzi) R. Mgr. men's dept. Santerians, Hatboro, Pa., 1972-77; sr. mgr. Webster Menswear, Plymouth Meeting, Pa., 1977-83; asst. mgr. Brooks Bros., Willow Grove, Pa., 1983-88; owner, chief exec. officer C.F.R. Constrn., Inc., Glenside, Pa., 1988-90; founder, owner Metropolis, Inc, Glenside, 1991—; cons. Retail Cons., Inc., Glenside, 1983—. Tchr. confraternity christian doctrine St. Luke's Ch., 1984—. Mem. Internat. Coun. Shopping Ctrs., AIA, Nat. Trust Historic Preservation, Key Club (lt. gov. Glenside chpt. 1970-71). Democrat. Roman Catholic. Office: Metropolis Inc PO Box 520 Glenside PA 19038

ROMEIS, RONALD ALAN, retirement and nursing home executive; b. Ft. Myers, Fla., May 13, 1947; s. Ludwig and Elizabeth Mina (Perry) R.; m. Margaret Elizabeth Whitworth, Oct. 19, 1968; children: Margaret Elizabeth, Sara Ellen. BA, Eckerd Coll., 1969; MDiv, Vanderbilt U., 1973. Assoc. pastor Towson (Md.) Presbyn. Ch., 1973-77; asst. to pres. Phila. Presbytery Homes, Villanova, Pa., 1977-83, v.p., 1984—; bd. dirs. Presbyn. Village, Rosemont, Pa., 1986—; trsutee Presbytery Phila., 1985—, pres., 1991—; pres. Presbyn. Assn. Homes for Aging, 1987-88. Editor: Directory of Presbyterian Homes In The United States, 1978—. Minister The Presbytery of Phila., 1977—, The Presbytery of Balt., 1973-77. Mem. Union League Phila. Republican. Office: Phila Presbytery Homes PO Box 607 Villanova PA 19085-0607

ROMELING, WALDEMAR BRIGGS, artist; b. Schenectady, N.Y., Feb. 26, 1909; s. Rudolph Carl and Sarah Anne (Friend) R.; m. Elizabeth Winbauer, Oct. 21, 1939; children: Crystel, Michael. Cert. in fine arts and illustration, Pratt Inst., 1932; BA in Art Edn., Syracuse U., 1942. Cert. art tchr., N.Y. Tchr. Owen D. Young Sch., Van Hornesville, N.Y., 1942-69. One man shows include Muggelton Gallery, Auburn, N.Y., 1975, 76, 77, Munson-Williams-Proctor, Utica, N.Y., 1982, Pioneer Gallery, Cooperstown, N.Y., 1989-91, Arts Guild of Old Forge, N.Y., 1991, Leighton Gallery, Schenectady, N.Y., 1992; exhibited in group show at Cen. N.Y./W.C. Soc., 1986, 87, 88, 89, 90, 91. With U.S. Army, 1943-45. Recipient Purebase award Schenectady Mus., 1971, Munson Williams Proctor Inst., 1988, Field & Streams medal Adirondack Nat. Exhbn., 1986, Pulsiver award Adirondack Nat. Exhbn., 1984. Mem. So. Vt. Artists, Cooperstown Art Assn. (bd. dirs. 1956-91, 5 awards), Arts Guild Old Farge. Republican. Home and Studio: Wiltsey Hill Rd Van Hornesville NY 13475

ROMEO, ROSS VICTOR, army officer; b. Detroit, Nov. 4, 1958; s. Salvatore Victor and Carol Ann (Kunart) R.; m. Mary Jo Cowdin, Dec. 21, 1983; children: Christian, Ross II. BA, U. Mich., 1981; MA, Boston U., 1987; postgrad., Averett Coll., 1990. Commd. 2d lt. U.S. Army, 1983, advanced through ranks to capt., 1987; co. commdr. U.S. Army, Heidelberg, Fed. Republic Germany, 1986-89; mgr. worldwide intercomputer network Def. Communications Agy., Washington, 1989—. Selected DCA Co. Grade Officer of Yr., 1990. Mem. Armed Forces Communications-Electronics Assn., Am. Assn. Individual Investors, Nat. Assn. Investors Corp., U. Mich. Alumni Assn. Home: 7753 Carrleigh Pky Springfield VA 22152-1303 Office: Def Communications Agy The Pentagon Washington DC 20303

ROMLEY, DEREK VANDERBILT, architect; b. Boston, June 16, 1935; s. Frederick Joseph and Cora-Marie (Sherman-Kenealy) R.; m. Elizabeth Colloredo-Mansfeld, Aug. 28, 1960 (div. June 1972). With various architects, N.Y., Paris, Lima, Milan, and Calif., until 1976; B.A., Harvard U., 1957; B.Arch., Yale U., 1964, M.Arch., 1965. Registered architect, Mass., Fla., Calif.; cert. Nat. Council Archtl. Registration Bds.; lic. contractor and real estate broker, Mass. instr. design Pratt Inst., 1969-70; vis. critic Sorbonne, Paris, U. Houston, UCLA, U. Calif.-Santa Barbara; prin. Derek Romley, Architects, Palm Beach, Fla. and Cape Cod, Mass., 1976—. Author: play The Men, 1987; work pub. in archtl. mags., Vogue, Life, Look, House Beautiful; features in Los Angeles Times, Paris Herald, N.Y. Times, Houston Chronicle, Cape Cod newspapers and periodicals. Chmn. Dennis Planning Bd., 1977-78, Dennis Archtl. Rev. Bd., 1977-81. Winner passive solar award cycle 5, HUD; design award; constrn. grantee. Mem. AIA, Boston Soc. Architects. Christian Scientist. Clubs: Harvard (Cape Cod, Mass.); Yale, Hyannis Yacht. Home and Office: 100 Center St # 1 South Dennis MA 02660-3626

ROMMEL, FREDERICK ALLEN, microbiologist, immunologist; b. Carlisle, Pa., Feb. 27, 1935; s. Norman Connely and Myra (Allen) R.; m. Constance Ann, Aug. 30, 1957; 1 child, Frederick Allen II. BS, U. Miami, 1957, PhD, 1967. Asst. prof. U. Tex. Health Sci. Ctr., San Antonio, 1970-75; assoc. prof. U. Mo., Kansas City Gen. Hosp., 1975-76; rsch. chemist USDA, Plum Island, N.Y., 1976-81; v.p. rsch. & devel. Immunogenetics Inc., Dover, N.H., 1981-83; dir. DACI lab. Johns Hopkins U. Sch. Medicine, Balt., 1984-89; dir. allergy ctr. Balt. Rh Typing Lab., 1989-91; vet. lab. mgr. diagnostic svcs. Commonwealth Pa., Summerdale, 1991—. With USAF, 1958-60, 61-62. Predoctoral fellow Howard Hughes Med. Inst., Miami, Fla., 1961-66, Postdoctoral fellow Johns Hopkins U. Med. Sch., Balt., 1966-67. Mem. Am. Acad. Allergy & Immunology, Am. Assn. Vet. Immunology, N.Y. Acad. Sci., World Aquaculture Soc., Clin. Ligand Assy Soc., Am. Soc. Microbiol. Home: 2811 Van Horn Rd Forest Hill MD 21050-2001

ROMMER, JAMES ANDREW, physician; b. Newark, Aug. 22, 1952; s. Thomas Colman and Hortense (Marsh) R.; m. Linda Joan Anderson, Oct. 7, 1979; children: Elizabeth Anne, Nicole Marie. BS, Haverford Coll., 1974; MD, Cornell U., 1978. Diplomate Am. Bd. Internal Medicine. Intern N.Y. Hosp., Cornell Med. Ctr., N.Y.C., 1978-79; resident in internal medicine N.Y. Hosp., Cornell Med. Ctr., 1978-81; fellow in internal medicine Johns Hopkins Med. Sch., Balt., 1981-82; pvt. practice internal medicine Livingston, N.J., 1982—; attending physician Newark Beth Israel Med. Ctr., 1982—, mem. exec. com., 1989; attending physician St. Barnabas Med. Ctr., Livingston, 1984—, mem. exec. com., 1990; asst. clin. prof. Univ. Medicine and Dentistry-N.J. Med. Sch., Newark, 1983—. Fellow Am. Coll. Physicians; mem. AMA, Am. Soc. Internal Medicine, Alpha Omega Alpha. Office: 349 E Northfield Rd Livingston NJ 07039-4802

RONAYNE, JOAN BERNICE, business strategy consultant; b. Needham, Mass., Sept. 23, 1966; d. Joseph Stephen and Joan Bernice (Mack) Ronayne. AB magna cum laude, Harvard U., 1988, MBA, 1991. Rsch. assoc. Ctr. for Strategic and Internat. Studies, Washington, 1985; analyst Union Francais de Banques-Locabail, Paris, 1986; cons. Alternative Investment Corp., Boston, 1987; cons., mgr. rsch. assocs. Monitor Co., Cambridge, Mass., 1988—; cons. in field; joint participant Washington Internat. Studies Ctr. Program and Harvard Summer in Washington Program, 1985. Bus. editor Harvard Crimson, Cambridge, Mass., 1984-88. mem. Needham Town Meeting, 1989—; religious edn. tchr. St. Joseph's Parish, Needham, 1989-90; mem. vis. fellows com. John F. Kennedy Sch. of Govt., Cambridge, 1985-87; exec. bd. mem. Harvard Crimson Key Soc., 1985-88. Kosciuszko Found. scholar, 1991; Cert. of Appreciation Archdiocese of Boston, 1990; John Harvard scholar, 1986, 87, 88; recipient Elizabeth Cary Agassiz award, Radcliffe Coll., 1986, 87, 88. Mem. NAFE, Radcliffe Club, Harvard Club, Rotary (Goodwill Ambassador to Soviet Union 1990), Phi Beta Kappa. Home: 15 Douglas Rd Needham MA 02192-4503 Office: Monitor Co 25 First St Cambridge MA 02140-1502

RONAYNE, MICHAEL RICHARD, JR., academic administrator; b. Boston, Apr. 29, 1937; s. Michael Richard and Margaret (Fahey) R.; m. Joanne Maria, Aug. 7, 1971; 1 child, Michelle Eileen. BS, Boston Coll., 1958; PhD, U. Notre Dame, 1962. Instr. chemistry Providence Coll., 1962-63, asst. prof. chemistry, 1963-64; rsch. chemist Panametrics, Inc., Waltham, Mass., 1964-66; asst. prof. chemistry Suffolk U., Boston, 1966-67, assoc. prof., 1967-70, prof., chmn. dept. chemistry, 1970-72, dean Coll. Liberal Arts and Sci., 1972—; reaccreditation vis. team mem. New Eng. Assn. Schs. and Colls., Winchester, Mass., 1974-80, Mass. Dept. Edn., Boston, 1975; mem. acad. adv. com. Mass. Bd. Higher Edn., Boston, 1977. Contbr. articles to sci. jours., profl. publs. Mem. Winchester Sch. Com., 1983-92, chmn., 1984-85, 86-87; mem. Winchester Town Meeting, 1983—, mem. town capital planning com., 1983-84, town coun. on youth, 1987-88, 89-90; mem. exec. com., bd. dirs. Mass. Bay Marine Studies Consortium, 1985-87; project dir. U.S. Dept. of Edn. Title III Grants. Shell Oil Corp. fellow, 1958-59, AEC fellow 1959-62; recipient Contbns. in Sci. and Edn. citation New Eng. Sch. Art and Design, Boston, 1991. Mem. AAAS, Am. Chem. Soc., Am. Conf. Acad. Deans, Coun. for Liberal Learning, Am. Assn. for Higher Edn., Sigma Xi, Phi Alpha Theta, Phi Gamma Mu, Sigma Tau Delta, Omicron Delta Epsilon, Sigma Zeta. Office: Suffolk U Beacon Hill Boston MA 02114

RONKIN, ALAN MARSHALL, mental health counselor; b. Boston, Nov. 4, 1941; s. Isadore Edward and Irene Mildred (Plotkin) R.; m. Sheila Joan Saltman, Mar. 12, 1966; children: Mikhail Scott, Jeremy Fredrick. AB, St. Anselm's Coll.; EdM, Briegewater State Coll.; EdD, Boston U., 1981. Lic. counselor. Health educator Brockton (Mass.) High Sch., 1970—; facilitator Brockton Community Schs., 1973-89; assoc. therapist Brookline Ctr. Personal Growth, Divorce Mediation Ctr., N.Y., 1980-82; exec. dir. Brockton Family Counseling Ctr. Inc., South Easton, Mass., 1981—; client cons. Parents Without Ptnrs., Mass., 1989—; client cons., therapist Transition Ind. Living Program for Homeless, Greater Brockton Area, 1987-92; adj. prof. Curry Coll., Milton, Mass., Bridgewater State Coll., 1974-80, guest lectr., 1987; guest lectr. Laboure Coll. Nursing Sch., 1981, St. Margaret's Hosp., 1981; EAP cons., therapist various police depts. Lt. USN. Mem. New Eng. Assn. Specialists in Group Work, Nat. Assn. Prevention Profls., APHA, AACD, Mass. Assn. Mental Health Counselors., Mass. Assn. Group Work, Am. Mental Health Counselors Assn., Mass. Mental Health Counselors Assn. (pres. 198-89, exec. bd. 1985-92), N.Y. Acad. Sci., Masons, Pi Lamba Theta. Jewish. Home: 35 Maple St Randolph MA 02192-2341 Office: Brockton Family Counseling PO Box 151 South Easton MA 02375-1128

RONKIN, BRUCE EDWARD, music educator, music publisher; b. Mt. Holly, N.J., Nov. 22, 1957; s. Seymour Martin and Flora (Ruder) R. MusB, Eastman Sch. Music, Rochester, N.Y., 1979; MusM, Ind. U., 1981; MusD, U. Md., 1987. Pres. Roncorp Publs., Cherry Hill, N.J., 1978—; prof. music bus. U. Mass., Lowell, 1987-91; dir. music industry studies Northeastern U., Boston, 1991—; lectr. in field; congress coord. concert series 8th World Saxophone Congress, Washington, 1985. Mem. Broadcast Music, Inc., Music and Entertainment Industry Educators Assn., Am. Fedn. Musicians, North Am. Saxophone Alliance. Office: Northeastern U Music Dept 351 Ryder Hall Boston MA 02115

RONNOW, ROBERT WILLIAM, finance educator, consultant; b. Hoboken, N.J., May 1, 1924; s. William Stanley and Clara Elizabeth (Lindenstruth) R.; m. Josephine Mary Nicastro, Sept. 9, 1950; children:

Robert W., David K., Lawrence R., Mark J. AB, Columbia U., 1949; MS, Stevens Inst. Tech., 1956. Food technologist Gen. Foods Corp., Hoboken, 1949-52; mgr. market rsch. and analysis The Borden Co., N.Y.C., 1954-56; dir. bus. rsch. and analysis Union Carbide Corp., Danbury, Conn., 1956-82; adj. prof. Western Conn. State U., Danbury, 1983—; cons. Union Carbide Corp./Amoco, Danbury, 1983-89. Vice chmn. Boy Scouts Am., N.J., N.Y. and Conn., 1946-90; vol. Danbury Sch. System, 1991, Literacy Vols., 1991. Staff sgt. U.S. Army, 1943-46, PTO. Named Vol. of the Yr., Union Carbide Corp., 1980. Mem. Nat. Assn. Bus. Economists (forecasting panel Conn. chpt. 1978-91). Home and Office: 7 Jarrod Dr Danbury CT 06811-3455

RONSON, RAOUL R., publishing executive; b. Fiume, Italy, Mar. 22, 1931; came to U.S., 1951; s. Mirko and Margaret (Fischer) Ruzicka; m. Susan Kohn, July 22, 1962; 1 child, Paul. DBA, U. Rome, 1950; MA, New Sch Social Research, 1957; postgrad., Inst. for Advanced Internat. Studies, U. Miami, 1967-68, NYU, 1974. Fgn. corr., freelance writer, 1953-59; treas. Daron Enterprises, Inc., 1959-63; pres. Seesaw Music Corp., N.Y.C., 1963—, Okra Music Corp., N.Y.C., 1963-77, Ulsyra Prodn. Corp., N.Y.C., 1963—; pres. The Composers Press, 1972-76; acad. lectr. Am., Australian, New Zealand univs. and conservatories; vis. lectr. Youngstown (Ohio) State U., 1985—. Producer documentary films, 1959—, classical music recs., 1963—, The Dana Recording Project. Mem. Emergency Control Bd. Office of Mayor, N.Y.C., 1973-82; rsch. analyst Office of the Sec. Def., Res. Affairs, The Pentagon, Washington, 1984-91; liaison officer U.S. Mil. Acad., West Point, N.Y., 1988—. With M.I., AUS, 1952-54, USAR, 1955-91, ret., 1991. Decorated Legion of Merit, Def. Superior Svc. medal; recipient numerous other awards and decorations. Mem. Am. Polit. Sci. Assn., Am. Acad. Polit. and Social Sci., Internat. Platform Assn., Civil Affairs Assn., Sibelius Soc. (bd. dirs. 1978-85), Nat. Acad. Rec. Arts and Scis., Masons. Home: 825 W End Ave New York NY 10025-5349 Office: 2067 Broadway New York NY 10023-2806

RONSON, SUSAN, administrative assistant; b. N.Y.C., June 30, 1940; d. Solomon Blondheim and Harriet (Lustbader) Kohn; m. Raoul Ronson, July 22, 1962; 1 child, Paul. Student, Miami U., Oxford, Ohio, 1958-60; cert., Katharine Gibbs, N.Y.C., 1960-61, Emergency Mgmt. Inst., Emmitsburg, Md., 1983, Nat. Def. U., Washington, 1988. Sec. Doubleday & Co., N.Y.C., 1961-65; freelance editor N.Y.C., 1965-73; exec. sec. Howard Needles Tammen & Bergendoff, N.Y.C., 1974-87; adminstrv. asst., office mgr. Capital Group, N.Y.C., 1987—; exec. sec., dir. Seesaw Music Corp., N.Y.C., 1988—; adminstrv. officer, Fed. Emergency Mgmt. Agy., N.Y.C. Mem. Nat. Def. Exec. Res., Assn. of Nat. Def. Exec. Reserve (exec. v.p. and dir. N.Y. met. chpt. 1988—). Republican. Club: Army Navy (Washington). Home: 825 W End Ave New York NY 10025-5349 Office: Capital Group 575 5th Ave # 21 New York NY 10017-2422

RONTY, BRUNO GEORGE, phonograph record manufacturing company executive, tenor; b. Lwow, Poland, June 10, 1922; came to U.S., 1946, naturalized, 1955; s. Leon and Hermine (Elsner) R.; m. Wanda von Rudolph, Nov. 3, 1943 (div. 1959); 1 child, Maria; m. Michele van Beveren, June 12, 1962 (div. 1972). Student, Lwow Lyceum of Humanities, 1938-40; BA, Conservatory, 1939, MA, MFA, 1941, PhD in History and Polit. Sci., 1945. Tenor USSR, Poland, Sweden, U.S., 1940-50; pres. Colosseum Records, Inc., N.Y.C., 1950—, Musicart Internat., Ltd., N.Y.C., Wilton, Conn., 1958—, Acropole Corp. Am., N.Y.C., 1972—; producer Bruno Hi-Fi Records; voice instr. N.Y.C.; tenor, gen. dir. cultural exchange program Musica Nostra et Vostra, Nat. Corp. Am., 1973—. Contrbr. articles to profl. jours. Bd. dirs. Ministry Culture, Art, Poland, 1945; pres. Narcolepsy and Cataplexy Found. Am., 1975—, Cultural Exchange Soc. Am., 1976—. With Polish Army, 1942-45. Decorated Grunwald Cross; Polonia Restituta; recipient 1st prize USSR Internat. Competition, 1940. Mem. YMCA Club Greater N.Y. (life mem.). Roman Catholic. Office: Acropole Corp Am 1410 York Ave New York NY 10021-3463

ROODIN, PAUL A., psychology educator; b. Brookline, Mass., June 1, 1943; s. Harry and Blossom (Sugarman) R.; m. Marlene Linda Lubarsky, Aug. 27, 1967; children: Neal D., Pamela L. AB, Boston U., 1965; MS, Purdue U., 1968, PhD, 1970. Asst. prof. psychology SUNY, Oswego, 1969-75, assoc. prof., 1975-81, prof., 1981—, assoc. dean, 1989-91, assoc. provost, 1991—. Co-author: Developmental Psychology, 1980, Adult Cognition and Aging, 1986, Adult Development and Aging, 1991; contbr. articles on devel. psychology to profl. jours. Jewish. Home: 122 Stanwood Ln Manlius NY 13104-1412 Office: SUNY Coll at Oswego Oswego NY 13126

ROOF, JAMES SHELDON, marketing executive; b. Springfield, Ohio, June 24, 1947; s. William E. and S. Barbara (Obley) R.; m. Mary Ellen Henneberry, June 20, 1970; children: Jason William, Kevin Andrew. BSBA, U. Mo., 1970. Positions including purchasing agt. to v.p. sci. products Mallinckrodt, Inc., St. Louis, 1970-88; pres., chief exec. officer Aspect Systems Corp., St. Louis, 1988-89; v.p. global sales and mktg. Shipley Co., Inc., Newton, Mass., 1989—. Republican. Roman Catholic. Home: 18 Shawnee Rd Medfield MA 02052-2940 Office: Shipley Co Inc 2300 Washington St Newton MA 02162-1469

ROOKEY, THOMAS JEROME, dean; b. Oswego, N.Y., Oct. 18, 1944; s. Ernest J. and Irene A. (Matthews) R.; m. Rosann Spohn, Mar. 30, 1967; children: Austin, Kristin, Dionna. Student, Siena U., Italy, 1964; BA, SUNY, 1966; MA, Bucknell U., 1968; PhD, Lehigh U., 1972. Rsch. assoc. Pa. Dept. Edn., Harrisburg, 1966-72; rsch. analyst Reach for Better Schs., Phila., 1971-72; assoc. prof. East Stroudsburg (Pa.) U., 1972-76; exec. dir. Ednl. Improvement Ctr., Princeton, N.J., 1976-83; dean Clarion U., Oil City, Pa., 1983-89; acad. dean Medaille Coll., Buffalo, 1989—. Contbr. articles to profl. jours. Councilman Town Coun., Hightstown, N.J., 1982-83; v.p. Oil City C. of C., 1984- 89; exec. bd. United Way, Venango, Pa., 1984-89; mem. County Planning Commn., Venango, 1985-89. With USAF, 1968-69. Named Citizen of Yr. Oil City, 1988; recipient Svc. awrd Venango Video, Oil City, 1989, Excellence award Nat. Assn. State Edn. Dept. Info. Officers, 1981. Mem. Am. Assn. Community and Jr. Coll., Nat. Assn. Campus Adminstrs., Rotary (Pres. 1987), Phi Delta Kappa (Kappan of Yr. 1976). Office: Medaille Coll 18 Agassiz Cir Buffalo NY 14214-2695

ROONEY, ANDREW AITKEN, writer, columnist; b. Albany, N.Y., Jan. 14, 1919; s. Walter S. and Ellinor (Reynolds) R.; m. Marguerite Howard, Mar. 21, 1942; children: Ellen, Martha, Emily, Brian. Student, Colgate U., 1942. Writer-producer CBS-TV News, 1959—; newspaper columnist Tribune Co. Syndicate, 1979—. Author: (with O.C. Hutton) Air Gunner, 1944, The Story of Stars and Stripes, 1946, Conquerors' Peace, 1947, The Fortunes of War, 1962, A Few Minutes with Andy Rooney, 1981, And More By Andy Rooney, 1982, Pieces of My Mind, 1984, Word for Word, 1986, Not That You Asked, 1989; TV programs include An Essay on War, Mr. Rooney Goes to Washington, Mr. Rooney Goes To Dinner; regular commentator-essayist: 60 Minutes, 1978—. Served with AUS, 1941-45. Decorated Air medal, Bronze Star.; recipient awards for best written TV documentary Writers Guild Am., 1966, 68, 71, 75, 76, Emmy awards, 1968, 78, 81, 82.

ROONEY, MARGARET LOUISE, success motivation institute distributor; b. St. Albans, Vt., July 10, 1951; d. Henry Carlton and Phyllis (Shedd) Ferguson; m. Robert Lawrence Rooney, Aug. 25, 1970 (div. Dec. 1985); children: Terry, Anne Marie, Matthew, Sara. Student, Miami U., Oxford, Ohio, 1969-71; BS, Community Coll. of Vt., 1991; BBA, Lyndon State Coll., 1991. Mgr. Yarn Cellar, St. Albans, Vt., 1973-74; co-owner Dunkin Donuts Franchise, Barre, St. Johnsbury, Vt., 1974-81; demonstrator, supr. House of Lloyd, Inc., Grandview, Mo., 1982—; dist. mgr. House of Lloyd, Inc., Grandview, 1985—; distbr. Success Motivation Inst., Waco, Tex., 1987—; mem. Pres.'s Honor Club, Kansas City, Mo., 1985-91. Mem. Washington County Rep. Com., 1990. Mem. Cen. Vt. Leads Club (dir. 1990), Small Bus. Network (v.p. 1991—), Cen. Vt. C. of C. Republican. Methodist. Home: 30 Bailey St Barre VT 05641-5215

ROONEY, MICHAEL, international software trading company executive; b. Ithaca, N.Y., Sept. 2, 1946; s. John F. Rooney and Patricia (Child) Fillingham. BSEE, Rutgers U., 1972. Mem. tech. staff Mitre Corp., Bedford, Mass., 1973-74; chmn., pres. Boston Systems Office, Inc., Waltham, Mass., 1974-89; chmn. Software Export Corp., Cambridge, Mass., 1989—, Productivity Solutions, Inc., Wellesley, Mass., 1987—. Mem. Cambridge Comprehensive Plan Com., 1985-86, Block grant Adv. Group, Cambridge, 1987—; dir. RCCC, Cambridge, 1985—. Office: Software Export Corp PO Box 32 Cambridge MA 02139-0901

ROONEY, MICHAEL J., banker; b. Dublin, Ireland, Aug. 10, 1941; came to U.S. 1959; s. Kevin Michael and Ann Thelma (Kelly) R.; m. Marilyn Joan Kolb, Oct. 13, 1962; children: Renee Irene, Robin Lynn. Vice-pres., dir. new ventures Citicorp Select Investments, Inc.; chmn., chief exec. officer Empire Nat. Securities, Inc.; pres., chief exec. officer EOA Investment Svcs. Corp.; sr. v.p. banking Meritor Bank FSB.

ROONEY, PATRICK MICHAEL, police officer; b. Balt., Dec. 27, 1957; s. Irving Joseph and Rita (Ruzicka) R.; m. Mary Susan Hurley, Aug. 1, 1981. AA in Criminal Justice, Essex Community Coll., Balt., 1989; BS in Phys. Geography, Towson State U.; grad. numerous tng. courses in field. Cert. safety inspector, hazardous materials specialist, Md., PR-24 police baton instr., EMT, radar operator, SCUBA diver. Police officer Balt. County Police Dept., 1978—; mem. Dignitary/Witness Protection Team. With USNR, 1987—. Recipient Amtrak Disaster award. Mem. Airborne Law Enforcement Assn., Aircraft Owners and Pilots Assn., Exptl. Aircraft Assn., Smithsonian Instn./Air and Space Assocs., Naval Enlisted Res. Assn., Nat. Geographic Assn., Fraternal Order of Police. Office: Baltimore County Police Dep 7607 Parkwood Rd Baltimore MD 21222-2222

ROORBACH, GEORGE BRETT, textile executive; b. Cambridge, Mass., Apr. 7, 1926; s. George Byron and Anne Elizabeth (Hubble) R.; m. Elizabeth Wood, Apr. 23, 1955; children: Emily Mathewson Roorbach Kelley, Gretchen Wood, Ashley Hubble. AB, Harvard Coll., 1951. Adminstrv. officer Fgn. Svc. U.S. Dept. State, Lagos, Nigeria, 1952-55; asst. mgr. Nat. Assn. of Engine and Boat Mfrs., N.Y.C., 1955-56; gen. mgr. Crown Worsted Mills Inc., Providence, 1956-62; pres. Crown Worsted Mills Inc., Central Falls, R.I., 1962-91, GEO Assocs., Franconia, N.H., 1991—; bd. advisors R.I. Hosp. Trust Nat. Bank, Providence, 1974—. Pres. Narragansett coun. Boy Scouts Am., 1976-79. Recipient Outstanding Vol. Svc. award United Way of South Eastern New Eng., Providence, 1982, Silver Beaver award Boy Scouts Am., Providence, 1979, Corning Community Action award Blackstone Valley C. of C., 1974. Mem. No. Textile Assn. (bd. dirs. 1984-88, 89—); To Kalon Club (bd. dirs.), Profile Club (pres. 1973), Providence Art Club. Office: GEO Assocs 208 Ridge Rd Franconia NH 03580

ROOS, RON, graphic designer; b. N.Y.C., July 27, 1952; s. Ernest R. and Marie (Kohler) R. BA, Hunter Coll., 1974; student, Sch. of Visual Arts, N.Y.C., 1976. Graphic designer Dept. of Commerce, Washington, 1976-77; exhibit designer Nat. Park Svc., Harpers Ferry, W.Va., 1977—; prin. Ron Roos design, Frederick, Md., 1986—. Creator graphic designs The Clustered Holsteins of Frederick, 1988, Frederick County Recycling Logo, 1991; contbr. articles to profl. jours. Mem. Frederick County Art Assn. (v.p. 1991—), Delaplaine Visual Arts Ctr. (design dir. 1988—). Home: 501 W 2d St Frederick MD 21701

ROOT, DAVID A., design consultant; b. St. Paul, Sept. 13, 1942; s. Morris J. and Sylvia (Tomash) R. BS, Ill. Inst. Tech., 1965. Designer Chapman/Goldsmith Design, Chgo., 1961-63, John Massey Design, Chgo., 1964-65; prin. David Root Design Office, Chgo., 1965-74; vis. prof. Va. Commonwealth U., Richmond, Va., 1975-76; pres. David Root Design, Washington, 1976-79, Root & Chester Design, Inc., Washington, 1979-85, Root & Co., Inc., Washington, 1985—; cons. White House Preservation Fund, Washington, 1983, Nat. Trust For Historic Preservation, Washington, 1987-91. One-person show includes Nat. Acad. of Sci., Washington; represented at permanent collections Libr. of Congress, Washington, Xerox Corp., Leesburg, Va. Officer Lambdd Light Spriritual Group, Washington, 1990-92; bd. dirs. Tiber Island Coop. Homes, Inc., 1983-86. Mem. 27 Chgo. Designers (pres. 1973). Home: 445 N St SW Washington DC 20024

ROOT, EDWARD LAKIN, dean of faculty, educator; b. Cumberland, Md., Dec. 5, 1940; s. Lakin and Edna Grace (Adams) R. BS, Frostburg (Md.) State Coll., 1962, MEd, 1966; EdD, U. Md., 1970. Cert. tchr., Md. Tchr. Allegany County Bd. of Edn., Cumberland, 1962-66; grad. fellow U. Md., College Park, 1966-67, fellow, 1967-69; with Frostburg State Coll., 1969—, prof., head edn. dept., 1980-87, dean, 1987—; adj. grad. prof. U. Md., 1980—; mem. Profl. Standards Bd. Md., Balt., 1980-87, Cert. Rev. Bd. Md., Balt., 1987-90, Md. Task Force Adminstrn., Balt., 1985-88, Md. Task Force: Essentials in Tchr. Edn. Mem. Nat. Assn. Secondary Sch. Prins., Nat. Soc. for the Study of Edn., Mensa, Elks, Shriners, Masons, Phi Delta Kappa. Democrat. Methodist. Home: 100 Pennsylvania Ave Cumberland MD 21502-4236 Office: Frostburg State U College Ave Frostburg MD 21532-1724

ROPER, JOHN JOSEPH, principal; b. Boston, Sept. 29, 1946; s. Alfred T. and Elizabeth L. (Flanagan) R.; m. Deborah A. DiCicco, Apr. 19, 1975; children: Brian C., Laurie A. BEd, Boston State Coll., 1968; MEd, Bridgewater State Coll., 1975; postgrad., Boston Coll., 1988—. Sci. tchr. Xaverian Bros. High Sch., Westwood, Mass., 1968-73, Assabet Valley Regional Vocat. Sch., Marlboro, Mass., 1974-87; project mgr. U. Mass., Boston, 1987-89; instr. Saginaw Valley State U., University Center, Mich., 1989-90; prin. North Shore Regional Vocat. Sch., Beverly, Mass., 1991—. Author: Principles of Technology, Vol. II, 1987, Applied Biology-Chemistry, Vol. 7, 1990, Vol. 4, 1991. Recipient Assoc. Commr.'s award Mass. Dept. Edn., 1987, Achievement cert. N.E. Network for Curriculum Coordination in Vocat. Tech. Edn., 1988, Disting. Svc. cert. Ctr. for Occupational R&D, 1985. Mem. Nat. Assn. Secondary Sch. Prins., Am. Vocat. Assn., Mass. Vocat. Assn., Mass. Assn. Vocat. Adminstrs., Essex County Prin.'s Assn., Phi Delta Kappa, Alpha Psi Omega. Home: 4 Sawmill Ln Georgetown MA 01833-1700 Office: North Shore Reg Vocat Sch 20 Balch St Beverly MA 01915-3099

ROSA, ALFRED FELIX, English educator; b. Waterbury, Conn., Feb. 7, 1942; s. Gerard and Lucy (Pilla) Rosa; m. Margaret Ann Shafran, Aug. 19, 1967; 1 child, Elizabeth Ann. BA, U. Conn., 1964; MA, U. Mass., 1966, PhD, 1971. Lectr. U. Mass., Amherst, 1969; instr. U. Vt., Burlington, 1969-71, asst. prof., 1971-74, assoc. prof., 1975-78, prof. English, 1978—; pres. New Eng. Press, Inc., Shelburne, Vt., 1978—; v.p. Regional Facts, Inc., Middlebury, Vt., 1989—. Author: Controversies, 1991, Outlooks and Insights, 1990, Subject and Strategy, 1990, Language Awareness, 1990, Models for Writers, 1989, Salem, Transcendentaliam and Hawthorne, 1980. NEH Vt. Writing Program grantee, 1977-82; Fulbright lectr., 1973-74. Mem. MLA, Authors Guild, Nat. Coun. Tchrs. English, Fulbright Assn., others. Home: 16 Juniper Rdg Shelburne VT 05482-7270 Office: U of Vt Dept English 321 Old Mill Burlington VT 05405

ROSA, GEORGE MACHADO, foreign language and literature educator; b. Madison, Wis., July 5, 1949; s. Alberto Machado da and Maria Aldegice (Machado) R.; m. Elizabeth Barron, July 26, 1986; 1 child, Meredith Barron Rosa. BA, UCLA, 1971; DPhil, Oxford (Eng.) U., 1981. Asst. prof. French and Italian, Tulane U., New Orleans, 1979-86, mem. grad. faculty, 1983-86; asst. prof. fgn. langs. and lits. Lafayette Coll., Easton, Pa., 1986-92, assoc. prof., 1992—; mem. Phi Beta Kappa election com. Tulane Univ., New Orleans, 1979-86; mem. La. Com. for Selection for Rhodes scholarships, 1981-85, sec., 1983-85; mem. Gulf Dist. Com. of Selection for Rhodes scholarships, 1983-85, Aydelotte-Kieffer-Smith Meml. Com., 1990—. Contbr. articles to profl. jours. Rhodes scholar, 1971-74; hon. mem. Royal Commonwealth Soc., 1971-74; Danforth fellow, 1974-79; grantee Zaharoff, Am. Phil. Soc., others. Mem. AAUP, MLA, Am. Assn. Tchrs. French, Soc. Interdisciplinary 19th Century Studies. Home: 116 N Main Nazareth PA 18064 Office: Lafayette College Dept Fgn Langs and Lits Easton PA 18042

ROSA, PETER MANUEL, higher education researcher, lobbyist; b. N.Y.C., Nov. 22, 1946; s. Pedro and Raquel (Ramirez) R.; m. Pamela Ann Greene, Aug. 10, 1968; children: Kimberly Ann, Peter Martin. BA, Cen. Conn. State U., 1968, MS, 1974; PhD, U. Conn., 1981. Tchr. Bristol (Conn.) Cen. High Sch., 1968-72; admission officer Cen. Conn. State U., New Britain, 1972-83; researcher, lobbyist Conn. Dept. Higher Edn., Hartford, 1983-87; higher edn. lobbyist Conn. State Univ. System, New Britain, 1987—; dean, mem. faculty Nat. Assn. Coll. Admission Counselors, Hampton (Va.) Inst., 1988—. Alderman, asst., majority leader New Britian Common Coun., 1989-91. Nat. Hispanic Leadership fellow N.J. Dept Higher Edn., 1985. Mem. Conn. Assn. Latin Ams. in Higher Edn. (pres. 1983), Nat. Assn. Coll. Admission Counselors. Democrat. Roman Catholic. Home: 154 Lewis Rd New Britain CT 06053-1411 Office: Conn State U PO Box 2008 New Britain CT 06050-2008

ROSAMOND, JOHN BELL, government official; b. West, Miss., Feb. 26, 1936; s. Denton Stribling and Grace Billie (Taylor) R.; m. Clare Mary Tully, July 28, 1968; 1 child, Ann. BS in Fin., Miss. State U., 1958; MBA, Syracuse U., 1970. Sales/pub. rels. staff Std. Life Ins. of the South, Jackson, Miss., 1958-59; commd. 2d lt. U.S. Army, 1959-87, advanced through grades to col., 1981; dep. asst. sec. def. res. affairs Dept. Def., Washington, 1987—. Decorated Legion of Merit, Purple Heart, Bronze Star for valor with 3 oak leaf clusters, Army Commendation medal, Air medal (2), Def. Superior Svc. medal, others. Mem. Assn. U.S. Army, Am. Def. Preparedness Assn., Army Navy Country Club (bd. govs. 1985-87), Omicron Delta Kappa, Delta Sigma Pi. Republican. Roman Catholic. Home: 825 Eden Ct Alexandria VA 22308-2034 Office: Dep Asst Sec Def Res Affairs The Pentagon Washington DC 20301-1500

ROSÀS, JOAN XICOTA, bank executive; b. Granollers, Barcelona, Spain, Mar. 5, 1958; d. Hilari Rosàs Mora and Mercè Xicota Olivé; m. Ma Carme Cañellas, July 27, 1985; children: Núria, Elisabet. JD, U. Barcelona, 1981, postgrad.; M in Internat. Affairs, George Washington U., 1986; cert. in fin. and internat. bus., NYU, 1989. Staff atty. legal dept. Banca Catalana, Barcelona, 1982; pvt. practice Granollers, 1983-84; fulbright trainee Banco de Bilbao, N.Y., 1986-87; mgr. planning and control Banco Bilbao Vizcaya, N.Y., 1987-90; v.p. planning and control Banco Bilbao Vizcaya, 1990—. Fulbright scholar, Madrid, 1984-85. Roman Catholic. Home: 24406 Van Zandt Ave Flushing NY 11362-1155 Office: Banco Bilbao Vizcaya 116 E 55th St New York NY 10022-4501

ROSATI, RICHIE, entertainer, music publishing executive, producer; b. Phila., Nov. 18, 1968; s. Domenic Michael and Joyce Josephine (DiFlorio) R. Student, Phila. Coll. Textiles and Sci., 1986-87. Profl. actor; singer, songwriter, owner, pres. Sunny Boy Music Pub. Div., Phila., 1991—; self mktg. profl., performance dir., self promotion profl., records producer Sunny Boy Music Pub. Div. Composer, pub., producer Fast and Nasty Girl, 1991, When Mama Ain't Watchin, 1992. Mem. ASCAP (writer, pub.). Republican. Roman Catholic. Office: Sunny Boy Mus Pub Div PO Box 18041 Philadelphia PA 19147

ROSATO, PETER CHARLES, special education administrator; b. Newark, Nov. 19, 1948; s. Peter C. and Josephine (Marchese) R.; m. Barbara A. Caruso, May 27, 1973; children: Jeffrey, Kevin. BA, Fairleigh Dickinson, 1970; MA, Montclair State Coll., 1975; PhD, Hofstra U., 1986. Lic. psychologist, N.J.; cert. sch. psychologist, prin. Rehab. counselor N.J. Div. Vocat. Rehab., Newark, 1973-77; personnel psychologist N.J. Dept. Civil Svc., Trenton, 1978; sch. psychologist Passaic County Vocat. Sch., Wayne, N.J., 1978-90; asst. prof. Kean Coll. of N.J., Union, 1989—; asst. dir. Bergen County Tech. Schs., Hackensack, N.J., 1990—; psychologist Achievement Ctr., Florham Park, N.J., 1988—; adj. prof. Coll. of St. Elizabeth, College Station, 1989—. Mem. Am. Psychol. Assn., N.J. Psychol. Assn., Nat. Assn. of Sch. Pscyhologists. Office: Bergen County Tech Schs 200 Hackensack Ave Hackensack NJ 07601-6195

ROSCH, PAUL JOHN, physician, educator; b. Yonkers, N.Y., June 30, 1927; s. Samuel Joseph and Mary (Gang) R.; m. Lorraine Marie Hunt, June 27, 1951; children: David Carl, Jonathan Hunt, Jane Ellen, Michael Edward, Richard Joseph, Donna Marie; m. Marguerite Delamater, Sept. 12, 1972. AB, Brown U., NYU, 1948; MA, NYU, 1950; MD, Albany Med. Coll., 1954. Diplomate Am. Bd. Internal Medicine. Fellow Inst. Exptl. Medicine and Surgery, U. Montreal, Que., Can., 1951; intern, asst. resident in medicine Johns Hopkins Hosp., 1954-56; resident in medicine, then chief dept. metabolism Walter Reed Med. Ctr., 1956-58; physician-in-charge nuclear medicine St. John's Riverside Hosp., Yonkers, 1959, vice chief of staff; chief endocrine clinic St. Joseph's Hosp., 1959, sr. cons. in medicine, 1980—; pres., chmn. Am. Inst. Stress, Yonkers, 1978—, sr. cons. in medicine, 1980—; clin. prof. medicine and psychiatry N.Y. Med. Coll., 1980—; adj. prof. medicine in psychiatry Sch. Medicine, U. Md. from asst. to assoc. editor Health Comm. and Informatics; mem. editorial bd. AMA ARchives Internal Medicine, Folia Clinica Internat.; contbg. editor Creative Living; contbr. articles to profl. jours. Bd. govs. Jewish Community Ctr.; bd. dirs. Family Svc. Soc., Mensana Clinic, 1980—; chmn. bd. Internat. Found. Biosocial Devel. and Human Health, 1980—; mem. adv. bd. Image Inst., 1980—. Capt. AUS, 1956-58. Fellow ACP, Am. Coll. Cardiology, Internat. Acad. Medicine, Am. Coll. Angiology, N.Y. Diabetes Assn.; mem. Westchester Diabetes Assn. (past pres.), Internat. Law Enforcement Stress Assn. (adv. bd. 1980—), Yonkers Acad. Medicine (bd. govs., past pres.), N.Y. Cardiology Soc., Acad. Psychosomatic Medicine, Soc. Behavioral Medicine, N.Y. Acad. Scis., Endocrine Soc., Am. Diabetes Assn., Westchester Soc. Internal Medicine (Past pres.), N.Y. State Soc. Internal Medicine (pres. 1981—), Soc. Nuclear Medicine (bd. dirs.), Am. Fedn. Clin. Rsch., Am. Soc. Internal Medicine, Am. Geriatrics Soc., Elmwood Country Club, Atlantis Country Club, Breakers Golf Club, St. Andrews Golf Club. Address: 124 Park Ave Yonkers NY 10703 also: 221 N Country Club Dr Atlantis FL 33462

ROSCHER, NINA MATHENY, chemistry educator; b. Uniontown, Pa., Dec. 8, 1938; d. Charles Kenneth and Wilma Pauline (Solomon) Matheny; m. David Roscher, Dec. 27, 1964. BS in Chemistry, U. Del., 1960; PhD in Chemistry, Purdue U., 1964. Phys. chemist Nat. Bur. of Standards, 1958-61; rsch. and teaching asst. Purdue U., West Lafayette, Ind., 1960-64, fellow in chemistry, instr. chemistry, 1964-65; instr. U. Tex., Austin, 1965-67; sr. staff chemist Coca-Cola Export Corp., 1967-68; asst. prof. Douglass Coll., Rutgers U., The State U., 1968-74, asst. dean, 1971-74; dir. acad. adminstrn. Am. U., Washington, 1974-76, assoc. prof. chemistry, 1974-79, prof., 1979—, assoc. dean grad. affairs Coll. Arts and Scis., 1976-79, vice-provost acad. svcs., 1979-82, vice provost for acad. affairs, 1982-85, dean faculty affairs, 1981-85; chair chemistry dept. U. Washington, 1991—; program dir. sci. edn., NSF, 1986—; lectr. in field. Contbr. articles to profl. jours. Standard Oil fellow, 1961-62, David Ross fellow, 1963-64, Rutgers U. Rsch. Fund, Biomed. Support grantee. Fellow AAAS, Am. Inst. Chemists (profl. opportunities for women com., pres. dist. inst. chemists 1978-79, sec. 1976-77, fin. com. 1983-87, exec. com., bd. dirs. 1986); mem. Am. Chem. Soc. (treas. Monmouth county sect. 1970-72, chmn. 1974, profl. programs planning and coord. com. 1976-78, adminstrv. com. 1981-89, Gen. Motors scholar 1956-60, Virgil F. Payne award, numerous others), N.Y. Acad. Scis., AAUA, Assn. Women in Sci., Soc. Applied Spectroscopy, Scientific Manpower Commn. Profls. in Sci. a. Home: 10400 Hunter Ridge Dr Oakton VA 22124-1616 Office: Am Univ Dept Chemistry Washington DC 20016-8014

ROSE, ABIGAIL JAYNE, artist, teacher; b. Buffalo, Nov. 25, 1960; d. Howard R. and Marilynn Louis (Jayne) R. BS in Sci., SUNY, Buffalo, 1983; MS in Edn., Nazareth Coll., 1986; student, U. Vt., 1987, Johnson State Coll., 1987. Cert. art tchr., spl. edn. tchr., elem. educator, early essential educator, early childhood educator. Art tchr. Albright Knox Gallery, Buffalo, 1980-81, Bd. Coop. Ednl. Svcs., Fairport, N.Y., 1983-86, Flemming Museum, Burlington, Vt.; art tchr., dir. after sch. program Shelburne (Vt.) Craft Sch., 1990—; tchr. pvt. art lessons, Burlington; tchr. painting and drawing Winooski (Vt. Jr.-Sr. High Sch., 1991. Exhbns. include Vt. Artist Collective, 1990, Famous Pearl St. Gallery, 1989, 90, Woodstock Gallery of Art, 1988, No. Wind Artisans Gallery, 1988; illustrator 3 Santas, 1991. Vol. reader, artist, Fletcher Free Libr., Burlington, 1990—; past bd. dirs. Assn. Retarded Children. Recipient Youth Cares award Gannett, 1979, Outstanding Vol. award ARC, 1974, 86, Reading to Children award Fletcher Free Libr., 1991; scholar Assn. Retarded Children, 1979, 80, Vt. Studio Sch., 1990. Mem. Vt. Coun. Arts. Home: 205 S Prospect St Apt 5 Burlington VT 05401-3547

ROSE, ANITA CARROLL, retired educator; b. New Bedford, Mass., Oct. 14, 1922; d. Louis Arthur and Aline (Chicoine) Carroll; m. Anthony E. Rose, Sept. 24, 1955 (dec.); children: Anthony David, Stephen Arthur. BA, U. Mass., Dartmouth, 1971; MAT, R.I. Coll., 1975. Exec. sec. Berkshire-Hathaway, Inc., New Bedford, 1941-55, New Bedford Cancer Soc., 1956-59;

tchr. French and English New Bedford Pub. Schs., 1971-88; ret., 1988; clk. Frineds of Coastline Elderly Svcs., Inc., 1991—. Pres. New Bedford Jr. Women's Club, 1950-51; v.p. Cath. Women's Club, 1957-59, del. Coun. of Women's Orgns., 1989—; pres. Fairhaven Mothers' Club, 1967-69, book chmn., 1989-91, sunshine chmn., 1991—; mem. Fairhaven Town Mtg., Mass., 1965—; trustee Millicent Libr., Fairhaven, 1980—; rec. sec. Fairhaven Improvement Assn., 1982—; sec. Fairhaven Rep. Town Com., 1980—; bd. dirs. St. Anne Credit Union, New Bedford, 1988—, asst. treas., mem. investment com. 1991—; mem. adv. coun. Coastline Elderly Svc. Inc., 1988-92; del. Mass. Rep. Conv., 1974, 82, 86, 90; mem. YWCA, Old Dartmouth Hist. Assn., Friends of the Zeiterion Theatre. Mem. AAUW (pres. Coll. Club New Bedford Inc. 1983-85, 1st v.p. 1989-91, del. nat. conv. 1981, 83, 85, chmn. nominating com. Mass. div. 1988-90), Tri-County Music Assn. (pres. 1992—, bd. dirs. 1988—), R.I. Coll. Alumni Assn., U. Mass.-Dartmouth Alumni Assn., Southeastern Mass. Assn. Social Studies, Mil. Order of the World Wars, Am. Ex-Prisoners of War, St. Joseph's Couples' Club (pres. 1987-88), Fairhaven Colonial Club (2d v.p. 1988-89). Home: 49 Laurel St Fairhaven MA 02719-2817

ROSE, CHARLES, television journalist. B in History, Duke U., JD; postgrad., NYU. Interviewer Sta. WPIX-TV, N.Y.C., 1972; mng. editor Bill Moyers Internat. Report, from 1974; exec. producer Bill Moyers Jour., from 1975; corr. U.S.A.: People in Politics, PBS, 1976; polit. corr. NBC News, 1976-77; co-host A.M. Chgo., 1978; host The Charlie Rose Show Sta. KXAS-TV, Dallas, Ft. Worth, 1979-81; host nationally syndicated The Charlie Rose Show Sta. WRC-TV, Washington, 1981-83; former host, interviewer CBS News Nightwatch, Washington, from 1984; now host The Charlie Rose Show Sta. WNET-TV, N.Y.C. Producer: (TV program) A Conversation with Jimmy Carter (Peabody award). Office: care WNET The Charlie Rose Show 356 W 58th St New York NY 10019

ROSE, GILBERT JACOB, psychiatrist, writer, psychoanalyst; b. Malden, Mass., May 9, 1923; s. M. Edward and Sara (Freedman) R.; m. Anne Kaufman, Mar. 10, 1946; children: Renee Rose Shield, Daniel Asa, Cecily Rose Itkoff, Aron Dana. AB, Harvard U., 1944; MD, Boston U., 1947. Diplomate Am. Bd. Psychiatry and Neurology. Asst. clin. prof. psychiatry Med. Sch. Yale U., New Haven, 1961-67; assoc. clin. prof. psychiatry Yale U. Med. Sch., New Haven, 1967-83, lectr. in psychiatry Med. Sch., 1983-87; instr. Western New Eng. Psychoanalytic Inst., New Haven, 1970-76; pvt. practice Rowayton, Conn., 1955—. Author: Power of Form: A Psychoanalytic Approach to Aesthetic Form, 1980, Trauma & Mastery in Life & Art, 1987. Capt. USAF, 1953-55. Fellow Am. Psychiat. Assn. (life), Am. Coll. of Psychoanalysts; mem. Am. Psychoanalytic Assn., Yale U. Muriel Gardiner Program for Psychoanalysis and the Humanities. Home and Office: PO Box 215 Norwalk CT 06853-0215

ROSE, GLORIA, gourmet cooking school administrator; b. Englewood, N.J.; d. Roland Harrington and Ethel (Schneider) Shaul; m. Hal Rose, Oct. 22, 1949; children: Hermyne, Barry Paul. BA, Allegheny Coll., Meadville, Pa., 1948; MA, NYU, 1949. Lectr. G. Rose, Antiques, Springfield, N.J., 1963-83; founder, dir. Gourmet Long Life Cooking Sch., Springfield, 1983—; nutritional food cons. Hilton Hotel, Short Hills, N.J., 1990—; cons. Campbell Soup Co., Camden, N.J., 1990, Best Foods Corp., Englewood Cliffs, N.J., 1990; host TV show Enjoying Good Health, 1988-90; pub. monthly newsletter Enjoying Good Health, 1990—. Author: Enjoying Good Health, 1990. Mem. Internat. Assn. Culinary Profls.

ROSE, MARIAN HENRIETTA, physics educator; b. Brussels, Belgium; (parents Am. citizens); m. Simon Rose, Oct. 20, 1948 (dec. Jan. 1981); children: Ann, James, David, Simon. BA, Barnard Coll., 1942; MA, Columbia U., 1944; PhD, Harvard U., 1947. Teaching fellow Harvard U., Cambridge, Mass., 1945-46; adj. asst. prof. Courant Inst., N.Y.C., 1947-48, rsch. assoc., 1951-65, sr. rsch. scientist, 1965-75; vis. fellow Yale U., New Haven, Conn., 1981—; bd. dirs. Minna-James-Heineman Stiftung, Essen, Fed. Republic of Germany. Contbr. articles to profl. jours. Mem. Wetlands Control Commn., Bedford, N.Y., 1991—, Conservation Bd., Bedford, 1989—. Mem. Sieera Club (conservation co-chair Atlantic chpt.), Phi Beta Kappa, Sigma Xi. Home: 9 Old Rd Bedford NY 10506 Office: Yale U Dept Physics 9 Hillhouse Ave New Haven CT 06511-6815

ROSE, MARK, management consultant; b. Missoula, Mont., Apr. 24, 1956; s. Daniel D. and Margaret (LeDoux) R.; m. Nancy Cogdill. BA, U. Mont., 1976. V.p., advt. mgr. Mont. Reconnaissance Project, Inc., Missoula, 1972-78; field coord. Idaho for Ch. Com., Boise, 1978-80; pres. Putnam Valley Retreat Ctr., N.Y.C., 1983-86; account exec. N.Am. Precis Syndicate, N.Y.C., 1981-84, Next West Mgmt., Inc., N.Y.C., 1984-87, Kreisel Co., Inc., N.Y.C., 1987; pres. Mark Rose Mgmt., Inc., N.Y.C., 1987—; bd. mem. Women's Liberation Writing Collective, N.Y.C., 1985—, Women Against Pornography, N.Y.C., 1985—; co-chair West 47th St. Residents' Com., N.Y.C., 1989—. Cons. Friends of Lance Fletcher, N.Y.C., 1986, Fletcher for City Coun., N.Y.C., 1989, Coalition for the Homeless, 1983-85, Camp Homeward Bound, N.Y.C., 1984-85; vol. Baucus for U.S. Senate, Missoula, 1978, Montanans for Safe Power, Missoula, 1976.

ROSE, RAYMOND DAVID, plant manager; b. Buffalo, Oct. 13, 1937; s. David F. and Mae (Potts) R.; m. Carol A. Donovan, May 21, 1960; children: Sharon, Sandra. BA, SUNY, Buffalo, 1960. Cert. protection profl. Security mgr. Eastman Kodak, Rochester, N.Y., 1972-78, plant svcs. mgr., 1978-86, loss prevention dir., 1986-90, Elmgrove property mgr., 1990—; bd. dirs. Asis Found., Washington, 1989—. Sponsor Atkinson project Wharton Sch., 1990-91. Maj. USAF, 1960-72. Mem. Am. Soc. Indsl. Security, U.S. Power Soc., Am. Legion, Nordic Ski Club, C. of C. Republican. Presbyterian. Home: 38 Round Trail Dr Pittsford NY 14534-3222 Office: Kodak Apparatus Div 901 Elmgrove Rd Rochester NY 14653-5505

ROSE, ROBERT LAWRENCE, lawyer, financial services company executive; b. N.Y.C., Mar. 10, 1945; s. Martin and Helen (Diamond) R.; m. Andrea Joan Hoffman, Dec. 27, 1964 (div. June 1972); 1 child, Dawn; m. Julia Frances Knipl, Jan. 2, 1974 (div. Mar. 1991; children—Justin, Adam, Andrew. B.S., Mich. State U., 1966; LL.B., U. Mich., 1969; LL.M. in Taxation, NYU, 1978. Bar: N.Y., Conn., Calif. Assoc. Kindel & Anderson, 1969-72; owner, mgr. Carol's Restaurant, N.Y.C., 1972-74; assoc. gen. counsel Equitable Life Ins. Co., N.Y.C., 1974-77; tax counsel Conn. Gen. Life Ins. Co., Bloomfield, 1977-80, assoc. gen. counsel, 1980-82; chief counsel employee benefits and fin. services CIGNA Corp., Bloomfield, 1982-84, sr. v.p., chief counsel investment group, 1984-89; v.p. corp. acctg. and planning CIGNA Corp., Phila., 1989—. Author: Group Insurance Tax, 1980, Annual Meeting-Annuity Taxation, 1983, Tax Shelters, 1984; editor U. Mich. Law Rev., 1968-69, Duke U. Law Jour., 1978. Mem. Leadership Greater Hartford, 1984, Am. Leadership Forum, 1986. Mem. Am. Council Life Ins. (fin. regulatory policy subcom.), U. Conn. Sch. of Law Ins. Inst. (chmn.), Assn. Life Ins. Counsel, Calif. Bar Assn., Conn. Bar Assn., N.Y. Bar Assn. Home: 735 S 2d St Philadelphia PA 19147 Office: CIGNA Corp 1 Liberty Pl PO Box 7716 1650 Market St Philadelphia PA 19192-1560

ROSE, ROBERT NEAL, brokerage house executive; b. Chgo., Feb. 27, 1951; s. James Allan Rose and Hazel (Gordon) Kaufman; m. Anna Yvette Trujillo, Aug. 23, 1981; children: David James, Michelle Elizabeth, Daniel Jonathan. BS, Georgetown U., 1973; postgrad., U. N.Mex., 1974. Trader Salomon Bros., N.Y.C., 1974-75; regional coord. Latin Am. Merrill Lynch Govt. Securities, N.Y.C., 1975-76; dir. fed. govt. affairs Pub. Service of N.Mex., Albuquerque, 1977-78; exec. dir. Gov. Jerry Apodaca, Washington, 1979-80; expert cons. U.S. Dept. Commerce, Washington, 1980-81; asst. treas. Am. Express Internat. Bank, N.Y.C., 1981-82; sr. v.p. Refco, Inc., N.Y.C., 1982-84; v.p., mgr. Thomson McKinnon Securities, N.Y.C., 1984-88; sr. v.p. Lehman Bros., N.Y.C., 1988-92; mng. dir. Credit Agricole Futures Inc., N.Y.C., 1992—; cons. BDM Corp., McLean, Va., 1981-88, Seminole Tribe of Hollywood, Fla., 1980-81, GFTA Trendanalysen, Feusisberg, Switzerland, 1988-92; mem. exec. com. N.Y. '92, N.Y.C., 1991-92. Mem. Nat. Bus. Coun., Washington, 1980-85, vice-chmn., 1989—; mng. trustee Dem. Nat. Com., 1989—, mem. conv. site selection com., 1989-90, mem. exec. com. N.Y. '92 Host Com., 1991-92; mem. arrangements com. Dem. Conv., San Francisco, 1984; founder Dem. State Treas.'s Assn., Washington, 1984, Nat. Dem. Party Hdqrs., Washington, 1984; exec. com. Nat. Jewish Dem. Coun., 1991, Wexner Heritage Found., N.Y.C., 1992—; governing com. Levitt Pavilion for the Performing Arts, Westport, Conn., 1989-90; mem. Dem. Town Com., Westport, Conn., 1990—. Mem. Delta Sigma Pi, Delta Phi Epsilon. Jewish. Home: 326 Bayberry Ln Westport CT 06880 Office: Credit Agricole Futures Inc 520 Madison Ave New York NY 10022

ROSE, ROSLYN, artist; b. Irvington, N.J., May 28, 1929; d. Mark and Anne Sarah (Green) R.; m. Franklin Blou, Nov. 26, 1950; 1 child, Mark Gordon Blue (dec.). Student, Rutgers U., 1949-51, Pratt Ctr. for Contemporary, Printmaking, N.Y.C., 1967; BS, Skidmore Coll., 1976. Artist. One-person shows include Midday Gallery, Caldwell, N.J., 1972, Caldwell Coll., 1972, Kean Coll., Union, N.J., 1973, Art Corner Gallery, Millburn, N.J., 1974, Brandeis U., Mass., 1974, Newark (N.J.) Mus., 1974, George Frederick Gallery, Rochester, N.Y.,1 981, Robbins Gallery, Washington, 1981, Signatures Gallery, Washington, 1981, Arnot Art Mus., Elmira, N.Y., 1982, Douglas Coll./Rutgers Univ., New Brunswick, 1987, Nathans Gallery, West Paterson, N.J., 1984, 86, 89; exhibited in group shows at Seattle Art Mus., Portland (Oreg.) Mus., NYU U. Small Works Show, Montclair Art Mus., N.J., Middlesex County Mus., Piscataway, N.J., and others; permanent collections include N.J. State Mus., Trenton, Citibank of N.Y., Moscow, N.J., State Libr., Trenton, Roddenbery Meml. Libr., Cairo, Ga., Rosenberg Libr., Galveston, Tex., Newark Mus., Newark Pub. Libr., AT&T, BASF Wyandotte Corp., Canon Calculator Systems, N.Y.C., First Fed. Bank, Rochester, Gulf & Western Industries, Irving Trust Co., N.Y., Kidder, Peabody & Co., N.Y., McAllen Internat. Mus., Tex., Nabisco Brands Corp., East Hanover, N.J., N.J. Bell, Readers Digest Collection, others; creator UNCIF cards, 1979-80. Recipient graphic award Westchester (N.Y.) Art Soc., 1973, Best-in-Show award Livingston (N.J.) Art Assn., 1971, N.J. Ctr. for Visual Arts, Summit, 1969; numerous others. Mem. Nat. Assn. Women Artists (Innovative Painting award 1990), N.Y. Artists Equity, Hoboken (N.J.) Creative Alliance, Associated Artists of N.J. (bd. dirs.). Office: Atelier Rose PO Box 5095 Hoboken NJ 07030-1501

ROSE, VINCENT CELMER, engineering educator, dean; b. Fall River, Mass., July 31, 1930; s. Vincent C. and Esther I. (Peckham) R.; m. Alberta Pauline Therrien; children: James, William, David. BS, U. R.I., 1952, MS, 1958; PhD, U. Mo., 1964. Registered profl. engr., R.I. Dir. pilot plant Lindsay Chem. Co., West Chicago, Ill., 1954-56; grad. asst. U. R.I., Kingston, 1956-58, prof. nuclear and ocean engring., 1963—, assoc. dean, 1971—; grad. asst. U. Mo., Columbia, 1958-63. Bd. dirs. Save the Bay, 1975—; commr. Kingston Water Dist., 1990—; warden Kingston Fire Dist., 1991—; mem. R.I. Atomic Energy Commn., 1980—; mem. R.I. Energy Advisor Commn., 1989—. Sgt. U.S. Army, 1952-54. Mem. North Eastern Assn. Grad. Sch. (sec.-treas. 1987—). Office: U RI Grad Sch Quinn Hall Kingston RI 02881

ROSE, WILLIAM ALLEN, JR., architect; b. Flushing, N.Y., Nov. 26, 1938; s. William Allen and Josephine (Grohe) R.; m. Sandra L. Latham, June 24, 1961; children: Lindsay E., Lesley A. BA cum laude, Harvard U., 1960; MArch, Columbia U., 1964. Architect Rose Beaton Corsbie Dearden & Crowe, N.Y.C. and White Plains, N.Y., 1964-69; ptnr. Rose Beaton & Rose, White Plains, 1969—. Chmn. White Plains Citizens Adv. Com., 1970-73; pres. Hillair Circle Civic Assn., White Plains, 1972-76, Am. Inst. Architects Rsch. Corp., 1980-81; mem. White Plains City Coun., 1974-78, pres., 1976-78; mem. White Plains Urban Renewal Agy., 1988—; bd. dirs. White Plains YMCA, 1970-73, chmn. bd. trustees, 1981-83; bd. govs. YMCA Cen. and No. Westchester, 1983—, vice-chmn., 1983-85, chmn., 1985-87; chmn. bd. mgrs. McBurney Sch., N.Y.C., 1973-76, trustee, 1981-85; trustee Rye Country Day Sch., N.Y., 1981-87; trustee Baldwin League of Ind. Schs., 1986-88; trustee Mercy Coll., 1980—, vice-chmn., 1982-88, chmn. 1988—; bd. dirs. Burke Rehab. Inst., 1979-84, v.p., 1981-84; chmn. Commn. Fed. Procurement of Archtl. and Engring. Svcs., 1983-84; mem. White Plains Urban Renewal Agy., 1988—. Recipient Robert Ross McBurney medal McBurney Sch., 1956; recipient Design award Bell System, 1971, 76, Honor award for Archtl. Excellence L.I. Assn., 1971, 76, award Westchester Easter Seals, 1976, Outstanding Citizenship award United Way White Plains, 1980, World Fellowship award YMCA, 1988. Fellow AIA (pres. chpt. 1975-76, regional dir. 1978-81, nat. v.p. 1982, trustee Polit. Action Com. 1981-82, bursar Coll. of Fellows 1986-88, vice chancellor, 1989, chancellor 1990, Gold medal Westchester chpt. 1983); mem. N.Y. State Assn. Architects (pres. 1977-78, trustee Polit. Action Com. 1981-84, Del Gaudio award 1982, James W. Kideney award 1988), Columbia Archtl. Alumni Assn. (v.p. 1969), Am. Archtl. Found. (regent 1990), St. Andrew's Soc. N.Y., Rotary, New York Athletic Club (N.Y.C.), Harvard of Westchester Club, Sunningdale Golf Club (U.K.), John's Island Club, Winged Foot Golf Club. Republican. Congregationalist. Office: Rose Beaton & Rose 100 First Stamford Pl Stamford CT 06902-6732

ROSEBAUM, PETER ANDREW, biology educator; b. N.Y.C., Sept. 11, 1952; s. Salo Rosenbaum and Selma (Stein) Cohen; m. Robin Edelstein, Sept. 15, 1979; children: Samantha, Sophia. BS, Tulane U., 1974, MS, 1976, PhD, 1980. Instr. Tulane U., New Orleans, 1979-80; rsch. assoc. La. State U. Med. Ctr., New Orleans, 1980-82, asst. prof., 1982-85; asst. prof. SUNY, Oswego, 1985-91, assoc. prof., 1991—. Contbr. articles to profl. jours. Pres., bd. dirs. Rice Creek Assocs., Oswego, N.Y., 1983—. Democrat. Jewish. Home: RR 5 Box 226 Oswego NY 13126-9230 Office: Biology Dept SUNY-Oswego Oswego NY 13126

ROSEBERRY, RICHARD LEE, coast guard officer; b. Davenport, Iowa, Aug. 17, 1953; s. Richard Robert and Billie Dawn (Lebkisher) R.; m. Susan June Bublin, June 23, 1989; children: Virginia Leigh, Dawn Marie. BS in History/Govt., U.S. Coast Guard Acad., 1975; MS in Mgmt. Engring., Rensselaer Poly. Inst., 1981. Commd. ens. USCG, 1975, advanced through grades to lt. comdr., 1986; deck officer USCG, Honolulu, 1975-77, Pearl Harbor, 1977-78; coast guard liasion officer Fleet Tng. Group, Pearl Harbor, 1978-80; asst. indsl. mgr. Support Ctr. Govs. Island, N.Y.C., 1981-84, indsl. mgr., 1988—; afloat ops. officer USCG Seattle, 1984-85; resident Inspector Office, Seattle, 1985-88; flotilla staff officer USCG Aux., Seattle, 1987-88, N.Y.C., 1988—, div. staff officer, 1991. Mem. Inst. Indsl. Engrs., U.S. Naval Inst., U.S. Sailing Assn., Yacht Racing Assn. L.I. Sound, Porsche Club Am., Gov.'s Island Boat Club (commodore 1988-90), N.Y. Yacht Club. Republican. Home: Quarters 944 Apt 1 Governors Island NY 10004-5534 Office: USCG Support Ctr NY Indsl Div Governors Island NY 10004

ROSEBURY, AMY L., psychologist; b. N.Y.C., Feb. 12, 1918; d. Martin J. and Anna (Lock) Loek; m. D. Theodor Rosebury, Nov. 21, 1949 (wid.). BA, NYU, 1938; MA in Psychology, Columbia U., 1939, MSW, 1942. Lic. psychologist, Mass. Pvt. practice N.Y.C., Miami, Amherst, Mass., and others, 1942—. Mem. Amherst Commn. on Middle East Crisis, 1990—; convener Gray Panthers, Amherst, 1988—. Mem. Am. Psychol. Assn., MPS. Office: 48 N Pleasant St Amherst MA 01002-1738

ROSELLE, DAVID PAUL, university administrator, mathematician; b. Vandergrift, Pa., May 30, 1939; s. William John and Esther Suzanne (Clever) R.; m. Louise Helen Dowling, June 19, 1967; children—Arthur Charles, Cynthia Dowling. BS, West Chester State Coll., 1961; PhD, Duke U., 1965. Asst. prof. math. U. Md., College Park, 1965-68; assoc. prof. math. La. State U., Baton Rouge, 1968-73, prof., 1973-74; prof. Va. Poly. Inst. and State U., Blacksburg, 1974—, dean grad. sch., 1979-81, dean research and grad. studies, 1981-83, provost, 1983-87; prof. U. Ky., 1987—, pres., 1987-90; pres. U. Del., 1990—; chmn. commn. on rsch. Va. Poly. Inst. and State U., 1981-83, commn. on grad. studies, 1979-83, commn. on undergrad. studies, 1983-87; pres. COMPA, Inc., Lexington, Mass., 1986—; bd. dirs. Diamond State Telephone Co., Wilmington Trust Corp. Editor: Proc. of the First Louisiana Conf. on Combinatorics, Graph Theory and Computing, 1970, Proc. of the Second Louisiana Conf. on Combinatorics, Graph Theory and Computing, 1971; mem. editorial bd. The Bicentennial Tribute to American Mathematics, 1977; contbr. numerous research articles to profl. jours. Mem. Del. Roundtable, 1990—, Bus./Pub. Edn. Coun., 1990—; trustee Winterthur Mus., 1991—; bd. dirs. Del. Acad. Medicine, 1991—, Med. Ctr. Del., 1991—. Named Outstanding Alumnus West Chester State Coll., 1979; Westinghouse Coop. scholar, 1957; NSF grantee, 1965-75; Teaching Excellence Cert., 1978; Digital Equipment grant, 1984; Nat. Coun. Tchrs. Math. Cert. of Appreciation, 1984; founding fellow of Inst. for Combinatorics and Its Applications, 1990; numerous invited addresses at univs. and profl. soc. meetings. Mem. Am. Math. Soc., Math. Assn. Am. (sec., fin. com., exec. com., com. on publs. 1975-84; com. on spl. funds 1985—; chmn. com. on accreditation 1985; numerous other coms.). Home: 47 Kent Way Newark DE 19711-5201 Office: U Del Hullihen Hall Newark DE 19716

ROSELLINI, ROBERT AMERIGO, psychology educator; b. Lucca, Tuscany, Italy, Oct. 14, 1946; came to U.S., 1958; s. Romeo and Michelina (Petroni) R.; m. Joanne Marie Horwath, June 20, 1970; children: Michael PierLuigi, Anthony Joseph. BS, U. Ill., 1970; PhD, DePaul U., 1974. NIMH postdoctoral fellow Dept. Psychology, U. Pa., Phila., 1974-77; asst. prof. Dept. Psychology, SUNY, Albany, 1977-83, assoc. prof., 1983-88, prof. psychology, 1988—, chairperson, 1989—; dir. Minor in Computing, SUNY, Albany, 1986-89. Author: (with others) Ethoexperimental Analysis of Behavior, 1989, The Psyhology of Learning and Motivation, 1989, Affect, Conditioning, and Cognition: Essays on the determinants of behavior, 1985, Psychopathology: Experimental Models, 1977; contbr. articles to numerous profl. jours. Grantee NIMH, 1978-79, NSF, 1979-82, NIDA, 1989-92; recipient Faculty Rsch. award SUNY, 1985-86. Fellow Am. Psychol. Soc.; mem. AAAS, APA (fellow div. 6),, Ea. Psychol. Assn., Midwestern Psychol. Assn., Psychonomic Soc. Office: Dept Psychology SUNY 1400 Washington Ave Albany NY 12222-0001

ROSEMAN, SUSAN CAROL, textile artist; b. Phila., June 20, 1950; d. Myer and Jeanette Maxine (Lewin) R.; m. James Robert Feehan, Feb. 21, 1985. Student, Art Inst. Pitts., 1967; 5-yr. cert., Pa. Acad. Fine Arts, 1973. Painter, printmaker, Pipersville, Pa., 1973—; sign painter Rose Moon Signs and Design, Pipersville, 1984—; curator Cafe Gallery, Rosemont, N.J., 1986—; textile designer So Fun Inc., Flourtown, Pa., 1991—; lectr. painting William Allen High Sch., Allentown, Pa., 1976; bd. dirs. Open Space Gallery, Allentown, 1980-81; mem. publicity and exhbn. com. Abington Art Ctr., Jenkintown, Pa., 1978-81; curator Gallery at Vineyards, New Hope, Pa., 1990; juror student show Pa. Acad. Fine Arts, Phila., 1990. One woman shows include Moravian Coll., Bethlehem, Pa., 1980, Gallery 500, Elkins Park, Pa., 1981, 20th Century Gallery, Phila., 1983, James A. Michener Art Mus., Doylestown, Pa., 1992; exhibited in group shows at Women in the Arts, William Penn Mus., Harrisburg, Pa., 1981-82, Japan Internat. Artists Soc., Prefectural Mus. of Nara and Chiba, Japan, 1981-82, Nat. Print Exhbn., Trenton (N.J.) State Coll., 1986, Fellowship of the Pa. Acad. of the Fine Arts, Port History Mus., Phila., 1988, Bucks Biennial I, James A. Michener Art Mus., Doylestown, Pa., 1992, others, including permanent collections. Juror Lambertville (N.J.) Shad Festival, 1990. Recipient 2d place award Allentown Art Mus., 1979, Warga award Princeton Art Assn., 1979, Critics Choice award Lehigh Art Alliance, 1983; scholar Pa. Acad. Fine Arts, 1972; fellow Baum Sch. Art, 1980-81. Mem. Woodmere Art Mus., Pa. Acad. Fine Arts Alumni Assn. (co-chmn. exhbns. 1990—, bd. dirs. 1991—). Home and Office: 6588 Groveland Rd Pipersville PA 18947-1402

ROSEN, BERNARD, psychologist, consultant; b. N.Y.C., Feb. 16, 1934; s. Samuel and Lilean Pearl (Bloom) R.; m. Elizabeth Catherine Flynn, Aug. 18, 1963; children: Delores Judith, Sara-Ann. BA in psychology, Bklyn. Coll., 1961; MA in psychology, Columbia U., 1966; PhD in psychology, Hofstra U., 1979. Rsch. psychologist Kings County Hosp. Ctr., Bklyn., 1960-66, rsch. assoc., 1975-77; rsch. assoc. L.I. Jewish - Hillside Med. Ctr., Glen Oaks, N.Y., 1967-77; cons. Kings County Hosp. Ctr., Bklyn., 1977-82; dir. program evaluation Kingsboro Psychiat. Ctr., Bklyn., 1982-91, acting dir. quality assurance, 1987-88, facility info. coord., 1987-91; dir. program evaluation Creedmoor Psychiat. Ctr., Queens Village, N.Y., 1991—; dir. program evaluation Central Islip (N.Y.) Psychiat. Ctr., 1977-82; clin. asst. prof. SUNY Downstate Med. Ctr., Bklyn., 1975-77; lectr. Adelphi U., Garden City, N.Y., 1970-75; cons. League Sch. for Seriously Disturbed Children, N.Y.C., 1967-77; co-project dir. Med. and Health Rsch. Assn., N.Y.C., 1964-66. Contbr. articles to profl. jours.

ROSEN, BERTRAM HOWARD, psychiatrist; b. N.Y.C., Mar. 16, 1933; s. Morris and Tillie (Roseman) R. AB, Cornell U., 1954; MD, Chgo. Med. Sch., 1958. Asst. resident in psychiatry Mt. Sinai Hosp., N.Y.C., 1959-60; resident in adolescent psychiatry Hillside Hosp., Glen Oaks, N.Y., 1960-61; resident in adult psychiatry Hillside Hosp., 1961-62, staff psychiatrist, 1962-65; staff psychiatrist Riverside Hosp., Bronx, 1962-64; attending psychiatrist Mt. Sinai Hosp., N.Y.C., 1962—; sr. instr. Mt. Sinai Med. Sch., 1969—; staff psychiatrist N.Y.C. Bd. Edn., 1964—. Comdr. USN, 1967-69. Fellow N.Y. Acad. Medicine; mem. Soc. for Adolescent Psychiatry (bd. dirs. 1987—), Am. Psychiatric Assn., Med. Soc. N.Y. Office: 4 E 95th St New York NY 10128-0705

ROSEN, CAROL MENDES, artist; b. N.Y.C., Jan. 15, 1933; d. Bram de Sola and Mildred (Bertuch) Mendes; m. Elliot A. Rosen, June 30, 1957. BA, Hunter Coll., 1954; MA, CUNY, 1962. Tchr. art West Orange (N.J.) Pub. Schs., 1959-85; co-curator exhibit Printmaking Coun. N.J., Somerville, 1981, bd. dirs., 1988-90; exhibit curator 14 Sculptors Gallery, N.Y.C., 1988, Collection: NCFA, Smithsonian Instn., Newark Mus., N.J. State Mus. Contbr. articles to arts mags. Fellow N.J. State Coun. on Arts, 1980, 83; recipient Hudson River Mus. award, Yonkers, 1983. Jewish. Home: Beavers Rd RR 3 Box 57 Califon NJ 07830

ROSEN, CHERYL HOPE, graphic designer; b. Worcester, Mass., Nov. 2, 1963; d. Marshall and Marilyn Joyce (Joseph) R. Student, Portland (Maine) Sch. Art, 1981-83; BFA, Clark U., Worcester, 1985. Asst. mgr. Paperback Trader, Portland, 1981-83; intern supr. Greater Media Cable, Worcester, 1984-85; studio mgr. Olan Mills Portrait Studio, Auburn, Mass., 1985-86; divsn. art dir. Sanford Advt., Worcester, 1986-87; graphic designer Palsons, Inc., Worcester, 1987-88; mgr. Sir Speedy Printing Ctr., Shrewsbury/Westborough, Mass., 1988-90; graphic designer Cheryl Rosen Graphic Design, Worcester, 1980-92; sales and mktg. rep. PrintSource, Worcester, 1991-92; owner, designer Designs Unltd., Shrewsbury, Mass., 1992—. Activist Soviet Jewry Day, Washington, 1984, 85. Mem. NAFE, Worcester C. of C., B'nai B'rith Women (sec. 1981-83), Ad Club of Greater Worcester. Office: Designs Unltd 180 Main St Shrewsbury MA 01545

ROSEN, DAVID MICHAEL, university administrator; b. Cambridge, Mass., Mar. 26, 1945; s. Maynard S. and Irma (Leavitt) R.; m. Nina J. Glick, Apr. 8, 1967; children: Michelle, Elisabeth. BA, Boston U., 1967, MS, 1977. Reporter The Day, New London, Conn., 1968-69, Boston Herald, 1969-73; polit. writer UPI, Boston, 1973-76, State House bur. chief, 1976-77; polit. commentator WGBH-TV, Boston, 1975-77; pub. affairs cons. Boston, 1977-79; pub. info. dir. U.S. Commodity Futures Trading Commn., Washington, 1979-80; dir. pub. rels. Harvard U., Cambridge, Mass., 1980-84; assoc. v.p. Harvard U., Cambridge, 1984-85, U. Chgo., 1986-88; v.p. Nicolazzo Assocs., Boston, 1988; chief of staff Office of Lt. Gov., Boston, 1988-89; v.p. Brandeis U., Waltham, Mass., 1989—; cons. U.S. GAO, Wshington, 1977-79, Mass. Ins. Div., Boston, 1977-78, Harvard U., 1977-80; substitute tchr. Boston Pub. Schs., 1967-68. Author: Protest Songs in America, 1977. Home: 28 Arapahoe Rd Newton MA 02165-2203 Office: Brandeis U 415 South St Waltham MA 02154-2700

ROSEN, DONALD JULES, stockbroker; b. Bronx, June 21, 1933; s. Morris and Gertrude (Katz) R.; (div. Jan. 1982); children: Melissa, Jeffrey Alan. BS in Bus. Mgmt., NYU, 1956; MA in Edn., CUNY, 1962, cert., 1966. Tchr. N.Y.C. Bd. of Edn., 1962-74, adminstr., 1974-89; account exec. Churchill Securities, Suffern, N.Y., 1989—; seminarist Churchill Securities, Suffern, 1985—, analyst, 1989—. Author: (coursebook) Motivotional Education, 1977. Organizer Tchrs. and Parents, Bronx, 1974. Mem. Getting It Together (pres. 1983). Office: Churchill Securities 120 Route # 59 Suffern NY 10901

ROSEN, FRANK STANLEY, pest control company executive; b. Phila., Apr. 2, 1937; s. Jacob and Pauline (Cohen) R.; m. Kathleen Rita Morabito, Sept. 10, 1977; children: Donna, Bruce. Cert. running engr. power plant, pest control operator. Plant helper Phila. Electric Co., 1969-71, aux. operator, 1971-75, asst. mech. operator, 1975-90, power plant operator, 1990; pres. Arrest-A-Pest, Inc., Swedesboro, N.J., 1990—; mng. ptnr. Aster Moline Assocs., Swedesboro, 1985—, StarCross Assocs., 1987—. Seaman 1st class USCG, 1955-57, Korea. Republican. Jewish. Home and Office: Arrest-A-Pest Inc 11 Hickory Ln Swedesboro NJ 08085-1431

ROSEN, GEORGE MICHEL, securities trading manager; b. Paris, Sept. 15, 1950; came to U.S., 1990; s. Melvin Stanley and Jeannette (Bosdure) R.; m.

Leticia Larios, Apr. 15, 1956 (div. Feb. 1990); 1 child, Luisa Jeannette. BS, U.S. Internat. U., 1974; MBA, Boston U., 1977. V.p. Smith Barney, Paris, 1978-79; account exec. Shearson Lehman, Paris, 1979-83; br. mgr., dir. Thomson McKinnon, Paris, 1983-85, Prudential Bache, Monte Carlo, Monaco, 1985-86, Shearson Hutton, Monte Carlo, 1986-88, Dominick & Dominick, Monte Carlo, 1989-90, Robert Thomas Securities, N.Y.C., 1990-91; br. mgr. stockbrokers Cantella & Co. Inc., N.Y.C., 1991—. Author (cassette tape) De La Musique Bien Wah, 1989. Home: 333 E 66th St # 1D New York NY 10021 Office: Cantella & Co Inc 20 Exchange Pl New York NY 10005

ROSEN, HARVEY SHELDON, economics educator; b. Chgo., Mar. 29, 1949; s. Edward and Eleanor (Altman) R.; m. Marsha E. Novick, June 20, 1976; children: Lynne, Jonathan. AB, U. Mich., 1970; AM, Harvard U., 1972, PhD, 1974. Asst. prof. Princeton (N.J.) U., 1974-80, assoc. prof., 1980-84, prof., 1984—; dep. asst. sec. U.S. Treasury, 1989-91; vis. fellow Inst. Advanced Studies, Hebrew U., Jerusalem, 1978; vis. scholar Hoover Intsn., Stanford, Calif., 1981. Fellow Econometric Soc.; mem. Phi Beta Kappa. Office: Princeton U Dept Econs Princeton NJ 08544

ROSEN, JAMES CARL, psychology educator; b. L.A., July 30, 1949; s. Robert Bert and Sandra (Brysha) R.; m. Julie Weston, Aug. 22, 1976; children: Emilia, Alexander. AB, U. Calif., Berkeley, 1971; PhD, U. Nev., 1976. Prof. psychology U. Vt., Burlington, 1976—. Contbr. articles to profl. publs. Office: U Vt Dept Psychology Burlington VT 05405-5000

ROSEN, JEFFREY SOLOMON, computer system analyst; b. Bklyn., Oct. 30, 1954; s. Ephraim and Lillian Rosalyn (Altstein) R.; m. Lynne Marie Huber, May 1, 1988; 1 child, Ayla Eve. BS in Biology, SUNY, Albany, 1976; MS in Oceanography, U. R.I., 1983, MS in Stats., 1986. Biologist U.S. EPA, Narragansett, R.I., 1976-82; computer programmer Univ. West Fla., Narragansett, 1982-85; system analyst Computer Scis. Corp., Narragansett, 1985—; cons. stats. Occupational Orthopaedic Systems, Pawtucket, R.I., 1989—; mgr. info. processing Environ. Monitoring Assessment Program Near Coastal, Narragansett, 1990—. Jewish. Office: Computer Scis Corp 27 Tarzwell Dr Narragansett RI 02882-1153

ROSEN, JEFFREY STUART, lawyer; b. Cin., July 18, 1946; s. Louis and Ruth Mae (Hornstein) R.; m. Sara Elaine Brown, May 26, 1974; children: Armin Richard, Louis Marcus. BA, Columbia U., 1968, JD, 1971. Bar: Ohio 1971, D.C. 1976, U.S. Dist. Ct. D.C. 1976, Md. 1976. Trial atty. U.S. Dept. Justice, Washington, 1971-73, SEC, Washington, 1973-76; pvt. practice Washington and College Park, Md., 1976-78; prin. De Martino Finkelstein Rosen & Virga, Washington, 1978—; lectr. Kent-IIT Commodities Law Inst., Chgo., 1982-88. Mem. bd. editors Commodities Law Letter, N.Y.C., 1985—; contbr. articles to profl. jours. Mem. lawyers com. Washington Opera, 1983-87, Silver Spring (Md.) Citizens Adv. Bd., 1978-80; bd. dirs. Mishkan Torah Synagogue, Greenbelt, Md., 1986-87. Mem. ABA (subchmn. adminstrv. proceedings futures com.), Fed. Bar Assn. (litigation chmn. futures regulation com.). Republican. Office: 1818 N St NW Ste 4400 Washington DC 20036-2406

ROSEN, JONATHAN MARTIN, artist; b. N.Y.C., Aug. 20, 1954; s. William and Helen (Martin) R. Student, SUNY, Purchase, 1972-74; BFA in Still Photography, Sch. Visual Arts N.Y.C., 1976. Author: (book of photography) Streets, 1981; represented in one person shows Midtown Photography Gallery, Bronx Mus. Satellite Gallery Program, 1984, 92, Neither Nor Gallery, N.Y.C., 1985, Dance Theater Workshop Gallery, N.Y., 1986, Sea Cliff Photo, 1986, Barry Gordin Gallery, West Village, 1986, Nicholas Roerich Mus., N.Y.C., 1987, Hudson Ctr. Photography, Nyack, N.Y., 1989, Helio Galleries, 1990, Focal Point Gallery, 1990, En Foco Gallery, N.Y.C., 1990, Edn. Testing Svc., Princeton, 1991, Execucom Gallery, Execucom Inc., Austin, 1991, Sarah Lawrence Coll., Bronxville, N.Y., 1992, others; two person shows Hudson Guild, N.Y.C., 1984, Bockley Gallery, Mpls., 1991, others; group shows Bronx Mus., 1984, Ammo Exhbn. Space, 1985, 86, 87, Hudson Ctr. Galleries, 1985, Now Gallery, N.Y.C., 1985, Eastman Wahmendorf Gallery, 1985, N.Y.C. Houston Ctr. Photography, 1986, Bridgewater Gallery, N.Y.C., 1987, 88, Sixtosix Gallery, N.Y.C., 1987, Pompidou Ctr. East, N.Y.C., 1988, Frank Bernarducci Gallery, N.Y.C., 1988, 89, 90, U. Minn., Morris, 1988, Helio Galleries, 1989, Carnegie Mus. Natural History, Pitts., 1990, 91, Cleve. Photographic Workshop, 1990, PepsiCo World Hdqrs. Gallery, Purchase, N.Y., 1991, Roberson Ctr. Arts and Scis., Binghampton, N.Y., 1991, Arnot Art Mus., Elmira, N.Y., 1991, Filmet Image Ctr., 1992 (Spl. Selection Carnegie Mus. show), others; represented in permanent collections including Mus. the City N.Y., Tampa (Fla.) Mus. Art, High Mus. Art, Atlanta, The L.A. County Mus., Picker Art Gallery Colgate U., Arthur Anderson Inc., Chgo., Capitol Corp., Stamford, Conn., Fierstein & Sturman, L.A., Mus. Modern Art, N.Y.C., Art Inst. Chgo., also pvt. collections; cinematographer, screenwriter Out of Space, 1971; dir., camera editor Jane, 1972, Untitled 1976, 1976, Pointless Gesture, 1983 (Best of Shorts award Filmex Film Festival 1983); assoc. producer, dir. cinematography Biblical Ecology, 1978, still photographer (PBS documentaries) The Free Voice of Labor, 1981, The Politics of Cancer, 1981, (NEH documentary) Homosexuality and the Law, 1981. B.R.I.O award Bronx Coun. of the Arts, 1990. Office: PO Box 630216 Bronx NY 10463-9992

ROSEN, LAWRENCE, sociology educator; b. Phila., June 20, 1937; s. Morris and Betty (Wadler) R.; m. Sonja Anne Brown (dec. 1978); children: Lise E., Rachel A.; m. Kathleen Ellen Neilson, Oct. 15, 1980. BS in Chemistry, Drexel U., 1960; MA in Sociology, Temple U., 1963, PhD in Sociology, 1968. Instr. Drexel U., Phila., 1960-63; teaching asst. Temple U., Phila., 1963-65, lectr., 1965-67, assoc. prof. sociology, 1969—; asst. prof. Smith Coll., Northampton, Mass., 1967-69; cons. Lea Assocs., Ambler, Pa., 1973-74, System Sci., Washington, 1972-74, Pa. Gov.'s Justice Commn., PHila., 1971-76, McCann Assocs., Phila., 1979-85. Author: City Life and Delinquency, 1987, The Delinquent and Non-Delinquent in a High Delinquency Area, 1978: editor: A Reader for Research Methods, 1973; editor Sociol. Viewpoints, 1991—; contbr. articles to profl. jours. Mem. Am. Crimilogical Assn. Office: Dept Sociology Temple U Philadelphia PA 19122

ROSEN, MICHAEL JORDON, fundraising firm executive; b. Bristol, Pa., July 1, 1961; s. Bernard S. and Evelyn (Seidman) R.; m. Lisa A. Rosenfeld, May 25, 1986. Student, Temple U., 1979-81. Reporter Jewish Exponent and Times, Phila., 1979-81; reporter and editor The Yardley (Pa.) News, 1981-82; cons. editor The Taft Group, Rockville, Md., 1990-91; pres. The Devel. Ctr. (formerly Telefund Mgmt.), Phila., 1982—; seminar speaker Telemktg. Expos, Developing a Membership Plan of Action, CUNY Devel. Dirs. Meeting, Pa. State Colls. and Univs. Annual Fund Dirs. Meeting, Vt./N.H. NSFRE Chpt. Conf., Assn. Am. Med. Colls. (Western/Midwestern), Resources for Religious Communities, Drexel U. MBA Arts Mgmt. Program, Greater Phila. NSFRE chpt. Contbr. articles to newletters and jours. Mem. Econ. Devel. Task Force, Falls Twp., Pa., 1985; bd. dirs. Phila. Direct Mktg. Telemarketing Coun., 1991—, Friends of Silver Lake Nature Ctr., Bristol, Pa., 1986-92, Phila. Area Repertory Theatre, 1984-86; mem. Congregation Rodeph Shalom, 1982—. Recipient Vol. recognition Friends of Silver Lake Nature Ctr., 1990. Mem. Nat. Soc. Fund-Raising Execs., Alpha Lambda Delta. Jewish. Office: The Devel Ctr 834 Chestnut St Ste 404 Philadelphia PA 19107

ROSEN, MILTON JACQUES, chemical consultant; b. N.Y.C., Feb. 11, 1920; s. Samuel and Fannie (Bernstein) R.; m. Ellen Doree, July 11, 1948; children: Leslie Sara, David Scott, Craig Steven. BS, CCNY, 1939; MS, U. Md., 1941; PhD, Poly. Inst. Bklyn., 1949. Tutor, instr. Bklyn. Coll., 1946-57, asst. prof., 1957-62, assoc. prof., 1962-66, prof. chemistry, 1966—, dir. surfactant rsch. inst., 1987—; vis. prof. in applied chemistry Hebrew U. Jerusalem, 1958-59, 64-65, 71-72, 80; cons. to numerous indsl. cos., including Colgate-Palmolive, Am. Cyanamid, Dow Chem., DuPont, GAF Corp., Marathon Oil, Texaco, and Westvaco; dir. undergrad. rsch. participation program in chemistry Bklyn. Coll., 1963-71, rsch. participation program for coll. tchrs. chemistry, 1970-71; mem. adv. panels NSF, 1960-62, 66, 70. Author: Surfactants and Interfacial Phenomena, 1978, 2d edit., 1989, Systematic Analysis of Surface-Active Agents, 1960, 2d edit., 1972; editor: Surfactants in Emerging Technologies, 1987, Structure/Performance Properties of Surfactants, 1984; assoc. editor: Jour. Am. Oil Chemists Soc., 1981—; editorial bd.: Colloids and Surfaces, 1979-87, Jour. Dispersion Sci. and Tech., 1983—; adv. bd.: Jour. Colloid and Interface Sci., 1990—. Nat. bd. Am. Friends of Lifeline for the Old, U.S., Israel, 1984—; chmn. scientists div. United Jewish Appeal Greater N.Y., 1961-62. With U.S. Army, 1944-46. NSF grantee, 1979-83, 84-85, 85-87, 87-90, 86-89; Pilot Chem. Co. grantee, 1976-78, Vista Chem. Co. grantee, 1984-85, Lever Bros. grantee, 1984-85, Alcon Labs. grantee , 1986-87, GAF grantee, 1987-89, Exxon Rsch. Engrs. grantee, 1988, Dow Chem. Co. grantee, 1989-90, Yamada Sci. Found. grantee, 1979, grantee Nat. Rsch. Coun. and Ministry of Trade and Industry of Israel, 1958-59. Mem. Am. Chem. Soc. (div. colloid and surface sci. 1975—), Am. Oil Chemists Soc. (exec. bd. surfactant and detergent div. 1990—), Sigma Xi (pres. Bklyn. Coll. chpt. 1963-64, treas. 1953-58), Phi Beta Kappa (pres. Bklyn. Coll. chpt. 1974-76, v.p. 1972-74). Jewish. Home: 20 Russell Woods Rd Great Neck NY 11021 Office: Surfactant Rsch Inst Brooklyn Coll City Univ NY Brooklyn NY 11210

ROSEN, MILTON WILLIAM, engineer, physicist; b. Phila., July 25, 1915; s. Abraham and Regina (Weiss) R.; m. Josephine H. Haar, Feb. 28, 1948; children: Nancy Elizabeth, Deborah Anne, Janet Suzanne. B.S. in Elec. Engring., U. Pa., 1937; postgrad., U. Pitts., 1937-38, Calif. Inst. Tech., 1946-47. Engr. Westinghouse Electric & Mfg. Co., 1937-38; engr., physicist Naval Research Lab., Washington, 1940-58; sci. officer Viking rocket Naval Research Lab., 1947-55, head rocket devel. br., 1953-55; tech. dir. Project Vanguard (earth satellite), 1955-58; engr. NASA, 1958-74, chief rocket vehicle devel. programs, 1958-59, asst. dir. for vehicles, 1959-60, dir. launch vehicle and propulsion, 1961-63, sr. scientist office def. affairs, 1963-72, dep. asso. adminstr. for space Sci. (engring.), 1972-74; exec. sec. Space Sci. Bd., Nat. Acad. Scis., Washington, 1974-78, Com. on Impacts Stratospheric Change, 1978-80, Com. on Underground Coal Mine Safety, 1980-83; exec. dir. Space Applications Bd., 1983-85; study leader Inst. for Learning in Retirement Am. U., Washington, 1987—. Author: The Viking Rocket Story, 1955. Chmn. Greater Washington Assn. Unitarian-Universalist Chs., 1966-68. Fellow Am. Rocket Soc. (dir. 1954, James H. Wyld Meml. award for application of rocket power 1954). Unitarian (chmn. trustees 1962-63). Home: 5610 Alta Vista Rd Bethesda MD 20817-3512

ROSEN, ROBERT LEWIS, television executive; b. N.Y.C., Oct. 7, 1935; s. Jules and Irma (Fischl) R.; m. Gloria Rosen, May 10, 1960 (div. 1970); children: Kimberly, Gary; m. Ann Ellen Slutsky, June 17, 1979. BSc, Lehigh U., 1956. Exec. asst. to v.p. United Artists Corp., N.Y.C., 1958-61; pres. RLR Assocs. Ltd., N.Y.C., 1961—; cons. C. Itoh & Co. Ltd., Tokyo, 1984—, PGA of Am., Palm Beach Gardens, Fla., 1988—. Com. mem. sports div. March of Dimes, N.Y.C., 1991; active Youth Suicide Prevention Program, N.Y.C., 1991. With U.S. Army, 1956-58. Recipient Gold award Internat. TV and Film Festival N.Y., 1987. Mem. NATAS (Emmy award 1976), City Athletic Club. Office: RLR Assocs Ltd 7 W 51st St New York NY 10019-6910

ROSEN, ROBERT STEPHEN, theatre arts and English educator; b. N.Y.C., Mar. 20, 1947; s. George Bernard and Elaine Lucille (Lavinsky) R.; m. Mary Patricia Bush; 1 child, David Michael. BA, U. Pitts., 1969, PhD in secondary edn., 1987; MA, California U. of Pa., 1980. Cert. secondary edn. tchr. in English and Speech, N.Y., secondary sch. prin., Pa. Studio dir. WQED-TV, Pitts., 1968-69; tchr. The Village Acad., Bethel Park, Pa., 1969-71; tchr. communication skills, English, humanities, theatre arts Mt. Lebanon (Pa.) Sch. Dist., 1976—; instr. edn. U. Pitts., 1986-89; mem. steering com. for arts Commonwealth of Pa., Pa. State U., 1988. Presenter Pitts. Assn. for Edn. of Young Children, 1988-90, Kennedy Ctr. for Performing Arts, AATE Think Tank on the Future of Theatre and Education, 1990, U. Pitts. Literacy Conf. 1991. Recipient Gift of Time Tributes Am. Family Inst., 1989, 90, First Place award for creativity and excellence for directing Romeo and Juliet, Nat. High Sch. Theatre Contest, 1992. Mem. ASCD, NEA, AFTRA, Am. Alliance Theatre and Edn. (secondary sch. chair for U.S. 1989, 90, 91, rsch. award 1989), Am. Ednl. Rsch. Assn., Inst. Ednl. Rsch. (Spl. Merit award 1989), Pa. Ednl. Rsch. Assn., Pa. Assn. Supervision and Curriculum Devel. (conf. presenter 1991), Phi Delta Kappa. Home: 552 Oxford Blvd Pittsburgh PA 15243-1562 Office: Mt Lebanon Sch Dist 155 Cochran Rd Pittsburgh PA 15228-1381

ROSEN, ROBERT THOMAS, analytical and food chemist; b. Concord, N.H., Nov. 5, 1941; s. Maurice J. and Miriam M. (Miller) R.; m. Sharon Lynne Beres, Apr. 23, 1972. BA (cum laude), Nasson Coll.; PhD, Rutgers U. Sr. rsch. scientist Chem. Rsch. and Devel. Ctr., FMC Corp., Princeton, N.J., 1966-84; program dir. analytical support facilities Ctr. for Advanced Food Technology, Rutgers U., New Brunswick, N.J., 1984—; chmn. North Jersey ACS Mass Spectrometry Topical Group, 1987-88. Assoc. editor The Mass Spec Source, 1988-90; contbr. articles and book reviews to profl. jours. Mem. Am. Soc. for Mass Spectrometry, Am. Chem. Soc., Am. Inst. Chemists, N.Y. Acad. Scis., North Am. Native Fishes Assn., Inst. Food Technologists. Home: Keats Rd # 293 Pottersville NJ 07979-9999 Office: Ctr for Advanced Food Tech Cook Coll Rutgers U New Brunswick NJ 08903

ROSEN, SEYMOUR, educator, author, optician; b. Bklyn., May 11, 1927; s. Louis and Fannie (Goldstein) R.; BA, Bklyn. Coll., 1966, MS, 1971; m. Mildred Jurman, Sept. 11, 1949; children—Dona Ann, Leslie Alan, Gary Frederick. Tchr. sci., mech. and ophthalmic optics Edward B. Shallow Jr. High Sch., Bklyn., 1963-91. Served with USNR, 1945-46. Author: Science Workshop Series, 12 vols., 1977, rev. edit., 1988, 92. Home: 211 Meredith Ln West Hempstead NY 11552-1243

ROSEN, SIDNEY, psychiatrist; b. Detroit, July 14, 1926. MD, U. Western Ontario, London, Can., 1948. Intern Lincoln Hosp., Bronx, N.Y., 1948-49; resident Syracuse (N.Y.) Psychopathic Hosp., 1949-52; coord., chief psychiatrist Community Mental Health Clinics Bklyn., 1955-63; psychiatrist in charge psychiat. svcs. Inst. Rehab. Medicine/NYU, N.Y.C., 1962-82; pvt. practice N.Y.C., 1950—. Author: My Voice Will Go With You: The Teaching Tales of Milton Erickson, 1982. Mem. Am. Psychiat. Assn. (life), N.Y. Milton H. Erickson Soc. Psychotherapy and Hypnosis (founding pres.). Office: 122 E 82nd St New York NY 10028-0822

ROSEN, THEODORE HOWARD, psychologist, human resources consultant; b. Balt., Aug. 25, 1947; s. Jerome and Mary (Schwartz) R.; m. Linda Peller, Oct. 21, 1973; children: Sara Michelle, Julia Diane. BA, George Washington U., 1969, PhD, 1984; MA, Temple U., 1971. Cons. Human Resources Rsch. Orgn., Alexandria, Va., 1972-76; psychologist U.S. Postal Svc., Washington, 1977-78; pers. psychologist U.S. Office of Personnel Mgmt., Washington, 1978-84; cons. CACI Internat., Arlington, Va., 1984-85; cons. indsl. and organizational psychologist Bethesda, Md., 1984—; adj. prof. U. Md. and George Washington U., 1983—. Assoc. editor Pers. Psychology; contbr. articles to profl. jours. Bd. trustees Green Acres Sch., Rockville, Md., 1989—; pres. Sonoma Citizens Assocs., Bethesda, Md., 1991—. Mem. APA, N.E. Ednl. Rsch. Assn., Soc. for Indsl. and Orgnl. Psychology (editorial bd. 1985-92), Pers. Testing Coun. of D.C. (pres. 1981-82), Met. Baseball Umpires Assn.

ROSENAU, JOHN RUDOLPH, engineering educator; b. Sheboygan, Wis., Feb. 25, 1943; s. Rudolph August and Elenora (Schlenvogt) R.; m. Marion Tenney, Aug. 14, 1965; children: Katherine, Paul. BS in Agr., U. Wis., 1965, BSME, 1966; PhD, Mich. State U., 1970. Registered profl. engr. Asst. prof. dept. food sci. U. Minn., St. Paul, 1970-73; assoc. prof. dept. food engring. U. Mass., Amherst, 1973-85, assoc. prof. and dept. head, 1985-87, prof., dept. head, 1987-90; prof. dept. forestry and wildlife mgmt. U. Mass., 1991—; tech. dir. Aqua Futura, Inc., Turners Falls, Mass., 1990-91. Mem. Am. Soc. Agr. Engrs., Am. Inst. Chem. Engrs., Inst. Food Technologists, Am. Fisheries Soc. Democrat. Episcopalian. Home: 127 Columbia Dr Amherst MA 01002-3107 Office: Dept Forestry/Wildlife Mgmt Univ Mass Amherst MA 01003

ROSENBAUM, ARTHUR SAUL, environmental company executive; b. Newark, Nov. 24, 1953; s. Leo and Lillian (Papier) R.; m. Ellen Janet Hertzoff, Aug. 7, 1983; children: Jamie Ann, Daniel Craig, Eric Scott. BS in Geol. Sci., Lehigh U., 1975; postgrad., L.I. U., 1975-76. Geologist Paulus, Sokolowski & Sartor, Warren, N.J., 1979-84, NUS Corp., Edison, N.J., 1984-84; tech. mgr. OH Matls. Corp., Windsor, N.J., 1984-87, CE Environ., Inc., Roseland, N.J., 1987-88; pres. Handex Environ. Mgmt., Morganville, N.J., 1988—; tech. adv. com. B.U.S.T., N.J. Dept. Environ. Protection, Trenton, 1988. Mem. environ. com. Washington Twp., 1988. Mem. Am. Inst. Profl. Geologists. Republican. Jewish. Home: 5 Perry Dr Cranbury NJ 08512-9793 Office: Handex Environ Mgmt 500 Campus Dr Morganville NJ 07751-1296

ROSENBAUM, BELLE SARA, personal property appraiser, interior designer, educator, museum director; b. N.Y.C., Apr. 1, 1923; d. Harry and Hinda (Sits) Heimowitz; m. Jacob H. Rosenbaum, Mar. 12, 1939; children: Linda Zelinger, Simmi Brodie, Martin, Arlene Levene. Cert. N.Y. Sch. Interior Design, 1945. Sr. mem. Am. Soc. Appraisers, Washington, 1979—; tchr./Judaica, Yeshiva U., 1984—; dir. Mus. Comtemporary Judaica; pres. Jarvis Designs, Inc., Union City, N.J., 1955-75, Design Assocs., BLS., Monsey, N.Y., 1970-78; v.p. Lord & Lady Inc., Union City, 1955-70, Cardio-Bionic Scanning, Inc., Spring Valley, N.Y., 1975-78; v.p., treas. Rapitech Systems, Inc., 1985. Author of short stories, 1947-48, Chronicle of Jewish Traditions, 1992; contbr. articles on interior design to profl. jours. Bd. dirs. Migdal Ohr Schs., 1971—; chmn. bd. of artifacts Rockland Holocaust Ctr., 1991—. Named Woman of Valor State of Israel, 1960; ambulance driver North Hudson chpt. ARC during WWII. Mem. Internat. Soc. Artists (founding mem.), Yeshiva of North Jersey Women (hon. pres. 1955); bd. govs. Yeshiva Univ. mus.; mem. N.Y. State Coun. of Judaic Arts and Letters; mem. editorial bd. Light Found. Clubs: Amit Women (pres. 1955-57) (N.J.), AMI Women (treas. 1948-78), Community Synogogue-Monsey (v.p. 1982—). Avocations: collector of art, antiques, Judaica, artist, gardening, communal and charity work.

ROSENBAUM, HOWARD STEWART, podiatrist; b. N.Y.C., Nov. 9, 1949; s. Benjamin andEsther (Cohen) R.; m. Donna Mae Sint, June 10, 1972; children: Elyssa Jill, Jamie Beth. BA cum laude, SUNY, Albany, 1971; DPM cum laude, N.Y. Coll. Podiatric Medicine, 1976. Diplomate Am. Bd. Podiatric Surgery, Am. Bd. Podiatric Orthopedics. Pvt. practice Bergen Podiatry Group, Rutherford, N.J., 1979—, Hillsdale, N.J., 1982—; mem. podiatric residency selection com. Englewood (N.J.) Hosp., 1988—. Active Temple Emmanuel, Woodcliff Lake, N.J. Fellow Am. Coll. Foot Surgeons; mem. Am. Podiatric Med. Assn., N.J. Podiatric Med. Soc. (chmn. no. div. 1986-88, vice-chmn. 1984-86, trustee 1981-84), B'nai B'rith, Psi Chi. Office: 31 Park Ave Rutherford NJ 07070-1795

ROSENBAUM, JOAN HANNAH, museum director; b. Hartford, Conn., Nov. 24, 1942; d. Charles Leon and Lillian (Sharasheff) Grossman; m. Peter S. Rosenbaum, July 1962 (div. 1970). A.A., Hartford Coll. for Women, 1962; B.A., Boston U., 1964; student, Hunter Coll. Grad Sch., 1970-73; cert., Columbia U. Bus. Sch. Inst. Non Profit Mgmt., 1978. Curatorial asst. Mus. Modern Art, N.Y.C., 1966-72; dir. mus. program N.Y. Council on Arts, N.Y.C., 1972-79; cons. Michal Washburn & Assocs., N.Y.C., 1979-80; dir. Jewish Mus., N.Y.C., 1980—; mem. adv. bd. Pub. Ctr., N.Y.C. Bd. dirs. Artists Space, 1980—; officer Council Am. Jewish Mus., 1981—; mem. policy panel Nat. Endowment Arts, 1982-83. Knighted (Denmark) 1983; European travel grantee Internat. Council Mus., 1972. Mem. Am. Assn. Mus. (cons. 1979—), Assn. Art Mus. Dirs., N.Y. State Assn. Mus. (mem. council). Office: Jewish Mus 1865 Broadway # 4 New York NY 10023-7503

ROSENBAUM, SHELDON A., lawyer; b. New Haven, Sept. 20, 1948; s. Norman and Arlene (Evans) R.; m. Zina Abramowitz, Oct. 16, 1988. BA in History, Rutgers U., 1970, JD, 1973. Bar: Conn. 1974, U.S. Dist. Ct. Conn. 1975, U.S. Ct. Appeals (2d cir.) 1980, U.S. Supreme Ct. 1980. Assoc. T.H. Goldstein, P.C., Danbury, Conn., 1974-80; ptnr. Goldstein & Rosenbaum, Danbury, 1990-89, Pinney, Payne, Van Lenten, Burrell, Wolfe and Dillman, P.C., Danbury, 1989—. Bd. dirs. Regional YMCA Western Conn., Danbury and Brookfield, 1977-87, sec., 1987-88, chmn., 1989—; bd. dirs. Regional Hospice Western Conn., Danbury, 1987—. Mem. Conn. Bar Assn., Danbury Conn. Office: Pinney Payne Ban Lenten Burrell Wolfe & Dillman PC 83 Wooster Hts # 3499 Danbury CT 06810-7548

ROSENBAUM, STEVEN IRA, public relations and publishing executive, photographer; b. N.Y.C., Feb. 8, 1946; s. Samuel Meyer and Mary (Slobodow) R.; m. Janet Marilyn Hart, July 12, 1970; children—Elizabeth Jean, Mark Edward. B.S., Rochester Inst. Tech., 1967. Tech. rep. E.I. DuPont de Nemours and Co., Inc., Wilmington, Del., 1967-72; pres. Photog. Pleasures, Inc., Great Neck, N.Y., 1972-75; East coast editor Photog. mag. Petersen Pub. Co., Los Angeles, Calif., 1975-77; account supr. Bozell & Jacobs Advt. Agy., N.Y.C., 1977-80; v.p., assoc. pub. Modern Photography mag. ABC Pub. Co., N.Y.C., 1980-81, v.p., pub. High Fidelity mag., Schwann Record and tape Guides, Mus. Am. Internat. Directory of Performing Arts, 1981-86, v.p. circulation, 1986, v.p., pub., editorial dir. Modern Photography mag., 1986-89; v.p., mgmt. supr. Bozell Inc. Pub. Rels., N.Y.C., 1990—; faculty Winona Sch. Profl. Photography, Winona Lake, Ind., 1972-75. Contbr. articles to profl. jours. Mem. Northport Bay Estates Civic Assn., N.Y., 1971—. Mem. Profl. Photographers Am., Soc. for Imaging Sci. and Tech., Am. Photog. Hist. Soc. (life), Mag. Pubs. Assn., Bay Boat Club. Home: 21 Hawkins Dr Northport NY 11768-1527 Office: Bozell Inc Pub Rels 75 Rockefeller Pla New York NY 10019

ROSENBERG, ALLISON ANNE, psychologist, researcher, policy analyst; b. Bowling Green, Ohio, July 15, 1959; d. B. G. and Peggy Lee (Hull) R. BA summa cum laude, U. Calif., Berkeley, 1981; PhD, Harvard U., 1987. Intramural rsch. fellow NIH, Bethesda, Md., 1987-89; postdoctoral rsch. fellow U. Calif., Berkeley, 1989-90; pub. policy fellow APA, Washington, 1990-91; AAAS congl. sci. fellow U.S. Senate Appropriations Com., Washington, 1991—. Guest editor Am. Psychologist, 1991; contbr. articles to profl. jours. Vol. counselor Women's Refuge, Inc., Berkeley, 1990; project coord. D.C. Cares, Washington, 1990—. G.C. Naumberg fellow Harvard U., 1982-87. Mem. AAAS, APA, Am. Psychol. Soc., Soc. for Rsch. in Child Devel., Soc. for Psychol. Study of Social Issue, Harvard Club of Washington (community svc. steering com. 1990—), Phi Beta Kappa, Sigma Xi. Office: AAAS Directorate Sci Policy Programs 1333 H St NW Washington DC 20005-4707

ROSENBERG, ARTHUR DONALD, writer, systems analyst; b. Spring Valley, N.Y., June 14, 1939; s. Joseph J. and Rose (Shargarofsky) R. BA in Psychology, UCLA, 1961; MA in English and French, U. Grenoble, France, 1968. Mgr. internat. mktg. Internat. Labor Office, Geneva, 1975-77; editor bus. Dun-Donnelley Pub. Co., N.Y.C., 1973-75; asst. mgr. internat. Harcourt Brace Jovanovich, N.Y.C., 1972-73; mktg. mgr. McGraw-Hill Book Co., N.Y.C., 1968-72; translator Organizing Com. Winter Olympics Games, Grenoble, France, 1965-68; instr. English Berlitz Sch., Paris, 1964-65, U. Stockholm, Sweden, 1963-64; pres. A.D.R. Documentation, Inc., Cliffside Pk., N.J., 1977—. Author: The Resume Handbook, 1987, 90, Paper Tiger, 1985, Chess for Children, 1977; contbr. articles to profl. jours. Instr. Chinese Am. Assn. N.Y., 1991. Mem. Authors Guild, Authors League, U.S. Chess Fedn., Cousteau Soc. Home: 250 Gorge Rd Apt 29I Cliffside Park NJ 07010-1313 Office: A D R Documentation Inc 250 Gorge Rd Apt 29I Cliffside Park NJ 07010-1313

ROSENBERG, BARBARA HATCH, molecular biologist, educator; b. N.Y.C., June 26, 1928; d. Arthur William and Evelyn (Schreiber) Hatch; m. John D. Rosenberg, Aug. 25, 1952 (div. 1969); m. Liebe F. Cavalieri, Sept. 5, 1970. BA, Cornell U., 1950, PhD, 1962; MA, Columbia U., 1957. With Meml. Sloan-Kettering Cancer Ctr., N.Y.C., 1962-89; assoc. prof. Cornell Med. Coll., N.Y.C., 1970-85; prof. environ. sci. SUNY, Purchase, 1989—; bd. dirs. Coun. for Responsible Genetics, Boston, 1976—; legis. chmn. Com. on Mil. Use of Biol. Rsch., Boston, 1986—; mem. coun. Fedn. Am. Scientists, 1992—, coord. expert working group on biol. and toxin weapons verification, 1989—. Contbr. articles to profl. jours. Congl. advisor Washington, 1986—; local organizer FREEZE campaign, 1981-86. Am. Cancer Soc. fellow, 1971; INSERM fellow, 1978, 85. Mem. Am. Soc. Biochemistry and Molecular Biology, Sigma Xi. Home: Old Church Ln Pound Ridge NY 10576 Office: SUNY/Purchase Div. Natural Scis Purchase NY 10577

ROSENBERG, CAROLE, art dealer, real estate broker; b. Bklyn., Nov. 16, 1936; d. Hugo and Mildred (Wilinsky) Clemente; m. Jerome A. Halsband; children: Michael S. Halsband, Kenneth L. Halsband; m. Alex J. Rosenberg, May 15, 1977. Student, Hunter Coll., 1954-56; BA, Bklyn. Coll., 1958; postgrad., NYU, 1961-62, 64-65. Tchr. N.Y.C. Sch. System, 1958-59, 61-63, Fla. Sch. System, Miami Beach, 1959-61; gallery owner and dir. Original

Graphics/Carole Halsband Gallery, N.Y.C., 1971-76; assoc. editor Transworld Art Inc., N.Y.C., 1974-78; exec. dir. Alex Rosenberg Gallery/Transworld Art Inc., N.Y.C., 1978-87; exec. dir., v.p. Ardmore Affiliates Ltd., N.Y.C., 1987—; real estate salesperson N.Y.C., 1986-91; real estate broker Carole Rosenberg Properties Internat. Ltd., 1992—; curator Alex Rosenberg Gallery, N.Y.C., 1978-87, Artist Rights Today, N.Y.C., 1976-78; treas. 3/69 Owners Corp., N.Y.C., 1984-87, pres., 1987-91, v.p., 1991—; chmn. bd. dirs. Friends of the Hofstra U. Arboretum, Hempstead, N.Y., 1991—. Editor: (art catalogs) Henry Moore, Howard Kanovitz, Mark Tobey, Lila Katzen, 1975; assoc. editor (portfolio) An American Portrait, 1976—. Com. mem. Friends of Upper East Side Hist. Dist., N.Y.C., 1983—; mem. art com. Lotos Club, N.Y.C., 1989—, chair art com., 1992—. Recipient Spl. Prize for Pub., 7th Internat. Triennial of Colored Prints, Grenchen, Switzerland, 1976, Mgmt. Achievement Award for Innovation, N.Y. Habitat Mag., N.Y.C., 1989. Mem. Real Estate Bd. N.Y.C., Parish Art Mus. (patron garden com.), Met. Mus. Art (sustaining), Whitney Mus. (friend), Mus. Modern Art (contbg.), Nat. Arts Club, Hort. Soc. N.Y., N.Y. Bot. Garden, Lotos Club (art com. 1989-92, chmn. 1992), City Gardens Club, Women's City Club. Democrat. Jewish. Home: 3 E 69th St New York NY 10021-4943

ROSENBERG, CHARLES HARVEY, otorhinolaryngologist; b. N.Y.C., June 10, 1919; s. Morris and Bessie (Greditor) R.; m. Florence Rich, Dec. 27, 1943; children: Kenneth, Ina Garten. BA cum laude, Alfred U., 1941; MD, U. Buffalo, 1944. Intern Jewish Hosp. Bklyn., 1944-45; resident otolaryngology Mt. Sinai Hosp., N.Y.C., 1945-46, 48-50; teaching faculty, sr. clin. asst. Mt. Sinai Hosp. and Med. Sch., N.Y.C., 1950-72; attending surgeon STamford (Conn.) Hosp., St. Joseph's Hosp., 1953—; dir. dept. otolaryngology Stamford Hosp. and St. Joseph's Hosp., 1973-79. Campaign chmn. United Jewish Fedn., Stamford, 1978-81, pres., 1981-83, exec. com. Capt. U.S. Army, 1945-46. Mem. Stamford Med. Soc., Fairfield Med. Soc., Conn. State Med. Soc., AMA, ACP, Am. Bd. Otolaryngology, Am. Acad. Ophthalmology and Otolaryngology. Democrat. Jewish. Home: 304 Erskine Rd Stamford CT 06903 Office: 180 Bedford St Stamford CT 06901

ROSENBERG, DAN, accountant, real estate agent; b. Haifa, Israel, Jan. 5, 1944; s. Peter M. and Rose (Oettinger) R.; m. Alele Nusblat, Aug. 29, 1965; children: Michelle, David J. BA, CUNY Queens Coll., 1974. CPA, N.Y. Supr. Mann Judd Landau, N.Y.C., 1969-79; controller Sam Goody, Inc., Maspeth, N.Y., 1979-82; audit mgr. BDO Seidman, Rockville Ctr., N.Y., 1982-86; controller Todd Products, Brentwood, N.Y., 1986-89; sole practitioner Dan Rosenberg CPA, Northport, N.Y., 1989—. Treas. Bayside Lodge Knights of Pythias, Bayside, N.Y., 1974-79; coach Northport (N.Y.) Youth Ctr. Soccer League, 1983-84. Democrat. Jewish. Home and Office: 11A Oelsner Dr Northport NY 11768-1228

ROSENBERG, DAVID ALAN, military historian, educator; b. N.Y.C., Aug. 30, 1948; s. Sidney and Fay (Breitman) R.; m. Deborah Lee Haines, July 1, 1973; 1 child, Rebecca Haines. BA in History, Am. U., 1970; MA in History, U. Chgo., 1971, PhD in History, 1983. Asst. historian, cons. Lulejian & Assocs., Inc., Falls Church, VA., 1974-75; instr. history U. Wis., Milw., 1976-78; pvt. practice cons., researcher Chgo., Washington, 1978-82; asst. prof. history U. Houston, University Park, 1982-83; sr. fellow Strategic Concepts Devel. Ctr., Nat. Def. U., Washington, 1983-85; prof. strategy and ops. U.S. Naval War Coll., Newport, R.I., 1985-90; assoc. prof. history Temple U., Phila., 1990—; mem. U.S. exec. com. Four Nation Nuclear History Program, project dir. Berlin Crisis, 1989—; cons. Office of Chief Naval Ops., Washington, 1974-78, 85—, Office of Sec. Def., 1990—. Co-editor: (15 vol. book set) U.S. Plans for War, 1945-1950, 1990; contbr. articles to Jour. Am. History (2 awards nat. hist. assns. 1980), 18 others; also book chpts. With USNR, 1982—. Advanced rsch. scholar U.S. Naval War Coll., 1974-79; Ford Found. grantee, 1985-86, MacArthur rsch. grantee, 1987-88; MacArthur fellow, 1988—. Mem. Orgn. Am. Historians (Binkley-Stephenson article prize), Soc. for Historians of Am. Fgn. Rels. (Bernath article prize), Am. Mil. Inst., U.S. Naval Inst., Internat. Inst. for Strategic Studies. Jewish. Office: Temple U Dept History Philadelphia PA 19122

ROSENBERG, FRED ALLAN, microbiology educator; b. Berlin, Germany, Mar. 19, 1932; came to U.S., 1939; s. Adolf and Lotte (Bieber) R.; m. Liane Balter, June 9, 1957; 1 child, Alysa Gail. AB, NYU, 1953; PhD, Rutgers U., 1960. Rsch. assoc. U. Pitts. Grad. Sch. Pub. Health, 1960-61; asst. to full prof. Northeastern U., Boston, 1961—; cons. Ford Found., 1962-63, Foods Rsch. Labs., Boston, 1963-91; adv. com. Bioxy Internat., Ltd., Ft. Worth, 1991—. Contbr. articles to profl. jours. Mem. Mass. Dept. Pub. Health Com. on Water Quality Standards, Boston, 1987-89; U.S. House Reps. subcom. on Bottled Water Standards. With U.S. Army, 1954-56. Recipient rsch. grant Dept. Health & Human Svcs., Sigma Xi, USPHS, 1957-60. Fellow Am. Acad. Microbiology; mem. Am. Soc. Microbiology (pres. northeast br. 1971), Boston Bacteriological Club (dir. 1969-81), Sigma Xi. Office: Northeastern Univ Dept Biology 360 Huntington Ave Boston MA 02115-5096

ROSENBERG, HENRY A., JR., petroleum executive; b. Pitts., Nov. 7, 1929; s. Henry A. and Ruth (Blaustein) R.; children: Henry A. III, Edward Lee, Frank Blaustein; m. Dorothy Lucibello, June 30, 1984. B.A. in Econs., Hobart Coll., 1952. With Crown Cen. Petroleum Corp., Balt., 1952—, pres., 1966-75, chmn. exec. com., 1966—, chmn. bd., 1975—, also chief exec. officer; dir. Am. Trading & Prodn. Corp., USF&G Corp., Signet Banking Corp.; mem. listed co. adv. com. Am. Stock Exchange. Bd. dirs. Johns Hopkins Hosp., Goucher Coll., McDonogh Sch., Nat. Flag Day Found., YMCA Greater Balt., United Way Cen. Md., Crohn's and Colitis Found., Md., Nat. Aquarium Balt.; mem. nat. exec. bd., mem. N.E. regional bd., v.p. program group nat. coun., past pres., exec. bd., adv. coun. Balt. Area coun. Boy Scouts Am.; past chmn., mem. adv. bd. William Donald Schaefer Ctr. for Pub. Policy. Mem. Nat. Petroleum Refiners Assn. (chmn., bd. dirs., exec. com.), Nat. Petroleum Coun., Balt. Area Convention and Visitors Assn. (chmn. bd. dirs.), 25 Yr. Club Petroleum Industry. Office: Crown Cen Petroleum Corp 1 N Charles St PO Box 1168 Baltimore MD 21203

ROSENBERG, JACOB JOSEPH, orthodontist; b. N.Y.C., July 15, 1947; s. Louis and Pearl (Flaster) R.; m. Marylynn Borteck; children: Jonathan, Carolyn, Hilary. BA, U. Vt., 1968; MS, Colo. State U., 1970; DDS with honors, SUNY, Buffalo, 1975; cert. in Orthodontics, Columbia U., 1977. Diplomate Am. Bd. Orthodontics. Practice dentistry specializing in orthodontics Bethesda, Md., 1977—; alumni admission rep. U. Vt. Mem. ADA, Md. State Soc. Orthodontists (pres. 1986-87), Am. Assn. Orthodontists, Am. Bd. Orthodontics (mem. Coll. Diplomates), Orthodontic Edn. of Research Found., Alpha Omega. Office: 4405 E West Hwy Bethesda MD 20814-4522

ROSENBERG, JAMES WILLIAM, marketing executive; b. Boston, Nov. 23, 1958; s. Sumner Harold and Ruth (Sheff) R.; m. Donna Gail Siskind, Oct. 23, 1982; children: Randall Alexandra, Bari Elizabeth. BBA, U. Mass., Amherst, Mass., 1980; MBA, Bentley Coll., Waltham, Mass., 1985. Fin. analyst Raytheon/Telex Data Systems, Norwood, Mass., 1980-85; direct mktg. dir. ISM, Strategic Mktg., Inc., Boston, 1985-92; exec. v.p. mktg. Berenson, Isham & Ptnrs., Boston, 1992—; bd. dirs. Leveathal-Siddman Jewish Community Ctr., Newton, Mass., 1991—; mem. judging com. Direct Mktg. Assn., N.Y., 1989-91; guest speaker Fla. Direct Mktg. Assn., Ft. Lauderdale, 1990. Contbr. articles to profl. jours.; speaker Integrated Direct Mktg. Am. Mktg. Assn., 1989. Mktg. chmn. Leventhal-Siddman Jewish Community Ctr., Newton, Mass., 1989-92. Recipient ECHO award, Direct Mktg. Assn. N.Y., 1989-90; NEDMA award, New England Direct Mktg. Assn., Boston, 1989-90. Mem. Direct Mktg. Assn., New England Direct Mktg. Assn. Office: Berenson Isham & Ptnrs 31 Milk St Boston MA 02109

ROSENBERG, JEROME LAIB, chemist, educator; b. Harrisburg, Pa., June 20, 1921; s. Robert and Mary (Katzman) R.; m. Shoshana Gabriel, Sept. 15, 1946; children—Jonathan, Judith. AB, Dickinson Coll., 1941; MA, Columbia U., 1944, PhD, 1948. Rsch. chemist S.A.M. Labs., 1944-46; Instr. chemistry Columbia U., 1946-48; rsch. assoc., asst. prof. Inst. Radiobiology and Biophysics, U. Chgo., 1950-53; mem. faculty U. Pitts., 1953-91, chmn. dept. biophysics and microbiology, 1976-91, prof. biol. scis., 1976-91, chmn. communication dept., prof. emeritus, 1991—, dean faculty arts and scis., 1970-86, vice provost, 1978-89, chmn. biol. scis., 1989-90, interim chmn. communication, 1991, assoc. dean faculty arts and scis., 1991-92, rsch. integrity officer, 1992—, chmn. communication dept., now prof. emeritus biol. scis., 1991—, acting dir. Jewish studies program, 1991—, rsch. integrity officer, 1992. Author: Photosynthesis, 1965; editor, reviser: Outline Theory and Problems of College Chemistry (Schaum), 1949, 58, 66, 80, 90; contbr. articles to profl. jours. NSF sr. fellow Technion Israel Inst. Tech., 1962-63, AEC fellow U. Chgo., 1948-50; recipient Pitts. award Am. Chem. Soc., 1987. Mem. AAUP (nat. coun. 1968-69, pres. Pa. div. 1968-69). Home: 1029 S Negley Ave Pittsburgh PA 15217-1045

ROSENBERG, JOSEPH LAWRENCE, accountant, consultant; b. Jersey City, Aug. 8, 1949; s. Victor Nathan and Louise (Gorovitz) R.; m. Sima Marian Schiff, June 21, 1981; children: Louis Gene, Mark Bennett, Nina Beth. BS, NYU, 1971. CPA, N.J., N.Y. Staff acct. Weiner & Co., East Orange, N.J., 1971-76; sr. acct. Clarence Rainess & Co., N.Y.C., 1976-78, Goldstein, Golub, Kessler & Co., N.Y.C., 1978-79; mgr. Friedman, Strulowitz & Buren, Livingston, N.J., 1980-82; supr. Main Hurdman, Roseland, N.J., 1982-83; ptnr. Levinston, Schwartz and Co., Livingston, 1985-86; prin. Joseph L. Rosenberg CPA, Livingston and Roseland, 1983-85, 86—; cons. N.J. Small Bus. Devel. Ctr., Newark, 1987—, Kean Coll. Small Bus. Devel. Ctr., 1989—. Treas. N.J. Pops Orch., Livingston, 1982-85, Congregation Agudath Israel West Essex, Caldwell, N.J., 1985-89; cabinet mem. United Jewish Fedn. Metro West, singles, keystone, young leadership divs. East Orange, 1978-86. Mem. AICPA, N.J. Soc. CPAs, Small Bus. Network, Metro Newark C. of C., Morris County C. of C., Bnai Brith. Democrat. Home and Office: 90 Elmwood Dr Livingston NJ 07039-2234

ROSENBERG, LAWRENCE JOSEPH, chiropractic physician, occupational healthconsultant; b. Bronx, N.Y., Dec. 19, 1941; s. Charles and Belle (Dubin) R.; m. Arline Enid Zalko, Aug. 27, 1967; children: Michael Jay, Stephanie Ann, Brad Allen. D in Chiropractic, Chiropractic Inst. N.Y., 1967. Pres. Tri County Chiropractic Assn., Lodi, N.J., 1980—, Nat. Incident Prevention Con., Lodi, 1989—; dir. chiropractic Prucare of No. N.J., Parsippany, N.J., 1989-92. Sgt. N.J. Air NG, 1962-68. Mem. Am. Chiropractic Assn., Internat. Acad. Occupational Health Cons., Am. Acad. Pain Mgmt. Democrat. Jewish. Home: 193 Geranium Ct Paramus NJ 07652-4418 Office: Tri County Chiropractic Asn PO Box 252 Lodi NJ 07644-0252

ROSENBERG, MICHAEL JOSEPH, financial executive; b. Passaic, N.J., Apr. 19, 1928; s. Emanuel and Sylvia Sarah (Schwartz) R.; m. Judith Ann Melnick, Dec. 6, 1964 (div. 1983); children: Ann Kirsten, Emily Jeanne; m. Kathleen Ann Jennings, Mar. 3, 1990. BS, Upsala Coll., 1951; MBA, NYU, 1955, postgrad., 1955-59. Asst. v.p. Meinhard & Co., N.Y.C., 1953-58, A.J. Armstrong Co., N.Y.C., 1958-59, Sterling Nat. Bank, N.Y.C., 1959-61; exec. v.p. Rosenthal & Rosenthal, Inc., N.Y.C., 1961—; bd. dirs. Del Val Fin., N.Y.C. Contbr. numerous articles on comml. fin. to newspapers and mags. Bd. dirs., treas. Town Hall Found., N.Y.C., 1982—; treas. Citizens for Clean Air, N.Y.C., 1984. Capt. U.S. Army, 1951-53, Korea. Decorated Silver Star, Bronze Star; recipient Meritorious Svc. award NYU, 1983; Albert Gallatin fellow, 1981. Mem. Albert Gallatin Assocs. (chmn. 1984-87), NYU Bus. Forum (pres. 1981-82), NYU. Grad. Sch. Bus. Adminstrn. Alumni Assn. (pres. 1978-79, co-chmn. 1987—), NYU Club (pres. 1975-77, 82-85). Office: Rosenthal & Rosenthal Inc 1370 Broadway New York NY 10018-7302

ROSENBERG, MILTON HERTZ, retired chemistry educator; b. N.Y.C., Apr. 16, 1912; s. Julius A. and Rebecca S. (Saltzman) R.; m. Beatrice Nelson, July 1938; children: Carol Ann Rosenberg Marsh, Gerald Nelson. BS, CCNY, 1933, MS in Edn., 1938. Cert. edn. adminstr., N.Y. Sci. tchr. N.Y.C. High Schs., 1935-51, asst. prin., supr. sci. and math., 1951-72; adj. prof. Pace U., Pleasantville, N.Y., 1972-86. Mem. Ret. Chemists Assn., Three Arrows Coop. Soc., Chemistry Tchrs. Club N.Y. Jewish. Home: 185 E 206th St Bronx NY 10458-1124

ROSENBERG, MORTON DAVID, program manager, chemical engineer; b. Bronx, N.Y., Aug. 26, 1929; s. Isaac Erik and Sophie (Bloom) R.; m. Marilyn Ruth Kleiner, May 7, 1952; children: Susan Jean, Kenneth Lee, Joan Miriam. B in Chem. Engring., NYU, 1950. Registered profl. engr., N.Y. Engr. Rose Iron Works, Uniontown, Pa., 1950; chem. engr. Liberty Powder Co., Connelsville, Pa., 1950-51, Stein Davies Co., L.I. City, N.Y., 1952-57; asst. project engr. Thiokol Chem. Corp., Elkton, Md., 1958-84; program mgr. Morton Thiokol Inc., Elkton, 1984-89, Thiokol Corp., Elkton, 1989—. Pres. Arbor Park Civic Assn., Newark, Del., 1970. Capt. C.C., U.S. Army, 1951-52, Korea. Fellow AIAA (assoc., chmn. Del. chpt. 1974-75, sec., treas., v.p., regional activities chmn., Shuttle Flag award 1984, nat. dep. dir. region I membership 1991).

ROSENBERG, PETER DAVID, lawyer, patent examiner, educator; b. N.Y.C., Aug. 2, 1942; s. Frederick and Martha (Grossman) R. BA, NYU, 1962, B in Chem. Engring., 1963; JD, N.Y. Law Sch., 1968; LLM, George Washington U., 1971. Bar: N.Y. 1970, U.S. Ct. Appeals (2d cir.) 1970, U.S. Dist. Ct. (so. and ea. dists.) N.Y. 1971, U.S. Supreme Ct. 1973, U.S. Dist Ct. (no. and we. dists.) N.Y. 1979, U.S. Ct. Appeals D.C. 1982, U.S. Ct. Internat. Trade 1982, U.S. Ct. Mil. Appeals 1982. Examiner U.S. Patent and Trademark Office, Washington, 1968—; assoc. professorial lectr. George Washington U.; Recipient Silver Medal award U.S. Dept. Commerce, 1981. Mem. ABA (antitrust and patent, trademark and copyright sects.). Author: Patent Law Fundamentals, 1975, 2d edit. 1980, rev. 1992, Patent Law Basics, 1992; asst. editor Jour. Patent and Trademark Office Soc.; contbr. articles to profl. jours. Home: 1400 S Joyce St Arlington VA 22202-1872

ROSENBERG, RAYMOND DAVID, educator; b. Jersey City, Apr. 25, 1951; s. Fabulous Sam and Arlene (White) R.; m. JoAnn Gabriella Simchera, June 10, 1984. BA, Boston U., 1974; MEd, William Paterson Coll., 1978. Cert. tchr., N.J. Child care worker Bergen Residential Ctr., Rockleigh, N.J., 1974; substitute tchr. aide South Cliff Elem. Sch., Ft. Lee, N.J., 1975-76; mgr. Betty Gercek Residence, N.Y.C., 1977-78; tchr. Lodi (N.J.) Boy's and Girl's Club Preschool, 1979-80; tchr. reading Passaic County Tech. Vocat. High Sch., Wayne, N.J., 1980-82; specialist learning disabilities North Jersey Devel. Ctr., Totowa, 1983-84, adaptive switch tchr., 1986—; ednl. specialist Div. Devel. Disabilities, Springfield, N.J., 1984-85. Editor: Common Sense Newsletter, 1972. Asst. scoutmaster Boy Scouts Am., Teaneck, N.J., 1980-83. Recipient Eagle Scout award Boy Scouts Am., Ridgefield, N.J., 1968. Mem. Nat. Eagle Scout Assn., Pi Lambda Theta (Beta Chi chpt.). Jewish. Lodge: Order of Arrow. Office: North Jersey Devel Ctr Minnisink Rd Totowa NJ 07512-1928

ROSENBERG, ROBERT ALLEN, psychologist, educator, optometrist; b. Phila., July 31, 1935; s. Theodore Samuel and Dorothy (Bailes) R.; m. Geraldine Bella Tishler, Sept. 3, 1961; children: Lawrence David, Ronald Joseph. BA, Temple U., 1957, MA, 1964; BS, Pa. Coll. Optometry, 1960, OD, 1961. Lic. optometrist, psychologist, Pa. Instr. Pa. Coll. Optometry, Phila., 1962-67, asst. prof., 1962-67; asst. prof. psychology Community Coll. Phila., 1967-76, assoc. prof., 1976—; pvt. practice optometry, Roslyn, Pa., 1965—. Contbr. articles to profl. jours. Named Humanitarian Chapel of Four Chaplains Bapt. Temple, 1980. Fellow Am. Acad. Optometry; mem. Am. Optometric Assn., Pa. Optometric Assn., Bucks-Montgomery Optometric Assn., Alumni Assn. Pa. Coll. Optometry (v.p. 1991—, sec. 1992—). Home: 970 Corn Crib Dr Huntingdon Valley PA 19006-3304 Office: Community Coll Phila 1700 Spring Garden St Philadelphia PA 19130-3991

ROSENBERG, ROBERT CRAIG, software consultant; b. Denver, June 15, 1951; s. Robert Calvin and Barbara Ann (Berkowitch) R.; m. Julia Sue Krekstein, Sept. 24, 1978 (div. May 1988); children: Rebecca Ann, Douglas Allen. BA, U. Pa., 1976. Computer operator Fin. Svcs. Inc., Bala Cynwyd, Pa., 1971-72, Gen. Accident Ins. Co., Phila., 1972-74; programmer United Engrs. & Constructors, Phila., 1974-75; sect. mgr. Computer Scis. Corp., Bryn Athyn, Pa., 1976-81; group mgr. CACI, Inc.-Fed., Ft. Washington, Pa., 1981-83; pres. Nat. Software Clearinghouse, Huntingdon Valley, Pa., 1983; bus. area dir. Keystone Computer Assocs., Ft. Washington, 1983—. Republican. Jewish. Office: Keystone Computer Assocs 1055 Virginia Dr Fort Washington PA 19034

ROSENBERG, RUDY, chemical company executive; b. Charleroi, Belgium, Feb. 26, 1930; came to U.S., 1949, naturalized, 1954; s. Hilaire and Frieda (Friedemann) R.; student in classical studies Atheneum Leon Lepage, Brussels, 1946; m. Rose H. Wauters, Nov. 7, 1953; 1 child, Rudy. Buyer, Lever Bros., Brussels, 1946-49; head Biochem. div. Mann Research Labs., N.Y.C., 1954-61, Gallard-Schlesinger, Carle Place, N.Y., 1961-75; pres. Accurate Chem. & Sci. Corp., Westbury, N.Y., 1975—; prin., v.p., Leeches U.S.A. Ltd. Served with U.S. Army, 1951-53. Mem. Reticuloendothelial Soc. Internat. Democrat. Clubs: Antique Automobile, Rolls Royce, Puppetry Guild Greater N.Y. Home: 68 Custer Ave Williston Park NY 11596-2301 Office: 300 Shames Dr Westbury NY 11590

ROSENBERG, SHIRLEY SIROTA, editor, writer; b. Bklyn.; d. Charles and Donia (Rudoy) Sirota; m. Jerome D. Rosenberg; children: Jonathan, Hindy. BA, Bklyn. Coll. Freelance writer, 1968—; contract writer-editor Dept. HEW, Washington, 1968-72; editor Smithsonian Instn., Washington, 1972-77; instr. George Washington U., 1979—, Georgetown U., Washington, 1979—; editor-in-chief, pres. SSR, Inc., Washington, 1977—; Washington corr. Parents' Mag.; cons. bd. dirs. NSF, Nat. Task Force on Minorities, Women and the Handicapped in Sci. and Engring., Joseph P. Kennedy Inst., Office of Communications, U.S. Holocaust Meml. Coun., Humanities mag. NEH. Author: The First Oil Rush, 1967; contbr. articles to profl. jours. Recipient 1st place award Soc. Tech. Communicators, 1983, Merit award Art Dirs. Club, 1984, Achievement award Soc. Tech. Communicators, 1990. Mem. Am. Soc. Journalists and Authors (former v.p.), Am. Editorial Businesses (v.p., bd. dirs.), Am. Med. Writers Assn., EdPress (v.p., bd. dirs.), Fed. Pubs. Com., Inst. of Diving, Internat. Assn. Bus. Communicators (1st place award 1983), Nat. Assn. Govt. Communicators (1st place award 1981, 2d place award 1990), Nat. Press Club, Women's Nat. Book Assn., Washington Women in Pub. Rels. (former bd. dirs.).

ROSENBERG, STEVEN MARK, behavioral therapist, consultant; b. Phila., Jan. 15, 1947; s. Theodore Samuel and Dorothy (Bailes) R.; 1 child, Jeffrey Scott. BA, Temple U., 1968, MA, 1973; PhD, Southwest U., 1982. Diplomate Acad. Pain Mgmt. Educator Pa. Dept. Edn., Harrisburg; psychotherapist Phila. Flyers Hockey Team; cons. to profl. hockey, golf, baseball, tennis and football players, 1988—. Creater: (no smoking program) Smokebreakers, 1985. Recipient Sealah award Hypnosis Hall of Fame, Blue Bell, Pa., 1991. Fellow Acad. Sci. Hypnotherapy (life); mem. AACD, Am. Bd. Med. Psychotherapy (assoc.), Am. Guild Hypnotherapists, Am. Assn. Nutritional Cons., Am. Bd. Nutritional Cert., Am. Assn. Behavior Therapists, Soc. Behavioral Medicine, Phila. C. of C., Phila Flyers Hockey Club (med. staff 1984-87). Office: 8080 Old York Rd #206 Elkins Park PA 19117

ROSENBERG, VICTOR I., plastic surgeon; b. N.Y.C., Nov. 15, 1936; s. Leonard C. and Sarah G. (Berger) R.; A.B., N.Y.U., 1957; M.D., Chgo. Med. Sch., 1961; m. Deborah Iskoe, Jan. 2, 1966; children—Spencer, Ria. Intern, Beth Israel Hosp., N.Y.C., 1961-62, resident, 1962-63, 64-66; resident Beekman Downtown Hosp., 1963-64, Bronx Mcpl. Hosp., 1966-67, Mt. Sinai Hosp., N.Y.C., 1967-68; practice medicine specializing in plastic surgery, N.Y.C., 1968—; assoc. attending surgeon Beth Israel Hosp., 1968—; assoc. attending surgeon Beekman Downtown Hosp., 1968—, chief plastic surgery, 1976-80, attending surgeon N.Y. Infirmary-Beekman Downtown Hosp., 1980—, dir. cosmetic surgery, 1984—; asst. attending surgeon Mt. Sinai Hosp., N.Y.C., 1968—; asst. clin. prof. Mt. Sinai Sch. Medicine CUNY. Served to comdr. USN, 1968-70. Diplomate Am. Bd. Plastic Surgery. Fellow ACS, Internat. Coll. Surgeons; mem. Am., N.Y. Regional socs. plastic and reconstructive surgeons, Am. Soc. Aesthetic Plastic Surgery, AMA, Am. Cleft Palate Assn., N.Y. Acad. Medicine, N.Y. State, N.Y. County Med. Socs., Pan Am. Med. Assn. (diplomate sect. plastic surgery). Club: Friars, Atrium. Office: 4 Sutton Pl New York NY 10022-3056

ROSENBERG, VICTOR LAURENCE, management and technology consultant, entrepreneur; b. Monroe, La., June 26, 1944; s. Leonard Herman and Gertrude Edna (Mazer) R.; m. Margaret States Miller, Aug. 15, 1965 (div. 1985); children: Michael Jerome, Ambriel States, Shamain Ilya, Arilim Gordon; m. Nina Greever Edwards, Apr. 30, 1988. BS in Engring., MIT, 1966; MS in Engring., Boston U., 1987, DBA in Strategy, 1991. V.p. Chesapeake Life Ins. Co., Balt., 1967-72, pres., 1979-82; program mgr. Xerox Co., Stamford, Conn., 1972-78; chmn. bd. dirs. Datatel, Alexandria, Va., 1978-79, 1978-79; asst. to pres. Atex div. Eastman Kodak, Bedford, Mass., 1982-85; cons. health care Boston U., 1985—; asst. prof. mktg. Keene State Coll., 1991—; founder, pres. Achiya Nursing Tech., Nashua, N.H., 1987—; lectr. Sch. Mgmt. Tech., Boston, 1987—, Northeastern U., U. Lowell; assoc. Ctr. Tech. Planning, 1985—; mgmt. cons. New Eng. Med. Ctr., Boston, 1986-87; vol. mgmt. cons. Roger Williams Hosp., Boston City Hosp., Mass. Gen. Hosp., Hahnemann Hosp.; bd. dirs. McIntyre Cons., 1991—. Contbr. articles to profl. publs. Founding dir. MIT Enterprise Forum of Washington, 1981; curriculum advisor Community Coll. Balt., 1972; active MIT Edn. Council, 1978. Mem. Clowns of Am., Phi Kappa Sigma. Republican. Jewish. Club: MIT of Balt. (pres. 1980-82). Home: 4 Bayberry Ln Framingham MA 01701-3031

ROSENBERG, WARREN, biologist, educator; b. N.Y.C., Nov. 30, 1954; s. Morris and Roslyn (Chalson) R.; m. Rosa Martinez, May 18, 1980; children: Melissa, Jessica, Olivia. BA, Lehman Coll., 1976; MS, NYU, 1979, PhD, 1982. Postdoctoral fellow Mt. Sinai Sch. Medicine, N.Y.C., 1982-83; asst. prof. biology Iona Coll., New Rochelle, N.Y., 1983-87, assoc. prof. biology, 1988—, chmn. biology dept., 1992—; biol. photographer Biol. Photo Svc., Moss Beach, Calif., 1980—; cons. N.Y. State Edn. Dept. Author: End Stage Renal Disease Monograph, 1991; contbr. articles to profl. jours. Trustee Briarcliff (N.Y.) Nursery Sch., 1988-91, exec. bd., 1986-88; adv. bd. No. Westchester Sch. Med. Tech., Mt. Kisco, N.Y., 1989—. Mem. Met. Assn. Coll. Univ. Biologists (pres. 1990—, sec. 1986-90), AAAS, Nat. Assn. Sci. Tech. and Soc. Office: Iona Coll Dept Biology 715 North Ave New Rochelle NY 10801-1890

ROSENBERG, WILLIAM HARRY, insurance company executive; b. Elizabeth, N.J., Dec. 19, 1949; s. Benson and Edith (Krouse) R.; m. Patricia Epstein, June 16, 1974; children: Alexander, Thomas. AB, Harvard Coll., 1971; MHA, U. Mich., 1976. Sr. planner R.I. Dept. of Health, Providence, 1976-79, chief program devel., 1979-81, chief med. care standards, 1981-83; statistical cons. Met. Life Ins., N.Y.C., 1983-84, mgr. health care resources and cost mgmt., 1984-85, dir. health care resource, 1985-87; asst. v.p. Met. Life Ins., Westport, Conn., 1991—; v.p. Corp. Health Strategies subs. Met. Life Ins., Westport, Conn., 1987-90, sr. vp., 1990-91. Trustee Temple B'nai Chaim. Mem. U. Mich. Program in Hosp. Adminstrn. Alumni, Harvard Club. Office: Met Life Ins Co 57 Greens Farms Rd Westport CT 06880

ROSENBLATT, JASON PHILIP, English educator; b. Balt., July 3, 1941; s. Morris D. and Esther (Friedlander) R.; m. Zipporah Marton, June 2, 1964; children: Noah David, Raphael Mark. BA, Yeshiva U., 1963; MA, Brown U., 1966, PhD, 1969. Asst. prof. English U. Pa., Phila., 1968-74; asst. prof. English Georgetown U., Washington, 1974-76, assoc. prof., 1976-83, prof. English, 1983—; vis. lectr. English lit. Swarthmore (Pa.) Coll., 1972-73; cen. exec. com. Folger Inst./Folger Shakespeare Libr., Washington, 1976-88. Co-editor: Not in Heaven: Coherence and Complexity in Biblical Narrative, 1991; contbr. articles to scholarly publs. Guggenheim Found. fellow, 1977-78; NEH fellow, 1990-91. Mem. MLA (del. assembly 1989-91, exec. com. div. religion and lit. 1982-86), Milton Soc. Am. (exec. com. 1977-80, James Holly Hanford award 1988), Milton Seminar, Phi Beta Kappa. Democrat. Jewish. Office: Dept English Georgetown Univ 37th St at O St Washington DC 20057

ROSENBLATT, JULIA CARLSON, journalist, psychology educator; b. Orange, N.J., Dec. 26, 1940; d. Harold S. and Anabel (Alberts) Carlson; m. Albert M. Rosenblatt, Aug. 23, 1970; 1 child, Betsy L. BA, Upsala Coll., East Orange, N.J., 1962; MA, U. Iowa, 1964, PhD, 1965. Postdoctoral fellow Ednl. Testing Svc., Princeton, N.J., 1965-67; asst. prof. psychology Vassar Coll., Poughkeepsie, N.Y., 1967-73; freelance journalist Pleasant Valley, N.Y., 1973—; instr. Mohawk Mountain Ski Sch., Cornwall, Conn., 1983—; bd. dirs. Poughkeepsie Savs. Bank, 1979-88. Co-author: Dining with Sherlock Holmes, 1976, rev., 1990; also articles. Bd. dirs. Dutchess County Assn. Sr. Citizens, Poughkeepsie, 1980-86, Mid-Hudson Civic Ctr., Poughkeepsie, 1982-91, Dorothy Albertson Fund for Little People, Pleasant Valley, 1984—; treas. Ret. Sr. Vol. Program, Poughkeepsie, 1980-81. USPHS fellow, 1962-65. Mem. APA, Eastern Ski Writers Assn., U.S. Ski

Writers Assn. Profl. Ski Instrs. Am. Avocations: photography, skiing. Home and Office: Freedom Rd Pleasant Valley NY 12569

ROSENBLATT, ROBERT JOHN, physician; b. Queens, N.Y., June 2, 1956; s. William and Naomi (Goldstein) R.; m. Frances Brown, June 23, 1991. BA, Queens Coll., 1977; MD, Universita di Roma, 1983. Intership and residency internal medicine Maimonides Med. Ctr., Bklyn., 1983-86; fellow critical care St. Michael's Med. Ctr., Newark, 1986-87; fellow pulmonary medicine Westchester County Med. Ctr., Valhalla, N.Y., 1987-89; pvt. practice Goshen (N.Y.) Med. Assocs., 1989—. Mem. Am. Coll. Physicians (assoc.), Am. Coll. Chest Physicians (affiliate), Am. Thoracic Soc.

ROSENBLATT, SIDNEY MARVIN, mental health services director, educator, psychoanalyst, psychologist; b. N.Y.C., May 24, 1939; s. Louis and Florence (Margolin) R.; m. Penelope Ann Robbins, Aug. 4, 1968; children: Bertram, Maya. BA, CCNY, 1961; MA, Columbia U., 1964, PhD, 1966. Lic. psychologist, N.Y. Intern in counseling psychology VA, 1962-63; rsch. asst. Office of Ednl. Rsch., Sch. of Edn. CCNY, 1964-65; sr. rsch. asst. safety rsch. and edn. project Tchr.'s Coll. Columbia U., N.Y.C., 1965; rsch. assoc. to asst. prof. dept. psychiatry Downstate Med. Ctr. SUNY, 1965-71; assoc. rsch. scientist dept. psychiatry Med. Sch. NYU, N.Y.C., 1971-72; chief psychologist Cath. Charities Guidance Clinic, Bronx, 1973-83; dir. mental health svcs. Lavelle Sch. for the Blind, 1983—; pvt. practice psychotherapist, 1967—; faculty supr., tng. analyst N.Y. Ctr. for Psychoanalytic Tng., 1982—; adj. clin. supr. Ferkauf Grad. Sch. of Psychology, Yeshiva U., 1985—; lectr. in statis. Baruch Sch., CCNY, 1966-68; psychotherapist Community Guidance Svc., 1967-75; cons., evaluator N.Y.C. Bd. of Edn., 1974-78; supr. psychotherpay Washington Sq. Inst. of Psychotherapy and Mental Health, 1976-77; psychol. cons. N.Y. State Div. Disability Determination, 1974—, Comprehensive Counseling Svc., 1986—; staff psychotherapist Arista Clinic, 1989—. Contbr. articles to profl. jours. Home: 755 W End Ave New York NY 10025-6238 Office: LaValle Sch 220th St Paulding Ave Bronx NY 10469

ROSENBLOOM, BERT, marketing educator, consultant, writer; b. Phila., Feb. 2, 1944; s. Max and Dora (Cohen) R.; m. Pearl Friedman, Aug. 18, 1968; children—Jack Alan, Robyn. B.S., Temple U., 1966, M.B.A., 1968, Ph.D., 1974. Instr. mktg. Rider Coll., Trenton, N.J., 1968-72, asst. prof., 1972-74; asst. prof. mktg. Baruch Coll. CUNY, 1974-76; assoc. prof. Drexel U., Phila., 1976-80, prof., 1980-85, G. Behrens Ulrich prof. mktg., 1985—; cons. editor mktg. Random House, N.Y.C., 1977—; cons. in field; mem. bd. dirs. Reality Lnadscaping Corp., 1991—, McKee Real Estate Devel. Corp., 1991—. Author: Marketing Channels, 1978, 3d edit., 1987, Market Functions and the Wholesaler Distribution, 1987, Marketing Channel: A Management View, 4th edit., 1991; Retail Marketing, 1981; editor: Journal of Marketing Channels, 1989—, Jour. Consumer Mktg., Jour. Global Mktg., Jour. Acad. Mktg. Sci.; contbr. articles to profl. jours. Named dist. Erskine fellow U. Canterbury, New Zealand, 1986; recipient outstanding educator award Chapel of Four Chaplains, 1984, rsch. award Distbn. Rsch. and Edn. Found., 1986, rsch. award Direct Selling Found., 1986, 91; Nat. Assn. Wholesaler Distbrs. grantee, 1991; honored as disting. prof Retail Mktg. Inst. of Australia, 1985. Fellow Acad. Mktg. Sci. (bd. govs. 1978-89); mem. Internat. Mgmt. Devel. Assn. (pres.-elect 1992), Am. Mktg. Assn. (v.p. Phila. chpt. 1978-79), Am. Collegiate Retail Assn., Beta Gamma Sigma. Office: Drexel U Sch Bus 32d and Market Sts Philadelphia PA 19104

ROSENBLUM, BERNARD WILLIAM, accountant, controller; b. Queens, N.Y., Mar. 26, 1948; s. Oscar and Sylvia Lee (Kronick) R.; m. Barbara Jean Galloway; 1 child, William P. BBA, U. Mass., 1971. Sales rep. Metro. Life Ins. Co., Northampton, Mass., 1971-73, GE Credit Corp., Weathersfield, Conn., 1973-74, Pitney-Bowes, Springfield, Mass., 1975-77; supr. acctg. Am. Bosch, Springfield, Mass., 1977-80; mgr. inventory acctg. Stanadyne, Inc., Windsor, Conn., 1980-81; mgr. cost acctg. Rexnord, Inc., Springfield, 1981-83; mgr. acctg. HBO & Co., Amherst, Mass., 1983-90; treas. H.B. Smith Co., Westfield, Mass., 1990-91; contr. William E. Wright, West Warren, Mass., 1991—; ind. fin. cons., South Hadley, Mass., 1978—. Chmn. Heart Sunday in South Hadley Am. Heart Assn., Springfield, 1975. Mem. Nat. Assn. Accts. (dir. communications 1982), Hickory Ridge Country Club (bd. dirs., treas. 1989—). Jewish. Home: 32 Westbrook Rd South Hadley MA 01075-2174 Office: William E Wright South St West Warren MA 01092

ROSENBLUM, LEONARD ALLEN, psychiatry educator; b. Bklyn., May 18, 1936; s. Samuel Abraham and Mae (Kotkin) R.; m. Marie Barbara Lopresti, Sept. 9, 1956 (div. Aug. 1988); children: Gianine, Douglas; m. June Machover Reinisch, Sept. 3, 1988. BA, Bklyn. Coll., 1956, MA, 1958; PhD, U. Wis., 1961. From instr. to prof. psychiatry SUNY Health Sci. Ctr., Bklyn., 1961-71, dir. primate behavior lab., 1963—; mem. adv. coun. Vol. Cons. Group, N.Y.C., 1991—; reviewer NIMH, NICHD, NIH, NSF, Washington; mem. adv. bd. new Eng. Regional Primate Rsch. Ctr., Southborough, Mass., 1989—; mem. exec. com. Ctr. for Sexuality and Religion, Phila., 1990—. Editor sci. books. Pres. Internat. Soc. Devel. Psychobiology, 1980. Grantee NIMH, NIH, NSF, Guggenheim Found.; recipient Rsch. Scientist Devel. award NIMH, 1964-71. Home: 1655 Flatbush Ave Brooklyn NY 11210-3276 Office: SUNY Health Sci Ctr 450 Clarkson Ave Brooklyn NY 11203-2098

ROSENBLUM, MARSHALL, architect; b. Newburgh, N.Y., May 25, 1947; s. Hyman and Evelyn L. R.; m. Rita E. Kreyl, Nov. 1984; 1 child, Nathan Louis. BArch, Ill. Inst. Tech., 1970. Registered architect, N.Y., N.J., R.I., Conn., Ill., Nat. Council Archtl. Registration Bds. With E.M. Cohon & Assocs., Chgo., 1970-73, Enviro-Technics, Ltd., Skokie, Ill., 1974; pvt. practice architecture, Newburgh, N.Y., 1975—. Mem. City of Newburgh Archtl. Rev. Commn., 1977-91, City of Newburgh Planning Bd., 1980-91; bd. dirs. Congregation Agudas Israel, Newburgh, 1987-89. Mem. AIA. Republican. Jewish. Club: Rotary (past pres.). Home: 139 Quassaick Ave New Windsor NY 12553-6636 Office: PO Box 2966 Newburgh NY 12550

ROSENBURGH, DWAYNE MAURICE, electronics engineer; b. Balt., Sept. 16, 1960; s. Samuel Boston and Lucille Anita (Hopkins) R.; m. Deborah Francine Muse, Mar. 23, 1985; 1 child, Lauren Stefanie. BS, Morgan State U., 1982; postgrad., Johns Hopkins U., 1989—. Profl. cryptologic engr., Md. Rsch. assoc., physics dept. Morgan State U., Balt., 1982-83; physicist Dept. of Def., Ft. Meade, Md., 1983-85; electronic engr. Dept. of Def., Ft. Meade, 1985—. Contbr. articles to profl. jours. Dep. comdr. for cadets, Civil Air Patrol, USAF Aux., Balt., 1984-86. Mem. IEEE, Internat. Freelance Photographers Orgn., Internat. Platform Assn., Am. Radio Relay League, Dep. Def. Sci. and Engring. Soc., Balt. Coun. on Fgn. Affairs, U.S. Chess Fedn., Mensa. Home: 8027 Greentree Ct Baltimore MD 21227-6106

ROSENFELD, BORIS ABRAMOVICH, mathematician; b. St. Petersburg, Russia, Aug. 30, 1917; came to U.S., 1990; s. Abram Samuilovich and Maria Semenovna (Jessilson) R.; m. Lucy Lvovna Davydova, Apr. 7, 1946; children: Svetlana Katok, Julia Rosenman. Degree in Math., Moscow State U., 1939, PhD, 1942, DSc, 1948. Prof. Azerbaijan State U., Baku, 1950-55; prof., chmn. Kolomna Pedagogical Inst., Moscow region, 1955-64; rsch. prof. Inst. for History of Sci. and Tech., Moscow, 1964-90, Pa. State U., State College, 1990—; adj. prof. Kolomna Pedagogical Inst., 1967-71, Moscow State Pedagogical Inst., 1971-87. Author: (Russian) Non-Euclidean Geometries, 1955, Multidimensional Spaces, 1966, Non-Euclidean Spaces, 1969, History of Non-Euclidean Geometry, 1976, (English) 1988; co-author: (Russian) Mathematicians and Astronomers of Medieval Islam, The Theory of Parallel Lines in the Arabic Literature of the 9-14th Centuries, 1983(Arab), 1989, Scientific Biographies of Khayyam, 1965, Al-Biruni, 1973, Al-Khwarizmi, 1983; contbr. over 350 articles to profl. jours. Sgt. USSR mil., 1944-45. Mem. Internat. Acad. History Sci., Am. Math. Soc., Moscow Math. Soc., History of Sci. Soc. Jewish. Home: 409 Martin Ter State College PA 16803-3426 Office: Pa State U University Park University Park PA 16802-1010

ROSENFELD, JEROLD CHARLES, chemist; b. New Haven, Conn., Apr. 13, 1943; s. Harry and Doris Elaine (Feldman) R.; m. Jane Deanne Berol, Feb. 12, 1967; children: Joanna Eve, Andrew Eric. BA, Clark U., 1965; PhD, Yale U., 1970. Sr. rsch. chemist Occidental Chem. Corp., Grand Island, N.Y., 1970—. Co-author: Encyclopedia of Composites, 1990. Mem. Am. Chem. Soc., Phi Beta Kappa. Jewish. Home: 18 Willow Green Dr Buffalo NY 14228-3420 Office: Occidental Chem Corp 2801 Long Rd Grand Island NY 14072-1244

ROSENFELD, JOSEPH, development corporation executive; b. Medway, Mass., Dec. 3, 1907; s. Abraham and Annie (Candleman) R.; student pub. schs., Milford, Mass. Mgr., Abraham Rosenfeld Sand & Gravel Co., Milford, 1925-32; former owner, operator Rosenfeld Washed Sand & Stone Co., Hopedale, Mass., 1932-85, also concrete plants, Dedham, Plainville, Ashland, Walpole, and Weymouth, Mass., pres. Rosenfeld Devel. Corp., Milford; dir. Milford Water Co., Milford Indsl. Com., 1966; chmn. Milford Indsl. Devel. Commn., 1966-76. Pres., Milford Combined Charities, 1958-59; mem. gifts com. Milford Hosp., 1961, mem. bd. mgrs., trustee; v.p., bd. dirs. Milford Whitinsville Hosp.; hon. chmn. Milford Heart Fund; mem. Milford Town Meeting, 1935-73; mem. men's assocs. Jewish Meml. Hosp., 1969; chmn. Milford area Mass. Assn. for Mental Health, 1967—; sponsor Nat. Jewish Hosp., 1969, Greater Boston Assn. Retarded Children, Milford and Hopedale Little League, Hopedale Women's Softball League, Babe Ruth League; mem. adv. bd. Algonquin council Boy Scouts Am., recipient Disting. Citizen award, 1974; mem. com. Speakers Ann. Charity Ball, 1965-67; mem. Milford Sch. Bldg. Com.; donor bldg. for Rosenfeld Hebrew Sch., Milford; hon. chmn. Milford Area March of Dimes campaign, 1970; Bd. dirs. Worcester chpt. Prevention Cruelty to Children, 1971, Central chpt. Mass. Heart Assn., 1967, Mass. 4-H Found. Recipient citation United Jewish Appeal, 1953, Milford Hebrew Assn., 1958, Milford Kiwanis Club, 1960, Community Service award V.F.W. Post 9373, 1961, citation Trustees Kiwanis-Rotary Pub. Service Trust, Greater Boston Assn. Retarded Children, Inc., Worcester chpt. Milford Heart Fund, 1966; Certificate of appreciation Nat. Found.-March of Dimes, 1968; Community leader of Am. award, 1969; State of Israel award, 1973; other awards. Mem. Asso. Gen. Contractors Am., Mass. Bldg. Congress, Utility Contractors New Eng., Home Builders Assn. Greater Boston, Nat. Assn. Home Builders U.S., Mass. Motor Truck Assn. Inc., Mass. Concrete Inst. (dir.), Milford (dir., mem. exec. bd., Distinguished Service award 1976), Greater Boston chambers commerce, A.I.M. (pres.'s council 1966), Milford Hebrew Assn. (trustee), Art Inst. Boston. Republican. Jewish religion. Lion (charter Milford, pres. 1956-57), Elk; mem. B'nai B'rith (25 year silver honor certificate for humanitarian programs 1961). Clubs: Century; Hopedale Country; Portuguese de Instrucao E Recreio Inc. (Milford) (hon. life mem.; citation 1965); Milford Sons of Italy. Home and Office: 34 Cedar St Milford MA 01757-1642

ROSENFELD, RONALD NORMAN, orthopaedic surgeon; b. Phila.; m. Amy Biener; children, Jonathan, Scott, Carl. AB, Temple U., 1968; DO, Phila. Coll. Osteopathy, 1973; MD, Med. Coll. Pa., 1974. Diplomate Am. Bd. Orthopaedic Surgery. Pvt. practice Haverford Orthopaedic Assocs., Broomall, Pa.; mem. staff Springfield Hosp., pres. med. staff, chief orthopedic svc.; mem. staff Mercy Haverford Hosp., Fitzgerald Mercy Hosp. Office: Haverford Orthopaedic Assoc 590 Reed Rd Ste 7 Broomall PA 19008

ROSENFELD, STEVEN IRA, artistic director, music publisher; b. Bklyn., May 24, 1949; s. Harry Allen and Rosina (DeStefano) R. BA, Southampton Coll., 1971; MFA, St. Francis Coll., Bklyn., 1975. V.p. mktg. JVC, Inc., Maspath, N.Y., 1972-74; dir. Yamaha Internat. Corp., Buena Park, Calif., 1974-75; v.p., gen. mgr. Audio Mktg. Cons., Yorktown, N.Y., 1976-88; pres. World Wide Mgmt., Yorktown, 1970—; dir. Parsec Electronics, Wilmington, Del., 1986-88; mng. dir. Westchester Shakespeare Festival, N.Y.C., 1987-90; dir. The Roger Hendricks Simon Studio, N.Y.C., 1987—. Editor (newspaper) The Windmill, 1968-69. Mem. Audio Engring. Soc. (cert.), Soc. Audio Cons. (cert.), Nat. Trust, Nat. Acad. Rec. Arts and Scis. Jewish. Address: PO Box 599 Yorktown Heights NY 10598

ROSENFIELD, ARTHUR TED, radiology educator; b. Waterbury, Conn., Dec. 7, 1942; s. Harry Nathan and Selina Sylvia (Glasser) R.; m. Nancy Schulkind, May 26, 1968; children: Wendy, Jonathan, Eric. BA cum laude, Brandeis U., 1964; MD, NYU, 1968; MA (hon.), Yale U., 1983. Diplomate Am. Bd. Radiology, Nat. Bd. Med. Examiners. Med. intern Montefiore Hosp., Pitts., 1968-69; instr. in medicine U. Pitts., 1968-69; resident, diagnostic radiology Beth Israel Hosp., Boston, 1971-73, chief resident, radiology, 1973-74; clin. fellow, radiology Harvard Med. Sch., Boston, 1971-74; various to attending radiologist Yale-New Haven Hosp., New Haven, Conn., 1975—; assoc. prof. diagnostic radiology Yale U. Sch. Medicine, New Haven, 1978-83, prof. diagnostic radiology, 1983—, prof. diagnostic radiology and surgery (urology), 1987-92; asst. resident internal medicine USPHS Hosp., Balt, 1969-70; affiliated resident, Armed Forces Inst. of Pathology, Washington, 1972, Children's Hosp. Med. Ctr., Boston, 1973, Tufts U. New Eng. Med. Ctr., Boston, 1973, Mass. Eye and Ear Infirmary, Boston, 1973; attending radiologist VA Hosp. West Haven, Conn., 1976—; cons. Norwalk (Conn.) Hosp., 1979—, The Yale Hereditary Renal Disease Clinic, New Haven, 1991; other. Contbg. author books in field; contbr. numerous articles to profl. jours. Recipient Editor's Recognition awards Radiology, 1986, 87, 90; grantee Squibb Med. Rsch. Found., Winthrop Labs., Gen. Electric Corp., others. Mem. New Eng. Roentgen Ray Soc., Mass. Med. Soc., Yale Soc. Urol. Surgeons, Am. Coll. Radiology, Assn. Univ. Radiologists, Radiol. Soc. N. Am., Am. Inst. Ultrasound in Medicine, Am. Roentgen Ray Soc., Soc. Uroradiology (award-winning paper 1988), Am. Urol Assn. (guest mem.), Sigma Xi. Office: Yale Univ Sch Medicine 300 Cedar St New Haven CT 08510

ROSENHOUSE, IRWIN, artist, designer; b. Chgo.. B.F.A., Cooper Union, N.Y.C., 1950. Designer Mus. Modern Art, 1954-57, Harcourt, Brace & Co., 1957, Dell Books, 1963; tchr. art Mus. Modern Art, 1967-69, Pratt Graphic Center, N.Y.C., 1972, 85, Bklyn. Coll., 1972-73, Bklyn. Mus. Art Sch., 1974, Nassau C.C., 1972-92, N.Y. Tech. Coll., 1983-86; owner Rosenhouse Gallery, N.Y.C., 1963-72; lectr. art, book illustration, design; preparer graphics for Arab-Israeli peace confs.: The Road to Peace, Convocation for Peace, N.Y.C., 1989-90; dir. monthly ednl. lecture series N.Y. Artist Equity, 1989-91. One-man shows N.Y.C., Bklyn., Easthampton, N.Y., Dance Theater Workshop Gallery, N.Y.C., 1992, also various colls. and mus. in U.S.; exhibited in group shows numerous mus., painting socs. exhbns. throughout U.S.; represented in permanent collections Met. Mus., N.Y. Pub. Libr., Everhart Mus., Cooper Union Mus., Bklyn. Coll. Collection; illustrator: (juvenile) Have You Seen Trees?. Served with U.S. Mcht. Marine, 1944-51. Recipient Louis Comfort Tiffany Found. award, 2 Huntington Hartford Found. awards, Billboard Ann. award, Illustrators Club award, 1st prize Rome Collaborative. Address: 256 Mott St New York NY 10012

ROSENHOUSE, MICHAEL ALLAN, editor, writer, lawyer; b. Chgo., Nov. 8, 1946; s. Seymour Samuel and Jeanne Mozette (Rosenthal) R. BA, Yale U., 1968; JD, U. Chgo., 1974. Bar: Ill. 1974, N.Y. 1982. Pvt. practice Chgo., 1974-80; mng. editor Lawyers Coop. Pub. div. Thomson Legal Pub. Inc., Rochester, N.Y., 1980—. Editor: Social Security Law and Practice, 1986-88, Goodrich-Amram - Procedural Rules Service, 1989—; contbg. editor Am. Law Reports, 1980-84, Am. Jurisprudence, 1988—; contbr. articles to legal publs. Active Vol. Legal Svcs. Project, Rochester, 1987—. Lt. (j.g.) USNR, 1968-71. Mem. ABA, Monroe County Bar Assn., Am. Judicature Soc., U. Chgo. Law Sch. Alumni Assn. (bd. dirs. 1977-80). Office: Lawyers Coop Pub div Thomson Legal Pub Inc 50 E Broad St Rochester NY 14694-0001

ROSENKRANZ, GERARDO MIGUEL, business development executive; b. Mexico City, Apr. 13, 1951; s. George and Edith (Stein) R. BSEE, Stanford U., 1972, MSEE, 1973, postgrad., 1977. Mgr., pub. network svcs. Telenet, L.A., 1977-79; dir., internat. systems GTE Telenet, Tysons Corner, Va., 1979-81; v.p., internat. bus. deve. GTE Telenet, Reston, Va., 1985-86; dir. European ops. GTE Telecommunications, Milano, Italy, 1981-85; v.p., internat. messaging U.S. Sprint, N.Y.C., 1986-88; pres., chief exec. officer Ventech Internat., N.Y.C., 1988—; bd. dirs. Pentamex Sa de CV, Mexico, Vencom, Inc., San Francisco; adv. bd. Kyros Corp., Butler, N.J.

ROSENKRANZ, HERBERT S., environmental toxicology educator, cancer researcher; b. Vienna, Sept. 27, 1933; came to U.S., 1948; s. Samuel and Lea Rose (Marilles) R.; m. Deanna Eloise Green, Jan. 27, 1959; children: Pnina Gail, Eli Joshua, Marguerite E., Dara V., Jeremy Emil, Sara C., Naomi, Cynthia. BS, CCNY, 1954; PhD, Cornell U., 1959. Research assoc. biochemistry U. Pa., Phila., 1960-61; asst. prof. microbiology Columbia U., N.Y.C., 1961-65, assoc. prof., 1965-69, prof., 1969-76; prof., chmn. microbiology dept. N.Y. Med. Coll., Valhalla, 1976-81; prof. Case Western Res. U., Cleve., 1981-90, dir. Ctr. Environ. Health Sci., 1981-84, chmn. dept. environ. health sci., 1985-90; prof., chmn. dept. environ. and occupational health U. Pitts., 1990—. Lalor Found. awardee, 1963; Nat. Cancer Inst. Research Career Devel. awardee, 1965-75. Mem. AAAS, Am. Assn. Cancer Research, Am. Soc. Biol. Chemists, Environ. Mutagen Soc., Soc. Toxicology. Jewish. Office: U Pitts Grad Sch Pub Health Dept Environ and Occup Health Pittsburgh PA 15261

ROSENMAN, STANLEY, psychologist; b. N.Y.C., May 29, 1923; s. Sigmund Zanvel and Bryna (Gross) R.; m. Muriel Cecile Zimmerman, 1952; 1 child, Peter. PhD, Harvard U., 1953. Lic. psychologist, N.Y. Psychologist N.Y.C., 1955—. Sgt. inf. AUS, 1945. Mem. APA, Nat. Psychol. Assn. for Psychoanalysis, Internat. Psychohist. Assn. Home and Office: 55 E 86th St New York NY 10028-1059

ROSENMAN, STEPHEN DAVID, physician, obstetrics, gynecology; b. Bklyn., Sept. 4, 1945; s. Bernard and Theresa (Marks) R. m. Arlette de Greet, Dec. 26m 1970; children: Burt, Joelle. BA in Biology, Hofstra U., 1967; MD, Cath. U. of Louvain (Belgium), 1972. Diplomate Am. Bd. Ob-Gyn., voluntarily re-cert. 1991; lic. N.Y., Conn. Rotating intern Dalhousie U., Canada, 1972-73; ob-gyn. resident Bridgeport (Conn.) Hosp., 1973-75, chief resident, 1976-77, sr. attending physician ob-gyn., 1986—; pvt. practice Fairfield, Stratford, Conn., 1978—. Named Tchr. of Yr., Bridgeport (Conn.) Hosp. 1977, '78, '80. Fellow Am. Bd. Obstetrics, Am. Coll. Ob.-Gyn. Office: Obs-gyn of Feld County 1725 Post Rd Fairfield CT 06430 Other: 2499 Main St Stratford CT 06400

ROSENN, HAROLD, lawyer; b. Plains, Pa., Nov. 4, 1917; s. Joseph and Jennie (Wohl) R.; m. Sallyanne Frank, Sept. 19, 1948; 1 child, Frank Scott. BA, U. Mich., 1939, JD, 1941; LLD (hon.), Coll. Misericordia, 1991. Bar: Pa. 1942, U.S. Supreme Ct. 1957. Ptnr. Rosenn & Rosenn, Wilkes Barre, Pa., 1948-54; ptnr. Rosenn, Jenkins & Greenwald, Wilkes Barre, 1954-87, of counsel, 1988—; mem. Pa. State Bd. Law Examiners, 1983—; asst. dist. atty. Luzerne County, Pa., 1952-54; mem. Pa. Gov.'s Justice Commn., 1968-73; mem. Pa. Crime Commn., 1968-73; mem. Fed. Jud. Nominating Com., Pa., 1977-79, Appellate Ct. Nominating Com., Pa., 1979-81; bd. dirs. Franklin 1st Fed. Savs. Bank, Wilkes-Barre, Keystone State Games, Inc. Chmn. ARC, Wilkes Barre, 1958-60; pres. Pa. Council on Crime and Delinquency, Harrisburg, 1969-71; bd. dirs. Coll. Misericordia, Dallas, Pa., 1976-86, Hoyt Library, Kingston, Pa., 1971-78, Nat. Council on Crime and Delinquency, N.Y.C., 1969-71; chmn. United Way Campaign of Wyoming Valley, 1975; pres. United Way, Wyoming Valley, 1978-80. Served to capt. USAAF, 1942-45, ETO. Recipient Erasmus medal Dutch Govt., Disting. Svc. award in Trusteeship, Assn. Governing Bds. Univs. and Colls., 1990; Disting. Community Svc. award Greater Wilkes-Barre Soc. Fellows Anti-Defamation League, 1991, Clara Baron honor award Wyoming Valley chpt. ARC, 1992, Lifetime Achievement award United Way of Wyoming Valley, 1992; honoree Wyoming Valley Interfaith Coun., 1986; named Golden Key Vol. of Yr., United Way of Pa., 1989. Mem. ABA, Pa. Bar Assn., Am. Judicature Soc., The Pa. Soc. Republican. Jewish. Clubs: U. Mich. (N.E. Pa.) (pres. 1946-76), Westmoreland (Wilkes Barre). Lodge: B'nai Brith (pres. Wilkes Barre 1952-53, Community Service award 1976). Home: 29 Hedge Pl Wilkes Barre PA 18704-4716 Office: Rosenn Jenkins & Greenwald 15 S Franklin St Wilkes Barre PA 18711-0075

ROSENN, MAX, federal judge; b. Plains, Pa., Feb. 4, 1910; s. Joseph and Jennie (Wohl) R.; m. Tillie R. Hershkowitz, Mar. 18, 1934; children: Keith S., Daniel Wohl. BA, Cornell U., 1929; LLB, U. Pa., 1932. Bar: Pa. 1932, U.S. Supreme Ct. 1955, Cts. of Philippines 1946. Spl. counsel Pa. Dept. Justice, 1939; asst. dist. atty. Luzerne County, 1942-44; also solicitor various mcpl. boroughs, ptnr. firm Rosenn & Rosenn, 1947-54, Rosenn, Jenkins & Grenwald, Wilkes-Barre, 1954-70; judge U.S. Ct. Appeals (3d cir.), 1970—, now sr. judge; sec. Pa. Dept. of Pub. Welfare, 1966-67; mem. criminal procedure rules com. Supreme Ct. Pa., 1958-85; mem. Pa. Commn. To Revise Pub. Employee Laws, 1968-69; chmn. White House Conf. on Children and Youth. Contbr. articles to legal publs. Mem. Pa. Bd. Pub. Welfare, 1963—; chmn. Pa. Gov.'s Hosp. Study Commn., Pa. Gov.'s Coun. for Human Svcs., 1966-67; mem. exec. bd. Commonwealth of Pa., 1966-67; chmn. Commn. Met. Govt., 1957-58; pres. Property Owners Assn. Luzerne County, 1955-57; chmn. Pa. Human Rels. Commn., 1969-70, Pa. Comm. Children and Youth, 1968-70, Legis. Task Force Structure for Human Svcs., 1970; alt. del. Rep. Nat. Conv., 1964; pres. Wyoming Valley Jewish Com., 1941-42; trustee Wilkes-Barre Jewish Community Ctr.;. Fellow Am. Coll. Trial Lawyers, Internat. Acad. Trial Lawyers; mem. ABA, Pa. Bar Assn., Luzerne County Bar Assn., Am. Law Inst., Am. Soc. Law and Medicine, Am. Judicature Soc., B'nai B'rith (pres. dist. grand lodge 1947-48, life bd. govs., pres. bd. dirs. Anti-Defamation League Pa., W.Va. and Del. 1955-58, nat. commr. 1964—), Westmoreland Club, Masons (33d degree), Alpha Epsilon Pi. Jewish. Office: US Ct Appeals 229 US Courthouse 197 S Main St Wilkes Barre PA 18701-1500

ROSENSAFT, MENACHEM ZWI, lawyer, author, community activist; b. Bergen-Belsen, Germany, May 1, 1948; came to U.S., 1958, naturalized, 1962; s. Josef and Hadassah (Bimko) R.; m. Jean Bloch, Jan. 13, 1974; 1 child, Joana Deborah. BA, MA, Johns Hopkins U., 1971; MA, Columbia U., 1975, JD, 1979. Bar: N.Y. 1980. Adj. lectr. dept. Jewish studies CCNY, 1972-74, professorial fellow, 1974-75; research fellow Am. Law Inst., 1977-78; law clk. to U.S. Dist. Ct. judge (so. dist.), N.Y.C., 1979-81; assoc. Proskauer, Rose, Goetz & Mendelsohn, N.Y.C., 1981-82, Kaye, Scholer, Fierman, Hays & Handler, N.Y.C., 1982-89; v.p., sr. assoc. counsel Chase Manhattan Bank, N.Y.C., 1989—. Author: Moshe Sharett, Statesman of Israel, 1966, Fragments, Past and Future (poetry), 1968, Not Backward to Belligerency, 1969; editor: Bergen Belsen Youth mag., 1965; book rev. editor Columbia Jour. Transnat. Law, 1978-79; co-editor (with Yehuda Bauer) Antisemitism: Threat to Western Civilization, 1988, Survivor's Son, 1990; contbr. to various publs. including N.Y. Times, Newsweek, N.Y. Post, L.A. Times, Internat. Herald Tribune, Jerusalem Post, Liberation, Paris, Davar, Tel Aviv, El Diario, Santiago de Chile, Columbia Human Rights Law Rev., Jewish Social Studies, Leo Baeck Inst. Year Book XXI, Columbia Jour. Environ. Law, (with Michael I. Saltzman) Tax Planning Internat. Rev., Fellowship, Reform Judaism, Midstream, Israel Horizons; subject of profile "Survivor's Son" in Present Tense mag., 1990. Chmn. Internat. Network Children Jewish Holocaust Survivors, 1981-84, founding chmn., 1984; pres. Labor Zionist Alliance, 1988-91; chmn. commn. human rights World Jewish Congress, 1986-91; chmn. exec. com. Am. sect., 1986-90; mem. Gen. Coun. World Zionist Orgn., 1987—; chmn. 2d Generation Adv. Com. U.S. Holocaust Meml. Coun., 1983-87; mem. N.Y.C. Holocaust Meml. Commn., 1982—, chmn. collections com., 1987-89; mem. Am. Zionist Tribunal, 1988-90, chmn., 1990; sec. Am. Zionist Fedn., 1990—; bd. dirs. Am. Jewish Joint Distbn. Com., 1988—, Mercaz, 1991—, N.Y. Met. region United Synagogue of Conservative Judaism, 1992—; organizer, leader demonstration against Pres. Reagan's visit to Bitburg Cemetery and Bergen-Belsen concentration camp, 1985; del. meeting on recognition of Israel between five Am. Jews and reps. of Palestine Liberation Orgn., Stockholm, 1988. Recipient Abraham Joshua Heschel Peace award, 1989, Parker Sch. recognition of achievement with honors in internat. and fgn. law, 1979; Harlan Fiske Stone scholar, 1977-79. Mem. ABA, Assn. Bar City N.Y., Phi Beta Kappa. Home: 179 E 70th St New York NY 10021-5154 Office: Chase Manhattan Bank 1 Chase Manhattan Pla New York NY 10081

ROSENSHINE, ALLEN GILBERT, advertising agency executive; b. N.Y.C., Mar. 14, 1939; s. Aaron and Anna (Zuckerman) R.; m. Suzan Weston-Webb, Aug. 31, 1979; children: Andrew, Jonathan. A.B., Columbia Coll., 1960. Copywriter J.B. Rundle (advt.), N.Y.C., 1962-65; copywriter Batten, Barton, Durstine & Osborn, N.Y.C., 1965, copy supr., 1967, v.p., 1968, asso. creative dir., 1970, sr. v.p., creative dir., 1975-77, exec. v.p., 1977-80, pres., 1980-82, chief exec. officer, 1981-86, chmn., 1983-86, also dir., mem. exec. com.; pres., chief exec. officer BBDO Internat., N.Y.C., 1984-86, also bd. dirs.; pres., chief exec. officer Omnicom Group, N.Y.C., 1986-88; chmn., chief exec. officer BBDO Worldwide, N.Y.C., 1988—; lectr. gen. studies Bklyn. Coll., 1961-65. Office: BBDO Worldwide 1285 Ave Of The Americas New York NY 10019-6028*

ROSENSTEIN, LAURENCE S., pharmacologist, toxicologist; b. Phila., Aug. 19, 1943; s. H. and Rosalyn (Slenn) R.; m. Bernice E. Zevin, June 17, 1964; children: Michael, Judith Anne. BSc, Drexel U., 1964, MSc, 1965; PhD, U. Cin., 1970. Supervising toxicologist EPA, Research Triange Park, N.C., 1972-79; mng. toxicologist EPA, Washington, 1979-85, chief br. chem. infor., 1984-85, chief sci. policy staff, 1985-87, chief br. risk analysis, 1987-90; asst. dir. div. antiviral drugs FDA, Rockville, Md., 1990-92, acting deputy dir. antiviral drugs, 1992—; adj. prof. N.C. State U., Raleigh, 1970-77, U. Miami, Coral Gables, Fla., 1970-77; preclin. dir. U.S. AIDS effort, FDA. Contbr. articles to profl. jours. Asst. dir. N.W. Potomac (Md.) Coalition, 1986-90. USPHS predoctoral fellow, 1965-70. Mem. Am. Coll. Toxicology, Internat. Antiviral Soc., Soc. Toxicology. Home: 10222 Yearling Dr Rockville MD 20850-3548 Office: US FDA 5600 Fishers Ln HFD-530 5600 Fishers Ln Rockville MD 20857-0001

ROSENSTOCK, MORTON, librarian; b. N.Y.C., Feb. 7, 1929; s. Samuel and Frieda (Hut) R.; m. Charlotte Smilon, July 11, 1954; children: Kenneth, Jason. BA, Harvard U., 1949; MA, Columbia U., 1951, MS, 1952, PhD, 1963. Libr. Bklyn. Pub. Libr., 1950-52, Bklyn. Coll., 1952-53, Queens Coll., Flushing, N.Y., 1955-57; chief libr., prof. history Bronx (N.Y.) Community Coll., 1958-66, assoc. dean, 1967-75, acting pres., 1976-77, chief libr., 1979—; dean CUNY, 1977-78; vis. prof. history Columbia U., N.Y.C., 1973-74. Author: Louis Marshall, Defender of Jewish Rights, 1965; contbr. articles to profl. jours. With U.S. Army, 1953-55. Mem. Am. Jewish Hist. Soc. (acad. coun. 1971—), Jewish Hist. Soc. N.Y. Home: 374 Murray Ave Englewood NJ 07631-1421 Office: Bronx Community Coll University Ave Bronx NY 10453-6994

ROSENSTREICH, DAVID LEON, medical educator, immunologist; b. N.Y.C., Nov. 16, 1942; s. Joseph S. and Gertrude (Tankenbaum) R.; m. Victoria Abokrek, June 13, 1965; children: Jonathan, Peter, Rebecca. BS in Chemistry, CCNY, 1963; MD, NYU, 1967. Internship, residency Bronx (N.Y.) Mcpl. Hosp. Ctr., 1967-69; intern, then med. resident Bronx Mcpl. Hosp. Ctr., 1968-69; clin. assoc. NIAID N.I.A.I.D., Bethesda, Md., 1969-72; sr. investigator NIDR, NIH, Bethesda, 1972-78; vis. assoc. prof. Rockefeller U., N.Y.C., 1978-80; prof. medicine Albert Einstein Coll. Medicine, N.Y.C., 1980—, dir. div. allergy and immunology, 1980—. Editor: Mitogens In Immunobiology, 1975, Cellular Functions in Immunity and Inflammation, 1980; assoc. editor Clin. Revs. in Allergy, 1987—. Comdr. USPHS, 1969-78. Fellow Am. Soc. Clin. Investigation, Am. Acad. Allergy and Immunology, Am. Coll. Allergy, Am. Assn. Physicians. Office: Albert Einstein Coll Med 1300 Morris Park Ave Bronx NY 10461-1924

ROSENTHAL, ABIGAIL LAURA, philosopher, educator; b. N.Y.C., Mar. 2, 1937; d. Henry M. and Rachelle (Tchernowitz) R. AB, Barnard Coll., 1958; MA, Columbia U., 1962; PhD, Penn State U., 1968. Grad. asst. dept. religion Columbia U., N.Y.C., 1960-61, sec. seminar on hermeneutics, 1960-61; teaching asst. dept. philosophy Penn State U., Univ. Park, Pa., 1962-64; editorial cons. various publishers, N.Y.C., 1967-80; asst. prof. philosophy SUNY, Stony Brook, 1968-71, Bklyn. Coll. of CUNY, N.Y.C., 1971-85; rsch. affiliate dept. traditional and modern philosophy U. Sydney, Australia, 1982-83; assoc. prof. philosophy Bklyn. Coll. of CUNY, 1986-88, prof. philosophy, 1989—. Author: A Good Look at Evil, 1987; editor: The Consolations of Philosophy, 1989; contbr. numerous articles to profl. jours. Named Fulbright scholar U.S. Govt., 1958-59. Office: Bklyn Coll of CUNY Dept of Philosophy Brooklyn NY 11210

ROSENTHAL, ARNOLD JOSEPH, chemical research and development consultant; b. N.Y.C., July 9, 1922; s. Morris R. and Evelyn (Wallach) R.; m. Dorothy Shaw, Feb. 9, 1947; children: Lawrence, Martin, Alan, Barbara. BS, CCNY, 1941; PhD, Poly. Inst., Bklyn., 1958. Rsch. chemist Celanese Corp., Cumberland, Md., 1941-46, Summit, N.J., 1946-82; pub., editor Exec. Sci. Inst., Inc., Whippany, N.J., 1955-87; cons. ESI Assocs., Whippany, 1987—; cons. to chem. and process industries, 1982—. Editor: Quality Control Yearbook, 1956-87, Operations Research Yearbook, 1961-87. 1st lt. AUS, 1944-46. Mem. IEEE, Am. Chem. Soc., Am. Soc. Quality Control, Am. Stats. Assn., Ops. Rsch. Soc. Am., Fiber Soc., Tech. Assn. of Pulp and Paper Industry. Home: 8 Ford Hill Rd Whippany NJ 07981-1817 Office: ESI Assocs 8 Ford Hill Rd Whippany NJ 07981-1817

ROSENTHAL, ARTHUR FREDERICK, biochemist, laboratory administrator; b. Bklyn., Aug. 3, 1931; s. Samuel J. and Pearl (Halpern) R.; m. Pili Pubul, Nov. 27, 1967; children: Paul, Alexander, Carolyn. BS, Antioch Coll., 1954; AM, Harvard U., 1956, PhD, 1960. Diplomate Am. Bd. Clin. Chemistry. Chief of biochemistry Long Island Jewish/Hillside Med. Ctr., New Hyde Park, N.Y., 1962-87; v.p. ops. Town Clin. Lab., Cedarhurst, N.Y., 1988-92; dir. chemistry Ren Labs., Ft. Lauderdale, Fla., 1992—; cons. in field, 1965—. Contbr. articles to profl. jours.; pantetee chromatographic applicator. Grantee NIH, 1963-75, Walter Reed Army Inst. Rsch., 1976-79. Home: 21 Radnor Rd Great Neck NY 11023-2227 Office: Ren Labs 5361 NW 33d Ave Fort Lauderdale FL 33309

ROSENTHAL, DAVID MICHAEL, musician, songwriter, composer, producer; b. N.Y.C., Jan. 1, 1961; s. Howard and Marylyn Joan (Vogel) R. BA in Music, Berklee Coll. Music, 1981. Multi-keyboardist Rainbow Polygram Records, N.Y.C., 1981-84; multi-keyboardist Little Steven EMI, N.Y.C., 1984; producer EMI Records, Cologne, Fed. Republic Germany, 1985; session musician various labels including Atlantic Records, Motown Records, CBS Records, Geffen Records, N.Y.C., L.A., 1985—; multi-keyboardist Cyndi Lauper, CBS Records, N.Y.C., 1986-87, 91, Robert Palmer, EMI Records, 1988-89; video instr. Hot Licks Video, Pound Ridge, N.Y., 1987—; music software cons. Apple Macintosh products, various synthesizer mfg. cos. Keyboardist (albums) Straight Between the Eyes, 1982 (Gold Album award 1983), Bent Out of Shape, 1983 (Gold Album award 1984), Finyl Vinyl, 1984, (Stacy Lattisaw) Personal Attention, 1988, (Donna Allen) Heaven on Earth, 1988, Will to Power, Will to Power, 1988, (Whitesnake) Slip of the Tongue, 1989 (Gold and Platinum album award 1990), (Steve Vai) Passion and Warfare, 1990 (Gold album award 1990), (singles) (Rainbow) Stone Cold, 1982, (Rainbow) Street of Dreams, 1983, (Rainbow) I Can't Let You Go, 1983, (Stacy Lattisaw) Let Me Take You Down, 1988, (Donna Allen) Joy & Pain, 1988, Will to Power, Baby I Love Your Way/Freebird Medley, 1988 (Gold Single award 1989); producer (album) Heart Made of Steel, 1985; contbr. columns and articles to Keyboards mag., Electronic Musician. Recipient Grammy award nomination, 1983. Mem. ASCAP, Am. Fedn. Musicians. Home and Office: 182 E Iselin Pky Iselin NJ 08830-1277

ROSENTHAL, DONNA MYRA, social worker; b. Rochester, N.Y., Feb. 23, 1944; d. Harry Lionel and Leila Estelle (Eber) Rosenthal; m. Thomas Robert Kolar, Aug. 5, 1979. BA, George Washington U., 1965; MS, Columbia U., 1967. Cert. social worker. Community organizer Health & Welfare Coun. Nassau County, Uniondale, N.Y., 1967-68; field rep. N.Y. State Office Aging, N.Y.C., 1968-73; asst. dir. United Neighborhood Houses, N.Y.C., 1973-84; exec. dir. Nat. Down Syndrome Soc., N.Y.C., 1984—; pres. Exec. Women in Human Svcs., N.Y.C., 1985-89. Pres. Congregation Beth Elohim, Bklyn., 1991—; pres. Columbia U. Social Work Alumni, N.Y.C., 1989-91; mem. adv. coun. Columbia U. Sch. Social Work, 1991—. Recipient Alumni medal Columbia U., 1991, NIMH fellowship, 1966-67, Regents scholarship, 1961. Mem. Ind. Sector, Am. Assn. Mental Retardation, Nat. Health Coun., Rsch. Am. Office: Nat Down Syndrome Soc 666 Broadway New York NY 10012

ROSENTHAL, FELIX, mechanical engineer; b. Munich, Germany, Feb. 6, 1925; came to U.S., 1936; s. Julius and Anny (Springer) R.; m. Mildrid Nyhamar, Apr. 14, 1960; children: Linda K., Fred J., Andy J. BSEE, Ill. Inst. Tech., 1947, MS in Math., 1948, PhD in Applied Mechanics, 1952. Instr., rsch. engr. Ill. Inst. Tech. Rsch. Inst., 1947-53; profl. engr., head math. scholar Clevite Corp. Rsch. Ctr., Cleve., 1953-60; asst. to mgr. engring. Raytheon Semiconductors, Newton, Mass., 1960-61; advisory engr. IBM Corp., Bethesda, Md., 1961-68; v.p. Oceanography, Inc., Santa Barbara, Calif., 1968-71; rsch. mech. engr., head applied mechanics Naval Rsch. Lab., Washington, 1971—; leader biomed. rsch. project Georgetown U. Hosp., Washington, 1990—. Contbr. over 50 papers to profl. publs.; patentee in field. Pres. World Federalist Assn. (Va. Chpt.), 1991—. With USN, 1944-46. Jewish. Home: 4020 Iva Ln Annandale VA 22003-3656 Office: Naval Rsch Lab Code 4223 Washington DC 20375

ROSENTHAL, LEONARD, finance educator; b. N.Y.C., Nov. 20, 1947; s. Jacob and Yetta (Hirsch) R.; m. Patricia Ann Adams. BA in Polit. Sci., Queens Coll., N.Y.C., 1968; MBA in Fin., Baruch Coll., 1971; PhD in Fin., CUNY, 1977. Asst. prof. fin. U. Wis., Madison, 1976-78, Boston U., 1978-83; assoc. prof. fin. Bentley Coll., Waltham, Mass., 1983—; cons. in field, 1981—. Contbr. articles to profl. jours. Mem. Am. Fin. Assn., Fin. Mgmt. Assn., Ea. Fin. Assn., So. Fin. Assn., Assn. for Investment Mgmt. Rsch., Boston Security Analysts Soc. Office: Bentley Coll 175 Forest St Waltham MA 02154-4705

ROSENTHAL, MARK LAWRENCE, art historian, curator; b. Phila., Aug. 9, 1945; s. Hyman and Lillian (Kononoff) R.; m. Laura J. Spilker, Sept. 17, 1967; children: Theo, Jess. AB, Temple U., 1966; MA, U. Iowa, 1971, PhD, 1979. Assoc. curator Wadsworth Atheneum, Hartford, Conn., 1974-76; curator U. Calif. Art Mus., Berkeley, 1976-83; curator 20th Century art Phila. Mus. Art, 1983-89; consultative curator Solomon R. Guggenheim Mus., N.Y.C., 1989—; freelance curator, 1989—. Author: Juan Gris, 1983, Jonathan Borofsky, 1984, Anselm Kiefer, 1987, Jasper Johns: Work Since 1974, 1988. Mem. Coll. Art Assn. Office: Solomon R Guggenheim Mus 1071 5th Ave New York NY 10128-0173

ROSENTHAL, MARVIN BERNARD, pediatrician, educator; b. Bklyn., Jan. 1, 1930; s. Robert Rosenthal and Elizabeth (Gartner) Rosenthal Dreyfuss; m. Janet H. Swerlick, dec. 31, 1959; 1 child, Robert G. BA, Alfred U., 1951; MD, Leiden U., The Netherlands, 1957. Diplomate Nat. Bd. Med. Examiners, Am. Bd. Pediatrics. Intern Kings County Hosp., Bklyn., 1957-58, resident in pediatrics, 1958-60; fellow in hematology Children's Hosp. Phila., 1962; pediatrician Somerset Pediatric Group, Bridgewater, N.J., 1963-84; chief pediatrics Somerset Hosp., Somverville, N.J., 1983-84; assoc. dir. family practice residency Warren Hosp., Phillipsburg, N.J., 1984—, chief pediatrics, 1991—, dir. med. edn., sec.-treas. hosp. staff; mem. cons. staff Morristown (N.J.) Meml. Hosp., 1989—; clin. asst. prof. Robert W. Johnson Med. Sch., New Brunswick, N.J., 1980—; mem. adj. faculty U. New England Coll. Osteopathics, Biddeford, Maine, 1988. Capt. USAF, 1960-62. Recipient Silver medallion Am. Heart Assn., 1976, 78. Fellow Am. Acad. Pediatrics; mem. Am. Acad. Family Practice, N.J. Med. Soc., Acad. Medicine N.J., N.J. Pediatric Soc., Warren County Med. Soc., Tchrs. Family Medicine, Ambulatory Pediatric Assn., Assn. Hosp. Med. Educators, Eagle Scout Assn. Home: 500 Spring Valley Rd Easton PA 18042-6872 Office: Warren Hosp Roseberry St Phillipsburg NJ 08865-1628

ROSENTHAL, SHIRLEY FLORENCE LORD, cosmetics magazine executive; b. London; came to U.S., 1971; d. Francis J. and Mabel Florence (Williamson) Stringer; m. A. M. Rosenthal, June 10, 1987; children from previous marriage: Mark, Richard. Matriculation, S.W. Essex Coll., London, 1948. Fiction editor Woman's Own, 1950-53; features editor Good Taste mag., 1953-56; features, fiction editor Woman and Beauty, 1956-59; fashion editor Star Evening newspaper, 1959-60; women's editor London Evening Standard, 1960-63, London Evening News, 1963-68; beauty editor Harper's Bazar, London, 1963-71, Harper's Bazaar, N.Y.C., 1971-73; beauty, health editor Vogue mag., Condé Nast Publs., N.Y.C., 1973-75; v.p. corp. rels. Helena Rubinstein, N.Y.C., 1975-80; beauty dir. Vogue mag., 1980—. Syndicated Field columnist on beauty, health; author 3 beauty books; also novels: Golden Hill, 1982; One of My Very Best Friends, (Lit. Guild Selection), 1985; Faces, 1989. City commr. Craigavon City, No. Ireland, 1963-68. Office: 350 Madison Ave New York NY 10017-3704

ROSENZWEIG, FRED, school system administrator; b. N.Y.C., Mar. 18, 1935; s. Louis and Sadie (Cohen) R.; m. Marcia Brooks, July 1, 1960; children: Lance, Andrew, Russ. BA, NYU, 1957, MA, 1958. Cert. chief sch. adminstr. Tchr. pub. schs., N.Y.C., 1958-60; dept. chmn. Island Trees Pub. Schs., Levittown, N.Y., 1960-69; adminstrv. asst. Westhampton Bch. (N.Y.) Pub. Schs., West Hampton Bch., N.Y., 1969-74; asst. supt. Morris Hills Regional Dist., Rockaway, N.J., 1974—. Recipient NDEA fellowship U.S. Dept. Edn. U. Maine and W.Va. U., 1960-62, Fulbright Hayes fellowship U.S. Dept. Edn. Paris, 1968-69, NSF fellowship Purdue U. and Ind. U., 1972-75, Inst. for Devel. of Ednl. Activities fellowship Harvey Mudd Coll., 1986-92. Mem. ASCD, Nat. Sch. Pub. Rels. Assn. (pres. 1985-87), Am. Assn. for Sch. Adminstrs., Phi Delta Kappa. Home: 16 Biscay Dr Parsippany NJ 07054 Office: Morris Hills Regional Dist 48 Knoll Dr Rockaway NJ 07866

ROSENZWEIG, STANLEY PAUL, clinical psychologist; b. N.Y.C., Oct. 15, 1928; s. Jacob Arthur and Edna (Braman) R.; m. Gloria Fay Braunstein, Aug. 3, 1958; children: Nancy Jean, Karen Lee. BS, CCNY, 1950, MA, 1951; PhD, Mich. State U., 1956. Lic. psychologist, Mass. Staff psychologist, asst. chief VA Outpatient Clinic, Boston, 1956-72, chief Day Treatment Ctr., 1964-88; assoc. in clin. psychology Boston U., 1967-84; psychol. cons. Mt. Ida Coll., Newton, Mass., 1977-79; psychologist Boston Family Svc., Needham, 1980-83; psychol. cons. Alpha Geriatric Svcs., Mass., 1986-90; group therapy supr. Beth Israel Hosp., Boston, 1989—; clin. assoc. Am. Geriatric Svcs., Mass., 1991—; adj. prof. Northeastern U., Boston, 1974-79; trustee Mass. Sch. Profl. Psychology, 1977—; clin. instr. psychology dept. psychiatry Harvard U., Cambridge, Mass., 1989—. Contbr. articles to profl. publs. Chmn. anti-defamation com. Mayflower lodge B'nai Brith, Boston, 1964-65, v.p., 1966. Fellow Mass. Psychol. Assn. (pres. 1970-72, Ezra Saul award 1975); mem. Am. Psychol. Assn. (coun. rep. 1973-76). Home: 41 Myerson Ln Newton MA 02159-3508

ROSENZWEIG, WILLIAM DAVID, microbiology educator; b. N.Y.C., Feb. 6, 1946; s. Manuel Edward and Anita Helen (Hochman) R. BS, St. John's U., Jamaica, N.Y., 1969; MS, L.I. U., 1971; PhD, NYU, 1978. Postdoctoral rsch. assoc. Rutgers U., New Brunswick, N.J., 1978-80; asst. prof. microbiology Drexel U., Phila., 1980-87, West Chester (Pa.) U., 1987—. Contbr. articles to profl. publs. Grantee U.S. EPA, 1984, NSF, 1986. Mem. Am. Soc. Microbiology, Am. Water Works Assn., Sigma Xi. Office: West Chester U Dept Biology West Chester PA 19383

ROSETT, RICHARD NATHANIEL, educator, economist; b. Balt., Feb. 29, 1928; s. Walter and Essie (Stofberg) R.; m. Madelon Louise George, June 24, 1951; children: Claudia Anne, Martha Victoria, Joshua George, Sarah Elizabeth, Charles Richard. B.A., Columbia U., 1953; M.A., Yale U., 1954, Ph.D., 1957. Instr. Yale U., 1956-58; mem. faculty U. Rochester, 1958-74, chmn. dept. econs., 1966-74, prof. econs., 1967-74, prof. preventive medicine and community health, 1969-74; prof. bus. econs. Grad. Sch. Bus., U. Chgo., 1974-84, dean, 1974-83; dean Faculty Arts and Scis. Washington U., 1984-87, prof. econs., 1984-90; dean Coll. Bus. Rochester (N.Y.) Inst. Tech., 1990—; pres. U.S. Bus. Sch. in Prague, Inc., 1990—; bd. dirs. Hutchinson Techs., Inc., Lumbermans Mut. Ins. Co., Nat. bur. Econ. Rsch. (chmn. 1986-89), Ctr. for Govtl. Rsch. Editor: The Role of Health Insurance in the Health Services Sector, 1976; Contbr. articles to profl. jours. Bd. dirs. Nat. Bur. Econ. Rsch., 1986-89. With USNR, 1944-45. Mem. Am. Econ. Assn., Mont Pelerin Soc., Phi Beta Kappa, Beta Gamma Sigma. Clubs: Cosmos; Chgo.; Yale (N.Y.C.); Valley (Rochester, N.Y.). Home: 26 Whitestone Ln Rochester NY 14618-4118 Office: Rochester Inst Tech Office of Dean One Lomb Memorial Dr Rochester NY 14623-0887

ROSHON, GEORGE KENNETH, manufacturing company executive, b. Pottstown, Pa., July 30, 1942; s. George Washington 3d and Ellen Eleanor (Knopf) R.; B.S. in Elec. Engring., Pa. State U., 1964; M.S., Drexel U., Phila., 1974, postgrad., 1974-75; m. Ella Maye Barndt, Nov. 21, 1964; 1 dau., Kirsten Renee. Sr. engr. Am. Electronics Labs., Inc., Colmar, Pa., 1966-69; v.p. engring. Acrodyne Industries, Inc., Montgomeryville, Pa., 1969-74; mgr. electric design W-J div. Hayes-Albion Corp., Norristown, Pa., 1974-78; mgr. quality assurance PSMBD, Gen. Electric Co., Phila., after 1978, mem. exec. com. electronics test council after 1980, mgr. advanced systems engring., 1983-84, mgr. communications engring., Malvern, Pa., 1984-86; v.p. quality assurance Hercules Aerospace Display Systems, Inc., Hatfield, Pa., 1986-88, v.p. engring., 1988-90; mgr. Electronics Group Westcode, Inc., Malvern, Pa., 1991—. Patentee in field. Served to lt. USNR, 1964-66. Registered profl. engr., Pa. Mem. Nat. Soc. Profl. Engrs., Am. Soc. Quality Control (cert. quality engr.), Pa. Soc. Profl. Engrs., Gen. Electric Mgmt. Assn., Elfun Soc., Drexel U. Alumni Assn., Pa. State U. Alumni Assn., Tri-County Arabian Horse Assn. Home: 454 Eagle Ln Lansdale PA 19446-1547 Office: 14 Lee Blvd Malvern PA 19355-1235

ROSIER, JAMES LOUIS, English philologist, educator; b. Chgo., Mar. 14, 1932; s. Escol MacFarland and Maudellen (Hamblin) R.; m. Katherine Lee Allen, Sept. 10, 1955; children: Meredith Lee, Paul Carrick, Jessica Holly. Student, De Pauw U., 1949-51; B.A., Stanford U., 1953, Ph.D., 1957; diploma, Freie U. Berlin, West Germany, 1955. Instr. Cornell U., Ithaca, N.Y., 1957-60; asst. prof. Cornell U., 1960-61, U. Mich., Ann Arbor, 1961-63; assoc. prof. English U. Pa., Phila., 1963-68; prof. English philology U. Pa., 1968—, chmn. grad. studies, 1977-79, mem. Outreach Program for Gifted Students; vis. assoc. prof. U. Chgo., 1965; honors examiner Manhattanville (N.Y.) Coll., 1970-71, Swarthmore (Pa.) Coll., 1972-73, 81-82, 88-89; cons. Binghamton Med. Studies, Can. Coun., Am. Philos. Soc.; external Ph.D. examiner U. Ottawa, 1979, Temple U., 1988; grad. Latin examiner; panelist NEH. Author/co-author: The Vitellius Psalter, 1962, Poems in Old English, 1962, The Norton Reader, 1965—, Philological Essays, 1970, Old English Language and Literature, 1972, Aldhelm: The Poetic Works, 1985; asst. editor: Middle English Dictionary, 1961-63; mem. editorial bd. Internat. Jour. Lexicography. Bd. dirs. Swarthmore Pub. Library, 1965-69, 1986—, v.p., 1987—; bd. dirs. Youth in Action, Chester, Pa.; mem. refugee com. Swarthmore Friends Meeting; mem., chmn. humanities panel Rsch. Found., U. Pa., 1989-91. Baker fellow, 1956-57; Am. Council Learned Socs. grantee, 1960, 72; Am. Philos. Soc. grantee, 1964, 71; Guggenheim fellow, 1964-65; U Pa. Research Found. grantee, 1983; mem. sr. common room Univ. Coll., Oxford (Eng.) U., 1961—. Fellow Soc. for Values in Higher Edn., Royal Hort. Soc.; mem. Modern Lang. Assn. Am. (chmn. Old English 1961-63), Medieval Acad. Am., Soc. Study Medieval Lang. and Lit., Dictionary Soc. Am. (co-founder, exec. bd. 1977—, pres. 1985-87, chmn. publs. com. 1988—), Renaissance Soc. Am. Home: 508 Cedar Ln Swarthmore PA 19081-1105 Office: U Pa Dept of English Philadelphia PA 19104-6273

ROSIN, ROBERT FISHER, software system architect; b. Chgo., Mar. 19, 1936; s. George Irving and Anna Gertrude (Rosenberg) R.; m. Rosalie Fay Lite, Apr. 7, 1963; children: Elizabeth, Alexandra. BS, MIT, 1957; MS, U. Mich., 1960, PhD, 1964. Assoc. prof. engring. Yale U., New Haven, 1964-68; prof. computer sci. SUNY, Buffalo, 1968-74, Iowa State U., Ames, 1974-76; mem. tech. staff Bell Labs., Holmdel, Lincroft, N.J., 1976-83; cons. mem. tech. staff Syntrex, Inc., Eatontown, N.J., 1983-86; dist. mgr. Bell Communications Rsch., Red Bank, N.J., 1986-89; v.p., prin. architect Enhanced Svc. Providers, Inc., Shrewsbury, N.J., 1989—; vis. prof. U. Aarhus (Denmark), 1972-74. Founding editor Annals of the History of Computing, 1978—. Program com. mem. History of Programming Langs. conf., 1978, 93; pres. Monmouth Reform Temple, Tinton Falls, N.J., 1983-85; commr. Environ. Commn., Fair Haven, N.J., 1990—; chmn. Fair Haven Sch. Long Range Plan Com., 1980-81. Mem. Assn. for Computing Machinery (chpt. pres.), IEEE Computer Soc. Jewish.

ROSINI, JOSEPH, contracting corporate executive; b. New Rochelle, N.Y., Nov. 25, 1939. Student, Fordham U., 1965-66, Iona Coll., 1972. Pres. Rosini Contracting Corp., New Rochelle, 1963—; prin. Rosini Devel. Co., Monticello, N.Y., 1965—; bd. dirs. Circuit Realty Corp., New Rochelle, 1970-71. Mem. planning bd. City of New Rochelle, 1986—, bldg. dept. adv. com., 1985; vol. instr. N.Y. State Dept. Environ. Conservation, Albany, 1968—; vice chmn. New Rochelle Conservative Party, 1984—; county committee-man Westchester County Conservative Party. Served with USN, 1959-61. Mem. Gen. Contractors Assn. N.Y., Constrn. Industry Council Westchester & Hudson Valley, Bldg. Trades Employers Assn., Soc. Explosives Engrs., Nat. Rifle Assn., Young Ams. for Freedom, Am. Lauretana Assn., Mensa. Roman Catholic. Office: Rosini Contracting Corp 113 Edison Ave Mount Vernon NY 10550

ROSNER, ANTHONY LEOPOLD, chemist, biochemist; b. Greensboro, N.C., Nov. 13, 1943; s. Albert Aaron and Elsie Augustine (Lincoln) R.; m. Ruth Francis Marks, June 19, 1966; 1 child, Rachel. BS, Haverford Coll., 1966; PhD, Harvard U., 1972. Staff fellow NIH-NINDS, Bethesda, Md., 1972-74; gen. dir. Receptor Lab. Beth Israel Hosp., Boston, 1976-81, tech. dir. Chem. Lab., 1981-83; tech. dir. New Eng. Pathology Svcs., Wilmington, Mass., 1983-86, cons., 1986—; dept. adminstr. Brandeis U., Waltham, Mass., 1986-91; rsch. ops. mgr. in newborn medicine Children's Hosp., 1991-92; dir. rsch. Found. for Chiropractic Edn. and Rsch., Arlington, Va., 1992—; vis. fellow Lab. Molecular Biology, CNRS, Gif-sur-Yvette, France, 1973. Contbr. articles to profl. jours. Harvard U. fellow, 1966. Mem. AAAS, Am. Chem. Soc. (auditor N.E. chpt. 1990—), N.Y. Acad. Scis., Clin. Ligand Assay Soc., Soc. Rsch. Adminstrs., Coun. for Chem. Rsch. Democrat. Jewish. Home: 1443 Beacon St Apt 201 Brookline MA 02146-4709 Office: Found for Chiropractic Edn & Rsch 1701 Clarendon Blvd Arlington VA 22209

ROSNER, DIANE A., academic administrator; b. New Haven, July 21, 1949; d. William A. and Clarice (Podheiser) Alderman; (div. May 1990); children: Jason E., Matthew L. BA, Clark U., 1970; MS, So. Conn. State U., 1984, profl. diploma, 1989. Lic. counselor, Conn. Asst. dir. coll. achievement program So. Conn. State U., New Haven, 1982-83, dir. coll. achievement program, 1983-86, coord. ednl. and summer ednl. opportunity program, 1986—; mem. univ. retention com. So. Conn. State U., 1983-84, mem. task force on racism, 1989, coord. stress opposition series, 1990-91. Author: (handbook) Surviving! A Handbook for College Survival, 1985. Member Temple Emanuel, PTA. Mem. AACD, Am. Coll. Pers. Assn., Conn. Assn. Ednl. Opportunity Programs, Conn. Coll. Pers. Assn., Nat. Acad. Advising Assn., New Eng. Assn. Ednl. Opportunity Program Pers. Home: 1008 Rainbow Trl Orange CT 06477-1041 Office: So Conn State U 501 Crescent St New Haven CT 06515-1355

ROSNER, MICHAEL JEFFREY, physician; b. Phila., Dec. 28, 1953; s. Albert and Evelyn (Scharf) R.; m. Sheryl Adler, Dec. 26, 1975; 2 children. MD, Hahnemann U., 1978. Diplomate Am. Bd. Internal Medicine, Am. Bd. Gastroenterology. Intern in Internal Medicine Hahnemann U., Phila., 1978-79, resident in Internal Medicine, 1979-81, fellow in Gastroenterology, 1981-83; pvt. practice Phila., 1983—; mem. staff in internal medicine and gastroenterology Frankford Hosp., Phila. Mem. AMA, Am. Gastroenterology Assn., Pa. Med. Soc., Montgomery County Med. Soc., Pa. Soc. of Gastroenterology. Office: 4242 Cottman Ave Philadelphia PA 19135

ROSNER, STANLEY, psychologist; b. Yonkers, N.Y., July 6, 1928; s. David Jacob and Rose (Meyers) R.; m. Blanche Muriel Altman, Feb. 20, 1955; children: David, Elisa, Adam, Jennifer. BA, NYU, 1950; MA, Boston U., 1951; PhD, New Sch. for Social Rsch., 1956. Diplomate Am. Bd. Profl. Psychology; cert. psychoanalysis; cert. neuropsychology. Psychology intern Grasslands Hosp., Valhalla, N.Y., 1951-52, jr. psychologist, 1952-55; clin. psychologist Manhattan State Hosp., N.Y.C., 1955-56; chief clin. psychologist Child Guidance Clinic of Greater Bridgeport, Conn., 1956-60; pvt. practice Fairfield, Stamford, Conn., 1958—; adj. med. staff Hall Brooke Hosp., Westport, Conn., 1959-84, Norwalk (Conn.) Hosp., 1978—; neuropsychology cons. Neuro-Rehab. Unit, Park City Hosp., Bridgeport, 1985—. Co-author: The Marriage-Gap, 1974; co-editor: The Creative Experience, 1970, The Creative Expression, 1976, Essays in Creativity, 1974; contbr. articles to profl. jours. Fellow Am. Psychol. Assn. (state psychol. affairs 1980), Am. Orthopsychiat. Assn., Soc. for Personality Assessment; mem. Conn. Psychol. Assn. (pres. 1972-73), Am. Group Psychotherapy Assn., Conn. Soc. of Psychoanalytic Psychologists (pres. 1984-88), Internat. Neuropsychol. Soc. Office: Counseling & Psychotherapy 1305 Post Rd Fairfield CT 06430-6016

ROSNER, WILLIAM, internist, educator, endocrinologist; b. N.Y., Jan. 7, 1933; children: Victoria, David; m. Karen Birnbaum, Oct. 16, 1983; 1 stepchild, Eric Birnbaum. BA, U. Wis., 1954; MD, Albert Einstein Coll. Medicine, 1961. Diplomate Am. Bd. Internal Medicine. Intern in medicine N.C. Meml. Hosp., 1961-62; resident in medicine Bellevue Hosp., N.Y.C., 1962-64; vis. fellow Coll. Physicians and Surgeons Columbia U., N.Y.C., 1964-66; asst. attending physician St. Luke's/Roosevelt Hosp. Ctr., N.Y.C., 1967-69, assoc. attending physician, 1969-72, sr. attending physician, dir. div. endocrinology, 1972—; instr. medicine Coll. Physicians and Surgeons Columbia U., 1967-69, assoc. in medicine, 1969-70, asst. clin. prof. medicine, 1970-72, asst. prof., 1972-73, assoc. prof., 1973-82, prof., 1982—; mem. endocrine study sect. NIH, Bethesda, Md., 1984-87. Assoc. editor Steroids, 1986—; contbr. over 80 articles and chpts. to scholarly and profl. jours. and books. With U.S. Army, 1954-56. Grantee NIH, 1967—. Fellow ACP; mem. AAAS, Am. Soc. Clin. Investigation, Am. Fedn. Clin. Rsch., Am. Soc.

Biol. Chemists, Endocrine Soc. (postgrad., membership, devel., pub. affairs coms., chmn. fin. com.), N.Y. Acad. Scis., Harvey Soc. Office: St Luke's Roosevelt Hosp Ctr 428 W 59th St New York NY 10019-1105

ROSNOW, RALPH LEON, psychology educator; b. Balt., Jan. 10, 1936; s. Irvin and Rebecca (Faber) R.; m. Mimi Medinger, Aug. 12, 1963. BS, U. Md., 1957; MA, George Washington U., 1958; PhD, Am. U., 1962. Asst. prof. Boston U., 1963-67; assoc. prof. Temple U., Phila., 1967-70, full prof., 1970-82; visiting prof. London Sch. Econs., 1973, Harvard U., Cambridge, Mass., 1978, 1988-89; Bolton professorship Temple U., 1982—; cons. editor Jours. in Psychology and Communication. Author: Paradigms in Transition, 1981, (with Robert Rosenthal) The Volunteer Subject, 1975, Essentials of Behavioral Research, 1984, 2nd edit., 1991, Contrast Analysis, 1985, (with Gary Fine) Rumor and Gossip, 1976, (with Mimi Rosnow) Writing Papers in Psychology, 1986, 2d edit., 1992, others; editor: (with Robert Rosenthal) Artifact in Behavioral Research, 1969, (with Marianthi Georgoudi) Contextualism and Understanding in Behavioral Science, 1986, others; contbr. articles to profl. jours. Fellow AAAS, Am. Psychol. Assn., Am. Psychol. Soc.; mem. Soc. Exptl. Social Psychology. Office: Temple Univ Psychology Dept 517 Weiss Hall Philadelphia PA 19122

ROSOFF, WILLIAM A., lawyer; b. Phila., June 21, 1943; s. Herbert and Estelle (Finkel) R.; m. Beverly Rae Rifkin, Feb. 7, 1970; children: Catherine D., Andrew M. BS with honors, Temple U., 1964; LLB magna cum laude, U. Pa., 1967. Bar: Pa. 1968, U.S. Dist. Ct. (ea. dist.) Pa. 1968. Law clk. U.S. Ct. Appeals (3d cir.), 1967-68; instr. U. Pa. Law Sch., Phila., 1968-69; assoc. Wolf, Block, Schorr & Solis-Cohen, Phila., 1969-75, ptnr., 1975—, chmn. exec. com., 1987-88; bd. dirs. Korman Co.; trustee RPS Realty Trust; guest lectr. confs. and seminars on tax law; mem. adv. bd. Commerce Clearing House, 1983—; mem. legal activities policy bd. Tax Analysts, 1978—. Editor U. Pa. Law Rev., 1965-67; mem. bd. contbg. editors and advisors Jour. Partnership Taxation, 1983—; author reports and papers on tax law. Bd. dirs. v.p. Phila. chpt. Am. Soc. for Technion; dir., mem. com. on law and social action, Phila. Council Am. Jewish Congress. Fellow Am. Coll. Tax Counsel; mem. Am. Law Inst. (cons. taxation of partnerships 1976-78, assoc. reporter taxation of partnerships, 1978-82, mem. adv. group, adv. group on fed. income tax project 1982—), Order of Coif, Beta Gamma Sigma, Beta Alpha Psi. Club: Locust. Office: Wolf Block Schorr Solis-Cohen Packard Bldg 12th Fl 15th & Chestnut Sts Philadelphia PA 19102

ROSOWSKY, ANDRE, chemist, educator; b. Lille, France, Mar. 3, 1936; came to the U.S., 1946; s. Vladimir and Tamara (Rajcyn) R.; m. Erlene Cohen, Aug. 26, 1962; children; David, Lisa, Jessica. BS, U. Calif., Berkeley, 1957; PhD, U. Rochester, 1961. Rsch. fellow Harvard U., Cambridge, Mass., 1961-62; rsch. assoc. Children's Cancer Rsch. Found., Boston, 1962-78; prin. assoc. Dana-Farber Cancer Inst., Boston, 1978-87; assoc. prof. Dana-Farber Cancer Inst., Harvard Med. Sch., Boston, 1987—; cons. NIH Study Sect. Editorial adv. bd.: Jour. Medicinal Chemistry, 1974-79, Pteridines, 1988—; contbr. articles to profl. jours. and chpts. to books; patentee in field. Mem. Am. Chem. Soc. (alternate councilor 1972-74, councilor 1979-83), Am. Assn. for Cancer Rsch. Office: Dana Farber Cancer Inst 44 Binney St Boston MA 02115-6084

ROSS, ALAN DALE, accountant; b. Franklin N.J., June 9, 1956; s. David Glendon and Barbara Louise (Dixon) R.; m. Michele P. Hughes, Sept. 3, 1983. B.S. in Acctg., Albright Coll., 1978. C.P.A., Pa. Staff acct. Samuel M. Fisher & Co., Reading, Pa., 1977-82; ptnr. Zuber, Close, Ross & Co., Reading, 1982-85; mng. ptnr., pres. Ross & Co., P.C., Reading, 1985—. Treas., Broadway Theater League of Reading Christ Ch. Mem. Pa. Inst. C.P.A.s (Alexander Loeb Silver Award, 1978, various coms., treas. Reading chpt.), Am. Inst. C.P.A.s, Muhlenberg Jaycees (pres. 1983-84), Breakfast Sertoma Club of Reading. Republican. Mem. United Church of Christ. Home: 4680 Pheasant Run Reading PA 19606-3530 Office: Ross & Co PC 1118 Penn Ave Reading PA 19610-2034

ROSS, ALAN MARSHALL, financial executive; b. Newark, Jan. 12, 1944; s. Bertram Chester and Lois (Kramer) R.; m. Eileen Marcia Wallach, Mar. 20, 1977; children: Hayley, Robyn. BA, Rutgers U., 1965; MBA, Xavier U., 1967. CPA. Auditor Haskins & Sells, CPA, N.Y.C., 1967-68, Arthur Young and Co., CPA, N.Y.C., 1971-72; mgr., fin. analysis CBS Inc., N.Y.C., 1973-76; dir. planning and analysis CBS Publs., N.Y.C., 1976-77; contr. Am. Family Publs. (joint venture of Time, Inc.), N.Y.C., 1977-79; v.p. finance Sat. Rev. Mag. Corp., N.Y.C., 1979-80; v.p. finance and adminstrn. MRCA Info. Svcs., Inc., Stamford, Conn., 1982-87; v.p. finance and planning Carol Wright Sales, Inc. subs. Dun & Bradstreet, Stamford, 1987-90; sr. v.p. finance Donnelley Mktg. Inc. subs. Dun & Bradstreet, Stamford, 1990—. Treas., bd. dirs. Walden Wood Homeowners Assn., Dobbs Ferry, N.Y., 1978-84. Lt. U.S. Army, 1968-70. Decorated Bronze Star (2), Air medal, Commendation medal. Mem. AICPA, N.Y. State Soc. CPAs, Fin. Execs. Inst., Planning Forum, Mag. Publs. Am. (tax com. 1979-80), Arthur Young Businessmen's Assn., Vietnam Vets. Am. Home: 114 Ogden Ave Dobbs Ferry NY 10522-3312 Office: Donnelley Mktg Inc 70 Seaview Ave PO Box 10250 Stamford CT 06904

ROSS, ALAN O(TTO), psychologist, educator, writer; b. Frankfurt am Main, Germany, Dec. 7, 1921; came to U.S., 1940, naturalized, 1943; s. Walter M. and Elizabeth L. (Keller) R.; m. Ilse Wallis, Sept. 2, 1950; children—Judith, Pamela. B.Social Sci., CCNY, 1949; M.S., Yale U., 1950, Ph.D., 1953. Diplomate: Am. Bd. Profl. Psychology.; Cert. psychologist, N.Y. Chief psychologist C. Beers Guidance Clinic, New Haven, 1956-59, Pitts. Child Guidance Center, 1959-67; prof. psychology SUNY, Stony Brook, 1967-91, prof. emeritus, 1991—; cons. VA, 1967-87; mem. N.Y. State Bd. Psychology, 1980-90. Author: The Practice of Clinical Child Psychology, 1959, The Exceptional Child in the Family, 1964, Psychological Disorders of Children, 1974, 2d edit., 1980, Psychological Aspects of Learning Disabilities, 1976, Learning Disability, 1977, Child Behavior Therapy, 1981, Personality, 1987, The Sense of Self, 1992, Personality Theories and Processes, 1992; bd. editors: Jour. Applied Behavior Analysis, 1980-83. Mem. Planning Bd., Village of Poquott, 1970-82. Served with U.S. Army, 1943-46, 51-56. Fellow Am. Psychol. Assn. (pres. div. clin. psychology 1969-70), Am. Psychol. Soc.; mem. Assn. for Advancement of Behavior Therapy (pres. 1983-84), Phi Beta Kappa, Sigma Xi.

ROSS, BRUCE, humanities educator, poet; b. Hamilton, Ontario, Canada, Mar. 1, 1945; s. Cecil and Esther (Spector) R. BA, Ohio U., 1968; MA, SUNY, Brockport, 1972; PhD, SUNY, Buffalo, 1982. Specialist in lang. Shandong U., People's Republic of China, 1983-84; asst. prof. English U. Rochester, N.Y., 1984-85, Prairie View (Tex.) A&M U., 1985-86; lectr. in English Webster U., St. Louis, 1986-87, Lindenwood Coll., St. Charles, Mo., 1987-88; lectr. humanities Draughons Coll., St. Louis, 1988-89; lectr. English, SUNY, Brockport, 1989-90; tutor in humanities Empire State Coll., Rochester, 1990—; lectr. in field. Author: The Inheritance of Animal Symbols, 1988, Thousands of Wet Stones, 1988, The Trees, 1991; author poetry; contbr. essays to profl. jours. Recipient Teaching fellowship U. Mannitoba, 1972-73; grantee SUNY, 1979, Tex. A&M U., 1985, Moroccan Govt., 1988, SUNY, 1990. Mem. MLA, Am. Comparative Lit. Assn., Internat. Soc. for Phenomenology and Lit. Home: 222 Culver Rd Rochester NY 14607-3012

ROSS, COLEMAN DEVANE, accountant; b. Greensboro, N.C., Mar. 18, 1943; s. Guy Matthews and Nancy McConnell (Coleman) R.; m. Carol Louise Morde, Aug. 26 1965; children: Coleman, Jonathan, Andrew. BS in Bus. Adminstrn., U. N.C., 1965; postgrad. Sch. of Banking of South, 1982-84. CPA, CLU, ChFC; chartered bank auditor. With Price Waterhouse, Tampa, 1965-76, Toronto, 1970, Hartford, Conn., 1976—, ptnr., 1977—, mng. ptnr. Nat. Ins. Svcs. Group, 1988—. Mem. exec. bd., Long Rivers Coun. Boy Scouts Am., 1978—, pres. 1985-88; mem. exec. bd. N.E. Region Boy Scouts Am., 1988—, pres. New Eng. area, 1988-91; div. campaign chmn. United Way of Capital Area, 1984; bd. dirs., treas. Family Svc. Soc. Greater Hartford, 1977-80; participant Leadership Greater Hartford, 1977. Recipient Silver Beaver award Boy Scouts Am., 1987, Silver Antelope award, 1991. Fellow Life Mgmt. Inst. Soc. Ctrl. New England; mem. AICPA (ins. cos. com. 1985-88, reins. auditing and acctg. task force 1979-85, rels. with actuaries com. 1982-85), N.C. Assn. CPAs, Conn. Soc. CPAs, Soc. Ins. Accts., Am. Soc. CLUs, Am. Soc. ChFCs., Internat. Ins. Soc., Nat. Soc. Chartered Bank Auditors, Assn. Mut. Ins. Accts., Soc. Ctrl. New England, Hartford Club (bd. govs. 1977-84). Home: 6 Wild Flower Ln West Simsbury CT 06092 Office: Price Waterhouse One Financial Pla Hartford CT 06103

ROSS, DANIEL MANUEL, insurance agent; b. N.Y.C., May 19, 1918; s. Max and Tillie (Klein) Rosenbaum; m. Norma Mandelbaum Ross, Nov. 24, 1949; children: Joan Carol, Paul. BS, Mich. State U., 1941. CLU. Life underwriter Equitable Life Assurance Soc., N.Y.C., 1941—; speaker Life Underwriters, 1950—, Top of the Table, Las Vegas, 1984, Mich. State U. Bus. Sch., 1989; tchr. life ins., 1960—. Fund raiser Am. Cancer Soc., N.Y.C., YMCA, Weizman, Inst. of Israel, ARC, 1950—, Am. Coll., Bryn Mawr, Pa., 1977-79; bd. overseers Hebrew Union Coll., N.Y.C., 1986—; bd. trustees Pritikin Rsch. Found., Santa Monica, Calif., 1987—; bd. dirs. Stamford (Conn.) Symphony, 1988—; mem. Vanderbilt YMCA; coll. advisor. Mem. Life Underwriters of N.Y. (v.p. 1950), Life Underwriters Conn., Million Dollar Roundtable (various coms. 1955—), Estate Planning Coun. of N.Y., Estate Planning Coun. of Conn., Charter Life Underwriter (fund raiser 1977-79), Top of the Table (speaker 1990), Hampshire Country Club (N.Y.), Masons. Office: Equitable Life 25 Valley Dr # 4630 Greenwich CT 06831-5203

ROSS, DAVID A., art museum director; b. Malverne, N.Y., Apr. 26, 1949; s. Joshua and Grayce R.; m. Margaret Gronner; children—Lindsay, Emily. B.A., Syracuse U.; postgrad. Grad. Sch. Fine Arts, Syracuse. Curator video art Everson Mus. Art, Syracuse, N.Y., 1971-74; dep. dir. program devel. and TV Long Beach Mus. Art, Calif., 1974-77; chief curator Univ. Art Mus., Berkeley, Calif., 1977-82; dir. Inst. of Contemporary Art, Boston, 1982-91; Whitney Mus. Am. Art., 1991—. Active Fed. Adv. Com. om Internat. Exbns., 1990—. Contbr. articles to profl. jours. Mem. Am. Assn. Mus. Dirs. Office: Whitney Museum Am Art 945 Madison Ave New York NY 10021-2705

ROSS, DAVID STANLEY, agricultural engineering educator; b. Du Bois, Pa., Apr. 16, 1947; s. Stanley Lorraine and Helen Lorne (Plyler) R.; m. Shirley Kay Garda, June 21, 1969 (div. 1986); children: Jason Patrick, Kelly Lauren. BS in Agrl. Engring., Pa. State U., 1969, MS in Agrl. Engring., 1971, PhD in Agrl. Engring., 1973. Rsch. asst. agrl. engring. dept. Pa. State U., State College, 1969-71, NSF trainee, 1971-72; asst. prof. U. Md., College Park, 1973-78, assoc. prof., 1978—, extension agrl. engr., 1973—; com. chmn. N.E. Regional Agrl. Engring. Svc., 1989—; treas. N.E. Agrl. and Biol. Engring. Conf., 1990—. Co-author Energy Conservation and Solar Heating for Greenhouses, 1978; co-author, editor Trickle Irrigation in Eastern United States, 1985; contbr. chpts. to USDA Yearbook of Agriculture, 1977, 78. Bd. dirs., treas. College Square Community Assn., Inc., 1976—; bd. dirs., officer Berwyn Dist. Civil Assn., College Park, 1981-92; troop com. chmn. College Park area Boy Scouts Am., 1986-92. Recipient Excellence in Extension award U. Md. Coll. Agr. Alumni Assn., 1983. Mem. Am. Soc. Agrl. Engrs. (coms., officer, Blue Ribbon awards 1977-80, 83, Young Engr. of Yr. award North Atlantic region 1983), Irrigation Soc., Coun. Agrl. Sci. and Tech. Republican. Presbyterian. Office: U Md System Agrl Engring Dept College Park MD 20742-5711

ROSS, DOLORES ANNE, health facility administrator; b. Bklyn., Apr. 4, 1952; d. John Joseph and Elizabeth Cecelia (Doonan) Ross. BS, CCNY, 1974; MA, NYU, 1982, postgrad., 1989—. Cert. rehab. registered nurse. Staff nurse Rusk Inst. NYU Med. Ctr., 1974-75, sr. staff nurse, 1975, team leader, 1975-76, asst. head nurse, 1976-77, head nurse, 1977-85, asst. dir., 1985-86, acting dir., 1986, asst. dir., 1986-91; rehab. nursing care coord. Victory Meml. Hosp., Bklyn., 1991—. Mem. Assn. Rehab. Nurses, Am. Assn. Spinal Cord Injury Nurses. Roman Catholic.

ROSS, DONALD EDWARD, engineering company executive; b. N.Y.C., May 2, 1930; m. Jeanne Ellen McKessy, Apr. 4, 1954; children: Susan, Christopher, Carolyn. BA, Columbia U., 1952, BS in Mech. Engring., 1953; MBA, NYU, 1960. Registered profl. engr., N.Y., 14 other states. Engr. Carrier Corp., N.Y.C., 1955-70; v.p. Dynadata, 1970-71; with Jaros, Baum & Bolles, N.Y.C., 1971—, ptnr., 1977—. Vice chmn. adv. coun. Columbia U. Sch. Engring. and Applied Sci. Lt. (j.g.) USN, 1953-55. Fellow ASHRAE; mem. ASME, NSPE, Am. Cons. Engrs. Coun., Nat. Bur. Engring. Registration, N.Y. Assn. Cons. Engrs. (pres. 1984-86), Coun. on Tall Bldgs. and Urban Habitat (vice chmn. N.Am., mem. steering group), Univ. Club (N.Y.C.), Nassau Country Club. Office: Jaros Baum & Bolles 345 Park Ave New York NY 10154-0004

ROSS, DORIS G., civic worker; b. Thompsonville, Conn.; d. Philip A. and Eva (Saffir) Sisitzky; student Barnard Coll., Max Reinhardt Drama Workshop, N.Y. U. Radio Workshop, Lee Strasberg Theatre Inst., Royal Acad. Dramatic Arts; m. Lewis H. Ross, Jan. 4, 1942; children—Phyllis, Allyne. Dir. New Eng. Zionist Youth Com., 1943-45; dir. theatre arts Manchester Inst. Arts and Scis., 1947-48; pres. Manchester Girls Clubs, 1950-51, dir., 1949-53, 54-58, 59-69, chmn. nat. adv. bd. Girls Clubs Am., 1955-57, v.p., 1956-57, pres., 1957-59, chmn. 15th Ann. Conf., 1960, first acting chmn. past pres. com., 1974, 1st pres. past pres. club, 1975-77, chmn. 15th ann. conf., 1960, chmn. silver jubilee com., 1969-70, chmn. directions and social concerns com., 1978-79, founder Children's Creative Theatre, 1978, chmn., 1979-81; hon. mem., 1981—; exec. com. Girls Clubs N.Y., 1970-73, bd. dirs., 1970-73, sustaining dir., 1973—, co-chmn. long range planning com., 1970-71; 1st pres. Theatre Art Players, Temple Emanuel, N.Y.C., 1970-71; trustee Actors Studio, 1978-82, 84, conceived Actors Studio Achievement awards celebration, 1981; dir. Manchester Settlement Assn., 1951-54, Manchester Vis. Nurses Assn., 1955-61; del. Nat. Soc. Welfare Assembly, 1957-59, White House Conf. on Children and Youth, 1960, voting del. nat. council state coms., 1960, mem. N.H. state exec. com., 1960, N.H. state sub-com. on Leisure Times Activities chmn., 1960; charter colleague Nat. Assembly Nat. Voluntary Health and Welfare Orgns., Inc., 1976—, mem. Nat. Juvenile Justice Program Collaboration, Mem. Pres.'s Citizens Adv. Com. on Fitness of Am. Youth, 1958-60; mem. exec. com. Gov.'s Com. on Children and Youth, 1961-63; Gov.'s rep. to Pres.'s Conf. on Youth Fitness, 1962; pres. Manchester Garden Club, 1963-64; dir. Opera League New Hampshire, Inc., 1964-69; trustee Actors Studio, 1978-82. Mem. Hadassah (pres. Manchester chpt. 1943-44, dir. Manchester chpt. 1942-49, New Eng. regional v.p. 1944-46). Address: 985 Fifth Ave New York NY 10021

ROSS, E. WAYNE, education educator; b. Greenville, S.C., Apr. 26, 1956; s. Bobby G. and Jean (Clutts) R.; divorced; 1 child, Rachel Layne. AB, U. N.C., 1978, MA in Teaching, 1979; PhD, Ohio State U., 1986. Cert. secondary social studies tchr., N.C., Ga., Ohio. Secondary social studies tchr. Fulton County Schs., Atlanta, 1979-81; dir. edn. Eastway Ch. of God, Charlotte, N.C., 1981-82; instr. Ohio State U., Columbus, 1982-86; asst. prof. edn. SUNY, Albany, 1986—; vis. prof. U. B.C., Vancouver, Can., 1991; chmn. editorial bd. SUNY Press, Albany, 1990—; pres. N.Y. State Coun. on Social Edn., Rochester, 1988-90; bd. dirs., mem. exec. com. Coll. and Univ. Faculty Assembly, Washington, 1990—; bd. dirs. N.Y. Coun. for Social Studies, White Plains, 1987—. Author, editor: Teacher Personal Theorizing, 1992; editor jour. Social Sci. Record, 1990—; contbr. articles to profl. publs., chpts. to books. Bd. dirs. Pierce Hall Day Care Ctr., Albany, 1989-90. Mem. John Dewey Soc., Am. Ednl. Rsch. Assn., Nat. Coun. for Social Studies, Am. Ednl. Studies Assn., Am. Fedn. Tchrs. Home: 201 Park Ave Albany NY 12202-1447 Office: SUNY Albany 1400 Washington Ave Albany NY 12222-0001

ROSS, EDWARD JOSEPH, architect; b. Everett, Mass., Dec. 13, 1934; s. Miriam (Rosenberg) R.; m. Gail Tishler, Feb. 2, 1963; children: Linda Joy, Melissa Carol. Student Boston Archtl. Ctr., 1952-55, 61-62, USAF Surveying Sch., 1955-56, Boston Soc. Civil Engrs., 1956-57, Carl Bolivar Structural Engring., 1962-63. Registered architect, Mass., Calif., N.Y., Fla., N.H., Vt.; cert. Nat. Coun. Archtl. Registration Bds.; lic. constrn. supr., Mass.; expert witness. Draftsman, assoc. William W. Drummey, Architect, Boston, 1952-59; job capt., designer Drummey-Rosane-Anderson, Boston, 1959-64; projects architect Maginnis & Walsh & Kennedy, Boston, 1964-69; v.p. William Nelson Jacobs Assocs., Inc., Boston, 1969-73; staff architect, Robert Charles Assocs., Inc., Architects, Boston, 1973-74; office mgr. Charles F. Jacobs Assocs., Inc., Cambridge, Mass., 1974-76; cons. architect Linenthal, Eisenberg & Anderson, Boston, 1976-77; staff architect Eisenberg Haven Assocs., Inc., Boston, 1977-78; chief architect, chief inspector Boston Housing Authority, 1978-83; prin. Edward J. Ross, AIA/FARA, Randolph, Mass., 1983-84; architect, sr. assoc., dir. constrn. adminstrn., Stull and Lee, Inc., Boston, 1984-91; part-time pvt. practice architecture, Randolph, 1963—; prin. Comprehensive Archtl. Svcs., Inc., Saugus, Mass., 1986—. Mem. Ancient and Honorable Arty. Co. of Mass. Staff sgt. USAF; lt. Mass. Def. Force. Fellow Soc. Am. Registered Architects; mem. Am. Arbitration Assn. (mem. nat. panel 1965—), AIA, Boston Soc. Architects (housing com. 1982-86), Mass. State Assn. Architects, Constrn. Specifications Inst., Air Force Assn. (pres. Boston chpt.), Ten of Us Club, Linderhof Golf Course Site One Assn. (pres. 1980-86), Elks, KP. Jewish. Home and Office: Eight Eagle Rock Rd Randolph MA 02368-3516 also: 99 Walnut St PO Box 1228 Saugus MA 01906

ROSS, GARY EARL, writing educator; b. Buffalo, Aug. 12, 1951; s. Earl Ross and Marlene (Edwards) Anderson; m. Katharyn Ellen Ketter, Dec. 23, 1970; children: Colleen, Timothy, David. BA in English, SUNY, Buffalo, 1973, MA in Humanities, 1975. Cert. English tchr., N.Y. Secondary English tchr. Buffalo Pub. Schs., 1973-76, Canisius High Sch., Buffalo, 1976-77; writing instr. Ednl. Opportunity Ctr. SUNY, Buffalo, 1977—; writing instr. Upward Bound SUNY, Buffalo, summers 1980-83, acting dir., summer 1984; presenter in field, U.S., Can., Europe, 1975—; reader various profl. fiction readings, 1985—. Contbr. articles, short stories, poems, essays to profl. publs.; videographer Writers on Video, Buffalo Pub. Libr., 1989. Local Incentive Funding Test fellow for fiction Buffalo Arts Coun., 1989; recipient Excellence award N.Y. State/United Univ. Professions, 1990. Mem. Niagara Erie Writers (chmn. bd. dirs. 1987-89), Just Buffalo, Inc. (fiction resident 1987, 92), Internat. Soc. for Exploration of Teaching Alternatives, United Univ. Professions. Home: 228 Highgate Ave Buffalo NY 14215-1024 Office: SUNY EOC Buffalo 465 Washington St Buffalo NY 14203-1707

ROSS, GEORGE MARTIN, investment banker; b. Phila., July 24, 1933; s. David L. and Beatrice (Rittenberg) Rosenkoff; m. Lyn Merry Goldberg, Nov. 26, 1959; children: Merry Beth, Michael John. BS, Drexel U., 1955. Mgmt. trainee Sears, Roebuck & Co., Phila., 1955-58; assoc. Goldman, Sachs & Co., Phila., 1959-68, v.p., 1968-70, gen. ptnr., 1971-90, ltd. ptnr., 1991—. Mem. Mayor's Cultural Adv. Council, Phila., 1987-91, campaign steering com. Bus. Leadership Organized for Cath. Schs., 1983-89, campaign policy com. United Way Southeastern Pa., 1983-84, We the People 200 com., 1984-86, Gov.'s Pvt. Sector Initiatives Task Force, 1983-84, Gov.'s Commn. on Financing Higher Edn., 1983-84, Wills Eye Hosp. Adv. Council, 1979-81, nat. bd. govs., exec. com., past pres., bd. dirs., past chmn. Phila chpt. Am. Jewish Com.; v.p., exec. com. Jewish Fedn. Greater Phila.; chmn. emeritus, bd. dirs., exec. com. Phila. Drama Guild; gov. Phila. Stock Exch., 1981-85; trustee Episcopal Acad., 1981-84; chmn. bd. trusts, mem. exec. com. Drexel U., Phila., 1981—; bd. dirs. Phila. Orch. Assn., and Acad. Music Phila., 1985-91, Cystic Fibrosis Found., 1978-83, Nat. Found. Jewish Culture, 1986-91; mem. nat. bd., Phila. co-chmn. One to One. Mem. Urban Affairs Partnership (bd. dirs. 1978-83), Greater Phila. C. of C. (mem. exec. com. 1989—), Fin. Analysts Phila., Phila. Securities Assn., Bond Club Phila., Union League, Sunday Breakfast Club (Phila.), Locust Club, Phila. Club. Home: 1116 Barberry Rd Bryn Mawr PA 19010-1908 Office: Goldman Sachs & Co Mellon Bank Ctr 26th Fl Philadelphia PA 19103

ROSS, GERALD ELLIOTT, lawyer; b. Chatham, Ont., Can., Aug. 9, 1941; s. Sanford Finlay and Helen Letitia Violet (Russell) R.; m. E. Sue Goetz, Dec. 29, 1963 (div. July 1975); m. Diana Guadalupe, Nov. 23, 1975; children: James Russell, Margaret Emily. BBA, U. Mich., 1962, MBA, 1963, JD cum laude, 1967. Bar: N.Y. 1968, U.S. Dist. Ct. (so. and ea. dists.) N.Y. 1969, U.S. Ct. Appeals (2d cir.) 1973, U.S. Ct. Appeals (8th cir.) 1973, U.S. Supreme Ct. 1973, U.S. Ct. Appeals (1st cir.) 1983. Assoc. Dewey Ballantine Bushby Palmer & Wood, N.Y.C., 1967-74, Dunnington, Bartholow & Miller, N.Y.C., 1974-77; sr. atty. J.C. Penney Co., N.Y.C., 1977-81; pvt. practice Law Offices Gerald Ross, N.Y.C., 1981-85; founding ptnr. Fryer, Ross & Gowen, N.Y.C., 1986—. Vestryman Christ and St. Stephen's Ch., N.Y.C., 1981-86, 88-89; mem. Commn. on Canons, Episcopal Diocese of N.Y., 1987—; bd. dirs. Corp. for the Relief of Widows and Children of Clergymen of the Protestant Episcopal Ch. in the State of N.Y.; pres. 160 West End Owners Corp., 1987—. 1st lt. U.S. Army, 1963-65. Mem. N.Y. State Bar Assn., Assn. of Bar of City of N.Y., Am. Arbitration Assn. (panel constrn. arbitrators), Univ. Club. Home: 160 W End Ave New York NY 10023-5601 Office: Fryer Ross & Gowen 551 5th Ave New York NY 10176-0001

ROSS, GLENN EVAN, financial executive, educator; b. New Haven, Conn., June 30, 1958; s. Robert Benjamin and Phyllis Mabel (Rowe) R.; m. Deborah Lynne Smith, May 27, 1978; children: Matthew Evan, Bradley Evan. BS, Towson State U., 1981; MBA, Loyola Coll., 1985. V.p. Mercantile Safe Deposit & Trust, Balt., 1975—; adj. prof. of fin. Towson (Md.) State U., 1989—. Statistician (book) The New Limited Partnership Investment Advisor, 1987, REITS, 1987, Understanding Real Estate, 1988. Mem. AAUP, Soc. Quantitative Analysts. Episcopalian. Office: Mercantile Safe Deposit & Trust PO Box 2257 Baltimore MD 21203-2257

ROSS, HEIDI A., comparative education educator; b. Kalamazoo, Jan. 3, 1954; d. Tom E. and Viola J. (Snip) R.; m. G. William Monaghan, Aug. 21, 1981. BA, Oberlin Coll., 1975; MA, U. Mich., 1978, PhD, 1987. Lectr. Providence Coll., Taichung, Rep. China, 1975-76, Shanghai (People's Republic China) Fgn. Lang. Sch., 1981-83; teaching and rsch. asst. U. Mich., Ann Arbor, 1978-81, teaching asst., 1983-86; vis. asst. prof. Ind. U., Bloomington, 1986-87; asst. prof. comparative edn. Colgate U., Hamilton, N.Y., 1987—; assoc. in rsch. program in East Asian studies Cornell U., Ithaca, N.Y., 1990—. Author: Making Foreign Things Serve China, 1992. Luce fellow U. Kans., 1989-90; grantee Spensor Found., 1991-92. Mem. Am. Ednl. Rsch. Assn., Am. Ednl. Studies Assn., Assn. Asian Studies, Comparative and Internat. Edn. Soc., Phi Beta Kappa, Phi Delta Kappa. Office: Colgate U 13 Oak Dr Hamilton NY 13346-1338

ROSS, HENRY, III, local government executive; b. San Antonio, Mar. 20, 1954; s. Henry Jr. and Birdie Marie R.; m. Marva Lynette Durden, Mar. 11, 1989. BS, S.W. Tex. State U., 1976, MPA, 1984. Adminstrv. resident Lutheran Gen. Hosp., San Antonio, 1982-83; adminstrv. intern City of San Antonio, 1983-84, budget analyst, 1984-89; dep. mgr. Township of Teaneck (N.J.), 1989—. Bd. dirs. YMCA, San Antonio, 1986. Am. Polit. Sci. Assn. grad. fellow, 1984. Mem. Internat. City Mgmt. Assn., Nat. Forum for Black Pub. Adminstrs., Tex. City Mgmt. Assn., N.J. Mcpl. Mgrs. Assn. Baptist. Home: 172 Washington Ave Apt 12 Little Ferry NJ 07643-2065 Office: Township of Teaneck The Municipal Bldg Teaneck NJ 07666

ROSS, JAMES J., college administrator; b. Niagara Falls, N.Y., Aug. 21, 1943; s. John P. and Elaine (Cuffe) R.; m. Lynn Russ; children: John J., James J., Erin. BS, Salem Coll., 1968; MS, Ill. State U., 1970; PhD, SUNY, Buffalo, 1978; postdoctoral, Harvard U., 1986. Cert. guidance and psychol. counselor. Dir. living/learning Ill. State U., Normal, 1969-71; grant assistantship Springfield (Mass.) Coll., 1971-72; dir. resident life N.C. State U., Raleigh, 1972-74; dir. student devel. and residence life SUNY, Buffalo, 1974-76, asst. v.p. student affairs, assoc. prof. sociology, 1976-79; dean student affairs, assoc. prof. sociology Phila. Coll. Textile Sci., 1979-87; dean, chief exec. officer Jamestown Community Coll., Olean, NY, 1987-91; pres. Mt. St. Claire Coll., Clinton, Iowa, 1991—; instr. adult edn. Bloomington (Ill.) Adult Orgn., 1970-71. Chmn. Spl. Purpose Parking Com., Olean, 1990; bd. dirs. Econ. Devel. Zone, Olean, 1990, Portville (N.Y.) Libr., 1990. Mem. Friends of Good Music (chmn. 1990-91), Portville Conservation. Office: Jamestown Community Coll Cattaraugus County Campus 244250 N Union St Olean NY 14760-9709

ROSS, JERROLD, music educator; b. N.Y.C., Feb. 8, 1935; s. James Murray and Alice (Gubernick) R. BS, NYU, 1955, PhD, 1963; M.S., Queens Coll., 1959. Music tchr. Syosset, N.Y., 1956-58, Great Neck, N.Y., 1958-61; instr. music edn. NYU, 1961-63; chmn. tchr. edn. dept. N.Y. Coll. Music, 1963-65, pres., 1965-67; head div. music edn. NYU, 1967-74, head div. arts and arts edn., 1974-82, assoc. dean, 1982—, acting vice dean, 1979, mem. senate, 1977-80, chmn. faculty council, 1979-80, dir. Nat. Ctr. for Research in Arts Edn., 1987—; dir. Town Hall of NYU, 1971-74; bd. dirs. Town Hall Found., 1973-75; asst. bd. examiners N.Y.C. Pub. Schs.; mem. Tchr. Edn. Certification and Practice Bd., State of N.Y.,1987—; cons. to and mem. music com. N.Y. State Edn. Dept. Coll. Proficiency Exam. Program; mem. adv. coun. on arts in edn.; participant various confs.Nat. Endowment for Arts, U.S. Office Edn., Am. Assn. Colls. Tchr. Edn., Getty Ctr. for Edn. in Arts; bd. dirs. various projects N.Y. State Edn. Dept., Nat. Found on

Arts and Humanities, N.Y. State Council on Arts, Andrew W. Mellon Found., Rockefeller Found., Reimann Found., Henry and Lucy Moses Found., Pinkerton Found., Rubin Scholars Program in Israel; instnl. rep. Holmes Group, 1987—. Author: Interpreting Music Through Movement, 1963. v.p. Concert Artists Guild N.Y., 1964-69; bd. dirs. Usdan Center for the Arts, chmn. bd., 1972-80, 85—; bd. dirs. Broadway Assn., Village Nursing Home, 1984-86; bd. dirs. Am. Assn. for Music Therapists, pres., 1978-80; mem. citizens adv. bd. Radio Sta. WNCN; bd. dirs. Alumni LaGuardia Sch. Music and Arts, N.Y.C.; mem. alumni bd. LaGuardia High Sch. of Arts. Mem. Music Educators Nat. Conf. (grad. commn.), Coll. Music Soc. (mem. council 1975-78), Nat. Assn. Schs. Music (govtl. relations com., mem. grad. commn. 1979-84), N.Y. Musicians Club, Phi Delta Kappa, Phi Mu Alpha Sinfonia (province gov. 1964-70). Club: Nat. Arts. Home: 2 Washington Square Vlg New York NY 10012-1711

ROSS, L. MICHAEL, county economic development official; b. Williamsport, Pa., Dec. 9, 1954; s. Larry Hoy and Mary Alice (Moyer) R.; m. Donna Jean Barkhymer, Aug. 4, 1979; children: Kira Michelle, Tracy Janelle, Alyssa Danielle. BA in Polit. Sci., Slippery Rock U., 1977; cert. basic edn. devel., Rochester Inst. Tech., 1985; postgrad. in econ. devel., U. Okla., 1987. Statis. analyst Stats., Research and Planning Pa. Dept. Commerce, Harrisburg, 1977-79, procurement specialist Minority Bus. Enterprise, 1979-83; indsl. devel. loan specialist Pa. Dept. Commerce, Pa. Indsl. Devel. Authority, Harrisburg, 1983-84; mktg. rep. Bur. Domestic and Internat. Commerce Pa. Dept. Commerce, Harrisburg, 1984-86; exec. dir. Franklin County Area Devel. Corp., Chambersburg, Pa., 1986—. Intern Pa. Ho. of Reps., Harrisburg, 1977; houseparent Milton Hersey (Pa.) Sch., 1979-80; mem. employer adv. panel Pa. Job Svc., 1986; mem. adv. panel curriculum devel. Franklin County Area Vocat. Tech. Sch., 1986; mem. adv. panel on entrepreneurial devel. svcs. Advanced Tech. Ctr. No. and Cen. Pa., 1986-87; mem. exec. com. Franklin-Adams Pvt. Industry Coun.; chmn. Punt Commn. on Bus.-Edn. Partnerships; grad. Leadership Pa. Recipient gov.'s letter of recognition State of Pa., 1977, commendation Congressman John P. Murtha, 1977, Disting. Alumni award Slippery Rock U., 1987, Transp. Partnership award CSX, Disting. Svc. award Franklin County Farmers Assn. Mem. Am. Econ. Devel. Coun., Pa. Econ. Devel. Assn. (bd. dirs., 1st v.p.), Cen. Pa. Internat. Bus. Assn., Active Corp Execs., Assn. U.S. Army, Soc. for Human Resource Mgmt. Republican. Lutheran. Office: Franklin County Area Devel Corp 1233 Lincoln Way E Chambersburg PA 17201

ROSS, LEONARD STANLEY, radiologist; b. Rockville, Conn., Sept. 8, 1928; s. Meyer Maurice and Lottie (Libby) R.; m. Muriel Kates, June 11, 1954; children: Mitchell Kenneth, Sheryl Lynn. BS, Trinity Coll., Hartford, Conn., 1950; MD, U. Pa., 1954. Diplomate Am. Bd. Radiology. Intern Hartford Hosp., 1954-55, resident in radiology, 1955-58; staff radiologist New Eng. Med. Ctr., Boston, 1960-61; staff radiologist Quincy (Mass.) City Hosp., 1961-86, chief dept. radiology, 1969-77, hon. mem. staff, 1986—; cons. Gen. Dynamics, N.Y.C., Boston, 1961-86, Norfolk County Hosp., Braintree, Mass., 1961-85; asst. clin. prof. radiology Boston U., 1965-75; pres. Quincy Radiology Assocs., 1969-85; cons. U.S. Army, 1982-85. Pres., co-founder Temple Sha'aray Shalom, Hingham, Mass.; trustee Hingham Civic Music Theater, 1977-84. Capt. U.S. Army, 1958-60. Mem. AMA (CME award 1978-87), Mass. Med. Soc., Mass. Radiol. Soc., Am. Coll. Radiology, Radiol. Soc. N. Am., New Eng. Roentgen Assn. Home: 61 Summer St Hingham MA 02043-1963

ROSS, MARY CASLIN, foundation executive; b. N.Y.C., Oct. 15, 1953; d. Michael John and Mary Rose (Harkins) C.; m. Alexander Barker Ross, Mar. 21, 1992. BA, St. John's U., 1975; MA, Manhattanville Coll., 1986; Doctorate (hon.), Marymount U., 1990. Exec. dir. The Fund for Am. Studies, Washington, 1976-77; library researcher Interbank Card Assn., N.Y.C., 1977-78; devel. cons. Martin J. Moran Co., N.Y.C., 1978-80; dir. devel. Internat. Ctr. for Disabled, N.Y.C., 1980-83; trustee, v.p. bd. ICD Internat. Ctr. for the Disabled, N.Y.C., 1984—; exec. dir. The Bodman/Achelis Found., N.Y.C., 1983—; trustee JM Found., N.Y.C., 1984—; bd. dirs. Philanthropy Roundtable, Indpls., 1988—; lectr. New Sch. Fundraising Inst., N.Y.C., 1988—; mem. adv. bd. A Different September Found., 1992. Recipient Pres. medal St. John's U., Jamaica, N.Y., 1975, Human Resources Ctr., Albertson, N.Y., 1991. Mem. Cold Spring Harbor Fish Hatchery. Republican. Roman Catholic. Office: Bodman Found/Achelis Found 767 3rd Ave New York NY 10017-2023

ROSS, MICHAEL FREDERICK, lawyer, magistrate; b. Coral Gables, Fla., Sept. 20, 1950; s. George Thomas and Frances (Brown) Skaro; m. Penny Lea Peninger, June 29, 1991. BA, Yale U., 1973; JD, U. Conn., 1979; MLS, So. Conn. State U., 1981. Bar: Conn. 1979, U.S. Dist. Ct. Conn. 1979, Fla. 1979, U.S. Ct. Claims 1980, U.S. Tax Ct. 1980, U.S. Ct. Customs and Patent Appeals 1980, U.S. Ct. Mil. Appeals 1980, U.S. Ct. Appeals (1st, 2d and D.C. cirs.) 1980, U.S. Ct. Appeals (5th, 9th and 11th cirs.) 1981, U.S. Ct. Appeals (Fed. cir.) 1982, U.S. Supreme Ct. 1982, N.J. 1983, U.S. Dist. Ct. N.J. 1983, U.S. Ct. Appeals (3d, 4th, 6th, 7th, 8th and 10th cirs.) 1983, Mass. 1984, U.S. Dist. Ct. Vt. 1984, V.I. 1985, U.S. Dist. Ct. V.I. 1985, Temp. Emergency Ct. Appeals 1985. Pvt. practice New Haven, Conn., 1979-82, Madison, Conn., 1985—; chief of adjudications Conn. Motor Vehicle Dept., Wethersfield, 1980-82; adminstrv. law judge State of Conn. Motor Vehicle Dept., Wethersfield, 1985—; asst. atty. gen. State of Conn., Hartford, 1982-84, Dept. of Law, St. Croix, V.I., 1984-85; magistrate Superior Ct. of Middlesex, New Haven and New London Counties, Conn., 1988—; mem. faculty Conn. Bar Assn. Acad. Profl. Devel. of Continuing Legal Edn., 1987, 91. Chmn. Madison Zoning Bd. Appeals, 1991. Mem. ABA, Conn. Bar Assn., V.I. Bar Assn., Mensa, Internat. Platform Assn., Conn. Def. Lawyers Assn., Madison Men's Club. Democrat. Jewish. Club: Fence, Morys Assn. (New Haven). Home: 49 Sandalwood Dr Madison CT 06443-2201 Office: PO Box 366 Madison CT 06443-0366

ROSS, NORMAN EVERETT, cultural organization administrator; b. Wilmington, Del., Aug. 1, 1930; s. Sidney James and Beulah Naomi (Glover) R.; m. Ruth Florence Fisher, Jan. 24, 1959; 1 child, Norman Reginald; stepchildren: Laverne Crawford, Kendall Crawford. BA, U. Del., 1953; Cert., Berkshire Music Ctr., 1964; MEd, U. Md., 1968; postgrad., Notre Dame Coll. Md., 1986-88. Tchr. music Queen Annes County Schs., Centreville, Md., 1955-56, Balt. Pub. Schs., 1956-70; dir. Cultural Arts Program, Balt., 1970-83; program coord. Urban Svcs. Cultural Arts, Balt., 1983—; part time instr., Coppin State Coll., Balt., 1978-81; chmn., Balt. County Commn. on Arts and Sci., 1975-82; bd. dirs., Ctr. Stage Md., Balt., 1988—. Contbr. to Book of Days encyc., 1988. Mem. exec. com., Mayor's Adv. Com. on Art and Culture, Balt., 1974-83; v.p., United Way Cen. Md., Balt., 1974-81; chmn. Afro-Am. Exposition, Balt., 1976—; mem. Ethnic Co-Coun., Balt., 1989. Mem. Assn. Performing Arts Presenters, Md. Alliance Arts Edn. (treas. 1980—), Assn. for Study of Afro-Am. Life and History (achievement award Balt. chpt.), Nat. Forum Black Pub. Adminstrs., Young Audiences Md. (past pres.), Masons, Kappa, Alpha Psi. Democrat. Episcopalian. Home: 9619 Winands Rd Randallstown MD 21133-2119 Office: Urban Svcs Cultural Arts 409 N Charles St Baltimore MD 21201-4405

ROSS, PAUL F(REDERIC), industrial psychologist; b. Ann Arbor, Mich., Dec. 31, 1926; s. Fred and Ethel M. (Moellenkamp) R.; m. Rita M. Thorp, June 6, 1953 (dec. Jan. 1983); children: Brenda L. Ross-Mathes, Sherri A. Ross Hruby, Frederic T.; m. Susanne A. Werner, Oct. 10, 1987. Student, U. Chgo., 1950-51; BA, Ohio Wesleyan U., 1950; MA, Ohio State U., 1952, PhD, 1955. Diplomate Indsl. and Orgnl. Psychology, Am. Bd. Profl. Psychology; lic. psychologist, Mass., N.Y. Human resources researcher Prudential Ins. Co. Am., Newark, 1955-57, Exxon Corp., N.Y.C., 1957-64; mgmt. cons. Arthur D. Little, Inc., Cambridge, Mass., 1964-71; rsch. and mgmt. cons. The Ross Co., Lincoln, Mass., 1971—; instr. Ohio State U., Columbus, 1952-55, Rutgers U., Patterson, N.J., 1958-59, U.S. Power Squadrons, Lexington, Mass., 1979—. Author (with Fahey & Love): Computers, Science, and Management Dynamics, 1969; bd. editors jour. in field; contbr. articles to profl. jours. Chair First Parish in Lincoln, 1969-70. Instr. USNR, 1944-46. Mem. APA (div. of evaluation and measurement), Am. Statis. Assn., Assn. for Computing Machinery, Psychometric Soc., Soc. for Indsl./Orgnl. Psychology, Phi Beta Kappa, Omicron Delta Kappa, Theta Alpha Phi, Psi Chi. Office: The Ross Co Todd Pond Lincoln MA 01773

ROSS, ROBERT EDGAR, food scientist; b. Trenton, N.J., Aug. 25, 1948; s. Edgar Hunter and Mildred (Brooks) R.; m. Nancy Handloser, May 27, 1979; children: Jillian, Allison. BS in food sci., Rutgers U., 1970; MS in food sci., U. Mass., 1972, PhD in food sic., 1973. Food scientist Hunt-Wesson Foods, Inc., Fullerton, Calif., 1973-77; group dir. biscuit R&D Nabisco Brands, East Hanover, N.J., 1978-86; v.p. gum and confection R&D Warner-Lambert, Morris Plains, N.J., 1986-87; group dir. tech. svcs. Internat. Nabisco Brands, Parsippany, N.J., 1987-89; v.p. R&D/ quality assurance Estee Corp., Parsippany, N.J., 1989-90; dir. R&D Pepperidge Farm, Norwalk, Conn., 1990—; newsletter editor So. Calif. Inst. of Food Technologists, 1975-77; exec. com. N.Y. Inst. of Food Technologists. Adv. bd. Dept. of Tech. Calif. State U., Long Beach, 1976-77; Capt. USAR, 1970-78. George H. Cook scholar Rutgers U., 1970. Mem. Inst. Food Technologists. Home: 102 Coventry Ln Trumbull CT 06611-1055 Office: Pepperidge Farm PO Box 5050 Norwalk CT 06856-5050

ROSS, ROBERT OBERHOLTZER, college administrator; b. Augusta, Ga., July 4, 1945; s. John Stevenson and Dorothy (Oberholtzer) R.; m. Sharon Anne Liada, June 3, 1967; children: Heather B., Stacie A. BS in Sec. Social Studies, SUNY, Oswego, 1963; MS in Instructional Comm., Syracuse U., 1969, MLS, 1979, postgrad., 1986—. Social studies tchr. Liverpool (N.Y.) High Sch., 1969; coord. edn. communications East Aurora (N.Y.) Pub. Schs., 1969-72; dir. learning resources Community Coll. of the Finger Lakes, Canandaigua, N.Y., 1972-75; div. head Inst. and Learning Resources Tompkins Courtland Community Coll., Dryden, N.Y., 1976-83, exec. asst. to pres., 1983-85, acting pres., 1986, dean coll. svcs., 1985—; bd. dirs. South Cen. Rsch. Libr. Coun., Ithaca, N.Y., 1982—. Lt. col. U.S. Army/USAR, 1968—. Methodist. Home: 3981 Northway Dr Cortland NY 13045-9317 Office: Tompkins Cortland Com Coll 170 North St Dryden NY 13053-9533

ROSS, ROBINETTE DAVIS, publisher; b. London, May 16, 1952; d. Raymond Lawrence and Pearl A. (Robinette) D.; m. William Bradford Ross III, Mar. 16, 1979; children: Nellie Tayloe, William IV, 1 stepchild, Aviza Tayloe. Student, Am. U., 1977-78. Asst. to editor The Chronicle of Higher Edn., Washington, 1978, advt. mgr., 1978-82, advt. dir., 1982-86, assoc. pub., 1986—; assoc. pub. The Chronicle of Philanthropy, 1988—. Mem. Am. Newspaper Pubs. Assn., Am. News Women's Club, City Tavern Club. Episcopalian. Home: 3908 Virgilia St Chevy Chase MD 20815-5026 Office: The Chronicle of Higher Edn 1255 23d St NW Washington DC 20037

ROSS, ROGER, publishing executive; b. Jan. 6, 1929; s. George and Sophia (Peck) R.; m. Lila Levy, Dec. 18, 1953; 1 child, Anthony. Student, Carnegie Mellon U., 1948; BS, Columbia U., 1950, MIA, 1952. Comptr. Coun. on Fgn. Rels., N.Y.C., 1952-58; dir. LTB Printing & Pub., Rio de Janeiro, 1958-65; dir., cons. Graphic Controls Corp., Buffalo, Brazil, 1965-77; pres., chief exec. officer Editora Tradicao/Opera Mundi, Rio de Janiero, 1965-77; chief exec. officer, mng. dir. Morrison & Gibb, Edinburgh, Scotland, 1977-81; dep. chmn., chief oper. officer British Printing Copr., Eng., Italy, Spain, Portugal, 1981-82; cons. Longman Pub. Group, Eng., Scotland, 1982; exec. v.p., chief oper. officer The Book Press, Brattleboro, Vt., 1983-84; pres. Roger Ross Assocs., South Orange, N.J., 1984—; exec. dir. Ctr. de Biblioteca-Franklin Book Programs, Rio de Janeiro, 1964-65; rep. of Brazil Nobel Prize ceremonies, Stockholm, 1974; lectr. in field. Editor in chief Jour. Internat. Affairs; contbr. articles to profl. jours. Vice chmn. joint meeting Essex and Union City, Elizabeth, N.J., 1987-91; village pres. City of South Orange, 1987-91. Mem. Coun. Fgn. Rels., Book Industry Study Group, Soc. Graphical and Allied Trades (hon.). Home and Office: 190 Montrose Ave South Orange NJ 07079-2415

ROSS, RONALD S., accountant, educator; b. Mexia, Tex., May 8, 1949; s. Jack R. and Betty (Blair) R. BBA, U. Tex., Austin, 1971, MPA, 1977, PhD, 1978. CPA, Tex. Asst. prof. Ind. U., Indpls., 1978-82; supr. Touche Ross & Co., Houston, 1982-85; mgr. Peat Marwick Mitchell, Houston, 1985-86; assoc. prof. U. Houston, 1986-88; asst. prof. Georgetown U., Washington, 1988—. Office: Georgetown U Sch Bus Washington DC 20057

ROSS, SCOTT LAMOND, criminal police investigator; b. Morristown, N.J., Mar. 4, 1948; s. Aubrey Thomas and Barbara (Lamond) R.; m. Kathleen Ann Prentiss, May 1, 1971; children: Matthew William, Erin Elizabeth. Student, Fairleigh Dickenson U., 1967, 73. Sr. assoc. Renaissance, Inc., 1988-92; criminal police investigator Borough of Madison (N.J.) Police Dept., 1992—. Pres. N.J. State Policeman's Benevolence Assn. # 92, Madison, 1983-85. With U.S. Army, 1967-69. Recipient Martin P. Jennings award Borough of Madison, 1990. Mem. Morris County Detective's Assn. (pres. 1990-92), Morris County Arson Investigators (pres. 1985-86, Ann. Achievement award 1991), Jaycees (sr. trustee Madison club 1986-89). Home: 183 Central Ave Madison NJ 07940

ROSS, SPENCER IRWIN, trade organization administrator; b. N.Y.C., Apr. 4, 1924; s. Morris William and Mary (Lippman) R.; m. Carolyn Sue Domeier, Mar. 25, 1935 (dec. Jan. 1979); children: Janet Marie, Michael Anthony. BSEE, Rutgers U., 1945. Mgr. telecommunications GE, N.Y.C., 1954-65; mgr. comml. and ednl. systems GTE Internat., N.Y.C., 1965-70; v.p. Bendix Internat. Mktg. Ops., N.Y.C., 1970-78; pres. Bendix Internat. Svc. Corp., N.Y.C., 1970-78; v.p. mktg. Sperry Corp., Great Neck, N.Y., 1978-86; pres., founder Nat. Inst. World Trade, Lloyd Harbor, N.Y., 1986—; trustee Friend World Coll., Lloyd Harbor, 1990-91; vice chmn. Dist. Export Coun., N.Y.C., 1972—; export advocate SBA, L.I., N.Y., 1990. Contbr. articles to New York Times, Long Island mag., Newsday, others. 2d lt. Signal Corps, U.S. Army, 1945-47. Mem. L.I. Assn. (dir. 1988-91, chmn. World Trade Coun. 1987—), Sagamore Rowing Assn. (trustee 1987-91). Home: 42 Turkey Ln Cold Spring Harbor NY 11724-1702 Office: Nat Inst for World Trade Plover Ln Huntington NY 11743-1037

ROSS, STANLEY CLARK, educator, consultant; b. Manchester, N.H., Aug. 16, 1948; m. Ellen Freshman, June 2, 1979; children: Justin, Jessica, Rebecca. BA, Boston U., 1973; MEd, U. Ariz., 1975; PhD, SUNY, Buffalo, 1988. Asst. prof. SUNY, Brockport, 1986; cons. Xerox Corp., Rochester, N.Y., 1988-90. Sgt. U.S. Army, 1967-70, Vietnam. Home: 61 Fairhaven Rd Rochester NY 14610-2229

ROSS, STEPHEN ADDISON, physician; b. Neptune, N.J., Jan. 2, 1940; s. Delbert Amos Ross and Evelyn Ernestine (Hutchinson) Bradway; m. Pamela Schrader Jensen, June 8, 1974. AB, Williams Coll., 1960; MD, Cornell U., 1964. Diplomate Am. Bd. Internal Medicine. Intern in internal medicine Yale-New Haven Hosp., New Haven, 1964-65, resident in internal medicine, 1965-66, 68-69; fellow in hematology Yale U., New Haven, 1969-70; chief resident in internal medicine VA Hosp., West Haven, Conn., 1970-71, fellow in hematology/oncology, 1971-73; mem. staff in internal medicine, hematology, oncology Community Health Care Ctr. Plan, New Haven, 1973-76; pvt. practice Rockland, Maine, 1976—; instr. Medicine Yale U., New Haven, 1970-72, asst. prof. Medicine, 1972-76; asst. clin. prof. Community Health Tufts U., Boston, 1983—, pres. med. staff, 1983—. Del. U.S. Pharmacopeial Conv., Washington, 1980-85; mem. adv. bd. Coastal Family Hospice, Rockland, 1984—. Capt. USAF, 1966-68. Fellow ACP; mem. Maine Med. Assn., Knox County Med. Soc., Am. Soc. of Clin. Oncology. Home: HCR 60 Box 3170 Camden NJ 04843 Office: 2 Glen Cove Dr Ste 103 Rockland ME 04841-2550

ROSS, STEPHEN CARL, alcohol/drug abuse services professional; b. Carroll, Iowa, Apr. 11, 1947; s. Dale Morris and Ethel Emma (Moore) R. BA in Psychology, U. Okla., 1969; MA in Counseling Psychology, Kutztown U., 1981. Cert. addiction counselor. Chief counselor P.G. County Drug Treatment Program, Cheverly, Md., 1971-73; sr. counselor No. Va. Family Svcs., Alexandria, 1973; counseling coord. counseling svcs. unit Community Gen. Hosp., Reading, Pa., 1973-90; program dir. Drug Treatment Program, Reading, 1990—; cons. to Family Life Svcs., Topton, Pa., 1981—, Concer, Cin., 1989—, Employee Sv cs., Wellsville, N.Y., 1986—; assessor, cons. to Pa. State Employee Assistance Program, Reading, 1989—; pvt. practice individual marriage and family therapy, 1971-91. Mem. Berks County Prison Soc., Reading, 1974-79; trainer People Against Rape, Reading, 1975-77; treas. Fort Northhill Jaycees, Shartlesville, Pa., 1978-79. With U.S. Army, 1969-71. Named Officer of Yr., Jaycees, Shartlesville, 1978-79; recipient Appreciation award Berks County Prison, 1990. Mem. ASCD, Am. Mental Health Counseelors Assn., Pa. Methodone Providers Assn. (sec. 1991-92), Phi Beta Kappa, Phi Kappa Phi, Phi Eta Sigma. Democrat. Lutheran. Home: RR 1 Box 260 Bernville PA 19506-9772

ROSS, STEVEN J., communications company executive; b. N.Y.C., 1927; married. Student, Paul Smith's Coll., 1948. Pres., dir. Kinney Services Inc., 1961-72; pres. Warner Communications Inc., N.Y.C., from 1972, chmn. bd., chief exec. officer, 1972—; co-chmn., co-chief exec. officer Time Warner Inc., N.Y.C., 1989-90, chmn., co-chief exec. officer, 1990—; bd. dirs. N.Y. Conv. and Visitors Bur., Mus. of TV and Radio; mem. sports medicine Lenox Hill Hosp. Office: Time Warner Inc 75 Rockefeller Pla New York NY 10019

ROSS, STUART DUNNING, sales manager; b. Lewiston, Maine, Feb. 24, 1936; s. Ronald Benjamin and Dorothy (Dunning) R.; m. Sonia Anne Barker (div. 1985); children: Deborah, Jennifer, Stephanie, Scott, Matthew, Michael; m. Merle A. Pushard, 1988; m. Rosemary A. Dobson, 1992. Student, Colby Coll., 1956-58, U. Md., 1959-60, U. Hartford, 1962-65. Internat. sales rep. United Techs., Hartford, Conn., 1961-71; NE sales mgr. Lincoln Controls Co., Pawtucket, R.I., 1971-78; gen sales mgr. Nichols Portland, Portland, Maine, 1979-88; dir. sales and mktg. Liquid Metronics div. Milton Roy Corp., Acton, Mass., 1990—. Served as cpl. USAF, 1956-60. Mem. Am. Mgmt. Assn., Nat. Fluid Power Assn., Am. Mktg. Assn., Assn. Water Technologies, Internat. Water Resources Assn., Water and Wastewater Equipment Mfrs. Assn. Republican. Clubs: Val Halla Country (Maine) (pres. 1972-74), Westminster Country. Office: LMI Div Milton Roy Corp 19 Craig Rd Acton MA 01720-5495

ROSS, THOMAS HUGH, business consultant, retired military officer; b. Pitts., May 18, 1927; s. Thomas Hugh and Anna Marie (Klaiber) R.; m. Ann Carolyn Sipp, Sept. 9, 1950; children: Thomas George, Douglas Alan, James William. BS, U.S. Naval Acad., 1950; BS in Aero. Engring., U.S. Naval Postgrad. Sch., 1957; grad., Command and Staff Naval War Coll., 1962; MS in Internat. Affairs, George Washington U., 1973, postgrad. internat. relations, 1975-78. Enlisted USN, 1945, commd. ensign, 1950, advanced through grades to capt., naval aviator, patrol plane comdr. worldwide, 1952-75, officer in charge 4th Unitas Air Group VP-56, S.Am., 1963, head dept. thermo/fluids U.S. Naval Acad., 1965-67, comdg. officer patrol squadron 16 Naval Air Sta., Jacksonville, Fla., 1968-69, ret., 1975; cons. Universal Systems, Inc. (Hadron, Inc.), Arlington, Va., 1979-82, Ecosystems, Internat., Inc., Gambrillis, Md., 1982-85; cons. then sr. v.p. engring. mgmt. Nat. Bus. Cons., Annapolis, Md., 1982-87. Decorated Air medal, Meritorious Service medal. Mem. DAV (life), Assn. Naval Aviation, Ret. Officers Assn. (life, bd. dirs. Annapolis chpt. 1988-92), U.S. Naval Acad. Alumni Assn. (life, pres. Annapolis chpt. 1978), Navy League (life), Am. Legion, Officers Christian Fellowship, Army-Navy Country Club, Officers and Faculty Club, U.S. Naval Acad. Republican. Presbyterian. Home and Office: 1928 Balt-Annopolis Blvd Annapolis MD 21401-6248

ROSS, THOMAS MCCALLUM, association executive; b. Hamilton, Ont., Can., May 5, 1931; s. Laverne Robinson and Della Louise (McCallum) R.; m. Marguerite Hilda Ross, Aug. 14, 1954; children: Thomas Wayne, Gregory (dec.), Karyn. Mgr. Sutherland Pharmacy, Hamilton, 1955-60; assoc. sec. Can. Pharm. Assn., Toronto, Ont., 1960-63; mem. research staff Royal Commn. Health Services Govt. Can., Ottawa, Ont., 1963-64; exec. dir. Can. Retail Hardware Assn., Toronto, 1964—. Bd. dirs. People for Sunday Assn., pres. 1987-88. Founding fellow Hardware Mgmt. Inst.; mem. Internat. Fedn. Ironmongers Assn. (coun. 1970—), Can. Soc. Assn. Execs. (chmn. edn. com. 1986-88, bd. dirs. 1990-92, Pinnacle award 1989), Am. Soc. Assn. Execs., Can. C. of C. Home: 59 Walby Dr, Oakville, ON Canada Office: 6800 Campobello Rd, Mississauga, ON Canada

ROSS, WILBUR LOUIS, JR., investment banker; b. Weehawken, N.J., Nov. 28, 1937; s. Wilbur Louis and Agnes (O'Neill) R.; m. Judith Nodine, May 26, 1961; children: Jessica, Amanda. AB, Yale U., 1959; MBA with distinction, Harvard U., 1961. Assoc. Wood, Struthers and Winthrop, N.Y.C., 1963-64; pres. Faulkner, Dawkins and Sullivan Securities Corp., N.Y.C., 1964-76; sr. mng. dir. Rothschild, Inc., N.Y.C., 1976—; bd. dirs. Aileen Inc., N.Y.C., Geo Internat. Corp., Stamford, Conn., Biocraft labs Inc., Rutherford, N.J., FurVault Inc., N.Y.C., Investors Ins. Co., Lawrence Harbor, N.J., Revere Copper and Brass Co., Stamford, Syms Corp., Secaucus, N.J., Am. Bankruptcy Inst., Washington, Allis Chalmers Corp., Milw., Mego Corp., Las Vegas, Nev.; fin. advisor equity holders com. Texaco Co., A.H. Robins Co., Pub. Service N.H. Treas. N.Y. State Dem. Com., 1980-83; vice chmn. Bklyn. Mus., 1981—; chmn. univ. coun. com. on art Yale U., 1983-88; chmn. NAD, N.Y.C., 1985—, Am. Art Forum, Smithsonian Instn., 1987—; trustee, vice chmn. Nat. Mus. Am. Art, Washington, 1986-91, chmn., 1991—; trustee Sarah Lawrence Coll., 1986—, chmn. art gallery, 1984—; pres. Parrish Art Mus., 1991—. With U.S. Army, 1961-63. Fellow Jonathan Edward Coll. of Yale U., Met. Mus. Art; mem. Fin. Analysts Fedn. (chartered), Century Assn. Home: The Dakota 1 W 72d St New York NY 10023 Office: Rothschild Inc 1 Rockefeller Pla New York NY 10020

ROSSELLO, JOSEPH ANTHONY, chiropractor, musician; b. Oyster Bay, N.Y., May 21, 1959; s. Anthony Joseph and Adele (Granese) R.; children: Leisa, Ina Mareé. D in Chiropractic, N.Y. Chiropractic Coll., 1984. Ptnr. Flushing (N.Y.) Plaza Family Chiropractic, 1984-89; ptnr. Pelham Bay Family Chiropractic, Bronx, N.Y., 1984-89, owner, 1989—. Mem. exec. bd. Bronx YMCA, 1989—, chmn. bd. and programs, 1991—; chmn. youth com. ARC, Bronx, 1989-91, chmn. bd., 1991—. Mem. Kiwanis (treas. Bronx chpt. 1988-90, sec. 1990-91, pres. 1991-92, Kiwanian of the Yr. 1988-89, editor Tocsin Newsletter 1990-91-hon. mention), Bronx C. of C. (bd. dirs). Office: Pelham Bay Family Chiropractic 3040 E Tremont Ave # 107 Bronx NY 10461-5733

ROSSETTOS, JOHN NICHOLAS, mechanical engineering educator; b. Nisyros, Dodecanese, Greece, Mar. 11, 1932; s. Nicholas John and Calliope Nicholas (Violis) R.; m. Elizabeth Joy Pureka, June 23, 1963; children: Nicholas, Linda. BS and MS, MIT, 1956; PhD, Harvard U., 1964. Staff engr. MIT Aeroclastic Lab., Cambridge, Mass., 1954-56; rsch. engr. United Aircraft Rsch. ctr., East Hartford, Conn., 1956-57; sr. engr. Am. Sci. & Engring., Cambridge, 1957-59; aerospace scientist NASA Langley Rsch. Ctr., Hampton, Va., 1964-66; sr. staff scientist Avco Corp., Wilmington, Mass., 1966-69; prof. mech. engring. Northeastern U., Boston, 1970—; cons. U.S. Army Matls. Tech. Lab., Watertown, Mass., 1987-88, Avco Systems Div., Wilmington, Mass., 1981-84; vis. assoc. prof. MIT, 1970; rsch. assoc. Harvard U., 1979. Author: Finite Element Method, 1977. Mem. parish coun. Greek Orthodox Ch., Lexington, Mass., 1974-77. Gordon M. McKay fellow, 1961; NASA Langley Rsch. Ctr. grantee, 1971; Transp. Systems Ctr. grantee, 1975; NASA Lewis Rsch. Ctr. grantee, 1989; named Outstanding Faculty Mem., Northeastern U., Dept. Mech. Engring., 1988, 89, 91. Fellow AIAA (assoc.), ASME; mem. Am. Acad. Mechanics. Home: 14 Dana Ave Winchester MA 01890-1010 Office: Northeastern Univ Dept Mech Engring Boston MA 02115

ROSS-GORDON, JOVITA M., education educator; b. Chgo., Nov. 11, 1952; d. William T. and Pauline (Jones) Martin; m. Stephen P. Gordon, Dec. 16, 1989. BS in Speech and Lang. Pathology, Northwestern U., 1974, MA in Learning Disabilities, 1975; EdD in Adult Edn., U. Ga., 1985. Learning disabilities tchr. Atlanta Speech Sch., 1975-76, Durham County (N.C.) Pub. Schs., 1976-78; learning skills counselor U. Pitts., 1978-81; grad. asst. Northwestern U., Evanston, Ill., 1981-82, U. Ga., Athens, 1982-85; asst. prof. Pa. State U., State College, 1985—. Cons. editor: Adult Edn. Quarterly, 1986—; author: Adults with Learning Disabilities: An Overview for the Adult Educator, 1989, (with others) Serving Culturally Diverse Populations: Adult Education Models, 1990; contbr. chpts. to books and articles to profl. jours. Named one of Outstanding Young Women Am., 1983; recipient Helmer Myklebust award Northwestern U., 1975, Levine award, 1974. Mem. Comm. Profs. Adult Edn. (exec. com. 1987-89, program co-chair nat. meetings for Adult and Continuing Edn. (selection com. for Imogene Oakes Rsch. award 1987, 88, chair membership unit on status of women/sex equity 1985-86). Home: 254 Gerald St State College PA 16801-7400 Office: Pa State U 403 S Allen St Ste 206 State College PA 16801-5252

ROSSI, COLUMBIA ROSE, foreign correspondent; b. Bklyn., Oct. 4, 1908; m. James Vincent Sileo, Sept. 20, 1928 (dec.); children: Gloria Sileo Smith, Joan V. Sileo Ziccardy, Felicia Sileo. Grad., Bay Ridge High Sch., Bklyn., 1926. Reporter, photographer Internat. News Svc., N.Y.C., 1939;

speaker various orgns., experiences as a newswoman in Latin Am. and Europe. Author: Tiajuana Susie, 1951, On a Mission to Danger, Even the Sugarcane Weeps, Bertie: Life After Death of H. G. Wells, 1973. Mem. Overseas Press Club of N.Y. Roman Catholic. Home: 2 Hunter Ln Levittown NY 11756-5114

ROSSI, FRANCIS VINCENT, civil engineer; b. Hartford, Conn., Aug. 31, 1925; s. Vincent Purcell and Carmen (Gallo) R.; m. Beatrice Ann Bujak, June 4, 1924. BSCE, U. Conn., 1951. Registered profl. engr., Conn., N.Y., Mass., R.I., Vt., N.H. Field/project engr. B. Perini Corp., Framingham, Mass., 1951-54; chief engr. Juno-Maskel Constrn. Co., East Hartford, Conn., 1954-58; v.p., sec. Maskel Constrn. Co., South Windsor, Conn., 1958-75; cons. F.V. Rossi, P.E., South Windsor, 1975-77; dir. pub. wks. Town of Simsbury, Conn., 1977—; cons. in field; constrn. arbitrator Am. Arbitration Assn., 1965—; bd. dirs. Conn. Call Before You Dig, Inc., Hamden, 1978—. Contbr. articles to profl. jours. 1st lt. USAF, 1943-46. Fellow ASCE; mem. NSPE (bd. dirs. 1970-74), Conn. Soc. Profl. Engrs. (pres. 1971-72), Profl. Engrs. in Constrn. (charter bd. govs. 1973-75), Nat. Utility Contrs. Assn., Mensa, Am. Pub. Works Assn. (dir. New Eng. chpt. 1990—). Democrat. Roman Catholic. Home: 412 Simsbury Rd Bloomfield CT 06002-2218 Office: Town of Simsbury 933 Hopmeadow St # 495 Simsbury CT 06070-1822

ROSSI, JOSEPH O., artist, educator; b. Paterson, N.J.; s. Pasquale and Marion (Stampone) R.; m. Joan O'Mara, 1949; children: Robert J., Donald J., Sharon M., Carolyn J. Student, Newark Sch. Fine-Indsl. Art, Columbia U. instr. watercolor, oil and life drawing Newark Sch. Fine and Indsl. Art, 1946, adminstrv. asst.; instr. watercolor Art Students League, N.Y.C., 1975. Exhibited in group shows Am. Watercolor Soc., NAD, N.Y.C., 1979, Allied Artists, 1979, Audubon Artists, 1979, Royal Acad., London, Rockport (Mass.) Art Assn., 1979; represented in permanent collections Salmagundi Club, Norfolk (Va.) Mus., Newark Hosp.; represented by Grand Central Galleries, N.Y.C.; work reviewed in various publs. Mem. Am. Watercolor Soc. (Lena Newcastle award 1979), Audubon Artists, Salmagundi Club (v.p. Malcolm Tuttle award 1974), Allied Artists Am. (former demonstration chmn.), Soc. Illustrators, N.J. Watercolor Soc. (past v.p., award 1978), North Shore Art Assn., Rockport (Mass.) Art Assn., Phila. Watercolor Soc. Home and Studio: 45 Lockwood Dr Clifton NJ 07013

ROSSI, RONALD ALDO, sports association administrator, Olympic athlete; b. Bronx, N.Y., Dec. 2, 1956; s. Aldo D. and Jeanette (Morretta) R.; m. Susan Veltman, Mar. 26, 1983. BEE, Manhattan Coll., 1978. Registered profl. engr., N.Y. Mem. computer ops. staff John Blair and Co., N.Y.C., 1978-83, communications engr., 1984; sports program dir. U.S. Luge Assn., Lake Placid, N.Y., 1984-85, exec. dir., 1985—; com. mem. U.S. Luge Assn., 1978—, athletes' rep., 1980-83; com. mem. U.S. Olympic Com., Colorado Springs, Colo., 1989-90. Mem. U.S. Olympic luge team, Sarajevo, Yugoslavia, 1984, Calgary, Can., 1988, Albertville, France, 1992. Office: US Luge Assn PO Box 651 Lake Placid NY 12946

ROSSI, STEVEN, automotive company executive; b. Bklyn., Sept. 5, 1954. BSME, Poly. Inst. Bklyn., 1976. With engine engring. group Ford Motor Co.; cert. engr. Saab Cars U.S.A., Inc., Orange, Conn., 1978-80, market adaptation engr., 1980-83, product devel. and compliance mgr., 1983-87, tech. planning mgr., 1987-89, dir. pub. rels., 1989-92; dir. industry, govt. and pub. rels. Saab Cars U.S.A., Inc., Norcross, Ga., 1992—. Office: Saab Cars USA Inc PO Box 9000 4405-A Trailmore Ct Norcross GA 30091

ROSSIGNOL, ROGER JOHN, coatings company executive; b. N.Y.C., Jan. 19, 1941; s. Willard and Claire (Tardif) R.; m. Gloria Jean Cone, Sept. 19, 1981; children: Vincent, Michael, David, Tricia. Salesman Bates Fabrics Inc., N.Y.C., 1964-75, Bates Mfg. Co., Lewiston, Maine, 1964-75; in mktg. Ethan Allen Co., Danbury, Conn., 1975-77; v.p. sales Internat. Flooring, Long Branch, N.J., 1977-80; sales mgr. Asbestos Corp., Long Branch, 1980-82; pres. Encapco Corp., Point Pleasant, N.J., 1982-84, Internat. Protective Coatings Corp., Ocean Twp., N.J., 1984—. Office: Internat Protective Coating 725 Carole Ave Oakhurst NJ 07755-1202

ROSSINGTON, DAVID RALPH, physical chemistry educator; b. London, July 13, 1932; s. George Leonard and Clara Fanny (Simmons) R.; children: Andrew, Carolyn, Nicholas, Philip. BSc with honors, U. Bristol, Eng., 1953, PhD, 1956. Postdoctoral research fellow N.Y. State Coll. Ceramics at Alfred (N.Y.) U., 1956-58; tech. officer Imperial Chem. Industries Ltd., Eng., 1958-60; asst. prof. phys. chemistry Alfred U., 1960-63, assoc. prof., 1963-69, prof., 1969—, head div. ceramic engring., 1976-79, 82-84, dean sch. engring., 1984-91. Editor: Advances in Materials Characterization, 1983; contbr. 32 articles to profl. jours. Town Justice, Alfred, 1976-86. Fulbright scholar, 1956, 58. Fellow Am. Ceramic Soc.; mem. Am. Chem. Soc., Ceramic Edn. Council, Materials Research Soc., Am. Soc. Engring. Edn. Democrat. Episcopalian. Office: Alfred U Sch of Engring Alfred NY 14802

ROSSKY, WILLIAM, English educator; b. Plainfield, N.J., July 11, 1917; s. Jacob and Esther (Kovitsky) R.; m. Evelyn Gross, Fb. 5, 1943; children: Ellen, Peter. BA, Lafayette Coll., 1938; MA, NYU, 1939, PhD, 1953. From instr. to prof. Temple U., Phila., 1946-82, chmn. dept. English, 1964-67, prof. emeritus, 1982—; vis. prof. NYU, 1957; advisor Jour. Modern Lit., 1968—. Mem. MLA, Renaissance Soc. Am., Soc. Study of So. Lit., Shakespeare Assn. Am., Phi Beta Kappa. Office: Temple U Dept English Broad St Philadelphia PA 19185-0002

ROSSMAN, HOWARD (DAVID), psychotherapist, psychologist, educator; b. Flushing, N.Y., June 6, 1945; s. Louis Harry and Gertrude (Ellenberg) R.; m. Linda F. Rossman, Nov. 18, 1967; 1 child, Julie Rebecca. BA, Queens Coll., 1967; MA in History, Brandeis U., 1969; MEd, Boston Coll., 1979, PhD, 1983. Lic. psychologist, Mass. Spl. needs tchr. Wayland (Mass.) Pub. Schs., 1974-79, guidance counselor, 1979-80; guidance counselor Newton (Mass.) Pub Schs., 1980-81; psychology intern Beaverbrook Guidance Ctr., Watertown, Mass., 1981-82, staff psychologist, 1985-87; staff psychologist Children's Friend & Family Svc. Soc., Salem, Mass., 1982-85; pvt. practic psychology Lexington, Mass., 1985—; clin. dir. Schs. for Children, Arlington, Mass., 1987-91, dir. ops. Dearborn Acad., 1991—. Mem. APA, Mass. Psychol. Assn., Assn. Spl. Educators. Office: 35 Bedford St Ste 7 Lexington MA 02173-4454

ROSSMAN, ISADORE, physician; b. Elizabeth, N.J., Mar. 29, 1913; s. Abraham and Lena (Roshonik) R.; m. Sylvia Weiner; 1 child, Paul Gordon. BA, U. Wis., 1933; PhD, U. Chgo., 1937, MD, 1942. Diplomate internal medicine. Rsch. assoc. anatomy U. Chgo., 1935-42; physician pvt. practice, N.Y.C., 1947—; med. dir. Montefiore Home Health Agy., N.Y.C., 1948—; assoc. clin. prof. medicine Einstein Coll. Medicine, 1970-84; commr. N.Y. State Moreland Commn., 1974-76; adv. coun. Nat. Inst. Aging, 1978-81; bd. dirs. Am. Geriatrics Soc., 1975-85, pres., 1982-83; asst. dir. Bur. Chronic Disease Control, N.Y.C. Dept. Health, 1971-75. Author: Looking Forward, 1989; editor: Clinical Geriatrics, 1970, 2d edit. 1979, 3d edit. 1986; contbr. articles to profl. jours. Capt. U.S. Army, 1943-46. Recipient Freeman award, Gerontologic Soc. Am., 1980, Leavitt award, Am. Geriatrics Soc., 1987. Fellow N.Y. Acad. Medicine, Phi Beta Kappa, Sigma Xi. Democrat. Jewish. Home: 50 W 96th St New York NY 10025-6526

ROSSMAN, ROBERT HARRIS, management consultant; b. Phila., Jan. 27, 1932; s. Benjamin Bernard Rossman; m. Roberta Ann Matisoff, May 30 1956 (div. 1976); children: Rodger Samuel, Robbi Jennifer, Ronni Esther; m. Wanda Ward, Aug. 9, 1980. BS, U.S. Merchant Marine Acad., 1953; MSME with honors, U.S. Naval Postgrad. Sch., 1963; cert. advanced naval architecture, MIT, 1973. Cert. mgr. human resources, value specialist. Commd. ensign USN, 1953, advanced through grades to comdr., 1967, shipboard engr., 1953-55, maintenance and repair officer Reserve Fleet, 1955-57; served as ship supt. Norfolk Naval Shipyard, Portsmouth, Va., 1957-60; maintenance and logistics planning officer Amphibious Squadron Twelve, Little Creek, Va., 1963-65; planning and estimating supt. U.S. Naval Ship Repair Facility, Yokosuka, Japan, 1965-67; design and planning advisor USN, Saigon, Republic Viet Nam, 1967-68; chief prodn. engring. Def. Contract Adminstrn. Svcs., Alexandria, Va., 1968-70; dir. cost reduction Naval Ship Systems Command, Washington, 1970-73; dep. program mgr. new ship class Naval Ship Engring. Ctr., Hyattsville, Md., 1973; ret. USN, 1973; ptnr. Kempter-Rossman Internat., Washington, 1974-91; owner Rossman Assocs. Internat., 1991—; cons. in field. Author: (textbook) Function Based Analysis, 1983, Total Cycle Time Reduction, 1992; editor mag. Performance, 1970-73; contbr. articles to profl. jours. Pres. PTA, Fairfax County, Va., 1969-70, Community Civic Assn., Fairfax County, 1970-71; chmn. Boy Scouts Am. and Weblos troops, 1969-71, del. at large 1st Congl. Dist. Rep. Com., N.C., 1989-90; chmn. Chowan County (N.C.) Rep. Com., 1990. Decorated Naval Commendation medals, Honor medal (Republic of Viet Nam Armed Forces), Combat Action Medal. Fellow Soc. Am. Value Engrs. (v.p. 1970-73, Disting. Svc. award 1976); mem. U.S. Merchant Marine Acad. Alumni Assn., Am. Legion, Sigma Xi. Jewish. Home: RR 2 Box 3 Edenton NC 27932-9602 Office: Rossman Assocs Internat Speight House Rt 2 Box 3 Edenton NC 27932

ROSTAMI, ABDOLMOHAMAD, neurologist, researcher; b. Bushehr, Fars, Iran, June 20, 1948; came to U.S., 1975; s. Abbas and Fatemeh Rostami; m. Nasrin Golshan. Pre-med. degree, Shiraz U., Iran, 1968, MD, 1974; PhD, U. Pa., 1981. Neurologist U. Pa., Phila., 1983—, dir. sect. neuroimmunology, 1991—. Mem. AAAS, Am. Neurol. Assn., Am. Acad. Neurology, Am. Assn. Immunologists, Nat. Multiple Sclerosis Soc., Guillain-Barre Syndrome Found. Office: U Pa Hosp Dept Neurology 3400 Spruce St Philadelphia PA 19104

ROSTOVSKY, ALLA GRIGORIEVNA, arts and sciences educator; b. Leningrad, USSR, June 18, 1941; came to U.S., 1980; d. Gregory and Lia Kravchik; m. Rostovsky Kiryll, June, 1967 (div. 1973); 1 child, Peter. MA, U. Theater, Music and Cinematography, Leningrad, 1965; MS, U. Precision Mechanics and Optics, Leningrad, 1972; D of Arts, SUNY, Stony Brook, 1991. Tenured scholar/researcher State Mus. Hermitage/Acad. of Sci. of USSR, Leningrad, 1969-79; lectr. SUNY, Stony Brook, 1982—; cons. in Russian/Soviet lit. and civilization, Main Libr./SUNY, Stony Brook, 1986—. Author: (script) Three Rice Grains, 1976. Recipient scholarship SUNY, 1982-89. Mem. Modern Lang. Assn.

ROSTROPROVICH, MSTISLAV, conductor. Mus. dir. Nat. Symphony Orch., Washington. Address: care Nat Symph Orch Concert Hall Kennedy Ctr Washington DC 20566*

ROSZKOWSKI, MICHAEL JOSEPH, psychologist; b. Szczawno-Zdroj, Poland, July 20, 1950; s. Michael and Elaine (Sichler) R.; m. Maryann Theresa Carolan, Dec. 28, 1974; children: Daniel M., John T. BS, St. Joseph's U., 1973; MEd, Temple U., 1975, PhD, 1981. Cert. sch. psychologist Pa., N.J.; licensed psychologist, Pa. Inland marine ins. underwriter Gen. Accident Assurance Co., Phila., 1973-74; rsch. asst. Woodhaven Ctr., Phila., 1976-78, rsch. assoc., 1978-81; rsch. psychologist Am. Coll., Bryn Mawr, Pa., 1981-88, dir. mktg. rsch., 1988—; test reviewer Buros Mental Measurements Yearbook. Cons. editor Jour. Genetic Psychology, 1984—, Genetic, Social and General Psychology Monographs, 1984—; contbr. articles to profl. jours. Mem. APA, Psi Chi. Home: 101 Cherry Tree Ln Cherry Hill NJ 08002-1006 Office: The Am Coll 270 S Bryn Mawr Ave Bryn Mawr PA 19010-2105

ROTA, MARIAN LOREN, translator, writer/editor; b. Hoboken, N.J., Jan. 28, 1958; d. Marino and Lida Rota. Student, U. Florence, Italy, 1978-79; BA, Rutgers U., 1980; cert., Georgetown U., 1987. Jr. credit analyst Irving Trust Co., N.Y.C., 1980-84; legal asst. Pillsbury Madison & Sutro, Washington, 1988; interpreter Chestnut Lodge Hosp., Rockville, Md., 1992; editorial cons. The World Bank, Washington, 1991-92, Nat. Acad. Scis., Washington, 1990, 92; freelance editorial proofreader The Brookings Inst., Washington, 1991-92, NSF, Washington, 1991-92. Bibliographer Am. Assn. of Mus., Washington, 1992. Mem. Washington Ind. Writers (workshop com. 1991-92, exec. bd. dirs. 1992—), am. Translators Assn., Phi Sigma Iota. Home and Office: 2000 F St NW # 815 2000 F St NW #815 Washington DC 20006-4238

ROTEMBERG, JULIO JACOBO, economist, educator, consultant; b. Buenos Aires, Argentina, Sept. 26, 1953; came to U.S., 1972; s. Salomon and Ellen (Wolf) R.; m. Analisa Lattes, Nov. 8, 1982; childrenL Veronica M., Martin S. BA, U. Calif., Berkeley, 1975; PhD, Princeton U., 1981. Researcher Banco Cen. De La Republica Argentina, Buenos Aires, 1976; from asst. prof. to assoc. prof. econs. Sloan Sch. Mgmt. MIT, Cambridge, 1980-89, prof., 1989—; rsch. assoc. Nat. Bureau of Econ. Rsch., Cambridge, 1986—. Mem. bd. editors Rev. Econ. Studies, 1985-88, Econometrica, 1987—, Quarterly Jour. Econs., 1989—; contbr. articles to profl. jours. Fellow Econometric Soc.; mem. Am. Econ. Assn. Office: MIT Sloan Sch Mgmt Cambridge MA 02139

ROTENBERG, MARC STEVEN, public interest advocate, lawyer; b. Boston, Apr. 20, 1960; s. Michael and Karen (Sethur) Rotenberg. AB, Harvard Coll., 1982; JD, Stanford U., 1987. Bar: Mass. 1987, D.C. 1990. Teaching fellow Harvard U., Cambridge, Mass., 1980-82; exec. dir. Pub. Interest Computer Assn., Washington, 1983-84; instr. Stanford (Calif.) U., 1986-87; counsel Senate Jud. Com., Washington, 1987-88; dir. Washington office Computer Profls. for Social Responsibility, 1988—; adj. prof. law Georgetown Law Ctr.; sec. Privacy Internat.; mem. adv. panels Office Tech. Assessment. Bd. editors Govt. Info. Quar.; contbr. articles to profl. jours. Mem. Assn. Computing Machinery, ABA, Am. Civil Liberties Union. Office: Computer Profls Social 666 Pennsylvania Ave SE Ste 303 Washington DC 20003-4319

ROTH, CHARLES FRANCIS, JR., communications educator; b. Allentown, Pa., Oct. 30, 1946; s. Charles Francis Sr. and Gloria M. (Mohry) R.; m. Sandra Ruth Steimling, June 29, 1968; children: Byron Jason, Jarrett Bryant, Kimberly Ann. BS in Edn., Kutztown U., 1968; MEd in Ednl. Media, West Chester U., 1972; PhD in Ednl. Media, Southern Ill. U., 1975. Cert. tchr., Pa. Tchr. Owen J. Roberts Sch. Dist., Pottstown, Pa., 1970-73; vis. asst. prof. Towson State U., Balt., 1975-78; asst. prof. SUNY, Fredonia, 1979-83; dir. learning resources U. Mich., Flint, 1983-88; dir. audiovisual svcs. Roger Williams Coll., Bristol, R.I., 1988-89; assoc. prof. Kutztown (Pa.) U., 1989—; asst. prof. U. Maine, Farmington, 1978; coord. audiovisual svcs. Chautaugua Instn., 1980; dir. instrl. activities WFUM-TV U. Mich., Flint, 1983-88; cons. GM, Flint, 1986; grant reviewer Nat. Inst. on Drug Abuse, Rockville, Md., 1990; workshop presenter Lehigh County Hist. Soc., Allentown, 1991, Patient Edn. and Community Health, South Cen., Pa., 1991. Contbr. articles to profl. jours. With USAF, 1968-70, Vietnam. Mem. Assn. Edn. Communication and Tech. (com. chair 1988—), Am. Ednl. Rsch. Assn., Pa. Assn. Edn. Communication and Tech., Pa. Ednl. Rsch. Assn. Lutheran. Home: 952 Lawrence Dr Emmaus PA 18049-1513 Office: Kutztown U Dept of Audiovisual Communication Kutztown PA 19530

ROTH, EDWARD EMIL, adult education specialist; b. St. James, Mo., July 13, 1945; s. Ernest Emil and Goldie May (Wilson) R. BA, Southeast Mo. State Coll., 1970, BS in Edn., 1970, MA, 1971; postgrad., Am. U., 1987—. Cert. tchr., Mo. With U.S. Postal Svc., 1977—; mgmt. edn. specialist, seminar leader U.S. Postal Svc., Potomac, Md., 1986—. Author: Postmaster Training, 1988; creator TV course Fin. Responsibility, 1990. With U.S. Army, 1966-70. Mem. Charcot Marie Tooth Assn. Democrat. Roman Catholic. Office: US Postal Svc 9600 Newbridge Dr Potomac MD 20858-4323

ROTH, JANE RICHARDS, federal judge; b. Phila., June 16, 1935; d. Robert Henry Jr. and Harriett (Kellond) Richards; m. William V. Roth Jr., Oct. 9, 1965; children: William V. III, Katharine K. BA, Smith Coll., 1956; LLB, Harvard U., 1965; LLD (hon.), Widener U., 1986. Bar: Del. 1965, U.S. Dist. Ct. Del. 1966, U.S. Ct. Appeals (3d cir.) 1974. Adminstrv. asst. various fgn. service posts U.S. State Dept., 1956-62; assoc. Richards, Layton & Finger, Wilmington, Del., 1965-73, ptnr., 1973-85; judge U.S. Dist. Ct. Del., Wilmington, 1985-91, U.S. Ct. Appeals (3d cir.), Wilmington, 1991—; adj. faculty Villanova U. Sch. Law. Mem. Chesapeake Bay coun. Girl Scouts U.S.; hon. chmn. Del. chpt. Arthritis Found., Wilmington; bd. overseers Widener U. Sch. Law; trustee Hist. Soc. Del. Recipient Nat. Vol. Service citiation Athritis Found., 1982. Mem. Fed. Judges Assn., Del. State Bar Assn. Republican. Episcopalian. Office: US Ct House 844 King St Lockbox 12 Wilmington DE 19801*

ROTH, JEROME ALLAN, pharmacology educator; b. N.Y.C., Aug. 20, 1943; s. Fred and Lillian Roth; divorced; children: Rachel, Evan; m. Patricia A. Kowal, Jan. 26, 1984; children: Chrissy A., Lyndsey B. BS, SUNY, New Paltz, 1965; M Nutritional Sci., Cornell U., 1967, PhD, 1971. Rsch. assoc. Vanderbilt U. Sch. Medicine, Nashville, 1971-72; asst. prof. Yale U. Sch. Medicine, New Haven, 1972-76; asst. prof. SUNY, Buffalo, 1976-80, assoc. prof., 1980-85, prof., 1985—, dir. med. scientist tng. program, 1990—. Mem. editorial bd. Biochem. Pharmacology. Office: SUNY Dept Pharmacology & Therapeutics Buffalo NY 14214

ROTH, LAURA MAURER, physics educator, researcher; b. Flushing, N.Y., Oct. 11, 1930; d. Keith Langden and Ruth (Oliphint) Maurer; m. Willard Dale Roth, June 6. 1952; children: Andrew Eric, Karen Elsa. AB, Swarthmore Coll., 1952; AM, Radcliffe Coll., 1953, PhD, 1957. Staff physicist Lincoln Lab., MIT, Lexington, Mass., 1956-63; lectr. Harvard U., Cambridge, Mass., summer 1959; assoc. prof., prof. physics Tufts U., Medford, Mass., 1963-67; physicist GE R & D Ctr., Schenectady, N.Y., 1967-72; lectr. Inst. for Theoretical Physics, U. Colo., Boulder, Colo., summer 1969; Abbey Rockefeller Mauze vis. prof. physics MIT, Cambridge, Mass., 1972-73; rsch. prof. SUNY, Albany, 1973-77, prof. physics, 1977—; cons. Lincoln Lab., MIT, Lexington, Mass., 1963,. Co-author: Women in Physics, 1975; co-editor: Fundamental Questions in Quantum Mechanics, 1984; contbr. 80 articles to physics jours., 1956—. Dir. Karma Thegsum Choling Buddhist Ctr., Albany, N.Y., 1979—; program dir. for publs. Karma Kagyu Inst., Woodstock, N.Y., 1988—. Recipient medal Radcliffe Grad. Soc., 1962; grantee Sloan Found., Tufts U., 1963-65, NSF, SUNY, Albany, 1976-81. Democrat. Buddhist. Home: 1270 Ruffner Rd Niskayuna NY 12309-4601 Office: SUNY Dept Physics 1400 Washington Ave Albany NY 12222-0001

ROTH, PHILIP, author; b. Newark, Mar. 19, 1933; s. Herman and Bess (Finkel) R.; m. Margaret Martinson, Feb. 22, 1959 (dec. 1968); m. Claire Bloom, Apr. 29, 1990. Student, Newark Coll. of Rutgers U., 1950-51; AB, Bucknell U., 1954; MA, U. Chgo., 1955. Tchr. English U. Chgo., 1956-58; short story writer, novelist, works pub. in Harper's, New Yorker, Epoch, Commentary, others, also reprints in Best Am. Short Stories of 1956, 59, 60, O'Henry Prize Stories of 1960; faculty Iowa Writers Workshop, 1960-62; writer in residence Princeton U., 1962-64; adj. prof. U. Pa., 1967-77; Disting. prof. Hunter Coll., CUNY, 1989—. Author: Goodbye, Columbus (Nat. Book award), 1959, Letting Go, 1962, When She Was Good, 1967, Portnoy's Complaint, 1969, Our Gang, 1971, The Breast, 1972, The Great American Novel, 1973, My Life as a Man, 1974, Reading Myself and Others, 1975, The Professor of Desire, 1977, The Ghost Writer, 1979, A Philip Roth Reader, 1980, Zuckerman Unbound, 1981, The Anatomy Lesson, 1983, Zuckerman Bound, 1985, The Prague Orgy, 1985, The Counterlife, 1987 (Nat. Book Critics Circle award for fiction, 1988), The Facts, 1988, Deception, 1990, Patrimony, 1991 (Nat. Book Critics Circle award 1992). Recipient Aga Khan prize for fiction, 1958, Nat. Book Critics Circle award for biography/autobiography, 1992; Guggenheim fellow, 1959-60, Rockefeller fellow, 1966; award Nat. Inst. Arts and Letters, 1960, Daroff award Jewish Book Coun. Am., 1960, Medal of Honor for Lit., Nat. Arts Club, 1991. Office: care Simon & Schuster Inc 1230 Ave Of The Americas New York NY 10020-1513

ROTH, PHYLLIS IRENE, social worker, psychotherapist; b. N.Y.C., Oct. 12, 1937; d. Maurice and Alice (Bader) Kleinman; m. Bernard S. Roth, Dec. 28, 1958 (div. Mar. 1980); children: Dana Alison, Bonnie Andrea; m. Louis S. Goldberg, Nov. 28, 1982. MS in Guidance-Counseling, Bklyn. Coll., 1963; MSW, Adelphi U., 1970. Diplomate Am. Bd. Examiners. Social worker Hillside Hosp., Glen Oaks, N.Y., 1970-71, Pride of Judea Treatment Ctr., Douglaston, N.Y., 1971-80, N.Y.C. Bd. Edn., Queens, 1980-83; supr. social worker North Shore Child and Family Guidance Ctr., Roslyn Heights, N.Y., 1983-92; pvt. practice psychotherapy Great Neck, N.Y., 1975—; therapist, cons. Parents of Murdered Children and Other Survivors of Homicide, Roslyn Heights, 1984-92; bd. dirs. Crime Victims Adv. and Support Program; coord. Single Parent Action Network, Roslyn Heights, 1984-92. Mem. crime victims L.I. Task Force; vice chairperson crime victims Nassau Suffolk Task Force. Fellow N.Y. State Soc. for Social Work Psychotherapists, Am. Orthopsychiatric. Jewish.

ROTH, ROBERT A., financial executive; b. Bklyn., Apr. 3, 1943; s. Harold L. and Catherine (Budway) R.; m. Myriam Munoz, June 15, 1969; children: Robert A., Karla. BA, CCNY, 1964; MS with hons., SUNY, Bronx, 1978. Asst. mgr. Pan Am. World Airways, Guatemala, 1968-70; area mgr. Pan Am. World Airways, Queens, N.Y., 1970-72; dir. cost controls Prudential Lines, Inc., N.Y.C., 1972-78; comptroller, gen. mgr. N.W. Johnsen & Co., Inc., N.Y.C., 1978-85; v.p. Contract Marine Carriers, Elizabeth, N.J., 1985; chief fin. officer Twp. of Middletown, N.J., 1985—; lectr. in field. Mem. Planning Bd., Middletown, N.J., 1986-91, Monmouth County Rep. Com., Middletown, 1983—. 1st lt. U.S. Army, 1964-66. Mem. Assn. Water Transp. Acctg. Officers (exec. v.p. 1985), Govt. Fin. Officers Assn. (bd. dirs. 1990—), Monmouth Ocean County Tax Collectors and Treas. Assn., Elks. Republican. Roman Catholic. Home: 6 Thompson Ave Leonardo NJ 07737-1458 Office: Township of Middletown 1 Kings Hwy Middletown NJ 07748-2594

ROTH, ROBERT HOWARD, psychologist; b. Newark, N.J., Jan. 15, 1933; s. Max and Marion (Gurkewitz) R.; m. Estelle Goldstein, June 16, 1957; children: Lisa C., Neil A. BS, Juilliard Sch., N.Y.C., 1953, MA, Columbia U., 1956, EdD, 1960. Lic. psychologist, N.Y., N.J. Instr. Union Coll., Cranford, N.J., 1959-60, Newark State Coll., Union, N.J., 1960-63; asst. prof. Hunter Coll. CUNY, N.Y.C., 1963-65; assoc. prof. Newark State Coll., Union, N.J., 1965-68, chmn. psychology dept., 1967-71; prof. psychology Kean Coll. N.J., Union, 1968—; cons. Marlboro (N.J.) Psychiat. Hosp., 1982—; pvt. practice clin. psychology Madison Med. Ctr. Editor: Contemporary Studies in Psychopathology, 1983, Contemporary Studies in Personality, 1986, Explorations in Mental Disorders, 1987, Personality Structures and Functions, 1989, Psychopathologies and Treatments, 1991. Fellow Am. Orthopsychiatric Assn.; mem. APA, AAAS, N.Y. Acad. Scis., N.J. Acad. Scis. (chmn. psychology sect. 1971-73). Home: 111 Gallinson Dr Nw Providence NJ 07974-2723 Office: Madison Med Ctr 28 Walnut St Madison NJ 07940-1631

ROTH, ROBERT STEELE, mathematician; b. Phila., July 3, 1930; s. Clyde Christian and Gerturde de la Barth (Steele) R.; m. Micheline Mary Mathews, May 13, 1966; 1 child, John Doguereau. AB cum laude, Kenyon Coll., 1953; MS, Carnegie Tech., 1954; PhD, Harvard U., 1962. Sr. staff scientist AVCO Corp., Wilmington, Mass., 1962-74; mem. tech. staff Charles S. Draper Lab., Cambridge, Mass., 1974—; mem. organizing com. Internat. Conf. on Computer and Math. Modeling, 1982—. Author: The Bellman Continuum, 1986; co-author: (with R.E. Bellman) Quasilinearization and the Identification Problem, 1983, The Laplace Transform, 1984, Methods in Approximation, 1986. Gordon McKay fellow Harvard U., 1960-61. Mem. Am. Acad. Mechanics. Office: C S Draper Lab 555 Technology Sq Cambridge MA

ROTH, SCOTT ALAN, information systems analyst, consultant; b. Harrisburg, Pa., Dec. 12, 1949; s. Robert Lynn and Lois Ann (Rider) R.; m. Kathleen Anne Hoak, Sept. 25, 1976; children: Robert Brenton, Shannon Kathleen. AS, Harrisburg Area Community Coll, 1969; cert. in data processing. Systems analyst Cen. Mgmt. Info. Ctr., Commonwealth of Pa., Middletown, Pa., 1969-80, Fleet Matl. Support Office, Dept. of the Navy, Mechanicsburg, Pa., 1980-81; sr. assoc. CACI Inc., Mechanicsburg, 1981-85; data processing mgr. Pa. Intergovernmental Coun., Harrisburg, Pa., 1985; data processing supr. Fruehauf Corp., Middletown, 1985-87; sr. assoc. CACI, Inc., Mechanicsburg, 1987-89; data processing mgr. Inst. of Modern Procedures, Mechanicsburg, 1989; sr. systems engr. Computer Task Group, Inc., Harrisburg, 1989—. Group leader Cub Scout Pack 196, Mechanicsburg, 1991. Mem. Info. Resources Mgmt. Assn. (sec. 1989—, bd. dirs. 1989—), Internat. Cobol User's Group, Harrisburg Bicycle Club. Home: 5500 Bearcreek Dr Mechanicsburg PA 17055-1983

ROTH, STANLEY W., electro-optical engineer; b. Bklyn., Aug. 7, 1932; s. Joseph S. and Bessie (Kofsky) R.; m. Harriet C. Otto, June 19, 1955; children: Scott, Eric, Caryn. BEE, CCNY, 1955, MEE, 1960. Sr. engr. Kollsman Instrument Corp., Woodside, N.Y., 1956-59; project engr. Bulova

Rsch. Labs., Woodside, 1959-63; prin. engr. Fairchild-Weston Systems, Syosset, N.Y., 1963-81, engring. group leader, 1987-91; applicaitons engr. Hartman Systems, Huntington Station, N.Y., 1981-86; chief engr. Espey Mfg. and Electronics Corp., Saratoga Springs, N.Y., 1991—. Contbr. articles to profl. jours. Mem. IEEE (chmn. profl. action com., sec. L.I. chpt. 1982-83, treas. 1983-84, asst. chmn. 1984-85), Am. Photogrametric Soc., AIAA. Home: 4 Ulster Dr Jericho NY 11753-1922

ROTH, WILLIAM V., JR., senator; b. Great Falls, Mont., July 22, 1921; m. Jane K. Richards; children: William V. III, Katharine Kellond. BA, U. Oreg.; MBA, LLB, Harvard U. Bar: Del., U.S. Supreme Ct. Mem. 90th-91st congresses at large from, Del., 1967-71; senator State of Del., 1971—; mem. fin., govt. affairs coms.; mem. fin., govt. affairs com., joint econ. com., com. on banking, housing and urban affairs; chmn. Del. Rep. State Com., 1961-64; mem. Rep. Nat. Com., 1961-64. Served to capt. AUS, 1943-46. Decorated Bronze Star medal. Mem. ABA, Del. Bar Assn. Episcopalian. Office: US Senate 104 Hart Senate Bldg Washington DC 20510*

ROTHBART, HERBERT LAWRENCE, chemist; b. Bklyn., Feb. 5, 1937; s. Abraham David and Doris (Mogulesky) R.; m. Marian Ilene Block, Mar. 12, 1961; 1 child, Bradley Ethan. BS, CUNY, 1958; PhD, Rutgers U., 1963. Asst. prof. Rutgers U., New Brunswick, N.J., 1963-66; rsch. scientist ARS-USDA, Phila., 1966-67; investigations leader USDA, Phila., 1967-74, lab. chief, 1975-80, ctr. dir., 1980-84, area dir., 1985—. Contbr. articles to profl. publs., chpts. to books.; patentee in field. Mem. John Scott awards com. City of Phila. Trusts, 1980—; mem. awards com. Franklin Inst. Arts and Scis., Phila., 1990—; mem. adv. com. dept. food sci. Rutgers U., 1980-89. Recipient Presdl. Rank award Office of Pres. U.S., Washington, 1989, Fed. Svc. award Phila. Fed. Exec. Bd., 1976. Mem. AAAS, Am. Chem. Soc., Inst. Food Technologists. Office: USDA Agrl Rsch Svc 600 E Mermaid Ln Philadelphia PA 19118-2598

ROTHBAUM, FRED MARK, psychologist; b. Washington, Dec. 24, 1949; s. Abraham and Esther (Fleisher) R.; m. Victoria Babbin, Jan. 23, 1972; children: Abraham, Maxwell. BA in Math. summa cum laude, U. Mich., 1971; MS in Devel. and Personality Psychology, Yale U., 1973, PhD in Clin. and Devel. Psychology, 1976. Clin. assoc. dept. psychology Yale U., 1974-75, rsch. assoc. with Dr. Edward Zigler, 1976; asst. prof. dept. edn. and child. devel. Bryn Mawr Coll., 1976-79; asst. prof. Eliot-Person dept. child study Tufts U., 1979-82, assoc. prof., 1982—, chair dept., 1986-89; psychotherapist Wilmington Family Counseling Ctr., 1980-89; coord. Child Devel. Clinic, 1976-79; clin. assoc. West Haven VA Hosp., 1974-75; psychol. cons. Prince Georges County Community Coll., 1974; psychotherapist St. Raphael Hosp., New Haven, 1973-74; clin. aide Yale Psychiat. Inst., 1973-74. Yale U. fellow, 1972-73; NIMH fellow, 1973-74; Child Devel. Tng. grantee Yale U., 1971-72; Madge Miller Fund grantee, 1978-79; Angell scholar U. Mich., 1971. Mem. Am. Psychol. Assn., Nat. Register Health Svc. Providers in Psychology (coun.). Office: Tufts U Eliot-Pearson Dept of Child Devel Medford MA 02155

ROTHENBERG, ALAN MILES, entrepreneur, investor; b. Bklyn., Dec. 8, 1941; s. Peter Louis and Lillian (Solomon) R.; m. Francine M. Jatlowsky, June 2, 1977. BA, Bklyn. Coll., 1963; LLB, NYU, 1966. Bar: N.Y. 1966, U.S. Supreme Ct. 1971, U.S. Dist. Ct. (so. and ea. dists.) N.Y. 1972, U.S. Ct. Appeals (2d cir.), 1972, U.S. Tx. Ct. 1972. Atty. U.S. Dept. Justice, Washington, 1967, Kroll Edelman Elser & Wilson, N.Y.C., 1971-72; risk arbitrage analyst Bache & Co., N.Y.C., 1968-70, Lazard Freres & Co., N.Y.C., 1970; arbitrageur Colin, Hochstin Co., N.Y.C., 1973-75, Wallach & Co., N.Y.C., 1976; corp. fin. exec. Muller and Co., Inc., N.Y.C., 1983-88; fin. cons. Merrill Lynch, Pierce, Fenner & Smith, Inc., N.Y.C., 1990; pvt. investor N.Y.C., 1989, 91—; ind. mem. N.Y. Stock Exch., N.Y.C., 1977-80, N.Y. Futures Exch., N.Y.C., 1980-84, Chgo. Mercantile Exch., 1983-86; registered rep. Philips, Appel & Walden, Inc., N.Y.C., 1982-88; corp. fin. coord. Enzon Inc., South Plainfield, N.J., 1984-88. Election insp. N.Y. City Bd. Elections, 1988—. With USCGR, 1966-72. Mem. Stock Exch. Lucheon Club. Republican. Jewish. Home and Office: 420 E 64th St New York NY 10021-7853

ROTHENBERG, JULIA CHRISTINE JOHNSON, psychology educator; b. Manning, Iowa, Feb. 15, 1941; d. Clifford Manning and Letha Nielsen (Boysen) Johnson; m. Albert Rothenberg, June 28, 1970; children: Michael, Mora Ruth, Rina Susannah. BA, Grinnell (Iowa) Coll., 1963; MA in Teaching, Yale U., 1964; PhD, SUNY, Albany, 1987. Tenured tchr. New Haven Pub. Schs., 1964-73; dir., tchr. Cedarhurst Sch. Yale Psychiat. Inst., New Haven, 1964-70; dir. of tng. Children's Ctr. Sch., Hamden, Conn., 1970-73; lectr., rsch. assoc. Yale U., New Haven, 1967-76; project dir. Conn. Child Svc. Demonstrationh Ctr., Trumbull, 1973-80; prof. ednl. psychology Russell Sage Colls., Troy, N.Y., 1988—; chair ednl. activities Boston Symphony Orch. Vols., Lenox, Mass., 1990—; flutist, pianist Aesculapian Players, Berkshire County, 1987—; flutist, pianist, vocalist Berkshire Chamber Group, 1986—. Author: (monograph) A Task- Analysis Program on Intervention, 1987, (manual) Make Every Child Capable of Achieving, 1978; contbr. articles to profl. jours. Mem. Dem. Party, Mass., 1987—, Construct, Great Barrington, Mass., 1987—. U.S. Office of Edn. grantee, 1971-78. Mem. APA, Am. Ednl. Rsch. Assn., Northeastern Ednl. Rsch. Assn., Assn. Univ. Profs., New Eng. Ednl. Rsch. Orgn., Am. Assn. Colls. of Tchr. Edn., Chamber Music Soc. Am., P.E.O. Home: PO Box 51 Canaan NY 12029-0051 Office: Russell Sage Colls Troy NY 12180

ROTHERMEL, JOSEPH JACKSON, retired manufacturing executive; b. Reading, Pa., Nov. 4, 1918; s. Joseph Alfred and Sara (Balthasar) R.; m. Daphne Margaret Land, Dec. 18, 1943; children: Pamela, Carol, Diana, Beverly, Faith. BS in Chemistry, Franklin & Marshall Coll., 1940; PhD in Chemistry, U. Pitts., 1948. Grad. asst. chemistry U. Pitts., 1940-44, 46-48; rsch. chemist Manhattan Project Sch. Medicine and Dentistry, Rochester, N.Y., 1944-46; devel. engr. Corning (N.Y.), Inc., 1948-68, sr. engring. assoc., 1968-83, ret., 1983. Patentee in field. Mem. Am. Chem. Soc. (sec. Corning sect. 1959, chmn. nominations and awards com. 1959-83, Eugene C. Sullivan award 1973), Am. Ceramic Soc., Soc. Glass Tech. Baptist. Home: 540 Powderhouse Rd Corning NY 14830-9416

ROTHLISBERGER, DANA JOHN, music educator, administrator; b. Durango, Colo., Aug. 27, 1952; s. John Alcid and Loretta Jean (Stocking) R.; m. Ann Rohde, Sept. 17, 1977; children: John Dana, Mark Peter, Heidi, Leisa, Laura, Luke James. BMEd, East Tex. State U., 1974, MMus, 1976; PhD, U. Md., 1992. Cert. tchr., Tex., Utah. Grad. asst. band dir. East Tex. State U., Commerce, 1975-76; dir. bands Davis High Sch., Kaysville, Utah, 1976-80; asst. dir. bands U. Ariz., Tucson, 1980-83; dir. bands Towson (Md.) State U., 1983—; adjudicator Md. State Solo and Ensemble, Towson, 1986-92. Mem. Md. Music Educators Assn., Nat. Band Assn., Music Educators Nat. Conf., Coll. Band Dirs. Assn. (sec., treas. ea. div. 1988-91), Md. Band Dirs. Assn. (pres. 1992). Mormon. Home: 137 W Chestnut Hill Ln Reisterstown MD 21136-3206 Office: Towson State U Dept Music Dir Bands Towson MD 21204

ROTHMAN, ALLEN S., neurosurgeon; b. N.Y.C., May 24, 1943; s. David and Sophie (Abo) R.; m. Helen Kahn, Sept. 8, 1967; children: Natalie, Philip. BA in Chemistry, Hofstra U., 1965, MA in Biology, 1967; MD, Chgo. Med. Sch., 1971. Intern Beth Israel Med. Ctr., N.Y.C., 1971-72; resident Mt. Sinai Med. Ctr., N.Y.C., 1974-78, asst. clin. prof., 1985—; chief neurosurgery New Rochelle Hosp., N.Y.C., 1990—; chief neurosurgery New Rochelle (N.Y.) Hosp., 1990—, mem. med. bd., 1990—. Contbr. articles to profl. jours. Maj. U.S. Army, 1972-74. Mem. AMA, Am. Assn. Neurol. Surgeons (pediatric sect.), Congress Neurol. Surgeons, N.Y. Neurol. Soc., N.Y. County Med. Soc., N.Y. Acad. Scis. Jewish. Office: 1160 Fifth Ave Ste 106 New York NY 10029

ROTHMAN, BERNARD, lawyer; b. N.Y.C., Aug. 11, 1932; s. Harry and Rebecca (Fritz) R.; m. Barbara Joan Schaeffer, Aug. 1953; children: Brian, Adam, Helene. BA cum laude, CCNY, 1953; LLB, NYU, 1959. Bar: N.Y. 1959, U.S Dist. Ct. (ea. and so. dists.) N.Y. 1962, U.S. Ct. Apls. (2d cir.) 1965, U.S. Supreme Ct. 1966, U.S. Tax Ct. 1971. Assoc. Held, Telchin & Held, 1961-62; asst. U.S. atty. U.S. Dept. Justice, 1962-66; assoc. Edward Gettinger & Peter Gettinger, 1966-68; ptnr. Schwartz, Rothman & Abrams, P.C., 1968-78; ptnr. Finkelstein, Bruckman, Wohl, Most & Rothman, N.Y.C., 1978—; acting judge Village of Larchmont, 1982-88, dep. Village atty., 1974-81, former arbitrator Civil Ct. N.Y.C., family disputes panel Am. Arbitration Assn., guest lectr. domestic rels. and family law on radio and TV, also numerous legal and mental health orgns. Author: Loving and Leaving-Winning at the Business of Divorce, 1991; contbr. articles to profl. jours. Mem. exec. bd., past v.p. Westchester Putnam coun. Boy Scouts Am., 1975—; past mem. nat. coun., 1977-81, recipient Silver Beaver award, Wood Badge award; pres. Congregation B'nai Israel, 1961-63, B'nai Brith, Larchmont chpt., 1981-83. Fellow Am. Acad. Matrimonial Lawyers (bd. govs. N.Y. chpt. 1986-87, 91—), Interdisciplinary Forum on Mental Health and Family Law (co-chair 1986—); mem. ABA (family law sect.), N.Y. State Bar Assn. (exec. com. family law sect. 1982—, co-chmn. com. on mediation and arbitration 1982-88, com. on legis. 1978-88, com. on child custody 1985-88, co-chmn. commn. on AIDS and matrimonial law), N.Y. State Bar Assn., Assn. of Bar of City of N.Y., N.Y. State Magistrate Assn., Westchestr Magistrate Assn., N.Y. Road Runners Club, Limousine 6 Track Club. Democrat. Co-author: Leaving Home, 1987; contbr. articles to profl. jours. Office: Finkelstein Bruckman Wohl Most & Rothman 575 Lexington Ave New York NY 10022-6102

ROTHMAN, ESTHER POMERANZ, social agency executive, psychologist; b. N.Y.C., Nov. 25, 1919; d. Max and Anne (Reiner) Pomeranz; m. Arthur M. Rothman, Apr. 13, 1946; 1 dau., Amy. B.A., Hunter Coll., 1942; M.A., Columbia U., 1944; M.A., CCNY, 1946; Ph.D., NYU, 1958. Cert. psychologist, N.Y. Tchr., N.Y.C. Bd. Edn., 1944-57, prin., 1957-80; exec. dir. Glie Youth Program, N.Y.C., 1980-85; exec. dir. Correctional Edn. Consortium, 1985—; research psychologist Tchrs. Hot Line, N.Y.C., 1972-74. Author: Angel Inside Went Sour, 1972; Troubled Teachers, 1974; co-author: Disturbed Child, 1967. Mem. Citizens Com. for Children, N.Y.C., 1972—. Recipient Valley Forge Freedom award, 1976. Fellow Am. Assn. Orthopsychiatry (sec. 1976-79); mem. Am. Psychol. Assn. Home: 200 E 16th St New York NY 10003-3707 Office: Correctional Edn Consortium 29-10 Thomson Ave Long Island NY 11101

ROTHMAN, LAURENCE SIDNEY, physicist; b. N.Y.C., Jan. 20, 1940; s. Jules A. and May Lucy (Winston) R. BS, MIT, 1961; AM, Boston U., 1964, PhD, 1971. Rsch. physicist Block Assocs., Inc., Cambridge, Mass., 1961-64; teaching fellow Boston U., 1964-68; physicist Geophysics Lab. (Air Force), Bedford, Mass., 1968—; co-chmn. working group Internat. Radiation Commn., Lille, France, 1990—; panel mem. Spectroscopy for NASA Satellites, 1986; panel mem. chlorofluorocarbon program Nat. Bur. Standards, Gaithersburg, Md., 1983; invited prof. U. Paris, 1985, 87, 90. Editor Proceedings SPIE Critical Rev., 1988; co-author: Geophysics Handbook, 1985, Atmospheric Ozone, 1985; contbr. articles to profl. jours. Bd. dirs. Aggasiz Community, Cambridge, 1978. Fellow Optical Soc. Am.; mem. Internat. Radiation Com. (ex-officio), Soc. PhotoOptical Inst. Engring., Boston Computer Soc., Sigma Xi (pres. local 1985). Office: Geophysics Lab OPS Hanscom AFB MA 01731

ROTHMAN, SIDNEY, art dealer, appraiser; b. N.Y.C., May 7, 1918; s. Bernard Herbert and Mollie (Baumoehl) R. Student, N.Y. Sch. Architecture Design, 1938-40; BA, Columbia U., 1940, Bklyn. Coll., 1940. Art dealer, appraiser Sidney Rothman-The Gallery, Barnegat Light, N.J., 1958—; chmn. art com., bd. dirs. Long Beach Island Found. of Arts and Scis., Loveladies, N.J., 1958—; chmn., vice-chmn. Ocean County Cultural and Heritage Com., Toms River, N.J., 1976-83. Active Barnegat Light First Aid Squad, 1968-83; chmn. Celebration of Pub. Events, Barnegat Light, 1976-86. Tech. sgt. U.S. Army, 1943-46. Recipient Mayor's award Coun. of Boro of Barnegat Light, 1985, Pres.'s award Long Beach Island Found., 1987, Supt.'s award So. Region High Sch., Manahawkin, N.J., 1987. Mem. U.S. Lighthouse Soc. Republian. Home and Office: 2105 Central Ave Barnegat Light NJ 08006-9999

ROTHOVIUS, ISKA, art director; b. Tampere, Finland, June 2, 1926; came to U.S., 1955; s. Sulo Richard and Maija Lempi Maria (Sparfven) R.; m. Anita Ritva Uggeldahl, Jan. 24, 1944 (div.); 1 child, Christine. Mainoshoitaja, Myynti ja Mainoskoulu, Helsinki, 1952. Copywriter, account exec. Erva Latvala, Helsinki, 1951-55; artist Hermon W. Stevens, Boston, 1955-57, Harold Cabot & Co., Boston, 1957-59; assoc. art dir. Kameny Assocs., N.Y.C., 1959-62; freelance artist N.Y.C., 1962-63; art dir. N.Y. Telephone Co., N.Y.C., 1963—. Mem. Soc. Illustrators (various awards), Art Dirs. Club, Finlandia Found. Office: NY Tel Co 605 41st St Brooklyn NY 11232

ROTHSCHILD, ANTHONY JOSEPH, psychiatrist; b. N.Y.C., Dec. 2, 1953; s. Ernest Leo and Edith Margot (Chan) R.; m. Judith Anne Shindul, May 19, 1985; children: Rachel Emma, Amanda Joan. AB, Princeton U., 1975; MD, U. Pa., 1979. Diplomate Am. Bd. Psychiatry and Neurology. Intern medicine/neurology Mass. Gen. Hosp., Mt. Auburn Hosp., Boston, 1979-80; resident psychiatry McLean Hosp., Belmont, Mass., 1980-83; instr. in psychiatry Harvard Med. Sch., Boston, 1983-85, asst. prof. psychiatry, 1985—; psychiatrist-in-charge depression research unit McLean Hosp., Belmont, 1983-88, assoc. dir. depression research facility, 1985—, clin. dir. affective disease program, 1988—; examiner Am. Bd. Psychiatry and Neurology, 1987—; reviewer Am. Jour. of Psychiatry, Washington, 1985—, Psychiatry Research, 1985—. Contbr. articles to profl. publs. Mem. Am. Psychiat. Assn., Am. Psychopath. Assn., Internat. Soc. of Psychoneuroendocrinology, N.Y. Acad. of Scis., Mass. Psychiat. Soc. Office: McLean Hosp 115 Mill St Belmont MA 02178-1048

ROTHSCHILD, CAROL LOUISE, science teacher; b. N.Y.C., Mar. 3, 1946; d. Leo and Nora (Thein) Schick; m. Steven James Rothschild, Dec. 18, 1966; children: Jeffrey Lee, Peter Elliot. BS, U. Vt., 1967; MEd, U. Md., 1968. Tchr. New Castle County (Del.) Sch. Dist., 1968-70, 78-85; tchr. sci. Brandywine Sch. Dist., 1974-78, William Penn High Sch., Wilmington, Del., 1985—. Bd. dirs. Jewish Community Ctr., Wilmington, 1983—. Mem. Scis. Alliance (chmn. 1990—), Kappa Gamma. Home: 402 Owls Nest Rd Wilmington DE 19807-1626

ROTHSCHILD, CAROLYN ANITA, art dealer; b. Mineola, N.Y., Apr. 3, 1939; d. Edwin Ephraim and Mildred Marie (Hausel) Kohl; m. John David Rothschild, Nov. 26, 1966. BS, SUNY, Potsdam, 1961; MS, So. Ill. U., 1963; postgrad., NYU, 1963-65, Internat. U. Santander, Spain, 1965. Copywriter various advt. agys., N.Y.C., 1965-76; pres., owner Rothschild Fine Arts Inc., N.Y.C., 1976—.

ROTHSCHILD, JAMES ALAN, management consultant; b. N.Y.C., Mar. 23, 1946; s. Lloyd David and Bernice Marjorie (Newmark) R.; B.S. in Chem. Engring., U. Pitts., 1967; M.B.A., Case Western Res. U., 1970; m. Vida Margurette Lauric, June 22 1968; children—Aaron, Haylee. Process engr. Olin Corp., Ashtabula, Ohio, 1968-70, fin. analyst, Stamford, Conn., 1971; mgmt. cons. Touche Ross & Co., N.Y.C., 1972-76; mgmt. cons. J. Rothschild Assoc., Georgetown, Conn., 1976-79; prin. Georgetown Cons. Group, Ridgefield, Conn., 1979-84; prin. Rothschild Fin. Cons., Wilton, Conn., 1985—. Home and Office: 115 Scarlet Oak Dr Wilton CT 06897-1016

ROTHSCHILD, JOHN ALBERT, nephrologist; b. Buffalo, Apr. 19, 1943; s. Alvin Raymond and Marjorie Dorothy (Breuer) R.; m. Rena Iris Miller, June 18, 1966; children: Sarah, Rebecca. BA, Cornell U., 1965, MD, 1969. Diplomate Am. Bd. Internal Medicine; cert. in nephrology, critical care medicine. Intern in medicine North Shore Hosp./Sloan Kettering Cancer Ctr., Manhassett, N.Y., 1969-70, resident in medicine, 1970-71; resident Pa. State U., Hershey, 1971-72, chief med. resident, 1972-73; renal fellow Hahneman Med. Coll. and Hosp., Phila., 1973-75; attending physician Wilkes Barre (Pa.) Gen. Hosp., 1975—, chief renal sect., 1978—. Mem. AMA, ACP, Pa. Med. Soc., Renal Physician Assn., Luzerne County Med. Soc. Office: Renal Cons Wyoming Valley 56 W Linden St Wilkes Barre PA 18702-2687

ROTHSCHILD, STEVEN JAMES, lawyer; b. Worcester, Mass., Mar. 23, 1944; s. Alfred and Ilse (Blumenfeld) R. B.A., U. Vt., 1965; J.D., Georgetown U., 1968. Bar: D.C. 1968, Del. 1969. Ptnr. Skadden Arps Slate Meagher & Flom, Wilmington; mem. Del. Bd. Bar Examiners, 1979-83; chmn. Del. Citizens Conf. on Adminstrn. of Justice, 1982. Campaign chmn. United Way Del., 1980, bd. dirs., 1978-85, v.p., 1981-84; bd. dirs. Milton & Hattie Kutz Home, 1972—, pres., 1982-84; bd. dirs. Del. region NCCJ, 1981-91, Hebrew Immigrant Aid Soc., 1986-91, Jewish Fedn. Del., 1989-91, Del. Hospice, 1989—; trustee Del. Art Mus., 1986—, pres., 1990-92. Mem. ABA, Bar Assn. D.C., Assn. of Bar of City of N.Y., Del. Bar Assn. Office: Skadden Arps Slate One Rodney Sq PO Box 636 Wilmington DE 19899

ROTHWARF, ALLEN, electrical engineering educator; b. Phila., Oct. 1, 1935; s. Max and Bessie (Dichter) R.; m. Bernice Cecelia Golansky, June 16, 1957; children: Richard, Jeanne, David. BA in Physics, Temple U., 1957; MS in Physics, U. Pa., 1960, PhD in Physics, 1964. Instr. Rutgers U., The State U., Camden, N.J., 1960-62; mem. tech. staff RCA Labs., David Sarnoff Rsch. Ctr., Princeton, N.J., 1964-72; postdoctoral fellow U. Pa., Phila., 1972-73; sr. scientist Inst. Energy Conversion, U. Del., Newark, 1973-79; prof. elec. engring. dept. Drexel U., Phila., 1979—; dir. Ben Franklin Superconductivity Ctr., Phila., 1989—; cons. RCA Labs., Princeton, 1979-83, Solarex Thin Film Div., Newtown, Pa., 1983—. Contbr. articles to profl. jours.; patentee in field. Recipient Rsch. award Drexel U., 1989. Fellow IEEE; mem. Am. Phys. Soc., Am. Vacuum Soc. Office: Drexel U Elec and Computer Engring Dept Philadelphia PA 19104

ROTHWELL, KENNETH SPRAGUE, JR., classics educator; b. Rochester, N.Y., Mar. 27, 1955; s. Kenneth S. and Marilyn Mae (Gregg) R.; m. Pamela Margaret Jones, Aug. 12, 1989. BA, U. Vt., 1977; PhD, Columbia U., 1985. Asst. prof. classics Holy Cross Coll., Worcester, Mass., 1984-91; asst. prof. Wellesley (Mass.) Coll., 1991—. Author: Politics and Persuasion in Aristophanes' Ecclesiazusae, 1990. Democrat. Episcopalian.

ROTMER, EDWARD DONALD, retail executive; b. Providence, Sept. 21, 1939; s. Samuel and Bessie (Bello) R.; m. Elayne E. Ackerman, Aug. 6, 1961 (div. 1979); children: Michelle E., Gregory C.; m. Lorraine Ann Cardillo. BA, Brown U., 1961. Salesman Paramount Office Supply Co., Providence, 1959-65, v.p., sales mgr., 1965-79, pres., 1979—. Mem. Nat. Office Products Assn. (gov. dist. one 1988-89), Masons. Home: 70 Sweetbriar Dr Cranston RI 02920-3527

ROTTER, STEVEN JEFFREY, accountant; b. Bklyn., May 21, 1955; s. Walter and Lillian (Needleman) R.; m. Robin A. Bass, May 3, 1980; children: Marc, Adam, Sara. BS in Acctg., Bklyn. Coll., 1976. CPA, N.Y. Staff acct. Margold, Ersken & Wang, N.Y.C., 1976-78, ptnr., 1980—; contr. Vanleigh Furniture Co., N.Y.C., 1978-80. Mem. AICPA, N.Y. State Soc. CPA. Office: Margold Ersken & Wang 880 3d Ave New York NY 10022-4730

ROTUNDA, DONALD THEODORE, corporate communications official; b. Blue Island, Ill., Feb. 14, 1945; s. Nicholas and Frances (Manna) R. B.A., Georgetown U., 1967; M.A., London Sch. Econs., 1968, Ph.D., 1972. Analyst NASA, Washington, 1972; lectr. in econs. U. D.C., 1973; legis. asst. Ho. of Reps., Washington, 1974-76, economist budget com., 1977; mgmt. analyst Office Mgmt. and Budget, Washington, 1977-81; cons., 1981-82; mgr. editorial svcs. United Technologies Corp., Hartford, Conn., 1982-87, Pepsico, Inc., Purchase, N.Y., 1987-89, Union Carbide Corp., Danbury, Conn., 1989-90; dir. editorial svcs. Martin Marietta, Bethesda, Md., 1990—. Contbr. numerous articles to Washington Post, New Republic, Saturday Rev. Roman Catholic. Home: 4431 Klingle St NW Washington DC 20016-3578 Office: Martin Marietta 6801 Rockledge Dr Bethesda MD 20817-1836

ROUBOS, GARY LYNN, diversified manufacturing company executive; b. Denver, Nov. 7, 1936; s. Dorr and Lillian Margaret (Coover) R.; m. Terie Joan Anderson, Feb. 20, 1960; children: Lyndel, Leslie. BSChemE with high honors, U. Colo., 1959; MBA with distinction, Harvard U., 1963. With Boise Cascade Corp., 1963-71, Dieterich Standard Corp., Boulder, Colo., 1971-76; exec. v.p., then pres. Dieterich Standard Corp. (co. acquired by Dover Corp. 1975), 1975-76; exec. v.p. Dover Corp., N.Y.C., 1976, pres., 1977—, chief exec. officer, 1981—, chmn., 1989—; bd. dirs. Omnicom Inc., N.Y.C., Scott Paper Co., Phila., Gabelli-O'Connor Treas. Fund, Greenwich, Conn.; mem. N.Y. adv. bd. Liberty Mut. Bd. dirs. Colo. U. Found., 1976-89; bd. govs. Bd. Rm., 1989—. 1st lt. C.E., U.S. Army, 1959-61. Mem. Tokeneke Club, Bd. Rm. Club, Winged Foot Golf Club, Econ. Club of N.Y. Office: Dover Corp 280 Park Ave New York NY 10017-1216

ROUDABUSH, AARON PAUL, insurance company executive; b. Pitts., Jan. 26, 1965; s. Glenn Earl and Barbara Phyllis (Bird) R. BS in Math., Rensselaer Poly. Inst., Troy, N.Y., 1987; MS in Math., Rensselaer Poly. Inst., 1989. Actuarial analyst Chubb Life Am., Concord, N.H., 1989—. Mem. Am. Math. Soc., Rensselaer Poly. Inst. Players (bus. mgr. 1988-89), Alpha Psi Omega, Alpha Phi Omega. Home: 23-6 Merrimack St Penacook NH 03303 Office: Chubb Life Am One Granite Pl Concord NH 03301

ROUHANA, WILLIAM JOSEPH, JR., investor, merchant banker; b. Bklyn., June 23, 1952; s. William Joseph and Anna Freida (Stephan) R.; m. Claudia Caruso, Aug. 27, 1972; children: Timothy, Rosemary. BA, Colby Coll., 1972; JD, Georgetown U., 1976. Bar: N.Y. 1977, U.S. Dist. Ct. (so. and ea. dists.) N.Y. 1977. Founding ptnr. Beinhauer, Rouhana & Pike, N.Y.C., 1977-80; sole practice N.Y.C., 1980-81; ptnr. Rouhana and Trinko, P.C., N.Y.C., 1981-85, Baer, Marks & Upham, N.Y.C., 1985-86; pres. WinStar Corp., N.Y.C., 1984-90; chief exec. officer WinStar Ptnrs., N.Y.C., 1989-90, WinStar Oil Ptnrs., N.Y.C., 1990-91; chmn. Manson Internat. L.A., 1986-87; vice chmn. Mgmt. Co. Entertainment Group, Inc., L.A., 1987-90; bd. dirs., chmn. Robern Apparel, Inc., 1989—; bd. dirs. Splty. Retail Ventures, 1990, Lancit Media Prodns., Ltd., 1991—, Found. Emmes, 1991—; bd. overseers Colby Coll., 1987-90; mem. adv. bd. KPMG Mid. Market, 1990; bd. dirs., chmn., chief exec. officer WinStar Cos., Inc., 1990—; pres. WinStar Svcs., Inc., 1990—; mem. adv. bd. UN Assn., 1992—. Mem. Nassau County Dem. Com., Jericho, N.Y., 1984, Bus. Execs. Nat. Security, 1991—. Grantee NSF, 1968, Thomas J. Watson Found., 1972-73. Mem. ABA (forum com. on entertainment and sports), N.Y. State Bar Assn., N.Y. County Lawyers Assn., Nat. Security Assn. (exec. and bus. coms.), U.N. Assn. (adv. bd.), Phi Beta Kappa. Roman Catholic. Club: Port Washington Democratic (N.Y.). Office: WinStar Svcs Inc 575 5th Ave Ste 24C New York NY 10017-2422

ROUKEMA, MARGARET SCAFATI, congresswoman; b. Newark, Sept. 19, 1929; d. Claude Thomas and Margaret (D'Alessio) Scafati; m. Richard W. Roukema, Aug. 23, 1951; children—Margaret, Todd (dec.), Gregory. B.A. with honors in History and Polit. Sci, Montclair State Coll., 1951, postgrad. in history and guidance, 1951-53; postgrad. program in city and regional planning, Rutgers U., 1975. Tchr. history, govt., public schs. Livingston and Ridgewood, N.J., 1951-55; mem. 97th-102nd Congresses from 5th N.J. dist., 1981—; vice pres. Ridgewood Bd. Edn., 1970-73; bd. dirs., co-founder Ridgewood Sr. Citizens Housing Corp. Trustee Spring House, Paramus, N.J.; trustee Leukemia Soc. No. N.J., Family Counseling Service for Ridgewood and Vicinity; mem. Bergen County (N.J.) Republican Com.; NW Bergen County campaign mgr. for gubernatorial candidate Tom Kean, 1977. Mem. Bus. and Profl. Women's Orgn. Clubs: Coll. of Ridgewood, Ridgewood Rep. Office: US Ho of Reps 303 Cannon House Office Bldg Washington DC 20515*

ROULEAU, MONIQUE LUCILLE, architectural designer; b. Woonsocket, R.I., Nov. 27, 1964; d. Maurice Joseph and Estelle Dora (Brunette) R. BS, R.I. Coll., 1986. Draft person Jim Lembo Civil Engr., East Providence, R.I., 1985-86; pres., owner Archtl. and Interiors, North Providence, R.I., 1986—. Mem. Woonsocket Jaycees, 1987—. Mem. Soc. of Mfg. Engrs. Roman Catholic.

ROULEAU, WILFRED THOMAS, mechanical engineering educator; b. Quincy, Mass., May 3, 1929; s. Wilfred Joseph and Sara (Wilkinson) R.; m. Ruth Eleanor Osborne, June 15, 1954; children: Richard, Keith. BS, Carnegie Inst. Tech., 1951, MS, 1952, PhD, 1954. Asst. prof. mech. engring. Carnegie Mellon U. (formerly Carnegie Inst. Tech., Pitts., 1954-60, assoc. prof., 1960-65, prof., 1965—; cons. to various industries, 1954—; reviewer tech. jours., 1954—. Contbr. articles on fluid mechanics, erosion of turbomachinery, wave propagation, stability, and lubrication theory to profl. jours. Asst. scoutmaster, scoutmaster, mem. troop com. Boy Scouts Am., Edgewood, Pa., 1969—. Recipient Dist. award of merit East Valley Area coun. Boy Scouts Am., 1983. Mem. ASME, AAUP, Sigma Xi, Tau Beta Pi, Phi Kappa Phi. Episcopalian. Home: 230 Race St Pittsburgh PA 15218-

1317 Office: Carnegie Mellon U Mech Engring Dept 4825 Frew St Pittsburgh PA 15213-3890

ROUPE, JAMES PAUL, accountant; b. Havre de Grace, Md., Apr. 20, 1957; s. Paul Clyde and Shirley Louise (Trivette) R. AA, Harford Community Coll., Bel Air, Md., 1977; BS, Towson (Md.) State U., 1979. CPA, 1989. Mgmt. asst. Loyola Fed. Savings and Loan, Balt., 1979-81; asst. treas. Legum Chevrolet-Nissan, Balt., 1983-89; controller Bob Bell Chevrolet-Nissan Inc., Balt., 1989-92; corp. sec.-treas. Bob Bell Chevrolet/Nissan, Inc., Balt., 1992—; sr. controller Bob Bell Chevrolet Geo of Bel Air (Md.) Inc., 1991-92, corp. sec.-treas., 1992—. Mem. AICPA, Md. Assn. CPA's, Inst. Mgmt. Accts. Republican. Baptist. Office: Bob Bell Chevrolet Nissan 7900 Eastern Blvd Baltimore MD 21224-2188

ROURKE, EVAN CHARLES, securities trader; b. Dundalk, Md., July 10, 1964; s. Donald Kenneth and Marionanne Helen (Mullins) R. BA, SUNY, Stonybrook, 1986. Coord. Bankers Trust Co., N.Y.C., 1986-87; assoc. Kidder Peabody & Co., N.Y.C., 1988, asst. trader, 1989, trader, 1991—.

ROUSE, ROBERT SUMNER, former college official; b. Northampton, Mass., Sept. 2, 1930; s. Charles Edward and Laura Elisabeth (Rowbotham) R.; divorced; children: R. Daniel, Roland, James, Katherine. B.S., Yale U., 1951, M.S., 1953, Ph.D. in Chemistry, 1957. Lab. asst., then asst. in instrn. Yale, 1951-56; asst. prof. chemistry Lehigh U., 1956-62; group leader, plastics div. Allied Chems. Corp., 1962-66, tech. supr., 1966-67; prof. chemistry Monmouth Coll., West Long Branch, N.J., 1967—; chmn. chemistry dept. Monmouth Coll., 1967-73, asso. dean faculty, 1968-73, dean faculty, v.p. acad. affairs, 1973-80, provost and v.p. acad. affairs, 1980-81, chmn. faculty coun., 1990—; mem. licensure adv. and approval bd. N.J. Dept. Higher Edn., 1973-82, chmn., 1980-81; bd. dirs. Assn. Ind. Colls. and Univs. N.J., 1978-81. Author: (with Robert O. Smith) Energy: Resource, Slave, Pollutant-A Physical Science Text, 1975. Recipient Disting. Tchr. award Monmouth Coll., 1991. Fellow N.Y. Acad. Scis.; mem. Am. Chem. Soc., AAUP, Sigma Xi. Home: 482 Cedar Ave West Long Branch NJ 07764-1806

ROUSH, ANNETTE MARIE, English educator; b. Paris, May 11, 1957; came to U.S., 1971; d. James Lee and Maria Katharine (Burck) R. BA in Polit. Sci., U. No. Colo., 1980; postgrad., George Mason U. Sch. of Law, 1982-83, George Mason U., 1985-90. Info. specialist Nat. Clearinghouse for Bilingual Edn., Arlington, Va., 1982-85; staff writer, adminstrv. asst. div. bilingual edn. Washington Pub. Schs., 1985-86; freelance editor and word processor, 1986-87; teaching asst. Alexandria (Va.) City Pub. Schs., 1987-88; tchr. spl. edn. and learning disabilities Alexandria City Pub. Schs./T.C. Williams High Sch., spring 1988; tchr. ESL Fairfax County (Va.) Pub. Schs., summer 1988, Montgomery County Pub. Schs./Wheaton (Md.) High Sch., 1988—; cons., proposal editor div. bilingual edn. D.C. Pub. Schs., Washington, 1986; cons., proposal reader Office for Bilingual Edn. & Minority Langs. Affairs, U.S. Dept. of Edn., Washington, 1986. Editorial asst. Peace in Action Mag., 1986-87, photographer, 1985; photographer: Wall of Silence-America's Drug Problem: A Different Perspective, 1990. Participant The Peace Ribbon, The Pentagon, Arlington, 1985; campaign asst. John Anderson Presdl. campaign, Greeley, Colo., 1980; vol. Arlington County Dems., 1990. Recipient Acad. Excellence award George Mason U., 1988. Mem. NEA, Washington Area Tchrs. of English to Speakers of Other Langs. Office: Wheaton High Sch 12601 Dalewood Dr Silver Spring MD 20906-4168

ROUSMANIERE, JOHN PIERCE, writer; b. Louisville, Mar. 10, 1944; s. James Ayer and Jessie (Pierce) R.; m. Jocelyn D. Hall, Apr. 25, 1970 (div. 1975); children: William Pierce, Dana Starr; m. Leah Ruth Robinson, May 21, 1989. BS, Columbia U., 1967, MA in History, 1968; MDiv, Union Theol. Sem., 1988. Asst. prof. history U.S. Mil. Acad., West Point, N.Y., 1970-72; assoc. editor Yachting Mag., N.Y.C., 1972-77; sr. editor Natural History Mag., N.Y.C., 1978; freelance writer Stamford, Conn., 1978—; adj. prof. Coll. of New Rochelle, 1980-83; tutor Union Theol. Sem., N.Y.C., 1985-88. Author: Annapolis Book of Seamanship, 1989, The Bridge to Dialogue, 1991, Fastnet, Force 10, 1980; contbr. numerous articles to profl. jours. Trustee St. John's Community Found., Stamford, 1990—; vestry St. John's Ch., Stamford, 1987-90; trustee Long Ridge Sch., Stamford, 1976-79. 1st lt. U.S. Army, 1969-72. Recipient Gold medal for Contbn. to Yachting, 1985, Disting. Alumnus award East Woods Sch., 1987, Lawton Boating Safety award Raytheon Co., 1989. Mem. Authors Guild, N.Y. Yacht Club, Am. Boat & Yacht Coun. Democrat. Episcopalian. Home and Office: 100-23 Hope St Stamford CT 06906

ROUSSEAU, IRENE VICTORIA, sculptor; m. Denis Lawrence Rousseau; children: Douglas, Scott. BA, Hunter Coll., N.Y.C.; MFA, Claremont (Calif.) Grad. Sch., 1969; PhD, N.Y. U., 1977. Tenured prof. William Paterson Coll., Wayne, N.J., 1970-74; invited speaker CAA-WCA Conf., L.A., 1985, N.J. Ctr. for Visual Arts, Summit, 1985. Exhbns. include Betty Parsons Gallery, N.Y.C., Claremont Colls., State Mus. Sci and Industry, L.A., Morris Mus. Arts an Scis., Morristown, N.J., The Bronx Mus. of Art, Galleri Sct. Agnes, Copenhagen/Roskilde, Denmark, Sculptors 5, Madison, N.J., Edmund Scientific Co., Barrington, N.J., AT&T World Headquarters, Basking Ridge, N.J., N.J. Ctr. for Visual Arts, The Brotherhood Synagogue Holocaust Meml. Gramercy Pk (mosaic), N.Y.C., 1986, painted aluminum wall reliefs Capital Sports Inc. headquarters Sports in Action, Stamford, Conn., 1989; represented in permanent collections Brit. Mus., Met. Mus., Guggenheim Mus., Walker Art Ctr., Nat. Mus. Am. Art, Smithsonian Instn. Recipient seven 1st prize awards for creative work in N.J., ER Squibb and Sons Sculpture award. Mem. AIA (profl. affiliate), Internat. Sculptors Assn., Am. Abstract Artists (exhbn. chmn. 1978-79, pres. 1979-82), Fine Arts Fedn. (bd. dirs.), Coll. Art Assn., Women's Caucus on Art (conf. speaker), Phi Delta Kappa. Home: 41 Sunset Dr Summit NJ 07901-2322

ROUSSEAU-FINELLI, SHARON, counselor; b. Waltham, Mass., Nov. 9, 1964; d. Wilfred Joseph and Margaret (Ryan) Rousseau; m. Robert Steven Finelli, June 4, 1988. BA, Framingham State Coll., 1986; MA, Lesley Coll., Cambridge, Mass., 1989. Cert. sch. guidance counselor. Spl. needs tchr. New Eng. Ctr. for Autism, Southboro, Mass., 1986-89; therapist Dearborn Acad., Arlington, Mass., 1989—. Participant AIDS action Com. fundraiser, Boston, 1990, 91. Mem. AACD, Assn. Humanistic Edn. and Devel. Democrat. Office: Dearborn Acad 34 Winter St Arlington MA 02174-6900

ROUSSEL, NORMAND LUCIEN, advertising executive; b. Bristol, Conn., July 15, 1934; s. Wilfred and Bernadette (Chaisson) R.; m. Barbara Rund, Dec. 3, 1960; children: Dean, Deena. BS, U. Hartford, 1962; MBA, U. R.I., 1967. Advt. salesman Hartford (Conn.) Courant, 1963; account exec. Bo Bernstein Advt., Providence, 1964-73; pres. Challenge Advt. Inc., Providence, 1973—. Served with USAF, 1952-56. Mem. R.I. Advt. Club, Epsilon Alpha Zeta. Home: 7 David Dr Johnston RI 02919-2215 Office: Challenge Advt Inc 178 Broadway Providence RI 02903-3091

ROUX, MILDRED ANNA, retired secondary educator; b. New Castle, Pa., June 1, 1914; d. Louis Henri and Frances Amanda (Gillespie) R. BA, Westminster Coll., 1936, MS in Edn., 1951. Tchr. Farrell (Pa.) Sch. Dist., 1939-55; tchr. Latin, English New Castle (Pa.) Sch. Dist., 1956-76; ret., 1976; chmn. sr. high sch. fgn. lang. dept. New Castle Sch. Dist., 1968-76, faculty sponsor sch. fgn. lang. newspapers, 1960-76, 71-76, Jr. Classical League, 1958-76. Mem. Lawrence County Hist. Soc., Am. Classical League, 1958-76. Mem. AARP, AAUW (chmn. publicity program com. Lawrence County chpt. 1992—), Nat. Ret. Tchrs. Assn., Lawrence County Br. Pa. Assn. Sch. Retirees (chmn. community participation com. 1978-81), Coll. Club New Castle (chmn. sunshine com. 1989-91, mem. social com. 1991-92), Woman's Club of New Castle (chmn. pub. affairs com. 1988-90, mem. internat. affairs com. 1990-92, program com. 1990-92). Republican. Roman Catholic. Home: 6 E Moody Ave New Castle PA 16101-2356

ROVEN, MILTON DEAN, podiatrist; b. Bklyn., Feb. 25, 1916; s. Harry and Ida R.; m. Ruth Katz, Dec. 18, 1955; children: Glen, Janice. DPM, L.I. U., 1938. Diplomate Am. Bd. Ambulatory Foot Surgery. Pvt. practice Bklyn., 1938—; spl. lectr. N.Y. Coll. Podiatric Medicine, Ohio Coll. Podiatric Medicine. Author: Non-Disabling Surgical Rehabilitation of the Forefoot, 1976; asst. editor Jour. Podiatric Medicine, Jour of Hosp. Podiatrists; editorial cons. Current Podiatry Jour.; contbr. numerous book revs. With USNR, 1942-46. Mem. Am. Podiatric Med. Assn., Acad. Podiatric Medicine (past pres.), Am. Podiatry Coun. (past pres.), Acad. Ambulatory Foot Surgery (past regional dir.). Home: 5 Caldwell Ter Marlboro NJ 07746-1778 Office: 1331 E 16th St Brooklyn NY 11230-6042

ROVETO, CONNIE IDA, financial services executive; b. Montreal, Que., Can.; d. Charles and Angela (Difruscia) R. BA in English & Lit., U. Toronto, Ont., Can., 1972, BEd, 1973. Cert. officer/dir. Investment Dealers Assn. Can. Mgr. human resources Can. Permanent Trust, Toronto, 1980-81, mgr. orgn. planning, 1981-82, mgr. trust bus. systems, 1982-84, project dir., 1984-85; asst. v.p. Can. Trust, Toronto, 1986; v.p. Cen. Capital Mgmt. Inc., Toronto, 1986-89; exec. v.p. United Fin. Mgmt. Ltd., Toronto, 1989—; v.p. Cen. Guaranty Trust, Toronto, 1988; chair, bd. dirs., chief exec. officer United Fin. Svcs. Ltd., Toronto, 1990—. Mem. senate U. St. Michael's Coll., Toronto, 1989—, mem. acad. planning com., 1991—, mem. capital campaign com., 1987—; mem. com. health care planning Archdiocese Toronto, 1986-90. Mem. Fitness Inst. Office: United Fin Mgmt Ltd, 200 King St W Ste 1202, Toronto, ON Canada M5H 3W8

ROW, CLARK, environmental and economics consultant; b. Washington, July 24, 1934; s. Lathe B. and Constance (Clark) R.; m. COnstance Foshay, May 21, 1972; children: Seth, Jess. BS, Yale U., 1956; MF, Duke U., 1958; PhD, Tulane U., 1973. Economist USDA Forest Svc., New Orleans, 1958-65; economist, rsch. adminstr. USDA Forest Svc., Washington, 1965-83; pvt. practice cons. Balt., 1984—. Contbr. numerous articles to profl. jours. Fellow Soc. Am. Foresters (policy com., Forest Sci. bd.); mem. Am. Econ. Assn., Forest Products Resource Soc. Home and Office: 5503 Boxhill Ln Baltimore MD 21210-2001

ROW, DAVID, artist; b. Portland, Maine, Aug. 31, 1949; s. Arthur Tracy Jr. and Ann Ogle (Shivers) R.; m. Kathleen Chorpenning. BS cum laude, Yale U., 1972, MFA, 1975. One-man shows include Yale U. Sch Art. New Haven, 1974, Rutgers U., Newark, 1977, SUNY, Purchase, N.Y., 1982, Art Galaxy, 1982, 55 Mercer St. Gallery, N.Y.C., 1984, John Good Gallery, N.Y.C., 1987, 89, 91, Ascan Crone, Hamburg, Germany, 1988, 91 Cava Gallery, Phila., 1989, Thaddaeus Ropac, Salzburg, Austria, 1990, Richard Feigen, Chgo., 1991, Thaddaeus Ropac, Paris, 1991, Fujii Gallery, Tokyo, 1991; exhibited in group shows at Yale U. Sch. Art, New Haven, 1973, 86, 112 Greene St. Gallery, N.Y.C., 1975, The Drawing Ctr., N.Y.C., 1978, 82, Sutton Place, Guilford-Surrey, Eng., 1982, Portland Mus. Art, 1983, Gallerie D'Arte Moderna, Venice, Italy, 1985, GE Corp. Hdqs., Stamford, Conn., 1985, The Pyramid Club, 1986, Condeso Lawler Gallery, N.Y.C., 1986, Pratt Inst. Gallery, Bklyn., 1986, John Good Gallery, N.Y.C., 1986, 87, 88, 89, 90, 91, One Penn Plz., N.Y.C., 1987, Jacob Javits Ctr., N.Y.C., 1988, Cava Gallery, Phila., 1988, Shea & Beker Gallery, N.Y.C., 1989, Inst. N.Am. Studies, Barcelona, Spain, 1989, Haines Gallery, San Francisco, 1989, J.B. Speed Art Mus., Louisville, 1989, Galerie Rahmel, Cologne, Germany, 1989, Marc Richards Gallery, L.A., 1989, Persons Lindell Gallery, Helsinki, Finland, 1989, Karl Bornstein Gallery, L.A., 1990, Baumgartner Galleries Inc., Wasington, 1990, High Mus. Art., Atlanta, 1990, Fernando Alcolea Barcelona, 1991, Feigen Gallery, Chgo., 1991, Wolff Gallery, N.Y.C., 1991, Tony Shafrazi, N.Y.C., 1991, Galerie Lelong, N.Y.C., 1991, Vrej Baghoomian, N.Y.C., 1991, Galeria in Arco, Turin, Italy, 1991, Sidney Janis Gallery, N.Y.C., 1991; represented in permanent collections Carnegie Mus. Art, Pitts, Cleve. Mus. Art, Bklyn. Mus; also represented in numerous exhbn. catalogues. Home: 38 Crosby St New York NY 10013 Office: 476 Broadway New York NY 10013

ROWAN, ARNOLD, accountant; b. N.Y.C., Apr. 21, 1954; s. Robert L. Rowan and Evelyn (Reinert) Britt. BA in Sociology, Haverford (Pa.) Coll., 1976; MBA in Fin., NYU, 1978, advanced profl. cert. acctg., 1981, advanced profl. cert. fed. taxation, 1985. CPA, N.Y. Jr. acct. Laventhol & Howarth, CPA, N.Y.C., 1980-81; tax sr. Bernard L. Dikman, CPA, N.Y.C., 1981-84, tax mgr., 1991—; tax supr. Grant Thornton, CPAs, N.Y.C., 1984-88; tax mgr. Phillips Gold & Co., CPAs, N.Y.C., 1988-90, Citrin Cooperman, CPAs, N.Y.C., 1990-91. Mem. AICPA, N.Y. State Soc. CPAs, NYU Grad. Sch. Bus. Adminstrn. Alumni Assn., Haverford Coll. Alumni Assn., CPA Club of New York. Home: 242 W 10th St Apt 22 New York NY 10014-2949 Office: Bernard L Dikman CPA 1841 Broadway # 500 New York NY 10023-7603

ROWDEN, GWEN ALISON, lawyer; b. Washington, July 17, 1954; d. Marcus Aubrey and Justine Leslie (Bessman) R.; m. John David Carton, Sept. 2, 1979; children: Pamela Carton, Emily Carton. BA, Brown U., 1976; JD, U. Mich., 1979; LLM in Tax, NYU, 1985. Assoc. Curtis, Mallet-Prevost, Colt & Mosle, N.Y.C., 1979-81, Gelberg & Abrams, N.Y.C., 1982-87; real estate counsel The Rockefeller Group, N.Y.C., 1987-90; v.p. Rockefeller Ctr. Mgmt. Corp. & Rockefeller Ctr. Devel. Corp., N.Y.C., 1989—; assoc. gen. counsel The Rockefeller Group, N.Y.C., 1990—; dir. Epode, Inc., N.Y.C. Editor Mich. Yearbook of Internat. Legal Studies, 1978-79. Mem. Comml. Real Estate Women N.Y. Home: 233 Madison Rd Scarsdale NY 10583 Office: The Rockefeller Group 1230 Ave of the Americas New York NY 10020

ROWE, DAVID LAWRENCE, bank executive; b. Hartsville, S.C., Dec. 6, 1952; s. E. Riley and Dorothy (Hine) R.; m. Virginia Heckenstaller, May 5, 1984; children: Nathan, Emily. BSEA, Clemson U., 1974; MBA, U. Tenn., 1978. Cert. fin. planner, cert. prodn. and inventory mgmt., cert. office automation profl. Cons. Westinghouse Electric, Pitts., 1979-84; productivity mgr. Mellon Bank, Pitts., 1984-87; sr. cons. LoBue Assocs., Fairlawn, N.J., 1987-90; founding dir. Polyrol Packaging Systems, Clearwater, Fla., 1988—; v.p. customer svc. ops. Citicorp/Citibank, Melville, N.Y., 1990—. Scoutmaster Boy Scouts Am.; conservationist Philmont Scout Ranch, Cimaron, N.Mex. Named Eagle award Boy Scouts Am.. Mem. Internat. Soc. Fin. Planners, Am. Assn. Indsl. Engrs. Home: 7 Alberta Ct Smithtown NY 11787-4709 Office: Citicorp/Citibank 2 Huntington Quad Huntington Station NY 11750-0001

ROWE, ELIZABETH WEBB, association administrator; b. Canton, Ohio, Dec. 2, 1957; d. Thomas Dudley Webb and Verity Elizabeth (Voight) O'Brien; m. David Lee Rowe, June 21, 1986. AB, Mt. Holyoke Coll., 1979. Legal asst. Willkie Farr & Gallagher, N.Y.C., 1979-82, legal asst. supr., 1983-88, adminstrv. asst., 1988-89—; outreach dir. St. Bartholomew's Ch., 1989—; legal asst. Community Law Offices, N.Y.C., 1980-82, St. Bartholomew's Ch.; clerical asst. 17th Precinct Police Detective, N.Y.C., 1981-82. Chair homeless shelter St. Bartholomew's Ch., N.Y.C., 1984-85; vol. Breakfast Feeding Program, 1983—, mem. Community Ministry Council, 1986-88; mem. N.Y. Jr. League, Pres.'s Council, 1988—; rep. Mt. Holyoke Coll. Alumnae Fund, 1986-89, class officer, 1989—, bd. dirs. Home: 167 E 67th St Apt 6E New York NY 10021-5916 Office: St Bartholomew's Ch 109 E 50th St New York NY 10022-6862

ROWE, KEVIN S., banker; b. Seldom come bye, Nfld., Can., Feb. 14, 1938; m. Valma Jean Rowe, Aug. 28, 1958; children: Todd, Michelle, Natalie, Scott. Student, Curtis Acad., St. Johns, Nfld. With The Bank of N.S., various locations, Can., U.S. and abroad, 1955-70; agt. N.Y.C., 1970-73; area mgr. V.I. and P.R., 1973-77; v.p., gen. mgr. Pacific Regional Office Manila, 1977-83; exec. v.p., gen. mgr. internat. Bank of N.S., Toronto, Ont., Can., 1983-86, exec. v.p. Pacific Region, 1987—; bd. dirs. BNS Internat. (Hong Kong) Ltd., The Bank of Nova Scotia Asia Ltd., Solidbank Corp., Poonpipat Fin. & Securities Co. Ltd. Office: Bank of Nova Scotia, 6th Fl Admiralty Ctr, Tower I 18 Harcourt Rd, Hong Kong Hong Kong

ROWE, LYNN TAYUL, telecommunications executive, educator; b. N.Y.C., Sept. 21, 1955; s. Kwang Wook and Hyo Suk (Lee) R.; m. Ana Cristina de Almeida Waack, Jan. 30, 1987. BA, Tufts U., 1977; MBA, NYU, 1982. Self employed cons. N.Y.C., 1979-83; mgr. telecommunications planning and adminstrn. Capital Cities/ABC Inc., N.Y.C., 1983-91; pres. Telecom Internat., Bklyn., 1991—; columnist Via Satellite, 1992—; lectr. NYU-Info. Techs. Inst., N.Y.C., 1985-86; affiliate rev. com. ABC, N.Y.C., 1986-88; judge Internat. Film & TV Festival, N.Y.C., 1989—. Mem. Internat. Communications Assn., Radio & TV News Dirs. Assn., Soc. for Satellite Profls. Internat., Internat. Computer and Communications (planning com. 1988—). Home and Office: 262 Forkner Dr Decatur GA 30030-6310

ROWE, WILLIAM JOHN, publishing executive; b. Detroit, Jan. 11, 1936; s. Howard Tiedeman and Thelma Irene (Fox) R.; m. Ellen McCabe, Nov. 28, 1959; children: Peter William, Susan Victoria. BA in Journalism and Advt., Mich. State U., 1958. With Chgo. Tribune, 1958-79, pres., gen. mgr. area publs. Suburban Trib subs., 1977-79; pres., gen. mgr. Merrill Printing Co., Chgo., 1977-79; pres., chief exec. officer Peninsula Times Tribune, Palo Alto, Calif., 1979-84; exec. v.p., chief operating officer Times Mirror Nat. Mktg., N.Y.C., 1984-85, pres., chief exec. officer, 1985-86; pres., pub., chief exec. officer The Advocate and Greenwich Time, Stamford, Conn., 1986—. Bd. dirs. United Way, Stamford and Greenwich, Conn., Conn. Bus. for Edn. Coalition. Served to 2d lt., inf. U.S. Army Res., 1959. Mem. Newspaper Assn. Am., New Eng. Newspaper Assn., Indian Harbor Yacht Club, Landmark Club. Home: 9 Hill Rd PO Box 4208 Greenwich CT 06830-4024 Office: Advocate So Conn Newspapers 75 Tresser Blvd Stamford CT 06901-3304

ROWELL, DAVID BENTON, publishing company executive, consultant; b. Hartford, Conn., Mar. 8, 1939; s. Harry George and Helen Myrtle (Krech) R.; m. Joanna Shreve Fortune, Aug. 4, 1962; 1 child, Andrew Fortune. BA, Amherst Coll., 1965. Lic. real estate broker, Calif., Mass. Exec. dir. Amherst (Mass.) C. of C., 1965-69; advt. and pub. rels. account exec. Daily Hampshire Gazette, Northampton, Mass., 1969-71, Santa Barbara (Calif.) News Press, 1971-77, InterMedia, Santa Barbara, 1977-84; cons. InterMedia, Niskayuna, N.Y., 1984-86, Schenectady, 1986—. Contbr. articles, poetry, jazz revs. and criticism to various publs. Bd. dirs. Old Spanish Days in Santa Barbara, Inc., 1982-84; pres. Santa Barbara-Puerto Vallarta Sister Cities Com., 1983. With USN, 1959-63. Mem. Albany Execs. Assn., Albany-Colonie C. of C., Advt. Club, Creative Club, Lions. Republican. Episcopalian. Office: InterMedia 915 Woodland Ave Schenectady NY 12309

ROWELL, HARRY BROWN, JR., corporate executive; b. Roberta, Ga., Sept. 21, 1941; s. Harry Brown Sr. and Essie Jewel (Sloan) R.; m. Mary Jeanette Hancock, Sept. 18, 1961; children: Harry Brown III, T. Scott. BBA, U. Ga., 1963, MA, 1964. Dir. cosmic U. Ga., Athens, 1964-69; dir. ops. Carnegie Mellon U., Pitts., 1969-74; v.p., treas. U. Bridgeport, Conn., 1974-79; v.p. corp. planning and devel., group v.p. Hubbell, Inc., Orange, Conn., 1985—; also exec. v.p. Hubbell, Inc., Orange, 1988—; bd. dirs. The Bank Mart, Bridgeport. Bd. dirs. Goodwill Industries, Bridgeport, 1976-87. Mem. Fin. Execs. Inst., Assn. for Corp. Growth. Club: Brokklawn Country (Fairfield, Conn.). Office: Hubbell Inc 584 Derby Milford Rd Orange CT 06477-2206

ROWELL, LESTER JOHN, JR., insurance company executive; b. Cleve., Apr. 2, 1932; s. Lester John and Francis Laureen (Corbett) R.; m. Patricia Ann Loesch, Jan. 16, 1953 (div. Sept. 1970); children: Deborah, Cynthia, Gregory, Maureen, Diane; m. Carol Ann Jankowski, Sept. 26, 1970. BS, Pa. State U., 1955; grad. Advanced Mgmt. Program, Harvard U. Bus. Sch., 1971. CLU. Second v.p., field mgmt. Mut. Life Ins. Co. N.Y., N.Y.C., 1969-70, v.p. agys., 1970-72, v.p. sales, 1972-78, sr. v.p., 1978-80; exec. v.p. Provident Mut. Life Ins. Co., Phila., 1980-84, pres., 1984-86, pres., chief oper. officer, 1987, pres., chief exec. officer, 1991—; bd. dirs. Provident Mut. Life Ins. Co., Provident Mut. Life and Annuity Co. Am., Continental Am. Life Ins. Co., Sigma Am. Corp. Vice chmn. major accounts United Way Southeastern Pa., Phila., 1986—; chmn. advt. book campaign Southeastern Pa. chpt. ARC, 1989, bd. dirs., Paoli Meml. Hosp., Phila. Drama Guild. Capt. USMC, 1953-62. Recipient Alumni award Pa. State U., 1972, Disting. Alumni award Pa. State U., 1988; Alumni Fellow Pa. State U., 1987. Mem. Life Ins. Mktg. and Rsch. Assn. (dir. 1980-83, mem. strategic mktg. issues com. 1987), NALU, Agy. Officers Round Table (chmn. 1980-81), Found. at Paoli, Life Underwriters Tng. Coun. (past trustee), Greater Phila. C. of C. (bd. dirs.). Republican. Office: Provident Mut Life Ins Co 1600 Market St Philadelphia PA 19103-4201

ROWEN, ROSE LEE, mathematician; b. Chgo., Feb. 11, 1917; d. Benjamin and Sarah (Browdy) Greenberg; widowed; children: William Edward, Celia Rowen Barash. AA, Woodrow Wilson Coll., 1936; BA, NYU, 1945. Cert. med. tech. With Army Map Service, Washington, 1947-49, Bur. Standards, Washington, 1949-50, Joint Chief of Staff, Washington, 1950-52; with aircraft and space divs. Hughes Aircraft Co., Culver City, Calif., 1953-60; with Horton project Aero. Corp., Los Angeles, 1961-63; earthquake researcher UCLA, 1963-65; with space contracts Hughes Aircraft Co., Hawthorne, Calif., 1965-67; with Watkins-Johnson Co., Gaithersburg, Md., 1976—. Contbr. over 50 articles on math., physics, and computer sci. to profl. jours. Mem. Soc. Applied Math., Am. Math. Soc., Soc. Women Engrs., Pi Mu Epsilon, Sigma Pi Sigma. Democrat. Lutheran. Club: Cosmos. Home: 1060 Pipestem Pl Rockville MD 20854-5548

ROWEN, RUTH HALLE, musicologist, educator; b. N.Y.C., Apr. 5, 1918; d. Louis and Ethel (Fried) Halle; m. Seymour M. Rowen, Oct. 13, 1940; children: Mary Helen Rowen, Louis Halle Rowen. B.A., Barnard Coll., 1939; M.A., Columbia U., 1941, Ph.D., 1948. Mgmt. ednl. dept. Carl Fischer, Inc., N.Y.C., 1954-63; assoc. prof. musicology CUNY, 1967-72, prof., 1972—, mem. doctoral faculty in musicology, 1967—. Author: Early Chamber Music, 1948, reprinted, 1974; (with Adele T. Katz) Hearing-Gateway to Music, 1959, (with William Simon) Jolly Come Sing and Play, 1956, Music Through Sources and Documents, 1979, (with Mary Rowen) Instant Piano, 1979, 80, 83; contbr. articles to profl. jours. Mem. ASCAP, Am. Musicol. Soc., Music Library Assn., Coll. Music Soc., Nat. Fedn. Music Clubs (nat. musicianship chmn. 1962-74, nat. young artist auditions com. 1964-74, N.Y. state chmn. Young Artist Auditions 1981, dist. coord. 1983, nat. bd. dirs. 1989—, rep. UN 1991—), N.Y. Fedn. Music Clubs (pres.), Phi Beta Kappa. Home: 115 Central Park W New York NY 10023-4153

ROWLAND, JAMES MORTEN, construction executive, electrical contractor; b. South Seaville, N.J., Aug. 19, 1948; s. James S. and Lillian T. (Olsen) R.; m. Danielle C. Meo, Mar. 19, 1973 (div. Oct. 1980); m. Joan J. Powell, Dec. 31, 1986; children: Darby, Lindsay, Stephen. BS in Mgmt., Rutgers U., Camden, N.J., 1983, MBA, 1985, postgrad., 1985-87. Project engr. E.C. Ernst, Inc., Atlantic City, 1983-85; gen. mgr., chief operating officer Scalfo Electric, Inc., Vineland, N.J., 1985-90; pres. Keystone Elec. Systems, Reading, Pa., 1990-91; mgr. bus. devel. Keystone Elec. Systems, Westville, N.J., 1991—, pres., CEO, 1992—; cons. J. Rowland & Assocs., South Seaville, 1990—; sec. Scalfo Electric, Inc., Vineland, 1987-90. Author seminar Electrical Contracting: Managing for Profit, 1989. Mem. Cape May County (N.J.) Planning Bd., 1992; bd. dirs. Cape May County Mental Health Svcs., 1985-87. Mem. Am. Arbitration Assn., Am. Soc. Profl. Estimators, Internat. Brotherhood Elec. Workers, Marine Corps Scholarship Found. Republican. Roman Catholic. Home: PO Box 522 South Seaville NJ 08246 Office: J Rowland & Assocs PO Box 522 South Seaville NJ 08246

ROWLAND, JOHN G., congressman; b. Waterbury, Conn., May 24, 1957; s. Sherwood L. and Florence (Jackson) R.; m. Deborah Nabhan; children: Kirsten Elizabeth, Robert John, Julianne Marie. B.S. in Bus. Adminstrn., Villanova U., 1979. Former mem. Conn. Ho. of Reps.; mem. 99th-101st Congress from 5th Conn. dist., 1985—; pres. Rowland Assocs. Ambassador, St. Mary's Hosp., Waterbury; bd. dirs. Am. Cancer Soc., Waterbury. Recipient Disting. Service award VFW, Holy Cross Alumni Assn. Republican. Home: 86 Cables Ave Waterbury CT 06710-1603 Office: US Ho of Reps 654 South St House Office Bldg Middlebury CT 06762

ROWLANDS, JUNE, mayor. Mayor City of Toronto, Can., 1992—. Office: City Hall, Office of Mayor, Toronto, ON Canada M5H 2N2*

ROWLEY, GLENN HARRY, lawyer; b. Hyannis, Mass., May 16, 1948; s. Harold Frederick and Olive Nellie (Jones) R.; m. Margene Elizabeth Munn, Oct. 12, 1986; 1 child, Brewster Westgate. BBA, U. Mass., 1970; JD with cum laude, Western New Eng. Coll., 1980. Bar: Mass. 1980, U.S. Dist. Ct. Mass. 1981, U.S. Tax Ct. 1981. Staff mem. Cape Cod Planning and Econ. Devel. Commn., Barnstable, Mass., 1975-76; staff, estate planning tax dept. Coopers and Lybrand, Springfield, Mass., 1980-81; legal assoc. Roberts and Farrell, West Chatham, Mass., 1982-84; ptnr. Roberts, Farrell & Rowley, West Chatham, 1984—; cons. Local Citizen Scholarship Trusts, Harwich and Chatham, Mass., 1985—. Contbr.: (weekly news column) The Cape Codder, The Enterprise, The Register, others.; contbr. articles to profl. jours. Founding mem. Brewster (Mass.) Conservation Trust, 1984; past elected mem. Brewster Hist. Dist. Com., 1975. With USN, 1971-74, Iceland.

Recipient Am. Jurisprudence awards Lawyers Co-op. Pub. Co., 1978, 79. Mem. Mass. Bar Assn., Ocean Edge Exec. Club, Profl. Writers of Cape Cod, Phi Delta Phi. Home: Annaniases Knoll/Sheep Pond Brewster MA 02631 Office: Roberts Farrell & Rowley The Marketplace 26 George Ryder Rd S West Chatham MA 02669

ROWLEY, JAMES MAX, retail fuel oil and rental property company executive; b. Milton, Vt., Oct. 26, 1943; s. Raymond George and Hope Valerie (Garrand) R.; m. Leslie Joan Dwinell, Aug. 27, 1966; children: Christina, Jo-Ellen. BS, U. Vt., 1966. Mkgt. trainee Mobil Oil Corp., Rochester, N.Y., 1966-67; shift supr. Champlain Container Group, Shelburne, Vt., 1967-69; co-owner J & J Assocs., Milton, Vt., 1968-71, Milton Lumber Co., 1969-72; pres. J.M. Rowley, Inc., Milton, 1970—, Rowley Fuels, Inc., Milton, 1980—; advisor Franklin-Lamoille Bank, Milton, 1989—. Bd. dirs. Milton Community News, 1990—; mem. sch. bd. Milton Graded Sch. Dist., 1977-86; pres. Milton Dem. Com., 1978; coach Milton Girls' Softball League, 1979-84, 87-90. Mem. Milton Bus. Assn. (charter, pres. 1987-88), Fraternal Order of Eagles (charter, pres. 1990-91), Alpha Zeta. Home and Office: Rowley Fuels Inc 472 W Milton Rd Milton VT 05468-3255

ROY, DELLA MARTIN, materials science educator, researcher; b. Merrill, Oreg., Nov. 3, 1926; d. Harry L. and Anna (Cacka) Martin; m. Rustum Roy, June 8, 1948; children: Neill R., Ronnen A., Jeremy R. BS, U. Oreg., 1947; MS, Pa. State U., 1949, PhD, 1952. Various rsch. positions Pa. State U., University Park, part-time 1952-60, sr. rsch. assoc. geochem., 1960-62, sr. rsch. assoc. materials sci. engr., 1962-69, assoc. prof. materials sci. engr., 1969-75, prof. materials sci. engr., 1975—; cons. in field. Editor: Instructional Modules in Cement Science, 1985; editor jour. Cement & Concrete Research, 1971—; contbr. articles to profl. publs. Chmn. status of cement, concrete Materials adv. bd., Washington, 1977-80; spl. adv. concrete durability Nat. Rsch. Coun., 1985—; mem. coun. Materials Rsch. Soc., 1988—; mem. exec. com. transp. rsch. bd. NAS, 1991—. Recipient award for outstanding slag rsch. Can. Ctr. Mineral and Energy Tech. Am. Concrete Inst., 1989. Fellow AAAS, Am. Ceramic Soc. (trustee 1990—, Jeppson Medal award 1982, Copeland award, 1987), Mineral. Soc. Am., Am. Concrete Inst. (keynote address 1980), Inst. Concrete Tech. (hon.); mem. NAS (exec. com., transp. rsch. bd. 1991—), Materials Rsch. Soc. (chmn. cement symposia 1980, 81, 86-88, trustee 1988-90), Nat. Acad. Engring. (elected mem. 1987, mem. acad. adv. bd. 1989—), Am. Ceramic Soc. (trustee 1990—). Democrat. Office: Pa State U 217 E Marylyn Ave State College PA 16801-6241

ROY, DELWIN ADAMS, development economist; b. Turlock, Calif., Apr. 3, 1937; s. Edward Tullio and Udell (Adams) R.; m. Corinne Eda Hemphill, Mar. 17, 1961; children: Eric Edward, Dana Anne, Kimberley Jeanette. Student San Francisco State U., 1955-56; BS, U. Calif., Berkeley, 1959, MBA, 1960; PhD, Purdue U., 1968. Personnel rep. Lawrence Radiation Lab., Berkeley, 1960-62; instr. Cornell U., Ithaca, N.Y., 1964-66; asst. prof. U. of Pacific, Stockton, Calif., 1966-67; program economist AID, Montevideo, Uruguay, 1967-69, sr. cons., Washington, 1977-78; planning officer Citicorp, N.A., N.Y.C., 1969-70; program advisor Ford Found., N.Y.C. and Cairo, Egypt, 1970-76; dir. Ga. World Congress Inst., Atlanta, 1978-81; chief exec. officer Devel. Decisions Internat., Atlanta, 1981-85; pres. The Hitachi Found., Washington, 1985—, also bd. dirs.; sr. fellow Wharton Applied Research Ctr., Phila., 1981—, So. Ctr. Internat. Studies, Atlanta, 1981—; mem. Assocs. for Middle East Research, Inc., U. Pa., Phila., 1980—; cons. World Bank, State Dept., Washington, 1978—; trustee Internat. Devel. Conf., 1984—. Co-author: Southeast Exporting, 1981, Arab Investors Sourcebook, 1987; Editor: Development Administration in the Middle East, 1975; Egyptian Economic Liberalization, 1984. Contbr. numerous articles on Middle East econ. issues to profl. jours. Served with U.S. Army, 1958-64. U.S. Steel Found. fellow, 1963; Harvard U. Ctr. Internat. Affairs fellow, 1976; CIC travelling scholar, 1964. Mem. Am. Econ. Assn., Middle East Studies Assn., AAAS. Democrat. Home: 1920 Belmont Rd NW Washington DC 20009-5402

ROY, DENNIS J., quality manager consultant; b. Boston, Nov. 24, 1954; s. Dolores C. Roy. LPN, Greater Lawrence Inst., Andover, Mass., 1975; BSN, U. Mass., Boston, 1984; MBA in Healthcare, Boston U., 1991. RN, Mass., Conn.; cert. in quality assurance. Nurse Peter Bent Brigham Hosp., Boston, 1975-78; nurse New Eng. Deaconess Hosp., Boston, 1978-85, utilization reviewer, 1985-87; quality assurance dir. The Arbour Hosp., Boston, 1987-88; quality mgr. Mass. Dept. Mental Health, Boston, 1988-91; quality cons. Aetna Health Plans, Hartford, Conn., 1991—; ind. cons., Boston, 1986-91. Mem. Nat. Assn. Healthcare Quality, Inst. Indsl. Engrs., Soc. for Health Systems, Am. Nurses Assn., Am. Soc. for Quality Control, Sigma Theta Tau. Home: 10 Spring St Chester CT 06412-1335 Office: Aetna Health Plans MC17 151 Farmington Ave Hartford CT 06156

ROY, RONALD DWAYNE, industrial hygienist; b. Logan, W.Va., Mar. 7, 1956; s. Basil W. and Lovey E. (Stevens) R.; m. Debra K. Triplett, Dec. 30, 1977; children: Heather Carissa, Sarah Lacy. BS, Marshall U., 1976; MS, W.Va. U., 1978. Cert. indsl. hygienist, safety profl. With safety mgmt. Austin Powder Co., McArthur, Ohio, 1979; indusl. hygienist Occupational Safety and Health Administn. U.S. Dept. Labor, Charleston, W.Va., 1979-84; sr. indusl. hygienist Motorola Inc., Phoenix, 1984-86; dir. safety, environ., and occupational health Allwash Syracuse, N.Y., 1986-90; asbestos program mgr. Galson Tech. Svcs., Inc., Syracuse, N.Y., 1990-91; v.p. environ. health safety AWI Environ., Syracuse, 1991—. Mem. Am. Indsl. Hygiene Assn. (pres. mountaineer sect. 1983-84, ergonomics com. 1984-87, sec. confined spaces com. 1987-91, mem. law com. 1989—), Am. Acad. Indsl. Hygiene, Am. Conf. Govtl. Indsl. Hygienists, Am. Soc. Safety Engrs., Nat. Fire Protection Assn., Internat. Platform Assn. Republican. Office: AWI Environ PO Box 605 Syracuse NY 13201-0605

ROYCE, PAUL C., medical administrator; b. Mpls., July 2, 1928. BA, U. Minn., 1948, MD, 1952; PhD, Case Western Res. U., 1959. Diplomate Am. Bd. of Internal Medicine. Intern U. Chgo. Clinics, 1952-53; fellow NSF Case Western Res. U., Cleve., 1953-54, 56-58, Upjohn fellow, 1958-59; resident internal medicine Bronx Mcpl. Hosp., N.Y., 1959-61; asst. prof. of medicine Albert Einstein Coll. of Med., N.Y.C., 1961-69; sr. staff endocrinologist Guthrie Clinic, Sayre, Pa., 1970-81; assoc. prof. of medicine Hahnemann Med. Sch., Phila., 1973-81; dean and prof. clin. sci. and physiology U. Minn., Duluth, 1981-87; sr. v.p., clin. dir. Monmouth Med. Ctr., Long Branch, N.J., 1987—; bd. dirs. Frank & Louise Groff Found., Red Bank, N.J., 1987—. Producer, host TV prgram Doctors on Call, 1983-87 (Nat. Friends of Pub. Broadcasting Hill award 1987). Lt. USNR, 1954-56. Mem. Harvey Soc., Am. Physiol. Soc., Fedn. Am. Scientists, Physicians for Social Responsibility, Am. Coll. Physician Execs., Sigma Xi, Alpha Omega Alpha. Office: Monmouth Med Ctr 300 2nd Ave Long Branch NJ 07740-6303

ROYCHOUDHURI, CHANDRASEKHAR, physicist; b. Barisal, Bengal, India, Apr. 7, 1942; s. Hiralal and Amiyabala (Sengupta) R.; m. Pamela Taren, Aug. 8, 1977; children: Asim, Onnesha. BS in Physics, Jadavpur U., India, 1963; MS in Physics, Jadavpur U., 1965; PhD, U. Rochester, 1973. Asst. prof. U. Kalyani, West Bengal, India, 1965-68; sr. scientist Nat. Inst. Astrophysics, Puebla, Mex., 1974-78; sr. staff scientist TRW Inc., L.A., 1978-86; mgr. laser systems Perkin-Elmer, Danbury, Conn., 1986-89; chief scientist Optics & Applied Tech. Lab., UTOS, West Palm Beach, Fla., 1990-91; dir. Photonics Rsch. Ctr. U. Conn., Storrs, 1991—. Author: chpt. Optical Shoptesting, 1978; contbr. articles to profl. jours. Fulbright scholar U. Vt., 1968. Mem. IEEE, Optical Soc. Am., Soc. Photo-optical Instrumentation, AAAS, Planetary Soc., Am. Phys. Soc. (life).

ROYDS, ROBERT BRUCE, physician; b. Harrogate, England, Oct. 3, 1944; came to U.S., 1974; s. John Edmund and Ailsa Dorothea (Williams) R.; m. Marilyn Maria Valerio, Apr. 28, 1948; children: Elizabeth Caroline, Leslie Alexandra. M.B., B.S., U. London, 1967, M.R.C.P., 1970. Sr. house officer Royal Northern Hosp., London, 1968; sr. house officer Luton and Dunstable Hosp., Beds, England, 1968-69; registrar St. Albans City Hosp., Herts, England, 1969-70; research fellow clin. pharmacology dept. St. Bartholomew's Hosp., U. London, London, 1970-72; chief asst., sr. registrar med. professorial unit St. Bartholomew's Hosp., U. London, 1972-74; assoc. dir. Merck, Sharp & Dohme, Inc., Rahway, N.J., 1974-75; sr. research physician Hoffmann-La Roche Inc., Nutley, N.J., 1976-78; v.p. Besselaar Assocs., Princeton, N.J., 1979-82; pres. Theradex Systems, Inc., Princeton, 1982—; cons. Ctr. for Rsch. Mothers/Infants Nat. Inst. Child Health & Human Devel., Washington, 1983. Bd. trustees Chapin Sch., Princeton, 1984-89, pres. bd. trustees, 1986-89; pres. Riverside Condominium Assn., Cranford, N.J., 1978-79. Fellow Royal Soc. Medicine; mem. Royal Coll. Physicians, Am. Coll. Clin. Pharmacology Therapeutics, Am. Soc. for Clin. Research (sr. mem.), Am. Soc. Microbiology. Home: 5 Quick Ln Plainsboro NJ 08536-1424 Office: Theradex Systems Inc CN5257 Princeton NJ 08540

ROYER, LINDA MARY, accountant; b. Allentown, Pa., Nov. 16, 1949; d. Norman Leon and Rita Mary (Shanaberger) Measler; m. Roy David Schadler, Aug. 21, 1970 (div. Sept. 1979); 1 child, R. David; m. George Leroy Royer Sr., Mar. 18, 1980; children: Kareen, Mary, George Jr., Karl. BS, Bloomsburg U., 1982, M in Bus. Sci., 1991. Office mgr. G&C Industries, Inc., Bloomsburg, Pa., 1982-86; gen. ledger supr. JDK Mgmt. Co., Inc., Bloomsburg, Pa., 1986—. Treas. Boy Scouts Am., Pack 25, Bloomsburg, 1989—, asst. scoutmaster Troop 25, 1991—. Mem. NAFE, Am. Mgmt. Assn. Republican. Roman Catholic. Home: 148 E 7th St Bloomsburg PA 17815-2730 Office: JDK Mgmt Co Inc RR 5 Box 290 Bloomsburg PA 17815-8905

ROYER, MARILYN ANN, accountant, educator; b. Buffalo, Sept. 25, 1948; d. Williams S. and Eugenia (Lorenc) R. BA, SUNY, Buffalo, 1970, MBA, 1980; MEd, Niagara U., 1975. CPA, N.Y. Acct. Conway Porter, Buffalo, 1979-81, Seidman & Seidman, Buffalo, 1981-84; ptnr. Rader & Royer, Tonawanda, N.Y., 1985-88; pvt. practice Tonawanda, 1988—; instr. part-time Niagara (N.Y.) U., 1991; commr. Niagara Frontier Transp. Authority, Buffalo, 1988—. Dir.-treas. Buffalo Area Coun. Alcoholism, 1982-84; prior sec. Zonta, North Tonawanda, N.Y., 1989. Recipient cert. Appreciation Daemen Coll., 1985. Mem. AICPA, Am. Soc. Women Accts., Nat. Assn. Accts. (dir. socioecon. projects 1984, dir. CMA affairs 1985, Disting. Svc. award 1984), N.Y. State Soc. CPA's. Home: 1328 Belling Pl North Tonawanda NY 14120 Office: 305 Delaware St Tonawanda NY 14150

ROYLANCE, PETER JAMES, executive medical director; b. Hull, Yorkshire, England, Oct. 3, 1928; came to U.S. 1979; s. James William and Muriel (Thompson) R.; m. Joan Margaret Hodgson, May 11, 1957; children: Katharine Margaret, Wendy Muriel. MB, BChir, U. Bristol, England, 1955; diploma in pharm. medicine, Royal Coll. of Physicians, Edinburgh, Scotland, 1976. Med. diplomate. Resident Southmead Gen. Hosp., Bristol, 1955-56; sr. resident United Bristol Hosps., 1956-58; demonstrator in anatomy Univ. Bristol, 1958-61; research haematologist Inst. of Cancer Research, London, 1961-70; med. adv. Beecham Pharmaceuticals, London, 1970-75; clin. research dir. Merck Sharp & Dohme Ltd., 1975-77, med. dir., 1977-78; sr. med. dir. Merck Sharp & Dohme Internat., Rahway, N.J., 1979-83; exec. med. dir. Merck Sharp & Dohme Internat., Rahway, N.J., 1982—; clin. prof. internal medicine Seton Hall U. Sch. Grad. Med. Edn., 1992—; fellow faculty pharm. medicine Royal Coll. Physicians, Eng., 1989. Author: New Essential First Aid 1967, New Advanced First Aid 1969, articles in profl. pubs. Surgeon Comdr., Royal Navy (Res.) 1957-82. Comdr. Order of St. John 1976; reserve decoration, H.M. Govt. U.K. 1967. Fellow Am. Coll. Physicians, Inst. of Biology; life mem., N.Y. Acad. Scis., livery man, Worshipful Soc. of Apothecaries. Home: 8 Magna Dr Gillette NJ 07933-1417 Office: Merck & Co Inc Rahway NJ 07065

ROZANSKI, RAPHAELA PATRICIA, dietitian; b. Boston, Mar. 1, 1945; d. Joseph and Antoinette Vendetti; m. Alfred H. Rozanski; children: Nicole, Alecia. BS, Simmons Coll., 1966; MS, Framingham State Coll., 1976. Registered dietitian. Dietitian N.E. Deaconess Hosp., Boston, 1966-67; chief of nutrition Norwood (Mass.) Hosp., 1967-670; dietitian ARA Mgmt. Corp., Waltham, Mass., 1971-74; cons. Area Nursing Homes, Medway, Mass., 1971—; area coord. Cons. Dietitians in Health Care Facilities, Chgo., 1991-92. Editor: Massachusetts Diet Manual LTC, 19889; contbg. author: Cons. Dietitians in Health Care Facilities newsletter, 1986-91; page-designer in-svc. manual, 1991. Vice-chmn. Conservation Commn., Medway, 1991-92. Mem. Am. Dietetic Assn., Mass. Dietetic Assn. (chmn. div. consultation, pvt. practicie 1986-88, 90-91), CD-HCF, Simmons Profl. Alumnae Network. Office: 5 Virginia Rd Medway MA 02053

ROZELLE, MARK ALBERT, company executive; b. Fairfield, Conn., Oct. 23, 1960; s. Warren J. and Patricia A. (Blake) R.; m. Susan C. Gasper, May 29, 1962. BS in Acctg. and Econs., U. Bridgeport, 1983, MBA, 1992. Intern Amax Inc., Greenwich, Conn., 1980-83; entry level. acct. UST Inc., Greenwich, 1983-84, investor rels. specialist, 1984-85, sr. investor rels. specialist, 1985-87, mgr. investor rels., 1987—. Tchr., cons. applied econs. program Jr. Achievement, Greenwich, 1983—; chpt. leader Guardian Angels, Bridgeport, Conn., 1989—. Mem. Nat. Investor Rels. Inst., Nat. Assn. Investors Corp. Republican. Home: 30 Nob Hill Cir Bridgeport CT 06610-1816 Office: UST Inc 100 W Putnam Ave Greenwich CT 06830-5342

ROZOVSKI, SAMUEL JAIME, biochemist, consultant; b. Santiago, Chile, Sept. 20, 1944; came to U.S., 1970; s. Leon and Ita (Narkunsky) R.; m. Michele Golodetz, May 28, 1977; children: David, Tama. Degree in biochemistry, U. Chile, Santiago, 1969; MSc, Columbia U., 1971, PhD, 1977. Rsch. fellow U. Chile, Santiago, 1969-70; postdoctoral fellow Boston U. Med. Sch., 1976-78; rsch. fellow Inst. Human Nutrition Columbia U., N.Y.C., 1978-81, asst. prof. pub. health, 1981-86, asst. clin. prof. pub. health, 1986; pres. Juniper Cons. Inc., N.Y.C., 1986—, also bd. dirs.; cons. World Bank, Washington, 1992. Contbr. articles to profl. jours. Muscular Distrophy Assn. fellow, 1977-79, Brookdale Inst. fellow Columbia U., 1984—; recipient Vis. Prof. and Lectr. award Lydia Roberts Meml. Lecture of U. P.R., 1986. Mem. AAAS, APHA, Am. Inst. Nutrition, N.Y. Acad. Scis., Soc. Latin Am. Nutrition, Harvey Soc., Sigma Xi. Home: 450 W End Ave New York NY 10024

RUASEN, AARON REUBEN, pediatric oncologist; b. Jersey City, June 30, 1930; s. David and Ruth (Schwartz) R.; m. Emalou Watkins, Apr. 7, 1968; children: David, Susan, Elisabeth. Degree, Dartmouth Coll., 1950; MD, SUNY, Bklyn., 1954. Intern, then resident in pediatrics Bellevue Hosp. Ctr., N.Y.C., 1954-56; chief resident in pediatrics Mt. Sinai Hosp., N.Y.C., 1958-59, asst., assoc. and attenging pediatrician, 1961-81; fellow in hematology Children's Hosp. and Harvard Med. Sch., Boston, 1959-61; chief of pediatrics City Hosp. Ctr., Elmhurst, N.Y., 1964-72; dir. pediatrics Beth Israel Med. Ctr., N.Y.C., 1972-81; dir. pediatric oncology NYU Med. Ctr., N.Y.C., 1981—; prof. pediatrics NYU Sch. Medicine, N.Y.C., 1981—; prof. pediatrics Mt. Sinai Sch. Medicine, N.Y.C., 1971-81; dir. Stephen D. Hassenfeld Children's Ctr. for Cancer and Blood Disorders, N.Y.C., 1990—; cons. Lenox Hill Hosp., N.Y.C., 1981—; vis. prof. Dartmouth Med. Sch., Hanover, N.HY., 1984-86. Contbr. articles to profl. jours. Bd. dirs. Am. Cancer Soc., N.Y.C., 1984—. Capt. med. corps U.S. Army, 1956-58. Fellow Am. Acad. Pediatrics; mem. Am. Pediatric Soc., Am. Soc. Hematology, Am. Soc. Clin. Oncology, Am. Assn. Cancer Rsch., Am. Soc. Pediatric Hematology-Oncology, N.Y. Pediatric Soc. (pres. 1974), Yale Club N.Y.C., Phi Beta Kappa, Alpha Omega Alpha. Office: NYU Med Ctr 550 1st Ave New York NY 10016-6402

RUBB, PEGGY-GRACE PLOURD, artistic director, dancer; b. Hartford, Conn., Sept. 27, 1931; d. Launcelot J. and Margaret (Feeney) Plourd; m. Milton Robert Rubb, June 6, 1953; children: Bonnie Leigh, Eric John, Michael Robert. Student, Hartt Conservatory of Music, Hartford, 1938-49; student, Shenandoah Conservatory, Winchester, Va., 1949-51, Froman Profl. Ballet Sch., New London, Conn., 1959-62, Hampton Acad. Ballet, Va., 1962-63, Nat. Ballet, Washington, 1963-66. Tchr. R.H. Lee Elem. Sch., Glen Burnie, Md., 1951-52; dancer Common Glory Jamestown Corp., Williamsburg, Va., 1963; accompanist Annapolis (Md.) Modern Dance Assn., 1973, Ballet Mistress Dance Studio, Crofton, Md., 1974-78; dance instr. gymnastics camp Washington Coll., Chestertown, Md., 1977; artistic dir. Crofton-Bowie (Md.) Sch. of Ballet and affiliated cos., 1978-92; choreographer Tom Thumb Players, Annapolis, 1972, Nat. Assn. for Regional Ballet, Inc. Choreography Conf., 1987; dancer Hampton Roads Civic Ballet, Va., 1962-63; composer, lyricist in field; dance coach Glen Burnie (Md.) Artistic Skate Club, 1980-81. Bd. dirs. Annapolis Children's Theatre, 1977-78. Mem. NAFE, Internat. Platform Assn., U.S. Naval Acad. Class '53 Wives Club (pres. San Diego cpt. 1957, pres. New London chpt. 1959), Severn Town Club, Md. Club, Gen. Fedn. Women's Club (co-mem.), Phi Beta Kappa. Home: 1 Pennsylvania Ave Edgewater MD 21037-1338 Office: 2411 Crofton Ln Ste 2 Chelsea House Crofton MD 21114

RUBEL, ARTHUR, fluid dynamicist, engineer; b. N.Y.C., Apr. 7, 1940; s. Sidney and Mina (Poris) R.; m. Frances Schulman, Dec. 19, 1964; children: Steven, Lance. BME, CCNY, 1960; MME, NYU, 1962, PhD, 1969. Engr. Curtiss Wright Corp., Wood Ridge, N.J., 1960-63; rsch. sci. Gen. Applied Sci. Labs., Westbury, N.Y., 1963-67, 69-77; head theoretical fluid dynamics lab. corp. rsch. ctr. Gruman Aerospace Corp., Bethpage, N.Y., 1977—. Contbr. articles to profl. jours.; reviewer for numerous sci. jours. Fellow AIAA (assoc.); mem. ASME, Am. Phys. Soc., Soc. Indsl. and Applied Math., Tau Beta Pi, Pi Tau Sigma. Home: 17 Seneca Pl Jericho NY 11753-1412 Office: Grumman Aerospace Corp Corp Rsch Ctr/MSA08-35 Bethpage NY 11714

RUBEN, RICHARDS, artist, educator; b. L.A., 1925; s. Frederick Edward and Eleanor (Barnett) R.; m. Ruth Lee Godley (div. 1948); 1 child, Raoul Ron Ruben; m. Gail Diven Ruben; 1 child, Caitlin Sara Ruben. Student, Chouinard Art Inst., L.A. Prof. Pomona Coll., 1958-62, Cooper Union, N.Y.C., 1962-65, Pratt Inst., Bklyn., 1967-71, Columbia U., N.Y.C., 1966-69; asst. prof., artist in residence NYU, 1963-72, asst. prof., 1974-76; prof. SUNY, New Paltz, 1979-80, Pratt Inst., Bklyn., 1982—; artist in residence Santa Barbara (Calif.) Mus. Art, 1964; vis. prof. Drew U., Madison, N.J., 1976. Fellow Nat. Endowment for Arts 1980, Ford Found. 1964, Am. Fedn. Art 1964, Tamarind 1961; grantee Tiffany 1954. Home: 85 Mercer St New York NY 10012-4438

RUBENSTEIN, ALLAN EARL, neurology educator; b. Buffalo, N.Y., Dec. 8, 1944. BA, Cornell U., 1966; MD, Tufts U., 1970. Assoc. prof. neurology Mt. Sinai Sch. Medicine, N.Y.C., 1974—; bd. dirs. Nat. Neurofibromatosis Found., N.Y.C. Editor: Neuro Fibromatosis: A Handbook, 1990. Fellow Am. Acad. Neurology; mem. Am. Soc. Human Genetics, Nat. Neurofibromatosis Found. (med. dir. 1978—). Office: Mt Sinai Sch Medicine 5 E 98th St New York NY 10029-6501

RUBENSTEIN, CHARLES PHILIP, electrical engineering educator; b. Bklyn., May 9, 1947; s. Morton and Maureen Rita (Herman) R.; m. Rose Lefkowitz, Nov. 15, 1969; children: Jaron, Adam, Scott. AS in Indsl. Lab. Tech., S.I. Community Coll., 1967; BS in Engring. Sci., CUNY, 1969; MS in Bioengring., Poly. Inst. of N.Y., 1971, PhD in Bioengring., 1980. Asst. prof. Pratt Inst., Bklyn., 1980-82; tenured assoc. prof. Bramson ORT Tech. Inst., N.Y.C., 1985—, chmn. elec. tech., 1982-85; adj. prof. engring. Cooper Union, N.Y.C., 1985-88; cons. Applied Rsch. Engring. Assoc., Massapequa, N.Y., 1968—; cons., tech. writer C.E.S. Industries, Inc., Farmingdale, N.Y., 1989-90. Author: Electrical Engineering Laboratory Manual, 1989; author, editor: Instructores Workbook for Technical Books I and II, 1980; editor IEEE newsletter Engring. Mgmt., 1990—; inventor electronic calendar display. Explorer adv. leader N.Y. coun. Boy Scouts Am., 1981—, cubmaster, 1981, asst. dist. commr. Suffolk County coun., 1985—. Recipient Dist. Merit award Boy Scouts Am., 1991. Mem. IEEE, Engring. Mgmt. Soc. (bd. govs. 1988—, Outstanding Teaching and Counseling award 1983, Outstanding Young Engr. 1984, Innovation award 1985), Electro Conf. and Exhbn. (bd. dirs. 1983-87), Tau Beta Pi, Eta Kappa Nu. Office: Pratt Inst Sch of Engring Brooklyn NY 11205

RUBENSTEIN, JOSHUA SETH, lawyer; b. Bklyn., Aug. 5, 1954; s. Seth and Elaine (Freedman) R.; m. Marta Johnson; children: Mary-Jane, Kenan. BA magna cum laude, Columbia U., 1976, JD, 1979. Bar: N.Y. 1980, N.J. 1980, U.S. Dist. Ct. (ea. dist.) N.Y. 1980, U.S. Dist. Ct. (so. dist.) N.Y. 1980, U.S. Dist. Ct. N.J. 1980, U.S. Tax Ct. 1986. Assoc. Fried, Frank, Harris, Shriver & Jacobson, N.Y.C., 1979-82; assoc. Rosenman & Colin, N.Y.C., 1982-88, ptnr., 1988—; mem. adv. bd. TE/DEC Systems, Inc., Jour. N.Y. Taxation; lectr. in field. Contbr. articles to legal publs. Pres. Brasch Farms Civic Assn., Middletown, N.J., 1982-84, 340 East 74th St. Owners Corp., 1990-91; dir. Irvington Inst. Med. Rsch., 1991, treas. 1991-92, sec., 1992—; chmn. estates and trust splty. group lawyers div. United Jewish Appeal-Fedn., 1989—; mem. legis. com., Madeleine Borg com., trustee Jewish Bd. Family and Children's Svcs., 1991—. Fellow Am. Coll. Trusts and Estate Counsel (state laws com.); mem. ABA (real property and probate sect.), N.Y. State Bar Assn. (trust and estate law sect., lectr. 1984—, vice chmn. legis. com. 1988, chmn. 1989-91, Pres.' Pro Bono Svc. award 1991, exec. com. award 1992, co-chmn. ad hoc com. to rev. proposals of EPTL adv. com. of N.Y. State 1991—, mem.-at-large exec. com. 1992—, exec. com. award 1992), N.J. Bar Assn. (real property and probate sect.), Assn. of Bar of City of N.Y., Practising Law Inst. (lectr. 1984—), Phi Beta Kappa. Democrat. Jewish. Office: Rosenman & Colin 575 Madison Ave New York NY 10022-2511

RUBENSTEIN, LEWIS W., artist; b. Buffalo, Dec. 15, 1908; s. Emil and Hannah (Hirschman) R.; m. Erica Beckh, June 28, 1942; children—Daniel B., Emily R. Morrow. A.B., Harvard, 1930, grad. fellow study painting in Europe, 1931-33. Mem. faculty Vassar Coll., 1939-74, prof. art, 1957-74. Mural commns. include Adolphus Busch Hall, Harvard U., 1935-37, Post Office, Wareham, Mass., 1940, Buffalo Jewish Ctr., 1949; originated: Time Painting, films Time Painting by Lewis Rubenstein, 1956; exhbns. include, NAD, Whitney Mus. Am. Art, Met. Mus., Am. Watercolor Soc., Library of Congress, Soc. Am. Graphic Artists, USIA, Harvard, Am. U., Vassar Art Gallery, Buffalo Jewish Center, Ford Found., Busch-Reisinger Mus., Fogg Art Mus., Albright-Knox Gallery, Schenectady Mus., Fleming Mus. Art, U. Vt., Barrett House, Poughkeepsie, N.Y.; video prodns. Dunes, 1982, Psalm 104, 1987. Served to lt. USNR, 1942-45. Fulbright grantee Japan, 1957-58; State Dept. grantee S. Am., 1961; recipient award Soc. Graphic Artists, 1952, 54, award Silvermine Artists, 1959, award Empire State Architects, 1950, Art award Dutchess County Execs., 1987. Mem. Soc. Am. Graphic Artists. Home: 153 College Ave Poughkeepsie NY 12603-2804

RUBENSTEIN, STANLEY ELLIS, public relations consultant; b. Balt., July 25, 1930; s. Albert B. and Lee (Goodman) R.; m. Ruth Anne Zinder, Feb. 8, 1953; children: Deborah C., Steven M., Michael L., Kenneth J., Andrew L. BA, U. Md., 1953. Writer, researcher Bozell & Jacobs, Inc., N.Y.C., 1953-54; reporter Jour. of Commerce, N.Y.C., 1954-56; writer, account exec. Ruder & Finn, Inc., N.Y.C., 1956-60; founder, prin. Rubenstein, Wolfson & Co., Inc., N.Y.C., 1960-91; pub. rels. cons. S. E. Rubenstein, N.Y.C., 1991—. Mem. Bd. Edn. Gt. Neck (N.Y.) Pub. Sch., 1968-74, pres. 3 yrs. Served with USN, 1948-49. Mem. Pub. Relations Soc. Am., N.Y. Fin. Writers Assn. (assoc.). Jewish. Clubs: Nat. Press; World Trade (N.Y.C.). Home: 51 Colgate Rd Great Neck NY 11023-1519 Office: Ste 300 420 Lexington Ave New York NY 10170

RUBIN, ARTHUR HERMAN, academic administrator, consultant; b. N.Y.C., Aug. 14, 1927; s. Samuel and Bessie (Moritt) R.; m. Janice Levy, Apr. 9, 1950 (div. 1965); children: Renee Ellen, Linda Joy; m. Audrey M. Schmidt, July 1, 1973. BS, NYU, 1950, MA, 1951. Adminstrv. asst. to asst. dean Sch. Edn. NYU, 1947-54, lab. asst. bus. edn. dept., 1950-54, instr., 1954-56, program dir. grad. students orgn., 1954-63, dir. tours, 1955-58, coord. summer sessions activities, 1959-64, dir. Bur. Pub. Occasions, 1963-74, dir. Bur. Conf. Facilities, 1968-69, asst. v.p. pub. occasions, 1974-75, dir. extramural affairs Coll. Dentistry, 1976, assoc. dean adminstrn., 1976-80, adj. asst. prof. behavioral scis. and community health, 1976-80, dir. alumni rels. Sch. of Med., 1980—, dir. spl. events med. ctr., 1988—; tchr. Patrick Henry Jr. High Sch., N.Y.C., 1949-58; acting asst. prin. Robert F. Wagner Jr. High Sch., N.Y.C., 1958-63; cons. in field. Trustee Agnew Found., 1967—. Recipient NYU Presdl. citation, 1971, GSO award, 1980, Ernest O. Melby award Sch. Edn. Alumni Assn., 1976, citation Bus. Edn. Assn. Met. N.Y., 1976, Sesquicentennial award NYU Alumni Fedn., 1982, Meritorious Svc. award, 1985. Mem. Eastern Bus. Tchrs. Assn. (chmn. exhibits 1953-74, exec. bd. 1969-71, pres. 1972-73, award 1974), Bus. Edn. Assn. of Met. N.Y. (mem. exec. bd. 1962-83), Bus. Edn. Securities Club, Inc. (pres. 1963-66, v.p. ops. 1967-68), Arch Securities Club, Inc. (pres. 1963-66, v.p. ops. 1967-68), Nat. Bus. Edn. Assn. (mem. exec. bd. 1972-74, conv. mgr. 1974-92), N.Y. Acad. Pub. Edn. (bd. dirs. 1979—), Educators Securities Club, Inc. (v.p. ops. 1966-68), N.Y. U. Edn. Alumni Assn. (v.p. 1961-62, 64-67), NYU Club (bd. govs. 1972-78, 79-89, v.p. 1983-86, chmn. bd. 1986-87), Princeton Club N.Y., Delta Pi Epsilon Rsch. Found., Inc. (bd. dirs. 1990-92), Delta Pi Epsilon (Svc. awards Alpha chpt. 1971, 81), Kappa Phi Kappa, Alpha Delta Pi Securities Club, Inc. (pres. 1963-66, v.p. ops. 1967-68). Home: 110 Bleecker St Apt 29E New York NY 10012-2107 Office: NYU Med Ctr 550 1st Ave New York NY 10016-6402

RUBIN, BENJAMIN ARNOLD, immunology educator, researcher; b. N.Y.C., Sept. 27, 1917; s. Eli and Helen Sarah (Arenoff) R.; m. Mae Koenig, Aug. 31, 1951. BS, CCNY, 1937; MS, Va. Polytech. Inst. & State U., 1938; PhD, Yale U., 1947. Asst. dir. Circle Analytical Lab., N.Y.C., 1938-40; chief lab. and radiology U.S. Army C.E., Nfld., also Cen. Am., 1940-44; asst. chief microbiologist Scherly Rsch. Lab., Lawrenceburg, Ind., 1944; rsch. asst. Yale U., New Haven, 1944-47; chief microbiologist Brockhaven Nat. Lab., L.I., 1947-52, Sytex, Mexico City, 1952-54; prof. Coll. of Medicine Baylor U., Houston, 1954-60; mgr. biol. rsch. Wyeth, Radnar, Pa., 1960-84; rsch. prof. Phila. Coll. Osteo. Medicine, 1984—; cons. GE, Valley Forge, Pa., 1972-80, U.S. Congressman Dingle, Washington, 1980-84. Contbr. over 150 articles to sci. jours. Named to Inventors Hall of Fame; recipient John Scott award and medal, 1982; named Inventor of Yr., 1985. Home: 50 Belmont Ave Apt 601 Bala Cynwyd PA 19004-2431 Office: Phila Coll Osteo Medicine 4150 City Ave Philadelphia PA 19131-1610

RUBIN, BERNARD, pharmacologist, consultant; b. N.Y.C., Feb. 15, 1919; s. Charles and Ann (Slutskin) R.; m. Betty R. Schindler, June 15, 1945; children: Stefi Gail, Robert Henry. BA, Bklyn. Coll., 1939; PhD, Yale U., 1951. Rsch. asst. various orgns., N.Y., 1940-48; rsch. pharmacologist E.R. Squibb & Sons, Inc., New Brunswick, N.J., 1951-65; group leader, pharmacology E.R. Squibb & Sons, Inc., Princeton, N.J., 1965-84; cons., licensing Bristol-Myers Squibb Co., Princeton, 1984—. Contbr. over 100 rsch. articles to profl. jours., 1948-85. With U.S. Army, 1942-43. Recipient A.E.C. pre-doctoral fellowship, Washington, 1949-50. Home: 2 Pin Oak Dr Trenton NJ 08648-3134

RUBIN, DAVID ALBERT, physician; b. Longbranch, N.J., Apr. 1, 1950; s. Samuel Harold and Audrey (Arndt) R.; m. Lorna Sacks, Dec. 23, 1973; children: Elizabeth, Geoffrey. AB, Brown U., 1971; MD, Columbia U., 1975. Resident in medicine Columbia-Presbyn. Med. Ctr., N.Y.C., 1975-78; fellow in cardiology Mount Sinai Hosp., N.Y.C., 1978-80; assoc. prof. medicine N.Y. Med. Coll., 1980—; dir. cardiology fellowship N.Y. Med. Coll., Valhalla, 1986—, dir. clin. electrophysiology Westchester Med. Ctr., Valhalla, 1980—. Contbr. articles to profl. jours. Fellow Am. Coll. Cardiology; mem. N.Am. Soc. of Pacing and Electrophysiology, Phi Beta Kappa, Sigma Xi, Alpha Omega Alpha.

RUBIN, DONALD BRUCE, statistician, educator, research company executive; b. Washington, Dec. 22, 1943; s. Allan A. and Harriet (Schainis) R.; m. Kathryn M. Kazarow; children: Scott Wilk, Paul Stuart. AB magna cum laude, Princeton U., 1965; MS, Harvard U., 1966, PhD, 1970. Rsch. statistician Ednl. Testing Svc., Princeton, N.J., 1971-75, chmn. stats., 1975-79, sr. statis. advisor, 1979-81; pres. Datamatrics Rsch. Inc., Waban, Mass., 1981—; prof. U. Chgo., 1982-84; prof. Harvard U., Cambridge, Mass., 1984—, chmn. stats., 1985—. Author: Handling Nonresponse in Sample Surveys by Multiple Imputation, 1980, Multiple Imputation for Nonresponse in Surveys, 1987; author: (with others) Imcomplete Data in Sample Surveys (Vol. 2): Theory and Bibliography, 1983; co-author: (with R.J.A. Little) Statistical Analysis With Missing Data, 1987; co-editor: (with P.W. Holland) Test Equating, 1982; contbr. over 160 articles to profl. jours. Woodrow Wilson Grad. fellow Woodrow Wilson Soc., 1965, NSF Grad. fellow, 1965, 68, John Simon Guggenheim fellow, 1977-78. Fellow AAAS (chmn. stats. 1992), Am. Statis. Assn. (editor jour. 1980-82), Inst. Math. Stats. (coun. mem. 1990-92); mem. NAS (mem. com. on nat. stats. 1989—, mem. panel on confidentiality data 1989—, mem. panel bilingual edn. 1990—, mem. working group on statis. analysis of com. on basic rsch. in behavioral and social scis., 1985-86, mem. other coms.), Biometric Soc., Internat. Assn. Survey Statisticians, Internat. Statis. Inst., Psychometric Soc., Royal Statis. Soc., Phi Beta Kappa. Office: Harvard U Dept Stats Cambridge MA 02138

RUBIN, DOROTHY MOLLY, educator, writer; b. N.Y.C., Feb. 11, 1932; d. Harry and Clara (Schweller) Schleimer; student CUNY, 1949-51; BA, Rutgers U., 1959, MEd, 1961; PhD in Ednl. Psychology, Johns Hopkins U., 1968; m. Arthur I. Rubin, Aug. 24, 1950; children—Carol Anne, Sharon Anne. Tchr., N.J. Schs., 1959-62; asst. prof. Coppin (Md.) State Coll., 1962-63; asst. prof. Towson (Md.) State Coll., 1963-66; adj. prof. Rollins (Fla.) Coll., 1968-69; assoc. prof. Trenton (N.J.) State Coll., 1969-73, prof., 1973—; cons. Harper & Row, 1983; cons., speaker, columnist. Recipient profl. awards. Mem. Internat. Reading Assn., Nat. Coun. Tchrs. of English, Kappa Delta Pi, Pi Lambda Theta, Phi Kappa Phi. Author: Teaching Elementary Language Arts, 1975, Gaining Word Power, 1978, rev. edit., 1986, 3rd edit., 1993, Reading and Learning Power, 1980, 2d edit., 1985, 3d edit. 1991, Teaching Elementary Language Arts, 1975, rev. edit., 1980, 3d edit., 1985, 4th edit. 1990, The Teacher's Handbook of Reading-Thinking Exercises, 1980, The Primary-Grade Teacher's Language Arts Handbook, 1980, The Intermediate-Grade Teacher's Language Arts Handbook, 1980, Gaining Sentence Power, 1981, The Teacher's Handbook of Writing-Thinking Exercises, 1980, The Teacher's Handbook of Primary-Grade Reading/Thinking Exercises, 1982, Vocabulary Expansion, vol. 1, 1982, vol. II, 1982, 2d edit., 1991, A Practical Approach to Teaching Reading, 1982, 2d edit., 1993, Diagnosis and Correction in Reading Instruction, 1982, 3d edit., 1991, Teaching Reading and Study Skills in Content Areas, 1983, 2d edit., 1991, Writing and Reading: The Vital Arts, 2d edit., 1983; (audio cassette) Passport to Power English, 1987; Power English: Basic Language Skills for Adults, 1989, rev. edit., 1990 (10 book series); Power Vocabulary: Basic Vocabulary for Adults, 1992-93 (5 book series); Mind Bind, Moon Master, Quick Scramble, ednl. video games; also numerous articles; syndicated columnist Word Games; producer, moderator ednl. TV shows; contbr. articles to USA Today. Home: 917 Stuart Rd Princeton NJ 08540-1212 Office: Hillwood Lakes CN550 Trenton NJ 08625

RUBIN, GABRIEL KEVI, psychiatrist; b. Bklyn., Feb. 9, 1927; s. Samuel and Augusta Gertrude (Katz) R.; m. Janis Lyn Millstein, June 27, 1988. BA, NYU, 1946; MD, Hahnemann Med. Coll., 1950. Diplomate Am. Bd. Psychiatry and Neurology. Resident psychiatrist Bellevue Hosp., N.Y.C., 1953-54, Pilgrim State Hosp., Brentwood, L.I., N.Y., 1954-56; clin. asst. psychiatrist Hillside Hosp., Queens, N.Y., 1956-58; chief psychiat. inpatient and outpatient svcs. Elmhurst (Queens, N.Y.) Gen. Hosp., 1958-60; med. dir. Fifth Ave Ctr. for Counseling and Psychotherapy, N.Y.C., 1960-76; chmn. faculty Met. Inst. Psychoanalytic Studies, N.Y.C., 1960-76; adj. psychiatrist Beth Israel Hosp. Med. Ctr., N.Y.C., 1960—; asst. attending psychiatrist Roosevelt Hosp., N.Y.C., 1963—; clin. assoc. psychiatrist Mt. Sinai Med. Coll., N.Y.C., 1980—; attending psychiatrist Forest Hills Gen. Hosp., Kew Gardens Gen. Hosp., Hillcrest Gen. Hosp., Blvd. Hosp., Astoria Gen. Hosp., Whitestone Gen. Hosp., Deepdale Gen. Hosp., Howard Park Hosp., Queens, 1958—. Hike leader Appalachian Mountain Club, N.Y.C., 1986—. 1st lt. USAF, 1951-53, Korea. Fellow N.Y. Acad. Medicine (life), N.Y. Acad. Sci. (life); mem. Island Peer Rev. Orgn., N.Y. County Peer Rev. Orgn., Bronx County Peer Rev. Orgn., Am. Contract Bridge League (life). Office: 71-36 110th St 1-M Forest Hills NY 11375

RUBIN, IRVIN I., plastics company executive; b. Bklyn., Feb. 27, 1919; children:Jesse, Julie. BS in Chemistry, CCNY, 1938; postgrad. Bklyn. Coll., 1939-40. Pres., Robinson Plastics Corp., Hoboken, N.J., 1940-42, 44—; engr. Montrose Chem., Newark, 1942-45; prin. Robinson, Lewis & Rubin, Inc., N.Y.C., 1957-70; adj. prof. plastics N.Y. Inst. Tech., 1960-63; mem. Plastics Ednl. Commn., Adv. Bd. Vocat. and Extension Edn., Bd. Edn. N.Y.C., 1960-71; cons. Dupont, Am. Optical, Kodex, Fellow Soc. Plastic Engrs. (pres. N.Y. sect.). Author: Injection Molding Theory and Practice, 1973; editor: Handbook of Plastic Materials and Processes, 1990. Office: 313 1st St Hoboken NJ 07030-2440

RUBIN, JACOB CARL, research engineer; b. N.Y.C., Nov. 22, 1926; s. Abraham and Bessie (Tockman) R.; m. Nancy Jean Weinstein, AUg. 2, 1952; children: Sara Lee, Jeffrey Daniel. BSME, CUNY, 1945; MMechE, NYU, 1947; MS of Applied Statistics, Rochester (N.Y.) Inst. Tech., 1969, MSEE, 1971, MS in Imaging Sci., 1975. Registered profl. engr., N.Y., D.C. Design group leader MacDonnell Aircraft Corp., St. Louis, 1955-56; mem. research staff U. Mich., Ann Arbor, 1956-57; staff engr. IBM, Vestal, N.Y., 1957-58; engr. advance design GE, Johnson City, N.Y., 1958-60; program engr. GE, Phila., 1960-62; mgr. standards engring. Martin-Marietta Corp., Balt., 1962-63; mgr. product design dept. Am. Car & Foundry Co., Rockville, Md., 1963-64; cons. reliability NASA, Greenbelt, Md., 1964-65; project engr. Eastman Kodak Co., Rochester, 1965-75, sr. rsch. assoc., 1975-90; staff mech. engr. Med. Lab. Automation, Inc., Pleasantville, N.Y., 1990-91; prin. engr. instrument div. Dresser Industries, Stratford, Conn., 1992—; course dir. Ctr. Profl. Advancement, East Brunswick, N.J., 1975—; adj. faculty Rochester Inst. Tech., 1965-90; faculty Bridgeport Engring. Inst., 1991—. Patentee artificial kidney, piezo-electric generator. Pres. Grove Place Neighborhood Assn., Rochester, 1984. Mem. NSPE (life), N.Y. State Soc. Profl. Engrs. Republican. Jewish. Home: 12-2 Foxwood Dr Pleasantville NY 10570 Office: Dresser Industries 250 E Main St Stratford CT 06497

RUBIN, JANE LOCKHART GREGORY, lawyer; b. Richmond, Va., May 27, 1944; d. Phillip Henry and Jane Ball (Lockhart) Gregory; m. Reed Rubin, Jan. 22, 1966; children: Lara Ross, Maia Ayers, Peter Lyon. BA, Vassar Coll., 1965; JD, Columbia U., 1975; LLM, NYU, 1984. Bar: N.Y, 1976. Of counsel Lankenau Kovner and Bickford, N.Y.C., 1985—; bd. dirs., treas. Reed Found., N.Y.C., 1985—; adv. bd. Vt. Studio Sch., 1985—, Assn. of the Bar of the City of N.Y. Fund, Inc.; mem. Mcpl. Archives Reference and Rsch. Adv. Bd., 1991—, N.Y.C. Commn. for Cultural Affairs. Author intro. and catalog for exhibit Temple of Justice: The Appellate Division Courthouse. Bd. dirs., vice chair Vol. Lawyers for the Arts. Harlan Fiske Stone scholar Columbia U. Sch. Law. Mem. ABA (sect. real property and probate law), N.Y. Bar Assn., Union Internationale des Avocats (mem. permanent commn. on tax law and intellectual property working group), Assn. of Bar of City of N.Y. (com. on no-profit orgns. 1984—), Am. Arbitration Assn. (mem. panel of Arbitrators), Copyright Soc. of the U.S.A. Home: 135 Central Park W New York NY 10023-2413 Office: Lankenau Kovner & Bickford 1740 Broadway Fl 25 New York NY 10019-4315

RUBIN, JEFFREY ZACHARY, psychologist, educator; b. N.Y.C., Jan. 21, 1941; s. Zoltan and Frances Evelyn (Sternberg) R.; m. Carol Milligan, May 27, 1972; children: David, Sally, Noah. BA, Antioch Coll., 1963; PhD, Columbia U., 1968. Asst. prof. psychology Tufts U., Medford, Mass., 1969-75, assoc. prof. psychology, 1975-81, prof. psychology, 1981—, adj. prof. internat. diplomacy Fletcher Sch. Law and Diplomacy, 1989—; dir. ctr. for study decision making Tufts, 1980-84; assoc. dir. program on negotiation Harvard U. Law Sch., Cambridge, Mass., 1985-89, 91—, exec. dir. program on negotiation, 1987-91; sr. lectr. Fulbright Fellowship Tel Aviv U., 1984-85. Co-author Social psychology of Bargaining and Negotiation, 1975, Social Psychology, 1983, Social Conflict: Escalation, Stalemate and Settlement, 1986, When Families Fight: How to Handle Conflict with Those You Love, 1989; editor: Dynamics of Third Party Intervention: Kissinger in the Middle East, 1981; co-editor: Leadership and Negotiation in the Middle East, 1988; editor Negotiation Jour., 1983—. Guggenheim fellow, 1977-78, U. Canterbury Vis. fellow, 1986. Fellow Am. Psychological Assn.; mem. Soc. for the Psychol. Study Social Issues (pres. 1987-88). Office: Harvard U Law Sch Program on Negotation Pound 500 Cambridge MA 02138

RUBIN, JOEL EDWARD, consulting company executive; b. Cleve., Sept. 5, 1928; s. Morris and Pearl (Jacobs) R.; m. Lucille Schutmaat, Dec. 18, 1953; children: Brian G., Jennifer L., Rebecca R. BS, Case Inst. of Tech., 1949; MFA, Yale U., 1951; PhD, Stanford U., 1960. Exec. v.p. Kliegl Bros. Lighting, N.Y.C., 1954-85; prin. cons. Joel E. Rubin & Assocs., N.Y.C., 1985—. Co-author: Theatrical Lighting Practice 1954; author: Technological Development of Stage Lighting 1960. Member Coll. of Fellows of Am. Theatre, John F. Kennedy Ctr. for the Performing Arts, Washington. Recipient Golden Triaga, Prague Quadrennial, 1987, Zlatou medal, 1991, 1st time award Bus. Com. for the Arts, Forbes Mag., 1987, Founders' award U.S. Inst. for Theatre Tech., 1972, 79, U.S. Inst. Tech. Nat. award, 1990. Fellow Am. Theatre Assn. (v.p. 1961-63), U.S. Inst. of Theatre Technology (pres. 1963-64); mem. Am. Nat. Theatre Acad. (bd. dirs. 1971-75), Internat. Theatre Inst. of the U.S. (bd. dirs. 1975-79), Nat. Coun. of Arts and Gov't (bd. dirs. 1975-79), Internat. Org. Theatre Architects and Scenographers (U.S. chmn., rep. 1968—, pres. 1971-79), Illuminating Engring. Soc. Home: 24 Edgewood Ave Hastings On Hudson NY 10706-2024 Office: Joel E Rubin & Assocs 119 W 57th St Ste # 820 New York NY 10019-2303

RUBIN, LENORE BORZAK, human resources executive; b. Chgo., Feb. 13, 1938; d. Philmour and Lillian (Lobelson) Fink; m. Jack Rubin, July 19, 1987; children by previous marriage: Steven Borzak, Peter Borzak. BA, U. Chgo., 1959; MA, Northwestern U., 1965, PhD, 1974. Instr. U. Ill., Chgo., 1966, Kendall Coll., Chgo., 1966-71; asst. prof., dir. office of field study Northwestern U., Evanston, Ill., 1971-82, pres. Ctr. for Human Resource Devel., 1980-82; dir. orgn. devel. and tng. Nynex Mobile Communications, Orangeburg, N.Y., 1988—. Editor: Field Study: A Sourcebook for Experiential Education, 1978. Mem. Am. Soc. for Tng. and Devel., Orgn. Devel. Network, Soc. for Human Resource Devel. Home: 459 Tenafly Rd Englewood NJ 07631-1785 Office: 2000 Corporate Dr Orangeburg NY 10962-2624

RUBIN, MARILYN RUTH, health educator; b. Boston, Nov. 25, 1946; d. Lawrence Leonard and Rose (Goldberg) Abrams; m. Richard Aaron Rubin, Sept. 1,1968; children: Lee Eric, Marissa Joy. BS summa cum laude, Montclair State U., 1976; EdM, Rutgers U., 1983. Med. technologist Commonwealth of Mass., Boston, 1966-67, to pvt. physicians, Boston, 1967-72; instr. Bryman Sch., Boston, 1969-70; assoc. prof., dir. med. lab. technician program Felician Coll., Lodi, N.J., 1973—; part-time instr. Career Acad., Boston, 1970-72, N.Y.C., 1972-73. Co-pres. Whittier Sch. Working Parents Assn., Teaneck, N.J., 1987-89, 91-92. AAUP grad. scholar, 1982. Mem. Am. Assn. Allied Health, Am. Soc. Clin. Pathologists, N.J. Soc. Med. Tech., Phi Kappa Phi, Kappa Delta Pi. Democrat. Jewish. Home: 440 Kensington Rd Teaneck NJ 07666-2713 Office: Felician Coll S Main St Lodi NJ 07644-2203

RUBIN, MARTIN N., meeting planner, consultant; b. N.Y.C., Aug. 9, 1928; s. Max and Esther (Chernow) R.; m. Shirley Anne Rubin, Aug. 22, 1954 (div. Aug. 1964); m. Karen Anne O'Brien, Sept. 21, 1981. AB, U. Mich.; AM, Miami U., Oxford, Ohio; PhD., Sussex U., Eng. Lic. psychologist. With Dayton (Ohio) Sch. System, 1951-60, West Alexandria (Ohio) Sch. System, 1961-63; instr. Wright State U., Dayton, 1961-63; with Devereux Found., Pa., N.Y. Dept. Corrections, Bklyn., 1971-73, Council for Retarded Children, Albany, N.Y., 1973-75; prin. M. Rubin & Co., Inc., Mount Vernon, N.Y., 1975—. Author: Developmentally Disabled, 1965. Candidate Dem. State Legis., 1982; adv. bd. Mt. Vernon Mental Health Bd., 1985. Master's degree scholar Miami U., 1958; Guidance Inst. grantee Miami U., 1959. Fellow Am. Assn. Mental Deficiency (pres. 1967); mem. Soc. Assn. Execs. (bd. dirs. 1985—). Lodge: Masons (sr. warden 1983).

RUBIN, MARVIN JOSEPH, podiatrist, educator; b. Jersey City, June 27, 1928; s. Eli Lazarus and Doris (Epstein) R.; m. Sherry Carrol, Oct. 1957 (div. July 1959); 1 child, Deidre Solonge; m. Barbara Ruth Goldberg Luers, Aug. 16, 1970; children: Robert Daniel, Evan Brian. D of Podiatric Medicine, Chgo. Coll. Podiatric Medicine, 1949. Diplomate Am. Bd. Podiatric Orthopedics. Intern Foot Clinics of Chgo., 1950; assoc. prof. podiatric medicine Pa. Coll. Podiatry Medicine, Phila., 1968-75; pvt. practice Hasbrouck Heights, N.J., 1953—; asst. attending Hackensack Med. Ctr., 1988-91; mem. podiatry staff Kennedy Meml. Hosp., Saddle Brook, N.J., 1984—; cons. Bergen County Dept. on Aging, Hackensack, 1968-88, Patient Care Mag., 1970, 73; mem. profl. com. United Jewish Community Assn. Developmentally Disabled, Tenafly, N.J., 1988—; resource person Office Minority Pub. Health Svc. U.S. Dept. Health Human Svc., 1989—. Vice chmn. bd. govs. exec. com. Bergen-Passaic Health Systems Agy., Rochelle Park, N.J., 1976-79; bd. dirs. Jewish Family Svcs. Bergen County, Hackensack, 1972-77, Jewish Fedn. Community Svc., Hackensack. Recipient Yr. of Miracles award Friends of Lubavitch of Bergen County, 1990; Appreciation award United Jewish Community Assn. Developmentally Disabled, 1988, 91, United Jewish Community of Bergen County, 1986, United Cerebral Palsy citation, 1961. Fellow Am. Coll. Foot Orthopedics (pres. 1968-69), Am. Assocs. Hosp. Podiatrists; mem. APHA (sects. podiatric health and community health planning and policy devel, Stephen P. Toth award 1991), Am. Podiatric Med. Soc., N.J. Podiatric Med. Soc. (bd. trustees, pres. No. div. 1964-66, Resolution award 1991, Ralph Zigler award 1966), N.J. Pub. Health Assn. (pres. 1992), Young Israel Ft. Lee (bd. dirs., pres. 1979-81). Office: 238 Boulevard Hasbrouck Heights NJ 07604-1937

RUBIN, MICHELE BARRIE, psychologist; b. Far Rockaway, N.Y., Dec. 29, 1944; d. Robert Lee and Blanche Rose (Rosen) Hirsch; m. Saul S. Rubin, Mar. 3, 1968; children: Rachel, Sarah, Jessica, Beth, Joshua. B.A. in Psychology, Syracuse U., 1966; M.A. in Tchrs. Coll., Columbia U., 1968, profl. diploma in sch. psychology, 1968; D.Ed. in Counseling, Lehigh U., 1974. Lic. psychologist, N.J.; cert. sch. psychologist. Dir. child study team, sch. psychologist Warren Twp. (N.J.) Public Schs., 1968-70; staff psychologist Somerset County Community Mental Health Center, Somerville, N.J., 1975-81, Family and Community Services, 1981-82, Raritan Valley Workshop, 1986-87; pvt. practice, Muhlenberg Regional Med. Ctr., 1987-88, Bridgewater, 1980—. Mem. Am. Psychol. Assn., N.J. Psychol. Assn., N.J. Assn. Sch. Psychologists, N.J. Acad. Psychology, Acad. Family Psychology. Home: PO Box 6450 Bridgewater NJ 08807-0450

RUBIN, NANCY RUTH ZIMMAN, journalist, author; b. Boston, Nov. 25, 1944; d. Stuart Wendell and Ethel Charlotte (Rabinovitz) Zimman; m. Peter H. Rubin, July 9, 1967; children: Elisabeth Kara, Jessica Ann. BA, Tufts U., 1966; MA in Teaching, Brown U., 1967. English tchr. Brighton High Sch., N.Y., 1967-68, N.Y. Schs., Pittsford, 1969-70; playwright, dir. Equity Library Theatre, Roundabout, Joseph Jefferson and St. Clement's theaters, N.Y.C., 1971-74; writer Westchester-Gannett newspapers and mags., 1975-77; free-lance reporter N.Y. Times, N.Y.C., 1977—; faculty affiliate Bush Ctr. in Child Devel., Yale U., New Haven, 1981—; mem. Westchester County Women's Adv. Bd., chair, 1988. Author: The New Suburban Women: Beyond Myth and Motherhood, 1982, The Mother Mirror: How a Generation of Women Is Changing Motherhood in America, 1984, Isabella of Castile: The First Renaissance Queen, 1991; contbg. editor Parents mag., 1987-91. Time, Inc.-Bread Loaf Writers' Colony scholar, 1979. Fellow MacDowell Colony; mem. Author's Guild, Am. Soc. Journalists and Authors (Author of Yr. award 1992), PEN, NOW. Office: care Agnes Birnbaum Bleecker St Assocs 88 Bleecker St New York NY 10012-1544

RUBIN, NORMAN JULIUS, columnist; b. New Haven, May 22, 1923; s. Louis and Ida (Levine) R. BA, Yale U., 1948. City hall police reporter Meriden (Conn.) Record, 1948-50; assoc. editor Meridan Jour., 1950-53; reporter news bur. Yale U., 1953-55, asst. dir. news bur., 1955-58; dir. pub. rels. New York Tuberculosis Health Assn., N.Y.C., 1958-61; pub. affairs assoc. Western Electric Co., N.Y.C., 1961-64, asst. mgr., pub. affairs, 1964-80; asst. mgr. community rels., 1980-86; asst. sec. Western Electric Fund, N.Y.C., 1974-80; mgr., com. rels. Western Electric Co., N.Y.C., 1980-86; columnist N.Y. Newsday, N.Y.C., 1986—. With Infantry U.S. Army, 1943-46, ETO. Recipient Humanitarian award for outstanding community svc. Jobs for Youth, 1989. Mem. Pub. Rels. Soc. Am. (accredited mem. N.Y. chpt.), Yale Club, Grads. Club. Home: 115 E 9th St Apt 14E New York NY 10003-5429 Office: NY Newsday Two Park Ave New York NY 10016

RUBIN, PAUL HAROLD, economist; b. Boston, Aug. 9, 1942; s. Joseph and Freda (Goldhagen) R.; m. Marcia Ann Claybon, June 15, 1964 (dec. Feb. 1973); children: Joseph Saul, Rachel Beth; m. Mariam Hope Moss, July 26, 1985. BA, U. Cin., 1963; PhD in Econs., Purdue U., 1970. Prof. econs. U. Ga., Athens, 1968-82; sr. staff economist Pres. Coun. Economic Advisers, Washington, 1981-82; prof. econs. Baruch Coll. and the Grad. Ctr., N.Y.C., 1982-83; head, consumer protection Bur. Econs., FTC, Washington, 1983-85; chief economist Consumer Product Safety Commn., 1985-87; v.p. Glassman-Oliver Economic Cons., Inc., Washington, 1987-91; prof. econs. Emory U., Atlanta, 1991—; adj. prof. George Washington U. Law Ctr., Washington, 1985-89. Author: Managing Business Transactions, 1990, Business Firms and the Common Law, 1983, Congressman, Constituents, and Contributors, 1982; contbr. articles to profl. jours. Mem. Am. Economic Assn., Soc. Economic Assn., ABA, Am. Law and Economics Assn., Pub. Choice Soc. Republican. Office: Emory U Dept Econs Atlanta GA 30322

RUBIN, SHARON GOLDMAN, university dean; b. Chgo., May 23, 1944; d. Leonard and Lorraine (Barshefsky) Goldman; m. David Lee Rubin, June 26, 1966; children: Ari Michael, Joshua Franklin. BA, U. Chgo., 1965, MA, 1966; PhD, U. Minn., 1972. Adminstr. Lindenwood Coll., St. Charles, Mo., 1976-78; dir. exptl. learning U. Md., College Park, 1978-84, asst. dean, 1984-87; dean Salisbury (Md.) State U., 1987—. Co-author: Strengthening Experiential Learning, 1986. Bd. dirs. Eastern Shore br. M.S. Soc., Salisbury, 1990—; Salisbury-Wicomico Arts Coun., Salisbury, 1989—, exec. v.p., 1991-92; mem. Gov.'s Bd. for Svc. and Citizens, Annapolis, Md., 1991-92; pres. Columbia Jewish Congregation, 1983. W.K. Kellogg Found. nat. fellow, Battle Creek, Mich., 1980-83. Mem. Nat. Soc. Internships and Experiential Edn. (mem. bd. 1986—, v.p. 1987-89, pres. 1990-91), Am. Assn. Higher Edn. Office: Salisbury State U Fulton Hall Salisbury MD 21801

RUBIN, STANLEY, insurance company executive; b. Bklyn., Feb. 9, 1943; s. Samuel Noah and Pearl (Friend) R.; m. Elaine Rosen, Aug. 21, 1966; children: Michael Lee, Brian Andrew. BS in Bus. and Fin., NYU, 1964; MBA, Adelphi U., 1967. Supervising security analyst Nat. Assn. of Ins. Commrs., N.Y.C., 1971-86; v.p. Presidential Life Ins. Co., Nyack, N.Y., 1986—. Bd. dirs. Rockland Community Coll. Found., Suffern, N.Y., 1990—. With U.S. Army, 1967.

RUBINO, JOHN ANTHONY, compensation specialist, consultant; b. Port Chester, N.Y., Nov. 22, 1956; s. Angelo J. and Ann (Posillipo) R.; m. Cynthia C. Corica, Nov. 9, 1980; 1 child, Sean Anthony. BA in Psychology magna cum laude, Wagner Coll., 1978; MBA with distinction, Pace U., 1985. Cert. compensation profl. Convention svc. mgr. Waldorf-Astoria Hotel, N.Y.C., 1978-80; compensation analyst County of Westchester, White Plains, N.Y., 1980-82; sr. compensation analyst Anaconda-Ericsson, Inc., Greenwich, Conn., 1982-83; compensation mgr. ASEA, Inc., White Plains, N.Y., 1983-84, Sterling Drug, Inc., N.Y.C., 1984-87; dir. exec. compensation, cons. The Equitable Life Insur. Co., N.Y.C., 1987—. Author: Developing Compensation Programs, 1990; contbr. articles to profl. jours. Mem. Am. Compensation Assn. (instr., course leader, guest speaker 1988—), Am. Mgmt. Assn. (instr., course leader, guest speaker 1988—). Home: 6B Scenic Vw Yorktown Heights NY 10598-5144 Office: The Equitable Life Ins Co 787 7th Ave # 42D New York NY 10019-6018

RUBINOVITZ, SAMUEL, diversified manufacturing company executive; b. Boston, Dec. 26, 1929; s. Benjamin Ephraim and Pauline (Kaufman) R.; m. Phyllis Ann Silverstein; children: David Jay, Robert Neal. BS, MIT, 1951, MS, 1952. Sales engr. Clevite Transistor Products, Waltham, Mass., 1954-63; sales mgr. EG&G Inc., Wellesley, Mass., 1963-72, div. mgr., 1972-79, v.p., 1979-86, sr. v.p., 1986-89, exec. v.p., 1989—; bd. dirs. KLA Instruments Inc., Santa Clara, Calif., Richardson Electronics Ltd., Chgo., Kronos Inc., Waltham, EG&G Inc., Wellesley, Mass. Served to 1st lt. USAF, 1952-54. Democrat. Jewish. Office: EG & G Inc 45 William St Wellesley MA 02181-4004

RUBINSTEIN, ARYE, pediatrician, microbiology educator, researcher; b. Tel Aviv, Oct. 2; came to U.S., 1971; s. Rueven and Kateh (Samson) R.; m. Orna Eisenstein, Dec. 7, 1965 (div. 1982); children: Ran, Yair, Avner, Noam; m. Charline Nezri, Dec. 27, 1984; children: Reuven, Rena, Rachel. MD, U. Berne (Switzerland), 1962. Bd. cert. Pediatrics, Israel, Switzerland, U.S.A.; allergy and immunology. Intern, pediatrics resident, fellow U. Tel Aviv, 1962-67; rsch. assoc., div. immunology Harvard Med. Sch., 1971-73; dir. div. immunology and bone marrow transplantation U. Berne, 1969-71; asst. prof. cell biology Albert Einstein Coll. Medicine, Bronx, 1973-80, asst. prof. pediatrics, 1973-77, assoc. prof. pedicatrics, 1977-82, assoc. prof. microbiology and immunology, 1981-85, prof. pediatrics, 1982—, prof. microbiology and immunology, 1985—; dir. div. clin. allergy and immunology Albert Einstein Coll. Med., Montefiore Med. Ctr.; dir. tng. program for allergy and immunology Albert Einstein Coll. Medicine; attending pediatrics Bronx Mcpl. Med. Ctr., Hosp. Albert Einstein Coll. Medicine; attending med. Hosp. Albert Einstein Coll. Medicine.; mem. NIH Study Section Gen. Clin. Rsch. Ctr. and AIDS Rsch. Editorial bd. mem. (jours.): AIDS, Internat. Jour. Pediatric Otorhinolaryngology, Annals of Allergy; reviewer: New England Jour. Medicine, Jour. for Clin. Investigation, Jour. of Pediatrice, Am. Journ. of Diseases of Children; contbr. over 100 articles to profl. jours. Lt. armed svcs., Israel, 1955-57. Recipient Lifetime award in Immunology, Humanitarian award DIFFA, Birch Svcs. for Children, Annual award U.S. Asst. Sec. of Health for excellence in AIDS rsch. and treatment, 1990; AIDS Rsch. Program grantee NIH, Bronx. Mem. Am. Acad. Allergy, N.Y. Acad. Scis., Soc. Pediatric Rsch., The Harvey Soc. Office: Albert Einstein Coll of Medicine 1300 Morris Park Ave Bronx NY 10461

RUBINSTEIN, BETSY ANNE, graphic designer; b. Washington, July 11, 1951; d. Eli Abraham and Minnie Sally (Seidenberg) R.; m. William Harrold

Thomas Jr., July 14, 1974 (div. 1984). BA, Grinnell (Iowa) Coll., 1973; MA, U. Ill., 1976. Psychologist NIMH, Bethesda, Md., 1972-74; dir. program distbn. Nat. Fedn. of Community Broadcasters, Champaign, Ill., 1976-81; dir. pubs. Nat. Fedn. of Community Broadcasters, Washington, 1981-85; prin., editorial dir. Page Designs Unltd. Inc., Bethesda, Md., 1986-91; owner BR Publs., Washington, 1991—. Editor Fast Forward, 1980-81, NFCB Newsletter, 1981-85; contbr. articles to profl. jours. Recipient Ozzie for best newsletter design, Mag. design & Prodn. Mem. Internat. Design by Electronics Assn., Am. Inst. Graphic Artists, Washington Apple Pi.

RUBINSTEIN, G. EDWARD, small business owner; b. Bryn Mawr, Pa., July 20, 1949; s. Mark and Judith Hadasah (Martin) R.; m. Judye Anne Rosewicz, Sept. 8, 1973 (div. 1985); children: Joshua Martin, Jacob Mathias. BFA, U. Minn., 1972. Cook The Bros., Mpls., 1972-73; salesman Fed. Copper & Aluminum, Mpls., 1973-74, M-R Photo Shop, Paoli, Pa., 1974-82; ptnr. M-R Color Lab./M-R Photo, Paoli, 1982-85; owner M-R Color Lab., Paoli, 1985-91, Custome Color Svc., Paoli, Pa., 1991—. Mem. Assn. Profl. Color Labs., Soc. Photo Finishing Engrs., Photo Mktg. Assn. Democrat. Jewish. Office: M-R Color Lab 20 Liberty Blvd Malvern PA 19355-1418 also: PO Box 506 Paoli PA 19301

RUCCIUS, ELIZABETH ANNE, music educator, organist, choir director; b. Valley Stream, N.Y., Mar. 18, 1952; d. Philip Sherwood and Dorothy Nell (Schirmer) Zipf; m. Frederick Edward Ruccius III, June 1, 1974; children: Peter Martin, Andrew David, Katherine Elizabeth. BS in Music Edn., West Chester U., 1974; Masters in Music Edn., Temple U., 1977, Doctors of Mus. Art, 1988. Music tchr. Florence (N.J.) Twp. Schs., 1974-80; asst. prof. music edn. Hunter Coll., N.Y.C., 1985—. Choir dir., organist St. Peter's Luth. Ch., Chester Springs, Pa., 1981—. State mini grantee State of N.J., 1978-79. Mem. Music Educators Conf. (collegiate advisor 1985—). Office: Hunter Coll Dept of Curriculum and Teaching 695 Park Ave New York NY 10021-5085

RUCH, WILLIAM VAUGHN, educator, consultant; b. Allentown, Pa., Sept. 29, 1937; s. Weston H. and Dorothy D. (Daubert) R. BA, Moravian Coll., 1959; MA in Communication, Syracuse U., 1969; MBA, Fairleigh Dickinson U., 1972; PhD, Rensselaer Poly. Inst., 1980; JD, Western State U. Coll. Law, 1983. Reporter Call-Chronicle Newspapers, Allentown, Pa., 1959-60; tchr. English conversation Jonan Sr. High Sch., Matsuyama, Japan, 1960-62; asst. editor Dixie News, Am. Can Co., Easton, Pa., 1964-65; fin. editor Pa. Power & Light Co., Allentown, 1967-69, advt. asst., 1966-67, sales promotion writer, 1965-66; tech. writer, editor Space Tech. Ctr., GE Co., King of Prussia, Pa., 1969; asst. editor Bell System Tech. Jour., Bell Telephone Labs., Murray Hill, N.J., 1969-71; field rep. N.W. Ayer & Son, Inc., N.Y.C., 1972-73; asst. prof. bus. communication Fairleigh Dickinson U., Madison, N.J., 1974-75, Bloomsburg (Pa.) State Coll., 1975-76; lectr. Sch. Bus. and Pub. Adminstrn., Calif. State U., Sacramento, 1977-79; asst. prof. bus. communication Coll. Bus. Adminstrn., San Diego (Calif.) State U., 1979-84; lectr. European div. U. Md., 1984-85; prof. mgmt. Monmouth Coll., West Long Br., N.J., 1985-88; cons. Corp. Communication, 1988-91; pres., owner WVR Assocs., 1991—; founder, exec. dir. Internat. Inst. of Corp. Communication, 1992—. Author: Corporate Communications: A Comparison of Japanese and American Practices, 1984, Business Reports: Written and Oral, 1988, International Handbook of Corporate Communication, 1990, The Manager's Complete Handbook of Communication, 1992. Named Outstanding Prof. of Yr. San Diego State U., 1983. Mem. Acad. Mgmt., Assn. for Bus. Communication, Internat. Assn. Bus. Communicators, Internat. Platform Assn. Republican. Mem. United Ch. of Christ. Home: PO Box 517 Rockaway NJ 07866-0517

RUCKDESCHEL HIBBARD, MARY JOSEPHINE, psychologist; b. N.Y.C., June 27, 1945; d. George and Dorothy V. (Holmer) R.; m. Thomas R. Hibbard, Nov. 15, 1975; children: Gregory Vaughn, Michael Hansen. RN, Lenox Hill Sch. of Nursing, 1965; MA, Columbia U., 1974, MEd, 1975; PhD, NYU, 1983. Lic. RN, lic. psychologist; cert. rehab. counselor. Head nurse neurology unit NYU Med. Ctr., N.Y.C., 1966-68, head nurse surgery unit, 1968-70; rsch. psychologist Rusk Inst.-NYU Med. Ctr., N.Y.C., 1975-77, sr. rsch. psychologist, 1978-85; clin. instr., dept. rehab. and psychiatry Mt. Sinai Med. Ctr., N.Y.C., 1986-87, asst. prof., dept. rehab. and psychiatry, 1987—; adj. prof. CUNY, N.Y.C., 1987—. Contbr. articles to profl. jours. Mem. Am. Psychology Assn., Am. Congress Rehab. Medicine. Office: Mt Sinai Med Ctr Box 1240 1 Gustave L Levy Pl New York NY 10029-6504

RUCKER, PAULA ELAINE, career counselor; b. Jacksonville, Fla., Nov. 28, 1964; d. Seabie P. and Letha (Edenfield) R. BS, Fla. State U., 1986, MS, 1989. Staff asst. Fla. Dept. Law Enforcement, Tallahassee, 1986-87; asst. dir. career planning and placement Fordham U., Bronx, N.Y., 1989—. Vol. Fla. AIDS Hotline, Tallahassee, 1987-89, WNYC, N.Y.C., 1989-91, N.Y. Cares, N.Y.C., 1991. Mem. AACD, Nat. Career Devel. Assn., Nat. Soc. Internships and Experiential Edn., Met. N.Y. Career Placement Officers Assn., Fordham Kiwanis, Omicron Delta Kappa. Democrat. Methodist. Home: 172 W 79th St Apt 17C New York NY 10024-6402 Office: Fordham U 219A McGinley Ctr Bronx NY 10458

RUCKMAN, MARK WARREN, physicist; b. Rolla, Mo., Dec. 26, 1954; s. Homer Leslie and Audrey (Warren) R. BS in Physics, Pa. State U., 1977; PhD in Physics, Rensselaer Polytechnic Inst., 1984. Asst. physicist Brookhaven Nat. Lab., Upton, N.Y., 1985-87, assoc. physicist, 1987-91, physicist, 1991—. Contbr. articles to profl. jours. Mem. Am. Phys. Soc., Am. Vacuum Soc., Am. Chem. Soc., Materials Rsch. Soc., Phi Beta Kappa, Phi Kappa Phi. Republican. Baptist. Office: Brookhaven Nat Lab 20 Pa Ave Upton NY 11973-9999

RUDD, DAVID WILLIAM, engineering consultant; b. Floral Park, N.Y., Dec. 31, 1931; s. Edward Lynn and Joanna (McSorley) R. m. Harriet Fay Sart, Aug. 8, 1953; children: Rebecca, Rachel. BA, Colby Coll., 1953; MS, Northeastern U., 1962. Rsch. chemist Monsanto Chem. Co., Everett, Mass., 1956-58, Kendall Co., Walpole, Mass., 1958-60, Metal Hydrides, Beverly, Mass., 1960-62; sr. staff engr. Western Electric Co., North Andover, Mass., 1969-78; mem. rsch. staff Engring. Rsch. Ctr., Princeton, N.J., 1978-80; co-founder, dir. David W. Rudd Assocs., mfg. cons., 1985—. Rsch. in surface chemistry, permeability of metals to hydrogen, rocket propellant synthesis infrared method of Q evaluation synthetic quartz, crystal growth, printed circuit tech., metal joining, computer-integrated mfg. techniques, statis. quality control, soldering tech., environ. modifications of mfg. processes. Served with U.S. Army, 1953-55. Recipient Western Electric Co. Engring. Excellence award, 1969, C.B. Sawyer Meml. award, 1974. Home: Valley Rd East Summer ME 04220

RUDDLEY, JOHN, art historian, artist, consultant; b. N.Y.C., Oct. 29, 1912; s. Anton and Katherine (Glusk) R.; m. Stella Elizabeth Subisky, Nov. 12, 1910. Grad., Cooper Union, 1941; B.S. in Art History, Columbia U., 1953, M.A. in Art Edn., 1954, postgrad., 1964. Architect, designer WOR-WOR-TV, N.Y.C., 1941-61; dean, head Corcoran Mus. Sch. Art, Washington, 1961-64; faculty George Washington U., 1961-64; dir. Westchester Art workshop, supr. art Westchester County, White Plains, N.Y., 1965-84; art faculty Pace U., Pleasantville, N.Y., 1973-74;arts cons., lectr. Finest Arts Inc., N.Y.C., 1984—; cons. staff Mus. Modern Art, N.Y.C., 1984; cons., lectr. in field. Author book reviews in field. Trustee Hammond Mus., 1970-74, Nippon Mus., N.Y.C., 1976-78. Served with U.S. Army, 1942-46, PTO. Mem. Washington Arts Club, Phi Delta Kappa (treas.-pres. Columbia U. chpt. 1953-56). Home: 97-40 62 Dr Flushing NY 11374 Office: Arts Club Washington DC 2017 I St NW Washington DC 20006-1804 Winter Address: Siesta Key 5600 Beachway Dr Sarasota FL 34242

RUDDY, FRANK S., lawyer, former ambassador; b. N.Y.C., Sept. 15, 1937; s. Francis Stephen and Teresa (O'Neil) R.; m. Kateri Mary O'Neill, Aug. 29, 1964; children—Neil, David, Stephen. A.B., Holy Cross Coll., 1959; M.A., NYU, 1962, LL.M., 1967; LL.B., Loyola U., New Orleans, 1965; Ph.D., Cambridge U., Eng., 1969. Bar: D.C., N.Y., Tex., U.S. Supreme Ct. Faculty Cambridge U., 1967-69; asst. gen. counsel USIA, Washington, 1969-72, 73-74; sr. atty. Office of Telecommunication Policy, White House, Washington, 1972-73; counsel Exxon Corp., Houston, 1974-81; asst. adminstr. AID (with rank asst. sec. state) Dept. State, Washington, 1981-84; U.S. ambassador to Equatorial Guinea, 1984-88; gen. counsel U.S. Dept. Energy, Washington, 1988-89; v.p. Sierra Blanc Devel. Corp., Washington, 1989—; vis. scholar Johns Hopkins Sch. Advanced Internat. Studies, 1990—. Author: International Law in the Enlightenment, 1975; editor: American International Law Cases (series), 1972—; editor in chief Internat. Lawyer, 1978-83; contbr. articles to legal jours. Bd. dirs. African Devel. Found., Washington, 1983-84. Served with USMCR, 1956-61. Mem. ABA (chmn. treaty compliance sect. 1991—), Am. Soc. Internat. Law, Internat. Law Assn., Hague Acad. Internat. Law Alumni Assn., Oxford and Cambridge Club (London), Conservative Club, Internat. Club, Dacor House. Republican. Roman Catholic. Home: 5600 Western Ave Chevy Chase MD 20815-3406 Office: Ste T-2 1718 P St NW Washington DC 20036

RUDENBERG, HERMANN GUNTHER, semiconductor engineer; b. Berlin, Aug. 9, 1920; came to U.S., 1938; s. Reinhold and Lily (Minkowski) R.; m. Joan Ritchie, Dec. 21, 1952; children: Elizabeth, Paul, James. SB, Harvard U., 1941, MS, 1942, PhD, 1950. Engr. Los Alamos Sci. Lab., Santa Fe, N.Mex., 1943-46; cons. Spencer-Kennedy Labs., Cambridge, Mass., 1946-50; scientist Raytheon Rsch. Lab., Waltham, Mass., 1948-52; dir. R&D Transitron Electronic Corp., Wakefield, Mass., 1952-62; sr. staff mem. Arthur D. Little, Inc., Cambridge, Mass., 1962-83; prin. Rudenberg Assocs., Beverly, Mass., 1983—; various positions Boston sect., NEREM, IRE, 1952-70. Contbr. articles to profl. jours.; patentee on electronic devices. Tech. sgt. U.S. Army, 1943-46. Mem. IEEE (life, bd. dirs., chmn. Electro Conv. 1976-80, Centennial medal 1984), Semicondr. Materials and Equipment Assn. Internat. Home: 3 Lanthorn Ln Beverly MA 01915-4721 Office: Rudenberg Assocs 3 Lanthorn Ln Beverly MA 01915-4721

RUDENSTINE, ANGELICA ZANDER, freelance curator and art historian; b. Berlin, May 24, 1937; came to U.S., 1960; d. Walter and Margaret (Magnus) Zander; m. Neil L. Rudenstine, Aug. 27, 1960; children: Antonia, Nicholas, Sonya. BA, Oxford (Eng.) U., 1959; MA, Smith Coll., 1961. Curator rsch. Mus. Fine Arts, Boston, 1961-68; rsch. curator Solomon R. Guggenheim Mus., N.Y.C., 1969-82; freelance curator, art historian various mus., 1982—; vis. prof. Inst. Fine Arts, NYU, 1986; guest curator Kazimir Malevich Exhbn., 1990-91; mem. publs. com. J. Paul Getty Trust, L.A., 1983-89; mem. vis. com. Ctr. for History Art and Humanities, L.A., 1986-90; chmn. vis. com. dept. fine arts Harvard U., Cambridge, Mass., 1984-90, J. Paul Getty Mus., L.A., 1990—. Author: (catalogs) The Guggenheim Mus. Collection of Paintings 1880-1945, 76, Peggy Guggenheim Collection, 1985 (Alfred H. Barr award 1987), Modern Painting, Drawing and Sculpture-Pulitzer Collection, 1988 (Mitchell prize for 10th century art 1988), Art of the Avant-Garde in Russia, exh. catalogue, Guggenheim Mus., 1981; author, editor: (monograph) Russian Avant Garde Art: The George Costakis Collection, 1981; mem. editorial bd. Am. Scholar. Trustee Am. Acad. in Rome, 1980-91. Guggenheim fellow, 1983-84. Mem. Coll. Art Assn., Internat. Coun. Museums (com. for Mus. Modern Art).

RUDENSTINE, NEIL LEON, academic administrator, educator; b. Ossining, N.Y., Jan. 21, 1935; s. Harry and Mae (Esperito) R.; m. Angelica Zander, Aug. 27, 1960; children: Antonia Margaret, Nicholas David, Sonya. B.A., Princeton U., 1956; B.A. (Rhodes Scholar), Oxford U., 1959, M.A., 1963; Ph.D., Harvard U., 1964. Instr. dept. English Harvard U., Cambridge, Mass., 1964-66; asst. prof. Harvard U., 1966-68; assoc. prof. English Princeton (N.J.) U., 1968-73, prof. English, 1973-88, dean of students, 1968-72, dean of Coll., 1972-77, provost, 1977-88; exec. v.p. Andrew W. Mellon Found., N.Y.C., 1988-91; pres. Harvard U., Cambridge, Mass., 1991—, prof. English, 1991—. Author: Sidney's Poetic Development, 1967; (with George Rousseau) English Poetic Satire, 1972; (with William Bowen) In Pursuit of the Ph.D., 1992. Served to 1st lt. arty. AUS, 1959-60. Fellow Am. Acad. Arts and Scis. Office: Harvard U Office of Pres Massachusetts Hall Cambridge MA 02138

RUDERMAN, IRVING WARREN, company executive; b. N.Y.C., Jan. 7, 1920; s. Jack and Mollie (Ettin) R.; m. Carol C. Ruderman, June 16, 1945; children: Barbara Lee, Clifford Eric, William Brandon, Genevieve Kathryn. PhD, Columbia U., 1949. Teaching fellow Columbia U., N.Y.C., 1946-47, lectr. chemistry, 1947-49, rsch. scientist, 1949-54; pres. Isomet Corp., Oakland, N.J., 1954-73; chmn., chief exec. officer Inrad, Inc., Northvale, N.J., 1973—. Contbr. articles to profl. jours. Fellow N.Y. Acad. Sci.; mem. Am. Phys. Soc., Am. Chem. Soc., Am. Optical Soc., Am. Ceramic Soc., Am. Soc. Quality Control, Sigma Xi, Phi Lambda Upsilon, Tau Beta Pi. Republican. Baptist. Home: 45 Duane Ln Demarest NJ 07627-1304 Office: Inrad Inc 181 Legrand Ave Northvale NJ 07647-2498

RUDIKOFF, MICHAEL T., internist, cardiologist; b. Bklyn., Nov. 9, 1946; s. Benuamin and Ethel (Epstein) R.; m. Paula Lerner, June 9, 1968; children: Bari, Robin. BA, Columbia U., 1967; MD, NYU, 1971. Diplomate Am. Bd. Internal Medicine, Am. Bd. Cardiology. Intern, resident, chief resident Bellevue Hosp., N.Y.C., 1971-75; fellow in cardiology Johns Hopkins Sch. Medicine, Balt., 1975-77; pvt. practice Balt., 1977—; instr. Johns Hopkins Sch. Medicine, Balt., 1977—. Mem. AMA, Am. Soc. Internal Medicine. Office: 222 W Cold Spring Ln Baltimore MD 21210

RUDINS, LEONIDS (LEE RUDINS), retired chemical company executive, financial executive; b. Linava, Latvia, Dec. 15, 1928; came to U.S., 1949; s. Leonids and Aleksandra (Zimins) R.; m. Galina Zakidalski, July 24, 1960; 1 child, Andrew. BS in Commerce, Rider Coll., 1953; MBA, Seton Hall U., 1967, cert. of internat. bus., 1968. Acct. Johnson & Johnson, New Brunswick, N.J., 1957-58; mgr. budget and cost LePage's, Johnson & Johnson, Gloucester, Mass., 1958-60; plant contr. Permacel, Johnson & Johnson, Decatur, Ill., 1960-62; asst. contr. Permacel, Johnson & Johnson, New Brunswick, 1962-63, treas., contr., 1963-70; div. contr. Titanium Pigments, NL Industries, Inc., Sayreville, N.J., 1970-71, group contr., 1971-76; dir. fin. and adminstrn. NL Pigments-U.S., NL Industries, Inc., Sayreville, N.J., 1976-77; dir. fin. and planning NL Pigments-Worldwide, NL Industries, Inc., Sayreville, N.J., 1977-79; v.p. fin., chief fin. officer NL Chemicals, Inc., Hightstown, N.J., 1979-89; pres. Internat. Bus. Mgmt. Assocs., Inc., Princeton, 1990-91; bd. dirs. Bentone-Chemie, GmbH, Nordenham, Federal Republic of Germany, Abbey Chemicals, Ltd., Livingston, England, Enenco, Inc., Memphis; guest speaker Planning Exec. Inst. Solicitor, budget com. mem. United Fund, New Brunswick, 1962-69. With U.S. Army, 1953-56, Korea. Mem. Nat. Assn. Accts., Fin. Exec. Inst., Forsgate Club, Battleground Club. Republican. Greek/Russian Orthodox. Home: 28 Tamarack Dr Englishtown NJ 07726-2734

RUDLOFF, ROBERT WILLIAM, JR., internal audit executive; b. Atlantic City, June 7, 1958; s. Robert William and Mary Elizabeth (McGowan) R.; m. Laurie Jean Ketcham, Aug. 9, 1980; children: Robert William III, Timothy Patrick, Andrew Jonathan. AS in Advt., Castleton State Coll., 1980, BS in Acctg., 1980. Cert. internal auditor, cert. fraud examiner. Staff acct. Ford, Scott & Assocs., CPA's, Ocean City, N.J., 1980; internal auditor Harrah's Atlantic City, 1980-82, sr. auditor, 1982-85, internal audit mgr., 1985-86; dir. internal audit Trump Pla. Hotel & Casino, Atlantic City, 1986-89, Trump Taj Mahal Casino Resort, Atlantic City, 1989—; pvt. practice acctg. and audit Somers Point, N.J., 1980—; adj. faculty bus. studies Stockton State Coll., Pomona, N.J., 1987—; adj. instr. acctg. Atlantic Community Coll., Mays Landing, N.J., 1991—; seminar instr. MIS Tng. Inst., Framingham, Mass., 1986-88. Author: Modern Auditing in the Hospitality Environment, 1986; contbr. articles to profl. pubs. Chmn. Community Standards Rev. Bd., Somers Point, 1986-88; gen. chmn. IIA 1989 Ea. Regional Conf., 1987-89; alumni recruiter Castleton State Coll., 1989—. Mem. Inst. Internal Auditors (chpt. sec. 1983-85, v.p. 1985-86, Outstanding Chpt. Mem. 1986, pres. 1986-87, Pres.'s award 1987, chpt. gov. 1987-91, N.Am. dist. dir. 1987-92, internat. bd. dirs. 1987-92, treas. 1991-93), Nat. Assn. Cert. Fraud Examiners. Republican. Roman Catholic. Office: Trump Taj Mahal Casino Resort 1000 Boardwalk at Virginia Ave Atlantic City NJ 08404

RUDMAN, REUBEN, chemistry educator, researcher; b. N.Y.C., Jan. 18, 1937; s. Joseph T. and Deborah N. (Hurwitz) R.; m. Idelle Menkes, June 26, 1958; children: Zave, Rachel, Benjamin, Ephraim, Sara. BA, Yeshiva U., 1957; PhD, Poly. Inst. Bklyn., 1966. Rsch. assoc. Brookhaven Nat. Lab., Upton, N.Y., 1966-67; asst. prof. chemistry Adelphi U., Garden City, N.Y., 1967-70, assoc. prof., 1971-75, prof., 1975—; vis. prof. Hebrew U., Jerusalem, 1973-74. Author: (monograph) Low Temperature X-ray Diffraction, 1976; also numerous articles. Rsch. grantee NSF, 1969-82. Mem. AAAS, Am. Crystallographic Assn. (com. chmn., editor Trans. 1983), Internat. Union Crystallography (chmn. crystallographic apparatus com. 1975-78), Assn. Orthodox Jewish Scientists (pres. 1978-80, chmn. bd. govs. 1990—). Office: Adelphi U Dept Chemistry Garden City NY 11530

RUDMAN, WARREN BRUCE, senator; b. Boston, May 18, 1930; s. Edward G. and Theresa (Levenson) R.; m. Shirley Wahl, July 9, 1952; children: Laura, Alan, Debra. B.S., Syracuse (N.Y.) U., 1952; LL.B., Boston Coll., 1960. Bar: N.H. 1960. Mem. firm Rudman & Gormley, Nashua, N.H., 1960-69; counsel to Gov. Walter Peterson, Concord, N.H., 1970; atty. gen. State of N.H., Concord, 1970-76; mem. firm. Sheehan Phinney Bass & Green, 1976-80; mem. U.S. Senate from N.H., 1980-92. Founder, chmn. bd. trustees Daniel Webster Jr. Coll., 1965—; chmn., founder New Eng. Aero. Inst. Capt. AUS, 1952-54, Korea. Decorated Bronze Star, Combat Inf. Badge. Mem. Am. Legion. Republican. Office: US Senate 530 Hart Senate Bldg Washington DC 20510*

RUDNICK, GARY WILLIAM, biochemist; b. Phila., Sept. 14, 1946; s. Martin I. and Libby Ruth (Perlmutter) R.; m. Hana Fishkes, Apr. 15, 1981; children: Tamar, Noam. BS in Chemistry, Antioch Coll., Yellow Springs, Ohio, 1968; PhD in Biochemistry, Brandeis U., 1974. Fellow Roche Inst. Molecular Biology, Nutley, N.J., 1973-75; asst. prof. dept. pharmacology Sch. Medicine, Yale U., New Haven, 1975-80, assoc. prof., 1980-91, prof., 1991—. Contbr. articles to pubs. Office: Yale U Sch Medicine 333 Cedar St New Haven CT 06510-3289

RUDO, FRIEDA GALINDO, pharmacology educator, researcher; b. N.Y.C., Nov. 13, 1923; d. Joseph Daniel and Rose (Falcon) Galindo; m. Alvin D. Rudo, Dec. 26, 1944 (dec. Oct. 1974); children: Sharon Rudo Schreter, Andrew Brent; m. Raynard F. Ruskin, Jan. 16, 1983. AB, Goucher Coll., 1944, DSc (hon.), 1976; MS, U. Md., 1960, PhD, 1963. Instr. surgery Sch. Medicine U. Md., Balt., 1960-61, rsch. fellow, 1961-63, asst. prof., 1963-68, asst. prof. Sch. Dentistry, 1968-70, prof., 1975-90, prof. emerita, 1990—; cons. Med., S.A., Cordova, Spain, 1974-84, Anaquest, Murray Hill, N.J., 1963-91. Contbr. video tapes on pharmacology; contbr. chpts. to books, articles to profl. jours. Active Cen. Scholarship Bur., 1950—, Balt. Mus. Art, 1950—, Art Seminar Group, 1981—. Grantee Ohio Med. Co., Madison, Wis., 1957-73, Ohio Med. Anesthetics, 1973-78, 78-83, Anaquest, 1983-92. Fellow Am. Coll. Office: U Md Sch Dentistry 666 W Baltimore St Baltimore MD 21201-1586

RUDOV, MELVIN HOWARD, risk management firm executive; b. Pitts, Aug. 27, 1933; s. David Joseph and Rose (Malin) R.; children: David, Cornell, Ted. BS, U. Pitts, 1955, MS, 1957; PhD, Ohio State U., Columbus, 1964. Registered profl. psychologist, Pa.; diplomate Am. Bd. Forensic Psychology, Am. Bd. Profl. Psychology. Research psychologist Aerospace Med. Research Labs., Wright-Patterson AFB, Ohio, 1958-65; head life scis. sect. Cornell Aero. Lab., Buffalo, 1965-69; dir. Pitts. Office Am. Inst. Research, 1969-72; dir. research Sec. Commn. on Med. Malpractice, HEW, Washington, 1972-73; cons. HEW, Washington, 1973-76; pres., dir. Ctrs. for Health, Edn. and Social Systems Studies, Pitts., 1972-77; pres. Affiliated Risk Control Adminstrs. Pa., Inc., Pitts., 1977—; vis. lectr. SUNY, Buffalo, 1968-69; adj. prof. Grad. Sch. Pub. Health, U. Pitts., 1972—. Assoc. editor Human Factors Soc. Jour., 1973-76; contbr. articles to profl. jours. Served to capt. U.S. Army, 1955-63. Home: 638 Poplar Ct Pittsburgh PA 15238-1344 Office: Affiliated Risk Control Adminstrs Pa Inc 128 N Craig St Pittsburgh PA 15213-2758

RUDZINSKI, KENNETH WILLIAM, financial planner; b. Phila., Aug. 23, 1947; s. Sigmund Michael and Nina R.; m. Mary Jane Hall Shaup, Aug. 16, 1969; children: Matthew Hylan, Alexander Hall. BA, Villanova U., 1969; MA, U. Del., 1971. CLU, cert. fin. planner, chartered fin. cons. Tchr. French Archmere Acad., Claymont, Del., 1970-73; mgr. sales Lincoln Nat. Sales Corp., Phila. and Bala Cynwyd, Pa., 1973-77, Aetna Life & Casualty, Wayne, Pa., 1977-80; v.p. mktg. Lincoln Nat. Sales Corp., Bala Cynwyd, 1980-85; dir. mktg. The Am. Group Ltd., Radnor, Pa., 1985-88, Wilmington, Del., 1988—; pres. Cardiac Perfusion Inc., Phila., 1986—; mem. adv. bd. Lincoln Nat. Agts., Ft. Wayne, 1983-84, SMA Life Agts., Worcester, Mass., 1987. Dupont Andelot fellow U. Del., Newark, 1969; recipient Nat. Sales Achievement award Million Dollar Round Table, Des Plaines, Ill., 1987; named One of Top 200 Fin. Planners in U.S. Money mag., 1987. Mem. Internat. Assn. Fin. Planners, Inst. Cert. Fin. Planners, Nat. Assn. Life Underwriters, Pa. Soc. Pub. Accts. (assoc.). Republican. Office: The Am Group 2036 Foulk Rd Ste 204 Wilmington DE 19810-3664

RUDZINSKY, LOUIS, business executive; b. Everett, Mass., June 16, 1933; s. Abraham Rudzinsky; m. Muriel P. Baltimore, June 11, 1957; children: Howard, Jeff, David, Lisa. BSBA, Northeastern U., Boston, 1956. Personnel dir. ITEK Corp., Lexington, Mass., 1958-66; dir. indsl. rels. Avco Corp., Everett, Mass., 1966-68; pres. Lra Inc., Lexington, 1968—; v.p. CSE-Corp., Everett, Mass., 1966-91; pres. XMX Corp., Montreal, Que., Can., 1991—, XMX Corp., Burlington, Mass., 1990—; sr. lectr. Northeastern U., Boston, 1969-85; bd. dirs. Laser Inst. of Am., Orlando, Fla. Chmn. personnel bd. Town of Belmont, 1971-73, mem. adv. com., 1973-75. 1st lt. U.S. Army, 1956-58. Office: XMX 6 New England Executive Park Burlington MA 01803-5018

RUDZKI, EUGENIUSZ MACIEJ, chemical engineer, consultant; b. Warsaw, Poland, Feb. 24, 1914; came to U.S., 1955.; s. Aleksander and Wanda (Łukaszewicz) R.; m. Fiorina Maria Di Vito, Feb. 23, 1952; children: Robert Alexander, Marcella Wanda Rudzki Meddick. Diploma with honors, Warsaw (Poland) Poly. Inst., 1937; Chem. Engr., The Polish U. Coll., London, 1951. Project devel. and field engr. Chance Bros. Ltd., Eng., 1951-54; head instr. chem. engring. dept. U. Toronto, Can., 1954-55; rsch. engr. T.C. Wheaton Co., N.J., 1955-56; rsch. engr. Bethlehem (Pa.) Steel Corp., 1956-61, supr. rsch. dept., 1961-82, ret., 1982; cons. Am. Flame Rsch. com., 1982—. Patentee in field, U.S., Eng., Can., Belgium; contbr. articles to profl. jours. Active The Polish Inst. Arts and Scis., N.Y.C., 1975, The Kosciuszko Found., N.Y.C., 1977; polit. prisoner Gulag Abis forced labor camp, Peczora, USSR, 1940-41. Maj. 2d Polish Army Corp. Gen. Anders, 1942-46. Decorated the Virtuti Militari Order, The Cross of Valor with bar, The Silver Order of Merit with Swords. Fellow The Inst. of Energy London, The Coun. Engring. Insts. London (chartered engr.); mem. AIME, Am. Inst. Chem. Engrs., The Combustion Inst., The Polish Vets. of World War II, Assn. Vets. of 2d Polish Army Corp. Roman Catholic.

RUE, THOMAS SCOTT, mental health therapist, educator; b. Plainfield, N.J., Oct. 27, 1958; s. Clyde Bieber and Bernette Ann (Woldin) R.; m. Carmen Betsabe Hernandez, Feb. 24, 1990; stepchildren: Janesa, Carolina, Eduardo. BA cum laude, Trenton State Coll., 1983; MA, Rider Coll., 1985. Nat. cert. counselor; cert. AIDS counselor, N.Y. Counseling intern St. Frances Med. Ctr. and Anchor House, Trenton, N.J., 1984-85; resident counselor Progress for Disabled Found., Ewing, N.J., 1985; clin. coord. Hunterdon Youth Svcs., Flemington, N.J., 1985; resident counselor Step-by-Step, Inc., Honesdale, Pa., 1985-86; houseparent Wayne County Group Home, Honesdale, 1986-87; probation officer Sullivan County Probation Dept., Monticello, N.Y., 1987-89; asst. prof. Sullivan County Community Coll., Loch Sheldrake, N.Y., 1988—; placement prevention worker Berkshire Farm Ctr. and Svcs. for Youth, Sullivan County, N.Y., 1989—; bd. dirs. Community Action Commn., Liberty, N.Y. Contbg. editor The River Reporter, 1985—; mem. book rev. bd. The Family Jour., 1992—; contbr. articles to various publs. Sec. Innisfree Corp., Milanville, Pa., 1974—; pres. Soc. Hist. Edn., Inc., Trenton, 1982-85; pres., bd. dirs. Del. Youth Ctr., Callicoon, N.Y., 1986-89; disaster vol. ARC, Sullivan County, 1987—; sec. Upper Del. Unitarian Universalist Fellowship, Milanville, 1987-89, pres., 1989-92; mem. Sullivan County Coun. Alcoholism and Drug Abuse. Mem. ACA, Am. Assn. Sex Educators, Counselors and Therapists, Assn. Humanistic Psychology, Internat. Assn. Marriage and Family Counselors, Am. Mental Health Counselors Assn., Internat. Soc. AIDS Edn., Upper Delaware River Assn. (sec.-treas. 1986—). Home: 23 Fisk Ave Monticello NY 12701

RUECKERT, FREDERIC, plastic surgeon; b. Boston, Oct. 24, 1921; s. Frederic and Elizabeth (Howe) R.; m. Joan Dodge, May 31, 1947; children: Nancy Lee, Patricia, William Dodge, Carolyn. AB, Hamilton Coll., 1945; MD, Columbia U., 1947. Diplomate Am. Bd. Plastic Surgery, Nat. Bd. Med. Examiners; lic. physician, N.Y., N.H. Intern internal medicine Bel-

levue Hosp., N.Y.C., 1947-48; resident gen. surgery Am. U. Hosp., Beirut, 1948-50; fellow surg. pathology Columbia-Presbyn. Hosp., N.Y.C., 1950-51; resident gen. surgery Dartmouth-Hitchcock Med. Ctr., Hanover, N.H., 1953-54, staff surgeon, 1956-86; resident plastic surgery, teaching fellow plastic surgery U. Pitts. Med. Ctr., 1954-56; mem. faculty Dartmouth Med. Sch., Hanover, 1956—, v.p. clin. surgery, 1974-86, prof. clin. surgery emeritus, 1986—; cons. VA Hosp., White River Junction, Vt., 1956—. Contbr. articles to profl. jours., chpts. to books. Mem. Sch. Bd. Edn., Hanover, N.H., 1964-67; bd. trustees Northfield (Mass.) Mt. Hermon Sch., 1969-71, 80-90. Capt. USAF, 1951-53. Recipient Lamplighter award Northfield Mt. Herman Sch., 1991. Mem. AMA, ACS, Am. Assn. Plastic Surgeons, Am. Assn. Med. Colls., Am. Soc. Plastic and Reconstructive Surgeons (bd. dirs. 1980-83, 84-86), Plastic Surgery Ednl. Found. (pres. 1985-86), Plastic Surgeons Assn. Am. (pres. 1984-85), Internat. Confederation Plastic and Reconstructive Surgeons, Am. Soc. Aesthetic Plastic Surgeons, New Eng. Surg. Soc., Northeastern Soc. Plastic Surgeons, New Eng. Soc. Plastic and Reconstructive Surgeons (pres. 1969-71), N.H. State Med. Soc., Grafton County Med. Soc. Republican. Home: 5 N Balch St Hanover NH 03755

RUEHL, MERCEDES, actress; b. Queens, N.Y.. BA in English, Coll. of New Rochelle; studied acting with Uta Hagen, Tad Danielewski. Stage appearances include Vanities, Cin., Indpls., 1977-78, Medea, Denver Ctr. Theatre Co., 1980-82, Three Sisters, Princeton, N.J., 1982-83, The Marriage of Bette and Boo, N.Y.C., 1985; Broadway stage work includes I'm Not Rappaport, 1985 (Obie Award from the Village Voice), Lost in Yonkers, 1991 (Tony Award, Drama Desk Award, Outer Critics Circle Award); film work includes Radio Days, 1987, Big, 1988, Married to the Mob, 1988, The Fischer King, 1991 (Academy Award for Best Supporting Actress). Office: care Susan Smith and Assocs 121 N San Vicente Blvd Beverly Hills CA 90211*

RUEHLE, CHARLES JOSEPH, pathologist, military officer; b. Boone, Iowa, May 26, 1943; s. John Donald and Alta (Brown) R. DVM, Iowa State U., 1967; MD, U. Iowa, 1973, MS, 1973; m. Nellie Backus, Aug. 5, 1972. Commd. 2d lt. USAF, 1964, advanced through grades to col., sr. flight surgeon, 1984, chief flight surgeon, 1987; chief Vet. Service, Grissom AFB, Ind., 1967-69; resident in aerospace medicine Brook AFB, Tex., 1973-75; resident in pathology Wilford Hall USAF Med. Ctr., Lackland AFB, Tex., 1975-79, with div. aerospace pathology Armed Forces Inst. Pathology, Washington, 1979-88, chief div. aerospace pathology, 1982-85, chmn. dept. forensic scis., 1985-88, sec. Joint Com. Aviation Pathology, 1984-88, exec. asst. to fed. air surgeon FAA, Washington, 1988—, sr. aviation med. examiner, 1989—; adj. asst. prof. preventive medicine Uniformed Services U. Health Scis. lectr. aerospace pathology; cons. USAF Sugeon Gen., 1987. Diplomate Am. Bd. Preventive Medicine, Am. Bd. Pathology. Fellow Am. Soc. Clin. Pathologists, Aerospace Med. Assn.; mem. Am. Acad. Forensic Scis. AMA, USAF Flight Surgeons, Nat. Sojourners, Assn. Mil. Surgeons U.S., Internat. Soc. Air Safety Investigators, Air Force Assn., Alpha Zeta, Gamma Sigma Delta, Omega Tau Sigma (gov. 1967-75), Cosmos Club, Masons. Republican. Presbyterian. Home: 1000 Lower Pindell Rd Lothian MD 20711-2704 Office: Fed Air Surgeon FAA 800 Independence Ave SW Washington DC 20591-0001

RUFF, LORRAINE MARIE, public relations executive; b. Washington, Feb. 13, 1947; d. William Stanley and Jeanne Ann (Murray) Charlton; m. R. Eugene Ruff, July 17, 1968; 1 child, David Michael. BS in Liberal Arts, Oreg. State U., 1976. Reporter The Oregonian, Corvallis, Oreg., 1976-79, Union-Bull., Walla Walla, Wash., 1979-80; dir. pub. rels. Strategic Mktg., Corvallis, 1980-82; gen. mgr. Campaigns Northwest, Corvallis, 1982-84; account supr. Arthur D. Little, Inc., Cambridge, Mass., 1985-87, mgr. corp. ID, 1988-89; dir. biotechnology New Eng. Hill and Knowlton, Waltham, Mass., 1989, v.p., dir. biotechnology, 1990, sr. v.p., mng. dir. internat. biotechnology practice, 1990-91; gen. mgr. Hill and Knowlton/New Eng., Waltham, 1991—. Mem. Pub. Rels. Soc. Am. (treas. Boston chpt. 1990—), Assn. of Biotech. Cos., Indsl. Biotechnology Assn., Mass. Biotechnology Coun., Oreg. Biotechnology Assn. Republican. Home: 7 Bigelow Rd Southborough MA 01772 Office: Hill and Knowlton 800 South St Waltham MA 02154-1439

RUGER, STEPHEN LEWIS, computer scientist; b. Bklyn., May 4, 1950; s. Robert William and Helen Paula (Boehmler) R.; m. Almeda Jane Pritchard, Nov. 3, 1973; children: Emily Kritina, Nathan Simon. BS, Drexel U., 1973; MBA, U. Pa., 1976. Mathematician FAA, Pomona, N.J., 1970-74; analyst Corning Glass Works, Greencastle, Pa., 1976-78; data processing supr. Corning Glass Works, Toronto, Ont., Can., 1978-80; analyst IU Internat., Phila., 1980-81, Cigna, Voorhees, N.J., 1981-84; data processing mgr. Harold Beck & Sons, Newtown, Pa., 1984-86; analyst Morgan, Lewis & Bockins, Phila., 1986-89; MIS mgr. Smiths Industries, Malvern, Pa., 1989—. Auditor Tabernacle Ch., Phila., 1975. Mem. Data Processing Mgmt. Assn. Democrat. Presbyterian. Home: 441 Apple Valley Dr Langhorne PA 19047-1907 Office: Smith Industries 255 Green St Malvern PA 19355-2721

RUGGIERI, PATRICIA, electronics executive; b. N.Y.C., Sept. 28, 1947; d. Sylvester Joseph and Clare Marie (Brett) R.; m. Karl Rathswohl, Dec. 31, 1986 (div. Apr. 1991). BA, Coll. Mt. St. Vincent, 1969. Document editor Netherlands U. Internat. Coop., Delft, 1972-76; ops. mgr. Automation House CNB-TV, N.Y.C., 1976-84; dir., TV ctr. St. John's U., Jamaica, N.Y., 1984-87; dir., telecon Steve Campus Prodn., Tuckahoe, N.Y., 1987-88; mgr. merchandising, promotions Sony Consumer Television Products Co., Park Ridge, N.J., 1988-91; nat. mktg. mgr. Watchman Products, Sony Consumer TV Products Co., Park Ridge, N.J., 1991—. Office: Sony Consumer TV Co 1 Sony Dr Park Ridge NJ 07656-8002

RUGGIERO, MURRAY ANTHONY, JR., computer company executive; b. New Haven, Mar. 4, 1963; s. Murray Anthony and Joanne Ann (Vestuti) R.; m. Diana Marie Bastura, Nov. 5, 1988. BA in Physics and Astronomy, Western Conn. State U., 1985; BA in Computer Sci., So. Conn. State U., 1988. Asst. engring. mgr. Harco Labs., Branford, Conn., 1985-87; programmer/analyst Olin Corp., New Haven, 1987-88; project dir. Travel Soft, New Haven, 1988; v.p. Promised Land Techs., Inc., New Haven, 1988—. Contbr. articles to profl. jours. Vol. Dem. Party, East Haven, Conn., 1991. Mem. AASS, Am. Meteorol. Soc., Sigma Xi. Roman Catholic. Home: 148 Meadow St East Haven CT 06512 Office: Promised Land Techs Inc 900 Chapel St New Haven CT 06511

RUGGIERO, RICHARD SALVADOR, former state legislator, marketing consultant; b. Utica, N.Y., Sept. 20, 1944; s. Thomas Joseph and Theresa (Passalacqua) R.; B.A. (N.Y. State Regents scholar), Niagara U., 1966; postgrad. Syracuse U., Colgate U., SUNY Coll. Tech.; m. Janis E. Zi-olkowski, July 2, 1966. Cert. secondary English, N.Y. Tchr. English, Utica City Sch. Dist., 1966-81; v.p., treas. T.J. Liberty Liquors, Inc., Utica., 1969-80, chmn. bd., 1974-80; assemblyman State of N.Y., 1981-86; mktg. cons. Gateway Trade Ctr., Inc. Buffalo, 1987—; ptnr. Glacier Ice Cream Co., Utica, 1971-73; chmn. task force on SUNY Coll. Tech., task force on univ./industry cooperation, mem. various coms. Mem. Buffalo Coun. on World Affairs, Utica City Coun., 1978-81; bd. dirs. Our Lady of Victory Hosp. Mem. Western N.Y. Internat. Trade Coun., Toronto Export Club, Niagara U. Alumni Assn., KC, Comity Club (v.p.), Phi Delta Kappa. Home: 40 S Meadow Dr Orchard Park NY 14127-2723 Office: 2544 Clinton St Buffalo NY 14224-1092

RUGINA, ANGHEL N., retired educator; b. Romania, May 24, 1913; came to U.S., 1950; s. Nicolae and Stefana (Corban) R.; m. Irene Rugina, June 28, 1958. PhD, Acad. of Econ. Studies, 1942, U. Freiburg, 1948. Prof. U. Portland, 1950-52; researcher Libr. of Congress, Washington, 1953; prof. Niagara U., Niagara Falls, N.Y., 1954-58; prof. Northeastern U., Boston, 1958-86, prof. emeritus, 1987; chmn. Bd. Econ. Advisors to Gov. Mass., Boston, 1965-70. Author: Geldtypen and Geldordnungen, 1949, American Capitalism At A Crossroads, 1976. Mem. Am. Econ. Assn., History of Econs. Soc., Can. Econ. Assn., British Royal Econ. Soc., Internat. Soc. for Intercommunication of New Ideas Inc. (pres. 1989-92). Home: 145 Moss Hill Rd Jamaica Plain MA 02130-3035

RUH, EDWIN, ceramic engineer, consultant, researcher; b. Westfield, N.J., Apr. 22, 1924; s. Harry John and Martha A. (Grasing) R.; m. Elizabeth J. Mundy, June 14, 1952; children: Edwin Jr., Elizabeth Jeanne. BS in Ceramic Engring. with honors, Rutgers U., 1949, MS in Ceramic Engring., 1953, PhD in Ceramics, 1954. Registered profl. engr., Pa. Rsch. engr. Harbison Walker Refractories Co., Pitts., 1954-57; asst dir. rsch. Harbison Walker Refractories Co., 1957-70; dir. rsch. Harbison Walker Refractories Div. Dresser Ind., Pitts., 1970-73; dir. advanced tech. Harbison Walker Refractories Div. Dresser Ind., 1973-74; v.p. rsch. Vesuvius Crucible Co., Pitts., 1974-76; adj. prof. Carnegie Mellon U., Pitts., 1976-84; rsch. prof. Rutgers U., New Brunswick, N.J., 1984—; pres. Ruh Internat., Inc., Pitts., 1976—. Editor Metallurgical Transactions, 1979-84; author chpts. to books; contbr. articles to profl. jours. With U.S. Army, 1943-46, ETO. Recipient ann. award Ceramic Assn. N.J., 1988. Fellow Am. Ceramic Soc. (pres. 1985-86, founders award Phila. sect. 1989, Bleininger award Pitts. sect. 1990), Inst. Ceramics; mem. Am. Soc. for Testing Materials, AAAS, AIME, Minerals, Metals and Materials Soc., ISS, Acad. Ceramics (profl.), Australasian Ceramic Soc., Keramos (nat. pres. 1970-72, Greaves-Walker Roll of Honor 1976). Republican. Presbyterian. Home: 892 Old Hickory Rd Pittsburgh PA 15243-1112 Office: Rutgers U Ctr for Ceramic Rsch Campus Busch Piscataway NJ 08855-0909

RUHM, THOMAS FRANCIS, lawyer, investor; b. Bridgeport, Conn., June 8, 1935; s. Herman David and Martica (Sturges) R.; m. Michele Wood, Oct. 5, 1974; children: Wendy Sturges, Thomas Wood. BA, Yale U., 1957; JD, Havard U., 1962. Bar: N.Y. 1963, U.S. Dist. Ct. (so. and ea. dists.) N.Y. 1964, U.S. Ct. Appeals (2nd cir.) 1969. Assoc. Shearman & Sterling, N.Y.C., 1962-70; asst. gen. counsel Bessemer Securities Corp., N.Y.C., 1970—, v.p., 1981—; chmn. legal aspects venture capital investing Practising Law Inst., N.Y. and San Francisco, 1979-81; lectr. on venture capital NYU Grad. Sch.; expert on fed. securities law and investment tax policy; frequent wtness during 1980's hearings, Senate Fin. Com., Ho. Ways and Means Com. Contbg. author: Technology and Economic Policy, 1986; contbr. articles to profl. jours. Commr. upper div. Eastchester (N.Y.) Youth Soccer League, 1990-91, coach, 1985-91; sr. warden Christ Ch., Bronxville, N.Y., 1991—; past v.p. Bronxville (N.Y.) Sch. PTA. Mem. ABA, Assn. of Bar of City of N.Y., Am. Council for Capital Formation (policy com.), Univ. Club, Bronxville Field Club, Quogue Field Club. Republican. Office: Bessemer Securities Corp 630 5th Ave New York NY 10111-0002

RUIBAL, CHARLES ADRIAN, chemical company executive; b. Habana, Cuba, Mar. 5, 1947; came to U.S., 1961; s. Evelino Arsenio and Maria Gloria (de Puzo) R.; m. Geraldine Catherine McNabb, Aug. 31, 1968; children: Gloria Lynne, Michael Charles. BSChemE, Villanova U., 1968. With Am. Cyanamid Co., 1968—; process engr. indsl. chems. div. Am. Cyanamid Co., Linden, N.J., 1968-69; tech. sales rep. paper chems. dept. Am. Cyanamid Co., Pittsfield, Mass., 1969-72, Montgomery, Ala., 1972-74; asst. to mktg. mgr. paper chems. dept. Am. Cyanamid Co., Wayne, N.J., 1974-75; dist. sales mgr. paper chems. dept. Am. Cyanamid Co., Ft. Washington, Pa., 1975-77; nat. sales mgr. paper chems. dept. Am. Cyanamid Co., Wayne, N.J., 1977-78, mktg. mgr. paper chems. dept., 1978-80, mktg. mgr. water treating chems. dept., 1980-81, dept. mgr. specialty polymers dept., 1981-83, dept. mgr. crop protection chems. dept., 1983-84, v.p. agrl. div., 1984, pres. indsl. products div., 1984-89, pres. indsl. and performance products div., 1990-92, group v.p. chem. bus., 1992—; bd. dirs. Am. Indsl Health Coun., vice chmn., 1990, chmn., 1991; bd. dirs. Mitsui Cyanamid, Ltd. Chmn. bd. dirs. United Way of Passaic Valley; bd. dirs. N.C. State U. Pulp and Paper Found. Mem. Soc. Chem. Industry, Paper Industry Mgmt. Assn. Republican. Roman Catholic. Office: Am Cyanamid Co 1 Cyanamid Dr Wayne NJ 07470-4000

RUIZ, EMILIO, grapic artist, design company executive; b. N.Y.C., July 25, 1944; s. Antonio and Petronila Ruiz; m. Brenda Jane Pridemore, June 21, 1964 (div. 1976); 1 child, Lisa Jane. Student, Famous Artist Sch., 1962-64, Cooper Union, 1966, New Sch. N.Y., 1979. Asst. advt. designer Will Kaplan Advt., N.Y.C., 1961-68; advt. designer sales div. Jerry Moss Assocs., N.Y.C., 1968-73; with sales div. Jonathan Leigh, N.Y.C., 1973-75, Transworld Mfg., Littleferry, N.J., 1975-76; account supr. Siebiel/Mohr Assoc., N.Y.C., 1976-80; creative dir. Promotion Devel. Corp., Westport, Conn., 1980-81; v.p. Paladin II Ltd., Norwalk, Conn., 1981—; pres. Emilio Ruiz & Assocs., Inc., 1992—; Inventee in field. Asst. scoutmaster ch. orgn., N.Y., 1962. Famous Artist Sch. scholar, 1962. Office: Paladin II Ltd 10 Byington Pl Norwalk CT 06850-3309

RUIZ, JOHN, firefighter; b. N.Y.C., Mar. 24, 1954; s. Bonifacio Ruiz and Luz Miranda; children: Yolanda, Johnny, Johnathan. Student, John Jay Coll., 1986-89, Lee Strasberg Inst., 1991. Firefighter N.Y.C. Fire Dept., 1984—; dir. The Rappin Fireman Project, N.Y.C., 1985—, Drugs Are Poison Program, N.Y.C., 1991—, Set It Straight Program, N.Y.C., 1992—; educator fire safety edn., 1989. Composer: Don't Play With Matches, 1985, Drugs Are Poison, 1992. Community leader Councilman Adam Clayton Powell, N.Y.C., 1992. Recipient Pub. Svc. award N.Y. Telephone, 1989, Cest Smile award Senator David Paterson, 1992, Thomas Jefferson award Couniclman Adam Clayton Powell, 1992, over 100 commendations from varous city and civic orgns., 1985—. Mem. Vulcan Soc., Hispanic Soc., Internat. Assn. Black Firefighters, Lee Strasberg Theater Inst., Downtown Community TV Ctr. Roman Catholic. Home: 1695 Madison Ave New York NY 10029 Office: NYC Fire Dept Engine 5 340 E 14th St New York NY 10029

RUKEYSER, LOUIS RICHARD, economic commentator; b. N.Y.C., Jan. 30, 1933; s. Merryle Stanley and Berenice Helene (Simon) R.; m. Alexandra Gill, Mar. 3, 1962; children: Beverley Jane, Susan Athena, Stacy Alexandra. AB, Princeton U., 1954; LittD (hon.), N.H. Coll., 1975; LLD (hon.), Moravian Coll., 1978, Mercy Coll., 1984, Am. U., 1991; DBA (hon.), Southeastern Mass. U., 1979; LHD (hon.), Loyola Coll., 1982, Johns Hopkins U., 1986, Am. U., 1991. Reporter Balt. Sun newspapers, 1954-65; chief polit. corr. Evening Sun, 1957-59; chief London bur. The Sun, 1959-63, chief Asian corr., 1963-65; sr. corr., commentator ABC News, 1965-73, Paris corr., 1965-66, chief London bur., 1966-68, econ. editor, commentator, 1968-73; host Wall St. Week with Louis Rukeyser PBS-TV, 1970—; nationally syndicated econ. columnist McNaught Syndicate, 1976-86, Tribune Media Services, 1986—; frequent lectr. Author: How to Make Money in Wall Street, 1974, 2d edit., 1976 (Literary Guild selection 1974, 76), What's Ahead for the Economy: The Challenge and the Chance, 1983, 2d edit., 1985 (Literary Guild selection 1984), Louis Rukeyser's Business Almanac, 1988, 2d edit., 1991; editor-in-chief monthly newsletter Louis Rukeyser's Wall Street, 1992/6. Served with AUS, 1954-56. Recipient Overseas Press Club award, 1963, Overseas Press Club citation, 1964, G.M. Loeb award U. Conn., 1972, Janus award for excellence in fin. news programming, 1975, George Washington Honor medal Freedoms Found., 1972, 78, N.Y. Fin. Writers Assn. award, 1980, Free Enterprise Man of the Yr. award Tex. A&M U. Ctr. for Edn. and Research in Free Enterprise, 1987, Women's Econ. Round Table award, 1990. Office: 586 Round Hill Rd Greenwich CT 06831-2724

RUMILLY, BERNARD SEBASTIAN, computer company executive; b. Chalon/Saone, France, Jan. 27, 1935; came to U.S., 1985; s. Louis Gabriel and Gabrielle (Gontier) R.; m. Idil Cizgen-Akad; children: Olivier, Mathias, Marc. Grad., Ecole Superieure de Commerce, Paris, 1957, Inst. de Haute Fin., Paris, 1975, Internat. Mgmt. Sch., Brussels, 1979. Asst. fin. dir. Commissariat Energie Atomique, Paris, 1959-60; sales rep. data processing IBM France, Paris, 1960-62; country mgr. IBM Far East, Phnom Phen, Cambodia, 1963-65; mktg. mgr. IBM France, Paris, 1966-75; br. office mgr. Strasbourg, 1976-78; mng. European edn. IBM Europe, Paris, 1979-81; regional mgr. IBM France, Marseille, 1982-84; mgr. product planning IBM USA, White Plains, 1985—. Served to lt. French Air Force, 1957-59. Home: 74 Kelley Grn New Canaan CT 06840-5805 Office: CMC Assocs PO Box 682 44 S Broadway New Canaan CT 06840

RUMSEY, R. DOUGLAS, manufacturing executive; b. Buffalo, Nov. 12, 1918; s. Dexter Phelps and Margaret (Ramsdell) R.; m. Elizabeth Frick Smith, Oct. 25, 1941; children: Margot R. Banta, Nicholas Perry, Theodore Brewster. Student, Harvard U., 1941. Land surveyor Niagara Mohawk Power, Buffalo, 1940; flight test engr. Bell Aircraft, Wheatfield, N.Y., 1941; design & project engr. Power Plant, Niagara Falls, N.Y., 1947; chief devel. engr. AMF, Buffalo, 1947-50; asst. chief engr. Stanley Aviation, Buffalo, 1950-56; chief engr., dir. engring. Houdaille Industries, Buffalo, 1956-71; pres. Daleng Corp., No. Tonawanda, N.Y., 1971—; trustee Forest Lawn Cemetery, Buffalo, 1967—. patentee in field. Usher Trinity Ch., Buffalo, 1950—; leader Cub Scouts Am., Buffalo, 1954-56. Named Inventor of Yr. Western N.Y. Engring Soc., 1980. Mem. Buffalo Canoe Club, Buffalo Tennis and Squash Club, Wianno Club. Republican. Episcopalian. Office: Daleng Corp 908 Niagara Falls Blvd North Tonawanda NY 14120-2016

RUMSFELD, DONALD HENRY, former government official, corporate executive; b. Chgo., July 9, 1932; s. George Donald and Jeannette (Husted) R.; m. Joyce Pierson, Dec. 27, 1954; 3 children. A.B., Princeton U., 1954; hon. degree, De Paul U. Coll. Commerce, Ill. Coll., Lake Forest Coll., Park Coll., Tuskegee Inst., Nat. Coll. Edn., Bryant Coll., Claremont (Calif.) Grad. Sch. Adminstrv. asst. U.S. Ho. of Reps., 1958-59; with A.G. Becker & Co., Chgo., 1960-62; mem. 88th-91st Congresses from 13th Ill. dist., Pres.'s Richard Nixon's Cabinet, 1969-73; dir. OEO, asst. to pres., 1969-70; counselor to Pres., dir. econ. stabilization program, 1971-72; U.S. ambassador and permanent rep. to NATO, 1973-74; White House chief of staff for Pres. Gerald Ford Washington, 1974-75; sec. Dept. Def., 1975-77; pres., chief exec. officer, then chmn. G.D. Searle & Co., Skokie, Ill., 1977-85; spl. envoy of Pres. Ronald Reagan to Mid. East, 1983-84; sr. advisor William Blair & Co., Chgo., 1985-90; chmn., chief exec. officer General Instrument Corp., Chgo., 1990—; bd. dirs. Rand Corp., Kellogg Co., Tribune Co., Gilead Scis., Inc. Chmn. Eisenhower Exch. Fellowships, 1986—. Naval Aviator USN, 1954-57. Recipient Presdl. Medal of Freedom, George Catlett Marshall award, Woodrow Wilson award. Office: Gen Instrument Corp 181 W Madison St Chicago IL 60602-4510

RUNCK, ROBERT RIDGWAY, publishing executive; b. Lincoln, Nebr., June 4, 1935; s. Roger John and Theodora May (Ridgway) R.; m. Sallie Ann Rowe, June 2, 1962; 1 child, Brian Christian. BA, Ohio State U., 1958. Sr. editor Holt, Rinehart & Winston, N.Y.C., 1962-67; exec. editor Scott, Foresman & Co., Glenview, Ill., 1967-79; editorial dir. D.C. Heath & Co., Lexington, Mass., 1979-82; pres., pub. Ballinger Pub. Co., Cambridge, Mass., 1982-84, Brick House Pub. Co., New Boston, N.H., 1984—. chmn. higher edn. com. Assn. Am. Pubs., N.Y.C., 1982-83. With USAR, 1959-62. Office: Brick House Pub Co Francestown Turnpike New Boston NH 03070

RUNDELL, JEFFREY EDWIN, public relations executive; b. Lakewood, Ohio, Apr. 30, 1951; s. Clinton Howard and Shirley Meagie (Brown) R.; m. Margaret Mary Marskik, Aug. 23, 1975; children: Meagan Jorienne, Chelsea Holland. BA magna cum laude, Ohio Wesleyan U., 1973. Sports editor Sun Newspapers, Cleve., 1974-75; reporter Elyria (Ohio) Chronicle-Telegram, 1975-77, Oakland Press, Pontiac, Mich., 1977-78; newswriter ABC-Sta. WXYZ-TV, Detroit, 1978-80; news editor Cable News Network, Atlanta, 1980-82; editor exec. communications Coca-Cola Co., Atlanta, 1982-88; sr. pub. rels. exec. Ocean Spray Cranberries, Inc., Lakeville-Middleboro, Mass., 1988—; cons. Atlanta Video, 1988. Producer videos and audio tapes; contbr. articles to profl. jours. Mem. Internat. Assn. Bus. Communicators, Atlanta C. of C. (life), Phi Gamma Delta (pres. Atlanta chpt. 1987-88), Phi Beta Kappa, Omicron Delta Kappa. Office: Ocean Spray Cranberries Inc 1 Ocean Spray Dr Middleboro MA 02349-1000

RUNKLE, ROBERT SCOTT, environmental company executive; b. Washington, Mar. 9, 1936; s. Lloyd Manor and Louise (Armstrong) R.; m. Betsy Grater, Mar. 26, 1960 (div. July 1983); children: Beth R. Mackey, Brynn A.; stepchildren: Lori Anne Thompson, Jay M. Thompson; m. Joan Lewis, Aug. 6, 1983 (dec. Nov. 1987); m. Mary Beth Jorgensen, July 12, 1992; stepchildren: Elizabeth Jorgensen Feild, David Jorgensen Feild. BS in Bldg. Constrn., Ga. Inst. Tech ., 1960. Draftsman Ted Englehardt AIA, Silver Spring, Md., 1960-62; engr. Research Facilties Planning BD. div. Research Service NIH, Bethesda, Md., 1962-64; vice chmn. biohazards sect. Nat. Cancer Inst., NIH, Bethesda, 1964-67; research contracts mgr. Becton Dickinson & Co., Rutherford, N.J., 1967-69; adminstrn. mgr. Becton Dickinson Research Ctr., Raleigh, N.C., 1969-73; dir. adminstrn. Huntington (Eng.) Research Ctr., 1974-75; dir. research Becton Dickinson Co, Rutherford, N.J., 1976-78; v.p. ops. BBL microbiology systems div., Becton Dickinson Co., Balt., 1978-85; pres., chief exec. officer, chmn. bd. Pharmplastics Closures Inc., Balt., 1985-88; v.p. EA Labs, EA Engring., Sci. and Tech., Inc., Balt., 1989-91, v.p. bus. devel., 1992—; cons. Am. Inst. Biological Scis., Bethesda, 1963-67, ind., Balt., 1982—. Author: Microbial Contamination Control Facilities, 1969, Biomedical Applications Laminar Airflow, 1973; contbr. articles to profl. jours. Mem. Assn. for Corp. Growth, Building Futures Coun., Balt.-Washington Venture Group, MIT Enterprise Forum., Ga. Tech. Nat. Alumni Assn., Raleigh (N.C.) C. of C. Democrat. Episcopalian. Home: 448 Five Farms Ln Lutherville Timonium MD 21093-2955 Office: EA Engring Science and Technology Inc 11019 McCormick Rd Cockeysville Hunt Valley MD 21031

RUNOLFSSON, THORDUR, electrical engineering educator; b. Reykjavik, Iceland, May 22, 1959; s. Runolfur and Hildur (Halldorsdottir) Thordarson; m. Anna Sigrunardottir, June 30, 1979; 1 child, Asdis. BS, U. Wis., 1983; PhD, U. Mich., 1988. Engr. RARIK, Iceland, 1983; cons. engr. Rafteikning, Iceland, 1988; lectr. U. Mich., Ann Arbor, 1988, rsch. assoc., 1988; asst. prof. elec. and computer engring. Johns Hopkins U., Balt., 1989—. Rackham fellow, 1987. Mem. IEEE. Office: Johns Hopkins Univ 105 Barton Hall Baltimore MD 21218

RUNYON, GUY ERIC, financial services company executive, lecturer, author; b. Bronx, N.Y., Feb. 9, 1945; s. Maurice B. and Mae (Steiner) R.; m. Diane Lynn Hyman; children: Michael , Adam, Todd, David, Brandon. BBA in Acctg., U. Cin., 1967. Pres. Runyon Orgn. Inc., Ramsey, N.J.; bd. dirs. Porky Products, Inc., Jersey City, N.J. Contbr. articles to profl. jours. Coach Little League and Soccer, Upper Saddle River, N.J., Jr. Basketball, Bergen County; foster parent Foster Parents Plan; lifetime mem., past chmn. Security Mut. Life Ins. Co. Pres.'s Cabinet. Named Salesman of Yr., Security Mut. Life Ins. Co., Binghamton, N.Y., 1983, 90, 91, Businessman of Yr., March of Dimes, 1992. Mem. Million Dollar Round Table (life, qualifying), Twenty Five Million Dollar Internat. Forum, The Top of the Table of the Internat. Million Dollar Round Table, Internat. Forum. Office: Runyon Orgn 500 N Franklin Tpke Ramsey NJ 07446-1160

RUNYON, MARVIN TRAVIS, federal utility executive; b. Ft. Worth, Sept. 16, 1924; s. Marvin T. and Lora Lee (Whittington) R.; children: Marvin, Elizabeth Anne, Paul, James. BS in Mgmt. Engring., Tex. A&M U., 1948. Staff mem. mfg. engring. areas assembly plants Ford Motor Co., 1943-60, asst., plant mgr. various assembly plants, 1960-70; mgr. assembly engring. automotive assembly div. gen. office Ford Motor Co., Dearborn, Mich., 1970-72; gen. mgr. automotive assembly div. Ford Motor Co., 1972-73, v.p. body and assembly ops., 1973-77, v.p. powertrain and chassis ops., 1977-78, v.p. body and assembly ops., 1979-80; pres., chief exec. officer Nissan Motor Mfg. Corp. U.S.A., Smyrna, Tenn., 1980-87; chmn. bd. TVA, Knoxville, Tenn., 1988-92; Postmaster Gen. U.S. Postal Svc., Washington, 1992—; mem. at large Nuclear Power Oversight Com., 1991-92. Bd. dirs. United Way Knoxville, 1988—, mem. campaign adv. com. 1990; bd. dirs. Downtown Orgn., Knoxville, 1988—, Tenn. Tech. Found., 1982, NCCJ, 1985-88, Nashville-Davidson County unit Am. Cancer Soc., 1986-88, United Way Rutherford County, 1986-89, Cumberland Mus., Nashville, 1986; participant Leadership Nashville Assn., 1982—, pres., 1986; participant Leadership Knoxville, 1989, Leadership Memphis, 1990-91; hon. chmn. Clinic Bowl, Nashville, 1986; mem. devel. adv. bd. Ctr. for Internat. Bus. Studies Tex. A&M U., 1987, mem. coll. bus. adminstrv. devel. coun., 1984-87; mem. outreach com. Knoxville Bicentennial '91 Coord. Coun.; mem. adv. bd. Inroads/Nashville, Inc., 1983—; mem. devel. adv. bd. Nashville State Tech. Inst., 1987; chmn. corp. adv. com. Middle Tenn. Regional Minority Purchasing Coun., 1982-83; mem. gov.'s adv. bd. to S.E./U.S. Japan Assn., 1981; gen. campaign chmn. United Way Nashville and Middle Tenn., 1985-86, trustee, 1984-86; trustee Automotive Hall of Fame, 1985—; chmn. Tenn. Minority Bus. Opportunity Fair, 1987-89, 1992 Trade Fair, Midsouth Minority Purchasing Coun., 1991-92;, Sr. Ptnrs. Bd. for May 1992 World Congress of Indsl. Devel. Rsch. Coun., 1991-92; bd. dir. Memphis in May Internat. Festival Inc., 1991-92, Met. Nashville Pub. Edn. Found., 1991-92; mem. U. Tenn. Devel. Coun., 1990—, Nucleus Fund Com. and Internat. Programs Resource Devel. Com., Tex. A&M U. Named Outstanding Man of Year Soc. Advanced Mgmt., 1968, Pres. slot on 1985 Model Yr. Automotive News All-Star Team, Automotive News; recipient Mgr. of Yr. award Avco Aerostructures chpt. Nat. Mgmt. Assn., 1985, CEO of Yr., Advantage mag., 1985, Disting. Service citation Automotive Hall of Fame, 1986,

Salesman of Yr., Nashville chpt. Sales and Mktg. Exec. Club, 1985, award Tenn.-Japan Friends in Commerce, 1989; hon. gen. com. Internat. Fedn. Automotive Engring. Socs. 1988 Congress; recipient Human Rels. award NCCJ Nashville chpt., 1990, Spl. Recognition award Minority Bus. Devel. Agy., 1990, Gold Knight of Mgmt. award Nat. Mgmt. Assn., 1992. Mem. Soc. Automotive Engrs., Engring. Soc. Detroit, Nashville Area C. of C. (bd. govs. 1983-85), Knoxville C. of C. (bd. dirs. 1988—), Memphis C. of C. (bd. dirs. 1990—), Tenn. Assn. Bus. (bd. dirs.), Soc. Internat. Bus Fellows, Belle Meade Country Club (Nashville). Episcopalian. Office: US Postal Svc Office of Postmaster Gen 475 L'Enfant Pla West SW Washington DC 20260

RUOF, RICHARD ALAN, clergyman; b. Lancaster, Pa., Oct. 11, 1932; s. Robert Jacob and Geneva May (Devers) R.; A.B., Franklin and Marshall Coll., 1954; M.Div., Lancaster Theol. Sem. and Union Theol. Sem. Va., 1960; STM Luth. Theol. Sem., Gettysburg, Pa., 1974; D.Min., McCormick Theol. Sem., 1981; m. Anne Margaret Demos; children: Mark Alan Demos Ruof, Anne Tracy Demos Ruof, Richard James Demos Ruof. Ordained to ministry United Ch. Christ, 1960; pastor Harrisville (Va.) Charge of United Ch. Christ, 1959-62, Thurmont (Md.) Charge, 1962-67, First Congl. Ch., Cortland, N.Y., 1967-77, St. Paul's United Ch. Christ of Hamlin, Fredericksburg, Pa., 1977-81, St. John's United Ch. of Christ, Egg Harbor City, N.J., 1982-87, St. John's United Ch. of Christ, Friedensburg, Pa., 1987—. Registrar-treas. Susquehanna Assn., N.Y. Conf., United Ch. Christ, 1968-74; mem. Egg Harbor City Bd. Edn., 1984. Served with USNR, 1954-56. Home: 1215 Geronimo Dr Lake Wynonah RR #1 Auburn PA 17922

RUPPERT, LEONARD HARVEY, association executive; b. New Brunswick, N.J., May 20, 1929; s. Henry Adam and Edith May (Cook) R.; m. Elizabeth Romano; children: Susan, Mark. BL in Journalism, Rutgers U., 1951. Editor Bound Brook (N.J.) Chronicle, 1951-52, Franklin Record, Somerset, N.J., 1950-52; corr. NEA Svcs., N.Y.C., 1952-55; exec. dir. N.J. Rep. State Com., Trenton, 1956-64, N.J. Petroleum Coun., Trenton, 1965-84, N.J. Conf. of Mayors, Trenton, 1985—; cons. N.J. Mcpl. Accts. Assn., Trenton, 1990-91; bd. dirs. Franklin State Bank, United Jersey Bank. Contbr. articles Inside Baseball mag., others. Mayor Franklin Twp., Middlebush, N.J., 1960, Montgomery Twp., Belle Mead, N.J., 1970; sec. Somerset County Bd. Elections, Somerville, N.J., 1960-64. With N.J. Nat. Guard. Mem. N.J. Hwy. Users Conf. (sec. 1960-65), Soc. Econ. Environ. Devel., N.J. C. of C. Republican. Methodist. Home: 32 Heather Ln Belle Mead NJ 08502-5124 Office: NJ Conf Mayors 180 Lower Ferry Rd Trenton NJ 08638-2422

RUPPERT, PAUL RICHARD, federal agency executive; b. Cleve., Aug. 30, 1958; s. Richard Arthur and Pierrette (Bougneteau) R.; m. Barbara Ann Mock, Jan. 30, 1988. AB, Washington U., St. Louis, 1982; MPA, Harvard U., 1989. Legis. asst. Senator John C. Danforth, Washington, 1983-85; elections dir. Nat. Conservative Polit. Action Com., Washington, 1985; dep. campaign mgr. Congressman Tom Kindness for Senate, Columbus, Ohio, 1986; campaign mgr. McIntee for Congress, Waterloo, Iowa, 1986; dir. govtl. affairs Computer Dealers & Lessors Assn., Washington, 1987; chief of staff Office Fed. Contract Compliance, U.S. Dept. Labor, Washington, 1988; legis. officer to Sec. Jack Kemp U.S. Dept. HUD, Washington, 1990—; mem. Rep. Congl. Leadership Coun., Washington, 1987. Contbr. articles to profl. publs. Dep. site coord. Bicentennial Presdl. Inaugural, Washington, 1988; mem. Mass. coalition devel. com. Bush-Quayle campaign, Boston, 1988. Mem. Am. Coun. Young Polit. Leaders, Kennedy Sch. Alumni Assn. (exec. coun. 1991), Washington U. Alumni Assn. (exec. coun. 1984-86), Capitol Hill Club, Harvard Club Boston, Harvard Club Washington (exec. com., membership com. 1990—). Episcopalian. Home: 250 S Reynolds St Apt 706 Alexandria VA 22304-4452 Office: US Dept HUD 451 7th St SW Ste 10120 Washington DC 20410

RUSCETTA, HAROLD PASQUALE, JR., customer services director; b. Brockton, Mass., Mar. 9, 1945; s. Harold P. and Olga Patricia (Carfagna) R.; m. Gail Ilene Donovan, Jan. 20, 1947; children: Lisa Marie, Karen Ilene. AS in Bus. Adminstrn., Massasoit Community Coll., Brockton, 1977; BS in Bus. Adminstrn., Stonehill Coll., 1983. Customer acct. supr. Ea. Utilities Assocs., Brockton, 1981-85; employee rels. mgr. Ea. Edison Co., Brockton, 1985-89; dir. customer svc. Ea. Utilities Assoc., West Bridgewater, Ma., 1990—; pres., chmn. Edico Credit Union, Brockton, 1976—; asst. treas., bd. dirs. Brockton Vis. Nurses, 1987—; sec., bd. dirs. Employee Assistance Program, Inc., Taunton, Mass., 1985—. Vice chmn. energy com. Town of Whitman (Mass.), 1981-82; mem. personnel com. Brockton YMCA, 1985—, Fuller Art Mus., Brockton, 1988—; mem. Dist. Atty.'s Civil Rights, Brockton, 1988. With USN, 1967-69. Mem. Am. Soc. Safety Engrs., Am. Mgmt. Assn., Metro South C. of C. (pres., chmn. pers. coun. 1987—), Beta Xi, Kiwanis Internat. (bd. dirs.). Roman Catholic. Office: Ea Utilities Assocs 750 W Center St PO Box 543 West Bridgewater MA 02379

RUSCIANO, ANTHONY, appraiser, consultant, auctioneer; b. Bronx, Nov. 14, 1944; s. Frank A. and Marie J. (Rose) R.; m. Joyce A. Palladino, Nov. 10, 1968; children: Hope, Frank, Anthony. BBA in Mktg., Pace U., 1967; postgrad., NYU, 1975-78. Real estate specialist U.S. Army C.E., N.Y.C., 1972; mgr. locations Reynolds Securities, Inc., N.Y.C., 1973-74; sr. appraiser Rusciano Appraisers & Cons., Inc., Mount Vernon, N.Y., 1975-78; pres., prin. Rusciano Realty Svcs., Ltd., White Plains, N.Y., 1979-87; pres. Benchmark Cons. Appraisers, Inc., Scarsdale, N.Y., 1979—; cons. Strook & Strook & Lavan, N.Y.C., 1982-83, N.Y. Urban Devel. Corp., 1982—, N.Y. Dept. Housing Preservation, N.Y.C., 1979—, N.Y. State Dormitory Authority, N.Y.C. Law Dept., U.S. Marshal So. Dist. N.Y., 1983—. Mem. Rep. Congl. Com., Washington, 1982-87, Rep. Nat. Com., 1991—. 1st lt. USAF, 1968-72. Mem. Internat. Platform Assn., Internat. Real Estate Inst. (internat. cons. team 1989—). Republican. Roman Catholic. Home: 1025 Post Rd Scarsdale NY 10583-4341

RUSE, PAUL WILLIAM, JR., state official; b. Springfield, Vt., Sept. 8, 1943; m. Carole Lemire; 2 children. Ed., Springfield High Sch. Fin. officer, treas. Town of Springfield, 1970-87, town mgr., 1983-87; dep. state treas. State of Vt., 1987-89, state treas., 1989—. With USCG, 1961-65. Mem. Govt. Fin. Officers Assn. of U.S. and Can., Vt. Mcpl. Clks. and Treas. Assn. (past pres.), Vt. Mcpl. Mgrs. Assn., VFW Post 771, Am. Legion Post 18. Democrat. Baptist. Home: Common Rd Springfield VT 05156 Office: Treasury Dept 133 State St 2nd Fl Montpelier VT 05602

RUSH, CECIL ARCHER, microchemist, consultant, researcher; b. Dillwyn, Va., Apr. 14, 1917; s. Archer Edward and Anne Elizabeth (Le Sueur) R.; m. Betty Anne Morgan; 1 child, Gordon David. BS, Coll. William and Mary, 1938; MS, U. Tex., 1940. Chief microanalytical rsch. lab. Aberdeen Proving Grounds, Edgewood, Md., 1940-70; microchemical cons., 1971—. Contbr. 40 articles to tech. jours. Recipient Sec. of Def. Outstanding Civilian Svc. award U.S. Dept. Def., 1950, First Peabody Sculpture award Md. Inst. Art, 1952. Mem. Am. Chem. Soc., Am. Crystallographic Soc., Rsch. Soc. Am. Home: 1410 Northgate Rd Baltimore MD 21218-1549 Office: Fine Books-Fine Arts 2605 N Charles St Baltimore MD 21218-4514

RUSH, DAVID, medical investigator, epidemiologist; b. N.Y.C., May 3, 1934; s. Samuel Hersh and Fannie (Dubin) R.; m. Catharine Ireland Dawson, June 24, 1957; children: Naomi Rush Olson, Hannah M., Leah D. BA cum laude, Harvard U., 1955, MD, 1959. Diplomate Am. Bd. Pediatrics. Resident in medicine U. Ill. Hosp., Chgo., 1959-61; resident in pediatrics Children's Hosp., Boston, 1963-64; registrar in pediatrics St. Mary's Hosp. Med. Sch., London, 1964-65; rsch. fellow, Harvard U. Med. Sch., Boston, 1965-66; asst. prof. preventive medicine and pediatrics, U. Rochester (N.Y.), 1967-69; asst. prof. pub. health (epidemiology) and pediatrics Columbia U., N.Y.C., also dir. prenatal project, 1969-76, assoc. prof., 1976-82; prof. pediatrics, social medicine and ob-gyn Albert Einstein Coll. Medicine, Bronx, N.Y., 1983-88; dir. epidemiology program USDA, Human Nutrition Research Ctr. on Aging, prof. nutrition, community health, Tufts U., Boston, 1988—; mem. human devel. and aging study sect. NIH, USPHS, 1982-86; prin. investigator nat. evaluation of spl. supplemental food program for women, infants and children U.S. Dept. Agr., 1981-86. Author: Diet in Pregnancy, 1980, Dead Reckoning, 1992; contbr. articles to profl. jours. Trustee, chmn. health services com. Children's Aid Soc., N.Y.C., 1971-86. Served as surgeon USPHS, 1961-63; capt. Res. Recipient career investigator award N.Y.C. Health Research Council, 1977; sr. internat. fellow Fogarty Ctr., NIH, USPHS, U. Bristol, Eng., 1977-78, U. Paris, 1984-85; research grantee Nat. Inst. Child and Human Devel., NIH, 1979-86. Fellow Am. Pub. Health Assn. (governing council 1976-79); mem. Soc. for Epidemiologic Research (pres. 1980-81), Soc. for Pediatric Research, Internat. Epidemiologic. Assn., Am. Epidemiol. Soc., Am. Pediatric Soc., Perinatal Research Soc., Am. Inst. of Nutrition, Am. Soc. Clin. Nutrition, Am. Coll. of Epidemiology. Office: Human Nutrition Rsch Ctr 711 Washington St Boston MA 02111-1524

RUSH, KENNETH WAYNE, academic administrator; b. Phila., Sept. 12, 1939; s. M. LeRoy and Vera May (Johnson) R.; m. Ruth Miller, Apr. 6, 1963; children: Nancy Jeanne, Stephen Todd. ABA, U. Pa., 1970, BBA, 1980. Actuarial clk. Presbyn. Mins. Fund, Phila., 1958-62, asst. sec., 1968-75, corp. sec., 1975-77; mgr. actuarial dept. Reliance Standard Life, Phila., 1965-68; controller Columbia (S.C.) Bible Coll., 1977-79; bus. mgr. Westminster Theological Sem., Phila., 1979—. Author: (with others) Human Resources Management in Religiously Affiliated Institutions, 1991. Treas. Phil. presbytery Presbyn. Ch. Am., 1986—; pres. Montgomery north camp Gideons Internat., Montgomery County, Pa., 1991—; dir. Covenant Counseling Ctr., Lansdale, Pa., 1991—. With USN, 1962-64. Republican. Office: Westminster Theological Sem 14321 N Pennsylvania Ave # B Oklahoma City OK 73134-6014

RUSHER, WILLIAM ALLEN, writer, commentator; b. Chgo., July 19, 1923; s. Evan Singleton and Verna (Self) R. A.B., Princeton, 1943; J.D., Harvard, 1948; D.Lit. (hon.), Nathaniel Hawthorne Coll., 1973. Bar: N.Y. bar 1949. Asso. firm Shearman & Sterling & Wright, N.Y.C., 1948-56; spl. counsel finance com. N.Y. Senate, 1955; asso. counsel internal security subcom. U.S. Senate, 1956-57; pub., v.p. Nat. Review mag., N.Y.C., 1957-88, also bd. dirs.; sr. fellow The Claremont Inst, 1989—; mem. Adv. Task Force on Civil Disorders, 1972. Author: Special Counsel, 1968, (with Mark Hatfield and Arlie Schardt) Amnesty?, 1973, The Making of the New Majority Party, 1975, How to Win Arguments, 1981, The Rise of the Right, 1984, The Coming Battle for the Media, 1988; Columnist: Universal Press Syndicate, 1973-82, Newspaper Enterprise Assn., 1982—; played role of Advocate in TV program The Advocates, 1970-73. Bd. dirs. Media Rsch. Ctr., Washington; chmn. bd. advisors Ashbrook Ctr., Ashland, Ohio; past vice chmn. Am. Conservative Union; trustee Pacific Legal Found., Sacramento. Served from 2d lt. to capt. USAAF, 1943-46. Recipient Distinguished Citizen award N.Y. U. Law Sch., 1973. Mem. Am. Bar Assn., Am.-African Affairs Assn. (past co.-chmn.). Anglican. Clubs: University (N.Y.C. and San Francisco); Metropolitan (Washington). Home and Office: 850 Powell St San Francisco CA 94108

RUSHING, BYRON, legislator; b. N.Y.C., Dec. 29, 1942; s. William and Linda (Turpin) R.; (div. 1972); 1 child: Osula Evadne. AA (hon.), Roxbury (Mass.) Community Coll., 1989. Pres. Mus. Afro Am. History, Boston, 1972-85; state rep. Commonwealth of Mass., Boston, 1983—. Mem. ACLU of Mass. (vice chmn.), Roxbury Hist. Soc. (pres. 1969—), Roxbury Heritage State Pk. Adv. Bd. (vice chmn.). Episcopalian. Office: Mass House Reps State House # 134 Boston MA 02133

RUSHTON, BRIAN MANDEL, chemical company executive; b. Sale, Cheshire, Eng., Nov. 16, 1933; came to U.S., 1957; s. Ronald Henry and Edith (Slater) Riley; m. Jean Wrigley, Apr. 1, 1958; children: Jacqueline, Lisa, Amy. A.R.I.C. in Chemistry, U. Salford, Eng., 1957; M.S. in Phys. Organic Chemistry, U. Minn., 1959; Ph.D. in Phys. Organic Chemistry, U. Leicester, Eng., 1963; postgrad. Sr. Exec. program, MIT, 1972. Prodn. mgr. trainee 3M Co. U.K., 1959-60; sr. research chemist Petrolite Corp., 1963-65, group leader, 1965-66; sect. mgr. Ashland Chem. Co., 1966-69; corp. research mgr. Hooker Chem. Corp. subs. Occidental Petroleum, 1969-72, dir. polymer and plastics research and devel., 1972-74, v.p. research and devel. chem. and plastics div., 1974-75; pres. Celanese Research Corp., 1975-80; corp. v.p. tech. Celanese Corp.; also pres. Celanese Research Corp., 1980-81; v.p. research and devel. Air Products & Chem., Inc., Allentown, Pa., 1981-92, sr. v.p. rsch. and devel., 1992—; pres., mem. exec. com., bd. dirs. Indsl. Rsch. Inst., 1990—, chmn. plans and policies com., 1988-90; bd. dirs. Diamonex, Inc., Mich. Molecular Inst., Supercritical Processing, Inc. Contbr. articles to profl. jours.; patentee in field. Mem. life scis., vis. com. Lehigh U., chmn. surface sci. vis. com., 1983-86; bd. dirs. WLVT Channel 39, Bethlehem, Pa., 1992—; trustee Summit YMCA, N.J., 1976-79; mem. nat. materials bd. NRC, 1980-84. Mem. Coun. Chem. Rsch. (dir., treas.), Am. Chem. Soc., Soc. Chem. Industry, Am. Mgmt. Assn. Episcopalian. Clubs: Saucon Valley Country (Bethlehem, Pa.). Home: RR 9 Bethlehem PA 18015-9805 Office: Air Products & Chems Inc 7201 Hamilton Blvd Allentown PA 18195-1501

RUSIN, WILLIAM ALOYSIUS, otolaryngologist; b. Wilkes-Barre, Pa., Jan. 16, 1938; s. Steven and Catherine (Halupka) R.; m. Elaine A. Jatkowski, June 24, 1961; children: William A. Jr., Christopher J. BS in Biology, King's Coll., Wilkes-Barre, 1959; MD, Temple U., 1963. Diplomate Am. Bd. Otolaryngology. Med. intern Geisinger Med. Ctr., Danville, Pa., 1963-64; otolaryngology resident Geisinger Med. Ctr., Danville, 1964-68; otolaryngologist E.N.T. Surg. Group, Wilkes-Barre, 1972—; pres. med. staff Wilkes-Barre Gen. Hosp. Maj. U.S. Army, 1968-71. Fellow Am. Acad. Otolaryngology, Head and Neck Surgery. Republican. Roman Catholic. Office: ENT Surg Group 35 W Linden St Ste 320 Wilkes Barre PA 18702

RUSINKO, FRANK, JR., tool company executive; b. Nanticoke, Pa., Oct. 12, 1930; s. Frank Sr. and Eva (Ruduski) R.; m. Lucy Geryak, June 1, 1957; children: Nancy, Lawrence. BS, Pa. State U., 1952, MS, 1954, PhD, 1958. Vice-pres., tech. dir. Airco Carbon, St. Mary's, Pa., 1959-76; pres. Electrotools Inc., Broadview, Ill., 1976-89, Intech EDM Electrotools, Broadview, Ill., 1989-91; sr. scientist, dir. Carbon Rsch. Ctr. Pa. State U., 1991—; bd. dirs., bd. chmn. Transor Filter USA, Park Ridge, Ill., C-Cor Electronics, State College, Pa. Contbr. articles to profl. jours. Mem. Hinsdale (Ill.) Plan Commn., 1986; mem. Region Campaign Pa. State U., 1989; pres. Sch. Bd. Edn., St. Marys, Pa., 1965-76. Fellow Pa. State Alumni Assn.; mem. Am. Chem. Soc., Am. Carbon Soc., Sigma Xi. Orthodox. Home: 2392 Pinehurst Dr State College PA 16803 Office: Pa State Univ 238 Research Bldg E University Park PA 16803

RUSK, BRIAN DWIGHT, public relations executive, consultant; b. Buffalo, May 2, 1955; s. Jerzy Thaddeus and Halina Elizabeth Ruszkowski; m. Maureen Beth Millane, Jan. 13, 1990; 1 child, Justine Halina. BA, U. Buffalo, 1974. corr. ABC, CBS, NBC TV affiliates, 1985—. Exec. asst. Ralph S. Harte Ctr., N.Y.C., Palm Beach, 1975-76; press coord. Com. to Elect K. Braun, Buffalo, 1976; mgr. Airport Indsl. Pk., Buffalo, 1977; field rep. N.Y. State Assembly, Albany, 1978-80; dir. pub. affairs Daemen Coll., Buffalo, 1981--; corr. ABC, CBS, NBC TV affiliates, 1985. Actor: Otto Frank, 1970 (outstanding achievement award 1971); interviewer Rusk Report radio program, 1979—; news columnist The Rusk Report, 1983—. Nat. dir. Polish Am. Congress, Chgo., Washington, 1980—; bd. dirs. U.S. Selective Svc., 1981—, Cystic Fibrosis, Buffalo, 1987—; pres. Pulaski Assn., Buffalo, 1987—; treas. Restoration Soc., Buffalo, 1988—; bd. dirs. Friendship Found., Buffalo, 1988—; mem. Erie County Rep. Exec. Com., 1988—. Recipient Pres. Plaque award 1979, Profl. and Bus. Assn., Pres. award Amherst (N.Y.) C. of C., 1981, Appreciation award, Nat. Polish Am. Congress, Chgo., 1982; named Man of Yr., Addicts in Distress, Buffalo, 1989. Mem. Kiwanis, Rotary (bd. dirs. 1984-87). Republican. Roman Catholic. Home: 275 Ranch Trl Buffalo NY 14221-2339 Office: Daemen Coll 4380 Main St Buffalo NY 14226-3592

RUSKIN, ADAM JAY, publishing executive, lawyer; b. Juneau, Alaska, May 29, 1963; s. David Barry and Evelyn Lois (Goodman) R.; m. Maura Freyer, Nov. 25, 1990. BA, U. Mich., 1985; JD, U. Colo., 1988. Bar: N.Y. 1989. Atty. Paul, Weiss, Rifkind, Wharton and Garrison, N.Y.C., 1989-91; exec. v.p. Edco Corp., N.Y.C., 1991-92; pub., editor-in-chief Ruskin's Israel Bus. Rev., N.Y.C., 1992—; assoc. Yerushalmi, Shiboleth, Yisraeli & Roberts, N.Y.C., 1992—. Author: (op-ed series) The Colo. Daily, 1987. Founder Am.-Israel Student Action Com., 1990—; mem. Am.-Israel Pub. Affairs Com., 1989—, Inst. for Pub. Affairs-Orthodox Union, 1989—, Nat. Jewish Outreach Program, 1989—. Mem. ABA, Am.-Israel C. of C. Republican. Home: 5 W 86th St Ste 90 New York NY 10024 Office: 350 Fifth Ave 60th Fl New York NY 10118

RUSKIN, ROBERT STERLING, association executive; b. Washington, Nov. 27, 1945; s. Robert Edward and Thelma (Gipe) R.; m. Rebecca Lynne Wilson, Aug. 11, 1967; 1 child, Brant Edward. BA, Washington Coll., Chestertown, Md., 1967; MA, W.Va. U., 1969, PhD, 1971. Lic. psychologist Va., D.C. Prof. dept. psychology Georgetown U., Washington, 1971-86, chmn. dept. psychology, 1976-85, dir. Ctr. for Personalized Instrn., 1977-80, dir. Teaching Resource Ctr., 1985-86; chief psychol. assessor leadership devel. U. Md., College Park, 1984—; prin. investigator and project dir. U.S. Army Rsch. Inst., Washington, Alexandria, 1985—; nat. rsch. fellow U.S. Dept. Edn., Washington, 1986-87; affiliate prof. psychology George Mason U., Washington, 1989—; prin. investigator Consortium & Office of Substance Abuse Prevention, Washington, 1990—; dir. programs and rsch. Consortium of Univs. of Washington Metro. Area, 1987-88, v.p., 1989—; psychol. cons. DuPont Corp., Seaford, Del., 1986-88; psychol. cons. Consortium of Univs. of D.C., 1984—; cons. in field; rep. of U.S. to UNESCO Planning Meeting, Paris, 1979. Co-author: Behavioral Instruction: An Evaluative Review, 1977; editor manuscript: Consortium Research Fellows Program; editor The Jour. of Personalized Instrn., 1975-81, Revista a Tecnologia Educativa, 1976-83. Battelle Inst. Disting. Acad. Rsch. fellow U.S. Army Rsch. Inst., 1984-86. Fellow APA, Am. Psychol. Soc. (charter); mem. AAAS, D.C. Psychol. Assn., Va. Psychol. Assn., Psi Chi. Methodist. Home: 309 W Alex Ave Alexandria VA 22302 Office: Consortium of Univs of Wash 1 Dupont Circle NW Washington DC 20036-2087

RUSNOCK, JAMES ALBERT, chemicals executive; b. Kingston, Pa., Sept. 25, 1946; s. Albert Joseph and Alice Marie (McHale) R.; m. Jane Elizabeth Majernick, Aug. 28, 1968 (div. 1985); children: Jeremy A., Thomas J. Cert. in Pedagogy, Orgn for Rehab through Tng Sch, Nathanya, Israel, 1966; BA in French, U. Scranton, 1971. Vol. Peace Corps, Man, Ivory Coast, Africa, 1966-68; sales mgr. Moduline Industries, Inc., Derry, N.H., 1971-72; systems specialist Sperry Remington, Wilkes Barre, Pa., 1973-75; contract adminstr. Coficomex, Riyadh, Saudi Arabia, 1976-77; pres. Indsl. Woodcraft, Inc., Scranton, Pa., 1978-84; account exec. Thomas Pub. Co., N.Y.C., 1985-86; v.p. Acton Techs., Inc., Pittston, Pa., 1986—; bd. dirs. New Eng. Mobilehome Assn., Boston, 1972. Mem. Soc. for Advancement of Materials Engring. Democrat. Roman Catholic. Home: 50 N Welles Ave Kingston PA 18704

RUSOFF, IRVING ISADORE, industrial food scientist, consultant; b. Newark, Jan. 29, 1915; s. Max and Rachel (Dodin) R.; m. Perle Greenspan, Sept. 12, 1941 (dec. Nov. 1986); children: Susan, Arnold; m. Lillian Louise Skora, Sept. 6, 1987. BS, U. Fla., 1937, MS, 1939; PhD, U. Minn., 1943. Dairy chemistry instr. U. Fla., Gainesville, 1939-40; Nat. Def. Coun. fellow U. Minn., Mpls., 1944-46; head of nutritional rsch. Standard Brands, Inc., N.Y.C., 1946-47; head of nutrition, fats and oils Gen. Foods Corp., Hoboken and Tarrytown, N.Y., 1947-62; mgr. rsch. DCA Food Industries, N.Y.C., 1962-63; dir. nutritional biochemistry Beech Nut Life Savers, N.Y.C., 1963-66; dir. basic studies Nabisco, Inc., Fairlawn, N.J., 1966-76; sr. scientist Nabisco Brands, Inc., East Hanover, N.J., 1976-85; cons. Brick, N.J., 1985—; membership chmn. indsl. liaison panel NRC, Washington, 1979-83; liaison chmn. for IFT, Nat. Inventors Hall of Fame, Akron, Ohio, 1980—; chmn. Gordon Rsch. Conf. on Food and Nutrition, 1981-82; rep. Grocery Mfrs. Assn.; mem. tech. com. for Nabisco, 1975-82; rep. Biscuit and Crackers Mfts. Assn. Nutrition Com., 1978-82. Contbr. articles to profl. jours.; patentee in field. Pres. Park Ridge (N.J.) Bd. Health, 1968. Nat. Found. for Infantile Paralysis fellow, 1943. Fellow Inst. Food Technologists (chmn. 1979-80); mem. Am. Assn. of Cereal Chemists (Charles N. Frey award 1984), Am. Chem. Soc., Am. Inst. Nutrition, Am. Oil Chemists Soc. (assoc. editor 1960-62), N.Y. Acad. Scis., Sigma Xi, Phi Tau Sigma. Jewish. Home: 65 Central Blvd Brick NJ 08724-2451

RUSS, GERALD ALLEN, radiopharmaceutical chemist; b. Washington, Oct. 17, 1936; s. David and Rosalie June (Herman) R.; m. Lana Cohen, Apr. 11, 1965; children: David Benjamin, Daniel Edward, Joseph Michael. BS, U. Md., 1964; PhD, Georgetown U., 1974. Rsch. assoc. USPHS, Rockville, Md., 1964; rsch. asst. Georgetown U., Washington, 1964-67, rsch. assoc., 1967-72; rsch. asst. Sloan-Kettering Inst. Cancer Rsch., N.Y.C., 1972-76, assoc., 1976-82; head radiopharmacy U. Rochester (N.Y.) Med. Ctr., 1982—. Contbr. articles to profl. jours. Pres. Springhill Lake Civic Assn., Greenbelt, Md., 1971-72; vice chmn. Park and Recreation Adv. Com., Greenbelt, 1972; precinct chmn. Dem. Party, Greenbelt, 1972; mem. Penfield (N.Y.) Vol. Ambulance. With U.S. Army, 1959-62. Recipient Outstanding Svc. award Cong. Sons of Israel, 1981. Mem. Soc. Nuclear Medicine, Am. Chem. Soc., Assn. Univ. Radiologists, N.Y. Acad. Scis., Am. Legion. Jewish. Home: 101 Heather Dr Rochester NY 14625-2511 Office: U Rochester Box 620 Medical Ctr Rochester NY 14642

RUSSELL, BARBARA DALTON, management consultant; b. New York, N.Y., Feb. 26, 1952; d. Stanley F. and Patricia C. (Flood) Dalton; m. David Russell, Jr., Dec. 4, 1981; children: Martha Louise, Peter Sargent. MS in Econs., Boston U., 1975, MIT, 1977; postgrad., Harvard U., 1976-77. Entertainment analyst Kidder Peabody, N.Y.C., 1977-83; sr. entertainment analyst Prudential Bache, N.Y.C., 1983-85, County-Nat. Westminster Securites, N.Y.C., London, England, U.S., 1985-87; pres. Cove Hill Consulting, N.Y.C., 1987—. Dir. Orpheus Chamber Orch. Mem. N.Y. Soc. Securities Analysts, Internat. Radio & TV Soc., Nat. Cable TV Assn. Home: 140 Cove Rd Oyster Bay NY 11771-3401

RUSSELL, DANIEL JOSEPH, JR., nonprofit organization executive; b. Elizabeth, N.J., Oct. 7, 1959; s. Daniel and Anne Patricia (Gleason) R. Student, Exeter (Eng.) U., 1979-80; BA, Coll. of Holy Cross, 1982. Project dir. Elizabeth (N.J.) Devel. Co., 1984-85; campaign mgr. Holzapfel for Assembly, Linden, N.J., 1985; dir. devel. Am. Cancer Soc.-Union, Elizabeth, 1986-89; exec. dir. Am. Cancer Soc.-Hudson, Secaucus, N.J., 1989—. Bd. dirs. Citizens League Elizabeth, 1986—, pres., 1988-89; dist. committeeman Union County Rep. Com., Roselle Park, N.J., 1986-90; sec. Juvenile Detention Bd. Union County, Elizabeth, 1987-89. Mem. Nat. Soc. Fund Raising Execs., Inst. Dirs. (London), Netherlands Inst., UN Assn., Hudson County C. of C., Elizabeth Town and Country Club (bd. dirs. 1987—, v.p. 1989-90). Home: 201 Shelley Ave Elizabeth NJ 07208-1061 Office: Am Cancer Soc 150 Meadowlands Pky Secaucus NJ 07094-2304

RUSSELL, DOMINIQUE See SOLER, TERRELL DIANE

RUSSELL, FABIAN LEVAN, resort company executive; b. Kingston, N.Y., July 4, 1953; s. Robert Snyder and Barbara Elizabeth (Haver) R.; m. Georgia May Hyde, Oct. 7, 1977; children: Fabian Ryan, Kimberly Hyde. BA, Alfred U., 1975; MS, Nova U., Davie, Fla., 1980. Mgr. prodn. control F.L. Russell Corp., Mt. Marion, N.Y., 1976-77, v.p. ops., 1981-84, pres., chief exec. officer, 1985-87; with Broward County Dept. Human Resource Svcs., Ft. Lauderdale, Fla., 1978-80; gen. ptnr. East Coast Resorts Am., Parish, N.Y., 1987—; advisor, cons. N.Y. State Coalition Camp Resorts, Parish, 1989—. Patentee Pocketab, Portfilio, Ultra. Cubmaster, chmn. Boy Scouts Am., North Syracuse, N.Y., 1988—; bd. advisor Home Sch. Orgn., North Syracuse, 1990—. Republican. Home: 6088 Hiller Dr Cicero NY 13039-9372 Office: East Coast Resorts Am Crim Rd Parish NY 13131

RUSSELL, FREDERICK WILLIAM, Canadian provincial official; b. St. John's, Nfld., Can., Sept. 10, 1923; s. Herbert J. and Jean (Campbell) R.; m. Margaret M. Cross, June 15, 1946; children: Douglas, Janice, James Peter. Student, Prince of Wales Coll., St. John's, Dalhousie U., Halifax, N.S., Can.; LLD (hon.), Meml. U. Nfld., St. John's, 1976. Pres. Blue Peter Steamships, St. John's, 1949-72, Terra Nova Motors Ltd., St. John's, 1962-79, Gen. Industries, St. John's, 1980-88, Delta Holdings Ltd., St. John's, 1980-88, Fremar Investments Ltd., St. John's, 1980-91; lt. gov. Province of Nfld., St. John's, 1991—; mem. Royal Trust Adv. Bd., St. John's, 1980-91. Mem. Nfld. Labour Rels. Bd., St. John's, 1953-58; chmn. United Ch. Sch. Bd., St. John's, 1958-67; chmn. bd. regents Meml. U. Nfld., 1974-82; bd. dirs. Atlantic Can. Opportunities Agy., Moncton, N.B., Can., 1986-91. Decorated Order of Can., knight of grace Order of St. John, 1991; recipient Order of Red Cross, Can. Red Cross Soc., 1992. Mem. Rotary (bd. dirs. St. John's). Mem. United Ch. of Canada. Home and Office: Govt House, Military Rd, Saint John's, NF Canada A1C 5W4

RUSSELL, GEORGE KEITH, biology educator, editor; b. Bronxville, N.Y., Dec. 13, 1937; s. Donald Keith and Anna (Kibitz) R.; m. Leonore Diane deSylva, Mar. 29, 1970. A.B., Princeton U., 1959; Ph.D., Harvard U., 1963. Asst. prof. biology Princeton U., 1965-67; asst. prof. Adelphi U., Garden City, N.Y., 1967-70, assoc. prof., 1970-77, prof. biology, 1977—. Editor ORION Nature Quar., 1982—. Author sci. monograph and lab. manual. Chmn. bd. trustees The Waldorf Sch. of Garden City, 1983—; bd. dirs. Am. Council for Drug Edn., N.Y.C., 1978—, The Myrin Inst., N.Y.C., 1977— . Mem. Am. Soc. Plant Physiologists, Sigma Xi. Club: Princeton (N.Y.C.). Avocations: gardening; hiking; reading. Office: Adelphi U Dept Biology South Ave Garden City NY 11530

RUSSELL, JOHN FINTAN, theology educator, editor; b. Springfield, Mass., July 19, 1934; s. David Joseph and Ellen Teresa (Shea) R. BA, St. Bonaventure U., 1957; STL, Lateran U., Rome, Italy, 1962; MA, Roosevelt U., 1968; STD, Cath. U., 1979. Dean of boys Carmel High Sch., Mundelein, Ill., 1962-67; dir. counseling Carmel Sem., Hamilton, Mass., 1967-70; dir. Whitefriars Hall, Washington, 1972-77; asst. prof. theology I.C.S. Sem., Mahwah, N.J., 1977-83; assoc. prof. theology Seton Hall U., South Orange, N.J., 1983-91, prof. theology, 1991—; theology cons. Nat. Office of Renew, Plainfield, N.J., 1988—. Author: (with others) Experiencing St. Therese Today, 1990; editor: Sword Mag., 1990—; contbr. articles to profl. jours. Mem. Com. for Ednl. Excellence, Cresskill, N.J., 1983-84. Faculty rsch. grantee Seton Hall U., 1989. Mem. Cath. Theol. Soc. Am. Roman Catholic. Home: 120 Monroe Ave Cresskill NJ 07626-1498 Office: Seton Hall U 444 S Orange Ave South Orange NJ 07079-2646

RUSSELL, JOHN WILLIAM, insurance executive; b. Springfield, Mass., May 24, 1952; s. John Jacob Jr. and Helen (Mullaly) R.; m. Beronica N. Trevino, Feb. 19, 1987. BS in Indsl. Engring., Western New Eng. Coll., 1975. Loss prevention rep. Liberty Mut. Ins. Co., Hamden, Conn., 1975-76; loss prevention rep. Liberty Mut. Ins. Co., Norwich, Conn., 1976-78, sr. loss prevention rep., 1978-80, loss prevention cons., 1980-81, loss prevention cons.-indsl., 1981; sr. loss prevention cons.-indsl. Liberty Mut. Ins. Co., East Hartford, Conn., 1981-85; tech. cons. indsl. Liberty Mut. Ins. Co., Glastonbury, Conn., 1985-88; div. tech. dir. indsl. Liberty Mut. Ins. Co., Weston, Mass., 1988-91; dir. indsl. svc. Liberty Mutual Ins. Co., Boston, 1991—; tchr. evening div. Hartford (Conn.) State Tech. Coll., 1982-87. Contbr.: Material Handling Handbook, 1985. Mem. planning com. City of Manchester, Conn., 1986-87; fin. bd. United Way, Groton, Conn., 1979; VIP com. Leukemia Soc., Hartford, 1984-85; mem. parish devel. team All Saints Episcopal Ch., East Hartford, 1987-88; mem. B11 parent com., B7, B24.1 coms. ANSI. Mem. Inst. Indsl. Engrs., Am. Soc. Safety Engrs., Internat. Material Mgmt. Soc. (cert.), Cert. Safety Profls., Nat. Fire Protection Assn., Nat. Welding Soc., Western New Eng. Coll. Alumni Assn. (v.p. 1987, pres. 1988), Indsl. Engring. Club (pres. 1973-74), Electronics Club (pres. 1969-70). Home: 40 Connolly St Randolph MA 02368-1511 Office: Liberty Mut Ins Co 175 Berkeley St Newton MA 02165-2637

RUSSELL, JUANITA RENNER, human resources executive; b. Washington, Pa., May 22, 1951; d. John D. and Dorothy (Balser) Renner; m. David D. Russell III, Feb. 23, 1980. BA, Slippery Rock State Coll., 1973; postgrad., Carnegie Mellon U., 1984-85. Benefits approver Equitable Life, Pitts., 1973-74, dental unit supr., 1974-77, group sales rep., 1978-80; group ins. supr. Koppers Co. Inc., Pitts., 1977-78; assoc. personnel dir. Carnegie Mellon U., Pitts., 1980-86; mgr. employee benefits Davy Corp., Pitts., 1986-88, dir. human resources, 1989—. campaign chair Davy United Way, Pitts., 1990-91. Mem. Pitts. Pers. Assn., Pitts. Engring. Assn. (equipment com. 1991—). Republican. Office: Davy Corp One Oliver Pla Pittsburgh PA 15222

RUSSELL, KEVIN PATRICK, account executive, writer, illustrator; b. Franklin Sq., N.Y., Sept. 21, 1952; s. William John and Adele Elizabeth (Gallagher) R. BA in Advt. Art, N.Y. Inst. Tech., 1974. Asst. art dir. PTN Pub., Hempstead, N.Y., 1973-75; graphic artist Vogue-Wright Studios, N.Y.C., 1978-81, account exec., 1981—. Author, artist: The Little People and the Garden, 1988, Tommy and Suzie Go To Zirock, 1989, The Mouse House, 1990, Who Stole the Necklace?, 1990. Republican.

RUSSELL, MARIANN BARBARA, English educator; b. N.Y.C., May 23, 1935; d. Theodore R. and Cecilia Ann (Chase) R. BA, St. John's U., Bklyn., 1955; MA, Columbia U., 1957, PhD, 1965. Tchr. N.Y.C. Pub. Schs., 1957-59; instr. Morgan State U., Balt., 1961-62; assoc. prof. English Cheyney (Pa.) State U., 1964-69; prof. English Sacred Heart U., Fairfield, Conn., 1969—; cons. Acad. of Am. Poets, 1975, Conn. Coun. Humanities, 1990. Author: Melvin B. Tolson's Harlem Gallery, 1980 (Coll. Lang. Assn. award 1983); contbr. articles to profl. jours. NEH fellow, 1974; John Hay Whitney fellow, 1955; St. John's U. scholar, 1951. Mem. Coll. Lang. Assn. (English area rep. 1984-86), MLA, Nat. Coun. Tchrs. English, Literary Vols. of Am. Democrat. Roman Catholic. Home: 334 S 7th Ave Mount Vernon NY 10550 Office: Sacred Heart Univ 5151 Park Ave Fairfield CT 06432-1000

RUSSELL, MASON WEBSTER, health facility administrator, economics educator; b. Beverly, Mass., July 28, 1956; s. Gordon Arthur and Elizabeth Mason (Webster) R.; m. Susanne Rachel Nadeau, Oct. 22, 1982. BA in Econs., Salem State Coll., 1978; MA in Polit. Economy, Boston U., 1981, postgrad., 1981-87. Lectr. econs. Boston U., 1979-82; asst. prof. econs. Bentley Coll., Waltham, Mass., 1982-85; sr. economist Policy Analysis Inc., Brookline, Mass., 1985-88; exec. dir. White Mountain Health Svcs., Gorham, N.H., 1988-91; dir. physician svcs. North Care Corp., Berlin, N.H., 1991—; dir., COO Mountain Health Svcs., Berlin, 1991—; faculty assoc. Sch. for Lifelong Learning, Univ. System N.H., Berlin, 1990—; sec., dir. Gorham Devel. Corp., 1991—. Contbr. articles to profl. jours. Pres., dir. United Way No. N.H., Berlin, 1990—; vice chmn. gt. no. dist. Daniel Webster coun. Boy Scouts Am., 1990—. Mem. Am. Coll. Healthcare Execs., Med. Group Mgmt. Assn., Rotary Internat. (chmn., membership dist. 7850 1991-93), Rotary Club Gorham (sec. 1989-90, pres. 1990-92), Phi Kappa Phi. Democrat. Roman Catholic. Office: NorthCare Corp 59 Page Hill Rd Berlin NH 03570-3531

RUSSELL, MICHAEL JAMES, lawyer; b. Northampton, Mass., May 19, 1958; s. John Michael and Celia (Jaskolka) R. Cert. in German, U. Vienna, 1979; BA summa cum laude, Gettysburg Coll., 1980; MA, JD, Vanderbilt U., 1984. Bar: Pa. 1984, D.C. 1985. Rsch. asst. Vanderbilt U., Nashville, 1982-84; legal intern U.S. State Dept., Washington, 1982; law clk. Stewart, Estes & Donnell, Nashville, 1983; atty. U.S. Dept. Agr., Washington, 1984-85; majority counsel subcom. on juvenile justice senate judiciary com. U.S. Senate, Washington, 1985-86, minority gen. counsel subcom. on constn., 1987, legislative dir. to Sen. Arlen Specter, 1987-90, chief of staff, 1988; senate staff mem. Congrl. Crime Caucus, 1987-90; dep. dir. Nat. Inst. Justice U.S. Dept. Justice, Washington, 1990—. Editorial staff Vanderbilt Jour. Transnat. Law, Nashville, 1982-83, contbr., 1983, rsch. editor, 1983-84 (editor award 1984). Mem. senate staff club, 1985-90, Bush/Quayle Campaign's Crime Adv. Com., 1988, Friends of the Nat. Parks at Gettysburg, Pa., 1989—; bd. fellows Gettysburg Coll., 1990—; vol. Nat. Constn. Ctr., Phila., 1990; mem. Bush/Quayle Adminstrn. S.E.S. Assn., 1990—; mem. com. to celebrate bicentennial of constn., Northampton, Mass., 1987. Recipient Voluntary Svc. award VA, Northampton, 1978, Trustees award Forbes Libr., Northampton, 1989, cert. of appreciation Correctional Edn. Assn., 1991, Phi Alpha Delta, 1989, Fed. Bur. Alcohol, Tobacco and Firearms, 1989, Gettysburg Coll. Career Svcs. Office, 1992, Young Alumni Achievement award Gettysburg Coll., 1992. Mem. ABA, Am. Soc. Internat. Law, Pa. Soc. of Washington, Phi Beta Kappa, Psi Chi (jr. award 1979). Office: Nat Inst Justice US Dept Justice 633 Indiana Ave NW Washington DC 20531-0002

RUSSELL, OLGA WESTER, language educator; b. Hartford, Conn., June 20, 1913; d. Thomas Nielsen and Olga S.K. (Iversen) Wester; m. Henry G. Russell, Mar. 8, 1938; 1 child, Lauren Rusk. Diploma, U. Paris, 1933; AB, Conn. Coll., 1934; MA, U. Calif., Berkeley, 1939; AM, PhD, Harvard U., 1944, 57. Asst. in French U. Calif., Berkeley, 1939; instr. Cambridge Jr. Coll., 1943-44, Wheaton Coll., Mass., 1944-46, Tufts U., 1946-48; asst prof. Chatham Coll., Pitts., 1956-61; tchr. WQED Ednl. TV, Pitts., 1956-60; asst. prof. U. South Fla., Tampa, 1961-63; prof., chmn. dept. fgn. langs. Longwood Coll., Va., 1963-65; assoc. prof. Ea. Ill. U., 1965-66; prof. emerita U. Maine, Orono, 1966—. Author: Etude historique et critique des Burgraves de Victor Hugo, 1962, Humor in Pascal, 1977. Fellow Radcliffe Coll., 1955. Mem. MLA, Phi Beta Kappa.

RUSSELL, RICHARD JOHN, textile executive; b. N.Y.C., June 24, 1953; s. Richard and Lucy (Nicodema) Miraglia. BA cum laude, Hofstra U., 1976, MBA magna cum laude, 1979; advanced profl. cert., Fordham U., 1987; postgrad., NYU, 1991, Real Estate Grad. Inst., 1991. Account exec. Burlington Industries, N.Y.C., 1980-88; dir. mktg. United Mchts. and Mfrs., N.Y.C., 1988-91; v.p. Mortgage One Corp., N.Y.C., 1991—. Mem. Am. Mktg. Assn., Ctr. Creative Leadership. Republican. Home: 728 10th Ave New York NY 10019-7111 Office: Mortgage One Corp 120 W 44th St Ste 309 New York NY 10036-4020

RUSSELL, RICHARD LAWSON, biology educator; b. Bar Harbor, Maine, Nov. 24, 1940; s. William Lawson and Elizabeth Buckley (Shull) R.; m. Stephanie Carhart Merton, June 16, 1962 (div. Nov. 1976); 1 child, Kerstin; m. Barbara Joan Furman Attardi, Dec. 18, 1977; children: Daniel, David. BA, Harvard Coll., 1962; PhD, Calif. Inst. Tech., 1967. Asst. prof. Cornell U., Ithaca, N.Y., 1966-67; postdoctoral fellow MRC Lab. Molecular Biology, Cambridge, Eng., 1967-70; asst. prof. Calif. Inst. Tech., Pasadena, Calif., 1970-76; assoc. prof. U. Pitts., 1976-84, prof. biology, 1984—; mem. study sect. NIH, Bethesda, Md., 1980-84. Contbr. articles to profl. jours. Commrs. recreation league Dynamo Soccer, Pitts., 1988-92. Rsch. grantee NIH, 1970-88, March of Dimes, 1976-78, Muscular Dystrophy Assn., 1978-80. Home: 310 S Lang Ave Pittsburgh PA 15208-2750 Office: U Pitts Dept Biol Scis 213 Clapp Hall Pittsburgh PA 15260-4402

RUSSELL, RINALDINA, linguist, educator; b. Ancona, Italy, Jan. 12, 1934; came to the U.S., 1961; m. Robert W. Russell, Sept. 24, 1960 (dec. 1992). PhD, Columbia U., 1971. Instr. Barnard Coll., N.Y.C., 1968-71; asst. prof. Queens Coll., Flushing, N.Y., 1971-79, assoc. prof., 1979-83, prof., 1984—. Author: Generi Poetici Medievali, 1982, Tre Versanti Della Poesia Stilnovistica, 1973; contbr. articles and revs. to profl. jours. Mem. Renaissance Soc. Am. Office: Queens Coll CUNY Flushing NY 11367

RUSSELL, ROBERT MITCHELL, gastroenterology educator; b. Boston, Apr. 9, 1941; s. Stanley Gordon and Martha Lillian (Johnson) R.; m. Sharon Stanton, Aug. 28, 1965; children: Kimberley, Brooke. BA cum laude, Harvard U., 1963; MD, Columbia U., 1967. Intern U. Chgo., 1967-69, resident, 1971-73, NIH fellow gastroenterology, 1973-75; from asst. to assoc. prof. medicine U. Md. Sch. Medicine, Balt., 1974-81; assoc. prof. medicine Tufts U., Boston, 1981-88, dir. human studies USDA Human Nutrition Rsch. Ctr. on Aging, 1981—, assoc. dir. USDA Human Nutrition Rsch. Ctr. on Aging, 1983—, sr. scientist USDA Human Nutrition Rsch. Ctr. on Aging, 1987—, prof. medicine and nutrition, 1988—; staff physician dept. medicine sect. gastroenterology New England Med. Ctr. Hosps., Boston, 1981—; chmn. sci. adv. bd. Nat. Dairy Coun., Chgo., 1987-91; mem. pretest com. Am. Bd. Internal Medicine, Phila., 1990—. Author: Nutritional Status of Boston Elderly, 1991; contbr. articles to profl. jours. Mem. Hyde Park Community Conf., Chgo., 1972-74, Famine Policy Ctr. Com., Boston, 1985-88; mem. So. Iraq cons. team UNICEF, N.Y.C., 1991. Major U.S. Army, 1969-71, Vietnam. Recipient Global Medicine award Assn. U.S. Army, 1971, rsch. award Chgo. Soc. Gastroenterology, 1974, Rsch. Devel. award VA Career Devel. Program, 1975-78. Fellow ACP; mem. Am. Gastroent. Soc., Am. Inst. Nutrition (grad. nutrition edn. com. 1989-90), Am. Coll. Nutrition, Am. Soc. Clin. Nutrition, Soc. for Internat. Nutrition Rsch. Democrat. Roman Catholic. Office: Tufts U USDA Human Nutrition Rsch Ctr on Aging 711 Washington St Boston MA 02111

RUSSELL, SCOTT CHARLES, program administrator; b. Kalamazoo, Feb. 18, 1936; s. Theodore Roosevelt and Ruth (Lowe) R.; m. Judith Ann Hagerman, June 14, 1958 (div. May 1976); children: Kristin Elizabeth, Theodore Lowe; m. Janet Marilyn Smith, Aug. 6, 1978. BS, Cen. Mich. U., 1957; MBA, Ohio U., 1983. Enlisted USN, 1959, advanced through grades to comdr., 1975, ret., 1981; mktg. rep. IBM Corp., Glendale, Calif., 1969-72; mgmt. systems analyst Gen. Dynamics Corp., San Diego, 1972-73; purchasing mgr. NCR Corp., San Diego, 1973-80; dir. purchasing NCR Corp., Cambridge, Ohio, 1980-85; dir. materials mgmt. NCR Corp., Ithaca, N.Y., 1985-87; dir. materials mgmt., bus. svcs. Cornell U., Ithaca, 1987—; tchr. San Diego State U., 1974-79. Bd. dirs. Challenge Industries, Ithaca, 1991. Mem. Am. Prodn. and Inventory Control Soc. (chpt. pres. 1977), Soc. for Preservation and Encouragement of Barbershop Quartet Singing in Am. (chpt. pres. 1990-91), Cambridge C. of C. (bd. dirs. 1980-82), Rotary. Republican. Episcopalian. Home: 311 Winthrop Dr Ithaca NY 14850-1736 Office: Cornell U 120 Maple Ave Ithaca NY 14850-4902

RUSSELL, SEENA, psychotherapist. BA in Edn., CUNY, 1972; MS in Counseling, L.I. Univ., 1974, Profl. Diploma in Psychol. Counseling, 1976; PhD in Organizational Behavior, Yeshiva U., 1984. Dir. Discovery Ctr. Long Island U., 1974-80; coord., program dir. Career Svcs. Ctr. Long Island U., 1980-84; assoc. prof. grad. sch. psychology Long Island U., 1985, faculty mem., 1986; dir., co-founder Mannaz Assoc., 1985—; pvt. practice, 1974—; inst. coord., faculty mem. Gestalt Synergy Inst., 1985, 86; faculty mem. SUNY, Empire State Coll., 1984, 85, Rubenfeld Synergy Tng. Inst., N.Y., 1984-85, Dowling Coll., 1983-84; adj. faculty mem. grad. counseling dept. Long Island U., 1980-82, C.W. Post campus, 1979-82; ednl. rsch. cons. Channel 67; mem. N.Y. State Task Force studying ednl. competencies for tchrs. Contbr. articles to profl. jours. Mem. Am. Assn. for Counseling and Devel., N.Y. State Counseling Assn., ASTD, Nat. Soc. for Exec. Women, Long Island Gestalt Inst., Assn. Humanistic Edn. and Psychology, Mental Health Assn. Nassau County. Home and Office: 181 Central Park Rd Plainview NY 11803-2036 also: Loews NY Hotel Lexington Ave at 51st St New York NY

RUSSELL, TED MCKINNIES, electronics technician; b. Marion, Va., Feb. 25, 1943; s. Frank and Virginia (Pollit) R.; m. Patricia Ann Gilroy, Feb. 25, 1979. B in Elec. Tech., Grantham Sch. Electronics, 1966. Sr. electronic technician DPL Svcs., 1965-76; ind. gen. contractor, 1976-78; electronics technician Teltronic Indsl. Systems, Silver Spring, 1978-80, Washington Met. Transit Authority, 1980—; pres. TMR Design, 1989—. Recipient Cert. Achievement Motorola Communications and Electronics, 1978. Home: 1414 17th St NW Apt 814 Washington DC 20036-6415 Office: Washington Met Transit Authority 600 5th St NW Washington DC 20001-2651

RUSSELL, TIMOTHY ROSS, pharmaceutical company executive; b. Hackensack, N.J., Mar. 17, 1942; s. Carl Ross and Patricia (Bradbury) R.; m. Lynn Vogel Holman, July 15, 1961; children: Patricia, Jill, Katherine, Karen, Brian. BS in Engring., Rensselaer Poly. Inst., 1964; MBA, U. Pa., 1987. Registered profl. engr., Pa. Market analyst Merck Sharp & Dohme, West Point, Pa., 1968-71, sr. engr. Rsch. Lab., 1971-72, mgr. ops. improvement, 1972-74, asst. to pres., 1974-75; dir. market info. McNeil Labs., Ft. Washington, Pa., 1975-77, exec. dir. planning, 1977-81; exec. dir. new products McNeil Pharm., Spring House, Pa., 1981-83, v.p. bus. devel., 1983-86, v.p. corp. rels., 1986-90; pres. Carlsson-Rensselaer Corp., Spring House, Pa., 1990—; bd. dirs. Barton & Pittinos Advt. Agy., Ft. Washington, Pa., Scandipharm, Inc., Birmingham, Ala.; mem. informal com. on prescription drug abuse AMA, Chgo., 1989; industry support collaborating Ctr. for Cancer Pain Rsch. U. Wis., 1988—; exec. in residence Temple U., Ambler, Pa., 1988. 1st lt. U.S. Army, 1964-68, lt. col. Res. Office: Carlsson Rensselaer Corp 921 Bethlehem Pike PO Box 774 Spring House PA 19477

RUSSELL, WILLIAM ALEXANDER, JR., environmental scientist; b. Hovre de Grace, Md., Nov. 12, 1946; s. William Alexander Sr. and Margaret Adams Webster (Scott) R.; m. Nancy Dion Stacey, Jan. 4, 1965 (div. June 1971); 1 child, Angela Dion; m. Lynne Allison Ertle, July 10, 1971; children: Sara Lynne, Brent William. AA, Harford Community Coll., 1973; BS, Towson State U., 1983, MA, 1991; grad., Army Mgmt. Staff Coll., 1991. Cert. EMT level III firefighter. Environ. coord. U.S. Army Aberdeen Proving Ground (Md.), 1976-81; environ. profl. protection Hdqrs. Dept. Army NAt. Guard Bur., Washington, 1981-85; environ. profl. specialist U.S. Army Environ. Hygiene Agy., Aberdeen Paving Ground, 1985—. Contbr. tech. papers. Bd. dirs. Md. Ornithological Soc., Balt., 1982—, Harford Glen Found., Bel Air, Md., 1989—; chmn. Harford County Environ. Adv. Bd., Bel Air, 1985—; vol., asst. chief, dir., others Aberdeen (Md.) Fire Dept., 1962—; asst. scout master Boy Scouts Am., 1989—. Mem. Nat. Assn. Environ. Profls., Nat. Wildlife Fedn. (life), Nat. Audubon Soc., Md. Conservation Fedn. (charter), Nature Conservancy, Internat. Geographical Honor Soc. Democrat. Home: 703 Beards Hill Aberdeen MD 21001-1776 Office: US Army Environ Hugiene Agy HSHB-MO-B Aberdeen MD 21010-5422

RUSSELL, WILLIAM B., finance executive. BA, Harvard U., 1956. Formerly sr. v.p. gen. fin. and real estate State Street Bank and Trust Co., Boston; now, pres. Fifty Assocs., Boston; treas. MASS Home Mortgage Fin. Agy., 1974-82; pres. MASS Mortgage Bankers Assn., 1979-80. Office: Fifty Assocs 160 Federal St Boston MA 02110-1702

RUSSO, ANTHONY MICHAEL, principal; b. Apr. 22, 1935; s. Domenic M. and Theresa (Calo) R. BA, U. Conn., 1957, student, 1971; MS, Cen. Conn. State U., 1963. Cert. elem. tchr., Conn. Tchr. Buncker Hill Sch., Waterbury, Conn., 1957-68, Walsh & Hyneville, Waterbury, Conn., 1970-72; prin. Duggan Elem. Sch., Waterbury, Conn., 1972-77, Antolini Elem. Sch., New Hartford, Conn., 1968-70, Maloney Elem. Sch., Waterbury, 1977-80, Barnard Elem. Sch., Waterbury, 1980-82, Carrington Elem. Sch., Waterbury, 1982—; prin. mentor Conn. Pines Acad., Hartford, 1990-91. Mem. Am. Fed. Sch. Adminstrs., Sch. Adminstrn. Waterbury (exec. bd., soc. chair 1988-92), Assn. Childhood Ednl. Internat. (pres. Waterbury chpt. 1969-70), Carrington PTA (pres. 1964-65), Bunker Hill PTA (pres. 1964-65). Republican. Roman Catholic. Home: 79 Suffolk St Waterbury CT 06704 Office: Carrington Sch 24 Kenmore Ave Waterbury CT 06708

RUSSO, DENNIS CHARLES, psychologist; b. Cleve., Feb. 11, 1950; s. Charles Martin and Helen Marie (Watrt) R.; m. Deborah Jillson, Oct. 26, 1985; children: Nicholas Charles, Amelia DeBogory. BA with honors, U. Calif., Santa Barbara, 1972, PhD, 1975. diplomate AM. Bd. Behavioral Psychology. Asst. prof. pediatrics and med. psychology Johns Hopkins U. Sch. Medicine, Balt., 1975-79; assoc. dir., dept. behavioral psychology John F. Kennedy Inst., Balt., 1975-79; assoc. prof. psychology Harvard Med. Sch., Boston, 1979-91; dir. behavioral medicine The Children's Hosp., Boston, 1979-89; dir. behavioral & pediatric programming New Medico Assocs. Inc., Boston, 1989-92; v.p. health and rehab. svcs. May Inst., Chatham, Mass., 1992—. Editor: Behavioral Pediatrics, 1982, Behavioral Medicine with the Developmentally Disabled, 1988; contbr. articles to profl. jours. Fellow APA, Am. Psychol. Soc., MAss. Psychol. Assn., Soc. Behavioral Medicine; mem. Assn. Advancement Behavior Therapy (pres. 1988-89). Office: May Inst 100 Sea View St Chatham MA 02633

RUSSO, FRANCIS BENNETT, electronics company executive; b. Bklyn., Dec. 12, 1948; s. Dante Vincent and Josephine Louise (Alessandra) R.; m. Susan Joan Russo, Mar. 10, 1974; children: Jema Nicole, Tara Jean, Cari Leah. BS in Acctg., St. Francis Coll., Loretto, Pa., 1970. Cost acct. Ozone Industries, Ozone Park, N.Y., 1972-74; cost/price analyst AIL, Deer Park, N.Y., 1974-76; controller PMI Motion Technologies, Commack, N.Y., 1976-81, v.p. fin., 1981-84, v.p. ops. and fin., 1984-89, pres., 1989-90; v.p. IMC Magnetics Corp., Jericho, N.Y., 1990—; bd. dirs. Cold Spring Harbor (N.Y.) Devel. Corp. Mem. Am. Electronics Assn. Republican. Roman Catholic. Home: 23 Hayes St Nesconset NY 11767-2635 Office: IMC Magnetics Corp 570 Main St Westbury NY 11590-4826

RUSSO, JOSEPH SALVATORE, elementary education educator; b. Fairfield, Conn., May 10, 1954; s. Joseph L. and Theresa C. (Gentile) R.; m. Nicole H. Vanderpol, Sept. 8, 1984; children: Alexander J., Julia L. BS, Northeastern U., 1977, MEd, 1980. Tchr. Kreb's Sch. Found., Lexington, Mass., 1977-80, Newton (Mass.) Pub. Schs., 1980-81, Brookline (Mass.) Pub. Schs., 1981—; organizer Brookline Tchr.'s Retreat, 1989. Named Outstanding Educator, Brookline Found., 1990. Mem. Brookline Educators Assn. (co-chmn. action team 1991). Democrat. Home: 17 Brookfield Rd Waltham MA 02154-8004 Office: Driscoll Sch 64 W Bourne Ter Jamaica Plain MA 02130-4603

RUSSO, ROBERT NICHOLAS, automotive educator; b. Weymouth, Mass., Nov. 19, 1936; s. Domenic John and Mary (Rosetti) R.; m. Mildred Diane Medeiros, Oct. 28, 1956; children: Virginia Mary, Tina Marie, Robert Nicholas Jr. Diploma, Weymouth Vocat. Inst.; cert. in auto mechanics, Fitchburg State U., 1982. Auto mechanic Connor Motors, Braintree, Mass., 1959-62, Swift & Bachmen, Quincy, Mass., 1962-71; instr., head dept. Blue Hills Regional Tech. Coll., Canton, Mass., 1971—; mem. curriculum devel. com. Pilgrim Youth Ctr., Braintree, 1980. Mem. East Weymouth Civic Assn., 1981-87; mem. South Shore Humane Soc., Weymouth, 1975—; sec., vice chmn. Weymouth Sch. Com., 1981-87; usher Immaculate Conception Parish, East Weymouth, 1980—. Recipient Contbns. Program award Ford Motor Co., 1991. Mem. NEA, Mass. Tchrs. Assn., Am. Vocat. Assn., Nat. Vocat. Assn., Cath. Charities Assns., Sons of Italy of Am., Elks. Democrat. Roman Catholic. Home: 53 Veronica Ln Weymouth MA 02189-2710 Office: Blue Hills Regional Vocat 800 Randolph St Canton MA 02021-1372

RUSSO, VINCENT FRANCIS, accountant; b. N.Y.C., Oct. 4, 1948; s. Salvatore and Marie V. (Bonacorsi) R.; m. Madeline Leykamm, June 21, 1969; children: Michael, Christopher. BBA, CUNY, 1969, MBA, 1974. CPA, Conn., N.Y. Auditor KMPG Peat Marwick, N.Y.C., 1969-70; mgr. acctg. Avis, Inc., Garden City, N.Y., 1970-75, Clairol div. Bristol-Myers, Inc., Stamford, Conn., 1979-82; internat. mgr. Xerox Corp., Greenwich, Conn., 1975-78; contr. div. N.Am. Philips Corp., Stamford, 1982-87; pvt. practice Monroe, Conn., 1987—; fin. cons. to municipalities, bus. and profls., Conn., 1987—. Mem. AICPA, Conn. Soc. CPAs, Monroe C. of C. (treas., dir.), So. Conn. Bus. Assn. (treas.), Greater Valley Bus. Assn., Bridgeport Regional Bus. Coun. Office: 158 Blackhouse Rd Trumbull CT 06611-2719

RUSSOM, PHILIP WADE, music educator; b. Dallas, Oct. 22, 1955; s. James Wallace and Ima Lodessa (Brewer) R.; m. Elisabeth Strenger, July 25, 1958. MusB, Univ. North Tex., 1978, MusM, 1980; M of Philosophy, Yale U., 1983, PhD in Music Theory, 1985. Asst. prof. Yale U., New Haven, Conn., 1985-86, Ind. U., Bloomington, 1986-87, Pa. State U., University Park, 1987-88, Brandeis U., Waltham, Mass., 1989—. Mem. Soc. for Music Theory, Am. Musicol. Soc., Coll. Music Soc., New Eng. Conf. of Music Theorists, Music Theory Soc. of N.Y. State. Office: Music Department Brandeis Univ Waltham MA 02254

RUSSOMANNO, LEE, stockbroker; b. Newark, Sept. 1, 1953; s. Leone and Carolyn (Caputo) R.; m. Nancy Joan Russell, Oct. 17, 1976; children: Scott, Jennifer. BS in Bus., Montclair State Coll., 1975. Sales rep. Burroughs, Elizabeth, N.J., 1975-77; account exec. Merrill Lynch, Toms River, N.J., 1977-84, E.F. Hutton, Shrewsbury, N.J., 1984-85; v.p. investments Dean Witter, Toms River, 1985—. Mgr. Toms River East Little League, 1986—; coach, Toms River Girls' Softball League, 1988—. Mem. Kiwanis Daybreak Club. Home: 1089 Dove St Toms River NJ 08753-3762 Office: Dean Witter 1433 Hooper Ave Toms River NJ 08753-2826

RUSSOTTO, THOMAS VINCENT, telecommunications company executive; b. Camden, N.J., Feb. 18, 1945; s. Thomas J. and Mary (DeLaurentis) R.; m. Nancy G. Teklin, Feb. 26, 1966; children: Matthew Thomas, Melanie Teklin, Marnie Tara. BS in Math, Stevens Inst. of Tech., 1966; MBA in Acctg., Loyola U., 1975; postgrad., George Washington U. Mathematician Applied Physics Lab., Laurel, Md., 1966-72; systems engr. Computer Rsch. Inc., Hyattsville, Md., 1972-74, Old Dominion Systems, Laurel, 1974-78; mgr. Tech. Svc. Corp., Suitland, Md., 1978-82; group mgr. Nmemos, Inc., Lawrenceville, N.J., 1982-83; v.p. Am. Computer and Electronics Corp., Gaithersburg, Md., 1983—; pres. Frederick Software Corp., Monrovia, Md., 1988—. Mem. IEEE. Office: Am Computer 209 Perry Pky Gaithersburg MD 20877-2143

RUST, DAVID EDWARD, museum curator; b. Normal, Ill., Dec. 30, 1929; s. Laurence Allen and Bernice (Brown) R.; m. Fiona Field, May 14, 1962 (div.); 1 dau., Marina. B.A., Harvard U., 1951; M.A. in Fine Arts, N.Y. U., 1963. With Bank of N.Y., 1951-53; mem. staff Nat. Gallery Art, Washington, 1961-83; curator French, Brit. and Spanish painting. Nat. Gallery Art; dir. exhbn. works of James Tissot; mem. profl. adv. panel Dade County Art for Pub. Places, Miami, Fla., 1987-90. Author: Small French Paintings from the Ailsa Mellon Bruce Collection, Drawings of Vincenzo Tamagni da San Gimignano, Catalogue of Old Master Paintings, Lowe Art Mus., U. Miami, 1990; co-author: Francois Boucher...100 Drawings. Mem. profl. adv.

com. Art for Pub. Places, Dade County, Fla., 1987-90. Clubs: Knickerbocker (N.Y.C.); 1925 F St. (Washington). Address: 2812 P St NW Washington DC 20007 also: 306 Elizabeth St Key West FL 33040

RUSTAGI, RAGHUVIR SHARAN, nuclear product manager; b. Rewari, India, June 7, 1936; came to U.S. 1984; s. Ratan Lal and Gomati Devi Rustagi; m. Vinod Rastogi, Jan. 30, 1963; children: Rajat, Saras. BSME, Delhi Polytechnic, Delhi, India, 1959; diploma nuclear engring., Oakridge Sch. Reactor Tech., Oakridge, Tenn., 1964; MBA, J.B. Inst. Mgmt., Bombay, India, 1974; doctoral student, Indian Inst. of Tech., Bombay, 1982. Registered profl. engr., N.J. Sci. officer Bhabha Atomic Research Ctr., Bombay, 1960-71; head safety and fuel design Nuclear Power Bd., Bombay, 1971-84; nuclear product mgr. Valcor Engring. Corp., Springfield, N.J., 1984—; vis. prof. Indian Inst. Tech., Bombay, Kanpur, India, 1980-84; author, speaker tech. seminar Inst. Engrs., India, 1980. Author tech. papers, conf. procs. Mem. sch. adv. com. South Plainfield (N.J.) Bd. Edn. Named Hon. Citizen State of Tenn., 1964. Mem. ASME (assoc.). Hindu. Home: 228 West Ave South Plainfield NJ 07080-1923 Office: Valcor Engring Corp 2 Lawrence Rd Springfield NJ 07081-3165

RUSTGI, EILEEN BOYLE, clinical psychologist; b. N.Y.C., Apr. 4, 1955; d. Francis Edward and Eileen Mary (Meagher) Boyle; m. Vinod Kumar Rustgi, Nov. 5, 1983; children: Sheila, Nina, Neil. BA, Yale U., 1977; MA, Cath. U. Am., 1980, PhD, 1986—. Intern Pacific Med. Ctr., San Francisco, 1982-83; rsch. asst. Chestnut Lodge, Rockville, Md., 1982; ednl. cons. Sidwell Friends Sch., Bethesda, Md., 1981-82. Mem. Am. Psychol. Assn. Roman Catholic.

RUSTGI, VINOD KUMAR, physician; b. Delhi, India, Jan. 24, 1954; came to U.S., 1957; s. Moti Lal and Kamla (Rohatgi) R.; m. Eileen Mary Boyle, Nov. 5, 1983; children: Sheila, Nina, Neil. BA, Yale U., 1975; MD, Johns Hopkins U., 1979. Dir. gastrointestinal rsch. Fairfax (Va.) Hosp., 1987—. Editor: Gastrointestinal and Hepatic Complications in Pregnancy, 1984, Hepatic Carcinoma, 1987, Liver Diseases, 1988, GI Infections in the Tropics, 1991; mem. editorial bd. Digestive Diseases and Scis. Jour., 1991—. Fellow Stanford U., NIH; recipient Fellowship award Am. Liver Found., 1984. Fellow ACP, Am. Coll. Gastroenterology; mem. William Earl Clark Soc. (pres. 1991—), Cosmos Club. Hindu. Office: 3027 Javier Rd Fairfax VA 22031-4607

RUSZKOWSKI, ROBERT LEE, city official, audit manager; b. Bklyn., Apr. 24, 1947; s. Leonard Stanley and Eleanor Joan (Buczkowski) R.; m. Kathleen Schmidt, Aug. 10, 1968; children: Dana, Jill, Robert Lee Jr. BS, St. John's U., Jamaica, N.Y., 1969; postgrad., Iona Coll., 1970-73. Tchr. math. and sci. Holy Name of Jesus Sch., Stamford, Conn., 1969-71; mgmt. analyst City of Stamford, 1972-73, internal auditor, 1973-81, auditor/budget dir., 1973-79, mgr. internal audit, 1981—; chmn. supervisory com. Stamford Mcpl. Employees Fed. Credit Union, 1985-86, v.p. bd. dirs., 1986. Coach Babe Ruth League Baseball, Pop Warner Football, Cath. Youth Orgn. Basketball, Stamford, 1969-71. Mem. Inst. Internal Auditors, Am. Mgmt. Assn., Internat. Assn., Assessing Officers, Omicron Delta Epsilon. Roman Catholic. Office: City of Stamford 888 Washington Blvd Stamford CT 06901-2930

RUTA, PHILIP RALPH, editor, publisher; b. N.Y.C., Oct. 7, 1931; s. Vincent and Delphina (Palumbo) R.; m. June 1, 1958; children: Doreen, Lisa, Vincent. BS in Banking and Fin., NYU, 1954. Mgr. loan dept. U.S. Trust Co. of N.Y., N.Y.C., 1956-66; pres. Joseph A. Schrager & Co. Inc., Bronx, 1966-81; stockbroker Kidder Peabody & Co., White Plains, N.Y., 1982-88; editor, pub. Ruta Fin. Newsletter, Bronxville, N.Y., 1988—. Republican. Roman Catholic. Home and Office: 49 Sunnybrook Rd Bronxville NY 10708

RUTGERS, KATHARINE PHILLIPS (MRS. FREDERIK LODEWIJK RUTGERS), dancer; b. Butler, Pa., Sept. 2, 1910; d. Thomas Wharton and Alma (Sherman) Phillips; m. Frederik Lodewijk Rutgers, Feb. 2, 1942; children: Alma, Corinne Tolles. Diploma Briarcliff Coll., 1928; student L'Hermiage, Versailles, France, 1929-30; pupil ballet Vera Trefilova, Paris, Carl Raimund, Vienna, Varga Troyanoff, Budapest; pupil modern dance with Iris Barbura, Bucharest Ballet, Vincenzo Celli, N.Y.C., Igor Schwezoff, N.Y.C., Jean Yazvinsky, N.Y.C. Performed dance concerts Bucharest, 1937-40, U.S., 1941—; repertoire includes patriotic, dramatic, poetical dances, religious interpretations; dance therapist St. Barnabas Hosp., N.Y.C., 1965-70; author numerous pamphlets on dance, verses for choreographies. Chmn. ethnol. dance dept. Bruce Mus. Assocs., Greenwich, Conn., 1970—. Bd. dirs. Bruce Mus. Recipient citation for promoting culture with dance programs Nat. Fedn. Music Clubs, 1973. Mem. DAR, Conn. Fedn. Music Clubs (chmn. dance dept. 1965-66), Nat. League Am. Pen Women (local pres. 1973-78), Alliance Francaise, Mayflower Soc., Colonial Dames Am., Federated Music Club N.Y.C. (dir., dance chmn.), Met. Farm and Garden Club (dir.), Indian Harbor Club. Home: La Cova Pecks Land Rd Greenwich CT 06830

RUTH, JOLINDA S., data transfer sales executive; b. Bklyn., Mar. 4, 1956; d. Emerson Ralph and Edith (Whitney) R. BA in Polit. Sci., Boston Coll., 1978. Cert. image cons. and color analyst The Color Workshop. Mktg. rep. Xerox Corp., Hartford, Conn., 1978-80, sr. mktg. rep., 1980-82; account exec. AT&T, N.Y.C., 1982-83; sr. major account rep. Wang Labs., Inc., N.Y.C., 1983-88; sr. sales rep. Dialcom, Inc. subs. British Telecom, Inc., N.J., 1989-90; pres. The JoLinda Ruth Cons. Group, Somerset, N.J., 1989—; mktg. rep. Infonet Internat., N.Y.C., 1990—; cons., coord. weddings Redeeming Love Christian Ctr., Nanuet. N.Y., 1987—; image cons. The Color Workshop, Lebanon, N.J., 1989—. Coordinator telethon United Negro Coll. Fund, N.Y.C., 1981-83, chair publicity, 1983-85, Ebony Annual Fahion Fair Show, N.Y.C; coordinator promotions Met. Area Minority Employees, N.Y.C., 1979-82; vol. campaign coord. David Dinkins N.Y.C. Mayoral Campaign, 1989—. Mem. Persons without Ptnrs. (events coordinator 1986—), Boston Coll. Alumni Assn. (N.Y. and N.J. chpt.), N.J. Assn. Women Bus. Owners. Republican. Mem. Evangelical Ch. Home: 43 Carlisle Ct Somerset NJ 08873-4403 Office: Infonet Internat 530 5th Ave New York NY 10036-5101

RUTH, RICHARD I., psychologist; b. New Haven, Sept. 15, 1953; s. Robert and Vivian (Hubelbank) R. BA, New Sch. Social Rsch., 1974; MA, Yeshiva U., 1977, PhD, 1986. Lic. psychologist, Md. Psychologist dept. preventive medicine Cornell U., Ithaca, N.Y., 1979-80; staff psychologist Gouverneur Hosp., N.Y.C., 1980-82, Elizabeth (N.J.) Gen. Med. Ctr., 1982-83; dir. P.R. Rsch. Inst., Washington, 1983—; clin. coord. emergency svc. mental health div. Arlington (Va.) County Dept. Human Svcs., 1984-88; pvt. practice Wheaton, Md., 1988—; cons. N.Y. State Mental Health Rsch. Found., N.Y.C., 1982-83; lectr. Trinity Coll., Washington, 1986—, U. Va., Falls Church, 1988-89, 91—; cons. psychologist Community Psychiat. Clinic, Gaithersburg, Md., 1988—. Contbr. articles to profl. jours. Mem. prevention, promotion adv. coun. Va. Dept. Mental Health, Mental Retardation and Substance Abuse Svcs., Richmond, 1987-90. Recipient cert. recognition Pres.'s Com. on Employment of Handicapped; fellow NIMH, 1975-77. Fellow Am. Orthopsychiat. Assn. (chair Study Group on Disability); mem. APA, Md. Psychol. Assn., Va. Psychol. Assn., Internat. Assn. Cross-Cultural Psychology, Latin Am. Studies Assn., Caribbean Studies Assn. Office: PR Rsch Inst PO Box 11204 Washington DC 20008-0404

RUTIGLIANO, DEBORAH GAIL, counselor; b. Lubbock, Tex., Dec. 6, 1964; d. Timothy Hart and Jane Ellen (Harris) Walsh; m. Peter Francis Rutigliano, Feb. 11, 1989. BS, Cen. Conn. State U., 1986, MS, 1991. Cert. secondary educator in social studies, guidance counselor. Asst. swim coach Naugatuck (Conn.) High Sch., 1988—, tchr., counselor, 1986—; counselor Student Assistance Team, Naugatuck, 1991—. EMT Woodbury (Conn.) Vol. Ambulance. Mem. NEA, ASCD, Am. Sch. Counselors Assn., Conn. Edn. Assn., Naugatuck Edn. Assn. Democrat. Congregationalist. Home: 20 White Deer Rocks Rd Woodbury CT 06798 Office: Naugatuck High Sch 543 Rubber Ave Naugatuck CT 06770-3797

RUTINS, KARLIS VISVALDIS, corporate executive; b. Riga, Latvia, May 17, 1937; s. Alfreds Karlis and Anna Lepik R.; student Brown U., 1955-58; B.S.M.E., Newark Coll. Engring., 1963; M.S.I.E., Columbia U., 1965; m. Margita Anderson, July 9, 1966; 1 son, Erik Karlis. Indsl. engr. Eastman Kodak, Rochester, N.Y., 1963-64; systems engr. IBM, N.Y.C., 1965-66; systems mgr. Am. Hoechst Corp., Somerville, N.J., 1966—, v.p. info. systems, 1980—, v.p. organizational planning, 1983-86, pres., Chief operating officer Strategic Procurement Group, Inc., Martinsville, N.J., 1986-90, pres. The Odin Group, Inc., Florham Park, 1990—. Mem. Am. Inst. Indsl. Engrs., Quality Productivity Mgmt. Assn.

RUTKIN, RICHARD, clinical psychologist; b. N.Y.C., May 27, 1938; s. Michael and Millie (Presseisen) R.; m. Pamela Hinckley Crabtree, Jan. 21, 1970; 1 child, Dorothy. BBA, CUNY, 1960, MS in Edn., 1962; PhD, U. Houston, 1966. Sr. psychologist Inst. for Rehab. Medicine, NYU, N.Y.C., 1966-68; mem. faculty, supr. postdoctoral program in psychoanalysis NYU, N.Y.C., 1991—; attending psychologist N.Y. Hosp., N.Y.C., 1968-70; asst. prof. Cornell Med. Coll., N.Y.C., 1968-72; assoc. prof. dept. sch. svcs. CUNY, 1970—; pvt. practice, N.Y.C., 1970—; mem. faculty, supr. Inst. for Contemporary Psychotherapy, N.Y.C., 1980—; psychol. cons. Columbia Grammar and Prep. Sch., N.Y.C., 1983—. Mem. APA, N.Y. State Psychol. Assn., Psychoanalyutic Soc. NYU Postdoctoral Program. Home: 328 Barr Ave Teaneck NJ 07666-3123 Office: 27 W 86th St New York NY 10024-3615

RUTLEDGE, ARTHUR CLAYTON, JR., electronics manufacturing executive; b. Lexington, Ky., Apr. 23, 1944; s. Arthur Clayton Sr. and Margaret E. (Bosley) R.; m. Judith Marie Miller, Sept. 1962 (div. June 1971); children: Melissa Lynn; m. Diane Morrissey, Nov. 6, 1971; Dawn Michelle. BS in Bus. Adminstrn., Towson State U., 1974. V.p. EOG Inc., Hunt Valley, Md., 1991—. Contbr. articles to profl. jours. Pres. Forest Hill (Md.) Recreation Coun., 1989—. Republican. Methodist. Home: 808 Stone Haven Dr Jarreytsville MD 21084 Office: EOG Inc 10947 Golden W Dr Hunt Valley MD 21030

RUTLEDGE, MYRA-ANN, historian; b. Muncie, Ind., Aug. 26, 1952; d. Myron Rutledge and JoAnn (Carmichael) Jones; m. Alan W. Johnson, Sept. 2, 1972 (div. Sept. 1977); m. Daniel Abbott Hinckley, Jan. 1, 1985. BA, Ind. U., 1973; postgrad., Ohio Inst. Photography, 1984-85. Bd. govs. Preservation Assn. for Tudor Hall, Bel Air, Md., 1988—, pres., 1992, 93, chmn. conf., 1990, 92; bd. dirs. Balt. County Hist. Soc., 1992-93. Mem. Surratt Soc., Samuel A. Mudd Soc., Lincoln Group N.Y., Lincoln Group Fla., Civil War Roundtable. Home: 39 Edgemoor Rd Lutherville Timonium MD 21093-3403

RUTMAN, ROBERT JESSE, biochemist, educator; b. Kingston, N.Y., June 23, 1919; s. Leon and Anne (Porringer) R.; B.S., Pa. State U., 1940; postgrad. U. Idaho, 1942, U. Calif., Berkeley, Ph.D., 1950; M.S., U. Pa., 1975; m. Geraldine Burwell, Jan. 1971; children—Rose, Randy, Steven, Brian, David, Ellen. Mem. teaching rsch. staffs Jefferson U., Phila., 1950-53; rsch. assoc. chemistry dept. U. Pa., 1954-60, assoc. prof., 1961-68, prof. biochemistry and molecular biology Sch. Vet. Medicine, 1968-87, prof. emeritus, 1987—, chmn. dept. biochemistry, 1976-80; vis. prof. U. Ibadan (Nigeria); coord. U. Pa.-U. Ibadan Exch. Agreement; expert witness on carcinogenesis. Mem. nat. steering com. Am. Found. Negro Affairs, also co-chmn. sci. and tech. div.; pres. C.W. Henry Home and Sch. Assn., 1960; pres. Phila. Citizens Com. on Pub. Edn., 1963; campaign fin. mgr. Mayoralty Campaign, Phila., 1978; bd. dirs. S.E. Pa. region Leukemia Soc., Southeastern Pa. Anti-Drug Symposium; chmn. bd. Ile-Ife Ctr. for Humanities, Parkside Human Svcs., Inc. (corp. sec.); v.p. Phila. region Martin Luther King Jr. Ctr., Pa. State Commn. Martin Luther King Celebration, Earth Regeneration Soc. (adv. bd. dirs.), Univ. Conversion Project. Served to capt. C.E., AUS, 1944-48, PTO. USPHS grantee, 1960-82. Mem. AAAS, AAUP, Am. Soc. Biol. Chemistry, Am. Chem. Soc., Am. Assn. Cancer Rsch., Phila. Cancer Club, Vet. Oncology Soc., Am. Assn. Vet. Educators, Phila. Biochemists Club (pres.), U.S. Fedn. Sci. Scholars (exec. bd.), World Fedn. Sci. Workers (exec. com.), Earth Regeneration Soc. (bd. dirs.). Office: 3900 Ford Rd Apt PH-P Philadelphia PA 19131

RUTSTEIN, HAZEL KLEBAN, journalist, publicist; b. N.Y.C., July 21, 1927; d. Milton and Mildred Ruth (Josephson) Kleban; m. Leonard Ralph Rutstein, Feb. 11, 1961 (dec. Sept. 1988). BA, Olivet Coll., 1949. Assoc. editor Haire Pub. Co., N.Y.C., 1956-58, mng. editor Giftwares and Home Fashions, 1959; ind. publicist home fashion industry N.Y.C., 1960-63; ptnr. Len Rutstein Advt., Sussex County, N.J., 1974-84; ind. editor Sussex County, N.J., 1984—. Mem. North West Jersey Assn. of Deaf, 1991—, Handicapped Svcs. Adv. Coun., Sussex County, 1990—, Task Force for Deaf and Hearing Impaired, Sussex County, 1990—, past chmn.; bd. dirs. Vis. Nurse Assn. Sussex County, 1991.

RUVOLO, LOUIS SALVATORE, surgeon; b. Bayonne, N.J., Aug. 1, 1940; s. Frank H. and Victoria (LaPilusa) R.; m. Clara A. Darcy, June 9, 1962; children: Loretta, Louis, Christine. BS, U. Notre Dame, 1962; MD, Ind. U., 1966. Chmn. dept. surgery Rancocas Hosp., Willingboro, N.J.; pres. Rancocas Valley Surgical Assocs., Willingboro, N.J. Capt. U.S. Army, 1969. Fellow Am. Coll. Surgeons; mem. Ea. Vascular Soc., N.J. Oncol. Soc., Soc. for Laparoscopic Surgery, AMA.

RUZEK, SHERYL BURT, health education educator; b. French Camp, Calif., June 15, 1945; d. Frederick Dent and DeEtte Carolyn (Hamsher) Burt; m. John B. Ruzek, Dec. 26, 1964 (div. 1979); 1 child, Jennifer Yael; m. James R. Griesemer, July 15, 1989. MA, U. Calif., Davis, 1971, PhD, 1977; MPH, U. Calif., Berkeley, 1982. Rsch. assoc. Inst. for Scientific Analysis, San Francisco, 1970-71; continuing edn. specialist U. Calif., San Francisco, 1977-81; postdoctoral fellow U. Calif., Berkeley, 1981-83; assoc. prof. health edn. Temple U., Phila., 1985-92, prof., 1992—; assoc. adj. prof. of sociology, U. Calif., San Francisco, 1983-85; consumer rep. Ob-Gyn Devices Panel, FDA, Washington, 1989—; mem. policy coun. Office of Maternal and Infant Health, Phila. Dept. Pub. Health, 1991—, policy and advocacy com. Maternity Care Coalition, Phila., 1989—. Author: The Women's Health Movement, 1978; editor: Health, Society and Policy series, Temple U. Press, 1982—; contbr. articles to profl. jours.; author/compiler/editor sci. bibliographies and other publs. in field. Adv. bd. Ctr. for Rsch. on Women, Memphis State U., 1986—, San Francisco Women's Health Ctr., 1979-84; charter mem. Nat. Women's Health Network, Washington, 1974—; founding mem. Calif. State Com. on Women and Drugs, 1974-75, founding chmn. Barbara Rosenblum Scholarship for the Study of Women and Cancer, Nat. Com. Sociologists for Women and Soc., 1988—; co-dir. Steps-in-Time Dance Co., Phila., 1988-90. Recipient prog. devel. fund for Improvement of Post-secondary Edn. for Women, Health and Healing Progs., U. Calif., San Francisco, 1983-86, rsch. grant Nat. Heart, Blood, Lung Inst., 1984-86, post-doctoral fellowship, 1981-83, rsch. fellowship Office of Edn., UCLA, 1980, grad. fellowship NSF, U. Calif., Davis, 1967-69. Mem. Am. Sociol. Assn. (med. sociology sect. 1971—), Sociologists for Women in Soc. (pres. Bay Area chpt. 1979-80, v.p. 1974-75), Soc. for Study of Social Problems (chmn., Lee Founders' award 1986-87, other offices), other. Unitarian. Office: Dept Health Edn Temple Univ 304 Seltzer Hall Philadelphia PA 19122

RUZICKA, MARY FRANCES, psychologist, educator; b. Balt., Dec. 4, 1943; d. Francis Frederick Jr. and Mary Margaret (Kernan) R. BA cum laude, Georgian Ct. Coll., 1966; PhD, Fordham U., 1975. Lic. psychologist, N.J.; lic. marriage and family counselor N.J. Guidance counselor N.J. Pub. Schs., Sayreville, 1971-73; tchr. Cath. schs., South Amboy and Edison, N.J., 1966-71; prof. psychology Seton Hall U., S. Orange, N.J., 1973—; pvt. practice psychology Maplewood, N.J., 1978—; conductor workshops in field; cons. in field. Co-author: A Manual Teaching the Use of APA Style, 1976; contbr. articles to profl. jours. Fellow Am. Acad. Sexology; mem. Am. Psychol. Assn., Am. Bd. Sexology (diplomate), Internat. Coun. Psychologists, Am. Assn. Sex Edn. Therapists and Counselors. Roman Catholic. Home: 12 Northview Ter Maplewood NJ 07040-3606 Office: Seton Hall U Dept Counseling Psychology South Orange NJ 07079

RYAN, DANIEL JOHN, college administrator; b. Buffalo, June 5, 1960; s. Michael E. and Joan F. (Walther) R.; m. Sandra Suffoleto, Aug. 19, 1989. BA in Pol. Sci., Canisius Coll., Buffalo, 1982, MS in Edn., 1992. Fin. cons. First Albany Corp., Buffalo, 1982-84; confidential investigator County of Erie, Buffalo, 1984-87; econ. mkt. analyst City of Buffalo, Buffalo, 1987-90; asst. dir. career planning Canisius Coll., Buffalo, 1990—; lectr. Buffalo and Erie County Pub. Libr., Buffalo, 1990—. Pres. Univ. Dist. N. Buffalo Civic Assn., Buffalo, 1990—; v.p. Kiwanis Club of N. Buffalo, 1987-88; vice chmn. City of Buffalo rep. Com., 1989-91; chmn. Delaware Ward Rep. Com., 1985-91. Mem. Nat. Assn. Student Personnel Admininstrn., Am. Assn. Counseling & Devel., Nat. Career Devel. Assn., Am. Coll. Personnel Assn., N. Buffalo Community Devel. Corp. Republican.

RYAN, DIANE PHYLLIS, nurse; b. Buffalo, June 19, 1954; d. Edward John and Helen (Pasko) Vnuk; m. Terrance Patrick Ryan, May 14, 1977; children: Kevin Daniel, Jaclyn Nicole, Amanda Leigh, Scott Michael. BSN, D'Youville Coll., 1976; MS in Nursing, SUNY, 1980. Cert. adult nurse practitioner. Staff nurse Buffalo VA Med. Ctr., 1976-79, nurse practitioner, 1980-83, community referral nurse coordinator, 1983-92, nurse practitioner, 1992—. Contbr. articles to profl. jours. Recipient continuing edn. award Homemaker's Upjohn, Buffalo, 1976, Carol Sinicki manuscript award Am. Diabetes Educators, 1984, 1st place award 11th Ann. Discharge Planning Symposium, Soc. Hosp. Social Work Dirs., Am. Hosp. Assn. Mem. Western N.Y. Discharge Planners Assn., Western N.Y. Nurse Practitioners, Sigma Theta Tau, Kappa Gamma Pi. Office: Buffalo VA Med Ctr 3495 Bailey Ave Buffalo NY 14215-1129

RYAN, DONALD FRANCIS, consumer products executive; b. Gainesville, Fla., Mar. 13, 1942; s. Donald Francis Ryan and Lorraine Mary (Sullivan) Prentice; m. Ellen Toby Siris, Dec. 2, 1972; children: Daniel Joseph, Elizabeth Rose. Warehouseman and clk. Crown Fabrics, N.Y.C., 1964-68; sales mgr. Abaco Fabrics, N.Y.C., 1968-70; div. sales mgr. Gold MIlls, N.Y.C., 1970-74; v.p. sales-retail Duplan Inc., N.Y.C., 1974-75; pres. A. J. Siris Products, Inc., Bronx, N.Y., 1975-80, Paterson, N.J., 1980—. Cpl. USMC, 1960-64. Mem. N.Y. Athletic Club. Office: A J Siris Products Inc 10 Essex St Paterson NJ 07501-1902

RYAN, JAMES FRANCIS, performing company executive, executive producer; b. N.Y.C., May 31, 1943; s. Patrick J. and Mary W. (Cunningham) R.; m. Rose Mary Cacciolo, June 5, 1965; children: Laura, Anthony. BA, St. Peter's Coll., Jersey City, N.J., 1965. Various editorial & communications mgmt. positions IBM Corp., N.Y.C., 1965-79; v.p., exec. producer Zacks & Perrier, Inc., N.Y.C., 1979-87, sr. v.p., 1987-90, pres., chief exec. officer, 1990—. Mem. Producer's Guild. Roman Catholic. Office: Zacks Perrier & Ryan Inc 475 10th Ave New York NY 10018

RYAN, KEVIN, optometrist, physics; b. Fitchburg, Mass., Aug. 1, 1952; s. Joseph Patrick and Hazel Clare (McGuane) R. BA in English, Villanova U., 1974, BS in Biology, 1974; BS, Pa. Coll. Optometry, 1975, D of Optometry, 1978; MA in Psycholgy, U. West Haven, 1990. V.p. Uncas Foods, Uncasville, Conn., 1978-89; clinician Conn. Visual Health Ctr., Bridgeport, Conn., 1978-88, Mobile Med. Testing Svc., Bloomfield, Conn., 1985—; adj. faculty mem. U. New Haven, West Haven, Conn., 1980—. Pres. Big Bros./Big Sisters S.E. Conn., New London, 1985; active Montville (Conn.) Bd. Edn., sec., 1987. Recipient Bd. Dirs. award, Big Bros./Big Sisters S.E. Conn., 1985. Mem. KC (gen. knight 1985-87, trustee 4th degree 1988-89), Pa. Coll. Optometry Alumni Assn. (treas. 1987—, v.p. 1991—), Montville Rotary, Elks (exalted ruler 1984-85, trustee, Grand Exalted Ruler award 1986), Friendly Sons St. Patrick (pres. 1986). Democrat. Roman Catholic. Home and Office: 2203 Norwich-New London Turnpike Uncasville CT 06382

RYAN, LEE THOMAS, ceramic tile company executive; b. Camden, N.J., May 3, 1949; s. Lee E. and Ruth L. (Webb) R.; m. Diane Evelyn Noe,. July 13, 1974; children: James G., Susan R. A.Bus. Mgmt., Peirce Jr. Coll., Phila., 1969. Customer svc. rep. Am. Olean Tile Co., Bellmawr, N.J., 1970-72, sales svc. ctr. mgr., 1972-86; warehouse mgr. Dal-Tile Corp., Mt. Laurel, N.J., 1986-90; sr. estimator Tuckahoe Ceramic Tile Co., Inc., Williamstown, N.J., 1990—. Mem., past pres. Welcome Vol. Fire Co., Oaklyn, N.J., 1967-76; mem., trustee, chief Oaklyn Fire Dept., 1976—. With USAR, 1969-76. Named Vol. of the Yr., Borough Coun., Oaklyn, 1990. Mem. Firemark Circle of Am., Union Hist. Fire Soc., N.J. Fire Chiefs Assn., N.J. State Vol. Firemen's Assn., Camden County Fire Chiefs Assn. (dir. 1985—). Home: 1001 Mansion Ave Collingswood NJ 08108-3227 Office: Tuckahoe Ceramic Tile Co 1184 N Tuckahoe Rd Williamstown NJ 08094

RYAN, MAUREEN ANN, educator; b. Newburgh, N.Y., Oct. 27, 1957; d. James Augustus and Elayne-Catherine (Frayne) R. BS, Mt. St. Mary Coll., 1979; MEd, Western Md. Coll., 1985; PD, Fordham U., 1988. Special edn. tchr. Orange/Ulster Bd. of Coop. Ednl. Svcs., Goshen, N.Y., 1979—; program supr. Orange/Ulster Bd. of Coop. Ednl. Svcs., 1989, cons., 1984-87. Cub Scout Leader Boys Scouts of Am., Goshen, 1988-89; program dir. Frost Valley YMCA, Olivera, N.Y., 1984-85. Roman Catholic. Home: 72 Sherman Ave Walden NY 12586-1528 Office: Orange/Ulster BOCES Gibson Rd Goshen NY 10924

RYAN, MAURICE WILLIAM, lawyer, electrical engineer; b. S.I., Feb. 19, 1924; s. Maurice William and Margaret Marie (Sullivan) R.; m. Amelia Ferretti, Sept. 9, 1950; children: Maurice W., John S., Robert M., Rosemarie A. BEE, Manhattan Coll., 1949; LLB, St. John's U., 1959, JD, 1960. Registered profl. engr., N.Y.; bar: N.Y. 1959. Elec. engr. Emerson Garden/L.K. Comstock, N.Y.C., 1949-51, Caldwell & Scott, N.Y.C. and Dominican Republic, 1951-54, J.G. White Engring., N.Y.C., 1954-59; patent atty. Union Carbide Corp., N.Y.C. and Danbury, Conn., 1959-83, U.S. Dept. of the Army, Ft. Monmouth, N.J., 1984-89; pvt. practice atty. N.Y.C., 1989—; parliamentarian, advisor Assn. Propietarios En Costambar, Puerto Plata, Dominican Republic, 1981—; cons. U.S. Dept. of Army, Ft. Monmouth, 1989—. Active numerous civic, profl., relgious and mil. orgns.; mem. Grasmere Civic Assn., 1966. Staff sgt. AAF, 1942-45, ETO. Mem. Am. Order French Croix Guerre, 320th Bombardment Group Assn. (past pres., Gavel award 1985), Monmouth Area Flying Club. Democrat. Roman Catholic. Home: 23 Leslie Ave Staten Island NY 10305-1527

RYAN, MICHAEL CLIFFORD, lawyer; b. N.Y.C., June 21, 1948; s. Cyril R. and Margaret (Glennon) R.; m. Patricia Dolan, Sept. 4, 1971; children: Bonnie, Cliff. AB, Boston Coll., 1970; JD, Harvard U., 1974. Bar: N.Y. 1975, U.S. Dist. Ct. (so. dist.) N.Y. 1975, U.S. Ct. Appeals (2d cir.) 1975. Assoc. Cadwalader Wickersham & Taft, N.Y.C., 1974-83, ptnr., 1983—; Bd. dirs. RHM Holdings USA, Inc., Nat. Ctr. For Health Edn. Office: Cadwalader Wickersham & Taft 100 Maiden Ln New York NY 10038-4818

RYAN, PAUL LOUIS, artist; b. N.Y.C., Mar. 15, 1943; s. James Edward Jr. and Margaret Mary (Roggeman) R.; m. Rosemary Padden, May 1968 (div. 1973); 1 child, Kyra. Student, Passionist Monastic Sem., 1960-65; BA, NYU, 1967; McLuhan fellow, Fordham U., 1968-69. Video cons. N.Y. State Coun. on Arts, 1969; founder, dir. Earthscore Found., High Falls, N.Y., 1971-78; founder, exec. editor Talking Wood Mag., North Jersey, 1979-80; dir. Gaia Inst. Cathedral of St. John the Divine, N.Y.C., 1986-87; cons. Dalton Sch. Video Program, N.Y.C., 1989—. Author: Cybernetics of the Sacred, 1974, Video Mind, Earth Mind, 1992; numerous video showings, video art, conceptual art work, publs., and presentations in field. Grantee N.Y. Coun. on Arts 1988-89, 84, 82. Mem. Environment '90, Earth Environ. Group (resident artist 1987—), Reality Club (pres. 1988-90). Office: Earth Environ Group 255 W 105th St # 42 New York NY 10025-3928

RYAN, PAUL PHILLIP, executive, chief information officer; b. Stancham, Mass., July 9, 1946; s. Phillip and Priscillia (Kitteridge) R.; m. Margaret McCormack, May 10, 1975; children: James Phillip, Tristan Marie. BBA, Boston U., 1968. Systems analyst New Eng. Life, Boston, 1968-72; asst. pres. Macro Svcs. Corp., N.Y.C., 1972-75; systems mgr. Digital Equipment Corp., Maynard, Mass., 1975-76; communications mgr. William M. Mercer Co., Boston, 1976-78; gen. mgr., dir. ops. Cole Surveys Inc., Boston, 1978-80; cons. self-employed Melrose, Mass., 1980-81; v.p. data svcs. Commonwealth Auto Reinsure, Boston, 1981-89, v.p. data svcs. & strategic planning, 1989-91, chief info. officer, 1991—; adv. bd. Norex Inc., Prior Lake, Minn., 1987—, co-founder, bd. Montvale Tire Co., Woburn, Mass., 1969-75; founder, owner Charles River Cons., Boston, 1970-76. Mem. Bellevue Golf Club (v.p. 1991—), Downtown Alumni Club, Colonial Club, Boston U. Friends of Crew, Boston U. Varsity Club, North Assn. Amateur Oarsman, Union Boat Club Boston. Republican. Office: Commonwealth Auto Reinsurer 100 Summer St Boston MA 02110-2104

RYAN, PAUL RYDER, JR., editor, writer; b. Mineola, N.Y., Jan. 5, 1932; s. Paul Ryder Ryan and Lillian (Roos) Doyle; m. Ruthann Tobin, Aug. 12, 1958; children—Liane, Bethann, Paul III, Michael. Student Boston U., 1954-55, Mex. City Coll., 1955-58; B.A., Harvard U., 1981. Editor, reporter Reuters, Eng., 1960-63, N.Y. Times, Paris and N.Y.C., 1964-68; asst. to news dir. Radio Free Europe, Munich, W.Ger., 1968-70; exec. editor Drama Rev., NYU, N.Y.C., 1970-75; editor Oceanus mag. Woods Hole Oceanographic Instn., (Mass.), 1975-90; dir. corp. communications Inst. for Sci. Info., Phila., 1990—. Editor: Seabirds, Sharks and Marine Animals, 1984; contbr. articles to profl. jours. and mags. Bd. dirs. Woods Hole Theater Co., 1979-83, also dir., actor, playwright; trustee Falmouth Theater Guild (Mass.), 1984. Served with USAF, 1950-54. Recipient Acad. award for Best Fgn. Film, Acad. Motion Picture Arts and Scis., 1967, 88—; Fulbright research scholar Japan, 1988. Mem. Am. Soc. Mag. Editors, Council Biology Editors, Soc. Scholarly Pub. Democrat. Roman Catholic. Clubs: Harvard; Harvard Faculty (Cambridge). Home: 1926 Spruce St Apt 4A Philadelphia PA 19103-6613 Office: Inst for Sci Info 3501 Market St Philadelphia PA 19104

RYAN, PHILIP GLENNON, public relations counselor; b. N.Y.C., Feb. 19, 1945. s. Cyril Richard and Margaret Virginia (Glennon) R. B.A., The Cath. U. Am., 1967; postgrad. Syracuse U., 1969-70; postgrad in Polit. Sci., CUNY, 1970-1975. Dep. press sec. N.Y.C. Planning Commn., 1974-76; Ruder & Finn, Inc., N.Y.C., 1977-79; v.p. Bozell & Jacobs Pub. Rels., N.Y.C., 1979-81; pres. Philip G. Ryan, Inc., N.Y.C., 1981—. Chmn. N.Y.C. Alcoholic Beverage Control Bd., 1984-91. Herbert H. Lehman fellow for pub. and internat. affairs N.Y. State Bd. Regents, 1970-75. Mem. Pub. Rels. Soc. Am. (accredited), Phi Beta Kappa. Home: 250 W 16th St New York NY 10011-6168 Office: 80 8th Ave New York NY 10011-5126

RYAN, RICHARD, electrical engineer; b. Urbana, Ill., Feb. 6, 1935; s. John Edward and Theresa Marie Ryan; m. Shirley Ann Phelon, Sept. 17, 1934; children: Michael Edward, Cynthia Ann, Timothy James, Patrick John. BSEE, U. Conn., 1963; MS in Adminstrv. Sci., U. Hartford, 1979. Registered profl. engr., Conn., Calif.; lic. real estate broker, Conn. Electronics engr. Dynamic Controls Corp., South Windsor, Conn., 1962-66; plant elect. engr. United Aircraft Corp. Systems Ctr., Farmington, Conn., 1966-69; supr. facilities engring. Hamilton Standard, Windsor Locks, Conn., 1969-70; mgr. plant engring. Hamilton Standard, Windsor Locks, 1970-92, R Squared Inc., South Windsor, Conn., 1992—; instr. U. Hartford, Conn., 1965-68; bd. dirs. Hamilton Standard Fed. Credit Union, 1988—. Contbr. chpts. in books, 1977, 83. Town coun. mem. Town of South Windsor, 1977—, planning and zoning com. mem. 1969-77. With USN, 1955-59. Mem. Constn. Inst. (bd. govs. 1988—), Rotary (pres. 1989—). Republican. Roman Catholic. Office: R Squared Inc PO Box 586 South Windsor CT 06074-0586

RYAN, WILLIAM JOHN, JR., bank executive; b. Newark, Oct. 22, 1954; s. William John and Louise Jennie (Badvini) R.; m. Marian Frances Finn, Mar. 27, 1976; children: William John III, Shannon Margaret, Dylan Vincent. AA in Bus. Adminstrn., Union Coll., Cranford, N.J., 1983; BS in Mgmt. with high honors, Rutgers U., 1985. Buyer J.L. Hammett Co., Union, N.J., 1974-76; dist. mgr. Valentine Assocs., Northridge, Calif., 1976-79; br. mgr. The Money Store, Springfield, N.J., 1979-82; asst. v.p. consumer lending City Fed. Savs. Bank, Somerset, N.J., 1982-91; asst. v.p., area mgr. First Fidelity Bank NA, N.J., Newark, 1991—. Coach Little League baseball, West Caldwell, N.J., 1987; mem. com. West Caldwell area Boy Scouts Am., 1987. Mem. Internat. Assn. Fin. Planning, Am. Mgmt. Assn. Roman Catholic. Office: City Fed Savs Bank 1057 Stuyvesant Ave Union NJ 07083-3697

RYBA, EARLE RICHARD, metallurgy educator; b. Elyria, Ohio, June 27, 1934; s. Joseph Walter and Edna Bertha (Senkbeil) R.; m. Ruth Alyea Murdick, Sept. 1954 (div.); chldren: Elizabeth Ann, David Mark; m. Kathy Ann Lansberry, Dec. 8, 1983; children: Beth Ann, Anya Krystyna, Janos Krystof. BS in Chemistry, MIT, 1956; PhD in Phys. Metallurgy, Iowa State U., 1960. Asst. then assoc. prof. metallurgy Pa. State U., University Park, 1960—; instr., course coord. ICDD X-ray Clinic, Pa. State U., 1990-91; instr. SUNY X-ray Clinic, Albany, 1983-89. Contbr. over 60 rsch. articles to profl. publs. Recipient Wilson award Coll. Earth & Mineral Scis., 1978; NASA-ASEE summer faculty fellow, 1984, 85. Mem. Am. Crystallographic Assn. (ann. meeting chmn. 1974), The Metall. Soc. (alloy phases com. 1962—), ASM Internat., Materials Rsch. Soc., Elks, Sigma Xi, Phi Lambda Upsilon, Kappa Sigma (alumnus advisor 1965-74, 78-84). Republican. Office: Pa State U 304 Steidle University Park PA 16802

RYCOMBEL, THOMAS J., secondary educator; b. Buffalo, Sept. 20, 1940; s. Stanley Thomas and Agnes Anastasia (Petraetis) R. BA, U. Buffalo, 1962; EdM in English, SUNY, Buffalo, 1966, postgrad., 1966-70. Cert. secondary English tchr., secondary supr., N.Y., Fla. Instr. English Lauderdale Lakes Middle Sch., Ft. Lauderdale, Fla., 1979-80; instr. English Niagara Wheatfield Sch. Dist., Sanborn, N.Y., 1962-79, 80—, chmn. dept., 1985-89; reading cons. Williamsville (N.Y.) Sch. Dist., 1969-70. Contbr. to Gt. Am. Poetry Anthology, 1988. N.Y. Regents scholar, 1958-62. Mem. N.Y. State United Tchrs., SAR. Democrat. Roman Catholic. Home: 400 Getzville Rd Buffalo NY 14226-2520 Office: Niagara-Wheatfield Sch Dist 2292 Saunders Settlement Rd Sanborn NY 14132-9336

RYDER, EDWARD BREYER, IV, public relations executive; b. N.Y.C., Sept. 21, 1955; s. Edward B. III Ryder and June Adair (Herz) Woods. BA in Polit. Sci., Am. U., Washington, 1977. Dir. govt. liaison Minuteman Press Internat., Inc., Farmingdale, N.Y., 1977-79; mgr. office svcs. Reliance Fed. Savings Bank, Garden City, N.Y., 1979-87; v.p. pub. rels. govt. affairs Minuteman Press Internat., Inc., Farmingdale, 1987-91, v.p. pub. affairs, 1991—. Mem. fin. devel. com. ARC, Mineola, N.Y., 1991; co-mgr. Bayne for County Legislature, Huntington, N.Y., 1991; vol. Friends of Congressman Bob Mrazek, Huntington, 1982, 84, 86, 88, 90; worker Pres. Ford Com., Washington, 1976. Mem. Internat. Real Estate Inst., Elks, K.C. (fin. sec. 1989-90), Kiwanis (sec. 1987, 88-90, pres. 1990-91, chmn. bd. 1991-92), Oyster Bay Desert Storm Support Group (pres. 1991—). Republican. Roman Catholic. Office: Minuteman Press Internat 1640 New Hwy Farmingdale NY 11735-1510

RYDER, EDWARD FRANCIS, secondary school teacher; b. Lynn, Mass., Mar. 25, 1931; s. Edward W. and Theresa (Callahan) R. BSBA, Salem State U., 1954, EdM in Edn., 1973; EdM in Bus. Edn., Boston U., 1956. Cert. tchr., Mass. Bus. tchr. North Quincy (Mass.) High Sch., 1968—; owner, pub. Sunnyside Pub. Co., 1975—. Author: The Art of Playing Bingo and Winning Consistently, 1980, The Art of Entering Sweepstakes and Winning Consistently, 1981, How To Save a Fortune Using Refunds and Coupons, 1983, How to Unlock the Secrets of Winning and Good Luck, 1983, How You Can Achieve Total Success Through Self-Hypnosis, 1984, Where to Buy Everything Wholesale--A Book of Lifetime Savings, 1984, A Guide to Over 1,000 Things You Can Get--For Free!, 1984, The Art of Betting Horses and Winning Consistently, 1985, Blackjack: How to Play and Win Like an Expert, 1985, Hot Dice! How to Leave the Table a Winner, 1986, Winning Secrets of a Poker Master, 1986, Picking Winners at the Harness Races, 1987, Winning Consistently at the Greyhound Races, 1987, Lucky Slots!! How to Beat the Casino Bandits, 1988, Secrets of Winning at Casino Roulette, 1988, Keno: The Art of Playing and Winning, 1989, How to Play and Win at Casino Baccarat, 1989, Secrets of Winning at Video Poker, 1990, Winning Secrets of a Master Sports Bettor--Football, 1991, Winning Secrets of a Master Sports Bettor--Basketball, 1992, Winning Secrets of a Master Sports Bettor--Baseball, 1992. Roman Catholic. Home: 28 Sunnyside Rd Lynn MA 01905-1105 Office: Sunnyside Pubs 51 Willow St Box 29 Lynn MA 01903

RYDER, THOMAS O., magazine publishing executive; b. Varnville, S.C., July 19, 1944; s. Floie Fritz and Helen Ryder; m. Darlene Wood, May 4, 1963; children: Shannon, Robert, Ashley, Alyson. BA, La. State U., 1966. Subscription mgr. Life Mag., N.Y.C.; group pub. edn. periodicals Xerox Pub., Conn.; founder Edn. Today, Palo Alto, Calif., Learning Today, Palo Alto; sr. v.p. CBS Mags., N.Y.C.; pres. Am. Express Pub. and Direct Mktg. Group, N.Y.C.; faculty mem. Stanford (Calif.) Pub. Course. Contbr. articles to mags. Named to Sch. Journalism Hall of Fame, La. State U., 1987. Mem. Mag. Pubs. Am. (vice chmn.), Young Pres. Orgn. (Gotham chpt.). Office: Am Express Pub Dir Mktg Group 1120 Ave of Americas New York NY 10036

RYDZEWSKI, ROBERT STANLEY, electrical engineer; b. Swoyerville, Pa., Mar. 17, 1931; s. Stanley and Mary R.; m. Joanne Nowak. BSEE, Pa. State U., 1957. Registered profl. engr., Pa. Design engr. Fed. Pacific Electric Co., Scranton, Pa., 1958-60, Weston Instruments, Archbald, Pa., 1961-63, Smith, Miller & Assocs., Kingston, Pa., 1964—. With USN, 1949-53, PTO. Mem. NSPE, K.C. Home: 7 Sunset Dr Wyoming PA 18644

RYERSON, W. NEWTON, association executive; b. N.Y.C., Sept. 29, 1902; s. William Newton and Martha (Taft) R.; m. Jean Hamilton, May 15, 1936 (dec. Sept. 1973); children: Timothy (dec.), Amy Ryerson Borer, Marjorie, William N.; m. Henriette Keil, July 13, 1974. BS in Engring., Yale U., 1925. Cadet engr. to pers. supr. Phila. Gas Works Co., 1927-44; various positions Sun Oil Co., Phila., 1944-67; dir. placement Vt. Tech. Coll., Randolph Center, Vt., 1967-82; exec. dir. Randolph C. of C., 1983—; bd. mem. Green Mountain Econ. Devel. Corp.; vis. instr. Pa. State U., University Park, 1962-68. V.p. Swarthmore (Pa.) Sch. Bd., 1956-62; chmn. troop Boy Scouts Am., Swarthmore, 1952-55; mem. Rep. Com., Swarthmore, 1951-55; jr. warden Trinity Ch. Vestry, Swarthmore, 1953-56. Named Randolph Bus. Exec. of Yr., 1988. Mem. Vt. Assn. Chamber Execs., Vt. Soc. Career Counselors, Vt. Soc. Assn. Execs., Tau Alpha Pi, Phila. Foremen's Club, Appalachian Mountain Club. Episcopalian. Home: Randolph Center VT 05061 Office: Randolph C of C PO Box 9 Randolph VT 05060-0009

RYERSON, WILLIAM NEWTON, not-for-profit fund raising consultant; b. Phila., Mar. 9, 1945; s. W. Newton and Jean (Hamilton) R.; m. Leta C. Finch, Dec. 6, 1975. BA, Amherst Coll., 1967; M.Phil., Yale U., 1971. Dir. student intern program Population Inst., Washington, 1971-73, dir. youth and student div., 1973-79; dir. devel. Planned Parenthood Southeastern Pa., Phila., 1979-81; assoc. dir. Planned Parenthood No. New Eng., Burlington, Vt., 1981-86; pres. Ryerson & Assocs., fund raising counsel, Shelburne, Vt., 1986—; exec. v.p. Population Communications Internat., N.Y.C., 1987—. Co-author: Population Activist's Handbook, 1974. NASA trainee in biology, Yale U., 1967-70. Mem. Phi Beta Kappa, Sigma Xi (assoc.). Home and Office: 2 Collamer Cir Shelburne VT 05482-7231

RYMER, JEANNE STOCKDALE, interior design educator; b. Morgantown, W.Va., Mar. 30, 1928; d. Charles E. and Bly (Schaffer) Stockdale. AB, W. Va. U., 1949, MS in Interior Design, 1970-72; postgrad., U. N.H., 1986, Ea. Ky. U., 1977. Instr. housing and design Fairmont State Coll., W.Va., 1972-76; asst. prof. interior design Ea. Ky. U., Richmond, 1976-77; dir. McAlpin's Design Studio, Lexington, Ky., 1977-79; assoc. prof. interior design U. Del., Newark, 1979—; cons. in interior design, W.Va. and Ky., 1970-76; cons. in interior and lighting design Wilmington, Del., 1980—; lectr. in field. Contbr. articles to profl. jurs. U. Del. Innovative Instrn. grantee, 1982, rsch. grantee for energy efficient window treatments, 1983; recipient Gov.'s award for energy innovation State of Del., 1985, Nat. Dept. of Energy award for energy innovation, 1985, Environ. Design award Am. Soc. Interior Design, 1986; Energy Power Ptnrs. rsch. grantee, 1988. Mem. Am. Soc. Interior Designers, Internat. Assn. Lighting Designers (bd. dirs.), Illuminating Engring. Soc., Interior Design Educators Coun. Office: U Del Alison Hall Newark DE 19716

RYON, JOHN WALKER, III, computer science educator, consultant; b. Akron, Ohio, Jan. 6, 1940; s. John Walker Jr. and Helen Augusta (Ehlert) R.; m. Gabrielle Judith Poole, June 11, 1966 (div. Nov. 1980); 1 child, John Walker IV. BS in Physics, MIT, 1962; MS in Physics, Stevens Inst. Tech., 1968, PhD in Physics, 1970. Engring. physicist Babcock & Wilcox, Lynchburg, Va., 1962-63; rsch. asst. Sci. Teaching Ctr. MIT, Cambridge, Mass., 1963-66; programmer Diecomp, South Plainfield, N.J., 1970-72, sect. head, sr. scientist, 1972-74; asst. prof. N.J. Inst. Tech., Newark, N.J., 1974-81; assoc. prof. N.J. Inst. Tech., Newark, 1981—; cons. Mfg. Techs., Hartford, Conn., 1974-76, RCA Globcom Systems, N.Y.C., 1977, Bendix Corp., N.J., 1979-81, Bell Labs., N.J., 1981-82. Author: Designing the User Interface, 1991; contbr. articles to profl. jours. Mem. Chancellor Search Adv. Com., Trenton, N.J., 1990; vice chmn. faculty coun. N.J. Inst. Tech., 1989, chmn., 1990. Home: 3 Pheasant Run Edison NJ 08820-2931 Office: NJ Inst Tech University Heights Newark NJ 07102

RYSKAMP, CARROLL JOSEPH, chemical engineer; b. Grand Rapids, Mich., Dec. 25, 1930; s. Henry C. and Edna E. (Robinson) R.; m. Joanne Ruth Winter, Nov. 17, 1951; children: Jan C., John M., Julie K., Jay A. BS in Chem. Engring., Wayne State U., 1953. Registered profl. control systems engr. Chem. engr. Reichhold Chem. Co., Ferndale, Mich., 1953-55; process supv. and specialist Marathon Oil Co., Detroit, 1955-65; process control coordinator Marathon Oil Co., Findlay, Ohio, 1965-70; control cons. Foxboro (Mass.) Co., 1970-85; owner Process Performance Co., Foxboro, 1986. Contbr. articles to profl. jours.; patentee in field. Bristol fellow, The Foxboro Co., 1985. Sr. mem. Instrument Soc. Am. (Philip T. Sprague award, 1981). Republican. Home and Office: 48 Prospect St Foxboro MA 02035-1724

RYTTER, LAWRENCE JENSEN, company executive; b. Balt., Jan. 14, 1945; s. Otto Jensen and Margaret (Rau) R.; m. Roberta Lange, June 21, 1968; children: Randall, Reginald. BSEE, Va. Poly. Inst., 1968; MEE, Johns Hopkins U., 1975, MAS, 1979. Program mgr. AAI Corp., Hunt Valley, Md., 1975-81, mgr. tng. and simulation, 1982-90, exec. v.p., 1990—; final rev. panel Dept. Transp./Nat. Advance Driving Simulator, NSF, Washington, 1991. Contbr. articles to profl. jours. Soccer coach Lutherville/Timonium (Md.) Recreation Coun., 1981-87. 1st lt. U.S. Army, 1969-71. Mem. Am. Def. Preparedness Assn., Am. Pub. Transp. Assn., Assn. of the U.S. Army, Assn. of Unmanned Vehicle Systems, Fire and Emergency Mfrs. and Svcs. Assn., Mfrs. Alliance for Productivity and Innovation, Nat. Security Indsl. Assn., Navy League of the U.S., Security Affairs Support Assn., Eta Kappa Nu. Lutheran. Office: AAI Corp 100 Industry Ln Cockeysville Hunt Valley MD 21030-3347

RYWKIN, MICHAEL, Russian studies educator; b. Wilno, Poland, Nov. 23, 1925; came to U.S., 1953; s. Solomon and Marie (Reznikov) R.; m. Liliane Carrie, 1950 (div. 1972); children: Richard, Monique, Robert; m. Christine De Lailhacar, 1978. MA, CCNY, 1955; PhD, Columbia U., 1960. Lectr. Columbia U., N.Y.C., 1956-58; instr. Colgate U., Hamilton, N.Y., 1959-60; asst. prof. NYU, N.Y.C., 1958-59, 60-62; prof. Russian studies CCNY, N.Y.C., 1963—; guide, interpreter, U.S. Dept. State, 1960-63, cons., 1978. Author: Russia in Central Asia, 1963, Moscow: Muslim Challenge, 1983, 2d edit., 1990, Soviet Society Today, 1989; editor: Russian Colonial Expansion to 1917, 1988; contbr. numerous articles to scholarly jours. IREX fellow USSR, 1984, 87; chevalier Palmes Academiques, French Ministry of Culture. Mem. Assn. for Study of Nationalities (pres. 1981—), Am. Assn. for the Advancement of Slavic Studies. Republican. Jewish. Home: 7 Walnut Ave East Quogue NY 11942-4348 Office: Russian Area Studies CCNY Convent Ave New York NY 10027-2604

RZEPKA, CHARLES JULIAN, English educator, author; b. Detroit, Sept. 24, 1949; s. Julian John and Lillian Ruth (Malinowski) R.; m. Jane Ranney, Aug. 29, 1970; children: Adam, Toby. BA, U. Mich., 1971; MA, U. Calif., Berkeley, 1975, PhD, 1979. Teaching fellow U. Calif., 1976-79; asst. prof. Boston U., 1979-89, assoc. prof., 1989—; dir. undergrad. studies English dept. Boston U., 1988—. Author: The Self as Mind, 1986 (Wilson prize 1986), Approaches To Teaching Shelley, 1990, Shelley: Twentieth Century Views, 1991; also articles. GM scholar, 1967-71; Regents fellow U. Calif., 1974-76, Boston U. fellow, 1986-87, NEH fellow, 1990. Mem. MLA, New Eng. MLA, Keats-Shelley Assn. Am., Byron Soc. Democrat. Home: 268 Bedford St Lexington MA 02173-3454 Office: Boston U English Dept 236 Bay State Rd Boston MA 02215-1403

RZEWNICKI, JANET C., state official; b. Akron, Ohio, May 21, 1953; d. Robert Myers; m. Victor Rzewnicki, June 3, 1972. B.S. in Acctg. and Fin. with distinction, U. Del. CPA. Sr. acct. Peat, Marwick Mitchell, Wilmington, Del., 1978-80; corp. acct. internat. sect. Hercules Inc., Wilmington, 1980-81; acctg. instr. U. Del., Newark, 1980-82; pvt. practice acctg., Wilmington, 1981-82; state treas. State of Del., Dover, 1983—; mem. Del. Econ. Adv. Coun. Leader People to People Del., People's Republic of China, 1985; v.p. Del. Children's Fire Safety Found.; treas., bd. dirs. March of Dimes, Newark, 1979—; bd. dirs. United Way of Del., Wilmington, 1980-82; active Gov.'s Coun. on Devel. Fin., 1982—. Mem. Nat. Assn. State Treas., AICPA, Del. Soc. CPAs, Pa. Inst. CPAs, Am. Soc. Women Accts. (bd. dirs. 1981), Beta Gamma Sigma. Republican. Office: Office of State Treas Thomas Collins Bldg PO Box 1401 Dover DE 19903-1401

SAAB, DEANNE KELTUM, real estate broker, shop owner; b. Allentown, Pa., Jan. 27, 1945; d. James A. and Agnes G. (Hanzlik) S. BA, Cedar Crest Coll., 1966; MS, U. Calif., Santa Barbara, 1973; realtors cert., Pa. State U., 1978. Cert. appraiser, Pa. Tchr. Ojai (Calif.) Unified Sch. Dist., 1966-74; real estate broker/appraiser pvt. practice, Allentown, Pa., 1978—; pres./treas. DeAnne & Assoc., Inc., Allentown, Pa., 1987—; owner Heritage Gardens, Allentown, Pa., 1981—. Mem. AAUW (various offices), Nat. Assn. Realtors, Pa. Assn. Realtors, Allentown (Pa.) Lehigh County Bd. Realtors (various offices), Soc. of Real Estate Appraisers, Cedar Crest Coll. Alumnae Assn. (various offices), Lehigh Valley Guild Craftsmen (various offices). Home: 1360 Dorney Ave Allentown PA 18103-9731

SAAD, EDWARD THEODORE, architect; b. Jerusalem, Palestine, Jan. 25, 1923; came to U.S., 1947, naturalized, 1954; s. Theodore and Kafa (Ghandour) S.; BA in Archtl. Engring., U. Nebr., 1953; m. Alice Ruth Harms, May 24, 1954; children: Roxana, Theodore, Lydia, Mark. Project mgr. Eero Saarinen & Assos., Bloomfield Hills, Mich., 1955-65; partner Harold Roth & Edward Saad, Hamden, Conn., 1965-72; prin. Edward Saad & Assos. Architects, Cheshire, Conn., 1973—. Cons. Upjohn Co., North Haven, Conn., 1966-67. Mem. AIA (corp. mem., Honor award New Eng. chpt. 1968, Honor award nat. council religious architecture div. 1970). Club: Rotary (bd. dirs. Hamden, pres. 1972-73). Important archtl. works include Mack House, Cheshire, 1966; Am. Field Service Hdqrs., N.Y.C., 1966; Surf Club West, Milford, Conn., 1967; Trinity Ch., Orange, Conn., 1967; No. Br. YMCA, Hamden, 1968; West Rock Nature Center, New Haven, 1968; Ridge Hill Sch., Hamden, 1970; Ernestine Stodelle Dance Studio, Cheshire, 1973; Cheshire Public Library, 1974; Cheshire Acad. Place Prof. Centre, 1976; Conn. 7-Up Bottling Co. Hdqrs., Meriden, 1979, R.T. Barba Hdqrs. Office Bldg., Greenwich, Conn., 1982, Cheshire Acad. Girls' Dormitory, 1984, Marshall Fisco Offices and Gymnastic Ctr., Cheshire, Conn., 1985, Dowling Ford Offices and Comml. Complex, Cheshire, 1986, A.C.E.S. Staff Devel. Ctr., Hamden, Conn., 1987, Church St. Sch., Hamden, 1987, Circuit-Wise Mfg. Fair Cities, Chihuahua, Mexico, 1988; cons. architect Cheshire Acad. Address: 608 S Brooksvale Rd Cheshire CT 06410

SAALBACH, WILLIAM FREDERICK, management consultant, economics expert witness; b. Pitts., Aug. 22, 1921; m. Betty Mae Paull; children: Christine, Pamela, Frederick. BS in Metal. Engring., U. Pitts., 1943, MLitt in Phychology, 1949, Phd in Bus. Adminstrn. and Econs., 1960; LLD (hon.), Washington and Jefferson Coll., 1985. Asst. to dean of men U. Pitts., 1946-52; pers. adminstr. rsch. div. Consol. Coal Co., Library, Pa., 1952-60, pers. cons., 1960-69; prof. econs. and bus. Washington and Jefferson Coll., Washington, Pa., 1960-84, chair dept., 1962-67, 77-84; pvt. practice Pitts., 1984—. Author: (textbook) The Consumer and the American Economy, vols. 1-5, 1974, 75; monthly columnist Coal Age, Mgmt. Forum, 1969-75; editor Washington Box Topics, 1968-83, Cargotainer Topics, 1970-76. With USNR, 1944-46. Mem. Am. Econ. Assn. Home and Office: 2513 Shenandoah Dr Pittsburgh PA 15241-2829

SABIDO, ALMEDA ALICE, mental health facility administrator; b. Blairsville, Pa., Sept. 24, 1928; d. George Jackson and Dora Irene (Byrd) McClellen; m. Frederick Lionel Harrison, Feb. 1, 1963; children: Frederick L.H., Derek M. BS in Secondary Edn., Indiana U. of Pa., 1950; MSW cum laude, U. Pitts., 1958. Staff psychiat. social worker S.I. Mental Health Soc., 1958-63, supr. psychiat. social worker, 1963-66, asst. dir. psychiat. social work, 1967-69, dir. psychiat. social work, 1969-81, acting dir. Children's Community Mental Health Ctr., 1981, dir. Children's Community Mental Health Ctr., 1982—. Mem. N.Y. Urban League, N.Y.C., 1991, Nat. Coun. Negro Women, S.I., 1991, NAACP, S.I., 1991. Mem. NASW, S.I. Com. on Child and Adolescent Mental Health (pres. 1984-86), S.I. Mental Health Coun. (sec. 1982-84), S.I. Mental Health Soc. (Richard M. Silberstein award 1991). Presbyterian. Home: 142 Benedict Ave Staten Island NY 10314-2315 Office: SI Mental Health Soc 669 Castleton Ave Staten Island NY 10301-2028

SABIN, MARC LESLIE, aerospace executive; b. Roswell, N.Mex., Mar. 25, 1944; s. Louis Simon Sabin and Sarah Francis Levine Freedman; m. Helen Marie Hill, June 30, 1974; children: Shanan Lorin, Ethan Evan. BS, USAF Acad., 1965; MS, Purdue U., 1966; postgrad., U. Fla., 1967; ScD, MIT, 1973. Commd. 2d lt. USAF, 1965, advanced through grades to lt. col., 1985; missile test controller 6555th ATW, Patrick AFB, Fla., 1966-69; lab. researcher/dir. FJ Seiler Rsch. Lab., USAF Academy, Colo., 1973-77; tech. mgr. Space div., L.A., 1978-80, program mgr., dir. Sec. of Air Force Spl. Projects, 1980-85; asst. to v.p. AIL div. Eaton Corp., Melville, N.Y., 1985-88; v.p. systems engr. Fairchild Space Co., Germantown, Md., 1988-89, v.p. adv. devel. and tech., 1989-91; mgr. spl. programs Space and Communications Group Hughes Aircraft Co., L.A., 1992—. Coach youth soccer and baseball, 1985-91. Decorated Joint Service Commendation medal. Mem. AIAA (tech. com. on space systems 1990-91), Am. Astron. Soc., Ret. Officers Assn., Am. Def. Preparedness Assn., Sigma Xi. Republican. Jewish.

SABLONE, FRANK ANTHONY, fund raising executive; b. Winthrop, Mass., May 14, 1946; s. Frank and Pearl Mary (Cotugno) S.; m. Julie Anne Laughlin, Nov. 4, 1972; children: Michael Patrick, Stephanie Anne, Christopher Andrew. AS, Mass. Bay Community Coll., 1967; BSBA, Suffolk U., 1970, MEd, 1971. Salesman Roper-Lanza, Inc., Boston, 1970-71; area mgr. Sperry & Hutchinson, N.Y.C., 1971-73; acad. dean Andover (Mass.) Jr. Coll., 1973-75; assoc. dir. devel. Suffolk Univ., Boston, 1975-79, Tufts Univ. Vet. Sch., Boston, 1979-80; dir. annual giving Joslin Diabetes Ctr., Boston, 1980-83, dir. devel., 1983-87; v.p. instnl. advancement Franklin Pierce Coll., Rindge, N.H., 1987—; trustee Suffolk Univ., Boston, 1982-85; mem. of the corp. Joslin Diabetes Ctr., Boston, 1987—. Named Outstanding Alumnus Suffolk Univ., Boston, 1985. Mem. Coun. for Advancement and Support of Edn., Nat. Soc. Fund Raising Execs., Planned Giving Group New Eng., Long Meadow Golf Club. Democrat. Home: 22 Erlin Rd Chelmsford MA 01824-2244

SABO, JACK CHARLES, surgeon; b. Bklyn., Sept. 26, 1936; s. Solomon and Nettie S.; B.A., Rutgers U., 1957; M.D., Jefferson Med. Coll., 1961; m. Marilyn Elaine Padgursky, June 21, 1959; children—Stephen, Robert, Elizabeth. Intern, Kings County Hosp., Bklyn., 1961-62, resident in gen. and thoracic surgery 1962-66, 68-70; USPHS fellow Downstate Med. Center, Bklyn., 1963-64; practice medicine specializing in surgery and thoracic surgery, Lakewood, N.J., 1970—, Whiting and Toms River, N.J., 1979—; mem. staff Paul Kimball Hosp., chmn. dept. surgery, 1982-84, sec. med. dental staff, 1978-81, pres. med. dental staff, 1984-86, staff Community Meml. Hosp. Adv. Med. Explorers Post 4, 1974—; mem. council Boy Scouts Am., 1975—; trustee Temple Beth Am, 1973—, v.p., 1976-78, pres., 1978-79. Served as capt. M.C., U.S. Army, 1966-68. Diplomate Am. Bd. Surgery, Am. Bd. Thoracic Surgery. Fellow ACS, Am. Coll. Chest Physicians, Acad. Medicine N.J.; mem. AMA, Ocean County Med. Soc., Am. Thoracic Soc., N.J. Thoracic soc., Alpha Omega Alpha, Phi Beta Kappa. Clubs: Rotary (dir. 1978-80, pres. 1983-84) (Lakewood); Woodlake Country (dir. 1976-78). Office: 5 Prospect St Lakewood NJ 08701

SABOT, RICHARD HENRY, economics educator, researcher, consultant; b. N.Y.C., Feb. 16, 1944; s. Arnold G. and Victoria (Gomberg) S.; m. Judith A. Plunkett, Sept. 9, 1969; children: Diana, Christopher, Oliver, Julia. BA, U. Pa., 1966, Oxford U., 1968; MA, Oxford U., 1970, DPhil, 1973. Rsch. officer Inst. Econs. and Stats. Oxford (Eng.) U., 1972-74; rsch. economist World Bank, Washington, 1974-84; prof. econs. Williams Coll., Williamstown, Mass., 1984—; sr. rsch. fellow Internat. Food Policy Rsch. Inst., Washington, 1987-92; sr. rsch. fellow country econs. dept. World Bank, 1992—; cons. OECD Devel. Ctr., Paris, 1971-74, Internat. Inst. Applied Systems Analysis, Vienna, Austria, 1972-73, Harvard Inst. for Internat. Devel., Cambridge, Mass., 1985-88, World Bank, 1985—, IFPRI, 1992—. Author: Economic Development and Urban Migration, 1979, Education Productivity and Inequality, 1990; editor: Migration and the Labor Market in Developing Countries, 1982, Unfair Advantage, 1991; contbr. numerous articles to scholarly jours. Trustee Nat. Child Rsch. Ctr., Washington, 1978-

8l; mem. nat. bd. Fund for Improvement Post-Secondary Edn., Washington, 1987—. Rsch. grantee Ford Found., Mellon Found., Rockefeller Found., World Bank; Fulbright fellow, Thouron fellow, Danforth fellow. Mem. Am. Econ. Assn., Royal Econ.l Soc., United Oxford and Cambridge U. Club (London), Williams Club (N.Y.C.), Mt. Greylook Ski Club (bd. dirs. 1984-85). Home: Birch Hollow Oblong Rd Williamstown MA 01267 Office: Williams Coll Fernald House Williamstown MA 01267

SABOURIN, STEVEN MARK, safety and environmental services manager; b. Holyoke, Mass., Jan. 22, 1960; s. Albert William and Irene Elizabeth (Hadvab) S.; m. Beverly Ann Hicks, May 13, 1979; children: Amanda Lee, Michael Steven, Kelly Lynn. AS in Engring. and Sci., Springfield (Mass.) Tech. Coll, 1981; BSME, Western New Eng. Coll., 1988. Cert. emergency response technician, hazard communication trainer, waste water operator, Mass. Quality control technician Advance Offset Plate, Holyoke, Mass., 1980-85, quality control mgr., 1985-87; prodn. mgr. Cookson Graphics, Holyoke, 1987-89, safety/environ. engr., 1989-91; safety/environ. engr. Anitec (Div. Internat. Paper), Holyoke, 1991—; mem. Holyoke Hazmat Task Force Com., 1990—, Mayor's Indsl. Devel. Adv. Com., Holyoke, 1990—; speaker Ams. with Disabilities Act Seminar/Return to Work Ctr., Holyoke, 1991; cons. Freundoffer, Elgin, Ill., 1990; liaison with pub. and regulatory ofcls. Author safety progs./policies in field. Sunday Sch. tchr. Tabernacle Bapt. Ch., Chicopee, Mass., 1984—; coach youth basketball/baseball, Granby, Mass., 1989—; equipment dir. Granby Athletic Assn., 1991; participant Elect Doug Dagarin/State Sen., Granby, 1990. Recipient Nat. Merit commendation Nat. Merit Scholarship Corp., 1977. Mem. ASME, Am. Soc. Safety Engrs., Nat. Fire Protection Assn. Republican. Office: Anitec PO Box 348 Holyoke MA 01041-0348

SACCENTE, VINCENT ULYSSES, dentist; b. N.Y.C., Oct. 16, 1946; s. John and Mary Dolores (Acciavatti) S.; m. Regina Marie Heuerman, Oct. 30, 1971; children: Kenneth, Carolyn. BS, Rensselaer Poly., 1968; MBA, Xavier U. Ohio, 1971; DDS, SUNY, Buffalo, 1976; cert. in prosthodontics, NYU, 1991; cert. in endodontics, Nassau County Med. Ctr., 1980, cert. in oral surgery, 1981. Engr. Procter & Gamble, Cinn., 1968-72; pvt. practice N.Y.C., 1976—; attending dentist Eger Nursing Home, S.I., N.Y., 1976—, dir. dental svcs., 1977-87; clin. asst. dentistry Seaview Hosp., S.I., 1978-80; jr. attending dentist Nassau County Med. Ctr., S.I., 1982-83; mem. med. bd. Eger Nursing Home, S.I., 1977—. Com. mem. Boy Scouts Am., S.I., 1988—. Fellow Acad. Gen. Dentistry; mem. ADA, Richmond County Dental Soc. Roman Catholic. Office: 1896 Richmond Rd Staten Island NY 10306

SACCO, JOHN MICHAEL, accountant; b. N.Y.C., Oct. 17, 1952; s. Anthony Carmine and Angelina (Pellegrino) S. BS, St. John's U., 1974. CPA, N.Y. Staff acct. Price Waterhouse & Co., N.Y.C., 1974-75; semi-sr. acct. Seidman & Seidman, CPAs, White Plains, N.Y., 1976-77; sr. acct. Diamond Internat. Corp., N.Y.C., 1977-79, Burns Internat. Security Services, Inc., Briarcliff Manor, N.Y., 1979-81; acctg. mgr. Burns Integrated Systems, Inc., Briarcliff Manor, N.Y., 1981-83; pvt. practice acctg. White Plains, N.Y., 1978—. Mem. AICPA, N.Y. Soc. CPAs. Republican. Roman Catholic. Home: 9 Tanglewood Rd Pleasantville NY 10570-2529 Office: 709 Westchester Ave White Plains NY 10604-3103

SACCO, RITA, corporate foundation administrator; b. N.Y.C., Aug. 8, 1937; d. Frank and Nisedy (Micheli) S.; m. Michael Aivaz, July 21, 1957 (div. June 1961); m. Robert Noonan, June 28, 1991. Grad. high sch., Union, N.J., 1955. Legal sec. Goldberg & Cerrato, Esquire, Freehold, N.J., 1957-60, Dominick A. Mirabelli, Esquire, Elizabeth, N.J., 1960-71; adminstrv. sec. Schering-Plough Corp., Kenilworth, N.J., 1971-75, assoc. community affairs, 1975-84; corp. officer, asst. sec. Schering-Plough Found., Madison, N.J., 1985—. Mem. adv. bd. St. Elizabeth Hosp., Elizabeth, 1991, mem. steering com. capital campaign, 1989-91; trustee St. Clares-Riverside Found., Denville, N.J., 1984. Mem. Roselle Golf Club (pool com.). Roman Catholic. Office: Schering-Plough Found 1 Giralda Farms Madison NJ 07940-1010

SACCO, RUSSELL, community employment coordinator, clergyman; b. East N.Y.C., June 3, 1944; s. Paul and Anna (Borgia) S.; m. Rose Ann Caruso, Oct. 5, 1969; children: Vincent Paul, Mark Russell. AAS in Advt., SUNY, Farmingdale, 1964; BS in Mgmt. and Communications, Adelphi U., 1983. Ordained minister East Meadow Assembly. Advt. artist Phillips, Miller, Speyer & Frost, Amityville, N.Y., 1968-73; mgr. creative svcs. dept. Doubleday Book & Music Clubs, Garden City, N.Y., 1973-82, mgr. customer svc., 1982-89; pres., founder Christiangram Ministries, Inc., Deer Park, N.Y., 1988—; employment tng. specialist United Cerebral Palsy Assn., Greater Suffolk, N.Y., 1991-92; community employment coord. United Cerebral Palsy Assn., Kings Park, 1992—. Author poem; producer, performer Cassettes First Fruit and Visitation Healing, 1987, 89. With U.S. Army, 1965-68. Mem. Am. Assn. Christian Counselors, L.I. Better Bus. Bur. (bd. dirs. 1987-89), Internat. Cops for Christ (adv. bd. 1991—, music dir. 1987—), Direct Mktg. Assn. (customer rels. coun. 1989), Internat. Platform Assn. Office: Christiangram Ministries Inc PO Box 724 Deer Park NY 11729

SACHAR, DAVID BERNARD, gastroenterologist, medical educator; b. Urbana, Ill., Mar. 2, 1940; s. Abram Leon and Thelma (Horwitz) S.; m. Joanna Maud Belford Silver, Aug. 29,1 961; children: Mark Benson, Kenneth Hulbert Belford. AB magna cum laude, Harvard U., 1959, MD cum laude, 1963. Diplomate Bd. Gastroenterology Am. Bd. Internal Medicine. Intern medicine Beth Israel Hosp., Boston, 1963-65, resident, 1967-68; asst. chief clin. rsch. Pakistan-SEATO Cholera Rsch. Lab., Dhaka, Bangladesh, 1965-67; resident in gastroenterology Mt. Sinai Hosp., N.Y.C., 1968-70; from instr. to prof. medicine Mt. Sinai Sch. Medicine, CUNY, N.Y.C., 1970-92, 1st Burrill B. Crohn prof. medicine, 1992—; dir. div. gastroenterology Mt. Sinai Hosp., N.Y.C., 1983—; co-chmn. work group on inflammatory bowel disease NIH, 1973-75; expert adv. panel on gastroenterology and nutrition U.S. Pharmacopeial Conv., 1980-85; chmn. rsch. devel. com. Nat. Found. for Ileitis and Colitis, 1984-89; co-founder, sec.-treas. Burrill B. Crohn Rsch. Foun., N.Y.C., 1984—; K.H. Koster meml. lectr. Danish Soc. of Gastroenterology, 1992. Author over 130 articles and chpts. on natural history and treatment of inflammatory bowel disease; editor 7 books and monographs on gastroenterology. Trustee Bangladesh Coun. of the Asia Soc., N.Y.C., 1972-75, Bd. Edn., Englewood Cliffs, N.J., 1973-75. Sr. surgeon, comdr. USPHS,1965-67. Fellow ACP, Am. Coll. Gastroenterology (program dirs. com. 1991—, Henry Baker Presdl. lectr. 1989); mem. Am. Gastroent. Assn. (chmn. subcom. on certification 1987, 1st chmn. clin. teaching project 1984-90), Crohn's and Colitis Found. Am. (grants rev. com. and coun. 1990—, Disting. Svc. award 1991), Internat. Orgn. for Study of INflammatory Bowel Disease (1st Am. elected chmn. 1989—), Phi Beta Kappa, Alpha Omega Alpha. Office: Mt Sinai Med Ctr One Gustave L Levy Pl New York NY 10029

SACHAROW, STANLEY, chemist, consultant, writer; b. N.Y.C., Oct. 8, 1935; s. Max and Fannie (Rosenberg) S.; m. Beverly Lynn Levy, June 18, 1961; children—Scott Hunter, Brian Evan. A.B., Hunter Coll., 1957, M.A., 1965. Engr. Standard Packaging Corp., Clifton, N.J., 1960-65; sales engr. Archer Aluminum, Winston-Salem, N.C., 1965-67; tech. service mgr. Reynolds Metals Co., Richmond, Va., 1967-84; exec. dir. The Packaging Group Inc., Milltown, N.J., 1984—; cons. world wide basis, The Packaging Group Inc., 1984—. Author: Food Packaging, 1970; Principles of Packaging Development, 1972; A Packaging Primer, 1979; Packaging Regulations, 1979. Contbr. articles to profl. jours. Recipient Golden Keys award Club Printing N.Y. 1969, Best Tech. Article award Chilton Press 1974. Mem. Packaging Inst., Am. Chem. Soc., Coblentz Soc., Inst. Dirs. (U.K.), Inst. Packaging (U.K.). Republican. Clubs: Napoleonic Soc. (Clearwater, Fla.), Victorian Soc. (Phila.). Avocations: antiques; writing; Napoleonic battles. Home: 70 Valley Forge Dr East Brunswick NJ 08816-3278 Office: Packaging Group Inc PO Box 345 Milltown NJ 08850-0345

SACHDEV, VED PARKASH, neurosurgeon; b. Mitranwali, India, Feb. 22, 1932; came to U.S., 1968; s. Girdhari Lal and Amar Kaur Sachdev; m. Ranjit Kaur Sachdev, Apr. 17, 1970; children: Ulka, Rivka. MB BS, Govt. Med. Coll., Amritsar, Panjab, India, 1955. Diplomate Am. Bd. Neurosurgery. Asst. prof. neurosurgery Med. Inst., Chandigarh, India, 1964-69; intern Lorain County Hosp., Ohio, 1969-70; resident in neurosurgery Mt. Sinai Med. Ctr., N.Y.C., 1970-73, from asst. to assoc. clin. prof. dept. neurosurgery, 1974-88, clin. prof. dept. neurosurgery, 1988—; vice chmn. dept. neurosurgery Mt. Sinai Med. Ctr., N.Y.C., 1988-92. Author chpts. in 7 med. books. Surgeon lt., Indian Navy, 1957-60. Fellow ACS, Royal Coll. Surgeons Eng. (diplomate laryngology and otology). Home: 128 Moorland Dr Scarsdale NY 10583 Office: Mt Sinai Med Ctr Dept Neurosurgery 1148 Fifth Ave New York NY 10028

SACHER, ALEX, chemical company executive; b. Bklyn., July 24, 1922; s. David and Dinah (Epstein) S.; m. May Goldstein, June 17, 1943; children: Joel, Stephen, Felice Arne Sacher Schneier, Lisa Ann Sacher Snyder. BS, CCNY, 1943; MS, Poly. Inst. Bklyn., 1946, PhD, 1948. Fellow Mellon Inst., 1949-51; asst. rsch. mgr. Irvington div. Minn. Mining & Mfg. Co., 1951-55; tech. dir. Standard Insulation Co., East Rutherford, N.J., 1955-58; v.p. comml. devel. Hudson Pulp & Paper Corp., N.Y.C., 1958-59; pres. Dimentional Pigments, Inc. subs. Cities Svc. Co., Bayonne, N.J., 1960-62, Universal Petrochems., Inc., Whippany, N.J., 1963—; adj. prof. chemistry N.Y. Inst. Tech., 1960; mem. Nat. Acad. Scis.-NRC Conf. on Elec. Insulation, 1955-60. Contbr. articles to profl. jours. With AUS, 1943-45. Fellow AAAS, Am. Inst. Chemists, N.Y. Acad. Scis.; mem. ASTM, Am. Chem. Soc., Chem. Spltys. Mfrs. Assn., Am. Soc. Biomechanics, Soc. Plastics Engrs., Assn. Rsch. Dirs., Sigma Xi, Phi Lambda Upsilon. Home: 92 Van Ness Ct Maplewood NJ 07040-3323 Office: Universal Petrochems Inc 156 Algonquin Pky Whippany NJ 07981-1687

SACHERE, ANDREW B., physician; b. Cleve.. BS, MIT, 1979; MD, Rutgers U., 1983. Diplomate Am. Bd. Family Practice; lic. N.Y. Bd. Med. Examiners, N.H. Bd. Registration, Commonwealth of Pa. Clin. instr. family medicine Robert Wood John Med. Sch. Rutgers U. Med. and Dentistry of N.J., 1986—; pvt. practice family medicine. Fellow Am. Acad. Family Physicians; mem. Am. Acad. Family Physicians, Physicians for Social Responsibility, N.Y. Acad. Scis., Union of Concern Scientists, MIT Alumni of Princeton (bd. dirs.). Office: 87 Brunswick Woods Dr East Brunswick NJ 08816-5601

SACHS, DAVID HOWARD, surgery and immunology educator, researcher; b. N.Y.C., Jan. 10, 1942; s. Elliot and Elsie (Hurvitz) S.; m. Kristina Olsson, Mar. 15, 1969; children: Michelle, Jessica, Karin, Teviah. AB, Harvard U., 1963; DES, U. Paris, 1964; MD, Harvard U., Boston, 1968. Intern in surgery Mass. Gen. Hosp., Boston, 1968-69, dir. transplantation biology rsch. ctr. surgery dept., 1991—; prof. surgery and immunology Harvard U. Med. Sch.; chief immunology br. Nat. Cancer Inst., Bethesda, Md., 1982-90. Capt. PHS, 1970-91. Office: Mass Gen Hosp TBRC Meigh Rd # 149 Chestnut Hill MA 02167-1327

SACHS, LEE ROBERT, writer; b. Phila., May 22, 1960; s. Herbert Stanley and Claire (Glynn) S.; m. Deborah Pangle, May 4, 1991. BA, Ithaca Coll., 1982; MFA, NYU, 1987. Location scout Woody Allen Film Prodns., N.Y.C., 1986-88; writer Nickelodeon TV Network, N.Y.C., 1988; writer, producer MTV Networks, N.Y.C., 1988; screen writer Goldigger Prodns., N.Y.C., 1989; screenwriter Grusskoff/Levy Prodns., L.A., 1990-91; music video dir. Rock Video Internat., N.Y.C., 1990; columnist Premiere Mag., N.Y.C., 1990—; columnist Metropolis. Mem. Tisch Sch. of the Arts Alumni Assn. Home: 56 W 11th St Apt 6re New York NY 10011-8625

SACHS, LORRAINE PHYLLIS, professional society administrator; b. Jersey City, Feb. 25, 1936; d. Abe and Ann (Beitel) S. BA, U. Mich., 1956; MA, Columbia U., 1958. Cert. assn. exec. Asst. dir. evaluation Nat. League for Nursing, N.Y.C., 1959-69, dir. evaluation, 1969-73, dir. test svc., 1973-83; dep. exec. dir. Nat. Assn. State Bds. Accountancy, N.Y.C., 1984—. Author: Measurement and Evaluation in Nursing Education, 1980; contbr. articles to Nursing Outlook, 1975-82. Scholar U. Mich. Alumni Assn., 1987-90. Mem. Am. Assn. for Counseling & Devel., Am. Psychol. Assn., Am. Psychol. Soc., Am. Soc. Assn. Execs., Nat. Coun. on Measurement in Edn., N.Y. Assn. for Applied Psychology, N.Y. Soc. Assn. Execs. Home: 420 E 55th St Apt 6C New York NY 10022-5141 Office: NASBA 380 Lexington Ave New York NY 10168-0002

SACHS, MENDEL, physics educator; b. Portland, Oreg., Apr. 13, 1927; s. Samuel and Florence Sarah (Farber) S.; m. Yetty Herman, June 22, 1952; children: Robert R., Daniel E., Carolyn T., Michael G. AB, UCLA, 1949, MA, 1950, PhD, 1954. Researcher ednl., radiation lab. U. Calif., Livermore, 1954-56; researcher Lockheed Missiles Lab., Palo Alto, Calif., 1956-61; asst. prof. San Jose (Calif.) State Coll., 1957-61; rsch. prof. McGill U., Montreal, Can., 1961-62; assoc. prof. Boston U., 1962-66; prof. SUNY, Buffalo, 1966—. Author: Einstein Versus Bohr, 1988, Quantum Mechanics from General Relativity, 1986, General Relativity and Matter, 1982, Ideas of the Theory of Relativity, 1974. With USN, 1945-46. Home: 95 Carriage Cir Buffalo NY 14221-2142 Office: SUNY Buffalo NY 14260

SACHS, MICHAEL LEO, physical education educator, sport psychologist; b. N.Y.C., Sept. 7, 1951; s. George and Eva Sachs; m. Fay Ades; 1 child, Rachel. BS in Psychology, Union Coll., Schenectady, N.Y., 1973; MA in Gen. and Exptl. Psychology, Hollins (Va.) Coll., 1975; PhD in Sport Psychology, Fla. State U., 1980; MS in Counseling Psychology, Loyola Coll., Balt., 1989. Prof. U. Que., Trois-Rivieres, Can., 1980-83; rsch. project coord. U. Md., Balt., 1983-89; assoc. prof. dept. phys. edn. Temple U., Phila., 1989—. Assoc. editor: The Psychology of Running, 1981; co-editor: Running As Therapy: An Integrated Approach, 1984; contbr. articles to profl. jours., also chpts. to books. Fellow Assn. Advanced Applied Sport Psychology (chmn. health psychology 1985-88, pres. 1991-92); mem. APA, AAHPERD, N.Am. Soc. for Psychology Sport and Phys. Activity, Am. Assn. Mental Retardation, N.Am. Soc. Sociology of Sport, Internat. Soc. Sport Psychology, Psi Chi, Phi Epsilon Kappa, Phi Kappa Phi. Office: Temple U Dept Phys Edn 048-00 Philadelphia PA 19122

SACHTJEN, WILBUR MANLEY, management consultant; b. Madison, Wis., Oct. 23, 1927; s. Wilbur P. and Kathryn M. (Manley) S.; m. Nancy O'Neil, Aug. 25, 1956; children: Barry, Brendan, Jeffrey, Brian Todd. BBA, U. Wis., 1950; MBA, Harvard U., 1955. Security analyst Harris Trust & Savs. Bank, Chgo., 1950-53; assoc. Morgan, Stanley & Co., N.Y.C., 1955-57, McKinsey & Co., Inc., N.Y.C., 1957-64; v.p. Pfizer Internat., N.Y.C., 1964-68; planning dir. Am. Can Co., Greenwich, Conn., 1969-72; v.p., dir. Owen, Webb Assocs., Inc., N.Y.C., 1972-75; pres. Wilbur M. Sachtjen Assocs., Inc., White Plains, N.Y., 1976—. Bd. govs. Lawrence Hosp., Bronxville, N.Y., 1973-88, pres., 1975-76. Mem. Harvard Club (N.Y.C.), Siwanoy Country Club. Home: 56 Oakledge Rd Bronxville NY 10708-4903 Office: Wilbur M Sachtjen Assoc Inc 50 Main St White Plains NY 10606-1920

SACK, ALVIN LEE, military officer; b. Berwyn, Ill., Apr. 21, 1949; s. Lee O'Neil and Verle Eleanor (Puscheck) S.; m. Nancy Marie Mitchem, Sept. 23, 1978. BS in Edn., No. Ariz. U., 1971; MA, Cen. Mich. U., 1975; MBA, U. North Fla., 1983. Commd. ensign USN, 1971, advanced through grades to comdr., 1986; intelligence officer Fleet Air Reconnaissance Squadron One, Agana, Guam, 1974-77, Def. Intelligence Agy., Washington, 1977; antisubmarine warfare officer Air Anti-Submarine Squadron 28, Jacksonville, Fla., 1977-80; tactical devel. and evaluation officer sea basd ASW Wings Atlantic, Jacksonville, 1980-82; ops. officer Air Anti-submarine Squadron 22, Jacksonville, 1984-86; budget officer Office of Chief of Naval Ops., Washington, 1986-89; comptroller Naval Air Engring. Ctr., Lakehurst, N.J., 1989-91; head manpower-personnel programs budget analysis sec. Office of Chief of Naval Ops., Washington, 1991—. Chmn. fin. com. Pointe O'Woods Condo Assn., Howell, N.J., 1990. Decorated Meritorious Svc. Medal, Navy Strike Flight medal, Vietnam, others. Mem. Am. Soc. Mil. Comptrollers, Army-Navy Country Club, Beta Gamma Sigma. Republican. Lutheran. Home: 1707 Hicks Dr Vienna VA 22182-2060 Office: Office of Chief Naval Ops OP-120C Washington DC 20370

SACK, GEORGE HENRY, JR., molecular geneticist; b. Balt., Apr. 17, 1943; s. George Henry and Sophia Ann (Philippi) S. BA, Johns Hopkins U., 1965, MD, 1968, PhD, 1974. Diplomate Am. Bd. Medical Examiners, Am. Bd. Medical Genetics. Intern Johns Hopkins Hosp., Balt., 1968-69, asst. resident, 1969-70, fellow genetics, 1975-76; rsch. fellow Johns Hopkins Sch. Medicine, Balt., 1970-73; asst. prof. dept. medicine Johns Hopkins U., Balt., 1976-84, assoc. prof. dept. medicine and biological chemistry, 1984—; molecular biologist Kennedy Inst., Balt., 1982—. Contbr. articles to profl. jours. Maj. USAR, 1973-75. Andrew W. Mellon scholar Johns Hopkins U., 1976, Kennedy Found. scholar, 1982. Mem. AAAS, Am. Soc. Human Genetics, Phi Beta Kappa. Office: Johns Hopkins Hosp Blalock 1008 600 N Wolfe St Baltimore MD 21205

SACK, LUCY ANN, dance educator; b. Grove City, Pa., Mar. 1, 1945; d. Antonio C. and Blanche A. (McConnell) Isacco; m. Anthony J. Sack, Jan. 10, 1970; children: Vanessa E., Andrea M. BS in Edn. in Health Phys. Edn., Slippery Rock U., 1967, MEd in Phys. Edn., 1970; postgrad, U. Utah, 1990—. Instr. Lee's Sch. Dance, Butler, Pa., 1962-72; tchr. Moniteau Sch. Dist., West Sunbury, Pa., 1967, Rochester (Pa.) Area Sch. Dist., 1967-68; grad. asst. Slippery Rock (Pa.) U., 1968-69, instr., 1969-74, asst. prof., 1974—, asst. chairperson dept. phys. edn., 1985-87, chairperson dept. dance, 1989—; dance dir., instr. Grove City YMCA, 1988-91. Choreographer: Sucre Crystallise, 1984, Carcinoma, 1984, Winter, 1985. Cons. Irene Stacey Mental Health Clinic, Butler, 1984-86. Mem. AAHPERD, Pa. Assn. Health, Phys. Edn., Recreation and Dance (v.p. for dance 1990-91, chair for the aging 1991), Dance and the Child Internat. Democrat. Roman Catholic. Home: 118 Chestnut Ridge Rd Grove City PA 16127-9750 Office: Slippery Rock U Pa 115G Morrow FH Slippery Rock PA 16057

SACK, MICHAEL ROLAND, protective services official; b. Pa., Oct. 23, 1957; s. William Albert and Marilyn (Hale) S.; m. Michelle Maria Vial, Dec. 26, 1981; 1 child, Michael Roland Jr. Entry level acctg. degree, Maryland Rehab., Balt., 1988. Security office We. Security & Investigation, Lubbock, Tex., 1982; communication officer Tex. Tech. Med. Sch. for Police, Lubbock, Tex., 1982-83. Active Right to LIfe Orgn., 1980-89; bowler for Cystic Fibrosis, Waldorf, Md., 1988; pack treas. Cub Scouts, Waldorf, 1989. With U.S. Army, 1976.77. Recipient Recognition award U.S. Congress, 1988. Republican. Roman Catholic. Home: PO Box 1182 Waldorf MD 20604-1182

SACKEIM, HAROLD, psychologist; b. Hackensack, N.J., July 13, 1951; s. Alexander and Ruth (Frymer) S.; BA, Columbia U., 1972; BA, MA, Oxford (Eng.) U., 1974; PhD, U. Pa., 1977; m. Donna Zucchi, Oct. 9, 1977. Asst. prof. psychology Columbia U., N.Y.C., 1977-79, lectr. psychiatry Coll. Physicians and Surgeons, 1980-87; asst. prof. psychology N.Y.U., N.Y.C., 1979-81, assoc. prof., 1981-87; assoc. prof. dept. psychiatry Columbia U., N.Y.C., 1987-90, prof. dept. psychiatry, 1990—, chief dept. biol. psychiatry, 1991—; assoc. attending psychologist N.Y. State Psychiat. Inst., N.Y.C., 1980—, research scientist and dep. chief dept. biol. psychiatry, 1980-91, chief dept. biol. psychiatry, 1991—; cons. WNET, 1978, 85 pvt. practice psychology, N.Y.C., 1977—. NIMH grantee, 1981—, N.Y.U. Research Challenge Fund grantee, 1981-82, McGraw-Hill grantee, 1979-80, NIA grantee, 1985—. Mem. AAAS, Am. Coll. Neuropsychopharmacology, Am. Psychol. Assn., Am. Psychopathol. Assn., Internat. Neuropsychol. Soc., Soc. Biol. Psychiatry. Assoc. editor Jour. Social and Clin. Psychology, 1982-87; cons. editor jour. Imagination, Cognition and Personality, 1981—, Convulsive Therapy, 1985—, Neuropsychiatry, Neuropsychol. and Behavior Neurology, 1987—; contbr. numerous articles to profl. jours. Office: Columbia U Dept Psychiatry 722 W 168th St # 72 New York NY 10032-2603

SACKETT, HUGH F., financial services executive; b. Tulsa, Sept. 6, 1930; s. Hubert F. and Frances (Cozier) S.; m. Claudette Despres, Aug. 31, 1968; children: Michael Stanton, Deborah Faye, Stephanie Frances. BS in Bus. Adminstrn., Ind. U., 1955. V.p., gen. mgr. vender products group Cornelius Co., Anoka, Minn., 1969-72; group v.p. automotive Stellar Industries, Inc., L.A., also pres. lawn care group, 1972-74; exec. v.p. Jefferson Mint, San Diego, 1974-79; pres. Graver Energy Systems, Inc., East Chicago, Ind., 1976-80, HFS, Inc., Guilford, Conn., 1976—, New H.S. Industries, Inc., 1980-82, Calif. Design Group, 1980-83, Am. Prins. Holdings, Inc.; chmn. Pvt. Ledger Fin. Svcs., Inc., 1982-84, also bd. dirs.; chmn. Pacific Capital Group, 1984—; chmn. bd. Quantum Holdings Ltd., Quantum Exploration, Inc., Quantum Plans, Inc., 1989-91; pres. KLI Ventures Ltd., 1990—; chmn. exec. com. Moore's Lumber Yards & Home Ctrs., 1991—. Mem. chancellors coun. Purdue U., Calumet, Ind., 1977. With USNR, 1951-52. Mem. Soc. Mayflower Desc., Alden Kindred Am., SAR, Ind. U. Alumni Assn. (life), Nat. Assn. Life Underwriters, Guilford Keeping Soc., Goodspeed Opera Assn., Rotary, Am. Legion, Delta Tau Delta. Republican. Presbyterian, Congregationalist. Home: 204 Northfield Rd Lunenburg MA 01462 Office: 22 W Main Ayer MA 01432

SACKLOW, STEWART IRWIN, advertising executive; b. Albany, N.Y., July 29, 1942; s. Jacob David and Freda Ruth (Pearlman) S.; A.A.S., N.Y.C. Community Coll., 1962; B.S., Western Mich. U., 1965; m. Harriette Lynn Cooperman, July 2, 1967; 1 son, Ian Marc. Asst. dist. office Humble Oil & Refining Co., Inc., Albany, 1963-65; dir. advt. and sales promotion Albany Pub. Markets div. Weiss Foods, 1965-68; Golub Corp., and dir. advt. Price Chopper Discount Foods, Schenectady, 1968-78; pres., creative dir. Wolkcas Advt., Inc., 1978—; exec. dir. Ski the Catskills, 1982-84; pres. Broadcast Creations, 1985—; pres. Testimonials, Inc., 1991—. Mem. Dist. Atty.'s readiness team; active Albany County Cerebral Palsy Telethons, 1966-68; mem. fund drive com. Sta. WMHT-TV ednl. TV, 1967-74; bd. dirs. N.E. Cystic Fibrosis Found., Video Spirit; bd. dirs., mem. exec. com. Upstate Leukemia Assn.; mem. bd. Gov. Clinton council Boy Scouts Am., leader, Voorheesville, N.Y.; pres. Takundewide Home Owners Assn., 1991—. Recipient certificate merit Nat. Research Bur., 1966, Freedoms Found., 1966, Amsterdam Recorder, 1968, Retail Advt. Conf., 1969, 70, Woman's Day Mag., 1971, 72, 73, 74, 75, 76; Grand Nat. award Am. Dairy Assn., 1969, Hunt Wesson Foods, 1970; recipient 4 1st place awards Am. Advt. Fedn., 1972, Crystal Prism award, 1973; Effie award Am. Mgmt. Assn., 1972; Silver medal award Am. Advt. Fed., 1973, Addy award, 1973, 74, 75; award excellence Retail Advt. Conf., 1971; Best 15 Internat. Ads award Internat. Newspaper Advt. Execs., 1972. Mem. N.Y. Art Dirs. Club, Ad Club N.Y. (dir., 1974-79, pres., 1976-77; Am. Advt. Fedn. (bd. govs. 1975), Profl. Pub. Rels. Coun. Albany Execs. Assn. Mem. B'nai B'rith (bd. dir. housing 1992—), Capital Dist. Creative Club, Mohawk Antique Auto Club, Albany Yacht Club, Schenectady Racquet Club, KP. Home: 716 St Marks Ln Niskayuna NY 12309-4843 Office: 435 New Karner Rd Albany NY 12205-3833

SACKS, DAVID GREGORY, judge; b. Holyoke, Mass., Jan. 19, 1950; s. Edward and Esther L. (Kramer) S.; m. Deborah Ann Leopold, Apr. 12, 1986. BA, Am. U., 1971; JD, Suffolk U., 1974. Bar: Mass. 1974, U.S. Dist. Ct. Mass. 1975, U.S. Supreme Ct. 1978. Pvt. practice law Holyoke, 1975-86; assoc. justice Trial Ct. of Mass. Probate and Family Ct. Dept., Springfield, 1986—. Former chmn. Holyoke Sch. Com.; former chmn. area adv. bd. Mass. Commn. Against Discrimination. Recipient Anti-Prejudice citation Greater Holyoke Coun. of Human Understanding, 1982, Friend of Edn. award Holyoke Tchrs. Assn., 1982. Mem. Mass. Bar Found., Holyoke Bar Assn. (treas.), Hampden County Bar Assn. (former chmn. Young Lawyers sect., former mem. exec. com.), Mass. Bar Assn. (former mem. bd. dels., Hampden County Probate Bench-Bar com. 1987—, family law sect. coun. 1988-91). Office: 50 State St Springfield MA 01103-2002

SADLER, BARBARA ANN, quality assurance professional; b. Bklyn., Nov. 27, 1955; d. Raymond Theodore Jr. and Elaine Mary (Bortscheller) S. Student, Suffolk Community Coll., 1978-79, 84. Various positions CEAG Electric Corp., Hauppauge, N.Y., 1981-87; indsl. engr., aide Hazeltine Corp., Greenlawn, N.Y., 1987-88; rep. quality assurance Def. Logistics Agy., Boston, 1988—; com. chmn. Hazeltine Corp., 1987-88, bldg. rep. Hazeltine Corp., Riverhead, N.Y., 1987-88, com. mem. Ceag Electric Corp., 1985-86. Author: Workmanship Manual STD Practices and Procedures, 1986, various process specification procedure manuals, 1986-87. Served with U.S. Army, 1975. Mem. Fellow Nat. Assn. Female Execs. Republican. Roman Catholic. Home: 333 Blodger St 333 Blodget St Manchester NH 03104 Office: DLA DCMAO-Boston-GFQND Bridge St Ste 265 Manchester NH 03101-1619

SADLER, CHARLES RANDOLPH, foreign service officer, lecturer; b. Anderson, S.C., Aug. 18, 1928; s. Hosea and Ollie (Ellis) S.; m. Jacquelyn Aline Walton, Nov. 26, 1966; children: Zara Ellis. BA, Claflin Coll., 1951; M in Pub. and Internat. Affairs, U. Pitts., 1970. Cert. secondary sch. tchr., Ga. French tchr. Ga. Sch. Systems, Macon, Ga., 1951-55; applied linguistics

educator Cultural Exchange Program Dept. State, Washington, 1955-57, Ministry of Edn., Tunis, Tunisia, 1957-62; devel. economist AID, Washington, 1962-85, fgn. service officer, 1987—. Sr. fgn. svc. officer Martin Luther King Fed. Holiday Commn., 1985-92; commd. Pres. Reagan, 1987; addressed Joint Legis. Session Okla. 3d Ann. Observance King Fed. Holiday, 1988, New England Fed. Aviation Adminstrn. King Day Observance, 1992; assisted U.S. Congress and White House prepare 5 yr. extension of Martin Luther King Commn., 1989; represented commn. vice-chmn. Congressman Ralph Regula at 15th ann. MLK Celebration 16th dist. Ohio, 1990. Recipient Martin Luther King Commn. Spl. Honors award, 1992; Smith-Mundt fellow U.S. Dept. State, Washington, 1955-67; named to the Order of the Republic, Tunisia, 1978. Mem. Freemasonry Assn., Claflin Coll. Alumni Assn., Omega Psi Phi. Presbyterian. Home: 7529 Morningside Dr NW Washington DC 20012-1554

SADLER, GLENN EDWARD, English educator, writer, consultant; b. Long Beach, Calif., Dec. 8, 1935; s. Glen O. Sadler and Winifred (Thomas) S. AB, Wheaton Coll., Ill., 1958; MA, UCLA, 1960; PhD, U. Aberdeen, Scotland, U.K., 1967. Jr. Coll. Cert. Instr. Long Beach City Coll., Long Beach, Calif., 1961-62; asst. prof. Wheaton Coll., Wheaton, Ill., 1967-69; vis. prof. Schiller Coll., London, England, 1968-69; vis. fellow Edinburgh U., Edinburgh, Scotland, 1969-70; asst. prof. Westmont Coll., Santa Barbara, Calif., 1969-70; prof. of English Point Loma Coll., San Diego, 1973-80; vis. prof. UCLA, L.A., 1979-80; vis. assoc. prof. U. Calif., San Diego, 1980-84; assoc. prof. Bloomsburg U., Bloomsburg, Pa., 1984—. Contbr. articles to profl. jours. Mem. Modern Lang. Assn., Children's Lit. Assn., Nat. Coun. Tchrs. English, Internat. Asn. U. Prof. English, George MacDonald Soc., Mervyn Peake Soc., Internat. Assn. for Fantastic in the Arts. Office: Bloomsburg U Bloomsburg PA 17815

SADOCK, VIRGINIA ALCOTT, psychiatrist; b. Sofia, Bulgaria, Nov. 25, 1938; came to U.S., 1941; d. Fred and Rica (Boni) Alcott; m. Benjamin James Sadock, Oct. 20, 1963; children—James, Victoria. A.B., Bennington Coll., 1960; M.D., N.Y. Med. Coll., 1970. Diplomate Am. Bd. Psychiatry and Neurology. Instr. N.Y. Med. Coll., N.Y.C., 1973-75, dir. program in human sexuality, 1973-80, asst. prof., 1975-80; assoc. prof. psychiatry NYU Med. Ctr., N.Y.C., 1980-88, clin. prof. psychiatry, 1988—, dir. grad. edn. in human sexuality, 1980—; mem. attending staff Bellevue Hosp., N.Y.C., 1980—, Tisch Hosp., NYU Med. Ctr., 1980—. Author and asst. to editors: (with others) Comprehensive Textbook of Psychiatry, 4th edit. 1985, 5th edit. 1989. Fellow Am. Psychiat. Assn., N.Y. Acad. Medicine; mem. AMA, Soc. for Sex Therapy and Research (founding 1976), Am. Assn. Sex Educators, Counselors, and Therapists. Avocations: travel; theatre. Office: 4 E 89th St New York NY 10128-0636

SADOVE, STEPHEN IRVING, consumer products company executive; b. Washington, July 25, 1951; s. A. Robert and Harriet (Tenenbaum) S.; m. Sandra Rozenberg, Feb. 24, 1982; children: Stacy, David. BA, Hamilton Coll., 1973; MBA, Harvard U., 1975. Asst. product mgr. Gen. Foods Corp.-Desserts Div., White Plains, N.Y., 1975-76; assoc. product mgr. Gen. Foods Corp.-Desserts Div., White Plains, 1976-77, product mgr., 1977-80, group product mgr., 1980-82, category mgr., 1982-84; mktg. mgr. Gen. Foods Corp.-Meals Div., White Plains, 1984-86, bus. unit mgr., 1986-88, v.p., gen. mgr., 1988-89; exec. v.p., gen. mgr. Gen. Foods Corp.-Desserts Div., White Plains, 1989-91; pres. Clairol, Inc., 1991—; alumni coun. Hamilton Coll., Clinton, N.Y.; sr. exec. adv. bd. U.S. Hispanic C. of C., Washington. Bd. trustees, exec. com. Coun. for the Arts in Westchester, White Plains, 1990—. Home: 6 Crest Ct Armonk NY 10504-2901 Office: Clairol Inc 345 Park Ave New York NY

SAEEDPOUR, VERA BEAUDIN, cultural organization administrator, educator; b. Barre, Vt., Mar. 27, 1930; d. Harry Meyer and Gertrude (Rosenthal) Fine; m. Marcel Beaudin, Nov. 26, 1948 (div. 1975); children: Marc, Paul, Rebecca Beaudin Winston, Adam, Jeb; m. Homayoun Saeedpour, 1975 (dec. 1981). BA magna cum laude, U. Vt., 1972, MEd, 1973; EdD, Columbia U., 1976. Founder, dir. Kurdish Program, N.Y.C., 1981—, Kurdish Libr., Bklyn., 1986—, Kurdish Mus., Bklyn., 1988—, Kurdish Heritage Found. of Am., Bklyn., 1990—. Author: (with others) Genocide Watch, 1992; jour. founder Kurdish Times, 1986, Kurdish Life Quar., 1991; mem. editorial bd. Jour. Polit. Comm., 1992. Mem. Bklyn. Borough Pres.'s Task Force on Cultural Understanding, 1990—. Tchrs. Coll. fellow Columbia U., 1973; Resident scholar AIA, 1975. Jewish. Office: The Kurdish Libr 345 Park Pl Brooklyn NY 11238

SAENZ, RODOLFO FORERO, environmental engineer, civil engineer; b. San Jose, Costa Rica, Sept. 23, 1934; came to U.S., 1987; s. Efraim C. and Isabel C. (Forero) S.; m. Agnes Bartorelli, Nov. 19, 1959; children: Gaston, Carmen, Agnes, Marianella. Diploma civil engring., U. Costa Rica, 1957; postgrad., U. Minn., 1959; cert. hydroelectric engr., Elec. Power Devel. Co., 1974; cert. sanitary engring., Internat. Inst. Hydraulic and Environ. Engring., Delft, The Netherlands, 1985. Registered profl. engr., Costa Rica. Sanitary engr. SCISP/ICA-USA/MSP-CR, San Jose, 1956-61; civil engr. Inst. Costarricense de Electricidad, San Jose, 1963-70; prof. U. Costa Rica, Tokyo, 1961-70; sanitary engr. Pan Am. Health Orgn., Quito, Ecuador, 1971-73; environ. engr. Pan Am. Health Orgn., Lima, Peru, 1979-87, Washington, 1987—; advisor to the pres. Govt. of Costa Rica, San Jose, 1974-76; vice minister Ministry Agr., San Jose, 1977-78. Author: novel CARIARI, 1983; contbr. articles to profl. jours. Mem. Smithsonian Inst., Washington, 1988. Mem. Colegio Ingenieros y Arquitectos Costa Rica, Assn. Interam. Ingen. Sanitaria (Gold medal 1974), Casa Italia. Roman Catholic. Home: 6060 California Cir Apt 403 Rockville MD 20852-4805 Office: PAHO/WHO 525-23d St NW Washington DC 20032

SAFE, KENNETH SHAW, JR., fiduciary firm executive; b. Providence, Oct. 13, 1929; s. Kenneth Shaw and Louise (King) S.; m. Elizabeth Kelley, Dec. 20, 1952; children: Hope, Elizabeth, Kenneth, Thorn and Edith (triplets). AB, Harvard U., 1951. Intelligence officer CIA, Washington, 1954-56; with trust dept. Old Colony Trust Co., Bank of Boston, 1956-59; registered rep. Tucker, Anthony & R.L. Day, Boston, 1959-68; ptnr. Welch & Forbes, Boston, 1968—, mng. ptnr., 1983—. Pres. Travelers Aid Soc. Boston, 1956-82, Community Workshops, Inc., Boston, 1968—; asst. treas. Wellesley (Mass.) Coll., 1970-80; trustee Georgiana Goddard Eaton Meml. Trust, Boston, 1975—, G. Howland Shaw Found., Boston, 1977—, Manomet Bird Observatory, Plymouth, Mass., 1984—; treas. Woods Hole (Mass.) Oceanographic Inst., 1981—; bd. dirs. Beverly Land Co., Providence, 1982—; corporator New Eng. Deaconess Hosp., Boston, R.I. Hosp., Providence; chmn. bd. dirs. Boys and Girls Camps, Inc., Boston; bd. dirs., asst. treas. Boston Port and Seaman's Aid Soc. With CIC, U.S. Army, 1952-54. Mem. Boston Security Analysts Soc., Somerset Club, Duxbury Yacht Club, Marshall St. Hist. Soc., Mason, Country Club. Republican. Episcopalian. Home: 207 King Caesar Rd Duxbury MA 02332-3912 Office: Welch & Forbes 45 School St Boston MA 02108-3204

SAFER, MORLEY, journalist; b. Toronto, Ont., Can., Nov. 8, 1931; came to U.S., 1964; s. Max and Anna (Cohn) S. Student, U. Western Ont., 1952. With Reuters, London, Eng., 1955; corr., producer Canadian Broadcasting Corp., 1955-60, writer, London corr., 1961-64; corr., producer BBC, 1961; Vietnam corr. CBS, 1964-71; co-host 60 Minutes news program CBS-TV, 1971—; writer-corr. news documentary The Second Battle of Britain, 1976. Author: Flashbacks: On Returning to Vietnam, 1990. Recipient Polk award L.I.U., 1965, Overseas Press Club award, 1965, 66, Sigma Delta Chi award, 1965, Peabody award, 1965, Paul White award Radio and TV, News Dirs. Assn., 1966, 4 Emmy awards, 1981, 82, 3 Emmy awards, 1985, George Foster Peabody award, 1983, 3 prestigious awards, George Foster Peabody, Alfred I. duPont-Columbia U., Emmy for "Lenell Geter's in Jail", 60 Min. broadcast, 1984. Fellow Royal Coll. Bloviation (Edinburgh). Office: care CBS News 524 W 57th St New York NY 10019-2902

SAFFRON, MORRIS HAROLD, medical history educator, dermatological educator; b. Passaic, N.J., Jan. 28, 1905; s. Abram N. and Bertha (Feder) S. AB, Columbia U., 1925, MA, 1949, PhD, 1967; MD, U. Md., 1928. Diplomate Am. Bd. Dermatology. Intern St. Mary's Hosp., Passaic, 1928-29; clin. asst. dermatology Dispensary Mt. Sinai Hosp., N.Y.C., 1934-38; asst. to dispensary Postgrad. Med. Sch., N.Y.C., 1938-40; chief of dermatology Gardiner Gen. Hosp., Chgo., 1942, Waltham (Mass.) Regional Hosp., 1943-44; cons. Cushing Gen. Hosp., Framingham, Mass., 1943-45; prof. history of medicine Seton Hall U., Jersey City, 1958-63; vis. prof. dept. med. history U. Medicine and Dentistry of N.J., Newark; adj. prof. med. info. Kean Coll., Union, N.J., 1970-78. Author: Samuel Clossy, 1967, Rowlandson Drawings Medical, 1972, Maurus of Salerno, 1972, Surgeon to Washington, 1977; editor various newsletters and jours.;contbr. articles to med. jours. Chmn. Friends of Columbia Librs., 1967-72; trustee N.J. Hist. Soc., 1970—. Flight surgeon AUS, 1940-42; lt. col. U.S. Army, 1940-45. Recipient Presdl. Citation for Excellence Columbia U., 1974; grantee Josiah Macy Found., 1975. Fellow Am. Antiquarian Soc., Morgan Libr., Century Assn., Grolier Club; mem. AMA, Am. Dermatology Acad., Acad. Medicine N.J. (past pres., editor bull., hon. fellow 1984), N.J. Acad. Sci. (pres. 1966), Passaic County Med. Soc., Am. Assn. History Medicine, Internat. Soc. History of Medicine, Medieval Acad. Am., Archeol. Soc. Am., Med. History Soc. N.J. (founder, cons., archivist 1983—), N.J. Dermatol. Soc. (pres. 1950). Home: 912 5th Ave New York NY 10021-4159 Office: NJ Med Sch Dept Medicine 185 S Orange Ave Newark NJ 07103-2714

SAFFT, STUART J., manufacturing company executive; b. Bklyn., May 21, 1941; s. Abe and Florence Dorothy (Greenberg) S.; m. Anne De Greef; children: Andrea, Kenneth. BSME, Swarthmore Coll., 1962; MBA with distinction, Harvard U., 1964. Analyst, mktg. devel. specialist Corning (N.Y.) Glass Works, 1964-66, supr. mktg., devel. and sales, 1967; mgr. pharm. planning Sandoz, Inc., East Hanover, N.J., 1967-70, gen. mgr. hosp. supplies div., 1970-74, dir. corp. planning, devel., data services, 1975-77, v.p., treas., 1978-80; v.p. fin. and adminstrn. Sandvik, Inc., Fairlawn, N.J., 1980-83; v.p. fin. Dianon Systems, Inc., Stratford, Conn., 1984-86; v.p. fin. Rogers (Conn.) Corp., 1986-90, sr. v.p. fin., 1990—. Mem. Ambulance Assn., Old Saybrook, Conn., 1988-91. Mem. Am. Mgmt. Assn., Am. Electronics Assn., Fin. Execs. Inst. Jewish. Office: Rogers Corp 1 Technology Dr Rogers CT 06263-9999

SAFIAN, LEROY SCHELLER, radiologist; b. N.Y.C., Dec. 15, 1916; s. Harry Markus and Frances (Scheller) S.; m. Helen Hoffman, Jan. 25, 1953 (div. Nov. 1962). BS, NYU, 1938; MD, Med. Coll. Va., 1943. Diplomate Am. Bd. Radiology. Instr. radiology N.Y. Med. Coll., N.Y.C., 1962-64; asst. radiologist Coney Island Hosp., Bklyn., 1965-69, assoc. radiologist, 1969-70; asst. radiologist Maimonides Med. Ctr., N.Y.C., 1966-70; attending radiologist Golden Isles Hosp., Hallendale, Fla., 1970-71; instr. radiology Columbia Coll. Physicians & Surgeons, 1972-75, Montefiore Med. Ctr., Bronx, 1975-87; asst. prof. radiology Albert Einstein Coll. Medicine, Bronx, 1975-88; asst. attending radiologist North Cen. Hosp., Bronx, 1975-84, assoc. attending radiologist, 1984-91; hon. radiologist North Cen. Hosp., Bronx, 1992—. Recipient Cert. of Merit, Mallinckrodt Pharms., 1981. Fellow Royal Soc. Medicine; mem. Am. Coll. Legal Medicine (assoc.), N.Y. Med. Soc. (grievance com.), Fla. Med. Soc., Univ. Club, various radiol. socs. Home: 301 E 66th St New York NY 10021

SAFIOL, GEORGE E., electronics company executive; b. Bklyn., Apr. 23, 1932; s. Charles and Effie (Patika) S.; m. Demetra Karambelas, July 12, 1958; children: Olympia Safiol Twomey, Peter, Christina. BS in Engring., NYU, 1954; postgrad. Sch. Engring., Columbia U., 1954-55. V.p., gen. mgr. No. Am. Telecom, ITT, Memphis, 1957-69; exec. v.p., chief operating officer Sycor, Inc., Ann Arbor, Mich., 1969-70; v.p. investments Heizer Co., Chgo., 1970-71; sr. v.p. Gen. Instrument Corp., Chicopee, Mass., 1971-77; pres., chief exec. officer Am. Biltrite, Framingham, Mass., 1977-83; various sr. exec. positions Gen. Instrument Corp., N.Y.C., 1984-87, chief operating offficer, pres., 1987—, also dir.; pvt. practice mgmt. cons., 1983-84. Served to 1st lt. U.S. Army, 1955-57. Mem. Alpha Omega. Republican. Greek Orthodox. Club: Metropolitan (N.Y.C.). Home: 64 Juniper Rd Weston MA 02193-1358 Office: Gen Instrument Corp 767 Fifth Ave New York NY 10153-0002

SAFIRE, WILLIAM, journalist, author; b. N.Y.C., Dec. 17, 1929; s. Oliver C. and Ida (Panish) S.; m. Helene Belmar Julius, Dec. 16, 1962; children: Mark Lindsey, Annabel Victoria. Student, Syracuse U., 1947-49. Reporter N.Y. Herald Tribune Syndicate, 1949-51; corr. WNBC-WNBT, Europe and Middle East, 1951; radio-TV producer WNBC, N.Y.C., 1954-55; v.p. Tex McCrary, Inc., 1955-60; pres. Safire Pub. Relations, Inc., 1960-68; spl. asst. to Pres. Nixon, Washington, 1969-73; columnist N.Y. Times, Washington, 1973—. Author: The Relations Explosion, 1963, Plunging into Politics, 1964, Safire's Political Dictionary, 1968, rev. edit., 1972-78, Before the Fall, 1975, Full Disclosure, 1977, Safire's Washington, 1980, On Language, 1980, What's the Good Word?, 1982, (with Leonard Safir) Good Advice, 1982, I Stand Corrected, 1984, Take My Word For It, 1986, Freedom, 1987, You Could Look It Up, 1988, Words of Wisdom, 1989, (with Leonard Safir) Leadership, 1990, Language Maven Strikes Again, 1990, Fumblerules, 1990, Coming to Terms, 1991, The First Dissident, 1992, Land Me Your Eavs, 1992. Served with AUS, 1952-54. Recipient Pulitzer prize for Disting. Commentary, 1978. Republican. Office: NY Times 1627 I St NW Washington DC 20006-4007

SAGAN, CARL EDWARD, astronomer, educator, author; b. N.Y.C., Nov. 9, 1934; s. Samuel and Rachel (Gruber) S.; m. Ann Druyan; children: Alexandra, Sam; children by previous marriages: Dorion Solomon, Jeremy Ethan, Nicholas. AB with gen. and spl. honors, U. Chgo., 1954, BS, 1955, MS, 1956, PhD, 1960; ScD (hon.), Rensselaer Poly. Inst., 1975, Denison U., 1976, Clarkson Coll. Tech., 1977, Whittier Coll., 1978, Clark U., 1978, Am. U., 1980, U. S.C., 1984, Hofstra U., 1985, L.I. U., 1987, Tuskegee U., 1988; DHL (hon.), Skidmore Coll., 1976, Lewis and Clark Coll., 1980, Bklyn. Coll., CUNY, 1982; LLD (hon.), U. Wyo., 1978, Drexel U., 1986. Miller research fellow U. Calif.-Berkeley, 1960-62; vis. asst. prof. genetics Stanford Med. Sch., 1962-63; astrophysicist Smithsonian Astrophys. Obs., Cambridge, Mass., 1962-68; asst. prof. Harvard U., 1962-67; mem. faculty Cornell U., 1968—, prof. astronomy and space scis., 1970—, David Duncan prof., 1976—, dir. Lab. Planetary Studies, 1968—, assoc. dir. Center for Radiophysics and Space Research, 1972-81, Johnson Disting. lectr. Johnson Grad. Sch. Mgmt., 1985; pres. Carl Sagan Prodns. (Cosmos TV series), 1977—; nonresident fellow Robotics Inst., Carnegie-Mellon U., 1982—; NSF-Am. Astron. Soc. vis. prof. various colls., 1963-67, Condon lectr., Oreg., 1967-68; Holiday lectr. AAAS, 1970; Vanuxem lectr. Princeton U., 1973; Smith lectr. Dartmouth Coll., 1974, 77; Wagner lectr. U. Pa., 1975; Bronowski lectr. U. Toronto, 1975; Philips lectr. Haverford Coll., 1975; Disting. scholar Am. U., 1976; Danz lectr. U. Wash., 1976; Clark Meml. lectr. U. Tex., 1976; Stahl lectr. Bowdoin Coll., 1977; Christmas lectr. Royal Instn., London, 1977; Menninger Meml. lectr. Am. Psychiat. Assn., 1978, Adolf Meyer lectr., 1984; Carver Meml. lectr. Tuskegee Inst., 1981; Feinstone lectr. U.S. Mil. Acad., 1981; Pal lectr. Motion Picture Acad. Arts and Scis., 1982; Dodge lectr. U. Ariz., 1982; Disting. lectr. USAF Acad., 1983; Lowell lectr. Harvard U., 1984; Poynter fellow, Schultz lectr. Yale U., 1984; Disting. lectr. Fla. State U., 1984; Jack Disting. Am. lectr., Ind. U., Pa., 1984; Keystone lectr. Nat. War Coll., Nat. Def. U., Washington, 1984-86; Marshall lectr. Nat. Resources Def. Coun., Washington, 1985; Gifford lectr. in natural theology U. Glasgow, 1985; Lilenthal lectr. Calif. Acad. Sci., 1986; Dolan lectr. Am. Pub. Health Assn., 1986; von Braun lectr. U. Ala., Huntsville, 1987; Gilbert Grosvenor Centennial lectr. Nat. Geog. Soc., Washington, 1988; Murata lectr., Kyoto, Japan, 1989; Bart Bok Centennial lectr. Astron. Soc. of the Pacific, 1989, James R. Thompson Leadership lectr. Ill. Math. and Sci. Acad., 1991, Nehru Meml. lectr. New Delhi, 1991; other hon. lectureships; mem. various adv. groups NASA and Nat. Acad. Scis., 1959—; mem. council Smithsonian Instn., 1975—; vice chmn. working group moon and planets, space orgn. Internat. Council Sci. Unions, 1968-74; lectr. Apollo flight crews NASA, 1969-72; chmn. U.S. del. joint conf. U.S. Nat. and Soviet Acads. Sci. on Communication with Extraterrestrial Intelligence, 1971; responsible for Pioneer 10 and 11 and Voyager 1 and 2 interstellar messages; mem. Voyager Imaging Sci. Team; judge Nat. Book Awards, 1975; mem. fellowship panel Guggenheim Found., 1976—; disting. vis. scientist Jet Propulsion Lab., Calif. Inst. Tech., 1986—; researcher physics and chemistry of planetary atmospheres and surfaces, origin of life, exobiology, Mariner, Viking and Voyager spacecraft observations of planets, nuclear winter. Author: Atmospheres of Mars and Venus, 1961, Planets, 1966, Intelligent Life in the Universe, 1966, Planetary Exploration, 1970, Mars and the Mind of Man, 1973, The Cosmic Connection, 1973, Other Worlds, 1975, The Dragons of Eden, 1977, Murmurs of Earth: The Voyager Interstellar Record, 1978, Broca's Brain, 1979, Cosmos, 1980, (novel) Contact, 1985, Comet, 1985, (with Richard Turco) Path Where No Man Thought: Nuclear Winter and the End of the Arms Race; also numerous articles; editor: Icarus: Internat. Jour. Solar System Studies, 1968-79, Planetary Atmospheres, 1971, Space Research, 1971, UFO's: A Scientific Debate, 1972, Communication with Extraterrestrial Intelligence, 1973; editorial bd.: Origins of Life, 1974—, Icarus, 1962—, Climatic Change, 1976—, Science 80, 1979-82. Mem. bd. advisors Children's Health Fund, N.Y.C., 1988—. Recipient Smith prize Harvard U., 1964; NASA medal for exceptional sci. achievement, 1972; Prix Galabert, 1973; John W. Campbell Meml. award, 1974; Klumpke-Roberts prize, 1974; Priestley award, 1975; NASA medal for disting. pub. service, 1977, 81; Pulitzer prize for lit., 1978; Washburn medal, 1978; Rittenhouse medal, 1980; Peabody award, 1981; Hugo award, 1981; Seaborg prize, 1981; Roe medal, 1981; Environment Programme medal UN, 1984; SANE Nat. Peace award, 1984; Regents medal Bd. Regents Univ. of State N.Y., 1984; Ann. award Physicians for Social Responsibility, 1985; Disting. Svc. award World Peace Film Festival, 1985; Honda prize Honda Found., 1985; Nahum Goldmann medal World Jewish Congress, 1986; Ann. award of merit Am. Cons. Engrs. Coun., 1986; Maurice Eisendrath award Cen. Conf. Am. Rabbis and Union Am. Hebrew Congregations, 1987; In Praise of Reason award Com. for Sci. Investigation of Claims of the Paranormal, 1987; Konstantin Tsiolkovsky medal Soviet Cosmonautics Fedn., 1987; George F. Kennan Peace award SANE/Freeze, 1988; Oersted medal Am. Assn. Physics Tchrs., 1990, Ann. award for Outstanding TV Script Writers Guild Am., 1991, UCLA medal UCLA, 1991; NSF fellow, 1955-60; Sloan research fellow, 1963-67. Fellow AAAS (chmn. astronomy sect. 1975), Am. Acad. Arts and Scis., AIAA, Am. Geophys. Union (pres. planetology sect. 1980-82), Am. Astronautical Soc. (council 1976-81, Kennedy award 1984), Brit. Interplanetary Soc., Explorers Club (75th Anniversary award 1980); mem. Am. Phys. Soc. (Leo Szilard award 1985), Am. Astron. Soc. (councillor, chmn. div. for planetary scis. 1975-76, Mazursky award 1991), Fedn. Am. Scientists (council 1977-81, bd. sponsors 1988—, Ann. award 1985), Am. Com. on East-West Accord, Soc. Study of Evolution, Genetics Soc. Am., Internat. Astron. Union, Internat. Acad. Astronautics, Internat. Soc. Study Origin of Life (council 1980—), Planetary Soc. (pres. 1979—), Authors Guild, Am. Com. on U.S.-Soviet Rels., Phi Beta Kappa, Sigma Xi. Office: Cornell U Space Sci Bldg Ithaca NY 14853

SAGE, JAY PETER, physicist; b. Pitts., Nov. 8, 1943; s. Charles Geldman and Shirley Sandra (Rigler) S.; m. Daphnah Dayag, May 23, 1971; children: Jesse Amos, Adele Daliah. AB, Harvard Coll., 1964; MA, Harvard U., 1965, PhD, 1969. Sr. rsch. scientist rsch. div. Raytheon Co., Waltham, Mass., 1968-81; Raytheon exch. scientist Toshiba R&D Lab., Kawasaki, Japan, 1973-74; staff mem. MIT Lincoln Lab., Lexington, 1981—. Contbr. articles to profl. jours.; patentee in field. Mem. IEEE (sec.-treas. robotics chpt. 1989—). Jewish. Home: 1435 Centre St Newton MA 02159-2469 Office: MIT Lincoln Lab PO Box 73 Lexington MA 02173-9108

SAGER, GILBERT LANDIS, bank executive; b. Harrisonburg, Va., June 28, 1947; s. Roy Franklin and Beatrice (Bradfield) S.; m. Esther Kendrick Brown, Nov. 8, 1969. BA in History, George Mason Coll., 1969; MBA in Finance, Fairleigh Dickinson U., 1978. Mgmt. trainee Chem. Bank, N.Y.C., 1969-73, credit investigation, 1973-74, mgr. credit, 1974-75, credit tng., 1975-76, group mgr. fin.-adminstrn. Europe-Canada, 1976-80, internat. human resources, 1980-81; v.p. human resources Midlantic Nat. Bank, Edison, N.J., 1981-90; sr. v.p. Human Resources, The Trust Co. N.J., 1990—. Bd. dirs. Princeton (N.J.) United Meth. Ch., 1988-90; Cpl. USMC, 1969-71. Named Bus. Coord. of Yr., Inroads/N.J., 1987-88. Mem. Internat. Assn. Corp. and Profl. Recruiters (co-pres. N.J. chpt. 1989-92), Soc. for Human Resource Mgmt. Methodist. Home: 9 Woodshire Way Belle Mead NJ 08502-3118

SAGHIR, ADEL JAMIL, artist, painter, sculptor; b. Beirut, Lebanon, May 27, 1930; came to U.S., 1973; s. Jamil Khalil and Aisha Rachid (Miril) S.; m. Jindriska Antonin Moucka, Aug. 24, 1968; children: Jamil, Ryan. BA, Am. U., Beirut, 1968, teaching diploma, 1973; MFA, Pratt Inst., 1975; postgrad., NYU, 1976-79. Asst. prof. Fine Arts Inst., Lebanese U., Beirut, 1963-73; lectr. Am. Beirut U. Coll., 1972-73; adj. prof. Western Conn. State U., Danbury, 1988—; instr., sculpture Silvermine Sch. Art, New Canaan, Conn., 1989—. artist various murals and tapestries. Recipient 4th Prize, Alexandria Beiennale, Egyptian Govt., 1963, 1st prize silk tapestries Nat. Contest Lebanon, 1965, 1st prize major monuments, 1966, Fine Arts Scholarship, German Fed. Republic, Munich Acad., 1958-60; Fulbright-Hays fellow NYU, N.Y.C., 1973-79. Mem. Internat. Soc. Advancement of Living Traditions in Art, Washington Pl. Artists Assn. (pres. 1977-80), Lebanese Artists Assn. (v.p. 1964-73). Home: 20 Newfane Rd New Fairfield CT 06812-4721 Office: Western Conn State U 181 White St Danbury CT 06810-6885

SAGL, NANCY LEIGH ANN, account executive, marketing consultant; b. Bayshore, N.Y., Dec. 9, 1958; d. Robert Richard and Joan Edna (Preston) S.; m. Mark Douglas Abrams, Sept. 6, 1986. BS, Oneonta U., N.Y., 1981; MBA, Baruch Coll., N.Y.C., 1992. Tchr. 7th grade English West Babylon (N.Y.) Jr. High Sch., 1982-83; account exec. Prestige Publs., N.Y.C., 1983-84, N.Y. Law Pub., N.Y.C., 1984—. Founder Learning Ctr., 1988. Mem. Profl. Pubs. Mktg. Group, Am. Mktg. Assn.

SAGO, ANTHONY E.W., financial service executive; b. Toronto, Ont., Can., Sept. 15, 1946; s. Antonio and Julie (Zawacki) S.; m. Judith Hamilton, May 31, 1949; children: Heather, Gregory. B in Bus. Adminstrn. with honours, York U., Toronto, 1975. Cert. mgmt. acct. Acct. Gray Coach Lines, Toronto, 1967-68; sr. analyst Borden Co., Toronto, 1968-72; contr. beaver homes Beaver Lumber Molson Group, Winnepeg, Man., Can., 1973-77, mgr. fin. planning Willson Off Spec, 1977-78; sr. contr. Qualico Devels., Winnepeg, 1978-80; single family divsn. mgr. Qualico Devels., Edmonton, Alta., Can., 1980-85; v.p. Jostens Can., Winnepeg, 1985-89; pres. Jostens Can., Mississauga, Ont., 1989—. Home: 403 Winston Blvd, Cambridge, ON Canada Office: Jostens Canada Ltd, 7145 W Credit Ave, Mississauga, ON Canada L5N 6J7

SAGOFF, MARK, philosopher, educator, academic administrator; b. Boston, Nov. 29, 1941; s. Maurice and Hazel Sagoff; m. Kendra Heymann, Oct. 14, 1984; children: Jared, Amelia. AB, Harvard U., 1963; PhD, U. Rochester, 1968. Lectr. dept. philosophy Princeton (N.J.) U., 1968-69; asst. prof. dept. philosophy U. Pa., Phila., 1969-75; vis. asst. prof. dept. philosophy U. Wis., Madison, 1975-76; asst. prof. sci., tech. and soc. program Cornell U., Ithaca, N.Y., 1976-79; rsch. scholar Inst. for Philosophy and Pub. Policy U. Md., College Park, 1979-86, sr. rsch. scholar, dir. Inst. for Philosophy and Pub. Policy, 1986—; mem. pub. advisor panel Chem. Mfrs. Assn., Washington, 1989-91; panelist, author Bergen (Norway) Conf. on Sci. and the Environment, 1990, ASCEND 21 Vienna (Austria) Conf., 1991; mem. adv. panel NSF, Washington, 1991-94; mem. sci. adv. bd. biotech. U.S. EPA, Washington, 1992-95; speaker in field. Author: The Economy of the Earth, 1988; contbr. articles to profl. jours. Pew scholar, 1991-94; NSF grantee, 1981—. Democrat. Jewish. Home: 6801 Carlynn Ct Bethesda MD 20817 Office: Inst for Philosophy & Pub Policy U Md College Park MD 20742

SAGRAVES, ALLAN TODD, business education educator; b. Louisville, Mar. 13, 1930; s. Crayton Glenn and Jennie (Goodlett) S.; m. Mary Anne Bokan, June 7, 1958; children: Scott Gary, Ann Denise. BA, Colo. State Coll., 1958; M of Retailing, U. Pitts., 1961; 6th yr. diploma, U. Conn., 1964; D in Humanitarian Svc. (hon.), Briarwood Coll., 1983. Cert. bus. edn. tchr., mktg. edn. tchr. coord. Mktg. edn. tchr. Grand Junction (Colo.) High Sch., 1958-60; mktg. edn. prof. Ctrl. Conn. State U., New Britain, 1961—; cons. G. Fox Dept. Store, Hartford, Conn., 1962-64, Elec. Supplies, Inc., Hartford, 1965-67; vis. prof. Univ. Ky., Lexington, 1972-75, Western Ky. Univ., Bowling Green, 1978-80, Colo. State Univ., Ft. Collins, 1981. Author: (teaching transparencies) Distributive Education, 1971, Principles of Selling, 1974. Youth chmn. Optimist Internat., Grand Junction, Colo., 1958-60; United Way capt. Cen. Conn. State Univ., New Britain, 1986-89. Sgt. USAF, 1951-54. Mem. AAUP, Nat. Bus. Edn. Assn., Vocat. Edn. Assn. Conn. (exec. bd. mem.), Nat. Assn. Distributive Edn. Tchrs. (hon. life mem.), Distributive Edn. Clubs Am. (nat. historian 1985—, outstanding svc. award 1976, hon. life mem. 1990), Conn. Assn. Distributive Edn. Tchrs. (hon. life mem.), Masons, Elks, Am. Legion. Democrat. Methodist. Home: 318 Commonwealth Ave New Britain CT 06053-2408 Office: Ctrl Conn State U 1615 Stanley St New Britain CT 06050-4010

SAHA, DEBABRATA, electrical engineering educator; b. Habra, West Bengal, India, Mar. 3, 1955; arrived in Can., 1980; s. Gopal Chandra and Minoti Saha; m. Namita Saha, Sept. 2, 1985; children: Anjan Kumar,

Debjani. BS, U. Calcutta, India, 1976; B. Tech., U. Calcutta, 1980; MASc, U. Toronto, Can., 1982; PhD, U. Mich., 1986. Teaching/rsch. asst. U. Toronto, 1980-82; teaching asst. U. Mich., Ann Arbor, 1983-84, rsch. asst. Cooley Electronics Lab., 1984-86; asst. prof. George Washington U., Washington, 1986—. Patentee in field; contbr. articles to profl. jours. Cultural sec. Mitali, Ann Arbor, 1984-85; mem. Sanskriti, Greater Washington, 1986—, India Cultural Coord. Com., Greater Washington, 1990—. Computer, Info., and Control Engrng. fellow U. Mich., 1983-84; Nat. scholar Gov. of India, 1973-76, 76-80, Overseas Merit scholar U. Calcutta, 1980-82. Mem. IEEE (officer Washington-North Va. chpt. 1987—), Assn. Computing Machinery. Home: 2947 Waterford Ct Vienna VA 22181-6050 Office: George Washington U Dept Electronic Engrng and Computer Sci Washington DC 20052

SAHANEK, TATANA, librarian, editor; b. Prague, Czechoslovakia, Nov. 2, 1922; d. Emanuel and Frances (Blovsky) S.; naturalized, 1969; JUDr., Masaryk U., Brno, Czechoslovakia, 1947; B.L.S., U. Toronto (Ont., Can.), 1953; Ph.D. (Higher Edn. Act fellow), U. Tex.-Austin, 1973. Cataloger, Toronto Pub. Library, 1953-55; law librarian, gen. reference librarian Ont. Legis. Library, Toronto, 1956-61; head catalog and classification div. Harvard Law Sch. Library, 1962-65; head catalog dept. Law Library, U. Mich., Ann Arbor, 1965-66; translator, interpreter Dow Chem. Internat., Midland, Mich., 1967-68; librarian-translator Dow Chem. Co., Tex. div., Freeport, 1968-70; asst. librarian Antioch Sch. Law, Washington, 1972-74; editor Index to Legal Priodicals, H.W. Wilson Co., Bronx, N.Y., 1974-78; coordinator Saginaw (Mich.) Med. Ctr., 1978-79; acquisitions librarian Exec. Office of Pres. Info. Ctr., Washington, 1980—. Recipient award U. Tex. Grad. Sch. Subvention Fund, 1972; spl. achievement award Exec. Office of Pres., 1981, Dir.'s award for Disting. Service Exec. Office of Pres., 1986. Mem. Assn. Am. Law Libraries, Spl. Libraries Assn., ALA, Canadian, Ont. library assns., Czechoslovak Soc. Arts and Scis. Club: Worldwide Sportmen's. Author: Entries for Provincial Publications, Province of Ontario, 1867-1960, 1960; editor Index to Legal Periodicals, 1973-79. Home: 205 S Yoakum Pky Apt 1602 Alexandria VA 22304-3840 Office: New Exec Office Bldg Washington DC 20503

SAHLEM, JAMES ROBERT, law librarian; b. Buffalo, Feb. 21, 1948; s. Lee M. and Mildred A. (Hibschweiler) S.; m. Susan Mary Schifferli, Aug. 9, 1969; children: Steven, Andrea, Gregory. BS in Mgmt., Canisius Coll., 1970; MLS, SUNY, Buffalo, 1971, ASC, 1985. Cert. pub. libr. profl., N.Y. State Edn. Dept. Libr. trainee Bus. Labor Dept. Buffalo-Erie County Pub. Libr., Buffalo, 1970-71; libr. I Mobile Librs. Buffalo-Erie County Pub. Libr., Buffalo, 1971-74; libr. II Amherst Pub. Librs., Williamsville, N.Y., 1974-78; libr. III, dir. North Park Crane Brs., Buffalo, 1978-81; prin. law libr. Supreme Ct. Libr., Buffalo, 1981—; cons. Lippes, Silverstein et al, Buffalo, 1985—. Mem. Am. Assn. Law Librs., Buffalo Curling Club (officer 1975—). Office: Supreme Ct Libr Buffalo 92 Franklin St Buffalo NY 14221

SAHOTA, GURCHARN SINGH, mechanical engineer; b. Talwandi Jattan, Punjab, India, Jan. 4, 1940; came to U.S., 1971; naturalized, 1980; s. Karam Singh and Amar Kaur (Nijjar) S.; m. Gurvindar Kaur Johal, May 4, 1966 (dec. Mar. 1978); 1 child, Saryadvinder Singh; m. Kamaljit Kaur Grewal, Jan. 10, 1979; 1 child, Parmeet Kaur. BS in Mech. Engring., Punjab U., 1957-61; MS in Mech. Engrin., N.J. Inst. Tech., 1975-77. Engr. Heavy Elecs., Bhopal, India, 1962-70; mnfg. engr. Engelhard Industries, Union, N.J., 1974-76; from sr. plant engr. to supr. plant engring. group Am. Cyanamid Co., Stamford, Conn., 1976—. Home: 34 Duke Dr Stamford CT 06905-1017 Office: Am Cyanamid Co 1937 W Main St Stamford CT 06902-4580

SAIDENBERG, REBECCA MARSHALL, food industry consultant; b. Arlington, Va., Feb. 17, 1958; d. Howard and Roxie (Breeden) Marshall; m. Steven Saidenberg, June 5, 1988. BA with high distinction, Univ. Va., 1980. Sous chef C & O Restaurant, Charlottesville, Va., 1977-79; garde manger Le Pavillon Restaurant, Washington, 1980; mgr. Am. Cafe Restaurants, Washington, 1981-82; designer Chanterelle Catering, Washington, 1983-85; instr. in French techniques Peter Kump's N.Y. Cooking Sch., 1985; cons. Barbara Kafka Assocs., N.Y.C., 1985-88; creative cons. Procter & Gamble Corp., Cin., 1985—; cons. The Mus. of Modern Art, N.Y.C., 1990-91. Bd. dirs. Mus. Observations, Inc. Julia Child Culinary fellow Permanent Charity Fund Boston, 1982. Mem. Les Dames d'Escoffier. Home and Office: 17 W 71st St New York NY 10023-4135

SAILER, WILLIAM FRANKLIN, engineering company executive, engineer; b. Reading, Pa., May 29, 1930; s. Franklin Rhoads and Ruth Matilda (Levengood) S.; m. Doris Larue Eberhart, June 23, 1962; children: Linda Ann, William Keith. Grad. high sch., Shillington, Pa. Registered profl. engr., Pa., Fla. Elec. engr. Gilbert Assocs., Inc., Reading, 1958-66, project elec. engr., 1966-71, project mgr., 1971-77, mgr. projects, 1977-82; mgr. program mgmt. div. Gilbert/Commonwealth, Inc. (formerly Gilbert Assocs., Inc.), Reading, 1982-83, v.p., gen. mgr. quality assurance div., 1983-88, v.p., dir. utility svc., 1988-90, sr. v.p., 1990—; bd. dirs. Drexelbrook Engrng. Co., Horsham, Pa. Participant Nuclear Mgmt. and Resource Coun. With USN, 1952-54. Mem. IEEE. Republican. Lutheran. Office: Gilbert/Commonwealth Inc PO Box 1498 Reading PA 19603-1498

SAINANI, RAM HARIRAM, civil engineer; b. Ratodero, Sind, India, Feb. 22, 1925; came to U.S., 1981; s. Hariram Gurdasmal and Radha Hariram (Ahuja) S.; m. Usha Ram (Devkaran-Nanjee), Jan. 16, 1956; 1 child, Devkumar Ram. BA in Math. with honors, U. Bombay, 1943, BA in Physics and Chemistry with honors, 1944, BS in Math. and Physics, 1945, BCE, 1948; MCE, U. Colo., 1958. Registered profl. engr., Ont., Can., Mass., Maine, N.H. Dep. dir. designs Cen. Water & Power Commn. Govt. India, New Delhi, 1951-59; sr. hydraulic engr. SNC Group, Montreal, Que., Can., 1959-65; asst. chief hydraulic engr. Tecsult Internat., Montreal, 1965-79; staff engr. Acres Internat., Niagara Falls, Ont., Can., 1979-81; prin. engr. Internat. Engring. Co. Inc., Norwalk, Conn., 1981-85; v.p. engring. Consol. Hydro Inc., Greenwich, Conn., 1985—. Pres. India Can. Assn., Montreal, 1974-77. Mem. ASCE (life), Rotary. Democrat. Hindu. Office: Consol Hydro Inc 1 Greenwich Plz Greenwich CT 06830-6352

SAINI, GULSHAN RAI, soil physicist; b. Hoshiarpur, India, Oct. 1, 1924; s. Ram Saran and Parmeshri Devi (Bhondi) S.; B.Sc., U. Panjab, 1945, M.Sc., 1956; Ph.D., Ohio State U., 1960; postgrad. Bus. Adminstrn. and Computers, U. N.B., 1983, Harvard, 1986. m. Veena Chaudhri, Jan. 14, 1950; 1 child, Vikas. Rsch. asst. Govt. Agrl. Coll., Ludhiana, India, 1945-57; rsch. assoc. Ohio State U., Columbus, 1957-60; asst. prof. Punjab Agrl. U., Ludhiana, India, 1960-61; rsch. scientist Can. Dept. Agr., Fredericton, N.B., 1962-84; adj. prof. Faculty of Forestry, U. N.B., Fredericton, 1968-76; vis. prof. Rutgers U., 1984-85; dir. fin./adminstrn. Lawyers Alliance for Nuclear Arms Control, Inc., 1985-90. Mem. Canadian Inst. of Internat. Affairs, 1974-82, treas. Fredericton br. 1979-81; mayor's com. on Languge and Culture, 1970-71. Mem. Indian Sci. Congress Assn. (life), Multicultural Assn. Fredericton (life pres. 1980-81), Profl. Inst. Pub. Svc. Can. (nat. v.p. 1980, 81, chmn. Atlantic regional coun. 1978, 79), Union Concerned Scientists, Lawyers Alliance for World Security (advisor nat. toxic campaign fund lab., coun. for planning and renewal tower of brookline), Fredericton Rotary Club (dir. internat. svc. 1967-68), Sigma Xi, Phi Lambda Upsilon. Contbr. articles to profl. jours. Home: 24 Brook St Brookline MA 02146-6914

SAINI, VASANT DURGADAS, computer software company executive; b. Bombay, Jan. 31, 1952; came to U.S., 1974; s. Durgadas D. and Pushpa (Sethi) S.; m. Sonia Juneja, May 20, 1983; 1 child, Isha. B Tech. Electronics, Ind. Inst. Tech., 1974; MSEE, U. Rochester, 1975, PhD in Elec. Engring., 1979. Asst. prof. elec. engring. U. Rochester (N.Y.), 1980-88; pres., chief exec. officer Advanced Computer Innovations, Inc., Pittsford, N.Y., 1988—; cons. All-Pro Printers, Rochester, 1986, W. Main Ultrasound Group, Rochester, 1986; software developer Dantec Electronics, Denmark, 1987-89. Co-author: Doppler Echocardiography, 1985, 2d edit., 1992; also articles. Mae Stone Goode Found. grantee, 1979-81. Home: 30 Burncoat Way Pittsford NY 14534-2216

ST. CLAIR, MICHAEL, art dealer; b. Bradford, Pa., May 28, 1912. Student, Kans. City Art Inst., Colo. Springs Fine Arts Ctr. Instr. Okla. Art Ctr. Sch., Oklahoma City; dir. Babcock Galleries, N.Y.C., 1959—. Named Vanderslice scholar Kansas City Art Inst. Mem. Art Dealers Assn. Am. (founding mem. 1962), Architecture & Am. Art Drawing Soc. Office: Babcock Galleries 724 5th Ave New York NY 10019-4106

ST. CLEMENT, COURTNEY TOLSON, international advertising executive; b. Fort Worth, Nov. 8, 1951; d. J.B. and Dorothy Allison (Marshall) Tolson; m. Reginald St. Clement, Sept. 13, 1981. Art dir. Bloom Advt., Dallas, 1973-77, Cunningham & Walsh, N.Y.C., 1977-82; pres., creative dir. St. Clement Group, N.Y.C., 1982-89; pres. Goodfriend/St. Clement, Inc., N.Y.C., Paris, London, 1990—. Bd. dirs. Major Circle Repertory Opera Ensemble. Mem. Snarks Club, Amateur Comedy Club, Societe d' Equitation de Paris. Mem. Dutch Reform Ch. Office: Goodfriend/St Clement Inc 151 W 19th St New York NY 10011-4116

ST. GERMAIN, JEAN MARY, medical physicist; b. N.Y.C.; d. Herbert and Mary J. (Newman) S.; BS, Marymount Manhattan Coll., 1966; MS, Rutgers U., 1967. Diplomate Am. Bd. Med. Physics. Fellow radiol. health USPHS, Rutgers U., New Brunswick, N.J., 1967; fellow dept. med. physics Meml. Hosp., N.Y.C., Cornell U. Med. Coll., 1967-68, asst. physicist, 1968-71, instr. radiology (physics), 1971-78, clin. asst. prof., 1979—; asst. attending physicist Meml. Sloan-Kettering Cancer Ctr.; cons. in field. Diplomate Am. Bd. Health Physics. Fellow Am. Assn. Physicists in Medicine (sec., bd. dirs.); mem. Am. Inst. Physics (gov. bd.), Am. Endocuric Therapy Soc., Health Physics Soc. (pres. N.Y. chpt.), Radiol. Soc. N.Am., N.Y. Acad. Scis., Radiol. & Med. Physics Soc. N.Y. (past pres.), Nat. Soc. Arts and Letters (regional dir., pres. N.Y. chpt.). Iota Sigma Pi (treas., pres. V chpt.). Author: The Nurse and Radiotherapy, 1978; contbr. articles, chpts. to med. jours., texts. Office: 1275 York Ave New York NY 10021-6094

ST. JACQUES, ROBERT H., food products executive; b. Mar. 3, 1924; s. Emile C. and Marie R. (Messier) St. J.; m. Beverly A. Trussel, June 29, 1975; children: Roberta, Elizabeth, Raymond, David. BME, Cornell U., 1948. Pres. Hayden Mfg. Co., Wareham, Mass., 1948—; chmn. Ocean Spray Cranberries Inc., Lakeville, Mass., 1984—; mem. exec. com. Plymouth Savs. Bank., 1975—. Mgr. community trust funds, Wareham, 1968-89. Sgt. U.S. Army, 1943-46, ETO. Republican. Roman Catholic. Home: 79 Oak St Wareham MA 02571-2091 Office: Ocean Spray Cranberries Inc 1 Ocean Spray Dr Middleboro MA 02349-0001*

ST. JAMES, RONALD LEON, psychiatric social worker; b. Barre, VT., Dec. 9, 1947; s. Leon Donat and Jeanette D. (Benoit) St. J.; m. Anne Marie Robichaud, July 11, 1970; children: Terri-Lee, Michelle Marie. BA, U. Vt., 1973; MSW, U. Conn. Sch. Social Work, 1981. Accredited clin. social worker. Therapist Bridge Inc., White River Junction, Vt., 1975-77; social work cons. State of N.H. DCYS, Claremont, 1977-84; faculty Community Coll. of Vt., White River Junction, 1986-88; caseworker N.H. Assn. for the Blind, Concord, 1984-88; clinician Lebanon, N.H., 1983-88; team leader Vietnam Vets. Outreach, New Haven, 1988-90; clinician West Haven, Conn., 1990-92; supervisory psychiat. social worker State of Maine Bur. Mental Health, 1992—. Contbr. articles to profl. jours. With U.S. Army, 1967-69. Mem. Soc. of Friends. Home: RR 3 Box 1895 Wells ME 04090

ST. LANDAU, NORMAN, lawyer; b. Vienna, Austria, Apr. 14, 1925; s. Henry M. and Anka (Nemirovska) St. L.; m. Maisie Dennis, July 18, 1942; children—Lorraine, Jon L., Norman D. B.S., A.B. with honors, U. Ill., 1941; LL.B., Rutgers U., 1948; LL.M., NYU, 1951. Bar: D.C. 1948, U.S. Supreme Ct. 1952, N.J. 1958. With Pitts. Plate Glass Co., Ohio, 1941-42; with Johnson & Johnson, New Brunswick, N.J., 1942-84, internat. counsel, 1957-84, chief trademark counsel, 1961-84; dir., officer numerous affiliates Johnson & Johnson Internat.; of counsel Lalos, Leeds, Keegan & Marsh, Washington, 1983-85, Durand, Gorman, Heher, Imbriaco & Morrice, Princeton, N.J., 1984-86, Brylawski, Cleary & Leeds, 1985-90; ptnr. Heher, Clarke & St. Landau, Princeton, 1987—; counsel counsel Tucker, Flyer, Lewis, Washington, 1990—; chmn. bd. Action Law Systems, Inc., 1987—; of counsel Tucker Flyen & Lewis, Washington, 1989—; prin. Law Offices of Norman St. Landau, Princeton, 1990—; mem. adv. com. Sec. State and Commr. Patents, 1975—; bd. dirs. Nika Ltd., Pulsair Ltd., BP Johnson. Co-author: Trademark Management, 1977, Guide to Patent Arbitration, 1987; fgn. editor Les Nouvelles, 1965—. Bd. dirs. N.Y. State Opera, 1990—. Mem. N.J. State Bar Assn. (chmn. patent, trade and unfair competionon sect. 1980-82, vice-chmn. immigration and nationality sect. 1988—), Nat. Fgn. Trade Council (chmn. indsl. property com.), N.J. Patent Law Assn. (past pres.), Nat. Council Patent Law Assns. (sec.-gen.), Nat. Panel Arbitrators, Am. Arbitration Assn., ABA, Am. Chem. Soc. (nat. councillor), Am. Patent Law Assn. (bd. mgrs.), Am. Immigration Lawyers Assn., Inter-Am. Assn. Indsl. Property (exec. com.), Internat. Patent and Trademark Assn., Lic. Execs. Lawyers. Club: Nassau. Lodge: Rotary. Home: 822 E Meadow Dr Bound Brook NJ 08805-1443 Office: St Landau PC 5 Independence Way Princeton Corporate Ctr Princeton NJ 08540

ST. ONGE, MARY FRANCES See BURKETT, MARY FRANCES

ST. PIERRE, BEVERLY JANE, information systems specialist; b. Springfield, Mass., Sept. 22, 1949; d. Peter Alfred and Dorothy Clark (Whitten) Roy; m. Dale A. St. Pierre, Apr. 11, 1970 (div. Oct. 1986). Student, Holyoke Community Coll., Mass., 1972-78, Am. Internat. Coll., 1979-89, St. Joseph Coll., West Hartford, Conn., 1990—. Cert. data processing. Keypunch operator Mass. Mutual Life Ins. Co., Springfield, 1967-72; computer operator Springfield Inst. for Savings, 1972-83; ops. supr. J.M. Ney Co., Bloomfield, Conn., 1983-89; dir. info. systems St. Joseph Coll., West Hartford, 1989—. Active Hartford Disaster-Recovery Group, 1983—; vol. Hartford Jaycee's. Office: St Joseph Coll 1678 Asylum Ave West Hartford CT 06117-2700

SAINT-PIERRE, GUY, agri-business executive; b. Windsor Mills, Que., Can., Aug. 3, 1934; s. Arm and Alice (Perra) Saint-P.; m. Francine Garneau, May 4, 1957; children—Marc, Guylaine, Nathalie. B.Applied Sci. in Civil Enging, Laval U., 1957; diploma, Imperial Coll., London, 1958; M.Sc., U. London, 1959. Registrar, Corp. Engrs. Que., 1964-66. Dir. Irnes Inc., 1966-67; v.p. Acres Que., 1967-70; minister of edn. Govt. Que., 1970-72, of industry and commerce, 1972-76; asst. to pres. John Labatt Ltd., Montreal, 1977-80; sr. v.p. John Labatt Ltd.; pres., chief operating officer Ogilvie Mills Ltd., Montreal, 1977-80; pres., chief exec. officer The SNC Group Inc., 1989—; dir. McGavin Foods, Popular Industries Ltd., Suncor Inc., Commerce Group Ins. Co., SNC, Inc. Bd. dirs. Clin. Rsch. Inst., Montreal. Served as officer C.E. Can. Army, 1959-64. Mem. Montreal Bd. Trade, Enging. Inst. Can., Can. Mfrs. Assn. (chmn. bd.), Order Engrs. Que., Council Can. Unity (v.p.), Mil. and Hospitalier Order St. Lazarus Jerusalem. Liberal. Roman Catholic. Clubs: Mt. Royal, St. Denis, Mt. Bruno, Forest and Streams. Office: SNC Group Inc, 2 Place Felix Martin, Montreal, PQ Canada H3B 2X2 also: John Labatt Ltd, 451 Ridout St N, London, ON Canada N6A 5L3

ST. PIERRE, RONALD LEO, radio broadcast executive; b. Pawtucket, R.I., Jan. 2, 1955; s. Leo Herbert and Harriet Lee (Simpson) St. P.; m. Patti Jean St. Pierre, June 5, 1982. AS in Communications, Graham Jr. Coll., Boston, 1976. News dir. Sta. WHIM Franks Communication, East Providence, R.I., 1978-81; program dir. Sta. WHJJ/WHJY Fed. Communication Corp., East Providence, 1981-88; program dir. Sta. WPRO Capital Cities/ABC, East Providence, 1988-89, ops. mgr. Sta. WPRO, 1989-90, pres., gen. mgr. Sta. WPRO, 1990—; bd. dirs. AP Broadcasters, Washington. Bd. dirs. R.I. Anti-Drug Coalition, Providence, 1991. Home: 37 Haswill St Warwick RI 02886 Address: Sta WPRO-AM 1502 Wampanaog Trail East Providence RI 02915

SAINTY, GUY STAIR, art dealer; b. Cuckfied, Sussex, England, Dec. 12, 1950; came to U.S., 1979; s. Christopher Lawrence and Virginia Cade (Stair) S.; m. Cynthia Holland Ash Volk, Feb. 4, 1983; children: Charles Henry Alastair, Clementine Virginia, Constance Della. LLB, Coll. of Law, London, 1975. Dir. M. Newman Ltd., London, 1976-79; cons. Stair & Co., N.Y.C., 1979-82; pres. Stair Sainty Matthiesen, N.Y.C., 1982—. Author: The Sacred Military Constantinian Order of Saint George, 1976, The Orders of Chivalry and Merit of the Bourbon Two Sicilies Dynasty, 1989, The Orders of Saint John, 1991; co-author: (exhibition catalog) The Macchiaioli, 1984, First Painters of the King, 1985, Francois Boucher, His Circle and Influence, 1985. Vice chancellor Sacred Mil. Constantinian Order of St. George, Madrid, 1989—; historiographer Most Venerable Order St. John of Jerusalem Am. Soc., N.Y.C., 1990—. Named Comdr. Most Venerable Order St. John of Jerusalem, 1989, Knight of Justice Constantinian Order of St. George, 1977, Knight Order of St. Januarius, 1979, Comdr. Order of Sts. Maurice & Lazarus, 1985. Mem. Art Dealers Assn. Am., Syndicat Nat. des Antiquaires, Turf Club. Roman Catholic. Home: 38 Hudson St Kinderhook NY 12106 Office: Stair Sainty Matthieson 42 E 74th St New York NY 10021-2735

SAIZON, ANTHONY L., book design and production manager; b. New Roads, La., Nov. 20, 1953; s. August and Gertrude (Ladmirault) S. MFA, U. Ill., 1980. Designer div. confs. and insts. U. Ill., Urbana, 1978-79; book designer William C. Brown Publishers, Dubuque, Iowa, 1980-83; sr. book designer, book design supr., coord., design mgr. Houghton Mifflin Co. Coll. Div., Boston, 1983—. Mem. Concord (Mass.) Minuteman Soc. Mem. AIGA, Am. Ctr. Design, N.Y. New England Bookbuilders, Art Dirs. Club Boston. Roman Catholic. Home: 170 Walden St Concord MA 01742-3622

SAJEWSKI, WILLIAM THOMAS CHRISTOPHER, insurance agent; b. Erie, Pa., Dec. 9, 1950; s. Henry Frank and Rita Mercedes (Duberow) S.; m. Diane Lynn Alfano, Sept. 15, 1984; 1 child, Christine Marie. BA in Econs., Gannon Coll., 1973. Cert. ins. counselor. Claims adjuster Erie Ins. Exch., 1973-75; agt. Armstrong Ins. Agy., Inc., Mercer, Pa., 1975-81, mgr., 1981-83, pres., 1983—. Bd. dirs. Mercer County Blind Assn., 1985-91, pres., 1990; lectr. Immaculate Heart of Mary Cath. Ch., 1981—, mem. parish coun. With Pa. Army Nat. Guard, 1970-76. Recipient Citation of Merit, Mercer Schs., 1980. Mem. Soc. Cert. Ins. Counselors, Profl. Ins. Agts. Assn. Pa., Md., Del., Mercer Area Jaycees (pres. Mercer chpt. 1979-80, Keyman and Jaycee of Yr. awards, JCI Senatorshp award 1986), Mercer Area C. of C. (1st and 2d v.p., pres. 1982-83, rep. to Mercer County Devel. Corp. 1982-84, Citizen of Yr. 1989), KC (4th degree, capt. Grove City 4th degree assembly, Grand Knight 1982-84). Democrat. Office: Armstrong Ins Agy Inc 111 Beaver St Mercer IA 16137

SAKHEIM, DAVID KURT, psychologist; b. Brockton, Mass., July 24, 1956; s. George A. and Ilse H. (Oschinsky) S.; m. Susan E. Devine, May 7, 1988. BS, Brown U., 1978; PhD, SUNY, Albany, 1984. Lic. psychologist, Mass., Conn. Inpatient team leader Bay State Med. Ctr., Springfield, Mass., 1984-85, cons. psychologist, 1985-86; dir. edn. and tng. Traumatic Stress Tx Program, South Windsor, Conn., 1986-87; pvt. practice Springfield, Mass., 1987—. Co-editor: Out of Darkness: Exploring Satanism and Ritual Abuse, 1991. Mem. Am. Psychol. Assn., Internat. Soc. Study Multiple Personality and Dissociative Disorders. Office: Maple Hill Psychology Assoc 852 Main St South Windsor CT 06074-3305 also: 20 Maple St Springfield MA 01103

SAKOWSKI, ROBERT JOSEPH, real estate company executive; b. Bklyn., July 8, 1942; s. Joseph and Regina Josephine (Oleneki) S. AAS in Bus. Adminstrn., Suffolk County Community Coll., 1979, BA, 1984. Program mgr. Unisys Corp., Great Neck, N.Y., 1972-92; pres. Robert J. Sakowski Enterprises Inc., Manorville, N.Y., 1991—; mortgage cons. Eastwood Mortgage Corp., Bellmore, N.Y., 1991-92. Scoutmaster Boy Scouts Am. With USN, 1964-70. Mem. Polish Town Civic Assn., KC. Home and Office: PO Box 359 Manorville NY 11949-0359

SAL, JACK, artist, educator; b. Waterbury, Conn., Mar. 28, 1954; s. Philip and Esther (Petrowver) S.; m. Mary K. Judge, July 8, 1989. BFA, Phila. Coll. Art, 1976; MFA, Art Inst. Chgo., 1978. Curator Light Gallery, N.Y.C., 1985; assoc. prof., chmn. Moore Coll. Art and Design, Phila., 1989—; vis. asst. prof. Rutgers U., New Brunswick, N.J., 1984-85; vis. artist Am. Acad., Rome, 1986-87. Exhibited in shows at Opera Perugia, Italy, 1991-92, Apt Art Moscow, 1991-92, Re/Action, 1992; author: Collected Writings, 1991. Mellon Found. grantee, 1984. Home: 53 Trenton Ave Frenchtown NJ 08825-1247 Office: 431 E 6th St New York NY 10009-6305

SALAMON, ITAMAR, psychiatry educator; b. Nov. 12, 1934; m. Linda Frank, 1959; children: Margaret, Elizabeth, Thomas. BS with high honors, Queens Coll., Flushing, N.Y., 1955; MD, Albert Einstein Coll. of Medicine, Bronx, N.Y., 1959. Intern Montefiore Hosp., Bronx, 1959-60; assoc. resident, chief resident psychiatry Strong Meml. Hosp. U. Rochester, 1960-63; surgeon St. Elizabeth's Hosp. USPHS, Washington, 1963-65; instr. psychiatry, attending psychiatrist Albert Einstein Coll. of Medicine and Bronx Mcpl. Hosp. Ctr., 1965-67, asst. prof. psychiatry, dir. inpatient psychiatry, 1967-70, asst. clin. prof. psychiatry, dir. geriatric psychiatry, 1970-71, asst. clin. prof., dir. psychiatry emergency svcs., 1971-77; assoc. clin. prof., dir. Sound View-Throg's Neck Community Mental Health Ctr. Albert Einstein Coll. Medicine, 1977—; pvt. practice Hartsdale, N.Y., 1970—; chmn. computer com. Dept. Psychiatry Albert Einstein Coll. of Medicine, 1985—. Contbr. articles and presentations to profl. jours. Mem. Nat. Coun. Community Mental Health Ctrs. (coun. on svcs.), Am. Psychiat. Assn. (steering com. to plan conf. on recruitment into psychiatry), Am. Assn. Geriatric Psychiatrists. Home: 1217 The Colony Hartsdale NY 10530-1723

SALAMON, RENAY, real estate broker; b. N.Y.C., May 13, 1948; d. Solomon and Mollie (Friedman) Langman; m. Maier Salamon, Aug. 10, 1968; children: Mollie, Jean, Leah, Sharon, Eugene. BA, Hunter Coll., 1969. Licensed real estate borker, N.J. Mgr. office Customode Designs Inc., N.Y.C., 1966-68; co-owner Salamon Dairy Farms, Three Bridges, N.J., 1968-86; assoc. realtor Max. D. Shuman Realty Inc., Flemington, N.J., 1983-85; pres., chief exec. officer Liberty Hill Realty Inc., Flemington, N.J., 1985—; cons. Illva Saronna Inc. (Illva Group), Edison, N.J. 1985—; real estate devel. joint venture with M.R.F.S. Realty Inc. (Illva Group), 1986—. Mem. Readington Twp. Environ. Commn., Whitehouse Sta., N.J., 1978-87; fundraiser Rutgers Prep. Sch., Somerset, N.J., 1984—; bd. dirs. Hunterdon County YMCA, 1987—; mem. N.J. Assn. Environ. Commrs., Trenton, 1978-87. Named N.J. Broker Record, Forbes Inc., N.Y.C. 1987. Mem. Nat. Assn. Realtors, N.J. Assn. Realtors, Hunterdon County Bd. Realtors (mem. chair 1986), Realtor's Land Inst. Republican. Jewish. Office: Liberty Hill Realty Inc 415 US Hwy 202 Flemington NJ 08822-9465

SALANT, NATHAN NATHANIEL, athletic conference executive; b. Bronx, N.Y., June 25, 1955; s. Benjamin B. and Marilyn (Balterman) S. BA cum laude, SUNY, Albany, 1976; JD, Boston U., 1979. Bar: N.J. 1981. Asst. athletic dir. SUNY, Albany, 1979-80, St. Francis Coll., Bklyn., 1981-85; spl. asst. athletic dir. Adelphi U., Garden City, N.Y., 1985-88; commr. Mid. Atlantic States Collegiate Athletic Conf., Chester, Pa., 1988—; adj. prof. English Widener U., Chester, 1988—; mem. men's basketball com. Eastern Collegiate Athletic Conf. Author: This Date in New York Yankees History, 1979, 81, 83, Superstars, Stars and Just Plain Heroes, 1982. Head coach Rockland (N.Y.) OTB Pirates Am. Legion Baseball Team, 1974-76, 77—. Named Coach of Yr., Rockland County Big League, 1979-81, 83, 85-86, 87, 89, N.Y. State Am. Legion, 1987, 89-91. Mem. ABA, N.Y. State Coll. Baseball Coaches Assn. (sec., publicist, bd. dirs. 1985-89), Ea. Coll. Athletic Conf. (men's basketball com. 1990—, ofcl. negotiating com. 1992—). Home: 7222 Hilltop Dr Chester PA 19015-1325 Office: Widener U MAC Office Schwartz Ctr Chester PA 19015

SALBERG, HOWARD J., advertising executive; b. Bklyn., Jan. 26, 1954; s. Arnold Jack and Hannah Libby (Roth) S.; m. Karen Susan Robinson, Aug. 23, 1975; children: Daniel Jared, David Matthew. BA, Hofstra U., 1976. Svc. desk Photo-Lettering, Inc., N.Y.C., 1977-83; type dir. Dancer, Fitzgerald, Sample, N.Y.C., 1983-87, McCann-Erickson, Inc., N.Y.C., 1987—. Art dir.: The Seed, 1970. Mem. Type Dirs. Club (bd. mem.). Democrat. Jewish. Office: McCann-Erickson Inc 750 3rd Ave New York NY 10017-2703

SALCMAN, MICHAEL, neurosurgeon; b. Pilsen, Czechoslovakia, Nov. 4, 1946; came to U.S., 1948; s. Arthur and Edith S.; m. Ilene Rebarber, July 27, 1969; children: Joshua, Dara. BA, Boston U., 1969, MD, 1969. Diplomate Am. Bd. Neurol. Surgery. Intern, surgery Boston U. Med. Ctr., 1969-70; fellow, neurophysiology NINDS NIH, Bethesda, Md., 1970-72; resident, neurosurgery Columbia Univ., N.Y.C., 1972-76; asst. to assoc. prof. Univ. of Md. Sch. Medicine, Balt., 1976-83, prof., head div. of neurosurgery, 1983-90; prof. Univ. Md., Balt., 1991—; pres. Congress of Neurol. Surgeons, 1990-91, sec., 1982-86; chmn. joint com. on edn., Chgo., 1991—; honored lectr. Wayne State U., Northwestern U., 1987, 88. Assoc. editor Neurosurgery

jour.; editor: (books) Neurologic Emergencies, 1980, 2nd edit. 1990, Neurobiology of Brain Tumors, 1991; inventor microwave hyperthermia for brain tumors, chronic microelectrode for brain recordings (patent 1974); contbr. articles to profl. jours. Pres. Friends of Modern Art, Balt. Mus. of Art, 1986. Maj. USPHS, 1970-72. Recipient Disting. Alumni award Columbia U., 1985; grantee NIH, 1980-82, Am. Cancer Soc., 1978, others. Fellow Am. Coll. Surgeons; mem. Soc. Neurol. Surgeons, Am. Assn. Neurol. Surgeons, So. Neurosurgical Soc., Soc. Univ. Neurosurgeons, Neurosurgical Soc. Am., Soc. for Neuroscience, N.Y. Acad. Scis., IEEE, Am. Physiol. Soc., Md. Neurol. Soc. (pres. 1983-84), Md. State Poetry Soc. (pres. 1978), Phi Beta Kappa, Alpha Omega Alpha. Jewish. Office: 7801 York Rd Ste 102 Baltimore MD 21204-7463

SALEE, ADRIAN MICHAEL, management consultant, software developer; b. Huntington, N.Y., May 9, 1936; s. Benjamin Louis and Edna (Horowitz) S.; m. Juliet Stein, June 9, 1957 (div. Apr. 1977); children: Linda R. Salee Perrella, Deborah J. Salee Chesbrough, Steven J.; m. Alice Levine, May 18, 1980. B Mech. Engring., Rensselaer Poly. Inst., 1957; MBA, NYU, 1961. Registered profl. engr., N.Y. Design engr. Fairchild Engine div. Fairchild Engine and Aircraft Corp., Deer Park, N.Y., 1957-58; project engr. Brookhaven Nat. Lab., Upton, N.Y., 1958-61; ops. rsch. analyst Ops. Rsch. Inc., Silver Spring, Md., 1961-63; salesman Huntington Materials, 1963-65; owner, mgr. Bayport (N.Y.) Lumber Co., 1972-76, Babylon Bldg. Supply, North Babylon, N.Y., 1976-78; head econometrics group Grumman Aerospace, Bethpage, N.Y., 1965-72; prin. The Emerson Cons., N.Y.C., 1979-87, assoc., 1987—; owner, pres. Salee Mgmt. Systems, N.Y.C., 1987—; dir. career devel. NYU, N.Y.C., 1986-89; assoc. The Omega Cons., Atlanta, 1987—; seminar lectr. Am. Mgmt. Assn., N.Y.C., 1989—. Author: CMMS Users Handbook, 1991, Directory of CMMS Systems, 1991; developer software Emmis, 1988, Mainroute, 1990. Bd. dirs. 3d Avenue Owners, N.Y.C., 1980-85, pres., 1987; committeeman New York County Dem. Com., 1989-90. N.Y. State Regents scholar, 1953. Mem. Inst. Mgmt. Cons. (cert., lectr. 1986-89), Am. Pub. Transit Assn. (assoc.), Am. Arbitration Assn., Yale Club N.Y., Delta Kappa Epsilon (bd. govs. N.Y. 1987—). Jewish. Home and Office: 205 3d Ave New York NY 10003

SALEM, DAVID ANDREW, lawyer, investment manager; b. Boston, Apr. 27, 1956; s. E.L. and Janet G. Salem; m. Eleanor Bosworth Shannon, Aug. 14, 1982; children: Caroline, Peter, Virginia. BA, Middlebury (Vt.) Coll., 1978; JD, Harvard U., 1983, MBA, 1983. Bar: D.C. 1983. Mng. dir. Cambridge Assocs., Boston, 1983-84, Washington, 1984-85, Charlottesville, Va., 1985-90; ptnr. Grantham, Mayo, Van Otterloo & Co., Boston, 1990—; mem. faculty Nat. Assn. Coll. and Univ. Bus. Officers, Washington, 1983—, Nat. Assn. Coll. and Univ. Attys., Washington, 1984; lectr. U. Va., Charlottesville, 1988; mem. adv. bd. Beyond Wall St. TV series, 1991—. Contbg. author, co-editor The Challenges of Endowment Investing, 1985; contbg. author College and University Business Administration, 1991; contbr. articles to profl. jours. Mem. ABA, D.C. Bar Assn., Harvard Club (N.Y., Boston), Longwood Cricket Club (Mass.), Mt. Auburn Club (Mass.), Boston Racquet Club. Home: 55 Devon Rd Chestnut Hill MA 02167-1851 Office: Grantham Mayo Van Otterloo & Co 40 Rowes Wharf Boston MA 02110-3327

SALEM, HARRY, toxicologist, pharmacologist, educator; b. Windsor, Ont., Can., Mar. 21, 1929; came to U.S., 1959; s. Oscar and Bessie (Pierce) S.; m. Florence Rosenbaum, June 30, 1957; 1 child, Jerome Sheldon. BA, U. Western Ont., London, 1950; BSc, U. Mich., 1953; MA, U. Toronto, Can., 1955, PhD, 1958. Registered pharmacist, Pa. Pharmacologist Air Shields, Inc., Phila., 1959-62; sr. pharmacologist Smith Kline & French, Phila., 1962-65; dir. respiratory rsch. labs. Nat. Drug Co., Phila., 1965-70; dir. pharmacolgy and toxicology Cooper Labs., Cedar Knolls, N.J., 1970-77; pres., chief toxicology Cannon Labs., Reading, Pa., 1977-80; pres., chief exec. officer ToxiGenics, Inc., Decatur, Ill., 1980-84; chief toxicology div. Chem. Rsch., Devel., and Engring. Ctr. U.S. Army, Aberdeen Proving Ground, Md., 1984—, dir. rsch. Chem. Rsch., Devel., and Engring. Ctr., 1989-90; assoc. prof. environ. health Temple U., Phila., 1965—; assoc. prof. pharmacology U. Pa., Phila., 1975-83; adj. prof. Drexel U., 1992—; cons. Med. Documentation Ctr. Coll. Physicians, Phila., 1968-80, Franklin Rsch. Ctr., Phila., 1978-80. Author: (with others) International Ency. of Pharmacology, 1970; editor: Inhalation Toxicology, 1987; editor-in-chief Jour. Applied Toxicology, 1988—; patentee in field. Curriculum adv. com. Harford C.C., Bel Air, Md. Fellow Am. Coll. Clin. Pharmacology, Acad. Toxicological Scis., N.Y. Acad. Scis.; mem. AAAS, ACGIH, Am. Soc. Clin. Pharmacology and Therapeutics, Am. Chem. Soc., Am. Soc. Pharmacology and Exptl. Therapeutics, Am. Coll. Toxicology (charter), Assn. Govt. Toxicologists (pres. 1988-89), Soc. Toxicology (chmn. tech. com., cert. appreciation 1990), Internat. Regulatory Pharmacology and Toxicology, European Soc. Toxicology, Internat. Soc. Toxinology, Soc. Comparative Ophthalmology. Home: 109-1D Idlewild St Bel Air MD 21014 Office: Chem Rsch Devel Engring Ctr US Army SMCCR-RST Aberdeen Proving Ground MD 21010-5423

SALEMBIER, VALERIE BIRNBAUM, publishing executive; b. Teaneck, N.J., July 2, 1945; d. Jack and Sara (Gordon) Birnbaum; m. David J. Salembier, June 23, 1968 (div. 1980); m. Paul J. Block, Dec. 9, 1990. Student, Fordham U., 1970-72; B.A., Coll. of New Rochelle, 1973. Merchandising mgr. Life Internat., Time, Inc., N.Y.C., 1964-69; merchandising copywriter Newsweek, Inc., N.Y.C., 1970; promotion prodn. mgr. Newsweek, Inc., 1971, adv. sales rep., 1972-76; advt. dir. Ms. Mag., N.Y.C., 1976-79, assoc. pub., 1979-81; pub. Inside Sports Mag., N.Y.C., 1982; v.p., pub. 13-30 Corp., N.Y.C., 1983; sr. v.p. advt. USA Today, 1983-88; pub. TV Guide, Radnor, PA, 1988-89; pres. N.Y. Post, N.Y.C., 1989-90; pub. Family Circle Mag., N.Y.C., 1991—; lectr. in field. Trustee Coll. New Rochelle, N.Y.C. Police Found.; mem. exec. com. United Jewish Appeal; bd. dirs. Supportive Children's Advocacy Network; chmn. bd. dirs. N.Y.C. Sports Commn.; pub. mentor Clairol Mentor Program; advisor Women, Men and Media. Recipient Woman of Distinction award United Jewish Appeal. Mem. Women in Comm., Orgn. for Rehab. Through Tng., Women's Forum, Women's City Club, Advt. Club N.Y., Hadassah. Home: 1075 Park Ave New York NY 10128 Office: Family Circle Mag 110 5th Ave New York NY 10011

SALEMME, ANTONIO, artist; b. Gaeta, Italy, Nov. 2, 1892; s. Nicholas Vincent and Felice (Fedele) S.; m. Elizabeth Hardy, July 1920 (div. June 1932); m. Martha Anna Blomgren, Aug. 5, 1941. Student, Eric Pape Art Sch., Boston Mus. Fine Arts Sch.; student sculpture, Rome, 1912-19. One man shows include Ferargil Gallery, Erich-Newhouse Gallery, Findlay Galleries, Wakefield Bookshop Gallery, Wellons Gallery, Sagittarius Gallery, Robert Schoelkopf Gallery, Fahlnaes Gallery, Gothenburg, Sweden, Hist. Cultural Ctr., Gaeta, Italy, State Theater Gallery, Easton, Pa.; exhibited group shows NAD, Pa. Acad. Fine Arts, Art Inst. Chgo., Archtl. League N.Y.C., Nat. Sculpture Soc., Allied Artists, Met. Mus. Art, Peitrantonio Gallery, J. and B. Weintraub Gallery, Kent State U., Salon des Tuileries, Paris, Salon d' Automne, Paris, others; represented in permanent collections Newark Mus., Syracuse Mus. Fine Arts, Beinecke Library Yale U., Met. Mus. Art, N.J. Coll. Women, Kleinhans Music Hall, Internat. Trade Ctr., Gothenburg, Columbia U., Rutgers U., Harvard U., Temple U., Kennedy Libr., also pvt. collections; tchr. sculpture Nat. Inst. Archtl. Edn., N.Y.C., 1921-22, Roerick Mus. Sch., N.Y.C., 1928-29, Spence Sch., N.Y.C., 1939. With Italian Army, World War I. Decorated War Cross; Guggenheim fellow, 1932, 36; recipient 1st prize sculpture Guild Hall, East Hampton, N.Y., 1958, other awards. Mem. Nat. Inst. Archtl. Edn., (hon. life). Home and Studio: 189 Gaffney Hill Rd Easton PA 18042

SALEMME, (AUTORINO) LUCIA, artist, writer; b. N.Y.C., Sept. 23, 1919; d. Salvatore and Teresa (Iovino) Autorino; m. Attilio Salemme, Sept. 26, 1943 (dec. 1955; children: Vincent, Lawrence. Student, Art Students League, N.Y.C. Instr. art Peoples Art Ctr., 1957-69, Mus. Modern Art, N.Y.C., 1957-69, Art Students League, N.Y.C., 1970-90; adj. asst. prof. NYU, 1959-72. Exhbns. in N.Y.C. galleries and mus. include 19 solo shows; author: Color Exercieses for the Painter, 1970, Compositional Exercises for the Painter, 1974, The Complete Book of Painting Techniques, 1983; represented in permanent collections including Guggenheim Mus., Whitney Mus. Am. Art, N.Y.C., Nat. Gallery Art, Washington. Grantee Solomon R. Guggenheim Found., 1942; resident at McDowell Colony, 1963. Mem. Pen and Brush Club (chmn. painting sect. 1989—). Democrat. Roman Catholic. Dance Studio: 55 Bethune St Apt 641-B New York NY 10014-1703

SALEMME, MARTHA ANNE CAROLINE, artist; b. Geneva, Ill., Aug. 30, 1912; d. John and Amanda (Carlson) Blomgren; m. Antonio Salemme, Aug. 5, 1941. RN, Augustana Hosp. Sch. Nursing, Chgo., 1934. From staff nurse to spl. duty nurse N.Y. Hosp., 1935, 43-72; painter oil and watercolor paintings, drawings; then nurse/sec. Dr. Mather, Cleve. and N.Y.C. Exhibited in group shows at Van Diemen-Lilienfeld Gallery, N.Y.C., 1949, Flamingo Gallery, Falkenburg, Sweden, 1975, Fahlnaes Gallery, Gothenburg, Sweden, 1975, Guild Hall, East hampton, N.Y., 1958, 59, Ctr. d'Art Contemporain, Paris, 1985, Jersey City Mus., 1959; exhibited in one-woman shows at Sagittarius Gallery, N.Y.C., 1963, Galerie Mouffe, Paris, 1974, Horred (Sweden) Libr. Gallery, 1980, Bach. & Co. Gallery, Emmaus, Pa., 1991, others. Mem. Artists Equity, Assn. Pour La Promotion Du Patrimoine Artistique Francais. Republican. Home and Office: 189 Gaffney Hill Rd Easton PA 18042-9510

SALEN, WAYNE LOUIS, insurance agency official, consultant; b. Hornell, N.Y., Oct. 18, 1954; s. Louis Delbert and Roselyn Ann (Muscarella) S.; m. Donna Mineva Piedmont, June 18, 1978; children: Wesley Louis, Janelle Ashley. Cert. internat. study, Lycée Rouget de Lisle, Lons-Le-Saunier, France, 1973; BA, SUNY, Buffalo, 1977; MBA, Canisius Coll., 1986. Lic. ins. broker, N.Y.; cert. hazard control mgr., product safety mgr. Exec. trainee Jones Chem. Co., Inc., Caledonia, N.Y., 1977-78; asst. to prodn. dir. FMC Corp., Middleport, N.Y., 1978-79; risk mgr. Twin Fair, Inc., West Seneca, N.Y., 1979-82, Peter J. Schmitt Co., Inc., West Seneca, 1987-90, Empire Soils Investigations, Inc., Middleport, 1990-91; loss control cons. Lansing B. Warner, Inc., Chgo., 1982-84; mgr., asst. to pres. Laverack & Haines, Inc., Buffalo, 1984-87; account exec. Teach, Ryan & Cable, Inc., Buffalo, 1991; risk mgr. County of Niagra, Lockport, N.Y., 1991—; com. mem. Bus. Coun. N.Y., Inc., Albany, 1985-91; mem. steering com. Food Mktg. Inst., Washington, 1988-90; cons. on risk mgmt. Mem. Royalton Hartland Cen. Sch. Bd., Middleport, 1984-89. Mem. Am. Soc. Safety Engrs. (profl.), Nat. Fire Protection Assn., Risk and Ins. Mgmt. Soc., N.Y. State Assn. Self-Insured Counties. Republican. Methodist. Office: County Courthouse 175 Hawley St Lockport NY 14094

SALGANICOFF, LEON, pharmacology educator; b. Buenos Aires, Sept. 11, 1924; came to U.S., 1964; s. Marcos Salganicoff and Ana Rosa Zelicson; m. Matilde Saffier, Dec. 11, 1957; children, Alina, Marcos. MSc in Pharmacy, U. Buenos Aires, 1948, DSc in Biochemistry, 1955. Instr. U. Buenos Aires, 1947-49; chief clin. pathologist Hosp. Mil. Cen., Buenos Aires, 1955-59; chief lab. Neurochem. Inst. Anatomy, U. Buenos Aires, 1959-64; rsch. asst. Nat. Coun. Investigation, Buenos Aires, 1959-64; rsch. fellow Johnson Found., U. Pa., Phila., 1964-65, Nat. Multiple Sclerosis Soc., 1965-68; assoc. prof. pharmacology Temple U., Phila., 1968-76, section leader Thrombosis Rsch. Ctr., 1971-80; prof. pharmacology Temple U. Med. Sch., Phila., 1976—; vis. prof. U. Rome la Sapienza, 1976—, NATO vis. prof., 1982. Grantee NIH, 1971-80; recipient W.W. Smith Charitable Trust award, 1980-83. Mem. AAAS., Fedn. Am. Socs. Exptl. Biology, Sigma Xi. Home: 556 N 23d St Philadelphia PA 19130 Office: Temple U Sch Medicine 3400 N Broad St Philadelphia PA 19140-5196

SALIM, HASSAN KAMAU, history educator; b. Newark, Jan. 23, 1950; s. William Hall and Bertha (Douglas) Hall-Shackleford; m. Cynthia Jennings, May 26, 1978 (div. Nov. 1988); children: Zuwena Iman, Hassan Iman. BA, Norfolk (Va.) State Coll., 1971; BA in African Studies, Rutgers U., 1973, MEd, 1978; PhD, Kemetic Inst., 1984. Asst. dir. Livingston Student Ctr. Rutgers U., Piscataway, N.J., 1973-76, asst. to dean Livingston Coll., 1976-79; head tchr. Nyerere Ednl. Inst., New Brunswick, N.J., 1976-90; prof. African history Kemetic Inst., Plainfield, 1987—, Middlesex County Coll., Edison, N.J., 1990-91; dir., founder after sch. program Maat Inst., Plainfield, 1987—; dir. founder Black Gold Afrakan Kulture Arts Ctr., Plainfield, 1979—. Author: (poems) Seven Shades of Black, 1982, A Treasury of Classical and Contemporary Love Poems, 1982 (1st Place award), In America, not of America, 1984, Kupigama Ngumi, 1991 (Outstanding Contbn. to Afrikan Studies award); author: Kupigana Ngumi Root Symbols of Civilzation and Ancient Kemet, 1992. African hist. and cultural adviser Plainfield Bd. Edn., 1987—, lectr., tchr. trainer, 1988—, chair multicultural com., 1989-90. Named Grand Champion Met. Open Karate Competition, 1988-89, Profl. Karate T-League, Inc., 1988-89, Somerset Kung Fu Sch. Tournament, 1984, 85, 86; recipient Tribute to Black Man in Am., Rutgers Student Alumni Assn., 1976, 77, 78, Martial Arts of Yr. award Rahway Karate Assn., 1982; named Cen. Jersey Black Entrepreneur of Yr. by Nat. Assn. Negro Bus. & Profl. Women, 1991. Mem. Sons and Daus. of the Sun (chpt. pres. 1985, high priest, lectr.), Shrine of Neb Hu (pres. 1984, high priest 1984—), Shrine of Ptah (priest, lectr., Big Brother-elder 1984), Pan Afrikan Kupigana Ngumi Fedn. (tchr. 1980—, nat. spokesman 1985—, grand master 1992), Shaolin Kung-Fu Fedn. (master 1971-80, 7th degree, tchr.), Hetep Heru Maat (Kemetic sr. priest 1992). Office: Black Gold Afrakan Kultural Arts Ctr 104 W Front St Plainfield NJ 07060

SALINGER, RUTH ANGIER, international trade company executive, environmental administrator; b. Newton, Mass., July 21, 1931; d. Ralph Loveland and Elizabeth (Chase) Angier; m. Richard Burtis Salinger, June 26, 1954; children: Peter Dennison, Jennifer Angier. BS in Edn., Wheelock Coll., Boston, 1953. Cert. in elem. edn. Tchr. Claflin Sch., Newton, 1953-54; dir. religious edn. Eliot Ch. of Newton, 1955-60; dist. case worker Mass. Senate Ways and Means Com., Boston, 1983-85; dir. constituent svcs. Congressman Chester G. Atkins, Lowell, Mass., 1985; pres., founder Greeley Found., Concord, Mass., 1986-90; pres., co-founder The Salinger Group, Gloucester, Mass., 1990—; chief exec. officer, co-founder Global Initiatives, Inc., Gloucester, 1990—; co-founder Just-A-Start, Boston and Cambridge, 1964-67; founder, pres. Concord-Carlisle Human Rights Council, 1979-83, Mass. Women Sch. Com. Mems., Boston, 1974-79. Co-editor: Forward Through the Ages, 1986. Chmn. Concord Sch. Com., 1972-79; trustee METCO, 1979-83; co-chmn. U.S./USSR Citizen Summit, Moscow, 1990; mem., adviser Women for Mut. Security, 1986—. Recipient Peace Day award Nat. Peace Day Com., 1986. Mem. Wheelock Coll. Alumnae Assn. (trustee 1979-83, chmn./pres. social action com. 1979-83, Centennial Alumnae award 1989). Democrat. Unitarian. Home: 53 Laurel St Concord MA 01742-3605 Office: The Salinger Group Inc 3 Crafts Rd Gloucester MA 01930-2135

SALIOLA, FRANCES, retired corporate assistant; b. Westfield, N.J., Oct. 27, 1921; d. Antonio and Maria (Chironna) Ponturo; m. Peter Saliola, Aug. 25, 1945; 1 child, George. Grad. high sch., Westfield, N.J., 1939. Sec., bookkeeper Pearsall & Frankenback, Inc., Westfield, 1939-45; legal sec. Dughi & Johnstone, Westfield, 1945-51; exec. sec. Arthur Venneri Co., Westfield, 1951-65; office mgr. Torcon, Inc., Westfield, 1965-77, dir. mgmt. risk and finance, 1977-86, dir. adminstrv. mgmt., 1983-86, corp. sec., dir., 1965-90. Sec. Solidarity of the Blessed Virgin, Westfield, 1938, Civic Club Westfield, 1944; mem. Union County Com. Boys' Towns of Italy, 1951-63. Roman Catholic.

SALISBURY, FRANKLIN CARY, lawyer, foundation executive; b. Cleve., Sept. 29, 1910. B.A., Yale U., 1932; J.D., Case Western Res. U., 1937; LL.D. (hon.), U. Wales, 1985. Bar: Ohio 1937, D.C. 1947. Adminstrv. asst. to commr. FCC, 1939-40; chief legal div. ammunition br. Office Chief Ordnance, U.S. Army, 1941-45; chief clearance div. WPB, Army Service Forces, 1945; dir. legal div. Office Fgn. Liquidation Commn., Rio de Janeiro, Brazil, 1945-46; asst. solicitor Indian legal activities Dept. Interior, 1956-61; gen. counsel Ams. United for Separation Ch. and State, 1963-72; pres., chief exec. officer Nat. Found. Cancer Research, Bethesda, Md., 1973—; hon. pres., hon. dir. Assn. for Internat. Cancer Research, St. Andrews, Scotland; chmn. Krebsforschung Internat., Dusseldorf, Federal Republic Germany; trustee, counsel Latin Am. Inst., 1943-75; sec., dir. Atlantic Research Corp., 1949-64, Dryomatic Corp., 1950-59; chmn. bd., sec., dir. Orbit Industries, Inc., 1960-68; co-founder, dir. Internat. Sch. Law (now George Mason Law Sch.), 1975-77. Named Pro Universitate Med. U. Debrecen, 1982; recipient Quantum Biology award Internat. Soc. Quantum Biology, 1983, Medal of Merit U. Turin, Italy, 1984; decorated Order of Leopold II (Belgium). Mem. Fed. Bar Assn.; associated fgn. mem. Institut de Biologie Physico-Chimique (Fondation Edmond de Rothschild). Office: 7315 Wisconsin Ave Rm 332 Bethesda MD 20814-3202

SALISBURY, HELEN HOLLAND, education educator; b. Bedford, Ind., Dec. 15, 1923; d. Deward Julius and Zella (Kinser) Holland; B.S. in Home Econs., Ind. U., 1957; M.Ed., U. Va., 1967; Ed.D., Temple U., 1979; m. Charles Jackson Salisbury, Jan. 10, 1942; children—Creggie Helen Salisbury Henderson, Charles Jackson II. Plating chemist Curtiss-Wright, Indpls., 1943; supr. sch. lunch program Charlottesville (Va.) Pub. Schs., 1963-65; dir. Harcum Jr. Coll. Lab. Sch., Bryn Mawr, Pa., 1966-68; prof. edn. Harcum Jr. Coll., Bryn Mawr, 1965-73; teaching assoc. Temple U., Phila., 1974; early childhood cons., 1979—; prof. edn. Harcum Jr. Coll., Bryn Mawr, 1982—, dir. infant devel. practice, 1982—; early childhood cons. Head Start, 1965. Mem. Nat. Assn. Edn. Young Children, Delaware Valley Assn. Edn. Young Children, Orgn. Mondiale pour L'Education Prescolaire, Assn. Supervision and Curriculum Devel., DAR, Kappa Alpha Theta, Episcopalian. Co-author: Diagnosing Individual Needs for Early Childhood Education, 1975. Home: 315 Strathmore Dr Bryn Mawr PA 19010-1230 Office: Harcum Jr Coll Montgomery Ave Bryn Mawr PA 19010-3403

SALISBURY, IRVING DANIEL, art educator; b. Sharon, Conn., Nov. 16, 1936; s. Jesse Walter and Helen Mae (Butler) S.; m. Margaretta Helen Bouw, Aug. 4, 1964 (div. May 1986); children: Roderick Byron, Christopher Brent. BS, SUNY, New Paltz, 1958, MS, 1968; postgrad., NYU, 1972. Cert. tchr. art, N.Y. Tchr. art Delaware Acad. and Cen. Sch., Delhi, N.Y., 1958-61, Newark Valley (N.Y.) Elem. Schs., 1964-66, Newburgh (N.Y.) Enlarged City Sch. Dist., 1966-70, Washington St. Sch. and Temple Hill Sch., Newburgh, 1970-73; tchr. art Newburgh Free Acad., 1973—, tchr. competitions Body Bldg. Club, 1986—. Designer logo Newburgh Free Acad., 1987, brochure, 1989; cover design St. Luke's Hosp. Ad Jour., 1992. Sgt. U.S. Armored Inf., 1961-64, Germany. Mem. Am. Fedn. Tchrs., N.Y. State United Tchrs., Newburgh Tchrs. Assn. Republican. Methodist. Home: 65 Townsend Ave # 2 Newburgh NY 12550-4319 Office: Newburgh Free Acad 201 Fullerton Ave Newburgh NY 12550-3798

SALISBURY, LUANN JOYCE, human resources professional; b. Hillsdale, Mich., Oct. 4, 1959; d. Jerry Franklin and Marjorie (Gale) S. BA in Psychology and Sociology, U. Mich., 1981; MS in Spl. Edn., Cen. Conn. State U., 1984, cert. in 6th yr. adminstrn.-supervision, 1987. Cert. spl. edn. tchr., Conn. Supervising tchr. Conn. Inst. for Blind, Hartford, 1985-89, staff devel. mgr., 1989—; trainer Peace Corps, Mansfield, Conn., 1991, Conn. Dept. Mental Retardation, 1990—; instr. phys. psychology Mgmt. Tng. Assn. First aid and CPR instr. ARC, Farmington, Conn., 1989—; instr. Nat. Safety Coun., 1990—. Mem. ASTD, Assn. for Severely Handicapped, Nat. Soc. Performance and Instrn., U. Mich. Alumni Assn. Office: Conn Inst for Blind 120 Holcomb St Hartford CT 06112-1529

SALKIN, MAUREEN ADA, arts administrator, management consultant; b. Chgo., Oct. 29, 1943; d. Harold and Dorothy (Kramer) Seligman; divorced; 1 child, Daniel. BA, Northwestern U., 1964; postgrad., SUNY, Albany, 1980—. Asst. to chmn. theatre dept. SUNY, Albany, 1973-77, mgr. Performing Arts Ctr., 1977-80; ops. mgr. Empire State Performing Arts Ctr., Albany, 1980-82; owner/pres. Events East, Inc., Albany, 1982-85; exec. dir. Albany League Arts, 1985-87; dir. bus. ops. Capital Repertory Co., Albany, 1987-88; gen. mgr. Heritage Artists Ltd., Cohoes, N.Y., 1988-89; freelance convention mgmt. cons. Guilderland, N.Y., 1988—; mng. dir. Empire State Performing Arts Ctr., Albany, N.Y., 1989-90; mgr. Palace Theatre, Albany, 1990—; cons. N.Y. State Office Gen. Svcs., Albany, 1977; com. coord. Assn. Community Univs. and Coll. Arts Adminstrs., Madison, Wis., 1981; adj. faculty Schenectady County Community Coll., 1983—. Vol. mgr. Sta. WMHT-TV, Schenectady, 1977-79. Mem. Theatre Communications Group, Nat. Assn. Female Execs., Albany League Arts (officer/bd. dirs. 1979-85), LWV (officer/bd. dirs. Albany County 1975-80). Democrat. Home: 1676 Western Ave Albany NY 12203-4231 Office: Palace Theatre 19 Clinton Ave Albany NY 12207

SALKIN, PAUL, psychiatrist; b. Bklyn., Dec. 22, 1932; s. Bernard David and Evelyn (Botnick) S.; m. Nesrin Bingöl, Nov. 20, 1959; 1 child, David. BA, NYU, 1954, MD, 1956. Intern Kings County Hosp., Bklyn., 1956-57; resident Bronx (N.Y.) Mcpl. Hosp., 1957-60; staff psychiatrist Hillside Hosp., Queens, N.Y., 1960-66; pvt. practice N.Y.C. and South Salem, N.Y., 1960—; med. dir. Ctr. for Therapeutic Arts, Patterson, N.Y., 1991—. Author: Assessment of Current Knowledge in Psychiatry, 1976. Fellow Am. Psychiat. Assn., N.Y. Acad. Medicine; mem. Am. Acad. Psychoanalysis, Westchester Psychiat. Soc. (chmn. pvt. practice com. 1988), Publicity Lodge, Masons. Jewish. Office: 200 East End Ave New York NY 10128

SALLANI, MRS. WERNER See DAVIS, MARION PEASE

SALLEN, IRA BRUCE, human resources executive, psychologist; b. Boston, Apr. 14, 1954; s. Melvin Julius and Lois Sheila (Margil) S.; m. Susan Laurie Lubarsky, Dec. 26, 1976; children: Marisa Beth, Amanda Joy, Joshua Andrew. BS in Edn. and Psychology, Bridgewater State U., 1976; MA in Clin. Psychology, New Sch. Social Research, 1978; MBA, Boston U., 1982. Research fellow Rockefeller U., N.Y.C., 1977-78; psychologist Counseling and Family Services, Inc., Brockton, Mass., 1978-81; staff cons. Arthur Young & Co., N.Y.C., 1981-82, sr. supr., 1982-83; mgr. human resource planning Computervision Corp., Bedford, Mass., 1983-85; mgr. human resources Ciba Corning Diagnostics, Medfield, Mass., 1985-88; v.p. human resources Clean Harbors, Inc., Braintree, Mass., 1988-89; v.p. employee relations BMG Internat, N.Y.C., 1989—; vis. lectr. Boston U., 1983—, Providence Coll., 1985; bd. dirs. Boston U. Grad. Sch. Mgmt.; faculty U. Conn., Storrs, 1981-83. Mem. Organizational Resources Internat. Roundtable, Human Resources Policy Inst., Human Resources Planning Soc. Office: BMG Internat 1133 Ave Of The Americas New York NY 10036-6710

SALLOUM, SALIM GEORGE, sales executive; b. Beirut, May 20, 1956; came to U.S., 1977; s. Georges Salim and Yamammeh (Farah) S.; m. Florinda Manolio, Apr. 2, 1978 (div. Oct. 1980); m. Laila S. Soussou, Apr. 27, 1985; 1 child, Christopher. AAS, Elizabeth Seton Coll., 1978; BA, Calif. Coast U., Santa Ana, 1982, MBA, 1984. Registered fin. planner. Asst. cashier fgn. exch. Republic Nat. Bank N.Y., N.Y.C., 1979-81; sales mgr. Prudential Ins., Paramus, N.J., 1985—. Mem. Masons (master 1987, fellow). Home: 120 Sussex St Hackensack NJ 07601-4149

SALOMON, LUCY, psychiatrist, educator; b. Zagreb, Yugoslavia, Jan. 25, 1925; came to U.S., 1950; d. Kornel and Jolanda (Schlesinger) Tarjan; m. Salomon M. Salomon, Feb. 4, 1950; children: Ronald M., Gary D., Melinda S. BS, Beloit Coll., 1962; MD, U. Wis., 1968. Diplomate Am. Bd. Psychiatry and Neurology, 1978. Rsch. assoc. in hematology and blood coagulation Tufts U.-New Eng. Med. Ctr., Boston, 1950-54; intern Madison (Wis.) Hosp., 1968-69; resident in psychiatry McLean Hosp., Belmont, Mass., 1969-71, fellow in psychiatry, 1969-72, assoc. attending psychiatrist, 1972-88, attending, 1989—; resident in psychiatry Beth Israel Hosp., Boston, 1971-72; pvt. practice Brookline, Mass., 1972—; clin. instr. psychiatry Harvard U. Med. Sch., Boston, 1972—. Contbr. numerous articles on hematology and psychiatry to med. jours. Mem. Am. Psychiat. Assn., AMA. Home and Office: 219 Buckminster Rd Brookline MA 02146

SALOP, ARNOLD, internist; b. N.Y.C., Oct. 19, 1923; s. Alexander and Anna (Lefrak) S.; m. Maryellen Kolt, June 27, 1979; children: Andrea, Holly, Evan Arnold. AB, Oberlin Coll., 1943; MB, Northwestern U., 1949, MD, 1950. Intern, resident in internal medicine Beth Israel Hosp., 1949-52; resident in internal medicine Goldwater Meml. Hosp., 1950-51, Kingsbridge VA Hosp., 1952-53; pvt. practice medicine specializing in cardiology and internal medicine, Ossining, N.Y., 1957-90; pres. med. staff affairs, sr. attending Phelps Meml. Hosp., North Tarrytown, N.Y, 1988-90; sr. v.p., med. dir. Phelps Meml. Hosp, North Tarrytown, 1991—. Served with AUS, 1943-45, 1st lt. USAF, 1953-54. Fellow ACP, Am. Coll. Cardiology; mem. Am. Heart Assn., Am. Geriatrics Assn., Am. Rheumatism Assn., Alpha Omega Alpha. Office: care Phelps Meml Hosp Ctr 701 N Broadway Tarrytown NY 10591-1096

SALTMAN, ROY GILBERT, computer scientist, consultant; b. N.Y.C., July 15, 1932; s. Ralph Henry and Josephine Yolanda (Stern) S.; children: David, Eve, Steven. BEE, Rensselaer Poly. Inst., 1953; SMEE, MIT, 1955; EE, Columbia U., 1962; MPA, Am. U., 1976. Sr. engr. Sperry Gyroscope Co., Great Neck, N.Y., 1955-64; regional rep. IBM Corp., Bethesda, Md., N.Y.C., 1964-69; computer scientist Nat. Inst. of Standards and Tech.,

Gaithersburg, Md., 1969—; cons. Fla. Joint Legis. Com. on Info. Mgmt. Resources, Tallahassee, 1990, State of Del., Dover, 1991. Author U.S. govt. reports on computerized voting; contbr. chpt. to book and articles to profl. jours. Pres. Whittier Woods Civic Assn., Bethesda, 1981-82; mem. The Archaeological Conservancy, Santa Fe, 1991, The Nature Conservancy, Arlington, Va., 1991. Recipient Commns. citation U.S. Bur. of Customs, Washington, 1971, Order of Paul Revere Patriots award State of Mass., Boston, 1977, Bronze medal U.S. Dept. Commerce, Washington, 1981, Rsch. grant John and Mary R. Markle Found., N.Y.C., 1986. Mem. IEEE, Assn. for Fed. Info. Resources Mgmt. Jewish. Office: Nat Inst of Standards & Tec B154 Technology Bldg Gaithersburg MD 20899

SALTON, GERARD, computer science educator; b. Nuremberg, Germany, Mar. 8, 1927; s. Rudolf and Elisabeth (Tuchmann) S.; m. Mary Birnbaum, Aug. 31, 1950; children: Mariann, Peter. B.A. magna cum laude, Bklyn. Coll., 1950, M.A., 1952; Ph.D., Harvard U., 1958. Mem. staff computation lab. Harvard U., 1952-58, instr., then asst. prof. applied math., 1958-65; prof. computer sci. Cornell U., 1965—, chmn. dept., 1971-77; cons. to industry. Author: Automatic Information Organization and Retrieval, 1968, The Smart System-Experiments in Automatic Document Processing, 1971, Dynamic Information and Library Processing, 1975, Introduction to Modern Information Retrieval, 1983, Automatic Text Processing, 1989; editor-in-chief: Assn. Computing Machinery Communications, 1966-68; Editor-in-chief: Assn. Computing Machinery Jour., 1969-72; editor: Info. Systems, 1974—, ACM Transactions on Data Base Systems. Guggenheim fellow, 1963; recipient Alexander von Humboldt award 1988. Fellow AAAS; mem. Assn. Computing Machinery (council 1972-78, Outstanding Contbn. award 1983), Am. Soc. for Info. Sci. (award of Merit 1989), Phi Beta Kappa. Home: 221 Valley Rd Ithaca NY 14850-6152 Office: Upson Hall Cornell U Ithaca NY 14853

SALTUS, PHYLLIS BORZELLIERE, music educator; b. Rochester, N.Y., Jan. 17, 1931; d. Nicholas and Sadie Veronica (Leone) Borzelliere; m. William Thomas Saltus, Aug. 21, 1965 (div. Apr. 1991); children: Julie Marie Nicole, William Nicholas. AA, Burlington County Coll., Pemberton, N.J., 1987; MEd in Measurement and Guidance, U. Maine, Orono, 1963; BS in Music Edn., SUNY, 1953, MS, 1957. Cert. student personnel svcs., music and guidance, N.J., N.Y. Music tchr., choral dir. Rochester Pub. Schs., 1953-56, 62-63, 1969-70, high sch. guidance counselor, 1963-65; asst. prof. music edn. SUNY, Geneseo and Fredonia, 1956-62; music tchr, choral dir. Concord (Mass.) Pub. Schs., 1965-66; owner, dir. Saltus Music Studio, Medford, N.J., 1982—; tchr. voice N.J. Sch. Arts, Glassboro (N.J.) State Coll., 1987-89; sr. adj. prof. Burlington County Coll., Pemberton, N.J. and Ft. Dix Mil. Post, 1989—; music coord., dist. tchr. for gifted and talented program Mt. Laurel (N.J.) Pub. Schs., 1989—; music dir. Triple Threat Prodns., Cherry Hill, N.J., 1991—, Kosciusko Boys Choir, Rochester, 1959-69, Young Adults Cath. Youth Orgn. Choir, Dunkirk, N.Y., 1960-62; lectr. in field. Contbr. poems to various publs.; soloist Rochester Philharm. Orch. Concert Series, Songsters, Inc., 1953-59. Choir dir., organist, soloist St. Philip Neri R.C. Ch., Rochester, 1949-65, St. Peter's Episc. Ch., Medford, 1989-90; vocal dir., accompanist Pineland Players of South Jersey Community Theatre, Medford, 1987-89, Cherry Hill East High Sch., N.J., 1991—; team capt. United Way, Rochester, 1953-56; membership chair Rochester Community Theater, 1955; bd. dirs., founding mem. Rochester Chamber Orch., 1964-65; judge preliminary Miss Am. contest Jr. C. of C., Jamestown, N.Y., 1962, vocal dir. Miss Dunkirk (N.Y.) pageant, 1962; active Welcome Wagon, Inc., pres., 1974, historian, 1981. NDEA grantee, 1964; EEOC scholar, 1986-87; recipient Jr. County Rifle Championship award Monroe County Dept. Health and Recreation, Rochester, 1948. Mem. AAUP (treas. 1960-62, state del. 1961), South Jersey Music Tchrs. Assn., Order Sons of Italy in Am., Kappa Delta Pi. Roman Catholic. Home: 112 Pine Valley Dr Medford NJ 08055-9214

SALTZBURG, STEPHEN ALLAN, law educator, consultant; b. Phila., Sept. 10, 1945; s. Jack Leonard and Mildrid (Osgood) S.; m. Susan Lee; children: Mark Winston, Lisa Marie, Diane Elizabeth, David Lee Mussehl. AB, Dickinson Coll., 1967; JD, U. Pa., 1970. Bar: Calif. 1971, D.C. 1972, Va. 1976. Law clk. U.S. Dist. Ct., San Francisco, 1970-71, U.S. Supreme Ct., 1971-72; asst. prof. law sch. U. Va., Charlottesville, 1972-74, assoc. prof. law sch., 1974-77, prof. law sch., 1977-82, Class of 1962 chairholder, 1987-90; Howrey prof. trial advocacy, litigation and profl. responsibility George Washington U. Nat. Law Ctr., Washington, 1990—; reporter Alaska Rules of Evidence, 1976-77, Alaska Civil Jury Instructions, 1979-81, Adv. Com. on Fed. Rules of Criminal Procedure, 1984-89, Virginic Rules of Evidence, 1984-85; dep. asst. atty. gen. criminal div. U.S. Dept. Justice 1988-89; mem. adv. com. on Fed. Rules of Criminal Procedure, 1989—. Author: American Criminal Procedure, 4th edit., 1992, Federal Rules of Evidence Manual, 5th edit., 1990, A Modern Approach to Evidence, 2d edit., 1982, Federal Criminal Jury Instructions, 1985, 2d edit., 1991, Evidence in America, 1987, Military Rules of Evidence Manual, 3d edit., 1991. Mem. ABA, Am. Law Inst. Office: George Washington U Nat Law Ctr 720 20th St NW Washington DC 20052-0001

SALTZER, JEROME HOWARD, electrical engineering educator; b. Nampa, Idaho, Oct. 9, 1939; s. Joseph and Helene (Scheuermann) S.; m. Marlys Anne Hughes, June 16, 1961; children—Rebecca, Sarah, Mark. B.S., MIT, 1961, M.S., 1963, Sc.D., 1966. Faculty dept. elec. engring. and computer sci. MIT, Cambridge, Mass., 1966—, now prof., tech. dir. project Athena; cons. Chem. Abstracts Service, 1968—, IBM Corp., 1970—. Fellow AAAS, IEEE; mem. NRC (computer sci. and telecommunications bd. 1991—), Assn. for Computing Machinery, Eta Kappa Nu, Tau Beta Pi. Home: 54 Gammons Rd Newton MA 02168-1216 Office: MIT Lab Computer Sci 545 Technology Sq Cambridge MA 02139-3539

SALTZMAN, BARRY, meteorologist, educator; b. N.Y.C., Feb. 26, 1931; s. Benjamin and Bertha (Burmil) S.; m. Sheila Eisenberg, June 10, 1962; children—Matthew David, Jennifer Ann. B.S., CCNY, 1952; S.M., Mass. Inst. Tech., 1954, Ph.D., 1957; M.A. (hon.), Yale, 1968. Research staff meteorologist MIT, 1957-61; sr. research scientist Travelers Research Center, Inc., Hartford, Conn., 1961-66; research fellow Travelers Research Center, Inc., 1966-68; prof. geophysics Yale U., 1968—, chmn. dept. geology and geophysics, 1988-91. Editor: Selected Papers on the Theory of Thermal Convection, 1962, Advances in Geophysics, 1977—; asso. editor Jour. Geophys. Research, 1971-74; mem. editorial bd. Climate Dynamics, 1986—, ATMOSFERA, 1987—; co-editor Milankovitch and Climate, 1984; contbr. articles to profl. publs. Fellow AAAS, Am. Meteorol. Soc.; mem. Conn. Acad. Sci. and Engring., Am. Geophys. Union, Acad. Scis. Lisbon (hon. fgn.), European Geophys. Soc., Phi Beta Kappa, Sigma Xi. Home: 9 Forest Glen Dr Woodbridge CT 06525-1420 Office: Yale U Dept Geology and Geophysics PO Box 6666 New Haven CT 06511-8101

SALTZMAN, LEE STEPHEN, real estate executive; b. N.Y.C., Oct. 6, 1948; s. Paul and Shirley (Spierer) S.; m. Suzanne C. Holstein, Oct. 30, 1977; children: Amanda K., Zachary K. BS in Econs., U. Pa., 1970, JD, 1974. Bar: N.Y. 1975. Acct. Price Waterhouse & Co., N.Y.C., 1970-71; atty. Paul, Weiss, Rifkind, Wharton & Garrison, N.Y.C., 1974-79; various positions, officer The Rockefeller Group, N.Y.C., 1979-87; v.p. Salomon Bros., Inc., N.Y.C., 1987-88; sr. v.p. Rockefeller Ctr. Devel. Corp., N.Y.C., 1988—; bd. dirs., exec. com. Nat. Realty Com., Washington. Bd. dirs. N.Y. Assn. for New Ams., N.Y.C., Times Square Bus. Improvement Dist., N.Y.; trustee Citizens Budget Commn., N.Y.C. With N.Y.N.G., 1970-76. Mem. Assn. of the Bar of the CIty of N.Y., Real Estate Bd. N.Y., Young Men's/Women's Real Estate Assn. N.Y., Urban Land Inst., City Athletic Club, Metropolis Country Club, Rockefeller Ctr. Club. Home: 115 Central Park West New York NY 10023 Office: Rockefeller Ctr Devel Corp 1230 Ave of the Americas New York NY 10020

SALTZMAN, RACHELLE HOPE, folklorist, educator; b. Wilmington, Del., June 2, 1956; d. Stanley Allen and Pearl C. (Sachs) S. BA in History, U. Del., 1977; MA in History, U. Tex., 1980, PhD in Anthrolopology, 1988. Dir. ethnic heritage project Ctr. for So. Folklore, Memphis, 1982-83; folklife coord. Fla. Folklife Programs, White Springs, 1988-89, folklife programs adminstr., 1989-91; asst. prof. English U. Del., Newark, 1991—; adj. faculty U. Del., 1987. Editorial bd.: Talking Folklore, 1986-88; contbr. articles to profl. jours. Mem. Am. Folklore Soc. (co-convenor women's section 1989—), Folklore Women's Communication (co-editor 1988-91), Am. Anthrop. Assn., MLA, Folklore Soc. England, Phi Beta Kappa.

SALTZMAN, RICHARD ALAN, jewelry store executive; b. Providence, Jan. 19, 1947; s. Joseph and Estelle (Friedman) S.; m. Andrea Gladstone, Jan. 5, 1975 (dec. Jan. 1991); children: Evan Brian, Brooke Stacey. BS, Bentley Coll., 1970. Pres. Providence Watch Hosp., Inc., 1978—. Pres. adv. coun. mem. Bentley Coll., Waltham, Mass., 1985—; bd. dirs. Temple Beth Shalom, Bentley Coll. Alumnae Assn. (pres. 1982); chmn. Providence Mchts. Assn., 1980. With USAF, 1967-73. Mem. Providence C. of C. (bd. dirs.), Govs. Crime Commn., Redwood Masonic Lodge. Office: Providence Watch Hosp Inc 50 Eddy St Providence RI 02903-1719

SALVADORE, MICHAEL ANDREW, JR., jewelry manufacturing consultant; b. Providence, R.I., June 26, 1957; s. Michael Andrew and A. Doris (Leone) S. BS in Mech. Engring., U. R.I., 1980, BSBA, 1980. Design engr. Salvadore Tool & Findings Inc., Providence, 1980-90; pres. Metal Findings Mfrs. Assn., Providence, 1989-92, Am. Jewelry Products Group, Warwick, R.I., 1990, Cons. Group Inc., Warwick, 1990. Com. mem. March of Dimes, Providence, 1987-89, Alex Daunis for Congress, Providence, 1986, 88, Deprete for Gov., Providence, 1986, 88, 90. Mem. Soc. Mfg. Engrs., Providence Jewelers Club, World Brotherhood Fashion Jewelry Mfrs., Aircraft Owners and Pilots Assn., Jewelers and Silversmiths Mgmt. Assn., Mfg. Jewelers and Silversmiths Am. (nat. govt. affairs com. 1990—, nat. trade show com. 1988—, expo Providence com. 1988—), Metacomet Country Club. Roman Catholic.

SALVATORE, FRANK A., state legislator; b. Phila., June 2, 1922; s. Peter and Dominia Salvatore; m. Gloria Leggiere, Aug. 1947; children: Elizabeth, Gloria Jean, Frank, John, Anthony. Student, St. Joseph's Coll. Indsl. Relations, Phila.; student Fells Inst., U. Pa. Field auditor Pa. Dept. Revenue, Harrisburg; mem. Pa. Ho. of Reps., Harrisburg, 1972-84, Pa. State Senate, Harrisburg, 1985—; Mem. Counselling or Referral Assistance Services, Phila. Mem. Frankford Hosp. Adv. Bd., Phila. Boosters Club, Sunshine Found., Edith R. Rudolphy Residence for Blind. Served with USMC, 1942-45. Mem. Phila. Assn. Retarde Children, Inc., Police Chiefs Southeast Pa. Republican. Roman Catholic. Club: The Greater Bustleton/Somerton Synagogue Men's. Lodges: Lions, KC, Knights of Pythias, B'rith Sholom, Sons of Italy. Office: Pa State Senate State Capitol Harrisburg PA 17120-0030

SALVESEN, ROBERT HENRY, petroleum researcher; b. S.I., N.Y., Jan. 31, 1924; s. Anton Elias and Annie Gunhilda (Nelson) S.; m. Alice Knutson, June 12, 1948; children: Diane, Susan, Robert A. BS, Wagner Coll., 1948; MA, SUNY, 1951; PhD, Poly. Inst. of Bklyn., 1958. Group leader Mobil Oil Corp., Tech. Svc. Labs., Bklyn., 1958-59; rsch. assoc. Exxon Rsch. and Engring. Co., Linden, N.Y., 1959-82; cons., pres. Robert H. Salvesen Assocs., Tinton Falls, N.Y., 1983—; mem. adv. com. Monmouth Country Hazard Waste, Freehold, N.J., 1984—. Author: (with others) Hazard Waste Minsn, 1990; contbr. articles to profl. jours.; patentee in field. Mem., pres. Bd. Edn., Clark, N.J., 1962-72. Sgt. U.S. Army, 1943-46. Home and Office: 4 Palermo Dr Eatontown NJ 07724-3824

SALWASSER, HAL, forest ecologist; b. Fresno, Calif., Aug. 4, 1945; s. Mervin James and Elizabeth Jean (Thonen) S.; m. Susan Louise Fite, July 12, 1969; 1 child, James Barrett. BA in Biology, Calif. State U., Fresno, 1971; PhD in Wildland Resource Sci., U. Calif., Berkeley, 1979. Cert. wildlife biologist. Rsch. assoc. U. Calif., Berkeley, 1976-79; regional wildlife ecologist Forest Svc., USDA, San Francisco, 1979-82; nat. wildlife ecologist Forest Svc., USDA, Washington, 1982-85, dep. dir. wildlife and fisheries, 1985-90, dir. new perspectives, 1990—. Contbr. articles to profl. jours. With U.S. Army, 1965-68. Mem. Soc. Am. Foresters, Wildlife Soc. (v.p. 1991-92), Ecol. Soc. Am., Soc. for Conservation Biology (bd. govs. 1985-91), Soc. for Ecol. Restoration. Republican. Office: USDA Forest Svc 14th and Independence Washington DC 20050

SALWEN, BARRY DAVID, concert pianist; b. N.Y.C., July 20, 1955; s. N. Steven and Rima (Lazare) S.; m. Tamar Gilad, Oct. 25, 1987; 1 child, Maya Leah. MusB, The Julliard Sch., 1976, MusM, 1977; MusD, The Juilliard Sch., 1982; Diploma with Highest Honors, Hochschule fü Musik, Vienna, Austria, 1984. Faculty Bklyn. Conservatory of Music, 1979-82, piano dept. chmn., piano faculty, 1984-88, profl. div. dir., 1988-92; asst. prof. music U. N.C., Wilmington, 1992—; exec. dir. The Roger Sessions Soc., New Hempstead, N.Y., 1988—; faculty San Diego Chamber Music Workshop. Recorded compact disks including The Complete Piano Works of Roger Sessions, 1992, Music of Maximilian Kreuz, 1989, Music of Frank Retzel and Ruth Shaw Wylie, 1993. Recipient Fulbright fellowship to Austria, 1982-83, Recording grant for Sessions Compact Disk, NEA, 1990, The Mary Flagler Cary Charitable Trust, 1990. Mem. Coll. Music Soc. Office: U of North Carolina Div of Music 601 S College Rd Wilmington NC 28403-3297

SALWIN, ARTHUR ELLIOTT, software engineer; b. Chgo., Feb. 18, 1948; s. Harold and Shirley Salwin; m. Nancy Kessler, July 31, 1977; children: Edward, Rebecca. BS, U. Md., 1970; MA, Princeton U., 1972, PhD, 1975. Tech. staff Applied Physics Lab., Laurel, Md., 1976-78; rsch. staff Riverside Rsch. Inst., Arlington, Va., 1978-80; system engr. MITRE Corp., McLean, Va., 1980-91, group leader, lead engr., 1983—; instr. Fairfax County Adult Edn., McLean, 1982—; lectr. Georgetown U., Washington, 1980, 82. Fellow NSF, 1970, Noxell Found., 1969, Woodrow Wilson fellow, 1969. Mem. Assn. for Computing Machinery (spl. interest group on Ada, reviewer computing revs. Canvassee Ada '9X), Phi Beta Kappa, Phi Kappa Phi, Phi Eta Sigma.

SALWIN, HAROLD, retired chemist; b. Kansas City, Mo., Nov. 24, 1915; m. Shirley Z. Minsk, June 20, 1943; children: Arthur E., Barbara C. Salwin Finkelstein. BS in Chemistry, U. Chgo., 1941. Chemist Tenn. Valley Authority, Wilson Dam, Ala., 1942-43, U.S. Bur. of Mines/Explosives Rsch. Lab., Bruceton, Pa., 1943-45, U.S. Customs Lab., Chgo., 1945-48; rsch. chemist Armed Forces/Quartermaster Food and Container Inst., Chgo., 1948-58, head, food biochemistry lab., 1958-61, acting chief, chemistry br., 1961; rsch. chemist, Div. Food Chemistry FDA, Washington, 1961-64, head, decomposition and preservation sect., 1964-71, chief, protein and cereal products br., 1971-79. Contbr. articles to profl. jours. Recipient Outstanding Employee award Dept. Army, 1960, Rohland A. Isker award Rsch. and Devel. Assocs., Food and Container Inst., Chgo., 1962. Fellow Assn. of Official Analytical Chemists; mem. Am. Chem. Soc., Inst. Food Technologists. Home: 706 Kerwin Rd Silver Spring MD 20901-4621

SALZBERG, ALLAN MICHAEL, hospital administrator, physician; b. N.Y.C., Apr. 21, 1939; s. N. Emanuel and Mona (Hirsch) S.; m. Carol Ann Wachtel, June 19, 1960; children: Deborah Holmes, David. BA, Cornell U., 1960; PhD, U. Minn., 1964; MD, U. Md., 1973. Intern Mt. Sinai Hosp., N.Y.C., 1973-75; resident VA Med. Ctr., Washington, 1980-81; sr. ops. analyst Ctr. Naval Analysis, Arlington, Va., 1965-68; sr. ops. analyst AFGOA/USAF Hdqrs. Pentagon, Washington, 1968-70; spl. asst. to v.p. Sci. Applications, Crystal City, Va., 1979-80; pvt. practice Springfield, Va., 1981-85; chief of medicine Miles City (Mont.) VA Med. Ctr., 1986-89; chief of medicine Bath (N.Y.) VA Med. Ctr., 1989-91, chief of staff, 1991—. Author: (med. software) CALCUDOS, 1986-91; contbr. articles to profl. jours. Testifier on AIDS, U.S. Congress, Washington, 1987; founder, chair Gen. Nelson A. Miles Found., Miles City, 1988-89. Lt. comdr. USN, 1975-79. Mem. Rotary. Jewish. Office: Bath VA Med Ctr Bath NY 14810

SALZINGER, KURT, psychology educator; b. Vienna, Austria, Nov. 15, 1929; came to U.S., 1940; AB in Psychology, NYU, 1951; AM in Psychology, Columbia U., 1952, PhD in Psychology, 1954. Cert. psychologist, N.Y. Research psychologist Linden Hill Sch. for Disturbed Adolescents, Hawthorne, N.Y., 1954-56; assoc. project dir. N.Y. State Psychiatric Inst., 1956-67, prin. rsch. scientist, 1967-91; rsch. assoc in med. psychology Columbia U., N.Y.C., 1961—; assoc. prof. psychology Polytech. U., Bklyn., 1964-68, prof., 1968-92, head dept. social scis., 1981-84; prof. psychology, dir. grad. program clin./sch. psychology Hofstra U., Hempstead, N.Y., 1992—; vis. investigator Roscoe B. Jackson Meml. Lab., Bar Harbor, Maine, 1959, 60 (summers); lectr. psychology dept. Columbia U., N.Y.C., 1959-70, grad. seminar in abnormal psychology Rutgers U., 1960; vis. prof. in learning theory CUNY, 1971; program officer Applied Exptl. Psychology Sect. NSF, 1979-81; mem. numerous editorial bds. for profl. jours. Author: Psychology: the Science of Behavior, 1969, Schizophrenia Behavioral Aspects, 1973; editor: Psychology in Progress: Annals of the New York Academy of Sciences, 1976; co-editor: Research in Verbal Behavior and Some Neurophysiological Implications, 1967, Studies in Verbal Behavior, 1973, The Roots of American Psychology: Historical Influences and Implications for the Future, 1977, others; contbr. numerous articles to profl. jours. and chpts. to books; consulting editor, reviewer profl. jour. Recipient Sustained Superior Performance award, NSF, 1981. Fellow AAS, APA (divs. 1, 9, 12, 25, numerous offices and coms.), Am. Psychopathol. Assn. (Stratton award 1964), N.Y. Acad. Scis. (pres., numerous offices), Behavior Therapy and Rsch. Soc. (clin. fellow); mem. Sigma Xi, Psi Chi. Home: 161 W 75th St New York NY 10023-1801 Office: Hofstra U Hempstead NY 11550

SALZMAN, EDWIN WILLIAM, surgery educator; b. St. Louis, Dec. 11, 1928; s. J. Marvin and Sophie (Brook) S.; m. Nancy Lurie Salzman, Nov. 27, 1954; children: Andrew, David, James. AB, Washington U., St. Louis, 1950, MD, 1953; MA (hon.), Harvard U., 1969. Resident in surgery Mass. Gen. Hosp., Boston, 1953-61, asst. surgeon, 1961-66; instr. in med. sci. Harvard Med. Sch., Boston, 1961-62, asst. prof. surgery, 1967-69, assoc. prof. surgery, 1969-72, prof. surgery, 1972—; assoc. dir. surgery Beth Israel Hosp., Boston, 1966-82. Author books; dep. editor New Eng. Jour. Medicine, 1981—; contbr. numerous articles to profl. jours. Capt. USAF, 1954-56. Vis. scholar Corpus Christi Coll., Cambridge, Eng., 1976-77; recipient Disting. Achievement award Am. Heart Assn., 1986. Mem. Am. Soc. Clin. Investigations, Am. Soc. Hematology, Am. Surg. Assn., Internat. Soc. Thrombosis and Haemostasis (Disting. Career award 1991), Internat. Cardiovascular Soc., Soc. Vascular Surgery, Am. Coll. Surgeons, New Eng. Surg. Soc. Jewish. Office: Beth Israel Hosp 330 Brookline Ave Boston MA 02215-5491

SALZMANN, GEORGE STEPHEN, biochemist, priest; b. Phila., June 19, 1948; s. George Edward and Jean Elizabeth (Bigley) S. BS in Math. and Physics, Allentown U., 1971; MS in Molecular Biophysics, Yale U., 1973; STL in Moral Theology and Bioethics, The Gregorian U., Rome, 1978; PhD in Biol. Chemistry, Harvard U., 1987. Ordained priest Roma Cath. Ch., 1977. Fellow dept. molecular biology, lectr. dept. religion Princeton (N.J.) U., 1987-91; chaplain profl. schs. Harvard U., Cambridge, Mass., 1992—; assoc. pastor St. Catherine Ch., Norwood, Mass., 1978-85, Holy Cross Ch., Wayne, N.J., 1986-87, St. Paul's Ch., Princeton, 1987-90, St. Anthony's Ch., Princeton, 1988-92. Founder A.W.N. Pugin Soc. N.Am.; trustee Allentown Coll. of St. Francis de Sales, Center Valley, Pa., 1991—. Nat. Merit scholar, 1966; NSF fellow, 1971-73. Home: St Paul's Rectory 29 Mt Auburn St Cambridge MA 02138 Office: Harvard-Radcliffe Cath Student Ctr 20 Arrow St Cambridge MA 02138

SAMACH, MICHAEL ALAN, gastroenterologist; b. N.Y.C., Mar. 10, 1947; s. Samuel and Rae (James) S.; m. Alice Blumberg, Nov. 27, 1969; children: Julie, David, Laurie. AB, Cornell U., 1967; MD, NYU, 1971. Diplomate Am. Bd. Internal Medicine, Am. Bd. Gastroenterology. Intern in internal medicine Montefiore Hosp., Bronx, N.Y., 1971-72, resident in internal medicine, 1972-74, fellow in gastroenterology, 1976-78; pvt. practice Denville, N.J., 1978-87; physician Affiliates in Gastroenterology, Morristown, N.J., 1987—; asst. clin. prof. Columbia U. Coll. Physicians and Surgeons, N.Y.C., 1989—. Contbr. articles to profl. jours. Trustee United Jewish Fedn., Metrowest, 1991-92, Temple B'nai Or., Morristown, 1986. Maj. USAF, 1974-76. Fellow Am. Coll. Physicians, Am. Coll. Gastroenterology; mem. Am. Gastroenterol. Assn., Am. Soc. Gastrointestinal Endoscopy, N.J. Gastro Soc. (pres. 1987-88), Morris County Med. Soc. (pres. 1989-90), AMA. Office: 101 Madison Ave Morristown NJ 07960

SAMAHA, RICHARD JOHN, oncologist; b. Boston, June 7, 1938; s. John Rosseller and Agnes (Maloof) S.; m. Christine Gonis. BS, MIT, 1960; MD, PhD in Biochemistry, Boston U., 1966. Diplomate Am. Bd. Internal Medicine, Am. Bd. Hematology and Med. Oncology. Intern Boston U. Sch. Medicine, 1966-67; resident Cornel Med. Coll., N.Y.C., 1967-68; clin. assoc. Nat. Cancer Inst., NIH, Bethesda, Md., 1968-70; asst. prof. medicine U. Mo. Sch. Medicine, Columbia, 1970-74; cons. hematology and oncology Cardinal Cushing Hosp., Brockton, Mass., 1974—; chief, div. oncology and hematology Cardinal Cushing Hosp., Brockton, 1981—. Contbr. articles to profl. jours. With Pub. Health Svc., 1968-70. Mem. Am. Soc. Clin. Oncology, Am. Soc. Hematology, New Eng. Cancer Soc., Internat. Soc. Hematology. Mem. Eastern Orthodox Ch. Office: Med Oncology & Hematology 225 Quincy Ave Brockton MA 02402

SAMAT, RAMKISHIN KANU, academic health program director; b. Shikarpur, Sind, Pakistan, Mar. 22, 1945; came to U.S., 1966; s. Lakhmichand Sobhraj and Gopi (Ahuja) S.; m. Anna Jaroslava Pizar, Dec. 29, 1973; children: Tara, Maya. BSEE, U. Poona, India, 1966; MS in Indsl. Engring., Rutgers U., 1970; MA in Philosophy, New Sch. Social Rsch., N.Y.C., 1980. Project cons. The Port Authority N.Y. and N.J., N.Y.C., 1968-81; dir. ops. analysis Thomas Jefferson U., Phila., 1981-84, exec. assoc. to v.p. adminstrn. and fin., 1984-87, exec. assoc. to sr. v.p. health svcs., 1987-91; cons. Paragon Mgmt. Group, Inc., Malvern, Pa., 1991—; project cons. Assn. Acad. Health Ctrs., Washington, 1983. Mem. United Way Southeastern Pa. Rev., Phila., 1986—, trustee, 1986-89; v.p. Vol. Action Coun., Phila., 1985-86, pres., 1986-89. Recipient Exc. Dirs. award Port Authority N.Y. and N.J., N.Y.C., 1979-80. Mem. Assn. Internal Mgmt. Cons. (pres. 1988-90, bd. dirs. 1990—, Outstanding Dir. 1984-85), Rotary (chmn. neighborhood corps 1990-91, Award for Community Svc. 1991). Office: Great Valley Corp Ctr 18 Great Valley Pkwy Ste 190 Malvern PA 19355

SAMBACH, WARREN AUSTIN, JR., architect; b. Bronx, N.Y., May 2, 1945; s. Warren Austin Sr. and Thalia (Gerhold) S.; m. Lani Marie Holdsworth, Dec. 21, 1974; children: Allyson, Elizabeth. AA, Concordia Coll., 1965; BS, N.Y. Tech., 1973. Registered architect, N.Y., Fla., Ariz. Designer, draftsman DeMarco & Sotis, architects, Farmingdale, N.Y., 1970-72; sr. designer Rice Engrs., Mineola, N.Y., 1972-73; office mgr. H.R. Fulton Assocs., Jamaica, N.Y., 1973-75; jr. ptnr. Otto J. & Warren Sambach Engrs., Williston Park, N.Y., 1975-83; prin. architect, owner Sambach Assocs., Levittown, N.Y., 1983—; bldg. com. chmn. West Gilgo Beach Assn., Babylon, N.Y., 1983-87. Mem. AIA, Nat. Coun. Archtl. Registration Bds., Am. Arbitration Assn. (arbitrator 1988)., L.I. Hist. Soc. Lutheran.

SAMENFELD, HERBERT WILLIAM, retired psychology educator; b. Newark, Mar. 7, 1924; s. Herbert and Estelle Bertha (Andrew) S.; m. Melanie Marie Maxwell, Jan. 21, 1948; children: Herbert Scott, Lisa Gae. BA, Drew U., 1949; MA, U. Minn., 1951, PhD, 1954. Lic. psychologist N.J. Asst. prof. psychology So. Conn. State U., New Haven, 1953-57; counselor Vocat. Counseling Svc., New Haven, 1953-57; assoc. prof. Kean Coll., Union, N.J., 1957-89, dean students, 1962-69, prof. chmn. psychology, 1977-89, prof. emeritus, 1989—. Pres. Am. Cancer Soc. Union County Unit, Elizabeth, N.J., mem. exec. com. 1964—; pres. Assn. Good Schs., Scotch Plains, 1959-61; v.p. Kean Coll. Fedn. Tchrs., Union, 1969-89. With USAF, 1943-46. Rose Honor scholar, Drew U., 1942; Rsch. fellow U. Minn., 1950-53. Mem. Am. Psychol. Assn., N.J. Acad. Psychol. Democrat.

SAMERS, BERNARD NORMAN, fund raising executive; b. N.Y.C., Jan. 25, 1934; s. Abraham and Edith (Slomack) S.; m. Edith Maralyn Rosenblum, Sept. 7, 1958; children: Audrey Meryl, Michael Eric, William David. BS, Queens Coll., 1956; BSIE, Columbia U., 1956; MBA, Harvard U., 1958; postgrad., Columbia U., 1958-68. Registered profl. engr., Calif. Cons. S.B. Littauer & Assocs., N.Y.C., 1956; asst. dir. spl. studies Hudson Pulp & Paper Corp., N.Y.C., 1957; sr. mgmt. scientist Dunlap & Assocs., Inc., Darien, Conn., 1958-66; v.p. Cooper & Co., Mgmt. Cons., Stamford, Conn., 1966-82; v.p. adminstrn. and regional ops. Am. Technion Soc., N.Y.C., 1982-86; exec. v.p. Am. Com. for the Weizmann Inst. of Sci., N.Y.C., 1986—; adj. asst. prof. mgmt. engring. U. Bridgeport, 1972-88; lectr. MBA program U. Conn., 1980-82. Pres. Jewish Edn. in media, N.Y.C., 1978—, United Jewish Fedn. of Stamford, 1978-79; dir. Coun. of Jewish Fedn., 1979-80; committeeman Dem. City Com., Stamford, 1980-82. Mem. Nat. Assn. Fund Raising Execs., Assn. Jewish Community Orgn. Pers., Ops. Rsch. Soc. of Am. Democrat. jewish. Home: 180 Big Oak Rd Stamford CT 06903-4608 Office: Am Com Weizmann Inst Sci 51 Madison Ave New York NY 10010-1603

SAMETZ, ARNOLD WILLIAM, financial educator; b. Bklyn., Dec. 4, 1919; s. Milton William and Natalie (Holland) S.; B.A., Bklyn. Coll., 1940; M.A., Princeton U., 1942, Ph.D., 1951; m. Agnes Baroth, Nov. 23, 1956; children: Margaret Rutherford, Laura. Instr., Princeton U., 1948-51, asst. prof. econs., 1951-57; assoc. prof. banking and fin. NYU, N.Y.C., 1957-62, prof. fin. Grad. Sch. Bus. Adminstrn. and Charles Simon and Sidney Homer dir. Salomon Bros. Ctr. for Study Fin. Instns., 1975-90; prof. emeritus, fin. econ. cons.; editor Studies in Banking and Fin. Lt. USN, 1942-46. Mem. Am. Econ. Assn., Am. Fin. Assn., Royal Econ. Soc. Author: Financial Management, An Analytical Approach, 1967, Financial Development and Economic Growth, 1972, Prospects for Capital Formation and Capital Markets, 1978, Securities Activities of Commercial Banks, 1981, The Emerging Financial Industry, 1984, The Battle for Corporate Control, 1990, Institutional Investors--Challenges & Responsibilities, 1991. Office: NYU 37 Washington Sq W New York NY 10011-9181

SAMII, ABDOL HOSSEIN, physician, educator; b. Rasht, Iran, June 20, 1930; came to U.S., 1978; s. Mehdi Ebtehaj and Zahra (Mojdehi-Akbar) S.; m. Shahla Khosrowshahi; children: Ali, Golnaz. Student, Stanford U., 1947-49; BA, UCLA, 1950, MA, 1952; MD, Cornell U., 1956. Intern N.Y. Hosp., N.Y.C., 1956, asst. in medicine, 1956-58; asst. in physiology Cornell U. Med. Sch., N.Y.C., 1958-59; resident and sr. resident N.Y. Hosp., Peter Bent Brigham Hosp. and Mass. Gen. Hosp., Boston, 1959-61; adj. prof. medicine Cornell U. Med. Sch., 1973-79, prof. clin. medicine, 1979—; rsch. fellow Harvard U., Boston, 1959-60; prof. medicine Nat. Univ. Iran, Tehran, 1963-68; med. dir. Pars Hosp., Tehran, 1968-73; dir. div. medicine N.Y. Hosp.-Cornell Med. Coll., White Plains, 1979—; chancellor Reza Shah Kabir Grad. Univ., Tehran, 1973-78; cons. med. rsch. WHO, Geneva, 1973-79; v.p. Imperial Acad. Sci., Tehran, 1974-78. Gen. editor: International Textbook of Medicine, 1981; author, editor: Medical Clinics of North America, 1983, Textbook of Diagnostic Medicine, 1987. Dep. minister, Ministry of Health, Tehran, 1963-65; minister, Ministry Sci. and Higher Edn., Tehran, 1973-75. Fellow Rockefeller Found., Helen Hay Whitney Found. Fellow Royal Soc. of Medicine; mem. N.Y. Acad. Medicine, Harvey Soc., Internat. Soc. Nephrology, Am. Fed. Clin. Rsch. Office: NY Hosp CMC WD 21 Bloomingdale Rd White Plains NY 10605-1596 also: 449 E 68th St New York NY 10021

SAMILOWITZ, HAZEL FAYE, psychiatrist; b. N.Y.C., Mar. 22, 1940; d. Emanuel and Mary (Sevebrenik) S.; children: Susan, Elizabeth Victoria. MD, NYU, 1964. Diplomate Am. Bd. Psychiatry. Intern Montefiore Hosp., Pitts., 1968; resident Western Psychiat. Inst. & Clinics, U. Pitts., Pitts., 1968; pvt. practice Pitts., 1968—; cons. to nursing homes and hosp. psychiatry. Fellow Am. Psychiat. Assn.; mem. Pitts. Psychiat. Soc. (pres. 1980), Pa. Psychiat. Soc. Office: 9102 Babcock Blvd Bldg 209 Pittsburgh PA 15237-5819

SAMMIS, STUART KEITH, information systems specialist; b. Ft. Devans, Mass., Apr. 8, 1954; s. Walter Stuart and Erna Jesse (Harrison) S.; m. Barbara Ann Badzinski, Aug. 30, 1980; children: Dane Wesley, Stephanie Elizabeth, Trevor Christian. BA, Fairleigh Dickinson U., 1977; MA, NYU, 1981. Nationally cert. records mgr. Archivist U. Medicine and Dentistry N.J., Newark, 1980-85; mgr. Corp. Records Corning (N.Y.) Inc., 1985—; project mgr. Jour. Med. Soc. N.J., 1984. Contbr. articles to periodicals. Mem. Soc. Am. Archivists, Med. History Soc. N.J., Assn. Records Mgrs. and Adminstrs., Assn. Info. and Image Mgrs., Mid Atlantic Regional Archives Conf. Republican. Presbyterian. Office: Corning Inc HP AB 00 1 Corning NY 14831

SAMMON, GRACE MARIE, educational consulting company executive; b. Rockville Centre, N.Y., Sept. 8, 1953; d. Robert Martin and Josephine T. (Caruso) S. BA, Cath. U. Am., 1975, MA, 1977. Admissions counselor Cath. U. Am., Washington, 1975-79, dir. grad. fin. aid, 1979-82, asst. acad. v.p., 1982-85; pres. GMS Ptnrs., Silver Spring, Md., 1985—; exec. dir. Bus. Inst. for Educators, Silver Spring, 1987—; advisor Montgomery (Md.) Edn. Connection, 1991-92, Explorers, Prince Georges County, Washington, 1991—. Author: (handbook) Shadows/Mentors, 1991. Leader Girl Scouts U.S., Silver Spring, 1987-91; mem. St. Andrew's Sch. Bd., Silver Spring, 1991—. Mem. NAFE. Roman Catholic. Office: GMS Ptnrs 1122 Kersey Rd Silver Spring MD 20902

SAMMONS, KRISTAN RODGER, volunteer; b. Ogdenburg, N.Y.; d. Rutherford David and Alice Edna (Miller) Rodger; m. William L. Sammons, 1975. AB, Wilson Coll., 1964. Rsch. assoc. Friends Med. Sci. Rsch., Balt., 1965-74; adminstrv. asst. Family Planning Onon Co. Health Dept., Syracuse, 1974-75; rsch. asst. St. Camillus Health and Rehab. Ctr., Syracuse, 1975-77; exec. dir. Consortium for Children's Svcs., Syracuse, 1981-84; pres. Fedn. of Woman's Exchs., Syracuse, 1988-92. Leader Girl Scouts Am., Balt., 1966-74; pres., bd. vol. The Consortium for Children's Svcs., Syracuse, 1979-91; bd. mem. Child and Family Svcs., 1985-90, Regional Learning Svcs., 1991—, Girls, Inc., 1991—; panel liaison United Way Cen. N.Y., 1991—; chair com. on ministry Cayuga-Syr. Presbyn., 1992—; elder Park Ctr. Presbyn. Ch., 1992—. Recipient Woman of Achievement award Post Standard and Syracuse Fed. Woman's Clubs, 1987. Mem. Daughters Am. Revolution. Presbyterian. Home: 231 Brattle Rd Syracuse NY 13203

SAMPLES, JERRY WAYNE, army officer; b. Staunton, Va., July 18, 1947; s. Wilmer Clark and Nellie Virginia (Price) S.; m. Kathleen Miller, Nov. 2, 1969; children: Christopher John, Steven Wayne. BS, Clarkson Coll., 1969; MS, Okla. State U., 1979, PhD, 1983. Registered profl. engr., Va. Lab. asst. Columbia Ribbon & Carbon, Glen Cove, N.Y., 1969-70; commd. 2d lt. U.S. Army, 1969, advanced through grades to col., 1991; asst. prof. mech. engring. U.S. Mil. Acad., West Point, N.Y., 1979-82; with Air Command and Staff Coll., Maxwell AFB, Ala., 1983; exec. officer 10th Engr. Bn., 1983-85, bn. comdr. 10th engr. bn. 3d inf. div., Fed. Republic Germany, 1987-89; assoc. prof. mech. engring. U.S. Mil. Acad., West Point, 1985-87, assoc. prof. dept. civil and mech. engr., 1989—. Author (with others) Fundamentals of Engineering Examination, 1991. Decorated Army Commendation medal, Meritorious Svc. medal. Mem. AIAA, ASME, Phi Kappa Phi. Home: 17 Wilson Rd # A West Point NY 10996-1706 Office: US Mil Acad Dept Civil and Mech Engring West Point NY 10996

SAMPSON, DAVID SYNNOTT, lawyer; b. Troy, N.Y., Oct. 2, 1942; s. Stephen Hastings and Ruth (Hall) S.; m. Arlene Mernit, July 1, 1967; children: Christopher Hastings, Jamie Everett. B.A., St. Lawrence U., 1965; J.D., Albany Law Sch., 1973. Bar: N.Y. 1975, D.C. 1977, U.S. Ct. Appeals (D.C. cir.) 1977. Reporter Troy Record, 1965-67; newsman AP, 1967-70; spl. asst. N.Y. State Dept. Environ. Cons., Albany, 1972-74; panel dir. Com. on Critical Choices for Ams., N.Y.C., 1974-75; chief legis. asst. U.S. Rep. H. J. Heinz, Washington, 1975-77; assoc. Boasberg, Hewes, Finkelstein & Klores, Troy, 1977-79; exec. dir. Am. Land Forum, Washington, 1978-79, Hudson River Valley Assn., Troy and Cold Spring, N.Y., 1987-89, Hudson River Valley Greenway Coun., Albany, 1989—; ptnr. Pattison, Sampson, Ginsberg & Griffin, Troy, N.Y., 1979—. Pres. Samaritan Hosp. Found., 1985—; bd. dirs. Samaritan Hosp., Troy, 1985—, St. Gregorys Sch., Loudonville, N.Y., 1982—. Troy Pub. Libr. Found., 1991—, Scenic Hudson, Poughkeepsie, N.Y., 1982—, vice-chmn., 1989—; bd. dirs. Preservation League N.Y., Albany, 1982—, adv. bd., 1989—; mem. N.Y. State Freshwater Wetlands Appeals Bd., 1980—, chmn., 1980—; active U.S./UK Countryside Stewardship Exch., Eng., 1989. Contbr. book revs., articles to profl. jours. Mem. Am. Conservation Assn. (bd. dirs. 1987—), N.Y. Pks. and Conservation Assn. (founding dir. 1986—), N.Y. State Bar Assn. (chmn. hist. preservation com. 1980—, exec. com. 1985—, chmn. environ. law sect.), Bar Assn. City of N.Y. Avocation: bicycling. Office: 22 1st St PO Box 208 Troy NY 12181 also: Hudson River Valley Greenway Coun PO Box 2080 Albany NY 12220-0080

SAMPSON, ROBERT CARL, JR., psychiatrist; b. Concord, N.H., June 6, 1948; s. Robert Carl Sr. and Alice May (Bedor) S. BA magna cum laude, Yale U., 1970; MD, U. Pa., 1974; CAc, New Eng. Sch. Acupuncture, Watertown, Mass., 1984. Diplomate Nat. Bd. Med. Examiners, Am. Bd. Psychiatry and Neurology, Child Psychiatry. Intern Bryn Mawr (Pa.) Hosp., 1974-75; resident in psychiatry U. Mich., Ann Arbor, 1975-77; resident in child psychiatry N.Eng. Med. Ctr., Boston, 1977-79; staff psychiatrist Beaverbrook Guidance Ctr., Waltham, Mass., 1979-89, med. dir., 1989—; med. dir. Sino-U.S. Qi Gong Health Scis. Devel. Ctr., Cambridge, Mass., 1985-87; psychiatrist Ctr. for Health, Newton Centre, Mass., 1986-89; instr. psychiatry Harvard U. Med. Sch., Boston, 1987-90; assoc. med. dir. Family Counseling and Guidance Ctrs., Inc., Marshfield, Mass., 1987-89; rsch. cons. Cambridge Hosp.-Psychiatry Dept., 1987-90; founder, cons. Stress Transformation Systems, Watertown, 1987—. Contbr. articles to profl. jours. Fellow Am. Acad. Child and Adolescent Psychiatry; mem. Am. Psychiat. Assn., Mass. Psychiat. Soc., New Eng. Coun. Child and Adolescent Psychiatry, Internat. Soc. Study of Subtle Energies and Energy Medicine, Phi Beta Kappa. Self-Realization Fellowship. Home: PO Box 333 Watertown MA 02272-0333 Office: 1126 Beacon St 2d Fl Newton MA 02161

SAMPUGNA, JOSEPH, chemist, biochemist, educator; b. Brewster, N.Y., Sept. 27, 1931; s. Anthony and Angela (Agusta) S.; m. Dorothy J. Leduc, June 1, 1957; children: Joseph Anthony, Theresa Ann. BA, U. Conn., 1957, MA, 1962, PhD, 1968. Rsch. assoc. U. Conn., Storrs, 1961-68; asst. prof. U. Md., College Park, 1968-72, assoc. prof., 1972—; treas. Chem. Assn. of Md., University Park, 1980—. Author: Molecules in Living Systems, 1972, 78; contbr. articles to profl. jours. With USAF, 1951-55. Mem. Am. Oil Chem. Soc., Am. Chem. Soc., Am. Inst. Nutrition. Office: U Md Dept Chemistry College Park MD 20742

SAMS, JAMES FARID, real estate development company executive; b. Bay City, Mich., Apr. 21, 1932; s. James and Adele (Abuismail) S.; m. Betty Suham Hamady, Aug. 17, 1957; children: James Karl, Alicia Diane, Victoria Saab. BA, Northwestern U., 1954; JD, U. Mich., 1957; LLM, Harvard U., 1959. Com. counsel ABA spl. com. World Peace/Law, Washington, 1960-63; ptnr. Reeves, Harrison, Sams & Revercomb, Washington, 1964-69, Brown & Sams, Washington, 1969-71, Kirkwood, Kaplan, Russin, Veechi & Sams, Beirut, 1971-74; cons. Universal Exchange Corp., Beirut, London, Washington, 1974-77; owner, prin. Am. Devel. Services Corp., Washington, 1978—; chmn. bd. DASI, Inc., Washington, 1974-90; rep. U.S. State Dept. Ams. Abroad, Washington, 1965; del. UN Com. on Internat. Trade Law, N.Y.C., 1970. Contbr. articles to profl. jours. Co-founder, dir. Am. Near East Refugee Aid, Washington, 1968—; adv. bd. Legacy Internat. Youth Program, Washington, 1983—; dir. U.S. Interreligious Com. for Peace in the Middle East, Washington. Served to lt. U.S. Army, 1957-58. Mem. ABA, Bar Assn. of Washington, Am. Soc. Internat. Law, Nat. Assn. Arab Ams. (pres. 1981, chmn. 1983), City Club, Georgian Club. Clubs: City (Washington); Georgian (Atlanta). Home: 8907 Fernwood Rd Bethesda MD 20817-3015 Office: Am Devel Svcs Corp 5454 Wisconsin Ave Ste 1260 Bethesda MD 20815-6901

SAMUEL, DAN JUDAH, management consultant; b. Jerusalem, Mar. 25, 1925; came to U.S., 1981; s. Viscount Edwin Herbert and Viscountess Hadassah (Grasovsky) S.; m. Esther Gordon, July 14, 1957 (div. 1977); children: Lia, Maia, Jonathan; m. Heather Macdonald Cumming, Mar. 10, 1981 (div. 1992); children: Sasha, Benjamin. BA and MA, Oxford U., Eng., 1950; postgrad., John Hopkins U., 1951. With Royal-Dutch Shell Group, 1952-86; gen. mgr., chief exec. officer Shell Co. of Thailand, Bangkok, 1962-66; pres., chief exec. officer Belgian Shell, Brussels, 1967-70; mktg. coord. Shell Internat. Petroleum Co., London, 1972-76, group pers. coord., 1976-77, regional coord. western hemisphere, 1977-81; bd. dirs. Shell Internat. Petroleum Co., London, 1973-81; pres., chief exec. officer Scallop Corp., N.Y.C., 1981-86; ret. Royal-Dutch Shell Group, 1986; mgmt. cons. Westport, Conn., 1986—; bd. dirs. Witco Corp., N.Y.C., 1985—, Can. Overseas Packing Industries, 1988—; mem. energy com. Cavenham Forest Industries, Inc., Portland, Oreg., 1985-87; mem. Latin Am. Trade Adv. Group, London, 1977-81; cons. Nat. Exec. Service Corps, 1988—. Trustee Asian Inst. Tech., Bangkok, 1962-68, 72-91; trustee Brit. Am. Ednl. Found., N.Y.C., 1984—; bd. dirs. Coun. of Ams., N.Y.C., 1981-86, Found. Mgmt. Edn. London, 1975-77. Maj. Yorkshire Hussars Brit. Royal Armored Corps, 1943-47. Decorated comdr. Order of Royal Crown (Thailand), officer Order of Crown (Belgium). Mem. Oxford and Cambridge U. Club (London), Spl. Forces Club (London), Hurlingham (London), Chichester Yacht Club (Eng.), Westhampton (LI) Yacht Squadron. Home: 154 Hillspoint Rd Westport CT 06880-6104

SAMUEL, STUART ALAN, physics research educator; b. Buffalo, N.Y., Aug. 8, 1953. BA, Princeton U., 1975; PhD, U. Calif. Berkeley, 1979. Mem. Inst. for Advanced Study, Princeton, N.J., 1979-81; paid sci. assoc. CERN, Geneva, Switzerland, 1985-86; asst. prof. physics Columbia U., N.Y.C., 1981-84; full prof. physics CCNY, N.Y.C., 1984—. Contbr. articles to profl. jours. Recipient PACER award, Control Data Corp., 1985; Sloan fellowship Alfred P. Slo an Found., 1984, Chester-Davis fellowship Ind. U., 1988; grantee: rsch. grant DOE, 1987-91, NATO, 1988-91. Office: CCNY 138th St and Convent Ave New York NY 10031

SAMUELS, CARL EUGENE, quality control engineer; b. Anchorage, Alaska, Apr. 6, 1953; s. Richard G. and Lillian L. (Stroud) S.; m. Chanda Coats, Apr. 22, 1989. BSEE, MIT, 1975. Devel. engr. Raytheon Co., Waltham, Mass., 1975-76; cons. ptnr. H & S Components, Cleve., 1976-78; design/devel. engr. Electronics Corp. Am., Cambridge, Mass., 1978-80; component engr. Wang, Tewksbury, Mass., 1980-82; quality control engr. Raytheon Co., Andover, Mass., 1982—; cons. quality, 1990—. Author: Receiving Quality, 1991; contbr. articles on quality to profl. jours. Mem. Black Alumni MIT, Cambridge, 1975, MIT Club N.H., 1984. Mem. Am. Soc. for Quality Control (cert. engr.), Mensa. Home: PO Box 102 Newton Junction NH 03859-0102

SAMUELS, JERALD M., accountant; b. N.Y.C., Dec. 12, 1936; s. Morris Schmulovitz and Mollie (Kalvariska) S.; m. Phyllis Ann Cosentino, Nov. 17, 1963; children: Karen, Michael. BBA, CCNY, 1958. CPA, N.Y. Acct. Benjamin Botowinick, CPA, N.Y.C., 1958-60, Joseph D. Blau and Co., CPA, N.Y.C., 1960-62, Eutectic, N.Y.C., 1962-66; budget dir. Eutectic, Brazil, 1966-67; sr. v.p. fin. Manhattan/Salant, N.Y.C., 1967—. Mem. AICPA, N.Y. Soc. CPAs. Office: Mahattan/Salant 1114 6th Ave New York NY 10036-7703

SAMUELS, RICHARD MEL, clinical psychologist, communications executive; b. Bklyn., Mar. 22, 1943; s. Murray and Rose S.; m. Linda Nersesian, Dec. 2, 1984; children: Lisa, David; stepchildren: Michelle, Michael. AAS, SUNY, 1961; BA, Hofstra U., 1965, MA, 1967; PhD, City U. N.Y., 1973; post-doctoral diploma Human Sexuality dept. Ob/Gyn N.J. Med. Sch. Diplomate Am. Bd. Clin. Psychology, diplomate in sexology ACS. Adj. assoc. prof. City U. N.Y., 1970-73; sr. clin. psychologist N.J. Med. Sch., Newark, 1973-74, sr. clin. prof. human sexuality program, dept. ob-gyn also adj. asst. prof. dept. psychiatry, 1974-76, dir. gender dysphoria clinic, 1974-76; clin. psychologist, creator 2d self discovery program; cons. in psychologically designed programming; dir. Human Insights Assocs.; pres., chief exec. officer Ambivision Inc., Oradell, 1986-90; pres. RMS Communications, N.J., 1990—; producer video programming which reduces perception of time; creator advt.-sponsored waiting room video programming with on-line data updates; chmn., exec. v.p. Travelvues, Oradell and Cin., 1986-90; dir. Intergalactic Trading Corp.; clin. dir. Biotech Resource Ctr. Corp.; mem. clin. faculty Sch., Applied and Profl. Psychology, Rutgers U. Grad. Sch.; internat. commodities trader; cons. Teaneck Group Home for Girls. Author: Sex During Pregnancy and the Postpartum Period, 1976, A Gender Dysphoria Clinic in New Jersey, 1977, Computers, An Extension of the Psychologist's Mind; cons. editor Behavior Therapy, 1973-80; editor Pvt. Practitioner, 1976-82; software rev. editor Jour. Psychotherapy and Pvt. Practice; inventor avist display system. Recipient Albert J. Harris award City U. N.Y., 1967; N.J. Med. Sch. fellow, 1973-74, clin. fellow Am. Acad. Clin. Sexologists. Fellow APA (past pres. div. ind. practice of psychology, chmn. com. on expanded psychol. practice), Behavior Therapy and Rsch. Soc., Eastern Assn. Sex Therapists (charter); mem. AAAS, Assn. Advancement of Behavior Therapy, N.J. Psychol. Assn., N.J. Assn. for Advancement Psychology (pres.), N.J. Acad. Psychology. Office: 354 Old Hook Rd Ste 205 Westwood NJ 07645

SAMUELSON, KENNETH LEE, lawyer; b. Natrona Heights, Pa., Aug. 22, 1946; s. Sam and Frances Bernice (Robbins) S.; m. Marlene Ina Rabinowitz, Jan. 1, 1980; children: Heather, Cheryl. BA magna cum laude, U. Pitts., 1968; JD, U. Mich., 1971. Bar: Md. 1972, D.C. 1980, U.S. Dist. Ct. Md. 1984. Assoc. Weinberg & Green, Balt., 1971-73, Dickerson, Nice, Sokol & Horn, Balt., 1973; asst. atty. gen. State of Md., 1973-77; pvt. practice Balt., 1978; ptnr. Linowes and Blocher, Silver Spring (Md.), Washington, 1979—. Author in field. 2d v.p., bd. dirs. D.C. Assn. for Retarded Citizens, Inc., 1981—. Capt. U.S. Army, 1976. Mem. ABA (vice-chmn. comml. leasing com., sect. real property, probate and trust law 1988—, moderator programs comml. leases 1981, 83, 88, 89, 90, 91), D.C. Bar (comml. real estate com., chmn. subcom. legal opinions 1987-91, moderator and speaker programs on real estate 1987, 89, 90), Md. State Bar Assn. (real property, planning and zoning sect., chmn. environ. subcom. legal opinions project, 1987-89, litigation sect. 1982-84, chmn. comml. trans. com.), Md. Inst. Continuing Profl. Edn. Lawyers (speaker on article 9 of Uniform Comml. Code, opinion letters and environ. considerations in real estate transactions and easements 1987, 88, 89, 91), Apt. and Office Bldg. Assn. (moderator of programs and speaker Met. Washington, 1989), East Coast Builders Conf. (moderator program on Asian financing 1990-91), Internat. Coun. Shopping Ctrs. (organized, co-faculty program "univ." 1988), Montgomery County Bar Assn. (jud. selections com. 1988-90), Phi Beta Kappa. Office: Linowes & Blocher 800 K St NW Ste 840 Washington DC 20001-3742

SAMUELSON, PAUL ANTHONY, economics educator; b. Gary, Ind., May 15, 1915; s. Frank and Ella (Lipton) S.; m. Marion E. Crawford, July 2, 1938 (dec.); children: Jane Kendall, Margaret Wray, William Frank, Robert James, John Crawford, Paul Reid.; m. Risha Eckaus, 1981. B.S., U. Chgo., 1935; M.A., Harvard U., 1936, Ph.D. (David A. Wells prize 1941), 1941; LL.D., U. Chgo., Oberlin Coll., 1961, Boston Coll., 1964, Ind. U., 1966, U. Mich., 1967, Claremont Grad. Sch., 1970, Seton Hall U., 1971, U. N.H., 1971, Keio U., 1971, Widener Coll., 1982, Cath. U. at Riva Aguero U., Lima, Peru, 1980; D.Sc., East Anglia U., Norwich, Eng., 1966; D.Litt. (hon.), Ripon Coll., 1962, No. Mich. U., 1973; L.H.D., Williams Coll., 1971; D.Sc., U. Mass., 1972, U. R.I., 1972; LL.D., Harvard, 1972, Gustavus Adolphus Coll., 1974, U. So. Calif., 1975, U. Pa., 1976, U. Rochester, 1976, Emmanuel Coll., 1977, Stonehill Coll., 1978; Doctorate Honoris Causa, U. Catholique de Louvain, Belgium, 1976, City U., London, 1980, New U. Lisbon, 1985; DLitt., Valparaiso U., 1987; DLitt, Columbia U, 1988; DSc, Tufts U., 1988; Doctor Honoris Causa, Univ. Nat. de Educacion a Distancia, Madrid, 1989, Univ. Politecnica de Valencia, Spain, 1991. Prof. econs. MIT, 1940-65, inst. prof., 1966, prof. emeritus, Gordon Y. Billard fellow, 1986; mem. staff Radiation Lab., 1944-45; prof. internat. econ. relations Fletcher Sch. Law and Diplomacy, 1945; cons. Nat. Resources Planning Bd., 1941-43, WPB, 1945, U.S. Treasury, 1945-52, 61-74, Bur. Budget, 1952, RAND Corp., 1948-75, Fed. Res. Bd., 1965—; council Econ. Advisers, 1960-68; econ. adviser to Pres. Kennedy; sr. adviser Brookings Panel on Econ. Activity; mem. spl. commn. on social scis. NSF, 1967-68; cons. int Econ. Council, Congl. Budget Office; inst. prof. emeritus, Gordon Y Billard Fellow MIT, Boston, 1986; vis. prof of polit. econ. Ctr. Japan-U.S. Bus. and Econ. Studies, NYU, 1987—; Stamp Meml. lectr., London, 1961, Wicksell lectr., Stockholm, 1962, Franklin lectr., Detroit, 1962; Carnegie Found. reflective year, 1965-66; John von Neumann lectr. U. Wis., 1971; Gerhard Colm Meml. lectr. New Sch. for Social Research, N.Y.C., 1971; Sulzbacher Meml. lectr. Columbia Law Sch., N.Y.C., 1974; J. Willard Gibbs lectr. Am. Math. Soc., San Francisco, 1974; John Diebold lectr. Harvard, 1976; Alice E. Blurneuf lectr. Boston Coll., 1981, Horowitz lectr. Jerusalem and Tel Aviv, 1984, Marschak Meml. lectr. UCLA, 1984, Tennenbaum lectr. Ga. Inst. Tech., 1985, Woodward lectr. U. British Columbia, 1987; lectr. Harvard 350 Symposium, Harvard U., 1986, commemorative lectr. Stonehill Coll., 1990, Lionel Robbins Meml. lectr. Claremont Coll., 1991; Vernon F. Taylor vis. disting. prof. Trinity U., San Antonio, Tex., 1989; Olin lectr. U. Va. Law Sch., 1989, many other lectureships. Author: Foundations of Economic Analysis, 1947, enlarged edit., 1983, Economics, 1948-85, Readings in Economics, 1955, 13th edit., 1989 (with R. Dorfman and R.M. Solow) Linear Programming and Economic Analysis, 1958, Collected Scientific Papers, 5 vols., 1966, 72, 78, 86; co-author numerous other books.; Contbr. numerous articles to profl. jours.; Columnist for, Newsweek, 1966-81; assoc. editor: Jour. Pub. Econs., Jour. Internat. Econs., Jour. Fin. Econs., Jour. Nonlinear Analysis; adv. bd. Challenge Mag.; editorial bd. Proceedings Nat. Acad. Scis. Chmn. Pres.'s Task Force Maintaining Am. Prosperity, 1964; mem. Nat. Task Force on Econ. Edn., 1960-61; econ. adviser to Pres. John F. Kennedy, 1959-63; mem. adv. bd. Nat. Commn. Money and Credit, 1958-60. Hon. fellow London Sch. Econs. and Polit. Sci. Guggenheim fellow, 1948-49; Ford Found. research fellow, 1958-59; recipient John Bates Clark medal Am. Econ. Assn., 1947, Alfred Nobel Meml. prize in econ. sci., 1970, Medal of Honor U. Evansville, Ill., 1970, Albert Einstein Commemorative award, 1971, Alumni medal U. Chgo., 1983, Britannica award, 1989, Gold Scanno prize, Naples, Italy, 1990. Fellow Brit. Acad. (corr.), Am. Philos. Soc., Econometric Soc. (v.p. 1950, pres. 1951), Am. Econ. Assn. (hon.; pres. 1961); mem. AAAS, Com. Econ. Devel. (commn. on nat. goals, research adv. bd. 1959-60), Am. Acad. Arts and Scis., Internat. Econ. Assn. (pres. 1966-68, hon. pres.), Nat. Acad. Scis., Leibniz-Akademie der Wissenschaften und der Literatur (corr. mem. 1987—) Nat. Assn. of Investment Clubs (Disting. Svc. award in Investment Edn. 1974), Club of Econ. and Mgmt. (medal, hon. Valencia, Spain 1990), Phi Beta Kappa, Omicron Delta Kappa (trustee), Omicron Delta Epsilon (trustee). Home: 94 Somerset St Belmont MA 02178-2010 Office: MIT Dept Econs Cambridge MA 02139

SAMUELSON, SYLVIA HELLER, retired elementary school principal; b. N.Y.C.; d. Louis and Sadie (Auerbach) Heller; m. Aaron Samuelson, Dec. 22, 1935 (dec. Mar. 1967); children: Herbert, Claire Samuelson Meadow; m. Noah Goldstein, Feb. 12, 1975 (dec. Jan. 1986). BA, CUNY, 1931; M in Supervision and Adminsrtn., NYU, 1960. Tchr. Jr. High Sch., N.Y.C., 1955-59, asst. prin., 1959-69; asst. examiner Bd. Edn., N.Y.C., 1960-69; prin. N.Y.C. Elem. Schs., Bklyn., 1970-80. Sec., bd. dirs. Bklyn. Jewish Community Coun., 1970-75; bd. dirs. Bronx House-Emmanuel Camps, N.Y.C., 1950—, Long Beach Coun. on Arts, 1976—; sec., treas., bd. dirs. YM/YWHA, Long Beach, 1976—. Mem. Ret. Sch. Suprs. (chmn. com. 1992). Democrat. Jewish. Home: 7502A Lido Blvd Long Beach NY 11561-5296

SANADI, D. RAO, research institute administrator; b. India, July 8, 1920. PhD in Biochemistry, U. Calif., 1949. Fellow Nat. Cancer Inst., 1949-52, rsch. assoc., 1952-53; asst. prof. biochemistry U. Wis., 1953-55; asst. prof. U. Calif., 1955-58; chief sect. comparative biochemistry NIH, 1958-66; dir. dept. cell physiology Boston Biomed. Rsch. Inst., 1966--, exec. dir., 1969-71, 75-77, 81-83; assoc. prof. dept. biol. chemistry Med. Sch. Harvard U., Boston, 1975—; chmn. Gordon Rsch. Conf. on Energy Coupling Mechanisms, 1969, 74, Gordon Rsch. Conf. on Biology of Aging, 1974; mem. adult devel. and aging rsch. and tng. com. Nat. Inst. Child Health and Human Devel., 1970-73; mem. adv. panel metabolic biology NSF, 1971-74; mem. cell transport and metabolism study com. Am. Heart Assn., 1990—. Editor Jour. Bioenergetics Biomembrane, 1975-91; mem. editorial bd. Arch. Biochem. Biophys., 1970-76, Biochim. Biophys. Acta, 1975-76. Established investigator Am. Heart Assn., 1954-58. Fellow Gerontol. Soc. Am.; mem. AAAS, Am. Chem. Soc., Am. Soc. Biol. Chemistry, Biophys. Soc., Am. Soc. Cell Biology. Office: Boston Biomed Rsch Inst Dept Cell/Molecular Biology 20 Staniford St Boston MA 02114-2500

SANANMAN, MICHAEL LAWRENCE, neurologist; b. Bklyn., Oct. 11, 1939; s. Jack and Sarey (Bykofsky) S.; m. Elisa Joan Freeman, Apr. 12, 1964; children: Amy, Peter. AB, Swarthmore Coll., 1960; MD, Columbia U., 1964. Diplomate Am. Bd. Psychiatry and Neurology. Intern, Univ. Hosp., San Francisco, 1964-65; resident in neurology N.Y. Neurol. Inst., N.Y.C., 1966-69; practice medicine specializing in neurology, Elizabeth, N.J., 1972—; cons. neurologist St. Elizabeth's Hosp., Elizabeth Gen. Hosp., Rahway (N.J.) Hosp.; instr. neurology Columbia U., N.Y.C., 1971-75; assoc. clin. prof. neurology U. Medicine and Dentistry N.J., Newark, 1975—; mem. adv. coun. N.J. chpt. Multiple Sclerosis Soc. Served to lt. comdr. M.C., USNR, 1969-71. Mem. AMA, Am. Acad. Neurology, Am. Epilepsy Soc. (adv. coun. N.J. chpt.), N.J. Acad. Medicine (chmn. neurology sect.), Am., Eastern EEG socs., Am. Assn. EMG and Electrodiagnosis. Office: 700 N Broad St Elizabeth NJ 07208

SAND, LEONARD B., federal judge; b. N.Y.C., May 24, 1928. B.S., NYU, 1947; LL.B., Harvard, 1951. Bar: N.Y. 1953, U.S. Supreme Ct. 1956, D.C. 1969. Clk. to dist. ct. judge N.Y., 1952-53; asst. U.S. atty. So. Dist. N.Y., 1953-54; asst. to U.S. Solictor Gen., 1956-59; mem. firm Robinson, Silverman, Pearce, Aronsohn Sand and Berman, N.Y.C., 1960-78; judge U.S. Dist. Ct. So. Dist. N.Y., 1978—; adj. prof. law NYU. Note editor: Harvard Law Rev, 1950-51. Del. N.Y. State Constl. Conv., 1967; v.p., treas. Legal Aid Soc. Fellow Am. Coll. Trial Lawyers; mem. Assn. Bar City N.Y., N.Y. State, Am. bar assns., Fed. Bar Council. Office: US Dist Ct US Courthouse Foley Sq New York NY 10007-1501

SANDBERG, ROBERT GUSTAVE, sales and marketing executive; b. Mpls., Mar. 20, 1939; d. Gustave Benhart and Edna (Leshefski) S.; m. Nancy Root Sandberg, Dec. 27, 1959; children: Kurt, Mark, Sarah. BSc, Hamline U., 1961; MSc, Ohio State U., 1963. Rsch. chemist Cargill, Inc., Mpls., 1963-66; sr. rsch. chemist Hoerner-Waldorf Corp., St. Paul, 1966-68; clin. chemist St. Johns Hosp., St. Paul, 1968-71; mktg. rep., new product analyst, mgr. DuPont Co., Wilmington, Del., 1971-81, tech. mgr., 1981-82, mgr. bus. devel., 1985-88; mgr. clin. diagnostics New Eng. Nuclear, Billerica, Mass., 1982-85; v.p. sales and mktg. Ohmicron Corp., Newtown, Pa., 1988—; presenter at profl. confs. Contbr. articles to profl. publs. Mem. Groton (Mass.) Bd. of Health, 1983, chmn., 1984. Mem. Am. Chem. Soc., Am. Assn. Clin. Chemists, Internat. Assn. Ofcl. Analytical Chemists, Inst. Food Technologists, Biomed. Mktg. Assn. (pres. 1979, bd. dirs. 1979-81), Moose. Lutheran. Home: 110 Hobson Dr Hockessin DE 19707 Office: Ohmicron Corp 375 Pheasant Run Newtown PA 18940

SANDELL, RICHARD ARNOLD, international trade executive, economist; b. Buenos Aires, Argentina, Oct. 22, 1937; s. Kurd Wolfcang and Isolde Mary (Josevich) S.; m. Phyllis H. Levinson, July 6, 1968; children: Laurie Alyssa, Karyn Joy, Sylvie Jennine. BA in Social Sci., U. Buenos Aires, 1957, JD, 1959; MS in Econs., U. San Marcos, 1960; LLM in Internat. Law, NYU, 1962; Ph.D., Columbia U., 1972, M.B.A., 1977. Dir. bus. planning Guerrero Merc. Internat. Ltd., Buenos Aires, 1954-62; gen. mgr. Acquatronic Universal, Inc., 1965-68; corp. v.p. indsl. econs. Mgmt. Analyst Group, Ins., Van Nuys, Calif., 1968-70; pres., chief exec. officer A.I.M. Internat. Corp., Alameda, Calif., 1970-76; pres., chief exec. officer, dir. Aurag Internat. Corp. and Aura Tech. Corp., Larchmont, N.Y., 1979—; bd. dirs. FerroCement Internat. Ltd. of Panama, Consorcio Pesquero Marmesa of Guayaquil, Ecuador, INTEX S.A., Buenos Aires, Export Marketeers Ltd., Auckland, N.Z., Aledo Transnat. Trading Corp., Panama, Geneva, Oakland, Calif., dir. Nexus Corp., Santa Rosa, Calif., Guanabara Mining Co., Rio De Janeiro, Brazil, Primax Electronics Ltd., Aimore Internat. Corp., Stockton, Calif., Premisa, S.A., Venezuela; former cons. U.S. Dept. State, govts. Ecuador, Nicaragua, Guyana, Zaire, Fiji, El Salvador, N.Z., Ghana, currently cons. to Taiwan, Chile, Venezuela, Brazil, 1972—; cons. Nat. Security Coun. during Desert Shield and Desert Storm Campaign, 1990-91; cons. on privatization Govt. Argentina; adj. prof. bus. adminstrn. Elbert Covell Coll. and Coll. Pacific at U. Pacific, 1972-77; adj. prof. internat. bus., mgmt. U. Am. States, Miami, Fla., 1977-79, prof. internat. trade and tech., chair bus. enterprise , 1987—; adj. prof. internat. bus., mgmt. U. Francisco Marroquin, Guatemala City, 1977-79; dir. Grad. Inst. Free Enterprise Studies, prof. internat. bus., govt. Mercy Coll. and L.I.U., Dobbs Ferry, N.Y., 1980-83; prof. internat. fin. and bus., chair bus. enterprise Ramapo Coll. of N.J., Mahwah, 1983-87. Author: The Politics of Marketing in Latin America, 1970, Private Investment in the Andean Block - A Study in Conflicts, 1970, Santa Cruz - Crossroads of Heaven and Hell, 1971, U.S.-Latin America - a Time for Reciprocity, 1972, Use of Consultants - How Valuable an Investment, 1972, The Role of U.S. Multinational Corporation, 1972, Summary of Controls on the International Movement of Capital, 1973, The Effects of Rising Energy Costs on LDC Development, 1974, Trade in the Andean Common Market, 1975, U.S. Private Investment - Its Future Role in Interamerican Development, 1976, Tourism in Latin America - Cornerstone of Development, 1976, Administration of Human Resources - Its Effectiveness in the Modern Organization, 1977, A System Called Capitalism, 1977, Marketing Plague - The Regulators, 1978; Prescription for Survival - Can Free Enterprise Make It?, 1979, The Intellectual Defense of Free Enterprise, 1980, Freedom at Bay - Government Controls in the Economy, 1982, American Values: the Economy, the Polity, the Society, 1986, The Debt Bomb: In the Shadow of Depression, 1987, Finance and Stress: The Market Crash of '87, 1988, Investment in Eastern Europe: Good Politics, Bad Finance! 1989, Socialism: The Accomplishment of a Nightmare, 1990, The House That Lenin Built: The Crash of the USSR, 1991, Special Interests: The Politics of Privilege, 1991; editor Interam. Econ. Journal, Univ. Am. States. Advisor Explorer post Alameda coun. Boy Scouts Am., 1969-71, post com. chmn. 1971-75; bd. dirs. San Francisco-Bay area coun. Girl Scouts U.S.A., m1975-80, v.p., 1978-80; trustee Amigos de las Americas, Houston, 1975-80, U. Am. States, Santiago, 1976-80, Am. Research Inst. for Social Environments, Alameda, 1975-82, Princeton Fund, 1976-82, Found. for Free Ent., 1983-87, Aura Tech. Found., 1987—, Electro-Bio-Scis., 1987-89, Am.-Pacific Found., 1989—; mem. Am. Rsch. Inst. for Soc. and Economy, Washington, 1990—, The Maldon Inst. Found., Washington, 1991— . With U.S. Army, 1962-65. Decorated BrStar; decorated Purple Heart; recipient medal Sagitario Found., 1962, Silver Condor award U. Andina, 1969, Kenneth Chilton Meml. award, 1972. Life fellow AAAS; mem. N.Y. Acad. Scis., Am. Numis. Assn., Inst. Mgmt. Cons. (dir., v.p. Latin Am. 1975-80), Am. Econs. Assn., Internat. Inst. Economists, Interam. Soc. Polit. Economists (trustee 1971-81, v.p. 1988-90, pres. 1991—), Inst. Mgmt. Sci., Internat. Execs. Assn., Fgn. Policy Assn., 2d Amendement Found., Am. Security Coun., Am. Soc. Internat. Execs., N.Am. Corp. Planning Assn., Soc. Internat. Trade Planning (dir. 1989—), Am. Sociol. Assn., Am. Psychol. Assn., Nat. Rifle Assn., Am. Radio Relay League (dir. 1990—), Soc. for Internat. Tech. Assessment, Mensa, many others. Clubs: Commonwealth (San Francisco) (chmn. sect. Latin Am. 1969-75); Oakland World Trade. Lodge: Rotary. Home: 2250 Boston Post Rd Larchmont NY 10538-3533 Office: 1 Chatsworth Ave Ste 508 Larchmont NY 10538-9998

SANDERS, BERNARD, congressman; b. Bklyn., Sept. 8, 1941; s. Eli and Dorothy (Glassberg) S.; B.A., U. Chgo., 1964; 1 son, Levi. Freelance writer, carpenter, youth counselor, 1964-76; with Govt. Vt., 1965-66; dir. Am. People's Hist. Soc., Burlington, Vt., 1976-81; mayor of Burlington, 1981-89; mem. U.S. House of Reps. from Vt., 1991—. Chairperson, Vt. Liberty Union Party, 1975-76, candidate for gov., 1972, 76, 86, U.S. Senate, 1971, 74. Mem. Vt. League Cities and Towns. Jewish. Author filmstrips and articles on social, hist. and polit. subjects. Office: PO Box 391 104 Church St Burlington VT 05402*

SANDERS, JAMES GRADY, biogeochemist; b. Norfolk, Va., June 10, 1951; s. Allen Buford and Maple Seretha (Myers) S.; m. Carmen Lee Nance, Aug. 19, 1972. BS in Zoology, Duke U., 1973; MS in Marine Scis., U. N.C., 1975, PhD in Marine Scis., 1978. Postdoctoral investigator Woods Hole (Mass.) Oceanographic Instn., 1978-80; vis. scientist Chesapeake Biol. Lab. U. Md., Solomons, 1980-81; asst. curator Benedict (Md.) Estuarine Rsch. Lab. Acad. Natural Scis., 1981-85, assoc. curator Benedict (Md.) Estuarine Rsch. Lab., 1985-89, curator Benedict (Md.) Estuarine Rsch. Lab., 1989—, dir. Benedict (Md.) Estuarine Rsch. Lab., 1983-91; cons. EPA Sweden, Stockholm, 1985-90; mem. Md. Sea Grant Adv. Com., College Park, 1983-90, Environ. Commn., Calvert City, Md., 1981-88; mem. enbiron. biology panel Office R & D EPA, Washington, 1986—; regional rep. Coastal Resources Adv. Commn., Md., 1983-86. Contbr. over 50 articles to sci. jours. Grantee NOAA, 1981—, EPA, 1983—. Mem. AAAS, Am. Soc. Limnology and Oceanography, Oceanography Soc., Soc. for Environ. Toxicology and Chemistry, Estuarine Rsch. Fedn. Office: Acad Natural Scis Benedict Estuarine Rsch Lab Benedict MD 20612

SANDERS, LOUISA ANN VILENSKY, dental educator, dentist; b. Atlantic City, N.J., Apr. 16, 1956; d. William Vilensky and Martha R. (Diamond) Shapiro; m. Robert Michael Sanders, Oct. 15, 1983; 1 child, Carlie Jillian. BS, Fairleigh Dickinson U., 1978; DMD, U. Medicine and Dentistry N.J., 1982; EdM, Rutgers U., 1990. Gen. dentist Marlton, N.J., 1982-83, Twp. Bloomfield (N.J.) Health Dept., 1983-89; gen. dental officer 194th med. detachment N.J. Army Nat. Guard, West Orange, 1980-90; clin. assoc. prof. U. Medicine and Dentistry N.J., Newark, 1983—; gen. dentist Daus. of Israel Geriatric Ctr., West Orange, 1991—. Contbr. articles to profl. jours. Mem. Am. Assn. Dental Schs., Fedn. Spl. Care Orgns. in Dentistry, Kappa Delta Pi. Jewish. Office: U Medicine and Dentistry NJ Dental Sch 110 Bergen St Newark NJ 07103-2400

SANDERS, RICHARD L., community college president; b. Clintonville, Wis., Jan. 2, 1937; s. Claude H. and Lucille B. (Wedde) S.; m. Janice Miles, Aug. 30, 1958; children: Scott, Todd, Zachary, Nicolle. BS, U. Wis., Eau Claire, 1959; MS, U. Wis., Milw., 1966; EdD, Marquette U., 1971. Tchr. music Milw. Pub. Schs., 1959-62, rsch. assoc., 1966-67; tchr. music West Allis (Wis.) Pub. Schs., 1962-66; registrar, asst. prof. Lakeland Coll., Sheboygan, Wis., 1967-71; dean Lakewood Community Coll., St. Paul, 1971-81; pres. Lincoln Trail Coll., Robinson, Ill., 1981-84, Mattatuck Community Coll., Waterbury, Conn., 1984—; sec. Mattatuck Community Coll. Found., Inc. Mattatuck Community Coll., Waterbury; chmn. adminstrv. coun. Cen. Naugatuck Valley Region Higher Edn. Ctr., Waterbury, 1989-91. Recipient Martin Luther King award Pearl Street Community Ctr., 1987, cert. of appreciation USN Recruiting Command, 1989, Meritorious Svc. award United Negro Coll. Fund, 1989. Mem. Am. Assn. Community and Jr. Colls., Conn. Coun. on Higher Edn., Coun. Conn. Community-Tech. Coll. Pres., Conn. Assn. on Latin Ams. in Higher Edn., Greater Waterbury C. of C. (employment at risk steering com.), Phi Delta Kappa (cert. outstanding membership 1990). Office: Mattatuck Community Coll 750 Chase Pky Waterbury CT 06708-3000

SANDERS, TERESSA IRENE, management consultant; b. Atlanta, May 29, 1951; d. Floyd Roscoe Jr. and Marian Teressa (Rutland) S.; m. John Christian Yoder, Apr. 23, 1983 (div. 1991). BS in Nursing, Duke U., 1973; MS in Nursing, Med. Coll. Ga., 1975. Psychiatric staff nurse Grady Meml. Hosp., Atlanta, 1973-74, adult health practitioner, 1975-77; cons., fed. liaison Ga. Dept. Human Resources, Atlanta, 1978-81; legis. asst. U.S. Sen. Sam Nunn, Washington, 1981-83; dir. mktg. and pub. affairs Nat. Rehab. Hosp., Washington, 1983-86; pres. Sanders & Co., Washington, 1986—, Pizzagram Inc., Washington, 1987—. Originator, assoc. producer, host TV series Lifelines, 1980-81. Founding dir., treas., chairperson legis. task force Ga. Assn. for Primary Health Care, Atlanta, 1978-81; co-chairperson Sesquicentennial Commn., Decatur, Ga., 1973-74; vice chairperson Bicentennial Commn., Decatur, 1976; bd. dirs. Samuel L. Jones Boys Club, Decatur, 1976-77; mem Ga. Drug Abuse Adv. Coun., Atlanta, 1976-77; mem. adv. bd. Nat. Assn. for Craniofacially Handicapped, Chattanooga, 1986-90. Fellow Johns Hopkin's U., 1987-88. Mem. U.S. C. of C. (pvt. sector task force on health care 1987-88, social security 1985-86, health care cost mgmt. task force 1985-86, health policy task force 1990-91). Democrat. Home: Rt 8 Box 244 Springs Rd Warrenton VA 22186 Office: Sanders & Co 1667 K St NW Ste 801 Washington DC 20006-1605

SANDERSON, ARTHUR CLARK, engineering educator, department chairman; b. Providence, Oct. 23, 1946; s. Robert Leroy and Julia Ayer (Oldham) S.; m. Susan Rita Walsh, Aug. 14, 1971; children: Angeline Mirada, Andrew McWain. BS, Brown U., 1968; MS, Carnegie-Mellon U., 1970, PhD, 1972. Rsch. engr. Westinghouse Electric Corp., Pitts., 1968-70; vis. rsch. scientist Delft (The Netherlands) U. Tech., 1972-73; prof. Carnegie-Mellon U., Pitts., 1973-87, co-dir. robotics inst., 1981-87; rsch. dir. Philips Rsch. Labs., Briarcliff Manor, N.Y., 1985-87; prof., dept. chmn. Rensselaer Poly. Inst., Troy, N.Y., 1987—; vis. prof. Univ. Iberoamericana, Mexico City, 1975-77. Contbr. over 180 chpts. to books, articles to profl. jours. Fellow AAAS, IEEE (pres. robotics and automation soc. 1989, 90); mem. AIAA (mem. space automation and robotics tech. com.), Am. Assn. Artificial Intelligence, Soc. Mfg. Engrs. Home: 523 Hancock Rd Williamstown MA 01267-3011 Office: Rensselaer Poly Inst Troy NY 12180-3590

SANDERSON, ERIC GEORGE (SANDY SANDERSON), broadcast executive; b. Toronto, Ont., Can., Oct. 10, 1948; s. George Douglas and Miriam W. (House) S.; m. Anne Chard, May 23, 1970; children: Timothy, Katherine. Student, U. Toronto, 1965-66, U. Western Ont., 1967-68. Morning announcer, program dir. Radio Sta. CKAR, Huntsville, Ont., 1970-73; prodn. dir. Radio Sta. CJBK, London, Ont., 1973; creative dir. Radio Sta. CKGM, Montreal, Que., Can., 1974-77; asst. program dir. Radio Sta. WABC, N.Y.C., 1977-80; program dir. Radio Sta. WLS, Chgo., 1980-81; dir. programming ABC Radio Network, N.Y.C., 1982; program dir. Radio Sta. CFTR, Toronto, 1983-85, v.p. programming, 1986, sr. v.p., gen. mgr., 1988-90; sr. v.p. programming Rogers Broadcasting Ltd., Toronto, 1987-88, exec. v.p., gen. mgr. stas. CFTR-AM and CHFI-FM, 1990—. Bd. dirs. Found. to Assist Canadian Talent on Record. Mem. Mayfair Lakeshore Tennis Club, Toronto Athletic Club. Office: Rogers Broadcasting Ltd, 44 Victoria St, Toronto, ON Canada M5C 1H3

SANDHU, RAJPAL, investor, venture capitalist; b. Calcutta, India, Feb. 6, 1962; came to U.S., 1976; s. Chani and Rajinder (Kaur) S. BS, Yale U., 1983; MBA, Harvard U., 1988. From project mgr. to mktg. mgr. Metaphor Computer Systems, Mt. View, Calif., 1983-86; asst. to dir. of acquisitions HMK Group Cos., Waltham, Mass., 1987; gen. ptnr. RKS Assocs., Providence, 1988—. Patentee in field. Office: RKS Assocs 2250 Hospital Trst Twr Providence RI 02903

SANDIDGE, KANITA DURICE, communications company executive; b. Cleve., Dec. 2, 1947; d. John Robert Jr. and Virginia Louise (Caldwell) S. AB, Cornell U., 1970; MBA, Case Western Res. U., 1979. Supr. assignments service ctrs. and installation AT&T, Cleve., 1970-78, chief dept. data processing and acctg., 1979-80; adminstrn. mgr. exec. v.p. staff AT&T, N.Y.C., 1980-83; sales forecasting and analysis mgr. resources planning AT&T, Newark, 1983-86; planning and devel. mgr. material planning and mgmt. AT&T Network Systems, Morristown, N.J., 1986-87; dir. adminstrv. services AT&T Network Systems, Lisle, Ill., 1987-89; dir. div. staff customer support and ops. AT&T Network Systems, Morristown, N.J., 1990—. Mem black exchange program Nat. Urban League, N.Y.C., 1986—. Named Black Achiever in Industry, Harlem YMCA, 1981; recipient Tribute to Women and Industry Achievement award YWCA, 1985. Mem. Nat. Black MBA's, Alliance Black AT&T Mgrs., Am. Mgmt. Assn., Nat. Assn. for Female Execs., NAACP, Beta Alpha Psi. Mem. African Meth. Episcopal Ch. Home: 10 Trade Winds Dr Randolph NJ 07869-1238 Office: AT&T Network Systems 475 South St Morristown NJ 07960-6440

SANDLER, GERALD HOWARD, aerospace executive; b. N.Y.C., Sept. 17, 1934; s. Irving and Sally S.; m. Ann Sandler; children: Eric, Steven. BS, CUNY, 1956, MS, 1957. Sr. v.p. Grumman Data Systems & Svcs., Bethpage, N.Y. Author: System Engineering, 1963. Home: 46 Bonnie Dr Westbury NY 11590-2804

SANDLER, KENNETH BRUCE, advertising executive; b. Newark, July 24, 1942; s. Ralph M. and Mae (Ness) S.; m. Denise Ann Brooks, May 8, 1973 (div. 1988); children: Todd, Brooke. BS in Pharmacy, Rutgers U., 1967, MBA, 1970. Registered pharmacist, N.J. Mgr. mktg. research E.R. Squibb and Sons, Princeton, N.J., 1970-73; account exec. Deltakos div. J. Walter Thompson, N.Y.C., 1973-75, exec. v.p., 1982-84; v.p., account group supr. Rolf Werner Rosenthal Inc., N.Y.C., 1975-82; pres. Sandler Communications Inc., N.Y.C., 1984—. Mem. Am. Pharm. Assn., Am. Mktg. Assn., Nat. Assn. Retail Druggists, Am. Soc. Hosp. Pharmacists. Office: Sandler Communications Inc 130 5th Ave 149 5th Ave New York NY 10010-6801

SANDNESS, ARNE OLAF, special machine design engineer, consultant; b. Syracuse, N.Y., Mar. 23, 1951; s. Arnold Everett and Enricheita (Fascia) S.; m. Karen Marie Brownell, July 4, 1970 (div. July, 1987); children: Karla Dawn, Dawn-Marie, Rebecca Anne; m. Christine V. Panelati, Dec. 4, 1987; 1 stepson, Andrew. Grad. mech. tech., Onandaga Community Coll., Syracuse, N.Y., 1986; BBA, Empire State Coll., 1989. Machinist Stone Machinery Co., Manlius, N.Y., 1970-73; machine assembler "A" White Sunstrand Inc., Liverpool, N.Y., 1973-77; sr. mech. designer Allen Tool Corp., Syracuse, N.Y., 1977-86; project engr. Vector Indsl. Svcs., Inc., Liverpool, N.Y., 1986-88; sr. tool and machine design engr. Pall Trinity Micro Corp., Cortland, N.Y., 1988-91; owner, consulting engr. Sandesign, Solvay, N.Y., 1991—; hon. faculty mem. Materials Engring. Inst., Metals Park, Ohio, 1989, '91; instr. ASM Internat., Metals Park, 1988, Soc. Mfg. Engrs., Dearborn, Mich., 1988. Author: (sci. fiction novella) Von Buhler's Cat, 1986. Mem. Taunton (N.Y.) Vol. Fire Co., 1986; pres. Western Area Vol. Emergency Svc., Fairmont, N.Y., 1987-89; assoc. mem. Am. Soc. Law Enforcement Trainers, Twin Lakes, Wis., 1990; cons. Village Bd. Trustees, Solway, N.Y., 1991. Recipient award of Honor, The Profl. Alliance, 1986, Cert. of Proficiency, Cen. N.Y. Shootists, Cert. of Proficiency, Lethal Force Inst., 1990, Cert. of Proficiency, Global Sch. of Investigations, Hanover, Mass. Mem. Soc. Mfg. Engrs. (chpt. sec. 1988, sr. mem.) Robotics Internat. (sr. mem.), Waves Ambulance, NRA, Dads Against Discrimination (chpt. pres.1991), Elbridge Rod and Gun Club. Home and Office: Sandesign 1007 3rd St Syracuse NY 13209-2534

SANDROW, HOPE, artist; b. Phila., Dec. 31, 1951; d. Harry Sandrow and Ruth Liebman Nanes; m. Ulf Skoosbergh. Student, Beaver Coll., 1970-71, Drexel U., 1971-72, Phila. Coll. of Art, 1972-75. Represented by T. Greathouse Gallery, N.Y.C., 1983-84, Gracie Mansion Gallery, N.Y.C., 1984-91. One-woman shows at T. Greathouse Gallery, 1983, 84, Gracie Mansion Gallery, 1986, 88, 89; solo show Phila. Coll. Art, 1984, Haggerty Mus., 1986; exhibited in group shows at Nat. Mus. Art, 1989, Herter Art Gallery, 1989, Haggerty Mus., Balt. Mus. Art, 1987, Whitney Mus. Art, 1987, Bard Coll., 1989, Hirshhorn Mus. Art, 1986, Indpls. Mus. Art, 1986, Alternative Mus., 1990, Inst. Contemporary Art, 1984; founder Artist and Homeless Collaborative, 1990. Grantee NEA, 1990, Andy Warhol Found., 1991, Art Matters, 1990; recipient Manhattan Borough Pres. award for Excellence in the Arts, 1991, award of Excellence for Vol. Svcs., N.Y.C. Human Resources Adminstrn., 1989-91.

SANDS, EDWARD A., wine and spirits retail company executive; b. Bklyn., Aug. 28, 1939; s. Max Wolf and Bess (Pinsky) Silverman; m. Roberta Ann Rosenfield, Dec. 19, 1964; children: David, Steven, Michael, Michele. BBA, CCNY, 1961; MS, U. Ill., 1963. Securities analyst Nat. Securities & Rsch., N.Y.C., 1963-64; fin. analyst SEC, Washington, 1964-66; pres. Woodley Wine & Liquor Inc., Washington, 1966—; dir. MacLachcen Nat. Bank, 1978-80; pres. T/A Calvert Woodley Wine & Liquor Inc., Washington, 1982—. Bd. dirs. Maclachlen Nat. Bank, 1978-79. With U.S. Army, 1961-62. Named One of Top 10 Retailers of Yr., Market Watch mag., 1983, Beverage Dynamics, 1992. Mem. Internat. Wine and Food Soc. (wine com. D.C. chpt. 1986—), D.C. Retail Liquor Dealers Assn. (bd. dirs. 1977-79, 91—, Wine Mcht. of Yr. award 1985). Office: Calvert Woodley Wine & Liquor Inc 4339 Connecticut Ave NW Washington DC 20008

SANDS, GARY LUTHER, government official; b. Waukegan, Ill., Feb. 18, 1962; s. Luther Aldine and Marilyn Ida (Ferguson) S. BS in Fin., U. Conn., 1984; MBA in Internat. Bus., George Washington U., 1989. Mgmt. trainee Citizens Bank of Md., Gaithersburg, 1985-86; fin. analyst Dept. of the Navy, Arlington, Va., 1986-87; budget analyst SBA, Washington, 1987-88; investment officer Overseas Pvt. Investment Corp., Washington, 1988—. Home: 2611 Key Blvd Arlington VA 22201-4001 Office: Overseas Pvt Investment 1615 M St NW Washington DC 20527-0002

SANDS, I. JAY, corporate, business, marketing and real estate consultant, lecturer, realtor; b. N.Y.C.; m. Kiti Reiner; children: Nelson, Tiffany, Summer Paige. B.A., NYU; J.D., Columbia U. Bar: N.Y., U.S. Supreme Ct. Mng. partner Korvette Bldg. Assocs., N.Y.C.; mng. dir., founder, chmn. bd. dirs., sec. First Republic Corp. Am.; chief exec. officer, sec. First Republic Corp., N.Y.; gen. partner Velvex Mid-City Parking Center, N.Y.C., Manhattan Parking Assocs.; dir., chmn. First Republic Underwriters, Inc.; pres., dir. Waltham Mgmt. Inc., Mass.; partner Cypress Parking Assocs., Cypress Plaza Shopping, Pompano Beach, Fla., Randolph House Co., Syracuse, N.Y., Beau Rivage Hotel Co., Bal Harbour, Fla., Gulf Assocs., Fla., Sahara Motel Assocs., Miami Beach, Fla.; chmn. Waltham (Mass.) Engring. & Research Co.; gen. partner Allstate Ins. Bldg. Co., N.Y.C., Fairfax Bldg. Assocs., Kansas City, Mo., Engring. Bldg. Assocs., Chgo., Manhattan Parking Co., Williamsbridge Assocs., N.Y.C., First Republic Funding Agy., N.Y.C., Atlantic Co., Miami, Syracuse-Randolph House Hotel, N.Y.C., Marchwood Realty Co., Phila., Video Film Center Assocs., N.Y.C., Hempstead Real Estate Enterprises, N.Y.C., Imperial Sq. Assocs., N.Y.C., DeMille Theatre Co., N.Y.C., Ohio Indsl. Assocs., Cleve., Pelham Park Assocs., Pa., Peoria (Ill.) Parking Assocs.; chmn., dir. Triple P Parking Corp., Peoria, Ill., Square Mgmt. Corp., N.Y.C., Park Circle Apts., Inc., N.Y.C., Holme Circle Apts., Inc., Phila.; sec. F.S. Mgmt. Corp., N.Y.C.; founder, chmn. exec. com., sec., dir. Imperial Sq. Mgmt. Corp., Hempstead, N.Y.; chmn. bd., chmn. exec. com., sec., dir. Nat. Med. Industries, Inc., Health Insts. Leasing Corp., Am. Med. Computer Corp.; pres. Med. Contract Supply Corp., City Capital Corp., N.J., Claredon Co.; vis. lectr., instr. mktg., real estate, comml. mktg. NYU, New Sch. for Social Research, U. Fla.; gen. agt. Northeastern Life Ins. Co., Patriot Life Ins. Co., Citizens Life Ins. Co. Past trustee Baldwin Sch., N.Y.C.; hon. trustee Pres. Harry S. Truman Libr. Served with AUS. Harlan Fiske Stone fellow, 1975; named Man of Yr., Real Estate Weekly. Mem. Nat. Real Estate Club, ABA, N.Y. Real Estate Bd., Columbia U. Law Sch. Alumni Assn. (class chmn. 1978). Clubs: Shriners, Masons (32 deg.), Merchants.

SANDS, MEREDITH BARBANELL, television production associate; b. N.Y.C., Nov. 26, 1965; d. Arthur Loren and June Ellen (Brown) Barbanell; m. David Clifton Sands, Oct. 18, 1990. BA, Goucher Coll., 1987. Scheduler VCA Teletronics, N.Y.C., 1987-88; assoc. producer ACTV Domestics Corp., N.Y.C., 1988-90; prodn. asst. Comedy Channel HBO, N.Y.C., 1990-91; control room prodn. asst. Image Workshop Lifetime TV, Astoria, N.Y., 1991-92; post prodn. coord. Commm. Techs., Inc., N.Y.C., 1992—. Mem. NAFE. Home: 182 E 95th St New York NY 10128-2539 Office: Com Tech Comm Techs 770 Lexington Ave 15th Fl New York NY 10021

SANDSTEDT, JOHN PHILIP, regulatory affairs specialist; b. Bklyn., Aug. 18, 1940; s. Harry Albert and Florence Gessina (Fetten) S.; m. Joan Lorraine Sim, Aug. 15, 1964; children: John Erik, David Michael. BSChemE, Princeton U., 1962; MS in Engring. Mgmt., N.J. Inst. of Tech., 1973. Cert. environ. profl.; cert. environ. auditor; cert. hazardous materials mgr. Chem. engr. FMC Corp., Princeton, N.J., 1962-65; devel. engr. UOP Chems., East Rutherford, N.J., 1965-69; group leader, pilot plant Tenneco Chems., Inc., Piscataway, N.J., 1969-72, mgr. environ. engr., 1972-76, mgr. environ. affairs, 1976-82; v.p. govt. affairs At-Sea Incineration, Inc., Parsippany, N.Y., 1982-86; v.p. and tech. dir. S&D Environ. Engring., Inc., Metuchen, N.J., 1987-90; dir. regulatory affairs Sybron Chems. Inc., Birmingham, N.J., 1989—; adj. prof. N.J. Inst. of Tech., Newark, 1989—, Burlington County Coll., Pemberton, N.J., 1990—, Brookdale Community Coll., Lincroft, N.J., 1990—. Contbr. articles to profl. jours. Mem. Am. Inst. Chem. Engrs., Inst. of Hazardous Materials Mgrs. (legis. com. chair 1986-87), Chem. Industry Coun. (chair environ. com. 1976-86, Award Merit), Air and Waste Mgmt. Assn., Nat. Assn. Environ. Profls. Home: 1306 Masoma Rd N Brunswick NJ 08902-1409 Office: Sybron Chems Inc Birmingham Rd # 66 Birmingham NJ 08011-9999

SANDSTROM, PHILIP WILLIAM, production manager; b. Chgo., Dec. 15, 1952; s. William A. and Marie C. Sandstrom. AB, Loyola U., 1974; postgrad., U. Ill., 1974-75, U. Wis., 1975-80. Prodn. mgr. and lighting designer dance dept. U. Wis., Madison, 1975-78, tech. dir., designer opera dept., 1978-79; prodn. mgr., lighting designer Movin On Prodns., Madison, 1979; project and tech. dir. Statute of Liberty II, 1980; prodn. mgr., resident lighting designer Dance Theater Workshop, N.Y.C., 1980—. Lighting designer (theater) Fools Fire, The Ghost Writer, The Harlot's Curse, The Mildred Piece, What Happened to Met, Watchtower; lighting designer (dance) Mark Morris Dance Group, 1982-90, Dance in America PBS, 1986, Joffrey Ballet, 1987, American Ballet Theater, 1988, and hundreds of dance cos., 1980-91. Recipient N.Y. Dance and Performance award, "The Bessies", 1985, 86. Home: 425 Prospect Pl # 2L Brooklyn NY 11238-4132 Office: Dance Theatre Workshop 219 W 19th St New York NY 10011-4076

SANDUSKY, HAROLD WILLIAM, physicist; b. Balt., Sept. 12, 1949; s. Howard Franklin and Edna May (Durham) S.; m. Patricia Anne Gorman, May 28, 1978; children: Heather, Timothy. B in Aero. Engring., Ga. Inst. of Tech., 1971; MSE, Princeton U., 1971, MA, PhD, 1976. Mech. engr. White Oak Lab. Naval Surface Warfare Ctr., Silver Spring, Md., 1976—. Contbr. articles to profl. jours. Office: Naval Surface Warfare Ctr Code R13 Silver Spring MD 20903-5000

SANDWEISS, MARTHA A., museum director, author; b. St. Louis, Mar. 29, 1954; d. Jerome Wesley and Marilyn Joy (Glik) S. BA magna cum laude, Radcliffe Coll., 1975; MA in History, Yale U., 1977, MPhil in History, 1981, PhD, 1985. Smithsonian-Nat. Endowment Humanities fellow, Nat. Portrait Gallery, Washington, 1975-76; curator photographs Amon Carter Mus., Ft. Worth, 1979-86, adj. curator photographs, 1987-89; dir. Mead Art Mus. Amherst Coll., 1989—, adj. assoc. prof. of fine arts and Am. studies, 1989—. Author: Carlotta Corpron: Designer with Light, 1980, Masterworks of American Photography, 1982, Laura Gilpin: An Enduring Grace, 1986, (catalogue) Pictures from an Expedition: Early Views of the American West, 1979; co-author: Eyewitness to War: Prints and Daguerreotypes of th Mexican War, 1989; editor: Historic Texas: A Photographic Portrait, 1986, Contemporary Texas: A Photographic Portrait, 1986, Denizens of the Desert, 1988, Photography in Nineteenth Century America, 1991. Fellow Ctr. for Am. Art and Material Culture, Yale U., 1977-79, Nat. Endowment for the Humanities, 1988. Office: Mead Art Mus Amherst Coll Amherst MA 01002

SANDY, LEO ROBERT, education educator, school psychologist; b. Lowell, Mass., Aug. 29, 1943; s. Leo Robert Sandy and Dorthy Victoria (Dickinson) Sandy Ling; m. Pearl Anne Sandy, Aug. 29, 1965; children: Kirsti A., Karl R. BA in Psychology, U. Mass., 1970; EdM in Counseling, Boston U., 1971, EdD in Human Devel., 1983. Tchr. spl. edn. Hermann Sch., Lowell, 1971-72; coord. guidance svcs. Bedford (N.H.) Pub. Schs., 1972-73; sch. psychologist Lowell Pub. Schs., 1973-83, Londonderry (N.H.) Pub. Schs., 1983-84; prof. edn. Rivier Coll., Nashua, N.H., 1984—; sch. psychologist Inter-Lakes Sch. Dist., Meredith, N.H., 1985—, Adult Learning Ctr., Nashua, 1988—. Vol. Lake Lay Monitoring Program, Gilford, N.H., 1985—; mem. N.H. State Dept. Edn. Coun., Concord, 1987. With USN, 1961-65. Named So. N.H. Peacemaker, Beyond War, 1988. Mem. ASCD (exec. bd. N.H. unit 1985), Nat. Assn. Sch. Psychologists, N.H. Assn. Peace and Lasting Security, Vets. for Peace, N.H. Educators for Social Responsibility, Nat. Assn. Supervision and Curriculum Devel., Assn. Tchr. Educators, Pi Lambda Theta. Democrat. Home: 46 Blueberry Hill Ln Laconia NH 03246-6609 Office: Rivier Coll 420 Main St Nashua NH 03060-5086

SANDYS, EDWINA KAPLAN, sculptor; b. London, Dec. 22, 1938; came to U.S., 1978; d. Duncan and Diana Spencer (Churchill) S.; m. Piers Dixon (div. 1972); children: Mark Pierson, Hugo Duncan; m. Richard D. Kaplan, Nov. 3, 1985. Sculptor: Paradise Regained, Breakthrough, Woman Free, Child, Family, Generations, Christa-1975. Mem. Women's Forum N.Y. Home: 131 E 66th St New York NY 10021-6129

SANG, HENG-KANG, transport economist, educator; b. Kucheng, Hebei, China; came to U.S., 1944; s. P.C. and Y.P. (Pei) S.; m. Nancy S. M. Sang, Aug. 18, 1949; 3 children. BA, Tsinghua U., Beijing, 1939; MA, Nankai U., Tianjin, China, 1943, Harvard U., 1946; PhD, Harvard U., 1947. Sr. economist UN, N.Y.C., 1947-78; sr. advisor African Devel. Bank, Abidjan, Ivory Coast, 1969-71; chief advisor Ministry of Transport and Communications, Sudan, 1976-78; chief economist Louis Berger Internat., Inc., Syria, 1980; vis. prof., dir. Inst. Transport Econ. Nankai U., Tianjin, China, 1985—; vis. prof. St. John's U., N.Y.C., 1980-82, Tsinghua U., Beijing, 1985, N.J. Inst. Tech., Newark, 1989—; UN advisor Bermuda, 1979, United Arab Emirates, 1979; UN cons. Beijing, 1983, 84, 85, 87-91. Author: Project Evaluation for Developing Countries-Techniques and Practices, 1988, China's Transportation Problems, 1992; contbr. numerous articles and reports to profl. jours. Mem. Royal Econ. Soc. (life mem.), Am. Econ. Assn., Atlantic Econ. Soc., Met. Econ. Assn.

SANGER, ALEXANDER CAMPBELL, family planning executive; b. N.Y.C., Nov. 25, 1947; s. Grant and Marjery Edwina (Campbell) S.; m. Lisa-Margaret Stevenson, Oct. 31, 1970, (div. July, 1978); m. Jeannette Kittredge Watson, Dec. 21, 1978; children: Ralph, Andrew, Matthew. AB, Princeton U., 1969; MBA, JD, Columbia U., 1974; LLM, NYU, 1985. Bar: N.Y. 1974, Fla. Ptnr., assoc. White and Case, N.Y.C., 1974-88; CEO Sanger Plastics, Union, N.J., 1988-90, Old Line Plastics, Forest Hill, Md., 1990; pres., CEO Planned Parenthood of N.Y.C., 1991—. bd. dirs. Planned Parenthood of N.Y.C., 1984-90, Pierpont Morgan Libr., 1988-90; active alumni coun. Princeton (N.J.) U., 1984-89. Sgt. Air N.G., 1969-70. Mem. Unitarian Ch. Home: 7 Gracie Sq New York NY 10028 Office: Planned Parenthood NYC 26 Bleecker St New York NY 10012

SANKNER, SHERI WARREN, marketing executive; b. Rock Island, Ill., May 22, 1959; d. Jerry Roger and Kay Constance (Smith) Warren. BS in Journalism, U. Ill., 1981. Reader mail corr., researcher CBS Mag.-Woman's Day, N.Y.C., 1981-82, editorial asst. to editor-in-chief, 1982, art dept. coord., asst. art dir., 1983; communications coord. Kable News Co., Inc., N.Y.C., 1984-85, advt. and promotion mgr., 1985-86; dir. promotions and communications Curtis Circulation Co., Inc., Hackensack, N.J., 1985-88; v.p. mktg. and promotions Network Design Studio, Inc., N.Y.C., 1989—. Recipient Scripps-Howard award, 1980, Hugh Hefner Mag. award, 1981. Mem. Women in Communications, Advt. Women N.Y. Democrat. Roman Catholic. Home: 277 Driggs Ave Brooklyn NY 11222-3916 Office: Network Design Studio Inc 276 Bowery New York NY 10012-3501

SANKS, CHARLES RANDOLPH, JR., psychotherapist, clergyman; b. Yonkers, N.Y., Feb. 14, 1928; s. Charles Randolph and Myrtle Elizabeth (Bunn) S.; m. Jacquelyn Gibson, Nov. 11, 1949; children—Charlene Cynthia Saunders, Valeri Ann. B.A. cum laude, Stetson U., 1956; B.Div., Southeastern Sem., 1960; M.Th., Union Sem., 1961; postgrad., U. Salamanca, Spain, 1975; D.Ministry, Wesley Theol. Sem., 1977. Ordained to ministry Baptist Ch., 1957. Minister Judson Meml. Bapt. Ch., Fayetteville, N.C., 1957-60; interim minister First Bapt. Ch. of South Miami, Fla., 1961-62, Sunset Heights Bapt. Ch., Hialeah, Fla., 1962; sr. minister Starling Ave. Bapt. Ch., Martinsville, Va., 1963-69; assoc. pastor 1st Bapt. Ch., Washington, 1969-82, minister to Pres. U.S., 1976-80; developer ministry to community foster-care patients, 1975; dir. Pastoral Counseling Ctr. Greater Marlboro, Md., 1982-87; sr. counselor Washington Pastoral Counseling Service, 1982—; dir. clin. mgmt. Washington Pastoral Counseling Service, 1988—; ptnr. Pastoral Psychotherapy Assocs., Washington, 1984—; fellow Am. Assn. Pastoral Counselors, 1984—; trainer Journeyman Program, Fgn. Mission Bd., So. Bapt. Convention, 1968; mem. exec. com. D.C. Bapt. Conv., 1971-77; leader, speaker in liturgics and worship N.C. Bapt. Conv. Conf., 1972, 75; cons. Pastoral Psychotherapy Assocs., Washington, 1981-84; lectr. on worship and liturgics So. Bapt. Theol. Sem., Louisville, 1978; lectr. Stetson U., Deland, Fla., 1978, So. Ecumenical Conf., Atlanta, 1978. Bd. dirs. Uplift House, Washington, 1970-73, Day Care Ctr., Martinsville, Va., 1963-69, Big Brother Orgn. and Sheltered Workshop, Martinsville, Va., 1963-69. Served to cpl. USMC, 1946-49. Fellow Interpreters' House, Lake Junaluska, N.C., 1968-79; guest Oxford U., Eng., 1981. Mem. Am. Digestive Disease Soc. (bd. dirs. 1979-87). Democrat. Baptist. Avocations: travel; horseback riding; music; art. Home: 1090 Larkspur Ter Rockville MD 20850-1002

SANNER, GEORGE ELWOOD, electrical engineer; b. Rockwood, Pa., Aug. 30, 1929; s. Dennis Charles and Alverda (Growall) S.; m. Marjorie Mary Hohman, July 1, 1951; children: George Bradley, Marjorie Rosalie, Cathy Ann. BS, U. Pitts., 1951; postgrad., Johns Hopkins U., 1957-59. Registered profl. engr., Md.; cert. cost acctg. mgmt. Supervisory engr. Westinghouse Electric Corp., Balt., 1952-58, chief scientist, cons. def. and space ctr., 1964-72; chief engr., program mgr. radio div. Bendix Corp., Balt., 1958-64; engring. mgr. jet propulsion labs. Bendix Corp., Pasadena, Calif., 1980-81; pres., gen. mgr. Santron Corp., Balt., 1972-79; v.p. engring. M-Tron Industries div. Curtiss Wright Corp., Yankton, S.D., 1979-80; sr. engring. specialist engring. ctr. Litton Data Systems, New Orleans, 1981-83; cons. engring. mgmt. AIL div. Eaton Corp., Deer Park, N.Y., 1983-87; sr. prin. engr. Am. Electronics Labs, Inc., Lansdale, Pa., 1987-92; pvt. practice cons. Chgo., 1992—; cons., Chgo., 1992—; rep. People to People Tour, various countries, 1978. Patentee in field. Ch. vestry Immanuel Ch., Sparks-Glencoe, Md., 1969-70, dir. advg. pony show, 1969-70; trustee St. Paul's Sch. for Boys, Balt., 1965-67; bishop's secretariat Diocese L.I., Garden City, N.Y., 1985-87; exec. com. Scriptural Coalition, Diocese, Phila., 1990-92. A.K. Mellon Found. scholar, 1947-50, Carnegie Inst. Tech. scholar, 1947-51. Mem. IEEE, Assn. Old Crows, Quarter Century Wireless Assn. Episcopalian. Home and Office: 1213 Easton Dr Carol Stream IL 60188-6099

SANOCKI, EDWARD JOHN, JR., lawyer; b. Detroit, Nov. 8, 1950; s. Edward John Sr. and Josephine (Gosk) S.; m. Sheila Gail Behar, Aug. 5, 1978; children: Michael David, Kenneth John. BA, U. Mich., 1972; MA, U. Tenn., 1974; JD, N.Y. Law Sch., 1977. Bar: N.Y. 1978, U.S. Dist. Ct. (so. dist.) N.Y. 1978. Assoc. Julien & Schlesinger, P.C., N.Y.C., 1978-84, ptnr., 1984-90; pvt. practice Law Office of Edward J. Sanocki, Jr., N.Y.C., 1990—; speaker Miss. Trial Lawyers Assn., Jackson, 1988, So. Trial Lawyers Assn., New Orleans, 1989. Co-writer Products Liability column N.Y. Law Jour., 1989-90. Mem. Assn. Trial Lawyers Am. (sustaining), N.Y. State Trial Lawyers Assn. (chmn. products liability com. 1987-88, bd. dirs. 1990—, speaker 1990—). Roman Catholic. Home: 17 Azalea Trl Westfield NJ 07090-1684 Office: 52 Duane St New York NY 10007-1207

SANSLONE, WILLIAM ROBERT, biochemistry educator, research executive; b. Vineland, N.J., Feb. 16, 1931; s. Fortunato and Rosa (Pelle) S.; m. Alice E. Koury, June 25, 1960; 1 child, Catherine. Biochemistry rsch. asst. U. Conn., Storrs, 1955-56; instr. biochemistry SUNY, Downstate Med. Ctr., Bklyn., 1961-64, asst. prof. biochemistry, 1964-70, assoc. prof., 1970-71; project scientist NIH, Bethesda, Md., 1971-72, sr. project scientist, 1972-73, exec. sec. biochemistry study sect., 1973-74, program dir. rev., 1974-83; assoc. dir. sci. program ops., 1983-87, dir. office of program planning and evaluation, Nat. Inst. Arthritis and Musculoskeletal and Diseases, 1987—; vis. assoc. prof. physiology and biophysics Med. Coll. Pa., Phila., 1970. Contbr. articles to profl. jours. Served to 1st lt. USAF, 1956-58. Mem. AAAS, Harvey Soc., Biophys. Soc., Am. Inst. Nutrition, Soc. Exptl. Biology and Medicine, Sigma Xi, Alpha Gamma Rho (chpt. treas. 1968-70). Home: 6835 Old Stage Rd Rockville MD 20852-4359 Office: NIH Bldg 31-4C11 Bethesda MD 20892

SANSONE, ERIC BRANDFON, environmental control and research professional; b. N.Y.C., Mar. 26, 1939; s. Philip Joseph and Lorraine (Brandfon) S.; m. Janet Patricia Stolorow, July 7, 1963 (div. May 1978); children: Judith, Jessica. BChemE, CCNY, 1960; MPH, U. Mich., 1962, PhD, 1967. Cert. safety profl., indsl. hygienist. Asst. prof. U. Pitts., 1967-73, assoc. rsch. prof., 1973-74; sect. head NCI Frederick (Md.) Cancer R&D Ctr., 1974-78, lab. chief, 1978-82, program dir., 1982—; cons. in field. Coauthor: Degradation of Chemical Carcinogens, 1980, Chemical Carcinogens, 1986, Destruction of Hazardous Chemicals in the Laboratory, 1990; contbr. articles to profl. jours. Mem. Am. Indsl. Hygiene Assn., Am. Biol. Safety Assn., British Occupational Hygiene Soc., Health Physics Soc., N.Y. Acad. Scis., Am. Conf. Gov. Indsl. Hygienists, Soc. Occupational and Environ. Health. Home: 1536 Dockside Dr Frederick MD 21701-4473 Office: NCI-FCRDC PO Box B Frederick MD 21702-1201

SANTAFERRARA, MICHAEL JOSEPH, art director; b. Syracuse, N.Y., Dec. 12, 1961; s. Joseph Francis and Joan Lorraine (Knickerbocker) S. BFA in Communications Design, SUNY, Buffalo, 1984. Design intern CBS, Inc., N.Y.C., 1984; designer Johnson & Higgins, N.Y.C., 1984-85; sr. art dir. Brecker & Merryman, Inc., N.Y.C., 1985—. Designer brochures Squibb, Conrail (Neographics award, 1990), Dun & Bradstree (Printing Industries of Am. award 1987), Ford (Assn. of Graphics Arts award 1990), Met. Life, N.Y. Telephone (N.J. Art Dir. Club award 1988), Chevron Corp. (Printing Industries of Am. award 1992). Mem. N.Y. Advt. and Communications Network. Roman Catholic. Home: 11 W 95th St New York NY 10025-6783 Office: Brecker and Merryman Inc 228 E 45th St New York NY 10017-3303

SANTA MARIA, DARIO ATEHORTUA, theologian, publishing executive; b. Medellin, Antioquia, Colombia, June 19, 1943; came to U.S., 1984; s. Juan De Jesus Athehortva and Maria (Altagracia) S. BD, BPh, Universidad St. Thomas, Bogota, Colombia, 1965; ThM, Asbury Sem., 1967; Licenciado en Comunicaciones, Univ. Complutense, Madrid, 1969; Cert. in Theology, Episcopal Sem., Alexandria, Va., 1971; Diploma in Palaeography, 1974; ThD, Universita Lateranense, Rome, 1975; postgrad., Ecole Biblique Francaise, Jerusalem, 1976, Oxford U., 1982-84. Ordained priest Roman Cath. Ch. Prof. N.T. Union Theol. Sem., Madrid, 1967-70; prof. Protestant theology Instituto Fe y Secularidad, Madrid, 1967-70; pastor Iglesia De Camillejas, Madrid, 1968-70; asst. editor Oikoumenikon, Vatican City, Italy, 1972-76; redactor News Bull. of Celam, Vatican City, 1975-76; editor reference books Editorial Clie, Barcelona, Spain, 1976-81; prof. liberation theology St. James Piccadilly Inst., London, 1981-84; pres. Santa Maria Pub. Co., Pitts., 1987—; cons. Secretariat for Christian Unity, Vatican City, 1972-84, Anglican Centre, Rome, 1972-83, United Bible Socs., London, 1976-85, Ch. World Svc., Geneva, 1980—; reader dept. manuscripts Brit. Libr., London, 1981—. Author: Diccionario Biblico Ilustrado, 1982, Yel Texto Griego Delabiblia, 1983, The World After Columbus 1492-1992, 1991; contbr. numerous articles to profl. jours.; chief editor Mag. pagina arierta, 1977-81. Ecumenical chaplain Inst. Italo Latino Americano, Rome, 1973-77; cons. Pa. Human Rels. Commn., 1988—. Sion Coll. fellow, 1982—; recipient Dr. of Letters, Lambeth, 1983. Mem. Asociacion de Periodistas De Colombia, Ordine Dei Giornalisti Rome, Asociacion De Criticos Literarios, Asociacion De Teologos Espanoles, Asociacion De Amigos De La Historia, Assn. Ministers of Western Pa. Office: Santa Maria Pub Co PO Box 2435 Pittsburgh PA 15230-2435

SANTAMARIA, PHILLIP, academic dean; b. Buffalo, Mar. 10, 1943; s. Anthony J. and Carmela (Gugliuzza) S.; m. Linda DeForno, Aug. 24, 1968; children: Michael, Christa. BA, St. Francis Coll., Loretto, Pa., 1966; MA, Niagara U., 1969; PhD, Kent State U., 1977. Area dir. Kent (Ohio) State U., 1968-74; asst. dir. career devel. ctr. Baldwin-Wallace Coll., Berea, Ohio, 1975-76, dir. career devel. ctr., 1976-78; v.p. for student affairs Daemen Coll., Amherst, N.Y., 1978-79; assoc. v.p. for student affairs, dean of students SUNY, Buffalo, 1979—; presenter in field. Author: The Question of Education in the Third Russian Duma, 1990; contbr. articles to profl. jours. Bd. dirs. Puerto Rican Am. Community Assn., Buffalo, 1987—, Western N.Y. Hispanic Friends & Civic Assn., Buffalo, 1989—, Buffalo Ballet Theatre, 1991; v.p. Buffalo Coun. on World Affairs, 1982—; mem. ho. of dels. United Way of Buffalo and Erie County, 1985—. Mem. Coll. Student Pers. Assn. N.Y. State (mem.-at-large 1988-89, membership chair 1989—), Western N.Y .Consortium Higher Edn. (chief student affairs officer coord. 1981—), Nat. Assn. Student Pers. Adminstrs., Ea. Assn. Counselors, Deans and Advisors of Students, Nat. Assn. Intercollegiate Athletics, Coll. Placement Coun., Ohio Assn. Sch., Coll. and Univ. Staffing (sec.-treas. 1977-78), Creative Problem Inst., Adelante Estudeiantes Latinos (advisor), Rotary, Tau Kappa Epsilon. Roman Catholic. Home: 228 Sherbrooke Ave Buffalo NY 14221-3423 Office: SUNY 1300 Elmwood Ave Buffalo NY 14222-1095

SANTEE, RICHARD ELLIS, JR., lawyer; b. Allentown, Pa., Oct. 29, 1951; s. Richard Ellis and Eleanor Gloria (Thomas) S.; m. Mollie Moore Mandell, Aug. 21, 1982; children: Richard Eugene, Madeline Moore, Katherine Mae. BA magna cum laude, Hofstra U., 1973; JD, U. Va., 1976. Bar: Pa. 1976, U.S. Dist. Ct. (ea. dist.) Pa. 1977, U.S. Ct. Appeals (3d cir.) 1980. Assoc. Sigmon, Littner & Ross, Bethlehem, Pa., 1976-77, ptnr., 1978-85; ptnr. Shay & Santee, Bethlehem, 1985-90, Shay, Santee & Kelhart, Bethlehem, 1990—; legal counsel local unit Am. Fedn. Musicians, 1978—. Chmn. bd. trustees Advent Moravian Ch., Bethlehem, 1987—, mem. Provincial Elders' Conf. Moravian Ch. Am., No. Province, 1990—. Mem. Northampton County Bar Assn. (chmn. civil procedural rules com. 1983—, bd. govs. 1986-87, sec. bd. 1989-90, v.p. 1990-91, pres. 1992), Bethlehem Club, Saucon Valley Country Club, Sigma Kappa Alpha. Democrat. Home: 1251 Biafore Ave Bethlehem PA 18017-1003 Office: Shay & Santee 44 E Broad St Bethlehem PA 18018-5920

SANTELLI, HEIDI LUX, communication director; b. Inglewood, Calif., Nov. 20, 1963; d. Robert Eugene and Dorothy (Burghdurf) Lux; m. Richard J. Santelli, Oct. 14, 1990. BS, Nazareth Coll. Rochester, 1985, art teaching cert., 1991. Features editor Wolfe Publs., Fishers, N.Y., 1985-89; decentralization grant coord. Wayne County Coun. for the Arts, Lyons, N.Y., 1989-91; communications dir. Myers Community Hosp., Sodus, N.Y., 1991—; chmn. pub. com. Seton Ball-St. Mary's Hosp., Rochester, 1985—; free-lance writer The Genesee Hosp., Rochester, 1990—, Strong Med. Ctr., Rochester, 1990—; vol. Wayne County Coun. for the Arts, Lyons, 1991—; mem. Twig Assn., Myers Community Hosp., 1992. Author poetry. Vol. Conservative Party, Wayne County, N.Y., 1991. Mem. Sigma Tau Delta. Home: 7581 Sixth St Sodus Point NY 14555 Office: Myers Community Hosp 6600 Middle Rd Sodus Point NY 14551

SANTEMMA, JON NOEL, lawyer; b. Oceanside, N.Y., Dec. 24, 1937; s. Esterino E. and Emilie E. (Davis) S.; m. Lynne Maurer, Dec. 27, 1960 (div. 1987); children: Suzanne, Deborah, Jon E., Christopher Jon, Jessica Noelle; m. Carol Marie Hoffman, July 16, 1988. BA, Cornell U., 1960; JD, Fordham U., 1963. Bar: N.Y. 1963, U.S. Ct. Mil. Appeals 1969, U.S. Ct. Claims 1969, U.S. Supreme Ct. 1969, U.S. Dist. Ct. (ea. dist.) N.Y. 1977. Assoc. Parnell Callahan, N.Y.C., 1963-64; assoc. Warburton, Hyman, Deeley & Connolly, Mineola, N.Y., 1964-66; law sec. to adminstrv. judge of Nassau County Mineola, 1966-71, sole practice, 1971-74, 89—; ptnr. Santemma & Murphy, P.C., Mineola, 1974-89; lectr. in field. Trustee Inc. Village of Laurel Hollow, N.Y., 1979—; mem. Nassau County Rep. Law Com., 1979—; mem. Nassau County Jud. Selection Com., 1992—. Recipient Outstanding Man of Yr. in Law award L.I. U., 1976. Mem. Am. Bar Found., N.Y. Bar Found., N.Y. State Bar Assn. (ho. of dels. 1980—, mem. exec. com. 1984-85, 89-90, v.p. 1986-88), Nassau County Bar Assn. (pres. 1979-80, pres.'s award for outstanding svc. 1981), N.Y. State Trial Lawyers Assn., Suffolk County Bar Assn., Assn. Bar City N.Y., Huntington Country Club, Cold Spring Harbor Club, Beach Club, Garden City Golf Club. Contbr. articles to profl. jours. Address: 200 Willis Ave Mineola NY 11501

SANTER, JAMES OWEN, research chemist; b. Benenden, Kent, Eng., May 3, 1931; came to U.S., 1955; s. Edward Owen and Emily (Symonds) S.; m. Eileen Mont, July 28, 1991; children: Judith A., Jeffrey O., Kenneth A., Hilary J. BSc, U. London, 1955; PhD, Ill. Inst. Tech., 1961. Sr. rsch. chemist Shawinigan Resins Corp., Springfield, Mass., 1961-64; from sr. rsch. chemist to prin. technologist Monsanto Co., Springfield, Mass., 1964—. Patentee in field. Served with British Army, 1949-51. Mem. Am. Chem. Soc. Office: Monsanto Co 730 Worcester St Springfield MA 01151-1089

SANTIAGO-NOA, VICTOR MANUEL, psychiatrist; b. San Juan, P.R., Feb. 29, 1944; s. Victor M. and Lydia M. (Noa) S.; m. Olga Carrion, June 15, 1968 (div. Aug. 1975); children: Cecile, Mara; m. Nancy Hernandez, Apr. 3, 1980; children: Vivienne, Joseph. Student, U. P.R., 1968, MD, 1972, postgrad., 1977. Instr. U. P.R., San Juan, 1977-80; asst. med. dir. P.H.P., Ft. Chaffee, Ark., 1980-81; clin. dir. geriatrics dept. Danville (Pa.) State Hosp., 1982-84; clin. dir. children Manchester (N.H.) Mental Health, 1984-87; staff psychiatrist Lakeshore Hosp., Manchester, 1987-88; med. dir. outpatient children York (Pa.) Hosp., 1988—; cons. P.R. Dept. Health, 1977-80, VA Hosp., San Juan, 1981-82, Union-Snyder Mental Health, Lewisburg, Pa., 1982-84. Author: short story Muneca, 1971, Labor de la noche a medias, 1971, The Wake, 1986. Vice pres. bd. Latin Am. Ctr., Manchester, 1986. Mem. Am. Psychiat. Assn. Office: 244 Center Rd Ste 201 Monroeville PA 15146-1789

SANTILLI, ARTHUR ATTILIO, chemist, researcher; b. Everett, Mass., July 25, 1929; s. Harry and Minnie (De Masi) S.; m. Kathryn Madenford, June 13, 1964; 1 child, David Arthur. AB in Chemistry, Boston U., 1951; MS in Chemistry, Tufts U., 1952; PhD in Chemistry, U. Mass., 1958. Postdoctoral fellow U. Mass., Amherst, 1957-58, Tufts U., Medford, Mass., 1958-60; sr. rsch. scientist Wyeth Labs., Radnor, Pa., 1960-65, group leader, 1965-86, rsch. supr., prin. scientist, 1986-87; rsch. fellow Wyeth-Ayerst Rsch., Princeton, N.J., 1987—. Contbr. more than 50 articles to profl. jours.; patentee in exptl. medicinal agts. field. V.p., pres. Holy Name Soc., St. Pius X Ch., Broomhall, Pa., 1970—, also ch. choir mem., 1985—. Sgt. U.S. Army, 1952-54. Named Man of Yr. Holy Name Soc., 1978. Mem. Am. Chem. Soc. (medicinal chemistry div.), Internat. Union Pure and Applied Chemistry, Phila. Organic Chemist's Club, Sigma Xi. Home: 1737 Sue Ellen Dr Havertown PA 19083 Office: Wyeth Ayerst Rsch CN 8000 Princeton NJ 08543-8000

SANTILLI, VINCENT EDWARD, banker; b. Bridgeport, Conn., June 5, 1962; s. Joseph Peter and Rose Florence (Tangredi) S.; m. Jeanine Alice Czajkowski, Sept. 19, 1987; 1 child, Joseph Peter. BA, U. Pa., 1984. V.p., br. mgr. People's Bank, Bridgeport, 1984—. Pres. adv. bd. Cath. Family and Social Svc., Bridgeport, 1990-91; treas. Crimestoppers of Bridgeport, 1989—; lector St. Raphael's-St. Margaret's Parish; vol. gen. bus. div. United Way; vol. Kennedy Ctr. for the Retarded, Bridgeport. Named Gen. Bus. Div. Outstanding Vol., United Way Ea. Fairfield County, 1991. Mem. Kiwanis (pres. 1990-91), KC (Pk. City Coun. #16, grand knight 1990-91, 91-92, Grand Knight of Yr., Conn., 1991-92). Democrat. Roman Catholic. Home: 35 Wood Ave Trumbull CT 06611-2352 Office: Peoples Bank 2772 Main St Stratford CT 06497

SANTOMASSO, ANTOINETTE THERESE, educator; b. New Haven, Oct. 1, 1949; d. Hugo Arthur and Theresa Nancy (Vellaccio) S.; m. Philip Thomas Ventre, Aug. 29, 1982. BS in Elem. Edn., So. Conn. State Coll., 1971, cert. in adminstrn.-supervision, 1986; MA in Social Scis., U. Chgo., 1972. Cert. elem. tchr., adminstr., Conn. Mid. sch. tchr. Branford (Conn.) Pub. Schs., 1973—; presenter ednl. workshop Branford Intermediate Sch., 1986, 87. Mem. profl. devel. com. Branford Intermediate Sch. Recipient Faculty Excellence award Branford Intermediate Sch., 1988, Celebration of Excellence award Conn. Dept. Edn., 1989, 91. Mem. NEA, Assn. for Supervision and Curriculum Devel., Conn. Edn. Assn., Adminstrn. Assn. So. Conn. State U.

SANTOPIETRO, JOSEPH C., educator; b. N.Y.C., Dec. 13, 1941; s. Carmine J. and Lucy G. S.; 1 child, Joseph. BS in Edn., Oswego State Coll., 1963; MS in Ednl. Guidance, Long Island U., 1968; MA in Adminstrn. and Supervision, NYU, 1980, ABD, 1982. Tchr. N.Y.C. Bd. Edn., 1963—. Mem. KC (grand knight 1983-86, 91-92), Elks (exalted ruler 1986-87, 1991-92, chmn. scholarship 1984-92, ritual chmn. 1986-89). Roman Catholic. Home: 11039 69th Rd Flushing NY 11375-3919

SANTORA, JOSEPH CHRISTOPHER, humanities and business administration educator; b. Newark, Dec. 25, 1950; s. Joseph A. and Angelina (Scannella) S.; m. Linda Monteverde, July 27, 1991. BS, Seton Hall U., 1972, MA, 1973; MA, NYU, 1978; EdD, Fordham U., 1981. Instr. humanities and bus. adminstrn. Essex County Coll., Newark, 1975-80, asst. prof., dir. Title III, 1980-81, assoc. prof., 1981-84, prof., 1990—, dir. program devel., 1981-84; assoc. prof., faculty coord. West Essex Campus Essex County Coll., West Caldwell, 1985-90; cons. to profit and non-profit orgns. Author 2 reference books and 20 monographs on bus. and pub. adminstrn.; contbr. book revs. to profl. jours. Mid-career fellow Princeton U., 1984-85. Mem. NEA, ASCD, Acad. Mgmt., Am. Ednl. Rsch. Assn., Urban Affairs Assn., Strategic Mgmt. Assn., Phi Delta Kappa. Office: Esssex County Coll 303 University Ave Newark NJ 07102-1798

SANTORO, ELISSA JEANNE, breast oncology surgeon; b. Newark, Oct. 18, 1938; d. James and Jean Santoro. AB in Chemistry, Coll. St. Elizabeth, 1960; MD, Woman's Med. Coll. Pa., 1965. Diplomate Am. Bd. Surgery, Nat. Bd. Med. Examiners. Straight surg. intern Hosp. of Woman's Med. Coll. Pa., Phila., 1965-66; asst. resident surgery Hosp. of Woman's Med. Ctr., N.Y.C., 1966-67; asst. resident surgery St. Vincent's Hosp. and Med. Ctr., N.Y.C., 1967-68, sr. asst. resident surgery, 1968-69, chief surg. resident, 1969-70; assoc. attending in surgery and oncology Irvington (N.J.) Gen. Hosp., 1971-77; asst. attending in surgery and oncology St. Barnabas Hosp. and Med. Ctr., Livingston, 1973-80, assoc. attending in surgery and oncology, 1980-81, attending physician, 1983—, clin. chief surg. oncology, 1984—; summer student rsch. fellow pathology Woman's Med. Coll. Pa., Phila., 1963; Am. Cancer Soc. fellow St. Vincent's Hosp. and Med. Ctr., N.Y.C., 1968-69; postdoctoral fellow in cancer tng. NIH, N.Y. Med. Coll. and Met. Hosp. Ctr., 1970-71; instr. surgery N.Y. Med. Coll., N.Y.C., 1970-72, assoc. clin. investigator cen. oncology group, 1970-72; clin. asst. prof. surgery Coll. U. Medicine and Dentistry, Newark, 1973-82; med. advisor Ruth Estrin Goldberg Meml. for Cancer Rsch., Reach to Recovery. Vice-chmn. svc. and rehab. com. State N.J. Am. Cancer Soc., 1976-78, chmn., 1978-80, chmn. exec. com., 1983, chmn., 1984, vice-chmn. nominating com., chmn. svc. and rehab. com. Essex County div., 1977-80, chmn. exec. com., 1981-83, v.p., 1983, bd. mgrs.; bd. trustees Regional Coun. Women in Medicine, Inc., 1984, Coll. St. Elizabeth, Convent Station, N.J., 1985-90. Recipient Physician of Yr. award N.J. div. Am. Cancer Soc., 1983, Friends of Hospice award Karen Ann Quinlan Ctr. of Hope, Newton, N.J., 1984, Hon. Chairperson of Yr. award N.J. Fedn. Bus. and Profl. Women's Clubs, Inc., 1984, Woman of Yr. award Irvington Bus. and Profl. Women's Club, 1985, Sister Miriam Teresa Demjanovich medal award N.J. Ladies Aux. Dept., Cath. War Vets., 1985, Woman of Yr. award Italian-Am. Columbus Day Celebration Com., 1986, Med. Appreciation award Reach to Recovery, 1988. Mem. AMA, Am. Med. Women's Assn., Am. Med. Writer's Assn., Am. Soc. Contemporary Medicine and Surgery, Assn. Am. Med. Colls., Assn. Acad. Surgery, Am. Assn. Cancer Edn., Am. Soc. Preventive Oncology, Am. Soc. Clin. Oncology, Acad. Medicine N.J., Surg. Soc. N.Y. Med. Coll., Inc., Essex County Med. Soc. (bd. mgrs.), N.J. Med. Women's Assn., N.J. Gastroent. Soc., N.Y. State Cancer Programs Assn., Inc., Oncology Soc. N.J., N.Y. Met. Breast Cancer Group, Inc., Am. Cancer Soc. N.J., Alpha Kappa Delta. Office: 315 E Northfield Rd Ste 3B Livingston NJ 07039

SANTORO, EUGENE ANTHONY, vocational school educator; b. Boston, Feb. 14, 1935; s. Giacomo Francis and Catherine Ann (Cogliano) S.; m. Bernadette Marie Dineen, June 4, 1955; children: Catherine Ann Santoro Breen, Susan Marie Santoro Twombly, James Eugene, Peter Charles. BS magna cum laude, Fitchburg State Coll., 1982, MEd, 1984; CAGS, U. Mass., 1991. Drafter Am. Machine & Foundry, Cambridge, Mass., 1953-54,

Assoc. Engrs., Waltham, Mass., 1954-58; sr. aero. design engr. ITEK Corp., Lexington, Mass., 1958-70; machine designer United Shoe Machinery Corp., Wakefield, Mass., 1970-71, B&M Contract Engring., Waltham, 1971-72, LeHigh Design Inc., Waltham, 1972-76; constrn. div. coord. Minuteman Regional Vocat. Tech. Sch., Lexington, 1976—; evening lectr. Northeastern U., Lexington, 1978—; cons. Cryovac, Woburn, Mass., 1978—, Digital Equip. Corp., Maynard, Mass., 1979. Patentee in field. Notary Rep. Party, Brockton, 1966. Mem. Mass. Assn. Occupational Edn. Dirs. (exec. coun. 1992), Am. Vocat. Assn., Mass. Vocat. Leadership Alumni Assn., Mass. Vocat. Assn. Roman Catholic. Home: 14 Peach Orchard Rd Burlington MA 01803 Office: Minuteman Reg Vocat Sch 758 Marrett Rd Lexington MA 02173

SANTORO, JOSEPH LEWIS, merchandise manager; b. Watertown, Mass., Oct. 14, 1936; s. Emidio Santoro and Rose Margaret (Corazzini) Tolleson. Student, Apparel Industry Sch. Design, 1954-58. Product engr. Wendy Watts, N.Y.C., 1974-87; pres. and owner JLS Studio, N.Y.C., 1987-88; mdse. mgr. Michael Marcella Ltd., N.Y.C., 1988—. Mem. Craftsmen of Ladies Apparel (pres. emeritus 1988-91). Republican. Roman Catholic.

SANTORUM, RICK, congressman; b. Winchester, Va., May 10, 1958; s. Aldo and Catherine (Dughi) S.; m. Karen Garver, June 2, 1990; 1 child, Elizabeth Anne. BA with honors, Pa. State U., State College, 1980; MBA, U. Pitts., 1981; JD, Dickinson Sch. Law, 1986. Bar: Pa. 1986. Adminstrv. asst. State Sen. Doyle Corman, Harrisburg, Pa., 1981-86; exec. dir. local govt. com. Pa. State Senate, Harrisburg, 1981-84, exec. dir. transp. com., 1984-86; assoc. atty. Kirkpatrick and Lockhart, Pitts., 1986-90; mem. U.S. Ho. of Reps. from 18th Pa. dist., 1991—, mem. budget, vets.' affairs coms., select com. on children, youth and families. Bd. dirs. Mt. Lebanon Extended Day Program, 1987-91; mem. Child Advocacy Project, 1987-91. Mem. Allegheny County Bar Assn., Tyrolean Soc. Western Pa., Italian Sons and Daus. Assn., Rotary. Republican. Roman Catholic. Home: 127 Seminole Dr Pittsburgh PA 15228-1528 Office: US Ho of Reps 1708 Longworth House Office Bldg Washington DC 20515

SANTOS, ARTHUR MAGNO, thoracic cardiovascular surgeon; b. Pasay City, Philippines, May 15, 1946; s. Regalado T. and Lily Santos; m. Lorna Perez Pantangco, Mar. 26, 1973; 1 child, Vladimir Allen Santos. BS in Premedicine, Far Eastern U., Manila, Philippines, 1967; MD, U. of the East, 1972. Cert. Am. Bd. Surgery, Am. Bd. Abdominal Surgery. Intern, 1973-74, resident in gen. surgery, 1974-79, resident in thoracic and cardiovascular surgery, 1979-81; pvt. practice Assn. of Thoracic Surgeons, Pitts., 1981—. Mem. AMA, Pa. Med. Soc., Soc. Philippine Surgeons in Am., Pa. Thoracic Soc., Allegheny County Med. Soc. Seventh-day Adventist. Office: Assn of Thoracic Surgeons 532 S Aiken Ave Pittsburgh PA 15232

SANTOS, EUGENE SY, JR., computer science researcher; b. Columbus, Ohio, Jan. 28, 1968; s. Eugene Sy and Evelyn (Wee) S. BS in Math. and Computer Sci. summa cum laude, Youngstown State U., 1985, MSc in Math., 1986; MSc in Computer Sci., Brown U., 1988, PhD in Computer Sci., 1992. Systems programmer and cons. Youngstown (Ohio) State U., 1983-86; design and rsch. cons. Integrated Profl. Systems, Youngstown, 1984—; rsch. asst. Brown U., Providence, 1986—; instr. Youngstown State U., 1986. Contbr. articles to profl. jours. Fellow Pi Mu Epsilon Nat. Math., 1984-86. Mem. Assn. for Computing Machinery, Am. Assn. for Articial Intelligence, Sigma Xi. Office: Dept of Computer Sci Box 1910 Brown U Providence RI 02912

SANTOS, GEORGE WESLEY, educator, physician; b. Oak Park, Ill., Feb. 3, 1928; s. George and Emma (Gast) S.; m. Joanne Agnes Corrigan, June 7, 1952; children: Susan Elizabeth, George Wesley II, Kelly Anne, Amy Coburn. SB, MIT, 1951, MS in Phys. Biology, 1951; MD, Johns Hopkins U., 1955; Doctoris Medicinae Gradum Honoris Cause, U. Munich, Fed. Republic Germany, 1989. Intern Johns Hopkins Hosp., Balt., 1955-56, asst. resident, 1958-60; scholar Leukemia Soc., N.Y.C., 1961-66; mem. faculty Johns Hopkins Sch. Medicine, Balt., 1962—, assoc. prof. medicine, 1968-73, prof. oncology and medicine, 1973—; asst. physician in chief Balt. City Hosp., 1963-77; mem. Cancer Clin. Investigative Rev. Com., 1969-73; mem. extramural sci. adv. bd. Meml. Sloan-Kettering Cancer Ctr., 1977-79; mem. Immunology-Epidemiology Spl. Virus Cancer Program, 1969-73; chmn. bone marrow transplant registry ACS, 1969-73; mem. Internat. Com. Organ Transplant Registry ACS, 1969-73; mem. cell biology-immunology-genetics rsch. evaluation com. VA, 1969-71. Assoc. editor Cancer Rsch., 1978-81; mem. bd. editorial advisors Jour. Immunopharmacology, 1978—; mem. editorial bd. Blood, 1983—. With USNR, 1956-58. Recipient Disting. Achievement in Cancer Rsch. award Bristol Meyers, 1988. Mem. Am. Soc. Hematology, Transplantation Soc. (counselor 1971-73), Am. Assn. Immunologists, Leukemia Soc. Am. (bd. dirs. 1973—), Internat. Soc. Exptl. Hematology (councillor 1973, pres. 1981), Am. Assn. Cancer Rsch., Am. Soc. Clin. Investigation, Nat. Multiple Sclerosis Soc. (chmn. adv. com. on drug devel. 1981-82, mem. adv. com. on drug devel. 1981—). Home: 13623 Bardon Rd Phoenix MD 21131-1517 Office: Johns Hopkins Hosp Baltimore MD 21205

SANTY, ALBERT CHRISTY, marketing executive; b. N.Y.C., Nov. 20, 1948; s. Albert Christy and Rosalyn (Walsh) S.; m. Stefani Glasgow, Oct. 14, 1978. BA, Duke U., 1971. Actor N.Y.C., 1971-77; assoc. cons. Bob Henabery Assocs., Inc., N.Y.C., 1977-86; computer cons. Travel Desk of N.Y., 1987-89; radio rsch. asst. Rantel Rsch., Laurel, Md., 1989-. Office: Rantel Rsch Corp PO Box 681 Laurel MD 20725-0681

SAPADIN, LINDA ALICE, psychologist, writer; b. N.Y.C., Mar. 20, 1940; d. Samuel Miles and Helen Leah (Bogen) Fink; m. Seymour Sapadin, Nov. 10, 1962 (div. 1980); children: Brian, Glenn, Daniel; m. Ronald J. Goodrich, May 15, 1983. BA, Bklyn. Coll., 1960; MA, Temple U., 1961, CUNY, 1986; PhD, CUNY, 1986. Lic. psychologist, N.Y. Sch. psychologist N.Y.C. Bd. Edn., 1962-66, rsch. cons., 1985-87; tchr. Hewlett-Woodmere (N.Y.) Adult Edn., 1975-84; devel. dir. Ctr. for Women and Achievement, Island Park, N.Y., 1984-89; dir. Biofeedback and Stress Reduction Ctr., Valley Stream, N.Y., 1990—; pvt. practice Valley Stream, 1987—; forum leader, adj. prof. Hofstra U., N.Y. Inst. Tech., Five Towns Coll., Nassau Community Coll., L.I., 1974-90; cons. Nassau County Town of Hempstead, N.Y., 1986; adj. prof. continuing edn. Hofstra U., Uniondale, N.Y., 1985—; talk show host Sta. WGBB Radio, Merrick, N.Y., 1987. Columnist Chanry Communications, 1987-90, Richner Publs., 1992; contbr. articles to profl. jours. Chmn. psychology com. Nassau County NOW, Uniondale, 1983; speaker L.I. Assn. Planned Parenthood, Econ. Opportunities Coun., L.I. Libr. System, B'nai Brith, Women's Forum, Nat. Coun. Jewish Women, 1984—. Recipient Outstanding Community Svc. award State Senator Carol Berman, 1984. Mem. APA (media div., psychology of women div.), Nassau County Psychol. Assn. (women's studies com.). Office: Biofeedback and Stress 19 Cloverfield Rd Valley Stream NY 11581-2421

SAPERSTON, HOWARD TRUMAN, JR., real estate broker; b. Buffalo, Oct. 4, 1939; s. Howard Truman and Nan (Basch) S.; m. Mary Bernard Franklin, Sept. 9, 1967; children: Howard T. III, W. Scott. BA, Franklin & Marshall, 1963. Chmn. Saperston Real Estate Corp., Buffalo, 1963—; dir. Buffalo Sabres, 1969—; chmn. Buffalo C. of C. Real Estate Coun., 1978-79. Former trustee Nichols Sch. of Buffalo; dir., past pres., trustee Boys and Girls Clubs of Buffalo; former dir. Y.M.C.A., Buffalo; dir. Buffalo Gen. Hosp. Found. Mem. Soc. Indsl. and Office Rels., Upstate N.Y. Soc. Indsl. and Office Realtors (pres. 1989-90). Republican. Jewish. Home: 100 Morris Ave Buffalo NY 14214 Office: Saperston Real Estate Corp 584 Delaware Ave Buffalo NY 14202

SAPHIR, RICHARD LOUIS, pediatrician; b. N.Y.C., May 1, 1933; s. Samuel and Grace (Greenberg) S.; m. Judith Schwartz, Dec. 6, 1958; 1 child, Steven. BA, NYU, 1954; MD, SUNY, N.Y.C., 1958. Diplomate Nat. Bd. Med. Examiners. Asst. attending physician Mt. Sinai Hosp., N.Y.C., 1965-71; chief, pediatric svcs. U.S. Naval Hosp., Newport, R.I., 1967-69; asst dir., pediatrics acute care clinic Mt. Sinai Hosp., 1970-78, asst. clin. prof. pediatrics, assoc. attending physician, 1971-82, assoc. clin. prof. pediatrics, 1982-88, attending physician, 1982—, clin. prof. pediatrics, 1988—; mem. bd. dirs. Mt. Sinai Childrens Ctr. Found., N.Y.C., 1987—. Contbr. articles to profl. jours. Chmn. community and adv. com. N.Y.C. Info. and Counseling Program for Sudden Infant Death Syndrome, 1979-81; med. bd. YMHA, N.Y.C., 1982-86. Comdr. USNR, 1967-69. Fellow N.Y. Acad. Medicine (treas. 1987-89), Am. Acad. Pediatrics; mem. N.Y. Pediatric Soc. (pres. 1978-79), N.Y. County Med. Soc. (vice chmn. com. child welfare 1974-85). Office: BSM Pediatrics PC 55 E 87th St New York NY 10128-1043

SAPHIRE, GARY STEVEN, podiatrist; b. Bklyn., July 10, 1952; s. Leonard and Dorothy (Henry) S.; m. Helene Frances Koolik, Sept. 12, 1982; children: Emily Laura, Erika Robyn. BS in Health & Sci., Bklyn. Coll., 1974; BS in Biol. Sci., Ill. Coll. Podiatric Medicine, 1978, D.P.M., 1978. Diplomate Am. Bd. Podiatric Surgery. Chief resident Coney Island Hosp., Bklyn., 1978-79; attending Coney Island Hosp., 1979-82, Maimonides Med. Ctr., Bklyn., 1979-86, Community Hosp., Bklyn., 1984—; dir. podiatric surgery Caledonian Hosp., Bklyn., 1986—; del. N.Y. State Podiatric Med. Assn., N.Y.C., 1988—; exec. bd. Kings County Podiatry Soc., Bklyn., 1987-88; chief podiatric surgery The Bklyn. Hosp. Ctr., 1989—. Author: Vascular Disease, 1982, Arthroscopy, 1989, Ankle Arthroscopy, 1989; editor, The Bull., 1988-89. Judge Sci. Fair, N.Y.C., 1985-89. Durlacher scholar Nat. Podiatric Honor Soc., 1978. Fellow Am. Coll. Foot Surgeons; mem. Am. Podiatric Med. Assn., Am. Diabetes Assn. Coun. Foot Health, N.Y. Acad. Sci., Westerliegh Tennis Club, Kappa Tau Epsilon (v.p. local chpt. 1977-78). Office: Parkway Podiatry Group 7516 Bay Pky Brooklyn NY 11214-1598

SAPOFF, MEYER, electronics component manufacturer; b. N.Y.C., June 2, 1927; s. Benjamin and Mary (Charney) S. Student, Mohawk Coll., 1946-48, Poly. Inst. Bklyn., 1948-50, 52-53; BS in Elec. Engring. magna cum laude, Poly. Inst. Bklyn., 1950, postgrad., 1952-53; postgrad., MIT, 1951, U. Pa., 1951-52; MS in Elec. Engring., Drexel Inst. Tech., 1952. Rsch. engr. Franklin Inst. Labs., Phila., 1950-52; rsch. fellow sr. grade Poly. Inst. Bklyn., 1952-53; dir. rsch. Victory Engring. Corp., Springfield, N.J., 1953-57; dir. engring. Victory Engring. Corp., Springfield, 1957-63, v.p., 1963-69; cons., sr. staff scientist Keystone Carbon Co., St. Mary's, Pa., 1969-70; pres. Thermometrics, Inc., Edison, N.J., 1970-86; chmn. bd., chief exec. officer Thermometrics, Inc., Edison, 1986—; bd. dir. Thermometrics, Inc.; cons. in field; program com., chmn. E20.08 Med. Thermometry subcom., chmn. session on thermistors 6th Symposium on Temperature, Measurement and Control in Sci. and Industry. Contbr. articles to profl. jours.; patentee in field. Active Citizens League West Orange, 1962-75, West Orange PTA, 1960-76. With USN, 1945-46. Recipient Indsl. Rsch. IR-100 award, 1974; State of NYU scholar, 1948-50; Poly. Inst. Bklyn. fellow, 1953. Mem. IEEE, ASTM, AAAS, Mfrs. Assn. of Union, N.J. Mfrs. Assn., Poly. Inst. Bklyn. Alumni Assn., Am. Ceramic Soc., Internat. Orgn. for Legal Metrology, Am. Nat. Standards Inst., Am. Vacuum Soc., Tau Beta Pi, Eta Kappa Nu. Home: 1137 Stuart Rd Princeton NJ 08540-1216 Office: 808 Us Hwy 1 Edison NJ 08817-4695

SAPONARA, EDUARDO MILLIGAN, hematologist, oncologist, internist; b. Lima, Peru, Mar. 6, 1948; s. Carlos Alberto Saponara and Norah (Milligan) Thaine; m. Jenny Esther Nagaro, June 12, 1974; children: Eduardo Carlos, Fiorella Karina. MD, Peruvian U., Lima, 1973. Intern medicine N.Y. Med. Coll., N.Y.C., 1973-74, resident medicine, 1974-76, fellow hematology/oncology, 1976-78; fellow neoplastic diseases Mt. Sinai Hosp., N.Y.C., 1978-79, clin. asst. attending neoplastic diseases, 1979—; sr. clin. instr. neoplastic diseases Mt. Sinai Sch. Medicine, N.Y.C.; clin. asst. prof. medicine, hematology, hemostasis N.Y. Med. Coll., Valhalla, N.Y., 1979—; chief hematology/oncology Lawrence Hosp., Bronxville, N.Y., 1980—; co-chmn. profl. edn. So. Westcheseter div. Am. Cancer Soc., 1987. Fellow ACP. Office: 77 Pondfield Rd Bronxville NY 10708

SARACHIK, MYRIAM PAULA, physics educator; b. Antwerp, Belgium, Aug. 8, 1933; came to U.S., 1947; d. Solomon and Sarah (Segal) Morgenstein; m. Philip E. Sarachik, Sept. 6, 1954; 1 child, Karen Beth. AB, Barnard Coll., 1954; MS, Columbia U., 1957, PhD, 1960. Rsch. assoc. IBM Watson Labs., Columbia U., N.Y.C., 1960-62; mem. tech. staff Bell Telephone Labs., Murray Hill, N.J., 1962-64; asst. prof. physics CCNY, 1964-67, assoc. prof., 1967-70, prof., 1970—; advisor NSF, former advisor NRC. Contbr. over 50 articles to profl. jours. Fellow Am. Phys. Soc. (various offices and coms.). Office: CCNY Physics Dept Convent Ave New York NY 10031

SARACHIK, PHILIP EUGENE, electrical engineering educator; b. N.Y.C., Dec. 3, 1931; s. Saul and Edith (Ochs) S.; m. Myriam Paula Morgenstein, Sept., 1954; 1 child, Karen. AB, Columbia U., 1953, BS, 1954, MS, 1955, PhD, 1958. Staff engr. IBM Rsch., Yorktown Heights, N.Y., 1958-60; asst. prof. Columbia U., N.Y.C., 1960-63, assoc. prof., 1963-64; assoc. prof. NYU, 1964-68, prof., 1968-73; prof. Poly. U., Bklyn., 1973—. Contbr. articles to profl. jours. Fellow IEEE. Office: Polytech U 333 Jay St Brooklyn NY 11201-2990

SARANTIDES, JAMES, warehouse executive, composer; b. Danbury, Conn., July 2, 1954; s. Edward and Penelope (Ganatsiou) S.; m. Joyce Ellen Merill, May 17,1980; children: Justin Edward, Christopher James. Diploma, Berklee Coll. Music, Boston, 1976. Salesman E.M. Adams Co., Medfield, Mass., 1978-82, exec. v.P., 1982—; pres. Tech Warehouse, Foxboro, Mass., 1991—. Designer ultrasound mini dopler, 1988; composer: Crazy Lover, 1991. Mem. ASCAP. Greek Orthodox. Home: 13 Young Rd Foxboro MA 02035

SARANTOS, SUSAN ELIZABETH, jewelry designer; b. Boston, May 3, 1958; d. George N. and Bettie J. (Deitrick) S. Basic silversmithing, with Corky Ackman, Newport, R.I., 1975; apprenticeship, C.L. Sherman & Co., Newport, R.I., 1978-81; enameling workshop, with Rebekah Laskin, Penland Sch., N.C., 1986; rendering workshop, with Sharon Church, Skidmore Coll., 1988. Pvt. practice Newport, 1981—. Exhibited in group shows at Nat. Ornamental Metal Mus., Memphis, 1988, Joan Michlin Gallery, Soho, N.Y., 1988, 89, Hydrangea House Gallery, Newport, 1991; one-woman show Deblois St. Gallery, Newport, 1989. Mem. Internat. Sculpture Ctr., Soc. N.Am. Goldsmiths (nomination and election coms. 1991, 92, conf. com. 1992), Mfg. Jewelers and Silversmiths Am. (membership guild com.), Am. Gem Trade Assn. (Spectrum award 1984), Am. Craft Assn. (Am. Craft Coun.), Soc. Jewelry Hist., Newport Art Mus. Studio: 1 Hope St Newport RI 02840

SARASOHN-KAHN, JANE, management consultant; b. Detroit, June 25, 1955; d. Charles Z. and Pauline (Greenberg) Sarasohn; m. Robert Hickey Kahn, June 8, 1986. BA in Econs. and Journalism, U. Mich., 1977, MA in Econs., MPH, 1983. Cons. Health Systems, Inc., Phila., 1983-86; sr. cons. Touche Ross Mgmt. Cons., London, Eng., 1986-88; mgr. Laventhol & Horwath, Phila., 1988-90; prin. The Kahn Group, Paoli, Pa., 1991—; speaker in field. Contbr. articles to profl. jours. Sec. Friendship Hill Civic Assn., 1990—. Fellow Inst. Health Svcs. Mgmt.; mem. APHA, Am. Econs. Assn, Am. Mktg. Assn. Democrat. Jewish. Home: 335 Friendship Dr Paoli PA 19301-1206

SARASON, ESTHER KROOP, clinical psychologist, consultant; b. N.Y.C., Dec. 14, 1918; d. Benjamin and Pauline (Gershfeld) Kroop; m. Seymour Sarason, May 22, 1943; 1 child, Julie. PhD, Clark U., 1950. Psychologist Southbury (Conn.) Tng. Sch., 1943-45; rsch. assoc. dept. psychology Yale U., New Haven, 1961-70, 88—, rssch. assoc. Inst. for Social and Policy Studies, 1970-88. Contbr. articles to profl. jours. Fellow Am. Orthopsychiat. Assn.; mem. Am. Psychol. Assn., Conn. Psychol. Assn. Home: 136 Hartley St North Haven CT 06473-4411

SARAZEN, RICHARD ALLEN, media company executive; b. Bklyn., June 27, 1933; s. Nicholas and Anna M. (Isacco) S.; m. Christine M. Horwith, July 27, 1974; children—Richard, Theresa, Mary, Barbara, David, Russell, Christina, Andrea. B.B.A., Hofstra U., 1955. CPA, N.Y., Pa., Calif. Acct. Arthur Young & Co., N.Y.C., 1955-58; ptnr. Alexander Grant & Co., N.Y.C., 1958-67; v.p. fin. Seeburg Corp., Chgo., 1967-69; mng. ptnr. Alexander Grant & Co., Pitts., Los Angeles, 1969-74; exec. v.p. News Am. Pub., Inc., N.Y.C., 1974-80; chmn. bd. XCor Internat., Inc., N.Y.C., 1980-82; sr. exec. v.p., bd. dir. The News Corp. Ltd., Sydney, Australia, 1982—. Bd. dirs. N.Y.C. Center Found. Mem. AICPA, N.Y. State Soc. CPAs. Republican. Roman Catholic. Club: Chgo. Athletic. Home: 233 E 69th St New York NY 10021-5414 Office: News Am Pub Inc 1211 Ave Of The Americas New York NY 10036-8701

SARBANES, PAUL SPYROS, senator; b. Salisbury, Md., Feb. 3, 1933; s. Spyros P. and Matina (Tsigounis) S.; m. Christine Dunbar, June 11, 1960; children—John Peter, Michael Anthony, Janet Matina. A.B., Princeton, 1954; B.A. (Rhodes scholar), Oxford (Eng.) U., 1957; LL.B., Harvard, 1960. Bar: Md. bar 1960. Law clk. to judge Morris Soper U.S. Ct. Appeals (4th cir.), 1960-61; asso. Piper & Marbury, Balt., 1961-62; adminstrv. asst. Walter W. Heller; chmn. Council Econ. Advisers, 1962-63; exec. dir. Charter Revision Commn., Balt., 1963-64; asso. Venable, Baetjer & Howard, Balt., 1965-70; mem. Md. Ho. of Dels., 1967-71, 92d Congress from 4th Dist. Md., 93d-94th congresses from 3d Dist. Md.; U.S. senator from Md., 1977—. Democrat. Greek Orthodox. Office: US Senate 309 Hart Senate Bldg Washington DC 20510 also: Fed Office Bldg Baltimore MD 21201

SARCHIO, ANDREW PHILIP, human resources director; b. Clifton, N.J., July 22, 1943; s. Andrew C. and Jessie V. (Cannici) S.; widowed, Oct. 1990; 1 child, Chad Thomas. BA, Montclair State Coll., 1970, MA, 1973. Cert. sr. profl. human resources. Dir. human resources North Jersey Devel. Ctr., Totowa, N.J., 1974—; bd. dirs. bus. coun. Occupational Ctr. Essex County, East Orange, N.J., 1985—; prof. pers. adminstrn. Seton Hall U., South Orange, N.J. Trustee Passaic County Community Coll., Paterson, N.J., 1988-90; bd. dirs. Wayne (N.J.) Bd. Edn., 1986-87. Mem. Soc. for Human Resources Mgmt. (placement chmn. 1990—), Cert. Pub. Mgr. Soc. N.J. (trustee 1990—), Internat. Pers. Mgmt. Assn. Office: NJ Devel Ctr 169 Minnisink Rd Totowa NJ 07512-1803

SARD, GEORGE, public relations company executive; b. N.Y.C., May 13, 1953. BA, Clark Univ., 1975. Pub. rels. writer Clark Univ., 1975-78; dir. pub. rels. East N.Y. Svgs. Bank, 1978-80; acct. exec. Adams & Rinehart, Inc. (now Ogilvy Adams & Rinehard), 1980-82, v.p., 1982-86; pres., chief operating officer Adams & Rinehart, Inc. (now Ogilvy Adams & Rinehard), N.Y.C., from 1986; now chmn./N.Y. Ogilvy Adams & Rinehart, N.Y.C. Office: Ogilvy Adams & Rinehart Inc 708 3rd Ave New York NY 10017-4103*

SARDI, MAURICE CHARLES, contract furniture industry executive; b. Jamestown, N.Y., Mar. 25, 1935; s. Charles John and Margaret Mary (Mistretta) S.; m. Jacqueline Ann Lawrence, May 3, 1958; children: Christopher Lawrence, Charles John, Elizabeth Ann, Maureen Rose. BSEE, U. Notre Dame, 1957; MBA, George Washington U., 1966. With Westinghouse Electric Corp., 1971-90, group mktg. mgr. Constrn. Group, 1973-74, div. gen. mgr. Semiconductor Div., 1974-77; gen. mgr. mktg. ops. Westinghouse Elevator Co., Short Hills, N.J., 1977-81; div. gen. mgr. Westinghouse Furniture System, Grand Rapids, Mich., 1981-84; v.p. corp. rels. Westinghouse Electric Corp., Pitts., 1984-88, exec. v.p. Comml. Group and Corp. Resources, 1988-90, chmn., chief exec. officer The Knoll Group, 1990—. Bd. dirs., past chmn. Allegheny County Commn. for Workforce Excellence, Pitts., 1986—; mem. steering com. Leadership Pitts, 1986; mem. Pa. State Job Tng. Coordinating Coun., 1987—; bd. dirs. Pitts. Ballet Theatre, 1989—. Mem. Pitts. Field Club, Laurel Valley Golf Club. Republican. Roman Catholic. Office: The Knoll Group 6 Gateway Ctr Pittsburgh PA 15222

SAREYAN, ALEXANDER, marketing consultant; b. New Haven, Nov. 18, 1913; s. George and Rose (Hagopian) S.; m. Mildred Belle Solez, Mar. 9, 1957; children: Roslyn Belle Dailey, Alexander Harold Sareyan. BSc in Econs., U. Pa., 1934. Bus. mgr. Econ. Forum, N.Y.C., 1934-35; statistician Anaconda Wire & Cable Co., N.Y.C., 1936-41; pub. rels. dir. Conn. State Hosp., Middletown, Conn., 1943-46, Nat. Mental Health Found., N.Y.C., 1946-50, Nat. Mental Health Assn., N.Y.C., 1950-52; exec. dir. Mental Health Materials Ctr., N.Y.C., 1953—; dir. The Healing Community, N.Y.C., 1978-88. Editorial cons. Nat. Ctr. for Health Edn., N.Y.C., 1982-86; editor: Education for Health - The Selective Guide, 1984; author: The Turning Point, 1992. Democrat. United Ch. of Christ. Office: Mental Health Materials Ctr PO Box 304 Bronxville NY 10708

SARFATY, WAYNE ALLEN, insurance agent, financial planner; b. Rochester, N.Y., Apr. 18, 1951; s. Benjamin and Grace (Rowan) S.; m. Karen Nugent, July 12, 1957, Apr. 18, 1951; children; Melissa A., Gabrielle M. Student, Parsons Coll., 1971-74. Cert. ins. agt. Sales rep. Met. Life, Rochester, N.Y., 1979-81; register rep. Prudential Fin. Svcs., Rochester, 1981-92; owner, broker Wayne A. Sarfaty & Assocs., Rochester, 1992—. Dir. tng. films. Mem. Eagle Club. Recipient Nat. Quality award Nat. Assn. Life Underwriters, 1982-90; named to Million Dollar Round Table, NALU, 1987. Home: 15 Kernwood Dr Rochester NY 14624-3310

SARGENT, DENNIS MICHAEL, retail executive; b. N.Y.C., Nov. 30, 1950; s. Alfred Francis and Grace Marion (Lovacco) S.; m. Linda Diane Silveri, May 17, 1975; children: Marisa Joleen, Lindsay Janine. BA, Queen's Coll., 1972. With Alexander's, Inc., N.Y.C., 1975—, mdse. mgr., v.p., 1991—. Coach girl's atheltic teams Catholic Youth Orgn. Mem. Holy Name Soc. Republican. Roman Catholic. Office: Alexander's Inc 500 7th Ave New York NY 10018

SARGENT, EDWARD VINCENT, toxicologist, epidemiologist; b. Norwalk, Conn., Nov. 12, 1951; s. Edward Porter and Verna Mae (Whitney) S.; m. Linda Anne Capodanno. BA, U. Conn., 1973; MPH, Yale U., 1975; PhD, NYU, 1981. lectr. Rutgers Coll. Nursing, Newark, 1988—, U. Medicine and Dentistry of N.J., Piscataway, 1989—; appointed N.J. Right to Know Adv. Coun., Trenton, 1988—; mem. Pharm. Mfrs. Assn. Occupational Safety and Health Com., Washington, 1988—. Assoc. rsch. scientist NYU, N.Y.C., 1976-81; corp. mgr. indsl. toxicology Merck and Co., Inc., Rahway, N.J., 1981-89; assoc. dir. toxicology and epidemiology Merck and Co., Inc., Rahway, 1989—; lectr. Rutgers Coll. Nursing, Newark, 1988—, U. Medicine and Dentistry of N.J., Piscataway, 1989—; appointed N.J. Right to Know Adv. Coun., Trenton, 1988—; mem. Pharm. Mfrs. Assn. Osh Comm., Washington, 1988—. Contbr. articles to profl. jours. Mem. Fanwood (N.J.) Rescue Squad. Mem. AAAS, Internat. Soc. for Environ. Epidemiology, Am. Coll. Toxicology, Soc. Toxicology (councilor Midatlantic chpt. 1988-91), Occupational Disease Adv. Group N.J., N.Y. Acad. Sci. Office: Merck and Co Inc PO Box 2000 Rahway NJ 07065

SARGENT, FRANCIS WILLIAMS, JR., science writer; b. Boston, June 1, 1946; s. Francis Williams and Jessie (Fay) S.; m. Claudia Praeger, Feb. 2, 1947 (div. 1982); 1 child, Benjamin; m. Kristina Lindborg, Oct., 1984; 1 child, Chappell. BA, Harvard U., 1970; postgrad., Tufts U., 1971. Asst. dir. Sci. Edn. Assn., Woods Hole, Mass., 1971-73; dir. Balt. Aquarium, 1973; lobbyist Sierra Club, N.Y.C., 1974; freelance sci. writer Woods Hole, 1979—; radio journalist Christian Sci. Monitor, Boston, 1987, TV journalist, 1988; cons. Norwalk (Conn.) Aquarium, 1983. Author: Shallow Waters, 1980, The Year of the Crab, 1987, America's Undersea World, 1990, (radio series) The Science Spot, 1988. Mem. AAAS, Signet Honor Soc., Nat. Assn. Sci. Writers. Unitarian. Home and Office: PO Box 331 Woods Hole MA 02543-0331

SARGENT, JOHN MORGAN, foundation administrator; b. Quincy, Mass., Oct. 27, 1939; s. Morgan and Margaret (Crane) S.; m. Susan Jane Walker, Aug. 22, 1964; children: Elizabeth, Katherine. BA, Williams Coll., 1963. With Exxon, USA, Pelham, N.Y., 1963-69, Paine, Webber, Jackson & Curtis, Providence, 1969-74, Brown U., Providence, 1975-82, Wheaton Coll., Norton, Mass., 1982-86; pres. Coast Guard Found., Stonington, Conn., 1986—. With USCGR, 1963-64. Mem. Namequoit Sailing Assn. (commodore 1985-87), Warwick Heights Tennis Club, Stonington Country Club. Office: Coast Guard Found 394 Taugwonk Rd Stonington CT 06378-1807

SARGENT, PAMELA, writer; b. Ithaca, N.Y., Mar. 20, 1948. BA, SUNY, Binghamton, N.Y., 1968, MA, 1970. Am. editor: The Bull. of the Sci. Fiction Writers Am., Johnson City, N.Y., 1983-91; mng. editor Binghamton, 1970-73, asst. editor, 1973-75; editor (anthology) Women of Wonder, 1975, Bio-Futures, 1976, More Women of Wonder, 1976, The New Women of Wonder, 1978, (with Ian Watson) Afterlives, 1986; author Starshadows, 1977, The Best of Pamela Sargent, 1987, Cloned Lives, 1976, The Sudden Star, 1979, Watchstar, 1980, The Golden Space, 1982, The Alien Upstairs, 1983, Earthseed, 1983, Eye of the Comet, 1984, Homesmind, 1984, Venus of Dreams, 1986, The Shore of Women, 1986, The Best of Pamela Sargent, 1987, Alien Child, 1988, Venus of Shadows, 1988. Office: PO Box 486 Johnson City NY 13790-0486

SARGENT, ROSE-MARY, philosophy educator; b. Haverhill, Mass., Jan. 30, 1950; d. William James and Rose Elizabeth (Buttrick) Godfrey. BA, Merrimack Coll., 1983; MA, U. Notre Dame, 1986, PhD, 1987. Asst. prof. Univ. N.Mex., Albuquerque, 1987-90; postdoctoral fellow Northwestern Univ., Evanston, Ill., 1989-90; asst. prof. Merrimack Coll., North Andover, Mass., 1990—; rsch. assoc. Boston (Mass.) Univ., 1990—. Contbr. articles to profl. jours. Recipient fellowship Mellon Fellowships in the Humanities, 1983-87, summer scholar's award NSF, 1989, 91. Mem. AAAS, Am. Philos. Assn., Philosophy Sci. Assn., History Sci. Soc. Home: 7 Crescent Dr Andover MA 01810-1528 Office: Merrimack College Dept Philosophy North Andover MA 01845

SARIDIS, GEORGE NICHOLAS, electrical, computers and system engineering educator, robotics and automation researcher; b. Athens, Greece, Nov. 17, 1931; came to U.S., 1961, naturalized, 1971; s. Nicholas and Anna (Tsofa) S.; m. Panayota Dimarogona, Apr. 10, 1985. Diploma in Mech. and Elec. Engring., Nat. Tech. U., Athens, 1955; MS in Elec. Engring., Purdue U., 1962, PhD, 1965. Instr. Nat. Tech. U., 1955-63, Purdue U., West Lafayette, Ind., 1963-65, asst. prof., 1965-70, assoc. prof., 1970-75, prof., 1975-81; prof. elec., computer and system engring. Rensselaer Poly. Inst., Troy, N.Y., 1981—, dir. Robotics and Automation Lab., 1982—; dir. NASA Ctr. for Intelligent Robotic Systems for Space Exploration, 1988—; engring. program dir. NSF, Washington, 1973. Author: Self-Organizing Control of Stochastic Systems, 1977; also numerous articles, reports. Co-editor, contbg. author: Fuzzy Automata, 1977; editor, contbg. author: Advances in Automation and Robotics, Vol. 1, 1985, Vol. 2, 1990. Fellow IEEE (founding pres. robotics and automation council 1981-84, Centennial medal 1984, Disting. Mem. award 1989); mem. ASME, Soc. Mfg. Engrs./Robotics Internat.-Machine Vision Assn. (sr.), Am. Soc. Engring. Edn., N.Y. Acad. Scis. Home: 38 Londonwood Ave Loudonville NY 12211 Office: Rensselaer Poly Inst NASA Ctr Intelligent Robotic Systems Troy NY 12180-3590

SARJEANT, WALTER JAMES, electrical and computer engineering educator; b. Strathroy, Can., Apr. 7, 1944; s. Walter Burns and Margaret (Laurie) S.; m. Ann Richards, June 30, 1972; children: Eric, Cheryl. BSc in Math, Physics, U. Western Ont., Can., 1966, MSc in Physics, 1967, PhD in Physics, 1971. Asst. dir. R&D Gen-Tec Inc., Quebec City, Que., Can., 1971-73; program mgr. Lumonics Rsch. Ltd., Ottawa, Ont., Can., 1973-75; staff scientist Nat. Rsch. Coun., Ottawa, Ont., Can., 1975-78; project leader Los Alamos (N.Mex.) Nat. Lab., 1978-81; James Clerk Maxwell prof. elec. and computer engring. SUNY, Buffalo, 1981—. Author: High Power Electronics, 1989. Fellow IEEE; mem. Electromagnetics Acad., Electrostatics Soc., N.Y. Acad. Scis., Rotary, Eta Kappa Nu. Office: SUNY Elec Engring Dept 312 Bonner Hall Buffalo NY 14260

SARKAS, ALBERT HARRY, artist, educator; b. Mahanoy City, Pa., Aug. 1, 1930; s. Harry L. and Julia D. (Demetriades) S.; B.S., Pa. State U., 1954; M.A., N.Y. U., 1958; student Scranton U., 1976-78, Coll. of Misericordia, 1977-78; m. Aliki Maria Liondou, Aug. 2, 1964; children—Harry, Alec. Instr. art Hazleton Area Sch. Dist., Hazleton, Pa., 1955-60, supr. art, 1961—; instr. art part-time Hazleton Art League, 1950—, Pa. State U., Hazleton, 1970—; nat. participant Getty Ctr. for Arts, 1985; advisor fine arts Northeastern Pa. Arts Alliance, Hazleton, 1978—; one man shows: Hazleton Art League, 1957, Berwick Art Center, 1959, Millbrook Art Gallery, 1962, Bloomsburg Art Gallery, 1965, Lock Haven State Coll., 1979, Wilkes U., 1990; group shows include: Eberhart Mus., Scranton, Pa., 1972, Robeson Meml. Center, 1972, Northeastern Pa. Arts Alliance, 1977—, also Moore Coll. of Art, Pa. Mus., 1986; represented in permanent collections: Pa. State U., Hazleton Art League, NYU, also numerous pvt. collections. Recipient awards Nat. Youth Arts Month, 1972-80; purchase awards in paintings Hazleton Art League, 1958, 1976; 1st prize in painting Scranton Fine Arts Festival, 1976; disting. svc. award, 1984; Nat. Adminstr. and Supervision award, 1992. Mem. Nat. Art Edn. Assn., Pa. Art Edn. Assn., Hazleton Art League (1st place award 1985), Am. Crafts Council, Pa. State Alumni Assn., Fine Arts Council, NE Pa. Arts Alliance. Mem. Greek Orthodox Ch. Club: Lions. Contbr. articles in field to profl. jours. Address: 695 Roosevelt Rd Hazleton PA 18201

SARKISIAN, RICHARD GABRIEL, financial engineer; b. N.Y.C., Aug. 1, 1952; s. Armen and Alice (Topalian) S. BS, Fairleigh Dickinson U., 1975; MA, SUNY, Buffalo, 1978; PhD in Math., CUNY, 1984. Postdoctoral fellow U. of Toronto, Toronto, Can., 1984-86; actuarial asst. The Equitable, N.Y.C., 1986-88; rsch. scientist Ocean and Atmospheric Sci., Dobbs Ferry, N.Y., 1988-89; fin. engr. The Options Group, N.Y.C., 1989-90, cons., 1991; fin. engr. James Capel, Inc., N.Y.C., 1992—. Home: 39 Beechwood Pl Harrington Park NJ 07640-1101 Office: James Capel Inc 405 Lexington Ave 39th Fl New York NY 10174

SARKODIE-MENSAH, KWASI, librarian, researcher; b. Ejisu, Ashanti, Ghana, June 13, 1955; came to U.S., 1982; s. Thomas Kwaku and Margaret Akua (Barnie) Mensah; m. Elizabeth Afua Sarkodie, Sept. 21, 1980; children: Kofi, Kwame, Nana Akua. Diploma, Complutense U., Madrid, 1978; BA with honors, U. Ghana, Legon, 1979; MLS, Clarion U, 1983; PhD, U. Ill., 1988. Tchr. English and French, Ahmadiyya High Sch., Kumasi, Ghana, 1979-80, Origbo Community High Sch., Ipetumodu, Nigeria, 1980-82; rsch. asst. Clarion (Pa.) U., 1982-84, U. Ill. Libr. Sch., Urbana, Ill., 1984-86; head pub. svcs. Xavier U. Libr., New Orleans, 1986-89; prof. French Xavier U., New Orleans, 1986-89, So. U., New Orleans, 1987-89; bibliog. instrn. coord. Northeastern U. Libr., Boston, 1989—; coord. New Eng. Bibliog. Instrn. Author: Foreign Students and United States Libraries, 1988; contbr. articles to profl. jours.; editor Libr. Instrn. Round Table News, 1990—. Recipient scholarship Ghana Govt., 1975-79, fellowship, U. Ill., 1986-88; named Best Tchr. Origbo Community High Sch. Ipetumodu, 1980-82. Mem. ALA, Acad. Rsch. Librs. Roman Catholic. Office: Northeastern U Libr 360 Huntington Ave Boston MA 02115

SARNI, VINCENT ANTHONY, manufacturing company executive; b. Bayonne, N.J., July 11, 1928; s. Alfred M. and Louise M. (Zoratti) S.; m. Dorothy Bellavance, Nov. 4, 1950; children: Louise Marie, Karen Lee, Vincent Anthony. B.S., U. R.I., 1949; postgrad., N.Y. U., 1950-52, Harvard U., 1973; LL.D. (hon.), Juniata Coll., 1979, U. R.I., 1985; DSc (hon.), New England Inst. Tech., 1991. Plant acct. Rheem Mfg. Co., Linden, N.J., 1950-53; dir. mfg. services Crown Can Co., Balt., 1953-57; dir. mktg. services Olin Corp., Stamford, Conn., 1957-68; with PPG Industries, Inc., Pitts., 1968—; v.p. mktg. indsl. chem. dept. PPG Industries Inc., Pitts., 1968-69, v.p., gen. mgr. indsl. chem. dept., 1969-75, v.p., gen. mgr. chem div., 1975-77, group v.p. chems. group, 1977-80, sr. v.p. PPG Industries Inc. (parent co.), Pitts., 1980-83, vice chmn., 1984, chmn., chief exec. officer, 1984—; bd. dirs. PNC Fin. Corp., Hershey Foods Corp., Pitts. Baseball Assocs.; chmn., chief exec. officer Inst. for Tng. of Handicapped in Advanced Tech. Chmn. Allegheny Conf. on Community Devel.; trustee U. R.I. Found., Juniata Coll., Carnegie-Mellon U.; bd. dirs. Pitts. Guild for Blind, 1980, Allegheny Gen. Hosp.; mem. bus. adv. coun. U. R.I., 1975—; chmn. Pitts. Opera Soc.; bd. dirs. River City Brass Band; chmn. Nat. Orgn. on Disability. Mem. Chem. Mfrs. Assn., Soc. Chem. Industry, Bus. Higher Edn. Forum, Bus. Roundtable, The Bus. Coun., Duquesne Club, Rolling Rock Club, Laurel Valley County Club, Chartiers Country Club, Allegheny Club, Point Judith Country Club. Office: PPG Industries Inc 3503 Wagon Wheel Wichita Falls TX 76310-1423

SARNO, PATRICIA ANN, biology educator; b. Ashland, Pa.; d. John Thomas and Anna (Harvest) S. BS, Pa. State U., 1966, MEd, 1971; postgrad. Bucknell U., 1967, Bloomsburg U., 1970. Programmer planetarium, tchr. sci. Pottsville (Pa.) High Sch., 1967; tchr. biology Schuylkill Haven (Pa.) Area High Sch., 1967-91, sci. chmn., coord. dist., 1973-91; lead tchr. sci. Pa. Acad. Suprs. and Curriculum Devel. Dist. Pa. Sch., 1991—; cons. Contbr. to profl. jours. Pa. Edn. Dept., career program Pottsville Hosp. Dow Chem. Co. grantee, 1971. Mem. AAAS, NEA, Pa. Edn. Assn. (exec. bd.), Nat. Assn. Biology Tchrs., Nat. Tchrs. Assn., Pa. Assn. Supervision and Curriculum Devel., N.Y. Acad. Scis., Pa. Tchrs. Assn., Am. Inst. Biol. Scis., Pa. Acad. Scis., Pa. State U. Alumni Assn., Schuylkill Haven Edn. Assn., Phi Sigma, Delta Kappa Gamma. Discoverer spider species Atypus snetzingeri, 1973. Home: 49 S Balliet St Frackville PA 17931-1703 Office: Schuylkill Haven High Sch Schuylkill Haven PA 17972

SARNOFF, PAUL, metals consultant, author, editor; b. Bklyn., Apr. 21, 1918; s. Nathan and Rose (Gelfand) S.; m. Lucille Levitt, Oct. 13, 1940; children: Alan Jan, Mitchell Ira, Steven Arthur. Various Wall St. positions, 1937-57; owner Sarnoff Co.-Stockbrokers, N.Y.C., 1955-57; sales mgr. Thomas Haab & Botts, N.Y.C., 1957-67; lectr.-in-fin. Hofstra U., Hempstead, N.Y., 1967-71; v.p. Herzog & Co., N.Y.C., 1972-76; research dir. ContiCommodity Services, N.Y.C., 1976-80, Rudolph Wolff, N.Y.C., 1980-82; corp. v.p. Paine Webber Jackson Curtis, N.Y.C., 1982-86; dir. The Metals Consultancy, Baldwin, N.Y., 1986—; history editor Banker's Mag., Boston, 1965-71; exec. editor Sci. & Tech., N.Y.C., 1968-71; dir. Inst. for Bus. & Urban Rsch., Hempstead, N.Y., 1969-70; curator econ. history U. Wyo., Laramie, 1966—; founding pres. Futures Industry Assn. options div. and rsch. div. Author more than 50 books, including biographies, histories, children's books, fin. volumes; editor spl. projects for Euromoney in London; columnist Japan Econ. Jour., 1981—; contbg. editor fin. newsletters and publs., 1987—. Founding dir. Oceanside (N.Y.) Jewish Ctr., Inst. for Children's Lit., Redding Ridge, Conn. Served to 2d lt. U.S. Army, 1944-46. Mem. Internat. Precious Metals Inst., Soc. Mining Engrs., N.W. Mining Assn., Authors Guild. Democrat. Jewish. Home: 3319 Poplar St Oceanside NY 11572-4516 Office: The Metals Consultancy PO Box 178 Baldwin NY 11510-0178

SARNOFF, WILLIAM, publishing company executive; b. Mt. Vernon, N.Y., May 22, 1929; s. Morris and Clara (Oppenheimer) S.; m. Pam Martin, Dec. 24, 1955; children—Jeffrey, Richard, Nancy. B.A., Stanford U., 1950; M.B.A., Harvard U., 1952. Treas. Club Razor Blade Mfg. Co., Newark, 1955-62; v.p. Warner Communications, Inc., N.Y.C., 1962-75; chmn. Warner Books Inc., and predecessor firms, 1975—. Trustee Horace Mann Sch., Beth Israel Hosp. Served with USAF, 1952-54. Office: Warner Books Inc 1271 Ave of the Americas New York NY 10020*

SAROFF, MARIE S., physician; b. Hydpraboda, India, Apr. 16, 1928; came to U.S., 1958; d. Syed Abdul and K. Hy (Guha) Jabbar; m. Jack Saroff (dec. Nov. 1977); children: David, Rahel Kitty. BBS, Christian Med. Coll., Vellore, South India, 1952; MD, SUNY, Buffalo, 1967. Diplomate Am. Bd. Pediatrics. Rotating intern Christian Med. Coll. Hosp., 1952-53; intern straight pediatrics Ottawa (Can.) Gen. Hosp., 1954-55; resident in pediatrics Children's Mercy Hosp., Kansas City, Mo., 1955-57; asst. dir. Salt Lake County Hosp., Salt Lake City, 1958-59; pediatric coord. child devel. program Children's Hosp. of Buffalo, 1959-64, mem. courtesy staff, 1966—; staff pediatrician Children's Neuromuscular Diagnostic Clinic, Cin., 1967; instr. dept. pediatrics Coll. Medicine U. Cin., 1967-72; mem. attending staff Erie County Med. Ctr., 1972-90; attending physician West Seneca Devel. Ctr., 1985—; physician well baby clinic Erie County Health Dept., Buffalo, 1990—; asst. dir. cerebral dysfunction program U. Affiliated Clin. Program for Mentally Retarded, U. Cin., 1967-72; mem. courtesy staff Children's Hosp., Cin., 1967, asst. attending staff mem., 1969-72; attending pediatrician Erice County Med. Ctr., 1972-85; pediatric cons. infant stimulation program, 1975—, N.Y. State Disability Bd.; mem. med. records com. Erice County Med. Ctr., 1980—. Mem. Buffalo Pediatric Soc., Am. Acad. Pediatrics, Women Physician's League, Am. Women Med. Assn., Am. Women's Med. Assn., Am. Pub. Health Assn., Ambulatory Pediatric Assn. Home: 501 Woodland Dr Buffalo NY 14223-1724

SARRAF, ROBERTA JEAN, planning consultant; b. Pitts., Nov. 9, 1945; d. Walter H. and Margaret E. (Ondof) S. BA, U. Pitts., 1967, M in Urban & Regional Planning, 1969. Intern Rep. James G. Fulton, Washington, 1965; planner Pa. Dept. Community Affairs, Pitts., 1970-76; dir. community devel. Twp. of Upper St. Clair, Pitts., 1976-82; cons. planning Pitts., 1982—; instr. Pa. Dept. Community Affairs, 1976—; del. Environ. Planning to People's Republic of China. Creator and performer (musical program), History of Am. Popular Music. Sec., bd. dirs. Chartiers Mental Health Ctr., Bridgeville, Pa., 1986-90; vol. U. Pitts. Ann. Giving Fund, 1973—; dem. committeewomen, Mt. Lebanon, Pa., 1965-68, 82-88; speaker civic and svc. clubs; mem. long range planning com. and choir Bower Hill Community Ch., elder, 1990-92; mem. devel. com. South Hills Family Hospice. Mem. Am. Planning Assn. (pres. Pitts. chpt. 1982-83), Nat. Assn. Housing and Redevel. Ofcls. (v.p. Pitts. chpt. 1980-81), Pa. Planning Assn. (bd. dirs. 1975-76, state conf. chmn. 1981), Women in Community Devel. (chartered), Am. Fedn. Musicians, Grad. Sch. Alumni Assn. (chmn. com. 1987-88), Am. Inst. Cert. Planners, Three Rivers Corvette Club (activities com. 1987), Lions Club (pres. 1990-91, zone chmn. 1991-92, region chmn. 1992-93). Democrat. Presbyterian. Home and Office: 1316 Bower Hill Rd Pittsburgh PA 15243-1308

SARRIS, ANDREW GEORGE, film critic; b. Bklyn., Oct. 31, 1928; s. George Andrew and Themis (Katavolos) S.; m. Molly Clark Haskell, May 31, 1969. A.B., Columbia, 1951. Film critic Village Voice, N.Y.C., 1960-89, N.Y. Observer, 1989—; editor-in-chief Cahiers du Cinema in English; instr. Sch. Visual Arts, 1965-67; asst. prof. N.Y. U., 1967-69; assoc. prof. films Columbia Sch. Arts, N.Y.C., 1969-81, prof., 1981—. Author: The Films of Josef Von Sternberg, 1966, Interviews with Film Directors, 1967, The Film, 1968 The American Cinema, 1968, Confessions of a Cultist, 1970, The Primal Screen, 1973, The John Ford Movie Mystery, 1976, Politics and Cinema, 1978. Served with Signal Corps AUS, 1952-54. Guggenheim fellow, 1969. Mem. Am. Film Inst. (dir.), Soc. Cinema Studies, Nat. Soc. Film Critics, N.Y. Film Critics. *

SARSFIELD, LUKE ALOYSIUS, school system administrator; b. Luzerne, Pa., July 29, 1925; s. Luke Aloysius and Margaret Ann (Conahan) S.; m. Nancy Ann Chiavacci, Aug. 19, 1961; 1 child, Luke Aloysius III. BA, King's Coll., Wilkes-Barre, Pa., 1952; MA, Montclair (N.J) State Coll., 1962; PhD, NYU, 1973. Diplomate Ednl. Adminstrn. Tchr. Ogdensburg (N.J) Pub. Schs., 1953-55, Luzerne Pub. Schs., 1955-60; tchr. Rutherford (N.J.) Pub. Schs., 1960-70, adminstrv. asst. to supt., 1970-72, supt. schs., 1972—. Trustee Rutherford Pub. Library, 1972—, Williams Inst. Inc., Rutherford, 1986—, Bergen County Tenn Arts, 1989—; pres. Jack Frost Jr. Racing Found., White Haven Pa., 1987—. Served with USN, 1943-46. Mem. Am. Assn. Sch. Adminstrs., N.J. Assn. Sch. Adminstrs., Bergen County Supts. Assn. (past pres.), Bergen County Assn. Sch. Adminstrs., Bergen County Audio-Visual Com., King's Coll. Alumni Assn. (past pres.), Rotary (past pres.), Phi Delta Kappa. Roman Catholic. Office: Rutherford Pub Schs 176 Park Ave Rutherford NJ 07070-2399

SARTORI, HELFRED EDWIN, environmental scientist; b. Graz, Styria, Austria, June 1, 1939; came to U.S., 1976; s. Erich E. and Maria A. (VonBodman) S. BS, Bea-Liebenau, Graz, 1957; MS, U. Med. Fac., Graz, 1961, MD, 1963, MPH, 1969. Demonstrator and scientist asst. Med. and Physiol. Chem. Inst., Graz, 1959-61; intern LKH Wagna, Leibnitz, Austria, 1963-64; resident First Med. U. Clinic, Graz, 1964-70; rsch. fellow C.H. Boehringer & Sohn, Ingelheim, Fed. Republic Germany, 1971-76; dir. rsch. and devel. Ams Laurel, Md., 1978—; dir. research and devel. Izone Int. Ltd., Vancouver, B.C., 1986—; pres. Life Sci. Universal, Washington, 1982—; dir. rsch. and devel. New Life Clinics, 1991—; dir. Am. Indsl. Svcs. Inc., Las Vegas, 1992—. Author: Cancer, 1985, Rheumatoid Disease, 1985, Multiple Sclerosis, 1985, AIDS, 1990; inventor Izone Enhanced Ozone Process. Lt. USNR, 1977-78. Recipient Physicians Recognition award AMA, 1982. Mem. Rotary Internat. (Paul Harris fellow 1982). Office: Am Indsl Svcs Inc PO Box 630 Logandale NV 89102

SARTORIO, ANTHONY THOMAS, process engineer; b. Queens, N.Y., Dec. 9, 1962; s. Sam Joseph and Jeanne Margaret (Rando) S.; m. Joan Theresa O'Leary, May 31, 1986. BE summa cum laude, Manhattan Coll., 1984; MBA with honors, NYU, 1990. Registered profl. engr., N.Y. Mgmt. intern Cons. Edison Co. of N.Y., N.Y.C., 1984-85, sr. mgmt. intern, 1985-87, assoc. engr., 1987-89; process engr. Pepsi-Cola Co., Valhalla, N.Y., 1989-91; sr. process engr. Pepsi-Cola Co., Valhalla, 1991—. Mem. Young Men's Hebrew Assn. North Jersey, 1987—. Mem. Am. Inst. Chem. Engrs., Am. Water Works Assn., Am. Filtration Soc., Soc. Soft Drink Technologists, Tau Beta Pi (pres. N.Y. Xi chpt. 1983-84).

SARTWELL, PHILIP EARL, retired epidemiology educator; b. Salem, Mass., Sept. 11, 1908; s. James Oliver and Blanche (Burpee) S.; m. Harriett E. Coffin (dec.); children: Peter Coffin, Nancy Blanche Sartwell Walker. MD, Boston U., 1932; MPH, Harvard U., 1938. Asst. dir. div. tuberculosis Mass. Dept. Pub. Health, Boston, 1938-42; from asst. prof. to prof. Sch. Pub. Health, Johns Hopkins U., Balt., 1947-73, prof. emeritus, 1973—, vis. lectr.; mem. various coms. U.S. Pub. Health Dept., FDA, Washington, 1948-73; vis. lectr. Sch. Pub. Health. Editor: Public Health and Preventive Medicine, 9th and 10th edits.; contbr. articles to profl. publs. Maj. U.S. Army, 1943-47. Mem. AMA, APHA, Am. Epidemiol. Soc., Mass. Med. Soc. Home: 38 Cloutmans Ln Marblehead MA 01945-1545

SARU, GEORGE, artist; b. Checea, Timis, Romania, Mar. 1, 1920; s. George and Zorca (Pavlov) S.; m. Semizaliana Brinzan, Aug. 31, 1945; children: Dorian, Horia. BFA, Acad. Fine Arts, Jassy, Romania, 1944; MFA, Acad. Fine Arts, Bucharest, Romania, 1948; Diplomate, Acad. Di Belle Arti, Perugia, Italy, 1963. editor-in-chief Arta Mag., Bucharest, 1950-64; dep. chancellor Inst. Fine Arts, Bucharest, 1966-67, prof., 1948-82. Exhibited in group shows at Biennale di Venezia, 1954, 56, Mus. of Modern Art, Szecin, Poland, 1965, 75, Vienna, Austria, 1956, Moscow, 1958, Geneva, 1961, Berlin, 1963, Paris, 1968, Leningrad, 1972, Orly, France, 1972, San Sebastian, Spain, 1973, Washington, 1973, Cairo, Egypt, 1974, Quebec, 1975, Prague, Czechoslovakia, 1979; one-man shows include Dalles Art Gallery, Bucharest, 1956, 70, 77, 81, Pushkin Mus., Moscow, 1960, LeMire Gallery, New Orleans, 1983, Alex Gallery, Washington, 1987, Morin Miller Gallery, N.Y.C., 1988, 89, 90, Dome Gallery, N.Y.C., 1991. Recipient Nat. award for Painting, Bucharest, 1950, Laureat of the State prize Bucharest, 1951, Internat. award for Painting, 1953, Gold medal Laureat or Triennial, Sofia, Bulgaria, 1976. Mem. UNESCO, Fine Arts Guild of Romania, Internat. Assn. Fine Arts, Assn. Internat. Arts Plastiques. Home and Office: 43-39 39th Pl #36 Long Island City NY 11104

SARVER, EUGENE, finance educator; b. N.Y.C., July 15, 1943; s. Edmund and Stella (Bodek) S.; m. Maria Teresa Diaz, Apr. 29, 1984 (div. 1989); Vivian J. Ortega, Jan. 1, 1992. BA, Haverford Coll., 1965; MA, Johns Hopkins U., 1967; postgrad., U. N.C., 1967-69; ArtsD, Idaho State U., 1973. Lectr. in polit. sci. U. N.C., Greensboro, 1969-72; chief economist, corp. fin. advisor Credit Lyonnais-U.S. Group (#2 French Bank), N.Y.C., 1974-79; v.p., mgmt. cons. Chemical Bank, N.Y.C., 1979-84; dir. banking programs N.Y. Inst. Fin., N.Y.C., 1984—; asst. chmn., assoc. prof. fin. Lubin Grad. Sch. Bus., Pace U., N.Y.C., 1985—; cons. INFORMASI Indonesian Bus. Data Ctr., Jakarta, Malaysian Indsl. Devel. Authority, World Trade Inst. of the Port Authority of N.Y. and N.J.; cross-cultural cons. Moran, Stahl and Boyer Internat. (subs. Prudential Ins. Co.). Author: The Eurocurrency Market Handbook, 1988, 2d edit., 1990; contbr. articles to Third World ann. edit., Currency Forecasters Digest, Jour. of Commerce, The World and I, Money and Investments; TV commentator on Financial Fitness. Pres., Haverford (Pa.) Young Democrats, 1964-65; candidate City Coun., Greensboro, 1971; elected bd. dirs. Am. Heritage (Mutual) Fund; elected gov. The Money Marketeers, 1990—. Mem. N.Y. Assn. Bus. Economists (chmn. conf. com. 1989), Money Marketeers, Met. Econs. Assn., Assn. Downtown Economists, AAUP (pres. Pace chpt. 1990—), Am. Arbitration Assn. (panel of comml. arbitrators 1980—), Am. Fin. Assn., Fin. Mgmt. Assn., Bradford Country Club. Democrat. Jewish. Home: 241 W 97th St Apt 8M New York NY 10025-6209 Office: Pace U Lubin Grad Sch Bus 1 Pace Plz New York NY 10038-1598

SASAYAMA, TAKAO, electronics company executive; b. Tokyo, June 29, 1937; s. Shigetaro and Kimiko (Tsudada) S.; m. Fumiko Waga; children: Tomoo, Mizuko. BS, Keio U., Tokyo, 1963; PhD, Keio U., 1983. Rsch. scientist Hitachi, Ltd., Hitachi, Japan, 1963-75; sr. researcher Hitachi Ltd., 1976-85; gen. mgr. Hitachi Am., Ltd., Tarrytown, N.Y., 1986—; v.p. Hitachi Am., Ltd., 1987—. Inventor automotive electronics and semiconductor devices; author sci. papers. Fellow Am. Soc Automotive Engrs., Japan Soc. Automotive Engrs. (Nakagawa prize 1983); mem. IEEE (sr.), Am. Phys. Soc., European Phys. Soc. Home: 50 Prospect Ave Tarrytown NY 10591-4625 Office: Hitachi Am Ltd 50 Prospect Ave Tarrytown NY 10591-4698

SASLAW, LEONARD DAVID, chemist; b. Bklyn., Aug. 27, 1927; s. Issay and Sara (Singer) S. BS, CCNY, 1949; MS, George Washington U., 1954; PhD in Chemistry, Georgetown U., 1963. Chemist Nat. Cancer Inst., NIH, Bethesda, Md., 1951-57, div. biophysics Sloan-Kettering Inst., N.Y.C., 1957-58, biochem. br. Armed Forces Inst. Pathology, Washington, 1958-65; dir. div. biochem. pharmacology, cancer chemotherapy dept. Microbiol. Assocs., Bethesda, 1965-68; sr. biochemist Nat. Drug Co., Phila., 1968-69; chief lab. cellular biochemistry Albert Einstein Med. Center, Phila., 1969-70; clin. lab. dir. Med. Diagnostic Ctrs., Inc., Norristown, Pa., 1970-71; lab. dir. and rsch. assoc., renal lab., dept. medicine N.Y. Med. Coll., 1971-73; mgr. biochem. investigation Bio/Dynamics, Inc., East Millstone, N.J., 1973-74; profl. assoc. Smithsonian Sci. Info. Exchange, Washington, 1975-77; physiologist FDA, Washington, 1978-82, Rockville, Md., 1983—, toxicologist, 1991—; lectr. residents' program in ophthalmology Washington Hosp. Ctr., 1967; cons. Burton, Parsons Co., Inc., Washington, 1978. Pres., Washington chpt. B'nai B'rith Young Men, 1954. With USN, 1945-46. Recipient Meritorious Achievement award Armed Forces Inst. Pathology, 1964. Mem. Am. Assn. Cancer Rsch., Am. Inst. of Biol. Scis., Am. Coll. Toxicology, Soc. of Toxicology (Mid-Atlantic chpt.), Am. Soc. Pharmacology and Exptl. Therapeutics, Sigma Xi. Democrat. Jewish. Contbr. articles to profl. jours. Achievements include establishment of colorimetric assay for deoxy sugar and related compounds; research in mechanism of action of cancer chemotherapeutic agents. Office: FDA Ctr for Veterinary Medicine 7500 Standish Pl Rm 355 Rockville MD 20855-2773

SASS, DANIEL BENJAMIN, geology educator; b. Rochester, N.Y., Mar. 28, 1919; s. Julius and Lillian (Gottlieb) S.; m. Mary Jane Moler, Aug. 29, 1959; children: Daniel Arthur Julius, Elizabeth Ellen. BA, U. Rochester, 1949, MS, 1951; PhD, U. Cin., 1959. Geologist Capitol Engring. Co., Dillsburg, Pa., 1951-52; asst. prof. Alfred (N.Y.) U., 1952-56, prof. environ. studies and geology, 1959-82, ret. prof. emeritus, 1982—; mus. curator U. Cin., 1956-59. Contbr. articles to profl. jours. With AUS, 1942-45, CBI. Fellow Danforth Found., 1980. Fellow Geol. Soc. Am.; mem. Lions Club, Phi Beta Kappa, Sigma Xi, Phi Kappa Phi. Home: 27 High St Alfred NY 14802-1302

SASS, DAVID WERNER, lawyer; b. Deusseldorf, West Germany, Dec. 24, 1935; s. Henry and Kate (Ries) S.; m. Evelyn, June 8, 1958; children: Jeffrey, Diane. BA, Ithaca Coll., 1957; JD, Temple U., 1960; LLM in Taxation, NYU, 1965. Bar: N.Y. 1960, U.S. Supreme Ct. 1972. Assoc. Singer, Levine & Petta, N.Y.C., 1960-65, Golenbock & Barell, N.Y.C., 1965-69; ptnr. McLaughlin, Stern, Ballen & Ballen, N.Y.C., 1969—; bd. dirs. Wildey, Inc.; sec., dir. JEC Lasers, Inc., Robotic Lasers, Inc., Stone Med. Supply Corp. Trustee Ithaca Coll., 1981—. Mem. ABA, N.Y. State Bar Assn. Home: 98-01 67th Ave Forest Hills NY 11374

SASSO, RUTH MARYANN, educator; b. Bridgeport, Conn., Dec. 9, 1928; d. Angelo Nicholas and Mildred Rita (Hayes) Sasso. BS in Edn., St. Joseph Coll., 1957, MA, 1968. Tchr. Catholic Schs. of Conn., 1950-68; founder, dir. Berkeley Primary Sch., Waterbury, Conn., 1969-71; from assoc. prof. to prof. early childhood edn., coordinator child care program Mattatuck Community Coll., Waterbury, 1971—, dir. early childhood edn., coordinator child care program, 1971—, dir. early childhood child devel. ctr., 1976—; mem. adv. council on early childhood edn. Conn. Dept. Edn.; cons. in field; adv. council Waterbury YMCA Day Care Ctr., 1980—; mem. adv. com. to Magnet Sch., Waterbury, Infant/Toddler Day Care, Wilson Sch., Waterbury; mem. adv. com. home cons. high sch. curriculum Conn. State Dept. Edn. Author: Field Placement Manual for Student Teachers, 1971, rev., 1980; Observation Manual in Early Childhood Edn., 1979. Bd. dirs. Child Care Ctr. Abused Children, Waterbury, 1971—; pres. St. Francis Sch. Bd., Naugatuck, 1989; chairperson Prek com. Office of Cath. Schs., Archdiocese of Hartford, Conn., 1990-91. Recipient Service award Head Start Policy Com., Danbury, Conn., 1973. Mem. Nat. Assn. Edn. Young Children (validator), Soc. Nutrition Edn., Action Children's TV, Nat. Council Campus Child Care Centers, Day Care and Child Devel. Council Am. Democrat. Roman Catholic. Home and Office: 96 Meadow Lark Rd Naugatuck CT 06770-4848

SASSOON, ANDRE GABRIEL, lawyer; b. Cairo, Apr. 13, 1936; came to U.S., 1959; s. Gabriel and Sarine (Tawil) S.; m. Barbara Dee Freedman, Aug. 15, 1965; children: DAniel, Gabriel, Sarina. GCE, Oxford & Cambridge, England, 1953; JD, Villanova U., 1969; LLM, Harvard U., 1970. Bar: Pa. 1969, N.Y. 1970. Product mgr. Rohm & Haas Co., Phila., 1960-66; law clk. Dist. Atty.'s Office, Phila., 1968; assoc. Weil, Gotshal & Manges, N.Y.C., 1970-73; pvt. practice N.Y.C., 1973—; dir. elem. Youth in Distress, N.Y.C., 1982—; v.p. dir. internat. Anti-Drug Abuse Found., N.Y.C., 1987—; sec.,

dir., mem. exec. com. Hebrew Immigrant Aid SOc., 1977—; internat. sec., gov. bd. internat. govs. World Sephardo Fedn., N.Y.C., 1988—; co-pres., chmn., U.S. com., dir. internat. Jewish Com. for Sephard '92, N.Y.C., 1989—; mem. N.Y. State Christopher Columbus Quincetenary Commn., Statewide Outreach Com, 1991—. Editor Villanova Law Rev.; contbr. articles to profl. jours. With USAR, 1960-66. Recipient Israel Trade award Govt. of Israel, 1985. Mem. ABA, Am. Arbitration Assn. (panel mem. 1971—), Am. Soc. Internat. Law, Order of the Coif, 0840 Internat. Pvt., 0860 Internat. Pub. Home: 888 Park Ave New York NY 10021-0235 Office: 600 Madison Ave New York NY 10022-1615

SATELL, EDWARD MICHAEL, publishing company executive; b. Springfield, Mass., Mar. 29, 1936; s. Murray and Sally (Gerstein) S.; m. Penny Strauss, June 29, 1958 (div. 1975); children: Steve, Scott, Glen, Greg, Todd; m. Margaret Cox, July 7, 1985; children: Matthew, Clifford. BS, U. Conn., 1957. Pres. First Nat. Acceptance, Bryn Mawr, 1965-88, Progressive Bus. Publs., Bryn Mawr, 1988—, Am. Foresight, Bryn Mawr, 1960—; bd. dirs. Am. Future Systems, Bryn Mawr; mem. adv. bd. Regal Ware Direct Sales Pr., Kewaskum, Wis., 1974-80. Bd. dirs. Better Bus. Bur., Phila., 1991—; mem. Phila. Pres. Orgn., 1986—, bd. dirs., 1990—, chmn., 1992—, Forum Groups Phila. Pres., 1986—. Recipient Outstanding Svc. award Save the Children Found., West Port, Conn., 1981. Mem. Direct Sales Assn. (bd. dirs. 1966-69), Sales and Mktg. Execs., Newsletter Pubs. Assn. (chmn. exec. com. Phila. chpt. 1991—). Office: Progressive Bus Publs 715 Lancaster Ave Bryn Mawr PA 19010

SATIN, ELAINE, educator; b. Wilmington, Del.; m. Steven P. Satin, Mar. 20, 1976; 1 child, Jenny. BA, Fairleigh Dickinson U., Teaneck, N.J., 1969; MS, Columbia U., 1975. Dental hygienist various locations, 1969—; rsch. cons. Hilltop Rsch., East Brunswick, N.J., 1981-85; assoc. prof. Bergen Community Coll., Paramus, N.J., 1973—. Mem Am. Assn. dental Hygiene, N.J. Edn. Assn., Columbia Alumni Assn. Home: 190 Edgemont Pl Teaneck NJ 07666-4619 Office: Bergen Community Coll 400 Paramus Rd Paramus NJ 07652-1508

SATINOVER, JEFFREY BURKE, psychiatrist, health science facility administrator; b. Chgo., Sept. 4, 1947; s. Joseph and Sena (Rotman) S.; m. Julie Rachel Leff, June 10, 1982; Sarah Katherine, Anne-Rebecca, Jenny Leigh. BS, MIT, 1971; EdM, Harvard U., 1973; MD, U. Tex., 1982; Diplomate, C.G Jung Institute, Zurich, Switzerland, 1976. Diplomate Am. Bd. Psychiatry and Neurology, C.G. Jung Inst. Fellow dept. psychiatry and child psychiatry Yale U., New Haven, 1982-86; founder, exec. dir. Sterling Inst., Stamford, Conn., 1985—; pres., bd. dirs. C.G. Jung Found. of N.Y., 1988—; med. dir., bd. dirs. Temenos Inst., Westport, Conn., 1985—; bd. dirs., mem. catchment area coun. S.W. regional Mental Health Bd., 1988-92; William James lectr. psychology and religion Harvard U., 1975; flight surgeon Conn. Army N.G., Hartford, 1987-90, USAR, 1990—; mem. Lower Fairfield County Regional Action Coun. Against Substance Abuse. Author: (book chpts.) Jungian Psychotherapy, 1984, Science and the Fragile Self, 1987, The Childhood Self, 1990; contbr. articles to profl. jours. Recipient Seymour Lustman Rsch. award Yale U., 1983, 85, Order of St. John of Jerusalem. Mem. AMA, Am. Psychiat. Assn. (Burroughs-Wellcome fellow 1983-85), Am. Psychosomatic Soc., Am. Acad. Psychomatics, Internat. Assn. Analytical Psychology (diplomate), N.Y. Assn. Analytical Psychology, Am. Coll. Physician Execs., Landmark Club, Alpha Omega Alpha. Republican. Home: 38 Steep Hill Rd Weston CT 06883-1800 Office: Sterling Inst 1250 Summer St Stamford CT 06905-5318

SATO, KAZUYOSHI, pathologist; b. Shibata, Niigata, Japan, Apr. 3, 1930; came to U.S., 1968; s. Katsueita and Kyo (Sakagawa) S.; m. Ann Marie Farrenkopf, July 5, 1964 (dec. Aug. 1983); children: P.T. Sachiko, P. Miyoko, Michael T., Phillip K. Student, Niigata U., Japan, 1954, MD, 1958. Diplomate Am. Bd. Pathology, Anatomic and Clin. Pathology. Intern USAF Hosp., Tachikawa, Japan, 1958-59; intern Ellis Hosp., Schenectady, N.Y., 1959-60, asst. resident in pathology, 1960-61; resident in pathology Free Hosp. for Women, Brookline, Mass., 1961-62; resident in pathology The Children's Hosp. Med. Ctr., Boston, 1962-63, resident in neuropathology, 1963-64; resident fellow in pathology Mayo Grad. Sch. Medicine, Rochester, Minn., 1968-70; dir. labs. Falmouth (Mass.) Hosp., 1972—; dir. Falmouth Hosp. Service Lab., Sandwich, Mass., 1986—; pathologist and rsch. assoc. Atomic Bomb Casualty Commn., Nagasaki, Japan, 1964-68; pathologist, chief of pathology USPHS Hosp., Norfolk Va., 1970-72, Falmouth (Mass.) Hosp., 1972—. Recipient Fulbright scholarship, 1959. Fellow Coll. Am. Pathologists, Am. Soc. Clin. Pathologists; mem. Assn. Mil. Surgeons U.S. Home: 88 Two Ponds Rd Falmouth MA 02540-2225 Office: Falmouth Hosp 100 Ter Heun Dr Falmouth MA 02540-2599

SATTERFIELD, TERRY LEE, psychology educator; b. Koscielsko, Miss., Aug. 28, 1948; s. Cicero and Freda Lee (Terry) S.; m. Brenda Travers, Sept. 15, 1972 (div.); 1 child, Terry Jr.; m. Nellie Erma Kerr, Sept. 3, 1981; 1 child, Dallas Allen. BS, Bowie State U., 1974; MA, U. No. Colo., 1982; EdD, George Washington U., 1990. Nat. cert. counselor. Instr. D.C. Pub. Schs., Washington, 1974—; counselor AACD, Nat. Bd. Cert. Counselors, Washington, 1983—. Author: Post-traumatic Stress Disorder in African-American Vietnam Veterans, 1990. Chmn. Order of Knights Pythagarus, Washington, 1987-91; sponsor Little League Athletics, Washington, 1987. Staff sgt. U.S. Army, 1978—. Named Emerging Leader, D.C. Assn. for Counseling & Devel., 1991. Mem. ASCD, D.C. Mental Health Counselors Assn. (pres.), D.C. Assn. for Counseling and Devel., Phi Delta Kappa, Omega Psi Phi. Baptist. Home: 1114 Oates St NE Washington DC 20002-3824 Office: Bowie State U Bowie MD 20715

SATTERFIELD-HARRIS, RITA, workers compensation representative; b. Bklyn., Oct. 14, 1949; d. Wilton Anthony and Hattie Eva (Tunstall) Satterfield; m. Sidney Harris, Jan. 5, 1973; 1 child, marcial A.H. BA in Psychology, Bernard Baruch Coll., N.Y.C., 1983; student, CCNY, 1971-74; Cert. in Paralegal Studies, L.I. U., Bklyn., 1982; cert. unemployment ins. benefits law, Cornell U., 1984. Lic. claimant's workers compensation rep. N.Y.; registered agt. N.Y. State Unemployment Ins. Dir. social svcs. Lincoln Sq. Neighborhood Ctr., N.Y.C., 1979-88; pvt. practice N.Y.C., 1988—; speaker The Workers' Def. League, N.Y.C., 1989—; writer proposals N.Y. Community Devel. Agy., 1980-82, N.Y.C. Dept. for Aging, 1984-88. Recipient Cert. of Appreciation for participation in vol. income tax assistance program Dept. Treasury, IRS, 1985, 86, Ptnrs. in Change award Nat. Displaced Homemakers Network, 1991. Mem. Workers' Def. League, Nat. Orgn. Social Security Claimant's Reps. Office: Workers Def League 218 W 40th St New York NY 10018-1509

SATTERTHWAITE, GEORGE, II, security director; b. San Jose, Costa Rica, Apr. 18, 1935; s. Livingston Lord andAdelaide (Bristol) S.; m. Helen Marie McCann, June 28, 1958 (div. July 1982); children: Patricia Ann, Livingston Lord, Frank Lord; m. Deanna Marie Kelliher, Apr. 30, 1983; 1 child, Kelley Elizabeth. BA in Internat. Rels., U. Pa., 1957; MA in History, Johns Hopkins U., 1965. Commd. 2d lt. U.S. Army, 1957, advanced through grades to col., 1979, retired, 1987; chief indsl. security Planning Rsch. Corp., McLean, Va., 1987-89; corp. dir. security PRC Inc., McLean, Va., 1989—. Mem. Am. Soc. Indsl. Security. Republican. Roman Catholic. Home: 513 Holly Rd Fort Washington MD 20744

SATTI, VENKATA SUBBIREDDY, psychiatrist; b. Veereswarapupam, India, Apr. 4, 1939; came to U.S., 1974; s. Surreddy and Manikyam (Gudimetla) S.; m. Savithri Ambur; children: Srinivasa Dinakar Reddy, Krishna Priya, Sudhakar Reddy. Student, Andhra Vet. Coll., India, 1958-60; MB, BS, Andhra Med. Coll., 1965. Pvt. practice India, 1965-74; resident in psychiatry Utica (N.Y.) Psychiat. Ctr., 1975-76, Mt. Sinai Hosp., N.Y.C., 1976-78; staff psychiatrist Willard (N.Y.) Psychiat. Ctr., 1978—, unit chief, 1986—, chief psychiatrist psychogeriatric svcs., 1989—; pvt. practice, Ithaca, N.Y., 1989-90; consulting psychiatrist, Auburn (N.Y.) Correctional Facility, 1981-90, Seneca County Mental Health Clinic, Waterloo, N.Y., 1986—. Mem. AMA, Am. Psychiat. Assn. Democrat. Hindu. Home: 17 Rosina Dr Ithaca NY 14850-9766 Office: Willard Psychiat Ctr Willard NY 14588

SATTLER, JOSEPH PETER, research physicist; b. N.Y.C., Oct. 19, 1940; s. Albert Joseph and Claire Josephine (Neal) S.; m. Jane Katherine Schoonover, July 1, 1968; children: Emily Neal, Timothy Joseph, Anna Margaret. BS in Physics, Iona Coll., 1962; MS in Physics, Georgetown U., 1966, PhD in Physics, 1969. Univ. fellow Georgetown U., Washington, 1962-64, rsch. asst., 1964-66; physicist Army Harry Diamond Labs., Adelphi, Md., 1966-88, chief scientist, 1988—; dep. for sci. and tech. Office Asst. Sect. Army, Washington, 1985-87. Contbr. numerous articles to profl. jours.; patentee test for R-E ion reaction, heterodyne indicial refractometer. Recipient R & D award Dept. Army, 1975, Wilbur S. Hinman award Army Harry Diamond Labs., 1978. Mem. IEEE, Am. Phys. Soc., Sigma Xi. Roman Catholic. Home: 1320 Woodside Pky Silver Spring MD 20910-1551 Office: Army Harry Diamond Labs 2800 Powder Mill Rd Hyattsville MD 20783-1197

SAUER, DAVID ANDREW, librarian; b. Urbana, Ill., Feb. 25, 1948; s. Elmer Louis and Frances (Hill) S. B.A., Northwestern U., 1970; M.S., Simmons Coll., 1975. Reference libr. Boston U., 1976-78, bibliographer, 1978-84, sci. bibliographer, 1984-88, head Stone Sci. Libr., 1988—. Mem. S.W. Corridor Project, Boston, 1977-87, Forest Hills Neighborhood Improvement Assn., Boston, 1977-90, Forest Hills/Woodbourne Neighborhood Group, 1991—. Mem. ALA, Spl. Librs. Assn., Assn. Coll. and Rsch. Librs., New Eng. Online Users Group, N.E. Map Orgn. Democrat. Home: 66 Weld Hill St Jamaica Plain MA 02130-4127 Office: Boston U Stone Sci Libr 675 Commonwealth Ave Boston MA 02215-1401

SAUER, GEORGE WILLIAM, mechanical engineer; b. Port Jervis, N.Y., May 31, 1931; s. George Conrad and Gladys (Hawkins) S.; m. Jean Marie Suderly, Aug. 31, 1956. BA, Hamilton Coll., Clinton, N.Y., 1953; MA, U. Ill., 1960. Designer Internat. Design Inc., Poughkeepsie, N.Y., 1960-64; mech. design coord. Automatic Systems Developers, Poughkeepsie, 1964-88; mech. design engr. Johnson & Williams Inc., Pleasant Valley, N.Y., 1988—. Cpl. U.S. Army, 1953-55. Mem. Scenic Hudson, Dutchess Land Conservancy, Nature Conservancy Eastern N.Y., Mohonk Preserve. Home: Maple Ave PO Box 296 Milton NY 12547-0296

SAUER, JEANNE MARIE, elementary school guidance counselor; b. Elmhurst, N.Y., Feb. 10, 1948; D. William M. and Lillian (Kenna) Leslie; m. Valentine Paul Sauer, Jan. 18, 1969; children: Jennifer Lynn, Mark Christopher. BA, Queens Coll., 1970; MS, L.I. U., Greenvale, N.Y., 1982, post-grad., 1987. nat. cert. counselor; nat. cert. sch. counselor. Claims adjudicator Social Security Adminstrn., Forest Hills, N.Y., 1970-71; pvt. tutor Queens County, N.Y., 1971-72; pre-vocat. counselor Hauppauge (N.Y.) Pub. Schs., 1982-85, elem. sch. counselor, 1985—. Active PTA, Hauppauge, 1977—. Mem. Am. Assn. Counseling and Devel., Am. Sch. Counselors Assn., Western Suffolk Counselors Assn., Anxiety Disorders Assn. Am., N.Y. State Elem. Counselors Network, WSCA Elem. Counselors Network, N.Y. State Assn. for Counseling and Devel., Hauppauge Sideliners Boosters Club. Democrat. Roman Catholic. Home: 36 Bluff Cir Hauppauge NY 11788-3437 Office: Bretton Woods Elem Sch Club Ln Hauppauge NY 11788-4453

SAUER, PAUL ALAN, educator; b. Lindenhurst, N.Y., June 11, 1945; s. Milton Adam and Jeanette Frieda (Bohne) S. BS in Meteorology and Oceanography, NYU, 1967; MS in Human Resource Mgmt., U. Utah, Ramstein, Germany, 1975; MA in Religion, Westminster Theol. Sem., Phila., 1983; MA in Philosophy, U. R.I., 1985; PhD in Philosophy, Syracuse U., 1991. Meteorologist Danac Inc., Thule, Greenland, 1979-81; teaching asst. U. R.I., Kingston, 1983-85; instr., teaching asst. Syracuse (N.Y.) U., 1985-89; adj. asst. prof. Hofstra U., Hempstead, N.Y., 1989-90; adj. asst. prof. logic and metaphysics Molloy Coll., Rockville Centre, N.Y., 1990—. Author: History of 3rd Weather Wing, 1977-79. Capt. USAF, 1967-79. Decorated Air Force Commendation medal, First Oak Leaf Cluster, Vietnam Svc. medal. Mem. Am. Philos. Assn. Eastern Orthodox. Home: 532 Washington Ave Lindenhurst NY 11757-5344 Office: Molloy Coll 1000 Hempstead Ave Rockville Centre NY 11570-1199

SAUER, ROBERT THOMAS, biochemistry educator; b. Cornwall, N.Y., July 13, 1948; s. Herbert George and Tommye Gaye (Miller) S.; m. Karen Ann Nestler, July 25, 1981; children: Jessica Ann, Rebecca Jane. BA, Amherst Coll., 1972; PhD, Harvard U., 1979. Asst. prof. MIT, Cambridge, Mass., 1978-82, assoc. prof., 1982-87, prof., 1987—, Whitehead prof., 1991—; cons. Collaborative Rsch., Waltham, Mass., 1981-88, Genentech, Inc., South San Francisco, Calif., 1988—. Editor: Protein-DNA Interactions, 1991; contbr. more than 100 articles to profl. jours. Rsch. grantee NIH, 1979-91. Mem. Protein Soc., Am. Chem. Soc., Am. Soc. Microbiology, Am. Soc. Biochemistry and Molecular Biology. Office: MIT 16-843 Dept Biology 77 Massachusetts Ave Cambridge MA 02139-4307

SAUL, GEORGE BRANDON, II, biology educator; b. Hartford, Conn., Aug. 8, 1928; s. George Brandon and Dorothy (Ayers) S.; m. Sue Grau Williams, Mar. 28, 1953. A.B., U. Pa., 1949, A.M., 1950, Ph.D., 1954. From instr. to assoc. prof. Dartmouth, 1954-67; prof. biology Middlebury (Vt.) Coll., 1967—, chmn. dept., 1968-76, 91—, v.p. acad. affairs, 1976-79; Research asso. Calif. Inst. Tech., 1964-65; NSF postdoctoral fellow U. Zurich, Switzerland, 1959-60; vis. scientist Boyce Thompson Inst. for Plant Research, Yonkers, N.Y., 1972-73. Author papers in field. Fellow AAAS; mem. Pa. Acad. Sci., Genetics Soc. Am., Am. Genetics Assn., Radiation Research Soc., N.Y. Acad. Scis., Sigma Xi. Club: Lion. Home: Munger St RD 3 Box 2575 Middlebury VT 05753 Office: Middlebury Coll Dept Biology Middlebury VT 05753

SAUL, MARK E., mathematics educator, consultant; b. N.Y.C., June 17, 1948; s. Sidney R. and Shura (Camenir) S.; m. Carol Portnoy, June 26, 1968; children—Susanna, Michael, Peter. BA, Columbia U., 1969; MS, Courant Inst. Math. Scis., NYU, 1975; PhD, NYU, 1987. Tchr. math. and computer sci. Bronx High Sch. Sci., N.Y., 1969-85; teaching fellow Adm. Hyman H. Rickover Found., 1985; computer cons./coord. Bronxville Schs., N.Y., 1985—; dir. Research Sci. Inst. Ctr. Excellence in Edn., McLean, Va., 1987, San Diego, 1990, Cambridge, Mass., 1992; mem. N.Y. State Com. on Problem Solving, 1985—; cons. computer graphics 1984 Olympics ABC-TV, N.Y.C., 1983-84; pres. N.Y.C. Interscholastic Math. League, N.Y.C., 1979-89, Am. Regions Math. League, 1989—; dir. ARML-Soviet Student Exch., 1991—; cons. Ednl. Testing Service, Princeton, N.J., 1980-82; panelist/cons. LaGuardia High Sch. Performing Arts, N.Y.C., 1977-86; tchr. trainer N.Y.C. Bd. Edn., 1981; tchr.-coord. computer sci. Hollingworth Ctr. for Gifted, Tchrs. Coll., Columbia U., 1984; instr. Lehman Coll., 1984-92, Johns Hopkins U. Ctr. Talented Youth, 1986, Sophie Davis Biomed. Ctr. CCNY, 1986—, Sarah Lawrence Coll., 1987—; mem. U.S. del. to Internat. Congress Math. Educators, Budapest, 1988. Author: Science/Mathematics Research Programs in the High School, 1982, The New York City Problem Book, 1986, Read the Questions: A Thinking Student's Guide to the SAT's, 1992; co-author: Advanced Placement Computer Science, 1985; author of enrichment problems in Leadership Manual for High School Supervisors in Mathematics, 1982; contbr. Jour. N.Y. State Assn. Computers and Tech. in Edn. Judge Internat. Math. Olympiad, Washington, 1981; author contest questions Mass. Math. League Ann. Contest, 1981; math. field editor Quantum, 1991—; mem. editorial bd. Mathematics and Informatics Jour., 1991—. Recipient Presdl. award for Excellence in Teaching Math., NSF, 1984. Mem. Assn. Tchrs. Math. (exec. bd. mem. 1980-85), Math. Assn. Am. (mem. com. on high sch. contests 1981-92), Nat. Council Tchrs. Math. Avocations: music, art. Home: 711 Amsterdam Ave Apt 27K New York NY 10025 Office: Bronxville UFSD Bronxville NY 10708

SAUNDERS, BEATRICE NAIR (MRS. DERO AMES SAUNDERS), editor, association executive; b. New Britain, Conn., Dec. 26, 1915; d. Frank and Sophie (Adler) Nair. B.A., Smith Coll., 1936; m. Dero Ames Saunders, May 23, 1936; children: David Nair, Richard Ames. Tchr. pub. schs., New Britain, 1936; editorial asst. Cordon Co., N.Y.C., 1937-39, Family Welfare Assn. Am., N.Y.C., 1939-42; supr. editorial div. publs. div. ARC, Washington, 1943-46; free-lance editor various publs. N.Y.C., 1946-50; editor-in-chief, publs. dept. Girl Scouts U.S., N.Y.C., 1950-55; dir. publs. dept., editor Social Work, Nat. Assn. Social Workers, N.Y.C., 1955-82, publs. cons., 1982—; mem. adj. faculty, editor-in-residence Grad. Sch. Social Svcs., Fordham U., Lincoln Ctr., N.Y.C., 1982—; vis. editor Sch. of Social Work, Rutgers U., New Brunswick, N.J., 1985—. Founding editor Affilia, Jour. Women and Social Work, 1986—. Vol. ARC, Freeport, L.I., 1946-47, Child Care Ctr., Freeport, 1946-47; chmn. parents assn. Downtown Community Sch., 1948-50; chmn. 22d-21st St. Community Coun., 1954-58, 62-63; chmn. com. on existing housing Chelsea Community Coun., 1957-60; vice chmn. Chelsea Com. for Neighborhood Devel., 1960-63, chmn., 1963-65; sec. West 400 Block Assn., 1987—. Clubs: Smith Coll., Heights Casino. Home: 446 W 22d St New York NY 10011

SAUNDERS, CATHERINE HOOVER, mental health services professional; b. Pickens, Miss., Oct. 12, 1948; d. Curtis and Henrene (Mitchell) Hoover; m. Lewis Henry Saunders (div. Mar. 1974); children: Jarod Dewayne, Lewis Keno. Cert. computer programmer system analyst, Computer Learning Ctr., Falls Church, Va., 1971; BS, Howard U., 1975, MS, 1977. Lic. sch. psychologist, D.C.; cert. jr. high sch. tchr., D.C. Sch. psychologist D.C. Pub. Schs., Washington, 1977-80; social svc. rep. Dept. Human Svcs., Washington, 1982-85; case mgmt. coord. Mental Retardation Devel. Disabilities Adminstrn., Washington, 1985—; asst. pres. Grad. Sch. Edn., Howard U., Washington, 1975-77; mem. Neighborhood ASvc. Com. Ward 4, Washington, 1986—; radio personality stas. WHUR-FM, WUST, WPFW, WINX, Rockville, Md.; poetry reader; TV appearances Sta. WDVM-TV, Sta. WTTG-TV. Author: Celebration of Life, 1987; author of poems on posters entitled, "My Friend" and "An Ode to Autumn", 1977. Sec. PTA Truesdale Elem. Sch., Washington, 1980-81; nat. assoc. Smithsonian Inst., 1978—; mem. The Am. Film Inst. John F. Kennedy Ctr. for Performing Arts, Washington, 1987; mem. WETA-TV Pub. Broadcasting, Washington, 1986—; mem. Mt. Pleasant Meth. Ch., 1987. Nat. Insts. Mental Health, Rockville, Md., 1975-76; grantee Howard U., 1973-74; recipient Vol.'s award Festival Am. Folklife Smithsonian Inst., 1982-85. Mem. Jerusalem-Mt. Pleasant United Meth. Ch. Baptist. Home: 780 Fairview Ave Apt 1 Silver Spring MD 20912-5978

SAUNDERS, ELIZABETH ANN, aerospace engineer; b. Greensboro, N.C., Oct. 4, 1965; d. Austin O. and Bessie R. (Maness) S. BS in Aerospace Engring., N.C. State U., 1987. Aerospace engr. Flight Test Engring. Group, Patuxent River, Md., 1987—. Mem. AIAA. Office: Flight Test Engring Group Naval Air Warfare Ctr SA86F Patuxent River MD 20670

SAUNDERS, GEORGE WENDELL, management consultant, retired government official; b. Hubbard, Ohio, Oct. 17, 1917; s. Phillip and Mary (Shafer) S.; m. Audrey Edna Bogue (dec. Nov. 1979); children: Wayne George, Wendy Jean; m. Virginia Hutson Baker, June 25, 1987; stepchildren: John Milton Jr., Kathee Eloise. B in Acctg., Rider Coll., 1937; postgrad, Harvard U., 1943; grad., Indsl. Coll. Armed Forces, 1955, Fgn. Service Inst., Naval War Coll.; student, Grad. Sch. Dept. Agr., Dept. Def. Computer Inst. Auditor, acct. U.S. Rubber Co., N.Y.C., 1937-39; acct., office mgr. S. King Fulton, Inc., Washington, 1939-40; with War Dept. and Civil Aero. Adminstrn., Washington, 1940-41; adminstrv. asst., sr. investigator Bur. Fed. Supply Treas. Dept., Washington, 1941-47; ops. planning analyst, orgn. and methods examiner, supply specialist Fed. Supply Services GSA, Washington, 1957-55, dep. dir. stores mgmt. div., 1955-61, dir. supply distbn. div., acting asst. dir. nat. buying div., 1956-61, dir. distbn. programs div., 1961-64, asst. commr. supply distbn., 1964-71, asst. commr. trans. and pub. utilities, 1971-73, dep. commr., 1973-75; v.p. Washington Mgmt. Group, Washington Mktg. Group, 1975-79; pvt. practice cons., 1979—; mem. Fed. Safety Council, Fed. Fire Council and Nat. Def. Trans. Bd., 1970-75. Contbr. to govt. publs. Chmn. bd. dirs., past pres. North Chevy Chase Swimming Pool Assn., 1960; vestryman, treas. Episc. Ch., Silver Spring, Md., 1950. Served with USN World War II, PTO, ATO, comdr. Res. ret., 1975. Recipient Adminstrs. Exceptional Service award GSA, 1975. Mem. Ret. Officers Assn., Am. Legion (exec. bd. Thad Dulin chpt. 1986-87, adj. 1988, vice comdr. 1989-91), Leisure World Golf Club, Kenwood Country Club, Montgomery Village Golf Club, Lions (pres. Rossmoor club Silver Spring 1988-89), Fireside Forum (v.p., bd. dirs.), Leisure World. Republican. Home and Office: 15107 Interlachen Dr Apt 812 Silver Spring MD 20906-5633

SAUNDERS, JAMES C., neuroscientist, educator; b. Elizabeth, N.J., May 8, 1941; s. Charles Oliver and Elizabeth Veronica (Drake) S.; m. Elaine Priscilla Edwards, Oct. 14, 1967; children: Breton Morris, Drew Charles. BA, Ohio Wesleyan U., 1963; MA, Conn. Coll., 1965, U. Pa., 1979; PhD, Princeton U., 1968. Lectr. dept. psychology Monash U., Victoria, Australia, 1969-72; rsch. assoc. Cen. Inst. for Deaf, St. Louis, 1972-73; asst. prof., then prof. dept. otorhinolaryngology U. Pa., Phila., 1973-92, acting dir. Inst. Neurol. Scis., 1980-83, prof., 1984—; guest scientist Karolinska Inst., Stockholm, 1984-85; exec. com. CHABA, Nat. Rsch. Coun., Washington, 1986-89; chmn. disorders rev. com. NIDCD, Bethesda, Md., 1987-89; mem. exec. coun. Assn. Rsch. Otolaryngology, Chgo., 1988-91; mem. com. on hearing and bioacoustics Nat. Inst. on Deafness and Other Communications Disorders. Contbr. chpts., rev. papers to books on biology of hearing; contbr. articles on auditory neurobiology to profl. jours; author abstracts of meeting presentations on hearing. Recipient Basic Sci. Rsch. award Am. Acad. Otolaryngology, 1978, 87, Pa. Acad. Otolaryngology, 1982, Basic Sci. Excellence award (Claude Pepper award) NIDCD, 1988, Lindback award for disting. teaching U. Pa., 1992. Mem. AAAS, Acoustical Soc. Am., Soc. Neurosci., N.Y. Acad. Sci., Sigma Xi (legal cons. effects of noise on hearing). Democrat. Office: U Pa 5 Silverstein ORL 3400 Spruce St Philadelphia PA 19104-4220

SAUNDERS, JOHN RICHARD, dentist; b. Stanislav, Poland, May 19, 1925; m. Annalie Deborah Bean, Sept. 6, 1959; children: Lesley Pauline, Andrea Elizabeth. DMD cum laude, U. Erlangen, Germany, 1949; DMD, Tufts U., Germany, 1952. With rsch. dept. Tufts Dental Sch., Boston, 1952; dentist health svcs. Harvard U., Boston, 1955-56; supervising dentist U. Bridgeport Sch. Dental Hygiene, Boston, 1955-56; practice dentistry Boston, 1955-89; dentist Harvard U., Boston, 1956-64; instr. prosthodontics grad. div. Tufts U. Dental Medicine, Boston, 1964-65, asst. clin. prof. dept. full denture prosthetics, 1980—; sponsor Hardy Prosthetic Conf.; lectr. dental meetings Research in viscosity of dental alloys. Served from 1st lt. to capt. USAF, 1952-55. Fellow Royal Soc. Health, Acad. Gen. Dentistry, Internat. Coll. Dentists, Am. Acad. Dental Sci.; mem. Am. Dental Assn., Mass. Dental Assn., Met. Dental Soc., Northeastern Dental Soc., Greater Boston Dental Soc., Boston In Town Dental Soc. Fed. Dentaire Internationale, Tufts U. Dental Alumni Assn., Acad. Gen. Dentistry, Am. Prosthodontic Soc., New Eng., Greater Boston Dental Socs. Home and Office: 23 Woodridge Rd Wellesley MA 02181-7018

SAUNDERS, JOSEPH ARTHUR, office products manufacturing company executive; b. Creston, Mont., July 9, 1926; s. Albert Henry and Edith Margaret (Rhodes) S.; m. Lois Evelyn White, June 19, 1948 (dec. Oct. 1986); children: Albert Henry II, Margaret Jean; m. Eva Homor, July 18, 1987; stepchildren: Rodney, Charmaine. Ed. pub. schs., Youngstown, Ohio and Winthrop, Maine. With Saunders Mfg. Co. Inc., Winthrop, 1947—, exec. v.p., 1967-77, pres., 1977-88 , chief exec. officer, 1967—, chmn. bd., 1988—; chmn. Saunders Internat. B.V., Netherlands, Saunders Southern Industires, Inc., Meridian, Miss.; co-founder, sec., bd. dirs. Dirigo Bank and Trust Co., Augusta, Maine, 1969-86; co-founder, dir. Cushnoc Bank and Trust Co., Augusta, Maine. With U.S. Army, 1945-47. Patentee in field. Mem. Maine C. of C. and Industry (bd. dirs. 1976-81, chmn. mfg. council 1978-82), Maine Metal Products Assn. (bd. dirs. 1983-84), Soc. Mfg. Engrs. (cert. new product engr.), Internat. Bus. Forms Industries (chmn. assocs. 1976-77, co-chmn. exhibits com. 1978-82), Nat. Bus. Forms Assn., Nat. Office Products Assn. (bd. govs. 1988—), Office Products Mfrs. Assn. (bd. govs. 1988—, v.p. 1990), Maine Metal Products Assn., Printing Industries New Eng. Am. Soc. Metals, Printing Industries Am., Am. Legion, Masons, Shriners, others. Home: PO Box 3068 Meridian MS 39305 Office: Saunders Southern 5122 Arundel Rd Meridian MS 39307

SAUNDERS, REBECCA ANN, educator, poet; b. Charlotte, N.C., Apr. 12, 1949; d. John Marshall Saunders and Barbara (Williams) Polk. BA in English, Music, U. Mass., 1978; MA, Tufts U., 1982, PhD, 1990. Tchr. Bay State Jr. Coll., Boston, 1979-81, U. Mass., Boston, 1976-79, 82; teaching asst. Tufts U., Medford, Mass., 1981-82, tchr.; cons., editorial asst. Bedford Books, Boston, 1985-87; rhetoric assoc. Boston U., 1986; lectr. English, U. Mass., Worcester, 1982—; seminar leader Syntax The Word Co., Milton, Mass., 1984—. Mem. MLA, New Eng. MLA, NOW, Can. Assn. Asian Studies, Am. Assn. Asian Studies, Southeastern Nineteenth Century Studies Soc. Democrat. Home: 71 Jay St Cambridge MA 02139-3124

SAUNDERS, ROBERT SAMUEL, investment company executive; b. Akron, Ohio, Dec. 3, 1951; s. Samuel Robert and Rose Annette (Schulman)

S.; m. Heidi Ruth Fulkerson, Mar. 18, 1978. AB with distinction, Stanford U., 1973; MSc with distinction, London Sch. Econs., 1974; diploma, U. Stockholm, 1976; MA, Harvard U., 1978. Cons. World Bank, Washington, 1975-77; sr. cons. Boston Cons. Group, 1978-82; dir. competitive strategy analysis Bain and Co., Boston, 1982-86; sr. v.p., chief planning officer Krupp Cos., Boston, 1986-88; chmn. Saunders Capital Group, Inc., Boston, 1988—; bd. dirs. Simon Boyle Group, Inc. Boston, Scand-Tech. Inc., Lincoln, Mass., The Walking Mag., Inc., Boston, Richey Impact Electronics, Inc., L.A. Editor Stanford Quar. Rev., 1973. Del. Mass. Dem. Nat. Conv., San Francisco, 1984; co-founder Weston Conservation Trust, Mass., 1988. Marshall scholar, 1973-75; NEH fellow, 1978; Swedish Govt. Fulbright grantee, 1975, U.S. Congress Profl. Devel. grantee, 1976. Mem. Am. Econ. Assn., Internat. Union for Sci. Study of Population. Unitarian.

SAUNDERS, STEVEN LAWRENCE, electronics company official; b. Manchester, N.H., July 4, 1955; s. Arthur Lawrence and Sylvia Florence (Moulton) S. BSBA, SUNY, Buffalo, 1977; MBA, Dartmouth Coll., 1982. Staff auditor Arthur Andersen and Co., Boston, 1977-78; chief acct. Saint John of God Hosp., Boston, 1978-80; from application specialist to phys. distbn. mgr. Hewlett-Packard, Andover, Mass., 1983-89; distbn. mgr. Hewlett-Packard, Andover, 1989—. Chmn. Hewlett-Packard campaign United Way, Andover, 1990—; bd. dirs. New Eng. Roundtable, Clm., 1992—. Mem. Coun. Logistics Mgmt., Appalachian Mountain Club, Tuck Alumni Club of Greater Boston. Home: 108 Main St # 302 Raymond NH 03077-2326

SAUNDERS, WILLIAM HUNDLEY, JR., chemist, educator; b. Pulaski, Va., Jan. 12, 1926; s. William Hundley and Vivian (Watts) S.; m. Nina Velta Plesums, June 25, 1960 (dec. June 1982); children: Anne Michele, Claude William. B.S., Coll. William and Mary, 1948; Ph.D., Northwestern U., 1952. Research assoc. Mass. Inst. Tech., 1951-53; mem. faculty U. Rochester, 1953—, prof. chemistry, 1964-91, faculty sr. assoc., 1991—, chmn. dept., 1966-70. Author: Ionic Aliphatic Reactions, 1965, (with A.F. Cockerill) Mechanisms of Elimination Reactions, 1973, (with L. Melander) Reaction Rates of Isotopic Molecules, 1980; contbr. articles to profl. jours. Guggenheim fellow, 1960-61; Sloan Found. fellow, 1961-64; NSF sr. postdoctoral fellow, 1970-71. Mem. Am. Chem. Soc., Chem. Soc. (London), Phi Beta Kappa, Sigma Xi, Phi Lambda Upsilon. Home: 15 Parkwood Ave Rochester NY 14620-3401

SAURO, JOSEPH PIO, physics educator; b. New Rochelle, N.Y., Apr. 4, 1927; s. Francesco Giovanni and Lucia (Arrivebene) S.; m. Elizabeth Joann Schellman, May 2, 1948; children: Brian, Michael, Joseph. BS, Poly Inst. Bkyn., 1955, MS, 1958, PhD in Physics, 1966. Dir. coll. sci. improvement program U. Mass. at Dartmouth, North Dartmouth, 1969-71, dean grad. sch., 1969-71, interim dean Coll. of Engring., 1978-80, dean Coll. Arts and Scis., 1969-80, prof. physics, 1965—. With USN, 1944-46. Sci. Faculty fellow NSF, 1964; State War Svc. scholar State of N.Y., 1953. Mem. Am Assn. Physics Tchr., Sigma Xi, Sigma Pi Sigma. Home: 8 Captain Wing Rd East Sandwich MA 02537-1122 Office: U Mass North Dartmouth MA 02747

SAUVÉ, JEANNE, former governor general and commander-in-chief of Canada; b. Prud'homme, Sask., Can., Apr. 26, 1922; d. Charles Albert and Anna (Vaillant) Benoît; m. Maurice Sauvé, Sept. 24, 1948; 1 son, Jean-François. Grad., U. Ottawa, D (hon.); diploma in French Civilization, U. Paris, 1952. Nat. pres. Jeunese etudiante catholique, Montreal, 1942-47; asst. to dir. youth sect. UNESCO, Paris, 1951; journalist, broadcaster, 1952-72; bd. dirs. Union des Artistes, Montreal, 1961, v.p., 1968-70; v.p. Canadian Inst. on Pub. Affairs, 1962-64, pres., 1964; mem. Can. Centennial Commn., 1967; gen. sec. Fedn. des Auteurs et des Artistes du Can., 1966-72; mem. Parliament for Ahuntsic, Montreal, 1972-79, Parliament for Laval-des-Rapides, 1980-84; advisor external affairs Sec. of State, 1978-79; min. sci. and tech., then min. environment and communications Govt. of Canada, Ottawa, Ont., 1972-79; speaker Ho. of Commons, Ottawa, 1980-84; gov. gen., comdr.-in-chief of Can., 1984-90. Founder, hon. chmn. Jeanne Sauvé Youth Found., 1990; sworn in mem. Privy Coun. P.C. Companion Order of Can.; decorated comdr. Order of Mil. Merit; recipient La Médaille de la Chancellerie des U. de Paris, Sorbonne U.; 1st woman to hold position of gov. gen. of Can. Fellow Royal Archtl. Inst. Can. (hon.), Royal Soc. Can. (hon.); mem. Inst. for Rsch. on Pub. Policy (founding). Mem. Liberal Party of Can. Roman Catholic.

SAVAGE, EUGENE ARNOLD, academic administrator; b. North Stratford, N.H., Aug. 29, 1934; s. Raymond A. and Harriet (Kennedy) S.; m. Joan Doyon, June 22, 1957; children: Suzanne, Deborah, Kathleen. BE, Plymouth State Coll., 1958; MEd, Boston U., 1963; LHD (hon.), Franklin Pierce Coll., 1990. Tchr., coach Pittsfield (N.H.) High Sch., 1958-60; guidance dir. Somersworth (N.H.) High Sch., 1960-61, Otter Valley Union High Sch., Brandon, Vt., 1961-63, Kingswood Regional High Sch., Wolfeboro, N.H., 1963-67; dir. admissions U. N.H., Durham, 1967-78, dean admissions, 1978-80, v.p. univ. rels., 1980-81; vice chancellor univ. system rels. Univ. System N.H., Lee, 1981—; cons. coll. admissions The Coll. Bd., Washington, 1981—, trustee 1977-81. Incorporator Wentworth-Douglass Hosp., Dover, N.H., 1983—; chmn. regional student program adv. coun. New England Bd. Higher Edn., 1987—; trustee Ea. States Exposition, West Springfield, Mass., 1988—; bd. dirs. Odyssey House, Inc., Hampton, N.H., 1989—. Recipient Profile of Svc. award U. N.H. Alumni Assn., 1977, Thomas More Ch., 1989, Disting. Svc. award New England Assn. Coll. Admissions Counselors, 1979, Plymouth State Coll. Alumni, 1989, N.H. Disting. Citizen award Daniel Webster Council of the Boy Scouts Am., 1992. Mem. Coun. for Advancement and Support Edn. Republican. Roman Catholic. Home: 45 Al Wood Dr Barrington NH 03825-3008 Office: Univ System NH Dunlap Ctr Lee NH 03824

SAVAGE, JAMES CATHEY, III, lawyer, educator; b. Nashville, June 26, 1947; s. James C. Jr. and Mary (Estes) S.; married, Aug. 5, 1975 (div.); children: Sean Patrick, Catriona Sarah; m. Clara Parra, Nov. 25, 1986; children: James C. IV, Anthony Joseph. BS, Austin Peay St. U., 1968; JD, Memphis State U., 1973; MS in Criminal Justice, Troy State U., 1977; LLM, John Marshall Law Sch., 1978, Georgetown U., 1981; LLD (hon.), North Tenn. Bible Inst., 1981. Bar: Tenn. 1973, U.S. Supreme Ct. 1977, D.C. 1981, Md. 1982; cert. tchr.; lic. min. Commd. 1st lt. U.S. Army, 1973, advanced through grades to lt. col, 1988; enlisted ranger and edn. dir. U.S. Army, Vietnam, 1969-70; ins. adjuster Tenn. Co., Molloy & Leary, Bituminious Casualty, 1971-73; judge advocate Ga., 1973-77, Germany, 1973-77; veterans and contracts atty. V.A. Gen. Counsel, Washington, 1978-82; fng. mil. sales atty. USAF Electronic Systems Div., Hanscom AFB, Mass., 1983-86; chief counsel U.S. Army Materials Tech. Lab., Watertown, Mass., 1986—; lt. col. civil air patrol Group I Mass, 1989—; adj. prof. several instns.; chmn. local acad. rev. com., Fed. Acquisition Ins., 1986-89, Higher Edn. Com., Nat. Contract Mgmt. Assn. Weekly show host Assembly (BCAT-TV), Burlington, Mass., 1989—; contbr. articles to profl. jours. Dep. dir. Internat. Rescue Com./Army Res. Project Resettlement for Refugees, Washington, 1980-82; canvasser Am. Heart Assn., Burlington, 1989-92; lay min., chmn. bd. deacons, Burlington Congl. Ch., Christian Chs. and Chs. of Christ, 1992-93; mem. Christian Legal Soc., 1980—, Inst. Religion and Democracy, 1980—, Christian Mil. Fellowship, 1984—. Decorated Bronze Star, Combat Infantryman Badge, Vietnam, 25 meritorious svc. medals and various mil. ribbons; named Mass. Citizen of Yr., Am. Legion, 1985; recipient Exceptional Profl. award, 1985, Boston Fed. Exec. Bd., 1st runner-up Community Svc. award, 1987, 92, Community Svc. Recognition Resolution, Mass. Ho. of Reps., 1992. Mem. Fed. Bar Assn. (nat. chmn. internat. procurement com. 1985-88, vice-chmn. 1979-90, past pres. and nat. del. Boston chpt., exec. com. 1983-90, Disting. Svc. award and others), New Eng. Chpt. Judge Advocates Assn. (pres./v.p. 1983-86), Res. Officers Assn. (state pres.-elect 1992—, state v.p. for Army 1990-92, state judge adv. 1985-86, pres. William Tudor and N.E. Civil Affairs Chpt. 1984-89, Nat. Disting. Svc. awards, dept. v.p. 1990—), DAV (life, Honor Guard Burlington chpt. 113 1985—), VFW (life, state judge adv. and sr. vice comdr.-All Am. Post 1982-83), AMVETS (life, post comdr.and state judge adv. 1982-83), 75th Ranger Regiment Assn. (nat. dir. 1987-90), Vietnam Vets. Am. (life, sec. D.C. chpt. 1980), Phi Delta Kappa (treas. Harvard U. chpt. 1990-92), Phi Alpha Delta. Home: 39 Purity Springs Rd Burlington MA 01803-2423 Office: Chief Counsel US Army Materials Tech Lab 495 Arsenal St Ste 215 Watertown MA 02172-5015

SAVAGE, JOSEPH GEORGE, hospital administrator; b. Bklyn.; s. Joseph George Jr. and Eileen (Schnell) S.; m. Lynn Ann Campbell; children: Kimberly, Patricia, Joseph IV. BA, Oswego Coll., 1977; postgrad., Seton Hall U., 1985. Pub. affairs dir. L.I. chpt. Nat. Multiple Sclerosis Soc., N.Y.C., 1977-79, exec. dir. Conn. chpt., 1979-80; dir. devel., mktg. Clara Mass Meml. Med. Ctr., Belleville, N.J., 1980-81; exec. dir. Found. of St. Joseph's Hosp. Med. Ctr., Paterson, N.J., 1981-89; sr. v.p. St. Francis Hosp. Heart Ctr., Roslyn, N.Y., 1989-92; v.p. St. Vincents Hosp. and Med. Ctr., N.Y.C., 1992—. Commr. health City of Clifton, 1990—; bd. dirs. N.Y. Heart Coun., Cath. Family and Community Svcs. Fellow Nat. Assn. Hosp. Devel. (communication chair 1982-85, edn. chair 1985-86, bd. dirs., regional dir. 1988-89), Ancient Order of Hibernians, Rotary (past pres. Clifton Club, Paul Harris fellow, Walter Head fellow). Roman Catholic. Home: 14 Abbe Ln Clifton NJ 07013-1447 Office: 153 W 11th St New York NY 11576-1346

SAVAGE, MICHAEL HOWARD, educational administrator, guidance counselor, educator; b. Bridgeport, Conn., June 12, 1938; s. Manuel Harvey and Lillian Rhoda (Jiler) S.; m. Mary Elizabeth Erb, May 8, 1988. BA, Dartmouth Coll., 1960; MA, NYU, 1967, PhD, 1981. Cert. sch. adminstr., N.Y., Conn.; nat. cert. counselor; cert. sch. dist. adminstrn., N.Y., Conn.; cert. in guidance, biology, chemistry, and gen. sci., N.Y.; cert. in student personnel svcs., N.J. Sales rep. Commodity Rsch. Bur., N.Y.C., 1960-64; tchr. sci. Jonas Salk Jr. High Sch., Levittown, N.Y., 1964-66, Gt. Neck (N.Y.) South Jr. High Sch., 1966-67; guidance counselor Engle Street Sch., Englewood, N.J., 1967-68, Dwight Morrow High Sch., Englewood, 1968-70, Baruch Jr. High Sch., N.Y.C., 1970-71, Intermediate Sch. 29M, N.Y.C., 1971-73; ednl. adminstr. N.Y. State Edn. Dept., Bklyn., 1973—; mem. Nat. Forum on Excellence, U.S. Dept. Edn., 1983. Mem. Am. Assn. Sch. Adminstrs., N.Y. State Coun. Sch. Supts., NYU Adminstrs. Roundtable, Sch. Edn., Health, Nursing & Arts Professions Alumni Fedn. NYU (v.p., bd. dirs.), Dartmouth Alumni Assn. N.Y.C. (exec. com.), Dartmouth Club N.Y.C. (trustee), Phi Delta Kappa. Home: 15 Hale Ln Darien CT 06820-4432 Office: NY State Edn Dept 55 Hanson Pl Rm 594 Brooklyn NY 11217-1580

SAVAGE, STEPHEN EDMAN, marketing company executive; b. Pontiac, Mich., Dec. 10, 1940; s. Robert Carlton and Wilda Zoe (Johnson) S.; m. Barrie Lane Thomas, Apr. 9, 1942; children: William, Cynthia, Allison, Lance, Matthew. BA, Wheaton Coll., 1962; MBA, Mich. State U., 1963. Exec. sec. Am. Bible Soc., Quito, Ecuador, 1964-66; sales mgr. Southwestern Co., Nashville, 1966-70; pres. Indian Lake Co., San Leandro, Calif., 1971-74; owner White River Designs, Randolph, Vt., 1974-79; v.p. Institutional Financing Svcs., Benicia, Calif., 1979—; pres. White River Farms, Reading, Vt., 1988—; bd. dirs., cons. IFS/Colgate Palmolive, Benicia, 1987—; v.p. IFS/Colgate Palmolive Internat., 1990. Author: A Fortune in Fund Raising, 1977, Rejoicing in Christ, 1990. Vestry, St. John's Ch., Randolph, 1977-80; treas. Vt. Morgan Horse Assn., Manchester, 1988—; group leader Sierra Club; chmn. lay readers St. James Episcopal Ch. Mem. Vt. Inst. Natural Sci. Home: RR 1 Box 101 Reading VT 05062

SAVAGE, STEPHEN WILLIAM, music educator; b. St. Louis, Aug. 18, 1953; s. John Nathan Moody and Marian (Hull) S.; m. Denise Ellen Nigrosh, July 12, 1981. MusB with honors, New Eng. Conservatory Music, 1975, MusM, 1980. Mem. faculty Berklee Coll. Music, Boston, 1975-80, New Eng. Conservatory Extension Div., Boston, 1980—, Groton (Mass.) Ctr. for Arts, 1982-85; mem. faculty, asst. dir. Indian Hill Arts Sch. Music, Littleton, Mass., 1985—. Composer, solo, chamber and orchestral works; compositions commd. by Mystic Valley Chamber Orch., Boston, 1978, Symphony Pro Musica, Hudson, Mass., 1986. Winner New Works composer competition, Mass. Coun. on Arts and Humanities, 1982. Mem. Am. Piano Tchrs.' Guild.

SAVANAUSKAS, LINDA SUE, management consultant; b. Norwood, Mass., Dec. 29, 1959; d. Steven Savanauskas and Marylou (Packard) Defeo. AS in Early Childhood Edn., Lasell Coll., 1980; BS in Edn. and Spl. Edn., Lesley Coll., 1982. Registered rep. Equitable Fin. Co., Wellesley, Mass., 1987; v.p. mktg. and new bus. devel. Knight Internat. Ins. Agy., Boston, 1988; prin. Savvan Assocs., Belmont, Mass., 1989—. Mem. NAFE, Nat. Assn. Life Underwriters, Life Underwriters Tng. Coun. Fellowship. Home: 43 Sherman St A-2 Cambridge MA 02138

SAVARINO, SAMUEL JOSEPH, construction company executive; b. Buffalo, May 2, 1958; s. Salvatore J. and Carol M. (Brown) S.; m. Paula Marie Schank, Jan. 13, 1983; children: Jenny, Julia. BA, U. Buffalo, 1982. Product mgr. ADF Constrn. Corp., Buffalo, 1979-82; gen. mgr. ADR Constrn. Corp., Buffalo, 1982-85, exec. v.p., 1985—. Mem. president's adv. coun. D'Youville Coll.; bd. dirs. Cystic Fibrosis Found. Western N.Y. Fellow Buffalo Exsecs. Assn.; mem. Parka Club, Saturn Club, Rotary. Roman Catholic. Home: 19 Bondcroft Dr Buffalo NY 14228 Office: ADF Construction Corp 455 Commerce Dr Buffalo NY 14228

SAVIANO, CARL ROCCO, psychiatrist, educator; b. N.Y.C., Mar. 28, 1940. BA, Columbia U., 196l; MD, N.Y. Med. Coll., 1965. Diplomate Am. Bd. Psychiatry and Neurology, Am. Bd. Child Psychiatry, Nat. Bd. Med. Examiners. Mixed med.-pediatrics intern Kings County Hosp.-Downstate Med. Ctr., Bklyn., 1965-66; resident in adult psychiatry N.Y. Med. Coll.-Met. Hosp. Med. Ctr., N.Y.C., 1966-68, resident in child psychiatry, 1968-70, cert. div. psychoanalytic tng. dept. psychiatry, 1979; pvt. practice Northampton, Mass., 1976—; dir. children and adolescent svcs. Ctr. for Children and Youth, Westfield, Mass., 1974-76, med. dir., 1976-80, 86-88, acting med. dir., 1980-86, staff psychiatrist, 1980-86, 88-90; assoc. med. dir. psychiat. program Cooley-Dickinson Hosp., Northampton, 1990—; courtesy staff psychiatrist Baystate Med. Ctr., Springfield, Mass.; cons. staff Noble Hosp., Westfield; psychiat. cons. Amherst (Mass.) Pub. Schs., 1980-83; asst. clin. prof. psychiatry Tufts U. Sch. Medicine, Boston, 1974-78; asst. clin. prof. U. Mass. Sch. Medicine, Worcester, 1978-82, assoc. in psychiatry, 1988-90. Contbr. articles to med. jours. Lt. col. M.C., U.S. Army, 1970-74. N.Y. State Regents scholar, 1957-6l. Fellow Am. Psychiat. Assn., Am. Acad. Psychoanalysis; mem. Mass. Psychiat. Soc., Western Mass. Psychiat. Soc. (sec. 1977-78, pres. 1979-80), Physicians for Social Responsibility (co-editor Pioneer Valley chpt. newsletter).

SAVIC, MICHAEL, electrical engineering educator; b. Belgrade, Serbia, Yugoslavia, Aug. 4, 1929; came to U.S. 1967; s. Miodrag and Jelena (Milisic) S.; m. Rose R. Micovic, June 4, 1961 (dec. Oct. 1989); 1 child, Alice. Dipl. Ing., U. Belgrade, 1955, Dr.Eng.Sc., 1965. Rsch. and devel. engr. Kretztechnick Zipf/Austria, 1956; rsch. engr. Tungsram Vienna/Austria, 1957-58; asst. prof. U. Belgrade, 1959-67; researcher Yale U., New Haven, 1967-68; prof. elec. engring. Western New Eng. Coll., Springfield, Mass., 1968-82, Rensselaer Poly. Inst., Troy, N.Y., 1982—; prin. investigator Rensselaer Poly. Inst., Troy, 1982—, dir. sginal and speech processing lab., 1989—. Contbr. articles to profl. jours.; patentee in field. Recipient Award of Appreciation for Achievements and Contbns., U. Belgrade, 1981, others. Mem. IEEE (sr. mem., Cert. of Appreciation 1972), IASTED, Sigma Xi, Beta Kappa Psi. Office: Rensselaer Poly Inst ECSE Dept Troy NY 12180-3590

SAVILLO, ROBERT LOUIS, physician; b. Bklyn., May 5, 1953; s. Carl and Olga (Martinez) S.; m. Denise Anne Silvasi, Sept. 23, 1989. BS with honors, SUNY, Stony Brook, 1975; MD, Albert Einstein Coll. Medicine, 1979. Surg. intern Montefiore Hosp., Bronx, 1979-80; med. resident Bronx Mcpl. Hosp., 1980-82; clin. instr. N.Y. Hosp.-Cornell U. Med. Ctr., 1982-85; asst. prof. Cornell U. Med. Coll., N.Y.C., 1985—; asst. attending physician N.Y. Hosp., N.Y.C., 1985—. Regents scholarship SUNY, 1971-75; Rsch. grant NSF, 1973, Bookhaven Lab., 1974, N.Y. Arthritis Found., 1976. Mem. Soc. of Gen. Internal Medicine, Am. Soc. Internal Medicine, Med. Soc. of the State of N.Y. Office: Cornell Med Practice 525 E 68th St Rm 142K New York NY 10021-4873

SAVITS, THOMAS H., mathematics educator; b. Williamsport, Pa., Sept. 27, 1938; s. Earl H. and Eva June (Croman) S.; m. Sheila M. Stratford, Aug. 15, 1965; children: Monique A., Renee M. BSEE, Pa. State U., 1961; MSEE, Stanford U., 1964, MS in Math., 1966, PhD in Math., 1968. Instr. Princeton (N.J.) U., 1968-70, lectr., 1970-71; asst. prof. U. Pitts., 1971-76, assoc. prof., 1976-84, prof., 1984—. Co-editor: Topics in Statistical Dependence, 1991; contbr. articles to profl. jours. Grantee NSF, 1977-80, Office Naval Rsch., 1980-87, U.S. Army, 1987-88, Air Force Office Sci. Rsrch., 1984-90, Nat. Security Agy., 1990-9. Fellow Inst. Math. Stats., Internat. Statis. Inst. Office: U Pitts Dept Math and Stats Pittsburgh PA 15206

SAVITZ, JOSEPH J., lawyer; b. Wilkes-Barre, Pa., Nov. 3, 1922; s. Julius H. and Sarah (Epstein) S.; m. Janice Weiss, Oct. 27, 1963; children: Lynne, Marc. BA, Wilkes U., 1948; LLB, JD, U. Pa., 1951. Bar: Pa. 1952, U.S. Dist. Ct. (mid. dist. Pa.) 1953, U.S. Ct. Appeals (3d cir.) 1956, U.S. Supreme Ct. 1958. Assoc. Rosenn & Rosenn, Wilkes-Barre, 1952-54; assoc. Rosenn, Jenkins & Greenwald, Wilkes-Barre, 1954-58, ptnr., 1958-91, of counsel, 1991—. Nat. judge adv. Jewish War Vets. USA, Washington, 1961-62; trustee Wilkes U., 1958—, chmn. bd. trustees, 1975-78. Recipient award of merit United Jewish Appeal, Jewish Fedn. Greater Wilkes-Barre, 1982, Pres.'s award Temple Israel, 1986, Heritage award State of Israel Bonds, 1991. Mem. Pa. Soc., Westmoreland Club, B'nai B'rith (Community Svc. award 1989), Masons, Shriners,. Home: 744 Milford Dr Kingston PA 18704 Office: Rosenn Jenkins & Greenwald 15 S Franklin St # 1000 Wilkes Barre PA 18711-0075

SAVITZ, MARTIN HAROLD, neurosurgeon; b. Boston, Jan. 20, 1942; s. Nathan and Bernice Beatrice (Segal) S.; m. Susan Rayna Gordon, June 23, 1968 (div. Sept. 1977); 1 child, Sean Isaac; m. Harmony Gwynne Keys, Oct. 28, 1979; 1 child, Ariel Austryn. AB, Harvard U., 1963; MD, Hahnemann, 1969. Diplomate Am. Bd. Neurol. Surgery, Am. Bd. Clin. Neurosurgery, Nat. Bd. Med. Examiners. Intern Boston City Hosp., 1969-70; resident Mount Sinai Hosp., N.Y.C., 1970-74; clin. instr. dept. neurosurgery Dept. Neurosurgery, Mount Sinai Sch. Medicine, Nanuet, N.Y., 1974-82, asst. clin. prof., 1982-86, assoc. clin. prof., 1986-91, prof., 1991—; attending neurosurgeon Nyack (N.Y.) Hosp., Good Samaritan Hosp., Rockland County, N.Y., 1974-91. Contbg. editor Mount Sinai Jour. Medicine, N.Y.C., 1976-90, asst. editor, 1990-91; mem. editorial bd. Jour. Orthopaedic Neurol. Medicine and Surgery, 1991; contbr. over 50 articles to profl. jours.; contbr. 2 chpts. to textbooks. Fellow ACS, Internat. Coll. Surgeons (chmn.-elect U.S. sect. neurosurgery 1992—), N.Y. Acad. Medicine, Phila. Coll. Physicians, Am. Acad. Neurol. Orthopaedic Surgery; mem. AMA, Am. Assn. Neurol. Surgeons, N.Y. Soc. Neurosurgery, Congress Neurol. Surgeons, N.Y. State Neurosurg. Soc., Am. Assn. Physicians, Internat. Soc. Minimal Intervention in Spinal Surgery, Hastings Ctr., Alpha Omega Alpha. Jewish. Home: Hobbit Hollow New City NY 10956 Office: 55 Old Turnpike Rd Ste 101 Nanuet NY 10954-2449

SAVOCA, CARMEN SALVATORE, opera director; b. Bklyn., Sept. 27, 1924; s. Santo and Carlotta (Armena) S. Student, Phila. Music Acad., 1946-50. Co-founder Tri-Cities Opera Co., Binghampton, N.Y., 1949, stage dir., vocal tchr., 1949—; also bd. dirs.; dir. opera dept. Deerwood Music Ctr., 1950; stage dir. Garden State Opera, 1951, Scranton Opera, 1953, N.Y.C. Opera, 1965; dir. Chautauqua, 1965, Wichita Opera, 1969-72, Oklahoma City Opera, 1973; cons. N.Y. State Coun. on Arts, 1963—. Producer, dir., singer world premiere Myron Fink's Jeremiah,1962; participant Title Three Tour, 1963-66; dir., singer, cons. High-Tor Opera, Co., 1964-64. Served with USAAF, 1943-46. Decorated Bronze Star. Mem. Opera Am., Cen. Opera Svc. Home: 79 Main St Binghamton NY 13905-2894 Office: Tri-Cities Opera Inc 315 Clinton St Binghamton NY 13905-2094*

SAVOCCHIO, JOYCE A., mayor; b. Erie, Pa.; d. Daniel and Esther S. BA in History, Mercyhurst Coll., 1965; MEd, U. Pitts., 1969; cert. secondary sch. adminstrn., Edinboro U., 1975; DHL (hon.), Gannon U., 1990. Tchr. social studies Erie Sch. Dist., 1965-85, asst. prin. Strong Vincent High Sch., 1985-89, tchr. coord. high sch. task force, 1971-75; pres. Erie Edn. Assn., 1975-76; mem. coun. City of Erie, 1981-90, pres. coun., 1983, mayor, 1990—; mem. various coms. Erie Sch. Dist. Past pres. Erie Hist. Mus.; past mem. editorial bd. Erie Hist. Soc.; mem. Pa. Gov.'s Flagship Commn., Community Task force on Drug and Alcohol Abuse. Named Woman of Yr., Dem. Women Erie, 1981, Italian Am. Women's Assn., 1987; recipient Disting. Alumna award Mercyhurst Coll., 1990, Community Svc. award Roosevelt Mid. Sch., 1990, Disting. Citizen award French Creek coun. Boy Scouts Am., 1991. Mem. Delta Kappa Gamma. Roman Catholic. Office: Office of Mayor Mcpl Bldg 626 State St Erie PA 16501-1128

SAWABINI, NABIL GEORGE, banker; b. Beirut, Sept. 11, 1951; came to U.S., 1980; s. George Issa and Yvonne (Slim) S.; m. Nadia Abdelnour, Dec. 15, 1973; children: Karim, Zina. BBA, Am. U. Beirut, 1973. Mgmt. trainee Bank Almashrek (affiliate Morgan GTY), Beirut, 1973-74, head corp. lending, 1977, head corp. lending, fgn. dept., 1978, head corp. lending, fgn. dept., treasury fgn. exch., 1979-80; with mgmt. tng. program Morgan Guaranty Trust Co., N.Y.C., 1974-75; with shipping and commodities dept. Morgan Guaranty Trust Co., London, 1976-77; petroleum banker Morgan Guaranty Trust Co., N.Y.C., 1980-81, unit head petroleum dept., 1981-84, govt. bond sales rep., 1984; head internat. sales and trading J.P. Morgan Securities, Inc., London, 1985-86; mng. dir., head domestic and internat. taxable sales J.P. Morgan Securities, Inc., N.Y.C., 1987-89, securities group mgmt., 1989, product mgr. global fin. svcs., 1990—. Greek Orthodox. Home: 88 Secor Rd Scarsdale NY 10583-6953 Office: JP Morgan 60 Wall St New York NY 10260-0001

SAWHILL, ISABEL VAN DEVANTER, economist; b. Washington, Apr. 2, 1937; d. Winslow B. and Isabel E. Van Devanter; m. John C. Sawhill, Sept. 13, 1958; 1 son, James W. B.A., NYU, 1962, Ph.D., 1968. Policy analyst Office Sec. HEW, 1968-69, Office Mgmt. and Budget, 1969-70; asst. prof. econs. Goucher Coll., Balt., 1969-73; sr. research assoc. Urban Inst., 1973-77, program dir., 1975-77, program dir., sr. fellow, 1980—; dir. Nat. Commn. Employment Policy, Washington, 1977-79; vis. prof. Georgetown U. Law Ctr., 1990-91. Author: The Reagan Record, 1984, Challenge to Leadership, 1988. Mem. Sec. of Labor's commn. on workforce quality and labor mkt. efficiency, 1989, Ctr. Strategic and Internat. Studies commn. on strengthening of Am., Nat. Res. Coun. bd. on sci., tech., and econ. policy; mem. bd. dirs. Assembly of Am. Mem. Am. Econ. Assn. (mem. exec. com.), Assn. Pub. Polit. Analysis and Mgmt. (pres. 1988), Resources of the Future (vice chair), Manpower Demonstration Res. Corp., Phi Beta Kappa. Office: Urban Inst 2100 M St NW Washington DC 20037-1207

SAWICKI, JOHN EDWARD, chemical engineer; b. Phila., Mar. 10, 1944; s. John Louis and Frances Theresa (Cimoch) S.; m. Geraldine Aileen Rogalski, Feb. 20, 1971; children—Christian John, Mara Beth. B.S.Ch.E., Drexel U., 1967, M.S. in Environ. Engring., 1968; Ph.D. in Chem. Engring., U. Va., 1972. Trainee NIH, 1968; sr. research officer C.S.I.R., Pretoria, Republic South Africa, 1972-74; research/devel. engr. J. Schlitz Brewing Co., Milw., 1974-78; sect. mgr. Air Products and Chems., Inc., Allentown, Pa., 1978-80, research group leader, 1980-82, tech. mgr., 1982-86, section mgr. research ops., 1986-87, process technologist engring., 1987—; former advisor chem. tech. program Lehigh County Community Coll., 1983; advisor Environ. Studies Inst., Drexel U., Phila., 1984—; liaison Environ. Solutions program U. Tex., Austin, 1990—. Contbr. articles to profl. jours. Patentee in field. Memminger fellow U. Va., 1969; NDEA fellow, 1970; U. Va. fellow, 1971. Mem. Sigma Xi. Roman Catholic. Avocations: fishing, shooting. Home: RR 2 Box 669 Breinigsville PA 18031-9756 Office: Air Products and Chems Inc PO Box 538 Allentown PA 18105-0538

SAWOROTNOW, PARFENY PAVLOVICH, mathematician, educator; b. Ust Medveditskaya, Russia, Feb. 20, 1924; came to U.S., 1949, naturalized, 1965; s. Pavel Ivanovich and Anna Davidovna (Soloview) S.; student U. Graz (Austria), 1946-49; M.A. (Peirce scholar), Harvard U., 1951, Ph.D. (Shattuck fellow), 1955. Teaching fellow Harvard U., 1953-54; instr. math. Cath. U. Am., Washington, 1954-57, asst. prof., 1957-62, assoc. prof., 1962-67, prof., 1967—. NSF grantee, 1967, 70; with Georgetown U. and George Washington U., 1971, 77. Mem. Am. Math. Soc., Math. Assn. Am., Calcutta Math. Soc., N.Y. Acad. Scis., AAUP, Sigma Xi. Mem. Eastern Orthodox Ch. Contbr. articles to and referred papers for math. rsch. jours. Home: 6 Avon Pl Hyattsville MD 20782-3328 Office: Cath U Am Dept Math 4th and Michigan Ave NE Washington DC 20064

SAWYER, ANNITA PEREZ, clinical psychologist; b. Yonkers, N.Y., May 7, 1943; d. Henry Taylor and Rosanna (Garrett) Perez; m. William Beaumont Sawyer, June 21, 1969; children: Genevieve Gruening, Garrett Beaumont. Student, Columbia U., 1967-69; BA in Sociology summa cum

laude, Yale U., 1971, M in Philosophy, 1974, PhD, 1981. Psychologist, supr. Associated Psychotherapy Ctrs., Madison, Conn., 1981-90; clin. psychologist Psychotherapy Endeavors, North Branford, Conn., 1990—; lectr. sch. of medicine Yale U., New Haven, 1985-87. Mem. New Haven Chorale, 1975—. Mem. Am. Psychol. Assn., Conn. Psychol. Assn., Mass. Psychol. Assn., Phi Beta Kappa. Soc. of Friends. Office: Psychotherapy Endeavors 72 Crossfield Rd North Branford CT 06471-1802

SAWYER, BONNIE LOUISE, construction company executive, nurse; b. Charleston, Ill., May 20, 1948; d. Robert Eugene and Helen Winona (Mowrer) Prince; m. W. Tom Sawyer, Mar. 28, 1970; children: Shannon Michelle, Patricia Winona. BS, U. Maine, 1970; MS, Boston U., 1982. RN, Maine. Med.-surg. RN St. Joseph Hosp., Bangor, Maine, 1973-74; cons. USAR, Bangor, 1982-83; med.-surg. RN Eastern Maine Med. Ctr., Bangor, 1975-76; clinician, tchr. USAR, Bangor, 1978-81; pres. Manor Mgmt. Inc., Bangor, 1989—, Classical Endeavors, Bangor, 1990—. Mem. aquatics com. YMCA, Bangor, 1984-85; bd. dirs. Edythe Dyer Libr., Hampden, Maine, 1980-83, Acadia Hosp., Bangor, 1991—; bd. dirs., v.p. Bangor Dist. Nursing Assn., 1984-91. 1st lt. U.S. Army Nurse Corp., 1969-71. Mem. NAFE, Nat. Assn. Women in Constrn., Patawa Club (civic chmn. 1986-91, v.p. 1990-91). Republican.

SAWYER, JAMES LAWRENCE, architect; b. Bangor, Maine, Nov. 24, 1947; s. Maynard Wallace and Adelma Irene (Pascal) S.; m. Debralee Standley, June 6, 1980; children: Jason, Beverly, Joshua, John, Joseph. Ind. study, Instituto di Urbanistica, Florence, Italy, 1971; BArch, Pratt Inst., 1973. Ordained to ministry Glad Tidings Ch., 1987. Designer Sawhawk Inc., Bklyn., 1973-75; state architect Farmers Home Adminstrn., Orono, Maine, 1975—. Producer MPBN-TV Energy Independence on the Rise, 1988. Pres. One Nation Under God, Inc., Lighthouse Prison Ministry; bd. dirs. Gospel Tent Ministry; mem. Nat. Trust Hist. Preservation, Maine Right To Life Com. Recipient Energy Innovation award U.S. Dept. Energy, 1984, Bangor Daily News Photography award, 1985. Mem. Maine Solar Energy Assn. (pres. 1988), Christian Civic League. Office: Farmers Home Adminstrn USDA Bldg 444 Stillwater Ave Bangor ME 04401

SAWYER-LAUÇANNO, CHRISTOPHER DAVID, writer, educator; b. San Mateo, Calif., Jan. 4, 1951; s. Geronimo Lauçanno and Anne Kathleen (high) Garcia; m. Patricia Lemora Pruitt, May 30, 1987; stepchildren: Sarah Diane Pruitt, Jessica Chelsea Pruitt. BA in English Lit., U. Calif., Santa Barbara, 1971; MA in French Lit., Brandeis U., 1976, PhD in Lit. Studies, 1983. Instr. French and Spanish Brandeis U., Waltham, Mass., 1975-77; instr. fgn. langs. Dean Jr. Coll., Franklin, Mass., 1977-80; staff writer Time-Life Books, Tokyo, 1980-82; lectr. fgn. langs. and lits. MIT, Cambridge, 1982-91, lectr. writing program, 1991—; communication cons. Impact Mktg. and Communications, Boston, 1983-85. Author: The Continual Pilgramage: American Writers in Paris, 1944-60, 92, Case Studies in International Management, 1987, An Invisible Spectator: A Biography of Paul Bowles, 1989; translator: Poems From the Books of Chilam Balam, 1987, Barbarous Nights (F. Garcia Lorca), 1991. Translation fellow Nat. Endowment for Arts, 1992. Mem. Internat. Simulation and Gaming Assn. (hon. internat. com. 1986). Democrat. Office: MIT Writing Program 14N 234 Cambridge MA 02139

SAXE, NATALIE, government consultant; b. Phila., May 11, 1923; d. Nathaniel and Lilian Paula (Weitzman) S.; m. David V. Randall, Sept. 5, 1981. BA, U. Pa., 1944. Staff person Dem. City Com., Pa., 1948-56; exec. asst. Mayor of Phila., 1956-62; adminstr. Dilworth for Gov. Pa. Campaign, 1962; cons. Auerbach Corp., Phila., 1963-64; spl. asst. to pres. Phila. Bd. of Edn., 1965-71; spl. asst. to supt. Sch. Dist. of Phila., 1971-74; cons. urban affairs Pa. Gen. Assembly, 1974-78; cons. pub. affairs U. Pa., 1978-80; cons. govt. relations Lincoln U., Pa., 1983—; coordinator Mus. Assn. of Pa., 1978—. Contbr. articles to profl. jours. Mem. Electoral Coll., Harrisburg, Pa., 1964; alt.-at-large Dem. Nat. Conv., Atlantic City, N.J., 1964; bd. dirs. Pa. Fedn. Dem. Women, 1951-55; bd. trustees Phila. Coll. of Textiles and Sci., 1980—. Mem. The Athanaeum, Phila. Club: Cosmopolitan.

SAXE, THELMA RICHARDS, educator; b. Ogdensburg, N.J., Apr. 21, 1941; d. George Francis and Evelyn May (Howell) Richards; m. Kenneth Elwood Meeker, Jr., June 22, 1957 (div. 1965); children: Sylvia Lorraine Meeker Hill, Michelle Louise Meeker Aromando, David Sean (dec.); m. Frederick Ely Saxe, Feb. 18, 1983; stepchildren: Jonathan Kent, Holly Harding. BA, William Paterson Coll., Wayne, N.J., 1972, MEd, 1975, postgrad., 1983-84; Paralegal Cert., Fairleigh Dickinson U., 1989. Tchr. handicapped Sussex (N.J.)-Wantage Regional Sch. Dist., 1972-75; resource rm. tchr. Sussex County Vo-Tech Sch., Sparta, N.J., 1975-77; learning cons. Sussex County Vo-Tech Sch., 1977-83; learning specialist Bennington-Rutland Supervisory Union, Manchester, Vt., 1986-87; learning cons. Stillwater (N.J.) Twp. Sch., 1987-88, Independence Twp. Cen. Sch., Great Meadows, N.J., 1989; learning cons., tutor in pvt. practice specializing dyslexia Sparta, 1986—; asst. prin. Harmony Twp. Sch., Harmony, N.J., 1989—; coordinator gifted/talented Sussex Vo-Tech, 1980-83; coordinator child study team Stillwater Twp. Sch., 1987-88. Mem. ASCD, Coun. for Exceptional Children, Assn. for Children and Adults with Learning Disabilities, Orton Dyslexia Soc., N.J. Prins. and Suprs. Assn., Masterwork Chorus, Kappa Delta Pi. Republican. Presbyterian. Home and Office: 17 Park Rd Sparta NJ 07871-2002

SAXON, JAMES, physician, actor; b. N.Y.C., Apr. 6, 1954; s. Peter Edward and Shelagh Maureen (Meenan) S.; m. Abby Lynn Levine, May 13, 1989; 1 child, Tyler James. BFA, NYU, 1977; MD, Columbia U., 1987. Actor N.Y.C., 1976—; intern Roosevelt Hosp., N.Y.C., 1987-88; resident internal medicine St. Vincent's Hosp., N.Y.C., 1988-90, fellow in critical care medicine, 1990-92; fellow in pulmonary medicine Roosevelt Hosp., N.Y.C., 1992—. With USN, 1972-73.

SAXTON, H. JAMES, congressman; b. Scranton, Pa., Jan. 22, 1943; s. Hugh R. and Helen M. (Billings) S.; m. Helen Jean Gadomski, June 9, 1965; children—Jennifer, James Martin. B.A., East Stroudsburg State Coll., 1965; postgrad. in elem. edn., Temple U., 1967-68. Tchr. Bordentown Pub. Schs., Bordentown, N.J., 1965-68; realtor Jim Saxton Realty Co., Bordentown, N.J., 1968-85; assemblyman N.J. State Assembly, Trenton, 1975-81; state senator N.J. State Senate, Trenton, 1981-84; mem. 99th-102nd Congresses from 13th N.J. Dist., Washington, 1984—; coms. include mcht. marine and fisheries, banking, finance, and urban affairs; select com. on aging; mem. travel and tourism caucus, maritime caucus, congl. port caucus environ. and energy study conf., Rep. study com., Stripers Ltd. (99th Congress); sec. N.J. Congl. Del., Washington, 1985-89. Active Boy Scouts Am., Burlington Council. Bordentown C. of C. Club: Leadership Found. N.J. Lodge: Elks. Office: US Ho of Reps 324 Cannon House Office Bldg Washington DC 20515*

SAYEN, DAVID WINPENNY, public official; b. Phila., May 10, 1955; s. Harvey Thomas and Dorothy Marie (Di Angelo) S.; m. Claudia Griffing, July 26, 1986. BA in Philosophy, Temple U., 1977, MBA, 1991. Data mgmt. specialist Health Care Financing Adminstrn. U.S. Dept. Health & Human Svcs., Phila., 1978-83, med. rev. program analyst Health Care Financing Adminstrn., 1983-85, spl. asst. to regional adminstr. Health Care Financing Adminstrn., 1985—. Mem. Am. Coll. Healthcare Execs. (assoc.). Republican. Roman Catholic. Office: US Dept HHS Health Care Fin Adminstrn PO Box 7760 Philadelphia PA 19101-7760

SAYEN, WILLIAM HENRY, newspaper columnist; b. Princeton, N.J., July 28, 1921; s. William Henry and Edith May (Conyers) S.; m. Isabelle Guthrie, June 29, 1946; children: William G., David C., George H., Henry L. AB, Princeton U., 1947. Interview mgr. Audience Research Inc. subs. Gallup Orgn., Princeton, 1947-49; with sales dept. Mercer Rubber Co., Trenton, N.J., 1949-53, v.p. sales, 1953-65, pres., chief exec. officer, 1965-81, chmn. emeritus, 1981-83; columnist The Times, Trenton, 1981—; interviewer radio program Sta. WHWH, 1983-87; mem. gov.'s spl. planning task force, 1991-92. Contbr. numerous articles to mags., newspapers. Chmn. Trenton Econ. Devel. Commn., 1986—, New Trenton Devel. Corp., 1983—, Mercer County GOP Com., 1970-75; vice-chmn. bd. govs. Rutgers U., 1971-75; pres. Planning MSM Regional Council, Princeton, 1981—; mem. exec. com. June Opera Festival, Lawrenceville, N.J.; bd. dirs. N.J. Art Mus.; mem. N.J. Bldg. Authority, 1979—, chmn., 1988—; vice chmn. Princeton Regional Planning Bd., 1979-81; mem. Princeton Consolidation Commn., 1980-81, Mercer County Govt. Commn., 1973-74, N.J. Gov.'s Spl. Regional Govt. Com., 1991-92. Served with U.S. Army, 1943-45, Brit. Army, 1942-43. Named Man of Yr. Cen. N.J., 1985. Presbyterian. Home and Office: 218 Prospect Ave Princeton NJ 08540-5304

SAYRE, NANCY ELLEN, early childhood education educator, consultant; b. Canton, Ohio, Aug. 3, 1943; d. George E. and Dorothy E. (Quinlan) Ressler; m. W.G. Sayre, Aug. 14, 1965; children: Kirk D., Kelly D. BS in Edn., Ea. Mich. U., 1967; MEd, Slippery Rock U., 1981; PhD, U. Pitts., 1988. Elem. tchr. Milan (Mich.) Sch. Dist., 1967-69; instr. Slippery Rock (Pa.) Park Comm., 1974-86; prof. early childhood edn. Clarion (Pa.) U., 1986—; mem. exec. bd. Head Start, Brookville, Pa., 1989—; dir. Earl R. Siler Children's Learning Complex, Clarion, 1990—. Grantee Clarion U. Coll. Edn., 1988, Clarion U. Found., 1989. Mem. AAHPERD, Nat. Assn. Young Children, Pitts. Assn. Young Children, Coun. for Nat. Cooperation in Aquatics, Phi Delta Kappa (pres. West Shortway chpt. 1990—). Home: RR 2 Box 208 Boyers PA 16020-8816 Office: Clarion U Stevens Clarion PA 16214

SAYRE, PHILIP ROBINSON, college dean; b. Phila., Apr. 5, 1946; s. Robert Wrigley and Lucy Babcock (McCoy) S.; m. Sarah Fox Vaughan, Dec. 30, 1972; children: Tobias Cloud, Hannah Vaughan. BA, Hamilton Coll., Clinton, N.Y., 1968; MEd, U. Mass., 1973; PhD, Boston Coll., 1980. Tchr. English Intermediate Sch. 55, N.Y.C., 1968-71; counselor Cambridge (Mass.) Talent Search, 1972-73; counselor North Shore Community Coll., Beverly, Mass., 1973-74, dir. ednl. opportunity ctr., 1974-76; coord. field placements Boston Coll., Chestnut Hill, 1977-79; instr. English Middlesex and North Shore Community Colls., Bedford and Beverly, Mass., 1974-81; dir. spl. svcs. Middlesex Community Coll., 1979-81; dean student affairs U. Maine, Fort Kent, 1981-84; v.p., dean student affairs Western Md. Coll., Westminster, Md., 1984—; cons. Bunker Hill Community Coll., Charlestown, Mass., 1978; conf. presenter Nat. Assn. Student Personnel Adminstrs. and Nat. Assn. Fgn. Student Advisors. Bd. dirs. Multiple Sclerosis Soc., Tri-County Br., Md., 1987-91; pres. Montessori Soc. Westminster, M.d, 1986-89. Mem. Nat. Assn. Student Personnel Adminstrs., Nat. Assn. Fgn. Student Advisors, Am. Assn. for Higher Edn. Democrat. Religious Soc. of Friends. Home: 169 Pennsylvania Ave Westminster MD 21157-4551 Office: Western Md Coll 2 College Hill Westminster MD 21157-4303

SBARRA, ROBERT ANTHONY, management consultant; b. Bklyn., May 20, 1934; s. Anthony H. and Rosemary (Dougherty) S.; m. Vita J. Zummo, May 23, 1959; children: Roseann, Joan, Robert. BBA, Manhattan Coll., 1956. With Met. Life Ins. Co., N.Y.C., 1956-60; dir. alumni fund Manhattan Coll., N.Y.C., 1960-61; sales rep. IBM Corp., N.Y.C., 1961-62; salary adminstr. Royal Globe Ins. Co., N.Y.C., 1963-65; asst. dir. Exec. Compensation Svc., Am. Mgmt. Assn., N.Y.C., 1965-68; v.p., cons. Sibson & Co., Inc., Princeton, N.J., 1968-73; v.p., dir. compensation consulting Handy Assocs., Inc., N.Y.C., 1973-75; pres. Sbarra & Co., Inc., Lyndonville, Vt., 1975—. Contbr. articles on compensation to various publs. With U.S. Army, 1957-58. Mem. Am. Compensation Assn. (regional bd. dirs. 1968-72), Am. Mgmt. Assn., Soc. for Human Resource Mgmt., N.Y. Personnel Assn., Vt. Personnel Assn. Republican. Roman Catholic. Home: RR 2 Lyndonville VT 05851-9802 Office: Sbarra & Co Inc PO Box 124 Lyndonville VT 05851-0124

SBRIGLIO, ROBERT PATRICK, psychiatrist; b. New Haven, Nov. 16, 1953; s. Robert and Margaret (Coccomo) S. BA, Boston U., 1976; MD, Rush Med. Coll., 1981; MPH, Yale U., 1989. Resident in psychiatry St. Vincent's Hosp. and Med. Ctr., N.Y.C., 1981-84; fellow in psychiatry and pub. health N.Y. Hosp.-Cornell Med. Ctr., N.Y.C., 1984-86; postdoctoral fellow in psychiatry Yale U. Sch. Medicine, New Haven, 1987-88; pvt. practice, Bridgeport, Conn., 1989—. Mem. AMA, Am. Psychiat. Assn., Phi Beta Kappa. Office: PLEXUS Health Svcs Conn World Trade Pla 350 Fairfield Ave Bridgeport CT 06604-6001

SBUTTONI, MICHAEL JAMES, orthodontist, building contractor; b. Albany, N.Y., Aug. 6, 1953; s. Michael Francis and Mary Susan (Walsh) S.; m. Karen Sbuttoni, Aug. 9, 1975; children: Michael Louis, Ashley Ryan. BS, SUNY, Albany, 1975; DDS, SUNY, Buffalo, 1979; cert. in orthodontics, Eastman Dental Ctr., Rochester, N.Y., 1981. Real estate salesman Tri City Realty-Albany Bd. Realtors, 1971—; bldg. contractor M. Sbuttoni Constrn., Albany, 1972-86; practice dentistry specializing in orthodontics Dr. Serling and Decker DDS. P.C., Albany, 1981—; bldg. contractor The Craftsmens Guild, Albany, 1987—; staff orthodontist St. Peter's Hosp., Albany, 1984—. Mem. ADA, Dental Soc. State of N.Y. (pub. rels. 1985-88), Third Dist. Dental Soc. (bd. dirs. 1985-89, v.p. 1987-88, pres. 1988-90, ADA rep. 1990—), Am. Assn. Orthodontists, Am. Assn. Lingual Orthdontists (charter mem. 1987—), Kiwanis (fund raising dir. 1985-87), Elks. Republican. Roman Catholic. Home: 92 Middlesex Ct Slingerlands NY 12159-9636 Office: Drs Serling & Decker DDS PC 1004 Western Ave Albany NY 12203-2743

SCAFFIDI, JUDITH ANN, school volunteer program administrator; b. Bklyn., Aug. 2, 1950; d. Anthony William and Rose Virginia (Nocera) S. BA, SUNY, Plattsburg, 1972, MS, 1973; postgrad. Kennedy Learning Ctr., Einstein Coll. Medicine, 1983. Cert. secondary edn. English. VISTA mem. ACTION, N.Y.C., 1976-77; coord. cultural resources N.Y.C. Sch. Vol. Program, N.Y.C., 1977-80; dist. coord. in Bklyn. N.Y.C. Sch. Vol. Program, 1980—; field supr., adj. faculty Coll. for Human Svcs., N.Y.C., 1984-86; adv. coun. chairperson Retired Sr. Vol. Program in Bklyn, 1983-86, adv. bd., 1986—; adv. bd. Retired Sr. Vol. Program in N.Y.C., 1983-86. Recipient award for svcs. in promotion literacy Internat. Reading Assn. and Bklyn. Reading Coun., 1986, award for outstanding leadership Ret. Sr. Vol. Program, 1986, cert. of appreciation Mayor City of N.Y., 1991. Mem. NAFE, Nat. Sch. Vol. Program Ptnrs. in edn., Cath. tchrs. Assn. Bklyn. (del. sch. dist. 18, 1982—), Am. Mus. Natural History, Internat. Platform Assn., World Found. Successful Women, Cath. Alumni Club N.Y. Roman Catholic. Home: 2330 Ocean Ave Apt 3H Brooklyn NY 11229-3036 Office: NYC Sch Vol Program 443 Park Ave S 9th Fl New York NY 10016

SCAIA, MARY JULIE, special education educator; b. Torrington, Conn., May 7, 1953; d. Geno William and Mollie Rose (Silano) S. BS, So. Conn. State U., 1975; MEd, Northeastern U., 1985. Cert. elem., secondary spl. edn. tchr., Conn. Spl. edn. resource room tchr. Ledyard Pub. Sch. System, Gales Ferry Sch., Gales Ferry, Conn., 1975-76; spl. edn. tchr., team coord. Torrington (Conn.) Pub. Sch. System, Vogel Jr. High Sch., 1976—; communications cons. deaf/blind group homes; mem. profl. sign lang., dance and mime troupe Cridders; area coord. Northwestern Conn. Spl. Olympics, Torrington, 1979-80; mem. sch. adv. panel Conn. Pub. TV, Hartford, 1978-79, Litchfield County Hike for the Handicapped Campaign, Torrington, 1981—, Handicapped Task Force on Learning Disabilities, Boston, 1984-85; instituted sign lang. program.; taught and designed courses for talented and gifted students. Contbr. to Conn. Pub. TV newsletter, 1978. bd. dirs. Litchfield County Assn. for Retarded Citizens, Torrington, 1980-82, Friendship Plus! - An Ind. Citizen Advocacy Network, Torrington, 1987—; master of ceremonies Telethons for local cable, Torrington, 1985-86. Recipient Tchr. of the Yr. award Probus Club of Torrington, 1987-89; finalist, runner-up Conn. Tchr. of the Yr., 1988-89. Mem. NEA, Conn. Edn. Assn. (del. to Washington NEA program), Torrington Edn. Assn. (v.p. 1980-82), Conn. Registry of Interpreters for the Deaf, Assn. for Children and Adults with Learning Disabilities, Zeta Delta Epsilon, Alpha Delta Kappa (v.p. 1982-84). Democrat. Roman Catholic.

SCALIA, ANTONIN, U.S. Supreme Court justice; b. Trenton, N.J., Mar. 11, 1936; s. S. Eugene and Catherine Louise (Panaro) S.; m. Maureen McCarthy, Sept. 10, 1960; children—Ann Forrest, Eugene, John Francis, Catherine Elisabeth, Mary Clare, Paul David, Matthew, Christopher James, Margaret Jane. A.B., Georgetown U., 1957; student, U. Fribourg, Switzerland, 1955-56; LL.B., Harvard, 1960. Bar: Ohio 1962, Va. 1970. Assoc. Jones Day Cockley & Reavis, Cleve., 1961-67; assoc. prof. U. Va. Law Sch., 1967-70; prof. law U. Va., 1970-74; gen. counsel Office Telecommunications Policy, Exec. Office of Pres., 1971-72; chmn. Adminstrv. Conf. U.S., Washington, 1972-74; asst. atty. gen. U.S. Office Legal Counsel, Justice Dept., 1974-77; vis. prof. Georgetown Law Center, 1977, Stanford Law Sch., 1980-81; vis. scholar Am. Enterprise Inst., 1977; prof. law U. Chgo., 1977-82; judge U.S. Ct. Appeals (D.C. cir.), 1982-86; justice U.S. Supreme Ct., Washington, 1986—; cons. CSC, 1969, 77, FCC, 1977, FTC, 1978, 80; bd. dirs. Nat. Inst. Consumer Justice, 1972-73, Ctr. Adminstrv. Justice, 1972-74; adv. coun. legal policy studies, Am. Enterprise Inst., 1978-88. Editor: Regulation mag, 1979-82. Sheldon fellow Harvard U., 1960-61. Mem. ABA (council, sect. adminstrv. law 1974-77, chmn. sect. adminstrv. law 1981-82, chmn. conf. sect. 1982-83). Office: US Supreme Ct 1 1st St NE Washington DC 20543

SCALIA, JOHN CAZES, steamship company executive; b. N.Y.C., May 16, 1947; s. Frank Anthony and Mae Francis (Weis); m. Laraine Ann Isoldi, May 9, 1948; children: Keith, John, Michael. BBA, Coll. of Ins., N.Y.C., 1970. Claims adjustor Hartford Ins. Group, N.Y.C., 1965-72; owner Good Time Jeans Inc., Merrick, N.Y., 1970-75; store mgr. The Image, Roosevelt Field, N.Y., 1975-77; risk mgr. Apex Marine Corp., Lake Success, N.Y., 1977-86; mgr. ins. claims and loss prevention Farrell Lines Inc., N.Y.C., 1986-89; ins. adjustor Maritime Overseas Corp., N.Y.C., 1989—; adv. bd. Marine Index Bur., N.Y.C. Tng. leader and commr. Boy Scouts of Am. Nassau City, N.Y. 1978—. Mem. Soc. Maritime Personal Injury Cons. (pres. 1982-86, Outstanding Achievement award 1987), Maritime Law Assn. (sub-com. chmn. 1981—). Roman Catholic. Home: 230 Hamilton Ave Massapequa NY 11758-4008 Office: Maritime Overseas Corp 43 W 42nd St New York NY 10036-8003

SCANES, COLIN GUY, animal sciences educator; b. London, July 11, 1947; s. Herbert Alfred and Marjorie Amy (Barltrop) S.; m. Carla Joy Turk, Apr. 25, 1976; children: Rosalind Amanda, Jaqueline Diana, Meredith Lyanne. BS, U. Hull, U.K., 1969; PhD, U. Wales, U.K., 1972; DSc, U. Hull, 1985. Lectr. U. Leeds, 1972-78; assoc. prof. Rutgers U., New Brunswick, N.J., 1978-82; prof. animal sci. Rutgrs U., New Brunswick, 1982—, chmn. dept. animal sci., 1981—; mgr. USDA Competitive Grants Program, Washington, 1989-90; cons. in field. Editor 5 books; contbr. over 200 articles to profl. jours., numerous chpts. to books. NATO fellow, 1990-91; recipient Rutgers U. Trustees award for research, 1986. Mem. Am. Soc. Animal Sci., Am. Physiol. Soc., Poultry Sci. Assn., Endocrine Soc., Internat. Com. for Avian Endocrinology (pres. 1984-88), Animal Sci. Depts. Heads/Chairs Assn. (exec. com. chmn. 1990-91). Republican. Home: 1601 Van Buren Rd New Brunswick NJ 08902-3028 Office: Rutgers U Lipman Dr Cook Campus New Brunswick NJ 08903

SCANLAN, JOHN THOMAS, writer, educator; b. Washington. AB, Rutgers Coll., 1979; AM, U. Mich., 1980, PhD, 1988. Vis. instr. English Vassar Coll., 1987-88; asst. prof. English Providence Coll., 1988—. Contbr. essays and revs. to profl. jours. Mem. Veblenians (sec.). Office: Providence Coll Dept English Providence RI 02918

SCANLAN, THOMAS JOSEPH, college president, educator; b. N.Y.C., Mar. 5, 1945; s. Thomas Joseph and Anna Marie (Schmitt) S. BA in Physics, Cath. U. Am., 1967; MA in Math., NYU, 1972; PhD in Bus. Adminstrn., Columbia U., 1978. Prin. Queen of Peace High Sch., North Arlington, N.J., 1972-75; dir. fin., edn. N.Y. Province, Bros. of Christian Schs., Lincroft, N.J., 1978-81; vice chancellor Bethlehem (Israel) U., 1981-87; pres. Manhattan Coll., Bronx, N.Y., 1987—. Trustee Lewis U., Romeoville, Ill., 1987—. Recipient Pro Ecclesia et Pontifice medal, Pope John Paul II, Vatican City, 1986. Mem. Bros. of Christian Schs., Am. Coun. Edn., Assn. Cath. Colls. and Univs., Assn. Am. Coll., Nat. Cath. Edn. Assn., Nat. Assn. Ind. Colls. and Univs., Nat. Collegiate Athletic Assn. (mem. pres. commn.), Phi Beta Kappa, Beta Gamma Sigma. Office: Manhattan Coll Manhattan College Pky Bronx NY 10471-3913

SCANLON, ANTHONY JOHN, association administrator; b. Bklyn., Nov. 26, 1951; s. Clifford J. and Nancy (Re) S. BA, Hunter Coll., 1973, MA, 1973. Bus. mgr. N.Y. Law Sch., N.Y.C., 1974-75, registrar, 1975-77, asst. dean, 1978-83, assoc. dean, 1983-84; asst. dean St. John's U. Law Sch., N.Y.C., 1984-88; dir. devel. Correctional/Osborne Assn., N.Y.C., 1989—. Contbr. articles to profl. publs. Democrat. Roman Catholic. Home: 7 E 14th St New York NY 10003-3115 Office: Correction/Osborne Assn 135 E 15th St New York NY 10003-3557

SCANLON, JANE CRONIN, mathematics educator; b. N.Y.C., July 17, 1922; d. John Timothy and Janet Smiley (Murphy) Cronin; m. Joseph C. Scanlon, Mar. 5, 1953 (div.); children: Justin, Mary, Emer, Edmund. Student, Highland Park Jr. Coll., 1939-41; B.S., Wayne State U., 1943; M.A., U. Mich., 1945, Ph.D., 1949. Mathematician Air Force Cambridge Research Center, 1951-54; instr. Wheaton Coll., Norton, Mass., 1954-55; asst. prof. Poly. Inst. Bklyn., 1957-58, asso. prof., 1958-60, prof., 1960-65; prof. math. Rutgers U., 1965—; cons. Singer-Kearfott Div., Naval Research Lab. Office Naval Research Fellow Princeton, 1948-49; Horace H. Rockham Postdoctoral fellow U. Mich., 1950-51, Rutgers Research Council fellow, 1968-69, 72-73; NSF vis. professorship for women Courant Inst., NYU, 1984-85. Author: Fixed Points and Topological Degree in Nonlinear Analysis, 1964, Advanced Calculus, 1967, Differential Equations: Introduction and Qualitative Theory, 1980, Mathematics of Cell Electrophysiology, 1980; Mathematical Aspects of Hodgkin-Huxley Neural Theory, 1987. Mem. Am. Math. Soc., Soc. for Indsl. and Applied Math., Internat. Soc. Chronobiology. Home: 110 Valentine St Highland Park NJ 08904-2106 Office: Dept Math Rutgers U New Brunswick NJ 08903

SCANNAPIECO, PASQUALE JOSEPH (PAT SCANNI), sales executive; b. Phila., June 28, 1942; s. Albert Joseph and Carmella (Trimarco) S.; div.; children: Carmella, Pasquale (Pat) Jr. BS in Edn., West Chester U., 1964; ABA in Mgmt. magna cum laude, U. Pa., 1973, BBA in Mktg. magna cum laude, 1975. Cert. secondary tchr., Pa. Sales rep. Royal Typewriter Co., Phila., 1964-66, territory mgr., 1967-69; account exec. R.H. Donnelley div. Dunn and Bradstreet, N.Y.C., 1969-80, account mgr., 1981-83; nat. acct. mgr. New Connections Mag. div. Dunn and Bradstreet, N.Y.C., 1983-85; regional v.p. Changing Homes Pub., Valley Stream, N.Y., 1985-88; pres. P.J.S. Enterprises, Trevose, Pa., 1988-89; sales exec. Treasure Chest Advt. Co., Inc., N.Y.C., 1989-90; regional sales mgr. Ad Cart div. T.V. Fanfare Publs., King of Prussia, Pa., 1990-92; sales mgr. Am. Home Rentals, Phila., 1992—. Coach baseball and football; mem. Royal Arcaum Integrity Council (pres. 1967-69). Mem. Am. Biog. Inst. (bd. advisors), Personalities of Am., Greater Phila. C. of C., Sigma Kappa Phi. Roman Catholic. Club: Flyers Fan. Home: 409 Merle Way Langhorne PA 19053-2426 Office: Trevose 524 S 3rd St Pittsburgh PA 19147

SCARBOROUGH, RUTH, medical school administrator; b. Phila., Mar. 18, 1939; d. Ransom Frederick and Janie Louise (Outing) S.; m. Pierce T. Ramsey, Sr., July 13, 1985. BS, St. Joseph's U., 1981; MEd, Temple U., 1987. Asst. dir. family planning Temple U. Sch. Medicine, Phila., 1969-91, dir. family planning, dir. project devel., 1992—. 1st v.p. Women's Christian Alliance Child Care and Adoption Agy., Phila., 1978—; trustee Holy Cross Bapt. Ch. Recipient Outstanding Svc. to Minority award Black Caucus of Am. Pub. Health, 1986, Recognition award State Senate of Pa., Phila., 1989. Mem. Family Planning Coun. S.E. Pa. (v.p. rsch. rev. bd., mem. fin. com. 1984—). Home: River Park House # 1912 3600 Conshohocken Ave Philadelphia PA 19131 Office: Temple U Sch Medicine Dept Obstetrics, Gynecology & Reproductive Scis Philadelphia PA 19140

SCARDERA, MICHAEL, research chemist, consultant; b. Providence, May 11, 1935; s. John and Anna (Caporicci) S.; m. Georgette Boilard, Apr. 28, 1962; children: Michael, Katherine, Maria, Mark. BS, Brown U., 1957; MBA, U. Bridgeport, 1963. Sr. rsch. assoc. Olin Corp., Cheshire, Conn., 1957-91; chem. cons. Hamden, Conn., 1991—; instr. So. Conn. State U., New Haven, 1965-75, 91—. Patentee chem. compositions. Mem. Am. Oil Chemists Soc., Sigma Xi. Home: 81 Manor St Hamden CT 06517-2319

SCARDINO, DON, actor, director, artistic director. Artistic dir. summer stock Playwrights' Horizon; profl. musician. Actor (plays) Godspell, King of Hearts, Johnny No Trump, As You Like It, (TV show) The Guiding Light; director (plays) Godspell, A Few Good Men, Making Movies, I'm Getting My Act Together and Taking It On the Road, Moon Children, How I Got That Story, Big Sister's Clothes, (films) The People Next Door,

Squirm, Cruising, He Knows You're Alone; director (TV) 27 Wagons Full of Cotton, The Days and Nights of Molly Dodd. Office: care Playwrights Horizons 416 W 42nd St New York NY 10036-6896*

SCARDINO, MARJORIE MORRIS, publishing company executive; b. Flagstaff, Ariz., Jan. 25, 1947; d. Robert Weldon and Addie Beth (Lamb) Morris; m. Albert James Scardino, Apr. 19, 1974; children: Adelaide Katherine Morris, William Brown, Albert Henry Hugh. BA, Baylor U.; JD, U. San Francisco. Ptnr. Brannen Wessels & Searcy, Savannah, Ga., 1976-85; pub. Ga. Gazette Pub. Co., Savannah, 1978-85; pres. The Economist Newspaper, Inc., N.Y.C., 1985—; mng. dir. Bus. Internat., Inc., N.Y.C., 1992—. Bd. dirs. Landmarks Conservancy, N.Y.C., 1986-90, New Sch. for Social Rsch., N.Y.C., 1989—. Office: The Economist 111 W 57th St 8th Fl New York NY 10019

SCARDOCCHIA, GAETANO, journalist; b. Campobasso, Molise, Italy, Mar. 7, 1937; s. Pasquale and Maria (Santone) S.; m. Rosemarie Zwerger, Apr. 7, 1965; children: Susy, Fabio. Student, U. Rome, 1960. East Europe corr. Il Giorno, Vienna, Austria, 1960-63; Germany corr. Il Giorno, Hamburg, Fed. Republic Germany, 1964-69; spl. corr. Il Giorno, Rome, 1970-75; spl. corr. Corriere Della Sera, Rome, 1976-77, bur. chief, 1977-80; Asia corr. Corriere Della Sera, Beijing, Peoples Republic China, 1980-83; bur. chief La Repubblica, N.Y.C., 1983-86; editor in chief La Stampa, Turin, Italy, 1986-89; USA corr. La Stampa, N.Y.C., 1990—. Co-author: Giornalismo E Vita Internazionale, 1988, L'Impero Riluttante, 1992. Office: La Stampa 235 West 56th St # 31-M New York NY 10019

SCARLATA, ANTONIA ELLEN L., rehabilitation psychologist; b. Woodbury, N.J., Jan. 5, 1944; d. Cornelius Anthony and Anne Elizabeth (Lyons) Lynch; m. Charles Francis Scarlata, Oct. 14, 1941; children: Joanna, Maurin, Celeste, Susan. BA, Duquesne U., 1965; MEd, U. Pitts., 1967. Lic. psychologist; cert. rehab. counselor. Counselor N. Va. Community Coll., Fairfax, Va., 1968-69; psychologist Mercy Hosp. Pittsburgh, 1970-74; prin. McCabe & Scarlata, Inc., Pitts., 1981-85; chief oper. officer OPTIONS, Pitts., 1985—. Bd. dirs. Mayview State Hosp., Bridgeville, Pa., 1981-85, Jud. Inquiry and Rev. Bd., Harisburg, Pa., 1986-90. Mem. Pa. Psychol. Assn., Greater Pitts. Psychol. Assn. (assoc.), Greater Pitts. C. of C. (bd. dirs. 1992—). Office: Options 1400 Penn Ave Pittsburgh PA 15222-4332

SCARPINO, JOHN J., financial information representative; b. Mineola, N.Y., Nov. 29, 1966; s. John J. and Irma H. (Rivera) S.; m. Kayla Ann Scarpino, Mar. 17, 1990. BA, Va. Mil. Inst., Lexington, Va., 1988. Account rep. Advest, N.Y.C., 1988-89; fin. advisor Prudential Bache, N.Y.C., 1989-90; account rep. Moody's Investors, Moody's Investors Svc., N.Y.C., 1990—, s.e. regional mgr., 1991—. With U.S. Army, 1985. Mem. U.S. Fencing Assn. Republican. Roman Catholic. Office: Moodys Investors Svc 99 Church St New York NY 10007

SCASTA, DAVID LYNN, psychiatrist; b. Austin, Tex., Dec. 13, 1949; s. Albert Ray and Helen Pearl (Hennessy) S. BA, Baylor U., 1972; MD, Baylor Coll. of Medicine, 1977. Diplomate Am. Bd. Psychiatry and Neurology. Staff physician U. Houston, 1977-78; adminstr. Temple U. Med. Sch., Phila., 1982-83; residency in psychiatry Temple U. Hosp., Phila., 1982; dir. consultation svcs. Grad. Hosp., Phila., 1983-84; dir. outpatient programs Phila. Psychiat. Ctr., 1983-84; pvt. practice Grad. Hosp. Phila. Psychiat. Ctr., 1984-89; med. dir. Phila. Consultation Ctr., 1987-89; attending psychiatrist Hunterdon Med. Ctr., Flemington, N.J., 1989—; vice chmn. dept. mental health Hunterdon Med. Ctr., Flemington, 1989—; pvt. practice New Hope, Pa., 1989—; clin. asst. prof. dept. psychiatry Temple U. Med. Sch., Phila., 1983—; researcher Assn. Gay and Lesbian Psychiatrists, Phila., 1989—; vice-chmn. dept. mental health Hunterdon Med. Ctr., Flemington, N.J. Editor Jour. of Gay & Lesbian Psychotherapy, 1987—, Newsletter of the Assn. of Gay & Lesbian Psychiatrists, 1984—. Dist. rep. Rep. Party of Tex., Houston, 1977, precinct sec., 1975-77. Named Ginsberg Fellow Group for Advancement of Psychiatry, 1980-82. Mem. Assn. Gay and Lesbian Psychiatrists, Am. Psychiat. Assn., Assn. Lesbian and Gay Psychologists, Parents and Friends of Lesbians and Gays. Republican. Baptist. Office: Dept Mental Health Hunterdon Med Ctr 2100 Wescott Dr Flemington NJ 08822-4603

SCEDROV, ANDRE, mathematics and computer science researcher, educator; b. Zagreb, Croatia, Aug. 1, 1955; came to U.S., 1977, naturalized, 1987; s. Oleg and Mira (Petric) S.; m. Bonnie Carol Hoke, July 23, 1983. BA, U. Zagreb, 1977; MA, SUNY, Buffalo, 1979, PhD in Math., 1981. T.H. Hildebrandt asst. prof. rsch. U. Mich., Ann Arbor, 1981-82; asst. prof. math. U. Pa., Phila., 1982-88, assoc. prof. math., computer and info. sci., 1988-92, prof. math., computer and info sci., 1992—; vis. scholar U. Milan, 1982, McGill U., Montreal, 1985, U. Sydney, Australia, 1986, U. Catholique de Louvain, Louvain-La-Neuve, Belgium, 1988, U. Paris, 1992; vis. scientist Math. Scis. Inst. Cornell U., Ithaca, N.Y., 1987; vis. assoc. prof. Stanford (Calif.) U., 1988-90; cons. Odyssey Rsch. Assocs., Ithaca, 1987, HP Labs, Palo Alto, 1990; program chair 7th ann. IEEE Symposium on Logic in Computer Sci., Santa Cruz, Calif., 1992; mem. program com. Logical Found. Computer Sci., Tver, Russia, 1992; invited speaker Math. Founds. Programming Semantics, Oxford U., Eng., 1992, Computer Sci. Logic, San Miniato, Italy, 1992. Author: (with P. Freyd) Categories, Allegories; editor Math. Structures in Computer Sci., 1989—; contbr. articles and rsch. papers to profl. publs. Recipient Young Faculty award Nat. Scis. Assn. U. Pa.; rsch. grantee math. NSF, 1985-87, rsch. grantee computer sci. NSF, 1987—, Office Naval Rsch., 1988—. Mem. Am. Math. Soc., Assn. Symbolic Logic (jour. editor 1988—, program com. 1988-90, coun. mem. 1990—), Assn. Computing Machinery, Math. Assn. Am. Office: U Pa Dept Math 209 S 33rd St Philadelphia PA 19104-6395

SCHAAB, ARNOLD J., lawyer; b. Newark, Dec. 26, 1939; s. Robert George and Pauline (Levine) S.; m. Marcia Stecker, 1964 (div. 1978); children: Emily Diana, Genevieve Elizabeth; m. Patricia Caesar, Mar. 7, 1981. BA, New Sch. for Social Rsch., 1962; LLB, Harvard U., 1965. Bar: N.Y. 1967, U.S. Dist. Ct. (so. and ea. dists.) N.Y. 1967. Assoc. Chadbourne & Parke, N.Y.C., 1966-69; ptnr. Anderson, Russell, Kill & Olick, N.Y.C., 1969-78; sr. ptnr. Pryor, Cashman, Sherman & Flynn, N.Y.C., 1978—; bd. dirs. Grove Press, Inc., N.Y.C. Bd. dirs. Literacy Vols. of N.Y.C., Inc., Netherlands-Am. Amity Trust, Washington, Shaker Mus. and Libr., Old Chatham, N.Y. Fulbright scholar Law Faculty U. Paris, 1966. Fellow N.Y. Bar Found.; mem. ABA (vice chair internat. fin. transactions com. , forum com. on constrn. industry), N.Y. State Bar Assn. (chair internat. law and practice sect., chmn. spl. com. free trade in the Ams., ho. of dels.), Univ. Club, Doubles, The Netherland Club, Old Chatham Hunt Club. Office: Pryor Cashman Sherman Flynn 410 Park Ave New York NY 10022-4407

SCHAAF, DONALD MARTIN, advertising executive; b. Lexington Park, Md., Dec. 27, 1961; s. Gordon Martin and Virginia Ann (Long) S. BS in Human Ecology, U. Md., 1985. Art dir. Jay Williams Design Co., Washington, 1985-86; pres., founder Pinnacle Design Group, Ltd., Bethesda, Md., 1986-91, Don Schaaf & Friends, Inc., Washington, 1991—; instr. design dept. Marymount U., Vienna, Va., 1991—; alumni advisor design dept. U. Md., College Park, 1986-90. Bus. advisor Montgomery County Pub. Schs., Rockville, Md., 1986-89; publ. com. Bethesda (Md.)/Chevy Chase C. of C., 1988. Recipient Outstanding Svc. to Edn. award Montgomery County Pub. Schs., 1987-88, Silver medal Strathmore Paper Co., 1990. Mem. Art. Dirs. Club Met. Washington, D.C. (Real Show award 1985). Republican. Roman Catholic. Office: Don Schaaf & Friends Inc 1010 Wisconsin Ave NW # 125 Washington DC 20007

SCHAAF, ERIC WILLIAM, photographic company executive; b. Rochester, N.Y., Nov. 2, 1956; s. William Ellsworth Jr. and Mary Ellen (Flickinger) S.; m. Paulette Ann Drabenstot, June 4, 1977; children: Kristin Noelle, Jaclyn Nicole, Ryan William, Erin Michelle. BS in Indsl. Engring., Purdue U., 1977; MBA, Ind. U., 1979. Indsl. engr. Eastman Kodak Co., Rochester, 1979-82; corp. auditor Eastman Kodak Co., 1982-86; dir. asset mgmt. Graphics Imaging Systems div. Eastman Kodak Co., 1987-90; v.p., dir. fin. and adminstrn. Anastar, A Kodak Co., Rochester, 1986-87; mgr. customer svc. Graphics Imaging Systems div. Eastman Kodak Co., 1990—, dir. strategic alliances, 1991—. Mem. Assn. MBAs. Home: 1 County Clare Cres Fairport NY 14450-9169 Office: Eastman Kodak Co G1SD 343 State St Rochester NY 14650-0001

SCHAAL, ALLYSON BROOKE, psychotherapist, researcher; b. Mt. Holly, N.J., Dec. 13, 1965; d. Walter Richard and Alice Mae (Robbins) S. BS, Chestnut Hill (Pa.) Coll., 1988; MA, Rider Coll., 1991. Account exec. Met. Life Ins. Co., Phila., 1988; ins. rater Harleysville Ins., Marlton, N.J., 1988-90; psychotherapist intern Family Svc. Burlington County, Moorestown, N.J., 1990; rsch. asst. Ctr. for Children's Support U. Medicine and Dentistry N.J., Stratford, 1990-91, coord. rsch., 1991—. Office: U Medicine Dentistry NJ Ctr for Children's Support 301 S Central Plz Ste 3400 Stratford NJ 08084-1504

SCHAAP, WILLIAM HERMAN, journalist, lawyer; b. N.Y.C., Mar. 1, 1940; s. Maurice William and Leah (Lerner) S.; m. Jill Gerson, Apr. 10, 1964 (div. 1973); m. Ellen Ray, Dec. 1, 1974. BA, Cornell U., 1961; JD, U. Chgo., 1964. Bar: N.Y. 1964, D.C. 1977. Pvt. practice N.Y.C., 1964-72; lawyer Asia Mil. Law Project, Okinawa, Japan, 1972-73, Lawyers Mil. Def. Commn., Heidelberg, Fed. Republic Germany, 1973-74, Ctr. for Constl. Rights, N.Y.C., 1975-76, 81; editor-in-chief Mil. Law Reporter, Washington, 1976-81; co-editor Covert Action Info. Bull., Washington, 1978—; dir. Sheridan Sq. Press, N.Y.C., 1981—, Inst. for Media Analysis, N.Y.C., 1986—; adj. prof. John Jay Coll., CUNY, N.Y.C., 1987, 88; expert witness U.S. and fgn. courts. Editor: (with others) The CIA in Western Europe, 1978, The CIA in Africa, 1980; mng. editor: Lies of Our Times, 1989—; editor numerous books; contbr. articles to profl. jours. and publs. Mem. Nat. Lawyers Guild (pres. D.C. chpt. 1978-79), Internat. Orgn. of Journalists. Democrat. Office: Inst Media Analysis Inc 145 W 4th St New York NY 10012-1054

SCHACHNE, GARY, steel company executive; b. Rehovot, Israel, May 24, 1950; came to U.S., 1954; s. Joseph and Dora Schachne; m. Esther A. Freitag, June 3, 1973; children: Erica, Sarah, Michael. BS in Econs., Bklyn. Coll., 1972. CPA, N.Y. Staff, sr. acct. John Addison & Co., N.Y.C., 1972-78; tax acct. J. Aron & Co., N.Y.C., 1978-83; treas., controller Oremco Inc., N.Y.C., 1983—; pvt. practice cons., N.Y.C., 1978—; co-developed computer tax applications, N.Y.C., 1982-84. Mem. Am. Inst. CPA's, N.Y. State Soc. CPA's. Office: Oremco Inc 261 Madison Ave New York NY 10016-2303

SCHACHNER, DIANNE JOYCE, marketing executive; b. Omaha; d. Saul William and Evelyn (Zweiback) Fellman; m. Stephen H. Schachner, June 7, 1961; children: Seth Andrew, Jill Elizabeth. BA, Creighton U., 1961. Edit. asst. Sperry Gyroscope, L.I., 1961-62; med. writer Med. Sch. U. Calif., San Francisco, 1962-63; freelance interior designer, 1964-81; dir. of bus. devel. Ward Hale Design Assoc., Washington, 1983-84; dir. of mktg. Allgeier Assoc., Washington, 1984-85, Leo A. Daly, Washington, 1985—. Patent for exercise bar. Rep. Youth Engaged in Svc., Arlington, Va., 1991; mem. Com. for Dulles, 1981—. Mem. Internat. Facilities Mgmt. Assn., Soc. Mktg. Profl. Svcs. (pres. Washington chpt. 1990-91), Comml. Real Estate Women, D.C. Bldg. Industries Assn., Japan Soc., Am. C. of C. Home: 10221 Sorbel Ave Potomac MD 20854

SCHACHTER, EDWIN NEIL, physician, educator; b. N.Y.C., May 10, 1943; s. Franz and Fay (Zeltzman) S.; m. Deborah Chase, Nov. 15, 1969; children: Karen Elizabeth, Lauren Beth. AB, Columbia U., 1964; MD, NYU, 1968. Intern Bellevue Hosp., 1968-69, resident, 1969-70, 72-73; asst. prof. Yale Sch. Medicine, New Haven, 1974-79, assoc. prof., 1979-84; prof. Mt. Sinai Sch. Medicine, N.Y.C., 1984-88, Maurice Hexter prof. pulmonary medicine, 1988—. Author: (with Lehnert) Respiratory Care Pharmacology, 1980, (with Witek) Advances in Repiratory Care Pharmacology, 1988, Current Issues in Respiratory Public Health, vols. 1 & 2, 1989, 90; contbr. over 130 peer reviewed articles and over 140 abstracts to profl. jours. Chmn. Smoking or Health Com. N.Y.C., 1988-89. Lt. comdr. USN, 1970-72. E.L. Trudeau fellow ALA, 1973. Fellow Am. Coll. Physicians, Am. Coll. Chest Physicians; mem. Nat. Assn. Med. Dirs. Respiratory Care (pres. 1988-90), Nat. Bd. Respiratory Care (bd. dirs. 1982—). Office: Mt Sinai Med Ctr 1 Gustave L Levy Pl # 1232 New York NY 10029-6504

SCHACHTER, MICHAEL BEN, psychiatrist; b. Bklyn., Jan. 15, 1941; s. Saul and Ann (Palestine) S.; m. Margaret Josephine Kavanagh, July 22, 1967 (div. Mar. 1979); children: Brian Joseph, Amy, Stefan James; m. Marlene Helen Brodsky, Aug. 22, 1982; children: Adam Elliot, Jason Neil. BA, Columbia Coll., 1961, MD, 1965. Diplomate Am. Bd. Psychiatry and Neurology in Psychiatry, Am. Bd. Chelation Therapy. Med., surg. and pediatric intern Hosp. for Joint Diseases and Med. Ctr., N.Y.C., 1965-66; resident psychiatry Downstate Med. Ctr., Kings County Hosp., Bklyn., 1966-69; staff psychiatrist Bklyn. Community Counseling Ctr., 1968-69; staff psychiatrist Rockland County Community Mental Health Ctr., Pomona, N.Y., 1971, dir. emergency and admissions, 1971-72, dir. outpatient clinic, 1972-74; founder, dir. Michael B. Schachter M.D., P.C. formerly Mountainview Med., Nyack, N.Y., 1974—. Author: (with David Sheinkin and Richard Hutton) The Food Connection, 1979, Food, Mind and Mood, 1980, 2d edit., 1987; contbr. articles to profl. jours. Maj. USAF, 1969-71. Recipient Appreciation award NHF, 1979, Carlos Lamar Pioneer Meml. award Am. Acad. Med. Preventics, 1979, Merit award Am. Acad. Craniomandibular Disorders, 1981, Physician's Recognition awards AMA. Fellow Am. Coll. of Advancement in Medicine (pres. 1989-91, v.p. 1985-87, pres.-elect 1987-89); mem. Am. Bd. Chelation Therapy (bd. dirs. 1983-88), Am. Psychiat. Assn., Am. Acad. Environ. Medicine, Am. Coll. Nutrition. Office: 2 Executive Blvd # 202 Suffern NY 10901

SCHACHTER, OSCAR, lawyer, educator, arbitrator; b. N.Y.C., June 19, 1915; s. Max and Fannie (Javits) S.; m. Mollie Miller, Aug. 9, 1936 (dec. July 1980); children: Judith (Mrs. John Modell), Ellen (Mrs. John P. Leventhal); m. Muriel L. Sackler, June 14, 1982. BSS, Coll. City N.Y., 1936; JD, Columbia, 1939. Bar: N.Y. 1939. Editor-in-chief Columbia Law Rev., 1938-39; pvt. practice N.Y.C., 1939-40; atty. U.S. Dept. of Labor, Washington, 1940; chief nat. defense sect. in law dept. FCC, 1941; sect. of law com. and adviser on internat. communications Bd. of War Communications, 1941-42; prin., divisional asst., adviser on wartime econ. controls and on European liberated areas U.S. Dept. State, 1942-43; asst. gen. counsel UNRRA, 1944-46; drafting officer UNRRA council sessions, 1944-45; legal adv. UNRRA del. to USSR and Poland, 1945; legal counselor UN, 1946-52, dir. gen. legal div., 1952-66; dep. exec. dir., dir. studies UN Inst. for Tng. and Research, 1966-75; lectr. law Yale U. Law Sch., 1955-71; Carnegie lectr. Hague Acad. Internat. Law, 1963-82; Rosenthal lectr. Northwestern U. Law Sch., 1974; prof. Law Sch. and Faculty Internat. Affairs Columbia U., 1975—, Hamilton Fish prof. internat. law and diplomacy Law Sch. and Faculty Internat. Affairs, 1980-85, prof. emeritus Law Sch. and Faculty Internat. Affairs, 1985—; vis. prof Harvard Law Sch., 1982; chmn. legal com. UN Maritime Conf., 1948; legal cons. UNESCO, 1948; past dir. Gen. Legal Div. of UN; served as legal adviser various internat. confs. and UN couns. and coms.; sec. legal adv. com. UN Atomic Energy Commn., 1946-47; vice chmn. Internat. Investment Law Conf., 1958; exec. sec. Internat. Arbitration Conf., 1958; mem. panel arbitrators Internat. Ctr. for Settlement of Investment Disputes, 1980-87; judge Ct. Arbitration in Canada-France Maritime Boundary dispute, 1989—; expert advisor UN com. on transnational sorps., 1990—. Author: Relation of Law, Politics and Action in the U.N, 1964, Sharing the World's Resources, 1977, International Law in Theory and Practice, 1985, rev. edit., 1991; co-author: Across the Space Frontier, 1952, Toward Wider Acceptance of UN Treaties, 1971, International Law Cases and Materials, 1980, 2d edit. 1987; contbr. articles and monographs on internat. law, internat. instns., legal philosophy, human rights, internat. peace and security, internat. resources to legal jours.; editor-in-chief Am. Jour. Internat. Law, 1978-84, hon. editor, 1985—; co-editor: Competition in International Business, 1981; editorial bd. Marine Policy. Bd. dirs. Internat. Peace Acad., 1970-82. Recipient Friedman award Columbia Law Sch., 1983; Carl Fulda award U. Tex. Law Sch., 1990, Columbia Law medal for excellence, 1991. Fellow Am. Acad. Arts and Scis., World Acad. Art and Sci.; mem. ABA, Am. Soc. Internat. Law (pres. 1968-70, hon. v.p., mem. exec. council, Manley Hudson medal 1981, Cert. Merit for Creative Scholarship 1992), Coun. on Fgn. Rls., Inst. de Droit Internat. (v.p. 1991—), Internat. Law Assn., Internat. Astronautical Acad., Phi Beta Kappa. Home: 11 E 86th St New York NY 10028-0548 Office: Columbia U Law Sch New York NY 10027

SCHAD, THEODORE MACNEEVE, science research administrator, consultant; b. Balt., Aug. 25, 1918; s. William Henry and Emma Margaret (Scheldt) S.; m. Kathleen White, Nov. 5, 1944; children: Mary Jane, Rebecca Christina. BSCE, Johns Hopkins U., 1939. Various positions water resources engring. U.S. Army C.E., U.S. Bur. Reclamation, Md., Colo., Oreg. Wash., 1939-54; prin. budget examiner water resources programs U.S. Bur. Budget, Exec. Office of Pres., 1954-58; sr. specialist engring. and pub. works, dep. dir. Congl. Research Service, Library of Congress, 1958-68; staff dir. U.S. Senate Com. Nat. Water Resources, 1959-61; exec. dir. Nat. Water Commn., 1968-73; exec. sec. Environ. Studies Bd., 1973-77; dep. dir. Commn. Natural Resources, Nat. Acad. Scis., Washington, 1977-83; exec. dir. Nat. Ground Water Policy Forum, 1984-86; sr. fellow Conservation Found., Washington, 1986-; U.S. commr. Permanent Internat. Assn. Nav. Congresses, Brussels, 1963-70, commr. emeritus, 1987—; cons. U.S. Senate Com. Interior and Insular Affairs, 1963, U.S. Ho. of Reps. Com. Sci. and Tech., 1964-65, Fed. Council Sci. and Tech., 1962-65, U.S. Office Saline Water, 1965-67, A.T. Kearney, Inc., Alexandria, Va., 1979-80, Chesapeake Research Consortium, 1984, Ronco Cons. Corp., 1986—, Gambia River Basin Devel. Commn., Dakar, 1986-87, Apogee Rsch. Corp., 1987—. Contbr. articles to Ency. Brit. and profl. jours. Treas. Nat. Speleol. Found., 1961-65, trustee, 1965—; bd. dirs. Vets. Coop. Housing Assn., Washington, 1958-81, v.p., 1960-72. Recipient Meritorious Svc. award U.S. Dept. Interior, 1950, Icko Iben award Am. Water Resources Assn., 1978, Henry P. Caulfield medal, 1990. Fellow ASCE (treas. Nat. Capital chpt. 1952-55, v.p. 1967, pres. 1968, Julian Hinds prize 1991); mem. AAAS, Nat. Speleol. Soc., Am. Water Works Assn. (hon.), Am. Geophys. Union, Am. Acad. Environ. Engrs., Nat. Acad. Pub. Adminstrn., Permanent Internat. Assn. Nav. Congresses, Internat. Commn. Irrigation and Drainage. Clubs: Potomac Appalachian Trail; Cosmos (Washington); Colo. Mountain (Denver); Seattle Mountaineers. Home: 4138 26th Rd N Arlington VA 22207-5115 Office: The Conservation Found 1260-24th St NW Washington DC 20037

SCHADLER, HARVEY WALTER, metal products executive; b. Cin., Jan. 4, 1931; s. Harvey George and Ida Helen (Beinert) S.; m. Margaret Eleanor Horsfall, Aug. 28, 1954; children: Janet A., Edward H., Linda S. BSMetE, Cornell U., 1954; PhD in Metallurgy, Purdue U., 1957. Metallurgist GE Co., Corp. R & D, Schenectady, N.Y., 1957-73, lab. mgr. metals and ceramics, 1973-85, mgr. materials rsch. ctr., 1985—. Co-author: Superconducting Materials, 1965. Sr. elder First Ref. Ch. of Schenectady, 1991—. Recipient Geisler award Eastern N.Y. Chpt. Am. Soc. for Metals, Menlo, Ohio, 1966; fellow Am. Soc. for Metals, Menlo, 1978, NAE, Washington, 1991. Mem. ABET, Tau Beta Pi. Republican. Office: Gen Electric Co Corp R & D 1 River Rd Schenectady NY 12301

SCHAEFER, GEORGE PETER, financial services executive; b. N.Y.C., Nov. 7, 1950; m. Lois Nancy Bedner, July 6, 1974; children: Lauren Jessica, Alexis Carmella. BA, Am. U., 1972; M in Pub. Adminstrn., Syracuse U., 1974. Budget analyst HEW, Washington, 1974-76; policy analyst U.S. Dept. Energy, Washington, 1976-78; assoc. Booz, Allen & Hamilton, Bethesda, Md., 1978-80; dir. energy program The Orkand Corp., Silver Spring, Md., 1980-81; dir. energy fin. Ultrasystems, Irvine, Calif., 1981-82; sr. v.p., mgr. energy project financing Gen. Electric Credit Corp., Stamford, Conn., 1982-88; sr. v.p. European ops. GE Capital Corp., London, 1988-91; sr. v.p. gas industry financing GE Capital Corp., 1991—; sr. v.p. internat. bus. devel. GE Capital Corp., Stamford, Conn., 1992—. Author: (with others) Biomass as Non Fossil Fuel Source, 1978, Energy Project Financing, 1986; also articles. Centennial scholar Case Western Res. U., Cleveland, 1978; named One of Outstanding Young Men of Am., U.S. Jaycees, 1982. Mem. Renewable Energy Inst., Internat. Assn. Energy Economists, Am. Soc. for Pub. Adminstrn. (co-founder sect. on budgeting and fin. 1975; co-founder, bd. govs. Jour. Pub. Budgeting and Fin. 1980). Home: 6 Knollwood Ln Darien CT 06820-2813

SCHAEFER, JOHN BOCK, physics educator; b. Pitts., May 16, 1937; s. John Paul and Ruth Helen (Bock) S.; m. Lois Leora Hinman, Aug. 28, 1962; children: Jonathan, Deborah, Paul, David, Mark. BS, MIT, 1959; MS, Carnegie-Mellon U., 1962. Instr. Indiana (Pa.) State U., 1960-61; asst.prof. Geneva Coll., Beaver Falls, Pa., 1962-63, 64-69, assoc. prof. physics, 1969—; rsch. physicist Carnegie-Mellon U., Pitts., 1963-65. Mem. IEEE, Acoustical Soc. Am., Am. Assn. Physics Tchrs., Sigma Xi. Office: Geneva Coll Dept Physics College Ave Beaver Falls PA 15010

SCHAEFER, MARCIA SONTZ, bank officer; b. Albany, N.Y., June 28, 1938; d. Myer and Anne (Forster) Sontz; m. Gerald Stephen Gordon, June 4, 1961 (div. Jan. 1979); children: Kara Lisa Gordon, Elyssa Kim Gordon, Marla Sheryl Gordon; m. Richard Joseph Schaefer, Oct. 19, 1991. BA in French, Boston U., 1960, postgrad., 1961-62. Lic. stockbroker, N.Y. French tchr. Brockton (Mass.) High Sch., 1961-63; dir. group sales Saratoga (N.Y.) Performing Arts Ctr., 1970-78; talk show moderator, host, producer WQBK Radio, Albany, 1975-78; stockbroker Merrill Lynch, Albany, 1978-81; dir. media N.Y. State Polit. Campaign, Albany, 1982; br. asst. mgr., sales trainer N.E. Savings, Albany, 1984-89; comml. mgr., officer Union Nat. Bank, Albany, 1989—. Author numerous poems. Facilitator Hill House Youth Substance Abuse, Albany, 1989-90; active Lions Club, Schenectady, N.Y., 1987; participant Capital Leadership, Albany, 1986—. Recipient Loaned Exec. award United Way, 1987. Mem. Albany Colonie C. of C., Guilderland C. of C. Democrat. Jewish. Home: 34 Windsor Ct Delmar NY 12054 Office: Union National Bank 2080 Western Ave Ste 101 Guilderland NY 12084

SCHAEFER, RHODA PESNER, educator; b. Bronx, N.Y., Mar. 15, 1947; d. Herman Pesner; m. Alan Jacob Schaefer, Sept. 23, 1967; children: Ira Marc, Melissa Anne. BA, Dominican Coll., Orangeburg, N.Y., 1980; MA in Edn., SUNY, New Paltz, 1987. Cert. tchr., N.Y. Teaching asst. East Ramapo Cen. Schs., Spring Valley, N.Y., 1984-87; tchr. East Ramapo Cen. Sch. Dist., Spring Valley, 1987—; instr. East Ramapo Tchrs.' Ctr., 1988—; adj. prof. L.I.U., 1989—. Pres., officer PTA, Spring Valley, 1972—. Mem. ASCD, Internat. Reading Assn., N.Y. Reading Assn., Rockland Reading Coun., Nat. Coun. English Tchrs. Office: Hillcrest Elem Sch Addison Boyce Dr Spring Valley NY 10977

SCHAEFER, ROBERT JAMES, physicist; b. New Rochelle, N.Y., June 9, 1939; s. Robert A. and Mary L. (Newhall) S.; m. Karin Wuertz, Oct. 15, 1974; 1 child, Sylvia. AB, Harvard Coll., 1960; PhD, Harvard U., 1965. Physicist Naval Rsch. Lab., Washington, 1964-79; physicist Nat. Inst. Standards and Tech., Gaithersburg, Md., 1979—; Contbr. articles to profl. jours. Office: Nat Inst Standards and Tech Materials A-153 Gaithersburg MD 20899

SCHAEFER, WILLIAM DONALD, governor of Maryland, former mayor; b. Balt., Nov. 2, 1921; s. William Henry and Tululu (Skipper) S. LLB, U. Balt., 1942, LLM, 1951, LLD (hon.), 1976; JD (hon.), Loyola Coll., 1976; D of Pub. Svc. (hon.), U. Md., 1979, LLD (hon.), 1981; JD, Goucher Coll., 1980; DHL (hon.), Towson State U., 1982; LLD (hon.), Morgan State U., 1983; D Pub. Svc. (hon), Gettysburg Coll., 1986; DHL (hon.), Villa Julie Coll., 1990; LLD (hon.), Coll. Notre Dame, 1991. Bar: Md. 1943. Practiced in Balt., 1943—; mem. Balt. City Coun., 1955-67, pres., 1967-71; mayor City of Balt., 1971-87; gov. State of Md., Annapolis, 1987—. Chmn. Chesapeake Bay Exec. Coun.; mem. Mayors Adv. Com., Nat. Coun. for Urban and Econ. Devel., U.S. Conf. Mayors. Served with AUS, 1942-45; col. Res. (ret.). Recipient numerous awards, including Alumni of Yr. award U. Balt., 1971, Man of Yr. award Jewish Nat. Fund, 1972, 1st ann. Civic Statesmanship award Citizens Planning and Housing Assn., Jefferson award for outstanding pub. svc., 1979, William Fell Pub. Svc. award Johns Hopkins U., 1980, Disting. Svc. award Nat. Coun. for Urban Econ. Devel., 1980, award of excellence Urban Land Inst., 1980, Michael A. DiNunzio award U.S. Conf. Mayors, 1981, Man of Decade award Advt. Club Balt., 1982, Nat. award Urban Energy Mgmt. Energy Task Force of Urban Consortium, 1982, Disting. Mayor award Nat. Urban Coalition, 1982, commendation for Exemplary Achievement Sister Cities Internat., 1985, Congl. cert. Merit for Outstanding Citizenship, 1986, Man of Yr. award Md. Soc. Acctg., 1987, award for Exec. Agy. Policy on Smoking Am. Heart Assn., 1987, Disting. Pub. Svc. award Brandeis U., The Doctor Henry P. and Page Laughlin award, 1988, commendation Pres'. Coun. Phys. Fitness and Sport, 1988, Gov. of Yr. Nat. Multiple Sclerosis Soc., 1989, Gov.'s award Nat. Assn. State Outdoor Recreation Liaison Officers, 1987, cert. Appreciation for Outstanding Record in Appointment of Women to State Cabinet Positions Nat. Women's Polit. Caucus, 1991, Making Marylanders Safe award Marylanders Against Handgun Abuse, 1991, Ann. Svc. award Outstanding Contrbn. to

Growth and Progress of Retail Industry Md. Retail Merchants Assn., 1991, award Outstanding Visionary Support of Arts in Md. Md. Citizens for Arts, 1991, Preservation award Hist. Annapolis Found., 1991, various others. Mem. AIA (hon.), Nat. League Cities (bd. dirs.), Md. Assn. Counties, Chesapeake Bay Exec. Coun. (chmn.), U.S. Conf. Mayors (Outstanding Leadership award 1979, Michael A. DiNunzio award 1981), Md. Mcpl. League, Balt. Bar Assn., Citizens Planning and Housing Assn. Balt., Nat. Hist. Soc., Balt. Ecol. Soc., Md. Ret. Officers Assn., Balt. Assn. Retarded Citizens, Md. Acad. Scis., VFW, Navy League U.S., Am. Inst. Banking (hon.), Am. Pub. Works Assn., Md. Law Enforcement Officers, Md. 4H Club., Md. Jaycees, Edgar Allen Poe Soc., Exchange Club Md. , Pres'. Club U. Md. (hon.), Md. Enlisted Assn. Nat. Guard Honorees (hon.), U. Balt. Alumni Assn., Rotary, Phi Delta Phi, Sigma Delta Kappa. Democrat. Home: Gov's Mansion Annapolis MD 21401 Office: Office of Gov State House Annapolis MD 21401

SCHAEFFER, INA ELAINE, counselor; b. Lebanon, Pa., Dec. 3, 1947; d. Paul Victor and Alice Mary (Hower) S. BA, Gallaudet Coll., 1973, MA, 1989. Dorm counselor Md. Sch. for Deaf, Frederick, 1973-81; computer programmer analyst Navy Ship Port Control Ctr., Mechcansburg, Pa., 1981-86; sch. counselor Austine Sch. for Deaf, Brattleboro, Vt., 1989-90, Scranton (Pa.) Sch. for Deaf, 1990-91; coord.-counselor challenge program for emotional students Austine Sch., Brattleboro, Vt., 1991—. Mem. Nat. Assn. for Deaf, Pa. Soc. for Advancement of Deaf. Home: RR 6 Box 16 B Brattleboro VT 05301-2631 Office: Austine Sch for the Deaf 120 Maple St Brattleboro VT 05301-2694

SCHAEFFER, NEIL JEROME, English literature educator; b. Bklyn., Nov. 30, 1940; s. David and Ann (Berkowitz) S.; m. Susan Fromberg, Oct. 11, 1970; children: Benjamin, May. BA, Columbia U., 1962, MA, 1964, PhD, 1971. Asst. prof. English Bklyn. Coll., 1971-75, assoc. prof., 1976-81, chmn., English Dept., 1982-85, prof. of humor, 1989-91, prof. of English, 1982—. Author: The Art of Laughter, 1981; contbr. articles to profl. jours. Home: 783 E 21st St Brooklyn NY 11210-1041 Office: Bklyn Coll Dept English Brooklyn NY 11210

SCHAFER, JOHN CHARLES, college administrator; b. Gary, Ind., June 26, 1948; m. Elisabeth A. Paeth, Aug. 19, 1972; children: Sommer, Brooke, Zachary. BS, Oreg. State U., 1970; MA, Ind. U., 1976. Dir. admissions, registrar Huntington (Ind.) Coll., 1978-83; dir. admissions West Suburban Coll. Nursing, Oak Park, Ill., 1983-86; dir. admissions and fin. aid Alaska Pacific U., Anchorage, 1986-90; dir. enrollment planning Utica (N.Y.) Coll. of Syracuse U., 1990—. Office: Utica Coll 1600 Burrstone Rd Utica NY 13502-4857

SCHAFER, LARRY W., fundraising executive; b. Trimont, Minn., Nov. 19, 1952; s. Wayne and Lois (Oien) S. BA, Manhattan Coll., 1979; MA, Columbia U., 1981. Promotion specialist City of N.Y., 1981-84; ind. cons. N.Y.C., 1984-87; devel. dir. Bklyn. Bur. Community Svc., N.Y.C., 1987—. Co-chmn. capital campaign First Unitarian Ch., Bklyn. With USN, 1972-76. Mem. Nat. Soc. Fundraising Execs. Office: Bklyn Bur Community Svc 285 Schermerhorn St Brooklyn NY 11217-1098

SCHAFER, SEYMOUR JAY, lawyer; b. Pitts., Dec. 28, 1933; s. Nathan and Lillian Shirley (Rivkees) S.; m. Loreen Rae Zavos, July 3, 1960; children: Todd David, Tracy Ellen, Douglas Eben. BA with honors, Univ. Pitts., 1955, LLB with honors, 1958; LLM, Univ. Mich., 1960. Bar: D.C. 1958, Pa. 1963, U.S. Supreme Ct. 1969. Asst. prof. law Western Res. U., Cleve., 1960-61; asst. prof. law Univ. Pitts., 1961-63, asst. research prof. of health law, 1961-63, adj. prof. law, 1963-65; ptnr. Markel, Schafer & Means, PC, Pitts., 1963—; legal counsel, The Hosp. Council of Western Pa. 1968—; lectr. in field. With USAF, 1958-64. Mem. Soc. of Hosp. Attys. of Western Pa. (founder, past pres.), Am. Acad. of Hosp. Attys. of Am. Hosp. Assn. Democrat. Jewish. Office: Markel Schafer & Means PC 1120 Grand Ave Pittsburgh PA 15212-2441

SCHAFFER, DEBRA SIMON, artist, sculpture educator; b. N.Y.C., Nov. 22, 1936; d. Louis and Fay (Soloway) Simon; m. Lewis Adam Schaffer, June 16, 1957; children: Michael Allen, Steven Carl. BA, Montclair State Tchrs. Coll., 1958. Cert. elem. and high sch. tchr. Tchr. English Collingswood (N.J.) High Sch., 1958-61; vol. tchr. Chidlren's Hosp. of Phila., 1961-64; tchr. sculpture Armonk, N.Y., 1980—, Heritage Hills, Somers, N.Y., 1982—. Sculptural works include Animal House, Flo's Family--Homage to Jane, 1987 (Jeffrey Childs Willis Meml. award), Animal House, 1989 (Gretchen Richardson Freelander Meml. award). Chmn. Fresh Air Fund, Armonk, 1970-73; bd. dirs. Middle Sch. Program, Armonk, 1973-76, Temple Design Sanctuary Commn., Armonk, 1980-82. Recipient Outstanding Artistic Achievement award Bedford (N.Y.) Art Show, 1988, Best in Show award St.Marks Art Festival, 1981, awards Armonk Art Show, 1990, 91. Mem. Nat. Assn. Women Artists, Stone Sculpture Soc. N.Y., Hudson Valley Art Assn., Working Artists. Democrat. Jewish. Home and Office: 10 Windmill Pl Armonk NY 10504-2828

SCHAFFER, MICHAEL J., educator; b. Dundalk, Md., May 29, 1944; m. Ellen Bond, Oct. 9, 1971; children: Kathryn J., Sarah L. BS, U. Md., 1971, MA, 1983. Health educator Prince George's County pub. schs., Upper Marlboro, Md., 1972-74; specialist in health edn. Prince George's County pub. schs., 1974-84; lectr. George Washington U., Washington, 1989—, U. Md., College Park, 1980—; supr. health edn. Prince George's County pub. schs., 1984—. With USN, 1962-66. Mem. Sex Edn. Coalition of Met. Washington, Eta Sigma Gamma. Home: 11502 Coralroot Ct Bowie MD 20721 Office: Prince Georges County Schs 7801 Sheriff Rd Hyattsville MD 20785-4497

SCHAFFER, ROBERT JAY, accountant; b. Kew Gardens, N.Y., June 24, 1960; s. Walter and Edith (Mintz) S. BBA, Pace U., 1983. CPA, N.Y. Acctg. intern Kaufman, Vanasco, Resnick & Co. CPAs, N.Y.C., 1979-80; office mgr. Safeguard Bus. Systems, Walt Schaffer Assocs. Distbr., Bayside, N.Y., 1981-83; staff acct. Kalish, Rubinroit & Co. CPAs, N.Y.C., 1983-87; mgr. Janover, Rubinroit & Co. CPAs, Valley Stream, N.Y., 1987—. Mem. AICPA, N.Y. State Soc. CPAs. Home: 84-20 Austin St Apt 7E Kew Gardens NY 11415-2233 Office: Janover Rubinroit & Co CPAs 65 Roosevelt Ave Valley Stream NY 11581-1106

SCHAFFER, ROSANNE STRUNSKY, motion picture film laboratory executive; b. N.Y.C., Jan. 3, 1922; d. Max and Ruth Ida (Heyman) Strunsky; m. Eugene Schaffer, Dec. 9, 1945; children: Eric Matthew, Meryl Sue. BA, Coll. William & Mary, 1943. Newspaper reporter The Sun, N.Y.C., 1943-47; from account exec., dir. sales & svc., to v.p. TVC Labs., Inc., N.Y.C., 1972-91; dir. sales & svc. Technicolor, East, N.Y.C., 1991—; bd. trustees Walden Sch., N.Y.C., 1968-71. Mem. N.Y. Women in Film (bd. dirs.). Office: Technicolor East 321 W 44th St New York NY 10036-5404

SCHAFFNER, ROBERT THOMAS, JR., municipal parking administrator; b. Sunbury, Pa., Jan. 9, 1937; s. Robert Thomas and Sarah Jane (Rupp) S.; m. Dorothy Ruth Gingrich, Mar. 23, 1962; (div. Dec., 1986) children: Melissa Anne, Melanie Beth. Student, Susquehanna U., 1958. Announcer several Pa. radio stations, 1959-63; news dir. WBPZ, Lock Haven, Pa., 1963-65; bus. editor Lancaster (Pa.) Newspapers, Inc, 1965-68; exec. dir. Lancaster Parking Authority, 1968-77, Harrisburg (Pa.) Parking Authority, 1975-77, Balt. Off-St. Parking Commn., 1977-91; chief parking mgmt div. Transp. Dept., Balt., 1991—. Pres. Lancaster (Pa.) Fed. of Musicians, 1974-75. With USN, 1954-58. Mem. Instl. and Mcpl. Parking Congress (pres. 1982-83), Middle Atlantic Parking Assn. (sec. 1988-89). Democrat. Office: 414 N Calvert St Baltimore MD 21202

SCHAFRAN, LYNN HECHT, lawyer, educator; b. N.Y.C., Oct. 11, 1941; d. David K. and Geraldine (Schaeffer) Hecht; m. L. G. Schafran, Aug. 28, 1966; children: David, Brooke. BA magna cum laude, Smith Coll., 1962; MA, Columbia U., 1965, JD, 1974. Bar: N.Y. 1975, U.S. Ct. Appeals (2d cir.) 1975, U.S. Supreme Ct. 1988. Asst. to the curator Gallery Modern Art, N.Y.C., 1964-66; instr. art history Smith Coll., Northampton, Mass., 1965-66; asst. dir., project assoc. Mus. Modern Art, N.Y.C., 1966-70; editorial assoc. Art News, N.Y.C., 1967-69; law clk. U.S. Dist. Ct., N.Y.C., 1974-75; assoc. atty. Weil, Gotshal and Manges, N.Y.C., 1975-77; rep. region II Fed. Regional Coun., N.Y.C., 1978; nat. dir. Fedn. Women Lawyers' Judicial Screening Bd., N.Y.C., 1979-81; dir. Nat. Judicial Edn. Program NOW Legal Def. and Edn. Fund, N.Y.C., 1981—; dir. Women's Forum, Inc., N.Y.C., 1991-93. Author: Promoting Gender Fairness in the Courts, 1990; contbr. articles to profl. jours., mags. and newspapers. Vice chair N.Y.C. Commn. on Status of Women, 1978-82, spl. counsel, 1982—; mem. N.Y. State Banking Bd., N.Y.C., 1983—. Recipient Gold medal Found. for Improvement of Justice, 1990, Centennial Honors award Smith Club N.Y., 1991, Smith Coll. medal, 1992. Fellow Am. Bar Found.; mem. ABA, Commn. on Women in the Profession, Nat. Assn. Women Judges (Disting. Svc. award 1990). Democrat. Jewish. Office: Nat Judicial Edn Program NOW Legal Def and Edn Fund 99 Hudson St 12th Fl New York NY 10013

SCHAFRANK, MICHAEL S., ophthalmologist; b. N.Y.C., Oct. 11, 1935; s. Benjamin and Betty (Alper) S.; m. Phyllis T. Solomon, June 7, 1958; children: Scott, Francine. BS, Queen's Coll., 1956; MD, SUNY, 1960. Internship internal medicine Jewish Hosp. Bklyn., 1960-61; resident ophthalmology NYU Med. Ctr., N.Y.C., 1961-64; chief ophthalmology John Moses Meml. Hosp., Minot, N.D., 1964-66; attending ophthalmology, clin. instr. ophthalmology NUY, 1966—; clin. instr. in ophthalmology Bellevue Med. Ctr. Hosp., N.Y.C., 1966—; attending in ophthalmology, teaching staff North Shore U. Hosp., Manasett, N.Y., 1970—. Fellow Am. Acad. Ophthalmology, ACS. Office: 72-35 112 St Forest Hills NY 11375

SCHAFTEL, ROBERT B., insurance agency executive; b. Balt., Sept. 9, 1940; s. Joseph B. and Jeanette B. Schaftel; m. Marilyn Saks, Aug. 9, 1964; children: Michael Scott, Julie Saks. BA, U. Md., 1962. Producing agt. J.B. Schaftel Co., Balt., 1962-70, producing v.p., 1970-80, producing exec. v.p., 1980-85, exec. v.p., chief exec. officer prodn., 1985-91, agy. head div. Am. Pheonix Corp., 1991—. Co-chmn. Associated Jewish Charities, Balt., 1982; dir. U. Md. Found., 1991—; mem. Balt. Hebrew Cong. Mem. Woodholme Country Club. Republican. Jewish. Office: JB Schaftel Co Div Am Phoenix Corp 38 South St Baltimore MD 21202-3291

SCHAIBLE, RONALD DAVID, environmental consultant; b. E. Stroudsburg, Pa., Nov. 18, 1947; s. Russell and Jeannette Concordia (Jacobs) Schaible; m. Gloriajean Aumack, Dec. 21, 1968; children: Kathy-Jean, Deborah Lynn. BSCE, Drexel U., 1971; MS, Westchester U., 1990. Diplomate Am. Acad. Indsl. Hygiene; registered profl. engr.; registered environ. profl.; cert. safety exec.; cert. indsl. hygienist, others. Loss prevention rep. Liberty Mut. Ins. Co., Bala Cynwyd, Pa., 1971-72; loss control rep. Hartford Ins. Group, Phila., 1972-75; supr. safety and security The Cooper Group, Phila., 1975-76; ea. region safety dir. NL Industries, Hightstown, N.J., 1976-77; mgr. safety and indsl. hygiene AMP Inc., Harrisburg, Pa., 1977—; prin. cons. Schaible Assocs., Mt. Joy, Pa., 1982—; adj. instr. Millersville (Pa.) U., 1984—. Contbr. articles to profl. jours. With USAR, 1970-76. Mem. Am. Indsl. Hygiene Assn., Am. Soc. Safety Engrs., Am. Conf. on Chem. Labeling, Human Factors Soc., Coun. Indsl. Hygiene, World Safety Orgn. Baptist. Home: 900 Center St Mount Joy PA 17552-9371

SCHAIBLE, STEVEN REINHOLD, mental health professional; b. Elgin, N.D., July 10, 1958; s. Reinhold and Helen (Lorenz) S.; m. Elizabeth Andresakis, July 25, 1986; 1 child, Rian Rita. BA in Sociology, U. N.D., 1981; MS in Pub. Adminstrn., Sage Coll., 1991; MS in Counseling, SUNY, Plattsburgh, 1991. Employment coord. Adirondack House, Westport, N.Y., 1986-87; family support worker Assn. Retarded Children, Plattsburgh, 1986-88; clinician Franklin Grand Isle Mental Health Inst., St. Albans, Vt., 1987-88; asst. mgr. Electronics Boutique, Plattsburgh, 1988-90; cons. Dept. Social Svcs., Plattsburgh, 1990—; ombudsman, client advocate Sunmount Devel. Ctr., Tupper Lake, N.Y., 1988—; coord., cons. Child Abuse Prevention Coun., Plattsburgh, 1990-91. Mem. AACD, Pub. Offender Counseling Assn., Am. Rehab. Assn., Am. Assn. Mental Retardation. Home and Office: RFD 1 PO Box 328 North Moffit Rd West Chazy NY 12992

SCHALL, JOSEPH JULIAN, zoology educator; b. Phila., June 18, 1946; s. August H. and Melania A. (Ziemek) S.; m. Rene W. Schall, July 29, 1972. BS, Pa. State U., 1968; MS, U. R.I., 1972; PhD, U. Tex., 1976. Postdoctoral assoc. U. Calif., Berkeley, 1977-80; assoc. prof. zoology U. Vt., Burlington, 1980—; adv. panel on population biology NSF, Washington, 1990—. Contbr. articles to profl. jours. NSF grantee, 1976—; NIH grantee, 1978-80; Nat. Geog. Soc. grantee, 1981—. Office: U Vt Dept Zoology Burlington VT 05405

SCHALLICH, TERRENCE JAMES, company executive; b. Salinas, Calif., Dec. 21, 1961; s. Richard Louis and Norma Jo (Ladra) S.; m. Lisa Marie Kollar. BA, Yale U., 1984. Systems cons. United Technologies, Hartford, Conn., 1984-85; mktg. dir. Cheshire Mgmt. Co., Inc., Wallingford, Conn., 1985-87; ptnr. Catalyst Group, New Haven, 1987-88; v.p. Salsbury Properties, Inc., New Haven, 1988-90; pres., founder T.S. Foresight, Inc., New Haven, 1990—; mem. Am. Bankruptcy Inst., 1992—; treas., dir. Artspace, Inc., New Haven, 1986-90. Mem. Leadership Greater New Haven, 1986-87, planning com. United Way of New Haven, 1987-88. Mem. The Mory's Assn., O-Wen-E-Go Beach and Tennis Club, Steinert Soc. New Haven Symphony Orch. Republican. Office: TS Foresight Inc 636 Quinnipiac Ave New Haven CT 06513-4003

SCHALTENBRAND, PHILIP EDWARD, art educator; b. Sunbury, Pa., Feb. 4, 1944; s. Walter E. and Ruth Catherine (Mengel) S. BS, U. Pa., Kutztown, 1964; MS, Temple U., 1967. Art tchr. Blue Mountain Sch. Dist., Schulkill Haven, Pa., 1964-67; cermaics instr. Gov. Thomas Johnson High Sch., Frederick, Md., 1967-68; art prof. Calif. Univ. Pa., 1968—; co. pres. Westerwald Corp. Am., Pitts., 1987—; cons. Pfaltzgraf Pottery, York, Pa., 1989-90. Author: Old Pots, 1978; contbr. articles to profl. jours. Mem. steering com. Nat. Rd. Heritage Pk. Commn., S.W., Pa., 1991. Named Pa. Disting. Teaching chair Pa. Dept. Edn.,1 980. Mem. AAUP. Republican. Methodist. Home: RR 1 Scenery Hill PA 15360-9801 Office: Calif Univ Pa California PA 15419

SCHAMBERGER, WILLIAM GEORGE, JR., data processing professional; b. Washington, July 15, 1943; s. William George and Betty (Litaker) S.; m. Judith Ann Dorsett, Jan. 27, 1973; children: Jason Scott, Scott Gray. BS in Math., Duke U., 1965. Dir. systems and programming Steuart Investment Co., Washington, 1969-82; account systems engr. Info. Systems Services, IBM, Bethesda, Md., 1982-85, project mgr., 1985-86, adv. project mgr., 1986-89; location mgr So. Va. IBM SID, 1989-91, mgr. fed. sector svcs., Rockville, Md., 1991—; tech. data processing U. Md. With USAF, 1964-69. Mem. Data Processing Mgmt. Assn., Am. Mgmt. Assn. Republican. Presbyterian. Office: 13101 Woodsboro Dr Gaithersburg MD 20878-2138

SCHANELY, PATRICIA ANN, early childhood educator, child care consultant; b. Quakertown, Pa., July 15, 1953; d. Harry Lawrence and Dorothy (Clark) Lees; m. John Richard Schanely, Sept. 9, 1973; children: Philip Lawrence, Carissa May. BS in Early Childhood, Pa. State U., 1976. Tchr. The Children's Hour, Seattle, 1077-78, Beechwood Sch., Haddonfield, N.J., 1981-82; head tchr. Indian Mills (N.J.) Presch., 1982-83; ednl. supr. Alpha Acad., Cinnaminson, N.J., 1984-85; head tchr. Pleasant Valley Nursery Sch., Mt. Laurel, N.J., 1985-86; dir. Woodland Children's Ctr., Cherry Hill, N.J., 1986-88; child care resource and referral specialist Burlington County Community Action Program, Burlington, N.J., 1988-89; owner, pres. Creative Child Care Enterprises, Inc., Moorestown, N.J., 1989—; cons. Child Care Solution, Inc., Lansdale, Pa., 1989, Southern Regional Child Care Resource Ctr., Sewell, N.J., 1989-90, J'N K Day Care Ctr., Willingboro, N.J., 1990-91; parent educator Rutgers U. Extension, New Brunswick, N.J., 1990—. Founding mem. Burlington County Coalition for Children, Westhampton, N.J., 1991, Burlington County Sch.-Age Child Care Coalition, Westhampton, 1990-91; founding mem. Women's Network, Cherry Hill, 1990-91. Mem. Assn. Child Care Consultants Internat., Nat. Assn. Edn. Young Children, Nat. Assn. Child Care Profls., Nat. Assn. Women Bus. Owners. Democrat. Lutheran. Office: Creative Child Care Enterprises 35 Red Leaf Rd Moorestown NJ 08057-1222

SCHANTZ, MICHAEL WILLIAM, museum director; b. Allentown, Pa., Mar. 6, 1948; s. John Philip and Mildred Laura (Katzaman) S.; m. Linda Susan Held, Aug. 22, 1970; 1 child, Michael Christopher. BA in Sociology, Muhlenberg Coll., 1971; MA in Art History, San Diego State U., 1975; PhD in Art History, UCLA, 1988. Tech. asst. Phila. Mus. Art, 1975-76, exhibition asst., 1976-77, project supr., 1977; curatorial asst. Grunwald Ctr. for Graphic Arts UCLA, 1977-78, asst. dir., 1978-81; dir. Woodmere Art Mus., Phila., 1981—; juror Internat. Art Competition, N.Y.C., 1990, Am. Color Print Soc. Annual, Phila., 1989; peer reviewer Inst. Mus. Svcs., Washington, 1991. Author various exhibition catalogs. Bd. dirs. Chestnut Hill Community Assn., Phila., 1987-91. Mem. Am. Assn. Mus., Mid-Atlantic Mus. Assn., Mus. Coun. Phila. (treas. 1987-89), Phi Kappa Phi. Office: Woodmere Art Mus 9201 Germantown Ave Philadelphia PA 19118-2618

SCHAPER, LOUISE LEVY, communications executive; b. Utica, N.Y., July 8, 1950; d. Harry and Helen (Toffler) L. BS, N.Y. State U., 1972; MSW, Syracuse U., 1982, MLS, 1984. Mktg. info. specialist AT&T Bell Labs., Murray Hill, N.J., 1984-87, info. alerting and document supply services mgr., 1987-90, dept. head librs., 1990-91; head systems dept. lbir. U. Calif., San Diego, 1991—. Contbr. articles to profl. jours. Mem. Am. Soc. for Info. Sci. (chmn. standards com. 1987-88), Copyright Clearance Ctr. User Group (chair 1990-91). Office: Univ Calif Ctrl Libr 9500 Gilman Dr La Jolla CA 92093-0175

SCHAPIRO, JEROME BENTLEY, chemical company executive; b. N.Y.C., Feb. 7, 1930; s. Sol and Claire (Rose) S.; B.Chem. Engring., Syracuse U., 1951; postgrad. Columbia U., 1951-52; m. Edith Irene Kravet, Dec. 27, 1953; children: Lois, Robert, Kenneth. Project engr. propellents br. U.S. Naval Air Rocket Test Sta., Lake Denmark, N.J., 1951-52; with Dixo Co., Inc., Rochelle Park, N.J., 1954—, pres., 1966—; lectr. detergent standards, drycleaning, care labeling, consumers standards, orgns., U.S., 1968—; U.S. del. spokesman on drycleaning Internat. Standards Orgn., Newton, Mass., 1971, Brussels, 1972, U.S. del. spokesman on dimensional stability of textiles, Paris, 1974, Ottawa, 1977, Copenhagen, 1981; chmn. U.S. del. com. on consumer affairs, Geneva, 1974, 75, 76, spokesman U.S. del. on textiles, Paris, 1974, mem. U.S. del. on care labeling of textiles, The Hague, Holland, 1974, U.S. del., chmn. del. council com. on consumer policy, Geneva, 1978, 79, 82, Israel, 1980, Paris, 1981; leader U.S. del. com. on dimensional stability of textiles, Manchester, Eng., 1984; fed. govtl. appointee to Industry Functional Adv. Com. on Standards, 1980-81. Mem. Montclair (N.J.) Sch. Study Com., 1968-69; co-founder Jewish Focus, Inc., 1991, pub. Sullivan County Jewish Star. 2d lt. USAF, 1952-53. Mem. Am. Inst. Chem. Engrs., Am. Nat. Standards Inst. (vice chmn. bd. dirs., 1983-85 , exec. com. 1979-81, 83-85 , bd. dir. 1979-85, fin. com. 1982-85 , chmn. consumer council 1976, 79, 80, 81, mem. steering com. to advise Dept. Commerce on implementation GATT agreements 1976-77, mem. exec. standards coun., 1977-79), internat. standards coun., chmn. internat. consumer policy adv. com. 1978-86), Am. Assn. Textile Chemists and Colorists (mem. exec. com on rsch. 1974-77, chmn. com. on dry cleaning 1976-88, vice chmn. internat. test methods com.) Am. Chem. Soc., Standards Engring. Soc. (cert.), ASTM (award 1970, chmn. com. D-12 Soaps and Detergents, 1974-79, mem. standing com. on internat. standards 1980-84, hon. mem. award com. D-13, textiles), Internat. Standards Orgn. (mem. internat. standards steering com. for consumer affairs 1978-81), Nat. Small Bus. Assn. (assoc. trustee 1983-85). Jewish (v.p., treas. temple). Lodge: Masons. Home: PO Box 771 Wurtsboro NY 12790-0771 Office: PO Box 7038 158 Central Ave Rochelle Park NJ 07662-4003

SCHAPIRO, ROLF LUTZ, physician; b. Duren, Rhineland, Fed. Republic of Germany, Sept. 16, 1933; came to U.S., 1949; s. Leo and Clara (Denniger) S.; m. Dolores Isabel Kison, June 19, 1954; children: Douglas A., Steven R., Sandra L. BA, Adelbert Coll., 1959; MD, Western Res. U., 1964. Diplomate Am. Bd. Radiology. Resident Hosp. of U. Pa., Phila., 1964-69; asst. prof. radiology U. Iowa, Iowa City, 1969-71, assoc. prof. radiology, 1971-73, prof. radiology, 1973-79, vice chmn. dept. radiology, 1974-79, chmn. dept. radiology, 1977-79; chmn. dept. radiology Allegheny Gen. Hosp., Pitts., 1979—; prof. radiologic scis. Med. Coll. of Pa., Pitts., 1988—; editor in chief Conn. Jour. of Computed Tomography, Balt., 1977-80; bd. dirs. Allegheny Gen. Hosp., Integrated Health Care Svcs., Inc., Pitts. Author: Clinical Radiology of the Pediatric Abdomen and Gastrointestianl Tract, 1974, Atlas of Body Computed Tomography, 1980; contbr. numerous scientific publs. With U.S. Army, 1955-57. Fellow Am. Coll. Radiology; mem. AMA, Radiol. Soc. of N.Am., Roentgen Ray Soc., Computerized Med. Imaging Soc., Pa. Med. Soc. Republican. Methodist. Office: Allegheny Gen Hosp 320 E North Ave Pittsburgh PA 15212-4772

SCHAPPERLE, ROBERT FRANCIS, accountant; b. Phila., Dec. 19, 1946; s. John Francis and Elizabeth Catherine (Monahan) S.; m. Frances L. Dougherty; children: Michele, Bryan. BS, Villanova U., 1968; MBA, U. Pa., 1970. CPA, Pa., Del. Staff acct. Haskins & Sells, Phila., 1968-70; sr. acct. Haskins & Sells, 1970-74; mgr. Haskins & Sells, N.Y.C., 1974-78; ptnr. Deloitte Haskins & Sells, Phila., 1978-89, Deloitte & Touche, Phila., 1989—. Author book chpt. Recipient Alexander E. Loab award Pa. Inst. CPAs, 1970. Mem. Nat. Assn. Corp. Dirs. (treas. 1984-86, pres. 1986-88), Internat. Soc. Bacchus (treas. 1982—), Overbrook Golf Club. Home: 716 Hamilton Rd Bryn Mawr PA 19010-1106 Office: Deloitte & Touche 1700 Market St Philadelphia PA 19103-4113

SCHAR, STUART, art association administrator; b. Chgo., Aug. 27, 1941; s. Sidney and Lillian (Lieberman) S.; m. Bonnie Gail Goodof; children: Reid, Daniel. BFA in Indsl. Design, Art Inst. Chgo., 1963; MFA in Printmaking, U. Chgo., 1964, PhD in Arts Adminstrn., 1967. Adminstrv. asst. to chancellor U. Ill., Chgo., 1969-71, acting dir. ctr. for urban studies, 1970-75; dir. sch. art Kent (Ohio) State U., 1975-83; prof. La. State U., Baton Rouge, 1983-86; interim dean Hartt Sch. of Music U. Hartford, Conn., 1989-90, dean Hartford Art Sch., 1986—, assoc. v.p. for the arts, 1990—; edn. cons. U. Mich. at Dearborn, 1972-74; rsch. cons. Found. of Interior Design Edn., N.Y., 1985. Recipient G.M. Purchase prize Art Inst. Chgo., 1974, Best of Show award Midway Studios, 1972. Office: U Hartford 200 Bloomfield Ave West Hartford CT 06117-1500

SCHARF, BERTRAM, acoustics educator, researcher; b. N.Y.C., Mar. 3, 1931; s. Louis Gershon and Nettie (Fink) S.; m. Anna-Liisa Pylvänen, Apr. 10, 1965; children: Riitta Liisa, Jonathan Lauri. BA, CCNY, 1953; diploma, U. Paris, 1955; PhD, Harvard U., 1958. Prof. psychology Northeastern U., Boston, 1958—; vis. researcher Nat. Ctr. for Sci. Rsch., Marseille, France, 1978—. Co-editor: Sensory Measurement, 1975; editor: Experimental Sensory Psychology, 1976. Fellow AAAS, Acoustical Soc. Am. (assoc. editor Jour. 1977-81); mem. Internat. Soc. for Psychophysics (exec. com. 1985-90). Home: 22 Chestnut Pl Brookline MA 02146-7565 Office: Northeastern U 413 MU Boston MA 02115

SCHARFF, CONSTANCE KRAMER, artist; b. Bklyn.; d. Charles and Rebecca (Blankfort) Kramer; m. Harry Scharff (dec.); 1 child, Matthew. Studied painting and printmaking with Adja Younkers, Louis Shanker, Bklyn. Exhibited in group shows at Libr. of Congress, Bklyn. Mus., Silvermine Guild, Einstein Coll. Medicine, Greenville Mus., Lenox Libr., maj. N.Y. galleries; represented in permanent collections Bkln. Mus., Smithsonian Archives, Butler Inst., Phila. Mus. Art, Norfolk Mus., Ga. Mus. Art, Columbia U., N.Y. Pub. Libr., Inst. Jamaica. Mem. Soc. Am. Graphic Artists, Nat. Assn. Painters in Consein Acrylic (rec. sec. 1977-89, Elsie Ject Key award 1988), Artists Equity, Audubon Artists (Medal of Honor. Home and Office: 115 Jaffrey St Brooklyn NY 11235-3022

SCHARFF, MONROE BERNARD, investor relations consultant; b. Boston, Sept. 8, 1923; s. Bernard Wertheimer and Minette (Switzer) S.; m. Edwina Kuhn, June 30, 1949; children: Peter Bernard, Stuart Monroe. BA, Columbia U., 1948. V.p. Cold Cathode Corp., N.Y.C., 1951-56; pres. Monroe B. Scharff & Co., N.Y.C., 1957—, Swofford & Scharff, N.Y.C., 1980-88; sr. cons. for investor rels. Doremus and Co. (merged with Swofford and Scharff), 1988—; bd. dirs. YMCA Greater N.Y., 1970-85, Ingalls Assocs., Boston, 1983—. Trustee Forman Sch., Litchfield, Conn., 1968—, Portland Mus. Art, 1985; bd. dirs. YMCA Greater N.Y., 1970-85, Found. for Blood Rsch., 1986—. 1st lt. USAF, 1943-46, 1951-52. MEM. Arundel Yacht Club, Camden Yacht Club, Kennebunk River Club, Army and Navy Club, Cumberland Club, City Midday Club. Republican.

SCHARFMAN, SCOTT PHILLIP, investment banker; b. N.Y.C., May 14, 1962; s. Melvin Allen and Helen (Brachfeld) S. AB cum laude, Princeton (N.J.) U., 1986. Co-founder, pres. Students for the Exploration and Devel. of Space, 1980-86; analyst The First Boston Corp., N.Y.C., 1986-88, assoc., 1988-91; assoc. The Blackstone Group, N.Y.C., 1991-92, v.p., 1992—. Mem. Princeton Club of N.Y., Sigma Xi. Office: Blackstone Group 345 Park Ave New York NY 10154-0004

SCHARY, EMANUEL, artist; b. Feb. 27, 1924; s. Harold and Aliza S.; m. Judith Schary, Sept. 23, 1951; children: Abby, David, Anne. Student, Carnegie Inst. Tech. Sch. Fine Arts, 1945-46, Art Students League, 1946-49, Pratt Graphics Ctr., 1962-63, Edwin Dickenson, Howard Trafton, Frank Reilly, Ivan Olinsky, Robert Hale, Jurgen Fischer. One-man shows, Guild Gallery, N.Y.C., 1978, 80, 81, group shows, Tel Aviv, Kean Coll., Bklyn. Mus., Kansas City Country Club Plaza, Mo., U. Mich., U. Miami, Fla., Nassau Community Coll., Lenox Square Art Festival, Ga., Guild Gallery, N.Y.; represented in permanent collections, Smithsonian Nat. Fine Art Collection, Met. Mus. Fine Art, N.Y., Vatican Mus., Rome, Bklyn Mus., Jewish Mus., N.Y.C., Spertus Mus., Chgo., Madison Art Mus., Wis., Fleming Mus., Vt., Wyo. Art Mus., Laramie, B'nai B'rith Mus., Washington, Mus. of Israel, Jerusalem, Mus. of Haifa, Israel, Bldg. of Chief Rabbinate, Jerusalem, New Britain Mus. Am. Art, Ind. Mus. Am. Art, Ga. Mus. Art, Hofstra U. Mus., Boston Pub. Library, N.Y. Pub. Library, Newark Pub. Library, U. Ariz. Art Mus., Kansas City Art Inst., Library of Congress, in pvt. collections, commns. include, N.Y. World's Fair Pavillion, Weizmann Inst. Sci., 1964; designed 4 stained glass painted windows for Synagogue, Rock Hill, N.Y., 1992. Address: 8 Nottingham Gate Rock Hill NY 12775

SCHARY, WILLIAM LEE, pharmaceutical executive, clinical researcher; b. San Francisco, July 31, 1948; s. Sigmund Lee Jr. and Thomasine Martha (Friday) S.; m. Deborah Graff, Aug. 2, 1975; children: Dawn Elizabeth, David Paul. BA, U. Calif., San Diego, 1971; MS, U. Calif., San Francisco, 1974; PhD, Victoria U., Manchester, Eng., 1978. Pharmacologist reviewer U.S. FDA, Rockville, Md., 1979-82; assoc. dir. E. I. DuPont deNemours, Wilmington, Del., 1982-86, Eastman Kodak Pharm., Rochester, N.Y., 1986-87; dir. Internat. Drug Registration, Rockville, Md., 1987-89; pres. Pharm. R&D Svcs., Frederick, Md., 1989-90; v.p. New Drug Svcs., Inc., Kennett Sq., Pa., 1990—. Contbr. numerous articles to profl. jours. Active in Rotary Club, Wilmington, Del., 1984-86. Fellow Am. Coll. Clin. Pharm.; mem. Am. Assn. Pharm. Scientists, AAAS, Assocs. Clin. Pharm., Drug Info. Assn., Regulatory Affairs Profls. Soc. Office: New Drug Services Inc 415 Mcfarlan Rd Ste 201 Kennett Square PA 19348-2454

SCHATTSCHNEIDER, DAVID ALLEN, religion educator; b. Phila., Mar. 30, 1939; s. Allen Wilbur and Naomi (Wartman) S.; m. Doris Jean Wood, June 2, 1962; children: Laura, Ellen. BA, Moravian Coll., Bethlehem, Pa., 1960; MDiv, Yale U., 1964; MA, U. Chgo. Div. Sch., 1966, PhD, 1975. Ordained to ministry, 1969. Instr. in hist. theology Moravian Theol. Sem., Bethlehem, 1968-71, asst. prof., 1971-78, assoc. prof., 1978-86, S. Morgan Smith and Emma Fahs Smith prof., 1986—, dean, v.p., 1988—; mem. investment policy com. Moravian Ch. in Am., Bethlehem, 1981—; cons. Gateway Films, 1982, 87. Author: (with others) Penn's Example to the Nations: 300 Years of the Holy Experiment, 1987; also articles; mem. editorial bd. James Burnside Bull., 1989—. Chmn. bd. Pinebrook Svcs. for Children/Youth, Whitehall, Pa., 1989—. Assn. Theol. Schs. grantee, 1981-82. Mem. Am. Hist. Assn., Am. Soc. Ch. History, Am. Soc. Missiology, Moravian Hist. Soc. (bd. mgrs. 1980—). Home: 2038 Sycamore St Bethlehem PA 18017-5118

SCHATTSCHNEIDER, DORIS JEAN, mathematics educator; b. N.Y.C., Oct. 19, 1939; d. Robert W. Jr. and Charlotte Lucille (Ingalls) Wood; m. David A. Schattschneider, June 2, 1962; 1 child, Laura E. AB, U. Rochester, 1961; MA, Yale U., 1963, PhD, 1966. Instr. in math. Northwestern U., Evanston, Ill., 1964-65; asst. prof. U. Ill., Chgo., 1965-68; prof. Moravian Coll., Bethlehem, Pa., 1968—. Author: Visions of Symmetry, 1990, book and models (with W. Walker) M.C. Escher Kaleidocycles, 1977, 87; co-author videos and activities: Visual Geometry Project, 1986-91. Exhbn. curator Allentown Art Mus., 1979, Payne Gallery, 1987. NEH rsch. grantee, 1988-90. Mem. Math. Assn. Am. (editor 1980-85, gov. 1980-89, Allendoerfer award 1979, Meritorious Svc. award 1991), Am. Math. Soc., Assn. for Women in Math., Pi Mu Epsilon (councillor 1990—). Mem. Moravian Ch. Office: Moravian Coll Math Dept 1200 Main St Bethlehem PA 18018-6650

SCHATZ, JULES LEONARD, marketing professional; b. Phila., Dec. 31, 1920; s. Harry A. and Rosalie (Abuhove) S.; m. Sylvia Lieberman, June 20, 1948; children: Ellen Pollack, Gordon B., Mark L., David R. BA, U. Pa., 1942, MBA, 1947. Market rsch. analyst Chilton Co., Inc., Phila., 1947-48; adminstrv. asst. to sales mgr. Penn Fruit Co., Inc., Phila., 1949-60; sr. rsch. analyst Pillsbury Co., Inc., Mpls., 1960-62; dir. rsch. Allied Supermarkets, Inc., Detroit, 1963-64, Stop and Shop Cos., Inc., Boston, 1964-69, Zayre Corp., Natick, Mass., 1969-73; pres. J.L. Schatz Rsch., Inc., Lexington, Mass., 1974—. Contbg. author: Marketing Practices, Vol. 1, 1985; author monthly column, New Eng. Real Estate Jour., 1985—. 1st lt. U.S. Army Signal Corps, 1943-46. Mem. Food Distbn. Rsch. Soc., Am. Mktg. Assn. (pres. Boston chpt. 1977-78), Retail Mktg. Soc. (pres. 1972-73), Internat. Coun. Shopping Ctrs. Democrat. Jewish. Office: J L Schatz Rsch Inc 135 Worthen Rd Lexington MA 02173-7019

SCHATZ, JULIUS, cultural organization consultant; b. N.Y.C., Aug. 3, 1915; s. Max and Freda (Chervin) S.; m. Sophie Sipser, July 2, 1944; children: William Paul, Eric Lawrence. BA, NYU, 1934, MA in Sci., 1936. Cert. tchr., N.Y. Dir. commn. on Jewish life and culature Am. Jewish Congress, dir. Martin Steinberg Ctr., dir. nat. commn. on youth, dept. community svcs., cons. fedns.; cons. media Am. Friends of Hebrew U.; cons. Commn. on Yiddish for the World Jewish Congree; mem. U.S. Holocaust Meml. Coun.; chmn. Com. on Acquistions and Arts for the U.S. Holocaust Meml. Mus. Contbr. numerous articles to profl. jours. Past sec. Friends of the Ida Kaminska Theatre Found.; past mem. exec. com. N.Y. Film Coun., Film Coun. Am.; bd. dirs. Jewish Nat. Fund, Yiddish Nath. Theatre, Congress for Jewish Culture; mem. cultural arts adv. com. Fedn. Jewish Philanthropies of N.Y. Mem. N.Y. State Ednl. Radio and TV Assn. Home: 92-31 57th Ave Elmhurst NY 11373 Office: Am Jewish Congress 15 E 84th St New York NY 10028

SCHAUBERT, DANIEL HAROLD, electrical engineering educator; b. Galesburg, Ill., Feb. 15, 1947; s. Robert Harold and Carolyn Virginia (Dunkle) S.; m. Joyce Marie Conard, June 15, 1968; 1 child, Karen Louise. BSEE, U. Ill., 1969, MS, 1970, PhD, 1974. Rsch. engr. U.S. Army Harry Diamond Labs., Adelphi, Md., 1977-80; rsch. engr., program mgr. U.S. Bur. Radiol. Health, Rockville, Md., 1980-82; prof. elec. enging. U. Mass., Amherst, 1982—. Patentee in field. 1st lt. U.S. Army, 1974-77. Fellow IEEE, IEEE Antennas and Propagation Soc. (membership chair 1980-82, editor newsletter 1982-84, sec.-treas. 1984-88). Office: U Mass Elec and Computer Enging Amherst MA 01003

SCHAUER, RICHARD COSTELLO, biology educator; b. Pitts., July 21, 1937; s. Elmer Costello and Lorene (Coleman) Forney; m. Ruth Vanstory, Jan. 30, 1969; children: Dana, Jason. MS, N.C. State U., 1968, PhD, 1972. High sch. tchr. Rich East High Sch., Park Forest, Ill., 1963-67; instr. U. N.C., Greensboro, 1971-72, asst. prof., 1972-78; assoc. prof. Gannon U., Erie, Pa., 1978—. Contbr. articles to profl. jours. Instructional equipment grant NSF, 1979, faculty rsch. grant Gannon U., 1982-90, rsch. coun. grants U. N.C., 1971-78, rsch. grant Sigmund Sterberger Found., 1975; recipient Excellence in Teaching award Sears Roebuck, 1991. Mem. AAAS, Pa. Acad. Sci., N.Y. Acad. Sci., Sigma Xi. Office: Gannon U University Square Erie PA 16541

SCHAUFELE, WILLIAM E., JR., retired U.S. ambassador; b. Lakewood, Ohio, Dec. 7, 1923; s. William Elias and Lillian (Bergen) S.; m. Heather Moon, Feb. 1, 1950; children: Steven W., Peter H. BA, Yale U., 1948; MIA, Columbia U., 1950. Resident officer Dept. of State, Pfaffenhofen, Ilm, Germany, 1950-52, Augsburg, Germany, 1952; vice consul Dept. of State, Duesseldorf, Germany, 1952-53, Munich, Germany, 1953-55; various positions Dept. of State, Washington, 1956-59; vice consul Dept. of State, Casablanca, Morocco, 1959-63; consul Dept. of State, Bukavu, Congo, 1963-64; Congo desk officer Dept. of State, 1964-65, alt. country dir. ctr. African affairs, 1965-67; U.S. amb. Ouagadougou (Upper Volta), 1969-71; amb. dep. U.S. rep. UN Security Coun., 1971-75; insp. gen. U.S. Fgn. Svc., 1975; asst. sec. of state for African affairs Dept. of State, 1975-77; U.S. amb. Poland, Warsaw, 1978-80; pres. Fgn. Policy Assn., 1980-83; dir. Inst. of World Affairs, 1983-89; sr. dir. for Africa Cath. Relief Svcs., 1985-87; ind. cons. Salisbury, Conn., 1987—; dir. Fgn. Policy Assn., N.Y.C., 1980-84, Helsinki Watch, N.Y.C., 1983—, Am. Forum for Global Edn., N.Y.C., 1983—. Author: Polish Paradox, 1981; contbr. articles to profl. jours. With AUS, 1943-46, ETO. Recipient Wilbur Carr award Dept. of State, 1980, Disting. Alumnus award Columbia U., 1981. Mem. Yale Club, Am. Acad. Diplomacy, Coun. on Fgn. Rels., Am. Fgn. Svc. Assn., Diplomatic and Consular Officers Ret. Democrat. Home and Office: Box 797 115 Undermountain Rd Salisbury CT 06068

SCHAUMBURGER, JOSEPH ZALMON, publishing executive; b. N.Y.C., June 28, 1930; s. Leo and Lillian Natalie (Fleck) S.; BA, CCNY, 1961; postgrad. NYU, 1971-72; m. Dorothy Constas, Sept. 11, 1959 (dec.); m. Nancy Engbretsen, Nov. 11, 1983. Head mail order dept. Haber & Fink, Inc., N.Y.C., 1953-55; sr. advt. billing exec. Gotham-Vladimir Advt., Inc., N.Y.C., 1955-56; asst. exec. sec. Synthetic Organic Chem. Mfrs. Assn., N.Y.C., 1956-61; asst. v.p., advt. mgr. Bus. & Profl. Books div. Prentice-Hall, Inc., Englewood Cliffs, N.J., 1961-81, asst. v.p., advt. mgr. Exec. Reports Corp., 1981-83, v.p., 1984-86; mng. editor DAW Books, Inc., 1986— . Committeeman 6th dist. Democratic Com., Closter, N.J., 1979-83. Served with U.S. Army, 1948-50. Mem. Direct Mail Mktg. Assn., Pascack Art Assn., Sci. Fiction Writers Am., N.J. Sci. Fiction Soc. (past pres.) Dickens Fellowship N.Y., Dickens Fellowship Westchester (pres., bd. dirs.), Nat. Fantasy Fan Fedn. Jewish. Author: Ultra-Psychonics, 1975. Home: 78 Westervelt Pl Cresskill NJ 07626-1620 Office: DAW Books Inc 375 Hudson St New York NY 10014-3672

SCHECHTER, CLIFFORD, financial executive, lawyer; b. N.Y.C., Feb. 14, 1958; s. Howard and Diana D. (Eiss) S.; m. Niely Okonsky, June 17, 1979; children: Dana Ann, Adam Hillel, Talia Beth. BS summa cum laude, U. R.I., 1979; JD, Fordham U. Sch. Law, 1982; MBA, L.I. U., 1988. Bar: N.Y. 1983, U.S. Tax Ct. 1983, U.S. Supreme Ct. 1986, D.C. 1990, U.S. Dist. Ct. (so. and ea. dists.) N.Y.; lic. Nat. Assn. Securities Dealers. Tax supr. Touche Ross & Co., Jericho, N.Y., 1982-86; sr. v.p., dir. taxes L.F. Rothschild & Co. Inc., N.Y.C., 1986-91, chief fin. officer, dir. adminstrn. and taxes, 1991—; adj. prof., Adelphi U., Garden City, N.Y., 1983-91, Pace U., N.Y.C., 1991—. Bd. dirs. P.A.D. Pub. Svc. Ctr., Washington, 1986—, Congregation Chabad of Rancho Bernardo and Poway. Recipient U. R.I. award for Scholastic Excellence in Fin., 1979, Uniroyal Found. Fellowship award, 1978, Am. Jurisprudence award Scholastic Excellence in Estate Planning, 1982; named to Dean's List, U. R.I. (8 times), 1975-79, Nat. Dean's List, 1978. Mem. ABA, Internat. Assn. Fin. Planning, N.Y. State Bar Assn., D.C. Bar Assn., Bar Assn. Nassau County, Securities Industry Assn. Fin. Mgmt. Div., Wall St. Tax. Assn. (elected mem.), Phi Alpha Delta (internat. hist. 1990—, internat. marshal 1988-90, internat. proctor 1986-88, dist. XV justice 1984-86, Stan P. Jones Meml. award 1984-85, Outstanding Active Mem. award 1981-82, Outstanding Alumnus mem. Wormser chpt. 1982-85), Beta Gamma Sigma, Phi Kappa Phi, Fin. Mgmt. Assn. Republican. Jewish. Home: 14376 Twisted Branch Rd Poway CA 92064 Office: L F Rothschild & Co Inc 55 Water St New York NY 10041-0002

SCHECHTER, JOSEPH MICHAEL, physics educator; b. N.Y.C., Sept. 28, 1938; s. David and Eva (Horowitz) S.; m. Virginia Anne Carson, June 30, 1973; children: David, Warren, Benjamin. BEE, Cooper Union, 1959; PhD, U. Rochester, 1965. Postdoctoral rsch. assoc. U. Chgo., 1965-67; asst. prof. physics Syracuse (N.Y.) U., 1967-70, assoc. prof., 1971-74, prof., 1974—. Contbr. articles to profl. jours. Fellow Am. Phys. Soc. Home: 205 Berkley Dr Syracuse NY 13210-3039 Office: Syracuse U Physics Dept Syracuse NY 13244-1130

SCHECHTER, MARSHALL DAVID, psychiatrist, educator; b. Chgo., Sept. 4, 1921; s. Joseph and Bessie (Czapler) S.; (div.); children: Judi, Cid, Nicole, Paul; m. Ann B., June 8, 1973. BS, U. Wis., 1942; MD, U. Cin., 1944; MS, U. Pa., 1980. Diplomate Am. Bd. Psychiatry and Neurology, diplomate Am. Bd. Psychiatry and Neurology Child Psychology. Assoc. clin. prof. psychiatry UCLA, L.A., 1953-64; prof. child and adolescent psychiatry U. Okla., Oklahoma City, 1964-73, prof. biol. psychiatry, 1964-73, prof. pediatrics, 1964-73; prof. child and adolescent SUNY Upstate Med. Ctr., Syracuse, 1973-76; prof. child and adolescent U. Pa., Phila., 1976-86, prof. emeritus child and adolescent psychiatry, 1986—; Author, editor: Psychology of Adoption, 1990, Being Adopted, 1991. Capt. USMC, 1945-47. Named Disting. profl. Wilford Hall USAF, San Antonio, 1966-89. Fellow APA (life), Am. Acad. Child and Adolescent Psychiatry; mem. Am. Psychoanalytic Assn. (life), Soc. for Rsch. in Child Devel., Soc. Profl. Child and Adolescent Psychiatry, Alpha Omega Alpha. Home and Office: 1142 Morris Rd Wynnewood PA 19096-2313

SCHECHTER, PETER DAVID, communications consultant; b. Rome, June 12, 1959; came to U.S., 1973; s. Edmund and Gerda (Frankley) S. BA, Johns Hopkins U., 1980, MA in Internat. Studies, 1982. Producer Nat. Pub. Radio, Washington, 1983; legis. asst. to Congressman Doug Bereuter of Nebr., U.S. Ho. of Reps., Washington, 1983-85, minority staff dir. subcom. on internat. devel. instns.-fin., 1985-87; mng. dir. Sawyer-Miller Group, Washington, 1987—. Contbr. articles to profl. jours. Campaign mgr. presdl. elections, Colombia, Ecuador, Chile, Argentina, 1987—. Home: 2716 P St NW Washington DC 20007-3064

SCHECTMAN, STEPHEN BARRY, investment banker; b. Washington, Oct. 20, 1947; s. Samuel and Rae (Tarnef) S.; m. Barbara Lea Butcher, Sept. 10, 1969; children: Christopher, Matthew. BS, Randolph-Macon Coll., 1969; postgrad., U. Tenn., 1969-74, Georgetown U., 1974-75. Staff scientist Enviro Control Inc., Rockville, Md., 1975-76; sr. cons. JRB Assocs. Inc., McLean, Va., 1976-78; dir. IMS Am. Ltd., Washington, 1979-81; pres., founder Alpha 1 Biomeds. Inc., Washington, 1981-84; pres. Research Data Corp., Haddenfield, N.J., 1984-85; pres., chief exec. officer Large Scale Biology Corp., Rockville, 1985-88; mng. ptnr. Encore Group, Inc., Rockville, Md., 1988—; mng. dir. Arrionga Capital Corp., Greenwich, Conn., 1989—, Rain Hill Group, N.Y., 1990—; cons. MEDCO Containment Svcs., Inc./ Med. Mktg. Group, Inc. Author: (with others) Biomedical Innovation, 1981. NIMH fellow U. Tenn., 1969-73. Mem. AAAS, Am. Mgmt. Assn., Beta Beta Beta. Jewish.

SCHEDLER, SPENCER JAIME, financial consultant; b. Manila, Philippines, Oct. 23, 1933; s. Edmund W. and Ruth (Spencer) S.; m. Judy Hamilton, Aug. 30, 1969; children: Ryan Edmund, Spencer Hamilton, Peter Joseph. BS, U. Tulsa, 1955; MBA, Harvard U., 1962. Petroleum engr. Humble Oil & Refining Co., 1957-60; fin. analyst Sinclair Oil Corp., Tulsa, 1963-65; asst. dir. budgets Sinclair Oil Corp., N.Y.C., 1965-66, mgr. budgets and fin. analysis for mfg. and mktg., 1966-67, corp. mgr. budget and analysis, 1968-69; asst. Sec. of Air Force, 1969-73; exec. v.p. Hycel Inc., Houston, 1973-74; gen. mgr., asst. to vice chmn. fin. and adminstrn. Continental Can Co., Inc., N.Y.C., 1974-76; gen. mgr. corp. bus. devel. Continental Group, Inc., N.Y.C., 1977-81, chief resources staff, 1981-82; v.p. Continental Resources Co., N.Y.C., 1982-83; pres. Maxam Corp. (cons. in U.S. acquisitions to maj. fgn. cos.), N.Y.C., 1984—; bd. dirs. Myers Group Inc., Hunneman Real Estate Corp. Served as pilot USAF, 1955-58. Office: PO Box 542 Old Greenwich CT 06870-0542

SCHEER, R. SCOTT, physician; b. N.Y.C., Oct. 24, 1938; s. Leonard and Josephine (Holtschl) S.; m. Beverly Joan Henry Scheer, Dec. 27, 1940; children: Kirsten Leigh, Laura Lynn. AB, Cornell U., 1960; MD, SUNY, Buffalo, 1965. Diplomate Am. Bd. Radiology, Am. Bd. Nuclear Medicine. Intern Santa Barbara (Calif.) Cottage Hosp., 1965-66; resident Cornell Univ.-N.Y. Hosp., 1966, Phila. (Pa.) Gen. Hosp., 1968-71; staff radiologist Meth. Hosp., Phila., 1971-72; assoc. dir. radiology Coatesville (Pa.) Hosp., 1972-77; dir. dept. of radiology Norristown (Pa.) State Hosp., 1973—; dir., chief exec. officer Med. Imaging Svcs., Exton, Pa., 1977—; cons. radiol. expert, 1981—; cons. radiologist Pottstown Meml. Med. Ctr., 1977—; cons. in magnetic resonance imaging Fonar Corp., 1990—. Capt. U.S. Army Med. Corps, 1966-68. Recipient N.Y. State Regents Med. scholarship, 1961. Mem. AMA, Am. Coll. of Radiology, Radiol. Soc. of N.Am., Pa. Med. Soc., Pa. Radiol. Soc., Phila. Roentgen Ray Soc., Soc. of Magnetic Resonance in Medicine, Chester County Med. Soc., Am. Inst. of Ultrasound in Medicine, Pa. Coll. Nuclear Medicine, Valley Forge Mountain Racquet Assn. Republican. Presbyterian. Office: Med Imaging Svcs 80 W Welsh Pool Rd Ste 101N Exton PA 19341-1233

SCHEIBEL, LEONARD WILLIAM, physician, pharmacologist, educator; b. Hays, Kans., Jan. 18, 1938; s. Raymond Philip and Thelma (Bane) S.; m. Melania Parada Valdes, May 1, 1976; children: Leonard William Jr., Raymond Philip. BS, Creighton U., 1960, MS, 1962; DS, Johns Hopkins U., 1967; MD, U. Fla., 1973. Diplomate Am. Bd. Clin. Pharmacology, Am. Bd. Preventive Medicine, Nat. Bd. Medical Examiners. Rotating intern Gorgas Hosp., Balboa Heights, Canal Zone, 1973-74, resident internal medicine, 1974-77; rsch. biochemist, capt. U.S. Army Walter Reed Army Inst. Rsch., Washington, 1967-70; rsch. assoc. dept. pharmacology U. Fla., Gainesville, 1970-73; asst. prof., lab. parasitology and staff physician Rockefeller U. and Hosp., N.Y.C., 1977-81; adj. assoc. prof. dept. microbiology U. Md., Balt., 1982-86; assoc. dept. immunology and infectious diseases Johns Hopkins U., Balt., 1982—; asst. prof. dept. preventive medicine and biometrics Uniformed Svcs. U. of the Health Scis., Bethesda, Md., 1981-82, assoc. prof. dept. preventive medicine and biometrics, 1982-86, prof. preventive medicine, biometrics, pharmacology depts., 1986—; cons. Pan American Health Orgn., Panama City, Panama, 1979, Environ. Applications Rsch., San Antonio, Tex., 1984—, Med. Svc. Cons., Inc., Arlington, Va., 1978, various other orgns. Contbr. over 45 articles to profl. jours. Recipient Cert. of Achievement Walter Reed Army Inst. of Rsch., 1970, Faculty Rsch. award U. Fla., 1973, Igor I. Sikorsky Helicopter Rescue award Republic of Panama, 1973. Fellow Infectious Diseases Soc. Am., Am. Coll. Physicians, Am. Coll. Preventive Medicine; mem. AMA (physicians recognition award 1979-93), Fedn. Am. Soc. Exptl. Biology, Am. Soc. Pharmacology and Exptl. Therapeutics (div. clin. pharmacology and drug metabolism), Am. Soc. Clin. Pharmacology and Therapeutics, Am. Soc. Tropical Medicine, Am. Soc. Parasitologists, N.Y. Soc. Tropical Medicine, numerous other orgns. Office: Uniformed Svc U Med Sch 4301 Jones Bridge Rd Bethesda MD 20814-4799

SCHEICH, JOHN F., lawyer; b. Bklyn., Aug. 6, 1942; s. Frank A. and Dorothy (O'Hara) S. BA, St. John's U., N.Y.C., 1963, JD, 1966. Bar: N.Y. 1967, U.S. Customs Ct. 1969, U.S. Dist. Ct. (ea. and so. dists.) N.Y. 1971, U.S. Ct. Appeals (2d cir.) 1971, U.S. Supreme Ct. 1975, Pa. 1980. Spl. agt. FBI U.S. Dept. Justice, Washington, 1966-69; asst. dist. atty. Queens County, Kew Gardens, N.Y., 1969-72; pvt. practice Richmond Hill and Hicksville, N.Y., 1972—, Milford, Pa., 1980—; mem. assigned counsel panel for indigent defendants in maj. felony and murder cases, 9th and 11th jud. dists. N.Y. State Supreme Ct., Queens County, 1972—; lectr. Lawyers in the Classroom, 1979—; chmn. arbitration panel Civil Ct. of City of N.Y., 1981-90; bd. dirs. Ra-Li Brokerage Corp., v.p., 1975—. Editor: Conashaugh Courier, 1989-92; mem. editorial bd., 1988-92; contbg. columnist, 1981-89. Mem. Com. for Beautification of East Norwich, N.Y., 1983—; pres. local chpt. Holy Name Soc., 1971-73; bd. dirs. Conashaugh Lakes Community Assn., 1981-90, organizing mem., interim com., 1977-81, pres., 1984-86; mem. St. Edward's Syosset Sch. Bd., 1986-90; mem. parish coun. Our Lady of Perpetual Help, 1976-82, pres., 1978-80, mem. fin. com., advisor to pastor, 1970-82, chmn. fin. com., 1979-82; bd. dirs. Northslope II Homeowners Assn., Shawnee-on-Delaware, Pa., 1988-90, 92—; v.p. East Norwich Rep. Club, 1987-89, pres., 1989—; mem. Internat. Wine Ctr., 1985—. Recipient J. Edgar Hoover award, 1967, award of appreciation, Civil Trial Inst., St. John's U. Sch. of Law, Disting. Svc. award, 1992, cert. of appreciation Conashaugh Lakes Community Assn., 1990, Dist. Svc. award Kiwanis Club, 1992, Cert. of Merit for Disting. Svc. award Hon. Thomas Gulotta, 1989, Presdl. Order of Merit award Pres. George Bush, 1991; named one of Best Trial Lawyers in the U.S., Town and Country mag., 1985. Mem. ABA (cert. of appreciation Am. Bar Endowment 1992), Pa. Bar Assn., Pike County Bar Assn., N.Y. State Bar Assn., Queens County Bar Assn., Nassau County Bar Assn., N.Y. State Trial Laywers Assn., Criminal Cts. Bar Assn., Internat. Platform Assn., John Marshall Lawyers Assn. (organizing), Soc. Former Spl. Agts. of FBI, N.Y. State Assn. Criminal Def. Lawyers, St. John's Coll. Alumni Assn., Asst. Dist. Attys. Assn. Queens County, St. John's U. Sch. of Law Alumni Assn., Friends of the Arts, Cath. Lawyers Guild, KC, Phi Alpha Delta. Home: 170 Sugar Toms Ln East Norwich NY 11732-1153 Office: 103-42 Lefferts Blvd Richmond Hill NY 11419-2012 also: 109 Newbridge Rd Hicksville NY 11801

SCHEIN, JONAH WALTER, psychiatrist; b. N.Y.C., Mar. 22, 1945; s. Stephen and Ethel (Barrett) S.; m. Carla Salomon, June 1, 1969; children: Alexandra, Gabrielle Jeremy. AB, Columbia U., 1965; MD, NYU, 1969. Diplomate Am. Bd. Psychiatry and Neurology. Intern Bellevue Hosp. Ctr., N.Y.C., 1969-70; resident N.Y. State Psychiat. Inst., 1970-73; asst. clin. prof. psychiatry Cornell Med. Coll., N.Y.C., 1980—; staff psychoanalyst Columbia U., N.Y.C., 1980—, tng. analyst, 1988—. Mem. Am. Psychiat. Assn., Am. Psychoanalytic Assn. Office: 1349 Lexington Ave New York NY 10128-1511

SCHEINER, LILLIAN CLAIRE, psychologist; b. N.Y.C., Oct. 15, 1937; d. Irving and Bertha (Feigenbaum) Solomon; m. Louis Scheiner, Aug. 24, 1955. BS in Sci., Bklyn. Coll., 1957; MS in Sci., U. of N.Y. State, 1960; D in Edn., Temple U., 1972. Supr. dr. interns, lectr. Temple U., Phila., 1971-75; sr. clin. psychologist City Health Svcs., Camden, N.J., 1973-83; pvt. practice Westmont, N.J., 1977—, Phila., 1977—. Office: 326 Haddon Ave Collingswood NJ 08108-2825

SCHEINKMAN, ALAN DAVID, legal educator; b. Newark, May 1, 1950; s. Henry R. and Gertrude (Einhorn) S.; m. Deborah Steinberg, July 1, 1978; children: Michael, Rebecca. BA, George Washington U., 1972; JD, St. John's U., Jamaica, N.Y., 1975. Bar: N.Y. 1976, U.S. Dist. Ct. (so. and ea. dists.) N.Y. 1977, U.S. Supreme Ct. 1990. Law clk. N.Y. Ct. Appeals, Albany, 1975-77; assoc. Marshall, Bratter, Greene, Allison & Tucker, N.Y.C., 1977-79, Golenbock & Barell, N.Y.C., 1979-82; assoc. prof. law St. John's U., Jamaica, 1983-90; assoc. counsel N.Y. State Temporary Commn. to Recodify Family Ct. Act, Albany, 1982; lectr. N.Y. State Annual Jud. Seminar, Law Sch., Pace U., Rutgers U. Contbr. to Practice Commentaries to McKinney's N.Y. Domestic Rels. Law, 1981—; reporter N.Y. Pattern Jury Instrns.; directing editor McKinney's Texts and Forms. Mem. ABA, N.Y. State Bar Assn. (exec. dir. adminstrn. adjudication task force, com. on appellate ct.), Assn. of Bar of City of N.Y. (coun. on jud. adminstrn., matrimonial com., spl. com. election law), Am. Acad. Matrimonial Lawyers. Home: 26 Chestnut Ridge Rd Armonk NY 10504-3001 also: 3 Barker Ave White Plains NY 10601

SCHEIRING, MICHAEL JAMES, academic administrator; b. Canton, Ohio, Oct. 11, 1949; s. Robert J. and Madonna L. (Geisigi) S.; m. Marcia L. Young, May 13, 1972; children: Kristy L., Lauren M. BA, Kent State U., 1971, MPA, 1972. Sect. supr. N.J. Dept. Treasury, Trenton, 1974-78; policy analyst to gov. Trenton, 1978-80; dir. adminstrn. N.J. Dept. Community Affairs, Trenton, 1980-82; dir. corp. budgeting N.J. Transit Corp., Newark, 1982-83; v.p. adminstrn. and fin. Thomas A. Edison Coll., Trenton, 1983—; exec. dir. Gov. Mgmt. Rev. Com., Gov.'s Office, Trenton, N.J., 1990—; trustee N.J. Ednl. Computer Corp., 1984-90; trustee, comptroller Edison Found., Trenton, 1984—. Contbg. author: N.J. Zero-Based Budgeting, 1979. Mem. Am. Soc. Pub. Adminstrn. (nat. coun., v.p. programs 1984, v.p. membership 1985, pres. 1987—), Coun. Coll. Fiscal Officers N.J., Laurence Rotary (pres. elect). Roman Catholic. Home: 2 Lotus Ln Trenton NJ 08648-3211 Office: Govs Office CN-001 State House Trenton NJ 08625

SCHELDE, PER, writer, educator; b. Copenhagen, Denmark, Sept. 23, 1945; came to U.S., 1978; s. Helge Jacob Schelde and Aase Schelde (Guldager Nielsen) Jacobsen. BA, CUNY, Queens, 1981; PhD, CUNY, 1985. Actor Svalegangen, Aarhus, Denmark, 1970-73, Fiolteatret, Copenhagen, 1974-77; asst. prof. York Coll., Jamaica, N.Y., 1985—. Author: Ibsen's Forsaken Merman: Folklore in the Late Plays, 1988, Androids, Humanoids and Other Folklore Monsters: Science and Soul in Science Fiction Films, 1991; contbr. articles to profl. jours. Fellow Royal Anthropological Soc.; mem. Am. Anthropological Soc., Phi Beta Kappa. Home: 333 E 69th St # 72 New York NY 10021-5549

SCHELLENBERG, PETER JOSEPH, electronics executive; b. Teaneck, N.Y., Aug. 19, 1931; s. Arnault George and Anne Cecilia (Hooney) S.; m.

Marjorie Poppens, Nov. 18, 1960; children: Ann M., Catherine L. BEE, CUNY, 1954; MBA, Boston U., 1969. Registered profl. engr., Mass., Conn. Pres. Electrical Co., Natick, Mass., 1962—, Control Assocs., Inc., Natick, 1970-71, Village Copy Ctr., Inc., Natick, 1975-79, Modular Motion, Inc., Natick, 1988—. Chmn. bd. pub. works Town of Natick, 1981-85. Mem. IEEE, Instrument Soc., Electrical Mfrs. Rep. Club, Rotary (pres. 1979, Paul Harris fellow). Democrat. Unitarian. Home: 11 Glen St Natick MA 01760-5601

SCHELLHASE, JODI ANN, chamber of commerce executive; b. Chambersburg, Pa., Oct. 19, 1966; d. Joseph G. and Louanne (Wentzel) S. BS, Wilson Coll., 1988. Asst. to dir. confs. Wilson Coll., Chambersburg, 1987-88; advt. rep. Greater Chambersburg C. of C., 1988-89, membership dir., 1989—. Mem. Cumberland Valley Mgmt. Coun., Women's Network, Wilson Coll. Franklin Country Club. Democrat. Methodist. Home: 308 Wendy Dr Fayetteville PA 17222-1140 Office: Greater Chambersburg C of C 75 S 2D St Chambersburg PA 17201

SCHELLHORN, ALICE HOPE, educator; b. Bklyn., Jan. 30, 1945; d. Irving M. and Sylvia K. (Hausner) Berger; m. John B. Schellhorn, Sept. 7, 1966; 1 child, Eric Michael. BA, Tufts U., 1966, MEd, 1974. Cert. tchr., guidance dir. French tchr. Reading (Mass.) Meml. High Sch., 1967-68; dir. admissions and student svcs. Lawrence Meml. Hosp. Sch. Nursing, Medford, Mass., 1975-84; vocat. guidance counselor Shawsheen Valley Tech. High Sch., Billerica, Mass., 1984-91; coord. vocat. student svcs. Stevens High Sch., Claremont, N.H., 1991—. Mem. exec. bd. Mass./R.I. League for Nursing, Charlestown, Mas., 1980-81. Mem. Bus. and Profl. Women's Club. Office: Stevens High Sch 175 Broad St Claremont NH 03743

SCHELLING, THOMAS CROMBIE, educator, economist; b. Oakland, Calif., Apr. 14, 1921; s. John M. and Zelda M. (Ayres) S.; m. Corinne T. Sapos, Sept. 13, 1947 (div. 1991); children: Andrew, Thomas, Daniel, Robert; m. Alice M. Coleman, Nov. 8, 1991. AB, U. Calif., Berkeley, 1943; PhD, Harvard U., 1951. U.S. govt. economist Copenhagen, Paris, Washington, 1948-53; prof. econs. Yale U., 1953-58, Harvard U., Cambridge, Mass., 1958—; prof. econs. and pub. affairs U. Md., College Park, 1990—; sr. staff mem. RAND Corp., 1958-59; chmn. research adv. bd. Com. Econ. Devel., 1978-81, 84-85; mem. sci. adv. bd. USAF, 1960-64, def. sci. bd., 1966-70; mem. mil. econ. adv. panel CIA, 1980-85; trustee Aerospace Corp. Author: National Income Behavior, 1951, International Economics, 1958, The Strategy of Conflict, 1960, Arms and Influence, 1966, Micromotives and Macrobehavior, 1978, Choice and Consequence, 1984; co-author: Strategy and Arms Control, 1961. Recipient Frank E. Seidman Disting. award in polit. economy, 1977. Fellow Am. Acad. Arts and Scis., AAAS, Assn. for Pub. Policy Analysis and Mgmt., Am. Econ. Assn. (pres. 1991, Disting. mem. award); mem. Nat. Acad. Scis., Inst. Medicine. Office: U Md Dept Econs College Park MD 20742

SCHEMAN, L. RONALD, lawyer; b. Bklyn., Aug. 9, 1931; s. Mac and Eleanor (Minkowitz) S.; divorced; children: Ann, Corinne, Jennifer, Daniel. BA with distinction cum laude (Rufus Choate scholar) Dartmouth Coll., 1953; JD, Yale U., 1956. Bar: N.Y., 1956, D.C., 1979. Pvt. practice law, Hartford, Conn., 1957, N.Y.C., 1958-59; Inter-Am. Cultural Conv. fellow, Brazil, 1959-61; atty. dept. legal affairs OAS, Washington, 1961-64, planning officer, 1966-70, asst. sec. gen. for mgmt., 1975-84; exec. dir. Pan Am. Devel. Found., 1964-68; pres. Porter Internat. Co., Washington, 1970-75; ptnr. Coudert Bros., Washington, 1984-85; exec. dir. Ctr. Advanced Studies of the Americas, 1985-87; ptnr. Kaplan, Russin and Vecchi, 1987—; secretariat Inter-Am. Commn. on Human Rights, 1961-64; exec. v.p., dir. Intercomp, S.A., 1971-74; v.p. fin. Robert R. Nathan Assocs., 1974-75; pub. Soviet Bus. and Trade, 1973-75; dir. Vision mag., 1973-74; assoc. dir. Coun. of Ams., 1976—; professorial lectr. in internat. orgn. George Washington U., 1979-83. Author: Foundations of Freedom, 1966, The Inter-American Dilemma, 1988, The Alliance for Progress, A Retrospective, 1989; bd. editors Mng. Internat. Devel. quar., 1984-86; contbr. articles on internat. orgn. and inter-Am. affairs to profl. jours. Trustee Inter-Am. Bar Found., 1967-74; trustee Pan Am. Devel. Found., 1987—, pres., 1976-83, 87—; mem. exec. com. Am. Jewish Com. of Washington; bd. dirs. East-West Trade Coun., 1974-75, Ctr. for Advanced Studies of the Ams., 1984-87, Inter-Am. Literacy Found., Inter-Am. Music Festival, 1979-82; mem. steering com. on governance in Western Hemisphere, Aspen Inst., 1981-82; mem. adv. panel on regionalism and devel. UNITAR, 1981-82; mem. Fed. City Coun. Decorated Order Bernardo O'Higgins (Chile), 1967. Mem. Washington Fgn. Law Soc. (bd. govs. 1965-67, pres. 1968), Am. Fgn. Law Assn. (v.p. 1971), Am. Soc. Internat. Law, Cosmos Club, Econ. Club of Washington, Phi Beta Kappa. Home: 4335 37th St NW Washington DC 20008-1901 Office: 1200 New Hampshire Ave NW Washington DC 20036-6802

SCHEMEL, DAVID JOSEPH, data processing professional; b. Granite Falls, Minn., Sept. 27, 1951; s. Gordon John and Kathleen Marie (Fisher) S. BS in Computer Sci. and Bus., Mankato State Coll., 1977, BA in Psychology, 1977. Cert. data processor, info. systems auditor. Programmer Sperry Univac, St. Paul, 1977-79; EDP auditor Coopers & Lybrand, Mpls., 1979-83, N.Y.C., 1983-87; EDP auditor Spicer & Oppenheim, N.Y.C., 1987-88, Coopers & Lybrand, Phila., 1988—. Author: (with others) Handbook of EDP Auditing, 1986-90. With USN, 1970-73. Republican. Home: 7411 Society Dr Claymont DE 19703-1774 Office: Coopers & Lybrand 2400 Eleven Penn Ctr Philadelphia PA 19103

SCHENCK, HARVEY NORMAN, engineer; b. East Orange, N.J., Sept. 7, 1937; s. Harvey Norman and Charlotte (Faatz) S.; m. Linda Phelps, July 20, 1963; children: Norman, Andy, Witt. BS in Mech. Engring., Stevens Inst. Tech., Hoboken, N.J., 1960. With rsch. applications dept. Lincoln Electric Co., Cleve., 1960-69; from engr. to exec. v.p. Rolfite, Stamford, Conn., 1969-84; v.p. engring. FuelTech, Stamford, 1984-89; dir. Omni Treatments Valorisation Dechets Compagnie Generale Des Baux, N.Y.C., 1989—; cons. IUS, Stamford, 1989—. Home: 12 Stanton Rd Darien CT 06820-5127

SCHENCK, HENRY PAUL, telecommunications executive; b. N.Y.C., Mar. 16, 1929; s. Mack and Helen (Newman) S.; m. Marjorie Mary Apgar, June 4, 1955; children: Kathleen Bauer, Colleen Tappan, Robert L. and Paul H. (twins). Student, Hofstra Coll., 1950-51; BS in Engring., U. Conn., 1955. Statis. analyst Borden Corp., N.Y.C., 1947-50; equipment engr. Western Electric, Newark, 1955-57; wire chief W. Jersey Telephone Corp., Blairstown, N.J., 1957-58; supr. Regal Corp., New Britain, Conn., 1958-70; chief exec. officer Businessmen's Svc. Bur., Grand Island, N.Y., 1970—; pres. Your Telephone Svc., Inc., Grand Island, 1985—. Sgt. USAF, 1951-53. Mem. IEEE (assoc.), Lions (pres. Grand Island Club 1969-70, dist. chmn. info. Erie County 1970-71). Office: Businessmens Svc Bur 1818 Bruce Ln Grand Island NY 14072-2602

SCHENCK, MARGARET ANNA, medical marketing executive; b. Camden, N.J., Apr. 25, 1938; d. John Richard and Margaret Nesbit (Ross) S. AB, Beaver Coll., 1960; cert. graphic design, The Cooper Union, N.Y.C., 1965. Writer, promotion Curtis Pub. Co., Phila., 1959-60, Forbes Mag., N.Y.C., 1960-62; copywriter Cummins, MacFail & Nutty, Somerset, N.J., 1967-69; sr. copywriter L.W. Frohlich/Intercon, N.Y.C., 1969-73; v.p., copy dir. Falcone & Assocs., Chatham, N.J., 1973-84; v.p., creative dir. McCann-Erikson/McCann Healthcare, Morristown, N.J., 1986-88; CEO, creative dir. Great Water Resources, Stockton, N.J., 1988—; cons. Siemens Corp., Iselin, N.J., 1991—, Bausch & Lomb Pharms., Tampa, Fla., 1990-91, ICI Pharms., Wilmington, Del., 1988—. Contbr. articles to trade mags. Instr. Bound Brook (N.J.) Adult Edn., 1980-82. Recipient numerous creative awards, 1974-84. Mem. Med. Mktg. Assn., ANSA Club (bd. dirs. 1974-76). Office: Great Water Resources PO Box 368 Stockton NJ 08559-0368

SCHENKER, HENRY HANS, research chemist; b. Vienna, Austria, June 19, 1926; came to U.S., 1939; s. Adolf and Olga (Strauss) S.; m. Verna Laura Kreider, Dec. 25, 1955; children: Constance, Jennifer, Laurie. BS, CCNY, 1949; PhD, Rutgers U., 1952. Teaching assoc. Rutgers U., New Brunswick, N.J., 1950-52; rsch. chemist E.I. Du Pont de Nemours & Co., Wilmington, Del., 1953-57, analytical supr., 1957-61, sr. rsch. chemist, 1961-90, rsch. assoc., 1990—. Contbr. numerous articles to sci. jours.; patentee nylon tire cord. President Green Acres Civic Assn., Wilmington, 1965-67, Congregation Beth Emeth, Wilmington, 1983-87, Delmarva Ecumenical Resource Ctr., Wilmington, 1984-86, Interfaith Lay Acad., Wilmington, 1990—. Sgt. AUS, 1944-46. Recipient cert. of merit Polymer and Textile, 1974. Mem. TAPPI, Soc. Automotive Engrs. (cons. clutch com. 1988—), Am. Chem. Soc., N.Y. Acad. Scis. Home: 1419 Bucknell Rd Wilmington DE 19803-5113 Office: EI Du Pont de Nemours & Co Fibers Dept 701 Chestnut Run Pla Wilmington DE 19880

SCHENKMAN, JOHN BORIS, pharmacologist, educator; b. N.Y.C., Feb. 10, 1936; s. Abraham and Theresa (Moses) S.; m. Deanna Owen, June 5, 1960; children: Jeffrey Alan, Laura Ruth. BA in Chemistry, Bklyn. Coll., 1960; PhD in Biochemistry, SUNY Upstate Med. Ctr., Syracuse, 1964. Postdoctoral fellow U. Pa. Johnson Found., Phila., 1964-67, Inst. Protein Research Osaka U., Japan, 1967-68, Inst. Toxicology Tübingen U., Fed. Republic Germany, 1968; asst. prof. Yale U. Sch. Medicine, New Haven, 1968-71, assoc. prof., 1971-78; prof., dept. head. U. Conn. Health Ctr., Farmington, 1978-87; prof. U. Conn., Farmington, 1987—. Contbr. articles to profl. jours. Served as sgt. U.S. Army, 1953-55. Research grantee NIH, NSF; recipient Research Career Devel award NIH, 1971-76. Mem. Am. Soc. Biol. Chemists, Am. Soc. Pharmacology Exptl. Therapeutics, Brit. Biochemistry Soc., Soc. Toxicology, Am. Med. Sch. Pharmacologists (councilor 1987—). Jewish. Club: Hillel Childrens Sch. (New Haven) (pres. 1976-78). Office: U Conn Sch Medicine Dept Phamacology Farmington CT 06032

SCHEPS, ESTHER, financial services company executive; b. N.Y.C., Nov. 25, 1941; d. Harold and Ethel Lynn (Bistritsky) Goldberg; m. Walter Scheps, Aug. 11, 1963; children: Robert, Andrew, Elizabeth. BA, City U. N.Y., 1963; MA, Ohio State U., 1975. Cert. fin. planner. Acct. exec. Merrill Lynch, Smithtown, N.Y., 1981-84; sales mgr. Shearson Lehman Bros., Melville, N.Y., 1984-88; v.p. investments Prudential Securities, Melville, N.Y., 1988—; lectr. adult edn. programs, N.Y.C., Long Island, 1981—. Trustee Lehman Coll. Art Gallery, pres. 1985-88; mem. Friends for Long Island Heritage. Mem. Mus. Stony Brook, Met. Mus. Art, Three Village Music Boosters. Home: 2 Jefferson Ct Setauket NY 11733 Office: Prudential Securities 445 BroadHollow Rd Melville NY 11747

SCHER, ALLAN JOSEPH, oncologist, consultant; b. Bklyn., June 2, 1935; s. David E. and Helen (Elbogen) S.; m. Linda Ronni Tash, Apr. 2, 1966; children: Michael B., Lauren J. BA, Yeshiva U., 1957; MD, Albert Einstein Coll. of Medicine, 1962. Diplomate Nat. Bd. Med. Examiners, 1963, Am. Bd. Radiology, 1967; lic. N.Y. 1963, Calif. 1966, N.J. 1968. Intern Bronx-Lebanon Hosp. Ctr., N.Y., 1962-63; resident in radiology Kings County Hosp., Bklyn., 1963-66; asst. chief radiation therapy USNR, San Diego, 1966-68; chief radiation oncology Morristown (N.J.) Meml. Hosp., 1968-86; cons. in radiation therapy Hackettstown (N.J.) Community Hosp., 1973-91; asst. adj. radiologist Beth Israel Hosp. Ctr., N.Y.C., 1966; clin. asst. instr. Kings County Hosp., 1969-71; clin. asst. prof. radiology Rutgers Med. Sch., 1974—; adj. asst. prof. allied health Fairleigh Dickinson U., Teaneck, N.J., 1975-85; cons. in radiation therapy Community Med. Ctr., Morristown, 1970-80. Presented numerous papers at various medical symposia. Mem. Coun. on Cancer, N.J., 1972-73, med. com. Riverside Hospice, 1976-79. Fellow N.J. Acad. Medicine (sec. radiation therapy sect. 1975-76, chmn. 1976-77), Am. Coll. Radiology (alternate councillor 1981-84, councillor 1984-87); mem. AMA, Am. Soc. Therapeutic Radiologists, Radiological Soc. of No. Am., N.J. Oncology Soc. (co-founder, treas. 1975-77, trustee 1984-86, treas. 1987-88, sec. 1988-89, v.p. 1989-90, pres. 1990-91), N.J. Med. Soc. (sec. radiology sect. 1971-72, chmn. 1972-73, mem. ad hoc com. on Atomic Energy Plants 1976), Radiology Soc. N.J. (sec. 1977-78, v.p. 1978-79, pres.-elect 1979-80, pres. 1980-81, mem. exec. com. 1982—, chmn. radiotherapy sect. 1972—), Morris County Med. Soc., Albert Einstein Coll. of Medicine Alumni Assn. (mem. bd. govs. 1975-78), N.J. Assn. Med. Specialty Socs. (v.p. 1980, pres. 1981), Acad. of Medicine of N.J. (mem. exec. com. 1991). Jewish. Office: Radiation Oncologists of NW NJ 100 Madison Ave Morristown NJ 07960

SCHER, DAVID LAWRENCE, power system executive; b. Albany, N.Y., Mar. 2, 1963; s. Paul and Elaine Joan (Alpart) S. BA, U. Rochester, 1985; MBA, U. Chgo., 1989. Analyst, corp. fin. The First Boston Corp., N.Y., 1985-87; v.p. devel. M. Scher & Son, Inc., Albany, N.Y., 1989—. Office: M Scher and Son Inc 136 N Lake Ave Albany NY 12206-2794

SCHER, ROBERT SANDER, manufacturing company executive; b. Cin., May 24, 1934; s. Stanford Samuel and Eva (Ordan) S.; m. Audrey Erna Gordon, Oct. 21, 1961; children: Sarahh, Alexander, Aaron. SB, MIT, 1956, SM, 1958, Diploma in Mech. Engring., 1960, ScD, 1963. Rsch. and teaching asst. MIT, Cambridge, Mass., 1957-62; control system engr. RCA, Hightstown, N.J., 1963-65; engring. mgr. Sequential Info. System, Elmsford, N.Y., 1965-71; tech. dir. Teledyne Gurley, Troy, N.Y., 1971-78, v.p. engring., 1978-86, pres., 1986—. Co-author patent Linear Digital Readout, 1975. Mem. ASME, Optical Soc. Am. Jewish. Home: 2 Laurel Oak Ln Clifton Park NY 12065-4712

SCHERAGA, JOEL DOV, economist; b. Bklyn., Mar. 29, 1955; s. Morton G. and Susanna (Rothberg) S. AB, Brown U., 1976, MA, 1979, PhD, 1981. Rsch. asst. Jet Propulsion Lab., summer 1974, 75; geophys. rsch. asst. Brown U., Providence, 1976-77, teaching asst., 1977-80; instr. U. R.I., Providence, 1979-80; asst. prof. Rutgers U., New Brunswick, N.J., 1981-87; vis. asst. prof. Princeton (N.J.) U., 1985-86; sr. economist U.S. EPA, Washington, 1987-91; br. chief EPA, Washington, 1991—; sr. economist Nat. Acid Precipitation Assessment Program, Washington, 1989-90; peer reviewer U.S. Man and Biosphere Program, Washington, 1988; editorial cons. to various publs.; tech. cons. Nat. Geographic Soc., 1988; panelist The Keystone Global Climate Change Dialogue, 1989—; participant Stanford Energy Modeling Forum #12, 1990—. Author: Problems and Issues in Microeconomics, 1985; contbr. articles to profl. publs. Hebrew tchr. Cong. Har Shalom, Potomac, Md., 1987. Mem. Am. Econs. Assn., Soc. Govt. Economists (book rev. editor 1988-90), Eastern Econs. Assn. (program com. 1985-88). Home: 13929 Castle Blvd # 31 Silver Spring MD 20904-4995 Office: EPA PM-221 401 M St SW Washington DC 20460-0002

SCHERBAN, DWIGHT MICHAEL, martial arts educator; b. Hartford, Conn., Dec. 3, 1948; s. Michael and Georgia Alma (Johnson) S.; m. Maria Elena Mendez, Apr. 14, 1991. BA, U. Hartford, 1970; MBA, U. New Haven, 1973; PhD, U. Conn., 1982. Instr. U. Hartford, West Hartford, Conn., 1975-77; assoc. prof. Cen. Conn. State U., New Britain, 1977—; pres. D.M.S. Assocs. Inc., Hartford, 1984—. Author: Bando Discipline-Boar System, 1983. Assistant steward Goodwill Grange # 127, 1980—. U. Conn. fellow, 1978, grantee, 1980. Mem. Am. Bando Assn. (bd. dirs. 1987-91). Office: Cen Conn State U 1615 Stanley St New Britain CT 06053-2439

SCHERER, A. EDWARD, nuclear engineering executive; b. Bklyn., May 23, 1942; s. Samuel M. and Margie Scherer. BS in Mech. Engring., Worcester Poly. Inst., 1963; MS in Nuclear Engring., Pa. State U., 1965; MBA, Rensselaer Poly. Inst., Hartford, Conn., 1978. Registered profl. engr., Mass. Asst. to project mgr. Combustion Engring., Inc., Windsor, Conn., 1968-70, reactor project engr., test evaluation engr., 1970-73, asst. project mgr., 1973-75, mgr. nuclear licensing, 1975-80, dir. nuclear licensing, 1980-90, v.p. nuclear quality ABB Combustion Engring. Nuclear Power, 1990-92, v.p. regulatory affairs ABB Combusting Engring. Nuclear Fuel, 1992—; mem. tech. adv. com., mem. issues mgmt. com., mem. standardization oversight com. NUMARC, Washington. Contbr. articles to profl. jours. Capt. U.S. Army, 1965-67, South Vietnam. Mem. ASME, Am. Nuclear Soc., Sigma Xi, Alpha Epsilon Pi (internat. pres. 1982-84, fiscal control bd. 1986—). Office: ABB Combustion Engring 1000 Prospect Hill Rd Windsor CT 06095

SCHERER, HAROLD NICHOLAS, JR., electric utility company executive, engineer; b. Plainfield, N.J., Apr. 5, 1929; s. Harold Nicholas and Nora (McDonough) S.; m. Jane Neely, Sept. 6, 1952 (div.); children—Anne Scherer McConnell, Peter; m. Patricia Condon, May 4, 1974; stepchildren: James, John, Joseph, Jeffery Ludwig, Jean Ludwig Ransdell. B.E., Yale U., 1951; M.B.A., Rutgers U., 1955. Registered profl. engr., Mass., N.J., Ohio. Various engring. positions Pub. Service Electric and Gas Co., Newark, 1951-63; various engring. positions Am. Electric Power Service Corp., N.Y.C., 1963-68, asst. chief. elec. engr., 1968-69, chief elec. engr., 1969-73, v.p. elec. engr., 1973-82; sr. v.p. elec. engring. Am. Electric Power Service Corp., Columbus, Ohio, 1982-90; also dir. Am. Electric Power Service Corp., until 1990; pres. Commonwealth Electric Co., Wareham, Mass., 1990—, Cambridge Electric Light Co., Canal Electric Co., Com/Steam Co., 1990—; bd. dirs. Commonwealth Electric Co., Cambridge Electric Light Co., Com/Steam Co., Commonwealth Svcs. Co., Canal Electric Co.; mem. joint U.S.-USSR working group on power transmission, 1975-81, joint U.S.-Italy working group on power transmission, 1979-88; vice-chmn. Am. Nat. Standards, N.Y.C., 1985-87; v.p. U.S. nat. com., 1985—, chmn. U.S. tech. com. Internat. Conf. on Large High Voltage Electric Systems, 1985-91, internat. adminstrv. coun., 1988—; mem. engring rev. bd. Bonneville Power Adminstrn., 1984—; chmn. elec. system and equipment com. Edison Electric Inst., 1989-90. Contbr. articles to profl. jours. Councilman, City of Plainfield, 1963-65; mem. Watchung (N.J.) Hills Regional High Sch. Bd. Edn., 1970-72; pres. Woods at Josephinum Civic Assn., Worthington, Ohio, 1983-84. Recipient Clayton Frost award U.S. Jaycees, 1961, Young Man of Yr. award Plainfield Jaycees, 1963, Lifetime Achievement award T&D Mag., 1990. Fellow IEEE (v.p. power engring. soc. 1988-89, pres. 1990-91, William Habirshaw award for transmission and distbn. engring. 1986); mem. NAE, Tau Beta Pi, Beta Gamma Sigma. Republican. Home: 467 Bay Ln Centerville MA 02632 Office: Commonwealth Electric Co 2421 Cranberry Hwy Wareham MA 02571-1091

SCHERR, MARVIN GERALD, psychologist; b. Balt., June 21, 1940; s. Harry and Fannie (Glazer) S. BA in Psychol. cum laude, U. Md., 1962; PhD in Indsl. Psychol., George Washington U., 1980, postdoctoral cert. in clin. psychology, 1984. Lic. psychol., Md. Disability claims examiner Social Security Adminstrn., Balt., 1962-66, sr. personnel psychol., 1967-71, policy analyst, 1972-74, exec. fellow, various posts, 1975-76, staff psychol., 1976-87; clin. psychol. Psychol. Scis. Inst., Balt., 1985-88; pvt. practice cons. and clin. psychology Columbia, Md., 1989—; cons. clin. psychology Office of Disability, Med. Evaluation Social Security Adminstrn., 1989—; Reviewer Journal of Applied Psychology, Washington, 1985-88. Recipient acad. grant U. Md., grant Cen. Scholarship Bur.; William Reiches scholar. Fellow Md. Psychol. Assn.; mem. Am. Psychol. Assn. (div. psychotherapy, consumer psychol., indsl. orgn. psychol., neuropsychology, independent practice). Home and Office: 10387 Barcan Cir Columbia MD 21044-2504

SCHERTZER, ROBERT JOHN, mathematics and science educator; b. Bklyn., Feb. 21, 1951; s. Robert Henry and Helen Marie (Brenwald) S. BA, Hofstra U., 1973. Sales svc. mgr. Mt. Vernon Mills Inc., N.Y.C., 1973-82; pruchasing agt. John Boyle and Co., Elmsford, N.Y., 1982-86; fabric mdser. Jest Textiles Inc., Haworth, N.J., 1986-87; tchr. jr. high sch. St. Ann Elem. Sch., Hoboken, N.J., 1987-88, Christopher Robin Acad., Queens, N.Y., 1988, Regina Pacis Rc Sch., Bklyn., 1988-89; med. records analyst Beth Israel Hosp., N.Y.C., 1989-90; Ursuline companion Community Action Agy. Inc., Malone, N.Y., 1990-91; vol. The Salvation Army, Syracuse, N.Y., 1991—; senator-at-large Hofstra Alumni Coll., Hempstead, N.Y., 1991—; pres. History Alumni Hofstra, 1988-91. Mem. Met. Mus. Art, N.Y.C., 1986—. Mem. Nat. Soc. Fund Raising (cen. N.Y. chpt.), Companions Mission. Roman Catholic. Home: 90 Amherst Rd Valley Stream NY 11581

SCHERZER, SAUL M., psychologist; b. N.Y.C., May 11, 1937; m. Leah Wallach. BEE, CUNY, 1959, MBA, 1962; PhD, NYU, 1969. Cons. Booz Allen, N.Y., 1962-67; sales mgr. Tex. Instruments, N.Y., 1964-67; mgr. Ford Motor Co., N.Y., 1967-69; mgr. orgn. devel. IT&T, N.Y., 1969-72; dir. orgnl. devel. GE, Conn., 1972-75; pres. Exec. Psychologists, Westport, Conn., 1975—. Mem. Am. Bd. Profl. Psychologists (trustee 1989—). Office: Cons Psychologists 6 Hidden Hill Westport CT 06880-1027

SCHETLIN, ELEANOR M., retired university official; b. N.Y.C., July 15, 1920; d. Henry Frank and Elsie (Chew) Schetlin; B.A., Hunter Coll., 1940; M.A., Tchrs. Coll., Columbia U., 1942, Ed.D., 1967. Playground dir. Dept. of Parks, N.Y.C., 1940-42; librarian Met. Hosp. Sch. Nursing, N.Y.C., 1943-44, dir. recreation, 1944-48, dir. recreation and guidance, 1948-59; coordinator student activities SUNY, Plattsburgh, 1959-63, asst. dean students, 1963-64; asst. prof., coordinator student personnel services CUNY, Hunter Coll., 1967-68; asst. dir. student personnel Columbia U., Coll. Pharm. Scis., N.Y.C., 1968-69, dir. student personnel, 1969-71; assoc. dean for students Health Scis. Center, SUNY, Stony Brook, 1971-73, asst. v.p. for student services, 1973-74, assoc. dean of students, dir. student services, 1974-85. Recipient Lifetime Achievement award Nassau NOW, 1992. Mem. Nat. Assn. Women Deans, Adminstrs. and Counselors. Contbr. articles to profl. jours. Home: 20 Barberry Ln Sea Cliff NY 11579-2052

SCHETZEN, MARTIN, electrical and computer engineer, educator; b. N.Y.C., Feb. 10, 1928; s. Harry and Mae (Brimberg) S.; m. Jeannine Miriam Desrochers, Sept. 2, 1984. BEE, NYU, 1951; SM, MIT, 1954, ScD, 1961. Registered profl. engr., Mass. Electronic scientist Nat. Bur. Standards, Washington, 1951-52; engr. Applied Physics Lab., Silver Spring, Md., 1954-56; rsch. asst. Rsch. Lab. of Electronics MIT, Cambridge, Mass., 1952-54, 58-60, teaching asst., 1956-58, instr., 1960-61, asst. prof., 1961-65, staff mem. Rsch. Lab. of Electronics, 1961-65; assoc. prof. Northeastern U., Boston, 1965-69, prof. system theory, signal theory, 1969—; vis. prof. U. Calif., Berkeley, 1977-078; vis. scientist Weizmann Inst. Sci., Rehovot, Israel, 1982, 84-85; cons. Atlantic Refining Co., Dallas, 1961-66, Instrumentation Lab., MIT, 1964-70, RCA, Burlington, Mass., 1968-71. Author: The Volterra and Wiener Theories of Nonlinear Systems, 1980; contbr. articles to profl. jours. With U.S. Army, 1946-48. Recipient Apollo Cert. of Commendation, NASA, 1970, Apollo Achievement award, 1970. Mem. IEEE, Sigma Xi, Tau Beta Pi, Eta Kappa Nu. Jewish. Home: 41 Centre St Brookline MA 02146-2803 Office: Northeastern U 409 Dana Rsch Bldg Boston MA 02115

SCHEUER, JAMES HAAS, congressman; b. N.Y.C., Feb. 6, 1920; s. S(imon) H. and Helen (Rose) S.; m. Emily Malino, Mar. 21, 1948; children: Laura Lee, Elizabeth Helen, James H(aas), John William. A.B., Swarthmore Coll., 1942; LL.B., Columbia U., 1948; I.A., Harvard U., 1943. Bar: N.Y. 1949. Economist FEA, 1945-46; mem. legal staff OPA, 1951-52; chmn. housing adv. council N.Y. State Commn. Against Discrimination, 1955-64; mem. N.Y. State Task Force Middle Income Housing, 89th-92d Congresses form 21st Dist. N.Y., 1965-73, 94th-97 Congresses from 11th Dist. N.Y., 1975-81, 98th-102nd Congresses from 8th Dist. N.Y., 1983—; cons. Pres. Kennedy and White House Staff on housing and human rights problems, 1960-64; pres. Renewal and Devel. Corp.; lectr. in field, 1950—; also writer, lectr. Del. UN Conf. Housing, Human Rights, City Planning and Urban Renewal in, Europe and Far East, 1958, 60, 61, 62; also mem. internat. seminars in field; pres. Citizens Housing and Planning Council N.Y.C., 1958-61; chmn. global com. Parliamentarians on Population and Devel.; exec. bd. Citizens Union N.Y.C., 1950-64; bd. dirs. Nat. Housing Conf., 1958—, pres., 1972-74; chmn. exec. com. Global Com. Parliamentarians on Population and Devel., 1983-86; chmn. Sci., Space and Tech. Subcom. on Natural Resources, Agr. Research and Environment; chmn. Joint Econ. Com. Sub-Com. on Edn. and Health. Author numerous articles in field. Pres. N.Y. chpt. Am. Jewish Com., 1960; chmn. exec. com. Met. council Am. Jewish Congress, 1964. Served with USAAF, 1943-45. Recipient 1st Walter White Meml. award Nat. Com. Against Discrimination in Housing, 1956, 1st Human Relations award Urban League Greater N.Y., 1962. Mem. Assn. of Bar of City of N.Y., Civil Rights Leadership Conf. Democrat. *

SCHEURING, DAVID KEITH, financial services company executive; b. Pitts., July 25, 1947; s. William A. and Elizabeth J. (Davis) S.; m. Kathleen Monahan, July 1, 1967; children: Jennifer Ann, David K. BA in Polit. Sci., U. Pitts., 1973. Prodn. mgr. U.S. Steel Corp., Pitts., 1974-75; zone sales mgr. Motorola Communications & Electronics, Pitts., 1975-77; mgr. adminstrn. and ops. Federated Investors Inc., Pitts., 1977-79; v.p., div. head Boston Fin. Data Svcs., North Quincy, Mass., 1979-85; sr. v.p. Putnam Investor Svcs., Boston, 1985-89; v.p. Mellon Bank N.A., Pitts., 1989-91; pres. Delaware Svc. Co. Inc., Phila., 1991—. Mem. Nat. Investment Co. Svc. Assn., Investment Co. Inst., Toastmasters Internat. Republican. Roman Catholic. Home: 930 Oak Ridge Dr Blue Bell PA 19422 Office: Delaware Svc Co Inc 1818 Market St Philadelphia PA 19103

SCHEUZGER, THOMAS PETER, audio engineer; b. Evanston, Ill., Nov. 19, 1960; s. Peter and Ruth Erica (Hadorn) S. MusB in Music Prodn. and Engring., Berklee Coll. of Music, 1985. Audio engr. Eiger Engring., Watertown, Mass., 1983—; dir. audio New Eng. Conservatory, Boston, 1985—; producer, dir. Continental Cablevision, Watertown, 1989—. Producer, dir. Music from the Source, 1991. Recipient USA Video Festival award Nat. Fedn. Local Cable Programmers, 1992. Mem. Audio Engring.

Soc. Home: 222 Palfrey St Watertown MA 02172-1836 Office: New Eng Conservatory 290 Huntington Ave Boston MA 02115-5000

SCHIAFFINO, S(ILVIO) STEPHEN, government official; b. Bklyn., Nov. 1, 1927; s. Stephen Anthony and Jane (DiDonato) S.; m. Josephine Rose Bovello, Apr. 25, 1954; children—Susan, Stephen. BS, Georgetown U., 1946, MS, 1948, Ph.D. in Biochemistry, 1956. Research biochemist div. nutrition FDA, Washington, 1948-50; asst. br. chief div. FDA, 1954-60; mgr. chemistry dept. Hazelton Labs., Vienna, Va., 1960-61; with NIH, 1961—; scientist adminstr. NIH (Nat. Cancer Inst.), 1961-64, asst. chief research grants rev. br., 1964-69, chief., 1969-72, asso. dir. for sci. rev., 1972-78, dep. dir. div. research grants, 1978-86; sr. sci. advisor office of extramural research and tng., office of dir. NIH, 1986-87; exec. officer, sci. officer Am. Soc. for Clin. Nutrition, Bethesda, Md., 1987—. Served with AUS, 1950-53. Recipient Superior Service award FDA, 1960, Superior Service award NIH, 1969. Mem. AAAS, Am. Soc. for Clin. Nutrition., Am. Inst. Nutrition. Office: Am Soc for Clin Nutrition 9650 Rockville Pike Bethesda MD 20814-3998

SCHIAVI, RAUL CONSTANTE, psychiatrist, educator, researcher; b. Buenos Aires, Argentina, Jan. 7, 1930; came to U.S. 1956; s. Constantino and Maria (Acquier) S.; m. Michelle deMiniac, Aug. 7, 1960; children: Isabelle, Nadine, Viviane. MD, U. Buenos Aires, 1953. Diplomate Am. Bd. Psychiatry and Neurology. Fgn. asst. psychiatry U. Paris, 1955-56; resident in psychiatry U. Pa., Phila., 1956-59; instr. psychiatry U. Pa., 1959-61; assoc. College de France, Paris, 1961-63; asst. prof. psychiatry Cornell U., N.Y.C., 1963-66; assoc. prof. psychiatry SUNY, Downstate Med. Ctr., Bklyn., 1966-71, Mt. Sinai Sch. Medicine, N.Y.C., 1971-78; prof. psychiatry Mt. Sinai Sch. Medicine, 1978—; fellow Found. Fund for Rsch. in Psychiatry, 1958-63; cons. NIMH, 1966-70, 77-81; dir. human sexuality program Mt. Sinai Sch. Medicine, 1973—; advisor World Health Orgn., 1989. Contbr. articles to profl. jours., chpts. to books; co-editor Jour. Sex and Marital Therapy; editorial bd. Archives of Sexual Behavior and Hormones and Behavior; mem. editorial bds. Revista Latinoamericana de Sexologia, Quaderni de Sessuologia Clinica, Revista Argentina de Sexualidad Humana. Recipient Rsch. Sci. Devel. award, 1966, Masters and Johnson award Soc. for Sex Therapy and Rsch., 1991; grantee NIH, 1977-89, 87—, NIMH, 1976—, others. Fellow Am. Psychopathol. Assn., Psychiat. Rsch. Soc.; mem. AAAS, Am. Psychiat. Assn. (cons. 1989), Acad. Behavioral Medicine Rsch., Am. Psychosomatic Soc. (coun. 1985-88), Internat. Acad. Sex Rsch., Soc. Sex Therapy and Rsch. (pres. 1984-86), Sex Info. and Edn. Coun. of U.S. (bd. dirs. 1979-83), Internat. Soc. Psychoneuroendocrinology, Sigma Xi. Home: 25 E 86th St New York NY 10028-0553 Office: Mt Sinai Sch Medicine 1 Gustave L Levy Pl New York NY 10029-6504

SCHIAVONI, ROBERT PATRICK, residence life director; b. Haverhill, Mass., Apr. 20, 1949; s. Patrick J. and Dora M. (Gaudet) S.; m. Ellen J. Gwinn, July 20, 1974; children: Gina M., Jenna L. BS, N.H. Coll., 1971; MEd, Springfield (Mass.) Coll., 1973. Intern counselor Springfield Community Coll., 1972-73; residence dir. Siena Coll., Loudonville, N.Y., 1973-76; dir. housing N.H. Coll., Manchester, 1976-81, dir. residence life, 1981—; mediator N.H. Child & Family Mediation Project, Manchester, 1989. Board dirs. Manchester Family Planning Ctr. (now Health Options), 1981-83, v.p. bd. dirs., 1983-85. Mem. Assn. Coll. and Univ. Housing Officers Internat. (vis. del.), Am. Coll. and Pers. Assn., N.H. Coll. Pers. Assn. (sec., treas. 1984-85), N.H. Mediation Assn. Roman Catholic. Home: 150 Mooresville Rd Manchester NH 03103-2206 Office: NH Coll 2500 River Rd Hooksett NH 03106-1045

SCHIAZZA, GUIDO DOMENIC (GUY SCHIAZZA), educational association administrator; b. Phila., May 17, 1930; s. Guido and Claudina (DiPrinzio) S.; m. Irmgard Heidi Reissmueller, May 15, 1954. BA, Pa. State U., 1952; postgrad., St. Joseph's U., 1954-55, Villanova U., 1954-55, Temple U., 1955-58. Cert. tchr., Pa.; cert. clinician, ednl. specialist, instructional specialist, sch. psychologist, guidance counselor, reading specialist. Speech therapist, lang. arts instr. Commonwealth of Pa., Dept. Edn., 1956-59; founder, clinician, instr., dir., bd. pres. Communicative Arts Ctr., Inc., Drexel Hill, Pa., 1958, Communication Skills Community Resources Ctr., Inc., Drexel Hill, Pa., 1958, 1964—; charter mem. exec. bd., bd. pres. United Pvt. Acad. Schs., Assn. of Pa., Drexel Hill, 1966—; exec. bd. govs., bd. chmn. The Accrediting Commn., Drexel Hill, 1971—; charter mem. Pa. State Univ. Radio and TV Guild, University Park, Pa., 1951—; mem. legis. action com., Pa. State U., Univ. Park, 1988—; cons. communications skills, The Accrediting Commn., 1971—, United Pvt. Acad. Schs. Assn., Pa., 1966—. Founder, chmn., chief exec. officer Am. Ednl. Group, 1991—; chmn., chief exec. officer Internat. Ednl. Group, 1991—; active Nat. Com. to Preserve Social Security and Medicare, Washington, 1986—, Am. Immigration Control Found., Monterey, Va., 1987—, English First, Springfield, Va., 1988—; mem. pres.'s coun. Rep. Nat. Com., 1989—, Nat. Rep. Senatorial Com., 1989—, Rep. Presdl. Task Force, 1989—. 1st Lt. Signal Corps, U.S. Army, 1952-54. Recipient Svc. award United Pvt. Acad. Sch. Assn. Pa., Monroeville, Pa., 1978, Disting. Achievement and Svc. award Bd. Govs. of the Accrediting Commn., Downington, Pa., 1980, Dr. Charles Boehm Edn. of Yr. award, University Park, Pa., 1990, Loyal and Dedicated Svc. award The Accrediting Commn., 1974. Mem. NEA, Libr. of Congress (chartered), Pa. Edn. Assn., Jefferson Ednl. Found., World Affairs Coun., Phila. Nat. Congl. Club, Penn State U. Nittany Lions Club, Penn State U. Alumni Assn., Penn State U. Football Letterman's Club. Republican. Roman Catholic. Office: The Accrediting Commn 436 Burmont Rd Drexel Hill PA 19026-3630

SCHICK, IRVIN HENRY, educator; b. Wilkes-Barre, Pa., Aug. 10, 1924; s. Irvin and Elizabeth (Valentine) S.; diploma Bliss Elec. Sch., 1947; B.E.E., George Washington U., 1958; M.S. in Elec. Engring. (NSF fellow), U. Md., 1961; m. Marilyn Freeman, July 17, 1954 (dec. Aug. 1961); m. 2d, Marjorie Bletch Beach, Dec. 23, 1967; 1 dau., Carolyn Patricia. Engring. asst. Jeddo-Highland Coal Co. (Pa.), 1942-43; instr. Bliss Elec. Sch., Washington, 1947-50; prof. math. and elec. engring., dept. head Montgomery Coll., Rockville, Md., 1950-65, dir. extension, 1965-67, dean adminstrn., 1967-75, adminstrv. v.p., 1975-78, prof. emeritus, adminstrv. v.p. emeritus, 1978—. Tchr., tutor, cons. indsl. cos. 1949—. Served with USAAF, 1943-46. Mem. AAUP, Montgomery County Edn. Assn., Md. State Tchrs. Assn., IEEE, Am. Assn. Sch. Adminstrs., Internat. Platform Assn., Bliss Elec. Soc. (bd. govs., past pres.), Theta Tau, Sigma Tau, Sigma Pi Sigma, Tau Beta Pi. Home: 105 Fleetwood Ter Silver Spring MD 20910-5512

SCHIER, ERNEST LEONARD, journalist, educator; b. Mar. 25, 1918; s. David and Celia (Reiss) S.; m. Marjorie Poore (div.); children: Johanna Hall, Jennifer Cole, Harry, William. Theatre critic Times-Herald, Washington, 1946-54, Daily News, Phila., 1956-58, The Bulletin, Phila., 1958-82; dramaturg Nat. Playwrights Conf., Waterford, Conn., 1983—; co-dir Nat. Theatre Inst.; dir. Nat. Critics Inst., 1968—, Nat. Critics Inst., Waterford; adj. profl. Villanova (Pa.) U., 1976-90. Recipient Medal of Excellence, Standard Oil, 1984. Mem. Am. Theatre Critics Assn. (founding mem. 1974, chmn. 1974-76). Office: Eugene O Neill Theatre Ctr 305 Great Neck Rd Waterford CT 06385

SCHIER, NEIL, accountant; b. Edison, N.J., Mar. 14, 1968; s. Lewis and Dorothy (Peretz) S. BA, U. N.C., 1989. Corp. acct. US RE Corp., N.Y.C., 1990—. Mem. Nat. Assn. Accts., Mensa. Home: 9 Watson Ct Edison NJ 08820-2306

SCHIFF, JAYNE NEMEROW, underwriter; b. N.Y.C., Aug. 8, 1945; d. Milton E. Nemerow and Shirley (Kaplan) Wachtel; m. Albert John Schiff, Mar. 7, 1971; children: Matthew Evan, Kara Anne. BS in Bus., Marymount Coll., 1981. Corporate sec., treas. Albert J. Schiff Assocs., Inc., N.Y.C., 1970-78; field underwriter MONY Fin. Svcs., Greenwich, Conn., 1973—; freelance employee benefit cons. Greenwich, 1979—; regional dir. mktg., MONY Fin. Services, N.Y.C., 1978-79. Bd. dirs. N.Y. League Bus. and Profl. Women, 1976-78, Temple Sinai, Stamford, Conn., 1979-84, N.Y. Ctr. Fin. Studies; leader Webelos Cub Scouts, 1977-78; treas. Ann. Mothers Bd. Benefit Greenwich Acad., 1988, upper sch. acquisitions chmn., 1989, chmn. spl. acquisitions Greenwich Acad. Benefit, 1990-91, chmn. advt., 1992. Named Conn.'s Outstanding Young Woman, 1979. Mem. LWV, Am. Soc. Chartered Life Underwriters, N.Y. Ctr. Fin. Studies (bd. dirs.), N.Y.C. Life Underwriters Assn. (bd. dirs. 1977-78). Jewish. Office: 30 Stanwich Rd Greenwich CT 06830-4860

SCHIFF, JEROME ARNOLD, biologist, educator; b. Bklyn., Feb. 20, 1931; s. Charles K. and Molly (Weinberg) S. BA in Biology and Chemistry, Bklyn. Coll. (summer scholar invertebrate zoology Woods Hole Marine Biol. Lab.), 1952; PhD in Botany and Biochemistry, U. Pa., 1956. Predoctoral fellow USPHS, 1954-56; fellow Brookhaven Nat. Labs., summer 1956; rsch. assoc. biology Brandeis U., Waltham, Mass., 1956-57, instr., 1957-58, asst. prof., 1958-61, assoc. prof., 1961-65, prof. biology, 1966—, chmn. dept., 1972-75, Abraham and Etta Goodman prof. biology, 1974—; dir. Inst. Photobiology of Cells and Organelles, 1975-87; summer instr. exptl. marine botany Marine Biol. Lab., Woods Hole, Mass., 1971; sr. investigator explt. marine botany Marine Biol. Lab., 1972-74; dir. programs Exptl. Marine Botany, 1974-79; cons. on devel. biology NSF, 1965-68, cons. on metabolic biology, 1982-86; vis. prof. Tel Aviv U., 1972, Hebrew U., 1972, Weizmann Inst., Israel, 1977; mem. biology grant rev. program U.S.-Israel Binat. Sci. Found., 1974—; mem. corp. Marine Biol. Lab., 1972—. Mem. editorial bd. Developmental Biology, 1971-74, Plant Sci., 1972-78, assoc. editor, 1978-81, chief co-editor, 1981—; asst. editor Plant Physiology, 1964-69, adv. editor, 1969-79; mem. editorial com. Ann. Rev. Plant Physiology, 1974-80; contbr. over 180 articles to profl. jours. Carnegie Instn. fellow in plant biology, 1962-63; Recipient Disting. Alumni award Bklyn. Coll., 1972. Fellow AAAS, Am. Acad. Arts and Scis.; mem. Soc. Devel. Biology (sec. 1964-66, mem. exec. com.), Am. Soc. Biol. Chemists, Am. Soc. Plant Physiologists (mem. exec. com. 1972-88, Disting. Svc. award N.E. sect. 1989), Biophys. Soc., Internat. Phycological Soc., Phycological Soc. Am., Soc. Cell Biology, Soc. Gen. Microbiology, Soc. Protozoologists, Am. Soc. Microbiology, Internat. Soc. Devel. Biologists, Brit. Phycological Soc., Am. Soc. Photobiology, Sigma Xi. Home: 37 Harland Rd Waltham MA 02154-7613 Office: Brandeis U Inst for Photobiology of Cells and Organelles Waltham MA 02254

SCHIFF, LAURENCE ELLIOT, psychiatrist; b. Bklyn., Nov. 12, 1950; s. Allan and Marjorie (Frauenglas) S.; 1 child, Zachary. BA, Kenyon Coll., 197l; MD, Autonomous U. Guadalajara, 1975. Diplomate Am. Bd. Psychiatry and Neurology. Intern Stamford (Conn.) Hosp., 1976-77; resident in psychiatry North Shore U. Hosp., Manhasset, N.Y., 1977-80; pvt. practice Bethpage, N.Y., 1984—; staff psychiatrist Creedmore Psychiat. Ctr., Queens, N.Y., 1980-81; attending psychiatrist Brunswick Hall, Amityville, N.Y., 1981-84; psychiatrist Jewish Community Svcs., Rego Park, N.Y., 1985-87, North Cen. Bronx (N.Y.) Hosp., 1987-88; dir. psychiatry Charles Gay Shelter, Ward's Island, N.Y., 1988—; cons. Dept. Social Svcs., Ward's Island, 1988—. Mem. Am. Psychiatric Assn. (chmn. L.I. com. on homeless). Republican. Office: 4230 Hempstead Tpke Bethpage NY 11714-5705

SCHIFF, LEONARD NORMAN, electrical engineer; b. N.Y.C., Dec. 7, 1938; s. Milton and Elsie (Sternberg) S.; m. Marilyn Claire Leiner, July 14, 1962; children: Michael, Laura. BEE, CCNY, 1960; MSEE, N.Y.U., 1962; PhD in Elec. Engring., Bklyn. Polytechnic Inst., 1968. Mem. tech. staff Bell Labs., Holmdel, N.J., 1960-67, RCA Labs., Princeton, N.J., 1967-78; group head RCA Labs., Princeton, 1978-83, lab. dir., 1983-87; lab. dir. David Sarnoff Rsch. Ctr., Princeton, 1987—. Patentee in field. Mem. IEEE (sr.), Eta Kappa Nu, Tau Beta Pi, Sigma Xi. Home: 184 Foch Ave Trenton NJ 08648-3720 Office: David Sarnoff Rsch Ctr Princeton NJ 08540

SCHIFF, LONNY, artist, papermaker, printmaker; b. Columbus, Ohio, Oct. 9, 1929; d. George V. and Grace (Teats) Clark; m. Daniel Schiff. Student Ohio State U., 1948; B.A., U. Ill., 1953; cert. Worcester Art Mus. Sch., 1964; student Impressions Workshop, Boston, 1965. One-woman shows Key Key Gallery, N.Y.C., 1981, Randall Beck Gallery, Boston, 1987-91, First Impression Gallery, Toronto, Ont., Can., 1990, Cambridge Multicultural Art Ctr., 1985; exhibited in group shows Chgo. Centre for the Print, Ringling Sch. of Art, Sarasota, Fla., 1991—, Greenhut Gallery, Portland, Maine, 1991—, Soc. Arts and Crafts, Boston, 1990-91, Phila. Print Club, 1986-92, NASA Space Mus., Cape Canaveral, Fla., 1989—, others; represented in permanent collection Fogg Art Mus., Harvard U., Bklyn. Mus., Nat. Mus. Am. Art, Washington, Am. Express Co., N.Y.C., Citicorp Bank, N.Y., Lipton Tea Co., Englewood Cliffs, N.H., Prudential Towers, Boston, FMC Corp., Chgo., Pubs. Clearing House, L.I. Conservator, Danforth Mus., Framingham, Mass., 1977—. Mem. aid bd. Framingham Union Hosp., 1977—; bd. dirs. Programs for People, Framingham. Studio: PO Box 2156 Framingham Centre MA 01701

SCHIFF, MARLENE SANDLER, entrepreneur; b. Great Barrington, Mass.; d. Jack and Lena Yetta (Klein) Sandler; m. Haskel Schiff (dec. Feb. 1967), 1 child, Melissa Robin. BA, U. Mass., 1970; OPM, Harvard U., 1985. Founder, chief exec. officer, chmn. Transceiver East Inc., N.Y.C., 1971-88. Mem. eye adv. com. N.Y. Hosp. Cornell Med. Ctr., 1988—; bd. dirs. Sol C. Schneider Entrepreneural Ctr. at Wharton Sch. U. Pa., Phila., 1987—, chairperson, 1990-92; mem. adv. bd. nutrition and fitness project Harvard U. Sch. of Pub. Health. Mem. Commn. of 200 (bd. dirs. 1990—, N.E. regional chair 1989-91, bd. dirs. found. 1991—), Am. Fedn. Arts (membership and spl. events com. 1990—). Home: 950 5th Ave New York NY 10021-1741

SCHIFF, MICHAEL, accountant, university dean, consultant; b. N.Y.C., Mar. 4, 1915; s. Moses and Clara (Fleisher) S.; m. Sylvia Schiffman, Dec. 25, 1939; children: Janet, Allen, Jonathan. BBA, CCNY, 1936, MBA, 1939; PhD, NYU, 1947. CPA, N.Y. Acct. in pvt. practice N.Y.C., 1939-60; instr. Hunter Coll., N.Y.C., 1941-46; prof. Grad. Sch. Bus. NYU, N.Y.C., 1946—; dean Sch. of Bus. Yeshiva U., 1988-92; bd. dirs. Ross Inst. Acctg. Rsch., N.Y.C., 1975-85; mem. N.Y. State Bd. for Pub. Accountancy, N.Y.C., 1973-81; cons. U.S. Dept. Energy, Washington, 1979; resercher NSF, 1975. Coauthor: Impairments and Writeoffs, 1989; editor: The Hayden-Stone Forums, 1980; contbr. chpts. to books, articles to profl. jours. Mem. AICPA, N.Y. State Soc. CPAs, Fin. Execs. Inst. Office: Yeshiva U 500 W 185th St New York NY 10033-3201

SCHIFFELBEIN, WAYNE LLOYD, architect; b. Chgo., Mar. 9, 1939; s. Walter Leo and Dora Schiffelbein; m. Patricia Kay Crawford, Sept. 1, 1962; 1 child, Jonathan. BArch, U. Mich., 1963; MArch, Columbia U., 1964, MS in Urban Planning, 1966; JD, George Washington U., 1971. Bar: D.C. 1972. Planner Keyes, Lethbridge & Condon, Washington, 1967-68; dir., fed. agy. liaison AIA, Washington, 1970-74; spl. asst. to commr. U.S. Consumer Products Safety Commn., Washington, 1974-78; cons., 1978-83; project mgr. Skidmore, Owings & Merrill, Washington, 1983—. Mem. AIA, ABA, D.C. Bar Assn. Home: 1660 Chimney House Rd Reston VA 22090 Office: Skidmore Owings & Merrill 1201 Pennsylvania Ave NW Washington DC 20004

SCHIFFMAN, ALAN THEODORE, accountant; b. N.Y.C., Feb. 18, 1942; s. Herbert and Lenore (Dick) S.; m. Sedra Gail Schiffman, June 30, 1963; children: Marc D., Lauren B. BS, Leigh U., 1963. CPA. Staff acct. Adler Faunce & Leonard, Phila., 1965-68; sr. acct. Main-Hurdman, Phila., 1968-71; ptnr. Laventhol Horwath, Phila., 1971-78; pres., dir. practice rev. Schiffman Hughes, Blue Bell, Pa., 1978—; pres., dir. Blue Bell Securities Corp., Blue Bell, Pa.; bd. chmn. Madison Bank, Blue Bell, Pa.; chmn. Madison Bank, Blue Bell, Pa.; chmn. Speakers Bur., Phila., 1976-78; pres. Lincoln Realty Mgmt. Co.; faculty Am. Inst. CPAs, N.Y.C. and Phila., 1970. Contbr. articles to various profl. jours. Chmn. adv. com. Montgomery Community Coll., 1986. Mem. AICPA (Phila. chpt.), Pa. Inst. CPAs, Home Builders Assn., Golden Slipper Club. Jewish. Home: 107 E Mill Rd Flourtown PA 19031-1628

SCHIFFMAN, DAVID, school administrator; b. Bronx, N.Y., Jan. 1, 1926; s. Solomon and Anna (Kopit) S.; div.; children: Paul Charles, Lawrence Bruce, Steven James. BA, Hunter Coll., 1950; MA, NYU, 1951. Cert. tchr., N.Y. Vice pres., assoc. dir. Spanish-Am. Inst., N.Y.C., 1955—. Author book and cassette program: Advanced English for the Foreign Born, 1958. Bd. dirs., pres. Nassau Ctr. for Developmentally Disabled, Woodbury, N.Y. Sgt. U.S. Army, 1944-46, ETO. Mem. Andiron Club, Phi Beta Kappa. Jewish. Office: Spanish Am Inst 215 W 43d St New York NY 10036

SCHIFFMAN, GERALD, microbiologist, educator; b. N.Y.C., May 22, 1926; s. Samuel and Mollie (Brookner) S.; m. Lillian Ebert, July 12, 1951; children: Stewart, Howard. B.A. cum laude, NYU, 1948, Ph.D., 1954. Asst. prof. microbiology Coll. Physicians and Surgeons, Columbia U., N.Y.C., 1960-63; asso. prof. dept. research medicine and microbiology U. Pa., Phila., 1963-70; prof. SUNY Health Sci. Ctr., Bklyn., 1970—; cons. Contbr. articles to profl. jours. Served in U.S. Army, 1943-45, ETO. Decorated Bronze Star; recipient Nichols award, 1947; Atomic Energy fellow, 1948-52; NIH grantee, 1974—. Mem. Am. Assn. Immunologists, Am. Chem. Soc., Am. Soc. Microbiology, AAAS, Harvey Soc., Soc. Complex Carbohydrates, Sigma Xi, Phi Beta Kappa, Mu Chi Sigma, Pi Mu Epsilon. Jewish. Office: 450 Clarkson Ave Brooklyn NY 11203-2098

SCHIFFMAN, JOSEPH HARRIS, literary historian, educator; b. N.Y.C., June 13, 1914; s. Samuel and Norma Minnie (Berger) S. B.A., L.I. U., 1937; M.A., Columbia U., 1947; Ph.D., NYU, 1951; m. Elizabeth Selsbee, Nov. 29, 1941; children: Jessica, Joshua. Instr. dept. English, L.I. U., 1945-49, asst. prof., 1949-51, assoc. prof., 1951-58, coord. grad. program Am. studies, 1956-58; prof. English Dickinson Coll., Carlisle, Pa., 1958-79, James Hope Caldwell prof. Am. studies, 1968-79, emeritus prof., 1979—, prof. continuing edn., 1979-86, 90-91, chmn. dept. English, 1959-69; sr. Fulbright vis. prof., India, 1964, U. Bordeaux (France), 1965-66, U. Indonesia, 1981-82; vis. prof. Grad. Sch. U. Pa., 1960, 67, New Coll., U. South Fla., spring 1981; lectr. U. P.R., 1984, Lifetime Learning, Sarasota, 1984-88; fgn. expert vis. prof. East China Normal U., Shanghai, 1985; founding dir. Am. Studies Rsch. Centre, India, 1964, Am. adv. com., 1990—; lectr. French Ednl. Radio System, 1966, acad. specialist program, Malaysia, Internat. Communication Agy., 1982; PhD theses examiner various univs., India, 1970—; lectr. numerous orgns. including Rotary, Pa. Writers Group, Jewish Community Ctr., Bosler Free Libr., AAUW, YWCA, Pa. Poetry Soc., Bethany Retirement Community, U.S.-China Peoples Friendship Assn., Sr. Action Ctr., Pa. Poets Soc., 1979—. With U.S. Army, 1942-45, ETO. Recipient Lindback Found. Disting. Teaching award, 1962, Fulbright-Hays award U.S. State Dept., 1964, 65, 81. Mem. Am. Studies Assn. (pres. Met. N.Y. chpt. 1958-59), MLA (head Am. lit. internat. bibliography com. 1961-64), Nat. Council Tchrs. English. Author: (with Lewis Leary) American Literature: A Critical History from Its Beginning to the Present, Ency. World Lit., 1973, William Faulkner, A Dramatic Evocation, 1981; contbr. articles on Am. writers to lit. jours.; contbr. introductions to Looking Backward (Edward Bellamy), 1959, Brook Farm (Lindsay Swift), 1961, Three Shorter Novels of Herman Melville, 1962; editor: Edward Bellamy, Selected Writings on Religion and Society, 1955; contbr. numerous book recs. including Idealist, Activist, The Haunted Chamber, The World a Ship, In Search of America, The Roaring Twenties, also revs. to scholarly jours. Home: 551 S Hanover St Carlisle PA 17013-3919 Office: Dickinson Coll Carlisle PA 17013

SCHIFFMAN, LAWRENCE STEVEN, internist, rheumatologist; b. Mineola, N.Y., Dec. 8, 1950; s. Carl Schiffman and Claire (Lynn) Baron; m. Susan Vera Friedman, Aug. 16, 1975; children: Theodore Carl, Celia Rose, Lucille Lynn. BA, SUNY, Stony Brook, 1973; MD, SUNY, Bklyn., 1977. Diplomate Am. Bd. Internal Medicine, Am. Bd. Rheumatology. Intern St. Vincent Hosp., Worcester, MA, 1977-78, resident in internal medicine, 1978-80; fellow rheumatology and immunology U. Mass. Med. Ctr., 1980-82; Practice medicine specializing in rheumatology Northampton, Mass., 1982—; mem. staff Cooley Dickinson Hosp., Northampton, 1982—; cons. in rheumatology VA Med. Ctr., Northampton, 1982—. Bd. dirs. Arthritis Found. of Springfield, Mass., 1989—. Rheumatology Immunolgy fellow U. Mass. Med. Ctr., 1980-82. Fellow Am. Coll. Rheumatology; mem. New Eng. Rheumatism Soc. Jewish. Office: Northampton Internal Medicine PC 190 Nonotuck St Northampton MA 01063-0001

SCHIFFMAN, LOUIS F., management consultant; b. Poland, July 15, 1927; s. Harry and Bertha (Fleder) S.;m. Mina R. Hankin, Dec. 28, 1963; children: Howard Laurence, Laura Lea. BChemE, NYU, 1948, MS, 1952, PhD, 1955. Rsch. engr. Pa. Grade Crude Oil Assn., Bradford, 1948-50; teaching fellow in chemistry NYU, 1950-54; rsch. chemist E.I. duPont de Nemours & Co., Wilmington, Del., 1954-56, Atlantic Refining Co., Phila., 1956-59; project leader, group leader, head corrosion sect. Amchem Products Inc., Ambler, Pa., 1959-70; pres. Techni Rsch. Assocs. Inc., Willow Grove, Pa., 1970—, real estate developer: ptnr. Bay Properties Co., Bay Club Marina, Margate, N.J., Willow Grove (Pa.) Assocs.; pub., editor Patent Licensing Gazette, 1968—, World Tech., 1975—; panelist on forum patents and inventions Delaware Valley Industry, 1973; mem. adv. oversight com. NSF, 1975, moderator energy conf. ERDA, Washington, 1976, Las Vegas, 1977. Editor: (with others) Guide to Available Technologies, 1985; contbr. to Encyclopedia of Chemical Technology, 1967; contbr. articles to profl. jours. Patentee in field. Recipient Founders Day award NYU, 1956. Fellow Am. Inst. Chemists; mem. Am. Chem. Soc., N.Y. Acad. Scis., Lic. Execs. Soc., Tech. Transfer Soc., Assn. Univ. Tech. Mgrs., Assn. Small Rsch. Cos. (editorial contbr. newsletter), Sigma Xi, Phi Lambda Upsilon. Home: 1837 Merritt Rd Abington PA 19001-4606 Office: Techni Rsch Assocs In Willow Grove Pla Willow Grove PA 19090

SCHIFFMAN, MINDY RAE, psychologist; b. N.Y.C., Mar. 31, 1952; d. William Louis and Barbara (Teck) S. BS, Simmons Coll., 1973, MBA, 1975; PhD, Columbia U., 1985. Lic. psychologist; cert. sex therapist. Psychotherapist Bklyn. Community Counseling Ctr., 1983-85; psychologist N.Y.C. Bd. Edn., 1983-86, Bronx Psychiat. Ctr., 1984-85; rsch. assoc. Meml. Sloan-Kettering, N.Y.C., 1985-86; clin. psychologist pvt. practice, N.Y.C., 1985—; psychologist IVF Australia, 1988-91; adj. asst. prof. Columbia U., N.Y.C., 1983-89; cons. in field. Psychology fellow Sloan-Kettering, 1986-88; Biomed. Sci. Rsch. grantee, N.Y.C. Psychiat. Inst., 1980. Mem. Am. Psychol. Assn., Am. Bd. Sexology, Am. Fertility Soc., N.Y. State Psychol. Assn. (mem. steering com. AIDS task force 1990—). Office: 1 Milligan Pl New York NY 10011

SCHIFFMAN, RICHARD GARY, otolaryngologist; b. Bklyn.. BS, Bklyn. Coll., 1973; MD, Tufts U., 1977. Internship MonteFiore Hosp., Bronx, N.Y., 1977-78, residency gen. surgery, 1978-79; residency otolaryngology Univ. Miami Med. Ctr., 1979-82; pvt. practice otolaryngology Bklyn., 1983—. Fellow Am. Acad. Otolaryngology-Head and Neck Surgery; mem. So. Med. Assn. Office: 2533 Batchelder St Brooklyn NY 11235

SCHIFFMAN, STEPHAN, management consultant; b. N.Y.C., June 14, 1946; s. Walter and Martha S.; B.S., Ithaca Coll., 1968; MSW, Cornell U., 1969; postgrad U. Md., 1971-72, Detroit U., 1971-73; m. Anne Feinglass, Aug. 25, 1974; children: Daniele Megan, Jennifer Ruth. Prin. Stephan Schiffman Assocs., N.Y.C., 1972—; dir. tng. United Jewish Appeal, N.Y.C., 1975—; practice psychotherapy, N.Y.C., 1976—; speaker on motivation and success, power sales, 1989; dir. D.E.I. Mgmt. Group, N.Y.C., 1979—; prin. Stephan Schiffman Telemarketing, 1992; mem. faculty Adelphi U., Garden City, N.Y., 1976-80; lectr. N.Y. U., 1977-80, New Sch. Social Research, 1978—, Queen's Coll., 1985—, Norwalk Community Coll., 1989;. Author: Cold Calling Techniques that Work, 1991, 3d edit., 1979, cassette edit. 1991, The Consultant's Handbook, 1988, 25 Sales Mistakes, 1990, Power Sales Presentations, 1989, Sales Habits of Highly Successful People, 1991; contbr. articles to profl. jours. Mem. Inst. Mgmt. Cons., Nat. Soc. Fund Raisers (dir.), Am. Mgmt. Assn., TC Acad. Arts and Scis., Soc. Profl. Mgmt. Cons., Am. Soc. Tng. and Devel., N.Y.C. Chamber Commerce and Industry (edn. chair, speaker), Cornell Club. Jewish. Home: 235 E 87th St New York NY 10128-3225 Office: 850 7th Ave Ste 1002 New York NY 10019-5230

SCHILDKRAUT, JOSEPH JACOB, psychiatrist, educator; b. Bklyn., Jan. 21, 1934; s. Simon and Shirley (Schwartz) S.; m. Elizabeth Rose Beilenson, May 22, 1966; children—Peter Jeremy, Michael John. A.B. summa cum laude, Harvard U., 1955, M.D. cum laude, 1959. Intern medicine U. Calif. Hosp., San Francisco, 1959-60; resident in psychiatry Mass. Mental Health Center, Boston, 1960-63; dir. neuropsychopharmacology lab., sr. psychiatrist, 1967—; research psychiatrist NIMH, Bethesda, Md., 1963-67; cons. NIMH, 1967-68; asst. prof. psychiatry Harvard Med. Sch., Boston, 1967-70; assoc. prof. Harvard Med. Sch., 1970-74, prof., 1974—; dir. psychiat. chemistry lab. New Eng. Deaconess Hosp., 1977—. Author: Neuorpsychopharmacology and the Affective Disorders, 1970; editor-in-chief Jour. Psychiat. Rsch., 1982—; mem. editorial bd. Psychophysiology, 1968-74, Jour. Psychiat. Rsch., 1968-82, Psychopharmacology, 1970-84, Sleep Revs., 1972-79, Communications in Psychopharmacology, 1974-81, Psychotherapy and

Psychosomatics, 1974-91, Rsch. Communications in Psychology, Psychiatry and Behavior, 1976—, Jour. Clin. Psychopharmacology, 1980, Integrative Psychiatry, 1982-89, 91—, others. Served as surgeon USPHS, 1963-65. Recipient Anna-Monika Found. prize, 1967, Hofheimer award Am. Psychiat. Assn., 1971, hon. mention award, 1968; McCurdy-Rinkel prize No. New Eng. Dist. br. Am. Psychiat. Assn., 1969; William C. Menninger award A.C.P., 1978. Mem. World Psychiat. Assn. (sec. sect. biol. psychiatry 1972-77), Psychiat. Research Soc., Am. Coll. Neuropsychopharmacology, Am. Psychiat. Assn., Am. Psychosomatic Soc., AAAS, Soc. Biol. Psychiatry, N.Y. Acad. Scis., Am. Psychopath. Assn., Am. Coll. Psychiatrists, Am. Soc. Pharmacology and Exptl. Therapeutics, Am. Soc. Neurochemistry, Group Without a Name, Assn. for Research in Nervous and Mental Disease, Collegium Internationale Neuropsychopharmacologicum, Soc. for Neurosci., Phi Beta Kappa. Home: 35 Jefferson Rd Chestnut Hill MA 02167-2341 Office: Mass Mental Health Ctr 74 Fenwood Rd Boston MA 02115-6106

SCHILDKRAUT, PETER JEREMY, congressional staff member; b. Boston, May 10, 1968; s. Joseph J. and Elizabeth (Beilenson) S. AB magna cum laude, Harvard Coll., 1990. Rsch. intern Dem. Congl. Campaign Com., Washington, 1988, Dukakis-Bentsen '88, Boston, 1988; rsch. assoc. Coun. on Hemispheric Affairs, Washington, 1989; rsch. asst. Dem. Congl. Campaign Com., Washington, 1990; legis. asst. U.S. Rep. Carl C. Perkins, Washington, 1991—. Contbr. articles to profl. jours. Bd. dirs. Harvard Internat. Rels. Coun., Inc., Cambridge, Mass., 1989-90, bd. auditors, 1988-90; polling pl. coord. Beilenson for City Coun., Balt., 1991; vol. Campaign for Mass. Future, Boston, 1990, Beilenson for Del., Balt., 1990, Clinton for Pres. Rsch. Dept., Washington, 1992. John Harvard scholar, 1989-90, Harvard Coll. scholar, 1987-89. Mem. Harvard Club of Washington. Democrat. Jewish. Home: 4600 Connecticut Ave NW 324 Washington DC 20008 Office: Hon Carl C Perkins MC 1004 Longworth HOB Washington DC 20515

SCHILLER, MARILYN, pediatric psychologist; b. Astoria, N.Y., Apr. 11, 1951; d. Harry and Margaret (Kremer) S. BA, Fordham U., 1971; MA, NYU, 1980, PhD, 1989. Lic. psychologist, N.Y. Sr. project asst. NYU Med. Ctr., N.Y.C., 1979-81; rsch. coord. Columbia Presbyn. Med. Ctr., N.Y.C., 1983-86; project dir. Am. Health Found., N.Y.C., 1986-88; rsch. asst. dept. pediatrics Mt. Sinai Sch. Medicine, N.Y.C., 1987-89, instr. dept. pediatrics, 1989-91, asst. prof. dept. pediatrics, 1991—; vis. rsch. assoc. div. pediatric hematology Cornell Med. Coll., N.Y.C., 1989—; mem. neuropsychology com. Hemophilia Growth and Devel. Study, L.A., 1989—. Author: (with others) Health Education in Schools, 1988; contbr. articles to profl. jours. Mem. Am. Psychol. Assn., Assn. for Care of Children's Health (Emma Plank scholar 1985), Soc. of Devel. Behavioral Pediatrics, Soc. Pediatric Psychology. Home: 382 Central Park W Apt 2V New York NY 10025-6045 Office: Mt Sinai Med Ctr Dept Pediatrics Annenberg 4-74 1 Gustave Levy Pl Box 1208 New York NY 10029-6504

SCHILLING, EDWARD GEORGE, statistician, educator, quality control consultant; b. Lancaster, N.Y., Nov. 9, 1931; s. Edward Frank and Mildred Regina (Frey) S.; m. Jean Catherine Bork, Sept. 5, 1959; children: Elizabeth Ann, Kathryn Jean. BA, U. Buffalo, 1953, MBA, 1954; MS, Rutgers U., 1962, PhD, 1967. Registered profl. engr., Calif. Instr. stats. U. Buffalo, 1957-59; engr. RCA, Somerville, N.J., 1959-61; sr. engr. Carborundum Co., Niagara Falls, N.Y., 1962-64; instr. Rutgers U., New Brunswick, N.J., 1964-67; assoc. prof. Rochester Inst. Tech., N.Y., 1967-69, prof., chmn. grad. stats., 1983-92, Paul A. Miller prof., 1983-92; dir. Ctr. for Quality and Applied Stats., 1992—; cons. statistician Gen. Electric Co., Cleve., 1969-74; mgr. stats. and quality systems operation Gen. Electric Lighting Bus. Group, Cleve., 1975-80, mgr. lighting quality operation, 1980-83; instr. stats. Case Western Res. U., 1969-70; lectr. math. U. Akron, 1974; adj. assoc. prof. math. Cleve. State U., 1976; series editor Marcel Dekker Inc., N.Y.C., 1984—. Author: Acceptance Sampling in Quality Control, 1982, Process Quality Control, 1990. Served with U.S. Army, 1955-57. Fellow Am. Statis. Assn. (pres. Cleve. chpt. 1973, Rochester chpt. 1990), Am. Soc. Quality Control (chmn. Edwards medal com. 1981-90, Shewhart medal com. 1990—, chmn. ANSI Z-1 com. quality assurance 1988-90, Brumbaugh awards 1973, 78, 79, 81, Shewhart medal 1983, Ellis R. Ott award Met. sect. 1984); mem. ASTM, Am. Econ. Assn., Inst. Math. Stats. Lutheran. Home: 71 Gateway Rd Rochester NY 14624-4433 Office: Rochester Inst Tech 1 Lomb Memorial Dr Rochester NY 14623-5603

SCHILLING, FRANKLIN CHARLES, JR., retail management professional; b. Balt., Apr. 17, 1958; s. Franklin Charles and Shirley Jean (Whitehurst) S.; m. Priscilla Lynn Stansbury, Apr. 16, 1983. Student, Dundalk Community Coll., 1975-77. Dept. mgr. Santonis Market, Inc., Balt., 1976-80; store mgr. A&P Plus Food Stores, Balt., 1980-82; area supr. Southland Corp/7-Eleven, Suitland, Md., 1982-85; mgr. retail ops. Moore Oil Co./Makin' Tracks Stores, Washington, N.C., 1986, Besche Oil Co./Quik Shop Stores, Waldorf, Md., 1987-89; dist. mgr. Cloverland Dairies/Royal Farm Stores, Balt., 1989—. Mem. Rep. Nat. Com. Mem. Mid-Atlantic Food Dealers Assn. Republican. Lutheran. Home: 6614 Marne Ave Baltimore MD 21224-6241 Office: Cloverland Dairies/Royal Farm Stores 2200 N Monroe St Baltimore MD 21217-1320

SCHILLING, JAMES JOSEPH, community relations professional; b. Kingston, Pa.; s. James Joseph and Bessmarie (Williams) S.; m. Susan Marie Pentrack, July 29, 1989; 1 child, Stephen Tyler. BA in Journalism, Pa. State U., 1981. Pub. rels. asst. Wilkes-Barre (Pa.) Gen. Hosp., 1981-86, dir. community rels., 1986—. Bd. dirs. Wyoming Valley (Pa.) unit Am. Cancer Soc., 1985—, Northeast Pa. chpt. Make-a-Wish Found., 1989—, Northeast Pa. unit Am. Heart Assn., 1990—. Cert. mem. Am. Soc. Health Care Mktg. and Pub. Rels. Office: Wilkes Barre Gen Hosp North River at Auburn St Wilkes Barre PA 18764

SCHIMIZZI, NED VINCENT, education educator; b. Mishawaka, Ind., Jan. 27, 1936; s. Anthony and Josephine (Miceli) S.; B.S., Ind. U., 1958, M.S., 1964, Ed.D., 1968. Classroom tchr. LaPorte County (Ind.) Schs., 1961-63, Bloomington (Ind.) Met. Schs., 1964-66; coordinator elem. student teaching program Ind. U., 1966-68; assoc. prof. dept. elem. edn. and reading SUNY, Coll. at Buffalo, 1968—; on sabbatical leave to study microcomputer instrnl. applications, 1981-83; cons. U.S. Senate com. on commerce, 1975; cons. on nat. metric conversion Gen. Dynamics, 1976, GAO, 1977; author and speaker in field. With USAR, 1959-64. Recipient numerous letters of commendation, polit., mil., ednl. and found. ofcls. Mem. Am. Ednl. Research Assn., Assn. Tchr. Educators N.Y. State, Assn. Supervision and Curriculum Devel. (speaker), Nat. Council Tchrs. Math., Research Council Diagnostic and Prescriptive Math., N.Y. State Assn. Tchrs. Math., Assn. Computing in Math. and Sci., Ind. U. Alumni Assn., Ind. U. Found., Phi Delta Kappa (pres. Buffalo State Coll. chpt. 1988-89, faculty advisor, past pres., faculty sponsor chpt. 165 1991—). Author: Mastering the Metric System, 1975; (studies) Microcomputers in the Schools, Microcomputers on Campus; contbr. articles to profl. jours. Patentee in field. Home: 1978 Delaware Ave Buffalo NY 14216-3539 Office: SUNY Buffalo Elmwood Hall 1300 Elmwood Ave Buffalo NY 14222

SCHIMMEL, ALLAN, rail company executive; b. Sioux Center, Iowa, June 18, 1940; s. Arie and Magdalena J. (Scheffer) S. BA, Northwestern Coll., 1962; MA, U. Iowa, 1966. Adminstrv. asst. Congressman Fred Schwengel, Washington, 1969-72, Congressman Howard W. Robison, Washington, 1973-74; asst. v.p. congl. relations U.W. Ry. Assn., Washington, 1975-76; dir. fed. relations Conrail, Washington, 1976-79; exec. dir. staff studies Conrail, Phila., 1979-80, corp. sec., asst. to chmn., 1980-90, v.p. adminstrv. svcs., corp. sec., 1990—; chmn. Monongahela Ry. Co., 1990—; bd. dirs. Belt R.R. Chgo., Peoria & Pekin Union Ry. Co., Creve Coeur, Ill. Trustee Northwestern Coll., Orange City, Iowa, 1971-81, 83-90; pres. bd. trustees First Presbyn. Ch., Phila., 1983-88, mem. session, 1990—. Mem. Am. Soc. Corp. Secs., The Com. of Seventy. Republican. Presbyterian. Office: Consol Rail Corp 1838 Six Penn Center Philadelphia PA 19104

SCHIMMEL, DAVID M., law educator; b. Balt., Mar. 30, 1934; s. Isidore William and Blanche (Sakols) S.; m. Barbara Barlin, June 18, 1961; children: Suzanne, Jonathan, Joanna. BA, Duke U., 1955; JD, Yale U., 1958; BHL, Hebrew Union Coll., 1962. Bar: Md. 1959, Mass. 1985, U.S. Supreme Ct. 1963. Assoc. Schimmel, Hettleman and Tatelbaum, Balt., 1959-60; ops. officer West African div. U.S. Peace Corps, Washington, 1962-63, exec. officer office of planning, evaluation and rsch., 1964-66; assoc. dir. Peace Corps Ethiopia, Addis Ababa, 1963-64; dir. Vols. to Am. U.S. Dept. State, Washington, 1966-67; dir. Peace Corps V.I. Tng. Ctr., 1967-68; assoc. prof. Sch. Edn. U. Mass., Amherst, 1968-72, prof., 1972—, dir. ednl. policy and adminstrn. program, 1989—; vis. scholar UCLA, 1975; lectr. Grad. Sch. Edn., Harvard U., Cambridge, Mass., 1984-85. Co-author: The Rights of Students and Teachers, 1982, Parents, Schools and the Law, 1987 (Am. Sch. Bd. Jour. "Must" book of 1988), Teachers and the Law, 3d edit., 1991, A Bicentennial Guide for Lawyers and Teachers, 1990; mem. authors com. Edn. Law Reporter, St. Paul, 1984—. Mem. Mass. Community Svc. Commn. 2d lt. U.S. Army, 1959. Grantee NEH, 1982. Mem. Mass. Assn. Law-Related Edn. (bd. dirs., pres. 1975-81, 86-90, Disting. Svc. award 1981), Am. Ednl. Rsch. Assn., Nat. Orgn. Legal Problems in Edn., Phi Alpha Delta. Democrat. Home: 200 W Pomeroy Ln Amherst MA 01002-3241 Office: U Mass 265 Hills S Amherst MA 01003

SCHIMMEL, PAUL REINHARD, biochemist, biophysicist, educator; b. Hartford, Conn., Aug. 4, 1940; s. Alfred E. and Doris (Hudson) S.; m. Judith F. Ritz, Dec. 30, 1961; children: Kirsten, Katherine. A.B., Ohio Wesleyan U., 1962; postgrad., Tufts U. Sch. Medicine, 1962-63, Mass. Inst. Tech., 1963-65, Cornell U., 1965-66, Stanford U., 1966-67, U. Calif., Santa Barbara, 1975-76; Ph.D., Mass. Inst. Tech., 1966. Asst. prof. biology and chemistry Mass. Inst. Tech., 1967-71, assoc. prof., 1971-76, prof. biochemistry and biophysics, 1976-92, John D. MacArthur prof. biochemistry and biophysics, 1992—; mem. NIH Study Sect. Physiol. Chemistry, 1975-79; indsl. cons. on enzymes and recombinant DNA. Author: (with C. Cantor) Biophysical Chemistry, 3 vols., 1980; contbr. numerous articles to profl. jours.; mem. editorial bd. Archives Biochemistry, Biophysics, 1976-80, Nucleic Acids Rsch., 1976-80, Jour. Biol. Chemistry, 1977-82, Biopolymers, 1979-88, Internat. Jour. Biol. Macromolecules, 1983-89, Trends in Biochem. Scis., 1984—, Biochemistry, 1989—, Accounts of Chem. Rsch., 1989—, European Jour. Biochemistry, 1991—, Protein Science, 1991—. Alfred P. Sloan fellow, 1970-72. Fellow AAAS; mem. NAS, Am. Chem. Soc. (Pfizer award 1978, chmn. div. biol. chemistry 1984-85), Am. Soc. for Biochemistry and Molecular Biology, Am. Acad. Arts and Scis., Protein Soc. Office: MIT Dept Biology Cambridge MA 02139

SCHINDLER, DONALD WARREN, biopharmaceutical engineer, consultant; b. Westfield, N.J., Apr. 2, 1925; s. Wilbur Vincent and Francis Lillian (Hollberg) S.; m. Scot N. Stahl, Sept. 7, 1947 (div. Aug. 1971); children: Leslie, Mark; m. Dorothy Jean Martin, July 1, 1980; children: William, Bruce, Judy, Patricia, Donna, Holly, Larry. AB in Biol. Scis., Marietta (Ohio) Coll. Dir. biol. mfg. Ortho Pharm. Corp., Raritan, N.J., 1951-59; mgr. biol. mfg. Warner-Lambert Pharm. Co., Morris Plains, N.J., 1959-74; gen. mgr. Fisher Sci. Diagnostics Div., Orangeburg, N.Y., 1978-82; pres. SRC Assocs., Park Ridge, N.J., 1982—; mem. adv. bd. Okla. Immunological Labs., Oklahoma City, 1972-78; cons. Serono Labs. Inc., Boston, 1982-91, U. Minn., Mpls., 1984-91. Pres. Passaic Twp. Sch. Bd., Stirling, N.J., 1964-70; trustee 1st Congl. Ch., Park Ridge, N.J., 1987-90; regional dir. tng. Boy Scouts Am. Watchung Area coun., Plainfield, N.J., 1968-71. With USNR, 1942-46, PTO. Mem. Am. Chem. Soc., Am. Inst. Chemists, Am. Legion, N.Y. ACad. Scis., Parenteral Drug Assn., Internat. Soc. Pharm. Engrs. Republican. Office: SRC Assocs 150 Upper Saddle River Rd Ste 101 Montvale NJ 07645-1027

SCHINE, JOAN GOLDWASSER, education center administrator; b. N.Y.C., Aug. 26, 1923; d. I. Edwin and Edith (Goldstein) Goldwasser; m. Harold L. Schine, Feb. 13, 1944; children: Judith Schine Seltz, James, Robert, Beth. BA, Smith Coll., Northampton, Mass., 1943. Program developer Higher Edn. Ctr. for Urban Studies, Bridgeport, Conn., 1972-74; project dir. Coop. Edn. Svcs., Fairfield County, Conn., 1974-76; program assoc. Nat. Commn. on Resources for Youth, N.Y.C., 1976-79, sr. program assoc., 1979-83; dir. Early Adolescent Helper Program, N.Y.C., 1983-91, Nat. Ctr. for Svc. Learning in Early Adolescence, N.Y.C., 1991—; mem. youth com. Lilly Endowment, Indpls., 1989—, adv. group Pub./Pvt. Ventures, Phila., 1988—, adv. com. Operation SMART, Girls Inc., N.Y.C., 1986, Edn. for Parenting, Phila., 1988—, Chancellor's Working Group on Community Svc., N.Y.C., 1990-91. Co-author: Connections: Service Learning in the Middle Grades, 1989. Mem. Bd. Edn., Westport, Conn., 1965-71, chmn. 1969-71. Recipient Woman of Valor award Ednl. Equity Concepts, 1991. Mem. Nat. Middle Sch. Assn. Office: Ctr Svc Learning Early Adolescence CASE 25 W 43rd St New York NY 10036

SCHIPITSCH, DOUGLAS ANTHONY, physician; b. Evergreen Park, Ill., Apr. 2, 1950; s. Julius J. and Mary L. (Jurenka) S.; m. Marilyn L. Maas, Mar. 1, 1981. BS, Ill. Benedictine Coll., 1972; MD, Loyola U., Maywood, Ill., 1975. Cert. Am. Bd. Surgery. Intern St. Francis Hosp., Evanston, Ill., 1975-76, resident, 1976-78; resident Loyola U. Med. Ctr., Maywood, Ill., 1978-80; staff surgeon Cumberland (Wis.) Med. Clinic, 1980-82, Redington-Fairview Hosp., Skowhegan, Maine, 1982—. Fellow ACS. Office: 21 Fairview Ave # 629 Skowhegan ME 04976-1403

SCHIPPERS, LOUIS, clinical psychologist, educator; b. Houston, Dec. 2, 1938; s. Louis and Margaret (Ude) S.; m. Patsy Park Patrick, June 10, 1960; children: Kimberly, Lori, Eric. BA, Phillips U., 1960; MDiv, Tex. Christian U., 1963; PhD, Boston U., 1970. Lic. psychologist, Mass. Prof. psychology Bridgewater (Mass.) St. Coll., 1965—; dir. group therapy Pembroke (Mass.) Hosp., 1985—; dir., co-owner Mass. Bay Counseling, Pembroke, 1988—. Editor Issues in Psychotherapy, 1983. Recipient Fulbright-Hayes fellowship Peoples Republic of China, 1990. Mem. APA, Am. Group Psychotherapy Assn., Mass. Psychol. Assn. Office: Mass Bay Counseling 31 Schoosett St Pembroke MA 02359-1821

SCHIRICK, EDWARD ARTHUR, insurance executive; b. Kingston, N.Y., Oct. 26, 1948; s. George F. and Mary M. (Fallon) S.; m. Cathleen M. Sorenson, Mar. 13, 1971; children: Scott, Michael, Elizabeth. BA, Villanova U., 1970. CPCU, cert. ins. counselor. Account exec. Beck & Levy-Tegeler, Inc., Liberty, N.Y., 1972-74; mgr. Lawrence A. Quilty, Inc., Kingston, 1974-76; sr. v.p. Markel Rhulen Underwriters & Brokers, Monticello, N.Y., 1976—; sr. v.p., bd. dirs. Markel Rhulen Ins. Co. Trustee Fund for Advancement of Camping, 1987-91. Mem. Am. Mgmt. Assn., Am. Camping Assn (spl. recognition for outstanding svc. 1986), Soc. CPCU (pres. Hudson Valley chpt. 1985-86), Soc. Cert. Inst. Counselors. Office: Markel Rhulen Underwriters & Brokers 217 Broadway Monticello NY 12701-1392

SCHIRICK, ROBERT JOHN, insulation manufacturer executive; b. Union City, N.J., Nov. 2, 1928; s. Harold Austin and Anne Janette (Whyte) S.; m. Dolores Irene Sofsky, June 21, 1952; children: Dave Michael, Susan Ann, John Alan. BSChemE, Lehigh U., 1952. Rsch. engr. Nat. Gypsum Co., Tonawanda, N.Y., 1952-55, rsch. group leader, 1956-62, sr. rsch. group leader, 1962-66; internat. v.p. Baldwin-Ehret-Hill Co., Trenton, N.J., 1967-68; internat. div. pres. Keene Corp., Princeton, N.J., 1969-75; v.p., gen. mgr. Jungers Corp., Clarks Summit, Pa., 1976-81; corp. and ind. sales mgr. U.S. Mineral Products Co., Stanhope, N.J., 1982-85, 91—; v.p., gen. mgr. Les Industries CAFCO Ltee, Thetford-Mines, Quebec, Can., 1986-90; dir. Soc. Italo Am. SpA, Lodi, Italy, 1967-75, Can. Assn. Man Made Mineral Fiber Mfgs., 1989-90; mem. Lic. Execs. Soc., N.Y.C., 1967-75. Patentee in field. Mem. Rotary, Trenton, 1967-75. With USN, 1946-48. Republican. Roman Catholic. Office: US Mineral Products Co 41 Furnace St Stanhope NJ 07874

SCHIVEK, ELAINE RONA, legal researcher; b. Boston, Mar. 9, 1930; d. Rueben and Sarah (Berch) Weinberg; m. James Schivek, Oct. 30, 1949 (dec. Feb. 1982); children: Helene Marcia Schivek Demeo, Alan Jay, Howard Richard. BA in Edn. cum laude, Suffolk U., 1953, MEd in Adminstrn. and Supervision magna cum laude, 1980; postgrad. Boston U., 1953, 65, 68, Boston State Coll., 1967-69, Simmons Coll., 1968-69, Lesley Grad. Sch., 1976-78, So. New England Sch. Law, 1983-90, 1976-78, Suffolk U., 1986—, U. Lowell (Mass.), 1989-90. Lic. tchr., cert. in adminstrn., spl. edn., Mass. Elem. tchr. Boston Sch. Dept., Boston and Roxbury, Mass., 1957-69, Westwood Elem. Sch., Mass., 1969-70, Revere Sch. Dept., Mass., 1970-71; office mgr. Storm/Check Aluminum Co., Hyde Park, Mass., 1971-79; elem. and secondary tchr. Cambridge (Mass.) Schs., 1979-84; legal researcher Registry of Motor Vehicles, Boston, 1984—, mgr., 1989; pvt. tutor Randolph Sch. Dept., Mass., 1983—. Mem. Randolph Clean Up Com., 1985-86, Dem. Town Com., Randolph, 1986—; candidate for sch. com. Randolph Sch. Dept., 1986, 88; mgr. candidate at large Boston City Coun., State Rep. Randolph and Canton, Mass, 1990-94; candidate for pres. Wheaton Coll., 1991—; active Mass. Polit. Caucus Women's Group, Boston, 1985-86, Women's Dem. Networking Group, Newton, Mass., 1985-86; fundraiser Senator John Kerry's Campaign, Boston, 1984-86, Gerald D'Amico for lt. gov., Mass., 1986—, Gov. Michael Dukakis for President, 1988, New Hampshire; fundraiser, campaign mgr. state rep. candidate, Mass., 1986—, candidate Boston City Coun., 1987; past v.p. and pres. Jewish War Vets. of Milton, Mass.; bd. dirs. Combined Jewish Philanthropies Career Div., 1985—; active Randolph Conservation Commn., 1986—. Five undergrad. scholars Suffolk U., Boston, 1948-53; teaching fellow Suffolk U. Grad. Sch., 1979-80; named Outstanding Woman Alumni Class of 1953 Suffolk U., 1988; Ednl. Coll. Greater Mass. intern, Brookline, Mass., 1984-85. Mem. Mass. Deans, Counselors and Adminstrs., Suffolk U. Alumnae Assn. (fundraiser), Mass. Caucus for Women, Knights of Pythias (bd. dirs., trustee, 1960-75), Brandeis U. Club (bd. dirs. 1976-80). Avocations: travel, reading, writing. Office: Registry Motor Vehicles 100 Nashua St Boston MA 02114-1106

SCHLABACH, TOM DANIEL, materials consultant; b. Cleve., July 4, 1924; s. Tom Daniel and Sarah (Gannon) S.; m. Ruth May McFadden, June 19, 1948; children: Timothy Daniel, Gretchen Ann. BS, Baldwin-Wallace Coll., 1948; PhD, Mich. State U., 1952. Mem. tech. staff AT&T Bell Labs., Murray Hill, N.J., 1952-56, supr., 1956-65, dept. head, 1965-89; pvt. practice materials cons. Whippany, N.J., 1989—; cons. Internat. Copper Assn., Inc., N.Y.C., 1965—; mem. coun. on energy engring. rsch. U.S. Dept. Energy, Washington, 1989—. Author: Printed and Integrated Circuitry, 1963; contbr. articles to profl. jours. Bd. dirs. Head Start, Morris County, N.J., 1992—. With USN, 1943-46 PTO. Mich. State U. fellow, 1951. Fellow AAAS, ASM Internat.; mem. Minerals, Metals and Materials Soc. (chmn. nonferrous metals com. 1980-84), Materials Rsch. Soc. Republican. Episcopalian. Home and Office: 4 Adams Dr Whippany NJ 07981-2050

SCHLACKMAN, NEIL, pediatrician, hematologist, oncologist, educator; b. Phila., Mar. 4, 1943; s. Harry and Rose (Strouss) S.; m. Cheryl I. Goldberg, June 20, 1965; children: Lisa, Keith. BA, U. Pa., 1964; MD, Hahnemann Med. Coll., 1968. Diplomate Am. Bd. Pediatrics, Am. Bd. Pediatric Hematology and Oncology. Resident and fellow in pediatrics St. Christopher's Hosp. for Children, Phila., 1968-71; pvt. practice, Sellersville, Pa., 1973-87; med. dir., v.p. med. delivery US Healthcare, Blue Bell, Pa., 1987—; assoc. prof. pediatrics Temple U. Med. Sch., Phila., 1973—. Maj. M.C., USAF, 1971-73. Fellow Am. Acad. Pediatrics (alt. chmn. Pa. chpt.); mem. AMA, Am. Coll. Physican Execs., Phila. Pediatric Soc. Office: US Healthcare PO Box 207 Blue Bell PA 19422-0207

SCHLAGER, MAYNARD MORTON, psychologist, consultant; b. Winthrop, Mass., Apr. 3, 1928; s. Saul and Rose Schlager; m. Nathalie Lewin, Dec. 30, 1966; children: Mason, Diane, David, Michael. BA, L.I. U., 1949; student, Yeshiva Ohr Yisroel, 1956, Mesivta Chaim Berlin, Jewish Theol. Sem., Hebrew Union Coll.; MA, Assumption Coll., 1976; D Ministry, Andover Newton Theol. Sch., 1978. Ordained rabbi, 1956; lic. psychologist, Mass.; accredited Coun. Nat. Register Health svc. and Providers in Psychology. Intern in clin. psychology U. Denver, 1953-54, Danvers State Hosp.-Tewksbury State Hosp.-Melrose-Wakefield, Mass., 1974-75; dir. Am. Counseling Ctrs., Peabody and Melrose, Mass., 1954—; dir. diet workshop div. Am. Counseling Ctrs., Peabody and Melrose, 1985—; supr. Worcester (Mass.) Pastoral Counseling Ctr., 1976-77. Author: Mixed Marriage, 1984. Acting chaplain USAF, 1950-54. Fellow Internat. Coun. Sex Edn. and Parenthood, Am. U., 1982. Mem. APA, Am. Assn. Marriage and Family Therapy (clin.), Mass. Assn. Marriage and Family Therapy, Mass. Psychol. Assn., Mixed Marriage Soc. U.S.A. (founder, bd. dirs. 1964—), Am. Legion (chaplain Malden 1978-83, Middlesex County 1983-85), Jewish War Vets. (vice comdr. 1965-66, Sugarman trophy 1966), B'nai B'rith (pres. Swampscott-Marblehead chpt. 1961-62, cert. of honor 1962), Masons. Office: Am Counseling Ctrs PO Box 3633 Peabody MA 01961-3633

SCHLAIN, DAVID, chemical engineer; b. Phila., July 21, 1910; s. Joseph and Anna (Klotka) S. BSChemE, U. Pa., 1932, MS in Edn., 1937; PhD in Chem. Engring., U. Md., 1951. Registered prof. engr., Md.; cert. chemist. Chemist U.S. Geol. Survey, Washington, 1937; metallurgist, chemist U.S. Bur. of Mines, Salt Lake City and, College Park, Md., 1937-48; electrochemist, sect. chief U.S. Bur. of Mines, College Park, 1948-55, project coord., 1955-70, rsch. supr., 1970-74; rsch. chem. engr. U.S. Bur. of Mines, College Park/Avondale, Md., 1974-81. Contbr. articles to profl. jours.; patentee in field. Recipient Meritorious Svc. award U.S. Dept. Interior, 1973. Fellow Am. Inst. Chemists, Wash. Acad. Scis.; mem. Am. Chem. Soc. (emeritus), Electrochem. Soc. (emeritus, gen. chmn. nat. meetings 1964, 71, various office local sects.), Electroplaters and Surface Finishers Soc. (Hanney award 1962, Precious Metals award 1970, emeritus), Am. Inst. Minerals, Metall. and Petroleum Engrs. (sr.), Nat. Assn. Corrosion Engrs. (accredited corrosion specialist). Home: 2A Gardenway Greenbelt MD 20770-1717

SCHLAKMAN, GEOFFREY CRAIG, information systems executive; b. Bklyn., Jan. 5, 1954; s. Irvine A. and Harriet (Kravet) S.; m. Jo-Anne C. DeCicco, Apr. 17, 1982; children: Ian Adrew, Michael Anthony. BS in Computer Sci., N.Y. Inst. Tech., Old Westbury, 1975, MBA, 1983. Systems analyst Grumman/CallData, Woodbury, N.Y., 1974-79; cons. Ernst & Young, N.Y.C., 1979-81; mktg. dir. Tekkon Computer Svcs., Syosset, N.Y., 1981-83; asst. v.p. Chemical Bank, N.Y.C., 1983-89; gen. mgr. info. systems Weight Watchers Internat./HJ Heinz, Jericho, N.Y., 1989-92; dir. software migration Actmedia, Inc., Norwalk, Conn., 1992—. Republican. Office: ACI Media Inc 301 Merritt 7 Norwalk CT 06856-5102

SCHLAM, MARK HOWARD, international marketing executive; b. Bklyn., Sept. 24, 1951; s. Murray J. and Sophia (Bonis) S.; B.S., Elec. Engring. (N.Y. State Regents scholar), Poly. Inst. Bklyn., 1972, M.S., 1973. Sales assoc. F.W. Madigan Real Estate Co., Flushing, N.Y., 1973-74; sales engr. Dayton T. Brown, Inc., Bohemia, N.Y., 1975-77; sr. mktg. rep. advanced systems Sperry Marine Systems, Gt. Neck, N.Y., 1977-80; pres. Mark H. Schlam Co. Internat., Melville, N.Y., 1980—, MHSCO Internat. Corp., East Northport, N.Y., 1987—; assoc. editor Poly. Press, Bklyn., 1969-76. Mem. Audio Engring. Soc., Acoustical Soc. Am., AIAA, Am. Soc. Naval Engrs., Armen Forces Communications and Electronics Assn., IEEE, Soc. Tech. Communication, Soc. Automotive Engrs., AAAS, Nat. Pilots Assn., Assn. Old Crows, Nat. Soc. Profl. Engrs., Realtors Nat. Mktg. Inst., Poly. Inst. N.Y. Alumni Assn. (asso. dir. 1973—), Tau Delta Phi. Club: Masons. Asst. editor: Computer Processing in Communications, 1970, Submillimeter Waves, 1971; assoc. editor Computers and Automata, 1971, Computer-Communications Networks and Teletraffic, 1972, Optical and Acoustical Micro-Electronics, 1975, Computer Software Engineering, 1976. Office: PO Box 97 East Northport NY 11731-0097

SCHLANG, DAVID, real estate executive, lawyer; b. N.Y.C., May 2, 1912; s. Alexander and Blanche (Cohen) S.; m. Arlene Roth, May 9, 1948. LLB, NYU, 1933. Bar: N.Y., 1935, U.S. Dist. Ct. (so. dist.) N.Y. 1940. Individual practice law, 1935-42; sec. Schlang Bros. & Co., Inc., N.Y.C., 1945—, pres., 1978—; gen. ptnr. 67 Wall St. Co., Maidgold Assocs.; pres. Corner Gold Realty Corp. Bd. trustees Brookdale Hosp., Bklyn., 1980—, v.p., 1983—; bd. dirs. Samuel Schulman Inst. Nursing and Rehab. of Brookdale Hosp., 1973—, sec. bd. dirs., 1976—; dir. Legion Meml. Sq., Inc., 1983—; sec. Schlang Found., 1945—; founding mem. U.S. Congl. Adv. Bd.; mem. U.S. Def. Com. Served with AUS, 1942-45. Decorated Croix de Guerre with palm (France); recipient Conspicuous Service award State of N.Y., 1965. Mem. Criminal Investigation Div. Agts. Assn., ABA, N.Y. State Bar Assn., N.Y. County Lawyers Assn., Real Estate Bd. N.Y., N.Y. State Assn. Realtors and Appraisers, Internat. Orgn. Real Estate Appraisers, Nat. Assn. Real Estate Appraisers. Clubs: New Nautilus Beach and Country (Atlantic Beach, N.Y.); U.S. Senatorial, Town (N.Y.C.), Metropolitan (N.Y.C.). Home: 737 Park Ave New York NY 10021-4256 Office: 67 Wall St New York NY 10005-3101

SCHLANG, JOSEPH, business executive; b. N.Y.C., Feb. 24, 1911; s. Alexander and Blanche (Cohen) S.; m. Bernice S. Breitbart, June 8, 1944; 1 son, Stuart Alexander. B.C.S., N.Y. U., 1931. Organized firm of Schlang Bros. & Co. (real estate), N.Y.C., 1934; controlled bldgs. 80, 89, 67 and 41 Broad St., 100 Gold St., 132 Nassau St., 30 Pine St., 67 Wall St., 15 Moore St., 27 William St.; co-owner others; part owner bldg. material co. of Candee, Smith & Howland Co., 1944-55; dir., part owner Fork Lift Truck Rental Corp., Bond Indsl. Maintenance Corp., 1956-57; owner 271 Central Park

West, 1958-59; ltd. ptnr. 975 Park Ave., 1957-60, 1165 Park Av., 1957-60, Majidot Realty Corp., 1958-68, Maidgold Realty Corp., 1960-81, 67 Wall St. Co., 1957-81, 80 Broad St., 1945-61, 1036 Park Ave. Assocs., 1960-61, N.Y. Stock Exchange firm Kalb, Voorhis & Co., 1958-85; pres. Schlang Manuscript Co., Inc., 1965-85, Internat. Opera Co., 1969-85, Opera Gems, Inc., 1971-85, Opera Presentations, Inc., 1972-88; founder, owner bank locations, N.Y, Fla., U.S.A.-Inc., Schlang Manuscript Co.; owner, contr. 125 ballet and art films, 1970-88; over 500 presentations of fims in U.S.A., Palm Beach, N.Y. Producer, sponsor, panelist weekly radio programs Opera Stars of Tomorrow, 1973-79, 100 and More Ways to Improve New York City, WNYC, 1973-74; assoc. pub. Graphic History Jewish Heritage, 1963, The Bible and Modern Medicine, 1963; author: booklet Survey of the Financial District of New York City, 1940, Financial District of New York City, 1956, also numerous newspaper and mag. articles. Asst. treas. Downtown Hosp., 1945-47; nat. council N.Y. Met. Opera, 1960—, 1st patron, 1962—; bd. dirs. Bklyn. Lyric Opera Co., 1972—, chmn. bd., 1991—; life mem. Concert Artists Guild, 1972—; sponsor N.Y.C. Opera, 1962-63; patron Cultural Film Club, Palm Beach, Fla., 1974, Palm Beach Opera, Greater Miami Opera, Norton Gallery of Art, Hist. Assn. Palm Beaches; life mem., patron Round Table Palm Beach, Soc. Four Arts; founder, 1st chmn. bus. Com. for Arts of Palm Beach County, 1979-82; founder, creator Met. Opera Co., patron 1962, 1st patron 1962—; adviser Library of Presdl. Papers, 1966-70; cons. Mayor's Cultural Com., Yonkers, 1972-74, Mamaroneck, 1972-73; sec., dir. Kehillah of N.Y.C. (Jewish community); sec., treas. Synagogue Council Am., 1953-57, mem. exec. com., dir., 1947-67; bd. dirs. Union Orthodox Jewish Congregations of Am., sec.-treas., 1944-74; pres. Schlang Found., Inc., Broad St. Found., Inc., Barclay Found., Inc., Joseph Schlang Found., Inc.; treas. Elias Cohen Found., Inc.; Found. For a Graphic History Jewish Lit., Inc.; trustee Cong. Kehilath Jeshurun N.Y., 1957-77; Founder Albert Einstein Coll. Medicine, 1961—; master builder Yeshiva U., 1975—; life mem. Technion Inst., Technion Inst. in Israel; charter mem. Rep. Presdl. Task Force, 1982—; life mem. Rep. Presdl. Cen. Task Force, 1988—; sponsor of GOP Victory Fund, 1987—, sustaining mem. Rep. Nat. Com., 1987—, mem. inner circle, 1991—; patron Ronald Reagan Libr. Found., 1986—. Recipient award Am. Jewish Lit. Found., 1960; Statesman award Synagogue Coun. Am., 1964—; proclamations for presentation of free opera festivals from Gov. N.Y. and mayors of 9 cities; certificate of appreciation Mayor Beame N.Y.C., 1974; proclamaitons County Exec. Nassau and mayors, N.Y.C.; proclamations County Exec. Nassau and mayors, Mamoroneck; proclamations Yonkers for Verdi Festival Periods, 1974. Mem. U.S. and N.Y. Power Squadron, N.Y. Real Estate Bd., Nat. Assn. Real Estate Bds., Numismatic Soc., Manuscript Soc. Am., nat. Assn. Owners, Mgrs. and Bldrs., Am. Biog. Inst. (life dep. gov., bd. dirs. Medal of Honor for lifelong achievement, Man of Yr. 1990), 100 Club (co-founder 1938, v.p. 1970-72, pres. 1972-74), Lancers Club (v.p., pres. 1960-75), City Club, Colonial Yacht Club, Palm Beach Poinciana Club, Gov.'s Club (founder Palm Beach chpt. 1984), Town Club (N.Y.C.). Republican. Home: 35 E 84th St New York NY 10028-0871 Office: 45 t New York NY 10038-3706

SCHLAPP, ANDREW THOMAS, JR., clinical hypnotherapist; b. N.Y.C., May 13, 1951; s. Andrew T. and Louise (Sgagragilo) S.; m. Patricia Ann, June 25, 1983; children: Thomas, Michael, Anne. Student, Hypnodyne Found., 1981, Nat. Guild of Hypnotists, 1981, The Focus Group, 1982. Cert. clin. hynotherapist. Analyst Smith Barney, 1972-76; pres. Teletron, 1976-79; sr. analyst Drexel Burhnham, 1979-81; communications analyst IBM/Rolm, 1981-90; dir. N.Y. Inst. Hypnotherapy, N.Y.C., 1990—. Mem. Huntington C. of C. Mem. Nat. Guild of Hypnotists, Am. Assn. Counseling and Devel., Internat. Assn. Counselors and Therapists. Office: 46 Green St Ste 200 Huntington NY 11748

SCHLECHT, MATTHEW FRED, research chemist; b. Milw., Nov. 26, 1953; s. William Arnold and Geraldine Anna (Hale) S.; m. Meryl Paula Gardner, Mar. 22, 1986; 1 child, Isaac Alexander. BS in Chemistry, U. Wis., 1975; MS in Chemistry, Columbia U., 1976, PhD in Chemistry, 1980. Postdoctoral researcher U. Calif., Berkeley, 1980-82; asst. prof. chemistry Poly. U., Bklyn., 1982-88; rsch. chemist agrl. products E.I. Dupont de Nemours, Newark, Del., 1988—. Postdoctoral Rsch. grantee NIH, 1980-82, NIH grantee, 1985-88. Mem. AAAS, Am. Chem. Soc., Am. Soc. Pharmacognosy, Internat. Soc. Heterocylic Chemistry, Sigma Xi, Phi Beta Kappa. Office: DuPont Stine-Haskell Rsch Ctr PO Box 30 Newark DE 19714

SCHLEGEL, JOHN FREDERICK, consultant management and health care associations; b. Ogden, Utah, Dec. 18, 1944; s. Max Joseph and Mary Georgia (Whittaker) S.; m. Priscilla Mary Hecht, Sept. 8, 1967. BS in Pharmacy, U. Pacific, 1967; D of Pharmacy, U. So. Calif., 1972, postdoctoral fellow, 1972-73, MS in Edn., 1980; ScD in Pharmacy (hon.), Mass. Coll. Pharmacy, 1984, L.I. U., 1985. Lic. pharmacist, Calif., Nev.; cert. assoc. exec. Chief pharmacist U. So. Calif. Sch. Pharmacy, Los Angeles, 1967-73, dir. pharmacy admissions, 1973-75; dir. office student affairs Am. Assn. Colls. Pharmacy, Alexandria, Va., 1975-77, asst. exec. dir., 1977-81, exec. dir., 1981-84; chief exec. officer Am. Pharm. Assn., Washington, 1984-89; exec. v.p., chief exec. officer Am. Acad. Facial Plastic and Reconstructive Surgery, Washington, 1989-92; pres. Schlegel & Assocs., Chevy Chase, Md., 1992—; cons. U.S. Govt., VA, HHS, various pharm. cos., assns. and schs. pharmacy. Contbr. over 60 articles on pharmacy, health care and assn. mgmt.; presenter in field. Nat. del. White House Conf. on Aging, Washington, 1981. Disting. alumnus U. So. Calif. Sch. Pharmacy, 1985, U. the Pacific Sch. Pharmacy, 1987. Fellow Am. Soc. Assn. Execs.; mem. Am. Pharm. Assn., Greater Washington Soc. Assn. Execs., Group Health Assn. Inc. (officer, trustee), Phi Delta Chi (charter, bd. counsellors). Office: 7423 Lynnhurst St Bethesda MD 20815-3101

SCHLEH, EUGENE PAUL ANDERSON, historian, educator; b. N.Y.C., Aug. 7, 1939; s. Eugene B. and Anna H. (Anderson) S.; children: Eugene R.R., Bruce G.W., Kristine A.M. BA, Union Coll., 1961; MA, Yale U., 1962, PhD, 1968. From asst. prof. to prof. U. So. Maine, Gorham, 1965—. Co-editor: Comsumable Goods II, 1988; editor, co-author: Mysteries of Africa, 1991; contbr. articles to profl. jours. John Anson Kittridge Edn. Fund Trust fellow, 1990, Republic of South Africa rsch.-travel fellow, 1980. Republican. Episcopalian. Home: 134 School St Gorham ME 04038-1027 Office: U So Maine College Ave Gorham ME 04038-1004

SCHLEICH, DONALD MAX, chemistry educator; b. Buffalo, Aug. 8, 1950; s. Herman and Margaret (Kaiser) S.; m. Jacqueline Godar, July 28, 1988; 1 child, Juliette. BS, SUNY, Fredonia, 1972; PhD, Brown U., 1977. Rsch. assoc. Nat. Ctr. for Sci. Rsch., Nantes, France, 1977-78, Ecole Poly., Paris, 1978-81; asst. prof. chemistry Poly. U., Bklyn., 1981-86, assoc. prof., 1986-89, prof., 1989—, head dept., 1988—; cons. Textron Splty. Materials, 1970—, Philip Morris USA, Richmond, Va., 1988—, Covalent Assocs., Boston, 1988—, Emcore, 1990-91. Author: (with Michael Russo) Fast Ion Transport in Solids, 1981; co-author: Disordered Semiconductors, 1987; also articles. Mem. Am. Chem. Soc., Electrochem. Soc., Materials Rsch. Soc. Office: Poly U 333 Jay St Brooklyn NY 11201-2990

SCHLEIF, ROBERT F., biology educator; b. Wenatchee, Wash., Nov. 22, 1940; s. Ferber R. and Wilma H. (Chittenden) S.; m. Nyuk Y. Ho, Nov. 25, 1970; 1 child, Kevin O. BS, Tufts U., 1963; PhD, U. Calif., Berkeley, 1967. Postdoctoral Harvard U., Cambridge, Mass., 1969-71; asst. prof. Brandeis U., Waltham, Mass., 1971-74, assoc. prof., 1974-81, prof., 1981-89; prof. biology Johns Hopkins U., Balt., 1989—. Author: Practical Methods Molecular Biology, 1981, Genetics and Molecular Biology, 1985; contbr. articles to profl. jours. Recipient Helen Hay Whitney award, 1970. Office: Johns Hopkins U Dept Biology 34th and Charles Sts Baltimore MD 21218

SCHLEIMER, JOSEPH, real estate developer; b. N.Y.C., Nov. 3, 1930; s. Harry and Clara (Schweller) S.; m. Joan T. Feinberg; Apr. 10, 1954; children: Lorraine Beth, Miriam Ethel. BS, CCNY, 1951, MA, 1959; postgrad., NYU, 1965. Chemist Ledele Labs., Pearl River, N.Y., 1953-56; tchr. chemistry, physics Yonkers (N.Y.) Pub. Schs., 1956-66; prof. physics Jersey City State Coll., 1966-69, dean dept. physics, 1966-69; pres. Nat. Health Inst., Yonkers, 1969-79; owner, mgr. Westchester Law Bldg., Yonkers, 1982—, Yonkers Med. Mall, 1978—; pres. Fishkill Properties Inc., Yonkers, 1984—; pres., bd. dirs. Yonkers Devel. Agy., 1985—. Mem. sch. bd. East Ramapo Cen. Sch. Dist., Rockland County, N.Y., 1968. Served with U.S. Army, 1951-52, Korea. NSF fellow, 1957-62. Mem. Downtown Yonkers Bus. and Profl. Assn. (pres., bd. dirs. 1983—). Democrat. Jewish. Home: 7 Old Phillips Hill Rd New City NY 10956-2107 Office: Westchester Law Bldg 33 S Broadway Yonkers NY 10701-3706

SCHLESINGER, DAVID HARVEY, medical educator, researcher; b. N.Y.C., Apr. 28, 1939; s. Philip T. and Fay (Margolis) S.; children: Sarah Jane, Karen Louise. BA, Columbia U., 1962; MS, Albany Med. Coll., 1965; PhD, Mt. Sinai Med. and Grad. Sch., 1972. Research fellow in medicine Mass. Gen. Hosp., Harvard Med. Sch., Boston, 1972-75, instr., 1975-77; asst. in biochemistry Mass. Gen. Hosp., Harvard Med. Sch., 1975-77; rsch. assoc. prof. U. Ill. Med. Ctr., Chgo., 1977-81; rsch. prof. exptl. medicine NYU Med. Ctr., N.Y.C., 1981—, co-dir. neuroscis. sect. mental health clin. rsch. ctr.; cons. Ortho Pharm. Co., 1977-91, Armour Pharm., 1979-81, Emisphere Techs., Inc., 1987—. cons. in drug delivery systems. Editor: monograph Neurobyphysical Peptide Hormones and Other Biological Active Peptides, 1981; editor and contbg. author: Macromolecular Sequencing and Synthesis: Selected Methods and Application, 1988. Recipient Lectureship award Fundacion Gen. Mediterranean, Madrid, 1975. Mem. N.Y. Acad. Scis., Am. Physiol. Soc., Am. Soc. Biol. Chemists, Am. Chem. Soc. Office: NYU Med Ctr 550 1st Ave New York NY 10016-6402

SCHLESINGER, SANFORD JOEL, lawyer; b. N.Y.C., Feb. 8, 1943; s. Irving and Ruth (Rubin) S.; divorced; children: Merideth, Jarrod, Alexandra. BS in Govt. with hons., Columbia U., 1963; JD, Fordham U., 1966. Bar: N.Y. 1966, U.S. Dist. Ct. (so. and ea. dists.) N.Y. 1967, U.S. Ct. Appeals (2d cir.) 1968, U.S. Ct. Internat. Trade 1969, U.S. Supreme Ct. 1978. Assoc. Frankenthaler & Kohn, N.Y.C., 1966-67; asst. atty. gen. trusts and estates bur. charitable found. div. State of N.Y., N.Y.C., 1967-69; ptnr. Rose & Schlesinger, N.Y.C., 1969-81, Goldshmidt, Oshatz, Powsner & Saft, N.Y.C., 1981-85; ptnr., head trusts and estates dept. Shea & Gould, N.Y.C., 1985—; adj. faculty Columbia U. Sch. Law, 1989—; adj. prof. N.Y. Law Sch., 1978—; mem. estate planning adv. com. Practising Law Inst., 1990—; bd. advisors and contbrs. Jour. of S Corp. Taxation, 1989—; lectr. in field; conductor workshops in field. Author: (text) Estate Planning for the Elderly Client, 1984; mem. editorial bd. Jour. Estate and Tax Planning for the Elderly and Disabled, 1989—; contbr. articles to profl. jours. Mem. adv. bd. Inst. Fed. Taxation NYU, 1988—; mem. legis. adv. com. Scarsdale (N.Y.) Sch. Bd., 1981-83, mem. nominating com., 1979-82; pres. Dist. 17 N.Y.C. Community Sch. Bd., 1970-71; mem. fin. and estate planning adv. bd. Commerce Clearing House, 1988—. Fellow Am. Coll. Trust and Estate Counsel; mem. ABA (chmn. social security and other govt. entitlements com. 1990—), Internat. Acad. Estate & Trust Law (academician 1992—), Nat. Acad. Elder Law Attys., Bklyn. Bar Assn., Westchester County Bar Assn., Assn. of Bar of City of N.Y., Consular Law Soc., N.Y. State Bar Assn. (treas. trusts and estates sect. 1991-92, sec. trusts and estates sect. 1992—, chmn. exec. com. 1st jud. dist. 1987-91). Office: Shea & Gould 1251 Ave Of The Americas New York NY 10020-1104

SCHLESSINGER, JOSEPH, pharmacology educator. BSc in Chemistry/Physics magna cum laude, The Hebrew U., Jerusalem, 1968, MSC in Chemistry magna cum laude, 1969; PhD, The Weizmann Inst. Sci., Rehovot, Israel, 1974. Postdoctoral assoc. dept. chemistry Sch. Applied Physics, Cornell U., 1974-76; vis. scientist immunology br. Nat. Cancer Inst., NIH, Bethesda, Md., 1977-78; sr. scientist dept. chem. immunology The Weizmann Inst. Sci., Rehovot, 1978-80, assoc. prof. dept. chem. immunology, 1980-84, prof. dept. chem. immunology, Ruth & Leonard Simon prof., 1984-91; dir. div. molecular biology Biotech. Rsch. Ctr. Meloy Labs., Inc., Rockville, Md., 1985-86, dir. Biotech. Rsch. Ctr., 1986-88; rsch. dir. Rorer Biotech., Inc., King of Prussia, Pa., 1988-90; prof., chmn. dept. pharmcology NYU Med. Ctr., N.Y.C., 1990—. Mem. editorial bds. European Molecular Biology Orgn. Jour., Jour. Cell Biology, Cell Regulation, Cancer Rsch., Receptors, Growth Factors, Cell Growth & Differentiation, Protein Engineering, Oncogenes and Growth Factor Abstracts; contbr. articles to profl. jours. Recipient Sara Leedy Prize, Weizmann Inst. Sci., 1980, Levinson Prize, 1984; Hestrin Prize, Biochem. Soc. Israel, 1983. Mem. European Molecular Biology Orgn. Office: NYU Med Ctr Dept Pharmacology 550 1st Ave New York NY 10016-6402

SCHLIERF, GREGORY NORBERT, college residence coordinator; b. Buffalo, N.Y., Sept. 26, 1964; s. Norbert H. and Arlene M. (Sweda) S.; m. Leslie K. Evans, May 26, 1991. BS, Slippery Rock U., 1988; MS, Shippensburg U., 1990. Cert. tchr., Pa. Resident advisor Slippery Rock (Pa.) U., 1986-88, coord. residence edn., 1989—; grad. residence hall dir. Shippensburg (Pa.) U., 1988-89; presentor Cable TV in Residence Hall/Regional Conf., 1990. Mem. Am. Assn. Counseling and Devel., Nat. Assn. Student Personal Adminstrn.

SCHLITT, JACOB, state official; b. Bronx, N.Y., Dec. 18, 1927; s. Louis and Celia (Goldstein) S.; m. Sylvia Feig, Dec. 22, 1951 (div. Feb. 1972); children: Carol, Lewis, Martha; m. Frances Mildred Morrill, July 26, 1981; 1 child, David. BS, CCNY, 1949, MA, 1951; postgrad., NYU, 1951-54. Tchr. pub. schs., N.Y.C., 1950; organizer Internat. Ladies Garment Workers Union, N.Y.C., 1951-54; nat. field sec. Jewish Labor Com., N.Y.C., 1956-62; dir. edn. Amalgamated Laundry Workers Joint Bd., N.Y.C., 1962-64; asst. dir. edn. and rsch. AFSCME, Washington, 1964-65; field rep., asst. dir., then dir. Mid-Atlantic Field Office, U.S. Commn. on Civil Rights, Washington, 1965-79; regional dir. U.S. Commn. on Civil Rights, Boston, 1979-86; mem. bd. rev. Mass. Dept. Employment and Tng., Boston, 1987—; exec. com. Jewish Labor Commn., 1981—; chmn. Boston Dist. Workmen's Circle, 1989—. Editor Labor Reports, 1956-62, Amalgamated Laundry Workers Bull., 1962-64. Mem. exec. com. Greater Boston Jewish Community Rels. Coun., 1984—. With Signal Corps, U.S. Army, 1954-56,. Mem. Nat. Assn. Unemployment Ins. Appellate Bds., Julius Bernstein Meml. Found. Democrat. Jewish. Home: 16 Greenough St Brookline MA 02146-6141 Office: Mass Dept Employment & Tng Bd Rev 19 Staniford St Boston MA 02114-2526

SCHLOBOHM, RAYMOND WILLIAM, human resources executive; b. N.Y.C., July 15, 1943; s. Howard William and Emily Jane (Stanton) S. BA, Mich. State U., 1965, MS in Labor Relations, 1970. Mgmt. trainee GTE Sylvania, Inc., N.Y.C., 1968-69; grad. asst. Mich. State U., East Lansing, 1969-70; indsl. relations assoc. Westinghouse Electric Corp., Edison, N.J., 1970-71; mgr. employee relations NL Industries, Inc., Hightstown, N.J., 1971-74; mgr. div. employee relations NL Industries, Inc., Wilmington, Del., 1974-76; dir. pension and employee benefit investments NL Industries, Inc., N.Y.C., 1976-80; dir. human resources adminstrn. NL Industries, Inc., Hightstown, 1980-83; dir. corp. employment and employee rels. ADP, Inc., Roseland, N.J., 1983-87, v.p. employee rels., 1987-90; v.p. human resources Givaudan-Roure Corp., Teaneck, N.J., 1990—. Contbr. articles to profl. jours. Vice pres., trustee Contact We Care, Inc., Westfield, N.J., 1991; v.p., bd. dirs. Raritan Sigma Phi Epsilon Corp., New Brunswick, N.J., 1981-83. Capt. U.S. Army, 1966-68. Decorated Army Commendation medal. Mem. ASTD, Internat. Assn. Corp. and Profl. Recruiters (v.p. regional planning and devel. 1987-88, exec. v.p. 1989, pres. 1990, chmn. bd. and chief exec. officer 1991), Employment Mgmt. Assn., Indsl. Rels. Rsch. Assn., Soc. Human Resource Mgmt., Nat. Assn. Human Resource Systems Profls., Sigma Phi Epsilon (sec. East Lansing chpt. 1964-65, MacDonough Counselor award 1983). Roman Catholic. Home: 311 Willowbrook Dr N Brunswick NJ 08902-1245 Office: Roure Inc 1775 Windsor Rd Teaneck NJ 07666-3018

SCHLOSS, WALTER AMSON, urologist; b. N.Y.C., Oct. 15, 1914; s. Irving Jay and Martha (Newman) S.; m. Ruth Doris Ginsberg, Feb. 1, 1942; children: Nancy Marks, Jane Phelan, Wendy Benger, Peggy Mendelson, W. Andrew, Barbara. BA, Amherst Coll., 1936; MD, NYU, 1940. Diplomate Nat. Bd. Med. Examiners, Am. Bd. Urology, ACS. Rotating intern Middlesex Hosp., Middletown, Conn., 1940-41; surg. intern Bellevue Hosp., N.Y.C., 1941; jr. asst. resident urology Beth Israel Hosp., N.Y.C., 1946-47, asst. resident urology, 1947-48, sr. resident urology, 1948-49; pvt. practice urology, chief urology Mt. Sinai Hosp., Hartford, Conn., 1949-76; med. dir. The Stanley Works, New Britain, Conn., 1976-85, Heublein Corp., Hartford, Conn., 1986—; med. cons. Hartford Health Dept., 1985—. Contbr. articles on urology to profl. jours. Maj., M.C., AUS, 1941-45. Mem. Occupational Med. Assn. Conn. (sec.-treas., v.p., pres. 1984-85), Hartford Med. Soc. (asst. sec. 1970), Phi Beta Kappa. Republican. Jewish. Home: 31 Brookside Blvd West Hartford CT 06107-1108 Office: Hartford Health Dept 112 Coventry St Hartford CT 06112

SCHLOSSER, PETER, geology educator; b. Speyer, Fed. Republic of Germany, Aug. 29, 1955; came to U.S., 1989; s. Alfons and Renate (Weber) S. Diplomprufung, U. Heidelberg, Fed. Republic of Germany, 1981, PhD, 1985. Rsch. asst. Inst. for Environ. Physics U. Heidelberg, 1981-86, asst. prof., 1986-89; assoc. prof. dept. geology Columbia U., N.Y.C., 1989—; mem. sci. steering group, chmn. geochem. tracer sci. panel World Ocean Circulation Experiment, 1989—, mem. exec. com., 1992—, mem. Sci. Steering Group exec. com. 1990-92, mem. U.S. World Ocean Circulation Experiment, Sci. Steering Com., 1991—. Contbr. articles and abstracts to profl. jours. Mem. Oceanography Soc., Am. Geophys. Union, German Phys. Soc. Office: Columbia U Lamont-Doherty Geol Obs Rte 9W Palisades NY 10964

SCHLOSSMAN, STUART FRANKLIN, physician, educator, researcher; b. N.Y.C., Apr. 18, 1935; s. Abe and Pearl (Susser) S.; m. Judith Seryl Rubin, Mar. 25, 1958; children: Robert, Peter. BA magna cum laude, NYU, 1955, MD, 1958; MA, Harvard U., 1975. Intern in medicine med. div. III Bellevue Hosp., N.Y.C., 1958-59, asst. resident in medicine med. div. III, 1959-60; Nat. Found. fellow dept. microbiology Coll. Physicians Columbia U., N.Y.C., 1960-62; asst. physician med. svc. Vanderbilt Clinic, Coll. Physician USPHS, Washington, 1960-62; Ward hematology fellow dept. internal medicine Sch. Washington U., St. Louis, 1962-63; rsch. assoc. lab. biochemistry Nat. Cancer Inst. USPHS, Washington, 1963-65; clin. instr. in medicine Sch. of Medicine George Washington U., 1964-65; assoc. in medicine, dir. blood bank Beth Israel Hosp., Boston, 1965-66; instr. Med. Sch. Harvard U., Boston, 1966-68, asst. physician, 1967-68, chief clin. immunology, 1971-73; physician Beth Israel Hosp., Boston, 1968—; from asst. to assoc. prof. medicine Harvard Med. Sch., Boston, 1968-77, prof., 1977—, Baruj Benacerraf prof. medicine, 1990—, chief div. tumor immunology and immunotherapy Dana-Farber Cancer Inst., 1973—; sr. physician Brigham and Women's Hosp., Boston, 1976—. Mem. editorial bd. Jour. of Immunology, 1969-74, Cellular Immunology, 1970—, Human Immunology, 1979-84, Clin. Immunology and Immunopathology, 1979—, Hybridoma, 1980—, Cancer Investigation, 1981, Stem Cells, 1981, Cancer Revs., 1984—, Internat. Jour. of Cell Cloning, 1983-86; mem. adv. bd. Cancer Treatment Reports, 1976-80; assoc. editor Human Lymphocyte Differentation, 1980-82; contbr. numerous articles to profl. jours. Recipient Solomon Berson Achievement award, 1984, Robert Koch prize and medal, 1984. Fellow AAAS; mem. NAS, Am. Soc. Hematology, Am. Soc. Immunologists, Am. Soc. Clin. Investigation, Assn. Am. Physicians, Alpha Omega Alpha. Office: Dana-Farber Cancer Inst 44 Binney St Boston MA 02115-6084

SCHLOTT, RICHARD WILLIAM, III, real estate, stock and insurance broker; b. Torrington, Conn., Dec. 16, 1939; s. Richard William Jr. and Marjorie (Vagnoit) S.; m. Karen Mary O'Connor, Apr. 20, 1968 (div. July 1983). Grad. high sch., Torrington, Conn. Prin. Richard W. Schlott III, Inc., Torrington, 1959-74; real estate broker Schlott Realtors, Torrington, 1972—; ins. broker Schlott Ins. Co., Torrington, 1977—; owner, chief exec. officer R.W. Schlott Mortgage, Torrington; fin. planner Richard W. Schlott III Fin. Planning, Torrington, 1978—; stock broker N.Am. Investment Corp., Torrington, East Hartford, Conn., 1980-88; commodity trading advisor N.Am. Investment Corp., East Hartford, 1983-88; chmn. TechniCast Inc., Glastonbury, Conn., 1985-88; stockbroker Forits Fin., 1988—. Pres. Fish, Inc., United Way Agy., Torrington, 1985-86; mem. Rep. Senatorial Inner Cir. Mem. Internat. Assn. Fin. Planning, Hartford Stock Broker Club, Litchfield County Bd. Realtors, Waterbury Realtors, C. of C. of N.W. Conn. Club: Hartford. Home: 43 Norton St Torrington CT 06790-5830 Office: Schlott Realtors 118 E Main St 1217 E Main St Torrington CT 06790-3963

SCHLUETER, JOHN WILLIAM, telecomunications executive; b. Muskegon, Mich., July 1, 1943; s. John William Sr. and Frances Elizabeth (Simpson) S.; m. Aloys Rosilind Black, June 22, 1963; children: Lisa Beth, Deann Lynn. Grad. high sch., Muskegon, Mich. Automatic electric equipment installer Automatic Electric Co., Northlake, Ill., 1962-67; technician GTE North, Portage, Ind., 1967-69; technician GTE North, Muskegon, Mich., 1969-86, adminstr. tech. support ctr., 1986-90; adminstr. centralized tech. support ctr. GTE North, Erie, Pa., 1990—. Republican. Methodist. Home: 1930 W 37th St Erie PA 16508-2016 Office: GTE North 20 E 10th St Erie PA 16532

SCHLUETER, JUNE MAYER, English educator, author; b. Passaic, N.J., Nov. 4, 1942; m. Paul Schlueter. BA in English magna cum laude, Fairleigh Dickinson U., 1970; MA in English, Hunter Coll., CCNY, 1973; PhD in English and Comparative Lit., Columbia U., 1977. Asst. prof. Lafayette Coll., Easton, Pa., 1977-84, assoc. prof., 1984-91, prof., 1991—, head English dept., 1992—; asst. to provost Lafayette Coll., Easton, 1986-90; Fulbright prof. Gesamthochschule Kassel Univ., Fed. Republic Germany, 1978-79; chmn. Shakespeare Seminar Columbia U., 1989-91, exec. bd., 1989—; active NEH summer seminar for coll. profs., 1981, lectr. Commonwealth Partnership Summer Lit. Inst., 1985-87, dir. summer seminar for sch. tchr.s, 1988, selection panel, 1989, 91, evaluator Instl. Grant Program, 1990. Author: Metafictional Characters in Modern Drama, 1979, The Plays and Novels of Peter Handke, 1981; (with James K. Flanagan) Arthur Miller, 1987; (with James P. Lusardi) Reading Shakespeare in Performance: King Lear, 1990; editor: Feminist Rereadings of Modern American Drama, 1989, Modern American Drama: The Female Canon, 1990; (with Paul Schlueter) The English Novel: Twentieth Century Criticism, Vol. 2: Twentieth Century Novelists, 1982, Modern American Literature, Supplement II, 1985, An Encyclopedia of British Women Writers, 1988; (with Enoch Brater) Approaches to Teaching Beckett's Waiting for Godot, 1991; editor Shakespeare Bull., 1984—; assoc. editor Stages, 1984-90; editorial bd. Studies in the Humanities, 1993—, Studies in the American Drama, 1945-Present, 1989—; editorial cons. Modern Drama, Theatre Jour., Pa. MLA, Studies in the Twentieth Century Lit., Thought, Mosaic, others; contbr. reviews, essays to profl. jours. Bd. govs. Fairleigh Dickinson U., Rutherford, N.J., 1985—; adv. com. Lehigh Valley Ednl. Coop., 1988-90; selection panel German Acad. Exch. Svc., Bonn, 1979. Rsch. grantee Lafayette Coll., 1977-91, NEH summer rsch. grantee, 1990, DAAD summer rsch. grantee, 1991. Mem. MLA, Shakespeare Assn. Am., Internat. Shakespeare Assn., Coll. English Assn., Samuel Beckett Soc., AAUP, N.Y. Shakespeare Soc. Home: 123 High St Easton PA 18042 Office: Lafayette Coll Easton PA 18042

SCHLUETER, PAUL, literary writer, editor, consultant; b. Chgo., May 10, 1933; m. Juen Mayer. BA in English, U. Minn., 1958; MA in English, U. Denver, 1963; PhD in English, So. Ill. U., 1968. With Coll. St. Thomas, St. Paul, 1959-60, U. Denver, 1962-63, So. Ill. U., Carbondale, 1963-66, Adrian (Mich.) Coll., 1966-68, U. Evansville, Ind., 1968-72, New Sch. for Social Rsch., N.Y.C., 1975-76; pub. rels. dir. Moorhead (Minn.) State U., 1960-62; dir. composition Kean Coll., Union, N.J., 1973-76; vis. prof. U. Hamburg, Fed. Republic Germany, 1973, U. Giessen, Fed. Republic Germany, U. Kassel, Fed. Republic Germany, 1978-79; selection com. German Acad. Exch. Svc., 1979; sec. Conf. Christianity and Lit., 1971-73; dir. Continuing Revolutionary Tradition: Bicentennial Conf. on N.J. Lit. Heritage, 1976; project dir. Yr. of Pa. Writer, Lehigh Valley, 1985; lectr. various U.S. and German colls. and univs. Author: The Novels of Doris Lessing, 1973, Shirley Ann Grau, 1981; editor: Literature and Religion: Wilder's "The Eighth Day," 1970, The Fiction of Doris Lessing, 1971, A Small Personal Voice: Essays, Reviews, Interviews (Doris Lessing), 1974, rev. edit., 1975, German edit., 1989, French edit., 1990; (with June Schlueter) The English Novel: Twentieth Century Criticism, 1982, Modern American Literature: Supplement Two, 1983, An Encyclopedia of British Women Writers, 1988; editor Procs. Sixteenth Nat. Conf. on Adminstrn. of Rsch., 1963, Christianity and Literature, 1971-72, Personalia, 1975-77; adv. bd. Virginia Woolf Quar., 1976-79, Doris Lessing Newsletter, 1978-88, editor, 1980-82, assoc. editor, 1982-85, editorial bd., 1985-88; presenter seminars and papers in field; contbr. revs., articles to various newspapers and mags. Mem. ACLU, MLA (exec. com. Religious Approaches to Lit. div. 1975-78, chmn. 1977-78), Am. Theater Critics Assn., Nat. Book Critics Circle, Coll. English Assn. (pres. Ind. chpt. 1972-73, v.p. 1971-72, sec.-treas. 1970-71, exec. bd. Pa. chpt. 1981-86, co-editor Pa. English 1981-86), Authors Guild, Doris Lessing Soc. (exec. coun. 1979-88, archivist 1988—), Pi Delta Epsilon (hon.). Home: 123 High St Easton PA 18042

SCHLUSSEL, JOSEPH LAZAR, diamond dealer, publisher; b. Munkacs, Czechoslovakia, Apr. 19, 1935; came to U.S., 1951; s. Charles C. and Fanny (Apfeldorf) S.; m. Rose Ickowitz, June 16, 1960; children: Fay,

Amy. Student, Bklyn. Coll., 1954-55, CCNY, 1956-59. Mgr. Gemcutters, N.Y.C., 1960-61; broker Diamond Dealers Club, N.Y.C., 1961-69; pres. The Diamond Registry, N.Y.C., 1969—; editor and publisher The Diamond Registry Bulletin, 1969—; cons. Nat. Westminster Bank USA, E.A.B., Merchants Bank, Bankers Trust, Solomon Bros. Columnist Nat. Jeweler, 1978, Jewel Mag., 1988--; lectr. in field; guest on NBC Today, 1978; quoted in many major publs. as leading authority in field. Mem. Gemological Assn. Gt. Britain, Jewelry Industry Coun., Jewelers Vigilance Com., Jewelers Bd. of Trade, Diamond Dealers Club. Office: The Diamond Registry 580 Fifth Ave New York NY 10036-4701

SCHLUTER, GERALD EMIL, economist; b. Carroll, Iowa, June 9, 1942; s. Emil and Violetta Marie (Witt) S.; m. Carolyn Jean Finnell, Apr. 27, 1968; 1 child, Deborah Jean. BS, Iowa State U., 1964, MS, 1966, PhD, 1971. Rsch. asst. econs. Iowa State U., Ames, 1964-66, rsch. assoc. econs., 1966-70; agrl. economist Econ. Rsch. Svc. USDA, Washington, 1970-84, supervisory economist Econ. Rsch. Svc., 1984—; econs. instr., Washington, 1983—, USDA Grad. Sch., Washington, 1979-83. Editor: (jour.) Agrl. Econs., 1984-87; author: (econs. series) Food & Fiber System, 1972—; contbr. over 80 articles to profl. jours. Mem. property com. Bethany Luth. Ch., Alexandria, Va., 1983-88; coach Lee-Mt. Vernon Soccer Assn., Alexandria, 1982-83. Mem. Am. Agr. Econs. Assn., So. Regional Sci. Assn., Ea. Econ. Assn., Atlantic Econ. Soc., Western Agr. Econs. Assn., N.E. Agr. Econs. Coun. Home: 3877 Manzanita Pl Alexandria VA 22309-1479 Office: USDA Econ Rsch Svc 1301 New York Ave NW Rm 912 Washington DC 20005-4708

SCHLUTER, PETER MUELLER, electronics company executive; b. Greenwich, Conn., May 24, 1933; s. Fredric Edward and Charlotte (Mueller) S.; m. Jaquelin Ambler Lamond, Apr. 18, 1970 (div. June 1990); children: Jane Randolph, Charlotte Mueller, Anne Ambler. BME, Cornell U., 1956; postgrad. Harvard U. Grad. Sch. Bus. Adminstrn., 1982. Sr. engr. Thiokol Chem. Corp., Brigham City, Utah, 1958-59; asso. Porter Internat. Co., Washington, 1960-65, v.p., 1965-66, pres., treas., dir., 1966-70; pres., treas. dir. Zito Co., Derry, N.H., 1970-72; internat. bus. cons., Washington, 1972-74; v.p., dir. Buck Engrng. Co. Inc., Farmingdale, N.J., 1975, pres., chief exec. officer, dir., 1975—; dir. Keystone Forging Co., Northumberland, Pa.; hon. mem. City and Guilds of London Inst. Mem. Republican Inaugural Book and Program Com., 1969; mem. community adv. bd. Monmouth council Girl Scouts U.S.; mem. adv. council Monmouth (N.J.) Coll. Sch. Bus. Admin.; bd. dirs. United Way of Monmouth County.; trustee Monmouth Med. Ctr.; N.Am. rep., mem. presidium WORLDDIDAC, Bern, Switzerland. Fellow City and Guilds of London Inst. (hon.); mem. World Assn. Mfrs. and Distributors of Ednl. Materials (N.Am. rep.), Metropolitan Club Washington, Rumson Country Club, Pi Tau Sigma. Home: 4 Quaker Ln Little Silver NJ 07739-1806 Office: PO Box 686 Farmingdale NJ 07727

SCHMALTZ, RICHARD ROBERT, investment counselor; b. Hartford, Conn., July 18, 1940; s. Henry Edward and Anna Mae (Starkel) S.; m. Joan Marie Dignam, Sept. 12, 1964; children: Heide, Dana. BA, Colby Coll., 1962, MA, 1976. Prin. Morgan Stanley, N.Y.C., 1973-83; mng. dir. Kidder Peabody, N.Y.C., 1983-87; exec. v.p. McGlinn Capital Mgmt., Wyomissing, Pa., 1987—; bd. dirs. Mfrs. Advisor Corp., Quaker City Ins.; trustee Colby Coll., Waterville, Maine, 1976—. Republican. Home: 133 Deborah Dr Reading PA 19610-3105 Office: McGlinn Capital Mgmt PO Box 6158 Reading PA 19610-0158

SCHMALZ, ROBERT FOWLER, geology educator; b. Ann Arbor, Mich., May 29, 1929; s. Carl Nelson and Esther Dorothy (Fowler) S.; m. Barbara Ann Leetch, July 18, 1964; children: Timothy F., Dorothy L. AB with honors, Havard Coll., 1951; AM, Harvard U., 1954, PhD, 1959. Cert. profl. geologist. Rsch. asst. Harvard/W.H.O.I., Cambridge, Mass., 1957-58; asst. prof. Pa. State U., University Park, 1968-63, assoc. prof., 1963-69, prof. of geology, 1969-91, chmn. geology, 1971-74, undergrad. coord., 1974-77, prof. of geology emeritus, 1992—; trustee Bermuda Biol. Sta., 1967-79; mem. adv. com. Appalachian Compact Users Radio Isotopes, University Park. Editor: Science Education in the United States, 1991, Environmental Radon, 1990; contbr. articles to profl. jours. Mem. vice chair State Coll. Borough Water Authority, State College, 1978—. With U.S. Army, 1955-57. Recipient Wilson Teaching award Earth and Mineral Sci. Coll., 1969, Lindback Teaching award Pa. State U., 1970. Fellow AAAS, Geol. Soc. Am.; mem. Am. Assn. Petroleum Geologists (disting. lectr. 1977-778), Soc. Econ. Mineralogists and Petrologists, Pa. Acad. Sci., Explorers Club, Sigma Xi. Home: 305 E Mitchell Ave State College PA 16803-3637 Office: Dept Geosciences 536 Deike Bldg University Park PA 16802

SCHMAUS, SIEGFRIED H. A., consulting engineer; b. Muelheim/Ruhr, W. Ger., Dec. 23, 1915; s. Wilhelm Friedrich and Hedwig (Flader) S.; student Staatliche Ingenieur Schule, Duisburg, W. Ger., 1940-41, Esslingen, W. Ger., 1945-46; m. A. Babette Schmid, Aug. 17, 1946. Apprentice-designer Demag A.G., Duisburg, 1930-36; designer/supr. Meissner, Cologne, W. Ger., 1936-38; designer aircraft engines Daimler-Benz A.G., Stuttgart, W. Ger., 1943-45; designer Fischer & Porter, Warminster, Pa., 1948-53, Ametek Inc., Sellersville, Pa., 1954-65; staff research engr. Fischer & Porter, Warminster, 1966-80; pres. Sensor Devel. Inc., Broomall, Pa., 1977-90, Sensor Research Inc., Phila., 1980-90. Patentee in field. V.p. Friends Hist. Rittenhouse Town. Served with German Luftwaffe, 1938-42. Recipient Hess Ingenuity award, 1962. Mem. Franklin Inst. (sr., silver mem.), Instrument Soc. Am. (sr.), Am. Soc. Mfg. Engrs., German Soc. Pa. (v.p. 1984, Founders medal 1987, Officer's Cross of the Gov. of Germany 1988), Masons. Republican. Lutheran. Home and Office: 806 Powder Mill Ln Penfield Downs Wynnewood PA 19096

SCHMEE, JOSEF, industrial management educator; b. Grieskirchen, Austria, Feb. 13, 1945; came to U.S. 1968; s. Martin and Elisabeth (Pill) S.; m. Marilyn Restifo, Sept. 22, 1967. Magister, U. Vienna, 1968; MSc in Ops. Rsch., Union Coll., Schenectady, 1970, PhD, 1974. Asst. prof. Union Coll., Schenectady, 1972-78, assoc. prof., 1978-82, prof. mgmt., 1982—, Kenneth B. Sharpe prof. mgmt., 1992—; dir. health stds. N.Y.State Dept. Health, Albany, 1978-79; adj. prof. dept. pathology Albany Med. Coll., 1981—; vis. scientist GE, Schenectady, 1988-89. Contbr. articles to profl. jours. Recipient Wilcoxon award Am. Soc. Quality Control, 1980, Brumbaugh award, 1980; Fulbright scholar 1981. Fellow Am. Statis. Assn.; mem. Inst. Math. Statistics, Biometric Soc. Office: GMI Union Coll Bailey Hall 300A Schenectady NY 12308

SCHMEIDLER, GERTRUDE RAFFEL, psychology educator; b. Long Branch, N.J., June 15, 1912; d. Harry B. and Clare (Holzman) R.; m. Robert Schmeidler, Aug. 27, 1937; children: James, Richard, Emilie, Katherine. BA, Smith Coll., 1932; MA, Clark U., 1933; PhD, Radcliffe/Harvard U., 1935. Instr. Monmouth Coll., Long Branch, N.J., 1935-37; rsch. assoc. Harvard U., Cambridge, Mass., 1942-45; rsch. officer Am. Soc. for Psychical Rsch., N.Y.C., 1946-47; instr. to prof. emeritus CUNY, N.Y.C., 1947—. Author: ESP and Personality Patterns, 1958, Parapsychology and Psychology: Matches and Mismatches, 1988; editor: Extrasensory Perception, 1974, Parapsychology: Its Relation to Physics Psychology, 1976. Rep. LWV, Hastings-on-Hudson, 1990. Recipient McDougall award Found. for Rsch. on the Nature of Man, 1964, Disting. Achievement in Parapsychology award So. Calif. Soc. for Psych. Rsch. Inc., 1981. Fellow AAAS, APA, Soc. for Psychol. Study of Social Issues; mem. Survival Rsch. Found. (adv. com.), Am. Soc. for Psychical Rsch. (pres. 1982-84, bd. dirs., 2nd v.p.), Parapsychol. Assn. (program chair conv., pres. 1959, 71, Career award 1988). Office: Dept Psychology City Coll Convent Ave # 138 New York NY 10027-2604

SCHMELTZ, EDWARD JAMES, engineering executive; b. Newark, June 22, 1949; s. Edward Leo and Loretta (Pittman) S.; m. Donna Hoppi Schmeltz, Sept. 28, 1974; children: Leigh Erin Wildes, Erik Edward. BS, N.J. Inst. Tech., 1971; M in Engring., Tex. A&M U., 1972. Registered profl. engr., N.Y., N.J., Conn. Rsch. asst. Tex. A&M U., College Station, 1971-72; coastal/ocean engr. F. R. Harris, Lake Success, N.Y., 1972-74; sr. coastal engr. PRC Harris, Lake Success, N.Y., 1974-76; dept. mgr. PRC Engring., Lake Success, N.Y., 1976-79; project mgr. PRC Engring., N.Y.C., 1980-87; deputy dir. N.Y. Ops., v.p. Frederic R. Harris, Inc., N.Y.C., 1987—; lectr. George Washington U., Lehigh U.; mem. Coastal Structures steering com., 1979, 83. Contbr. articles to technical and profl. jours. Mem. Flood and Erosion Control Bd., Rep. Town Meeting, Greenwich, Conn., 1988—. Recipient Adm. Harris award Frederic R. Harris, Inc., N.Y.C., 1989. Mem. Am. Soc. Civil Engring., Soc. Am. Mil. Engring., Permanent Internat. Assn. Navigation Congresses, Nat. Soc. Profl. Engrs. Roman Catholic. Office: Frederic R Harris Inc 300 E 42nd St New York NY 10017-5947

SCHMERLING, ERWIN ROBERT, government official; b. Vienna, Austria, July 28, 1929; came to U.S., 1955, naturalized, 1962; s. Heinrich H. and Lily (Goldsmith) S.; m. Esther M. Schmerling, Apr. 5, 1957; children: Susan D., Elaine M. BA, Cambridge U., 1950, MA, 1954, PhD in Radio Physics, 1958; grad., Advanced Mgmt. Program, Harvard, 1969, Fed. Exec. Inst., 1975. Asst. prof. elec. engring. Pa. State U., University Park, 1955-60, assoc. prof., 1960-62, 63-64; staff scientist NASA-Hdqrs., Washington, 1962-63, program chief ionospheric physics, magnetospheric physics, space plasma physics, 1964-82; asst. dir. space and earth scis. Goddard Space Flight Ctr., NASA, Greenbelt, Md., 1984-86; chief data system scientist Office Space Science and Applications NASA Hdqrs., Washington, 1986-88; SAIS program scientist NASA, Washington, 1988-89; data system scientist solar system exploration div. NASA Hdqrs., Washington, 1989-90, program mgr. astrophysics data systems, 1991—; mem. U.S. coms. III and IV Internat. Sci. Radio Union, 1985—, sec. U.S. Com. III, 1966-69, chmn., 1969-72; chmn. subcom. C1 Com. Space Rsch. (COSPAR), 1984-88; mem. Adv. Group Aerospace Research and Devel.; vis. scholar Stanford U., 1983; cons. RCA, Gen. Electric, 1959-62. Contbr. papers to profl. jours. Fellow IEEE (mem. wave propagation standards com.); mem. Am. Geophys. Union, AAAS, Sigma Xi. Home: 9917 La Duke Dr Kensington MD 20895-3140 Office: NASA-Hdqrs Code SZ Washington DC 20546

SCHMEYER, JON ERIC, ophthalmologist; b. N.Y.C., Jan. 25, 1955; s. Frank Felix and Felice Enid (Breslaw) S.; m. Monica Laskowich, June 4, 1981; children: Veronica Matilda, Elsa Amelia. BA, Hamilton Coll., 1977; MD, N.Y. Med. Coll., 1981. Diplomate Am. Bd. Ophthalmology. Resident in Ophthalmology Nassau County Med. Ctr., East Meadow, N.Y., 1982-85; mem. staff in Ophthalmology Hanover (Pa.) Gen. Hosp., 1985—; dir. Hanover Surgi-Ctr., Hanover, 1990—. Mem. AMA, Pa. Med. Soc., Pa. Acad. Ophthalmology, Am. Acad. of Ophthalmology, South Pa. Road Runners Club, Hanover Elks Lodge, Hanover Lions Club. Office: 250 E Walnut Hanover PA 17331

SCHMID, ANDREW MICHAEL, JR., advertising executive; b. Nanticoke, Pa., Aug. 19, 1957; s. Andrew Michael Sr. and Shirley Mae (Lasher) S. A in Applied Sci. in Communication Design cum laude, Luzerne County Community Coll., 1977; BFA in Communication Design, Kutztown State Coll., 1979. Designer, artist Conner Comml. Co., Bloomsburg, Pa., 1979-80; owner Schmid Advt., Bloomsburg, 1980—; adj. prof. Bloomsburg State Coll., 1983-84. Bd. dirs. Children's Oncology Svcs. Danville, Inc.; operators of Danville Ronald McDonald House. Recipient Addy Certs. of Merit and Excellence Am. Advt. Fedn., 1986. Republican. Roman Catholic.

SCHMID, CALVIN ERIC, social psychologist; b. Ft Payne, Ala., Sept. 2, 1950; s. Robert Paul and Jeane (Day) S.; m. Janis Ellen Pouche, June 25, 1972; 1 child Gregory Keith. BA in Psychology, Boston U., 1976; MA in Psychology, Boston coll., 1979; PhD in Psychology, Boston Coll., 1987. Cons. Solomon Mental Health Ctr., Lowell, Mass., 1977-79; instr. Lesley Coll., Cambridge, Mass., 1979-82, Boston Coll., Chestnut Hill, Mass., 1979-82; dir. edn. & tng. Gen. Motors, B.O.C. Wentzville, Mo., 1982-87; sr. cons. Marion Labs., Inc., Kansas City, Mo., 1987-88, mgr. corp. tng. and devel., 1988-89; pres., dir. orgn. and mgt. resources Warner-Lambert Co., Morris Plains, N.J., 1989—; pres. HRD, Inc., St. Louis, 1983-85. Co-author, presenter: MMPI Profiles of Success Fearers, 1978; author: dissentation The Effects of Performance Feedback, Social Acceptance and Cooperative competitive Group Structure on the Performance of Success Fearing Persons. Mem. Phi Beta Kappa. Home: 26 Concord Ln Morristown NJ 07960-6135

SCHMID, JAMES ADDISON, environmental consultant; b. Dallas, Jan. 24, 1945; s. James Addison and Julia Marie (Hengy) S.; m. Wendy Lee Wollwoge, June 20, 1971; children: James Addison, Jonathan Chapman Abraham. Student, Rice U., Houston, 1962-63; BA cum laude, Columbia Coll., 1966; MA, U. Chgo., 1969, PhD, 1972. From instr. to asst. prof. biol. scis. Barnard Coll./Columbia U., N.Y.C., 1970-73; chmn., v.p. Jack McCormick & Assocs., Inc., 1973-79; prin. scientist WAPORA, Inc., Devon, Pa., 1979-81; prin. environ. scientist TERA Corp., Valley Forge, Pa., 1981-82; pres. Schmid & Co., Inc., Cons. Ecologists, Media, Pa., 1981—. Author: Urban Vegetation: A Review and Chicago Case Study, 1975, Checklist and Synonomy of New Jersey Higher Plants, 1990. Chmn. Marple Twp. Environ. Adv. Bd., Broomall, Pa., 1983—. NDEA Title VI fellow, 1966, Columbia Coll. scholar, 1963-66. Mem. Ecol. Soc. Am., Brit. Ecol. Soc., Assn. Am. Geographers, N.J. Acad. Sci., Wetland Scientists, Soc. Ecol. Restoration and Mgmt., Phi Beta Kappa. Home and Office: Schmid & Co Inc Consulting Ecologists 1201 Cedar Grove Rd Media PA 19063-1044

SCHMID, WILFRIED, mathematician; b. Hamburg, Germany, May 28, 1943; came to U.S., 1960; s. Wolfgang and Kathe (Erfling) S. BA, Princeton U., 1964; MA, U. Calif., Berkeley, 1966, PhD, 1967. Asst. prof. math. U. Calif., Berkeley, 1967-70; prof. math. Columbia U., 1970-78, Harvard U., 1978—; vis. mem. Inst. for Advanced Study, Princeton, 1969-70, 75-76; vis. prof. U. Bonn, 1973-74. Editor Springer Ergebnisse der Mathematik, Jour. Am. Math. Soc.; contbr. articles to profl. jours. Home: Silver Hill Rd Lincoln MA 01773-3404 Office: Harvard U Dept Math Cambridge MA 02138

SCHMIDLIN, FRED WILLIAM, physicist, consultant; b. Maumee, Ohio, Aug. 28, 1925; s. Fred J. and Anna M. (Kuhlman) S.; m. Helene T. McDonald, Aug. 22, 1959; children: Anne, Edward, Janet. BS in Engring. Physics, U. Toledo, 1950; PhD, Cornell U., 1956. Sr. scientist Space Tech. Labs., Redondo Beach, Calif., 1956-60, Gen. Tech. Corp., Torrance, Calif., 1960-63; prin. scientist Xerox Corp., Webster, N.Y., 1963—. Contbr. over 50 articles to profl. jours; over 36 patents in field. Cpl. U.S. Army, 1945-46, Japan. Corning Glass fellow Cornell U., 1954. Mem. IEEE (sr.), Am. Phys. Soc. Home: 8 Forestwood Ln Pittsford NY 14534-3410

SCHMIDT, ALFRED OTTO, international engineering consultant; b. Mogilno, Germany, May 12, 1906; came to U.S., 1939, naturalized, 1945; s. Oskar and Emma (Schulz) S.; Mech.Engr., Ingenieurschule Ilmenau, Germany, 1928; M.S.E., U. Mich., 1940, D.Sc., 1943; m. Dorothy Lancaster, Dec. 19, 1941; children—Elsa, Margaret. Mech. engr. Carl Zeiss Jena, Germany, 1929-38; chief research engr. Kearney & Trecker Corp., Milw., 1943-61; prof. mech. engring. and indsl. engring. Colo. State U., Ft. Collins, Marquette U., Milw., Roorkee (India) U., U. Wis., Milw., U. R.I., Kingston, Pa. State U., University Park, 1963-71; adv. machine tools UN Indsl. Devel. Orgn., Israel, 1967, Argentina, 1968, 73, 78, 79, Brazil, 1972, Pakistan, 1970, Kenya, 1970, Sri Lanka, 1974; cons. Korea, 1979, China, 1980, 89, India, 1981, Sri Lanka, 1981, Taiwan, 1982, 89. Recipient Gold medal Am. Soc. Tool Engrs. Fellow ASME (life), Soc. Mfg. Engrs., Sigma Xi. Unitarian-Universalist. Author: Effective Use of Machine Tools, 1972; patentee in field; contbr. research papers to engring. jours. Home: PO Box 342 Jackson NH 03846-0342

SCHMIDT, CAROLYN MARIE, vocational educator, consultant; b. Jacksonville, Fla., Sept. 1, 1948; d. Leonard Stephen and Marianne Vesta (Ruscher) S. EdB, SUNY, Buffalo, 1980, MEd, 1981; cert. advanced study, SUNY, Brockport, 1988. Cert. tchr., N.Y., SDA Work Study Coord. Instr. Erie Bd. Coop. Edn. Svcs., Lancaster, N.Y., 1977-82, Orleans-Niagara Bd. Coop. Ednl. Svcs., Medina, N.Y., 1982—; adj. instr. State U. Coll., Buffalo, 1988-90; cons. N.Y. Dept. Edn., Albany, 1982—, facilitator, 1982-85, regional resource person, 1985—. Leader Girl Scouts U.S.A., Buffalo. Tchr. Intern award Tchrs. Ctr., Lockport, N.Y., 1989; N.Y. Disting. Occupational edn. award, 1991. Mem. ASCD, Am. Vocat. Assn., Vocat. Indsl. Clubs Am. (advisor), N.Y. State Tchrs. Vocat. Assn. (regional rep.), Phi Delta Kappa, Epsilon Pi Tau, Iota Lambda Sigma. Home: 4803 Cambridge Dr Apt B Lockport NY 14094-3447 Office: Orleans-Niagara Bd Ednl Svc 4232 Shelby Basin Rd Medina NY 14103-9515

SCHMIDT, CHARLES, art educator; b. Pitts., Mar. 4, 1939; s. Charles Samuel and Elizabeth (McComb) S.; m. Nancy Hurlston, Mar. 25, 1941; children: John Martin, Carrie. BFA in Painting, Carnegie Mellon U., 1960; MFA in Painting, Cranbrook Acad. Art, 1967. Calligrapher social staff The White House, Washington, 1961-62; instr. Atlanta Coll. Art, 1963-65; prof. Tyler Sch. Art, Temple U., Phila., 1967—; chair painting Temple Abroad, Tyler Sch. Art in Rome, Temple U., 1970-72. Painter (NASA commn.) Spacelab I, 1983 (presented to European Space Agy., Paris), 9th Launch of Space Shuttle, 1983, Mariner 9 Flyby of Mars, 1986, Hubble Space Telescope, 1987. With U.S. Army, 1960-62. Recipient commn. (through competition) Meml. Mural of Challenger Astronauts, Brumidi Corridor of U.S. Capitol for U.S. Senate, 1986, purchase award Art and the Law, The West Collection, St. Paul, 1984, Dana Watercolor medal Pa. Acad. Fine Arts, 1969, others. Office: Temple U Tyler Sch Art Beech and Penrose Aves Philadelphia PA 19126

SCHMIDT, DEBORAH THYNG, academic administrator; b. Augusta, Maine, Oct. 6, 1955; d. William Joseph Thyng and B. Arlene (Hayes) Landon; m. Douglas Alan Schmidt, Oct. 7, 1978; 1 child, Sarah Thyng Schmidt. BA in English, Bates Coll., Lewiston, Maine, 1977; MA in English Lit., U. Wis., 1980. Tchr. New Canaan (Conn.) Country Sch., 1977-78; devel. officer Bates Coll., Lewiston, 1978-79; editor U. Wis., Madison, 1981; coll. adminstr., admissions officer Carleton Coll., Northfield, Minn., 1981-85; devel. officer Ithaca (N.Y.) Coll., 1985-86; univ. adminstr., admissions officer Cornell U., Ithaca, 1986—. Vice chairwoman Literacy Vols., Broome-Tioga Counties, Endwell, N.Y., 1988. U. Wis. grad. fellow, Madison, 1979-80. Mem. Nat. Assn. Coll. Admissions Counselors, N.Y. State Assn. Coll. Admissions Counselors, Bates Coll. Alumni Assn. (exec. bd. 1990—, pres. 1992—). Office: Cornell U Admissions Office 410 Thurston Ave Ithaca NY 14850-2488

SCHMIDT, FREDERICK EBERHARD, policy research educator; b. Bklyn., July 23, 1940; s. Eberhard Winter and Lorraine (Beckerman) S.; m. Ann Victoria Warren, June 22, 1963; children: Kathryn Ann, Amy Suzanne, David Christopher. BA in Secondary Edn., Antioch Coll., 1963; MS in Rural Sociology, Cornell U., 1968, PhD in Devel. Sociology, 1973. Vol. community devel. office U.S. Peace Corps, Sungaitiang, Malaysia, 1963-65; asst. prof. sociology dept. Univ. Vt., Burlington, 1970-79, assoc. prof. sociology and agrl. depts., resource econs., 1980—, dir. Ctr. for Rural Studies, 1979—; dir. Office of Info. Office of Info. U. Vt. Extension System, Burlington, 1990—; 1st v.p. bd. dirs. Community Transp. Assn. of Am., Washington, 1981—; sec. bd. dirs. Rural Voice, Washington, 1986-90. Co-author: (booklet) From the Grassroots, 1991. Mem. Sewer com. Fire Dist. #1, Shelburne, Vt., 1985-90, Bd. Civil Authority, Shelburne, 1986—, Shelburne (Vt.) Planning Commn., 1989—; chmn. Govs. Commn. on Agrl. Rsch., Vt., 1987-89. Recipient Self Devel. Rsch. grant ERS, USDA, Washington, 1989-90, Head Start Demo grant HHS, Washington, 1991—, Job Start Demo grant HHS, Washington, 1990—, Population Estimates grant Vt. State Health Dept., Burlington, 1990-91. Fellow Ctr. for Rsch. on Vt. (dir. 1979-82); mem. Nat. Organic Farm Assn., Vt. Honduras Ptnrs. of the Ams. (v.p. 1989-90), Rural Sociol. Soc. (program com. 1987), Vt. Nat. Resource Com., N.E. Rural Sociol. Soc. (v.p. 1986-91), Extension Leadership Coun. Vt. (v.p. 1990-91). Office: U Vt Ctr for Rural Studies 207 Morrill Hall Burlington VT 05405-0106

SCHMIDT, RAYMOND PAUL, naval career officer, historian, government official; b. Western, Nebr., Sept. 14, 1937; s. Reuben Edward and Angeline Agnes (Kudlik) S.; m. Roberta Ruth Schrom, June 11, 1961; 1 child, Douglas Craig. B in Edn., History and Social Sci., U. Nebr., 1958; postgrad., U. Md., 1960-62, The Am. U., 1975-81; M in History, U. Wis., 1966. Instr. math. and social sci. Sr. High Sch., Bellevue, Nebr., 1958-59; ensign USN, 1959, advanced through grades to capt., 1981; historian, archivist Naval Security Group Command USN, Washington, 1968-81, sr. congl. security policy rev. officer Office Naval Intelligence, 1981-82, sr. res. forces advisor Dept. Def., 1982-88, head info. security policy, 1988—; history instr. James Madison Meml. High Sch., Madison, Wis., 1966-68. Author: (with others) Naval Officers Guide, 1983, And I Was There, 1985; contbr. articles to profl. jours. Pres. North Ashburton Citizens Assn., Bethesda, Md., 1982—; Merit badge counselor Boy Scouts Am., 1974—; info. officer U.S. Naval Acad., Annapolis, Md., 1978—; speaker Pearl Harbor Symposium Adm. Nimitz Found., Tex., 1991, symposium moderator, 1992; active Montgomery County Planning Bd. Citizens Adv. Com., Md., 1989—. Mem. DAV (life), Nat. Classification Mgmt. Soc. (editor Viewpoints 1991—), Nat. Trust Hist. Preservation, Am. Hist. Assn., U.S. Naval Inst. (life, contbr.), Acad. Pol. Sci., Res. Officers Assn. (life), Ret. Officers Assn. (life), Naval Res. Assn. (life, sec./treas. 1966-68), U. Nebr. Alumni Assn. (life). Unitarian. Home: 6205 Lone Oak Dr Bethesda MD 20817-1743

SCHMIDT, SANDRA JEAN, auditor; b. Limestone, Maine, Mar. 21, 1955; d. Dale Laban and Marie Audrey (Bailey) Winters; m. Lee Lloyd Schmidt, Oct. 20, 1973; children: Colby Lee, Katrina Leesa. AA, Anne Arundel Community Coll., 1987; BS, U. Balt., 1990. CPA, Md. Enlisted U.S. Army, 1973, traffic analyst, 1973-85, resigned, 1985; legis. auditor Md. State Div. Audits, Balt., 1990—. Tutor Anne Arundel County Literacy Coun., Pasadena, Md., 1990—; mentor U. Balt., 1991. Mem. AICPA, Am. Soc. Women Accts., Md. Assn. CPAs, U. Balt. Alumni Assn., Alpha Chi, Beta Gamma Sigma, Phi Theta Kappa. Republican. Baptist. Home: 7716 Pinyon Rd Hanover MD 21076-1585

SCHMIDT, WERNER A., chemical company executive, physician; b. Gelsenkirchen, Fed. Republic Germany, Feb. 3, 1925; came to U.S., 1964; s. Hubert and Maria (Oeldemann) S.; m. Ursula Knickmeyer, Oct. 26, 1957; children: Hans-Joachim, Klaus-Dieter. BS, Grillo Gymnasium, Gelsenkirchen, Fed. Rep. Germany, 1943; MD, U. Freiburg i.Br., 1951, Diplom Chemiker, 1957. Rsch. fellow U. Freiburg, 1952, U. Zurich, Switzerland, 1952-54, U. Oxford, England, 1952, U. Lund, Sweden, 1953; clin. rsch. E. Merck, Darmstadt, Fed. Rep. Germany, 1957; dir Internat. Div. E. Merck, Hartsdale, N.Y., 1964-70; pres. E.M. Lab. Co., Elmsford, N.Y., 1970-74; chmn. of bd. E.M. Ind. Inc., Hawthorne, N.Y., 1974-85. Pres. German Sch., White Plains, N.Y., 1980-84. Decorated with Officers Cross of Fed. Rep. of Germany, Pres. of Fed. Rep. of Germany, Bonn, 1982. Mem. German Med. Soc., German Club N.Y. (pres. 1988-90, 1992—), German Club N.Y.C. (pres. 1976-78), German Forum (bd. dirs. 1980—), Hercynia (pres. 1954). Home: 9 John Jay Pl Rye NY 10580-2222 Other Address: Elperweg 101, 02361 26307 Recklinghausen Federal Republic Germany

SCHMIDT, WILLIAM JAMES, artist; b. Bayonne, N.J., Mar. 18, 1932; s. John and Agnes Cecilia (Sweeney) S.; m. Dorothy Joan Radil, Sept. 1, 1956; children: William, Barbara, Karen. BChemE, Cornell U., 1958. Engr. Stone & Webster Engring., Boston, 1958-61, Yankee Atomic Electric Co., Rowe, Mass., 1961-63, Niagara Mohawk Power Co., Buffalo, 1963-67; engr., asst. mgr. NUS Corp., Gaithersburg, Md., 1967-77; pres., founder Indsl. Tng. Corp., Rockville, 1977-82; cons. Rockville, 1982-84, artist, 1984—. One-man shows include Venable-Neslage, Washington, 1988, 89, Bendann Galleries, Towson Town Centre, 1989, McBride's Gallery, Annapolis, Md., 1990, Loretta Goodwin Gallery, Birmingham, Ala., 1991; exhibited in group shows at McNichols Gallery, Naples, Fla., Miller Gallery, Cin., DeVille Galleries, L.A. Named to Top 100 Arts for the Parks Nat. Park Acad. Arts, 1990, 91; placed 58th Grand Nat. Exhbn. Am. Artists Profl. League, 1986, 60th, 1988. Mem. Washington Soc. of Landscape Painters (pres. 1988-90). Home: 13404 Bartlett St Rockville MD 20853-2938

SCHMIDTLEIN, FRANK ALLEN, educator; b. San Francisco, June 20, 1932; s. Frank Michael and Grace (Herr) S.; m. PatriciaJane Sidford, Oct. 10, 1964 (dec. Oct. 1987); m. Toby He, Mar. 18, 1989. BS, Kans. State U., 1954; MA, Berkeley, 1970, PhD, 1979. Spl. asst. U.S. Bur. Budget, Washington, 1962-64; exec. officer div. rsch. U.S. Office Edn., Washington, 1964-65, sr. program specialist, 1965-71; sr. researcher Ford Found., U. Calif., Berkeley, 1971-73; research specialist CRDHE, U. Calif., Berkelely, 1973-76; dir. Div. Acad. Fin. Planning, Md. Bd. for Higher Edn., Annapolis, 1976-80; asst. to chancellor U. Md., College Park, 1980-84, assoc. prof. higher edn., 1984—; cons. Tex. Higher Edn. Coordinating Bd., Austin, 1989, 91, Peat, Marwick and Main, Ames, Iowa, 1988, Mgmt. Sci. Corp., Washington, 1984, La. State Bd. Regents, Baton Rouge, 1981. Author: State Budgeting for Higher Education, 1977; contbr. chpts. to books. Capt. USAF, 1961-62. Mem. Am. Assn. Higher Edn., Assn. Instnl. Rsch., Assn. Study of Higher Edn., Am. Edn. Rsch. Assn., Md. Assn. for Higher Edn., Soc. Coll. and Univ. Planning, Washington Higher Edn. Group. Democrat. Home: 164 Berrywood Dr Severna Park MD 21146-2032

SCHMIDTMANN, LUCIE ANN, systems and software engineer; b. Jamaica, N.Y., Oct. 22, 1963; d. Otto Stanislaus and Nancy Dorothy (Koonmen) S. BS in Computer Sci., Siena Coll., Loudonville, N.Y., 1985; MS in Computer Sci., Stevens Inst. Tech., Hoboken, N.J., 1989; student, U.S. Coast Guard Acad., New London, Conn., 1981-82, St. John's U., 1980-81, 83; postgrad., Polytech U. Bklyn., Bklyn., 1990—. Computer cons. dept. computer sci. Siena Coll., Loudonville, N.Y., 1984-85; figure clk. King Kullen Grocery Co., Westbury, N.Y., 1983-85; project mgr. AT&T Bell Labs., Whippany, N.J., 1985-88; asst. to rsch. and devel. mgr. AT&T Bell Labs., 1988-89, system/software engr., 1990—; source selection cons. Highpoint Condominium Assn., Stanhope, N.J., 1989-92, bd. dirs. 1990-92; computer cons. Champcare Inc., Davenport, Iowa, 1989-91; head math judge North Jersey Regional Sci. Fair, 1990, head math and computer sci. judge, 1991, math. and computer sci. judge, 1992. Vol. N.J. Spl. Olympics, Area 3, Flanders, N.J., 1985—, vol. coord., 1985—, design/graphic artist, 1989. With USCG, 1981-82. Recipient Vol. award, N.J. Spl. Olympics Area 3, 1989. Mem. ACM (vice chmn. 1984-85, capt. programming team 1984-85), IEEE, IEEE Computer Soc., Math. Assn. Am., Performance Mgmt. Assn. (mem. North Jersey chpt. planning com. 1990, sec. 1990-91), Upsilon Pi Epsilon. Republican. Roman Catholic. Home: 10-186 Dell Pl Stanhope NJ 07874 Office: AT&T Bell Labs 1 Whippany Rd Whippany NJ 07981-1500

SCHMIEDEKER, RONALD EDWARD, insurance company executive; b. Cin., May 26, 1946; s. William John and Lois Ann (Knapp) S.; m. Ruth Ann Ramsey, Aug. 24, 1968. BA, U. Cin., 1968. Underwriter Great Am. Ins., Cin., 1971-74, sr. underwriter, 1974-78, underwriting mgr., 1978-82, staff underwriting mgr., 1982-88; br. underwriting mgr. Great Am. Ins., Chgo., 1988-90; v.p. underwriting Erie (Pa.) Ins. Group, 1990—. Sgt. U.S. Army, 1969-70, Vietnam. Republican. Home: 1650 Mulberry Ln Fairview PA 16415 Office: Erie Ins Group 100 Erie Insurance Pl Erie PA 16530

SCHMINCKE, DONALD RANDOLPH, JR., management consultant; b. Balt., Mar. 27, 1956; s. Donald Randolph Sr. and Audrey May (Jones) S. AA in Computer Sci., Essex Community Coll., Balt., 1976, AA in Engring., 1977; B in Engring. and Sci., MIT, 1979; M in Adminstrn. Sci., Johns Hopkins, 1984. Researcher Johns Hopkins Applied Physics Lab., Laurel, Md., 1977; engr. Charles Stark Draper Labs., Cambridge, Mass., 1978-79; intern Schlumberger Internat., Paris, 1979; tech. asst. Harvard/MIT Biomed., Cambridge, 1979-80; R&D scientist Pfizer Med. Systems, Columbia, Md., 1980-81; sr. mgmt. strategies cons. IBM, Washington, 1981-90; pres. Methods Internat., Inc., Balt., 1990—; chmn. Atlantic U., Virginia Beach, Va., 1992—. Contbr. articles to profl. jours. Mem. IEEE, AAAS, NSS, Am. Mgmt. Assn. Home: 29 S Stricker St Baltimore MD 21223 Office: Methods Internat Inc Legg Mason Tower 111 S Calvert St Baltimore MD 21202

SCHMITT, ROBERT LEE, computer scientist, system acquisition manager; b. Astoria, N.Y., Oct. 1, 1948; s. Edward and Margaret Louise (Gleason) S.; AAS in Data Processing, SUNY, Farmingdale, 1972; student Hofstra U., 1972-73; BS in Computer Sci., SUNY, Stony Brook, 1974, MS in Computer Sci., 1975; postgrad. in gen. adminstrn. U. Md., 1979-80;grad. diploma in strategic planning U.S. Naval War Coll., 1991. Cert. computer programmer, data processor. Computer programmer U.S. Army Environ. Hygiene Agy., Aberdeen Proving Ground, Md., 1976; data systems programmer Dept Def., Ft. George G. Meade, Md., 1976-78, data systems analyst, 1978-83, computer systems analyst, 1983-85, sr. computer system analyst, 1985-86, computer scientist, 1986-89, system acquisition mgr., 1989—. With USNR, 1968-79. Mem. Toastmasters. Home: 1211 Scattered Pines Ct Severn MD 21144-1814 Office: 9800 Savage Rd Fort George G Meade MD 20755

SCHMITT, ROLAND WALTER, academic administrator; b. Seguin, Tex., July 24, 1923; s. Walter L. and Myrtle F. (Caldwell) S.; m. Claire Freeman Kunz, Sept. 19, 1957; children: Lorenz Allen, Brian Walter, Alice Elizabeth, Henry Caldwell. BA in Math, U. Tex., 1947, BS in Physics, 1947, MA in Physics, 1948; PhD, Rice U., 1951; DSc (hon.), Worcester Poly. Inst., 1985, U. Pa., 1985; DCL (hon.), Union Coll., 1985; DL (hon.), Lehigh U., 1986; DSc (hon.), U. S.C., 1988, Universite De Technologie De Compiegne, 1991. With GE, 1951-88; R & D mgr. phys. sci. and engring. GE, Schenectady, 1967-74; mgr. energy sci. and engring. R & D GE, 1974-78, v.p. corp. R & D, 1978-82, sr. v.p. corp. R & D, 1982-86, sr. v.p. sci. and tech., 1986-88, ret., 1988; pres. Rensselaer Poly. Inst., Troy, N.Y., 1988—; bd. dirs. Gen. Signal Corp., 1987—; mem. tech. adv. bd. Chrysler Corp., 1990—; past pres. Indsl. Rsch. Inst.; mem. energy rsch. adv. bd. U.S. Dept. Energy, 1977-83; chmn. CORETECH, 1988—; mem. Com. on Japan, NRC, 1988-90, Comml. Devel. Ind. Adv. Group, NASA, 1988-90; exec. com. Coun. on Competitiveness, 1988—; chmn. NRC Panel on Export Controls, 1989-91; mem. Dept. Commerce Adv. Commn. on Patent Law Reform, 1990—. Trustee N.E. Savs. Bank, 1978-84; bd. advisors Union Coll., trustee Schenectady, 1981-84, Argonne Univs. Assn., 1979-82, RPI, 1982-88; bd. govs. Albany Med. Ctr. Hosp., 1979-82, 88-90; bd. dirs. Sunnyview Hosp. and Rehab. Ctr., 1978-86, Coun. on Superconductivity for Am. Competitiveness, 1987-89; mem. exec. com. N.Y. State Ctr. for Hazardous Waste Mgmt., 1988-89, chmn. OTA adv. panel on industry and environment. With USAAF, 1943-46. Recipient RPI Community Svc. award, 1982, award for disting. contbns. Stony Brook Found., 1985, Rice U. Disting. Alumni award, 1985, IRI Medalist award, 1989, Royal Swedish Acad. of Engring. Sci., 1990; named Fgn. Assn. of Engring. Acad. of Japan. Fellow AAAS, IEEE (Centenial medal 1984, Engring. Leadership award 1989), Am. Phys. Soc., Am. Acad. Arts and Scis.; mem. NAE (coun.), A. Inst. Physics (chmn. com. on corp. assocs., governing bd. 1979-83), Nat. Sci. Bd. (past chmn. 1982), Dirs. Indsl. Rsch., Cosmos. Office: Rensselaer Poly Inst Office of Pres Troy NY 12180-3590

SCHMITT, SARA GREEN, clinical psychologist; b. Rahway, N.J., Sept. 22, 1962; d. Philip Stanley Green and Roma Helen (Gizang) Green; m. Ralph Henry Schmitt, Jan. 6, 1985. BA magna cum laude, Rutgers U., 1984; PhD, Fairleigh Dickinson U., 1988. Lic. psychologist, N.J. Staff psychologist CPC Mental Health Svcs., Freehold, N.J., 1987-90; psychologist pvt. practice Holmdel, N.J., 1988—; staff psychologist Women's Resource Survival Ctr., Keyport, N.J., 1987-88; cons. Prudential, Holmdel, 1989-90; co-dir. Premenstrual Mgmt. Svcs., Holmdel, 1990—. Mem. Am. Psychol. Assn., N.J. Psychol. Assn. (children, youth and families com. 1985—, student affiliate com. 1985-88), Monmouth Ocean County Psychol. Assn., N.J. Acad. Psychology, Phi Beta Kappa, Psi Chi. Jewish. Home: 160 Smithburg Rd Englishtown NJ 07726-8118 Office: Associated Psychol Svcs 717 N Beers St Ste 2B Holmdel NJ 07733-1503

SCHMOKE, KURT, mayor; b. Balt., Dec. 1, 1949; m. Patricia Schmoke; children: Katherine, Gregory. BA, Yale U., 1971; JD, Harvard U., 1976. Former assoc. Piper & Marbury; former pvt. practice; asst. U.S. atty Balt.; state's atty. Maryland, 1982-87; mayor Baltimore, 1987—; apptd. mem. White House Domestice Policy Staff, 1977-78; former mem. Gov.'s Commn. on Prison Overcrowding; former mem. Md. Criminal justice Coord. Coun. & Task Force to Reform Insanity Def.; founder Balt. Community Devel. Financing Corp., 1988—. Rhodes Scholar Yale U. Office: 250 City Hall Baltimore MD 21202*

SCHMOLL, HARRY F., JR., lawyer, educator; b. Somers Point, N.J., Jan. 20, 1939; s. Harry F. Sr and Margaret E. Schmoll; m. Rita L. Miescier, Aug. 29, 1977. BS, Rider Coll., 1960; JD, Temple U., 1967. Bar: Pa., D.C. 1969, N.J. 1975. With claims dept. Social Security Adminstrn., Phila., 1960-67; staff atty. Pa. State U., State College, 1968-69; regional dir. Pa. Crime Commn., State College, 1969-70; campaign aide U.S. Senator Hugh Scott, Harrisburg, Pa., 1970; pvt. practice law, State College, 1970-74, Manahwkin, N.J., 1975—; instr. criminal justice Pa. State U., University Park, 1969-74, assoc. prof. criminal justice Burlington County Coll., Pemberton, N.J., 1974-92, prof., pres. elect edn. assn., 1992—; judge mcpl. ct., Stafford Twp., 1982-85. Gen. counsel German Heritage Coun. of N.J., Inc.; mem. Barnegat Twp. Rent Control Bd. Author: New Jersey Criminal Law Workbook, 1976, 2nd edit. 1979. Mem. Stafford Twp. Com., 1979-81, dep. mayor, 1979. Trustee Pheasant Run Homewoners Assn., Barnegat, N.J., 1992. Mem. Pa. Bar Assn., N.J. Bar Assn., Ocean County Bar Assn., German-Am. Club of So. Ocean County (pres.). Office: 6 Citrus Ct Barnegat NJ 08005-3126

SCHNAKENBERG, DONALD G., financial administrator; b. Queens, N.Y., Dec. 6, 1939; s. Herman G. and Rose (Conte) S. BS in Acctg., Bklyn. Coll., 1960; MBA in Mgmt. with honors, Pace U., 1969. Acct. Rosen, Futterman & Berylson CPA's, N.Y.C., 1960-62; sr. acct. Fluhr, Massen & Light CPA's, N.Y.C., 1963; tax examiner N.Y. State Tax Commn., N.Y.C., 1963-65; acct. N.Y.C. Housing and Redevel. Bd., N.Y.C., 1965-67; sr. acct. N.Y.C. Bd. Edn., N.Y.C., 1967-68, N.Y.C. Housing and Redevel., N.Y.C., 1968; prin. budget examiner Bur. of Budget Office of Mayor, N.Y.C., 1968-76; fin. dir. N.Y.C. Coun., 1976-89; chief fin. officer Lower Eastside Svc. Ctr., N.Y.C., 1989-90, Promesa Inc., Bronx, 1990—. Mem. Am. Mgmt. Assn., Govt. Fin. Officers Assn., JFK Dem. Club, Manhattan Chess Club. Democrat. Roman Catholic. Home: 123-35 82d Rd 7K Kew Gardens NY 11415

SCHNALL, EDITH LEA (MRS. HERBERT SCHNALL), microbiologist, educator; b. N.Y.C., Apr. 11, 1922; d. Irving and Sadie (Raab) Spitzer; AB, Hunter Coll., 1942; AM, Columbia U., 1947, PhD, 1967; m. Herbert Schnall, Aug. 21, 1949; children: Neil David, Carolyn Beth. Clin. pathologist Roosevelt Hosp., N.Y.C., 1942-44; instr. Adelphi Coll., Garden City, N.Y., 1944-46; asst. med. mycologist Columbia Coll. Physicians and Surgeons, N.Y.C., 1946-47, 49-50; instr. Bklyn. Coll., 1947; mem. faculty Sarah Lawrence Coll., Bronxville, N.Y., 1947-48; lectr. Hunter Coll., N.Y.C., 1947-67; adj. assoc. prof. Lehman Coll., City U. N.Y., 1968; asst. prof. Queensborough Community Coll., City U. N.Y., 1967, assoc. prof. microbiology, 1968-75, prof., 1975—, adminstr. Med. Lab. Tech. Program, 1985—; vis. prof. Coll. Physicians and Surgeons, Columbia U., N.Y.C., 1974; advanced biology examiner U. London, 1970—. Mem. Alley Restoration Com., N.Y.C., 1971—; mem. legis. adv. com. Assembly of the State of N.Y., 1972. Mem. Community Bd. 11, Queens, N.Y., 1974—, 3d vice-chmn., 1987-92, 2nd vice chmn., 1992—; public dir. of bd. dirs. Inst. Continuing Dental Edn. Queens County, Dental Soc. N.Y. State and ADA, 1973—. Rsch. fellow NIH, 1948-49; faculty rsch. fellow, grantee-in-aid Rsch. Found. of SUNY, 1968-70; faculty rsch. grant Rsch. Found. City U. N.Y., 1971-74. Mem. Internat. Soc. Human and Animal Mycology, AAAS, Am. Soc. Microbiology (coun., N.Y.C. br. 1981—, co-chairperson ann. meeting com. 1981-82, chair program com. 1982-83, v.p. 1984-86, pres. 1986-88), Med. Mycology Soc. N.Y. (sec.-treas. 1967-68, v.p. 1968-69, 78-79, archivist 1974—, fin. advisor 1983—, pres. 1969-70, 79-80, 81-82), Bot. Soc. Am., Med. Mycology Soc. Americas, Mycology Soc. Am., N.Y. Acad. Scis., Sigma Xi, Phi Sigma. Clubs: Torrey Botanical (N.Y. State); Queensborough Community Coll. Women's (pres. 1971-73) (N.Y.C.). Editor: Newsletter of Med. Mycology Soc. N.Y., 1969-85; founder, editor Female Perspective newsletter of Queensborough Community Coll. Women's Club, 1971-73. Home: 21406 29th Ave Flushing NY 11360-2622

SCHNAPF, ABRAHAM, aerospace engineer, consultant; b. N.Y.C., Aug. 1, 1921; s. Meyer and Gussie (Schaeffler) S.; m. Edna Wilensky, Oct. 24, 1943; children: Donald J., Bruce M. BSME, CCNY, 1948; MSME, Drexel Inst. Tech., 1953. Registered profl. engr., N.J. Devel. engr. on lighter-than-air aircraft Goodyear Aircraft Corp., Akron, Ohio, 1948-50; mgr. fire control system def. electronics RCA, Camden, N.Y., 1950-55, mgr. airbourne navigation system, aerospace weapon system, 1955-58; program mgr. TIROS/TOS weather satellite systems RCA Astro-Electronics, Princeton, N.J., 1958-70, mgr. satellite programs, 1970-79, prin. scientist, 1979-82; cons. Aerospace Systems Engring., Willingboro, N.J., 1982—; lectr., presenter on meteor. satellites, space tech., communication satellites. Sgt. USAF, 1943-46. Recipient award Nat. Press Club Washington, 1975, award Am. Soc. Quality Control-NASA, 1968, Pub. Svc. award NASA, 1969, cert. of appreciation U.S. Dept. Commerce, 1984. Fellow AIAA; mem. Am. Astro. Soc., Am. Meterol. Soc., Space Pioneers, N.Y. Acad. Scis. (mem. think tank week sessions 1980's), N.J. Arbitration Soc. Home and Office: 41 Pond Ln # 160 Willingboro NJ 08046-2756

SCHNAPF, DONALD JEFFREY, neuroradiologist, educator; b. Bronx, N.Y., Mar. 19, 1946; s. Abraham and Edna (Wilensky) S.; m. Carole Elaine Shaub, June 9, 1973; children: Rebekah Susan, Jared Matthew, Joshua Nathanael, Abigail Jean, Danielle Sarah. BA in Biology, Ithaca Coll., 1969; DO, Phila. Coll. Osteopathic Medicine, 1973. Diplomate Am. Bd. Radiology; cert. neuroradiologist. Resident in radiology Met. Hosp., Springfield, Pa., 1977; fellow in neuroradiology Thomas Jefferson Hosp., Phila., 1978; asst. prof. radiology Georgetown U., Washington, 1978—; chief, neuroradiology Walter Reed Med. Ctr., Washington, 1978-80; lectr. Armed Forces Inst. Pathology, Washington, 1978—; practice medicine specializing in radiology Washington County Hosp., Hagerstown, Md., 1980-83, Community Hosp., Lancaster, Pa., 1983—; asst. clin. prof. Pa. State U. Med. Sch., Hershey, 1983—; med. dir. York (Pa.) Magnetic Imaging Ctr., 1985—; rep. Nat. Council Radiation Protection Measurement, 1981—; rep. com. N-44 Am. Nat. Standards Inst., 1982—. Contbr. articles to profl. jours. Recipient Kenneth L. Wheeler award Phila. Coll. Osteo. Medicine, 1973; Am. Coll. Osteo. Radiology fellow, 1988. Fellow Am. Coll. Osteo. Radiology; mem. AMA, Am. Radiol. Soc. N.Am., Am. Roentgen Ray Soc., Soc. Magnetic Resonance in Medicine, Am. Soc. Neuroradiology (sr. mem.). Home: 132 Sandstone Dr Willow Street PA 17584-9440

SCHNATTERLY, ROBERT CHRISTOPHER, marketing specialist, consultant; b. Uniontown, Pa., Nov. 3, 1952; s. Robert J. Schnatterly and Sarah F. (TenCate) Wallace; m. Jean E. Whitehill, July 17, 1982; children: Robert J., James K. BS, U. Pitts., 1975; MBA, Katz Grad. Sch. Bus., Pitts., 1977. Tech. sales rep. Koppers Co., West Orange, N.J., 1977-78; supr. sales Copperweld Co., Pitts., 1978-80, export mgr., 1980-83, mgr. mktg. svcs., 1983-84, internat. mgr. sales and mktg., 1984-85; sr. mktg. mgr. Calgon Carbon Corp., Pitts., 1987-88; mng. dir. Internat. Mktg. Assocs., Pitts., 1985—. Office: Internat Mktg Assocs 549 Clemson Dr Pittsburgh PA 15243-1735

SCHNECK, ERIC MILO, computer consultant; b. N.Y.C., Feb. 5, 1954; s. William and Beverly Schneck. BA in Maths., Rutgers Coll., 1976; MSEE, Columbia U., 1980; MBA in Fin., NYU, 1983. Cert. data processor. Programmer Interactive Market Systems, Inc., N.Y.C., 1976-79; teaching cons. ADP, Clifton, N.J., 1979-80; systems analyst W.R. Grace & Co., N.Y.C., 1980-83; pres. Eric M. Schneck, Inc., N.Y.C., 1983—; instr. Courant Inst., NYU, N.Y.C., 1983-85. Mem. Ind. Computer Cons. Assn., Tudor City Assn. Home and Office: Eric M Schneck Inc 333 E 43 St Ste 1014 New York NY 10017

SCHNECK, JAMES ANTHONY, principal; b. Canton, Ohio, Dec. 30, 1953; s. Vernon Abraham and Ida Marie (Nussbaum) S.; m. Rosalee Diffenbach, Sept. 15,1 979; children: Peter, Annika, James Abram, Katrina. BS in Spl. Edn., U. Akron, 1982, MS in Spl. Edn., 1988. Data processor Fame Beverage Co., Canton, 1970-72; tchr. aide to deaf mentally retarded Apple Creek (Ohio) State Instn., 1972-74; interpreter for deaf U. Akron (Ohio), 1974-76; adminstr., founder New Life Homes, Inc., Massillon, Ohio, 1976-80; instr. U. Akron, 1980-90, Weaver High Sch., Cuyahoga Falls, Ohio, 1983-89; prin., adminstr. Hinkletown Mennonite Sch., Ephrata, Pa., 1989—; cons. Ft. Wayne State Devel. Inst., 1990, Agy. for Instructional Tech., 1991; tchr. workshops. Rotating interpreter deaf person Alcoholics Anonymous, Wooster, Ohio, 1980-89; mem. First Deaf Mennonite Ch., Smoketown, Pa.; mem. Nat. Right to Life; treas. Lancaster Area Coun. of Mennonite Schs.; mem. steering com. Coordinated Sch.-Community Intervention Program for Non-Public Schs.; former bd. dirs. Stark County Coun. for Retarded Citizens, 1978-80; former mem. adv. bd. Community Svcs. for the Deaf, Akron. Recipient Jefferson award TV 8, Cleve., 1980, Liberty Bell award Stark County Bar Assn., 1979, Outstanding Young Man of Am. award U.S. Jaycees, 1975; mini-grantee Mid-Eastern Ohio Regional Resource Ctr., 1988, Akron Coun. for Exceptional Children, 1987, grantee Martha Holden Jennings Found., 1986, Ohio Dept. Transp., 1980, Ohio Dept. Mental Retardation and Developmental Disabilities, 1979, 80. Mem. Registry of Interpreters for the Deaf. Republican. Home: 407 Fairview St PO Box 509 Terre Hill PA 17581 Office: Hinkletown Mennonite Sch 272 Wanner Rd Ephrata PA 17522-9314

SCHNEE, DAVID Z., data processing consultant; b. Bklyn., July 8, 1941; s. Nathan and Edythe (Shapiro) S.; m. Elaine S. Landau, June 29, 1969 (div.); children: Hal, Dennis, Matthew, Mark. BEE, The Cooper Union, N.Y.C., 1962; MSEE, U. Pa., 1964. Mgmt. trainee Gen. Electric, Valley Forge, Pa., 1962-65; assoc. engr. Sperry Gyroscope Co., Lake Success, N.Y., 1965-69; software mgr. Western Union Telegraph Co., N.Y.C., 1969-70; ptnr. DN James Co., N.Y.C., 1970-71, Dynax Resources, Inc., Jericho, N.Y., 1971—. Fin. sec. Old Westbury (N.Y.) Hebrew Congregation, 1988-89, recording sec., 1987-88. N.Y. Regents scholar, 1958. Mem. L.I. Systems User Group (dir., v.p. 1984—), Mensa. Jewish.

SCHNEIDER, DAVID THEODORE, financial executive; b. Upland, Pa., June 11, 1949. BS, MIT, 1970; MBA, Harvard U., 1972. V.p. fin., chief fin. officer Formica Corp., Wayne, N.J., 1989—. Office: Formica Corp 155 State Rt 46 Wayne NJ 07470-6831

SCHNEIDER, FREDERICK HOWARD, pharmacologist; b. Detroit, Nov. 19, 1938; s. Fred and Evora (Hanson) S.; m. Leslie Ann Smith, July 10, 1971; children: Catherine Ann, Phillip Andrew, Mark Brian. MS, Ariz. State U., 1962; PhD, Yale U., 1966. Chemist Merck Sharp Dohme, Rahway, N.J., 1961-63; prof. Med. Sch. U. Colo., Denver, 1966-72, Emory U., Atlanta, 1972-74; pres. Bioassay Systems Corp., Cambridge, Mass., 1971-85; v.p., cons. Bogart Delafield Ferrier, Morristown, N.J., 1985-91; sr. v.p. tech. Dynagen Inc., Cambridge, Mass., 1991—. Contbr. articles to profl. jours.

SCHNEIDER, GERTRUDE, academic placement director, association executive; b. Vienna, Austria, May 27, 1928; d. Pinkas and Charlotte (Le Winter) Hirschhorn; m. Eric Schneider, July 8, 1951; children: David, Barbara, Peter. BS, CCNY, 1970, MS, 1972; PhD, CUNY, 1973. Prof. edn. CCNY, 1970-80; prof. Fordham U., N.Y.C., 1975-80; assoc. placement dir. Grad. Sch. CUNY, 1980—, pres. PhD alumni assn., 1983—; cons. Dept. State, Washington, German Cts., Hamburg, Cologne and Düsseldorf. Author: Journey into Terror: Story of the Riga Ghetto, 1979; editor: Muted Voices: Jewish Survivors of Latvia Remember, 1987 (Jewish Book award 1988), The Unfinished Road: Jewish Survivors of Latvia Look Back, 1991. Lehman fellow N.Y. State Dept. Edn., 1971, Touro Coll. fellow, 1972; grantee CUNY Rsch. Found., 1989. Mem. Jewish Survivors of Latvia (v.p. 1984—). Office: CUNY PhD Alumni Assn GC 33 W 42nd St New York NY 10036-8003

SCHNEIDER, GRETA SARA, ergonomics consultant; b. Bklyn., May 26, 1954; d. Irving Victor and Anne Joyce (Goldberg) S. BA, MA, CUNY, 1975, MA, 1976, PhD, 1977. Writer, cons. Pitts., 1972-73; cons. Flushing, N.Y., 1973-85; sr. writer, cons. Buck Cons. Inc., N.Y.C., 1985-86; chmn., chief exec. officer Schneider Cons Inc., N.Y.C., 1986—. Mem. Little Theatre Group, Marathon Community Ctr., Little Neck, N.Y., 1980-83. Mem. AFTRA, Nas. Assn. Women Bus. Owners, Nat. Assn. Bus. Communicators, Employee Assistance Profls. Assn., Soc. Human Resource Mgmt., Writers Guild Am., Rotary. Home: 25237 60th Ave Flushing NY 11362-2423 Office: Schneider Cons Inc 124 W 30th St New York NY 10001-4009

SCHNEIDER, HERBERT C(ARPENTER), oil products distribution company executive; b. Newburgh, N.Y., Nov. 20, 1945; s. Floyd R. and Katharyn (Carpenter) S.; m. Judith S. Seidowitz, Feb. 14, 1976; 1 child, Victoria. BA, Dartmouth Coll., 1967; MBA, Columbia U., 1969. Researcher Iran Nat. Tourist Orgn. Peace Corps., Tehran, 1969-71; trainee Carpenter & Smith, Inc., Monroe, N.Y., 1972-75, treas., 1975-82, pres., 1982—; bd. dirs. Met. Energy Coun., N.Y.C., 1986—, v.p., 1990—; bd. dirs. Hudson Valley Oil Heat Coun., Middletown, N.Y., 1985—. Sec., Hudson Valley Oil Heat Coun., 1987-89, v.p., 1989-91, pres., 1991—; bd. dirs. Orange County Community Coll. Ednl. Found., 1988—. Republican. Lodge: Rotary (pres. Monroe-Woodbury 1987-88, Paul Harris fellow 1986). Home: 51 Laurel Hill Rd Croton On Hudson NY 10520-1209 Office: Carpenter & Smith Inc 100 Spring St # 686 Monroe NY 10950-3612

SCHNEIDER, JACK, accountant; b. Boston, Apr. 1, 1917; s. Harry and Mollie (Chuves) S.; m. Doris Orkin, Dec. 26, 1948; children: Ronald Mark, Marjorie Lee. BBA, Boston U., 1939; student, Northeastern U. Sch. Law, Boston, 1951-52. LPA, Mass. Pvt. practice Boston, 1939—. Tech. sgt. U.S. Army, 1943-45. Home and Office: 16 Wendell Park Milton MA 02186-3118

SCHNEIDER, JOHN K., financial administrator; b. Bryn Mawr, Pa., June 30, 1964; s. Arnold C. Jr. and Dorothy A. Schneider. BS in Fin. summa cum laude, Lehigh U., 1986. Cert. chartered fin. analyst, 1989. V.p. Wilmington (Del.) Capital Mgmt., 1986-91; sr. securities analyst DuPont Pension Fund, Wilmington, 1991; v.p. Newbold's Asset Mgmt., Bryn Mawr, 1991—. Mem. Phila. Fin. Analysts Soc. (speakers com. mem.), Fin. Analysts of Wilmington, Kappa Alpha Soc., Beta Gamma Sigma (v.p. 1986). Republican. Episcopalian.

SCHNEIDER, MARTIN AARON, photojournalist, ecologist, engineer, writer; b. N.Y.C., Sept. 23, 1926; s. Morris and Florence (Frohlich) S. Student, CUNY, 1946-52. Freelance artist, 1941—, freelance photographer, 1954—; photojournalist Life, Time, Newsweek, Sports Illustrated, Mpls. Tribune, 1960—; lectr. NYU, Cornell U., Ithaca, N.Y., New Sch. Social Rsch., N.Y.C., 1969—; TV and radio commentator NBC, CBS, ABC, PBS, FOX, 1970—; ecologist USPHS, U.S. Senate, U.S. EPA, N.Y. EPA, 1964—; pub. intervenor N.Y.C. Health Dept., N.Y. State Health Dept., N.Y. State Dept. Environ. Conservation, People of N.Y.C., 1970—; TV news guest NBC Today, CBS, ABC, 1970—; radio news guest NBC, NPR, 1970—; lectr. in field. Author: Consumer Genocide, 1992; co-author: America-- Photographic Statements, 1972, Eye of Conscience, 1974; dir., writer, producer, videographer TV documentaries: No Justice for Victims--Criminals Only, 1992, Environment Crusade, 1970, The Poisoned Air, 1970, Killers of the Environment, 1971, Censorship of Pollution Solutions by Media and Government, 1974; contbr. N.Y. Times, Ency. Britannica, 1970—; engr., builder crash-safety, pollution and radiation-monitoring vehicle; photography exhibited in group shows at N.Y. Mus. Modern Art, 1958—, Libr. Congress, 1970, Art Inst. Chgo., 1973, Whitney Mus., 1978. With U.S. Army, 1944-46, PTO. Creative Artists Pub. Svc. grantee, 1977, 78; recipient TV Franny Consumer Advocacy award, 1978. Mem. Am. Soc. Mag. Photographers. Jewish. Office: 1501 Broadway Rm 2907 New York NY 10036-5600

SCHNEIDER, PHILIP ALLEN, government agency executive; b. St. Louis, Oct. 26, 1938; s. John Henry and Elizabeth (Stellwagen) S.; m. Mary Linda Brown, June 28, 1963; children: Martha Glenn, Mary Elizabeth, John Mahlon, Linda Anne, David Allen, Patrick Brown. AB, Cornell U., 1961; PhD, Duke U., 1968. Intelligence officer U.S. Army Security Agy., Arlington, Va., 1962-64; programming group leader Def. Communications Agy., Arlington, Va., 1964; software cons. Duke U. and U. N.C., Durham, 1964-68; dir sci. svcs. U.S. Army Systems Analysis Group, Ft. Belvoir, Va., 1968-72; chief manpower statistics div. U.S. Civil Svc. Commn., Washington, 1972-75; asst. dir. workforce info. U.S. Office of Personnel Mgmt., Washington, 1975—; asst. prof. U. Va., Charlottesville, 1968-72, assoc. prof., No. Va. Community Coll., Annandale, 1973-85; prof. George Mason U., Fairfax, Va., 1986—. Author: New Foundations for Confirmation in Science, 1968, Measures of Effectiveness for Combat Developments, 1971, Digital Topographic Mapping for Combat Simulation, 1972, Privacy Act Regulations, 1975; editor: Federal Civilian Workforce Statistics, 1974-91, The Guide for Processing Personnel Actions, 1976-91, Personnel Records and Files Systems, 1976-91, Federal Personnel Data Standards, 1976-86; dir. The Bureaucrat Mag., 1987—. Mem. Fairfax County (Va.) Citizens Commn. on Declining Enrollment in sec. Schs. Capt. U.S. Army, 1962-64. NDEA fellow, 1964-67; NSF fellow, 1968. Mem. U.S. Sr. Exec. Svc. (charter mem.), Fed. Exec. Inst. Alumni Assn. (dir. 1982-86, v.p. 1986), Am. Statis. Assn., Am. Philos. Assn., Delta Tau Delta. Episcopalian. Home: 8511 Browning Ct Annandale VA 22003-2218 Office: US Office Pers Mgmt Rm 7494 Washington DC 20415

SCHNEIDER, PHILIP JAMES, research institute executive; b. Bronx, June 28, 1949; s. Wilbur Henry and Lurline J. (Smith) S.; m. Gail Elizabeth Brown, Feb. 6, 1981; 1 child, Theodore Arthur. BArch, U. Notre Dame, 1972; postgrad., Ohio State U., 1979-80. Registered architect Va., Md. Bldg. rsch. officer dept. pub. wks. Fiji ACTION, Washington, 1977-79; researcher Dept. of City and Regional Planning, Ohio State U., Columbus, 1979-80, Program for Energy Rsch., Edn. and Pub. Svc., Columbus, 1980-81; project architect Austin Spriggs Assocs., Washington, 1981-84; project dir. Basco Assocs., Inc., York, Pa., 1984-85; project mgr. Kann & Ammon, Inc., Balt., 1985-87; program mgr. Nat. Inst. Bldg. Scis., Washington, 1987-89, dir. tech. programs, 1989—; cts. cons. Archtl. Rsch. Collaborative, Balt., 1991—. Project dir. book: U.S. Courts Design Guide, 1991. Mem. AIA,

ASTM, Arch. for Justice Com. Home: PO Box 22927 Baltimore MD 21203 Office: Nat Inst Bldg Scis 1201 L St NW Washington DC 20005

SCHNEIDERMAN, BOB ALLEN, real estate excutive; b. N.Y.C., Sept. 15, 1963; s. Michael M. and Gail V. (Gordon) S.; married. BSBA, Washington U., St. Louis, 1985; MBA, George Washington U., Washington, 1986. Assoc. v.p. Julien J. Studley, Inc., McLean, Va., 1987—. Office: Julien J Studley Inc 8180 Greensboro Dr # 750 Mc Lean VA 22102

SCHNEIDERMAN, HOWARD GARY, sociologist, educator; b. N.Y.C., Jan. 11, 1949; s. Sol and Adele (Korb) S.; m. Nancy Trayes, Aug. 10, 1974; 1 child, Benjamin Charles. BA, CCNY, 1970; MA, U. Pa., 1971, PhD, 1978. Lectr. U. Pa., Phila., 1972-73; instr. Lafayette Coll., Easton, Pa., 1973-78, asst. prof., 1978-80, assoc. prof. sociology, 1980—. Author, editor introduction to book: The Protestant Establishment Revisited, 1991, Judgement and Sensibility, 1992, Hindrances to Good Citizenship, 1992; assoc. editor jour. Society, 1991—, book rev. editor, 1992—; contbr. articles to profl. jours. NSF fellow, 1970-73; Mellon Found. fellow, 1978; Lafayette Coll. rsch. fellow, 1986; Sloan Found. seminar fellow, 1984, 87, 89; NSF seminar fellow, 1990. Mem. Am. Sociol. Assn., Soc. for Sci. Study of Religion, Orgn. Am. Historians, Ea. Sociol. Soc. (chmn. Candace Rogers com. 1987-89), Am. Culture Assn., Nat. Assn. Scholars, Tocqueville Soc. Jewish. Office: Lafayette Coll Dept Sociology Easton PA 18042

SCHNEIDER-MAUNOURY, MICHEL, petroleum company executive; b. Vert-le-Petit, Essone, France, May 26, 1931; came to U.S., 1982; s. Jacques and Odette (Dubernet de Garros) S.; m. Brigitte Dupuy, Nov. 24, 1958 (dec. Apr. 1964); children: Guillaume, Sylvie; m. Maryllis Tenaille, Aug. 14, 1975; children: Eglantine, Romain. Student, Ecole Polytechnique, Paris, 1950-52, Ecole Nationale Superieure des Mines de Paris, 1953-54; engring. student, Ecole Superieure de Petrole, Paris, 1955. Sr. geophysicist BRP, Paris, 1957-59, v.p. industry and commerce, 1963-65; asst. to dir. SEREPT, Tunis, Tunisia, 1960-62; v.p. econs. and fin., exploration and prodn. ERAP, Paris, 1966-73; sr. v.p. planning and trading SNEA, Paris, 1973-79, sr. v.p. chems., 1980-82; chmn. Elf Aquitaine, Inc., N.Y.C., 1982—, Texasgulf Inc., Raleigh, N.C.; bd. dirs. French Am. Banking Corp., SCOR, U.S. ELF Atochem N.Am., Am. Mining Congress. Mem. adv. com. Ctr. for French Civilization and Culture, NYU. Served as lt. arty. French Army. Decorated officer L'ordre Nat. du Merite, chevalier de la Legion d'Honneur. Mem. Assn. Francaise des Technicens du Petroles, Societe de Chimie Industrielle. Home: 1199 Park Ave Apt 15A New York NY 10128-1787 Office: Elf Aquitaine Inc 280 Park 36th Ave New York NY 10017-1216

SCHNEIER, ARTHUR, rabbi; b. Vienna, Austria, Mar. 20, 1930; m. Elisabeth Nordmann; children: Marc, Karen Schneier Dresbach. BA, Yeshiva U., 1951; MA in Psychology and Edn., NYU, 1953; DHL (hon.), Fordham U., 1981, L.I. U., 1981; PhD (hon.), U. Budapest, 1984; DD (hon.), Yeshiva U., 1986; ThD (hon.), Reformed Ch. Theol. Sem., 1988; LLD (hon.), Susquehanna U., 1988. Ordained rabbi, 1955. Rabbi Park East Synagogue, N.Y.C., 1962—; founder Park East Day Sch. and Sam and Esther Minskoff Cultural Ctr. (renamed Rabbi Arthur Schneier Park East Day Sch.), N.Y.C.; founder, pres. Appeal of Conscience Found., N.Y., 1965; chmn. Am. sect. World Jewish Congress, 1979-84, hon. chmn., 1984—; alt. rep. of U.S. to Gen. Assembly of UN, 1988; mem. Coun. of Fgn. Rels.; mem. U.S. Presdl. Delegation for Return of Crown of St. Stephen to Hungary, 1978; chmn. bd. dirs. Am.-Romanian Flood and Earthquake Relief, 1970-74; leader Armenian Earthquake Relief, 1988; founding trustee U.S.-Japan Found.; apptd. chmn. U.S. Commn. for Preservation Am.'s Heritage Abroad, 1991. Bd. dirs. UN Devel. Corp., N.Y., 1973-80; mem. exec. com., bd. dirs. Am. Joint Distbn. Com.; bd. dirs. Hebrew Immigration Aid Soc.; vice chmn. Am. Gathering of Holocaust Survivors; hon. vice chmn. Jewish Nat. Fund. Leader 1st Jewish prayer svc. in Kremlin, 1990; only Jewish leader to address Millenium of Russian Orthodox Ch., Moscow, 1988; recipient Clergyman of Yr. award Protestant Coun. Chs., 1983, Religious Liberty award, 1989, Torch of Freedom award Internat. League for Repatriation of Russian Jews, 1989, Ellis Island medal of Honor, 1990, Defender of Jerusalem award Jabotinsky Found., 1990, Am.-Israel Friendship award, 1991. Mem. Rabbinical Coun. Am., N.Y. Bd. Rabbis (bd. govs. 1966—), Union Orthodox Jewish Congregations (bd. dirs.), World Fedn. Hungarian Jews (spiritual leader). Home: 251 E 71st St New York NY 10021-4501 Office: 163 E 67th St New York NY 10021-5964

SCHNELLING, ANTHONY HENDRIK NEHEMIAH, lawyer; b. N.Y.C., June 3, 1947; s. Moritz Schnelling and Emily (Stern) Leeser. BA, Swarthmore Coll., 1969; MBA, Harvard U., 1972; JD, Fordham U., 1989. Sales mgr. Colora Printing Inks Ltd., London, 1969-70; exec. v.p. Colora Printing Inks Inc., L.I., 1972-74; assoc. Internat. Licensing Assocs., N.Y.C., 1974-75; officers asst. Morgan Guaranty Trust, N.Y.C., 1975-78; chmn., pres. Colora Printing Inks, Ltd., S.A., Inc., U.S., U.K., and France, 1978-86; assoc. Warburg Paribas Becker, N.Y.C., 1980-81, Stroock & Stroock & Lavan, N.Y.C., 1989—. Mem. Harvard Club (N.Y.C.), Reform Club (U.K.). Office: Stroock & Stroock & Lavan 7 Hanover Sq New York NY 10004-2616

SCHNERING, PHILIP SCOTT, insurance brokerage executive; b. Evanston, Ill., Nov. 29, 1947; s. Philip B. and Ruth (Scott) S.; m. Susan Parrish; children: Brian Parrish, Anne Pendleton. Student, U. Denver, 1972. Underwriter Chubb & Son, Inc., 1971-77; v.p. Johnson & Higgins, Denver, 1977-82, Alexander & Alexander, Balt., 1982—. Dir. major gift campaign Greater Balt. coun. Boy Scouts Am., 1988; elder Towson Presbyn. Ch., 1987; pres. bd. dirs. Towson Presbyn. Kindergarten. Mem. Am. Soc. Safety Engrs. Republican.

SCHNITZER, JESHAIA, rabbi, marriage and family therapist; b. Phila., Jan. 25, 1918; s. Philip and Jennie (Galler) S.; m. Hilde Maier, Mar. 9, 1947; children: Jonathan Aaron, Lisa Judith. BA, U. Del., 1940; rabbi, Jewish Inst. Religion Hebrew Union Coll., 1944; MA in Social Work, Columbia U., 1949; EdD, Tchrs. Coll., Columbia U., 1954; M.H.L. (hon.), Hebrew Union Coll., 1969; D.Div. (hon.), Jewish Theol. Sem., 1975. Diplomate Am. Bd. Sexology. Rabbi B'nai Abraham, Hagerstown, Md., 1943-44; chaplain U.S. Army Chaplain Corps., Korea, 1944-47; rabbi Free Synagogue, N.Y.C., 1947-49, 92d St. YMHA, N.Y.C., 1949-51, Congregation Shomrei Emunah, Montclair, N.J., 1951-79; rabbi emeritus Congregation Shomrei Emunah, Montclair, 1979—; adj. prof. Seton Hall U., South Orange, N.J., 1978-88; chaplain Montclair State Coll. Author: New Horizons for the Synagogue-A Counseling Program for the Rabbi and the Synagogue, 1956; contbg. author: Marriage Counseling, 1967. Mem. Montclair Civil Rights Commn., 1960-68; bd. dirs. ARC, Montclair chpt., 1953-55, 80-85; mem. Mayor's Montclair Youth Com., 1953-56; pres. Essex County Bd. Rabbis, 1959-61; bd. dirs. Council Social Agys., Montclair, 1960-63; bd. dirs. Child Guidance Clinic, Montclair, 1955-60, N.J. chpt. UN Assn., Montclair, 1955-65, Council Social Agys., Montclair, 1957-60, Jewish Community Council Essex County, 1953-56, Sex Info. and Edn. Council U.S., N.Y.C., 1968-72, Urban Coalition Montclair and Vicinity, 1969-74; exec. bd. mem. Tri-State Family Relations Council, 1955-60; co-chmn. Joint Chaplaincy Com. Metrowest, 1959—; v.p. Coordinating Coun. Compassionate Care of the Sick, 1991—. Recipient award for meritorious svc. B'nai B'rith, 1955, Disting. Svc. award Nat. Jewish Welfare Bd., 1948, Samuel W. and Rose Horowitz award Fedn. Jewish Philanthropies N.Y.C., 1977, Saul Schwarz Disting. Svc. award N.J. chpt. Conf. Jewish Communal Svc., 1990. Fellow Am. Assn. Marriage and Family Therapy (approved supr.); mem. Am. Assn. Sex Educators, Counselors and Therapists, Nat. Assn. Social Workers, Rabbinical Assembly Am. (pres. No. N.J. chpt. 1962-64), N.J. Assn. Marriage and Family Counselors (pres. 1960-63, 80-83), Jewish War Vets, Jewish Chaplains Assn., Ministerial Assn. Montclair and Vicinity (pres. 1971-72), Am. Bd. Sexology (clin. supr.), Internat. Acad. of Profl. Counseling and Psychotherapy Inc. (diplomate in profl. psychotherapy). Home and Office: 144 Midland Ave Montclair NJ 07042-3023

SCHNITZER, ROBERT BRUCE, academic administrator; b. Bklyn., May 22, 1949. BBA, CUNY, 1971; MBA, St. John's U., Queens, N.Y., 1976. CPA, N.Y. Supervising auditor N.Y. State Comptr.'s Office, N.Y.C., 1971-82; asst. to dir. fin. Albert Einstein Coll. Medicine, Bronx, N.Y., 1982-83; assoc. v.p. fin. affairs Nassau Community Coll., Garden City, N.Y., 1983—; instr. N.Y. State Comptr.'s Office, 1975-82. Contbr. articles to profl. publs. Mem. parents' com. Nassau County area Boy Scouts Am., Rockville Centre, N.Y., 1989-91; mem. com., 1990-91. Mem. AICPA, N.Y. State Community Coll. Bus. Officers Assn. (mem. com. 1985—), N.Y. State Soc. CPAs. Office: Nassau Community Coll One Education Dr Garden City NY 11530-6793

SCHNITZLER, RONALD MICHAEL, academic administrator, biology educator; b. Providence, Jan. 13, 1939; s. Hans Michael and Evelyn Helen (Wilk) S.; m. Ute Vogel, May 17, 1968; children: Micaela, Aletta. BA, Brown U., 1962, BSc. 1962; MS, U. Vt., 1964, PhD, 1969. Rsch. asst. Marine Biol. Lab., Woods Hole, Mass., 1963-64; instr. U. Vt., Burlington, 1969-70, rsch. assoc., 1971-75; Alexander von Humboldt Found. fellow Technische Hochschule, Aachen, Fed. Republic Germany, 1970-71; chairperson, prof. Bay Path Coll., Longmeadow, Mass., 1975-85; dir. div. acads. Mattatuck Community Coll., Waterbury, Conn., 1985—. Contbr. articles to profl. jours. Contract mediator Congress of Conn. Community Colls., Hartford, 1989; campaigner Liz Brown Hdqrs., Waterbury, 1991. Postdoctoral rsch. fellow NIH, 1971, spl. fellow, 1971; Title III grantee U.S. Dept. Edn., 1987; rsch. grantee Am. Muscular Dystrophy, 1975; recipient Curriculum Improvement award NSF, 1977. Mem. AAAS, Nat. Sci. Tchrs. Assn., Sigma Xi. Democrat. Home: 75 Cobblestone Rd Longmeadow MA 01106 Office: Mattatuck Community Coll 750 Chase Pky Waterbury CT 06708-3000

SCHNYDER, SANDRA ELIZABETH EDDY, writer; b. N.Y.C., Feb. 1, 1939; d. Edwyn Alen and Claire Elizabeth (Baum) Eddy; m. Eugene Alfred Schnyder, Sept. 28, 1965; children: John E., Michael E. Student, Pa. State U., 1961. Tech. writer Computer Assocs. Internat., Mt. Laurel, Princeton, N.J., 1984—; computer book writer Medford Lakes, N.J., 1990—. Author: The First Book of Q & A, 1991, (with John E. Schnyder) The First Book of Microsoft Word for Windows 2.0, 1992. Mem. Soc. for Tech. Communication.

SCHOCK, WILLIAM WALLACE, pediatrician; b. Huntingdon, Pa., Aug. 15, 1923; s. Clarence and Mabel (Decker) S.; m. Doris Ann Wilson, Ju.y 1, 1944; 1 child, William Wallace. Student, Juniata Coll., 1941-43; MD, Temple U., 1947. Intern Conemaugh Valley Meml. Hosp., Johnstown, Pa., 1946-48; resident Women AFB, Cheyene, Wyo., 1951-52; pvt. practive medicine Huntingdon, 1948-50; pediatrician Warren AFB Hosp., 1951-52; chief outpatient svc. USAF, Cheyenne, Wyo., 951-52; pvt. practice medicine specializing in pediatrics Huntingdon, 1952—; pediatrician J. C. Blair Meml. Hosp.; local pub. health pediatrician. Pres. Huntingdon chpt. Am. Cancer Soc., 1955-57; bd. dirs. local chpt. Am. Heart Assn., 1955-62; mem. Am. Security Coun., Rep. Nat. Com., 2d Amendment Found. With AUS, 1942-45, USAF, 1950-52. Recipient Wisdom award Leon Gutterman, Wisdom Hall of Fame, 1970. Fellow Royal Soc. Health; mem. AMA, Pa. Med. Soc. Huntingdon County Med. Soc. (past pres.), Med. Alumni Assn. Temple U., Pa. Pediatric Soc., Huntingdon Pediatric Soc., Am. Assn. Mil. Surgeons U.S., Am. Acad. Gen. Practice (past pres. Huntingdon), Am. Acad. Pediatrics (assoc.), Internat. Platform Assn., Phi Rho Sigma, Huntingdon Country Club, Hiedelburg Country Club (Altoona, Pa.), U.S. Senatorial Club, Rotary. Republican. Presbyterian. Home and Office: RR 2 Box 69 Huntingdon PA 16652-9115

SCHOEN, ALLEN HARRY, aerospace engineering executive; b. N.Y.C., Mar. 10, 1936; s. Harry Alfred and Dorothy Julia (Browne) S.; m. Patricia Alice O'Madigan, June 1, 1958 (div. 1989); children: Theresa Mary, James Allen, Karen Linda. SB in Aero. Engring., MIT, 1958. Aerodynamicist Douglas Aircraft Co., Santa Monica, Calif., 1958-61, United Aircraft Co., Farmington, Conn., 1961-66; with Boeing Helicopters, Phila., 1966—; technology mgr. Boeing Helicopters, 1980-84, dir. technology, 1984-86, dep. tech. dir. V-22 Osprey joint program, 1986-88, dir. preliminary design, 1988—; mem. aero. adv. com., NASA, Washington, 1985-90. Patentee propulsion system; author tech. papers. Fellow AIAA (assoc.); mem. Am. Helicopter Soc. (pres. Phila. chpt. 1983-84, v.p. Mideast region 1986-88, dir.-at-large 1988-90). Republican. Episcopalian. Home: 17 Mullray Ct Deptford NJ 08096-6713 Office: Boeing Helicopters PO Box 16858 Philadelphia PA 19142-0858

SCHOEN, BARBARA TAYLOR, educator, writer; b. N.Y.C., July 4, 1924; d. Howard Canning and Caroline Bayard (Colgate) Taylor; m. Donald R. Schoen, Nov. 9, 1946; children: Robert, John, Claire, Susan. AB, Bryn Mawr Coll., 1946; MA, Boston U., 1948. Instr. SUNY, Purchase, 1970-74, asst. prof., 1974-78, assoc. prof. lit., 1978—. Author: (novels) A Place and a Time, 1969, A Spark of Joy, 1971; contbr. articles to jours. Office: SUNY Anderson Hill Rd Purchase NY 10577-2002

SCHOEN, HERBERT MARTIN, engineering executive, chemical engineer; b. L.I., N.Y., Oct. 2, 1928; s. Herbert Carl and Martha Anna (Dietrich) S.; m. Christina Erne Eisen, Sept. 8, 1951; children: Karen Christine, Linda Marie, William Herbert, Eric Martin. BSChemE, Syracuse (N.Y.) U., 1952, MSChemE, 1953, PhD in Chem. Engring., 1957. Prodn. engr. U.S. Rubber Internat. Corp., Cuba and P.R., 1953-54; rsch. chem. engr. Am. Cyanamid Corp., Stamford, Conn., 1957-60; dir. rsch. Radiation Applications, Inc., N.Y.C., 1960-62; prin. investigator N.E. Rsch. Inst., N.Y.C., 1960-62; pres. Separations Tech. Inc., Stamford, Conn., 1962; dir. contracts Quantum, Inc., Wallingford, Conn., 1962-64; mgr. lab. Birdseye div. Gen. Foods Corp., White Plains, N.Y., 1964-68, dir. basic sci., 1972-79, corp. scientist, 1979-82, fellow, 1982-86; prin. HMS Assocs., Stamford, Conn., 1986—; vis. prof. U. Tex., 1967, Cornell U., Ithaca, N.Y., 1968-69, lectr., 1969, NYU, 1966, MIT, Cambridge, 1975, Va. Poly. Inst. & State U., 1976, Ohio State U., 1976; cons. Ctr. for Advanced Food Tech., Rutgers U., New Brunswick, N.J., 1990—. Editor: (book) New Chemical Engineering Separation Techniques, 1962, (book series) Interscience Library of Chemical Engineering and Processing, 1962-68; contbr. numerous articles to profl. jours. With USNR, 1946-48. Fulbright fellow Tech. U., Braunschweig, Germany, 1956-57. Fellow Am. Inst. Chem. Engrs. (chmn. Fairfield County, Conn. chpt. 1963, chmn. food, pharm. and bioengring. div. 1973); mem. Am. Chem. Soc., History of Sci. Soc. Home: 73 Clay Hill Rd Stamford CT 06905-1727 Office: HMS Assocs 73 Clay Hill Rd Stamford CT 06905-1727

SCHOEN, ROY MILES, physician; b. Staten Island, N.Y., Sept. 24, 1940; s. Herbert Edvane and Mary Ann (Levenstein) S.; m. Linda Nan Rosen, Sept. 5, 1964. AB, Dartmouth Coll., 1962; DDS, NYU, 1966; MD, Hadassan Med. Sch., Jerusalem, 1971. Diplomate Am. Bd. Psychiatry and Neurology. Intern Booth Meml. Med. Ctr., Flushing, N.Y., 1969-71; resident in psychiatry Payne Whitney clinic N.Y. Hosp., N.Y.C., 1971-73; resident in child psychiatry N.Y. Psychiatric Inst., N.Y.C., 1973-75; resident in ob-gyn. Lenoxhill Hosp., N.Y.C., 1979-82; physician Orlando & Schoen, MD, PC, N.Y.C., 1982—. Maj. Army Res. N.G., 1971-81. Fellow Am. Coll. Ob-Gyn., N.Y. Gynecologic Soc. Office: Orlando and Schoen MD PC 17 E 82nd St New York NY 10028-0346

SCHOENBORN, BENNO P., biophysicist, educator; b. Basel, Switzerland, May 2, 1936; came to U.S., 1955; s. Wilhelm and Maria (Dobler) S.; m. Catherine Cowie Kay, Oct. 26, 1962. BA, UCLA, 1958; PhD, U. New South Wales, Australia, 1962; DSc (hon.), N.J. Inst. Tech., 1982. Teaching fellow U. New South Wales, Sydney, 1958-61; postdoctoral fellow U. Calif. Med. Coll., San Francisco, 1962-63; visiting scientist Molecular Biology Lab., Cambridge, Eng., 1964-66; biophysicist dept. biology Brookhaven Lab., Upton, N.Y., 1967-74, sr. biophysicist dept. biology, 1974—, assoc. chmn. dept. biology, 1984-90; adj. prof. biochemistry Columbia U., N.Y.C., 1978—; adj. scientist biophysics, U. N.Y., Stonybrook, 1988—; editorial bd. Biophys. Jour., 1977-80; mem. Reactor Safety com., 1972-79. Editor: Neutrons in Biology, 1976, 84; contbr. articles to profl. jours.; patent in multilager monochromator, 1975. Recipient E.V. Lawrence award Dept. of Energy, 1980. Mem. Nat. Com. for Crystallography, Biophys. Soc. (coun. mem. 1976-79). Republican. Office: Brookhaven Nat Lab Upton NY 11973

SCHOENBRUNN, ERWIN FREDERICK, chemical engineer; b. Newark, N.J., July 15, 1921; s. Erwin O. and Katherine (Stetter) S.; m. Dorothy M. Rinehart, Nov. 21, 1948; children: Carol R., Mary R., Laura R., Frederick R. BS in Engring., Princeton U., 1947; MS in Engring., U. Pa., 1949. Project engr. Sharples Corp., Phila., 1947-51; project mgr. Nat. Rsch. Corp., Cambridge, Mass., 1951-58; dept. head process and exploratory rsch. Escambia Chem. Co., Wilton, Conn., 1958-68; sr. rsch. chem. engr. Am. Cyanamid, Stamford, Conn., 1968-91; cons. Ridgefield, Conn., 1991—. Patentee in field. Sgt. U.S. Army, 1943-46, PTO. Mem. Am. Chem. Soc. (chmn. Southwestern Conn. chpt. 1973-74), Am. Inst. Chem. Engrs. Democrat. Lutheran. Home and Office: 22 Christopher Rd Ridgefield CT 06877

SCHOENFELD, HENRY F., insurance executive; b. Germany, May 1, 1928; came to U.S., 1938; s. Solomon and Alice (Cohen) S.; children: Judith A. Morrison, Betsey L. Collins. BS in Indsl. Engring., Pa. State U., 1951. CLU; CPCU. Inds. engr. The Martin Co., Balt., 1951, Markel Svc., Richmond, Va., 1954-55; ins. agy. The Apple & Bond Co., Balt., 1955-60; ptnr. Hecht Schoenfeld Ins. Agy., Balt., 1960-62; v.p. Wolman Hecht & Schoenfeld, Balt., 1962-64; pre. Schoenfeld Ins. Assocs. Inc., Balt., 1964—; instr. Johns Hopkins U., Balt., 1966-68; mem. nat. agts. adv. bd. Hartford, 1972, Atlantic Ins. Co., 1982-85, Zurich Am. Ins. Co., 1987-90, Northbrook Inc. Co., 1991—. Mem. Har Sinai Congregaton Balt., treas. 1982-84, 90—. 1st lt. U.S. Army. 1951-54. Mem. Am. Soc. CLU, Soc. CPCU, Balt. Assn. Ind. Ins. Agts., Balt. Assn. Life Underwriters, Profl. Ins. Agts., Ind. Ins. Agts. Assn., Nat. Assn. Casualty & Surety Atgs., Balt. Assn. Ind. Ins. Agts., Mt. Nittany Soc., Million Dollar Roundtable, Suburban Club of Baltimore County, Ctr. Club (Balt.). Home: 2001 Wiltonwood Rd Stevenson MD 21153 Office: Schoenfeld Ins Assocs Inc 110 E Lombard St Baltimore MD 21202

SCHOENFELD, MICHAEL P., lawyer; b. Bronx, N.Y., Oct. 17, 1935; s. Jack and Anne S.; B.S. in Acctg., N.Y.U., 1955; LL.B., LL.D., Fordham U., 1958; m. Helen Schorr, Apr. 3, 1960; children—Daniel, Steven, Tracy. Admitted to N.Y. bar, 1959, U.S. Supreme Ct., 1963; atty. Am. Home Assurance Co., N.Y.C., 1958-62; ptnr. firm Schoenfeld & Schoenfeld, Melville, 1959—; v.p. Interstate Brokerage Corp., 1965-84, pres., 1984—; ptnr. Melville Realty Co., 1977—; legal adv. various bus. orgns. Vice pres., trustee Temple Beth David, Commack, N.Y., 1972-75; chmn. Community Action Com. of Dix Hills and Commack, 1970-72, Dix Hills Planning Bd., 1972-74; treas. Dix Hills Republican Club, 1976-80; mem. Huntington (N.Y.) Zoning Bd. Appeals, 1980-91, chmn., 1986-89. Recipient United Jerusalem award Israel Bond Drive, 1977; City of Hope Service award; George Bacon award Fordham Law Sch. Mem. N.Y. State Bar Assn., Suffolk County Bar Assn. Home: 14 Clayton Dr Dix Hills NY 11746 Office: 60 Broad Hollow Rd Melville NY 11747

SCHOENHEIT, EDWARD WILLIAM, JR., internist, hospital administrator, lawyer; b. Asheville, N.C., Mar. 10, 1926; s. Edward William and Elizabeth (Kimberly) S.; m. Carol Straehley, Sept. 23, 1950 (div. 1966): children: John William, Thomas Edward, Susan, Ruth; m. Marian Ruth Zintek, Dec. 30, 1976. MD, Harvard U., 1950; JD, Syracuse U., 1984. Diplomate Am. Bd. Internal Medicine. Intern Pa. Hosp., Phila., 1950-52; resident internal medicine Columbia div. Bellevue Hosp., N.Y.C., 1955; resident in chest svc. Columbia div. Bellevue Hosp., 1956; resident in cardiology Columbia Presbyn. Hosp., N.Y.C., 1957; pvt. practice Syracuse, N.Y., 1957-81; med. dir. Oswego (N.Y.) Hosp., 1987-89, Lee Meml. Hosp., Fulton, N.Y., 1987-89; ret., 1989; past pres. med. staff Community Hosp., Syracuse; mem. N.Y. State Bd. Profl. Med. Conduct, 1986—. Lt. M.C., USNR, 1592-54. Fellow ACP, Am. Coll. Legal Medicine; mem. Am. Coll. Physician Execs., Oswego County Med. Soc. Republican. Episcopalian. Home and Office: 74 W 5th St Oswego NY 13126-1528

SCHOENHEIT, MARIAN BEAUCHAMP, academic administrator; b. Milw., Dec. 24, 1927; d. Sylvester Stephen and Pearl Evelyn (Petrowski) Zintek; m. William Dudley Beauchamp, Nov. 1, 1952 (dec. Aug. 1968); m. Edward W. Schoenheit Jr., Dec. 30, 1976. BA, U. Wis., 1948; MA, Syracuse U., 1957, EdD, 1972. Cert. ednl. adminstr., N.Y.; cert. tchr., N.Y. Dir. occupational therapy unit Vanderbilt U. Hosp., Nashville, 1949-54; tchr. N.Y., 1954-58; prin. West Genesee Cen. Sch., Camillus, N.Y., 1958-74; dir. elem. edn. Liverpool (N.Y.) Cen. Sch., 1974-86; assoc. dean, assoc. prof. ednl. adminstrn. SUNY, Oswego, 1986-89, prof., 1989—. Bd. dirs. Community Gen. Hosp., Syracuse, 1989—; pres., bd. dirs. Skaneateles (N.Y.) Savs. Bank, 1978—. Mem. ASCD (sec. and treas. curriculum tchrs. network 1985-89, bd. dirs. 1988—; exec. sec. N.Y. affiliate 1988—; pres. Cen. N.Y. affiliate chpt. 1986-88). Home: 74 W 5th St Oswego NY 13126-1528 Office: SUNY 210 Rich Hall Oswego NY 13126

SCHOENHERR, DAVID WILBERT, bank executive; b. Niagara Falls, N.Y., Sept. 17, 1939; s. Wilbert Otto and Mildred Magdalena (Guinther) S.; m. Mary Ann Harlow, June 16, 1962; children: Beth Ann, Andrew David. BS, Purdue U., 1961; MBA, Temple U., 1971. Asst. treas. Girard Bank, Phila., 1969-71, asst. v.p., 1971-74, sr. banking officer, 1974-75, v.p., 1975-79; v.p. Lincoln Bank (now Continental Bank), Phila., 1979-82, Continental Bank, Phila., 1982—; vice chmn., trustee Christian Heritage Endowment Fund, Mountainside, N.J. Editor (newsletter) Robert Morris Assocs. Spreadsheet, 1986-87. Lt. U.S. Coast Guard, 1962-65. Mem. Robert Morris Assocs. Republican. Office: Continental Bank 1500 Market St Philadelphia PA 19102-2148

SCHOENWANDT, THOMAS RAYMOND, video production company executive; b. N.Y.C., Aug. 29, 1944; s. Raymond and Anne (Gallagher) S. Diploma in Tech. Engring., RCA Inst., N.Y.C., 1972. Chief engr., instr. RCA Inst., N.Y.C., 1972-74; broadcast opers. engr. ABC-N.Y., N.Y.C., 1974-76; v.p., owner Manhattan Video Prodns., N.Y.C., 1979—. Tech. dir. TV prodn. Profit and Laws, 1986 (TV Acad. award), Hands Off to Crime, 1986 (TV Acad. award). With U.S. Navy, 1961-65. Mem. Internat. TV Assn. Office: Manhattan Video Prodn 1210 27th St New York NY 10001-1106

SCHOFIELD, GEORGE H., corporate executive; b. Newark, Nov. 18, 1929; s. George H. and Louise (Minder) S.; m. Barbara Shimmin; children—George, Linda, Lauren, Robert. B.S., U. Vt., 1951. Various fin. positions gen. mgmt. Gen. Electric Co., 1951-85, v.p., 1978-85; pres., chief exec. officer Zurn Industries Inc., Erie, Pa., 1985-86, chmn., chief exec. officer, 1986—; bd. dirs. Autoclave Engrs., Inc., Nat. Fuel Gas, Inc., Goodyear Tire and Rubber Co. Trustee Gannon U.; bd. dirs. Erie Conf. Community Devel., United Way Erie County; chmn. Leadership Giving, 1990-91; pres. N.W. Pa. Coalition for Health Cost Containment. Mem. Pa. Bus. Roundtable, Pa. Chamber Bus. and Industry (bd. dirs.). Office: Zurn Industries Inc 1 Zurn Pl Erie PA 16505

SCHOLES, CYNTHIA MARIE, marketing professional; b. Phila., May 3, 1958; d. James Stevenson and Florence Regina (Watson) Cuthbert; m. James Raymond Scholes Jr., June 16, 1979. B. in Mktg., Neumann Coll., 1983. List mgr. Clement Communications, Inc., Concordville, Pa., 1980-83; mktg. mgr. Enterprise Pub., Inc., Wilmington, Del., 1983-90; v.p. Creative Mktg. Co., Inc., Boothwyn, Pa., 1990-91; cons. Media Mgmt. Group, Inc., Plainsboro, N.J., 1991—; bd. dirs. J.S. Cuthbert Co., Yeadon, Pa. Mem. Direct Mktg. Assn., Phila. Direct Mktg. Assn., Washington Direct Mktg. Assn. Am. Booksellers Assn., Direct Mktg. Alternative Media Coun., Direct Mktg. List Coun. Republican. Roman Catholic. Home and Office: 123 Crosskeys Dr Marcus Hook PA 19061-1316

SCHOLSKY, MARTIN JOSEPH, priest; b. Stafford Spring, Conn., Jan. 16, 1930; s. Sigmund Felix and Mary Magdalen (Wysocki) S. BA, St. John's Sem., 1952, MA in History, 1956; MA in Classical Greek, Cath. U. of Am., 1966. Ordained priest Roman Cath. Ch., 1956. Asst. pastor St. Peter's Ch., Hartford, Conn., 1956-61; prin. St. Peter's Sch., Hartford, 1956-58; instr. St. Thomas Sem., Bloomfield, Conn., 1961-67; admissions dir. St. Thomas Sem., Bloomfield, 1965-67; vocations dir. Archdiocese of Hartford, 1967-78; chaplain Newington (Conn.) Children's Hosp., 1961-78; weekend asst. St. Mary's Ch., Newington, 1961-78; pastor St. Bartholomew Ch., Manchester, Conn., 1978-90; dean Manchester Deanery, 1989-91; spiritual dir. St. Thomas Aquinas High Sch., New Britain, Conn., 1991—; weekend asst. St. Francis of Assisi Ch., South Windsor, Conn., 1991—; instr. Holy Apostle's Sem. & Coll., Cromwell, Conn., 1988—. Contbr. articles to profl. jours. Home: 36 Griswold St Manchester CT 06040-3928 Office: St Francis of Assisi Ch South Windsor CT 06074

SCHONBACH, BERNARD HARVEY, engineering company executive; b. Phila., Oct. 1, 1948; s. Frederik and Jeannette (Goldberg) S.; m. Sara Shnaper, Aug. 22, 1970; children: Joel Michael, Addie Lynn. BSME, Pa. State U., 1971; MBA, Lehigh U., 1982. Registered profl. engr., Pa. Design

engr. Link-Belt Co., Colmar, Pa., 1971-72; mgr. product devel. Fuller Co., Bethlehem, Pa., 1972-85; dir. engring. Allen-Sherman-Hoff Co., Malvern, Pa., 1985-87; gen. mgr. product devel. Fuller Co., Bethlehem, 1987-90; v.p. engring. Pa. Crusher Corp., Broomall, Pa., 1990—. Patentee in field; contbr. articles to profl. jours. Home: 1732 Brandywine Rd Allentown PA 18104-1704 Office: Pa Crusher Corp 600 Abbott Dr PO Box 100 Broomall PA 19008-0100

SCHONBACH, DAVE IRWIN, electrical engineer; b. Phila., Sept. 20, 1947; s. Frederik and Jeannette (Goldberg) S.; m. Ellen Wise, June 8, 1975; children: Mark, Lisa. BSEE, Northeastern U., 1970; MSEE, Carnegie-Mellon U., 1971, PhD in Elec. Engring., 1975. Engr. Bell Telephone Labs., Holmdel, N.J., 1972-76, Autotote, Ltd., Newark, Del., 1976-79; engring. assoc. E.I. DuPont de Nemours & Co., Wilmington, Del., 1979—; pres. WS/EDL Fed. Credit Union. Former pres. West Riding Civic Assn.; fin. advisor local sch. dist.; treas. Piedmont Little League; fellowship selection com. Hertz Found. Mem. IEEE, Tau Beta Pi, Eta Kappa Nu, Phi Kappa Phi.

SCHONEBAUM, ALFRED, food company executive; b. Dortmund-Horde, Westfalen, Germany, Nov. 27, 1914; came to U.S., 1947; s. Emil and Bertha (Muller) S.; m. Margaret Karliner, July 13, 1939; 1 child, Reuben-Max. Abitur, Real Gymnasium, Dortmund-Horde, 1930. Dept. mgr. Wollwaren House Saxonia, Dresden, Germany, 1934-35, buyer, 1936-38; sales rep. Import Firm, Soerabaia, Java, 1938-40; exec. Import Firm, Semarang, Java, 1940-47; dept. mgr. textile firm N.Y.C., 1948-52; exec. Specialty Food Co., N.Y.C., 1952-80; cons. in field. Pres. condo bd., Jackson Heights, N.Y., 1986—; vol. Light House, Rego Park, N.Y., 1982—. Recipient Mgmt. Achievement award N.Y. Habitat, 1988. Mem. Coun. N.Y. Coops. Democrat. Jewish. Home: 76-15 35th Ave Jackson Heights NY 11372

SCHONFELD, IRVIN SAM, psychologist, educator; b. N.Y.C.; s. George and Ruth (Berson) S.; children: Emily Aviva, Daniel Reuben; m. July 12, 1981. BS, Bklyn. Coll., 1969; MA, New Sch. for Social Rsch., 1974; PhD, CUNY, 1980; MPH, Columbia U., 1987. Cert. psychologist, N.Y. Math. tchr. N.Y.C. Bd. Edn., 1969-75; rsch. assoc. Columbia U., N.Y.C., 1981-85; prof. CUNY, 1985—. Contbr. articles on stress and psychopathology rsch., child, adolescent rsch. to profl. jours. Office: EDFN City Coll NY New York NY 10031

SCHONHOLTZ, GEORGE JEROME, orthopaedic surgeon; b. Bklyn., June 9, 1930; s. Morris and Rose (Stofsky) S.; m. Joan S. Hirsh, Aug. 21, 1951; children: Margot, Steven, Barbara. BA, NYU, 1950; MD, N.Y. State U., 1954. Diplomate Am. Bd. Orthopaedic Surgery, Nat. Bd. Med. Examination; lic. physician, Md. Intern, resident gen. surgery and orthopaedic surgery Walter Reed Gen. Hosp., Washington, 1956-59; asst. chief orthopaedic surgery Martin Army Hosp., Ft. Benning, Ga., 1960-63, asst. dir., dir. med. edn., 1962, 63; instr. human biology Am. U. Undergrad. Sch., Ft. Benning, 1962, 63; asst. clin. prof. orthopaedic surgery Howard U., Washington, 1964-66, Georgetown U., Washington, 1966-67; asst. clin. prof. orthopaedic surgery George Washington U., Washington, 1968—, chmn., dir., 1983—; pvt. practice Silver Spring, Md., 1964—; orthopaedic cons. VA Hosp., Martinsburg, W.Va., 1964-68; civilian cons. orthopaedic surgery Walter Reed Army Hosp., Washington, 1968—; chief orthopaedic surgery Holy Cross Hosp., Silver Spring, 1971-74, chmn. infection control com. 1975-76; v.p. med. and dental staff Washington Adventist Hosp., 1988-89, chmn. credential com., 1988-89; rep. Coun. of Musculoskeletal Soc., 1987-90. Author: Arthroscopy of the Shoulder, Elbow and Ankle, 1986, An Atlas of Arthroscopic Surgery of the Knee, 1988. Maj. U.S. Army, 1960-64. Mem. AMA, ACS, Am. Acad. Orthopaedic Surgery (mem. resolutions com. 1989—), Assn. Hosp. Dirs. Med. Edn., Soc. Mil. Orthopaedic Surgeons, Internat. Arthroscopy Assn., Ea. Orthopaedic Assn. (bd. incorporators, bd. dirs. 1970-79), Arthroscopy Assn. N.Am. (pres. 1988-89, bd. dirs. 1983-90), Montgomery County Med. Soc., Med. and Chirurgical Faculty Med., Washington Orthopaedic Soc., Internat. Soc. Knee. Republican. Office: Schonholtz & Magee 8830 Cameron St Silver Spring MD 20910-4114

SCHONHORN, HAROLD, chemist, researcher; b. N.Y.C., Apr. 2, 1928; s. Benjamin and Dorothy (Gitlin) S.; m. Esther Matesky, Jan. 17, 1954; children: Deborah, Jeremy. BS, Bklyn. Coll., 1950; PhD, N.Y. Polytech. U., 1959. Mem. tech. staff Bell Labs., Murray Hill, N.J., 1961-84; v.p. R & D Polyken Tech. div. Kendall Co., Lexington, Mass., 1984—. Contbr. over 100 articles to profl. jours. Pres. B'nai B'rith Lodge, Summit, N.J., 1970. With U.S. Army, 1953-55, Korea. Mem. Am. Chem. Soc. Home: 12 Heathwood Ln Chestnut Hill MA 02167-2685 Office: Kendall Co Polyken Techs Div 17 Hartwell Ave Lexington MA 02173-3195

SCHOOLS, RANDOLPH ROBERT, association executive; b. Balt., Jan. 28, 1945; s. Walter Robert and Evelyn Mildred (Greenstreet) S.; m. Dianne Barbara Stephens, Nov. 2, 1969 (div. June 1974); m. Barbara Anne Mannix, Aug. 16, 1980; children: Bradley Shane, Alexandra Maria. BS, U. Balt., 1967; MA, Georgetown U., 1977. Ops. mgr. Garfinckels, Washington, 1972-77; gen. mgr. NIH Recreation and Welfare Assn., Bethesda, Md., 1977—; pres. Spl. Love, Inc., Winchester, Va., 1983—; adminstr. Friends of the Clin. Ctr., Bethesda, 1985—; treas. Children's Inn at NIH, Bethesda, 1988—; pres. Nat. Employee Svcs. and Recreation, Chgo. Contbr. articles to profl. jours. Chair of devel. Leadership Montgomery, Rockville, Md. Sgt. U.S. Army, 1967-70. Named Washingtonian of the Yr., Washingtonian Mag., 1988. Mem. Greater Washington Soc. Assn. Execs. (Chmns. award 1985, 88, bd. mem.), NIH Alumni Assn. (bd. mem. 1988—). Roman Catholic. Office: NIH Recreation & Welfare 9000 Wisconsin Ave Bethesda MD 20892-0001

SCHOON, CRAIG GERALD, service executive; b. Monticello, Iowa, Mar. 2, 1942; s. Gerald Schoon and Marie (Gerdes) Schoon-Till; m. Susan Wiley, Dec. 20, 1968; 1 child, Sara. BA, U. Iowa, 1966, MA, 1970; PhD, NYU, 1974. Lic. psychologist, N.Y. Asst. dir. rsch. and tng. Inst. of Rehab. Medicine, N.Y.C., 1974-75, dir. of licensure, 1975-76; v.p. Profl. Exam. Svc., N.Y.C., 1976-77, exec. v.p., 1977-79, pres., 1979—; mem. adv. panel W.K. Kellogg Found./Pa. State U., University Park, 1981-85, Bur. of Health Professions, Washington, 1984-85. Contbr. articles to profl. jours. Mem. APA, Am. Ednl. Rsch. Assn., Am. Pub. Health Assn., Nat. Coun. on Licensing, Enforcement and Regulation, Nat. Orgn. Competency Assessment (bd. dirs. Washington chpt. 1988-90). Office: Profl Exam Svc 475 Riverside Dr New York NY 10115-0099

SCHOONOVER, NICHOLAS JEROME, III, high school guidance counselor, consultant; b. Waverly, N.Y., Jan. 24, 1961; s. Nicholas Jerome and Sally Josephine (Willmot) S.; m. Tammy Bell, Aug. 20, 1983. AA, Louisburg Coll., 1982; BA, Eastern Coll., St. Davids, Pa., 1986; MEd, West Chester U., 1991. Cert. secondary edn. guidance counselor. Dairy farmer The Bell Farm, Barton, N.Y., 1983-84; office asst. NACSW, St. Davids, 1984-86; dir. Christian edn. Prospect Presbyn. Ch., Mooresville, N.C., 1986; resident program dir. ACCESS, Inc., Conshohocken, Pa., 1987-89; asst. pastor Christ United Meth. Ch., Lansdale, Pa., 1987-91; guidance counselor Liberty High Sch., Bethlehem, Pa., 1991—; cons. ACCESS, Inc., 1989-91. Asst. scoutmaster Boy Scouts Am., Tioga Ctr., N.Y., 1982-83; vol. Habitat for Humanity, Morristown, Pa., 1991; crew chief Appalachia Svc. Project, Ky., W.Va., 1989, 91; bd. dirs. ACCESS, Inc., 1992—. Mem. AACD, Am. Sch. Counselors Assn., Pa. Sch. Counselors Assn., Kappa Delta Pi. Democrat. Mennonite. Home: 715-A Forty Foot Rd Hatfield PA 19440 Office: Liberty High Sch 1115 Linden St Bethlehem PA 18018

SCHOR, LAURENCE, lawyer; b. Bklyn., May 3, 1942; s. Julius and Ruth (Zackowitz) S.; m. Susan Leslie Gurevitz, Dec. 26, 1965; children: Meredith Nan, Joseph Sanford, Wendy Claire, Samuel Julius. BBA, So. Meth. U., 1963; JD, U. Tex., 1966; LLM, George Washington U., 1972. Bar: Tex. 1966, D.C. 1970, U.S. Ct. Appeals (D.C., 4th, 5th and 11th cirs.). Atty. NASA, Huntsville, Ala., 1966-68; asst. gen. counsel NASA support, U.S. Army C.E., Washington, 1968-70; assoc. Sellers, Conner & Cuneo, Washington, 1970-73; assoc., then ptnr. Max E. Greenberg, Trayman, Cantor, Reiss & Blasky, Washington, 1974-80; ptnr. Schnader, Harrison, Segal & Lewis, Washington, 1981-86, ptnr.-in-charge, 1986-88; mem. Miller & Chevalier, Washington, 1991—; lectr. George Washington U., other orgns. Author: The Right to Stop Work, 1991, (manual) Delays, Suspensions and Acceleration, Workplace Safety and Health in the 1990's, 1992, Claims Against Bonding Companies, Construction Contractor's Handbook of Business and Law, 1992. Founder, pres. Manor Lake Civic Assn., Montgomery County, Md., 1969-71; precinct chmn. Montgomery County Dem. party, 1972-76. Mem. D.C. Bar Assn. (chmn. div. 10 govt. contracts and litigation 1981-85), ABA (chmn. region III pub. contracts sect. 1982-86, chmn. constrn. com. 1986-90, sect. budget and fin. 1990—), Fed. Bar Assn., Am. Coll. Constrn. Lawyers (founder, bd. dirs.), Phi Alpha Delta (pres. T.C. Clark chpt. 1965-66), Jewish. Avocations: reading, travel. Home: 7021 Mountain Gate Dr Bethesda MD 20817 Office: Miller & Chevalier Metropolitan Sq 655 15th St NW Washington DC 20005-5701

SCHORR, JEFFREY MICHAEL, manufacturer's representative, owner; b. Schenectady, N.Y., June 25, 1963; s. Marvin Michael and Patricia Ann (Restifo) S. BS, Northeastern U., 1986, MBA, 1991. Registered engr. in tng., Mass. Sales engr. Alpine Am. Corp., Natick, Mass., 1986-88; tech. marketer Toxikon, Woburn, Mass., 1988-89; owner, mfr. rep. Shorelines, Boston, 1989—. Mem. World Footbag Assn., Surfrider Orgn., New Eng. Ski Reps. Assn., Ea. Ski Reps. Assn. Home and Office: Shorelines 8 Monument Sq Ste 4 Charlestown MA 02129-3446

SCHORR, JUSTIN, artist, educator; b. N.Y.C., June 10, 1928; s. Harry and Ethel Helen (Samuels) S.; m. Betty Claire Lieber, June 16, 1957 (dec. Mar. 1974); 1 child, Mark L.; m. Sharon Ann Winter, July 4, 1976; 1 child, Tiara. BSS, CCNY, 1950; MA, Columbia U., 1951, EDD, 1962. Instr. art Lyndon (Vt.) St. Coll., 1954-57; prof. art and edn. Tchrs. Coll. Columbia U., N.Y.C., 1962-75, full prof. Tchr.'s Coll., 1975—. Author: Aspects of Art, 1966, Toward Transformation of Art, 1972, Godwrighting, 1989; exhbns. Nat. Acad., Bklyn. Mus., Butler Inst., others. With U.S. Army, 1952-54. Office: Tchrs Coll Columbia U 525 W 120th St New York NY 10027-6625

SCHORR, MARTYN LAURENCE, public relations executive; b. N.Y.C., Mar. 28, 1936; s. Herbert and Regina (Fingerman) S.; m. Sharon A. Atos, Sept. 28, 1986; children: Patrice, Stuart. Editor Magnum Communications, N.Y.C., 1961-67, editorial dir., 1967-71, v.p. auto group, 1971-73; pres. Performance Media Pub. Rels., Haworth, N.J., 1973—. Author: Buick GNX, 1987 (Automotive Journalism Conf award 1988). Mem. Internat. Motor Press Assn. (bd. dirs. 1988-90, chmn. activities com. 1991—). Home: 62 Eckerson Rd Harrington Park NJ 07640-1408 Office: Performance Media 167 Terrace St Haworth NJ 07641-1835 also: 988 Blvd of the Arts Ste 1212 Sarasota FL 34236

SCHOTT, HOWARD MANSFIELD, lawyer, musicologist; b. N.Y.C., June 17, 1923; s. Simon Leopold and Rebecca Louise (Landay) S. BA, Yale U., 1943, JD, 1948; PhD, Oxford (Eng.) U., 1978. Bar: N.Y. 1949, Mass. 1986. Assoc. Fried, Frank, Shriver & Kampelman, Washington, 1948-51; atty. AEC, N.Y.C., 1951-54; ptnr. Duncombe, Oltarsh & Schott, N.Y.C., 1954-60; internat. counsel Schering Corp., Bloomfield, N.J., 1961-67; musicologist Victoria & Albert Mus., London, 1976-81; pvt. practice law and mediation, Boston, 1981—; cons. Ashmolean Mus., Oxford, 1969-79, Met. Mus. Art, N.Y.C., 1981. Author: Playing the Harpsichord, 1971, 3d edit., 1979, Catalogue of Keyboard Instruments in Victoria and Albert Mus., 1984. Sec., dir. Walter W. Naumburg Found., Inc., N.Y.C., 1961-76. With U.S. Army, 1943-46, ETO. Mem. Oxford and Cambridge Soc. New Eng. (pres. 1990—), United Oxford and Cambridge U. Club London, Glyndebourne Sunday Club. Home and Office: 19 Prospect St Charlestown MA 02129-3428

SCHOTT, JOHN (ROBERT), international consultant, educator; b. Rochester, N.Y., Jan. 30, 1936; s. John and Ellen (Waite) S.; m. Diane Elizabeth Dempsey, June 19, 1963; children: Elizabeth Anne (dec.), Jennifer, Jared Reed, George Kermit Alexander. BA magna cum laude, Haverford Coll., 1957; postgrad., Oxford U., 1957-59; PhD, Harvard U., 1964. Resident tutor in govt. Eliot House, Harvard Coll., Cambridge, Mass., 1960-64; inst. polit. sci. Wellesley (Mass.) Coll., 1964-66; policy planning specialist AID, Washington, 1966-67; chief Title IX div. AID, Washington, 1967-68; vis. prof. polit. devel. Fletcher Sch. Law & Diplomacy, Tufts U., Medford, Mass., 1968-70; sr. v.p. Thunderbird Grad. Sch. Internat. Mgmt., Phoenix, 1970-71; cons. internat. affairs Francestown, N.H., 1971-74; pres. Schott & Assocs., Inc., Francestown, Jaffrey Center, N.H., 1974—; mem. U.S. Del. World Assembly Internat. Secretariat for Voluntary Service, New Delhi, 1967; advisor Office Prime Minister Royal Thai Govt., Bangkok, 1978-80, Minister Cooperatives Govt. of Indonesia, Jakarta, 1983-84; research asst. spl. appointment The Brookings Inst., Washington, 1960-61;. Author: Kenya Tragedy: European Colonization in East Africa, 1964, Frances' Town: History of Francestown, N.H., 1972, A Five-Year Comprehensive Plan for Development of Agricultural Cooperatives in Thailand, 1979, Recana-Komprehensip Pengembangan Kud, Jakarta, Indonesia, 1985; editor: An Experiment in Integrated Rural Development, 1978; contbr. articles to govt. reports, speeches, profl. jours. and regional publs. Member Bd. of Selectmen, Francestown, N.H., 1975-78; trustee Spaulding Youth Ctr., Tilton, N.H., 1971-82, 85-89, pres. bd. trustees, 1972-75; trustee Internat. Inst. Rural Reconstrn., N.Y.C., 1979-89, mem. exec. com., 1985-89, N.H. Pub. Radio, 1990—; mem. spl. study commn. Coop. Extension Svc., State of N.H., 1980-81; forestry rep. County Extension Coun., Hillsboro County, N.H., 1979-82; pres. N.H. Timberland Owner's Assn., 1989-90, bd. dirs., 1988-91; chmn. N.H. chpt. The Nature Conservancy, 1990—; vice-chmn. Profl. Foresters Lic. Bd. State of N.H., 1990—. Rotary Found. fellow, 1957-58, Coslett Found. fellow, 1958-59, Harvard Arts & Scis. fellow, 1959-60, Fulbright scholar, 1962-63. Mem. Am. Forestry Inst. (cert. tree farmer). Home: PO Box 660 Jaffrey NH 03452-0660 Office: Schott & Assocs Inc Mountain Rd Jaffrey NH 03452-2116

SCHOWALTER, ELLEN LEFFERTS, financial planner; b. Milw., Apr. 23, 1937; d. William George and Alice (Virgin) Lefferts; m. John Erwin Schowalter, June 11, 1960; children: Jay, Bethany. BS, U. Wis., 1958, MS, 1959; MA, Yale U., 1982. Cert. fin. planner. Tchr. English West Allis (Wis.) Bd. Edn., 1959-60, New Haven (Conn.) Bd. Edn., 1960-61, Cin. Bd. Edn., 1961-63; dir. Bethesda Nursery Sch., New Haven, 1971-80; registered rep. First Investors Corp., Hamden, Conn., 1982-85; sr. rep. Jonathan Alan and Co., Inc. (name changed to Schowalter & Seymour Assocs.), White Plains, N.Y., 1985-90; cert. fin. planner Titan Value Equities Group, Inc., New Haven, 1990—; seminar leader, tchr., Fairfield, Conn., 1987-90. Bd. dirs. Bethesda Nursery Sch., 1981-87. Mem. Internat. Assn. Fin. Planners, Women in Sales Assn., Coll. Fin. Planning, Mortar Bd. Democrat. Lutheran. Home: 606 Ellsworth Ave New Haven CT 06511-1636 Office: Schowalter & Seymour Assocs 211 Schraffts Dr Waterbury CT 06705

SCHOWALTER, TONI LEE, graphic designer; b. Phila., Mar. 23, 1948; d. Sidney Stanley and Gladys (Scherdorf) Silber; m. David Thomas Schowalter, June 11, 1967; 1 child, Amber Portia. Student, Phila. Coll. Art, 1968; BA, Kean Coll., Elizabeth, N.J., 1974. Designer Aron & Falcone, Chatham, N.J., 1976-78; prin. Environments, Graphics & Goodies, Summit, N.J., 1978-79; designer Werbin & Morrill, N.Y.C., 1979-80, Robert P. Gersin Assocs., N.Y.C., 1980-81, CBS, N.Y.C., 1981-83; design dir. MuirCorneliusMoore, N.Y.C., 1983-86; prin. Schowalter2 Design, Short Hills, N.J., 1986—. Mem. Jr. League of the Oranges & Short Hills, 1987-88. Mem. Am. Inst. Graphic Artists, Soc. for Mktg., Profl. Svcs., Women in Design, Art Dirs. Club of N.J., N.J. League Women Voters. Home: 21 The Cres Short Hills NJ 07078-2813 Office: Schowalter2 Design 21 The Cres Short Hills NJ 07078-2813

SCHRADER, DAVID EUGENE, philosophy educator; b. Northfield, Minn., Oct. 1, 1947; s. Eugene Maurice and Joyce Elaine (Bestul) S.; m. Cathy Lynn Buchanan, Dec. 20, 1975 (div. Sept. 1979); m. Sandra Jo Thompson, July 11, 1980; children: Sara Michele, Tami LeAnn. BA, St. Olaf Coll., Northfield, 1969; MTS, Harvard U., 1971; MA, U. Mass., 1974, PhD, 1975. Instr. philosophy Loras Coll., Dubuque, Iowa, 1975-77, asst. prof., 1977-79; asst. prof. philosophy Austin Coll., Sherman, Tex., 1979-84, assoc. prof., 1984-89; assoc. prof. philosophy Washington and Jefferson Coll., Washington, Pa., 1989—; assoc. Ctr. for Philosophy of Sci., U. Pitts., 1990—. Editor: Ethics and the Practice of Law, 1988; contbr. articles to profl. jours. Mem. Grace Presbytery Commn. on Exams., Dallas, 1989, S.W. Pa. Synod ELCA Commn. on Ch. in Soc. NEA grantee, 1977, 81, 85, 91, Am. Coun. Learned Socs. travel grantee, 1989; Ctr. for Study of Values fellow, 1986. Mem. AAUP (v.p. Austin Coll. chpt. 1983-84, sec. 1987-89, pres. W & J Coll. chpt. 1992), Am. Philos. Assn., Philosophic Soc. Study of Sport (exec. com. 1990—), Philosophy of Sci. Assn., Soc. for Bus. Ethics, Soc. for Philosophy and Pub. Affairs, Soc. for Philosophy of Religion (exec. com. 1989-92, v.p. 1992—), SAR (sec. 1986-89, v.p. 1990—). Republican. Lutheran. Home: 424 Leonard Ave Washington PA 15301-3370 Office: Washington and Jefferson Coll Washington PA 15301

SCHRADER, HENRY CARL, civil engineer, consultant; b. Chgo., Jan. 5, 1918; s. Henry Fred and Helene (Arkenberg) S.; m. Marium Warner, Aug. 22, 1942; children: Henry Carl, Gary Warner. BS in Civil Engring., U. Ill., 1940, MS in Civil Engring., 1959; diploma Indsl. Coll. Armed Forces, Ft. McNair, D.C., 1962. Registered profl. engr., Ill., Va., Md., D.C., Pa., Mass., N.C. Commd. 2nd lt., U.S. Army, 1940; advanced through grades to maj. gen., 1971; dist. engr. Corps of Engrs., Okinawa, Ryukus Island, 1962-64; chief systems analysis Office Chief Staff Dept Army, Washington, 1966-67, dir. mgmt. info. systems, 1967-70; comdr. 18th Engr. Brigade, Vietnam, 1970-71, comdr. Computer Systems Command, Ft. Belvior, Va., 1971-73; ret., 1973; prin. mktg. Dalton Dalton Newport, Washington, 1973-84; v.p. URS Dalton, 1984-86; v.p. URS Cons., 1986—; bd. dirs. GTE. Decorated Air Medal with 2 clusters, Disting. Svc. medal with cluster, Legion of Merit with 3 clusters; Engr. Yr. award Dept. Civil Engring. U. Ill., 1971. Fellow Am. Soc. Civil Engrs., Soc. Am. Mil. Engrs. (dir. 1979-86); mem. Nat. Soc. Profl. Engrs., Am. Rd. and Transportation Bldrs. Assn. (bd. dirs. 1982—, pres. planning and design div. 1988-90, pres. pub./pvt. ventures div. 1990-92, railroads adv. coun. 1987—), HighSpeed Rail Assn. (bd. dirs. 1982—, vice chmn. 1990—), Army and Navy Club, Bethesda Country Club (dir. 1983-86), Farmington Country Club. Republican. Episcopalian.

SCHRADER, MARTIN HARRY, retired publisher; b. Queens, N.Y., Nov. 26, 1924; s. Harry F. and Ida (Spiess) S.; m. Cecelia Sofer, July 7, 1957; children: Howard, Daniel, Esther. B.A., Queens Coll., 1946. Vice pres. Alfred Auerbach & Co., 1950-60; dir. mktg. House Beautiful mag., N.Y.C., 1960-65; pub. spl. publs. div. House Beautiful mag., 1965-69; pub. Town and Country mag., N.Y.C., 1969-77, Harpers Bazaar, 1977-91; retired, 1991—; v.p. Hearst Mags., 1983-91; lectr. merchandising Fairleigh Dickenson U., 1958-61, Parsons Sch. Design, 1976—; lectr. Merchandising New Sch. Grad. Center, 1984. Former nat. adv. bd. Salk Inst., La Jolla, Calif.; bd. govs. Coty Fashion Critics Awards.; bd. dirs. Mother's Day Found., Ednl. Found. Fashion Industries. Recipient Human Relations award Am. Jewish Com., 1979. Mem. U.S. Lawn Tennis Assn. (umpire's com. 1961—). Jewish (trustee temple 1965—).

SCHRADER, PETER HARMON, contractor; b. Schenectady, N.Y., Nov. 22, 1945; s. Henry Matthew and Jeanette Grant (Swart) S.; m. Christy Lynne Jones, Dec. 29, 1972; children: Erin Christine, Silas Peter, Nicholas Steven. AA, Indian River Jr. Coll., 1966; postgrad., Fla. Atlantic U., 1967-68. Cert. grad. remodelor. Foreman Suburban Contractors, Schenectady, 1970-73; pres. Schrader and Co., Inc., Burnt Hills, N.Y., 1973—; owner Homecheck, Inc.; instr. career awareness workshop for jr. high sch., 1985, sr. high sch., 1988; instr. Scotia-Glenville Continuing Edn. Program, 1988-89. Mem. endowment com. 1st Reformed Ch. Glenville; vol. West Glenville Vol. Fire Dept. With USN, 1968-70, Vietnam. Named to Top 500 Leaders list Qualified Remodeler Mag., 1989-90, Top 50 Remodelers in the U.S., Remodeling Mag.; recipient Housing Industry award, 1991. Mem. Nat. Assn. Home Builders (bd. dirs. 1987-92, Life Spike award), N.Y. State Builders Assn. (exec. com. 1985-92, chair remodelers coun. 1987-89, alt. trustee then trustee legal def. fund 1987-89, 2d v.p.-sec. 1988, 1st v.p.-treas. 1989, pres. 1990, chair consumer contracts working group 1991-92), Home Builders Assn. Schenectady (bd. dirs. 1979—, treas. 1982, 2d v.p. 1983, 1st v.p. 1984, pres. 1985, founding chair remodelers coun. 1992, membership com. 1992). Republican. Mem. Reformed Ch. in Am.

SCHRADER, RICHARD JAMES, English educator; b. Canton, Ohio, Aug. 24, 1941; s. A. W. and Margaret Louise (Karcher) S. BA, U. Notre Dame, 1963; MA, Ohio State U., 1965, PhD, 1968. Prof. Princeton (N.J.) U., 1968-75, John Witherspoon Bicentennial Preceptor, 1972-75; prof. Boston Coll., Chestnut Hill, Mass., 1975—. Author: Reminiscences of Alexander Dyce, 1972, God's Handiwork: Images of Women in Early Germanic Literature, 1983; translator: Arator's On the Acts of the Apostles, 1987; also articles. Grantee Mellon Found., 1980-81. Mem. MLA, Medieval Acad. Am., Assn. for Scottish Literary Study, Mencken Soc., Soc. for Am. Baseball Rsch., New Chaucer Soc. Roman Catholic. Office: Boston Coll Dept of English Chestnut Hill MA 02167

SCHRAGE, MARTIN HENRY, computer company executive; b. Atlanta, Feb. 22, 1941; s. William Egon and Augusta (Saul) S.; m. Andrea Paula Bleichmar, June 20, 1987; 1 child, Seth Alexander. SB, MIT, 1963. Sr. engr. EG&G, Inc., Boston, 1963-69; v.p. CSP, Inc., Billerica, Mass., 1969-86; pres., founder Xanalog Corp., Woburn, Mass., 1986—; bd. dirs. Nihon Xanalog Co., Ltd., Tokyo. Named one of Boston's Most Eligible Bachelors, The Boston Herald, 1984, Elected MIT Class of 1963 Devel. Officer, 1988. Mem. MIT Club of Boston (bd. govs. 1990—). Home: 370 Clyde St Chestnut Hill MA 02167-2924 Office: Xanalog Corp 300 Wildwood St Woburn MA 01801-6815

SCHRAIBMAN, SANDRA MARGUERITE MILNER, lawyer; b. Charleston, S.C., Aug. 18, 1947; d. Edward Hampton and Sybil Jeanette (Karesh) Milner; m. Julian Stanley Schraibman, July 1, 1969; children: Jessica Hayley, Erin Caitlin. BA in Polit. Sci., U. S.C., 1969, JD, 1973; LLM, Georgetown U., 1978. Bar: S.C. 1973, D.C. 1974, Fla. 1975. Prettyman fellow Georgetown U. Law Ctr., Washington, 1973-75; asst. prof. law Holland Law Ctr., U. Fla., 1975-76; trial atty. Fed. Programs Branch, Civil Div., U.S. Dept. of Justice, Washington, 1976-80, asst. dir., 1980—. Mem. Women's Bar Assn. D.C., D.C. Bar Assn., S.C. Bar Assn., Fla. Bar Assn. Office: US Dept Justice Civil Div 901 E St NW Washington DC 20530

SCHRAMM, GUNTER, economist, researcher; b. Beuthen, Silesia, Germany, Feb. 15, 1929; came to U.S. 1969; s. Kurt Herrmann and Maria (Scheffczyk) S.; m. Adelheid (Heidi) Martha Honisch, Dec. 3, 1955; children—Eileen Suzanne, Barbara Michelle. B.A. in Econs., U.B.C., Vancouver, Can., 1964; M.A. in Econs., U. Mich., 1965, Ph.D. in Natural Resources Econs., 1967. Regional rep. PHB, Western Can., 1959-64; research assoc. U. Mich., Ann Arbor, 1964-67, assoc. prof. resources econs., 1969-73, prof., 1975-83; rsch. assoc. U. Manitoba, Winnipeg, Can., 1967-69; sr. economist World Bank, Washington, 1983-87; chief energy devel. div., 1987-91, adviser industry and energy dept., 1991—; sr. econ. adv. Nat. Water Plan, Mex., 1973-75; co-team leader Asian Energy Survey Asian Devel. Bank, Manila, 1980-81; mem. econ. council State of Alaska, 1982. Author: Role of Low-Cost Power in Economic Development, 1979; Energy Economics, Demand Management and Conservation, 1983; co-author: Asian Energy Problems, 1982; editor, co-author: Environmental Management and Economic Development, 1989; contbr. articles to profl. jours., chpts. to books. Mem. Western Regional Sci. Assn. (bd. dirs. 1975-83, pres.-elect 1985—, pres. 1986), Can. Econs. Assn. (bd. dirs. 1969-72), Am. Econs. Assn., Internat. Assn. Energy Economists. Home: 4004 N Tazewell St Arlington VA 22207-4640 Office: World Bank 1818 H St NW Washington DC 20433-0002

SCHRAMM, PATRICIA CAIN, construction equipment company executive; b. Kansas City, Kans., Mar. 25, 1937; d. William Howard and Helen (Pospisil) Cain; m. Richard E. Schramm, June 4, 1960. BA, Bryn Mawr Coll., 1959, PhD, 1971; MA, U. Chgo., 1963. Reporter, writer Chgo. Sun Times, 1959-61, Phila. Bull., 1961-63; rsch. dir. Greater Wilmington (Del.) Devel. Coun., 1963-67; dir. social planning City of Wilmington, 1970-73, dir. devel. and planning, 1973-77; sec. health and social svcs. State of Del., Wilmington, 1977-85; pres. Schramm & Assocs., Wilmington, 1985-87, Pneumatic & Electric Equipment Co., West Chester, Pa., 1987—. Vol. United Way, West Chester; mem. adv. bd. Del. Nature Conservancy, Dover. Office: Pneumatic & Electric Equipment Co 501 Garfield Ave West Chester PA 19380-4446

SCHRANKEL, KENNETH REINHOLD, toxicologist, biologist; b. Rice Lake, Wis., Mar. 26, 1945; s. R. W. and M. K. (Soldner) S.; m. Dawn Porter, Sept. 19, 1970; children: Peter, Stephan. BA, Wartburg Coll., Waverly, Iowa, 1967; MS, Ill. State U., 1973, PhD, 1978. Grad. researcher Ill. State U., Normal, 1967-68, 72-78; vis. asst. prof. dept. biology and Inst. Devel. Tex. A&M U., 1978-79; postdoctoral trainee Ctr. for Environ. Toxicology U. Wis., 1979-81; rsch. toxicologist Internat. Flavors & Fragrances, Inc., Union Beach, N.J., 1981-84, sr. rsch. toxicologist, 1984-85, dir. flavor and fragrance safety assurance, 1985-91, v.p., 1992—. Author study guide; contbr. articles to profl. jours.; patentee in field.

SCHRATZ, WALTER ALFRED, university official; b. Pitts., May 19, 1922; s. John and Susanna (Haas) S.; m. Helen A. Budnick, July 14, 1951; children: Cheryl Finlay, Walter Wayne, Caryl Goeller. AB, U. Pitts., 1947, MLitt, 1948, PhD, 1954. Instr. labor rels. Sch. Bus. U. Pitts., 1947-52, asst. prof. indsl. mgmt., 1952-57; supr. tng. Westinghouse Electric Corp., East Pittsburgh, Pa., 1957-59; mgr. employee rels. Westinghouse Electric Corp., East Pittsburgh, 1959-65; dir. tng. and devel. Westinghouse Electric Corp., Pitts., 1965-70, gen. mgr. tng. and devel., 1970-80, mgr. univ. rels., 1980-83; exec. dir. Westinghouse Ednl. Founds., Pitts., 1983-87; sr. cons. Carnegie-Mellon U., Pitts., 1988—; mem. tng. com. Ednl. TV, Pitts., 1970-80; bd. visitors U. Pitts., 1975—; condr. seminars various internat. orgns. in 10 countries for Westinghouse Electric Corp., 1971-81. Trustee Foreman's Found., N.Y.C., 1960-65; v.p. Pitts. Blind Assn., 1980—; chmn. Forest Hills Youth Commn., Pitts., 1970-80. Sgt. USAAF, 1943-46. Mem. Am. Econ. Assn., Assn. Tng. and Devel., Soc. for Advancement of Mgmt. (pres. 1963-64, nat. gov. 1964-70, profl. mgr. citation 1975), Syria Temple. Republican. Lutheran. Home: 219 Castlegate Rd Pittsburgh PA 15221-4415

SCHREIBER, ELLIOTT HAROLD, psychologist, educator; b. Newark, N.J., Apr. 28, 1933; s. Harry and Sylvia (Schwartz) Schreiber; m. Louise F. Bossio, June 18, 1961; chidlren: Andrea, Pamela, David, Karen. BA, Upsala Coll., 1956; Ma, Bradley U., 1959; EdD, W.Va. U., 1967. Diplomate Am. Bd. Profl. Psychology; lic. clin. psychologist, N.J., Pa. Sch. psychologist Burlington (N.J.) City Schs., 1965-67; prin. psychologist Bordentown (N.J.) Reformatory, 1967, 68; assoc. prof. psychology Glassboro (N.J.) State Coll., 1967—; pvt. clin. psychologist, Moorestown, N.J., 1965—. Author: Violence and Aggression in Human Behavior, 3d edit., 1988, Abnormal Behavior, 5th edit., 1991; contbr. articles to profl. jours. Pres. S. Jersey chpt. United Nations Assn., USA, N.Y.C., 1975—. Mem. Am. Psychol. Assn., N.J. Edn. Assn., N.J. Psychol. Assn., Pa. Psychol. Assn., Men of Achievement (Hon. award 1968), Kappa Delta Pi. Home: 708 Camden Ave Moorestown NJ 08057-2228 Office: Glassboro State Coll Rte 322 Glassboro NJ 08028

SCHREIBER, EUGENE RALPH, financial planner; b. Jersey City, Jan. 31, 1939; s. Eugene Leo and Leah Teresa (Moreton) S.; m. Ellen Louise Paulson, Sept. 2, 1961; 1 child, Steven Keith. BA, Rutgers U., 1966. Reg. rep. N.Y. Stock Exch. (series 7), lic. ins. rep. N.J. Investment portfolio analyst Merrill Lynch, Pierce, Fenner & Smith, N.Y.C., 1966-67, asst. mgr. investor rels. dept., 1967-68, mgr. investor rels. dept., 1968-70, corp. rels. dept. mgr., 1970-72, asst. to dir. instl. div., 1972-76, rep. instl. corp. bond mktg., 1976-77, rep. retirement plans, 1977-78; mgr., v.p. retirement plans dept. Thomson McKinnon Securities, Inc., N.Y.C., 1980-86; v.p. instl. capital markets E.F. Hutton, N.Y.C., 1986-88; personal fin. planner IDS, Am. Express, Parsippany, N.J., 1989-92; telemarketer sales dept. Reed Reference Pub., New Providence, N.J., 1992—. Author (pamphlets) Retirement Plans Questions and Answers, 1981-86; contbr. articles on retirement to newspapers and fin. papers including Wall St. Jour., N.Y. Times. Group leader Indian Guides, Madison, N.J. chpt. YMCA, 1973-74, Webelos leader Pack 226 Cub Scouts, Madison, 1975-78: advancement com. Boy Scouts Am., Troop 25, Madison, 1978-85. With U.S. Army, 1962-68. Home: 16 Fen Ct Madison NJ 07940-2317

SCHREIBER, H. MARK, public relations communications specialist; b. Sharon, Pa., June 16, 1950; s. Eugene and Eva (Weiss) S.; m. Karen Pomerantz, Nov. 27, 1971; children: Emily Ida, Julie Lynn, David Aaron. BSJ, Northwestern U., 1972, MS, 1973. News producer WWSW Radio, Pitts, 1973-75; reporter, talk show host, news dir. KQV News Radio, Pitts, 1975-83; reporter, producer WPXI TV, Pitts., 1983-87; exec. dir. Pa. Dem. Party, Harrisburg, 1987-89; dir. pub. rels. Pa. State Lottery, Harrisburg, 1989—; cons. video prodn. Pa. Dept. Aging, 1990—; adj. prof. communications Shippensburg (Pa.) U., 1990—. Jewish. Home: 1421 Smokehouse Ln Harrisburg PA 17110-3131 Office: Pa Lottery 2850 Tpke Indsl Dr Middletown PA 17057

SCHREIBER, JUDY ANN, counselor; b. St. Marys, Pa., Apr. 22, 1952; d. Francis John and Agnes (Meyer) S. BS in Edn./Music, Edinboro U. Pa., 1974, MA in Counseling, 1991; postgrad., Notre Dame U., 1981-82; grad. nursing program, Erie Tech./Hamot Hosp., 1979. Cert. music tchr., elem. sch. counselor, secondary sch. counselor. Tchr. Erie (Pa.) Diocese, St. Mary's, 1974-77, Clearfield, Pa., 1977-78; missionary Young People Who Care Ctr., Clearfield, 1977; sr. mem. Mercy, Erie, Pa., 1977-86; nurse Hamot Hosp./DuBois Hosp., Erie and DuBois, Pa., 1978-81; tchr., coord. pastoral music St. George Parish Sch., Erie, 1981-87; tchr. Millcreek Sch. Dist., Erie, 1987-91, sch. counselor, 1991—; mem. Erie Philharmonic Chorus, 1987-89, Presque Isle Choral, 1991—; soloist Erie Parishes, 1974—; cantor St. George Ch., Erie, 1981—; musician Erie Playhouse, 1990—; cons. Mem. Great Erie Excellence Coun., 1990—; mem. Community Awareness Coun., J.S. Wilson Mid. Sch., Erie, 1991. Nominee for Pa. Tchr. of Yr. award, 1990-91. Mem. Music Educators Nat. Conf., Am. Sch. Counselors Assn., Erie County Sch. Counselors Assn. Roman Catholic. Office: Millcreek Schs Westlake Mid Sch 4330 W Lake Rd Erie PA 16505-1498

SCHREIBER, KURT CLARK, chemistry educator; b. Vienna, Austria, Feb. 23, 1922; s. Morris and Jeffie Clark (Hayek) S.; m. Lillian Berger, Aug. 18, 1951; children: Emanuel, Celia Anne, Samuel. BS, CCNY, 1944; AM, Columbia U., 1947, PhD, 1950. Rsch. assoc. UCLA, 1949-51; asst. prof. chemistry Duquesne U., Pitts., 1951-54, assoc. prof., 1954-58, chmn. dept. chemistry, 1957-72, assoc. dean for sci. Coll. Arts and Sci., 1961-66, acting dean Grad. Sch. Arts and Sci., 1981-84, prof. chemistry, 1959—. Contbr. chpt. to book, articles to profl. jours. Mem. sci. adv. bd. Regional Indsl. Devel. Co. of Allegheny County, 1962-72; unit commr. Three Rivers dist. Boy Scouts Am., 1968-78; mem. adv. bd. Internat. Poetry Forum, Pitts., 1966-74; dir. Pa. Sci. Talent Search, 1977-87. Sgt. U.S. Army, 1944-46, ETO. Recipient Shofar award Boy Scouts Am., 1979. Mem. AAAS, Pa. Acad. Sci. (pres. 1987-89, editor newsletter 1980-87), Am. Chem. Soc. (chmn. Pitts. sect. 1967-68, Pitts. award 1986, councillor 1980—), Am. Inst. Chemists (chmn. Pitts. sect. 1970-72), Pa. Assn. Coll. Chemistry Tchrs. (chmn. 1971-72). Democrat. Jewish. Home: 1812 Wightman St Pittsburgh PA 15217-1536 Office: Duquesne U Dept Chemistry Pittsburgh PA 15282

SCHREIBER, STEVEN L., film editor, film company executive; b. Bklyn., June 6, 1942; s. Harry D. Schreiber and Leonora (Ackerman) Silverstein; m. Sherry Berkowitz, May 1964 (div. 1974); children: Mitchell K., Lisa D.; m. Diane P. Hills, Sept. 8, 1985; children: Danielle L., Nicole A. Student, Ohio U., 1960-61. Expeditor Synchrofilm and Tape Films/MPO, N.Y.C., 1964; apprentice editor Eue Screen Gems, N.Y.C., 1965, asst. editor, 1965-66; asst. editor Wilde Films, Inc., N.Y.C., 1966-67, editor, 1967-69; editor, pres., co-founder, dir. Editors Gas, Inc., N.Y.C., 1969—; v.p., dir. They Shoot Films, Inc., N.Y.C., 1986—. Editor, dir. comml. films, 1985-87. With USAR, 1960-64. Recipient Bronze Lion award Cannes Film Festival, 1986, 2 Gold Lion awards, 1987, 2 Silver Lions, 1988; winner Silver Telly award for directing, 1992. Republican. Office: Editors Gas Inc 16 E 48th St New York NY 10017-1017

SCHREICK, JOSEF A., marketing executive; b. Columbus, Ohio, Jan. 25, 1951; s. Joseph and Rosemary (McGee) S. BS, Ohio State U., 1973, MBA, 1974, MA, 1974. Mgmt. supr. Revlon Grey Advt., N.Y.C., 1975-80; v.p. Noxell-Cover Girl Lintas, N.Y.C., 1980-85; sr. v.p. Pfizer-Coty Ketchum Advt., N.Y.C., 1985-90; v.p. mktg. and creative svcs. Aramis, Inc., N.Y.C., 1990—; vis. prof. NYU; cons. in field.

SCHREINER, CHRISTOPHER STEPHEN, writer, literature educator; b. Glen Cove, N.Y., Mar. 28, 1956; s. Robert L. and Hope (Trepass) S.; m. Andrea Streit, Aug. 24, 1985; 1 child, Phaedra. BA, Hobart Coll., 1978; MS, Rensselaer Poly. Inst., 1984; PhD, Pa. State U., 1991. Cons. AT&T Info. Systems, Somerset, N.J., 1983-84; Edmund Ramsur scholar U. S.C., Columbia, 1984-86, rsch. editor, 1985-86; educator, writer Pa. State U., University Park, 1986—, intellectual mentor U. Scholars Program, 1991—. Contbr. articles to profl. jours. Recipient McKinney Writing award Rensselaer Poly. Inst., 1983, 84. Mem. Internat. Assn. Philosophy and Lit., Internat. Assn. Phenomenology and Lit., Modern Langs. Assn. Home: 155 Scholar's House Atherton Hall University Park PA 16802

SCHRIBER, JONATHAN DAVID, television producer; b. Buffalo, May 10, 1951; s. Edward Clay and Julia (Kehr) S.; m. Jane Susan Ross, Sept. 27, 1986. BA in Econs., SUNY, Cortland, 1973; MA in Econs., New Sch. for Social Rsch., 1979; MS in Journalism, Columbia U., 1980. Trainee Swiss Bank Corp., N.Y.C., 1974-75, FX advisor, 1976-77; fgn. exch. trader United Calif. Bank Internat., N.Y.C., 1975-76; reporter Forbes Mag., N.Y.C., 1980-82; producer Fin. News Network, N.Y.C., 1982-84, Sta. WNBC-TV, N.Y.C., 1984-86, ABC News, N.Y.C., 1986—; cons. Population Coun., N.Y.C., 1980; assistantship dept. rsch. East Asian Inst.Columbia U., 1980. Home: 250 W 103rd St Apt 2D New York NY 10025-4472 Office: ABC News 157 Columbus Ave Fl 4 New York NY 10023-5907

SCHRIER, JACK JOSEPH, advertising executive, marketing consultant; b. N.Y.C., June 21, 1932; s. Wolfgang Von Schrier and Florence (Kanfer) Schrier; m. Daphne Norma Elizabeth Gee, May 25, 1974; children: Stephen David, Samantha Alexandra Clementine. BS in Chemistry, Fairleigh Dickinson U., 1955. Advt. copywriter Frank Vos & Co., Inc., N.Y.C., 1960-62; copywriter, account exec. Schwab & Beatty, Inc., N.Y.C., 1962-64; copy chief, mktg. dir. The Free Press Macmillan Pub., N.Y.C., 1964-66; copy chief record clubs RCA, N.Y.C., 1966-68; founder, pres. The Copy Shoppe/CataLogistics, Inc., Mendham, N.J., 1972—; cons. Hanover House Industries, N.Y.C., 1974-90, SONY Corp. Am., Park Ridge, N.J., 1986—, Maxell Corp. Am., Fair Lawn, N.J., 1974—; assoc. Orlan & Assocs., La Crosse, Wis., 1989—. Founder Coalition for a Sane Jail Site, Morristown, N.J., 1990; liaison Bd. Health and Recreation Commns., Mendham, 1992—; councilman Mendham Twp., 1992—, chmn. Pub. Works Com., 1992—. With USNR, 1951-55. Republican. Home: 186 Mendham Rd Mendham NJ 07945 Office: The Copy Shoppe/CataLogistics Inc PO Box 304 Mendham NJ 07945-0304

SCHROEDER, DAVID LAWRENCE, electrical technician; b. Louisville, July 24, 1945; s. Arthur Newton and Rita (Myers) S. BS, No. Ariz. U., 1970, MA with honors, 1971. Cert. 1st class broadcast engr.; cert. pvt. tchr. Coord. therapeutic svcs. No. Ariz. U. Inst. for Human Devel., Flagstaff, 1969-72; lectr. U. Hawaii, Hilo, 1973-83; dept. chmn. St. Joseph High Sch., Hilo, 1983-86; assoc. prof. Jefferson Community Coll., Louisville, 1987-89; elec. technician Komori Am., Allendale, N.J., 1989—. Editor: (booklet) Biolongevity, 1984; also articles. Campaign mgr. Friends of Wendell Kaehuea, Hilo, 1978. With USNR, 1962-66. Mem. Big Island Amateur Radio Club (treas. 1979-80, pres. 1980-81), Phi Kappa Phi. Home: 28 Homestead Village Dr Warwick NY 10990-4210 Office: Komori Am 6 Pearl Ct Allendale NJ 07401-1611

SCHROEDER, HENRY, JR., dermatologist; b. N.Y.C., Nov. 2, 1932; s. Henry Paul and Irmgard Helene (Roggenkamp) S.; m. Doris Helen Olde, Oct. 14, 1961; children: Susan, Henry, Peter, Sandi. AB, Johns Hopkins U., 1954; MD, N.Y. Med. Coll., 1958. Diplomate Am. Bd. Dermatology. Resident in dermatology NYU Med. Ctr., N.Y.C., 1961-64; dermatologist Fishkill (N.Y.) Med. Ctr., 1984—. Capt. U.S. Army, 1959-62. Recipient 1st prize Consultations in Dermatology, Pfizer Corp., 1980. Mem. Am. Soc. Dermatologic Surgery, Internat. Soc. Dermatologic Surgery, Internat. Soc. Tropical Dermatology. Office: Fishkill Med Ctr 333 Rte 52 Fishkill NY 12524

SCHROEDER, NEIL ROLF, theater educator; b. Cleve., Nov. 12, 1930; s. Gilbert Henry and Anna Louise (Findling) S.; m. Sylvia Lou Dowden, Sept. 15, 1931 (dec. 1981); children: Rolf, Melissa, Kenneth. AB, Brown U., 1952; PhD, Yale U., 1962. Asst. prof. to assoc. prof. Clark Univ., Worcester, Mass., 1960—. Mem. Internat. Fedn. for Theatre Rsch., Am. Soc. for Theatre Rsch., Soc. for Theatre Rsch., Ibsen Soc. Am. Home: 1029 Pleasant St Apt 32 Worcester MA 01602-1357 Office: Visual & Performing Arts Clark Univ Worcester MA 01610

SCHROEDER, RICHARD PHILIP, electronics company executive, consultant; b. Scranton, Pa., Mar. 10, 1951; s. Philip Richard and Pearl Marion (Maier) S.; m. Donna Lee Elliott; children: Derek, Kyle. BSBA and Engring., Pa. State U., 1973, BA, 1974. Bus. mgr. H.R. Imbt, Inc., Lake Ariel, Pa., 1973-75; quality engr. Fisher Body div. GM, Trenton, N.J., 1975-77; asst. quality control mgr. Pitts. Forgings, Phila., 1977-78; divisional quality assurance mgr. Bindery Systems div. Harris Corp., Melbourne, Fla., 1978-83; corp. dir. productivity and quality Harris Graphics Corp., Melbourne, 1978-85; dir. operational and total quality improvement practice Coopers and Lybrand, Boston, 1985-86; v.p. corp. quality assurance and customer svc. Fed. Govt. Compliance, Codex Corp. subs. Motorola, Inc., Canton, Mass., 1986-91; v.p. quality, time-based mgmt. ABB, Stamford, Conn., 1991—; sr. examiner Malcolm Baldridge Award, Washington, 1987-92. Contbr. articles to profl. publs.; inventor 3D inspection for CMM. Mem. ASTM, Am. Soc. for Quality Control (cert. quality engr.), Machine Vision Assn. (charter), Soc. Mfg. Engrs., Am. Gear Mfrs. Assn., Pa. State U. Alumni Assn. (alumni advisor 1980—), Pi Kappa Phi. Republican. Home: 34 Shadow Ln Wilton CT 06897-3529 Office: ABB 900 Long Ridge Rd Stamford CT 06902-1194

SCHROER, RICHARD ALLEN, pathologist; b. Celina, Ohio, July 10, 1944; s. Clarence Eldo and Esther W. (Tostrick) S.; m. Patricia Ann Trippet, Feb. 26, 1972 (div. Mar. 1990); children: Michael Allen, Arthur Warren. BS, Kent (Ohio) State U., 1966, PhD, 1970. Postdoctoral fellow U. Calif., Irvine, 1970-73; dir. biology dept. Nelson R&D, Irvine, 1973-74; sr. rsch. scientist Am. Cyanamid Co., Pearl River, N.Y., 1975-76, group leader clin. pathology, 1976-88, mgr. clin. pathology, 1989—. Patentee in field; contbr. articles to profl. jours. Kent State U. fellow, 1969, NIH fellow, 1971-73. Mem. Assn. for Clin. Chemistry (chmn. div. animal clin. chemistry 1990-91). Office: Am Cyanamid Co Med Rsch Div N Middletown Rd Pearl River NY 10965-2650

SCHROFF, PETER DAVID, biochemical executive; b. Munich, Apr. 19, 1926; came to U.S., 1948; s. David and Bonnie (Gora) S.; m. Brenda Llewellyn, Oct. 20, 1971; children: James, John. MS in Biochemistry, U. London, 1948, MSChemE, 1949; PhD, Mich. State U., 1951; PhD in Clin. Chemistry, Ga. State U., 1972. Registered profl. engr., Ill., Mich., Calif. Chief devel. engr. Fluor Products, Los Angeles, 1951-55; dir. reliability N.Am. Rockwell, Los Angeles, 1955-70; dir. new products and quality control Gen. Diagnostics, Morris Plains, N.J., 1972-79; dir. advanced devel. Coulter Corp., Hialiah, Fla., 1979-82; dir. life scis. Janssen Life Scis. (J & J Corp.), Piscataway, N.J., 1982—. Author: Advances in Petroleum Chemistry and Refining, 1955; contbr. over 43 articles to profl. jours.; patentee in field. Rhodes scholar, 1948-49, Setnam scholar, 1949-51. Mem. Am. Soc. Clin. Pathology, Am. Assn. Cost Engrs., Am. Soc. for Med. Tech., Am. Soc. for Cell Biology, Am. Soc. for Microbiology, Nat. Soc. Histotech., Nat. Soc. Profl. Engrs. Club: Toastmasters (Los Angeles) (pres. 1956). Lodge: Kiwanis (pres. Los Angeles club 1958). Home: 956 Concord Way Neshanic Station NJ 08853 Office: Janssen Life Scis 40 Kingsbridge Rd Piscataway NJ 08854-3998

SCHROLL, EDWIN JOHN, theater educator, stage director; b. Watertown, N.Y., Feb. 14, 1941; s. Clarence Edwin and Frances Lucille (Snyder) S. BS, Lyndon State Coll., 1966; MS, Oswego State U., 1971. Cert. tchr. N.Y. English tchr. jr. high sch. Watertown (N.Y.) Sch. System, 1966-67; English tchr. high sch. Belleville (N.Y.) Cen. Sch., 1967-71; English tchr. high sch. Massena (N.Y.) Cen. Sch., 1971—, drama and speech tchr., 1988—, drama coach, 1975—; engr., announcer, programmer Pathways to Peace program Sta. WNCQ, Watertown, 1967-92. Cinematographer, writer, narrator, prodr. (documentaries) The United States: A Bicentennial Tour, 1976, Europe on $100 a Day, 1986; cinematographer (TV film) Partying, 1989; dir. various high sch. prodns.; actor various community prodns. Republican. Mem. LDS Ch. Home: 9559 Murray St Box 216 Cape Vincent NY 13618 Office: Massena Sch System 290 Main St Massena NY 13662

SCHROPFER, DAVID WALDRON, advertising executive, educator, consultant; b. Plainfield, N.J., Oct. 27, 1939; s. Frank Jeremiah and Edna Mae (Mueller) S.; m. Gloria Weaver, Aug. 10, 1963; children: Suzanne, David Jr., Kathleen. BS, NYU, 1961; postgrad., Hunter Coll., 1972-74. Asst. product mgr. Procter and Gamble, Cin., 1961-63; account exec. Ted Bates, N.Y.C., 1963-65; sr. account exec. Ogilvy and Mather, N.Y.C., 1965-68; v.p., mgmt. supr. SSC&B, N.Y.C., 1969-72, D'Arcy McManus and Masius Inc., N.Y.C., 1973-75; exec. v.p. James Neal Harvey, Inc., N.Y.C., 1976-79; exec. v.p., ptnr. Mike Sloan, Inc., Miami, Fla., 1980-82; pres., chief exec. officer Knudsen Moore Schropfer Advt., Inc., Stamford, Conn., 1983-88; pres. DWS Assocs., Inc., Stamford, 1988—; adj. prof. Fla. Internat. U., Miami, 1982; lectr. U. Mass., Amherst, 1985-86, U. New Haven, 1985, Providence Coll., 1987. Author: What Every Account Executive Should Know About Marketing Plans, 1990, Fundamentals of Marketing: Basic Concepts and Applications, AMA, 1990. Chmn. Charter Revision Commn., Stamford, 1986-87; mem. Stamford Bd. Fin., 1987—; chmn. ARC, Stamford, 1987-89, bd. dirs. 1984—, Jr. Achievement, Miami, 1982-83. Mem. Am. Assn. Advt. Agys. (lectr. 1982-85), Am. Mktg. Assn., Am. Mgmt. Assn. (lectr. 1984—). Democrat. Roman Catholic. Office: DWS Assocs Inc 957 Sunset Rd Stamford CT 06903-2400

SCHROTE, JOHN ELLIS, government executive; b. Findlay, Ohio, May 6, 1936; s. Millard L. and Alberta (Ellis) S.; m. Rachel Daly, Mar. 2, 1957; children: James D., Gretchen Schrote Kent. BS in Agriculture, Ohio State U., 1958; MBA, Xavier U., 1964. Buyer-expediter McGraw Constrn. Co., Middletown, Ohio, 1958-59; buyer Armco Corp., Middletown, 1959-66; adminstrv. asst. Congressman D.E. Lukens, Washington, 1967-71; prin. asst. dir. OEO, Washington, 1971-72; spl. asst. sec. USDA, Washington, 1972-76, nat. rep. congl. com., 1976-79, acting asst. sec., 1981-82; adminstrv. asst. Congressman F.J. Sensenbrenner, Jr., Washington, 1979-81, 1984-89; dep. dir. presdl. pers. office The White House, 1982-83; exec. v.p. Bishop Bryant & Assocs., Washington, 1983-84; asst. to sec. and dir. congl. affairs Dept. Interior, Washington, 1989, dep. asst. sec. policy mgmt. and budget, 1991, asst. sec. policy mgmt. and budget, 1991—; mem. Congl. staff adv. com. USDA Grad. Sch. Advance hotel chmn. Citizens for Reagan, Topeka, 1968; spl. rep. Com. to Re-Elect Pres., Washington, 1972; midwest regional dir. Pres. Ford Com., Washington, 1976. Mem. Adminstrv. Assts. Assn. Episcopalian. Home: 1744 Preston Rd Alexandria VA 22302 Office: US Dept Interior 1849 C St NW Washington DC 20240-9996

SCHROTH, PETER W(ILLIAM), lawyer, educator; b. Camden, N.J., July 24, 1946; s. Walter and Patricia Anne (Page) S.; children: Laura Salome Erickson-Schroth, Julia James. AB, Shimer Coll., 1966; JD, U. Chgo., 1969; M in Comparative Law, U.Chgo., 1971; SJD, U. Mich., 1979; postgrad., U. Freiburg, Fed. Republic Germany, Faculté Internationale pour l'Enseignement de Droit Comparé; MBA, Rensselaer Poly. Inst., 1988. Bar: Ill. 1969, N.Y. 1979, Conn. 1985, Mass. 1990. Asst. prof. So. Meth. U., 1973-77; fellow in law and humanities Harvard U., 1976-77, vis. scholar, 1980-81; assoc. prof. N.Y. Law Sch., 1977-81; prof. law Hamline U., St. Paul, 1981-83; dep. gen. counsel Equator Bank Ltd., 1984-87; v.p., dep. gen. counsel Equator Holdings Ltd., 1987—; adj. prof. law U. Conn., 1985-86, Western New Eng. Coll., 1988—, adj. prof. of mgmt. Hartford Grad. Ctr., 1988—. Author: Foreign Investment in the United States, 2d edit., 1977, (with Stiefel) Products Liability: European Proposals and American Experience, 1981, Doing Business in Sub-Saharan Africa, 1991; bd. editors Am. Jour. Comparative Law, 1981-84, 91—, Conn. Bar Jour., contbr. articles to profl. jours. Mem. ABA (editor in chief ABA Environ. Law Symposium 1980-82), Am. Soc. Comparative Law (bd. dirs. 1978-84, 91—), Am. Fgn. Law Assn., Internat. Bar Assn., Internat. Law Assn. (com. multinat. banking), Acad. Internat. Bus., Conn. Civil Liberties Union (bd. dirs. 1985-92), Environ. Law Inst. (assoc.), Columbia U. Peace Seminar (assoc.), Univ. Club. Office: Equator House 111 Charter Oak Ave Hartford CT 06106-5102

SCHUBERT, RONALD WALTER, marketing and sales executive; b. Pitts., Apr. 21, 1937; s. Walter Anthony Schubert and Rosemond Spada; m. Norma Kromer, May 30, 1959 (div. June 1980); children: Jennifer, Eric; m. Barbara Freeland, July 11, 1980. BE magna cum laude, Duquesne U., 1959. Cert. elem. tchr., Pa. Tchr. Chartiers Valley Joint Schs., Pitts., 1959-60; mgr. staff svcs. Alcoa, Pitts., 1960-68; nat. sales mgr. Xerox Corp., Rochester, N.Y., 1968-76; mgr. div. mktg. and sales Internat. Paper, N.Y.C., 1976-84; v.p. Allnet Corp., Chgo., 1984-85; dir., owner Miracle-Ear Ctr. of Greater Macon (Ga.), 1985—. Cpl. U.S. Army, 1960-61. Recipient Chgo. Tribune Silver medal, 1959. Mem. Internat. Tape Assn. Roman Catholic. Home: 157 Saddle Run Macon GA 31210 Office: Miracle Ear Ctr Sears Macon Mall 3661 Eisenhower Pkwy Macon GA 31206

SCHUCK, VICTORIA, political science educator; b. Oklahoma City, Mar. 16, 1909; d. Anthony B. and Anna (Priebe) S. A.B. with great distinction, Stanford U., 1930, M.A., 1931, Ph.D., 1937; L.H.D. (hon.), Mt. Vernon Coll., 1980. Univ. fellow Stanford U., 1931-33, teaching asst., 1934-35, acting instr., 1935-36, instr., 1936-37; asst. prof. Fla. State Coll. Women, 1937-40; mem. faculty Mt. Holyoke Coll., 1940-77, prof. polit. sci., 1950-77; pres. Mt. Vernon Coll., Washington, 1977-80, ret.; vis. lectr. Smith Coll., 1948-49; vis. prof. Stanford U., summer 1952, vis. scholar polit. sci., 1982—; guest scholar Brookings Instn., 1967-68, summers 68, 70, Woodrow Wilson Ctr. Internat. Scholars, 1980; Prin. program analyst, planning for local bds. OPA, 1942-44; rep. Am. Polit. Sci. Assn. UN World Conf. of UN Decade for Women, Nairobi, Kenya, 1985; sponsor Women's Fgn. Policy Council, N.Y., 1986; cons. Office Temporary Controls, 1945-47; mem. internat. secretariat UN Conf. San Francisco, 1945; mem. Mass. Commn. Interstate Coop., 1957-60, U. Mass. Bldg. Authority, 1960-68; Mass. adv. com. U.S. Commn. Civil Rights, 1962-78; cons. GAO, 1980-82; non-govtl. rep. UN Commn. on Status of Women, Vienna, Austria, 1988. Regional editor: Ency. Brit., 1958-61; co-editor and contbr.: Women Organizing: An Anthology, 1979, New England Politics, 1981; contbr. articles to profl. jours. Mem. Pres.'s Commn. Registration and Voting Participation, 1963; mem. Berkshire Community Coll. Planning Com., 1964-68, Greenfield Community Coll. Planning Com., 1965-68, Mass. Bd. Higher Edn., 1976-77; mem. Town of South Hadley Planning Bd., 1959-67, chmn., 1961-67; trustee U. Mass., 1958-65. Grantee Haynes Found., 1951-52; Grantee Asia Soc., 1971-72. Mem. ASPA, AAUW (pres. Mass. 1946-50, nat. chmn. legis. prog. com., bd. dirs. 1965-69), AAUP (pres. Mt. Holyoke 1962-64), Am. Polit. Sci. Assn. (sec. 1959-60, v.p. 1970-71), New Eng. Polit. Sci. Assn. (pres. 1950-51), Northeastern Polit. Sci. Assn. (pres. 1972-73), Internat. Polit. Sci. Assn., Acad. Coun. on UN System, Supreme Ct. Hist. Soc., Fed. City Coun., Internat. Studies Assn., Mortar Bd. (hon.), Cosmopolitan Club, Cosmos Club, Phi Beta Kappa, Chi Omega. Home: 4000 Cathedral Ave NW Washington DC 20016-5249

SCHUCKER, CHARLES, artist, educator; b. Gap, Pa., Jan. 19, 1908; s. Gabriel and Carrie (Musgrove) S.; m. Margaret Hamilton Rust, Apr. 16, 1938; children—Cheryl Chang, Carrie Schucker Gerowitz. Grad. Md. Inst. Fine and Mech. Arts, 1934. Instr. NYU, 1947-54, CCNY, 1955-56; prof. Pratt Inst., 1956-74, emeritus, 1974—; one-man shows include: Chgo. Art Inst., 1947, Macbeth Gallery, N.Y.C. 1946, 49, 53, Passedoit Gallery, N.Y.C., 1955, 58, Howard Wise Gallery, N.Y.C., Whitney Mus. Am. Art, 1971, Max Hutchinson Gallery, N.Y.C., 1972, 74, 78, Katonah Mus., 1955, 73, 78, 90, Gallery Camino Real, Boca Raton, Fla., 1980, 81, 84, 90, Rotunda Gallery Inaugural, Bklyn. Borough Hall, 1981, Solomon Downtown, Los Angeles, 1984; exhibited group shows including Mus. Modern Art, Bertha Schaefer Gallery, Carnegie Inst., Walker Art Ctr., Contemporary Am. Painting, Met. Mus. Art, Art in 20th Century, Phila. Acad. Fine Art, Calif. Palace Annual, Chgo. Art Inst., San Francisco Mus. Art, Whitney Mus. Am. Art, Bklyn. Mus., Amherst Coll., Contemporary Arts Ctr., SUNY-Potsdam, Hotel Stamford Plaza, Gallery Camino Real, Boca Raton, Fla., Pratt Inst., 1988, 91, others; represented in permanent collections Am. Acad. Arts and Letters, Bklyn. Mus., Bklyn. Heights Library, Newark Mus., New Britain (Conn.) Mus., Whitney Mus. Am. Art, Harcourt, Brace Jovanovitch, Louisa and John I. H. Baur, Roy Neuberger, Percy Uris, Paul Ferber, Howard Wise, Woodhull Hosp., Dr. Janna Claire Collins, Archtl. Digest, Katonah Village Library, Pratt Inst., 1991, others. Recipient Henry Walters Traveling Fellowship, Guggenheim Found. Fellowship, 1953, Audubon prize for Oil Painting, 1949; Childe Hassam prize, AAAL, 1952, Bklyn. and L.I. Biennial award for Oil Painting, 1948, 50; subject of video documentary Schucker, Portrait in Color, 1986, 88, Christopher Chang; Images/Art, N.Y., Bill Page, 1991, Carter Ratcliff, catalog essay, 1990. Address: Studio 33 Middagh St Brooklyn Heights NY 11201-1339

SCHUCKER, GERALD DELANO, chemist; b. McConnellstown, Pa., Oct. 29, 1936; s. Paul Raymond and Freda May (Noel) S.; m. Joann Pastrick, July 28, 1984; stepchildren: Harold, Melissa, Carrie. BS, Juniata Coll., 1958; MS, U. Mo., Rolla, 1967. Chemist PRR Test Dept., Altoona, Pa., 1958-62; rsch. tech. Cornell U., Ithaca, N.Y., 1962-65; grad. asst. U. Mo., Rolla, 1965-67; sr. rsch. scientist Corning (N.Y.) Inc., 1967-92, ret., 1992. Mem. Am. Chem. Soc., Soc. Applied Spectroscopy, Found. Chem. Rsch. Home: 468 Main St Big Flats NY 14814 Office: Corning Inc HP-ME-03-070 Corning NY 14831

SCHUELE, ALBAN WILHELM, chemical company executive; b. Stuehlingen, Baden-Wuerttemberg, W. Ger., Apr. 28, 1944; came to U.S., 1963; s. Wilhelm and Emma (Utz) S.; m. Grayce Winifred LaGrotta, Jan. 25, 1969; children: Jason Alban, Kathleen Marie. B.S. in Econs., Ariz. State U., 1969; B. Internat. Mgmt., Am. Grad. Sch. Internat. Mgmt. Thunderbird, Glendale, Ariz., 1970. V.p. Chase Manhattan Bank, N.Y.C., 1970-80; treas. Am. Hoechst Corp. (now Hoechst Celanese Corp.), Somerville, N.J., 1980—, v.p., treas., 1985-88; treas. Hoechst-Roussel Pharms., Inc., 1985—, Hoechst-Roussel Agri-Vet Co., 1985—; v.p. quality and communications Hoechst Celanese Corp., 1988—, corp. v.p. and pres. splty. products group, 1989—; treas. P.B. Diagnostics, Inc., 1985—; pres. Hoechst Can., Inc., 1991—, Celanese Can. Inc., 1991—. Roman Catholic. Office: Celanese Can Inc 800 Rene Levesque Blvd W, Montreal, PQ Canada H3B 1Z1

SCHUELLEIN, ROBERT JOSEPH, health science administrator, consultant; b. N.Y.C., Feb. 22, 1920; s. Jacob John and Wilma (Metzner) S.; m. Wilma Linkins, June 12, 1970. BS, U. Dayton, 1944; MS, U. Pitts., 1946, PhD, 1956; postdoctoral, Columbia U., 1956-57. Assoc. prof. Univ. Dayton, Ohio, 1953-64; health scientist adminstr. Nat. Heart and Lung Inst., Bethesda, Md., 1964-66; dir. grants assoc. program NIH, Bethesda, 1966-67; chief periodontal and soft tissues diseases program Nat. Inst. Dental Rsch., Bethesda, 1967-73, spl. asst. for man power rsch., 1973-83, rsch. cons., 1983—; dir. McTye Inc., Fairfax, Va., 1964-66. Author: Genetics, 1955, Radiation Lab Manual, 1960, Genetics Lab Manual, 1963. Mem. Am. Genetics Soc., Human Genetics Soc., Sigma Xi., Phi Sigma (v.p. 1965). Democrat. Roman Catholic. Home: 5626 Lamar Rd Bethesda MD 20816-1350 Office: Nat Inst Dental Rsch 5333 Westbard Ave Bethesda MD 20894-0001

SCHUESSLER, RICHARD JAY, insurance broker; b. Bklyn., Dec. 18, 1938; s. Oscar Joseph and Doris Lesly (Altenbrand) S.; m. Sarah Alexander Foster, Feb. 11, 1961; children: Richard J. Jr., Kemp Foster. BS in Bus. Adminstrn., Stetson U., 1962. V.p. Davis, Dorland & Co., N.Y.C., 1965-82, Jardine, Emett & Chandler, Parsippany, N.J., 1982-86; pres. CPI Brokerage, Inc., Morristown, N.J., 1986—; bd. dirs. Ardmore Minerals Corp., Ardmore, Okla., N.J. Mktg. Assocs., Whippany, N.J. Mem. Morris County Golf Club. Republican. Presbyterian. Home: Village Rd PO Box 457 New Vernon NJ 07976 Office: CPI Brokerage Inc 1201 Mt Kemble Ave Morristown NJ 07960-6626

SCHUETH, STEVEN J(EROME), marketing professional; b. New Hampton, Iowa, Aug. 27, 1954; s. James Jerome and Sue Jane (Petrie) S.; m. Darla Luann Olney, July 30, 1977; children: Samuel, Dayna. BA in Journalism, Marquette U., 1976. Real estate broker Province Realty, Green Bay, Wis., 1977-82; account exec. Shearson Am. Express, Indpls., 1982-83; v.p. mktg. Prescott Realty Svcs., Pitts., 1983-87; dir. devel. Wharton Sch. U. Pa., Phila., 1987-89; v.p. socially responsible investing, dir. corp. comm. ach, Bethesda, Md., 1989—; exec. v.p., bd. dirs. Social Investment Forum, Mpls. Office: Calvert Group 4550 Montgomery Ave Bethesda MD 20814

SCHUETZ, MICHAEL DAVID, communications manager; b. Detroit, Mar. 28, 1959; s. Rudy Ludwig and Shirley Jean (Engel) S.; m. Nancy Brand, Jan. 9, 1984; 1 child, Benjamin Michael. BS in Indsl. Design, U. Cin., 1984. Artist, graphic designer Just Your Type, Upper Saddle River, N.J., 1984-86; art dir. Image Works, Ramsey, N.J., 1986-89; corp. communications mgr. The Texwipe Co., Upper Saddle River, 1989—; freelance designer MS Design, Allendale, N.J., 1982—. Mem. Am. Ctr. for Design (corp.), Art Dirs. Club N.J. Republican. Methodist. Office: The Texwipe Co 650 E Crescent Ave Saddle River NJ 07458-1827

SCHUETZE, FREDERIK EDWIN, music educator; b. Monroe, Wis., Nov. 25, 1947; s. Edwin William and Helen Elizabeth (Spencer) S.; m. Joy Talbert, June 13, 1976; 1 child, Nora. BA, Lawrence U., 1969; MusB, MA, Calif. State U., Northridge, 1979; D Mus. Arts, U. Mo., Kansas City, 1984. Tchr. Baraboo (Wis.) High Sch., 1969-70; grad. teaching asst. U. Mo., 1979-81; prof. music Washburn U., Topeka, 1981-86; prof. music Bradford (Mass.) Coll., 1986—, dir. coll. honors program, 1991—. Trustee Universalist-Unitarian Ch., Haverhill, Mass., 1988-90. Sgt. USAF, 1970-74, Vietnam. Mem. Sonneck Soc., Music Tchrs. Nat. Assn., Coll. Music Soc., Nat. Assn. Tchrs. Singing. Office: Bradford Coll 320 S Main St Haverhill MA 01835-7393

SCHUG, RIC ANDREW, consultant; b. Upton, Mass., Sept. 4, 1951; s. Richard Schug and Chestin A. (Heald) Tinker; m. Leta M. Gordon, Sept. 22, 1991. BSEE, Lowell Tech. Inst., 1973. Prodn. engr. Hewlett Packard, Waltham, Mass., 1974-76, design engr., 1976-78, svcs. mgr., 1978-80, PC design mgr., 1980-90, productivity engr., 1990-91; CAEE cons. Hewlett Packard, Chelmsford, Mass., 1991—. Mem. HP Design Ctr. Users Group (chmn. 1987-91). Office: Hewlett Packard 300 Apollo Dr Chelmsford MA 01568

SCHUKER, ELEANOR SHEILA, psychiatrist, educator; b. N.Y.C., Jan. 3, 1941; d. Louis Aaron and Millicent (Milchman) S.; m. Alan Melowsky, Dec. 26, 1974; 1 child, Julie Millicent. BA, Swarthmore Coll., 1961; MD, Columbia U., 1965; cert. in psychoanalytic medicine, Columbia U. Ctr. for Psychoanalytic Training and Rsch., 1975. Diplomate Am. Bd. Psychiatry and Neurology. Intern Mt. Sinai Hosp., N.Y.C., 1965-66; resident in psychiatry N.Y. State Psychiat. Inst., Columbia U., N.Y.C., 1966-69; attending psychiatrist Columbia U. Health Svc., N.Y.C., 1969-90; co-dir. psychiat. emergency svcs. St. Luke's Hosp., N.Y.C., 1970-72, founder, dir. rape intervention program, 1977-80, assoc. attending psychiatrist, 1978—; collaborating psychoanalyst Columbia U. Psychoanalytic Ctr., N.Y.C., 1975-85, training and supervising analyst, 1985—; asst. clin. prof. psychiatry Columbia U., 1980-90, assoc. clin. prof. psychiatry, 1990—; cons. Women's Counseling Project, N.Y.C., 1974-89. Editor: (with Nadine Levinson) Female Psychology: An Annotated Psychoanalytic Bibliography, 1991; contbr. articles to profl. jours. Fellow Am. Acad. Psychoanalysis, Am. Psychiatric Assn. (cert. in psychoanalysis); mem. Am. Psychoanalytic Assn. (cert., alt. del. to exec. coun. 1986—), Alumni Assn. Columbia Psychoanalytic Ctr. (pres. 1978-80). Office: 150 W End Ave # 26A New York NY 10023-5743

SCHUKRAFT, SCOTT ALAN, agronomist; b. Fleetwood, Pa., Sept. 22, 1960; s. Albert E. and Roberta A. (Hilbert) S. BS in Agronomy, Del. Valley Coll., 1982. Asst. grounds dir. Glade Springs, Daniels, W.Va., 1982-84; golf course supt. Rolling Hills Country Club, Wilton, Conn., 1984-91, Hunstville Golf Club, Lehman Twp., Pa., 1992—. Recipient Oustanding Agronomy Sr. award, 1982. Mem. Golf Course Supts. Assn. Am., Am. Soc. Agronomy, Met. Golf Course Supt. Assn., Conn. Assn. Golf Course Supts. Democrat. Lutheran. Home and Office: 147 Hayfield Rd Shavertown PA 18708-9748

SCHULBERG, ARNOLD L., lawyer, landman; b. Pitts., June 28, 1952; s. Irwin Harris and June (Schilit) S.; m. Mary Sue Weekley, Feb. 14, 1988. BS, U. Pitts., 1974; JD, Duquesne U., 1977. Bar: Pa. 1977, U.S. Dist. Ct. (we. dist.) Pa. 1977, U.S. Ct. Appeals (3rd cir.) 1978, U.S. Supreme Ct. 1987; cert. profl. landman. Pvt. practice Pitts., 1977-83, 90—; pub. defender Allegheny County, Pitts., 1980-83; sr. contracts landman CNG Devel. Co., Pitts., 1983-90. Mem. Am. Assn. Profl. Landmen, Pa. Bar Assn. Home and Office: 135 Huron Dr Carnegie PA 15106-1826

SCHULBERG, HERBERT CHARLES, psychologist; b. N.Y.C., Feb. 10, 1934; s. Philip and Sarah (Bookin) S.; m. Phyllis Gitelman, June 23, 1957; children: Mark Ira, Michelle Tobi. BA, Yeshiva Coll., 1955; PhD, Columbia U., 1960; MS, Harvard U., 1963. Prof. of psychiatry, psychology and medicine Sch. Medicine U. Pitts., 1976—; vis. scientist NIMH, Rockville, Md., 1986. Office: U Pitts 3811 Ohara St Pittsburgh PA 15213-2593

SCHULER, DORTHY ANN, college director; b. Monroe, Wis., Nov. 19, 1927; d. Jacob John and Claire Virginia (Pryce) Zimmerman; m. Robert Toelle, Jan. 5, 1952 (separated); 1 child, John Toelle Schuler. BS, U. Wis., 1949; MPA, SUNY, Albany, 1972. Dir. scheduling Coll New Paltz SUNY, 1972—. Chair com., vol. Hudson Valley (N.Y.) Philharmonic Chamber Series, 1987—; vol. Ulster Performing Arts Ctr. Guild, 1989—; treas. League Women Voters Mid-Ulster County, Kingston, N.Y., 1990-92. Democrat. Methodist. Office: SUNY Coll New Paltz New Paltz NY 12561

SCHULER, JAMES TERRY, human resources specialist; b. Cin., Aug. 5, 1948; s. James William and Alma Lucille (Mullenix) S.; m. Mary Ann Bermudes; children: Jennifer Anne, Corinne Terese, Catherine Noelle. BA, U. Calif., Riverside, 1970; MPA, UCLA, 1977. Sr. personnel analyst City of L.A., 1970-78; mgr. employment and affirmative action Avery Label Group Avery Dennison, Pasadena, Calif., 1978-81; dir. personnel rels. Avery Label Group Avery Dennison, Azusa, Calif., 1981-85, group dir. human resources, 1986-88, group dir. human resources converted products group, 1989-90; group dir. human resources office products group Avery Dennison, Milford, Mass., 1991—. Mem. personnel com. Weingart Ctr. Assn., L.A., 1986-90; mem. Pasadena Pvt. Industry Coun., 1980-82; regional commr. Hacienda Heights, Calif. chpt. Am. Youth Soccer Assn., 1988-90. Staff sgt. USAF, 1970-76. Mem. Am. Soc. Personnel Adminstrs. Democrat. Office: Avery Dennison 321 Fortune Blvd Milford MA 01757-1723

SCHULER, RICHARD EDWARD, economics educator, consultant; b. Allentown, Pa., Nov. 22, 1937; s. Edward John and Clare May (Moyer) S.; m. Mary Patricia Callaghan, May 12, 1962; children: Richard E. Jr., Anne E., Judith M. BE, Yale U., 1959; MBA, Lehigh U., 1969; MA, Brown U., 1972, PhD, 1972. Registered profl. engr., Pa. Engr., mgr. Pa. Power and Light Co., Allentown, Pa., 1959-67; sr. energy economist Battelle Meml. Inst., Columbus, Ohio, 1968-69; dir., Office Rsch., N.Y. State Dept. Pub. Svc., Albany, N.Y., 1977-78; commr., deputy chmn. N.Y. State Pub. Svc. Commn., Albany, N.Y., 1981-83; prof. econ. and civil engring. Cornell U., Ithaca, N.Y., 1972—, assoc. dir. Cornell Ctr. for Environ., 1988—; vis. prof. Fuqua Sch. Mgmt., Duke U., Durham, N.C., 1987; vis. scholar Ctr. for Ops. Rsch. and Econometrics, Louvain-la-Neuve, Belgium, 1988; cons. World Bank, numerous regulatory bodies, ind. and utilities, 1976—; chmn. adv. panel study increased competition in elec. supply U.S. Office Tech. Assessment, Washington, 1987-89. Co-author: The Future of Electrical Energy, 1986; contbr. numerous articles to profl. jours. Named one of twelve Stars of State Govt., Washington Monthly, 1982. Mem. Am. Econ. Assn., Regional Sci. Assn. Democrat. Office: Cornell U 465 Hollister Hall Ithaca NY 14853

SCHULHOF, MICHAEL PETER, electronics company executive; b. N.Y.C., Nov. 30, 1942; s. Rudolph B. and Hannelore (Buck) S.; m. Paola Nissim, Apr. 17, 1969; children: David Kenneth, Jonathan Nissim. BA, Grinnell Coll., 1964, DSc (hon.), 1990; MS, Cornell U., 1967; PhD (NSF fellow), Brandeis U., 1970. Lic. comml. pilot. Am. research fellow Brookhaven Nat. Lab., Uptown, N.Y., 1969-71; asst. to v.p. mfg. CBS Records, Inc., N.Y.C., 1971-73, mem. exec. com., bd. dirs., 1987—; gen. mgr. bus. products div. Sony Corp., N.Y.C., 1973-77, v.p., 1977-78, sr. v.p., 1978-86; pres. Sony Industries, N.Y.C., 1978-86; chmn. Digital Audio Disc Corp., Terre Haute, Ind., 1986—; pres. Sony Software Corp., 1991—; chmn. bd. dirs. Quadriga Art Inc., 1980—, Sony Video Software; vice chmn. Sony USA, Inc., 1990—; bd. dirs. Sony Corp., Japan, Sony Corp. Am. (name change to Sony Music Entertainment), Columbia Pictures Entertainment, Materials Rsch. Corp.; chmn. CBS Records. Contbr. articles to profl. jours. Patentee audio disc apparatus, 1986. Trustee Brandeis U., 1990—. NSF fellw Brandeis U. Mem. Am. Phys. Soc. (dir. 1978), Computer and Bus. Equipment Mfrs. Assn. (dir.), Am. Radio Relay League, Coun. on Fgn. Rels., Aircraft Owners and Pilots Assn., Guggenhiem Mus., Whitney Mus., Harmony Club, Gipsy Trail Club, East Hampton Tennis Club, Profile Club, Fenway Golf Club. Home: 770 Park Ave New York NY 10021-4153 Office: Sony USA Inc 9 W 57th St New York NY 10019-2600

SCHULLER, DIANE ETHEL, allergist, immunologist, educator; b. Bklyn., Nov. 27, 1943; d. Charles William and Dorothy Schuller. AB cum laude with honors in Biology, Bryn Mawr Coll., 1965. Diplomate Am. Bd. Allergy and Immunology, Am. Bd. Pediatrics, Nat. Bd. Med. Examiniers. M.D., SUNY Downstate Med. Sch., Bklyn., 1970. Intern, then resident in pediatrics Roosevelt Hosp., N.Y.C., 1970-72, resident in allergy Cooke Inst. Allergy, 1972-74; asso. in pediatrics Geisinger Med. Center, Danville, Pa., 1974—, dir. dept. pediatric allergy, immunology and pulmonary diseases 1978—; asst. clin. prof. pediatrics Hershey Med. Coll., Pa. State U., 1974-79, assoc. clin. prof., 1979-88; clin. prof. Jefferson Med. Coll., Phila., 1989—; mem. Columbia-Montour Home Health Services Adv. Group of Profl. Personnel, 1975—. Bd. dirs. Central Pa. Lung and Health Assn.; bd. dirs., exec. com. Am. Lung Assn. of Pa., sec., 1992— ; chmn. Susquehanna Valley Lung Assn., 1983—; mem. scholarship com. Bryn Mawr Club, N.Y., 1970-75. Recipient Physicians Recognition award AMA, 1973-76, 74-76, 75-78, 79-82, 83-86, 1987-90, 91—. Fellow Am. Acad. Pediatrics, Am. Coll. Allergy and Immunology (2d v.p., bd. regents 1989-92, exec. com. 1990-92, treas. joint coun. of allergy and immunology 1991—, editorial bd. annals of allergy), Am. Assn. Clin. Immunology and Allergy (regional dir., exec. com.), Joint Coun. Allergy and Immunology (bd. dirs. 1986—), Am. Acad. Allergy and Immunology; mem. Pa., N.Y. State allergy socs., N.Y. State, N.Y. County med. socs. Office: Geisinger Med Ctr Danville PA 17821

SCHULMAN, BRUCE DAVID, investment banker; b. Chgo., Aug. 16, 1950; s. Leonard and Berneice (Weiner) S.; m. Sandra Jo Evans, July 16, 1983; 1 child, Barri Skyler, July 11, 1985. BA, U. Colo., 1972; MBA, So. Meth. U., 1975. Chief exec. officer Chesters, Salt Lake City, 1975-77; v.p. A. David Silver & Co., N.Y.C., 1972-73, 77-78; pres. B.D. Schulman Inc., N.Y.C., 1978-81; pres. Niederhoffer & Niederhoffer, Inc., N.Y.C., 1981—; bd. dir. Ludwig Industries, Inc., Bklyn.; bd. dirs., pres. R.B. Studio, N.Y.C.; cons. small businesses. Jewish. Avocations: skiing, aikido. Home: 170 E 88th St Apt 4C New York NY 10128-2277 Office: Niederhoffer & Niederhoffer Inc 635 Madison Ave New York NY 10022-1009

SCHULMAN, LAWRENCE S., physics educator; b. Newark, N.J., Nov. 21, 1941; s. Louis Leon and Anna (Susser) S.; m. Claire Frangles Sherman; children: Leonard, Linda, David. BA, Yeshiva U., 1963, BHL, 1963; PhD, Princeton U., 1967. From asst. prof. to prof. Ind. U., Bloomington, 1967-78; NATO postdoctoral fellow, 1970; assoc. prof., then prof. Technion, Haifa, Israel, 1970-88; prof. of physics Clarkson U., Potsdam, N.Y., 1985—; cons. IBM, Yorktown Heights, N.Y., 1975—; vis. prof. U. Paris VI, 1985—, Columbia U., 1992; vis. scientist CEA Saclay, Gif-sur-Yvette, France, 1986—; Donders prof. U. Utrecht, the Netherlands, 1990. Author: Techniques and Applications of Path Integration, 1981. Mem. Am. Phys. Soc., Israel Phys. Soc., Internat. Assn. Math. Physicists. Office: Clarkson U Physics Dept Potsdam NY 13699-5820

SCHULMAN, MARTIN FRED, ophthalmologist; b. N.Y.C., Dec. 23, 1943; s. Samuel and Sylvia (Schwartz) S.; m. Susan Brotman, July 15, 1967; children: Robin, Andrew, Aimee. BA, NYU, 1964; PhD in Chemistry, Rutgers U., 1968; MD, George Washington U., 1976. Diplomate Am. Bd. Ophthalmology. Sr. applications chemist Varian Assocs., Springfield, N.J., 1969-72; postdoctoral rsch. fellow Fla. State U., Tallahassee, 1968-69; resident in medicine George Washington U., Washington, 1976-77; resident and chief resident in ophthalmology Mt. Sinai Sch. Medicine, N.Y.C., 1977-80; pvt. practice ophthalmology Hackensack, N.J., 1980—. Contbr. articles to profl. jours. Trustee Gimbel Multiple Sclerosis Clin. Care Ctr., Teaneck, N.J., 1985. Fellow ACS; mem. William Beaumont Med. Rsch. Hon. Soc., Sigma Xi. Office: 75 Essex St Hackensack NJ 07601-4036

SCHULMAN, MARVIN, executive, mathematician; b. Bklyn., Nov. 13, 1927; s. Elias and Lena (Finger) S.; m. Beatrice Ludwig, Feb. 14, 1954; children: Karen, Robert, David, Tracy. BA in Math., Bklyn. Coll., 1953. Br. head Naval Air Engring. Ctr., Phila., 1957-71, Naval Air Devel. Ctr., Warminster, Pa., 1971-85; cons. Ketron, Warminster, 1985-86; tech. advisor, cons. Human Factors Engrs., Warminster, 1985-86; v.p. sr. tech. advisor LME Inc., Warminster, 1986—; cons. Naval Air Devel. Ctr., Warminster, 1986—, Naval Air Systems Command, Washington, 1985-86. 5 patents in field; contbr. over 30 articles to profl. jours. Cpl. U.S. Army, 1946-47. Recipient Disting. Svc. Award USN, 1976, Meritorious Civilian award USN, 1976. Mem. Safety & Flight Equipment, Soc. Automotive Engrs., East Coast Chpt. Safety & Flight Equipment Engrs. Home: 448 Candlewood Rd Broomall PA 19008-1735 Office: LME Inc 444 Jacksonville Rd Warminster PA 18974-4861

SCHULMAN, ROBERT GLEN, graphic art company executive; b. Long Beach, N.Y., Jan. 18, 1952; s. Harry and Natalie Schulman; m. Nancy Winicki, June 10, 1979 (div. 1988). BS in Mktg. and Mgmt., L.I. U., 1974. Pres. Advent Composition, Inc., N.Y.C., 1975-81, Dunshaw Press, N.Y.C., 1982—; dir. printing The Equitable, N.Y.C., 1990—, cons., 1990-91. With U.S. Army, 1976-78. Mem. Printing Industries Assn., Nat. Bus. Form Assn. Office: Dunshaw Press 360 W 31st St New York NY 10001-2727

SCHULMANN, HORST, international economist; b. Frankfurt am Main, Germany, Apr. 13, 1933; came to U.S., 1984; s. Eugen Max and Johanna Hermine (Hübner) S.; m. Uli Wagner, Mar. 13, 1973; children: Daniel, Anja. MA in Econs., J.W. Goethe U., Frankfurt am Main, 1958; PhD in Econs., U. Saarbrücken, Fed. Republic Germany, 1964. Rsch. assoc. U. Saarbrücken, 1959-64; bd. asst. Hoesch A.G., Dortmund, Fed. Republic Germany, 1965-66; sec.-gen. Coun. Econ. Experts, Wiesbaden, Fed. Republic Germany, 1967-69; dep. dir. World Bank, Washington, 1970-75; dir. European Community, Brussels, 1976-77; chmn. monetary com. Econ. Commn., Brussels, 1982; dir. gen. Ministry Fin., Chancellor's Office, Bonn, Fed. Republic Germany, 1977-80, sec. state, 1981-82; dep. mng. dir. Inst. Internat. Fin., Washington, 1984-86, mng. dir., 1987—; pers. rep. Chancellor H. Schmidt, Bonn, 1978-82. Author books; contbr. articles to profl. jours. Decorated Legion of Honor (France). Mem. Am. Econ. Assn. Roman Catholic. Home: 7917 Cypress Grove Ln Cabin John MD 20818-1001 Office: Inst Internat Fin Ste 8500 2000 Pennsylvania Ave NW Washington DC 20006-1812

SCHULTE, JEFFREY LEWIS, lawyer; b. N.Y.C., July 24, 1949; s. Irving and Ruth (Stein) S.; m. Elizabeth Ewan Kaiser, Aug. 13, 1977; children: Andrew Riggs, Ian Garretson, Elizabeth Alexandra. BA, Williams Coll., 1971; postgrad., Harvard U., 1971-72; JD, Yale U., 1976. Bar: Pa. 1978. Law clk. to judge U.S. Ct. Appeals (3d cir.), Newark, 1976-77; assoc. Schnader, Harrison, Segal & Lewis, Phila., 1977-84, ptnr., 1985—. Contbr. articles to profl. jours. Bd. dirs. North Ardmore (Pa.) Civic Assn., pres., 1990; bd. dirs. Main Line YMCA, chmn., 1989-91; active Ardmore (Pa.) Alliance Project. Mem. ABA, Pa. Bar Assn., Phila. Bar Assn., Yale Club (bd. dirs. Phila. chpt.), Williams Club Phila., Phila. Racquet Club, Merion Cricket Club, Phi Beta Kappa. Office: Schnader Harrison Segal & Lewis 1600 Market St Ste 3600 Philadelphia PA 19103-4247

SCHULTER, ALBERT JACK, illustrator, graphic designer; b. Newark, Feb. 13, 1933; s. Benjamin and Rose (Kirsch) S.; m. Nancy Ruth Lipson, Mar. 15, 1959; children: Hilary Blair, Heidi Mae, Jill Ann, Vikki Lynn. Student, Newark Sch. Fine & Indsl. Arts, 1952-53, Art Students League, N.Y.C., 1955, Parsons Sch. Design, 1955-57, Phila. Coll. Art, 1959, 60. Illustrator Picatinny Arsenal, Dover, N.J., 1956, Western Elec. Co., Winston-Salem, 1957-59, GE Aerospace, Moorestown, N.J., 1959—. Designer Submarine Operational Automation System logotype and folder (Winner 38th Internat. Tech. Communication Conf. 1991). With U.S. Army, 1953-55. Home: 118 Chaucer Pl Cherry Hill NJ 08003-3543 Office: GE Aerospace ATL Bldg 145-2 Moorestown NJ 08057

SCHULTHEIS, CARL FRANK, JR., pediatrician; b. Woodbury, N.J., Nov. 5, 1930; s. Carl Frank and Rose Estelle (Redmond) S.; m. Ella Ruth Katkowski, Sept. 6, 1952; children: Melissa, Carl III, Christopher, Eric. BS, Haverford Coll., 1955; MD, Jefferson Med. Coll., 1959. MD. Physician Pediatric Assoc. Inc., Rosemont, Pa., 1962-72; sec., treas. King of Prussia Med. Assoc., 1969—; pres. Pediatric Assoc. Inc., King of Prussia, Pa., 1972—; med. cons. Vis. Nurse Assn., Norristown, Pa., 1970; bd. dirs. The Pathway Sch., Jeffersonville, Pa., 1986—. Producer (TV series) Doctor's Notebook, 1987, 88, 89, 90. Mem. King of Prussia Hist. Soc., 1976-80, pres., 1980—; scouter Boy Scouts Am., Valley Forge Coun., 1972— (Dist. award Merit 1979); mem. Em. Legion, Valley Forge Post, 1986—. Sgt. U.S. Army, 1948-51. Fellow Am. Acad. Pediatrics; mem. AMA, Pa. Med. Soc., Montgomery County Med. Soc., Valley Force Pediatric Soc. (pres. 1988), King of Prussia C. of C. Office: Pediatric Assoc Inc 491 Allendale Rd King Of Prussia PA 19406-1426

SCHULTHEIS, EDWIN MILFORD, business educator; b. N.Y.C., Apr. 15, 1928; s. Milford Theodore and Lillian May (Hill) S.; BS, Hofstra Coll., 1950; MBA, N.Y. U. Grad. Sch. Bus. Adminstrn., 1958, EdD, Sch. Edn., 1972; m. Joan Edna Bruckner, June 23, 1956. Officer mgr., sales rep. Topton Rug Mfg. Co., N.Y.C., 1950-54; area mgr., trainer Mobil Oil Co., N.Y.C., 1954-62; coord. distributive edn. North Babylon (N.Y.) Pub. Schs., 1962-88; prof. bus. adminstrn. SUNY, Farmingdale, 1970—; asst. prof. edn. N.Y. U., 1973—; dir. edn. Syracuse (N.Y.) U., 1973-78; chmn. bus. mktg. and indsl. edn. depts. North Babylon (N.Y.) Pub. Schs., 1988-91, chmn. dept. bus. adminstrn. Five Towns Coll., Seaford, N.Y., 1991—; test writer, cons. N.Y. State Dept. Edn., Albany, 1965—; textbook reviewer McGraw-Hill Book Co., N.Y.C., 1967-69; cons. Cornell U., 1975; dist. adviser Distributive Edn. Clubs N.Y., 1970, bd. govs. , trustee, 1975-78; mem. curriculum adv. council Suffolk County (N.Y.) Distributive Edn. Assn., 1967—. Author: Content and Structure of Belief-Disbelief Systems, 1972. Elder Presbyn. Ch., U.S.A. Named N.Y. State Tchr. of Yr., 1976; Outstanding Tchr. in N.Y. State, 1978; recipient Outstanding Svc. award Distributive Edn. Clubs. N.Y., Suffolk County Distributive Edn. Assn., Tchr. Excellence award N.Y. State, 1980, Citation for Excellence in Edn. Gov. Mario Cuomo N.Y., 1991, Citation Excellence in Teaching Babylon Twp., 1991. Mem. Acad. Mgmt., Am. Petroleum Inst., Am. Security Coun., Suffolk County Assn. Distributive Edn. Tchrs. (mem. exec. bd. 1962-74), N.Y. State (pres. 1975-78), L.I. Distributive Edn. Assns. (hon. life, exec. bd. 1972-75), N.Y. State Occupational Edn. Assn. (v.p. 1975-78), L.I. Bus. Edn. Chmns. Assn. (hon. life), Distributive Edn. Clubs Am. (regional leader 1972-75, hon. life 1991), Phi Delta Kappa, Kappa Delta Pi, Sigma Alpha Lambda. Presbyterian (ordained ruling elder). Club: Bellport (N.Y.) Golf. Author: Modern Petroleum Marketing, 1971. Home: 10 Brendan Ave Massapequa Park NY 11762-3306 Office: Five Towns Coll Seaford NY 11783

SCHULTZ, ANDREW EDWARD, educator, editor; b. Schuyler, Nebr., Jan. 21, 1949; s. Lumir Edward and Jean Monteith (Rathbone) S.; m. Mary Clare Sutton, June 21, 1986. BS, U. Nebr., 1978, MA, 1983, PhD, 1985. Instr. Region Office of Retardation, Lincoln, Nebr., 1973-78; tchr. York (Nebr.) High Sch., 1978-79; engring. draftsman Square D Corp., Lincoln, 1979-80; tchr. Gresham (Nebr.) High Sch., 1980-82; researcher U. Nebr., Lincoln, 1982-85; prof. Calif. State U., San Bernardino, 1985-89; editor Taunton Press, Newtown, Conn., 1989—. Dir., writer: (video) Vocational Education in Times of Transition, 1984; contbr. articles to profl. jours. With USN, 1969-73. Grantee Nebr. State Adv. Com., 1984, U. Nebr. Rsch. Com., 1984, Nebr. Dept. Edn., 1984, Dept. Consumers Affairs, 1985; Cobb Meml. fellow U. Nebr., 1984-85. Mem. Internat. Tech. Edn. Assn. (chair rsch. com. 1986-88), Am. Vocat. Assn. (lobbyist, intern, 1983, 85), Assn. Psychol. Type, Phi Delta Kappa. Home: Lakeview Ter Sandy Hook CT 06482-1410 Office: Taunton Press 63 S Main St Newtown CT 06470-2344

SCHULTZ, BARBARA TOWNSEND, English educator; b. Anderson, Ind., June 1, 1929; d. Charles and Emma May (Wilson) Funkhouser; m. Marion Mayo Townsend, June 26, 1949 (dec. Dec. 1985); children: Barbara Kristin Hoover, Marion Mayo II, Paul Aaron; m. John Duncan Schultz (dec. Nov. 1989). BA, Ball State U., 1950, MA, 1954, PhD, 1972. Cert. elem. and secondary tchr., Ind. Tchr. Madison County Schs., Anderson, 1950-51, Anderson City Schs., 1951-58, Muncie (Ind.) Community Schs., 1958-68; asst. prof. English, Ball State U., Muncie, 1968-73; assoc. prof. Salisbury (Md.) State U., 1973—; adj. prof. U. Del., Georgetown. Contbr. chpt. in book. Pres. Widowed Persons Svcs., Salisbury, 1986-87. Memm. Nat. Coun. Tchrs. English, Internat. Reading Assn., Md. Assn. Tchr. Educators, Diamond State Reading Assn., Md. Libr. Assn., Mensa, Phi Delta Kappa, Kappa Delta Pi (counselor Rho Eta chpt. 1987-91, Outstanding Counselor award 1991). Home: 1505 Rose Dr Salisbury MD 21801-7230 Office: Salisbury State U 1101 Camden Ave Salisbury MD 21801-6800

SCHULTZ, DOUGLAS GEORGE, art museum director; b. Oakland, Calif., Oct. 3, 1947; s. Leon H. and Teresa (deMonte) S. A.B., U. Calif., Berkeley, 1969, M.A. in History of Art, 1972; grad., Inst. Arts Adminstrn., Harvard U., 1971. Summer intern Nat. Gallery of Art, Washington, 1970; curatorial intern Albright-Knox Art Gallery, Buffalo, 1972; asst. curator Albright-Knox Art Gallery, 1973-75, asso. curator, 1975-76, curator, 1977-79, chief curator, 1980-83, dir., 1983—; adj. prof. art history SUNY, Buffalo, 1975-79; mem. adv. bd. Arts Council of Buffalo and Erie County 1975—. Office: Albright-Knox Art Gallery 1285 Elmwood Ave Buffalo NY 14222-1096

SCHULTZ, GERALD ALFRED, chemical company executive; b. Lockport, N.Y., Jan. 22, 1941; s. Alfred Henry and Lucy Vivian (Proctor) S.; m. Barbara Joan Beals, July 13, 1962; children: Amy Lynn Schultz Poole. AAS, Erie County Tech. Inst., Buffalo, 1961; student, SUNY, Buffalo, 1975-76, Harvard U., 1979. Rsch. technician Occidential Chem. Corp., Niagara Falls, N.Y., 1961-63; rsch. engr. Nat. Gypsum Co. Inc., Buffalo, 1963-66; chemist, devel. mgr., gen. mgr. to v.p. Akzo Chems., Burt, N.Y. and Chgo., 1966-86; exec. v.p. VandeMark Chem. Co. Inc., Lockport, N.Y., 1986—. Contbr. articles to profl. jours; patentee in field. Fund raiser United Way, Newfane, N.Y., 1982-84; treas., bd. dirs. Newtane Intercommunity Meml. Hosp., 1980-84; bd. dirs. ARC, Lockport, N.Y., 1980-84. Mem. Soc. Plastic Engrs., Soc. Plastics Industry (bd. dirs. 1974-76), Organic Peroxide Prodn. Safety Div. (chmn. 1974-76),Tuscawar Club, Olcott Yacht Club (past commdr. 1975), Synthetic Organic Chem. Mfrs. Assn. (bd. dirs. 1991—), N.Y. State Bus. Coun., N.Y. State Chem. Alliance, Lockport Indsl. Coun. (treas. 1991), Ea. Niagara C. of C. Republican. Episcopalian. Home: 4025 Hartland Rd Gasport NY 14067-9318 Office: VanDeMark Chem Co Inc One North Transit Rd Lockport NY 14094

SCHULTZ, JANE SCHWARTZ, academic research administrator; b. N.Y.C., July 28, 1932; d. Jacob and Helene (Rosenthal) Schwartz; m. Jerome Samson Schultz, Sept. 1, 1955; children: Daniel S., Judith Schultz Nyquist, Kathryn Schultz Hubbard. BA in Chemistry cum laude, CUNY, 1953; MS in Chem. Engrng., Columbia U., 1955; MS in Human Genetics, U. Mich., 1968, PhD, 1970. Rsch. scientist USDA Forest Products Lab., Madison, Wis., 1955-58; sci. tchr. Pearl River (N.Y.) High Sch., 1958-64; sr. rsch. investigator dept. immunohaematology U. Leiden, Holland, 1971-72; geneticist, prin. investigator VA Med. Ctr., Ann Arbor, Mich., 1972-83; asst. prof., then assoc. prof. dept. human genetics U. Mich., Ann Arbor, 1975-83; asst. dean curriculum, then asst. dean student affairs U. Mich. Med. Sch., Ann Arbor, 1979-83; chief genetics and transplantation biology br. Nat. Inst. Allergy and Infectious Diseases/NIH, Bethesda, Md., 1983-88; dir. rsch. adminstrn. health scis. U. Pitts., 1988—, rsch. integrity officer, 1991-92; chief div. program devel. and rev. VA, Washington, 1977-79; VA liaison rep. genetics study sect. NIH, Bethesda, 1973-77; com. mem. Fed. Interagy. Com. on Recombinant DNA Rsch., Behtesda, 1977-83; VA rep. Nat. Insts. Gen. Med. Scis. Coun./NIH, Bethesda, 1979-83; mem. Organ Transplantation task force Med. Scis. Coun., NIH, Bethesda, 1985-86. Contbr. over 30 rsch. papers to peer-reviewed jours.; contbr. book revs. to profl. jours. Grantee NIH/Nat. Cancer Inst., 1975-78; recipient Pub. Health Svc. Spl. Achievement award NIAID, 1988. Mem. Am. Soc. Human Genetics, Genetics Soc. Am., Am. Assn. Immunologists, Am. Soc. Histocompatibility and Immunogenetics, Soc. Rsch. Adminstrs., Phi Beta Kappa. Office: U Pitts Oxford Bldg Rm 813 3501 Forbes Ave Pittsburgh PA 15213-3306

SCHULTZ, K. DAVID, clinical psychologist; b. Mt. Pleasant, Iowa, June 19, 1949; s. Kenneth Darrell and Virginia (Rosa) S.; m. Deborah Boettger, Jan. 6, 1980; children: Sarah, Leah. BA, U. Mich., 1971; MS, Yale U., 1973, PhD, 1976. Lic. clin. psychologist, Conn. Psychotherapist Highland Heights, New Haven, 1971-73; psychologist assoc. VA Med. ctr., West Haven, Conn., 1973-76; staff psychologist Waterbury (Conn.) Hosp. Health Ctr., 1976-85; dir. psychology Grand View Psychiat. Resource Ctr., Waterbury, 1985-90; psychologist Dept. Children and Youth Svcs., Newtown, Conn., 1990—, Grandview Psychiat. Resource Ctr., Waterbury, 1990—; pvt. practice Woodbury, Conn., 1979—; asst. clin. prof. Yale U. Sch. Medicine, 1977—. Contbr. articles to profl. jours., chpts. to books. Deacon 1st Congl. Ch., Woodbury, 1980-81; personnel com. North Congl. Ch., Woodbury, 1988—, usher ministry, 1990—. Mem. Am. Psychol. Assn., Conn. Psychol. Assn. (key psychologist 1985—), Am. Orthopsychiat. Assn., Am. Bd. Profl. Psychology. Home: 15 Laurel Wood Rd Woodbury CT 06798-2516 Office: Grandview Psychiatric Resource Ctr 88 Grandview Ave Waterbury CT 06708-2509

SCHULTZ, MICHAEL VICTOR, international trade and export promotion company executive, consultant; b. Teaneck, N.J., July 11, 1951; s. Michael Paul and Heléne Elizabeth (Ringler) S.; m. Nancy L. Grieme, June 20, 1986 (div. Oct. 1988). BS in Fgn. Svc. in Internat. Affairs, Georgetown U., 1973; MBA in Internat. Bus. Fin., Pace U., 1989. Mgr. ops. Cargo Brokerage Corp., N.Y.C., 1973-75, St. John Internat., Washington, 1975-79; regional dir. Africa and Middle East U.S. Wheat Assocs., Casablanca, Morocco, 1979-80, Cairo, 1980-87; profl. tutor Orange County Community Coll., Middletown, N.Y., 1989-90; dir. internat. svcs. Sporicidin Internat., Rockville, Md., 1991—; cons. trade and agribus., Washington, 1990—; cons. Fgn. Agrl. Svc., Nairobi, Kenya, 1979-86, Shah Enterprises, Kisumu, Kenya, 1983-86. Sec. 2720 Wisconsin Ave. Coop., Washington, 1990-91; tchr. Vol. English to Latinos, N.Y.C., Washington, 1989-91. Mem. Soc. for Internat. Devel., Georgetown U. Alumni Assn., Pace U. Alumni Assn. Democrat. Roman Catholic. Home: 2720 Wisconsin Ave NW # 205 Washington DC 20007-2313 Office: Sporicidin Internat 5901 Montrose Rd Rockville MD 20852-4753

SCHULTZ, THOMAS S., neurosurgeon; b. Cambridge, Mass., Jan. 2, 1944; s. Henry C. and Leocadia A. S. AB in Chemistry, Cornell U., 1965; MS in Biophys. Chemistry, Purdue U., 1967; MD, St. Louis U., 1970. Diplomate Am. Bd. Neurol. & Orthopaedic Surgery, Am. Bd. Disability Evaluating Physicians. NIH rsch. fellow St. Louis U. Med. Sch., 1970-72; intern, then asst. resident Harvard Surg. Svc., Boston, 1972-74; resident in neurol. surgery Neurol. Inst. Columbia Presbyn. Med. Ctr., N.Y.C., 1974-78; pvt. practice West Roxbury, Mass., 1978—. Fellow Am. Trauma Soc., Am. Acad. Sports Medicine; mem. Am. Acad. Disability Evaluating Physicians (bd. dirs., sec., v.p. 1987-92), Am. Coll. Emergency Medicine, Pewter Collecting Club Am., Cornell Club N.Y., Harvard Club Boston, Internat. Wine and Food Soc. (Mass. chpt.), U.S. Amateur Ballroom Dancers Assn. (bd. dirs. 1992). Office: 540 Vfw Pky West Roxbury MA 02132-1332

SCHULTZE, ANTOINETTE PRIEN, sculptor, political activist; b. Portsmouth, N.H., June 1, 1944; d. Alfred Gustave and Mary Ann (Marconi) Prien; m. Frederick Ralph Schultze, Nov. 24, 1961; children: Carla Schultze Spencer, Pamela, Sarah, Abel. Student, Columbia U.; studies with Felix Wolfes, Boston; studies with Roy King, Maine. Sculptor, exhibitor Maine Coast Artists, Rockport, 1983, York Inst. Mus., Saco, Maine, 1984, Fitchburg (Mass.) Mus., 1985, Concord (Mass.) Art Assn., 1986, Barn Gallery Sculpture Ct., Ogunquit, Maine, 1986, Bowdoin Coll., Brunswick, Maine, 1986, Killian Gallery, Sharon, N.H., 1987, Ariel Gallery, N.Y.C., 1985-90, Mast Cove Galleries, Kennebunkport, Maine, 1980-92, City of Stamford (Conn.)-Latham Park, 1990-92; artist in residence Berwick (Maine), 1990-91, Marshwood High Sch., Eliot, Maine, 1987, U. N.H., Durham, 1981; art tchr. Arts Inst. Manchester, N.H., 1989. Public commd. sculpture: The Mill Girl, 1988, EverGreen, 1990, Black Panther, 1984, Life Entwined, 1990. Spokesperson Maine Conservation Rights Inst., Lubec, 1991-92; video recorder Constitutional Advancement & Literacy League of Maine, Limerick, 1991-92; chmn. land use com. Comprehensive Planning Com., Eliot, Maine, 1988-92; mem. Eliot Planning Bd., 1991-92. Recipient Cert. of Excellence in Sculpture, Art Horizons Internat. Art Competition, 1988, Judge's Choice Best in Show, Kennebunk River Club Show, Kennebunkport, 1989, Juror's Choice award Copley Soc. Boston, 1991. Mem. New Eng. Sculpture Soc., N.H. Art Assn., Maine Women in Arts (bd. dirs. 1981-83), Ogunquit Art Assn. (bd. dirs. 1990-91), Copley Soc. Boston. Home: 335 Goodwin Rd Eliot ME 03903

SCHULZ, HELMUT WILHELM, chemical engineer, environmental executive; b. Berlin, July 10, 1912; came to U.S., 1924; s. Herman Ludwig Wilhelm and Emilie (Specka) S.; m. Colette Marie Francoise Prieur, Mar. 6, 1954; children: Raymond A., Caroline P., Roland W., Robert B., Thomas F. BS, Columbia U., 1933, ChE, 1934, PhD, 1942. Rsch. engr. to mng. dir. Union Carbide Corp., Charleston, W.Va., 1934-69; spl. asst. to dir. def. rsch. and engring. U.S. Dept. of Def., Washington, 1964-67; spl. asst. to U.S. commr. of edn. U.S. Dept. of Edn., Washington, 1971; sr. rsch. scientist, adj. prof. Columbia U., N.Y.C., 1972-85; pres., chief exec. officer Dynecology, Inc., Harrison, N.Y., 1974—. Contbr. articles to profl. jours. Mem. N.Y.C. Mayor's Sci. and Tech. Adv. Coun., 1973-74; bd. dirs. Charleston Symphony Orch., 1956-62, Am. Cancer Soc., W.Va., 1954-58; chmn. W.Va. AEC, Charleston, 1962-64. Grantee in field. Fellow Am. Inst. Chem. Engrs.; mem. N.Y. Acad. Sci., Am. Chem. Soc. (emeritus), N.Y. Yacht Club, Cosmos Club. Home: 611 Harrison Ave Harrison NY 10528-1406

SCHULZ, JUERGEN, art history educator; b. Kiel, Germany, Aug. 18, 1927; came to U.S., 1938; s. Johannes Martin Askan Schulz and Ilse (Lebenbaum) Hiller; m. Justine Hume, Sept. 1951 (div. 1968); children: Christoph (dec.), Ursula, Catherine; m. Anne Markham, May 19, 1969; 1 child, Jeremy. BA, U. Calif., Berkeley, 1950; PhD in Art, U. London, 1958. Reporter San Francisco Chronicle, 1950-51; copy editor UPI, London, 1952-53; from instr. to prof. history of art U. Calif., 1958-68; prof. Brown, Providence, 1968-90, Andrea V. Rosenthal prof. history art and architecture, 1990—; mem. Inst. for Advanced Study, Princeton, N.J., 1971-72. Author: Venetian Painted Ceilings of the Renaissance, 1968, Printed Plans and...Views of Venice, 1971, La cartografia tra scienza e arte, 1990; also articles. Staff sgt. U.S. Army, 1945-48. Decorated grande ufficiale Ordine della Stella della Solidarieta della Repubblica Italiana; Guggenheim fellow, 1966-67. Mem. Ateneo Veneto. Office: Brown U Dept History Art and Architecture PO Box 1855 Providence RI 02912-0001

SCHULZE, RICHARD TAYLOR, congressman; b. Phila., Aug. 7, 1929; s. John L. and Grace (Taylor) S.; m. Nancy Lockwood, May 14, 1955 (dec. Feb. 1989); children: Karen, Richard Taylor, Michael, Linda. Student, U. Houston, 1948, 50, Villanova U., 1952, Temple U., 1968. Propr. Home Appliance Ctr., Paoli, Pa., 1950—; register of wills clk. Orphans Ct., Chester County, 1967-69; mem. Pa. Ho. of Reps. from 157th dist., 1969-74; mem. 94th-102nd congresses from 5th Pa. dist., 1975—, regional whip.; mem. com. on ways and means, subcoms. on trade, oversight (ranking)and social security, com. on Interior, subcoms. on Nat. Pks. and Water, poverty, of f-shore energy resources 94th-102nd congresses from 5th Pa. dist.; exec. com., vice chmn. Congl. steel caucus, exec. com. Rep. study com. 94th-101st congresses from 5th Pa. dist.; chmn. Congl. Sportsmens Caucus. Pres., Upper Main Line Jaycees, 1956; scoutmaster local Boy Scouts Am., 1954; chmn. Chester County coun. Philmont Com., 1956; chmn. advancement com. Conestoga Dist., 1957; chmn. Paoli Meml. Hosp. Day, 1970, Tredyffrin Twp. Rep. Com., 1966; pres. Upper Main Line Young Rep. Club, 1963, Chester County Fedn. Rep. Clubs, 1965; mem. Pa. Young Reps., 1965; chmn. nominating com. Pa. Young Rep. Biennial Conv., 1966; exec. com. Chester County Rep. Com., 1965, campaign chmn., 1964, 66, 69, 70. With U.S. Army, 1951-53. Recipient Scoutmaster Key award Boy Scouts Am., 1957, Disting. Merit award, 1958, Disting. Eagle award, 1986, Retail Promotion of Yr. award Nat. Elec. Mfrs. Assn., 1965, Disting. Mcht. award GE., 1967, 68; named Outstanding Jaycee of Yr. Upper Main Line chpt. Jr. C. of C., 1955. Mem. Paoli Bus. Assn. (past v.p., dir.), Hillside Sch. PTA (charter), Great Valley Jr. C. of C., Archaeol. Inst. Am., Great Valley Assn., Register of Wills Assn. Pa., Am. Legion, Circus Saints and Sinners, Green Valleys Assn. Presbyterian. Club: Maxwell Football (Phila.). Lodge: Masons. Home: PO Box 85 Berwyn PA 19312-0085 Office: 2267 Rayburn Bldg Washington DC 20515

SCHUMACHER, JOHN WILLIAM, military officer, chaplain; b. Elkhart, Ind., June 21, 1934; s. Herman John and Julia Beatrice (Needham) S.; m. Martha Ann Catching, June 8, 1957; children: Laurie Ann Schumacher Huesmann, Julia Diane, John Christian, Eric Paul. BS, Bob Jones U., Greenville, S.C., 1957; MDiv, Grace Theol. Sem., 1963; MS in Counseling, Long Island U., 1973. Asst. prin. Whittier (Calif.) Brethrew Elem. and Jr. High Sch., 1957-60; assoc. pastor Patterson Park Brethren Ch., Dayton, Ohio, 1963-65; commd. U.S. Army, advanced through ranks to col., 1984; bn. and squadron chaplain U.S. Army, U.S. and Vietnam, 1965-69; brigade chaplain U.S. Army, various camps, 1973-78; bridgade chaplain U.S. Army, Ft. Ord, Calif., 1981-83; comman chaplain U.S. Army, Alaska, 1985-89; mem. staff and faculty War Coll. U.S. Army, 1989—; mem. bd. trustees Grace Coll. and Sem., Winona Lake, Ind., 1987—; course developer and dir. U.S. Army War Coll. Ethical Devel. Programs, 1989—. Mem. Mayor's Prayer Breakfast Com., Anchorage, Alaska, 1985-89, Gov. Prayer Breakfast Com., 1986-89; mem. advisory bd. Salvation Army, Anchorage, 1985-89. Recipient two Bronze Stars U.S. Army, Viet Nam, 1966, 1969, Meritorious Svc. Medal, 1978-89, Army Commendation medal, Army Achievement medal, Germany, 1982, Vietnamese Cross of Gallantry, Viet Nam, 1969; Named Seminary Alumnus of the Year Grace Coll. and Sem., Winona Lake, Ind., 1990. Mem. Army of the U.S., Josephson Inst. Ethics. Republican. Home: 19A Garrison Ln Carlisle PA 17013-5001 Office: US Army War Coll PO Box 505 Carlisle PA 17013-0505

SCHUMAN, CHESTER D., admissions director; b. Williamsport, Pa., Sept. 29, 1949; m. Pamela G. Schuman, May 12, 1973; children: Sarah, Lauren. AB, Susquehanna U., 1972; MEd, Memphis State U., 1974. Adminstrv. asst. Memphis State U., 1973-75; dir. of admissions Pa. Coll. of Tech., Williamsport, 1975—. Active Turbotville (Pa.) Borough Zoning Commn., 1979—; sch. dir. Warrier Run Sch., Turbotville, 1983—; dir. intermediate unit Centra Susquehanna I.V.,Montandon, Pa., 1989-91. Mem. Pa. Sch. Counselors Assn., Pa. Sch. Bd. Assn., Pa. Vocat. Edn. Assn., Nat. Audubon Soc., Ducks Unltd., Lions. Home: PO Box 169 Turbotville PA 17772-0169 Office: Pa Coll of Tech One College Ave Williamsport PA 17701

SCHUMAN, DAVID FELLER, government studies educator; b. Tulsa, Apr. 24, 1942; s. Joseph Joel and Sophie (Feller) S.; m. Barbara Ann Meyer, Sept. 30, 1976; 1 child, Benedict. BA, Tulsa U., 1964; PhD, U. Calif., Berkeley, 1971. Researcher Inst. Govt. Studies, Berkeley, 1966-68; teaching assoc. U. Calif., Berkeley, 1968-70; prof. U. Wash., Seattle, 1970-75, U. Mass., Amherst, 1975—; Cons. State of N.Y., Albany, 1990. Author: Bureaucracies, Organizations and Administration, 1976, The Ideology of Form, 1978, Policy Analyses, Education and Everyday Life, 1981, American Government: The Rules of the Game, 1984, A Preface to Politics, 5th edit., 1991; co-author: Public Administration of the United States, 1988. Recipient Disting. Teaching award U. Mass., 1980. Home: 276 Elm St Northampton MA 01060-2850

SCHUMAN, DIANA C., educator; b. N.Y.C.; d. Clarence H. and Edith (Sakellarios) Hansing; m. Robert E. Schuman; children: Kimberly, Kirt. BA, Hunter Coll., 1967; postgrad., Lehman Coll., 1968-70; postgrad, NYU, 1969. Cert. bus. tchr., Maine. Tchr. Hesser Coll., Manchester, N.H., 1972-73; sec. Spaulding High Sch., Rochester, N.H., 1974; tchr. Portsmouth (N.H.) High Sch., 1974-76, McIntosh Coll., Dover, N.H., 1974-75, 79-82, Dover (N.H.) Adult Learning Ctr., 1978-79; owner Univ. Secretarial Assocs., Dover, 1976-81; tchr. Noble High Sch., Berwick, Maine, 1982—. Active Dover Parents Music Club, 1985—, v.p., 1988-89; den leader Boy Scouts Am., 1985-89, Camp Fire Girls, Dover, 1982, 86; trustee St. John's United Meth. Ch., 1983-88, women's retreat com., 1979—, assoc. lay leader, 1992—. Mem. Maine Tchrs. Assn. (negotiation rep.), Bus. Edn. Assn. Maine.

SCHUMAN, ROBERT JAMES, psychiatrist; b. Manhasset, N.Y., Jan. 10, 1956; s. David L. and Harriet Elizabeth (Klein) S.; m. Sheri Lynn Katz, Aug. 21, 1983; children: Michael Leigh, Elisha Rebecca. BA in Psychiatry summa cum laude, Adelphi U., 1978; MD, Jefferson Med. Coll., 1984. Resident in psychiatry Westchester Med. Ctr., Valhalla, N.Y., 1984-88; attendant on staff Riverview Med. Ctr., Red Bank, N.J., 1988-90; cons. Children's Psychiat. Ctr., Monmouth County, 1988—; pvt. practice Red Bank, 1988—. Mem. Monmouth Med. Soc., Delta Tau Alpha. Jewish. Office: 225 Hwy 35 Red Bank NJ 07701-5919

SCHUMAN, SANDOR PAUL, management consultant, business executive; b. N.Y.C., Dec. 15, 1951; s. Samuel and Annette (Borstein) S.; m. Martha Louise Healy, Sept. 6, 1981; children: Benjamin Paul, Samuel Joseph, Anna Louise. BS, Cornell U., 1973; MPA, SUNY, Albany, 1979. Marine extension specialist N.Y. Sea Grant Inst., Ithaca, 1973-77; energy extension specialist N.Y. State Energy Office, Albany, 1978-79, program devel. and evaluation coord., 1980-83; decision analyst Decision Techtronics Group, Albany, 1983-85, exec. dir., 1986—; pres. Exec. Decision Svcs., Inc., Albany, 1987—; chmn. Software Chief Execs. Network, Albany, 1991-92. Contbr. articles to profl. jours. Named to Quill and Dagger Cornell U. Svc. Hon. Soc., 1972, Pi Alpha Alpha, SUNY, 1978. Mem. AAAS, Am. Soc. Pub. Adminstrn., Assn. for Computing Machinery, N.Y. State Forum for Info. Resources Mgmt., Soc. for Judgment and Decision Making, Inst. Mgmt. Scis., Alpha Phi Omega (Gamma chpt. pres. 1971-72, sectional chmn. 1973-77); Pi Alpha Alpha. Office: Exec Decision Svcs Inc PO Box 9102 Albany NY 12209-0102

SCHUMANN, CAROLE ANN, financial consultant; b. Greenwich, Conn., July 19, 1959; d. Frank Schumann and Sheila (Rooney) Schumann Hiler. BS in Mgmt., Syracuse U., 1981; Cert. Spl. Studies in Mgmt., Harvard U., 1983. Investment exec. Bear Stearns & Co., Boston, 1985; nat. sales mgr. Wang Devel. Capital Corp., Boston, 1988; investment exec. Paine Webber, Boston, 1989; fin. cons. Shearson Lehman Bros., Boston, 1990—; bd. dirs. Strategic Acctg., Boston, 1990—. Fund raiser Hunger Project, Boston, 1988; mem. com. Friends of Boston Philharmonic, 1988-91; cons. Jr. League, Boston, 1990; bd. vol. rep. Boston Ballet, 1991—. Mem. Amex Club, Boston Stock Brokers Club, Chi Omega (Rush chair, alumni cons. 1987). Republican. Home: 283 Ocean Ave Marblehead MA 01945 Office: Shearson Lehman Bros 53 State St Boston MA 02109

SCHUMER, CHARLES ELLIS, congressman; b. Bklyn., Nov. 23, 1950; s. Abraham and Selma (Rosen) S.; m. Iris Weinshall, 1980; 1 child, Jessica Emily. BA magna cum laude, Harvard U., 1971, J.D. with honors, 1974. Bar: N.Y. 1975. Mem. staff U.S. Senator Claiborne Pell, 1973; assoc. Paul, Weiss, Rifking, Wharton and Garrison, 1974; mem. N.Y. State Assembly, 1975-80, chmn. subcom. on city mgmt. and governance, 1977, chmn. com. on oversight and investigation, 1979; mem. 97th-98th Congresses from 16th N.Y. Dist.; mem. 99th-102nd Congresses from 10th N.Y. Dist., 1985—, mem. banking, interior and judiciary coms. Mem. B'nai Brith, Phi Beta Kappa. Democrat. Jewish. Office: US House of Reps Rayburn House Office Bldg Rm 2412 Washington DC 20515*

SCHUR, PETER HENRY, internist; b. Vienna, Austria, May 9, 1933; came to U.S., 1939; s. Max and Helen (Kraus) S.; m. Susan Dorfman, Sept. 3, 1963 (div. 1984); children: Diana, Erica. BS, Yale U., 1955; MD, Harvard U., 1958. Diplomate Am. Bd. Internal Medicine, Am. Bd. Allergy and Clin. Immunology. Intern, then resident Bronx (N.Y.) Mcpl. Hosp., 1958-62; postdoctoral fellow Rockefeller U., N.Y.C., 1964-67; instr., then assoc. prof. Harvard Med. Sch., Boston, 1967-81, prof. medicine, 1981—; sr. physician Robert B. Brigham Hosp., Boston, 1967-81, dir. clin. labs., 1970-81; dir. Clin. Immunology Lab. Brigham and Women's Hosp., Boston, 1981—; sr. physician, dir lupus clinic & rsch. Brigham & Women's Hosp., Boston, 1981—; Bd. dirs. Lupus Found. Am., Washington, 1979-89, pres. Mass. unit, 1989—; bd. dirs. Arthritis Found., Atlanta, 1980-85. Editor: Clinical Management of Systemic Lupus Erythematosus, 1983; co-author: In Search of the Sun, 1989; editor Arthritis and Rheumatism, 1990—; contbr. over 150 articles to med. and sci. jours. Capt. U.S. Army, 1962-64. Grantee NIH, 1967—, Lupus Found., 1975—. Fellow ACP; mem. Am. Soc. Clin. Investigation, Assn. Am. Physicians. Office: Brigham and Womens Hosp 75 Francis St Boston MA 02115-6195

SCHUR, WALTER ROBERT, physician; b. Webster, Mass., June 17, 1914; s. Robert O. and Alma L. (Gatzke) S.; student Valparaiso U., 1931-34; M.D., Middlesex U., Waltham, Mass., 1940; m. Delta Jean Newman, June 17, 1944; children—Paul, David, Jonathan, Ruth, Timothy, Peter, Stephen, Mary, Joel, Daniel, Rhoda. Resident, Milford (Del.) Meml. Hosp., 1940-41, Grace Hosp. Cleve., 1942-43; intern Lutheran Hosp., Cleve., 1941-42; pvt. practice, Oxford, Mass., 1944—; bd. dirs., pres. Doctors Hosp., Worcester, Mass., chmn. bd., 1978-87; bd. dirs. AdCare Hosp., 1987—, chmn. bd. dirs., 1987-91, Atlantic dist. Luth Ch.-Mo. Synod, 1978-87, mem., sec. edn. com., missions com., 1960-77, mem. stewardship com., youth com., edn. com., 1951-57, chmn. edn. com. Atlantic dist., 1954-57, mem. commn. on mission and ministry in ch., named Dist. Layman of Year, 1966, chmn. com. on ministry Atlantic dist., 1970; , bd. dirs. Luth. Assn. Works of Mercy, Assn. Evang. Luth. Chs.; bd. dirs. Valparaiso U., 1969—, sec., 1984—; pres., scholarship chmn. N.E. dist. Luth. Laymen's League, 1946-57; nat. bd. govs. Nat. Luth. Laymen's League, 1957; vice chmn. Luth. Hour Oper. Com., 1958, chmn. 1959-61; New Eng. bd. dirs. Assn. Evang. Luth. Chs., 1977-87, trustee East Coast Synod, 1977-87, mem. nat. bd. dirs., 1979-88; mem. council New Eng. Synod Evangelical Lutheran Ch. Am. 1988—; bd. dirs., vice chmn. French River Edn. Ctr., 1985—; mem. Oxford Sch. Com., 1961-86, Mass. Commn. on Christian Unity; assoc. charter mem. Park Ridge Ctr., 1986. Recipient award of Merit, Internat. Luth. Laymen's League, 1963. Fellow Am. Acad. Gen. Practice, Am. Acad. Family Physicians (charter); mem. AMA, Mass., Worcester Dist. med. socs., Am. Geriatrics Assn., New Eng. Obstet. and Gynecol. Soc., Valparaiso U. Alumni Assn. (past pres.), Luth. Acad. for Scholarship (bd. dirs. 1977-86), Concordia Hist. Inst., New Eng. Luth. Hist. Soc. (charter), Internat. Platform Assn., Rotary (past pres.). Home: Charlton Rd Oxford MA 01540 Office: 367 Main St Oxford MA 01540

SCHURGAST, ANSELM W., psychiatrist; b. Berlin, Germany, Mar. 7, 1921; came to U.S., 1926; s. Lothar W. and Gertrude D. (Bernstein) S. BS, U. Cin., 1943, MD, 1945. Diplomate Am. Bd. Psychiatry and Neurology. Resident R.I. State Hosp. for Mental Disease, Warwick, 1948-50; pvt. practice Providence, 1950-52, N.Y.C., 1952-53; sr. physician Conn. State Hosp., Middleton, 1953-57; pvt. practice Meriden, Conn., 1957—; dir. psychiatric svcs., WWII Meml. Hosp., Meriden, 1979-82, chief of psychiatry, 1976, 80, 81. Vol. United Fund, Meriden, 1987, 88. Capt. U.S. Army, 1946-48. Mem. AMA, Am. Psychiat. Assn. (life), New Haven County Med. Assn., Conn. Psychiat. Soc., New Eng. Soc. Clin. Hypnosis, Am. Assn. Clin. Hypnosis. Baha'i Faith. Office: Anselm W Schurgast MD PC 236 W Main St Meriden CT 06450-4026

SCHURIN, RONALD CHARLES, college administrator; b. N.Y.C., Oct. 31, 1949; s. Herman David and Evelyn Louise (Lund) S.; m. Emily Sheean Van Ness, Sept. 9, 1979; children: Zachary David, Matthew Avery. BA, U. Mich., 1971; MA in U.S. History, U. Minn., 1976; MPA, Princeton U., 1977. Speechwriter U.S. Postmaster Gen., Washington, 1970-72; cons. Rockefeller Pub. Svcs. Awards, Princeton, N.J., 1975-76, N.J. Commr. Edn., Trenton, 1976-77; policy analyst, speechwriter U.S. Dept. HEW, Washington, 1977-78; asst. to provost Baruch Coll.-CUNY, N.Y.C., 1979-81, dir. inst. rsch., 1981-88, dir. acad. planning, 1988—; cons. Hunter Coll., N.Y.C., 1988—, Rutgers Univ. Div. Consumer Health Edn., New Brunswick, N.J., 1990—. Mem. state exec. com. Minn. Dem.-Farmer-Labor Party, Mpls., 1973-75; mem. county com. Mercer County Dem. Com., Trenton, 1981—; vice-chair Affordable Housing Com., West Windsor, N.J., 1988—; mem. Unitarian Ch. of Princeton. Mem. Princeton Club N.Y. Home: 6 Springwood Dr Princeton Junction NJ 08550-1312

SCHUSSLER, THEODORE, lawyer, physician, consultant; b. N.Y.C., July 27, 1934; s. Jack and Fannie (Blank) S.; m. Barbara Ann Schussler, June 18, 1961; children—Deborah, Jonathan, Rebecca. B.A. in Polit. Sci., Bklyn. Coll., 1955; LL.B., Bklyn. Law Sch., 1958; J.D., Bklyn. Law Sch., 1967; M.D., U. Lausanne (Switzerland), 1974. Bar: N.Y. 1959, U.S. Dist. Ct. (so. and ea. dists.) N.Y. 1975, U.S. Tax Ct. 1961, U.S. Ct. Appeals (2d cir.) 1962, U.S. Supreme Ct. 1975. Clerkship and practice, N.Y.C., 1956, 58-59; legal editor tax div. Prentice-Hall, Inc., Englewood Cliffs, N.J., 1956; vol. criminal law div. Legal Aid Soc., N.Y.C., 1959; atty. legal dept. N.Y.C. Dept. Welfare, 1959-60; sole practice, N.Y.C., 1960—; sr. staff asst. IBM-Indsl. Medicine Program, 1969-70, 74-76; intern in medicine St. Vincent's Med. Center of Richmond, S.I., N.Y., 1976-77, resident emergency medicine, 1977-79, resident in gerontology, chief house physician Carmel Richmond Nursing Home, S.I.; 1978-80; surg. rotation emergency dept. Met. Hosp. Ctr., 1979; house physician dept. medicine Richmond Meml. Hosp. and Health Ctr., 1979-80; gen. practice medicine, 1980—; attending physician, chief dept. family practice, chmn. med. care evaluation, med. records and by-laws coms., former physician, advisor emergency dept., former mem. blood transfusion, credential's, emergency dept. coms., former mem. exec. com., mem. med. staff Community Hosp. of Bklyn., 1980—; attending physician Meth. Hosp., Bklyn., 1984—; supervising emergency dept. physician, dept. ambulatory care Meth. Hosp., Bklyn., 1980-83; attending physician Kings Hwy. Hosp., 1981-88, coord. emergency dept., 1981; Methodist Hosp., Bklyn., 1984—; clin. instr. dept. preventive medicine and community health, Downstate Med. Ctr. SUNY, Bklyn., 1981-88; clin. asst. prof. dept. of Preventive Medicine and Community Health, SUNY, 1988—; SUNY Health Service Ctr. med. dir. Mishkon JBFCS, Bklyn., 1982—; cons. in gerontology Palm Beach Home for Adults, Bklyn., 1980—; cons. indsl. medicine IBM, 1990-92; med.-legal cons. to professions of medicine and law. Capt. (med. corp.) USAR. Fellow Am. Coll. Legal Medicine; mem. Am. Coll. Emergency Physicians (past bd. dir. N.Y. chpt., past chmn. medico-legal com. N.Y. chpt.), Bklyn. Law Sch. Alumni Assn. (bd. dirs.), Delta Sigma Rho. Author: Torts; Jurisdiction and Practice in Federal Courts; Constitutional Law; Conflict of Laws; contbr. articles to profl. jours. Home and Office: 760 E 10th St Apt 6H Brooklyn NY 11230-2355

SCHUSTER, RICHARD LOUIS, human service agency executive, clergyman; b. Waterbury, Conn., Apr. 5, 1945; s. Robert Bryan and Mabel Margaret (Bristol) S.; m. Carolyn Schumacher, Sept. 14, 1968 (div. Dec. 1984); children: Wendi Ann, Alyson Rebecca; m. Angela Stovall, June 9, 1989. BA in Bus. and Econs., Nasson Coll., Springvale, Maine, 1968; MDiv, Yale U., 1971. Ordained priest Episcopal Ch., 1972. Curate Ch. Holy Trinity, Middletown, Conn., 1971-75; rector Joint Ministry Immanuel and St. James' Episcopal Chs., Ansonia and Derby, Conn., 1975-84; asst. dir. Episcopal Social Svc., Inc., Bridgeport, Conn., 1984-86; acting dir. St. Luke's Community Svcs., Inc., Stamford, Conn., 1986-87, exec. dir., 1987—; mem. standing com. Episcopal Diocese Conn., 1983-88, pres. 1988. Founder Lower Naugatuck Valley Community Mental Health Ctr., Ansonia, 1979; chmn. Inter-Faith Emergency Housing Project, Derby, 1981-84; pres. Conn. Coalition for Homeless, 1984-85; bd. dirs. Lower Fairfield County Coalition for Homeless, Stamford, 1987—, pres., 1988; bd. dirs. Person to Person, Darien, Conn., 1988-91, Conn. AIDS Residence Coalition, Hartford, 1988-91. Recipient Gold Seal award Lower Naugatuck Valley C. of C., 1981, Charles H. Flynn Humanitarian award Valley United Way, Ansonia, 1983, Good Neighbor award Lower Naugatuck Valley Mental Health Ctr., 1984. Office: St Luke's Commmunity Svcs 8 Woodland Pl Stamford CT 06902-6963

SCHUTTE, GILES W., mail order company executive; b. Erie, Pa., Dec. 5, 1931; m. Joan G. Todaro, June 12, 1954; children: Sharon, Anna. BA in Bus. Adminstrn, Pa. State U., 1954. C.P.A., Pa. Exec. v.p., treas., mem. exec. com. Blair Corp., Warren, Pa., 1974—; bd. dirs. Blair Corp., Warren; dir. Pennbank. Bd. dirs. Warren Gen. Hosp. Lt. (j.g.) USCG, 1955-58. Mem. AICPA, Pa. Inst. CPAs. Home: 7 Quaker Cir Warren PA 16365-4125 Office: Blair Corp 220 Hickory St Warren PA 16366-0001

SCHUTZER, DANIEL M., bank executive, researcher; b. N.Y.C., Apr. 25, 1940; s. Henry E. and Alice Schutzer; m. Myra L. Schutzer, Sept. 25, 1966; children: Eric, Richard, Pamela. BSEE, CCNY, 1961; MSEE, Syracuse U., 1962, PhD, 1965. Engr. IBM, Poughkeepsie, N.Y., 1960-62; instr. Syracuse (N.Y.) U., 1962-65; mem. tech. staff Bell Telephone Labs., Whippany, N.J., 1965-67; program mgr. Sperry Rand, N.Y.C., 1967-72; br. chief Def. Communications Agy., Reston, Va., 1972-76; tech. dir. naval intelligence, navy command and control USN, Washington, 1976-83; v.p. Citibank, N.Y.C., 1983—. Author: Military Communications, 1985, Artificial Intelligence, 1986, Computers in Business, 1990; editor: Military Command and Control, 1982. Mem. IEEE, Am. Assn. Artificial Intelligence, Sigma Xi. Office: Citibank 909 3rd Ave New York NY 10022-4731

SCHUYLER, JANE, fine arts educator; b. Flushing, N.Y., Nov. 2, 1943; d. Frank James and Helen (Oberhofer) S. BA, Queens Coll., 1965; MA, Hunter Coll., 1967; PhD, Columbia U., 1972. Asst. prof. art history Montclair State Coll., Upper Montclair, N.J., 1970; coord. fine arts, asst. prof. York Coll., CUNY, Jamaica, 1973-77, 78-87, assoc. prof., 1988—, C.W. Post Coll., L.I. Univ., Greenvale, N.Y., 1971-73, adj. assoc. prof., 1977-78. Author: Florentine Busts: Sculpted Portraiture in the Fifteenth Century, 1976; contbr. articles on occult and art to Cakes and Ale, 1978, Italian Quar., 1982, Secac Jour. on Italian Renaissance art, 1983, 85, Source, 1986-90, Studies in Iconography, 1987. Mem. Fine Arts Com. Internat. Women's Arts Festival, 1974-76; pres. United Community Dems. of Jackson Heights, 1987-89. N.Y. Columbia U. Summer Travel and Rsch. grantee, 1969; recipient PSC-CUNY Rsch. award, 1990-91. Mem. AAUP, Coll. Art Assn. Am., Women's Caucus for Art, Nat. Trust Hist. Preservation, Renaissance Soc. Am. Roman Catholic. Home: 35-37 78th St Jackson Heights NY 11372

SCHWAAR, PIERRE GEORGES, retired aerospace research engineer; b. Hauteville, Vaud, Switzerland, Apr. 30, 1921; came to U.S., 1959; s. Georges André and Bertha Emma (Bersot) S.; m. Elisabeth Marguerite Grütter, Aug. 11, 1945; children: Pierre-Yves, Fabienne, Corinne. BS, Gymnasium, Porrentruy, Berne, Switzerland, 1940; MS, diploma in Mech. Engring., Swiss Fed. Inst. Tech., Zürich, 1945. Sci. collaborator Inst. Aerodynamics, Zürich, 1953-54; mgr. Soc. Nat. d'Etudes, et de Constrn. de Moteurs d'Aviation, Paris, 1954-59; initiated/directed devel. transonic axial compressor tech.; rsch. engr. AVCO Lycoming, Stratford, Conn., 1959-62; project engr. Pratt and Whitney Aircraft, East Hartford, Conn., 1962-65; prin. engr. Textron Lycoming, Stratford, 1965-87. Contbr. articles to profl. jours. Fellow AIAA (assoc.).

SCHWAB, GEORGE DAVID, social science educator, author; b. Nov. 25, 1931; s. Arkady and Klara (Jacobson) S.; BA, City Coll. N.Y., 1954; MA, Columbia, 1955, PhD, 1968; m. Eleonora Storch, Feb. 27, 1965; children: Clarence Boris, Claude Arkady, Solan Bernhard. Lectr., Columbia Coll., N.Y.C., 1959; lectr. CUNY, 1960-68, asst. prof. history, 1968-72, assoc. prof. history, 1973-79, prof., 1980—. Mem. Columbia U. Seminar on Legal and Polit. Thought; dir. Conf. History and Politics, CUNY. Bd. dirs., sr. v.p., mem. exec. com. Nat. Com. Am. Fgn. Policy. Mem. Am. Hist. Assn., Am. Polit. Sci. Assn., Authors Guild, Conf. for Study Polit. Thought, Internat. Conf. for History 2d World War, Internat. Platform Assn. Author: Dayez: Beyond Abstract Art, 1967; Enemy oder Foe, 1968; Switzerland's Tactical Nuclear Weapons Policy, 1969; The Challenge of the Exception: An Introduction to the Political Ideas of Carl Schmitt, 1970, 2d edit., 89; Appeasement and Detente, 1975, 81; Carl Schmitt: Political Opportunist?, 1975; translator: The Concept of the Political with Comments by Leo Strauss (Carl Schmitt), 1976, Legality and Illegality as Instruments of Revolutionaries in their Quest for Power: Remarks Occasioned by the Outlook of Herbert Marcuse, 1978, The German State in Historical Perspective, 1978, Ideology: Reality or Rhetoric?, 1978, Ideology and Foreign Policy, 1978, 81, The Decision: Is the American Sovereign at Bay?, 1978; State and Nation: Toward a Further Clarification, 1980, American Foreign Politics at the Crossroads, 1980, Carl Schmitt: Through a Glass Darkly, 1980, From Quantity and Heterogeneity to Quality and Homogeneity: Toward a New Foreign Policy, 1980, Toward an Open-Society Bloc, 1980; Eurocommunism: The Ideological and Political Theoretical Foundations, 1981; American Foreign Policy at the Crossroads, 1982; A Decade of the National Committee on American Foreign Policy, 1984; Political Theology: Four Chapters on the Concept of Sovereignty (Carl Schmitt), 1985, 88, Elie Wiesel: Between Jerusalem and New York, 1990, The Destruction of a Family, 1987, The Broken Vow, the Good Obtained, 1991, Thoughts of a Collector, 1991; editor Am. Fgn. Policy Newsletter; series Global Perspectives in History and Politics. Home: 140 Riverside Dr New York NY 10024-2605 Office: CUNY New York NY 10036

SCHWAB, HAROLD LEE, lawyer; b. N.Y.C., Feb. 5, 1932; s. Harold Walter and Beatrice (Braverman) S.; m. Rowena Vivian Strauss, June 12, 1953; children: Andrew, Lisa, James. B.A., Harvard Coll., 1953; LL.B., Boston Coll., 1956. Bar: N.Y. 1957, U.S. Ct. Mil. Appeals 1958, U.S. Dist. Cts. (so. and ea. dist.) N.Y. 1967, U.S. Ct. Appeals (2d cir.) 1971, U.S. Supreme Ct. 1971, U.S. Dist. Ct. (no. dist.) N.Y. 1974, U.S. Ct. Appeals (D.C. cir.) 1986, U.S. Dist. Ct. (we. dist.) N.Y. 1988, U.S. Ct. Appeals (11th cir.) 1988, U.S. Ct. Appeals (5th cir.) 1991. Vice pres. H.W. Schwab Textile Corp., N.Y.C., 1959-60; assoc. Emile Z. Berman & A. Harold Frost, N.Y.C., 1960-67, ptnr., 1967-74; sr. ptnr. Lester Schwab Katz & Dwyer, N.Y.C., 1974—; lectr. N.Y. State Bar Assn., N.Y. County Lawyers Assn. Served to lt. col. USAFR. Mem. ABA, Soc. Automotive Engrs., Assn. for Advancement of Automotive Medicine, Product Liability Adv. Council, N.Y. State Bar Assn. (chmn. trial Lawyers sect. 1980-81), Am. Bd. Trial Advs. (pres. N.Y. chpt. 1982-83), Fedn. Ins. and Corp. Counsel (v.p. 1979-80), Assn. of Bar of City of N.Y. (subcom. product liability), N.Y. County Lawyers Assn., N.Y. State Trial Lawyers Assn., Def. Assn. N.Y. Clubs: Harvard of N.Y., Governors Island Officers, Drug and Chem., Mason. Contbr. articles to legal jours.; editor Trial Lawyers Sect. Newsletter-N.Y. State Bar Assn., 1981-84; mem. editorial bd. Jour. Products Liability, 1976—. Home: 205 Beach 142d St Neponsit NY 11694 Office: Lester Schwab Katz & Dwyer 120 Broadway New York NY 10271-0002

SCHWAB, LARRY, ophthalmologist; b. W.Va., Sept. 12, 1940; s. I. Wayne and Helen Ruth (Tidd) S.; m. Martha Harris, June 4, 1966; children: Eric, Mark, Angela. BA, W.Va. U., 1962, MD, 1966. Internship Charity Hosp. of La., New Orleans, 1966-67; residency in ophthalmology W. Va. U., 1969-72; ophthalmologist Internat. Eye Found., Ethiopia, 1972-74; asst. prof. ophthalmology W.Va. U., Morgantown, 1975, 80-82; assoc. dir. Internat. Eye Found., Kenya, 1976-80; project dir. Internat. Eye Found., Malawi, 1982-85, Internat. Eye Found., Royal Commonwealth Soc. for Blind, Zimbabwe, 1986-89; med. adviser Internat. Eye Found., Bethesda, Md., 1989—; adj. assoc. prof. W.Va. U., Morgantown, 1991—; cons. VA Hosp., Clarksburg, W.Va., 1991—. Author: Eye Care of Developing Nations, 1987, 2d edit., 1990; contbr. over 60 sci. articles to profl. jours. Capt. U.S. Army, 1967-69. Named Disting. Alumnus, 1985; recipient Internat. Eye Found. Honor award, 1989; decorated Bronze Star for Valor and Heroism, Rep. of Vietnam, 1968. Fellow Am. Acad. Ophthalmology, W.Va. Acad. Ophthalmology. Home: 3333 Collins Ferry Rd Morgantown WV 26505-2301 Office: Internat Eye Found 7801 Norfolk Ave Bethesda MD 20814-6015

SCHWAB, LEONARD CHARLES, manufacturing executive; b. N.Y.C., May 19, 1922; s. Samuel and Sylvia (Rosembaum) S.; m. Jane Holstein, Mar. 31, 1951; children: L. Tadd, Douglas S. BSME, Lehigh U., 1944. Ptnr. S. Schwab Co., Cumberland, Md., 1946-68; v.p. S. Schwab Inc., Cumberland, 1968-85, exec. v.p., 1985—. Patentee in field; inventor. Pres. Potomac council Boy Scouts Am., Cumberland, mem. NE regional bd., Edison, N.J., 1980—; bd. dirs. Lions Manor Nursing Home, Cumberland, 1977-88. Served as 1st lt. U.S. Army, 1943-52, Korea. Recipient Silver Beaver award Boy Scouts Am., Cumberland, 1969, Silver Antelope award, 1989. Mem. Am. Apparel Mfg. Assn. (com. chmn. 1975—), Allegany County Enterprise Zone Commn., Lions (local pres. 1972-73, dep. dist. gov. 1974-75, Melvin Jones fellow), Masons (33 degree Scottish Rite), Shriners. Democrat. Jewish. Office: S Schwab Co Inc Upper Potomac Industrial Pk Cumberland MD 21502

SCHWAB, THOMAS CHARLES, physician; b. Darby, Pa., Aug. 12, 1953; s. Julius Charles and Margaret (Ernst) S.; m. Anne Tyson, May 19, 1978; children: Edward, Laura. BS, Ursinus Coll., 1975; MD, Hahnemann U., 1979. Diplomate Am. Bd. Internal Medicine. Intern, resident Hahnemann Univ., Phila., 1979-82; pvt. practice internal medicine Parkesburg, Pa., 1982—. Mem. AOA Med. Honor Soc. Office: 351 W 1st Ave Parkesburg PA 19365-1201

SCHWABSKY, BARRY, arts magazine editor, poet; b. Paterson, N.J., Oct. 26, 1957; s. David and Irene (Steinberg) S.; m. Carol Szymanski, Nov. 9, 1990. BA, Haverford Coll., 1979; MA, Yale U., 1981. Mng. editor Flash Art, Milan, Italy, 1987-88; editor Arts Mag., N.Y.C., 1988—; mem. nat. profl. coun. Awards in the Visual Arts, 1989—. Author poetry chapbooks, art exhbn. catalogs. Office: Arts Mag 561 Broadway New York NY 10012-3918

SCHWANAUER, FRANCIS, philosopher, educator; b. Zsámbék, Hungary, Jan. 20, 1933; came to U.S., 1959; s. Georg and Maria (Keller) S.; m. Johanna Maria Koelln, Sept. 29, 1957; children: Stephan Michael, Miriam Frances. Maturum, Ulrich von Hutten Gymnasium, Korntal, Germany, 1954; PhD, U. Stuttgart, Germany, 1959. Asst. prof. Lebanon Valley Coll., Annville, Pa., 1960-62, U. Maine, Orono, 1962-65; assoc. prof. U. So. Maine, Portland Gorham, 1965-69, prof., 1969—. Author: Truth is a Neighborhood with Nothing in Between, 1977, Those Fallacies by Slight of Reason, 1978, No Many is not a One (For the Case is Comparison), 1981, The Flesh of Thought is Pleasure or Pain, 1982, To Make Sure is to Cohere, 1982, Philosophical Fact and Paradox, 1987, Fables from the Fox, 1991. Mem. New England Philos. Assn. Democrat. Roman Catholic. Home: 4 Woodmont St Portland ME 04102-2709

SCHWARTZ, ANTHONY, veterinary surgeon, educator; b. Bklyn., July 30, 1940; s. Murray and Miriam Sarah (Wittes) S.; m. Claudia Rosenberg, July 21, 1963; children: Thomas Frederick, Eric Leigh. Student, Mich. State U., 1957-58; DVM, Cornell U., 1963; PhD, Ohio State U., 1972. Diplomate Am. Coll. Vet. Surgeons (bd. of regents 1989-92). Gen. practice vet. medicine Huntington, N.Y., 1963-66; resident in surgery Animal Med. Ctr., N.Y.C., 1968-69; resident in surgery Ohio State U., Columbus, 1969-70, asst. prof., head sect. small animal surgery, 1973; asst. prof., then assoc. prof. Yale U. Sch. Medicine, New Haven, 1973-79; assoc. prof. then prof., chmn. dept. surgery, assoc. dean Tufts U. Sch. Vet. Medicine, Boston, 1979-89; prof., chmn. dept. surgery, assoc. dean clin. edn. Tufts U. Sch. Vet. Medicine, 1989—; cons. U.S. Surg. Corp., Norwalk, Conn., 1975—. Author: (with others) Small Animal Surgery, 1989; mem. editorial bd. Vet. Surgery, 1986-89, Jour. Investigative Surgery; assoc. editor: Text Book of Small Animal Surgery, 1985; contbr. articles to profl. jours. Capt. U.S. Army Vet Corps., 1966-68. Recipient 1st prize N.Y. State Vet. Med. Soc., 1963; Robert Wood Johnson Health Policy fellow, Washington, 1988-89; NIH grantee, 1975-84. Mem. AVMA (legis. planning com. 1989-92), AAAS, Am. Assn. Immunologists, Am. Assn. Vet Clinicians, Mass. Vet. Med. Assn. (chmn. animal welfare com. 1990-91), Sigma Xi, Phi Kappa Phi, Phi Zeta. Democrat. Jewish. Office: Tufts U Sch Vet Medicine 200 Westboro Rd North Grafton MA 01536-1895

SCHWARTZ, ARTHUR IRA, periodontist; b. Lynn, Mass., Jan. 6, 1950; s. Israel Max and Bertha (Bernstein) S.; m. Cheryl Ann Young, Sept. 3, 1972; children: Mark, Naomi, Scott. AB, Clark U., 1971; DMD, Harvard U., 1975; Cert. advanced grad. study, Boston U., 1976. Pvt. practice Stoneham, Mass., 1976—; clin. instr. sch. grad. dentistry Boston U., 1976-78, Harvard Sch. Dental Medicine, Boston, 1978-90; gen. chmn. Yankee Dental Congress, Natick, Mass., 1992. Fin. sec. Temple Israel, Swampscott, Mass., 1985-86, bd. dirs., 1981—. Fellow Pierre Fauchard Acad., 1989, Am. Coll. Dentists, 1991, Internat. Coll. Dentists, 1991. Mem. ADA, Am. Acad. Periodontology (ethics com. 1985-88), Mass. Dental Soc. (trustee 1987-91, asst. sec. 1991—), Greater Boston Dental Soc. (bd. dirs.), Harvard Odontological Soc. (bd. dirs. 1983-87). Office: 61 Main St Stoneham MA 02180

SCHWARTZ, BRUCE F., writer; b. Bklyn., Nov. 1, 1952; s. Paul I. and Mildred H. (Herman) S.; m. Cheryl A. Ferrer, July 24, 1983; children: Jason Scott, Lindsay Robyn. BA, So. Conn. State U., 1975; MS, U. Bridgeport, 1977. Broadway producer Bruce Schwartz Entertainment, N.Y.C., 1978-82; prof. U. Bridgeport, Conn., 1990-92. Author: A Tangled Web, 1986, The RH Factor, 1992; actor, dir. various prodns., 1970-78. Recipient Lincoln Ctr. award for performing arts, N.Y.C., 1969-70. Democrat. Jewish.

SCHWARTZ, CHARLES J., gastroenterologist; b. N.Y.C., July 31, 1944. BS, Tufts Coll., 1966; MD, SUNY, Bklyn., 1970. Diplomate Am. Bd. Internal Medicine. Dir. endoscopy Univ. Hosp., Boston Univ. Med. Ctr., 1975-77; dir. gastroenterology Quincy (Mass.) Hosp., 1992—. Contbr. articles to profl. jours. Mem., bd. dirs. Temple Beth David, Westwood, Mass. Capt. USAR, 1971-77. Mem. Am. Coll. Gastroenterology, ACP, AMA, Am. Soc. Gastrointestinal Endoscopy. Office: 500 Congress St Ste 3C Quincy MA 02169

SCHWARTZ, DAVID HOWARD, investment banker; b. Lake Success, N.Y., Jan. 21, 1957; s. Solomon and Florence (Zwecker) S. BA, Hofstra U., 1979, MBA, 1981; CFP, Adelphi U., 1982. Cert. fin. planner. Sales rep. Port Clyde Foods, Inc., Rockland, Maine, 1975-79; lending rep. NatWest U.S.A., N.Y.C., 1980-82; pres. First Capital Equities, Ltd., Great Neck, N.Y., 1982—, F.C.E. Realty Corp., Great Neck, 1984—; v.p. F.J.B. Devel. Corp., Great Neck, 1987—; pres. First Capital Pension Advisors Corp., Great Neck, 1985—; ptnr. First Capital Cons. Inc., 1990—; v.p. MFA Contrn. Inc., 1990—; bd. dirs. C.A.P., Inc., Westbury, N.Y., 1984—; bd. dirs. Tri-State Ins. Co., C.A.P., Inc., Westbury, N.Y. Contbr. numerous articles to newspapers and profl. jours. Mem. Inst. Cert. Planners, Internat. Assn. Cert. Planners, Real Estate Bd. of N.Y., Albert Einstein Coll. Medicine, Hadassah U. Med. Ctr., Nat. Assn., Security Dealers. Office: First Capital Equities Ltd 175 Great Neck Rd Ste 402 Great Neck NY 11021-3313

SCHWARTZ, EDWARD, health facility executive, researcher; b. Phila., Dec. 25, 1932; s. Harry and Sylvia Schwartz; m. Harriet M. Cohen, June 15, 1958; children: Lisa, Elaine, Daniel. BS in Pharmacy, Phila. Coll. Pharmacy & Sci., 1955; VMD, U. Pa., 1959; PhD in Pharmacology, Jefferson Med. Sch., 1963. Sr. toxicologist Hoffman LaRoche Inc., Nutley, N.J., 1962-65; dir. toxicology Warner Lambert Co., Morris Plains, N.J., 1965-77; sr. dir. pathology and toxicology Schering Plough Corp., Lafayette, N.J., 1977-89; v.p. rsch. White Eagle Toxicology Lab., Doylestown, Pa., 1989—. Mem. Am. Coll. Toxicology, Am. Vet. Med. Assn., Can. Soc. for Study of Toxicology, Soc. of Toxicology, Am. Soc. Pharmacology and Exptl. Therapeutics, European Soc. Toxicology. Office: White Eagle Toxicology Lab 2003 Lower State Rd Doylestown PA 18901-2603

SCHWARTZ, EDWARD A., paralegal educator, administrator; b. Paterson, N.J., Jan. 22, 1955; s. Jesse and Ida Sarah (Linevsky) S.; m. Kerry Reardon (div.); 1 child, Jeremy Daniel. BS in Bus./Mktg., Ramapo Coll. N.J., 1984. Dir. Camden Mercer County Bill Bradley for Senate, 1977-78; mgr. WAWA, Inc., 1979-82; v.p. opers. Nat. Acad. Paralegal Studies Inc., Middletown, N.Y., 1982—; news corr. Sta. WZAD Radio, Wurstboro, N.Y., 1991—; talk show host Sta. WALL Radio, Middletown, 1992—. Mem. adv. planning com. Thomas Edison State Coll., Trenton, N.J., 1990—; ednl. adv. com. 22d Congl. Dist., Middletown, 1987—. Recipient Recognition award Program on Non-Collegiate Sponsored Instrn., Trenton, 1991. Mem. Am. Vocat. Assn., Am. Assn. Adult and Continuing Edn., Nat. Paralegal Assn., Nat. Fedn. Paralegal Assn., Nat. Assn. Legal Assts., Internat. Assn. Continuing Edn. and Tng. Jewish. Home: PO Box 506 Harriman NY 10926 Office: Nat Acad Paralegal Studies 28 Industrial Dr PO Box 907 Middletown NY 10940

SCHWARTZ, GARY RAY, business educator; b. DuBois, Pa., Nov. 18, 1939; s. William Raymond Schwartz and Margaret Alice (May) Schwartz Dusch; m. Constance Lucille Whipple, Dec. 9, 1960; children: Cynthia, Gregory. BS, Ind. U. Pa., 1965; MS, Syracuse U., 1966. Div. mgr. Sears Roebuck & Co., Ind., Pa., 1961-65; instr. Auburn (N.Y.) Community Coll., 1965-66; sr. prof. Harrisburg Area Community Coll., 1966—; cosn. Schwartz Assocs., Harrisburg, 1966—. Author: (booklet) Accounting for Auctioneers, 1991. Cubmaster Boy Scouts Am.; coach elem. sch. basketball, West Hanover Twp.; sponsor parolees Camp Hill (Pa.) Correctional Instn. Named Outstanding Young Man Am. U.S. Jaycees, Pa., 1973; Corine Menk Wahr scholar Ind. U., 1965. Mem. Nat. Bus. Edn. Assn., Internat. Soc. Bus. Edn., Am. Bus. Law Assn., Pa. Bus. Edn. Assn. (state pres. 1972-73). Republican. Lutheran. Home: 7731 Valleyview Ave Harrisburg PA 17112-3872 Office: Harrisburg Area Community Coll 3300 N Cameron Street Rd Harrisburg PA 17110-2999

SCHWARTZ, GERALD ARTHUR, safety engineering consultant; b. Bklyn., May 27, 1946; s. Robert and Phyllis (Gabriel) S.; m. Sandra Joan Rappoport, June 20, 1970 (div. June 1984); children: Michael, Neil; m. Linda Sheryl Jaffe, Apr. 21, 1985; 1 child, Wendy. BAChemE, CCNY, 1970; MS, Newark Coll. Engring., 1973. Project engr. Sun Chem. Co., Staten Island, N.Y., 1970; engring. assoc. Western Electric, Princeton, N.J., 1971-74; chem. process engr. DIVA, Inc., Eatontown, N.J., 1974-76; staff engr. Ionac Chem. Co., Birmingham, N.J., 1976-79; safety specialist FMC Corp., Princeton, 1979-84; cons. Profl. Safety & Health Cons., Morrisville, Pa., 1984—; bd. dirs. Tri-Tech Labs. Inc., Gap Pa.; cons. Apex Environ. Inc., Rockville, Md., 1979-91, Atlantic Environ. Inc., Dover, N.J., 1987-82, Hillmann Environ. Inc., Union, N.J., 1991-92. Mem. Am. Indsl. Hygiene Assn. (cert.), Am. Soc. Safety Engrs. (cert.), Am. Acad. Indsl. Hygiene. Office: Profl Safety & Health Cons Inc PO Box 1059 Morrisville PA 19067-9059

SCHWARTZ, HAROLD LLOYD, business executive; b. Bklyn., June 27, 1936; s. Daid and Frieda (Streigold) S.; m. Rochelle Applebaum, Nov. 24, 1960; children: Michael, Bernard. B.S. in Acctg., Bklyn Coll., 1964. Credit analyst Dunn & Bradstreet, N.Y.C., 1959-62; sr. acct. Leon, Tarlow & Saper, N.Y.C., 1962-66; divisional controller Better Homes & Gardens, N.Y.C., 1966-72; v.p. Fince Names Unltd., N.Y.C., 1972-77; pres. Hanover House Industries, Pa., 1977—; exec. v.p. Horn & Hardart; pres. Leavitt Advt. Agy., Inc. Author: Creative Product Selling Through Catalogs, 1982. Pres. Men's Club Gt. Neck Synagogue, N.Y., 1980; bd. dirs. Bklyn. Coll., 1983. Served with U.S. Army, 1957-59. Recipient Judea award Israeli Bond Com., 1983. Mem. Direct Mktg. Assn. (bd. dirs. N.Y. chpt. 1983), Direct Mktg. Club (bd. dirs. N.Y. chpt. 1982 Direct Marketer of Yr. award), Direct Mail Info. Exchange (bd. dirs. N.Y. chpt. 1980), Third Class Mail Assn. (Officer 1980). Democrat. Jewish. Lodge: K.P. Office: Hanover House Industries Inc 340 Poplar St Hanover PA 17331-2358

SCHWARTZ, HARVEY JOEL, psychiatrist; b. N.Y.C., Mar. 29, 1951; s. Donald Schwartz and Gloria (Harris) Sackett; m. Jan Ellen Felman, June 21, 1981; 1 child, Eric Felman. BA, NYU, 1972; MD, Hahnemann Med. Coll., Phila., 1976. Diplomate Am. Bd. Psychiatry and Neurology. Pvt. practice Phila., 1979-82; dir. residency tng. Jefferson Med. Coll., Phila., 1982—. Editor three profl. books, 1984, 88, 90; contbr. articles to jours., 1987-88. Fellow Am. Psychiat. Assn.; mem. Am. Psychoanalytic Assn. (affiliate mem.), Am. Assn. Dirs. Psychiat. Residency Tng. (exec. com. 1987). Jewish. Office: Jefferson Med Coll 1015 Walnut St Philadelphia PA 19107-5005

SCHWARTZ, HENRY, artist, educator; b. Winthrop, Mass., Oct. 27, 1927; s. John and Anna (Goldberg) S. Student, Sch. of Mus. of Fine Arts, 1948-53, Yale U., summer 1953; studied with, Oskar Kokoschka, Salzburg, Austria, 1954. Tchr. Sch. of the Mus. Fine Arts, Boston, 1956—, Newton (Mass.) Arts Ctr., 1980-87. One man shows include Boris Mirski Gallery, Boston, 1956, 58, 62, 65, 68, Harvard U. Law Sch. Libr., Cambridge, Mass., 1976, Newton Arts Ctr., 1981, Fuller Mus of Art, Brockton, Mass., 1990; exhibited in group shows Chgo. Art Inst., 1952, Boston Arts Festival, 1952-64, Carnegie Inst., 1961, Parke-Bernet, N.Y., 1964, Boston U. Art Gallery, 1984, Inst. of Contemporary Art, 1986, Boston Pub. Libr., 1987; represented in pub. collections Boston Pub. Libr., DeCordova Mus. and Sculpture Park, Fuller Mus. Art, Brockton, Mass., Mus. Fine Arts, Boston, Brandeis U., Waltham, Mass., Rose Art Mus. Brandeis U., Wheaton Coll. North, Norton, Mass. With U.S. Army, 1946-47, CBI. Democrat. Jewish. Home: 8 Garrison St Boston MA 02116-5701 Office: Boston Mus Sch 230 Fenway Boston MA 02115-5534

SCHWARTZ, HILDA G., retired state judge, judicial hearing officer; b. N.Y.C.; d. Solomon and Anna Leah (Rubin) Ginsburg; m. Herman N. Schwartz, Feb. 21, 1930; 1 child, John Michael. BS, Washington Sq. Coll. of NYU; LLB, NYU, 1929. Bar: N.Y. 1930. Pvt. practice, 1930-46; sec., bur. head, trial commr. Bd. Estimate, N.Y.C., 1946-51; city magistrate City of N.Y., 1951-58, city treas., head dept. finance, 1958-62, dir. finance, 1962-64, judge civil ct., 1965-71; justice state supreme ct. State of N.Y., 1972-83; ret., 1983; jud. hearing officer State of N.Y., 1984—; counsel to law firm, 1984; chmn. law com. Bd. Magistrates, 1953-58; chmn. home term panel judges, 1954-56; judge adolescent ct., 1953-58. Mem. welfare adv. bd. N.Y. Jr. League, 1953-56; bd. mgrs. Greenwich House, 1946-48; v.p. Young Dem. club 1935-37; trustee Village Temple, 1956-61, chair dedication com., 1957; chair exec. bd. Coun. Org. Am. Jewish Congress, 1958; hon. chair, bd. dirs. Women's League for Histadrut, 1959; vice-chair Greenwich Village Fresh Air Fund, 1962; co-chair community breakfast State of Israel Bonds, 1956; bd. dirs. Washington Sq. Outdoor Art Exhibit, 1950-58, Washington Sq. Coll. Alumni Assn., 1967. Recipient Citation by Women for Achievement, 1951, Award of Merit Women Lawyers Assn. State of N.Y., 1957, Scroll of Key award Key Women, 1959, Honor award Am. Jewish Congress Coun. of Orgns., 1959, Honor award Greenwich Village Community for State of Israel Bonds, 1960, Mother of Yr. award Justice Lodge Masons, 1960, First Egalitarian award Aegis Soc., Fed. Negro Civil Svc. Orgns., 1961, Honor award B'nai B'rith, 1963, Interfaith award, 1963, Alumni Achievement award NYU Washington Sq. Coll. Alumni Assn., 1968; named Woman of Achievement Fedn. Jewish Women Orgns., 1959, Patron ann. bridge, Cath. Ctr. NYU, 1960. Mem. ABA, Assn. of Bar of City of N.Y. (mem. lectr., legal aid, matrimonial law, profl. and jud. ethics coms.), N.Y. State Assn. Women Judges (hon. mem., bd. dirs., Outstanding Jud. Achievement award 1983), Supreme Ct. Judges Assn. of City of N.Y. (bd. dirs. 1976-89), Ins. Arbitrator Forums (arbitrator), N.Y. County Lawyers Assn. (profl. ethics com.), N.Y. State Bar Assn. (jud. sabbaticals com.), N.Y. Women's Bar Assn. (past pres., founder, mem. adv. bd., scroll of honor 1958, Disting. Svc. award 1977, Lifetime Contbn. to Justice award 1984), Nat. Assn. Women Judges, Assn. Supreme Ct. Justices State of N.Y. (community rels., retirement and pensions, jud. sabbaticals coms.), Hadassah (hon. mem. N.Y. chpt. 1961), United HIAS Women's Div. (life), Emerald Soc. (hon. mem. 1961), Histradrut (hon. mem. 1960), Iota Tau Tau (hon.). Office: 43 5th Ave New York NY 10003-4368

SCHWARTZ, HOWARD ALAN, periodontist; b. Paterson, N.J., Dec. 27, 1944; s. Samuel and Ruth (Dimond) S.; m. Rita Blumenthal, Dec. 29, 1968; children: Andrew David Schwartz, Steven Austin Schwartz. BS, Fairleigh Dickinson U., 1967, DDS, 1970; cert. in periodontology, Georgetown U., 1972. State Dental Lic. N.J., N.Y., Mass., Pa., Md., Conn., Washington.

Clin. instr. in periodontics Georgetown U., 1970-72; chief resident Periodontal Section Dept. Dentistry Veteran's Adminstrn. Hosp., Washington, 1972; asst. prof. Periodontics and Oral Medicine Fairleigh Dickinson U. Sch. Dentistry, Hackensack, N.J., 1972-73, part time clin. asst. prof. Periodontics and Oral Medicine, 1973-79, part time clin. assoc. prof. Periodontics and Oral Medicine, 1979-87, part time clin. prof. Periodontics and Oral Medicine, 1987-89; pvt. practice Periodontics and Oral Medicine, 1972-91. Author: (with W.A. Gibson) Immunofluorescent Demonstration of IgG, IgM, and IgA in Human Dental Plaque, (with others) Histochemical Localization of Selected Dehydrogenases in Frozen Sections of Human Dental Plaque, (with others) Salvary Composition as related to Dental Calculus Formation in Humans. Mem. Dentist's Div. Com., Hon. Cabinet, United Jewish Community of Bergen County, 1984-85. Fellow Am. Coll. Dentists, Internat. Coll. Dentists. Mem. Am. Dental Assn., Am. Acad. Periodontology, N.J. Dental Assn., Internat. Assn. Dental Rsch., Northeastern Soc. Periodontists, Am. Acad. Oral Medicine, N.J. Soc. Periodontology, Bergen County Dental Soc., Am. Coll. Dentists, Internat. Coll. Dentists. Jewish. Home: 10 Wood Hollow Trl Saddle River NJ 07458-1346 Office: 97 N Dean St Englewood NJ 07631-2806

SCHWARTZ, JACK, physicist, consultant; b. N.Y.C., May 4, 1931; s. Aaron and Jeanette (Levine) S.; m. Joan D. Rosef, June 23, 1957; children: Gary D., Linda G. BS in Physics, CUNY, 1953; AM in Physics, Harvard U., 1954, PhD, 1958. Registered profl. engr., N.H. Rsch. assoc. Brookhaven Nat. Lab., Upton, N.Y., 1957-60; mem. tech. staff RCA Labs./Sarnoff Ctr., Princeton, N.J., 1960-64, Sanders Assocs., Nashua, N.H., 1964-83, Mitre Corp., Bedford, Mass., 1983-90; pres. Touchstone Tech., Inc., Arlington, Mass., 1983—; bd. dirs. Computer Optics, Inc., Hudson, N.H. Mem. IEEE, Soc. for Imaging Sci. & Tech. (councilor 1983—), Phi Beta Kappa, Sigma Xi. Home and Office: 147 Ridge St Arlington MA 02174-1733

SCHWARTZ, JAMES HARRIS, neurobiologist, educator; b. N.Y.C., Apr. 20, 1932; s. Milton An. and Marjorie A. (Bloom) S.; m. Frances Messik, June 30, 1963 (dec. 1984); children: Peter Joseph, Margaret Clare; m. Catherine Bing Lipkin, 1988. AB, Columbia U., 1954; MD, NYU, 1959; PhD, Rockefeller U., 1964. Asst. prof. microbiology NYU Sch. Medicine, 1964-67, assoc. prof., 1967-72, prof., 1972-74; assoc. mem. Pub. Health Rsch. Inst. City of N.Y., 1969-74; prof. physiology Columbia U. Coll. Physicians and Surgeons, 1974-76, prof. physiology and cellular biophysics, prof. neurology, 1976—; investigator Howard Hughes Med. Inst., 1984-92; vis. scholar N.Y. Psycho Analytic Inst., 1990—; vis. prof. Weitzmann Inst., 1987, Nat. Inst. Dental Rsch., 1991; cons. Nat. Inst. Neurol. and Communicative Disorders and Stroke; Wesley Spink lectr. in comparative medicine U. Minn., 1989; Jenssen disting. lectr. Soc. Neirosurg. Anesthesia and Critical Care, 1981, 89, 91. Co-editor: Principles of Neural Science, 1981; mem. edit. bd. of Brain Rsch., 1975-84, Jour. Neurophysiology, 1980-83, Jour. Neurosci., 1980-86, sect. editor, 1986-92; mem. edit. bd. Molecular Brain Rsch., 1985—; contbr. articles to profl. jours. Bd. dirs. Hebrew Free Loan Soc., 1976—. Recipient Selman A. Waksman lectureship award Theobald Smith Soc., 1968, Lucy G. Moses prize in basic neurology, 1980, Solomon A. Berson Med. Alumni Achievement award in basic sci. NYU Sch. Medicine, 1988. Fellow Am. Numis. Soc.; mem. AAAS, Am. Soc. Biochemistry and Molecular Biology, Soc. Neurosci., Am. Soc. Neurochemistry, N.Y. Acad. Scis., Harvey Soc., Sigma Xi. Office: 722 W 168th St New York NY 10032-2603

SCHWARTZ, JEFFREY STEPHEN, physician, educator; b. Paterson, N.J., May 27, 1943; s. Herbert Joseph and Anne (Fabian) S.; m. Susan Hellmann, May 7, 1967; children: Rachel, Jonathan. BA, Rutgers U., 1964; MD, Albert Einstein Coll. Medicine, 1968. Diplomate Am. Bd. Internal Medicine, Am. Bd. Cardiovascular Disease. Resident Lincoln Hosp. Albert Einstein Coll. Medicine, 1968-71; cardiology fellow Univ. Chgo., 1971-72, 74-75; asst. prof. medicine U. Minn., Mpls., 1977-83, assoc. prof. medicine, 1983-87; prof. medicine SUNY, Buffalo, 1987—; also head div. cardiology, 1991—. Contbr. articles to profl. jours. Maj. U.S. Army, 1972-74. Recipient Henry Rutgers scholarship Rutgers U., 1963-64, Young Investigator Rsch. award NIH, 1977-83, Rsch. grant NIH, 1984-87, 88-92. Mem. Am. Heart Assn., Am. Fedn. for Clin. Rsch., Phi Beta Kappa, Alpha Omega Alpha. Office: Buffalo Gen Hosp 100 High St Buffalo NY 14203

SCHWARTZ, JOEL, social worker; b. Bklyn., June 13, 1955; s. Emmanuel and Selma (Roth) S.; m. Judy Ziegler, June 21, 1978; children: Tzvi, Chavie, Tova, Mindy. BA, Bklyn. Coll., 1977; MSW, Yeshiva U., 1979. Program dir. Coun. of Jewish Orgns. of Boro. Park, Bklyn., 1979—; exec. dir. Assn. of Orthodox Jewish Scientists, Bklyn., 1982—; pub. rels. cons. Assemblyman Dov Hikind, Bklyn., 1983-84; coord. Human Svcs. Task Force, Bklyn., 1979—; cons. Bensonhurst Coun. Jewish Orgns., Bklyn., 1987-88; instr. Sch. for Lifelong Edn. Touro Coll., N.Y. Editor (resource manual) Boro Prk Guide for Human Svc. Agys., 1982. Mem. Assn. Orthodox Jewish Scientists. Home: 718 Westwood Ave Staten Island NY 10314-4108 Office: Assn Orthodox Jewish Scientists 1364 Coney Island Ave Brooklyn NY 11230-4120

SCHWARTZ, JOHN JAMES, association executive, consultant; b. New Rochelle, N.Y., Aug. 28, 1919; s. Edwin Benner and Marjorie Helen (James) S.; m. Katharine S. Sprackling, Jan. 6, 1942; children: Christopher Louis. Grad. high sch., New Rochelle; student, Mercersburg Acad., 1938. Campaign dir. John Price Jones Inc., N.Y.C., 1946-50; dir. pub. relations and fund raising Travelers Aid Soc. N.Y., N.Y.C., 1950-55; dir. devel. Community Service Soc., N.Y.C., 1955-57, Near East Found., N.Y.C., 1957-60; v.p. G.A. Brakeley & Co. Inc., N.Y.C., 1960-61; dir. devel. Fgn. Policy Assn., N.Y.C., 1962-64; asst. v.p. for crusade Am. Cancer Soc., N.Y.C., 1964-66; exec. dir. Am. Assn. Fund Raising Counsel, N.Y.C., 1966-68, exec. v.p., 1968-72, pres., 1972-87; founding bd. mem. Ind. Sector, Washington, 1980-85, mem. com. to measurably increase giving; mem., former pres. Com. on Nat. Ctr. for Charitable Stats.; spl. cons. to Com. on Pvt. Philanthropy and Pub. Needs., 1973; chair pvt. adv. group Nat. Assn. Attys. Gen. Model Law Project. Mem. adv. bd. mgmt. fund-raising NYU Cert. Program; mem. adv. coun. Grad. Sch. Mgmt. & Urban Professions, New Sch. Social Rsch.; active formation of 5 borough coalition Daring Goals for Caring Soc., N.Y.C., 1987; voting mem. N.Y. Blue Cross/Blue Shield, 1978-92; cons. Ind. U. Ctr. on Philanthropy, 1988-91, Community Counselling Svc. Co., Inc., 1988-91; pres. Nat. Philanthrophy Day, 1988-90, mem. hon. com., 1991; bd. dirs. at-large USA World Fund Raising Coun., 1992. Capt., U.S. Army Air Corps, PTO, 1941-46. Recipient Disting. Profl. Service to Philanthropy award Am. Assn. Fund-Raising Counsel, N.Y., 1976, Outstanding Agy. Profl. award United Way Am., Alexandria, 1982. Mem. Nat. Charities Info. Bur. (bd. dirs. 1978-92), Nat. Soc. Fund-Raising Execs. (bd. dirs. 1964-90, past pres.), Am. Assn. Ret. Persons (bd. dirs. Andrus Found. 1983-90), 501C-3 Soc., Princeton Club (N.Y.C.). Democrat. Unitarian.

SCHWARTZ, KOVE JEROME, lawyer, podiatrist; b. Hartford, Conn., Sept. 1, 1938; s. Maurice and Mollie (Hurwitz) S.; m. Kathleen Rossi, Apr. 26, 1972; children: Jeffrey Michael, Andrew Eric. DPM, Ohio Coll. Podiatric Medicine, 1961; BA, Cen. Conn. State U., 1972; JD, U. Conn., 1976. Bar: Conn. 1977. Practice medicine specializing in podiatrics Newington, Conn., 1961—; sole practice Newington, 1977—. Contbr. articles on med. malpractice risk mgmt. to profl. jours. Named Podiatrist of Yr. Conn. Podiatric Med. Assn., 1977. Mem. ABA, Am. Podiatric Med. Assn. (spl. editor jour. 1979, pres. 1986-87). Republican. Jewish. Home: 45 Reverknolls Avon CT 06001-2038 Office: 1247 Main St Newington CT 06111-3031

SCHWARTZ, LEONARD, psychiatrist; b. Pitts., July 10, 1925; s. Harry Morris and Jeannette (Harris) S.; m. Mildred Bernstein, Sept. 8, 1946; children: Debra Lynn Schwartz Bailey, Jodi Sue Schwartz Lindner. BS, U. Pitts., 1948, MD, 1952, cert. in psychiatry, 1956, cert. in psychoanalysis, 1968. Diplomate Am. Bd. Psychiatry and Neurology. Intern Montefiore Hosp., 1952-53; resident Western Psychiat. Inst., U. Pitts., 1953-56; pvt. practice Pitts., 1956-87; chmn. dept. psychiatry Montefiore Hosp., Pitts., 1963-87; adj. clin. prof. Dept. Health and Edn., U. Pitts. Author: heavyhands, the Ultimate Exercise, 1982, heavyhands Walking, 1987, The Heavyhands Walking Book, 1989; inventor hand weights for exercise. With USN, 1943-46. Mem. Am. Psychiat. Assn., AMA, Allegheny County Med. Soc., Am. Coll. Sports Medicine, Alpha Omega Alpha. Home: PO Box 81867 Pittsburgh PA 15217-0867

SCHWARTZ, LOUIS O., sport association executive; b. Bklyn., Apr. 20, 1927; s. Samuel and Sarah (Binder) S.; m. Elaine E. Schwartz, Sept. 5, 1968; 1 child, Scott. Grad., Latin Am. Inst., N.Y.C. and Chgo., 1946-48. Sec. of dept. Dept. Pub. Works, N.Y.C., 1962-66; asst. to v.p. McLean Svc. Co., N.Y.C., 1966-67; v.p. All Bldg. Constrn. Corp., N.Y.C., 1967-68; pres., chief exec. officer Harvard Constrn. Corp., N.Y.C., 1969-84; pres., gen. mgr. Finger Lakes Broadcasting Corp., Geneva, N.Y., 1984-88; founder, pres. Am. Sportscasters Assn., N.Y.C., 1981—; trustee Am. Sportscasters Charitable trust, N.Y.C., 1984—; insp. N.Y. State Athletic Commn., 1985—. Editor, pub. Insider Broadcasting, 1981—. With AUS, 1944-45. Mem. Nat. Assn. Broadcasters, N.Y. State Broadcasters Assn. Home: 130 Water St New York NY 10005-1637 Office: Am Sportscasters Assn 5 Beekman St New York NY 10038-2206

SCHWARTZ, LOUIS WINN, ophthalmologist; b. Pa., Apr. 19, 1942; s. Edward and Sylvia Beatrice (Winn) S.; m. Linda Weinberg, June 14, 1964; children: Joanne Karen, Geoffrey Paul. AB, Bowdoin Coll., 1963; MD, Jefferson Med. Coll., 1967. Diplomate Am. Bd. Ophthalmology. Intern Phila. Gen. Hosp.-U. Pa., 1967-68; resident in ophthalmology Wills Eye Hosp., Phila., 1970-73; ophthalmologist Ophthalmic Assocs., Lansdale, Pa., 1973—; attending surgeon Wills Eye Hosp. Glaucoma Svc., Phila., 1984—; clin. assoc. prof. ophthalmology Jefferson Med. Coll., Phila., 1984—. Coauthor: Laser Therapy of Anterior Segment, 1988, 7 other books; assoc. editor Contact Lens Assn. Ophthalmology Jour., 1988; contbr. 18 articles to profl. jours. Recipient Honor award Am. Acad. Ophthalmology, 1988. Mem. AMA, InterCounty Ophthalmol. Soc. (pres. 1985-86), Ophthalmic Club Phila. (pres. 1985-86). Office: Ophthalmic Assocs 1000 N Broad St Lansdale PA 19446

SCHWARTZ, MEL M., metallurgy and materials engineer; b. Phila., Nov. 7, 1929; s. Samuel and Bess S.; m. Carolyn Klein, Jan. 17, 1954; 1 child, Anne-Marie. BA in Metallurgy, Temple U., 1951; postgrad., U. Md., 1951-53, 57-60; MS in Engring. Mgmt., Drexel U., 1965. Metallurgist U.S. Bur. Mines, College Park, Md., 1951-52; program mgr., staff scientist, chief labs. Martin-Marietta Corp., Balt., 1954-70; dir. mfg. devel. and rsch., engring. staff Rohr Industries, Chula Vista, Calif., 1970-78; mgr. mfg. technology, materials engring. Sikorsky Aircraft, Stratford, Conn., 1978—; cons. in field; presenter lectrs., workshops, seminars for profl. socs., ednl. instns. Author: Modern Metal Joining Techniques, 1969, Metal Joining Technology, 1979, Composites, 1983, Brazing, 1988, Ceramics Structure, 1991; contbr. articles to profl. publs.; patentee, brazing paste, braze processes. Cpl., U.S. Army, 1952-54. Fellow SAMPE Internat. (George Lubin award 1986), ASM Internat.; mem. Am. Welding Soc. (com. chmn.; R.D. Thomas Meml. award 1979, Comfort Adams lectr., 1975), Welding Rsch. Coun. Home: 80 Rolling Meadow Rd Madison CT 06443-2329 Office: Sikorsky Aircraft 35 Nutmegland 6900 Main St Trumbull CT 06611

SCHWARTZ, MICHAEL ALLEN, cardiologist; b. Kansas City, Mo., Jan. 27, 1946; s. Harry and Esther (Braigan) S.; m. Diane Decher, Nov. 27, 1970; children: David, Kaben. BA, U. Mo., 1968; MD, U. So. Calif., L.A., 1972. Intern Georgetown U. med. div., D.C. Gen. Hosp., 1972-73; Resident medicine Georgetown U. Med. div. D.C. Gen. Hosp., Washington, 1973-75; fellow in cardiology U. Vt., Burlington, 1975-77; pvt. practice Cardiology Specialists, Greenbelt, Md., 1978—; med. advisor Assn. Am. RRs, Washington, 1985—. Fellow ACP, Am. Coll. Cardiology, Am. Heart Assn.; mem. AMA (physician recognition award 1984—). Office: 7500 Hanover Pky Ste 103 Greenbelt MD 20770-3634

SCHWARTZ, MURRAY MERLE, federal judge; b. 1931. BS, Wharton Sch. U. Pa., 1952; LLB, U. Pa., 1955; LLM, U. Va., 1982. Bankruptcy judge Dist. of Del., 1969-74; judge U.S. Dist. Ct. Del., 1974—, chief judge, 1985-89. Author: The Exercise of Supervisory Power by the Third Circuit Court of Appeals, 1982. Mem. ABA, Del. State Bar Assn., Am. Judicature Soc. Office: US Dist Ct 844 N King St Ste 44 Wilmington DE 19801-3578

SCHWARTZ, PAUL ARTHUR, conductor, composer; b. N.Y.C., Aug. 20, 1956; s. Arthur and Mary Emily (O'Hagan) S.; m. Charlotte Seely, Dec. 10, 1980 (div. July 1986); m. Lisa Lee Lockwood, July 10, 1988; 1 child, Matthew. MusB, Royal Coll. of Music, London, 1977. Guest condr. Ballet Rambert, Eng., 1977-79; asst. conr., music adminstr. Washington Opera, 1981-82; Steinberg fellow Pitts. Symphony, 1982-84; condr. On Your Toes, N.Y.C., 1982-84, Song and Dance, N.Y.C., 1985-86, Carrie, N.Y.C., 1988, Phantom of the Opera, N.Y.C., 1988—; cons. for music N.Y.C. Ballet, 1985-87. Composer: Trio, 1984, Virgin Forest, 1987, Arctic Fire, 1987, Archetypes, 1988, Carpenter Sonata, 1988, and the White Wind Blew, 1989, Trilogies, 1990, Olympic Fanfare, 1992. Recipient Composition prize Royal Ballet, 1980; N.Y. Found. for the Arts fellow, 1986, 90, Gulbenkian Found. fellow, 1978; Adrian Boult Conducting scholar Royal Coll. of Music, 1977.

SCHWARTZ, PAULA, French civilization and language educator; b. Washington, Sept. 18, 1953; d. Morey and Margaret (Mottillo) S. BA, Duke U., 1975; MA, Columbia U., 1981; postgrad., NYU, 1981—. Rsch. asst. Select Com. on Intelligence Activities, U.S. Senate, Washington, 1989—; asst. prof. French civilization Middlebury (Vt.) Coll., 1979—; tchr., prof. various instns., including U. Paris VIII, 1984-88; speaker on oral history, women's and French studies to nat. and internat. prof. confs. Contbr. articles to scholarly jours., chpt. to book. ITT fellow, Paris, 1977-78, Bourse Chateaubriand, Govt. of France, 1983-84, others. Mem. MLA, AAUP. Home: 105 S Main St Middlebury VT 05753-1324 Office: Middlebury Coll French Dept Middlebury VT 05753

SCHWARTZ, PERRY THOMAS, theatre, film and speech educator; b. Hartford, Wis., Aug. 14, 1940; s. Henry Herman and Helen Audrey (Wells) S.; divorced; children: Jillian (dec.), Nathan. BS speech and Theatre, Wis. State U., 1962; MA in Theatre, U. Kans., 1965; MFA Theatre Directing and Filmmaking, Ohio U., 1985. Prof. theatre Ft. Hays (Kans.) State Coll., 1965-69; prof. theatre and film St. Leo (Fla.) Coll., 1970-71; prof. theatre Bowie (Md.) State Coll., 1971-74; prodn. mgr. Washington Theatre Club, 1975-76, Am. Theatre, Washington, 1976-78; dir. Square Root of Soul Adolph Caesar Prodns., Washington and N.Y.C., 1977-79; dir., producer Playwright's Coop., Bowie, 1973-80; producing dir. Washington Theatre Wing, Silver Spring, Md., 1984-86; dir., producer Ol Black Bear Prodns., Silver Spring, 1988—; prof. theatre and speech Montgomery Coll., Takoma Park, Md., 1978—. Author: I Know What I Like, 1990; dir., producer video prodns.: Shizumi Dance Theater, 1988, Soap Opera, 1991; dir. theatre prodns. over 100 colls./communities, 1965—. Md. Arts Coun. grantee, 1989. Mem. Assn. Md. Area Media Artists (v.p. 1991—), Washington Video and Film Coun. Democrat. Office: Montgomery Coll 7600 Takoma Ave Silver Spring MD 20912-4199

SCHWARTZ, RICHARD FREDERICK, electrical engineering educator; b. Albany, N.Y., May 31, 1922; s. Frederick William and Mary Hoyle (Holland) S.; m. Ruth Louise Feldman, Oct. 25, 1945 (div. Oct. 1977); children: Kathryn Gail, Frederick Earl, Karl Edward, Eric Christian, Frieda Dianne; m. Margaret Owen Camp Boes, May 29, 1982. BSEE, Rensselaer Poly. Inst., 1943, MSEE, 1948; PhD, U. Pa., 1959. Registered profl. engr., Pa., Mich. Teaching asst., then instr. Rensselaer Poly. Inst., Troy, N.Y., 1946-48; engr. Radio Corp. of Am., Camden, N.J., 1948-51; rsch. staff mem. U. Pa., Phila., 1951-59, mem. faculty, 1959-73; prof. elec. engring., head dept. Mich. Technol. U., Houghton, 1973-79, prof. elec. engring., 1979-85; prof. elec. engring. SUNY, Binghamton, 1985—; vis. asst. prof. U. Mich., Ann Arbor, 1960; con. Pa. Bar Assn. Endowment, Armstron Cork Co., Am. Electronics Labs. Inc., IBM. Contbr. articles to profl. jours. Active Delaware County Symphony, Pa., 1867-72, Keeweenaw Symphony Orch., Houghton, 1973-85. With U.S. Army, 1942-46. Mem. IEEE, Am. Soc. Engring. Edn., AAAS, NSPE, Audio Engring. Soc., Acoustical Soc. Am., Catgut Acoustical Soc., Order of Engr., Kiwanis, Eta Kappa Nu, Sigma Xi, Tau Beta Tau. Unitarian-Universalist. Office: SUNY Sch Engring and Applied Sci Binghamton NY 13902-6000

SCHWARTZ, RICHARD HAROLD, mathematics educator; b. N.Y.C., Apr. 10, 1934; s. Joseph and Rose (Larks) S.; m. Loretta R. Susskind, Feb. 14, 1960; children: Susan Esther, David Elliot, Deborah Ann. BCE, CCNY, 1956, MCE, 1958; PhD, Rutgers U., 1967. Registered engr., N.Y. Lectr. CCNY, N.Y.C., 1956-59; instr. Rutgers Univ., New Brunswick, N.J., 1961-66; asst. prof. Pratt Inst., Bklyn., 1966-70; assoc. prof. S.I. (N.Y.) Community Coll., 1970-76, Coll. of S.I., N.Y., 1976—. Author: Judaism & Global Survival, 1984, Judaism & Vegetarianism, 1988, Math & Global Survival, 1989. Pvt. U.S. Army, 1959. Named Jewish Vegetarian of the Yr., Jewish Vegetarians of N.Am., 1987; recipient Outstanding Achievement in Math Edn. award N.Y. State Math Assn. of Two Yr. Colls., N.Y., 1991. Democrat. Office: Coll S I 715 Ocean Ter Staten Island NY 10301-4547

SCHWARTZ, RICK, importer; b. Bklyn., Apr. 1, 1948; s. David B. and Sunny (Garfunkel) S.; m. Gail Osterwell, Aug. 8, 1971; Gary, Robyn, Brian. BBA, U. Wis., 1970; MBA, NYU, 1973. V.p. Avon Glove Corp., Farmingdale, N.Y., 1970—. Bd. dirs. Manetto Hill Jewish Ctr., Plainview, N.Y., 1973—, Mid Island YM & YWHA, Plainview, 1984—. Recipient Ketem Torah, Manetto Hill Jewish Ctr., Plainview, 1991. Home: 52 Joyce Ln Woodbury NY 11797-2113

SCHWARTZ, ROBERT BERNARD, physicist; b. N.Y.C., Sept. 2, 1929; s. Jack and Lillian Gertrude (Vogel) S.; m. Rita Frances Bagley, Sept. 20, 1956; children: David, William. BS, Union Coll., 1951; MS, Yale U., 1952, PhD, 1955. Asst. physicist Brookhaven Nat. Lab., Upton, N.Y., 1955-58, 59-60; rsch. assoc. Atomic Energy Rsch. Establishment, Harwell, Eng., 1958-59; rsch. physicist Naval Rsch. Lab., Washington, 1960-62; physicist Nat. Inst. Standards and Tech., Gaithersburg, Md., 1962-74, 75—; guest scientist Atomic Energy Rsrch. Establishment, 1974-75. Contbr. 45 articles to profl. jours. Mem. Am. Phys. Soc., Health Physics Soc. Jewish. Office: Nat Inst Standards & Tech Bldg 235 Gaithersburg MD 20899

SCHWARTZ, ROBERT GEORGE, insurance company executive; b. Czechoslovakia, Mar. 27, 1928; came to U.S., 1929, naturalized, 1935; s. George and Frances (Antoni) S.; m. Caroline Bachurski, Oct. 12, 1952; children: Joanne, Tracy, Robert G. BA, Pa. State U., 1949; MBA, NYU, 1956. With Met. Life Ins. Co., N.Y.C., 1949—, v.p. securities, 1962-70, v.p., 1970-75, sr. v.p., 1975-78, exec. v.p., 1979-80, vice chmn. bd., 1980-83, chmn. investment com., 1980—, chmn. bd., 1983—, chmn. bd., pres., chief exec. officer, 1989; bd. dirs. Potlatch Corp., San Francisco, Lowe's Cos., Inc., North Wilkesboro, N.C., Communications Satellite Corp., Washington, Mobil Corp., N.Y.C., Reader's Digest Assn., Inc., Consolidated Edison Co. of N.Y., CS First Boston, Inc., Am. Quality Found., Am. Coun. Life Ins., Bus. Coun. N.Y. State. Trustee Com. for Econ. Devel., Econ. Club N.Y., Found. for Malcolm Baldridge Nat. Quality Award, Inc.; mem. bd. overseers Leonard Stern Sch. Bus., NYU. With AUS, 1950-52. Mem. Bus. Coun., Bus. Roundtable, N.Y. State Bus. Roundtable, Alpha Chi Rho. Clubs: Seaview Country (Absecon, N.J.); Springdale Country (Princeton, N.J.); Sky (N.Y.C.), Blind Brook Country. Office: Met Life Ins Co 1 Madison Ave New York NY 10010-3603

SCHWARTZ, ROBERT WILLIAM, management consultant; b. N.Y.C., Oct. 23, 1944; s. Edward and Bertha R. S.; m. Gail Beth Greenbaum, Mar. 18, 1967; children: Jill, Evan. BS, Cornell U., 1967; postgrad., SUNY, Albany, 1970. Assoc. IBM, 1967-68; cons. Peat, Marwick, Mitchell & Co., Albany, 1970-71; v.p. Security Gen. Svcs., Inc., Rochester, N.Y., 1971-73; v.p. fin. and adminstrn. Gardenway Mfg. Co., Troy, N.Y., 1973-77; exec. v.p. United Telecommunications Corp., Latham, N.Y., 1977-79; pres. United Telecommunications Corp., Latham, 1980-82; also bd. dir. United Telecommunications Corp.; pres., chmn. Winsource, Inc., Albany, 1982-85, Schwartz, Gordon, Haslin & Assoc., Inc., 1985—; bd. dirs. Caddim Corp., Union Nat. Bank, Albany, ESARCO Internat., Inc., Springfield, Mo., LBO Capital Corp., Detroit; adj. prof. Rochester Inst. Tech., 1971-73. Bd. dirs. United Cerebral Palsy of Capital Dist., 1973—; trustee Newman Found., Rensselaer Poly. Inst., 1974-78, Gov. Clinton coun. Boy Scouts Am. Mem. Am. Mgmt. Assn., Esarco Internat., Assoc. Video Hut, N.Am. Tel. Assn., Assn. for Systems Mgmt., Ft. Orange Club, Econ. Club, Corenell Club (N.Y.C.). Republican. Home: 2 Myton Ln Albany NY 12204-1310 Office: 120 Defreest Dr Troy NY 12180-8360

SCHWARTZ, SHEILA RUTH, educator; b. N.Y.C., Mar. 15, 1936; d. Mark Philip and Sylvia (Schwartz) Frackman; children: Nancy (dec.), Jonathan, Elizabeth. BA, Adelphi U., 1956; MA, Columbia U., 1958; EdD, NYU, 1964. Prof. SUNY, New Paltz, 1963—. Author: Earth in Transit, 1977, Like Mother, Like Me, 1978, Growing Up Guilty, 1978, Teaching Reading Through Adolescent Literature, 1978, Teaching Adolescent Literature, 1979, The Solid Gold Circle, 1980, One Day You'll Go, 1981, Jealousy, 1982, The Hollywood Writers' Wars, 1982, Bigger is Better, 1987, Sorority, 1987, The Most Popular Girl, 1987, and others; producer, writer (documentary film) The Children of Izieu; contbr. over 100 article, book reviews, commentaries in jours. and mags. Mem. PEN (prison writing com., children's book com. 1988—, women's com. 1987—), Authors' Guild (dir. children's book rev. svc. 1970—, dir. high/low report 1979—). Democrat. Jewish. Office: State Univ Coll New Paltz NY 12561

SCHWARTZ, SORELL LEE, pharmacologist, toxicologist, educator; b. Buffalo, Sept. 13, 1937; s. Jacob M. and Rosalind (Greenberg) S.; m. Marsha Kohlenstein, June 9, 1963; children: Joanne Beth, Rebecca Lynn. B.S., U. Md., 1959; Ph.D., Med. Coll. Va., 1963. Pharmacologist, U.S. Naval Med. Research Inst., Bethesda, Md., 1963-66, head pharmacology div., 1966-68; prof. pharmacology Georgetown U. Sch. Medicine, 1968—; sci. dir. Ctr. for Environ. Health and Human Toxicology, Washington, 1983—. Contbr. numerous articles to sci. jours. Served with USNR, 1963-66. Mem. Am. Soc. Pharmacology and Exptl. Therapeutics, Soc. Toxicology, Am. Coll. Toxicology, Am. Acad. Clin. Toxicology, Soc. Risk Analysis. Jewish. Address: Georgetown U Dept Pharmacology Sch Medicine Washington DC 20007

SCHWARTZ, STEPHEN EUGENE, physical chemist; b. St. Louis, June 18, 1941; s. Alfred Seymour and Ellen Jane (Freund) S.; m. Carolyn Rosenberg, Aug. 23, 1964 (div. 1977); 1 child, Arielle; m. Sherry R. Blick, June 29, 1980; 1 child, David Blick. AB, Harvard U., 1963; PhD, U. Calif., Berkeley, 1968. Postdoctoral fellow U. Cambridge (Eng.) Dept. Phys. Chemistry, 1968-69; asst. prof. dept. chemistry SUNY, Stony Brook, 1969-75; assoc. chemist Dept. Applied Sci. Brookhaven Nat. Lab., Upton, N.Y., 1975-77, chemist, 1977-90, sr. chemist, 1991—; mem. com. atmospheric chemistry U.S. Nat. Rsch. Coun., 1988-91. Assoc. editor Atmospheric Environment, 1984—, Jour. Geophys. Rsch. Atmospheres, 1986-89; mem. editorial adv. bd. Internat. Jour. Chem. Kinetics, 1990—; N.Am. editor chemistry Urban Atmosphere, 1991—; editor: Trace Atmospheric Constituents, 1983; contbr. articles to profl. jours. Mem. AAAS, Am. Chem. Soc., Am. Phys. Soc., Am. Geophys. Union, Am. Meteorol. Soc. (com. atmospheric chemistry 1985-91). Home: 12 Mallard Dr Center Moriches NY 11934-3106 Office: Brookhaven Nat Lab Dept Applied Sci 51 Bell Ave Bldg 426 Upton NY 11973-9999

SCHWARTZ, STEVEN HARVEY, dentist; b. Queens, N.Y., Feb. 5, 1948; s. Michael M. and Adele (Zweig) S.; m. Helen R. Schulberg, June 14, 1970; children: Daniel, Jill, Jonathan. BS, SUNY, Binghamton, N.Y., 1968; DMD, Tufts U., 1972. Dental surgeon USAF, Hampton, Va., 1972-74; ptnr. Drs. Jerome Cohen-Steven Schwartz, Budd Lake, N.J., 1975—; cons. in field. Pres. Hebrew Acad. of Morris County, Randolph, N.J., 1986-88; area chmn. UJA Nat. Youth Leadership Cabinet, N.Y.C., 1987—; bd. dirs. United Jewish Fedn. Metro West, E. Orange, N.J., 1989. Fellow Acad. Gen. Dentistry; mem. Am. Dental Assn., N.J. Dental Assn., Tri County Dental Assn., N.Am. Jewish Forum. Republican. Jewish. Home: 30 Deer Run Dr Randolph NJ 07869-4333 Office: Cohen & Schwartz DMD PA Village Green Shopping Ctr Budd Lake NJ 07828

SCHWARTZ, SUSAN ELISABETH BRALOFF, executive search consultant; b. N.Y.C., June 14, 1956; d. Max E. and Lillian (Braloff) S. BA, Harvard U., 1978. Account exec. Grey Advt., N.Y.C., 1981-85; sr. account exec. Doyle Dane Bernbach, N.Y.C., 1985-86; v.p. client svcs. Arbeit and Co., N.Y.C., 1986-87; cons. Korn/Ferry Internat., N.Y.C., 1988—. Mem. Nat. Speleological Soc. (cave diving sect.), Harvard Club N.Y.C. (admissions com. 1975—, program com.). Home: 308 E 79th St New York NY 10021-0904 Office: Korn/Ferry Internat 237 Park Ave New York NY 10017-3142

SCHWARTZ, TERI J(EAN), clinical psychologist; b. N.Y.C., Dec. 30, 1949; d. Jerome and Shirley Ruth (Dushkind) Kraus; m. Raymond C. Schwartz; children: Rachel, Michael, Daniel. BA, Queens Coll., 1971; MS, C.W. Post Ctr., 1974; MA, New Sch. for Social Rsch., 1977, PhD, 1980. Staff psychologist to chief psychologist New Hope Guild, Howard Beach, N.Y., 1982-85, 85—; staff psychologist Queens Child Guidance Ctr., Flushing, N.Y., 1985-88; staff psychotherapist Adelphi Univ.-Postdoctoral Psychotherapy Ctr., Garden City, N.Y., 1984—; pvt. practice, clin. psychologist Briarwood and Floral Park, N.Y., 1984—; adj. clin. supr. Yeshiva Univ., Bronx, 1987—; clin. supr. Adelphi Univ., Garden City, 1991—, assoc. clin. prof., 1992—. Mem. exec. bd. Briarwood (N.Y.) Civic Assn., 1984—; adv. bd. Queens Community Mental Health Ctr. and Area D Subcom.-Queens Hosp. Ctr., Jamaica, N.Y., 1984—. Mem. Am. Psychol. Assn., N.Y. State Psychol. Assn., Adelphi Soc. for Psychoanalysis and Psychotherapy, Nassau County Psychol. Assn., Queens County Psychol. Assn.

SCHWARTZ, THOMAS ALAN, civil engineering consultant; b. Plainfield, N.J., Jan. 31, 1951; s. Herbert M. and Carolyn (Lowe) S.; m. Mary Ada Morris, Aug. 12, 1979; children: Carolyn, Trevor, Kevin. BSCE, Tufts U., 1973; SM, MIT, 1977. Registered profl. engr., Mass., N.H., Md., Fla., N.J., Va. Prin. Simpson Gumpertz & Heger Inc., Arlington, Mass., 1973—. Patentee ski binding. Mem. ASTM (chmn. subcom. 1980—), Sigma Xi, Tau Beta Pi. Office: Simpson Gumpertz & Heger 297 Broadway Arlington MA 02174-5394

SCHWARTZ, VALERIE BREUER, interior designer; b. Senica, Czechoslovakia, May 13, 1912; came to U.S., 1928, naturalized, 1928; d. Jacob and Ethel (Weiss) Breuer; m. Leo Schwartz, Feb. 5, 1939; children—Catherine, Robert, William. Student States Real Gymnazium, Prague, 1925-28; Parsons N.Y. Sch. of Fine and Applied Arts, 1930-32. Cert. Am. Soc. Interior Designers. Self-employed interior designer, N.J., 1932—. Contbr. to various mags. including N.Y. Times, House & Garden, Cue Mag., Confort, Argentina; guest radio talk shows. Mem. Hadassah (life). Designed Holocaust Room, Kean Coll., N.J.

SCHWARTZ, WILLIAM, lawyer; b. Providence, May 6, 1933; s. Morris Victor and Martha (Glassman) S.; m. Bernice Konigsberg, Jan. 13, 1957; children: Alan Gershon, Robin Libby. A.A., Boston U., 1952, J.D. magna cum laude, 1955, M.A., 1960; postgrad., Harvard Law Sch., 1955-56. Bar: D.C. 1956, Mass. 1962, N.Y. 1989. Prof. law Boston U., 1955-91, Fletcher prof. law, 1968-70, Roscoe Pound prof. law, 1970-73, dean Sch. of Law, 1980-88, dir. Ctr. for Estate Planning, 1988-91; Univ. Prof. Yeshiva U., N.Y.C., 1991—; of counsel firm Swartz & Swartz, Boston, 1973-80; counsel Cadwalader, Wickersham and Taft, N.Y.C., Washington, L.A., Palm Beach, 1988—; mem. faculty Frances Glessner Lee Inst., Harvard Med. Sch., Nat. Coll. Probate Judges, 1970, 77, 78, 79, 88; gen. dir. Assn. Trial Lawyers Am., 1968-73; reporter New Eng. Trial Judges Conf., 1965-67; participant Nat. Met. Cts. Conf., 1968; dir. Mass. Probate Study, 1976—; chmn. spl. com. on police procedures City of Boston, 1989, 91; vice chmn. bd. UST Corp.; bd. dirs. Viacom Inc., Viacom Internat. Inc., U.S.T. Corp.; mem. legal adv. com. N.Y. Stock Exch. Author: Future Interests and Estate Planning, 1965, 77, 81, 86, Comparative Negligence, 1970, A Products Liability Primer, 1970, Civil Trial Practice Manual, 1972, New Vistas in Litigation, 1973, Massachusetts Pleading and Practice, 7 vols., 1974-80, Estate Planning and Living Trusts, 1990, others; note editor: Boston U. Law Rev., 1954-55; property editor: Annual Survey of Mass. Law, 1960—; contbr. articles to legal jours. Bd. dirs. Kerry Found.; trustee Hebrew Coll., 1975—, Salve Regina Univ.; rep. Office Public Info., UN, 1968-73; chmn. legal adv. panel Nat. Commn. Med. Malpractice, 1972-73; examiner of titles Commonwealth of Mass., 1964—; spl. counsel Mass. Bay Transp. Authority, 1979; trustee Yeshivah U. Recipient Homer Albers award Boston U., 1955, John Ordronaux prize, 1955; Disting. Service award Religious Zionists Am., 1977; William W. Treat award; William O. Douglas award. Fellow Am. Coll. Probate Counsel; mem. ABA, Am. Law Inst., Mass. Bar Assn. (chmn. task force tort liability), Nat. Coll. Probate Judges (hon. mem.), Phi Beta Kappa. Office: 100 Maiden Ln New York NY 10038-4818

SCHWARTZMAN, JACK, lawyer, educator, writer; b. Vinnitsa, Ukraine, Mar. 22, 1912; came to U.S., 1925; s. Solomon and Anna (Toporoff) S.; m. Vivian Reicher (dec. 1988); children: Steven, Marcia, Robert. BS, CCNY, 1936; LLB, Bklyn. Law Sch., 1936, JSD, 1953; PhD, NYU, 1970. Bar: N.Y. 1938. Instr., Henry George Sch., N.Y.C., 1938-40, 46-49, 68-72, Rhodes Sch., N.Y.C., 1956-60; editor, writer Fragments Quar., Floral Park, N.Y., 1963—; prof. English, philosophy Nassau Community Coll., SUNY, Garden City, 1964—; pvt. practice law, N.Y.C., L.I., 1938—; lectr. in field. Author: Rebels of Individualism, 1949; Alleged Rights to Organize Under the Soviet Constitution, 1953, The Philosophy and Politics of Paul N. Miliukov, 1970; contbr. chpts. to books and over 400 articles to profl. jours. Served to capt. AUS, 1942-46. Decorated Citation for the Army Commendation; recipient Founders Day award NYU, 1971; N.Y. State Chancellor's award for excellence in teaching SUNY, 1974. Mem. N.Y. State Bar Assn., Disting. Teaching Professorship (rev. com.), MLA, Thoreau Soc., Albert Jay Nock Soc., Council of Georgist Orgns., Univ. Profs. Acad. Order, Acad. of Polit. Sci., Found. for Econ. Edn., Albert Keith Chesterton Soc., Christopher Morley Knothole Assn., Internat. Platform Assn., N.Y. Acad. of Sci., Walt Whitman Assn. (Camden chpt.), Walt Whitman Birthplace Assn. (Huntington chpt.), Henry George Inst. (bd. dirs.), Walden Forever Free (bd. sponsors), Townsend Harris Alumni Assn., Bklyn. Law Sch. Alumni Assn., NYU Alumni Assn., CCNY Alumni Assn., Pi Sigma Alpha, Phi Theta Kappa. Office: 87-16 Winchester Blvd Ste 3E Bellerose NY 11427

SCHWARTZMAN, RONALD NEIL, lawyer; b. Hagerstown, Md., Sept. 28, 1953; s. Samuel L. and Doris H. (Greenwald) S.; m. Susan F. Strauss, May 31, 1987. AB, Vassar Coll., 1975; JD, U. Fla., Gainesville, 1977. Bar: Fla. 1978, N.Y. 1980. Assoc. Stuzin & Camner, Miami, Fla., 1978-79; ptnr. Pollner, Mezan & Stolzberg, N.Y.C., 1979-90, Gold & Wachtel, N.Y.C., 1990—. Sr. articles and tax editor U. Fla. Law Rev., 1976-77. Mem. Vol. Lawyers for the Arts, N.Y.C., 1983-90, Jr. Friends Lenox Hill Hosp., N.Y.C., 1987-90; bd. dirs. Watery Star Theatre, N.Y.C., 1986-88. Mem. Alumnae/i Assn. of Vassar Coll. (1st nat. v.p. 1992—), Vassar Club of N.Y. (pres. 1988-90), Order of the Coif, Phi Kappa Phi. Office: Gold & Wachtel 110 E 59th St New York NY 10022-1304

SCHWARZ, DANIEL ROGER, English educator; b. Rockville Centre, N.Y., May 12, 1941; s. Joseph Alexander and Florence (Rimler) S.; m. Marcia Mitson, Sept. 1, 1963 (div. 1986); children: David K., Jeffrey C. BA, Union Coll., 1963; MA, Brown U., 1965, PhD, 1968. Asst. prof. Cornell U., Ithaca, N.Y., 1968-74, assoc. prof., 1974-80, prof., 1980—, dir. undergrad. studies in English, 1976-82; disting. vis. Cooper prof. U. Ark., Little Rock, 1988; vis. citizen's prof. lit. U. Hawaii, 1992-93; dir. Summer Seminars for Coll. Tchrs. on Modernism, NEH, 1984, 86, 88, 90, Summer Seminars for Secondary Tchrs. on James Joyce, 1985, 87, 89, 91. Author: Narrative and Representation in Poetry of Wallace Stevens, The Case for a Humanistic Poetics, 1991, The Transformation of the English Novel, 1890-1930, 1989, Reading Joyce's Ulysses, 1987, rev. 1991, The Humanistic Heritage; Critical Theories of the English Novel from James to Hillis Miller, 1986, rev., 1989, Conrad; The Later Fiction, 1982, Conrad: Almayer's Folly to Under Western Eyes, 1980, Diraeli's Fiction, 1979. Bd. mem. Freeville Planning Bd., 1968-74, Freeville Zoning Bd., 1968-74. Grantee, Am. Philos. Soc., 1981, NEH, 1984, 85, 86, 87, 88, 89, 90, 91. Mem. Internat. Narrative Soc. (pres. 1990-91), MLA, James Joyce Soc. Jewish. Home: 925 Mitchell St # 3 Ithaca NY 14850-4936 Office: Cornell Univ 304 Rockefeller Hall Ithaca NY 14853

SCHWARZ, EKKEHART RICHARD JOHANNES, architect, urban designer; b. Stettin, Fed. Republic Germany, Sept. 12, 1938; came to U.S., 1970; s. Walter and Barbara Elisabeth (Doberman) S.; m. Elaine Carmella Wong, Sept. 12, 1982; children: Elisabeth Barbara Alicia, Patricia Kathrina. Diploma in architektur, T.U. Berlin, 1969; MArch, U. Calif., Berkeley, 1971. Registered architect, N.Y. Draftsman Hans Scharoun, West Berlin, Fed. Republic Germany, 1964, J.P. Kleihues, Architect, West Berlin, 1970; urban design cons. The Architects Renewal Com. in Harlem, N.Y.C., 1972; urban designer Urban Design sect. NYC Dept. of Transp., 1972, architect-in-charge Urban Design sect., 1977-84, dir. Office of Urban Design, 1984-86; prin. Schwarz and Zambanini, P.C. Architecture Engring., N.Y.C., 1987—. Mem. Tribeca Community Orgn., N.Y.C., 1984. Mem. AIA, Am. Inst. Cert. Planners. Lutheran. Office: Schwarz and Zambanini PC 28 Hubert St New York NY 10013-2041

SCHWARZ, KARL OTTO, physician; b. Arad, Romania, Feb. 12, 1949; came to U.S., 1980; s. Andreas and Juliana (Hönig) S.; m. Susan Chi-Ching Shen, Dec. 21, 1982; 1 child, Charlotte Maria. MD, Tel-Aviv U., 1975. Resident Mt. Sinai Med. Ctr., N.Y.C., 1980-83, Albert Einstein Coll. Medicine, Bronx, 1983-84, U. Health Ctr., Pitts., 1984-85, Allegheny County Coroner's Office, Pitts., 1985-86; chief lab. svc. Highland Dr. VA Med. Ctr., Pitts., 1988; chief, sect. of neuropathology Robert Wood Johnson Med. Sch., New Brunswick, N.J., 1988—. Home: 327 N 8th Ave Edison NJ 08817-2914 Office: Robert Wood Johnson Med Sch Dept Pathology One Robert Wood Johnson Pl New Brunswick NJ 08903-0019

SCHWARZ, KATHLEEN ANN BROGAN, pediatrics educator, physician; b. Des Moines, Feb. 6, 1942; d. Griffith Elihu Brogan and Carolyn (Chaney) Green; m. Frederick Henry Schwarz, Dec. 27, 1966; children: Kurt Frederick, Arthur Axel. BA in Biology, Scripps Coll., 1964; MAT in Biology and French, Northwestern U., 1965; postgrad., Univ. Cen. de Venezuela, 1968-70; MD, Washington U., St. Louis, 1972. Intern in pediatrics St. Louis Children's Hosp., 1972-73, asst. resdient in pediatrics, 1973-74, fellow in pediatric gastroenterology and nutrition, 1974-76; instr. pediatric gastroenterology dept. pediatrics Washington U., St. Louis Children's Hosp., 1977-78; NIH trainee in gastroenterology Barnes Hosp., St. Louis, 1976; instr. in medicine dept. internat. medicine Washington U., Barnes Hosp., St. Louis, 1977-78; asst. prof. pediatrics St. Louis U. Sch. Medicine, 1978-83; asst. prof. pediatrics Div. Pediatric Gastroenterology and Nutrition Johns Hopkins U. Sch. Medicine, 1987-89; chmn. div. pediatric gastroenterology St. Louis U. Sch. Medicine, 1978-87; mem. staff Cardinal Glennon Childrens Hosp., 1978-87, St. Louis U. Hosp., 1987, U. Md. Med. Systems, 1987—; assoc. prof. pediatrics St. Louis U. Sch. Medicine, 1983-87; assoc. prof. Johns Hopkins U. Sch. Medicine, 1989—. Author: (with others) Textbook of Gastroenterology and Nutrition in Infancy Vol. 2, 1981, Nutrition in Pediatrics - Basic Sciences and Clinical Applications, 1985, Textbook of Gastroenterology and Nutrition in Infancy, 1989, Practical Gastroenterology, 1989, Primary Pediatric Care, 1990; contbr. numerous articles and abstracts to profl. jours. Recipient Thomas Wilson Sanitarium award, 1991; grantee Washington U. Clin. Rsch. Ctr., 1978, biol. sci. rsch. grantee Johns Hopkins/NIH, 1989-90. Mem. Am. Acad. Pediatrics, N.Am. Soc. for Pediatric Gastroenterology (chmn. by-laws com., coun. mem. 1989—), Am. Inst. Nutrition, Am. Soc. Clin. Nutrition, Am. Assn. for the Study of Liver Diseases, Soc. for Pediatric Rsch., Am. Gastroenterology Assn. Episcopalian. Office: Johns Hopkins Hosp Brady 320 600 N Wolfe St Baltimore MD 21205-2104

SCHWARZ, MAURICE JACOB, pharmaceutical company executive; b. Northampton, Eng., Sept. 13, 1939; came to U.S., 1939; s. Ernst L. and Guste Elaine (Cohen) S.; m. Sandra Ann Murray, Apr. 3, 1965; children: Rachel Lisa, Jessica Eden. BA in Chemistry, U. Oreg., 1962, PhD in Chemistry, 1965; postgrad., Columbia U., 1981. Various positions Ciba-Geigy Corp., various locations, 1967-75; v.p. pharm. R & D, Ciba-Geigy Corp., Summit, N.J., 1975—; chmn. R & D Coun. N.J., 1991-93. Capt. U.S. Army, 1965-67. Mem. Pharm. Mfrs. Assn. (steering com. pharm. devel. subsect. 1990).

SCHWARZ, PETER KARL, secondary educator; b. Unterhammer, Fed. Republic of Germany, Aug. 24, 1944; came to U.S., 1974; s. Peter and Anna Schwarz. BA, Paedagogische Hochschule, Kaiserslautern, Fed. Republic Germany, 1969; MA, U. Richmond, 1976, U. Md., 1979. Cert. ESL tchr., Md. Tchr. State Schs. Rhineland-Palatinate, Mainz, Fed. Republic Germany, 1969-74; instr. German U. Richmond (Va.), 1975-76, U. Md., College Park, 1978-84, George Mason U., Fairfax, Va., 1983—; tchr. German and French Winston Churchill High Sch., Potomac, Md., 1985-90; tchr. Richard Montgomery High Sch., Rockville, Md., 1990-91; lectr. George Washington U., Washington, 1982-85; coord. U. Md. Exch. Program, U. Kassel (Federal Republic Germany), 1983; co-producer CHASCO, ednl. TV, Waldorf, Md., 1984. Co-author: (anthology) Women in German Literature, 1986; editor: (bibliography) German Teaching Material, 1979; contbr. to Women Writers in Germany, Austria and Switzerland, 1989; translator: Humanismus Germanicuss, 1981. Holt scholar, 1977; Prahl fellow, 1980. Mem. Am. Assn. Tchrs. German (v.p. Md. chpt. 1981-83, pres. 1983-86, chmn. 1986-90), Phi Kappa Phi. Home: 1016 Robroy Dr Silver Spring MD 20903

SCHWARZWALDER, DANIEL ROBERT, retail executive; b. Bklyn., Aug. 6, 1948; s. Gus and Elfrieda (Mann) S.; m. Susan Denise Silver; children: Michael, Dana, Sara. BA, Queens Coll., Flushing, 1970; MBA, Wharton Grad. Sch., 1972. Mdse. v.p. Abraham and Straus div. Federated Dept. Stores, Bklyn., 1972-82; asst. to pres. Miller Wohl Co., Secaucus, N.J., 1982-84; pres., chief exec. officer Mothercare Stores, Inc., Secaucus, 1984—. Mem. Young Pres. Orgn., Queens Coll. Alumni Assn. (bd. dirs. 1972-74, trustee 1972—), Kiwanis (award 1970). Home: 106 Van Riper Ln Westwood NJ 07675-8221 Office: Mothercare Stores Inc 80 Enterprise Ave S Secaucus NJ 07094-1902

SCHWEBEL, MILTON, psychologist, educator; b. Troy, N.Y., May 11, 1914; s. Frank and Sarah (Oxenhandler) S.; m. Bernice Lois Davison, Sept. 3, 1939; children—Andrew I., Robert S. A.B., Union Coll., 1934; M.A., SUNY, Albany, 1936; Ph.D., Columbia U., 1949; certificate in psychotherapy, Postgrad. Center for Mental Health, 1958. Diplomate: Am. Bd. Examiners Profl. Psychology; licensed psychologist, N.Y., N.J. Asst. prof. psychology Mohawk Champlain Coll., 1946-49; asst. to prof. edn., dept. chmn., assoc. dean NYU, 1949-67; dean, prof. Grad. Sch. Edn., Rutgers U., New Brunswick, N.J., 1967-77; prof. Grad. Sch. Applied and Profl. Psychology, 1977-85, prof. emeritus, 1985—; sr. rsch. scholar Ctr. for Psychol. Studies in the Nuclear Age, Harvard U.; vis. prof. U. So. Calif., U. Hawaii; lectr. psychologist Postgrad. Ctr. for Mental Health, 1958-60; cons. NIMH, U.S., state, city depts. edn., ednl. ministries Europe, Asia, UNESCO, univs. and pub. schs.; pvt. cons. psychologist and psychotherapist, 1953—. Author, co-author numerous books including A Guide to a Happier Family, 1989, Personal Adjustment and Growth, 1990, Student Teachers Handbook, 2d edit., 1992; editor: Mental Health Implications of Life in the Nuclear Age, 1986, Facilitating Cognitive Development, 1986, Promoting Cognitive Growth over the Life Span, 1990; co-editor Bull. Peace Psychology, 1992—; mem. editorial bd. Am. Jour. Orthopsychiatry, Readings in Mental Health, Jour. Contemporary Psychotherapy, Jour. Counseling Psychology, Jour. Social Issues, others. Mem. sci. adv. bd. Internat. Ctr for Enhancement of Learning Potential, 1988—; trustee Edn. Law Center, 1973-81; trustee Nat. Com. Employment Youth, Nat. Child Labor Com., 1967-75, Union Exptl. Colls. and Univs., 1976-78; pres. Nat. Orgn. for Migrant Children, 1980-85, Art Found. N.D., 1984—. Served with AUS, 1943-46, ETO. Postdoctoral fellow Postgrad. Center for Mental Health, 1954-56; Met. Applied Research Council fellow, 1970-71. Fellow APA, Am. Psychol. Soc., Am. Orthopsychiatry Assn., Soc. POsychol. Study Social Issues, Jean Piaget Soc. (trustee), Am. Ednl. Rsch. Assn., N.Y. Acad. Scis., Psychologists for Social Responsibility (pres.). Home: 1050 George St Apt 17L New Brunswick NJ 08901-1011 Office: Rutgers U Grad Sch Applied and Profl Psychology Piscataway NJ 08854

SCHWEIGER, ANTHONY WALTER, mortgage company executive; b. Phila., Nov. 25, 1941; s. Jerome Walter and Hannah (Zinman) S.; m. Sally Jane Grossman, Aug. 4, 1964 (div. 1972), m. Katherine M. Dratt, 1984; children: David Michael, Suzanne, Jonathan Landau, Philip Miguel. BS in Econs., U. Pa., 1964; MBA, Temple U., 1968. With South Jersey Mortgage Co., Camden, N.J., 1959-75, Assoc. Mortgage Cos., Camden, 1959-75; v.p. Bowest Corp., Los Angeles, 1975-77; pres. Mortgage Investment Securities, Clearwater, Fla., 1977-78; sr. v.p. Arvida Mortgage Co., Miami, Fla., 1978-80; mng. ptnr. Schweiger and Assocs., Cherry Hill, N.J., 1980-83; exec. v.p., chief operating officer Meridian Mortgage Corp., Wayne, Pa., 1983-87, pres., chief exec. officer, 1987—. Gen. chmn. Jaycee Football Classic, Princeton, 1969; asst. sec. N.J. Jaycees, Princeton, 1969; active Fedn. Jewish Agys. Mem. MBA Am. (bd. govs. 1988—). Republican. Jewish. Lodge: Masons. Home: 958 Derring Ln Bryn Mawr PA 19010-1749 Office: Meridian Mortgage Corp 744 W Lancaster Ave Wayne PA 19087-2523

SCHWEIKERT, EDGAR OSKAR, dentist; b. Heidelberg, Fed. Republic Germany, Aug. 30, 1938; came to U.S., 1972; s. Oskar and Priska (Zehr) S.; m. Mary Lou Como, Apr. 7, 1969; 1 child, Marisa. Degree, Hamburg Dental Sch., 1966; Dr. Med. Dentistry, U. Munich, 1969. Lic. dentist, Calif., N.Y. Dentist, U.S. Army, Frankfurt, Fed. Republic Germany, 1969-72; gen. practice dentistry, L.A., 1972-73, Bklyn., 1973—; lectr. in field. Author Multiple Cantilevers in Fixed Prosthesis, 1988, Spanish edit., 1990; contbr. articles to profl. jours. Served as capt. German Air Force, 1967-69. Mem. ADA, German Dental Assn., Second Dist. Dental Assn., Bay Ridge Dental Soc., Guild Dental Craftsmen. Home and Office: 429 77th St Brooklyn NY 11209

SCHWEITZER, BARBARA MICHELE, mental health therapist; b. Butler, Pa., Aug. 17, 1965; d. Raymond Joseph and Patricia Ann (Kerin) S. BA, Edinboro (Pa.) U., 1986; MEd, Auburn U., 1990. Appointment sec. Office of the Mayor, Montgomery, Ala., 1987-90; mental health therapist Turtle Creek (Pa.) Valley Mental Health/Mental Retardation, 1990—; sec. Student Govt. Assn., Edinboro, 1983-86; intern Pa. State Bd. of Probation and Parole, Pitts., 1986, Julia Tutwiler Prison fro Women, Wetumpka, Ala., 1989-90. Mem. Montgomery (Ala.) Young Reps., 1987-90; vol. Emory Folmar for Mayor, Montgomery, 1987, George Bush for Pres., Montgomery, 1988. Mem. AACD, Pub. Offender's Counselor's Assn., Ala. Assn. for Counseling and Devel., Marriage and Family Counselor's Assn. Roman Catholic. Home: 174 Senate Dr Pittsburgh PA 15236-4416

SCHWEITZER, PAUL JEROME, operations research specialist, educator; b. N.Y.C., Jan. 16, 1941; s. Louis and Martha Schweitzer; children: Tzvia, Seth, Yonatan. BS, MIT, 1961, DSc, 1965. Rsch. staff Inst. for Def. Analyses, Arlington, Va., 1965-70; vis. faculty Technion-IIT, Haifa, Israel, 1970-72; rsch. staff IBM, Yorktown Heights, N.Y., 1972-77; faculty U. Rochester, N.Y., 1977—. Assoc. editor: Ops. Rsch. Letters, IIE Transactions; contbr. numerous articles to profl. jours. Mem. Ops. Rsch. Soc. Am., Beta Gamma Sigma, Sigma Xi. Office: U Rochester Simon Sch Rochester NY 14627

SCHWEIZER, CHARLES THOMAS, food/pharmaceutical executive; b. Rutherford, N.J., Nov. 15, 1935; m. Oct. 3, 1959; children: Douglas, Diane. BS, F.D.U., 1959; MBA, NYU, 1968. Mgr. CPC Internat., Englewood, N.J., 1973-79; gen. mgr. Borden Internat., N.Y.C., 1979-84; mktg. mgr. Cardi Foods, Rockaway, N.J., 1980-84; v.p. Pharbita, Parsippany, N.J., 1984—, also bd. dirs.; bd. dirs. Cardi Foods, Wenzhou-Pharbita Joint Venture, Pharbita. With U.S. Army, 1957-59. Home: 46 Rainbow Trl Denville NJ 07834-3208

SCHWEIZER, PAUL DOUGLAS, museum director; b. Bklyn., Nov. 26, 1946; s. Alvin Charles and Marie Gertrude (Scholtz) S.; m. Jane Kulczycki, June 10, 1978. BA, Marietta Coll., Ohio, 1968; MA, U. Del., 1975, PhD, 1979; postgrad. Mus. Mgmt. Inst., U. Calif., Berkeley, 1990. Instr. art history St Lawrence U., Canton, N.Y., 1977-78; asst. prof. St. Lawrence U., Canton, N.Y., 1978-80; curator St. Lawrence U. (Brush Gallery), Canton, N.Y., 1977-78; dir. St. Lawrence U., Canton, N.Y., 1979-80, Munson-Williams-Proctor Inst. Mus. Art, Utica, N.Y., 1980—. Author exhbn. catalog; contbr. articles to profl. jours. Bd. dirs. Remington Art Mus., Ogdensburg, N.Y., 1979-80; bd. dirs. Williamstown (Mass.) Regional Art Conservation Lab., 1981-92, pres., 1988-92. Ensign USN, 1968-69. Rsch. grantee Nat. Endowment for Arts, 1978. Mem. Coll. Art Assn., Assn. Art Mus. Dirs., Alpha Sigma Phi, Omicron Delta Kappa. Clubs: Ft. Schuyler (Utica); Otsego Sailing (Cooperstown, N.Y.). Office: Munson-Williams-Proctor Inst Mus Art 310 Genesee St Utica NY 13502-4799

SCHWEMMER, GEARY KARL, electronics engineer; b. Balt., May 16, 1953; s. Karl and Audrey Francis (Jett) S.; m. Sharon Weems Bland, Sept. 17, 1977; children: Justin Karl, Daniel Robert, Marshall Austin. BSEE, U. Md., 1976. Program analyst U. Md., College Park, 1974-77; electronic engr. NASA Goddard Space Flight Ctr., Greenbelt, Md., 1977—; cons. in field; vis. scientist Inst. Phys. Sci. and Tech., U. Md., 1986-88. Co-author: Optical and Laser Remote Sensing, 1983, Tunable Solid State Lasers for Remote Sensing, 1986; contbr. articles to profl. jours.; patentee and inventor in field. Cub scout den leader Boy Scouts Am., Hampstead, Md., 1988—. Mem. AIAA, Optical Soc. Am. Office: NASA Goddard Space Flight Code 917 Greenbelt MD 20771

SCHWENSFEIR, ROBERT JAMES, JR., physicist; b. Hartford, Conn., June 27, 1934; s. Robert James and Elizabeth Mary (Condron) S.; m. Margaret Mary Gagosz, June 17, 1967; children: Thomas Michael, Michael Patrick, Mary Elizabeth. BA in Physics with distinction, Wesleyan U., 1956; MS in Physics, Trinity Coll, Hartford, Conn., 1960; PhD in Physics, Brown U., 1966. Exptl. nuclear physicist Pratt & Whitney Aircraft, Middletown, Conn., 1956-60, rsch. assoc., 1966-68; grad. rsch. asst. Brown U., Providence, 1960-66; asst. prof. physics Bucknell U., Lewisburg, Pa., 1968-74; nuclear criticality safety engr. United Nuclear Corp., Uncasville, Conn., 1974-76, nuclear criticality safety specialist, 1976-79; mgr. nuclear safety and materials Tex. Instruments Inc., Attleboro, Mass., 1979-81, mem. tech. staff, 1981-85; dir. tech. svcs. Cook-Horton div. Stern-Leach, North Attleboro, Mass., 1986-89, Polymetall. Corp. div. Stern-Leach, North Attleboro, 1990—; cons. United Nuclear Corp., Uncasville, 1979—; presenter in field. Contbr. articles to profl. jours. Grantee NSF, 1970, Bucknell U., 1969-70. Mem. AAAS, ASTM, ASM Internat. (vice chmn. R.I. chpt. 1988-89, chmn. 1989-90, mem. exec. com. 1987—), Am. Phys. Soc., Am. Assn. Physics Tchrs., Sigma Xi, Phi Beta Kappa. Roman Catholic. Home: 54 Marlise Dr Attleboro MA 02703-6535 Office: Polymetall Corp PO Box 3249 North Attleboro MA 02761-3249

SCHWEPPE, HENRY NELSON, III, management consultant; b. Alton, Ill., Apr. 10, 1963; s. Henry Nelson Jr. and Janet (Schranz) S.; m. Elaine McCurdy, Oct. 11, 1986. BSBA in Acctg., Wash. U., 1985. Sr. fin. analyst Centerre Bank NA, St. Louis, 1985-88; cons. Price Waterhouse, St. Louis, 1988-89, N.Y.C., 1989—; trustee Monticello Coll. Found., Godfrey, Ill., 1986—. Mem. Nat. Assn. Accts., Am. Mgmt. Assn.

SCHWERDT, LISA MARY, language professional, English; b. Coral Gables, Fla., Feb. 7, 1953; d. Henry G. and Dilys Doris (Bandurske) S. BS, Fla. Internat. U., 1973, BA, 1977; MA, Purdue U., 1979, PhD, 1984. Cert. secondary educator English, spl. edn., Fla. English instr. Green Sch. of English, Tokyo, Japan, 1973-75; spl. edn. tchr. Carol City (Fla.) Elem. Sch., 1975-77; grad. instr. Purdue U., West Lafayette, Ind., 1977-85; asst. prof. U. North Ala., Florence, 1985-89; adj. lectr. U. Cen. Fla., Orlando, 1989-90, Rollins Coll., Winter Pk., Fla., 1989-90; asst. prof. English Calif. U. of Pa., 1990—. Author: Isherwood's Fiction, 1989; contbr. articles and book revs. to profl. jours. Mem. ACLU, Pitts., 1990—, Sierra Club, Pitts., 1990—, Planned Parenthood, Pitts., 1986—. Grantee Purdue Found., 1982; recipient Excellence in Teaching award Purdue U., 1979, 81. Mem. MLA, Coll. English Assn., Nat. Coun. Tchrs. English, Mid. Atlantic MLA, Soc. for the Study Narrative Lit., Soc. for Health and Human Values. Unitarian. Home: 620 Royal Dr Library PA 15129-8509 Office: Calif Univ of Pa Dept of English California PA 15419

SCHWERT, G(EORGE) WILLIAM, III, finance educator; b. Durham, N.C., Jan. 26, 1950; s. George William Jr. and Margaret (Houlton) S.; m. Camille Matthews, Dec. 19, 1970 (div. 1983); 1 child, Lisa Margaret; m. Patricia Michel, Dec. 23, 1983; children: Michael William, Andrew Patrick. AB in Econs. with honors, Trinity Coll., 1971; MBA, U. Chgo., 1973, PhD in Fin., 1975. Asst. prof. Grad. Sch. Bus. U. Chgo., 1975-76; asst. prof. to prof. Grad. Sch. Mgmt. U. Rochester, N.Y., 1976-86, Gleason prof. fin., 1986—; chmn. Knollwood Cons. Group, Inc., Rochester, 1987—. Co-editor Jour. Fin. Econs., 1979-86, 89—, adv. editor, 1986-89; assoc. editor Jour. Fin., 1983—, Jour. Monetary Econs., 1984—; contbr. articles to econs. jour. Recipient Smith-Breeden Disting. Paper prize Jour. Fin., 1990, Gahamand Dodd plaque Fin. Analysts Jour., 1990. Mem. Am. Fin. Assn. (bd. dirs. 1987-89), Am. Econs. Assn., Econometrics Soc., Am. Statis. Assn. (chair bus. econs. sect. 1990-91). Home: 71 Knollwood Dr Rochester NY 14618-3512 Office: U Rochester W E Simon Grad Sch Bus Adminstrn Rochester NY 14627

SCHWESIG, CLAUDE RUDOLF EMIL, accountant; b. Montreal, Que., Can., Sept. 20, 1945; came to U.S., 1981; s. Friedrich Wilhelm and Luise Meta

(Dirschauer) S.; m. Patricia Netherwood, June 25, 1976; children: Evianne Angelica, Lianna Victoria.. BComm with honours, Sir George Williams U., Montreal, 1973; diploma French studies, U. Neuchatel (Switzerland), 1977. CPA, Vt. Various positions Assoc Textiles Can., Montreal, 1963-7l; compt. Viva Mills Ltd., Granby, Que., 1971-74; sec.-treas. Municipality Canton and La Ville, Sutton, Que., 1974-76; pvt. practice Sutton, 1978-81; ptnr. Herrick Ltd., CPA's, Burlington, Vt., 1982—; cons. Paramount Farms Ltd., Sutton, 1979-81; co-ptnr. 29 de la Rue Principale, Sutton, 1980-83; lectr. acctg. Dist. Bedford Continuing Edn., Cowansville, Que., 1978-81. Contbr. articles to profl. publs. and newspapers. First reader 1st Ch. Christ, Scientist, Montreal, 1972-74, chmn. exec. bd., Burlington, 1988-92; mcpl. councillor Canton of Sutton, 1979-81; mem. planning com. Vt. Mozart Festival, Burlington, 1988, 91—; fin. chmn. Parc Sutton, 1980-82; acct. Oriana Singers, Burlington, 1985—. Protestant Sch. Bd. Excelsior scholar, Montreal, 1962. Mem. AICPA, Vt. Soc. CPAs (chmn. ethics com. 1988-91, treas. 1991—), Nat Assn. Profl. Accts. Home: PO Box 44 Charlotte VT 05445-0044 Office: Herrick Ltd CPA's 72 Main St Burlington VT 05401-8419

SCHWISTER, JAY EDWARD, portfolio manager; b. Milw., Apr. 16, 1962; s. Jerome Charles and Carol Christina (Keeler) S.; m. Theresa Marie Pierce, Oct. 27, 1990. BS in Fin. cum laude, Marquette U., 1984. Chartered fin. analyst. Sr. investment officer First Wis. Trust Co., Milw., 1984-87; sr. v.p., sr. portfolio mgr. The Putnam Cos., Boston, 1987—; fin. com. mem. Hills Residence Adv. Com., Wayland, Mass., 1990—; investment cons. Menomonee Mut. Ins., Menomonee Falls, Wis., 1984—. Fund raising com. Marquette U. Alumni Fund, Boston, 1989—. Mem. Assn. for Investment Mgmt. and Rsch., Boston Security Analysts Soc., Inc., Bond Analysts Soc., Inc., Beta Gamma Sigma. Home: 83 Hillside Dr Wayland MA 01778-3826 Office: The Putnam Cos One Post Office Sq 9th Fl Boston MA 02109

SCIACCA, KATHLEEN, psychologist; b. N.Y.C., Jan. 19, 1943; d. Rosario and Angela (Pucciarelli) S.; children: Kenneth Mortellaro, Cheryl Ann Mortellaro. BS in Psychology, SUNY, Empire State, 1976; MA in Psychology, New Sch. for Social Rsch., 1980, postgrad., 1980. Pvt. practice, 1976—; primary therapist, vocat. coord., program developer Bronx-Lebanon Hosp., South Bronx, N.Y., 1977-84; mental health program specialist N.Y. State Office of Mental Health, various cities, 1984—; founding exec. dir. Sciacca Comprehensive Svc. Devel. Mental Illness, Drug Addiction and Alcoholism, N.Y.C., 1990—, nat. lectr., program developer for multiple disorders; cons. program devel. Am. Assn. for Partial Hospitalization, Washington, 1987-91, Columbia U., N.Y.C., 1991, numerous mental health depts. across the country; nat. presenter and cons. in field. Author/developer: (manual-book) Mental Illness, Drug Addiction and Alcoholism Svc. Manual, 1990; contbr. articles to profl. jours. Mem. APA (assoc.), N.Y. State Psychol. Assn. (assoc., com. on Alcoholism, Drug Abuse and other Addictions), Soc. Psychologists in Addictive Behaviors. Home and Office: 299 Riverside Dr #3E New York NY 10025-5278

SCIALABBA, ARTHUR JOSEPH, systems analyst; b. N.Y.C., Apr. 14, 1966; s. Vincent Joseph and Elizabeth Ruth (Costa) S. Student, Western Conn. State U., 1984-87. Tech. support person MCI, Rye Brook, N.Y., 1986-87, product mgr., 1987-88, systems analyst, 1989—; v.p., treas. Creative Computer Systems, Inc., Danbury, Conn., 1986-88; cons. Creative Computer Systems, Inc., 1986-88. Author: (computer program) Reducing Fractions, 1978. Constable Danbury Police Dept., 1985-88; Rep. candidate for 3rd Ward Common Coun., 1989. Mem. Am. Radio Relay League, IEEE, Computer Soc. Republican. Episcopalian. Home: 54 Danbury Rd Ste 170 Ridgefield CT 06877

SCIAME, JOSEPH, university administrator; b. Bklyn., Sept. 9, 1941; s. Joseph and Sophie (Pintacuda) S. EdB, St. John's U., 1971. Fin. aid officer, asst. to dean of admissions St. John's U., Jamaica, N.Y., 1967-71, dir. fin. aid, 1971-82, dean fin. aid, 1982, v.p., 1982—; pres. N.Y. Assoc. Student Fin. Aid Adminstrn., 1980-82, Ea. Assoc. Student Fin. Aid Adminstrn., 1986-87; chmn. Nat. Assoc. Student Fin. Aid Adminstrn., 1987-88. Chmn. bd. ethics Town of North Hemps, N.Y., 1984—; nat. chmn., bd. dirs. Garibaldi-Meucci Mus., N.Y., 1987-93. Recipient Disting. Svc. award Nat. Assn. Student Fin. Aid Adminstrs., 1988, Achievement award N.Y. State Fin. Aid Adminstrs., 1982, Congl. Record award Congress, 1979, 91. Mem. Knights of the Equestrian Order of the Holy Sepulchre (Knight with Grand Cross elevated 1991, Knight invested 1980), Order Sons of Italy in Am. (pres. 1974-75, state v.p. 1989—). Roman Catholic. Home: 6 Jones St New Hyde Park NY 11040-1616 also: Trout Ln Southampton NY 11969 Office: St John's U Jamaica NY 11439

SCIANDRA, MARIA THERESA, accountant; b. Pittston, Pa., Feb. 16, 1967; d. Ross John and Lucy Ann (Krukowski) S. BS in Acctg., U. Scranton, 1989. Jr. acct. Tinsley & Co., P.C., Wilkers-Barre, Pa., 1989-90; asst. contr. Suburban Publishers, Exeter, Pa., 1990-91; asst. to chm. bd., chief exec. office Gruen Mktg. Corp., Exeter, 1991—; Active Vol. Income Tax Assistance Program, mem. 1988, sr. coord. 1989, cert. 1989, 90. Donor to ARD; active St. Rocco's Roman Cath. Ch., Pittston. Recipient Presdl. scholarship U. Scranton, 1985-89, Redginton Gen. scholarship, 1985-89, Gunster scholarship, 1985-89. Democrat. Home: 131 Market St Pittston PA 18640-1436 Office: Gruen Mktg Corp 150 Susquehanna Ave Pittston PA 18643-2668

SCIANNA, COSIMO, photographer, commercial director; b. N.Y.C., Jan. 13, 1941; s. Mario and Anna (Palumbo) S.; m. Carole DiGiorgio, May 27, 1961 (div. 1965); 1 child, Lisa; m. Irene Flaxman, June 12, 1971; children: Paul, Stephanie. Student sch. art and design, Pratt Inst. Comml. dir., photographer Cosimo's Studio Inc., N.Y.C., pres., 1972—; adj. instr. Sch. Visual Arts; lectr, conductor seminars in field. Contbg. photographer to profl. publs. including Backstage , CA mag. Millimeter mag., Photo Dist. News; exhibited in shows at Kodak Pavilion, EPCOT Ctr., Fla., Neikrug Photographic Gallery, Nikon Gallery, APA Gallery, ICP/Midtown; juror Canadian Advt. Photographers, Toronto. Recipient numerous awards including 8 Clios, 17 Andys, 3 Tellys, Grand award Internat. Film Festivals, Chgo., N.Y.C., Best TV Comml. Advt. Age mag., 10 Creativity awards Art Direction mag., 8 Merit awards Art. Dirs. Club. Mem. Am. Soc. Mag. Photographers, Am. Photographers Assn., Soc. Illustrators (Merit award), Dirs. Guild Am., Image Bank, Broadcast Employees and Technicians, Internat. Photographers of Motion Picture and TV Industries (local). Office: Cosimo's Studio Inc 43 W 13th St New York NY 10011-7910

SCIARRATTA, PATRICK LOUIS, director, educator, artistic director; b. Bklyn., Dec. 5, 1951; s. Pasquale Joseph and Antoinette (Angeleri) S.; m. Jane Goodrich Searle, Oct. 19, 1991. BA in Theatre, Queens Coll./CUNY, 1974; MA in Theatre Anthropology, NYU, 1983. Movement program dir. for performing arts dept. Adelphi Univ., Garden City, N.Y., 1976-79; theatre dept. faculty L.I. Univ., Brookdale, N.Y., 1979-81; campus events dir. Iona Coll., Seton Campus, Yonkers, N.Y., 1986-87; performing arts dir. Hunter College, N.Y.C., 1987—; founder, artistic dir., pres., bd. dirs. Bond St. Theatre, N.Y.C., 1976—; founder, dir. Palenville N.Y. Interarts Colony, 1983—; resident dir. Israel Festval, Jerusalem, 1985; artistic dir. Barondess Theatre Lab, N.Y.C., 1988—; critic Show Bus. Mag., 1978-82. Playwright: The Hunger Artist, 1977; lead actor in Emmy-award-winning prodn. Great Performances Spl.: The Orch., PBS-TV, 1990. Mem. Yorkville Civic Coun. (art com.), N.Y.C., 1991—. Recipient MacArthur award John D. and Catherine MacArthur Found., 1990. Office: Hunter Coll 695 Park Ave New York NY 10021-5085

SCIGLIANO, J. MICHAEL, chemicals executive; b. Omaha, Nov. 22, 1941; s. Joseph and Irene Carol (Campbell) S.; m. Beverly Carol King, June 23, 1964; children: Julie Ann, David Michael. BSChemE and Indsl. Adminstrn., Iowa State U., 1964, MS in Indsl. Engring., 1965; DSc in Chem. Engring., Washington U., St. Louis, 1971. Process engr. Monsanto Co., St. Louis, 1965-68, project mgr., 1969-71, engring. supr., 1972-75; devel. mgr. Air Products & Chems., Allentown, Pa., 1975-76, process design mgr., 1977-82; corp. engring. mgr. Johnson Matthey Inc., Valley Forge, Pa., 1983-86, catalyst bus. mgr., 1987-90; tech. dir. Rodel, Inc., Newark, Del., 1990—. Coauthor book chpt.; contbr. articles to profl. jours. Lay leader Grove United Meth. Ch., 1986-89. Mem. Am. Inst. Chem. Engrs., Phi Kappa Phi. Home: 2 Karrington Dr Newark DE 19711-2800 Office: Rodel Inc 451 Bellevue Rd Newark DE 19713-3473

SCIOCCHETTI, PETER AUGUSTO, real estate property manager; b. Niskayuna, N.Y., May 27, 1957; s. Augusto and Josephine Sciocchetti; m. Marie Ravaioli, Apr. 17, 1982; children: Alyssa, Christopher. AAS in Mktg., Hudson Valley Community Coll., Troy, N.Y., 1979; BSBA, Coll. of St. Rose, 1982. Gen. mgr. Brook Fin. Corp., Albany, N.Y., 1985-86; regional property mgr. United Realty Mgmt. Corp., Albany, 1986-92; v.p. real estate Fulton County Econ. Devel. Corp., Johnstown, N.Y., 1992—; pvt. cons. State of N.Y., 1985—, cert. instr., 1991. Mem. Inst. Real Estate Mgmt., Bldg. Owners and Mgrs. Assn., Albany County Bd. Realtors, Inc., Nat. Ctr. for Housing Mgmt. (cert.). Office: Fulton County Econ Devel Corp Crossroads Indsl Park RR 1 9 Balzano Rd Johnstown NY 12095

SCIORTINO, J. PAUL, hospital representative; b. Huntington, N.Y., Nov. 26, 1958; s. John Paul and Maryellen (Duquette) S.; m. Vanessa Sue Dunderman, Sept. 30, 1988. BS, SUNY, Oswego, 1980. Cert. secondary tchr., N.Y. Tchr. Ballston Spa (N.Y.) High Sch., 1980-81, Berlin (N.Y.) High Sch., 1981-82; gen. mgr., wholesale dir. DBA Fish Restaurant, Saratoga Springs, N.Y., 1982-84; direct sales rep. Weather Shield Mfg., Camp Hill, Pa., 1984; regional sales rep. Weather Shield Vt., Burlington, 1984-86; profl. sales rep., focus group leader, dist. trainer Key Pharms., Kenilworth, N.J., 1986-89; sr. clin. hosp. rep. Genentech, Inc., So. San Francisco, 1989—. Dir. team Champlain Valley (Vt.) Soccer League.

SCIRICA, ANTHONY JOSEPH, federal judge; b. Norristown, Pa., Dec. 16, 1940; s. A. Benjamin and Anna (Scalfani) S.; m. Susan Morgan, May 6, 1966; children—Benjamin, Sara. B.A., Wesleyan U., 1962; J.D., U. Mich., 1965; postgrad., Central U., Caracas, Venezuela, 1966. Bar: Pa., 1966, U.S. Dist. Ct. (ea. dist.) Pa., 1984, U.S. Ct. Appeals (3d cir.), 1987. Ptnr. McGrory, Scirica, Wentz & Fernandez, Norristown, Pa., 1966-80; asst. dist. atty. Montgomery County, Pa., 1967-69; mem. Pa. Ho. of Reps, Harrisburg, 1971-79; judge Montgomery County Ct. Common Pleas, Pa., 1980-84, U.S. Dist. Ct. (ea. dist.) Pa., Phila., 1984-87, U.S. Ct. Appeals (3d cir.), 1987—; chmn. Pa. Sentencing Commn., 1980-85. Fulbright scholar Central U., Caracas, Venezuela, 1966. Mem. Montgomery Bar Assn., Pa. Bar Assn., ABA. Roman Catholic. Office: US Courthouse Independence Mall W #22614 601 Market St Philadelphia PA 19106-1510

SCIUBBA, JAMES JOHN, oral pathology educator, dental administrator; b. Jersey City, Dec. 12, 1942; s. Fiorino James and Angela (DiLorenzo) S.; m. Dolores Ann Citta, June 25, 1967; children: Dana, James. BS in Biology, Fairleigh Dickinson U., 1964, DMD, 1967; PhD in Pathology, U. Ill., Chgo., 1974. Diplomate Am. Bd. of Oral Pathology. Instr. Coll. Dentistry U. Ill., Chgo., 1973-74, asst. prof. Coll. Dentistry, 1974-75; assoc. prof. Sch. Dental Medicine SUNY, Stony Brook, 1978-83; assoc. chmn. dept. dental medicine L.I. Jewish Med. Ctr., New Hyde Park, N.Y., 1977-83; prof. oral pathology SUNY, Stony Brook, 1983—; chmn. dept. dental medicine L.I. Jewish Med. Ctr., New Hyde Park, 1983—; cons. Armed Forces Inst. of Pathology, Washington, 1978-89, Vets. Adminstrn. Hosp., Northport, N.Y., 1976—. Author: (monograph) Tumors of Major Salivary Glands, 1981 (book) Oral Pathology Clinical-Pathologic Correlations, 1989; editor Jour. Oral Surgery Oral Medicine Oral Pathology, 1982-88, Jour. Oral Pathology & Medicine, 1988—; co-editor Manual of Dental Therapeutics, 1991. Bd. dirs. Little Village Sch., Garden City, N.Y., 1983; chmn. med. adv. bd. Sjogren's Syndrome Found. Maj. U.S. Army, 1967-78. Recipient Alumni Recognition award Fairleigh Dickinson U. Sch. Dentistry, 1981, Pinnacle award Fairleigh Dickinson U., 1990. Fellow Am. Coll. Dentists, Internat. Coll. Dentists, Am. Acad. Oral Pathology (pres.-elect 1990), Am. Acad. Oral Pathology (pres. 1991-92). Republican. Roman Catholic. Home: 27 Robbins Dr Williston Park NY 11596-2009 Office: LI Jewish Med Ctr Dept Dental Medicine New Hyde Park NY 11042

SCLAFANI, ACCURSIO PETER, lawyer; b. N.Y.C., July 1, 1947; s. Nick and Marie (Cossu) S. B.S., Poly. Inst. Bklyn., 1968; J.D., St. John's U., 1976. Tchr. math. N.Y.C. schs., 1968-76; admitted to N.Y. State bar, 1977, U.S. Dist. Ct. bars, 1977, Fla. bar, 1979, D.C. bar, 1980, U.S. Tax Ct. bar, 1977, U.S. Supreme Ct. bar, 1980, D.C. Ct. Appeals bar, 1980; corp. officer Harvard Security Service, 1969—; pres. Quick Response Svc., N.Y.C., 1979—, Rapid Service Team, 1979-81; impartial arbitrator Local 363, Indsl. and Allied Trades Workers Union, 1980-85. Panel arbitrator Suffolk County Alternative Dispute Resolution by Arbitration Program, 1980-83. Cert. scuba diver; 1st degree black belt Chung Do Kwan Karate. Mem. Am. Bar Assn., N.Y. County Lawyers Assn., N.Y. State Bar Assn., Assn. Bar City N.Y., Fla. Bar Assn., D.C. Bar Assn. Roman Catholic. Home and Office: 80 Park Ave New York NY 10016-2541

SCLUFER, NICHOLAS GEORGE, builder; b. Elmer, N.J., Oct. 31, 1919; s. George and Helen (Laurantos) S.; m. Anne Helene Sprague, Nov. 15, 1963; children: Karen Anne, Evelyn Helene. Student, U. Pa., 1946-47. Pres. Pa. Aircraft Works, Upper Darby, 1942-46; co-founder Container Rsch. Assocs., Glenn Riddle, Pa., 1956-60; pres. Sclufer Constrn. Co., Newtown Square, Pa., 1950-86, Penn Springton Corp., Newtown Square, 1954-86, Gen. Leasing and Mgmt. Co., Newtown Square, 1970—; mng. ptnr. Penton Co., Newtown Square, 1986—. Inventor Apparatus for Confining Fusion Plasma, 1981, Magneto Hydro Dynamic Electric Power Generation, 1987; contbr. articles to profl. jours. Bd. dirs. Commonwealth Fed. Savs. Bank, Malvern, Pa., 1963—, chmn. internal audit com. 1980—; bd. trustees People's Light and Theatre Co., Malvern, 1976—. With USAF, 1943-45. Mem. Fusion Power Assocs. Home: 725 Dodds Ln Gladwyne PA 19035

SCOBBO, JAMES JOSEPH, physicist, engineer; b. Morristown, N.J., Mar. 13, 1962. BSChemE, U. Akron, 1984, MS in Polymer Engring., 1986, MS in Physics, PhD in Polymer Engring., 1989; MBA, Union Coll., 1992. Rsch. asst. Va. Inst. Polymer Engring., Akron, Ohio, 1984-89; staff engr. GE Corp. R&D, Schenectady, N.Y., 1989-91; advanced engr., physicist GE Plastics, Selkirk, N.Y., 1991—. Patentee in field; contbr. articles to profl. jours. Mem. Soc. for Advancement of Material and Process Engring. (treas. 1990-92, Edward Horne award 1988), Soc. Rheology, Soc. Plastic Engrs., Am. Chem. Soc. (rubber div.), Sigma Pi Sigma. Office: GE Plastics 1 Noryl Ave Selkirk NY 12158

SCOLNICK, EDWARD MARK, science administrator; b. Boston, Aug. 9, 1940; s. Barbara (Chasen) Scolnick; m. Barbara Bachrach; children: Laura, Jason, Daniel. AB, Harvard U., 1961; MD, Harvard U. Med. Sch., 1965. Intern Mass. Gen. Hosp., 1965-66, asst. resident internal medicine, 1966-67; research assoc. USPHS, 1967-69; sr. staff fellow lab. biochem. genetics NIH, 1969-70; instr. NIH Sem., 1970; sr. staff fellow viral leukemia and lymphoma br. Nat. Cancer Inst., 1970-71, spl. advisor to spl. virus cancer program, 1973-78, mem. coordinating com. for virus cancer program, 1975-78, chief. lab. tumor virus genetics, head. molecular virology sect., 1975-82; exec. dir. basic research virus and cell biology research Merck Sharp & Dohme Rsch. Labs., West Point, Pa., 1982-83, v.p. virus and cell biology research, 1983-84, sr. v.p., 1984, pres., 1985-91; sr. v.p., pres. rsch. Merck & Co., Inc., 1991—; adj. prof. microbiology Sch. Medicine U. Pa., 1983-86. Editor-in-chief Jour. Virology; mem. editorial bd. Virology; contbr. numerous articles to profl. jours.;. Served with USPHS, 1965-67. Recipient Arthur S. Fleming award, 1976, PHS Superior Svc. award, 1978, Eli Lilly award, 1980, Indsl. Rsch. Inst. Medal award, 1989. Am. Soc. Biol. Chemists, Am. Soc. Microbiologists, Nat. Acad. Scis. Home: 811 Wickfield Rd Wynnewood PA 19096-1610 Office: Merck Sharp & Dohme Rsch Labs PO Box 2000 Rahway NJ 07065-0900

SCONFITTO, GERARD CARL, real estate broker, real estate executive; b. Rochester, N.Y., Feb. 1, 1942; s. Joseph Sconfitto and Mary D'Agata; m. Estella Ann McMindes, Sept. 11, 1971. Student, Empire State U., 1987, 89. Lic. real estate broker, N.Y. Broker Gallery of Homes, Rochester, N.Y., 1975-76; broker 111 East Ave. Assocs., Rochester, 1976-78; property mgr. Norry Co., Rochester, 1978-86; owner One Eleven Realty, Rochester, 1978-88; pres. Comml. Design Consultants, Rochester, 1986-87, Sconfitto Group Ltd., Rochester, 1987—, Com-Pro Realty Inc., Rochester, 1988—. Bd. dirs. Brighton Rep. Com., Rochester, 1988; mem. Monroe County Rep. Fin. Com., 1991, Brighton Rep./Town Leader 1992; co-chair membership com. Nathaniel Rochester Soc. of Rochester Inst. Tech., 1992. Home: 193 Georgian Court Rd Rochester NY 14610-3416 Office: Com Pro Realty Inc 193 Georgian Court Rd Rochester NY 14610-3416

SCONYO, PHILIP, engineering consultant; b. Phila., Dec. 14, 1951; s. Joseph J. and Susie A. (Minghinelli) S.; m. Coleen A. Murphy, Apr. 3, 1972; children: Pamela, Diana. BEE, Villanova U., 1973. Registered profl. engr., N.J., Pa., Del. Field engr. Factory Mut. Engring. Assocs., Phila., 1974-76; sr. engr. Phila. Mfrs. Mut. Ins. Co., Valley Forge, Pa., 1977-85; unit engring. mgr. Arwkwright Mut. Ins. Co., Malvern, Pa., 1985-87; pres. Phiscon Enterprises Inc., Audubon, N.J., 1987—. Candidate for commr., Borough of Audubon, 1989. Mem. Soc. Fire Protection Engrs., Nat. Fire Protection Assn., Order Sons of Italy, Audubon PTA. Home and Office: Phiscon Enterprises Inc 213 S Davis Ave Audubon NJ 08106-1115

SCOPPECHIO, ROBERT ANTHONY, stockbroker, educator; b. Buffalo, Aug. 12, 1948; s. Anthony Caesar and Concetta (LaMonte) S.; m. Elizabeth Mighton, Feb. 15, 1991. BBA, Niagara U., 1970. Cost acct. Union Carbide, Inc., Niagara Falls, N.Y., 1970-72; sr. staff auditor Nat. Gypsum, Inc., Buffalo, 1972-75; chief fin. officer Krehbiel Assocs., Tonawanda, N.Y., 1975-85; fin. cons. Shearson Lehman Bros., Buffalo, 1985-87; acct. exec. Dean Witter Reynolds, Williamsville, N.Y., 1987—; part-time instr. investment workshops Erie Community Coll., 1989—. Author numerous poems. Com. mem. Am. Cancer Soc., Amherst, 1989, Am. Heart Assn., Amherst, 1989, Amherst C. of C., 1990—, Amherst Youth Found., 1990—, Bond Club Buffalo, 1985-91; loaned exec. United Way, Buffalo, 1990, mem. allocation funds com., 1992. Home: 110 Chateau Ter Buffalo NY 14226-3928 Office: Dean Witter Reynolds 4701 Transit Rd Buffalo NY 14221-6021

SCORZELLI, JAMES FRANCIS, counseling psychology educator; b. Detroit, June 19, 1943; s. Joseph Ernest and Loretta Barbara (Wolynski) S.; m. Mary Margaret Reinke, Nov. 27, 1970; children: Christopher, Miriam, Caroline, Jonathan. BS, Mich. State U., 1965, MA, 1967; PhD, U. Wis., 1973. Lic. psychologist, Mass.; cert. rehab. counselor. Counselor for deaf Mich. Assn. for Better Hearing, East Lansing, 1965-66; vocat. evaluator, counselor Nev. Rehab. Svcs., Las Vegas, 1967-68; program coord. Ighamn County Jail Rehab. Program, Mason, Mich., 1969-70; rsch. assoc. U. Wis., Madison, 1972-73; prof. dept. counseling psychology, rehab. and spl. edn. Northeastern U., Boston, 1973—; cons. psychologist, Newton, 1976—. Author: Drug Abuse: Prevention and Rehabilitation in Malaysia, 1987; contbr. articles to profl. jours. Sgt. U.S. Army, 1968-69. Fulbright scholar Coun. Internat. Exch. of Scholars, Malaysia, 1984-85; WHO fellow, Malaysia, 1987, 90. Mem. AACD (ad hoc editor 1990—), AAAS, APA, Am. Rehab. Counselors Assn. (newsletter editor, rsch. award 1974), Nat. Rehab. Assn., Nat. Rehab. Counseling Assn., Mass. Psychol. Assn., Fulbright Alumni Assn. Lutheran. Home: 19 Adella Ave Newton MA 02165-1901 Office: Northeastern U 207 Lake Hall Boston MA 02115

SCOTT, ANNETTA ELIZABETH, clinical psychologist; b. R.I., Jan. 28, 1960; d. Brian Frank and Janet Lee (Van Hoeve) Burke; m. Jeffrey David Scott, June 18, 1988; children: David Jeffrey, Michael Joseph. BA, Bryn Mawr (Pa.) Coll., 1982; PhD, SUNY, Albany, 1987. Lic. psychologist, N.Y. Grad. rsch. asst. SUNY, Albany, 1982-85; psychology asst. St. Colman's Home for Boys and Girls, Watervliet, N.Y., 1985-86; psychology intern The Astor Home for Children, Rhinebeck, N.Y., 1986-87, psychologist, 1987—. Contbr. articles to profl. jours. SUNY-Albany Benevolent Assn. Rsch. grantee, 1985. Mem. Am. Psychol. Assn., Hudson Valley Psychol. Assn. Presbyterian. Home: 3 Thayer Ln Red Hook NY 12571-1017 Office: The Astor Home for Children 36 Mill St # 5005 Rhinebeck NY 12572-1495

SCOTT, BLAINE WAHAB, III, insurance executive; b. Phila., Apr. 22, 1927; s. Blaine W., Jr., and Dorothy (Fox) S.; ed. Friends' Central Sch.; m. Mary L. Howe, Nov. 14, 1964; 1 child, Robert P.; children by previous marriage: M. Kathleen, Bruce K., Sharon L., Linda, Blaine Wahab, Carol. Registered Health Underwriter. past pres. bd., 1962-91; chmn. bd. Worlco Inc., also chmn., dir. all affiliates and subsidiaries; pres. Upper Merion Investment Corp.; dir. Gen. Devices, Inc., Agy. Rent-A-Car, Madison Bank. Mem. Upper Merion Bd. Suprs., 1960-66, chmn., 1961-66; trustee Temple U., 1969-73, Valley Forge Mil. Acad. and Jr. Coll., 1978-84, 86—; treas. Valley Forge Country Convention Vis. Bur., past dir., 1965-91; dir. emeritus King of Prussia C. of C.; mem. Pa. Rep. State Com., 1986-90. Served in U.S. Army, World War II, Korea. Named one of 5 outstanding young men of commonwealth, Pa. Jr. C. of C., 1962, Republican of Yr. Upper Merion Rep. Com., 1984. Mem. VFW, Am. Legion, Nat. Assn. Health Underwriters, Greater Delaware Valley Assn. Health Underwriters (dir.), Ins. Fedn. of Pa., Inc. (chmn. 1985-86, bd. dirs. 1964-91), Greater Valley Forge Hotel Assn. (Man of the Yr. 1987), Union League (Phila.). Home: 480 General Washington Rd Wayne PA 19087-2164 Office: 215 W Church Rd Ste 200 King of Prussia PA 19406

SCOTT, CAROLYN ALICE, counselor; b. Chicopee, Mass., Nov. 5, 1965; d. Allan E. and Dorothy L. (Carroll) Sittard; m. Bryan Drake Scott, Oct. 5, 1990. AS, Becker Jr. Coll., Worcester, Mass., 1985; BS, Rivier Coll., Nashua, N.H., 1988, MA, 1991. Head resident dir. Rivier Coll., 1988-90; grad. asst., counselor U. Lowell, Mass., 1989-90; dir. student devel. Wilcox Coll. Nursing, Middletown, Conn., 1990—. Advisor food drive Wilcox Coll. Student Orgn., 1990; entertainment chair Rivier Coll., 1988-89. Mem. Am. Assn. for Counseling and Devel., Am. Coll. Personnel Assn. Roman Catholic. Office: Wilcox Coll Nursing 28 Crescent St Middletown CT 06457

SCOTT, DAVID WILLIAM, immunology educator, researcher; b. Trenton, N.J., Feb. 4, 1943; s. Jack and Rose (Zuts) S.; m. Judith Gold, June 17, 1967; children—Jason Adam, Joshua Alan. Student, Antioch Coll., 1960-63; M.S., U. Chgo., 1964; Ph.D., Yale U., 1969. Postdoctoral fellow Yale U., New Haven, 1969, Oxford U., Eng., 1969-70; asst. prof. Duke U., Durham, N.C., 1971-74, assoc. prof, 1974-79, prof. immunology, 1979-83; Dean's prof. immunology U. Rochester, N.Y., 1983—; mem. study sect. NIH; chmn. immunology adv. com. Am. Cancer Soc., 1985—. Co-author: Key Facts in Immunology, 1984; co-editor: Immunologic Tolerance to Self and Nonself, 1982; contbr. numerous articles to sci. jours., chpt. to book. Coach and edn. dir. Central Carolina Youth Soccer Assn., Chapel Hill, 1979-83. Research grantee, NIH, Am. Cancer Soc., other orgns.; Jane Coffins Childs fellow, 1969-70; recipient Eleanor Roosevelt award Internat. Union against Cancer, 1976-77, 86, research career devel. award NIH, 1975-80. Mem. Am. Assn. Immunologists (edn. com. 1981—), Brit. Soc. for Immunology, Fedn. Am. Soc. for Exptl. Biology (edn. com. 1982—, chmn. 1987—), N.Y. Acad. Sci. Jewish. Home: 49 Hunters Pt Pittsford NY 14534-2479 Office: U Rochester Cancer Ctr PO Box 704 Rochester NY 14642-0001

SCOTT, GERALD DAVID, aluminum company executive; b. Meshoppen, Pa., Dec. 1, 1952; s. Gerald Leo and Jean (Strickland) S.; m. Lynn Tracy, Dec. 22, 1977; children: Alexander Tracy, Philip Nicholas, Karl Vincent. AA, Keystone Jr. Coll., 1973; BS, Wilkes Coll., 1980; MS, U. Va., 1983, PhD, 1985. Rsch. assoc. U. Va., Charlottesville, 1980-85; sr. engr. Alcoa Tech. Ctr., Alcoa Center, Pa., 1985-87, sr. scientist, 1987-88; staff application engr. Alcoa Wire, Rod & Bar Div., Massena, N.Y., 1988-89, sr. staff application engr., 1989; mgr. application engring., 1989-91, mgr. market devel., 1991—; mem. strategic steering com. NASA, Washington, 1988-89; internat. market devel. Alcoa Asia, Massena, 1987—; cons. Automotive Racing, Charlottesville, Va., 1980-85. Author: Electrocatalytic Materials, 1985; inventor, patentee internal combustion piston alloy, 1988, aluminum foundry alloys, 1988, aluminum die casting, 1989, lightweighting automobile, 1991, abrasion resistant aluminum alloy, 1991, high temperature aluminum forging alloy, 1992. Judge Pa. Jr. Acad. Sci., Pitts., 1985-86; vol. Friends of Charlottesville Libr., 1983-85; mem. N.Y. Polit. Action Com., Massena, 1988-91; bd. dirs. North County Pub. Radio, 1992. U. Va. fellow, Dow Chem. Corp., 1980-85. Mem. Nat. Screw Machine Products Assn (strategic steering com. 1989), Am. Soc. Metals (assoc.), Am. Defence Preparedness Assn., AIAA, Soc. Automotive Engrs. (sr. mem.), Soc. Mfg. Engrs. (sr. mem.). Office: Aluminum Co Am Park Ave E PO Box 150 Massena NY 13662

SCOTT, GLORIA ROMONA, childcare administrator; b. N.Y.C., Feb. 24, 1927; d. Thomas Frederick and Mary (Smith) Ashby; m. Elmer Gross, Aug. 18, 1945; children: Craig, Debra, Keith, Michelle. BA, SUNY, Old Westbury, 1974; postgrad., L.I. U., 1975. Adminstrv. dir. Internat. Child Creative Edn. Ctr., South Floral Park, N.Y. Home and Office: Internat Child Creative Ednl Ctr SUNY/Old Westbury Campus PO Box 11568 Old Westbury NY 11001-3522

SCOTT, HARLEY EARLE, publisher, historian; b. Buffalo, Oct. 17, 1934; s. Earle Marcus and Grayce Etta (Scheffler) S. BA, U. Buffalo, 1960; AM, Clark U., 1963; EdD, Ind. U., 1976. Tchr. geography Col. E. Brooke Lee Jr. High Sch., Kemp Hill, Md., 1965-66; instr. in geography Chgo. State U., 1966-71; asst. prof. geography SUNY, New Paltz, 1976-77; pres. Cayuga Creek Hist. Press, Lancaster, N.Y., 1981—; town hist. Lancaster, 1982—. Author: Tales of the Muskoka Steamboats, 1969, More Tales of the Muskoka Steamboats, 1980, Tales of Old Lancaster, 1981, Steamboats Today, 1986, Steam Tugs and Supply Boats of Muskoka, 1987. Member com. Boy Scouts Am. Troop 551, Lancaster, 1987; writer Lancaster Enterprize, 1982—; active Muskoka Sun, Ontario, 1969—. Clark U. scholar, 1961, 62. Mem. AAUP, Assn. Am. Geographers. Lutheran. Home: 22 Brookfield Pl Lancaster NY 14086

SCOTT, HOWARD WINFIELD, JR., temporary help service company executive; b. Greenwich, Conn., Feb. 24, 1935; s. Howard Winfield and Janet (Lewis) S.; B.S., Northwestern U., 1957; m. Joan Ann MacDonald, Aug. 12, 1961; children—Howard Winfield III, Thomas MacDonald, Ann Elizabeth. With R.H. Donnelly Corp., Chgo., 1958-59; sales rep. Masonite Corp., Chgo. also Madison, Wis., 1959-61; sales rep. Manpower Inc., Chgo., 1961-63, br. mgr., Kansas City, Mo., 1963-65, area mgr., Mo. and Kans., 1964-65, regional mgr. Salespower div., Phila., 1965-66; asst. advt. mgr. soups Campbell Soup Co., Camden, N.J., 1966-68; pres. PARTIME, Inc., Paoli, Pa., 1968-74; dir. marketing Kelly Services Inc., Southfield, Mich., 1974-78; pres. CDI Temporary Services, Inc., 1978-91; pres. Dunhill Pers. System, Inc., Woodbury, N.Y. Trustee Internat. House Phila. Served with AUS, 1957-58. Mem. Nat. Assn. Temporary Services (sec. 1970-71, pres. 1971-73, bd. dirs. 1982-91), Kappa Sigma. Republican. Episcopalian. Home: PO Box 237 Paoli PA 19301-0237 also: 1204 Annapolis Sea Colony E Bethany Beach DE 19930 Office: Dunhill Pers System Inc 1000 Woodbury Rd Woodbury NY 11797

SCOTT, I. B., railroad executive; b. Feb. 2, 1930. Student, McGill U., Montreal, Que., Can. Joined Can. Pacific Ltd., Montreal, 1949, gen. mgr. pub. relations and advt., 1973-81, v.p. adminstrn. and pub. affairs, 1981-85; chmn., chief exec. officer CP Rail div. Can. Pacific Ltd., Montreal, 1985-88; chmn., pres., chief exec. officer CP Rail div. Can. Pacific Ltd., 1989-90; exec. v.p. Can. Pacific Ltd., Montreal, 1988—; chmn., chief exec. officer CP Rail div. Can. Pacific Ltd., Montreal, 1990—; bd. dirs. Montreal Trust, Can. Pacific Ltd., United Dominion Industries, Inc., United Dominion Industries Ltd., Assn. Am. R.R.s, Can. Trust Co., Montreal Trust Co. Can., Montreal Trustco Inc., Soo Line Corp. Mem. adv. com. Concordia U., Montreal, Alliance For Drug Free Can.; bd. dirs. Royal Victoria Hosp. Found. Mem. Conf. Bd. Can. (past chmn. pub. affairs coun.), Nat. Freight Transp. Assn., Ry. Assn. Can. (bd. dirs.). Office: CP Rail Windsor Sta, Box 6042 Sta A, Montreal, PQ Canada H3C 3E4

SCOTT, JAMES HUNTER, JR., investment executive; b. Balt., Jan. 28, 1945; s. James Hunter and Marialice (Short) S.; m. Katheen Ann Bilderback, Sep. 1, 1973; children: Andrew James, Elizabeth Ann. BA, Rice U., 1967; MS, Carnegie Mellon U., 1970, PhD, 1975. Instr. Carnegie Mellon U., Pitts., 1969-71; rsch. fellow Fed. Res. Bank of Cleve., 1971-72; asst. prof. U. Wis., Milw., 1972-75; from asst. prof. to prof./divisional rep. fin. Columbia U., N.Y.C., 1975-87; mgn. dir. Prudential Ins. Co., Newark, 1987—; pres. PTC Svcs., Newark, 1991—; vis. asst. prof. Stanford (Calif.) U., 1974-75, assoc. prof., 1979; adj. prof. grad. sch. bus. Columbia U., 1988—; rsch. coord./prize com. Inst. for Quantitative Rsch. in Fin., N.Y.C., 1976—; with Goldman, Sachs, Kinsey & Co., 1981-82; trustee adminstrv. com. Eastern Air Lines Pilots Investment Plan, Miami, 1985-91. Contbr. over 25 articles to profl. jours. Pres. bd. trustees Alpine (N.J.) Community Ch., 1986-89; v.p. bd. trustees Tenafly (N.J.) Bd. Edn., 1989—. Mem. Am. Econ. Assn., Am. Fin. Assn., Tenafly Swim Club, Englewood Field Club. Methodist. Office: PDI Strategies 20 Prudential Pla Newark NJ 07102

SCOTT, JOHN CLARK, JR., art conservator, consultant; b. Winfield, Kans., June 13, 1953; s. John Clark Sr. and Virginia Lee (Huffman) S.; m. Linda Marie Kenepaske, Dec. 23, 1977. BA in Philosophy, U. Kans., 1975, MA in History of Art, 1979, MBA, 1982; MA in Art Conservation, N.Y. State Univ. Coll., Buffalo, 1984. Exhbns. asst. Spencer Mus. of Art, Lawrence, Kans., 1977-78; contracting conservator trainee Nelson-Atkins Mus. of Art, Kansas City, Mo., 1978-81; fellow Cooperstown (N.Y.) Tng. Program for Conservation, 1981-84; intern conservator Nat. Gallery of Art, Washington, 1983, Phila. Mus. Art, 1983-84; conservator John Scott Conservators, N.Y.C., 1984-90; conservator/dir. N.Y. Conservation Ctr., Inc., N.Y.C., 1991—; cons. and contractor Princeton (N.J.) U. Putnam Collection Modern Sculpture, 1984—; cons., contractor bd. edn., health and hosps. corp., parks and recreation, art commn., City of N.Y., 1985—, Pa. State Capitol Preservation Com., Harrisburg, 1986—, Whitney Mus. Am. Art, N.Y.C., S.R. Guggenheim Mus., Mus. Am. Folk Art, Columbia U., Cornell U.; lectr., instr. local schs. of restoration and conservation. Mellon Found. fellow, 1981-84, Nat. Endowment for the Arts, 1981-84; Nat. Gallery of Art grantee, 1983. Mem. Internat. Inst. for Conservation, Nat. Inst. for Conservation, Am. Inst. for Conservation, Nat. Assn. Corrosion Engrs., N.Y. Conservation Assn. (treas.), Am. Inst. Conservation Conservators in Pvt. Practice. Office: NY Conservation Ctr 519 W 26th St New York NY 10001-5503

SCOTT, JOHN LENARD, broadcast executive; b. Morrisville, Pa., May 19, 1921; s. John Lawrence and Toretta Amelia (Block) Silverstein; m. Frances Allen, Sept. 16, 1944 (div. 1960); children: Lawrence Lee, Amelia Dorothy Scott Cozart. BA, Kent State U., 1943. Anchorman, reporter, and correspondent Sta. WOR and WOR-TV div. Mut. RKO Broadcasting System, N.Y.C., 1943-78; pres. Infocom Broadcast Services, Inc., N.Y.C. and Princeton, N.J., 1978-90, Media Resource Ctr., Inc., Princeton, 1981—; producer, host N.J. Pub. TV, Princeton, 1990—. Author: Treasured Volume, 1968, Treasured Volume of Thoughts, 1969, Treasured Volume of Prayer, 1970. Trustee Found. Thanatology, Coll. Physicians and Surgeons, Columbia U., N.Y.C., Greater Trenton, N.J., Symphony Soc.; bd. dirs., v.p. Hemlock Farms Com. Assn., Hawley, Pa., 1984-86; bd. dirs. Greater Trenton Symphony Orch., 1991—. Mem. NATAS, Overseas Press Club, Nat. Press Club, N.Y. Press Club, Soc. Silurians, Sigma Delta Chi. Home and Office: Media Resource Ctr Inc 202 Salem Ct # 1 Princeton NJ 08540-7040

SCOTT, LOTTIE BELL, civil rights administrator; b. Ridgeway, S.C., Nov. 5, 1936; d. Joe and Estelle (Stone) Bell; m. Charles Wright, 1961 (div. 1965); 1 child, Clyburn. AS, Mohegan Community Coll., Norwich, Conn., 1982; B of Gen. Studies, U. Conn., Storrs, Conn., 1986. Clerk-typist Conn. Dept. of Mental Health, Norwich, 1962-70; neighborhood resource worker Conn. Commn. on Human Rights & Opportunities, Norwich, 1970-73, investigator, 1973-79, regional mgr., 1979—. Dir. Thames Valley coun. for Community, Jewett City, Conn., 1965-68; br. sec. NAACP, Norwich, 1967-74, br. pres., 1974-86; asst. sec. Conn. State Conf. of the NAACP, 1971-73, v.p., 1973-79; bd. dirs. Conn. Civil Liberties, Hartford, 1972-76; vice chmn. Norwich Redevelopment Agy., 1974; vice moderator, Unitarian Universalist Ch., 1977-81; bd. dirs. United Community Svc., 1977-80, 1985-88; com. chmn. William W. Backus Hosp. Long Range Planning, 1981-88, bd. dirs, 1981-88, chmn. bd. dirs., 1988-90; bd. dirs. Conn. Hosp. Assn., Wallingford, Conn., 1990—, YMCA, Norwich, 1991—. Mem. Rotary. Democrat. Home: 85 Church St Norwich CT 06360-5001 Office: Comm on Human Rights & Opportunities 100 Broadway Norwich CT 06360-4431

SCOTT, MARY JANE GOMEZ, human resources executive; b. Hartford, Conn., Aug. 12, 1944; d. Juan and Marion Priscilla (Jewett) Gomez; m. Jeffery Anderson Scott, Jan. 27, 1967. BS in Edn., U. Conn., 1966. Tchr. elem. schs. Stamford (Conn.) Bd. Edn., 1966-69; coll. relations asst. Olin Corp., Stamford, 1969-73, compensation analyst, 1973-77, mgr. salary programs, 1977-78, mgr. internal placement, 1978-80; mgr. salaried personnel Olin Corp., New Haven, 1980-82; mgr. staffing GTE Communication Systems Corp., Stamford, 1982-84; dir. personnel TransKrit Corp., Brewster, N.Y., 1984-89; v.p. human resources TransKrit Corp., Brewster, 1989—. Bd. dirs. Brewster Edn. Found. Mem. Am. Compensation Assn., Soc. for Human Resource Mgmt. Home: 285 N Salem Rd Ridgefield CT 06877-3125 Office: TransKrit Corp PO Box 500 Brewster NY 10509-0500

SCOTT, MICHAEL DAVID, sales executive; b. Columbus, Ohio, June 24, 1963; s. Henry Clay and Mary Elizabeth (Doherty) S.; m. Janet C. Wertz, May 4, 1991. BSBA, Ohio State U., 1987. Student mgr. The Southwestern Co., Nashville, 1983-86; leasing officer BancNew Eng. Leasing Group, Boston, 1987-89; regional sales mgr. Assocs. Corp. of N.Am., Boston, 1989—. Vol. Big Brother/Big Sister Program, Columbus, 1984-87. Republican. Roman Catholic. Home: 1 Madel Ln Bedford MA 01730-1521 Office: Assocs Corp of North Am 101 Federal St Ste 1900 Boston MA 02110-1848

SCOTT, MILTON LEONARD, nutrition educator; b. Tempe, Ariz., Feb. 21, 1915; s. Squire Milton and Ione Frances (Greenleaf) S.; m. Dorothy Marie Jaeger, July 1, 1938; children: Grace Ione Scott Saroka, June Marie Scott Kopald. AA, Riverside (Calif.) Jr. Coll., 1934; AB, U. Calif., Berkeley, 1937; PhD, Cornell U., 1945. Vitamin chemist Coop. GLF Feed Mills, Buffalo, 1937-42; rsch. assoc. Cornell U., Ithaca, N.Y., 1945-46, asst. prof., 1946-48, assoc. prof., 1948-53, prof., 1953-79, chmn. dept. poultry sci., Jacob Gould Schurman prof., 1976-79, Jacob Gould Schurman prof. emeritus, 1979—. Author: (textbook) Nutrition of Humans, 1986; co-author: Nutrition of the Chicken, 1982, Nutrition of the Turkey, 1987, Nutrition & Mgmt. of Ducks, 1991. Recipient AFMA award, 1952, Rsch. award Nat. Turkey Fedn., 1958, N.Y. Farmer's award, 1971, Klaus Schwartz award, 1980. Fellow AAAS, Inst. of Nutrition, Poultry Sci. Assn. (Borden award 1965); mem. Rotary. Republican. Home: 16 Spruce Ln Ithaca NY 14850-1765

SCOTT, MIMI KOBLENZ, psychotherapist; b. Albany, N.Y., Dec. 15, 1940; d. Edmund Akiba and Tillie (Paul) Koblenz; m. Barry Stuart Scott, Aug. 13, 1961 (dec. Nov. 1991); children: Karen Scott Zantay, Jeffrey B. BA in Speech, English Edn., Russell Sage Coll., 1962; MA in Speech Edn., SUNY, Albany, 1968; M in Social Welfare, SUNY, 1985; PhD in Psychology, Pacific Western U., Encino, Calif., 1985. Cert. tchr., social worker. Tchr. English, speech Albany Pub. Schs., 1961-63; hostess, producer talkshow Sta. WAST-TV 13, Albany, 1973-75; freelance actress N.Y.C., 1975-77; producer, actress Four Seasons Dinner Theater, Albany, 1978-82; instr. of theatre Albany Jr. Coll., 1981-83; pvt. practice psychotherapy Albany, N.Y., 1985—; exec. producer City of Albany Park Playhouse, 1989—; cons. Kairos Counseling Ctr, Albany, 1982-84, Mid. Earth Counseling Ctr., 1982-83, Parsons Child & Family Treatment Ctr., 1984-85; actor, performer Mental Health Players, 1982-84. Columnist Metroland mag., 1986; scriptwriter, dir., actress TV movie, 1984. Event organizer AmFar, 1985; co-chmn. March of Dimes Telethon, 1985-86; fundraiser Leukemia Found., 1987, Aids Benefit, N. Miami Beach, Fla., 1988; elected to SUNY Albany U. Found., 1990. Recipient FDR Nat. Achievement award March of Dimes, 1985, Recognition Cert. Capital Dist. Psychiat. Ctr., 1983, 84, 85; named Woman of Yr. YWCA, 1986, Commr. Albany Tricentennial Celebration, 1986; Mimi Scott Day proclaimed by Mayor of Albany, 1989. Mem. Doctorate Assn. N.Y. Educators, N.Y. State Soc. Clin. Psychotherapists, Nat. Assn. Social Workers, Actors Equity Assn., Screen Actors Guild, Am. Fedn. Radio & TV Artists. Democrat. Jewish. Club: Turnberry Isle Yacht & Racquet (N. Miami Beach, Fla.). Home and Office: 36 Willett St Albany NY 12210-1145

SCOTT, NANCY ELLEN, psychotherapist; b. El Paso, Tex., Nov. 1, 1960; d. Robert Churchill and Annie Jo (Schmidt) S. BS, U. Tex., El Paso, 1982; MS, Springfield Coll., 1985; MA, Columbia U., 1987, EdM, 1989. Cert. tchr., Tex. Assoc. Occupational Health Consulting Inc., West Nyack, N.Y., 1985-88; psychiat. rehab. counselor Met. Hosp., N.Y.C., 1988-91; psychotherapist Met. Ctr. for Mental Health, N.Y.C., 1991—; psychology intern Albert Einstein Coll. of Medicine, Bronx, Bronx, 1991-92; psychotherapist Metro Ctr. for Mental Health, N.Y.C., 1991—. Contbr. articles to profl. jours. Mem. APA (student affiliate group div. 17). Office: Metro Ctr for Mental Health 130 W 97th St New York NY 10025-6450

SCOTT, RICHARD ALBERT, JR., credit union executive; b. N.Y., Nov. 1, 1957; s. Richard Albert and June (Burge); m. Jo-Ann Prior, 1979; children: Kimberly, Heather, Amanda. BBA, SUNY, Binghamton, 1979. Internal auditor Endicott (N.Y.) Johnson Corp., 1979, Kason Industries, Inc., Binghamton, N.Y., 1980-81; contr. Kason Industries, Fixtureware, Binghamton, N.Y., 1981-82; exec. v.p. LICU Corp. Fed. Credit Union, Endicott, 1984-85; v.p. fin. IBM Endicott/Owego EFCU, N.Y., 1982-90, v.p. mgmt. info. systems, 1990—; sec., bd. dirs. Endicott Owego Mem. Svc. Corp., 1987-88, Real Estate Svcs. Corp., 1987-88; v.p., bd. dirs. N.Y. State Credit Union League So. Tier, Binghamton, 1988-89, pres., 1989—, pres. of dist. pres.'s, 1991—. Republican. Roman Catholic. Office: IBM Credit Union 24 Mckinley Ave Endicott NY 13760-5491

SCOTT, RICHARD EUGENE, international migration organization executive; b. Ft. Dodge, Iowa, Sept. 30, 1950; s. Gordon Eugene and Josephine Jean (Engler) S. BS, Iowa State U., 1973. Ops. officer Internat. Orgn. for Migration, Hong Kong, 1978-79, Bangkok, 1979-80; chief of mission Internat. Orgn. for Migration, N.Y.C., 1980—; exec. dir. Soviet/Pan Am Travel Effort, Moscow, 1991. Recipient Honor award Refugee Appreciation Day Com., Rayburn House Office Bldg., Washington, 1991.

SCOTT, ROBERT ALLYN, college administrator; b. Englewood, N.J., Apr. 16, 1939; s. William D. and Ann. F. (Waterman) S.; m. Phyllis Virginia Brice, Mar. 23, 1963; children: Ryan Keith, Kira Elizabeth. BA, Bucknell U., 1961; PhD, Cornell U., 1975. Mgmt. trainee Procter & Gamble Co., Phila., 1961-63; asst. dir. admissions Bucknell U., Lewisburg, Pa., 1965-67; asst. dean Coll. Arts and Scis. Cornell U., Ithaca, 1967-69, assoc. dean, 1969-79, prof. anthropology, 1978-79; dir. acad. affairs Ind. Commn. for Higher Edn., Indpls., 1979-84, asst. commr., 1984-85; pres. Ramapo (N.J.) Coll., 1985—; lectr. U. Philippines, 1964-65; cons. to Sta. WSKG Pub. TV and Radio, 1977-79; cons. to various colls. and univs., pubs. 1966—; mem. curriculum adv. com. Ind. Bd. Edn., 1984-87; mem. Lilly Endowment Thinktank, 1984-86; nat. adv. panel Ind. 21st Century Schooling Project, 1990-92; bd. dirs. United Jersey Bank, N.J. World Trade Coun., N.J. Ctr. for Internat. Bus. Edn., Hackensack Med. Ctr., Hillcrest Health Svc. Systems, Am. Ednl. Products, Inc., NCO Investors II, L.P.; chmn. coll. and univ. ednl. satellite systems of PBS and AM. Assn. State Colls. and Univs. Author books and monographs; editorial bd. Cornell Rev., 1976-79; book rev. editor Coll. and Univ., 1974-78; cons. editor Change mag., 1979—; cons. editor Jour. Higher Edn., 1985—; exec. editor Saturday Evening Post book div. Curtis Pub. Co., 1982-85; contbr. articles to sociols., ednl. and popular publs. Mem. bd. Bergen coun. Boy Scouts Am.; trustee, Bucknell U., 1976-78, First Unitarian Ch., Ithaca, 1970-73, 78-79, chmn., 1971-73, Unitarian Universalist Ch. of Indpls., 1980-85. With USNR, 1963-65. Spencer Found. rsch. grantee, 1972, Exxon Edn. Found. rsch. grantee, 1977; recipient Sagamore of the Wabash award, 1985, Prudential Found. Leader of Yr. award, 1987, Disting. Svc. award West Bergen Mental Health Ctr., 1991. Fellow Am. Anthrop. Assn.; mem. Assn. Study Higher Edn., Am. Sociol. Assn., Am. Assn. Higher Edn., Am. Assn. State Colls. & Univs. (com. on internat. edn.), O.E.C.D. (higher edn. program, Paris), Am. Coun. on Edn. Commn. on Internat. Edn., Am. forum, Higher Edn. Colloquium (chmn. 1982-84), N.J. Assn. of Coll. and Univs. (chair), Bucknell U. Alumni Assn. (bd. dirs. 1971-80, pres. 1976-78, Outstanding Achievement 1991), Indpls. Com. on Fgn. Rels., Ithaca Yacht Club, Econs. Indpls. Club, Indian Trails Club, Phi Kappa Psi, Phi Kappa Phi. Office: Ramapo Coll 505 Ramapo Valley Rd Mahwah NJ 07430-1623

SCOTT, ROBERT MONTGOMERY, museum executive, lawyer; b. Bryn Mawr, Pa., May 22, 1929; s. Edgar and Helen Hope (Montgomery) S.; m. H. Gay Elliot, June 30, 1951; children: Hope Tyler Scott Rogers, Janet Pauling, Elliot Montgomery. AB, Harvard U., 1951; LLB, U. Pa., 1954. Ptnr. Montgomery McCracken Walker & Rhoads, Phila., 1961-82, of counsel, 1982-88; spl. asst. to U.S. Amb. to Ct. of St. James, London, 1969-73; hon. Brit. consul Phila., 1979-83; pres., chief exec. officer Phila. Mus. Art, 1982—; bd. dirs. First Fidelity Bancorp, Fidelity Bank, Phila. Trustee Phila. Mus. Art, 1965—, Royal Oak Found., 1978-86, Inst. Cancer Rsch., Fox Chase Cancer Ctr., 1960-86, Lankenau Hosp., 1959-86, William Penn Found., 1986-91; bd. dirs. Glyndebourne Assn. Am., Inc. Recipient Superior Honor award Dept. State, 1973. Fellow Am. Bar Found.; mem. Am. Assn. Mus., Phila. Club, Union League, Knickerbocker Club, Locust Club, White's Club. Republican. Home: 705 Church Rd Wayne PA 19087-4712 Office: Phila Mus Art Benjamin Franklin Pkwy PO Box 7646 Philadelphia PA 19101-7646

SCOTT, RONALD JOHN, mechanical engineer; b. Ogdensburg, N.Y., May 17, 1936; s. Howard Dawley and Agnes Ann Scott; m. JoAnne Marie Bartman, July 6, 1958; children: Richard, David. ME, Clarkson U., Potsdam, N.Y., 1958. Office engr. Uhl, Hall & Rich, Niagara Falls, 1958-60; asst. plant engr. Diamond Nat. Corp., Ogdensburg, 1960-66; dir. physical plant State U. Coll., Potsdam, 1966-91; bldg. constrn. cons. Canton, N.Y., 1991—. Trustee Village of Canton, N.Y. Mem. Assn. Phys. Plant Adminstrs. Republican. Presbyterian. Home: Outer Riverside Dr PO Box 141 Canton NY 13617

SCOTT, RUSSELL WILLIAM, analytical laboratory manager; b. Buffalo, Aug. 25, 1957; s. Kenneth Richard and Elizabeth Willette (Miller) S.; m. Tonya Belle Blackwell, June 25, 1988. BS in Chemistry, Howard U., 1979; MPH, Yale U., 1983. Chemist Triangle Resource Industries, Laurel, Md., 1979-81; rsch. asst. U.S. EPA, Washington, 1982; environ. scientist Dynamac Internat., Inc., Rockville, Md., 1983-84; assoc. safety engr. IBM Corp., Endicott, N.Y., 1984-88, sr. assoc. safety engr., 1988, mfg. mgr., 1988—. Active Broome County Urban League, Binghamton, N.Y., 1986—. Amoco Book grantee, 1975; named one of Outstanding Young Men Am., 1985. Mem. Am. Chem. Soc., Am. Soc. Safety Engrs., Am. Indsl. Hygiene Assn., Alpha Phi Alpha (v.p. 1987-88). Democrat. Lutheran. Home: 818 Jennifer Ln Endicott NY 13760-1228 Office: IBM Corp 1701 North St Endicott NY 13760-5598

SCOTT, STANLEY DEFOREST, real estate executive, lithography company executive; b. Hudson County, N.J., Nov. 2, 1926; s. Stanley DeForest and Anne Marie (Volk) S.; B.A., U. So. Calif., 1950; m. Mary Elizabeth Hazard, Dec. 30, 1953. Gen. mgr. Alfred Scott Publishers, N.Y.C., 1951-56; chmn., pres. S.D. Scott Printing Co., Inc., N.Y.C., 1956—; gen. ptnr. 145 Hudson St. Assocs. Mem. Mayor's Industry Adv. Coun.; bd. dirs. Bus. Relocation Commn., art mus. hist. socs.; past co-chmn. Fraunces Tavern Mus.com., 1973-87. With USNR, 1944-46. Frick Collection fellow. Mem. Assn. Graphic Arts (past dir.), Am. Inst. Graphic Arts, Printers League (past v.p.), Soc. Mayflower Descs., Soc. Colonial Wars, S.R. (bd. mgrs., 1969—, treas. 1972-73, 3d v.p. 1975-77, 2d v.p. 1977-79, chmn. mus. and art com. 1987), N.Y. Hist. Soc., Met. Mus. Art, Mus. Modern Art, Morgan Libr., rare book librs., Am. Mus. in Britain (coun. 1986—), Mt. Vernon (Va.) Ladies Assn. (adv. com.), Knickerbocker Club, Union Club, Downtown Athletic Club, Merchants Club (v.p.1985—). Republican. Episcopalian. Home: 1 Sutton Pl S New York NY 10022-2471 Office: 145 Hudson St New York NY 10013-2103

SCOTT, WALTER NEIL, physiologist, educator; b. Evansville, Ind., Mar. 2, 1935; s. Paul Kruger and Pauline Virginia (Kimbley) S.; m. Margaret Ann Simon, Nov. 21, 1959; children: Walter David Kimbley, Benjamin Bray. B.S., Western Ky. State Coll., 1956; M.D., U. Louisville, 1960. Intern New Eng. Ctr. Hosp., Boston, 1960-61; resident New Eng. Ctr. Hosp., 1961-62; NIH fellow medicine Mass. Meml. Hosps., Boston, 1962-63; USPHS fellow biophys. lab. Harvard Med. Sch., Brookline, Mass., 1963-65; spl. NIH fellow biochemistry MIT, Cambridge, 1965-66; biochemist Sch. Aerospace Medicine, San Antonio, 1966-68; acting chief biochem. pharmacology div. Sch. Aerospace Medicine, 1967-68; asst. prof. Mt. Sinai Grad. Sch., N.Y.C., 1968-71; mem. grad. faculty CUNY, N.Y.C., 1968-82; asst. prof. ophthalmology Mt. Sinai Med. Sch., N.Y.C., 1971-74; assoc. prof. ophthalmology Mt. Sinai Med. Sch., 1974-79, research prof. ophthalmology, 1979-82, asst. dean research, 1976-81, assoc. dean, 1981-82; chmn. dept. biology NYU, N.Y.C., 1982-87, prof., 1982—; Lancaster vis. prof. Western Ky. U., 1980; mem. cornea task force Nat. Eye Inst., 1972, vision research program com., 1975-79; cons. metabolic biology program NSF, 1976—; established investigator Am. Heart Assn., 1971-76; Molly Berns sr. investigator N.Y. Heart Assn., 1976-80; chmn. Gordon Conf. Biology and Chemistry of Peptides, 1978; mem. organizing com. 3d Gordon Conf. on Peptides, 6th Am. Peptide Symposium. Contbr. articles to sci. publs. Served to capt. USAF, 1966-68. Fellow N.Y. Acad. Scis. (gov. 1978-82, pres. 1983, chmn. conf. organizing com. 1980-81, 87-88); mem. Am. Physiol. Soc., Am. Soc. Biol. Chemists, Biophys. Soc., Soc. Exptl. Biology and Medicine (editorial bd. procs.), Am. Heart Assn., AAAS, Am. Chem. Soc., Am. Soc. Nephrology, N.Y. Acad. Medicine (com. pub. health 1986—), Endocrine Soc., Soc. Cell Biology, Sigma Xi, Alpha Omega Alpha. Office: NYU Dept Biology 1009 Main Bldg Washington Sq E New York NY 10003

SCOTT, WILEY ANTHONY, JR., financial consulting company executive, consultant; b. Washington, Feb. 8, 1955; s. Wiley Anthony and Ethel Catherine (Holmes) S.; m. Deborah McCusker Bennett, Oct. 12, 1985; children: Katherine Breckenridge, Caroline Bennett. BS in Econs., BS in Mgmt., U. Utah, 1977. Dir. mktg. Clif Taylor Enterprises, South Bend, Ind., 1977-78; account exec. Oscar Mayer, Madison, Wis., 1978-81; sales mgr. Browning-Ferris Industries, L.A., 1981-83; sales mgr. Wast Mgmt., Inc., L.A., 1983-85, dir. acquisitions, 1985-89; valuation cons. Marshall and Stevens Inc., L.A., 1989-91; v.p. sales Marshall and Stevens Inc., Phila., 1991—. Mktg. mgr. L.A. Olympic Organizing Com., 1983-84, fundraiser, 1985-88; dir. mkt.g L.A. Beautiful, 1988-89. Republican. Methodist. Office: Marshall and Stevens Inc 1700 Market St Ste 1510 Philadelphia PA 19103-9977

SCOTT, WILLIAM A(DDISON), III, pharmaceutical executive, researcher; b. Indpls., Apr. 27, 1940; s. William Addison Jr. and Mildred Lois (Cameron) S.; m. Lonna Sue Lagreco, Aug. 28, 1966; 1 child, Erin Marie. BS in Chemistry, U. Ill., 1962; PhD in Biochemistry, Calif. Inst. Tech., 1967; postgrad., Rockefeller U., 1967-69. Rsch. investigator Rockefeller U., N.Y.C., 1969, asst. prof., 1970-77, assoc. prof., 1978-83, assoc. dean, 1979-82; dir. cellular biology E.R. Squibb & Sons, Lawrenceville, N.J., 1983-86, v.p. molecular and cellular biology, 1986-89; sr. v.p. exploratory and drug discover rsch. Bristol-Myers Squibb, Lawrenceville, 1989—; cons. Squibb Inst. for Med. Rsch., Lawrenceville, 1982-83; mem. sci. bd. Procepts, Inc., Cambridge, Mass., 1990—. Contbr. numerous articles to profl. jours. Mem. Am. Soc. Biol. Chemists, Am. Soc. Immunologists, Harvey Soc., Phi Lambda Upsilon, Sigma Xi. Office: Bristol Myers Squibb PO Box 4000 Princeton NJ 08543-4000

SCOTT, WILLIAM JAMES, analytical chemist; b. Coleraine, No. Ireland, Oct. 28, 1944; s. William and Jean (Morgan) S. BSc 1st class, Queen's U., Belfast, No. Ireland, 1967, PhD, 1970. Rsch. assoc. Clarkson U., Potsdam, N.Y., 1970-73; scientist Technicon Inst. Corp., Tarrytown, N.Y., 1973-76, sr. scientist, 1976-80, project scientist, 1980-90; sr. staff scientist Miles Inc., Tarrytown, 1990—. Contbr. (book series) CRC Handbook in Electrochemistry, 1984; patentee carbonate selective electrode, mercury-free buffer for ISE. Presbyterian. Office: Miles Inc 511 Benedict Ave Tarrytown NY 10591-5097

SCOTT, WINFIELD ALLEN, safety and health manager; b. Atlantic City, June 16, 1934; s. Winfred Savanna and Amanda Mildred (Nehr) S.; m. Dorothy Ann, Sept. 18, 1952 (div. May 1960); m. Oct. 1, 1960 (div. Apr. 1973);m. Serita Bredin Brous, Sept. 8, 1974; children: Gregory, Alison, Leslie, Daryl, William, Julia. BA with honors, Rutgers U., 1974; MS, Ind. U., 1987. Cert. safety mgr. Rsch. engr. technician Frankford Arsenal, Phila., 1956-71; rsch. engr. technician Naval Air Propulsion Ctr., Trenton, N.J., 1976-83, safety and occupational health mgr., 1983-87; safety and occupational health mgr. FAA Tech. Ctr., Atlantic City, 1987-91; pres. SAHRA, Inc., Barnegat, N.J., 1991—. Inventor precipitating hood, 1979. Chair Mercer County Mental Health Bd., Trenton, 1985. Sgt. USMC, 1956-58. Balwin and Univ. fellow Lehigh U., Bethlehem, Pa., 1975. Fellow Am. Soc. Safety Engrs.; mem. World Safety Orgn. Home: PO Box 546 Teton Village WY 83025-0546 Office: SAHRA Inc 3 Mediterranean Ct Barnegat NJ 08005-2519

SCOTT-FINAN, NANCY ISABELLA, government administrator; b. Canton, Ohio, June 13, 1949; d. Milton Kenneth and Gertrude (Baker) Scott; m. Robert James Finan II, Aug. 23, 1986. Student, Malone Coll., 1970-73; BA magna cum laude, U. Akron, 1976, postgrad., 1976; postgrad., Kent State U., 1977, George Mason U., 1992—. Legal sec. Krugliak, Wilkins, Griffiths & Dougherty, Canton, 1969, Amerman, Burt & Jones, Canton, 1970-77; legal sec., paralegal Black, McCuskey, Souers & Arbaugh, Canton, Ohio, 1977-81; adminstrv. staff mem. com. on judiciary U.S. Senate, Washington, 1981-86; adminstrv. asst. to counsel to Pres., The White House, Washington, 1986-89; adminstrv. asst. to former counsel to pres. O'Melveny

& Myers, Washington, 1989; asst. dir. congl. rels. Office Legis. Affairs, U.S. Dept. Justice, Washington, 1989-91, spl. asst. to asst. atty. gen., 1991—; substitute tchr. North Canton City Sch. System, 1979-80; residential tutor Canton City Sch. System, 1980-81, Fairfax (Va.) County Sch. System, 1983;instr. dance and exercise Siffrin Home for Developmentally Disabled, Canton, 1980. East coast regional v.p. for spl. projects Childhelp U.S.A., Washington, 1988-90; mem. Rep. Women of Capitol Hill, Washington, 1984—; bd. mem. Have a Heart Homes for Abused Children, Washington, 1990-91. Mem. AAUW. Presbyterian. Home: 2056 Hopewood Dr Falls Church VA 22043-1836

SCOTT-WILLIAMS, NIGEL SIMON, interior designer; b. Durban, Natal, South Africa, Aug. 29, 1955; came to U.S., 1979; s. Leslie and Gladness Adele (Muller) Scott-Williams; m. Wendy Lee Schutt, Feb. 29, 1980. B in Commerce, U. Natal, Durban, South Africa, 1975, LLB, 1977; LLM, U. Cambridge, Eng., 1979; cert. in interior design, Parsons Sch. of Design, N.Y.C., 1986. Tax atty. Deloitte Haskins & Sells, N.Y.C., 1982-84; v.p. Interdimensional Design Assocs., N.Y.C., 1985-88; sr. interior designer Ellerbe Becket, N.Y.C., 1988—; dir. Deepa Textiles, Calif. Home: 41-16 47th Ave Long Island City NY 11104 Office: Ellerbe Becket 200 Madison Ave New York NY 10016

SCOVIL, H. RAYMOND, agricultural consultant; b. Queenstown, N.B., Can., Nov. 8, 1925; s. Walter Harold and Gladys Eva (Mayes) S.; m. Elizabeth Eleanor Jonsson; children: Mary, Jean, Joan, Catherine. BS in Agr., McGill U., 1949; MS, Cornell U., 1967. Asst. dist. agriculturist N.B. Dept. Agr., Gagetown, 1949-54, markets specialist, Fredericton, N.B., 1954-59, asst. dir. extension br., 1959-60; sec. Royal Commn. N.B. Potato Industry, Province of N.B., Fredericton, 1960-61; classification officer N.B. Civil Svc. Commn., Fredericton, 1961-62; adminstrv. asst. N.B. Dept. Agr., Fredericton, 1964-65, asst. dep. minister agr., 1966-73, dep. minister agr., 1973-83; chmn. N.B. Farm Products Mktg. Commn., Fredericton, 1983-88; agrl. cons., Fredericton, 1988—; pres. Scovil Assocs., 1988—. Past pres. Can. Agrtl. Hall Fame, Toronto. Author bull.: Mktg. N.B. Christmas Trees, 1966. Agrl. Inst. Can. fellow, 1986. Mem. Agrl. Inst. Can. (dir. 1973-75), N.B. Inst. Agrologists, Inst. Pub. Adminstrn. Can. Anglican. Club: Rotary (dir. 1982-83). Home: 135 Edinburgh St, Fredericton, NB Canada E3B 2C8 Office: Scovil Assocs, 135 Edinburgh St, Fredericton, NB Canada E3B 2C8

SCOVILLE, JONATHAN ARMSTRONG, artist; b. N.Y.C., Nov. 13, 1937; s. Samuel Armstrong and Laura (Richardson) S. Student, Art Students League, 1956-57, 64-65, NYU, 1960-62. Assoc. for circulation Am. Fedn. Arts, N.Y.C., 1961-62; assoc. dir. Dintenfass Gallery, N.Y.C., 1962-64; pub. writer Dell Pub. Co., N.Y.C., 1965-66; dir. Dorsky Gallery, N.Y.C., 1966-67; editor Reader's Digest Condensed Books, Pleasantville, N.Y., 1967-74; tchr. Regional Art Ctrs., Conn., 1968-91. One-man shows include New Britain (Conn.) Mus. Am. Art, Mattatuck Mus., Waterbury, Conn., Condeso/Lawler Gallery, N.Y.C., 1968-91; group shows at Am. Acad. and Inst. Arts and Letters, N.Y.C., 1987-91, Aldrich Mus., Ridgefield, Conn., Old State House, Hartford, Conn., Nat. Acad. Design, N.Y.C., others. Recipient grants in painting, Conn. Commn. the Arts, Hartford, 1975-79, 91, fellowships Yaddo, 1967, MacDowell Colony, 1969, 74, 75, 80, Millay Colony for Arts, 1977, Va. Ctr. for Arts, 1978. Democrat. Episcopalian. Home: Old Town Rd West Cornwall CT 06796

SCOWCROFT, BRENT, retired air force officer, government official; b. Ogden, Utah, Mar. 19, 1925; s. James and Lucile (Ballantyne) S.; m. Marian Horner, Sept. 17, 1951; 1 dau., Karen. B.S., U.S. Mil. Acad., 1947; M.A., Columbia U., 1953, Ph.D., 1967; postgrad., Georgetown U., 1958. Commd. 2d lt. USAAF, 1947; advanced through grades to lt. gen. USAF, 1974; asst. prof. dept. social sci. U.S. Mil. Acad., 1953-57; asst. air attache Am. Embassy, Belgrade, Yugoslavia, 1959-61; assoc. prof. dept. polit. sci. U.S. Air Force Acad., Colo., 1962-63; prof., head dept. U.S. Air Force Acad., 1963-64; mem. staff long range planning div. Office Dep. Chief Staff Plans and Ops., Washington, 1964-67; assigned Nat. War Coll., 1967-68; staff asst. Western Hemisphere region Office Asst. Sec. Def. Internat. Security Affairs, Washington, 1968-69; dep. asst. dir. plans for nat. security matters office Dep. Chief Staff Plans and Ops., 1969-70; spl. asst. to dir. Joint Staff, Joint Chiefs of Staff, 1970-71; mil. asst. to Pres., 1972-73, dep. asst. to Pres. for nat. security affairs, 1973-75, asst. to Pres. for nat. security affairs, 1975-77; mem. Pres.'s Gen. Adv. Com. on Arms Control, 1977-80; asst. to Pres. Nat. Security Coun., Washington, 1989—; dir. Nat. Bank of Washington; vice chmn. Kissinger Assocs., Inc.; chmn. Pres.' Commn. on Strategic Forces; mem. Pres.' Commn. on Def. Mgmt., Pres. Spl. Rev. Bd. on the Iran/Contra Affair. Bd. dirs. Atlantic Council U.S.; Bd. visitors U.S. Air Force Air U., 1977-79; mem. adv. bd. Georgetown Center for Strategic and Internat. Studies. Decorated D.S.M. with two oak leaf clusters, Legion of Merit with oak leaf cluster, Air Force Commendation medal, D.S.M. Dept. Def., Nat. Security medal. Mem. Council Fgn. Relations (bd. dirs.), UN Assn. U.S. (vice chmn.), Am. Polit. Sci. Assn., Acad. Polit. Sci. Mem. Ch. Jesus Christ of Latter-day Saints. Office: 1600 Pennsylvania Ave NW Washington DC 20500*

SCOWCROFT, RICHARD MARK, English educator, mediaevalist; b. Palo Alto, Calif., June 2, 1951; s. Richard Pingree and Anne Means (Kendall) S. BA, Cornell U., 1972, MA, 1977, PhD, 1982. Lectr. Cornell U., Ithaca, N.Y., 1983; asst. prof. U. Va., Charlottesville, 1983-90; assoc. prof. English, Cath. U. Am,, Washington, 1990—; rsch. assoc. Dublin Inst. for Advanced Studies, Dublin, Ireland, 1990—. Contbr. articles to profl. jours. and book. Grad. fellow Ford Found., 1972-75, Lane Cooper Found., 1975-76; scholar Dublin Int. for Advanced Studies, 1978-79, 80-82. Mem. MLA, Medieval Acad. Am., Mediaeval Acad. Ireland, Royal Soc. Antiquaries of Ireland, Celtic Studies Assn. North Am., Early English Text Soc., Irish Texts Soc. Home: 1002 N Carolina Ave SE Washington DC 20003-3908 Office: Cath Univ of Am Dept of English Washington DC 20064

SCRASE, DAVID ANTHONY, German language educator; b. Upton, Dorset, Eng., Nov. 27, 1939; came to U.S., 1969; s. Robert Stanley and Dorothy Adelaide (Ridgewell) S.; m. Mary Ellen Martin, May 5, 1973 (div. Apr. 1985); 1 child, Anna Rachel Martin-Scrase. BA, Bristol U., 1962; PhD, Ind. U., 1972. Lectr. Zurich U., Switzerland, 1964-68; asst. prof. Oxford Poly., Eng., 1968-69; prof. U. Vt., Burlington, 1971—. Author: Wilhelm Lehmann, A Critical Biography, 1984; also articles, translations. Recipient fellowships Brit. Acad., London, 1973, Humboldt Found., Bonn, Fed. Republic Germany, 1974, 79. Office: U Vermont Dept German Waterman Bldg Burlington VT 05405

SCREPETIS, DENNIS, consulting engineer; b. Hoboken, N.J., Feb. 12, 1930; s. George and Athanasia (Stasinos) S.; m. Betty Pravasilis, Sept. 17, 1960. Student, Stevens Inst. Tech., Bklyn. Poly. Inst., Cooper Union, Rutgers U. Registered profl. engr., N.J., N.Y. Nuclear engr. Vitro Corp. Am., N.Y.C., 1957-60; project engr. Gen. Cable Corp., Bayonne, N.J., 1960-63; project mgr. AMF Atomics, York, Pa., 1963-65; sr. staff engr. nuclear div. Combustion Engring. Corp., Windsor, Conn., 1965-66; corp. engr. Standard Packaging Corp., N.Y.C., 1966-68; v.p. engring. Eastern Schokbeton, Bound Brook, N.J., 1968-74; cons. engr., Ft. Lee, N.J., 1974—. Patentee in nuclear sci. Mem. Am. Concrete Inst., Pre-Stressed Concrete Inst., Concrete Reinforcing Inst., Nat. Safety Coun., Am. Nat. Standards Inst., Nat. Fire Protection Assn., Internat. Platform Assn., Am. Water Works Assn., Am. Inst. Steel Constrn., ASTM, Am. Welding Soc., Concrete Industry Bd., Bldg. Ofcls. and Code Adminstrs. Soc. of Am. Mil. Engrs., Nat. Forensic Ctr., Am. Biog. Inst. Rsch. Assn. (bd. dirs.), Internat. Biog. Ctr. (bd. dir.), Masonry Soc. Greek Orthodox. Home and Office: 2200 N Central Rd Fort Lee NJ 07024-7523

SCRIABINE, ALEXANDER, pharmacologist; b. Yelgava, Latvia, Oct. 26, 1926; came to U.S., 1950; s. Constantine and Helene (Gorstkine) S.; m. Kira Kosbun, Jan. 10, 1949 (div. 1963); 1 child, Raisa; m. Christine Brendel, Oct. 24, 1964; 1 child, Nicholas. MD, U. Mainz, 1958; MS in Pharmacology, Cornell U., 1954. Rsch. mgr. Pfizer & Co., Groton, Conn., 1954-56, 59-66; chief pharmacologist Phila. Gen. Hosp., 1966-67; exec. dir. pharmacology Merck Inst., West Point, Pa., 1967-78; assoc. dir. Wyeth Labs., Radnor, Pa., 1978-79; dir. Inst. for Preclin. Pharmacology, Miles Inc., West Haven, Conn., 1979—; adj. assoc. prof. pharmacology U. Pa., Phila., 1967-84. Editorial bd. Jour. Cardiovascular Pharmacology, 1978—; editor: New Drugs Annual: Cardiovascular Drugs, 1983-84, Cardiovascular Drug Reviews, 1989—; editor 9 books; contbr. over 200 articles to profl. jours., chpts. to books; patentee in field. Mem. German Pharmacol. Soc., Am. Soc. for Pharmacology and Exptl. Therapeutics, Physiol. Soc. Phila. (pres. 1972-73), Am. Soc. for Clin. Pharmacology and Therapeutics, Sigma Xi. Russian Orthodox. Office: Miles Inc Pharm West Haven CT 06516

SCRITCHFIELD, RANDY LAWRENCE, financial planner; b. Harrisburg, Pa., Mar. 25, 1956; s. William Lawrence and Gladys (Etnoyer) S.; m. Katherine Gilroy, June 16, 1979; children: Joseph Martin, Jennifer Lynne. Cert. fin. planner, 1985. Mgr. Marriott Corp., Washington, 1972-80; sales rep. Aetna Life Inc., Washington, 1980-81, Acacia Group, Washington, 1981-87, Benicor, Silver Spring, Md., 1987-91; pres. Montgomery Fin. Group, Gaithersburg, Md., 1991—. Co-chmn. Libr. Adv. Com., Damascus, Md., 1990-92. Mem. Nat. Assn. Life Underwriters, Suburban Md. Life Underwriters (pres. 1990-91), Million Dollar Round Table (zone chmn. Chgo. 1991-92). Home: 10105 Nightingale St Gaithersburg MD 20882 Office: Montgomery Fin Group 10105 Nightingale St Gaithersburg MD 20882-4019

SCROCCO ZRZAVY, PHYLLIS ANN, mass communications educator; b. Dayton, Apr. 14, 1960; d. Anthony John and Christina Ann (Hall) Scrocco; m. Helfried Christian Zrzavy, Aug. 17, 1991. PhB, Miami U., Oxford, Ohio, 1982, BS in Edn., 1982, MEd, 1983. Cert. tchr. English and reading, N.H. Asst. prof. mass communications Franklin Pierce Coll., Rindge, N.H., 1988—; prof. media studies Regent's Coll., London, 1991. Active N.H. Women's Lobby, Concord, 1989—. Mem. Am. Studies Assn., Popular Culture Assn., Speech Communication Assn., Am. Folklore Soc. Home: 316 Greenfield Rd Bennington NH 03442-4000 Office: Franklin Pierce Coll College Rd Rindge NH 03461-3114

SCRUGGS, JOHN FLOYD, lobbyist; b. Everrett, Wash., Jan. 14, 1955; s. Floyd Leon and Marilyn (McVay) S.; m. Nancy Ellen Warner, June 25, 1983; children: Cari Michelle, Sarah Jane. BA, Biola U., 1978; JD, Am. U., 1986. Subcom. counsel Ho. Rules Com. U.S. Congress, Washington, 1979-80; floor asst. U.S. Congress, 1980-81; spl. asst. to Pres. for legisl. affairs The White Ho., Washington, 1982-83; asst. sec. HHS, Washington, 1984; ptnr. Gold and Liebengood, Inc., Washington, 1984—. Republican. Presbyterian.

SCRUITSKY, ROBERT LEE, project engineer; b. Kingston, Pa., Apr. 22, 1963; s. Robert Stanley and Mildred Mae (Katchmar) S. BS, Pa. State U., 1985. Electronics engr. USN Civil Svc., St. Inigoes, Md., 1985—. Recipient Aegis Excellence award 1991. Mem. AIAA. Home: 100 Dipon Ct Lexington Park MD 20653-1159 Office: USN (DOD) Code 2481 NESEA Saint Inigoes MD 20684-0010

SCUDERI, ANTHONY JOSEPH, psychotherapist/addictions counselor; b. Phila., Aug. 25, 1958. AA, Bucks County (Pa.) Community, 1978; BS, East Stroudsburg U., 1981; MDiv, Cath. Theol. Union, 1987; postgrad., Liberty U., 1989—. Cert. addictions counselor, cert. hypnotherapist. Judo/self-def. instr. Bucks Community Coll., Bucks County, 1977-78; Roman Cath. priest Franciscan Friars of Pulaski (Wis.), 1981-90; quality assurance chmn. Phila. Ctr. for Human Devel., 1989-91, outpatient coord., 1989-90, addictions svc. coord., 1989-90, partial hosp. coord., 1989-92; in-svc. lectr. Phila. Ctr. for Human Devel., 1989—. Notary pub., Phila., 1990-94. Mem. AACD, Am. Assn. Profl. Hypnotherapists, Nat. Bd. Hypnotherapist Examiners, Am. Assn. Behavioral Therapists, Pa. Chem. Abuse Certification Bd. Democrat. Home: Green Manor Apts # A-2 Philadelphia PA 19144 Office: Phila Ctr for Human Devel 10360 Drummond Rd Philadelphia PA 19154-3804

SCUDIERI, LORRAINE ALBERTO, mathematician, educator; b. Montclair, N.J., Apr. 25, 1940; d. Harry and Evelyn C. (Palmerie) Alberto; m. Bart Scudieri, Aug. 14, 1965; children: Laura, Matt, Chris, Tim, Patrick. B.A., Montclair State Coll., 1962; M.A., Rutgers U., 1966, M.S. in Statistics, 1987; postgrad. in mgmt., Rutgers U., Newark, 1988—. Tchr., Pascack Valley High Sch., Hillsdale, N.J., 1962-65, Pascack Hills High Sch., Montvale, N.J., 1976-77, Montclair State Coll., Upper Montclair, N.J., 1966-68, 69-70, 71, 74, 79-83, 85-87; stat. studies analyst bus. research div., Bell Atlantic Corp., Newark, 1987-92; mem. tech. staff measurement rsch. Bellcore, 1992—; instr. Fairleigh Dickinson U., 1969-72, 79-81, William Paterson Coll., Wayne, N.J., 1974-76, 82-83, Wyckoff (N.J.) Community Learning Center, 1979, Upsala Coll., East Orange, N.J., 1979-81; instr. decision scis. Rider Coll., Lawrenceville, N.J., 1983-85. Den mother Boy Scouts Am. NSF grantee, 1962-66. Mem. Ops. Rsch. Soc. Am., Soc. Indsl. and Applied Math., Soc. Computer Simulation.

SCULCO, LOIS JEAN, English educator; b. New Kensington, Pa., Nov. 12, 1938; d. L. Alexander and Rose Carmella (Condelli) S. BA, Seton Hill Coll., 1960; MA, Duquesne U., 1969, Azusa Pacific U., 1985. Faculty English dept. Seton Hill Coll., Greensburg, Pa., 1970-77; campus ministry Seton Hill Coll., Greensburg, 1975-77, dean student svcs., 1977-85, coord. freshman sem., 1981-85, sec. bd. trustees, 1988—, exec. asst. to pres., 1988-90, assoc. prof. English, 1989, v.p. for adminstrn. and student life, 1990—; campus ministry officer Sisters of Charity, Greensburg, 1985-89; sec. bd. trustees Seton Hill Coll., Greensburg, 1986—, cons. devel. edn. leader, 1987—; presenter on Holocaust, Shippensburg (Pa.) Univ., 1991. Bd. mem. Women's Svcs. of Westmoreland County, Greensburg, 1985-91, sec. bd., 1987-89, vol. training, 1989-91; mem. Greensburg (Pa.) Civic and Cultural Ctr., 1985-87. Named Outstanding Freshman Adv. Freshman Yr. Experience, Univ. S.C., 1990; recipient Outstanding Profl. Achievement award in Edn. and Adminstrn., Arnold (Pa.) C. of C., 1991. Mem. NAACP, Nat. Assn. Student Pers. Adminstrn., Nat. Assn. Women Deans and Councilors, Leadership Conf. Women Religious. Democrat. Roman Catholic. Office: Seton Hill College Greensburg PA 15601

SCULLEY, DAVID W., food company executive; b. N.Y.C., July 17, 1946; s. John and Margaret Blackburn (Smith) S.; m. Paula Cook; children—Heather Kahrl, David. B.A. in Econs. cum laude, Harvard U., 1968. Group product mgr. Lever Bros. Co., N.Y.C., 1971-73; gen. mgr. mktg. H.J. Heinz-U.S.A., Pitts., 1974-77, v.p. mktg., 1978-81; dep. mng. dir. H.J. Heinz-U.K., Middlesex, Eng., 1982-85; pres., chief exec. officer Heinz U.S.A., Pitts., 1985-89, sr. v.p., 1989—, also bd. dirs. Trustee Sewickley Valley Hosp., Pa., 1981, Allegheny Gen. Hosp., Pitts., 1986—; chmn. D.T. Watson Home Charity Golf Tournament, Sewickley, 1986, Young Pres.'s Orgn. Republican. Episcopalian. Clubs: Allegheny Country (Sewickley); Duquesne (Pitts.); Laurel Valley Golf (Ligonier, Pa.). Office: H J Heinz Co PO Box 57 Pittsburgh PA 15230-0057

SCULLY, MONYA FRANCES, clothing designer, inventor; b. Nirvana, Mich., July 31, 1921; d. Sylvester and Frances Elizabeth (Puburka) Horujko; m. Cornelius Andrew Thomas Scully, Feb. 28, 1950; 1 child, Cornelia Frances. BA, Ferris Inst., Big Rapids, Mich., 1942; philosophy student, New Sch. Social Rsch., 1948-51; student, Yogi Gupti Found., N.Y.C., 1955-58, Silva Mind Control, N.Y.C., 1972-74. Photographic model Conover Agy., N.Y.C., 1944-52; actress David O. Selznick, N.Y.C., 1945-50; writer New Sch. Social Rsch., N.Y.C., 1948-51; model Cy Perkins Agy., N.Y.C., 1975-77. Patentee in field; clothing designer. Activist in peace movement, Greenwich Village, N.Y.C., 1966-70; vol. Channel 13 TV, N.Y.C., 1978-84; mem. Greenwich Village Community Orgn., 1988—. Democrat. Roman Catholic.

SCULLY, ROGER TEHAN, lawyer; b. Washington, Jan. 10, 1948; s. James Henry and Marietta (Maguire) S.; m. Martha Anne Seebach, Dec. 29, 1979. BS, U. Md., 1977; JD, Cath. U., 1980. Bar: Md. 1980, D.C. 1981, U.S. Tax Ct. 1982, U.S. Supreme Ct. 1988. V.p. Bogley Related Cos., Rockville, Md., 1971-75; law clk. to presiding justice Superior Ct. of D.C., Washington, 1979-81; assoc. Lerch, Early & Roseman, Bethesda, Md., 1981-82; gen. counsel Laszlo N. Tauber, M.D. & Assocs., Bethesda, 1982—, Jefferson Meml. Hosp., Alexandria, Va., 1982—; spl. counsel Venable, Baetjer, Howard & Civiletti, Washington, 1991—; cons. in real estate Order of Friar Minor, N.Y.C., 1977—; lectr. Mortgage Bankers Assn., Washington, 1984—; bd. dirs. Jefferson Hosp. Corp., Alexandria, Va., Nozzoli Constrn. Co., Washington. Author: (with Quarles & Howard) Summary Adjudication Dispositive Motions and Summary Trials, 1991. Chmn. univ. adv. coun. St. Bonaventure U., Olean, N.Y., 1986—; trustee Edmund Burke Sch., Washington, 1984—; bd. dirs. Nat. Children's Choir, Washington, 1980—. Recipient First Order Affiliation Order of Friars Minor, 1985; named one of Outstanding Young Men in Am., 1982. Fellow D.C. Bar Assn.; mem. ABA, Fed. Bar Assn., Md. Bar Assn. (chmn. corp. counsel sect.), Assn. Trial Lawyers Am., Am. Judicature Soc., Selden Soc. (permanent mem.), U.S. Jud. Conf. of 4th Cir. (del.), U.S. Jud. Conf. Fed. Cir., Nat. Press Club, Univ. Club (Washington), Realty Club (N.Y.C.), Phi Delta Phi. Republican. Roman Catholic. Home: 10923 Wickshire Way Rockville MD 20852-3220 Office: 5110 Ridgefield Rd Ste 408 Bethesda MD 20816-3346

SCULLY, SUSAN, artist; b. Phila., Aug. 3, 1950; d. Francis J. and Eileen (O'Connor) S. BA in English, Chestnut Hill Coll., 1972. Designer of life-like masks, costumes, art work.

SEADLE, MICHAEL STEVEN, data processing executive, writer; b. Detroit, June 16, 1950; s. Peter Stephan Seadle and Ruth Mary (Stevens) Knight; m. Joan Louise Luft, May 18, 1984. BA, Earlham Coll., 1972; MA, U. Chgo., 1973, PhD, 1977. Supr. U. Chgo. Libr., 1976-81; applications programmer Washington Nat. Ins., Evanston, Ill., 1981-83, Bankers Life and Casualty, Chgo., 1983-84; data base adminstr. Am. Dental Assn., Chgo., 1984-87; asst. dir. U. Computing Eastern, Mich. U., Ypsilanti, Mich., 1987-89; systems programmer Network Resources Cornell U., Ithaca, N.Y., 1989-90; online ops. mgr. Cornell U. Libr., Ithaca, N.Y., 1990—; treas. Midwest Region Am. Friends Svc. Com., Chgo., 1979-85; mem. Allocations Oversight Com., AFSC, Phila., 1985—. Author: Quakers in Nazi Germany, 1979, Automating Mainframe Management, 1991; contbr. articles to profl. jours. Mem. Nat. Systems Programmers Assn., Phi Beta Kappa. Mem. Soc. of Friends. Office: Cornell University 501 Olin Library Ithaca NY 14853

SEADLER, STEPHEN EDWARD, business and computer consultant, social scientist; b. N.Y.C., 1926; s. Silas Frank and Deborah (Gelbin) S.; AB in Physics, Columbia U., 1947, postgrad. in atomic and nuclear physics, 1947; postgrad. in relativity, cosmology and quantum mechanics, George Washington U., 1948-50; m. Ingrid Linnea Adolfsson, Aug. 7, 1954; children: Einar Austin, Anna Carin. Legal rsch. asst., editor AEC, Washington, 1947-51; electronic engr. Cushing & Nevell, Warner, Inc., N.Y.C., 1951-54; seminar leader, leader trainer Am. Found. for Continuing Edn., N.Y.C. 1955-57; exec. dir. Medimetric Inst., 1957-59; mem. long range planning com., chmn. corporate forecasting com., mktg. rsch. mgr. W. A. Sheaffer Pen Co., Ft. Madison, Iowa, 1959-65; founder Internat. Dynamics Corp., Ft. Madison and N.Y.C., 1965, pres., 1965-70; orginator DELTA program for prevention and treatment of violence, 1970; founder ID Center, Ft. Madison, now N.Y.C., 1968, pres., 1968—; mgmt. cons. in human resources devel. and conflict reduction, N.Y.C., 1970-73; pres. UNICONSULT computer-based mgmt. and computer scis., N.Y.C., 1973—; speaker on decision support systems, internat. affairs and ideological arms control; author/speaker (presentation) Holocaust, History and Arms Control; originator social scis. of ideologics and computer based knowledge systems sci. of ideotopology; spl. works collection accessible via On-line Computer Libr. Ctr. Instr. polit. sci. Ia. State Penitentiary, 1959-62. Served with AUS, 1944-46. Mem. Am. Phys. Soc., Am. Statis. Assn., Acad. Polit. Sci., Am. Sociol. Assn., IEEE, N.Y. Acad. Sci., Am. Mgmt. Assn. (lectr. 1963-68), Internat. Platform Assn. Unitarian. Lodges: Masons (32 deg.), Shriners. Author: Savagery in Modern Marriage and Its Relation to Social and International Violence, 1990, Holocaust, History and Arms Control II, 1990; contbr. Ideologics and ideotopology sects. to Administrative Decision Making, 1977, Societal Systems, 1978; Management Handbook for Public Administrators, 1978; also articles profl. jours. Testimony on ideological arms control in Part 4 of Senate Fgn. Relations Com. Hearings on Salt II Treaty, 1979. Office: 521 5th Ave Ste 1700 New York NY 10175-0003

SEAL, JOHN S., JR., consulting company executive; b. Phila., May 20, 1944; s. John S. Sr. and Gertrude Eva (Abbott) S.; m. Anna M. Salcedo; children: Kathryn, Ashley and Kristen (twins), Heather. BS in Econs., Drexel U., 1967; MBA, Dartmouth Coll., 1971. CPA, N.Y. Asst. to exec. v.p. fin. Gould Inc., Chgo., 1971; dir. electronics group fin. planning Gould Inc., Newton Upper Falls, Mass., 1972-73; pres., treas., chief exec. officer Nat. Communications Industries Co., Greenwich, Conn., 1973-76, chmn., 1973-79; exec. v.p. Boyerton (Pa.) Burial Casket Co., 1976-77; v.p., gen. mgr. communications products div. FSC Corp., Pitts., 1977-79; sr. v.p. Butcher and Singer Inc. subs. Butcher and Co. Inc., Phila., 1979-85; pres. Sovereign Group Inc. subs. Butcher and Co. Inc., Phila., 1983-85, Seal Devel. Co., Phila., 1985-88; mng. dir. Essex Fin. Group, Phila., 1988—; bd. dirs. Rittenhouse Sq. Fitness Club, Phila. Trustee Please Touch Mus., Phila., 1987-90; bd. dirs. alumni bd. Drexel U., Phila., 1983—. Served U.S. Army, 1967-68. Mem. Am. Inst. CPAs, N.Y. Soc. CPAs, Conn. Soc. CPAs. Republican. Mem. Ch. of Christ. Club: Union League (Phila.). Home: 208 Llanfair Rd Ardmore PA 19003-3306 Office: Essex Fin Group Essex House 1708 Locust St Philadelphia PA 19103-6107

SEALL-SASIAIN, JORGE, lawyer; b. Asuncion, Paraguay, Oct. 20, 1952; came to U.S., 1982; s. Enrique and Luisa (Sasiain) S. Abogado, Nat. U. Law Sch., Asuncion, 1977; sociologist, CATH. U., Asuncion, 1979; LLM, Harvard Law Sch., 1984, D. in Juridical Scis. all but dissertation, 1987. Bar: Paraguay 1978. Atty. pvt. practice, Asuncion, 1978-82; case cons. Comité Iglesias/Legal Aid Orgn., Asuncion, 1978-82; dir. internat. law dept. Orgn. Am. States, Washington, 1987-89, human rights specialist, 1989—; v.p. constrn. law com. Inter-Am. Bar Assn., Washington, 1989—. Bd. dirs. Ayuda, Washington, 1987—. Mem. Inter-Am. Bar Assn. (v.p. constitutional law com. 1989—), Harvard Club, Potomac Boat Club. Roman Catholic. Home: 730 24th St NW Apt 716 Washington DC 20037 Office: Orgn Am States Inter-Am Com Human Rights 1889 F St Rm 830-D Washington DC 20006

SEAMAN, PEGGY JEAN, lawyer; b. New Orleans, Nov. 21, 1949; d. William David and Leah Catherine (Bourdet) Smith; m. Terry Noako Seaman, Dec. 22, 1970; children: Vanya Lianne, Ember Catherine. BA, Rutgers U.-Camden, 1974; JD, N.Y. Law Sch., 1978. Bar: N.Y. 1978, Va. 1980, U.S. Dist. Ct. Va., 1980, U.S. Dist. Ct. (so. and ea. dists.) N.Y. 1978. Assoc. Carol Lilienfeld, Esq., N.Y.C., 1978-79; gen. atty. Merit Systems Protection Bd., Office of Appeals, Washington, 1980-82, presiding ofcl., Washington regional office, Falls Church, Va., 1982-85, adminstrv. judge St. Louis regional office, 1985-87; atty. Office of Dep. Exec. Dir. for Regional Ops., Washington, 1987—; gen. atty. Office of Appeals Counsel, Washington, 1987—. Recipient Sustained Superior Performance award Merit Systems Protection Bd., 1982, 84, 90, Spl. Act award, 1988, Chmn.'s Honor award, 1991). Mem. ABA, Athenaeum Honor Soc., Mensa. Democrat. Home: 8302 Crown Court Rd Alexandria VA 22308-1526 Office: Merit Systems Protection Bd 1120 Vermont Ave NW Washington DC 20419-0002

SEAMANS, ANDREW CHARLES, editorial and public relations consultant, columnist, author; b. Hillside, N.J., Sept. 10, 1937; s. Thomas Randall and Marie Josephine (Mazur) S.; m. Marion Gloria Lufbery, Aug. 25, 1956 (div. June 1985); children: Andrew Charles, Darryl Wayne, Marion Gloria Seamans Raynor, Dawn Louise. AS cum laude, No. Va. Community Coll., Annandale, 1989. Lic. real estate salesman, Va. Editorial writer U.S. Press Assn., McLean, Va., 1968-70; pub. rels. asst. Nat. Right to Work Com., Washington, 1970; assoc. editor Human Events, Washington, 1970-81; mng. editor Heritage Features Syndicate, Washington, 1981-91; syndicated columnist The Answer Man Creators Syndicate, L.A., 1985—; bd. dirs., pub. rels. cons. Marine Learning Inst., St. Louis, 1980—. Author: Who, What, When, Where, Why In the World of American History, 1991, Who, What, When, Where, Why In the World of World History, 1991, Who, What, When, Where, Why In the World of Nature, 1992; co-author: Whose FBI?, 1974. Bd. dirs. McLean Little League Baseball, Inc., 1975-83, pres., 1982-83; pres. Rahway (N.J.) Young Rep. Club, 1964-66; chmn. platform com. Union County Young Reps., N.J. Young Reps., various other Rep. orgns. Recipient cert. of appreciation McLean Little League Baseball, 1978, named to Hall of Fame, 1985. Mem. Pub. Rels. Soc. Am., Soc. Profl. Journalists (bd. dirs. D.C. chpt. 1986-87, membership dir. 1986-87, 89-90, dir. pub. info. 1988), No. Va. Assn. Historians, Va. Hist. Soc., Internat. Platform Assn., Nat. Press Club. Episcopalian. Home and Office: 1921 Westmoreland St Mc Lean VA 22101-4325

SEAMANS, ROBERT CHANNING, JR., astronautical engineering educator; b. Salem, Mass., Oct. 30, 1918; s. Robert Channing and Pauline (Bosson) S.; m. Eugenia Merrill, June 13, 1942; children: Katherine (Mrs. Louis Padulo), Robert Channing III, Joseph, May (Seamans Baldwin),

Daniel M. BS, Harvard U., 1939; MS, MIT, 1942, ScD, 1951; grad. exec. program bus. adminstrn., Columbia U., 1959; DSc, Rollins Coll., 1962, NYU, 1967; DEng, Norwich Acad., 1971, Notre Dame U., 1974, Rensselaer Poly. Inst., 1974, U. Wyo., 1975, George Washington U., 1975, Lehigh U., 1976, Thomas Coll., 1980, Curry Coll., 1982. Successively instr. dept. aero. engring., staff engr. instrumentation lab., asst. prof., project leader instrumentation lab., asso. prof. Mass. Inst. Tech., 1941-55; chief engr. Project Meteor, 1950-53, dir. flight control lab., 1953-55; mgr. airborne systems lab., chief systems engr. airborne systems dept. RCA, 1955-58, chief engr. missile electronics and controls div., 1958-60; asso. adminstr. NASA, 1960-65, dep. adminstr., 1965-68, cons., 1968-69; vis. prof. MIT, 1968, Hunsaker prof., 1968-69; sec. air force, 1969-73; pres. Nat. Acad. Engring., 1973-74; adminstr. ERDA, Washington, 1974-77; Henry R. Luce prof. environment and pub. policy MIT, 1977-84, sr. lectr. dept. aeros. and astronautics, 1984—, dean Sch. Engring.,, 1978-81; mem. sci. adv. bd. USAF, 1957-62, assoc. adviser, 1963-67. Mem. bd. overseers Harvard U., 1968-74; trustee Mus. of Sch., Boston, Sea Edn. Assn., Nat. Geog. Soc., Carnegie Inst., Washington. Recipient Naval Ordnance Devel. award, 1945; Godfrey L. Cabot award Aero Club New Eng., 1965; Distinguished Service medal NASA, 1965, 69; Robert H. Goddard Meml. trophy, 1968; Distinguished Pub. Service medal Dept. Def., 1973; Exceptional Civilian Service award Dept. Air Force, 1973; Gen. Thomas D. White U.S. Air Force Space Trophy, 1973; Ralph Coats Roe medal ASME, 1977; Achievement award Nat. Soc. Profl. Engrs.; Thomas D. White Nat. Def. award, 1980; Exceptional Service award Dept. Air Force, 1985. Fellow Am. Acad. Arts and Scis., Am. Astron. Soc., IEEE, AIAA (hon., Lawrence Sperry award 1951); mem. Internat. Acad. Astronautics, Am. Soc. Pub. Adminstrn., Nat. Acad. Engring., AAAS, Air Force Acad. Found., Fgn. Policy Assn., Coun. on Fgn. Rels., Sigma Xi. Clubs: Harvard (Boston); Manchester Yacht (Mass.); Essex County (Mass.); Chevy Chase, Metropolitan (Washington); Cruising of Am. (Boston Sta.). Office: 33-406 MIT Cambridge MA 02139

SEARLE, NIGEL HILTON, management consultant; b. Manchester, Eng., Oct. 30, 1946; s. Robert Frederick Southgate and Nellie (Kirby) S.; m. Madeline Wood, Sept. 16, 1967 (div. 1978). BA, Lancaster U., Eng., 1967; PhD, Edinburgh U., Scotland, 1970. Computer scientist Arthur D. Little, Cambridge, Eng., 1970-72; tech. dir. Sinclair Radionics Ltd., Cambridge, Eng., 1972-74; exec. v.p. Sinclair Radionics Inc., N.Y.C., 1974-77; pres. GFN Ind., Inc., N.Y.C., 1977-80; exec. v.p. Sinclair Rsch. Inc., Boston, 1980-82; mng. dir. Sinclair Rsch. Ltd., Cambridge, Eng., 1982-85; pres. The Mktg. Clinic, Keene, N.H., 1986—; adj. faculty Keene State Coll., 1987-91. Author: Successful Investments, 1972; inventor voice recognition, 1991, math. functions "Searle" operators; contbr. articles to profl. jours. Home: 16 Church St Keene NH 03431-3884 Office: The Marketing Clinic 16 Church St Keene NH 03431-3884

SEARLES, THOMAS DANIEL, society administrator; b. New Orleans, Aug. 6, 1937; s. Eugene Harve and Mary Louise (Swan) S.; m. Edna Winifred Lowe, Mar. 10, 1956; children: Thomas Daniel II, Laura Louise, Carol Gay, Prentiss Eugene. BS, La. Tech. U., 1960; postgrad., Montgomery Coll. Field rep. So. Pine Inspection Bur., Pensacola, Fla., 1960-65, Am. Lumber Standards Com., Germantown, Md., 1965-70; exec. v.p. Am. Lumber Standards Com., Germantown, 1970—; U.S. rep. to lumber com., UN ECE, Geneva, 1974—; appointee to Industry Sectory Adv. Com., Sec. Commerce, Washington, 1986—, Industry Functional Adv. Com., Sec. Commerce, Washington, 1986—. Vice pres. Clarksburg (Md.) Community Assn., 1988. Mem. Standards Engring. Soc., Greater Washington Soc. Assn. Execs. Republican. Methodist. Office: Am Lumber Standards Com PO Box 210 Germantown MD 20875-0210

SEARLES, WILLIAM HARRIS, processing engineering company administrator; b. Marlborough, Mass., June 26, 1956; s. Clarence Eugene and Rita (Scally) S. BS, Worcester State Coll., 1985; MA, Harvard U., 1989. Acctg. asst. Cen. Mass. Magnetic Imaging, Worcester, Mass., 1987-89; gen. mgr. Oliver M. Dean, Inc., Worcester, Mass., 1990—. Mem. Harvard Club Boston. Republican. Home: 43 Santoro Rd Worcester MA 01606

SEARLS, JAMES PAUL, mineral economist; b. Madison, Wis., Aug. 11, 1937; s. Edward Marlborough and Anna Mary (Haughey) S.; m. Thea Marie Waldrop, Oct. 11, 1967 (div. Nov. 1986); children: Christopher Kerry, Damion Thomas. BS in Physics, St. Louis U., 1966; MA in Econs., Pa. State. U., 1977. Physicist Munitions Command U.S. Army, Aberdeen, Md., 1966-74; mineral economist Electric Power Rsch. Inst., Palo Alto, Calif., 1976-78; prog. analyst Resource Applications Dept. Energy, Washington, 1978-79; mineral economist Bur. Mines Dept. Interior, Washington, 1979—. Home: 20407 Shadow Oak Ct Gaithersburg MD 20879-1127 Office: Bur Mines Washington DC 20241

SEARLS, ROBERT LOUARN, biology educator; b. Madison, Wis., Oct. 26, 1931; s. Edward Marlborough and Anna Mary (Haughey) S.; m. Ellen Donovan, June 10, 1961; children: Timothy, David, Paul, Anne. BS, U. Wis., 1953; PhD, U. Calif., 1960. Postdoctoral Brandeis U., Waltham, Mass., 1960-63; asst. prof. U. Va., Charlottesville, 1963-68; from assoc. prof. to prof. Temple U., Phila., 1968—. Contbr. numerous articles and abstracts to profl. jours. 1st lt. U.S. Army, 1954-56. Mem. Am. Soc. Cell Biologists, Am. Assn. Anatomists, Am. Soc. Zoologists, Internat. Soc. Devel. Biologists, Soc. Devel. Biology. Home: 1306 Jericho Rd Abington PA 19001-3313 Office: Temple U Dept Biology Philadelphia PA 19122

SEARS, JOHN WINTHROP, lawyer, administrator; b. Boston, Dec. 18, 1930; s. Richard Dudley and Frederica Fulton (Leser) S.; m. Catherine Coolidge, 1965 (div. 1970). AB magna cum laude, Harvard U., 1952, JD, 1959; MLitt, Oxford U., 1957. Bar: Mass. 1959, U.S. Dist. Ct. Mass. 1982. Rep. Brown Bros. Harriman, N.Y.C., 1959-63, Boston, 1963-66; mem. Mass. Ho. Reps. 1965-68; sheriff Suffolk County, Mass., 1968-69; chmn. Boston Fin. Commn., 1969-70, Met. Dist. Commn., 1970-75; councillor-at-large Boston City Coun., 1980-82; trustee Sears Office, Boston, 1975—; apptd. bd. dirs. Fulbright Scholarship, 1991. Contbr. articles to profl. jours. Trustee Christ's Ch., Longwood, Brookline Mass., 1965—, Sears Trusts, Boston, 1975—; hon. trustee J.F. Kennedy Libr., 1991—; bd. dirs. Crime and Justice Found. Corp., Boys and Girls Clubs Boston, Middlesex Club, Ripon Soc., Mus. Am. Textile Heritage, 1987—; assoc. Boston Pub. Libr.; Rep. candidate Mayor of Boston, 1967, Sec. State, Mass., 1978, Gov. of Mass., 1982; vice chmn. Ward 5 Rep. Com., 1965-69, 75-85; chmn. Rep. State Com., 1975-76, mem., 80-85; del. Rep. Nat. Conv., 1968, 76, State Conv., 1966—; mem. U.S. Electoral Coll., 1984; bd. dirs. United South End Settlements, 1966—, chmn., 1977-78. Lt. comdr. USN, 1952-54, 61-62. Rhodes scholar, 1955; recipient Outstanding Pub. Servant award Mass. Legis. Assn., 1975. Mem. Mass. Bar Assn., New Eng. Hist. and Geneal. Soc. (bd. dirs., councillor 1977-82), Mass. Hist. Soc., Handel and Haydn Soc. (gov. 1982-87), Spee Club (pres., trustee, Cambridge), Tennis and Racquet Club, Somerset Club, The Country Club (Brookline), St. Botolph Club, Wed. Evening Club of 1777, Phi Beta Kappa. Republican. Home: 7 Acorn St Boston MA 02108-3501 Office: 15 Court Sq Rm 830 Boston MA 02108

SEARS, MARVIN, ophthalmologist, educator; b. N.Y.C., Sept. 16, 1928; s. Louis and Blanche Sears; m. Myra Sears, July 30, 1951 (div.); children: Anne, David, Jonathan, Edward; m. Francine Moss, July 31, 1979; 1 child, Benjamin. AB, Princeton U., 1949; MD, Columbia U., 1953. Intern Bellevue Hosp., N.Y.C., 1954; resident in ophthalmology Johns Hopkins Hosp., 1954-61; fellow NIH, 1959-60; chmn. sect. ophthalmology Yale-New Haven (Conn.) Hosp., 1961-71; asst. prof. dept. ophthalmology and visual sci. Yale U. Sch. Medicine, 1961-64, assoc. prof., 1964-69, prof., 1969—, chmn., 1971—; cons. Vets. Meml. Med. Ctr., Meriden, Conn., 1986—, Princess Margaret Hosp., Nassau, 1982—, Waterbury (Conn.) Hosp., 1975—, William W. Backus Hosp., Norwich, Conn., 1974—, Hosp. Albert Schweitzer, Des Chapelles, Haiti, 1968-83, Jenkins (Ky.) Clinic Hosp., 1968, Hosp. St. Raphael, New Haven, New Britain (Conn.) Gen. Hosp.; chief cons. VA Med. Ctr., West Haven, Conn., 1961—; instr. Johns Hopkins Hosp., 1959-61; vis. prof. dept. ophthalmology U. Puerto Rico; mem. numerous adv. coms. Editorial bd.: Am. Jour. Ophthalmology, 1967-82, Investigative Ophthalmology, 1968-78, Jour. Ocular Pharmacology, 1985—; contbr. articles to profl. jours. Recipient McKosh prize/Epistemology Princeton U., 1949, Schwentker medal Johns Hopkins Hosp., 1958, Alcon Rsch. Inst. award, 1985, Merit award Nat. Eye Inst., 1990—; named Gifford lectr. Chgo. Ophthal. Soc., 1985. Fellow ACS, Pierson Coll. Yale U.; mem. Am. Acad. Ophthalmology, Am. Ophthal. Soc., Assn. for Rsch. in Vision and Ophthalmology (Jonas S. Friedenwald award 1977), Assn. Univ. Profs. Ophthalmology, Conn. State Med. Soc., Internat. Agy. for Prevention Blindness, Internat. Soc. for Eye Rsch., New England Ophthal. Soc. (award 1969), Pan Am. Assn. Ophthalmology, Soc. Eye Surgeons, Wilmer Residents Assn., Appalachian Mountain Club, Audubon Soc., Lions (Melvin Jones fellow). Jewish. Home: 51 Flying Point Rd Branford CT 06405-5703 Office: Yale Eye Ctr 330 Cedar St # 3333 New Haven CT 06510-3218

SEARY, LAWRENCE ANTHONY, cinematographer; b. N.Y.C., June 13, 1951; m. Phyllis Cole, Oct. 2, 1976; children: Tara Ann, Paul Anthony. BFA, NYU, 1973. News cameraman NBC, N.Y.C., 1974—. Recipient N.Y. State Broadcast award UPI, 1987. Mem. NATAS (Emmy award nominations, 1978, 82, Emmy award 1978), N.Y. Press Photographers Assn., Mensa, N.Y. Press Club. Democrat. Roman Catholic. Office: NBC 30 Rockefeller Pla New York NY 10112

SEASON, JAMES HOBSON, trading company executive; b. Savannah, Ga., Mar. 8, 1944; s. Edwin Herbert Jr. and Hazel Margaret (Hobson) S.; m. Randi Tangen Loftsgaarden, Oct. 17, 1981; children: Jonathan Hale, Tyler Welles. AB, Dartmouth Coll., 1966; MBA, U. Mich., 1967; JD, U. Va., 1971. Bar: N.Y. 1972. Assoc. corp. fin. Kuhn, Loeb & Co., N.Y.C., 1971-74; mgr. corp. fin. policy Exxon Corp., N.Y.C., 1974-77; v.p. Corp. Capital Cons., N.Y.C., 1977-80; exec. v.p., chief fin. officer Logan (Utah) Mfg. Co., N.Y.C., 1980-82; mng. dir. Chase Investment Bank, N.Y.C., 1982-86; v.p. Golodetz Trading Corp., N.Y.C., 1986—; bd. dirs. MemTech Tech. Corp., Santa Clara, Calif., Am. Homestead, Inc., Mt. Laurel, N.J., Am. Builders Hardware Corp., L.A. Republican. Home: 18 Brookside Park Greenwich CT 06831-5316 Office: Golodetz Trading Corp 666 5th Ave New York NY 10103-0001

SEATS, PEGGY CHISOLM, marketing executive; b. Lisman, Ala., Oct. 12, 1951; d. William H. and Bernice (Berry) Chisolm; m. Melvin Seats (div.). BA in Communications cum laude, Lewis U., 1974. Account exec. Globe Broadcasting, Chgo., 1976-78, Merrill Lynch, Chgo., 1978-79, Transp. Displays, Inc., Chgo., 1979-81; nat. accounts mgr. Soft Sheen Products Co., Chgo., 1981-83; mktg. cons. Reverie, Inc., Chgo., 1983-85, Atlanta, 1987—; pub. rels., mktg. mgr. Proctor & Gardner Advt., Chgo., 1985-86; dir. pub. rels., mktg. Morris Brown Coll., Atlanta, 1986-87; mgr. mktg. Howard U. Press, Washington, 1989-90; cons. White House Initiative on Historically Black Colls., Univs., 1990—; founder Black Pub. Rels. Soc., Atlanta, 1987. Contbr. numerous articles to newspapers and mags. Bd. dirs Lewis U. Alumni, Ill., 1979; state advisor U.S. Congl. Adv. Bd., Ill. 1982. Recipient Kizzie award Black Women Hall of Fame, Chgo., 1981, Svc. award Nat. Assn. Women in Media, Chgo., 1982; inductee Outstanding Women of Am., 1975, 87. Mem. Internat. Platform Assn., Internat. Assn. Bus. Commmunicators, Pub. Rels. Soc. Am., Black Pub. Rels. Soc. (pres. emeritus), Nat. Assn. Market Developers. Republican. Baptist. Home: 2020 Pennsylvania Ave NW Washington DC 20006-1846

SEBOLD, THOMAS EDWARD, company executive; b. Hartford, Conn., Jan. 7, 1951; s. Hubert Elwood and Viola Ann (Gayeski) S.; m. Barbara Ann Coughlin, Oct. 19, 1974; children: Melissa Ann, Matthew Thomas. AS in Gen. Studies, Middlesex Community Coll., 1982. Cert. indsl. electronics. Ops. mgr., v.p. S&S Motors, Inc., Cromwell, Conn., 1972; multi-machine operator Pratt & Whitney Aircraft div. United Technologies, East Hartford, Conn., 1972-75, indsl. electronics apprentice, 1975-78; electronic technician Pratt & Whitney Aircraft div. United Technologies, North Haven, Conn., 1978-82; audio-visual coord. mktg. support Sikorsky Aircraft div. United Technologies, Stratford, Conn., 1982-83, sr. coord. shows and exhibits, 1983-89, exhibit mgr. Boeing Sikorsky, 1989-90; sr. coord. tech. presentations corp. United Technologies, Hartford, Conn., 1990-91, internal communications rep./total quality mgmt. coord., 1991—. Editor, author Chronos, 1969. Aux. state trooper Conn. State Police, Colchester, 1975-77; mem. Rep. Town Com., Middletown, 1986-87. Mem. Internat. Exhibitors Assn., Am. Soc. Quality Control, Xavier High Sch. Alumni Assn. (bd. mem. 1991-94). Roman Catholic. Home: 56 Acorn Dr Middletown CT 06457-6122 Office: United Technologies Corp United Technologies Bldg Hartford CT 06457

SECCAFICO, JOHN, clinical social worker; b. Jersey City, Oct. 2, 1948; s. James Anthony and Lucille (Mastronardi) S.; m. Alice O'Neill, June 10, 1989; stepchildren: Robert, Sarah. BA, Seton Hall U., 1971, MA, 1974; MSW, Rutgers U., 1983. Diplomate Am. Bd. Med. Psychotherapists, Am. Bd. Examiners in Clin. Social Work; cert. sch. social worker, N.J.; lic. marriage and family therapist, N.J. Income maintenance specialist Ocean County Bd. Social Svcs., Toms River, N.J., 1974-81; clin. social worker Shore Mental Health Ctr., Lakewood, N.J., 1978-87, Ocean Inst., Manahawkin, N.J., 1983-84; pvt. practice Brick, N.J., 1983—; chief ops. officer Personamax Internat. Ltd.; dir. gerontology Georgian Court Coll., Lakewood, 1987—; dir. home psychotherapy program Medex Home Health Care, Inc., Toms River, 1988—. Weekly mental health columnist, 1987. Dir. Toms River Jaycees, 1978. Mem. Acad. Cert. Social Workers, Nat. Assn. Social Workers. Baptist. Home: 821 Bay Ave Toms River NJ 08753 Office: 35 Beaverson Blvd Ste 3 Brick NJ 08723-7895

SECKEL, CORNELIA, publisher; b. N.Y.C., June 28, 1946; d. Robert Samuel and Elsie (Teich) Seckel; m. Raymond J. Steiner, Oct. 12, 1980. BA, Queens Coll., CUNY, Flushing, 1968; MA, Mich. State U., 1973. Tchr. N.Y.C. Bd. Edn., 1968-69, Lansing (Mich.) Sch. Dist., 1969-76; career educator Ulster County C. of C., Kingston, N.Y., 1979-85; pub. Art Times, cultural and creative jour., Saugerties, N.Y., 1984—. Pres. Ulster County NOW Chpt., Kingston, 1983; legis. cand. Ulster County, 1984; arts commentator WAMC Pub. Radio Network, Albany, 1988—. Mem. Artists Fellowship, Nat. Arts Club. Office: CSS Publications Inc PO Box 730 Mount Marion NY 12456-0730

SECOLA, JANE AUSTIN, marketing consultant; b. Orange, N.J., July 1, 1929; d. Dondald Drysdale and Grace (Gibson) Austin; m. Theodore A. Secola, Sept. 22, 1951; children: Sheryl Secola Young, Wendy Robin. Student, Fairleigh Dickinson Jr. Coll.; BA, Berkeley Coll., Little Falls, N.J., 1947; Cert. Mktg. Dir., Calif. Poly. U., 1950. With sales promotion dept. ABC, N.Y.C., 1948-53; radio rep. John Blair & Co., 1953-54; ptnr. Tyndall Assocs., pub. rels., N.Y.C., 1955-70; dir. mktg. The Mall at Short Hills, N.J., 1970-73; sr. mktg. dir. The Rouse Co., Wayne, N.J., 1973-78; regional mktg. dir. Pembrook Mgmt., Rockaway, N.J., 1978-80; corp. mktg. dir. Federated Stores Realty, Cin., 1980-85, Enterprise Devel. Co., Columbia, Md., 1985-90; mktg. cons. Solutions by Secola, Inc., Fairfield, N.J., 1990—. Contbr. articles to mags. Bd. dirs., trustee Berkeley Sch., 1981—; trustee Berkeley Coll. Bus., 1981—. Named Alumni of Yr., Berkeley Coll., 1969; recipient Anny award Advt. Club N.Y., 1983, also civic and community awards, Maxi Awards, ICSC. Mem. Internat. Coun. Shopping Ctrs. (N.J., N.Y. Shopping Coun., cert. mktg. dir. com., 7 Maxi awards 1978-90). Republican. Baptist. Home and Office: 31 Stag Trl Fairfield NJ 07004-1527

SECOR, GLEN MICHAEL, publishing executive; b. Salem, Mass., Aug. 27, 1960; s. John Ralph Secor and Sally Ann (Bayley) Secor Moniz; m. Rosheen Margaret Murphy, Jan. 30, 1980; children: Patrick, Catherine, Andrew, Elisabeth. BA in Psychology, Stonehill Coll., 1982; MS in Acctg., N.H. Coll., 1988; Student, Suffolk U. Law Sch., 1989—. Cert. mgmt. acct. Exec. v.p. Yankee Book Peddler, Inc., Contoocook, N.H., 1981—. Mem. Nat. Assn. Accts. (N.H. chpt.), Am. Mgmt. Assn., Bus. and Industry Assn. N.H. Republican. Roman Catholic. Home: 14 Drawbridge Rd Westford MA 01886-2614 Office: Yankee Book Peddler Inc Maple St Contoocook NH 03229

SEDELMAIER, J. J., film producer and director; b. Chgo., Mar. 11, 1956; s. John Josef and Marie S.; m. Patrice Estella Masters, Nov. 4, 1981; 1 child, Chloe Jordan. Student, Millikin U., 1974-75; BS in Art, U. Wis., 1979. Asst. animator Perpetual Motion Pictures, N.Y.C., 1981-82; asst. animator, animator Buzzco Prodns., N.Y.C., 1982-84; asst. animator, animator The Ink Tank Corp., N.Y.C., 1984-85, producer, 1985-86, exec. producer, 1986-88, assoc. dir., dir., exec. producer, rep., 1989-91; pres., producer, dir. J. J. Sedelmaier Prodns., White Plains, N.Y., 1991—. Mem. Assn. Internat. Film Animation, Acad. TV Arts and Scis., Art Dirs. Club, Shore Line Interurban Hist. Soc., Eastchester Hist. Soc. Office: 199 Main St White Plains NY 10601-3200

SEDLACEK, KEITH WAYNE, psychiatrist, educator; b. Grand Island, Nebr., Oct. 24, 1944; s. John J. and Vivian M. (Barney) S.; m. Diane K. Roth, Sept. 3, 1987; children: John Daniel, Heather Jean. BA, Harvard Coll., 1966; MD, Columbia U., 1972. Intern, then psychiat. resident St. Lukes Hosp., N.Y.C., 1972-75, attending physician, 1972-83; instr. clin. psychiatry Columbia Coll. Physicians and Surgeons, N.Y.C., 1972—; attending physician St. Lukes-Roosevelt Hosp. Ctr., N.Y.C., 1983—; med. dir. Stress Regulation Inst., N.Y.C., 1981—; bd. dirs. Biofeedback Soc. Am., Denver, 1982-85, Biofeedback Certification Inst. Am., Denver, 1983-87. Author: The Sedlacek Technique, 1989; co-author: How to Avoid Stress Before it Kills You; asst. editor Biofeedback & Self Regulation, 1985—. Rockefeller fellow Rockefellow Fund, Harvard U., 1966-68, Noble fellow in fgn. affairs Noble Found., Columbia U., 1972-73. Mem. AMA, Am. Psychiat. Assn., Am. Psychiat. Assn. (chmn. behavioral therapy N.Y.C. area 1984—), Behavioral Medicine Soc. Office: Stress Regulation Inst 239 E 79th St Ste 1 New York NY 10021-0810

SEDLAK, VALERIE FRANCES, English educator; b. Balt., Mar. 11, 1934; d. Julian Joseph and Eleanor Eva (Pilot) Sedlak; 1 child, Barry. AB in English, Coll. Notre Dame, Balt., 1955; MA, U. Hawaii, 1962; PhD, U. Pa., 1992. Tchr. Sacred Heart Sch., Pensacola, Fla., 1955-56; grad. teaching fellow East-West Cultural Ctr. U. Hawaii, 1959-60; adminstrv. asst. Korean Consul Gen., 1959-60; tchr. Boyertown (Pa.) Sr. High Sch., 1961-63; asst. prof. English U. Balt., 1963-69; asst. prof. Morgan State U., Balt., 1970—, sec. to faculty, 1981-83, faculty research scholar, 1982-83, communications officer, 1989-90, dir. writing for TV program, 1990—. Author poetry and lit. criticism. Coord. Young Reps., Berks County, Pa., 1962-63; chmn. Md. Young Reps., 1964; election judge Baltimore County, Md., 1964-66; regional capt. Am. Cancer Soc., 1978-79; mem. adv. bd. Md. Our Md. Anniversary, 1984, The Living Constitution: Bicentennial of the Fed. Constitution, 1987. Fellow Morgan-Penn Faculty, 1977-79, Nat. Endowment Humanities, 1984; named Outstanding Teaching Prof., U. Balt. Coll. Liberal Arts, 1965, Outstanding Teaching Prof. English, Morgan State U., 1987. Mem. MLA, AAUW South Atlantic MLA, Coll. Lang. Assn., Coll. English Assn. (v.p. Mid.-Atlantic Group 1987-90, pres. 1990-92), Women's Caucus for Modern Langs., Md. Council Tchrs. English, Md. Poetry and Literary Soc., Md. Assn. Depts. English (bd. dirs. 1992—), Mid. Atlantic Writers' Assn. (founding 1981), U. Auburn Club, Delta Sigma Epsilon (v.p. 1992—). Roman Catholic. Home: 102 Gorsuch Rd Lutherville Timonium MD 21093-4318 Office: Morgan State U Dept English Baltimore MD 21239

SEEFF, ADELE, faculty administrator; b. Johannesburg, South Africa, Apr. 16, 1938; came to U.S., 1964; d. Sam and Beryl Simler; m. Leonard Seeff, Dec. 20, 1959; children: Amanda, Laura, Daniel. PhD, U. Md., 1979. Cert. secondary edn. tchr. Interim pres. Internat. U. Consortium, College Park, Md., 1985-86, v.p., 1983-85, assoc. pres., 1979-83; exec. dir. Ctr. for Renaissance and Baroque Studies, College Park, 1986—; cons. Md. Pub. TV, 1981—. Author: Exploring Language, 1981; author TV scripts; contbr. articles to jours. Mem. Shakespeare Assn. Am., Modern Lang. Assn.

SEEGER, JOHN ADAM, business educator, consultant; b. Evanston, Ill., July 11, 1933; s. Gerald Paul and Jeannette (Bresnan) S.; m. Martha Frances Adelle Negus, Dec. 22, 1956 (div. 1968); 1 child, Jeffrey John; m. Sue Fisher, Sept. 6, 1981. SB, MIT, 1956; D in Bus. Adminstrn., Harvard U., 1978. Pres., dir. The Slencil Co., Orange, Mass., 1959-71; exec. v.p., treas. Data Service, Inc., Boston, 1963-67; asst. dir. Sponsored Research div. MIT, Cambridge, Mass., 1967-70; adminstrv. officer System Dynamics group MIT, Cambridge, 1970-72; assoc. prof. mgmt. Northeastern U., Boston, 1978-83; assoc. prof. mgmt. Bentley Coll., Waltham, Mass., 1983-87, prof. mgmt., 1987—, exec. dir. Inst. for Rsch. & Faculty Devel., 1990-91; vis. scholar MIT, 1991—; bd. dirs. Applied CAD Knowledge, Inc.; writer Mott & Reid Assocs., El Paso, 1951-53; ind. cons., Boston, 1956-59; cons. CAV Ltd. div. Joseph Lucas, London, 1972-77; mem. adv. bd. Tech. and Mgmt. Systems, Burlington, Mass., 1983—, Atlantic Flyways, Winchendon, Mass., 1985-89. Editor Case Rsch. Jour., 1991—; contbr. articles to profl. mgmt. jours.; contbr. numerous chpts. and cases in mgmt. textbooks. Organizer Alewife/Grace Residents' Orgn., Cambridge, 1984. Recipient University award for excellence in teaching Northeastern U., Boston, 1982. Mem. AAAS, Acad. Mgmt., Strategic Mgmt. Soc., N.Am. Case Rsch. Assn. (regional dir. 1988-91), System Dynamics Soc. (chmn. ann. meetings arrangements 1983), Ea. Casewriters Assn. (pres. 1988-91), Kappa Sigma (chpt. adviser, dist. officer), Beta Gamma Sigma.

SEELEY, BENJAMIN JACKSON, controller; b. Scranton, Pa., Aug. 18, 1945; s. Benjamin Jackson and Janice Carolyn (Yuhas) S.; m. Pamela Warner, July 20, 1968 (div. Feb., 1991); children: Heather, Jason; m. Mary Ann McHale, Aug. 2, 1991; 1 child, Kimberly. Student electronic tech., U.S. Naval Tng. Sch., Great Lakes, Ill., 1964; BS in Acctg. cum laude, U. Scranton, 1973, MBA, 1976. Sr. acct. RCA, Dunmore, Pa., 1968-79; controller, bd. sec. Suckle Corp., Scranton, 1979—; bd. dirs. Learning Window Day Care, Moosic, Pa. , 1990—. Cert. lay speaker United Meth. Ch., 1987—; adminstrv. bd. chmn. United Meth. Ch., Moosic, 1976—; dir. Moosic Youth Ctr., 1973; umpire Moosic Little League, 1991. Mem. Delta Mu Delta, Omicron Delta Epsilon, Alpha Sigma Lambda. Republican. Home: 407 Phoenix St Pittston PA 18642-1223 Office: Suckle Corp 733 Davis St Scranton PA 18505-3594

SEELEY, JOHN GEORGE, horticulture educator; b. North Bergen, N.J., Dec. 21, 1915; s. Howard Wilson and Lillian (Fiedler) S.; m. Catherine L. Cook, May 28, 1938; children: Catherine Ann, David John, Daniel Henry, George Bingham, Thomas Dyer. B.S., Rutgers U., 1937, M.S., 1940; Ph.D., Cornell U., 1948. Research asst. N.J. Agrl. Exptl. Sta., 1937-40, foreman ornamental gardens, 1940-41; instr. floriculture Cornell U., Ithaca, N.Y., 1941-43, 45-48, asst. prof., 1948-49, prof. floriculture, 1956-83, prof. emeritus, 1983—, head dept. floriculture, 1956-70; prof. floriculture Pa. State U., 1949-56; D.C. Kiplinger chair floriculture, prof. horticulture Ohio State U., 1984-85; asst. agronomist Bur. Plant Industry Dept. Agr., 1943-44; chemist Wright Aero. Corp., Paterson, N.J., 1944-45. Trustee Kenneth Post Found., 1956-84, Fred. C. Gloeckner Found., 1970—. Recipient S.A.F. Found. for Floriculture Rsch. & Edn. award, 1965, Cornell Edgerton Career Teaching award, 1983. Fellow AAAS, Am. Soc. Hort. Sci. (pres. 1982-83, chmn. bd. 1983-84, Leonard H. Vaughan rsch. award 1950, Bittner Extension award 1982); mem. Am. Acad. Floriculture (hon.), Soc. Am. Florists (Hall of Fame 1979), Mass. Hort. Soc. (Silver medal 1980), Am. Hort. Soc., Internat. Soc. Hort. Sci. (Appreciation award 1986), Am. Carnation Soc., N.Y. Acad. Scis., N.Y. Flower Growers Assn., Pa. Flower Growers Assn., Sigma Xi, Phi Kappa Phi, Alpha Zeta, Pi Alpha Xi (pres. 1951-53), Epsilon Sigma Phi, Phi Epsilon Phi. Presbyterian. Lodge: Rotary Internat. (dist. gov. 1973-74). Home: 1344 Ellis Hollow Rd RD2 Ithaca NY 14850-9601

SEELY, SAMUEL, electrical engineering educator, retired; b. N.Y.C., May 7, 1909; s. Abraham and Celia (Strulovici) S.; m. Helen E. Anderson; children: Kittredge, Martha Ann. EE cum laude, Poly. Inst. Bklyn., 1931; MS, Stevens Inst. Tech., 1932; PhD, Columbia U., 1936. Asst. prof. CCNY, 1936-41; mem. staff radiation lab. MIT, 1941-46; assoc. prof. electronics U.S. Naval Postgrad. Sch., 1946-47; prof. elec. engring. Syracuse U., 1947-56, chmn. dept., 1951-56; prof. elec. engring. Case Inst. Tech., 1956-64, head dept., 1956-59; prof. elec. engring., coord. rsch., assoc. dean Grad. Sch. U. Mass., 1968-70; prof. elec. engring. U. Conn., 1970-72; vis. prof. Johns Hopkins U., 1965, CCNY, 1966, Okla. State U., 1967, U. R.I., 1972-79 (ret. 1979); guest prof. Chalmers U. Tech., Sweden, 1967-68; mem. com. computers in elec. engring. Commn. on Engring. Edn., 1965-72; head engring. sect. NSF, 1961-63; Fulbright lectr. advance sch. telecommunication and electronics Hellenic Army Gen. Staff, Athens, Greece, 1959-60; expert cons. to R & D Bd., Dept. Def., 1950; sci. cons. Office Chief Signal Officer, 1952-53, others. Author: Electronics, 1941, 2d edit., 1951, Electron Tube Circuits, 1950, 2d edit., 1958, General Network Analysis, 1951, Electronic Engineering, 1956, Radio Engineering, 1956, Introduction to Electromagnetic Fields, 1958, Modern Network Analysis, 1959, Electromechanical Energy Conversion, 1962, Dynamic Systems Analysis, 1964, Electronic Circuits, 1968, Digital Computers in Engineering, 1970, An Introduction to Engineering Systems, 1972, others; co-author: (with A.D. Poularikas) Electromagnetics, Classical and Modern Theory and Applications, 1979, Signal and Systems, 1985, 2d edit., 1991, Elements of Signals and Systems, 1988, numerous others. Recipient Army-Navy cert. Appreciation, 1947; decorated Silver Cross Royal Order Phoenix, Greece. Fellow IEEE (past bd. dirs.),

Am. Phys. Soc.; mem. Am. Soc. Engring. Edn., Sigma Xi, Tau Beta Pi, Eta Kappa Nu.

SEEMAN, NADRIAN CHARLES, chemistry educator; b. Chgo., Dec. 16, 1945; s. Herman and Emma (Klaman) S. BS, U. Chgo., 1966; PhD, U. Pitts., 1970. Rsch. assoc. biology Columbia U., N.Y.C., 1970-72; postdoctoral fellow biology MIT, Cambridge, 1972-77; asst. prof. biology SUNY, Albany, 1977-83, assoc. prof. biology, 1983-88; prof. chemistry NYU, N.Y.C., 1988—; sr. cons. Molecular Biophysics Tech., Inc., Phila., 1983-87; cons. Lifecodes Corp., Inc., Elmsford, N.Y., 1983-87, Datascope, Malvern, Pa., 1989—. Contbr. articles to profl. jours. Recipient Sidhu award Pitts. Diffraction Soc., 1974, Rsch. Career Devel. award NIH, 1982-87; Basil O'Connor fellow March of Dimes, 1978-81; rsch. grantee NIH, 1979—, ONR, 1989—. Mem. Am. Crystallographic Assn., Biophys. Soc., Am. Chem. Soc., Am. Soc. Biochemistry and Molecular Biology. Office: NYU Dept Chemistry New York NY 10003

SEGAL, ALLAN, surgeon; b. Phila., Aug. 3, 1948; s. Maxwell and Jeanette (Snyder) S.; m. B.J. Segal, June 27, 1976; children: Blake H., James D. BS cum laude, St. Joseph's U., 1970; MD, Temple U., 1974. Asst. instr. surgery U. Pa., Phila., 1974-77; chief resident surgery Temple U., Phila., 191978-79; chief of surgery The Med. Ctr., Beaver, Pa., 1990—. Fellow ACS.

SEGAL, BERNARD GERARD, lawyer; b. N.Y.C., June 11, 1907; s. Samuel I. and Rose (Cantor) S.; m. Geraldine Rosenbaum, Oct. 22, 1933; children: Loretta Joan Segal Cohen, Richard Murry. A.B., U. Pa., 1928, LL.B., 1931, LL.D., 1969; LL.D., Franklin and Marshall Coll., 1953, Temple U., 1954, Dropsie U., 1966, Jewish Theol. Sem. Am., 1977, Vt. Law Sch., 1978, Villanova U., 1980, Georgetown U., 1983; J.S.D., Suffolk U., 1969; D.H.L., Hebrew Union Coll., 1970. Bar: Pa. 1932, D.C. 1976. Mem. faculty U. Pa., 1928-35, 45-47, coach varsity debate team, 1929-32; Am. reporter on contracts Internat. Congress of Law, The Hague, The Netherlands, 1932; asst. dep. atty. gen. Commonwealth of Pa., 1932-33, dep. atty. gen., 1933-34; cofounder Schnader Harrison Segal & Lewis, Phila., 1935—, sr. ptnr., 1986-88, counsel, 1988—; instr. grad. bus., govt. Am. Inst. Banking, 1936-39; mem. Bd. Law Examiners, Phila., 1940-46; chmn. Commn. Jud. and Congl. Salaries, U.S. Govt., 1953-55; mem. Atty. Gen.'s Nat. Com. to Study Antitrust Laws, 1953-55; mem. exec. com. Atty. Gen.'s Nat. Conf. on Ct. Congestion, 1958-61; mem. standing com. on rules of practice and procedure Jud. Conf. U.S., 1959-76; co-chmn. Lawyers Com. on Civil Rights Under Law, 1963-65 (Founder award, 25th Anniversary, 1988); chmn. Pa. Jud. Nominating Commn., 1964-66; mem. Nat. Citizens Com. on Community Rels., 1964-74; mem. adv. com. U.S. mission to UN, 1967-68; mem. adv. panel internat. law U.S. Dept. State, 1967-79; mem. Adminstrv. Conf. U.S., 1968-74; chmn. nat. adv. com. on legal svcs. U.S. OEO, 1968-76, chmn. exec. com., 1971-74; chmn. bd. Coun. Legal Edn. Opportunities, 1968-71; mem. Jud. Coun. Pa., 1968-71; coun. World Peach Through Law Ctr., chmn. 1st demonstration trial, Belgrade, Yugoslavia, 1971, coun., 1973—, participant world confs., Athens, Greece, Washington, Geneva, Bangkok, Abidjan, Ivory Coast, Manila and Cairo, chmn. com. on internat. communications, world chmn. World Law Day, Madrid, 1979, Berlin, 1985; mem. U.S. Commn. on Exec., Legis. and Jud. Salaries, 1972-73, 76-77; mem. Appellate Ct. Nominating Commn., 1973-79; mem. U.S. Commn. Revision Fed. Ct. Appellate System, 1974-75; chmn. World Conf. on Peace and Violence, Jerusalem, 1979. Editor-in-chief: Pennsylvania Banking and Building and Loan Law, 3 vols., 1941; editor: The Belgrade Spaceship Trial, 1972; mem. internat. hon. bd. Ency. Judaica; contbr. articles to law revs., other publs. Life trustee, mem. exec. bd. U. Pa., 1959-77, life trustee emeritus, 1977—; mem. bd. overseers U. Pa. Law Sch., 1959—; mem. Commn. on Anti-Poverty Program for Phila., 1967-71, Bus. Leadership Organized for Cath. Schs., 1979—, Commonwealth Commn. on Bicentennial of U.S. Constn., 1986-87; chmn. bd. Coun. Advancement Legal Edn., 1972-77; coun. trustees Hebrew U. Jerusalem; bd. dirs. So. Africa Legal Svcs. and Legal Edn. Project, 1979—, NAACP Legal Def. and Ednl. Fund, Found. Fed. Bar Assn.; bd. govs. emeritus, past v.p., past treas. Dropsie Coll.; trustee emeritus, former exec. com. Albert Einstein Med. Ctr.; trustee Phila. Martin Luther King, Jr. Ctr. Nonviolent Social Change (Drum Major award for legal justice, 1984), 1984—, Found. for the Commemoration of the U.S. Constn., 1986-88, Found. for U.S. Constn., 1988—, bd. dirs. Chapel of Four Chaplains; mem. planning commn. Miracle at Phila., 1986-87. Recipient Arthur von Briesen medal Nat. Legal Aid and Defender Assn., 1970, Nat. Human Rels. award NCCJ, 1972, Herbert Lewis Harley award, Am. Judicature Soc., 1974, World Lawyer award World Peace through Law Ctr., 1975, Judge William H. Hastie award NAACP Legal Def. Fund, 1986, Legion Honor Gold Medallion award Chapel of Four Chaplains, 1988, Nat. Civil Rights award U.S. Atty. Gen. and Lawyers Com. for Civil Rights Under Law, 1969, Ford Found. award to our Counselor on Pub. Interest, 1979, Nat. Award of Merit Fed. Adminstrv. Law Judges Conf., 1984, Pa. Bar Assn. award for Dedicated and Disting. Service, Field of Jurisprudence and Admin. of Justice, 1962, 10rsary award Pub. Interest Law Ctr. Phila., 1944; co-recipient Nat. Neighbors Disting. Leadership in Civil Rights award, 1988, ACLU Civil Liberties award, 1991, U. Pa. Law Alumni award of Merit, 1991. Fellow Am. Coll. Trial Lawyers (pres. 1964-65), ABA (pres. 1969-70, Gold medal 1976), Inst. Jud. Adminstrn. (bd. dirs. 1968—), Am. Bar Found. (pres. 1976-78); mem. Jewish Fed. Greater Phila. (mem. emeritus exec. com.), Pa. Bar Assn., Phila. Bar Assn. (chancellor 1952, 53), Pa. Urban Affairs Partnership, Fed. Bar Assn. (nat. coun.), Assn. of Bar of City of N.Y., D.C. Bar Assn., Am. Arbitration Assn. (former dir.), Am. Law Inst. (1st v.p. 1976-86, 2nd v.p. 1970-75, treas. 1955-69, counselor emeritus 1987—), Am. Judicature Soc. (chmn. 1958-61, bd. dirs. 1956—), Coun. Legal Edn. for Profl. Responsibility (dir.), Fed. Jud. Conf. 3d Cir. (life), World Assn. Lawyers (pres. for Ams. 1976-86), Nat. Conf. Bar Pres., Taxpayers Forum Pa. (past pres.), Allied Jewish Appeal (past pres., hon. pres.), Legal Aid Soc. Phila. (bd. dirs.), Jewish League Israel (nat. bd.), Jewish Pub. Soc. Am. (life trustee, mem. exec. com.), Jewish Family Svc. (hon. dir.), Order of Coif, Tau Epsilon Rho, Delta Sigma Rho. Republican. Clubs: Locust, Union League, Faculty, Metropolitan (Washington). Home: The Philadelphian Apt 19-C-44 2401 Pennsylvania Ave Philadelphia PA 19130 Office: 1600 Market St Ste 3600 Philadelphia PA 19103-4247

SEGAL, DONALD HENRY GILBERT, real estate developer; b. Phila., Mar. 20, 1928; s. A. Louis and Harriet B. Segal; children: Susan, John. BS in Econs., U. Pa., 1950. V.p. Sandee Constrn. Co., Brookhaven, Pa., 1951-59; pres. Segal Constrn. Co., Cinnaminson, N.J., 1959-76, Segal Assocs., Inc., Bellmawr, N.J., 1976-90; chmn. bd. Hotel Devel. Assocs., 1985—; commr. Lower Merion Twp., Pa., 1972-80, pres. bd. commrs., 1974-80. Bd. dirs. Phila. All Star Forum, 1980—, Atlantic City Ballet Co., 1981-84, Phila. Child Guidance Clinic, 1981—, chmn. bd., 1989-92; mem. bd. mgrs. Moore Coll. Art, 1981-88, trustee, 1989—; mem. Mid-Atlantic Ctr. for the Arts, Internat. Visitors Coun. Mem. Hotel Motel Assn., U.S. Yacht Racing Union. Republican. Jewish. Club: Corinthian Yacht (Cape May, N.J.). Home: 422 Garden Ln Bryn Mawr PA 19010-3626 also: 1830 Maryland Ave Cape May NJ 08204

SEGAL, GERALDINE ROSENBAUM, sociologist; b. Phila., Aug. 26, 1908; d. Harry and Mena (Hamburg) Rosenbaum; m. Bernard Gerard Segal, Oct. 22, 1933; children: Loretta Joan Cohen, Richard Murry. BS in Edn., U. Pa., 1930, MA in Human Rels., 1963, PhD in Sociology, 1978; MS in Libr. Sci., Drexel U., 1968; Dr. Letters (Hon.), Franklin & Marshall Coll., 1990. Social worker County Relief Bd., Phila., 1931-35; sociologist, Phila., 1935—; cons. and lectr. in field. Author: In Any Fight Some Fall, 1975; Blacks in the Law, 1983. Bd. dirs. NCCJ, 1937-47, 82—, sec., 1983—; bd. overseers U. Pa. Sch. Social Work, 1983—; bd. dirs., Juvenile Law Ctr., 1984—; chair Phila. Tutorial Project, 1966-68; 1st v.p. U. Pa. Alumnae Assn., 1967-70. Co-recipient Nat. Neighbors Disting. Leadership in Civil Rights award, 1988; recipient Drum Major award for Human Rights, Phila. Martin Luther King, Jr. Assn. for Nonviolence, 1990. Democrat. Jewish. Home: Apt 19C44 2401 Pennsylvania Ave Philadelphia PA 19130-3061

SEGAL, KAREN R., exercise physiologist; b. Boston, Oct. 25, 1954; d. Alexander Michael and Selma Hilda (Hyde) Rutenburg. BA, Conn. Wesleyan U., 1976; MA, Columbia U., 1981, MEd, EdD, 1982. Postdoctoral fellow Columbia U., N.Y.C., 1982-83; rsch. assoc. St. Luke's Roosevelt Hosp., N.Y.C., 1983-85; asst. prof. Mt. Sinai Sch. of Medicine, N.Y.C., 1985-89, assoc. prof., 1989-92; assoc. prof. Cornell U. Med. Coll., N.Y.C., 1992—. NIH grantee, 1989—. Fellow Am. Coll. Sports Medicine; mem. Am. Fedn. for Clin. Rsch., Am. Physiol. Soc., Am. Soc. for Clin. Nutrition. Home: 10 W 66th St New York NY 10023

SEGAL, PETER WYMAN, lawyer; b. Boston, Apr. 17, 1943; s. Maurice S. and Sylvia C. (Wyman) S.; m. Carole Elizabeth Williams, Sept. 4, 1971; 1 child, Jonathan. BA, Tufts Coll., 1965; JD, Boston U., 1968. Bar: D.C., 1968. Atty. HUD, Washington, 1968-70, Melrod, Redman & Gartlan, Washington, 1970-72, Colton & Boykin, Washington, 1972—. Club: Congl. Country (Washington). Office: Colton & Boykin 1025 Thomas Jefferson St NW Washington DC 20007-5201

SEGAL, SANFORD LEONARD, mathematics educator; b. Troy, N.Y., Oct. 11, 1937; s. Joseph and Bessie (Katz) S.; m. Rima Maxwell, Sept. 3, 1959; children: Adam, Joshua, Zoë. BA, Wesleyan U., 1958; PhD, U. Colo., 1963. Instr. U. Rochester, N.Y., 1963-64, asst. prof., 1964-70; rsch. fellow U. Vienna, Austria, 1965-66; assoc. prof. U. Rochester, N.Y., 1970-77, assoc. chmn., maths., 1969-79; vis. lectr. U. Nottingham, Eng., 1972-73; prof. U. Rochester, N.Y., 1977—, chmn. maths., 1979-87. Author: (book) Nine Introductions in Complex Variables, 1981; contbr. numerous articles to profl. jours. Fulbright fellow, Mainz, Germany, 1958-59, Fulbright Rsch. fellow, Vienna, Austria, 1965-66; fellow Inst. Math. Para e Applicada, Brazil, 1982, Alexander Von Humboldt Found., Fed. Rep. Germany, 1988. Mem. Am. Maths. Soc., Math. Assn. Am. (various coms. and chmn.) , History Scis. Soc. Democrat. Home: 511 Rockingham St Rochester NY 14620-2519 Office: U Rochester Wilson Blvd Rochester NY 14627

SEGAL, STEPHEN MARTIN, advertising executive; b. N.Y.C., Mar. 22, 1938; s. Abraham and Elsie (Dinberg) S. AB, Cornell U., 1959; postgrad., Columbia U. Grad. Sch. Bus., 1959-60. Media research supr. Grey Advt., N.Y.C., 1962-65; v.p. bus. and media research Marschalk Co., N.Y.C., 1965-70; v.p. mktg. intelligence services McCann-Erickson, Inc., N.Y.C., 1970-74; mgr. mktg. services Lever Bros., N.Y.C., 1976-78; v.p. Tinker Campbell & Ewald, N.Y.C., 1978-80; v.p., dir. media planning Lowe-Marschalk, Inc., N.Y.C., 1980-84, sr. v.p., media dir., 1984, exec. v.p., media dir., 1985—, also bd. dirs., 1984—. Jewish. Office: Lowe-Marschalk Inc 1345 Ave Of The Americas New York NY 10105-0099

SEGALL, JULES PETER, public affairs counselor; b. Dec. 26, 1954; s. Sydney and Lisl (Gotlieb) S. BA, Princeton U., 1976; JD, Georgetown Law Ctr., 1982. Bar: D.C. 1982. Spl. counsel Coun. of Energy Resource Tribes, Washington, 1981-84; v.p. Gray & Co./Hill & Knowlton, Washington, 1984-87; exec. v.p. Madison Pub. Affairs Group, Washington, 1987-89; sr. v.p., gen. mgr. Dorf & Stanton/Washington, D.C., 1990—; bd. dirs. Am. League Lobbyists, D.C. Co-editor: Student Political Involvement in the 1970's, 1976. Co-mgr. Kostmayer for Congress campaign, Bucks County, Pa., 1976. Named Woodrow Wilson scholar Woodrow Wilson Sch. Pub. and Internat. Affairs, Princeton, 1976. Jewish. Office: Dorf & Stanton 1750 K St NW #1200 Washington DC 20006

SEGALMAN, JOEL SCOTT, podiatrist; b. Bayside, N.Y., Feb. 26, 1963; s. Ira George and Marilyn (Goldbaum) S. BS, SUNY, Stonybrook, 1985; BS, D of Podiatric Medicine, Ill. Coll. Podiatric Medicine, Chgo., 1989. Dir. Chase Parkway Podiatry Group, Waterbury, Conn., 1991—, also bd. dirs.; attending podiatrist Boston Marathon, Boston Athletic Assn., 1990-92. Mem. Am. Coll. Foot Orthopedics (assoc.), Am. Acad. Podiatric Sports Medicine (assoc.), Am. Podiatric Circulatory Soc. (assoc.), Am. Podiatric Med. Assn., Conn. Podiatric Med. Soc. Home: 19 Frostfield Pl Melville NY 11747-1608 Office: Chase Pkwy Podiatry Group 714 Chase Pky Waterbury CT 06708-3012

SEGAR, JAMES HENRY, accounting educator; b. Marshall, Mich., Mar. 20, 1938; s. Fred Edgar Segar and Lela Elvina (Gray) Campbell; m. Mary Lou Claypool, Dec. 28, 1958; children: Jamie, Laurie. BA, Andrews U., 1961; MA, Cen. Mich. U., 1968. Tchr. Wis. Acad., Columbus, 1961-63; auditor Lake Union Conf. of SDA, Berrien Springs, Mich., 1963-65; bus. mgr. Cedar Lake (Mich.) Acad., 1965-68; prof. Middle East Coll., Beirut, Lebanon, 1968-75, Columbia Union Coll., Takoma Park, Md., 1975-77, Atlantic Union Coll., South Lancaster, Mass., 1977—; acct. Lancaster (Mass.) Sewer Dist., 1980—. Mem. Nat. Assn. Accts. Seventh-Day Adventist. Home: 302 George Hill Rd Lancaster MA 01523-2117 Office: Atlantic Union Coll Main St South Lancaster MA 01561

SEGARRA, ROBERT, jewelry designer, artist, writer; b. Bronx, N.Y., Aug. 3, 1959. BS, St. John's U., Queens, N.Y., 1985; student, Ultissima Beauty Inst., Bklyn., 1985, The Clairol Sch., N.Y.C., 1985, N.Y.C. Tech. Coll., 1990. Mus. cons. Internat. Hwy. Music Co., Bklyn., 1986; mem. staff distbn. and quality inspection Putumayo, N.Y.C., 1989; mem. designer staff Gerard Yosca Designer Jewelry, N.Y.C., 1990—. Contbg. author: American Poets and Their Poems, 1982, American Poetry Anthology, 1986; designer logo Wicked Mystic Mag., 1991; artist, writer (mags.) Ash, 1992, Wicked Mystic, 1990-92. Home: 236 15th St Brooklyn NY 11215

SEGATTO, PETER RICHARD, chemist; b. N.Y.C., June 4, 1928; s. Peter and Norma (Aroni) S.; m. Jean Meriam Spahr, June 12, 1954; children: Patricia, Linda, Helen. BS in Chemistry, Adelphi U., 1953; PhD in Chemistry, Rutgers U., 1958. Assoc. chemist Corning (N.Y.) Inc., 1957-60, rsch. chemist, 1960-69, sr. chemist, 91969-72, mgr. devel., 1972-78, dir. tech. svcs., 1978-80, dir. devel., 1980—. Patentee in field. Mem. IEEE, Am. Chem. Soc., Am. Ceramic Soc., Sigma Xi. Home: 1060 W Water St Elmira NY 14905-2022 Office: Corning Inc RD&E Div SP DV-02-1 Corning NY 14831

SEGEL, ARNOLD LESTER, surgeon; b. Cambridge, Mass., May 6, 1911; s. Sydney and Celia (Kramer) S.; m. Ruth Cohn, 1948; children: William, Margaret, James, Arthur, Anne. AB, Harvard U., 1932, MD, 1936. Diplomate Am. Bd. Surgery. Intern Beth Israel Hosp., Boston, 1936-38; asst. resident and resident Beth Israel Hosp., 1938-40; surgery asst. to instr. Harvard Med. Sch., 1946-74; asst. prof. Tufts Univ. Med. Sch., Boston, 1983—; pvt. practice Beth Israel Hosp., 1946-74; asst. surgeon to surgeon Beth Israel Hosp., 1946-74; assoc. chief of staff Boston VA Hosp., 1974-88. Contbr. articles to profl. pubs. Decorated Bronze Star, 7 Battle Stars, Presidential citation, Croix de Guerre with Palm (France). Mem. AMA, Mass. Med. Soc., ACS, Mass. chpt. ACS, Boston Surg. Soc.

SEGGEV, MEIR, radiologist, educator; b. Burgas, Bulgaria, Jan. 23, 1939; came to U.S., 1969, naturalized, 1976; s. Bouco and Helen (Bejerano) S.; m. Ruth Lerner, Dec. 30, 1964 (div. Apr. 1978); 1 child, Yael.; m. Sandra Lee Slarsky, Apr. 7, 1979. MD, Hebrew U. Hadassah, Jerusalem, 1966. Diplomate Am. Bd. Radiology. Radiology resident Harvard Med. Sch., Beth Israel Hosp., Boston, 1970-73; radiologist Peter Bent Brigham Hosp., Boston, 1973-74, Hale Hosp., Haverhill, Mass., 1974—; assoc. radiologist Beth Israel Hosp., Boston, 1974—; clin. instr. radiology Harvard Med. Sch., Boston, 1973—. Mem. AMA, Am. Inst. Ultrasound in Medicine, Am. Roentgen Ray Soc., Radiol. Soc. N.Am., Am. Coll. Radiology, Mass. Med. Soc., Harvard Club. Home: 35 Morton St Andover MA 01810-2037

SEGMEN, JOHN ROBERT, psychologist, educator; b. Chgo., Dec. 19, 1937; s. B. Robert and Ann (Mircheva) S.; m. Patricia K. Hill (div.). BA in Math., U. Buffalo, 1960; PhD in Psychology, SUNY, Buffalo, 1978. Lic. psychologist. Grad. asst. psychology dept. SUNY, Buffalo, 1960-65; instr. psychology dept. Daemen Coll., Amherst, N.Y., 1965-68, asst. prof., 1968-72, assoc. prof., 1972—; cons. in psychology, Kenmore (N.Y.) Mercy Hosp., 1988—, Mid-Erie Mental Health Svcs., Lancaster, N.Y., 1987-89. Author/presenter: (lecture) On Being A Man Amongst Changing Women and Perplexed Men, 1990. Mem. Am. Psychol. Assn., Ea. Psychol. Assn., Psychol. Assn. of Western N.Y. (past pres.), Analytical Psychology Soc. of Western N.Y. (bd. dirs. 1985—, past pres.), Mental Health Assn. of Erie County (past bd. dirs.). Office: Daemen Coll Psychology Dept Bos 762 PO Box 762 Amherst NY 14226-3592 also: 208 North St Rm 211 Buffalo NY 14201-1529

SEHLMEYER, RICHARD GEORGE, real estate broker, educator; b. Mineola, N.Y., July 4, 1934; s. Ernest Ferdinand and Anna Francis (Wighaus) S.; m. Joanne Elizabeth Hanlon, Nov. 30, 1957; children: Richard George Jr., Deborah Ann, James Joseph, Daniel David, Elizabeth Joanne. Grad., Realtor's Inst., Albany, N.Y., 1976. Cert. real estate appraiser, Ariz.; cert. environ. insp., N.Y.; lic. and cert. gen. real estate appraisals, N.Y. Electrician Local #25, Internat. Brotherhood Elec. Workers, Westbury, N.Y., 1952-63; real estate broker Lake Luzerne Real Estate Co., Lake Luzerene, N.Y., 1969—, Sacandaga Real Estate, Day, N.Y., 1986—, Corinth Real Estate, Corinth, Lake George, 1986—; real estate instr. Adirondack Community Coll., Queensbury, N.Y., 1974—; instr. Nat. Assn. Real Estate Appraisers, Scottsdale, Ariz., 1991—; training dir., pres. Sellmeyer Inc., Hadley, N.Y., 1987—; hearing officer N.Y. State Supreme Ct., 4th Jud. Dist., 1985—, N.Y. Author: Sure-Sell System, 1989. Br. chmn. ARC, Glen Falls, N.Y., 1982—; planning bd. Town of Hadley, N.Y., 1974; Dem. chmn. Town of Hadley, 1986; mem. Great Sacandaga Lake Assn., Edinburg, N.Y., 1985. Mem. Nat. Assn. Real Estate Appraisers (cert. instr., chmn. Adirondack chpt. 1991—), Lake Luzerne C. of C. (bd. dirs. 1970—, Man of Yr. award). Democrat. Roman Catholic. Home: 11154 Old Corinth Rd Hadley NY 12835 Office: Lake Luzerne Real Estate 5791 Bridge St Lake Luzerne NY 12846-0040

SEHRING, HOPE HUTCHISON, library science educator; b. Akron, Ohio; d. Wesley Harold and Jane (Brown) H.; m. Frederick Albert Sehring, July 15, 1978. BS, Slippery Rock U., 1968; MEd, U. Pitts., 1973, MLS, 1984. Cert. instructional media specialist. Reference libr.-intern Carnegie Mellon U., Pitts., 1981; libr. media specialist Gateway Sch. Dist., Monroeville, Pa., 1968—. Contbr. articles to profl. jours. Active Pa. Citizens for Better Libraries. Recipient Henry Clay Frick Found. U. of London scholarship, 1969, 73, Gift of Time tribute Am. Family Inst., 1992; U. Pitts. Evaluation Inst. grantee, 1976. Mem. NEA, Pa. Sch. Librarians Assn. (treas. 1982-84), Pa. Stte Edn. Assn., Gateway Edn. Assn., Alpha Xi Delta. Home: PO Box 74 Delmont PA 15626-0074 Office: Gateway Sch Dist Mosside Blvd Monroeville PA 15146

SEIBERT, MARY LEE, college official; b. Evansville, Ind., Jan. 30, 1942; d. Ernest Hensley and Lillian (Schmadel) S.; BS, Ind. U., 1963, MS, 1973, EdD, 1979. Cert. med. technologist, med. asst. Lab. supr. Wishard Meml. Hosp., Indpls., 1964-67; chmn. life scis. div. Ind. Vocat. Tech. Coll., Indpls., 1967-73; assoc. prof., program dir. Ind. U. Sch. Medicine, Indpls., 1973-79; assoc. project coordinator Am. Assn. State Colls. and Univs., Washington, 1979-81; dean coll. allied health professions Temple U., Phila., 1981-90; assoc. provost Ithaca (N.Y.) Coll., 1990—; vis. prof. U. Tex. Med. Br., Galveston, 1985. Assoc. editor Jour. Med. Tech., 1985-86. Fellow Am. Soc. Allied Health Profls. (hon., chmn. forum on allied health data, rsch. com. 1983-89, bd. dirs. 1999-92, Outstanding Mem. award 1986); mem. Am. Soc. Med. Technologists (profl. affairs com. 1986-889), Am. Assn. Med. Assts. (hon.), Nat. Coun. on Health Professions Edn., Phi Delta Kappa, Pi Lambda Theta. Republican. Home: 16 Bean Hill Ln Ithaca NY 14850 Office: Ithaca Coll Provosts Office 3307 N Broad St Ithaca NY 14850

SEIBERT, PETER SWIFT, curator; b. Harrisburg, Pa., Nov. 22, 1965; s. Gladys Jane (Swift) Seibert. BHumanities, Pa. State U., 1987, M Am. Studies, 1992. Assoc. curator photography Ft. Hunter Mansion, Harrisburg, 1986-87; curator Cumberland County Hist. Soc., Carlisle, Pa., 1987-88; exec. dir., curator Dauphin County Hist. Soc., Harrisburg, 1988—; cons. Ft. Hunter Mansion, Harrisburg, 1990—; curator various exhibits; instr. adult edn. Harrisburg Area Community Coll. Mem. awards com. Pa. Fedn. Mus. and Hist. Orgns., 1992; reviewer Inst. Mus. Svcs. Grants Program U.S. Govt. Mem. Am. Assn. Mus., Can. Mus. Assn., Masons (sr. master of ceremonies 1989). Republican. Presbyterian. Home: 204 Miller Rd Harrisburg PA 17109-2914

SEIDEL, SELVYN, lawyer, legal educator; b. Longbranch, N.J., Nov. 6, 1942; s. Abraham and Anita (Stoller) S.; m. Deborah Lew, June 21, 1970; 1 child, Emily. B.A., U. Chgo., 1964; J.D., U. Calif.-Berkeley, 1967; Diploma in Law, Oxford U., 1968. Bar: N.Y. 1970, U.S. Dist. Ct. (so. and ea. dists.) N.Y. 1970, D.C. Ct. Appeals, 1982. Ptnr. Latham & Watkins, N.Y.C., 1984—; adj. prof. Sch. Law, NYU, 1974-85; instr. Practicing Law Inst., 1980-81, 84. Mem. ABA, New York County Bar Assn., N.Y.C. Bar Assn. (mem. fed. cts. com. 1982-85, internat. law com. 1989-92), Boalt Hall Alumni Assn. (bd. dirs. 1980-82), Contbr. articles to profl. jours. Home: PO Box 31 Litchfield CT 06759-0031 Office: Latham & Watkins 885 3d Ave New York NY 10022

SEIDEN, BILL A., marketing executive; b. N.Y.C., Jan. 10, 1955; s. Ralph Edward and Elaine Rita (Weinbrand) S.; m. Jill Marlene Cohen, Aug. 20, 1977; children: Russell, Eric. BS, Cornell U., 1976; MBA in Mktg., St. John's U., N.Y.C., 1979. Mgmt. engr. Am. Cyanamid-Lederle Lab., Pearl River, N.Y., 1976-79; product mgr. Sterling Drug-Glenbrook Labs., N.Y.C., 1979-84; sr. product mgr. Am. Home Products-Whitehall Labs., N.Y.C., 1984-87; dir. Colgate Palmolive Co., N.Y.C., 1987—; instr. The New Sch., N.Y.C., 1988-89. Office: Colgate Palmolive Co 300 Park Ave New York NY 10022-7402

SEIDEN, HENRY (HANK SEIDEN), advertising executive; b. Bklyn., Sept. 6, 1928; s. Jack S. and Shirley (Berkowitz) S.; m. Helena Ruth Zaldin, Sept. 10, 1949; children: Laurie Ann, Matthew Ian. B.A., Bklyn. Coll., 1949; M.B.A., CCNY, 1954. Trainee Ben Sackheim Advt. Agy., 1949-51; nat. promotion mgr. N.Y. Post Corp., 1951-53; promotion mgr. Crowell-Collier Pub. Co., Inc., 1953-54; copy group head Batten, Barton, Durstine & Osborn, Inc., 1954-60; v.p., creative dir. Keyes, Madden & Jones, 1960-61; sr. v.p., assoc. creative dir. McCann-Marschalk, Inc., 1961-65, chmn. plans bd., 1964-65; creative dir., dir., prin. Hicks & Greist, Inc., N.Y.C., 1965—, sr. v.p., 1965-74, exec. v.p., 1974-83, chief operating officer, 1983—, pres., 1986—; chief exec. officer Ketchum/Hicks & Greist Inc., 1987-89; chmn., chief exec. officer Ketchum Advt., 1989-91; exec. v.p. Ketchum Communications Inc.; bd. dirs. Ketchum Communications Inc., Ketchum Internat. Inc.; vice chmn. Jordan, McGrath, Case & Taylor, Inc., 1992—; chmn., CEO The Seiden Group, Inc.; exec. v.p., dir. Ketchum Communications, Inc., 1990-91, Ketchum Internat., Inc., 1990-91; vice chmn. Jordan, McGrath, Case & Taylor, Inc., 1992—; chmn., CEO The Seiden Group, Inc., 1992—; guest lectr. Bernard M. Baruch Sch. Bus. and Pub. Adminstrn., CCNY, 1962—, Baruch Coll., 1969—, New Sch. Social Scis., 1968, 72, 73, Sch. Visual Arts, 1979, 80—, Lehman Coll., CCNY, 1980—, Ohio U., 1981, Newhouse Grad. Sch., Syracuse U., 1981, NYU, 1983; cons. pub. rels. and communication to mayor of New Rochelle, N.Y., 1959—, also; mktg. dept. Ohio State U.; Cons. to pres. N.Y.C. City Coun., 1972-73, to postmaster Gen. U.S., 1972-74; communications adviser to Police Commr. N.Y.C., 1973—; hon. dep. commr. N.Y. Police Dept., 1991—, spl. cons. to police commr., 1992—. Author: Advertising Pure and Simple, 1976, Advertising Pure and Simple: The New Edition, 1990; contbg. editor: Madison Ave. mag, 1966—, Advt. Age, Mag. Age; guest columnist: N.Y. Times, 1972. Vice commr. Little League of New Rochelle.; bd. dirs. Police Res. Assn. N.Y.C., 1973—, pres. exec. com. ; bd. dirs. Cancer Research and Treatment Fund, Inc., Transmedia Network, Inc; bd. dirs., exec. v.p N.Y.'s Finest Found., 1975—. Recipient award Four Freedoms Found., 1959, award Printers Ink, 1960, promotion award Editor and Publisher, 1955, Am. TV Commls. Festival award, 1963-69, Effie award Am. Marketing Assn., 1969, 70, award Art Directors Club N.Y., 1963-70, award Am. Inst. Graphic Arts, 1963, Starch award, 1969; spl. award graphic art lodge B'nai B'rith Greater N.Y., 1971, 87. Mem. A.I.M. (assoc.), Nat. Acad. TV Arts and Scis., Advt. Club N.Y. (exec. judge Andy awards, award 1963-65), Advt. Writers Assn. N.Y. (Gold Key award for best newspaper and mag. advts. 1962-64), Copy Club (co-chmn. awards com., Gold Key award for best TV comml. 1969), Alpha Phi Omega. Home: 1056 5th Ave New York NY 10028-0112 Office: Jordan McGrath Case & Taylor 445 Park Ave New York NY 10022

SEIDEN, KATIE, artist, sculptor, newspaper editor; b. N.Y.C., Sept. 4, 1936; d. Maxwell Geismar and Anne Rosenberg; m. Larry Seiden, July 14, 1957; children: Jonathan, Matthew, Tara. BA, Sarah Lawrence Coll., 1958; MA, NYU, 1960. Editor-in-chief Boulevard mag., 1986-89; exec. editor Country Plaza mag., 1989-91; art editor, staff writer Gold Coast Gazette, Sea Cliff, N.Y., 1991—. One-woman shows, 1981—, including Sensory Evolution Gallery, N.Y.C., 1987, 88, Washington County Mus. Fine Arts, Hagerstown, Md., 1988, Gallery 10 Ltd., Washington, 1990; exhibited in numerous group shows, including Heckscher Mus., 1978, 81, Long Beach (N.Y.) Mus., 1980, Schenectady Mus., 1986, Islip Art Mus., 1986, 87, 89, 90, USIA, Mex., S.Am., Europe, 1989, 90, Queens Mus., 1990, Hillwood Art Mus., 1982, 83, 86, 90, 91; represented in permanent collections Grand Manan Mus., N.B.,

Can., Washington County Mus. Fine Arts, Helen Keller Nat. Ctr., Mid-Hudson Arts & Sci. Ctr., Islip Art Mus., House of Humour & Satire, Gabrova, Bulgaria, others. Recipient award of excellence Heckscher Mus., 1978, 1st grand award 5 Towns Music and Art, 1979, spl. opportunity stipend N.Y. Found. for Arts, East End Arts Coun., 1992; grantee Artists Space, 1988, 90, 91. Mem. Nat. Assn. Women Artists, Women's Caucus for Art. Office: Gold Coast Gazette 321 Sea Cliff Ave Sea Cliff NY 11579-1239

SEIDEN, RICHARD STEVEN, interior designer; b. Albany, N.Y., May 7, 1938; s. Henry Wallace and Beatrice (Olshein) S.; m. Roberta Cohen, Apr. 3, 1960; children—Terri B., Sharon L., Melinda B. Grad. Interior Design, N.Y. Sch. Interior Design, 1959. Interior designer Sharlet Furniture, Latham, N.Y., 1962-67; design dir. Concord House, Schenectady, 1967-74; owner R.S.I. Interiors, Albany, N.Y., 1974—; pres. Seiden Realty. Pres. Colonie Village PTA, 1968; dir. B'nai Brith Parkview Home, 1986—; adv. interior design program Jr. Coll. Albany; co-chmn. adv. network interior design Capitol Dist. Psych. Ctr.; bd. dirs. Albany Jewish Community Ctr., 1991—. Mem. Nat. Soc. Interior Designers (sec.-treas. 1968-74), Internat. Soc. Interior Designers, Am. Soc. Interior Designers (bd. dirs.). Democrat. Jewish. Clubs: Automobilists of Hudson Valley, Antique Auto Am., Elks, B'nai B'rith (v.p. Gideon lodge), K.P. Home: 164 Vly Rd Niskayuna NY 12309-2034 Office: RSI 238 N Allen St Albany NY 12206

SEIDEN, SHARON LYNN, sales manager; b. Albany, N.Y., Dec. 19, 1963; d. Richard Stephen and Roberta Gloria (Cohen) S. AAS in Mktg., Monroe Community Coll., Rochester, N.Y., 1984. Sales mgr. Equifax, Albany, 1986—; speaker in field. Judge Distributive Edn. Clubs of Am., N.Y., 1987—. Mem. Credit Mgmt. Assn. (pres. N.Y. chpt. 1990—), Health Care Receivables Assn., Northeastern Subcontractors Assn., Health Care Fin. Mgrs. Assn. Jewish. Office: Equifax 1 Park Pl 4th Fl Albany NY 12205

SEIDEN, STEVEN JAY, lawyer; b. N.Y.C., June 21, 1960; s. Martin S. and Rita (Glazer) S.; m. Kathryn LaRussa, Sept. 30, 1984; children: Robert B., Daniel M. BA, SUNY, Oneonta, 1981; JD, Hofstra U., 1984. Bar: N.Y. 1985, U.S. Dist. Ct. (ea. and so. dists.) N.Y. 1985. Assoc. Shapiro, Baines, Saasto & Shainwald, Mineola, N.Y., 1984-88; ptnr. Seiden & Kaufman, Carle Place, N.Y., 1988—. Mem. ABA, N.Y. State Bar Assn., N.Y. State Trial Lawyers Assn., Assn. Trial Lawyers Am., Nassau County Bar Assn., L.I. Trial Lawyers Assn. (bd. dirs.), Civil Justice Found. (founding sponsor). Jewish. Office: Seiden & Kaufman 1 Old Country Rd Carle Place NY 11514-1801

SEIDER, JULIA LIANE, lawyer; b. N.Y.C., Oct. 4, 1907; d. Nathan and Anna (Mollis) Tennenbaum; m. Morris Seider, Dec. 16, 1928; children: Norman Richard, Paula Sydney. LLB, Washington Sq. Coll., 1928; LM, NYU, 1929; JSD, St. John's U., 1936, LLD (hon.), 1936. Bar: N.Y. 1931, U.S. Dist. Ct. (ea. dist.) N.Y. 1932, U.S. Supreme Ct. 1938. Pvt. practice Bay Shore, N.Y., 1931—. Chair N.Y. div. Legal Aid Soc. Suffolk County, Bay Shore, 1941—; atty., Vet.'s Counseling Svc.; mem. Hoover Commn. Sullolk County Rep., del. judicial convs. Mem. Suffolk Acad. Law, Nat. Assn. Women Lawyers (del. with Eleanor Roosevelt to com. on human rels. of U.N.), N.Y. State Bar, Nat. Assn. Legal Aid Orgns., Navy Relief Soc., Am. Judiciary Soc., Nat. Bar Assn., Matrimonial Bar Assn., Inter-Am. Bar Assn., Nassau County Lawyers Conf., Am. Acad. Matrimonial Lawyers. Republican. Hebrew. Home: 8 Garner Ln Bay Shore NY 11706-8610 Office: 134 4th Ave Bay Shore NY 11706-7978

SEIDL, FREDRICK WILLIAM, school dean, social work educator; b. Buffalo, Sept. 29, 1940; s. Wolfgang and Anna Clara (Schneider) S.; m. Ann Jane Hazlewood, Apr. 19, 1963; children: Andrew, Barbara. AB, Ohio U., 1962; MSW, SUNY, Buffalo, 1964; PhD, U. Wis., 1970. Asst. prof. U. Minn., Morris, 1964-68; assoc. prof. Wilfred Laurier U., Waterloo, Ont., Can., 1970-72; assoc. prof. U. Wis., Madison, 1972-78, prof., 1978-84, dir. Sch. Social Work, 1980-82; dean, prof. Sch. Social Work SUNY, Buffalo, 1985—; resident Toynbee Hall, London, England, 1991. Author: The Wisconsin Experiment, 1984; contbr. articles on social issues, edn., to jours., 1964—; author, performer: (musical) Hull House: A Folk Music Celebration, 1988, Songs of New Horizons, 1989, Letter From America, 1992, 3 albums of Folk Revival music, 1990-92. Bd. dirs. Child and Family Svcs., Buffalo, 1989—, Gateway Youth and Family Svcs., Williamsville, N.Y., 1989—, United Way, Buffalo, 1989—, Urban League, Buffalo, 1989—; bd. visitors Ohio U., Athens; chair edn. div. Buffalo Philharm. Ann. Appeal; mem. editorial com. Social Work Encyclopedia. Recipient Alumnus of Yr. award SUNY, Buffalo, 1985. Mem. Nat. Assn. Social Workers, Nat. Assn. Deans and Dirs. Social Work Schs., Coun. Social Work Edn. Democrat. Home: 69 Symphony Cir Buffalo NY 14201-1203 Office: SUNY Buffalo Sch Social Work 285 Alumni Ave Buffalo NY 14260

SEIDLING, SUSAN MARY, state official; b. Duquesne, Pa., July 24, 1929; d. John and Maria (Sokolovsky) Boronkay; m. Jack Cleon Seidling, Sept. 18, 1949 (dec. 1979); children: Cheryl Susan, Janet Marie, David John. Student, LaSalle Inst., Pitts., 1949, N.Y. Inst. Fin., 1964. Lic. ins. agt.; stock broker. Paralegal A.J. Rosenbleet, Esq., McKeesport, Pa., 1949-51, Stokes & Lurie, Clairton, Pa., 1952-56; asst. mgr. Bernstein & Co., McKeesport, 1963-64; stockbroker Chaplin-McGuiness Co., Pitts., 1965-66; account exec. Bache & Co., Pitts., 1966-75; employment rep. Pa. Office Employment Security, McKeesport, 1975-91; ret., 1991. Author/editor newsletter Sr. Ams. Newsletter, 1981—. Founder, dir., past pres. Sr. Ams., Inc., North Versailles, Pa., 1981-91; pres. St. Stephens Ladies Guild, 1983. Recipient Senatorial Citation Pa. Senate, 1988, Lt. Gov.'s Proclamation State of Pa., 1988, People Who Care award Sec. of Labor, 1990. Mem. Am. Legion (founder, travel chmn. post 701 srs. 1982—, v.p. 1982-83), Rotary. Home: 1000 Taylor St North Versailles PA 15137-2130

SEIFMAN, ELI, social science educator; b. Bklyn., Aug. 4, 1936; s. Alex and Lillian (Menoff) S. BA, Queens Coll., 1957, MS, 1959; PhD, NYU, 1965. Cert. secondary edn. tchr. social studies, N.Y. Tchr. social studies Campbell Jr. High Sch., Flushing, N.Y., 1957-63; lectr. edn. Queens Coll., Flushing, 1963-64; lectr. edn. SUNY, Stony Brook, 1964-65, asst. prof., 1965-68, assoc. prof., 1968-71, prof., 1971-75, prof. social scis., 1975—, prof. history, chmn. dept. social scis., 1978—; vis. prof. Durham (Eng.) U., 1977, Jiangsu Inst. Edn., Nanjing, People's Republic of China, 1980, N.W. Tchrs. U., Lanzhou, People's Republic of China, 1982, Kuming (People's Republic of China) Med. Coll., 1983; bd. dirs. Internat. Act of Jazz, Inc. Co-author: The Social Studies, 1969, The Teacher's Handbook, 1971, Toward a New World Outlook, 1976, Education & Socialist Modernization, 1987; mem. editorial bd. Asian Thought and Soc., 1985—, Social Sci. Record, 1990—, Jour. L.I. History, 1991—. Recipient Outstanding Book for 1971-1972 award Phi Lambda Theta, 1973. Mem. Royal Soc. Asian Affairs, Kappa Delta Pi, Phi Beta Kappa, Phi Alpha Theta. Office: SUNY Dept Social Scis Stony Brook NY 11794-4333

SEIFORD, LAWRENCE MARTIN, industrial engineering educator, management consultant; b. Houston, Feb. 1, 1945; s. Frank Martin and Wanda May (Tripp) S. BA, U. St. Thomas, Houston, 1969; MA, U. Tex., 1972, PhD in Math., 1977. Asst. prof. U. Kans., Lawrence, 1979-80; assoc. prof. U. Tex., Austin, 1980-86; prof. indsl. engring. and ops. rsch. U. Mass., Amherst, 1986—; mgmt. sci. cons. Editor Jour. Productivity Analysis, The Netherlands, 1991—, Math. Jour., San Francisco, 1990—; contbr. articles to profl. jours. Lilly Endowment teaching fellow U. Mass., 1987. Mem. Ops. Rsch. Soc. Am., Inst. Mgmt. Sci., Am. Soc. for Quality Control, Math. Assn. Am., Inst. Indsl. Engrs., Prodn. and Ops. Mgmt. Soc., Decision Scsi. Inst., Omega Rho (founding mem.). Office: U Mass IEOR 114 Marston Hall Amherst MA 01003

SEIGEL, ALLEN S. (BUDDY SEIGEL), computer company executive; b. Balt., Apr. 26, 1942; s. Myer and Tobye Faye (Frank) S.; m. Donna Gail Rasinsky, Sept. 18, 1942; children: Rachel, Michael, Laura. BA, U. Miami, 1964. Social worker Dept. Pub. Welfare, Balt., 1965-66; programmer, analyst Vitro Labs., Silver Spring, Md., 1965-72; computer specialist Social Security Adminstrn., Woodlawn, Md., 1972-80; sr. computer scientist Computer Scis. Technicolor Assn., Goddard Space Flight Ctr., 1980-82; data systems mgr. Lockhead EMSCO, Goddard Space Flight Ctr., 1982-84; software systems mgr. Computer Sci. Corp., Balt., 1984-88, Infonet Corp. Split, 1988—. Spiritual leader B'nai Israel Congregation, Westminster, Md., 1978-90. Mem. Am. Mgmt. Assn., Metro DC Users Group (pres. 1977). Democrat. Jewish. Home: 6405 Taper Ct Sykesville MD 21784-8136 Office: Infonet 11700 Montgomery Rd Beltsville MD 20705-1192

SEIGEL, ARTHUR MICHAEL, neurologist; b. Rochester, N.Y., Oct. 1944; s. Hyman and Judith (Hyman) S.; B.A. in Biology with distinction, SUNY, Buffalo, 1966, M.D, 1970; m. Ellen May Streitfeld, June 1, 1969; children—Daniel Aaron, Mark Louis. Intern, SUNY Affiliated Hosps., Buffalo, 1970-71; resident Yale-New Haven Hosp., 1973-76; asst. prof. pediatrics and neurology Yale U. Sch. Medicine, New Haven, 1976-77, clin. instr., 1977-81, clin. asst. prof., 1981—; cons. in neurology Gaylord Rehab. Hosp., Wallingford, Conn., 1976-86; practice medicine specializing in neurology, New Haven, 1977—; attending physician Hosp. St. Raphael, New Haven, Yale-New Haven Hosp. Served with USPHS, 1971-73. Diplomate Am. Bd. Psychiatry and Neurology. Mem. Conn. Neurol. Soc. (v.p. 1987-92), Royal Soc. Medicine (affiliate), Am. Acad. Neurology, Conn. Med. Soc., New Haven County Med. Soc. Home: 38 Vineyard Ave Guilford CT 06437-3235 Office: 60 Temple St New Haven CT 06510

SEILER, GEORGE ROBERTS, marketing professional, consultant; b. Berkeley, Calif., June 27, 1934; s. George Atwood and Virginia May (Roberts) S.; m. Pemberly Ann Cole, Aug. 27, 1955 (div. 1970); children: George Matthew, Thomas Roberts; m. Jean Whiting Loft, Nov. 19, 1972; 1 child, Mark Lincoln. BS in Physics, William and Mary Coll., 1957; BSChemE, MIT, 1957, MSChemE, 1958. Sr. rsch. engr. Stauffer Chem. Co., N.Y.C. and Richmond, Calif., 1958-65; mgr. rsch. adminstrn. Stauffer Chem. Co., N.Y.C., 1965-66, asst. to v.p. and gen. mgr. Plastics Div., 1966-68, product mgr. Plastics Div., 1968-69, dir. fin. and adminstrn. Plastics Div., 1969-71; dir. fin. adminstrn. Vinyl Products Group WR Grace and Co., Inc., N.Y.C., 1971-73; asst. to v.p. and gen. mgr. Ch. and Dwight Co., Inc., N.Y.C., 1973-74; v.p., gen. mgr. Precision Gas Products, Inc., Rahway, N.J., 1974-78; mng. ptnr. Profit Planning Assocs., Montclair, N.J., 1978—; v.p. Tom Jones & Co., Inc., Ridgewood, N.J., 1985—; dir. Multilevel System Desings, Inc., Union, N.J., 1989-92. Author: Control: The Key to Successful Planning, 1981. chmn., bd. dirs. The Cage Teen Ctr., Inc., White Plains, N.Y., 1963-68; vice chmn. Glen Ridge Civic Conf. Com., 1975-78; bd dirs. League for Family Svcs. of Bloomfield, N.J., 1987-89. Mem. AICE, Comml. Devel. Assn., The Planning Forum, Colloquium of Cons. on Strategy (chmn. 1983-85, treas., 1983—). Mem. Soc. of Friends. Home: 30 Burnett St Glen Ridge NJ 07028 Office: Profit Planning Assocs PO Box 1265 Montclair NJ 07042

SEITELMAN, LEON HAROLD, mathematician; b. N.Y.C., May 27, 1940; s. Solomon and Yetta (Greenberg) S.; m. Brenda Auerbach, Sept. 1, 1962; children: David Jeffrey, Ellen Rachel. BEE, Cooper Union, 1960; SM in Math., U. Chgo., 1963; PhD, Brown U., 1967. Asst. project engr. Pratt & Whitney, East Hartford, Conn., 1967-71, assoc. research scientist, 1971-73, sr. applied mathematician, 1973—; vis. prof. Brown U., 1984-85, mem. exec. com. math. competition in modeling, 1984—; mem. exec. com. Project to Increase Mastery of Math. and Sci. in Conn., 1980—; active Glastonbury Ad Hoc Com. on Computing, 1977-78. Patentee. Cooper Union scholar 1956-60; Brown U. fellow 1963-64. Mem. Am. Math. Soc., Math. Assn. Am., Soc. Indsl. and Applied Math. (nat. chmn. vis. lectr. program 1980-84, mem. edn. com. 1984—), AAAS, N.Y. Acad. Scis., Sigma Xi, Tau Beta Pi. Office: Pratt & Whitney 400 Main St East Hartford CT 06108

SEITZ, DAVID FRANCIS, hospital official; b. Johnstown, Pa., Mar. 28, 1954; s. William Charles and Helen Wiberta (Hite) S.; m. Susan Elaine Zakula, Aug. 4, 1979; children: Zachary David, Benjamin William, Nicholas Patrick. BS, Edinboro (Pa.) State Coll., 1976; MA, St. Francis Coll., Loretto, Pa., 1988. Tchr. spl. edn. Commonwealth of Pa., Ebensburg, 1978-81, mgr. mental retardation unit, 1981-85; pers. analyst Commonwealth of Pa., Harrisburg, 1986-88; dir. pers. Somerset (Pa.) State Hosp., 1988—; cons., Johnstown, 1990—. Mem. Internat. Pers. Mgmt. Assn., Cambria-Somerset Soc. for Human Resource Mgmt.(program com. 1990-92). Home: 801 Linden Ave Johnstown PA 15902-2857 Office: Somerset State Hosp PO Box 631 Somerset PA 15501-0631

SEITZ, JAY ALFRED, education educator, psychologist; b. Princeton, N.J., Jan. 8, 1954; s. John Alfred and Gloria Emily (Valdessari) S. AB, Rutgers U., 1978; MA, New Sch. for Social Rsch., 1981, CUNY, 1983; MPhil, CUNY, 1986, PhD, 1987. Lic. psychologist, N.Y. Staff psychotherapist Washington Sq. Inst., N.Y.C., 1985-87; psychologist-in-term St. Lukes Hosp., N.Y.C., 1987; staff psychologist Children's Community Mental Health Ctr.-S.I. Mental Health Soc., 1987-89; assoc. psychologist South Beach Psychiatric Ctr., S.I., 1989; asst. prof. psychology St. Peter's Coll., Jersey City, 1989-90; asst. prof. edn. Adelphi U., Garden City, N.Y., 1991—; chair bd. dirs. child activity ctr. Adelphi U., Garden City, N.Y.; cons. psychologist First Steps Program Vis. Nurse Svc., N.Y., 1990-91, Outpatient Dept. St. Vincent's Svcs., Bklyn., 1990-91, Project Return, N.Y.C., 1992—, Northside Ctr. for Child Devel., N.Y.C., 1990—, N.Y.C. Bd. Edn., Spl. Edn., 1991—; devel. psychologist harlem Hosp. Ctr., N.Y.C., 1990-91; clin. psychologist pvt. practice, Manhattan, N.Y., 1990—. Contbr. articles to profl. jours. Vol. Coalition for Homeless, N.Y.C., 1987—. Mem. APA, AAUP, Am. Ednl. Rsch. Assn., Soc. for Rsch. in Child Devel., N.Y. Acad. Scis., N.Y. Neuropsychology Group, Jean Piaget Soc. Home: 220 E 24th St # 61 New York NY 10011 Office: Adelphi U Sch Edn Harvey Hall Garden City NY 11530

SEITZ, RAYMOND CARLTON, property manager; b. Balt., Sept. 19, 1936; s. Raymond Albright and Dorothy Sumner (Cook) S.; m. Phyllis Gail Evans, Dec. 23, 1959 (div. 1966); 1 child, Raymond Clayton. BA, St. John's U., Annapolis, Md., 1962; MA, Johns Hopkins U., 1965, PhD, 1972; MBA, Hofstra U., 1977. Rsch. asst. Chesapeake Bay Inst., Balt., 1965-72; asst. prof. Ft. Schuyler Maritime Coll., N.Y.C., 1973-76; student fellow Woods Hole (Mass.) Oceanographic Inst., 1963, 65. Contbr. articles to profl. jours. With U.S. Army, 1956-58. Mem. Balt. Area Conservation Group, Masons. Republican. Home: 502 Highland Ave Baltimore MD 21204-4222

SEKERKA, ROBERT FLOYD, scientist, educator; b. Wilkinsburg, Pa., Nov. 27, 1937; s. John Jacob and Vivian Mae (Smith) S.; m. Dianne Thompson, Apr. 30, 1960 (div. Apr. 1981); children: Lee Ann, Robert Thompson; m. 2d Carolyn Lee Confer, May 24, 1981. B.S. in Physics, U. Pitts., 1960; A.M., Harvard U., 1961, Ph.D., 1965. Engr. Westinghouse Research Labs., Pitts., 1965-68, mgr. materials growth and properties dept., 1968-69; lectr. Carnegie-Mellon U., Pitts., 1967-69, assoc. prof., 1969-72, prof. metallurgy and materials sci., 1972-82, dept. head, 1976-82, prof. physics and math., dean Mellon Coll. Sci., 1982-91; Univ. Prof. Carnegie Mellon U., Pitts., 1991—; mem. space studies bd. NRC, 1989-91. Assoc. editor Jour. Crystal Growth, Metallurgical Trans., 1970-76; mem. editorial bd. Applied Microgravity Tech., 1987—. Past bd. dirs. Forbes Health System, Pitts.; past vice chmn. bd. dirs. NMR Inst.; past mem. rsch. com. Allegheny Singer Rsch. Inst., Pitts.; past bd. dirs. Pitts. Regional Ctr. for Sci. Tchrs. Recipient A.G. Worthing award U. Pitts, 1959; Woodrow Wilson fellow, 1960; NSF fellow, 1962-65; Am. Soc. Metals fellow, 1980; recipient Philip M. McKenna Meml. award, 1980. Fellow Am. Soc. Metals; mem. AIME, Am. Assn. Crystal Growth (exec. com.), Internat. Assn. Crystal Growth (co-v.p.), Am. Phys. Soc., Edgewood Country Club, Club One, Phi Beta Kappa, Sigma Xi, Omicron Delta Kappa. Home: 307 S Dithridge St Apt 407 Pittsburgh PA 15213-3514 Office: Carnegie Mellon U Dept Physics 6319 Wean Hall Pittsburgh PA 15213

SEKOVSKI, BLAZE, physician; b. Macedonia, Sept. 12, 1954; came to U.S., 1969; s. Risto and Tonka (Surgunova) S.; m. Jasna Gojkovic, Apr. 22, 1977; children: Katerina, Lauren, Jessica. BS, Yale U., 1977; MD, Stanford U., 1981. Diplomate Am. Bd. Internal Medicine, Am. Bd. Cardiovascular Diseases. Intern, resident, then fellow in cardiology SUNY-Buffalo Affiliated Hosps., 1981-86; dir. ECMC Non-Invasive Cardiovascular Lab., 1988—; assoc. clin. prof. SUNY/Buffalo Sch. Medicine, 1988—. Fellow Am. Coll. Cardiology; mem. AMA, Am. Coll. Physicians. Democrat. Macedonian Orthodox. Home: 7 Hummingbird Ct Orchard Park NY 14127 Office: Erie County Med Ctr 462 Grider St Buffalo NY 14215

SEKULER, ROBERT WILLIAM, educator, scientist; b. Elizabeth, N.J., May 7, 1939; s. Sidney and Marian (Siegel) S.; m. Susan Pamela Nemser, June 25, 1961; children: Stacia, Allison, Erica. A.B., Brandeis U., 1960; Sc.M., Brown U., 1963, Ph.D., 1964; postgrad. (NIH postdoctoral fellow), M.I.T., 1964-65. Prof. psychology Northwestern U., Evanston, Ill., 1973-89, chmn. dept., 1975-79, prof. ophthalmology Med. Sch., 1978-89, prof. neurobiology and physiology, 1982-89, assoc. dean Coll. Arts and Scis., 1985-89, John Evans prof. neurosci., 1986-89; v.p. Optronix, Inc., 1980-82; provost, dean of faculty Brandeis U., Waltham, Mass., 1989-91, Louis and Frances Salvage prof. psychology, 1989—; mem. Ctr. for Study Complex Systems, 1990—; rsch. prof. of biomedical engring. Boston U., 1992—; rsch. prof. biomed. engring. Boston U., 1992—; cons. NSF, NIH, AAAS, USAF, U. Calif.; chmn. NRC-Nat. Acad. Sci. Vision Com.; chmn. NRC Working Group on Visual Function and Aging; chmn. NRC Working Group on Aging Workers and Visual Impairment. Author: (with D. Kline and K. Dismukes) Aging and Human Visual Function, 1981, (with R. Blake) Perception, 1985, 2d edit., 1990; editor: Perception & Psychophysics, 1971-86, Jour. Exptl. Psychology, 1973-74, Vision Research Jour, 1974-79, 80—, Optics Letters, 1977-79, Am. Jour. Psychology, 1979-81, Sensory Processes, 1979-81, Ophthalmic and Physiological Optics, 1986—, Intelligent Systems, 1986—, Psychology and Aging, 1987—; contbr. other sci. jours. Grantee Nat. Inst. Neurol Diseases and Stroke; Grantee U.S. Air Force; Grantee NSF; Grantee Nat. Eye Inst.; Grantee Nat. Inst. Aging; U.S. Navy, U.S. Army contractor. Fellow AAAS, Optical Soc. Am., Am. Acad. Optometry, Am. Psychol. Soc.; mem. Assn. Research in Vision and Ophthalmology, Neurosci. Soc., Psychonomic Soc., Knowles Inst. for Hearing Rsch. (bd. dirs.), Sigma Xi. Home: 64 Strawberry Hill Rd Concord MA 01742-5502 Office: Brandeis U Psychology Dept Waltham MA 02254

SELBY, ROBERT NORMAN, metal products executive, treasurer; b. Watervliet, N.Y., July 15, 1932; s. William Wallace and Olive (Kins) S.; m. Shirley Mary Duffney, Apr. 25, 1954; children: Deborah, Karen, Stephen, Bryan, Matthew. Grad. high sch., Watervliet. Trustee Union Health Fund, Albany, N.Y., 1960-64; founder, treas. Selby & Smith, Inc., Watervliet, 1965—. Mem. Nat. Com. on Sheet Metal Tng., 1989-92; bd. dirs. C. of C., Troy, 1980-83; chmn. Apprentice Trust, Albany, 1980-92, N.Y. State Sheet Med. Edn., 1985-92; pres. Rotary, Watervliet, 1984-85, fundraiser, 1988. With U.S. Army, 1949-56. Mem. ASHRAE, Eastern Conf. on Sheet Metal Tng. (chmn. 1985-92), Sheet Metal Contractors Assn. (pres. 1991-92). Democrat. Home: Oxford Heights Essex # A5 Albany NY 12203 Office: Selby & Smith Inc 2431 3d Ave Watervliet NY 12189

SELCHOW, ROGER HOFFMAN, artist, sculptor; b. Greenwich, Conn., Feb. 13, 1911; s. Paul Hoffman and Alice Allen (Mills) S. Student Grand Central Sch. Art, 1931-33, Columbia U., 1947-48, Academies Andre Lhote, Fernand Leger, Paris, 1949, 50, 53, Instituto Statale d'Arte, Florence, Italy, 1951. Dir. Atelier du Vieux Vaison, Vaison-la-Romaine, France, 1953-60. 19 one-man shows in Germany, Belgium, France and U.S. including N.Y.C., 1983, Thematic Assemblages, 1987.; 25 group shows in Belgium, Germany and U.S.A.; represented in several mus. and numerous pvt. collections in Europe and U.S.A.; 2 hist. maps of Greenwich, Conn., 1939, 48; contbr. hist. articles to Greenwich Time. Custodian records 2d Congl. Ch., Greenwich; bd. dirs. Greenwich Hist. Soc. before 1949. Recipient numerous prizes for art. Served with USNR, 1942-45. Avocation: writing memoirs of 1949-70 in Europe. Home: Madison Green 5 E 22d St Apt 7-C New York NY 10010

SELDEN, DAVID EDWARD, law librarian; b. Rochester, N.Y., Jan. 16, 1960; s. Sherman and Irene (Bauerle) S.; m. Karen Elaine Slagle, Aug. 22, 1987. BS, Appalachian State U., 1983; MLS, Simmons Coll., Boston, 1987. Law librarian Orr & Reno P.A., Concord, N.H., 1987—; instr. N.H. Tech. Inst., Concord, N.H., 1989—. Mem. Assn. of N.H. Law Librarians, Am. Assn. Law Librarians, Law Librarians of New Eng. Democrat. Office: Orr & Reno PA 1 Eagle Sq Concord NH 03301-4903

SELDEN, LAWRENCE V., physician, surgeon; b. Springfield, Mass., Jan. 2, 1922; s. Ruben and Rose Selden; m. Claire G. Casler, June 1, 1946; children: Reid, Patricia, Stacey. BS, Tulane U., 1942, MD, 1945. Diplomate Am. Bd. Surgery. Intern Beth Israel Hosp., Boston, 1945-46; resident in surgery Alexander Blain Clinic, Detroit, 1948-49, 50-52, Cooley Dickinson Hosp., Northampton, Mass., 1949-50; fellow in surgery Univ. Hosp., Ann Arbor, Mich., 1950—; instr. Tufts Med. Sch., Medford, Mass.; chief of surgery Wesson Meml. Hosp., 1959-60, 61-63; staff Baystate Med. Ctr., Mercy Hosp., Springfield, Mass., 1952—. Capt U.S. Army, 1946-48. Fellow ACS, Internat. Coll. Surgeons; mem. Parlor Med. Soc. (past pres.), Maimonides Med. Soc. (past pres.), John Hunter Med. Soc. (past pres.). Home: 140 Chestnut St Springfield MA 01103 Office: Surgeons Inc 34 Mulberry Ln Springfield MA 01105

SELIG, DAVID GEORGE, podiatrist; b. Amityville, N.Y., Aug. 30, 1955; s. Joseph Lewis and Janet Lucille (Stern) S.; m. Linda J. Soled, Mar. 30, 1980. BS, U. Md., 1977; D of Podiatric Medicine, N.Y. Coll. Podiatric Medicine, 1983. Preceptorship in sports medicine and foot surgery Foot Care Group, N.Y.C., 1983-84; pvt. practice N.Y.C., 1984—; asst. attending podiatrist Mt. Sinai Hosp., N.Y.C., 1989—; attending podiatrist Med. Arts Ctr. Hosp., N.Y.C., 1984—; panel podiatrist Union 1199, N.Y.C., 1987—. Contbr. articles to profl. jours. Med. vol. N.Y.C. Marathon, 1979-82, 86-90; found. mem. Town Club of N.Y.C., 1989—. Fellow Am. Coll. Foot Orthopedists, Am. Acad. Podiatric Sports Medicine; mem. Am. Coll. Foot Surgeons (assoc.), Am. Podiatric Med. Assn., N.Y. State Podiatric Med. Assn., Am. Running and Fitness Assn. (clinic advisor), Phi Sigma, Psi Chi. Office: 353 E 72nd St New York NY 10021-4671

SELIG, KENNETH MISHARA, psychiatrist, lawyer; b. Boston, Sept. 24, 1950; s. Robert Belmont Selig and Marilyn (Mishara) Seligman; m. Colleen Ann Farrell, Aug. 1, 1979; children: Brian Farrell, Amanda Farrell. BA, U. N.C., 1972; MD, Boston U., 1977; JD, Yale U., 1987. Diplomate Nat. Bd. Med. Examiners, Am. Bd. Psychiatry and Neurology; bar: Conn. 1987. Resident psychiatry N.C. Meml. Hosp., Chapel Hill, 1977-81; med. staff Inst. Living, Hartford, Conn., 1981-83; cons. staff Hartford Hosp., 1982—; pvt. practice Hartford, 1983-84; co-dir. forensic psychiatry cons. program Inst. Living, Hartford, 1987-90; pvt. practice adult and forensic psychiatry Glastonbury, Conn., 1990—; cons. Cts. Diagnostic Clinic, Hartford, 1987—. Assoc. editor Jour. Contemporary Psychiatry, 1981-91. Treas. Mental Health Assn. Conn., 1988—, chmn. bd. dirs., 1991—; bd. dirs. Intercommunity Mental Health Group, Glastonbury, 1986—. Mem. Am. Psychiat. Assn. (Falk fellow 1979-81), ABA, Am. Coll. Legal Medicine, Am. Acad. Psychiatry and Law, Phi Beta Kappa, Phi Eta Sigma. Democrat. Office: 257 New London Turnpike Glastonbury CT 06033

SELIGSON, FRANCES HESS, nutrition scientist; b. Phila., Sept. 6, 1949; d. John Henry Sr. and Rita (Schoener) H.; m. Michael Edward Seligson, June 21, 1975. BS, Drexel U., 1971; PhD, U. Calif., Berkeley, 1976. Asst. prof. U. N.C., Chapel Hill, 1976-77; scientist Procter & Gamble Co., Cin., 1977-87; sr. mgr. Hershey (Pa.) Foods, 1987—. Patentee in field. Mem. Am. Dietetic Assn., Am. Inst. Nutrition, Inst. Food Technology, Internat. Life Scis. Orgn. (chmn. fatty acid sub-com. 1989—, vice chair food, nutrition and safety coms. 1991—). Office: Hershey Foods Corp PO Box 805 Hershey PA 17033-0805

SELIN, IVAN, federal official; b. N.Y.C., Mar. 11, 1937; s. Saul and Freda (Kuhlman) Selin; m. Nina Kallet, June 8, 1957; children: Douglas, Jessica. B.E., Yale U., 1957, M.E., 1958, Ph.D., 1960; Dr. es Sciences, U. Paris, 1962. Rsch. engr. Rand Corp., Santa Monica, Calif., 1960-65; systems analyst Dept. Def., Washington, 1965-67, dep. asst. sec. def., 1967-69, acting asst. sec. for systems analysis, 1969-70; founder, chmn. bd. Am. Mgmt. Systems, Inc., Arlington, Va., 1970-89; undersec. state Dept. State, Washington, 1989-91; chmn. NRC, Washington, 1991—; lectr. UCLA, 1961-63; chmn. mil. econ. adv. panel to CIA, 1978-89. Author: Detection Theory, 1964; contbr. articles to profl. jours. Pres. Corp. Against Drug Abuse, 1988—; bd. dirs., gov. UN Assn. U.S., 1979-89; mem. exec. com. Greater Washington Research Ctr., Fed. City Council. Decorated Disting. Civilian Svc. medal, 1970; recipient Disting. Svc. medal Sec. of State, 1991; Fulbright scholar, 1959-61; Ford Found. grantee, 1952-54. Mem. Council Fgn. Relations, Fed. City Council Washington (trustee), IEEE (editor Trans. on Ifo. Theory 1960-65), Sigma Xi, Tau Beta Pi. Clubs: Yale, Cosmos. Home: 2905 32nd St NW Washington DC 20008-3526 Office: Nuclear Regulatory Commn Washington DC 20555

SELKE, WILLIAM AUGUST, chemical engineer, consultant, educator; b. Newburgh, N.Y., June 16, 1922; s. August Frank and Catherine Louise

(McAree) S.; m. Martha Whitney Floyd, Oct. 4, 1952; children: William August Jr., Whitney Floyd, Edward Delavan. SB, MIT, 1943, SM, 1947; D in Engring., Yale U., 1949. Engr. Conn. State Water Commn., New Haven, 1947-48; asst. prof. chem. engring. dept. Columbia U., N.Y.C., 1949-54, mgr. AEC heat transfer facility, 1953-55; dir. rsch. Peter J. Schweitzer, Inc., Lee, Mass., 1955-57; dir. R&D Peter J. Schweitzer div. Kimberly-Clark Corp., Lee, 1957-81; v.p. group R&D Kimberly-Clark Corp., Roswell, Ga., 1981-84, v.p. tech. assessment, 1984-86; prin. Meetinghouse Assocs., Stockbridge, Mass., 1986—; prof. Lenox (Mass.) Inst. for Rsch., 1987—; chmn. tech. adv. group 126 Am. Nat. Standards Inst., N.Y.C., 1988—. Contbr. articles to profl. jours., chpts. to books; 19 patents in field. Trustee Boston Symphony Orch., 1980-84; mem. State Bd. Edn., Mass., 1969-71. Lt. USNR, 1943-45, PTO. Fellow N.Y. Acad. Scis.; mem. Am. Inst. Chem. Engrs., Tech. Assn. Pulp and Paper Industry, Assn. Environ. Engring. Profs., Lenox Club (bd. dirs., pres. 1989-90), Mahkeenac Boating Club (bd. dirs., pres. 1982). Episcopalian. Home: Meetinghouse Stockbridge MA 01262-0506

SELKOW, PAULA, psychologist; b. N.Y.; m. Maurice Jay Rosenstraus, May 22, 1977. BA, SUNY, New Paltz, 1967; MEd, Boston U., 1969; PhD, Fordham U., 1978. Lic. psychologist, N.J., N.Y. Tchr. N.Y.C. Bd. Edn., 1967-68, 69-70; employment counselor N.Y. State Employment Svc., N.Y.C., 1970-71; sch. psychologist Bur. Child Guidance, N.Y.C., 1971-76, Princeton (N.J.) Regional Schs., 1977-78; asst. prof. William Paterson Coll., Wayne, N.J., 1979-84; pvt. practice, Somerset, N.J., 1981—; adj. instr. Trenton (N.J.) State Coll., 1977-79; cons. psychologist Laurie Neurodevel. Inst., New Brunswick, N.J., 1981-87. Author: Assessing Sex Bias in Testing, 1984; also articles. Grantee HEW, 1979. Mem. APA, Ea. Psychol. Assn., N.J. Psychol. Assn., N.J. Acad. Psychology, Cen. N.J. Women's Profl. Network (founder). Home and Office: 40 Smith Rd Somerset NJ 08873-2726

SELKOWITZ, JUDITH, art advisor, dealer; b. Pittsfield, Mass., Dec. 21, 1944; d. Milton M. Selkowitz and Molly L. Levitt. BA, Skidmore Coll., 1966. Pres. Art Adv. Services Inc., N.Y.C., 1969—; lectr. Grad. Sch. Design Harvard U., 1979-80; lectr. in field. Author: Art in Interiors, 1981. Fulbright scholar, 1967. Mem. Art Table, Appraisal Assn. Am. Office: Art Advisory Services 530 Park Ave New York NY 10021-8015

SELL, ROBERT DEMEUSY, business development executive; b. Phila., May 8, 1954; s. James Robert and Alice Marie (Demeusy) S.; m. Judy Melissa Kahle, May 31, 1975; children: Christi Ann, Rebecca Lynn, Michael Demeusy, Brian Kahle. BS in Chemistry, U. Va., 1975; MBA, West Va. U., 1987. Shift supr. Corning Inc., Parkersburg, W.Va., 1979-81, sr. process engr., 1981-82, supr. process engr., 1982-84, supr. quality assurance, 1984-85, project mgr., 1985-87, dept. mgr., 1987-89, bus. devel. mgr., 1989—; instr. Glenville State Coll., Parkersburg, 1985-88. Elder 1st Presbyn. Ch., Horseheads, N.Y.; treas. Cub Scouts Am., Horseheads, 1989-91, com. chmn., Vienna, W.Va., 1987-89. Lt. USN, 1975-79. Mem. ASTM, Am. Mktg. Assn., Am. Chem. Soc., Am. Water Works Assn., Am. Sci. Glassblowers Soc., AOAC Internat., Phi Beta Kappa, Alpha Chi Sigma. Office: Corning Inc HP AB 03 11 Corning NY 14831

SELLA, EDWARD GERARD, telephone company executive; b. Bound Brook, N.J., Feb. 24, 1933; s. John Joseph and Mary Catherine (Gavornick) S.; m. Jeanne Marilyn Geyer, June 3, 1930; children: Edward Geoffrey, Mary Louise, David Gerard, Mary Jeanne, John Lester. BS, Ursinus Coll., 1957. Analyst Nat. Security Agy., Washington, 1957-59; salesman Mutual of N.Y., Washington, 1959-62; sales mgr. Mutual of N.Y., 1962-78, agy. mgr., 1978—; prin. Sella, Kinkel & Sella, Rockville, Md., 1982—; pres. Capital Pay Telephone Corp., Rockville, 1987—; v.p. Columbia (Md.) Life Underwriters, 1983. Chmn., bd. dirs. Jr. Achievement, Chevy Chase, Md., 1976-77; bd. dirs. Rockville Scholarship Found., 1987-91, v.p. Holy Cross Hosp. Men's Guild, Silver Spring, Md., 1988—, fundraiser Harden & Weaver Golf Tournament, 1977-78; com. mem. Heart Assn. Pro-Am Golf Tournament, 1983-84; program chmn. Make-A-Wish Golf Tournament, 1989; bd. dirs. Rockville Chamber Commn., 1988-91. Mem. Rotary. Republican. Roman Catholic. Home: 14901 Rocking Spring Dr Rockville MD 20853-3636 Office: Capital Pay Telephone Corp 3200 Tower Oaks Blvd # 300 Rockville MD 20852-4216

SELLA, EMMANUEL, investment company executive; b. Vilno, Lithunia, July 24, 1924; came to U.S., 1952; s. Ephriam and Lea (Kelman) Solchanski; m. 1947 (div. 1950); 1 child, Gour; m. Aviva Freidis, Dec. 17, 1952; children: Ephriam, Gideon, Shelley, Carmel. Student, Hasscala Coll., Tel Aviv, Israel, 1942-47; BS, Syracuse U., 1954; MA, Harvard U., 1956. Founder, chmn. bd., chief executive officer, pres. Amivest Corp., N.Y.C., 1958—. Mem. bd. govs. Haifa U., Israel, 1989; dir. non-traditional employment for women NEW; bd. dirs. Am. Israel Friendship League. Mem. Am. Israel Pub. Affairs Com. (nat. exec. com., chmn. leadership project com.), Economic Club N.Y., Harvard Club. Democrat. Jewish. Home: 131 E 64th St New York NY 10021-7004 Office: Amivest Corp 767 5th Ave New York NY 10153-0002

SELLER, STEVEN MARK, pharmacist; b. Buffalo, June 2, 1952; s. Marvin Philip Seller and Molly (Kramer) Lettman. BS in Natural Sci., Niagara U., 1974; BS in Pharmacy, Mass. Coll. Pharmacy, 1976. Clin. rotation Beth Israel Hosp., Boston, 1976; pharmacist CVS Pharmacy, Braintree, Mass., 1977-78; pharmacy mgr. Mall Drugs, Boston, 1978; store and pharmacy mgr. Wagner Leader Drugs, Buffalo, 1978-80; pharmacy mgr. James Super Drug, Buffalo, 1980-83; pharmacist Buffalo RX Ctr., 1983-85; clin. instr. Sch. Pharmacy SUNY, Buffalo, 1984-87; pharmacist Health Care Plan, Buffalo, 1985—; cons. Beechwood Nursing Home and Residence, Buffalo, 1985—; cons. pharmacist. Bd. rev. jour. Cons. Pharmacist, 1990. Mem. Mason, Albright-Knox Art Gallery. Fellow Am. Soc. Cons. Pharmacist (upstate dir. N.Y. state chpt. 1985—, mem. orgnl. affairs coun. 1990—), Alumni Assn. Mass. Coll. Pharmacy, Nat. Alumni Assn. Niagara U. Democrat. Jewish. Home: 75 Groton Dr # B Buffalo NY 14228-2545 Office: Health Care Plan 2075 Sheridan Dr Buffalo NY 14223-1491

SELLERS, ALFRED MAYER, physician; b. Phila., Feb. 23, 1924; s. Philip A. and Rebecca (Feinberg) S.; m. Helen Obermayer, June 22, 1952; children: Joseph Marc, David Alan. BS in Medicine, Duke U., 1951, MD, 1951; MA (hon.), U. Pa. Diplomate Am. Bd. Internal Medicine. Staff physician U. Pa. Hosp., Phila., 1951—; assoc. prof. U. Pa. Med. Sch., Phila., 1966—; rsch. in field. Contbr. articles to profl. jours. Staff sgt. U.S. Army, 1942-46. Fellow Am. Coll. Physicians, Am. Coll. Cardiology, Am. Coll. Chest Physicians, Am. Coll. Clin. Pharmacology. Republican. Home: 718 Arlington Rd Narberth PA 19072-1503 Office: U Pa Hosp 3400 Spruce St Philadelphia PA 19104-4283

SELLERS, DONNA REIMAN, counselor, educator; b. Bethlehem, Pa., Nov. 5, 1954; d. Delbert Reiman and Frances (Long) Pagano; m. Joseph G. Sellers Jr., June 28, 1980; children: Alyssa Ann, Christopher Joseph. BE, East Stroudsburg (Pa.) U., 1976; MEd, Lehigh U., 1979, EdS in Elem. Counseling, 1990. Tchr. spl. edn. Bethlehem Area Schs., 1977-91; counselor, educator social and emotion maladjusted students Bethlehem Schs., 1991—; edn. cons. Bethlehem Area Schs., 1990; homebound instr. Bethlehem Schs., 1989—. Kitchen coord. St. Theresa Ch., Hellertown, Pa., 1990—; pres. Marine Sch. PTO, 1983-88; bus. econs. coord. Marine Sch., 1983-88, 91—. Recipient Apple Tchr. award Lehigh Valley Assn. for Children with Learning Disabilities, 1979, Class Favorite award Bethlehem Schs. Parents, 1988. Mem. AACD, NEA, Pa. Edn. Assn., Bethlehem Edn. Assn., PTA Saucon Valley Schs. Democrat. Roman Catholic. Office: Bethlehem Area Sch Dist 1516 Sycamore St Bethlehem PA 18017-6099

SELLERS, KAREN ANNE, graphic designer; b. Woodbury, N.J., Nov. 30, 1945; d. Raymond George Sr. and Pearl Elva (Smith) Strable; m. Vincent DePaul McGarry, Jr. (div. Jan. 1972); m. David Thomas Sellers, May 26, 1980 (div. Dec. 1991); children: Thomas Raymond, Stephen David. BFA in Graphic Design, Phila. Coll. of Art, 1969; postgrad., U. of the Arts, Phila., 1990—. Mech. artist H.S. Goodsett Advertising, Inc., Phila., 1971-73, art dir., 1973-77; traffic mgr. Elkman Advertising, Inc., Bala Cynwyd, Pa., 1977-80; freelance artist Ambler, Pa., 1980—; staff artist Smith Simon Co., Ft. Washington, Pa., 1985, art dir., 1986-87. Republican. Home and Office: 733 Alene Rd Ambler PA 19002-2606

SELLIG, ROBERT GEORGE, orthopedist; b. Webster, Mass., May 14, 1941; s. George A. and Marion G. (Melican) S.; m. Sara Grafton; children: Thomas, Elizabeth, Kathryn. BA, Harvard U., 1962; MD, U. Vt., 1966. Cert. Am. Bd. Orthopedic Surgery, 1975. Resident in orthopedic surgery U. Pitts., 1971-73; active staff Glens Falls (N.Y.) Hosp., 1974—. Fellow Am. Acad. Orthopedic Surgeons, ACS, AMA. Office: 88 Broad St Glens Falls NY 12801

SELLINGER, ELAINE, psychologist, lawyer; b. N.Y.C., Jan. 27, 1931; d. Louis Nathan and Fanny (Seitel) Katz; m. Norman Moore, Jan. 28, 1953 (div. 1971); children: David N., Charles, Martha Moore Monroy; m. Stuart Sellinger, June 29, 1973. Pre-law cert., U. Vt., 1950; LLB, Bklyn. Law Sch., 1953; MA, Fairfield (Conn.) U., 1962, cert. in advanced studies, 1963; PsyD, Yeshiva U., 1989. Asst. clk. Ct. of Common Pleas, Bridgeport, Conn., 1956-59; pvt. practice Fairfield, 1959-62; sch. psychologist New Canaan (Conn.) Schs., 1962-63, Westport (Conn.) Pub. Schs., 1963—; treatment coord. Hall Brooke Hosp., Westport, 1989—. Mem. Hurllutt Fund Com., Westport, 1971—. Recipient Spl. Recognition award Yeshiva U., 1987; Classical scholar U. Vt., 1948. Mem. APA, Conn. Assn. Sch. Psychologists, Audubon Soc., Sierra Club. Office: Westport Pub Schs Kings Hwy Westport CT 06880-4710

SELLINGER, JOSEPH ANTHONY, college president; b. Phila., Jan. 17, 1921; s. Frank and L. Caroline (Wiseman) S. Ph.L., Spring Hill Coll., 1945, B.S. in Chemistry, 1945; postgrad. in theology, Weston Coll., 1948-49, Woodstock Coll., 1949-50; S.T.L., Facultes St. Albert, Louvain, Belgium, 1952. Joined S.J., 1938, ordained priest, Roman Catholic Ch., 1951. Assoc. dean Coll. Arts and Scis. Georgetown U., Washington, 1955-57; dean Georgetown U., 1957-64, sec. corp., instnl. dir., 1957-64; pres., rector Loyola Coll., Balt., 1964—. Mem. Am. Council Edn. (vice-chmn.), Assn. Higher Edn., Middle States Assn., Nat. Cath. Ednl. Assn., Cath. Theol. Soc., Assn. Am. Colls., Phi Beta Kappa (hon.), Nat. Assn. of Ind. Colls. and Univs. (bd. dirs.). Office: Loyola Coll Office of Pres 4501 N Charles St Baltimore MD 21210-2601*

SELLKE, FRANK WILLIAM, cardiothoracic surgeon, researcher; b. Ft. Wayne, Ind., Feb. 5, 1956; s. Erwin A. and Anna Luise (Schumacher) S.; m. Amy Marie Brill, Jan. 31, 1987; children: Michelle, Eric. AB summa cum laude, Wabash Coll., 1978; MD, Ind. U., Indpls., 1981. Diplomate Am. Bd. Thoracic Surgery, Am. Bd. Surgery. Intern Ind. U. Hosp., Indpls., 1981-82; emergency physician Culver Union Hosp., Crawfordsville, Ind., 1982-83; resident in surgery Akron (Ohio) City Hosp., 1983-87; postdoctoral fellow cardiac surgery U. Iowa, Iowa City, 1987-90; instr. Harvard Med. Sch., Boston, 1990-92, asst. prof. surgery, 1992—; cardiothoracic surgeon Beth Israel Hosp., Boston, 1990—. Contbr. rsch. articles to profl. jours. Fellow Am. Coll. Cardiology; mem. AMA, Am. Heart Assn., Am. Physiol. Soc., Am. Coll. Chest Physicians, Phi Beta Kappa. Lutheran. Home: 129 Beaumont Ave Newton MA 02160-2315 Office: Beth Israel Hosp 330 Brookline Ave Boston MA 02215-5491

SELSKI, WILLIAM E., architect; b. Bridgeport, Conn., Mar. 18, 1953; s. Edward and Amelia (Fensky) S.; m. Deborah Rick Selski, Oct. 30, 1983. B.Arch., Syracuse U., 1975; postgrad., Cen. Conn. State U., 1980. Lic. architect. Draftsman Fletcher-Thompson, Bridgeport, Conn., 1969-72; designer Hill & Harrigan, New Haven, 1973, Whitcomb Assocs., Danbury, Conn., 1974-76, J.L. Elovitz Architect, Fairfield, Conn., 1977; architect/educator State of Conn. Bullard Havens, Bridgeport, 1978—, U. Bridgeport, 1982—. Editor The Spexpert, 1988. Mem. CSI (bd. dirs. 1988—), BOCA (bd. dirs. 1988—). Republican. Roman Catholic. Home: 8 Harwood Ter Trumbull CT 06611-2819 Office: Bullard Havens Tech Sch 500 Palisade Ave Bridgeport CT 06610-3499

SELTMAN, MARK ALLAN, industrial designer; b. Pitts., June 16, 1947; s. Cy and Miriam (Fagen) S.; m. Joanna Brotman, Oct. 13, 1985; 1 child, Cassandra Brotman Seltman. BFA, Carnegie Mellon U., 1969. Pres. Dac Mktg. Inc., Pitts., 1969-71; v.p. Universal Media, Inc., Pitts., 1972; owner Mark Seltman Assocs., N.Y.C., 1973—; mem. faculty New Sch. Social Rsch., N.Y.C., 1978-81, Parsons Sch. Design, N.Y.C., 1983-88, Cooper Union for the Advancement of Sci. and Art, N.Y.C., 1987-92. Mem. Nat. Coun. Geocosmic Rsch., Hubbard Hall, Environ. Action Coalition, Nat. Resources Def. Coun., Wilderness Soc., The Nature Conservancy, Coop Am.

SELTZER, JEFFREY LLOYD, lawyer, investment banker; b. Bklyn., July 27, 1956; s. Bernard and Sue (Harris) S.; m. Ana Isabel Sifre, Aug. 24, 1985; children: Ian Alexander, Pamela Allison. BS in Econs. cum laude, U. Pa., 1978; JD, Georgetown U., 1981. Bar: N.Y. 1982. Assoc. Austrian, Lance & Stewart, N.Y.C., 1981-85; assoc. gen. counsel, asst. v.p. Shearson Lehman Bros., N.Y.C., 1986; mng. dir. Lehman Bros., N.Y.C., 1986—. Author: The U.S. Greeting Card Market, 1977, Starting and Organizing a Business, 1984, Swap Risk Management: A Primer, 1988. Mem. U.S. Trade Adv. Com. on Svc. Industries, Washington, 1990—; mem. nat. adv. coun. SBA, Washington, 1982-87; mem. small bus. adv. coun. Rep. Nat. Com., Washington, 1984-90; advisor Friends of Giuliani, N.Y.C., 1989, New Yorkers for Lew Lehrman, N.Y.C., 1981-82; policy analyst Reagan-Bush Com., Arlington, Va., 1980. Mem. ABA, Re. Nat. Lawyers Assn., Federalist Soc., Ctr. for Study of Presidency, Am. Assn. Polit. Cons., Securities Industry Assn. (chmn. swap and derivative products com. 1990—), Jericho Athletic Assn. (coach 1991-92). Home: 3 Yates Ave Jericho NY 11753-1418 Office: Lehman Bros Am Express Tower World Fin Ctr New York NY 10285-1200

SELTZER, MITCHELL SHERMAN, hotel executive; b. Abington, Pa., June 10, 1948; s. Larry and Mary Ellen (Gallagher) S.; m. Lucille M. Bartleson, May 22, 1975 (div. May 1989). BA, Pa. State U., 1971. Chef Valley Forge Hilton Hotel, King of Prussia, Pa., 1974-77, Cutillo's Restaurant, Pottstown, Pa., 1977-79; gen. mgr. Unisys Edn. Ctr., Malvern, Pa., 1984-88; gen. mgr. Dave Thomas Ctr. Duke U., Durham, N.C., 1988-90; gen. mgr. Am. Coll. Marriott Corp., Bryn Mawr, Pa., 1990—. Home: #1 Drummers Ln Wayne PA 19087 Office: Am Coll Gregg Ctr 270 Bryn Mawr Ave Bryn Mawr PA 19010

SELTZER, RICHARD WARREN, JR., writer, editor, consultant; b. Clarksville, Tenn., Feb. 23, 1946; s. Richard Warren and Helen Isabella (Estes) S.; m. Barbara Ann Hartley, July 28, 1973; children: Robert, Heather, Michael, Timothy. BA, Yale U., 1969; MA in Comparative Lit., U. Mass., 1972. Editor Benwill Pub., Boston, 1973-79; sr. communications cons. Digital Equip. Corp., Maynard, Mass., 1979—. Author: Name of Hero, 1981, Lizard of Oz, 1974; author short stories. With USAR, 1969-75. Mem. Internat. Assn. Bus. Communicators, U.S. Chess Fedn. Office: Digital Equip Corp 111 Powerdermill Rd MS02-1/D1 Maynard MA 01754-1418

SELTZER, SAMUEL M., psychologist; b. Bklyn., Nov. 5, 1926; s. Jacob and Elizabeth (Maclaire) S.; m. Evelyn P. Mandel, Sept. 17, 1949; children: Stanley Eric, Allen Jeffrey, Margo Ilene. BS, CCNY, 1948, MS, 1950; postgrad., Alfred U., 1950, SUNY, Buffalo, 1956-57. Lic. psychologist, N.Y.; cert. sch. psychologist, N.Y. Cons. Des Moines Pub. Schs., 1949-51; clin. psychologist Clarinda Mental Health Inst., Clarindo, Iowa, 1951-53, Milw. County Hosp. Mental Diseases, Milw., 1953-54; chief psychologist Buffalo Psychiat. Ctr., 1954-55, Attica (N.Y.) Prison, 1955-58; pvt. practice, 1958—; chief psychologist Craig Devel. Ctr., Sonyea, N.Y., 1958-67, 68-71, chief of svc., 1971-81; dir. Masten Park Rehab. Ctr., Buffalo, 1967-68. Dist. chair Genesee (N.Y.) coun. Boy Scouts Am., 1959-62. Mem. Psychol. Assn. West N.Y. (editor newsletter 1986-91), Attention Deficit Hyperactive Disorder Assn. West N.Y. (editor newsletter 1991—), Rotary (pres. elect Tonawandas 1991—, pres. Mount Morris chpt. 1962-63), Shriners. Home: 66 Longmeadow Rd Buffalo NY 14226-2808

SELTZER, SHERWIN PAUL, sales executive; b. Bklyn., Nov. 3, 1934; s. Irving Martin and Lillian (Goldfarb) S.; m. Iris Meryl Wolf, June 26, 1960; children: Melanie Gwen, Andrew Ian. BS in Mgmt., NYU, 1956. Salesman Brown & Williamson, Louisville, 1957-58, Faber Coe & Gregg, Newark, 1958-77; western regional mgr. Faber Coe & Gregg, L.A., 1958-77; nat. sales mgr. Nat Sherman Co., N.Y.C., 1977-78; v.p. mktg. and sales Danby-Palizio div. Villazon & Co., Upper Saddle River, N.J., 1978—. Mem. Tobacco Merchants Assn. (bd. dirs., treas. 1990—). Home: 39 Mabro Dr Denville NJ 07834

SELWOOD, PETER JOHN, mortgage company executive; b. Horsham, Sussex, Eng., July 3, 1942; came to U.S., 1947; s. John Leslie Baker and Helen Eileen (Neylon) S.; m. Beverly JoAnne Crouch, July 29, 1967; children: Christopher Michael, Amy. BA, Am. U., 1967, MS, 1973. Exec. v.p. Selwood Rsch., Inc., Kensington, Md., 1966-67; bd. govs. Mortgage Bankers of Washington, 1982-84; mem. exec. com. B.F. Saul Co., Chevy Chase, Md., 1989—. Pres. Edgewood-Glenwood Citizens, Bethesda, Md., 1976-80, Montgomery County Pub. Schs. PTA, Bethesda, 1980-81, The Real Estate Group, Washington, 1982-83; pres., founder Bethesda Soccer Club, Inc., 1979-90. Lt. USN, 1967-71. Recipient Appreciation award Montgomery County Pub. Schs., 1981. Mem. Nat. Assn. Office Parks, Md. State Soccer Assn. (exec. v.p. Balt. chpt. 1979—), Ann Tyler Book Club (founder). Office: LEGG-MASON Real State Svcs 8401 Connecticut Ave Chevy Chase MD 20818

SELYA, BRUCE MARSHALL, federal judge; b. Providence, May 27, 1934; s. Herman C. and Betty (Brier) S.; m. Ellen Hazel Barnes, Feb. 27, 1965; children: Dawn Meredith Selya Sherman, Lori Ann. B.A. magna cum laude, Harvard U., 1955, J.D. magna cum laude, 1958. Bar: D.C. 1958, R.I. 1960. Law clk. U.S. Dist. Ct. R.I., Providence, 1958-60; assoc. Gunning & LaFazia, Providence, 1960-62; ptnr. Gunning, LaFazia, Gnys & Selya, Providence, 1963-74, Selya & Iannuccillo, Providence, 1974-82; judge U.S. Dist. Ct. R.I., Providence, 1982-86, U.S. Ct. Appeals (1st cir.), Providence, 1986—; judge Lincoln Probate Ct., R.I., 1965-72; mem. R.I. Jud. Council, 1964-72, sec., 1965-70, chmn., 1971-72; mem. Gov.'s Commn. on Crime and Adminstrn. Justice, 1967-69; del. Nat. Conf. on Revisions to Fed. Appellate Practice, 1968-82; mem. various spl. govtl. commns. and adv. groups. Chmn. bd. trustees, Bryant Coll., Smithfield, R. I., 1986—; bd. trustees, R. I. Hosp. Recipient Louis Dembitz Brandeis medal for disting. legal svc. Brandeis U., 1988. Mem. ABA, Fed. Bar Assn., Fed. Judges Assn., R.I. Bar Assn. (chmn. various coms.), R.I. Bar Found., U.S. Jud. Conf. (com. on jud. br.), Am. Arbitration Assn., Am. Judicature Soc. (dir.). Jewish. Home: 137 Grotto Ave Providence RI 02906-5720 Office: US Ct Appeals 311 Fed Bldg & US Courthouse Providence RI 02903 also: 1704 McCormack Boston MA 02109

SEMBER, JUNE ELIZABETH, educator; b. Apr. 3, 1932; d. Charles Benjamin and Cora Emma (Miller) Shoemaker; m. Eugene Sember, Oct. 18, 1975. BS with honors, Ea. Mennonite, 1957; postgrad., Columbia U., 1958, U. W.Va., 1960. Tchr. grades 1-6 Coss Road and Pvt. Sch., Salisbury, Pa., 1953-55; tchr. grade 5 Connellsville (Pa.) Area Schs., 1957-58, tchr. grade 2, 1958-66, tchr. grade 1, 1967—; supervising tchr. California (Pa.) U., 1970-90. Mem. Delta Kappa Gamma (pres. 1978-80). Presbyterian. Home: 1125 W Pittsburgh St Scottdale PA 15683 Office: Connellsville Area Schs 7th Ave Connellsville PA 15425

SEMEDO, JOAN DELLA, fine arts and U.S. history educator; b. Boston, Nov. 12, 1938; d. Arthur William and Eleanor (Miles) Beattie; m. John Homer Semedo; 1 child, Sara-Ann. BS in Elem. Edn., U. Mass., 1977, MEd, 1987, postgrad., 1987—. Cert. art and elem. edn. tchr., Mass. Tchr. Boston Pub. Sch., 1979-88, prin., tchr. art and history, 1988—; artist-in-embassy U.S. Dept. of State, Washington, 1976-89. Artist Tegusagarpah-Honduras Embassy, 1976-90, N.Z. Embassy, Wellington, 1977-90. Episcopalian. Home: 42 Menlo St Brockton MA 02401-6130

SEMEGRAM, HARRIET RITA (HARRIET RITA BARRY), vocalist, educator; b. N.Y.C., June 29, 1933; d. Maxwell and Mildred (Goldberg) Semegram; divorced; children: Milina Mia Barry, Marlan Frederick Barry. BA in Mus., Hunter Coll. Art dealer, film producer Albert Barry & Assocs.ocs., Bklyn., 1955-61; concert singer WonderWomen Enterprises, N.Y.C., 1966—, entrepreneur, 1987—; childbirth preparation educator, edn. cons. Brookdale Hosp. Med. Ctr., Bklyn., 1973-83; exec. dir. Wholistic Childbirth Preparation, N.Y.C., 1973-81; exec. asst. Associated Actors and Artists of Am., N.Y.C., 1989—. Contbr. chpts. to books: The Pregnant Body, 1977, The Pregnant Father, 1977; producer film: Memories of the Shtetl, 1961 (award Edinburgh Film Festival). Vol. FDC, Bklyn., 1970-83. Mem. Am. Soc. Psychoprophylactics in Obstetrics (v.p. edn. 1987, editor N.Y.C. chpt. 1976). Office: Associated Actors & Artists 165 W 46th St Brooklyn NY 11226

SEMERJIAN, HRATCH GREGORY, research and development executive; b. Istanbul, Turkey, Oct. 22, 1943; came to U.S., 1966; s. Krikor and Diruhi (Semerciyan) S.; m. Sona Kohar Kurkciyan, July 12, 1969 (dec. 1983); children: Tamar, Ara; m. Ayda Karabal, Feb. 8, 1986. BSME, Robert Coll., Istanbul, 1966; MSc in Engring., Brown U., 1968, PhD in Engring., 1972. Rsch. asst. div. engring. Brown U., Providence, 1966-70; lectr. chemistry U. Toronto, Ont., Can., 1971-73; rsch. engr. Pratt & Whitney Aircraft United Technologies Corp., East Hartford, Conn., 1973-77; group leader Ctr. for Chem. Tech. Nat. Bur. Standards (now Nat. Inst. Standards and Tech.), Gaithersburg, Md., 1977-87, div. chief Chem. Sci. and Tech. Lab., 1987—; organizer tech. sessions, confs. and symposiums for various profl. orgns., 1978—. Contbr. rsch. articles to profl. publs.; editor numerous conf. procs. Mem. parish coun. St. George Armenian Apostolic Ch., Hartford, Conn., 1975-77; chmn. parish coun., dir. choir St. Mary Armenian Apostolic Ch., Washington, 1977—; coach youth soccer Montgomery Soccer, Inc., Rockville, Md., 1978-81; mem., treas. Ani Armenian Choral Group, Washington, 1988—. Hagopian scholar Robert Coll., 1961-64, A.M.&F. corp. fellow, 1965, C.B. Keen fellow Brown U., 1969; recipient Silver medal Dept. Commerce, Washington, 1984; named Fed. Engr. of Yr., NSPE, Washington, 1991. Mem. AAAS, AIAA, ASME, Am. Inst. Chem. Engrs., Am. Chem. Soc., Combustion Inst. Office: Nat Inst Standards & Tech Bldg 221 Rm B306 Gaithersburg MD 20899

SEMLA-PULASKI, HALINA MARIA, podiatric medicine physician; b. Chorzów, Poland; came to U.S., 1976; d. Emill and Maria (Jadamik) Semla; m. Anthony F. Pulaski, Jan. 27, 1973; children: Marta, Ania. MS in Analytical Medicine, Profl. Med. Sch., Warsaw, Poland, 1972; MS in Toxicology, St. John's U., N.Y.C., 1984; D Podiatric Medicine, N.Y. Coll. Podiatric Medicine, 1989. Med. lab. dir. Glubczyce Dist. Hosp., Kietrz, Poland, 1972-76; researcher dept. endocrinology Queens (N.Y.) Coll., 1979-80; researcher Winthrop U. Hosp., Mineola, N.Y., 1980-85; mem. staff dept. orthopedics Winthrop U. Hosp.; pvt. practice podiatry Mineola, 1989—. Contbr. articles to profl. jours. Fellow Am. Soc. Podiatric Medicine; mem. Am. Acad. Podiatric Sports Medicine, Fed. Svcs. Podiatric Med. Assn., Am. Soc. Podiatric Dermatology, Am. Podiatric Med. Assn., mem. N.Y. Acad. Sci., Mus. Natural History, Smithsonian Inst. Office: Winthrop U Hosp 211 2d St Mineola NY 11501 also: 117 Nassau Ave Brooklyn NY 11222

SEMMELMEYER, KRISTIN LEIGH, computer consulting executive; b. Chapel Hill, N.C., Oct. 8, 1958; d. John Albert III and Eloise Ann (Blue) S. BS in Psychology, Tufts U., 1981. Rsch. assoc. Cambridge (Mass.) Survey Rsch., 1980-81; adminstrv. asst. Bank of New Eng., Boston, 1981-83; accts. payable coord. Esquire Mag. Group, N.Y.C., 1983-84, fin. group supr., 1985-86; officer mgr. NYU, N.Y.C., 1987-88; dir. ops. Maier Group, Inc., N.Y.C., 1988-89, v.p. ops., 1990-92; pres. Med. Computer Cons., N.Y.C., 1992—. Office: Med Computer Cons 310 E 12th St # 4G New York NY 10003

SEMONIAN, ROBERT ALEXANDER, energy and lighting consultant; b. Boston, May 17, 1939; s. Leon Astor and Veron (Agojian) S. BBA, U. Miami, Fla., 1964. Editor The Miami Sunlight, 1962-64; adminstr. cost acctg. Raytheon Co., Bedford, Mass., 1964-68; acct. corp. staff L.F.E. Corp., Boston, 1968-70; cons. Watertown, Mass., 1970-73; mktg. rep. Cenebal Corp., Dedham, Mass., 1973-75; energy/lighting cons. No. Am. Philips Corp., Boston, 1975—; dir. Communications Engring. Inc., Cambridge, Mass., 1972—, Systems and Analytical Scis., Bedford, 1981—; advisor to newspaper The Impartial Observer, 1985; mem. rsch. bd. advisors The Am. Biog. Inst. Inc., Raleigh, 1992—. Exec. dir. Mass. Conservative Caucus, Marlborough, Mass., 1984—, membership chmn., 1984, program chmn., 1983; chmn. Watertown Rep. Town Com., Mass., 1980-88, advisor, 1972-80, 88—, vice chmn., 1968-72; trustee Cambridge Emergency Relief Trust, 1972—; treas. Reps. for Middlesex County, Weston, Mass., 1972—; treas. Armenian-Am. Rep. Club Mass., Watertown, 1972—, Conservation Commn., Watertown, 1966-69, Reagan Dinner, Waltham, Mass., 1975, Boxborough, Mass., 1977; Mass. state co-chmn. Bush/Quayle, 1988; nat. vice chmn. Armenian Ams. for Bush-Quayle '88 Com., Washington; mem.

exec. com. Am. Bicentennial Presdl. Inaugural Com. for Mass., Washington, 1988-89; Mass. chmn. Nat. Conservative Alliance, Waterloo, Iowa, 1985—, Am. Freedom Coalition Mass., Peabody, 1987—; bd. govs. conv. Am. Freedom Coalition, Washington, 1988, 89; treas. Greater Boston Young Rep. Club, 1968, v.p., 1969-70; mem. exec. com. Mass. Reagan for Pres. Com., 1975-76, state nationalities chmn., 1979-80, state vice chmn., 1979-80, exec. com., 1979-80; del. Rep. Nat. Conv., Detroit, 1980, Dallas, 1984, New Orleans, 1988; mem. Watertown Town Mtg., 1965-75; state committeeman Mass. Rep. State Com., Boston, 1972-80, dep. chmn., 1972-80, heritage chmn., 1972-80, exec. com., 1972-80; del. Mass. Rep. Conv., 1972, 74, 78, 82, 86, 90, chief page, 1974; Mass. state nationalities co-chmn. Reagan/Bush Com., Mass., 1980; Watertown chmn. Reagan/Bush Com., 1980, 84, State Legislators Conf., Scottsdale, Ariz., 1985, Washington, 1986, World Media Conf., 1986; Am. Leadership Confs., Washington, 1986, 87, 88; state chmn. Robertson for Pres., 1988; co-chmn. East Coast Conservative PAC, Marlborough, 1986—; mem. Appalachian Nat. Scenic Trail Commn., Harpers Ferry, W.Va., 1986-88; dir. Watertown Better Govt. Assn., 1966—, World Info. Network/N.E. Team, Mt. Vernon. N.H., 1986—; exec. com. Zoryan Inst. Support Com., Cambridge, Mass., 1989—; human resources chmn. Armenia Earthquake Fund, N.E. Relief Ctr., Boston, 1988—; exec. com. Armenia Earthquake Relief Coalition Greater Boston, 1988—; bd. advisors Doctors to The World, Denver, 1989—; mem. exec. com. Watertown/JRASHEN Armenia Friendship Assn., Watertown, 1990—, Watertown chmn. Pierce for Gov. primary election, 1990, Weld for Gov./Cellucci for lt. gov., 1990; co-chmn. Mass. State Buchanan for Pres. com., 1992. Subject 120th Anniversary Bachrach Photographers Exhibit of Successful People, Boston, 1990. Watertown chmn. Pierce for Gov., 1990, Weld for Gov./Cellucci for Lt. Gov., 1990; state co-chmn. Buchanan for Pres. Com., Mass., 1992. Rsch. adv. bd. Am. Biog. Inst., Inc., Raleigh, N.C., 1992—. Recipient Svc. award N.Am. Philips Corp., 1978, Merit award for svc. to Armenian victims of earthquake, 1988; hon. Lt. Col. Aide-de-Camp in Ala. State Militia, 1986. Advisor The Improper Bostonian, 1991—. Mem. Am. Policy Adv. Council (treas., exec. com. 1983—), Fed. Emergency Mgmt. Agy. (Nat. Def./Exec. Res. 1982—), Nat. Assn. Armenian Studies & Rsch., Watertown/Jrashen Armenia Friendship Town Assn. (exec. com. 1990—), U. Miami Alumni Assn., Armenian Students Assn. (nat. v.p. 1971-72, pres. Boston br. 1970-71, 77-78), Delta Sigma Pi. Mem. Armenian Apostolic Ch. Lodge: Masons. Avocation: politics. Home: 11 Howe St Watertown MA 02172-4210

SEMOWICH, CHARLES JOHN, art historian, curator, artist; b. Binghamton, N.Y.; s. Zeekie and Alice (Osgood) S. BA, SUNY, Binghamton, 1971; MFA, Cath. U., 1972; PhD, Internat. Coll., L.A., 1981. Owner, operator Semowich Fine Arts, Albany, N.Y., 1982—; adj. prof. Empire State Coll., Albany, Saratoga Springs, N.Y., 1987—; instr. Chautauqua (N.Y.) Instn., 1988-90; curator Susquehanna County Hist. Soc., Montrose, Pa., 1976; guest curator SUNY, Albany, 1991. Exhibiting artist, author: Am. Furniture, 1984; co-editor: Dorothy Lathrop-A Centenary Celebration, 1991; contbr. articles and revs. to profl. jours. Chair art com. Empire State Aerosci. Mus., Schenectady, N.Y., 1991—; mem. Chenango Town Bicentennial Commn., Chenango Bridge, N.Y., 1976, Mayor's Task Force for Arts, Albany, 1990; mem. visual arts com. Albany-Tula Alliance, 1992. Recipient 1st place award Regina Bell Ringers, 1987, 2d and 3d art prizes N.Y. State Fair, 1970. Mem. AAOMS (organist 1992, flying fezes 1992), Am. Guild Organists (historian Eastern N.Y. 1986—), Pub. Employees Fedn. (steward 1991—, chair membership com. 1992—), Soc. Historians Am. Art, Coll. Art Assn., Assn. Ind. Historians Art, N.Y. State Archaeol. Assn. (officer Triple Cities chpt. 1977-81), Artist Action Group (co-chairperson 1975-76), Print Club Albany (pres. 1989—), Mus. Print Club Albany (pres. 1990—), Capital Area Archivists (sec. 1992—), Broome County Landmark Soc. (pres. 1975-76), Masons (jr. deacon 1992, capt. of guard 1992). Home: 168 N Allen St Albany NY 12206-1704

SEMPLE, CECIL SNOWDON, retired manufacturing company executive; b. Assam, India, Aug. 12, 1917; came to U.S., 1927, naturalized, 1948; s. Fordyce B. and Anne (Munro) S. B.A., Colgate U., 1939. Buyer R.H. Macy & Co., 1939-42, 46-48; buyer, div. supt. Montgomery Ward, 1948-50; v.p. Nachman Corp., Chgo., 1950-55; sales mgr. radio receiver dept. Gen. Elec. Co., Bridgeport, Conn., 1955-60; mktg. cons. merchandising Gen. Elec. Co., N.Y.C., 1966-67, gen. mgr. audio products dept., 1967-68, dep. div. gen. mgr. housewares div., 1968-69, gen. mgr. housewares div., 1969, v.p., 1969-71, v.p. corp. customer relations, 1971-85; v.p. Rich's Inc., Atlanta, 1960-62, sr. v.p., dir., 1962-66; trustee Peoples Savs. Bank., Bridgeport, 1975-89, trustee emeritus. Bd. dirs. Nat. Jr. Achievement Inc., 1974-86, Bridgeport Area Found., 1970-91, dir. emeritus, 1991—; bd. dirs. Bridgeport Hosp., chmn. 1983-89; vice chmn. bd. trustees Colgate U., 1978-84; trustee emeritus, past pres., bd. dirs. Alumni Corp.; chmn. So. Conn. Health Svc. Inc. Served to maj. USAAF, 1942-46. Mem. St. Andrews Soc. State N.Y. (chmn. bd. mgrs. 1968-70), Delta Kappa Epsilon. Clubs: Brooklawn Country (Fairfield, Conn.), Fairfield Country. Home: 25 Cartright St Bridgeport CT 06604-2023

SEMPLE, NATHANIEL MEACON, association executive; b. St. Louis, Aug. 15, 1946; s. Robert Baylor and Isabelle (Neer) S.; m. Patricia Maguire, Sept. 9, 1976; children: Nathaniel Jr., Carter Fitzhugh. AB, Columbia U., 1968; postgrad., MIT, 1969-71. Spl. asst. to U.S. Sen. Robert R. Griffin Washington, 1971-72; sr. legal asst. to U.S. Congressman Marvin Lesch Marvin L. Esch, Washington, 1972-74; legis. counsel con. on edn. and labor U.S. Congress, Washington, 1974-81; v.p., sec., dir. Com. Econ. Devel., Washington, 1981—; vis. scholar SUNY, Buffalo, 1984-85. Author: Path of Progress, 1981; editor: Work and Change, 1987; contbr. articles to profl. jours. Pres. Mich. State Soc., 1974-76, Andover (Mass.) Abbot Alumni Assn., Washington, 1983-87, mem. Alumni coun., 1984-88; mem. nat. governing bd. Ripon Soc., Washington. Lt. USNR, 1969-70. Clubs: Metropolitan (Washington); Gibson Island (Md.); Old Dominion Hunt (Orlean, Va.). Home: 3604 Davis St NW Washington DC 20007-1427 Office: Com Econ Devel 2000 L St NW Ste 700 Washington DC 20036-4907

SEMYONOV, ALEXEY I., computer programmer; b. Leningrad, USSR, July 27, 1956; came to U.S. 1978; s. Ivan Vassilievich and Elena (Bonner) S.; m. Olga A. Lyovshina, Nov. 1974 (div.); 1 child, Keity; m. Liza K. Alekseyeva; children: Alexanoza (Sasha), Igor. MA in Maths., Brandeis U., 1981. Gen. systems analyst TRW, Lexington, Mass. Human rights activist Sakharov Found., N.Y., 1970—. Office: TRW 430 Bedford St Lexington MA 02173-1548

SEN, TAPAS KUMAR, communications company executive; b. Calcutta, India, Mar. 1, 1933; came to U.S. 1959; s. Pulin Behari and Parul Bala (Gupta) S.; m. Sondra Lee Kotzin, July 3, 1966; children: Raji, Monisha. BSc, Calcutta U., 1951, MSc, 1954; PhD, Johns Hopkins U., 1963. Rsch. scholar Indian Statis. Inst., Calcutta, 1955-59; assoc. psychologist Johns Hopkins Applied Physics Lab., Balt., 1960-63; mem. tech. staff Bell Labs., Murray Hill, N.J., 1963-72; dist. mgr. human resources and strategic planning AT&T, Basking Ridge, N.J., 1973-78, dist. mgr. human resources and indsl. rels., 1979-90, human resources and indsl. rels. dir., 1991—; adv. bd. Work in Am. Inst., Scarsdale, N.Y., 1985—; adv. bd. sci., tech. and pub. policy Kennedy Sch. of Harvard U., Cambridge, 1988-91. Chair Nat. Adv. Coun. of S. Asian Affairs, 1988-89; founding chair Assn. of Indians in Am., 1967-69. Recipient Leadership award The Mayflower Group, 1985. Fellow Human Factors Soc. (pres. Metro. chpt. 1970, 80, chair coun. of tech. groups 1972-77); mem. Am. Psychol. Assn., Toastmasters (Disting. Area Gov. 1967). Office: AT&T 100 Southgate Pkwy Morristown NJ 07960

SENA, DONALD THOMAS, electric utility company executive; b. Lakeville, Mass., Jan. 23, 1948; s. Mathew Donald and Irma (Chute) S.; m. Susan Elizabeth Cooper, Feb. 20, 1980; 1 child, Scot Alexander. BS in Acctg., Southestern Mass. U., 1973, MBA, 1977. Internal auditor Ea. Utilities Assocs. Svc. Corp., Boston, 1978-80; rate analyst Ea. Utilities Assocs. Svc. Corp., Lincoln, R.I., 1980-81; revenue analyst Ea. Utilities Assocs. Svc. Corp., Boston, 1981-84; sr. revenue analyst Ea. Utilities Assocs. Svc. Corp., Lincoln, 1984-86; supr. fin. svcs. Ea. Utilities Assocs. Svc. Corp., Boston, 1986-88, mgr. treasury svcs., 1988-90; mgr. rate dept. Ea. Utilities Assocs. Svc. Corp., West Bridgewater, Mass., 1990—. With USN, 1970-72. Mem. Edison Elec. Inst. (chmn. subcom. fin. forecasting 1987-90), Mass. Revenue Requirement Forum (chmn. 1990—). Office: EUA Svc Corp 750 W Center St West Bridgewater MA 02379

SENDERS, VIRGINIA LOFTUS, psychologist, educator; b. N.Y.C., Apr. 21, 1923; d. Frank Richardson and Ruth (Russell) Loftus; m. John W. Senders, Feb. 26, 1920 (div. 1976); children: Warren Russell, Stefan John. AB magna cum laude, Mt. Holyoke Coll., 1943; AM, HArvard U., 1945, PhD, 1947. Lic. psychologist, Mass. Teaching fellow Harvard U., Cambridge, Mass., 1944-47; instr. psychology Wellesley Coll., Mass., 1947-50; dir. aviation psychology project, assoc. prof. psychology Antioch Coll., Yellow Springs, Ohio, 1950-56; lectr. psychology U. Minn., Mpls., 1957-62, co-founder, co-dir., coordinator Women's Continuing Edn. Program, 1960-62; assoc. dir. New Eng. Bd. Higher Edn., Winchester, Mass., 1963-66; dir. career planning and counseling ctr., prof. Simmons Coll., Boston, 1966-68; postdoctoral fellow McLean Hosp., Belmont, Mass., 1968-71; pvt. practice psychology Framingham, Mass., 1982-86; prof. Framingham State Coll., 1971-84; pvt. practice psychology Shutesbury, Mass., 1986—; vis. prof. U. Toronto, Ont., Can., 1973-74; mem. field faculty human studies Goddard Coll., Plainfield, N.J., 1976-78; acad. coun. monitor Beacon Coll., Boston, 1975-81; cons. on women's edn. 1960-67; dir. Wainwright Ho., Rye, N.Y., 1985-89, Temenos, Shutesbury, Mass., 1987-91. Author: Measurement and Statistics, 1958; contrbr. articles to profl. jours. Mem. edn. com. Pres. Kennedy's Commn. on Status of Women, 1962-63; active various charitable orgsn., polit. orgns. Named Woman of Conscience of Yr. Nat. Council of Women of U.S., 1965. Fellow Am. Psychol. Assn. Mass. Psychol. Assn.; mem. New Eng. Psychol. Assn. (pres. 1974-75), Assn. for Humanistic Psychology, Guild for Spiritual Guidance. Democrat. Home: Pelham Hill Rd Shutesbury MA 01072-9702

SENFT, MASON GEORGE, musician; b. Bklyn., Nov. 1, 1942; s. Arthur and Ann (Nagel) S. BA cum laude, Adelphi U., 1964. Self employed accompanist Roslyn Heights, N.Y., 1964—; cons. Glimmerglass Opera, 1992—; tchr. Adelphi U., Garden City, N.Y., 1964-73; dir. Nat. Scholastic Aptitude Tng. Inst., Garden City, 1966-69; musical dir. Tibbits Opera House, Coldwater, Mich., 1972-73, Canal Fulton (Ohio) Playhouse, 1974-84, Island Lyric Opera, Garden City, 1980—, A Small Co. in America, Glen Cove, N.Y., 1984—; cons. Island Chamber Symphony Orch., Glen Head, N.Y., 1985—, Nat. Grand Opera, Tilles Ctr., Greenvale, N.Y., 1988—, PBS TV spl. Christmas with Flicka, 1988, Dark Summer debut by Christine Berl, Lincoln Ctr. Chamber Soc., Alice Tully Hall, N.Y., 1989; accompanist to Frederica von Stade 350th Convocation Celebration, Harvard U., Cambridge, Mass., 1986; accompanist ARC benefit concert In Concert, Carnegie Hall, 1989; music coach The Aspern Papers, Dallas Opera, debut 1988; cons. N.Y. Virtuoso Chamber Symphony, 1989—; music coach DiCapo Opera Co., 1975—; accompanist concert in honor of Queen Margrethe II of Sweden, The White House, 1991, hist. gala concert at Steinway Hall, N.Y., 1991; cons., accompanist Glimmerglass Opera, 1992. Mem. Musicians Union Local 802, L.I. Singers Soc. (accompanist 1985—), MENSA. Home: 300 Edwards St Roslyn Heights NY 11577-1131

SENGSTACK, DAVID KELLS, publisher; b. Bklyn., June 22, 1922; s. John Fred and Edna Josephine (Maloney) S.; m. Anita Elizabeth Browne, Aug. 12, 1944 (div. 1975); children: Jeffrey Scott, Lynn Ann, Gregg Clift; m. Arlene M. Rambaum Dec. 30, 1978 (div. 1986); m. Alice H. Fleischman, Sept. 30, 1988; adopted children: Michele Amy, Elizabeth Anne. BSME, Rutgers U., 1944. Mktg. dir. Birch Tree Group Ltd., Princeton, N.J., 1947-57, pres., chmn., 1957-89; owner, pres. The Sengstack Group, Ltd., 1989—. Trustee Bucknell U., Lewisburg, Pa., 1980-84, McCarter Ctr. for Performing Arts, Princeton, 1983-90, Carrier Clin. Devel. Fund, 1987—; mem. vis. com. Eastman Sch. Music, Rochester, N.Y., 1984—. With C.E., AUS, 1942-47, 50-52, Korea. Mem. Union League Club, Cliff Dwellers Club, Nassau Club, N.Y. Athletic Club. Office: The Sengstack Group Ltd 180 Alexander St Princeton NJ 08540

SENICA, CARL GERARD, purchasing agent, public transportation director; b. Newark, Aug. 31, 1933; s. Carlo and Lena (Liparulo) S.; m. Gilda DiRuggiero, Sept. 16, 1956 (div. Jan. 1989); children: Maria Senica Outten, Michael G. Senica; m. Judith Domenico Senica, Feb. 9, 1991. AA in Pharmacy, Rutgers U., 1954; AA in Bus. Adminstrn., Fairleigh-Dickinson Coll., 1958. Regional purchasing agt. Prudential Ins. Co., Newark, 1952-79; dir. procurement Union Fidelity Corp., Trevose, Pa., 1979-82; corp. purchasing mgr. John Wanamaker Co., Phila., 1982-83; dir. transp. Bucks County, Doylestown, Pa., 1983-89; councilman Borough of New Britain, Pa., 1973-76; supr. Township of New Britain, Pa., 1981-91; dir. receivables Phoenix Mktg. Group, Lincoln Park, N.J., 1990—; pres., Cen. Atlantic Recreation Assn., Ft. Washington, Pa., 1973-74, New Britain (Pa.) Civic Assn., 1975-77; state adjutant Italian/Am. War Vets., Phila., 1972-73; dir. Lenape Valley Mental Health Found., Chalfont, Pa., 1973-75. Mem. Tri Mcpl. Planning Commn., New Britain, Pa., 1981-89; vice chmn. New Britain (Pa.) Twp. Bd. Suprs., 1981-90; loaned exec. Greater Phila. United Way Campaign, 1973; bd. mem. Bucks County Assn., Twp. Suprs., New Britain, Pa., 1981-90. With U.S. Army 1954-56. Recipient Community Svc. award Prudential Ins. Co., Ft. Washington, Pa., 1975; named Citizen of Yr., New Britain (Pa.) Civic Assn., 1975. Mem. New Britain Lions Club (past pres.), Toastmasters Internat. (v.p.), Italian/AM. War Vets. (v.p.), Am. Legion Post 5205, Vets. Fgn. Wars, Holy Name Soc. (pres.), Cen. Atlantic Recreation Assn. (dir.). Republican. Roman Catholic. Home: 21 Independence Way Rockaway NJ 07866 Office: Phoenix Mktg Group Inc One Phoenix Dr Lincoln Park NJ 07035

SENIOR, JOHN ROBERT, internist, gastroenterologist, consultant; b. Phila., July 17, 1927; s. John Henry and Catherine (Cumming) S.; m. Sara Elizabeth Spedden, Dec. 27, 1952; children: John Ormond, Laura Bruns Council, Lisa Ann. BS in Physics, Pa. State U., 1950; MD, U. Pa., 1954. Diplomate Am. Bd. Internal Medicine, Am. Bd. Gastroenterology. Intern Hosp. U. Pa., Phila., 1954-55, resident in medicine, 1955-57, clin. fellow in gastroenterology, 1957-59; rsch. fellow in gastroenterology Mass. Gen. Hosp.-Harvard U., Boston, 1959-62; rsch. fellow Harvard U., Cambridge, Mass., 1959-62; dir. gastrointestinal rsch. lab. Phila. Gen. Hosp.-U. Pa., 1962-70; clin. prof. of medicine U. Pa., 1970-79, adj. prof. medicine, 1980—; dir. regulatory affairs E.R. Squibb & Sons, Princeton, N.J., 1979-81; v.p. clin. affairs Sterling-Winthrop Rsch. Inst.-Sterling Drug Corp. Worldwide, N.Y.C. and Rensselear, N.Y., 1981-84; pres. pers. cons. corp. Merion, Pa., 1984—; prin. cons. med. editor for internat. pharm. R&D G. H. Besselaar Assocs., Princeton, N.J., 1986—; mem. gastrointestinal rsch. staff (without compensation) VA Med. Ctr., Phila., 1991—; mem. adv. coun. Nat. Inst. Diabetes and Kidney and Digestive Diseases, Bethesda, Md., 1981-85; senatorial liaison Nat. Commn. Digestive Diseases, Washington, 1978-80. Author: Towards Evaluation of Competence in Medicine, 1976; author, editor: Medium Chain Triglycerides, 1968; contbr. articles to profl. jours. With USNR, 1945-84, rear adm. USNR, 1984—. Fellow ACP; mem. Am. Assn. Study of Liver Diseases (pres. 1973-74), Am. Soc. Clin. Investigation, Am. Gastroenterol. Soc., Cosmos Club, Phi Beta Kappa, Phi Kappa Phi, Sigma Pi Sigma, Alpha Omega Alpha. Republican. Episcopalian. Home: 54 Merbrook Ln Merion Station PA 19066-1618 Office: G H Besselaar Assocs 101 College Rd E Princeton NJ 08540-6681

SENSENIG, DAVID MARTIN, surgeon; b. Gladwyne, Pa., May 4, 1921; s. Wayne and Elizabeth Long (Crawford) S.; B.S., Haverford Coll., 1942; postgrad. Sch. Medicine, U. Pa., 1942-43; M.D., Harvard U., 1945; children—Philip Campbell, David Martin, Andrew Wilson, Thomas O'Brien; m. 2d, Bernice Evans, Dec. 20, 1975. Rotating intern Allentown (Pa.) Hosp., 1945-46; surg. house officer, jr. asst. resident Peter Bent Brigham Hosp., Boston, 1948-50; sr. asst. resident, resident surgeon New Eng. Center Hosp., Boston, 1950-52; surg. resident Westfield (Mass.) State Sanatorium, 1952-53; asst. chief surg. service, dir. surg. research lab. VA Med. Teaching Group Hosp., Memphis, 1953-55; asst. chief surg. service VA Hosp., Albany, N.Y., 1955-57; resident in thoracic and cardiac surgery Univ Hosp., State U. Iowa, Iowa City, 1957-59, instr. in surgery, 1957-58, asso. in surgery, 1958-59, asst. prof., asso. prof. surgery, 1960-62; chief thoracic surgery sect. VA Hosp., Phila., 1959-60, asst. chief surg. service, 1963-66; cardiothoracic surgeon Pa. Hosp., Phila., 1962-63; asst. prof. surgery U. Pa., Phila., 1962-66, supr. Animal Research Lab., 1963-66; pvt. practice medicine specializing in surgery, Bangor, Maine, 1966-88; attending surgeon Eastern Maine Med. Center, Bangor, 1966-88; attending surgeon St. Joseph Hosp., Bangor, 1966-88, chief surg. service, 1974-79, chief thoracic surgery sect., 1979-88; chief surg. service VA Hosp., Togus, Maine, 04330, 1988—. Served to capt. M.C., U.S. Army, 1943-48. Diplomate Am. Bd. Surgery, Am. Bd. Thoracic Surgery. Mem. ACS (gov. at large 1985-91), Pa. Assn. Thoracic Surgery, Penobscot County Med. Soc. (pres. 1974), Maine, Am. thoracic socs., AAAS, Internat. Cardiovascular Soc., Am. Geriatric Soc., Iowa Acad. Surgery, Phila. Acad. Surgery, Am. Coll. Chest Physicians, Bangor Med. Club (pres. 1970), Maine Vascular Soc. (pres. 1978), New Eng. Surg. Soc., N.Y. Acad. Scis., New Eng. Soc. Vascular Surgery. Republican. Episcopalian. Contbr. articles to sci. publs. Home: 55 Ridgewood Dr Augusta ME 04330-4337 Office: VA Hosp Togus ME 04330

SENTAK, GERTRUDE ROSE, builder; b. Trenton, N.J., Dec. 30, 1945; d. Edwin P. and Emma Mae (Cole) MacNicoll; m. Raymond John Sentak, oct. 26, 1974; children: Daniel, Jessica. Student in appraising, Mercer County Coll., Trenton, 1985; student realtor, Mercer City Coll., Trenton, 1988. Lic. N.J. contractor. Pres. Sen-Tri Enterprises, Bordentown, N.J., 1985-91, Attisen Realty, Bordentown, 1985-91, Sentak & Malloy, Inc., Bordentown, 1985-91, Attisen Profl. Bldg. Assocs., Bordentown, 1988—; realtor Million Dollar Sales, Mercer County Realtors, 1985-91. Recipient Pres.' Circle award Ryland Homes, N.E. Md., 1985-89. Mem. N.J. Bldg. Trades Assn., Burlington County Realtor, Mercer County Realtor. Republican. Roman Catholic. Home: 46 Sykesville Rd Wrightstown NJ 08562 Office: Sentak & Malloy Inc 146 Route 130 Bordentown NJ 08505-2219

SENTELLE, DAVID BRYAN, federal judge; b. Canton, N.C., Feb. 12, 1943; s. Horace Richard, Jr., and Maude (Ray) S.; m. Jane LaRue Oldham, June 19, 1965; children: Sharon Rene, Reagan Elaine, Rebecca Grace. AB, U. N.C., 1965, JD with honors, 1968. Bar: N.C. 1968, U.S. Dist. Ct. (we. dist.) N.C. 1969, U.S. Ct. Appeals (4th cir.) 1970. Assoc. Uzzell & Dumont, Asheville, N.C., 1968-70; asst. U.S. atty. City of Charlotte, N.C., 1970-74, dist. judge, 1974-77; ptnr. Tucker, Hicks, Sentelle, Moon & Hodge, P.A., Charlotte, 1977-85; judge U.S. Dist. Ct. (we. dist.) N.C., Charlotte, 1985-87, U.S. Ct. Appeals D.C., 1987—; adj. prof. dept. criminal justice U. N.C., Charlotte. Contbr. articles to profl. jours. Chmn. Mecklenburg County Rep. Com., 1978-80; chmn. N.C. State Rep. Conv., 1979-80. Dameron fellow, 1967. Mem. ABA, Fed. Bar Assn. (chpt. pres. 1975), Mecklenburg County Bar Assn. Baptist. Lodges: Masons, Scottish Rite, Shriners. Office: 333 Constitution Ave NW Washington DC 20001-2802

SEOW, CHOONG HUEI, computer engineer; b. Melaka, Malaysia, Oct. 29, 1967; came to U.S., 1986; s. Kim Swee and Hong Pheik (Yin) S. BS in Computer Sci., MIT, 1990. Assoc. software engr. Syncsort Inc., Woodcliff Lake, N.J., 1990-91; software engr. Syncsort Inc., Woodcliff Lake, 1991—. Tchr. Role Models, Inc., Englewood, N.J., 1990—; vol. Vol. Ctr. of Bergen County, Hackensack, N.J., 1990—. Mem. Assn. for Computing Machinery, Mensa Soc. Malaysia, MIT Club of Northern N.J. (bd. govs. 1990—). Office: Syncsort Inc 50 Tice Blvd Cn 18 Woodcliff Lake NJ 17670

SEPE, CAROLE JAAR, architectural consultant; b. Port-au-Prince, Haiti, Nov. 2, 1957; d. Georges and Denise Jaar; m. Gerardo Sepe, June 1, 1985; children: Daniel, Natasha. BS in Architecture, Cath. U., 1981, MArch, 1984. Ptnr. Perspective 26 Archtl. Cons. & Designers, Silver Spring, Md., 1987—. Mem. NAFE, Rockville C. of C., W.B.O. of Montgomery Co. Home: 117 Finale Ter Silver Spring MD 20901-5037

SEPEZ, PETER VINCENT, psychologist, educator; b. Bklyn., June 30, 1929; s. Rudolph and Esmerelda (Huntley-Gordon) S.; m. Lois-ann Larson, June 18, 1955; children: Thomas Vincent, Jeniffer Anne. BS, Adelphi U., 1952; MS in Edn., Hofstra U., 1956; EdD, Columbia U., 1971. Lic. psychologist, N.Y.; cert. tchr. and adminstr., N.Y. Tchr. Valley Stream (N.Y.) Sch., 1955-62; sch. psychology New Hyde Park (N.Y.) Schs., 1964-69; asst. instr. Columbia U., N.Y.C., 1962-63; psychol. asst. Morton Prince Clinic, N.Y.C., 1964-67, sch. psychologist Huntington (N.Y.) Pub. Schs., 1969—; prof. psychology Pace U., N.Y.C., 1975—; head counselor Ramapo Anchorage Camp, Rhineneck, N.Y., 1954-61; cons. Asthma/Allergy Assoc., Hauppauge, N.Y., 1972-73; in-svc. instr. Hillcrest Nursery Sch., Huntington, N.Y., 1973; prof. psychology Fla. Inst. Tech., Melbourne, Fla., 1975-80; adj. assoc. prof. St. John's U., Queens, N.Y., 1978-82; dir. spl. edn. Huntington Sch., 1988-90; speaker in field. Contbr. articles to profl. jours. Cpl. U.S. Army, 1952-54. Recipient Svc. award Town of Huntington, 1988. Mem. APA, N.Y. Psychol. Assn. (pres. sch. div. 1979-80, Sch. Psychologist of Yr., award 1985), Suffolk County Psychol. Assn. Unitarian. Home and Office: 8 Rocklyn Ct Huntington NY 11743-3856

SERAFIN, JAMES ADAM, organization executive, management consultant; b. Redruth, Cornwall, Eng., July 26, 1945; came to U.S., 1949; s. Adam Mieczyslaw and Donna Josephine (Szarnagiel) S.; m. Barbara Ann Waligora, May 2, 1975 (div. Oct. 1983); children: Mara Sonya, Adam James. BA, U. Buffalo, 1969; MA, Syracuse U., 1972. Regional planner Comprehensive Health Planning Coun. Western N.Y., Buffalo, 1971-74; fin. planning cons. Niagara County Mental Health Dept., Lockport, N.Y., 1974-76; dir. planning and allocations United Way Niagara, Niagara Falls, N.Y., 1976-80; exec. dir. Amarillo (Tex.) Community Coun., 1980-83; v.p. ops. Opinions Unltd., Amarillo, 1983-84; dir. mktg. and planning High Plains Bapt. Hosp., Amarillo, 1984-87; dir. planning and bus. devel. St. Joseph Hosp., Denver, 1988-89; mgmt. cons., pres. Svcs. and Mgmt. Planning assocs., Buffalo, 1990—; exec. dir. Cath. Worker Niagara Falls, 1991—; cons. Human Svcs. Planning Assocs., Lockport. 1974-76; pres. Svcs. & Mgmt. Planning Assocs., Tex., Colo., N.Y., 1974—; vis. guest lectr. Amarillo Coll., West Tex. State U., U. Denver, SUNY, Buffalo, 1974—; grad. instr. U. Denver, 1989; state, regional and nat. conf. and workshop presenter. Contbr. articles to profl. jours. Pres. bd. dirs. Neighborhood Info. Ctr., Buffalo, 1971-73; mem. steering com. Erie County Execs. Task Force, Buffalo, 1974-76; chmn. Panhandle Drug Abuse Consortium, Amarillo, 1981-85; bd. dirs. Buffalo-Rzeszow Sistr Cities, Inc., 1990—. Mem. Acad. Health Svcs. Mktg. (pres. Colo. chpt. 1989-90), Am. Hosp. Assn. (nat. com. 1988-89), Rotary (program chmn. Amarillo 1983-84). Home: 115 Avery Pl Buffalo NY 14225 Office: Cath Worker Niagara Falls PO Box 297 Niagara Falls NY 14305

SERAFINI, RICHARD ALDO, lawyer; b. Passaic, N.J., Jan. 27, 1954; s. Aldo and Mary Elizabeth (Schultz) S. BA, U. Pa., 1976; JD, Temple U., 1979. Bar: N.Y. 1980, Pa. 1979. Examining atty. N.Y.C. Dept. Investigation, 1979-82; asst. dist. atty. County of N.Y., N.Y.C., 1982-83; asst. atty. gen. Atty. Gen.'s Office State of N.Y., N.Y.C., 1983-86; chief Br. of Enforcement SEC, N.Y.C., 1986-89; trial atty. U.S. Dept. of Justice, Washington, 1990—. Home: 500 23d St NW Washington DC 20037 Office: US Dept of Justice 1400 New York Ave NW Washington DC 20005-2107

SERCHUK, IVAN, lawyer; b. N.Y.C., Oct. 13, 1935; s. Israel and Freda (Davis) S.; children: Camille, Bruce Mead, Vance Foster. BA, Columbia U., 1957, LLB, 1960. Bar: N.Y. 1961, U.S. Dist. Ct. (so. dist.) N.Y. 1963, U.S. Ct. Appeals (2d cir.) 1964, U.S. Tax Ct. 1966. Law clk. to judge U.S. Dist. Ct. (so. dist.) N.Y., 1961-63; assoc. Kaye, Scholer, Fierman, Hays & Handler, 1963-68; dep. supt., counsel N.Y. State Banking Dept., N.Y.C. and Albany, 1968-71; mem. Berle & Berle, 1972-73; spl. counsel N.Y. State Senate Banks Com., 1972; mem. Serchuk & Siwek, White Plains, N.Y., 1974; sr. ptnr. Serchuk & Zelermyer, White Plains, 1976—; lectr. Practising Law Inst., 1968-71. Mem. Assn. of Bar of City of N.Y., N.Y. State Bar Assn. Home: Mead St Waccabuc NY 10597 Office: Serchuk & Zelermyer 81 Main St White Plains NY 10601-1711

SERENBETZ, WARREN LEWIS, financial management company executive; b. N.Y.C., Mar. 27, 1924; s. Lewis E. and Estelle (Weygand) S.; m. Thelma Randby, Apr. 10, 1948; children: Warren Lewis, Paul Halvor, Stuart Weygand, Clay Raymond. B.S., Columbia U., 1944, M.S., 1949. Cons. Emerson Engrs., N.Y.C., 1949-51; with Oliver Corp., 1951-53; with REA Express, 1953-68, sr. v.p., 1966-68; v.p., dir. REA Leasing Corp., 1961-68; chmn. exec. com., chief exec. officer Interpool, Ltd., 1968-86; pres., chief exec. officer Radcliff Group, Inc., 1986—; pres. Containerization and Intermodal Inst., 1986-87; bd. dirs. Home Savs. Bank, Containerization and Intermodal Inst., Interpool Ltd., Trac Leasing Corp. Inc., Microtech Corp., Bowery Savs. Bank. Trustee St. Cabrini Nursing Home. Served to lt. (j.g.) USNR, World War II. Mem. Am. Mgmt. Assn., Larchmont Yacht Club, Univ. Club, Union League Club. Presbyterian. Home: Hunter Hill West St Harrison NY 10528 Office: Radcliff Group Inc W St Harrison NY 10528

SERGI, ANTHONY ROBERT, physician, surgeon; b. Elizabeth, N.J., May 1, 1963; s. Martin and Agnes (Kraus) S. BS in Biology, Fairleigh Dickinson

U., 1985; DPM, Pa. Coll. Medicine, 1989. Surg. resident Kennedy Meml. Hosp., Saddle Brook, N.J., 1989-91; chief surg. resident Kennedy Meml. Hosp., Saddle Brook, 1990-91; physician surgeon Foot and Ankle Treatment Ctr. of N.J., Paramus, N.J., 1991—. Contbr. articles to profl. jours. Named one of Outstanding Young Men of Am., 1989. Roman Catholic. Office: Foot and Ankle Treatment Ctr 241 Oradell Ave Paramus NJ 07652-4808

SERGI, ROSE ANNE, journalism educator; b. Somerville, Mass., Feb. 28, 1946; d. Guy John and Adeline (Ministeri) S.; children:Guy Doyon, Matthew Doyon. BA, Northeastern U., 1968, MA, 1970. Asst. prof. Bryant-McIntosh Jr. Coll., Lawrence, Mass., 1970-72; instr. Daniel Webster Jr. Coll., Nashua, N.H., 1971-74; tchr. Billerica (Mass.) Meml. High Sch., 1972-75; instr. U. Lowell, Mass., 1975-77; gen. assignment reporter, then investigative reporter Lowell Sun, 1985-87; instr. Regis Coll., Weston, Mass., 1987-88; sr. lectr. Northeastern U., Boston, 1971—; assoc. prof. journalism Middlesex Community Coll., Bedford, Mass., 1988—. Appointee Svc. Acad. Rev. Bd., Boston, 1983. Mem. NEA, Mass. Tchrs. Assn., Northeastern U. Journalism Alumni Assn. (pres. 1990—). Roman Catholic. Office: Middlesex Community Coll Springs Rd Bedford MA 01730-1655

SEROTTA, EDWARD BARRY, software company executive; b. Boston, May 20, 1951; s. Norman and Marion (Goldstein) S.; m. Linda Jean Cleasby, May 21, 1978; children: Rachel, Andrew. AB, Harvard Coll., 1973; MBA, Clark U., 1988. Officer Old Stone Bank, Providence, 1977-79; treas., asst. v.p. Guild Loon & Investment, Providence, 1979-82; asst. v.p. Old Stone Corp., Providence, 1982-88; chief fin. officer, sr. v.p. Femcon Assocs., Westford, Mass., 1988-91, chief exec. officer, 1991—; also bd. dirs. Femcon Assocs., Westford; bd. dirs. AFT Europe, Ltd., Athens, Greece. Mem. Harvard Club Worcester. Office: Femcon Assocs Inc 6 Olde Boston Sq Westford MA 01886

SERRANO, BASILIO, educator; b. San Sebastian, P.R., May 7, 1948; s. Victor Basilio and Rosario (Hernandez) S.; m. Norma Perez, June 2, 1974 (div. 1985). BS, CCNY, 1970, MS, 1974; PhD, NYU, 1989. Tchr. N.Y.C. Bd. Edn., 1970-73; instr. Bklyn. Coll., 1973-77; prof. Dept. Tchr. Edn. Coll. at Old Westbury-SUNY, 1978—, chmn. tchr. edn., 1990—, project dir. tchr. edn., 1979—. Chmn. bd. dirs. P.R. Heritage House, N.Y.C., 1989—. Title VII grantee, 1979-82, 84-91, U.S. Office Spl. Edn. Tng. grantee, 1982-85. Mem. Am. Ednl. Rsch. Assn., Am. Assn. Higher Edn., Nat. Assn. Bilingual Edn., Congress for P.R. Rights. Democrat. Roman Catholic. Office: SUNY Coll at Old Westbury Tchr Edn Box 210 Old Westbury NY 11568

SERRANO, JOSE, congressman; b. Mayaguez, P.R., Oct. 24, 1943; s. Jose E. and Hipolita (Soto) S.; m. Mary Serrano; children: Lisa Marie, Jose Marco, Justine, Jonathan, Benjamin. With Mfrs. Hanover Trust Co., 1961-69; mem. Bd. Edn. N.Y., 1969-74; former N.Y. State Assemblyman Albany, from 1975; now mem. 102nd Congress from 18th Dist. N.Y., Washington, 1990—; mem. edn. and labor, small bus. coms. Roman Catholic. Office: 890 Grand Concourse Bronx NY 10451-2898 also: US House of Reps Offices of House Members Washington DC 20515 also: 1217 Longworth HOB Washington DC 20515

SERVEDIO, DOMINICK MICHAEL, engineering executive; b. N.Y.C., Aug. 7, 1940; s. Daniel and Margaret (Ingenito) S.; m. Patricia L. Filatro, July 26, 1969; children: Dominique, Daniel. BEE, NYU, 1962; MBA, St. John's U., 1972. Registered profl. engr., N.H., Mass. Engr. in tng. N.Y. Cen. R.R., N.Y.C., 1962-63, engr., 1965-67; elec. engr. Citizen Utility Co., N.Y.C., 1967-68; project engr. L.I. R.R., N.Y.C., 1968-73; asst. dir., supervising engr. Met. Transp. Authority, N.Y.C., 1973-77; from v.p. to pres., chief operating officer Seelye Stevenson Value & Knecht, N.Y.C., 1977—; exec. v.p. STV Group, Pottstown, Pa. Mem. Columbus Citizens Found., Inc., N.Y.C., 1990, N.J. Alliance for Action, Edison, 1991; active Greater N.Y. March of Dimes, 1991, Greater N.Y. Couns. Boy Scouts Am., 1991. 1st lt. U.S. Army, 1963-65. Mem. NSPE, Soc. Am. Mil. Engrs., N.Y. R.R. Club Inc., Soc. for Mktg. Profl. Svcs., Moles. Office: STV/Seelye Stevenson & Knecht 225 Park Ave S New York NY 10003-1604

SERVICE, KENNETH PATRICK, public relations executive; b. N.Y.C., Sept. 6, 1946; s. Albert and Margaret Ann (Feddis) S.; m. Rhys Elaine Downing, Nov. 30, 1968; children: Jennifer Ann, Amy Elaine. BA in English, Canisius Coll., 1969. Tchr. English All Sts. High Sch., Bklyn., 1969-70; dir. news bur. Canisius Coll., Buffalo, 1970-71; dir. pub. rels. Rosary Hill Coll., Buffalo, 1971-73; dir. news bur. SUNY, Buffalo, 1973-76; dir. pub. rels. Carnegie Mellon U., Pitts., 1976-79; asst. v.p. pub. affairs U. Cin., 1979-83; v.p. univ. rels. Duquesne U., Pitts., 1983-87; dir. corp. info. Duquesne Light Co., Pitts., 1987—. Mem. editorial bd. Carnegie Mellon U., 1989—. Bd. dirs. Cin. Chamber Orch., 1982-83, Divine Providence Hosp., Pitts.; active Cin. Area Red Cross, 1982-83; mem. Bethel Park (Pa.) Sch. Bd., 1986-87; mem. Bethel Park Historic Architecture Rev. Bd.; pres. Pitts. Internat. Folk Theatre, 1988—; mem. univ. rels. adv. bd. U. Pitts., 1990—. Recipient Leadership Pitts. award C of C, 1985. Mem. Pub. Rels. Soc. Am. (exec. com. 1982-85, bd. dirs. Pitts. chpt. 1984-86), Pub. Rels. Person of Yr. 1989), Nat. Trust for Historic Preservation, Pitts. Club, Bulgarian-Macedonian Beneficial Assn. Democrat. Roman Catholic. Home: 6024 Ramsgate Dr Bethel Park PA 15102-2620 Office: Duquesne Light Co 301 Grant St Pittsburgh PA 15279-0001

SERVICE, THOMAS HOWARD, mechanical engineer; b. Balt., Dec. 13, 1952; s. Gordon Thomas and Caroline (Crockett) S.; m. Kathryn Francis Pekala, Sept. 14, 1974. BSME, U. Mass., 1977, MSME, 1979, PhD, 1984. Registered profl. engr., Mass. Engr. Owens Corning Fiberglass, Granville, Ohio, 1979-80; rsch. asst. U. Mass., Amherst, 1980-83, sr. rsch. engr., 1983-90; owner, founder Svc. Engring. Lab., Greenfield, Mass., 1990—. Contbr. articles to profl. jours. East German Exch. fellow Nat. Acad. Sci., 1988. Mem. ASME, NSPE, Am. Ceramic Soc. Home: 19 Butler Pl Northampton MA 01060-3307 Office: Svc Engring Lab 324 Wells St Greenfield MA 01301-1628

SERY, THEODORE WILSON, radiation safety consultant, microbiologist; b. N.Y.C., Feb. 5, 1924; s. John and Rhoda (Saddler) S.; m. Doris Anne Dragner, Nov. 2, 1957; children: Paul, Matthew, Elizabeth, Katherine. BS, Columbia U., 1949; PhD, Cornell U., N.Y.C., 1954. Instr. Cornell U. Med. Sch., 1954-55; head microbiology Wills Eye Hosp., Phila., 1955-89, dir. rsch., 1972-80, dir. basic rsch., 1980-89, ret., 1989, cons. on radiation safety,, 1989—. Contbr. numerous articles to ophthal. jours. With AUS, 1943-46, ETO. Grantee NIH, 1957-1989. Mem. Assn. for Rsch. in Vision Ophthalmology (sec. 1956-61), Am. Soc. Microbiology, Am. Assn. Immunologists. Office: Wills Eye Hosp 9th and Walnut Sts Philadelphia PA 19107

SESSLER, JOHN CHARLES, federal agency official, physicist; b. Newark, Feb. 14, 1932; s. John Charles and Theresa Dorothy (Nowak) S.; m. Alma Regina, Dec. 20, 1954 (div. 1984); children: John, Gabrielle, Kevin, Karen, Beverly, Susan, Keith. AB in Physics, Rutgers U., 1956; MA in Physics, U. So. Calif., 1961; PhD in Physics, Georgetown U., 1970. Engr. N.Am. Aviation, Rocketdyne Div., Canoga Park, Calif., 1956-60; assoc. scientist Tech Ops., Washington, 1960-62; mem. staff Ctr. for Naval Analysis, Arlington, Va., 1962-72, The Drug Abuse Coun., Inc., Washington, 1972-78; evaluation coord. USPHS, Washington, 1978-82; prof. U. So. Calif., L.A., 1982-85; analyst Hdqrs. USAF Europe, Fed. Republic of Germany, 1986-90, Hdqrs. USAF, Washington, 1990-91, Strategic Def. Initiative Orgn., Washington, 1991—. Author: (with others) The Evaluation of Social Programs, 1976, Facts About Drug Abuse, 1980; co-inventor high temperature thermocouple. Cpl. U.S. Army, 1949-53. Franklin Inst. fellow, 1968. Mem. Washington Ops. Rsch. Coun., Sigma Xi. Roman Catholic. Office: SDIO The Pentagon Washington DC 20301-7100

SESSLER, JOHN GEORGE, mechanical engineer, consultant; b. Syracuse, N.Y., Apr. 8, 1920; s. John Michael and Helen (Young) S.; m. Phyllis Anne Long, May 2, 1953; children: Laurels, Robert, Michael, John, Marita. BS in Mech. Engring., Syracuse U., 1950, MS in Metallurgy, 1962. Rsch. tech. Syracuse (N.Y.) U., 1950-52, rsch. engr., 1952-56, sr. rsch. engr., 1956-66; sr. metallurgist Syracuse Rsch. Corp., 1966-72; cons. engr. M.E. Barzelay, P.E., P.C., Syracuse, 1972-76; tech. cons. Syracuse, 1976—. Editor: Aerospace Structural Metals Handbook, 1963, NASA Materials Data Handbooks, 1965. Staff sgt. USMC, 1942-46, PTO. Recipient Minor award NASA, 1968. Mem. ASTM, Am. Soc. Metals, N.Y. Sheriff's Assn. Roman Catholic. Home and Office: 121 Jean Ave Syracuse NY 13210-4235

SETHI, DEEPAK, marketing executive; b. Jhelum, India, July 1, 1945; s. Siriram and Prakash (Kathuria) S.; m. Anita Johar, May 15, 1973; children: Ripka, Reeti. BSME, MS U., Baroda, India, 1968; MBA in Mktg., Pa. State U., 1977. Sales engr. Indian Oil Corp., Bombay, 1968-73; mktg. rep. Control Data Corp., N.Y.C., 1977-79; mem. staff domestic and internat. mktg. AT&T, Basking Ridge, N.J., 1979-88; dir. exec. edn. AT&T, Morristown, N.J., 1979—. Co-editor: (co. publ.) Marketing Spectrum. Fellow Rotary Found., 1973. Mem. Am. Mktg. Assn., Am. Soc. Tng. Devel. Home: 92 Beaufort Ave Livingston NJ 07039-1703 Office: AT&T 100 Southgate Pky Morristown NJ 07960-6442

SETRAKIAN, BERGE, lawyer; b. Beirut, Lebanon, Apr. 14, 1949; came to U.S. 1976; s. Hemayak and Arminee S.; m. Vera L. Nazarian, Nov. 22, 1975; children: Ani, Lara. Diplome d'Etudes de Doctorat, U. Lyons, France, 1973; Diplome d'Etudes de Doctorat Droit Compare, F.I.E.D.C., Strasbourg, France, 1974; Licence en Droit Francais, U. St. Joseph, Beirut, 1972, Licence en Droit Libanais, 1972. Bar: Beirut 1972, N.Y. 1983. Assoc. Tyan & Setrakian, Beirut, 1972-76; ptnr. Whitman & Ransom, N.Y.C., 1976—; bd. dirs. Bank Audi (Calif.), 1987—, Bank Audi (USA), 1991; fgn. law cons., N.Y., 1978. Bd. dirs., sec. Armenian Gen. Benevolent Union, N.Y.C., 1977—, pres. Worldwide Youth orgns., 1978—; bd. dirs. Armenian Assy. of Am., Washington, 1978-87; mem. Am. Task Force for Lebanon, 1988—. Mem. ABA, N.Y. Bar Assn., Beirut Bar Assn., Am. Fgn. Law Assn., Englewood (N.J.) Field Club. Office: Whitman & Ransom 200 Park Ave New York NY 10166-0005

SETTINERI, CYRUS, food broker executive; b. Garfield, N.J., Apr. 9, 1952; s. Cyrus and Ann (Marino) S.; m. Susanne Witte. Student, U. St. Louis, 1970-71, Rutgers U., 1971-74. Pres. CTR Food Svc., Milford, Conn., 1978-81, CS Brokers, Milford, 1982—. Named Broker of Yr. Bahlsen USA, 1987, AL Bazzini Co., 1985, ASA Beverage Co., 1988, Select Origins Corp., 1991, Annes Original Farmhouse Foods, one of Outstanding Young Men in Am., 1987. Mem. Nat. Food Brokers Assn., Nat. Assn. for Speciality Food Trade, Nat. Assn. Specialty Food and Confection Brokers, Boston Confectionary Salesmen's Club, Milford C. of C. Republican. Roman Catholic. Office: CS Brokers 151 Platt Ln Milford CT 06460-2057

SETTLE, GEORGE WARREN, orthopaedic surgeon; b. Balt., Oct. 4, 1926; s. Norman Charles and Charolett (Sanger) S.; m. Geraldine Ann Waybright, May 31, 1953; children: George, Anne, Beth, Thomas. BA, Johns Hopkins U., 1950, MD, 1953. Diplomate Am. Bd. Orthopaedic Surgery. Intern King County Hosp., Seattle, 1953-54; jr. asst. resident in orthopaedic surgery Johns Hopkins U., Seattle, 1954-55, asst. resident in orthopaedic surgery, 1956-57; chief resident in orthosurgery N000, 1957-58, mem. staff, 1958-59; pvt. practice Annapolis, Md., 1959-77, 79—; med. dir. Potomac Electric Power Co., Washington, 1977-78; chief orthopaedic surgery Anne Arundel Gen. Hosp., 1962-67, 81-82, chmn. med. bd., 1965-66, pres. med. staff, 1975-77. Contbr. articles to profl. jours. Mem. jud. nominating commn. Appellate Div., State of Md.; mem. com. and health planning Med & Chi Faculty of Md.; mem. med. rev. bd. City of Annapolis. With USN, 1944-46, PTO, World War II. Fellow Am. Acad. Orthopaedic Surgeons; mem. AMA, Md. Orthopaedic Soc., Anne Arundel County Med. Soc. Office: 195 Duke of Gloucester Annapolis MD 21401

SETTLE, RAY LEONARD, secondary school educator, computer consultant; b. Frostburg, Md., Mar. 11, 1944; s. Ray Leonard and Margaret Alice (Seibert) S.; m. Nora Elizabeth Schleicher, July 27, 1985; 1 child, Christa Rae. BS, Frostburg State U., 1966. Cert. tchr., Md. Tchr. Balt. County Pub. Schs., Towson, Md., 1966—, curriculum writer, 1970—, dept. chmn., 1983—, computer liaison, 1984—. Contbr. articles to profl. jours. Pres. Annapolis Apple Slice User Group, 1990. Mem. NEA, Internat. Soc. Tech. Edn., Am. Vocat. Assn. (Tchr. Yr. award 1990), Md. Assn. Coop. Edn. (pres. 1989), Md. State Tchrs. Assn., Tchrs. Assn. Balt. County, Assn. Balt. County Dept. Chmn. (pres. 1988-91). Office: Chesapeake High Sch 1801 Turkey Point Rd Baltimore MD 21221-1799

SETTLE, ROBERT BURTON, marketing educator; b. Princeton, Minn., Aug. 5, 1934; s. Robert R. and Kathryn M. (Luby) S.; m. Pamela L. Alreck. BA, Dominican Coll., 1965; MBA, U. Wis., Milw., 1967; PhD, UCLA, 1970. Staff announcer WPRE Radio, Prairie Du Chien, Wis., 1958-59; prodn. mgr. WBEL Radio, Beloit, Wis., 1959-60; sta. mgr. WRAC Radio, Racine, Wis., 1960-67; asst. prof. mktg. U. Fla., Gainesville, 1970-72; asst. prof. mktg. San Diego (Calif.) State U., 1972-76, assoc. prof., 1976-81, prof., 1981-88, prof. emeritus, 1988; prof. mktg. Bentley Coll., Waltham, Mass., 1988-90, Salisbury State U., Md., 1990—; bd. dirs. Psychometric Systems Inc., San Diego, 1975-86; pres. Associated Bus. Cons., San Diego, Boston, 1987—. Author: Survey Research Handbook, 1985, Why They Buy: American Consumers Inside and Out, 1986, Niche Marketing: How to Pinpoint Target Markets, 1990; contbr. articles to profl. jours. Mem. Am. Mktg. Assn., Assn. Consumer Rsch., Acad. Mktg Sci., Southwestern Mktg. Assn., Am. Psychol. Assn., Beta Gamma Sigma. Home: PO Box 2014 Salisbury MD 21802-2014 Office: Salisbury State U 1101 Camden Ave Salisbury MD 21801-6800

SETZER, HERBERT JOHN, chemical engineer; b. N.Y.C., Oct. 23, 1928; s. Leo and Barbara (Hafner) S. m. Elizabeth Bernadette Curran, May 30, 1957; children: Stephen Lawrence, Robert Drew, John Herbert, Brian Edmund. BChemE, CUNY, 1951; MChemE, NYU, 1958. Engr. U.S. Army Ordnance Corps Redstone Arsenal, Huntsville, Ala., 1955-57; rsch. asst. NYU, 1958-61; rsch. engr. Internat. Fuel Cells (joint venture United Techs. Corp., Hartford, Conn. and Toshiba Corp., Tokyo), 1962—. Holder 21 U.S. patents chem. processing and hydrogen generation, other patents in Can., Europe, Africa, Asia, Australia; contbr. tech. papers in field to publs. Chmn. troop com. Long Rivers coun. Boy Scouts Am., 1971-81, com. mem., 1973-81. With U.S. Army, 1951-56. Recipient Mason award, NYU, 1962, Spl. award United Techs. Corp., 1980. Mem. Catalyst Soc. New Eng., Sigma Xi, Elks. Roman Catholic. Home: 17 Virginia Dr Ellington CT 06029-3432 Office: PO Box 109 South Windsor CT 06074-0109

SEVERINGHAUS, CHARLES WILLIAM, wildlife biologist; b. Ithaca, N.Y., Sept. 3, 1916; s. Wilbur Clinton and Jane Margaret (Barden) S.; m. Ethel Long, Dec. 12, 1941 (div. 1971); children: Jane Raena, William Daniel, Charles Long; m. Jacqueline Degraff, Aug. 13, 1971; 1 child, Mark R. BS in Agr., Cornell U., 1939. Conservation laborer N.Y. State Conservation Dept., 1935-41; asst. game rsch. investigator N.Y. State Conservation Dept., Delmar, 1941, game rsch. investigator, 1941-61; dist. game mgr. N.Y. State Conservation Dept., Albany, 1941-44; leader deer mgmt. rsch., leader big game mgmt. rsch. N.Y. State Conservation Dept., Delmar, 1944-61, sr. wildlife biologist, 1961-62, supervising wildlife biologist, 1962-74, prin. wildlife biologist, 1974-77; cons. wildlife biologist Cornell U., Ithaca, N.Y., 1977-86; cons. wildlife biologist in pvt. practice Voorheesville, N.Y., 1986—; discussion leader Big Game session No. Am. Wildlife Conf., 1950; chmn. big game session N.E. Wildlife Conf., 1953, others; co-chmn. N.E. Deer Study Group, 1968. Editorial bd. Jour. Wildlife Mgmt., 1960-67, reviewer, 1972. Active in past numerous civic orgns. including Boy Scouts Am., Meth. Ch. Recipient Conservation award Am. Motors Corp., The Wildlife Soc., 1962, Wildlife Conservationist award Nat. Wildlife Fedn. and Sears Roebuck Found., 1965, Conservation award Sullivan County Sportsmen's Fedn., N.Y., 1966, Outstanding Svc. award Adirondack Deer Forum, 1973, Disting. Svc. award N.Y. State Conservation Coun., 1974, others. Mem. The Wildlife Soc. (founding orgn. mem. 1936, co-chmn. N.E. sect. 1959, awards com. 1962, chmn. 1963, N.Y. state rep. 1962-71, N.Y. chpt. v.p. 1972, pres. 1973-74), Am. Soc. Mammalogists, Alumni Assn. of N.Y. State Coll. of Agr. and Life Scis., Cornell U. (Outstanding Alumni award 1987), Gamma Sigma Delta. Home and Office: 4665 Martin Rd Voorheesville NY 12186

SEVERS, WILLIAM FLOYD, actor; b. Britton, Okla., Jan. 8, 1932; s. Harry Lysander Fletcher and Katherine Lucinda (McAuliffe) S.; m. Mary Anne Proctor, Jan. 18, 1964 (div. 1971); 1 child, Pilar; m. Barbara Alice Schonger, Sept. 9, 1978; children: Katherine Meghan, Erin Christine. AA, Pasadena Playhouse Coll., 1956. Appeared on Broadway in Cut of the Axe, 1959-60, On Borrowed Time, 1991-92, nat. tour Look Homeward, Angel, 1960; co-star nat. tour Spoon River, 1964; actor Secret Storm, All My Children, One Life To Live, Guiding Light, Texas, Search for Tomorrow, Another World, 1965-88; other TV appearances include Armstrong Circle Theatre, 1963, The Defenders, 1964, World War II, A GI Diary, 1978, Nurse, 1980, Muggable Mary, 1986, Law and Order, 1990, recurring role as Hon. Henry Fillmore, 1991; appeared in film Funny Farm, 1988, Regarding Henry, 1991; actor European tour West Side Story, 1990—; actor, voice artist numerous commls., 1964—. Staff sgt. USAF, 1946-53. Mem. Actors Equity Assn., Screen Actors Guild, Am. Fedn. Television and Radio Artists, Pasadena Playhouse Alumni Assn., Concerned Actors Network. Democrat. Home: 21 Stuyvesant Oval Apt 12H New York NY 10009-2035 Office: J Michael Bloom Assocs 233 Park Ave S New York NY 10003-1606

SEVON, WILLIAM DAVID, III, geologist; b. Andover, Ohio, July 22, 1933; s. William David and Ethel Matilda (Smith) S.; m. Joan Eleanor Johnson, Sept. 7, 1957 (div. 1982); children: Douglass William, David Hugh; m. Cecilia Louise Miller, June 25, 1988. BA, Ohio Wesleyan U., 1955; MA, U. S.D., 1955; PhD, U. Ill., 1961. Lectr. geology U. Canterbury, Christchurch, New Zealand, 1961-65; geologist Pa. Geol. Survey, Harrisburg, 1965—; Co-editor: The Catskill Delta, 1985, Appalachian Geomorphology, 1989; contbr. articles and abstracts to profl. jours. Mem. Geol. Soc. Am., Harrisburg Area Geol. Soc., Soc. for Sedimentary Geology. Office: Pa Geol Survey PO Box 2357 Harrisburg PA 17105-2357

SEWALL, WARREN, radiologist; b. Hartford, Conn., July 10, 1941; s. Joseph L. and Edna (Shakin) S.; m. Phyllis Nan Vogelhut, Apr. 29, 1970. BS, MIT, 1963; B in Med. Sci., Dartmouth U., 1965; MD, Harvard U., 1967. Diplomate Am. Bd. Radiology. Intern Mt. Auburn Hosp., Cambridge, MA, 1967-68; resident Mass. Gen. Hosp., Boston, 1970-73; therapeutic radiologist SE Radiology, Ltd., Chester, Pa., 1974—. Served to capt. U.S. Army, 1968-70. Named to Legion Membership Chapel of Four Chaplains. Mem. Am. Soc. Therapeutic Radiology and Oncology, Keystone Area Soc. for Radiation Oncology, Am. Coll. Radiology, Pa. Radiologic Soc., Am. Soc. Clin. Oncology, MIT Ednl. Coun. (regional vice-chmn. 1989—), Dartmouth Med. Sch. Alumni Coun. (rchmn. resource com. 1989-91). Office: Crozer-Chester Med Ctr Chester PA 19013

SEXTON, MARK, publishing consultant; b. N.Y.C., Nov. 20, 1930; s. Joseph James and Mary Winifred (Cahill) S.; m. Marie Kathleen McCarthy, Apr. 9, 1957; children: Mark, Adam, James. AB, Haverford Coll., 1953; postgrad., Syracuse U. Reporter, editor UP, N.Y.C., 1953-54; mgr. Macmillan Co., Midwest, N.Y., 1954-63; editor, mgr. Cornell U. Press, Ithaca, N.Y., 1963-65; field mgr. McGraw-Hill, Ithaca, 1965-67; mktg. dir. Random House, N.Y.C., 1967-73, Cambridge U. Press, N.Y.C., 1973-84; pres. Mark Sexton Assocs., Pelham, N.Y., 1984—; adv. bd. Univ. Press Books, N.Y.C., 1987-91, Gill Libr., New Rochelle (N.Y.) Coll., 1989—; seminar leader Folio Mag., N.Y.C. Contbr. articles to profl. jours. Trustee Pelham (N.Y.) Sch. Bd., 1965-70, Pelham Pub. Libr., 1990—. Mem. Soc. Scholarly Pub., ALA. Home and Office: Mark Sexton Assocs 152 Corlies Ave Pelham NY 10803-1902

SEXTON, MIRIAM ELAINE, clinical child psychologist; b. Akron, Ohio, July 26, 1949; d. Clifford C. and Eileen (Neer) S. BA, Manchester Coll., 1971; MA, Clark U., 1974, PhD, 1978. Lic. psychologist, Mass. Predoctoral intern Children's Hosp., Boston, 1975-76; psychologist cons. Millbury (Mass.) Pub. Schs., 1976-78, West Boylston (Mass.) Pub. Schs., 1977-79; psychologist U. Mass. Med. Ctr., Worcester, 1979—; family therapist Chandler St. Assocs., Worcester, 1989—; cons. day care ctrs. in Westborough, Webster, and Norwell, Mass., 1989—. Contbr. articles to profl. jours. NIMH fellow Clark U., 1971-75; recipient Interdisciplinary award in Mental Health MacArthur Found., U. Mass. Med. Ctr., 1981-82. Mem. APA, Soc. Pediatric Psychology. Democrat. Office: U Mass Med Ctr Dept Devel Pediatrics 55 Lake Ave N Worcester MA 01655-0001

SEYBOLD, KAREN COLAPIETRO, university administrator; b. Endicott, N.Y., May 21, 1964; d. Bruno and Jane (Larson) Colapietro; m. Eric Arnold Seybold, Aug. 2, 1991. BS, Cornell U., 1986; MS in Counseling, Syracuse U., 1992. Asst. dir. allocations United Way of Tompkins County, Ithaca, N.Y., 1986-87; asst. dean of admission Hamilton Coll., Clinton, N.Y., 1987-88; program coord. Maurice Horowitch Career Ctr. of Hamilton Coll., Clinton, N.Y., 1988-90; placement counselor and asst. dir. counseling/programming Syracuse U. Placement Ctr., 1990-92; assoc. dir. admissions Grad. Sch. of Mgmt., Clark U., Worcester, Mass., 1992—; English conversation group leader Office of Internat. Svcs., Syracuse U., 1990-91; aslumni admissions ambassador Cornell U., 1990—. Burton Blatt scholar, 1989-90. Mem. AACD, Am. Coll. Pers. Assn., Nat. Career Devel. Assn., Pi Lambda Theta, Omicron Nu, Phi Kappa Phi. Office: Clark Univ 950 Main St Worcester MA 01610-1477

SEYMOUR, CHARLES, microbiologist; b. Washington, June 11, 1944; s. Charles and Charlotte (Ball) S.; m. Laura Dean Kramer, Sept. 1, 1970 (div. July 1, 1980); m. Roberta Ann Williamson, Sept. 3, 1986; children: Lee, Alexander. BA, Yale U., 1966; PhD, Cornell U., 1975; MA, Tufts U., 1992. Diplomate Am. Bd. Med. Microbiology. Postdoctoral fellow Gorgas Lab., Panama, 1974-77, U. Wis., Madison, 1977-80; staff virologist Inciensa, Tres Rios, Costa Rica, 1981-82; postdoctoral fellow, clin. microbiologist U. Conn. Ctr. Health Sci., Farmington, 1983-85; chief clin. microbiology Carney Hosp., Boston, 1985-86; researcher bacteriology Boston City Hosp., 1986-89; staff virologist MIT, Cambridge, 1989-90; adj. asst. prof. Boston U., U. R.I., 1986—; cons. Biotek, Wilmington, Mass., 1989-90, Ciba-Corning, Walpole, Mass., 1988, BBI, Bridgewater, Mass., 1990-92. Contbr. over 15 articles to profl. jours. and 2 chpts. to books. Mem. Am. Soc. for Microbiology, Am. Soc. Tropical Medicine & Hygiene, N.E. Assn. for Clin. Microbiology and Infectious Disease. Home: 510 Harland St Milton MA 02186

SEYMOUR, EVERETT HEDDEN, JR., lawyer; b. Tuxedo Park, N.Y., Apr. 16, 1958; s. Everett Hedden and Deborah (Robinson) S. BA, Yale U., 1980; JD, U. Va., 1986. Bar: N.Y. 1988, U.S. Dist. Ct. (so. and ea. dists.) N.Y. 1988, Conn. 1988, U.S. Dist. Ct. Conn. 1988. Law clk. to justice U.S. Dist. Ct., New Haven, 1986-87; assoc. Davis Polk & Wardwell, N.Y.C., 1987—. Articles rev. editor U. Va. Law Rev., 1984-86.

SEYMOUR, GERALD, public relations executive; b. Bklyn., July 10, 1933; s. Edward Ferguson and Marian Elizabeth (Langdon) S.; m. Georgette Khouri, Sept. 8, 1963; 1 child, Elizabeth Anne. Student, U. Md., 1953-55, NYU, 1955-56. News editor N.Y. Herald Tribune, N.Y.C., 1958-66, N.Y. World Jour. Tribune, N.Y.C., 1966-67; prodn. editor Book Week, N.Y.C., 1967-69; news editor N.Y. Bur. Newsday, N.Y.C., 1969-70; assoc. editor Book World, N.Y.C., 1970-72; correspondent N.Y. Chgo. Tribune Book World, N.Y.C., 1972-73; asst. bus. editor N.Y. Daily News, N.Y.C., 1973-82; copy editor Newsweek Mag., N.Y.C., 1982-87; v.p. Gavin Anderson & Co., N.Y.C., 1987—; adj. asst. prof. journalism L.I. Univ., 1987-89; lectr. in journalism Baruch Coll. City Univ., N.Y.C., 1986, NYU, 1990. Contbr. articles to profl. jours. Sgt. USAF, 1951-55, Germany. Mem. Overseas Press Club, Soc. of Silurians, Soc. Profl. Journalists, Publicity Club of N.Y. Home: 580 84th St Brooklyn NY 11209-4731 Office: Gavin Anderson & Co 11 W 42nd St Fl 8 New York NY 10036-8094

SFORZA, PASQUALE MICHAEL, aerospace engineering educator; b. N.Y.C., Mar. 5, 1941; s. Michael and Lucia (Marzocchi) S.; m. Mary Ann Aufmuth, June 2, 1963; children: Laura, Michael, Julia. B.Aero.Engring., Poly. Inst. Bklyn., 1961, MS, 1962, PhD, 1965. Asst. prof. Poly. Inst. Bklyn., 1965-67, assoc. prof., 1968-76; prof. mech. engring. Poly. Inst. N.Y., Bklyn., 1977—, dept. head mech. and aerospace engring., 1983-86, 88—; dir. Flowpower Inc., Huntington, N.Y. Patentee (3) on fluid power; inventor vortex augmentor for wind power; contbr. articles to World Book Ency., McGraw-Hill Ency. Sci. & Tech. Mem. adv. bd. N.Y. State Legislature Commn. on Sci. and Tech., 1976-87. Mem. AIAA (assoc. fellow, Tech. Achievement award 1977, editor jour. 1980-82, 83—), ASME, N.Y. Acad. Scis. Office: Polytechnic U Rte 110 Farmingdale NY 11735

SGROI, DONALD ANGELO, obstetrician-gynecologist; b. Newark, Aug. 20, 1943; s. Joseph and Mary (Desimone) S.; m. Phyllis Ann Intorelli, Nov. 19, 1967; children: Donna, Felisa, Chela, Gabriela, Alexandria. BS, Fairleigh Dickinson U., 1970; MD, Autonomous U. Guadalajara, Mex.,

1974. Diplomate Am. Bd. Ob-Gyn. Sr. tech. aide Bell Labs., Berkley Heights, N.J., 1967-70; intern St. Michael's Med. Ctr., Newark, 1974-76; resident in ob-gyn. St. Joseph's Med. Ctr., Paterson, N.J., 1976-78, chief resident, 1978-79; assoc. attending physician Wayne (N.J.) Gen. Hosp., 1980-84, co-chmn. dept. ob-gyn., 1980-84, attending physician, 1984—, chmn. tissue rev. com., 1984-88, mem. tissue rev. com., 1988—, chmn. dept. ob-gyn., 1988-91, co-chmn. dept. ob-gyn., 1991—; sec., treas. med. exec. com., 1988-91, mem. peer assessment com., 1988-91, quality assurance com., 1988, credentials com., 1988—; mem. Peer Rev. Orgn. of N.J., 1991—. Fellow Am. Coll. Ob-Gyn., Am. Fertility Soc. (jr.); mem. Internat. Assn. Gynelogic Laparoscopist, Internat. Corr. Soc. Obstetricians and Gynecolgists. Roman Catholic. Home: 231 Indian Trail Dr Franklin Lakes NJ 07417-1014 Office: 401 Hamburg Tpke Ste 104 130 Skyline Dr Wayne NJ 07470

SGROI, ROSEMARY JANE, educational administrator; b. Albany, N.Y., Jan. 18, 1940; d. Salvadore Rocco and Anna Catherine (Urbano) S. AA in Liberal Arts, Maria Coll., 1963; BA in English, Coll. of St. Rose, 1968; MS in Ednl. Adminstrn., SUNY, Albany, 1973. Cert. tchr., N.Y. Elem. and secondary tchr. Albany Diocese schs., 1965-71; prin. Sacred Heart of Mary Sch., Watervliet, N.Y., 1971-73; dir. admissions Maria Coll., Albany, 1973-79; assoc. campus minister Siena Coll., Loudonville, N.Y., 1980-88; dir. campus ministry Siena Coll., Loudonville, 1988—. Editor: Potpourri of Prayers, 1990. Bd. dirs. Mercy High Sch., Albany, 1982-84, Arbor House, Albany, 1984-90, St. Peter's Hosp., Albany, 1984-90; co-dir. Franciscan Vol. Ministry, Loudonville, 1989—; del. 1st inst. chpat. Sisters of Mercy, Buffalo, 1991; mem. Capital Leadership Program, Albany, 1990-91. Mem. Nat. Assembly of Religious Women, Women's Ordination Conf., Cath. Campus Ministry Assn. Office: Siena Coll 515 Loudon Rd Albany NY 12211-1462

SHACKELFORD, CHARLES LEWIS, electrical engineer; b. Wagoner, Okla., Oct. 19, 1918; s. Ralph Lewis and Mary Roselle (Beck) S.; m. Harriet Margurite Roll, May 12, 1945; 1 child, Charles, Jr. BSEE, Okla. State U., 1941; MSEE, U. Mo., 1942. Engr. Westinghouse, Pitts., 1942, Bloomfield, N.J., 1952; engr. Chatham Electronics, Livingston, N.J., 1952-62; chief engr. Tung-Sol Div./Wagner Electronics, Livingston, 1962-67; sr. engr. ITT Electron Tech. Div., Easton, Pa., 1967—. Contbr. articles to profl. jours. Home: 3916 Oakland Rd Bethlehem PA 18017-1457

SHACKELTON, NORMAN JOHN, JR., naval officer; b. Syracuse, N.Y., Oct. 30, 1939; s. Norman John and Jane Aileen (Wood) S.; m. Judith Ann Offiler, Sept. 18, 1965; children: Holly Ann, Cory Matthew. BS, US Naval Acad., 1963; MS in Ops. Rsch., Naval Postgrad. Sch., Monterey, Calif., 1971, PhD, 1973. Commd. ensign USN, 1963, advanced through grades to capt., various engring. and ops. officers positions, 1965-79; asst. program mgr. Naval Sea Systems Command USN, Washington, 1979-83; attack submarine program coord. Office Naval Ops. USN, Washington, 1983-85, trident program mgr. Naval Sea Systems command, 1985-89; supr. shipbuilding USN, Groton, Conn., 1989-91; asst. to dep. comdr. Naval Sea Systems Command USN, Washington, 1991—. Vestry mem. All Hallows Episcopal Ch., Birdsville, Md., 1982-88. Mem. Ops. Rsch. Soc. Am., Inst. Indsl. Engrs., Inst. Mgmt. Scis., Am. Soc. Naval Engrs., Rotary, Sigma Xi. Home: 231 Chatham Ln Annapolis MD 21403-1017 Office: Naval Sea Systems Command SEA 071 Washington DC 20362

SHADOIAN, HOLLY LYNN, academic administrator; b. Providence, Feb. 12, 1952; d. Forrest Barton and Barbara Holly (Oldham) Marty; m. Charles John Shadoian, Jr., July 24, 1976; 1 child, Jeffrey Charles. BA, R.I. Coll., 1973, MEd, 1975; PhD, U. Conn., 1989. Admissions officer R.I. Coll., Providence, 1974-75, grad. program officer, 1975-79, acting affirmative action officer, 1979, dir. alumni affairs, 1979—. Bd. dirs. Kaleidoscope Theatre, Providence, 1980—, pres., 1980-82, featured performer, singer, 1980—; judge Miss R.I./Miss Am. Pageant, Providence, 1988. Recipient Spl. award R.I. Coll. Alumni Assn., Providence, 1988, Faculty Rsch. award R.I. Coll., 1988-89. Mem. Coun. Advancement and Support of Edn. (silver medal periodicals improvement, 1987). Office: RI Coll Providence RI 02908

SHAFER, JONATHAN STICKLEY, advertising executive; b. Highland Park, Ill., Sept. 23, 1936; s. Frederick Webber and Louise (Stickley) S.; m. Margot Van Gilder, June 6, 1959; children: Jonathan Jr., Peter Dell, Sheridan Lee. BS, U.S. Air Force Acad., 1959. Commd. 2d lt. USAF, 1959, advanced through grades to capt., 1963, resigned, 1965; mgr. sales Container Corp. Am., Carol Stream, Ill., 1965-70; sales mgr. Fed. Paper Bd. Am., Oak Brook, Ill., 1970-72; mem. mktg. mgmt. staff Gen. Printing Ink div. Sun Chem. Co., Northlake, Ill., 1972-74; v.p. sales and mktg. Clevepak, White Plains, N.Y., 1974-76; nat. acct. sales rep. Garber Co., N.Y.C., 1976-82; v.p. sales Procorp, Framingham, Mass., 1982-84; pres., chief exec. officer Shafer Enterprises, Inc., Stratford, Conn., 1984-90; pres. C-Com, Inc., Fairfield, Conn., 1990—. Republican. Episcopalian.

SHAFFER, DAVID CLARENCE, university administrator; b. Du Bois, Pa., June 4, 1955; s. Forrest I. and Amelia R. (Rockey) S.; m. Evelyn K. Evans, Jan. 29, 1983; 1 child, Nicole Ann. BA in Journalism, Pa. State U., 1977. News dir. Tri-County Broadcasting Co., Inc., Du Bois, 1977-85; dir. univ. rels. Pa. State U., Du Bois, 1985—; bd. dirs. Keystone West Pubs. Bd. dirs. Du Bois Regional Med. Ctr. Devel. Coun., 1985—, Du Bois Area United Way; actor, dir. Du Bois Community Theatre Group, 1980-88. Recipient Cert. of Appreciation, DuBois Job Svc., 1984, DuBois Am. Legion, 1983. Mem. Coll. and Univ. Pub. Rels. Assn. Pa., Pa. State U. Alumni Assn. (life), Du Bois Area C. of C. (bd. dirs. 1985-88), Du Bois Campus Alumni Soc. (pres. 1980-86, Outstanding Alumni award 1986), Rotary (v.p. Du Bois chpt. 1988-89, pres. 1990-91). Home: 402 Berkley St Philipsburg PA 16866-1808 Office: Pa State U Du Bois Campus College Place Du Bois PA 15801

SHAFFER, DONALD STEPHEN, educator; b. Ottumwa, Iowa, May 22, 1929; s. Emery Jay and Rose Rachel (Channel) S.; m. Patricia Louise Hemm, Oct. 16, 1953; children: Mark, Lee, Jean, Beth. BS, Sophia U., Tokyo, 1962; MLA, Johns Hopkins U., 1969. Commd. 2d lt. U.S. Army, 1948, advanced through grades to chief warrant officer, ret., 1973; assoc. prof. Dundalk Community Coll., Balt., 1973—; lectr. Harford Community Coll., Bel Air, Md., 1972—, Essex Community Coll., Balt., 1972—, Jewish Community Ctr., Balt., 1976—; evaluator Am. Coun. on Edn., Washington, 1980—; dir. internat. edn. Dundalk Community Coll. 1980—; trustee Eastern Christian Coll., Bel Air, 1980-90, chmn., 1979-80. Co-author: People's Republic of China, 1967. Sponsor Polit. Sci. Club Dundalk Community Coll., 1974—; workshop presenter Dem. Cen. Com., Md., 1980-86; elder Joppatowne Christian Ch., Joppa, Md., 1970—. Recipient Commendation Md. Ho. of Dels., 1976, Excellence in Teaching award Md. Bd. for Community Colls., 1987. Mem. DAV (life). Office: Dundalk Community Coll 7200 Sollers Point Rd Baltimore MD 21222-4649

SHAFFER, GAIL S., state government official; b. Kingston, N.Y., Aug. 1, 1948; d. Robert E. and Marion (Gallagher) S. BA summa cum laude, Elmira Coll., 1970; student, U. Paris, 1968-69. Editor Sam Har Press, 1972-76; legal asst. Rahmas Law Firm, 1973-76; spl. asst. to commr. N.Y. State Environ. Conservation, 1977-79; exec. dir. N.Y. State Rural Affairs Council, 1979-80; mem. N.Y. State Assembly, 1981-83; sec. state State of N.Y., Albany, 1983—. Mem. N.Y. State Dem. Com., 1976—; chair Yonkers Emergency Fin. Control Bd., 1985—. Mem. Women Execs. in State Govt., N.Y. State Assn. Women Officeholders (pres.). Presbyterian. Office: Sec of State NY 162 Washington Ave Albany NY 12231-0001*

SHAFFER, NANCY L., nursing educator; b. Niagara Falls, N.Y., Sept. 13, 1938; d. Gilbert and Gertrude Louise (Angell) Johnston; 1 child, Margaret L. Clark; m. Bruce R. Shaffer, Apr. 1, 1983; stepchildren: Scott, Steven, Gregory. BS, U. Buffalo, 1959; MS, SUNY, Buffalo, 1972. Cert. nurse practitioner. Nursing instr. Niagara (N.Y.) U., 1968-74, asst. prof., 1974-78, assoc. prof., 1978-84, prof., 1984—; chairperson jr. and advanced nursing Niagara U., 1988—; dir. RN Completion Program Niagara U., 1991—; developer orientation programs Niagara Falls Meml. Ctr., 1980-81. Co-presenter Nat. Nursing Conv., 1990; contbr. articles to profl. jours. Home: 2227 Bedell Rd # A Grand Island NY 14072-1659 Office: Niagara U Coll of Nursing Niagara University NY 14109

SHAFFER, NELSON JAY, transportation consulting company executive; b. Mechanicsburg, Pa., Aug. 12, 1951; s. Perry Mason and Frances Geraldine (Kreiser) S.; m. Diane DiPersio, June 17, 1978; children: Ashleigh Brooke, Nikandra Lee, Dustin Fielding, Jenna Alexandra. BA in Sociology, Western Md. Coll., 1973; MS in Transp. Engring., Villanova U., 1981. Engr. asst. John Comiskey and Assocs., Newtown Square, Pa., 1973-79; recreation counselor Devereux Found., Devon, Pa., 1973-78; co-founder, dir. The Champs Camp, Drexel Hill, Pa., 1977-82; project engr. Pennoni Assocs. Inc., Phila., 1979-82, project mgr., 1982-87, div. mgr. transp. svcs., 1987—, v.p., 1988—, chmn. strategic planning com., 1989—, also bd. dirs. Head girls intramural coach Aston (Pa.) Youth Soccer Assn., 1990, asst. coach travel team, 1991. Mem. Am. Soc. Hwy. Engrs., Inst. Transp. Engrs. (transp. planner and cons. coun., newsletter editor Mid-Atlantic sect. 1986-89, treas. 1988-89, sec. 1989-90, 2d v.p. 1990-91). Republican. Lutheran. Home: 1715 Hillcrest Ln Aston PA 19014-1041 Office: Pennoni Assocs Inc 1600 Callowhill St Philadelphia PA 19130-4112

SHAFFER, SHERRILL LYNN, economist; b. Tyler, Tex., Aug. 1, 1952; s. Douglas Marsene and Ethel Elizabeth (Green) S.; m. Margaret Jane Ahrens, Jun 20, 1987; 1 child, David Carsten. BA, Rice U., 1974; MA, Stanford U., 1978, PhD, 1981. Rsch. asst. Stanford (Calif.) U., 1976-79, instr., 1979-80; from economist to chief Fed. Res. Bank N.Y., N.Y.C., 1980-88; from rsch. officer and economist to asst. v.p. and economist Fed. Res. Bank Phila., 1988—; violinist solo and with orchs., Calif., N.Y., 1976-88; cons. asst. Rosse & Olszewski, Palo Alto, Calif., 1978-80. Contbr. numerous articles to profl. jours. Sec. bd. dirs. N.Y. Arts Group, N.Y.C., 1982-83. Mem. Am. Econ. Assn., Am. Math. Soc., Math. Assn. Am., Indsl. Orgn. Soc. Episcopalian. Home: 403 Atwood Rd Philadelphia PA 19118-1005 Office: Fed Res Bank Phila 10 Independence Mall Philadelphia PA 19106

SHAFIR, MICHAIL KLEYNER, medical educator; b. Shanghai, China, July 16, 1943; came to U.S., 1974; s. George and Isabella (Kleyner) S.; m. Adela Fruhling, May 6, 1967; children: Alan, Daniela. MD, U. Chile, 1967. Surgeon Lopez Perez Cancer Inst., Santiago, Chile, 1970-74; resident Mt. Sinai Hosp., N.Y.C., 1974-79, attending surgeon, 1979—; assoc. prof. surgery, neoplastic diseases Mt. Sanai Sch. Medicine, N.Y.C., 1985—; cons. in field. Jr. Faculty fellow Am. Cancer Soc., N.Y.C., 1982. Fellow Am. Coll. Surgeons; mem. Am. Soc. Clin. Oncology, N.Y. Surg. Soc., Soc. Surg. Oncologists. Jewish. Office: 1021 Park Ave New York NY 10028

SHAFTEL, OSCAR HAMILTON, foreign studies educator; b. N.Y.C., May 5, 1912; s. Maurice B. and Anna (Stoll) S.; m. Ruth Marra, Feb. 10, 1945; children: Anthony E., Ann Marra, Eve. BA, CCNY, 1931; MA, Harvard U., 1932, PhD, 1936. Tutor to asst. prof. of English Queens Coll.-CUNY, N.Y.C., 1937-53; asst. prof. to prof. of English and oriental studies Pratt Inst., Bklyn., 1963-77, prof. emeritus, 1977—; vis. prof., adj. prof. religious studies Queens Coll., Flushing, N.Y., 1973-92; prof. emeritus, vis. prof. Pratt Inst., 1977-90. Author: An Understanding of the Buddha, 1974; contbr. to Good Reading. Candidate state senate Am. Labor Party, Queens, N.Y., 1952. Capt. USAF, 1942-46. Home: 3915 45th St Long Island City NY 11104-2103

SHAFTO, ROBERT AUSTIN, insurance company executive; b. Council Bluffs, Iowa, Sept. 15, 1935; s. Glen Granville and Blanche (Radigan) S.; m. Jeanette DeFino, Dec. 17, 1954; children: Robert, Dennis, Teri, Shari, Michael. BS in Actuarial Sci., Drake U., Des Moines, 1959. Mgr. computer svcs. Guarantee Mut. Life Ins. Co., Omaha, 1959-65; v.p. Beta div. Electronic Data Systems, Dallas, 1965-71; from 2d v.p. to v.p. for computer systems devel. and info. svcs. The New Eng., Boston, 1972-75, sr. v.p. policy holder and computer svcs., 1975-81, adminstrv. v.p., 1981-82, exec. v.p. individual ins. ops., 1982-86, exec. v.p. ins. and employee benefits ops., 1986-88, pres. ins. and personal fin. svcs., 1988-90, pres., chief oper. officer, 1990-92, pres., CEO, 1992—, also bd. dirs.; bd. dirs., pres. New Eng. Variable Life. Bd. overseers Children's Hosp., Boston, 1989—; mem. corp. Dana Farber Cancer Inst.; bd. dirs. United Way of Mass. Mem. Am. Coun. Life Insurers, Commn. on Fin. Svcs. Integration, IBM Ins. Industries Customer Adv. Coun., Life Underwriters Tng. Coun. (bd. trustees), Life Office Mgmt. Assn. (bd. dirs.). Roman Catholic. Office: New Eng Mut Life Ins Co 501 Boylston St Boston MA 02116-3706

SHAGIN, TRACY DEAN, investment management firm executive; b. Paterson, N.J., Jan. 20, 1952. BA in Econs. magna cum laude, Boston U., 1975; MBA in Fin., Fairleigh Dickinson U., 1980. Chartered fin. analyst. V.p. Trascott, Alyson, Craig Inc., Fair Lawn, N.J., 1977—. Contbr. articles to newspapers. Mem. N.Y. Soc. Securities Analysts, Fin. Analysts Fedn., Investment Co. Inst., Internat. Fin. Analysts Fedn. Office: Trascott Alyson Craig Inc 16-00 Rt 208 Fair Lawn NJ 07410

SHAH, ANWAR MUHAMMAD CHAUDRY, economist; b. Faisalabad, Punjab, Pakistan, Jan. 29, 1948; came to U.S., 1986; s. Shah M. and Nazir Fatima Chaudry; m. Ghazala Shaheen Shah, Apr. 23, 1981; children: Furhawn, Sana. BA, Punjab U., 1965, postgrad. diploma in stats., 1966, MA in Econs., 1967; MA in Econs., Vanderbilt U., 1972; PhD, U. Alta., Can., 1983. Economist, demographer U.S. Agy. for Internat. Devel., Islamabad, Pakistan, 1974-75; economist govt. of Alta., Edmonton, 1979-82; sr. economist Fin. Dept. Govt. of Can., Ottawa, 1982-86, The World Bank, Washington, 1986—. Contbr. several articles to profl. jours. Hon. Sgt.-at-Arms of the Tenn. Senate, 1973. Mem. Econometric Soc., Nat. Tax Assn., Am. Econ. Assn., Can. Econs. Assn. Office: The World Bank 1818 H St NW # 10053 Washington DC 20433-0002

SHAH, DAKSHA RAJNIKANT, pathologist; b. Broach, Gujarat, India, July 3, 1945; came to U.S. 1970; d. Kanchanlal C. and Bachugauri K. Kansupada; m. Rajnikant S. Shah, Dec. 12, 1969; children: Ami, Ameesh, Anand. M.B.B.S., B.J. Med. Coll., India, 1969. Diplomate Am. Bd. Pathology. Intern Roxborough Meml. Hosp., Phila., 1970-71; resident in pathology Fitzgrald Mercy Hosp., Darby, Pa., 1971-75; dir. Ami Lab., Yardley, Pa., 1979-85, Medilab., Penddell, Pa., 1985—; med. examiner Mercer County, Trenton, N.J., 1980—; dir. pathology Women's Diagnostic Ctr., Langhorne, Pa., 1989—; dir. Cardiology Assocs. of Bucks County, Inc., Levittown, Pa., 1978—. Fellow Am. Coll. Pathologists. Hindu. Home: 1177 University Dr Morrisville PA 19067-2861 Office: 1723 Woodbourne Rd Bldg 10 Levittown PA 19057-5203

SHAH, MUBARIK AHMAD, surgeon; b. Lahore, Punjab, Pakistan, Dec. 19, 1949; came to U.S., 1976; s. Tufail Mohammad and Amna (Bibi)) S.; m. Mansoora Nazli, Nov. 10, 1974; children: Rizwan, Maliha, Numaan. FSc, T.I. Coll., Rabwah, Pakistan, 1966; MBBS, Punjab U., Multan, Pakistan, 1971. Diplomate Am. Bd. Surgery. Instr. King Edward Med. Coll., Paskistan, 1975-76; house surgeon N.Y. Polyclinic Hosp., N.Y.C., 1976-77; resident surgery St. Mary Hosp., Waterbury, Conn., 1977-78, New Rochelle (N.Y.) Hosp., 1978-79; resident surgery Presbyn.-U. Pa. Med. Ctr., Phila., 1979-82, fellow vascular surgery, 1982-83; clin. instr. U. Pa. Sch. Medicine, Phila., 1979-83; attending physician, surgeon St. Mary Hosp., Langhorne, Pa., 1983—; dir. trauma svcs. Med. Coll. Hosps., Bucks County Campus, Warminster, Pa., 1988-90. Med. advisor Trevose (Pa.) Rescue, 1988-90; pres. Ahmadiyya Youth Orgn., Phila., 1989-90. Capt. Pakistan Army, 1971-75. Fellow ACS, Internat. Coll. Surgeons, Am. Soc. Abdominal Surgeons; mem. AMA, Am. Trauma Soc., Pa. Med. Soc., Bucks County Med. Soc. Office: St Mary Med Office Bldg 1205 Langhorne Newtown Rd Langhorne PA 19047

SHAH, NAREN NATWARLAL, cardiologist; b. Ahmedabad, India, Jan. 12, 1934; came to U.S., 1959; s. Natwarlal G. and Kanta M. Shah; m. Mary Ann Iafolla; children: Jennifer, Jeffrey, Jason. Student, M.G. Sci. Inst., Ahmedabad, 1951; MD, B.J. Med. Coll., Ahmedabad, 1957. Intern Elgin Gen. Hosp., St. Thomas, Ontario, Can., 1959-60; resident in medicine Union Meml. Hosp., Balt., 1960-62; resident in cardiology Phila. Gen. Hosp., 1962-63, fellow in cardiology, 1965-66; resident in cardiology Hahnemann Med. Ctr., Phila., 1963-64, fellow in kidney disease, 1964-65; fellow in medicine Hamilton (Ontario) Gen. Hosp., 1966-67; fellow in cardiology St. Michael's Hosp., Toronto, 1967-68; with Group Health Assn., Washington, 1968-72; chief medicine VA Med. Ctr., Montrose, N.Y., 1980—; attending cardiologist Lincoln Hosp., Bronx, N.Y., 1972-73, Met. Hosp., Manhattan, N.Y., 1973-80; clin. assoc. N.Y. Med. Coll., Valhalla, 1980—. Contbr. articles to profl. jours.; rsch. panel: Sports Medicine, The Medical News. Lt. col. USAR, 1980—. Recipient Physician's Recognition Award AMA, 1979—. Fellow Am. Coll. Physicians, Am. Coll. Angiology; mem. Am. Coll. Cardiology, Am. Soc. Echocardiography, Am. Heart Assn., N.Y. Med. Soc. Home: 67 Tarry Hill Rd Tarrytown NY 10591

SHAH, RAJNIKANT S., cardiologist, consultant; b. Mehsana, Gujarat, India, Sept. 1, 1946; came to U.S., 1970; s. Shantilal M. and Kamalaben S. (Shah) S.; m. Daksha K. Kansupada, Dec. 12, 1969; Ami, Ameesh, Anand. MB, BS, The M.S. U., Baroda, India, 1969. Diplomate Am. Bd. Internal Medicine; diplomate in cardiovascular disease. Attending physician The Lower Bucks Hosp., Bristol, Pa., 1975—, Frankford Hosp., Phila., 1977—; assoc. prof. clin. medicine Med. Coll. of Pa., Phila., 1977; chief, cardiology sect. St. Mary's Hosp., Langhorne, Pa., 1977—; pres., chief cardiologist Cardiology Assocs. of Bucks County, Levittown, Pa., 1977—; pres., cardiologist Oxford Valley Diagnostic Ctr., Fairless Hills, Pa., 1985—; pres. Internat. Tech. Inc., Yardley, Pa., 1987—; assoc. prof. clin. medicine Hahneman U., Phila., 1988—. Contbr. articles and abstracts to profl. jours. Fellow Am. Coll. Cardiology, Am. Heart Assn. (clin. council), Am. Coll. Physicians, Am. Fed. for Clin. Rsch., Am. Coll. Chest Physicians. JAIN. Home: 1177 University Dr Morrisville PA 19067-2861 Office: Cardiology Assocs 1723 Woodbourne Rd Levittown PA 19057-1501

SHAH, SHIRISH KALYANBHAI, computer science educator, chemistry and environmental science educator; b. Ahmedabad, India, May 24, 1942; came to U.S., 1962, naturalized, 1974; s. Kalyanbhai T. and Sushilaben K. S.; B.S. in Chemistry and Physics, St. Xavier's Coll., Gujarat U., 1962; PhD in Phys. Chemistry, U. Del., 1968; cert. in bus. mgmt. U. Va., 1986; PhD in Cultural Edn. (hon.) World U. West, 1986; m. Kathleen Long, June 28, 1973; 1 son, Lawrence. Asst. prof. Washington Coll., Chestertown, Md., 1967-68; dir. quality control Vita Foods, Chestertown, 1968-72; asst. prof., assoc. prof. sci., adminstr. food, marine sci. and vocat. programs Chesapeake Coll., Wye Mills, Md., 1968-76; assoc. prof., prof. sci., chmn. dept. tech. studies Community Coll. of Balt., 1976-91; assoc. prof. chemistry Coll. Notre Dame of Md., 1991—; chmn. computer systems and engring. techs., 1982-89, coord. tech. studies, 1989-91; mem. Balt. City Adult Edn. Adv. Com., 1982-89; chmn. Coll. wide computer user com., 1985-91; permanent mem. Rep. Senatorial Com.; charter mem. Rep. Presdl. Task Force. Mem. com. Am. Lung Assn., 1971-80; mem. Congl. Adv. Com., 1983—. Fellow Am. Inst. Chemists; mem. IEEE, Am. Chem. Soc., Data Processing Mgmt. Assn., Nat. Environ. Tng. Assn., Nat. Sci. Tchrs. Assn., Nat. Assn. Indsl. Tech. (dir. local region, bd. accreditors), Am. Vocat. Assn., Am. Tech. Edn. Assn., Am. Fedn. Tchrs., Md. State Tchrs. Assn., Md. Assn. Community and Jr. Colls. (v.p. 1977-78, pres. 1978—), Sigma Xi, Epsilon Pi Tau, Iota Lambda Sigma Nu. Roman Catholic. Contbr. articles on sci. and tech. to profl. jours. Home: 5605 Purlington Way Baltimore MD 21212-2950 Office: Coll Notre Dame Dept Chem 4701 N Charles St Baltimore MD 21210

SHAHANI, COMILA, industrial psychologist, educator; b. Bombay, India, Dec. 26, 1961; came to U.S., 1983; d. Indru and Sheila Shahani. BA, St. Xaviers Coll., Bombay, 1983; MA, Rice U., 1986, PhD, 1988. Asst. prof. psychology Hofstra U., Hempstead, N.Y., 1988—. Contbr. articles to profl. jours. Dem. campaign vol., N.Y., 1988—. Mem. Am. Psychol. Assn., Am. Psychol. Soc., Soc. Indst. Psychology (sub com. head 1990-91), Indsl. Psychology Inst. (mem. exec. bd. 1990—). Democrat.

SHAH-JAHAN, M. M., economist; b. Dacca, Bangladesh, June 30, 1943; came to U.S., 1975; s. M.M. Serajul Hoq and Ayesha A. Khaton; m. Mahmuda Khatun, Aug. 14, 1972; children: Al M., Nydia. BA in Bus., Dacca U., 1963, MA in Bus., 1964; MA in Econs., Georgetown U., 1982; PhD in Econs., Georgetown-Pacific Western U., 1987. Asst. prof. edn. dept. Dacca Coll., 1965-75, sec. gen. prof. staff coun., 1971-75; audit supr. Marriott Corp., Arlington, Va., 1975-81; economist Potomac Electric Power Co., Washington, 1981—; cons. economist World Bank, Washington, 1988—. Author: (with M.R. Khan) Principles of Income Tax, 1970, Principles of Banking, 1974, An Econometric Forecasting Model, 1988, Jordan: A Macroeconomic Projection, 1988, U.S. Macroeconomic Outlook, 1989, Empirical Open Economy Macromodel for Developing Countries, 1992. Govt. of Pakistan scholar, 1964. Mem. Am. Econ. Assn., WH Swimming Club. Democrat. Islam. Home: 1223 S Buchanan St Arlington VA 22204 Office: Potomac Electric Power Co 1900 Pennsylvania Ave NW Washington DC 20068

SHAHON, LAURIE MERYL, holding company executive; b. Boston, Jan. 28, 1952; m. Kenneth Meister. AB, Wellesley Coll., 1974; MBA, Columbia U., 1976. Assoc. Morgan Stanley and Co. Inc., N.Y.C., 1976-80; dir. retailing and consumer products group Salomon Bros., N.Y.C., 1980-88; with '21' Internat. Holdings Inc., N.Y.C., 1988—.

SHAIEVITZ, SIDNEY, lawyer; b. N.Y.C., Mar. 21, 1935; s. Simon Shaievitz and Rose (Uberman) Breitman; m. Rhoda Joan Vogel, July 11, 1959; children: Jacqueline I., Sondra A. B Chem. Engring., CCNY, 1957; M Chem. Engring., NYU, 1968; JD cum laude, Seton Hall U., 1974. Bar: N.J. 1974, N.Y. 1988; U.S. Dist. Ct. N.J. 1974. Rsch. engr. Air Products & Chemicals, Inc., Trexlertown, Pa., 1957-60, Philips Labs., Briarcliff Manor, N.Y., 1960-66; process engr. Am. Messer Corp., N.Y.C., 1966-68; process engr. Lummus Crest, Inc., Bloomfield, N.J., 1968-75, corp. atty., 1975-78; pvt. practice Bloomfield, N.J., 1978-82; ptnr. Shaievitz & Berowitz, Bloomfield, N.J., 1982—; cons. Maskaleris & Assocs., Morristown, N.J., 1975-78. Patentee in field cryogenic processing. Pres. Livingston (N.J.) Dem. Club, 1982-83; mem. Essex County Dispute Resolution Project, Roseland, N.J., 1989-90. Recipient Am. Jurisprudence award Seton Hall U., Newark, 1974. Mem. N.J. State Bar Assn., Essex County Bar Assn. Jewish. Office: Shaievitz & Berowitz 299 Glenwood Ave Bloomfield NJ 07003-2412

SHAIKH, ZAHIR AHMAD, toxicologist, educator; b. Jullundur, India, Mar. 31, 1945; came to U.S., 1972; s. Zafer Ahmad and Mehmooda Begum (Chohan) S.; m. Mary Butterfield, Aug. 23, 1975; children: Faraz, Kashan, Summur. BSc, U. Karachi, Pakistan, 1965, MSc, 1967; PhD, Dalhousie U., 1972. Rsch. assoc. environ. health U. Okla., Oklahoma City, 1972-73; sr. postdoctoral fellow toxicology U. Rochester, N.Y., 1973-75, asst. prof., 1975-81, assoc. prof., 1981-82; assoc. prof. pharmacology and toxicology U. R.I., Kingston, 1982-86, prof., 1986; chmn. dept. pharmacology and toxicology U. R.I., Kingston, 1985—, mem. toxicology study sect., 1985-89. Contbr. articles to profl. jours. NIH fellow, 1973-75; NIH grantee, 1975—. Mem. AAAS, Am. Soc. Pharmacology and Exptl. Therapeutics, N.Y. Acad. Scis., Soc. Toxicology (past pres. metal sect.), Tissue Culture Assn. Office: U RI Dept Pharmacology and Toxicology Kingston RI 02881

SHAINE, FREDERICK MORDECAI, newspaper executive; b. Cambridge, Mass., Feb. 5, 1916; s. Joseph and Mollie (Prescott) S.; m. Sylvia Pollack, Mar. 21, 1944; 1 child, Frederick Mordecai Jr. (Rick). Student, U. Vt., 1934-35; BS, Columbia U., 1970. From copy boy to advt. sales rep. Boston Herald, 1933, 36-41; advt. rep. O'Mara & Ormsbee, N.Y.C., 1946-58; advt. dir. Book Rev. N.Y. Herald Tribune, 1958-63; bus. mgr. Book Week Nat. Sun newspaper, 1963-66; bus. mgr. Book World, Sun. book rev. Washington Post/Chgo. Tribune, N.Y.C., 1966-72; dir. N.Y. ops. European Stars and Stripes, N.Y.C., 1972—; Transl. from Italian: And No Quarter, 1972; reviewer and translator various publs. Mem. adv. coun. Casa Italiana, Columbia U., 1967-70. With USCG, 1941-45. Mem. Soc. for Italian Hist. Studies, P.E.N., The Players. Home: 930 5th Ave Apt 12F New York NY 10021-2651 Office: European Stars and Stripes 201 Varick St New York NY 10014

SHAINMAN, JACK, art gallery owner; b. Pittsfield, Mass., July 21, 1957; s. Irwin and Bernice (Cohen) S. BS, Am. U., 1980. Asst. dir. Osuna Gallery, Washington, 1981-83; dir. Massimo, Provincetown, Mass., 1983-84; owner, dir. Jack Shainman Gallery, Washington, 1984-88, N.Y.C., 1986—. Office: Jack Shainman Gallery 560 Broadway Fl 2D New York NY 10012-3938

SHAKESPEARE, EASTON GEOFFREY, insurance broker, consultant; b. Mar. 20, 1946; s. Easton Gladstone George and Leonie (Phillips) S.; m. Maria Adina Prescott, Apr. 20, 1968; children: Christpher Geoffrey, Collin Maurice. Group rep. The Guardian Life Ins. Co., N.Y.C., 1979-87; ins. cons. Easton Shakespeare & Assocs. Ins. Agy., Matawan, N.J., 1987—; real estate assoc. Century 21 Iavarone Realty and Era Teitel/Reich Realtors, Matawan, N.J., 1990—, ERA Tietel/Reich Realtors, Matawan, 1990-91, Prudential N.J. Realty, Matawan, 1991; dir., treas. F.F. & G. Assocs.,

Newark, 1991—; cons. Met. LIfe Ins. Co., 1991. Mem. NAACP, Am. Soc. CLU's and Chartered Fin. Cons., N.J. Soc. CLU's amd Chartered Fin. Cons., Nat. Assn. Life Underwriters, Monmouth County, N.J. Bd. of Realtors. Home: 91 Atlantic Ave Matawan NJ 07747-2598

SHALES, THOMAS WILLIAM, writer, journalist, television and film critic; b. Elgin, Ill., Nov. 3, 1948; s. Clyde LeRoy and Hulda Louise (Reko) S. B.A., Am. U., 1973. Entertainment editor Washington Examiner, 1968-71; arts reporter Washington Post, 1971-77, TV editor and chief TV critic, 1977—; film critic, modular arts service Nat. Public Radio, 1970-79, film critic, Morning Edit., 1979—; adj. prof. Am. U., 1978; syndicated columnist On the Air, Washington Post Writers Group, 1979—. Author: The American Film Heritage, 1972, On the Air!, 1982, Legends, 1989. Recipient Disting. Alumnus award Am. U., 1978. Recipient Pulitzer Prize, 1988. Home: 4655 23rd Rd N Arlington VA 22207-3508 Office: Washington Post Co 1150 15th St NW Washington DC 20071-0002

SHALIT, BERNARD LAWRENCE, dentist; b. Quincy, Mass., Feb. 17, 1920; s. L. Melville and Mildred (Kolb) S.; m. Helen L. Shoener, Oct. 11, 1951; children: Barbara L., William L. DMD, Tufts U., 1944; grad. East Coast Aero Tech. Sch., 1981. Pvt. practice dentistry, Quincy. Dir. maintenance Manning Aviation. Served from lt. (j.g.) to lt. Dental Corps. USNR, 1944-46. Life fellow seminars on Hypnosis Found.; mem. Mass. Dental Soc. (life), Am. Dental Assn. (life), Am. Soc. Clin. Hypnosis (life), New Eng. Soc. Clin. Hypnosis, NRA (life), Norfolk County Beekeepers Assn., Masons. Home and Office: 14 Walker St Quincy MA 02171-1924

SHALIT, HANOCH, imaging scientist, executive; b. Tel-Aviv, July 1, 1953; came to U.S., 1982; s. Mordechai and Yael (Bryskier) S. BSc with honors, Poly. of Cen. London, 1978; PhD in Physics, London U., 1981. Asst. photographic scientist John Hadland Ltd., Bovingdon, Eng., 1977-78; demonstrator London U., 1978-81; asst. prof. Rochester (N.Y.) Inst. of Tech., 1981-82; sr. photographic scientist Chemco Photo Products, Glen Cove, N.Y., 1982-83, sr. rsch. project mgr., 1984-87; dir. of photographic sci. Fonar Corp., Melville, N.Y., 1987-88; pres. IMATEC Ltd., Roslyn, N.Y., 1988—. Contbr. articles to profl. jours; patentee in field. With M.C. Israeli Army, 1971-74. Recipient scholarship, London U., 1978-81. Mem. Soc. for Imaging Sci. and Tech., Brit. Assn. for Crystal Growth, Soc. Motion Picture and TV Engrs. (voting mem., subcom. on med. imaging). Home: 86 Edwards St #2a Roslyn Heights NY 11577

SHALLCROSS, DORIS JANE, educator; b. Cranford, N.J., Feb. 28, 1933; d. John William and Ethel Belle (Ruth) S. BA, Montclair State Coll., 1955; MA, Wesleyan U., Middletown, Conn., 1962; EdD, U. Mass., 1973. Tchr. Hunterdon Cen. High Sch., Flemington, N.J., 1955-61, Roosevelt Jr. High Sch., Cleveland Heights, Ohio, 1961-65, Cleveland Heights High Sch., 1965-67; adminstr. Cleveland Heights Pub. Schs., 1967-69; dir. humanistic edn. Montague (Mass.) Pub. Schs., 1972-75; program devel. specialist Tchr. Corps., SUNY, Oneonta, N.Y., 1976-78; asst. prof. edn. Div. Home Econs., U. Mass., Amherst, 1978-82; prof., dir. grad. studies in creativity U. Mass., Amherst, 1982—; pres. bd. trustees Creative Edn. Found., Buffalo, 1989—; bd. dirs. Ctr. for Critical and Creative Thinking, Hartford, Conn., 1989—. Author: Teaching Creative Behavior, 1981; co-author: The Growing Person, 1985, Leadership: Making Things Happen, 1987, Intuition: An Inner Way of Knowing, 1989; cons. editor Jour. Creative Behavior, 1967—; contbr. articles to profl. jours. Mem. Planning Bd., Town of Williamsburg, 1981-89. Recipient Disting. Leader award, Creative Edn. Found., 1986; grantee, NSF, 1987-89, U. Mass., 1987-89. Mem. NEA, Mass. Soc. of Profs., Assn. for Transpersonal Psychology, Inst. for Noetic Scis., World Coun. for Gifted Chidlren, Am. Creativity Assn. (bd. dirs. 1990—). Home: 26 S Main St Haydenville MA 01039-9735 Office: Univ of Mass 361 Hills S Amherst MA 01003

SHAMBERG-WEISBERG, BARBARA A(NN), psychologist; b. Atlantic City, July 22, 1953; d. Martin and Margaret (Fox) S.; m. Allan Weisberg, Aug. 29, 1987; 1 child, Lauren Margaret. BA, New Coll., 1975; MA, Hofstra U., 1979, PhD, 1984. Lic. psychologist, N.Y. Mem. faculty Fairleigh Dickinson U., Madison, N.Y., 1977; psychologist Hofstra U., Hempstead, N.Y., 1978-84, SUNY, Farmingdale, 1981-82, Bd. of Coop. Ednl. Svcs., Yorktown, N.Y., 1982-83, N.Y.C. (N.Y.) Bd. Edn., 1983-88; supervising psychologist Childrens' Village, Dobbs Ferry, N.Y., 1989—; pvt. practice clin. psychology N.Y.C. and Scarsdale, N.Y., 1984—; sr. clin. cons. psychologist Ctr. for Behavior Therapy, Scarsdale, 1989—; lectr., workshop leader in field; expert interviewee ABC News, N.Y.C., Sta. WMID, Atlantic City. Author: Wives' Marital Satisfaction, 1984. Bd. dirs. 218 E. 29th St. Owners' Corp., 1984-89. Mem. Am. Psychol. Assn., N.Y. State Psychol. Assn., Westchester County Psychol. Assn., Am. Assn. Behavioral Therapists. Home: 4 Hidden Glen Rd Scarsdale NY 10583-1229 Office: Ctr for Behavior Therapy 1495 Weaver St Scarsdale NY 10583-7018

SHAMES, ERVIN RICHARD, footwear executive; b. Des Moines, July 6, 1940; s. David S. and Evelyn (Grund) Williams; m. Louise Ginson, May 24, 1964; children: Allyson, Steven. B.S.B.A., U. Fla., 1962; M.B.A., Harvard U., 1966. With Gen. Foods Corp., White Plains, N.Y., 1967-89; group exec. external devel., info. services and corp. planning, successively group v.p., coffee and food service, pres. Maxwell House div., group v.p. Gen. Foods Europe, Brussels, 1979-82, exec. v.p., pres. internat. ops., 1982-86, sr. exec. v.p. U.S. grocery bus., 1986-87; pres., chief exec. officer Gen. Foods U.S.A., 1987-89; pres. Kraft USA, 1989; chmn., pres., chief exec. officer The Kendall Co., 1989-90; pres., chief exec. officer The Stride Rite Corp., 1990—, chmn. bd., 1992—; bd. dirs. First Brands Corp., 1987—. Vice chmn. Alvin Alley Am. Dance Theater, 1985-89; bd. visitors Fugua Sch. Bus., Duke U., 1988—, Coll. Bus. Adminstrn., Northeastern U., 1990—; bd. overseers New Eng. Med. Ctr., Inc., 1992—; bd. trustees Com. for Econ. Devel., 1992—. Mem. Harvard Bus. Sch. Alumni Assn. (bd. dirs. 1991—).

SHAMES, GEORGE HERBERT, former psychology educator; b. Pitts., May 16, 1926; s. Harry and Hilda (Julius) S.; m. Joan Carol Kramer, June 15, 1966; children: Hilary, Matthew. BS, U. Pitts., 1948, MS, 1949, PhD, 1952. Lic. psychologist, Pa., speech pathologist, Pa. Instr. psychology U. Pitts., 1950-52, from asst. prof. to prof., 1962-90, prof. emeritus, 1991—; vis. prof. Med. Ctr. U. Miami (Fla.), 1966—, U. NSW, Sydney, Australia, 1976—; cons. VA hosps., Pitts. area, 1967-90, Vocaltech, Inc., St. Claire, Pa., 1985-90, others; cons. workshops, U.S., Mex., Can.; appeared on various programs including Today Show, ABC Health Show, CBS Evening Mag., others; featured in Newsweek Mag., Parade Mag., others. Developer therapy stutter-free speech therapy, vocal feedback therapy, 1988; patentee vocal feedback device; contbr. articles to profl. jours. Fellow Am. Speech, Lang., Hearing Assn.; mem. Pa. Speech and Hearing Assn., Am. Psychol. Assn., Sigma Xi. Home: 216 Gladstone Rd Pittsburgh PA 15217-1112

SHAMES, JORDAN NELSON, health care executive, consultant health services; b. Malden, Mass., June 27, 1949; s. Abraham and Annette (Harris) S.; m. Joni Schechter, Apr. 15, 1984; children: Robert Zachary, Rebecca Naomi. BS in Polit. Sci., Allegheny Coll., 1971; postgrad., U. Ky., 1973-74, New Sch. for Social Rsch., N.Y.C., 1983-85. Real estate and nursing home property mgr. H.R.F. Co., Triplex Ltd., Bethpage, N.Y., 1974-77; L.I., N.Y.C. area mgr. Quality Care, Rockville Centre, N.Y., 1977-80; exec. dir. Health Force, East Meadow, N.Y., 1980-82; adminstr. Med. Personnel Pool, White Plains, N.Y., 1982-83; exec. dir. Continental Health Affiliates, White Plains, 1983-85; exec. dir. Community Home Care, Bronx, N.Y., 1985-88, pres., 1989—; cons., pres. Jordan Shames Enterprises, Forest Hills, N.Y., 1985—; mem. profl. adv. bd. Beth Abraham Hosp. Home Health Agy., Bronx, 1986—; bd. dirs. Home Health Mgmt., Inc.; chmn. bd. Bronx Community Home Care, Inc., 1989—; interviewee Nat. Pub. Radio, 1989; bd. dirs. Bedford Park Multi-Svc. Ctr., Bronx, 1991—. Co-author: Home Health Services Quarterly, 1985, Caring Mag., 1987. Bd. dirs. Bedford Park Multi-Svc. Ctr., Bronx, 1991—; mem. lobby renovation com. Gerard Owners Corp. Coop., Forest Hills, 1986-87, chmn. fin. com., 1991-92; mem. community affairs com. Forest Hills Jewish Ctr., 1990—. Recipient Army Commendation medal, 1974, Cert. Appreciation, Am. Heart Assn., 1976. Mem. Nat. Assn. Home Care (presenter ann. meeting 1985, 89), N.Y. State Home Care Assn. (ann. meeting com. 1990, presenter ann. meeting 1990, 91, svcs. com. 1991, nominating com. 1992), Hospice Assn. Am., Masons. Republican. Jewish. Office: Community Home Care 2532 Boston Rd Bronx NY 10467-9004

SHAMOS, MORRIS HERBERT, physicist educator; b. Cleve., Sept. 1, 1917; s. Max and Lillian (Wasser) S.; m. Marion Jean Cahn, Nov. 26, 1942; 1 son, Michael Ian. A.B., NYU, 1941, M.S., 1943, Ph.D., 1948; postgrad., MIT, 1941-42. Faculty NYU, 1942—, prof. physics, 1959-83, prof. emeritus, 1983—; chmn. dept. Washington Sq. Coll., 1957-70; sr. v.p. research and devel. Technicon Corp., 1970-75, chief sci. officer, 1975-83, also dir., prin. sci. cons., 1983—; pres. M.H. Shamos & Assocs., 1983—; chmn. Protein Databases, Inc., 1985-90, Sci. Imaging Corp., 1985-88; dir. Anagen Ltd., 1989—, Nat. Assn for Sci., Tech. & Soc., 1990-91; Cons. pvt. industry; cons. Office Armament Center, USAF, 1955-57, Tung-Sol Electric, Inc., 1949-65, Office Pub. Information, UN, 1958, NBC, 1957-67, AEC, 1957-70, N.Y. Eye and Ear Infirmary, 1961-64, 79—, L.I. Jewish Hosp., 1962—, N.Y.C. Health Dept., 1961-70, Technicon Instruments Corp., 1964-70, U.S. Office Edn., 1964-72. Author: Great Experiments in Physics, 1959; co-editor: Recent Advances in Science, 1956, Industrial and Safety Problems of Nuclear Technology, 1950; cons. editor, Addison-Wesley Pub. Co., 1965-69; adv. bd.: Jour. Coll. Sci. Teaching, 1971-75, 76-80, Clin. Lab. Guide, Am. Chem. Soc, 1972-76. Dir. tng., N.Y.C. Office Civil Def., 1950-54; subscribing mem. N.Y. Philharmonic Soc.; mem. adv. council Pace U., 1971—, N.Y. Poly. Inst., 1980—; trustee Hackley Sch., 1971-80, Westchester Arts Council. Poly. U. fellow. Fellow N.Y. Acad. Scis. (past chmn. phys. scis., bd. govs. 1977-83, rec. sec. 1978-80, v.p. 1980-81, pres. 1982), AAAS; mem. Nat. Assn. Ednl. Broadcasters, Am. Phys. Soc., IEEE, AAUP, AFTRA, Am. Chem. Soc., Nat. Sci. Tchrs. Assn. Am. (pres. 1967), Assn. Physics Tchrs. Britain, Chemist's Club, Am. Assn. Clin. Chemists, Phi Beta Kappa, Sigma Xi, Pi Mu Epsilon, Sigma Pi Sigma. Club: Cosmos. Home: 3515 Henry Hudson Pky Bronx NY 10463-1326

SHAMY, ROBERT GEORGE, education educator; b. New Brunswick, N.J., June 8, 1945; s. Frank and Rose (Boutros) S. BS in Edn., U. N. Ala., 1968; MEd, Rutger's U., 1974. Tchr. Monroe Twp. (N.J.) Bd. of Edn., 1968—; dir. Monroe Twp. High Sch. Archaeology Mus., 1974—. Contbr. articles to profl. jours. N.J. State mini-grantee N.J. Dept. of Edn., 1974, N.J. Govs. and Tchr. grantee, 1987; named Middlesex County Tchr. of Yr., N.J. State Dept. Edn., 1989. Mem. N.J. Council for Social Studies (pres. 1991-92), Southeastern Social Studies Coun. Home: 59 Carriage Ln Englishtown NJ 07726-1640 Office: Monroe Twp High Sch Perrineville Rd Jamesburg NJ 08831-1604

SHANBACKER, FRANK MORSE, III, television news producer; b. Bryn Mawr, Pa., Oct. 2, 1946; s. Frank M. Jr. and Adele (Sislian) S. BA in English, U. Pa., 1968; MA in English, NYU, 1970. Page NBC, N.Y.C., 1970, awards writer, 1970-72, researcher news spl. broadcasts, 1972-73, writer news spl. broadcasts, 1973-79, producer Nightly News, 1979-90, producer Expose, 1990-91, producer Dateline NBC, 1992, sr. producer news spl. programs, 1990. Treas. Midtown North Precinct Community Coun., N.Y.C., 1991—. Emmy nominee TV Acad. Arts and Scis., 1989. Office: NBC News 30 Rockefeller Plaza Rm 510 New York NY 10112

SHANBACKER, KIAMIL EDWARD, association executive; b. Bryn Mawr, Pa., Oct. 8, 1952; s. Frank Morse and Adele (Sislian) S.; m. Noreen C. O'Meara, May 21, 1977; 1 child, Elizabeth Ellen. BA, NYU, 1974; MPA, Am. U., 1983. Social worker S.S. Day Care Ctr., Bronx, N.Y., 1974-76, Vis. Nurse Svc., N.Y.C., 1976-77; region supr. Capitol Hill Homemaker and Home Health Aid Svc., Washington, 1977-78; program specialist U.S. Dept. Labor, Washington, 1979-80; asst. exec. dir. Montgomery County Med. Soc., Rockville, Md., 1980-86, exec. dir., 1986—; dir. Community Clinics Md., Rockville, 1984-86. Commr. Adv. Neighborhood Com. 3-E, Washington, 1985-87. Mem. Am. Soc. Assn. Execs., Am. Assn. Med. Soc. Execs., Greater Washington Soc. Assn. Execs., Pi Alpha Alpha. Democrat. Episcopalian. Home: 4615 Alton Pl NW Washington DC 20016-2039 Office: Montgomery County Med Soc PO Box 5689 Rockville MD 20855-0689

SHANE, ROBERT SAMUEL, chemical engineer; b. Chgo., Dec. 8, 1910; s. Jacob and Selma (Shayne) S.; m. Jeanne Felice Lazarus, Aug. 21, 1936; children: Stephen H., Susan R., Jacqueline G. SB, U. Chgo., 1930, PhD, 1933. Plant supt. Amecco Chems., Rochester, N.Y., 1941-42; plant chemist Bausch & Lomb Optical Co., Rochester, 1942-46; project supr. Wyandotte (Mich.) Chems. Corp., 1952-54; assoc. dir. rsch. Davis & Geck div. Am. Cyanamid, Danbury, Conn., 1954-55; mgr. chem., ceramics, powder metals Westinghouse Atomic Power, Forest Hills, Pa., 1955-57; nucleonics specialist Bell Aircraft Co., Niagara Falls, N.Y., 1958-59; mgr. parts, materials, process engring. GE, Valley Forge, Pa., 1959-69; staff cons. Nat. Materials Adv. Bd., Washington, 1969-80; prin. Shane Assocs., Wynnewood, Pa., 1980—; cons. in field; editor material engring. Marcel Dekker, Inc., N.Y.C., 1983—. Author, editor: Space Radiation Effects on Materials, 1962, Predictive Testing, 1972, Materials and Processes, 1985; author: Technology Transfer & Innovation, 1982; mem. editorial bd. Jour. Testing and Evaluation, 1985—; editor: Testing for Prediction of Material Performance, 1972; contbr. articles to profl. jours. Adult leader Boy Scouts Am.; organizer Literacy Coun., Ardmore, Pa., 1988. Recipient Joseph Stewart award Am. Chem. Soc., 1976. Fellow ASTM (award of merit 1973), Am. Inst. Chem. Engrs.; mem. Am. Soc. for Metals Internat. (life), Sigma Xi. Office and Home: 238 Hemlock Rd Wynnewood PA 19096-1115 Office (winter): 10701 S Ocean Dr Jensen Beach FL 34957-2634

SHANEBROOK, JOHN RICHARD, mechanical engineering educator, consultant; b. Syracuse, N.Y., July 10, 1938; s. John Abraham and Lois Levine (Doss) S.; m. Joan Faith Eisler, Dec. 9, 1967; children: Jill Faith, Julie Marie. BSME, Syracuse U., 1960, MSME, 1963, PhD in Mech. Engring., 1965. Instr. Syracuse U., 1964-65; asst. prof. mech. engring. Union Coll., Schenectady, 1965-69, assoc. prof., 1969-75, prof., 1975—, chmn. dept., 1974-79; cons. N.Y. State Dept. Edn., Albany, 1978, A.W. Proskin, Albany, 1978, Cowan & Latman, P.C., N.Y.C., 1989, Houghton Mifflin Co., Boston, 1991. Author: Energy One, 1990; co-patentee heart valve, blood pump, catheter. Co-chmn. campaign United Way, Union Coll., 1982-84; mem. adv. com. Niskayuna (N.Y.) Schs., 1982-83; advisor Big Bros. and Big Sisters, Union Coll., 1985-87. Rsch. grantee NSF, 1967-72, Engring. Found., 1973-75. Mem. ASME, Union Concerned Scientists, Tau Beta Pi (faculty advisor 1966-74), Pi Tau Sigma (faculty advisor 1991—). Office: Union Coll Mech Engring Dept Schenectady NY 12308

SHANEFIELD, DANIEL JAY, ceramics engineering educator; b. Orange, N.J., Apr. 29, 1930; s. Benjamin and Nan (Leichter) S.; m. Elizabeth Davis, June 28, 1964; children: Alison, Douglas. BS in Chemistry, Yale U., 1952; PhD in Chemistry, Rutgers U., 1962. Sr. project engr. ITT Group, Nutley, N.J., 1962-67; sr. mem. tech. staff AT&T Bell Labs., Princeton, N.J., 1967-86; disting. prof. Rutgers U., New Brunswick, N.J., 1986—; chmn. standards com. IEEE, Piscataway, N.J., 1984—. Co-author: Defects in Gold Plating, 1981; Contbr. 4 chpts. to tech. books; co-inventor 17 patents; assoc. editor Jour. Am. Ceramic Soc., 1987—. With U.S. Army, 1952-54, Korea. Fellow Am. Inst. Chemists; mem. Am. Chem. Soc., Am. Ceramics Soc. Republican. Home: 119 Jefferson Rd Princeton NJ 08540-3373 Office: Rutgers U Ceramics Engring Dept PO Box 909 Piscataway NJ 08855-0909

SHANK, BRENDA M., radiation oncologist; b. Cleve., Sept. 25, 1939; d. John Frederick and Dorothy May (Zieburtz) Buckhold; m. Charles V. Shank, June 16, 1969. BA in Chemistry, Case Western Res. U., 1961, PhD in Biophysics, 1966; MD, U. Medicine & Dentistry N.J., 1976. Diplomate Am. Bd. Radiology. Resident Meml. Sloan-Kettering Cancer Ctr., N.Y.C., 1976-79, fellow in radiation oncology/immunology, 1979-80, clin. asst. attending radiation oncologist, 1980-81, asst. attending radiation oncologist, 1981-85, assoc. attending radiation oncologist, 1985-89; assoc. attending radiation oncologist NYU, N.Y.C., 1980-89; dir., attending radiation oncologist Mt. Sinai Hosp., N.Y.C., 1989—; instr. Cornell U. Med. Ctr., N.Y.C., 1980-82, asst. prof., 1982-85, assoc. prof., 1985-89; chmn., prof. Mt. Sinai Sch. Medicine, 1989—. Contbr. articles to profl. jours. Fellow Am. Cancer Soc., 1976-84. Fellow Am. Coll. Radiology; mem. Am. Soc. Therapeutic Radiol. Oncology, Radiation Rsch. Soc., European Soc. Therapeutic Radiol. Oncology. Office: Mt Sinai Hosp Radiation Oncol Dept Box 1236 1 Gustave L Levy Pl New York NY 10029-6574

SHANK, PETER RABE, virologist, educator; b. Ithaca, N.Y., Feb. 17, 1946; s. Donald Jay and Ruth (Rabe) S.; m. Kathleen Ryan, Aug. 15, 1970; children: Jonathan Ryan, Jeffrey Stephen. BS, Cornell U., 1968; PhD, U. N.C., 1973; MS (hon.), Brown U., 1983. Postdoctoral fellow dept. microbiology U. Calif., San Francisco, 1974-77, vis. asst. prof. microbiology, 1977-78; asst. prof. med. sci. Brown U., Providence, 1978-83, assoc. prof., 1983-92, prof., 1992—; cons. NIH, Nat. Inst. Allergy and Infectious Diseases, Nat. Cancer Inst., Bethesda, Md., 1983—; vis. scientist NIH, Nat. Cancer Inst. Lab. Molecular Virology, Bethesda, 1986-87. Assoc. editor: Virology, 1991—; contbr. over 50 articles to profl. jours. Grantee NIH, 1978—, Am. Found. AIDS Rsch., 1988. Mem. AAAS, Am. Soc. Microbiology, Am. Soc. Virology, Soc. Gen. Microbiology. Office: Brown U PO Box G-B 629 Providence RI 02912-0001

SHANKAR, RATNASWAMY, manufacturing company executive, engineer; b. Coimbatore, Madras, India, Aug. 19, 1942; s. Subramanian and Pattu (Gangadharan) Ratnaswamy. B.S. in Engring., Poona U., Maharashtra, India, 1963; MS in Indsl. Engring. Indian Inst. Tech., Madras, 1968. Jr. engr. Dastur & Co., Calcutta, India, 1964-65, M & M Ltd., Bombay, India, 1966-67; asst. engr. Larsen & Toubro Ltd., Bombay, 1968-73; prodn. engr. Tork, Inc., Mt. Vernon, N.Y., 1973-75, materials mgr., 1975-79, v.p., 1979-85, exec. v.p., 1986-87, pres., chief operating officer, 1987—. Recipient Merit award Indian Inst. Tech., Madras, India, 1968. Mem. Inst. Indsl. Engrs. (v.p. Tappanzee chpt. 1981-82, pres. 1982-84), Am. Prodn. and Inventory Control Soc. Office: Tork Inc 1 Grove St Mount Vernon NY 10550-2450

SHANKMAN, GARY CHARLES, art educator; b. Washington, Sept. 30, 1950; s. Bernard and Barbara Emeline (Robertson) S. BFA, Boston U., 1972; MFA, Am. U., 1975; postgrad., Koninklijke Academie, Antwerp, 1975-76, Skowhegan Sch. Painting and Sculpture, Maine, 1978. Instr. No. Va. Community Coll., Woodbridge, Va., 1978-85; instr. continuing edn. dept. U. D.C., Washington, 1978-86, Md. Coll. Art and Design, Silver Spring, 1981-86, Smithsonian Instn., Washington, 1978—; assoc. prof. Sage Jr. Coll., Albany, N.Y., 1986—; judge Ea. N.Y. State regional scholastic art exhbn. N.Y. State Mus., Albany, 1987—. One-man shows include Seta House, Antwerp, Belgium, 1976, H.C. Dickens, London, 1982, Mickelson Gallery, Washington, 1981, 85, 88, 92, Shelnutt Gallery, RPI, Troy, N.Y., 1989; represented in permanent collections Mabee-Gerrer Mus. of Shawnee, Okla., Superior Ct. Art Trust, Washington. Home: 157 S Lake Ave # 2 Albany NY 12208-3202 Office: Sage Jr Coll of Albany 140 New Scotland Ave Albany NY 12208-3425

SHANKS, JUDITH WEIL, editor; b. Montgomery, Ala., Nov. 2, 1941; d. Roman Lee and Charlotte (Alexander) Weil; m. Hershel Shanks, Feb. 20, 1966; children: Elizabeth Jeannette, Julia Emily. BA in Econs., Wellesley Coll., 1963; MBA, Trinity Coll., 1980. Econs. asst. Export-Import Bank, Washington, 1963-68; cons. econs. and social sci., 1968-76; researcher Time-Life Books, Alexandria, Va., 1976-80, prin. researcher, 1980-83, illustrations editor, 1983, editorial adminstr., 1984—. Vol. dinner program for homeless women; bd. dirs. Anne Frank House, for formerly homeless women. Mem. Garden Writers Am., Internat. Alliance, Washington Alliance Bus. Women, Leadership Greater Washington, Washington Wellesley Club (career caucus). Democrat. Jewish. Home: 5208 38th St NW Washington DC 20015-1812

SHANMAN, JAMES ALAN, lawyer; b. Cin., Aug. 1, 1942; s. Jerome D. and Mildred Louise (Bloch) S.; m. Marilyn Louise Glassman, June 11, 1972; 1 child, Ellen Joan. BS, U. Pa., 1963; JD, Yale U., 1966. Bar: N.Y. 1967, U.S. Ct. Mil. Appeals 1971, U.S. Supreme Ct. 1971, U.S. Ct. Appeals (2d cir.) 1972, U.S. Dist. Ct. (so. and ea. dists.) N.Y. 1972, U.S. Ct. Internat. Trade 1976, U.S. Ct. Appeals (fed. cir.) 1987, U.S. Dist. Ct. (ea. dist.) Mich. 1989. Assoc. Cahill Gordon & Reindel, N.Y.C., 1971-74, Freeman, Meade, Wasserman, Sharfman & Schneider, N.Y.C., 1974-76; mem. firm Sharfman, Shanman, Poret & Siviglia, P.C., N.Y.C., 1976—; speaker on reins. law topics. Capt. USAF, 1966-71. Mem. ABA, N.Y. State Bar Assn., Assn. of Bar of City of N.Y. (com. ins. law, 1985-88, 1990-92, com. profl. liability ins. 1988-92, com. on assn. ins. plans 1989—), Am. Arbitration Assn. (comml. panel arbitrators), Air Force Assn., Lotos Club. Office: Sharfman Shanman Poret & Siviglia PC 750 Lexington Ave New York NY 10022-1200

SHANN, MARY HALLIGAN, education educator; b. Albany, N.Y., Aug. 23, 1945; d. John Phillip and Katherine (McLaughlin) H.; m. Robert Allen Shann, Dec. 28, 1968; children: Ryan Patrick, Derek Thomas. BS, Boston Coll., 1966, MEd, 1967, PhD, 1969. Cert. secondary sci. and math. tchr., Mass. Asst. prof. Boston U., 1969-75, assoc. prof., 1975-80, assoc. dean, 1980-85, prof. edn., 1986—; prof. in residence overseas grad. programs Boston U., Europe, 1971-72; project dir. NSF, 1973-77, World Bank, Cairo U., 1981-89; prin. investigator U.S. Dept. Edn., Boston, 1986-90; evaluator NSF applications of advanced technology, rsch. on teaching and learning, 1988—, Minority Scholars Program, Boston, 1990—; designer, adviser preparation of Portuguese tchr. educators program, Lisbon, 1980-85; proposal reviewer NSF, Washington, 1975—, U.S. Dept. Edn., Washington, 1989—; advisor Boston Compact, 1989—; chair faculty awards screening com. Fulbright Found., 1987-90. Guest columnist Boston Tchrs.' Union Newsletter, 1991—; contbr. articles, reports to profl. pubLs. Fulbright scholar Fed. U. Ceara, Brazil, 1985-86. Fellow Phi Delta Beta; mem. Am. Ednl. Rsch. Assn. (internat. com. 1988-91, govt. and profl. liaison com. 1984-87, exec. com. instnl. affiliates 1981-84, 87-90). Office: Boston U 605 Commonwealth Ave Boston MA 02215-1605

SHAPER, CHRISTOPHER THORNE, sales executive; b. Columbus, Ohio, Sept. 6, 1955; s. Charles R. and M. Caroline (Garringer) S. BA, Wake Forest U., 1977; MA in Mgmt., Coll. of Notre Dame, 1992. Sales rep. Intex Products Inc., Winston-Salem, N.C., 1977-78; tech. sales rep. Am. Can Co., Oak Brook, Ill., 1979-81, J.T. Baker Chem. Co., Atlanta, 1981-83; corp. accts. rep. Chemetals, Inc., Glen Burnie, Md., 1983-84, industry sales mgr., 1984—. Mem. Am. Chem. Soc., Nat. Feed Ingredient Assn., Am. Feed Industries Assn. Republican. Roman Catholic. Home: PO Box 663 Pasadena MD 21122-0104 Office: Chemetals Inc 711 Pittman Rd Baltimore MD 21226-1788

SHAPIRO, ARTHUR JOSEPH, sales executive; b. Cape May Courthouse, N.J., Oct. 5, 1952; s. Sandy and Phyliss Shapiro. BSME, Drexel U., 1976; MS, Johns Hopkins U., 1990. Registered profl. engr., Md., Fla. Mgr. filter products Environ. Elements Corp., Balt., 1975-87; capital projects mgr. State of Md., Balt., 1987-90; mgr. mcpl. sales Katadyn Systems Inc., Bedford Hills, N.Y., 1990-91, v.p. mktg. & sales, 1992—. Mem. ASME, NSPE, Md. Soc. Profl. Engrs. (pres. 1990-91, v.p. Balt. chpt. 1989-90). Home: 3123 Walnut Ave Owings Mills MD 21117-1113 Office: Katadyn Systems Inc 299 Adams St Bedford Hills NY 10507

SHAPIRO, ASCHER HERMAN, mechanical engineer, educator, consultant; b. Bklyn., May 20, 1916; s. Bernard and Jennie (Kaplan) S.; m. Sylvia Charm, Dec. 24, 1939 (div. 1959); children: Peter Mark, Martha Ann, Bernett Mary; m. Regina Julia Lee, June 4, 1961 (div. 1972); m. Kathleen Larke Crawford, Sept. 6, 1985. Student, CCNY, 1932-35; S.B., MIT, 1938, Sc.D., 1946; D.Sc. (honoris causa), Salford U., Eng., 1978, Technion-Israel Inst. Tech., 1985. Asst. mech. engring. MIT, 1938-40, faculty, 1940—, prof. mech. engring., 1952—, prof. charge fluid mechanics div., mech. engring. dept., 1954-65, Ford prof. engring., 1962-75, chmn. faculty, 1964-65, head dept. mech. engring., 1965-74, inst. prof., 1975-86, inst. prof. emeritus, sr. lectr., 1986—; vis. prof. applied thermodynamics U. Cambridge, Eng., 1955-56; Akroyd Stuart Meml. lectr. Nottingham (Eng.) U., 1956; editor Acad. Press, Inc., 1962-65; cons. United Aircraft Corp., M.W. Kellogg Co., Arthur D. Little, Inc., Hardie-Tynes Mfg. Co., Carbon & Carbide Chems. Corp., Oak Ridge, Rohm & Haas Co., Ultrasonic Corp., Jackson & Moreland (Engrs.), Stone & Webster, Bendix Aviation, Oak Ridge Nat. Lab., Acushnet Processing Co., Kennecott Copper Co., Welch Sci., Sargent-Welch, Bird Machine Co., Organogenesis, Inc.; others; served on sub-coms. on turbines, internal flow, compressors and turbines NACA; mem. Lexington Project to study and report on nuclear powered flight to AEC, summer 1948; dir. Project Dynamo to study and report to AEC on technol. and econs. nuclear power for civilian use, 1953, Lamp Wick study Office Naval Research, 1955; mem. tech. adv. panel aeronautics Dept. Def.; cons. ops. evaluation group Navy Dept.; sci. adv. bd. USAF, 1964-66; founder, mem. Nat. Com. for Fluid Mechanics Films, 1962—, chmn., 1962-65, 71—; chmn. com. on ednl. films Commn. on Engring. Edn., 1962-65; dir. lab. for devel. power plants for use in torpedoes Navy Dept., 1943-45; mem. ad hoc med. devices com. FDA, HEW, 1970-72; mem. com. Nat. Council for Research and Devel., Israel, 1971—; mem. com. sci. and pub. policy Nat. Acad. Scis., 1970-74. Author: The Dynamics and Thermodynamics of Compressible Fluid Flow,

vol. 1, 1953, vol. 2, 1954 (with Chinese tranls.), Shape and Flow, 1961 (Japanese, Italian, German and Spanish transls.); also 3 ednl. films, 39 videotape lecture series: Fluid Dynamics, 1984; contbr. 125 articles to scientific jours.; editorial bd.: Jour. Applied Mechanics, 1955-56; editorial com.: Ann. Rev. Fluid Mechanics, 1967-71; mem. editorial bd.: MIT Press, 1977-87, chmn., 1982-87. Mem. Town Meeting Arlington, Mass.; chmn. 1st Mass. chpt. Atlantic Union Com., 1951-52, mem. council, 1954—; bd. govs. Technion, Israel Inst. Tech., 1968-89. Recipient Naval Ordnance Devel. award, 1945; joint certificate outstanding contbn. War and Navy depts., 1947; Richards Meml. award ASME, 1960; Worcester Reed Warner medal, 1965; Fluids Engring. award, 1981; Townsend Harris medal Coll. City N.Y., 1978. Fellow AIAA, Am. Acad. Arts and Scis. (councillor 1967-71), ASME; mem. Am. Sci. Films Assn., Nat. Acad. Scis. (com. on sci. and pub. policy 1973-77), Nat. Acad. Engring. (adv. com. on edn. 1985-89), Biomed. Engring. Soc. (charter mem. 1968), AAAS, Am. Soc. Engring. Edn. (Lamme medal 1977), MIT Faculty Club, Cavendish Club (Brookline, Mass.), Sigma Xi, Tau Beta Pi, Pi Tau Sigma. Home: 111 Perkins St # 86 Jamaica Plain MA 02130-4313

SHAPIRO, BENNETT MICHAELS, biochemist, educator; b. Phila., July 14, 1939; s. Simon and Sara (Michaels) S.; m. Fredericka Foster, Mar. 13, 1982; children: Lisa, Lise, Jonathan. BS, Dickinson Coll., 1960; MD, Jefferson Med. Coll., 1964. Research assoc. NHLI, NIH, 1965-68, med. officer, 1970-71; vis. scientist Inst. Pasteur, Paris, 1968-70; from assoc. prof. to full prof. biochemistry U. Wash., 1971-90, chmn. biochemistry dept., 1985-90; exec. v.p. for worldwide basic rsch. Merck, Sharp and Dohme Rsch. Labs., Rahway, N.J., 1990—. Contbr. articles to profl. jour. Served as surgeon USPHS, 1968-70. John S. Guggenheim fellow, 1982; Japan Soc. for Promotion Sci., 1984. Mem. Am. Soc. Biol. Chemists, Am. Soc. Cell Biology, Am. Soc. Devel. Biology, Phi Beta Kappa, Alpha Omega Alpha. Office: Merck Sharp and Dohme Rsch Labs PO Box 2000 Rahway NJ 07065-0900

SHAPIRO, DAVID JOEL, poet, art critic, educator; b. Newark, Jan. 2, 1947; s. Irving Shapiro and Fraida Chagy; m. Lindsay Stamm, Aug. 30, 1970; 1 child, Daniel Jonathan Stamm. BA magna cum laude, Columbia U., 1968, PhD in English with distinction, 1973; BA with 1st honours, Cambridge (Eng.) U., 1970, MA, 1974. Lectr., instr., asst. prof. Columbia U., N.Y.C., 1972-81, vis. prof., 1987, 88; assoc. prof. William Paterson Coll., N.J., 1980—; vis. prof. creative writing Bklyn. Coll., CUNY, 1979; vis. lectr. visual arts Princeton (N.J.) U., 1982-83; vis. adj. prof. Cooper Union, N.Y.C., 1980—; editorial assoc. Res, Harvard mag. in anthropology and aesthetics. Author: January, 1965, Poems from Deal, 1969, A Man Holding an Acoustic Panel, 1971, The Page Turner, 1973, Lateness, 1977, House (Blown Apart), 1988, Introduction to John Ashbery's Poetry, (chapbook, with Terry Winters) After a Lost Original, numerous others; author critical books on Jasper Johns, Mondrian's Flowers, Jim Dine; mem. editorial bd. Blvd., Architectures; former mem. editorial bd. Little Mag. Bd. advisors Poet's House, N.Y.C. Recipient poetry prize Gotham Book Mart, 1962, Triennial Zabel prize Nat. Acad. and Inst. Arts and Letters, 1977; grantee Merrill Found., 1967, NEH and Nat. Endowment for the Arts, 1978-80; Kellett fellow Cambridge U. Jewish. Home: 3001 Henry Hudson Pky Bronx NY 10463-4717

SHAPIRO, ELAINE, psychologist; b. N.Y.C., July 25, 1925; d. Abraham and May (Meyerson) Schlaffer; children: Peter T., Moira D. Shapiro Tollefson, Kaethe S. BA, CUNY, 1953; PhD, U. Chgo., 1963. Intern in clin. psychology U. Ill., Chgo., 1954-55; clin. psychologist Mass. Mental Health Ctr., Boston, 1956-57; rsch. asst., asst. instr. Harvard U., Cambridge, Mass., 1957-58; sr. psychologist Mt. Vernon (N.Y.) Mental Health Ctr., 1964-67; asst. clin. prof. psychology in psychiatry Payne Whitney Clinic, N.Y. Hosp., Cornell U., N.Y.C., 1968-77; co-dir. Tourette and Tic Lab. and Clinic, N.Y.C., 1977-87, 1987—; med. adv. bd. Tourette Syndrome Assn., 1975-86; exec. dir. Tourette Rsch. Found., 1980—; assoc. clin. prof. psychiatry Mt. Sinai Sch. Medicine, N.Y.C., 1977—. Author: Gilles de la Tourette Syndrome, 1978, 2d edit., 1988. Mem. Am. Psychol. Assn., Sigma Xi. Home and Office: Tourette and Tic Lab/Clinic 17 Colvin Rd Scarsdale NY 10583-1407

SHAPIRO, ELI, business consultant, educator, economist; b. Bklyn., June 13, 1916; s. Samuel and Pauline (Kushel) S.; m. Beatrice Ferbend, Jan. 18, 1946; 1 child, Laura J. A.B., Bklyn. Coll., 1936; A.M., Columbia U., 1937, Ph.D., 1939. Instr. Bklyn. Coll., 1936-41; rsch. assoc. Nat. Bur. Econ. Rsch., 1938-39; cons. Nat. Bur. Econ. Research, 1939-42; mem. rsch. staff Nat. Bur. Econ. Rsch., 1955-62; asst. prof. fin. U. Chgo., 1946-47, asso. prof., 1948-52, prof., 1952; prof. fin. Mass. Inst. Tech., 1952-61; assoc. dean Mass. Inst. Tech. (Sch. Indsl. Mgmt.), 1954-58, Alfred P. Sloan prof. mgmt., 1976-84, Alfred P. Sloan prof. emeritus, 1984—; prof. fin. Harvard Bus. Sch., 1962-72, Sylvan C. Coleman prof. fin. mgmt., 1968-72; chmn. fin. com., dir. Travelers Ins. Cos., Hartford, Conn., 1971-78; vice chmn. bd., dir. Travelers Ins. Cos., 1976-78; chmn. bd. Mass. Co., 1971-72; pres. Nat. Bur. Econ. Research, 1982-84; chmn. bd. Fed. Home Loan Bank Boston, 1970-89; econ. analyst div. monetary rsch. U.S. Dept. Treasury, 1941-42; economist rsch. div. OPA, 1941-42; staff cons. Com. Econ. Devel., 1950-51, mem. rsch. adv. com., 1961-64, 69—, project dir., 1966-69; cons. to sec. treasury; mem. enforcement commn. WSB, 1952-53; cons. Inst. Def. Analyses; dep. dir. Rsch. Com. on Money and Credit, 1959-61. Author: (with others) Personal Finance Industry and Its Credit Standards, 1939, (with Steiner) Money and Banking, 1941, Development of Wisconsin Credit Union Movement, 1947, Money and Banking, 1953, (with others), 1958, (with D. Meiselman) Measurement of Corporate Sources and Uses of Funds, 1964, (with others) Money and Banking, 1969, (with Wolf) The Role of Private Placement in Corporate Finance, 1972; Editor: (with W.L. White) Capital for Productivity and Growth, 1977. Served from ensign to lt. USNR, 1942-46. Recipient Econ. Dept. award Bklyn. Coll., 1936, Honors Day award for distinguished alumni, 1949. Fellow Am. Acad. Arts and Scis.; mem. Nat. Bur. Econ. Research (pres.), Am. Econ. Assn., Council Fgn. Relations, Am. Fin. Assn. Home and Office: 180 Beacon St Boston MA 02116-1455

SHAPIRO, GEORGE M., lawyer; b. N.Y.C., Dec. 7, 1919; s. Samuel N. and Sarah (Milstein) S.; m. Rita V. Lubin, Mar. 29, 1942; children: Karen Shapiro Spector, Sanford. BS, LIU, 1939; LL.B. (Kent scholar), Columbia U., 1942; LL.D. (hon.), L.I. U., 1986. Bar: N.Y. 1942. Mem. staff gov. N.Y., 1945-51, counsel to gov., 1951-54; ptnr. Proskauer, Rose, Goetz & Mendelsohn, N.Y.C., 1955—, mem. exec. com., mng. ptnr., 1974-84, co-chmn. corp. dept., 1980-90; pres. Edmond de Rothschild Found., 1964-92; dir. Bank of Calif., 1973-84; counsel, majority leader N.Y. Senate, 1955-59; counsel N.Y. Constl. Revision Commn., 1960-61. Chmn. council State U. Coll. Medicine, N.Y., 1955-71; mem. Gov.'s Com. Reapportionment, 1964, Mayor's Com. Jud. Selection, 1966-69; chmn. Park Ave. Synagogue, 1973-81; mem. Coun. on Fgn. Rels., 1974-92. Served with USAAF, 1943-45. Club: Harmonie. Home: 1160 Park Ave New York NY 10128-1212 also: The Stratford Arms 2600 S Ocean Blvd Apt 16F Boca Raton FL 33432 Office: 1585 Broadway New York NY 10036-8200

SHAPIRO, HAROLD TAFLER, university president, economist; b. Montreal, Que., Can., June 8, 1935; s. Maxwell and Mary (Tafler) S.; m. Vivian Bernice Rapoport, May 19, 1957; children: Anne, Marilyn, Janet, Karen. BComm, McGill U., Montreal, 1956; PhD in Econs. (Harold Helm fellow, Harold Dodds sr. fellow), Princeton U., 1964. Asst. prof. econs. U. Mich., 1964-67, assoc. prof., 1967-70, prof., 1970-76, chmn. dept. econs., 1974-77, prof. econs. and pub. affairs from 1977, v.p. acad. affairs, 1977-79, pres., 1980-87; research adv. Bank Can., 1965-72; prof. econ. and pub. affairs, pres. Princeton U., 1988—; bd. dirs. Dow Chem.; trustee Univs. Rsch. Assn., 1988—; mem. exec. com. Assn. Am. Univs., 1985-89, N.J. Commn. on Sci. and Tech., 1988-91; mem. Pres.'s Coun. Advisors on Sci. and Tech., 1990—; chmn. com. on employer-based health benefits Inst. Medicine, 1991. Trustee Alfred P. Sloan Found., 1980—, Interlochen Ctr. for Arts, 1988—; dir. Am. Coun. Edn., 1989-92; chmn. Spl. Presdl. Com., The Research Libraries Group, 1980-91; mem. Gov.'s High Tech. Task Force, Mich., 1980-87; mem. Gov.'s Commn. on Jobs and Econ. Devel. (Mich.), 1983-87; mem. Carnegie Commn. on Coll. Retirement, 1984-86. Recipient Lt. Gov.'s medal in commerce McGill U., 1956. Fellow Am. Acad. Arts and Scis., Mich. Soc. Fellows (sr.); mem. Inst. Medicine of NAS, Am. Philos. Soc., Nat. Bur. Econ. Rsch. (bd. dirs.). Home: 83 Stockton St Princeton NJ 08540-6821 Office: Princeton U 1 Nassau Hall Princeton NJ 08544

SHAPIRO, HARVEY, poet; b. Chgo., Jan. 27, 1924; s. Jacob J. and Dorothy (Cohen) S.; m. Edna Lewis Kaufman, July 23, 1953; children—Saul, Dan. B.A., Yale U., 1947; M.A., Columbia U., 1948. Instr. English Cornell U., 1949-50, 51-52; creative writing fellow Bard Coll., 1950-51; mem. editorial staff Commentary, New Yorker, 1955-57; editorial staff N.Y. Times mag., N.Y.C., 1957; asst. editor N.Y. Times mag., 1964-75; editor N.Y. Times Book Rev., 1975-83; dep. editor N.Y. Times Mag., 1983—. Author: The Eye, 1953, The Book and Other Poems, 1955, Mountain, Fire, Thornbush, 1961, Battle Report, 1966, This World, 1971, Lauds, 1975, Nightsounds, 1978, The Light Holds, 1984, National Cold Storage Company, 1988. Served with USAAF, World War II. Decorated D.F.C., Air medal with 3 oak leaf clusters.; Rockefeller Found. grantee in poetry, 1967. Club: Elizabethan (New Haven). Office: NY Times 229 W 43d St New York NY 10036

SHAPIRO, HARVEY, sales manager, journalist, writer, lyricist; b. Bklyn., Mar. 18, 1937; s. Louis and Pauline (Watson) S.; m. Judith Shapiro, June 16, 1962 (div. Dec. 1982); children: Eric, Elyse; m. Eileen Strachman, Apr. 20, 1985. BA in Journalism, L.I. Univ., 1958. Enlisted USAR, 1954; honorably discharged U.S. Army, 1962; reporter, editor various publs., 1958-1982; sports writer, sports slotman Dayton (Ohio) Daily News, 1974-79; founder, editor, pub. World of Speed, Dayton, 1979-81; copy editor Lake County Telegraph, Painesville, Ohio, 1982; gen. sales mgr. Del Rey Plastics Corp., N.Y.C., 1982—. Author: Faster Than Sound, 1975 (named 1st in book div. 1976), Sports Stars Cookbook, 1978; composer: (with Hanan Harchol) A Simple Silver Band, 1989, We Love You, Welcome Home, 1991, Where Are You America?, 1992; contbr. articles to profl. jours. Recipient numerous writing awards AP, 1972-82; mag. named Top Nat. Motorsports Mag., Dayton Auto Racing Fan Club, 1980. Mem. Am. Automobile Racing Writers and Broadcasters Assn. (writing awards 1974-79), Vietnam Vets. Am. (assoc. chpt. 151), Nat. Forget-Me-Nots, L.I. Song Writers Assn. Home: 508 Meisel Ave Springfield NJ 07081

SHAPIRO, HOWARD IRWIN, engineering consultant; b. Bklyn., Apr. 16, 1932; s. Charles M. and Rose (Smith) S.; m. Dorothy Arluck, June 20, 1953; children: Jay P., Lawrence K., Gail S., Daniel A. BCE, Poly. Inst. Bklyn., 1953. Registered profl. engr., N.Y., N.J., Ohio, Md., Va., Mo. Engr. Charles M. Shapiro, P.E., Bklyn., 1957-60; ptnr. Charles M. Shapiro & Sons, Bklyn., 1960-74; v.p. Charles M. Shapiro & Sons, P.C., Bklyn., 1974—; pres. Howard I. Shapiro & Assocs. Consulting Engrs., P.C., Bklyn., 1989—. Author: Cranes and Derricks, 1980, 2d edit. (with Jay P. Shapiro and Lawrence K. Shapiro), 1991. 1st lt. CE, U.S. Army, 1953-56. Mem. Nat. Soc. Profl. Engrs., ASCE, Soc. Automotive Engrs., Am. Inst. Steel Constrn., Concrete Industry Bd. Office: Howard Shapiro & Assocs 6315 Mill Ln Brooklyn NY 11234-5512

SHAPIRO, JAMES ELIOT, economist; b. Boston, Apr. 13, 1957; s. Leon Nathan and Rose (Kurhan) S.; m. Tia Powell, July 29, 1984; 1 child, Sophia Rose. BA magna cum laude, Harvard Coll., 1980; MA in Econs., Yale U., 1985, MPhil, 1986, postgrad. Lectr. Yale U., New Haven, 1987-88; sr. economist N.Y. Stock Exchange, N.Y.C., 1988-89, dir., 1989-90, mng. dir., 1990-91. Mem. Am. Econ. Assn., Am. Fin. Assn., Western Fin. Assn. Office: NY Stock Exchange 11 Wall St New York NY 10005-1916

SHAPIRO, JONATHAN, psychologist; b. N.Y.C., Jan. 2, 1949; s. Irwin and Edna (Richter) S.; m. Nanette Gordon, Mar. 27, 1970; children: Natasha, Mia. BA, Queens Coll., 1970; MSW, SUNY, Albany, 1976; PsyD, Antioch U., 1986. Lic. psychologist, N.Y.; cert. social worker, N.Y. Supervising social worker Capital Dist. Psychol. Ctr., Schenectady, N.Y., 1977-85, supervising psychologist, 1985-88; co-dir., pvt. practice Opening Doors Counseling Ctr., Albany, 1988—; cons. Troy (N.Y.) Assn. for Retarded Children, 1990; workshop facilitator Singles Outreach Support, Albany, 1990—, First United Ch. of Albany, 1991. Active various community orgns. Mem. Am. Assn. Marriage and Family Therapy, Am. Psychol. Assn., Psychol. Assn. of Northeast N.Y. Jewish. Home: 60 Elliot Ave East Greenbush NY 12061-1709 Office: Opening Doors Counsel Ctr 321 Hamilton St Albany NY 12210-1707

SHAPIRO, KENNETH PAUL, insurance company executive, actuary; b. New York, N.Y., Mar. 20, 1946; s. Harry and Esther (Forman) S.; m. Hazel Paula Neuwirth, Sept. 20, 1970; children: Seth, Matthew, Elissa. BS in Math., Bklyn. Coll., 1967; MS in Math., U. Mich., 1968. Actuary Penn Mutual Life Ins. Co., Phila., 1971-74; v.p. Hay/Huggins Co., Inc., Phila., 1974-82, pres., chief exec. officer, 1982—; bd. dirs. The Hay Group, 1987—. Columnist Bus. Insur., 1980-85. Lt. USPH, 1968-71. Fellow Soc. Actuaries, Conf. Actuaries; mem. Am. Acad. Actuaries, Acutaries Club of Phila. (pres. 1982-83). Home: 412 Country Club Dr Cherry Hill NJ 08003-3312 Office: Hay/Huggins Co Inc 229 S 18th St Philadelphia PA 19103-6144

SHAPIRO, LESLIE ALAN, ophthalmic surgeon; b. Bklyn., Aug. 21, 1945; s. Sidney Joseph and Betty (Miller) S.; m. Carolyn Bresnick, June 23, 1968; children: Jordan David, Jennifer Elaine. BA, NYU, 1967; MD, George Washington U., 1971. Surg. resident Beth Israel Med. Ctr., N.Y.C., 1971-73, ophthalmology resident, 1973-76; pvt. practice Bayside, N.Y., 1976—; attending surgeon North Shore U. Hosp., Manhasset, N.Y., 1986—, St. Joseph's Hosp., Flushing, N.Y., 1985—, Beth Israel Med. Ctr., N.Y.C., 1976—. Dep. mayor Village of Kensington, Great Neck, N.Y., 1984-88. Fellow ACS, Am. Acad. Ophthalmology, Am. Soc. Cataract and Refractive Surgeons. Office: 200-14 44th Ave Bayside NY 11361

SHAPIRO, LYNN HUBERMAN, alumni director; b. Phila., July 14, 1942; d. Ralph Huberman and Vivian (Spiegleman) Manekin; m. Ronald M. Shapiro, Mar. 22, 1964 (div. Jan. 1988); children: Mark, Julie, Laura, David. BA in English with honors, U. N.C., Greensboro, 1964. Bus. office mgr. Material Equip. Handling Co., Bala Cynwyd, Pa., 1964; social sci. rsch. asst. Harvard U., Cambridge, Mass., 1964-67; owner, dir. day care ctr. Balt., 1970-73, freelance lectr., 1986-88; alumni dir. Villa Julie Coll., Stevenson, Md., 1988—; mem. CASE, 1988—. Mem. Com. on Jewish-Christian Rels., Balt., 1988-91, Nat. Com. on Holocaust, Washington, 1989-91; counselor Planned Parenthood, 1986-88; bd. trustees The Bryn Mawr Sch., 1979-87. Democrat. Jewish. Home: 2404 W Rogers Ave Baltimore MD 21209-4322 Office: Villa Julie Coll Greenspring Rd Stevenson MD 21153

SHAPIRO, MARIAN KAPLUN, psychologist; b. Lexington, Mass., July 13, 1939; d. David and Bertha Rebecca (Pearlman) Kaplun; m. Irwin Ira Shapiro, Dec. 20, 1959; children: Steven, Nancy. BA, Queens Coll., 1959; MA in Teaching, Harvard U., 1961, EdD, 1978. Cert. psychologist. Tchr. North Quincy High Sch., Quincy, Mass., 1962-64; instr. Carnegie Inst., Boston, 1968-74; staff psychologist South Shore Counselling Assn., Hanover, Mass., 1978-80; pvt. practice psychologist Lexington, Mass., 1980—; adj. instr. Mass. Sch. Profl. Psychology, Dedham, 1985—. Author: 2nd Childhood: Hypnoplay Therapy with Age-Regressed Adults, 1989; contbr. articles on teaching reading, hypnotherapy, multiple personality and other clin. issues to profl. jours. Fellow Am. Orthopsychiat. Assn.; mem. Am. Psychol. Assn., Mass. Psychol. Assn., Northeast Soc. Group Psychotherapy, Am. Soc. Group Psychotherapy, Am. Soc. Clin. Hypnosis, New Eng. Soc. for the Study Multiple Personality Disorders, Internat. Soc. for the Study Multiple Personality Disorders, New Eng. Soc. Clin. Hypnosis, Sigma Alpha, Pi Lambda Theta. Jewish. Home and Office: 17 Lantern Ln Lexington MA 02173-6029

SHAPIRO, MARK, gastroenterologist; b. N.Y.C., Aug. 18, 1955; s. Pincus Phillip Shapiro and Martha (Helfman) Levine. BA, U. Chgo., 1977; MS, U. Mich., 1978, PhD, 1982; MD, U. Cin., 1986. Diplomate Am. Bd. Internal Medicine. Intern medicine Columbia-Presbyn. Med. Ctr., N.Y.C., 1986-87, resident medicine, 1987-89; rsch. fellow Liver Ctr., Albert Einstein Coll. Medicine, Bronx, N.Y., 1989-90; clin. fellow div. gastroenterology Albert Einstein Coll. Medicine, Montefiore Med. Ctr., Bronx, 1990-92; attending physician emergency medicine Booth Meml. Med. Ctr., Flushing, N.Y., 1989-92, attending physician gastroenterology med. svc. and ICU Bronx Mcpl. Hosp. Ctr., 1991—; attending physician gastroenterology Jack Weilen Hosp. of Albert Einstein Coll. Medicine; pvt. practice gastroenterology and internal medicine Tenbroeck Med. Assocs., Bronx. Contbr. articles and abstracts to profl. jours. Martin Rsch. fellow Albert Einstein Coll. Medicine, 1989, Cheryl Purkey Rsch. fellow Am. Liver Found., 1989. Mem. Am. Coll. Physicians, N.Y. Acad. Scis., AAAS, N.Y. State Med. Assn., AMA, Alpha Omega Alpha. Home: 4705 Henry Hudson Pky Apt 2C Bronx NY 10471-3232 Office: Tenbroeck Med Assocs PC 1180 Morris Park Ave Bronx NY 10461

SHAPIRO, NEIL ROBERT, lawyer; b. N.Y.C., Sept. 21, 1962; s. Herman and Ruth (Zuckerandel) S.; married. BA, SUNY, Albany, 1984; JD, U. Pa., 1987. Bar: N.Y. 1988. V.p. Hyru Corp., Bklyn., 1980-92; assoc. Weil, Gotshal & Manges, N.Y.C., 1987—. Mem. ABA, N.Y. State Bar Assn., N.Y. County Lawyers Assn., U. Pa. Alumni Assn. (mem. reunion com., class com., firm solicitor), Phi Alpha Theta. Jewish. Office: Weil Gotshal & Manges 767 5th Ave New York NY 10153-0002

SHAPIRO, NELLA IRENE, surgeon; b. N.Y.C., Nov. 13, 1947; d. Eugene and Ethel (Pearl) S.; m. Jack Schwartz, Oct. 16, 1977; children: Max, Molly. BA, Barnard Coll., 1968; MD, Albert Einstein Coll., 1972. Diplomate Am. Bd. Surgery. Resident in gen. surgery Montefiore Hosp., N.Y.C., 1972-76; mem. staff North Cen. Hosp., Bronx, N.Y., 1976-77, Bronx Mcpl. Hosp., Bronx, 1977-87, mem. staff in gen. surgery Albert Einstein Coll. Hosp., Bronx, 1977—, chief gen. surgery, 1991—; asst. prof. surgery Albert Einstein Coll., Bronx, 1980—; assoc. dir. gen. surgery Weller Hosp., Bronx, 1991—; co-founder Whaecom Breast Ctr., Bronx, 1991—. Fellow Am. Coll. Surgeons. Office: Weiler Hosp 1825 Eastchester Rd Bronx NY 10461

SHAPIRO, NORMA SONDRA LEVY, federal judge; b. Phila., July 27, 1928; d. Bert and Jane (Kotkin) Levy; m. Bernard Shapiro, Aug. 21, 1949; children: Finley, Neil, Aaron. BA in Polit. Theory with honors, U. Mich., 1948; JD magna cum laude, U. Pa., 1951. Bar: Pa. 1952, U.S. Supreme Ct. 1978. Law clk. to presiding justice Pa. Supreme Ct., 1951-52; instr. U. Pa. Law Sch., 1951-52, 55-56; assoc. Dechert Price & Rhoads, Phila., 1956-58, 67-73; ptnr. Dechert Price & Rhoads, 1973-78; judge U.S. Dist. Ct. (ea. dist.) Pa., 1978—; assoc. trustee U. Pa. Law Sch., 1978—; former trustee Women's Law Project, Albert Einstein Med. Ctr.; v.p. Jewish Pub. Soc.; trustee Fedn. Jewish Agys. 1980—; mem. lawyer's adv. panel Pa. Gov.'s Commn. on Status of Women, 1974; legal adv. regional Coun. Child Psychiatry. Guest editor: Shingle, 1972. Mem. Lower Merion County (Pa.) Bd. Sch. Dirs., 1968-77, pres., 1977, v.p., 1976; v.p. Jewish Community Relations Council of Greater Phila., 1975-77; chmn. legal affairs com., 1978; pres. Belmont Hills Home and Sch. Assn., Lower Merion Twp.; legis. chmn. Lower Merion Sch. Dist. Intersch. Council; mem. Task Force on Mental Health of Children and Youth of Pa.; treas., chmn. edn. com. Human Relations Council, Lower Merion; v.p., parliamentarian Nes Ami Penn Valley Congregation, Lower Merion Twp. Named Woman of Yr., Oxford Circle Jewish Community Center, 1979, Woman of Distinction, Golden Slipper Club, 1979; Gowen fellow, 1954-55; recipient Hannah G. Solomon award Nat. Coun. Jewish Women, 1992. Mem. Am. Law Inst., Am. Bar Found., ABA (ho. dels. 1990—, coun./chmn. conf. fed. judges 1986-87, vice-chmn. com. law and mental health sect. family law), Pa. Bar Assn. (ho. of dels. 1979-81), Phila. Bar Assn. (chmn. com. women's rights 1972, 74-75, chmn. bd. govs. 1977-78, chmn. pub. rels. com. 1978), Fed. Bar Assn. (Bill of Rights award 1991), Nat. Assn. Women Lawyers, Phila. Trial Lawyers Assn., Am. Judicature Soc., Phila., Fellowship Commn., Order of Coif (chpt. pres. 1973-75), Tau Epsilon Rho, Jurisprudence. Office: US Dist Courthouse Rm 10614 US Courthouse Independence Mall W Philadelphia PA 19106

SHAPIRO, RASHI YISROEL, clinical psychologist; b. Washington, Feb. 25, 1953; s. Aharon and Marta (Berl) S.; m. Charline Carron Rosenbloom; children: Elkana, Ohra. BA, Bklyn. Coll., 1973; MSW, Barry U., 1982; MA in Psychology, L.I. U., 1984, PhD in Psychology, 1986. Ordained rabbi, 1977. Dir. Kibbutz Shaalvim Israel) U. Level Religious Tng., 1973-75, Horeb Coll. Women Talmudic U. Fla.; exec. dir. Hypno Therapy Counseling Ctrs., Miami Beach, Fla., 1979-79; psychotherapist Tikvah New Hope Guild, Bklyn., 1982-84; clin. dir. Tikvah New Hope Guild, 1984-87; dir. day hosp. Pesach Tikvah Hope Devel., Bklyn., 1987-89; assoc. exec. dir. Pesach Tikvah Hope Devel., 1990—; lectr., L.I. U., 1984-86. Composer, producer Rashi and the Rishonim, 1970, Best Jewish Folk Rock Record, 1971. Mem. APA, Assn. Orthodox Jewish Scientists (lectr. 1987-88). Home and Office: 52 Dekoven Ct Brooklyn NY 11230

SHAPIRO, RUTH, career development and communications consultant; b. N.Y.C., Oct. 22, 1926; d. Isaac Jacob and Leonora (Rosenfeld) S. BS in Retailing, NYU, 1947, M of Vocat. Guidance, 1973. Advt. copywriter various orgns., N.Y.C., 1948-60; dir. merchandising Simplicity Pattern Co., N.Y.C., 1960-62; promotion writer, asst. account exec. Ralf Shockey & Assocs., N.Y.C., 1962-64; promotion writer House and Garden mag., N.Y.C., 1964-68; advt. promotion mgr. Ethan Allen, Inc., N.Y.C., 1968-71; dir. pub. rels. Conso Products Co., N.Y.C., 1971-74; pres., counselor, cons. Ruth Shapiro Assocs., N.Y.C., 1974—; instr. adult edn. NYU, Fashion Inst. Tech., also others, 1976—; cons. Swain & Swain, Inc., N.Y.C., 1987—; bus. writing trainer McGraw Hill, Inc., N.Y.C., 1984; speaker in field. Contbr. articles to numerous profl. publs. Mem. NAFE, ASTD, Am. Women's Econ. Devel., Career Devel. Specialists Network, N.Y. Assn. Counseling and Devel., NOW, Hadassah. Office: 200 E 30th St New York NY 10016-8274

SHAPIRO, SANDRA LIBBY ROSENBERG, dean, business education educator; b. Passaic, N.J., May 19, 1946; d. Saul and Helen (Blickstein) Rosenberg; m. Edward David Shapiro, June 22, 1968; 1 child, Stephanie Anne. BS in Bus. Edn., Rider Coll., 1967; MA in Bus. Edn., Montclair (N.J.) State Coll., 1972. Cert. bus. edn. tchr. and supr., N.J. Tchr. Jersey City Bd. of Edn., 1967-74; tchr. Katharine Gibbs Sch., Montclair, 1974-76, dean of edn., 1987—; adj. instr. Rockland Community Coll., Suffern, N.Y., 1980-81, Bergen Community Coll., Paramus, N.J., 1981-87; part-time job developer, placement specialist spl. projects in coop. edn. dept., 1985-87; mem. sec. adv. com. Edn. Testing Svc., Princeton, N.J., 1990—. Leader Troop 334 Girl Scouts U.S., Fair Lawn, N.J., 1973-75. Mem. Nat. Bus. Tchrs. Assn., N.J. Bus. Tchrs. Assn., N.J. Coll. and Univ. Coalition on Women's Edn., Eastern Bus. Tchrs. Assn., Jersey City Edn. Assn., B'nai B'rith (life, pres., counselor, program v.p., fin. sec., aid to Israel chmn., installation chmn.), Delta Pi Epsilon, Pi Omega Pi, Delta Phi Epsilon. Jewish. Home: 41-12 Christine Ct Fair Lawn NJ 07410 Office: Katharine Gibbs Sch 33 Plymouth St Montclair NJ 07042-2699

SHAPIRO, STUART CHARLES, computer scientist, educator; b. N.Y.C., Dec. 30, 1944; s. Louis M. and Bertha (Rubinstein) S.; m. Caren Dee Knight, July 16, 1972. BS, MIT, 1966; MS, U. Wis., 1968, PhD, 1971. Lectr. computer scis. dept. U. Wis., Madison, 1971; vis. asst. prof. Ind. U., Bloomington, 1971-72, asst. prof., 1972-77, assoc. prof., 1977-78; asst. prof. SUNY, Buffalo, 1977-78, assoc. prof., 1978-83, prof., 1983—, chmn., 1984-90; cons. Calspan UB Rsch. Ctr., Buffalo; rsch. scientist Nat. Ctr. for Geographic Info. and Analysis, 1989—. Author: Techniques of Artificial Intelligence, 1979, LISP: An Interactive Approach, 1986, Common Lisp: An Interactive Approach, 1992; editor: Encyclopedia of Artificial Intelligence, 1987, paperback edit., 1990, 2d edit., 1992; contbr. articles to profl. jours. Grantee NSF, 1971—; recipient numerous grants for computer sci. research, 1971—. Mem. IEEE, Assn. for Computing Machinery (chmn. spl. interest group on artificial intelligence 1991—), Am. Assn. Artificial Intelligence, Assn. Computational Linguistics, Cognitive Sci. Soc. Home: 142 Viscount Dr Buffalo NY 14221-1770 Office: SUNY at Buffalo Dept of Computer Sci 226 Bell Hall Buffalo NY 14260

SHAPIRO-ROSS, DEBRA, chemical company manager; b. Phila., Feb. 27, 1955; d. Harold Hirsch and Edith Frances (Wishnefsky) Shapiro; m. Andrew Marc Ross, June 26, 1983. BSChemE, Drexel U., 1977; MBA, Fairleigh Dickinson U., 1981. Registered profl. engr., N.J. Jr. engr. BASF Corp., Parsippany, N.J., 1977-78, process engr. II, 1978-81, process engr. I, 1981-84, sr. project engr. II, 1984-87, sr. project engr. I, 1987-89, spl. projects mgr., 1989-90, mgr. site master planning, 1990—. Mem. Am. Inst. Chem. Engrs. Office: BASF Corp 100 Cherry Hill Rd Parsippany NJ 07054-1146

SHARFMAN, WILLIAM LEE, interviewer, writer, management consultant; b. Washington, Oct. 11, 1942; s. Warren Leonard and Amalie (Schenthal) S.; m. Caroline Sharp, Sept. 5, 1964 (div. 1985). BA, U. Mich., 1964; MA, Columbia U., 1965, PhD, 1969. Lectr., preceptor Columbia U., N.Y.C., 1966-70; founder Courses for Coll. Credit, Sun Valley, Idaho, 1971; vice chmn. dept. English Idaho State U., Pocatello, 1970-72; pres. Time-Sharing Info. Svcs., Phila., 1972-73; v.p. mktg. Metagraphic Systems, N.Y.C., 1973-76; sr. v.p. strategic planning Brouillard Communications div.

J. Walter Thompson Co., N.Y.C., 1978-82, J. Walter Thompson U.S.A., N.Y.C., 1982-85; prin. Sharfman & Co., N.Y.C., 1985—. Contbg. writer Automobile Mag., 1986—; contbr. articles to profl. jours. Mem. U. Mich. Alumni Assn. (life), Columbia U. Grad. Faculties Alumni Assn. Home: 50 Riverside Dr New York NY 10024-6508 Office: Sharfman & Co 50 Riverside Dr New York NY 10024-6508

SHARGAL, SUSAN K. Y., psychologist; b. N.Y.C., Mar. 12, 1948; d. Alexander and Helen (Jaffe) Katz. BA, U. Chgo., 1968; PhD, CUNY, 1980. Cert. psychologist, N.H.; lic. psychologist, Mass. Psychologist Greater Manchester (N.H.) Mental Health Ctr., 1980-82, Potentia, Auburn, N.H., 1982—; cons. Notre Dame Coll., Manchester, N.H., 1982-83. Contbr. articles to profl. jours. Candidate for v.p. Dem. Primary, N.H., 1992. Fellow Am. Orthopsychiatric Assn.; mem. APA, Soc. Family Therapy and Rsch. Office: Potentia PO Box 184 Auburn NH 03032-0184

SHARGEL, LEON DAVID, pharmacy educator, consultant; b. Balt., Nov. 18, 1941; s. Earl and Irene (Singer) S.; m. Sharon Lee Fine, June 10, 1967; children: Deborah Ann, Jeffrey Reuben. BS in Pharmacy, U. Md., 1963; PhD in Pharmacology, George Washington U., 1969. Registered pharmacist, Mass., Md., D.C. Group leader Sterling Rsch. Group, Rensselaer, N.Y., 1969-75; assoc. prof. pharmacy Northeastern U., Boston, 1975-82, Mass. Coll. Pharmacy and Allied Health Scis., Boston, 1982-91; dir. pharmacokinetics Chelsea Labs., West Hempstead, N.Y., 1991—; cons. to pharm. industry, 1975—; adj. prof. pharmacy; mem. Mass. Drug Formulary Commn., 1988—. Author: Applied Biopharmaceutics and Pharmacokinetics, 2d edit., 1985; editor: Pharmacy Review, 1989; assoc. editor Pharmacy Practice Exam, 1990; contbr. chpt. to Biopharmaceutics, 1990. Vol. ARC, Framingham, Mass. Mem. AAAS, Am. Soc. Pharmacology and Exptl. Therapeutics, Am. Assn. Pharm. Scientists, Am. Pharm. Assn., Sigma Xi, Rho Chi. Office: Chelsea Labs Inc 896 Orlando Ave West Hempstead NY 11552-3939

SHARIFY, NASSER, librarian, educator, author; b. Tehran, Iran, Sept. 23, 1925; came to U.S., 1953, naturalized, 1972; s. Ebrahim and Eshrat (Saghafy) S.; m. Homayoun Taslimy, June 14, 1950 (div. 1978); children: Sharareh, Shahab. Licencie es Lettres, U. Tehran, 1947; M.S., Columbia U., 1954, Dr. L.S., 1958. Editorial staff Teheran jours. Rah-e Now, Jahan-e Now, Saba, Jonb va Jush, 1943-51; translator, announcer All India Radio, 1948-49; librarian, dep. dir. Library of Parliament Iran, Tehran, 1949-53; cataloger Library of Congress, 1954-55; program asst. libraries devel. sect. UNESCO, Paris, 1959-61; acting chief servicing sect. Dept. Edn., 1962-63; dir. gen. Ministry Edn., Tehran, 1961-62; asst. prof. library and info. scis. and internat. edn. U. Pitts., 1963-66; founder, dir. Internat. Library Info. Center, 1964-66; vis. lectr. SUNY Albany Sch. Library Sci., summer, 1966; dir. internat. librarianship and documentation, internat studies and world affairs SUNY, Oyster Bay, 1966-68; dean, prof. grad. sch. library and info sci. Pratt Inst., Bklyn., 1968-87, chmn. inst. research council, 1971-89, disting. prof., dean emeritus sch. computer, info. and library scis., 1987-89, dean emeritus, 1987—; pres. B.E.L.T., Inc., internat. planning cons., 1981—; Dir. Grad. Library Tng. Program, UNESCO Mission, Nat. Tchrs. Coll., Tehran, 1960; Iran's Ofcl. del. to UNESCO Conf. Ednl. Pubs., Geneva, 1961, SE Asia Edn. Secs. Conf., Murree, Pakistan, 1961, Internation Conf., on Cataloging Prins., Paris, 1961, CENTO Libr. Devel. Conf., Ankara, Turkey, 1962; chmn. standing com. for preparation reading materials for new literates UNESCO, Tehran, 1961-62; mem. U.S. AID Mission, Turkey, Pakistan, 1966; dir. Conf. on Internat. Responsibility Coll. and Univ. Librarians, Oyster Bay, 1967; U.S. del. 33d Conf. and Internat. Congress on Documentation, Tokyo, 1967; ALA del. UN Conf. on Non-Govtl. Orgn., 1969; cons. U.S. AID, Conf. on Book Devel., 1967; mem. adv. bd. Ency. Libr. and Info. Scis., 1969—; chmn. Pre-Am. Library Assn. Conf. Inst. on Internat. Libr. Manpower, Edn. and Placement in N.Am., Detroit, 1970; mem. Am. del. Internat. Fedn. Libr. Assn. Conf., Liverpool, Eng., 1971, Budapest, 1972, Grenoble, France, 1973, Washington, 1974, Brussels, 1977, Montreal, 1982, Chgo., 1985; bldg. cons. Learning Resources Center, Nat. Tchrs. Coll., Iran, 1972-73, cons. campus planning, 1972-73; UNESCO cons. missions to plan and evaluate Nat. Sch. Info. Sci., Morocco, 1973-74, 79-81, 89; cons. U.S. Info. Agy., Morocco, 1991; chmn. Conf. on Orgn. and Control of Info for Islamic Research, 1982; chmn. bd. cons. to Nat. U. Iran, 1974-75, Pahlavi Nat. Library of Iran, 1975-77; speaker Symposium Internat. sur l' information Economique, Casablanca, Morocco, 1990. Author: cataloging of Persian works Including Rules for Transliteration Entry and Description, 1959, Book Production, Importation and Distribution in Iran, Pakistan and Turkey, 1966; Beyond the National Frontiers: The International Dimension of Changing Library Education for a Changing World, 1973; The Pahlavi National Library of the Future, 17 vols., 1976; other books; contbr. to Ency. of Library and Info. Sci., 1969, ALA World Ency. Library and Info. Services, 1980, 86, library jours., 1973—, Bookmark, 1972; contbr. poetry to various jours., 1947-51, 67, lyrics to Iranian motion pictures and recs., 1948-52; works on display at Archieves of Hoover Inst. on War Revolution and Peace, Stanford U.; Contbr. to: film script for motion picture Morad, 1951-52. Trustee Bklyn. Public Library, 1970-82; pres. Maurice F. Tauber Found., 1981—. Recipient Taj (crown) medal and citation for disting. svc. Mohammad Reza Shah Pahlavi, Shah of Iran, 1978, Kaula Gold medal and citation for disting. svc. to internat. librarianship, 1985; named for Annual Nasser Sharify Lecture Series, Sch. of Computer Info. and Libr. Scis., Pratt Inst., 1988—; writings by and about Nasser Sharify are preserved at Archives of Hoover Instn. on wars, revolutions nd peace., Stanford U., Stanford, Calif. Mem. ALA (chmn. com. equivalencies and reciprocity 1966-71, mem. UNESCO panel, mem. nominating com. 1970-71, chmn. Pakistan and Middle East Resource panels, internat. library edn. com., mem. com. internat. library schs. div. library edn. 1968-72, coordinator country resources panels, internat. library edn. com. library edn. div. 1973-78), N.Y. Library Assn. (dir. library edn. sect. 1969-72), Pub. Library Assn. (task force on internat. relations 1981-86), Am. Assn. Library Schs. (chmn. govtl. relations com., 1984-88), Am. Soc. Info. for Sci., Spl. Librarian Assn., Internat. Fedn. Library Assns. (adv. group library edn. 1971-73, v.p. library schs. sect. 1973-77). Home: 252 Jericho Tpke Westbury NY 11590-1213 Office: Pratt Inst Sch Info and Libr Sci 200 Willoughby Ave # 4 Brooklyn NY 11205-3899

SHARKEY, JOHN BERNARD, chemistry educator, dean; b. Elizabeth, N.J., Sept. 5, 1940; s. Owen and Betty (Given) S.; m. Dolores Dorothy Passiatore, May 30, 1964; children: Laura, Ian, Brian. BA, NYU, 1964, MS, 1967, PhD, 1970. Chemist Engelhard Industries, Newark, 1962-66; asst. prof. chemistry Pace U., N.Y.C., 1970-77, assoc. prof., 1977-81, prof. chemistry, 1981—, chmn. dept. chemistry, 1978-90, assoc. dean, 1990—; cons. World Book, Inc., Chgo., 1985—, Am. Coun. Learned Socs., N.Y.C., 1992—. Recipient Kenan Award for teaching excellence Pace U., 1987-88. Mem. Am. Chem. Soc. (chmn. N.Y. sect. 1987, councilor 1986—), History of Sci. Soc., Sigma Xi, Omicron Delta Epsilon. Office: Pace Univ Pace Plaza New York NY 10038

SHARMA, RAN S., biostatistician; b. Rupapura, Gujara, India, June 9, 1937; s. Shankarbhai C. and Dahiben S. (Valad) S.; m. Sudha R. Mistry, Apr. 2, 1967; children: Mona, Satyan. BA with honors, Gujarat U., India, 1959, MA with honors, 1961; PhD, UCLA, 1966. Biostatistician Riker Labs., Calif., 1966; sr. statistician E.R. Squibb & Sons, Inc., New Brunswick, N.J., 1966-68, Syntex Lab., Palo Alto, Calif., 1969-70; asst. prof. Temple U., Phila., 1970-74, assoc. prof., 1974-80, assoc. prof. and chmn. biostatistics, 1975-80; mgr. pre-clin. biostatistics Ortho Pharm. Co., Raritan, N.J., 1980-84, asst. dir., 1984-85; dir. pre-clin. biostatistics RWJ-PRI, Raritan, 1985—; cons. Merck Sharp & Dohm, 1976-80, Sandoz, 1976-80, Shering Plough, 1976-80. Reviewer Am. Jour. Pub. Health, 1975-80, Jour. Am. Med. Assn., 1970-80. Mem. Am. Statis. Assn., Biometrics Assn., Drug Info. Assn. Democrat. Hinduism. Home: 1815 Cynthia Ln Langhorne PA 19053-3301 Office: RWJ-PRI 202 South Raritan PA 19053

SHARMA, SUSHIL, hospital administrator; b. Feb. 2, 1956; s. Chandra Dhar and Sushila Sharma; m. Heena Sharma, Feb. 19, 1988; children: Shefali, Sangita. MBA in Fin., Gannon U., 1978, MS in Health Adminstrn., 1981. Internal auditor Hamot Med. Ctr., Erie, Pa., 1977-80; contr. and dir. fin. Community Health Services Crawford County, Meadville, Pa., 1980-82; dir. fin. Jamestown (N.Y.) Gen. Hosp., 1982-83; dir. fin. and ops. Buffalo Columbus Hosp., 1983-85, pres., chief exec. officer, 1985—; bd. dirs. Mountainview Nursing Rehab. Ctr., Duncannon, Pa.; mem. corp. Blue Cross Western N.Y., Buffalo, 1984—; developer Preventive Health Svcs. Wellness Wagon, 1985—. Mem. Congress U.S., 1987, N.Y. State senator, 1987. Recipient resolution Erie County, 1987, City of Buffalo, 1987, Hispanics United of Buffalo Community Svc. award, Community Svc. award Kiwanis Internat., 1990, Community Svc. awrd West Side Sportsmen's Assn., 1990; named Up and Comer, Modern Healthcare Mag., 1990; New Diagnostic and Treatment Ctr. at Buffalo Columbus Hosp. named in his honor. Mem. Western N.Y. Hosp. Assn. (govt. relations com. 1986—), Am. Hosp. Assn. Ambulatory Soc., Am. Coll. Health Execs., Statue of Liberty Found., Pres. Assn., Village Glen Club (Williamsville, N.Y), Waterfront Club, Rotary (civic affairs com. Buffalo 1987—). Office: Buffalo Columbus Hosp 300 Niagara St Buffalo NY 14201-2197

SHARON, YITZHAK YAAKOV, physicist, educator; b. Tel Aviv, Feb. 29, 1936; came to U.S., 1948; s. Abraham Sharon Schwadron and Dina Freidenberg; m. Sandra Brook, Jan. 13, 1991. AB with highest honors, Columbia U., 1958; MA in Physics, Princeton U., 1960, PhD in Physics, 1966. Asst. Inst. for Advanced Study, Princeton, N.J., 1965-66; asst. prof. Northeastern U., Boston, 1966-72; assoc. prof. Stockton State U., Pomona, N.J., 1972-75; prof. physics Stockton State U., Pomona, 1975—; cons. Ednl. Svcs., Inc. Phys. Sci. Study Commn., 1962-63; vis. prof. Temple U., Phila., 1970-71, U. Montreal, 1970; vis. fellow Princeton U., 1980-82, 91-92; summer physicist Nat. Bur. Standards, Washington, 1971, Oak Ridge (Tenn.) Nat. Lab., 1969, Lawrence Radiation Lab., Berkeley, Calif., 1968. Contbr. articles to profl. jours. Grantee NSF, N.J. Dept. Higher Edn. Mem. Am. Phys. Soc., Am. Assn. Physics Tchrs., Sigma Xi, Phi Beta Kappa. Jewish. Home: 6 Petunia Dr Apt 1F New Brunswick NJ 08902 Office: Stockton State Coll Dept Physics Pomona NJ 08240

SHARP, ALFRED JAY, personnel relations executive; b. Elmira, N.Y., Oct. 18, 1929; s. Albert Jay Sharp and Berneita May (Doughty) Purdy; m. Alberta Marie Rohring, Dec. 27, 1948 (div.); children: Dannie Neil, Sharon Eileen. Machine operator Eastman Kodak Co., Rochester, N.Y., 1951-71; technician Eastman Kodak Co., Rochester, 1971-82; staff asst. Mfg. Materials Mgmt., Rochester, 1982-86; systems analyst Corp. Relations, Rochester, 1986-87; retired, 1988. Dir. Teen Session Youth Group, Rochester, 1973-78; pres. 36 West Avenue Inc., Fairport, N.Y., 1979-87. Master sgt. USAFR, 1952-89. Mem. Air Force Sgts. Assn. (Div. 1 pres. 1974-81, cons. 1981-87, treas. 1981-90, conv. mgr. 1984-91, numerous awards 1981, 82, 87), Assn. Bus. Mgmt. (instr., scholarship chmn. 1986—), Am. Legion, Moose. Republican. Home: 54 Red Bud Rd Rochester NY 14624-4718 Office: 343 State St Rochester NY 14650-0001

SHARP, GEORGE BALDWIN, banker; b. N.Y.C., Mar. 3, 1941; s. George Clough Sharp and Ruth Baldwin; m. Lucy Hufstader, June 8, 1963; children: Ruth Sloan Keilty, George Anderson, Carolyn. BA, Yale U., 1963; MBA, Columbia U., N.Y.C. Asst. v.p. KLH Rsch., Cambridge, Mass., 1964-67; asst. casier Citibank, N.A., N.Y.C., 1968-71, asst. v.p., 1971-73, v.p., 1973—, sr. credit officer, 1980—, also tng. dir. Bd. dirs. Columbia Bus. Sch., N.Y.C., 1983-87. 1st lt. USAR, 1963-69. Mem. Bankers Assn. Fgn. Trade (edn. com. 1987—), Robert Morris Assocs., Fin. Mgmt. Assn., Pilgrims of the U.S., Knickerbocker Club, Bedford Golf & Tennis. Democrat. Episcopalian. Office: Citibank NA 153 E 53d St New York NY 10043

SHARP, J(AMES) FRANKLIN, finance educator, academic administrator; b. Johnson County, Ill., Sept. 29, 1938; s. James Albert and Edna Mae (Slack) S. B.S. in Indsl. Engring., U. Ill., 1960; M.S., Purdue U., 1962, Ph.D., 1966, cert. mgmt. acctg., 1979. Chartered fin. analyst, 1980. Asst. prof. engring., econs. Rutgers U., New Brunswick, N.J., 1966-70; assoc. prof. NYU Grad. Sch. Bus., N.Y.C., 1970-74; supr. bus. research AT&T, N.Y.C., 1974-77, dist. mgr. corp. planning, 1977-81, dist. mgr. fin. mgmt. and planning, 1981-85; prof. fin. Grad. Sch. Bus. Pace U., N.Y.C., 1975-91; chmn. Sharp CFA Rev. & Inst. for Investment Edn., 1987—; speaker, moderator meetings, 1965—; cons. Sharp Investment Mgmt., 1967—. Contbr. numerous articles to profl. publs.; corr.: Interface, 1975-78; fin. editor: Planning Rev., 1975-78. Mem. N.Am. Soc. Corp. Planning (treas. 1976-77, bd. dirs. at large 1977-78), Inst. Mgmt. Sci. (chpt. v.p. acad. 1972-74, chpt. v.p. program 1974-75, chpt. v.p. membership 1975-76, chpt. pres. 1976-77), Internat. Affiliation Planning Socs. (coun. 1978-84), N.Y. Soc. Security Analysts (CFA Rev. 1985-87), Ops. Rsch. Soc. Am. (pres. corp. planning group 1976-82), AAUP (v.p. Pace U. chpt. 1988-90), Theta Xi. Republican. Office: 315 E 86th St # 7H New York NY 10028

SHARP, JAMES ROGER, historian, educator; b. Troy, Kans., Aug. 8, 1936; s. Francis Wilson and Shirley Maureen (Carlson) S.; m. Nancy Anne Weatherly, Dec. 18, 1957; children: Sandra Lynn, Matthew Edward. BA, U. Mo., 1958, MA, 1960; PhD, U. Calif., Berkeley, 1966. Asst. prof. dept. history Syracuse (N.Y.) U., 1966-70, assoc. prof., 1970-79, chair history dept., 1976-83, 90—, prof., 1979—; cons. Courage Found., N.Y.C., 1986-90, NEH, Washington, 1972-78. Author: The Jacksonians Versus the Banks, 1970, The New Nation on Trial: Opposition Politics in the U.S., 1978-1801, 1993; bd. editors Jour. Early Republic, 1981-85, 89—. Capt. U.S. Army, 1958-59. Fellow Am. Coun. Learned Socs., 1979-80, NEH, 1970-71; grantee Social Sci. Rsch. Coun., 1969, Am. Philosoph. Soc., 1967. Mem. Am. Hist. Soc., Orgn. Am. Historians, Soc. Historians for Early Republic (program chair 1981, adv. bd. 1981-85). Democrat. Episcopalian. Home: 4846 Briarwood Ln Manlius NY 13104-1306 Office: Syracuse U Dept History Syracuse NY 13244

SHARPE, ROOSEVELT, JR., photographer; b. Miami, Fla., Mar. 7, 1951; s. Roosevelt and Gusteen (Smith) S.; m. Marian Yvonne Roundtree, June 18, 1977; children: Roosevelt III, Alexis Yvonne, Brian Demetrius. BS in Pharmacy, Howard U., 1975. Pharmacist mgr. Rite Aid Drug Stores, Balt., 1975-84; owner, photographer Roosevelt Sharpe Photographer, Silver Spring, Md., 1981—. Mem. Internat. Spl. Events Soc. (communication bd. Washington chpt. 1991—), Nat. Assn. Catering Execs. (Washington chpt.), Md. Profl. Photographer (Best-in-Show award 1989), Profl. Photographers Soc. (D.C. chpt.), Profl. Photographers Am., Wedding Photographers Internat. Office: 11406 Classical Ln Silver Spring MD 20901-5023

SHARPLESS, JOSEPH BENJAMIN, county official; b. Takoma Park, Md., Feb. 4, 1933; s. William Raiford and Julia Maude (Rouse) S.; m. Nancy Kathleen Steffen, July 28, 1962 (dec. Feb. 1988); 1 child, Carole Marie. BA, Earlham Coll., 1955; MS, Pa. State U., 1960. Instr. recreation Montgomery County Recreation Dept., Rockville, Md., 1957-58; from program supr. to dir. Recreation and Parks Dept., Livingston, N.J., 1959-70; chief recreation svc. Md.-Nat. Capital Park and Planning Commn. Prince George's County, Riverdale, Md., 1970-77, parks and recreation div. chief, 1977—. Contbr. articles to profl. jours. V.p. Montpelier Community Assn., South Laurel, Md., 1983-84, pres., 1985; mem. Md. Sports Adv. Com., 1988-92. With U.S. Army, 1955-57. Mem. U.S. Volleyball Assn. (bd. dirs. 1973—, mem. exec. com. 1976-80, 85-89, 92—, v.p. 1973-90, regional commr. 1965-78, nat. ofcl. 1967—, exec. cons. 1989-91, numerous awards), Nat. Recreation and Parks Assn. (disting. svc. award, Mid-Atlantic fellow), Am. Park & Recreation Soc. (bd. dirs. 1977-79, nat. coun., coun. affiliate pres.), N.J. Recreation and Parks Assn. (pres. 1967), Md. Recreation and Park Assn. (v.p. 1975-77, pres. 1977-78, named mem. of yr. 1975, citation 1985). Republican. Mem. Soc. of Friends. Home: 8754 Oxwell Ln Laurel MD 20708 Office: Md Nat Capital Park & Planning Com 10701 Livingston Rd Fort Washington MD 20744

SHARSHAN, RANDALL JOHN, civil engineer; b. Youngstown, Ohio, Oct. 9, 1955; s. John and Ann (Tirpack) S.; m. Richylee Amelia McNurlin, July 7, 1979. BS in Civil Engring., USCG, New London, 1977; MS in Systems Mgmt., U. So. Calif., L.A., 1982. Registered profl. engr., Utah, Md. Facilities engr. Tex. Instruments, Dallas, 1982-85, Morton Thiokol, Brigham City, Utah, 1985-88; facilities project mgr. Fairchild Space and Def., Germantown, Md., 1988-90; asst. dir. facilities Washington County Hosp. Assn., Hagerstown, Md., 1990—. Lt. (j.g.) USCG, 1977-82. Recipient Silver Snoopy award, NASA, 1987. Mem. ASCE, Internat. Facilities Mgmt. Assn., Nat. Mgmt. Assn., Am. Inst. Plant Engrs. Byzantine Catholic. Home: 7131 Bradshaw Ct E Frederick MD 21701-7162 Office: Washington County Hosp 251 E Antietam St Hagerstown MD 21740-5771

SHASHAANI, AVIDEH, educational organization administrator. Degree in psychology, U. Md.; degree in ednl. planning and mgmt., The Hague, Netherlands. Dir. pub. rels. rep. East Coast M.T.O. Shahmaghsoudi, 1981—; cons., trainer, 1982—; mng. dir. East Coast Wayfinders, Inc., 1991—; guest lectr. in field. Translator: Al'Rasa'el, 1986, The Mystery of Humanity, 1986, Dawn, 1989, The Secret Word, 1989, The Approaching Promise, 1989, Masnavi Ravayeh, 1990; contbr. articles to profl. jours. Chair, bd. dirs. Refugee Women in Devel. Inc.; v.p., literary advisor Literary Friends of D.C. Pub. Libr.; mem. Rehab. Internat. Assembly, 1976-79, Rehab. Internat. Tech. Aids Commn., 1976-79; mem. Poetry Com. of Greater Washington. Mem. NAFE, Writer's Ctr.'s, Mid. East Inst., Internat. Platform Assn. Home: 4601 N Park Ave # 1410 Chevy Chase MD 20815-4519

SHATTO, JOHN FREDERICK, court administrator; b. Frederick, Md., July 5, 1957; s. Paul Frederick and Dell (Napier) S.; m. Elizabeth Vandiver Scott, Aug. 16, 1980; children: Julia Reed, Scott Napier. BS in Psychology, Armstrong State Coll., 1985; MS in Adminstrn., Cen. Mich. U., 1988. Dep. ct. adminstr. County of Chatham, Savannah, Ga., 1986-91; ct. adminstr. Howard County Cir. Ct., Ellicott City, Md., 1991—. Bd. dirs. Mental Health Assn., Savannah, 1990; Gov.'s intern State of Ga., 1983. Jim Droege scholar Nat. Assn. Pretrial Agys., 1989. Mem. Nat. Assn. for Ct. Mgmt., Nat. Assn. Pretrial Agys., Sigma Iota Epsilon. Episcopalian. Home: 9796 Chestnut Oak Ct Frederick MD 21701-6724 Office: Howard County Cir Ct 8360 Court Ave Ellicott City MD 21043-4550

SHATZKY, JOEL LAWRENCE, playwright, educator; b. Vancouver, Wash., Nov. 30, 1943; s. Benjamin and Bessie (Yackira) S.; m. Dorothy Frances Shustin, July 1, 1967; children: Benjamin, Judith. BA, CUNY, 1964; MA, U. Chgo., 1965; PhD, NYU, 1970. Mem. faculty SUNY, Cortland, 1968-79, prof. English, 1979—; playwright-in-residence 1st St. Playhouse, Ithaca, N.Y., 1983-84; drama tchr. Salt City Ctr. for Performing Arts, Syracuse, N.Y., 1983-87. Playwright It's a Clean, Well-light Place, 1976, The Day They Traded Seaver, 1979, Nazi, 1982, Lessons in Flying, 1989. Grantee Puffin Found., 1989. Mem. Dramatists Guild. Democrat. Jewish. Home: 11 Melvin Ave Cortland NY 13045-1815 Office: SUNY Coll at Cortland PO Box 2000 Cortland NY 13045-0900

SHATZMAN, AARON MARK, dean, writer, historian; b. St. Louis, Aug. 31, 1946; s. Ben and Miriam Leah (Levin) S.; m. Karen Michelle Kaplan, May 29, 1988; 1 child, Aliza Rose. AB summa cum laude, Washington U., St. Louis, 1968; MA, Stanford U., 1970, PhD, 1981. Asst. dean Coll. Arts & Scis. Washington U., 1973-85; assoc. dir. Atlanta Hillel Found., 1985-88; contbr., staff writer Fanfare mag., Tenafly, N.J., 1985-88; writer, reviewer The Absolute Sound, Sea Cliff, N.Y., 1987—; dean student programs, adj. assoc. prof. Franklin & Marshall Coll., Lancaster, Pa., 1988—; judge, head Italian panel, best of show panel Atlanta Internat. Wine Festival, 1986, 87. Author: Servants into Planters, 1989; contbr. numerous articles to profl. jours. Woodrow Wilson Found. fellow, 1968, James Birdsall Weter fellow Stanford U., 1972-73; Ford Found. grantee, 1967. Mem. Inst. Early Am. History and Culture, Sommelier Guild Atlanta, Lancaster Bicycle Club, Phi Beta Kappa. Jewish. Office: Franklin & Marshall Coll PO Box 3003 Lancaster PA 17604-3003

SHAUGHNESSY, JAMES MICHAEL, lawyer; b. Rockville Centre, N.Y., Feb. 1, 1945; s. James Gregory and Frieda Louise (Brosche) S.; m. Linda Ann Bonfiglio, Aug. 17, 1968; m. 2d, Kari Marie Thoring, Nov. 19, 1977; children—Brendan Michael, Megan Ann. B.A., Adelphi U., 1967; J.D., NYU, 1969. Bar: N.Y. 1970, U.S. Dist. Ct. (so. and ea. dists.) N.Y. 1971, U.S. Ct. Appeals (2d cir.) 1974, Calif. 1977, U.S. Dist. Ct. (so. dist.) Calif. 1977, U.S. Ct. Appeals (9th cir.) 1977, U.S. Ct. Appeals (5th cir.) 1983, U.S. Supreme Ct. 1979, U.S. Dist. Ct. (no. dist.) N.Y. 1982, N.J. 1983, U.S. Dist. Ct. N.J. 1983, U.S. Tax Ct. 1983, U.S. Dist. Ct. (we. dist.) N.Y. 1987. Assoc. Casey, Lane & Mittendorf, N.Y.C., 1969-76, ptnr., 1976-82; ptnr. Haythe & Curley, N.Y.C., 1982-87, Windels, Marx, Davies & Ives, N.Y.C., 1987—. Served with N.Y. N.G., 1969-70. Recipient Benjamin F. Butler award Sch. Law NYU, 1969. Mem. ABA, Assn. Bar City of N.Y., N.Y. State Bar Assn., Fed. Bar Council, N.J. State Bar Assn. Republican. Roman Catholic. Office: Windels Marx Davies & Ives 156 W 56th St New York NY 10019-3800

SHAVER, PHILLIP ROBERT, psychologist, educator; b. Iowa City, Iowa, Sept. 7, 1944; s. Robert Richard and Frances Magdalene (Quinn) S. BA in Psychology, Wesleyan U., Middletown, Conn., 1966; PhD in Social Psychology, U. Mich., 1971. Asst. prof. psychology Columbia U., N.Y.C., 1971-75; assoc. prof. NYU, 1975-80; assoc. prof. U. Denver, 1980-84, prof. psychology, 1984-87; prof. psychology SUNY, Buffalo, 1988—; coord. doctoral program in personality and social psychology NYU, 1978-80; pres. Societal Data Corp., N.Y.C., 1977-82; head experimental and social areas dept. psychology U. Denver, 1981-84, 87—; vis. prof. U. Hawaii, Manoa, 1986; mem. grad. fellowship evaluation panel NSF, 1990—; cons. to numerous orgns. Editorial bd.: Jour. Social and Personal Relationships, 1988—, Personality and Social Psychology Bull., 1985—, Rev. Personality and Social Psychology, 1979-82, 86—, Jour. Personality and Social Psychology, 1978-80, 85—, Behavioral Sci., 1972-80, Jour. Experimental Social Psychology, 1972-75; contbr. reviews and articles to profl. jours. Fundraiser Arthritis Found., Buffalo, 1991. Grantee NIMH, Russell Sage Found., Spencer Found., NSF, Nat. Inst. Alcoholism, Nat. Ctr. for Child Abuse and Neglect; Woodrow Wilson fellow, NSF fellow. Fellow Am. Psychol. Assn.; mem. Am. Psychol. Soc., Eastern Psychol. Assn., Soc. for Experimental Social Psychology, Soc. for Psychol. Study Social Issues, Internat. Soc. for Rsch. on Emotion, Internat. Soc. for Study Personal Relationships, Internat. Network Personal Relationships, Phi Beta Kappa, Phi Kappa Phi, Sigma Xi. Democrat. Home: 317 Ruskin Rd Buffalo NY 14226-4238 Office: SUNY Buffalo Dept Psychology Park Hall Buffalo NY 14260

SHAW, ANTHONY EDWARD, municipal official, restaurant design consultant; b. Queens, N.Y., July 18, 1955; s. Carleton and Edna Lorraine (Pernell) S.; m. Bonnie Lee Weissberg, Mar. 25, 1979 (div. Mar. 1991); m. Elizabeth Frances Kates, Oct. 12, 1991. B in Pub. Adminstrn. magna cum laude, CUNY, 1978; cert., U.S. Dept. Agr. Grad. Sch., 1987. Adminstrv. asst. Boss Realty Co., Bklyn., 1976-79; account mgr. Dun & Bradstreet Internat., N.Y.C., 1979; community planner region 2 GSA, N.Y.C., 1979-81, mgmt. analyst region 2, 1981-83, sr. mgmt. analyst region 2, 1983-85; dep. dir. corruption prevention unit N.Y.C. Dept. of Investigation, 1985-90, dir. internal control unit, 1990—; corp. sec. Penn Restaurant Assocs., Inc., N.Y.C., 1986—; mem. Mayor's Parking Violations Bur. Task Force, N.Y.C., 1986, Mayor's Collection Agy. Coun., N.Y.C., 1986-87. Associate editor (sports mags.) Countrywide Publs., 1974-75. Campaign dir. Cory/Boss Ind. Com., Bklyn., 1977; bd. dirs. West Bklyn. Ind. Dems., Brooklyn Heights, N.Y., 1990—, pres. bd. dirs. Brooklyn Heights SANE/Freeze, 1984—. Recipient Spl. Svc. award GSA, 1984, Community Svc. Cert. Bklyn Borough Pres., 1989, Vol. Svc. award L.I. Coll. Hosp., 1991, Outstanding Achievement award N.Y.C. Commr. Investigation, 1992. Jewish. Home: 131 Joralemon St Brooklyn NY 11201-4069 Office: NYC Dept Investigation 80 Maiden Ln New York NY 10038-4811

SHAW, BARRY N., lawyer; b. Newark, July 31, 1940; s. Harry G. and Evelyn (Kruger) S.; m. Cheryl Lynn Rosen, Mar. 24, 1963; children: Jennifer B., Jonathan M. BS in Acctg., Rutgers U., 1962, JD, 1965. Bar: Pa. 1966, U.S. Dist. Ct. (ea. dist.) Pa. 1966, U.S. Dist. Ct. N.J. 1974, U.S. Ct. Appeals (3d cir.) N.J. 1974, U.S. Supreme Ct. 1988; CPA, Pa. Acct. Coopers & Lybrand, Phila., 1965-68; corp. counsel Lincoln Bank, Phila., 1968-72, Waste Resources Corp., Phila., 1972-74; ptnr. Spivack, Dranoff & Shaw, Phila., 1974-75, Dranoff & Shaw, Phila., 1975-79, Jubanyik, Varbalow Tedesco Shaw & Shaffer, Cherry Hill, N.J., 1979—; lectr. in banking law. Author: Selected Decisions in Lender Liability Law, 1990. Chmn. Shamong Twp. (N.J.) Planning Bd., Local Civic Assn. Mem. ABA, AICPA, N.J. Bar Assn., Phila Bar Assn., Camden County Bar Assn. Republican. Home: 113 Shadow Lake Dr Vincentown NJ 08088-8948 Office: Jubanyik Varbalow Tedesco Shaw & Shaffer 1701 Rte 70 E PO Box 2570 Cherry Hill NJ 08034

SHAW, BERNARD, television journalist; b. Chgo., 1940; m. Linda Shaw; children: Anil, Amar. Corr. Washington bur. CBS News, 1971-77; fgn. corr., bur. chief ABC News, 1977-80; anchor Cable News Network, Washington, 1980—. Served with USMC. Office: CNN 820 1st St NE Washington DC 20002-4205

SHAW, GRACE GOODFRIEND (MRS. HERBERT FRANKLIN SHAW), publisher, editor; b. N.Y.C.; d. Henry Bernheim and Jane Elizabeth

(Stone) Goodfriend; m. Herbert Franklin Shaw (dec. 1992); 1 son, Brandon Hibbs. Student, Bennington Coll.; BA magna cum laude, Fordham U., 1976, MS, 1991. Reporter Port Chester (N.Y.) Daily Item; editorial coordinator World Scope Ency., N.Y.C.; assoc. editor Clarence L. Barnhart, Inc., Bronxville, N.Y.; freelance-writer for reference books; editing supr. World Pub. Co., mng. editor, sr. editor; mng. editor Peter H. Wyden Co., N.Y.C., 1969-70; assoc. editor Dial Press, N.Y.C., 1971-72; sr. editor Dial Press, 1972, David McKay Co., N.Y.C., 1972-75, Grosset & Dunlap, 1975-79; chief editor Today Press (Grosset), 1977-79; sr. editor, coll. dept. Bobbs-Merrill, N.Y.C., mng. editor, exec. editor trade div., 1979-80; pub. Bobbs-Merrill, 1980-84; mng. editor Rawson Assocs. div. Macmillan Pub., 1985-91; pres. Grace Shaw Assocs., Scarsdale, N.Y., 1991—. Mem. Overseas Press Club (bd. dirs. 1984-88, chmn. fgn. policy book awards 1983-87, mem. com. 1987-91). Home and Office: 85 Lee Rd Scarsdale NY 10583-5212

SHAW, HERBERT WELLER, psychotherapist, educator; b. N.Y.C., Feb. 8, 1935; s. Herbert W. and Mary Edna (Smith) S.; m. Judith Shiscak (div.); children: Suzanne Dengler, Christopher Weller; m. Moira Buxton, Sept. 19, 1974. BA in Chemistry, Haverford (Pa.) Coll., 1956. Assoc. creative dir. Marsteller, Inc., N.Y.C., 1961-65; v.p., creative dir. Muller, Jordan, Herrick, Inc., N.Y.C., 1965-67; pres. Shaw Elliott Inc., N.Y.C., 1967-78; trustee and exec. dir. The Pathwork Inc., N.Y., 1972-83; psychotherapist Lake Hill, N.Y., 1978—; bus. cons.; trainer and tchr. Pathwork, Inc.; workshop leader for couples and successful men. Contbr. articles to profl. jours. Chez Aimee Found. grantee, 1991. Home: PO Box 221 Lake Hill NY 12448-0221

SHAW, ISABEL, sculptor, layout designer; b. N.Y.C.; d. Louis and Clara (Slutsky) Goldburt; m. J. Carol Summers, 1952 (div. 1953); m. Henry Shaw, Jan. 12, 1961; children: Frank Jeffrey Shaw, Andrea Shaw. BFA, Bard Coll., Annendale-on-Hudson, N.Y., 1952; student, Sch. Visual Arts, N.Y.C., 1953, Cooper Union, 1954. One-woman shows include Kennedy Coun. for the Arts, Cork Gallery, Lincoln Ctr., N.Y.C., 1988, Contemporary Artists Gallery, Nyack, N.Y., 1981, Mari Gallery, Mamaroneck, N.Y., 1981, MAG Gallery, Larchmont, N.Y., 1981, Anaya Gallery, Scarsdale, N.Y., 1980; exhibited in group shows at The Bruton St. Gallery, London, 1991-92, Broome St. Gallery, N.Y.C., 1991-92, Sandra Neustadter Gallery, Delray Beach, Fla., 1989-90, Roslyn Sailor Fine Arts, Margate, N.J., 1988-92, MAG Gallery, Larchmont, 1980-92. Recipient first prize for sculpture, Beaux Arts Finale, Westchester County, 1974, Lyla J. Weiss Meml. award Mamarneck Artists Guild Nat. Juried, White Plains, N.Y., 1984. Mem. Art Studio Club, N.Y. Soc. Women Artists, Contemporary Artists Guild, Hudson Valley Contemporary Artists, Sculptors League, Mamarneck Artists Guild, Working Artists.

SHAW, JAMES RENFREW, music educator; b. Phila., Aug. 27, 1930; s. Alexander Renfrew and Marion Hesther (Richardson) S.; m. Barbara Ann Kindig, June 4, 1955 (div. 1968); children: Debra Lee, Bryan Richard, Gretchen Kristina, Leslie Anne; m. Joanna Gibbs Miller, Nov. 21, 1969. MusB, Pa. State U., 1954; MusM Edn., Temple U., 1959; student, U. Arizona, 1961-62, U. Ind. Tchr. Scott High Sch., Coatesville, Pa., 1954, Pennridge High Sch., Perkasie, Pa., 1956-61, Niagara-Wheatfield High Sch., Sanborn, N.Y., 1962-63; prof. music Glassboro (N.J.) State Coll., 1963—. Composer (opera) The Minion and the Three Riddles, 1988, (children's shows) Penny and The Magic Medallion, 1974, Beanstalk, 1975, Legend of the Sun Child, 1976, Showdown at the Sugarcane Saloon, 1979, Once Upon A Shoe, 1981, The Princess, The Poet, and the Little Gray Man, Legend of the Sun Child, (adult mus.) Ashes, Ashes, All Fall Down, 1983, Dear Me, The Sky is Falling, 1991, (cantata) The Lovely Shall Be Choosers, 1990. Served as 1st lt. Signal Corp., 1954-56. Mem. Nat. Assn. Tchrs. Singing (N.J. and nat. chpts.). Home: 450 Lake Ave Pitman NJ 08071-1854 Office: Glassboro State Coll Music Dept Glassboro NJ 08028

SHAW, (GEORGE) KENDALL, artist, educator; b. New Orleans, Mar. 30, 1924; s. George Kendall and Florence Gladys (Worner) S.; m. Frances Glenn Fort, Oct. 31, 1955. Student, Ga. Inst. Tech., 1944-46; B.S. in Chemistry, Tulane U., 1949, M.F.A. in Painting, 1959; postgrad., La. State U., 1950. instr. Columbia U., 1961-66, Hunter Coll., 1966-68, Parsons Sch. Design, N.Y.C., 1966-86, Lehman Coll., 1968-70, Bklyn. Mus. Art Sch., 1970-76. One-man shows include Columbia U., 1965, Bienville Gallery, New Orleans, 1968, Tibor de Nagy Gallery, N.Y.C., 1964, 65, 67, 68, Southampton Coll., 1969, John Bernard Myers Gallery, 1972, Alessandra Gallery, 1976, Lerner/Heller Gallery, N.Y.C., 1979, 81, 82, Bernice Steinbaum Gallery, N.Y.C., 1991, Artists Space, N.Y.C., 1992; group shows include P.S.I., N.Y.C., 1977, Gladstone-Villani Gallery, N.Y.C., 1978, Galerie Habermann, Cologne, 1979, Modern Art Gallery, Vienna, 1980, Jacksonville Art Mus. (Fla.), 1983, others; represented in permanent collections Peter Ludwig, Aachen, Bklyn. Mus., Albright-Knox Gallery, Buffalo, Mus. Contemporary Art, Nagaoka, Japan, Everson Mus., Syracuse, Chase Manhattan Bank, N.Y.C., Chem. Bank, N.Y.C., N.Y. U., N.Y.C. Served with USN, 1943-46. Mem. Coll. Art Assn., Artists Equity Assn. Democrat. Address: 458 Broome St New York NY 10013

SHAW, LAWRENCE EVERETT, engineering and construction company executive; b. Elkton, Md., Mar. 2, 1947; s. William Lesley and Helen (Everett) S.; m. Rebecca Louise Batson, June 13, 1970; 1 child, R. Tyler. BS in Nuclear Engring., N.C. State U., 1970; MBA in Mgmt., NYU, 1975. Registered profl. engr., Pa., N.Y. Engr. Ebasco Svcs. Inc., N.Y.C., 1970-76; engring. mgr. Ebasco Svcs. Inc., Princeton, N.J., 1976-83; project mgr. Ebasco Svcs. Inc., N.Y.C., 1983-86, v.p. mktg., 1986—; cons. Superconduction Supercollider Lab., Tex., 1990—. Contbr. articles to profl. jours. Mem. Am. Nuclear Soc., Am. Vacuum Soc. (fusion com.). Home: 183 Carriage Way Princeton NJ 08540 Office: Ebasco Svcs Inc 2 World Trade Ctr New York NY 10048

SHAW, MARTIN ANDREW, clinical and research psychologist; b. N.Y.C., Jan. 27, 1944; s. Aaron S. and Betty Shaw; m. Dorothy Korot, Nov. 7, 1971; 1 child, Anatole Bernard. BS, NYU, 1966; MA, Dalhousie U., 1972; PhD, U. Wis., 1977; postgrad. Advanced Inst. Analytic Psychotherapy, 1977-82. Art tchr. N.Y.C. Schs., 1966-69; art therapist Kingsbridge VA Hosp., Bronx, N.Y., 1969-71; grad. teaching asst. Dalhousie U., 1971-72, Killam Children's Hosp., Halifax Sch. for Blind, N.S., Can., 1971-72; psychometrician, cons. N.Y.C. Bd. Edn., 1977-80; staff therapist, staff psychologist Advanced Ctr. for Psychotherapy, Jamaica, N.Y., 1977-82; clin./child psychologist Health Ins. Plan, Mental Health Service, N.Y.C., 1980-84; pvt. practice clin. and clin. child psychology, N.Y.C., 1981-83, Gt. Neck, N.Y., 1981—; cons. psychologist Hearing and Speech Ctr. of L.I. Jewish-Hillside Med. Ctr., New Hyde Park, N.Y., 1986-87, Trinity-Pawling (N.Y.) Sch., 1986—; founder, pres. ORT Inst., Inc.; trustee Signal Hill Edn. Ctr., Inc., 1983-87. Recipient Founders Day award, N.Y.U., 1966, VA commendation, 1970; lic. psychologist, N.Y. State. Fellow Soc. for Personality Assessment, Brit. Soc. for Projective Psychology (hon.); mem. Am. Psychol. Assn., N.Y. State Psychol. Assn., N.Y. Soc. Clin. Psychologists, Nassau County Psychol. Assn., AAAS, N.Y. Acad. Scis., Internat. Rorschach Soc., Soc. Psychoanalytic Rsch., Pi Lambda Theta. Contbr. papers to profl. jours. and confs. Office: 29 Barstow Rd Ste 102 Great Neck NY 11021-2209

SHAW, MONTGOMERY THROOP, chemical engineering educator; b. Ithaca, N.Y., Sept. 11, 1943; s. Robert William and Charlotte (Throop) S.; m. Stephanie Habel, Sept. 5, 1966 (dec. 1989); 1 child, Steven Robert. B-ChemE, Cornell U., 1966, MS, 1966; MS, Princeton (N.J.) U., 1968, PhD, 1970. Engr., project scientist Union Carbide Corp., Bound Brook, N.J., 1970-76; assoc. prof. Dept. Chem. Engring., U. Conn., Storrs, 1977-83, prof., 1983—; sabbatical prof. Sandia Nat. Labs., Albuquerque, 1983-84; adv. bd. Jour. of Applied Polymer Sci., 1984—. Co-author: Polymer-Polymer Miscibility, 1977. Grantee Alcoa Found., 1985, Exxon Edn. Found., 1986. Mem. IEEE, Soc. Rheology (sec. 1977-81), Am. Chem. Soc., Am. Phys. Soc. Office: U Conn IMS 97 S Eagleville Road Ext Storrs Mansfield CT 06269-0001

SHAW, RICHARD JOHN, horticulture educator; b. Fall River, Mass., Jan. 15, 1939; s. Gilbert B. and Doris (Gleason) S.; m. Loretta Hagemann, Aug. 21, 1965; children: Cynthia, Deborah. BS, U. R.I., 1961; MS, U. Mo., 1963, PhD, 1966. Rsch. asst. U. Mo., Columbia, 1961-66; asst. prof. La. State U., Baton Rouge, 1966-70; asst. prof. U. R.I., Kingston, 1970-76, assoc. prof., 1976—. Mem. Am. Horticulture Therapy Assn. (treas. New Eng. chpt. 1989—), Am. Soc. for Hort. Sci., Am. Horticulture Soc., Profl. Plant Growers Assn., Ohio Florists Assn. Office: U RI Dept Plant Scis Kingston RI 02881

SHAW, RICHARD PAUL, civil engineer, educator; b. N.Y.C., June 23, 1933; s. Thomas Henry and Margarete (Knaack) S.; m. Heather Gaye Stern, May 4, 1961; children: Deirdre Ellen, Melissa Lee. BS in Math., Poly. Inst. Bklyn., 1954; MCE, Columbia U., 1955, PhD in Civil Engring., 1960. Registered profl. engr., N.Y. Asst. prof. dept. engring. sci. Pratt Inst., Bklyn., 1957-62; assoc. prof. sch. engring. and applied sci. SUNY, Buffalo, 1962-69, prof. sch. engring. and applied sci., 1969—; program assoc. NSF, Washington, 1977-78; postdoctoral fellow Joint Tsunami Rsch. Effort, Honolulu, 1973-74, 69-70. Contbr. over 100 articles to profl. jours. and chpts. to books; co-editor: Advancements in BEM in Japan and USA, 1990. Am. Coun. Edn. fellow, 1973, NOAA fellow, 1973, 69, NSF fellow, 1955, Guggenheim fellow, 1954; named Eminent Scientist Wessex Inst. Tech., 1988. Mem. Internat. Soc. for Innovative Numerical Analysis (pres. 1980—). Unitarian. Office: SUNY-Buffalo Buffalo NY 14260

SHAW, RICHARD WALLACE, JR., insurance marketing representative; b. Olney, Md., Aug. 26, 1962; s. Richard W. and Doris (Cole) S. B of Gen. Studies, U. Md., 1984. Sales rep. Washington Nat., Columbia, Md., 1984-86, The Fred Weaver Agy., Columbia, Md., 1986-87; account rep. PaineWebber Risk Mgmt., Columbia, Md., 1987-89; supr. Hobbs Group, Inc., Columbia, Md., 1989-90, mktg. rep., 1990—. Mem. Ellicott City Jaycees (pres. 1989), Terrapin Club, Md. Alumni Assn., Howard County Rep. Club. Republican. Methodist. Home: 11768 Stonegate Ln Columbia MD 21044 Office: Hobbs Group Inc 10400 Little Patuxent Pky Columbia MD 21044-3510

SHAW, ROBERT SAMUEL, psychologist; b. Pitts., Jan. 29, 1952; s. Matthew J. and Margaret R. (Greathouse) S.; m. Karen Trimble, Aug. 5, 1972; children: Matthew R., James J. AA, Northeastern Christian Coll., Villanova, Pa., 1971; BA, Abilene Christian U., 1974, MA, 1981; MA, Marywood Coll., Scranton, Pa., 1986. Ordained to ministry Ch. of Christ, 1978. Minister Harding Ch. of Christ, Pittston, Pa., 1978—; dir. pastoral care The Wesley Village, Pittston, 1988-91; psychologist, pvt. practice Dallas, Pa., 1990—. Recipient Eugene Raymond scholarship Marywood Coll., 1984, 85, Immaculate Heart of Mary scholarship, 1982. Mem. Am. Psychol. Assn. (assoc.), Pa. Psychol. Assn., Northeastern Pa. Psychol. Assn. (exec. com.), Rotary (past pres. Pittston club, Paul Harris fellow), Wyoming Valley Coun. of Chs. (chmn. pastoral care com.), Wyo. Conf. United Meth. Ch. (assoc.). Office: Back Mountain Profl Bldg Rte 309 Dallas PA 18612

SHAW, STEVEN, stage manager; b. Bklyn., Feb. 2, 1937; s. Harold Alexander and Mary Ellen (Daken) S.; m. Diana Kerew, Aug. 5, 1973; children: Merideth, Christopher, Jennifer. Grad., Ft. Hamilton High Sch., Bklyn., 1955. Stage mgr. Deathtrap, N.Y.C., 1980-81; dir. Deathtrap, Mexico City, 1982, Amadeus, Mexico City, 1984; stage mgr. Sunday in the Park with George, N.Y.C., 1985-86, Rumors, N.Y.C., 1989, Broadway Bound, N.Y.C., 1988-89, Orpheus Descending, N.Y.C., 1990, Mule Bone, N.Y.C., 1991, Death and the Maiden, N.Y.C., 1992; cons. Masur Theatre at Asphalt Green, N.Y.C., 1985. Author (reference) Prop Shopper Guide, 1972. Mem. Actors' Equity Assn. (com. mem. 1987—), Stage Mgrs. Assn. (exec. bd. 1989—), Broadway Show League (bd. advisors 1985-91).

SHAY, PHILIPP WENDELL, management consultant, professional writer, educator; b. Elberta, Utah, Apr. 17, 1914; s. Robert Martin and Ida Beth (Kelly) S.; m. Agnes Cecilia Schaefer, July 22, 1940; children: Katherine Ann, Philip Brian, Mary Eleanor, Robert Joseph, Peter Fabian, Brooke Elizabeth, Philip W. Jr. BA, Seattle U., 1935; MA, Cath. U., 1937; PhD, U. Toronto, 1941. Prof. Stanford U., Calif., 1941-42, NYU and Columbia U., 1962-66; nat. program asst. dir. USO, N.Y.C., 1942-46; mgmt. cons. Harry Hopf & Co., Ossining, N.Y., 1946-49; ednl. cons. U.S. Army of Occupation, Tokyo, 1949-50; research dir. Am. Mgmt. Assns., N.Y.C., 1950-54; exec. dir. Inst. Mgmt. Cons. of U.S., 1969-75, Assn. Cons. Mgmt. Engrs., N.Y.C., 1954-77; pres. Shay Assocs., Inc., Yonkers, N.Y., 1977—; cons. part-time Assn. Exec. Recruiting Cons., Inst. Mgmt. Cons. of Ont., Can., Mgmt. Cons. Assn. of Australia, Japan, N.Z., India and S.Africa. Editor of 14 publs. on mgmt. cons. published by Assn. Cons. Engrs.; also articles. Recipient Outstanding award 6th Annual N.Am. Conf. Mgmt. Cons., 1977. Democrat. Roman Catholic. Home and Office: 119 Hawthorne Ave Yonkers NY 10701-3553

SHAY, ROBERT MICHAEL, manufacturing company executive, consultant; b. Phila., Sept. 14, 1936; s. Harry and Bertha (Shaivitz) S.; m. Elaine Lee Rosenthol-Kushner, June 8, 1956; children: Susan, Lauri, Robert Michael Jr., Heather. BS in Econs., U. Pa., 1958, JD, 1961. Bar: Pa. 1962, U.S. Supreme Ct. 1962. Chief operating officer, sec., treas. Montefiore Cemetery Co., Phila., 1952-88, pres., 1988—; dir., sec., treas. Metachron Rsch. Corp., Phila., 1955-59; assoc. Fox, Rothschild, O'Brien & Frankel, Phila., 1961-74, ptnr., 1973; treas., dir. Forest Hills Cemetery Corp., Phila., 1964-83; pres., chief exec. officer Nat. Crematory Corp., Luna, N.Mex., 1988—, also bd. dirs.; chmn. bd., chief exec. officer, officer, dir. various oper. subs. Morlan Internat., Inc. and its domestic and fgn. subs., Phila., 1969-83; chmn. bd. Superior Holding Corp., Cleve., 1981—, Internat. and Commerce Bank, Phoenix, 1988-90; chmn. bd., chief exec. officer, bd. dirs. Innovative Bicycle Products Inc. (formerly Bike-O-Matic Ltd.), Eagleville, Pa., 1987—, Regal Corrugated Box Co., Inc. (name changed to Camelback Internat., Inc.), 1986—; chmn. bd., chief exec. officer Terraplex Corp. and subs., Phila., 1983—, Eagle Communications Inc., Eagleville, Pa., 1990; chmn. ALS, Inc., Phila., 1988—; bd. dirs. Am. Cemetery Svcs., Inc., 4-U Corp., also various fin. corps.; lectr. Am. Coll. Life Underwriters, Bryn Mawr, Pa.; cons. in health care field. Contbr. articles to profl. publs. Shelter mgr., mem. Abington CD and Race Network, Pa., 1960-61; co-leader Sawmill Hill coun. Boy Scouts Am., 1974; co-pres. Huntingdon Jr. High Sch. PTO, Abington, 1973-74; fin. chmn. Coyle for State Rep. Com., Abington, 1978, Swan for State Rep. Com., Abington, 1980, Greenleaf for State Senate Com., Abington, 1982, 86, 88; co-fin. chmn. Fox for State Rep. Com., Abington, 1984, 86, 88; alt. del. Rep. Nat. Conv., 1988, 92; chmn. Century Club, Abington Twp. Rep. Orgn., 1983-86; chmn. bd. dirs. Contemporary Opera Co. Am., Phila., 1983-84; bd. dirs. Mann Music Ctr., Phila., 1975—, Nat. Mus. Am. Jewish History, Phila., 1982-84, Am. com. Phila. br. Shaare Zedek Hosp., 1982—; bd. dirs. Moss Rehab. Hosp., Phila., 1989—, Moss Rehab., Inc., 1991—, vice chmn., 1991—; bd. dirs. RehabVentures, Inc., 1991—; trustee Shay Found., Phila., 1989—, Pa. Coll. Optometry, 1992—, Einstein Health-Care Systems, 1992—; bd. dirs., sec. Phila. br. Am. Friends of Haifa U., 1982-86, pres., 1986—, also bd. dirs.; treas., trustee Abington Free Libr., 1981-88, Young Pres. Orgn., 1974-87; mem. adv. coun. William Feinbloom Vision Rehab. Ctr., Phila., 1991—; mem. bd. govs. Albert Einstein Med. Ctr., 1992—. Mem. ABA, World Bus. Coun., Phila. Pres. Orgn., Am. Cemetery Assn. (bd. dirs. 1979-81, chmn. spring conf. 1982), Cemetery Consumer Svc. Coun. (pres. 1982-83), Keystone State Assn. Cemeteries, Cemetery Assn. Greater Phila. and Vicinity, Jewish Cemeteries Assn. Greater Phila. and Vicinity (pres. 1967), Cremation Assn. N.Am., Tech. Assn. Pulp and Paper Industry, Aircraft Owners and Pilots Assn., Locust Club Phila., Philmont Country Club, Ariz. Club, Beta Gamma Sigma, Beta Alpha Psi. Home: 1326 Panther Rd Rydal PA 19046-2420 Office: Terraplex Corp Church Rd Philadelphia PA 19117-2206

SHAY, STEPHEN ELLIOTT, lawyer; b. Bangor, Maine, May 9, 1951; s. Robert P. and Esther (Cunningham) S.; m. Wendy A. Weiss, May 31, 1982; children: David, Rachel. BA, Wesleyan U., 1972; JD, Columbia U., 1976, MBA, 1976. Bar: N.Y. 1977, Mass. 1991. Assoc. Reavis & McGrath, N.Y.C., 1976-79, Coudert Bros., N.Y.C., 1979-81; mem. staff office of internat. tax counsel U.S. Dept. Treasury, Washington, 1982-85; internat. tax counsel U.S. Dept. Treasury, Washington, $D, $D, 1985-87; ptnr. Ropes & Gray, Boston, 1987—. Contbr. author: American Law Institute/Federal Income Tax Project: U.S. Income Tax Treaties; contbr. articles to jours. Mem. ABA (chmn. subcom. on sect. 367 and 1491 trans.), Am. Law Inst., N.Y. State Bar Assn., Boston Bar Assn. Home: 27 Manns Hill Rd Sharon MA 02067-2210 Office: Ropes & Gray One International Place Boston MA 02110-2624

SHAYNER, JOHN ANTHONY, English educator, executive assistant; b. Ipswich, Suffolk, Eng., Aug. 27, 1945; came to U.S., 1950; s. Benny Anthony and Gladys Muriel (Pluckrose) S.; m. Katie Celesta Lenig, Aug. 13, 1983. BA in Latin, Columbia U., 1967; PhD in Classics, Stanford U., 1973. Instr. Raritan High Sch., Hazlet, N.J., 1973-74, Middlesex Coll., Edison, N.J., 1974-79; assoc. prof. Centenary Coll., Hackettstown, N.J., 1979—, exec. asst. to pres., 1986—; treas. Morningside Assocs., Del., 1991—. Co-author: (chpt.) Empowering Women, 1988; author, producer (video program) Origins of English, 1985, Triumph of English, 1986. Officer Panther Valley Ecumenical Ministry, Hackettstown, 1990—. N.J. Dept. Higher Edn. grantee, 1984, 85, 86, 87. Mem. Am. Philological Assn., Classic Assn. Atlantic States, Columbia Club of N.Y.C., Panther Valley Golf and Country Club. Episcopalian. Home: 17 Wood Duck Ct Hackettstown NJ 07840-3312 Office: Centenary Coll 400 Jefferson St Hackettstown NJ 07840-2184

SHAYS, CHRISTOPHER, congressman; b. Stamford, Conn., Oct. 18, 1945; m. Betsi deRaisnes, 1968; 1 child. BA, Principia Coll.; MBA, MPA, NYU. Vol. U.S. Peace Corps, 1968-70; state rep. State of Conn. (Dist. 147), Stamford, 1974-87; mem. 100th-102nd Congresses from 4th Conn. Dist., Washington, 1987—. Republican. Office: Ho of Reps 1531 Longworth Bldg Washington DC 20515

SHEA, ANN MARIE, educational theatre instructor, actress, theatre director; b. Worcester, Mass., Dec. 17, 1939; d. Michael Joseph and Ellen Mary (Greney) S. AB in English, Anna Maria Coll., 1961; MA in Drama, The Cath. U. Am., 1964; postgrad. internat. stage movement inst., So. Meth. U., Dallas and London, 1971, 72; postgrad., Tufts U., 1973, U. Mass., 1973-74, 79-80; PhD in Ednl. Theatre, NYU, 1984; attended, Shakespeare and Co., 1990. Tchr. speech, acting, theatre history Coll. Misericordia, 1966-68; prof. ednl. theatre Worcester State Coll., 1969—; coord. summer youth theatre Worcester Children's Theatre, 1984, coord. coop. venture with Summer's World Theatre in the Pks., 1987; mem. adv. bd. Program Enrichment for Able Kids Worcester Pub. Schs., 1985-86, curriculum cons. to design theatre magnet programs; adjudicator drama festival Tantasqua Regional High Sch., 1989; adjudicator regional festival Mass. High Sch. Drama Guild, 1983, state finals, 1982; festival adjudicator Community Theatre Assn., Springfield, Mass., 1982. Dir. Worcester State Coll. plays including The Unknown Soldier and His Wife, 1971, The Good Doctor, 1978, Raised in the Faith, 1989, Twelfth Night, 1992; Coll. Misericordia plays include The Red Shoes, 1965, Royal Gambit, 1966; plays various community theatres include The American Dream, 1967, Glass Menagerie, 1977, As You Like It, 1985; Worcester Children's Theatre plays include Step on A Crack, 1989, The Arkansaw Bear, 1990, The Velveteen Rabbit, 1991; appeared in plays including A Streetcar Named Desire, 1966, What the Butler Saw, 1988; also TV commls., voice overs, and radio commls. founder Worcester Children's Theatre, 1969, pres., 1984-86, v.p. edn., 1988-89; sec. Worcester Forum Theatre Ensemble, 1987-89, bd. dirs., 1986—; mem. edn. com. Higgins Armory Mus., 1989; mem. band pavilion com. City of Worcester Pks. and Recreation Dept., 1988-89; mem. fundraising cabinet Ctr. for the Performing Arts, 1985; organizer festivals, bd. dirs. Very Spl. Arts, 1987-88; former v.p., bd. dirs. Summer's World, 1979-87. Winner Moss Hart Meml. award New Eng. Theatre Conf. Mem. Assn. for Theatre in Higher Edn., Am. Assn. Theatre for Youth, Alpha Epsilon Rho, Delta Kappa Gamma. Home: 5 Fairview Rd # 2A Sturbridge MA 01566-1208 Office: Worcester State Coll Dept Media Arts and Philosophy 486 Chandler St Worcester MA 01602-2597

SHEA, EMMETT ANDREW, historian, educator; b. Worcester, Mass., Oct. 24, 1930; s. Emmett A. and Linda C. (Lis) S.; m. Margaret F. Carr, Aug. 19, 1961; 1 child, Carolyn A. BS, Boston U., 1955, EdM, 1956, AM, 1961; AM, Boston Coll., 1971; PhD, Internat. Inst. for Advanced Studies, St. Louis, 1982. Lect. Wellesley (Mass.) Coll., 1957-62; prof. Worcester State Coll., 1962--; prof. Coll. of Holy Cross, Worcester, 1962-73, Regis Coll., Westen, Mass., 1964-70; TV analyst, Worcester, 1966-73; chmn. Worcester State Coll., 1970-76, chmn. dept. hist. and poli. sci., 1987-90. Lt. USMC, 1950-53, Korea. Recipient Ford Found. grant, 1957. Mem. Am. Hist. Assn., Am. Assn. for Slavic Studies, Am. Asian Assn., Soc. Historians of Fgn. Rels., N.E. Slavic Assn., N.E. Asian Assn., Phi Alpha Theta, Pi Gamma Mu. Democrat. Roman Catholic. Home: 9 Philip Rd Framingham MA 11701 Office: Worcester State Coll 486 Chandler St Worcester MA 01602-2597

SHEA, JOHN EDWARD, advertising executive; b. Chgo., July 13, 1943; s. Lester Albert and Corinne Margret (Lang) S.; m. Doris Scharfenberger, May 12, 1991. BA, Marshall U., 1965; postgrad., Columbia U., 1966-67, Hunter Coll., 1968—. Dir. mem. svcs.m United Community Funds & Couns. Am., N.Y.C., 1968-69; v.p., ptnr. The Assignment Group, 1969-73; contbg. editor Packaging Design Mag., N.Y.C., 1970-77; ptnr., cons. The SMC Group, N.Y.C., 1973-76; ptnr. Corp. Resources for Mktg., N.Y.C., 1974-79; pres. Canon & Shea Assocs. Inc., N.Y.C., 1978—; mem. Am. Mktg. Assn., N.Y.C., 1972-79. Contbg. editor, guest editor to several jours. Advance man Rep. Com. to Elect Pres., N.Y.C., 1968, pub. rels. com., 1968; pub. rels. com. Cecil Underwood Gov. election com., W.Va., 1965; mem., fellow Mus. Modern Art, N.Y.C., 1973—, Witney Mus. Am. Art, N.Y.C., 1984—; mem. adv. bd. nat. com. pub. rels. dirs. Community Funds & Coun. Am., N.Y.C., 1966. Mem. Bus. Profl. Advt. Assn., Publicity Soc. N.Y., Am. Chem. Soc. (Rubber div.), Soc. Plastics Engrs., Marshall U. Alumni Assn. Episcopalian. Home: 424 E 52d St Apt 2G New York NY 10022 also: 118 New St New Hope PA 18938 Office: Canon & Shea Assocs Inc 224 W 35th St Ste 1500 New York NY 10001-2507

SHEA, THOMAS JAMES, human resources executive; b. Springfield, Mass., Feb. 14, 1949; s. Thomas Andrew and Anne Marie (Kane) S.; m. Marthe Roberts, Mar. 9, 1991; 1 child, Michael W. BSEd, Westfield (Mass.) Coll., 1970, MEd in Counseling, 1976. Tchr. Springfield (Mass.) Pub. Schs., 1971-81; tng. specialist Mass. Mutual Life Ins. Co., Springfield, 1981-83; tng. adminstr. Advo-System, Inc., Hartford, Conn., 1984-85; mgmt. devel. cons. CIGNA Corp., Hartford, Conn., 1985-87; dir. tng. The Kasten Co., Phila., 1987-88; tng. and devel. mgr. GMAC Mortgage Corp., Elkins Park, Pa., 1988-89, v.p. human resources, 1989—. Sgt. ARNG, 1970-76. Mem. ASTD (nat. conf. design com. fin. svcs. conf. 1989, nat. conf. design com., 1990, bd. dirs. banking industry group 1990—). Office: GMAC Mortgage Corp 8360 Old York Rd Elkins Park PA 19117-1590

SHEAFFER, CAREY NELSON, human resource management executive; b. McAlisterville, Pa., Sept. 22, 1947; s. Herman Clarence and Gladys Elaine (Losch) S.; m. Carol Jean Reigle, Oct. 23, 1965; children: Christopher, Jeffery. AS, Susquehanna U., 1974. Cert. sr. profl. in human resources Human Resource Cert. Inst. Ops. supr. Tri-County Nat. Bank, Middleburg, Pa., 1969-75; v.p., dir. human resources First Nat. Trust Bank, Sunbury, Pa., 1975—. Sgt. U.S. Army, 1966-69. Mem. Soc. Human Resource Mgmt., Am. Bankers Assn., Pa. Bankers Assn., Bank Adminstrn. Inst., Am. Inst. Banking, Susquehanna Pers. Mgmt. Assn. (pres. 1987-88), Sunbury C. of C., Am. Legion, Moose, Rotary (bd. dirs. Sunbury 1987-88). Democrat. Home: 203 Baldwin Blvd Selinsgrove PA 17870-9511

SHEALY, ALAN WARDWELL, investor; b. Fitchburg, Mass., Aug. 15, 1953; s. Austin Craig and Marin (Jones) S.; m. Laura Johnson, Dec. 27, 1980; children: Scott, Grant, Roxie. AB, Harvard U., 1975; BA, MA, Oxford (Eng.) U., 1978. Vice pres., head U.S. dollar interest rate swaps Citibank, N.A., N.Y.C., 1982-90; 1st v.p., head fgn. exch. Union Bank Switzerland, N.Y.C., 1990-91; pvt. investor N.Y.C., 1991—. Mem. Olympic rowing team, 1976, 80, world champion, 1974. Mem. Fgn. Exch. USA, Power Ten Soc. Office: 3 Pickwick Plz Ste 200 Greenwich CT 06830

SHEAR, CHARLES ROBERT, anatomist, educator; b. Chgo., Jan. 20, 1942; m. Carol Justine Gardner, Dec. 18, 1966. BS, U. Ill., 1965; MS, Columbia U., 1967, PhD, 1969. Asst. prof. Emory U. Sch. Medicine, Atlanta, 1970-75, assoc. prof., 1975-76; assoc. prof. U. Md. Sch. Medicine, Balt., 1976—; mem. nat. adv. coun. VA, 1980-84, ad hoc study sect. reviewer NIH, 1983-86. NIH grantee, 1973-89. Mem. AAAS, AAUP, Am. Soc. for Cell Biology, Am. Assn. Anatomists, Sigma Xi. Home: 579 Stocketts Run Rd Davidsonville MD 21035-2606 Office: U Md Sch. Medicine Anatomy 655 W Baltimore St Baltimore MD 21201-1509

SHEAR, IONE MYLONAS, archaeologist; b. St. Louis, Feb. 19, 1936; d. George Emmanuel and Lella (Papazouglou) Mylonas; B.A., Wellesley Coll., 1958; M.A., Bryn Mawr Coll., 1960, Ph.D., 1968; m. Theodore Leslie Shear, June 24, 1959; children—Julia Louise, Alexandra. Research asst. Inst. for

Advanced Study, Princeton, N.J., 1963-65; mem. Agora Excavation, Athens, 1967, 72—; lectr. art and archaeology Princeton U., 1983-84; also excavator various other sites in Greece and Italy. Mem. Archaeol. Inst. Am., Greek Archaeol. Soc. (hon.). Author: The Panagia Houses at Mycenae, 1987; contbr. articles to profl. jours. Address: 87 Library Pl Princeton NJ 08540

SHEAR, NATALIE PICKUS, public relations executive, consultant; b. N.Y.C., Oct. 18, 1940; d. Sam and Mildred (Shulman) Pickus; m. Daniel H. Shear, Dec. 14, 1968 (dec. Apr. 1989); children: Adam Brian, Tamara Beth. BA in Journalism, Fairleigh Dickinson U., 1962. Editorial asst. Show Bus. Newspaper, N.Y.C., 1962-64, The Jewish News, Newark, 1964-66; dir. Manhattan women's div., program asst. Am. Jewish Congress, N.Y.C., 1966-68; mng. editor The Jewish Week, Washington, 1968-71; dir. pub. rels. United Jewish Appeal, Washington, 1973-74; pub. affairs dir. Leadership Conf. on Civil Rights, Washington, 1977-83; pres. Natalie P. Shear Assocs., Inc., Washington, 1983—. Editor (newspaper) Books Alive, 1973-74; editor, pub. (newsletter) Trends, Inc., 1989—. Vol. Dem. Nat. Com., Washington, 1991—; chairperson women's task force Am. Jewish Congress, Washington, 1984-86, mem. nat. women's task force, 1989—; v.p. Nat. Child Rsch. Ctr., Washington, 1974-76; pres. Ohr Kodesh Sisterhood, Chevy Chase, Md., 1980-82. Mem. Am. Jewish Pub. Rels. Soc., Greater Washington Soc. Assn. Execs. Home: 4701 Willard Ave Bethesda MD 20815-4635 Office: 1629 K St NW # 802 Washington DC 20006-1632

SHEAR, VIRGINIA MARGUERITE, computer operator; b. Rochester, N.Y., Apr. 2, 1950; d. James Rodney and Arloine Jeanne (Weidman) S. B Music Edn., Madison Coll., 1972; postgrad., SUNY-Brockport, 1988. Tchr. instrumental music Rochester (N.Y.) City Sch. Dist., 1974-77; mechanic Batavia (N.Y.) Kawasaki, Inc., 1977-78, Wehner Mower Co., Rochester, 1978-80; computer programmer, operator Eastman Kodak Co., Rochester, 1980—. Co-editor Chrome Rose's Rev., LeRoy, N.Y., 1986—. Co-organizer Women's Motorcycle Festival, LeRoy, 1984—. Mem. Women Motorcyclists Found. (co-chmn. LeRoy chpt. 1984—), Moving Violations Motorcycle Club, Gay Alliance Genesee Valley (past sec.), Sigma Alpha Iota. Baptist. Home: 7 Lent Ave Le Roy NY 14482-1009

SHEARD, CHARLES, III, dermatologist; b. Toronto, Ontario, Can., Nov. 22, 1914; came to U.S., 1945; s. Charles Jr. and Alice Elizabeth (Ramsay) S; m. Katherine Patricia Murphy, Nov. 19, 1938; children: Joan Virginia Sheard Cumming, Pamela Carol Sheard McGuiness, Wendy Alice Sheard Geyer. Sr. matriculation, Upper Can. Coll., Toronto, 1933; MD, U. Toronto, 1939. Diplomate Am. Bd. Dermatology. Intern Toronto Gen. Hosp., 1939-40; instr. physiology, anatomy U. Toronto Med. Faculty, 1940-41; surgical asst. resident Hosp. for Sick Children, Toronto, 1945; asst. to chief resident dermatologist Columbia Presbyn. Hosp., N.Y.C., 1945-49; assoc. prof. medicine Cornell U. Med. Coll., N.Y.C., 1950—. Author: (textbook) Treatment in Dermatology, 1948; contbr. articles to profl. jours. Flight lt. RCAF, 1941-45. Fellow ACP, Royal Coll. Physicians of Can.; mem. Metro-Manhattan Dermatol. Soc.N.Y.C. (sec. 1970-80), Can. Club of N.Y., Royal Can. Yacht Club, St. George's Club, Wee Burn Golf & Country Club Darien. Republican. Episcopalian. Office: Charles Sheard MD PC 440 Bedford St Stamford CT 06901-1599

SHEARD, WENDY STEDMAN, art historian; b. New Haven, July 24, 1935; d. Frank Owen Heywood and Geraldine Stickney (Swift) Williams; m. Arthur K. Stedman, Sept. 1958 (div. 1966); children: Amanda Keeney Stedman Bourque, Anthony Owen Stedman; m. Michael H. Sheard, Oct. 10, 1969. BA, Vassar Coll., 1957; MA, Yale U., 1965, PhD, 1971. Instr. art history Yale U., New Haven, 1966-67, vis. lectr., 1972-73; lectr. Smith Coll., Northampton, Mass., 1974-75; lectr., asst. prof. Mt. Holyoke Coll., South Hadley, Mass., 1978-79; vis. asst. prof. U. Hartford, Conn., 1979-80; vis. asst. prof. Boston U., 1983-84, vis. adj. assoc. prof., 1988; freelance art historian, 1988—. Author: Antiquity in the Renaissance, 1980; co-editor: Collaboration in Italian Renaissance Art, 1978; contbr. articles to symposiums and jours. Mem. Renaissance Soc. Am., Coll. Art Assn., Assn. Ind. Historians of Art, Phi Beta Kappa. Home and Office: 693 Leetes Island Rd Branford CT 06405

SHEARIN, KATHRYN KAY, lawyer, humor writer; b. Norfolk, Va., Dec. 24, 1946; d. John Willis and Kathryn (Riecken) S.; m. James Charles Bray, June 1, 1969 (div. May 1973). BA, U. N.C., Greensboro, 1968; MA, Boston U., 1972; MS, N.C. State U., 1978; JD, Rutgers U., Newark, 1980; LLM in Taxation, Georgetown U., 1983. Bar: N.J. 1980, U.S. Dist. Ct. N.J. 1980, D.C. 1981, Md. 1982, U.S. Tax Ct. 1982, U.S. Supreme Ct. 1984, Del. 1986, U.S. Dist. Ct. Del. 1986, U.S. Cir. Ct. (3d cir.) 1987. Law clk. to magistrate U.S. Dist. Ct. N.J., Newark, 1978-79; prin. stat. State of N.J., Trenton, 1979-80; atty., adviser U.S. Dept. of Justice, Washington, 1982-83; editor tax law BNA Tax Mgmt., Washington, 1983-84; editor, pub. Common Law Revue CapriComp, Wilmington, Del., 1984—; pvt. practice law, 1986—; cons. LibraComp, 1982-84, 86—; trust counsel, v.p., corp. sec. E.F. Hutton Trust Co., Wilmington, 1984-86, lectr., 1986—; mng. atty. Hyatt Legal Svcs., 1986; lectr. in field; leader tax seminar SBA/SCORE. Writer Del. Corp. Law Update, 1987—. Libertarian candidate for atty. gen., Del., 1990. Mem. ABA, D.C. Bar Assn., Del. Bar Assn., Md. Bar Assn., N.J. Bar Assn., Fed. Bar Assn., Am. Chem. Soc., Geol. Soc. Am., Am. Math. Soc., Marine Tech. Soc., AAAS, Del. Acad. Sci. (pres. 1990), Wilmington Tax Group, Estate Planning Counsel Del., Smithsonian Assocs., Mensa. Libertarian. Home: 1301 Maple Ave Wilmington DE 19805-5036 Office: 501 Silverside Rd Ste 88 Wilmington DE 19809-1376

SHEARMAN, JEFFREY LYNN, safety manager; b. Johnstown, Pa., June 17, 1957; s. Jay Irvin and Elizabeth Virginia (Rhoades) S.; m. Bonnie Marie Furlong, Aug. 21, 1982; children: Heather Marie, Bradley Jordan, Justin Alexander. AAS in Fire Sci., Westmoreland County Coll., Youngwood, Pa., 1986; BS in Fire Svc. Adminstrn., SUNY, Saratoga Springs, N.Y., 1989. Cert. safety specialist, hazardous materials supr., asbestos bldg. insp. and mgmt. planner. Lab tech. Kenna Metal Inc., Latrobe, Pa., 1976-77; lab tech. SCM Metal Products, Johnstown, 1977-80, prodn. tech., 1980-82, prodn. supr., 1982-88, safety supr., 1988-89; safety mgr. Crown Am. Corp., Johnstown, 1989—; asst. chief, tng. officer Cambria County Hazardous Materials Team, 1988—. Fire chief Solomon Run Vol. Fire Dept., Johnstown, 1988—, active, 1982—, Cambria County 911 Adv. Bd., Johnstown, 1990—. Mem. Nat. Fire Protection Assn., Am. Soc. Safety Engrs., World Safety Orgn., Greater Johnstown Fire Chiefs Assn. (pres. 1992—). Democrat. Methodist. Office: Crown Am Corp Pasquerilla Pla Johnstown PA 15907-0879

SHECHTMAN, GEORGE HENOCH, art dealer; b. Paterson, N.J., Dec. 8, 1941; s. Abraham and Sadye (Fenster) S. BA, Rutgers U., 1964. Owner, dir. Christopher St. Gallery, N.Y.C., 1966-72, Christopher Gallery, N.Y.C., 1972-82, Gallery Henoch, N.Y.C., 1982—. Home: 112 E 73rd St New York NY 10021-4208

SHECHTMAN, MICHAEL ALAN, lawyer; b. Phila., Dec. 16, 1951; s. Leon Shechtman and Suzanne (Lieberman) Koplin; m. Donita Jane Art, Nov. 19, 1972 (div. 1976); m. Emily Kate Haber, June 24, 1979; children: Benjamin Lee, Samantha Allyn. BA, Pa. State U., 1972; JD, Villanova U., 1976. Bar: Pa. 1976, U.S. Dist. Ct. (ea. dist.) Pa. 1976, U.S. Ct. Appeals (3d cir.) 1982, U.S. Supreme Ct. 1985. Assoc. Gold, Bowman & Unterberger, Phila., 1976-78, Wolov & Rosenberg, Phila., 1978-79, Joseph S. Aronstein, Phila., 1979-81, Pepper, Winderman, Gordon & Breen, Phila., 1982-88; pvt. practice, Phila., 1988—. Mem. ABA, Pa. Bar Assn., Phila. Bar Assn., Am. Trial Lawyers Assn., Pa. Trial Lawyers Assn., Phila. Trial Lawyers Assn., Variety Club, B'nai B'rith. Jewish. Office: 1346 Chestnut St Ste 917 Melrose Park PA 19107

SHEDD, DONALD POMROY, surgeon; b. New Haven, Aug. 4, 1922; s. Gale and Marion (Young) S.; m. Charlotte Newson, Mar. 17, 1946; children—Carolyn, David, Ann, Laura. B.S., Yale U., 1944, M.D., 1946. Diplomate Am. Bd. Surgery. Intern Yale New Haven Hosp., 1946-47, asst. resident, resident, 1949-53; instr. surgery Yale U. Med Sch., New Haven, 1953-54, asst. prof., 1954-56, assoc. prof., 1956-67; chief dept. head and neck surgery Roswell Park Meml. Inst., Buffalo, 1967—. Co-editor: Surgical and Prosthetic Speech Rehabilitation, 1980, Head and Neck Cancer, 1985; contbr. numerous articles to profl. jours. Founding bd. dirs. Hospice Buffalo, Inc., 1973-83. Served to capt. U.S. Army, 1947-49. Mem. Soc. Univ. Surgeons, New Eng. Surg. Soc., Soc. Head and Neck Surgeons (pres. 1976-77). Home: 671 Lafayette Ave Buffalo NY 14222-1435 Office: Roswell Park Meml Inst 666 Elm St Buffalo NY 14263-0001

SHEDD, FRANCIS WILLIAM, lawyer; b. Niagara Falls, N.Y., July 29, 1922; s. Will D. and Agnes E. (Choate) S.; m. Barbara Jane Conger, Dec. 10, 1945 (div. 1970); children: Jonathan W., Jennifer Allen, Rebecca Greenberg; m. Audrey Donner, Mar. 24, 1973. LLB, Syracuse U., 1948. Atty. Niagara Falls; counsel joint legis. com. on regional and area studies, N.Y. Senate and Assembly, 1966-72; rep. plaintiff and co-counsel, Niagara Counsel Charter case/U.S. Supreme Ct., Washington, 1975. Republican candidate for State Assembly, Lewiston and Niagara Falls Dist., 1963. Sgt. U.S. Army, 1943-45, ETO. Decorated Bronze Star (2), Purple Heart. Mem. Niagara Club (pres. 1966, 89), Niagara Falls Country Club (bd. govs. 1991). Methodist. Office: 724 Division Ave Niagara Falls NY 14305-2587

SHEDD, GEORGE JOEL, artist, educator; b. Yonkers, N.Y., Sept. 19, 1922; s. Alfred Oswald and Gladys Fern (Butler) S.; m. Janice Mary Brailey, Nov. 10, 1962; children: David George, Carolyn Elizabeth. Student, Mass. Coll. Art, 1950. Asst. Li'l Abner Comic Strip, Boston, 1951-53; creator and cartoonist Marlin Keel comic strip N.Y.C., 1953-54; staff artist Rust Craft Pubs., Dedham, Mass., 1954-75, art dir., 1975-81; freelance comml. artist Jan Studio, Burlington, Mass., 1981—. One-man shows include Guild Boston Artists, 1988, 90, Orleans (Mass.) Art Gallery, 1985, 89, Priscilla Hartley Gallery, Kinnebunkport, Maine, Lexington (Mass.) Arts and Crafts Soc.; exhibited in group shows at Am. Watercolor Soc., N.Y.C., Allied Artists Am., N.Y.C., Salmagundi Open Shows, N.Y.C., Hudson River Valley Show, Yonkers, N.Y., Mus. of Fine Arts, Boston; author watercolor page Am. Artist Mag., 1988, paintings on cover of Yankee Mag., 1983, 90. 1st lt. USAAF, 1945-46, PTO. Recipient Philip Isenberg award Salmagundi Club, 1992, Sharon Orslip award Salmagundi Club, N.Y.C., 1987, Salmagundi award for watercolor, 1988. Mem. Am. Watercolor Soc. (Carolyn Stern award 1979), Allied Artists Am. (Gold medal for watercolor 1974, award of distinction 1977, John Hunter Meml. award 1991), New Eng. Watercolor Soc. (sec., treas. 1975-77, bd. dirs.), Guild Boston Artists. Home: 46 Paulson Rd Burlington MA 01803-2842

SHEDLAWSKI, JOSEPH FERDINAND, materials manager, educator; b. Wilkes-Barre, Pa., Mar. 13, 1954; s. Joseph F. and Mary Catherine (Boinski) S. BS in Biology, Bucknell U., 1976; MBA in Fin. cum laude, Iona Coll., 1982. Cert. prodn. and inventory mgr., 1986. Chemist Lederle Labs, Pearl River, N.Y., 1976-77, 78-79, biologist, 1977-78, quality assurance, 1979-80, dist. planner, 1981-82, mfg. scheduler, 1982-83, material requirements planner, 1983-85, master scheduler, 1985-86, planning mgr., 1987-89, materials mgr., 1990—; Am. prodn. and inventory control cer. program instr. Bloomfield (N.J.) Coll., 1987—. Mem. Am. Prodn. and Inventory Control Soc. (editor 1987, program v.p. 1988, exec. v.p. 1989, pres. 1990; Platinum award 1987, 88, 89, 90). Republican. Roman Catholic. Home: 34 New Holland Village Nanuet NY 10954 Office: Lederle Labs 401 N Middletown Rd 43D/301 Pearl River NY 10965

SHEEDY, JANICE LIBERATOR, educator; b. Buffalo, Apr. 30, 1951; d. Victor Anthony and Jane Mildred (De Falco) L.; m. David Lawrence Sheedy, June 30, 1973. AA, Villa Maria Jr. Coll., Buffalo, 1971; BA in Psychology and Spl. Edn., D'Youville Coll., Buffalo, 1974; MS in Learning Behavioral Disorders, SUNY, Buffalo, 1990. Cert. spl. edn. and elem. tchr., N.Y. Tchr. spl. edn. Buffalo Bd. Edn., 1974—. Vol. Roswell Park Meml. Inst., Buffalo. Mem. Assn. for Supervision and Curriculum Devel., Nat. Assn. Mental Retardation. Office: City of Buffalo City Hall Buffalo NY 14202

SHEEDY, KENNETH JOHN, finance executive; b. Jersey City, Feb. 28, 1945; s. Joseph and Anne (Rakowski) S.; married; children: Sharon, Deirdre, Erin. BS, St. Peters Coll., 1967; MBA, Fairleigh Dickinson U., 1973. Banker N.J. Bank, N.A., Paterson, 1967-71; acct. Interpace Corp., Parsippany, N.J., 1971-73; controller Plessey Frenchtown, N.J., 1973-79; asst. corp. controller Plessey, Inc., White Plains, N.Y., 1979-82; corp. controller ILC Data Device Corp., Bohemia, N.Y., 1982-85, v.p. fin., 1985—; adj. prof. fin. St. Joseph's Coll. Republican. Roman Catholic. Office: ILC Data Device Corp 105 Wilbur Pl Bohemia NY 11716

SHEEDY, MADELON UNKOVIC, museum curator; b. Pitts., Oct. 6, 1936; d. Nicholas and Mary (Clark) Unkovic; m. John C. Sheedy, Jr., Jan. 20, 1963 (div. 1982); children: Catharine Clare, Christopher Clark, Anne Morgan, Mary Cray. BA, Manhattanville Coll., 1958; BS, Carnegie Mellon U., 1959. Asst. to dir. Carnegie Mus. Art, Pitts., 1959-62; rsch. asst. to author Mrs. James H. Beal, Pitts., 1962-64; curator, dir. Johnstown (Pa.) Art Mus., 1985—; curator Jenner Art Gallery, Jennerstown, Pa., 1989—. Author: (slide program) Allegheny Adventures, 1965; lecture Compass Inn, 1970; contbr. to profl. jours. Bd. dirs. Westmoreland County Assn. for Blind, Greensburg, Pa., 1977-84, Valley Sch. of Ligonier, Ft. Ligonier, Pa., 1985-90, activities com. chair, 1986-90; chmn. edn. com. Ligonier Valley Libr., 1986—. Mem. Rolling Rock Club (swimming com. 1982-84). Office: Johnstown Art Mus 430 Main St Johnstown PA 15901-1819

SHEEHAN, GERARD FRANCIS, dean; b. Salem, Mass., Aug. 4, 1952; s. Jeremiah Richard and Mary Margaret (McManus) S.; m. Marilyn Kay Kuhar, Jan. 5, 1980; children: Caitlin Kuhar, Jeremiah Edward. BA, Holy Cross Coll., 1974; MS, Georgetown U., 1979. Dep. dir. grad. programs Sch. Fgn. Svc. Georgetown U., Washington, 1979-85; assoc. dean Fletcher Sch. Law & Diplomacy Tufts U., Medford, Mass., 1985—; cons. in field. Editor: Careers in International Affairs, 1982, 2d edit., 1986. Mem. nat. adv. com. program on internat. and pub. affairs Woodrow Wilson Nat. Fellowship Found., Princeton, 1989—; vol. Peace Corps Cent. African Republic, 1974-76. Mem. Assn. Profl. Sch. Internat. Affairs (chair task force on admissions and data base 1990—), Boston Com. Fgn. Affairs, Internat. Studies Assn., Phi Beta Kappa. Democrat. Roman Catholic. Home: 25 Greenleaf Ave Medford MA 02155 Office: Tufts U Fletcher Sch Medford MA 02155

SHEEHAN, JOHN MICHAEL, construction company executive; b. Newark, Sept. 13, 1929; s. Matthew Joseph and Marie (Coyle) S.; m. Janet M. Purcell, Jan. 26, 1930; children: Matthew, Michael A., Dennis P., Terence J., Joseph D., MaryAnne, Kathleen. Student, U.S. Mil. Acad., 1950-53; BCE, Newark Coll. Engring., 1958. Registered profl. engr., N.J., Pa. Project engr., mgr. Damon G. Douglas Co., Newark, 1956-75, chief engr., 1975-80; v.p. Damon G. Douglas Co., Springfield, N.J., 1980-84; sr. v.p. Damon G. Douglas Co., Cranford, N.J., 1984-87, exec. v.p., 1987—. Master troop 29 Boy Scouts Am., Newark, 1956-70; pres. Arrowhead Br. Community YMCA, Marlboro, N.J., 1969-71; coach Little League baseball and basketball, Hazlet, N.J., 1966-72. Fellow ASCE (pres. N.J. br. 1969-70, come com. on masonry 1982—); mem. NSPE (vice chmn. Profl. Engrs. in Constrn. 1987—), Assn. Contractors Essex County (pres. 1981-82), Am. Concrete Inst. (code com. on concrete masonry 1982—), N.J. Bldg. Contractors Assn. (legis com. 1982—, bd. dirs. 1984—). Republican. Roman Catholic. Home: 15 Irwin Pl Hazlet NJ 07730-2209 Office: Damon G Douglas Co 245 Birchwood Ave Cranford NJ 07016-2599

SHEEHAN, JOHN WILFRED, JR., operations manager; b. L.A., Sept. 11, 1941; s. John Wilfred Sr. and Mary Urma (Sheerin) S.; m. Joyce Linda Santoro, May 26, 1973; children: Christopher Michael, Corey Daniel. BS, U.S. Naval Acad., 1963; MBA, Rensselaer Polytech Inst., 1987. Commd. ensign USN, 1964, advanced through grades to capt., 1975, various positions, 1964-75; exec. officer SSN COMSUBGRU TWO, Subase Nlon, Groton, Conn., 1975-79, comdg. officer SSBN, 1980-83; dir., officer FBM tng. Submarine Sch./Subase Nlon, Groton, 1983-85; exec. officer Submarine Base Nlon, Groton, 1985-87; retired USN, Groton, 1988; ops. mgr. Ortronics, Inc., Pawcatuck, Conn., 1988—. Mem. Dem. Town Com., Waterford, Conn., 1989-91; rep. Waterford Representative Town Meeting, 1989-91, majority leader, 1991-92. Mem. Am. Prodn. and Inventory Control Soc., Ret. Officers Assn., U.S. Naval Inst., Am. Legion, DAV, U.S. Submarine League, USN League, U.S. Naval Acad. Alumni Assn. Roman Catholic. Home: 19 Laurel Crest Dr Waterford CT 06385-3305 Office: Ortronics Inc 595 Green Haven Rd Pawcatuck CT 06379-2055

SHEEHAN, MARY ANDERSON, college official; b. Pitts., Jan. 26, 1932; d. Donald C. and Dorothy (Fagan) Anderson; m. Thomas E. Sheehan, Nov. 25, 1961; children: Mark, David. BA, Chatham Coll., Pitts., 1954. Copy writer Sta. WQED, Pitts., 1954-60; trainer Gimbel's, Pitts., 1960-61; spl. events staff United Way, Pitts., 1961; mem. fund raising staff Harmarville Rehab. Ctr., Pitts., 1979-80; dir. devel. and alumnae rels. Chatham Coll., 1980-84; exec. asst. to pres. Chatham Coll., Pitts., 1984-92. Chmn. Mercy Hosp. Found. Bd., Pitts., 1990—; sec. Harmarville Rehab. Ctr., Pitts., 1990—. Mem. Nat. Soc. Fund-Raising Execs. Office: Chatham Coll Woodland Rd Pittsburgh PA 15232-2814

SHEEHAN, NEIL, journalist; b. Holyoke, Mass., Oct. 27, 1936; s. Cornelius Joseph and Mary (O'Shea) S.; m. Susan Margulies, Mar. 30, 1965; children—Maria Gregory, Catherine Fair. AB cum laude, Harvard, 1958; LittD, Columbia Coll., Chgo., 1972; LHD (hon.), Am. Internat. Coll., 1990, U. Lowell, 1991. Vietnam Bur. chief U.P.I., Saigon, 1962-64; reporter N.Y. Times, N.Y.C., Djakarta, Saigon, Washington, 1964-72. Author: The Arnheiter Affair, 1972, A Bright Shining Lie: John Paul Vann and America in Vietnam, 1988 (Nat. Book award 1988, Pulitzer prize for general nonfiction 1989, Robert F. Kennedy book award 1989, Vetty award Vietnam Vets. Ensemble Theatre Co. 1989, Spl. Achievement award Vietnam Vets. Am. 1989, Outstanding Investigative Reporting award Investigative Reporters and Editors, Inc. of U. Mo. Sch. Journalism 1989, Amb. award English-Speaking Union 1989, John F. Kennedy award, Holyoke, Mass 1989), After the War Was Over: Hanoi and Saigon, 1992, also articles and book revs. for popular mags.; contbr. to The Pentagon Papers, 1971. Served with AUS, 1959-62. Recipient Louis M. Lyons award for conscience and integrity in journalism, 1964, Silver medal Poor Richard Club, Phila., 1964, certificate of appreciation for best article on Asia Overseas Press Club Am., 1967, 1st Ann. Drew Pearson prize for excellence in investigative reporting, 1971, Columbia Journalism awards, 1972, 89, Sidney Hillman Found. awards, 1972, 88, Page One award Newspaper Guild N.Y., 1972, Distinguished Service award and Bronze medallion Sigma Delta Chi, 1972, citation of excellence Overseas Press Club, 1972; Guggenheim fellow, 1973-74; Adlai Stevenson fellow, 1973-75; Lehrman Inst. fellow, 1975-76; Rockefeller Found. fellow in humanities, 1976-77; Woodrow Wilson Center for Internat. Scholars fellow, 1979-80. Mem. Soc. Am. Historians, Am. Acad. Achievement. Home: 4505 Klingle St NW Washington DC 20016-3580

SHEEHAN, PAUL ROBERT, technical services consultant; b. Cambridge, Mass., Mar. 28, 1951; s. Robert Francis and Lorraine Theresa (McCool) S.; m. Patricia Ann Duprey (div. 1988). BSBA, Bentley Coll., 1975. V.p. Interstate Tech. Svcs., Nashua, N.H., 1980—. Mem. Nat. Tech. Svcs. Assn., New Eng. Design Drafting Mgrs. Assn. Home: 10 Mt Laurels Dr Nashua NH 03062 Office: Interstate Tech Svcs 2 Wellman Ave Nashua NH 03060

SHEEHAN, ROBERT JAMES, II, economics and management consultant; b. Pitts., May 13, 1937; s. Regis James and Helen Lillian (O'Leary) S.; A.B. in Econs., U. Pitts., 1967, M.A., 1970; postgrad. Am. U.; m. Marie Elizabeth Yoskovich, Apr. 24, 1964; children: Stephanie Ann, Robert James, III. Cer. mgmt. cons. Rsch. analyst Action Housing Inc., Pitts., 1960-63; from project rep. to dir. rehab. Urban Redevel. Authority Pitts., 1963-73; assoc. chief economist, dir. econ. rsch. Nat. Assn. Homebuilders, Washington, 1973-82; v.p. econ. policy analysis Nat. Assn. Homebuilders, 1982-83; v.p. Regis J. Sheehan & Assocs., McLean, Va., also Pitts., 1983—; vice-chmn. Fairfax County Housing and Redevel. Authority, 1988—; cons. in field. Pres., Kent Gardens Elem. Sch. PTA, McLean, Va., 1974-76, Longfellow Intermediate Sch. PTA, McLean, 1979-81, Kent Gardens Recreation Club, 1979-82; bd. dirs. Touchstone Theatre Co., 1984—. Mem. Am. Econ. Assn., Nat. Economists Club, Inst. Mgmt. Cons. (v.p. Washington chpt. 1989—), Adminstrv. Mgmt. Soc., Nat. Assn. Bus. Economists, KC. Roman Catholic. Avocations: walking, jogging, reading. Author: The Basics of Land Acquisition, 1985; contbr. articles to profl. jours. also: 291 Foxcroft Rd Pittsburgh PA 15220

SHEEHAN, THOMAS FRANCIS, JR., advertising agency executive; b. Clearfield, Pa., Mar. 12, 1958; s. Thomas Francis Sr. and Suzanne Freda (Goebert) S.; m. Patricia Ann Yanisko, Sept. 25, 1982; children: Christopher Thomas, Lauren Elizabeth. BA in Advt., Pa. State U., 1979. Ind. profl. musician Reading, Pa., 1975—; writer Gilbert/Commonwealth, Reading, 1980-82, dir. mktg., 1983-85; v.p. Ruhe & Co., Reading, 1985-89; pres. Media One, Reading, Pa., 1989-91, Tom Sheehan, Inc., 1992—. Writer, producer, musician (album) 9 Years Gone, 1986, Can't Escape the Noise, 1992; contbg. editor GIG mag., 1987-89. Mem. ASCAP, Nat. Acad. Rec. Arts and Scis. Democrat.

SHEEHAN, THOMAS GERARD, financial executive; b. Bridgeport, Conn., Oct. 4, 1956; s. Gerard Arthur and Catherine Lee (Fekete) S.; m. Barbara Ann Beckerle, May 31, 1980; children: Emily Catherine, Meghan Elizabeth. BA, Fairfield (Conn.) U., 1978. Regional dir. Nat. Assn. of Realtors, Washington, 1980-82; dep., pvt. sector liason Office of the U.S. Trade Rep. Exec. Office of the Pres., Washington, 1982-83; N.E. dir. Rep. Nat. Com., Washington, 1983-85; agt., registered rep. Nationwide Ins. & Fin. Svcs., Newtown, Conn., 1985—; owner Thomas G. Sheehan Agy., Newtown, 1985—. Mem. St. Rose Roman Cath. Ch. Adv. Coun., fin. com., sch. devel. com. Mem. Nat. Assn. of Life Underwriters, N.E. Conn. Assn. Life Underwriters (polit. action com chair 1990—), Newtown Kiwanis, K.C. (mem. Pope John XXIII Coun. 1978—, dep. grand knight 1985-86). Office: 19 Church Hill Rd Newtown CT 06470-1651

SHEERAN, MAUREEN FLYNN, secondary education educator; b. Lewiston, N.Y., May 10, 1946; d. Edward and Ursula (Trank) Flynn; m. Thomas J. Sheeran, June 27, 1970; children: Meaghan, Brendan. BA in English, Niagara U., 1968, MSEd, 1973, CEA, 1975. Cert. tchr. elem. edn., secondary English, counseling, adminstrn., N.Y. Secondary English tchr. Niagara Falls (N.Y.) City Sch. Dist., 1968-87, 90—, tchr. on spl. assignment, instructional team leader, 1987-90. Publs. chmn./editor: College Club, Niagara Falls, 1986-88. Mem. Niagara Falls C. of C., Phi Delta Kappa. Home: 5230 Newitt Pky Lewiston NY 14092 Office: Niagara Falls Bd Edn Walnut Ave Niagara Falls NY 14301-1024

SHEERIN, WILLIAM EUGENE, educator; b. Bklyn., Oct. 30, 1946; s. William Vincent and Elizabeth (Fuller) S.; m. Patricia Ann Irwin, Oct. 9, 1971; 1 child, Christopher. BA, Fordham Coll., 1969; MA, Fordham U., 1971, PhD, 1981. Econs. tchr. Yorktown High Sch., Yorktown Heights, N.Y., 1971—; adj. instr. edn. Fordham U. Grad. Sch. of Edn., N.Y.C., 1977-78. Contbr. articles to newspapers, mags., profl. jours. Bd. trustees, v.p. Yonkers Pub. Libr., 1989-91. Mem. Larchmont Shore Club, Phi Delta Kappa. Democrat. Roman Catholic. Home: 18 Thornbury Rd Scarsdale NY 10583

SHEETZ, RALPH ALBERT, lawyer; b. Dauphin County, Pa., June 13, 1908; s. Harry Wesley and MaNora (Enders) S.; m. Ruth Lorraine Bender, May 19, 1938; 1 son, Ralph Bert. PhB, Dickinson Coll., 1930; JD, U. Ala., 1933. Bar: Pa. 1934, U.S. Dist. Ct. (mid. dist.) Pa. 1944. Solicitor, East Pennsboro Twp., Pa., 1937-53, Peoples Bank of Enola (Pa.), 1935-75; atty. Lawyers Title Ins. Corp., Richmond, Va., 1956—, Commonwealth Land Title Ins. Co., Phila., 1957—; atty. Employees Loan Soc., 1966-76. Ofcl. Appeal Area no. 4, SSS, Pa., assoc. legal adviser to Draft Bd. No. 2, adviser to registrants to Local Bd. No. 55, Harrisburg, Pa., 1974—; counselor Camp Kanestake, Huntingdon County, Pa., Methodist Ch.; treas., atty. Enola Boys Club, from 1950; pres. East Pennsboro Twp. PTA, 1951-52; atty. hon. mem. Citizens Fire Co. No. 1, Enola, 1951; apptd. bd. gov's. Am. Biog. Inst. Rsch. Assn.; del. arts and communications 15th Internat. Congress, Singapore, 16th Internat. Congress Willard Inter-Continental Hotel, Washington, 1989, 17th Internat. Congress Safari Park Hotel, Nairobi, Kenya, 1990, 18th Internat. Congress Harbour Castle Westin Hotel, Toronto, Can., 1991; sec., treas. West Shore Regional Coordinating Com., Cumberland County, 1956-66; mem. bd. adjustments East Pennsboro Twp., 1959, chmn., 1959, mem. planning commn, 1956-59, vice-chmn., mem. zoning commn., 1958, chmn., 1959; mem East Pennsboro Twp. Republican Club, from 1936; dep. dir. gen. Internat. Biog. Ctr. for the Ams., 1989. Recipient numerous awards and honors from Pres. of U.S. for service to SSS; Order of the Silver Trowel, Council of Anointed Kings Commonwealth of Pa., Altoona, 1948. Mem. ABA, Dauphin Bar Assn. (social com. 1934—), Cumberland County Bar Assn., Pa. Bar Assn., Tall Cedars Club of Lebanon (historian Harrisburg Forest No. 43 1980-89, exec. com. 1980-89), Shriners, Masons (York cross of honor), K.T. (comdr. 1946).

SHEFFE, EDWARD DEVEREUX, III, writer, editor, editorial consultant; b. San Diego, Aug. 10, 1950; s. Edward Jr. and Frances (Buck) S; m. Mary Ann Davis Wilson, Oct. 3, 1975 (div. Nov. 1981). Student, U. Tenn., 1969-70, U. Fez (Morocco), 1973; BA magna cum laude, U. Fla., 1978; postgrad., Fla. Internat. U., 1979-80. Spl. projects asst. USIA, Dept. State, Fez, 1973-75; polit. and legis. reporter Tenn. Democrat, Nashville, 1976; editor Jacksonville (Fla.) Herald, 1977; sr. editor Sport Diver mag., Miami, Fla., 1978-79; editor-in-chief Ski X-C mag. and Backpacker mag., N.Y.C., 1980-82, Adventure Travel mag., N.Y.C., 1981-82; group editorial dir. Ziff-Davis Pub. Co., N.Y.C., 1982; writer, editorial cons. E. Devereux Sheffe Assocs., N.Y.C., 1983—; contbg. editor Madison Ave. mag., N.Y.C., 1983-84, Outside mag., Chgo., 1983-87, PC Computing mag., Boston, 1988-89; lectr. editorial writing Pratt Inst., N.Y.C., 1987—; bd. dirs. Riverside Symphony Orch., N.Y.C. Contbr. over 200 articles to nat. publs. including Esquire, Frequent Flyer, Chgo. Tribune, Phila. mag., Washingtonian, PC Computing, AutoWeek. Bd. dirs. Found. for Ednl. Devel., N.Y.C., 1987—; del. 17th ann. U.S.-Soviet Conf., Moscow, 1989. With USN, 1971-73. Mem. Am. Soc. Journalists and Authors, Soc. Profl. Journalists, Appalachian Mountain Club (Boston, bd. edn. 1987—), Phi Beta Kappa. Office: 247 E 28th St New York NY 10016-8508

SHEFFIELD, JAMES ROCKWELL, foundation executive; b. N.Y.C., Dec. 15, 1936; s. Frederick and Carolyn (Blair) S.; m. Jill Wilkinson, June 27, 1964; children: James, Sarah. BA, Yale Coll., 1959; MAT, Harvard U., 1960; EdD, Columbia U., 1964. History tchr. Groton (Mass.) Sch., 1960-61, Bronxville (N.Y.) High Sch., 1961-62; rsch. assoc. Edn. and World Affairs, N.Y.C., 1964-65; project asst. Ford Found., Nairobi, Kenya, 1965-67; prof. Columbia U., Tchrs. Coll., N.Y.C., 1967-81; pres. U.S. Com. for UNICEF, N.Y.C., 1981-84, Concern for Dying, N.Y.C., 1988-89, African Med. Rsch. Found., N.Y.C., 1989—; cons. World Bank, Washington, 1986-87, Johnson and Johnson, New Brunswick, N.J., 1985-87; trustee Groton Sch., 1985-91, Renee Dubos Ctr. for Human Environments, N.Y.C., 1989-92. Author: Education in Kenya, 1972, Non-Formal Education in African Development, 1971. Mem. Century Assn. Home: 105 E 29th St New York NY 10016 Office: AMREF 420 Lexington Ave New York NY 10170

SHEFT, PETER IAN, lawyer; b. N.Y.C., Jan. 11, 1956; s. Leonard Alvin and Monique Inge (Eisinger) S. BA cum laude, Duke U., 1977; JD, Georgetown U., 1980. Bar: La. 1980, U.S. Dist. Ct. (ea. dist.) La. 1981, U.S. Ct. Appeals (5th and 11th cirs.) 1985, N.Y. 1985, D.C. 1990, U.S. Dist. Ct. (so. and ea. dists.) N.Y. 1990, U.S. Dist. Ct. (no. dist.) N.Y. 1990. Assoc. Phelps, Dunbar Marks, Claverie & Sims, New Orleans, 1980-84; assoc. Sheft & Sheft (formerly Sheft, Wright & Sweeney), N.Y.C., 1984-88, ptnr., 1988—. Mem. ABA, Assn. of Bar of City of N.Y., Maritime Law Assn., N.Y. State Bar Assn., La. Bar Assn., Fed. Ins. & Corp. Counsel, India House, Univ. Club, Downtown Athletic Club, Whitehall Club. Office: Sheft & Sheft 11 Broadway New York NY 10004-1302

SHEFTEL, HARRY BERNARD, retired economist; b. Clinton, Mass., July 9, 1906; s. Morris Sheftel and Molly Siff; m. Alice Naistat, Sept. 21, 1935; children: Janice C., Rosalyn L. AB, Clark U., Worcester, Mass., 1927; MA, Am. U., Washington, 1935. Statistician Dept. Labor, Washington; economist War Prodn. Bd., Washington; chief economist Fed. Works Agy., Washington; clearance officer Office of Mgmt. and Budget, Exec. Office of the Pres., Washington. Author: Quotations from My Questing, Of Truths and Wonderments, From Alpha to Omega (poetry). Mem. World Lit. Soc., Fed. Poets of Washington, Ellicot St. Poets, Am. Acad. Poets. Jewish. Home: 5813 3d Pl NW Washington DC 20011

SHEFTEL, ROGER TERRY, merchant banking executive; b. Denver, Sept. 10, 1941; s. Edward and Dorothy (Barnett) S.; m. Phoebe A. Sherman, Sept. 7, 1968; children: Tisha B., Ryan B. BS in Econs., U. Pa., 1963. Comml. lending officer Provident Nat. Bank, Phila., 1963-65; asst. to pres. Continental Finance Corp., Denver, 1965-68; v.p. Eastern Indsl. Leasing Corp., Phila., 1968-71, exec. v.p., dir., 1971-73; exec. v.p., dir. HBE Leasing Corp., Phila., 1971-73; dir. Kooly Kupp, Inc., Boyertown, Pa., 1974-77, pres., dir., 1977; prin. Trivest, Phila., 1973-77; pres. Trivest, Inc., Phila., 1977-78, 1670 Corp., mgmt. cons.'s, 1978-82; pres. Am. Cons. Group, Inc., 1982-83; exec. v.p., dir. Argus Rsch. Labs., Inc., 1982-83; pres. Leasing Concepts, Inc., 1983-87, Brice Capital Corp., 1987—. Mem. Nantucket Yacht Club, Friars Club, Rotary. Home: 414 Barclay Rd Bryn Mawr PA 19010-1218 Office: Brice Capital Corp 1016 W 9th Ave # 1 King Of Prussia PA 19406-1221

SHEID, CHRISTIANE VALENTINE, investment banker; b. Glen Cove, N.Y., Feb. 14, 1957; d. Louis Xavier and Michele (Herant) S. BA in Econs., UCLA, 1978, MBA, 1981. Registered rep. Assoc. to asst. v.p. Warburg Paribas Becker, N.Y.C., 1981-84; v.p. mortgage fin. The Bear Stearns Cos., N.Y.C., 1984-87; v.p. to sr. v.p. Lehman Bros., N.Y.C., 1987—. Republican. Roman Catholic. Office: Lehman Bros 200 Vesey St New York NY 10285-0001

SHEIMAN, RONALD LEE, tax lawyer; b. Bridgeport, Conn., Apr. 26, 1948; s. Samuel Charles and Rita Doris (Feinberg) S.; m. Deborah Joy Lovitky, Oct. 16, 1971; children: Jill, Laura. BA, U. Mich., 1970; JD, U. Conn., 1973; LLM in Taxation, NYU, 1974. Bar: Conn. 1973, U.S. Ct. Appeals (2d cir.) 1975, U.S. Dist. Ct. Conn. 1975, U.S. Tax Ct. 1975, U.S. Supreme Ct. 1977, D.C. 1978, N.Y. 1981. Sr. tax atty. Office of Regional Counsel, IRS, Phila., 1974-78; pvt. practice, Westport, Conn., 1978—. Adv. bd. Early Childhood Resource and Info. Ctr., N.Y. Pub. Library, N.Y.C., 1984. Mem. ABA, Fed. Bar Assn., Conn. Bar Assn., Westport Bar Assn. Home: 128 Random Rd Fairfield CT 06432-1408 Office: 1804 Post Rd E Westport CT 06880-5683

SHEIN, SAMUEL T., clinical psychologist; b. Salem, Mass., Mar. 19, 1932; s. William and Bessie (Resnick) S.; m. Susan Lamer; children: Pamela, Karen, Meredith, Danielle. AB, Boston U., 1954; MA, PhD, NYU, 1961; postgrad., Psychoanalytical Tng. Inst. Nat. Psychol. Assn. for Psychoanalysis, N.Y.C., 1962-70. Lic. psychologist, N.J., Pa., N.Y. Instr. psychology NYU, N.Y.C., 1957-58; intern Bergen Pines County Hosp., Paramus, N.J., 1958-59, staff psychologist, 1959-61, supervising psychologist, 1961-63; chief psychologist, adminstrv. dir. Community Mental Health Ctr., Dumont, N.J., 1963-66; psychologist Learning Lab., Spl. Edn., Wood-Ridge, N.J., 1966-69; pvt. practice Teaneck, N.J., 1962—; founding bd. dirs., officer Delta Inst. for Prevention of Violence, Abuse and Victimization, Essex and Bergen Counties, N.J., 1990—; guest clin. psychologist TV show Nine Broadcast Plaza, Cabel and Sta. WWOR, N.Y.; guest lectr. Bergen County Conf. on Learning Disabilities, Paramus, 1991, JCC-on-Palisades, Tenafly, N.J., 1988—. Sec., v.p. profl. adv. com. Bergen County Mental Health Bd., 1978-81; bd. dirs., co-founder Cliffwood Community Mental Health Ctr., Englewood, N.J., 1980-82. Mem. APA, N.J. Psychol. Assn., N.J. Acad. Psychology, Assn. Lic. Psychologists, Bergen County Psychol. Assn., Wilton Psychotherapy Ctr. (past pres., founder, dir. 1982—). Office: 757 Teaneck Rd Wilton Med Bldg N Teaneck NJ 07666

SHEIN, SIMRA EZRA, surgeon; b. N.Y.C., May 23, 1931; s. Nathan and Leah (Weinstein) S.; m. Elaine Rosalind Manuel, Aug. 20, 1966; children: David, Hilary, Warren, Jordan, Jeremy. AB, Columbia U., 1952; MD, SUNY, 1956. Diplomate Am. Bd. Surgery. Intern Beth Israel Hosp., N.Y.C., 1956-57; surg. resident Bklyn. Jewish Hosp., 1959-63; pvt. practice surgery Bklyn., 1963-72, Cedarhurst, N.Y., 1971—; medico-legal cons., 1989-92, surg. devices cons., 1987-92. Pres. Congregation Chab Zedek, Belle Harbor, N.Y., 1982-84. Lt., M.C., USNR, 1957-59. Fellow ACS. Jewish. Home: 212 Beach 141st St Belle Harbor NY 11694 Office: 97 Cedarhurst Ave Cedarhurst NY 11516 also: 431 Beach 129th St Belle Harbor NY 11694

SHELDON, DAVID FREDERICK, museum director, headmaster; b. N.Y.C., Feb. 2, 1929; s. Seward Ross and Zue Mac (Bronaugh) S.; m. Judith West, June 18, 1954; children: Frederick William, Charles Seward, James Nias. A.B., Amherst Coll., 1951; M.B.A., Harvard U., 1953, M.A.T., 1958. Trainee, then account exec. McCann-Erickson Inc. (advt.), 1953-57; tchr. history and English Middlesex Sch., Concord, Mass., 1957-59; dir. admissions Middlesex Sch., 1961-64, headmaster, 1964-90; exec. dir. Shelburne (Vt.) Mus., 1990—; Pres. Sch. Scholarship Service, 1963-65. Trustee Charles River Sch., Dover, Mass., 1965-68, Carroll Sch., Lincoln, Mass., 1972—, Interalp, Princeton, N.J., 1973—, Ind. Schs. Coun. for Religion; mem. corp. Emerson Hosp., Concord, Mass., 1970—; mem. overseers vis. com. Harvard U., 1966—; exec. com. Ind. Schs. Found. Mass., 1981—; mem. commn. for ind. schs. New Eng. Assn. Schs. and Colls., 1985-88; exec. dir. Shelborne (Vt.) Mus. Mem. Headmasters Assn., New Eng. Assn. Schs. and Colls. (commn. ind. schs. 1985—, overseas schs. 1985—, pres. 1990—). Episcopalian (vestryman). Address: Shelburne Museum 18 Heritage Ln Shelburne VT 05482

SHELDON, ERIC, physics educator; b. Pilsen, Bohemia, Oct. 24, 1930; s. Robert Bernard and Martha (Martin) S.; m. Sheila Harper, July 8, 1959; 1 child, Adrian. B.Sc., London (Eng.) U., 1951, B.Sc. in Physics, with honors, 1952, Ph.D., 1955, D.Sc., 1971. Chartered chemist; chartered physicist. Lectr., rsch. assoc. Acton Tech. Coll., London, 1952-55; assoc. physicist IBM Rsch. Lab., Switzerland, 1957-59; rsch. assoc. E.T.H., Zurich, Switzerland, 1959-62, lectr., 1962-64, prof., 1964-69; prof. physics and applied physics Lowell (Mass.) Technol. Inst. and U. Lowell, 1970-91, U. Mass. at Lowell, 1991—; prof. U. Lowell, 1985-88; vis. prof., NSF sr. sci. fellow U. Va., 1968-69; vis. prof. U. Tex., 1969-70, U. Oxford (Eng.), 1989. Author: (with R. Szostak and P. Marmier) Kernphysik I, 1960, Kernphysik II, 1961, (with P. Marmier) Physics of Nuclei and Particles, Vol. I, 1969, Vol. II, 1970; editor Procs. Internat. Conf. on Interactions of Neutrons with Nuclei, 1976; contbr. articles to books, encys. and profl. jours. Mem. Convocation London U., 1951—. Decorated Order of Merit (Poland). Fellow AAAS, Am. Phys. Soc. (chmn. New Eng. sect. 1985-86, mem. exec. com. 1983-87), Inst. Physics, Royal Soc. Chemistry, Royal Astron. Soc.; mem. Zurich Physics Soc. (life), Royal Instn. Gt. Britain, Am. Assn. Physics Tchrs., Mensa. Anglican/Episcopalian (lay reader). Office: U Mass at Lowell Dept Physics 1 University Ave Lowell MA 01854-2881

SHELDON, GEORGE WILLIAM, III, real estate developer; b. N.Y.C., June 22, 1957; s. George William S. and Suzanne (Moffatt) Jackson; m. Elizabeth Winthrop Bowen, Sept. 9, 1989. BA, U. Va., 1979; MBA, Am. U., 1982. Sr. cons. Arthur Andersen, Washington, 1982-85; sr. v.p. Hadid Devel. Cos., Rosslyn, Va., 1985-91; exec. v.p. Sienna Assocs., McLean, Va., 1991—. Mem. Internat. Real Estate Inst. Home: 5212 Macarthur Blvd NW Washington DC 20016-2506 Office: Sienna Assocs 7927 Jones Branch Dr Ste 600W Mc Lean VA 22102

SHELDON, J. MICHAEL, public relations/communications executive; b. Mt. Carmel, Pa., Sept. 1, 1951; s. Lloyd Loomis and Helen Roberta (Sosnoski) S. AA, Harrisburg (Pa.) Community Coll., 1978; BS, Pa. State U., 1980; M in Journalism, Temple U., 1991. News announcer Sta. WNUE-AM, Ft. Walton Beach, Fla., 1974-76, Sta. WFEC-AM, Harrisburg, 1977-78; announcer Sta. WCMB-AM, Wormleysburg, Pa., 1979-80; writer newspaper Pa. Beacon, Harrisburg, 1982-85; media specialist Commonwealth Media Svcs., Harrisburg, 1982-86; dir. communications Pa. Poultry Fedn., Harrisburg, 1986-89; news anchor Sta. WGAL-TV, Lancaster, Pa., 1989-90; dir. pub. rels. Profl. Ins. Agts. - Pa., Md., Del., Mechanicsburg, Pa., 1990-92; v.p. comm. and mktg. United Way of the Capital Region, Harrisburg, Pa., 1992—; mem. adj. faculty dept. journalism Temple U., 1992. Contbr. articles to profl. jours. Pub. rels. advisor Cen. Pa. Leukemia Soc., Harrisburg, 1989-90; media advisor Polit. Campaign, Hershey, Pa., 1990. With USAF, 1969-73. Mem. VFW, Pa. Soc. Assn. Execs., Pub. Rels. Soc., Chi Gamma Iota, Delta Tau Kappa, Am. Legion. Republican. Roman Catholic. Office: One United Way Harrisburg PA 17112

SHELESKI, STANLEY JOHN, accountant, comptroller, consultant; b. Harleigh, Pa., Feb. 20, 1931; s. Stanley Joseph and Agnes Rose (Yeshmond) S.; m. Sandra Lee Atkins. BS in Fin. Acctg., Rider Coll., 1958. Treas., mgr. United Savs. and Loan, Trenton, N.J., 1958-62; mgr. acctg. dept. Allstates Engring. Co., Trenton, 1962-85, asst. treas., asst. sec., comptroller, 1985—; v.p. fin. Allstates Design and Devel. Co., Trenton, 1988—; bd. dirs. Allstates Credit Union, Trenton, 1966—, treas. and gen. mgr. Allstates Credit Union, 1968—. Planner Jr. C. of C., Trenton, 1959. Served to sgt. USMC, 1952-54, Korea. Mem. Nat. Assn. Accts., Ewing Bus. Assn. (treas. 1959-62). Republican. Roman Catholic. Lodge: North Star Club (v.p. 1953-58).

SHELTON, BONNIE LEE, foundation administrator, consultant; b. Waterloo, Iowa; d. Darrell Lee and Leona (Brown) S.; children: Jeffrey David Blankenship, Daniel James Blankenship. BS in Communications with high honors., U. Ill., 1971, MS in Journalism, 1974; CSS in Adminstrn. and Mgmt., Harvard U., 1989. Staff writer, columnist The News-Gazette, Champaign, Ill., 1965-71; asst. to pres. Internat. Features Enterprises, Inc., Rome, 1971-75; dir. publs. News Bur., exec. editor Grad. Sch. Bus. Ind. U., Bloomington, 1975-78; dir. programs Nat. Fedn. Bus. and Profl. Women, Washington, 1978-83; exec. dir. Unitarian Universalist Women's Fedn., Boston, 1983-88; communications cons., property mgr. Boston, 1988-90; exec. dir. Nat. Assn. Rehab. Profls. Pvt. Sector, Brookline, Mass., 1990—. Presenter paper 1984 Congress Internat. Assn. Religious Freedom, Tokyo. Mem. Mus. of Fine Arts. Recipient Dudley McAllister Meml. award Excellence in Pub. Affairs reporting. Mem. Am. Soc. Assoc. Execs., New England Soc. Assn. Execs., World Affairs Coun., Philosophy Found. Boston, Kappa Tau Alpha.

SHEN, STEVE YU-LIANG, physician, researcher; b. Taiwan, Republic of China, Feb. 14, 1946; s. Shui-Yun and Chih-Yu (Hsu) S.; m. Mei-Jung Lee, Aug. 31, 1975; children: Elaine Joan, Jonathan Michael. MD, Taipei (Taiwan) Med. Coll., 1971. Diplomate Am. Bd. Internal Medicine, Am. Bd. Medicine in Subsplty. of Nephrology. Intern St. Francis Hosp., Pitts., 1973-74; resident Wayne State U.-Harper Hosp., Detroit, 1974-76; clin. and rsch. fellow in nephrology U. Md. Hosp., Balt., 1976-79; dir. transplant clinic U. Md. Med. System., Balt., 1983-89; med. dir. trans. svc. U. Md. Med. System, 1982-89; assoc. prof. medicine U. Md., Balt., 1988—; med. dir. acute hemodialysis svc. Ch. Hosp., Balt., 1990—, chief of nephrology, 1991—; mem. med. adv. bd. Md. Organ Procurement Ctr., Balt., 1982—; mem. med. rev. bd. Mid-Atlantic Renal Coalition, Richmond, Va., 1988—. Author: (booklet) Kidney Transplantation: An Information Booklet for Patients and their Family, 1984; contbr. articles to profl. jours. Rep. United Network for Organ Sharing, Richmond, Va., 1988—. Fellow ACP; mem. Am. Fedn. Clin. Rsch., Am. Soc. Transplant Physicians, Internat. Soc. Nephrology, Internat. Transplantation Soc. Home: 307 Meadowcroft Ln Lutherville Timonium MD 21093-6422

SHEN, YUAN-YUAN, mathematics educator; b. Yenchao, Taiwan, Republic of China, June 30, 1954; came to U.S., 1979; s. Wu-Hsing and Jin-Fon (Kung) S.; m. Joan Chyong-Jue Chen, June 25, 1988; 1 child, Angela Rachel. BA, Tunhai U., Taiwan, 1976; PhD, U. Md., 1988. Asst. prof. Cath. U. of Am., Washington, 1988—. 2d lt. Republic of China mil., 1976-78. Mem. Am. Math. Soc., Math. Assn. Am., Phi Tau Phi. Home: 3149 Beethoven Way Silver Spring MD 20904-6860 Office: Cath U of Am 620 Michigan Ave NE Washington DC 20064-0001

SHEN, YUJIN, mathematics educator; b. Shanghai, China, Oct. 11, 1949; came to U.S., 1981; s. Hengyou and Xiaju (Wang) S.; m. Zhaole Luo, Jan. 26, 1978; 1 child, Ming. BS, Kirin U., Changchun, People's Republic of China, 1977; MA, U. Del., 1983, PhD, 1986. Rsch. asst. Inst. Math. Academia Sinica, Beijing, 1977-81; asst. prof. maths. Stockton State Coll., Pomona, N.J., 1986-91, assoc. prof. math., 1991—. Contbr. articles to profl. jours. Mem. Am. Math. Assn., Soc. Actuaries (assoc.). Office: Stockton State Coll Jimmie Leeds Rd Pomona NJ 08240-9999

SHENKIN, HENRY ARNOLD, retired neurosurgeon; b. Phila., June 25, 1915; s. Julius and Rose (Rosenbaum) S.; m. Renee Friedenberg, Jan. 12, 1940 (dec. Nov. 1989); children: Budd, Robert, Katherine Shenkin Seal, Emily Shenkin Simon. AB, U. Pa., 1935; MD, Jefferson Med. Coll., 1939. Diplomate Am. Bd. Neurol. Surgery. Pvt. practice, 1946-88; internship Phila. Gen. Hosp., 1939-41; fellow dept. of Physiology Yale U. Sch. Medicine, 1941-42; residency Hosp. Univ. of Pa., 1942-45; instr., asst. prof. neurosurgery U. Pa. Sch. Medicine, Phila., 1945-60, assoc. prof., 1960-67; clin. prof. Temple U. Sch. Medicine, Phila., 1967-74; prof. Med. Coll. Pa., Phila., 1974-82; ret., 1982; dir. neurosurgery and residence program in neurosurgery Episcopal Hosp., Phila., 1960-82. Author: Clinical Practice and Cost Containment, 1986, Medical Ethics: Evolution, Rights and the Physician, 1991. Home: 3300 Darby Rd Apt 3101 Haverford PA 19041-1069

SHENOUDA, GEORGE SAMAAN, engineering executive, consultant; b. Alexandria, Egypt, June 7, 1943; came to U.S., 1972; s. Samaan and Sania S. Shenouda. BSc, Alexandria U., 1963, MSc, 1969. Rsch. assoc. Dept. Rsch., Cairo, 1963-72; engr. Unitrode Corp., Watertown, Mass., 1973-78; mgr. Raytheon Corp., Waltham, Mass., 1978-80, Analog Devices Inc., Wilmington, Mass., 1980-81, Kollsman Instrument Co., Merrimack, N.H., 1981-85; br. mgr. precision products div. Northrop Corp, Norwood, Mass., 1985-89; sect. mgr. Northrop Corp., PPD, Norwood, Mass., 1989-90; sr. mgr. electronic systems div. Northrop Corp., ESD-N, Norwood, Mass., 1990—. Mem. IEEE, Am. Soc. Safety Engrs., Inst. Environ Scis. (sr.). Office: Northrop Corp ESD-N PO Box Bu Norton MA 02766-0987

SHEPARD, GEORGE LEO, sales and marketing executive, consultant; b. Balt., Sept. 18, 1947; s. George Wesley and Naomi Shepard; m. Eleanor Sheila Fitzpatrick, June 29, 1985; children: Jeffrey Stewart, David George. BS, U. Md., 1974; MS in Pub. Rels., Am. U., 1979; MBA, U. Balt., 1990. Key account rep. Chesebrough-Ponds Inc., Greenwich, Conn., 1969-71, Armour-Dial Inc., Phoenix, 1971-74; ter. mgr. Am. Optical Corp., Southbridge, Mass., 1974-76, Norton Co., Worcester, Mass., 1976-83; dist. mgr. Childs Corp., Newport, Del., 1983-86; sales and mktg. mgr. Nat. Capital Industries, Bladensburg, Md., 1987-90; mgr. sales adminstrn. Locke Insulators, Balt., 1990—; asst. prof. mgmt. U. Balt., 1990—. Vol. Balt. Symphony Orch., 1985—. Mem. U. Balt. Alumni Assn. (mentor 1991—), U. Md. Alumni Assn., Am. U. Alumni Assn., Blue Key, Phi Kappa Phi, Alpha Sigma Lambda, Sigma Iota Epsilon. Home: 11 Haylock Ct Apt 303 Baltimore MD 21236-1311

SHEPARD, SCOTT, journalist; b. Macon, Ga., Dec. 26, 1948; s. John Arthur and Betty (Butler) S.; m. Deborah Gail Matthews, May 9, 1987; 1 child, Aliana Matthews Shepard. BA, U. Ga., 1971; student, Auburn U., 1977-78. Reporter Tifton (Ga.) Gazette, 1975-76; reporter AP, Montgomery, Ala., 1976-77, capitol corr., 1978-81; reporter AP, Atlanta, 1981-82; corr. AP, Albany, Ga., 1982-83, Washington, 1983-85; southeastern news editor AP, Atlanta, 1985-86; corr. Atlanta Jour. Constn., Atlanta, Washington, 1986-90; sr. nat. polit. corr. Cox Newspaper, Washington, 1990—. Foster parent Fairfax County, Va., 1987—. With U.S. Army, 1972-75. Home: 7904 Candlewood Dr Alexandria VA 22306-3218 Office: Cox Newspapers 2000 Pennsylvania Ave NW Washington DC 20006-1812

SHEPARDSON, ELIZABETH PRENTISS (BETSY SHEPARDSON), artist; b. Salt Lake City, July 13, 1953; d. John Whitney and Joan Prentis (Baker) S. Cert., Art Students League, 1986. Librarian Nightingale-Bamford Sch., N.Y.C., 1980-81; tchr. presch. art Friends Sem. Sch., N.Y.C., 1982-83; exec. sec. Delta Capital Corp., N.Y.C., 1988—. Mem. Soc. Illustrators, Met. Post Card Collectors Club. Office: Delta Capital Corp 500 3d Ave New York NY 10022

SHEPARDSON, JOHN UPHAM, chemist, consultant; b. Winchendon, Mass., May 4, 1920; s. Donn Clifford and Agnes Gertrude (Upham) S.; m. Camille Jane Comstock, Dec. 25, 1942; children: Ann, Sallie, Roy Michael. BS in Chemistry, U. Mass., 1942; MS in Organic Chemistry, Rensselaer Poly. Inst., 1948, PhD in Analytical Chemistry, 1950. Quality mgr. Mallinckrodt Chem. Works, Weldon Springs, Mo., 1950-64; quality dir. Winthrop Labs., Rensselaer, N.Y., 1964-76; tech. dir. CIS Radiopharmaceuticals, Bedford, Mass., 1976-80; chief chemist Astro Cir. Corp., Lowell, Mass., 1980-84; pvt. practice cons. Lowell, 1984-89, ret., 1989. Contbr. Uranium Production Technology, 1959. Member Ferguson (Mo.) City Coun., 1956-60. Mem. Am. Chem. Soc. Home: 11 Hitching Post Rd Chelmsford MA 01824-1919

SHEPHERD, JACK EDWIN, editor, author, educator; b. Summit, N.J., Dec. 14, 1937; s. John Edwin and Grace Jean (Anderson) S.; m. Kathleen Kessler, Sept. 3, 1960; children: Kristen, Caleb. BA, Haverford Coll., 1960; MS, Columbia U., 1961; PhD, Boston U., 1989. Sr. editor, asst. mng. editor Look mag., N.Y.C., 1963-71; gen. editor Newsweek mag., N.Y.C., 1971-73; sr. assoc. Carnegie Endowment, N.Y.C., 1974-76, 84-86; mng. editor South-North News Svc., Hanover, N.H., 1985-88, pres. of trustees; prof. war and peace studies and conflict resolution Dartmouth Coll., Hanover, 1988—; pres. Shepherd Assocs. Inc., 1968—; sr. fellow Dickey Endowment, Dartmouth Coll. Author: The Forest Killers, 1974, The Adams Chronicles, 1974, The Politics of Starvation, 1975, The Runner's Handbook, 1977, Cannibals of the Heart: The Biography of Louisa and John Quincy Adams, 1981; (with Christopher S. Wren) Quotations from LBJ, 1969, Poor Richard Nixon's Almanac, 1970, The Super Summer of Jamie McBride, 1971; (with Bob Glover) The Family Fitness Book, 1989; contbr. numerous articles to N.Y. Times, Washington Post, Harpers, Atlantic, Reader's Digest, Newsweek, Esquire. Mem. Norwich (Vt.) Conservation Commn., 1982-84; del. Vt. Dem. Conv., 1988; clk. Hanover Soc. of Friends Meeting, 1988-90; mem. exec. coun. Haverford Coll., 1990—, Quaker Office of UN, 1992—. Recipient Haverford Coll. award, 1977. Home: RR 1 Norwich VT 05055-9801

SHEPHERD, SAUNDRA DIANNE, pediatrician, educator, consultant; b. N.Y.C., July 16, 1945; d. Archibald Ethelbert and Sylvia Marguerite (Allman) Shepherd; m. Peter John Payne Finch, Nov. 24, 1973; 1 dau., Abi Jean Shepherd-Finch. B.S., CCNY, 1968; M.A., Hunter Coll., 1971; M.D., Yale U., 1975. Intern NYU/Bellevue Pediatrics, 1975-76, resident, 1976-78, fellow, 1978-79; fellow in pediatric hematology and oncology, Bellevue Hosp., N.Y.C., 1978-79, Columbia-Presbyn. Med. Ctr., N.Y.C., 1979-80, staff assoc. responsible for pediatric sickle cell clinic, Columbia-Presbyn. Med. Ctr., 1980-81, clin. instr. pediatrics, 1981-84; attending physician St. Luke's Roosevelt Hosp. Ctr., 1980-90, Harlem Hosp. Ctr., N.Y.C., 1982-84; dir. pediatric tng. residency program in social medicine, 1986—; asst. prof. pediatrics and community medicine residency program in social medicine Montefiore Hosp., 1984-86; mem. adj. faculty Sophie Davis Sch. Biomed. Edn., CCNY, 1980—; adj. lectr. Fordham U. Grad. Sch. Social Work, 1982-86; social medicine residency program preceptor Martin Luther King Health Ctr., N.Y.C.; cons. physician Family Ct., N.Y.C., 1972—; cons. pediatrician Legal Aid Soc., 1972—, advisor for project for homeless families, 1983—; cons. pediatrician Legal Service Corp., N.Y.C.; mem. Emergency Com. to Aid Lebanon; vol. physician, El Salvador; delivered med. aid to Mozambique, 1986; mem. First U.S.-Nicaragua Colloquium on Health, 1983. Bd. dirs. United Meth. City Soc., advisor on med. aid for Mozambique, 1986; mem. pres.'s adv. com. for housing plans for homeless Borough of Bronx. Regents Coll. scholar, 1963, Woods Found. scholar, 1963, Nat. Med. Fellowship award, 1971-73, NIH Postdoctoral Tng. grantee, 1978, 79; recipient Luth. Brotherhood award, 1963, Fannie Lou Hammer award Fannie Lou Hammer Ednl. Organ. and Women for Racial and Econ. Equality, 1989, 90. Mem. Physicians for Social Responsibility, Am. Acad. Pediatrics, N.Y. Acad. Scis., Am. Med. Women's Assn., Am. Pub. Health Assn., Pub. Health Assn. NYC, Am. Orthopsychiat. Assn., N.Y. Acad. Scis., Ambulatory Pediatrics Assn. Home: 59 W 94th St New York NY 10025-7113

SHEPPARD, JOSEPH SHERLY, painter, sculptor; b. Owings Mills, Md., Dec. 20, 1930; s. Joseph Ensor Sheppard and Edna Grace (Marquis) Kenny; children: Jonthan, William, Joseph. Student, Md. Inst. of Art, Balt., 1948-52. Artist in residence Dickinson Coll., Carlise, Pa., 1955-57; tchr. Md. Inst. of Art, 1960-75. Author: Anatomy, 1975, Drawing the Male Figure, 1976, Drawing the Female Figure, 1975, Learning from the Masters, 1979, The Work of Joseph Sheppard, 1982, Drawing the Living Figure, 1984, Bringing Textures to Life, 1987. Guggenheim fellowship, 1957, John F. and Anna Lee Stacey scholarship 1958; recipient John J. McDonough Prize Butler Inst. of Art, 1967, Tallix Foundry Prize Nat. Sculpture Soc. Exhbn., 1983, Agop Agopoff Meml. Prize, 1986. Fellow Nat. Sculpture Soc. (Agop Agopoff prize 1986, Tallix Foundry prize 1983); mem. Soc. of Animal Artists (Award of Merit 1983), Allied Artists of Am. (Bronze medal of honor 1963, Paul Puzinas award 1984, William Meyerowitz Meml. award 1985, Silver medal of honor 1986).

SHEPPARD, POSY (MRS. JEREMIAH MILBANK), social worker; b. New Haven, Aug. 23, 1916; d. John Day and Rose Marie (Herrick) Jackson; m. John W. Sheppard, May 16, 1936 (dec. Apr. 1990); children: Sandra S. (Mrs. Allan Gray Rodgers), Gail G. (Mrs. Gail Bidwell), Lynn S. (Mrs. William Muir Manger), John W.; m. Jeremiah Milbank, May 4, 1991. Student, Vassar Coll., 1938. Vol. field cons. Conn. A.R.C., 1955-60;

vice chmn. bd. govs. Am. Nat. Red Cross, 1962-66; rep. League Red Cross Socs. to UN, 1957-80, Am. Nat. Red Cross to com. internat. social welfare Nat. Social Welfare Assembly, 1957-61; chmn. Non-Govtl. Orgn. Com. for UNICEF, 1963-64, 71-73; chmn. Non-Govtl. Orgn. Com. exec. com. for Office Pub. Information, UN, 1964-66; pres. conf. non-govtl. orgns. in consultative status with UN Econ. and Social Council, 1966-69. Mem. Am. Soc. Polit. and Social Sci., Soc. Internat. Devel., Nat. Soc. Colonial Dames, Descs. Signers of Declaration Independence, Round Hill Club, River Club (N.Y.). Home: 535 Lake Ave Greenwich CT 06830-3831 also: 1 E 66th St New York NY 10021

SHEPPARD, RONALD JOHN, business education administrator; b. New Rochelle, N.Y., Apr. 13, 1939; s. Lester John and Louise Marie (Cox) S.; B.S., Rensselaer Poly. Inst., 1961; M.S., Howard U., 1962, Ph.D., 1965; M.B.A., Rochester Inst. Tech., 1974; student Detroit Coll. Law; m. Shirly Christine Saddler, June 8, 1963; children: Jeffrey Brandon, Mark Justin. Systems analyst RCA, Moorestown, N.J., 1965-66; mgr. strategic planning Booz Allen Hamilton, Inc., Washington, 1966-69; program mgr. space research Teledyne Brown Engring. Co., Huntsville, Ala., 1969-71; planning mgr., asst. group program mgr. Xerox Corp., Rochester, N.Y., 1971-77; later with Gen. Motors Corp., Warren, Mich.; now dir. Ctr. Bus. and Industry, U. Toledo; cons. Rensselaer Human Dimensions Center, 1975—; coll. student adviser Keuka Coll., 1975—; vis. faculty So. U., 1975, Empire State Coll., 1975-76, Rochester Inst. Tech., 1974-75. Pres., Rochester Montessori Sch. Bd., 1975-76; bd. dirs. Easter Seal Soc., Rochester Better Contractors Bur.; chmn. S.I Urban League; mem. market com. Snug Harbor Cultural Ctr. NDEA fellow, 1962-64, Howard U. Trustee fellow, 1964-65, NATO fellow U. Newcastle, Eng., 1964; recipient K.B. Weissman Meml. Found. Human Relations award, 1957. Mem. Am. Mktg. Assn., Assn. Masters in Bus. Adminstrn. Execs., Nat. Black Masters Bus. Adminstrn. Assn. Republican. Episcopalian. Clubs: Rensselaer Alumni, Rotary, Cornell of N.Y., Shriners. Home: 2456 Parliament Sq Toledo OH 43617-1285 Office: CUNY 715 Ocean Ter Staten Island NY 10301-4547

SHEPPARD, SHERRI YVONNE, federal agency administrator; b. Dallas, Dec. 30, 1949; d. M.T. and Johnnye Jewel (Davis) S. BA, Howard U., 1972, ME, 1974-75. Research analyst office of sec. U.S. Dept. Transp., Washington, 1972-74, program analyst, 1974-79; supervisory mgmt. analyst U.S. EEOC, Birmingham, Ala., 1979-80; program mgr. U.S. EPA, Washington, 1980—, fed. womens program mgr., 1985-89. Mem. Nat. Coalition of 100 Black Women (Capital City chpt. 1986-89), Nat. Council Negro Women (life, program coordinator mid-atlantic bethune recognition program 1984-86), Blacks in Govt. (life, nat. sec. 1983-86, nat. nominating chair 1990—), Nat. Assn. Female Execs., Alpha Kappa Alpha. Democrat. Baptist. Office: US EPA 401 M St SW (H7502C) Washington DC 20460-0002

SHEPPARD, WALTER LEE, JR., chemical engineer, consultant; b. Phila., June 23, 1911; s. Walter Lee and Martha Houston (Evans) S.; m. Dorothy Virginia Cosby Vanderslice, Oct. 17, 1942 (div. Mar. 1947); m. Boudinot Atterbury Oberge Kendall, Mar. 24, 1953; stepchildren: Charles H. Kendall Jr., John Atterbury Kendall. BChem, Cornell U., 1932; MS, U. Pa., 1933. Registered profl. engr., Del., Calif.; diplomate Am. Acad. Environ. Engrs.; ordained priest Liberal Cath. Ch., 1955. Control chemist various cos., 1933-35; advt. writer N.W. Ayer & Son, 1936-37; asst. to editor The Houghton Line, 1937-38; salesman Atlas Mineral Products, 1938-48; plant mgr., cons. engr. Tanks & Linings, Ltd., Droitwich, Eng., 1948-49; sales engr., dist. mgr. ElectroChem. Engring. & Mfg., and successor cos., 1949-68; field sales mgr. Corrosion Engring. div. Pennwalt Corp., Phila., 1968-76; pres. C.C.R.M., Inc.; cons. on chemically resistant masonry, 1976—; profl. genealogist, 1936—. Author: Ancestry and Descendants of Thomas Stickney Evans and Sarah Ann Fifield, His Wife, 1940, Chemically Resistant Masonry, 1977, 2d edit., 1982, Ancestry of Edward Carleton and Ellen Newton, His Wife, 1978; author, editor: Corrosion and Chemical Resistant Masonry Materials Handbook, 1986; editor: Ships and Passengers, Ancestral Roots of 60 New England Colonists, 6th edit., 1988, Magna Charta Sureties, 4th edit., 1991; contbg. editor Am. Genealogist, 1941-79, Nat. Geneal. Quar., 1961—; mem. publs. com. Pa. Geneal. Mag., 1960-76; contbr. articles on corrosion resistant masonry constrn. to profl. jours. Dir. displaced persons camps UNRRA, also staff Chief of Mission, Vienna, Austria, 1945-46; founding trustee Bd. Cert. Genealogists, 1965-82, pres., 1969-78, chmn., 1978-79. Served to maj. U.S. Army, 1941-45; lt. col. Res. (ret.). Named hon. mem. Class of 1928 U.S. Naval Acad. Fellow Am. Soc. Genealogists (sec. 1958-61, 66-67, v.p. 1967-70, pres. 1970-73), Nat. Geneal. Soc., Pa. Geneal. Soc.; mem. ASTM (membership sec. 1975-83, C-3 com.), NSPE, Am. Acad. Environ. Engrs., Welcome Soc. (pres. 1969-76), Illegitimate Sons and Daus. of Kings and Queens of Britain (founder, sec. 1950-68, pres. 1968-88), Flagon and Trencher Soc. (co-founder, pres. 1967-73), Nat. Assn. Corrosion Engrs. (cert. competence in corrosion engring., chmn. Phila. sect. 1962), New Eng. Historic Geneal. Soc., Nat. Geneal. Soc. (contbg. editor quar.), Geneal. Soc. Pa., Soc. Genealogists (London), Yorkshire Archeol. Soc., Savoy Co., Gilbert and Sullivan Soc. (founder, pres. Phila. br. 1957-63), Sovereign Order St. John of Jerusalem, Mil. Order Fgn. Wars, Mayflower Descs., Order of Three Crusades, Order of the Crown of Charlemagne in Am. (3rd v.p. 1989—), Ret. Officers Assn., Phi Kappa Psi (nat. v.p. 1964-68, pres. 1968-70), Alpha Chi Sigma. Home and Office: 923 Old Manoa Rd Upper Darby PA 19083-2610

SHEPPARD-GOERKE, CARROL SAHODRA, financial executive; b. Guyana, S.Am., July 28, 1947; d. Joseph and Stella (Morrison) Dookram; m. Osmond Sheppard, Sept. 14, 1968 (div. 1982); m. Richard Goerke, June 29, 1991; children: Christine, Doug. Assoc. Bus. Adminstrn., Borough of Manhattan Coll., 1984. Sec., office mgr. Michael Fain Advt., N.Y.C., 1968-72; sr. sec. Ted Bates Advt., N.Y.C., 1972-76, exec. sec., 1976-85, account coord., 1985-86; asst. account exec. Backer, Spielvogel, Bates, N.Y.C., 1986-87; account exec. Jamison & Leary Advt., Inc., N.Y.C., 1987-90; fin. dir. Jamison & Assoc. Advt. Inc., N.Y.C., 1991—. Pres. Young Women Club, Grace Luth. Ch., 1987. Home: 52 1st Ave Medford NY 11763-3837 Office: 1500 Broadway New York NY 10036-4015

SHER, MICHAEL STEPHEN, university official; b. Kansas City, Mo., Jan. 8, 1941; s. Abe A. and Ann (Kramer) S.; m. Gloria Lynn Kraft, Aug. 19, 1962; children: Barbara E. Weiss, Karen M., David E. AB in Physics, Washington U., St. Louis, 1962; MS in Atmospheric Sci., U. Mo., 1964; MS in Physics, Mich. State U., 1966, PhD in Physics, 1968. Rsch. asst. prof. computer sci. dept. U. Ill., Urbana, 1969-70, assoc. dir. Ctr. for Advanced Computation, 1970-74; pres. Ill. Ednl. Consortium, Springfield, 1974-79; dep. dir. info. scis. directorate, mgr. Office Policy, Planning & Controls EG&G Idaho Nat. Engring. Lab., Idaho Falls, 1979-82; staff officer for computing UCLA, 1982-87; spl. asst. to chancellor U. Calif., Santa Barbara, 1988; dir. acad. computing SUNY, Buffalo, 1988—; cons. President's Office, U. Calif., Berkeley, 1988. Contbr. articles to profl. jours. Home: 168 Brenridge Dr East Amherst NY 14051-1383 Office: Acad Computing 201 Computing Ctr Buffalo NY 14260

SHERBON, JOHN WALTER, agriculture educator; b. Lewiston, Idaho, Oct. 31, 1933; s. Ollis W. and Agnes G. (Jones) S.; m. Ruth Fern Poppens, Mar. 4, 1934; children: Barbara Elaine, William Ollis. BS, Wash. State U., 1955; MS, U. Minn., 1958, PhD, 1963. Asst. prof. Cornell U., Ithaca, N.Y., 1963-69, assoc. prof., 1969-77, prof. dairy sci., 1977—; cons. UN Devel. Project ID/708/020, Karnal, India, 1986, Maritime Province Higher Edn. Commn., Halifax, N.S., 1981; vis. rsch. officer N.Z. Dairy Rsch. Inst., Palmerston North, 1970-71. Contbr. over 60 articles to profl. jours. Fulbright scholar, 1955-56. Mem. Am. Dairy Sci. Assn., Inst. of Food Technologists, Assn. Milk, Food and Environ. Sanitarians, Lions. Lutheran. Office: Dept Food Sci Cornell U Wing Dr Ithaca NY 14853

SHEREDOS, CAROL ANN, rehabilitation agency director; b. N.Y.C., Jan. 29, 1944; d. Robert J. and Margaret M. (Adams) Ross; m. Saleem J. Sheredos, July 14, 1973; children: Emily Joy, Douglas Joseph. BS, Ithaca Coll., 1967; postgrad., Coll. of Notre Dame, Balt., 1990—. Lic. phys. therapist, N.Y., Md., Fla., N.J. Staff phys. therapist Glen Cove (N.Y.) Community Hosp., 1967-68, Nassau County Health Dept., Mineola, N.Y., 1968-70; rsch. phys. therapist VA, N.Y.C., 1970-71, prosthetics rsch. and edn. specialist, 1971-73; chief phys. therapist Medicus, Wappingers Falls, N.Y., 1983-88; dir. Meridian Rehab. Svcs., Towson, Md., 1989—; pvt. practice phys. therapy, N.Y., 1967-83; cons. in disability and aging Alliance, Inc., Balt., 1990—. Contbr. articles to profl. jours. Host minister St. Joseph's Ch., Texas, Md., 1990—. Named One of Ten Most Outstanding Handicapped Americans, Pres.' Com. on Employment of Handicapped, 1971. Mem. Am. Phys. Therapy Assn., Md. Coalition for Assistive Tech., Assn. Christian Therapists, Nat. Coun. Aging, Am. Soc. Aging, Resna. Republican. Roman Catholic. Office: Meridian Rehab Svcs 515 Fairmount Ave Baltimore MD 21204-5466

SHERER, SAMUEL AYERS, lawyer, urban planning consultant; b. Warwick, N.Y., June 17, 1944; s. Ernest Thompson and Helen (Ayers) S.; m. Dewi Sudewinahidah, June 28, 1980. AB magna cum laude, Oberlin Coll., 1966; JD, Harvard U., 1970; M in City Planning, MIT, 1970. Bar: D.C. 1972, U.S. Supreme Ct. 1979. Atty., advisor Boston area office HUD, 1970; sr. cons. McClaughry Assoc., Washington, 1970-71, 74-76; cons. Urban Inst., Washington, 1971-72; atty., urban planner IBRD Jakarta (Indonesia) Urban Devel. Study, 1972-74; atty., advisor Office Minority Bus. U.S. Dept. Commerce, Washington, 1976-77; ptnr. Topping & Sherer, Washington, 1977-90; pres. Sherer-Axelrod-Monacelli, Inc., Cambridge, Mass., 1978—; prin. The Washington Team, Inc., 1992—; bd. dirs. Optical Communications Corp., Washington, PADCO, Inc.; rep. Internat. Devel. Law Inst., Washington, 1983-90; sr. fellow Climate Inst., 1988—; cons. in field. Co-author: Urban Land Use in Egypt, 1977; editor: Important Laws and Regulations Regarding Land, Housing and Urban Development in the Arab Republic of Egypt, 1977, Important Laws and Regulations Regarding Land, Housing and Urban Development in the Hashemite Kingdom of Jordan, 1981. Bd. dirs. MIT Enterprise Forum of Washington-Balt., 1980-82; mem. D.C. Rep. Cent. Com., 1984-88; mem. nat. governing bd. Ripon Soc., Washington, 1977-83. Urban Studies fellow HUD, 1969-70. Mem. ABA, D.C. Bar Assn., Am. Planning Assn., Inst. Land Info., Tech. Transfer Soc., Asia Soc., Phi Beta Kappa. Home: 4600 Connecticut Ave NW Apt 205 Washington DC 20008-5702 Office: 316 Pennsylvania Ave SE # 202 Washington DC 20003

SHERIDAN, SISTER ANN LOUISE, school administrator; b. Lowell, Mass., July 26, 1940; d. Edward James and Laura (Burke) S. BA in Am. History, Cath. U., 1964; MS in Edn., SUNY, Buffalo, 1973. Cert. tchr., N.Y. Tchr. St. Paul Sch., Kenmore, N.Y., 1961-62, Blessed Sacrament Sch., Kenmore, 1964-67, St. John the Baptist Sch., Kenmore, 1967-69; prin. St. Mary Sch., Lockport, N.Y., 1969-70; supervising prin. Lockport Cath. Schs., 1970-77; prin. Holy Spirit Sch., Buffalo, 1977-81; dir. ednl. planning Diocese of Buffalo, 1982-91, coord. community residence for aged and ret. sisters, 1991—; mem. provincial adminstrn. Sisters of St. Mary of Namur, Kenmore, 1973-77, 81-87, 90—, devel. dir. 1986—; mem. academic coun. Mt. St. Mary High Sch. Bd. Trustees, Kenmore, 1984—. Coord. criteria for sch. consolidation Diocese of Buffalo, 1983-84. Mem. Nat. Cath. Edn. Assn. Office: Diocese of Buffalo Dept Cath Edn 795 Main St Buffalo NY 14203

SHERIDAN, CHARLES FITZGERALD, JR., lawyer; b. Syracuse, N.Y., May 31, 1928; s. Charles F. and Millicent (McElvare) S.; m. Ellen Sisson, July 4, 1953; children: Amy, Timothy, Cornelia. BA, Amherst Coll., 1948; LLB (hon.), Harvard U., 1951, JD (hon.), 1951. Bar: N.Y. 1951, R.I. 1951, Mass. 1958, N.H. 1962. Assoc. Edwards & Angell, Providence, 1951-57; from asst. gen. counselt to gen., counsel Avis Rent-A-Car, Boston, 1957-62; Sulloway & Hollis Sulloway Hollis & Soden, Concord, N.H., 1962—; dir. First Capital Bank, Concord, 1972-91; adv. dir. First N.H. Bank, 1992—; bd. dirs. Globe Mfg. Co., Pittsfield, N.H. Trustee N.H. Civil Liberties Union, N.H. Symphony Orch., Manchester, 1986—; past pres. United Way, Merrimack County, YMCA, Concord C. of C. Fellow Am. Coll. Trusts and Estates; mem. N.H. Bar Assn. (past chmn. sections of taxation and corp. and banking and bus. section), Lake Sunapee Yacht Club. Home: 9 Fiskill Farm Concord NH 03301 Office: Sulloway & Hollis 9 Capitol St Concord NH 03301

SHERIDAN, DIXIE M., academic administrator; b. Ardmore, Okla., Oct. 19, 1943; d. Richard Monsor and Mary Sue (Cantrell) Massad; m. James Davern Sheridan, Apr. 16, 1966 (div.). AB, Vassar Coll., 1965; MA, U. Okla., 1969. Reporter, editor So. Dutches News, Wappingers Falls, N.Y., 1975-77; editor Vassar Quarterly, Poughkeepsie, N.Y., 1977-80; asst. to pres. Vassar Coll., Poughkeepsie, N.Y., 1980-84, pres. sec., 1984-88, v.p. coll. rels., 1988—; dir. SPIN Theater, N.Y.C., 1991—, Cummington (Mass.) Community of Arts, 1987-91. Photographer: (book) Main to Mudd, 1987; contbr. photographs and articles to profl. jours. Dir. C. of C., Poughkeepsie, 1986-90. Mem. Coun. Advancement and Support Edn., PRSA. Office: Vassar Coll Raymond Ave Poughkeepsie NY 12603-2312

SHERIDAN, JOAN RUTH, publishing executive; b. Forest Hills, N.Y., July 3, 1956; d. Thomas Patrick and Ruth B. (Stalzer) S. BS in Communication Arts, St. John's U., Jamaica, N.Y., 1978. Media planner BBDO, N.Y.C., 1978-81; media supr. Ted Bates & Co., N.Y.C., 1982-84; v.p., assoc. media dir. FCB Leber Katz Ptnrs., N.Y.C., 1985-87; assoc. ad dir. Woman's Day, N.Y.C., 1987—. Office: Woman's Day 375 Hudson St New York NY 10014-3658

SHERIDAN, NEIL WALLACE, marketing professional; b. N.Y.C., Sept. 25, 1941; s. Wallace Moore and Helen Christine (Meyer) S. AB in Liberal Arts, Franklin and Marshall Coll., 1964. Mktg. rep. Scott Paper Co., Phila., 1964-65; mktg. mgr. Richardson-Vick, N.Y.C., 1965-71, Chesebrough-Ponds Inc., Greenwich, Conn., 1971-74, Warner-Lambert, Morris Plains, N.J., 1974-76; dir. corp. planning Sterling Drug, N.Y.C., 1976-89; v.p. The Travelers, Hartford, Conn., 1989-91; dir. Advanced Med. Devices, Branford, Conn., 1991—. Chmn. Conn. River Watershed Coun., Hartford, 1990—; dir. Middlesex County Extension Svc., Haddam, Conn., 1990—. Republican. Congregationalist. Home: Bayberry Farm East Haddam CT 06423

SHERLOCK, GARY FULLER, newspaper publisher; b. Avalon, Catalina Island, Calif., May 3, 1945; s. Jay Robert and Dorothy Marilyn (Bryant) S.; m. D. Joyce Conrad, Aug. 24, 1966; children—Blake Edward, Regan Jay; m. 2d, Susan Paounoff, Jan. 2, 1982. B.S. in Bus. Adminstrn., U. Idaho, 1968. With Idaho Statesman, Boise, 1967-86, advt. sales intern, 1968, retail advt. account exec., 1968-72, retail advt. mgr., 1972-76, advt. dir., 1976-81, pub., 1981-86; pres. sales Gannett Nat. Newspaper, 1986-90; exec. v.p. advt. Gannett Co., Inc., Rosslyn, Va., 1987-90; pres., pub. Gannett Suburban Newspapers, White Plains, N.Y., 1990—. Bd. dirs. Westchester County Assn., Westchester Arts Coun., Hudson Valley Regional Blood Svcs., Regional Plan Assn. Trustee Albertson Coll. Idaho. Mem. Newspaper Assn. Am., Am. Advt. Fedn. (past state lt. gov.), Phi Delta Theta. Methodist. Clubs: Westchester Country, Hillcrest Country, Arid, Landmark. Office: Gannett Suburban Newspapers One Gannett Dr White Plains NY 10604

SHERMAN, BURTON STUART, medical educator, researcher, consultant; b. Bklyn., Nov. 12, 1930; s. Samuel and Mary (Bloom) S.; m. Eileen Iris Chanin, Aug. 30, 1952; children: Steven, Lisa, Cari, Keith. BA, NYU, 1951, MS, 1956; PhD, SUNY, Bklyn., 1960. Rsch. asst. Sloan-Kettering Inst., N.Y.C., 1951-52; rsch. chemist Jewish Hosp. of Bklyn., 1952-56, rsch. assoc., 1959-60; from instr. to assoc. prof. SUNY-Downstate Med. Ctr., N.Y.C., 1960-85, assoc. prof. emeritus, 1986—; prof., dean Sch. Health Scis. Touro Coll., Dix hills, N.Y., 1986-89, prof., dean emeritus, 1989—; cons. Tobacco Chem. Corp., Wilmington, Del., 1967-74, Hoffman-LaRoche Inc., Basel, Switzerland, 1968-71; vis. scientist, Strangeways Rsch. Lab., Cambridge, Eng., 1964-65; exec. dir., N.Y. Biomed. Cons. Co., Valley Stream, N.Y., 1978—. Co-author: Techniques of Medication, 1969; contbr. articles to profl. jours. Trustee Congregation Beth Emeth, Hewlett, N.Y., 1969—, pres., chmn. bd. trustees, 1971-73. Mem. AAAS, Am. Assn. Anatomists, Am. Assn. Clin. Anatomists, Soc. Sigma Xi. Home: 184 Elmwood St Valley Stream NY 11581-2636

SHERMAN, GEOFFREY KIMMETT, psychotherapist; b. Allentown, Pa., June 24, 1961. Mt. St. Mary's Coll., Mt. St. Mary's Coll., Emmitsburg, Md., 1984; MA magna cum laude, Kutztown U. of Pa., 1989. Bd. cert. med. psychotherapist. Adminstr. Allentown Osteopathic Med. Ctr., 1985-87; psychologist intern Counseling Assocs., Allentown, 1988; psychotherapist Springhaven Counseling Ctr., Allentown, 1989—; med. psychotherapist Orefield (Pa.) Med. Ctr., 1990—, Maulfair Med. Ctr., Mertztown, Pa., 1990—; clin. assoc. Am. Bd. Med. Psychotherapists. Mem. APA, AACD, Pa Psychol. Assn., Am. Mental Health Counselors Assn., Pa. Counseling Assn., Christian Assn. for Psychol. Studies, Pa. Assn. Counselor Educators and Suprs., Pa. Career Devel. Assn., Pa. Mental Health Counselors Assn., Pa. Assn. for Counselors Specializing in Couples and Families, Pa. Assn. for Adult Devel. and Aging. Office: Brookside Profl Counseling Springhaven Counseling Ctr Brookside Profl Pk Box 3434 Allentown PA 18106-0434

SHERMAN, LARRY RAY, chemistry educator; b. Easton, Pa., June 26, 1934; s. Ray Earl and Estella Mary (Wirebach) S.; m. Irene Helen Price, Aug. 27, 1966. BS in Chemistry, Lafayette Coll., 1956; MS in Chemistry, Utah State U., 1961; PhD in Analytical Chemistry, U. Wyo., 1969. Engr. GE, Cleve., 1956-58; analyst Weyerhauser Co., Seattle, 1962-64; mem. faculty No. Ill. U., Dekalb, 1964-66, N.C. Agrl. and Tech. State U., Greensboro, 1969-74, U. Miss., Oxford, 1976-78, U. Akron, Ohio, 1978-81, 87-88; rsch. scientist Hillyard Chem. Co., St. Joseph, Mo., 1974-76; mem. faculty dept. chemistry U. Scranton, Pa., 1981—; rsch. cons. JHL Industries, York, Pa.; guest prof. U. Dortmund, Germany, summer 1986; faculty fellow Brooks AFB, San Antonio, summer 1988, 92; dir. Internat. Symposium on Effect of Organotins upon Malignant Cell Growth, Chapman Lake, Pa., 1984, 85, 88. Author: Chemistry in the Bible, 1976, Introduction to Chemistry, Parts I and II, 1990, (with M. Brdar) A Manual for Balancing Chemical Equations, 1980; contbr. articles to sci. and religion jours., chpts. to books. Mem. nat. com. Eastern Orthodox Com. on Scouting Boy Scouts Am., Avoca, Pa. Recipient Merck award Lafayette Coll., 1958, Silver Beaver award Forest Lakes coun. Boy Scouts Am., 1986, Prophet Elisha award Orthodox Ch. in Am., 1986; NASA rsch. fellow U. Wyo., 1968. Fellow Royal Soc. for Chemistry; mem. Am. Chem. Soc. (com. 1963-64, 67, 71, 73-74, summer fellow analytical div. 1967), Controlled Release Soc. (com. 1981), Pa. Acad. Scis. (life), Fedn. Russian Orthodox Clubs (lt. gov.), Sigma Xi. Home: 1035 Quincy Ave Scranton PA 18510-1121 Office: U Scranton Dept Chemistry Scranton PA 18510-4626

SHERMAN, PHILIP MARTIN, computer systems consultant; b. Norwalk, Conn., July 10, 1930; s. Robert and Anne (Margulies) S.; m. Doris G. Sherman, Apr. 3, 1955; children: Judith Schwartz, Alan, Emily. B.Engring. Physics, Cornell U., 1952; MEE, Yale U., 1956, PhD, 1959. Dept. head Bell Telephone Labs., Murray Hill, N.J., 1959-69; mgr. info. systems Xerox Corp., Rochester, N.Y., 1969-84; pres. Sherman Data Systems, Rochester, N.Y., 1984—. Author: Programming Digital Computers, 1963, Techniques in Computer Programming, 1969, Strategic Planning, 1982; contbr. articles to profl. jurs. Pres. Town Libr. Bd., Rochester, 1975-84. Mem. IEEE (sr. mem., founding chmn.). Home and Office: Sherman Data Systems 471 Claybourne Rd Rochester NY 14618-1201

SHERMAN, ROBERT MARTIN, information systems executive; b. Lakewood, N.J., Aug. 22, 1949; s. Robert Coleman and Evelyn Clara (Woodington) S.; m. Lorraine LaRue Pilger, A ug. 19, 1972; children: Amanda Nicole, David Robert. BA History, Polit. Sci., Kans. Wesleyan U., Salina, 1972. Cert. systems profl., office automation profl., data processor. Computer programmer N.J. Treasury Data Ctr., Trenton, 1978-82; systems analyst N.J. Treasury Data Ctr., 1981-82, sr. systems analyst, 1982-83; project ldr. Continental Data Ctr., Neptune, N.J., 1983-84; project mgr. N.J. Div. Pensions, Trenton, 1984-87; MIS dir. Ancora Hosp., Hammonton, N.J., 1987—; cons. Manahawkin Bapt. Ch., N.J., 1983—. Mem. Data Processing Mgmt. Assn., Assn. for Systems Mgmt., Assn. of Inst. for Cert. Computer Profls., Healthcare Info. and Mgmt. Systems Soc., N.J. Healthcare Data Processing Mgmt. Assn. Republican. Baptist. Home: 1093 Prospect Ave Manahawkin NJ 08050-3049 Office: Ancora Hosp Hammonton NJ 08037

SHERMAN, RUTH TENZER, artist, fixtures company executive; b. Chgo., Sept. 11, 1920; d. Philip and Jennie (Greitzer) Tenzer; m. Samuel Sherman, May 18, 1946 (dec. Nov. 1974); children: Patricia (dec.), Randy Mitchell. Art student, Pratt Inst., 1938-42, Art Students League, N.Y.C., 1942-45; studies with Raphael Soyer, N.Y.C., 1943, studies with Harold Baumbach, 1947-49; studies with Ruth Connery, Mamaroneck, N.Y., 1955; studies with Rudolph Baranik, White Plains, N.Y., 1961-63, studies with George Koras, 1966. Cert. artist Dept. Cultural Affairs. Pres. Pioneer Fixture Corp., Paterson, N.J., 1975-86. Exhbns. include Mamaroneck Artists Guild, 1963, Jr. League Artists of North Westchester, 1964, Westchester C.C., Valhalla, N.Y., 1964, The New Rochelle (N.Y.) Art Assn., 1964, Union Carbide Bldg. Christmas Show, N.Y.C., 1964, Silvermine Guild Artists, New Canaan, Conn., 1964, Westchester Art Soc., White Plains, 1964-72, Hudson River Mus., Yonkers, N.Y., 1965, Sisterhood Temple Israel New Rochelle, 1966, First Westchester Nat. Bank, New Rochelle, 1967, Conn. Acad. Fine Arts, Hartford, 1967, Stern Bros., N.Y.C., 1967, Nat. Jewish Hosp. Denver, Woodmere, N.Y., 1968, Quaker Ridge Sch., Scarsdale, N.Y., 1970, Gallery Shop, Westport, Conn., 1976, Mari Gallery, Woodstock, N.Y., 1978, The Village Gallery, Ardsley, N.Y., 1979, Todd Gallery, Kiamesha Lake, N.Y., 1980, Norwalk Mchts. Bank, New Canaan, 1980, Mchts. Bank, Norwalk, 1980, Emery Air Freight Hdqs., Conn., 1981, Mari Hube Gallery, N.Y., 1990, Helio Gallery, N.Y.C., 1991, Maska Gallery, Seattle, 1991. Recipient Merit award Westchester Art Soc., 1964. Home: 211 W 71st St New York NY 10023

SHERMAN, STEVEN LLOYD, secondary educator; b. Bklyn., Oct. 19, 1947; s. Jack and Gertrude (Apatov) S.; m. Vonabell Lee Roocke, Aug. 15, 1982; children: Matthew, Rachel, Jaime, Jesse. BS in Phys. Edn., Bklyn. Coll., 1968, MS in Phys. Edn., 1972, cert. in sch. adminstrn., 1974. Phys. edn. tchr. N.Y.C. Bd. Edn., 1968—. Exec. dir., pres. Just Pray No to Drugs, East Rockaway, N.Y., 1990—; mem. East Rockaway Drug Abuse and Control Com., 1991. Recipient Citation U.S. Congress, 1991, Proclaimation Nassau County Exec. Dir., 1991. Messianic believer. Office: Just Pray No Ltd 124 Garfield Pl East Rockaway NY 11518-1017

SHERMAN, STRATFORD PRESSLEY, reporter, editor, writer; b. Norwalk, Conn., Aug. 21, 1952; s. Herbert Allen and Margaret (Elliott) S.; m. Meredith Chandler Davis, Sept. 21, 1985; children: Spencer Davis, Chandler Elliott. BA in English, Harvard U., 1974. Tchr. St. Maarten, Saint Maarten, 1974-75; COO Colonial Gardens Corp., Bridgeport, Conn., 1975-76; editorial asst. William Morrow & Co., N.Y.C., 1976-77; reporter, assoc. editor, bd. of editors Fortune Mag., N.Y.C., 1977—. Author: (screenplay) SOUL, 1989, (book with Noel Tichy) Control Your Destiny or Someone Else Will, 1992. Chmn. Ridgefield (Conn.) Homeowners Assn., 1992. Mem. Harvard Club. Office: Fortune Mag 1271 6th Ave New York NY 10020

SHERMAN, THOMAS BROOKS, stockbroker; b. Evanston, Ill., Oct. 17, 1950; s. James Garfield Sherman and Elizabeth (Brooks) Granger; m. Elizabeth Cornman, May 1, 1986; children: Brooks Miller, Hannah Elizabeth. AB in Econs., Boston U., 1975; postgrad. in Acctg., Northeastern U., Boston, 1982. Banker Provident Bank, Boston, 1970-75; mgr. Edison Bros., Inc., St. Louis, 1975-82; stockbroker A. G. Edwards & Sons, Pittsfield, Mass., 1983—. Dir. Girls Club, Pittsfield, 1986—; chmn. Lenox Town Fin. Com., 1986—; chmn. of trustees Ch. on the Hill, Lenox, 1990. Mem. Cen. Berkshire C. of C. (vice chmn. 1983—), Rotary (dir. 1990—). Congregationalist. Home: PO Box 1717 19 Old Stockbridge Rd Lenox MA 01240 Office: A G Edwards & Sons Inc Berkshire Common Pittsfield MA 01201

SHERMAN, ZACHARY, civil and aerospace engineer, consultant; b. N.Y.C., Oct. 26, 1922; s. Harry and Minnie (Schulsinger) S.; m. Bertha Leikin, Mar. 23, 1947; children: Gene Victor, Carol Beth. BCE, CCNY, 1943; MCE, Polytech. U. N.Y., Bklyn., 1953, PhD in Civil Engring. & Mechanics, 1969; MME, Stevens Inst. Tech., 1968. Registered profl. engr., N.Y., N.J. Stress analyst Gen. Dynamics, San Diego, 1943-45; sr. stress analyst Republic Aviation, Farmingdale, N.Y., 1945-47, 59-62; prof. civil engring. U. Miss., Oxford, 1954-59; lectr. civil engring. Stevens Inst. Tech., Hoboken, N.J., 1962-67, CUNY, 1967-69; assoc. prof. aerospace engring. Pa. State U., State College, 1969-73; prin. Dr. Zachary Sherman Cons. Engrs., Long Beach, N.Y., 1973—; aerospace engr. FAA, N.Y.C., 1980-86; designated engr. rep., FAA. Contbr. articles to profl. jours. NSF grantee, 1972. Fellow ASCE; mem. AIAA (v.p. Western Conn. chpt. 1977-78), N.Y. Acad. Scis., Sigma Xi. Home and Office: 25 Neptune Blvd Apt 7H Long Beach NY 11561-4657

SHERRICK, CARL EDWIN, research psychologist, consultant; b. Carnegie, Pa., Oct. 28, 1924; s. Carl Edwin and Ruth Hunter (Clark) S.; m. Patricia Ames Daily, Oct. 15, 1954; children: Kathleen, Diana, Molly

Clark. BS in Chemistry, Carnegie-Mellon U., 1948; MA in Psychology, U. Va., 1950, PhD in Psychology, 1952. Asst. prof. psychology Washington U., St. Louis, 1953-59; rsch. assoc. Cen. Inst. for Deaf, St. Louis, 1959-61, U. Va., Charlottesville, 1961-62; rsch. psychologist Princeton (N.J.) U., 1962-70, sr. rsch. psychologist, 1970—; mem. communicative scis. study sect. NIH, Bethesda, Md., 1967-71, mem. adv. coun. Nat. Adv. Neurol. and Communicative Disorders and Stroke, 1985-89, Nat. Inst. on Deafness and Other Communication Disorders, 1989-91. Contbr. articles and revs. to sci. jours. Sgt. AUS, 1944-46. Rsch. grantee NIH, 1972-91. Fellow APA, Am. Psychol. Soc., Acoustical Soc. Am.; mem. Psychonomic Soc., Raven Soc., Sigma Xi. Unitarian. Home: 44 Maclean Cir Princeton NJ 08540-5621 Office: Princeton U Green Hall Princeton NJ 08544-1010

SHERROD, LONNIE RAY, foundation administrator, researcher, psychologist; b. Knoxville, Tenn., Sept. 7, 1950; s. Raymond O. and Jane L. (Lambdin) S.; m. Barbara A. Cornblatt, Jan. 31, 1981; 1 child, Sara Raye. BS, Duke U., 1972; MA, U. Rochester, N.Y., 1974, Yale U., 1976; PhD, Yale U., 1978. Rsch. assoc. Yale U., New Haven, 1978; staff assoc. Social Sci. Rsch. Coun., N.Y.C., 1979-85; sr. program assoc. William T. Grant Found., N.Y.C., 1986-89, v.p. programs, 1990—; asst. dean grad. faculty New Sch. for Social Rsch., N.Y.C., 1986-89; mem. adj. faculty psychology dept. NYU, N.Y.C., 1980-85, grad. faculty, 1986-91. Co-author: Infant Social Cognition, 1981; contbr. articles to profl. jours.; assoc. editor: Human Nature, 1989-91. Mem. program com. Grantmakers of Children and Youth, 1990, N.Y. Regional Assn. of Grantmakers, 1991—; mem. adv. bd. Ctr. Study of Child and Adolescent Devel., Pa. State U., 1992—; bd. dirs. Life Trends, Inc., 1992—, Timber Trails Community Assn., 1992—. Mem. APA, Am. Psychol. Soc., Soc. Study of Social Biology (sec., treas. N.Y.C. chpt. 1984-90), Internat. Soc. for Study of Behavior Devel., Soc. Rsch. on Adolescence, Soc. for Rsch. in Child Devel. (mem. com. on pub. policy, pub. info and child devel., chmn. subcom. on pub. info, 1992—. Office: William T Grant Found 515 Madison Ave New York NY 10022-5403

SHERRY, SOL, physician, scientist, educator; b. N.Y.C., Dec. 8, 1916; s. Hyman and Ida (Greenman) S.; m. Dorothy Sitzman, Aug. 7, 1946; children—Judith Anne, Richard Leslie. A.B., NYU, 1935, M.D., 1939; D.Sc. (hon.), Temple U., 1980. Successively fellow, intern, resident 3d med. div. Bellevue Hosp., N.Y.C., 1939-42, 46; asst. prof. medicine NYU Coll. Medicine, 1946-51; dir. May Inst. Med. Research, Cin., 1951-54; dir. medicine Jewish Hosp., St. Louis, 1954-58; prof. medicine Washington U. Sch. Medicine, St. Louis, 1958-68; co-chmn. dept. Washington U. Sch. Medicine, 1964-68; chmn. dept. Temple U. Sch. Medicine, 1968-84, disting. univ. prof., 1983-87, Disting. prof. emeritus, 1987—, dean, 1984-86; dir. Thrombosis Research Center, 1970-79, dir. emeritus, 1979—; cons. emeritus surgeon gen. army; past chmn. com. thrombolytic agts., past chmn. com. on thrombosis USPHS; chmn. council on thrombosis Am. Heart Assn.; past mem. com. blood, past chmn. task force on thrombosis NRC; mem. Internat. Commn. on Hemostasis and Thrombosis; past chmn. and pres. Internat. Socs. on Thrombosis and Hemostasis; past mem. sci. adv. com. St. Louis Heart Assn., also St. Louis Multiple Sclerosis Soc. Contbr. articles to profl. jours. Mem. bd. Hillel, 1961-67; pres. S.E. Pa. chpt. Am. Heart Assn., 1978-79. Served as flight surgeon USAAF, 1942-46, ETO. Recipient medal for typhus control Lower Bavaria U.S. Army Typhus Commn., 1946; Research Career award USPHS, 1962; Disting. Achievement award Modern Medicine, 1963; Disting. Achievement award A.C.P., 1968; Disting. Achievement award Am. Coll. Cardiology, 1971; Disting. Achievement award Internat. Soc. Thrombosis and Haemostasis, 1978, Disting. Achievement award Tex. Heart Inst., 1990; Gold medal Internat. Soc. Thrombosis and Hemostasis, 1983; Disting. Achievement award Phila. County Med. Soc., 1985; Disting. Achievement award APDIM, 1992. Fellow Royal Coll. Physicians; mem. AMA (past mem. and chmn. council drugs, chmn. sect. exptl. medicine and therapeutics), Assn. Am. Physicians, Assn. Profs. Medicine (council 1973-75, pres. 1976), Am. Soc. Clin. Investigation, Am. Heart Assn., Central Soc. Clin. Research (council 1962-64), Am. Physiol. Soc., Soc. Exptl. Biology and Medicine, A.C.P. (master), Phi Beta Kappa, Sigma Xi (pres. Washington U. chpt. 1962-63), Alpha Omega Alpha. Home: 4 Promenade Pl Voorhees NJ 08043-4169

SHERTUKDE, HEMCHANDRA MADHUSUDAN, electrical engineering educator; b. Bombay, Apr. 29, 1953; came to U.S., 1983; s. Madhusudan Gajanan and Sulabha Madhusudan (Lanjekar) S.; m. Rekha Hemchandra Mathkar, Jan. 22, 1981; children: Amola, Karan, Rohan. B Tech. in Elec. Engring. with honors, Indian Inst. Tech., Kharagpur, 1975; diploma in mgmt. studies, U. Bombay, 1980; MS in Elec. and Systems Engring., U. Conn., 1985, PhD in Elec. and Systems Engring., 1989. Asst. engr. Tata Engring. and Locomotive Co. Ltd., Pune, India, 1975-77; mgmt. trainee Crompton Greaves Ltd., Kanjurmarg, Bombay, 1977-78, asst. design officer, 1978-79, design officer, 1979-81, sr. exec., 1981-83; assoc. prof. elec. engring. U. Hartford, West Hartford, 1988—; prin. investigator Engring. Application Ctr., U. Hartford, West Hartford, Conn., 1990—. Co-author: Multitarget-Multisensor Tracking: Applications and Advances, Vol. II, 1991; contbr. articles to profl. jours. Doctoral dissertation fellow U. Conn., 1988; Vincent B. Coffin grantee U. Hartford, 1990; grantee Canberra Industries, Inc., 1990, 91. Mem. AIAA (sr.), IEEE (sr.), Soc. Optical Engrs., Tau Beta Pi, Eta Kappa Nu. Republican. Hindu. Home: 246 Willowcrest Dr Windsor CT 06095-3869 Office: U Hartford 200 Bloomfield Ave West Hartford CT 06117-1500

SHERWIN, JOHN MARTIN, orthopaedic surgeon; b. White Plains, N.Y., July 2, 1929; s. Martin Hutchinson and Barbara (Laimbeer) S.; m. Marjorie Richardson, Feb. 23, 1952; children: Elizabeth, James, Jane. BA, Colgate U., 1951; student, Union Theol. Sem., 1951; MD, Albany Med. Coll., 1960. Resident Yale U., New Haven, 1965; pvt. practice orthopaedic surgery Manchester, N.H., 1965—; pres. med. staff Elliot Hosp., Manchester, 1975; del. to AMA, Chgo., 1984—. Inventor Sherwin knee retractor, 1971. Capt. USMCR, 1951-56. Fellow ACS, Am. Acad. Orthopaedic Surgeons; mem. AMA, N.H. Med. Soc. (pres. exec. com. 1982), Hillsborough County Med. Soc. Republican. Presbyterian. Home: 246 N Gate Rd Manchester NH 03104-1825 Office: NH Orthopaedic Surgery PA 700 Lake Ave Ste 1 Manchester NH 03103-2776

SHERWOOD, JAMES WEBSTER, III, limousine company owner; b. Hollywood, Calif., May 18, 1936; s. James Webster Sherwood Jr. and Vesta Graybeal Hughes; m. Valdi Hiesinger, Apr. 17, 1964 (div. 1972); m. Marylou Coddington Lemke, July 4, 1972 (div. 1989); m. Karyn Virginia Lindig, Mar. 18, 1990; children: Veronica E.C. Sherwood Wright, Alexandra C.E., Roxanna Z.S.R., Christopher Michael De Santis, James Webster IV, George Marshall De Santis. Student, Choate Sch., U. Chgo., 1954-55; BL, U. Paris, 1963. Reporter, columnist San Mateo (Calif.) Times, Burlingame Advance, 1951-52; mng. editor Chgo. Rev. Mag., 1954-55; producer Myers-Sherwood Pictures, Inc., Chgo., 1955; editor Trans World Pictures, Inc., Chgo., 1955; editor, columnist Westchester News-Advertiser, L.A., 1956-57; prodn. asst. Cecil B. DeMille-Paramount Pictures, Hollywood, Calif., 1957-59; v.p., gen. mgr. Smith Limousine, N.Y.C., 1977-85; pres., owner Sherwood Justice & Barton Limousine Corp., N.Y.C., 1985—; producer, dir. Sherwood Films, Hollywood, 1958-60; cons. on Tom Jones, 1961; adaptor The Sicilian Clan, 1966; producer After Laughter, 1968, others. Syndicated columnist 11 western states for Christian Sci. Monitor, Hungry Horse (Mont.) News, Hellenic Rev., 1956-58; editor Popular Libr., 1970-72; biographic researcher Holt, Rinehart & Winston, 1970-72; journalist Ladies Home Jour., Village Voice, N.Y., 1972-73; author: (verse play) The Wooed Wife, 1957; author: 101 Sonnets of Sex, God, The Circus and Love, 2d edit., 1959, (novel) Stradella, 1961, others. Recipient Nat. Book award for best translation preface to (with Ralph Manheim/Castle to Castle), 1970, John Dos Passos award for Creative Writing, 1987. Republican. Episcopalian. Home: Grand Central Five Central Dr Plandome NY 11030-1408 Office: Sherwood Limousines PO Box 257 New York NY 10044-0205

SHERWOOD, KENNETH PARKER, JR., aquarium program director; b. New Milford, Conn., May 31, 1945; s. Kenneth Parker Sr. and Florence (Kelly) S.; m. Mary Ellen Melillo, Aug. 24, 1968; children: Kristin Kelly, Evan Matthew. BS, U. Cin., 1968; MA, Fairfield (Conn.) U., 1972. Phys. edn. tchr. Kings Hwy. Elem. Sch., Hillspoint Elem. Sch., Westport, Conn., 1968-72; fifth grade tchr. Hillspoint Elem Sch., Westport, 1972-77, Kings Hwy. Elem. Sch., Westport, 1977-81; dir. edn. Mystic (Conn.) Marinelife Aquarium, 1981—; asst. summer sch. prin. Westport Bd. Edn., 1980; adj. instr. U. Conn., Storrs, 1984—. Contbr. articles to profl. jours. Mem. Am. Assn. Mus., Am. Assn. Zool. Parks and Aquariums, Conn. Sci. Tchrs. Assn., Nat. Marine Educators Assn., New Eng. Mus. Assn. Democrat. Congregationalist. Office: Mystic Marinelife Aquarium 55 Coogan Blvd Mystic CT 06355-1997

SHERWOOD, LOUIS MAIER, physician, scientist, pharmaceutical company executive; b. N.Y.C., Mar. 1, 1937; s. Arthur Joseph and Blanche (Burger) S.; m. Judith Brimberg, Mar. 27, 1966; children: Jennifer Beth, Arieh David. AB with honors, Johns Hopkins U., 1957; MD with honors, Columbia U., 1961. Diplomate Am. Bd. Internal Medicine, Subsplty. Bd. in Endocrinology and Metabolism. Intern Presbyn. Hosp., N.Y.C., 1961-62, asst. resident in medicine, 1962-63; clin. assoc. research fellow Nat. Heart Inst., NIH, Bethesda, Md., 1963-66; NIH trainee endocrinology and metabolism Coll. Physicians and Surgeons, Columbia U., N.Y.C., 1966-68; assoc. medicine Beth Israel Hosp. and Harvard Med. Sch., Boston, 1968-69; chief endocrinology Beth Israel Hosp., 1968-72; asst. prof. medicine Harvard U., 1969-71, assoc. prof., 1971-72; physician-in-chief, chmn. dept. medicine Michael Reese Hosp. and Med. Ctr., Chgo., 1972-80; prof. medicine, div. biol. scis. Pritzker Sch. Medicine, U. Chgo., 1972-80; Ted and Florence Baumritter prof. medicine and biochemistry Albert Einstein Coll. Medicine, 1980-88, vis. prof. medicine and biochemistry, 1989—, chmn. dept. medicine, 1980-87; physician-in-chief Montefiore Hosp. and Med. Ctr., N.Y.C., 1980-87; sr. v.p. med. and sci. affairs Merck, Sharp & Dohme Internat., 1987-89; exec. v.p. worldwide devel. Merck, Sharp & Dohme Rsch. Labs., 1989-92' sr. v.p. U.S. Med. and Sci. Affair, Merck Human Health, 1992—; bd. dirs. Physicians and Surgeons Corp., Michael Reese Med. Ctr., 1973-80, Barren Found., 1974-80; Josiah Macy Jr. Found. fellow and vis. scientist Weizmann Inst., Israel, 1978-79; assoc. mem. bd. on subcom. endocrinology and metabolism Am. Bd. Internal Medicine, 1977-83. Editor: Beth Israel seminars New Eng. Jour. Medicine, 1968-71; mem. editorial bd. Endocrinology, 1969-73; assoc. editor Metabolism, 1970-85, Gen. Medicine B Study Sect., NIH, 1975-79; mem. editorial bd. Yr. in Endocrinology, 1976-86, Calcified Tissue Internat., 1978-80, Internal Medicine Alert, 1979-89; contbr. numerous articles on endocrinology, protein hormones, calcium metabolism and ectopic proteins to jours. Trustee Michael Reese Med. Ctr., 1974-77; mem. vis. council CUNY Med. Sch., 1986—; mem. alumni council Columbia Coll. Physicians and Surgeons, 1986—. Served as surgeon USPHS, 1963-66. Recipient Joseph Mather Smith prize for outstanding alumni research Coll. Physicians and Surgeons, Columbia U., 1972, Sr. Class Teaching award U. Chgo., 1976, 77; grantee USPHS, 1968-88. Fellow ACP (Outstanding Contbn. to Internal Medicine award 1987); mem. AAAS, Am. Fedn. Clin. Rsch. (bd. dirs. Found. 1989-92), Am. Inst. Chemists, Am. Soc. Biol. Chemists, Am. Soc. Clin. Investigation (pres. 1982-83), Assn. Am. Physicians, Endocrine Soc., N.Y. Acad. Medicine (bd. dirs. 1991—), Mass. Med. Soc., Cen. Soc. Clin. Rsch., Assn. Program Dirs. Internal Medicine (coun. 1979-85, pres. 1983-84), Assn. Profs. Medicine, Chgo. Soc. Internal Medicine, Interurban Clin. Club, Phi Beta Kappa, Alpha Omega Alpha. Office: Merck & Co US Human Health Sumneytown Pike West Point PA 19486

SHERWOOD, MARY PASCO, environmentalist; b. Hartford, Conn., May 1, 1906; d. Arthur Joseph and Mary (Lundy) Pasco. BS in Forestry, U. Conn., 1934; MS in Wildlife, Cornell U., 1937. Jr. forester State of Wis., Madison, 1944-45; ecologist State of Conn., Storrs, 1934-35, 38-44; creator, chmn. Walden Forever Wild Work, Concord, Mass., 1980—; owner native plant nursery Falls Village, Conn., 1945—; curator Conn. State Forest Mus., 2 summers; program dir. Mass. Audubon Soc., 1961-62; worker herbarium, Nantucket, Mass. Creator, editor The Saunterer, 1967-68, Thoreau Jour. Quar., 1968-78. Creator Thoreau Lyceum, Concord, 1967, Thoreau Fellowship, Old Town Maine, 1968-80. Grantee Colson, Corcord, 1936-37, Women's Farm and Garden, 1961-62; recipient Plaque, EPA, 1987, E-Mag. award, 1992, Medallion, U. Conn., Storrs, 1992. Mem. Thoreau Soc. (nominating com. 1992), New Eng. and Wildflower Soc. (book reviewer 1984-91). Home: Juniper Hill Village C101 Storrs CT 06268 Office: Walden Forever Wild Inc PO Box 275 Concord MA 01742

SHERWOOD, WILLIAM BRADLEY, human resources professional; b. Nashua, N.H., 1946; m. Betsy Delman; three children. BA in Social Rels., Harvard U., 1969; EdM, Rutgers U., 1971, EdD in Counseling Psychology, 1974. Dir. counseling and personal devel. svcs. Pace Univ., 1972-80, adj. prof., 1972-80; pvt. practice mgmt. cons., 1978-80; sr. tng. specialist The Am. Mgmt. Assn., 1980-82; exec. tng. specialist Reader's Digest Assn., 1982-84; mgr. mgmt. edn. and tng. SCM Corp., 1984-86; mgr. of human resources devel. N.Am. Philips Corp., N.Y.C., 1986-88, dir. human resources devel., 1988-91; dir. adminstrv. and tech. svcs. N.Am. Philips Corp., Briarcliff Manor, 1991—, Philips Rsch. Labs., Briercliff, N.Y.; adj. prof. L.I. Univ., 1972-80. Office: Philips Rsch Labs 345 Scarborough Rd Briarcliff Manor NY 10510-2099

SHERZER, WILLIAM MARTIN, foreign language educator; b. Phila., Aug. 22, 1946; s. Benjamin and Edna S.; m. Carmen Gea, Jan. 3, 1983; 1 child, David Sherzer-Gea. BA, Oberlin (Ohio) Coll., 1967; PhD, Princeton (N.J.) U., 1974. Instr. Bklyn. Coll. of CUNY, 1971-74, asst. prof. fgn. lang., 1974-81, assoc. prof., 1981-92, prof. fgn. lang., 1992—. Author: Religion, Morals and Ethics in the Contemporary Novels of Benito Perez Galdos, 1978, La novelistica de Juan Marse', 1982; contbr. articles to profl. jours. Mem. Am. Assn. Tchrs. Spanish and Portuguese, Spanish and Spanish-Am. Soc. Am.

SHESTACK, ALAN, museum director; b. N.Y.C., June 23, 1938; s. David and Sylvia P. (Saffran) S.; m. Nancy Jane Davidson, Sept. 24, 1967. BA, Wesleyan U., 1961, DFA (hon.), 1978; MA, Harvard U., 1963. Mus. curator graphic art Nat. Gallery Art, Washington, 1965-67; assoc. curator prints and drawings Yale Art Gallery, New Haven, 1967-68; curator prints and drawings Yale Art Gallery, 1968-71, dir., 1971-85; adj. prof. history of art Yale U., 1971-85; dir. Mpls. Inst. Art, 1985-87, Boston Mus. Fine Arts, 1987—; mem. adv. com. Art Mus., Princeton, 1972-75; mus. panel Nat. Endowment for the Arts, 1974-77; mem. com. prints and illustrated books Mus. Modern Art, N.Y.C., 1972—; mem. Fed. Arts and Artifacts Indemnification Panel, 1979-83. Author: Fifteenth Century Engravings of Northern Europe, 1967, The Engravings of Martin Schongauer, 1968, Master LCZ and Master WB, 1971, Exhibitions Organized and Catalogued: Master E.S, 1967, The Danube School, 1969, Hans Baldung Grien, Prints and Drawings, 1981; contbr. articles to profl. jours. Woodrow Wilson fellow Harvard U., 1963, David E. Finley fellow, 1963-65. Mem. Print Coun. Am. (bd. dir., v.p. 1970-71), Coll. Art Assn. (bd. dir. 1972-76), Am. Assn. Mus., Assn. Art Mus. Dirs. (pres. 1983-84), Am. Fedn. Arts (trustee 1981—), Alpha Delta Phi, Phi Beta Kappa. Office: Mus Fine Arts 465 Huntington Ave Boston MA 02115-5519

SHETH, NILA AMARISH, physician; b. India, May 16, 1946; came to U.S., 1972; d. J.C. and Kala J. Shah; m. Amarish R. Sheth, Nov. 21, 1971; children: Anish, Aarti. MD, N.H.L. Mcpl. Med. Coll., India, 1971. Cert. Am. Bd. Psychiatry and Neurology; cert. geriatric psychiatry. Internship U.S. Gen. Hosp., India, 1970-71; residency Phila. Psychiat. Ctr., 1976-78; med. dir. Trenton (N.J.) Psychiat. Hosp., 1984-88, Albert Einstein Med. Ctr., Phila., 1978-79; chief dept. psychiatry Trenton Psychiat. Hosp., 1988—, pres. med. staff, 1990—; clin. dir. Trenton Psychiatric Hosp., 1991—. Mem. Am. Psychiat. Assn., N.J. Psychiat. Soc. Home: 1263 Knox Dr Morrisville PA 19067-4423

SHETTY, ASHOK KOLKEBAIL, physician; b. Nov. 19, 1945; s. Sheenappa M. and Rajeevi Shetty; m. Rajani Shetty, May 5, 1974; 1 child, Amit. MB, Govt. Med. Coll., Mysore, India, 1970, MD, 1971. Diplomate Am. Bd. Internal Medicine, Am. Geriatric Bd. Sr. house officer infectious disease Castle Hill Hosp., Hull, Eng., 1972-74, sr. house officer respiratory medicine, 1974-75; registrar respiratory medicine Monsall Hosp., Manchester, Eng., 1975-76; resident Shadyside Hosp., Pitts., 1976-78, chief resident internal medicine, 1978-79; pvt. practice Monroeville, Murrysville, Pa., 1979—. Fellow ACP; mem. AMA, Am. Geriatric Soc., Pa. Med. Soc. Home: 3125 Treeline Dr Murrysville PA 15668-1521 Office: 4212 Old William Penn Hwy Murrysville PA 15668-1901

SHEVACH, ETHAN MENAHEM, immunologist; b. Brookline, Mass., Oct. 16, 1943; s. Benjamin Jacques and Anne (Pollack) S.; m. Ruth Schneider, May 30, 1967; children: Matthew, Seth. BA, Boston U., 1967, MD, 1967. Diplomate Am. Bd. Internatl Medicine, Am. Bd. Allergy/Immunology. Resident physician Bronx (N.Y.) Mcpl. Hosp. Ctr., 1967-69; fellow Lab. Clin. Investigation, NIH, Bethesda, Md., 1969-72; sr. staff fellow Lab. of Immunology, NIAID, Bethesda, 1972-73, sr. investigator, 1973-87, head cellular immunology sect., 1987—; Adv. bd. Am. Leprosy Found., Rockville, Md., 1988. Author: Immunophysiology, 1990; editor: Current Protocols in Immunology, 1990; editor-in-chief Jour. of Immunology, Bethesda, 1987-92. Capt. USPHS, 1973—. Recipient Pub. Health Svc. Commendation medal, 1978, Pub. Health Svc. Meritorious Svc. medal, 1986. Mem. Am. Assn. Immunologists, Am. Soc. Chem. Investigation, Assn. Am. Physicians, Am. Fedn. Clin. Rsch., Coun. Biology Editors. Office: NIH Niaid Bldg 10 Rm 11 N 315 Bethesda MD 20892

SHEVCHUCK, HARRY, image systems consultant; b. Jerome, Pa., Sept. 24, 1924; s. Nickolai and Anastana (Emilianovich) S.; (div.), remarried Joyce E. Shevchuck; children: Robert N., Gregory A., Cathleen E., Susan D., Ivan P., Lisa M. BS in Geology, W.Va. U., 1949; AS, Temple U., 1960. Warehouse supr. Owens Ill. Glass Co., Fairmont, W.Va., 1949-50; polymer structural analyst E.I. DuPont de Nemours & Co., Wilmington, Del., 1950-73, electronic imaging equipment specialist, 1973-86, cons., 1986—. Asst. to scout master Boy Scouts Am., Wilmington, 1960. Served with inf. U.S. Army, 1943-45, ETO, prisoner of war, Germany. Roman Catholic. Lodge: Ceasar Rodney. Home: 602 Stanton Rd Wilmington DE 19804-3636

SHEWCHUK, ROBERT JOHN, television executive; b. Passaic, N.J., Oct. 2, 1950; s. Frank Russell and Adele (Sweetman) S. BFA, Rochester Inst. Tech., 1972; Cert in Advt., Fairleigh Dickinson U., 1972. Assoc. producer, tech. dir. TV Ctr. Rochester (N.Y.) Inst. Tech., 1970-72; prodn. cons., writer ABC TV Network/Daphne Don Lipp Prodns., N.Y.C., 1975-76; pres., producer, dir. Bob Shewchuk Prodns., Clifton, N.J., 1972-76; dir., editor, prodn. mgr. AT&T Long Lines, Bedminster, N.J., 1976-80; sr. producer, prodn. mgr. Gen. Foods Corp., White Plains, N.Y., 1980-82; v.p., dir. TV services, pub. affairs dept. Citicorp/Citibank, N.Y.C., 1982—; producer, dir. World Cycling Championships, 1986; pres., chief exec. officer Bob Shewchuk Enterprises/Video Vanguard Prodns., 1988—. Mem. editorial adv. bd. Internat. TV Orgn., Corp. TV Mag., 1987-89; producer, photographer Penthouse and Playboy mags., 1974-75; contbr. articles to profl. jours. Recipient medals Chgo. Indsl. Film Festival, 1985, Internat. Film and TV Festival, N.Y.C., 1985-87, Telly awards, Cin., 1986; recipient Cine Gold Eagle, Council Internat. Non-Theatrical Events, Washington, 1987. Mem. Internat. TV Assn. (medal winner), Soc. Motion Picture and TV Engrs., Nat. Acad. TV Arts and Scis. (2 Emmy awards 1987). Home: 52 Woodland Dr West Paterson NJ 07424 Office: Citicorp/Citibank 1 Court Square Long Island City NY 11120

SHIAW, EMMA, executive; b. Taiwan, Republic of China, July 27, 1954; came to U.S., 1976; BA, Chinese Culture Coll., 1976; MA, SUNY, Binghamton, 1980. Realtor assoc. Lewis and Silverman Realtors, Bethesda, Md., 1979-81, Merrill Lynch Realtors, Bethesda, Md., 1981-82, Long and Foster Realtors, Potomac, Md., 1983-85; exec. v.p. DIGICON Corp., Bethesda, 1985—. Mem. NAt. Assn. Minority Bus., U.S. Pan Asian Am. C. of C., Nat Contract Mgmt. Assn., Armed Forces Communication and Electronics Assocs. Office: DIGICON Corp 6707 Democracy Blvd Ste 402 Bethesda MD 20817-1129

SHIBIB, M. AYMAN, electronics engineer; b. Damascus, Syria, Feb. 14, 1953; came to U.S., 1975; s. Subhi and Lutfieh (Sharkatili) S.; m. Reem E. Estwani, Mar. 30, 1982; children: Dena R., Kareem A. BS in Physics, Am. U., Beirut, Lebanon, 1975; MSEE, U. Fla., 1976, PhD in Elec. Engring., 1979. Grad. rsch. asst. in elec. engring. U. Fla., Gainesville, 1976-78, grad. rsch. assoc., 1978-79, asst. prof. elec. engring., 1979-80; mem. tech. staff AT&T Bell Labs., Reading, Pa., 1980-87, disting. mem. tech. staff, 1987—; gen. chmn. Internat. Symposium on Power Semiconductor Devices, 1989, 91, mem. adv. com., Tokyo, 1990, 92. Editor: High Voltage and Smart Power ICs, 1989, Power Semiconductor Devices & ICs, 1991; contbr. articles to profl. publs.; patentee in field. Mem. IEEE (sr., sect. vice chmn. Lehigh Valley sect. 1987-88, chmn. 1988-89, chmn. electron devices chpt. 1986-91, Cert. of Appreciation 1986, mem. exec. com. 1986—). Muslim. Office: AT&T Bell Labs 2525 N 12th St Reading PA 19605-2749

SHICK, BRADLEY ULLIN, construction company executive; b. Upper Darby, Pa., Dec. 26, 1956; s. Charles David and Jeanette Vivian (Reuter) S.; m. Lucille Marie DeSanto, Oct. 31, 1981. BSCE, U. Pitts., Johnstown, Pa., 1978; MBA, U. Scranton, 1981. Project mgr. Sordoni Constrn. Co., Forty Fort, Pa., 1978-83; project mgr. PepsiCo site Sordoni Constrn. Co., Somers, N.Y., 1983-86; mgr. procedures and controls Sordoni Skanska Constrn. Co., Parsippany, N.J., 1986-89, adminstr. project site Hoffman-La Rouche Sci. & Tech. Ctr., 1990—. Mem. ASCE, Delta Chi. Republican. Presbyterian. Home: RD 5 Box 5580 Spring Lake Estates East Stroudsburg PA 18301 Office: Sordoni Skanska Constrn Co 119 Cherry Hill Rd Parsippany NJ 07054-1114

SHIEH, FRANCIS, economics educator, consultant, researcher; b. Shanghai, People's Republic of China, Feb. 7, 1926; came to U.S., 1947; s. Wei-yu and Pei-ying (Chen) S.; m. Agnes Li, Nov. 26, 1955; chldren: Grace, Joseph, Michael, F. Christopher. Instr. Loyola Coll., Shanghai, 1945-47; statistician Farmers Ins. Group, L.A., 1951-52; instr. Chinese lang. U.S. Army Lang. Sch., Monterey, Calif., 1953-56; acct. IBM, San Jose, Calif., 1957-58; instr. bus. adminstrn. Immaculate Heart Coll., L.A., 1958-61; asst. prof. Aquinas Coll., Grand Rapids, Mich., 1961-64; mem. rsch. staff RAND Corp., Santa Monica, Calif., 1964-65; chief compiler project NSF, 1965-66; assoc. prof. econs. Prince George's Coll., Largo, Md., 1966-71; head econs. dept. Prince George's Coll., Largo, 1967-69, prof., chmn. dept. econs., 1971-73, prof., 1973-84; adj. prof. Montgomery Coll., Takoma Park, Md., 1987—; Fulbright sr. scholar Lingnan Coll., Hong Kong, Coun. Internat. Exch. of Scholars, USIA, 1989-90; cons. GE TEMPO, Santa Barbara, 1966; economist U.S. Dept. Labor, Washington, 1967. Author: Economics, 1971, 76, 78; 10 works listed in the Libr. of Congress, Washington. Mem. Atlantic Econ. Soc. Democrat. Roman Catholic. Home and Office: 11201 Woodlawn Blvd Upper Marlboro MD 20772-2361

SHIEH, YANG TAUR, research and development executive; b. Taiwan, Feb. 19, 1953; came to U.S., 1980, naturalized 1991; s. Song-Ling and Chung-Ning (Chu) S.; m. Betty Shieh, June 26, 1982; children: Angus C., Christine Y. BS in Chemistry, Nat. Chung-Kung U., Taiwan, 1976; PhD in Polymer Physics, Case We. Res. U., 1988. Sr. polymer scientist Beloit Corp., Clarks Summit, Pa., 1988-91; mgr. R&D Advanced Materials Corp., Phila., 1991—. Contbr. articles to profl. jours. Mem. Am. Chem. Soc., Soc. Polymer Engr., Material Rsch. Soc. Home: 101 Garnet Ln Wallingford PA 19086 Office: Advanced Materials Corp 10 Industrial Hwy Lester PA 19086

SHIEL, THOMAS WILLIAM, safety and health consultant; b. Syracuse, N.Y., June 22, 1941; s. James and Margaret Ellen (Hammond) S.; 1 child, Lisa Beth. BS, SUNY, Binghamton, 1972. TV dir. Pub. TV WSKG, Binghamton, N.Y., 1966-69; asst. instr. Broome Community Coll., Binghamton, 1972-73; field supr. Lawler, Matusky & Skelly Engrs., Pearl River, N.Y., 1973-76; ptnr. Great Lakes Co., Oswego, N.Y., 1976-78; staff dir. Broome County Environ. Mgmt. Council, Binghamton, 1978-81; safety and health inspector N.Y. State Dept. Labor, Binghamton, 1981-87, sr. safety and health cons., 1987—. Committeeperson Dem. Party, Chenango County, N.Y., 1988—, Binghamton, 1980-82; chpt. pres. Huntington's Disease/Am., Binghamton, 1977-81; crusade chairperson Am. Cancer Soc., Binghamton, 1979-84; port comdr. Yegotta Regotta Annual Event, Binghamton, 1979-83. Mem. Am. Soc. Safety Engrs., Coyote Club (Bakersfield, Calif.). Democrat. Roman Catholic. Home: PO Box 594 Binghamton NY 13902 Office: NY State Dept Labor 30 Wall St Binghamton NY 13901

SHIELDS, BARBARA MARIA, health facility administrator; b. Bklyn., May 26, 1945; d. Hugo Alfred and Rose (Marino) Casolaro; children: Brian, Maria, Cristiana. BS, Marymount Manhattan U., 1966; postgrad., NYU. Corp. contbns. dir. McGraw-Hill, Inc., N.Y.C., 1974-79, mng. editor, 1981-86; devel. dir. Winthrop U. Hosp., Mineola, N.Y., 1987—. Columnist Rockville Centre Herald, 1990—; contbr. articles to N.Y. Times. Mem. Nat. Soc. Fundraising Execs., Nat. Assn. Hosp. Devel., Internat. Women's

Writing Guild. Home: 30 Knollwood Rd Rockville Centre NY 11570-3215 Office: Winthrop U Hosp 259 1st St Mineola NY 11501-3987

SHIELDS, BRUCE MACLEAN, management consultant; b. Wilkinsburg, Pa., Sept. 27, 1922; s. Edwin Bruce and Edith Barbara (Kennedy) S.; m. Nancy Garwood Adams, June 2, 1951; children: Duncan, Gordon A. B-SMetE, Carnegie-Mellon U., 1944; MS in Metallurgy, MIT, 1952; cert., U. Pitts., 1959, U.S. Steel Adv. Mgmt. Sch., 1976. Registered profl. engr., Pa. Chief metallurgist U.S. Steel Corp., Duquesne, Pa., 1956-60, Chgo., 1960-65; mgr. process metallurgh U.S. Steel Corp., Pitts., 1965-68, mgr. tubular product metallurgy, 1968-72, gen. mgr. product metallurgy, 1972-76, gen. mgr. customer tech. svc., 1976-77, gen. mgr. metall. svcs., 1977-78, dir. metall. engring., 1978-83; pvt. practice mgmt. cons. Pitts., 1983—; presenter to tech. confs. Contbr. articles to profl. jours.; patentee in field. Cubmaster, scoutmaster, dist. chmn., mem. exec. bd., bd. dirs. Boy Scouts Am., Chgo. and Pitts., 1962-87; elder, deacon, budget chmn., pres. bd. trustees Southminster Ch., Pitts.; pres. USS Goodfellowship Club, Pitts., 1983. 1st lt. U.S. Army Corps Engrs., 1942-46. Recipient Silver Beaver award Boy Scouts Am., 1978. Fellow Am. Soc. Metals (life); mem. AIME (life), Am. Iron and Steel Inst. (life, chmn.'s award 1983), Am. Petroleum Inst. (mem. pipe standardization com.), Am. Iron and Steel Engrs. Republican. Presbyterian. Home and Office: 240 Glen Abbey Ct Presto PA 15142

SHIELDS, JAMES JOSEPH, JR., educator, educational administrator, author; b. Phila., Feb. 11, 1935; s. James Joseph and Lena Josephine (Dyer) S. BS in Polit. Sci., Saint Joseph's U., 1956; EdM, Temple U., 1959; EdD, Columbia U., 1963. Social studies tchr. Phila. Pub. Sch. System, 1956-59; asst. to dir., internat. studies Tchers. Coll., Columbia U., N.Y.C., 1961; researcher, Tchrs. for East Africa Program Tchrs. Coll., Columbia U., N.Y.C. and Kampala, Uganda, 1961-62; asst. prof. history and philosophy of edn. SUNY, New Paltz, 1962-64; asst. prof. comparative and politics of edn. CUNY, 1964-69; assoc. prof. comparative and politics of edn. CUNY, N.Y.C., 1969-75, prof. comparative and politics of edn., 1975—, head, Sch. Adminstrn. Program, 1983-85, chair, dept. social and psychol. founds., 1988-90, dir., Japan Initiative Com., 1986—; cons. Inst. for Ednl. Devel., N.Y.C., 1968-71, Equitable Life Ins. Co., N.Y.C., 1981; vis. rsch. prof. Tokyo Met. U., 1986—; mem. evaluation bd. Nat. Coun. on Accreditation of Tchr. Edn., Washington, 1970-75; assoc. Columbia U., Univ. Seminar on Modern Japan, N.Y.C., 1987—, chair, 1990-91. Author: Education in Community Development: Its Function in Technical Assistance, 1967; editor: Problems and Prospects in International Education, 1968, Foundations of Education: Dissenting Views, 1974, Japanese Schooling: Patterns of Socialization Equality and Political Control, 1989 (nominated for Books on Japan award); author numerous book chpts., monographs and book reviews; contbr. numerous articles to profl. jours. Mem. Pub. Edn. Assn. Task Force on a Reconstructed Ednl. System, N.Y.C., 1977-78, Pub. Edn. Assn. Task Force on Tchr. Selection, N.Y.C., 1981; adv. bd. Infant and Toddler Learning Program, N.Y.C., 1983-87; mem. N.Y. Urban Coalition, 1982-84. With USAR, 1958-59. Grantee Japan-U.S. Friendship Commn., 1986-89, The City Coll. Provost, 1988-89, 89-90, Rsch. Found. CUNY, 1980-81, N.Y. State Edn. Dept., 1969-72, SUNY Rsch. Found., 1964; Fulbright travel grantee, 1964; recipient Higher Edn. award Holy Family Coll., Phila., 1990, Wyo. Governor's Youth Coun. award, 1974; Postdoctoral fellow, Yale U., New Haven, Conn., 1967-68. Mem. Am. Ednl. Studies Assn. (pres. 1973-74, exec. coun. 1970-75), Carnegie Coun. on Ethics and Internat. Affairs, Comparative and Internat. Edn. Soc. (N.E. region conf. coord. 1984), Japan Soc. of N.Y., Internat. House of Japan, Soc. for Ednl. Reconstruction (exec. com. 1973—), Am. Ednl. Rsch. Assn. Home: 562 W End Ave Apt 4D New York NY 10024-2718 Office: City Coll, CUNY 138th St and Convent Ave New York NY 10031

SHIELDS, LAWRENCE THORNTON, orthopedic surgeon; b. Boston, Oct. 2, 1935; s. George Leo and Catherine Elizabeth (Thornton) S.; AB, Harvard U., 1957; MD, Johns Hopkins U., 1961; m. Karen S. Kraus, Sept. 21, 1968; children: Elizabeth Coulter, Laura Thornton, Sarah Daly, Michael Lawrence. Intern, Barnes Hosp., Washington U., St. Louis, 1961-62, resident, 1962-63; resident orthopedic surgeon Children's Hosp. Med. Ctr., Boston, 1966-67, Mass. Gen. Hosp., Boston, 1967-68, Peter Bent Brigham, Robert Breck Brigham hosps., Boston, 1968-69; resident orthopedic surgeon Harvard Med. Sch., Boston, 1965-69, instr., 1969—; orthopedic surgeon Peter Bent Brigham & Women's Hosp., Children's hosps., 1969—; orthopedic surgeon Waltham (Mass.) -Weston Hosp. and Med. Ctr., 1969—, also chief orthopedic surgery, pres. med. staff; mem. Waltham-Weston Orthopedic Assos.; proprietor Boston Athenaeum; mem. staffs Hahnemann Hosp., Boston, Newton-Wellesley (Mass.) hosps.; cons. orthopedic surgeon VA Hosp., Boston; mem. faculty Harvard Med. Sch.; bd. dirs. Wal-West Health Systems, 1986—; pres. Massachusetts Bay Investment Trust; dir. Waltham Investment Group. Bd. dirs. Mass. Acad. Emergency Med. Technicians, Waltham Boys' Club; trustee, exec. com. Waltham-Weston Hosp. and Med. Ctr. Lt. M.C., USNR, 1963-65. Diplomate Am. Bd. Orthopedic Surgery. Fellow ACS, Am. Acad. Orthopedic Surgeons, Mass. Hist. Soc. Libr., Mass. Hist. Soc.; mem. Royal Soc. Medicine, Mass. Orthopaedic Assn. (bd. dirs., sec. 1986—), New Eng., Boston orthopedic clubs, Charles River Dist. (treas., exec. com., pres. 1982-83) Mass. (councillor; v.p. 1982-83) med. socs., R. Austen Freeman Soc. (v.p.), Thomas B. Quigley Sports Medicine Soc., Titanic Hist. Soc., Boston Opera Assns. (bd. dirs.), Trollope Soc. (founding mem., London), Handel and Hayden Soc. (bd. overseers), Waltham Hist. Soc., St. Botolph Club (Boston), Harvard Club, Algonquin Club of Boston (bd. dirs., pres. 1990—), English Speaking Union (bd. dirs.), Union Club of Boston, St. Botolph Club of Boston, Rotary, Pi Eta (Harvard). Contbr. articles to med. jours. Home: 9 Beverly Rd Newton MA 02161-1112 Office: 721 Huntington Ave Boston MA 02115 also: 20 Hope Ave Ste 314 Waltham MA 02154

SHIELDS, PATRICIA LYNN, educational broker, consultant; b. Bklyn.. BS in Biology, Bucknell U., 1984; postgrad., Rutgers U., 1985—. Mgmt. trainee Alexander's World Trade Ctr., N.Y.C., 1985; supr. Saks Fifth Ave., N.Y.C., 1985-87; vis. lectr. Rutgers U., Newark, 1987-88; supr., coord., (intern) Middletown (N.J.) Pub. Libr., 1987-88; home instrn. tchr. Middletown Bd. Edn., 1988-89; advisor/counselor Essex County Coll., Newark, 1989-91; bilingual parenting educator Union County Coll., Elizabeth, N.J., 1991-92; educational broker Career and Life Counseling Ctr. Bergen County Tech. Schs., Hackensack, N.J., 1992—; pres., chief exec. officer Buttercup's Internat., Inc., Middletown, 1988—. Author: Seeing with Others' Hearts, 1987; author ednl. literary essays. Lifetime mem. Nat. Coun. Sr. Citizens, Washington, 1990—; assoc. mem. Nat. Coun. La Raza, Washington, 1990; participating mem. Am. Mus. Natural History, N.Y.C., 1988—, Smithsonian Mus., Washington, 1992—; sustaining mem. Friends of the Middletown Pub. Libr., 1987—. Recipient Gold Card Honor Roll award Nat. Coun. Sr. Citizens, Washington, 1990, Citation of Leadership N.J. State Dept. Higher Edn., Jersey City State Coll. and Nat. Conf. Christians and Jews, 1990. Mem. ACA, Assn. Humanistic Edn. and Devel., Assn. Multicultural Counseling and Devel., N.J. Ednl. Opportunity Fund Profl. Assn., N.J. Community Coll. Counselors Assn. Home: 12 Dorothy Ct Middletown NJ 07748-1817 Office: Buttercup's Internat Inc PO Box 148 Middletown NJ 07748-0148

SHIELDS, RANDY JOE, medical writer; b. Columbus, Ohio, Oct. 13, 1953; s. Paul Clair and Viola Louise (Germer) S.; m. Karen Elaine Irland, Nov. 3, 1984 (div. Sept. 1991); children: Peter, Timothy, Anna. BA, Ohio State U., 1975, MA, 1980. Communications specialist Ohio State U. Hosps., Columbus, 1975-77; mgmt. svcs. dir. Printing Industry of Cen. Ohio, Columbus, 1977-78; editor Sudler & Henhessey Advt., N.Y.C., 1984-86; account supr. Hill and Knowlton Pub. Rels., N.Y.C., 1984-86; pres. Pharm. Communications, Old Westbury, N.Y., 1986—. Home and Office: Pharm Communications 27 Radcliff Ave Port Washington NY 11050

SHIELDS, ROBERT MICHAEL, state agency administrator; b. Buffalo, Nov. 14, 1952; s. George Henry and Rose Mary (Reznik) S.; m. Michele Jean Kantor, Sept. 18, 1982. BA, U. Notre Dame, Ind., 1974; M of Regional Planning, Syracuse (N.Y.) U., 1976. Assoc. planner Dept. Devel. and Planning, Gary, Ind., 1976-78; sr. planner Dept. Urban and Econ. Devel., Utica, N.Y., 1978-79, dep. planning dir., 1980-82, planning dir., 1982-84; rep. housing and community devel. N.Y. State Div. Housing and Community Renewal, Albany, 1984-85, program mgr., 1985-89, dir. contract adminstrn., 1989-91, asst. dir. Housing Assistance programs, 1992—. Bd. dirs. Sculpture Space, Inc., Utica, 1980-84. Mem. Am. Planning Assn., Am. Inst. Cert. Planners, Notre Dame Club of Mohawk Valley (sec., treas. 1979-81, v.p. 1981-83, pres. 1983-85), Notre Dame Club of N.E. N.Y. (sec. 1990—), Optimists (bd. dirs. Downtown Utica club 1980-83, v.p. 1980-82). Democrat. Roman Catholic. Home: 5 Linda Ln Niskayuna NY 12309-1911 Office: NY State Div Housing and Community Renewal 38-40 State St Hampton Pla Albany NY 12207

SHIELDS, THOMAS FORD, orthopaedic surgeon; b. Paragould, Ark., Nov. 22, 1930; s. James Thomas and Ollie Belle (Jones) S.; m. Bethel Bragdon, Oct. 12, 1957; children: Leslie Elizabeth, Dana Alison, Thomas Bragdon, Ford Davies, James Bryant. BA, Westminster Coll., 1952; MD, St. Louis U., 1956. Diplomate Am. Bd. Orthopedic Surgery. Commd. capt. USAF, 1958, advanced through grades to Maj., 1964, resigned, 1966; intern Milwaukee County Gen. Hosp., Milw., 1956; resident in gen. surgery Passavant Meml. Hosp., Chgo., 1957-58; resident in orthopedic surgery Wilford Hall USAF Hosp., San Antonio, 1959-62; chief orthopaedic surgery St. Mary's Regional Med. Ctr., Lewiston, Maine, 1984—. Fellow Am. Acad. Orthopaedic Surgeons; mem. AMA, Maine Med. Assn. (speaker Ho. of Dels. 1985-91, pres.-elect 1991-92, pres. 1992—), New Eng. Orthopaedic Assn., Ea. Orthopaedic Assn. Presbyterian. Home: 375 Maple Hill Rd Auburn ME 04210 Office: 137 East Ave Lewiston ME 04240

SHIHADEH, STEVE, healthcare software marketing manager; b. Bryn Mawr, Pa., Oct. 30, 1954; s. William and Eleanor (Beltz) S.; m. Aimee Shihadeh, Oct. 14, 1978; children: Maggie, Ellie. BS in Bus. Mgmt., Shippensburg U., 1977. Assoc. sales rep. Shared Med. Systems, Malvern, Pa., 1977-79; sales rep. Shared Med. Systems, N.Y.C., 1979-83, mktg. mgr., 1984-86; mktg. mgr. Shared Med. Systems, San Francisco, 1987-89; nat. sales mgr. Shared Med. Systems, Oakland, Calif., 1989-91. Coach Tredyrrin/Eastown Youth Soccer Assn., Berwyn, Pa., 1991. Mem. Hosp. Fin. Mgmt. Assn. (assoc.). Republican. Episcopalian. Home: 1950 Standiford Malvern PA 19355

SHIH CARDUCCI, JOAN CHIA-MO, cooking educator, biochemist, medical technologist; b. Rukuan, Chunghua, Republic of China, Dec. 21, 1933; came to U.S., 1955; d. Luke Chiang-hsi and Lien-chin (Chang) Shih; m. Kenneth M. Carducci, Sept. 30, 1960 (dec. July 1988); children: Suzanne R., Elizabeth M. BS in Chemistry, St. Mary Coll., Xavier, Kans., 1959; intern in med. tech., St. Mary's Hosp., Rochester, N.Y., 1960. Med. researcher Strong Meml. Hosp. (U. Rochester), 1960-61; pharm. chemist quality control Strasenburgh Labs., Rochester, 1961-62; cooking tchr. adult edn. Montgomery County Pub. Schs., Rockville, Md., 1973-79; cooking tchr. The Chinese Cookery Inc., Rockville, 1975-86; cooking tchr. The Chinese Cookery Inc., Silver Spring, Md., 1986—, pres., bd. dirs., 1975—; chemist NIH, Bethesda, 1987—. Author: The Chinese Cookery, 1981, Hunan Cuisine, 1984. Mem. Internat. Assn. Cooking Profls. Republican. Roman Catholic. Home and Office: The Chinese Cookery Inc 14209 Sturtevant Rd Silver Spring MD 20905-4448

SHILDNECK, BARBARA JEAN, accounting magazine editor; b. Waynesboro, Pa., Apr. 1, 1937; d. Barry Price and Helen Matilda (Armstrong) S. B.A. in English Lit., Wilson Coll., Chambersburg, Pa., 1959. With AICPA, N.Y.C., 1959—, jr. prodn. asst., 1959-62, sr. prodn. asst., 1962-66, editor The CPA, 1969-73, asst. editor to manuscript editor Jour. of Accountancy, 1966-79, from mng. editor to exec. editor, 1979—; editor Centennial issue AICPA, May, 1987; panelist edn. program video tapes in Can. and U.S.; lectr. in field. Contbr. articles to profl. jours. Recipient Gold Circle award Am. Soc. Assn. Execs., 1986, Bronze Ozzie for spl. issue Mag. Design and Prodn., May 1987, Soc. Nat. Assn. Publs. award, 1987, award of distinction Soc. Tech. Communication, 1987. Mem. NAFE, Am. Soc. Bus. Press Editors, Am. Acctg. Assn. Democrat. Office: Harborside Fin Ctr 201 Plaza III Jersey City NJ 07311-3881

SHILEPSKY, ARNOLD CHARLES, mathematics educator, computer consultant; b. Norwalk, Conn., Dec. 10, 1944; s. Morris Jacob and Rose (Pfeffer) S.; m. Carol Irene Carter, June 15, 1968; children: Lisa Ruth, Beth Carter. AB, Wesleyan U., Middletown, Conn., 1966; PhD, U. Wis., 1971. Asst. prof. Ark. State U., Jonesboro, 1971-74; asst. prof. Wells. Coll., Aurora, N.Y., 1974-79, assoc. prof., 1979-85, prof., 1985—, Herbert E. Ives prof. of scis., 1985-91. Pres. Community Devel. Fedn., Southwest Cayuga County, N.Y., 1987—. Mem. Am. Math. Soc., Math. Assn. Am., Assn. for Women in Math., Assn. for Computer Machinery. Home: Main St # 295 Aurora NY 13026 Office: Wells Coll Aurora NY 13026

SHILKOFF, MARILYN LEADER, gerontologist; b. N.Y.C., June 18, 1932; d. Maurice and Augusta (Singer) Leader; m. Paul Shilkoff, Oct. 23, 1960; children: William, Jacqueline. SB, MIT, 1954; MA, NYU, 1976; EdD, Columbia U., 1979. Specialist in engring. communications small aircraft engines GE Co., Lynn, Mass., 1954-58; tech. editor, contbg. editor Soc. Automotive Engrs., N.Y.C., 1959-68; rsch. assoc. Dept. of Aging City of New York, 1976-79; dir. rsch. Aging in Am., Bronx, 1980-83; coord. curriculum Ctr. for Geriatrics and Gerontology Columbia U., N.Y.C., 1984-87; grants adminstr. Mainstream the Retirement Inst. Westchester Community Coll., Valhalla, N.Y., 1985-86; rsch. analyst, dir. pub./pvt. initiatives Westchester County Office for Aging, White Plains, N.Y., 1986—; exec. bd. Group for Rsch. on Older Women, 1985-91, co-chmn., 1989-90; mem. adv. bd. Project Transition, Valhalla, 1986-90. Pub., editor The Women's Letter (newsletter), 1986-90. Mem. ednl. coun. MIT, 1983—; mem. adv. bd. Mainstream the Retirement Inst., Westchester Community Coll., Valhalla, 1985—; adv. bd. Westchester Libr. System Outreach Program, White Plains, 1989—; mem. Congresswoman Lowey's Adv. Com. on Aging, 20th Congl. Dist., Westchester, 1989—. Brookdale fellow, 1978-79. Mem. APA, N.Y. State Soc. Aging (Chair Task Force on Older Women 1988—), Northeastern Gerontol. Soc. (co-chmn. social policy com. 1989-92, mem. nominating com. 1991-92, pres.-elect 1992—), Gerontol. Soc. Am. Home: 25 Larchmont Ave Larchmont NY 10538-4205 Office: Westchester County Aging Office 214 Central Ave White Plains NY 10606

SHILL, TODD JEFFREY, computer consultant; b. Phila., Nov. 30, 1967; s. Ronald Irving and Sharyn M. (Abramson) S. BS in Computer Infosystems cum laude, Drexel U., 1990; postgrad., Widener U., 1990—. Asst. to fin. supr. Duane, Morris & Heckscher Law Firm, Phila., 1987-89, network cons., developer, 1989-90, network and computer cons., 1991—; systems cons. Ronald Castille for Dist. Atty. Com., Phila., 1989-90. Reporter Drexel U. Triangle newspaper, 1988-89; contbr. Widener U. Law Rev. Assoc. mem. Phila. Leadership Coun., 1989-90; mem. Rep. Nat. Com., 1990—. Mem. ABA, Harrisburg Leadership Coun. (founder, pres. 1990—), Dauphin City Young Reps. Jewish. Home: 1523 High Point Dr # F Harrisburg PA 17110-9241

SHIMANSKY, RICHARD ANTHONY, mechanical engineering educator; b. Riverdale, Md., Jan. 15, 1959; s. Anthony Robert and Frances Mae (Stull) S.; m. Peggy Elizabeth Ruckle, Mar. 30, 1985; children: Robert Charles, Alexander Warren. BSME, U. Md., 1982; MSME, Bucknell U., 1987; PhD in Engring. Sci. and Mechanics, Pa. State U., 1989. Assoc. engr. Dominion Engring., McLean, Va., 1982-85; asst. prof. mech. engring. Bucknell U., Lewisburg, Pa., 1989—, cons. Bucknell Small Bus. Devel. Ctr., 1989—; cons. E.I. DuPont de Nemours & Co., Wilmington, Del., 1989—, Boeing Helicopter, Phila., 1990; rsch. engr. Ben Franklin Partnership Program, Harrisburg, Pa., 1989—. Contbr. articles on ceramic matrix composites and powdered metals to profl. jours. Mem. ASME, Am. Soc. for Composites, Soc. for Advanced Materials and Process Engring. Republican. Roman Catholic. Home: RR 1 Box 127A Mifflinburg PA 17844-9801 Office: Bucknell U Mech Engring Dept Lewisburg PA 17837

SHIMER, ALICE MARIE, retired educator; b. Decatur, Ill., Apr. 24, 1926; d. George Henry and Grace Lovawn (Burkard) S. Student, Milliken U., 1944-46; BS, U. Ill., 1948; MS, SUNY, Buffalo, 1963. Chemist Clarks Microanalytical Lab., Urbana, Ill., 1949-51; rsch. microanalytical chemist Olin Mathieson Labs., Niagara Falls, N.Y., 1951-60, Thiokol Labs., Huntsville, Ala., 1960-61; tchr. Niagara Falls Bd. Edn., 1961-84. Tax counselor AARP, Niagara Falls, 1984—; vol. St. Mary's Hosp., Lewiston, N.Y., 1986—. Mem. Niagara Falls Ret. Tchrs. Assn. (pres. 1988—), Delta Kappa Gamma (past treas.). Republican. Lutheran. Home: 5105 Dana Dr Lewiston NY 14092-2015

SHIMKONIS, DEBORAH ANN, financial executive; b. Methuen, Mass., June 14, 1957; d. Julius J. Shimkonis. BS in Acctg. with honors, U. Lowell, 1979; MST in Taxation, Bentley Coll., 1987, postgrad., 1988—; student, Lambers CPA Rev. Course, 1989. Sr. acct. Lechmere Sales, Woburn, Mass., 1979-81; tax specialist Compugraphic Corp., Wilmington, Mass., 1981-83; tax supr. Nixdorf Computer Corp., Burlington, Mass., 1983-85; tax specialist Standex Internat. Corp., Salem, N.H., 1986-88; tax sr. Purdy, Bornstein, Hamel & Burrell, CPAs, Portsmouth, N.H., 1989; corp. cons. Londonderry, N.H., 1989-91; supr. tax/audit Cabletron Systems, Inc., Rochester, N.H., 1991—; bd. dirs. Career Network Group, Londonderry. Recipient Standex Internat. Corp. Profit Incentive Program award, 1987, 88. Mem. Nat. Assn. Accts. (bd. dirs.), N.H. Soc. CPAs, Bentley Coll. Alumni Assn. (bravo com.), Manchester Toastmasters, CPA Club. N.H. Home: 4 Fairfax Ave Derry NH 03038

SHINAGEL, MICHAEL, educator, university dean; b. Vienna, Austria, Apr. 21, 1934; came to U.S., 1941; s. Emanuel and Lilly (Hillel) S.; m. Ann Birdsey Mitchell, Sept. 1, 1956 (div. 1970); children—Mark Mitchell, Victoria Stuart; m. Rosa Joanne Bonanno, Dec. 6, 1973. A.B., Oberlin Coll., 1957; A.M., Harvard U., 1959, Ph.D., 1964. Teaching fellow Harvard U., Cambridge, Mass., 1958-59, tutor in English, 1962-64, assoc. dir. career office, 1959-64, dean continuing edn., 1975—, lectr. extension, 1976—, sr. lectr. English., 1983—, master Quincy House, 1986—; asst. prof. English, Cornell U., Ithaca, N.Y., 1964-67; prof., chmn. dept. English, Union Coll., Schenectady, 1967-75; pres. bd. dirs. Ednl. Exchange of Boston, 1982-87. Author: Defoe and Middle-class Gentility, 1968; co-author: (handbook) Summer Institutes in English, 1965; editor: Concordance to Poems of Swift, 1972, Critical Edition of Robinson Crusoe, 1975; co-editor: Harvard Scholars in English (1890-1990), 1991. Served with U.S. Army, 1952-54, Korea. Woodrow Wilson fellow, 1957; NEH grantee, 1965. Mem. Nat. Univ. Continuing Edn. Assn., Assn. Continuing Higher Edn., Mass. Hist. Assn., Old South Meeting House, Harvard Faculty Club (Cambridge) (pres. 1985-8 7), Phi Beta Kappa. Clubs: Harvard Faculty (pres. 1985-87) (Cambridge). Home: Masters' Residence Quincy House 58 Plympton St Cambridge MA 02138-6609 Office: Harvard U Div Continuing Edn 51 Brattle St Cambridge MA 02138-4925

SHINE, ROBERT JOHN, chemistry educator, computer science educator; b. Orange, N.J., May 21, 1941; s. Elmer Paul and Mary Agnes (Price) S.; m. Dorothy Loretta McCaffrey, Sept. 16, 1967; children: Robert John, Daniel Paul, Margaret Christine. BS, Seton Hall U., 1962; PhD, Pa. State U., 1966; MS, Stevens Inst., Hoboken, N.J., 1985. Asst. prof. chemistry Trinity Coll., Washington, 1969-71; prof. chemistry Ramapo Coll., Mahwah, N.J., 1971—. Contbr. articles to profl. jours. Sci. mentor Ridgewood (N.J.) Sch. System, 1976-81. Capt. U.S. Army, 1967-69. Recipient Mayor's award for excellence Ridgewood, 1980. Mem. Am. Chem. Soc., Assn. for Computing Machinery, Sigma Xi. Democrat. Roman Catholic. Home: 268 Eastside Ave Ridgewood NJ 07450-5313 Office: Ramapo Coll 505 Ramapo Valley Rd Mahwah NJ 07430-1623

SHINE, WILLIAM MORTON, chemical consultant; b. St. Louis, Nov. 24, 1912; s. Charles Haskell and Leah Libby (Cohen) S.; m. Katherine Seims, Sept. 1, 1946 (div. 1971); children: Carol J., Lynn E. Shine Linde, Elizabeth Anne Shine Bishop, Katherine L.; m. Marjorie Lois Dack, Dec. 18, 1971 (dec. Mar. 1991). BSChemE, Washington U., St. Louis, 1934; MS in Chemistry, U. Ill., 1937. Rockefeller Found. grantee in biochem. rsch. Washington U. Med. Sch., 1934-36; mfg. chemist Pfanstiehl Chem. Co., Waukegan, Ill., 1937-41; rsch. sect. leader plastics dept. GE, Pittsfield, Mass., 1941-45; comml. devel. engr. GAF Corp., N.Y.C., 1945-50; dir. market devel. ICI Organics, N.Y.C., 1950-53; v.p. devel. Celanese Devel. Co., Celanese Corp., N.Y.C., 1953-63; cons. W.M. Shine Cons. Svcs., Southbury, Conn., 1963—. Trustee Heritage Village, Southbury, 1987-90, chmn. landscape com., 1989, chmn. structural com., 1990. Mem. Am. Chem. Soc. (emeritus), Am. Inst. Chemists (emeritus), Comml. Devel. Assn. (life), Chem. Mktg. Rsch. Assn. (life), Soc. Plastics Engrs. (sr.), Chemists Club N.Y. (emeritus). Home: 854B Heritage Vlg Southbury CT 06488-1334 Office: PO Box 2069 Heritage Village Southbury CT 06488

SHINN, ROGER LINCOLN, minister, educator; b. Germantown, Ohio, Jan. 6, 1917; s. Henderson L.V. and Carrie Margaret (Buehler) S.; m. Katharine Cole, Nov. 6, 1943; children: Carol Katharine Shinn Wheeler, Marybeth. BA, Heidelberg Coll., 1938, DLitt (hon.), 1963; MDiv summa cum laude, Union Theol. Sem., 1941; PhD, Columbia U., 1951; DD (hon.), Mission House Theol. Sem., 1960, Franklin and Marshall Coll., 1963; LHD(hon.), Drury Coll., 1984; HHD (hon.), Blackburn U., 1985. Ordained to ministry United Ch. of Christ, 1946. Pvt. practice horticulture, 1932-37; student asst. 2d Presbyn Ch., N.Y.C., 1938-41; instr. Union Theol. Sem., N.Y.C., 1947-49; chmn. Depts. Philosophy and Religion Heidelberg Coll., Tiffin, Ohio, 1949-54; prof. theology Vanderbilt U. Div. Sch., Nashville, 1954-57, prof. Christian Ethics, 1957-59; William E. Dodge Jr. prof. Applied Christianity Union Theol. Sem., N.Y.C., 1960-70, Reinhold Niebuhr prof. Social Ethics, 1970-85, dean of instruction, 1963-70, acting pres., 1974-75, counselor to grad. students, 1975-85; adj. prof. religion and society, Columbia U., 1962-86; adj. prof. econs., NYU Grad. Sch. Bus. Adminstrn., 1979; vis. prof. Philosophies of Judaism, Jewish Theol. Sem. Am., 1982; lectr. Pacific Sch. Religion, 1957, Harvard U., 1960, Garrett Theol. Sem., 1967, Assn. Am. Colls., 1970, Princeton Theol. Sem., 1971, U.S. Army Chaplain Sch., 1974, Woodstock Coll., 1971-74; occasional lectures in over 250 schs., colls. and univs. in N.Am. and abroad. Author: Beyond This Darkness, 1946, Christianity and the Problem of History, 1953, Life, Death and Destiny, 1957, The Existentialist Posture, 1959, rev. edit., 1970, The Educational Mission of Our Church, 1962, Moments of Truth, 1962, Tangled World, 1965, We Believe, 1966, Man: The New Humanism, 1968, Wars and Rumors of Wars, 1972, Forced Options: Social Decisions for the 21st Century, 1982, 3rd edit. 1991; editor, co-author: The Search for Identity: Essays on the American Character, 1964, Restless Adventure, 1968, The Thought of Paul Tillich, 1985; contbr. articles to religious jours., chpts. to books; writer, narrator TV series Tangled World; assoc. editor Bull. Sci., Tech. and Soc.; contbg editor Christianity and Crisis; mem. editorial bdd. Jour. Religious Ethics. Served to maj. U.S. Army, 1941-45, ETO. Decorated Silver Star; recipient Excellence award Grad. Faculties Alumni, Columbia U., 1981; named to U.S. Army Inf. Sch., Hall of Fame, 1973. Mem. ADA, NAACP, Am. Theol. Soc.(pres. 1975-76), Soc. Christian Ethics (pres. 1974-75), Soc. for Values in Higher Edn. (Kent fellow 1946), Conf. on Sci., Philosophy and Religion (fellow 1966), Am. Vets Com., Am. Assn. for UN, League for Indsl. Democracy. Home: 288 Cowles Rd Woodbury CT 06798-1726 Office: 501 W 123rd ST #6A New York NY 10027 also: Union Theol Sem 3041 Broadway New York NY 10027

SHIPLER, DAVID KARR, journalist, author; b. Orange, N.J., Dec. 3, 1942; s. Guy Emery Jr. and Eleanor (Karr) S.; m. Deborah S. Isaacs, Sept. 17, 1966; children: Jonathan Robert, Laura Karr, Michael Edmund. AB, Dartmouth Coll., 1964; LittD (hon.), Middlebury Coll., 1988, Glassboro (N.J.) State Coll., 1988. News clk. N.Y. Times, 1966-67, news summary writer, 1968, reporter met. staff, 1968-73, fgn. corr. Saigon bur., 1973-75, fgn. corr. Moscow Bur., 1975—, bur. chief Moscow Bur., 1977-79, chief Jerusalem bur., 1979-84, corr. Washington bur., 1985-87, chief diplomatic corr., 1987-88; sr. assoc. Carnegie Endowment for Internat. Peace, Washington, 1988-90; guest scholar Brookings Instn., 1984-85; adj. prof. Sch. Internat. Svc., Am. U., Washington, 1990; Ferris prof. journalism and pub. affairs Princeton U., 1990-91; Woodrow Wilson vis. fellow, 1991—. Author: Russia: Broken Idols, Solemn Dreams, 1983 (Overseas Press Club award); author: Arab and Jew: Wounded Spirits in a Promised Land, 1986 (Pulitzer Prize for General Non-fiction, 1987), exec. producer, prin. writer, narrator documentary film made from book, 1989 (Alfred DuPont-Columbia U. award for Broadcast Journalism, 1990); contbr. articles to New Yorker and other nat. mags. Served with USNR, 1964-66. Recipient award for disting. reporting Soc. Silurians, 1971; award for disting. pub. affairs reporting Am. Polit. Scis. Assn., 1971; award N.Y. chpt. Sigma Delta Chi, 1973; co-recipient George Polk award, 1982. Mem. Mid. East Watch (bd. dirs.).

SHIPLEY, KARL L., safety engineer; b. Washington, Jan. 13, 1953; s. Edward George and Barbara (Fiddick) S.; m. Kristie Ruth Sehnert, Aug. 26, 1978. Student, U. Md., 1974-76. Asst. dir. safety and health AGC of Am., Washington, 1977-79; project safety supr. Aluminum Co. of Am., Davenport, Iowa, 1979-81, Mobile, Ala., 1981-82; project safety engr.

Gilbane Bldg. Co., Trenton, Ohio, 1982-83, Clinton, N.J., 1983; reg. safety mgr. Gilbane Bldg. Co., Princeton, N.J., 1983—. Mem. Am. Soc. Safety Engrs., N.J. Safety Council, Nat. Safety Council (exec. com. 1978-82). Office: Gilbane Bldg Co 125390 Village Blvd Princeton NJ 08540-5736

SHIPLEY, REGINALD ALDEN, medical educator; b. Dayton, Ohio, Oct. 15, 1905; s. Bernis Melvin and Grace Isabelle (Trone) S.; m. Louise Joanna Zschiesche, June 1, 1935 (dec. 1977); children: Richard M., Anne E., Roger D. BS, Otterbein Coll., 1927; MD, Western Res. U., 1931. Diplomate Am. Bd. Internal Medicine. Instr. Sch Medicine Western Res. U. (now Case Western Res. U.), Cleve., 1938-40, asst. prof., 1941-48, assoc. prof., 1949-62, prof. medicine, 1963-73, prof. emeritus, 1974—; cons. NIH, Bethesda, Md., 1957-63; mem. editorial bd. Steroids, 1963-66, Am. Jour. Physiology, 1967-74. Author: The Androgens, 1956, Tracer Methods, 1972; contbr. articles to sci. jours. Mem. AAAS, Am. Soc. Clin. Investigation, Endocrine Soc., Soc. for Exptl. Biology and Medicine, Am. Physiol. Soc., Cen. Soc. for Clin. Rsch. Republican. Home: 35 Lyman St Easthampton MA 01027-1037

SHIPLEY, WALTER VINCENT, banker; b. Newark, Nov. 2, 1935; s. L. Parks and Emily (Herzog) S.; m. Judith Ann Lyman, Sept. 14, 1957; children: Barbara, Allison, Pamela, Dorothy, John. Student, Williams Coll., 1954-56; BS, NYU, 1961. With Chem. Bank, N.Y.C., 1956—, exec. v.p. in charge internat. div., 1978-79, sr. exec. v.p., 1979-81, pres., 1982-83, chmn. bd., 1983-91, pres., chief oper. officer, 1992—; Bd. dirs. Champion Internat. Corp., NYNEX Corp., Reader's Digest Assn., Inc. Bd. dirs. Japan Soc., Lincoln Ctr. for Performing Arts Inc., Goodwill Industries Greater N.Y. Inc., United Way Tri-State; trustee NYU. Mem. The Bus. Coun., Bus. Roundtable, Coun. Fgn. Rels., Links, Augusta Nat. Golf Club, Baltusrol Golf Club (Springfield, N.J.), Blind Brook Golf Club. Office: Chem Banking Corp 270 Park Ave New York NY 10017-2070

SHIPMAN, STEPHANIE LOUISE, government official; b. Bellefonte, Pa., July 4, 1954; d. William Gibson and Virginia Irene S. AB, Princeton U., 1975; PhD, Columbia U., 1981. Teaching asst. Tchrs. Coll. Columbia U., N.Y.C., 1978, rsch. asst. Inst. Urban and Minority Edn., 1977-79; social sci. analyst U.S. Gen. Acctg. Office, Washington, 1981-90, asst. dir., 1990—. Mem. editorial bd. Am. Jour. Orthopsychiatry, 1981-89; contbr. articles to profl. jours., chpts. to books. Mem. Evaluation Rsch. Soc., Am. Evaluation Assn., Sigma Xi. Office: Gen Acctg Office 441 G St NW Washington DC 20548-0002

SHIPULA, ANTHONY JAMES, II, university administrator; b. Wilkes-Barre, Pa., Dec. 12, 1956; s. Anthony and Phyloretta (Horoshko) S.; m. Christine Hudak, June 16, 1979; children: Jennifer Ann, Anthony Joseph, Joseph James. BS in Commerce and Fin., Wilkes Coll., 1978. Life ins. salesman Home Life Ins. Co. Am., Wilkes-Barre, 1978-79; nat. acct. rep. underwriting/mktg. Aetna Life & Casualty, Phila. and Hartford, Conn., 1979-83; ins. salesman and svc. Chamberlin Ins., Scranton, Pa., 1983-84; corp. underwriter WVIA TV Channel 44, Wilkes-Barre and Scranton, Pa., 1984-85; alumni dir. Wilkes U., Wilkes-Barre, 1985—. Bd. dirs. Cystic Fibrosis Found., Allentown, 1987—. Mem. Wyoming Valley Country Club (sec. 1990-91), Wyoming Valley "Mickey Noonan" Football chpt. (football ofcl.). Home: 19 Grandview Ave Wilkes Barre PA 18702-3104 Office: Wilkes U Alumni Office PO Box 111 Wilkes Barre PA 18766-0001

SHIRA, GERALD DEE, II, retired financial executive; b. Cortland, N.Y., Mar. 14, 1933; s. Gerald Dee and Ruth Irene (Lugar) S.; m. Coral Lynne Faulring, June 16, 1956; children: Donna Lee, Scott Dee. BS, Syracuse U., 1955. With Eastman Kodak Co., Rochester, N.Y., 1957-67; adminstrv. mgr. Kodak Venezuela S.A., Caracas, 1967-72, Kodak Argentina S.A.I.C., Buenos Aires, 1972-74; dir. fin. svcs. Latin Am. Eastman Kodak, Rochester, 1974-76; dir. fin. and adminstrn. Kodak Brasileira Ltda., Sao Paulo, 1976-84; dir. fin. svcs. Europe Eastman Kodak Co., London, 1984-87; dir. fin. planning Latin Am. Eastman Kodak Co., Rochester, 1987-92. Bd. dirs. Colegio Internacional de Caracas, 1967-72. With Army, 1955-57. Mem. Brazil/Am. C. of C., Council of Ams., Caracas Sports Club, Caracas Theatre Club, Beta Alpha Psi. Republican. Home: 317 Greenwood Dr Hilton Head Island SC 29928

SHIRLEY, LAWRENCE HOYT, educator; b. Flagstaff, Ariz., Nov. 13, 1947; s. Robert Albert and Shirley Amelia (Hoyt) S.; m. Alberta Ohenewah, Aug. 31, 1974; children: Jefferson, Emily. BS in Math., History, Calif. Tech., 1969; MEd in Comparative Edn., U. Ill., 1973; PhD in Math. Edn., Ahmadu Bello U., Zaria, Nigeria, 1984. Tchr. math. Bonthe (Sierra Leone) Secondary Sch./Peace Corps, 1969-71; advisor, peace corps math. Sierra Leone Ministry Edn., Bo, 1971-72; prof. math. edn. Ahmadu Bello U., 1974-88, dept. head., 1978-88; prof., math. edn. No. Ill. U., DeKalb, 1988-89, Towson State U., Balt., 1989—; cons., Nigeria Edn. Rsch. Coun., Lagos, 1978-88, Fed. U. Tech., Minna, Nigeria, 1986, Nat. Edn. Tech. Ctr., Kaduna, Nigeria, 1986-88. Co-author, editor: Nigerian Primary Math, 1981; contbr. articles to profl. jours. Mem. Nat. Coun. Tchrs. Math., Md. Coun. Tchrs. Math., Internat. Study Group Ethnomath., Internat. Study Group History Pedagogy Math., Amnesty Internat., Planetary Soc. Democrat. Home: 854 Bosley Ave Baltimore MD 21204-2610 Office: Towson State U Dept Math Towson MD 21204-7079

SHIRLEY, NORMA, librarian, bibliographer; b. Chatham, N.Y., Mar. 22, 1935; d. George and Bertha (Shattuck) Shirley. B.A., Russell Sage Coll., 1962; M.L.S., SUNY-Albany, 1963, M.S. in Ednl. Adminstrn., 1980. Asst. reference librarian Jr. Coll. Albany, 1963-65; librarian Hudson Area Library (N.Y.), 1966-67; reference librarian Russell Sage Coll., Troy, N.Y., 1967-69; librarian Poughkeepsie High Sch. (N.Y.), 1970-71; library media specialist Spl. Edn. Ctr., Dutchess County BOCES, Poughkeepsie, 1971—. Co-author: Checklist of Serials in Psychology and Allied Fields, 1969; Serials in Psychology and Allied Fields, 1976. Mem. Dutchess County Library Assn. (past pres.), Sch. Library Media Specialists Southeastern N.Y. (past pres.), ALA, N.Y. Library Assn., NEA, Dutchess County Mental Health Assn., N.Y. State Tchrs. Handicapped. Home: PO Box 2401 Poughkeepsie NY 12603-0881

SHIVANANDAN, MARY, family life consultant and researcher; b. Rangoon, Burma, Jan. 6, 1932; came to U.S., 1960; d. John Francis and Jean Newton (Simpson) Sheehy; m. Kandiah Shivanandan, Sept. 17, 1960; children: John Uthya-surian, Marianne Gauri. BA with honours, Cambridge (Eng.) U., 1954, MA, 1967; STL, John Paul II Inst., Washington, 1991. Asst. producer CBC, Toronto, Montreal, 1956-60; writer and broadcaster Washington, India, 1960-70; assoc. editor Am. Friends Mid. East, 1968-69; assoc. rsch. scientist fgn. area studies Am. U., 1969-70; writer and researcher, 1973-79; dir. KM Assocs., cons., researchers, Bethesda, Md., 1980-91; faculty John Paul II Inst. for Studies on Marriage and Family, 1990—; editor Internat. Fedn. Family Life Promotion, Washington, 1983, Nat. Core Coalition Nat. Family Planning, Washington, 1985; rsch. cons. Ednl. Guidance Inst., Arlington, Va., 1988-89; researcher Office of Population, HHS, Washington, 1987. Author: Natural Sex, 1979; contbg. author fgn. area handbooks, 1970-75; editor Breastfeeding and Natural Family Planning, 1986; contbr. articles to profl and popular publs. Vice pres. Asian-Am. Forum, Washington, 1986-87, pres., 1987-88. Scholar Newnham Coll., Cambridge U., 1951; McGivney fellow KC and John Paul II Inst., 1988. Mem. Nat. Coun. on Family Rels. (cert. family life educator). Home: 4711 Overbrook Rd Bethesda MD 20816-3029

SHIVE, RICHARD BYRON, architect; b. Cleve., Jan. 16, 1933; s. Roy Allen and Mary Elizabeth (Thompson) S.; m. Patricia Butler, Aug. 28, 1954; children: Lisa Ann, Laura Mary, John Thompson, Nancy Butler. BS, Rensselaer Poly. Inst., Troy, N.Y., 1954; postgrad., Newark (N.J.) Coll. Engring., 1957, Rutgers U., 1960-63. Registered architect, N.J., N.Y., Pa., Vt.; lic. profl. planner, N.J. Field engr. Wigton-Abbott Corp., Plainfield, N.J., 1954-55, The Glenwal Co., Rochelle Park, N.J., 1955; asst. supt. Wigton-Abbott Corp., Plainfield, 1955-57; archtl. draftsman Raymond B. Flatt, Architect, Bloomfield, N.J., 1957-58; chief draftsman Raymond B. Flatt, Architect, 1958-60; project architect Scrimenti/Swackhamer/Perantoni Architects, Somerville, N.J., 1960-66; assoc. Scrimenti/Swackhamer/Perantoni Architects, 1966-69; ptnr. Scrimenti, Shive, Spinelli, Perantoni Architects, Somerville, 1969-86, Shive/Spinelli/Perantoni & Assocs., Architects & Planners, Somerville, 1986—; adv. com. First Fidelity Bank, Bound Brook, N.J., 1989-91; chmn. bd. Somerset Health Care Corp., 1987—. Contbr. articles to profl. jours. Bd. dirs., exec. com. N.J. Hosp. Assn., Princeton, 1986-92; chmn. bd. trustees Somerset Med. Ctr., Somerville, 1973—; mem. Nat. Trust for Hist. Preservation; bd. dirs. Ctr. for Health Affairs, Inc., 1992—. Recipient James F. Lincioln ArcWelding Found. award, 1973; Pres.'s award for outstanding svc. Rolling Hills Girl Scout Council, 1988. Mem. AIA, N.J. Soc. Architects, ACI (chpt. bd. dirs. 1978-83), ASHRAE, Illuminating Engring. Soc., ASTM, Nat. Congress of Hosp. Trustees of Am. Hosp. Assn., Nat. Fire Protection Assn., Greater Somerset County C. of C. (v.p. 1985-86, 92—), Rotary (pres. 1969-70), Wash. Campground Assn. (pres. 1975-76, v.p. 1977-78, sec. 1979—), Chi Phi (sec. 1973—). Republican. Congregationalist. Home: 1001 N Mountain Ave Bound Brook NJ 08805-1451 Office: Shive Spinelli Perantoni & Assocs PO Box 758 Somerville NJ 08876-0758

SHLIEN, HELEN SNOWER, curator; b. Kansas City, Mo., May 13, 1919; d. William and Henrietta (Berkowitz) Snower; m. John M. Shlien, Dec. 4, 1943; children: Andrea, Laura, David. BA, Sarah Lawrence Coll., 1941; MA, U. Chgo., 1964. Asst. editor Big Table mag., Chgo., 1958-60; dir. Contemporary Prints & Drawings Gallery, Chgo., 1965-67, Boston Visual Artists Union, 1974-76, Helen Shlien Gallery, Boston, 1978-85; asst. curator Inst. Contemporary Art, Boston, 1969-71; ind. curator, Boston, 1985—; bd. dirs. The Space, Boston, 1988—; mem. acquisitions com. Danforth Mus. Art, Framingham, Mass., 1989—. Author: (catalog) Fiber Arts; editor: Directory of Artists Associations in USA, 1977; contbr. articles and revs. to profl. jours. Grantee Nat. Endowment Arts, 1976. Mem. Women's Caucus for Art. Home: 14 Reservoir Rd Wayland MA 01778-3713

SHOCKLEY, ALONZO HILTON, JR., school system administrator; b. Milford, Del., Sept. 30, 1920; s. Alonzo Hilton Sr. and Elizabeth (Hilton) S.; m. Kay Marilyn Falke, Aug. 13, 1979; children: Novella Lela Shockley Randolph, Cheryl Emmelyn Shockley Durant, Alonzo Hilton III. BS, Del. State Coll., 1943; MA, Mich. State U., 1947; cert., NYU, 1956, postgrad., 1980; postgrad., Queens Coll., 1961-62, U. Maine, 1963. Cert. tchr., N.Y., Pa., Del. Tchr. sci. Brooks High Sch., Prince Frederick, Md., 1948; prin. elem., jr. high schs., dept. public instrn., Dover, Del., 1948-58; rsch. assoc. Del. State Coll., Dover, 1958-60; elem. sch. tchr. Cen. Sch. Dist. 4, Plainview, N.Y., 1960-62; asst. elem. prin. Union Free Sch. Dist., Wyandanch, N.Y., 1962-64; assoc. adminstrn. ofcl. N.Y. State Edn. Dept., Albany, 1964-65; edn. coord. Nassau County Commn. Econ. Opportunity, Garden City, L.I., 1965-66; dir. state and fed. programs Freeport (N.Y.) Pub. Schs., 1966-67; coord. state and fed. programs Amityville Pub. Schs., L.I., N.Y., 1985-88; ednl. cons., 1988—. Contbr. articles in field of ednl. adminstrn. to profl. jours. Pres. mid L.I. chpt. UN Assn. of U.S., bd. dir. so. N.Y. div., mem. coun. pres. steering com. Served with U.S. Army, 1942-45, NATOUSA. Mem. Am. Assn. Sch. Adminstrs., NEA, N.Y. State Tchrs. Edn., Assn. Childhood Edn. Internat., Assn. Supervision and Curriculum Devel., Nat. Assn. Elem. Prins., Amityville Sch. Dist. Adminstrs., Am. Acad. Polit. and Social Sci., NYU Alumni Assn. (bd. dirs., v.p.), Sch. Health, Edn. and Nursing Arts Professions (pres.). Home: 49 Gaymore Rd Port Jefferson Station NY 11776-1354

SHOCKLEY, SUSAN EVELYN, artist; b. Nashville, Sept. 3, 1957; d. John Nichol and Anne Holt (Sexton) S.; m. Nels Anders Swanson, July 2, 1983; children: Chelsea Susan Swanson, Hannah Holly Swanson. BFA, Memphis Coll. of Art, 1981; MFA in Painting, Cornell U., 1983. Two person shows at Cumberland Gallery, Nashville, 1982, Memphis Coll. of Art, 1990; one woman shows at Belmont Coll., Nashville, 1981, Cornell U., Ithaca, N.Y., 1983. Pollock Krasner Found. grantee, 1985-86. Home and Office: PO Box 286 East Pembroke NY 14056-0286

SHOEMAKER, ELEANOR BOGGS, television production company executive; b. Gulfport, Miss., Jan. 20, 1935; d. William Robertson and Bessie Eleanor (Ware) Boggs; m. D. Shoemaker, April 9, 1955 (div. 1987); children: Daniel W., William Boggs. Student in protocol, Southeastern U., 1952-53; student, George Washington U., Washington, 1953-56; BA in Communications and Polit. Sci. with honrs, Goucher Coll., 1981; postgrad., Villanova U. Feature writer Washington Times Herald, 1951-54; dir. Patricia Stevens Modeling Agy., Washington, 1955-56; free-lance model Julius Garfinkel, Woodward & Lothrop, Washington, 1951-56; research analyst Balt. County Council, Towson, Md., 1980-81; feature news reporter Sta. WGCB-TV, Red Lion, Pa., 1980—; pub. speaker, protocol The Reliable Corp., Columbia, Md., 1982-86; media cons. The Enterprise Found., Columbia, Md., 1985-86; faculty, TV prodn. and communication St. Francis Prep Sch., Spring Grove, Pa., 1985-88; owner Windswept Prodns. Co., Felton, Pa., 1989—; mem. conservation bd. Pa. Parks and Recreation Soc., 1984—; producer The Pa. County TV Prodn., 1981; producer, host Westar 4 Channel 9 half hour weekly news program Keystone Report. Producer: The Pa. County TV prodn., 1981, documentary Human Rights: A Special Report, Sta. WGCB-TV, 1989; producer, host, weekly news program Keystone Report, 1990. Bd. dirs. York (Pa.) County Parks and Recreation, 1972-87, YWCA, York, 1957-82, Hist. York, 1990—; mem. exec. com. York County Reps., 1972-82; accreditation adv. com. York Coll. of Pa.; instr. YWCA Women in Politics; founder, mem. Child Abuse Task Force, York, 1983—; mem. select com. Pa. Agrl. Zoning, 1988; mem. steering com. York Forum, 1989—; co-chmn. Cross Mill Restoration, 1987—; mem. Displaced Homemaker's Bd., 1989—; bd. dirs. Hist. York, 1990—; founder, host Old Rose Tree Pony Club, 1967—; chair Spring Valley County Pk. Task Force, 1972; master of fox hounds Mrs. Shoemaker's Hounds, 1969—; master of beagles Mrs. Shoemaker's Weybright Beagles, 1988—. Recipient pro bono child legal representation grant Pa. Bar Assn., 1983, Pa. Tree Farmer of Yr. award, 1987, Lay Person of Yr. award Pa. Recreation and Parks Assn. and Gov. Thornburg, 1982, Jefferson award, 1992, Achievement award Am. Women in Radio and TV Broadcasting; selected journalist Novosti Press USSR-U.S. Press Exch. program, 1989. Mem. Am. Polled Hereford Assn., York Area C. of C., York County C. of C. (publicity com. 1985—, agri. bus. com.), Masters of Foxhounds Assn. Episcopalian. Home and Office: PO Box 167 Felton PA 17322-0167

SHOEMAKER, RICHARD D., editor, financial consultant; b. Brwn Mawr, Pa., Nov. 24, 1947; s. Frank A. and Mary K. (Kuller) S.; m. Elizabeth Walters, Jan. 5, 1983. BA, Pa. State U., 1971. Owner Collegiate Enterprises, State College, Pa., 1967-74, Richard Shoemaker & Assoc., State College, 1971—; owner, editor Nat. Epson User Group, Lemont, Pa., 1983—; cons. in field. Author: American Bicentennial Covers and Cachets and Cards, 1984; editor (newsletter) The Epson Life Boat, 1981—; writer Life Ins. Selling Mag., St. Louis, 1983-86. Founder Pa. State Liberal Arts Alumni Soc., Pa. State U., 1979, sec. 1981-82; chmn. Pa. State U. Class 69 Spring Week Project, 1969, Class 70 Spring Week Project, 1970. With USAF, 1967-74. Mem. NRA, Am. Legion, North Shore Animal League, Pa. State Alumni Assn., Pa. State Liberal Arts Alumni Soc., Nittany Lion Club, State Coll. Boosters. Republican. Office: PO Box 1076 Lemont PA 16851-1076

SHOEMAKER, WILLIAM EDWARD, financial executive; b. Charleston, W.Va., Sept. 17, 1945; s. Robert Edward and Janet Elizabeth (Hoglund) S. BBA, U. Notre Dame, 1967. Assoc. buyer Proctor & Gamble, Cin., 1971; gen. mgr. Eastwind Inc., Anchorage, 1972-73; pres., operator Golden Horn Lodge, Inc., Bristol Bay, Alaska, 1973-79; treas. Hawley Resource Group, Inc., Anchorage, 1979-88; treas., chief fin. officer Golden Zone Resources, Inc., Campbell, Calif., 1988-90; ptnr. Resort Mgmt. Corp., Anchorage, 1987-90; pres. Foremost Group Inc., Montvale, N.J., 1991—; bd. dirs. Golden Zone Resources, Inc. Bd. dirs. Anchorage Econ. Devel. Corp., 1988-90. Served to lt. (j.g.) USN, 1967-71. Mem. Quarter Deck Club (Anchorage). Republican. Home: 145 River Rd Grand View on Hudson NY 10960

SHOEMATE, CHARLES RICHARD, agricultural products executive; b. LaHarpe, Ill., Dec. 10, 1939; s. Richard Osborne and Mary Jane (Gillette) S.; m. Nancy Lee Gordon, Sept. 16, 1962; children: Steven, Jeffrey, Scott. BS, Western Ill. U., 1962; MBA, U. Chgo., 1973. Supr. Corn Products Co., Summit, Ill., 1962-72; comptroller Corn Products Unit of CPC Internat., Englewood Cliffs, N.J., 1972-74; plant mgr. Corn Products Unit of CPC Internat., Corpus Christi, Tex., 1974-76; v.p. ops. Corn Products Unit of CPC Internat., Englewood Cliffs, 1976-81; pres. Can. Starch Co., Montreal, Que., 1981-83; v.p. Corn Refining div. CPC Internat., Englewood Cliffs, 1983-86, pres., 1986-88; corp v.p. CPC Internat., Englewood Cliffs, 1983-88, pres., 1988—, chmn., chief exec. officer, 1990. Office: CPC Internat Inc International Pla Englewood Cliffs NJ 07632

SHOFFNER, MARY BARBARA, campus registrar; b. Wilkes-Barre, Pa., Jan. 12, 1963; d. Paul Leo and Alexandra Victoria (Woronowicz) Winterhalter; m. Gregg Robert Shoffner, Sept. 22, 1984; children: Caitlin Elizabeth, Alexandra Victoria. BS in Microbiology, Pa. State U., 1983. Sr. rsch. technician Heraeus Cermalloy, Conshohocken, Pa., 1984-88; records clk. Pa. State U. Great Valley Ctr. for Grad. Studies, Malvern, 1988, mktg. asst., 1988, registrar, 1989—; chair child care task force Pa. State U. Great Valley Ctr. for GRad. Studies, 1989—. Mem. Am. Assn. Coll. Registrars and Admissions Officers. Presbyterian. Office: Pa State U Great Valley Ctr 30 E Swedesford Rd Malvern PA 19355-1480

SHOLES, DAVID H., state senator, lawyer; b. Providence, June 1, 1943; s. Leonard and Anna S. BA, Brown U., 1965; JD, Boston U., 1968. Bar: R.I. 1968, Mass. 1968. Pvt. practice law, Providence and Warwick, R.I., 1969-72; sr. ptnr. Sholes & Sholes, Warwick, 1972—; former lectr. U. R.I. Extension; mem. R.I. State Senate, 1976—, chmn. senate com. on health, edn. & welfare; mem. permanent legis. oversight commn. Dept. Children, Youth and Families; mem. state adv. com. U.S. Civil Rights Commn.; mem. Def. Civil Preparedness Adv. Council. Incorporator Cranston Gen. Hosp. Mem. R.I. Bar Assn., Cranston Hist. Soc., Phi Alpha Delta. Democrat. Jewish. Clubs: K.P., Masons, Kiwanis, Touro Fraternal Assn. (bd. dirs.). Home: 32 Mauran St Cranston RI 02910-1818 Office: 1375 Warwick Ave Warwick RI 02888-5032 Other: RI State Senate State Capitol Providence RI 02903

SHOLL, HOWARD ALFRED, electrical engineer; b. Northampton, Mass., Oct. 14, 1938; s. Alfred Evolt and Florence Ann (Lownds) S.; m. Beverly Beatty, June 4, 1960; children: Pamela Ellen, Lisa Ann. BEE, Worcester Poly. Inst., Worcester, Mass., 1960; MEE, WPI, Worcester, Mass., 1963; PhD, U. Conn., 1970. Sr. engr. Sylvania Electric Co., Waltham, Needham, Mass., 1963-66; instr. U. Conn., Storrs, 1966-70, asst. prof., 1970-75, assoc. prof., 1975-83, prof. computer sci. and engring., 1983—; dir. Booth Rsch. Ctr. U. Conn., 1986—. Contbr. articles to profl. jours. NSF grantee; Leverhulme fellow United Kingdom Rsch. Coun., 1973-74, Fulbright Rsch. fellow, 1981-82. Mem. IEEE (sr.), Assn. for Computing Machinery, Sigma Xi, Eta Kappa Nu, Tau Beta Pi, Upsilon Pi Epsilon. Office: U Conn Booth Rsch Ctr 233 Glenbrook Rd Storrs Mansfield CT 06268

SHOLLENBERGER, BRADLY SCOTT, podiatrist; b. Reading, Pa., Oct. 27, 1959; s. Lewis Irvin and Shirley Jane (Wagner) S.; m. Cynthia Kay Hoover, June 18, 1983; children: Michael Scott, Michelle Lynn. BS in Biology, Pa. State U., 1981; DPM, Pa. Coll. Podiatric Medicine, 1985. Diplomate Am. Bd. Podiatric Surgery. Pvt. practice Hamburg, Pa., 1986—; mem. staff St. Joseph Hosp., Reading, 1986—, Reading Hosp., 1991; mem. courtesy staff Community Gen. Hosp., Reading, 1986—; mem. assoc. Brandywine Hosp., Coatesville, Pa., 1988—. Fellow Am. Coll. Foot Surgeons; mem. Am. Podiatric Med. Assn., Sterling-Harford Hon. Anatomical Soc., Berks County Podiatry Soc., Pi Delta. Republican. Lutheran. Home: 6 Antietam Dr Birdsboro PA 19508-9316 Office: 6 Hearthstone Ct # 103 Reading PA 19606-3037

SHOOLMAN, ALAN ROBERT, medical services executive; b. Boston, May 29, 1929; s. David Leveton and Jane Florence (Hurwitz) S.; m. Barbara Carol Perlmutter, Aug. 26, 1956; children: Amy Shoolman Gordon, Nina, Jennifer. BS, Tufts U., 1950; MBA, Boston U., 1961. Engr. Puritan Distbg. Co., Boston, 1953; chief engr. Jet Spray Cooler Corp., Boston, 1953-54; sect. leader Lincoln Lab. MIT, Lexington, 1954-58; dept. head Mitre Corp., Bedford, Mass., 1958-68; v.p. Unitrode Corp., Billerica, Mass., 1968-86; pres., chief exec. officer Med. Area Svc. Corp., Boston, 1986—. Bd. dirs. Jewish Meml. Hosp., Boston, 1986—. Lt. (j.g.) USN, 1950-53. Office: Med Area Svc Corp 333 Longwood Ave Boston MA 02115-5711

SHOOTER, TOM, artist, educator; b. Williamsport, Pa., Aug. 18, 1941; s. Charles Preston and Grace Marie (Beiter) S.; children: Heather, Eric. AA, Lycoming Coll., 1961; diploma, Sch. Mus. Fine Arts, Boston, 1965, MA, 1966; BFA, Tufts U., 1971. Asst. instr. tech. painting Boston Mus. Sch., 1966, instr. painting, 1976-77, lectr., 1977-78; instr. drawing and painting Tufts U., Naples, Italy, 1968; instr. Cambridge (Mass.) Ctr. for Adult Edn., 1970-80, Boston Ctr. for Adult Edn., 1974-80; instr. drawing and painting Ednl. Alliance, N.Y.C., 1992—. Exhibited in group shows Fogg Mus., Harvard U., Cambridge, 1974, Inst. Contemporary Art, 1975, Rose Art Mus., Waltham, Mass., 1979, Wetherholt Gallery, N.Y.C., 1991, also others; one-man shows include Modern Art Agy., Naples, Italy, 1968, Harbor Gallery, Boston, 1975, Sunne Savage Gallery, Boston, 1977, 78, 79, George DePaul Gallery, N.Y.C., 1987; works in permanent collections Boston Bicentennial Art collection, Comml. Assurance Union, Boston, Spaulding & Sly Corp., Boston, others. James W. Paige fellow Boston Mus. Fine Arts, 1966; grantee Nat. Endowment for Arts, 1966, Mass. Coun., 1979, Adolph and Esther Gottleib Found., 1985. Home and Studio: 463 West St # 107H New York NY 10014

SHORB, ROBERT DAVID, college administrator, financial aid consultant; b. Gettysburg, Pa., Nov. 5, 1955; s. Richard and Irene Louise (Boyd) S.; m. Janice Marie Olsen, May 1, 1982; children: Meredith, Kimberly. BS in Edn., Mansfield (Pa.) State Coll., 1976; MS in Edn., Alfred (N.Y.) U., 1979. Asst. dir. fin. aid Clark U., Worcester, Mass., 1979-81, dir. fin. aid, 1981-84, dir. annual giving, 1984-85; dir. fin. aid Wheaton Coll., Norton, Mass., 1985-88; dir. student aid and family fin. Skidmore Coll., Saratoga Springs, N.Y., 1988—; fin. aid instr. U.S. Dept. Edn., Washington, 1991—; cons. Coll. Bd. Phila., 1991—. Author: (booklet) How to Pay for Your College Education, 1990. Trustee mem. Saratoga Springs Bd. Edn., 1991—. Recipient Outstanding Young Alumnus award Mansfield (Pa.) U., 1992. Mem. N.Y. Student Fin. Aid Adminstrn. Assn., Nat. Assn. Student Aid Adminstrs., Saratoga Springs Jaycees, Tau Kappa Epsilon. Democrat. Lutheran. Home: 26 Hearthstone Dr Gansevoort NY 12831-2506 Office: Skidmore Coll N Broadway Saratoga Springs NY 12866

SHORE, CAROLE JEAN, nutritionist; b. Dayton, Ohio, Dec. 7, 1948; d. Erroll Victor and Mabell B. (Pallanch) Black; m. Michael J. Shore, June 5, 1976; 1 child, Victoria Jean. BS, Ohio State U., 1971, MS, 1975. Intern Harvard U. Med. Ctr., Boston, 1971-72; pub. health nutritionist Polk County (Fla.) Health Dept., Winter Haven, 1972-73; asst. prof., program dir. Hood Coll., Frederick, Md., 1975-76; nutrition analyst USDA Consumer and Food Econs. Inst., Hyattsville, Md., 1976-79, USDA Human Nutrition Info. Service, Hyattsville, 1979-82; tech. info. specialist USDA Nat. Agrl. Library, Beltsville, Md., 1982-90; chief of quality mgmt. for clin. nutrition-computer programs Dept. Vets. Affairs, Washington, 1991—; coordinator Nat. Food Irradiation Info. Ctr. Author: (with others) Promoting Nutrition Through Education, 1985; contbr. articles to profl. jours. Mem. Am. Dietetic Assn. (Recognized Young Dietitian 1979, treas. Community Nutrition Rsch. Group 1981-83, chair 1984-85), D.C. Met. Area Dietetic Assn. (chair coun. on practice 1980-82, 87-88, treas. 1982-84, pres. elect. 1988-89, pres. 1989-90, chair state adv. com. Am. Dietetic Assn. conv. 1991), Soc. for Nutrition Edn., Inst. Food Technologists, ASTD, Omicron Nu, Phi Upsilon Omicron. Republican. Roman Catholic. Home: 6356 Crosswoods Dr Falls Church VA 22044-1210 Office: Dept Vets Affairs Washington DC 20420

SHORE, ERIC EUGENE, physician, consultant; b. Phila., Feb. 12, 1948; s. Reuben and Mary (Osinoff) S.; m. Mona Diane Cherry, Oct. 23, 1977; children: Brett Ian, Matthew Adam. Student, Temple U., 1965-67; BS in Biology, Widener U., 1969; DO, Phila. Coll. Osteopathic Med., 1973. Med. diplomate Nat. Bd. Examiners, diplomate Am. Bd. Utilization Rev. and Quality Assurance. Intern Botsford Gen. Hosp., Farmington, Mich., 1973-74; resident Phila. (Pa.) Gen. Hosp., 1974; instr. in medicine Hahnemann Med. Coll., Phila., 1975-78; treas. med. staff West Park Hosp., Phila., 1986-87, chief of geriatrics, 1986-88; sec. of med. staff Jefferson Park Hosp., Phila., 1987-91, chief of family medicine, 1988—; pres. Gen. Medicine Assocs., Ltd., Phila., 1987—, Bala Clin. Assocs., P.C., 1989—; instr. medicine Phila. Coll. Osteopathic Medicine, Phila., 1987—; clin. asst. prof. medicine Med. Coll. Pa., Phila., 1991—; med. dir. Fairmount Geriatric Ctr., Phila., 1985-88, Bala Nursing & Retirement Ctr., Phila., 1990—; chmn. bd. UniMed Systems, Inc., Phila., 1989—; cons. in medicine and geriatrics Phila. Psychiat. Ctr., Phila., 1987—. Med. officer Civil Air Patrol, Phila., 1976-78. Recipient Legion of Honor, Chapel of Four Chaplains, Phila., 1981. Fellow Am. Acad. Family

Physicians, Am. Coll. Utilization Rev. Physicians; mem. AMA (physician's recognition award 1990), Royal Soc. Medicine, Am. Geriatrics Soc., Am. Coll. Physician Execs., N.Y. Acad. Scis. Office: Gen Medicine Assocs Ltd 7516 City Ave # 8 Philadelphia PA 19151-2102

SHORE, HARVEY HARRIS, business educator; b. Cambridge, Mass., Apr. 14, 1940; s. Jacob and Freda Edna (Pearlman) S.; m. Roberta Ann Rogers, Jan. 29, 1967; children: Nina Ellen, Elissa Amy. BA cum laude, Harvard U., 1961; MS, MIT, 1963; DBA, Harvard U., 1966. Asst. prof. indsl. adminstrn. U. Conn., Storrs, 1966-72; assoc. prof. indsl. adminstrn. U. Conn., 1972-77; dir. Hartford MBA prog. U. Conn., Hartford, 1977-82; assoc. prof. mgmt. U. Conn., Storrs, 1982—. Contbr. articles to profl. jours.; editor Cubic Rev., 1975-78; author: Arts Administration and Management, 1987. Chmn. bus. adv. com. Tunxis Community Coll., Farmington, Conn., 1983-85; bd. dirs. Temple Beth Sholom, Manchester, Conn., 1987-90. Mem. Coll. and Univ. Bus. Instrs. in Conn. (pres. 1975-76), Employee Assistance Soc. N.Am., Acad. Mgmt., Harvard Bus. Sch. Club of No. Conn., MIT Ednl. Coun., Masons. Democrat. Jewish. Office: U Conn 368 Fairfield Rd Storrs CT 06269

SHORT, JANET MARIE, principal; b. Boston, Sept. 18, 1939; d. Robert Emmet and Getta Agnes (Mills) S. BS in Edn., Boston State Coll., 1962, MEd, 1967; LLD (hon.), Regis Coll., 1991. Tchr. Boston Pub. Schs., 1962-70, acting asst. dir. staff devel., 1970-71, tchr.-in-charge, 1971-75; prin. D.L. Barrett Sch., Boston, 1976-81; tchr. Boston Pub. Schs., 1981-82; prin. Maurice J. Tobin Sch., Boston, 1982—; lectr. in field. Adv. bd. DiMaiti Stuart Found., Boston, 1990—; adv. bd. Mission Hill and Camp Mission Possible, 1984-87; community adv. bd. Harvard Sch. Pub. Health, Boston, 1990—; adv. bd. Boston Against Drugs, 1990—. Recipient Thankful Recognition Channel 5, Boston, 1987, Recognition Boston Women's Mag., 1988, Pub. Svc. award Henry L. Shattuck, Bus. Mcpl. Bur. Rsch., 1988, Freedom's Found. Honor medal, 1990, others; movie based on J.M. Short, "A Matter of Principal," 1990. Mem. ASCD, Mass. Middle Level Adminstrs. Assn., Boston Assn. Sch. Adminstrs. (exec. bd. 1984—), Boston Middle Sch. Assn., Boston Elem. Prins. Assn., MESPA, Delta Kappa Gamma (chpt. pres. 1978-80). Roman Catholic. Home: 39 Ridgeway Dr Quincy MA 02169 Office: Maurice Tobin Sch 40 Smith St Roxbury MA 02120-2799

SHORT, JOSEPH NORTON, college president; b. Kingsville, Tex., Oct. 28, 1939; s. Hubert Irvin and Edith Alvena (Mueller) S.; m. Marilyn Won, June 28, 1968; 1 child, Erich. BA, Tex. Christian U., 1961; MA, Columbia U., 1963, PhD, 1974. Instr., adminstr. Ranche House Adult Edn. Coll., Salisbury, So. Rhodesia, 1963-64; tchr., adminstr. adult edn. ctr., exec. asst. African-Am. Inst., Tanzania and U.S., 1966-69; vis. instr. Upsala Coll., East Orange, N.J., 1972-73; asst. to pres. NYU, 1973-76; exec. dir. Oxfam Am., Boston, 1977-84; cons. internat. and econ. devel. orgns. Boston, 1984-89; pres. Bradford (Mass.) Coll., 1989—, also bd. dirs. Author: American Business and Foreign Policy: Cases in Coffee and Cocoa Trade Regulation, 1961-74, Diversity in Development: U.S. Voluntary Assistance to Africa, 1986. Mem. Interlink Press Svc., 1980-83; bd. dirs. Oxfam Am., 1977-84, Internat. Devel. Conf., Washington, 1983—, Mgmt. Edn. Inst., Arthur D. Little, Inc., 1984-89. Mem. Greater Haverhill C. of C. (bd. dirs. 1990—). Office: Bradford Coll Office Pres 320 S Main St Haverhill MA 01835-7393

SHORT, R. ALASTAIR, private investor; b. Toronto, Aug. 8, 1953; s. John and Anneliese (Bechler) S. BA magna cum laude, Queens U., Kingston, Ontario, Can., 1975; student, London Sch. Econs., Eng., 1974-75; LLB magna cum laude, York U., Toronto, 1979; cert. de matrise mention bien, U. Paris, 1980-81. Bar: N.Y. Atty. Rogers & Wells, N.Y.C., 1981-83; v.p. Quadrex Securities Corp., N.Y.C., 1983-87; ptnr. Apex Capital Ptnrs. L.P., N.Y.C., 1988—; bd. dirs. Rostone Corp., Ind., 1990—. Mem. N.Y. State Bar Assn. Office: Apex Ptnrs LP 40 W 57th St Ste 1500 New York NY 10019

SHORT, WILLIAM LEIGH, engineering consultant; b. Calgary, Alta., Can., Jan. 30, 1935; s. William Smith and Ada Iola (Matchett) S.; m. Patricia Macbeth, Aug. 4, 1979; children: Keith Jones, Steven Jones, laura Jones Kobrin, Jane Fisher, Michael Short. BSc, U. Alta., Edmonton, 1956, MSC, 1957; PhD, U. Mich., 1962. Registered profl. engr., Tex. Project engr. Can. Industries Ltd., Edmonton, 1957-59; sr. process engr. Chevron Rsch., Richmond, Calif., 1962-67; from asst. prof. to prof., head dept. chem. engring. U. Mass., Amherst, 1967-79; v.p. ERT, Houston, 1979-85; sr. program mgr. Radian Corp., Herndon, Va., 1985-88; prin. Woodward Clyde Cons., Wayne, N.J., 1988—; mem. sci. adv. bd., mem. peer rev. panels EPA, Washington, 1976—. Contbr. chpt. to book; patentee in field. Granteee, EPA, USPHS. Mem. Am. Inst. Chem. Engring., Am. Chem. Soc., Air Waste Mgmt. Assn. Presbyterian. Home: 2 Johnston Dr Morristown NJ 07960-6043 Office: Woodward Clyde Cons 201 Willowbrook Blvd Box 290 Wayne NJ 07470

SHORTESS, EDWIN STEEVIN, marketing consultant; b. Cedar Rapids, Iowa, Oct. 31, 1920; s. Edwin Stephen and Rita (Clemente) S.; m. Jane Elizibeth Gallagher, Dec. 27, 1941 (div. Apr. 1970); children: E. Stephen, Richard J., Mark Andrew, Cathy Shortess Pool; m. Mary Francis Kerns, May 28, 1970; children: Dana Menshing, Emil Bartsche, Roger Bartsche, Lisa Bartsche, Vincent Bartsche, Kirsten Bartsche. Student, North Iowa U., 1938-39; BSEE, Chgo. Tech. Coll., 1942. Engring. rsch. analyst Douglas Aircraft Corp., El segundo, Calif., 1942-44; liaison engr. Martin Aircraft Corp., Omaha, 1944-45; chief engr., dir. Burlington (Iowa) Instrument co., 1945-53; adminstrv. engr., dir. Hickok Elec. Instrument Co., Cleve., 1953-59; ea. sales mgr. Hickok Elec. Instrument Co., Paramus, N.J., 1960-65; v.p., gen. mgr., dir. Wacline, Dayton, Ohio, 1959-60; v.p., gen. mgr. Colo. Hickok, Grand Junction, 1965-69; pres. Shortess Rawson & Assocs., Allenwood, N.J., 1969-86; mktg. cons. Shortess Rawson & Assocs., Allenwood, N.J., 1986—; bd. dirs. Federated Purchasers Inc., Kenelworth, N.J. Author: Design and Application of Electrical Industrial Instruments, 1964. Mem. Instrument Soc. Engrs. (sr.). Republican. Methodist. Home and Office: PO Box 152 Allenwood NJ 08720-0152

SHORTT, RAE MICHAEL, mathematician, educator; b. Hartford, Conn., Dec. 9, 1957; s. Hugh Mungo and Rose Marie (Massaro) S.; m. Catherine Louise Frick, June 1980 (div. Feb. 1983). BA, Amherst Coll., 1978; PhD in Math., MIT, 1982. Asst. prof. Mich. Technol. U., Houghton, 1982-85; asst. prof. Wesleyan U., Middletown, Conn., 1985-88, assoc. prof., 1988—; cons. Conn. Chief State's Attorney's Office, 1988-90; speaker, lectr. various colls., confs. and symposiums. Reviewer, referee various jours. and orgns.; contbr. over 40 articles to profl. jours. Edler Grace Evangelical Luth. Ch., Middletown, 1988—. Recipient grant NSF, 1984-86, 1988, Shell Found., 1983, Fulbright Found., 1991-92. Mem. Math. Assn. Am. (com. on consultants 1988—), Phi Beta Kappa, Sigma Xi. Office: Wesleyan Univ Dept Math Middletown CT 06459

SHOSKY, JOHN EDWIN, government official; b. Colorado Springs, Colo., Nov. 1, 1955; s. Alexander Matthew and Barbara Marie (Middelkamp) S. BA in Polic. Sci., Colo. Coll., 1979; MA in Philosophy, U. Wyo., 1987; PhD in Philosophy, Am. U., 1992. Dep. dir. Media and Sports Commns., White House Conf. for Drug Free Am., Washington, 1987-88; sr. policy analyst White House Office Pub. Affairs, 1988; cons. to sec. HHS, Washington, 1984-87, 88-91, cons. to Surgeon Gen., 1991—; speech writer for govt. ofcls., corp. execs., profl. athletes, congressmen, senators; lectr. in philosophy Am. U., 1987—; adj. prof. philosophy George Mason U., 1990—. Contbr. numerous articles to acad. and profl. jours., trade publs., newsletters, regional and nat. newspapers. Recipient spl. svc. award HHS, 1986, cert. of commendation, 1988, 89, cert. of appreciation, 1988, 89. Mem. Mind Assn., Colo. Coll. D.C. Alumni Assn., Washington Philosophy Club, Capitol Hill Squash Club. Republican. Roman Catholic. Home: 1806 Rollins Dr Alexandria VA 22307-1657

SHOSTAK, ED BENNETT, sculptor; b. N.Y.C., Aug. 23, 1941; s. Joseph V. and Edna Shostak. Student, Ohio U., 1960-61, Cooper Union, 1961-62. One-man shows include Fischbach Gallery, N.Y.C., 1971, 73, Sch. of Visual Arts Gallery, 1974, Holly Solomon Gallery, 1975, 79; exhibited in group shows at Whitney Mus. Am. Art, N.Y.C., 1973, 90, Mus. Modern Art, N.Y.C., 1975, Leo Castelli Gallery, 1980. Grantee Creative Artists Pub. Svcs., N.Y. State Coun. on the Arts, 1973; Guggenheim fellow, 1974. Home: 303 E Houston St New York NY 10002-1103

SHOTWELL, CHARLES BLAND, air force officer, lawyer; b. Tucson, Jan. 10, 1955; s. William Bedford and Pauline (Bainbridge) S.; m. Jeannene V. Brooks, Aug. 10, 1988. BA, U. Puget Sound, 1977, JD, 1980, LLM, 1991. Bar: Hawaii 1980, U.S. Dist. Ct. Hawaii 1980, U.S. Ct. Mil. Appeals 1981, D.C. 1989, U.S. Ct. Appeals D.C. 1989. Commd. 2d lt. USAF, 1980, advanced through grades to maj., 1989; chief civil law USAF, K.I. Sawyer AFB, Mich., 1980-83; mil. justice reviewer USAF, Sembach Air Base, Fed. Republic Germany, 1983-84, area def. counsel, 1984-85; desk officer Internat. Negotiations Div. USAF, Ramstein Air Base, Fed. Republic Germany, 1985-88; chief legis. sect., dir. internat. programs Pentagon USAF, Washington, 1988-91; adj. instr. aviation law and ins. Embry-Riddle Aero. U., Ramstein Air Base, 1985-88; USAF Nat. Def. fellow Tufts U., 1991-92; instr. USAF Acad., 1992—. Newsletter editor; contbr. to profl. publs. Mem. ABA, Hawaii State Bar Assn., D.C. Bar Assn., Air Force Assn. Home: 19715 Top O' The Moor Dr Monument CO 80132 Office: Dept Polit Sci U S A F Academy CO 80840

SHOUB, EARLE PHELPS, chemical engineer; b. Washington, July 19, 1915; m. Elda Robinson; children: Casey Louis, Heather Margaret Shoub Dills. BS in Chemistry, Poly. U., 1938, postgrad. 1938-39. Chemist, Hygrade Food Products Corp., N.Y.C., 1940-41, Nat. Bur. Standards, 1941-43; regional dir. U.S. Bur. Mines, 1943-62; chief div. Accid Prev & Health, 1962-70; dep. dir. Appalachian Lab. Occupational Respiratory Diseases, Nat. Inst. Occupational Safety and Health, Morgantown, W.Va., 1970-77, dep. dir. div. safety research, 1977-79; mgr. occupational safety, indsl. environ. cons., safety products div. Am. Optical Corp., Southbridge, Mass., 1979, cons., 1979—; assoc. prof. dept. anesthesiology W.Va. U. Med. Center, Morgantown, 1977-82, prof. Coll. Mineral and Energy Resources, 1970-79. Recipient Disting. Service award Dept. Interior and Gold medal, 1959. Registered profl. engr.; cert. safety profl. Fellow Am. Inst. Chemists; mem. Am. Indsl. Hygiene Assn., Vets. of Safety, AIME, Am. Soc. Safety Engrs., Nat. Fire Protection Assn., Nat. Soc. Profl. Engrs., Am. Conf. Govtl. Indsl. Hygienists, Internat. Soc. Respiratory Protection (pres.), ASTM, Am. Nat. Standards Inst., Sigma Xi. Methodist. Contbr. articles to profl. jours. and texts. Home: 5850 Meridian Rd Apt 202C Gibsonia PA 15044-9605

SHOUP, CARL SUMNER, retired economist; b. San Jose, Calif., Oct. 26, 1902; s. Paul and Rose (Wilson) S.; m. Ruth Snedden, Sept. 27, 1924; children: Dale, Paul Snedden, Donald Sumner (dec.). AB, Stanford U., 1924; PhD, Columbia U., 1930; PhD (hon.), U. Strasbourg, 1967. Mem. faculty Columbia U., 1928-71; dir. Internat. Econ. Integration Program and Capital Tax Project, 1962-64; Editor Bull. Nat. Tax Assn., 1931-35; staff mem. N.Y. State Spl. Tax Commns., 1930-35; tax study U.S. Dept. Treasury, June-Sept. 1934, Aug.-Sept. 1937, asst. to sec. Treasury, Dec. 1937-Aug. 1938, research cons., 1938-46, 62-68; interregional adviser, tax reform planning UN, 1972-74; sr. Killam fellow Dalhousie U., 1974-75; staff Council of Econ. Advisers, 1946-49; dir. Twentieth Century Fund Survey of Taxation in U.S., 1935-37, Fiscal Survey of Venezuela, 1958, Shoup Tax Mission to Japan, 1949-50, Tax Mission to Liberia, 1969; co-dir. N.Y.C. finance study, 1950-52; pres. Internat. Inst. Pub. Finance, 1950-53; cons. Carnegie Ctr. for Transnat. Studies, 1976, Harvard Inst. for Internat. Devel., 1978-83, Venezuelan Fiscal Commn., 1980-83, Jamaica Tax Project, 1985, World Bank Value-Added Tax Study, 1986-87, Duke U. Tax Missions Study, 1987-88; vis. prof. Monash U., 1984. Author: The Sales Tax in France, 1930, (with E.R.A. Seligman) A Report on the Revenue System of Cuba, 1932, (with Robert M. Haig and others) The Sales Tax in the American States, 1934, (with Roy Blough and Mabel Newcomer) Facing the Tax Problem, 1937, (with Roswell Magill) The Fiscal System of Cuba, 1939, Federal Finances in the Coming Decade, 1941, Taxing to Prevent Inflation, 1943, Principles of National Income Analysis, 1947, (with others) Report on Japanese Taxation, 1949, (with others) The Fiscal System of Venezuela, 1959, Ricardo on Taxation, 1960, The Tax System of Brazil, 1965, Federal Estate and Gift Taxes, 1966, Public Finance, 1969 (transl. into Japanese 1974, Spanish 1979), (with others) The Tax System of Liberia, 1970; Editor: Fiscal Harmonization in Common Markets, 1966. Decorated Order Sacred Treasure (Japan), Grand Cordon. Disting. fellow Am. Econ. Assn.; mem. Nat. Tax Assn. (pres. 1949-50, hon. mem.), Phi Beta Kappa. Address: 48 Heard Rd Center Sandwich NH 03227

SHOWE, JONATHAN, snack food company executive; b. Yonkers, N.Y., Sept. 14, 1945; s. Raymond Julian and Grace (Kent) S.; m. Elena Kornetchuk, July 4, 1975. BA, Grinnell Coll., 1967; MA, John Hopkins U., 1972. Spl. asst. Trade Rep. Office, White House, Washington, 1972-76; pub. issues advisor FMC Corp., Chgo., 1976-78; pres. Theatre Candy Co., Inc., Pitts., 1978-88, Leisurepro, Inc., Pitts., 1988—; bd. dirs. Internat. Images, Ltd., Pitts. Chmn. Planning Commn., Sewickley, Pa., 1986-90; trustee Pitts. (Pa.) Ballet Theatre, 1988—. 1st lt. U.S. Army, 1968-71, Vietnam. Decorated Bronze star U.S. Army, Vietnam, 1971. Mem. Soc. Profl. Journalists, Young Pres.' Orgn. (chpt. chair 1992—). Office: Leisurepro Inc 2800 Smallman St Pittsburgh PA 15222

SHPUNTOFF, ALBERT FRANK, computer scientist; b. N.Y.C., Mar. 15, 1950; s. Harry and Ann (Klauber) S.; m. Karen Marie Caskey, July 28, 1985. SB, U. Chgo., 1971; MA, U. Ill., 1973. Asst. prof. Morningside Coll., Sioux City, Iowa, 1977-80, U. Nebr., Omaha, 1980-86; vis. asst. prof. Oberlin (Ohio) Coll., 1986-87, U. Akron, Ohio, 1987-88; mgr., tng. Stardent Computer, Concord, Mass., 1988-91; sr. cons. Sci. Visualization Assocs., Concord, Mass., 1991—. Author: UNO VAX Book, 1985. Mem. IEEE (chmn. Nebr. sect. IEEE Computer Soc. 1984-86), Am. Math. Soc., Assn. for Computing Machinery.

SHREM, CHARLES JOSEPH, metals corporation executive; b. Cairo, May 9, 1930; came to U.S., 1959; s. Joseph C. and Paula (Cadranel) S.; m. Vivian L. Chalom, Jan. 30, 1955; children: Jeff, Leslie Allen. Degree in bus. and economy, Coll. Français, Cairo, 1951. Export mgr. Stanton Ironworks U.K., Middle East, 1950-57; comml. mgr. Soc. Sovibor, Paris, 1957-59; purchasing dir. Montanore, Inc., N.Y.C., 1959-65; exec. v.p. Commonwealth Metal Corp., Englewood Cliffs, N.J., 1965-85, pres., chief exec. officer, 1985—. Bd. dirs. Adult Edn., Pequannock, N.J., 1970-80. Office: 560 Sylvan Ave Englewood Cliffs NJ 07632-3104

SHREVE, JACK, English educator; b. Youngstown, Ohio, Feb. 6, 1949; s. John F. and Evelyn (Sarcinella) S. BA, Pa. State U., 1970; MA, U. Pitts., 1972, PhD, 1976. Prof. English and Spanish Allegany Community Coll., Cumberland, Md., 1975—, chmn. dept. lang. and lit., 1977-78; chmn. dept. humanities Allegany Community Coll., Cumberland, 1984-85. Contbg. author: Magill Critical Survey of Literature, 1983-85, Beacham Research Guide and Fiction Series (5), 1985-86, Research Guide to American Historical Research, 1988-91, Dictionary of Literary Biography: 20th Century Italian Poetry, 1992; contbr. over 100 book revs. in Choice, Libr. Jour., Modern Lang. Jour., Hispania, The Md. Hist. Mag., Book Rev. Digest. NEH seminar, 1979-80, 87, others. Mem. Am. Assn. Tchrs. of Spanish, Am. Lit. Translators Assn., Md. Hist. Soc., Allegany County Arts Coun. Democrat. Home: 308 Cumberland St Cumberland MD 21502-2008 Office: Allegany Community Coll Willowbrook Rd Cumberland MD 21502-2541

SHRIDHARANI, VASANT NANALAL, quality control engineer; b. Bombay, Sept. 25, 1937; came to U.S., 1968; s. Nanalal Nathubhai and Chaturlaxmi S.; m. Rasila Vasant, Feb. 8, 1961; children: Kanan, Kaushik. BCE, Birla Engring. Coll., Anand, India, 1959; MCE, Northeastern U., Boston, 1971. Registered profl. engr., Mass., N.Y. Lead structural engr. Chas T. Main Inc., Boston, 1973-77; structural engr. Ebasco Svcs. Inc., Jericho, N.Y., 1977-81, N.Y.C., 1985-88; structural engr. Burns & Roe Inc., Woodbury, N.Y., 1981-83, United Engrs. Inc., Phila., 1983, Stone & Webster Inc., Niantic, Conn., 1984; constrn. engr. Passive Solar Homes Inc., Irving, Tex., 1985; quality control engr. Shah Assocs. P.C., Bellmore, N.Y., 1988—. Mem. ASCE. Democrat. Home: 96 Cedar Dr W Plainview NY 11803-2824

SHRIVER, DAVID A., pharmacologist; b. Syracuse, N.Y., May 29, 1942; s. Harry J. Shriver and Elizabeth (Allen) Jones; m. Sharon L. Shriver, Aug. 30; children: Amy E., Carrie J. Student, Union Coll., Cranford, N.J., 1960-62; BS, Purdue U., 1966; MS, U. Iowa, 1968, PhD, 1970. Rsch. scientist Wyeth Pharm., Radnor, Pa., 1970-74, sr. rsch. scientist, 1974-77; group leader Ortho Pharm. Corp., Raritan, Pa., 1977-82, rsch. mgr., 1982-91; asst. dir. R.W. Johnson Pharm. Rsch. Inst., Spring House, Pa., 1991—. Contbr. over 50 articles and abstracts to profl. jours.; patentee in field. Pres. Bridgewater-Raritan Sch. Bd., 1987; exec. dir. Bridgewater Youth Svc. Commn., 1988; mem. grant mgmt. com. N.J. Dept. Edn., 1989—. Home: 2051 Lynne Way PO Box 8 Martinsville NJ 08836 Office: RW Johnson Pharm Rsch Inst Welsh and McKean Rd Spring House PA 19477-0776

SHROEDER, JANET GREGG WALLACE, sculptor; b. St. Louis, May 4, 1902; d. Cecil Dudley and Jesse Marian (Howard) Gregg; m. Asa Brookings Wallace, 1922 (dec. 1942); children: Marian Ney, Janet Jones, Eugenie Darrow; m. Henry Alfred Schroeder, May 20, 1949 (dec. 1975). Student, Byrn Mawr Coll., 1920-21, Washington U. Sch. Art, 1929-30. Tchr. sculpture John Burroughs Sch., St. Louis, 1937-38, Hickory Ridge Sch., Putney, Vt., 1946-47. Exhibits include Feragils, Brit. Am. Gallery, St. Louis Art Mus., Julius Polk, Inc., St. Louis, Manchester (Vt.) Art Gallery, Book Cellar Gallery, Brattleboro, Vt., 1959, Black Starr, Gorham (N.Y.C.) 1948-49; permanent collections include portraits in bronze Robert S. Brookings, Dr. Arthur H. Compton, Rt. Rev. Father Alphnose Schwitalla, Rev. Mother Concordia, Pierre Laclede; exhibited permanent collections six portraits Nat. Portrait Gallery Smithsonian Instn., Washington; portrait Malboro (Vt.) Coll.; works include bronze portraits Ambassador Carol Bunker, 1974, Walter Muir Whitehill, 1977, Gardner Cox, What is Man?; represented by Things Finer Gallery, Santa Fe. Home and Studio: 44 Concord Ct Bedford MA 01730

SHU, CHI-WANG, mathematics educator, researcher; b. Beijing, People's Republic of China, Jan. 2, 1957; came to U.S., 1982; s. Kuang-Yao and Ding-Zhen (Shi) S.; m. Din-Sui Loh, May 1, 1984; 1 child, Hai-Shuo. BS, U. Sci. and Tech. of China, 1982; PhD, UCLA, 1986. Rsch. assoc. U. Minn., Mpls., 1986-87; asst. prof. applied math. Brown U., Providence, 1987-91, assoc. prof., 1992—; cons. ICASE, NASA Langley Rsch. Ctr., Hampton, Va., 1988—. Contbr. articles to profl. jours. Grantee NSF, NASA, Army Rsch. Office. Mem. Am. Math. Soc., Soc. for Indsl. and Applied Math. Home: 135 Woodbury St Providence RI 02906-3511 Office: Brown U Div Applied Maths Providence RI 02912

SHUART, JAMES MARTIN, university president; b. College Point, N.Y., May 9, 1931; s. John and Barbara (Schmidt) S.; m. Marjorie Strunk, Apr. 5, 1953; children: James Raymond, William Arthur. BA, Hofstra U., 1953, MA, 1962; PhD, NYU, 1966. Group rep. Home Life Ins. Co., 1955-57; N.Y. Life Ins. Co., 1957-59; adminstr. Hofstra U., Hempstead, N.Y., 1959-70, asst. dir. admissions, asst. dean faculty, asst. pres., exec. dean student services, assoc. dean liberal arts scis., trustee, 1973-75; v.p. adminstrv. services Hofstra U., 1975-76, pres., 1976—; trustee Commn. on Ind. Colls. and Univs., N.Y. State, 1982-89, chmn., 1986-89, sec. exec. com., 1982-86; mem. higher edn. adv. com. N.Y. State Senate, 1979—; bd. dirs. European Am. Bank. Trustee Molloy Coll., 1973-77; mem. adv. bd. Adelphi U. Sch. Social Work, 1973-84; dep. county exec. Nassau County, 1973-75, commr. social svcs., 1971-73, commr. L.I. Reg. Planning Bd., 1978-83, chmn., 1981-83; bd. dirs L.I. Assn., 1986-90; trustee Uniondale (N.Y.) Pub. Libr., 1967-78, L.I. Hosp. Planning Coun., 1971-75; pres., bd. dirs. Health Welfare Coun. Nassau County, 1971-80; chmn. Nassau Bd. Social Svcs., 1971-73; bd. dirs. Winthrop U. Hosp., 1979-86, others. Recipient Founders Day award NYU, 1967, Outstanding Alumnus of Yr. award Hofstra U., 1973, George M. Estabrook Disting. Svc. award Alumni Assn., 1974, Leadership in Govt. award C. W. Post Coll., L.I. U., 1978, Man of Yr. award Hempstead C. of C., 1978, L.I. Pers. and Guidance Assn. award, 1977, Lincoln Day award Syosset-Woodbury Rep. Club, 1981, L.I. Disting. Leadership award 1982, Joseph Giacalone award, 1986, others; decorated Officer in the Order of Orange Nassau, The Netherlands, 1991. Home: 25 Cathedral Ave Garden City NY 11530-4412 Office: Hofstra U Office of Pres Hempstead NY 11550

SHUBERT, DUANE DOYLE, psychiatrist, researcher; b. New Castle, Pa., Mar. 24, 1962; s. Doyle George and Betty Ellen (Huffman) S. BS, Geneva Coll., 1984; MD, Pa. State U., 1988. Resident psychiatrist dept. psychiatry Milton S. Hershey Med. Ctr., Hershey, Pa., 1988-92; staff psychiatrist Wernersville (Pa.) State Hosp., 1992—; cons. Chase-Brexton Clinic, Balt., 1985—. Recipient Roche award Roche Pharms. Co., 1988. Mem. AMA, Am. Psychiat. Assn., Pa. Med. Soc., Pa. Psychiat. Physicians, Dauphin County Med. Soc. Office: Wernersville State Hosp Wernersville PA 19565

SHUEBROOK, RONALD LEE, artist, educator; b. Fort Monroe, Va., July 29, 1943; s. George Albert and Ruth Ellen (Nowling) S.; m. Frances Gallagher, Mar. 2, 1968; children: Paul David, Meghan Sara. BS in Art Edn., Kutztown State Coll., 1965, MEdn, 1969; postgrad. Haystack Mountain Sch. Crafts, 1965, 67; MFA, Kent State U., 1972. Instr., U. Saskatchewan, Saskatoon, Can., 1972-73; asst. prof. Acadia U., Wolfville, N.S., Can., 1973-77; assoc. prof., coord. art edn. York U., Downsview, Ont., Can., 1977-79; assoc. prof. of studio N.S. Coll. Art and Design, Halifax, Can., 1979-80, chmn. studio div., 1980-83, coord. painting and drawing, 1983-85, assoc. prof., 1983-87; exec. dir. Ottawa (Ont.) Sch. Art, 1987-88; chmn., prof. dept. fine art, U. Guelph, Ont., 1988—; vis. artist, lectr. numerous art depts. and galleries across Can., U.S. and U.K., 1974—; mem. visual arts awards juries Can. Coun., Ottawa, 1977—, Social Sci. and Humanities Coun., 1991; curriculum cons. Acadia U., Wolfville, N.S., Bishop's U., Lennoxville, Quebec, 1984; BFA cons. Emily Carr Coll. Art and Design, Vancouver, B.C., 1989; cons. Ont. Ministry Culture and Communications, 1989, U. Victoria, B.C., 1991, Concordia U., Montreal, 1992; advisor Georgian Coll., Barrie, Ont., 1991. Contbr. articles to profl. jours., essays to catalogues. Exhibited internationally in one-man shows; represented in numerous public and pvt. collections. Bd. dirs. Visual Arts Ont., 1988—; mem. founding exec. com. Visual Arts N.S., Halifax, 1975-77, chmn., 1986-87, hon. life mem., 1987—; mem. N.S. Art Bank Com., Dept. of Culture, N.S., Halifax, 1975-77; mem. task force for art history in pub. schs. N.S. Dept. Edn., Halifax, 1975; bd. dirs. Eye Level Gallery, Halifax, 1977, 81-83, Art Gallery N.S., 1986-87. Fellow Fine Arts Work Ctr., 1969-70, MacDowell Colony, 1981; Can. Coun. grantee, 1980, 81, 83, 85, 88, 90, New Faculty Rsch. grantee U. Guelph, 1989. Mem. Can. Assn. Univ. Tchrs., Visual Arts N.S. (hon.), Univ. Art Assn. Can., Faculty Assn. N.S. Coll. Art and Design (pres. 1984-85), Visual Arts Ont. Home: 540 St David St, North Fergus, ON Canada NIM 2K4 Office: U Guelph, Chmn Dept Fine Art, Guelph, ON Canada N1G 2W1

SHUELL, THOMAS JOHN, educational psychology educator; b. Kansas City, Mo., Apr. 28, 1938; s. Gerald Joseph and Beulah Marie (Palmer) S.; m. Anne L. Bougher, June 6, 1960; children: Kathryn Anne, Lisa Marie. BS, Oreg. State U., 1960; PhD, U. Calif., Berkeley, 1967. Prof. ednl. psychology SUNY, Buffalo, 1967—; numerous presentations at profl. confs. Co-author: Learning and Instruction, 1976; editor Ednl. Psychologist, 1978-84; contbr. articles to profl. jours., chpts. to books. Lt. (j.g.) USN, 1960-63. Recipient Outstanding Tchr. Educator award Confederated Orgn. for Tchr. Edn., 1987. Fellow APA (exec. com. div. 15, 1978—, pres. 1990-91); mem. Am. Ednl. Rsch. Assn., Northeastern Ednl. Rsch. Assn. (bd. dirs. 1982-88, pres. 1986-87). Office: SUNY Dept Counseling and Ednl Psychology 409 Baldy Hall Buffalo NY 14260

SHUEY, ELAINE M., speech pathologist, educator; b. Harrisburg, Pa., Nov. 22, 1956; d. Mark W. and Doris M. (Campbell) S. BS in Speech Pathology, Clarion U., 1978; MA in Speech Pathology, Kent State U., 1980, PhD, 1990. Cert. clin. speech pathologist. Speech lang. pathologist Children's Rehab. Ctr., Warren, Ohio, 1980-81; assoc. prof. East Stroudsburg U., Pa., 1984—. Contbr. articles to profl. jours. Mem. Antoine Dutot Sch. & Mus., 1989, sec., 1991; visitor Monroe County Area Agy. on Aging, 1985-89; deacon Zion United Ch. of Christ, 1990—. Grantee East Stroudsburg U., 1988, 91, East Stroudburg U. Found., 1990-91. Mem. Am. Speech & Hearing Assn. (Continuing Edn. award 1988), Pa. Speech Lang. Hearing Assn. (CUE subcom. 1984-91), Northeastern Speech & Hearing Assn. Pa. (exec. coun. 1984—, v.p. program 1986-88, 90-92, CUE chairperson 1985-86), Phi Delta Kappa. Office: East Stroudsburg U LaRue Hall East Stroudsburg PA 18301

SHUFRO, SALWYN, investment company executive; b. N.Y.C., Feb. 1, 1905; s. Jacob J. and Rebecca (Phillips) S.; m. Edna Epstein, May 29, 1930; children: Edward G., Joan Shufro Silverman. BS, CCNY, 1924; MBA, Harvard U., 1926. With investments dept. Mfrs. Trust, N.Y.C., 1926-28; salesman Salomon Bros. & Hutzler, N.Y.C., 1928-38; ptnr. Shufro, Rose &

Ehrman, N.Y.C., 1938—. Home: 200 E 64th St New York NY 10021-7497 Office: Shufro Rose & Ehrman 745 5th Ave New York NY 10151-0002

SHUGARS, ANNE O'DONNELL, investment management firm executive; b. Balt., Aug. 13, 1961. BBA, Loyola Coll., 1983. Chartered Fin. Analyst. Investment officer Md. Nat. Bank, Balt., 1982-87; asst. v.p. ASB Capital Mgmt., Inc., Washington, 1987—. Mem. Assn. Investment Mgmt. and Rsch., Washington Soc. Investment Analysts, Washington Assn. Money Mgrs. Office: ASB Capital Mgmt Inc 655 15th St NW Ste 800 Washington DC 20005

SHUGHART, DALE FRANKLIN, academic administrator; b. South Middleton, Pa., July 21, 1913. PhB, Dickinson Coll., 1934; postgrad., Shippensburg State Tchrs. Coll., 1934; LLB, Dickinson Sch. Law, 1938, LLD (hon.), 1969; LLD (hon.), Gettysburg Coll., 1984, Shippensburg State U., 1990, Dickinson Coll., 1990. Tchr., coach Boiling Springs (Pa.) High Sch., 1934-36; pvt. practice law, 1938-42, 45-46; dist. atty. Cumberland County, Pa., 1946; pres. judge Common Pleas Ct., Pa., 1947-83; adj. prof. law Dickinson Sch. Law, Carlisle, Pa., 1958—, pres., 1962—; of cousel Fowerler, Addams, Shughart and Rundle, 1984—; mem. legal staff Pa. Turnpike Comm., 1940-41. Author: Selected Cases on Pennsylvania Practice, 1963, 69, 71, 81, Pennsylvania Civil Practice, 1988. Mem. Grace United Meth. Ch. Carlisle, past mem. ch. coun.; mem. com. bus. and industry Lebanon Valley Coll., adv. com. Little League Baseball, com. children and youth region III Gov.'s Coun. Human Svcs., planning bd. Holy Spirit Hosp.; past bd. dirs., Carlisle chpt. ARC, United Cerebral Palsy Dauphin, Cumberland, and Perry Counties, Tri-County Heart Assn.; commr. Boy Scouts Am.; trustee Dickinson Sch. Law, 1949—, Carson Long Inst.; state bd. dirs. YMCA, various coms., past pres., bd. dirs. Carlisle chpt.; past trustee Pa. Indsl. Sch. White Hill. With U.S. Army, 1942-45, ETO. Decorated Bronze Star; recipient Outstanding Alumni award Dickinson Sch. Law, 1969, Molly Pitcher award for Citizen of Yr. 1982, Carlisle Exchange Club, Outstanding Svc. award State Juvenile Ct. Judges Commn., 1982. Mem. Nat. Assn. Probate Judges, Pa. Bar Assn. (adminstrn. sect. 1981—), Masons, Am. Legion (Citation Appreciation 1983). Office: Dickinson Sch Law 150 S College St Carlisle PA 17013-2848

SHUGOLL, JOAN S., market research executive; b. June 16, 1928; d. Jerry I. and Lucille (Unger) Simons; m. Eugene L. Shugoll, Oct. 10, 1948; children: Mark, Robert. Student, Bklyn. Coll., 1945-47. Pres. Shugoll Rsch., 1970—. Mem. Am. Mktg. Assn., Marketing Rsch. Assn. (co-founder Washington chpt., 1980, program chmn. 1980-81, membership chmn. 1981-83). Home: 4701 Willard Ave Chevy Chase MD 20815

SHUKAN, DONALD CRAINE, pediatrician; b. Newark, Aug. 27, 1937; s. Leo Z. and Sylvia (Gross) S.; m. Elinor Barbara Gellar, June 11, 1967; children: Brian, Evan, Scott, Zachary. AB, Temple U., 1959; MD, Chgo. Med. Sch., 1963. Diplomate Am. Bd. Med. Examiners, Am. Bd. Pediatrics. Intern Newark Beth Israel Hosp., 1963-64; resident Children's Meml. Hosp., Chgo., 1964-66; pediatrician Pioneer Valley Pediatrics, Longmeadow, Mass., 1969—. Sch. physician East Longmeadow (Mass.) Pub. Schs., 1979—. Capt. U.S. Army, 1966-68. Fellow Am. Acad. Pediatrics; mem. Mass. Med. Soc., N.E. Adolescent Medicine Soc., Maimonides Med. Club. Office: Pioneer Valley Pediatrics 123 Dwight Rd East Longmeadow MA 01106-1748 Office: 146 Hazard Ave Apt A Enfield CT 06082-4520

SHULER, MICHAEL LOUIS, biochemical engineering educator, consultant; b. Joliet, Ill., Jan. 2, 1947; s. Louis Dean and Mary Clara (Boylan) S.; m. Karen Joyce Beck, June 24, 1972; children: Andrew, Kristin, Eric, Katherine. BSChemE, U. Notre Dame, 1969; PhDChemE, U. Minn., 1973. Asst. prof. biochem. engring. Cornell U., Ithaca, N.Y., 1974-79, assoc. prof., 1979-83, prof., 1984-91; Samuel E. Beckett prof. chem. engring. Cornell U., Ithaca, 1992—; vis. scholar U. Wash., Seattle, 1980-81; vis. scientist U. Wis., Madison, 1988-89; mem. adv. coun. biochem. engring. program Dartmouth Coll.; bd. dirs. Phyton Catalytic Inc., Ithaca, N.Y. Editor 5 books; contbr. numerous articles to profl. jours. and chpts. to books. Bd. dirs., treas., sec., v.p. Advs. for the Handicapped, Ithaca, 1978-88; sec., bd. dirs. Tompkins County Human Rights Commn., Ithaca, 1985-87; mem. adv. bd. Md. Biotech. Inst., Carnegie-Mellon Chem. Engring. Recipient Outstanding Paper award Am. Oil Chemist Soc., 1984, Coll. of Engring. Honor award U. Notre Dame, 1989. Founding fellow Am. Inst. of Med. and Biol. Engrs.; mem. NAE, Am. Chem. Soc. (M. J. Johnson award 1986), Am. Inst. Chem. Engrs. (editor Biotech. Progress 1985-88, cons. editor jour. 1986—, mem. publ. com. 1988—, Food, Pharm. and Bioengring. award 1989, Profl. Progress award 1991), Am. Soc.Microbiology, Am. Soc. Pharmacognosy. Roman Catholic. Office: Cornell U Dept Chem Engring 340 Olin Hall Ithaca NY 14853

SHULL, FRANK TAYLOR, IV, financial executive; b. Washington, Oct. 22, 1967; s. Frank Taylor and Mary Anne (Goodyear) Shull III. BA, U. Md., 1991. Fin. engr. Frank T. Shull & Assocs., Bethesda, Md., 1991—. Mem. Young Terrapins Club (pres. 1991—), Order of Omega, Sigma Alpha Epsilon (v.p. 1990-91). Republican. Episcopalian. Home: 1405 Bernard Pl Rockville MD 20851 Office: Frank T Shull & Assocs 6500 Rock Spring Dr Bethesda MD 20817

SHULMAN, JACK ARNOLD, computer research scientist; b. Plainfield, N.J., June 30, 1952; s. Sam and Helen (Kramer) S. BA, BS, Rutgers U., 1974, BSEE, 1975. Computer scientist Apollo Computer, Inc., Chelmsford, Mass., 1980-83; engring. mgr. Nat. Intelligence Machines, Armonk, N.Y., 1984-87; cons. MCI Corp., Rye Brook, N.Y., 1987-88, AT&T Bell Labs., Lincroft, N.J., 1988-89, R.J. Nabisco Corp., Parsippany, N.J., 1989-91, Prudential Corp., Newark, 1991, IBM, Armonk, 1991-92, David Sarnoff Labs., Penns Neck, N.J., 1992; owner, mgr. Cons. Office Jack A. Shulman, Mountainside, N.J., 1992—; bd. dirs. Tech. Internat. Corp., Princeton, N.J.; tech. advisor Nat. Sec. Agy., McLean, Va., 1973—. Patentee software Relational Spreadsheet, Overlapping Windowed G.U.I., hardware Symmetrical Multiprocessor, hardware and software Massively Parallel AI Supercomputer. Tech. advisor U.S. Exec. Dept., Washington, 1989—, High Definition TV, Washington, 1989—. Recipient outstanding invention award NSF, 1973, sci. award IBM Sci. Fellows, 1982, Outstanding Achievement award AGS Info. Systems, 1988. Fellow TECUS Sci. Coloquium (pres. 1985-86); mem. Nat. Space Soc., Am. Artificial Intelligence Assn., Inst. for Imaging Sci. (founder), Delaware Valley Artificial Intelligence Assn. Office: PO Box 1221 Mountainside NJ 07092

SHULMAN, LAWRENCE EDWARD, biomedical research administrator, rheumatologist; b. Boston, July 25, 1919; s. David Herman and Belle (Tishler) S.; m. Pauline K. Flint, July 19, 1946; 1 son, Lawrence E.; m. Reni Trudinger, Mar. 20, 1959; children: Kathryn Verena, Barbara Corina. A.B., Harvard U., 1941, postgrad., 1941-42; Ph.D., Yale U., 1945, M.D., 1949. Nat. Bd. Med. Examiners. Intern Johns Hopkins Hosp., 1949-50, resident and fellow in internal medicine, 1950-53; dir. connective tissue div. Johns Hopkins U., 1955-75, assoc. prof. medicine, 1964—; assoc. dir. div. arthritis, musculoskeletal and skin diseases NIH, Bethesda, Md., 1976-82, dir., 1982—; dir. Nat. Inst. Arthritis and Musculoskeletal and Skin Diseases NIH, 1986—; chmn. med. adminstrn. com. Arthritis Found., Atlanta, 1974-75, exec. com., 1972-77; dir. Lupus Found. Am.; med. adv. bd. United. Scleroderma Found., Watsonville, Calif., 1977-88. Discoverer: Eosinophilic Fasciitis, 1974, new med. sign friction rubs in scleroderma, 1961. Recipient Sr. Investigator award Arthritis Found., 1957-62, Disting. Service award, 1979; Heberden medal for research, London, 1975; Superior Service award USPHS, 1985; W.R. Graham Meml. lectr., 1973. Fellow ACP; mem. Am. Rheumatism Assn. (pres. 1974-75, master 1987—), Soc. Clin. Trials, Pan-Am. League Against Reumatism (pres. 1982-86). Home: 6302 Swords Way Bethesda MD 20817-3350 Office: NIH Rm 4C32 9000 Rockville Pike Bethesda MD 20892-0001

SHULTZ, LEONARD DONALD, research scientist; b. Boston, Apr. 16, 1945; s. Samson and Jean (Korim) S.; m. Kathy Louise Jacobs, Aug. 31, 1969; children: David Benjamin, Sarah Natalie. BA, Northeastern U., Boston, 1967; PhD, U. Mass., 1972. Rsch. asst. Tufts U. Sch. of Med., Boston, 1967-68; from grad. teaching asst. to predoctoral fellow U. Mass., 1968-72; from postdoctoral fellow to sr. staff scientist The Jackson Lab., Bar Harbor, Maine, 1972—; editorial bd. In Vivo, 1991—. Contbr. numerous rsch. papers. Bd. Dirs. YMCA, Bar Harbor, Maine, 1989—. Mem. Am. Assn. Immunologists, Am. Soc Microbiology, Internat. Assn. Comparative Rsch. on Leukemia and related diseases. Home: Box 2545 RFD 1 Bar Harbor ME 04609 Office: The Jackson Lab Main St Bar Harbor ME 04609-1842

SHUMAKER, JOHN WILLIAM, university president; b. Pitts., Aug. 21, 1942; s. Thomas E. Shumaker and Sara Jane (Giffn) Cobun; m. Michele Deasy, June 3, 1972; children: Timothy, Brian. BA, U. Pitts., 1964; MA, U. Pa., 1966, PhD, 1969; LLD hon., Briarwood Coll., 1989. Asst. assoc. prof. classics Ohio State U., Columbus, 1969-77, asst. dean coll. humanities, 1971-72, acting chmn. dept. classics, 1972-73, assoc. dean coll. humanities, 1973-77; dean coll humanities and fine art SUNY, Albany, N.Y., 1977-83, v.p. rsch. and ednl. devel., 1983-85, v.p. academic planning and devel., 1985-87; pres. Cen. Conn. State U., New Britain, 1987—; bd. dirs. Conn. World Trade Assn., Bridgeport; exec. dir. Capital Dist. Humanities Program, Albany, 1978-83; trustee, chmn. Conn. Inst. for the Arts in Edn., New Britain, 1988-91; trustee Nat. Commn. for Coop. Edn., Boston, 1987—. Bd. dirs. New Britain Gen. Hosp., 1988—, Hartford chpt. ARC, 1988—, A.W. Stanley Found, New Britain, 1988—, Mcpl. Econ. Devel. Agy., New Britain, 1988—. Mem. Internat. Assn. Univ. Pres. (exec. com. 1987—, vice chmn. N.Am. coun. 1990—), Internat. Assembly Coop. Educators, Am. Assn. State Colls. and Univs. (com. on internat. programs 1987-88, com. state reps. 1988—), New England Bd. Higher Edn. (bd. govs. 1990—), Conn. Inst. for European and Am. Studies (chmn. bd. dirs.), Conn. Inst. for Asian and Am. Studies (chmn. bd. dirs.), Interdist. Edn. Action Corp. (bd. dirs.), New Britain C. of C. (bd. dirs.), Phi Beta Kappa. Office: Cen Conn State U 1615 Stanley St New Britain CT 06053-2439

SHUMAN, EARL STANLEY, songwriter, music publisher; b. Boston, Aug. 2, 1923; s. Benjamin Morris and Mildred Judith (Kaplan) S.; m. Margaret Stein, Nov. 25, 1956; children: Cathy Elizabeth, Daniel James, Steven Lewis. BA, Yale U., 1947. Owner, pres. Earl/Peg Music Co., N.Y.C., 1957—; pub. BMI, ASCAP, N.Y.C., 1977—. Composer (lyric writer) popular songs include Seven Lonely Days, 1953 (Country and Western award 1970), Hey There Lonely Girl, 1970 (Gold record), (musicals) Secret Life of Walter Mitty, 1964 (award 1965), (country song) Leaves are the Tears of Autumn, 1968 (County and Western award 1969); pub. Bat Out of Hell album, 1977 (platinum award 1979). Capt. USMCR, 1943-46, 50-51. Mem. ASCAP. Home and Office: 111 E 88th St New York NY 10128-1111

SHUMAN, JAMES BURROW, writer, consultant; b. N.Y.C., Sept. 8, 1932; s. Ik and Elizabeth Frances (Davies) S.; m. Victoria Grove, Oct. 4, 1958 (div. 1976); children: James Burrow Jr., Robert Grove. BA, Wesleyan U., 1954. Reporter The Sharon (Pa.) Herald, 1956-60, UPI, Washington, 1960-61; assoc. editor The Reader's Digest, Washington and Pleasantville, N.Y., 1961-71; cons. to John D. Rockefeller 3d, N.Y.C., 1971-73; pvt. practice writer, cons. Lahaska, Pa., 1973-75; asst. press sec. The White House, Washington, 1975-77; cons. Gerald R. Ford, Palm Springs, Calif. and Washington, 1977-80; pres. Allegheny Found., Pitts., 1980-81; chmn. James B. Shuman and Assocs., Lahaska, N.Y.C., Washington, 1981—. Author: (with others) The Kondratieff Wave, 1972, In Constant Fear, 1974; contbr. numerous articles to mags. Lt. (j.g.) USN, 1954-56. Recipient Best Spot News Story award Pa. Newspaper Pubs. Assn., 1959. Mem. Phillips Mill Assn., Pisces Club, Lav Club Paris, Gilgit Polo Club (Pakistan). Republican. Mem. Soc. of Friends. Home and Office: Box 403 Lahaska PA 18931

SHUMAN, MICHAEL HARRISON, lawyer, policy analyst; b. N.Y.C., June 4, 1956; s. Jack Jacob and Bernadine Sydelle (Fine) S. AB, Stanford U., Palo Alto, Calif., 1979; JD, Stanford U., 1982. Bar: Calif. 1983, D.C. 1990. Intern NRDC, San Francisco, 1981-82; pres. Ctr. for Innovative Diplomacy, Irvine, Calif., 1982-91; fellow Inst. for Policy Studies, Washington, 1991—; bd. dirs. Eart Vote PAC, Brussels, 1988—, Exploratory Project on Peace, Washington, 1989-92. Author: Citizen Diplomats, 1987. Kellogg Found. fellow, 1987. Office: Inst Policy Studies 1601 Connecticut Ave NW Washington DC 20009-1035

SHUMATE, JOHN PAGE, diplomat; b. El Paso, Tex., Sept. 18, 1934; s. John Page and Elizabeth (McWilliams) S.; m. Caroline Taylor, June 16, 1978. BA in Polit. Sci., UCLA, 1956; MAin Internat. Rels., U. So. Calif., 1970. Counsellor of Embassy, U.S. Embassy, Quito, Ecuador, 1970-72; dir. exec. tng. Fgn. Service Inst., Washington, 1972-75; dir. U.K. Affairs, Dept. State., 1975-78, exec. dir. Bur. Ednl. and Cultural Affairs, 1978-80, exec. dir. Bur. Adminstrn., Washington, 1981-84; staff dir. Sec. of State's Adv. Panel on Overseas Security, 1984-85; exec. v.p., chief exec. officer Am. Fgn. Service Protective Assn., 1986—; co-pres. U.S.-Mexico Cultural Commn. com., 1978-80. Recipient Superior Honor award U.S. Dept. State., 1981; Phi Kappa Phi Cert. of Honor, 1970. Mem. Am. Fgn. Service Assn., Assn. Fed. Health Orgns. (chmn. bd. dirs. 1992—), Nat. Assn. Sr. Living Industries, Phi Kappa Phi. Clubs: Ft. Meyer Officers, Fgn. Service, Dacor Bacon House, Bethany West Tennis. Office: Am Fgn Svc Protective Assn 1716 N St NW Washington DC 20036-2907

SHUMWAY, DAVID ROBERT, language professional, English; b. Fremont, Ohio, Mar. 25, 1952; s. Robert Carl and Harriet Jean (Melcher) S.; m. Linda Susan Colantonio. BA, New Coll. of Hofstra U., 1974; MA, Ind. U., 1978, PhD, 1983. Instr. English and Am. Studies Miami U., Oxford, Ohio, 1979-84; asst. prof. English Bradley U., Peoria, Ill., 1984-85; asst. prof. literary and cultural studies Carnegie Mellon U., Pitts., 1985-91, assoc. prof. literary and cultural studies, 1991—; exec. dir. Group for Rsch. into Institutionalization and Professionalization of Lit. Studies, Pitts., 1985—; series co-editor Univ. Press Va., 1990—. Author: Michel Foucault, 1989, Creating American Civilization, 1992; co-editor: Knowledges, 1992; contbr. articles to profl. jours. Founding mem. Tchrs. for a Dem. Culture, Evanston, Ill., 1991—. Recipient Rsch. fellowship Ctr. for Humanities, 1990. Mem. MLA (div. exec. com. 1986-91, del. assembly 1988-90), Popular Culture Assn. (chmn. philosophy sect. 1988-89), Soc. for Cinema Studies, Nat. Coun. Tchrs. English, Midwest MLA, Soc. for Critical Exch. (bd. dirs. 1984-90). Home: 1114 Winterton St Pittsburgh PA 15206-1732 Office: Carnegie Mellon U English Dept Pittsburgh PA 15213

SHUR, IRENE GINSBURG, history educator; b. Cleve., May 14, 1921; d. William and Edna Ginsburg; 1 child, Ronald Shur. BSc, Ohio State U., 1943; MEd, U. Del., 1956; EdD, U. Pa., 1976. Faculty West Chester (Pa.) U., 1956-77, prof. history, 1977—; vis. faculty Peking (China) U., summer 1980, Hebrew U., Jerusalem, summer 1978; lectr. in field. Author: In Answer--History, Holocaust, 1989, Let Schoolbells Ring, 1979, Reflections on the Holocaust, 1981, Mr. Puckles Hat, 1991. Mem. West Chester Sch. Bd., 1979—. Fulbright fellow, 1964, Freedom Found. fellow, 1966; Rockefeller grantee, 1956, U. Pa. dissertation grantee, 1973. Mem. Am. Assn. for chinese Studies (trustee 1977), Ethnic Studies Inst., Nat. Inst. on the Holocaust, Assn. for Pakistan and India-Islamic Studies, Anne Frank Inst., Pi Gamma Mu. Republican. Jewish. Office: West Chester Univ Dept History West Chester University PA 19383

SHURKIN, LORNA GREENE, academic official; b. N.Y.C., Mar. 5, 1944; d. Morris and Rita Rose (Cohen) Greene; m. Joel N. Shurkin, July 4, 1966 (div. Nov. 1981); children: Jonathan Greene, Michael Robert. BA, Bklyn. Coll., CUNY, 1964; postgrad., NYU, 1965-66. English tchr. N.Y.C. Schs., 1963-64; asst. to articles editor Womans Day mag., N.Y.C., 1964-66; reporter, columnist News-Herald, Willoughby, Ohio, 1966-68; pub. rels. rep. and editor Phila. Inquirer, Reuters and others, 1974-76; pub. rels. rep., editor Thomas Jefferson U., Phila., 1976-79; account exec. Sommers/Rosen Pub. Relations, Phila., 1979-81; dir. pub. relations Swarthmore (Pa.) Coll., 1981—. Dem. candidate Radnor Twp. (Pa.) Sch. Bd., 1987; sec. Radnor Dem. Com., 1988—; v.p. Footlighters Theater, Berwyn, Pa., 1985-88; ofcl. pronouncer Delaware County (Pa.) Spelling Bee, 1986—; mem. adv. bd. Eastern Pa. Theater Coun., 1986—; bd. dirs. Families of Murder Victims, Phila., 1989—, Delaware County Press Club, 1991—. Mem. Coun. for Advancement and Support of Edn. (conf. speaker, panelist 1983, 86-87, program com. and track chair 1993), Pub. Rels. Soc. Am., Women in Communications, Phila. Pub. Rels. Assn. Coll. and Univ. Pub. Rels. Assn. Pa. (co-chair conf. 1993), Del. County Press Club (bd. dirs., program chair 1991—). Jewish. Home: 435 E Lancaster Ave Apt 110 Saint Davids PA 19087-4221 Office: Swarthmore Coll Pub Rels Office 500 College Ave Swarthmore PA 19081-1110

SHUSTER, E. G. BUD, congressman; b. Glassport, Pa., Jan. 23, 1932; s. Prather and Grace (Greinert) S.; m. Patricia Rommell, Aug. 27, 1955; children: Peg, Bill, Debbie, Bobby, Gia. B.S., U. Pitts., 1954; M.B.A., Duquesne U., 1960; Ph.D. in Econs. and Mgmt., Am. U., 1967. Nat. account mgr. Univac div. Sperry Rand, 1956, Univac div. Remington Rand Co. (name now Sperry Rand), 1956-60; dist. mgr. Western Pa. RCA, 1960-62; mgr. ops. RCA, Washington, 1962-65; v.p. EPD div. RCA, 1965-68; pres. computer terminal co., 1968-72; mem. 93d-102nd Congresses from 9th Dist. Pa., 1973—; former mem. budget com., chmn. House Republican policy com., 1979; vice chmn. surface transp. subcom., sr. mem. com. on public works and transp., aviation subcoms House Select Intelligence Com., vice chmn. oversight a nd evaluation subcom.; pres. 93d Congress Republican Freshman Class; chmn. Nat. Transp. Policy Study Commn., 1976. Author: Believing in America, 1983. Del. Republican Nat. Conv., 1976, 80, 84, 88; co-chair Energy, Environment & Transp. Platform Subcom.; sr. transp. advisor Bush-Qualyle campaign; also mem. platform com.; chmn. Reagan-Bush Campaign in Western Pa.; sr. adviser to transition team for Dept. Transp., 1980-81. Served with inf. and CIC AUS, 1954-56. Recipient Watchdog of Treasury award, Guardian of Small Bus. award, Golden Age Hall of Fame award. Mem. Pa. Soc., Chowder and Marching Soc., Phi Beta Kappa, Omicron Delta Kappa, Sigma Chi (Significant Sig award). Club: Capitol Hill. Office: US Ho of Reps 2188 Rayburn House Office Bldg Washington DC 20515*

SHUSTER, MARC RONALD, planning consultant; b. Phila., June 1, 1946; s. Abraham and Sylvia R. (Wilder) S.; m. Susan Staley, Aug. 22, 1970; children: Lisa M., Kara M. BA, Rutgers Coll., 1969, MCRP, 1973. Lic. planner, N.J. Social worker N.J. Bur. of Children's Svcs., Camden, 1969-71; planner/assoc. Taylor, Wiseman & Taylor, Mt. Laurel, N.J., 1973-82; project mgr. Adams, Rehmann & Heggan, Hammonton, N.J., 1983-85; dir. community devel. Twp. of Cherry Hill, N.J., 1985-88; ptnr. Shuster/Abbington-Ney, Cherry Hill, 1988-91; pvt. practice Marlton, N.J., 1991—. Mem. Cherry Hill Planning Bd., 1988; trustee South Jersey Devel. Coun., 1988—. Mem. Am. Planning Assn., N.J. Fedn. of Planning Officials, N.J. Am. Planning Assn. (exec. com. 1987-92). Office: 9 E Stow Rd Marlton NJ 08053-3159

SIBAL, LOUIS RICHARD, science administrator; b. Chgo., Aug. 6, 1927; s. Louis and Betty H. (Hrdina) S.; m. Patricia M. Gardner, June 27, 1964; children: L. Gregory, Christopher R. BS, U. Ill., 1951; MS, U. Colo., 1954, PhD, 1957. Instr. to assoc. prof. U. Ill. Med. Sch., Chgo., 1957-65; rsch. microbiologist, then sci. adminstr. NIH, Bethesda, Md., 1965—. Contbr. numerous articles to reviewed jours. Mem. Am. Assn. Immunologist, Fedn. of Am. Socs. for Experimental Biology.

SIBLEY, LEWIS BRANCH, tribologist; b. Lyons, N.Y., Apr. 13, 1931; s. Lewis Schollenberger and Hattie Elizabeth (Branch) S.; m. Clara Mary Carle, Oct. 17, 1953 (div. 1977); children: Russell Carle, Daniel Lee. Student, Ohio Wesleyan U., 1948-51; BSME, Rensselaer Poly. Inst., 1953; postgrad., Ohio State U., 1953-57. Prin. mech. engr. Battelle Meml. Inst., Columbus, Ohio, 1953-57, project leader, 1957-61; supr. mech. test SKF Industries, Inc., Phila., 1961-68; mgr. rsch. dept. SKF Tech. Svcs., King of Prussia, Pa., 1968-76, mgr. tribology, 1976-82; prin. Tribology Cons., Paoli, Pa., 1982—; tech. dir., owner Tribology Systems, Inc., Paoli, 1989—; chmn. Computerized Tribology Info. Svcs. Planning Workshop, Gaithersburg, Md., 1985. Author: (with others) Role of Viscosity in Lubrication, 1960, Computer-Aided Design of Bearings and Seals, 1976, Wear Control Handbook, 1980 (ASME Centennial project award 1980); editor: Achievements in Tribology, 1990; contbr. articles to profl. jours.; patentee in field. Fellow ASME (chmn. rsch. com. on tribology 1981), Soc. Tribologists and Lubrication Engrs. (Alfred E. Hunt medal 1962); mem. Am. Soc. Testing and Materials, Am. Ceramic Soc. Home: 504 Foxwood Ln Paoli PA 19301-2010 Office: Tribology Systems Inc 225A Plank Ave Paoli PA 19301-1726

SICHEL, ARTHUR GUTMAN, psychologist; b. Biloxi, Miss., July 18, 1945; s. Walter Samuel and Amelia Sondheimer (Gutman) S.; m. Gail Lynn Clark, Feb. 25, 1984; children: Corianna, Amarynth. BA, The New Sch. Social Rsch., N.Y.C., 1972; MS, Yeshiva U., 1978, PhD, 1982; cert. in psychotherapy, Greenwich Inst. Psychoanalytic Studies, 1979. Lic. psychologist, N.Y., N.J. Psychotherapist Fifth Ave. Ctr. Counseling and Psychotherapy, N.Y.C., 1975-84; pvt. practice N.Y.C., 1984-91; psychologist Kessler Inst. Rehab., Saddle Brook, N.J., 1986, dir. psychology, 1987-90; dir. psychology St. Lawrence Rehab. Ctr., Lawrenceville, N.J., 1990—. Contbr. articles to profl. jours. Mem. APA, Am. Congress Rehab. Medicine, Am. Pain Soc., Pre- and Perinatal Psychology Assn. N.Am., N.J. Psychol. Assn., Soc. Clin. and Exptl. Hypnosis, Internat. Primal Assn. (pres. 1985-87, v.p. 1983-85, bd. dirs. 1980-90). Office: St Lawrence Rehab Ctr 2381 Lawrenceville Rd Lawrenceville NJ 08648

SICHEL, ENID KEIL, physicist; b. Burlington, Vt., May 14, 1946; d. Ferdinand J.M. and Elsa (Keil) S. AB, Smith Coll., 1967; PhD, Rutgers U., 1971. Vis. scientist Nat. Magnet Lab., Cambridge, Mass., 1970-71; tech. staff RCA Labs., Princeton, N.J., 1973-79, GTE Labs., Waltham, Mass., 1979-85; cons. Lincoln, Mass., 1986—; program dir. NSF, Washington, 1988-89; vis. prof. MIT, Cambridge, 1986-88. Contbr. articles to profl. jours.; patentee in field. Chair Recycling Com., Lincoln, 1988-92. Mem. Am. Phys. Soc., Materials Rsch. Soc., AAAS. Home: PO Box 236 Lincoln MA 01773-0011

SICULAR, TERRY, economics educator; b. San Jose, Feb. 5, 1955; d. George Myer and Alice (Greene) Sicular; m. Robin Arthur Cowan. BA, Pomona Coll., Claremont, Calif., 1976; PhD, Yale U., 1983. Instr. U. Wis., Madison, 1982-83; asst. prof. Stanford (Calif.) U., 1983-87; assoc. prof. econs. Harvard U., Cambridge, Mass., 1987—. Editor: Food Price Policy in Asia, 1989; contbr. articles to profl. jours. Mem. Am. econ. Assn., Am. Agrl. Econs. Assn. Office: Dept Econs Harvard Univ Cambridge MA 02114

SIDAR, THOMAS WILSON, retail executive; b. New Brunswick, N.J., Nov. 21, 1949; s. Alexander George Jr. and Jean (Wilson) S.; m. Ellen Elizabeth Woods,. BA, Colby Coll., 1972. Sales rep. L.L. Bean, Inc., Freeport, Maine, 1975, retail buyer, 1976-82, asst. product mgr., 1982-85, product mgr., 1985-88, sr. product mgr., 1988-89, dir. product devel., 1990-91; v.p. creative dept., 1991—. Mem. Maine Audubon Soc., Nature Conservancy, Ducks Unltd., Ruffed Grouse Soc. Democrat. Episcopalian. Home: Middle Rd # 1490 Woolwich ME 04579 Office: LL Bean Inc Casco St Freeport ME 04033-0002

SIDARE, LYNN CATHERINE, public relations executive; b. Rochester, N.Y., July 25, 1958; d. Frank John and Catherine (Ferro) S. BA in Psychology, SUNY, Buffalo, 1979, MSW, 1981. Social worker Children's Hosp. Buffalo, 1981-83, Hemophilia Ctr. Western N.Y., Buffalo, 1983-85; dir. Family Planning Clinic, SUNY, Buffalo, 1982-85; account exec. Community Blue div. Blue Cross Western N.Y., Inc., Buffalo, 1985-86; pub. info. specialist Community Blue div. Blue Cross Western N.Y., Inc., Buffalo, 1986-88, pub. rels. specialist, 1988-89, mgr. pub. rels., 1989-91; dir. advt. and pub. rels., 1991—. Named Best in Category Buffalo Club Printing House Craftsmen, 1986, 87, Internat. Assn. Printing House Craftsmen, 1986, 87. Mem. Pub. Rels. Soc. Am., Internat. Assn. Bus. Communicators. Office: Blue Cross Western NY 1901 Main St Buffalo NY 14208-1036

SIDARWECK, WILLIAM JOHN, educational psychologist; b. Bridgeport, Conn., Oct. 15, 1950; s. John and Mary (DeNigris) S.; m. Corinne Sidarweck; children: William Jr., Christopher, Sarah. BA, Sacred Heart U., 1972; MS, U. Bridgeport, 1975. Cert. sch. psychologist, Conn. Instr. Found. Sch., Orange, Conn., 1972-75, sch. psychologist, 1975-77; assoc. dir., co-founder Elizabeth O'Hara Walsh Sch., Stratford, Conn., 1977—; co-founder, assoc. dir., sch. psychologist Quaezar, Inc., Bridgeport, 1977-83, pres., exec. dir., 1983—. Coach North End Little League, Bridgeport, 1985-91. Mem. Coun. Assn. Pvt. Ednl. Facilities (sec.-treas. 1986-90), Ct. Assn. Residential facilities, Conn. Assn. Autistic Children. Democrat. Roman Catholic. Office: Quaezar Inc 555 Madison Ave Bridgeport CT 06604-2730

SIDDALL, PATRICIA ANN, English educator; b. North Adams, Mass., May 20, 1947; d. William W. and Shirley M. (Ogert) Hartman; m. Stephen B. Siddall, Apr. 18, 1970; 1 child, Michael William. BA in English, North

Adams State Coll., 1969. Cert. secondary edn. tchr., English, Social Studies. English tchr. Bay Path Regional Vocat. Tech. High Sch., Charlton, Mass., 1977—, humanities cluster chmn., 1987-91; sec. Mass. Vocat. Assn. Cen. Chpt., 1982-85. Del. Mass. Dem. State Conv., 1986, 87, 89, 90. Mem. ASCD, NEA, Am. Vocat. Assn., Nat. Coun. Tchrs. of English, Mass. Tchrs. Assn. (exec. com. 1988—). Roman Catholic. Home: Pinewood Dr Webster MA 01570

SIDDAYAO, CORAZON MORALES, economist, educator; b. Manila, July 26, 1932; came to U.S., 1968; d. Crispulo S. and Catalina T. (Morales) S. Cert. in elem. teaching, Philippine Normal Coll., 1951; BBA, U. East, Manila, 1962; MA in Econs., George Washington U., 1971, MPhil, PhD, 1975. Tchr. pub. schs. Manila, 1951-53; asst. pensions officer IMF, Washington, 1968-71; cons. economist Washington, 1971-75; rsch. assoc. Policy Studies in Sci. and Tech. George Washington U., Washington, 1971-72, teaching fellow dept. econs., 1972-75; natural gas specialist U.S. Fed. Energy Adminstrn., Washington, 1974-75; sr. rsch. economist, assoc. prof. Inst. S.E.A. Studies, Singapore, 1975-78; sr. rsch. fellow energy/economist East-West Ctr., 1978-81, acad. staff coord. energy and industrialization, 1981-86; vis. fellow London Sch. Econ., 1984-85; sr. energy economist in charge energy program Econ. Devel. Inst., World Bank, Washington, 1986—; vis. prof. U. Montpellier, France, 1992; affiliate prof. econs. U. Hawaii, 1979—; cons. internat. orgns.; vis. prof. econs. U. Phlippine, intermittent 1989—. Author: Increasing the Supply of Medical Personnel, 1973, The Offshore Petroleum Resources of Southeast Asia: Some Potential Conflicts and Related Economic Factors, 1978, Round Table Discussion on Asian and Multinational Corporations, 1978, The Supply of Petroleum Reserves in Southeast Asia: Economic Implications of Evolving Property Rights Arrangements, 1980, Critical Energy Issues in Asia and the Pacific: the Next Twenty Years, 1982, Criteria for Energy Pricing Policy, 1985, Energy Demand and Economic Growth, 1986; editor various publs. on energy policy/planning and energy environment issues, 1990-91; contbr. chpts. to books, articles to profl. jours. Grantee in field. Mem. Am. Econ. Assn., Internat. Assn. Energy Economists, Pan Am. Clipper Club, Alliance Francaise, Omicron Delta Epsilon. Roman Catholic. Office: Econ Develop Inst Energy Div The World Bank 1818 H St NW Washington DC 20433-0002

SIDDON, THOMAS EDWARD, Canadian government official; b. Drumheller, Alta., Can., Nov. 9, 1941; s. Ronald Victor and Gertrude Violet (Humfrey) S.; m. Patricia Audrey Yackimetz, Sept. 1, 1962; children—Charles, David, Robert, Elizabeth, Katherine. BSME with distinction, U. Alta., 1963; MS in Aerospace Engring., U. Toronto, 1965, PhD in Aerodyn Noise, 1968. Assoc. prof. mech. engring. U. B.C., 1968-79; mem. House of Commons, Ottawa, Ont., Can., 1978—; minister of state for sci. and tech. House of Commons, Ottawa, Ont., 1984-85, minister of fisheries and oceans, 1985-90, minister Indian Affairs and Northern Devel., 1990—; mem. Queen's Privy Coun., 1984; founder acoustical engring. firm and audiometric testing bus.; acoustical cons., Can., U.S.; mem. priorities and planning com., 1988—, environment, fed.-provincial rels. com., 1988—, human rels. com., cultural affairs com., 1988—. Alderman Twp. of Richmond, B.C., 1975-77. Recipient Assn. Profl. Engrs. award, 1978. Fellow Acoustical Soc. Am. Anglican. Office: Ho of Commons, Parliament Bldgs, Ottawa, ON Canada K1A 0A6

SIDEL, ENID RUTH, educator; b. N.Y.C., Apr. 15, 1936; d. Jerome and Mae (Sklaroff) Lipskin; m. H. David Sidel (div. May 1970). AB, Hunter Coll., 1958; MEd, U. Buffalo, 1961; postgrad., Rutgers U., 1978--. Grad. asst. U. Buffalo (N.Y.), 1958-59; English tchr. Buffalo City Bd. Edn., 1959-60; tchr. Matawan (N.J.) Bd. Edn., 1969-70; prof., coord. honors program Brookdale Community Coll., Lincroft, N.J., 1970--; field faculty Goddard Coll., Plainfield, Vt., 1977-78; freelance cons. Matawan, 1970—; speaker Am. Assn. Higher Edn. Author, editor Bayshore Community Hosp. Newsletter, Holmdel, 1968-70. Mem. Nat. Council Tchrs. English, Pi Lambda Theta. Democrat. Hebrew. Office: Brookdale Community Coll 765 Newman Springs Rd Lincroft NJ 07738-1543

SIDEL, VICTOR WILLIAM, social medicine educator; b. Trenton, N.J., July 7, 1931; s. Max and Ida (Ring) S.; m. Ruth Grossman, June 3, 1956; children: Mark, Kevin. AB, Princeton U., 1953; MD, Harvard U., 1957. Intern, then resident in medicine Peter Bent Brigham Hosp., Boston, 1957-62; instr. biophysics Harvard Med. Sch., Boston, 1962-64; head community medicine unit Mass. Gen. Hosp., Boston, 1964-69; chair dept. social medicine Montefiore Med. Ctr., Bronx, N.Y., 1969-84; prof. community health Albert Einstein Coll. Medicine, Bronx, 1969-84, disting. prof. social medicine, 1984—; chair tech. adv. com. Community Childhood Hunger Identification Project, Washington, 1987—. Author: Serve the People, 1973, A Healthy State, 1978, The Health of China, 1982; editor: Reforming Medicine, 1984; mem. editorial bd. PSR Quar., 1990—, Jur. Prison and Jail Health, 1980—, Health and Environ. Digest, 1985—. Member N.Y. State Pub. Health Coun., 1984—. With USPHS, 1959-61. Recipient Poiley award N.Y. Acad. Scis., 1978. Fellow Am. Pub. Health Assn. (pres. 1984-85, award for excellence 1987), Royal Soc. Health; mem. N.Y. Pub. Health Assn. (Biggs award 1986), Pub. Health Assn. N.Y.C. (Emerson award 1990), Assn. Tchrs. of Preventive Medicine (Clark award 1989), Physicians for Social Responsibility (pres. 1987-88), Physicians Forum (pres. 1971-72). Office: Montefiore Med Ctr 111 E 210th St Bronx NY 10467-2490

SIDNAM, CAROLINE NORTHCOTE, architect; b. N.Y.C., June 23, 1952; d. Alan Northcote Sidnam and Shirley Lazo (Steinman) Katzenbach; m. Myer S. Berlow, July 9, 1973 (div. 1975); m. Carl Joseph Pucci, Oct. 15, 1983; children: Emma X, Samuel Northcote. Student, Kenyon Coll., 1970-72; BA, Sarah Lawrence Coll., 1974; BArch, The Cooper Union, 1979. Registered architect, N.Y., N.J. Designer Eisenman Robertson, N.Y.C., 1979-80; prin. Caroline N. Sidnam Design, N.Y.C., 1980-82, Caroline N. Sidnam Architect, N.Y.C., 1982-84; co-owner Sidnam Halsey Architects, N.Y.C., 1984-91, Sidnam Petrone Architects, N.Y.C., 1991—; curator exhibition of women architects AIR Gallery, N.Y.C., 1984. Office: Sidnam Petrone Architects 7 W 22d St 10th Fl New York NY 10011

SIDOR, ELLEN SUTHERLAND, sculptor; b. Concord, Mass., Oct. 26, 1940; d. Charles Woodward and Mary Elizabeth (Frost) Sutherland; m. Reinhard Sidor, Aug. 28, 1968; children: Inga Frost, Anna Leopold. AB, Mt. Holyoke Coll., S. Hadley, Mass., 1962; EdM in Counseling, Boston U., 1967. Reporter Holyoke (Mass.) Transcript/Telegraph, 1963; office mgr./trainee Little Brown & Co., Waltham, Mass., 1964-65; counselor Boston U Counseling Svc., 1967-69; psychologist in pvt. practice Newton, Mass., 1971-73; ptnr. Sidor Vineyards, Gilmanton, N.H., 1973-79; Dharma tchr. Providence Zen Ctr., Cumberland, R.I., 1983—; founding editor Primary Point Press, Cumberland, R.I., 1986-88; editor-in-chief and founding editor Primary Point Kwan Um Sch. of Zen, Cumberland, R.I., 1983-88; copyeditor Providence Jour.-Bull., 1990; founder, tchr. The Meditation Place, Providence, 1985—; sr. Dharma tchr. Kwan Um Sch. Zen, 1988—; co-organizer retreat/workshops Revisioning the Future, 1988; founder Zen Artisans Coop, 1982-85. Author, editor: A Gathering of Spirit, 1987; solo exhbn. Tennyson Gallery, Provincetown, Mass., 1988; group shows include Water St. Gallery, Mystic, Conn., 1988, Hera Ednl. Found., Wakefield, R.I., 1989, Provincetown Art Assn. and Mus., 1989, R.I. Mus. Natural History, 1991, Schoharie Arts Coun., N.Y., 1991, Springfield (Mass.) Art League, 1991, Cape Mus. Fine Arts, Dennis, Mass., 1991; represented in pvt. collections including Zen ctrs., pres. of Portugal. Coun. pres. Temenos Inc., Shutesbury, Mass., 1990—; bd. dirs. Providence Zen Ctr., 1983-87. Mem. New Eng. Sculpture Assn., N.H. Grapegrowers Assn. (sec. 1974-76). Democrat. Buddhist.

SIDOTI, CHRISTOPHER ALEXANDER, lawyer; b. Jersey City, Dec. 26, 1952; s. Anthony J. and Catherine L. (Tomasulo) S.; m. Kathleen Marie Pagley, July 4, 1980; children: Giancarlo, Vincenzo, Cristoforo, Marissa. BA, Rutgers Coll., 1974; JD, Seton Hall U., 1977. Bar: Pa. 1978, N.J. 1979, N.Y. 1990. Atty. trademark office U.S. Dept. Commerce, Washington, 1977-80; attorney trademark office Bristol-Myers Corp., N.Y.C., 1980; lead atty. trademark office U.S. Dept. Commerce, Washington, 1981-88; atty. Mathews, Woodbridge & Collins, Princeton, N.J., 1988—; legal counsel Ellypsis Mag., New Brunswick, N.J., 1991—. Author: Protecting Intellectual Property under N.J. Law, 1989-90. V.p. Young Dems. Club, Rutgers Coll., New Brunswick, 1973-74; pres. Italian Club, Rutgers Coll., 1973-74. Recipient Award of Excellence, Am. Collegiate Theater Festival, 1974. Mem. N.J. State Bar Assn. (entertainment and arts sect. sec. 1989-90, vice chmn. 1990-91, chmn. 1991-93), Am. Bar Assn. (subcom. state trademark chmn. 1990-91), N.Y. Bar Assn., Pa. Bar Assn. Roman Catholic. Office: Mathews Woodbridge and Collins 100 Thanet Cir Ste 306 Princeton NJ 08540

SIDRANSKY, HERSCHEL, pathologist; b. Pensacola, Fla., Oct. 17, 1925; s. Ely and Touba (Bear) S.; m. Evelyn Lipsitz, Aug. 18, 1952; children: Ellen, David Ira. BS, Tulane U., 1948, M.D., 1953, M.S., 1958. Diplomate: Am. Bd. Pathology. Intern Charity Hosp. La., New Orleans, 1953-54; vis. asst. pathologist Charity Hosp. La., 1954-58; practice medicine, specializing in pathology Washington, 1977—; pathologist Nat. Cancer Inst., NIH, Bethesda, Md., 1958-61; instr. pathology Tulane U., 1954-58; prof. pathology U. Pitts., 1961-72; prof., chmn. dept. pathology U. South Fla., Tampa, 1972-77, George Washington U., 1977—; cons. VA Hosp. and Children's Hosp., Washington. Mem. editorial bd. Jour. Nutrition, 1973-77, Cancer Research, 1974-77, Human Pathology, 1979-91, Am. Jour. Clin. Nutrition, 1979-82, Am. Jour. Pathology, 1980-85, Jour. Exptl. Pathology, 1982—, Exptl. Molecular Pathology Jour., 1987—; contbr. articles to profl. jours. Served with AUS, 1944-46. Life Ins. Med. Research fellow, 1956-57; USPHS fellow, 1957-58, 67-68; NIH research grantee, 1961—. Mem. Am. Assn. Pathologists, Soc. Exptl. Biology and Medicine, Am. Assn. Cancer Research, Am. Inst. Nutrition, Am. Soc. Clin. Nutrition, Internat. Acad. Pathologists, Med. Mycology Soc. of Americas, Reticuloendothelial Soc., N.Y. Acad. Scis., AAAS, Washington Acad. Medicine, Washington Soc. Pathologists, Assn. Pathology Chmn., Intersoc. Com. on Pathology Info., Sigma Xi. Home: 5144 Macomb St NW Washington DC 20016-2612 Office: 2300 I St NW Washington DC 20037-2337

SIEBENBERG, HENRY NORMAN, engineering manager; b. Balt., Feb. 24, 1940; s. William annd Ida (Sugan) S.; m. Judy Adler, June 7, 1959; children: Susan, Scott. BS, U. Md., 1961; MS, Renesselaer Poly. Inst., 1964. Registered profl. engr., Md. Engr., analyst Pratt & Whitney Aircraft, East Hartford, Conn., 1961-64; project mgr. Ops. Rsch. Inc., Silver Spring, Md., 1964-69; pvt. practice cons. Silver Spring, 1969-71; sr. staff mem. System Assocs., Inc., Arlington, Va., 1971-72, Doty Assocs., Inc., Rockville, Md., 1972-73; sr. engr. Vitro Labs., Silver Spring, 1973-77; pres. Applied Mgmt. Tech., Inc., Arlington, 1977-87; sr. program mgr. Gen. Scis. Corp., Laurel, Md., 1987-91; div. mgr. Rsch. & Data Systems Corp., Greenbelt, Md., 1991—; co-founder, dir. Image Matrix, Inc., Alexandria, Va., 1981-86. Co-inventor matrix construction for fuel cells. Mem. ASME, AIAA, NSPE, Armed Forces Communications andn Electronics Assn., U.S. Naval Inst., U. Md. Alumni Assn. Office: Rsch & Data Systems Corp 7855 Walker Dr Greenbelt MD 20770-3212

SIEBER, JAMES LEO, mathematics educator; b. New Glasgow, N.S., Can., Nov. 3, 1936; s. H. Wilson Sieber and Mary L. Speer McClure. BS, Shippensburg (Pa.) U., 1958; MA, Pa. State U., 1961, PhD, 1963. Grad. asst. Pa. State U., University Park, 1958-63; asst. prof. Shippensburg U., 1963-65, assoc. prof., 1965-67, dept. chmn. math. and computer sci., 1964-85, prof. math. and computer sci., 1967—. Mem. ACM (chmn. Susquehanna Valley chpt. 1983-84), Cen. Pa. Math. Assn. (pres. 1979-81), Pa. Coun. Tchrs. Math. (exec. com. 1973-74), Gen. Alumni Assn. of Shippensburg U. (pres. 1990-91), Tall Cedars of Lebanon, Masons (33 degree). Republican. Presbyterian. Home: 126 Park Pl Shippensburg PA 17257-9214 Office: Shippensburg U Dept Math and Computer Sci Shippensburg PA 17257

SIEBERT, DONALD ROBERT, physicist, program manager; b. Oak Ridge, Tenn., July 6, 1946; s. Robert Fredrick and Annetta Heisler (Maneval) S.; m. Lynn Ellen Laitman, June 22, 1968; children: Arielle Justine, Asher Benjamin. BS in Gen. Sci., Union Coll., 1968; PhD in Phys. Chemistry, Columbia U., 1973. Rsch. chemist Photon Chemistry Dept. Allied-Signal, Inc., Morristown, N.J., 1978-79, rsch. physicist Electro-Optical Products, 1980-81; project engr. Allied-Signal, Inc., Mt. Bethel, N.J., 1981-82; project leader Apollo Lasers Allied-Signal, Inc., Mt. Bethel, 1982-83; sr. rsch. physicist Allied-Signal Corp. Technology, Morristown, 1983-84, rsch. assoc., program mgr., 1984-90; program mgr. laser systems Guidance Systems Div. Allied-Signal, Inc., Teterboro, N.J., 1990—; cons. in field. Contbr. articles to profl. jours. and chpts. to books. Home: 178 Hillcrest Ave Morristown NJ 07960-5059 Office: Allied-Signal Aerospece Co Bendix Guidance & Control Systems Rte 46 Teterboro NJ 07608

SIEBERT, DOUGLAS KENT, dental management consultant; b. Fresno, Calif., Jan. 27, 1943; s. Menno Walter and Agnes (Klassen) S.; m. Dorothy Lou Kenyon, Mar. 30, 1962 (div. Sept. 1986); children: Sandra LaRee, Daniel Kevin, Douglas James, Kristin Lynn; m. Mary Lee Elkins, Nov. 1, 1986; children: Donna Siebert, Leonard Michael, Aleck Russell, Anthony Joseph, Michael John Warren. BBA, U. Oreg., 1968. CPA, Calif., Oreg., Utah., Ariz., N.H. Owner Douglas K. Siebert Bookkeeping and Tax Svcs., Springfield, Oreg., 1966-68; v.p. Profl. Practice Sales, Inc., Tustin, Calif., 1968-69; owner Douglas K. Siebert, CPA, El Toro, Calif., 1969-73, Salem, Oreg., 1973-80, Laguna Hills, Calif., 1982-84, Provo, Utah, 1984-85, Concord, N.H., 1985-89; pres. Douglas Pacific Corp., Salem, 1980-82, Siebert & Baer, CPAs; founder Doug Siebert Co., Concord, 1989—. Author: Open Wide...This Won't Hurt a Bit!, 1991. Mem. AICPA, Practice Valuation Study Club. Republican. Mem. LDS Ch. Office: Doug Siebert Co PO Box 727 Concord NH 03302-0727

SIEBERT, STEPHEN WARNER, psychiatrist; b. Chicago Heights, Ill., Feb. 14, 1957; s. Warner Holman and Joyce Alair (Johnson) S.; m. Noël Gibson Hardwick, Nov. 21, 1981; children: Warner Hardwick, Stephanie Whelan. BA, Kalamazoo Coll., 1977; MD, Johns Hopkins U., 1981, MPH, 1981. Diplomate Am. Bd. Psychiatry & Neurology. From staff psychiatrist to supt. of psychiatry, chief exec. officer Clifton T. Perkins Hosp., Jessup, Md., 1986-90; med. dir. NeuroPsych Systems, Balt., 1989—; coord. inpatient managed care Sheppard Pratt Hosp., Towson, Md., 1990-91. Mem. AMA, Am. Psychiat. Assn., Am. Acad. of Psychiatry and Law, Phi Beta Kappa, Delta Omega. Democrat. Episcopalian. Home: 5312 Tilbury Way Baltimore MD 21212-3541 Office: NeuroPsych Systems 3901 Greenspring Ave Baltimore MD 21211-1340

SIEFERT-KAZANJIAN, DONNA, corporate librarian; b. N.Y.C.; d. Merrill Emil and Esther (Levins) S.; m. George John Kazanjian, June 15, 1974; 1 child, Merrill George. BA, NYU, 1969; MSLS, Columbia U., 1973; MBA, Fordham U., 1977. Asst. librarian Dun & Bradstreet, N.Y.C., 1969-73; research assoc. William E. Hill & Co., N.Y.C., 1973-76; sr. info. analyst Info. for Bus., N.Y.C., 1976-77; librarian Handy Assocs., N.Y.C., 1979-90; mgr. Infoserve Fuchs Cuthrell & Co., Inc., N.Y.C., 1991—. Mem. Spl. Librs. Assn., Rsch. Roundtable, Am. Mensa Ltd. Roman Catholic. Office: Fuchs Cuthrell & Co Inc 555 Madison Ave Fl 14 New York NY 10022-3301

SIEGEL, ALAN ROGER, association manager, consultant; b. Bklyn., Dec. 22, 1931; s. Leo and Charlotte (Fingerhut) S.; m. Joyce Bernhardt, June 22, 1953; children: Marjorie, Barbara, Adam. BS in Engring., Princeton U., 1953. Aeros. engr. Glenn L. Martin Co., Balt., 1953-62; project mgr. Martin-Marietta, Balt., 1962; aerospace tech. NASA, Washington, 1962-69; dir. govt. rsch. U.S. Dept. Housing and Urban Devel., Washington, 1969-83; pres. Al Siegel Assocs., Bethesda, Md., 1983—; exec. sec. Nat. Assn. County Adminstrs., Bethesda, Md., 1987—. Co-author: Let's Eat Out in Montgomery County, 1987, 90; author pub. fire protection coll. courses, 1990. Comme. Fire & Rescue Commn., Monrgomery County, Md., 1991—; bd. dirs. Citizens for Quality Civilization, Bethesda, 1991. Mem. ASPA (Stone award 1979), ICMA. Office: Al Siegel Assocs PO Box 34667 Bethesda MD 20827

SIEGEL, ERIKA JANET, graphic designer; b. N.Y.C., Apr. 26, 1962; d. Joel Robert and Anne (Shuttleworth) S. AB in Art History with distinction, Swarthmore Coll., 1984. Asst. Galerie St. Etienne, N.Y.C., 1984-86; asst. art dir. Promotion Solutions, N.Y.C., 1986-87; designer Corp. Graphics, Inc, N.Y.C., 1987-89, Lintas Mktg. Communications, N.Y.C., 1989-91; sr. designer Sparkman & Assocs., Washington, 1991—. Recipient award Am. Inst. Graphic Arts, Type Dirs. Club. Mem. Phi Beta Kappa.

SIEGEL, FRED, management consultant; b. Gloversville, N.Y., Apr. 17, 1941; s. Leon and Sarah (Madora) S. BS, L.I. U., 1970. Asst. to mayor City of N.Y., 1968-74; recruitment mgr. Arthur Young & Co., N.Y.C., 1974-76; assoc. dean Grad. Sch. Bus. NYU, 1976-80; ptnr. Consulting Assocs., Inc., N.Y.C., 1980-88; pres. Conex, Inc., N.Y.C., 1988—; mem. acctg. program adv. coun. N.Y.C. Tech. Coll., Bklyn., 1980-88; mem. pres.' adv. coun. Fgn. Policy Assn., N.Y.C., 1988-91; mem. Jan Peerce Found. Bd. With USAF, 1961-65. Mem. Assn. for Better N.Y. Office: Conex Inc 919 3d Ave New York NY 10022

SIEGEL, GEORGE LEWIS, endocrinologist; b. Bklyn., June 2, 1934; s. Harry and Bertha (Safier) S.; m. Jean Gellis, May 29, 1964; children: Robert, Steven, Laura. AB, Colgate U., 1955; MD, Albany Med. Coll., 1959. Diplomate Am. Bd. Internal Medicine, Am. Bd. Endocrinology and Metabolism. Asst. clin. prof. Hahneman Sch. of Medicine, Phila., 1968-71, Mt. Sinai Sch. Medicine, N.Y.C., 1971—; attending physician of endocrinology Beth Israel Med. Ctr., N.Y.C., 1971—; chief endocrinology sect. Beth Israel North, N.Y.C., 1989—. Contbr. articles to profl. jours. Capt. med. corps., U. S. Armyu, 1966-68. Mem. ACP, Endocrine Soc., N.Y. County Med. Soc., Am. Diabetes Assn., Clin. Diabetes Soc. N.Y., Am. Fedn. Clin. Rsch., N.Y. Acad. Scis., Am. Assn. Clin. Endocrinologists. Home: 40 E 80th St New York NY 10021 Office: 240 E 82nd St New York NY 10028

SIEGEL, GLENN ERNEST, lawyer; b. Bklyn., May 31, 1958; s. Stanley Gerald and Emily Marsha (Levenson) S.; m. Sandra Goyeneche, June 14, 1987. BA, Bklyn. Coll., 1979; JD, Boston U., 1982; LLM, NYU, 1984. Bar: Mass. 1982, N.Y. 1983, N.J. 1983. Assoc. Horwitz & Assocs., N.Y.C., 1982-84; assoc. Glass & Howard, N.Y.C., 1984-86; assoc. Shea & Gould, N.Y.C., 1986-91; assoc. Winthrop, Stimson, Putnam & Roberts, N.Y.C., 1991—. Mem. ABA, N.Y. State Bar Assn., Mass. Bar Assn., Bankruptcy Lawyers Bar Assn., Am. Bankruptcy Inst. Democrat. Jewish. Office: Winthrop Stimson et al One Battery Park Pla New York NY 10004-1490

SIEGEL, HERBERT JAY, communications executive; b. Phila., May 7, 1928; s. Jacob and Fritzi (Stern) S.; m. Ann F. Levy, June 29, 1950; children: John C., William D. B.A., Lehigh U., 1950. Sec., dir. Official Films, Inc., N.Y.C., 1950-55; v.p., dir. Bev-Rich Products, Inc., Phila., 1955-56, Westley Industries, Inc., Cleve., 1955-58, Phila. Ice Hockey Club, Inc., 1955-60; chmn. bd. Fort Pitt Industries, Inc., Pitts., 1956-58, Seeburg Corp., 1958-60, Centlivre Brewing Corp., Ft. Wayne, Ind., 1960-67, Baldwin-Montrose Chem. Co., 1960-67; chmn. United TV, Inc., 1982—, chief exec. officer, 1983—; pres. Gen. Artists Corp., 1963-65; chmn. bd., pres. Chris-Craft Industries, Inc., 1967—; dir. Baldwin Rubber Co., Pontiac, Mich., Mono-Sol Corp., Gary, Inc., Piper Aircraft Corp., 1967-77; Warner Communications, Inc., 1984-89; chmn. bd., pres. BHC Communications Inc., 1977—, United TV Inc, 1982—; bd. dirs. Paramount Pictures, 1963-64. Bd. dirs. Phoenix House, 1978-81, United TV, Inc., 1981—; bd. advisors Vets. Bedside Network, 1980—; v.p. Friars Nat. Assn. Found., 1980—; trustee Lehigh U., Blair Acad., 1985. Club: Friars. Home: 190 E 72nd St New York NY 10021-4370 Office: Chris-Craft Industries Inc 600 Madison Ave New York NY 10022-1615

SIEGEL, IRA THEODORE, publishing executive; b. N.Y.C., Sept. 23, 1944; s. David Aaron and Rose (Minsky) S.; m. Sharon Ruth Sacks, Sept. 5, 1965; children: Melissa Ann, Allison Kim, Jessica Fay. BS, NYU, 1965; MBA, L.I. U., 1968. Bus. mgr. Buttenheim Pub. Co., N.Y.C., 1965-72; corp. v.p. rsch. Cahners Pub. Co. div. Reed Pub. USA, Boston, 1972-86; pres. R.R. Bowker Pub. Co. div. Reed Pub. USA, New Providence, N.J., 1986-91, Martindale-Hubbell div. Reed Pub. USA, New Providence, N.J., 1990-91, Reed Reference Pub. (includes R.R. Bowker Co., Martindale-Hubbell, Nat. Register Pub. Co., The Salesman's Guide, Marquis Who's Who), New Providence, N.J., 1991—. Mem. Am. Mktg. Assn., Am. Mgmt. Assn., ALA, Am. Booksellers Assn., Info. Industry Assn. Democrat. Jewish. Office: Reed Reference Pub 121 Chanlon Rd New Providence NJ 07974-1544

SIEGEL, JEFF K., financial analyst; b. Washington, Dec. 11, 1958; s. Stanley Ernest and Mildred S. BS in Indsl. Enging., Va. Poly. Inst., 1981; MBA in Fin., George Washington U., 1987. Indsl. engr. Koppers Co., Balt., 1981-82; electric system engr. Potomac Electric Power Co., Washington, 1982-86; retail, restaurant, hotel/gaming equity analyst Donaldson, Lufkin, & Jenrette, Pershing Div., N.Y.C., 1987-88, McManus and Miles, N.Y.C., 1989-90, Georgeson and Co., N.Y.C., 1990, Arcus/Dataport Co., N.Y.C., 1990—. Bd. dirs. Terrace Townhouses of Beverly Hills, Alexandria, Va., 1985-87; vol. algebra tutor Higher Achievement Program, Washington; vol. Referral Ctr., N.Y.C. Mem. Am. Inst. Indsl. Engrs., Am. Assn. Individual Investors, Merchandising Analysts Group. Clubs: Va. Tech. Alumni Assn. (N.Y.C. chpt.), George Washington U. Alumni Assn. (N.Y.C. chpt.), Walker Pk. Tennis Club. Avocations: tennis, physical fitness, various other athletics, chess, investing. Home: 4 Lincoln Ave Staten Island NY 10306-2437 Office: World Trade Ctr 302 Concourse Level New York NY 10048

SIEGEL, JEREMY JAMES, finance educator, consultant; b. Chgo., Nov. 14, 1945; s. Bernard G. and Gertrude (Levitt) S.; m. Ellen Ruth Schwartz, Jan. 14, 1980; children: Andrew M., Jeffrey Eric. BA, Columbia U., 1967; PhD, MIT, 1971. Asst. prof. bus. econs. Grad. Sch. Bus. U. Chgo., 1972-76; assoc. prof. fin. Wharton Sch. U. Pa., Phila., 1976-86, prof. fin. Wharton Sch., 1986—; macroecons. coord. The Morgan Bank, N.Y.C., 1984—. Contbr. numerous articles to profl. jours. NSF fellow, 1971-72, NSF grantee, 1983-86. Mem. Am. Econ. Assn., Am. Fin. Assn. Office: U Pa Wharton Sch Dept Fin Philadelphia PA 19104

SIEGEL, JEROME HAROLD, internist, gastroenterologist; b. Atlanta, Mar. 2, 1932; s. Isadore Meyer and Eva Dell (Felson) S.; m. Beverly, Dec. 19, 1955; children: Dori Gayle, Brian David. BS in Pharmacy, Mercer U., 1954; BS in Chemistry, U. Ga., 1956; MD, Med. Coll. of Ga., 1960. Diplomate Am. Bd. Internal Medicine and Gastroenterolgy. Intern Allentown (Pa.) Hosp., 1960-61; asst. resident VA Hosp., Bronx, N.Y., 1963-64, resident, 1964-65, chief resident gastroenterology, 1965-66; physician pvt. practice Atlanta, 1966-73; vol. prof. N.Y. Med. Coll., N.Y.C., 1975-79, Mt. Sinai Sch. Medicine, CUNY, N.Y.C., 1979—; chief gastroenterology St. Clare's Hosp., N.Y.C., 1981-86, Doctors Hosp., N.Y.C., 1986-89; chief endoscopy Beth Israel Hosp. North, N.Y.C., 1989—. Contbr. over 80 abstracts and 73 sci. articles to profl. jours.; author: Endoscopic Retrograde Cholangiopangreatography. Capt. USAF, 1961-63. Fellow Am. Coll. Physicians, Am. Coll. Gastroenterology (chmn. com. 1987-89), N.Y. Acad. Medicine, N.Y. Acad. Scis.; mem. AAAS, Am. Soc. Gastrointestinal Endoscopy (editorial bd. 1981-85), Am. Gastroenterological Assn., N.Y. Soc. Gastrointestinal Endocsopy (pres. 1981-82). Democrat. Jewish. Office: 60 East End Ave New York NY 10028

SIEGEL, JEROME SAMUEL, trucking company executive; b. Newark, Dec. 16, 1944; s. Harry Charles and Pauline Ruth (Schwartz) S.;m. Janet Iris Lukes, Oct. 18, 1975; children: Laura Anne, Jason Henry. BS in Hotel Adminstrn., Cornell U., 1967; MS in Bus., Am. U., Washington, 1971. Co-owner Whitby's Restaurant, Washington, 1969-73; v.p. Siegel & Cohen Express, Newark, 1973-78; co-owner Halo Optical Products, Inc., Johnstown, N.Y., 1978-84; owner, founder SLA Transport, Inc., Gloversville, N.Y., 1981—. Bd. dirs. Jewish Community Ctr., Gloversville, 1982—, Promote Gloversville Devel. Corp., 1986—. Mem. Fulton County C. of C. (dir. 1983—, pres. 1992—), Eccentric Club. Republican. Jewish. Office: SLA Transport Inc PO Box 993 Gloversville NY 12078-0993

SIEGEL, LAWRENCE J., university administrator, development professional; b. Bklyn., June 18, 1943; s. Max and Etta Vivian (Horowitz) S.; m. Patricia Carol Minikes, Feb. 5, 1972; children: Laura, Karen. BS, Cornell U., 1964; MBA, Columbia U., 1969, JD, 1969. Bar: N.Y. 1969. Atty. firm Aranow, Brodsky, Bohlinger, Einhorn & Dann, N.Y.C., 1969-70; asst. dir. employment svcs., human resources adminstrn. City of N.Y., 1971-77; program officer Edna McConnell Clark Found., N.Y.C., 1977-79; dir. Inst. for Consumer Policy Rsch. Consumers Union, Mt. Vernon, N.Y., 1979-82; dir. nat. field ops. Am. Jewish Congress, N.Y.C., 1982-86; exec. dir. Stony Brook (N.Y.) Found. Realty, Inc., 1987-90; devel. dir. Sch. Edn., Health, Nursing and Arts Professions NYU, N.Y.C., 1990—. Editor: Home Energy Conservation: Strategies for the 1980s, 1981; editor nat. newsletter Advance Notice, 1980-82; editor various policy studies on domestic issues. Mem. Temple Beth-El Brotherhood, Phi Kappa Phi. Jewish. Home: 23 South Dr Great Neck NY 11021-1959 Office: NYU Devel Office 25 W 4th St New York NY 10012-1199

SIEGEL, MARVIN IRA, pharmaceutical executive; b. Bklyn., July 11, 1946; s. Morris and Ray Norma (Goldman) S.; m. Frances L. Greenstein, Nov. 20, 1970 (div. Aug. 1983); 1 child, Deborah Genevieve; m. Debra F. Miller, Dec. 29, 1987; 1 child, Rachel Leigh. BS in Chemistry magna cum laude, Lafayette Coll., 1967; MA in Chemistry, Columbia U., 1968; PhD in Physiol. Chemistry, Johns Hopkins U., 1973. Postdoctoral fellow Sch. of Medicine Johns Hopkins U., Balt., 1973-75; rsch. scientist Burroughs Wellcome Co., Research Triangle Park, N.C., 1975-82; assoc. dir. biol. rsch. Schering Plough Co., Bloomfield, N.J., 1982-84, dir. biol. rsch., 1985-88, sr. dir. biol. rsch., 1988-92; v.p. Schering Plough Rsch. Inst., Bloomfield, 1992—; adj. asst. prof. U. N.C. Sch. Medicine, Chapel Hill, 1976-81, adj. assoc. prof., 1982; adj. prof. Rutgers U., Newark, 1987—. Contbr. articles to profl. jours.; patentee in field. Columbia U. fellow, 1967-68, NIH fellow, 1973-75. Mem. Am. Acad. Allergy and Immunology, Am. Chem. Soc., Am. Soc. Biochemistry and Molecular Biology, Am. Assn. Immunology, Am. Soc. Pharmacology and Exptl. Therapeutics, Am. Inst. Chemists, Info. Rsch. Assn., Soc. for Leukocyte Biology, N.Y. Acad. Scis. Office: Schering Plough Rsch Inst 60 Orange St Bloomfield NJ 07003-4795

SIEGEL, MARY-ELLEN, social worker, psychotherapist, author; b. N.Y.C., Feb. 12, 1932; d. Monroe E. and Miriam (Baum) Greenberger; m. Edgar Kulkin, Nov. 4, 1951 (div. 1978); children: Betsy Kulkin Baldwin, Peter, Vicki Kulkin Beckerman; m. Walter Siegel, Aug. 24, 1980. BS, CUNY, 1974; MSW, Columbia U., 1976. Lic. social worker, N.Y. Pvt. practice N.Y.C., 1978—; social worker Mt. Sinai Hosp., N.Y.C., 1976-82; lectr. dept. community medicine Mt. Sinai Sch. Medicine, N.Y.C., 1983—; cons. Chemotherapy Found., N.Y.C., 1978—; bd. dirs. Found. of Thanatology, N.Y.C. Author, co-author: Her Way, revised edit., 1984, More than a Friend: Dogs with a Purpose, 1984, Reversing Hair Loss, 1985, The Cancer Patient's Handbook, 1986, The Nanny Connection, 1987, Finger Tips, 1988, Dr. Greenberger's What Every Man Should Know About His Prostate, 1989, Safe in the Sun, 1990, Behind the 8-Ball, 1992; editorial bd. numerous jours. Mem. NASW, Nat. Assn. Pvt. Geriatric Care Mgrs., Nat. Assn. Oncology Social Workers, Am. Soc. Journalists and Authors, Am. Med. Writers Assn., Authors Guild. Home and Office: 75-68 195th Fresh Meadows NY 11366

SIEGEL, MICHAEL ERIC, judicial center official; b. Newark, June 1, 1950; s. Aaron and Mindy (Schulman) S.; m. Anne Paula Solotar, Nov. 11, 1984; 1 child, Sophie Elaine. BA, Am. U., 1972; MA, Tufts U., 1975, PhD, 1976. Asst. prof. govt. U. Va., Wise, 1977-78; asst. prof. govt. Am. U., Washington, 1978-82, dir. credit programs and continuing edn., 1982-84; coordinator faculty devel. U. Md., College Park, 1984-87, asst. dean faculty devel., 1987-88; sr. tng. specialist div. ct. edn. and tng. Fed. Jud. Ctr., Washington, 1988—; cons. Council of Ind. Colls., Washington, 1986-87, Am. Coll. of Cardiology, Bethesda, Md., 1986-87, Loyola U., Balt., 1987—. Contbr. articles to profl. jours. Chmn. commn. on internat. affairs Am. Jewish Congress, Washington, 1985—. Recipient Teaching Excellence award U. Tex., 1985. Mem. Nat. U. Continuing Edn. Assn. (sec. region II 1986-87), Am. Polit. Sci. Assn. Democrat. Home: 10500 Rockville Pike Apt 702 Rockville MD 20852-3342 Office: Fed Jud Ctr Div Court Edn and Tng 1520 H St NW Washington DC 20005-1003

SIEGEL, NORMAN JOSEPH, pediatrician, educator; b. Houston, Mar. 8, 1943; m. Rise Joan Ross, Dec. 24, 1967; children: Andrew, Karen. BA, Tulane U., 1964; MA, U. Tex. Med. Br., Galveston, 1968, MD, 1968. Intern, then resident Yale-New Haven Hosp., 1968-70; fellow Sch. Medicine, Yale U., New Haven, 1970-72, asst. prof. pediatrics and medicine, 1972-76, assoc. prof., 1976-82, prof., 1982—, vice chmn. pediatrics, 1979—; chmn. rsch. awards com. Hood Found., Boston, 1986-88. Contbr. articles to profl. jours., chpts. to books. Grantee NIH, Am. Heart Assn., Hood Found. Mem. Am. Pediatric Soc., Am. Soc. Clin. Investigation, Am. Soc. Pediatric Nephrology (pres. 1988-89), Nat. Kidney Found. (chmn. con. on pediatric nephrology and urology 1987-91, grantee), Soc. Pediatric Rsch. (membership sec. 1979-85), Phi Beta Kappa, Mu Delta. Office: Yale U Sch Medicine Dept Pediatrics 333 Cedar St New Haven CT 06510-3289

SIEGEL, RICHARD A., foundation executive; b. Pitts., Aug. 2, 1947; s. Ralph R. and Frieda S. (Stein) S.; m. Jeanne Bakst, July 1, 1979; children: Andrew, Ruth. BA, Brandeis U., 1969, MA, 1972; MA, Jewish Theol. Sem., 1974. Dir. B'nai B'rith Hillel Found. SUNY, Stony Brook, 1974-78; assoc. dir. Nat. Found. for Jewish Culture, N.Y.C., 1978-89, exec. dir., 1989—. Co-editor: The Jewish Catalog, 1973, The Jewish Almanac, 1981. Office: Nat Found Jewish Culture 330 7th Ave Fl 2 New York NY 10001-5010

SIEGEL, RICHARD ALLEN, economist; b. Chgo., Mar. 11, 1927; s. Mandel Irving and Mary Marsha (Shulman) S.; m. Shirley Platin, Dec. 17, 1950 (dec. 1980); children: Joel, Robert, Peter; m. Rosalyn Sandra Miller, June 28, 1981. AB, UCLA, 1953, MBA, 1959, PhD, 1961. Asst. prof. econs. SUNY, Buffalo, 1962-64; economist Bank of Am., San Francisco, 1964-66, Calif. Dept. Fin., Sacramento, 1967-68, Arthur D. Little, Inc., Cambridge, Mass., 1968-70; pres., economist Richard Siegel Assocs., Boston, 1970-79; prin., economist Econ. Research Assocs., Boston, 1979-83; pres., economist Applied Econs., Inc., Boston, 1983—. Contbr. articles to profl. jours. Served with USN, 1945-46, PTO. Jewish. Club: Appalachian Mountain (chmn. Boston chpt. 1983-84). Office: Applied Econs Inc 2 Liberty Sq Boston MA 02109-4867

SIEGEL, RITASUE, business owner; b. Bklyn.; d. Ruban Louis and Blanche (Weintraub) Bernstein. B of Indsl. Design, Pratt Inst., Bklyn., 1961, M of Indsl. Design, 1963. Dir. placement Pratt Inst., 1961-69; chmn. RitaSue Siegel Assocs, Inc., N.Y.C., 1969—; instr. Pratt Inst., 1962-69; bd. dirs. Design Mgmt. Inst., Boston, Design Coun., San Francisco; juror I.D.E.A. Awards, Alexandria, Va., N.Y.C., 1992. Author: American Graphic Design, 1985; contbr. articles to profl. jours. Mem. Am. Inst. Graphic Design, Indsl. Designers Soc. Am., Soc. Environ. Graphic Design. Office: Rita Sue Siegel Assocs 18 E 48th St New York NY 10017

SIEGEL, ROBERT, broadcaster. Grad., Columbia U., 1968. Reporter, host, dir. news and pub. affairs Sta. WRVR Radio, N.Y.C., 1971-76; assoc. producer Nat. Pub. Radio, 1976-77, pub. affairs editor, 1977-78, sr. editor, 1978-83; dir. news and info. dept. Nat. Pub. Radio, Washington, 1983-87; host All Things Considered evening newsmag. Western and Ea. Europe and Israel Nat. Pub. Radio, 1987—; morning newsman, telephone talk show host Sta. WGLI Radio Babylon, N.Y. Recipient Alfred I. duPont-Columbia U. award for excellence in broadcast journalism, 1984, Nat. Mental Health Assn.'s Mental Health award 1991. Office: Nat Pub Radio 2025 M St Washington DC 20036*

SIEGEL, SCOTT ADAM, biochemist; b. Bronx, N.Y., Jan. 27, 1957; s. Morton J. and Marilyn S. (Helfman) S.; m. Sandra H. Rosovsky, Aug. 5, 1979; children: Justin Ian, Daniel Jared. BS in Biology, SUNY, New Paltz, 1978; PhD in Biochemistry, Downstate Med. Ctr., 1982. Postdoctoral fellow Yale U. Sch. Medicine, New Haven, 1982-85; scientist and project leader Becton Dickinson & Co., Rsch. Triangle Pk., N.C., 1985-88; sr. rsch. scientist Centocor, Inc., Malvern, Pa., 1988-89, asst. dir., 1989-90, assoc. dir., 1990—; adj. assoc. prof. U. Pa. Sch. Dental Medicine Dept. Microbiology, Phila., 1989—. Contbr. articles to profl. jours. Bd. mem. Newton Parish Homeowners Assn., Raleigh, N.C., 1986, Beth Meyer Synagogue, Raleigh, N.C., 1988. Recipient Nat. Cancer Inst. fellowship, 1985. Mem. N.Y. Acad. Sci., Am. Soc. for Microbiology. Democrat. Jewish. Office: Centocor Inc 200 Gt Valley Pkwy Malvern PA 19355

SIEGEL, SEYMOUR LOUIS, assistant principal; b. N.Y.C., May 23, 1933; s. Sol and Helen (Gorfinkel) S.; m. Aug. 17, 1980. BA in History, CCNY, 1954, MA in Internat. Rels., 1957. Tchr. social studies and math. Niles Jr. High Sch., Bronx, 1954-60; tchr. social studies, student govt. advisor Walton High Sch., Bronx, 1960-67; asst. prin. Charles R. Drew Intermediate Sch., Bronx, 1967-68, Michelangelo Intermediate Sch., Bronx, 1968-87, Intermediate Sch. 180, Bronx, 1987-90; asst. examiner Bd. of Examiners, Bd. of Edn. City of N.Y.; mem. social studies com. Dist. 11, Bronx; presenter 5 consecutive ann. cons. Law, Youth and Citizenship Program, N.Y. State Dept. Edn., N.Y. State Bar Assn. and N.Y. State Bd. Edn. Author introductory chpt. in A Handbook for the Teaching of Social Studies, 1977, Social Science Record, vol. IX, 1972; contbr. articles to profl. jours. Mem. Nat. Assn. Secondary Sch. Prins., N.Y. Acad. Pub. Edn. Democrat. Jewish. Home: 3777 Independence Ave Apt 12G Bronx NY 10463-1409

SIEGEL, THOMAS JOSEPH, marketing executive; b. Erie, Pa., Feb. 17, 1935; s. James Edward and Marie Amelia (Will) S.; m. Karen Ann Shaffer, Nov. 2, 1958; children: Michael, Stacey. BS in Acctg., Gannon U., 1960. Telegrapher N.Y. Cen. R.R., Erie, 1952-55, dispatcher, 1956-61; cost analyst Bessemer & Lake Erie R.R., Pitts., 1961-64; mgr. pricing Duluth (Minn.) Missabe & Iron Range Rwy., 1965-66; dir. mktg. Elgin, Joliet & Eastern Rwy., Chgo., 1967-76; v.p. mktg. BLE, DMIR, EJ & E, Monroeville, Pa., 1977-88, Transtar, Monroeville, 1989—. 1st lt. U.S. Army, 1960. Office: Transtar 135 Jamison Ln Monroeville PA 15146-2330

SIEGERT, BARBARA (MARIE), health care administrator; b. Boston, May 22, 1935; d. Salvatore Mario and Mary Kathleen (Wagner) Tartaglia; m. Herbert C. Siegert (dec. Apr. 1974); children: Carolyn Marie, Herbert Christian Jr. Diploma, Newton-Wellesley (Mass.) Hosp. Sch. Nursing, 1956; MEd, Antioch U., 1980. Diplomate Am. Bd. Med. Psychotherapists. Supr. nursing Hogan Regional Ctr., Hathorne, Mass., 1974-78; community mental health nursing advisor Cape Ann area office Dept. Mental Health, Beverly, Mass., 1978-79; dir. case mgmt. Dept. Mental Health, Beverly, 1979-87, dir. case mgmt. north shore area office, 1988-91; dir. case mgmt. Dept. Mental Health-north shore area-Lynn (Mass.) site, Lynn, Mass., 1991-92; mem. interdisciplinary faculty, profl. cons. com., lecture staff clin. pastoral counseling program Danvers State Hosp./Hogan/Berry Regional Ctrs., Hathorne, Mass., 1982-86; nursing edn. adv. com. North Shore Community Coll., Beverly, 1983-91; tng. staff Balter Inst., Ipswich, Mass., 1987-88. Mem. Internat. Cultural Diploma Honor, 1989—. Recipient Spl. Recognition award Lexington (Mass.) Pub. Schs., 1973, Peter Torci award Lexington Friends of Children in Spl. Edn., 1974; named Internat. Biog. Roll. of Honor, 1989—. Fellow Am. Biog. Inst. (life, Woman of Yr. 1990); mem. ANA, Mass. Nurses Assn., World Inst. Achievement. Home: 63 Willow Rd # B Boxford MA 01921-1218

SIEGLER, MORTON ABRAHAM, real estate and construction company executive; b. Jersey City, N.J., Nov. 24, 1922; s. George and Freda (Steierman) S.; m. Carol B. Shapiro, Nov. 26, 1947; children: Jan Ellen Siegler Kliger, Kim Laurie Siegler Schaffer, Meg Allison Siegler Callahan. B of Civil Engring., Cornell U., 1944. Instr. civil engring. Cornell U., Ithaca, 1946-47; v.p. George Siegler Co., 1947-64, pres., chief exec. officer, 1978-86; pres. Siegler Constrn. Co., 1964-74; prin. Morton A. Siegler Assocs., Hopatcong, N.J., 1975—; dir. N.J. State Div. Bldg. and Constrn., Trenton, 1982-83; chmn. N.J. State Bldg. Authority, Trenton, 1983-88; pres. Mid Ea. Funding, Ltd., 1964-74; dir. Three D Depts. Vice chmn. bd. trustees St. Barnabas Med. Ctr., N.J.; past chmn. bd. trustees Essex County Coll., Newark. 1st lt. U.S. Army, 1943-46. Mem. Am. Soc. Real Estate Counselors (lic. real estate broker), Mountain Ridge C. of C. (bd. govs.), Met. Pres. Orgn., World Pres. Orgn. Home: Elba Pointe Hopatcong NJ 07843 Office: 19 Elba Ave Hopatcong NJ 07843-1866

SIEGMUND, WALTER PAUL, optics scientist, consultant; b. Bremen, Germany, Aug. 26, 1925; came to U.S., 1930; s. Heinrich Oskar and Meta Louise (Osmers) S.; m. Lois Schramm, June 29, 1950; children: Paul, Lisa, Kurt. AB, U. Rochester, 1945, PhD, 1952. Sci. aide Am. Optical Co., Southbridge, Mass., 1952-58, asst. dir. rsch., 1958-64, tech. mgr. fiber optics, 1964-86; dir. R & D, Schott Fiber Optics, Southbridge, 1986-91, chief scientist, 1991—. Over 50 patents in field. With USNR, 1944-45. Fellow Soc. Photo-Optical Instrumentation Engrs. (Karl Fairbanks award 1970); mem. Optical Soc. Am. (David Richardson medal 1977), Phi Beta Kappa. Home: 31 Cassidy Rd Pomfret Center CT 06259-1400 Office: Schott Fiber Optics 122 Charlton St Southbridge MA 01550-1960

SIEH, DAVID HENRY, pharmaceutical chemist; b. Columbus, Nebr., Aug. 21, 1947. BS, U. Nebr., 1969, PhD, 1979. Chemist Frederick (Md.) Cancer Rsch. Ctr., 1979-81; rsch. investigator Squibb Pharm. Co., New Brunswick, N.J., 1981-86, sr. rsch. investigator, 1986-88, group leader, 1988-90; assoc. dir. Bristol-Myers Squibb, New Brunswick, 1990—. Contbr. articles to Jour. Analytical Chemistry, Jour. Pharm. Sci., Jour. Am. Chem. Soc., Mutation Rsch.; author: (with others) Analytical Profiles of Drug Substances, 1982, 89. Staff sgt. USAF, 1969-73. Mem. Am. Assn. Pharm. Sci., Am. Chem. Soc. Mem. United Ch. of Christ. Home: 36 Coachlight Dr Chatham NJ 07928-1790 Office: Bristol Myers Squibb One Squibb Dr New Brunswick NJ 08903-0191

SIEKMANN, FRANK HERMAN, musician; b. Staten Island, N.Y., June 20, 1925; s. Emil and Emma (Blum) S.; m. Doris May Pelletier, Nov. 4, 1950; children: Ellen Claire, Bruce Frank, Matthew Emil. BS, NYU, 1948, MA, 1949; EdD, Columbia U., 1959. Instr. music Smyrna (Del.) schs., 1949-52; instr. music Ramsey (N.Y.) schs., 1952-54, Chappaqua (N.Y.) schs., 1954-64; asst. prof. music U. Vt., Burlington, 1964-65; prof. music Kutztown (Pa.) U., 1966-90; pvt. practice Kutztown, 1990—; pres. Reading (Pa.) Pops Orch., 1987—. Composer Concerto Bass Trombone, 1983, Scenes of the Mind, 1987, Triunity for Strings, 1989, Richmond Concerto, 1991. Bd. dirs. Reading Musical Found., 1987; mem. Berks Camera Club, 1977—; commencement speaker Kutztown State Coll., 1971. Petty Officer 1st class USNR, 1943-46, PTO. Recipient Kutztown State Coll. Exceptional Acad. Svc. award, 1980. Mem. ASCAP. Republican. Mem. United Ch. of Christ. Home and Office: 241 Kohler Rd Kutztown PA 19530-9639

SIEMANKOWSKI, FRANCIS THEODORE, geology educator; b. Buffalo, Nov. 12, 1914; s. Frank and Rose (Rusinski) S.; m. Stephanie Theresa Zajaczek, May 16, 1942; children: Raymond, Michael. BS, Buffalo State Tchrs. Coll., 1939; MEd, U. Buffalo, 1950; EdD, SUNY, Buffalo, 1970. Cert. secondary tchr., N.Y. Sci., English tchr. Sloan (N.Y.) High Sch., 1939-41; sci. tchr. J.F. Kennedy High Sch., Cheektowaga, N.Y., 1946-63; coord. East European and Slavic studies program State U. Coll., Buffalo, 1974-79, prof. dept. geoscience, physics, interdisciplinary sci., 1964-79, prof. emeritus, 1979—; cons. U.S. Tchr. Corps, Buffalo, 1971-73, U.S. Peace Corp, Afghanistan Sci. program, Buffalo, 1971-73, Individualized Instrn., Buffalo, 1970-79. Author: College Geology Textbook, 1976, Study Guide to College Geology, 1976, Physical Geology Laboratory Manual, 1971; contbr. articles to profl. jours. Pres. St. Vincent de Paul Soc., 1960-65. Capt. U.S. Army, 1941-45. Recipient L'Ordre Du Merite Culturel, Ministry of Culture, Warsaw, Poland, 1975. Mem. Nat. Assn. Geology Tchrs., N.Y. Acad. Sci, Polish Am. Hist. Assn., Polish Inst. Arts and Scis. in Am., Kosciuszko Found. Western N.Y. (dir. 1990), Phi Delta Kappa (pres. 1962). Democrat. Roman Catholic. Home: 50 Cayuga Creek Rd Buffalo NY 14227-1704

SIENER, WILLIAM HAROLD, museum director, historian, consultant; b. Silver Creek, N.Y., Feb. 24, 1945; s. Harold Edwin and Christian (Dovesmith) S.; m. Estelle Minervino, Dec. 27, 1968; children: Alison Louise, Christian Dovesmith, Geoffrey David. AB, U. Rochester, 1967; MAT, U. Chgo., 1970; MA, U. Southampton, Eng., 1973; PhD, College William & Mary, 1982. Cert. social studies tchr., N.Y. Tchr. Cen. YMCA High Sch., Chgo., 1968-71; dir. youth svcs. City of Niagara Falls (N.Y.) Youth Bd., 1973; historian Gloucester County (Va.) Hist. Bicentennial Com., 1976; exec. dir. Wyo. Hist. and Geol. Soc., Wilkes-Barre, Pa., 1976-82; curator of history Rochester (N.Y.) Mus. and Sci. Ctr., 1982-86; exec. dir. Buffalo and Erie County (N.Y.) Hist. Soc., 1986—; curator various gallery exhibits, 1976—; mem. adv. bds. Pa. State Hist. Records, 1982, Documentary Heritage Program, Buffalo, 1986—; adj. assoc. prof. Dept. History Buffalo State Coll., 1987—; historian County of Erie, Buffalo, 1988—; cons. Arts Devel. Svcs., Buffalo, 1983, OAS, The Bahamas, 1984, 85, St. Lucia, 1985, 89; mem. Buffalo Preservation Bd., 1986—. Author: (brochure) Silent Sentinel of the Shallow Seas, 1988; (catalog) The Lake Erie Shore: Views from Across the Border; co-author: (exhibit catolog) Children and Their Samplers, 1790-1850, 1983; co-editor: (manuscript guide) A Guide to Gloucester County Virginia, Historical Manuscripts, 1650-1865, 1976.; book and exhibit reviewer profl. jours., 1981—. Mem. Leadership Buffalo, 1991, Buffalo Preservation Bd., 1986-91; clk. of session Westminster Presbyn. Ch., Buffalo, 1991—. Mem. Am. Assn. Mus. (panel mem. 1985), Mid-Atlantic Assn. Mus. (chmn. internat. com. 1987-88), Am. Assn. for State and Local History, Nat. Trust for Hist. Preservation, Inst. Early Am. History and Culture (assoc.), Mid-Atlantic Assn. Mus's (vice-chmn. small mus. com. 1981-82, panel mem. 1982), Rotary. Democrat. Home: 264 Middlesex Rd Buffalo NY 14216-3118 Office: Buffalo/Erie County Hist Soc 25 Nottingham Ct Buffalo NY 14216-3199

SIENICKI, DENNIS J., secondary education educator; b. Passaic, N.J., Feb. 22, 1949; s. Henry F. Sienicki and Lillian (Legath) Spengler; m. Darlene Lois Dempsey, Apr. 3, 1971; children: Dawn, Darryl John. BA, Newark State Coll., 1971; MA, Montclair State Coll., 1974; postgrad., Trenton/Jersey City State Coll, 1982. Cert. tchr., N.J. Tchr. Montville (N.J.) High Sch., 1971-80; CETA tchr. Morris County Vocat.-Tech., Denville, N.J., 1972-78; tchr. adult edn. Morris County Adult Edn., Montville, 1972-80; tchr. North Hunterdon High Sch., Annandale, N.J., 1980—; tchr. adult edn. Raritan Valley Coll., Somerset, N.J., 1980-88; master automotive technician Nat. Inst. Automotive Svc. Excellence, Washington, 1973—; evaluation team leader Nat. Automotive Tech. Educators Found., Alexandria, 1990—. Advisor Vocat.-Indsl. Clubs of Am., 1980—, Nat. Plymouth Troubleshooting Contest, 1981—; pres., dir. N.J. Quar. Horse Assn., 1985—. Mem. NEA, Am. Vocat. Edn. Assn., N.J. Vocat. Edn. Assn., Epsilon Pi Tau. Roman Catholic. Home: 33 Winters Rd Phillipsburg NJ 08865-7614 Office: North Hunterdon High Sch 14 Route # 31 Annandale NJ 08801

SIESS, ALFRED ALBERT, JR., engineering executive, management consultant; b. Bklyn., Aug. 16, 1935; s. Alfred Albert and Matilda Helen (Suttmeier) S.; m. Gale Murray Scholes, Dec. 17, 1966; children: Matthew Alan, Daniel Adam. BCE, Ga. Inst. Tech., 1956; postgrad. in bus. Boston Coll., 1968; MBA, Lehigh U., 1972. With fabricated steel constrn. div. Bethlehem Steel Corp. (Pa.), 1958-76, project mgr., 1969-76, engr., projects and mining div., 1976-86; sr. cons. T.J. Trauner Assocs., Phila., 1986-87; assoc. S.T. Hudson Internat., Phila., 1987—; dir. mktg. SWIN Resource Systems, Inc., Bloomsburg, Pa., 1989—; mem. adj. faculty Drexel U., 1976—. Weekly columnist Economic and Environmental Issues, East Pa. edit. The Free Press, 1981-86; co-patentee suspension bridge erection equipment. Founder S.A.V.E. Inc., Coopersburg, Pa., 1969, pres., 1970, 75, 81, bd. dirs, 1970—. Served with C.E., USN, 1956-58. Recipient Environ. Action award S.A.V.E. Inc., 1975. Mem. ASCE (chmn. environ. tech. com. Lehigh Valley sect. 1971-83), Chi Epsilon. Republican. Mem. United Church of Christ. Lodge: Lions. Home: 6460 Blue Church Rd Coopersburg PA 18036-9357 Office: Swin Resource System Inc 29 Frosty Valley Rd Bloomsburg PA 17815-9553

SIEWERT, RAYMOND FRANCIS, JR., federal official; b. Chgo., Mar. 14, 1931; s. Raymond Francis Sr. and Martha Lilian (Hrody) S.; m. Maureen Elizabeth Smith, Jan. 22, 1955; children: Mary Camilla, Joan Marie, Margaret Ann, Raymond Francis III, William Charles, Maureen Elizabeth, Patrick James. BS in Aero. Engring., U. Ill., 1954; MS in Pub. Adminstrn., George Washington U., Washington, 1975. Engr. Martin Co., Balt., 1954-55; aviator U. S. Army, Ft. Riley, Kans., 1955-58; engr. N.Am. Aviation, Columbus, Ohio, 1958-66, Naval Air Systems Command, Washington, 1966-79; dir. engring. tech. Office of The Sec. of Def., Washington, 1979-90, acting dep. dir. def. rsch. and engr., 1990—. Contbr. articles to profl. jours. Mem. AIAA. Home: 8210 Langbrook Rd Springfield VA 22152-1228

SIFF, MARLENE IDA, artist; b. N.Y.C., Sept. 20, 1936; d. Irving Louis and Dorothy Gertrude (Lahn) Marmer; m. Elliott Justin Siff, July 11, 1959; children: Bradford Evan, Brian Douglas. BA, Hunter Coll., 1957. Cert. elem. tchr., N.Y., N.J. Tchr. Stewart Manor (N.Y.) Sch. System, 1957-59, Teaneck (N.J.) Sch. System, 1959-60; free-lance interior designer Westport, Conn., 1966-70; designer indsl. plant Varo Inertial Products, Trumbull, Conn., 1970; corp. sec., treas. Belmar Corp., Westport, 1972—, also bd. dirs.; chmn. bd. Marlene Designs Inc., Westport, 1973-77; owner Marlene Siff Design Studio, Westport, 1978—; designer Signature Collections, J.P. Stevens & Co., Inc., 1974-78, J.C. Penney Co., N.Y.C., 1978, C.R. Gibson Co., Norwalk, Conn., 1980; aesthetic cons. ALCIDE Corp., Norwalk, 1980-88. One-woman shows include David Segal Gallery, N.Y.C., 1987, Conn. Pub. TV Gallery 24, Hartford, 1987, Paul Mellon Art Ctr. at Choate Rosemary Hall, Wallingford, Conn., 1989, Conn. Nat. Bank Hdqrs., Norwalk, 1990. Decorator ann. charity ball Easter Seal Home Svc., 1976; bd. dirs. United Jewish Appeal, Westport, 1982-86; mem. com. Levitt Pavillion Performing Arts, Westport, 1982-89. Recipient award Lower Conn. Mfrs. Assn., 1970. Mem. Kappa Pi. Home: 15 Broadview Rd Westport CT 06880-2303

SIFFLARD, NANCY NICHOLS, school counselor; b. Boston, Feb. 13, 1964; d. Charles Richard and Patricia (Bowman) N. BA (summa cum laude), Stonehill Coll., 1986; MEd, Boston Coll., 1988; postgrad., Bridgewater State Coll. Cert. early childhood educator, guidance counselor, Mass. Dir. primary activities Recreation Dept., Norwell, Mass., 1983; tutor Norwell, 1984—; asst. tchr. spl. edn. Norwell High Sch., 1985; substitute tchr. Norwell, 1984-88; elem. sch. counselor Manomet Elem. Sch., Plymouth, Mass., 1988-89, Cole and Sparrel Elem. Sch., Norwell, 1989—. Named to Lambda Epsilon Sigma Honor Soc., Ames Soc. Mem. Mass. Sch. Counselor Assn., Am. Assn. Counseling Devel., Am. Sch. Counselor Assn. Home: 216 East St Hanover MA 02339-1602 Office: Norwell Pub Schs Main St Norwell MA 02061-2439

SIGEL, LOUIS PAUL, JR., insurance executive; b. Phila., Mar. 26, 1921; s. Louis Paul and Julia (Klein) S.; m. Shirlee Van Voorhis, Feb. 12, 1944; children: Louis Paul III, Eric C., Karen Sigel McDonald. BS in Econs., U. Pa., 1948. CPCU, CLU. Commd. 2d lt. USAF, 1942, advanced through grades to capt., ret., 1952; chmn. Sigel Ins. Group, Phila., 1948—; adj. prof. St. Joseph's U., Phila., 1953-73. Mem. Nat. Soc. CPCU (sec./treas. Malvern, Pa., chpt. 1975-81), Phila. Soc. CPCU (pres. 1970-71), Ins. Soc. Phila. (pres. 1974), Ins. Agents Pa. (pres. 1964-66,) Ins. Agents Phila. (pres. 1959-62). Office: Sigel Ins Group 709 Main St Schwenksville PA 19473-1051

SIGLER, ANDREW CLARK, forest products company executive; b. Bklyn., Sept. 25, 1931; s. Andrew J. and Eleanor (Nicholas) S.; m. Margaret Romefelt, June 16, 1956; children: Andrew Clark, Patricia, Elizabeth. A.B., Dartmouth, 1953; M.B.A., Amos Tuck Sch., 1956. With Champion Papers Co., Hamilton, Ohio, 1957—; pres. Champion Papers div. Champion International Corp., 1972, exec. v.p., dir. parent co., 1972-74, pres., chief exec. officer, Stamford, Conn., 1974-79, chmn. bd., chief exec. officer, 1979—; dir. Bristol-Myers Squibb Co., Chem. Bank, Gen. Electric Co. Trustee Dartmouth Coll. Served from 2d lt. to 1st lt. USMCR, 1953-55. Office: Champion Internat Corp 1 Champion Plz Stamford CT 06921-6000

SIGMAN, KARL, engineering educator; b. Buffalo, N.Y., Mar. 21, 1957; s. Eugene Marvin and Lois (Swados) S. BA in Math., U. Calif., Santa Cruz, 1979; MA in Math., U. Calif., Berkeley, 1983, MS in Ops. Rsch., 1984, PhD in Ops. Rsch., 1986. Postdoctoral assoc., math. scis. inst. Cornell U., Ithaca, N.Y., 1986-87; asst. prof., dept. indsl. engring. and ops. rsch. Columbia U., N.Y.C., 1987-91, assoc. prof., 1991—; rsch. assoc. Ctr. for Telecommunications Rsch. Ctr., Columbia U., N.Y.C., 1987—; rsch. fellow Tokyo Japan Soc. for the Promotion of Sci., 1990-91. Recipient Presidential Young Investigator award, NSF, 1989, Bernard Friedman Meml. prize, Dept. Math. U. Calif., Berkeley, 1986, George Nicholson prize, Ops. Rsch. Soc. Am., 1987. Mem. Am. Math. Soc., Inst. Math. Statistics, Ops. Rsch. Soc. Am. Office: Columbia U Dept IEOR Mudd Bldg New York NY 10027

SIGMAN, STUART JAY, speech educator; b. Bklyn., Jan. 29, 1955; s. Harvey Morton and Pauline (Balasiano) S. BA, CUNY, 1976; MA, U. Pa., 1979, PhD, 1982. Asst. prof. Pa. State U., State College, 1982-84, SUNY, Buffalo, 1984-87; assoc. prof. communications/linguistics SUNY, Albany, 1987—; vis. scholar UCLA, 1990; vis. assoc. prof. Bond U., Gold Coast, Australia, 1991; cons. N.Y. State Jud. Seminars, Unified Cts., N.Y.C., 1985, 90; presenter workshops Harrison County Ednl. System, Shinnston, W.Va., 1981, Milton Hershey Med. Ctr., Hershey, Pa., 1984, 85, Lake Area Health Edn. Ctr., Erie, Pa., 1986. Author: A Perspective on Social Communication, 1987; spl. issue editor Rsch. on Lang. and Social Interaction, 1987; contbr. articles to profl. publs. Vol. Compeer Program, Albany, 1991. CBS Found. fellow, 1978-80; grantee NATO Advanced Study Insts., 1979, Green Island Found., 1982. Mem. Speech Communication Assn., Internat. Communication Assn. Office: SUNY Albany 1400 Washington Ave Albany NY 12222-0001

SIGMOND, RICHARD BRIAN, lawyer; b. Phila., Dec. 7, 1944; s. Joseph and Jean (Nissman) S.; children: Michael, Catherine, Alina; m. Susan Helen Peteraf, Dec. 24, 1984. BS, Phila. Coll. Textiles & Sci., 1966; JD, Temple U., 1969. Bar: Pa. 1969, U.S. Supreme Ct. 1973, U.S. Dist. Ct. (ea. dist.) Pa. 1975, U.S. Ct. Appeals (3d cir.) 1975, N.Y. 1982. Atty. Pub. Defender Assn., Phila., 1969-70; ptnr. Meranze, Katz, Spear & Wilderman, Phila., 1970-84; sr. ptnr. Spear, Wilderman, Sigmond, Borish & Endy, Phila., 1985-89, Sagot, Jennings & Sigmond, Phila., 1989—; chmn., bd. dirs. Gatehouse Phila., 1972-83; lectr. Pvt. Industry Coun., Phila., 1985—, labor studies div., Pa. State U., 1978-82, 85-86. Mem. ABA (labor law com.), Pa. Bar Assn., Phila. Bar Assn. (labor law com.), AFL-CIO (lawyers coordinating com.), Phi Alpha Delta. Office: Sagot Jennings & Sigmond 1172 Pub Ledger Bldg Philadelphia PA 19106

SIGNOR, SHARON SMITH, educator; b. Kinderhook, N.Y., Mar. 17, 1943; d. Lyman Theodore and Eva May (Wormwood) Smith; m. Gene Daniel Signor, July 20, 1968; children: Aaron Gene, Jason Earl (twins). AAS, SUNY, Farmingdale, 1963; BS cum laude, SUNY, Cortland, 1983, MS in Edn., 1988. Cert. dental hygiene, nursery, and k-6 tchr., N.Y. Dental hygienist Dr. Raymond Ripp, DDS, Garden City, N.Y., 1963-65; tchr. dental hygiene Brentwood Pub. Schs., 1965-68; dental hygienist Drs. A. Scholnik and A. Hirschman, Brentwood, 1967-68; pub. health dental hygienist, supr. dental hygiene Onondaga County Health Dept., Syracuse, N.Y., 1968-70; dental hygienist Opportunities for Cortland County (N.Y.), Inc., 1970, Joseph J. Speicher, DDS, Cortland, 1970-71; substitute tchr. Cortland Madison Bd. of Coop. Ednl. Svcs., 1978; computer aide SUNY, Cortland, 1981-82; substitute tchr. various schs., N.Y., 1983-84; reading tchr. asst. Groton (N.Y.) Elem. Sch., 1984-85, kindergarten tchr., 1985—. Sunday sch. tchr. United Presbyn. Ch., Cortland, deacon, 1976-78; active Com. on Spl. Edn., Homer Cen. Schs., N.Y., 1976-78; mem. Homer-Scool Community Assn., Homer, 1975-78; mem. Seven Valley Reading Coun.; organizer Parent Orgn., 1989-90; liason Groton Elem. and PTO, 1990—. Mem. NEA, N.Y. State Reading Assn., N.Y. State Edn. Assn., Groton Faculty Assn. (negotiation com. 1987—), Twins Mothers Club (chmn. 1972-73), Music Boosters (chmn. membership com. 1988-90), Nat. Orgn. Albinism and Hypopigmentation, N.Y. State Dental Hygiene Tchrs. Assn., L.I. Dental Hygiene Tchrs. Assn. (10th dist. 1964-68), Nat. Dental Hygiene Assn., N.Y. State Dental Hygiene Assn. (10th dist. del. to conv. 1966, 67), Bretwood Sch. Tchrs. Assn., Health, Phys. Edn. and Recreation Assn. Republican. Home: 3835 Highland Rd Cortland NY 13045-9326 Office: Groton Elem Sch Elm St Groton NY 13073-1116

SIGNORELLI, LINDO A., university official; b. Troy, N.Y., Sept. 15, 1937; s. John A. and Jessie (Pagura) S.; m. Marilyn Frances LeClair, June 20, 1959; children: Jeffrey, Jodi, Jacquelyn, Janet, James. BS, SUNY, Saratoga Springs, 1981. Sr. draftsman N.Y. State Dept. Pub. Works, Albany, 1962-65; coord. facilities program Cen. Adminstrn. N.Y. State Dept. Mental Hygiene, Albany, 1965-67; asst. architect Cen. Adminstrn., N.Y. State Dept. Social Svcs., Albany, 1967-70; assoc. vice chancellor facilities mgmt. Cen. Adminstrn., SUNY, Albany, 1970—. Mem. bldg. and grounds com. St. Jude's Sch. and Ch., Wynantskill, N.Y. Staff sgt. USAF, 1955-62. Mem. Assn. Phys. Plant Adminstrs. Home: 15 Fairfax St Wyantskill NY 12198

SIGNORILE, VINCENT ANTHONY, lawyer; b. Jersey City, Mar. 22, 1959; s. Ralph R. and Rita (DeRosa) S. BS, St. Peter's Coll., Jersey City, 1981; JD, Seton Hall U., 1985. Bar: N.J. 1985, Pa. 1985. Aide Jersey City Mcpl. Coun., 1980-81, Office of Mayor, City of Jersey City, 1981; law clk. Corp. Counsel Jersey City, 1981-85; law sec. Superior Ct. N.J. for Hudson County, Jersey City, 1985-86; assoc. atty. Jersey City, 1986-89; ptnr. Signorile & Saminski, Jersey City, 1989—. Mem. Hudson County Dem. Com., 1977-81, Jersey City Environ. Com., 1989—, Jersey City Planning Bd. Com., 1991—, Jersey City Ins. Fund Com., 1989—; co-chmn. Hudson County Columbus Parade, 1984-85; elected to Mcpl. Coun. Jersey City, 1989—. Mem. ABA, N.J. Bar Assn., Pa. Bar Assn., Hudson County Bar Assn. (treas. Young Lawyer's Assn. 1987-88, scholar 1984-85), Assn. Trial Lawyers Am. Roman Catholic. Home: 1691 Kennedy Blvd Jersey City NJ 07305 Office: Jersey City Mcpl Coun City Hall 280 Grove St Jersey City NJ 07302-3698

SIKES, ALFRED C., communications executive; b. Cape Girardeau, Mo., Dec. 16, 1939; s. William Kendall and Marcia (Weber) S.; m. Martha Pagenkopf, Aug. 19, 1961; chldren: Deborah Sue, Christine Louise, Marcia Cay. AB, Westminster Coll., 1961; LLB, U. Mo., 1964. Asst. atty. gen. Senator John Danforth, State of Mo., Jefferson City, 1970-72; campaign mgr. Bond. for Gov. Com., Jefferson City, 1972; dir., gov.-elect transition staff Bond for Gov. Com., Jefferson City, 1972; dir. dept. community and consumer affairs State of Mo., Jefferson City, 1973-76; exec. v.p. Mahaffey Enterprises, Springfield, Mo., 1977-78; pres., CEO Sikes & Assocs., Springfield, Mo., 1978-86; asst. sec. nat. telecom. and info. adminstrn. U.S. Dept. Commerce, Washington, 1986-89; chmn. FCC, Washington, 1989—. contbr. articles to profl. jours. Pres. Springfield Coun. Chs., 1984. Recipient Alumni Achievement award Westminster Coll., 1987. Mem. Mo. Bar Assn., Orgn. Mo. Jaycees (pres. 1968-69), U.S. Jaycees (v.p. 1969-70), Orgn. Internat. Jaycees (legal counsel 1971-72). Republican. Methodist. Home: 5907 Aberdeen Rd Bethesda MD 20817-3805 Office: FCC 1919 M St NW Washington DC 20554-0002

SILANO, ROBERT ANTHONY, defense analyst, educator; b. Bklyn., Sept. 10, 1942; s. Ralph Henry and Charlotte Tecla (Borst) S. BA, Cathedral Coll., 1964; postgrad., New Sch., 1965-66, U. Louvain, 1971-72, U. Kent, Canterbury, 1972-74. Tchr. Bd. of Coop. Ednl. Svcs., Patchogue, N.Y., 1964-65; instr. U.S. Army Spl. Warfare Sch., Ft. Bragg, N.C., 1967-69; rsch. scientist Human Scis. Rsch., Inc., Saigon, Vietnam, 1969-71; plans officer Hdqrs. Dept. of the Army, Washington, 1975-77; R&D coord. Army Materiel Systems Analysis Agy., Aberdeen Proving Grounds, Md., 1977-79; rsch. scientist Mission Rsch. Corp., Washington, 1979-80; staff mem. Office of the Sec. of Def., Washington, 1980-81; exec. dir. Coun. on Econs. and Nat. Security, Washington, 1982-85; faculty mem. Inst. of Higher Def. Studies Nat. Def. U., Washington, 1986—; lectr. U. Saigon, 1969-70, Georgetown U., Washington, 1985; cons. U.S. Synthetic Fuels Corp., Washington, 1982, Human Sci. Rsch., Inc., Saigon, 1972. Bd. dirs. The Thomas More Soc. of Am., Washington, 1984-88; dep. dir. of planning commn. on the Bicentennial of the U.S. Constn., Washington, 1986; mem. ABA Working Group on Chem. Weapons, Washington, 1984. Capt. U.S. Army, 1966-69, 75-79, 80-81. Mem. Internat. Inst. for Strategic Studies (London). Republican. Roman Catholic. Office: Nat Def U Fort Lesley J NcNair Washington DC 20319-6000

SILBER, DAVID E., clinical psychologist, educator; b. Detroit, Sept. 19, 1935; s. Morris and Ethel (Kraunz) S.; m. Doris J. Kendler, Apr. 29, 1962 (div. Mar. 1987); children: Barry I., Alan M., Daniel J. BA, Wayne State U., 1958; MA, Ohio U., 1960; PhD, U. Mich., 1965. Lic. clin. psychologist, D.C. Asst. prof. psychology George Washington U., Washington, 1965-70, assoc. prof. psychology, 1970-76, prof. psychology, 1976—; chair dept. psychology U. Washington, Washington, 1991—; vis. assoc. prof. Hebrew U. of Jerusalem, Israel, 1972-73; cons. U.S. Secret Svc., Washington, 1986—. Co-author: Apperceptive Personality Test, 1989; contbr. articles to profl. jours. Fellow Soc. Personality Assessment; mem. Am. Psychol. Assn. Office: George Washington U Dept of Psychology Washington DC 20052

SILBER, JOHN ROBERT, university president; b. San Antonio, Aug. 15, 1926; s. Paul G. and Jewell (Joslin) S.; m. Kathryn Underwood, July 12, 1947; children: David Joslin, Mary Rachel, Judith Karen, Kathryn Alexandra, Martha Claire, Laura Ruth, Caroline Jocasta. B.A. summa cum laude, Trinity U., 1947; postgrad., Northwestern U., summer 1944, Yale Div. Sch., 1947-48, U. Tex. Sch. Law, 1948-49; M.A., Yale, 1952, Ph.D., 1956; L.H.D., Kalamazoo Coll., 1970, others. Instr. dept. philosophy Yale U., 1952-55; asst. prof. U. Tex., Austin, 1955-59, asso. prof., 1959-62, prof. philosophy, 1962-70, chmn. dept. philosophy, 1962-67, Univ. prof. arts and letters, 1967-70, chmn. (Comparative Studies Program), 1967, dean (Coll. Arts and Scis.), 1967-70; Univ. prof., prof. philosophy and law Boston U., 1971—, pres., 1971—; vis. prof. U. Bonn, 1960; fellow Kings Coll. U. London, 1963-64; mem. Nat. Adv. Bd. on Internat. Edn. Programs, 1982—, Mass. Corp. for Ednl. Telecommunications, 1983—. Author: The Ethical Significance of Kant's Religion, 1960, Straight Shooting: What's Wrong With America and How to Fix It, 1989; editor: Religion Within the Limits of Reason Alone, 1960, Works in Continental Philosophy, 1967—; assoc. editor: Kant-Studien, 1968—; Contbr. to profl. jours. Chmn. Tex. Soc. to Abolish Capital Punishment, 1960-69; mem. Nat. Commn. United Methodist Higher Edn., 1974-77; exec. bd. Nat. Humanities Inst., 1975-78; trustee Coll. St. Scholastica, 1973-85, U. Denver, 1985-89, WGBH Ednl. Found., 1971—, Adelphi U., 1989—; bd. visitors Air U., 1974-80; bd. dirs. Greater Boston Council Boy Scouts Am., 1981—, Nat. Humanities Faculty, 1968-73, Nat. Captioning Inst., 1985—; bd. advisors Matchette Found., 1971—; mem. Nat. Bipartisan Commn. on Central Am., 1983-84, Presdl. Adv. Bd. Radio Bradcasting to Cuba, 1985—; adv. bd. Schurman Library of Am. Hist., Ruprecht-Karl U., Heidelberg, 1986—, Jamestown Found., 1989—; mem. def. policy bd. U.S. Dept. of Def., 1987-90; mem. internat council advisors Inst. for Humanities at Salado, 1988—; bd. dirs. New Eng. Holocaust Meml. Com., 1989—, Brit. Inst. of U.S., 1989—; Dem. gubernatorial candidate of Mass., 1990. Recipient E. Harris Harbison award for disting. teaching Danforth Found., 1966, Wilbur Lucius Cross medal Yale Grad. Sch., 1971, Outstanding Civilian Service medal U.S. Army, 1985, Disting. Pub. Svc. award Anti-Defamation League of B'nai B'rith, 1989, Am.-Swiss Friendship award, 1992, Horatio Alger award, 1992; Fulbright Research fellow Germany, 1959-60; Guggenheim fellow Eng., 1963-64; decorated with Knight Comdr.'s Cross with Star of Order of Merit Fed. Republic of Germany, 1983; commandeur Nat. Order of Arts and Letters (France), 1985. Fellow Royal Soc. Arts; mem. Am. Philos. Assn., Am. Soc. Polit. and Legal Philosophy, Royal Inst. Philosophy, Am. Assn. Higher Edn., Nat. Assn. Ind. Colls. and Univs. (dir. 1976-81), Phi Beta Kappa. Office: Boston U 147 Bay State Rd Boston MA 02215-1789

SILBERG, CAROL ANN SCHWARTZ, cultural organization administrator, consultant; b. Balt., June 8, 1948; d. Aaron Huron and Reba Isabel (Gottlieb) Schwartz; m. Steven Edward Silberg, Aug. 10, 1968; 1 child, Elizabeth Ellis Silberg. BS, U. Md., 1971, PhD, 1990; MA, Cen. Mich. U., 1980. Freelance journalist, 1968-74; sci. editor Raytheon Svc. Co., Hyattsville, Md., 1974-75; press sec. U.S. Congress, Washington, 1975; pres. Silberg & Assocs., Inc., Balt. and Washington, 1976-82; dir. coll. rels. Prince George's Community Coll., Largo, Md., 1982-86; exec. dir. Prince George's County Parks and Recreation Found., Bowie, Md., 1986—, Nat. Fund for Patuxent Wildlife Visitor Ctr., Largo, Md., 1988-92; mgmt. cons. in field, 1982—; fundraising cons. in field, 1986—. Author, co-author: Talking the Mystery Out of Cable TV, 1984. Member Israeli friendship com. Sisters Cities Program, Upper Marlboro, Md., 1991; pres. College Park (Md.) Bus. and Profl. Women, 1980; bd. dirs. Prince Georgians on Camera, Largo, 1982-87; chair local bd. Selective Svc. System, Bowie, 1991. Exxon Corp. grantee, 1985, Ind. U. grantee, 1991; recipient Citation, Gov. of Md., 1982. Mem. Nat. Soc. Fund Raising Execs., Ind. Soc. Fund Raising Execs. (assoc.), Nat. Fedn. Bus. and Profl. Women (Nat. Program award 1983, 84), Prince George's County Pub. Rels. Assn., Prince George's C. of C. Jewish. Home: 13203 Marthas Choice Cir Bowie MD 20720-4705

SILBERGELD, SAM, psychiatrist; b. Wengrov, Poland, Mar. 1, 1918; came to U.S., 1923; s. Hyman and Frieda (Orenstein) S.; m. Mae Ann Driscoll, June 22, 1952; children: Sandra Sue, Daniel Lance, Janet Joy, Nancy Ann. AA, Blackburn Coll., 1938; BS, U. Chgo., 1939; PhD in Chemistry, U. Ill., 1943; MD, Duke U., 1955. Cert. specialist in psychiatry, Md. Instr. biochemistry Mayo Found., Rochester, Minn., 1942-44; instr., asst. prof. chemistry U. Ill., Chgo., 1945-46, 46-52; med. officer U.S. Pub. Health Svcs., Bethesda, Md., 1956-88; staff asst. to dir. Div. Biologic Standards, NIH, Bethesda, 1956-59; rsch. grants specialist Div. Gen. Med. Sci., NIH, Bethesda, 1959-60; chief gen. clin. rsch. NIH, Bethesda, 1960-64; various rsch. positions NIMH, Md., 1964-81; staff psychiatrist, adminstr. geriatric program St. Elizabeth Hosp., Washington, 1981-87; staff psychiatrist Sheppard & Enoch Pratt Hosp., Balt., 1988-89; clin. prof. dept. psychiatry Uniformed Svcs. of the Health Scis. Sch. of Medicine, Bethesda, 1982—; adj. prof. U. Md., College Park, 1979—. Contbr. numerous articles to profl. jours. Mem. vis. com. in scis. Blackburn Coll., Carlinville, Ill., 1986, trustee, 1987—; ad hoc mem. Eagle Scout Review Bd., Bethesda, 1987—; chmn. Boy Scout Troop Com., Kensington, Md., 1973-80. Recipient Leadership Citation Blackburn U., 1989; rsch. grantee Dept. Psychiatry Stanford Sch. Medicine, 1966-67. Mem. AMA, AAAS, Am. Chem. Soc., Am. Psychiat. Assn., Am. Psychosomatic Soc., N.Y. Acad. Scis. Home: 10704 Clermont Ave Box 377 Garrett Park MD 20896

SILBERMAN, H. LEE, public relations executive; b. Newark, Apr. 26, 1919; s. Louis and Anna (Horel) S.; m. Ruth Irene Rapp, June 5, 1948; children: Richard Lyle, Gregory Alan, Todd Walter. B.A., U. Wis., 1940. Radio continuity writer Radio Sta. WTAQ, Green Bay, Wis., 1940-41; reporter Bayonne (N.J.) Times, 1941-42; sales exec. War Assets Adminstrn., Chgo., 1946-47; copy editor Acme Newspictures, Chgo., 1947; reporter, editorial writer Wichita (Kans.) Eagle, 1948-55; reporter Wall St. Jour., N.Y.C., 1955-57; banking editor Wall St. Jour., 1957-68; 1st v.p., dir. corporate relations Shearson-Hamill & Co., N.Y.C., 1968-74; N.Y. corr. Economist of London, 1966-72; contbg. editor Finance mag., 1970-74, editor in chief, 1974-76; v.p., dir. Fin. Services Group, Carl Boyir & Assos., Inc., N.Y.C., 1976-78, sr. v.p., 1978-80, exec. v.p., 1981-86; sr. counselor Hill & Knowlton, Inc., N.Y.C., 1986—. Contbr. articles to profl. jours. Served to capt. C.E. AUS, 1942-46. Recipient Loeb Mag. award U. Conn., 1965; Loeb Achievement award for distinguished writing on fin. Gerald M. Loeb Found., 1968. Mem. N.Y. Fin. Writers Assn., Deadline Club N.Y., Overseas Press Club, Soc. Profl. Journalists, Pub. Rels. Soc. Am., Soc. Silurians, Sigma Delta Chi, Phi Kappa Phi, Zeta Beta Tau. Republican. Home: 80 Miller Rd Morristown NJ 07960-5237 Office: 420 Lexington Ave New York NY 10170-0002

SILBERMAN, JAMES HENRY, editor, publisher; b. Boston, Mar. 21, 1927; s. Henry R. and Dorothy (Conrad) S.; m. Selma Shapiro, Aug. 26, 1986; children by previous marriage: Michael, Ellen. A.B., Harvard U., 1950. Asst. to pub. Writer, Inc., 1950-51; asst. to advt. mgr. Little, Brown & Co., 1951-53; publicity dir. Dial Press, Inc., 1953-55, editor, 1954-55, exec. editor, 1955-59, v.p., editor-in-chief, 1959-63; editor The Dial, 1959-62; sr. editor Random House, Inc., N.Y.C., 1963-65, exec. editor, 1965-66, exec. editor, v.p., 1966-68, v.p., editor in chief, 1968-76, also pub., 1975-76; pres., editor-in-chief Summit Books div. Simon & Schuster, 1976-91; v.p., sr. editor Little Brown & Co., N.Y.C., 1991—; judge First Novel, Am. Book Awards, 1982; mem. adv. com. George Polk Meml. Awards, 1980—. Served as pfc. AUS, World War II. Mem. PEN, Assn. Am. Pubs. (Freedom to Read com. 1971-80, Freedom to Pub. com. 1982), Book Table, Pubs. Lunch Club, Corp. of Yaddo (bd. dirs. 1987—, exec. com. 1989—). Clubs: Harvard (N.Y.C.); Century Assn. Home: 315 E 70th St New York NY 10021-8657 Office: Little Brown & Co Inc 1271 Avenue of the Americas New York NY 10020

SILBERMAN, LAURENCE HIRSCH, circuit judge; b. York, Pa., Oct. 12, 1935; s. William and Anna (Hirsch) S.; m. Rosalie G. Gaull, Apr. 28, 1957; children: Robert Stephen, Katherine DeBoer Balaban, Anne Gaull. AB, Dartmouth Coll., 1957; LLB, Harvard U., 1961. Bar: Hawaii 1962, D.C. 1973. Assoc. Moore, Torkildson & Rice and Quinn & Moore, Honolulu, 1961-64; ptnr. Moore, Silberman & Schulze, Honolulu, 1964-67; atty. appellate div. gen. counsel's office NLRB, Washington, 1967-69; solicitor of labor U.S. Dept. Labor, Washington, 1969-70, undersec. labor, 1970-73; ptnr. Steptoe & Johnson, Washington, 1973-74; dep. atty. gen. U.S. Washington, 1974-75; ambassador to Yugoslavia, 1975-77; mng. ptnr. Morrison & Foerster, Washington, 1978-79, 83-85; exec. v.p. Crocker Nat. Bank, San Francisco, 1979-83; judge U.S. Ct. Appeals (D.C. cir.), Washington, 1985—; lectr. labor law and legis. U. Hawaii, 1962-63; adj. prof. adminstrv. law Georgetown U., Washington, 1987—; Pres.' spl. envoy on ILO affairs, 1976; mem. gen. adv. com. on Arms Control and Disarmament, 1981-85; mem. Def. Policy Bd., 1981-85; vice chmn. State Dept.'s Commn. on Security and Econ. Assistance, 1983-84. Bd. dirs. Com. on Present Danger, 1978-85, Inst. for Ednl. Affairs, 1981-85; vice chmn. adv. council on gen. govt. Rep. Nat. Com., 1977-80. Served with AUS, 1957-58. Am. Enterprise Inst. sr. fellow, 1977-78, vis. fellow 1978-85. Mem. ABA (labor law com. 1965—, corp. and banking com. 1973, law and nat. security adv. com. 1981—), Hawaii Bar Assn. (ethics com. 1965-67), D.C. Bar Assn. (council fgn. relations).

SILBERMAN, MICHAEL JAY, engineering executive; b. Phila., Sept. 7, 1954; s. Aron Morris Silberman and Joan (Andrusser) Abramson. Grad. high sch., Phila. Founder, pres., chief exec. officer MS Electric & Sound, Inc., Warminster, Pa., 1984—. Mem. Ind. Elec. Contractors Assn., Nat. Geographic Soc., Phila. Zool. Soc., N.J. State Aquarium, Smithsonian Instn., Divers Alert Network. Office: MS Electric & Sound Inc 892 W Street Rd # 126 Warminster PA 18974

SILBERMAN, REBECCA LOUISE, psychologist; b. L.A., Apr. 15, 1957; d. Max and Mildred (Lapidus) S. BA, U. Calif., Santa Cruz, 1979; MA, Duquesne U., 1980, PhD, 1989. Lic. psychologist, Pa. Mental health counselor YWCA, Pitts., 1983-86; psychologist in pvt. practice Pitts., 1990—; clin. therapist Western Psychiat. Inst. and Clinic, Pitts., 1986—. Mem. Am. Psychol. Assn. Office: Western Psychiat Institute and Clinic 3811 Ohara St Pittsburgh PA 15213-2593

SILBERSACK, WALTER ROY, marketing consultant; b. Cin., June 6, 1926; s. Walter Frank and Eleanor Rose (Stoeckle) S.; m. Joan Small, Feb. 3, 1951; children: John Walter, James Davis. BS, U.S. Mcht. Marine Acad., 1946. Mktg. cons. Mktg. Support Group, Port Washington, N.Y. Lt. (j.g.) USNR, 1944-48. Mem. Manhasset Bay Yacht Club. Episcopalian. Home and Office: 11 Cornwells Beach Rd Port Washington NY 11050-1305

SILBERT, THEODORE H., banker; b. Boston, July 5, 1904; m. Nadia S. Stark, May 6, 1984; 1 child from previous marriage, Arthur Frederick (dec.). LLB (hon.), Bard Coll., Western State U., Anaheim, Calif. With Standard Fin. Corp., 1934—, pres., 1945—, bd. dirs., pres., bd. dirs. various subs. cos.; pres., chief exec. officer, dir. Sterling Bancorp. (formerly Standard Prudential Corp.), until 1968, chmn., chief exec. officer, dir., 1968—; chmn. Sterling Nat. Bank & Trust Co. N.Y.; moderator small bus. Columbia U. Contbr. articles to Harvard Bus. Rev., other bus. publs. Past pres. and former chmn. Assn. Comml. Fin. Cos.; former trustee Bronx-Lebanon Hosp. Ctr.; trustee, founder, chmn. Jewish Assn. for Svcs. for Aged; hon. vice chmn. Anti-Defamation League Nat. Commn.; nat. chmn. Anti-Defamation League Appeal, N.Y.C., nat. treas., mem. exec. com., bd. dirs. N.Y.C. div.; also life mem. Am. Cancer Soc.; bd. dirs., life trustee, mem., bd. dirs., bd. overseers United Jewish Appeal Fedn.; assoc. trustee, mem. pres.'s council Bard Coll., Annandale-on-Hudson, N.Y.; trustee emeritus Brandeis U.; treas., trustee emeritus, Jewish Communal Fund, N.Y.C.; founder Albert Einstein Coll. Medicine; past pres. Soc. Founders; moderator small bus. Columbia U.; trustee Am. Jewish Hist. Soc.; past trustee Park Ave. Synagogue; bd. dirs., mem. exec. com. Jewish Theol. Sem. Am.; bd. dirs. Fashion Inst. Tech., Hebrew Free Loan Soc.; leadership chmn. United Way Harrison, 1987-88. Mem. Fgn. Policy Assn. (assoc.), Def. Orientation Conf. Assn., Assn. Theatrical Press Agts. and Mgrs., Sponsor Ann. Econ. Forecasting Award, Standard Club (Chgo.), Board Room, Harmonie Club, Friars (N.Y.C.), Old Oaks Country Club, Purchase Club (past pres.), Hillcrest Country Club (L.A.). Home: 936 5th Ave New York NY 10021-2653 Office: 540 Madison Ave New York NY 10022-3213

SILER, TODD LAEL, visual artist, author, researcher, lecturer; b. Long Island, N.Y., Aug. 21, 1953; s. Bernard O. Siler and Gloria (Kates) Haberman. BA, Bowdoin Coll., 1975; MS in Visual Studies, MIT, 1981, PhD in Interdisciplinary Studies in Psychology and Art, 1986. Hon. rsch. affiliate Ctr. for Advanced Visual Studies MIT, 1981-83, vis. artist Computer-Aided Design Lab. Dept. Mech. Engring., 1986-88, 90—. Author: Cerebreactors, 1981, The Biomirror, 1983, The Art of Thought, 1987, Neurocosmology, 1985, Metaphorms: Forms of Metaphor, 1988, Breaking the Mind Barrier, 1990; patentee in field; one man show include O.K. Harris Gallery, N.Y.C., 1978, Ronald Feldman Fine Arts Gallery, N.Y.C., 1981, 83, 87, 90, , Galerie France Morin, Montreal, Que., Can., 1982, MIT Mus. and Hist. Collections, Cambridge, 1982, Compton Gallery, MIT, 1983, N.Y. Acad. Scis., N.Y.C., 1988; exhibited in group shows Ars Electronica Internat. Brucknerfestes, Linz and Munich, 1982, Musee D'Art Moderne De La Ville De Paris, 1982, Chrysler Mus., Norfolk, Va., 1984, Mcpl. Art Gallery, L.A., 1985, Festival Steirishcher Herbst, Graz, Austria, 1985, Hokin Gallery, Miami, Fla., 1985, Sao Paulo Biennale, 1985, Ctr. Internat. D'Art Comtemporain, Montreal, 1986, 90, others; represented in permanent collections at Solomon R. Guggenheim Mus., N.Y.C., The Met. Mus. Art, N.Y.C., The Mus. Modern Art, N.Y.C., Pushkin Fine Arts Mus., Moscow, Tel Aviv Mus. Art; represented in numerous pub. and pvt. collections. IBM Thomas J. Watson fellow, Paris, 1975-76, Fulbright fellow, India, 1985-86, Mass. Artists Found. fellow, 1987, Meitec fellow Meitec Corp., Tokyo, 1990-91; William Zorach Painting scholar, 1972; Coun. for Arts grantee MIT, 1979, 83, 87, 88. Office: MIT Ctr Advanced Visual Studies 40 Massachusetts Ave Cambridge MA 02139-4312

SILK, ALVIN JOHN, business educator; b. Winnipeg, Manitoba, Can., Dec. 31, 1935; came to U.S., 1959, naturalized, 1975; s. John Edward and Bertha Lena (Kirton) S.; m. Diane D. Wilson; children: Jonathan, Andrea, Stephanie. BA, U. Western Ont., 1959; MBA, Northwestern U., 1960, PhD, 1968. Asst. prof. mgmt. UCLA, 1963-66; asst. prof. U. Chgo., 1966-68; from assoc. prof. to prof. Sloan Sch. Mgmt., MIT, Cambridge, 1968-88; dep. dean MIT Sloan Sch. Mgmt., Cambridge, 1981-87; Lincoln Filene prof. Grad. Sch. Bus. Adminstrn. Harvard U., Boston, 1988—; vis. rsch. fellow Mktg. Sci. Inst., Cambridge, Mass., 1970-71, trustee, 1984—; Ford Found. vis. prof. European Inst. for Advanced Studies in Mgmt., Brussels, 1975-76, Harvard Bus. Sch., 1987—; bd. dirs. Bay Bank Systems Inc., Waltham, Mass., 1987—, Reed and Barton, Inc., Tauton, Mass., 1990—. Co-editor: Behavioral and Management Science in Marketing, 1978; assoc. editor: Management Science, 1969-77; mem. editorial bd.: Jour. Marketine Research, 1969-73, Jour. Marketing, 1978-81, Marketing Science, 1980—; author, coauthor numerous articles to profl. jours. Mem. Am. Mktg. Assn. (O'Dell award 1983), Am. Statis. Assn., Assn. for Consumer Rsch., Econometric Soc., Inst. for Mgmt. Scis. (Achievement award 1982, 83), Psychometric Soc., Beta Gamma Sigma, Zeta Psi. Home: 327 Commonwealth Ave Boston MA 02115 Office: Harvard U Grad Sch Bus Adminstrn Soldiers Field Rd Allston MA 02134-1805

SILK, GERALD DOUGLAS, art educator; b. Fall River, Mass., Dec. 29, 1947; s. Nathan and Esther Rose (Fine) S.; m. Marguerite Helen O'Brien, Apr. 15, 1983; 1 child, Caitlin Natalie. AB, Brandeis U., 1970; PhD, U. Va., 1976. Instr. U. Va., Charlottesville, 1974; lectr. Columbia U., N.Y.C., 1975-76, asst. prof. Art, 1976-83; asst. prof. Art U. Pa., Phila., 1983-87; assoc. prof. Art Tyler Sch. of Art Temple U., Phila., 1988—; assoc. editor Arts mag. N.Y.C., 1983-88; mem. adv. bd. Ctr. for Advanced Study in Art & Culture, L.A., 1990—; cons. in field. Author: Museums Discovered, 1982; contbg. author: Automobile and Culture, 1984, Futurism and Futurisms, 1986; mem. editorial bd. Art Jour., 1990—. Smithsonian Inst. predoctoral fellow, 1974-75, Rome Prize fellow, 1982, Ailsa Bruce Mellon Sr. fellow, 1987-88. Fellow Am. Acad. in Rome; mem. Coll. Art Assn., Soc. for Historic Preservation. Home: 3718 Hamilton St Philadelphia PA 19104 Office: Tyler Sch Art Temple U Beech & Penrose Aves Philadelphia PA 19126

SILK, JOHN KEVIN, physicist; b. Cambridge, Mass., May 6, 1938; s. John Leo and Margaret Mary (Lynch) S.; m. Laura Pearce Wright, nov. 26, 1960; children: Catherine C., Sean C. AB, Harvard Coll., 1960; PhD, MIT, 1969. Engr. Rytheon Co., Waltham, Mass., 1960-64; pvt. bus., cons. Weston, Mass., 1964-69; sr. scientist Am. Sci. and Engring., Cambridge, 1969-88; chief scientist Contraves/Block Engring., Boston, 1988—. Inventor in field; contbr. articles to profl. publs. Recipient Skylab Achievement award, NASA, 1972, Group Achievement award, NASA, 1974. Mem. Am. Phys. Soc. Ind. Unitarian. Home: 992 Memorial Dr Cambridge MA 02138-4872

SILKA, LINDA KAY, psychology educator; b. Creston, Iowa, Dec. 31, 1951. PhD in Social Psychology, U. Kans., 1978. With Dept. Psychology U. Lowell, Mass. Author: Intuitive Judgements of Change, 1989. Mem. Am. Psychol. Assn., Soc. Exptl. Social Psychology. Home: 4 Pinewood St Orono ME 04473 Office: U Lowell Dept Psychology Lowell MA 01854

SILLIN, LELAN FLOR, surgeon; b. Camp Lejeune, N.C., July 26, 1945; m. Katharine G. Shevenell, June 17, 1967; children: Peter, Katharine, Elizabeth. MD, Tulane U., 1973. Intern in pathology Charity Hosp., New Orleans, 1974, intern in surgery, 1974-75; resident surgery Med. Coll. Wis., Milw., 1975-80; asst. prof. surgery SUNY Health Sci. Ctr., Syracuse, 1980-85, assoc. prof. surgery, 1985—. Contbr. numerous articles to profl. jours. Med. adv. com. Cen. N.Y. chpt. Nat. Found. for Ileitis and Colitis, Syracuse, 1990—. Fellow ACS; mem. Am. Gastroenterol. Assn., Assn. of VA Surgeons, Soc. for Surgery of the Alimentary Tract, Soc. of Am. Gas-

trointestinal Endoscopic Surgeons, Collegium Internationale Chirurgiae Digestivae. Office: SUNY Health Sci Ctr 750 E Adams St Syracuse NY 13210

SILLMAN, EMMANUEL, zoologist, educator; b. Phila., Dec. 7, 1915; s. Maxwell and Esther K. Sillman. BS, Bucknell U., 1937; MA in Zoology, U. Mich., 1948, PhD in Zoology, 1954. Teaching fellow U. Mich., Ann Arbor, 1951-53; from instr. to asst. prof. U. Guelph, Guelph, Ont., Can., 1953-58; asst. prof. U. Manitoba, Winnipeg, Can., 1958-60; asst. prof., prof. Duquesne U., Pitts., 1960-80; liaison Pa. Coun. Sci. Edn., Pitts., 1981—. Contbr. articles to profl. jours. Bd. dirs. Group Against Smog and Pollution, Pitts., 1971-89; v.p. Pitts. Secular Humanists, 1990—. Capt. U.S. Army, 1943-47. Rsch. grantee Nat. Rsch. Coun. Can., 1954-60; recipient Commendation medal U.S. Army. Mem. AAAS, Ams. United for Separation of Ch. and State, Ams. for Religious Liberty, Nat. Ctr. Sci. Edn., Natural Resources Def. Coun., People for the Am. Way, Environ. Def. Fund. Home: 623 Burton Dr Pittsburgh PA 15235-4423

SILLS, JUDITH ROBIN, psychologist; b. Phila.; d. Harold and Gerry (Adelman) S.; m. Lynn Hoffman, Sept. 12, 1981; 1 child, Spencer Maeve. BA, Boston U., 1968; MA, PhD, New Sch. of Social Rsch., 1974. Dir. Outpatient Psychiatric Svcs. Pacific Presbyn. Hosp., San Francisco, 1976-79; dir. The Inst. of the YM/YWHA, Phila., 1983-85; pvt. practice Phila., 1981—. Author: How to Stop Looking for Someone Perfect and Find Someone to Love, 1984, A Fine Romance, 1987; contbr. articles to popular jours. Fellow NSF, 1968-69, 69-70, 70-71, Alvin Johnson fellow New Sch. for Social Rsch., 1972. Mem. APA. Office: Lincoln Rittenhouse 222 W Rittenhouse Sq Philadelphia PA 19103-5705

SILLS, RICHARD REYNOLDS, scientist, educator; b. N.Y.C., Sept. 19, 1946; s. Leonard Harold and Carol (Rudin) S. BA, Boston U., 1968. Tchr. N.Y.C. Pub. Schs., 1968-70, 79-81; v.p. Plutronics, Inc., N.Y.C., 1981-85; pvt. practice N.Y.C., 1985—. Author: (children's book) Jonny the Jester, 1977; contbr. articles to profl. jours.; patentee method and apparatus for encoding and decoding signals. Mem. Rep. Nat. Com., Washington, 1981—; rep. Presdl. Task Force, Washington, 1982—. Named Educator of Decade, Found. for Universal Brotherhood Inc., 1978.

SILVA, LAURA J. M., transpersonal psychotherapist, educator, researcher; b. Boston, May 6, 1949; d. Joseph V. and Amelia (Ianucci) S. BA in Polit. Sci., U. Mass., 1972; MA in Psychology, Assumption Coll., Worcester, Mass., 1979. Lic. mental health counselor; cert. advanced clin. hypnotherapist. Dir. vol. svcs. Rutland Heights Hosp., Rutland, Mass., 1972-82; acad. adviser Cen. New Eng. Coll., Worcester, 1978-84; transpersonal educator, staff psychotherapist Amethyst Point Holistic Ctr., Worcester, 1989; ind. transpersonal psychotherapist Worcester and Petersham, Mass., 1983—; referral therapist Inst. Parapsychology, Durham, N.C., 1991—,organizer Sacred Earth journeys and tours, 1989—; guest local regional radio programs. Mem. Assn. for Past Life Therapy and Rsch. (referral therapist 1987—), Worcester Profl. Women's Network, Nat. Guild Hypnotists, Nat. Assn. Counseling and Devel. Home: Flat Rock Rd RR01 Box 38 Petersham MA 01366 Office: 78 Burncoat St Petersham MA 01366

SILVA, MARK ROBERT, insurance agency executive; b. Hyannis, Mass., Feb. 19, 1954; s. Robert F. and Veronica M. (Lenord) S.; m. Candace T. Casala, Sept. 17, 1989. BS, U. Bridgeport, 1976. Ins. agt. Benson & Young, Provincetown, Mass., 1976-81; pres. Benson, Young & Downs Ins. Agy. Inc., Provincetown, Wellfleet, Mass., 1981—. Mem. Provincetown Dem. Com., 1985-89. Fellow Ind. Ins. Agts. Mass. (Local Agt. Assoc. of Yr. 1984), Cape Cod Ins. Agts. Assn. (pres. 1983-84); mem. Profl. Ins. Agts. New Eng. (bd. dirs., v.p., sec., treas. 1982—, pres. 1990-91, chmn. Mass. steering com. 1985-87, Chmn. of Yr. 1987), K.C. (grand knight Provincetown 1981-82), Lions (pres. Provincetown 1981-82, zone chmn. 1982-83). Democrat. Roman Catholic. Home: 71 Race Point Rd Provincetown MA 02657-1529 Office: Benson Young & Downs Ins Provincetown MA 02657

SILVA, PATRICIO, medicine educator, hospital administrator; b. Santiago, Chile, July 7, 1939; came to U.S., 1969; s. Mario Julio and Luisa Emma (MacIver) S.; m. Vjera Maritza Bakovic, Nov. 21, 1964; children: Patricio, Jose Pablo, Marcela Cecilia. MD, U. Chile, Santiago, 1964; LM, Cath. U. Chile, Santiago, 1964. Instr. Med. Sch., Harvard U., Boston, 1972-74, asst. prof., 1974-78, assoc. prof., 1978; staff physician Beth Israel Hosp., Boston, 1973—, assoc. dir. renal div., 1981-90; staff physician Joslin Diabetes Ctr., Boston, 1990; staff physician, chief div. nephrology Joslin Diabetes Ctr. New Eng. Deaconess Hosp., Boston, 1990—; trustee Mt. Desert Island Biol. Lab., Salisbury Cove, Maine, 1978-84. Contbr. numerous articles to profl. jours. Mem. Am. Soc. Nephrology, Am. Soc. Renal Biochemistry and Metabolism (pres. 1991—), Am. Physiol. Soc., Am. Soc. for Clin. Investigation, Am. Soc. for Exptl. Biology and Medicine, Internat. Soc. Nephrology. Office: New Eng Deaconess Hosp 110 Francis St Boston MA 02215-5501

SILVER, ALVIN M., management consultant; b. N.Y.C., Oct. 20, 1931. BS, Columbia U., 1958; MS, Steven Inst. Tech., 1962; ScD in Engring., Columbia U., 1972. Registered profl. engr., N.Y. Prin. A. Silver Assocs., Northport, N.Y. Office: A Silver Assocs 1302 Pulaski Rd East Northport NY 11731-2099

SILVER, BARRY WILLIAM, banker; b. Great Lakes, Ill., Dec. 28, 1946; s. Dean Silver and Margaret (Howe) Gray; m. Heidi Eftekhar, June 15, 1972; children: Garrick, Justin, Darren. BBA, Nichols Coll., Dudley, Mass., 1968; MBA, Am. U., 1974. Vol. Peace Corps, Huacho, Peru, 1968-70; bank rev. examiner Fed. Res. Bd., 1974-77; asst. v.p. Am. Security Bank, Washington, 1977-80; sr. v.p., sr. credit officer Nat. Coop. Bank, Washington, 1980—; mem. fin. com. Group Health-HMO, Washington, 1990—. With U.S. Army, 1970-72, Iran. Mem. Am. Mktg. Assn., Robert Morris Assocs., Nat. Soc. Accts. for Corps. Home: 2887 Melanie Ln Oakton VA 22124 Office: Nat Coop Bank 1401 I St Washington DC 20005

SILVER, BRIAN QUAYLE, broadcast journalist, educator, musician; b. Denver, Sept. 8, 1942; s. Harold Farnes and Madelyn Cannon (Stewart) S.; m. Shubha Sankaran, Dec. 4, 1988; 1 adopted child, Laila Benazir Robinson. BA, Harvard Coll., 1964; postgrad., Sch. Oriental and African Studies U. London, 1969-70; PhD., U. Chgo., 1980. Asst. prof. Urdu U. Minn., 1971-74; assoc. prof. Urdu & Indo-Muslim studies Harvard U., 1974-83; dir. internat. house, asst. dean study abroad Duke U., 1983-86; exec. dir. Internat. Music Assocs., Washington, 1982—; chief, Urdu svc. Voice of Am., Washington, 1986—; dir. internat. exchange programs Pan Orient Arts Found., Manchester, N.H., 1968—; bd. dirs. Archive Rsch. Ctr. Ethnomusicology, New Delhi, India; South Asia coun. Assn. Asian Studies, Ann Arbor, Mich., 1983-86. Sitar and surbahar performance in India, Pakistan, England, Canada and U.S., 1966—; contbr. numerous publs. on South Asian Music and Urdu Lit. Dir. Durham Chpt. UNICEF, 1984-86. Fulbright grantee Inst. Internat. Edn., India, 1964-66, grantee in aid Washington Coun. for Arts and Humanities/Nat. Endowment for the Arts, 1991-92; Ford fellow Am. Coun. Learned Socs., Pakistan, India, 1969-71, Am. Inst. Indian Studies, India, 1982-83; named Khansahib, All-Pakistan Music Conf., Lahore, 1988, Gold medal, 1989. Mem. Soc. Ethnomusicology (New England chpt. v.p. 1978-80), Assn. Asian Music, Internat. Coun. Tradition Mus., Middle East Studies Assn., Asia Soc., Assn. Asian Studies, Folklore Soc. Greater Washington. Home: 1730 C St NE Washington DC 20002-6661 Office: Internat Music Assoc PO Box 15526 Washington DC 20003-0526

SILVER, EDWARD LAWRENCE, accountant; b. N.Y.C., Mar. 3, 1969; s. Sheldon and Rosa Silver. BS, Yeshiva U., 1989. Sr. acct. Anchin, Block & Anchin CPAs, N.Y.C., 1989—. Bd. dirs. Pirchei of Am. Youth Orgn., N.Y.C., 1989—. Home: 550 Grand St # G New York NY 10002-4225 Office: Anchin Block & Anchin 1375 Broadway Fl 18 New York NY 10018-7086

SILVER, HOWARD IRA, electrical engineering educator; b. N.Y.C., June 2, 1939; s. Sidney and Shirley (Jacobs) S.; m. Ronnie Brenner, Aug. 19, 1962; children: Sharon, Michael. BEE, CCNY, 1961; MEE, NYU, 1964; student, U. Pa., Phila., 1961-62; PhD, NYU, 1968. Elec. engr. GE, Phila., 1961-62, ITT Labs., Nutley, N.J., 1962-64, Sperry Gyroscope Co., Great Neck, N.Y., 1964-66; instr. elec. engring. NYU, N.Y.C., 1966-68; prof. elec. engring. Fairleigh Dickinson U., Teaneck, N.J., 1968—; instr., cons. Devenco Rsch., N.Y.C., 1969, AT&T, Holmdel, N.J., 1971-88, 92—, Allied Signal, Teterboro, N.J., 1990. Author: 32 Bit Microprocessing, 1988; cons. editor: Modular Fortran 77, 1989, MathCAD for Scientists and Engineers, 1992. Vol. Meals on Wheels, Westwood, N.J., 1989—. Grantee NSF, 1976, AT&T. 1985. Home: 10 Clairmont Dr Westwood NJ 07675-7607

SILVER, HOWARD JOEL, social science advocate; b. Bronx, Mar. 25, 1949; s. Milton and Mollie (Vogel) S.; m. Marilyn Brick Silver, Dec. 1, 1974; 1 child, Mark Steven. BA, CCNY, 1969; MA, Ohio State U., 1971, PhD, 1975. Instr. Franklin U., Columbus, Ohio, 1970-74; asst. prof. Washington Coll., Chestertown, Md., 1975-80; legis. analyst U.S. Dept. Edn., Washington, 1980-82; cons. Nat. Conf. State Legis., Nat. Alliance of Bus., Washington, 1982-83; assoc. dir. govt. rels. Consortium of Social Sci. Assns., Washington, 1983-88, exec. dir., 1988—; bd. dirs. Nat. Commn. on Social Studies in the Schs., Washington, 1988-90. Contbr. articles to profl. jours. Pres. Sch. Aged Child Care, PAG, Fairfax, Va., 1985-87; campaign mgr. Gubernatorial campaign, Md., 1978, congl. campaign, Del., 1980. Inst. for Ednl. Leadership Edn. Policy fellow, 1980-81. Mem. Coun. of Profl. Assns. on Fed. Statistics (exec. com. 1988-89), Am. Polit. Sci. Assn. (pres. applied polit. sci. 1987—). Home: 9105 Windflower Ln Annandale VA 22003 Office: Consortium Social Sci Assns 1522 K St NW Washington DC 20005

SILVER, KENNETH ALAN, government official; b. N.Y.C., Feb. 9, 1927; s. Harold Ivan and Leah Etta (Waters) S.; m. Miriam Goodman, Nov. 4, 1956; children: David Franklin, Daniel Ivan. BS, U. Calif., Berkeley, 1948; postgrad., NYU, 1969-70. Gen. mgr. Outlook Prodns., Inc., N.Y.C., 1952-54; exec. v.p., gen. mgr. Automatic Projection Corp., N.Y.C., 1954-56; v.p. internat. Alexander Film Co., Colorado Springs, Colo., 1957-65; sales exec. Columbia Pictures Corp., N.Y.C., 1965-66; sales mgr. Caedmon Records, Inc., N.Y.C., 1966-67; exec. officer region II FDA, Bklyn., 1967-71, program mgr. for intergovt. affairs, 1971-74, dir. state programs br. region II, 1974-80, asst. regional food and drug dir. for intergovt. affairs, 1980-89, ret., 1989; speaker on food and drug regulation. Editor, writer. Mem. Montclair (N.J.) Civil Rights Commn., mem. environ. adv. com.; sec. Programs for Parents, Inc. With USNR, 1944-45. Recipient Disting. Pub. Service award Fed. Exec. Bd., 1973, Commendable Service award FDA, 1984. Mem. Assn. Food and Drug Ofcls. (editor Jour. 1987-91), Cen. Atlantic States Assn. Food and Drug Ofcls. (pres. 1972, CASA award 1979, Spl. award 1987). Jewish. Home and Office: 16 Waterbury Rd Montclair NJ 07043-1714

SILVER, MONTY, artists' representative; b. Bklyn., Aug. 7, 1933; s. Irving and Lillian (Rock) S.; m. Pamela S. Burrell, July 18, 1965 (div. 1976); children: Deirdre Silver, Emily Silver. BA, Bklyn. Coll., 1957. Pres. Monty Silver Agy., Ltd., N.Y.C., 1962-89, Silver, Kass & Massetti/West, Ltd., Hollywood, Calif., 1989—, Silver, Kass & Massetti/East, Ltd., N.Y.C., 1989—; sec. Nat. Assn. Talent Reps., N.Y.C., 1980—. With U.S. Army, 1952-54. Mem. Turf and Field Club. Home: 28 Baiting Hollow Rd East Hampton NY 11937 Office: Silver Kass & Massetti 145 W 45 St New York NY 10036

SILVER, NINA GAIL, writer, singer-songwriter; b. Roslyn, N.Y., Oct. 15, 1951; d. David Louis Silverman and Dianne Kaplan; m. Paul Siver-Fox. BA magna cum laude, Queens Coll., Flushing, N.Y., 1975. Performer (singer) Hosp. Audiences, Inc., N.Y.C., 1976—; cons., writer, founder, dir. Healing Heart Music, N.Y.C., 1979—. Contbr. articles to profl. jours.; author poems: Women's Glib, 1991. Meet the Composer grantee, 1982, 83; Broadcast Music Inc. scholar/grantee, 1976-77. Mem. Poets and Writers, Nat. Writers Union, Broadcast Music Inc. Office: Healing Heart Music PO Box 293 New York NY 10025

SILVER, PATRICIA ANN, advertising executive; b. Allentown, Pa., Aug. 28, 1955; d. Sidney James and Margaret Ann (McKewen) S.; m. Jeffrey Trauberman, Nov. 10, 1990. BS, Franklin and Marshall Coll., 1977. Asst. promotion and advt. dir. Congl. Quar., Washington, 1977-82; account exec. Richardson Myers & Donofrio Advt., Balt., 1982-83; account supr. Earle Palmer Brown Advt., Bethesda, Md., 1983-84; pres. Silver & Co., Bethesda, 1984—. Mem. young leadership bd. United Jewish Appeal, Bethesda, 1985-86; mem. bus. com. Overseas Ednl. Found., Washington, 1989, 90; bd. dirs. Washington Adventist Hosp., Takoma Park, Md., 1987—, Jewish Nat. Fund, Washington, 1985—. Mem. Direct Mktg. Assn. Washington (bd. dirs. 1990—, bd. dirs. Ednl. Found. 1989-91, silver medal 1986, 91, bronze medal 1988, gold medal 1989), Bd. Trade Washington, Advt. Club Washington.

SILVER, PAUL JOSEPH, pharmaceutical executive; b. Akron, Ohio, Dec. 11, 1951; s. Max and Atilia Marion (Dini) S.; m. Cynthia Jean Schmidt, Sept. 15, 1979; children: Joanna Jean, Julia Angeline, Jessica Michelle. BS in Biology cum laude, U. Akron, 1974, MS in Biology, 1976; PhD in Med. Physiology, U. Cin., 1979. Rsch. assoc. U. Tex. Health Sci. Ctr., Dallas, 1980-82; mgr. cardiovascular biochemistry Wyeth Labs., Inc., Phila., 1982-86; dir. cardiovascular/cardiopulmonary rsch. Sterling Drug, Inc., Rensselaer, N.Y., 1986—. Guest editor (supplement) Jour. Cardiovascular Pharmacology, 1986; reviewer, mem. editorial bd. Jour. Pharmacology and Exptl. Therapeutics, 1988—, Drug Devel. Rsch., 1991—; contbr. numerous articles to profl. jours. Baseball coach New Scotland (N.Y.) Kiwanis, 1991. Ryan Found. fellow U. Cin., 1978-79. Mem. Am. Soc. Pharmacology and Exptl. Therapeutics, Phi Sigma Alpha, Phi Eta Sigma, Omicron Delta Kappa. Office: 81 Columbia Tpke Rensselaer NY 12144-3411

SILVER, PAUL ROBERT, market executive, consultant; b. Balt., Mar. 15, 1931; s. Harry and Freida (Rosengarten) S.; m. Natalie Nessa Nechamkin, May 17, 1957; children; Geri Ellen, Steven Marc, Lawrence Alan. BA, U. Md., 1949; BS, U. Balt., 1958; postgrad., Eckerd Coll., 1984. Pres. chief exec. officer Sterling Prodns. Inc., Balti., 1950-51; advt. mgr. Hecht Co., Washington, 1951-53; pres., chief exec. officer Artists & Models, Inc., Washington and Balt., 1974-76, The Charles Agy. Inc., Washington and Balt., 1955-80, The Golden Triangle Agy., Clearwater, Fla., 1980-82; chief operating officer Bridgman Assocs. Inc., Annapolis, Md., 1985-86; dir. promotions Internat. Beverage Expn., Washington, 1986; pres., chief exec. officer Prasco Inc., Tampa and Miami, Fla., and Balt., 1982—; cons. Lewis and Ptnrs. Inc. San Francisco, Corp. Vision Inc., Los Angeles, Computer Response Inc. Balt., Themes and Schemes Inc., Dunedin, Fla. and San Diego, 1984—, J&B Mgmt. Co., 1991; v.p. Coupon Am., Bel Air, Md., 1987-88. Active in Radio Free Asia, 1972, Pinellas County Heart Savers, Clearwater, 1981; campaign mgr. for candidates for Balt. City Coun., U.S. Senate and U.S. Congress, 1968, 88, Fla. Commr. Agr., 1990. With U.S. Army, 1953-55, 72. Democrat. Jewish. Office: Prasco Inc PO Box 402443 Miami Beach FL 33140-0443

SILVER, RICHARD TOBIAS, physician, educator; b. Jan. 18, 1929; m. Barbara Silver; 1 son, Adam Bennett. Diploma, A.B., Cornell U., 1950, M.D., 1953. Diplomate: Nat. Bd. Med. Examiners, Am. Bd. Internal Medicine, Am. Bd. Clin. Oncology. Intern N.Y. Hosp.-Cornell Med. Ctr., N.Y.C., 1953-54, asst. resident in medicine, 1956-57, resident in hematology, 1957-58; clin. assoc. gen. medicine br. Nat. Cancer Inst., NIH, Bethesda, Md., 1954-56; asst. in medicine Cornell U. Med. Coll., N.Y.C., 1956-58, instr. medicine, 1958-62, clin. asst. prof., 1962-67, clin. assoc. prof., 1967-73, clin. prof., 1973—; physician to out-patients N.Y. Hosp., 1958-64, asst. attending physician, 1964-67, assoc. attending physician, 1967-73, attending physician, 1973—; asst. vis. physician 2d Cornell Med. div. Bellevue Hosp., N.Y.C., 1963-66; vis. Fulbright prof. U. Bahia Sch. Medicine, Brazil, 1958-59; vis. prof. Hershey Hosp.-Pa. State Hosp., 1976, Mayo Clinic, 1977, Upstate Med. Ctr., Binghamton, N.Y., 1977, Med. Coll. Va., 1979, Med. Sch. Colubia U., 1982, N.J. Coll. Medicine, New Brunswick, 1983, Meml. Med. Ctr. U. Ga., 1984, 86; invited lectr. Med. Coll. Shanghai and Chengchow, 1979, VIII Brazilian Hematology Congress, Salvador, 1981, 14th Internat. Congress Chemotherapy, Kyoto, Japan, 1985, XI Brazilian Congress of Cancerology, Florianopolis, Santa Catarina, , 1987; mem. rev. bd. NIH, Nat. Cancer Inst.; cons. Cancer Chemotherapy Investigative Rev. Bd., 1980, clin. trials com., 1979-81; mem. Cornell U. COuncil, 1987—. Author: Morphology of the Blood and Marrow in Clinical Practice, 1970; co-author: (with R.D. Lauper, C.I. Jarowski) A Synopsis of Cancer Chemotherapy, 1977, ed edit., 1987; editor, contbr.: Topics in Cancer, 1982; contbr. chpts. to books and articles to profl. jours., to nat. and internat. profl. confs., seminars and workshops in medicine. Fellow ACP; mem. N.Y. State Soc. Med. Hematologists and Oncologists (pres. 1991—), Cornell U. Med. Coll. Alumni Assn. (pres. 1973-76, sr. advisor 1976—), Am. Soc. Clin. Oncology, Internat. Soc. Hematology, Am. Soc. Hematology, N.Y. Soc. Study of Blood, N.Y. County Med. Soc., N.Y. State Med. Soc. Oncologists and Hematologists (pres. 1991), Harvey Soc., Am. Fedn. Clin. Rsch., Am. Assn. Cancer Rsch., Explorers Club (bd. dirs., chmn. sci. adv. com. 1987), Sigma Xi. Office: NY Hosp Cornell Med Ctr 525 E 68th St New York NY 10021-4873 also: 1440 York Ave New York NY 10021

SILVER, SHEILA JANE, composer, music educator; b. Seattle, Oct. 3, 1946; d. Robert Eugene and Fannie (Horowitz) S.; m. John Feldman, Dec. 11, 1988. BA, U. Calif., Berkeley, 1968; postgrad., Hochschule fur Musik, Stuttgart, Fed. Republic Germany, 1969-71; MFA, Brandeis U., 1972, PhD, 1974. Assoc. prof. music SUNY, Stony Brook, 1979—. Composer classical works for orch., string orch., opera, chamber orch., string quartet, various instruments, also vocal and choral compositions and feature film scores. Radcliffe Inst. fellow, 1977-78, Koussevitzky fellow, 1972; recipient Composer award Am. Inst. and Acad. Arts and Letters, 1986, Prix de Rome, Am. Acad. in Rome, 1978-79; winner Nat. Composers' Competition, Internat. Soc. Contemporary Music., 1981-82, winner competition Indpls. Symphony Orch., 1977, IV Internat. Wettbewerb fur Komponistinnen, 1976. Mem. Fellows of Am. Acad., Am. Music Ctr., N.Y. Women Composers. Jewish. Home and Office: 68-37 Dartmouth St Forest Hills NY 11375

SILVER, STEPHEN CHAITT, colon and rectal surgeon, educator; b. Harrisburg, Pa., July 1, 1946; s. Morris A. and Mollie (Chaitt) S.; m. Susan C. Silver; children: Chuck, Beth, Aaron, Alan. BS, Dickinson Coll., 1967; MD, Jefferson Med. Coll., 1971. Diplomate Am. Bd. Surgery, Am. Bd. Colon and Rectal Surgery. Surg. resident Cleve. Clinic Edn. Found., 1972-73, 75-77, colon and rectal surgery fellow, 1977-78; chief colon and rectal surgery Del. County Meml. Hosp., Drexel HIll, Pa., 1978—; asst. prof. surgery Jefferson Med. Coll., Phila., 1978—. Contbr. articles to profl. jours. Maj. USAF, 1973-75. Fellow ACS, Am. Soc. Colon and Rectal Surgeons, Pa. Soc. Colon and Rectal Surgery (pres.-elect), Phila. Acad. Surgery. Office: 1010 Chester Pike Ste 201 Havertown PA 19083

SILVERLIGHT, TERRY BENNET, musician, composer, arranger, drummer, producer; b. Newark, Jan. 15, 1957; s. Arthur Max and Hermine (Klein) S. Student, Princeton U., 1975-76. Drum instr. Drummers Collective Inc., N.Y.C., 1981-85; professional musician worldwide, 1969—; influential fusion drummer Barry Miles and Silverlight, 1971-81; drummer with Roberta Flack, 1986-88. Author drum instrn. book: The Featured Drummer, 1981; composer: Chasin' A Dream (recorded by Nancy Wilson), All I Wanna Do (recorded by Carl Anderson), Christmastime Won't Be the Same This Year (recorded by Judy Torres), Listen to Love, Take My Love for Real, Dancing to the Beat, Chain of Events, Vic's Theme, Tandoori, Buck Rogers, Someday Beneath The Sun, So What (all songs); drummer on albums including: Suddenly (by Billy Ocean), Twice the Love (by George Benson), Miracles (by Change), Torme - A New Album (by Mel Torme), many others; contbr. articles to profl. jours. Home and Office: 339 E 58th St Apt 6B New York NY 10022

SILVERMAN, BENNET HUGH, lawyer; b. Bklyn., Oct. 6, 1938; s. Morris and Belle (Marcus) S.; m. Linda Dresden, July 15, 1962; children: Valerie, Marjorie, Pamela. AB, Columbia Coll., 1959; JD, Columbia U., 1962. Bar: N.Y. 1963, U.S. Dist. Ct. (so. dist.) N.Y. 1964, U.S. Dist. Ct. (ea. dist.) N.Y. 1971, U.S. Ct. Appeals (2d cir.) 1971, U.S. Ct. Internat. Trade 1970, U.S. Ct. Mil. Appeals 1967, U.S. Supreme Ct. 1967. Assoc. Katz, Wittenberg, Levine & Silverman and predecessors, N.Y.C., 1963-70, ptnr., 1970—. Sec., bd. dirs. Hebrew Inst. White Plains, N.Y., 1981—. Lt. USN, 1962-70. Mem. ABA, Union Internat. d'Avocats, Internat. Bar Assn. (co-chmn. commodities arbitration subcom. sale of goods com. bus. law sect.), N.Y. State Bar Assn., Assn. of Bar of City of N.Y., N.Y. County Lawyers Assn., N.Y. State Trial Lawyers Assn., Customs and Internat. Trade Bar Assn., Pi Lambda Phi (nat. councilman, v.p.). Office: Katz Wittenberg Levine & Silverman 370 Lexington Ave New York NY 10017-6503

SILVERMAN, DAVID IRVING, cardiologist; b. New Bedford, Mass., Aug. 24, 1954; s. Seymour and Roslyn (Feldman) S.; m. Adrienne Bentman, May 26, 1985; children: Gabriel, Alexandra. BA, Yale Coll., 1976; MS, U. Chgo., 1977; MD, U. Ill., 1982. Diplomate Am. Bd. Internal Medicine in medicine and cardiovascular disease. Resident Boston City Hosp., 1982-85; fellow West Roxbury (Mass.) VA/Harvard Med., 1985-87; rsch. fellow Beth Israel Hosp., Boston, 1987-90; asst. prof. U. Conn. Health Ctr., Farmington, 1990—; dir. Lipid Disorders Clinic, U. Conn., Farmington, 1991—. Fellow Am. Coll. Cardiology; mem. ACP, Am. Heart Assn., Mass. Med. Soc. Office: U Conn Health Ctr Cardiology Div Farmington CT 06030

SILVERMAN, ELLEN LOUISE, advertising and public relations agency executive; b. Jersey City, Nov. 1, 1940; d. Herman and Rose (Goldberg) Drogin; m. Irwin N. Silverman, Dec. 18, 1960; chidlren: Ronald Marc, Shari Cyd. BS in English Edn. magna cum laude, Jersey City State Coll., 1964. Tchr. Jersey City, 1966-68; photographer Sch. Pictures, Balt., 1970-71; real estate agt. Grempler Realty, Balt., 1972-74; mktg. mgr. A.S. Barnes Pub. Co., Cranbury, N.J., 1974-75; dir. mktg. Transaction Pub., Rutgers U., New Brunswick, N.J., 1975-77; dir. advt. Eisenhower Gallery of Homes, Bridgewater, N.J., 1977-80; dir. Crossroads Ltd., Bedminster, N.J., 1980-81; owner, pres. Ellen Silverman Advt., East Brunswick, N.J., 1981—. Author: Real Estate Relocation Coloring Book, 1980; author, editor quar. Relocation Homes Book Homeward Bound, 1978-79; contbr. articles to jours. Mem. pub. rels. com. LWV, East Brunswick, 1974-76; dir. adult edn. Temple B'nai Shalom, East Brunswick, 1981-82, trustee, bd. dirs., 1980-82. Recipient 1st Place Gold award Advt. Pub. Rels. Assn. N.J., 1990. Mem. Middlesex County C. of C. (pub. rels. com. 1990), N.J. Assn. Women Bus. Owners (Middlesex County bd. dirs., pub. rels. com. 1990-91, v.p. mktg. 1991-92, newsletter editor 1990-91, state pub. rels. chmn. 1991-92, state v.p. mktg. 1992—). Office: Ellen Silverman Advt 6 Oakcrest Dr East Brunswick NJ 08816-4041

SILVERMAN, HAROLD I., pharmaceutical executive; b. Lawrence, Mass., Apr. 27, 1928; s. Jack David and Norma (Illman) S.; m. Arlene Jacobowitz, Nov. 25, 1951; children: Robert L., Richard L. BSc, Phila. Coll. of Pharmacy, 1951, MSc, 1952, DSc, 1956. Instr. Phila. Coll. of Pharmacy, 1952-56; prof. pharmaceutics L.I. U., Bklyn., 1956-64; sr. scientist Warner Lambert Rsch. Inst., Morris Plains, N.J., 1958-60; v.p. sci. dir. Knoll Pharm. Co., West Orange, N.J., 1964-68; prof., assoc. dean Mass. Coll. of Pharmacy, Boston, 1968-85; sr. v.p. Thompson Med. Co., N.Y.C., 1985—; lectr. Boston U. Sch. Medicine, 1971-73, New Eng. Coll. of Optometry, Boston, 1971-80. Contbr. numerous articles to sci. jours. Mem. human subcom. Peter Bent Brigham, Boston, 1980-85, Boston U., 1983-85; cons. Mass. Bd. Optometry, Boston, 1974-80, WHO, Washington, 1985. Named Man of the Yr., Boston Assn. Druggists, 1977; recipient Disting. Svc. award Am. Optometric Assn., 1974. Fellow Soc. Cosmetic Chemists; mem. AAAS, Am. Pharm. Assn. (Phytochemistry award 1956), Am. Chem. Soc., Am. Soc. Hosp. Pharmacists, Am. Oil Chemists Soc., Am. Assn. Pharm. Scientists. Home and Office: 45 Crest Rd Framingham MA 01701-5606

SILVERMAN, IRA NORTON, news producer; b. Bklyn., May 17, 1935; s. Joseph and Mildred (Axelrod) S.; m. Elizabeth Parsons Aspray, June 16, 1979; children by previous marriage: Gary, Bruce; stepchildren: Elizabeth, Aime, Alison. AB, Columbia U., 1957. Newspaper, mag. and book editor, 1957-67; producer, writer NBC News, 1967-79; sr. producer spl. projects NBC Nightly News, Washington, 1979—. Co-author: The Pleasant Avenue Connection, 1976. Recipient Nat. Headliner award, 1977, 78, 81, 87, Alfred I. DuPont-Columbia U. award, 1983-84, 85-86, Emmy award for news and documentary, 1985, 87, award Overseas Press Club Am., 1987, 90, George Polk award L.I. U., 1988, Excellence in TV award Channels mag., 1990, George Foster Peabody award U. Ga., 1991. Office: NBC News 4001 Nebraska Ave NW Washington DC 20016-2795

SILVERMAN, JACK JACOB, podiatrist; b. N.Y.C., Mar. 7, 1911; s. Charles and Molly (Cohen) S.; children: Kenneth, Charles. DPM, N.Y. Coll. Podiatric Medicine, 1936. Podiatrist Workman's Cir. Geriatric Ctr., Bronx, N.Y., 1955—; pres. Tru Fit Shoes, New Rochelle, N.Y., 1990—. Inventor molded shoes, heel stabilizators. Director New Rochelle Com-

munity, 1970, Westchester Teen Age Blind, New Rochelle, 1973. Mem. Am. Podiatry Assn. (Gold and Silver medals 1970, 71, 76). Home and Office: 38 Stratton Rd New Rochelle NY 10804-1416

SILVERMAN, LESTER PAUL, economist, energy industry consultant; b. N.Y.C., Feb. 28, 1947; s. Eli and Irene B. (Karp) S.; m. Janit Roslyn Smith, June 14, 1969 (dec.); 1 child, Leigh. BS in Adminstrn. and Mgmt. Sci., Carnegie-Mellon U., 1969, MS in Indsl. Adminstrn., 1969, PhD in Econs., 1973. Economist Ctr. for Naval Analyses, Arlington, Va., 1969-74; assoc. exec. dir. NAS, Washington, 1974-78; dir. policy analysis Dept. Interior, Washington, 1978-80; prin. dep. asst. sec. Dept. Energy, Washington, 1980-81; exec. v.p. Dist. Heat & Power, Inc., Washington, 1981-82; dir. McKinsey & Co., Inc., Washington, 1982—; cons. in field, 1966-78. Author (with others) govt. report: Reducing U.S. Oil Vulnerability, 1981; editor: Population Redistribution and Public Policy, 1978; contbr. articles to profl. publs. Mem. exec. coun. Am. Jewish Com., Washington, 1983-84. Recipient Spl. Achievement award Dept. Interior, 1979, Outstanding Svc. award Dept. Energy, 1981. Mem. NAS (panel on natural gas stats., 1983-84, exploratory com. on future of nuclear power, 1984, alternative energy R&D com., 1989), Am. Econ. Assn., Internat. Assn. Energy Economists, Omicron Delta Epsilon, Omicron Delta Kappa. Home: 3728 Military Rd NW Washington DC 20015-1766 Office: McKinsey & Co Inc 1101 Pennsylvania Ave NW Washington DC 20004-2504

SILVERMAN, MARTIN BERNARD, secondary school educator; b. Boston, May 27, 1936; s. Joseph Lazarus and Sonya Lillian (Feldman) S.; m. Joseph Harvey. BS in Chemistry, U. Mass., 1960, MEd, 1962; MEd, Columbia U., 1974, EdD, 1985. Math./sci. tchr. Northampton (Mass.) Pub. Schs., 1960-62, U.S. D.O.D., Korea and Bermuda, 1963-66; math.-sci. tchr. N.Y.C. Bd. Edn., 1966-91; ret.; rsch. scholar biophysics NYU, 1986—; biochemistry rsch. asst. Harvard U. Med. Sch., Boston, 1960; cons. in field. Writer, musician, composer and performer; photographer Explorers Jour., U. Mo. Archives collection. Recipient scholarship Itneratn. Ctr. Photography, N.Y.C., 1975. Mem. Explorers Club, Mensa. Home: 25 Montgomery St New York NY 10002-6557

SILVERMAN, MARY DELSON, international co-production executive; b. N.Y.C.; d. Max and Dorothy (Haupt) Delson; children: Sarah, Benjamin. BA, Sarah Lawrence Coll., 1960. Exec. producer Lenox (Mass.) Arts Ctr., Music Theatre Performing Group, 1972-78; dir. acquisitions Phoenix Films, N.Y.C., 1978-81; v.p. co-prodn. BBC/Lion Heart, 1981—; v.p. program acquisitions Lifetime Cable TV, Astoria, N.Y., 1986—. Producer theater: The Club, Dr. Selavy's (Obie award 1977), Magic Theater, Nightclub (Obie award 1972), Cantata; assoc. producer movie Mandy's Grandmother; producer movie What Do Children Think of When They Think of the Bomb?. Bd. dirs. Women in Need, N.Y.C. Mem. Women in Film, Women's Forum. Office: Lifetime Cable TV 36-12 35th Ave Astoria NY 11106

SILVERMAN, MICHAEL HARRIS, physician, regulatory affairs director; b. Chgo., May 25, 1949; s. Paul and Anna Harriet (Socol) S.; m. Brenda Hope Kurtz, June 27, 1971; 1 child, Rebecca Sydney. BS, U. Ill., 1969; MD, U. Chgo., 1973. Diplomate Am. Bd. Internal Medicine, Am. Bd. Rheumatology. Pvt. practice Portland, Oreg., 1978-83; physician Palm Springs Med. Ctr., Palm Springs, Calif., 1984-85; dir. clin. research Sterling Research Group, Rensselaer, N.Y., 1986-89; dir. med. rsch. Sandoz Rsch. Inst., East Hanover, N.J., 1989-91; dir. regulatory affairs Sandoz Rsch. Inst., 1992—. Author: (with others) Conn's Current Theray, 1979, Clinical Internal Medicine, 1979; contbr. articles to profl. jours.; copyright holder Joint Examination teaching slide collection, 1983. Fellow Am. Coll. Physicians, Am. Coll. Rheumatology; mem. Morris Area Freewheelers, Phi Beta Kappa, Phi Kappa Phi. Jewish. Office: Sandoz Rsch Inst RR 10 East Hanover NJ 07936

SILVERMAN, MORRIS, educational administrator; b. Bronx, N.Y., Mar. 20, 1924; s. Samuel and Lena (Fridson) S.; m. Esther Shapiro Horowitz, Feb. 19, 1984; m. Gilda Ruth Semmel, 1948 (dec. 1982); children: Samuel, Elliot, Gail Kety. BA, Yeshiva U., N.Y.C., 1945, BRE, 1953, MS, 1960; MA, Bklyn. Coll., 1949. Faculty mem., adminstr. Yeshiva U., 1945-89. Contbr. numerous articles to profl. jours. Recipient Bernard Revel Mem. award Yeshiva U. Alumni, 1982. Mem. Am. and Middle States Assns. Collegiate Registrars (chmn. various coms.). Jewish. Home: 1271 E 9th St Brooklyn NY 11230-5107 Office: Yeshiva Univ 500 W 185th St New York NY 10033-3201

SILVERMAN, PAUL LEONARD, clinical psychologist; b. Newark, Apr. 29, 1937; s. Samuel and Ann (Schwam) S.; m. Judith Shapiro, June 18, 1961; children: Michael, Noah. BA, Rutgers U., 1959; MA, U. Md., 1962, PhD, 1964. Clin. psychologist Bur. Mental Health, Washington, 1964-67, dir. psychology tng., 1967-68; chief psychologist Youth Svcs. Adminstrn., Washington, 1968-87, chief office program svcs., 1987-88; chief office program svcs. Kensington, Md., 1988—; bd. appeals Nat. Register Health Svc. Providers, Washington, 1985-87; vis. assoc. psychologist Taylor Manor Hosp., Ellicott City, Md., 1989—; cons. Cooksville (Md.) Acad. for Boys, 1989-90; ind. examiner St. Elizabeth Hosp., Washington, 1989-91; provider Blue Cross/Blue Shield Md., Blue Cross/Blue Shield Nat. Capital Area, Medicare. Contbr. articles to profl. jours. Chmn. ACLU, Montgomery County, Md., 1971-72; bd. dirs. Nat. Capital Area Cello Club, Washington, 1985-91. Fellow Md. Psychol. Assn.; mem. Am. Psychol. Assn., D.C. Psychol. Assn. (cert. recognition 1982). Democrat. Jewish. Home: 14315 Bauer Dr Rockville MD 20853-2345 Office: Kensington Mental Health 10400 Connecticut Ave Kensington MD 20895-3910

SILVERMAN, RICHARD, marketing consultant; b. Manchester, N.H., Feb. 21, 1925; s. Abraham B. and Bess (Finman) S.; m. Rosemary Arico, July 18, 1964; 1 child, Eileen. BJ, U. Mo., 1948; Diploma in Acctg., N.H. Sch. of Bus./Fin., Manchester, 1943. Account exec. Mailograph Co., Inc., N.Y.C., 1948-51; dir. mail copywriter Remington Rand, N.Y.C., 1951-52; sales promotion dir. Advance Patterns Co., N.Y.C., 1953; dir. mktg. Universal Products Corp., Westbury, N.Y., 1954-58; copywriter Harrison Home Products, N.Y.C., 1958-60; sr. copywriter Schwab, Beatty & Porter, N.Y.C., 1960-65; editor-in-chief Sophisticated Investing, Palisades Park, N.J., 1967-73; cons., pvt. practice Kew Gardens, N.Y., 1965—; bd. dirs., chmn. Casino Digest, Inc., Glen Cove, N.Y. Author: $100 Gets You Started: Market Secrets for the Small Investor, 1965, The Insurance Industry, 1968. With U.S. Army, 1943-46, ETO. Recipient Best-of-Industry awards Direct Mail Advt. Assn., 1950, 52, 53. Mem. Newsletter Assn. (pres. N.Y. chpt. 1983), Direct Mail Creative Guild (v.p. publicity 1975).

SILVERMAN, ROBERT ALAN, real estate consultant, historian; b. Phila., Dec. 22, 1947; s. Milton Edward and Rhoda (Pasternack) S.; m. Fran Stukelman, Mar. 30, 1969; 1 son, David. B.S., Drexel U., 1969; M.A., Harvard U., 1973, Ph.D., 1977. Fin. analyst Harvard U., Cambridge, Mass., 1977-78, v.p. Harvard Real Estate, 1978-84; dir. planning Harvard U., 1984-88; sr. v.p. Watch Hill Co., 1988-89; mng. dir. Keystone Advisors, Inc., St. Cambridge, Mass., 1990—; cons. With U.S. Army, 1969-72. Author: Law and Urban Growth, 1981; editor: The Corporate Real Estate Handbook, 1987. Jewish. Office: Keystone Advisors Inc 124 Mt Auburn St Cambridge MA 02138-5758

SILVERMAN, SAM MENDEL, physicist, lawyer; b. N.Y.C., Nov. 16, 1925; s. Moshe Aaron and Gitel (Korenbaum) S.; B.Ch.E., CCNY, 1945; Ph.D., Ohio State U., 1952; J.D., Suffolk U., 1982; m. Jacqueline Greenberg, Sept. 12, 1948 (div. Apr. 1965); children—Ann, William, Nancy; m. 2d, Phyllis Rolfe, June 26, 1966; children—Gila, Aaron. Bar: Mass. 1982, N.Y. State 1983, U.S. Ct. Appeals (1st cir.) 1982, U.S. Dist. Ct. Mass. 1982, U.S. Supreme Ct. 1986. Assoc. Ohio State U., Columbus, 1952-55; asst. prof. chem. physics U. Toledo, 1955-57; research physicist Air Force Cambridge Research Labs. (named changed to Air Force Geophysics Lab. 1975), Bedford, Mass., 1957-80, chief polar atmospheric processes br. and dir. geopole obs., 1963-74, cons., 1980—; vis. research assoc. Queens U., Belfast, 1963-64; vis. prof. Osmania U., Hyderabad, India, 1965-66; mem. adv. bd. Inst. Space and Atmospheric Studies, U. Sask. (Can.), 1965-69; sr. research physicist Boston Coll., 1981—; co-chmn. interdivisional commn. history Internat. Assn. Geomagnetism and Aeronomy, 1987-91. Mem. Town Meeting Lexington (Mass.), 1973-79, 84—. Served with USAAF, 1945-46. Fellow Am. Phys. Soc., Explorers Club; mem. Am. Geophys. Union (editor, History of Geophysics newsletter 1983-91), Internat. Assn. Geomagnetism and Aeronomy (co-chmn. intradivisional comm. History). Contbr. articles to profl. jours. Home: 18 Ingleside Rd Lexington MA 02173-2522

SILVERMAN, STEPHEN MEREDITH, editor, author; b. L.A., Nov. 22, 1951; s. Raymond and Shirley (Garfein) S. BA, U. Calif., Irvine, 1973; MS, Columbia U., 1975. Editor-in-chief Coast Mag., L.A., 1975-77; chief entertainment writer New York Post, 1977-88; editor-in-chief Hollywood Mag., L.A., 1989-90; adj. prof. Hunter Coll., N.Y.C., 1978, Marymount Manhattan, 1979. Author: Public Spectacles, 1981, The Fox That Got Away: The Last Days of the Zanuck Dynasty, 1988, David Lean, 1989, Where There's a Will: Who Inherited What and Why, 1991; contbr. numerous articles to nat. mags. Mem. Dramatists Guild. Office: Authors and Artists Group 14 E 60th St New York NY 10022-1006

SILVERS, ROBERT BENJAMIN, editor; b. Mineola, N.Y., Dec. 31, 1929; s. James J. and Rose (Roden) S. A.B., U. Chgo., 1947; grad., Ecole des Sci. Politiques, Paris, France, 1956. Press sec. to Gov. Bowles of Conn., 1950; mem. editorial bd. Paris Rev., 1954—; assoc. editor Harper's mag., 1959-63; co-editor N.Y. Rev. Books, 1963—. Editor: Writing in America, 1960; translator: La Gangrene, 1961; mem. editorial com. Rivista dei Libri, Italy, 1991—. Served with AUS, 1952-53. Mem. Council on Fgn. Relations. Clubs: Century Association (N.Y.C.), Coffee House (N.Y.C.). Office: NY Rev of Books 250 W 57th St New York NY 10107-0001

SILVERSTEIN, ALVIN, biology educator; b. N.Y.C., Dec. 30, 1933; s. Edward and Fannie (Wittlin) S.; m. Virginia Barbara Opshelor, Apr. 3, 1937; children: Robert Alan, Glenn Evan, Carrie Lee, Sharon Leslie, Laura Donna Nunn, Kevin Andrew. BA, Bklyn. Coll., 1955; MS, U. Pa., 1959; PhD, NYU, 1963. Asst. instr. U. Pa., Phila., 1956-58; sci. tchr. Jr. High Sch. 60, N.Y.C., 1959; instr. S.I. Community Coll., 1959-63, asst. prof., 1963-66, assoc. prof., 1966-70, prof., 1970-78; chmn., prof. Coll. S.I., CUNY, 1978-79, prof., 1979—. Author: The Biological Sciences, 1974, Human Anatomy and Physiology, 1980, 2d edit., 1983; co-author numerous books in field. Mem. AAAS, Am. Chem. Soc., Authors Guild. Home: PO Box 537 Lebanon NJ 08833-0537 Office: Coll SI 715 Ocean Ter Staten Island NY 10301-4547

SILVERSTEIN, EMANUEL, medical educator, biochemist and molecular biologist; b. N.Y.C., Feb. 14, 1930; s. Israel Isidore and Raize Rose (Rubock) S.; m. Shoshana Shame Tubi, Mar. 25, 1965; children: Roselle Rama, Daniel Doron. BS magna cum laude, CUNY, 1950; MD, SUNY, 1954; PhD in Biochemistry, U. Minn., 1963. Diplomate Nat. Bd. Med. Examiners. Intern in medicine U. Minn. Hosps., Mpls., 1954-55, resident and NIH fellow in medicine NIH, 1958-59, postdoctoral fellow Biochemistry Am. Cancer Soc., 1959-63; intern in pathology Sch. of Medicine Yale U., New Haven, 1955-56; sr. asst. surgeon USPHS lab. pathology and histochemistry Nat. Inst. Arthritis & Metabolic Diseases, Bethesda, Md., 1956-58; with dept. biology MIT, Cambridge, 1963-64; asst. prof. medicine SUNY Health Sci. Ctr., Bklyn., 1964-69, assoc. prof. medicine and grad. program in biochemistry, 1970-77, prof. medicine and grad. program in biochemistry, 1977—; vis. scientist Weizmann Inst. Sci., Rehovoth, Israel, 1971. Contbr. articles to profl. jours. Sr. asst. surgeon USPHS, 1956-58. N.Y. State Regents scholar, 1950-54. Mem. Am. Soc. Biochemistry and Molecular Biology, Am. Assn. Pathologists, Phi Beta Kappa. Office: SUNY Health Sci Ctr 450 Clarkson Ave Brooklyn NY 11203-2098

SILVERSTEIN, JO ANN, health policy analyst; b. N.Y.C., May 7, 1935; d. Max and Mary (Stoler) Kleinman; m. Samuel Charles Silverstein, Apr. 2, 1967; children: David Paul, Jennifer Kate. BA, Cornell U., 1956; MPH, Yale U., 1972. Dir. pub. info. N.Y.C. Model Cities, 1968-70; mem. transition task force N.Y.C. Dept. Hosps., 1970; staff dir. health task force N.Y. State Study Commn. for N.Y.C., 1972-73; freelance cons. and writer N.Y.C., 1975-89; dir. spl. projects, program reporting Bur. AIDS Program Svcs., N.Y.C. Dept. Health, 1987-91; sr. analyst for AIDS United Hosp. Fund, N.Y.C., 1991—; mem. city hosp. vis. com. United Hosp. Fund, 1976-80, vice chmn., 1978-80. Contbr. articles to profl. publs. Bd. dirs. Rockefeller U. Children's Sch., N.Y.C., 1976-80, chmn., 1979-80. Mem. APHA, Pub. Health Assn. N.Y.C. Home: 325 E 79th St Apt 6B New York NY 10021-0982 Office: United Hosp Fund 55 5th Ave New York NY 10003

SILVERSTEIN, JUDITH LYNN, clinical psychologist; b. Phila., Oct. 19, 1946; d. Arthur J. and Ruth L. (Lieberman) Handelsman. PhD, Tufts U., 1975. Lic. psychologist; cert. sex therapist. Psychotherapist Boston Psychol. Ctr. for Women, 1977-81, New Eng. Inst., Framingham, Mass., 1977-81, Next Step Conseling, Newton, Mass., 1983-86; psychologist Boston Inst. Psychotherapies, 1986-91; pvt. practice psychologist Cambridge and Needham, Mass., 1981—; coord. continuing edn. Boston Inst. for Psychotherapies, 1985-92. Author: Sexual Enhancement for Women, 1978, Sexual Enhancement for Men, 1986. Mem. Mass. Psychol. Assn. Am. Psychol. Assn., Am. Group Psychotherapy Assn. Democrat. Jewish. Home: 29 Briarwood Cir Needham MA 02194-1829

SILVERSTEIN, MELVIN SAUL, counselor; b. Hartford, Conn., Oct. 30, 1925; s. Samuel and Dora S.; m. Florence Elizabeth Heath, June 26, 1948; children: Lucy Kate, Jeffrey, Timothy, Melanie. BA, U. Hartford, 1950, MEd, 1956. Nat. cert. counselor; nat. cert. career counselor. Counselor Glastonbury (Conn.) Bd. Edn., 1953-60; counselor Darien (Conn.) Bd. Edn., 1960-67; counselor Westport (Conn.)üBd. Edn., 1967-85, adult edn. counselor, 1987—; pvt. practice counseling Norwalk, Conn., 1987—; adj. prof. U. Bridgeport (Conn.), 1974-80; com. mem. Conn. Edn. Assn. Human Rights Commn., Hartford, 1989-91, career edn. adv. com. chairperson, Westport, 1973—. Sgt. USAF, 1944-46. NDEA fellow Boston U., 1964, GE fellow, Boston, 1969; named Counselor of Yr., State of Conn., 1975. Mem. AACD, Am. Sch. Counselors Assn. Home: 12 Newtown Ter Norwalk CT 06851-3021 Office: Westport Continuing Edn Dept 70 North Ave Westport CT 06880-2799

SILVERSTEIN, SETH, physician; b. N.Y.C., May 20, 1939; s. Reuben B. and Mollie (Silver) S. BS, L.I. U., 1963; MS, Hofstra U., 1967; MD, U. Cen. Del Este, Dominican Republic, 1980. Lic. physician N.Y., Pa., La. Diagnostic radiologist Queens Hosp. Ctr., Jamaica, N.Y., 1983-84, Newark (N.J.) Beth Israel Med. Ctr., 1984-85; nuclear medicine VA Med. Ctr., Northport, N.Y., 1985-86, SUNY U. Hosp., Stony Brook, 1986-87; diagnostic radiologist La. State U., New Orleans, 1987-89; pvt. practice in diagnostic radiology nuclear medicine Roslyn, N.Y., 1990—; parole officer N.Y.C.; tchr. N.Y. City Bd. Edn. Mem. AMA, Radiol. Soc. N.Am., N.Y. Med. Soc., N.Y. Roentgen Soc., King's County Med. Soc., Soc. Nuclear Medicine. Hebrew. Home: PO Box 136 Roslyn NY 11576

SILVERSTEIN, VIRGINIA BARBARA, translator; b. Phila., Apr. 3, 1937; d. Samuel Wolf and Gertrude (Bresch) Opshelor; m. Alvin Silverstein, Dec. 30, 1933; children: Robert Alan, Glenn Evan, Carrie Lee, Sharon Leslie, Laura Donna Nunn, Kevin Andrew. Student, McGill U., Montreal, 1955; BA, U. Pa., 1958. Analytical chemist Am. Sugar Co., Bklyn., 1958-59; translator of Russian sci. lit. N.Y.C., 1960—. Translator jours. Biokhimiya, 1970-92, Immunologiya, 1982-90, Molekyularnaya Genetika, Mikrobiologiya i Virusologiya, 1986—; co-author syndicated column Tales from Dr. A., 1972-74; co-author numerous books in field; contbr. entries to encycs. Mem. Am. Translators Assn., Authors Guild. Address: PO Box 537 Lebanon NJ 08833

SILVERSTONE, DAVID EDWARD, ophthalmologist; b. N.Y.C., Feb. 16, 1948; s. Sidney Milton and Estelle (Cohen) S.; m. Linda Carol Thalberg, June 19, 1969; 1 child, Scott. AB, Columbia Coll., 1969; MD, NY Med. Coll., 1973. Cert. Ophthalmology, Am. Bd. Ophthalmology, 1977. Acad. internat. eye fellow Albert Schweitzer Hosp., Deschapples, Haiti, 1976; instr. Dept. Ophthalmology and Visual Scis. Yale Sch. Medicine, Newhaven, Conn., 1976-77, asst. clin. prof. Dept. Ophthalmology and Visual Scis., 1977-86, assoc. clin. prof. Dept. Ophthalmology and Visual Scis., 1986-91, clin. prof. Dept. Ophthalmology and Visual Scis., 1991—; chief ophthalmology VA Hosp., West Haven, Conn., 1977-85; attending physician Yale-New Haven Hosp., New Haven, Conn., 1976—, asst. chief ophthalmology, 1988—; dir. continuing edn. Am. Soc. Cataract and Refractive Surgery, Washington, 1991—; mem. Bd. Permanent Officers Yale Sch. Medicine, New Haven, 1991—. Author: Automated Visual Field Testing, 1986; contbr. articles to profl. jours. Recipient Med. Student Essay award Am. Sc. Pharmacology and Experimental therapeutics, 1971, Moshy Book award N.Y. Med. Coll., N.Y.C., 1973, Physician's regognition award AMA, Chgo., 1976, 79, 82, 85, Honor award Am. Acad. Ophthalmology, San Francisco, 1990. Fellow Am. Acad. Ophthalmology; mem. New England Ophthalmological Soc., AMA, Conn. State Med. Soc., Conn. Soc. Eye Physicians, New Haven County Med. Assn., Yale Alumni Ophthalmology, Assn. for Rsch. in Vision and Ophthalmology. Office: Temple Eye Physicians 60 Temple St New Haven CT 06510

SILVERSTONE, FELIX ABRAHAM, geriatrician, diabetologist; b. N.Y.C., Aug. 27, 1919; m. Bella Karell. MD, George Washington U., 1942. Diplomate Nat. Bd. Med. Examiners. Intern Univ. div. Kings County Hosp., Bklyn., 1942-43, resident in medicine, 1944-46; instr. physiology George Washington U. Sch. Medicine, Washington, 1943-44; internal medicine trainee univ. div. Kings County Hosp., Bklyn., 1942-49; pvt. practice internal medicine Bklyn., 1949-77; attending physician in charge of diabetes Maimonides Med. Ctr., Bklyn., 1951-77; investigator in gerontology Nat. Heart Inst., NIH, Bethesda, Md., 1953-55; assoc. med. dir., dir. rsch. Parker Jewish Geriatric Inst., New Hyde Park, N.Y., 1977—; chair, participant sci. symposia, cons., 1956-90. Contbr. articles to profl. jours. Lectr., symposia chair sr. citizens, PTA, health ctrs., lay chpt. N.Y. Diabetes Assn., N.Y.C., Bklyn., Herricks, N.Y., 1956-90. Surgeon full grade USPHS, 1953-55. Emma K. Carr scholar George Washington U., 1938-41; recipient 1st prize rsch. award Maimonides Med. Ctr., Bklyn., 1974, N.Y. Acad. Scis., 1990. Fellow Am. Coll. Physicians, Gerontol. Soc. Am., Am. Geriatrics Soc.; mem. AMA, Am. Diabetes Assn. Office: Parker Jewish Geriatric Inst 271-11 76th Ave New Hyde Park NY 11042

SILVERSTONE, PAUL HAROLD, naval historian, author, travel agency executive; b. London, June 8, 1931; s. Arthur Silverstone and Pearl (Finkelstein) Newsom (parents Am. citizens). AB, Yale U., 1953; JD, Harvard U., 1956. Sec.-treas. Travel Near & Far Inc., N.Y.C., 1965-71; exec. v.p. Dunwell Travel Ltd., N.Y.C., 1977-84; v.p., exec. dir. ATA Travel Inc., N.Y.C., 1990—. Author: U.S. Warships of World War II, 1965, U.S. Warships of World War I, 1970, Dictionary of the World's Capital Ships, 1984, U.S. Warships Since 1945, 1986, Warships of the Civil War Navies, 1989. With U.S. Army, 1956-58. Mem. Internat. Naval Rsch. Orgn., World Ship Soc., U.S. Naval Inst., Yale Club of N.Y.C. Home: 330 W 58th St New York NY 10019

SILVESTRO, JOHN RICHARD, publishing company executive; b. Medford, Mass., Sept. 26, 1946; s. John Joseph and Adeline Ann (Battista) S.; m. Emily Sue Brown, June 20, 1970; children: Anne, Thomas. AB, Boston Coll., 1968; MS, Pa. State U., 1970, PhD, 1974. Instr. of psychology and edn., asst. to dean Western New Eng. Coll., Springfield, Mass., 1971-73; assoc. prof. ednl. psychology SUNY, Fredonia, 1973-83; NIMH postdoctoral fellow U. Ky./Coll. of Medicine, Lexington, 1980-82; project dir. Psychol. Corp., Cleve., 1983-85; area dir. Nat. Evaluation Systems, Amherst, Mass., 1986—. Contbr. articles to profl. jours.; author two books in field. Chmn. Hadley (Mass.) Elem. Sch. Bldg. Commn., 1989—; bd. dirs. Hampshire Community United Way, Northampton, 1989—. Recipient Chancellor's award for Excellence in Teaching, SUNY, 1980, NIMH postdoctoral fellowship, U. Ky. Coll. of Medicine, Lexington, 1980, NDEA grad. fellowship, Pa. State U., University Park, 1968. Mem. Am. Psychol. Assn., Am. Ednl. Rsch. Assn. Home: 141 Rocky Hill Rd Hadley MA 01035-9743 Office: Nat Evaluation Systems Inc PO Box 226 Amherst MA 01004-0226

SILVIA, WILLIAM FRANK, civil engineer, consultant; b. East Providence, R.I., Dec. 27, 1933; s. Frank Perry and Mildred Helen (Lisbon) S.; m. Pauline Therese Senecal, Oct. 8, 1955; children: William J., Michele, Stephen, Suzanne, Thomas, Judithe. BS in Civil Engring., U. R.I., 1955; MBA, SUNY, Buffalo, 1967. Registered profl. engr., N.Y. Engr. Bell Aerosystems, Niagara Falls, N.Y., 1955-56; from engr. to div. pres. Union Carbide Corp., Danbury, Conn., 1956-86; mgmt. cons. Silvia Assocs., Darien, Conn., 1986-88; pres., chief operating officer Batts, Inc., Zeeland, Mich., 1988-89; mgmt. cons. Warren Co., Providence, R.I., 1989—; bd. dirs. Internat. Oxygen Mfrs. Assn., Cleve., 1980-83; pres. Western N.Y. sect. Am. Assn. Cost. Engrs., 1961-65. 1st lt. U.S. Army Corps Engrs., 1956-61. Mem. Presidents Assn., Am. Mgmt. Assn. Roman Catholic.

SIMIC, CHARLES, English language educator, poet; b. Beograd, Yugoslavia, May 9, 1938; came to U.S., 1954, naturalized, 1971; s. George and Helen (Matijevich) S.; m. Helen Dubin, Oct. 1964; children: Anna, Philip. B.A., NYU, 1967. Editorial asst. Aperture, Quar. of Photography, N.Y.C., 1966-69; prof. English Calif. State U., Hayward, 1970-73, U. N.H., Durham, 1973—; vis. tchr. Boston U., spring 1975, Columbia U., fall 1979. Author: poems What the Grass Says, 1967, Somewhere Among us a Stone is Taking Notes, 1969, Dismantling the Silence, 1971, White, 1972, Return to a Place Lit by a Glass of Milk, 1974, Biography and a Lament, 1976, Charon's Cosmology, 1977, Classic Ballroom Dances, 1980, Austerities, 1982, Weather Forecast for Utopia and Vicinity, 1983, Selected Poems, 1985, Unending Blues, 1986, The World Doesn't End, 1989 (Pulitzer Prize 1990), The Book of Gods and Devils, 1990, Hotel Insomnia, 1992; prose The Uncertain Certainty, 1985. Wonderful Words, Silent Truth, 1990; translator, editor: (with C.W. Truesdale) poems Fire Gardens, 1970, (with Mark Strand) Another Republic, 1976, (with others) Selected Poems of Tomaz Salamun, 1987, RollCall of Mirrors, 1987; translator: Four Modern Yugoslav Poets, 1970, (with P. Kastmiler) Atlantis, 1983; contbr. poems to mags. and anthologies. Served with U.S. Army, 1961-63. Recipient PEN Internat. award for translation, 1970, 80, Edgar Allan Poe award Am. Acad. Poets, 1975, Nat. Inst. Arts and Letters and AAAL award, 1976, Harriet Monroe poetry award U. Chgo., 1980, DiCastignola award Poetry Soc. Am., 1980, Pulitzer prize for poetry, 1990; Guggenheim fellow, 1972-73; Nat. Endowment for Arts fellow, 1974-75, 79-80; Fulbright Travelling fellow, 1982, Ingram Merrill fellow, 1983-84; Mac Arthur fellow, 1984-89. Home: PO Box 192 Strafford NH 03884-0192 Office: U NH Dept English Durham NH 03824

SIMICSAK, ROBERT ALLEN, civil engineer; b. Trenton, N.J., Jan. 9, 1948; s. Frank George and Alma (Szilagyi) S.; m. Anne DeAngelis, Apr. 17, 1982; children: Anthony DeAngelis, Tracy DeAngelis. AAS, Mercer County Coll., Trenton, N.J., 1975; BS, Thomas Edison Coll., Trenton, N.J., 1980. Registered profl. engr., N.J.; cert. pub. mgr. Surveyor N.J. Dept. Environ. Protection, Trenton, 1969-75, staff engr., 1975-84, sect. chief permits, 1984-89; regulatory affairs mgr. Schoor & Canger Group, Manalapan, N.J., 1989-91; mcpl. engr. Twp. of Woodbridge, N.J., 1991—. Author/editor: N.J. Wastewater Treatment Trust Technical Regulations, 1987. Mem. NSPE, N.J. Soc. Profl. Engrs., N.J. Builders Assn. (environ. com. 1989-90), Water Pollution Control Fedn., Engrs. Club Trenton (program com.), Bently Drivers Club (sec. N.E. region), Rolls Royce Owners Club. Roman Catholic. Office: Township of Woodbridge 1 Main St Woodbridge NJ 07095-3352

SIMKIN, THOMAS EDWARD, geologist; b. Auburn, N.Y., Nov. 11, 1933; s. William Edward and Ruth Helen (Commons) S.; m. Sharon Marie Russell, July 3, 1965; children: Shona Kathleen, Adam Javier. BS, Swarthmore Coll., 1955; PhD, Princeton U., 1964. Instr. SUNY, Binghamton, 1964-65; postdoctoral fellow U. Chgo., 1965-67; supr. geology Smithsonian Oceanographic Sorting Ctr., Washington, 1967-71; curator Nat. Mus. Natural History, Smithsonian Instn., Washington, 1972—, dir. Global Volcanism Program; sec. for the Americas (sci.) Charles Darwin Found. for Galapagos Isles, 1970-90. Author: (with others) Volcanoes of the World, 1981; editor Catalog of Active Volcanoes of the World, Internat. Assn. Volcanology, 1980—; contbr. articles to profl. jours. Mem. Arlington County (Va.) Environ. Improvement Commn., 1981-91. With U.S. Coast and Geodetic Survey, 1956-58. Grantee NSF, Smithsonian Instn., NASA. Mem. Am. Geophys. Union, Internat. Assn. Volcanology. Office: Nat Mus Natural History Stop 119 Smithsonian Instn Washington DC 20560

SIMMONS, BARRY PUTNAM, orthopaedic physician, educator; b. Boston, Dec. 18, 1939; s. Arthur Maxwell and Kathleen Beverly (Perlis) S.; m. Laura Maureen Matheson, Oct. 9, 1968; children: Quincey Rebecca, Sara Putnam, Molly MacMathin. BA, Harvard U., 1961; MD, Columbia U., 1965. Cert. Am. Bd. of Orthopaedic Surgery. Resident Combined Harvard

Orthopaedic Program, Boston, 1969-73; fellow hand surgery Group de l'Etude de la Main, Paris, 1973; fellow trauma Swiss Assn. for Internat. Fixator, Basel, 1974; assoc. orthopaedic surgeon Children's Hosp., Boston, 1974—, Brigham and Women's Hosp., Boston, 1974-89; asst. prof. Med. Sch. Harvard U., Cambridge, Mass., 1982-87; assoc. prof. orthopaedic surgery Med. Sch. Harvard U., Cambridge, 1988—; orthopedic surgeon Brigham Orthopedic Assocs. Inc., Boston, 1974—; chief hand surgery svc. Children's Hosp. Boston, 1981—, Brigham and Women's Hosp., Boston, 1981—. Assoc. editor Jour. Hand Surgery, 1985-91, Chirurgie de la Main, Paris, 1985; editor: Yearbook of Orthopedics, 1992; contbr. numerous articles to profl. jours. Marshall Harvard 25th reunion, 1986; vis. prof. many univs., co-chmn. residency selecton Combined Harvard Orthopaedic Residency Program . Lt. comdr. USN 1967-69 (Vietnam). Fellow Am. Acad. Orthopaedic Surgery; mem. Am. Soc. for Surgery of the Hand, British Soc. for Surgery of the Hand, French Soc. for Surgery of the Hand, Harvard Club, Hand Study Soc. of Minn., Acad. Orthopedic Soc., Am. Acad. of Orthopedic Surgery (sec. coun. of muscule skeltal specialties 1992—). Jewish. Office: Brigham and Womens Hosp 75 Francis St Boston MA 02115-6195

SIMMONS, EDWIN HOWARD, marine corps officer, historian; b. Paulsboro, N.J., Aug. 25, 1921; s. Edwin Lonsdale and Nettie Emma (Vankirk) S.; m. Frances Bliss, Apr. 25, 1962; children: Edwin Howard, Clarke Vankirk, Bliss, Courtney. B.A., Lehigh U., 1942; M.A., Ohio State U., 1955; postgrad., Amphibious Warfare Sch., 1949-50, Nat. War Coll., 1966-67. Commd. 2d lt. USMC, 1942, advanced through grades to brig. gen., 1967; asst. prof. NROTC, Ohio State U., 1952-55; with Hdqrs. Marine Corps, 1955- 59; naval attache Dominican Republic, 1959-60; with Hdqrs. Marine Corps and Joint Staff, 1962-65, 3d Marine Div., 1965-66, 1st Marine Div., Vietnam, 1970-71; dep. fiscal dir. Marine Corps, 1967-70; dir. Marine Corps history and museums USMC Hdqrs., Arlington, Va., 1971—; pres. Am. Mil. Inst., 1979*72; v.p. U.S. Commn. Mil. History, 1979-83, exec. v.p. Marine Corps Hist. Found., 1979-88; pres. Coun. Am.'s Mil. Past, 1991—. Author: The United States Marines, 1974, Marines, 1987; Mng. editor: Marine Corps Gazette, 1946-49; sr. editor: Publs. Group, Marine Corps Schs., 1960-61; Contbr. to numerous books, encys., mags., jours. and annuals. Pres. Am. Mil. Inst., 1979-83; v.p. U.S. Commn. Mil. History, 1979-83; exec. v.p. Marine Corps Hist. Found., 1979-88; pres. Coun. on Am.'s Mil. Past, 1991—. Decorated D.S.M., Silver Star, Legion of Merit with two gold stars, Bronze Star with gold star, Meritorious Service medal, Navy Commendation medal, Purple Heart; knight Nat. Order of Vietnam, Vietnamese Cross of Gallantry with 2 palms and silver star; recipient Centennial Disting. Grad. medallion Ohio State U., 1970. Fellow Co. Mil. Historians; mem. Am. Soc. Mil. Comptrollers (nat. v.p. 1967-69, pres. 1969-70), Nat. War Coll. Alumni Assn. (v.p. 1969-70, 74-75), Phi Beta Kappa, Omicron Delta Kappa, Phi Sigma Kappa. Home: 9020 Charles Augustine Dr Alexandria VA 22308-2822 Office: USMC Mus MC Hist Ctr Navy Yard Washington DC 20374-0580

SIMMONS, EUGENE, military personnel; b. N.Y.C., June 14, 1943; s. James Christopher and Annie (Whitfield) S.; m. Barbara Ann Whittaker, May 5, 1966; children: Eugene Jr., Stuart, Darrell, Earl, Desmonda Altovise. Grad. high sch., Bronx, N.Y.; diploma, AFCC NCO Acad., Keesler AFB, Miss., 1982. Enlisted USAF, 1962; telecomm. technician 1962nd Communication Squadron, Okinawa, Japan, 1964-66; telecomm. crew chief 1909th Communication Squadron, Andrews AFB, Md, 1966-67, 1876th Communication Squadron, TonSon Nhut AFB, Viet Nam, 1967-68, 2164th Communication Squadron, RAF Bentwaters, England, 1968-72; non-commissioned officer in charge 2045th Communication Squadron, Bolling AFB Washington, 1972-73, 2045th Communication Group, Andrews AFB, Md., 1973-80, 27th Communication Group, Anderson AFB, Guam, 1980-82, 1925th Communication Group, Edwards AFB, Calif., 1982-84; mgr. telecommunications The Fairfax Hosp., Falls Church, Va., 1984—. Democrat. Home: 7213 Havre Turn Upper Marlboro MD 20772-4256 Office: The Fairfax Hosp 3300 Gallows Rd Washington DC 20206-0001

SIMMONS, HEATHER PATRICIA, public relations administrator; b. Phila., Mar. 7, 1969; d. J. Earl Jr. and Linda (Palermo) S. BA in Internat. Rels., St. Joseph's U., Phila., 1991. External rels. asst. St. Joseph's U., 1989-91; pub. rels. specialist, exec. alumni dir. Gloucester County Coll., Deptford, N.J., 1991—. Contbr. articles to profl. jours. Mem. Phi Theta Alpha. Home: 6419 Sherwood Rd Philadelphia PA 19151 Office: Gloucester County Coll RR# 4 Box 203 Deptford Twp Tanyard Rd Sewell NJ 08080

SIMMONS, HOWARD L., academic administrator; b. Mobile, Ala.. BS in Secondary Edn., Spring Hill Coll., 1960; MAT in Slavic langs. and Lit., Ind. U., 1965; PhD in Design and Mgmt. of Postsecondary Edn., Fla. State U., 1975. Assoc. dir. , asst. exec. sec. Commn. on Higher Edn. Middle States Assn. of Colls. and Schs. Phila., 1974—, exec. dir., 1988—; vis. lectr. in Russian Lafayette Coll., Easton, Pa., 1970-71; part-time Russian/Spanish instr. Clayton (Mo.) High Sch., 1965-67; dean instructional svcs. Northampton Community Coll., Bethlehem, Pa., 1969-74; chmn. dept. fgn. lang. Forest Park Community Coll., Mo., 1964-69; sr. researcher Ariz. State U., nat. Ctr. for Postsecondary Governance and Fin., 1986-87; cons. in field; keynote speaker in field; researcher on accreditation and blacks in higher edn. Contbr. articles to profl. jours. NDEA grantee Spring Hill Coll., 1958-60; NDEA fellow Ind. U., 1963-64, EPDA fellow Fla. State U., 1973-75, ACE fellow, 1972-73; Given Faculty Merit award St. Louis Community Coll., 1967, 68. Mem. Am. Ednl. Rsch. assn., Am. Assn. for Community and Jr. Colls. (assoc.), Assn. for the Study of Higher Edn., Assn. of Tchrs. of Slavic and East European Langs., Am. Assn. for Higher Edn. (exec. bd. black caucus, nat. cultural diversity award by caucuses 1992), Phi Delta Kappa, Kappa Delta Pi. Home: 1420 Locust St Apt 12D Philadelphia PA 19102-5024 Office: Mid State Assn of Colls and Schs Commn on Higher Edn 3624 Market St Philadelphia PA 19104-2611

SIMMONS, JOHN DEREK, financial consultant; b. Essex, Eng., July 17, 1931; came to U.S., 1952; s. Simon Leonard and Eve (Smart) S.; m. Rosalind Wellish, Mar. 5, 1961; children: Peter Lawrence, Sharon Leslie. BS, Columbia, 1956; MBA, Rutgers U., 1959; postgrad. NYU, 1959-62.Chief cost acct. Airborne Accessories, Hillside, N.J., 1952-57; sr. cost analyst Curtiss-Wright Corp., Wood Ridge, N.J., 1957; sr. fin. analyst internat. group Ford Motor Co., Jersey City, N.J., 1958-60; rsch. assoc. Nat. Assn. Accts., N.Y.C., 1960-64; asst. to v.p. fin. Air Reduction Co., Inc., 1965-67; mgr. corp. planning Anaconda Wire & Cable Co., N.Y.C., 1968; ind. fin. cons., 1968-71; assoc. cons. Rogers, Slade and Hill, Inc., N.Y.C., 1969-71; v.p., security analyst, economist Moore & Schley, Cameron & Co. (name now changed to Fourteen Rsch. Corp.), 1972-81; v.p., security analyst Merrill Lynch Capital Markets, N.Y.C., 1981-88; security analyst Arnhold and S. Bleichroeder, Inc., N.Y.C., 1988-89; v.p., security analyst, corp. fin. specialist Smith Barney, Harris Upham & Co., Inc., N.Y.C., 1989-90; sr. cons. Carl Byoir & Assocs., N.Y.C., 1991—; lectr. profl. socs. and confs.; lectr. econs., mgmt., polit. sci. Rutgers U., 1957-64. Contbr. articles on econs. of underdeveloped nations, polit. sci., mgmt., fin. to U.S. and fgn. publs. Served to 1st lt. Brit. Army, 1950-52. Granted personal coat of Arms By Queen Elizabeth II: manorial Lord of Ash., Suffolk, Eng. Mem. Am. Econ. Assn., Royal Econ. Soc., N.Y. Soc. Security Analysts. Home: 360 E 72d St New York NY 10021 Office: 420 Lexington Ave New York NY 10017

SIMMONS, MARVIN GENE, geophysics educator; b. Dallas, May 15, 1929; s. Burt H. and Mable (Marshall) S.; divorced; children—Jon Eric, Debra Lynn, Sandra Kay, Pamela Jean. B.S., Tex. Agrl. and Mech. Coll., 1949; M.S., So. Methodist U., 1958; Ph.D., Harvard U., 1962. Petroleum engr. Humble Oil Co., 1949-51; propr. gravel business, 1953-58; asst. prof. So. Meth. U., 1962-65; prof. geophysics MIT, 1965-89, prof. emeritus, 1989—; prin. Hager-Richter Geoscience Inc., 1989—; Cons. NASA, 1965-72; chief scientist NASA (Manned Spacecraft Center), Houston, 1969-71; cons. on siting of nuclear facilities; sec. Internat. Heat Flow Com., 1967-71; chmn. com. drilling for sci. purposes Nat. Acad. Scis., 1965; Mem. geophysics panel NSF. Served with USAF, 1951-53. NSF postdoctoral fellow, 1961-62. Fellow Geol. Soc. Am., Am. Geophys. Union; mem. ASTM (com. C-18 on dimension stone 1986—), Boston Geol. Soc. (pres. 1967-68), Soc. Exploration Geophysicists, Sigma Xi, Tau Beta Pi. Home: 180 N Policy St Salem NH 03079-1916 Office: 8 Industrial Way Unit 10D Salem NH 03079-2837

SIMMONS, NORMAN SARNEY, jazz pianist; b. Chgo., Oct. 6, 1929; s. Sarney and Blanche (Gibson) S.; m. Betty Sparrow, Oct. 16, 1949 (div. Sept. 1973); 1 child, Deborah; m. Karen Beatrice Hodge, Oct. 28, 1987. Student, Chgo. Sch. Music, 1945-50. Arranger Riverside Records, N.Y.C., 1960-61; musical dir. Carmen McRae, 1961-69; accompanist Betty Carter, 1970-72; instr. JazzMobile Sch., N.Y.C., 1973—; pres., owner Milljac Rec. Co., N.Y.C., 1979—; adj. prof. William Patterson Coll., Wayne, N.J., 1982—, Parson's New Sch., N.Y.C., 1986—; house band leader Chgo. Bee-Hive, 1953-58. Arranger/composer Big Soul Band, 1960; arranger Lover Man, 1961; artist/producer I Am the Blues, 1981, 13th Moon, 1986; mem. Eddie Davis/Johnny Griffin Quintet,1960; accompanist Anita O'Day, 1979-81, musical dir. Joe Williams, 1980—. Grantee Nat. Endowment for Arts 1973, 77. Mem. Broadcast Music, Inc., Mechanical Copyright Protection Soc., Harmony Lodge No. 88. Office: Milljac Pub Co 106 Forest Ave W Teaneck NJ 07666

SIMMONS, PAUL ALLEN, retired federal judge; b. Monongahela, Pa., Aug. 31, 1921; s. Perry C. and Lilly D. (Allen) S.; m. Gwendolyn O. Gladden, Sept. 2, 1950; children—Paul A., Gwendolyn Dale, Anne Marie. B.A., U. Pitts., 1946; J.D., Harvard U., 1949. Mem. faculty dept. law S.C. State Coll. Law, 1949-52; prof. law N.C. Central U., 1952-56; pvt. practice law Monongahela, 1956-73; judge Ct. of Common Pleas, Washington County, Pa., 1973-78; sr. judge U.S. Dist. Ct. (we. dist.) Pa., Pitts., 1978-91; ret., 1991. Mem. Pa. Human Relations Commn., 1963-68; mem. Pa. Minor Jud. Edn. Bd., 1970-86, Washington County Redevel. Authority, 1970-73. Mem. Pa. Bar Assn., N.C. Bar Assn., Am. Bar Assn., Washington County Bar Assn., Pa. Bar Assn., Am. Judicature Soc., NAACP. Democrat. Mem. African Meth. Episcopal Ch. Clubs: Masons, Elks. Home: 700 Meade St Monongahela PA 15063-2200

SIMMONS, PETER, university dean, law educator; b. N.Y.C., July 19, 1931; s. Michael L. and Mary A. S.; m. Ruth J. Tanfield, Jan. 28, 1951; children: Sam, Lizzard. A.B., U. Calif., Berkeley, 1953, LL.B., 1956; postgrad. (Alvord fellow), U. Wis., 1956-58. Prof. SUNY, Buffalo, 1963-67; mem. faculty Ohio State U., 1967-75, U. Ill., 1972, Case Western Res. U., 1974-75; prof. law and urban planning Rutgers U. Coll. Law, Newark, 1975—, dean, 1975—. Contbr. articles to profl. jours. Mem. Ohio Housing Commn., 1972-74; commr. Ohio Reclamation Rev. Bd., 1974-75; chmn. N.J. Criminal Disposition Commn., 1983-84; mem. N.J. Law Revision Commn., 1987—. Mem. Am. Planning Assn., Urban Land Inst., Am. Law Inst., AAUP (nat. council 1973-75). Office: Rutgers U Law Sch 15 Washington St Newark NJ 07102-3192

SIMMONS, RICHARD DE LACEY, mass media executive; b. Cambridge, Mass., Dec. 30, 1934; s. Ernest J. and Winifred (McNamara) S.; m. Mary DeWitt Bleecker, May 20, 1961; children: Christopher DeWitt, Robin Bleecker. Grad., 1951; AB, Harvard Coll., 1955; LLB, Columbia U., 1958. Bar: N.Y. 1959. V.p., gen. counsel Dun & Bradstreet Corp., N.Y.C., 1969-73, exec. v.p., 1976-79, vice chmn., 1979-81; vice chmn. Moody's Investors Svc., N.Y.C., 1973-75; pres. Dun & Bradstreet, Inc., N.Y.C., 1975; pres., chief oper. officer Washington Post Co., Washington, 1981-91; pres. Internat. Herald Tribune, Paris, 1989—; bd. dirs. The Washington Post Co., J.P. Morgan & Co., Inc., Morgan Guaranty Trust Co. of N.Y., Union Pacific Corp.; equity adv. bd. GE Investment Corp., Drug Screening Systems, Inc. Mem. coun. White Burkett Miller Ctr. Pub. Affairs, U. Va. Office: Internat Herald Tribune 1150 15th St NW Washington DC 20071-0002

SIMON, ANNE ELIZABETH, biochemist; b. Manhasset, N.Y., June 8, 1956; d. Mayo and Sandra (Fingerman) S.; m. Clifford D. Carpenter, June 29, 1980. BA, U. Calif., San Diego, 1978; PhD, Ind. U., 1982. Rsch. assoc. Ind. U., Bloomington, 1982-84; rsch. assoc. U. Calif. San Diego, La Jolla, 1984-87; asst. prof. U. Mass., Amherst, 1987—; panel mem. NSF, Washington, 1991. Author several papers including proceeding Nat. Acad. Scis., 1989, 82. NSF rsch. grantee, 1987, 88, 90, 91. Democrat. Jewish. Office: U Mass Dept Biochemistry LGRT Amherst MA 01003

SIMON, CHARLOTTE TULCHIN, psychology educator; b. N.Y.C., Dec. 10, 1925; d. Sam and Celia (Kamin) Tulchin; m. Ralph Simon, Sept. 5, 1947; children: Ellen, Randy, Lisa, Russell. BA, Bklyn. Coll., 1945; PhD, Syracuse U., 1953. Instr. psychology Syracuse (N.Y.) U., 1947-50; social psychologist VA Hosp., Perry Point, Md., 1958-59; asst. prof. psychology U. Md., College Park, 1959-60; cons. NIMH, Rockville, Md., 1964, Montgomery County Dept. Health, Rockville, 1966-69; prof. Montgomery Coll., Rockville, 1969—. Mem. Am. Psychol. Assn., Psychology of Women Div. 35, AAUP. Home: 6213 Hollins Dr Bethesda MD 20817-2348 Office: Montgomery Coll Dept Psychology Rockville MD 20850

SIMON, DAVID F., lawyer; b. El Paso, Tex., Apr. 14, 1953; s. Maurice and Susan (Bendekovits) S.; m. Deborah Hart, Mar. 1, 1980; children: Alison Mallory, Joshua Alan, Rebecca Elizabeth. BS magna cum laude, U. Buffalo, 1974; JD cum laude, U. Pa., 1977. Bar: Pa. 1977, N.J. 1978. Law clk. to presiding judge Phila. Ct. Common Pleas, 1977-79; assoc. Wolf, Block, Schorr & Solis-Cohen, Phila., 1979-85, ptnr., 1985-90; sr. v.p. U.S. Healthcare, Inc., Blue Bell, Pa., 1990—. Mem. Phila. Bar Assn. (exec. com. young lawyers sect. 1983-85, chmn. computer law com. 1984-85). Home: PO Box 551 Gwynedd Valley PA 19437-0551 Office: US Healthcare Inc PO Box 1180 Blue Bell PA 19437

SIMON, DAVID JUDAH, reporter; b. Washington, Sept. 2, 1960; s. Bernard and Dorothy (Ligeti) S.; m. Kayle Tucker, 1991. BS in Gen. Studies, U. Md., 1983. Editor in chief Besthesda-Chevy Chase (Md.) High Sch. Tattler, 1977-78; editor U. Md., Diamondback, College Park, 1978-81; editor in chief U. Md. Diamondback, College Park, 1981-82; corr. Balt. Morning Sun, 1982-83, city reporter, 1983—. Author: Homicide: A Year on the Killing Streets, 1991. Recipient 5 nat. and 13 regional newspaper writing awards. Jewish. Office: Balt Sun 501 N Calvert St Baltimore MD 21278-0001

SIMON, HERBERT A(LEXANDER), social scientist; b. Milw., June 15, 1916; s. Arthur and Edna (Merkel) S.; m. Dorothea Pye, Dec. 25, 1937; children: Katherine S. Frank, Peter Arthur, Barbara. AB, U. Chgo., 1936, PhD, 1943, LLD (hon.), 1964; DSc (hon.), Case Inst. Tech., 1963, Yale U., 1963, Marquette U., 1981, Columbia U., 1983, Gustavus Adolphus U., 1984, Mich. Tech. U., 1988, Carnegie-Mellon U., 1990; Fil. Dr. (hon.), Lund U., Sweden, 1968; LLD (hon.), McGill U., Montreal, Que., Can., 1970, U. Mich., 1978, U. Pitts., 1979, U. Paul Valery, France, 1984, Harvard U., 1990; Dr. Econ. Sci. (hon.), Erasmus U. Rotterdam, Netherlands, 1973, Duquesne U., 1988; DSc (hon.), LHD (hon.), Ill. Inst. Tech., 1988; D in Polit. Sci. (hon.), U. Pavia, Italy, 1988. Research asst. U. Chgo., 1936-38; staff mem. Internat. City Mgrs.' Assn.; also asst. editor Pub. Mgmt. and Municipal Year Book, 1938-39; dir. adminstrv. measurement studies Bur. Pub. Administrn., U. Calif., 1939-42; asst. prof. polit. sci. Ill. Inst. Tech., 1942-45, asso. prof., 1945-47, prof., 1947-49; also chmn. dept. polit. and social sci., 1946-49; prof. administrn. and psychology Carnegie-Mellon U., Pitts., 1949-65, Richard King Mellon univ. prof. computer scis. and psychology, 1965—; head dept. indsl. mgmt. Carnegie-Mellon U., Pitts., 1949-60; asso. dean Grad. Sch. Indsl. Adminstrn., 1957-73, trustee, 1972—; cons. to Internat. City Mgrs. Assn., 1942-49, U.S. Bur. Budget, 1946-49, U.S. Census Bur., 1947, Cowles Found. for Research in Econs., 1947-60; cons. and acting dir. Mgmt. Engring. br. Econ. Cooperation Adminstrn., 1948; Ford Distinguished lectr. N.Y. U., 1959; Vanuxem lectr. Princeton, 1961; William James lectr. Harvard, 1963, Sigma Xi lectr., 1964, 76-78, 86; Harris lectr. Northwestern U., 1967; Karl Taylor Compton lectr. MIT, 1968; Wolfgang Koehler lectr. Dartmouth, 1975; Katz-Newcomb lectr. U. Mich., 1976; Carl Hovland lectr. Yale, 1976; Ueno lectr., Tokyo, 1977; Gaither lectr. U. Calif., Berkeley, 1980; Camp lectr. Stanford U., 1982; Gannon lectr. Fordham U., 1982; Oates vis. fellow Princeton U., 1982; Marschak lectr. UCLA, 1983; Auguste Comte lectr. London Sch. Econs., 1987; Lee Kuan Yew lectr. U. Singapore, 1989, Hitchcock lectr. U. Calif., Berkeley, 1990; hon. prof. Tianjin (China) U., 1980, Beijing (China) U., 1986; hon. research scientist Inst. Psychology, Chinese Acad. Scis., 1985; chmn. bd. dirs. Social Sci. Research Council, 1961-65; chmn. div. behavioral scis. NRC, 1968-70; mem. President's Sci. Adv. Com., 1968-72; trustee Carnegie Inst., Pitts., 1987—; cons. bus. and govtl. orgns. Author or co-author books relating to field, including Administrative Behavior, 1947, 3d edit., 1976, Public Administration, 1950, Models of Man, 1956, rev. edit., 1991, Organizations, 1958, New Science of Management Decision, 1960, rev. edit., 1977, The Shape of Automation, 1965, The Sciences of the Artificial, 1968, 2d edit., 1981, Human Problem Solving, 1972, Skew Distributions and Business Firm Sizes, 1976, Models of Discovery, 1977, Models of Thought, Vol. I, 1979, Vol. II, 1989, Models of Bounded Rationality, 1982, Reason in Human Affairs, 1983, Protocol Analysis, 1984, Scientific Discovery, 1987, Models of My Life, 1991. Chmn. Pa. Gov.'s Milk Inquiry Com., 1964-65. Recipient adminstrs. award Am. Coll. Hosp. Adminstrs., 1957, Frederick Mosher award Am. Soc. Pub. Adminstrn., 1974, Alfred Nobel Meml. prize in econ. scis., 1978, Dow-Jones award, 1983, scholarly contbns. award Acad. Mgmt., 1983, Nat. Medal of Sci., 1986, Pender award U. Pa., 1987, Fiorino d'Oro City of Florence, Italy, 1988, Am. Psychol. Found. Gold medal, 1988, award for excellence in the scis. Gov. of Pa., 1990. Fellow AAAS, Am. Econ. Assn. (Ely lectr. 1977, disting.), Econometric Soc., Am. Acad. Arts and Scis., Am. Psychol. Assn. (Disting. Sci. Contbn. award 1969), Am. Sociol. Soc., Inst. Mgmt. Scis. (life, v.p. 1954, Von Neumann Theory award 1988), Brit. Psychol. Assn. (hon.); mem. IEEE (hon.), N.Y. Acad. Scis. (hon.), Jewish Acad. Ars Scis., Am. Polit. Sci. Assn. (James Madison award 1984), Assn. for Computing Machinery (A.M. Turing award 1975), NAS (mem. com. sci. and pub. policy 1967-69, 82-90, chmn. com. air quality control 1974, chmn. com. behavioral scis. NSF 1975-76, coun. 1978-81, 83-86, chmn. com. scholarly communication with PRC, 1983-87 co-chmn. com. behavioral sci. in prevention of nuclear war, 1986-90), Soc. Exptl. Psychologists, Am. Philos. Soc., Royal Soc. Letters (Lund) (fgn. mem.), Orgnl. Sci. Soc. (Japan, hon.), Yugoslav Acad. Scis. (fgn.), Indonesian Economists Assn. (hon.), Cosmos Club, Univ. Club Pitts., Phi Beta Kappa, Sigma Xi (Procter prize 1980). Democrat. Unitarian. Office: Carnegie-Mellon U Dept Psychology Schenley Park Pittsburgh PA 15213-3830

SIMON, JACQUELINE ALBERT, political scientist, journalist; b. N.Y.C.; d. Louis and Rose (Axelroad) Albert; m. Pierre Simon; children: Lisette, Orville. BA cum laude, NYU, MA, 1972, PhD, 1977. Adj. asst. prof. Southampton Coll., 1977-79; mng. editor Point of Contact, N.Y.C., 1975-76; assoc. editor, U.S. bur. chief Politique Internationale, Paris, 1979—; rsch. assoc. Inst. French Studies, NYU, 1980—, asst. prof. govt., 1982-83; assoc. Inst. on the Media for War and Peace; frequent appearances French TV and radio. Contbg. editor Harper's, 1984—; contbr. numerous articles to French mags., revs., books on internat. affairs. Bd. dirs. Fresh Air Fund, 1984—. Mem. Ams. for Dem. Action, Overseas Press Club (bd. dirs.), Phi Beta Kappa. Home: 988 5th Ave New York NY 10021-0143

SIMON, JOHN LEWIS, health care executive; b. Bayonne, N.J., Mar. 10, 1947; s. Marvin Charles and Charlotte (Blaustein) S.; m. Marylu Shore (div. 1982); 1 child, Julie Keren. BA in Psychology, U. Rochester, 1968; MPA, Cornell U., 1971. Rsch. assoc. Inst. Medicine, Washington, 1971; co-founder Kaiser-Georgetown U. Health Plan, Washington, 1971-76; clin. fellow preventive medicine Harvard U. Med. Sch., 1974-75; program officer The Robert Wood Johnson Found., Princeton, N.J., 1976-79; dir. clin. programs Johnson & Johnson Spl. Rsch. Group, New Brunswick, N.J., 1979-81; dir. mktg. Technicare, Cleve., 1981-82; dir. consumer/profl. mktg. Johnson & Johnson Health Mgmt., Inc., New Brunswick, 1982-86; pres. Profl. Postgrad. Svcs., Secaucus, N.J., 1986-88, The Keren Group, Princeton, N.J., 1988—; vis. lectr. Harvard Sch. Pub. Health, Boston, 1975-79; chmn. N.J. State Commn. on Health Svc. Corps., Trenton, N.J., 1988-89. Author: Student Guide to HMO's, 1977, Role Guide for Clinical Preceptors, 1977. Pres. Washington Knoll Homeowners Assn., Rocky Hill, N.J., 1985-86; trustee Bellemead (N.J.) Jewish Community Ctr., 1985-86. With Med. Svc. Corps, U.S. Army Res., 1968-74. Mem. Am. Pub. Health Assn. Jewish. Office: The Keren Group 301 N Harrison St Ste 208 Princeton NJ 08540-3512

SIMON, LINDA, writer, educator; b. Bklyn., Dec. 12, 1946; d. Samuel and Kay (Pacula) Perlin; 1 child, Aaron. BA, Queens Coll., 1967; MA, NYU, 1972, Brandeis U., 1981; PhD, Brandeis U., 1983. Instr. Emory U., Atlanta, 1982-83; head preceptor Harvard U., Cambridge, Mass., 1983—, dir. Writing Ctr., 1986—. Author: Biography of Alice B. Toklas, 1977, Thornton Wilder: His World, 1979, Of Virtue Rare: Margaret Beaufort, Matriarch of the House of Tudor, 1982, Good Writing: A Guide and Sourcebook for Writing Across the Curriculum, 1988; editor: Gertrude Stein: A Composite Portrait, 1974, Contexts: A Thematic Reader, 1991. Mem. Nat. Book Critics' Circle. Office: Harvard Univ 12 Quincy St Cambridge MA 02138-3879

SIMON, MARILYN W., art educator, sculptor; b. Chgo., Aug. 25, 1927; d. William and Caroline Mabel (Bergman) Weintraub; m. Walter E. Simon, Mar. 19, 1950 (div. Sept. 1990); children: Nina Fay Simon-Rosenthal, Jacob Aaron, Maurine Joy Simon Rubinstein, Linda Gay Simon Shapiro. PhB, U. Chgo., 1947; MEd, Temple U., 1969. Cert. tchr., Pa. Bd. sec. Delaware Valley Smelting Corp., Bristol, Pa., 1957-89; art tchr. Calumet Sch. Dist., Ill., 1951-53; art tchr., chmn. elem. art program Cheltenham (Pa.) Sch. Dist., 1969—; real estate agt., Tullytown, Pa.; speaker in field. One woman show include Hahn Gallery, Phila., 1985; also represented in med. offices, pvt. colls.; author publs. on using art reproductions in edn. chmn. Phila. chpt. U. Chgo. Alumni Fund. Assn., 1978-84. Recipient numerous art awards including 1st prize Doylestown Art League, 1986-87, Best Sculpture award Mummers's Mus. Phila., 1987, Juror's award Cheltenham Art Ctr., 1987-88, 3d prize Abington Art Ctr., 1988, 1st prize for sculpture Art Assn. of Harrisburg, 1989. Mem. Nat. Art Edn. Assn., Pa. Art Educators Assn. (regional rep. 1988-89, Outstanding Art Educator of Yr. award 1987), Oil Pastel Assn. N.Y.C. (invited mem.). Democrat. Jewish. Office: PO Box 29722 Philadelphia PA 19117-0922

SIMON, MYRON SYDNEY, chemist, consultant; b. Burlington, Vt., Sept. 23, 1926; s. Louis Abelheim and Gertrude Gussie (Yette) S.; m. Rose Reguera, Aug. 30, 1950; children: Laurel, Amy, Ethan. BA, Harvard U., 1946, MA, 1948, PhD, 1949. Scientist Polaroid Corp., Cambridge, Mass., 1949-51, group leader, 1951-55, co-mgr. dept., 1955-65, mgr., assoc. dir., 1965-81, sr. staff mem., rsch. fellow, 1981-88; pres. Image-Ination Assocs., West Newton, Mass., 1989—. Contbr. articles to profl. publs.; patentee in field. Mem. Am. Chem. Soc. (chmn. Northeastern Sect. 1985, alternate councilor 1985—), Assn. Harvard Chemists. Home and Office: Image-Ination Assocs 20 Somerset Rd Newton MA 02165-2722

SIMON, NEIL, playwright, television writer; b. N.Y.C., July 4, 1927; s. Irving and Mamie Simon; m. Joan Balm, Sept. 30, 1953 (dec.); m. Marsha Mason, 1973 (div.); m. Diane Lander, 1987. Student, NYU, 1946; LLD (hon.), Hofstra U., 1981, Williams Coll., 1984. Author materials for Tamiment (Pa.) revues, 1952-53; author: (with brother Danny) sketches Catch a Star, 1955, (with brother Danny) for New Faces of '56; book for musicals Little Me, 1962, Sweet Charity, 1966, Promises, Promises, 1968, They're Playing Our Song, 1979, Little Me (rev. version), 1982; plays include Come Blow Your Horn, 1961, Barefoot in the Park, 1963, The Odd Couple, 1965, The Star-Spangled Girl, 1966, Plaza Suite, 1968, Last of the Red Hot Lovers, 1969, The Gingerbread Lady, 1970, The Prisoner of Second Avenue, 1971, The Sunshine Boys, 1972, The Good Doctor, 1973, God's Favorite, 1974, California Suite, 1976, Chapter Two, 1977, I Ought to be in Pictures, 1980, Fools, 1981, Brighton Beach Memoirs, 1983, Biloxi Blues, 1985, The Odd Couple (female version), 1985, Broadway Bound, 1986, Rumors, 1988, Lost in Yonkers, 1991 (Pulitzer Prize for Drama, Tony award Best Play 1991), Jake's Women, 1992; wrote screenplays adapted from own plays: Barefoot in the Park, 1967, The Odd Couple, 1968, Plaza Suite, 1971, Last of the Red Hot Lovers, 1972, The Prisoner of Second Avenue, 1975, The Sunshine Boys, 1975, California Suite, 1978, Chapter Two, 1979, Only When I Laugh (adapted from play The Gingerbread Lady), 1981, I Ought to be in Pictures, 1982, Brighton Beach Memoirs, 1986, Biloxi Blues, 1988; other screenplays include After the Fox, 1966, The Out-of-Towners, 1970, The Heartbreak Kid, 1973, Murder by Death, 1976, The Goodbye Girl, 1977, The Cheap Detective, 1978, Seems Like Old Times, 1980, Max Dugan Returns, 1983, The Lonely Guy (adaptation), 1984, The Sluggers Wife, 1984, The Marrying Man, 1991, Broadway Bound, 1992; other motion pictures based on his stage plays: Come Blow Your Horn, 1963, Sweet Charity, 1969, The Star-Spangled Girl, 1971; wrote for TV shows: The Phil Silver Arrow Show, 1958, The Tallulah Bankhead Show, 1951, The Sid Caesar Show, 1956-57, Phil Silvers Show, 1958-59, Garry Moore Show, 1959-60; also NBC spl. The Trouble with People, 1972; (Recipient Emmy award nominations for Sid Caesar Show, 1956-57, Phil Silvers Show 1958-59, Tony award nominations for Little Me, 1963, Barefoot in the Park, 1963, Plaza Suite, 1968, Promises, Promises, 1969, Last of the Red Hot Lovers, 1970, The Prisoner of Second

Avenue, 1972, Brighton Beach Memoirs, 1984, Broadway Bound, 1987, Tony award for The Odd Couple, 1965, Tony award for Best Play Biloxi Blues, 1985, Best Play Lost in Yonkers, 1991, Sam S. Shubert award 1968, Writers Guild screen awards 1968, 70, 75, Writers Guild Laurel award 1979). Served to cpl. USAAF, 1945-46. Mem. Dramatists Guild, Writers Guild Am. (Laurel award 1979). Address: care A DaSilva 502 Park Ave New York NY 10022

SIMON, PHILIPPE JEAN-MARIE, management consultant; b. Paris, Mar. 29, 1954; came to U.S., 1982; s. Louis Félix and Marie-Thérèse Rose (Degraeve) S.; m. Catherine Marie-Françoise Michel, Mar. 29, 1983. BS in Engring., Ecole Nationale Supérieure des Mines de Paris, 1975; MBA, U. Chgo., 1977. Engring. diplomate, France, 1975. Asst. to v.p. mktg. Aluminum Pechiney, Paris, 1978-82; sr. market research analyst Howmet Aluminum Corp., Greenwich, Conn., 1982-83; mktg. and bus. devel. mgr. Aluminum Pechiney Corp., N.Y.C., 1983-86; U.S. mktg. and bus. devel. mgr. Aluminum Pechiney Corp., Greenwich, 1986-88; mgmt. cons. Bain & Co., Paris, 1988-89, Boston, 1989-; mentor and career cons. U. Chgo. Grad. Sch. Bus. Mentor Program, N.Y.C., 1985—; liaison officer MIT Indsl. Liaison Program, Cambridge, 1984-87. Dist. organizer Giscard D'Estaing's Presdl. Election Campaign, France, 1974. Served to ensign French Air Force, 1977-78. Mem. Am. Soc. Metals, Soc. Automotive Engrs., Soc. Mfg. Engrs. Roman Catholic. Clubs: Fontainebleau Golf. Home: 920 Us Highway 202 # 300 Raritan NJ 08869-1420

SIMON, THOMAS HASKELL, management consultant; b. Bklyn., May 23, 1936; s. Stanley H. and Marian B. (Stadin) S.; m. Paula Friedman, June 10, 1957 (div. July 1982); m. Gloria R. Richter, Oct. 18, 1989; children: Beth E., Stacy F. BS, Columbia U., 1959; MS, Purdue U., 1961, PhD, 1963. Scientist Cramer-Lambert, Morris Plains, N.J., 1963-67; assoc. dir. phys. pharmacy Warner-Lambert, Morris Plains, N.J., 1967-72; dir. pharmaceutics Cramer-Lambert, Morris Plains, N.J., 1972-82, dir. solids formulation, 1982-86, dir. rsch. and devel., 1986-91; pres. T.H. Simon Assocs., Cedar Knolls, N.J., 1992—. Mem. Rho Chi, Sigma Xi. Home: 2C Yacenda Dr Morris Plains NJ 07950 Office: TH Simon Assocs 14 Ridgedale Ave Ste 105 Cedar Knolls NJ 07927

SIMON, THOMAS SHAHEAN, marketing professional; b. Olean, N.Y., Sept. 17, 1952; s. Thomas Shahean and Caroline Dawn (Limerick) S.; m. Diane Jean Moszak; children: Matthew, Lauren. BSChemE, Clarkson U., 1974. Devel. chemist Dexter Corp., Olean, N.Y., 1974-77; market devel. mgr. Dexter Corp., Olean, 1987—; sales engr. Dexter Corp., Anderson, Ind., 1977-82, market devel. specialist, 1983-84, sr. sales engr., 1984-87; officer Fusion Bonded Coaters Assn., Chgo., 1983-84, Epoxy Resin Formulators Div., Washington, 1988-89. Mem. Rep. Senate Action Com., Indpls., 1985-87. Recipient Outstanding Svc. award Hysol Fed. Credit Union, 1989. Mem. Rep. Senatorial Action Com., Indpls., 1985-87. Republican. Roman Catholic. Home: 527 York St Olean NY 14760-3933 Office: Dexter Electronic Materials 211 Franklin St Olean NY 14760-1297

SIMONE, ELIZABETH ORTIZ, brokerage firm executive; b. Manhattan, N.Y., July 24, 1951; d. Crescencio and Filiamor (Hernandez) Ortiz; m. Joseph Francis Simone, Dec. 22, 1979; children: Michael Joseph, Edward Correa, Michelle Deana, Brad Joseph. Student, Montclair (N.J.) State Coll., 1973-74, Coll. S.I., N.Y., 1974-77. Registered ops. prin., gen. securities prin., gen. securities rep., uniform securities agt., fin. and ops. prin. Acctg. clk. Am. Express Co., N.Y.C., 1974-78; sales asst. Kingsley, Boye & Southwood, N.Y.C., 1978-79; account exec. William M. Cadden & Co., Summit, N.J., 1979-82; v.p., gen. prin., corp. sec. Dolan & Pitcher, Inc., Summit, N.J., 1982-85; gen. and options prin. Lauria Guerin Horowitz, Inc., S.I., 1985-86; asst. v.p. Waterhouse Securities, Inc., N.Y.C., 1986-87; chief fin. officer, v.p., corp. sec. Marsh Block & Co., Inc., N.Y.C., 1987—. Recipient Berkeley award Berkeley Sch. Bus., 1969, 70. Nat. Assn. Securities Dealers. Roman Catholic. Home: 730 Craig Ave Staten Island NY 10307-1510 Office: Marsh Block & Co Inc 50 Broad St New York NY 10004-2307

SIMONE, GAIL ELISABETH, research analyst; b. Boston, Dec. 3, 1944; d. Hugh Nelson and Louise Amelia (Shedrick) Saunders; m. Edburnne R. Hare, Sept. 7, 1968 (div. 1974); m. Joseph R. Simone, June 27, 1987. BA, The King's Coll., 1966; postgrad., Harvard U., 1976-77, N.H. Coll., 1991—. Placement dir. Boston Bar Assn., 1966-67; pub. relations Emerson Coll., Boston, 1967-69; asst. to v.p. Vance, Sanders, Inc., Boston, 1969-70; office mgr. Trans. Displays, Inc., Boston, 1970-71; seminar coordinator Assn. Trial Lawyers Am., Cambridge, Mass., 1971-74; writer, researcher Ednl. Expeditions Internat., Belmont, Mass., 1975-76; analyst United Brands Co., N.Y.C., 1976-80; analyst Mil. Sealift Commd., USN, Washington, 1980-84, legis. affairs officer, 1984-88; rsch. analyst Bath (Maine) Iron Works, Shipbuilders, 1988—; free-lance writer, editor, Boston, 1970-73. Vol. Mass. Pax, Boston; active Childreach, Warwick, R.I., 1986—; mem. Amnesty Internat., N.Y.C., 1987—, and various other orgns. Mem. Nat. Assn. Female Execs., Women's Trans. Seminar. Office: Bath Iron Works 700 Washington St Bath ME 04530

SIMONS, RICHARD DUNCAN, state judge; b. Niagara Falls, N.Y., Mar. 23, 1927; s. William Taylor and Sybil Irene (Swick) S.; m. Muriel E. Genung, June 9, 1951 (dec. 1992); children: Ross T., Scott R., Kathryn E., Linda A. A.B., Colgate U., 1949; LL.B., U. Mich., 1952; LLD (hon.), Albany Law Sch., 1983. Bar: N.Y. 1952. Pvt. practice law Rome, N.Y., 1952-63; asst. corp. counsel City of Rome, 1955-58, corp. counsel, 1960-63; justice 5th jud. dist. N.Y. Supreme Ct., 1964—, assoc. justice appellate div. 3d dept., 1971-72, asso. justice appellate div. 4th dept., 1973-82; assoc. judge N.Y. Ct. Appeals, 1983—; mem. Law Sch. Admission Svcs., Bar Study Group. Editorial staff: N.Y. Pattern Jury Instructions, 1979-83. Chmn. Republican City Com., 1958-62; vice chmn. Oneida County Rep. Com., 1958-62; bd. mgrs. Rome Hosp. and Murphy Meml. Hosp., 1953. Served with USN, World War II. NEH fellow U. Va. Law Sch., 1979. Fellow Am. Bar Found., N.Y. State Bar Found.; mem. ABA, N.Y. State Bar Assn., Oneida County Bar Assn., Rome Bar Assn., Am. Law Inst., Inst. Jud. Adminstrn. Home: 1410 N George St Rome NY 13440-2704 Office: NY Ct Appeals Hall 20 Eagle St Albany NY 12207-1095

SIMONS, SAMUEL STONEY, JR., health science research director; b. Phila., Sept. 13, 1945; s. S. Stoney Sr. and Virginia Simons; m. Cyrena Goude, Apr. 25, 1970; children: C. Torrey, Caroline S. AB, Princeton (N.J.) U., 1967; PhD, Harvard U., 1972. Postdoctoral fellow in biochemistry U. Calif., San Francisco, 1972-75; staff fellow NIH, Bethesda, Md., 1975-80, rsch. chemist, 1980-85, sect. chief, 1985—. Mem. editorial bd. Receptors, 1991—, Jour. Biol. Chem., 1992—; author 15 chpts. in books; contbr. numerous articles to profl. jours.; patentee in field. Regional co-chmn. ann. giving campaign Princeton U., 1982—. Temple U. scholar, 1984. Mem. Am. Chem. Soc., Am. Soc. Biochemistry and Molecular Biology, Phi Beta Kappa. Office: NIH Bldg # 8 Rm # B2A-07 Bethesda MD 20892

SIMONSON, LEE J., small business owner; b. Niagara Falls, N.Y., Sept. 5, 1953; s. Marvin W. and Mamie C. (Maroon) S.; m. Brenda J. Wright, July 3, 1976; children: Jill, Robin. AAS Bus. Adminstrn., Niagara County Community Coll., 1974; BS in Commerce, Niagara U., 1978. Asst. to dir. United Way Niagara, Niagara Falls, 1973; dir. small bus. program Medaille Coll., Buffalo, 1977-79; pub. Investible Growth Letter, Lewiston, 1977-89; owner, pres. Am. Collectibles, Lewiston, 1979—; bd. dirs. Niagara Ednl. Found., Niagara Falls, Bipartisan Alliance Western N.Y. County Legislators, Williamsville. Author: How to Run for Public Office, 1977. County legislator Niagara County, Lockport, N.Y., 1974—, chmn. jud. and laws and legis. com., 1978, chmn. edn. com. 1979, 87-88, chmn. social svcs. com. 1982, chmn. waste mgmt. com., 1989, chmn. of the legis., 1990—; bd. dirs. sml. bus. resource ctr. Niagara County Community Coll., 1986—; chmn. western N.Y. Chalk Walk, Lewiston Coun. on the Arts, 1984—. Named Rep. of Yr. Lewiston Rep. Com., 1984, 92, Leader of the Yr. Leadership Niagara, 1991; recipient WHLD Top Hat award Sta. WHLD Radio and Tops Supermarkets, 1975. Mem. N.Y. State Assn. Counties (medicaid and welfare task force). Roman Catholic. Office: Am Collectibles 504 Morgan Dr Lewiston NY 14092-1106

SIMON-SPADA, SUSAN MINDY, lawyer, real estate consultant; b. Newark, July 10, 1957; d. Bernard and Sara (Mintz) S. BA with honors, Rutgers U., 1979; JD, John Marshall Law Sch., Chgo., 1982. Bar: N.J., 1982, U.S. Dist. Ct. (dist. of N.J.) 1982, N.J. Supreme Ct., 1982. Atty. Rachlin Residential Realty Corp., Orange, N.J., 1982-83, Natalie Devel., Inc., Orange, 1983-86, Yankowitz & Goldsmith, East Orange, N.J., 1986-88, Weiner Lesniak, Roseland, N.J., 1988—; seminar speaker on legal banking topics to major N.J. fin. instns. Recipient Outstanding Svc. award, Essex-Newark Legal Svcs., Vol. Lawyers Project, 1987. Mem. N.J. State Bar Assn. Democrat. Jewish. Office: Weiner Lesniak 425 Eagle Rock Ave Roseland NJ 07068-1720

SIMOPOULOS, ARTEMIS PANAGEOTIS, physician, educator; b. Kampos-Avias, Greece, Apr. 3, 1933; came to U.S. 1949, naturalized 1955; d. Panageotis L. and Nena P. (Konteas) S.; m. Alan Lee Pinkerson, Jan. 10, 1957; children—Daphne, Lee, Alexandra. B.A., Barnard Coll., 1952; M.D., Boston U., 1956. Diplomate Am. Bd. Pediatrics. Pediatric intern Kings County Hosp., Bklyn., 1956-57; resident Kings County Hosp., 1957-58; fellow in hematology Children's Hosp., Washington, 1960-61, asst. chief resident in pediatrics, 1961-62, mem. acad. staff, 1962-67, assoc. staff in pediatric nursery service, 1967-71; spl. lectr. pediatrics Ewha Woman's U. Sch. Medicine, Seoul, Korea, 1958-59; asst. prof. pediatrics George Washington U. Sch. Medicine, 1962-67, clin. asst. prof., 1967-71; dir. nurseries George Washington U. Hosp., 1965-67; staff pediatrician Nat. Heart and Lung Inst., NIH, 1968-71, cons. endocrinology br., 1971-78; with div. med. scis. Nat. Acad. Scis., NRC, Washington, 1971-74; exec. sec. Nat. Acad. Scis., NRC, 1974-76, exec. dir. bd. maternal, child and family health research, 1974-76; cons. to dir. Nat. Inst. Child Health and Human Devel., NIH, Bethesda, Md, 1976-77; chief devel. biology and nutrition br., ctrs. for research for mothers and children Nat. Inst. Child Health and Human Devel., NIH, 1977; vice chmn. and exec. sec. nutrition coordinating com. NIH, 1977-78; cons. nutrition and health to spl. asst. to the Pres. for Consumer Affairs The White House, Washington, 1978-81; chmn. nutrition coordinating com. office of the dir. NIH, 1978-86; dir. Ctr. for Genetics, Nutrition and Health, Washington, 1989-90, pres., 1990—; co-chmn., exec. sec. joint subcom. Human Nutrition Rsch., Office Sci. and Tech. Policy, Exec. Office of the Pres., 1979-83; dir. div. nutritional sci. Internat. Life Scis. Inst. Rsch. Found., 1986-88. Editor World Rev. Nutrition and Dietetics, 1989—; contbg. editor Nutrition Revs., 1979—; mem. editorial bd. Jour. Nutrition, Growth, and Cancer, 1982—, Internat. Jour. Vitamin and Nutrition Research, 1986—, n=3 News, 1986-90, Annals Nutition and Metabolism, 1991—; cons. editor Nutrition Research, 1983—, Annals Internal Medicine, 1984—, Jour. AMA, 1985—; contbr. articles in endocrinology, genetics, nutrition and fitness, omega-3 fatty acids, and obesity to profl. jours. Recipient Disting. Alumna award Sch. Medicine, Boston U., 1991; NIH grantee, 1960-61. Fellow Am. Acad. Pediatrics, Am. Coll. Nutrition; mem. Soc. Pediatric Rsch., Endocrine Soc., Maternity Ctr. Assn. (rsch. adv. com.), Am. Pediatric Soc., Am. Inst. Nutrition, Am. Soc. Clin. Nutrition, Am. Assn. for World Health (v.p. 1981-90, asst. treas. 1981-90, nat. chmn. for World Health Day 1982—, vice chmn. bd. 1991—, dir. Ctr. for Genetics, Nutrition and Health 1989-90, pres. 1990—), D.C. Med. Soc., N.Am. Assn. for Study Obesity, Internat. Life Scis. Inst. (trustee 1982-88, exec. com. 1982-85, trustee Nutrition Found. 1985-87). Greek Orthodox. Home: 4330 Klingle St NW Washington DC 20016-3577 Office: Ctr Genetics Nutrition and Health 2001 S St NW #530 Washington DC 20009

SIMOVICI, DAN, computer science educator; b. Lasi, Romania, Feb. 15, 1943; came to U.S., 1981; s. Avram and Adelina (Herscu) S.; m. Doina Brauner, June 15, 1965; 1 child, Alex. MSEE, Poly. Inst., Lasi, Romania, 1965; MS, U. Lasi, 1970; PhD, U. Bucharest, Romania, 1974. Researcher U. Lasi, 1965-70, instr., 1970-74, asst. prof., 1974-78, assoc. prof., 1978-81; assoc. prof. U. Miami, Fla., 1981-82; assoc. prof. U. Mass., Boston, 1982-85, program dir., prof., 1985—. Author: Formal Languages and Compiling Techniques, 1978, Math. Foundations of Computer Science, 1990. Mem. Computer Soc. of IEEE (chair tech. com. multiple-values logic 1987-89). Republican. Jewish. Home: 407 Washington St # 3 Brookline MA 02146-6115 Office: U Mass Dept Computer Sci Boston MA 02125

SIMPKINS, LUCILLE ANGELIQUE, personnel administrator; b. New Orleans, May 26, 1944; d. Robert Aunding and Addie Grace (Frazier) Elmore; m. Leonard W. Simpkins, Jr., Nov. 22, 1960; children: Terri, Leonard W. BA, Coppin State Coll., 1979; MEd, Temple U., 1982. Cert. pers. adminstr. Clk. stenographer Unemployment Compensation Bd. Rev., Phila., 1964-66; sec. to br. mgr. West Br. OIC, Phila., 1967-69; adminstrv. asst. to pres. external affairs U. Pa., Phila., 1969-70; sec. III fiscal dept. Nat. Progress Assn. Econ. Devel., Phila., 1970-72; office mgr., pers. adminstr. Opportunities Acad. Mgmt. Tng. Inc./Opportunities Industrialization Ctrs. Am., Inc., Phila., 1975—. Bd. mem. YWCA North Cen. Br., 1984—; v.p. St. Barbara's Parish Coun., 1989—. Mem. ASTD, Soc. Human Resource Mgmt., Educators' Roundtable Inc. (co-editor 1985-88), Indsl. Human Svcs. Coun. (bd. mem. 1985-89). Roman Catholic. Home: 2235 Georges Ln Philadelphia PA 19131-2326 Office: OAMT Inc 1415 N Broad St Philadelphia PA 19122-3323

SIMPSON, BARBARA L., library director; b. Cleve., Apr. 6, 1947; d. Curley and Cora (Chambliss) Brown; children: Michelle, Crystal, Twilla. BS, Ohio State U., 1967; MS in Ednl. Media, Kent. State U. (Ohio), 1971, MLS, 1971. Adminstrv. supr. Cleve. pub. schs., 1968-72; libr. Cuyahoga Community Coll., Cleve., 1972-75, coord., 1975-77, interim dir., 1977-78, asst. dean, 1978-80, dir., 1980-84; dir. libr. Kean Coll., Union, N.J., 1984—; cons. Dembsy Assocs., Boston, 1967-81; editorial cons. Max Pub. Co., N.Y.C., 1967-81; cons. reader U.S. Office Edn., Washington, 1979-80; editorial cons. Jossey-Bass Pub. Co., 1979. Cons. editor Probe, 1975, Sch. Media Ctr., 1968, Booklist, 1969; contbr. articles to profl. jours. Bd. dirs. N.J. Adv. Bd. on the Status of Women, 1988, Africana Studies, 1988, N.J. State Libr. Adv. Bd., 1987; chairperson N.J. Acad. Libr. Network, N.J. Ednl. Activities Task Force Libr. Com. Recipient Phillips award Kent State U., 1970. Mem. ALA, Higher Edn. Reps., N.J. Acad. Libr. Network (chmn. 1987), Council N.J. Coll. Librs. (pres. 1987—), N.J. Libr. Assn., Oral History Soc., N.J. Hist. Soc., Jr. League (Cleve. vice chmn. 1981, 83), Concerned Parents Club (pres. 1984), Women's City Club. Avocations: music, reading. Office: Kean Coll Libr Morris Ave Union NJ 07083-7117

SIMPSON, CAROL LOUISE, executive; b. Phila., Jan. 30, 1937; d. William Huffington and Hilda Agnes (Johnston) S. Student, Community Coll., 1985, 86, 87, U. Minn., 1986, 87, 88. Cert. Nat. Assn. Securities Dealers, Inc., Washington; registered options, mcpl. securities, gen. securities, fin. and ops. prin.; lic. life, accident, health ins. Exec. asst. Germantown Fed. Savs., Phila., 1954-67; asst. sec. Am. Med. Investment Co., Inc. (formerly Cannon and Co., Inc.), Blue Bell, Pa., 1967-91; also bd. dirs. Cannon & Co., Inc., 1986; v.p., sec. AMA Investment Advisers, Inc. (formerly Pro Svcs., Inc.), Blue Bell, Pa., 1967-91; also bd. dirs. AMA Investment Advisers, Inc. (formerly PRO Svcs., Inc.), Blue Bell, Pa., 1984-86; fin. svcs. compliance cons., 1991; exec. v.p., sec. Rutherford Fin. Corp., Phila., 1991—, Rutherford, Brown & Catherwood Inc., Phila., 1991—, Walnut Asset Mgmt. Inc., Phila., 1991—. Mem. World Affairs Coun., Investment Co. Inst. (fed. legis. com. 1984-91, investment advisers com. 1988—, compliance com. 1990—), Internat. Assn. Fin. Planners, Investment Women's Club, Nat. Notary Assn., Pa. Assn. Notaries, Nat. Soc. Compliance Profls. (assoc.), Whitemarsh Valley Country Club. Republican. Home: 7701 Lawnton St Philadelphia PA 19128-3105 Office: Rutherford Fin Corp Ste 500 1617 John F Kennedy Blvd Philadelphia PA 19103-1823

SIMPSON, GEORGE CHARLES, licensing company executive; b. Yonkers, N.Y., Mar. 31, 1961; s. George Charles and Marion Nancy Simpson. BS, Fordham U., 1983. Media specialist Dancer Fitzgerald Sample, N.Y.C., 1983-86; asst. account exec. Lowe Marschalk, N.Y.C., 1986-87; account exec. new bus., writer Osborn & Assocs., Portland, Oreg., 1987-89; account exec. Wieden & Kennedy, Portland, 1989; market analyst Calet Hirsch & Spector, N.Y.C., 1989-90; freelance writer N.Y.C., 1991—; pres., creative dir. Sarcastic Remarks, Inc., N.Y.C., 1991—.

SIMPSON, JAMES ROGER, songwriter, poet, commercial writer; b. Bklyn., Oct. 5, 1945; s. Floyd Norman and Jeanette (Readey) S.; m. Joan M. White, Sept. 23, 1973; children: James Roger Jr., Sean Patrick, Deborah Ann, Linda Marie. Cert., Art Students League, N.Y.C., 1972, Am. Art Sch., N.Y.C., 1972; student, U.S. Sch. Music, N.Y.C., 1959-61, Amb. Coll., Pasadena, Calif., 1989-91. Comml. writer Rogers Advt., Lake grove, N.Y., 1975-79, Sta. WJJF, R.I., 1989; lyrics writer Coltrain Records, Nashville, 1988-91; writer CRS Records, Lewiston, N.Y., 1989-90, Chapel Rec. Co., Wallaston, Mass., 1990; owner, mgr. JRS Records, Lake Grove, 1989—. Composer songs; author: (poetry) Lonely, 1991. With USAF, 1966-72. Meml. scholar Art Students League, 1972. Mem. ASCAP, Audubon soc., Smithsonian Assocs. Office: PO Box 104 Lake Grove NY 11755-0104

SIMPSON, KENNETH LEE, food science educator; b. L.A., June 24, 1931; s. Harry B. and Marguerite F. (Mounts) S.; m. Jill E. Morris, Aug. 31, 1957; children: Pamela M. Simpson Winchell, Valerie A. Simpson Criman, Andrew K. BS, U. Calif., Davis, 1954, MS, 1960, PhD, 1963. Rsch. asst. U. Calif., Davis, 1956-63; postdoctoral fellow NSF, Aberyshwyth, Wales, 1963-64; asst. prof. U. R.I., Kingston, 1964-69, assoc. prof., 1969-72, prof. food sci., 1972—; researcher dept. biochemistry U. Liverpool, Eng., 1971-72; researcher Embrapa, Brazil, Rio de Janeiro, 1990; cons. in field. Contbr. articles to profl. publs., chpts. to books. Trustee Barrington (R.I.) Coll., 1968-71; elder West Kingston (R.I.) Bapt. Ch., 1979-85. With U.S. Army, 1954-56. Recipient Sci. medallion Acad. Sci., Cluj, Romania, 1976. Mem. Am. Chem. Soc., Inst. Food Technologists, World Aquaculture. Republican. Home: 73 North Rd Peace Dale RI 02883-2103 Office: U RI Food Sci & Nutrition Dept Kingston RI 02881

SIMPSON, MICHAEL MARCIAL, congressional science specialist; b. Honolulu, Sept. 24, 1954; s. Marcial Tolentino and Beatrice (Martin) S. AB in Biol. Scis., U. Calif., Berkeley, 1976; MS in Biol. Scis., U. San Francisco, 1977; MS in Energy and Resources, U. Calif., Berkeley, 1979; PhD in Environ. Scis. and Engring., UCLA, 1986. Assoc. researcher NASA, Moffett Field, Calif., 1973; radio program host, producer Sta. KUSF-FM, San Francisco, 1976-78; rsch. asst. Lawrence Berkeley Lab., Berkeley, Calif., 1977-79; rsch. assoc. UCLA/U.S. Dept. Energy, 1979-81; congl. fellow, environ. health U.S. Congress, Washington, 1981-82; head, biomed. policy sect. and specialist in life scis. U.S. Congl. Rsch. Svc., Washington, 1982—; adv. bd. Banbury Ctr., Cold Spring Harbor, N.Y., 1985—. Contbr. articles to profl. jours. Youth educator, Westminster Community, Alexandria, Va., 1985—. Fellow AAAS (Named Congl. Sci. fellow 1981-82); mem. Washington Acad. Sci., Library of Congress Profl. Assn., UCLA in Washington (exec. steering com. 1986—). Office: US Congl Rsch Svc CRS-SPR-LM413 Washington DC 20540

SIMPSON, MURRAY, engineer, consultant; b. N.Y.C., July 21, 1921; s. George and Sonia (Vernov) S.; m. Ethel Gladstein, June 29, 1947; children: Anne Simpson Everett, David, Mindy, Jonathan. BEE, CCNY, 1942; MEE, Polytech. Inst. of N.Y., 1952. Engr. Internat. Tel.&Tel., N.Y.C., 1942-44; sr. engr. Raytheon Co., Waltham, Mass., 1946-48; sect. mgr. Fairchild Guided Missles div., Farmingdale, N.Y., 1948-50; v.p. Maxson Elec. Co., N.Y.C., 1950-62; pres. SEDCO Systems Inc. subs. Raytheon Co., Melville, N.Y., 1963-86; cons. M. Simpson Assocs., West Hempstead, N.Y., 1986—; chmn. bd. dirs. Raydyne Corp. Contbr. articles to profl. jours. Bd. dirs. United Way of L.I., N.Y., 1984-87. Served to lt. (j.g.) USNR, 1944-46, PTO. Fellow IEEE (chmn. L.I. sect. 1963-64); mem. Air Force Assn., Anchorage Yacht Club (Lindenhurst, N.Y.). Club: Anchorage Yacht.

SIMPSON, RICHARD VERNON, visual information specialist; b. Providence, Oct. 31, 1935; s. William Vernon and Elsie Mary (Couillard) S.; m. Irene V. Godfrey, Sept. 11, 1959. Sch. Practical Art, Boston, 1957. Visual info. specialist Dept. Def. Naval Undersea Weapons Ctr., Newport, R.I., 1968—. Author: Independence Day-How the Day is Celebrated in Bristol, Rhode Island, 1989, The Day That We Celebrate, 1991, The Torpedo Boats of Bristol, Rhode Island, 1990; contbr. numerous articles to profl. jours. Mem. Fourth of July Commn, Bristol, R.I., 1966-76; charter mem. Housing for Bristol Citizens, Inc.; mem. Citizens Adv. Commn., Bristol. Recipient Aldrich prize Providence Art Club, 1959, Margaret nerone award Bristol Art Mus., 1965, Antique Dealer of the Yr. award Southeastern New Eng. Antique Dealers Assn., 1976. Roman Catholic. Home: 332 High St Bristol RI 08809 Office: NUWG Code 0252 Bldg 1272/2 Newport RI 02840

SIMPSON, SAMUEL FORD, JR., international sales and marketing executive; b. Patuxent River, Md., May 19, 1950; s. Samuel Ford and Dorothy Louise (Truslow) S.; m. Debra Ann Lehrl, Apr. 23, 1977; children: Taryn Debra, Lauren Louise. BS in Computer Sci., Va. Commonwealth U., 1970; MBA, UCLA, 1979. Graphics mgr. L. Grief & Co., Fredericksburg, Va., 1971-73; cons. Hydrospace Challenger Inc., Dahlgren, Va., 1973-75; product mgr. Hughes Aircraft Co., Carlsbad, Calif., 1975-80; dir., gen. mgr. Gerber Garment Technology, Inc., Tolland, Conn., 1980—; dir. apparel, design rsch. com. Va. Poly. Inst., Blacksburg, 1987—. Youth leader United Meth. Ch., Vernon, Conn., 1988—. Mem. Am. Mktg. Assn., IEEE. Republican. Home: 30 Austin Dr Tolland CT 06084-2423 Office: Gerber Garment Tech Inc 24 Industrial Park Rd W Tolland CT 06084-2806

SIMPSON, WILLIAM HENRY, minister; b. Fredrick, Md., Nov. 22, 1924; s. Walter Albaugh and Leah Mae (Michael) S.; m. Martha Ann Benner, Nov. 7, 1955 (dec. 1982); 1 child, Timothy Benner; m. Margaret Catherine Horgan, Oct. 9, 1983. AB, Western Md. Coll., 1951; BD, Lancaster Sem., Pa., 1955; PhD, Boston U., 1968; postgrad., U. Edinburgh, Scotland, 1952-53. Ordained to ministry United Ch. of Christ, 1955. Tchr. music Westminister (Md.) High Sch., 1951-52; asst. pastor St. Andrew Ch., Lancaster, Pa., 1955; sr. pastor St. Andrew Ch., Lancaster, 1956-60; part-time pastor Bethany United Ch. of Christ, Lynn, Mass., 1960-83; counselor Ea. Jr. High Sch., Lynn, 1967-70; counselor, tchr. Lynnfield (Mass.) High Sch., 1970-83; sr. pastor Bethany United Ch. of Christ, Lynn, 1983—; tchr./adminstr. Release Time Religious Edn., Lancaster, Pa., 1956-59, Lynn, 1961-64; clk. Essex Assn. United Ch. of Christ, Haverhill, 1985-87; pres. Greater Lynn Coun. of Chs., 1984-86; bd. dirs. Regional Ecumenical Network (MCC), Boston, 1984-88, Strategic Action Commn. (MCC), 1987. Composer song: Come, Come, Everybody, 1974; contbr. articles to newspapers. Bd. mgmt. Camp Rotary, Lynn, 1986—; sr. league mgr. East Lynn Little League, 1970-72; bd. dirs. Family & Children's Svcs., Lynn, 1984-91, Greater Lynn YMCA, 1985-90; bd. dirs. North Shore Human Rights Com. With U.S. Army, 1946-48. Recipient Bates award Western Md. Coll., 1951; Rotary Found. fellow 1952; Recognition for Svc. City of Lynn, 1990. Mem. ASCD, Am. Mental Health Counselors Assn., Mass. Sch. Counselors Assn., Nat. Assn. Clergy Hypnotherapists, Greater Lynn Clergy and Religious (treas.), Rotary (asst. sec.-treas., 2d v.p., Paul Harris fellow 1989). Home: 420 Eastern Ave Lynn MA 01902-1632 Office: Bethany United Ch of Christ 410 Eastern Ave Lynn MA 01902-1632

SIMSON, ROSALIND SLIVKA, philosophy educator; b. N.Y.C., Apr. 3, 1952; d. Norman Slivka and Brenda (Spiewak) Guterman; m. Gary Joseph Simson, Aug. 15, 1971; children: Nathaniel, Jennie Anne. BA, Yale U., 1973, MA, 1974, PhD, 1979. Instr. in philosophy S.W. Tex. State U., San Marcos, 1978-79; asst. prof. philosophy Hobart & William Smith Coll., Geneva, N.Y., 1979—. Contbr. articles to profl. jours. Mem. AAUP, Am. Philos. Assn., Phi Beta Kappa. Office: Hobart & William Smith Coll Dept Philosophy Geneva NY 14456

SINATRA, RICHARD CHARLES, education educator, consultant, director reading; b. N.Y.C., Dec. 19, 1938; s. Salvatore Charles and Elizabeth Patricia (Kelly) S.; m. Mary Snodgrass, Sept. 3, 1961 (div. Aug. 1971); children: Christina M., Melissa A.; m. Camille Sinatra, July 25, 1985. BA, Lafayette Coll., 1960; MS, Hofstra U., 1970, PhD in Reading Ed., 1972. Tchr. English Riverhead (N.Y.) Jr. High Sch., 1963-65; reading specialist U.S. Dep. Schs. of Europe, Germany and Italy, 1965-68; diagnostic reading specialist Shelter Rock Sch., Manhasset, N.Y., 1970-73; dist. reading coord. Manhasset Schs., 1973-76; prof. grad. reading Sch. of Edn. St. John's U., Jamaica, N.Y., 1976—, chmn. div. human svcs. Sch. of Edn., 1984-88, dir. reading clinic, 1980—; cons. Dist. 24, Moss Point, Miss., 1986—; v.p. Think Network, Inc., N.Y.C., 1985—. Author: Visual Literacy Connections to Thinking, Reading & Writing, 1986; co-author: Using the Right Brain in the Language Arts, 1982; theme editor Jour. reading Psychology and the Reading & Writing Quar., 1988, 91; lead author: (computer programs) Thinking Networks for Reading & Writing, 1985-91, Start-A-Story, 1992, MacMapper, 1991. 1st lt. inf. U.S. Army, 1960-63. Mem. ASCD (chmn. arts edn. network 1985-81, network adv. bd. 1991—), N.Y. State Reading Assn. (del. 1984-91, chmn. 1986-91), Nassau (N.Y.) Reading Coun. (pres. 1988-89). Office: St Johns U 308 Marillac Hall Jamaica NY 11439

SINCERBEAUX, ROBERT ABBOTT, lawyer, foundation executive; b. N.Y.C., July 22, 1913; s. Frank Huestis and Jessie Marian (Batterson) S.; m. Elizabeth Morley, Apr. 19, 1940; children—Richard M., Suzanne Sincerbeaux Brian, Charles M. B.A. cum laude, Princeton U., 1936; LL.B., Yale U., 1939. Bar: N.Y. 1940. Assoc. White & Case, N.Y.C., 1939-42, Simpson, Thacher & Bartlett, N.Y.C., 1942-43; assoc. Sincerbeaux & Shrewsbury, N.Y.C., 1946-52, ptnr., 1952-72, of counsel, 1972—. Pres., Eva Gebhard-Gourgaud Found., N.Y.C., 1959—, trustee, 1947—; mng. trustee Cecil Howard Charitable Trust, N.Y.C., 1968—; hon. trustee Woodstock Hist. Soc., Vt., 1972—; trustee Woodstock Found., 1976-91, Preservation Trust Vt., 1980—; chmn. design rev. bd. Village of Woodstock, 1983-91, Fund for Vt.'s Third Century, 1988-91. Served to lt. comdr. USNR, 1943-65. Recipient Preservation award Preservation Trust Vt., 1983, Honor award Nat. Trust for Historic Preservation, 1984, Thomas award Vt. Land Trust, 1991. Fellow Met. Mus. Art (life); mem. Soc. Col. Wars. Episcopalian. Clubs: Woodstock Country, Lakota, Round Table; Nassau (Princeton), Belleair Country (Fla). Home: 80 Lyme Rd Apt 1010 Hanover NH 03755 Office: One The Green Woodstock VT 05091

SINCHE, ROBERT MILLER, economist; b. Oceanside, N.Y., July 11, 1952; s. Robert Raymond and Edna Jane (Miller) S.; m. Judith Ellson, Dec. 27, 1975. B.A. in Econs., Hamilton Coll., 1974; M.A. in Econs., Brown U., 1976. Vice pres., economist Paine Webber, N.Y.C., 1976-79; economist Bear Stearns & Co., N.Y.C., 1979-81, chief economist, ltd. ptnr., 1981-85; mng. dir. Simms Capital Mgmt., N.Y.C., 1985-88; sr. v.p., dir. internat. Alliance Capital Mgmt., N.Y.C., 1988—. Mem. Nat. Assn. Bus. Economists, N.Y. Assn. Bus. Economists, Phi Beta Kappa. Office: Alliance Capital Mgmt 1345 Ave Of The Americas New York NY 10105-0099

SINCLAIR, JOHN LUTHER, manufacturing company executive; b. Attleboro, Mass., Dec. 30, 1960; s. John Champion and Virginia Luther (Clark) S. BA, Dartmouth Coll., 1983. Mgmt. asst. Sinclair Mfg. Co., Chartley, Mass., 1983-84, mktg. mgr., 1984-85, exec. v.p., dir., 1985—; also chmn. Sinclair Mfg. (GB) Ltd., Cambridge, Eng. Mem. Royal Automobile Club, Stone Horse Yacht Club (Harwichport, Mass.), Dartmouth Club (N.Y.C.), Yale Club of N.Y.C., Queen's Club (London). Republican. Episcopalian. Address: 30 Hans Pl, London SW1, England Office: Sinclair Mfg Co 12 S Worcester St Chartley MA 02712-9999

SINCLAIR, ROLF MALCOLM, physicist; b. N.Y.C., Aug. 15, 1929; s. Nathan and Elizabeth (Stout) S.; m. Margaret Lee Andrews, June 13, 1959 (div. 1978); children: Elizabeth Ann, Andrew Caisley; m. Allyn J. Miner, July 29, 1991. B.S., Calif. Inst. Tech., 1949; M.A. (Reade scholar), Rice U., 1951, Ph.D. (Inst. fellow), 1954. Physicist, Westinghouse Research Labs., 1953-56; vis. scientist U. Hamburg, Germany, 1956-57, U. Paris, 1957-58, U.K. Atomic Energy Authority, Culham Lab., Eng., 1965-66; research physicist Princeton U., 1958-69; program dir. NSF, Washington, 1969—; rep. U.S. solar eclipse expdn. to India, 1980; mem. Solstice Project, 1978-91 ; Disting. vis. prof. N.Mex. State U., 1985; vis. prof. No. Ariz. U., 1986; vis. scientist Los Alamos Nat. Lab., 1988-89, guest scientist, 1989—; cons. to industry, 1960-69. Fellow Am. Phys. Soc. (panel pub. affairs 1976-77, nominating com. 1988-90), AAAS (sec. physics sect. 1972—, mem. coun. 1972-73, nominating com. 1982-83), Sigma Xi. Home: 7508 Tarrytown Rd Bethesda MD 20815-6027 Office: Nat Sci Found Physics Div Washington DC 20550

SINCOFF, JAY MITCHELL, accountant; b. N.Y.C., May 17, 1949; s. Sidney Louis and Edith Peace (Budnick) S.; m. Marcia F. Bodack, July 2, 1978; children: Shawn, Rachel, Shara, Scott. BS in Bus. Adminstrn., SUNY, Buffalo, 1972. CPA, N.Y. Mgr. Trager, Glass & Co., N.Y.C., 1979-81; prin. Jay M. Sincoff CPA, Spotswood, N.J., 1981—. Trustee Free Sons of Israel, 1985—. Mem. Nat. Soc. Pub. Accts., N.J. Soc. CPAs, KP. Jewish. Home and Office: Jay M Sincoff CPA 41 S Rhoda St Spotswood NJ 08884-1947

SINDALL, TERESA LEE, administrative assistant; b. Casper, Wyo., June 13, 1954; d. Richard Eugene and Helen Elma (Kelly) Chubb; m. John Offerman Sindall, June 16, 1975. AAS in Secretarial, Casper Coll., 1974. Program coord. Met. State Coll., Denver, 1975-77; sec., receptionist Zephyr Archtl. Partnership, Honolulu, 1977-79; office mgr. Universal Graphics, Inc., Provo, Utah, 1979; exec. sec. Southern Pacific Petroleum N.L., Sydney, Australia, 1979-84; office mgr. Leigh Stowell & Co., Seattle, 1985; adminstrv. asst. Abt Assocs. Inc., Boston, 1986—. Home: 115 W Squantum St Apt 616 Quincy MA 02171-2115

SINDELAR, JODY LOUISE, economics educator; b. Oak Park, Ill., June 17, 1951; s. Joseph C. and Margaret (Faulkner) S.; m. Roger G. Ibbotson, July 5, 1983; children: Tyler Ibbotson-Sindelar, Timothy Ibbotson-Sindelar. BA, MA, Stanford U., 1973, PhD, 1980. Economist HEW, Washington, 1975-77, Pub. Svc. Lab., Georgetown U., Washington, 1978; lectr. econs. U. Chgo., 1979; vis. asst. prof. Boston U., 1980; asst. prof. U. Chgo. Grad. Sch. Bus., 1980-84; asst. prof., assoc. prof. health Yale U., New Haven, 1985—. Mem. Panel of Health Economist, N.Y.; bd. dirs. Shirley Frenchy Alcohol Treatment, New Haven, 1985—, Calvin Hill Daycare, New Haven, 1989—. NIMH postdoctoral fellow, Chgo., 1978-80; grantee Rockefeller Found., 1989-90, S.S. Huebner Found., 1982-83, Nat. Inst. Alcohol, 1989—, Nat. Ctr. for Health Statistics, 1990. Mem. Am. Econ. Assn., Am. Assn. Pub. Health. Home: 75 Old Hartford Tpke Hamden CT 06517-3524 Office: Yale U Sch Pub Health PO Box 3333 New Haven CT 06510

SINDELAR, WILLIAM FRANCIS, surgeon, researcher; b. Cleve., Mar. 13, 1945; s. William Frank and Josephine Ann (Storkan) S.; m. Aleta Beth Merkel, May 8, 1982 (div. July 7, 1987). A.B., Western Res. U., 1967; M.A., Case Western Res. U., 1968, Ph.D., 1970, M.D., 1971. Diplomate Am. Bd. Surgery. Instr. Marine Biol. Lab., Woods Hole, Mass., 1966-67; fellow in biology Western Res. U., Cleve., 1966-67; fellow in surgery Johns Hopkins U., Balt., 1971-73; clin. assoc. Nat. Cancer Inst., Bethesda, Md., 1973-75, sr. investigator, 1977—; fellow in surgery U. Md., Balt., 1975-77, cons. in surgery, 1980-91. Contbr. articles to profl. jours., chpts. to books. NSF grantee; NIH grantee; recipient President's Scholar award Western Res. U., 1967, Thwing Throphy Leadership award Western Res. U., 1967, J.D. Lane Research award USPHS Profl. Assn., 1983, Brian Bednarz Lectureship Worcester Meml. Hosp., 1983, Curts Lectureship Dartmouth Med. Sch., 1990. Fellow ACS, Internat. Coll. Surgeons; mem. AAAS, Am. Assn. Cancer Research, Am. Fedn. for Clin. Rsch., Am. Pancreatic Assn., Am. Radium Soc., Am. Soc. Cell Biology, Am. Soc. Clin. Oncology, Am. Soc. for Microbiology, Assn. Acad. Surgery, Assn. Mil. Surgeons of U.S., Commn. Officers Assn. of USPHS, Internat. Assn. Pancreatology, Internat. Hepatobiliary Pancreatic Assn., Internat. Photodynamic Assn., Johns Hopkins Med. and Surg. Assn., N.Y. Acad. Scis., Pancreas Club, Res. Officers Assn. of U.S., Soc. Surgery of Alimentary Tract, Soc. Surg. Oncology, Soc. Univ. Surgeons, Southeastern Surg. Congress, So. Assn. for Oncology, So. Med. Assn., Univ. Md. Surg. Soc., Phi Beta Kappa, Alpha Omega Alpha, Omicron Delta Kappa, Pi Delta Epsilon, Phi Rho Sigma. Republican. Roman Catholic. Home: 8009 York Rd Baltimore MD 21204-7025 Office: NIH Nat Cancer Inst Surgery Br Bethesda MD 20892

SING, ROBERT FONG, physician; b. Camden, N.J., May 29, 1953; s. William Fong and Elizabeth (Maxwell) S.; m. Lauren McNamee, May 11, 1991. BS in Biology, Ursinus Coll., 1975; DO, Coll. Osteo. Medicine, Surgery, 1978. Intern, then resident Met. Hosp., Phila.; dir. Emergency Dept. Springfield (Pa.) Hosp., 1984—, dir. sports medicine, 1987—; sch. and team physician Springfield Sch. Dist., 1989—, Rose Tree-Media (Pa.) Sch. Dist., 1987—. Author: Dynamics of the Javelin Throw, 1984. Med. dir. Springfield Ambulance Corp., 1988—. Named to Athletic Hall of Fame, 1985. Fellow Am. Coll. Emergency Physicians, Am. Coll. Sports Medicine, Am. Coll. Osteo. Emergency Physicians. Home: 1274 Gradyville Rd Glen Mills PA 19342 Office: Springfield Hosp 190 W Sproul Rd Springfield PA 19064

SINGEL, MARK STEPHEN, state official; b. Johnstown, Pa., Sept. 12, 1953; s. Stephen and Jean Ann (Mertle) S.; m. Jacqueline Lynn Schonel; children: Allyson Jean, Jonathan Albert, Christopher Mark. BA, Pa. State U., 1974, postgrad., 1975; postgrad., George Washington U., 1979. Legis. intern Pa. Ho. of Reps., 1972-73; legis. asst. to U.S. Rep. Helen S. Meyner, 1975; adminstrv. asst. to U.S. Rep. Helen S. Mayner, 1976-79, to U.S. Rep. Peter A. Peyser, 1979; U.S. senator from Pa., 1980-87; lt. gov. State of Pa., 1987—; Chmn. Pa. Energy Office, Pa. Emergency Mgmt. Coun., Pa. Heritage Affairs Commn.; mem. Pa. Econ. Devel. Partnership Bd.; trustee Pa. State U.; mem. Nat. Gov.'s Task Force on Hazardous Materials; mem. adv. bd. U. Pitts.-Johnstown, Indiana U. of Pa.; bd. dirs. Johnstown Flood Mus. Recipient Man of Yr. award Archdiocese of Pitts. Byzantine Rite, 1982, Community Achievement award Johnstown Lodge 214 Order Italian Sons and Daughters Am., 1986, Disting. Svc. award Pa. Industries for Blind and Handicapped, 1988, Humanitarian award Chapel of Four Chaplains, Valley Forge, 1990. Mem. adv. bd. U. Pitts.-Johnstown, Indiana U. of Pa.; bd. dirs. Johnstown Flood Mus. Recipient Man of Yr. award Archdiocese of Pitts. Byzantine Rite, 1982. Mem. Cambria County Young Dems., Travelers Protective Assn., Johnstown Sportsmen's Assn., Greek Catholic Union, Elks, Pi Kappa Phi (alumni bd. dirs.), Phi Kappa Phi, Omciron Delta Kappa. Democrat. Office: Office of Lt Gov Capitol Bldg Harrisburg PA 17120

SINGER, DAVID MICHAEL, marketing and public relations company executive; b. Bklyn., N.Y., Feb. 11, 1957; s. Seymour Allen and Ellen Sybil (Pavnick) S.; m. Pamela Rae Silton, July 20, 1986; 1 child, Max Ira Benjamin. BA in History, NYU, 1978; MA in Communications, Syracuse U., 1979; MA in Media, New Sch. Social Research, 1983; JD, Yeshiva U., 1981. Cons. pub. rels. Burson-Marsteller, N.Y.C., 1979-81, The Haas Group, N.Y.C., 1981-84, Braff & Co., N.Y.C., 1987-89; pub., editor-in-chief Lodestone Pub., N.Y.C., 1984-87; chief oper. officer Pentagon Ltd., N.Y.C., 1989-91; v.p. pub. rels. Braff & Co., N.Y.C., 1991—; lectr. evening div. NYU, 1982-83; dir. media rels. Braff & Co. Contbr. articles and poems to profl. and consumer jours. and mags. Pres. Jewish Cultural Found., N.Y.C., 1976. Named Mem. of Yr., N.Y. State Kiwanis, 1976, Outstanding Young Man of Am., Jaycees, 1977; recipient Cert. Recognition Am. Film Inst., 1982, ANDY Design award Advt. Club N.Y., 1983, Proclamation Bklyn. Borough Pres., 1987. Mem. Alpha Epsilon Pi (Bro. of Yr. 1976).

SINGER, HOWARD JACK, biology educator; b. Newark, Sept. 4, 1940; s. Nat I. and Rose (Alboum) S.; m. Helena Liisa Niskanen, May 29, 1986; children: Jamie Alexander Niskanen-Singer. BA, Oberlin Coll., 1962; MS, U. Minn., 1966; PhD, Tufts U., 1970. Prof. biology Jersey City State Coll., 1970—; cons. Proforma Base Corp., Jersey City, 1985-87, Instructivision, Inc., Livingston, N.J., 1988-89; researcher SUNY Downstate Med. Ctr., Bklyn., 1987-89. Contbr. articles to profl. jours. Pres. Van Vorst Pk. Assn., Jersey City, 1977-78; treas. Environ. Voters Alliance, N.J., 1984-90; dir. Hudson County (N.J.) Toxic Task Force, 1980-86; active Scientists Com. for Pub. Info., N.Y.C., 1976-80. Am. Chem. Soc. scholar, 1958-62; fellow NIH, 1966-70, NSF, 1961. Mem. Am. Soc. for Microbiology, Theobald Smith Soc., Am. Fedn. Tchrs. (membership chmn. 1989—). Home: 297 York St Jersey City NJ 07302 Office: Jersey City State Coll 2039 Kennedy Blvd Jersey City NJ 07305

SINGER, JUDITH D., statistics educator; b. N.Y.C., Oct. 17, 1955; d. Milton H. and Hilda (Gabin) S. BA, SUNY, Albany, 1976; MA, Harvard U., 1977, PhD, 1983. Rsch. analyst Abt Assocs., Inc., Cambridge, Mass., 1977-82; sr. rsch. assoc. Children's Hosp., Boston, 1982-88; asst. prof. Harvard U., Cambridge, 1984-89, assoc. prof. Grad. Sch. Edn., 1989—. Author: By Design, 1990, Who Will Teach?, 1991. Spencer postdoctoral fellow Nat. Acad. Edn., 1989. Mem. Am. Statis. Assn. (rsch. fellow 1991—), Am. Ednl. Rsch. Assn. (Palmer Johnson award 1989), Phi Beta Kappa. Office: Harvard Univ Grad Sch Edn Cambridge MA 02138

SINGER, MATTHEW ROSS, computer engineer; b. Huntington, N.Y., Feb. 16, 1961; s. Irvin and Florence (Hoffenberg) S.; m. Linda Marie Burns, May 13, 1984; children: Debra Rose, Joseph Zachary. BS in Physics, Audio Tech, Am. U., 1983. PC specialist Nat. Hwy. Traffic Safety Adminstr., Washington, 1985; software engr. U.S. Naval Rsch. Lab., Washington, 1983-86; staff engr. Lincoln Lab. MIT, Lexington, 1986—. Jewish. Home: 50 Eaton Rd Framingham MA 01701-2729 Office: MIT Lincoln Lab 244 Wood St Lexington MA 02173-6499

SINGER, MAX, lawyer; b. N.Y.C., Oct. 8, 1931; s. Sumer Wolf and Jeanne Florence (Goodstein) S.; m. Suzanne Lois Fried, Feb. 12, 1959; children: Saul H., Alexander L. (dec.), Daniel A., Benjamin S. BA, Columbia Coll., 1953; JD, Harvard U., 1956. Bar: N.Y. 1956, D.C. 1958. Acting pres., counsel, pres. Hudson Inst., Croton-on-Hudson, 1961-73; dep. dir. Hudson Inst., Washington, 1979-80; researcher, mng. dir. World Inst., Jerusalem, Israel, 1973-76; dir. Inst. for Jewish Policy Planning-Rsch., Washington, 1978-79; scholar in residence Russell Sage Found., N.Y.C., 1980-81; pres. The Potomac Orgn., Chevy Chase, Md., 1981—. Author: Passage to a Human World, 1984; (with others) Beyond Containment, 1983. With U.S. Army, 1957. Republican. Jewish. Home and Office: The Potomac Orgn 5400 Greystone St Bethesda MD 20815-5536

SINGER, MICHAEL NORMAN, actuarial analyst, consultant, educator; b. N.Y.C., July 28, 1946; s. Irving F. and Miriam N. (Wolf) S.; children: Deborah, Sarah. BS, Cornell U., 1968; PhD, U. Rochester, 1976; MBA, Adelpha U., 1986. Chartered property casualty underwriter. Rsch. assoc. U. Mass., Amherst, 1974-75, Southeastern Mass. U., North Dartmouth, Mass., 1975-77; sr. systems analyst KLD Assocs., Huntington, N.Y., 1977-78; sr. cons. Anistics, Inc., N.Y.C., 1978-80, v.p., 1981-88; mgr. systems and applications Landart Systems, Inc., N.Y.C., 1980-81; pres. Risk Info. Systems Cons., Inc., Huntington, from 1988; now sr. actuarial analyst Reliance Nat. Risk Specialists, N.Y.C. Contbr. articles to Phys. Rev. D. Mem. Soc. of CPCU, Am. Phys. Soc. Home: 45 Summit Ave Northport NY 11768-1636 Office: Reliance Nat Risk Specialists 77 Water St New York NY 10005-4401

SINGER, STEVEN RICHARD, university administrator; b. Bklyn., Dec. 29, 1956; s. Robert Paul and Florence (Silverman) S.; m. Kimberly E. Borman, July 2, 1989. BA, Colby Coll., 1979; MPA, Harvard U., 1986. Assoc. writer New Haven Advocate, 1979-81; communications dir. Conn. Citizen Action Group, Hartford, 1979-81; press sec. State Sen. William Curry, New Britain, Conn., 1981-82, U.S. Rep. William Ratchford, 1983-84, U.S. Rep. Chester Atkins, 1985; dir. press rels. Kennedy Sch. Harvard U., Cambridge, Mass., 1986-90, dir. comm. and pub. affairs, 1990—; guest lectr. Harvard U. Extension, 1987—, Simmons Coll., Boston, 1988-89. Contbr. articles to profl. jours. Mem. Arlington (Mass.) Dem. Town Com.

SINGH, AMRITJIT, English educator; b. Rawalpindi, India, Oct. 20, 1945; came to U.S., 1968; s. Kesar Singh and Balbir Kaur (Bhandari) Uberoi; m. Premjit Seth, Mar. 24, 1968; children: Samir, Reshma. BA, Panjab U., India, 1963; MA, Kurukshetra U., India, 1965; AM, NYU, 1970, PhD, 1973. Lectr. in English U. Delhi, India, 1965-68; instr. in English NYU, 1971-72; lectr., asst. prof. Lehman Coll., Bronx, N.Y., 1970-71, 73-74; rsch. assoc. Amer Studies Rsch. Ctr., Hyderabad, India, 1974-77; assoc. prof. English U. Hyderabad, 1977-78; prof. English U. Rajasthan, India, 1978-83; assoc. prof. English Hofstra U., 1984-86; assoc. prof., now prof. English R.I. Coll., Providence, 1986—, Mary Tucker Thorp disting. prof. arts and sci., 1991-92. Author: The Novels of the Harlem Renaissance, 1976, rev. edit., 1992; editor: Afro-American Poetry and Drama 1760-1975, 1979, Indian Literature in English, 1927-1979, 1981, India: An Anthology of Contemporary Writing, 1983, The Harlem Renaissance: Revaluations, 1989, The Magic Circle of Henry James, 1989. Fulbright-Smith-Mundt fellow NYU, 1968-69, Ford Found. fellow in ethnic studies NYU, 1972-73, ACLS fellow Yale U., 1983-84, NEH fellow DuBois Inst. Harvard U., 1991-92. Mem. MLA (del. assembly), Soc. for Study of Multi-Ethnic Lit. U.S. (book rev. editor 1989—), Asian Studies Assn., Am. Studies Assn., Am. Studies Rsch. Ctr. India. Office: Rhode Island Coll 600 Mt Pleasant Ave Providence RI 02908-1924

SINGH, DHANWANT, supermarket chain executive; b. Jammu, India, June 27, 1946; came to U.S., 1975; m. Kamal Jeet, Apr. 25, 1974; children: Surbparkash K., Perdeep. BSc, Jammu U., LLB; postgrad., West Indies. Lawyer Jammu, 1974-75; pres. Fair Deal Food Store; pres. Surbdeep Inc., Cinnaminson, N.J., 1985-90; chmn. Global Link Cons., Pensauken, N.J., 1990-91; owner four shopping strips. Mem. SWS Soc. Jammu (founder, dir.). Home: 202 Devin Rd Cinnaminson NJ 08077

SINGH, JYOTI SHANKAR, political organization director; b. Pathalgaon, India, Apr. 15, 1935; came to U.S., 1972; s. Brijnath Kumar and Tirthmani (Singh) S.; m. Maria Luz Molares, 1962; children: Anil, Rajeev, Ajit. BA, Banaras U., India, 1952, MA, 1954, LLB, 1955; MA, NYU, 1979; D (hon.), Inst. Internacional de Integracion, Bolivia, 1980. Assoc. sec. coordinating secretariat Leiden, The Netherlands, 1960-61, sec. gen. coordinating secretariat, 1961-64; programme cons. Internat. Youth Centre, New Delhi, 1965-66; sec. gen. World Assembly of Youth, Brussels, 1966-72; liaison officer Fund for Population Activities UN, N.Y.C., 1972-73, asst. exec. sec. World Population Yr., 1973-74, dep. chief info. and pub. affairs, 1975-80, chief info. and external rels., 1980-85, dir. info. and external rels., 1986-90; dir. tech. and evaluation div. UN Population Fund, 1990—; hon. prof. Cen. Am. U., Managua, Nicaragua, 1975; exec. coord. UN Internat. Conf. on Population, 1982-84; exec. coord. Internat. Conf. on Population and Devel., 1994. Author: A New International Economic Order, 1977; editor: World Population Policies, 1979; editor-in-chief Populi, 1980-90. Mem. Soc. for Internat. Devel. Home: 10 Waterside Plz Apt 26D New York NY 10010-2606 Office: UN Population Fund 220 E 42d St New York NY 10017

SINGHAL, JAYA ASTHANA, management science educator; b. Hyderabad, India, Apr. 8, 1952; came to U.S., 1977; d. Rajendra Narain and Suvira Asthana; m. Kalyan Singhal, Dec. 13, 1975. BSc, Marathwada U., Aurangabad, India, 1972, MSc, 1974; PhD, U. Ariz., 1982. Asst. prof. mgmt. sci. U. Balt., 1983-89, assoc. prof., 1989—. Lead author: (software package) Zero-One Optimization Methods; contbr. articles to profl. jours. Mem. Inst. Mgmt. Sci., Math. Programming Soc., Ops. Rsch. Soc. Am. Home: 11317 Ridermark Row Columbia MD 21044-5704 Office: U Balt 1420 N Charles St Baltimore MD 21201-5720

SINGHAL, KALYAN, business administrations educator; b. Mhow, Madhya Pradesh, India, June 3, 1946; came to U.S., 1969; s. Dwarkadas and Dhapubai (Mody) S.; m. Jaya Asthana, Dec. 13, 1975. B in Tech. with honors, Indian Inst. Tech., Bombay, 1967; MBA, Kent State U., 1970, D of Bus. Adminstrn., 1972. Indsl. engr. Union Carbide India Ltd., Calcutta, West Bengal, 1968-69; asst. prof. bus. admstrn. Kent (Ohio) State U., 1972-73; asst. prof. U. Houston, 1973-74; assoc. prof. Indian Inst. Mgmt., Bangalore, 1974-78, U. N.C., Greensboro, 1978-79; from assoc. prof. to prof. U. Ariz., Tucson, 1979-82; prof. U. Balt., 1983—; cons. Govt. of India, New Delhi, 1975-77, Coromondel Fertilizers, Vizag, India, 1975-77. Special editor Interfaces Jour., 1987; contbr. articles to profl. jours. Recipient Best Paper award N.E. Decision Scis. Inst., 1985. Mem. Inst. Mgmt. Scis. Coll. Prodns. and Ops. Mgmt. (founder, chmn. 1987-98), Prodns. and Ops. Mgmt. Soc. (founder, pres. 1989—, editor-in-chief jour. 1992—). Home: 11317 Ridermark Row Columbia MD 21044 Office: U Balt 1420 N Charles St Baltimore MD 21044

SINGHVI, SAMPAT MANAKCHAND, pharmaceutical scientist; b. Jodhpur, India, Oct. 14, 1947; came to U.S., 1968; s. Manakchand R. and Jethi (Balai) S.; m. Usha Sampat Mutha, July 17, 1971; children: Nikhil, Nilima. B Pharm, Birla Inst. Tech. and Sci., Pilani, India, 1967; MS, Phila. Coll. Pharmacy, 1970; PhD, SUNY, Buffalo, 1974; MBA, Rider Coll., 1979. Rsch. investigator E.R. Squibb & Sons, Princeton, N.J., 1974-78, sr. rsch. investigator, 1978-79, rsch. group leader, 1979-88, sr. rsch. group leader, 1988; assoc. dir. Bristol-Myers Squibb Co., Princeton, 1988—. Contbr. articles, abstracts and book chpts. to profl. publs. Mem. Am. Soc. Pharmacology and Exptl. Therapeutics, Am. Assn. Pharm. Scientists, Am. Pharm. Assn., Drug Info. Assn., Regulatory Affairs Profl. Soc., Rho Chi. Office: Bristol Myers Squibb Co PO Box 4000 Princeton NJ 08543-4000

SINGLETARY, MICHAEL JAMES, television executive; b. N.Y.C., Jan. 23, 1950; s. Elmer Dewitt and Lucille (Williams) S.; m. Michelle Jan Nero, Aug. 11, 1973; 1 child, Monique Janelle. Student, U. West Africa, Ghana, 1969, Fountainbleau (France) Music and Fine Arts Conservatory, 1970; BFA, Syracuse U., 1972; postgrad., R.I. Sch. Design, 1972-73; film cert., WNET Tng. Sch., N.Y.C., 1974. Assoc. dir. CBS News and Sports, N.Y.C., 1975—; producer Global Village Prodn., N.Y.C., 1982; dir. Melting Film, N.Y.C., 1987; prodn. supr. CBS Radio, N.Y.C., 1989—; tchr. Mus. Contemporary Craft, N.Y.C., 1973-74, Met. Mus. Art, N.Y.C., 1974, Coun. for Art in Westchester, White Plains, N.Y., 1989, Sarah Lawrence Coll., 1989—; lectr. Barach Coll., 1986, Am. Cancer Soc., Syracuse U., 1987, Arts and Entertainment Alliance, N.Y., 1989, Iona Coll., 1989. One-man exhbns. include U.S. Fed. Ct. House, Kenco Gallery, NY, Gicchinelli Gallery, Alain Bilhaud Gallery (Soho), N.Y., 1984-82, Greenburgh (N.Y.) Pub. Libr., 1985, Barauch Coll, N.Y., 1986, Mayors Mini Gallery, Washington, 1987, S.U. Lubin House Gallery, N.Y., 1988, Gallery 50, Bridgeton, N.J., 1989, Dalcour Fine Arts and Collectabels, Soho, 1990, Avon Products Incs., N.Y.C., 1990, NYU, N.Y.C., 1990, Iona Coll., New Rochelle, N.Y., 1990, Mercy Coll., Dobbs Ferry, N.Y., 1990, Bridge Gallery, White Plains, 1990, 112 St. Gallery, Soho, Brooke Alexander Gallery, Soho, Francis Laterman Salon Gallery, N.Y.C., Iona Coll., Newark Mus., Shark Bar Restaurant, Lee Solomon Pvt. Exhbn., N.Y.C. Basketball Hall of Fame, Readers Digest, 1992; group shows include Gallery of Western Art Washington, Bronx Mus. of Art, State Office Bldg., N.Y., Nuegerger Mus., U. of Guadalajra, C.B.S., Inc., 1985-80, Bridgeport Mus. of Art and Sci., Kuros Gallery, Madison Ave., N.Y., Folk Art Mus., Syracuse, Acabaw Gallery, Mt. Vernon, N.Y., 1986-87, Women Ctr., N.Y., 1988, Savacou Gallery, N.Y., 1988, Harlem Renaissance Gallery, N.Y., 1988, Adept Mus., Westchester, N.Y., 1988, Grace Bapt. Ch., Mt. Vernon, 1989, Bedford Stuyvesant Ctr. for the Arts and Clture, Bklyn., 1989, Ted Gallery, Albany, N.Y., 1989, Acbaw Gallery, Mt. Vernon, 1989, Flushing (N.Y.) Art Gallery, 1989, Bridge Gallery, 1990, Am. Express Gallery, N.Y.C., 1990, Kent State U., 1990, Dalcour Fine Art Gallery, 1990, Bayly Art Mus., 1990, Brooke Alexander Gallery, Francis Laterman Salon Gallery, others; represented in pvt. collections include Joe Dumars, Vince Williams, Amelia Marshall, Earl Davis, Dieter Jungman Emden; commns. include (portraits) N.Y.C. Basketball Hall Fame, Mickey Mantle Restaurant, N.Y.C. Police, (record covers) Capitol/Blue Note Records, Guiding Light TV series, Bill Saxton Quartet; numerous TV appearences; paintings appeared in segments of (TV show) The Cosby Show, (movies) Mo Better Blues, 1990, Jungle Fever, 1991, also The Slide Libr. of the Mus. of Modern Art, N.Y., 1990; contbr. articles to profl. jours. Bd. dirs. Green Chimneys, Brewster, N.Y., 1987; mem. artists adv. com. Art Coun. of Rockland and Westchester Counties; mem. artists adv. com. art installation, pub. art com. Westchester Community Coll. Mem. Dirs. Guild of Am., Writers Guild of Am., Soc. Motion Pictures and TV Engrs., Univ. Film Assn., Nat. Assn. Community of Artist, POW WOW Internat., Coll. Art Assn., Arts Internat., The Assn. of Am. Cultures, Allied Artist of Am., Art Internat. of N.Y.C., N.Y. Artist Equity Assn. Home: 375 Hawthorne Ter Mount Vernon NY 10552-2429

SINGLETARY, ROBERT LOMBARD, marine biologist; b. Atlanta, Mar. 21, 1941; s. Robert Edgar and Dorothy Louise (Lombard) S.; m. Virginia Ann Lloyd, June 21, 1964; children: James Robert, David Bradford. AB in Zoology, U. N.C., 1963; MS in Zoology, U. R.I., 1967; PhD in Marine Biology, U. Miami, 1970. Asst. prof. U. Bridgeport, Conn., 1970-74, assoc. prof., 1974-82, prof. marine biology, 1982—; cons. Regional Vocat. Aquaculture Program, Bridgeport, 1988—; mem. Conn. D.E.P. Standing Com. for Marine Rsch., Hartford, Conn., 1989—. V.p. Housatonic Coun. Boy Scouts of Am., Darby, Conn., 1981—. Mellon Faculty fellow Yale U., 1981; named one of Am. Men & Women of Scis., 1972. Mem. Internat. Oceanographic Found., Am. Soc. Limnology and Oceanography, New Eng. Estuaries Rsch. Soc., Estaurine Rsch. Fedn., Sigma Xi, Phi Kappa Phi. Office: U Bridgeport Univ Ave Bridgeport CT 06601

SINGLETON, JOHN, education and anthropology educator; b. Phila., Aug. 7, 1930; s. William Francis and Janet (Anthony) S.; m. Anne Haase Singleton, Dec. 22, 1953; children: Mark, William, Peter. AB, Oberlin Coll., 1952; AM, Haverford Coll., 1953; PhD, Stanford U., 1965. High sch. tchr. Bur. Indian Affairs, Fort Totten, N.D., 1953-55; edn. specialist U.S. Trust Ter. of the Pacific Islands, Truk, Fed. State of Micronesia, 1955-59; adminstr. East-West Ctr., U. Hawaii, Honolulu, 1963-66; prof. U. Pitts., 1966—; cons. AID, Peace Corps, Govt. of Malaysia, China, and others, 1966-90; field dir., Yr. in Japan Program, Konan U., Kobe, Japan, 1981-82; chair Internat. and Devel. Edn. Program, U. Pitts., 1968-71, 76-81. Author: Nichu: A Japanese School, 1967, (book in Chinese) Lectures on Applied Anthropology, 1984; founding editor: Anthropology and Education Quarterly, 1970-73; contbr. numerous articles to profl. jours. and books. Bd.

dirs. Internat. Ctr. for Conflict Resolution, Pitts., 1968-88. Foreign Area fellow, Ford Found., Tsuchiura, Japan, 1961-63, Profl. fellow, Japan Found., Mashiko, Japan, 1987. Fellow Soc. for Applied Anthropology (pres. 1979-80), AAAS; mem. Coun. on Anthropology and Edn. (pres. 1970-71), Am. Anthrop. Assn., Assn. for Asian Studies, Comparative and Internat. Edn. Soc., Soc. for the Anthropology of Work. Office: U Pitts FQ 5M32 Pittsburgh PA 15260

SINGLETON, ROYCE A(LAN), JR., sociology educator; b. Norman, Okla., Apr. 11, 1944; s. Royce Alan and Rebecca Rachel (Caldwell) S.; m. Nancy Jean Goerss, Aug. 20, 1966; children: Robert Brent, Katherine Anne. BS, Okla. State U., 1966, MS, 1968; PhD, Ind. U., 1973. From lectr. to asst. prof. U. Calif., Riverside, 1972-77; from asst. prof. to prof. Holy Cross Coll., Worcester, Mass., 1977—. Co-author: Oppression, 1984, Approaches to Social Research, 1988, rev. edit., 1993; assoc. editor: Teaching Sociology, 1989—; contbr. articles to profl. jours. 1st lt. U.S. Army, 1971. Mem. Am. Sociol. Assn. Democrat. Home: 6 Slipper Hill Ln Jefferson MA 01522-1406 Office: Holy Cross Coll 1 College St Worcester MA 01610-2322

SINNREICH-LEVI, DEBORAH MARGARET, medieval literature educator; b. N.Y.C., May 9, 1957; d. Jan Jiri and Leonore (Wachtel) Sinnreich; m. Ronald Alan Levi, July 2, 1989. BA, CUNY, 1978, MPhil, 1985, MA, 1986, PhD, 1987. Adj. lectr., English dept. Queens Coll., CUNY, N.Y.C., 1980-83; faculty coord., Romance Lang. dept. C. W. Post, Greenvale, N.Y., 1984-87; asst. prof., chief reader, English dept. Baruch Coll., CUNY, N.Y.C., 1983-89; asst. prof., English dept. N.Y. Inst. Tech., Greenvale, N.Y., 1989-90; asst. prof., dir. writing program and writing ctr. Steven's Inst. Tech., Hoboken, N.J., 1990—; deputy dir. CUNY Medieval City Conf., CUNY Grad. Ctr., N.Y.C., 1985, Intersession Basic Skills Immersion Program, Baruch Coll., N.Y.C., 1989. Author, translator: Eustach Deschamps' L'Art de Dictier, 1991; editor, contbr.: Voices in Translation, 1991. Mem. Nat. Coun. Tchrs. English, N.J. Coll. English Assn., CUNY Assn. Writing Suprs., Soc. for Textual Scholarship, Medieval Club N.Y., Modern Lang. Assn., N.E. Modern Lang. Assn. Democrat. Jewish. Office: Stevens Inst Tech Humanities Dept Castle Point on the Hudson Hoboken NJ 07030

SINTES, JORGE LUIS, health products company executive, researcher; b. San Juan, P.R., Dec. 8, 1948; s. Pedro Juan and Carmen Manuela (Belmonte) S.; m. Marilyn Yallen, Apr. 6, 1980; children: Amanda Ruthe, Isadora Raquel. BS, U. P.R., 1968, D of Dental Medicine, 1973, MPH, 1975; PhD, Mass. Inst. Tech., 1978. Cert. Dentistry, Nutrition, Dietetics. Clin. instr. U. P.R., Rio Peidras, 1972-74; dir. rsch. Comm P.R. Dept. Health, San Juan, 1974-75; clin. instr. Tufts U., Boston, 1975-78; cariologist Fairleigh Dickinson U., Hackensack, N.J., 1978-82, assoc. prof., chair, 1979-82; community dental educator Project HOPE, Natal, RN, Brasil, 1982-84; assoc. prof., chair Meharry Med. Coll., Nashville, 1984-88; prof., chair Calif. State U., San Bernardino, 1988-90; assoc. dir. The Colgate Palmolive Co., Piscataway, N.J., 1990—; cons. Colgate Palmolive Co., 1974-90; exec. dir. Y & S Cons., 1980—; dir. grad. program Fed. U. Rio Grande do NOrte Project HOPE, Natal, 1982-84; statewide dir. Area Health Edn. Ctrs. Oral Program, Nashville, 1985-88. Sec. Am. Soc. Preventive Dentistry, San. Juan, 1973; vol. Dental Vols. for Israel, Jerusalem, 1990; trustee, sec., treas. Hispanic Dental Assn., Chgo., 1990—. Grantee NIH, Bethesda, Md., 1974, post doctoral fellow, 1975-78; recipient Mario Badan award Brasilian Dental Assn. Fellow Acad. Gen. Dentistry; mem. ADA (Internat. award human svcs., Chgo., 1978), APHA, Internat. Assn. Dental Rsch., Tenn. Dental Assn. (Int. award human svcs. 1988), Acad. Oral Med., Colegio de Cirujanos Dent PR. Home: 7 Leeds Rd Flemington NJ 08822 Office: The Colgate Palmolive Co 909 River Rd Piscataway NJ 08854

SION, EDWARD MICHAEL, astrophysicist, educator; b. Wichita, Kans., Jan. 18, 1946; s. Michael Elias and Ramze Rae (Ayesh) S.; m. Miriam Kay Kangas, Sept. 7, 1968; children: Michael E., Melanie K. BA, U. Kans., 1968, MA, 1969; PhD, U. Pa., 1975. Assoc. prof. then prof. astron. astrophysics Villanova U., Pa., 1975—; vis. assoc. prof. physics Ariz. State U., Tempe, 1983-85, Chercheur Associé Ctr. Nat. de la Recherche Sci. Obs. Pic du Midi U. Toulouse, France, 1990; vis. scientist Hubble Space Telescope Sci. Inst. Johns Hopkins U., Balt., 1991; mem. NASA Internat. Ultraviolet Explorer Users com., peer rev. panels, 1981-90; guest investigator Kitt Peak Nat. Obs., Multiple Mirror Telescope Obs., Einstein Heao-B, EXOSAT, Cerro Tololo Inter-Am. Obs. Contbr. articles to profl. jours. Grantee NASA, 1978—, NSF, 1978, 86, 88, 90. Recipient Outstanding Faculty Rsch. award Villanova U., 1989; fellow Royal Astron. Soc.; mem. Internat. Astron. Union, Am. Astron. Soc., Astron. Soc. of the Pacific, Sigma Xi, Sigma Pi Sigma. Republican. Eastern Orthodox. Avocations: 18th and 19th Century American and European history.

SIPP, G. ROBERT, engineering and manufacturing company executive; b. Pitts., July 5, 1950; s. George Anthony and Jane Helen (Keraitis) S.; m. Madeleine Fay Cassidy, June 23, 1979; children: R. Nathan, Abbey Lundy. BS in Indsl. Engring., Purdue U., 1972; MBA, U. Pitts., 1980. Sales engr. The Timken Co., Canton, Ohio, 1972-74; v.p., gen. mgr. DMI Corp., N.Y.C., 1974-78; regional mgr. Dresser Industries, Inc., Pitts., 1978-83; v.p. ATP, Inc., Pitts., 1983-87; pres. Omnitec Enterprises, Inc., Pitts. and Coral Springs, Fla., 1985—. Chief, Indian Guides, YMCA, Coral Springs, Fla., 1989-90. Mem. Am. Def. Preparedness Assn., Abrasives Engring. Soc. (exec. v.p. 1980-87, jour. editor 1986-87; Man of Yr. 1986), Soc. Automotive Engrs., Soc. Mfg. Engrs., Inst. Food Technologists, Rep. Club Coral Springs. Roman Catholic. Home: 1104 1st St Canonsburg PA 15317-1840 Office: Omnitec Enterprises Inc 5335 Baptist Rd #ist Rd Pittsburgh PA 15236-1735

SIRACUSANO, LUCIANO VINCENZO, III, writer; b. N.Y.C., May 14, 1965; s. Luciano J. and Louise J. (Lombardi) S. BA, Columbia U., 1987. Asst. to Gov. Mario M. Cuomo for communications State N.Y., Albany, 1988-92. Founding editor, pub. Newman Jour., 1986, 87, 88. Democrat. Roman Catholic. Home: 120 Hamilton St Albany NY 12207

SIRMANS, DAN LAMAR, personnel administrator; b. Durham, N.C., July 13, 1941; s. Horace Lamar and Juanita (Fort) S.; B.B.A., Ga. State U., 1967; m. Sandra Elaine Bridges, Dec. 27, 1962; children—Todd Anthony, Elizabeth Anne. Asso. engr. Western Electric Co., Inc., Atlanta, 1962-67, sr. tng. specialist, St. Louis, 1968-74; dir. tng. and devel. ITT Aetna Corp., Denver, 1975-77; dir. personnel ITT Fin. Corp., St. Louis, 1978-79, dir. adminstrn., 1979-81; dir. employment Gen. Dynamics Communications, St. Louis, 1981-82; dir. human resources United Techs. Communications Co., 1982-83; v.p. human resources United Tech. Communication Co., 1983-85; dir. tng.and orgn. devel. United Techs. Carrier Corp., Syracuse, N.Y., 1989—. cons. program on analyzation and resolution of conflicts Syracuse U. Mem. Am. Soc. for Tng. and Devel., Am. Soc. Personnel Adminstrn., Am. Mgmt. Assn. for Quality and Participation, Assn., St. Louis Indsl. Relations Assn., Ind. Telephone Pioneer Assn., N.Am. Telephone Assn. Personnel Council, Assn. Human Resources Mgmt. and Orgn. Behavior, Orgn. Devel. Inst., Organ Devel. Network, Soc. for Human Resources Mgmt. Office: UTC/Carrier Corp 6311 Court St Rd East Syracuse NY 13057

SIROIS, ALLEN LOUIS, computer graphics artist; b. Bridgeport, Conn., Mar. 14, 1950; s. Louis Alexander and Mildred (Hoffman) S.; m. Linda Kathryn Jackson, June 27, 1977 (div. 1984); m. Paula Robin Warsh, Oct. 19, 1991; children: Daniel Stein, Kira Alexandra Sirois. Student, U. Bridgeport, 1968-70. Film technician Acigraf Ltd., Guilford, Conn., 1979-83; art and animation dir. Compu-Teach Inc., New Haven, 1983-85; sr. graphic artist Prodigy Svcs. Co., White Plains, N.Y., 1985—. Author: (children's book) Dinosaur Dress Up, 1992; author short stories. Mem. Sci. Fiction and Fantasy Writers of Am. Home: 66 Sanfordville Rd Warwick NY 10990 Office: Prodigy Svcs Co 445 Hamilton Ave White Plains NY 10601

SIROIS, HERMAN ARNOLD, school superintendent; b. Hartford, Conn., Sept. 11, 1945; s. Herman Clinton and Lois (Wood) S.; m. Barbara Reneē Grossman, Oct. 20, 1984. BA, U. Hartford, 1970; MS, Cen. Conn. State U., 1972; PhD, U. Conn., 1978. Tchr. W. Hartford Pub. Schs., W. Hartford, Conn., 1970-75; instr. U. Conn., Storrs, 1975-76; sch. prin. Warren Pub. Schs., Warren, Mass., 1976-78; dir. instruction Middletown Pub. Schs., Middletown, Conn., 1978-81; asst. supt. schs. Levittown Pub. Schs., Levittown, N.Y., 1981-86; supt. schs. Levittown Pub. Schs., 1986—; v.p. Sch. and Mgmt. Resource Group, N.Y.C., 1983—. Author: Error-Free Math, 1984, School Improvement, 1985; editor: Impact: Instructional Design, 1989; contbr. articles to profl. jours. Named to Exec.-Educator 100 N. Am., Nat. Sch. Bd. Assn., 1985. Mem. Am. Assn. Sch. Adminstrs., Assn. for Supervision and Curriculum Devel., Levittown C. of C., Kiwanis, Phi Delta Kappa (pres. Hartford chpt. 1976). Home: 245 E 19th St New York NY 10003-2639 Office: Levittown Pub Schs Abbey Ln Levittown NY 11756-4007

SIROWER, BONNIE FOX, fundraising executive; b. Bklyn., Jan. 9, 1949; d. Stanley S. and Harriet (Fischer) Fox; m. Martin Alan Sirower, Sept. 20, 1970; children: Kenneth, Daniel. AB, Barnard Coll., 1970; MA, Columbia U., 1971. Tchr. United Cerebral Palsy, N.Y.C., 1970-73, Bergen County Bd. Spl. Svcs., Paramus, N.J., 1973-76; spl. events coord. Am. Heart Assn., Glen Ridge, N.J., 1979-81; dir. devel. Goodwill Industries, Astoria, N.Y., 1981-83; pres. Access Unltd., 1984-85; dir. devel. Cheshire Home, Inc., 1986-89, Barnert Hosp., Paterson, N.J., 1989—. Mem. N.J. Soc. Fund Raising Execs. (bd. dirs. 1989, chmn. mentoring com.), Women in fin. Devel., Assn. Fund Raisers for Disabled (pres. 1981-83), N.J. Puzzlers' League (pres.), Barnard Coll. Class of '70 (pres. 1990—), YMCA of Paterson, N.J. (trustee 1991), Rotary Internat. (bd. dirs.), Phi Beta Kappa. Jewish. Home: 69 Godfrey Ter Glen Rock NJ 07452-3510

SIRY, JOANNE MICHAELE, psychologist, educator; b. Washington, July 18, 1947; d. Joseph William and Jennie (DiPietro) S. BA, Am. U., 1969; MA, U. Md., 1971, PhD, 1983. Instr. Dunbarton Coll., Washington, 1971-73, Cath. U., Washington, 1973-75; lectr. No. Va. Community Coll., Alexandria, 1975-76, instr., 1976-78, asst. prof., 1978-81, assoc. prof., 1981-86, prof., 1986—; asst. div. chmn. No. Va. Community Coll., 1980-82, 88—. Contbr. articles to profl. jours. Mem. Am. Psychol. Assn. Congregationalist. Office: No Va CC 3001 N Beauregard St Alexandria VA 22311-5065

SISK, PAUL DOUGLAS, lawyer; b. Colorado Springs, Colo., Mar. 30, 1950; s. Charles Ray Sisk and Patricia Joann (Linville) Botzler; m. Patricia Rizzo, Aug. 8, 1981; 1 child, Hannah Elizabeth. AB, Brown U., 1972; JD, Temple U., 1979; MA in Govt. Adminstrn., U. Pa., 1989. Bar: Pa. 1979, U.S. Ct. Appeals (3d cir.) 1980, U.S. Supreme Ct. 1983, U.S. Dist. Ct. (ea. dist.) Pa. 1985. Atty. U.S. Ct. Appeals (3d cir.), Phila., 1979-80, supervising atty., 1980-81, sr. staff atty., 1981—; lectr. law U. Pa., 1989—; reporter Joint Supreme Ct.- 3d cir. Death Penalty Task Force, 1989—. Acctg. Warden Episc. Ch., Springfield, Pa., 1979-81; bd. dirs. Springfield Pastoral Care Found., 1979-82; vestry St. Giles Ch., Upper Darby, Pa., 1991—. Mem. ABA, Am. Judicature Soc., Com. Appellate Staff Attys. (exec. bd. 1986—). Republican. Home: 8 Windsor Cir Media PA 19064-1422 Office: US Ct Appeals 3d Cir 601 Market St Philadelphia PA 19106-1510

SISKA, PETER EMIL, chemistry educator; b. Evergreen Park, Ill., Apr. 11, 1943; s. Emil Thomas and Marie Clara (Wintercorn) S.; m. Jeanne Cathy Artman, June 24, 1967; children: David, Sarah. BS, DePaul U., 1965; PhD, Harvard U., 1970. Rsch. assoc. U. Chgo., 1970-71; asst. prof. U. Pitts., 1971-76, assoc. prof., 1976-91, prof., 1991—; chmn. Gordon Rsch. Conf. on Atomic and Molecular Interactions, Wolfeboro, N.H., 1984. Sloan rsch. fellow, 1975. Mem. Am. Chem. Soc., Am. Phys. Soc. Office: U Pitts Dept Chemistry Pittsburgh PA 15260

SISKIND, GREGORY WILLIAM, medical educator, academic administrator; b. N.Y.C., Mar. 3, 1934; s. Jesse and Zenaida (Drabkin) S. BA, Cornell U., 1955; MD, NYU, 1959. Intern in medicine 3d med. div. Bellevue Hosp./NYU Sch. of Medicine, 1959-60, asst. resident in medicine 3d med. div., 1960-61; rsch. fellow dept. microbiology Sch. of Medicine Washington U., 1961-62; rsch. fellow in biology Harvard U., 1962-64; rsch. fellow dept. of medicine Sch. of Medicine, NYU, 1964-65, instr., 1965-66, asst. prof., 1966-68; asst. attending physician Bellevue Hosp., 1964-68; assoc. prof. Med. Coll., Cornell U., N.Y.C., N.Y., 1969-76, head div. allergy and immunology dept. medicine, prof., 1976—; assoc. dean rsch. and sponsored programs Med. Coll., Cornell U., Ithaca, N.Y., 1983-84, 1985—; attending physician dept. of medicine N.Y. Hosp., 1976—; mem. AIDS rsch. rev. com. NIH, Bethesda, Md., 1989-91. Editor: Immune Depression and Cancer, 1975, Clinical Evaluation of Immune Function in Man, 1976, Immune Effector Mechanisms in Disease, 1977, Developmental Immunobiology, 1979; editor, chief Proceedings of Soc. Exptl. Biology and Medicine, 1989—; contbr. numerous articles to profl. jours. Fellow Am. Acad. Allergy; mem. Am. Assn. Immunologists, Am. Soc. Clin. Investigation, N.Y. Allergy Soc. (pres. 1979). Office: Cornell U Med Coll 1300 York Ave New York NY 10021-4896

SISLEY, EMILY LUCRETIA, psychologist, medical writer; b. North Charleroi, Pa., May 7, 1930; d. Frederick William and Harriet Watkins (Litman) S. PhD in Clin. Psychology, L.I. U., 1972. Diplomate Am. Bd. Med. Psychotherapists. Mng. editor Med. Jours., Harper & Row, N.Y.C., 1960-67; freelance med. writer-editor N.Y.C., 1967—; supervising psychologist, dept. psychiatry Roosevelt Hosp., N.Y.C., 1972-77; clin. instr. Columbia Univ. Coll. Physicians and Surgeons, N.Y.C., 1975-77; chief psychologist Gramercy Park Inst., N.Y.C., 1978-84; counselor, cons. PPC, Inc., N.Y.C., 1984—; cons. Internat. Jour. Group Tensions, N.Y.C., 1968-72. Illustrator: You and Your Brain, 1963, Thomas Alva Edison award, 1963; co-author: The Vitamin C Connection, 1983; contbr. articles to profl. jours. Fellow Am. Bd. Med. Psychotherapists; mem. APA, N.Y. Acad. Scis. Democrat. Episcopalian.

SISSON, BRETA CORA, academic official; b. Wellsbridge, N.Y., Sept. 29, 1935; d. Bert Samuel and Josephine Lucia (Cuyle) S. Student bus. adminstrn., Albany Bus. Coll., 1955; BA in Geography, SUNY, Cortland, 1968. Account clk. SUNY, Binghamton, 1955-57; sr. account clk. SUNY, Cortland, 1958-62; cons., staff asst. SUNY, 1966-68, 72-77, bursar, 1968-72, budget control officer, 1977—; adminstrv. asst. contracts unit, Cornell U., Ithaca, N.Y., 1962-66; mem. acctg. and budgeting com., SUNY, Albany, 1978—. Mem. allocations com., Cortland County United Way, 1980-86; bd. dirs., Cortland Arts Coun., 1988. Mem. AAUW (corp. rep. 1980-87), SUNY-Cortland Alumni Assn. (treas. 1979-83, bd. dirs. 1988), Cortland County Hist. Soc. (various coms.). Democrat. Methodist. Home: 19 Melvin Ave Cortland NY 13045-1815 Office: SUNY Coll at Cortland PO Box 2000 Cortland NY 13045-0900

SISTERSON, JANET MARGOT, physicist, educator; b. Edinburgh, Scotland, July 7, 1940; came to U.S. 1968, naturalized, 1985; d. Thomas James and Lucy Margaret (Smith) Brownlee; m. L. Keith Sisterson, Oct. 23, 1965; children: James, Mark. BS, U. Durham, 1961; PhD, Imperial Coll. Sci. and Tech., U. London, 1965; Cert. in Advanced Mgmt. Studies Radcliffe Coll., 1989. Basic grade physicist London Hosp., 1964-66; sr. physicist Chelsea Hosp. for Women, London, 1966-68; rsch. fellow Cambridge (Mass.) Electron Accelerator, 1968-73; rsch. assoc. Harvard Cyclotron Lab., 1973—. Contbr. articles to profl. jours. Mem. exec. bd. Harrington Sch. PTA 1977-83. Mem. Am. Phys. Soc., Am. Assn. Physicists in Medicine, Am. Nuclear Soc., Am. Women in Sci., Meteoritical Soc. Office: 44 Oxford St Cambridge MA 02138-1998

SISTO, DONATO, surgeon; b. Verona, Italy, Apr. 22, 1950; came to U.S., 1976; s. Alfonso and Amelia (Frosandi) S.; m. Joan Mae Skinner, May 11, 1991. MD magna cum laude, Padua (Italy) U., 1974. Diplomate Am. Bd. Surgery and Thoracic Surgery. Resident surgery Albert Einstein Coll. Medicine, N.Y.C., 1976-81, resident cardiac surgery, 1981-83, attending surgeon dept. cardiac surgery, 1983—, assoc. prof. cardiothoracic surgery, 1992—; chief div. cardiac surgery Weiler Hosp. of Albert Einstein Coll. Medicine, N.Y.C., 1990—. Author sci. publs. on exptl. and clin. cardiac surgery. Fellow Am. Coll. Chest Physicians, ACS, Soc. Thoracic Surgeons; mem. Am. Soc. for Artifical Internal Organs, Denton Cooley Soc., Internat. Soc. for Heart Transplantation. Office: Weiler Hosp 1825 Eastchester Rd Bronx NY 10461

SISTO, ELENA, artist, educator; b. Boston, Jan. 11, 1952; d. Fernando Jr. and Grace Sisto; m. John David Kirkpatrick. BA, Brown U., 1975; grad., N.Y. Studio Sch., 1977; postgrad., Yale U., Norfolk, Conn., 1975, Skowhegan (Maine) Sch., 1976. Gallery artist Vanderwoude Tanabaum, N.Y.C., 1983-89; gallery artist Damon Brandt Gallery, N.Y.C., 1989-91; Gallery artist Genmans Van Ecil, N.Y.C., 1991—; tchr. Bates Coll., Maine, 1986, Colby Coll., Maine, 1986, SUNY-Purchase, 1988, R.I. Sch. Design, Providence, 1987—, N.Y. Studio Sch., N.Y.C., 1987—, Bard Coll., summer, 1990, Columbia U., N.Y.C. Represented in various pub. and pvt. collections. Fellow Skowhegan Sch., 1970, Yale Norfolk, 1975, NEA, 1983-83, 1989-90, Millay Colony, 1987.

SITTEL, KARL, physicist; b. Frankfurt, Federal Republic of Germany, Oct. 10, 1916; came to the U.S., 1947; s. Karl Wilhelm and Helene (Schmitt) S.; m. Edith Emilia Ecker, May 16, 1953; 1 child, Frederick Karl. PhD, Goethe U., 1940. Rsch. assoc. Max Planck Inst. for Biophysics, Frankfurt, 1939-47; dir. aerological instrumentation lab. German Marine Observatory, Greifswald, 1941-45; physicist, group leader Naval Air Experimental Sta., Phila., 1947-50; sr. staff physicist Franklin Inst. Rsch. Lab., Phila., 1950-59; staff scientist, leader RCA, Moorestown, N.J., 1959-67; cons. scientist Gen. Electric Co., Phila., 1967-81; staff cons. Jefferson Med. Coll., Phila., 1953-56; ptnr. Walsco Corp., Trenton, N.J., 1960-66; mem. radar workshop Def. Atomic Support Agy., Washington, 1962-67; assoc. mem. Albert Einstein Med. Ctr. Rsch. Lab., Phila., 1969-71. Contbr. articles to profl. jours.; contbr.: Handbooks in Physics and Rheology. Active Rep. Nat. Com., Washington, 1978—. Woehler Found. scholar, 1939-41. Mem. Physics Soc. Am. (emeritus), Scientific Rsch. Soc. Am. (emeritus), Elfun Soc. Lutheran. Home: Normandy Farm Estates Apt B-112 1801 Morris Rd Box 1108 Blue Bell PA 19422

SITTER, KATHRYN ANNE, academic administrator; b. Erie, Pa., Dec. 15, 1965; d. Frederick Michael and Arlene Carol (Kneidinger) S. BFA in Art, Carnegie Mellon U., 1987. Exhbn. coord. Carnegie Mellon Art Gallery, Pitts., 1987-89, student affairs/outreach coord., 1989—. Home: 2100 Mary St # 5D Pittsburgh PA 15203-2106 Office: Art Dept Carnegie Mellon Univ Pittsburgh PA 15213-3890

SITVER, ROBIN SUSAN, finance and systems executive; b. N.Y.C.; d. Herbert and Helen (Wishnia) S.; m. Jeffrey Mermelstein, Mar. 25, 1978; children: Scott, Jamie. AB, Brandeis U., 1977; MBA, U. Pa., 1979. Systems analyst Pfizer Pharms., N.Y.C., 1979-80, assoc. project analyst, 1980-81; mgr. fin. analysis Pfizer Agrl. Div., N.Y.C., 1981-83, mgr. fin. analysis and systems devel., 1983-87, asst. contr., 1987-88; dir. U.S. and hdqrs. fin. ops. Pfizer Animal Health Group, N.Y.C., 1988—. Bd. trustees N.J. Zool. Soc., West Orange, 1990—. Home: 464 Lenox Ave South Orange NJ 07079-1227

SIVULICH, STEPHEN, academic administrator, educator; b. Dixonville, Pa., Jan. 9, 1936; s. Michael and Mary (Taczak) S.; m. Alice Bilewicz, Sept. 1, 1968. BA, Mt. Union Coll., 1962; MA, Kent (Ohio) State U., 1973; EdD, Lehigh U., 1975. Dir. student conduct Kent State U., 1969-72; adminstrv. asst. to v.p. Lehigh U., Bethlehem, Pa., 1972-75; dean of students Allentown Coll., Center Valley, Pa., 1975-85, William Paterson Coll., Wayne, N.J., 1985-87; rsch. assoc. Coll. Placement Coun., Bethlehem, 1987-88; ednl. specialist Lehigh County Community Coll., Schnecksville, Pa., 1987-88; v.p. student affairs La Roche Coll., Pitts., 1988—. Sgt. U.S. Army, 1953-56, Korea and PTO. Mem. Nat. Assn. Student Pers. Adminstrs., Pa. Assn. Student Pers. Adminstrs. (pres. 1982-83), Coun. Eastern Orthodox Youth Leaders of Americas (pres. 1975-77), Ukranian Orthodox League of U.S. (pres. 1965-68, 1st v.p. 1991—, Orthodox of the Yr. 1978). Home: 120 Deer Valley Dr Sewickley PA 15143-9501 Office: La Roche Coll 9000 Babcock Blvd Pittsburgh PA 15237-5898

SJOLUND, PER-A., market research consultant; b. Ornskoldsvik, Sweden, Mar. 24, 1942; came to U.S. 1977; s. Erik Oskar and Astrid Margareta (Naeslund) S.; m. Kerstin Margareta Bring, July 5, 1967; children: Martin, Andreas, John. MSc in Mech. Engring., Royal Tech. Inst., Stockholm, 1966; MBA, Stockholm Sch. Econs., 1967; postgrad., UCLA, 1967-68. Asst. trade commr. Swedish Trade Commn., L.A., 1967-68; project mgr. Swedish Trade Commn., Vancouver, B.C., Can., 1968-70; sales mgr. Haegglund, Ornskoldsvik, Sweden, 1970-71; mktg. mgr. Swedish Steel AB/Plannja, Lulea, Sweden, 1971-74; pres. Shipman AB/Marco Materials, Hameling AB, Angelholm, Sweden, 1974-77; Swedish trade commr. Swedish Trade Commn., Chgo., 1977-83, N.Y.C., 1983-86; pres. Online Mktg. Co., Greenwich, Conn., 1986—. Mem. Swedish Am. C. of C. (dir.), Finnish Am. C. of C. (chmn.), Swedish MBAs in U.S., Swedish Ski Club (Alpine chmn. 1986-88). Home: 49 Hillside Rd Greenwich CT 06830 Office: Online Mktg Co PO Box 1608 Greenwich CT 06836

SKAGGS, CALVIN LEE, film, television and stage producer, director; b. Perryville, Mo., June 29, 1937; s. Roy Raymond and Ruby A. (Hand) S.; m. Merrill Ann Maguire, Aug. 19, 1960; children: Sylvia Merrill, J. Adam. BA, Henderson State U., 1957; MA, Duke U., 1960, PhD., 1966. Tutor of English Duke U., Durham, N.C., 1960-62; prof. English and cinema Drew U., Madison, N.J., 1962-75, dir. arts, 1976; v.p. Learning in Focus, Inc., N.Y.C., 1976-84; pres. Lumiere Prodns., N.Y.C., 1984—. Editor/writer: The American Short Story, 1976, 80, TV series producer, 1975-80; producer (TV movie) Go Tell It on the Mountain, 1980, (films) On Valentine's Day, 1986, The Wash, 1988, Fly by Night, 1992, (play) From the Mississippi Delta, 1991. Recipient Alumnus of Yr. award Henderson State U., 1989. Office: Lumiere Prodns Inc 26 W 17th St 8th Fl New York NY 10011

SKAGGS, MERRILL MAGUIRE, university dean; b. Florala, Ala., Oct. 1, 1937; d. John Henry and Clyde Louise (Merrill) M.; m. Calvin Lee Skaggs, Aug. 19, 1960; children: Sylvia Merrill, John Adam. BA, Stetson U., DeLand, Fla., 1958, LLD, 1988; MA, Duke U., 1960, PhD, 1965. Tutor Duke U., 1961-62; lectr. Bklyn. Coll., 1965; assoc. editor The MacMillan Co., N.Y.C., 1966-67; adj. asst. prof. English Drew U., Madison, N.J., 1975-76, adj. assoc. prof., 1976-79, assoc. prof., 1979-85, prof., 1985-86, dean Grad. Sch., 1988-92. Author: The Folk of Southern Fiction, 1972 (Edd Winfield Parks award), After the World Broke in Two: The Later Novels of Willa Cather, 1990; co-author: The Mother Person, 1975. Bd. dirs. Willa Cather Pioneer Meml., Red Cloud, Nebr., 1991—, N.J. Coun. for the Humanities, New Brunswick, 1990—. Mem. Soc. for Values in Higher Edn. (bd. dirs. 1988—), Soc. for Study of So. Lit. (bd. dirs. 1982, 83-85, 87-89). Democrat. Quaker. Home: 9 Woodcliff Dr Madison NJ 07940-2006 Office: Drew U Madison NJ 07940

SKANDERA-TROMBLEY, LAURA ELISE, language professional, English; b. L.A., Nov. 1, 1960; d. John and Mary Ruth (Chaney) S.; m. Nelson Edmund Trombley, July 13, 1991. BA, Pepperdine U., 1981, MA, 1983; PhD, U. So. Calif., 1989. Asst. lectr. U. So. Calif., L.A., 1983-87; vis. prof. U. Eichstatt, Bavaria, Germany, 1985-87, Pepperdine U., Malibu, Calif., 1988-90; asst. prof. Potsdam Coll., SUNY, 1990—. Author: Mark Twain's Literary Marriage, 1992; editor: Poetry and Epistemology, 1986. Named Quarry Farm fellow Ctr. for Mark Twain Studies, 1988, Finklestein fellow U. Soc. Calif., 1988. Office: Potsdam Coll Dept of English Potsdam NY 13676

SKATES, RONALD LOUIS, computer manufacturing executive; b. Kansas City, Mo., Sept. 25, 1941; s. Raymond and Suzanne (Lispi) S.; m. Mary Austin; children: Melissa, Elizabeth. AB cum laude, Harvard U., 1963, MBA, 1965. Acct. Price Waterhouse, Boston, audit ptnr., 1976-86; sr. v.p. fin. and adminstrn. Data Gen. Corp., Westboro, Mass., 1986-88, exec. v.p., chief oper. officer, 1988-89; dir., pres., chief exec. officer Data Gen. Corp., 1989—. Trustee Brigham and Women's Hosp., Boston; overseer Mus. Fine Arts, 1989. Mem. AICPA, Mass. Soc. CPAs. Office: Data Gen Corp 4400 Computer Dr Westborough MA 01580-0001

SKEBE, STANLEY ANDREW, aerospace and acoustical engineer; b. Euclid, Ohio, June 23, 1953; s. Stanley Gregor and Anna Angela (Urankar) S. BS in Fluid & Thermal Scis., Case Western Res. U., 1975, MS in Mech. Engring., 1978, PhD in Mech. Engring., 1983. Registered profl. engr., Ohio. Grad. rsch. asst. Case Western Res. U., Cleve., 1975-83; assoc. rsch. engr. United Techs. Rsch. Ctr., East Hartford, Conn., 1984-88, rsch. engr., East Asian rep., 1988—; participant 1st Japan-Am. Grassroots Summit, 1991. Mem. AIAA, Chinese Culture Ctr., Japan Soc. Conn. (chmn. pub. rels. 1987—), World Affairs Coun. Office: United Techs Rsch Ctr 17ms Silver Ln East Hartford CT 06118-1004

SKEER, MARTIN HENRY, management consultant; b. N.Y.C., May 16; s. Abraham and Freda (Smith) S.; m. Susan Fox, Aug. 20, 1967; children: Craig, Michael, Margie. BSCE, Cooper Union, N.Y.C.; MBA in Fin., Am.

U., 1972; PhD, Carnegie-Mellon U., 1968. Registered profl. engr., N.Y., N.J. Supr. Bell Labs., Murray Hill, N.J., 1971-83; mgr. AT&T Corporate, N.Y.C., 1983-86; pres. Martin Skeer Assocs., Berkeley Heights, N.J., 1986—. Carnegie-Mellon U. rsch. assistantship. Mem. Summit Jr. C. of C. (pres. 1982-83), Sigma Xi. Office: Martin Skeer Assocs 36 Rutherford Rd Berkeley Heights NJ 07922-2014

SKELLY, RICHARD FRANCIS, merchandising brokerage executive; b. RockvilleCenter, N.Y., Dec. 14, 1937; s. E. Frank and Mary Agnes (Kiernan) S.; m. Barbara Lee Friemonth, Apr. 4, 1964; children: David Kiernan, Megan Friemonth. BS, Am. U., 1960. Sales rep. GE, N.Y.C., 1960-66; sales mgr. Schick, Inc., Lancaster, Pa., 1966-68; v.p. Clairol, Inc., N.Y.C., 1968-71; pres. Meteor/Skelly, Inc., Larchmont, N.Y., 1971—; former mem. bd. dirs. Regina Corp., Rahway, N.J., Gold Medal, Inc., Richmond, Va., Westport Labs., Inc., Fairfield, Conn., Housewares Club, N.Y.C. Industry chmn. N.Y. div. Am. Cancer Soc., 1986-89; past mem. Wilton (Conn.) Rep. Town Com. Mem. Nat. Assn. Gen. Mdse. Reps. (bd. dirs. 1983-90, pres. 1986-87), Conn. Golf Club (bd. dirs. 1983—, pres. 1992—). Republican.

SKELLY-GONZALEZ, RALPH THOMAS, lawyer; b. San Juan, P.R., Jan. 7, 1945; s. Hubert Skelly and Esther González; divorced; 1 child, Ramses. BS, King's Coll., Wilkes-Barre, Pa., 1966; JD, U. P.R., 1969. Bar: P.R. 1970. Fed. Dist. Ct. P.R. 1970, U.S. Ct. Appeals 1970, U.S. Supreme Ct. 1974, Pa. 1991; cert. notary public 1970. Spl. prosecutor Dept. of Justice of P.R., 1970-73; asst. exec. dir. San Juan Legal Svcs. Inc., 1974-77; dir. anti-trust office, dep. atty. gen. Dept. of Justice of P.R., 1977-82; dep. adminstr. P.R. State Ins. Fund Adminstrn., 1982-85; individual practice law P.R., 1985-89; asst. mgr. for field ops. Holicong Dist. Office, U.S. Dept. Commerce, Bucks County, Pa., 1989-90; dist. mgr. Pa. State Workmen's Ins. Fund, Pa. Dept. Labor and Industry, Phila., 1991—. Mem. Congreso Borricua, Washington, 1990, Latino Scholarship Fund, Phila., 1991; v.p. Centennial Health Ctr., Warminster, Pa., 1990-92. Mem. ABA, Phila. Bar Assn., Colegio Abogado de P.R. Roman Catholic. Home: PO Box 66 Morrisville PA 19067

SKELTON, DENNIS LEE, aerospace engineer; b. Pontiac, Mich., June 17, 1951; s. Walter Kenneth and Phyllis Elaine (Walter) S.; m. Helen Demetrios Gioka, June 8, 1983; children: Anastasia Danae, Alexander Demetrios. BS, U. Mich., 1973; MS, U. Colo., 1978. Mem. tech. staff Ball Aerospace Systems Div., Boulder, Colo., 1978-82; sr. optical engr. Itek Optical Systems, Lexington, Mass., 1982-86; sr. engr. Hughes Danbury (Conn.) Optical Systems (formerly Perkin-Elmer Electro-Optical Systems div.), 1986-90; staff engr. McDonnell Douglas Space Systems Co., Seabrook, Md., 1991—. Author, co-author conf. proc. and abstracts. Mem. Am. Astron. Soc., Optical Soc. Am. (sec. New Eng. sect. 1984-85, sec.-treas. Rocky Mountain sect. 1981-82), Soc. Photo-Optical Instrumentation Engrs., AIAA. Methodist. Office: McDonnell Douglas Space Systems Co 7404 Executive Pl Lanham Seabrook MD 20706-0001

SKELTON, EARL FRANKLIN, research physicist, engineering educator; b. Hackensack, N.J., Apr. 8, 1940; s. Floyd and Frances (Rucker) S.; m. Anita Patton, June 17, 1962 (div. 1984); children: Diana Lynn, Isaac Patton; m. Thelma Francesca Fried, Oct. 19, 1986. BS in Physics, Fairleigh Dickinson U., 1962; PhD in Physics, Rensselaer Polytechnic Inst., 1967. Rsch. physicist Benet Weapons Lab. Watervliet Arsenal, 1961-62; rsch. assoc. Rensselaer Polytechnic Inst., Troy, N.Y., 1967; postdoctoral assoc. NAS-Nat. Rsch. Coun. Naval Rsch. Lab., Washington, 1967-68, rsch. physicist, 1968-76, supervisory rsch. physicist, 1976—; liaison scientist Office Naval Rsch., Tokyo, 1978; lectr. physics Prince George's C.C., 1968-73; assoc. professorial lectr. engring. George Washington U., 1974-79, professorial lectr., 1979—; lectr. grad. sch. dept. chem. engring. U. Md., 1975-80, assoc. mem. lab. high presure sci., 1977-80; vis. scholar synchrotron radiation lab. Stanford U., 1980-81, elected mem. users exec. com., 1983; elected mem. users exec. com. nat. synchrotron light source Brookhaven Nat. Lab., 1989, 90, 91; rsch. affiliate Hawaii Inst. Geophysics U. Hawaii, 1982-86. Contbr. over 200 articles to tech. and sci. jours. Recipient Yuri Gargaran Satellite Communication award Fed. Commn. Radiosport, U.S.S.R., 1979, Best Family History Writing award Nat. Geneal. Soc., 1992; predoctoral scholar NIH, 1964-67. Fellow Am. Physical Soc.; mem. SAR (Washington D.C. chpt.), Am. Crystallographic Assn., Sigma Xi. Home: 6311 29th Pl NW Washington DC 20015-2221 Office: US Naval Rsch Lab Code 4680 5000 Overlook Ave SE Washington DC 20375-5320

SKELTON, J(AMES) A(NDERSON), II, psychology educator; b. Ft. Campbell, Ky., Sept. 29, 1949; s. James Anderson and Elizabeth Ann (Harlinger) S.; m. Melinda Ann Matthews, May 17, 1969. BA, Washington & Lee U., 1976; postgrad., Duke U., 1976-77; MA, U. Va., 1979, PhD, 1981. Asst. prof. psychology Dickinson Coll., Carlisle, Pa., 1981-87; assoc. prof. psychology Dickinson Coll., Carlisle, 1987—. Author: Mental Representation in Health and Illness, 1991; contbr. articles to profl. jours. Mem. AAUP, Union of Concerned Scientists, Soc. for Psychophysiological Rsch., Soc. for Advancement Social Psychology, Soc. for Personality and Social Psychology, Am. Psychol. Soc., Am. Psychol. Assn. Office: Dickinson Coll Dept Psychology PO Box 1773 Carlisle PA 17013-2896

SKEMER, DON CORNEL, librarian; b. N.Y.C., Jan. 31, 1948; s. Alex and Lillian S.; m. Margaret S. Stein, Apr. 6, 1973; children: Philip, Andrew. BA, CUNY, 1968; PhD, Brown U., 1972; MLS, Columbia U., 1978. Keeper manuscripts N.J. Hist. Soc., Newark, 1974-79, dir. publs., 1979-86, assoc. exec. dir., 1986; head spl. collections and archives, adj. lectr. U. Albany, SUNY, 1986-91; curator manuscripts Princeton (N.J.) U. Librs., 1991—. Author: American History in Belgium, 1975; mng. editor: New Jersey History, 1983-86; contbr. articles to profl. jours. NDEA fellow, 1969-72, Fulbright fellow Medieval Acad. of Am., 1974-74. Mem. ALA, Soc. Am. Archivists. Office: Princeton U Libr Dept Rare Books and Spl Collections One Washington Rd Princeton NJ 08544

SKENDERIAN, DONALD ERWIN, data technology company executive, engineer; b. Boston, Nov. 21, 1941; s. Emil Edward and Alice (Moranian) S.; m. Sept. 10, 1967 (div. Dec. 1980); m. Janice Anne Bogosian, Oct. 15, 1982; children: Donald Hagup, Elyse De Anna. BSEE, Northeastern U., 1967. Industry engr. GE, Schenectady, N.Y., 1967-69; sales engr. Data Tech., Watertown, Mass., 1969-71; OEM mgr. Data Tech., Woburn, Mass., 1971-78; gen. sales mgr. Data Tech., Woburn, 1978-85, v.p. sales mktg., 1985—. Mem. TAPPI, Am. Indsl. Corrugated Converters, Nat. Assn. Diemakers, Nat. Paper Box Assn. Roman Catholic. Office: Data Tech Inc 4 Gill St Woburn MA 01801-1750

SKIADOS, DEBORAH ANN, insurance company executive; b. Meriden, Conn., Feb. 9, 1958; d. Charles Christopher and Nancy Jean Skiados. BA in Speech Communications, So. Conn. State U., 1980, MS in Social Sci. Edn., 1990, postgrad., 1983-85. Med. asst./accounts receivable Gen. Practitioners of Hamden, Conn., 1981-84; med. claim processor The Hartford Ins. Group, 1984-86; with Revere Corp., Wallingford, Conn., 1986-87; underwriting supt. Aetna Life & Casualty, Hartford, 1987—; faculty So. Conn. State U., New Haven, 1991. Sexual assault counselor YWCA of Meriden, 1983-85. Mem. Orgn. Am. Historians. Office: Aetna Casualty & Surety 151 Farmington Ave Hartford CT 06156-0001

SKIBINSKI, MARIE ANNE, systems analyst, computer programmer; b. Wilkes-Barre, Pa., July 1, 1947; d. Leo Stanley and Rose Delores Skibinski; m. Kenneth Michael Gresko, Apr. 26, 1980 (div. Sept. 1988). BA in Math., Wilkes U., 1969. Programmer analyst IBM, Kingston, N.Y., 1969-72; computer scientist Am. Mgmt. Systems, Arlington, Va., 1973-74; standards analyst Potomac Electric Power Co., Washington, 1974-75; computer specialist Nat. Credit Union Adminstrn., Washington, 1975-76; systems analyst City of Falls Church, Va., 1976-77; computer programmer Am. Temps at Burroughs Corp., McLean, Va., 1978; computer specialist FCC, Washington, 1978-83; computer asst. Social Security Adminstrn., Phila., 1992; computer specialist FCC, Washington, 1978-83; computer asst. Social Security Adminstrn., Phila., 1992. Recipient commendation Nat. Credit Union Adminstrn., 1976, outstanding rating FCC, 1980, 81. Home: 1377 Stairville Rd Mountain Top PA 18707

SKIDMORE, DAVID THEODORE, service executive; b. Williamson, W.Va., July 31, 1952; s. Theodore Roosevelt and Frances Margaret (Shamblin) S.; m. Donna Joy Burgess, Feb. 6, 1970; children: Suzette Lynn, Christopher David. Lineman C & P Telephone Co., Huntington, W.Va., 1970-71, splicer, 1971-76, engr., 1976-78; engr. Tesinc, Columbia, S.C., 1978-79, area mgr., 1979-80; with Volt Info. Scis., N.Y.C., 1982—, regional mgr., 1982-84, div. mgr., 1987-91; v.p. The Maxima Corp., Lanham, Md., 1991—. Recipient Glass Fiber Splicer award Anaconda Corp., 1984. Mem. Am. Mgmt. Assn., Assn. Field Svc. Mgrs. Republican. Home: 4909 Rockvue Pass Bowie MD 20715-1059

SKIDMORE, KENNETH FRANKLIN, metallurgical engineer; b. Nutter Fort, W.Va., Aug. 24, 1929; s. John Morgan and Flossie Juanita (Hopkins) S.; m. Linda Lee Gillespie, July 18, 1959; children: Laura Lee, Thomas John. Student in elec. engring., W.Va. U., 1947-50; BS/MMS, Carnegie Inst. Tech., Pitts., 1969. Dist. matls. inspector W.Va. Dist. 4 Constrn. Div., Clarksburg, 1950-52; mech. equip. developer U.S. Steel Applied Rsch. Lab., Monroeville, Pa., 1957-69; corp. staff metall. engr. Rockwell Internat. Corp., Pitts., 1969-88; sr. metall. engr. Sensus Technologies, Inc., Uniontown, Pa., 1988—; pres., owner Metall. Tech. Svc., Monroeville, 1976—; bd. trustees Die Casting Rsch. Found., Chgo., 1979-84. Contbr. articles to profl. jours. Recipient Award of Honor, VFW, 1947, Nyselius award, Die Casting Rsch. Found., Chgo., 1982. Mem. N. Am. Die Casting Assn. (tech. editor 1991—), Nat. Assn. Corrosion Engrs., Pa. Soc. Profl. Engrs. (bd. dirs. 1974-76), ASM (bd. dirs. 1975-77), Am. Chem. Soc., ASTM, NSPE, Am. Foundrymen's Soc. Home: 312 Oliver Dr Monroeville PA 15146-4643 Office: Metall Tech Svc 312 Oliver Dr Monroeville PA 15146-4643

SKIDMORE, LEMUEL, III, data processing consultant; b. N.Y.C., Dec. 23, 1947; s. Lemuel Jr. and Anne (Kinkead) S.; m. Susan Jane McDonald, Jan. 15, 1972; children: Sara Lynn, Emily Elizabeth. BA, Hawthorne Coll., Antrim, N.H., 1972; MS, Ind. State U., 1975. Programmr analyst Marion County, Indpls., 1975-77, Lane Bryant Inc., Indpls., 1977-79; sr. systems analyst Pfizer, Inc., Groton, Conn., 1979-82; cons. New Eng. Data Svcs., Madison, Conn., 1982-84; pres. Skidmore Resource Mgmt. Co., Clinton, Conn., 1984-89; cons. IBM, Southbury, Conn., 1989—. Contbr. articles to profl. jours. Pres. Clinton Jaycees, 1980-81; mem. Clinton Planning and Zoning Commn., 1981, Computer Study Commn., Clinton, 1983. Mem. Hartford Data Processing Mgmt. Assn. (bd. dirs. 1982-84), Toastmasters (adminstrv. v.p. Essex 1980). Office: IBM 150 Kettletown Rd Southbury CT 06488

SKIFF, PETER DUANE, physics educator; b. Pitts., Dec. 16, 1938; s. Walter B. and Mary A. (Tallman) S.; m. Katherine Louise White, Oct. 16, 1965. AB, U. Calif., Berkeley, 1959; MS, U. Houston, 1961; PhD, La. State U., 1966. Instr. La. State Univ., Baton Rouge, 1964-66; asst. to full prof. Bard Coll., Annandale On Hudson, N.Y., 1966—; adj. faculty various colls. and univs.; lectr. in field. Reviewer Choice Mag., 1981—; contbr. book reviews and articles to profl. jours. Mem. Am. Phys. Soc., Am. Assn. Physics Tchrs., British Assn. for Philosophy of Sci., British Soc. for the History of Sci., History of Sci. Soc., Philosophy of Sci. Assn., The Oriental Inst. Office: Bard Coll Annandale On Hudson NY 12504

SKILLMAN, JOHN HAROLD, educational exchange executive; b. Norwich, N.Y., Oct. 8, 1927; s. Frank Martin and Olive May (Stewart) S.; m. Verlie-Anne McKenzie; children: Alan McKenzie, Jenny-Lynn, Theodore Martin, Elizabeth Joanne, Andrew Mark. BA, Syracuse U., 1949, MA, 1950, PhD, 1958. Ednl. missionary Bd. of Missions, United Meth. Ch., Tokyo, 1951-72; instr. Aoyama Gakuin U., Tokyo, 1952-58; from asst. prof. to assoc. prof.; prof. Aoyama Gakuin U., Tokyo, 1971-72; asst. exec. dir. Coun. Internat. Ednl. Exch., N.Y.C., 1972-78, dep. exec. dir., Asia dir., 1978—; Bd. dirs. Taiyo Kobe Bank and Trust Co., N.Y.C., 1988—, Japanese Ednl. Inst., N.Y.C., 1974—. Editor: Edn. Abstracts, Japan Edn. Assn., 1958-72; contbr. articles to profl. jours. Bd. dirs. Aoyama Gakuin, Tokyo, 1958-72, Am. Sch. in Japan, Tokyo, 1962-72. With U.S. Army, 1944-47, Philippines. Recipient N.Y. State Regents scholarship, 1956-58. Mem. Assn. for Asian Studies. Democrat. Home: 146 Secor Ln Pelham Manor NY 10803-2211 Office: Coun on Internat Ednl Exch 205 E 42d St New York NY 10017-3204

SKINNER, MAURICE EDWARD, IV, information security system specialist; b. Balt., Aug. 31, 1962; s. Maurice Edward III and Patricia U. (O'Connor) S. BSc in Computer Sci., BBA, Lynchburg (Va.) Coll., 1986. Cert. info. systems auditor. Systems analyst Lynchburg Coll., 1985-86; ptnr. Bates Marine Basin, Oxford, Md., 1985-87; mgr. info. tech. audit svcs. Coopers & Lybrand, Washington, 1986-92; systems mgr. faculty practice info. systems Pasquerilla Healthcare Ctr., Georgetown U., Washington, 1992—; chmn. Mid-Atlantic area Security Local Users Group of Digital Equipment Corp. Users Soc. Mem. Assn. for Computing Machinery, Electronic Data Processing Auditors Assn., Info. Systems Secrity Assn. Republican. Methodist. Home: 5818 Inman Park Cir # 200 Rockville MD 20852-5474 Office: Pasquerilla Healthcare Ctr Faculty Practice Info 3800 Reservior Rd NW Washington DC 20007

SKINNER, ORIN ENSIGN, retired artist, foundation executive; b. Sweden Valley, Pa., Nov. 5, 1892; s. Enos Eton and Catherine Ines (Dunbar) S.; m. Frances Van Arsdale, 1916 (dec. 1979); 1 child, Charles Van Arsdale (dec.). Student, Rochester Athenaeum and Mechanics Inst., 1912-16. Craftsman, artist, sec. Charles J. Connick Studio, Boston, 1920-86, pres., 1945-86; pres. The Charles J. Connick Stained Glass Found., Ltd., Newtonville, Mass., 1985—; lectr. on stained glass throughout U.S., 1926—, Columbia U., N.Y.C., 1949. Contbr. articles on stained glass to profl. publs. Fellow Stained Glass Assn. Am. (pres. 1948-50, editor Quar. 1933-48), Soc. Arts and Crafts (master craftsman), Tuesday Club. Office: Charles J Connick Stained Glass Found Ltd 37 Walden St Newton MA 02160-2133

SKINNER, PAUL ELLIOT, electronics executive; b. Boston, Apr. 12, 1943; s. Roy Elliot and Mabel Katherine (Lemay) S.; m. Sheila Mary Magee, Apr. 16, 1966; children: Michael Elliot, Paul Douglas. AAS, USAF, 1963; student, U. Maine, 1961-63, Northeastern U., 1977-79. Adminstr. bus. loan 1st Nat. Bank Boston, 1963-64; retail mgr. Herman Inc., Avon, Mass., 1964-67; auditor Cumberland Farms Inc., Canton, Mass., 1967-69; gen. mgr. Goodick Industries Inc., Weymouth, Mass., 1969-71; counselor Snelling & Snelling, Boston, 1971; asst. mgr. Rex Fulton Inc., Weymouth, 1971-78; planner, coord. mfg. Merriman Div. Litton Industries, Hingham, Mass., 1978-80; planner, coord. engring. Loral Infrared Imaging Systems (formerly Honeywell Electro-Optics Div.), Lexington, Mass., 1980—. Pres. North Weymouth Civic Assn., 1982, v.p., 1981; tchr. religion Archdiocese of Boston, Weymouth, 1964-84; active on July 4th Com. Town of Weymouth, 1988. With USAF, 1961-63. Mem. Am. Prodn. and Inventory Control Soc. Democrat. Roman Catholic. Home: 45 Canacum Rd Weymouth MA 02191-2221 Office: Loral Infrared Imaging System 2 Forbes Rd Lexington MA 02173-7393

SKINNER, SAMUEL KNOX, political organization executive, lawyer; b. Chgo., June 10, 1938; s. Vernon Orlo and Imelda Jane (Curran) S.; m. Mary Jacobs, 1989; children: Thomas, Steven, Jane. B.S., U. Ill., 1960; J.D., DePaul U., 1966. Bar: Ill. 1966. Asst. U.S. atty. No. Dist. Ill., Chgo., 1968-74, 1st asst. U.S. atty., 1974-75, U.S. atty., 1975-77; ptnr. Sidley & Austin, Chgo., 1977-89; chmn. Regional Transp. Authority, Chgo., 1984; U.S. sec. of transp., 1989-91; chief of staff White House, Washington, 1991-92; gen. chmn. Republican Nat. Com., Washington, 1992—. Chmn. Ill. Capitol Devel. Bd., 1977-84. Served as 1st lt. U.S. Army, 1960-61. Mem. ABA, Ill. Bar Assn., Chgo. Bar Assn., Chgo. Shoreacres Club. Republican. Presbyterian. Office: Rep Nat Com 310 1st St SE Washington DC 20003

SKIRNICK, ROBERT ANDREW, lawyer; b. Chgo., Apr. 23, 1938; s. Andrew and Stella (Sanders) S.; children: Rebecca, David; m. Maria Ann Castellano, Oct. 4, 1974; 1 child, Gabriella. BA, Roosevelt U., 1961; JD, U. Chgo., 1966. Bar: U.S. Dist. Ct. (no. dist.) Ill. 1966, U.S. Ct. Appeals (7th cir.) 1968, U.S. Supreme Ct. 1970, U.S. Ct. Appeals (5th and 9th cirs.) 1982, N.Y. 1982, U.S. Ct. Appeals (3d cir.) 1983, U.S. Dist. Ct. (ea. dist.) Mich. 1988, (so. dist. and ea. dist.) N.Y. 1989, U.S. Ct. Appeals (2nd cir.) 1990, U.S. Dist. Ct. (no. dist.) Calif. 1992, U.S. Ct. Appeals (11th Cir.) 1992, U.S. Dist. Ct. (so. dist.) Tex. 1992. Atty. office gen. counsel honors program HEW, Washington, 1966-68; ptnr. Fortes, Eiger, Epstein & Skirnick, Chgo., 1975-77, Much, Shelist, Freed, Chgo., 1977-79, Wolf, Popper, Ross, Wolf & Jones, N.Y.C., 1979-87, Kaplan, Kilsheimer & Foley, N.Y.C., 1988-89, Wechsler, Skirnick, Harwood, Halebian & Feffer, N.Y.C., 1989—; instr. NYU, 1979-80; cons. Nat. Legal Aid and Def. Assn., Chgo., 1968-69; spl. asst. atty. gen. Ill. Atty Gen. Office, Chgo., 1972-73; spl. antitrust counsel State of Conn., 1976-77; mem. adv. bd. Small Bus. Legal Def. Commn., San Francisco, 1982—; lectr. Practicing Law Inst., N.Y.C., 1986-87; spl. master So. Dist. N.Y., 1988-91; bd. dirs., exec. com., selection com., investment and fin. com. Nat. Assn. for Pub. Interest Law Fellowships, Washington. Author: (with others) Federal Subject Matter Jurisdiction of U.S. District Courts, Federal Civil Practice, 1974, Antitrust Class Actions-Twenty Years Under Rule 23, 1986, The State Court Class Action-A Potpourri of Differences in the ABA Forum, Summer 1985; bd. editors Ill. Bar Antitrust Newsletter, 1969-73; topic & articles editor Jour. Forum Com. on Franchising, 1981-86. Atty. Office Gen. Counsel Honors Program, U.S. Dept. HEW, 1966-68; chmn. Ill. Legis. Com. Antitrust Section Ill. Bar., 1970-71; Topic and Articles Editor, Jour. Forum Com. on Franchising, 1981-86; mem., bd. dirs., Nat. Assn. for Pub. Interest Law fellowships, Washington, 1991—. Mem. ABA (co-chair securities law subcom., litigation sect. 1987, com. on futures regulation, forum com. on franchising), Am. Trial Lawyers Assn., Fed. Bar Coun. (com. on second cir. cts. 1983-86), N.Y. State Bar Assn. (class action com.), N.Y. State Trial Lawyers Assn., Ill. Bar Assn. (chmn. antitrust sect. Ill. legis. com. 1970-71), Nat. Assn. for Pub. Interest Law Fellowships (bd. dirs. 1991—), Plandome Country Club. Office: Wechsler Skirnick Harwood Halebian & Feffer 555 Madison Ave New York NY 10022-3301

SKLAR, SCOTT, association executive; b. Astoria, N.Y., Nov. 12, 1950; s.Phillip and Ruth B. (Frost) S.; m. Kathleen H. Zwicker, May 23, 1986. BA in Internat. Affairs, George Washington U., 1973. Legis. aide U.S. Senator Jacob Javits, Washington, 1970-79; Washington dir. Nat. Ctr. Appropriate Technology, 1980; acting dir. rsch. Nat. Ctr. Appropriate Technology, Butte, Mont., 1981; polit. dir. Solar Lobby, 1983-84; exec. dir. Solar Energy Industries Assn., Washington, 1984—, U.S. Export Coun. Renewable Energy, Washington, 1987—, Nat. Wood Energy Assn., Washington, 1987—. Co-author: The Forbidden Fuel, 1984, Consumer Guide to Solar Energy, 1991. Mem. Am. Solar Energy Soc. (bd. dirs. 1988—), Coun. Renewable Energy Edn. (officer, bd. dirs.1988—). Home: 706 N Ivy St Arlington VA 22201-2208 Office: Solar Energy Industries Ste 805 777 N Capitol St NE Washington DC 20002-4239

SKOHLNIK, MARTEN, commercial design executive; b. Newark, Aug. 10, 1951; s. Sid and Muriel (Schafler) Skolnik. BA in Philosophy, Montclair State Coll., 1978; MS in Elem. Edn., Bank Street Coll. Edn., 1979. Cert. life tchr., N.Y. Tchr. B'Nai Or, Morristown, N.J., 1972-77, Emmanuel Community Day Sch., Beverly Hills, Calif., 1979-83; assoc. dir. Communications Works, West Hollywood, Calif., 1983-85; project coord. APLA AIDS Project L.A., Calif. Dept. Health, West Hollywood, 1985-86; designer, adminstr., owner Vega Planners Ltd., Tamarac, Fla., 1985—; master tchr. Bd. Jewish Edn., L.A., 1978-83; dir. edn. G/L Community Svcs. Ctr., Hollywood, Calif., 1985. Contbr. articles to profl. jours. Office: Vega Planners Ltd 7154 N University Dr Ste 180 Tamarac FL 33321

SKOLER, CELIA REBECCA, art gallery director; b. Sioux City, Iowa, Apr. 7, 1931; d. Jacob and Flora (Gorchow) Stern; m. Louis Skoler, Aug. 24, 1952; children: Elisa Anne, Harry Jay. BFA in Art and Music magna cum laude, Syracuse U., 1976. Fin. planner Architects' Partnership, Syracuse, N.Y., 1969-71; bus. mgr. Skoler & Lee Architects P.C., Syracuse, 1971-89; owner, dir. New Acquisitions Gallery, Syracuse, 1981—; ptnr. Gallery Metro, Syracuse, 1991—, mng. ptnr., 1992—; contbg. writer Syracuse Herald and Syracuse Newtimes, Syracuse, 1989-91; art cons. IBM, Syracuse, Rochester, Albany, 1983-86, Costello, Cooney & Fearon, Syracuse, 1981—, Menter, Rudin & Trivelpiece, Syracuse, 1987-88; supr. community internship program Syracuse U., 1981-87, commn. of mayoral portrait City of Syracuse, 1983, Gelling Meml. Portrait U. Coll., 1984, Levine Meml. Commn. Temple Concord, 1984; TV producer Syracuse U. Friends of Art, 1979-80; curated 45 exhibits, 1981-90; panelist for art critique Everson Mus. Art, Syracuse, 1989; lectr. on gallery mgmt. Syracuse U. Sch. Art., 1989; juror Fine Art N.Y. State Fair, 1989. One-man shows include Camillus Plaza, 1972, The Associated Artists Gallery, Syracuse, 1973, Pub. Library of Fayetteville, N.Y., 1974; exhibited in group show at N.Y. State Fair (1st prize 1974), U. Coll, 1967, 69, 71, Rochester Meml. Gallery, 1969, 70, 71, 72, 74, The Associated Artists, 1971, 72, Cen. N.Y. Art Open, 1970, 71, (Purchase prize 1970, 71), Munson Williams Protor Inst, Utica, N.Y., 1971, 72, Cayuga Mus., Auburn, N.Y., 1972, Oneida (N.Y.) Art Festival, 1969, (1st prize), Jewish Community Ctr., Syracuse, 1968 (1st prize 1969), St. David's Invitational, Dewitt, N.Y., 1970, 71, 72, 73, 74, 75, Cooperstown Art Inst., Nat. Show, 1973, 74, Arena Nat. Show, Binghamton, N.Y., 1975 (Purchase prize 1975). Peer counselor Univ. Coll., Syracuse, 1980-85; Tel-auc auctioneer Sta. WCNY-TV, Liverpool, N.Y., 1982; mem. steering and implementation com. Gelling Meml. Lounge U. Coll., 1984-85; exec. bd. Syracuse U. Friends of Art, 1977-80; fine art juror N.Y. State Fair, Syracuse, 1982, Downtown Com., Syracuse, 1982, Oswego (N.Y.) Art Guild, 1984. Recipient Purchase prize Marine Midland Bank, 1974, Crouse-Irving Hosp., 1974. Mem. Everson Mus. Art (corp.) mem. Phi Kappa Phi, Alpha Sigma Lambda (pres. 1980-81). Home: 213 Scottholm Ter Syracuse NY 13224-1737 Office: New Acquisitions Art Adv 120 E Washington St Ste 1004 Syracuse NY 13202-4000

SKOLNEKOVICH, DOROTHY ANN, counselor; b. Hopewell, Pa., Aug. 8, 1941; d. John and Dorothea (McNally) S. AA, DeKalb Community Coll., Clarkston, Ga., 1982; BS, U. Steubenville, Ohio, 1984; MS in Edn./Counseling, U. Dayton, 1986; postgrad., Duquesne U. LPN Grady Meml. Hosp., Atlanta, 1967-75; resident U. Dayton, Ohio, 1984-86; LPN Little Sisters of the Poor, Pitts., 1989-90; counselor Counseling and Spiritual Direction Ctr., Pitts., 1990—; caseworker John Kane Ross Twp., Pitts., 1991—, Children and Youth Svc., Pitts., 1988-91; cons. Mercy Sch. Nursing, Pitts., 1991, Doorway, Pitts., 1991; lectr. U. Dayton, 1984-86. Nurses aide, instr. ARC, Atlanta, Pitts., 1969-91. Named Den Mother of Yr. Boy Scouts Am., 1978-79. Mem. Am. Assn. Counselors, Pa. Assn. Counselors, Nat. Assn. Licensed Nurses. Roman Catholic. Home: PO Box 41007 Pittsburgh PA 15202-0007 Office: Counseling Spiritual Direction 814 4th Ave Coraopolis PA 15108-1547

SKOLNICK, PHIL, pharmacologist, psychiatry educator; b. N.Y.C., Feb. 26, 1947; s. David Louis and Gertrude (Gewirtzman) S.; m. Nancy Louise Ostrowski, July 17, 1985; children: Michael, Stephen. BS summa cum laude, L.I. U., 1968; PhD, George Washington U., 1972. Staff fellow NIH, Bethesda, Md., 1972-75, sr. staff fellow, 1975-77, sr. investigator, 1977-83, chief neurobiology sect., 1983-86, chief Lab. of Neurosci., 1986—; Wellcome prof. Burroughs-Wellcome Trust, 1988, 92; prof. dept. psychiatry Uniformed Svcs., U. of Health Scis., Bethesda, 1989—. Recipient A.E. Bennett award Soc. Biol. Psychiatry, 1981, Mathilde Solowey award, 1983, Sci. Achievement award Washington Acad. Sci., 1984. Fellow Am. Coll. Neuropsychopharmacology; mem. Am. Soc. Pharmacology and Exptl. Therapeutics, Soc. Neurosci., Internat. Soc. Neurochemistry. Office: NIH/NIDDK/LN Bldg # Rm # 111 Bethesda MD 20892

SKOLNIK, HERMAN, retired chemist; b. Harrisburg, Pa., Mar. 22, 1914; s. Morris and Edith (Locke) S.; m. Ida Kopp, Dec. 24, 1938 (dec. July 1973); children: Carol Deanna Skolnik Czitrom, Susan Jean. BSChemE, Pa. State U., 1937; MS in Organic Chemistry, U. Pa., 1940, PhD in Phys. Organic Chemistry, 1942. Chemist Petroleum Refining Lab., State College, Pa., 1935-37, Pa. Testing Lab., Harrisburg, 1938-39, Barrett div. Allied Chem. So., Phila., 1939-42; chem. engr. Roosevelt Oil Co., Mt. Pleasant, Mich., 1937-38; rsch. chemist, supr. and mgr. Hurcules Inc. Rsch. Ctr., Wilmington, Del., 1942-79; ret., 1979; former cons. Nat. Bur. Standards, Washington, Nat. Lab. Medicine, Washington. Author: Multi Sulfur and Sulfur and Oxygen Five-and Six-Membered Heterocycles, 1966, A Century of Chemistry, 1976, Literature Matrix of Chemistry, 1980; editor terpene chem. sect. Chem. Abstracts, 1968—, Jour. Chem. Info. and Computer Sci., 1961-83; also over 200 articles. Bd. dirs. Del. Symphony Orch., Wilmington, 1957-80; sci. edn. advisor Del. Pub. Schs., New Castle County, 1980—. Recipient Patent Communication award Phila. Patent Assn., 1978, Terpene Chemistry awad Assn. Engrs. and Technologists Perfumes, 1986. Mem. Am. Chem. Soc. (chmn. div. chem. info. 1961, chmn. Del. sect. 1962, councilor

1962-84, former cons. membership activities com., cons. div. chem. info. 1988, Crane/Patterson award Dayton-Columbus sects. 1969, Chem. Info. award 1976, svc. award Del. sect. 1986). Unitarian. Home: 239 Waverly Rd Wilmington DE 19803-3134

SKOLNIK, JINNY, small business owner; b. N.Y.C., July 29, 1934; d. Maxie and Bella (Cohen) Weitzman; m. I. Arthur Skolnik, Dec. 24, 1955; children: Neil S., Heidi B. BS in Edn., CCNY, 1954. Elem. sch. tchr. Bronx, N.Y., 1954-58; pres. Fads & Fashion, Inc., Englewood Cliffs, N.J., 1972—. Chairperson singles group under 39 JCC Fort Lee, 1983-91. Jewish. Office: Fads & Fashion 18 Sylvan Ave Englewood Cliffs NJ 07632-2419

SKOLNIK, RICHARD ALAN, plastic surgeon; b. N.Y.C., Jan. 7, 1951. BA in Biology summa cum laude, C.W. Post Coll., 1972; MD, Cornell U., 1976. Cert. Am. Bd. Plastic and Reconstructive Surgery. Resident gen. surgery Mt. Sinai Med. Ctr., N.Y.C., 1976-79, resident plastic surgery, 1979-82; clin. instr. Mt. Sinai Sch. Medicine, N.Y.C., 1982-84, asst. clin. prof., 1985—; assoc. attending Mt. Sinai Med. Ctr., N.Y.C., 1982—, Beth Israel Med. Ctr., N.Y.C., 1984—; courtesy staff Beth Israel North (Doctor's Hosp.), N.Y.C., 1987—; fellow cleft lip and palate Children's Hosp., Lima, Peru, 1982; vis. prof. Reconstructive Surgery Found., Maceo, Brazil, 1990. Fellow ACS; mem. Am. Soc. of Plastic and Reconstructive Surgeons, N.Y. Regional Soc. Plastic and Reconstructive Surgeons, AMA, Barsky Soc., N.Y. State Med. Soc. Office: 21 E 87th St New York NY 10128

SKOLNIKOFF, EUGENE B., political science educator; b. Phila., Aug. 29, 1928; s. Benjamin H. and Betty (Turoff) S.; m. Winifred S. Weinstein, Sept. 15, 1957; children: David, Matthew, Jessica. B.S., M.I.T., 1950, M.S., 1950, Ph.D., 1965; B.A., Oxford (Eng.) U., 1952, M.A., 1955. Registered profl. engr. Rsch. asst. in elec. engring. Uppsala U., Sweden, 1950; prof. polit. sci. M.I.T., 1965—, chmn. polit. sci. dept., 1970-74; dir. Center for Internat. Studies, 1972-87; vis. rsch. prof. Carnegie Endowment for Internat. Peace, Geneva, 1969-70; vis. fellow Balliol Coll., U. Oxford, 1989; systems analyst Inst. for Def. Analyses, Washington, 1957-58; mem. White House staff Office Spl. Asst. to Pres. for Sci. and Tech., Washington, 1958-63; adj. prof. Fletcher Sch. Law and Diplomacy, Tufts U., Medford, Mass., 1965-72; sr. cons. White House Office of Sci. and Tech. Policy, 1977-81, also vice chmn. adv. com. on sci., tech. and devel.; mem. policy rev. com. on nat. low-level nuclear waste mgmt., 1980-86; cons. Dept. State, Office of Tech. Assessment, AID, OECD, Resources for the Future, Am. Soc. Internat. Law, Ford Found., Inst. Def. Analyses; chmn., pres. Sci. and Public Policy Studies Group, 1967-73; mem. Internat. Council Sci. Policy Studies; Montague Burton vis. prof. U. Edinburgh, 1977. Author: Science, Technology and American Foreign Policy, 1967, International Imperatives of Technology, 1972; co-editor: World Eco-Crisis, 1972, Visions of Apocalypse, End or Rebirth?, 1985; contbr. articles to publs.; chmn. editorial bd.: Public Sci., 1971-75; editorial bd.: Tech. Rev., 1967-78, Social Studies of Sci., 1970-75, Internat. Orgn., 1974-80. Trustee German Marshall Fund, 1979-87, chmn., 1980-86; trustee UN Rsch. Inst. for Social Devel., 1979-85; bd. dirs. Saco Def., 1984-86; mem. Overseas Devel. Coun.; mem. U.S. del. UN Commn. for Social Devel., 1979; mem. State Dept. Adv. Com. on Sci. and Tech., 1987—. Served with U.S. Army Security Agy., 1955-57. Rhodes scholar, 1950-52; Rockefeller Found. fellow, 1963-65; decorated Comdr.'s Cross Fed. Republic Germany, Order of Rising Sun, Golden Rays, Neck Ribbon, Japan. Fellow Am. Acad. Arts and Scis. (councillor 1973-77), AAAS (sec. sect. K 1967-69, mem. com. on sci. and pub. policy 1973-74, com. on sci., engring. and pub. policy 1984-89); mem. UN Assn., Am. Coun. on Germany, Fedn. Am. Scientists, (coun. 1981-85), Coun. Fgn. Rels., Am. Assn. Rhodes Scholars, Soc. for Internat. Devel., Soc. for Social Studies of Sci., Sigma Xi, Tau Beta Pi, Eta Kappa Nu. Home: 3 Chandler St Lexington MA 02173-3601 Office: MIT Cambridge MA 02139

SKOOG DE LAMAS, LISA MARIE, public policy analyst; b. Anchorage, July 3, 1957; d. Ronald O. and Patricia A. (O'Keefe) Skoog; m. Luis F. Lamas, June 24, 1983. BA in Econs. with high distinction, U. Va., 1979; diploma in Japanese, Osaka U. Fgn. Studies, 1981; MPA in Econs. and Pub. Policy, Princeton U., 1985. Editor econs. and fgn. policy Am. Enterprise Inst., Washington, 1979-80; grad. rsch. fellow Kobe (Japan) U., 1981-83; jr. econ. officer U.S. Embassy, Lima, Peru, 1984; policy analyst internat. corp. affairs Am. Express, N.Y.C., 1985-86, mgr., 1986-89, dir., 1989—. Active adv. coun. Fgn. Exec. Devel. Program Princeton (N.J.) U. Mem. Japan Soc., Phi Beta Kappa. Office: Am Express Co World # 200 New York NY 10285-0001

SKOPIC, BEVERLY JANE, insurance company executive; b. Phila., June 16, 1959; d. Frederick Joseph and Jane Beverly (Snyder) Cook; m. Stephen Ellis Skopic, May 6, 1978; children: Emily Susanne, Stephen Joseph. Cert. profl. ins. woman; CPCU. Clk. typist Swigart Assocs., Huntingdon, Pa., 1977-78, comml. lines underwriter, 1978-83, supr. casualty lines, 1984-89, supr. comml. lines, 1989-90; under mgr. comml. lines, 1990—. Sch. dir. South Huntingdon County Sch. Dist., Orbisonia, Pa., 1985-91. Lodge: Order Eastern Star. Home: HC 60 Box 145 Orbisonia PA 17243-9708 Office: Swigart Assocs Inc 409 Penn St Huntingdon PA 16652-1622

SKOU, BENT, diplomat, public information officer; b. Silkeborg, Denmark, Sept. 27, 1931; s. Soren and Marie (Nielsen) S.; m. Martha Christine B. Petersen, Apr. 20, 1957; children: Lene Skou Moynihan, Lise Ringland. Degree in journalism, U. Aarhus, Denmark, 1956. Journalist Danish Newspapers, Denmark, 1949-61; press attache Fgn. Ministry, Denmark, 1961-63; press counselor Danish UN Mission, N.Y.C., 1963-69; cultural and press counselor Danish Embassy, Bonn, Germany, 1970-73, Danish Mil. Mission, Berlin, 1970-73; counselor of embassy Danish Embassy, Washington, 1973-79; min. counselor Danish Embassy, London, 1980-83; head of press. dept. Fgn. Ministry, Copenhagen, 1983-86; min. counselor Danish Embassy, Washington, 1986-92; head Internat. Press Ctr., Copenhagen, 1992—. Home: Solbakkevej 8, 3050 Humlebaek Denmark

SKOULTCHI, MARTIN MILTON, research chemist; b. N.Y.C., Oct. 27, 1933; s. Irving and Berty (Gelsky) S.; m. Illene Rochelle Strom, July 3, 1960 (dec.); children: Barry I., Alan J., Gail S. BA, N.Y. U., 1954, MS, 1957, PhD, 1960. Chemist N.Y. State Dept. Labor, N.Y.C., 1954-57; chemist, rsch. div. N.Y. U. Coll. Engring., N.Y.C., 1957-60; sr. rsch. assoc. Nat. Starch and Chem. Co., Bridgewater, N.J., 1960—; computer cons. Franklin Twp., Somerset, N.J., 1983-87; instr. Adult Sch., Somerset, 1983-87. Contbr. articles to sci. jours. Mem. AAAS, Am. Chem. Soc., N.Y. Acad. Scis., Sigma Xi, Phi Lambda Epsilon. Democrat. Jewish. Home: 6 Lilac Ln Somerset NJ 08873-2808 Office: Nat Starch and Chem Co 10 Finderne Ave Bridgewater NJ 08807-3300

SKRAJEWSKI, DENNIS JOHN, hospital administrator; b. Trenton, N.J., Jan. 19, 1954; s. Raymond Joseph and Philomena Florence (Zook) S.; m. Debra Ann Fortin, Oct. 25, 1980; children: Diana Nicole, Danielle Marie, Dominic Raymond. BA in Biology, Lafayette Coll., 1977; cert. physician asst., Yale U., 1980; MBA in Health Care Mgmt., Boston U., 1985. Physician asst. Masonic Home and Hosp., Wallingford, Conn., 1980-84; adminstrv. resident/fellow Charlton Meml. Hosp., Fall River, Mass., 1984-86, mgr. clin. resource utilization, 1986-87; mgr. constrn. project Lakes Region Gen. Hosp., Laconia, N.H., 1987-88; v.p. adminstrv. svcs. Lakes Region Gen. Hosp., Laconia, 1988—. Mem. pastoral adv. bd. St. Joseph's Parish, Belmont, N.H., 1987—, vice chmn. pastoral adv. bd., 1988-91, chmn. pastoral adv. bd., 1991—; bd. dirs. Lakes Region Community Health Agy., Laconia, 1988—, chmn. pers. com., 1989-90, chmn. bd. dirs., 1990—. With USN, 1972-74. Mem. Am. Coll. Healthcare Execs., Am. Hosp. Assn., N.H. Hosp. Assn., New Eng. Hosp. Assembly, Boston U. Health Care Mgmt. Alumni Assn., Lakes Region Rotary, Beta Gamma Sigma. Republican. Home: Ridgewood Rd RR 1 Box 124 Gilmanton NH 03237-9211 Office: Lakes Region Gen Hosp Highland St Laconia NH 03246-3210

SKRAPEC, CANDICE ANN, criminological psychologist, consultant; b. Kamsack, Sask., Can., June 29, 1952; came to U.S., 1984; d. Albert and Martha Anne (Loucks) S. BSc, U. Calgary, Alta., Can., 1976, MSc, 1980; MPhil, CUNY, 1988, postgrad., 1988—. Cert. and chartered psychologist, Alta. Coord. Police Crisis Unit Calgary Police Svc., 1981-83; psychologist in pvt. practice, 1980-84; rsch. assoc. Am. Correctional Assn./Nat. Ctr. Pub. Productivity, N.Y.C., 1986-87; coord. Diagnostic Ctr. N.Y.C. Dept. Correction/John Jay Coll. Criminal Justice, 1987-90; criminological psychologist N.Y.C., 1985—; psychol. cons./trainer N.Y.C. Police, N.Y.C. Transit Police, N.Y.C. Health and Hosps. Corp., Police Acad., N.Y.C. Dept. Mental Hygiene; adj. faculty in criminology John Jay Coll. Criminal Justice, 1988—; cons. on serial murder and investigative profiling of crime scenes to police, authors, film makers, others, 1986—. Author: Introduction to The Sadist, 1992; contbr. chpts. to books. Grad. Sch. CUNY disting. scholar and dissertation fellow, 1989-90. Mem. Psychologists Assn. Alta. (chartered), Can. Psychol. Assn., Am. Soc. Criminology, Acad. Criminal Justice Scis., N.Y. Acad. Scis. Home: PO Box 20770 Columbus Cir New York NY 10023

SKROUMBELOS, NICHOLAS GEORGE, management consulting company executive, accountant; b. Flemington, N.J., Feb. 8, 1952; s. George Athan and Georgia (Kannellis) S. AA, Mercer County Coll., 1973; BS in Acctg., Fairleigh-Dickinson U., Madison, N.J., 1976. Adminstrv. analyst to exec. v.p. Beneficial Mgmt., Morristown, N.J., 1976-78; dir. mgmt. adv. services Nowalk & Assoc., Cranbury, N.J., 1979-88; pres. PCMC, Inc., Lawrenceville, N.J., 1983—; charter founder 1st Constn. Bank, Cranbury, 1989. Mem. com. to celebrate 50th Anniversary of War of the Worlds Broadcast, Grover's Mill and West Windsor, N.J., 1986—. Recipient Merger Plaque, RT/Katek, Inc., 1983; named to Honorable Order of Ky. Cols. Mem. Pa. Soc. Pub. Accts., N.J. Assn. Pub. Accts. Greek Orthodox. Home: 4093 Quakerbridge Rd Trenton NJ 08648-4701

SKULSKY, HAROLD LAWRENCE, English educator; b. Bklyn., Apr. 12, 1935; s. Samuel and Ida (Greenberg) S.; children: Sabina, Livia, Eva, Eli. BA, Columbia U., 1956; MA, Harvard U., 1957, PhD, 1961. Asst. prof. Johns Hopkins Univ., Balt., 1961-63, Univ. Wis., Madison, 1963-65; prof. Smith Coll., Northampton, Mass., 1965—. Author: Spirits Finely Touched, 1976, Metamorphosis, 1984, Language Recreated, 1991. Office: Smith College Northampton MA 01060

SKURDENIS, JULIANN VERONICA, librarian, educator, writer, editor; b. Bklyn., July 13, 1942; d. Julius J. and Anna M. (Zilys) S.; A.B. with honors, Coll. New Rochelle, 1964; M.S., Columbia U., 1966; M.A., Hunter Coll., 1974; m. Lawrence J. Smircich, Aug. 21, 1965 (div. July 1978); m. 2d, Paul J. Lalli, Oct. 1, 1978; 1 adopted dau., Kathryn Leila Skurdenis-Lalli. Young adult librarian Bklyn. Pub. Library, 1964-66; periodicals librarian, instr. Kingsborough Community Coll., Bklyn., 1966-67; acquisitions librarian Pratt Inst., Bklyn., 1967-68; acquisitions librarian, asst. prof. Bronx (N.Y.) Community Coll., 1968-75, head tech. services, assoc. prof., 1975—. N.Y. State fellow, 1960-66, Columbia U. fellow, 1964-66, Pratt Inst. fellow, 1965. Mem. AAUP, NOW, Library Assn. CUNY (chairwoman numerous coms.), Archaeol. Inst. Am., CUNY Women's Coalition. Author: Walk Straight Through the Square, 1976, More Walk Straight Through the Square, 1977; contbg. editor Internat. Travel News, 1989—; travel editor Archaeology mag., 1986-89; contbr. over 125 travel, hist., and archaeol. pieces. Avocations: archaeology, travel, travel writing. Office: CUNY Bronx CC University Ave Bronx NY 10453-6994

SKWARYK, ROBERT FRANCIS, judge; b. Erie, Pa., Nov. 4, 1948; s. Frank and Gloria (Hinkle) S. BS, Pa. State U., 1973; JD, U. Kans., 1977. Bar: Pa. 1977, U.S. Dist. Ct. (we. dist.) Pa. 1977. Legal intern legal svcs. Clallum and Jefferson Counties, Port Angeles, Wash., 1977; assoc. Galbo, McNelis, Restifo & Held, Erie, 1977-80; instr. bus. law Behrend Coll. Pa. State U., Erie, 1978-80; appeals referee Commonwealth of Pa., Harrisburg and Pottsville, 1981, Pitts. and Erie, 1985-88; adminstrv. law judge Commonwealth of Pa., Allentown, 1988—. Contbg. author ct. opinions Pa. Liquor Control Bd., 1988—. Mem. Behrend Coll. Soccer Alumni Assn., Erie, 1974-90. Sgt. USMC, 1967-70, lt. (j.g.) USN, 1981-85, lt. USNR, 1986-92, Saudi Arabia, lt. comdr. USNR, 1992—. Mem. ABA, Pa. State Bar Assn., Erie County Bar Assn., Pa. Conf. Adminstrv. Law Judges, First Marine Air Wing Assn., Pa. State U. alumni Assn., Sierra Club. Home: 3 Maryland Cir Apt 226 Whitehall PA 18052-6302 Office: Commonwealth Pa Office Adminstrv Law Judge 22 N 7th St Fl 4 Allentown PA 18101-1311

SKYLER, MARC NORMAN, biology educator; b. Newark, Sept. 28, 1945; s. Morris and Ethel (Rabinowitz) S.; m. Aine Bray, June 11, 1972; children: David, Alexandra. BS, CCNY, 1967; MA, Hofstra U., 1969; MPhil, St. John's U., Queens, N.Y., 1984, PhD, 1986. Cert. soccer coach. Rsch. asst. Coll. Phys. and Surgs., N.Y.C., 1969; prof. biology N.Y.C. Tech. Coll., Bklyn., 1969—; bd. mem., advisor Acad. Sci. and Math., N.Y.C., 1990—. Resource person N.Y.C. Pub. Schs.; sci. resource judge N.Y. Acad. Sci., 1990. Mem. AAAS, N.Y. Acad. Sci., N.Y. State Assn. Two-Yr. Colls., Acad. for Humanities and Scis. CUNY. Democrat. Jewish. Office: NYC Tech Coll 300 Jay St Brooklyn NY 11201-2902

SLABE, JAMES F., business executive; b. Johnstown, Pa., Nov. 29, 1940; s. Frank and Antoinette Marie (Draksler) S.; m. Elaine Werner, July 14, 1973. BA, Washington and Jefferson Coll., 1962; postgrad., U. Md., 1962-64. Div. contr. Pfizer, Inc., N.Y.C., 1967-72; treas., contr. Pharmacaps, Inc., Elizabeth, N.J., 1972-73; dir. profit planning McGraw-Hill, Inc., N.Y.C., 1973-78; v.p. fin. Parade Publs., Inc., N.Y.C., 1978-79; pres. Exec. Enterprises, Inc., N.Y.C., 1979—, bd. dirs.; bd. dirs. The 21 Bldg. Corp., N.Y.C., Jersey Shore Properties, Lair Realty Co. Inc. Pub. Nat. Productivity Rev., Baks in Ins. Report, S Corp. Strategies, Employee Rels. Today, Employment Rels. Law Jour., Fed. Facilities Environ. Jour., Loan Officers Legal Alert, Pollution Prevention Rev., Jour. Environment Regulation, Total Quality Environ. Mgmt. and Jour. Environ. Permitting. Capt. U.S. Army, 1964-66. Capt. U.S. Army, 1964-66. Mem. Fin. Execs. Inst., Assn. Am. Planners, Assn. Am. Contrs., Phi Beta Kappa. Roman Catholic. Home: 17 Mountainview Dr Mountainside NJ 07092-2510 Office: Exec Enterprises Inc 22 W 21st St New York NY 10010-6904

SLABON, ROLAND MICHAEL, author; b. Breslau, Germany, Oct. 31, 1941; came to U.S., 1950; s. Hans Josef and Else Adelheid (Stadtlander) S.; m. Susan Mary Boudo, Dec. 24, 1978; children: Stephanie Helene, Alena Michelle, Michael Patrick. BA, Cornell U., 1964; law student, Boston Coll., 1964-65. Editor, pub. Vintage BMW Bull., Exeter, N.H., 1973—; treas. Vintage BMW Motorcycle Owners, Ltd., Exeter, 1985—, pres., 1986—; contbg. editor On the Level, BMW Riders Assn., Lufkin, Tex., 1984—; author Classic Motorbooks, Osceola, Wis., 1990—. Author: Illustrated BMW Buyers Guide, 1990, BMW Motorräder, 1992; contbr. articles to mags. Lt. USN, 1966-69. Mem. Owl's Head (Maine) Mus. of Transp. (life), Vintage Sports Car Club Am., Antique Motorcycle Club Am., BMW Veteranen Club Deutschland, Tau Kappa Epsilon. Republican. Congregationalist. Office: Vintage BMW Motorcycle Owners Ltd PO Box 67 Exeter NH 03833

SLABY, ANDREW EDMUND, psychiatrist, epidemiologist; b. Milw., July 14, 1942; s. Andrew and Evelyn (Herde) S. BS, U. Wis., 1964; MD, Columbia U., 1968; MPH, Yale U., 1974, PhD, 1977. Intern medicine Boston City Hosp., 1968-69; resident psychiatry Yale U., 1969-72; aast. prof. psychiatry Yale Univ., New Haven, 1974-77; dir. emergency psychiat. svcs. Yale-New Haven (Conn.) Hosp., 1975-77; psychiatrist-in-chief Dept. Psychiatry-R.I. Hosp., Providence, 1978-87; prof. psychiatry Brown Univ., Providence, 1979-87; psychiatrist-in-chief Women & Infants Hosp., Providence, 1981-87; clin. prof. psychiatry NYU, N.Y.C., 1987—; med. dir. Fair Oaks Hosp., Summit, N.J., 1987-92; psychiatrist-in-chief The Regent Hosp., N.Y.C., 1988—; pres. Am. Assn. Suicidology, 1990-91; chmn. dir. Am. Wine Alliance for Rsch. and Edn., San Francisco, 1990—; dir. CONTACT, USA, 1991—. Author: The Handbook of Emergency Psychiatry, 1985, Adapting to Life Threatening Illness, 1985, Sixty Ways to Make Stress Work for You, 1989, Aftershock, 1990. Bd. mem. The Samaritians of R.I., Providence, 1980-86; trustee Thomas Bechet Found., Providence, 1984-86; bd. mem. Summit (N.J.) Jr. League, 1987-90. Lt. comdr. USPHS, 1972-74. Elected Top 20 Lectrs. in psychiatry The Psychiat. Times, 1988. Fellow Am. Psychiat. Assn., Am. Coll. Psychiatrists, N.Y. Acad. Medicine; mem. Am. Assn. Gen. Hosp. Psychiatrists (coun. mem. 1984-92), Am. Assn. Emergency Psychiatrists (trustee 1985—), Internat. Soc. Law and Mental Health, Am. SUicide Found. (pres. Ea. div. 1989—, nat. v.p. 1989—), N.J. Assn. Suicidology, N.J. Psychiat. Soc., Tri-County Psychiat. Soc. (pres. 1991-92). Roman Catholic. Home: 50 New England Ave Summit NJ 07901-1827 Office: The Regent Hosp 425 E 61st St New York NY 10021-8722

SLACHTA, MICHAEL, JR., auditor; b. Homestead, Pa., Nov. 20, 1944; s. Michael Robert and Pauline (Haverlitz) S.; m. Sharron Bennick, Nov. 26, 1977; children: Dougals, Michael, David Alan. BS in Biology, U. Pitts., 1970. Adjudicator VA, Detroit, 1971-74; mgmt. analyst VA, Washington, 1974-77, audit mgr., 1977-78; dir. VA, Hyattsville, Md., 1978-80; dep. asst. inspector gen., auditor Dept. Vet. Affairs, Washington, 1980—; bd. dirs. Mymats Inc., Annandale, Va.; participant Leadership VA, Washington, 1978. Bd. dirs. Grandview Community Assn., Springfield, Va., 1974-78; chmn. archtl. rev., Beacon Ridge Community Assn., Springfield, 1987—. With USN, 1966-70, Vietnam. Decorated Bronze Star with Combat V, USMC, Vietnam; named Meritorious Exec., Dept. Vet. Affaris, 1991. Mem. Assn. of Govt. Accts. (treas. 1977-78), Inst. Internal Auditors. Russian Orthodox. Home: 8802 Shadowlake Way Springfield VA 22153-2100 Office: Office of Inspector Gen 810 Vermont Ave NW Washington DC 20420-0002

SLACK, FREDERICK FORD, retired electronic scientist, writer; b. Lawrence, Mass., June 16, 1917; s. Harold Jay and Grace Regina (Charnley) S.; 1 child, Frederick F., Jr. Grad. high sch. Factory worker J.O. Whitten Co., Winchester, Mass., 1938-40; radio technician Nat. Co., Malden, Mass., 1940-41; electronic technician MIT, Cambridge, Mass., 1941-45; electronic scientist USAF Hanscom Field, Bedford, Mass., 1945-76, ret., 1976; freelance writer, 1976—. Discoverd universal paradigm that places all mass and energy in the frequency domain, providing physical link to paranormal activity; co-inventor electronic circuitry translator of scanning positions; inventor display earth satellites, light gun; contbr. articles to profl. jours. Home: 72 Church St West Newbury MA 01985

SLADE, BERNARD NEWTON, management consultant; b. Sioux City, Iowa, Dec. 21, 1923; s. William Charles and Katherine Gertrude Slotsky; m. Margot Friedlein, Aug. 18, 1946; children: Steven P., Eric J. BSEE, U. Wis., 1949; MS, Stevens Inst. Tech., 1954. Devel. engr. tube div. RCA, Harrison, N.J., 1948-55; devel. engr. RCA Labs., Princeton, N.J., 1955-56; mgr. tech. program IBM, Pouthkeepsie, N.Y., 1956-60; mgr. product ops. IBM, Hopewell Junction, N.Y., 1960-64; dir. mfg. tech. IBM World Trade Corp., Armonk, N.Y., 1964-65, IBM, Armonk, 1965-84; sr. cons. Arthur D. Little, Inc., Cambridge, Mass., 1984-86, Gemini Consulting, Morristown, N.J., 1986—. Co-author: Winning the Productivity Race, 1985; author: Compressing the Product Develompment Cycle, 1992; contbr. numerous articles to tech. jours.; patentee in field. 2d lt. AUS, 1943-46. Mem. IEEE (sr.), Sigma Xi. Home: 12 Merry Hill Rd Poughkeepsie NY 12603-3214

SLADE, CORINNE SUE, health facility administrator, occupational therapist; b. Boston, Mar. 27, 1945; d. Fred and Paula (Szejnik) Kampler; m. Michael S. Slade, June 26, 1966; children: Daphne, David, Danielle. BS in Psychology, U. Mass., 1966; cert. in occupational therapy, Columbia U., 1968. Staff occupational therapist U. Minn., Mpls., 1968-70; cons. U.S. Ctr. for Fed. Prisoners, Springfield, Mo., 1970-72; cons. in occupational therapy Mpls., 1972-77; pvt. practice N.J., 1977-83; pres., dir. Rehab. Specialists, Hawthorne, N.J., 1983—. Pres. Community Adv. Bd., Hawthorne, 1991-92; mem. Mayor's Adv. Com. Handicapped, Hawthorne, 1989-91. Mem. Am. Occupational Therapy Assn., N.J. Occupational Therapy Assn., N.J. Head Injury Assn. (co-chmn. annual conf. 1990-91), N.J. Head Injury Profl. Coun. (sec. 1991—), Hawthorne C. of C. Office: Rehab Specialists 484 Lafayette Ave Hawthorne NJ 07506-2529

SLADKUS, HARVEY IRA, lawyer; b. Bklyn., Mar. 5, 1929; s. Samuel Harold and Charlotte Dorothy Sladkus; m. Harriet Marcia Barske, Dec. 31, 1940 (div.); children: Steven David, Jeffrey Brandon; m. Roberta Frances Pope, Oct. 24, 1986. AB, Syracuse U., 1950; JD, N.Y.U., 1961. Bar: N.Y. 1962, Conn. 1981, U.S. Supreme Ct. 1967. Assoc. Morris Ploscowe, N.Y.C., 1961-66; sole practice, N.Y.C., 1966-67; ptnr. Dweck & Sladkus and Feiden, Dweck & Sladkus, N.Y.C., 1968—; lectr. family and matrimonial law; small claims ct. arbitrator N.Y.C. civil ct. 1977—; matrimonial master Supreme Ct., N.Y. County, 1987—; amicus Supreme Ct., Westchester County. Served to 1st lt. U.S. Army 1952-53; Korea. Decorated Bronze Star medal; recipient George Washington Honor medal Freedoms Found. Valley Forge, 1953. Mem. ABA, N.Y. State Bar Assn., Assn. Bar City N.Y., Conn. Bar Assn., Am. Acad. Matrimonial Lawyers, Am. Judges Assn., Am. Arbitration Assn. (nat. panel arbitrators). Jewish. Contbg. author: Practice under New York's Matrimonial Law, 1971-79; editor-in-chief Family Law Practice, 1982; contbr. articles on family and matrimonial law to legal publs. Office: 295 Madison Ave New York NY 10017

SLADZINSKI, MARIANNE, executive, consultant; b. Wilkes-Barre, Pa., Nov. 23, 1942; d. Peter Anthony and Anna (Turinski) S. B.S. in Elem. Edn. and English, Misericordia Coll., 1963; M.Ed. in Ednl. Psychology, Rutgers U., 1967; postgrad. Temple U., 1977, U. Mich., 1984, George Washington U., 1985; MA in Applied Psychology, U. Santa Monica, 1988. Tchr. Hillsborough Twp., N.J., 1963-67; counselor, coordinator RCA Service Co., Drums, Pa., 1967-68, mgr. various depts., 1968-75, administr. orgn. devel. and tng., Cherry Hill, N.J., 1975-77, dir. orgn. and devel., 1977-80, dir. orgn. and employment, 1980-84, corp. dir. quality edn. and communication, 1984-87; pres. Sladzinski Assocs., Cherry Hill, N.J., 1987—; external cons. Monet Jewelry, N.Y.C., 1982, Barra Internat., RMR Assocs., RCA, Thompson S.A., Gen. Electric, U. Pa., AT&T, other cos., also internat. cons. Korea, Taiwan, The Netherlands, Spain, England, Brazil, Japan, Singapore. Rep. of Voorhees Twp. to County Democratic Com., Camden County, N.J., 1981—. Recipient Acad. Women Achievers award YWCA of N.Y.C., 1982; Pres.'s Seal, RCA Service Co., 1983-84. Mem. Orgn. and Devel. Network, Orgn. Transformation Network, Phila. Women's Network, Am. Soc. Tng. and Devel., Am. Soc. Quality Control, Assn. Internal Mgmt. Cons. Club: Fall Line Ski (Cherry Hill) (pres. 1982-83, bd. dirs. 1980-83). Office: PO Box 3850 Cherry Hill NJ 08034-0595

SLAGLE, JACOB WINEBRENNER, JR., homeowners service company executive; b. Balt., Jan. 18, 1945; s. Jacob Winebrenner and Anna Dorothea (Vernon-Williams) S.; m. Sharon Carol Muth, Nov. 18, 1973 (div. 1982); children: Alexander, Dylan. Student, U. Ariz., 1963-65; BA in Sociology, U. Md., 1969; diploma, Broadcasting Inst. Md., balt., 1975. Claims adjuster Govt. Employees Ins. Co., Towson, Md., 1969-71; exec. Slagle & Slagle, Inc., Balt., 1971-81, pres., 1981-92; bd. dirs., v.p. H.S.A., Inc., Balt., 1992—; freelance writer for various newspapers and mags., 196-83; monthly columnist Jake About Town, Balt. Chronicle, 1989—; mem. bd. advisors Broadcasting Inst. Md., 1990—, Freedom Svcs., Inc., Balt., 1991—. Contbg. author: Baltimoer: A Living Renaissance, 1981. Bd. dirs. Hist. Balt. Soc., 1979—, v.p., 1989-92; bd. dirs. Intervention with Pact, Balt., 1982-89; pres. Hanover House Condominium Assn., Balt., 1983—; arbitrator Better Bus. Bur. Greater Md., Balt., 1983-91. Mem. Homebuilders Assn. Md. (bd. dirs. remodelers coun. 1989—), Balt. Blues soc. (bd. dirs. 1992—), Rotary (bd. dirs. Balt. 1992—). Address: Village of Cross Keys Ste 208 Village Square II Baltimore MD 21210

SLAGLE, LARRY B., federal government executive; b. Templeton, Pa., Dec. 17, 1934; s. William Harry and Luella (Armstrong) S. AB, Wabash Coll., 1956; postgrad., Am. U., 1967-71. Dep. adminstr. for mgmt. and budget USDA Animal & Plant Health Inspection Svc., Washington, 1978-88, assoc. adminstr., 1988-90; dir. pers. USDA, Washington, 1990—. With U.S. Army, 1957-59, Korea. Named Meritorious Exec. President Reagan, 1985, President Bush, 1991. Home: 208 Sixth Ave SE Washington DC 20003 Office: USDA Office of Pers Washington DC 20250

SLAGLE, STEVE BRYCE, composer, saxophonist; b. L.A., Sept. 18, 1952; s. Bryce and Joan (Forestel) S. MusB, Berklee Music, 1971; MusM, Manhatten Sch. Music, 1989. Prof., instr. saxophone, leader sax quartet Manhatten Sch. Music, N.Y.C., 1989—; musical dir. Ray Baretto Band (grammy award winner); alto sax Charles Mingus Big Band; mem. Steve Slagle Quartet; benefit concert Oreg. Indian Edn. Assn. Scholarship Fund, Sybarite Club, N.Y.C., 1992; clinician, performer Slagle Music Publ., 1989, 90—. Lead alto Machito Afro-Cuban Orch.; mem. Steve Kuhn's Quartet; lead alto Lionel Hampton; tenor Woody Herman; guest artist with Milton Nascimento; recording artist: Rio Highlife, High Standards, Smoke Signals, Motility, Non-Fiction, Live in Switzerland, Live in Harlem, That's the Way I Feel Now, Carla Bley Live, Heavy Heart, Mortelle Randonnee, Ballad of the Fallen, Encontros and Despedidas, First Strike, Strike Zone. Recipient Jazz Scholarship, Downbeat Mag., 1970. Mem. Nat. Jazz Edn. Assn., Am.

Mechanic Rights Assn., Broadcast Music, Inc., Music Union. Home: 33 S Elliott Pl Brooklyn NY 11217

SLAP, JOSEPH WILLIAM, psychiatrist; b. N.Y.C., Aug. 27, 1927; s. Leonard and Elizabeth (Goodman) S.; m. Elizabeth Draper Sagle, Oct. 23, 1954; children: Laura, Robert, Leonard, Edward. BS, CCNY, 1948; MD, Hahnemann Med. Coll., 1952. Diplomate Am. Bd. Psychiatry and Neurology. Intern Phila. Gen. Hosp., 1952-53, resident in psychiatry, 1953-54; resident in psychiatry Hillside Hosp., Glen Oaks, N.Y., 1954-56; pvt. practice Phila., 1956—; tng. analyst Inst. of Phila. Assn. for Psychoanalysis, Bala Cynwyd, Pa., 1976—; clin. prof. psychiatry Hahnemann Med. Coll., Phila., 1974-90, Jefferson Med. Coll., Phila., 1990-91. Author: (with L. Slap Shelton) The Schema in Clinical Psychoanalysis, 1991; contbr. articles to profl. jours. With U.S. Army, 1946-47. Mem. AMA, APA, Am. Psychiatric Assn., Phila. Assn. for Psychoanalysis, Phi Beta Kappa, Alpha Omega Alpha. Home: 553 Heath Rd Merion Station PA 19066-1422 Office: Psychiatric Assocs 1601 Walnut St Ste 1312 Philadelphia PA 19102-2994

SLATE, FLOYD OWEN, chemist, materials scientist, civil engineer, educator, researcher; b. Carroll County, Ind., July 26, 1920; s. Ora George and Gladys Marie (Miller) S.; m. Margaret Mary Magley, Oct. 14, 1939; children: Sally Lee Slate McEnteer, Sandra Kay Slate Miller, Rex Owen. B.S., Purdue U., 1941, M.S., 1942, Ph.D., 1944. Chemist Manhattan Project, N.Y.C., Oak Ridge and Decatur, Ill., 1944-46; asst. prof. civil engring. Purdue U., Lafayette, Ind., 1946-49; v.p., dir. Geotechnics & Resources Inc., White Plains, N.Y., 1959-63; prof. engring. materials Cornell U., Ithaca, N.Y., 1949—; internat. lectr., cons. concrete, low-cost housing. Author books, research papers on concrete, low-cost housing, soil stabilization, 1944—. Recipient Excellence in Teaching award Cornell U., 1976, sr. fellow East-West Center, 1976, NSF research grantee, 1960-86. Fellow Am. Concrete Inst. (hon., Wason Research medal 1957, 65, 74, 86, Anderson award 1983), Am. Inst. Chemists; mem. ASCE, ASTM, Am. Chem. Soc. Home: 255 The Esplanade N Apt 306 Venice FL 34285-1518 Office: Hollister Hall Cornell U Ithaca NY 14853

SLATER, ALAN T., banking executive; b. Bklyn., Dec. 9, 1945; s. Moe H. and Miriam (Greenfield) S.; m. Lois Black, Aug. 19, 1967; children: Terri, Douglas. BS, Bklyn. Coll., 1966; MBA, NYU, 1972. Cert. tchr., N.Y., regulatory compliance mgr. Tchr. Stuyvesant High Sch., N.Y.C., 1966-73; banking exec. Citibank, N.A., N.Y.C., 1973—; speaker at profl. meetings; TV panelist, Assn. State Bank Assns., 1988. Author: How a Check is Processed; author policy manuals; author, producer tng. films. Blood drive organizer, ARC, 1984—. Mem. N.Y. State Benkers Assn. (chmn. ops. and payment systems com. 1989—), Am. Soc. Indsl. Security. Home: 10 Jefferson Rd East Brunswick NJ 08816-4552 Office: 1 Court Square 41st Fl Long Island City NY 11120

SLATER, C. STEWART, chemical engineering educator; b. Atlantic City, Feb. 24, 1957; s. Clarence S. and Elizabeth H. Slater. BS, Rutgers U., Piscataway, N.J., 1979, MS, 1981, MPh, 1982, PhD, 1983. Cert. chem. labs. mgr., N.Y. Process devel. engr. Procter & Gamble Co., Cin., 1979-81; teaching asst., project mgr. Rutgers U., 1981-83; prof. chem. engring. Manhattan Coll., Riverdale, N.Y., 1983—; cons. to major U.S. corps. Contbr. articles to profl. jours. Recipient Ralph R. Teetor award Soc. Automotive Engrs., 1986. Mem. Am. Chem. Soc., Am. Inst. Chem. Engrs., N.Am. Membrane Soc., Am. Soc. for Engring. Edn. (program chmn. 1990, New Engring. Educator Excellence award 1987, Dow Outstanding Faculty award 1989, John Fluke award 1992), Sigma Xi, Tau Beta Pi, Omega Chi Epsilon. Home: 680 Newcomb Rd Ridgewood NJ 07450-5523 Office: Manhattan Coll Chem Engring Dept Manhattan College Pkwy Riverdale NY 10471

SLATER, JAMES ALEXANDER, entomologist, educator; b. Belvidere, Ill., Jan. 10, 1920; s. Ray Alvin and Gladys (Banks) S.; m. Elizabeth Thackston, Feb. 20, 1943; children: James Alexander, Jacquelyn, Samuel, Lydia. BA, U. Ill., 1942, MS, 1947; PhD, Iowa State U., 1950. Asst. prof. Iowa State U., Ames, 1950-53; asst. prof. U. Conn., Storrs, 1953-55, assoc. prof., 1955-60, prof., 1960-87, emeritus prof., 1987—, head dept. zoology, entomology, 1962-67, head sect. systematics, evolutionary biology, 1970-82. Contbr. articles to profl. jours., chpts. to books. State ornithologist, Conn., 1955-80; commr. Conn. Geol. and Natural History Survey, 1960s; mem. Conn. Accrediting Bd. Higher Edn., 1960s. Served to lt. USN, 1943-46. Recipient Faculty rsch. award U. Conn. Alumni Assn., 1972, Harriet Forbes Meml. award Assn. Gravestone Studies, 1981, L.O. Howard Disting. Rsch. award Entomol. Soc. Am., 1986. Mem. Royal Entomol. Soc. London, Entmol., Soc. Am. Entmol. Soc. South Africa, Assn. Gravestone Studies, Nat. Milk Glass Collectors Soc. (pres. 1987-91), Soc. Systematic Zoology (pres. 1983-85). Democrat. Avocation: antique glass collector. Home: 373 Bassetts Bridge Rd Mansfield Center CT 06250-1305 Office: U Conn 75 S Eagleville Road Ext Storrs Mansfield CT 06269-0001

SLATER, RALPH EVAN, lawyer; b. Bklyn., July 14, 1948; s. Ralph Groff and Silvia Helen (Montanelli) S.; m. Cynthia Elaine Mahn, Aug. 29, 1970; children: Robert Evan, Andrew Montgomery, Steven Edward. AB, Princeton U., 1970; JD, U. Pa., 1973. Bar: Conn. 1973, U.S. Dist. Ct. Conn. 1984, U.S. Tax Ct. 1984, U.S. Supreme Ct. 1987. Assoc. Gregory & Adams, Wilton, Conn., 1973-79, ptnr., 1980—; chmn. bd. The Wilton Bank; atty. Planning and Zoning Commn., Zoning Bd. Appeals, Ridgefield, Conn., 1979-81. Chmn. bd. edn. 1st Congl. Ch., Ridgefield, Conn., 1982-84, chmn. bd. trustees, 1985-87. Mem. Conn. Bar Assn. (exec. com. estates and probate sect. 1984-86), Western Conn. Estate and Tax Planning Coun. Inc. Republican. Mem. Ch. of Christ. Home: 30 Strawberry Ridge Rd Ridgefield CT 06877-6019 Office: Gregory & Adams PO Box 190 190 Old Ridgefield Rd Wilton CT 06897-0190

SLATER, SCHUYLER GEORGE, chemist, retired educator; b. New Haven, Feb. 22, 1923; s. Matthew Adam and Bertha Adeline (von Runnen) S. BS, U. Conn., 1944, MS, 1947; EdD, Boston U., 1965. Instr. sci. U. Conn., 1946-49; asst., instr. sci. Boston U., 1950-52, instr. phys. sci., 1952-54; instr. phys. sci. Cen. Conn. State U., 1953-54; assoc. prof. phys. sci. U. Maine, Presque Isle, 1954-56, prof. chemistry, 1954-56; prof. chemistry Salem (Mass.) State Coll., 1956—, chmn. dept. chemistry, 1960-71, 77-86, prof. emeritus, 1986—; coord. pre-engring. program; hon. fellow Queen Elizabeth Coll., London, 1971-72. Active Arnolda Improvement Corp.; town moderator, Charleston, R.I., 1987-90. Fellow Am. Inst. Chemists; mem. N.Y. Acad. Scis., Am. Chem. Soc., Am. Civil Liberty Union, Internat. Platform Assn., Masons, Phi Delta Kappa, Theta Xi. Republican. Episcopalian. Home: PO Box 689 Charlestown RI 02813

SLATKIN, DANIEL NATHAN, pathologist; b. Montreal, Que., Can., Aug. 5, 1934. BSc, McGill U., Montreal, 1955, MD, 1959. Licentiate Med. Coun. Can., 1961; diplomate Am. Bd. Med. Examiners, 1962, Am. Bd. Pathology, 1965. Intern Mt. Sinai Hosp., N.Y.C., 1959-60; assoc. medicine Hosp. Med. Rsch. Ctr., 1960-61; resident gen. pathology, neuropathology Montefiore Hosp., Bronx, N.Y., 1961-64; resident pediatric pathology Presbyn. Hosp., N.Y.C., 1964-65; registrar morbid anatomy Hammersmith Hosp., London, 1965-66; biochemistry fellow Anna Fuller Fund Centre de Recherches Scientifiques sur le Cancer, Villejuif, France, 1966-67; assoc. pathologist McKellar Gen. Hosp., Ft. William, Ont., Can., 1968-69; from instr. to asst. prof. pathology SUNY, Stony Brook, 1969-83; assoc. clin. prof., depts. pediatrics and neurol. surgery Albert Einstein Coll. Medicine, Bronx, 1988—; cons. VA Med. Ctr., Northport, N.Y., 1972-89; attending pathologist Hosp. Med. Rsch. Ctr., 1973-85; dir. clin. lab. Clin. Rsch. Ctr., 1985—; scientist med. dept. Brookhaven Nat. Lab., Upton, N.Y., 1972—. Home: PO Box 701 Upton NY 11973 Office: Brookhaven Nat Lab Med Rsch Ctr Upton NY 11973

SLATON, GWENDOLYN CHILDS, librarian; b. Phila., June 19, 1945; d. George Alexander and LaFronia (Dunbar) Childs; m. Harrison Allen Slaton, Sept. 17, 1966; children: Kimberly Dawn, Leigh Alison. BA in History, Pa. State U., 1970; MA in Edn., Seton Hall U., 1976; MLS, Rutgers U., 1981. Lic. profl. librarian, N.J. Tchr. Project A.C.T.I.O.N., New Brunswick, N.J., 1969-70; prodn. coord. Essex County Coll., Newark, 1972-75, non-print media spl., 1975-81, dir. libr., 1981—. Sec. Maplewood Cultural Commn., 1983—; mem. adv. bd. Family Svc. Child Guidance Ctr. of the Oranges, Maplewood and Millburn, 1976-82. Mem. ALA, N.J. Libr. Assn., Essex Hudson Regional Libr. Coop (sec. exec. bd. 1988-89), Assn. Two Yr. Coll. Libr. Dirs. (pres. 1984), Delta Sigma Theta. Office: Essex County Coll 303 University Ave Newark NJ 07102-1798

SLATTERY, JAMES ARTHUR, educator, retired; b. Northampton, Mass., Dec. 1, 1930; s. James Arthur and Beatrice Irene (LaPlante) S.; m. Nancy Jean Kenyon; children: Neal P., James A., Thomas, Brian K., Christopher J., Amy Jean. BS in Edn., Westfield State Coll., Mass., 1953; MS in Elem. Edn., Hofstra U., 1963. Tchr. Roe-Jan Cen. Sch., Hillsdale, N.Y., 1955-57, Levittown (N.Y.) Sch., 1957—; cons. in outdoor edn. Nassau County BOCES, Westbury, N.Y., 1974—. Dist. commr. Boy Scouts Am., 1960-64; pres. Levittown Community Ctr., 1978-81, 91-92, Levittown Men's Athletic Assn., 1982-90. With U.S. Army, 1953-55.

SLAUGHTER, LOUISE MCINTOSH, congresswoman; b. Harlan County, Ky., Aug. 14, 1929; d. Oscar Lewis and Grace (Byers) McIntosh; m. Robert Slaughter, 1956; children: Megan Rae, Amy Louise, Emily Robin. BS, U. Ky., 1951, MS, 1953. Bacteriologist Ky. Dept. Health, Louisville, 1951-52, U. Ky., 1952-53; market researcher Procter & Gamble, Cin., 1953-56; mem. staff Office of the Lt. Gov. N.Y., Albany, 1978-82; state rep. N.Y. Gen. Assembly, Albany, 1983-86; U.S. congresswoman from 30th Dist. N.Y., Washington, 1987—; mem. Ho. Rules Com., Ho. Budget Com. Del. Dem. Nat. Conv., 1972, 76, 80, 88; mem. Monroe County Pure Water Adminstrn. Bd., Nat. Ctr. for Policy Alternatives Adv. Bd., League of Women Voters, Nat. Women's Polit. Caucus. Office: US Ho of Reps Office of House Mems 1424 Longworth Office Bldg Washington DC 20515

SLAVINSKAS, DARIUS DOMAS, physicist; b. Akmene, Lithuania, July 28, 1933; came to U.S., 1966; s. Domas and Stasé (Vaičaitis) S.; divorced; children: Andrew Darius, Gintara Dana. BA, U. Toronto, 1956; MS, McMaster U., 1962, PhD, 1966. Researcher Imperial Oil, Ltd., Calgary, Alberta, Can., 1956-63; supr. AT&T Bell Labs., Whippany, N.J., 1967-72; mem. tech. staff AT&T Bell Labs.; mem. tech. staff AT&T Bell Labs., Holmdel, N.J., 1978-82, disting. mem. tech. staff, 1982—; chmn. physics sessions Lithuanian Symposium Arts & Scis., Chgo., 1985. Inventor various algorithms for Satellite Sta.-Keeping and ABM systems; co-inventor a new energy source for seismic exploration, planning and designing transoceanic undersea fiber optic communications systems. Children's choir conductor Lithuanian Ethnic Saturday Sch., Elizabeth, N.J., 1967-72. Republican. Roman Catholic. Home: 69 Bonnie Dr Keansburg NJ 07734-2287

SLAVUTIN, LEE JACOB, pension and estate planning insurance executive; b. Melbourne, Victoria, Australia, Mar. 10, 1951; came to U.S., 1978; s. Nathan Jacob and Irene (Fishman) S.; m. Debra C. Schwartz, Nov. 11, 1979; children: Aaron, Lydia. BSc in Medicine with honors, Monash U., Melbourne, 1972, MB, BS with honors, 1974. Diplomate Am. Bd. Pathology. Pathologist Lenox Hill Hosp., N.Y.C., 1978-82; pension and estate planning specialist Stern, Slavutin & Slavutin, N.Y.C., 1983-87, chmn., 1987—. Contbr. articles to profl. jours. Mem. Am. Soc. Pension Actuaries (cert.), Am. Assn. Advanced Life Underwriters, Million Dollar Round Table. Home: 321 W 78th St New York NY 10024-6513 Office: 530 5th Ave New York NY 10036-5101

SLAYMAN, CLIFFORD LEROY, JR., biophysicist, educator; b. Mt. Vernon, Ohio, July 7, 1936; s. Clifford Leroy and Ethel May (Stantz) S.; m. Carolyn Ruth Walch, Dec. 26, 1959; children: Andrew Lowell, Rachel Whitehouse. AB, Kenyon Coll., 1958; PhD, Rockefeller Inst., 1963; DSc (hon.), Kenyon Coll, 1991. NSF fellow Cambridge (Eng.) U., 1963-64; asst. prof. Western Res. U., Cleve., 1964-67; from asst. prof. to prof. physiology Yale U., New Haven, 1967—; mem panel on pre-doctoral fellowships NSF, Washington, 1969-71; DOE-DOA-NSF panel on Plant Sci. Ctrs., Washington, 1988. Editor: Electrogenic Ion Pumps, 1982; contbr. articles to profl. jours. and revs.; editorial bd. Bio Sci. Jour., 1985-88, Jour. Membrane Biology, 1982—. Mem. Hamden (Conn.) Neighborhood Preservation Com., 1980-82. Grantee NIH, 1964-91, NSF, 1979-82, DOE, 1985—. Mem. AAAS, Am. Physiol. Soc., Am. Soc. Plant Physiologists, N.Y. Acad. Scis., Soc. Gen. Physiologists. Office: Yale Sch Medicine 333 Cedar St New Haven CT 06510-3289

SLAYTON, RONALD ALFRED, artist; b. Barre, Vt., Dec. 16, 1910; s. Oscar and Mary Elsie (Cowles) S.; m. Dorothy Kennedy, June 20, 1936 (dec.); children: Thomas, Peter, Gail; m. Mariette Paine. Student, Pratt Inst., 1931-33, U. Vt., 1935-36; BS, Columbia U., 1945; postgrad., U. Tenn., 1947. Cert. art tchr., Vt. With Works Progress Adminstrn., Burlington, Vt., 1936-39; dir. Burlington Arts Ctr., 1938-39; advt. mgr. Sears Roebuck & Co., Burlington, 1941-43; advt. layout artist D.B. Hopkins Co., N.Y.C., 1944-45; assoc. prof. arts and crafts, crafts specialist U. Tenn., Knoxville, 1945-52; copy writer, layout artist Miller's Dept. Store, Knoxville, 1955; tchr. indsl. arts Northfield (Vt.) High Sch., 1959-60; dir. Fletcher Farm Craft Sch., Ludlow, Vt., 1959-61; tchr. art Montpelier (Vt.) Pub. Schs., 1959-62; curator W.T. Wood Art Gallery Vt. Coll., Montpelier, 1962-84; acting dir. Vt. Guild Old Time Crafts and Industries, Weston, 1939; founder Dog River Art Sch., 1968; spl. instr. various colls. in Vt. One man shows include Vt. Coun. Arts, 1992; exhibited in group shows in Bonn, Fed. Republic Germany, 1989, Moscow, 1989; retrospective exbhns. include T.W. Wood Art Gallery, 1989, Valley Performing Arts Ctr., 1990. Pres. Montpelier Theatre Guild, 1968-70; trustee T.W. Wood Art Gallery, 1968-89; bd. dirs. Artists for Social Responsibility, 1984-89; chmn. art Internat. Conf. on Arts and Communications, Florence, Italy, 1976. Recipient award of merit Vt. Coun. on Arts, 1971. Mem. Am. Assn. Ret. Persons, Ret. Tchrs. Assn., Parents and Tchrs. for Social Responsibility, Art Resource Assn., Vt. Art Tchrs. Assn. (pres. 1956-67), The Club (pres. 1985). Democrat. Unitarian. Home and Studio: RFD 2 Montpelier VT 05602

SLAYTON, THOMAS KENNEDY, editor, writer; b. Burlington, Vt., July 29, 1941; s. Ronald Alfred and Dorothy (Kennedy) S.; m. Elizabeth Craig Wilson; 1 child, Ethan Augustus. BA, U. Vt., 1963. Reporter Rutland (Vt.) Herald newspaper, 1964-72; reporter, bur. chief Vt. Press Bur., Montpelier, 1972-79; asst. editor, editor Times-Argus newspaper, Barre, Vt., 1979-85; editor in chief Vt. Life Mag., Montpelier, 1985—; mem. adv. bd. confs. Windham Found., Grafton, Vt., 1986-89; adj. prof. journalism dept. St. Michael's Coll., Winooski, Vt., 1988—. Author: Finding Vermont, 1986; author introduction to book The Vermont Experience, 1987; contbr. articles and revs. to profl. jours. Bicentennial fellow U. Vt., Burlington, 1988-91. Mem. Vt. Press Assn., Regional Pubs. Assn. (bd. dirs.). Mem. Soc. of Friends. Office: Vt Life Mag 61 Elm St Montpelier VT 05602-2713

SLEASE, CLYDE HAROLD, III, lawyer; b. Pitts., May 2, 1944; s. Clyde Harold and Eleanor (Cunningham) S.; m. Marcia Ethel Coleman, Aug. 6, 1966 (div. 1975); children: Eleanor Carolyn, Gretchen Coleman; m. Ann Miller Adams, June 25, 1990. BA, Duke U., 1966; JD, U. Pitts., 1969. Assoc. Thorp Reed and Armstrong, Pitts., 1969-71; adminstrv. asst. Dist. Atty. Allegheny County, Pitts., 1971-72; staff atty. Fed. Communications Commn., Washington, 1972-74; gen. counsel R.M. Scaife Assocs., Pitts., 1974-86; pvt. practice Pitts., 1988—; mem. Pa. Fed. Jud. Nominating Commn.; bd. dirs. Saltworks, Inc. Mem. Pa. Rep. State Fin. Commn., Harrisburg, 1986-92. Mem. Pa. Bar Assn., D.C. Bar Assn., Allegheny County Bar Assn., Duquesne Club, Rolling Rock Club, Burning Tree Club, Oakmont County Club. Home: PO Box 323 Ligonier PA 15658 Office: 2550 One PPG Pl Pittsburgh PA 15222

SLEDGE, REGINALD LEON, senior industry analyst; b. Balt., July 8, 1954; s. Herbert Clifton and Juanita (Brantley) S. Grad., Lawrence Acad., 1972; student, Dartmouth Coll., 1968; BS, Boston U., 1976; MBA, Columbia U., 1984; student, Dartmouth Coll., 1968, Columbia U., 1988. Fin. analyst West Point-Pepperell, Inc., N.Y.C., 1976-77; fin. futures trader European Am. Bank, N.Y.C., 1978-82; portfolio mgr. Fuji Bank, N.Y.C., 1984-85; fin. cons. Control Assocs., N.Y.C., 1986-87; acct., fin. analyst Spicer & Oppenheim, N.Y.C., 1987-88; sr. industry analyst BankAm. Bus. Credit Inc., N.Y.C., 1988—. Mem. Rep. Nat. Com., 1986—. Mem. Assn. for Investment Mgmt. and Rsch., Fin. Analysts Fedn., N.Y. Soc. Security Analysts, Columbia Bus. Sch. Club N.Y. (past v.p.). Republican. Roman Catholic. Home: 282 E 35th St Apt 6W Brooklyn NY 11203-3979 Office: BankAm Bus Credit Inc 228 E 45th St New York NY 10017-3303

SLEEPER, FRANK HAROLD, journalist; b. Worcester, Mass., Aug. 4, 1927; s. Francis Harper and Ruth Lydia (Putnam) S.; m. Joan Garland Weeks, Aug. 14, 1954 (div.); children: Frank Bruce, Eric Warren, Keith Garland (dec.). AB in Govt. cum laude, Harvard U., 1949; MA in Internat. Rels. and Orgn., Am. U., 1950; MA in Politics, Princeton U., 1952. Reporter Portland (Maine) Press Herald, Gannett Pub. Co., 1953-61, 86-91, bus. editor, 1961-86. Maine corr. Time mag., 1958-84, 91—, Wall St. Jour., 1964-80; Maine corr. Sports Illustrated, 1958-91, Maine, N.H., Vt. corr., 1991—; contbr. articles to publs. Chmn. newspaper publicity com. Maine chpt. March of Dimes, Cumberland County (Maine) chpt. March of Dimes, 1955, 58-59; dir. pub. rels. First Internat. Conf. Mental Retardation, 1959, First Tri-State Bus. Show, Portland, 1957; bd. dirs. World Affairs Coun. Maine, 1977-80, v.p. 1981-83; vestryman St. Alban's Episc. Ch., Cape Elizabeth, Maine, 1954-72; mem. 150th anniversary Augusta (Maine) Mental Health Inst., 1990-91. Recipient Outstanding Merit cert. 2nd Ann. Ind. Natural Gas Assn. Am., 1966, U. Mo. Writing awards, Econ. and Indsl. Devel. award Indsl. Devel. Coun. Maine, 1980; Fulbright fellow, 1952-53. Mem. Assn. Former Intelligence Officers (life), Masons (32d degree). Home: 55 Lambert St # 7 Portland ME 04103-2130

SLEIGHT, THOMAS PERRY, applied physics educator; b. Glens Falls, N.Y., May 15, 1943; s. Hollis Decker and Elizabeth (Smith) S.; m. Dorothea Schmidt, July 16, 1966; children: Kristen, Ketti, Randall, Ryan. BS in Chemistry, Ohio U., 1965, BS in Math., 1965; PhD in Chemistry, SUNY, Buffalo, 1969. Postdoctoral fellow Leichester (Eng.) U., 1968-69; group supr. Applied Physics Lab., Johns Hopkins U., Laurel, Md., 1969-83; dir.'s asst. for computing Applied Physics Lab., Johns Hopkins U., 1983-88, program mgr., 1988—; teaching lectr. Johns Hopkins U., Laurel, Md., 1972—, prin. profl. staff applied physics lab., 1976—; guest editor tech. digest Computing at APL, 1984. Recipient cert. appreciation, Am. Soc. Naval Engrs., 1980. Mem. Computer Soc. of IEEE, Am. Chem. Soc. Office: Applied Physics Lab Johns Hopkins Univ Laurel MD 20723-6099

SLENKER, RICHARD DREYER, JR., broadcasting executive; b. New Rochelle, N.Y., June 2, 1957; s. Richard D. and Ellen (Mullins) S.; m. Maria Pope, July 10, 1982; children: Scarlett Anne, Jessica Martha, Elizabeth Ellen, Martha Maria. BA in Communications, Colgate U., 1979; MS in Tech. Mgmt., N.Y. Poly. U., 1986. Engr. WPIX, Inc., N.Y.C., 1979-82, engring. supr., 1982-86, dir. tech. ops., 1986-91; v.p. ops. and engring. Sta. WTTG-TV, Fox TV, Washington, 1991—; cons. Archdiocese of N.Y., N.Y.C., 1987—. Sr. mem. CAP, Westchester, N.Y., 1989. Mem. NATAS, Soc. Motion Picture and TV Engrs., Aircraft Owners and Pilots Assn. Office: Sta WTTG-TV, Fox TV 5151 Wisconsin Ave NW Washington DC 20016-4124

SLESINGER, JACQUES ISIDORE, management executive; b. Antwerp, Belgium, Feb. 22, 1930; came to U.S., 1941; s. Charles and Helen (Alfus) S.; m. Irene Polk, June 21, 1970; 1 child, Andrew. BEE, CCNY, 1951; MSEE, Columbia U., 1953. V.p. Charles Slesinger, Inc., N.Y.C., 1951—; fin. mgr. Ramsgate, Inc., N.Y.C., 1987—, Denning, Inc., N.Y.C., 1988—. Bd. dirs. 115 Central Park West Corp., N.Y.C., 1991-92. Mem. Zionist Orgn. Am. (v.p. 1958-67). Democrat. Jewish. Home: 115 Central Park West New York NY 10023 Office: Charles Slesinger Inc 609 Fifth Ave New York NY 10017

SLESINGER, LARRY HOWARD, nonprofit executive; b. Pitts., Feb. 1, 1954; s. William and Maxine (Shermer) S.; m. Francesca Maria Piemonte, May 28, 1983; children: Sophie, Eric, Nina. BA, Carleton Coll., 1977; MBA, Stanford U., 1980. Spl. asst. to pres. Inter-American Foundation, Arlington, Va., 1980-84; program officer John and Mary Markle Foundation, N.Y.C., 1985-87; deputy dir. National Center for Nonprofit Boards, Washington, 1988—; bd. dirs. Iona Sr. Svcs., Washington; cons. various nonprofit orgns., 1984—. Recipient Thomas J. Watson fellowship, Thomas J. Watson Found., 1977-78. Office: Nat Ctr for Nonprofit Bds 2000 L St NW # 411 Washington DC 20036-4907

SLESNICK, WILLIAM ELLIS, mathematician, educator; b. Oklahoma City, Feb. 24, 1925; s. Isaac Ralph and Adele (Miller) S. B.S., U.S. Naval Acad., 1945; B.A., U. Okla., 1948; B.A. (Rhodes scholar), Oxford (Eng.) U., 1950, M.A., 1954; A.M., Harvard, 1952; A.M. (hon.), Dartmouth, 1972. Math. master St. Paul's Sch., Concord, N.H., 1952-62; vis. instr. Dartmouth Coll., 1958-59, mem. faculty, 1962—, prof. math., 1971—; asst. dir. ednl. uses Kiewit Computation Center, 1966-69; mem. N.H. Rhodes Scholar Selection Com.; mem. advanced placement exam. com. math. Coll. Entrance Exam. Bd., 1967-71; mem. Nat. Humanities Faculty, 1972—. Co-author: 12 math. textbooks including (with R.H. Crowell) Calculus With Analytic Geometry, 1968. Active Boy Scouts Am., 1937—, attache world bur., 1955, 67, council exec. bd., 1964—, dist. chmn., 1974-76; mem. nat. com. Order of Arrow, 1965—, mem. internat. com., 1974—; mem. Nat. Jewish Com. Scouting, 1973—; mem. assembly of overseers Mary Hitchcock Meml. Hosp., Hanover; trustee Lawrence L. Lee Mus., Hanover-Norwich Youth Fund, New Hampton (N.H.) Sch., 1975-81; mem. selection com. Okla. Found. for Excellence, 1986-91. Served with USN, 1942-47. Recipient Vigil Honor, 1948, Nat. Disting. Svc. award Order of Arrow, 1967, Silver Beaver award Boy Scouts Am., 1967, Silver Antelope award, 1972, Disting. Eagle Scout award, 1979, Wendall E. Badger award for contbn. to rowing Dartmouth Coll., 1978, Shofar award, 1980, Silver Buffalo award, 1990, Presdl. medal Dartmouth Coll., 1991. Mem. Nat. Council Tchrs. Math., Math. Assn. Am., Assn. Tchrs. Math. in New Eng., Assn. Am. Rhodes Scholars, Phi Beta Kappa (chpt. pres. 1974-77), Phi Eta Sigma, Pi Mu Epsilon, Alpha Phi Omega. Home: 19 S Park St Hanover NH 03755-2135

SLEVIN, JOSEPH RAYMOND, editor, publisher; b. N.Y.C., Nov. 27, 1918; s. Theodore and Katherine (Bluh) S.; m. Zillah Katherine Day, Dec. 8, 1943; children: Ann Day, Michael Scott, Jonathan Day, Peter Day. BA, Yale U., 1939; student, Yale U. Law Sch., 1939-40, U. Nebr., 1940-41, U. Ill., 1941-42; MA, U. Nebr., 1942. Staff editor Changing Times mag., Washington, 1946-47; econ. corr. Jour. of Commerce, Washington, 1947-55; Washington corr. Fin. Times, London, England, 1952-57; nat. econs. editor N.Y. Herald Tribune, Washington, 1955-66; syndicated econs. columnist Newsday, Times Mirror and Phila. Inquirer, 1966-85; econs. commentator Westinghouse Broadcasting, Washington, 1974-77; editor, pub. Washington Bond Report, 1962-89, Washington Bond and Money Market Report, Washington, 1990—; fin. sec. Nat. Press Club, Washington, 1979, v.p., 1980, pres., 1981, Nat. Press Bldg. Corp., 1981-82; bd. dirs. Nat. Press Found., Inc., pres., 1983-87. Lt. USNR, 1942-45, PTO. Mem. Am. Polit. Sci Assn., White House Corr. Assn., Overseas Writers, Periodical Press Gallery, Nat. Press Club, Yale Club, Fed. City Club. Home: 16 E Melrose St Bethesda MD 20815-4204 Office: Washington Bond Report Nat Press Bldg Washington DC 20045

SLEVIN, PATRICK JOSEPH, engineer; b. Orange, N.J., Nov. 28, 1951; s. John Francis and Bridie (Devaney) S.; m. Jacqueline Eileen Cavalero, July 29, 1978; children: Patrick Joseph, John, Daniel. BS in Indsl. Engring., N.J. Inst. Tech., 1976; MSME, L.I. U., 1980. Engr. Fairchild Rep. Corp., Farmingdale, N.Y., 1977-79; engr. Kearfott (formerly Singer Kearfott), Little Falls, N.J., 1979-84, mem. engring. mgmt. staff, 1984-89, mgr. telecommunications, 1989-91; v.p. Internat. Mktg. Law Enforcement Products Internat., Orange, N.J., 1991—. Mem. Am. Prodn. and Inventory Control Soc., Am. Assn. Individual Investors, Glen Ridge Country Club N.J. Roman Catholic. Home: 10 Sutherland Rd Montclair NJ 07042-2443 Office: LEPI Box 580 171 Parron St Orange NJ 07051-0580

SLEWITZKE, CONNIE LEE, retired army officer; b. Mosinee, Wis., Apr. 15, 1931; d. Leo Thomas and Amelia Marie (Hoffman) S. BSN, U. Md., Balt., 1971; MA in Counseling and Guidance, St. Mary's U., San Antonio, 1976. Commd. 1st lt. U.S. Army, 1957, advanced through grades to brig. gen., 1987; ret., 1987; chief dept. nursing Letterman Army Med. Ctr. U.S. Army, San Francisco; asst. chief nurse Army Nurse Corps U.S. Army, Washington; chief brigadier gen. U.S. Army, 1983-87. Contbr. articles to profl. jours. Decorated D.S.M., Legion of Merit, Bronze Star medal, Meritorious Service Medal with 2 oak leaf clusters, Joint Services Commendation medal, Army Commendation Medal, Nat. Def. Service medal, Vietnam Service medal with 4 devices, Overseas Service ribbon with 4 devices, Republic of Vietnam Campaign medal. Mem. ANA, Va. State Nurses Assn., Alumni Assn. U.S.A. War Coll., Nat. Orgn. Nurse Execs., Assn. U.S. Army, Women in Mil. Svc. for Am. Found., Sigma Theta Tau.

SLEZAK, STEVEN EUGENE, trade unionist; b. West Covina, Calif., Apr. 19, 1959; s. Steve and Ruth Marie (Gansenhuber) S. BS in Fgn. Svc., Georgetown U., 1981. Researcher Sta. WETA-TV, Washington, 1981-82, Coalition for Democratic Majority, Washington, 1982; constrn. worker Drywall Plastering and Framing, 1983; program officer Free Trade Union Inst. AFL-CIO, Washington, 1983-86, rep. Dept. Internat. Affairs, 1986—. Contbr. articles to profl. jours. Office: AFL-CIO 815 16th St NW Washington DC 20006-4104

SLIMMER, JOHN EARL, counselor; b. Chambersburg, Pa., Feb. 24, 1940; s. John E. and Elsie J. (Avinger) S.; m. Carol Heckman Slimmer; stepchildren: Shari, Matthew, Andrew. BS in Edn., Shippensburg U., 1961, MEd in Guidance and Counseling, 1965. Cert. supr. sch. guidance svcs., Pa. Elem. tchr. Chambersburg (Pa.) Area Sch. Dist., 1961-66, counselor, 1966—; pvt. practice Chambersburg, 1985—; adj. asst. prof. Millersville (Pa.) U., 1971-73; vis. asst. prof. Shippensburg U., 1973-74; cons. and workshop leader in field; mem. Franklin County Children Youth Adv. Bd., 1984—. Contbr. articles to profl. jours. Named Disting. Tchr. of the Yr. Chambersburg Svc. Clubs, 1965; recipient Gov.'s citation State of Pa., 1976, Cert. of Appreciation Pa. Pers. and Guidance Assn., 1976, Citizen of the Yr. award Chambersburg Elks Lodge, 1977, Cert. of Appreciation The Easter Seal Soc. Franklin County, 1986. Mem. AACD (mem. bd. cons. editors 1978-82, Cert. of Recognition 1982), Am. Sch. Counselors Assn. (state coord. 1972-76, mem. editorial bd. Elem. Sch. Guidance and Counseling Jour. 1973-76, com. mem.), Nat. Vocat. Guidance Assn., Assn. Counselor Edn. and Supervision (com. mem. 1982-83), Pa. Sch. Counselors Assn. (unit rep. 1970-72, task force chmn. 1972-75, bd. govs. 1975-77), Pa. Counselors Assn. NEA (Pa. and Chambersburg chpts.), Phi Delta Kappa. Lutheran. Home: 2109 Independence Dr Chambersburg PA 17201-1422

SLIPPEN, MICHAEL, otolaryngologist; b. N.Y.C., Feb. 2, 1942; s. Morton and Eleanor (Weinstock) S.; m. Carol Susan Goldman; children: Jeffrey, Mark, Daniel. MD, Cath. U. Louvain (Belgium), 1969. Chief otolaryngology Parker Jewish Geriatric Inst., New Hyde Park, N.Y., 1978—. Pres. L.I. Soc. of Otolaryngology, 1986. Maj. USAF, 1975-77. Fellow ACS, Am. Acad. Otolaryngology.

SLIVINSKI, ROBERT MICHAEL, human resources consultant; b. Phila., June 14, 1949; s. Joseph Ludwig and Veronica (Czarnecki) S.; m. Tamara Kristowicz, Oct. 10, 1976; children: Luke Matthew, Kristina Marie. BS in Commerce, Rider Coll., 1971. Claims adjuster Liberty Mus. Ins. Co., Bala Cynwyd, Pa., 1971-72; personnel mgr. Chamberlain Mfg. Corp., Burlington, N.J., 1972-74, Scranton, Pa., 1974; adminstrv. asst. to equipment mgr. Lavino Shipping Co., Phila., 1975-77; supr. employment and employment svcs. Gould Inc., Phila., 1977-78; personnel dir. Frankford-Quaker Grocery Co., Phila., 1978-86, personnel dir. Fleming Cos. Inc. div., 1986-89; prin., pres. Robert Michaels Assocs. Inc., Mt. Laurel, N.J., 1987—; personnel mgr. Port Authority Transit Corp., Lindenwold, N.J., 1990—; bd. dirs. Frankford-Quaker Fed. Credit Union, Phila., past chmn. credit com. Mem. Men of Malvern, Pa., 1990—, St. John Neumann Ch. Ministry for Drug and Alcohol Dependency, Mt. Laurel, 1987—; past asst. den leader Cub Scouts Am., Mt. Laurel, 1989-90. With USN, 1968-70. Mem. Tri-State Personnel Assn., Am. Soc. Safety Engrs. (assoc.), 5 State Survey Group (chmn. personnel com. 1990—), St. John Neumann Holy Name Soc. (v.p. 1989-91, pres. 1991—). Republican. Roman Catholic. Home: 33 Boothby Dr Mount Laurel NJ 08054-1901 Office: Port Authority Transit Corp Adminstrv Offices Lindenwold NJ 08021

SLOAN, F(RANK) BLAINE, lawyer, educator; b. Geneva, Nebr., Jan. 3, 1920; s. Charles Porter and Lillian Josephine (Stiefer) S.; m. Patricia Sand, Sept. 2, 1944; children—DeAnne Sloan Riddle, Michael Blaine, Charles Porter. AB with high distinction, U. Nebr., 1942, LLB cum laude, 1946; LLM in Internat. Law, Columbia U., 1947. Bar: Nebr. 1946, N.Y. 1947. Asst. to spl. counsel Intergovtl. Com. for Refugees, 1947; mem. Office Legal Affairs UN Secretariat, N.Y.C., 1948-78, gen. counsel Relief and Works Agy. Palestine Refugees, Beirut, 1958-60, dir. gen. legal div., 1966-78, rep. of Sec. Gen. to Commn. Internat. Trade Law, 1969-78, rep. to Legal Sub-com. on Outer Space, 1966-78; rep. UN Del. Vietnam Conf., Paris, 1973; rep UN Conf. on Carriage of Goods by sea, Hamburg, 1978; prof. internat. law orgn. and water law Pace U., 1978-87, prof. emeritus, 1987—. Author: United Nations General Assembly Resolutions in Our Changing World, 1991; contbr. articles to legal jours. Cons. UN Office of Legal Affairs, 1983-84, UN Water Resources Br., 1983; supervisory com., Pace Peace Ctr. Navigator AC, U.S. Army, 1943-46. Recipient Outstanding Prof. award Pace Law Sch., 1987. Decorated Air medal. Mem. Am. Soc. Internat. Law, Am. Acad. Polit. and Social Sci., Am. Arbitration Assn. (panel of arbitrators), Order of Coif, Phi Beta Kappa, Phi Alpha Delta (hon.). Roman Catholic. Home: HCR-68 Box 72 Foxwind-forbes Park Fort Garland CO 81133 Office: 78 N Broadway White Plains NY 10603-3796

SLOAN, ROBERT HOOD, JR., insurance agent; b. Albany, N.Y., Feb. 2, 1953; s. Robert Hood and Valerie Frances (Mauss) S.; m. Janet Marie Schultz, June 21, 1975 (div. 1983); m. Catherine Barringer Brown, July 21, 1984; children: James Michael, Catherine Elizabeth. BSBA, Rochester Inst. Tech., 1975. CLU, chartered fin. cons. Agt. PMA Ins. Co., Wilmington, Del., 1975-76, Mut. of Omaha, Broomall, Pa., 1976-78, Bankers Life Nebr., King of Prussia, Pa., 1978-80; exec. v.p. Shevlin Assocs., Nat. Life Vt., Broomall, 1980-88; gen. agt. Sloan Assocs., Nat. Life Vt., Warwick, R.I., 1988—. Mem., grandee Life Underwriters Polit. Action Com., 1975—; mem. scout troop leadership com. Troop 2, East Greenwich; charter mem. United Ch. of Christ, East Greenwich, R.I., 1990. Mem. Am. Soc. CLU and ChFC (Golden Key soc.), Gen. Agts. and Mgrs. Assn. (bd. dirs. Providence chpt. 1988—), Nat. Assn. Life Underwriters, U.S. Jaycees (pres. Exton chpt. 1978-79), Mensa, Turk's Head Club, Rotary. Republican. Office: Sloan Assocs Nat Life Vt 875 Centerville Rd Bldg 1 Warwick RI 02886

SLOAN, ROBERT SMULLYAN, artist, art appraiser; b. N.Y.C., Dec. 5, 1915; s. Albert and Clara (Freeman) Smullyan; m. Irene Lapouse; children: Daniel Peter, Deborah Ann. AB, CCNY, 1936. One-man shows include Leger Gallery, White Plains, N.Y., 1956, Herbert F. Johnson Mus., Ithaca, N.Y., 1974, Capricorn Gallery, Bethesda, Md., 1974; group shows include Nat. Gallery, Washington, 1945, Kennedy Art Ctr., 1991; permanent collections include IBM Coll., U.S. Treasury Dept., Nat. Portrait Gallery, Washington, Herbert F. Johnson Mus. With U.S. Army, 1943-46. Recipient Disting. Achievement award "The Seasoned Eye", Modern Maturity Mag., 1990. Mem. Appraisers Assn. Am. Home: 1412 Arlington St Mamaroneck NY 10543-1301

SLOAN, ROBERT WESLEY, retired mathematics educator; b. Rankin, Ill., July 18, 1924; s. Roscoe Stirling and Pauline Laura (Bone) S.; m. Marilyn Margaret Pfingsten, Dec. 25, 1949: children: Abigail Elizabeth Cole, Priscilla Margaret Beese. BS, U.S. Naval Acad., 1946; MS, U. Ill., 1951, PhD, 1955. Asst. prof. U. N.H., Durham, 1955-56, Carleton Coll., Northfield, Minn., 1956-59; prof. SUNY, Oswego, 1959-65; prof., chmn. Alfred (N.Y.) U., 1965-86, prof. emeritus, 1986—. Author: Introduction to Modern Mathematics, 1960. Active Alfred Village Bd., 1982-84; mayor Village of Alfred, 1984-87. Lt. USNR, 1946-49, 52-54. Mem. Math. Assn. Am. (chmn. seaway sect. 1972). Republican. Home: 4 Spruce St Alfred NY 14802-1319

SLOANE, DAVID EDWARD EDISON, language professional, educator; b. West Orange, N.J., Jan. 19, 1943; s. Thomas Edison and Elaine Bernice (Levy) S.; m. Bonnie Lee Fiedorek, June 18, 1968 (div. June 1977); m. Bonnie Gayle Fausz, Aug. 12, 1985; children: Rachel Edison, David Edison. BA with honors, Wesleyan U., Middletown, Conn., 1964; MA, Duke U., 1966, PhD, 1970. Grad. tutor, dept. English Duke U., Durham, N.C., 1966-68; instr. to asst. prof. Lafayette Coll., Easton, Pa., 1968-74; HEW-Trio Writing Instr. Fashion Inst. of Technology, N.Y.C., 1974-75; assoc. prof. Medgar Evars Coll./CUNY, Bklyn., 1975-76; assoc. prof. to prof. Univ. New Haven, West Haven, Conn., 1980—; cons. in writing, KPMG, Peat Marwick, Montvale, N.J., 1982—. Author: Mark Twain As a Literary Comedian, 1979, Adventures of Huckleberry Finn: American Comic Vision, 1989; editor: Country Dance and Song, 1983—, Essays in Arts and Sciences, 1990—, The Literary Humor of the Urban Northeast, 1830-1890, 1982, American Humor Magazines and Comic Periodicals, 1987, others. Bd. dirs. Eli Whitney Mus., Whitneyville, Conn., 1980-88, pres. 1984-86; bd. dirs. New Haven Country Dancers, 1979—. Recipient Winchester fellowship Wesleyan U., 1964, Mellon Conn. fellowship, Yale U., New Haven, 1982; named Disting. Vis. Prof. Univ. Miss., Oxford, 1986, Saybrook Assoc. Fellow, Yale U., 1988-92, USIA Lectr./Brazil, 1987. Mem. MLA, N.E. MLA, Am. Humor Studies Assn. (exec. dir. 1990—, pres. 1989), Mark Twain Circle (pres. 1992—, v.p. 1989-91). Office: U New Haven 300 Orange Ave West Haven CT 06516-1999

SLOANE, ROBERT LINDLEY, retail chain store executive; b. Presque Isle, Maine, Oct. 5, 1940; s. William James and Alexina Laura (Michaud) S.; m. Ada Marjorie Hersey, July 11, 1964; children: Lynn Ellen, Susan Lenor. BS in Engring., U.S. Mil. Acad., 1963; MS in Phys. Edn., U. Wis., 1969; MBA, Fairleigh Dickinson U., 1972; grad., Army War Coll., Carlisle, Pa., 1980. Commd. 2d lt. U.S. Army, 1963, advanced through grades to col., 1983; U.S. exchange officer to Brit., 1973-75; sr. exec. to dep. comdr. NATO, 1975-77; sr. ops. mgr., 1977-79; sr. ops. exec. U.S. Mil. Acad., West Point, N.Y., 1980-83; dir. profl. and exec. devel. Army War Coll., 1983-86; ret., 1986; v.p. for human resources Bank N.Y., N.Y.C., 1986-88; v.p. adminstrn. and human resources Rite Aid Corp., Harrisburg, Pa., 1988—. Editor: The Recourse to War, 1988; contbr. articles to profl. jours. Bd. dirs. Met. Arts, Harrisburg, 1988—, Fed. Credit Union, 1989—. Decorated Legion of Merit. Office: Rite Aid Corp PO Box 3165 Harrisburg PA 17105-3165

SLOANE, THOMAS EDISON, JR., medical industry consultant; b. Orange, N.J., May 10, 1940; s. Thomas Edison and Elaine Bernice (Levy) S.; m. Ann Marie DellaSelva, Nov. 4, 1967; children: Michelle, Thomas Edison III. BS in Indsl. Engring., U. New Haven, 1962, BSEE, 1964. Dir. voice engring. Mattel Inc., Hawthorne, Calif., 1968-72; dir. prodn. and devel. Childguidance Toy Co., Bronx, 1972-74; dir. mfg. devel. Baxter Labs., Deerfield, Ill., 1974-77; dir. engring. U.S. Surg. Corp., Norwalk, Conn., 1977-79; gen. mgr. Sonin Inc., North Haven, Conn., 1980-81; v.p. engring. Promark Inc., Seymour, Conn., 1981-83; v.p. strategic market devel. Pfizer Hosp. Prodn. Group, N.Y.C., 1983-87; cons. The Alva Group, West Redding, Conn., 1987—; dir. Dynamic Digital Displays Inc., St David's, Pa., 1988-92. Inventor in field. Commr., treas. Lake Barrington (Ill.) Park COmmn., 1975-77. Mem. Soc. Advancement Med. Product Devel. and Engring. (dir., treas. 1991-92).

SLOANE, WILLIAM MARTIN, lawyer, legal educator; b. Harrisburg, Pa., Nov. 28, 1951; s. William and Margaret Mater (Martin) S.; m. Susan Marie Ankney, June 16, 1984; 1 child, Sara Marie. BA, York Coll. of Pa., 1972; cert. in English Law, London Poly., Eng., 1973; JD, Widener U., 1975; LLM in Labor, Temple U., 1979; D in Juridical Sci., Heed U., 1982. Bar: Pa. 1976, U.S. Dist. Ct. (mid. dist.) Pa. 1980, Md. 1985. Lectr. St. Francis Coll., Harrisburg, 1979-83; asst. prof. Millersville (Pa.) U., 1985; instr. Elizabethtown (Pa.) Coll., 1987—; pres. Profl. Edn. Rsch. Group, Carlisle, Pa., 1975—; legal counsel Ho. of Reps., Harrisburg, 1976—; exec. dir. House Local Govt. Com., Harrisburg, 1987—; adj. asst. prof. Heed U., Christiansted, V.I., 1982—, pres. sch. theology, 1991—; lectr. Wilson Coll., Chambersburg, Pa., 1981—; adj. faculty Newport U., Newport Beach, Calif., 1983—, Greenwich U., Hilo, Hawaii, 1988—; mem. faculty Fairfax U., New Orleans, 1987—, assoc. dean 1988—, dean bus. sch., 1989-91; adj. prof. Widener U. Sch. Law, 1991—. Author: Feasability of a Harrisburg Law School, 1986; co-author: Feasability of a Harrisburg University, 1990. Exec. com. mem. Cumberland County Dems., Carlisle, Pa., 1976-84, Pa. Dem. State Com., Harrisburg, 1976-84; gen. counsel Young Dems. of Pa., Harrisburg, 1976-86; chmn. Am.-European Community Youth Assn., London, 1980-91; chmn. Acad. for Rsch. in Chiropractic Scis., 1984-86, 88—; trustee Pa. Coll. Straight Chiropractic, 1991—; mem. commn. on accreditation Straight Chiropractic Acad. Standards Assn., 1991—. Recipient Citizen in Action award Sta. WSBA Radio, 1972. Mem. ABA (3d cir. Brass Key award student div. 1973), Md. Bar Assn., Pa. Bar Assn., Assn. Trial Lawyers Am., Pa. Trial Lawyers Assn., Am. Soc. Internat. Law, Mansfield Law Club, Mensa, Scottish Lawyers, Phi Alpha Delta. Democrat. Anglican. Home and Office: 26 Shepherd Rd Newville PA 17241-1102

SLOAT, JANE ROBERTS DEGRAFF, government official, civic worker, consultant; b. N.Y.C., Dec. 31, 1939; d. John Wynne and Agnes (Murton) Roberts; m. Elliott Dodd DeGraff, June 28, 1959 (div.); children: Pamela DeGraff Porter, Jill Katherine; m. Jonathan Welsh Sloat, June 19, 1983. Active Hospitality and Info. Svc., Washington, 1964-70, sec. bd., 1971-73; spl. asst. to ambassador-at-large for cultural affairs Dept. State, Washington, 1981; spl. asst. to U.S. coord. refugee affairs, Washington, 1982-85, coord. conf. on Ethical Issues and Moral Principles in U.S. Refugee Policy, 1983; real estate broker Samuel P. Padoe Real Estate, Washington, 1986—. Tour lectr. Corcoran Gallery Art, Washington, 1965-70; vice chmn. UN Concert, Washington, 1971, 50th Jubilee Nat. English Speaking Union, 1971; spl. asst. to chmn. United Givers Fund, Washington, 1971-72; chmn. ball Opera Soc. Washington, 1972; bd. dirs. Jr. League, 1970-71, Nat. Ballet Soc., 1972-74, Washington Performing Arts Soc., 1972-75; mem. D.C. Mayor's Com. on Internat. Visitors, 1972-77; trustee Hosp. for Sick Children, Washington, 1973-76; editor Washington Antiques Show Catalogue, 1972-75; mem. D.C. Rep. Fin. Com., 1972-75; trustee Meridian House Internat. Ctr., Washington, 1964-82, sec. 1974-75, vice chmn. bd., 1976-82; mem. bd. advisers D.C. Lung Assn., 1975—; active fund-raising drive for Washington Cathedral, 1976; bd. dirs. Washington Home for Incurables, 1976-89, Nat. Eye Found., 1976-78, Children's Hosp. Nat. Rsch. Found., 1978-81, D.C. chpt. ARC, 1976-84, Travelers Aid Soc., 1976-90; chmn. Washington Antiques Show, 1976-78, Washington Cathedral Flower Mart; dir. fin. devel. YWCA of Nat. Capital Area, 1979; vice chmn. Reagan Bush Inaugural, Washington, 1981; mem. transition team for Reagan Bush for NEA, 1981; bd. dirs. Family Stress Services, 1981-84; founder, chmn. Entertaining People, 1982-91; bd. dirs. All Hallows Guild, Washington br. English Speaking Union, 1987-90, Woodrow Wilson House, Washington; chmn. Bush-Quayle Inaugural Ball, 1989; fundraiser Ann. Fund kennedy Ctr. Performing Arts, 1987, 90; v.p. bd. Washington Home, 1990-92; appointed mem. Pres.'s Commn. Arts & Humanities, 1990-91. Mem. Million Dollar Club, Sulgrave Club, Chevy Chase Club. Episcopalian. Avocations: art, design, tennis, opera.

SLOBADIN, STEPHEN, retired foundation executive; b. N.Y.C., July 25, 1918; s. Maxsym and Alexandra (Triuda) S.; m. Elizabeth A. Rogers, Nov. 6, 1976. BA, U. Mich., 1940; MBA, NYU, 1942. Exec. dir. Prescott Neighborhood House, N.Y.C., 1947-58; pres., bd. dirs. Prescott Fund for Children and Youth, Inc., N.Y.C., 1954—; bd. dirs. Day Care Coun. N.Y., N.Y.C., 1947—, v.p., treas., 1973-77; bd. dirs. Christodora Found., N.Y.C., 1983—. Mem. Nat. Arts Club. Republican. Episcopalian. Home: 9 Marigold Ln Somerset NJ 08873-2935 Office: Prescott Fund for Children and Youth Inc 15 Gramercy Park S New York NY 10003

SLOBODIEN, HOWARD DAVID, surgeon; b. Perth Amboy, N.J., July 25, 1923; s. Albert Leo and Anna Frances (Sontag) S.; B.S., Rutgers Coll., 1943; M.D., N.Y.U., 1947; m. Sally Doris Yerkes, May 9, 1950; children—David, Donald, Daniel, Douglas. Intern, Morrisania City Hosp., N.Y.C., 1947-48, resident, 1948-52; practice medicine specializing in surgery, Perth Amboy, 1955—; pres. John F. Kennedy Med. Center, Edison, N.J., 1967-70, dir. surgery, 1975-79; attending surgeon Gen. Hosp., Perth Amboy, dir. surgery, 1970-74; chief gen. surgery, past pres. med. staff Roosevelt Hosp., Edison; cons. surgery Meml. Hosp., South Amboy; clin. asst. prof. surgery Rutgers U. Med. Sch., 1971-84, mem. adv. council Office Consumer Health Edn., 1973-81; mem. adv. council Middlesex County Coll., 1968-78; v.p. Regional Health Facilities Planning Council, 1970-73. Editor N.J. Medicine, 1988—. Pack committeeman Cub Scouts, 1960-64; active steering com. Metuchen YMCA, 1962. Served with USNR, 1943-45, USAF, 1952-54. Diplomate Am. Bd. Surgery. Fellow ACS; mem. AMA, World, Pan-Am. med. assns., N.J. (trustee 1972-84, chmn. pub. relations council 1973-76, pres. 1982-83), Middlesex County (pres. 1970-71) med. socs., Pan-Pacific Surg. Assn., Am. Geriatric Soc., Royal Soc. Health, Am. Acad. Med. Adminstrs., Royal Soc. Medicine, N.J. Acad. Medicine (trustee 1974-78), Middlesex County Med. Assts. Assn. (county med. adviser 1973-80), N.J. Soc. Surgeons, Phi Beta Kappa. Clubs: Metuchen Country, Innisbrook. Home: 34 Linden Ave Metuchen NJ 08840-1418 Office: 500 Lawrie St Perth Amboy NJ 08861-3090

SLOCHOWER, JOYCE ANNE, psychologist, psychoanalyst, educator; b. N.Y.C., May 6, 1950; d. Harry and Muriel (Zimmerman) S.; m. Bruce Rodin, July 20, 1975; children: Jesse, Alison, Avi. Student, Clark U., 1968-70; BA, NYU, 1970-72; PhD, Columbia U., 1975. Cert. psychoanalyst, N.Y. Asst. prof. psychology Hunter Coll. CUNY, 1975-82, assoc. prof. Hunter Coll., 1982—; pvt. practice N.Y.C., 1976—; supr. Nat. Inst. for Psychotherapies, 1991—; pvt. practice, N.Y.C., 1976—. Author: Excessive Eating, 1983; contbr. numerous articles to profl. jours. NIMH grantee, 1980-82, CUNY grantee, 1981-83. Mem. APA, Eastern Psychol. Assn., N.Y. Psychol. Assn., NYU Postdoctoral Soc., Phi Beta Kappa. Jewish. Home and Office: 15 W 75th St New York NY 10023

SLOCUM, ROBERT BIGNEY, retired librarian; b. Brockton, Mass., Apr. 6, 1922; s. George Wheaton and Florence Alice (Heustis) S.; m. Christine Stanfield, Aug. 23, 1953; children: Robert Stanfield, Kathryn Slocum Goodwin. BA, Boston U., 1946; MA, Columbia U., 1947; BS in Libr. Sci., Simmons Coll., 1949. Libr. intern Libr. of Congress, Washington, 1949-50; asst. to dir. librs. Simmons Coll., Boston, 1950-51; libr. cataloger, instr. U. Ill. Libr., Urbana, 1951-54; assoc. catalog libr. Cornell U. Libr., Ithaca, N.Y., 1954-88. Author: Sample Catalog Cards, 1962, Biographical Dictionaries and Related Works, 1967, rev. edit. 1986, Sample Cataloging Forms, 1968, rev. edit. 1980; editor Manual of Cataloging Procedures, 1959, rev. edit. 1969; contbr. articles to profl. jours. With U.S. Army, 1942-45, ETO. Mem. AAUP, Am. Libr. Assn., Am. Hist. Assn., Common Cause, Smithsonian Assocs., Dryden Hist. Soc., Sane/Freeze. Democrat. Presbyterian. Home: 92 W Main St Dryden NY 13053-9706

SLOCUM, RUSSELL HUNTINGTON, advertising executive; b. N.Y.C., June 10, 1949; s. Herrick Huntington and Helen Marjorie (Henderson) S.; m. Ann Hippensteel, Oct. 7, 1972; 1 child, Matthew Huntington. BA in English, BA in Art, Lycoming Coll., 1971. Copywriter, artist Prentice-Hall, Englewood Cliffs, N.J., 1971-72; copywriter Ted Black Advt. Co., Reading, Pa., 1972-75; freelance writer Reading, 1975-76; v.p. Arnold Advt., Reading, 1976-85; pres. Slocum Advt., Reading, 1985-88; ptnr. Slocum/Blatt Advt., Fleetwood, Pa., 1988—; instr. Albright Coll., Office of Continuing Edn., Reading, 1983-85; ptnr. Photolith Graphics Co., Fleetwood, 1990—, Max Grafix, Fleetwood, 1990—. Co-author: (real estate manual) How to Get Top Dollar For Your Home, 1991; contbr. articles to consumer mags. and profl. jours. Home: 2610 Hollywood Ct Reading PA 19606-2127 Office: Slocum/Blatt Advt 1 S Franklin St Fleetwood PA 19522-1612

SLONEM, HUNT, artist; b. Kittery, Maine, July 18, 1951; s. Charles and Louise W. Slonem. Student, Skowhegan Sch. Painting and Sculpture, 1972; BA, Tulane U., 1973. Numerous one-man shows, 1977—, including Tilden-Foley Gallery, New Orleans, 1991, Helander Gallery, N.Y.C., 1991, Charlotte Milburn Fine Art Mus., Oslo, 1991, Pulitzer Gallery, Amsterdam, 1991, Witteveen Gallery, Amsterdam, 1991, numerous others; exhibited in numerous group shows, 1977—, including Laguna Gloria Mus., Austin, Tex., 1990, Bergen Mus. Art & Sci., Paramus, N.J., 1990, Meredith Long Gallery, Houston, 1990, Ctr. for Religion and Art, Washington, 1991, N.Y. Acad. Art, 1991, Delgado U., New Orleans, 1991, numerous others; represented in numerous permanent collections including Met. Mus. Art, N.Y.C., Contemporary Mus., Honolulu, Chrysler Mus., Norfolk, Va., Columbus (Ohio) Mus. Art, Oklahoma Art Ctr., Oklahoma City, Portland (Maine) Mus. Art, Wichita (Kans.) Art Mus., many others. McDowell fellow, 1983, 84, 86, Ragsdale Found. fellow, 1983; Elizabeth T. Greenshields Found. grantee, 1976, NEA grantee, 1991; recipient award Millay Colony, 1982. Home and Studio: 87 E Houston New York NY 10012

SLOSBERG, MYLES JOSEPH, prosecutor; b. Cambridge, Mass., Jan. 29, 1937; s. Charles and Mildred Harriet (Dizon) S.; m. Joyce Gail Shemin, Aug. 28, 1960; children: John, Jessica, Thomas. BA, Dartmouth Coll., 1958, MBA, 1959; JD, Harvard Law Sch., 1989. Bar: Mass. 1989. Exec. v.p. Stride Rite Corp., Cambridge, 1959-71, pres., 1971-74; pres. Stride Rite Footwear, Cambridge, 1974-80, Keds Corp., Cambridge, 1980-85, Stride Rite Internat. Corp., Cambridge, 1985-86; law clk. U.S. Dist. Ct., Boston, 1989-90; assoc. Stoneman, Chandler & Miller, Boston, 1990-91; asst. atty. gen. Office of Atty. Gen., Boston, 1991—; bd. dirs. Stride Rite Corp., 1962—. Mem. ABA, Mass. Bar Assn., Boston Bar Assn. Home: 145 Monadnock Rd Chestnut Hill MA 02167 Office: Office of Atty Gen 1 Ashburn Pl Boston MA 02108

SLOT, LARRY LEE, molecular biologist; b. Grand Rapids, Mich., Nov. 8, 1947; s. Russell Lee and Vivian June (Wolfert) S.; m. Pamela Chronis, Nov. 25, 1948; children: Franchot, Jason, Lara. AS, Grand Rapids Jr. Coll., 1971; BS, Mich. State U., 1982. Pub. Grand Rapids Interpreter, Mich., 1971-75; bush pilot Palacios, Honduras, 1978-80; pres. Genemsco Corp., Kingston, Mass., 1984—. Sculpture include The Pontibus, 1986; inventor in field; designer, mfr. first Tandem Cortege horizontal gel electrophoresis system; designer over 90 different mutant clones of the Moloney Leukemia Virus; creator, copywriter (cell cloning and gene splicing module) The Dr. Cloner's Genetic Engineering Home Cloning Kit, 1984; designer, builder molecular-level structural models of sea water carbonate and silicate crystals impregnated in fibrous proteins of conchiolin; researcher of biological structures, processes and functions associated with the production of carbonate-silicate-impregnated fibrous proteins. With USMC, 1966-69. NSF fellow, 1982. Mem. AAAS, Am. Soc. Microbiology, Airplane Owners and Pilots Assn., Pontibus Soc. (founder 1986, pres. 1986-87), Golden Key Soc., Phi Kappa Phi. Home: 10 Braintree Ave Kingston MA 02364-1714 Office: Genemsco Corp Genemsco Beach Kingston MA 02364-1714

SLOWICK, DANIEL WILLIAM, fire and explosion investigator, detective; b. Ware, Mass., Apr. 21, 1952; s. Albert William and Mary Alice (Szado) S. AS in Fire Sci., Springfield Tech. Coll., 1974; BS in Fire Sci. and Adminstrn., John Jay Coll., 1976. Structural firefighter Palmer (Mass.) Fire Dist. 1, 1969-76; sales mgr., svc. rep. Fire Fighting Equipment Ltd., Palmer, 1970-74; dir. fire sci. State of S.C., Columbia, 1976-78; staff analyst fire loss control Nationwide Mut. Ins. Co., Columbus, Ohio, 1978-79; fire and explosion investigator Connell Consultants Ltd., Great Neck, N.Y., 1979-81; pres. Fire Sci. Techs., Inc., Palmer, 1981—; cons. S.C. Fire Adv. Bd., Columbia, 1977-78, Franklin County Sheriff's Dept., Columbus, 1978-79; instr. Minutemen Fire Vols., Inc., Ware, 1973-76; assoc. prof. Midlands Tech. Coll., Columbia, 1976-78. Ch. organist, choir dir. Mem. Coun. Internat. Investigators (sec.-treas. 1989—, Internat. Investigator of Yr. 1991), Nat. Fire Protection Assn., Internat. Assn. Arson Investigators, Inst. Profl. Investigators, Downtown Palmer Assn., Quaboag Valley C. of C. (bd. dirs. 1981-89). Home: 12 Pleasant St Palmer MA 01069 Office: Fire Sci Techs Inc PO Box 149 Palmer MA 01069-0149

SLUD, ERIC VICTOR, mathematics educator; b. Buffalo, N.Y., Feb. 8, 1953; s. Maurice Howard and Frances Dorothy (Ferris) S.; m. Lynne Judy Levy, July 14, 1978; children: Francesca, Natalie. BA, Harvard U., 1972; PhD, MIT, 1976. From asst. prof. to assoc. prof. U. Md., College Park, 1976-89, prof., 1989—, dir. statistics, 1989—; statistician Info. Mgmt. Svcs., Inc., Rockville, Md., 1984—; vis. asst. prof. N.Mex. State U., Las Cruces, 1975-76; cons. NASA/Goddard, Greenbelt, Md., 1979-81. Contbr. over 30 articles to profl. jours. Grantee Air Force Office Sci. Rsch., 1979-80, 82-83, Office of Naval Rsch., 1985—. Mem. Am. Statis. Soc., Am. Math. Soc., Inst. Math. Statistics, Biometric Soc. Office: U Md Dept Math College Park MD 20742

SLURZBERG, ELIHU (LEE SLURZBERG), marketing professional; b. Newark, Mar. 22, 1929; s. Herman Harry and Mildred (Nemhauser) S.; m. Nancy Hope Miller, Dec. 30, 1956; children: Michael, Wendy. BS, NYU, 1952, MBA, 1956. Dir. mktg. services J.B. Williams Co., N.Y.C., 1962-65; v.p. div. direct survey Audits & Survey Inc., N.Y.C., 1965-68; exec. v.p., chief exec. officer Alfred Politz Research div. Computer Scis. Corp., N.Y.C., 1968-70; pres. Lee Slurzberg Research, Ft. Lee, N.Y., 1970—; adj. instr. mktg. Baruch Coll. CUNY, 1972-75. Contbr. articles to profl. jours. Named Outstanding Young Man of Yr. Jaycees, Englewood, N.J., 1963. Mem. Am. Mktg. Assn., Pharm. Advt. Club, Delta Pi Sigma. Jewish. Home: 379 Windsor Rd Englewood NJ 07631-1424 Office: 158 Linwood Plz Fort Lee NJ 07024-3704

SLUSSER, EUGENE ALVIN, electronics manufacturing executive; b. Denver, Mar. 13, 1922; s. Jesse Alvin and Grace (Carter) S.; m. Anne L. Longley, Oct. 2, 1943; children: Robert, Jon, Carolyn. BS in Physics, U. Denver, 1947. Registered profl. engr., N.H. Staff mem. MIT Radiation

Lab., Cambridge, 1942-45; project engr. Heiland Research Co., Denver, 1945-47; cons. Gen. Telephone System, N.Y.C., 1947-51; project engr. Airborne Inst. Lab., Mineola, N.Y., 1951-53; v.p. N.E. Electronics Corp., Concord, N.H., 1953-58; pres. Aerotronic Assocs., Inc., Contoocook, N.H., 1958-84, N.H. Automatic Equipment Corp., Concord, 1962-90, N.H. Realty Corp, 1990—, E.A. Slusser & Assocs., Concord. Patentee electronics field. Chmn. Hopkinton (N.H.) Water Bd., 1962-69, Hopkinton Planning Bd., 1971-77, Hopkinton Precinct Bd. Adjustment, 1977. Mem. Aircraft Owners and Pilots Assn. Lodge: Masons (32 degree). Home: RFD-5 Box 254 Hopkinton Village NH 03229 Office: 16 Centre St Concord NH 03301-6302

SLUTZKY, JACK, communications educator; b. N.Y.C., May 20, 1937; s. Samuel Morris and Lillian (Laner) S.; m. Adriana Ippel, Aug. 25, 1990; children: Stuart, Cathy, Helena, Bill, Elizabeth. BA, Bradley U., Peoria, Ill., 1959; MFA, UCLA, 1961, PhD, 1963. Animator Walt Disney Prodns., Burbank, Calif., 1959-60; producer Charisma Prodns., N.Y.C., 1965; prin. Miller/Slutzky Assocs., N.Y.C., 1965-67; pres., creative dir. Stewart, Adams and Bartell, N.Y.C., 1967-69; prin. Meta Imaging Assocs., Rochester, N.Y., 1990-91; prof. Rochester Inst. Tech./Nat. Tech. Inst. for Deaf, 1969—; cons. in field; vis. prof. Universidad Metro. Autonoma, Mexico City, 1988. Named Outstanding Tchr. of the Yr., Rochester Inst. Tech., 1982; named Citizen of the Yr., Kiwanis, 1983. Mem. Nat. Assn. Neuro Linguistic Programming, Arts for Greater Rochester, Ky. Cols. Home: 53 Clio St Rochester NY 14612-2045 Office: Rochester Inst Tech One Lomb Meml Dr Rochester NY 14623

SLUTZKY, RICHARD OWEN, endowment administrator; b. Omaha, May 11, 1956; s. Ben and Charlotte (Nogg) L.; m. Alyson Wolens, June 14, 1981; children: Diane Rebecca, Beth Michelle. AB in Urban Studies, Washington U., St. Louis, 1978; JD, Emory U., 1981. Dir. Jewish Community Found. of MetroWest, N.J., East Orange; bd. dirs. Congregation Oheb Shalom. NSF grantee, 1976; Sherman fellow, Brandeis U., 1990. Mem. Planned Giving Group of Greater N.Y., Assn. of Jewish Communal Profls., Coun. of Jewish Fedns. (endowment adv. coun.), Unity Club. Office: Jewish Community Found 901 Rte 10 Whippany NJ 07981

SLY, JOHN EUGENE, advertising and marketing consultant; b. N.Y.C., Feb. 14, 1917; s. Frederick Sanford and Alberta Belle (Coy) S.; m. Ethel Elizabeth Weldon, May 22, 1943; children: John E. Jr., Warren F. AB in Econs., Cornell U., 1938; cert. in Engring., N.C. State U., 1943. Salesman Diamond Match Co., N.Y.C., 1939-40; info. specialist Ea. State Farmers Exchange, West Springfield, Mass., 1940-41; asst. dir. info. svcs. So. States Coop., Richmond, Va., 1946; various positions to mktg. communications mgr. Du Pont Co., Wilmington, Del., 1946-81; pres. The John Sly Group, Inc., Wilmington, 1983-91; advt. and mktg. cons., Wilmington, 1991—; exec. dir. Del. Com. for Effective Justice, 1982; pres. Ea. Indsl. Advertisers, Phila., 1958-60; dir. Tech. and Mgmt. Svcs., U. Del., Newark, 1983-87. Dir. Arthritis Found. Del., Wilmington, 1986—. Lt. comdr. USNR, 1941-45, ATO, 1950-52, Korea. Mem. Greenville Country Club (pres. 1968-69), Du Pont Country Club. Republican. Presbyterian. Home: 4031 Kennett Pike Wilmington DE 19807-2032

SLYTER, LEONARD LEROY, microbiologist; b. Fontana, Kans., Nov. 13, 1933; s. Elmer Jess and Anna Dorothea (Rodewald) S.; m. Dolores Jean Reifel, Sept. 6, 1958; children: Susan Lynn, Sandra Jean. BS in Dairy Prodn. Agr., Kans. State U., 1955; MS in Agr., U. Mo., 1958; PhD in Nutrition, N.C. State U., 1963. Rsch. asst. U. Mo., Columbia, 1957-58; resident asst. N.C. State U., Raleigh, 1959-62; rsch. assoc. U. Ill., Urbana, 1963-64; rsch. chemist Agrl. Rsch. Svc., USDA, Beltsville, Md., 1965-78, microbiologist, 1979—; coop. scientist Office Internat. Coop. and Devel., New Delhi, 1986-91, dept. animal sci. and agrl. biochemistry U. Del., Newark, 1988-90, Colo. State U., Ft. Collins, 1974-76. Contbr. articles to profl. publs. 1st lt. U.S. Army, 1955-57. Flood fellow, 1951-52. Mem. Am. Soc. Microbiology, Am. Soc. Animal Sci. Republican. Lutheran. Office: USDA Agrl Rsch Svc Bldg 200 Rm 123 BARC-EAST Beltsville MD 20705

SMAHA, FRANCIS WALTER, pension consultant; b. Springfield, Mass., July 19, 1959; s. Walter and Phyllis (Goodwin) S. BA, St. Anselm Coll., 1981; MBA, Babson Coll., 1990. Cert. employee benefit specialist. Plan cost analyst John Hancock Mutual Life Ins. Co., Boston, 1981-84, pension underwriter, 1984-86; pension analyst Hills Dept. Stores, Canton, Mass., 1986-89; pension cons. Bank of Boston, 1990—; mem. MBA coun. Babson Coll. Vol. John Glenn for Pres., Boston, 1984, John Kerry for Senate, Boston, 1984. Office: Bank of Boston 100 Federal St Boston MA 02110-1802

SMAHA, JOSEPH JOHN, therapist; b. Manhattan, N.Y., May 17, 1951; s. Joseph and Celestine (Repetti) S.; m. Pamela Naomi Eckler, June 29, 1974; children: Jeremiah Joseph, Timothy Daniel, Jonathan David. BS magna cum laude, Nyack Coll., 1978; MEd, Cambridge Coll., Mass., 1989. Ordained to ministry Christian and Missionary Alliance Ch., 1980. Assoc. pastor Hope Alliance Ch., Utica, N.Y., 1978-82; pastor Christian & Missionary Alliance Ch. of Laconia (N.H.), 1982-86; house coord. Northshore Assn. Retarded Citizens, Beverly, Mass., 1987-88; rehab. counselor Northshore Assn. Retarded Citizens, Danvers, Mass., 1988-89; counselor, outreach dir. Good News Christian Counseling Ctr., Swanzey, N.H., 1989—; clin. mgr. Beech Hill Hosp., Dublin, N.H., 1989-91; clin. coord. Mentor Clin. Care, Keene, N.H., 1991—; cons. Hennesey Human Svcs. Specialists, Beverly, 1988-89; field svc. rep. Christian & Missionary Alliance Nat. Office, Nyack, 1980-82. Family advocate Vols. in Protective Svcs., Laconia, 1985-86; group leader Parents Annonymous, Laconia, 1985-86; chmn. Christian Edn. Com. of C&MA, New Eng. Dist., 1985-86; bd. dirs. Lakes Region Mental Health Ctr., Laconia, 1986. Recipient N.H. Gov.'s award for Vol. Svcs., 1985, 86. Mem. Am. Assn. Counseling & Devel., Nat. Assn. Drug and Alcohol Counselors, Assn. for Religious and Value Issues in Counseling. Democrat. Christian & Missionary Alliance. Home: 238 Base Hill Rd Keene NH 03431-5914

SMALDONE, EDWARD MICHAEL, composer; b. Wantagh, N.Y., Nov. 19, 1956; m. Karen Ajamian, Aug. 5, 1979; children: Laura, Gregory. PhD in Music, CUNY, 1986. Lectr. SUNY, Purchase, 1986-90; adj. asst. prof. Hofstra U., Hempstead, N.Y., 1988-90; vis. asst. prof. New Sch. for Social Rsch., N.Y.C., 1988; adminstrv. dir. Speculum Musicae, N.Y.C., 1988-89; artistic dir. Sounds for the Left Bank, Rego Park, N.Y., 1985—; asst. prof. Copland Sch. of Music, CUNY, Flushing, 1990—. Composer in field. Recipient Standard award ASCAP, 1986—, Creative Incentive award CUNY Rsch. Found., 1992; recipient Residency fellowship Yaddo Corp., 1986, 87, Composer's fellowship Charles Ives Ctr. for Am. Music, 1990. Home: 228 Manhasset Ave Manhasset NY 11030 Office: Copland Sch of Music Queens Coll Flushing NY 11030

SMALDONE, GERALD CHRISTOPHER, physiologist; b. N.Y.C., Sept. 1, 1947; s. Gerald J. and Theresa (Petrolino) S.; m. Arlene Merne, July 29, 1972; children: Marc, Lauren. BSChE, NYU, 1969, MD, PhD, 1975. Intern, resident Strong Meml. Hosp. U. Rochester, N.Y., 1975-77; fellow in medicine Johns Hopkins U., Balt., 1977-80, fellow in environ. health sci., 1977-80; asst. prof. medicine, physiology and biophysics SUNY, Stony Brook, 1980-86, assoc. prof., 1986—; cons. to pvt. industry and govt., 1988—. Contbr. articles to profl. jours.: editor: Jour. Aerosol Medicine, 1987—. Mem. Internat. Soc. for Aerosols in Medicine (bd. dirs. 1991—). Office: SUNY Pulmonary Critical Care Div HSC T-17040 Stony Brook NY 11794-8172

SMALKIN, FREDERIC N., judge. BA, Johns Hopkins U., 1968; JD, U. Maryland, 1971. Pvt. practice Monkton, Md., 1976; magistrate U.S. Dist. Ct. Md., Balt., 1976-86, judge, 1986—; lectr. comml. law U. Md., Balt., 1978—, SMH bar rev., Balt., 1985-86, BRI/Modern Bar Rev. Course, Inc., Balt., 1980-81; faculty MICPEL, Va. Trial Advocacy Inst., 1982—; panel speaker on Utilization of Magistrates at the 1985 fourth cir, Judicial Conf. Capt. U.S. Army, 1968-76. Mem. Fed. Bar Assn., Order of Coif, Phi Beta Kappa. Office: US Dist Ct 101 W Lombard St Baltimore MD 21201-2626

SMALL, KENNETH LAWRENCE, chemical technician, researcher; b. Wilmington, Del., Mar. 14, 1941; s. Alfred Gabriel and Mae (Orchow) S.; m. Patricia Anne Dombal, July 2, 1965; children: Naomi, Rebecca, Kim-Su. Student, Fairleigh Dickinson U., 1962-65. Rsch. technician Rohm and Haas Co., Springhouse, Pa., 1969—. Sch. dir. Upper Perkiomen Sch. Dist., East Greenville, Pa., 1981—; mem. East Greenville Zoning Bd., 1980-81, East Greenville Borough Coun., 1981; sch. dir., officer Montgomery County Intermediate Unit, Erdenheim, Pa., 1982—. Fellow Inst. Devel. Ednl. Activities. Republican. Home: 313 Blaker Dr East Greenville PA 18041

SMALL, PARKER ADAMS, III, investment banker; b. Phila., Feb. 1, 1958; s. Parker Adams Jr. and Natalie (Settimelli) S.; m. Katherine Currier, Aug. 24, 1985; children: Margaret Edmea, Elizabeth Parker. BA, Dartmouth Coll., 1980; MBA, Harvard U., 1985. Account exec. Leo Burnett Advt., Chgo., 1980-83; assoc. Merrill Lynch-Becker Paribas, N.Y.C., 1984; product mgmt. The Gillette Co., Boston, 1985-86; mgmt. cons. Arthur D. Little Inc., Cambridge, Mass., 1986-89; v.p. Butler Capital Corp., N.Y.C., 1989—; pres. S.R.S. Sera Co., Gainesville, Fla., 1976—; bd. dirs. Julius Koch USA Inc., Strine Printing Co., Lancaster Press Inc.; reunion chmn. Dartmouth Coll., 1990. Author: Understanding Immunology, 1976; producer Dartmouth Coll. video, 1980. Home: 11 Westwood Rd New York NY 02181 Office: Butler Capital Corp 767 5th Ave New York NY 10153-0002

SMALL, SARAH MAE, volunteer; b. Salisbury, N.C., Nov. 16, 1923; d. Clint and Lillie Mae (Wilbourn) Evans; m. Jesse Small Sr., May 4, 1941; children: Jesse Jr., Jean Carol Small Bell. Cert., Cortez Bus. Sch., 1948. File clk. gen. acctg. office Fed. Govt., Washington, 1941-47; sec., stenographer CIA, Washington, 1948-52; adminstrv. asst. CIA, McLean, Va., 1952-65; ret. CIA, 1965. Pres. Youth Triumph Ch., Washington, Md., S.C. and Ga., 1965-76; bd. dirs. ARC, Washington, 1986-87; mem. adv. bd. D.C. Gen. Hosp., 1985-86; bd. dirs. Children's Edn. Found., Inc., 1989—. Recipient Outstanding and Dedicated Vol. Svc. award Kiwanis Club of Capital Centre, 1985, Plaque in Recognition of Dedicated and Outstanding Vol. Svc. to the Corps and Washington D.C., Community Jr. Citizen's Corps., 1989, Appreciation award for Outstanding and Dedicated Vol. Svc. to Corps, Jr. Citizens Corps., Inc., 1990, Appreciation award Jr. Citizens Corp., Inc., 1990, Community Svc. award for leadership and youth advocacy Bus. and Profl. Women's League, Inc., 1991, others. Mem. Jr. Citizens Corps (life, pres. 1985—, Dedicated Community Svc. award 1983, Bus. and Community Svc. award 1986), Bus. and Profl. Women's League (treas. 1982-86), Women in Arts (chartered, pres. 1984—), Nat. Coun. Negro Women, World Affairs Coun. Washington, Agrl. Coun. Am., Exec. Travel Club Riverdale. Democrat. Baptist. Home: 2010 Upshur St NE Washington DC 20018-3244

SMALLACOMBE, ROBERT JOSEPH, company executive; b. West Chazy, N.Y., May 26, 1933; s. Bert Henry and Flossie Jean (Relation) S.; children: Daniel M., Melissa J., Margaret M., James F., Andrew B. BS, SUNY, Plattsburgh, 1960. Foreman composing room Plattsburgh Press-Rep., 1953-60; asst. mgr. prodn. Wall Street Jour. subs. Dow Jones & Co., Mass., Ill., 1960-64; dir. prodn. Washington Daily News, 1964-68; pres. MILGO/IDAB, Miami, Fla. and East Patterson, N.J., 1968-71, Tal-Star Computer Systems, Princeton Junction, N.J., 1971-79; pres., ptnr. Ferag, Inc., Bristol, Pa., 1979-80; pres., chmn. bd. Delta Data Systems Corp., Trevose, Pa., 1981-86; pres., founder Exec. Intervention, Inc., Pennington, N.J., 1986—; pres., chief exec. officer Applied Packaging Tech., Vineland, N.J., 1989-91; bd. dir. Emons Industries Inc., York, Pa., Quipp Inc., Miami, Fla., Tech. Mktg. Inc., Irvine, Calif., Cardinal Pub., Inc., Pennington, N.J. Trustee Am. Boychoir Sch., Princeton, N.J., 1979-80, Solebury (Pa.) Sch., 1985. Served with USMC, 1951-53, Korea. Mem. Nat. Assn. Corp. Dirs. (adv. com. small bus.), World Bus. Coun., Phila. Pres.'s Orgn., Am. Inst. Indsl. Engrs., Confrerie de la Chaine des Rotisseurs, Les Amis d'Escoffier. Republican. Roman Catholic. Home: 423 Lawrenceville Rd Apt 415 Lawrenceville NJ 08648 Office: Exec Intervention Inc PO Box 732 Pennington NJ 08534-0732

SMALLEY, CHRISTOPHER JOSEPH, pharmaceutical company professional; b. Phila., June 26, 1953; s. Charles Wilfred and Verna May (Coulter) S.; m. Maria Visniskie, Aug. 7, 1974; children: Christa Maria, Mark Charles. BS, Phila. Coll. Pharmacy and Sci., 1976; MBA, Temple U., 1982; PhD, LaSalle U., 1991. Mfg. pharmacist supr. McNeil Labs., Fort Washington, Pa., 1976-77; mfg. pharmacist group supr. McNeil Consumer Products Co., 1978-79, mfg. pharmacist mgr., 1980-85; tech. svcs. mgr. Janssen Pharmaceutica, 1985-88, plant mgr., 1988—. Mem. Rep. Nat. Com., 1979—. With the USNR Med. Corps., 1986—. Mem. Am. Pharm. Assn., Assn. Mil. Surgeons of U.S., Am. Assn. Pharm. Scientists, Internat. Soc. Pharm. Engrs., Aerospace Med. Assn., Am. Acad. Med. Adminstrs., Naval Res. Assn., Assn. Med. Svc. Corps Officers, Pa. Pharm. Assn., Inst. Environ. Scis., Eastern Assn. GMP Trainers, Parenteral Drug Assn. (tng. com.), Pharm. Mfrs. Assn. (prodn. section), Phila. Pharm. Forum, USn Inst., Am. Numismatic Assn., NRA, Kappa Psi. Presbyterian. Home: 421 Drayton Rd Oreland PA 19075-2010 Office: McNeil Consumer Products Co Camp Hill Rd Fort Washington PA 19034-2902

SMALLEY, JAMES CARL, photographer, producer; b. Little Rock, Oct. 7, 1947; s. Carl Steward and Lorene Gertrude (Cloninger) S.; m. Teresa Jo Nix, Aug. 9, 1968; children: Jana Leigh, Jennifer Anne. AS, So. Ark. U., Camden, 1978; BS in Edn., U. Ark., 1969. Tchr. Rogers (Ark.) Pub. Schs., 1969-76; asst. dir. Ark. Fire Tng. Acad., Camden, 1976-78, acting dir., 1978-79; fire edn. specialist U.S. Fire Adminstrn., Washington, 197982; dir. communications tech. Nat. Fire Protection Assn., Quincy, Mass., 1982—; cons. Pvt. Satellite Network, N.Y.C., 1990; dir. ub. Svc. Satellite Consortium, Washington, 1986-89. Author: Funding Sources for Fire Departments, 1983; contbr. articles to profl. jours.; producer over 24 video programs. Recipient Meritorious Svc. award, Fed. Emergency Mgmt. Agy., Washington, 1982. Mem. Am. Soc. Mag. Photographers, Soc. Fire Protection Engrs. Episcopalian. Home: 7 Jackson Rd Scituate MA 02066-4703 Office: Nat Fire Protection Assn Batterymarch Park Quincy MA 02169-7452

SMALLWOOD, GENEVIEVE CHARLENE, rail transportation executive, information systems specialist; b. Gauley Bridge, W.Va., Jan. 6, 1942; d. Charles Walker and Genevieve (Jones) S. BS in Math., W.Va. Inst. Tech., 1964; diploma in mgmt. studies, Ins. Inst. Am., 1971; diploma in organizational behavior, U. Hartford, 1978. Cert. Data Processor. From trainee programmer to systems engr. Ins. Co. N.Am., Phila., 1964-69, asst. dir. MIS, 1969-73; mgr. applications programming Xerox Corp., Rochester, N.Y., 1973-76; asst. dir. data processing strategic planning The Hartford (Conn.) Ins. Group subs. ITT, 1976-80, dir. human resources devel., 1980-82; mgr. Griffin Office Ctr. The Hartford Ins. Group subs. ITT, Windsor, Conn., 1982-83; dir. orgn. planning The Hartford (Conn.) Ins. Group subs. ITT, 1983-86; systems devel. mgr. AGS Info. Svcs., Inc., Wappingers Falls, N.Y., 1986-87; asst. dir. info. resource mgmt. The L.I. R.R., Jamaica, N.Y., 1987—; speaker, lectr. U. Hartford, 1980-84, Clark Coll., Atlanta, 1980-84, Howard U., Washington, 1980-84, others; seminar facilitator Urban League of Hartford, 1981-83; mem. State of Conn. Video Display Terminal Task Force, Hartford, 1981-83. Bd. dirs, exec. com., v.p. Better Bus. Bur., Hartford, 1980-85; tutor, supr. Literacy Vols. Am., Hartford, 1981-83; bd. dirs. Jr. Achievement North Cen. Conn., Hartford, 1983-85, Community Coun. for the Capitol Region, Hartford, 1985-86. Named Alumnus of Yr. W.Va. Inst. Tech., 1985. Mem. Data Processing Mgmt. Assn., Conf. Minority Transp. Ofcls., W.Va. Inst. Tech. Alumni Assn. (bd. dirs. 1979-81), Order Ea. Star (sec. Stella chpt. 16, 1982-84), Daus. of Isis. Baptist. Office: The LI RR 14802 Archer Ave Jamaica NY 11435-4379

SMALLWOOD, ROBERT ALBIAN, JR., teacher; b. Phila., Oct. 3, 1946; s. Robert Albian and Mildred May (Miller) S.; BSC, Rider Coll., 1969, MA, 1976; EdS, Rutgers U., 1986; m. Geraldine Ann Boozan, May 27, 1972; children: Amy Lynn, Daniel James. Cert. social studies tchr., secondary sch. prin., supr. curriculum and instrn., Pa.; cert. social studies and gen. bus. tchr., prin., supr., sch. bus. adminstr.; asst. supt. bus., sch. adminstr. (supt.) N.J. Tchr. social studies Trenton Bd. Edn., 1973-76, tchr. bus. edn., 1975-76, sch. disciplinarian, 1976-84, acting asst. prin. Jr. High Sch. 2, 1980-83, tchr. U.S. history, 1983-87, chmn. social studies dept., 1984-85; acting asst. prin. Carroll Robbins Elem. Sch., Jr. High Sch. #1, Jr. High Sch. #5, 1987-88; tchr. gifted and talented social studies Dunn Jr. High Sch., 1989—. Mem. Dist.'s Affirmative Action Adv. Council; mem. Nat. Tchr. Corps Project, Trenton Area. Asst. ops. officer Trenton CD Unit, 1974-76, asst. disaster analysis officer, 1976, disaster analysis officer, 1976-79; trustee N.J. Council for Alcohol/Drug Edn., 1983—, mem. exec. com., 1985—, chmn. nominating com., 1985, 86, treas. 1987—; chmn. membership com. Hamilton Square Baptist Ch., 1981-82, chmn. Christian edn. com., 1982-85, supt. ch. sch., 1982-85, vice chmn. exec. bd., 1981-85, chmn., 1985-89. Served with U.S. Army, 1969-72. Decorated Bronze Star medal, Army Commendation medal with oak leaf cluster, Joint Service Commendation medal. Mem. NEA, Nat. Council Social Studies, Vietnam Vets. Am., Am. Legion, Nat. Bus. Edn. Assn., Va. Geneal. Soc., Md. Geneal. Soc., Md. Hist. Soc., Geneal. Soc. Pa., Nat. Geneal. Soc., Phi Delta Kappa. Home: 2 Leese Ave Trenton NJ 08609-1828

SMARDON, RICHARD CLAY, landscape architecture/environ studies educator; b. Burlington, Vt., May 13, 1948; s. Philip Albert and Louise Gertrude (Peters) S.; m. Anne Marie Graveline, Aug. 19, 1973; children: Regina Elizabeth, Andrea May. BS cum laude, U. Mass., 1970, MLA, 1973; PhD in Environ. Planning, U. Calif., Berkeley, 1982. Environ. planner, landscape architect Wallace, Floyd, Ellenzweig, Inc., Cambridge, Mass., 1972-73; assoc. planner Exec. Office Environ. Affairs, State of Mass., Boston, 1973-75; environ. impact assessment specialist USDA extension svc. Oreg. State U., Corvallis, 1975-76; landscape architect USDA Pacific S.W. Forest and Range Expt. Sta., Berkeley, 1977; rsch. landscape architect U. Calif., Berkeley, 1977-79; prof. landscape architecture, sr. rsch. assoc. SUNY Coll. Environ. Sci. and Forestry, Syracuse, 1979-86, prof. environ. studies, 1987—, dir. Inst. for Environ. Policy and Planning, 1979-89; co-dir. Gt. Lakes Rsch. Consortium, Syracuse, 1986—; guest lectr. numerous univs.; adj. asst. prof. U. Mass., Amherst, 1974-75; Sea Grant trainee Inst. for Urban and Regional Devel., Berkeley, 1976; condr., presenter numerous seminars and workshops; cons. to numerous orgns.; mem. com. on environ. design and landscape Transp. Rsch. Bd.-NAS, 1985; mem. tech. adv. bd. Wetlands Rsch., Inc., Chgo., 1985; mem. adv. bd. Wetlands Fund, N.Y., 1985; v.p. Integrated Site Inc., Syracuse. Co-editor: Out National Landscape, 1979, spl. issue Coastal Zone Mgmt. Jour., 1982, The Future of Wetlands, 1983, Foundations for Visual Project Analysis, 1985, The Legal Landscape, 1992; mem. editorial bd. Northeastern Environ. Sci. Jour., 1981, Landscape and Urban Planning, 1991; contbr. more that 100 articles to profl. jours. Bd. dirs. Sackets Harbor Area Hist. Preservation Found., Watertown, N.Y., 1984—; pres. Save the County, Inc., Fayetteville, N.Y., 1986-88; appointed to Great Lakes (N.Y.) Adv. Commn.. N.Y. Recipient Beatrice Farrand award U. Calif., 1979, Am. Soc. Landscape Architects awrd, 1972. Mem. AAAS, Am. Land Resource Assn. (charter), Internat. Assn. for Impact Assessment, Coastal Soc., Alpha Zeta (life), Sigma Lambda Alpha. Office: SUNY Inst for Environ Policy and Planning Syracuse NY 13210 Office: Integrated Site Inc 886 E Brighton Ave Syracuse NY 13205

SMART, MARY-LEIGH CALL (MRS. J. SCOTT SMART), civic worker; b. Springfield, Ill., Feb. 27, 1917; d. S(amuel) Leigh and Mary (Bradish) Call; m. J. Scott Smart, Sept. 11, 1951 (dec. 1960). Diploma, Monticello Coll., 1934; student, Oxford U., 1935; B.A., Wellesley Coll., 1937; M.A., Columbia U., 1939, postgrad., 1940-41; postgrad., N.Y. U., 1940-41; painting student, with Bernard Karfiol, 1937-38. Dir. mgmt. Cen. Ill. Grain Farms, Logan County, 1939—; owner Lowtrek Kennel, Ogunquit, Maine, 1957-73, Cove Studio Art Gallery, Ogunquit, 1961-68; art collector, patron, publicist, 1954—, cons., 1970—. Editor: Hamilton Easter Field Art Found. Collection Catalog, 1966; originator, dir. show, compiler of catalog Art: Ogunquit, 1967; Peggy Bacon-A Celebration, Barn Gallery, Ogunquit, 1979. Program dir., sec. bd. Barn Gallery Assocs., Inc., 1958-69, pres., 1969-70, 82-87, asst. treas., 1987—, hon. dir., 1970-78; curator Hamilton Easter Field Art Found. Collection, 1978-79, curator exhbns., 1979-86; mem. acquisition com. DeCordova Mus., Lincoln, Mass., 1966-78; mem. chancellor's coun. U. Tex., 1972—, U. N.H., 1978—; bd. dirs. Ogunquit C. of C., 1966, treas. 1966-67, hon. life mem., 1968—; bd. overseers Strawbery Banke, Inc., Portsmouth, N.H., 1972-75, 3d vice chmn., 1973, 2d vice chmn., 1974; bd. advisors Univ. Art Galleries, U. N.H., 1973-89, v.p., bd. overseers, 1974-81, pres., 1981-89; bd. dirs. Old York Hist. and Improvement Soc., York, Maine, 1979-81, v.p., 1981-82; mem. adv. com. Bowdoin Coll. Mus. Art Invitational Exhibit, 1975, '76 Maine Artists Invitational Exhbn., Maine State Mus., Maine Coast Artists, Rockport, 1975-78, All Maine Biennial '79, Bowdoin Coll. Mus. Art juried exhbn.; mem. jury for scholarship awards Maine Com. for the Skowhegan Sch. Painting and Sculpture, 1982-84; mem. nat. com. Wellesley Coll. Friends of Art, 1983—; adv. trustee Portland Mus. Art, 1983-85, fellow, 1985—; mem. mus. panel Maine State Commn. on Arts and Humanities, 1983-86; mem. adv. com. Maine Biennial, Colby Coll. Mus. Art, 1983; mem. coun. advisors Farnsworth Libr. and Art Mus., Rockland, Maine, 1986—; mem. collections com. Payson Gallery, Westbrook Coll., Portland, Maine, 1987-91; dir. Greater Portsmouth Community Found., N.H. Charitable Fund, 1991—; mem. corp. Mus. of Art Ogunquit, 1988-90. Served to lt. jg. WAVES, 1942-45. Recipient Deborah Morton award Westbrook Coll., 1988. Mem. Am. Fedn. Arts, Am. Coun. for Arts, Mus. Modern Art, Springfield Art Assn., Boston Mus. Fine Arts, Solomon R. Guggenheim Mus., Whitney Mus. Am. Art., Jr. League of Springfield, Western Maine Wellesley Club. Republican. Episcopalian. Address: 30 Surf Point Rd York ME 03909

SMETANA, ANDREW FRANK, quality/safety engineer; b. Paterson, N.J., June 1, 1930; s. Andrew A. and Marian (Walls) S.; m. Marilyn Davey, June 30, 1956; children: Regina, Susan, Andrew D., Paul, Catherine, Tracey. BS, Seton Hall U., 1954. Chemist Picatinny arsenal, Dover, N.J., 1955-56; rsch. chemist Rsch. Labs. Picatinny Arsenal, Dover, N.J., 1958-77, quality engr. product assurance, 1977-85; mng. ptnr. Sparta (N.J.) Communications Systems, 1986-89; quality and safety engr. Applied Ordnance Tech., Inc., Sparta, 1989—. contbr. articles to reports and profl. jours. Chmn. Recreation Commn., Wharton, N.J., 1964-77; pres. St. Marys Holy Name Soc., Wharton, 1972, Little League, Wharton, 1975-76. Recipient Appreciation award Wharton Coun., 1975. Mem. Am. Def. and Preparedness Assn., Sigma Xi. Home: 440 Glen Rd Sparta NJ 07871

SMIALEK, THOMAS WALTER, JR., musician, educator; b. Newport, R.I., July 16, 1955; s. Thomas Walter and Beatrice (Botelho) S.; m. Lisa Logrande. BA, Westfield (Mass.) State Coll., 1977; MusM, Northwestern U., 1979; DMA, U. Ga., 1991. Vis. artist N.C. Vis. Artist Program, various cities, 1981-85; lectr. U. Ga., Athens, 1988-89; asst. prof. Pa. State U., Hazleton, 1989—; founder, alto saxophonist Fantasy Duos, N.C., 1981-82; tenor saxophonist Verismo Saxophone Quartet, 1988—. Contbg. editor for articles in profl. jours. Recipient Performance award Saxophone Jour., 1978, 80. Mem. Am. Fedn. Musicians, Coll. Music Soc., North Am. Saxophone Alliance, Pi Kappa Lambda. Roman Catholic. Office: Pa State U High Acres Hazleton PA 18201

SMIDT, SEYMOUR, economics educator; b. Chgo., Nov. 2, 1928; s. Joseph and Harriet (Morrison) S.; m. Rita Barbara Liss, Jan. 28, 1951; children—Tamar Rachelle, Stanley Adam. A.B., U. Chgo., 1948; M.A., 1952, Ph.D., 1954. Asst. prof. econs. and fin. Cornell U. Johnson Grad. Sch. Mgmt., Ithaca, N.Y., 1956-59; assoc. prof. Cornell U. Johnson Grad. Sch. Mgmt., 1959-65, prof., 1965-78, Nicholas H. Noyes prof., 1978—; assoc. dir. Instl. Investor Study, SEC, 1969-70. Author: (with Harold Bierman, Jr.) The Capital Budgeting Decision, 1960, 66, 71, 75, 80, 84, 88 (with others) Management Decision-Making Under Uncertainty, 1969; contbr. articles to profl. jours. Mayor Village of Lansing, N.Y., 1975-81. Served with U.S. Army, 1954-56. Mem. Am. Econ. Assn., Am. Fin. Assn., Fin. Mgmt. Assn. Home: 120 Oakcrest Rd Ithaca NY 14850-1037 Office: Cornell U Grad Sch Mgmt Ithaca NY 14853-4201

SMIGEL, IRWIN ELLIOT, dentist; b. N.Y.C., Oct. 9, 1924; m. Lucia Shvetz, Sept. 30, 1956; children: Bellanca Smigel Rutter, Robert. WSC, NYU, 1950, DDS, 1950. Dentist pvt. practice, N.Y.C., 1950—; vis. prof. Pitts. Dental Sch., 1980-83, Case Western U., 1990—; cons., lectr. in field. Author: Dental Health, Dental Beauty, 1978; contbr. editor Dentistry Today, 1980—. With INF., 1943-45. Irwin Smigel Chair in Aesthetic Dentistry established NYU Sch. Dentistry. Fellow Am. Soc. Dental Aesthetics (pres. 1979—); mem. Am. Dental Assn., Acad. Gen. Dentistry, Fedn. Dentaire, First Dist. Dental Soc., Acad. Oral Medicine. Office: 635 Madison Ave New York NY 10022-1009

SMILEY, ALBERT KEITH, economist, resort executive; b. Mohonk Lake, N.Y., June 30, 1944; s. Keith and Ruth (Happel) S.; m. Nina Sue Feldman, June 29, 1974. BA in Math. magna cum laude, Syracuse U., 1966; PhD in Econs., Princeton U., 1978. Mem. rsch. staff Courant Inst. Math. Scis., N.Y.C., 1967-71; systems analyst Shared Ednl. Computer System,

Poughkeepsie, N.Y., 1971-73; rsch. assoc. Ctr. for Energy and Environ. Studies, Princeton (N.J.) U., 1978-80; economist econ. analysis group antitrust div. U.S. Dept. Justice, Washington, 1980-85, dir. rsch., 1986-90; pres., chief exec. officer Smiley Bros., Inc., New Paltz, N.Y., 1990—; bd. dirs. Smiley Bros., Inc., New Paltz, N.Y., chmn. exec. com., 1987—; trustee Mohonk Mountain House, New Paltz, 1986—; cons. sec.'s outer continental shelf adv. bd. U.S. Dept. Interior, Washington, 1976-77. Author: Competitive Bidding under Uncertainty, 1979. Bd. dirs. Mohonk Preserve, New Paltz, 1988—. Sloan Found. grantee, 1976-78; Harold W. Dodds fellow, 1977; award of Merit Antitrust Div., 1985. Mem. Am. Econ. Assn., Soc. Family Hoteliers, N.Y. State Hospitality and Tourism Assn. (bd. dirs.), Phi Beta Kappa. Mem. Soc. of Friends. Home and Office: Lake Mohonk New Paltz NY 12561

SMILEY, IRWIN, insurance agency executive; b. N.Y.C., Jan. 16, 1928; s. Max and Henriette Smiley; student Columbia U., 1948; B.S., U. Ill., 1950; M.S. in Fin. Service, Am. Coll., 1983; m. Cecilia Sahlman, Apr. 16, 1972; children: David, Michael, Jonathan, Daniel, James. Acct., S.D. Leidesdorf & Co., Chgo., 1950-52, asst. to pres., 1952-55, v.p., N.Y.C., 1955-63; life underwriter Mut. Benefit Life, N.Y.C., 1963-67; gen. agt. Nat. Life Ins. Co., N.Y.C., 1967-87, chmn. joint com. on strategic issues, 1987; pres., chmn. bd. dirs. Smiley Assocs., Inc., N.Y.C., 1972—; adj. assoc. prof. Coll. Ins., N.Y.C., 1968-78, C.W. Post Coll., 1977-78, N.Y. Ctr. for Fin. Studies, 1983-84. Pres. Greater Port Washington Civic Council, 1965-67; bd. dirs. Ctr. for African Art, 1989—, treas., 1991. Mem. CLUs (chmn. estate planning sect. 1985-87, 91, N.Y. chpt.), CLUs and Chartered Fin. Cons. (bd. dirs. N.Y. chpt. 1988-89), Gen. Agts. Assn. (pres.-elect 1981-82), Gen. Agts. Mgrs. Conf, Town Tennis Club (gov. 1980-83). Home: 300 E 56th St New York NY 10022-4136 Office: 380 Lexington Ave New York NY 10168-0002 also: Hillside Rd Southampton NY

SMILEY, RONALD MICHAEL, communications executive; b. Phila., Mar. 12, 1949; s. Frank Edward and Regina Ellen (Maquire) S.; m. Kathryn Augusta Giemza, Sept. 16, 1978. BS in Communication, Temple U., 1974. Studio dir. Delaware County Community Coll., Media, Pa., 1974-78; sports producer Sta. WQIQ, Aston, Pa., 1978-80; co-founder, v.p. Videosmith, Phila., 1980-83; founder, pres., chief exec. officer RSVP, Inc., Phila., 1983—; pres. Good Day Sunshine Co., Inc., Avalon, N.J., 1988-92; cameraman for CBS Nightly News, CBS Sunday Morning, Entertainment Tonight, Lifestyles of the Rich and Famous, Fox Broadcasting, Walt Disney's Epcot mag.; dir. photography AM Phila., 1982-92. Mem. NATAS, Internat. TV Assn. (v.p. 1985-86).

SMILOWITZ, HENRY MARTIN, pharmacology educator; b. Bklyn., Sept. 25, 1946; s. Benjamin and Doris (Prager) S.; m. Connie Dollin, June 17, 1979; children: Benjamin, Talya, Joshua. AB, Reed Coll., 1968; PhD, MIT, 1972. Postdoctoral fellow Tufts U. Med. Sch., Boston, 1972-73, Harvard Med. Sch., Boston, 1973-76; asst. prof. U. Conn. Health Ctr., Farmington, 1976-82, assoc. prof., 1982—. Contbr. 25 articles and 30 abstracts to profl. publs. Mem. Ad Hoc Adv. Com. on Electric and Magnetic Fields, State of Conn. Dept. Environ. Protection, Hartford, 1991—. Rsch. grantee NIH, 1977-90; fellow Woodrow Wilson Found., 1968, Muscular Dystrophy Found., 1973-75. Office: U Conn Health Ctr 263 Farmington Ave Farmington CT 06030-0001

SMITH, ALAN LAMONT, marketing professional, consultant; b. Glen Ridge, N.J., Sept. 13, 1925; s. Alan Philbrook and Edith Evelyn (Igou) S.; m. Jeanne Marion Fornoff, Jan. 1, 1948 (dec. 1985); children: Sydney Alison, Scott Edward; m. Vivienne Elvira Vilardi, Apr. 10, 1987. BA, U. N.C., 1948. Asst. editor East Orange (N.J.) Record, 1948-50; advt. writer N.Y. Telephon, N.Y.C., 1953-54; advt. asst. Bklyn. Union Gas Co., 1951-52, pub. supr., 1955-60, dir. pub. rels., 1960-75, mgr. pub. rels. and advt., 1976-82, asst. v.p., 1983-89, v.p., 1989-90; pres. Environ. Plus, North Salem, N.Y., 1991—; sr. v.p., dir. N.Y. Bd. Trade, N.Y.C., 1960—; founder, pres. Nat. Energy Found., N.Y.C. 1965-75. Author, dir.: (film) 20th Century Miracle, 1973, and others. Pres. Bklyn. Arts Coun., 1970-90; bd. dirs. Am. Lung Assn. Bklyn., 1990-91; chmn. Hammond Mus. Lt. (j.g.) AC, USN, 1943-46, PTO. Recipient Tree of Life award Jewish Nat. Fund, N.Y.C., 1987, community svcs. award Am. Lung Assn., Bklyn., 1988. Mem. Princeton Club. Republican. Home: 497D Heritage Hills Dr Somers NY 10589-1920 Office: Bklyn Union Gas Co One Metrotech Ctr Brooklyn NY 11201-3684

SMITH, ALBERT MATTHEWS, animal science educator; b. Bangor, Maine, Dec. 25, 1927; s. Albert William and Helen (Matthews) S.; m. Patricia Anne Gray, Sept. 10, 1950; children: Margaret Anne, Kathryn Smith Haslam. BS, U. Maine, 1952; MS, Cornell U., 1954, PhD, 1956. Asst. prof. animal sci. Cornell U., Ithaca, N.Y., 1956-57; asst. prof. animal sci. U. Vt., Burlington, 1957-61, assoc. prof., 1961-67, prof., 1967—, dept. chair, 1962-79, assoc. dean coll., 1978-89, dir. agrl. expt. sta., 1978-89. Fellow AAAS; mem. Am. Dairy Sci. Assn., Am. Assn. Animal Sci., Vt. Feed Dealers and Mfr. Assn. (sec.-treas. 1987—), Masons, Kiwanis Internat. (sec. 1989—), Sigma Xi, Alpha Zeta, Alpha Gamma Rho. Home: 1807 Spear St S Burlington VT 05403-7906 Office: U Vt Coll Agrl and Life Sci 204 Carrigan Hall Burlington VT 05405

SMITH, ALLAN, psychologist; b. Bklyn., May 13, 1949; s. Philip and Stella (Silverstein) S.; m. Robin Gail Tivoli, July 26, 1980; children: Stephen, Adam. BA, Queens Coll., 1971, MA, 1974; PhD, Hofstra U., 1988. Lic. psychologist, N.Y. Psychology asst. III Pilgrim Psychiat. Ctr., West Brentwood, N.Y., 1976-79; psychologist I Sagtikos Intermediate Care Facility/Mental Retardation, Melville, N.Y., 1979-86; psychologist II Kings Park (N.Y.) Psychiat. Ctr., 1986—; pvt. practice Levittown, N.Y., 1990—; ind. contractor Cath. Psychoednl. Svcs., Williston Park, N.Y., 1990-91, South Manor Sch. Dist., Manorville, N.Y., 1991. Coach Levittown-South Wantagh Baseball, Levittown, 1991. Mem. APA, Nassau County Psychol. Assn. Democrat. Jewish. Home: 162 Tardy Ln Wantagh NY 11793-1931

SMITH, ALTHEA MARIE, health and hospital executive, psychologist, nurse; b. Boston, Sept. 29, 1950; d. David and Mary (Cannady) S. BSN, U. Mass., 1972; MA in Clin. Psychology, Boston U., 1982, PhD in Clin. Psychology, 1986; postgrad., Boston Neurobehavioral Inst., 1988. RN, Mass. Nurse practitioner U. Mass. Health Svcs., Amherst, 1974; aftercare coord. Greater Lynn (Mass.) Community Mental Health Program, 1974-77; head nurse inpatient psychiat. unit Boston (Mass.) U. Med. Ctr., 1977-80; charge nurse neuropsychiatric unit Boston (Mass.) City Hosp., 1980-83; unit dir. maximum secure unit McLean/Bridgewater Program Bridgewater (Mass.) State Hosp., 1983-86; assoc. area dir. Dr. Solomon Carter Fuller Mental Health Ctr., Boston, 1986-87, area dir., supt., 1987-89, ctr. dir., supt., 1989-90; v.p. for corp. nursing N.Y.C. (N.Y.) Health and Hosps. Corp., 1990, sr. v.p. corp. nursing svcs. and spl. health initiatives, 1991—; cons. Casa Myrna Vasquez Shelter for Battered Women, 1986; cons. Dept. Mental Health, Forensic Unit MCI Framingham-Women's Prison, 1986; teaching asst. Boston (Mass.) U., 1981-82; sr. instr. Cambridge (Mass.) Coll., 1986, 87, 90; clin. fellow psychology Adolescent & Family Treatment Unit, Harvard Med. Sch., McLean Hosp., Belmont, Mass., 1983-84, clin. fellow psychology, law and psychiatry, 1984-86, asst. attending psychologist dept. psychiatry, 1986—; presenter in field. Bd. dirs. Casa Myrna Vasquez, Shelter for Battered Women; mem. adv. com. for acute care nursing in the adult NYU Grad. Sch. of Nursing. Mem. APA, Am. Coll. Health and Execs. (nominee), Assn. Black Psychologists, Nat. Black Nurses Assn., New Eng. Regional Black Nurses Assn., N.Y. Coalition 100 Black Women, Sigma Theta Tau. Office: NYC Health & Hosp Corps 125 Worth St New York NY 10013

SMITH, ANDREW ALFRED, JR., urban planner; b. Lynchburg, Va., Oct. 3, 1947; s. Andrew Alfred and Josephine (Vaughan) S. BArch (cum laude), Howard U., 1972; M in City Planning, MIT, 1980. Archtl. designer The Architects Collaborative Inc., Cambridge, Mass., 1972-76; archtl. coordinator Fay, Spofford & Thorndike Inc., Boston, 1977-79; city planner N.Y.C. Planning Commn., 1980—. Active Briarwood (N.Y.) Community Assn., 1985—, Cen. Queens YMCA, Jamaica, N.Y.; Newark Area Planning Assn., 1968, Peoples Involvement Corp., Washington, 1971-72, Mission Hill Planning Commn., Boston, 1978-80. HUD grantee, 1978-80; recipient Hallmark medal, 1989. Mem. Am. Planning Assn., Inst. Urban Design, Nat. Assn. Housing and Redevel. Ofcls. (sec. N.Y. Metro chpt. 1991—), Urban Land Inst. (assoc.), Howard U. Alumni Assn. (regional rep. 1978-79, 82-86, pres. L.I. chpt. 1983-85), Sierra Club, Nat. Travel Club. Democrat. Home: 84-55 Daniels St Briarwood NY 11435 Office: NYC Planning Commn 22 Reade St New York NY 10007-1216

SMITH, ANNE BOWMAN, academic administrator, editor; b. Craigsville, Va., Dec. 17, 1934; d. Joseph Benjamin and Louise Frances (Smith) Bowman; m. William Jerry Smith, June 29, 1957; children: Stacey Anne, Joan Elizabeth. Student, James Madison U., 1951-54, Old Dominion U., 1979-82; BA, Cath. U. Am. Reporter The Richmond (Va.) Times-Dispatch, 1955-56, The Miami (Fla.) Herald, 1965-68, 70-72, The Virginian-Pilot, Norfolk, 1968-70, 72-78; Portsmouth-Chesapeake city editor The Virginian-Pilot, 1978, govt. editor, 1978-80, asst. met. editor, 1980-82; dir. pub. info. Cath. U. Am., Washington, 1982-84, exec. dir. pub. affairs, 1984—; exec. editor Cath. U. Am. mag.; lectr. journalism Cath. U. Am., Washington, 1988—. Editor: Century Ended, Century Begun, 1990. Bd. dirs. Summer Opera Theatre Co., Washington, 1990—. Recipient numerous journalism awards including Va. Press Assn., Va. Press Women, Nat. Fedn. Press Women, Cath. Press Assn. Mem. Soc. Profl. Journalists, Cath. Press Assn. Office: Cath U Am Washington DC 20064

SMITH, BARBARA DARLING, religion instructor; b. Albion, Mich., Sept. 23, 1954; d. Harold William and Ollie (Black) Darling; m. Sydney Smith III, July 23, 1977. BA, Spring Arbor Coll., 1975; MA, Boston U., 1981, PhD, 1989. Instr. religion Wheaton Coll., Norton, Mass., 1981-82, 83-84, 1986-87, asst. prof., 1990—; instr. in philosophy and religious studies Curry Coll., Milton, Mass., 1985-90, Bridgewater (Mass.) State Coll., 1987—; asst. to dir. Boston U. Inst. for Philosophy and Religion, 1980—. Contbr. articles to profl. jours. Mem. North Weymouth (Mass.) Civic Assn., 1987-90, Friends of Webb State Park, North Weymouth, 1990—. Named one of Outstanding Young Women of Am., 1986, Young Leader of Yr. Spring Arbor Coll., 1991. Mem. AAUP, Mass. Tchrs. Assn., NEA, Am. Acad. Religion. United Church of Christ. Office: Wheaton Coll Norton MA 02766

SMITH, BARRY DAVID, obstetrician-gynecologist, educator; b. Suffern, N.Y., July 3, 1938; s. Alexander N. and Beatrice (Morris) S.; m. Maryann Blair, Oct. 11, 1963; children: Gillian, Adam. AB, Dartmouth Coll., 1959; MD, Cornell U., 1962. Diplomate Am. Bd. Ob-Gyn. Resident in ob-gyn N.Y. Hosp. Cornell U. Med. Ctr., N.Y.C., 1963-67, chief resident, instr., 1967-68; staff obstetrician/gynecologist Mary Hitchcock Meml. Hosp., Hanover, N.H., 1970—; asst. prof. Dartmouth Coll., Hanover, 1970-78, assoc. prof., 1979—; chief sect. ob-gyn Mary Hitchcock Clinic, 1977—, bd. govs. 1975-85, bd. dirs. 1980-86; chief sect. ob-gyn Dartmouth Med. Ctr., 1977—. Treas., pres. Norwich (Vt.) Recreation and Conservation Council, 1975-77. Served to comdr. USNR. Fellow Am. Coll. Ob-Gyn (v.p. 1991—), Am. Fertility Soc., Am. Soc. Colposcopy. Office: Dartmouth Hitchcock Clinic 1 Medical Center Dr Lebanon NH 03756

SMITH, BARRY DECKER, psychology educator; b. Harford, Pa., June 12, 1940; married; 2 children. BS in Psychology, Pa. State U., 1962; MA in Psychology, Bucknell U., 1964; PhD in Psychology, U. Mass., 1967. Predoctoral fellow pub. health svc., then rsch. assoc. U. Mass., 1966-67; asst. prof. psychology U. Md., College Park, 1967-71, assoc. prof., 1971-80, prof., assoc. chair psychology, 1981—, asst. chair psychology, 1979-80, acting chair psychology, 1983-84, 88-89, 91-92; cons. D.C. Pub. Schs., VA, U.S. Gen. Acctg. Office, Howard U. Coll. Medicine, NIH. Author: (with Teevan) Motivation, 1967, (with Vetter) Personality Theory: A Source Book, 1971, (with Vetter) Theoretical Approaches to Personality, 1982, Theories of Personality, 1991; contbr. articles to profl. jours. Chmn. adv. com. Boy Scouts Am.; cons. ARC. Recipient Hon. Mention, Creative Talents Award Program; grantee Biomed. Scis. Support Com., Nat. Inst. Mental Health, NSF, Pub. Health Svc., Gen. Rsch. Bd. Fellow Internat. Orgn. Psychophysiology; mem. AAAS, APA, Am. Psychol. Found., Biofeedback Soc. (D.C./Md. chpt.), Ea. Psychol. Assn., Soc. Psychophysiol. Rsch., Phi Kappa Phi, Psi Chi, Pi Gamma Mu. Office: Univ Md Dept Psychology College Park MD 20742

SMITH, BERNICE DRISKELL, educator, writer; b. Fort Gaine, Ga., Feb. 27, 1916; d. Joseph A. Stanford and Mary (Agusta) Mount-Stanford; m. Abner Guy Smith (dec. 1934); 1 child, Marline Virginia Smith (dec.); m. William J. Smith, Apr. 19, 1947. BS, Fla. A&M U., 1970; cert., Oxford U., Eng., 1985. Cert. reading specialist, Tallahassee Bd. Edn. Magnetflux inspector USAF, Middletown, Pa., 1943-44; tchr. typing and shorthand Phila. Bus. Sch., 1945-50; asst. to dean of men Del. State Coll., Dover, 1960; girls counselor Morgan U., Balt., 1962, Bowie (Md.) State Coll., 1963; tchr. Phila. Bd. Edn., 1970-83; creative writing tchr. Bartlett Elem. Sch., 1978-79; lectr. poetry writing various schs. Author: (children's books) Pink Satin, 1963 (Writer of Yr. 1963), Company for Thanksgiving, 1967, Bonny Squirrel and Mrs. Boyette, 1980, Shellbby Rumford, The Happy Rabbit, 1984, (poems) Shadopa, 1989; songwriter: Man and His Mountain, 1987, Rthym of Love, 1988, Ticket In My Pocket, 1990, Give Me Extended Time, 1990, (songs) My Rainbow of Love, 1991, The Stranger Who Called, 1990, Fight for Victory, 1991, The Battle is Over, 1991, It's Christmas, Holy Christmas, Whisper of Love, 1992 (Golden Eagle award 1992). Named Writer of Yr. WWRL Radio and Sackstore, 1963, Community Hall of Fame WWRL Radio, 1963; recipient 2 awards for community svc. Chapel of Four Chaplains, 1963, 2 awards for svc. to children and schs. Belmont and Pallumbo Schs. Bds. of Edn., 1973. Mem. AAUW, Internat. Platform Assn. (books on display Bodleian Libr., Univ. Oxford, Eng., 1985, Phila. Libr., 1985), Nat. Profl. Writer's Club, Women's Way, Ea. Star Lodge, Cyrenes, Zeta Phi Beta (sec., Woman of Yr. 1988), Kappa Omega Zeta (sec.), World Found. Interlectural Women. Republican. Baptist. Home: 6003 W Columbia Ave PO Box 12512 Philadelphia PA 19151

SMITH, BERTRAND DEAN, safety consulting company executive; b. Bryn Athyn, Pa., Nov. 20, 1929; s. Bertrand L. and Dorothy (Winderan) S.; m. Catharine Arrington, June 20, 1953; children: Stewart Dean, Christopher J., Matthew A., Aaron L. BS, U.S. Naval Acad., 1953; MBA, George Washington U., 1968. Commd. 2d lt. USAF, 1953, advanced through grades to col., ret., 1974; v.p. Cranston Rsch., Alexandria, Va., 1974-77; pres. Capital Safety, Mitchellville, Md., 1977—, Smith Consol. Svcs., Crofton, Md., 1989—; mem. Nat. Safety Standards Com., 1986—. Bd. dirs. Acad. of the New Church, Bryn Athen, 1990—; trustee Gist Blair Fund, Washington, 1986—; v.p. Acton Park Citizens, Mitchellville, 1965—; comdr. region IV Mil. Order, Md., Va., Washington, 1990. Decorated Air medal, Bronze Star; recipient Joint Commendation, Joint Chiefs of Staff, 1974. Mem. Am. Soc. Safety Engrs., Mil. Order World Wars (asst. treas. gen. Hann-Busewll meml. chpt., adjutant 1988). Republican. Home: 11907 Progress Ln Bowie MD 20721-2108 Office: Smith Consol Svcs Corp 10 Village Grn Crofton MD 21114-2014

SMITH, BETTY, writer; b. Bonham, Tex., Sept. 16; d. Sim and Gertrude (Dearing) S. Student, Stephens Coll., 1939-40; BJ, U. Tex., 1940-43. Pres. Hope Assocs. Corp., N.Y.C., 1948-50; pres., owner Betty Smith Assocs., N.Y.C., 1950—. Author: A Matter of Heart, 1969. Pres. Melchior Heldentenor Found., N.Y.C., 1987—. Office: 322 E 55th St New York NY 10022

SMITH, BONNIE LOU, chemistry educator; b. Chester, Pa., Dec. 13, 1944; d. Warren D. and Florence Lillian (Justison) Edwards; m. Laurance Ensor, Apr. 24, 1964; children: Steven Laurance, Amy Lynne. BS in Med. Tech., U. Del., 1966, Cert. in Secondary Edn., 1972, MEd in Sci. Curriculum, Instrn., 1986. Cert. tchr.; cert. med. technologist. Med. technologist Wilmington (Del.) Med. Ctr., 1966-75, hematology supr. gen. div., 1970-72; tchr. math. and chemistry Wilmington Christian Sch., Hockessin, Del., 1977-80, tchr. chemistry and sci., 1980-84, tchr. chemistry, physiology, head sci. dept., 1984—; tchr. Sunday sch. Bethel Bapt. Ch., Wilmington, 1972-84. lunar rocks specialist. Tchr. Sunday sch. Bethel Bapt. Ch., Wilmington, 1972-84; block capt. Am. Heart Assn., Wilmington, 1985-86. Nat. Tandy scholar, 1991. Mem. Nat. Sci. Tchr.'s Assn. (Nat. Aeros. and Space Assn./Nat. Sci. Tchr.'s Assn. NewMast winner 1989), Am. Soc. Clin. Pathologists, Del. Tchrs. Sci., Am. Chem. Soc., Nat. Right To Life Assn., U. Del. Alumni Assn. (mentor 1987—). Republican. Baptist. Home: 1114 Graylyn Rd Wilmington DE 19803-3335 Office: Wilmington Christian Sch PO Box 626 Hockessin DE 19707-0626

SMITH, BRIAN RICHARD, hematologist, oncologist, immunologist; b. Glen Cove, N.Y., May 7, 1952; s. Frank C. and Gloria R. S.; A.B. in Chemistry summa cum laude, Princeton U., 1972; M.D., Harvard U., 1976. Clin. fellow in medicine Harvard U., also med. house officer Peter Bent Brigham Hosp., Boston, 1976-77, asst. resident physician, 1977-78, clin. fellow in hematology-oncology, 1978-81; instr. medicine Harvard Med. Sch. and asso. Brigham and Women's Hosp., Children's Hosp., Dana-Farber Cancer Inst., Boston, 1981-88; asst. prof. medicine Harvard Med. Sch., 1985-88; assoc. prof. medicine, lab. medicine and pediatrics Sch. of Medicine Yale U., New Haven, 1988—; dir. rsch. Yale Bone Marrow Transplant Unit, dir. clin. immunohematology. Recipient George A. Howe prize Princeton U., 1976; Am. Cancer Soc. fellow, 1981-84; Leukemia Soc. fellow, 1982-88, scholar Leukemia Soc. Am., 1989—. Diplomate Am. Bd. Internal Medicine. Fellow ACP; mem. AAAS, N.Y. Acad. Sci., Phi Beta Kappa, Sigma Xi, Alpha Omega Alpha. Roman Catholic. Office: Yale U Sch Medicine 333 Cedar St New Haven CT 06510-3289

SMITH, BRIAN WILLIAM, lawyer, former government official; b. N.Y.C., Feb. 3, 1947; s. William Francis and Dorothy Edwina (Vogel) S.; m. Donna Jean Holverson, Apr. 24, 1976; children: Mark Holverson, Lauren Elizabeth. BA, St. John's U., N.Y.C., 1968, JD, 1971; MS, Columbia U., 1981. Bar: N.Y. 1972, D.C. 1975, U.S. Dist. Ct. (ea. and so. dists.) N.Y. 1975, U.S. Supreme Ct. 1976, U.S. Dist. Ct. D.C. 1986. Atty. Am. Express Co., N.Y.C., 1970-73, CIT Fin. Corp., N.Y.C., 1973-74; assoc. counsel, mng. atty. Interbank Card Assn. (named changed to Master Card Internat., Inc.), N.Y.C., 1974-75, sr. v.p., corp. sec., gen. counsel, 1975-82; chief counsel Compt. of Currency, Washington, 1982-84; ptnr. Stroock & Stroock & Lavan, Washington, 1984-92, mng. ptnr., 1986-92; ptnr. Mayer, Brown & Platt, Washington and N.Y.C., 1992—. Capt., USAR, 1970-78. Mem. ABA, N.Y. State Bar Assn., D.C. Bar Assn., Assn. Bar City N.Y., Fed. Bar Assn., N.Y. Athletic Club, Met. Club N.Y. Home: 35 W Lenox St Bethesda MD 20815-4208 Office: 2000 Pennsylvaina Ave NW Washington DC 20006

SMITH, CARL DEAN, JR., management consultant; b. Denver, Sept. 12, 1949; s. Carl Dean and Jean Beth (Hitz) S.; m. Patricia Ann O'Donnell, Aug. 18, 1973; children: Amanda Paige, Grant Carlton. BA, Springfield Coll., 1972; postgrad., Goethe Inst., Munich, 1972-73, Gordon Conwell Theol. Sem., Hamilton, Mass., 1986-88. Bus. analyst Dun & Bradstreet, Inc., Boston, 1974-77; Western U.S. credit mgr. Salomon/N.Am., Inc., Peabody, Mass., 1977-81; regional credit mgr. Stride Rite Corp., Cambridge, Mass., 1981-82; sales mgr., franchisee V.R. Bus. Brokers of Chestnut Hill, Mass., 1982-85; pres. C.D. Smith Assocs., Wakefield, Mass., 1985-90; ind. cons. Swampscott, 1990—. Pres. coun. Gordon Conwell Theol. Sem., 1988—; Boston coord. Fellowship of Cos. for Christ, 1988—; leadership gifts solicitor United Way, 1987, 88, 89—. Home and Office: 314 Forest Ave Swampscott MA 01907

SMITH, CARL HOFLAND, physicist; b. Mpls., June 6, 1942; s. Howell Kurtz and Synneva (Hofland) S.; m. Margaret Elizabeth Heinsohn, Sept. 3, 1966; children: Benjamin Allan, Katrina Elizabeth. AB in Physics, Hamilton Coll., 1964; MA in Solid State Physics, U. Minn., 1969, PhD in Solid State Physics, 1971. Vis. asst. prof. Macalester Coll., St. Paul, 1969-71; rsch. assoc. U. Minn., Mpls., 1971; entrepreneur Port Star Industries, Nyack, N.Y., 1971-72; chief scientist Auto Rsch. Corp., Oakland, N.J., 1972-79; tech. supr. Allied Chem. Corp., Morristown, N.J., 1979-81; sr. devel. assoc. Allied Metglas Products, Parsippany, N.J., 1981-83; sr. rsch. assoc. Allied Corp., Morristown, 1983-85; supr. magnetic alloys rsch. Allied-Signal Inc., Morristown, 1985—. Author chpts. in books; patents for electronic controls. Instructor in first aid and CPR, ARC, Minn., N.Y. and N.J., 1965—; sr. patroler Nat. Ski Patrol, Minn., Wis., N.J. and N.Y., 1965—. Mem. IEEE (sr.), Am. Phys. Soc., Sigma Xi. Home: 115 Lafayette Ave Chatham NJ 07928-2005 Office: Allied-Signal Inc PO Box 1021 Morristown NJ 07962-1021

SMITH, CARMELA VITO, counselor; b. Riverdale, Md., Aug. 2, 1950; d. Samuele G. and Bertha Gray (McNeil) V.; m. Rodney Charles Smith, Nov. 25, 1983. BS, Frostburg State Coll., 1972; MEd, U. Md., 1978. Nat. cert. counselor; cert. profl. counselor, Md. Tchr. Prince George's County Bd. Edn., Upper Marlboro, Md., 1972-78, counselor, 1978-91, tchr. coord. talented and gifted magnet sch., 1991—; pvt. practice counseling Bowie, Md., 1982-90. Mem. AACD, ASCD (profl. conf. com. Md. unit), Am. Sch. Counselors Assn., Md. Assn. Counseling and Devel. (sec., exec. bd. 1989-90, com. chair profl. conf. 1990), Md. Mental Health Counselors, Phi Delta Kappa, Alpha Xi Delta. Office: Heather Hills Elem 12605 Heming Ln Bowie MD 20716-1199

SMITH, CAROLYN J(ANE) HOSTETTER, psychologist, educator; b. Indpls., Mar. 29, 1938; d. John Daniel and Louise Margaret (Reiber) Hostetter; m. Thomas Tomasian, June 18, 1988. BA, DePauw U., 1959; MS in Teaching-Guidance & Counseling, U. Chgo., 1962, PhD, 1981. Lic. psychologist, Mass. Guidance counselor Blue Island (Ill.) High Sch., 1962-63, Univ. Chgo. (Ill.) Lab. Schs., 1963-66; counseling dir. Upward Bound, Mundeline Coll., Chgo., 1966-68; assoc. prof. counseling Kennedy-King Coll., Chgo., 1968-82; psychotherapist Worcester County Counseling Assocs., Bolton, Mass., 1982-87; clin. supr. Valley Adult Counseling Svc., Bellingham, Mass., 1982-84; cons. psychologist Mass. Dept. Edn., Bur. of Instnl. Schs., Boston, 1984-90; dir., psychotherapist Ea. Shore Assocs., Shrewsbury, Mass., 1987—; psychologist Dept. Pediatrics and Psychiatry, St. Vincent's Hosp., Worcester, 1986—; cons., educator various schs. and orgns., Mass., Ill., 1962—; workshop presenter. Bd. mem., chair children's com. Worcester (Mass.) Area Mental Health & Retardation Bd., 1984-87. Recipient Improvement Edn. grant Ford Found., Univ. Chgo., 1962. Fellow Am. Assn. Orthopsychiatry; mem. APA, AACD, Mass. Pschol. Assn., Internat. and New England Society for Study of Multiple Personality Disorder and Dissociation, Pi Lamda Theta, Psi Chi, Delta Theta Chi. Episcopalian. Office: Ea Shore Assocs 586 Main St Shrewsbury MA 01545

SMITH, CEDRIC MARTIN, pharmacology and therapeutics educator; b. Stillwater, Okla., Feb. 1, 1927; s. Otto Mitchell and Mary Catherine (Carr) S.; m. Mary Ella Wylie, Dec. 21, 1948 (div. June 1983); children: Cristine Renell, Michael Cedric, Celia Louise. BS, Okla. State U., Stillwater, 1949; BS in Medicine, U. Ill., Chgo., 1950, MD, 1953, MA in Pharmacology, 1953. Lic. to practice medicine, N.Y., Ill., Pa. Intern Phila. Gen. Hosp., 1953-54; instr., asst., assoc. prof. U. Ill., 1954-63; prof. pharmacology U. Ill. Coll. Medicine, 1963-66; chmn. dept. pharmacology and therapeutics SUNY, Buffalo, 1966-73, prof., 1966—; founding dir. N.Y. State Rsch. Inst. on Alcoholism, 1970-79, rsch. assoc., 1979—; med. staff Erie County Med. Ctr., Buffalo, 1976—, resident in psychiatry, 1983—; staff scientist Inst. for Def. Analyses, Arlington, Va., 1964-65; editorial bd. Jour. Pharmacology and Exptl. Therapeutics, 1959-65, Alcoholism: Clin. Exptl. Rsch., 1977-83, Rsch. Communications in Substance Abuse, 1979—, Jour. Studies on Alcohol, 1983-92, Clin. Pharmacology and Therapeutics, 1988—; cons. in field. Editor: (with A.M. Reynard) Textbook of Pharmacology, 1992; author: (with others) Textbook of Pharmacology, 1992; contbr. articles to profl. jours. Bd. dirs. Alcoholism Svcs. Erie County, 1983-90, profl. svcs. adv. com., 1979-83, Erie County Mental Hygiene Community Svcs., 1989-90; drug abuse adv. com. N.Y. State Dept. health and Div. Substance Abuse Svcs., 1979-91; chmn. vital task force com. on rsch. N.Y. State Task Force on Alcohol Problems, 1972-74; med. adv. com. Alcoholism Coun. Erie County, 1975-77, bd. dirs., 1971-77. Recipient Borden Award for Undergrad. Rsch., 1953; grantee Nat. Inst. Neurol. Diseases and Stroke, 1958-72; named mem. rsch. rev. orgns. NIH, 1965-88, VA Program Evaluation in Nervous and Sensory Diseases, 1969-70, Nat. Inst. on Drug Abuse, 1984-88, N.Y. State Health Rsch. Coun., 1975-91, Alcoholic Beverage Med. Rsch. Found., 1987-89. Mem. AMA, AAAS, AAUP, Am. Soc. for Clin. Pharmacology and Therapeutics, Am. Soc. for Pharmacology and Exptl. Therapeutics, Am. Coll. Clin. Pharmacology, Am. Soc. Addiction Medicine (cert.), Assn. Chemoreception Scis., Western N.Y. Psychiat. Assn., Internat. Brain Rsch. Orgn., Internat. Soc. for Biomed. Rsch. on Alcoholism, Med. Soc. County of Erie, N.Y. State Med. Soc., Med. Soc. State N.Y. (com. on alcoholism 1981—), Sigma Xi (pres. Buffalo chpt. 1987-88), Alpha Omega Alpha. Home: 1011 W River Rd Grand Island NY 14072-2422 Office: SUNY Main St Campus Buffalo NY 14214

SMITH, CHARLES EVAN, continuous inprovement consultant; b. Pitts., Oct. 7, 1960; s. Max Charles III and Janet Yvonne (Baumgartel) S. BS and

BA, Pa. State U., 1983; M of Pub. and Pvt. Mgmt., Yale U., 1989. Assoc. indsl. engr. IBM, East Fishkill, N.Y., 1981, 82; info. systems mgmt. program GE Aerospace, Valley Forge, Pa., 1983-85, systems support cons., 1986, systems support mgr., 1987; mgmt. devel. program Dexter Corp., Windsor Locks, Conn., 1989-91, total quality coord., 1991—. Supporter Boston Chamber Ensemble, 1991—; supporter Amnesty Internat., Conn. chpt., 1991—, Nature Conservancy, Conn. chpt., 1991—. Mem. Am. Soc. Quality Control, Am. Prodn. and Inventory Control Soc. Home: PO Box 552 Windsor Locks CT 06096 Office: The Dexter Corp 2 Elm St Windsor Locks CT 06096

SMITH, CHARLES QUINTON, employment agency executive; b. Reading, Pa., July 19, 1939; s. Charles Quinton Sr. and Jessica Gehr (Weaver) S. BSME, Lafayette Coll., 1961; MBA in Fin., U. Chgo., 1963. Owner, pres. Charles Q. Smith Ins. Assocs., Chambersburg, Pa., 1966-88, Adia Pers. Svcs., Chambersburg, 1988—; mng. ptnr. Sailing Vacations, Chambersburg, 1986—, C&D Realty, Chambersburg, 1988—; bd. dirs. United Nat. Bancorp., Chambersburg. Contbr. guest editorials to local newspaper. Scoutmaster Chambersburg area Boy Scouts Am., 1966-91; bd. dirs., past chair Chambersburg Hosp., 1985-90, Chambersburg Health Svcs., 1989—; bd. dirs. Chambersburg Coun. for Arts, 1986—. Capt. U.S. Army, 1964-66. Recipient Silver Beaver award Keystone Area coun. Boy Scouts Am., 1977, God and Svc. award Presbyn. Ch. and Boy Scouts Am., 1991; named Citizen of Yr. Wilson Coll., Chambersburg, 1987. Mem. Chambersburg C. of C. (past chair, bd. dirs.), Chambersburg Rotary (pres. 1979-80, Rotarian of Yr. 1986), Chambersburg Club (life), Masons, Phi Beta Kappa, Tau Beta Pi. Republican. Presbyterian. Home: 1627 Alexander Ave Chambersburg PA 17201 Office: Adia Pers Svcs 983 Lincoln Way E Chambersburg PA 17201

SMITH, CHARLES WILLIAM, secondary education educator, actor; b. Wheeling, W.Va., June 27, 1936; s. Harold F. and Bessie M. (Magill) S.; m. Mary Anna D. Richardson, Nov. 18, 1967; 1 child, Ian David. BS, Millersville U., 1959; student, Montclair Coll., 1965, Tex. A&M U., 1966. Cert. tchr., N.J. Tchr., dir. Gibbstown (N.J.) Sch., 1959-63; tchr. Pennsauken (N.J.) Jr. High, 1963-64; tchr., dir. theatre Salem (N.J.) High Sch., 1964-67; dir. theatre Salem Tech., 1967; tchr., theatre dir. Edgewood Regional Sr. High Sch., Atco, N.J., 1967—. Appeared in TV series Texas, 1982; film Fidelito, 1991 (Best Actor 1991). Adv. coun. Camden County Arts Soc., Cherry Hill, N.J., 1968-82; bd. dirs. Shakespeare '70, Trenton, N.J., 1970—. Ford Found. fellow, 1967. Mem. NEA, AFTRA, NATAS, N.J. Edn. Assn., Nat. Judges Assn. (visual judge), Actor's Equity Assn., Actor's Equity Assn. (liaison com. 1985-87). Home: 1208-207 Clements Bridge Rd Barrington NJ 08007 Office: Edgewood Regional Sr High 250 Coopers Folly Rd Atco NJ 08004

SMITH, CHRISTINE DONOHUE, academic director; b. St. Louis, Aug. 6, 1948; d. Carroll John and Juanita (Maire) Donohue; m. Charles Robert Smith, June 13, 1970; children: Brian Donohue, Christopher Norwood. BA, Tulane U., 1970; MS, Purdue U., 1974. Program coord. Purdue U., West Lafayette, Ind., 1974-78; cons. Poly. Inst. N.Y., Bklyn., 1978-79; asst. dean students Moravian Coll., Bethlehem, Pa., 1979-80; asst. dir. devel. Lehigh U., Bethlehem, 1980-83, dir. corp. and found. rels., 1983-90, campaign dir., 1991—; cons. U. Notre Dame, South Bend, Ind., 1977. Pres. Boys and Girls Club, Bethlehem, 1991—; bd. dirs. YMCA, Bethlehem, 1990-91. Mem. Nat. Computer Graphics Assn. Found. (bd. dirs. 1988-90), Quota Internat. Unitarian Universalist. Home: 1683 Pleasant Dr Bethlehem PA 18015-9311 Office: Lehigh U Alumni Meml Bldg 27 Memorial Dr W Bethlehem PA 18015-3086

SMITH, CHRISTOPHER HENRY, congressman; b. Rahway, N.J., Mar. 4, 1953; s. Bernard Henry and Katherine Joan (Hall) S.; m. Marie Hahn, July 2, 1977; children: Melissa, Christopher, Michael Jonathan, Elyse. Student, Worcester Coll., Eng., 1973-74; B.A. in Bus. Adminstrn., Trenton State Coll., 1975. Exec. dir. N.J. Right to Life Com., 1976-77; dir. instl. sales Leisure Unltd. Inc., Woodbridge, N.J., 1978-80; mem. 97th-102nd Congresses from 4th N.J. dist., Washington, 1981—; U.S. rep. to UN internat. conf. immunizing world's children. Active human rights movements Romania, China, USSR, Vietnam. Named Legislator of Yr. VFW, Legislator of Yr. Internat. Assn. Chiropractors, Legislator of Yr. KC, 1989; recipient Leader for Peace award Peace Corps. Mem. Nat. Fedn. Ind. Bus. Republican. Roman Catholic. Office: 2440 Rayburn House Office Bldg Washington DC 20515*

SMITH, CHRISTOPHER ROBIN, actor, arts administrator, screenwriter; b. Cleve., May 14, 1959; s. Lawrence Barrett III and Mary A. (Prinios) S.; m. Tamara Wilcox, Aug. 1, 1986; children: Sean Damien, Christopher Barrett. BA, Kenyon Coll., 1981. Actor Interplay, N.Y.C., 1983—; co-founder Nat. Improvisational Theatre, Inc., N.Y.C., 1984—, exec. dir., 1984-89, dir. community outreach, 1989—; exec. dir. The Wilcox Group Exec. Tng., N.Y.C., 1989—; artist-in-residence N.Y.C. Bd. Edn., 1989—. Author: (play) The One, The Only Groucho, 1978, (documentary) Scandinavia: There's Only One Place Like It, 1991, (screenplays) What's Wrong With This Picture, 1990, The Gasp, 1991. Recipient Betty Padden Meml. Drama prize U. Exeter, Eng., 1980. Mem. AFTRA. Home: 484 W 43d St #40-S New York NY 10036 Office: Nat Improvisational Theatre 223 8th Ave New York NY 10011

SMITH, CHRISTOPHER RUSSELL, environment and natural resources specialist; b. Rochester, N.Y., Nov. 19, 1953; s. Warren Greenwood and Margaret (Donoghue) S.; m. Angela Walton, June 11, 1983; children: Christopher, Ryan, Nicole. BS in Forestry, Syracuse U., 1975; BS in Environ. Sci., SUNY, Syracuse, 1975. Natural resources coord. CARE, Quiche El Quiche, Guatemala, 1977-78; arid land forestry specialist CARE, Amman, Jordan, 1978-80; project adminstr. Chemonics Internat., Washington, 1980-83; natural resources and environ. specialist Chemonics Internat., Panama City, Panama, 1984-86; project supr. Chemonics Internat., Washington, 1987-91, dep. dir. Near East, 1991—; cons. USAID, Panama, Honduras, Egypt, Nepal, 1981-91. Environ. Protection grantee Save the Children, Guatemala, 1977. Mem. Soc. Am. Foresters, Internat. Soc. Tropical Foresters, Soil and Water Conservation Soc. Home: 9707 Water Oak Dr Fairfax VA 22031 Office: Chemonics Internat 2000 M St NW Ste 200 Washington DC 20036

SMITH, CLAYTON ALEXANDER, college administrator; b. Flemington, N.J., Sept. 16, 1959; s. Howard A. and Frances E. (Deitz) S.; m. Shannon M.E. Griffith, Aug. 9, 1986. BA, U. So. Maine, Portland, 1981; MA, Drew U., Madison, N.J., 1982; MPA, U. Maine, 1991. Teaching fellow Drew U., 1981-82; instr. Baldridge Study Skills, Inc., Greenwich, Conn., 1982-83; legis. asst. Tabor & Assocs., Washington, 1983-85; town mgr. Town of Brownville, Maine, 1985-86; asst. dir. admissions U. Maine, Augusta, 1986-88, acting dir. admissions, 1988-89, interim dir. admissions, 1989-90, dir. admissions, 1990—. Pres. Gardiner (Maine) Area Fed. Credit Union Bd., 1987-89; del. Maine Dem. Party Conv., 1988; mem. Maine Sch. Adminstrv. Dist. 11 Aspirations Compact, Gardiner, to 1990. Mem. New Eng. Assn. Coll. Admissions Officers and Registrars (exec. coun. 1990—), New Eng. Assn. Coll. Admissions Counselors, Cen. Maine Assn. Counseling and Devel., Maine Assn. Counseling and Devel., Am. Assn. Coll. Admissions Officers and Registrars. Episcopalian. Home: 11 1/2 Spring St Augusta ME 04330 Office: U Maine at Augusta University Hts Augusta ME 04330

SMITH, CORINNE ROTH, psychologist; b. Reading, Pa., May 22, 1945; d. Zoltan and Elizabeth (Foldes) Roth; m. Lynn Helden Smith, June 9, 1968; children: Juliette Sarah, Rachael Eliza. BA in Psychology cum laude, Syracuse U., 1967, PhD, 1973; MA, Temple U., Phila., 1969. Lic. psychologist, N.Y. Psychologist reading clinic Syracuse (N.Y.) U., 1969-70, coordinator lab. sch. and clinic, 1971-72, founder, dir. psychoednl. teaching lab., 1972—, founder, dir. comprehensive assessment ctr., 1981-83; psychologist experimental presch. program Syracuse City Schs., 1970-71; assoc. prof. Syracuse U., 1971—; mem. Council for Exceptional Children; reviewer Aspen, Ablex, Mc Graw Hill, Little Brown & Co., N.Y., Allyn & Bacon, Pergammon, 1985—; apptd. mem. Gov. N.Y. Council for Youth, Albany, 1984—; speaker in field. Author: Learning Disabilities: The Interaction of Learner, Task and Setting, 1983, 2d edit., 1991; contbr. articles to profl. jours. and chpts. to books. Bd. dirs. Cen. N.Y. United Way, 1987—; pres. Jewish Community Ctr., Syracuse, 1978-81; bd. dirs., chairperson career women's network Syracuse Jewish Fedn., 1985-87, women's campaign chairperson, 1987-89, gen. campaign chair, 1991—. Recipient Disting. Svc. award Jewish Community Ctr., 1976, Community Leadership award Syracuse Jewish Fedn., 1986, 89, Jewish Family Svc. Humanitarian award, 1991; N.Y. State Office Mental Retardation and Devel. Disabilities grantee, 1985-90; named Woman of Yr. Post Standard, 1990. Mem. Am. Psych. Assn., Nat. Assn. Sch. Psychologists, N.Y. State Assn. for Children and Adults with Learning Disabilities, Learning Disabilitiy Assn. of Am. Office: Syracuse U 805 S Crouse Ave Syracuse NY 13244-0001

SMITH, DALE AUSTIN, air force officer; b. Honolulu, Jan. 14, 1952; s. Russell Lynn Jr. and Jean Margaret (Austin) S.; m. Leslie Cahterine Leach, June 1, 1976; children: Erin Cecily, Lauren Stephanie, Sean Ashford, Ian Edward Russell. BA in Geography, U. Colo., 1974; postgrad., Air U., Montgomery, Ala., 1987, Cen. Mich. U., 1987-89, SUNY, Plattsburgh, 1992—. Cert. instrument flight instr. FAA. Field engr. Gt. Western Sugar Co., Denver, 1975; v.p. Russ Smith Corp., Honolulu, 1975-77; commd. 2d lt. USAF, 1977, advanced through grades to maj., 1988; geodetic survey officer Def. Mapping Agy. USAF, F.E. Warren AFB, Wyo., 1977-78; instr., flight navigator USAF, various locations, 1979-84; command post contr., then asst. flight comdr. USAF, Wurtsmith AFB, Mich., 1984-86, chief current ops. 379 bombardment wing, 1986-90; dep. wing tactician USAF, Plattsburgh, 1991—; USAF liaison, chief check pilot CAP, Broomfield, Colo., 1974-79, Rapid City, S.D., 1979-83, Oscoda, Mich., 1983-90, Peru, N.Y., 1990—. Inventor infant flight safety capsule; contbr. articles to Navigator Mag. Vol. local couns. Girl Scouts U.S., 1986—; vol. Peru Cen. Sch., 1991—. Decorated Air Force Commendation medal, Air Force Meritorius Svc. medal. Mem. Air Force Assn., Aircraft Owners and Pilots Assn. Home: 26 Ormsby Cir Peru NY 12972-9200 Office: 380 AREFW/OSS/DOJ Plattsburgh AFB Plattsburgh NY 12903-5000

SMITH, DANIEL ALBERT, controller; b. Dayton, Ohio, Aug. 4, 1951; s. Donald Albert and Eleanor Ann (Panepento) S.; m. Rebecca Victoria Toledo, May 7, 1985; children: Daniel, Sean. Assoc. of Occupational Studies, Bryant & Stratton Inst., 1976; BSBA, SUNY, Buffalo, 1978. Acct., auditor Erie County Comptroller, Buffalo, 1977-79; sr. acct. Samuel Goldman & Co., CPAs, Buffalo, 1979-83; controller Great Lakes Cons., Tonawanda, N.Y., 1983-85, A.W. Miller Tech. Sales, Inc., East Aurora, N.Y., 1985—. Member K.C., Buffalo, 1983, U. Buffalo Alumni Assn., Amherst, N.Y., 1985, Philippine Health & Med. Campaign, Toronto, Can., 1988. Home: 1164 Maple Rd Buffalo NY 14221-3440 Office: AW Miller Tech Sales 7661 Seneca St East Aurora NY 14052-9407

SMITH, DANIEL JAMES, immunologist, educator; b. Rochester, N.Y., June 17, 1944; s. James Elbridge and Margaret Marie (Fowler) S.; m. Danice Marie; children: Jessica Koren, Rachel Elisabeth, Andrea Noelle. BS, Houghton Coll., 1966; PhD, N.Y. Med. Coll., 1972. Staff assoc. Forsyth Dental Ctr., Boston, 1972-74, asst. staff mem., 1974-78, assoc. staff mem., 1979-84, sr. staff mem., 1984—; clin. instr. Sch. Dental Medicine Harvard U., Boston, 1976-80, asst. clin. prof., 1980-87; assoc. clin. prof. Harvard U., 1987—. Office: Forsyth Dental Ctr 140 The Fenway Boston MA 02115

SMITH, DAVID CLAYTON, historian; b. Lewiston, Maine, Nov. 14, 1929; s. William G. and Ella (Churchill) S.; m. Sylvia White Smith, July 9, 1953; children: Clayton W., Katherine L. BSEd, U. Maine, Farmington, 1955; MEd, U. Maine, Orono, 1956, MA, 1958; PhD, Cornell U., 1965. Prof. history Hobart & William Smith Coll., Geneva, N.Y., 1960-65, U. Maine, Orono, 1965—; chmn. history dept. U. Maine, Orono, 1980-84; pres. N.E. Historic Films, Inc., Blue Hill, Maine, 1985-89; bd. dirs. Forest History Soc., Durham, N.C., 1982-89. Author: biography H.G. Wells: Desperately Mortal, 1985; (with others) Miss You: World War II Letters, 1990, Since You Went Away: World War II Letters From the Home Front, 1991. Chmn. Bangor (Maine) Dem. Com., 1972-80; pres. Pres. Heritage Museum, Bangor, 1975-79. With USN, 1948-52. Named Disting. Rsch. Prof. U. Maine, 1985, Disting. Alumni, 1987. Mem. Orgn. Am. Historians, So. Hist. Assn., Agrl. History Assn., Forest History Assn. Democrat. Home: 39 Cortland Cir Bangor ME 04401 Office: Univ Maine 150 Stevens Orono ME 04469

SMITH, DAVID LARRY, music educator; b. Johnson City, N.Y., Oct. 1, 1943; s. Edgar Lee and Thelma Bell (Forsythe) S.; m. Judith Elizabeth Werthner, Apr. 6, 1969; children: David L. Jr., Karen, Christopher, Kevin. BS in Music Edn., Mansfield U., 1967; M of Music Performance, East Carolina U., 1970. Music tchr. Elmira (N.Y.) City Schs., 1967-69; prof. music Western Conn. State U., Danbury, 1970—; percussionist New Haven (Conn.) Symphony Orchestra, 1976—, Bridgeport (Conn.) Symphony Orchestra, 1971-88, Ives Symphony Orchestra, Danbury, 1988—, N.Y.C. Symphony, 1988-90. Performance of premier solo pieces, 1988, 89; contbr. articles to profl. jours. With U.S. Army, 1961-64. Mem. Percussive Arts Soc. (state pres. 1978-85), Am. Fedn. Musicians, Music Educators Nat. Conf., Conn. Music Educators Assn., Phi Mu Alpha Sinfonia. Home: 5 Macalpine Way Danbury CT 06811-3605 Office: Western Conn State Univ 181 White St Danbury CT 06810-6885

SMITH, DAVID LIONEL, American literature educator; b. Tuskegee, Ala., Feb. 3, 1954; s. David Alexander and Thelma Leontine (Crockett) S.; m. Vivian A. Cooke-Buckhoy, June 15, 1980; 1 child, Nikita Lynne Buckhoy. BA, New Coll., 1974; MA, U. Chgo., 1975, PhD, 1980. Asst. prof. Williams Coll., Williamstown, Mass., 1980-87, assoc. prof., 1987-92, prof., 1992—; panelist media program Nat. Endowment for Humanities, Washington, 1986—; cons. on comics Smithsonian Instn., Washington, 1988; chair faculty steering com. Williams Coll., Williamstown, 1990-91. Author: (poetry book) Cowboy Amok, 1987; compiler Molten Truths, 1989; mem. editorial bd.: Encyclopedia of African-American Culture, N.Y.C., 1990—; disk jockey: (radio show) Let the Music Speak, 1981—. Mem. Zoning By-Laws Com., Lanesborough, Mass., 1987-91. Recipient grad. fellowship Nat. Fellowships Fund, 1974-79, fellowship NEH, 1987-88, Am. Coun. Learned Socs., 1991-92, Nat. Humanities Ctr., 1991-92. Mem. Am. Studies Assn., Popular Culture Assn., Modern Lang. Assn. (exec. com. So. literature discussion group 1991—). Home: 131 Old State Rd Berkshire MA 01224 Office: Williams Coll Dept English Williamstown MA 01267

SMITH, DEAN, communications advisor, arbitrator; b. N.Y.C., Aug. 10, 1925; s. Franklin Grant and Anna Lucille (Kranebell) S.; m. Andree Marie Praileur, Aug. 9, 1947; children—David F., Christopher P. Student, NYU, 1945-46, Columbia U., 1946-47, N.Y. Sch. Printing, 1946-47. Editor ShowBill Mag., N.Y.C., 1945-47; news editor Boulder City (Nev.) Daily News, 1947-49; owner, pub., editor Tucson Sun-News, N.Y.C., 1949-51; dir. radio and TV news Sta. WBEN/WBEN-TV, Buffalo, 1951-53; dir. pub. svc. and promotion Indpls. Times, Buffalo, 1953-56; v.p., gen. mgr Kendall Assocs., Inc., N.Y.C., 1956-60; dir. Office Publs. and Info., Commerce Dept., Washington, 1961-70, dir. publs. div., 1970; asst. dir. Nat. Tech. Info. Svc., Springfield, Va., 1971-81, dir. office of market devel., 1982-83; assoc. dir. NTIS, Springfield, Va., 1984-85, self-employed communications advisor, 1986—. Chmn. for fed. mail list policy Vice Pres.'s Com. on Right of Privacy; chmn. presdl. domestic policy rev. work group on fed. acquisition of fgn. tech., 1979; bd. dirs. Commerce Fed. Credit Union. Served with AUS, 1943-45. Decorated Silver Star with oak leaf cluster, Bronze Star, Purple Heart with oak leaf cluster; recipient award Ariz. Newspaper Assn., 1950, Ind. Photo Journalism award, 1954. Mem. Am. Arbitration Assn. (mem. panel arbitrators), Soc. Mayflower Descendants, Sons of Revolution, Flagon and Trencher. Democrat. Home and Office: 2325 49th St NW Washington DC 20007-1002

SMITH, DENISE GROLEAU, data processing professional; b. Worcester, Mass., Feb. 7, 1951; d. Edmond Laurence and Audrey Mildred (Paquin) Groleau; m. Wayne Marshall Smith, Apr. 17, 1976; 1 child, Andrew. BSBA, Fitchburg State U., 1983. Bindery worker Atlantic Bus. Forms, Hudson, Mass., 1969-73; proofreader New Eng. Bus., Townsend, Mass., 1974-75; computer operator New Eng. Bus., Groton, Mass., 1975-80, adminstrv. asst. bus. systems, 1980-82, adminstrv. asst. info. ctr., 1982-85; info. ctr. analyst Wright Line Inc., Worcester, 1985-88; personal computer coord. Thom McAn Shoe Co., Worcester, 1988-91; cons. personal computer Buckingham Transp., Groton, 1987-92. Mem. Nat. Assn. Female Execs. Home: 14 Cedar Cir Townsend MA 01469-1336

SMITH, DENNIS EDWARD, property management executive; b. Balt., May 28, 1945; s. Edward Albert and Ella Jeanette (Hartlove) S.; m. Patricia A. Draayer, Nov. 16, 1969; 1 child, Jeffrey Scott. BS in Mktg., U. Balt., 1967. Br. mgr. 1st Nat. Bank Md., Balt., 1968-71; retail sales supr. BP Oil Corp., Balt., 1971-72; property mgr. Monumental Properties, Inc., Balt., 1972-74, automated rent systems coord., 1975-79; br. mgr. 1st Nat. Bank of Md., Balt., 1974-75; v.p. The Town and Country Mgmt., Balt., 1979—. Mem. Citizen's Adv. Com. on Gifted and Talented Edn., Baltimore County, 1987-91; bd. dirs. Apt. Builders and Owners Coun., 1992—. Mem. Nat. Assn. Home Builders. Democrat. Lutheran. Home: 6 Kingston Park Ln W Baltimore MD 21220-4914 Office: Town and Country Mgmt Corp 100 S Charles St Ste 1700 Baltimore MD 21201-2750

SMITH, DONALD C., artist; b. Dexter, Mo., July 10, 1935; s. Walter C. and Elsa Louise (Shearon) S.; m. Joyce L. Forsee; children: Matthew Sean, Grantham Scott, Hannah Claire. AB, U. Mo., 1957, MA, 1959. Dir. Spiva Art Ctr., Joplin, Mo., 1960-64; prof. art R.I. Coll., Providence, 1964—; vis. artist Harvard U.; lectr. Yale Summer Sch. for Art and Music; lectr. and researcher on Am. painter Edwin Dickinson. Exhibited paintings extensively in midwestern and northeastern U.S. Univ. fellow U. Mo., 1958. Home: 12 Pine Hill Ave Johnston RI 02919-1452 Office: RI Coll 600 Mt Pleasant Ave Providence RI 02908-1924

SMITH, DONALD CHARLES, communication educator; b. Derby, Conn., Mar. 27, 1957; s. Bernard and Rita (Conway) S. BA, So. Conn. State Coll., 1980; MS, Emerson Coll., 1981; PhD, U. Mass., 1987. Grad. asst. Emerson Coll., Boston, 1980-81; teaching asst. U. Mass., Amherst, 1981-84; faculty-in-residence dept. communication U. N.H., Durham, 1984-87; asst. prof. dept. communication U. New Haven, West Haven, Conn., 1987-91, assoc. prof. with tenure, 1991—; chmn. faculty senate U. New Haven, 1990-91, dir. freshman advising, 1991—, chmn. presdl. search adv. com., 1990-91; communication cons., 1985—. Contbr. articles to profl. jours. Record holder for winning over 300 inter-collegiate speaking awards, 1976-79. Mem. Ea. Communication Assn., Speech Communication Assn. Office: Dept Communication Univ of New Haven 300 Orange Ave West Haven CT 06516-1999

SMITH, DONALD HUGH, education educator; b. Chgo., Mar. 20, 1932; s. William Henry and Madolene F. (Franklin) S.; m. Gloria Valentine, Aug., 1965 (div. 1970). AB, U. Ill., 1953; MA, DePaul U., Chgo., 1959; PhD, U. Wis., 1964. High sch. tchr. pub. schs. Chgo., 1956-63; asst. prof., assoc. prof. Northeastern Ill. U., Chgo., 1964-67; prof., dir. U. Pitts., 1968-69; exec. assoc. The Urban Coalition, Washington, 1969-70; prof., chmn. dept. edn. Baruch Coll., CUNY, N.Y.C., 1970—; cons. Rockefeller Found., N.Y.C., 1975-80, N.Y. State Black and Puerto Rican Legis. Caucus, 1986-87, pub. sch. systems and univs. Contbr. articles to profl. jours. Bd. mem. N.Y. Svcs. to Older People, N.Y.C., 1986-91; chmn. CUNY African Am. Network, N.Y.C., 1988—. With U.S. Army, 1954-56. Recipient Teaching Excellence award Chgo. Pub. Schs., 1962; U.S. Office Edn. tchr. fellowship grantee, Washington, 1966. Mem. Nat. Alliance Black Sch. Educators (pres. 1983-85, Ida B. Wells risk-taker 1987), Nat. Black Child Devel. Inst., Am. Assn. Colls. Tchr. Edn. Office: Baruch Coll 17 Lexington Ave # 505 New York NY 10010-5526

SMITH, DOUGLAS JAMES, juvenile probation officer; b. East Orange, N.J., Dec. 10, 1965; s. Albert G. and Virginia E. (Pa Jer) S. BS in Criminal Justice, Xavier U., 1988; MS in Counseling, West Chester U., 1991. Counselor Talbert House-Victim Svc. Ctr., Cin., 1986-88, New Dominion Sch., Richmond, Va., 1988; probation officer Delaware County Juvenile Ct., Chester, Pa., 1990—; chef Tonik's Restaurant, Wilmington, Del., 1989—. Mem. Big Bros., Inc., Cin., 1986-88. Mem. AACD, Nat. Employment Counselors Assn. Home: 1117 Concord Rd Chester PA 19014-1410 Office: Delaware County Juvenile Probation 112 E 5th St Chester PA 19013-4508

SMITH, EARL HAROLD, college dean, educator; b. Waterville, Maine, Oct. 6, 1939; s. Clarence Dean and Anita (Crockett) S.; m. Barbara Diane Hubbard, Sept. 10, 1959; children: Jeffrey, Kelly Ann, Michael. BA, U. Maine, 1962. News asst. Colby Coll., Waterville, 1962-65, dir. news bur., 1965-68, dir. student activities, 1968-70, assoc. dean of student, 1970-74, asst. to pres., 1974-75, dir. communications, 1975-76, dean of students, 1976-81, dean of coll., 1981—; bd. dirs. Mid-Maine Med. Ctr., Waterville, chair, 1985-86. Contbr. articles to profl. jours. City councilor Waterville, 1965-71; state rep. State of Maine, 1970-72; mem. Waterville Bd. Edn., 1978-80. Recipient U.S. Jaycees Disting. Svc. award, 1970, named One of Outstanding Young Men of Yr., 1971. Office: Colby Coll Waterville ME 04901

SMITH, EDWARD K., retired economist, consultant; b. Buffalo, Apr. 12, 1922; s. Clifford Kershaw and Helen (Baro) S.; m. Mary Alice Pendergast, Dec. 20, 1948; children: Benjamin, Christopher, Mrs. Loretta Christopher, Katherine, Alice, Margarita, James, Daniel. B.A., Hobart Coll., 1946; M.A., U. Buffalo, 1950, Harvard U., 1955; Ph.D., Harvard U., 1960. From asst. to assoc. prof. econs. Boston Coll., 1956-64; dep. asst. sec. U.S. Dept. Commerce, Washington, 1965-68; prof., chmn. dept. econs. Colo. State U., Ft. Collins, 1968-70; v.p. Nat. Bur. Econ. Research, N.Y.C., 1970-77; sr. econ. cons. Brimmer & Co. Inc., Washington, 1977-83; dir. Internat. Banking Ctr., Fla. Internat. U., Miami, 1982, Bur. Ind. Econs., U.S. Dept. Commerce, Washington, 1983; assoc. dir. Bur. Econ. Analysis, 1984-88; cons. economist, 1988—; vis. prof. econs. U. Colo., 1965, Yale U., New Haven, 1971, Fla. Internat. U., Miami, 1982. Author: The Economic State of New England, 1954. Fiscal advisor Lt. Gov. Mass., Boston, 1955; mem. Pres.'s Task Force on Environ., 1966, Pres.'s Task Force on Housing, 1968, Gov. Carey's Task Force on Unemployment, N.Y.C., 1974; trustee St. Mary's Coll., Newburgh, N.Y., 1972-77. Served with U.S. Army, 1943-46. Mem. Am. Econs. Assn., Nat. Assn. Bus. Economists, So. Regional Sci. Assn., Nat. Economists Club (v.p. 1984, bd. dirs. 1985-86). Democrat. Episcopalian.

SMITH, EDWIN LEE, land surveyor, civil engineer; b. Charleston, W.Va., Nov. 9, 1956; s. Homer Lee and Margaret Anne (Smith) S. BS in Civil Engring., W.Va. Inst. Tech., 1978, MS in San. Engring., 1985. Lic. surveyor, Md. W.Va., lic. engr., Md. W.Va. Hydraulic engr. Huntington (W.Va.) Dist. Corps of Engrs., 1978-83; rsch. asst. Va. Water Resouces Rsch. Inst., Blackburg, 1983-85; hydraulic engr. Dewbery & Davis, Inc., Fairfax, Va., 1986; hydraulic engr. pub. works dept. Harford Co., Bel Air, Md., 1986-88; engr. and surveyor Beavin Co., Balt., 1988-91; owner Edwin L. Smith Surveyor and Engr., Inc., Balt., 1991—. Active Nature Conservancy. Mem. Greenpeace, W.Va. Assn. Land Surveyors, Balti. Bird Club (bd. dirs. 1988—), Union Concerned Scientists, Brooks Bird Club, Sierra Club. Quaker. Home and Office: Edwin L Smith Surveyor and Engr Inc 1020 Boyd St Baltimore MD 21223-2563

SMITH, ELIZABETH, artist; b. New Britain, Conn., Aug. 13, 1943. BS, Cen. Conn. State U., 1969, MS, 1974; student, U. Vt., U. Hartford. Exhibited in group shows at Nat. Acad. Design, N.Y.C., 1988, Mus. Fine Arts, Springfield, Mass., 1988, 90, 92, Bergen Mus. Art and Sci., Paramus, N.J., 1990, Allied Artists Am., N.Y.C., 1988-89, 91, Pastel Soc. Am., N.Y.C., 1990, 91, 92, Silvermine Guild Arts Ctr., New Canaan, Conn., 1992. Mem. Am. Artists Profl. League (Coun. Am. Artists Socs. award 1988), Audubon Artists, Acad. Artists Assn. (award 1991), Nat. Assn. Women Artists (Nydia Preede award 1987, C. L. Mason and A.V. Mason Meml. award 1989), Conn. Acad. Fine Arts (bd. dirs. 1991-92, pres. 1992—), Knickerbocker Artists N.Y. (Silver medal of Honor 1986, 91), Katharine Lorillard Wolfe Art Club (medal of honor 1986, IBM award 1987, Ida Becker Meml. award 1989). Home: 10 Ardsley Way Avon CT 06001-4031

SMITH, EMERSON WARFIELD, postal service executive; b. Charlottesville, Va., Nov. 30, 1922; s. Rockwell Emerson and Jean Macdonald (Dunnington) S.; m. Elizabeth Ann Calkins, Sept. 3, 1924; children: Ann Kelso, Elizabeth Macdonald, Rockwell Emerson, Raub Warfield, Lyman Dunnington. BSMechE, U. Va., 1943; BSMechE, Calif. Inst. of Technology, 1949. Registered mech. engr., Calif. Asst. prof. mech. engring. U. Va., Charlottesville, 1949-52; chief, group leader propulsion design N.Am. Rockwell Corp., Columbus, Ohio, 1952-62, chief advanced engring., 1962-64, dir. OV-10 engring., 1964-70; v.p. Teleflex, Inc., North Wales, Pa., 1970-71; mgr. process engring. div. U.S. Postal Svc., Washington, 1971-74, dir. office of bldg. and design, 1974-76; gen. mgr. engring. div. ea. region hdqrs. U.S. Postal Svc., Phila., 1976-86; field dir. ops. support Harrisburg (Pa.) div. U.S.

Postal Svc., 1986—; mem. indsl. and profl. adv. council Pa. State U., 1982-87. Dir. engring. OV-10A Counter Insurgent Aircraft, 1968; dir. design and constrn. of first U.S. postal office heated and cooled by solar energy, 1976; author and speaker in field. Pres. Yorktown Crew Boosters, Arlington, Va., 1973-74, Greenhouse Condominium Assn., Bala Cynwyd, Pa., 1980-83. Served with USNR, 1944-46. Fellow AIAA (sect. affairs com. 1968); mem. Inst. Indsl. Engrs. (sr.), Internat. Mgmt. Soc., ASME (subcom. on guided indsl. vehicles 1984—). Presbyterian. Home: 549 Windsor Ct Hummelstown PA 17036-9119 Office: US Postal Svc Harrisburg Div 501 King Blvd Harrisburg PA 17105-9993

SMITH, ERIC PARKMAN, retired railroad executive; b. Cambridge, Mass., Mar. 23, 1910; s. B. Farnham and Helen T. (Blanchard) S.; A.B., Harvard U., 1932, M.B.A., 1934. Staff fed. coordinator transp., Washington, 1934; with traffic and operating depts. N.Y. New Haven & Hartford R.R., Boston and New Haven, Conn., 1934-53; with Maine Central R.R., Portland, 1953-82, sec. adv. bd. retirement trust plan, 1958-82, asst. treas., dir. cost analysis, 1970-82. Trustee parish donations 1st Parish in Concord, Unitarian-Universalist Ch., 1960—. Mem. New Eng. R.R. Club (pres. 1973-74), Louisa May Alcott Meml. Assn. (dir. 1984—, treas. 1987—), The Thoreau Soc. (dir. 1987—, treas. 1987—). Author: Verses on an Icelandic Vacation, 1965, The Church in Concord and its Ministers, 1971, In All That Dwell Below the Skies, 1972; contbr. The Meeting House on the Green, 1985. Home and Office: 35 Academy Ln Concord MA 01742-2431

SMITH, EUGENE WILLIS, elementary educator; b. Beals, Maine, Apr. 21, 1947; s. Vinton Franklin and Violet Belle (Alley) S.; m. Clara Ellen Sawyer, June 18, 1970; children: James Eugene, Franklin Charles, Richard Thomas. BS in Edn., U. Maine, 1970. Cert. type 34 profl. tchr., Maine. Social studies and sci. tchr. Elm St. Sch., East Machias, Maine, 1970-72; tchr. grades 5-8 George L. Bucknam Sch., Holmes Bay, Maine, 1972-87; grade 5 tchr. Fort O'Brien Sch., Machiasport, Maine, 1987—; income tax preparer Gene's Income Tax Svc., Beals, Maine, 1973—. Ambulance attendant Beals Ambulance Svc., 1980-90, EMT, 1991—; CPR instr. Am. Heart Assn., Augusta, Maine, 1991—. Democrat. Home: Back Field Rd Beals ME 04611-9999

SMITH, EZRA SHELDON, secondary school educator; b. N.Y.C., May 4, 1931; s. Ezra Sheldon Jr. and Virginia Rose (Fernandez) S.; m. Edith Alice McNary, Dec. 25, 1951; children: Shelley Jean, Joseph Lyman, Jennifer Lee. BS, Bridgewater State Coll., 1955, MEd, 1957; cert. advanced grad. study in Physics, Boston Coll., 1965; postgrad., Brown U., Rutgers U., MIT, U. R.I., U. Mass. at Dartmouth. Cert. sci. tchr., Mass. Optical lab technician Bay State Optical Co., Attleboro, Mass., 1948-49; tchr. sci. Attleboro Pub. Schs., 1955-61, Swansea (Mass.) Pub. Schs., 1961—; head dept. sci. Joseph Case High Sch., Swansea, 1963—; orthopedic technician Sturdy Meml. Hosp., Attleboro, 1967—; tech. and edl. cons., 1960—; med. researcher MIT Reactor, Cambridge, Mass., 1989. Author: (with others) Teaching Tips for Science Teachers, 1970, (monograph) Study of Emerging Technologies for Detection of Land Mines From the Air, 1989; contbr. articles to profl. jours. Dir. pub. rels. Parents Guild for Hard of Hearing, 1955; leader Boy Scouts Am., Attleboro, 1959-69. With U.S. Army, 1951-59, Korea. Newsmast/NASA scholar Goddard Space Flight Ctr., 1987. Mem. NSTA, NEA, Mass. Tchrs. Assn., Kappa Delta Pi, Sigma Psi (Sci. Tchr. of Yr. 1987). Home: 58 Bank St Attleboro MA 02703-2313 Office: Joseph Case High Sch 70 School St Swansea MA 02777-4599

SMITH, FRANK ACKROYD, biochemical toxicologist, educator, retired; b. Winnipeg, Man., Feb. 14, 1919; came to U.S., 1919; s. Frank and Doris A. (Babcock) S.; m. Helen Jane McGuire, Apr. 15, 1944; children: Susan Jane, Deborah Ackroyd. BA, Ohio State U., 1940, MSc, 1941, PhD, 1944. Fellow Mellon Inst. for Ind. Rsch., Pitts., 1944, U. Rochester (N.Y.) Manhattan Project, 1944-46, U. Rochester (N.Y.) Atomic Energy Project, 1946-84; instr. toxicology U. Rochester (N.Y.) Sch. Medicine & Dentistry, 1946-54, asst. prof. toxicology, 1954-58, assoc. prof. toxicology, 1958-84, ret., 1984, part time assoc. prof. toxicology, 1984-85, prof. emeritus, 1985—; cons. World Health Orgn., Geneva, 1969-73, Nat. Inst. Dental Rsch. NIH, Bethesda, Md., 1969-73, Nat. Rsch. Coun., Nat. Acad. Sci., Washington, 1971, Workers Compensation Bd. B.C., Vancouver, Conn. Dept. Health, U.S. EPA; mem. panel on water fluoridation U.S. Surgeon Gen., Washington. Co-author: Fluorine Chemistry, Vol. III, 1963, Vol. IV, 1965; contbr. chpts. to books and articles to profl. jours. Vol. Rochester (N.Y.) Mus. and Sci. Ctr. Recipient Adolph Kammer award for merit-in-authorship Am. Occupational Med. Assn., 1978. Mem. AAAS, AAUP, Am. Chem. Soc., Am. Indsl. Hygiene Assn., Am. Soc. for Pharmacology and Experimental Therapeutics, Soc. Toxicology (charter), Sigma Xi. Home: 84 Raleigh St Rochester NY 14620

SMITH, FRANKLIN L., school system administrator; b. Cape Charles, Va., May 26, 1943; s. Frank and Margaret (Dixon) S.; m. Gloria Hall, July 30, 1977; children: Franklin L. Jr., Frederick L., Ericka, Delvin L., Kristy L. BS, Va. State U., 1967, MEd, 1972; EdD, Nova U., 1980. Tchr. health, phys. edn., drivers edn. Petersburg (Va.) Pub. Schs., 1968-72, asst. prin., 1972-74, prin., 1975-82, asst. supt., 1982-85; asst. supt. Dayton (Ohio) Pub. Schs., 1985, interim supt., 1985-86, supt., 1986-91; supt. D.C. Pub. Schs., Washington, 1991—. Bd. dirs. Am. Youth Found.; chmn. membership com., mem. exec. com. of bd. dirs., co-chair AIDS edn. task force Coun. of Great City Schs.; charter mem. nat. exec. coun. Nat. Alumni Bd. Nova U., Ft. Lauderdale, Fla.; bd. dirs. Nat. Conf. Christians & Jews. Recipient Exemplary Leadership award for Region IX State of Ohio, BASA, 1988, Smitty award Miami Valley chpt. Pub. Rels. Soc. Am., 1989; named Ohio Supt. of Yr. Am. Assn. Sch. Adminstrs., 1988. Mem. NAACP (life), Am. Assn. Sch. Adminstrs., Nat. Alliance Black Sch. Adminstrs., Nat. Assn. Elem. Sch. Prins., Nat. Assn. Secondary Sch. Prins., Kappa Alpha Psi (polemarch Petersburg Alumni chpt. 1976-78, achievement award 1987), Phi Delta Kappa, Sigma Pi Phi. Democrat. Baptist. Office: DC Pub Schs 415 12th St NW Washington DC 20004-1905

SMITH, FRED CLIFTON, JR., media sales executive; b. Anderson, S.C., July 8, 1961; s. Fred Clifton Sr. and Harriet Veronica (George) S. Student, Winthrop Coll., Rock Hill, S.C., 1979-81; BA, George Washington U., 1984. Treas. Am. Conservative Trust, Washington, 1984-87; dir. advt. Campaigns and Elections Mag., Washington, 1989-91; regional sales mgr. Mil. Grocery and Mil. Lifestyle Mags., Bethesda, Md., 1991—. Mem. Am. Advt. Fedn., Advt. Club Met. Washington. Home: PO Box 57246 Washington DC 20037-0246

SMITH, GAIL HUNTER, artist; b. Nashville, Mar. 18, 1948; d. Walter Gray Smith and Eleanor Theresa (Cregar) Egan. Student, Memphis State U., 1966-67; BFA in Advt. Design, Memphis Acad. Arts, 1971. Prodn. asst. Visual Studios, Phila., 1970; asst. art dir. Eric Ericson and Assocs. and Ken White Design, Inc., Nashville, 1971-72; art dir. Contemporary Mktg., Inc., Ivan Stiles Advt., Bala Cynwyd (Pa.), Phila., 1972-74; specialist publs. design Temple U., Phila., 1974-75; represented by Quester Gallery, Stonington, Conn., 1992—, Mystic (Conn.) Maritime Gallery, 1984-90, Capricorn Gallery, Bethesda, Md., 1986-92, Cumberland Gallery, Nashville, 1982-83, The Studio L'Atelier, Nashville, 1983-85, Ambiance Fine Arts, Nashville, 1985, Arnold Art Gallery, Newport, R.I., 1986-92, Quester Gallery, Stonington, Conn., 1992—; judge Haddonfield (N.J.) Artists Exhbn., 1976; tchr. in field. Editor: Artists USA, 7th edit., Yacht Portraits, 1987; one-woman show Dow Jones & Co., Inc., Princeton, N.J., 1987, Johnson & Johnson, Inc., New Brunswick, N.Y., 1990; exhibited in group shows at 12th and 17th Tenn. All-State Artist Exhbn., Nashville, 1972, 77, Arnold Art Gallery, Newport, 1986, 87, 88, 89, 90, 91, Wildfowl Festival, Easton, Md., 1987, Mystic Maritime Gallery, 1984-86, 88-90, Capricorn Gallery, 1987, Quester Gallery, 1992. Editor: Artists USA, 7th edit., Yacht Portraits, 1987; one-woman show Dow Jones & Co., Inc., Princeton, N.J., 1987, Johnson & Johnson, Inc., New Brunswick, N.Y., 1990; exhibited in group shows at 12th and 17th Tenn. All-State Artist Exhbn., Nashville, 1972, 77, Arnold Art Gallery, Newport, 1986-91, Wildfowl Festival, Easton, Md., 1987, Mystic Maritime Gallery, 1984-86, 88-90, Capricorn Gallery, 1987, Quester Gallery, 1992. Recipient awards Nashville Ad Fedn., 1973. Mem NAFE, Artists Equity Assn., Am. Inst. Graphic Arts, Am. Soc. Marine Artists, Am. Coun. Arts, Soc. Illustrators, Soc. Scribes, Mus. Women in Arts. Office: PO Box 2602 Westfield NJ 07091-2602

SMITH, GALE EUGENE, physical chemist, retired printing technologist; b. Van Wert County, Ohio, Feb. 11, 1933; s. Lewis Frank and Olive Gertrude (Parmer) S. BA, Bowling Green State U., 1955; PhD, Mich. State U., 1963. Rsch. chemist Eastman Kodak, Rochester, N.Y., 1963-83, printing technologist, 1983-91; ret., 1991. Active Rochester (N.Y.) Theater Organ Soc., 1964—. With U.S. Army, 1956-57. Mem. Am. Chem. Soc., Soc. Photog. Scientists and Engrs., Tech. Assn. of Graphic Arts. Home: 299 Seneca Park Ave Rochester NY 14617

SMITH, GARY F., lawyer, minister; b. N.Y.C., Feb. 15, 1948; s. Seba F. and Cecelia Maryann (Ambrosio) S.; m. Eileen Marie Grosso, Aug. 23, 1969; 1 child, Evan Gary Smith. BA summa cum laude, Iona Coll., 1966-70; JD, Fordham U., 1970-73. Atty. Met. Life Ins. Co., N.Y.C., 1973-74; assoc. Koozman & Hartman, Esq., N.Y.C., 1974-77, ptnr., 1977-79; pvt. practice Westbury, N.Y., 1979-86, Hauppauge, N.Y., 1986-91. Ordained minister Jehovah's Witnesses, Westbury, N.Y., 1973-85, Port Jefferson, N.Y., 1985—. Recipient Phi Beta Kappa award Long Island Phi Beta Kappa Alumni Assn., Hempstead, N.Y., 1966, Cornelian Honor Soc. Iona Coll., New Rochelle, N.Y., 1970. Mem. Am. Bar Assn., N.Y. State Bar Assn., Suffolk County Bar Assn., Phi Alpha Delta Frat. Jehovah's Witness. Home: 2 Birch Hollow Ct Stony Brook NY 11790-1846 Office: 1363-44 Veterans Memorial Hwy Hauppauge NY 11788-3046

SMITH, GARY H., podiatrist; b. Rahway, N.J., May 6, 1949; s. Sidney and Mildred (Brown) S.; m. Judith Lynn Rhoads; children: Evan Marc, Ryan James. BA, Rutgers U., 1971; DPM, Pa. Coll. Podiatric Medicine, 1975. Diplomate Am. Bd. Podiatric Surgery. Podiatric surg. resident Parkview Hosp., 1976, Cherry Hill Hosp., 1977; pvt. practice Phila. and Mt. Laurel, N.J., 1977—; chief cons. in biomechanics Prescription Podiatry Lab., 1984—; mem. faculty Pa. Coll. Podiatric Medicine, 1980—, Calif. Coll. Podiatric Medicine, 1986—, Barry U. Coll. Podiatric Medicine, 1986—; dir. podiatric edn. Parkview Hosp., 1981-86, dir. risk mgmt. seminar, 1988, 91, 92; dir. sports medicine seminar Parkview Hosp., 1979-84; chief of podiatry Meml. Hosp. of Burlington County, Mt. Holly, N.J., 1983—, Episcopal Hosp., Phila., 1986—, Parkview Hosp., Phila., 1986—. Author: (chpt.) Out Patient Surgery, 1989, Current Topics Podiatric Surgery, 1989; contbr. articles to profl. jours.; inventor biobalancing system of three med. instruments. Named one of Outstanding Young Men in Am., 1975; recipient Disting. Physician's award, 1990. Fellow Am. Coll. Foot Surgeons; mem. APHA, Am. Podiatric Med. Assn., Am. Acad. Podiatric Sports Medicine, Pa. Podiatric Med. Assn., Am. Diabetes Assn. Office: Mayfair Med Bldg 6921 D Franford Ave Philadelphia PA 19135 Office: Route 38 And Ark Rd Mount Laurel NJ 08054

SMITH, GERALD STEVEN, aerospace engineer; b. Middletown, Conn., Feb. 13, 1962; s. Jarvis Elmer S. and Maria Josefina (Salgado) Coleman. AAS in Airport Ops., USAF Community Coll., 1985; BS in Decision Sci., George Mason U., 1986; postgrad., U. Denver, 1990, U. Md., 1991. EDP analyst govt. info. svcs. group Boeing Computer Svcs., Vienna, Va., 1986-87; systems analyst space sta. freedom Boeing Computer Svcs., Reston, Va., 1987-89; engr., analyst command and control group RJO Enterprises, Lanham, Md., 1987; sr. tech. specialist flight dynamics tech. group Computer Sci. Corp., Goddard Space Flight Ctr., Md., 1989; satellite controller Intelsat Satellite Control Ctr., Washington, 1989-90, ops. analyst, 1990-91, spacecraft engr. flight ops. sect., 1991—. Staff sgt. ANG, 1980-86. Mem. AIAA (space ops. and support tech. com. 1991—), Nat. Space Soc. Home: 4241 Columbia Pike Apt 404 Arlington VA 22204 Office: Intelsat Box 34 3400 International Dr NW Washington DC 20008-3098

SMITH, GRAHAM MONRO, chemist, researcher; b. Bayshore, N.Y., Nov. 11, 1947; s. Charles Edward and Ruth Elizabeth (Hildreth) S.; m. Peggy Goethals Bason, Nov. 27, 1971; children: Kenneth, Karen. BA, Adelphi U., 1969; PhD, SUNY, Buffalo, 1974. Postdoctoral fellow Princeton U., N.J., 1974-75, U. Santa Cruz, Calif., 1975-76; sr. rsch. chemist Merck Sharp & Dohme Rsch. Labs., Rahway, N.J., 1976-81; rsch. fellow Merck Sharp & Dohme Rsch. Labs., Rahway, 1981-85; sr. rsch. fellow Merck Sharp & Dohme Rsch. Labs., West Point, Pa., 1985-88; sr. investigator Merck Sharp & Dohme Rsch. Labs., West Point, 1988—. Author (with others): Molecular Modeling in Drug Discovery, 1987. Mem. AAAS, Am. Chem. Soc., N.Y. Acad. Scis. Office: Merck Sharp & Dohme Rsch Labs WP 42-3 PO Box 4 West Point PA 19486-0004

SMITH, GREGORY DEAN, academic administrator; b. Decatur, Ill., Aug. 18, 1948; s. Harold Roy and Evelyn Anna (Sulleng) S.; m. Margaret Ann Capozzola, Jan. 2, 1982; 1 child, Stephane. BA, U. Ill., 1970, MA, 1971; MPhil, NYU, 1985. Asst. budget officer City of Newark, N.J., 1971-74; div. chief City of New York, 1974-80; dep. controller D.C., Washington, 1980-83; budget officer New Sch. for social Rsch., N.Y.C., 1983-89, v.p., 1989—. Mem. Phi Beta Kappa. Democrat. Episcopalian. Home: 120 Center Ave Chatham NY 07982

SMITH, MONSIGNOR GREGORY MICHAEL, priest, adult education administrator; b. Danbury, Conn., May 25, 1941; s. Michael Paul and Helen Marie (McFarland) S. MA, Fairfield U., 1973; MDiv, St. Mary U., Balt., 1976; MS, Fordham U., 1976; EdD, NYU, 1982. Assoc. pastor St. Teresa Ch., Trumbull, Conn., 1967-69, St. Joseph Ch., Danbury, Conn., 1969-72; asst. dir. rel. edn. Diocese of Bridgeport, Conn., 1972-75, dir. rel. edn., 1975-83, chancellor, 1983-90, sec. edn., 1985-89; adminstr. Office for Catechesis, Bridgeport, 1990-92; dir. Inst. for Religious Edn. and Pastoral Studies Sacred Heart U., Fairfield, Conn., 1990—; bd. dirs. Conn. Cath. Conf. Author: Pilgrims in Process, 1978, The Fire in Their Eyes, 1984, (with others) Priming the Pump, 1989; contbr. articles to profl. jours. Bd. dirs. Fairfield Found., Bridgeport, 1983—, Danbury Assn. to Aid Handicapped/Retarded, 1970-72, com. on edn. and morality NYU, 1990—; commr. Youth Coun. City of Danbury, 1970-72. Mem. Am. Assn. Adult and Continuing Edn., Nat. Conf. Diocesan Dirs. (bd. dirs. 1974-77), Nat. Catholic Ednl. Assn., Religious Edn. Assn., New England Conf. Diocesan Dirs. (pres. 1977-79), Nat. Assn. Ch. Pers. Adminstrs., Assn. Grad. Programs in Ministry. Roman Catholic. Home: 163 Ortega Ave Bridgeport CT 06606-3053 Office: Sacred Heart U 5151 Park Ave Fairfield CT 06432-1000

SMITH, HAMILTON OTHANEL, molecular biologist, educator; b. N.Y.C., Aug. 23, 1931; s. Bunnie Othanel and Tommie Harkey S.; m. Elizabeth Anne Bolton, May 25, 1957; children: Joel, Barry, Dirk, Bryan, Kirsten. Student, U. Ill., 1948-50; A.B. in Math, U. Calif., Berkeley, 1952; M.D., Johns Hopkins U., 1956. Intern Barnes Hosp., St. Louis, 1956-57; resident in medicine Henry Ford Hosp., Detroit, 1959-62; USPHS fellow dept. human genetics U. Mich., Ann Arbor, 1962-64; rsch. assoc. U. Mich., 1964-67; asst. prof. molecular biology and genetics Sch. Medicine Johns Hopkins U., Balt., 1967-69; assoc. prof. Johns Hopkins U., 1969-73, prof., 1973—; asso. Inst. für Molekularbologie der U. Zurich, Switzerland, 1975-76; assoc. Rsch. Inst. Molecular Pathology, Vienna, 1990-91. Contbr. articles to profl. jours. Served to lt. M.C. USNR, 1957-59. Recipient Nobel Prize in medicine, 1978; Guggenheim fellow, 1975-76. Mem. Am. Soc. Microbiology, AAAS, Am. Soc. Biol. Chemists, Nat. Acad. Sci. Office: Johns Hopkins U Sch Med Dept Molecular Biology/Gen 725 N Wolfe St Baltimore MD 21205-2105

SMITH, HAROLD CHARLES, private pension fund executive; b. N.Y.C., Jan. 11, 1934; s. Harold Elmore and Hedwig Agnes (Gronke) S. BA cum laude with honors, Ursinus Coll., 1955; MBA, NYU, 1958; M in Div., Union Theol. Sem., N.Y.C., 1958. Ordained minister United Ch. of Christ, 1959. Vice pres. YMCA Retirement Fund, Inc., N.Y.C., 1958-69, portfolio mgr., 1960—, assoc. sec., 1969-77, v.p., 1977-80, exec. v.p., 1980-82, pres. elect, 1982-83, pres., 1983—; pastor 1st E&R Ch., Bridgeport, Conn., 1958-88, Unity Hill United Ch. of Christ, 1988—; assoc. prof. bus. and fin. L.I. U., 1969-71; trustee Bank Mart, Bridgeport, Conn., 1983-91; bd. dirs. Y Mut. Ins. Co., treas. 1988—, United Ch. Residencies, 1962-65. Trustee YWCA Greater Bridgeport, 1975-79, Pension Funds United Ch. of Christ, 1968—, Springfield Coll. (Mass.), 1983—; bd. dirs. YMCA Greater N.Y., 1983—, Bridgeport Area Found., 1989—. Cert. fin. analyst. Mem. N.Y. Soc. Security Analysts, Am. Econs. Assn., Fin. Analysts Fedn., World and Trade Club, Mcht's Club, Masons, Marco Polo Club, Order Eastern Star. Author: Getting it All Together for Retirement, 1977. Office: YMCA Retirement 225 Broadway New York NY 10007-3001

SMITH, HARRY JOSEPH, publisher, writer; b. N.Y.C., Oct. 15, 1936; s. Harry Joseph and May Anna (Dinkelmeyer) S.; m. Marion Camilla Petschek, Feb. 21, 1958; children: Tristram, Lisa, Rebecca. AB, Brown U., 1958. Reporter Southbridge (Mass.) Evening News, 1958-59, Worcester (Mass.) Telegram, 1959; mng. editor Modern Server, N.Y.C., 1960-62; editor-in-chief Recess, N.Y.C., 1962-64; pub. The Smith, N.Y.C., 1964—; chmn. COSMEP-The Internat. Assn. of Ind. Pubs., San Francisco, 1972-74, bd. dirs., past bd. dirs. Author: Trinity, 1975, Me, The People, 1980, Ballads for the Possessed, 1988, (with Menke Katz) Two Friends, 1989. Mem. PEN (Medwick award 1975). Democrat. Office: The Smith Pubs 69 Joralemon St Brooklyn NY 11201

SMITH, HELENE CATHERINE, publisher, writer, researcher; b. Youngstown, Ohio, Feb. 6, 1935; d. John Bowie and Frances Cecilia (Arthur) Snyder; m. Wayne E. Smith Jr., June 8, 1958; children: Cheryl Helene Smith Genovesi, Michael Wayne (dec.), Gregory Martin, Jennifer Lynn Smith Benzer, Laurel Ann. BA, Westminster Coll., 1958. Cert. Pa. historian. Freelance artist and musician Pa., 1960—, freelance writer, 1973—; owner, pres. McDonald/Swärd Pub. Co. (subs. Am. North East House Pub.), Greensburg, Pa., 1986—; researcher for Edgar J. Kaufmann, Jr. Author: Getting Down to Earth, 1980, Export, A Patch of Tapestry out of Coal Country America, 1986, (children's book) Rings, Springs and Thingamajigs, 1990, (novel) So Circles the Eagle, 1992, (play) Carry A Nation, 1984, rev. edit., 1989, (screenplay) Ethelbert (Nevin), 1980, (folk art) Tavern Signs of America--A Catalog, 1988, Tavern Signs of America--A History, 1989; co-author: A Guidebook to Historic Western Pennsylvania, 1976, rev. edit., 1991, The Carnegie Nobody Knows, 1989, (plays) Lest We Forget, Wellspring of Power, A Place of Consequence; co-author, illustrator: (children's novel) Hannah's Town, 1973; contbg. author: Rolling Rivers: An Encyclopedia of American Rivers, 1984, (dictionary) Big City Mayors, 1980; illustrator: The Governors of Pennsylvania, 1990. Co-dir. historic survey light rail transit, Pitts.; co-dir. historic site survey Westmoreland County, Pa., 1979-81; Rep. minority insp., Westmoreland County, 1987—; mem. fife and drum corps., 1980—. Named hon. life mem. Westmoreland County Hist. Soc., 1980. Office: McDonald/Swärd Pub Co Preservation Hill Box 104A RD3 Greensburg PA 15601

SMITH, HERBERT CHARLES, political science educator; b. Phila., June 13, 1946; s. Charles Joseph and Margaret Carolyn (Goessman) S.; m. Elise Ann Hopkins, Sept. 14, 1968; children: Megan Meredith, Tyler Hopkins. BA, Ursinus Coll., 1968; MA, Johns Hopkins U., 1971, PhD, 1976. Asst. prof. Western Md. Coll., Westminster, Md., 1973-81, assoc. prof., 1981-89, prof. polit. sci., 1989—; dir. polling Sta. WBAL-TV (CBS), Balt., 1986—; cons. Bd. Elections Suprs., Balt., 1987—; rsch. assoc. Schaefer Ctr. for Pub. Policy, Balt., 1988—; sec. of the faculty Western Md. Coll., Westminster, 1989—. Author: Baltimore Votes, Vol. I, 1988, Vol. II, 1989, Vol. III, 1990; contbr. periodic columns to Balt. Sunpapers. Pres. Oakenshawe Improvement Assn., Balt., 1976-80; bd. dirs. Greater Homewood Community Corp., Balt., 1976-80; mem. adminstrv. bd. Grace United Ch., Balt., 1988—; coach Roland Park Little League, Balt., 1988—, pres., 1992—. Mem. Am. Polit. Sci. Assn., Am. Assn. Pub. Opinion Rsch. Home: 310 Southway Baltimore MD 21218-2517 Office: Western Md Coll Main St Westminster MD 21157-5007

SMITH, HOKE LAFOLLETTE, university president; b. Galesburg, Ill., May 7, 1931; s. Claude Hoke and Bernice (LaFollette) S.; m. Barbara F. Walvoord, June 30, 1979; children by previous marriage—Kevin, Kerry, Amy, Glen. B.A. (Harold fellow), Knox Coll., 1953; M.A., U. Va., 1954; Ph.D. (fellow 1958), Emory U., 1958. Asst. prof. polit. sci. Hiram Coll., Ohio, 1958-64; assoc. prof. polit. sci. Hiram Coll., 1964-67; asst. to pres., prof. polit. sci. Drake U., Des Moines, Iowa, Md., 1967-70; chmn. interim governing com. Drake U., 1971-72, v.p. acad. adminstrn., 1970-79; pres. Towson (Md.) State U., 1979—; mem. univ. adv. council Life Ins. Council Am., 1969-71. Chmn. exec. com. Coun. Econ. Edn., Md., Towson, 1979—; mem. Balt. County Econ. Devel. Commn., 1988—; bd. dirs. Balt. Coun. on Fgn. Rels. Served with U.S. Army, 1954-56. Recipient Eileen Tosney award Am. Assn. Univ Administrs., 1991; Congl. fellow Am. Polit. Sci. Assn., 1964-65. Mem. Am. Assn. State Colls. and Univs. (bd. dirs. 1984-88, bd. dirs. found. 1985-87, chmn.-elect 1985-86, chmn. 1986-87, past chmn. 1987-88), Am. Coun. Edn. (bd. dirs., exec. com. 1988—, chmn.-elect 1991-92, chmn. 1992—), Am. Assn. Higher Edn., Soc. for Coll. and Univ. Planning (bd. dirs. 1986-88), Balt. C. of C. (adv. coun.), Phi Beta Kappa, Phi Kappa Phi, Omicron Delta Kappa, Delta Sigma Rho, Gamma Gamma, Pi Sigma Alpha. Office: Towson State U Office of Pres Baltimore MD 21204

SMITH, HOWARD ALAN, astrophysicist; b. Boston, June 1, 1944; s. Edward W. and Sarah Smith; m. Nancy Rigelhaupt; children: Avi, Sarah. BS in Humanities, Sci., MIT, 1966, BS in Physics, 1966, postgrad., 1966-67; PhD in Physics, U. Calif., Berkeley, 1976. Rsch. asst. dept. physics U. Calif., Berkeley, 1968-76; rsch. assoc. lunar and planetary lab. U. Ariz., Tucson, 1976-79, rsch. assoc. Steward obs., 1979-81; astrophysicist Naval Rsch. Lab., Washington, 1981-89; chm. lab. for astrophysics Nat. Air and Space Mus., Smithsonian Instn., Washington, 1989—. Contbr. articles to profl. jours. Active environ., civic and synagogue groups. Mem. AAAS, Am. Phys. Soc., Am. Astron. Soc., Optical Soc. Am., Internat. Astron. Union, Astron. Soc. of the Pacific. Office: Smithsonian Instn Nat Air and Space Mus Lab for Astrophysics Washington DC 20560

SMITH, HOWARD FRANKLIN, real estate executive; b. N.Y.C., Feb. 17, 1930; s. Alexander and Sadie (Weiner) S.; m. Jeannette Trotta, July 12, 1957; children: Shawn, Moira, Amanda. BS, NYU, 1955. Real estate salesman C.B. Snyder Realty Co., Hoboken, N.J., 1955-56; real estate mgr. IBM Corp., N.Y.C., 1956-61; v.p. Uris Bldgs. Corp., N.Y.C., 1961-62; sr. v.p. Cushman & Wakefield, Inc., N.Y.C., 1962-78; pres. Dailey Smith & Co., Inc., N.Y.C., 1978-80; exec. v.p. Cross and Brown Co., N.Y.C., 1980-88, Pearce Perrone & Co., Inc., N.Y.C., 1988-90; sr. v.p. Helmsley-Noyes Co., Inc., N.Y.C., 1990—; instr. Real Estate Licensees Continuing Edn. program. Mem. spl. real estate task force Westchester County Bd. of Legislators, White Plains, 1986. With U.S. Army, 1951-53. Recipient William L. Scott Meml. award Westchester County Bd. Realtors, 1986. Mem. Mil. Order of Purple Heart (life), Am. Arbitration Assn., Soc. Indsl. and Office Realtors, N.Y. State Assn. Realtors (bd. dirs. 1984-91, pres. comml. and investment div. 1986), Nat. Assn. Realtors (bd. dirs. 1987-88). Office: Helmsley Noyes Co Inc 22 Cortlandt St New York NY 10007

SMITH, J. OTIS, management consultant, educator; b. Wilmington, N.C., Aug. 30, 1941; s. J. Otis and Karey (Bailey) S.; m. Theresa Hill, Aug. 14, 1965; children: J. Otis III, Karen Michelle, J. Ryan. BA, Oberlin Coll., 1963; MA, Temple U., 1965, EdD, 1971. Asst. dean of students Temple U., Phila., 1966-71; assoc. prof. then prof. psychology Cheyney (Pa.) U., 1973—, v.p. student affairs, 1973-75; treas. Stand By Systems II Inc., Phila., 1978—, pres., 1976-78. Treas. Phila. Swimming Adv. Coun., 1981—. Mem. Am. Assn. Counseling and Devel. (treas. 1984, chmn. profl. devel. directorate 1990-91), Assn. Multicultural Counseling and Devel. (treas. 1982-83), Alpha Phi Alpha. Episcopalian. Office: Stand By Systems II Inc PO Box 8222 Philadelphia PA 19101-8222

SMITH, JACK LOUIS, biochemistry educator, academic administrator; b. Huntington, W.Va., July 15, 1934; s. William Baughman Smith and Violet Ruby (Roberts) York; m. Carol L. Schroherloher, Jan. 7, 1961; children: Karen, Michael. BS in Pharmacy, U. Cinn., 1956, PhD in Biochemistry, 1961. Asst. prof. biochemistry Tulane U., New Orleans, 1965-71, assoc. prof., 1971-74; assoc. prof. biochem. U. Nebr. Med. Ctr., Omaha, 1974-83; assoc. prof. dept. human nutrition and food svc. mgmt. U. Nebr., Lincoln, 1975-84; clin. prof. preventive medicine and pub. health Creighton U., Omaha, 1976-84; Swanson prof. biochemistry U. Nebr. Med. Ctr., Omaha, 1983-84; exec. v.p. Strategic Mktg. Assn., Inc., Mt. Laurel, N.J., 1984-87; prof. and chair dept. nutrition and dietetics U. Del., Newark, 1989—; dep. dir. Swansons Ctr. For Nutrition, Inc., Omaha, 1976-84; adj. prof. U. Nebr. Med. Ctr., 1984-85; pres. J. Smith and Assocs., Inc., Newark, 1981—; dir. Network Ctr. Contemporary Nutrition U. Del., Newark, 1988—. Bd. dirs. Internat. Dietary Info. Found., 1979-82, pres. bd. dirs., 1982—. Fellow Am. Coll. Nutrition; mem. Am. Bd. Nutrition (cert. specialist human nutrition sci.), Am. Dietetic Assn., Am. Soc. Clin. Nutrition, Inc., N.Y. Acad. Sci., Nutrient Databank Assn., Sigma Xi.

SMITH, JAMES ALAN, physicist, researcher; b. Detroit, Nov. 19, 1942; s. Robert S. Hogan and Mildred (Markwick) Wentz. BS in Math., U. Mich., 1963, MS in Math., 1965, PhD in Physics, 1970; MS in Computer Sci., Johns Hopkins U., 1992. Rsch. asst. Willow Run Labs., Ann Arbor, Mich., 1964-66; rsch. assoc. dept. physics U. Mich., Ann Arbor, 1966-70; from asst. prof. to prof. Colo. State U., Ft. Collins, 1970-85, assoc. dir. Computer Ctr., 1974-76; br. head biospheric scis. NASA, Greenbelt, Md., 1985-90, assoc. chief sci. info. systems Goddard Space Flight Ctr., 1990, staff scientist lab. for terrestrial physics Goddard Space Flight Ctr., 1990—; cons. numerous fed. agys. and industries, 1970-85; prin. investigator NASA, Army Rsch. Office, U.S. Forest Svc., U.S. Geol. Survey, U.S. Fish and Wildlife Svc., others, 1970-90. Author, editor book chpts. and monographs; contbr. articles to profl. jours. Mem. IEEE (sr., assoc. editor Transactions on Geoscis. and Remote Sensing 1983-91, editor 1991—), Am. Geophys. Union. Office: NASA Goddard Space Flight Ctr Code 920 Greenbelt MD 20771

SMITH, JAMES ALMER, JR., psychiatrist; b. Montclair, N.J., May 30, 1923; s. James Almer and Carrie Elizabeth (Moten) S.; m. Elsie Mae Brooks; children: James III, Roger, Margo, Melanie. BS, Howard U., 1947, MD, 1948. Diplomate Am. Bd. Psychiatry and Neurology. Staff psychiatrist Hartley Salmon Child Guidance Ctr., Hartford, Conn., 1955-60; assoc. psychiatrist Child Guidance Clinic Springfield (Mass.), 1960-83; cons. psychiatrist Gandara Mental Health Ctr., Springfield, 1984—; med. dir. Kolburne Sch., New Marlborough, Mass., 1969—; bd. dirs. Hampden Mental Health Dist., Springfield, 1968—; cons. psychiatrist Childrens' Services Hartford, 1956-60, Childrens' Study Ctr., Springfield, 1960—, W.W. Johnson Ctr., Springfield, 1979—. Bd. dirs. Springfield Commn. on Human Relations, 1961-62, Negro Cath. Scholarship Fund of Springfield, 1976—. Served to capt. M.C., U.S. Army, 1953-55. Recipient Dr. Anthony Brown award W. W. Johnson Ctr., 1987. Fellow Am. Orthopsychiat. Assn., Am. Assn. Psychoanalytic Physicians (pres. 1979-81), Soc. Psychoanalytic Physicians; mem. Am. Psychiat. Assn., Am. Soc. Psychoanalytic Physicians, Sigma Pi Phi. Baptist. Club: Squires of Springfield (pres. 1980-81). Home and Office: 96 Dartmouth St Springfield MA 01109-3909

SMITH, JAMES BIGELOW, SR., electrical engineer; b. Hamilton, Ont., Can., Dec. 18, 1908; s. Percy Merrihew and Ethel Burgess (Torrey) S.; m. Elizabeth Perry Dane, Mar. 1936 (div. 1954); children: James Bigelow Jr., Sylvia Perry, David Prentiss; m. Catharine Dean Temple, Jan. 17, 1959. BSEE, MIT, 1932, MSEE, 1933. Registered profl. engr., Mass. Quality control engr. Sylvania Electric Products Co., Salem, Mass., 1933; claims adjuster Liberty Mutual Ins. Soc., N.Y.C. and Lynn, Mass., 1933-35; lab. engr. engr.-in-charge sect. Factory Mutual Rsch. Corp., Norwood, Mass., 1935-74, asst. chief engr. to chief engr., v.p., mgr. applied rsch.; assoc. cons. engr. Lement & Assocs., Waltham, MA, 1974—; chair black liquor recovery boiler adv. com. for pulp and paper industry, 1960's. Patentee fire protection methods and systems apparatus. Fellow Soc. Fire Protection Engrs. (life, charter mem., pres. New Eng. chpt. 1962-63, historian 1980—, bd. dirs. 1980—, Richard E. Stevens award 1985), Nat. Fire Protection Assn. (life, past chair oven and furnace com.), Fire Detection Inst. (past chair). Home and Office: 25 Mitchell Grant Way Bedford MA 01730-1258

SMITH, J(AMES) BRIAN, school system administrator; b. Camden, Maine, Dec. 13, 1943; s. Clifford Russell and Ruth Melvina (Alexander) S.; m. Cynthia V. Cashman, Aug. 5, 1967 (div. 1971); m. Negar Paydar, Nov. 19, 1978; children: Negin, Vahid, Tristan, James. Student, Coll. Wooster, 1962-63, U. Hawaii, 1963-64; BA in English, U. Maine, 1967; postgrad., Va. Poly. and State U., 1977-78; MS in Ednl. Adminstrn., U. So. Maine, 1982; postgrad., Boston Coll. Cert. sch. supt., Maine. Owner, dir., operator pvt. summer boys camp, 1962-65; asst. sailing instr. Camden Yacht Club, 1966-67; jr. high sch. English & social studies tchr. Bath, Maine, 1967; sr. high sch. English and U.S. history tchr. Old Town (Maine) Schs., 1967-68; jr. high sch. English and U.S. history tchr. Union (Maine) Schs., 1968-71; entrepreneur, broker, fin. planner, 1971-75; tchr. English Wishaw (Scotland) Sr. Secondary Sch., 1975-77; tchr. high sch. English, U.S. history, govt., econs. Iran Electronics Industries Sch., Shiraz, 1977-78; tchr. English Portland (Maine) High Sch., 1977-78; tchr. English and world history Falmouth (Maine) High Sch., 1979-82; teaching prin. Palermo (Maine) Consol. Sch., 1982-84; supt. schs. Maine Sch. Union # 104, 1984-86, Maine Indian Edn., Indian Island, 1986—; invited keynote speaker Maine Dept. Edn., 1991; apptd. del. to White House Conf. on Indian Edn., 1992; chmn. edn. com. United South and Eastern Tribes, Nashville. Mem. drug and alcohol and exec. coms. Maine Sch. Supts. Assn.; mem. program rev. and comment com. div. alcohol and drug ednl svcs Maine Dept. Edn.; sch. bd. mem. South and Eastern Tribes Agy. Sch. Bd., Bur. Indian Affairs, Dept. Interior. Mem. ASCD, Am. Assn. Sch. Adminstrs. (past mem. resolutions com.), New England Assn. Supts. Schs., Maine Sch. Supts. Assn. (chmn. ad hoc com. on Maine ednl. assessment program), New England Supts. Leadership Coun. (mem. adv. bd.), Washington County Supts. Assn., The Grange, Phi Delta Kappa. Office: Maine Indian Edn River Rd PO Box 412 Calais ME 04619

SMITH, JAMES DONALDSON, geology and mining consultant; b. Wilkes-Barre, pa., Aug. 23, 1922; s. Donald Noah and Helen Louise (Marshall) S.; m. Mary Ann Hyson, June 29, 1947 (dec. Nov. 1990); children: Kathryn, Laurie Susan, Jane. BS in Geology and Mining, Pa. State U., 1949. Registered profl. engr., Pa., geologist, Va., Calif., land surveyor, Pa.; lic. blaster, Pa. Mining geologist U.S. Bur. Mines, Wilkes-Barre, 1950-51; mng. and safety engr. Lehigh Navigation Coal Co., Lansford, Pa., 1951-54; chief geologist pa. Turnpike Commn., Highspire, 1954-65; dir. geotech. engring. Michael Baker Corp., Beaver, Pa., 1965-73; pvt. practice geotech. engring. cons. Beaver, 1973-74; geologist, engr. Pullman-Swindell div. Pullman Corp., Pitts., 1974-81, John T. Boyd Co., Pitts., 1981-82; pvt. practice geol. and mining cons. Beaver, 1982—; presenter symposium in field. Author publs. in field. Pres. Lions Club, Lansford, 1962. Lt. (j.g.) USN, 1942-46, PTO. Fellow Geol. Soc. Am.; mem. AIME, Assn. Engring. Geologists, Am. Inst. Profl. Geologists (charter mem.), Brit. Tunnelling Soc. (charter mem.),. Republican. Home and Office: 111 Crest Dr Beaver PA 15009-9353

SMITH, JAMES ERVIN, research company executive, research demographer; b. Phila., May 16, 1949; s. John E. and Elaine L. (Hurtt) S.; m. Margaret Smith. BS in Sociology, Brigham Young U., 1975; MA in Sociology, U. So. Calif., 1975, PhD, 1979. Asst. prof. Brigham Young U., Provo, Utah, 1976-82; rsch. scientist Cambridge Group for History of Population, 1982-84; mgr., exec. Westat Inc., Rockville, Md., 1985—. Contbr. chpts. to books, articles to profl. jours. Mem. Population Assn. Am., Internat. Union for the Sci. Study of Population. Office: Westat Inc 1650 Research Blvd Rockville MD 20850-3195

SMITH, JAMES FREDERICK, securities executive; b. N.Y.C., Jan. 6, 1944; s. James Arthur and Agnes Rose (Kollenz) S.; m. Joan Ann Kelly, June 18, 1966; children: James Patrick, John Michael. BBA in Accountancy Practice, Pace U., 1970. CPA, N.Y.; registered fin. & operational prin., registered rep. Mgmt. trainee Chase Manhattan Bank, N.Y.C., 1965-67; internal auditor MW Kellogg & Co., N.Y.C., 1967-69; sr. acct. Price Waterhouse, N.Y.C., 1969-72; asst. treas. and contr. Henderson Bros. Inc., N.Y.C., 1972-80; pvt. practice Clearwater, Fla., 1980-82; sr. audit mgr. Price Waterhouse, N.Y.C., 1982-84; v.p. & contr. Integrated Resources, N.Y.C., 1984-86; sr. v.p., chief fin. officer Freeman Securities, Jersey City, 1986—. With USN, 1961-65. Mem. AICPA, Internat. Soc. CEBS (charter mem.), N.Y. State Soc. CPA, Securities Industry Assn., Pub. Securities Assn., Wall St. Tax Assn. Home: 3 Greenfield Ter Congers NY 10920-2606 Office: Freeman Securities 30 Montgomery St Jersey City NJ 10732

SMITH, JAMES HOWARD, accountant; b. Charleston, W.Va., Feb. 11, 1947; s. James Carlisle and Charlene Louise (Jones) S.; m. Kimberley Ann Johnson-Smith, Jan. 1, 1977; children: James Lloyd Woodward, Stephen Adam Carlisle. Student, Duke U., 1965-67, U. Tenn.-Nashville, summers 1970-72; BS, Belmont Coll., 1973; MBA, So. Ill. U., 1979. CPA, Tenn., D.C. Adminstr. Williams, Shields & Wildman, Attys., Nashville, 1973-75; tax law specialist IRS, Washington, 1975-77; supr. Ernst & Young, Washington, 1977-79, nat. dir. tax and fin. services Utility Group, Washington, 1979-91, internat. utility and fin. cons., 1991—. Speaker on utility's coop. fin. and taxation. Author: Federal Income Taxation of Rural Electric Cooperatives, 1982, Depreciation, Salvage, and Cost of Removal: A Critical Analysis, 1982. Mem. Boy Scouts Am., 1988—, chmn. project sales nat. capital area coun., 1990—; treas. Waverly Hills Homeowners Assn., Arlington, Va., 1983, spokesman before county bd., 1983; treas. Animal Welfare League of Arlington (Va.), 1975-83, Animal Welfare Found. Arlington, 1983; v.p. Adam Walsh Child Resource Ctr. Greater Washington; bd. dirs. Missing Children of Greater Washington, 1985-88. With USN, 1967-70. Decorated with two Bronze Star medal with cluster, Purple Heart; recipient Spl. Achievement award U.S. Dept. Treasury, 1977. Fellow D.C. Inst. CPA's; mem. AICPA, Tenn. Soc. CPAs, Nat. Assn. Accts. for Coops., Nat. Acctg. Assn., Arlington C. of C., Duke U. Alumni Assn., So. Ill. U. Alumni Assn., Tower Club, James B. Duke Club. Republican. Presbyterian. Home: 3131 N Piedmont St Arlington VA 22207-5330 Office: Ernst & Young Utility Group 1225 Connecticut Ave NW Washington DC 20036-2604

SMITH, JAMES PARKER, accountant; b. N.Y.C., July 5, 1959; s. John Patterson and Georgina (Budd) S.; m. Karen Ann Ahrens, June 3, 1989. AS in acctg., Suffolk County Community Coll., Riverhead, N.Y., 1979; BS in acctg., SUNY, Plattsburgh, 1981. Accountant Fink Rainer and Nickl, Lindenhurst, N.Y., 1983-84, Fenelon Crowley and Tutino, E. Hampton, N.Y., 1984-86, Markowitz Preishe and Stevens, E. Hampton, N.Y., 1987-89; sr. acct. Advanced Healthcare Resources, Inc., Hauppauge, N.Y., 1989—; tax preparer, 1982—. Mem. Nat. Soc. Tax Profls., Alpha Sigma. Methodist.

SMITH, JAMES PEMBROKE, service industry and franchising executive; b. Beaver County, Pa., Aug. 11, 1950; s. Gilbert Oscar and Louise E. (McCowan) S.; m. Nancy Strella, Aug. 29, 1970; children: Yvonne Rene', James Pembroke Jr. Student, Clarion U. Pa., 1968-70; AA in Bus. Adminstrn. and Mktg., Fullerton Coll., 1977; student, U. N. Fla., 1979-80, U. Pitts., 1983-84. Sales engr. N.E. U.S. consumer products div. Thetford Corp., Ann Arbor, Mich., 1974; sales engr. S.W. U.S. appliance div. Thetford Corp., Anaheim, Calif., 1975-77; sales and mktg. mgr. svc. div. Thetford Corp., Jacksonville, Fla., 1977-78, v.p. sales and mktg. svc. div., 1979-81; tng. mgr. The Linc Corp., Pitts., 1981-83, nat. sales mgr. and tng. mgr., 1984, dir. ops. and devel., 1985, v.p. mktg. and ops., 1986-87, v.p. franchise devel., 1988-90, v.p. new bus. rsch. and devel., 1991—; instr. negotiation course Community Coll. Allegheny County, 1985; mem. exec. rev. com. The Linc Corp., Pitts., 1985—, mem. exec. reorgn. com., 1988. Author: Service Management and Operations, 1979, Customer Relations in Service Industry, 1982, Project Pricing, 1983; (franchise devel. package) We Are Looking, 1980 (Outstanding Franchise Package, Internat. Franchise Assn. 1980); (sales tng. program) Linc Service Sales Training, 1982; (tng. program) Effective Negotiation Skills, 1985; contbr. articles to profl. jours. Sgt. Shriver Peace Corps scholar Peace Corps, 1968. Mem. Internat. Franchise Assn. (trade and pub. rels. com. 1980-83, franchise rels. com. 1984), Am. Soc. Tng. & Devel., Boy Scouts Am., Masons (charities com. 1983—). Republican. Lutheran. Home: 1797 Locust Rd Sewickley PA 15143-8556

SMITH, JANET SUE, systems specialist; b. Chgo., Jan. 15, 1945; d. Curtis Edwin and Margaret Louise (Yost) Smith; B.A., Ind. U., 1967. Sales mgr. Marshall Field & Co., Chgo., 1968-70, programmer, 1970-72; sr. programmer, analyst Trailer Train Co., Chgo., 1972-75; mgr. data base and systems devel. RAILINC-Assn. Am. R.R., Washington, 1975-85, asst. v.p. to pres., corp. sec., 1985—. Nat. student v.p. YWCA, 1966-67; bd. dirs., v.p. planning and fin. Guide Internat., Friends of the Nat. Zoo; advisor Jr. Achievement. Mem. Am. Council R.R. Women, Ind. U. Alumni Assn. (life), Women's Transp. Seminar. Home: 2000 N St NW Washington DC 20036-2336 Office: 50 F St NW Washington DC 20001

SMITH, JAY LESTER, government executive; b. Washington, May 18, 1945; s. Lester Thomas and Virginia Katherine (Murphy) S.; m. Wendy Haimes, Oct. 1, 1983. BS, Georgetown U., 1968. Internat. project mgr. Internat. Trade Adminstrn., U.S Dept. Commerce, Washington, 1975—. Author: Enemy in View, 1991. Home: 5000 Nebraska Ave Washington DC 20008 Office: ITA US Dept Commerce Rm 2015 Washington DC 20230

SMITH, JEFFERY STEVEN, psychiatrist; b. Palo Alto, Calif., Oct. 28, 1945; s. Harold Jeffery and Elizabeth (Driscoll) S.; m. Claude Marguerite (Driscoll) S.; m. Claude Marguerite Penaud, July 22, 1967; children: Anne, Matthew, Colin. BA, Stanford U., 1968; MD, UCLA, 1972. Diplomate Am. Bd. Psychiatry and Neurology. Intern in internal medicine SUNY Upstate Med. Ctr., Syracuse, 1972-73; residen in psychiatry Albert Einstein Coll. Medicine, Bronx, N.Y., 1973-76; chief physician outpatient psychiatry Bronx-Lebanon Hosp. Ctr., Bronx, N.Y., 1977-80; dir. alcoholism svcs. N.F.W. York Med. Coll., Valmalla, N.Y., 1981-89; founding med. dir. Cortland Med. Ouptatient Rehab. Ctr., Hawthorne, N.Y., 1989—; asst. prof. psychiatry N.Y. Med. Coll., Valhalla, N.Y., 1990—. Roman Catholic. Office: Cortland Med Outpatient Rehab Ctr 4 Skyline Dr Hawthorne NY 10532

SMITH, JERI LYNN, program director; b. Cleve., Dec. 7, 1952; d. Edward and Lillian Barbara (Smejkal) Donat; m. Bradford L. Smith, Apr. 30, 1977; children: Nathan Edward, Noah Lee. BA, Syracuse U., 1975. Dir., community rels. City of Syracuse (N.Y.) Parks & Recreation, 1974-77; edit. assoc. SUNY, Syracuse, 1977-85, assoc. dir. community rels., 1985-90, dir. coll. news & publs., 1990—; news rm. mgr. First Nat. Urban Forestry Conf., Washington, 1979; news dir. IV Internat. Congress Ecology, Syracuse, 1985; chair Syracuse Press Club Scholar Com., 1984— (Bernard S. Newer Svc. award 1989). Mem. parent adv. com. Kids Unltd., Syracuse, 1989-90, 90-91. Mem. Nat. Assn. Sci. Writers, Soc. Environ. Journalists. Office: SUNY Coll Environ Sci 1 Forestry Dr Syracuse NY 13210-2778

SMITH, JERRY EDWIN, counselor, psychologist, administrator; b. Pitts., June 27, 1944; s. John Edwin and Joy Helen (Wagner) S. BS in Psychology, Ball State U., 1967, MA, 1968; PhD in Counselor Edn., U. Pitts., 1978. Instr. Ellsworth Coll., Iowa Falls, Iowa, 1968-70; psychologist, supr. Community Mental Health/Mental Retardation Ctr. St. Francis Med. Ctr., Pitts., 1970—; instr. Pa. State U., University Park, 1980—; psychotherapist Ruth P. Kane, M.D., and Assocs., Pitts., 1985—. Guest on numerous radio, TV pub. affairs programs, 1985-90; mem. Pitts. AIDS Task Force, Pa. Ednl. Network for Eating Disorders. Mem. Am. Psychol. Assn., Am. Counseling Assn., Nat. Bd. Cert. Counselors (cert.). Office: St Francis Med Ctr CMH/MRC 45th St off Pennsylvania Ave Pittsburgh PA 15201

SMITH, JOHN BRUCE, JR., protective services official; b. Clearfield, Pa., May 16, 1942; s. John Bruce and Ruth Naomi (Pike) S.; m. Beverly Sue Brown, July 27, 1968; 1 child, John B. III. Lic. fire subcode offcl.; cert. fire offcl., N.J. Draftsman F.L. Smidth Co., Inc., Lebanon, N.J., 1965-68, asst. purchase agt., 1968-70; office mgr. Wm. Stothoff Co., Inc., Flemington, N.J., 1970-77; communications operator County of Hunterdon, Flemington, 1977—; fire marshal Township of Raritan, Flemington, 1982—, dep. coordinator office of emergency mgmt., 1988—; instr. Warre County Fire Sch., Belvidere, N.J., 1980-82, Hunterdon County Office of Emergency Mgmt., Flemington, 1978-80; fire code adv. coun. State of N.J., 1983—. Fire chief., asst. chief Lebanon Vol. Fire Co., 1965-76; treas. Fire Adv. Coun., Fort Dix., N.J., 1974-76, sec. Sergeantsville Vol. Fire Co., 1991—. Mem. N.J. Fire Prevention and Protection Assn. (exec. bd. 1990—), Hunterdon Warren Fire Prevention and Protection Assn., (pres. 1989—). Methodist. Home: 9 Delaware Dr Stockton NJ 08559 Office: Township of Raritan 1 Raritan Ave Flemington NJ 08822

SMITH, JOHN STANDBRIDGE, JR., podiatrist, consultant; b. Summit, N.J., Mar. 14, 1955; s. John Standbridge and Pamela (Scull) S.; m. Robin R. Wilson, Apr. 7, 1979; children: Sarah, Emily, Rebecca. BS, Muhlenberg Coll., Allentown, Pa., 1977; D of Podiatric Medicine, Pa. Coll. Podiatric Medicine, 1981. Diplomate Am. Bd. Podiatric Surgery. Resident Kern Hosp. Spl. Surgery, Warren, Mich., 1981-83; pvt. practice Princeton, N.J., 1983—; mem. staff Princeton Med. Ctr.; cons. sports medicine Princeton U., 1984—, Rutgers U., 1989—, Trenton State Coll., 1985—; dir. podiatry Sports Medicine Princeton, 1986—. Councilman Borough of Hightstown, N.J., 1988, pres. coun., 1990—. Recipient Lewis Newman award Pa. Coll. Podiatric Medicine, 1981. Fellow Am. Coll. Foot Surgeons. Office: 153 S Main St Hightstown NJ 08520-3341

SMITH, JOHN T., JR., special education educator; b. Columbia, Mo., Feb. 21, 1944; s. John T. and Jeannette L. (Cottrill) S.; m. Donna Kwall, Aug. 22, 1968; 1 child, Lauren S. BS, U. Pitts., 1966, MEd, 1967, PhD, 1971. Cert. supr. spl. edn., supr. pupil pers. svcs., psychologist, Pa. Adminstr., instr. U. Pitts., 1968-72; dir. spl. edn. ARIN Intermediate Unit, Shelocta, Pa., 1973—; mem. adj. faculty Indiana U. Pa., 1972—; pvt. practice psychology, Indiana; cons. in field, 1978—. Chmn. adv. bd. Armstrong-Indiana Mental Health and Mental Retardation. Named to Owl Hall of Fame, U. Pitts.; fellow U. Pitts. Mem. ASCD, Am. Psychol. Assn., Coun. for Exceptional Children, Assn. for the Gifted, Coun. Adminstrs. Spl. Edn., Phi Delta Kappa. Office: PO Box 175 Shelocta PA 15774-0175

SMITH, JOSEPH JUDSON, III, communications executive; b. Washington, Dec. 29, 1938; s. Joseph Judson and Harriet S. (Schmaltz) S.; m. Katherine Hill Carter, June 9, 1962 (div. 1983); children: Joseph Judson IV, Christine Howell; m. Joan Beverly Uhlenhaut, Sept. 28, 1985. BA, Washington & Lee U., Lexington, Va., 1960; MBA, Harvard U., 1962. First lt. U.S. Army, Ft. Eustis, Va., 1962-64; registered rep. Ferris & Co., Washington, 1964-67; v.p. Legg Mason & Co., Washington, 1967-76; pres., owner Swift Mailing Svc., Washington, 1976-87; v.p., dir. reseller program TCOM Systems, Washington, 1987-88; v.p. ops. FKB Direct, Nashville, 1989-90; v.p. sales and mktg. KCMS (a Kiplinger Co.), Hyattsville, Md., 1990—; chmn. Met. Washington Postal Customer Counsul 1983-85; dir. Mail Advt. Svc. Assn., Washington, 1983-87. Mem. Direct Mktg. Assn. Washington, Mail Advt. Svc. Assn. (bd. dirs. 1983-86), Alumni Frat. Coun. Washington & Lee U. (pres. 1987-89), Civitan Club Washington (Pres. 1972), Met. Club Washington, Chevy Chase Club Md., Soc. Cin. Va. Republican. Episcopalian. Home: 401 Wilkes St Alexandria VA 22314-3721 Office: KCMS A Kiplinger Co 3401 E West Hwy Hyattsville MD 20782-1915

SMITH, JULIAN CLEVELAND, JR., chemical engineering educator; b. Westmount, Que., Can., Mar. 10, 1919; s. Julian Cleveland and Bertha (Alexander) S.; m. Joan Elsen, June 1, 1946; children: Robert Elsen, Diane Louise Smith Brook, Brian Richard. B.Chemistry, Cornell U., 1941, Chem. Engr., 1942. Chem. engr. E. I. duPont de Nemours and Co., Inc., 1942-46; mem. faculty Cornell U., 1946—, prof. chem. engring., 1953-86, prof. emeritus, 1986—, dir. continuing engring. edn., 1965-71; assoc. dir. Cornell U. (Sch. Chem. Engring.), 1973-75, dir., 1975-83; vis. lectr. U. Edinburgh, 1971-72; cons. to govt. and industry, 1947—; UNESCO cons. Universidad de Oriente, Venezuela, 1975. Author: (with W. L. McCabe and P. Harriott) Unit Operations of Chemical Engineering, 1976, 4th edit., 1986; also articles; sect. editor: Perry's Chemical Engineers Handbook, 1963. Fellow Am. Inst. Chem. Engrs.; mem. Am. Chem. Soc., Sigma Xi, Tau Beta Pi, Phi Kappa Phi, Alpha Delta Phi. Clubs: Ithaca Country, Statler (Ithaca). Home: 711 The Parkway Ithaca NY 14850-1546

SMITH, JUNE, graphic arts equipment company executive; b. N.Y.C.; d. Ermino Benitez and Mary Magdalen (Piniero) Borges; m. C. Michael Smith, Aug. 26, 1967 (dec. Sept., 1989); children: Christopher, Patrick, Jennifer. Acct. coord. Farly Manning Assocs., N.Y.C., 1964-70; office mgr., pub. affairs rep. Mt. Sinai Med. Ctr., N.Y.C., 1979-81; prin. Caviar Etc., Inc., Woodbury, N.Y., 1981-82; gen. mgr. Lane Assocs., Island Park, N.Y., 1982-84; exec. v.p., gen. mgr. Bidco, Inc., Bidco Mfg. Corp., Hicksville, N.Y., 1984—. Home: 169 Chichester Rd Huntington NY 11743-6526 Office: Bidco Inc 8 Commercial St Hicksville NY 11801-5212

SMITH, KATHERINE E., management consultant; b. Hudson, N.Y., Apr. 14, 1954; d. George Richard and Iris Glorian (Downs) Eger; m. Bruce P. Smith, Aug. 22, 1982; 1 child, Andrew P. BS, SUNY, Albany, 1974; MBA, SUNY, 1976; postgrad., Stanford U., 1980. Office mgr. Shop-Rite, Hudson, Troy, N.Y., 1970-75; mgr. human resources Western Pub./Mattel Toy, N.Y.C., 1975-76; dir. human resources San Francisco State U., 1976-78, Times Mirror Pub., L.A., 1978-80; v.p. human resources ICL Am., Stamford, Conn., 1980-81; pres. 1st Mgmt. Svcs., Stamford, 1981—; docent recruiter Olana Historic Site, Hudson, 1971-76; recruitment mgr. Family Ct. Dutchess County, N.Y., 1973-75. Author Folio mag. Named Small Bus. Entrepreneur of Yr. SACIA, 1988, 89, 90. Mem. IAPW, WIM, AQP (bd. dirs.), ASTD, EWN, WID. Office: 1st Mgmt Svcs 992 High Ridge Rd Stamford CT 06905-1603

SMITH, KEITH DRYDEN, JR., education administrator; b. Bronx, N.Y., June 8, 1951; s. Keith Dryden Sr. and Isolene (Hart) S.; m. Sharon Benson, Aug. 5, 1983 (div. Dec. 1990). BA, SUNY, Potsdam, 1973; MS, Syracuse U., 1978. Tchr. 8th grade sci. Red Creek (N.Y.) Cen. Schs., 1974-75; outdoor recreation specialist N.Y. State Dept. Parks and Recreation, Fair Haven, 1974; program counselor higher edn. opportunity program Utica (N.Y.) Coll. Syracuse U., 1975-78, coord. acad. supportive svcs., 1978-79, project dir., 1979-81; project dir. ednl. opportunity program SUNY, Plattsburgh, 1981-92, Cortland, 1992—; chmn. pres. adv. com. affirmative action SUNY, 1991-92, sec., 1986-87; senator Faculty senate SUNY, 1990-91; human rights chmn. Coll. Student Personnel Assn., Oswego, N.Y., 1986-87. Contbr. articles to mags. Mem. City of Plattsburgh Martin Luther King Com., 1987—; vol. worker Jesse JAckson Presdl. Campaign, Plattsburgh, 1984, 88; advisor SUNY Plattsburgh African-Am. Orgn., Plattsburgh, 1982-86. Mem. Coun. Ednl. Opportunity Program Dirs. (sec. 1989-91). Democrat. Home: 420 Hayts Rd Ithaca NY 14850 Office: 116D Cornish SUNY-Cortland Cortland NY 13045

SMITH, LAPREAL MONSON, government official; b. Logan, Utah, Oct. 11, 1920; d. Ezra Parkinson and Roxie LaPreal (Clapp) M.; m. William J. Farmer, Oct. 11, 1939 (div. 1951); children: William James, Bonnie Jeanne Lambdin, Susan Elaine La Melle; m. Frank Miller Smith, Aug. 15, 1968 (dec. Feb. 1985). Student, Am. U., Washington Internat. Coll. Sec. Sen. John Marshall Butler (Md.), Washington, 1952-53, Sen. Henry Dworshak (Idaho), Washington, 1953-54; sec. polit. office VA, Washington, 1955, sec., adminstrv. asst. Office of Asst. Adminstrn., 1955-56, sec., adminstrv. asst., Info. Svc.-Pub. Relations, 1956-73, spl. asst., Office Asst. Adminstrn. for Personnel, 1973-75; chmn. publicity VA Alumni Assn., Washington, 1987—; vis. tchr. Relief Soc. Women's Organ., Washington. Contbr. articles to profl. publs. Mem. Daus. Utah Pioneers (sec. 1987-89), NRA, BYU Mgmt. Soc. Washington, Beta Sigma Phi. Republican. Mormon. Home: 5432 Connecticut Ave NW Washington DC 20015-2860

SMITH, LARRY DENNIS, paper mill stores executive; b. Altoona, Pa., Dec. 12, 1954; s. Bernard Robert and Dollie Edith (Nofsker) S. BS in Art Edn., Ind. U. Pa., 1977. Audio artist, 1974—; artist Mail Art Network, 1980—; organizer, curator Manifesto Shnn Archives, East Freedom, Pa., 1982-86. Author: Manifesto Shnnalchemy, 1981, In the Wake of the Disaster Machine, 1981; editor: Artcomnet, 1981-87; artist The Labours of Grimnlaek, 1984; one-man shows in Rome, Stockholm, Zurich, Brusque and Helsinki. Mem. Sons of Am. Revolution. Republican. Home: RR1 Box 704-A East Freedom PA 16637-9770 Office: Appleton Papers Inc 100 Papermill Rd Roaring Spring PA 16673

SMITH, LAURENCE ROGER, management consultant; b. N.Y.C., Sept. 30, 1939; s. John and Edith (Haabestad) S.; m. Betty Ann Larsen, Oct. 9, 1965; children: Erik Lars, Alesa Ann. AAS, Staten Island Community Coll., 1962; BS, SUNY, Oswego, 1965; MBA, St. John's U., 1975. Dir. community devel. Staten Island (N.Y.) C. of C., 1965-77; exec. v.p., chief exec. officer Yonkers (N.Y.) C. of C., 1977-78; chief exec. officer Greater Lawrence (Mass.) C. of C., 1978-91; pres. The LeaderShip, North Andover, Mass., 1991—; dir., clk. Lawrence Downtown Parking Assocs., 1979—; dir., asst. treas. Greater Lawrence Revolving Loan Fund, 1979—; apptd. Mass. Dept. of Edn. Sch. Bus. Partnership Com., 1991—, U.S. C. of C. Com. on Edn. and Tgn., 1990-91. Author: Godfidence, 1991. Chmn. Lower Merrimack Valley Pvt. Industry Coun., Lawrence, 1981; treas. Lawrence YMCA, 1985; pres. leadership div. Mass. Bus. Adv., Inc., 1990; vice-chmn. literacy com. Mass. Regional Employment Bd., 1989-90; bd. dirs. Greater Lawrence Red Cross; apptd. to Mass. Dept. Edn. Sch.-Bus. Ptnrship. Com., 1990—. Served with USCG, 1958-60. Recipient Pvt. Sector award Presdl. Commn., 1985, Flood Relief award ARC, 1987; named to U. Notre Dame Acad. Orgn. Mgmt., 1989, CUNY Hall of Fame. 1990. Mem. Am. C. of C. Execs., New Eng. Assn. C. of C. Execs. (pres., 1986), Mass. Assn. C. of C. Execs. (pres. 1984). Democrat. Episcopalian. Home: 233 Osgood St North Andover MA 01845-4025 Office: The LeaderShip 233 Osgood St North Andover MA 01845

SMITH, LAWRENCE BARRETT, IV, art gallery director and curator; b. Cleve., Aug. 29, 1952; s. Lawrence Barrett III and Mary Andrew (Prinios) S. BA, Baldwin Wallace Coll., 1974. Program dir. Nat. Pub. Radio, Cleve., 1974-77; producer, dir. CitiCorp Ctr.-Treatre at Noon, N.Y.C., 1977-81; dir., curator La Ma Ma La Galleria, N.Y.C., 1981—, also trustee; curator poetry and fiction Fordham U., N.Y.C., 1991; producer N.Y. Meets Cleve., Cleve. Performance Arts Festival, 1990, Monday Nights Comedy Series Levitt Pavillion, Westport, Conn., 1988; curator Ken Burgess-A Retrospective, Springfield (Mass.) Coll. Gallery, 1989; cons. grant com. Merrill G. Emita E. Hastings Found., 1987-89. Producer, creator radio series Portraits of Eve, 1978 (Twyla M. Conway Radio/TV Excellence award). Mem. community bd. N.Y.C. Div. Neighborhood Improvement. Grantee Hastings Found., 1988. Mem. SAG, Theta Alpha Phi (life). Democrat. HOme: 537 W 49th St Apt 9 New York NY 10019-7168 Office: La Ma Ma La Galleria 6 E 1st St New York NY 10003-8902

SMITH, LEAH JOHNSON, economist, college official; b. Ft. Worth, Feb. 1, 1943; d. Francis Bonneau and Leah Townsend (Zeigler) Johnson; m. Woollcott Keston Smith; children: Amelia, Keston. BA, Stanford U., 1964; PhD, Johns Hopkins U., 1972. Instr. econs. N.C. State U., 1969-72; economist 1st Nat. Bank Boston, 1972-73; with Woods Hole Oceanographic Instn., 1973-82, assoc. marine policy and ocean mgmt., 1982; asst. prof. Haverford (Pa.) Coll., 1981-82; asst. prof. Swarthmore (Pa.) Coll., 1982-85, asst. to pres., dir. instl. rsch., 1985—, acting dean, 1991—; mem. sci. and statis. com. New Eng. Fishery Mgmt. Coun.; mem. adv. bd. Dept Interior; cons. in field. Contbr. articles to profl. jours. Trustee Woods Hole Library, 1976-81, pres., 1978-80; mem. vestry Trintiy Episcopal Ch., Swarthmore, 1987-89. Rsch. grantee Nat. Marine Fisheries Svc. Mem. Am. Econ. Assn., AAAS, Assn. Instl. Rsch. Episcopalian. Office: Swarthmore Coll Dean's Office Swarthmore PA 19081

SMITH, LIZ, newspaper columnist; b. Ft. Worth, Feb. ; d. Sloan and Sarah Elizabeth (McCall) S. B.J., U. Tex., 1948. Editor Dell Publns., N.Y.C., 1950-53; assoc. producer CBS Radio, 1953-55, NBC-TV, 1955-59; assoc. on Cholly Knickerbocker newspaper column, N.Y.C., 1959-64; film critic Cosmpolitan mag., 1966; columnist Chgo. Tribune-N.Y. Daily News Syndicate (now Tribune Media Services), 1976-91, New York Newsday, L.A. Times Syndicate, 1991—; TV commentator WNBC-TV, N.Y.C., 1978-91; commentator Fox-TV, N.Y.C., 1991—; freelance mag. writer, also staff writer Sports Illus. mag. Author: The Mother Book, 1978. Office: New York Newsday 2 Park Ave New York NY 10016

SMITH, MANNING LEE, student services director, priest; b. Winston-Salem, N.C., Jan. 7, 1943; s. C. Manning and Martha Lee (Myers) S.; m. Katharine Llewellyn Squibb, June 14, 1969; children: Courtney Llewellyn, Ashley Manning. BA, Wake Forest U., 1964; MDiv, Va. Theol. Sem., Alexandria, 1968; MA, U. W.Va., 1977; Advanced Grad. Specialist, U. Md., 1989. Cert. profl. counselor, Md. Vicar Emmanuel Ch., Moorefield, W.Va., 1968-70; asst. rector Calvary Ch., Ashland, Ky., 1970-71; vicar St. James Ch., Charleston, W.Va., 1971-74; chaplain W.Va. State Coll., Institute, 1971-74; rector St. Matthew's Ch., Oakland, Md., 1974-86; adj. prof. Garrett Community Coll., McHenry, Md., 1982—, dir. student svcs., 1986—. Dir. Oompah Band, Oakland. Chaplain Oakland Vol. Fire Dept., 1976—, Garrett Meml. Hosp., Oakland, 1985—; health adv. Garrett County Health Dept., Oakland, 1990—; mem. GCC Found., McHenry, 1990—. Mem. ASCD, Am. Assn. Pastoral Counselors (assoc.), Nat. Bd. Cert. Counselors (cert.). Republican. Episcopalian. Office: Garrett Community Coll PO Box 151 Mc Henry MD 21541-0151

SMITH, MARCIA JEAN, accountant, tax specialist, financial consultant; b. Kansas City, Mo., Oct. 19, 1947; d. Eugene Hubert and Marcella Juanita (Greene) S. Student, U. Nebr., 1965-67; BA, Jersey City State Coll., 1971; MBA in Taxation, Golden Gate U., 1976, postgrad., 1976-77; MS in Acctg., Pace U., 1982; Cert. of completion, Cours Commerciaux de Geneve, 1985-86. Legal intern Port Authority, N.Y., N.J., N.Y.C., 1972; legis. aide to Senator Harrison A. Williams Washington, 1973; tax accountant Bechtel Corp., San Francisco, 1974-77; sr. tax accountant Equitable Life Assurance Soc. U.S., N.Y.C., 1977, sec., 1977-79; tax sr. Arthur Andersen & Co., N.Y.C., 1979-82; pres. M.J. Smith Co., N.Y.C., 1983-85; prin. owner MJS Cons. Svcs. Internat. Tax Cons., Boston, Mass., 1988—; cons. U.N., specialized agys., Geneva, 1985-87; asst. sec. Equico Lessors, Inc., Mpls., 1977-78, Equitable Gen. Ins. Group, Ft. Worth, 1977-79, Heritage Life Infield Assurance Co., Toronto, Ont., Can., 1978-79, Informatics, Inc., L.A., 1978-79, Heritage Life Assurance Co., L.A., 1978-79; sec. Equico Capital Corp., N.Y.C. 1977-79, Equico Personal Credit, Inc., Colorado Springs, Colo., 1978-79, Equico Securites, Inc., N.Y.C., 1977-79, Equitable Environ. Health, Inc., Woodbury, N.Y., 1977-79; tax cons., real estate salesperson. Spl. advisor U.S. Congl. Adv. Bd.; human rights chmn. YWCA, Lincoln, Nebr., 1966-67. Recipient Certificate of Recognition, Central Mo. State Coll., 1965, Unicameral award State Neb., 1967, Mary McLeod Bethune award Jersey City State Coll., 1971. Mem. AAAS, AAUW, NAA (Swiss Romande chpt.), Am. Mgmt. Assn., Nat. Soc. Pub. Accts., Inst. Mgmt. Accts., Am. Acctg. Assn., Internat. Assn. Fin. Planners, Internat. Fin. Mgmt. Assn., Am. Women's Club of Geneva, Nat. Assn. Women Bus. Owners, Am. Assn. Individual Investors, Inst. Internal Auditors, N.Y. Acad. Scis., Nat. Hist. Soc., Nat. Assn. Tax Practitioners, Assn. Managerial Economists, Postal Commemorative Soc., Am. Mus. Natural History, Nat. Trust Historic Preservation, Internat. Tax Inst., Am. Econs. Assn., UN Assn. USA, EDP Auditors Assn., Mass. Soc. Ind. Accts., Acad. Legal Studies in Bus., Am. Bus. Law Assn., Internat. Platform Assn., U.S. Senatorial Club. Office: MJS Cons Svcs Internat Tax Cons 25 Huntington Ave Ste 605 Boston MA 02116-5713

SMITH, MARGARET PHYLLIS, editor, consultant; b. Plymouth, Pa., Aug. 24, 1925; d. Harold Dewitt and Mae Elmira (Bittenbender) S. AB magna cum laude, Bucknell U., 1946, AM, 1947; postgrad., U. Pa., summer 1951-54. Instr. English Bucknell U., Lewisburg, Pa., 1947-52, asst. prof., 1952-55; personnel asst. RCA Labs., Princeton, N.J., 1955-58, staff writer pub. affairs dept., 1958-76, adminstr. communications, 1976-87; editor spl. projects David Sarnoff Rsch. Ctr. (formerly RCA Labs.), Princeton, 1987—; mng. editor Vision mag. David Sarnoff Rsch. Ctr., 1987—, editor UPDATE newsletter, 1969—. Editor: 1942-67 Twenty-five Years at RCA Laboratories, 1968. Mem. corp. communications com. United Way, Princeton, 1976-88. Mem. AAUW, N.J. Press Women (publicity dir. 1985-86), Internat. Assn. Bus. Communicators. Episcopalian. Office: David Sarnoff Rsch Ctr 201 Washington Rd Princeton NJ 08540-6492

SMITH, MARILYN PATRICIA, aviator, aviation consultant and educator; b. Jamaica, N.Y., July 5, 1942; d. Raymond Lionel and Katherine Marie (Doepp) Cowan; m. Adrian Roy Smith, Dec. 7, 1991; 1 child, Paul William Hibner. Student various aviation schs., St. Joseph's Coll., N.Y.; cert. in Leadership and Human Resources Devel. Goldratt Inst., Conn., JONAH, cert. Exec. sec. to chief design Wiedersum Assocs., architects and engrs., Valley Stream, N.Y., 1960-61; officer mgr., interior designer Keith I. Hibner, architect, Hicksville and Garden City, N.Y., 1961-73; owner, pres. Hibner Atelier, Ltd., interior design and gen. constrn., Garden City, 1968-75; office mgr. Ward Assocs./Planning Assocs., architects and engrs., Bohemia, N.Y., 1975-76; flight/ground aviation instr. Islip Aviation, Ltd. (N.Y.), 1974-77; exec. asst. to pres. Arkay Packaging Corp., Hauppauge, N.Y., 1977-86, inhouse constrn. mgr., 1980-82, adminstrn. and human resources mgr., 1986-89, dir. corp. devel., 1989, dir. materials mgmt., 1989-90; cert. assoc. Goldratt Inst. for L.I./Metro N.Y. area, 1990-92; owner Concepts for Constructive Change, Educators and Facilitators for Continuous Improvement, Lake Grove, N.Y., 1990-92; ind. aviation flight/ground instr. airplane and instrument, 1977—; safety counselor FAA, 1974—, Eastern region counselor coord., 1985-86; past bd. dirs., officer Aviation Council L.I.; founder Seminar on Air Travel for Everyone (S.A.F.E.), 1975, Fly-C-Cure/We Air Condition People, 1979. Author articles, seminar syllabus. Mem. nat. panel Consumer arbitrators Nat. Consumer Arbitration Program, Better Bus. Bur. Lic. comml. pilot, flight and ground instr. Mem. NAFE, Ninety-Nines (past chmn. L.I. chpt., founding internat. chmn. safety edn., Amelia Earhart Bronze medal 1975), Aircraft Owners and Pilots Assn., Nat. Assn. Flight Instrs., Silver Wings, Exptl. Aircraft Assn. Specialist on fear of flying, Specialist on Theory of Constraints Mgmt. Methodology. Home and Office: 1 Teal Ln Smithtown NY 11787-3318

SMITH, MARK ALAN, management consultant; b. Lafayette, Ind., May 15, 1934; s. Mark Andrew and Sarah Fredissa (Palin) S.; children by previous marriage: Michelle Renee, Janene Marie. BA in Mus. Edn., BS in French, Ind. State U., 1957; MS in Adminstrn., George Washington U., 1976; postgrad., U. Pa. Wharton Sch., U. Denver Coll Law, U. Md. Coll. Law. Tech. writer Douglas Aircraft Co., Santa Monica, Calif., 1961-62; editor Copyright Law Office, Library Congress, Washington, 1963-64; asst. dir. personnel Holy Cross Hosp., Silver Spring, Md., 1964-65, dir. personnel adminstrn., 1965-80, dir. human resources adminstrn., 1980-82, asst. v.p., 1982-88; pres. Mark Smith & Assocs., Rockville, Md., 1989—; instr. personnel mgmt. and labor rels. Strayer Coll., Washington, 1970-73, bus. adminstrn. Cen. Mich. U. Grad. Sch., Washington extension, 1975-80; vis. lectr. George Washington U. Grad. Sch. Bus. Adminstrn., Washington, 1969, 70, 76; cons. to various hosps. in Md., Va. and Washington, 1975—. contbr. articles on orgn. devel. to profl. jours. Served with CIC, U.S. Army, 1957-60. Mem. Am. Hosp. Assn., Am. Soc. for Hosp. Personnel Dirs. (mem. labor rels. com. 1970), Soc. for Human Resource Mgmt. (accredited, sr. profl. in human resources, mem. pub. affairs com. 1975), Am. Mgmt. Assn., Washington Personnel Assn., Hosp. Council of Nat. Capital Area (pres. personnel dirs. div. 1969, 71), Md. Hosp. Personnel Adminstrn. Assn., Am. Soc. Law and Medicine, Phi Delta Kappa, Phi Mu Alpha Sinfonia, Blue Key. Home and Office: 872 New Mark Esplanade Rockville MD 20850-2750

SMITH, MARY ALICE, non-profit administrator; b. Milledgeville, Ga., Nov. 6, 1944; d. Woodson Harris and Landyce Miriam (Little) Beall; m. Ben Lewis Jones, Oct. 1967 (div. 1972); 1 child, Rachel Virginia Landyce Jones; m. Norman Clark Smith, Jan. 22, 1976. AA, Oxford Coll. of Emory U., 1964; BA, U. N.C., 1966. Devel. writer Emory U., Atlanta, 1972-76; ptnr. Smith & Venezky, Newark, Del., 1977-79; dir. devel. Mystic (Conn.) Community Ctr., 1980-83; dir. devel. and alumni affairs The Williams Sch., New London, Conn., 1983-85; asst. dir. devel. Conn. Coll., New London, 1986-87; dir. community rels. and devel. The Westerly (R.I.) Hosp., 1987—. fund-raising counsel Mystic River Hist. Soc., 1986-87, Denison Pequotsepos Nature Ctr., Mystic, 1987-88; mem. Commn. on Devel. and Pub. Rels., Conn. Assn. Ind. schs., 1983-85; study chair Thames East League of Women Voters, Groton, 1990—, v.p., 1979-80. Recipient Distinctive Merit award Advt. Club Del., 1978. Mem. Assn. for Healthcare Philanthropy, Am. Soc. Healthcare Mktg. and Pub. Rels., Westerly/Pawcatuck C. of C. (dir. 1989-92). Home: 161 Pequot Ave Mystic CT 06355-1728 Office: The Westerly Hosp 25 Wells St Westerly RI 02891-2934

SMITH, MICHAEL PETER, banking executive; b. Terre Haute, Ind., Jan. 2, 1949; s. Charles Wallace and Muriel (Baker) S.; m. Marie Catherine Murphy, Sept. 29, 1973; children: Amy, Tara, Christie, Michael, Jennifer. BA in Govt., Cornell U., 1971; sr. exec. program, Stanford U., 1986. Spl. asst. Office of Congressman Stewart B. McKinney, Washington, 1971-74; dist. coord. Office of Congressman Stewart B. McKinney, Bridgeport, Conn., 1974-75; fed. affairs rep. N.Y. State Bankers Assn., N.Y.C., 1975-77, dir. govt. rels., 1977-79, v.p. govt. rels., 1979-81, group v.p., 1981-89, exec. v.p., 1989—, also bd. dirs.; bd. dirs. Trustees Life Ins. Co., Phoenix, Corp. for Am. Banking, Washington; trustee Retirement System, N.Y. State Bankers Assn., N.Y.C., 1989—. Mem. Gov. Cuomo's Task Force on Schs. and Bus., N.Y.C., 1990—, Real Estate Coun., Cornell Univ., Ithaca, N.Y., 1990—. Mem. Cornell Club of N.Y. Roman Catholic. Home: 14 Grace Church St Rye NY 10580-3925 Office: New York State Bankers Assn 485 Lexington Ave New York NY 10017-2630

SMITH, MICHAEL VINCENT, surgeon; b. Athens, Ga., Mar. 30, 1957; s. Thomas Allen and Lucile Vivian (Jackson) S.; m. Jeralyn Demetria Scott, July 28, 1979; 1 child, Demetria Joy. BS in Agr., U. Ga., 1979; MD, Med. Coll. of Ga., 1983. Diplomate Nat. Bd. Med. Examiners, Diplomate Bd. Surgery. Intern in surgery U. Ky. Med. Ctr., Lexington, 1983-84, resident in surgery, 1984-89, chief resident in gen. surgery, 1988-89; clin. asst. prof. surgery Sch. Medicine Morehouse Coll., Atlanta, 1989-90; assoc. vascular surgeon Midtown Vascular Surgery, Atlanta, 1989-90; attending surgeon Ga. Bapt. Med. Ctr./Crawford Long Hosp. of Emory U., Atlanta, 1989-90, Northlake Regional Med. Ctr./S.W. Community Hosp. and Med., Atlanta, 1989-90; fellow in cardiothoracic surgery Coll. of Medicine Mt. Sinai Med. Ctr., N.Y.C., 1990-91; fellow cardiovascular rsch. U. Mass. Med. Ctr., Worcester, 1991-92, resident cardiothoriac surgery, 1992—; mem. ICU S.W. Community Hosp., Atlanta, 1989-90. Sunday sch. tchr. 1st African Meth. Episcopal Ch., Athens, Ga., 1975-79, Bethel African Meth. Episcopal Ch., Augusta, Ga., 1980-83, St. Paul African Meth. Episcopal Ch., Lexington, Ky., 1985-89. Sunday sch. tchr. First A.M.E. Ch., Athens, Ga., 1975-79, Bethel African Meth. Episcopal Ch., Augusta, Ga., 1980-83, St. Paul A.M.E. Ch., Lexington, Ky., 1985-89. Nat. Achievement scholar, 1974; named one of Outstanding Young Men of the Yr., Jaycees, 1983. Mem. ACS (mem. candidate group), AMA, Atlanta Med. Assn., Southeastern Surg. Congres (assoc.), Assn. Acad. Surgery, Soc. Black Acad. Surgeons, Nat. Med. Assn., Mass. Med. Soc., Am. Heart Assn. (affiliate in tng.), Am. Coll. Cardiology, NAACP (Worchester chpt.), Alpha Phi Alpha.

SMITH, MILDRED FREE, agriculturist, educator; b. Altha, Fla., Aug. 4, 1942; d. Leonard Lawrence and Susan Mary (Chason) Free; m. Wayne Hilry Smith, June 16, 1962 (div. Mar. 9, 1990). AA, Chipola Jr. Coll., Marianna, Fla., 1961; BS, Miss. State U., 1964; MS, U. Fla., 1967; PhD, U. Md., 1978. Tchr. Gainesville (Fla.) High Sch., 1967-69; tchr. P. K. Yonge Lab. Sch., U. Fla., Gainesville, 1969-70, chmn. middle sch., 1971-72; dir. project grant Coll. Edn., U. Fla., Gainesville, 1970-73; coord. design and evaluation J. Hillis Miller Health Ctr., U. Fla., Gainesville, 1977-79; asst. to assoc. prof. Coll. Agriculture, U. Fla., Gainesville, 1979-85; assoc. prof. to full prof., coord. program planning/eval. Coll. Agriculture, Coop. Extension Svc., U. Md., College Park, 1985—; cons. in curriculum and program planning for various orgns., 1973-77, 85-89. Author: Evaluability Assessment, 1989; (with others) The Valuing Approach to Career Education, K-2 Series, 1973, The Valuing Approach to Career Education, 3-5 Serie, 1973, The Valuing Approach to Career Education, 6-8 Series, 1974; editor: Evaluation in Cooperative Extension, 1982, Current Issues/Problems in Evaluating Cooperative Extension Programs, 1991; contbr. over 100 articles to profl. jours., papers to profl. confs., symposiums; editor profl. jour. 1989—. Mem. U. Md. Faculty Club, 1986—, Univ. Fla. Women's Club, 1964-85; bd. trustees Hippodrome, State of Fla. Theatre, Gainesville, 1984, 85; design com. Heritage Club, Gainesville, 1985; bd. dirs. U. Fla. Faculty Club, 1983-84; pres. Forestry Student/Faculty Club, U. Fla., 1965, 67. Recipient grant EExt. Svc./USDA, 1984, 86, 87, 88-89, Sustained Excellence in Ext. Edn. award, 1990; recipient Nat. Excellence in Rsch. award Nat. Assn. Home Economists, 1990. Mem. Am. Assn. Adult and Continuing Edn., Am. Evaluation Assn., Rural Sociol. Soc., Epsilon Sigma Phi, Phi Delta Kappa. Office: Univ Md 2115 Symons Hall College Park MD 20742

SMITH, NELSON F., psychology educator, behavioral consultant; b. Leominster, Mass., Feb. 15, 1937; s. A. Fay and Katherine M. (Sheehan) S.; m. Virginia A. Kotowski, Jan. 27, 1966; children: Kevin J., Beverly A. BA in Psychology, Colgate U., 1959; MA in Psychology, Coll. William and Mary, 1961; PhD in Psychology, Princeton U., 1963. Rsch. assoc. Princeton (N.J.) U., 1964-65; from asst. prof. to assoc. prof. psychology U. R.I., Kingston, 1965-75, prof. psychology, 1975—, chair psychology dept., 1984-90; cons. in field. Contbr. articles to profl. jours. Home: 13 Rose Cir Peace Dale RI 02883-2416 Office: Univ R I 306 Chafee Ctr Kingston RI 02881

SMITH, OLIVER, theatrical producer, designer; b. Waupun, Wis., Feb. 13, 1918; s. Larue F. and Nina (Kincaid) S. B.A., Pa. State U., 1939; Dr. (hon.), Bucknell U., L.I. U. Master tchr. NYU; co-dir. Am. Ballet Theatre, 1945-80, 90—. Co-producer, designer plays On the Town, 1945, Billion Dollar Baby, 1945, No Exit, 1946, Me and Molly, 1947, Gentlemen Prefer Blondes, 1949, Bless You All, 1950, In The Summer House, 1952, Clearing in the Woods, 1957, Time Remembered, Romulus, 1961, The Night of the Iguana, Lord Pengo, 1962, Barefoot in the Park, 1963, 110 in the Shade, 1963, The Girl Who Came to Supper, 1963, Dylan, 1963, The Chinese Prime Minister, 1964, Ben Franklin in Paris, 1964, Luv, 1964, Poor Richard, 1964, Odd Couple, 1965; designer of musicals Brigadoon, 1946, High Button Shoes, 1946, Miss Liberty, 1949, Paint Your Wagon, 1952, Pal Joey, 1952, On Your Toes, 1955, My Fair Lady, 1956, Candide, 1955, Auntie Mame, 1956, West Side Story (Antoinette Perry award 1958), Jamaica, Destry, Flower Drum Song, Camelot, Beckett; on Broadway Rosalinda, 1942, First Monday in October, Clothes for a Summer Hotel; for Met. Opera Traviata, 1958, Martha, 1961; Hello Dolly, 1963 (Tony award), I Was Dancing, 1964, Candide, 1971, The Little Black Book, 1972, The Time of Your Life, 1972, Lost in The Stars, 1972, Lunch Hour, 1980, Mixed Couples, 1980, A Talent for Murder, 1981, 84, Charing Cross Road, 1982; off-Broadway The Golden Age, 1984; Naughty Marietta, N.Y.C. Opera, 1978; designer movies Band Wagon, 1952, Oklahoma, 1955, Guys and Dolls, 1955, Porgy and Bess; broadway mus. Sound of Music, Unsinkable Molly Brown, 1960; co-dir. Am. Ballet Theatre, 1945-80; designer ballets Rodeo, 1942, Fancy Free, 1943, Fall River Legend, 1946, Swan Lake, Les Noces; exhbns. Pa. State Coll., Mus. Modern Art, Bklyn. Mus., Chgo. Art Inst., Cocoran Gallery, Yale U., interior, Nat. Theatre, Washington; produced On the Town, London, 1962-63. Recipient Donaldson award 1946, 47, 49, 53, Antoinette Perry award 1957, 58, 60, 61, 64, 65, Shubert award 1960, N.Y. Handel medallion 1975; Disting. Alumni award Pa. State U., 1962, Gt. Tchr. award NYU, 1981. Mem. Triangle Soc., Acacia, Nat. Council Arts. Office: care Am Ballet Theatre 890 Broadway New York NY 10003-1211*

SMITH, ORIN ROBERT, chemical company executive; b. Newark, Aug. 13, 1935; s. Sydney R. and Gladys Emmett (DeGroff) S.; m. Stephanie M. Bennett-Smith; children: Lindsay, Robin; 1 stepchild, Brendan. B.A. in Econometrics, Brown U., 1957; M.B.A. in Mgmt., Seton Hall U., 1964; PhD (hon.), Centenary U., 1991. Various sales and mktg. mgmt. positions Allied Chem. Corp., Morristown, N.J., 1959-69; dir. sales and mktg. Richardson-Merrell Co., Phillipsburg, N.J., 1969-72; with M&T Chems., Greenwich, Conn., 1972-77, pres., 1975-77; with Engelhard Minerals & Chems. Corp., Menlo Park, Edison, N.J., 1977-81, corp. sr. v.p., 1978-81, pres. div. minerals and chems., 1978-81, also bd. dirs., 1979-81, pres., dir. various U.S. subs., 1979-81; exec. v.p., pres. div. minerals and chems. Engelhard Corp., Menlo Park, Edison, 1981-84; pres., chief exec. officer Engelhard Corp., Iselin, N.J., 1984—, also bd. dirs.; bd. dirs. Summit Trust Co., The Summit Bancorp, Vulcan Materials Co., La. Land. and Exploration Co., N.J. Mfrs. Ins. Co., N.J. Reins. Co. Trustee Mfrs. Alliance for Productivity and Innovation; bd. overseers N.J. Inst. Tech.; vice chmn. bd. trustees Centenary Coll.; mem. adv. bd. Watchung Area coun. Boy Scouts Am.; trustee Welkind Rehab. Hosp.; past chmn. Ind. Coll. Fund N.J.; past dir.-at-large U. Maine Pulp and Paper Found. Lt. (j.g.) USN, 1957-59. Mem. Chem. Mfrs. Assn. (past bd. dirs.), Am. Mgmt. Assn. (gen. mgmt. coun.), N.J. State C. of C. (bd. dirs.), Bus. Higher Edn. Forum, N.J. Bus. and Industry Assn. (trustee), Econ. Club N.Y.C., Union League Club N.Y.C., Roxiticus Golf Club (Mendham, N.J.), N.Y. Yacht Club. Office: Engelhard Corp 101 Wood Ave Iselin NJ 08830-0770

SMITH, PAUL DAVID, electrical engineer, administrator; b. Omaha, Sept. 30, 1936; s. James Posley and Dorothy (Rosicky) S.; m. Martha Anne MacDonald, Sept. 12, 1964; children: Kara Anne, Samantha Anne, todd David. BSEE, U. Nebr., 1959; SMEE, MIT, 1961. Mem. staff Lincoln Lab. MIT, Lexington, 1961-69; regional mgr. PERTEC Peripheral Equipment Co., Chatsworth, Calif., 1969-76; pres., owner Cape Cod Electronics, Chatham, Mass., 1976-78; v.p. product devel. ITT Courier, Tempe, Ariz., 1978-84; sr. v.p., chief tech. officer Summagraphics, Seymour, Conn., 1984—. Contbr. articles to profl. jours. Mem. IEEE, Sigma Xi, Eta Kappa Nu, Tau Beta Pi, Pi Mu Epsilon, Sigma Tau. Home: 567 Carter St New Canaan CT 06840-5018 Office: Summagraphics 60 Silvermine Rd Seymour CT 06483-3926

SMITH, PETER, podiatrist; b. Yonkers, N.Y., Feb. 17, 1962; s. Thomas W. and Arlene T. (Maglietta) S.; m. Kathleen M. Hughes, Jan. 14, 1989. BS, Boston Coll., 1984; D in Podiatric Medicine, N.Y. Coll. Podiatric Medicine, 1988. Pvt. practice Stony Brook, 1989—. Mem. Am. Podiatric Med. Assn., N.Y. State Podiatric Med. Assn., N.Y. Acad. Scis. Roman Catholic. Office: 207 Hallock Rd Stony Brook NY 11790-3033

SMITH, PHILIP DODD, JR., publishing executive; b. Berkeley, Calif., Feb. 22, 1933; s. Philip and Dorothy LePage (Gibbs) S.; m. Shirley Irene Grant, Jan. 29, 1954; children: Philip D. III (dec.), Corrine L. Smith Garrison, Edward A. BA, Pepperdine U., 1954; MA, U. Nev., Reno, 1959; PhD, Ohio State U., 1967; diploma, Gaelic Coll., An Teanga, Skye, Scotland, 1981. Tchr., prin. Lander County (Nev.) Schs., Battle Mountain, 1956-60; supr. fgn. langs. Nev. State Dept. Edn., Carson City, 1960-64; assoc. dir. NDEA French Inst. U. Nev., Reno, 1964-65; prof. langs. West Chester U. of Pa., 1967-91, chair lang. dept., 1972-74, assoc. provost, v.p. acad. affairs, 1983-85, asst. dean grad. studies, 1985-87; dean Japan campus West Chester U. of Pa., Fukuoka, 1988-90; author, pub. Heinle & Heinle, Enterprises, Concord, Mass., 1990—. Author: Sagebrush Soldiers, 1965, Comparison of Cognitive and Audiolingual Approaches to Foreign Language Instruction, 1971, Vida y Voces, 1976, numerous other lang. books; contbr. articles to profl. publs. Pres. bd. dirs. La Comunidad Hispana, Kennet Square, Pa., 1980-89; mem. Pa. Standards and Practices Commn., 1983-89. With USN, 1954-56. Recipient Gov.'s award for Excellence, Commonwealth of Pa., 1967, Acad. Svc. award State System Higher Edn., 1979, Disting. Svc. award State System Higher Edn., 1980. Fellow Scottish Tartans Soc.; mem. Am. Coun. Teaching Fgn. Langs., Tchrs. of Enlgish to Speakers of Other Langs., Phi Delta Kappa. Republican. Mem. Ch. of Christ. Home: 372 Churchtown Rd Narvon PA 17555-9650

SMITH, PRESTON GIBSON, management consultant, engineering executive; b. Long Beach, Calif., Aug. 4, 1941; s. Preston Gibson and Arlene Frances (Lamar) S.; m. Judy Anne Conkling, Dec. 18, 1966; children: Christina, Marjorie. BSME magna cum laude, U. So. Calif., 1963, MSME, 1964; PhD, Stanford U., 1967. Cert. mgmt. cons. Mem. tech. staff Bell Telephone Labs., Washington, 1967-71; group leader Gen. Motors Rsch. Labs., Warren, Mich., 1971-76; program mgr. Ensco, Inc., Springfield, Va., 1976-80; project leader Inst. for Def. Analyses, Alexandria, Va., 1980-84; mgr. corp. tech. Emhart Corp., Farmington, Conn., 1984-86; pres. New Product Dynamics, West Hartford, Conn., 1986—. Author: Developing Products in Half the Time; contbr. articles to mags., jours. Mem. ASME, Product Devel. and Mgmt. Assn., Inst. Mgmt. Cons., AIAA, Sigma Xi, Phi Kappa Phi, Tau Beta Pi. Office: New Product Dynamics 240 N Main St West Hartford CT 06107-1261

SMITH, RAYMOND LEIGH, plastic surgeon; b. Norristown, Pa., Sept. 27, 1940; s. Walter Joseph and Pauline C. (Wolfskill) S.; m. Coralynn Elder, Jan. 8, 1966; children—Susan, Elizabeth, Christine. B.S., Ursinus Coll., 1962; M.D., Temple U., 1966. Diplomate Nat. Bd. Med. Examiners, Am. Bd. Plastic Surgery. Active staff Reading Hosp., Pa., 1976—, St. Joseph Hosp., Reading, 1976—, Community Gen. Hosp., Reading, 1976—. Mem. Am. Security Council, Republican Majority Found., Washington Legal Found. Mem. Am. Soc. Plastic and Reconstructive Surgery, Robert H. Ivy Soc., A.C.S., Am. Assn. Hand Surgery, AMA. Lutheran. Office: 926 Penn Ave Wyomissing PA 19610

SMITH, RAYMOND W., telecommunications company executive; b. Pittsburgh, PA, 1937. B.S., Carnegie-Mellon U., 1959; M.B.A., U. Pitts., 1967. Dir. budget planning and analysis comptroller dept. AT&T, 1976-77; with Bell of Pa., Phila., 1959-75, 77-85, div. ops. mgr. Western area, 1971-74; asst. v.p. pub. relations Bell of Pa. and Diamond State Telephone, Phila., 1974-75; v.p., gen. mgr. Eastern region Bell of Pa. and Diamond State Tel., Phila., 1977-81, v.p.-regulatory, 1981-83, pres., chief exec. officer, 1983-85; vice chmn., chief fin. officer, dir. parent co. Bell Atlantic Corp., Phila., 1985-88; pres., chief oper. officer Bell Atlantic Corp., 1988; chmn., chief exec. officer Bell Atlantic Corp., Phila., 1989—; mem. bd. USAir Group, Core States Fin. Corp.; mem. Bus. Roundtable, 1990—; mem. nat. adv. bd. Pvt. Sector Coun., 1990—; mem. James Madison Nat. Coun. Libr. of Congress, 1990—; bd. overseers Sch. Engring. and Applied Scis., U. Pa., 1989—. Pub. playwright. Trustee U. Pitts. With Signal Corps, U.S. Army, 1959-60. Mem. Bus. Roundtable, Pvt. Sector Coun. (nat. adv. bd. 1990—), James Madison Nat. Coun. Libr. Congress. Office: Bell Atlantic Corp 1717 Arch St Philadelphia PA 19103-4201

SMITH, RAYMOND WALTER, antiquarian bookseller; b. Newark, Oct. 26, 1942; s. Aloysius J. and Ruth Caroline (Varhley) S. BA, Stetson U., 1964; MA, Yale U., 1966, MPhil, 1968. Proprietor R.W. Smith-Bookseller, New Haven, Conn., 1975—; curator John Slade Ely House, New Haven, 1986—. Contbr. articles to profl. jours. Named Woodrow Wilson fellow, Woodrow Wilson Found., Yale U., 1964-65, Ford Found. fellow in Afro-

Am. Studies, Ford Found., 1971-72. Mem. Antiquarian Booksellers Assn. Am. Office: John Slade Ely House 51 Trumbull St New Haven CT 06510-1004

SMITH, RICHARD ANTHONY, investment banker; b. St. Louis, July 17, 1939; s. Jack and Ruth Smith; children: Richard Adam, Jonathan. Student, Yale U., 1961. With Salomon Bros., N.Y.C., 1969-75, Morgan Stanley & Co., N.Y.C., 1975—; mng. dir. Morgan Stanley, N.Y.C., 1983, mem. mgmt. com., 1988—. Mem. Bd. Am. Jewish World Svc., Shelter Island Yacht Club, Yale Club (N.Y.C.). Office: Morgan Stanley 1251 Ave of the Americas 33d Fl New York NY 10020

SMITH, RICHARD AUSTIN, writer; b. Clarksburg, W.Va., Dec. 3, 1911; s. Silas Morris and Mildred Margaret (Johnson) S.; m. Kathleen Knox, May 20, 1939; children: Richard Austin, Roderick Sheldon. Student, Mercersburg Acad., 1927-31, Duke U., 1931-34; DLitt, Salem (W.Va.) Coll., 1955. Writer indsl. and occupational analyses U.S. Dept. Labor, 1934-38; staff writer Think Mag., pub. IBM Corp., 1939, assoc. editor, 1939-42; fin. writer Time Mag., 1946; S.C. corr. Time, Life and Fortune Mags., 1946-48; assoc. editor Dixie Mag., 1946-48; econ. corr. Time and Fortune Mags., Washington, 1948-50; assoc. editor Fortune Mag., 1950-58, mem. bd. editors, 1958-66; mem. editorial bd. Duke Mag.; mem. adv. com. Groton/New London (Conn.) Airport. Author: The Sun Dial, 1942, Corporations in Crisis, 1963, Alaska and Hawaii: The Frontier States, 1968; editor: President's Report, Aviation Adv. Commn., 1971-72, The Long-Range Needs of Aviation 1972-2000; contbr. to profl. publs. Trustee Gunston Sch., Centreville, Md., 1962-70; dir. Salem (W.Va.) Coll., 1963-69. With AUS, 1943-46, mil. corr. ETO, 1944-45. Recipient Loeb award U. Conn., 1962; named Ferris lectr. Trinity Coll., Hartford, 1966. Mem. Sigma Upsilon, Phi Eta Sigma, Nat. Press Club (Washington), Authors Guild, Army Navy Club, Sons of the Am. Revolution, Princeton Club. Home: PO Box 9191 Noank CT 06340-9191

SMITH, RICHARD WARREN, venture capitalist; b. Boston, July 18, 1952; s. James Stuart and Ruth Ann (Jarvis) S.; m. Charlotte Vivienne Hayles, July 5, 1980; children: Emily Wyndham, Nicholas James, Alastair, Davis, Penelope Ann. BA cum laude, Harvard U., 1974. Asst. treas. Morgan Guaranty Trust Co., London, N.Y., 1974-79; sr. investment mgr. Citicorp Venture Capital, N.Y.C., 1979-81; gen. ptnr. WestVen, Lawrence WPG Ptnrs., Lawrence, Tyrrell, Ortale & Smith, N.Y.C., 1981—. Author: Treasury Management: A Practitioner's Handbook, 1981. Office: Lawrence Tyrrell Ortale & Smith 515 Madison Ave Fl 29 New York NY 10022-5403

SMITH, ROBERT ALLEN, trust company executive; b. Bronx, N.Y., Mar. 27, 1936; s. Lewis and Anne (Gorelick) S.; m. Carmen de los Angeles Acevedo Serrano; stepchildren: Jorge M. Santiago, Ivan M. Gutierrez, Wilson M. Gutierrez. AAS, N.Y.C. Community Coll., 1956; cert. in hotel mgmt., N.Y.C. Bd. Edn., 1957; cert., N.Y. Inst. Criminology, 1958. Mgr. credit and hotel bus. Sheraton, Zeckendorf, Bossert Hotel, Bklyn., 1954-56, Louisville, 1962-65; mgr. credit Am. Express Co., N.Y.C., 1965-69; credit officer Mfrs. Hanover Trust Co., N.Y.C., 1969—; survey assoc. statis rsch. police problems Bristol twp., Pa., 1964; instr. credit and hotel law N.Y. Inst. Criminology, N.Y.C, 1958-60; bd. dirs. Camp de Wolfe and Conf. Ctr., Wading River, N.Y., Hispanic Am. Career Edn. Resources Inc., N.Y.C., Friends P.R. Inc., N.Y.C. Contbr. articles to profl. jours. Bd. dirs. N.Y.C. Fire Mus., 1990—, Friends P.R. (Mus. Contemporary Hispanic Art); hon. bn. chief N.Y.C. Fire Dept., 1989; 1st lt. Civil Air Patrol, 1960—. Named to Hon. Order of Ky. Cols., 1962, Hon. Dep. Sheriff County Jefferson, Ky., 1962, Col. Ky. State Police, 1962, Ky. Athletic Hall Fame, 1962; recipient key to City of Louisville, 1962, key to My Old Ky. Home, 1962. Mem. Am. Philatelic Soc., Am. Stamp Dealers Assn., Am. Air Mail Soc., Fire Bell Club N.Y., Masonic Stamp Club N.Y. (pres. 1971), Masons (master 1968). Episcopalian. Home: 110-55 72d Rd Forest Hills NY 11375 Office: Mfrs Hanover Trust Co 270 Park 45th Ave New York NY 10017-2014

SMITH, ROBERT CLINTON, senator; b. Trenton, N.J., Mar. 30, 1941; s. Donald and Margaret (Eldridge) S.; m. Mary Jo Hutchinson, July 2, 1966; children: Jennifer L., Robert Clinton, Jason H. A.A., Trenton Jr. Coll., 1963; B.A., Lafayette Coll., 1965; postgrad., Long Beach State U., 1968-69. Tchr., realtor Wolfeboro, N.H., 1975-85; chmn. Gov. Wentworth Dist. Sch. Bd., 1978-84; mem. 99th-101st Congresses from 1st N.H. dist., 1985-90; mem. U.S. Senate, 1990—; mem. vets., armed svcs., sci. and tech. coms., chmn. House Task Force on Acid Rain; mem. armed svcs., environ. and pub. works, joint econ. com., vice-chmn. select com. on POW/MIA affairs, dep. minority whip. With USN, 1965-67, Vietnam; with USNR, 1962-65, 67-69. Decorated campaign medal (Republic of Vietnam). Mem. VFW, Am. Legion, NRA, Theta Xi. Republican. Roman Catholic. Office: US Senate 332 Dirksen Senate Office Washington DC 20510

SMITH, ROBERT JAMES, clinical psychologist; b. Hartford, Conn., Aug. 31, 1960; s. Robert James and Diane Grace (Zaino) S.; m. Pilar Pueyo, Apr. 21, 1990. Student, Trinity Coll., 1979-81; BA in Psychology, U. Wis., 1983; MA in Psychology, U. Cin., 1985, PhD in Clin. Psychology, 1988. Lic. psychologist, Conn., Mass. Route merchandiser Coca-Cola Bottling Co., East Hartford, Conn., 1982-85; mental health worker Mt. Sinai Hosp., Hartford, Conn., 1985; psychology intern U. Cin., 1984-87; psychologist acute inpatient and day hosp. svcs. Greater Bridgeport (Conn.) Community Mental Health Ctr., 1988-91; clin. psychologist and sport performance cons. Bridgeport, 1990-91; pvt. practice Wellesley, Mass., 1991—; cons. Fairfield U. Athletic Dept., 1990—, Kolbe Cathedral High Sch., Bridgeport, 1990—, Warren Harding High Sch., Bridgeport, 1988-90. Author videotape screenplay: Survival Skills for Student Athletes, 1991; contbr. articles to profl. jours. U. Cin. rsch. fellow, 1987. Mem. APA, Conn. Psychol. Assn., Assn. for the Advancement of Applied Sport Psychology (charter), U.S. Tae Kwon Do Assn., Phi Kappa Phi. Democrat. Roman Catholic. Office: 70 Walnut St Wellesley MA 02181

SMITH, ROBERT LUTHER, management educator; b. Kutztown, Pa., Feb. 18, 1927; s. Paul Luther and Esther Florence (Schwoyer) S.; m. Canda Eure Banks, Aug. 18, 1951; children: Kimberley Smith Kidd, Valerie Smith Eudy, Alexandra. BS, U.S. Naval Acad., 1949; MSA, George Washington U., 1975, DBA, 1984. Commd. USN, 1949-72, advanced through grades to comdr.; commanding officer USS Grouper, 1962-65; engr. and repair officer U.S. Submarine Base, Groton, Conn., 1965-67; supt. of test Portsmouth Naval Shipyard, Portsmouth, N.H., 1967-70; asst. project mgr. Naval Systems Submarine Acquisition, Washington, 1970-72; project mgr. EG&G, Washington Analytical, Rockville, Md., 1972-80; pres. Interface Resources Ltd., Alexandria, Va., 1980—; lectr. George Mason U., Fairfax, Va., 1981-84; assoc prof. Coll. of Notre Dame of Md., Balt., 1984—; seminar leader various pvt. cos., 1980-85; faculty Dealer Mgmt. Inst., Columbus, Ohio, 1981-83; cons. in field. Contbr. articles to profl. jours. Sr. warden St. Paul's Episcopal Ch., Alexandria, 1980-81; mem. Alexandria Health Svcs., 1983—. Mem. Acad. of Mgmt., Ea. Acad. of Mgmt., Alexandria Health Svcs. Corp., U.S. Naval Inst., Kiwanis of Alexandria (pres. 1985-86, del. to internat. 1985), Masons, Beta Gamma Sigma. Republican. Home: 1102 Bayliss Dr Alexandria VA 22302 Office: Coll of Notre Dame of Md 4701 N Charles St Baltimore MD 21210

SMITH, ROGER POWELL, pharmacology and toxicology educator, consultant; b. Hokuchin, Korea, July 16, 1932; came to U.S., 1938; s. Burton Powell and Mary Hannah (McMullen) S.; m. Rena Joan Pointer, Nov. 1, 1956; children: Sam Fitzgerald, Joan Bartlett, Ben Holbrook. BS, Purdue U., 1953, MS, 1955, PhD, 1957; MA (hon.), Dartmouth Coll., 1975. Instr. Dartmouth Med. Sch., Hanover, N.H., 1960-63, asst. prof., 1963-68, assoc. prof., 1968-73, prof., 1973—, chmn., 1976-87; adj. prof. Dartmouth Coll., Hanover, 1984—; cons. Toxicoloty Study Sect., NIH, Bethesda, Md., 1969-72, Pharmacology-Toxicology Program, Bethesda, 1972-76, Environ. Health Scis., Research Triangle Park, N.C., 1985-87; mem. cons. staff Mary Hitchcock Meml. Hosp., Hanover, 1968—. Author: Primer Environmental Toxicology, 1992; co-author: Clinical Problems Basic Pharmacology, 1989, Clinical Toxicology Commercial Products, 1984; contbr. over 100 articles to profl. jours. Cubmaster Boy Scouts Am., Hanover, 1968-71, scoutmaster, 1971-75; active com. Youth Hockey, Hanover, 1975-85; deacon United Ch. of Christ, Hanover, 1981-83. 1st lt. USAR. Recipient Career Devel. awards USPHS, NIH, Bethesda, Md., 1966-71, Disting. Alumnus award Purdue U., 1986; grantee Nat. Heart, Lung and Blood Inst., NIH, 1962—, Nat. Inst. Environ. Health Scis., NIH, Research Triangle Park, 1979—. Fellow AAAS; mem. Acad. Toxicol. Sci. (cert.), Am. Soc. Pharm. Exptl. Therapy, Am. Assn. Poison Control Ctrs. (treas.), Soc. Toxicology (edn. com.), Sigma Xi, Alpha Omega Alpha. Republican. Home: 12 Kingsford Rd Hanover NH 03755-2210 Office: Dept Pharmacology Dartmouth Med Sch Remsen 7650 Rm 519 Hanover NH 03755-3835

SMITH, RONA, real estate developer, consultant; b. N.YC., Dec. 10, 1944; d. Harry and Edith (Stern) Silberman; m. Barry Martin Smith, Aug. 29, 1965; children: David Evan, Letty Chandra. BA, CUNY, 1965; MA, NYU, 1968, PhD, 1977. Cons. N.Y.C., 1977-80; broker Douglas Elliman Gibbons & Ives, N.Y.C., 1980-85; mng. dir. 1st London Properties Fund, N.Y., London, 1985-91, 1st London Group, N.Y., London, 1988—. Mem. Reform Club, Sloane Club. Home: 290 W End Ave New York NY 10023-8106

SMITH, RONALD LEE, psychologist, consultant; b. Nashville, Apr. 29, 1951; s. Emory William and Mary Ellen (Cowan) S. BS, U. Tenn., 1978; MEd in Guidance and Counseling, Mid. Tenn. State U., 1988. Human svc. counselor Tenn. State Dept. Human Svcs., Nashville, 1980-88; psychologist Young Adult Inst., N.Y.C., 1988-89, Westchester Assn. Retarded Citizens, White Plains, N.Y., 1989—; exec., sr. therapist Behavior Mgmt. Consultants, White Plains, 1990—. Ednl. dir. Mt. Vernon (N.Y.) Ch. of Christ, 1990, youth dir., 1991. Mem. Am. Psychol. Assn., N.Y. State Psychol. Assn. Home: 4111 Gunther Ave Bronx NY 10466 Office: Westchester Assn Retarded Citizens 39 Westmoreland Ave White Plains NY 10606-1937

SMITH, ROY LEONARD, psychology educator, psychotherapist; b. Santa Cruz, Calif.; s. Raymond Woodrow and Nola May (Walker) S.; m. Geraldine Marie Moran; children: Stacey Raeleen, Rebecca Louise, Bruce Edward, Michelle Kathleen. BA, Seattle Pacific U., 1958; postgrad, Fuller Theol. Sem., 1959-60; MEd, Wash. U., St. Louis, 1970, PhD, 1970. Lic. psychologist, N.Y. Asst. min. Fairview Heights Bapt. Ch., Inglewood, Calif., 1959-60; tchr. elem. North Monterey County S.D., Moss Landing, Calif., 1959-60; tchr. Watsonville (Calif.) Union, 1962-63; tchr., counselor Ramey (P.R.) Base Schs., (Dept. of Def.), 1963-64; counselor Tacoma Pub. Schs., 1964-67; instr. psychology Wash. U., 1969-70; asst. prof. Smith Coll., Northampton, Mass., 1970-72; prof. psychology L.I.U., Brookville, N.Y., 1972—; cons. in field; pvt. practice, Bayshore, N.Y., 1986—. Co-author: Educational Psychology, 1972; contbr. articles to profl. mags. Mem. APA (div. neuropsychology), APA-Psychologists Interested in Religious Issues. Mem. Church of Christ. Home: 268 Windsor Ave Brightwaters NY 11718-1402 Office: CW Post Campus Northern Blvd Brookville NY 11718

SMITH, ROY PHILIP, judge; b. S.I., N.Y., Dec. 29, 1933; s. Philip Aloysius and Virginia (Collins) S.; m. Elizabeth Helen Wink, Jan. 23, 1965; children: Matthew P., Jean E. BA, St. Joseph's Coll., Yonkers, N.Y., 1956; JD, Fordham U., 1965. Bar: N.Y. Asst. reg. counsel FAA, N.Y.C., 1966-79; adminstrv. law judge U.S. Dept. Labor, Washington, 1979-83; adminstrv. appeals judge Benefits Rev. Bd., Washington, 1983-88; chmn. and chief adminstrv. appeals judge Benefits Rev. Bd., 1988—; adj. prof. aviation law Dowling Coll., Oakdale, N.Y., 1972-79; adj. prof. transp. law Adelphi U., Garden City, N.Y., 1975-79; vis. prof. Georgetown U. Law Sch., 1989—. With U.S. Army, 1957-59. Mem. Assn. of Bar of City of N.Y. (sec.-treas. aeronautics com. 1978-79), Fed. Adminstrv. Law Judges Conf. (treas. 1983-84, exec. com. 1982-83), Internat. Platform Assn., Friendly Sons of St. Patrick, Edgemoor Club. Home: 6700 Pawtucket Rd Bethesda MD 20817-4836 Office: Benefits Rev Bd 800 K St NW Washington DC 20001-3742

SMITH, RUSSELL AUBREY, mechanical engineer, educator; b. Little Rock, June 8, 1936; s. Russell Davenport and Frances Caroline (Reynolds) S.; m. Maureen Polk, Feb. 27, 1960; children: Annemarie, Thomas, Claudine. BA, Rice U., 1958, BSME, 1958; MME, Catholic U. Am., 1964, PhD, 1969. Assoc. prof. Catholic U. Am., Washington D.C., 1966-76; supervisory mech. engr. U.S. Dept. Transp., Washington D.C., 1976-82; prof. U.S. Naval Acad., Annapolis, Md., 1982—; cons. Forensic Technologies Internat., Annapolis, Md., 1983—. Lt. U.S. Navy, 1958-63. Mem. Am. Soc. Mech. Engrs., Soc. Automotive Engrs., Am. Soc. for Engring. Edn., Sigma Xi. Roman Catholic. Office: US Naval Academy Mech Engring Dept Annapolis MD 21402

SMITH, RUSSELL DAVID, oil company executive; b. Mexico, Mo., Feb. 7, 1950; s. Harlan D. and Eula N. S.; m. Rita M. Hunn, May 20, 1972; children: Annette, Timothy. BS in Ceramic Engring., U. Mo., Rolla, 1972; MS in Ceramic Engring., U. Mo., 1974; Diploma in Chem. Engring., Univ. Mich., 1974. Devel. engr. Dow Chemical, Midland, Mich., 1973-77; rsch. engr. Carborundum, Niagara Falls, N.Y., 1977-80, product devel. mgr., 1980-83, tech. mgr., 1984-89, gen. mgr., 1989—; adv. bd. SUNY/Buffalo, MBA Mfg. Option, 1990—. Author: Alumina As Ceramic Material, 1990; patentee in field. Mem. Grand Island (N.Y.) Little League, 1989—. Recipient fellowship ALCOA, U. Mo., Rolla, 1972-73. Mem. Am. Ceramic Soc., Keramos, Ishm. Office: Carborundum PO Box 2467 Niagara Falls NY 14302-2467

SMITH, SAMUEL DAVID, pediatric surgeon, educator; b. Magnolia, Ark., Aug. 20, 1955; s. Samuel Denny and Nancy Jane (Rogers) S.; m. Nancy Gail Marbury, June 2, 1985. MD, U. Ark., Little Rock, 1980. Cert. gen. surgery, pediatric surgery, surgery-critical care Am. Bd. Surgery. Surg. intern U. Ark. for Med. Scis., 1980-81, resident gen. surgery, 1981-82; resident pediatric surgery Children's Hosp. Med. Ctr., Boston, 1983-84; sr. resident gen. surgery U. Ark. for Med. Scis., 1983-85, chief resident gen. surgery, 1984-85; fellow pediatric surgery Children's Hosp. of Pitts., 1985-87, pediatric surg. critical care fellow, 1987-88; resident in surgery U. Ark. for Med. Scis.; asst. prof. pediatric surgery U. Pitts., 1988—; pediatric surgeon, dir. nutritional support svc. Children's Hosp. Pitts., 1988—. Contbr. chpts. to med. books. Recipient Resident of Yr. award 1984-85 Med. Student Coun., U. Ark. for Med. Sci., 1985. Fellow ACS, Am. Acad. Pediatrics; mem. Surg. Infection Soc., Am. Pediatric Surgery Assn. Office: Children's Hosp Pitts 3705 5th Ave Pittsburgh PA 15213-2524

SMITH, SHARON PATRICIA, dean; b. Jersey City, Nov. 6, 1948; d. Vincent C. and Dorothy (Linehan) S. AB, Rutgers U., 1970, MA, 1972, PhD, 1974. Rsch. assoc. Princeton (N.J.) U., 1974-76, vis. sr. rsch. economist, 1988-90; economist Fed. Res. Bank, N.Y.C., 1976-81, sr. economist, 1981-82; dist. mgr. AT&T, N.Y.C. and Piscataway, N.J., 1982-90; dean Coll. of Bus. Adminstrn. Fordham U., Bronx, 1990—; vis. assoc. prof. N.Y. State Sch. Indsl. and Labor Rels., Ithaca, N.Y., 1981; adj. assoc. Drew U., Madison, N.J., 1984. Author: Equal Pay in the Public Sector: Fact or Fantasy, 1977, (with Albert Rees) Faculty Retirement in the Arts and Sciences, 1991; contbr. articles to profl. jours. NDEA fellow, 1970-73. Mem. Am. Econ. Assn., N.Y. Human Resource Planners Assn., Indsl. Rels. Rsch. Assn., Am. Assn. for Higher Edn., Princeton Club of N.Y. Democrat. Roman Catholic. Home: 45 Wellington Ave Short Hills NJ 07078-3307 Office: Fordham U Coll of Bus Adminstrn 101 Thebaud Hall Bronx NY 10458

SMITH, SHARRON WILLIAMS, chemistry educator; b. Ashland, Ky., Apr. 3, 1941; d. James Archie and May (Waggoner) Williams; m. William Owen Smith, Jr., Aug. 16, 1964; children: Leslie Dyan, Kevin Andrew. BA, Transylvania U., 1963; PhD, U. Ky., 1975. Chemist, Procter & Gamble, Cin., 1963-64; tchr. sci. Lexington pub. schs., Ky., 1964-67; chemist NIH, Bethesda, Md., 1974-75; asst. prof. chemistry Hood Coll., Frederick, Md., 1975-81, assoc. prof., 1981-87, prof. 1987—; chair dept. chemistry, physics and astronomy, 1982-86, acting dean grad. sch. 1989-91. NDEA fellow, 1967-70, Dissertation Yr. fellow U. Ky., Lexington, 1970-71; grantee Hood Coll. Bd. Assocs., 1981, 85, 91, Beneficial-Hodson faculty fellow Hood Coll., 1984, 92; grantee NSF, 1986. Mem. AAAS, AAUP, Am. Chem. Soc., Am. Assn. Higher Edn., Middle Atlantic Assn. Liberal Arts Chemistry Tchrs. (pres. 1984-85). Democrat. Office: Hood Coll Dept Chemistry Frederick MD 21701

SMITH, STACEY ELLEN, public relations executive; b. Bklyn., Apr. 29, 1958; d. Jerome and Shirley (Zinn) S. BS in Communication, U. Tenn., 1980; MS in Mgmt., Antioch/New Eng. Coll., 1989. Assoc. counsel Jackson, Jackson & Wagner, Exeter, N.H., 1981-85, counsel, 1986—; adj. instr. pub. rels. Antioch-New eng. Grad. Sch., New Eng. Coll., Henniker, N.H., U. sagrado Corazon, Santurce, P.R. Mgr. Seacost Concert Band, N.H., Maine, 1986-87; bd. dirs. A Safe Place, Battered Women's Shelter, Portsmouth, N.H., 1991-93. Mem. Pub. Rels. Soc. Am. (bd. dirs. Yankee chpt. 1984—, pres. 1989-90, assembly del. nat. governing body 1990—, dir. nat. social svcs. sect. 1986-89, juried presenter nat. conf. 1989), Am. Assn. Pub. Opinion Rsch., Orgn. Devel. Network. Office: Jackson Jackson & Wagner 14 Front St Exeter NH 03833-2747

SMITH, STANDISH HARSHAW, non-profit company executive; b. Germantown, Pa., Dec. 28, 1931; s. Standish Oscar and Kathryn Jeanette (Harshaw) S.; m. Joan H. Lallou, Dec. 29, 1956; children: Hamilton, Robertson. BA, Kenyon Coll., 1956; postgrad., State U. Iowa, 1956-58, Villanova U., 1959-61, U. Pa., 1963, Temple U., 1967. Rsch. analyst Rowland and Lo., Haddonfield, N.J., 1961, Franklin Inst., Phila., 1961-63, RCA Svc. Co., Moorestown, N.J., 1963-64, Fed. Aviation Agy., Pomona, N.J., 1964-66, Gen. Elec., Phila., 1966-70; founder, treas. Aqua Systems, Inc., Villanova, Pa., 1970-72; founder, owner Auto. Bus., Phila., 1970-84; ret., 1984-91; founder Heirs, Inc., Villanova, 1991-92; human factors engr. Burroughs Corp., Paoli, Pa., 1959-61; lectr. Burroughs Night Sch., Paoli, 1960. Inventor Marine pipelaying system, 1973; contbr. articles to profl. jours. Mem. Merion Cricket Club, Plays and Players, Wissahickon Skating Club, Orpheus Club, Wistar Inst. Office: 1744 Cedar Ln Villanova PA 19085

SMITH, STEPHEN CHARLES, economist, educator; b. Waterbury, Conn., Apr. 24, 1955; s. Charles Lynn Jr. and June Emma (Wilkins) S.; m. Renee Jakobs, Aug. 24, 1984; children: Martin Wilkins, Helena Christine. BA in Liberal Arts, Goddard Coll., 1976; MA in Econs., Cornell U., 1981, PhD in Econs., 1983. Rsch. writer, lobbyist rsch. groups Ralph Nader, 1976-78; grad. teaching, rsch. asst. Cornell U., Ithaca, N.Y., 1978-83; asst. prof. George Washington U., 1983-88; vis. asst. prof. European U. Inst., Florence, Italy, 1984; vis. asst. prof., fellow Cornell U., Ithaca, 1986; assoc. prof. econs. George Washington U., Washington, 1988—; rsch. assoc. Econ. Policy Inst., Washington, 1987—; rsch. advisor Progressive Policy Inst., Washington, 1990—; cons. European Commn., U.S. HHS, 1984, U.S. Info. Agy., 1988, World Bank, 1991-92. Author: Industrial Policy in Developing Countries, 1991; contbr. articles to profl. jours. Nat. Inst. Pub. Fin. and Policy scholar, 1986-87, U. Belgrade and Inst. Ind. Econ. scholar, 1988; Dilthey Soc. fellow, 1989, Fulbright fellow, 1989-90, Jean Monnet Rsch. fellow, 1989-90, Banneker fellow, 1991. Mem. Am. Econ. Assn., Assn. Comparative Econ. Studies, Univ. Club. Democrat. Unitarian Universalist. Home: 2422 Silver Fox Ln Reston VA 22091 Office: George Washington U Econ Dept 2201 G St NW Washington DC 20052-0001

SMITH, STEPHEN ROSS, physician; b. Iowa City, Iowa, Mar. 5, 1938; s. Wendell Ross and Ruth Anne (Frudenfeld) S.; m. Elaine Cashman Frazier, July 4, 1964 (div. Dec. 1990); children: Julia Helene, Stuart Ross; m. Regina Alilada Clarito, Dec. 26, 1990; 1 child, Alexander Ross. AB, Princeton U., 1959; MD, Harvard Med. Sch., 1963. Asst. prof. medicine Johns Hopkins U. Sch. Medicine, Balt., 1970-73, 82—; chief endocrinology Kern County Hosp., Bakersfield, Calif., 1973-76; assoc. prof. medicine Tex. Tech. U. Sch. Medicine, El Paso, 1977-80; chief medicine Thomason Gen. Hosp., El Paso, 1977-80, Bon Secours Hosp., Balt., 1980-83, Security Forces Hosp., Riydah, Saudi Arabia, 1984-88; physician internal medicine, endocrinology pvt. practice, Balt., 1988—; med. dir. Nat. Clin. Rsch. Ctrs., Bethesda, 1988—; rsch. assoc. Johns Hopkins Ctr. Med. Rsch. and Tng., Calcutta, India, 1970-72; bd. dirs. El Paso Diabetes Assn., 1978-80; cons. Liberty Med. Ctr. Diabetes Mgm. Ctr., Balt., 1991—. Contbr. articles to profl. jours. Capt. USAF, 1965-67. Fellow Am. Coll. Physicians; mem. Am. Diabetes Assn., Am. Fedn. Clin. Rsch., Princeton Club Md., Hampton Swim Club. Republican. Home: 1104 Temfield Rd Towson MD 21204 Office: 8709 Harford Rd Baltimore MD 21234

SMITH, STEWART EDWARD, physical chemist; b. Balt., Oct. 5, 1937; s. Ambrose Jefferson and Gladys Ruth (Stewart) S.; m. Marguerite Carmelita Grier, June 23, 1962; children: Nicole Catherine, Stewart Bradford. BS, Howard U., 1960; PhD, Ohio State U., 1969. Chemist Du Pont, Gibbstown, N.J., 1963-64; rsch. chemist Du Pont, Wilmington, Del., 1972-74; tech. svc. rep. Du Pont, Wilmington, 1974-78; rsch. chemist Sun Oil, Marcus Hook, Pa., 1969-71; coal chemist Exxon Rsch. and Engring., Baytown, Tex., 1976-81, group head, 1981-82; relocation coord. Exxon Rsch. and Engring., Clinton, N.J., 1982-84; sr. staff chemist Exxon Rsch. and Engring., Baytown, 1984-86; advisory engr. Westinghouse-Bettis, West Mifflin, Pa., 1986—. Contbr. articles to profl. jours. Mem. jr. high sch. adv. bd., Wilmington, 1975; coach Little League Baseball, Clear Lake City, Tex., 1979. Lt. U.S. Army, 1961-63. Recipient Pres.'s award Howard U. Alumni, Wilmington, 1976. Mem. AAAS, Am. Chem. Soc., Sigma Xi, Kappa Alpha Psi. Home: 125 Amberwood Ct Bethel Park PA 15102-2252 Office: Westinghouse Elec Corp PO Box 79 West Mifflin PA 15122-0079

SMITH, S(TEWART) GREGORY, ophthalmologist; b. Wyandotte, Mich., Jan. 24, 1953; s. Stewart Gene and Veronica (Latta) S. BA in Econs. with distinction, U. Mich., 1974; MD, Wayne State U., 1978. Diplomate Am. Bd. Ophthalmology, Nat. Bd. Med. Examiners. Intern, Sacred Heart Med. Ctr., Spokane, Wash., 1978; resident in ophthalmology U. Minn., Mpls., 1979-82, fellow cornea and anterior segment surgery, 1982-83; practice medicine specializing in cornea and anterior segment surgery, and ophthalmology Wilmington, Del., 1983—; clin. prof. ophthalmology U. Pa., Hershey Med. Ctr., 1984—; assoc. surgeon Wills Eye Hosp., Phila., 1984—; mem. sr. faculty 3M Vision Care Dept., Mpls., 1984—, research cons., 1984, lectr., 1983—; lectr. in field, Korea, Hong Kong, Thailand, Malaysia, Phillipines, 1986. Author: Complications of Intraocular Lenses and Their Management, 1988; contbr. articles to profl. publs. Patentee investigational device. Recipient award for Best Sci. Poster, Contact Lens Assn. of Ophthalmologists, 1980; Best Film award Internat. Congress of Cataract Surgeons, 1985; Grand Prize Am. Soc. Cataract and Refractive Surgeons Film Festival, 1986. Fellow Am. Intraocular Implant Soc., Castroviejo Soc. (Best Paper award 1984), AMA, Eye Bank Assn. Am., Internat. Intraocular Implant Club. Avocations: fly fishing, hunting, saxophone. Home: Cloud Farm Rd Yorklyn DE 19736 Office: 1700 Shallcross Ave Suite 2 Wilmington DE 19806

SMITH, SURVILLA MARIE, outreach worker; b. Chattanooga, Oct. 17, 1933; d. Charlie and LeGusta (Robinson) Prater; children: Charles, Calvin, Robin. Student, Mass. Bay Community Coll., Boston, 1965-66, Northeastern U., 1967-79, Mus. Sch. of Fine Arts, 1989-90, U. Mass., 1989-91. Exec. sec. The Ecumenical Ctr., Roxbury, Mass., 1965-67, Roxbury Fedn. of Neighborhoods, 1965-68; bus. mgr. Coun. of Elders, Inc., Boston, 1969-72; exec. sec., asst. bookkeeper Edn. Renewal, Inc., Boston, 1972-73; asst. dir. METCO Inter-Dist. Transfer Inc., Roxbury, 1973-75; pupil pers. coord. Met. Coun. for Ednl. Opportunity, Roxbury, 1975-78; with Vis. Nurse Assn. of Boston, 1978-79; sec. Bay State Banner Newspaper, Roxbury, 1980; sr. outreach coord. Mattahunt Community Sch Sr. Outreach, Mattapan, Mass., 1989—. Mem. Mass. Sr. Action, Boston, 1990—; chmn. health campaign Grove Hall/Franklin Park AARP, Boston, 1990—. Home: 4 Wentworth St Dorchester MA 02124-3517

SMITH, SUSANNA SCHAEFFER, career development executive; b. Cortland, N.Y., Oct. 29, 1966; d. Daniel Herbert and Sondra (Lundy) S. BA in Polit. Sci., Hood Coll., 1988; MEd in Counseling and Student Devel., Am. U., 1990. Myers-Briggs type indicate cert. Legis. corr. Congresswoman Beverly B. Byron, Washington, 1988; interview coord. Am. U. Law Sch., Washington, 1988-90; asst. dir. recruitment Crowell and Moring, Washington, 1990-91; asst. dir. career devel. George Washington U. Nat. Law Ctr., Washington, 1991—; cons. Peace Corps-Returning Vols., Washington, 1991—. Mem. AACD, Nat. Assn. for Law Placement, Washington Area Legal Recruiters Assn. Democrat. Roman Catholic. Office: George Washington U Nat Law Ctr 716 20th St NW # 303B Washington DC 20052-0001

SMITH, TERRY EDWARD, research and development manager; b. Evansville, Ind., Aug. 23, 1940; s. Russell Trent and Mabel LaRue (Wright) S.; m. Linda Lee Newsom; children: Jeffrey Russell, Virginia Lynn, Stacey Lee. BA, David Lipscomb U., 1962; PhD, Ga. Inst. Tech., 1967. Rsch. chemist Am. Cyanamid Co., Stamford, Conn., 1967-72; rsch. specialist, analytical GAF Corp., Wayne, N.J., 1972-76, group leader, analytical, 1976-

85, mgr., R & D adminstrn., 1979-82; R & D sect. mgr. Internat. Splty. Products (formerly GAF), Wayne, N.J., 1985—. Contbr. articles to profl. jours.; patentee Polymer compositions and processes. Tchr., deacon and elder in various chs., 1965—. Mem. Am. Chem. Soc. (polymer div.).

SMITH, THOMAS CLAIR, manufacturing company executive; b. Indiana, Pa., Mar. 14, 1925; s. William Bryan and Edna Louise (Thomas) S.; m. Marilyn Louise Globisch, May 29, 1948; children: Claudia Lynn Smith Holtry, Craig Randall. BSME, Pa. State U., 1946; A, Alexander Hamilton Bus. Inst., 1949. Registered profl. engr., Pa. Structural test engr. Chance Vought Aircraft Co., Bridgeport, Conn., 1946-48; test engr. Fed. Mogul Bearings Co., Lancaster, Pa., 1949-51; fuse engr. to mgr. materials Hamilton Watch Co. (name now Hamilton Tech.), Lancaster, Pa., 1952-70; plant mgr. Woodstream Corp., Lititz, Pa., 1970-79, v.p. mktg., 1980—; faculty, coach Lacrosse Franklin and Marshall Coll., Lancaster, 1950-53. Pub. Smith, Bryan, Allison & Morris Geneal. Chart, 1989; author and pub. of 1600 person geneal. chart in Libr. of Congress, 1989; patentee electric watch, 1957, swivel snap, 1975. Pres., bd. dirs. Lancaster County Mental Health Assn., 1952-60, Lancaster County Community Svc. Ctr., 1968-78, Am. Cancer Soc., 1968—; bd. dirs. Hearing Conservation Assn., Lancaster, 1955-60, ARC, Lancaster, 1967—, United Way Lancaster, 1968-72, Ephrata (Pa.) Area Rehab. Ctr., 1986—; mem. Heritage Ctr. Lancaster, 1980—, Lancaster County Hist. Soc., 1983—, Ind. County Hist. Soc., 1984—, Greene County Hist. Soc., Waynesburg, Pa., 1985—, Selective Svc. Bd., 1992; mem. all-Am. Lacrosse Team, 1945. With USMC, 1951. Recipient Outstanding Svc. award Mental Health Assn., Lancaster, 1961, Edward D. Eshelman award as Humanitarian of Yr., Am. Cancer Soc., Lancaster, 1991; named Boss of Yr. Am. Bus. Womens Assn., 1978, Man of Yr. Am. Cancer Soc., 1984, Tennis Family of Yr., Pa., N.J., Del., 1970. Mem. Order of Crown of Charlemagne in U.S.A. (life), Pa. State U. Alumni Club (life), Pa. Sons. Revolution (bd. dirs. 1985—), Phi Delta Theta (pres. Pa. State U. chpt. 1945), Wheatland Tennis Club (v.p. 1990). Republican. Presbyterian. Club: Lancaster Country (chmn. tennis com. 1960-75). Home: 1420 Quarry Ln Lancaster PA 17603-2426 Office: Woodstream Corp 69 N Locust St Lititz PA 17543-1714

SMITH, THOMAS WALTER, political economist; b. Rochester, N.Y., Sept. 28, 1955; s. William Herbert and Jean (Hagen) S.; m. Frances Miller, May 26, 1979. BA, Duke U., 1977; MA in Law and Diplomacy, Tufts U., 1980. Rsch. asst. Nat. Assn. Attys. Gen., Raleigh, N.C., 1977-78, 79; instr. English, Lang. Inst. Japan, Odawara, 1980-83, editor, 1981-83; editor Environ. Systems Rsch. Inst., Redlands, Calif., 1984; rsch. analyst Link Resources Corp., N.Y.C., 1984-85; polit. economist Yamaichi Rsch. Inst., N.Y.C., 1985—. Guest commentator politics and econs. CNBC and FNN cable TV networks; contbr. books revs. on U.S.-Japan topics to various publs. Mem. Nat. Assn. Bus. Economists, Assn. for Investment Mgmt. and Rsch., N.Y. Soc. Security Analysts. Home: 35 Clark St Apt 5A Brooklyn NY 11201-2374 Office: Yamaichi Rsch Inst 2 World Trade Ctr Ste 9846 New York NY 10048-0203

SMITH, VIRGINIA ELEANORE, mental health counselor, educator; b. Bklyn., Aug. 12, 1940; d. Valentine A. and Katherine V. (Angold) Pajer; m. Albert G. Smith, Aug. 12, 1961; children: Daniel, Douglas, Andrew, Katherine, James. BA, Neumann Coll., 1978; MS, Drexel U., 1984; postgrad., Union Inst., Cin., 1990—; postgrad. clin. tng., Gestalt Therapy Inst. Phila., 1991—. Lic. mental health counselor, Del., Pa. Med. social worker Delaware County Commn. Nursing Svc., Chester, Pa., 1983-84; counselor Manatee County Mental Health Agy., Bradenton, Fla., 1984-85; pvt. practice Wilmington, Del., 1990—; mental health counselor Correctional Med. Systems, Wilmington, Del., 1990—; adj. prof. Delaware County Community Coll., Media, Pa., 1985—, Widener U., Goldey Beacon Coll., Wilmington, 1987—. Mem. AACD, Am. Sociol. Assn., Mental Health Counselors Assn., Assn. Humanistic Psychologists. Roman Catholic. Home: 4201 Fox Point Ct Glen Mills PA 19342

SMITH, WALTER ARNOLD, insurance consultant; b. Allentown, Pa., Aug. 19, 1943; s. Harold A. and Margaret A. (Klimek) S.; m. Suzanne J. Pancottine, Jan. 9, 1965; children: Kristine, David, Jay. BS in Math., Lafayette Coll., 1965. Actuarial student Prudential Ins., Newark, 1965-69; mgr. Nat. Health and Welfare Retirement, N.Y.C., 1969-75; cons. Nutley, N.J., 1975—. Commr. Twp. Nutley, N.J., 1988—, planning bd., 1986—; bd. dirs. Nutley Red Cross, Nutley Sr. Citizen Housing Corp., 1982—, Nutley Sr. Baseball League Nutley Cen. Little League, pres. 1980-87, coach; head Montclair YM-YWCA Indian Guides and Princesses, Nutley, 1977-80; active Yantacaw, Franklin High Sch. PTA, 1979-89, Mayor's UN com., 1967-68, Cerebral Found., 1966-67, March of Dimes; Republican committeeman Essex County. Recipient Jerseyan of Week award Star Ledger, 1975. Mem. Rotary (pres. Nutley chpt. 1989-90), Jaycees (v.p. U.S. 1976-77, Senator award 1970), Nutley Elks. Lutheran. Home: 568 Prospect St Nutley NJ 07110-1520 Office: Twp of Nutley One Kennedy Sq Nutley NJ 07110

SMITH, WALTER JOSEPH, JR., lawyer, educator; b. N.Y.C., Feb. 23, 1936; s. Walter J. and Florence W. (Watson) S.; m. Felicitas U. Von Zeschau, Oct. 5, 1968; children—Caroline, Alexandria, Christopher. A.B., Hamilton Coll., 1958; LL.B., Columbia U., 1961. Bar: U.S. Ct. Mil. Appeals 1967, U.S. Dist. Ct. (D.C. dist.) 1967, U.S. Ct. Appeals (D.C. cir.) 1967, U.S. Supreme Ct. 1974, U.S. Ct. Claims 1975. Mem. Judge Advocate Gen.'s Office, U.S. Navy, Washington, 1966-68; trial atty., Washington, 1968-75; ptnr. Wilson, Elser, Moskowitz, Edelman & Dicker, Washington, 1975—; mng. ptnr., 1979—; adj. prof. law Antioch Sch. Law, 1981—. Pres. Dogwood Assn., 1982-83. Served to lt. USN, 1962-67. Recipient Pres.'s award Am. Soc. Pharmacy Law, 1984. Mem. ABA, Def. Research Inst., Counsellors, D.C. Bar Assn. Democrat. Roman Catholic. Clubs: Tuckahoe. Author: Insurance Protection in Product Liability. Office: 1341 S G St NW Washington DC 20005

SMITH, WALTER JULIUS, JR., real estate company executive; b. Bklyn., Apr. 4, 1911; s. Walter J. and Emma Van Rennsalaer (Wilson) S.; m. Dorothy Groser, Dec. 1, 1940 (dec. 1964); 1 child, Walter J. III; m. Joan Faye, 1965 (dec. 1988). Student, Hofstra U. Real estate salesman, appraiser N.Y.C., 1930-50, Walter J. Smith Co., Inc., N.Y.C., 1950—; founder appraisal divs. various bds. N.Y. State, 1970—. Contbr. articles on real estate to profl. jours. Pres. polit. orgns., L.I., 1968—. Named Realtor of Yr., N.Y. State-L.I. Bd., 1968. Mem. Am. Soc. Real Estate Appraisers, N.Y. State Soc. Real Estate Appraisers (past pres., dir. 1966-80), L.I. Bd. Realtors (dir., pres. 1960-80). Office: Walter J Smith Co Inc 12 Railroad Ave Glen Head NY 11545-1814

SMITH, WARREN L., electrical engineer, physicist; b. Wayne, Nebr., July 6, 1924; s. James M. and Mattie M. (Meng) S.; m. Frances M. Dowd, June 18, 1948; children: Marjory, Catherine, James, Gerald, Janine. BSEE, U. Wis., 1944. Rsch. asst. U. Wis., Madison, 1947-51; mem. tech. staff Bell Telephone Labs., Murray Hill, N.J., 1954-87; ret., 1987; tech. cons. to Tech. Com. 49 of IEC, 1973—. Contbr. 17 publs. to confs. and symposium proceedings; contbr. 3 chpts. to books. Lt. USN, 1942-46, 51-54. Fellow IEEE; mem. AAAS, Electronic Industries Assn. (quartz devices sect.). Home: 3046 Meadowbrook Cir S Allentown PA 18103-5422

SMITH, WILLIAM KEVIN, investment banker; b. Suffern, N.Y., May 10, 1951; s. Daniel Endy and Patricia (McTernan) S.; m. Kathleen Shelton, Oct. 25, 1980; children: William Kevin Jr., Patricia. BSEE, Villanova U., 1973; MBA in Fin., U. Pa., 1978. Cert. mgmt. cons., Series 7 securities rep. Mktg. engr. Gould, Inc., Indpls., 1973-76; sr. mgr. Touche Ross & Co., N.Y.C., 1978-87; v.p. Bear Stearns & Co., Inc., N.Y.C., 1987-89; sr. v.p. Kidder, Peabody & Co., Inc., N.Y.C., 1989-91; pres., chief exec. officer Renaissance Capital Corp., N.Y.C., 1991—. Author: Strategic Growth Through Mergers and Acquisitions, 1985. Mem. Nat. Assn. Securities Analysts (registered broker/dealer), Eta Kappa Nu. Republican. Roman Catholic. Home: 124 Pecksland Rd Greenwich CT 06831-3650

SMITH-HEFNER, NANCY JOAN, English educator; b. Youngstown, Ohio, Nov. 22, 1952; d. William Thomas and Joan Duane (Muir) Smith; m. Robert William Hefner, Sept. 6, 1980; 1 child, Claire-Marie. BA in Comparative Lit., U. Mich., 1974, MA in Linguistics, 1976, PhD in Linguistics, 1983. Vis. asst. prof. English, U. Mass., Boston, 1984-88, asst. prof., 1988—; mem. Fulbright ASEAN Rsch. Grants and Teaching Awards Area Rev. Com., 1991. Contbr. articles to profl. jours. Rsch. grantee Social Sci. Rsch. Coun., Java, Indonesia, 1985, Fulbright Commn., Java, 1985, Spencer Found., 1988, 90, Inst. for Study Econ. Culture, Boston U., 1991. Mem. Assn. for Asian Studies (Indonesian studies com. 1986-90), Am. Anthrop. Assn., Assn. Tchrs. ESL, Nat. Assn. for Bilingual Edn., Mass. Assn. for Bilingual Edn. Home: 350 Tappan St Apt 3 Brookline MA 02146-4352 Office: U Mass Dept English Boston MA 02125-3393

SMITH-YOUNG, ANNE VICTORIA, health services professional; b. Long Beach, Calif., Aug. 25, 1947; d. James Warren and Jeanne Anne (Cooney) Wright; m. Lynn Walker Smith, Aug. 11, 1968 (div. Feb. 1980); children: Amy Lyanne and Caroline Walker (twins); m. Stephen Nicholas Young, May 29, 1982. AS, Long Beach City Coll., 1967; BS, Marymount Coll., 1984. Diplomate Am. Bd. Urologic Allied Health Professions (cons., adminstrv. sec. 1987—). Mgr. office Williams-Brinton Med. Corp., Huntington Beach, Calif., 1975-80; adminstr. Westchester Urol. Assocs., White Plains, N.Y., 1980-82; adminstr. Pediatric Urol. Assocs. Westchester County Med. Ctr., Valhalla, N.Y., 1982-86; clin. coord. urodynamics lab. cystocopy ste. dept. urology Westchester County Med. Ctr., Valhalla, 1986—, chairperson exec. com. employee adv. coun., 1987—; cons. Office Career Svcs., Marymount (N.Y.) Coll., 1984—; cons. to mfrs., individuals and healthcare providers on urinary incontinence and urodynamics. Mem. editorial bd. Sex Over Forty; contbr. articles to profl. jours. Mem. NAFE, Am. Urol. Assn. (allied, nat. fundraiser 1980-86, bd. dirs. N.Y. chpt. 1988—, recognition award 1985), Assn. Urinary Continence Control (bd. dirs. 1988—), Am. Assn. Med. Assts., Nat. Trust for Hist. Preservation, Internat. Platform Assn., Mothers of Twins Club (pres. Long Beach 1974-75), Lions (bd. dirs. White Plains, N.Y. 1989, editor Lions Roar newsletter, 1st v.p. 1990-91, pres. 1991—, Lion of Month award 1990, Officer of Yr. award 1991). Democrat. Home: 407 Strawberry Hill Ave Stamford CT 06902-2513 Office: Westchester County Med Ctr Dept Urology Valhalla NY 10595

SMITS, EDWARD JOHN, museum director; b. Freeport, N.Y., Dec. 11, 1933; s. Karl M. and Jennie (Spring) S.; m. Ruth K. Hall; children: E. John, Robert K., Theodore R. BA, Hofstra U., 1955; MA, NYU, 1959. Curator Nassau County Hist. Mus., East Meadow, N.Y., 1956-70; dir. mus. svcs. Div. Mus. Svcs. Nassau County, Syosset, N.Y., 1971—; Nassau County historian, 1985—. Author: Long Island Landmarks, 1970, Creation of Nassau County, 1959, Nassau, Suburbia U.S.A., 1974. Trustee Friends for L.I.'s Heritage, Nassau County Hist. Soc. 1st. lt. U.S. Army, 1955-56. Fulbright grantee, 1965; recipient Nassau County Disting. Svc. award County of Nassau, 1970, Alumni Disting. Svc. award Hofstra U. 1970, H. Sherwood Historic Preservation on L.I. award Soc. for the Preservatioin of L.I. Antiquities, 1975. Mem. Am. Assn. Mus. Home: 14 Wavy Ln Wantagh NY 11793-1202

SMOCK, ARTHUR RESEAU, JR., retired airline economist; b. Lakewood, N.J., Apr. 28, 1920; s. Arthur Reseau and Ethel Merle (Worden) S.; m. Virginia Harriet Ste. Marie, Sept. 18, 1943. BA, Rutgers Coll., 1943. Staff analyst TWA, N.Y.C., 1952-56, mgr. revenue forecasting, 1956-59, dir. revenue forecasting, 1959-62, dir. market rsch., 1962-65, dir. econ. rsch., 1965-70, dir. tariff studies, 1970-72, staff economist, 1973-83; ret., 1983; panelist, speaker World Congress of Travel Agts., Mexico City, 1963; instr. SRI Round Table on Airport Planning, Washington, 1966; panelist, speaker Northwestern U. Transp. seminar, Evanston, Ill., 1969. Contbr. articles De Halve Maen Mag., 1985—. Pres. Community Svc. Assn., New Providence, N.J., 1956-60; sec. svc. unit Salvation Army, New Providence, 1950-91. Mem. SAR, Holland Soc. N.Y. (trustee 1974—, chmn. centennial celebration 1984-85, pres. 1987-90, gold medal 1983), New Netherland Festival (bd. dirs. 1988-91), Friends New Netherland Project N.Y. State Libr. (charter), N.J. Hist. Soc., Ocean County Hist. Soc., Nat. Trust Historic Preservation, Circumnavigators Club, Lambda Chi Alpha (trustee New Brunswick chpt. 1960-86, emeritus 1987—, disting. svc. award 1983), Masons. Republican. Episcopalian. Home: 11 Greenwood Rd New Providence NJ 07974-2302

SMOKE, RICHARD, political scientist, political psychologist; b. Huntington, Pa., Oct. 21, 1944; s. Kenneth Ludwig and Lillian Duerer (Harbaugh) S. B.A., Harvard Coll., 1965; Ph.D., MIT, 1972. Asst. dean, lectr. Kennedy Sch. Govt. Harvard U., Cambridge, Mass., 1971-73; postdoctoral fellow Inst. Personality Assessment and Research U. Calif.-Berkeley, 1973-74; fellow Ctr. Advanced Study Behavioral Scis., Palo Alto, Calif., 1974-75; research assoc., prof. Wright Inst., Berkeley, 1975-81; interim dean Wright Inst., 1981-82; exec. dir., co-founder Peace and Common Security, San Francisco, 1982-84; prof. polit. sci., dir. Ctr. for Fgn. Policy Devel. Brown U., Providence, 1984—. Author: National Security and the Nuclear Dilemma, 1984, 2d edit., 1987, War: Controlling Escalation, 1977; co-author: (with Alexander L. George) Deterrence in American Foreign Policy: Theory and Practice, 1974 (winner Bancroft prize 1974); (with Willis Harman) Paths to Peace, 1987; editor: (with Andrei Kortunov) Mutual Security, 1991; assoc. editor Polit. Psychology, 1978-81. Mem. Internat. Soc. Polit. Psychology (governing council 1980-82), Am. Polit. Sci. Assn. (Helen Dwight Reid award), Am. Psychol. Assn. Office: Brown U Ctr for Fgn Policy Devel PO Box 1948 Providence RI 02912-0001

SMOLEV, TERENCE ELLIOT, lawyer, educator; b. Bklyn., Oct. 5, 1944; s. Lawrence and Shirley (Lebowitz) S.; m. Sherry Gale Rosen, Nov. 24, 1968; children: Cindy, Scott. BBA, Hofstra U., 1966; JD, American U., 1969; LLM, NYU, 1974. Bar: N.Y. 1970. Acct. Peat Marwick & Mitchell, N.Y.C., 1969-70; dir. deferred giving Hofstra U., Hempstead, N.Y., 1971-74; editor Panel Publishers, Greenvale, N.Y., 1970-71; ptnr. Naidich & Smolev, P.C., Bellmore, N.Y., 1972-92; mem. bd. trustees Hofstra U., 1992—; adj. prof. Hofstra U., Hempstead, N.Y., 1971—; dist. counsel North Merrick (N.Y.) UFSD, 1975—; bd. dirs. Hofstra U. Club, Hempstead, 1981—. Author of book chpt. Mem. Nassau County, N.Y. Dem. Com., 1972-80; mem. IRS Small Bus. Adv. Com., Washington D.C., 1975-77. Recipient Hofstra U. George M. Estabrook award, 1991; named Senator of Yr., Hofstra U., 1985. Mem. ABA, N.Y. State Bar Assn., Nassau County Bar Assn., N.Y. State Assn. Sch. Attys. (pres. 1984), Hofstra U. Alumni Senate (pres. 1987-89). Office: Two Hillside Ave Williston Park NY 11596-2335

SMULLEN, HAROLD ARTHUR, JR., insurance agent; b. New Haven, Apr. 5, 1954; s. Harold Arthur and Irene Mary (Quigley) S.; m. Mary Margaret Quish, May 24, 1986; children: Jeffrey, Brandon. BA, Trinity Coll., Hartford, Conn., 1976; MBA, U. Conn., 1985. CPCU. Account analyst, account mgr., then asst. sec. Travelers Ins. Co., Hartford, 1976-85, dir., 1985-86, regional mgr., 1986-87; account exec. R.C. Knox and Co., Inc., Hartford, 1987-90, v.p., 1990—, also bd. dirs. Contbr. articles to industry publs. Mem. Soc. CPCU, Conn. Soc. CPCU, Exch. Club West Hartford (bd. dirs. 1992), Wampanoag Country Club, Univ. Club Hartford (bd. dirs. 1990—, activities chmn. 1988-89, membership chmn. 1989-90), Trinity Club Hartford (exec. com. 1991-92), Pi Gamma Mu, Beta Gamma Sigma. Roman Catholic. Office: RC Knox and Co Inc 300 Pearl St Hartford CT 06117

SMYER, MICHAEL ANTHONY, university official, human development educator; b. New Orleans, Oct. 21, 1950; s. Anthony and Alyce Mary (McGraw) S.; m. Patricia Ellen Piper, May 24, 1975; children: Brendan Piper-Smyer, Kyle Piper-Smyer. BS in Psychology, Yale U., 1972; PhD in Psychology, Duke U., 1977. Lic. psychologist, Pa. Asst. to pres. S.I. Community Coll., CUNY, 1970-71, Duke U., Durham, N.C., 1976-77; asst. prof. human devel. Pa. State U., University Park, 1977-82, assoc. prof., 1982-87, prof., 1987—, assoc. dean rsch. and grad. studies, 1988—; assoc. chmn. gerontology ctr., Pa. State U., 1979-86, prof.-in-charge individual and family studies, 1982-87, grad. prof.-in-charge individual and family studies, 1983-85; peer rev. com. mem. NIMH, 1991—. Co-author: (books) Mental Health and Aging, 1983, Mental Health Consultation in Nursing Homes, 1988; mem. editorial bd. Psychology and Aging, 1985-88, 92—, Internat. Jour. of Geriatric Psychiatry, 1992—, Jour. of Gerontology, 1981-83; co-author more than 40 sci. articles on gerontol. health. Mem. adv. com. Centre Region Sr. Citizens, State College, 1983-86; bd. dirs. The Meadows Clinic, State College, 1983-85, Foxdale Village Continuing Care Retirement Community, State College, 1986-91. Am. Coun. on Edn. fellow, 1985-86, W.K. Kellogg Found. fellow, 1982-85; rsch. grantee NIMH, Nat. Inst. Aging, Adminstrn. on Aging, Health Care Financing Adminstrn. Fellow APA (pres.-elect div. 20 1991-92), Gerontol. Soc. Am., Sigma Xi; mem. AAAS, APHA, Soc. Behavioral Medicine. Mem. Soc. of Friends. Home: 215 Ridge Ave State College PA 16803-3525 Office: Pa State U 201 Henderson Bldg University Park PA 16802

SMYTH, DAVID, editor, author; b. Buenos Aires, Feb. 7, 1929; came to U.S. 1962, naturalized 1970; s. Currell Hutchinson and Jessie Rodger (Dodds) S.; m. Elli Helene Dusterhoft, Nov. 9, 1968; 1 child, Clifford Dieter. BA, Cambridge (Eng.) U., 1951, MA, 1967. Tech. writer, copywriter, 1953-55, movie promotion writer, 1956; owner Ace Translation Agy., Buenos Aires, 1957-58; sec. Found. Econ. Edn., 1959; cables editor Buenos Aires Herald, 1960; lexicographer Simon & Schuster English-Spanish Dictionary, 1961; Latin Am. desk editor UPI, N.Y.C., 1962-63; Latin Am. desk editor AP, N.Y.C., 1963-73, world svcs. fin. editor, 1973—. Author: You Can Survive Any Financial Disaster, 1977, Worldly Wise Investor, 1988; co-author: The Speculator's Handbook, 1974, Unusual Investments That could Make You Rich, 1978, No Cost/Low Cost Investing, 1987. Served with Argentine Army, 1952. Mem. N.Y. Fin. Writers Assn. Home: 8 Beechwood Ave Metuchen NJ 08840-2107 Office: AP 50 Rockefeller Pla New York NY 10020

SMYTH, PETER HAYES, radio executive; b. Apr. 25, 1952; s. Arthur and Irene (McNamara) S; m. Catherine Comerford Smyth, Aug. 8, 1976; children: Nancy, Colin, Kathleen. BA, Holy Cross Coll., Worcester, Mass., 1975; postgrad., Fordham U., 1975-76. Retail sales man Sta. WROR Radio, Boston, 1975-76, gen. sales mgr., 1976-83; gen. sales mgr. Sta. WOR Radio, N.Y.C., 1983-86; v.p., gen. mgr. Sta. WMEX-AM/WMJX-FM, Boston, 1986—; cons. Greater Media Cable, North Oxford, Mass., 1988-89. Bd. dirs. Holy Cross Coll., Worcester, Univ. Club, Boston. Mem. New England Broadcast Assn. (bd. dirs. 1987, v.p., pres. 1992—). Republican. Roman Catholic. Office: WMEX-AM/WMJX-FM 330 Stuart St Boston MA 02116-5229

SMYTHE, KYM CORSCADDEN, university administrator; b. Phila., Feb. 12, 1963; d. Jack Charles and Charlotte Ruth (Wagner) Corscadden; m. Douglas Stewart Smythe, June 13, 1987; 1 child, Kyle Kastle. BA, LaSalle U., Phila., 1985; MEd, U. Vt., 1987. Prof. hall dir. U. Del., Newark, 1987-88, asst. area coord., 1988-89, area coord., 1989-90; asst. dir. student activities Widener U., Chester, Pa., 1990-91, dir. residential programs and housing ops., 1991—; new profls. coord. NASPA Region II, 1990—; presenter workshops in field. Foster parent Christian Children/Plan Internat., Indonesia/Haiti, 1986—; vol. United Way campaign, Newark, 1987-89; crisis counselor Sexual Assault Support Group, Newark, 1988-90; co-chmn. U. Del. Sexual Assault Awareness Wk., 1990. Mem. Nat. Assn. Student Personnel Adminstrs. (adv. bd. 1990—, Outstanding New Profl. award 1990), Nat. Assn. for Women in Edn., Am. Coll. Personnel Assn., Nat. Assn. Campus Activities. Democrat. Methodist. Home: 5 Beacon Ln New Castle DE 19720 Office: Widener Univ 1 University Pl Chester PA 19013

SMYTHE, SHEILA MARY, graduate school health sciences dean; b. N.Y.C., Nov. 1, 1932; d. Patrick John and Mary Catherine (Gonley) S. Student, Creighton U., 1952; BA, Manhattanville Coll., 1952; MS, Columbia U., N.Y.C., 1956; LHD (hon.), Manhattanville Coll., 1974. From rsch. assoc. to asst. dir. of rsch. and planning Blue Cross Assn., Chgo., 1957-63; exec. assoc. to pres. Empire Blue Cross & Blue Shield, N.Y.C., 1963-72, v.p., 1972-74, sr. v.p., 1974-78, exec. v.p., 1978-82, pres., chief oper. officer, 1982-85; health fin. and mgmt. cons. N.Y.C. and Washington, 1986-87; chief health policy advisor GAO, Washington, 1987—; dean grad. sch. health scis. N.Y. Med. Coll., N.Y.C., 1990—. Trustee Manhattanville Coll., Purchase, N.Y., 1981—; bd. dirs. Cath. Charities-U.S.A., 1989—, Mut. Am., 1990—, Nat. March of Dimes, 1989—, Nat. Health Coun., 1989—; dir. Greater N.Y. March of Dimes, 1985-89. Recipient Elizabeth Cutter Morrow award YWCA, N.Y., 1977, Disting. Alumni award Manhattanville Coll., 1981, Excellence in Leadership award Greater N.Y. March of Dimes, 1989. Mem. Nat. Arts Club N.Y.C. Roman Catholic. Office: NY Med Coll Grad Sch Health Scis Valhalla NY 10595

SNAPPER, ERNST, mathematics educator; b. The Netherlands, Dec. 2, 1913; came to U.S., 1938, naturalized, 1942; s. Isidore and Henrietta (Van Buuren) S.; m. Ethel Lillian Klein, June 1941; children—John William, James Robert. MA, Princeton U., 1939, PhD, 1941; AM (hon.), Dartmouth Coll., 1964. Instr. Princeton, 1941-45, vis. asso. prof., 1949-50, vis. prof., 1954-55; asst. prof. U. So. Calif., 1945-48, asso. prof., 1948-53, prof., 1953-55; NSF post-doctoral fellow Harvard, 1953-54; Andrew Jackson Buckingham prof. math. Miami U., Oxford, Ohio, 1955-58; prof. math. Ind. U., 1958-63; prof. math. Dartmouth, 1963—, Benjamin Pierce Cheney prof. math., 1971—. Mem. Am. Math. Soc., Math. Assn. Am. (pres. Ind. sect. 1962-63, Carl B. Allendoerfer award 1980), Assn. Princeton Grad. Alumni (governing bd.), Soc. for Preservation Bridges of Konigsburg, Phi Beta Kappa (hon.), Pi Mu Epsilon (hon.). Home: PO Box 67 Norwich VT 05055-0067

SNAVELY, RICHARD MELLINGER, communications executive, religious administrator; b. Strasburg, Pa., June 4, 1931; s. Abram Herr and Anna Mary (Mellinger) S.; m. Jacqueline DeVere, June 21, 1952; children: Carol, Rick, Randy, Ron. BA in Christian Edn., Bob Jones U., 1954. Field rep. Billy Graham Film Assn., Va., Md., Del., W.Va., 1954-56; founder, exec. dir. Family Life Ministries, Inc., Bath, N.Y., 1957—; eastern v.p. trustee Youth For Christ Internat., Wheaton, Ill., 1972-73; founder, exec. dir. New Life Homes, Inc., Bath, 1973—; exec. v.p. Youth Evangelism Assn., Kansas City, Kans., 1980-83; pres. Youth Evangelism Assn., Bath, 1985-87; also bd. dirs. Youth Evangelism Assn., Kansas City, Kans.; pres., gen. mgr. Sta. WCIK-FM, Bath, 1983—; pres., gen. mgr. Family Life Network, Sta. WCIK-FM, Bath, Sta. WCIH-FM, Elmira, Sta. WCID-FM, Friendship, Sta. WCII-FM, Spencer, N.Y. Fellow Nat. Religious Broadcasters Assn., Rotary (Paul Harris fellow). Republican. Home: PO Box 38 Avoca NY 14809-0038 Office: Family Life Ministries PO Box 506 Bath NY 14810-0506

SNEIRSON, GREGG ABNER, economic consultant; b. N.Y.C., July 8, 1953; s. Lester Sumner and Loretta Ida (Segel) S. AB summa cum laude, Northeastern U., Boston, 1984; M Pub. Policy, Harvard U., 1986. Pres. Diversified Musical Enterprises, N.Y.C., 1976-80; exec. fellow Robert Bosch Found., Stuttgart, Germany, 1986-87; spl. cons. Combined Jewish Philanthropies, Boston, 1987-88; v.p. Council for Econ. Action, Inc., Boston, 1988-90; pres. ISI Svcs. Group, Boston, 1990—; cons. Combined Jewish Philanthropies, 1988-90, Harvard U. Hillel, Cambridge, Mass., 1988-91, DATAR/Invest in France, Devon-Cornwall, U.K., North Rhine-Westfalia, Germany, 1990—. Co-founder Council on German-Jewish/Am. Relations, Boston, 1988; active Repub. Nat. Com., 1987—, Camera, Boston, 1987; adj. lectr. MPA program Northeastern U. Harry S. Truman scholar, 1983, John F. Kennedy fellow, 1984. Mem. German-Am. Bus. Club, German-Am. C. of C., Robert Bosch Alumni Assn. (v.p., treas. 1988-90), Harvard Club. Jewish. Office: ISI Svcs Group 1873 Central St Stoughton MA 02072

SNELBECKER, GLENN EUGENE, psychologist, educator; b. Dover, Pa., Sept. 24, 1931; s. William S. and Anna M. Snelbecker; m. Janice C. Fixler, Sept. 23, 1962; children: David M., Karen A., Laura B. BS in Bus. Edn., Elizabethtown Coll., 1957; MS in Guidance and Counseling, Bucknell U., 1958; PhD, Cornell U., 1961; diploma in Acctg., Thompson coll., 1952. Lic. psychologist, Pa. Postdoctoral intern VA Hosp., Brockton, Mass., 1961-62, clin. psychologist, Behavior Rsch. Lab. supr., 1962-67; assoc. prof. psychol. studies Temple U., Phila., 1967-72, prof. psychol. studies, 1972—; cons., author in pvt. practice Mgmt. Assocs. for Tech., Communications and Health, 1963—; investigator NSF computer project Retraining High Sch. Tchrs. Temple U., Phila., 1985-92. Author: Learning Theory, Instructional Theory, 1985; contbr. articles to profl. jours. Sgt. U.S. Army, 1952-55. Mem. Am. Edn. Rsch. Assn., Am. Psycholog. Assn., Phila. Area Computer Soc., Phila. Soc. Clin. Psychologists. Office: Temple U RA217 TU-004-00 Philadelphia PA 19122

SNELL, CORINNE MARIE, university administrator; b. Hazleton, Pa., Aug. 17, 1961; d. Richard Edward and Irene Marie (Hoppy) S. BA in Psychology, Lock Haven U., 1983; MA in Student Pers., Indiana U. of Pa., 1985. Resident dir. Old Dominion U., Norfolk, Va., 1985-88; coord. career/counseling svcs. Temple U., Ambler, Pa., 1988-92; assoc. dir. career svcs. Temple U., Phila., 1992—. Author: (booklets) Resume Writing, 1989, Cover/Thank You Letters, 1989, Interview Techniques, 1991. Roman Catholic. Office: Temple U Career Svcs Mitter Hall 2d Fl Philadelphia PA 19122

SNELL, GEORGE DAVIS, geneticist; b. Bradford, Mass., Dec. 19, 1903; s. Cullen Bryant and Katharine (Davis) S.; m. Rhoda Carson, July 28, 1937; children: Thomas Carleton, Roy Carson, Peter Garland. B.S., Dartmouth Coll., 1926; M.S., Harvard U., 1928, Sc.D., 1930; M.D. (hon.), Charles U., Prague, 1967; LL.D. (hon.), Colby Coll., 1982; Sc.D. (hon.), Dartmouth Coll., 1974, Gustavus Adolphus Coll., 1981, U. Maine, 1981, Bates Coll., 1982, Ohio State U., 1984. Instr. zoology Dartmouth Coll., 1929-30, Brown U., 1930-31; asst. prof. Washington U., St. Louis, 1933-34; research asso. Jackson Lab., 1935-56, sr. staff scientist, 1957—, emeritus, 1969—, sci. adminstr., 1949-50. Author: Search for a Rational Ethic, 1988, (with others) Histocompatibility, 1976; also sci. papers in field; editor: The Biology of the Laboratory Mouse, 1941. Recipient Bertner Found. award in field cancer research, 1962; Griffin award Animal Care Panel, 1962; career award Nat. Cancer Inst., 1964-68; Gregor Mendel medal Czechoslovak Acad. Scis., 1967; Internat. award Gairdner Found., 1976; Wolf Found. prize in medicine, 1978; award Nat. Inst. Arthritis and Infectious Disease-Nat. Cancer Inst., 1978; Nobel prize in medicine (with Dausset and Benacerraf), 1980; NRC fellow U. Tex., 1931-33; NIH health research grantee for study genetics and immunology of tissue transplantation, 1950-73 (allergy and immunology study sect. 1958-62); Guggenheim fellow, 1953-54. Mem. Nat. Acad. Scis., Transplantation Soc., Am. Acad. Arts and Sci., French Acad. Scis. (fgn. asso.), Am. Philos. Soc., Brit. Transplantation Soc. (hon.), Phi Beta Kappa. Home: 21 Atlantic Ave Bar Harbor ME 04609-1703

SNELL, JOHN THOMAS, architect, civil engineer; b. Chgo., Mar. 1, 1947; s. Ralph William and June Bertha (Buendgen) S.; m. Jod Rosen, Jan. 6, 1974; children: Ashleigh Jane, Christopher John; m. Mary Frances Rooney, Dec. 6, 1986. BArch, U. Ill., Chgo., 1970; M of Adminstrv. Sci., Johns Hopkins U., 1983; student, Howard Community Coll., Columbia, Md. Registered architect, Ill.; registered profl. engr., Md. Draftsman A.H. Ramp, Oak Park, Ill., 1968-71; engr. asst. U.S. Army, Washington, 1971-74; architect Gen. Svc. Adminstrn., Washington, 1974-78, FDA, Rockville, Md., 1978-84; chief archtl. engring. Crawford & Russell/John Brown, Inc., Stamford, Conn., 1984-86; dir. design Schumacher & Forelle, Great Neck, N.Y., 1986-91; v.p. Fletcher Thompson Inc., Bridgeport, Conn., 1991—. Contbr. articles to profl. jours. Mem. Boat U.S., Alexandria, Va., 1986. Mem. Nat. Soc. Profl. Engrs. Republican. Lutheran. Office: Fletcher Thompson Inc 2 World Trade Plz Bridgeport CT 06604-3944

SNIBBE, PATRICIA MISCALL, advertising agency executive; b. Hackensack, N.J., June 1, 1932; d. Jack and Margaret Lois (Drake) Miscall; m. Richard Wilson Snibbe, Sept. 8, 1962; stepchildren: John Robinson, Paul Clor. BFA, R.I. Sch. Design, 1954; postgrad., New Sch. for Social Rsch., 1975-80, U. London, 1989. Art dir., film producer Peckham Prodns., N.Y.C., 1960-64; dir. art, ptnr. Stallman and Snibbe, N.Y.C., 1964-66; dir. art Shevlo Advt., N.Y.C., 1966-72, Bernard Hodes Advt., N.Y.C., 1972-77; owner, creative dir. Designstuff, N.Y.C., 1978-88; creative dir. Archtl. Film Libr., N.Y.C., 1980—; pres. Crommelin and Bliss, Parfumier, 1988—. Author and artist: Feminist Funnies, 1981—. Recipient Golden Cir. award Affiliated Advt. Agys. Internat., 1975-77, Creativity award of Distinction, 1978. Mem. NOW (bd. dirs. N.Y.C. 1983-84), Graphic Artists Guild (steering com. Cartoonists Guild div. 1984-85), NATAS, Archael. Inst. Am. Home: 139 E 18th St New York NY 10003-2470

SNIDER, JAMES HARRY, writer, consultant, lecturer; b. Boston, Dec. 26, 1958; s. Stanley Walter and Mary Ann (Kane) S.; m. Terra Ziporyn, June 22, 1986; children: Pallas Amita, Sage Tivona. AB, Harvard Coll., 1981; MBA, Harvard U., 1987. Pres. Omnimedia, Burlington, Vt., 1987—. Author: Future Shop, 1992. Home: 70 Van Patten Pky Burlington VT 05401-1133

SNIDER, WILLIAM ALAN, broadcast journalist; b. Providence, Apr. 8, 1967; s. Stephen Harvey and Esta Fruma (Greenberg) S. BS Broadcast Journalism, Syracuse U., 1989; postgrad., Western New Eng. Coll., 1991, Western New Eng. Coll., 1990—. Asst. mgr. Cromwell (Conn.) Pharmacy, 1982-86; loan analyst Conn. Nat. Bank, E. Hartford, 1987; tech. engr. Sta. WVIT-Channel Thirty, W. Hartford, Conn., 1988; videographer, editor Sta. WWLP-TV, Springfield, Mass., 1990-91; salesperson video store Suncoast Motion Picture Co., Farmington, Conn., 1991—. Foster parent Foster Parents Plan, Warwick, R.I., 1983-91. Foster parent, Foster Parents Plan, Inc., Warwick, R.I., 1983-91. Democrat. Jewish. Home: 48 Fuller Dr West Hartford CT 06117-1324

SNIDERMAN, MARVIN, dentist; b. Pitts., Oct. 23, 1923; s. Abraham and Rebecca (Hecht) S.; B.S. in Pharmacy, U. Pitts., 1943, D.M.D., 1947; m. Eleanore Jessie Cohen, Dec. 25, 1947; 1 child, Abby Milstein. Pvt. dental practice Pitts., 1947-50, 53—; chief oral surgery dept. Pitts. Skin and Cancer Found., 1947-67. Mem. dental adv. com. Allegheny County Dept. Health, div. dental health, 1958-70; mem. undergrad. and postgrad. faculty U. Pitts. Sch. Dental Medicine, 1962—, assoc. prof. oral medicine, 1972-89, clin. assoc. prof. diagnostic svcs., 1989—; mem. charter council, 1986—; chief dental service Rehab. Inst. Pitts., 1948—. Mem. health adv. com. Pitts. Bd. Pub. Edn., 1965-70, dental health com. Mayor's Com. on Human Resources, Operation Head Start, 1965, adv. com. on health Mayor's Com. on Human Resources, 1965-70, charter council U. Pitts., 1986—; dental cons. USPHS, 1965-78; bd. dirs. Delta Dental of Pa., 1971-78; health edn. com. Allegheny County Adv. Council, 1972-74, 78—; mem. dental adv. com. Office Med. Programs Pa. Dept. Pub. Welfare, 1976-89; bd. dirs., sec. editorial com. Jewish Chronicle of Pitts., 1987—; vis. lectr. Emory U., U. Pa., Polyclinic and French Med. Sch., N.J. Coll. Medicine Dentistry, Temple Dental Sch. Albert Einstein Coll. Medicine, NYU Dental Sch., N.Y.C.; bd. dirs. Health/Edn. Commn. of Allegheny County, 1978—. Served with AUS, 1943-44, to capt., Dental Corps, 1950-53. Recipient Bicentennial Medallion of Distinction, 1987 U. Pitts. Fellow Am. Coll. Dentists (pres. Pitts. sect. 1972), Acad. Dentistry for Handicapped (charter), Acad. Gen. Dentistry (master), (charter), Soc. Oral Physiology and Occlusion, Internat. Coll. Dentists (dep. regent 1970-76, counselor 1981—), Am. Endodontic Soc. (charter), Internat. Coll. Applied Nutrition, Acad. Oral Medicine (academic, charter), Acad. Dentistry Internat. (charter), Am. Soc. Dentistry for Children, Am. Acad. Craniomandibular Orthopedics (charter), Acad. Stress and Chronic Disease (charter), Am. Equilibration Soc.; mem. AAUP, ADA (councils on journalism and dental rsch. and coun. on dental practice 1989, cons. editor jour.), Pa. Dental Assn. (vis. lectr.), Pierre Fauchard Acad., Am. Soc. Acupuncture, Am. Assn. Functional Orthodontics, Am. Acad. Oral Medicine (charter), Am. Soc. Assn. Execs., N.Y. Acad. Scis., Am. Assn. Dental Editors, Internat. Assn. Study Pain, Am. Pain Soc. (Charter), Odontological Soc. Western Pa. (pres. 1965, Albert R. Pechan award of excellence, 1981), Am. Internat. Acad. Preventive Medicine, Am. Prosthodontic Soc., Internat. Assn. Dental Research, AAAS, Am. Assn. Hosp. Dentists, Am. Assn. Dental Sch., Am. Acad. Implant Dentistry, Fedn. Prosthodontic Assns., Am. Endodontic Soc., Am. Dental Soc. Anesthesiology, Am. Analgesia Soc., Am. Acad. Dental Practice Adminstrn., Internat. Coll. of Oral Implantologists, U. Pitts. Dental Alumni Assn. (pres. 1973-74, Alumnus Distinction 1986), Am. Med. Writers Assn. Jewish. Editor: Odontological Bull. Western Pa., 1960-70, Pa. Dental Assn., 1970—; cons. editor Jour. Dental Practice Adminstrn., 1980—; also articles in field; abstractor Jour. Oral Research Abstracts. Home: 5633 Callowhill St Pittsburgh PA 15206-1452 Office: 204 5th Ave Pittsburgh PA 15222

SNIFFEN, MICHAEL JOSEPH, hospital administrator; b. Ossining, N.Y., June 16, 1949; s. John Francis and Mary Agnes (Madden) S.; m. Anne Marie Gillick; children: Kevin, Kristina. BS, Fordham U., 1971; MBA in Hosp. Adminstrn., Baruch Coll., 1977. Dir. of fin. planning Westchester div. N.Y. Hosp., White Plains, N.Y., 1971-74; assoc. dir. N.Y. Hosp., N.Y.C., 1974-80, sr. assoc. dir., assoc. dean Cornell Med. Ctr., 1980-87; pres., chief exec. officer Overlook Hosp., Summit, N.J., 1987—; exec. dir. Cornell Health Policy Program, N.Y.C., 1984-87; adminstr. program Commonwealth Fund, N.Y.C., 1978-81; adv. bd. Robert Wood Johnson Found.-Teaching Nursing Home Program, Princeton, N.J., 1980-86. Vol. March of Dimes, Tarrytown, N.Y., 1984-88; bd. dirs. St. Columbans Sch., Peekskill, N.Y., 1981-84; mem. various Father's Clubs, Westchester County, N.Y., 1976—. Mem. Am. Coll. Healthcare Execs., Hosp. Fin. Mgmt. Assn. (advanced mem.), Echo Lake Country Club (Westfield, N.J.), Beacon Hill Country Club, Lake Isle Country Club (Eastchester, N.Y.), Rotary. Roman Catholic. Home: 49 Drum Hill Rd Summit NJ 07901-3141 Office: Overlook Hosp 99 Beauvoir Ave Summit NJ 07901-3595

SNINCHAK, FAYE RITA, educator; b. Ilion, N.Y., Aug. 18, 1947; d. John Michael and Rita Anna (Bass) S. BA in Classics, Coll. of St. Rose, Albany, N.Y., 1969; postgrad. in English, Russell Sage Coll., 1970-74. Cert. permanent Latin and English tchr., N.Y. Tchr. English, Chatham (N.Y.) Cen. High Sch., 1969—, also coord. dept.; English item writer N.Y. State Edn. Dept., Albany, 1985—; mem. policy bd. greater Capital Region Tchr. Ctr., Schodack, N.Y., 1986—. Chmn. Village of Nassau (N.Y.) Planning Bd., 1979-85. N.Y. State Regents scholar, 1965; Activities Devel. Fund grantee, 1988-89. Mem. ASCD, NEA (del. region 10 1987—), Nat. Coun. Tchrs. English, Chatham Cen. Sch. Tchrs. Assn. (pres. 1981-87, chief negotiator 1987-91). Republican. Office: Chatham Cen High Sch 50 Woodbridge Ave Chatham NY 12037-1310

SNITOW, CHARLES, lawyer; b. N.Y.C., Feb. 7, 1907; m. Virginia Levitt, Nov. 2, 1935; children: Ann Barr, Alan Mark. AB, Cornell U., 1928, JD, 1930. Ptnr. Pomerance & Snitow, N.Y.C., 1931—; pres. Nat. Hardward Show Inc., N.Y.C., 1945-70, World Hobby Exposition, Chgo., Phila., 1948-53, Charles Snitow Orgn., N.Y.C., 1950-79, Internat. Auto Show, N.Y.C., 1952-80, Nat. Fancy Food Conf. Show, N.Y.C., 1955-70, U.S. World Trade Fair Inc., N.Y.C., San Francisco, 1957-66, Internat. Photography & Travel Show Inc., N.Y.C., 1960-72, Consumer Electronics Show, N.Y.C., 1967-77, Snitow Show Consultants, Inc., N.Y.C., 1975—; cons. Soviet Expn. Sci. and Tech., N.Y.C., 1959, N.C. Internat. Fair, Charlotte, 1959, British Expn., N.Y.C., 1960, Cahners Expn. Group divsn. Reed Exhbn. Cos., N.Y.C., 1970-87, Brazil Expo, N.Y., Chgo., L.A., Dallas, Atlanta, Miami, 1981, Greater N.Y. Internat. Auto Show, 1982—. Contbr. articles to Cornell Law Quar. Bd. dirs. Bill of Rights Found., N.Y.C., 1980; mem. Met. Opera Chorus, Schola Cantorum, Collegiate Chorale. Recipient cert. honor March of Dimes, Gold Key-Medal Honor City of N.Y., 1960-62, Gran Prix Americain, France, 1965, Garcia Moreno medal Equador, 1966, Award for Excelence N.A.E.M. Kings Glove, 1991, named Knight of Order of Merit, Republic of Italy, 1963; named to Order Honorable Ky. Cols., La. Cols. Mem. Latin Am. C. of C. (hon.), Nat. Assn. Expn. Mgrs. (hon.), Cornell Club, Savage Club, Phi Beta Kappa, Alpha Kappa Delta. Home: 81 Walworth Ave Scarsdale NY 10583-1140 Office: Snitow Show Cons Inc 4 Sniffen Ct New York NY 10016-3505

SNODDY, CHARLES EDISON, JR., real estate investment company executive; b. Buies Creek, N.C., Aug. 11, 1923; s. Charles Edison and Martha Arabella (Newton) S.; m. Olga Melockoff, Dec. 20, 1947 (dec. 1985); children: Charles Edison III, Gale Deborah Snoddy Margulies; m. Jean Green, June 5, 1987. BS, NYU, 1952. Real estate rep. Shell Oil Co., N.Y., Vt., 1954-63; v.p. Met. Life Ins. Co., N.Y.C., 1963-88; chief exec. officer Charles E. Snoddy & Co., Inc., N.Y.C., 1988—; chief exec. officer Assoc. Real Estate Advisors, Inc., N.Y.C., 1988—, also dir. Lt. USN, 1942-54. Mem. Internat. Coun. Shopping Ctrs. (com. mem. 1986-88), N.Y. Geneal. and Hist. Soc. (contbr. 1987—), Nat. Assn. Real Estate Appraisers, Pension Real Estate Assn., Urban Land Inst., Real Estate Bd. N.Y. (com. mem. 1986-88), Beacon Hill Country Club (Atlantic Highlands, N.J.), Masons. Republican. Methodist. Office: Assoc Real Estate Advisors 141 E 33d St New York NY 10016-4650

SNODGRASS, JEANNE ELLEN, adult education educator; b. Springfield, Ohio, Nov. 10, 1930; d. Harry Williams and Fontabelle (Baker) S. BA, Ohio Wesleyan U., 1952; MS, Smith Coll., 1953; EdD, U. N.C., Greensboro, 1975. Instr. Wellesley (Mass.) Coll., 1953-57; tchr. Newton (Mass.) Pub. Schs., 1957-59; prof. George Washington U., Washington, 1960-91, clinician movement edn. Am. Coun. for Internat. Sports, 1975-91; tchr. YWCA, Springfield; coord. Elderhostel, 1989—; presenter in field. Contbr. articles to profl. jours. Former coach (field hockey) Wellesley Coll., George Washington Univ., (swimming) Sunnyland Swim Club, Ohio, (squash) George Washington Univ.; mem. recreation and pk. adv. bd. City of Rockville, Md., 1977-78, commn. on aging, Montgomery County, Md., 1985—, chair, 1989-90; coord. adult ministries North Bethesda United Meth. Ch., 1985—. Mem. Ea. Assn. Phys. Edn. for Coll. Women (past pres. and various other positions and coms.), Nat. Assn. Phys. Edn. for Coll. Women (exec. bd., others), Nat. Assn. for Phys. Edn. in Higher Edn. (fin. com. 1979-82), AAHPERD (various positions and coms. locally and nationally), Ea. Assn. for Intercollegiate Athletics for Coll. Women (pres., others), Health Promotion Inst. (regional del.), Nat. Coun. on Aging. (various coms.), Kappa Delta Pi, Alpha Xi Delta, Alpha Delta Kappa.

SNOPKOWSKI, RICHARD RAYMOND, telecommunications service executive; b. Pittston, Pa., May 29, 1942; s. Adam B. and Veronica (Sekerchak) S.; m. Ann M. Manganiello, Feb. 1, 1964 (div. 1990); children: Michelle, Michael, Susan; m. Jean S. Swaim, Apr. 28, 1990. BS in Commerce and Fin., Wilkes U., 1963; MBA in Mgmt., U. Scranton, 1967; A in Engring., Pa. State U., 1984. Dist. comml. mgr. Commonwealth Telephone Co., Dallas, Pa., 1963-66, various mgmt. postions in ops. and mktg., 1971-85; facilities planner RCA Corp., Montaintop, Pa., 1966-71; gen. mgr. Yadkin Valley Telephone Membership Corp., Yadkinville, N.C., 1985-89; dir. industry rels. Nat. Exch. Carrier Assoc., Inc., Whippany, N.J., 1989—. Bd. dirs. Towanda Area C. of C., 1972-75; co-chmn. Bradford County Heart Assn., 1974. Mem. KC, Rotary. Republican. Roman Catholic. Home: 19 Georgian Rd Randolph NJ 07869

SNOW, DEAN RICHARD, anthropology educator, archaeologist; b. Sleepy Eye, Minn., Oct. 18, 1940; s. Roger Pershing and Gloria Jane Snow; m. Janet Charlene Keller, Dec. 21, 1963; children: Katherine, Barbara, Joshua. BA, U. Minn., 1962; PhD, U. Oreg., 1966. Asst. prof. anthropology U. Maine, Orono, 1966-69; asst. prof. SUNY, Albany, 1969-74, assoc. prof., chmn., 1974-80, prof., assoc. dean, 1980-83, prof., 1983-89, prof., dept. chmn., 1989-91, prof., 1991—. Author: The Archaeology of North America, 1976, Archaeology of New England, 1980, Archaeology of North American Indians, 1989; editor: Fondations of Northeast Archaeology; co-author: (with Michael Coe and Elizabeth Benson) Atlas of Ancient America. Pres. N.Y. Archaeol. Coun., 1987-89; active N.Y. State Bd. for Hist. Preservation, v.p., 1985. Grantee Nat. Geog. Soc., 1983, 85, NEH, 1984-85, 85-86, 87-89, 91-93, NSF, 1991-92. Fellow AAAS, Am. Anthrop. Assn., N.Y. State Archaeol. Assn.; mem. Am. Soc. Ethnohistory (pres. 1978-79), N.E. Anthrop. Assn. (pres. 1984-86). Office: SUNY at Albany 1400 Washington Ave Albany NY 12222-0001

SNOW, EDWARD LEON, small business owner; b. Chelsea, Mass., July 2, 1931; s. Benjamin and Cecilia (Mitchell) S.; m. Barbara Joan Levy, June 27, 1954; children: Nancy Diane, Linda Ellen, Michael Alan. BA, Harvard Coll., 1953. Mgmt. trainee Inland Steel Co., Chgo., 1955-56; sales mgr. Indsl. Distbrs., Lynn, Mass., 1956-75; pres., owner Creative Indsl. Supply, Lynn, 1975—; guest lectr. Tuft Coll., Medford, Mass., 1960. Pres. Marblehead (Mass.) Little Theater, 1962-64; v.p., bd. mem. Temple Emanu-El, Marblehead, 1970-80, bd. dirs., 1975-76; bd. dirs. North Shore Jewish Fedn., Marblehead, 1980—. Cpl. U.S. Army, 1953-55. Mem. Indsl. Distbn. Assn., Materials Handling Equipment Distbrs. Assn., Lynn C. of C. (bd. dirs. 1975—), Masonic Lodge (Lynn). Jewish. Home: 70 Weatherly Dr # 208 Salem MA 01970-6631 Office: Creative Indsl Supply Co 106 Oakville St Lynn MA 01905-2817

SNOW, JAMES BYRON, JR., physician, research administrator; b. Oklahoma City, Mar. 12, 1932; s. James B. and Charlotte Louise (Andersen) S.; m. Sallie Lee Ricker, July 16, 1954; children: James B., John Andrew, Sallie Lee Louise. B.S., U. Okla., 1953; M.D. cum laude, Harvard U., 1956; M.A. (hon.), U. Pa., 1973. Diplomate: Am. Bd. Otolaryngology (dir. 1972-90). Intern Johns Hopkins Hosp., Balt., 1956-57; resident Mass. Eye and Ear Infirmary, Boston, 1957-60; prof., head dept. otorhinolaryngology Sch. Medicine U. Okla., Oklahoma City, 1962-72; prof., chmn. dept. otorhinolaryngology and human communication U. Pa. at Phila., 1972-90; dir. Nat. Inst. on Deafness and Other Communication Disorders, Bethesda, Md., 1990—; mem. nat. adv. council neurol. and communicative disorders and stroke NIH, 1972-76, 82-86 ; chmn. Nat. Com. Research Neurol. and Communicative Disorders, 1979-80. Editor: Am. Jour. Otolaryngology, 1979-83; Contbr. articles to sci. and profl. jours. Served with M.C. AUS, 1960-62. Recipient Regents award for superior teaching U. Okla., 1970, Golden award Internat. Fedn. Otorhinolaryngological Socs., 1989; named to Soc. of Scholars Johns Hopkins U., 1991. Fellow Japan Broncho-Esophagological Soc. (hon.); mem. ACS (regent 1982-90), AMA (coun. on sci. affairs 1975-86), Soc. Univ. Otolaryngologists (pres. 1975), Am. Acad. Otolaryngology-Head and Neck Surgery, Assn. Acad. Depts. Otolaryngology (pres. 1981-82), Am. Laryngol., Rhinol., and Otol. Soc., Am. Otol. Soc., Am. Laryngol. Assn. (editor 1983-89, pres. 1990-91), Am. Broncho-esophagol. Assn. (editor trans. 1973-77, pres. 1979), Collegium Otorhinolaryngologicum, Soc. Scholars of Johns Hopkins U., Phi Beta Kappa, Alpha Omega Alpha. Home: 119 Discoll Way Gaithersburg MD 20878 Office: Nat Inst on Deafness and Other Communication Disorders Bethesda MD 20892

SNOW, ROBERT BRIAN, lawyer, educator; b. Rochester, N.Y., Apr. 9, 1953; s. Warren Buffington and Betty (Thrash) S.; m. Laura Rudman, May 11, 1976 (div. Sept. 1981); m. Patricia M. Lindsay, April 29, 1984; children: Robert Kyle, Alyssa Lindsay. BA in Polit. Sci. and Communications, U. N.H., 1975; postgrad., Suffolk U., 1975-76; JD, Boston Coll., 1978. Bar: N.H. 1979, U.S. Dist. Ct. N.H. 1979, U.S. Supreme Ct. 1982, Mass. 1985, U.S. Dist. Ct. Mass. 1985, U.S. Ct. Appeals (1st, D.C. and Fed. cirs.) 1985, D.C. 1985, U.S. Ct. Claims 1985. Asst. supr. Dept. Atty. Gen., Boston, 1977-78; dir. crime prevention and pub. info. State Dept. of Safety, Concord, N.H., 1978-79; atty., adminstr. subcontracts Kollsman Inst. Co. div. Sun Chem. Corp., Merrimack, N.H., 1979-81; sole practice Nashua, N.H., 1982—; atty. contracts divs. youth and adult svcs. State Dept. Human Svcs., Concord, 1983-88; instr. faculty Hesser Coll., Manchester, N.H., 1983-86, U. N.H., 1986—, Rivier Coll., 1991—; chmn. bd. dirs., legal counsel Mt. Hope Bd. of Edn., Nashua, N.H., 1983—; chmn. appellate div. State Dept. Employment, Concord, 1983-85; prosecutor p.t. Hudson (N.H.) Police Dept., 1985-86; chmn. Juvenile Parole Bd., 1987-88; judge Goffstown Dist. Ct., 1988—; counsel N.H. Supreme Ct. Commn. on Character and Fitness, 1990—. Author rules N.H. Motor Vehicle Title, 1979, N.H. Fire Code, 1979, N.H. Profl. Code of Conduct, 1984, N.H. D.E.S. Appellate Rules, 1986, N.H. Juvenile Parole Rules, 1988, Rules for Commn. on Character and Fitness. Candidate N.H. Reps., Concord, 1982; candidate State Senate, Merrimack, 1983; del. State Constl. Conv., Concord, 1983. Named one of Outstanding Young Men in Am., 1985, 86, 87. Mem. ABA, N.H. Bar Assn. (profl. code rev. com., criminal practice rev. com.), N.H. Trial Lawyers Assn., Assn. Trial Lawyers Am. (real estate standards rev. com.), N.H. Trial Lawyers Assn., So. N.H. Bus. and Indsl. Club, Merrimack C. of C. Republican. Clubs: Merrimack Exchange (chartered), Soc. N.H. Bus. and Industry. Home: 6 Valleyview Dr Merrimack NH 03054-3103 Office: 2 Wellman Ave Nashua NH 03060-1463

SNYDER, ARNOLD LEE, JR., retired air force officer, research director; b. Washington, Oct. 12, 1937; s. Arnold Lee and Frances May (Humbert) S.; B.C.E., George Washington U., 1960; M.S., U. Colo., 1966; Ph.D., U. Alaska, 1972; m. Patricia Dorine Ward, July 6, 1963; children: Heinrick Jason, Sonya Doreen, Ross Nansen. Commd. 2d lt. USAF, 1960, advanced through grades col., 1981, ret., 1987; chief space environ. support system devel. sect. Air Force Global Weather Central, Offutt AFB, Nebr., 1972-76; chief ionospheric dynamics br. Geophysics Lab., Hanscom AFB, Mass., 1976-80; test dir. CONUS OTH-B radar system, Columbia Falls AFS, Maine, 1980-81; program dir. CONUS OTH-B radar System, Hanscom AFB, 1981-85; dir. Office of Tech. Support, 1985-87; tech. dir. U. Lowell Ctr. Atmospheric Rsch., 1987-89; with The Mitre Corp., 1989—; instr. Western New Eng. Coll., 1978-80; adj. prof. U. Lowell, 1987-89. Recipient Legion Merit, Meritorious Service medal with one oak leaf cluster, Commendation medal USAF, research and devel. award, 1981; Def. Value Engring. award, 1984; Henry Harding scholar, 1955-56. Mem. Am. Geophys. Union, Am. Meteorol. Soc., Air Force Assn., Sigma Xi. Methodist. Contbr. articles to sci. jours. Home: RR 2 Box 135 Orrington ME 04474 Office: The Mitre Corp Burlington Rd Bedford MA 01730-1306

SNYDER, DONALD BENJAMIN, biology educator; b. N. Manchester, Ind., Oct. 6, 1935; s. Benjamin Franklin and Eva Katherine (Speicher) S.; m. Wilma Frankie Simpson, Aug. 8, 1965; children: Douglas, Jonn. BS, Manchester Coll., Ind., 1957; MS, Ohio State U., 1959, PhD, 1963; postgrad., U. Puerto Rico, 1966. Cert. wildlife biologist. From grad. asst. in zoology to rsch. fellow in wildlife Ohio State U., 1957-63; biology instr. Houghton (N.Y.) Coll., 1963; asst. prof. biology Central (S.C.) Wesleyan Coll., 1963-64, Geneva Coll., Beaver Falls, Pa., 1964-69; prof. biology Edinboro (Pa.) U., 1969—, Pymatuning Lab. of Ecology U., Pitts., 1982, 88, 89; bird records com. Presque Isle Audubon Soc., Erie, Pa., 1975—; vol. for wildlife Pa. Game Commn., Harrisburg, 1990—; ornithol. tech. com. Pa. Biol. Survey, Harrisburg, 1991—. Contbr. numerous articles to profl. jours. Committeeman Boy Scouts Am., Laketon, Ind., 1965-70; elder Christian & Missionary Alliance Ch., Erie, 1987-90; trustee Purple Martin Conservation Assn., Edinboro, Pa., 1988—. Equipment grantee Atomic Energy Commn., Oak Ridge, Tenn., 1966; recipient Meritorious Svc. award Edinboro U. Pa., 1974. Mem. Wildlife Soc., Assn. Field Ornithologists, Assn. Pa. State Coll. and Univ. Faculty, Beta Beta Beta. Home: 13190 Cambridge Rd Edinboro PA 16412-2837 Office: Dept of Biology Edinboro Univ Edinboro PA 16444

SNYDER, G(ARY) DEAN, sales and marketing executive; b. Coudersport, Pa., Mar. 19, 1960; s. Gary Laverne Snyder and Sue Ann (Tauscher) Bowman; m. Deborah Louise Ferguson, Oct. 21, 1987; 1 child, Kristi Ann. BS in Mktg., Bloomsburg U., 1981; MBA in Mgmt., Loyola Coll., Balt., 1989. Lic. life and accident and health ins. Owner, mgr. Mister G's Clothing, Coudersport, 1981-86; br. mgr., lender Commonwealth Bank, N.A., Williamsport, Pa., 1982-86; v.p., regional mgr. Equitable Bank, N.A., Balt., 1986-90; ea. regional dir. Household Bank Bus. Banking, Balt., 1990-91; part owner, v.p. sales and mktg. Egypt Farms Inc., White Marsh, Md., 1991—. Asst. treas. Tau Kappa Epsilon Fraternity, Bloomsburg, 1980; pres. Coudersport (Pa.) Area Merchants Assn., 1984; bd. dirs. Clarion County ARC, 1986; treas. Pen-Mar Mental Health Mental Retardation Orgn., Maryland Line, Md., 1990, 91, 92. Mem. Am. Mgmt. Assn., Pa. Interscholastic Athletic Assn. (basketball and football official 1981-86), Coudersport Consistory, Masons, Shriners, Tau Kappa Epsilon. Office: Egypt Farms Inc PO Box 223 White Marsh MD 21162

SNYDER, JANE PETERS, public relations executive; b. Manassas, Va., July 23, 1925; d. James Walker and Alma Dorothy (Cross) Peters; student George Washington U., 1943-45, Columbia U. Sch. Public Health, 1962; div.; children: Susan Leland, James Peters. Reporter, Montgomery County (Md.) Sentinel, 1952-54, Chatham (N.J.) Courier, 1956-59, Morris County (N.J.) Daily Record, 1959-61; pub. rels. asst. East Orange (N.J.) Gen. Hosp., 1962-64, United Hosp., Newark, 1964-65; dir. community rels. Georgetown U. Hosp., Washington, 1966-68; dir. pub. rels. Hosp. Coun. and Met. Regional Med. Program, Washington, 1968-70, Washington Hosp. Ctr., Washington, 1970-82; v.p. pub. relations The Pathfinder Corp., Washington, 1982-88 ; v.p. pub. and govt. affairs Delaware Valley Hosp. Council, Phila., 1984-90; appointed to adv. bd. Nat. Insts. of Health's Nat. Kidney and Urological Diseases, 1987—, active Information Clearinghouse coordinating panel, 1989—; lectr. George Washington U. Sch. Health Care Adminstrn., 1973, 78, 79, 80, 82; mem. coordinating panel NKUD Info. Clearing House, 1990—. Recipient Excellence award Assn. Am. Med. Colls., 1981. Mem. Am. Soc. Hosp. Public Relations (dir. 1973-75), Acad. Hosp. Public Relations (treas. 1973, dir. 1973-78, MacEachern awards 1963, 72-81). Home: 5235 Elliott Rd Bethesda MD 20816-2910

SNYDER, JED COBB, foreign affairs specialist; b. Phila., Mar. 24, 1955; s. David and Lynn S. BA, Colby Coll., 1976; MA, U. Chgo., 1978, postgrad., 1978-79. Rsch. asst. U. Chgo., 1979; asst. researcher Pan Heuristics div. R&D Assocs., Marina del Rey, Calif., 1979-80, assoc. researcher, asst. div. mgr., 1980-81, cons., 1982-83; cons. Sci. Applications, Inc., 1979-81, Rand Corp., Santa Monica, Calif., 1979-81, Los Alamos Nat. Lab., 1984; sr. spl. asst. to dir. Bur. of Politico-Mil. Affairs, Dept. State, Washington, 1981-82; rsch. assoc. Internat. Security Studies Program, Woodrow Wilson Internat. Ctr. for Scholars, Smithsonian Instn., Washington, 1982-84; founder, chmn. Washington Strategy Seminar, 1984-90, pres., 1984—; dep. dir. nat. security studies Hudson Inst., 1984-87; sr. rsch. fellow Nat. Strategy Info. Ctr., 1988-90; pres. Washington Strategy Seminar, 1984—; appointee v.p. Bush's adv. task force on Mid. East; appointee sr. fellow Inst. for Nat. Strategic Studies, Nat. Def. U., 1992—; cons. Office of Sec. of Def., 1988-92, Rand Corp., 1983-88; fellow Brit.-Am. Project for Successor Generation, 1991—; apptd. sr. fellow Inst. for Nat. Strategic Studies Nat. Def. U., 1992—. Contbr. articles on U.S. fgn. policy and mil. def. to profl. pubs. Trustee Kents Hill (Maine) Sch. Guest scholar Sch. Advanced Internat. Studies, Johns Hopkins U., 1982-83; fellow U. Chgo., 1979, Inter-Univ. Seminar on Armed Forces and Soc., 1980, MacArthur Sr., 1985-86, Herman Kahn, 1985-86, Smith

Richardson, 1987-88, John M. Olin, 1987-88, British-Am. Successor Generation Project, 1991; selected as a Young Am. Leader, Am. Coun. on Fed. Republic of Germany, 1984. Mem. Internat. Inst. for Strategic Studies, Internat. Studies Assn., Coun. on European Studies, Mil. Ops. Rsch. Soc., U.S. Naval Inst., Fgn. Policy Rsch. Inst., AIAA, Am. Polit. Sci. Assn., Coun. on Fgn. Rels. Home: 2201 L St NW Apt 602 Washington DC 20037-1412 Office: Nat Def UInst Nat Strategies Studies Ft Lesley McNair Washington DC 20319-6000

SNYDER, JOHN MENDENHALL, medical administrator, retired thoracic surgeon; b. Slatington, Pa., Aug. 1, 1909; s. James Wilson and Gertrude Winifred (Mendenhall) S.; m. Betty June Wiltrout, Feb. 14, 1942 (dec. May 1991); children: Sue Anne Snyder-Alexy, John Sanford. BS in Biology, Bucknell U., 1930; MD, U. Pa., 1934; MS in Surgery, U. Minn., 1941. Diplomate Am. Bd. Surgery, Am. Bd. Thoracic Surgery. Rotating intern Bryn Mawr (Pa.) Hosp., 1934-35; asst. resident in medicine Univ. Hosps. of Cleve.-Western Res. U., 1935-36; fellow in surgery Mayo Clinic, Rochester, Minn., 1936-41; practiced thoracic surgery Pa., 1945-77; emeritus asst. chief surg. svc., in charge thoracic surgery St. Luke's Hosp., Bethlehem, Pa., 1977—; med. dir. Bur. of Health, Bethlehem, 1981—; formerly on staff St. Luke's Hosp., Sacred Heart Mt. Trexler San.; formerly thoracic surg. cons. Sacred Heart Hosp., Allentown, Pa., Allentown State Hosp., Easton (Pa.) Hosp., Graden Huetten Hosp., Lehighton, Pa., Muhlenberg Med. Ctr., Bethlehem. Contbr. articles to profl. jours. Dir. med. sect. Bethlehem CD; mem. Bethlehem Air Pollution Coun.; chmn. Lehigh Valley Med. Adv. Com.; chmn. case finding com. Lehigh Valley Tb and Health Assn., pres., 1978-80. Lt. col. U.S. Army, 1942-45, ETO, Col. USAR, 1945-58. Decorated Silver Star, Legion of Merit, Bronze Star. Mem. Masons. Republican. Episcopalian. Home: 139 E Market St Bethlehem PA 18018-6225 Office: Bur of Health 10 E Church St Bethlehem PA 18018

SNYDER, JUDITH BEVERLY, historical society administrator; b. Paterson, N.J., Nov. 24, 1947; d. N. Ralph and Frances B. (Walter) S.; m. J. O'Boyle (div.); 1 child, Jonathan Daniel. BFA, Moore Coll. Art, 1969. Asst. to curator Phila. Mus. Art, 1969-76; membership dir. Victorian Soc. Am., Phila., 1980-84; exec. dir. Victorian Soc. Am., 1984—; interior design cons. Assoc. editor Classic Am. mag., 1987-90; editor Nineteenth Century mag., 1990—. Mem. Am. Assn. State and Local History, Nat. Trust Historic Preservation, Am. Friends Brit. Heritage. Republican. Episcopalian. Home: 786 S 2d St Philadelphia PA 19147 Office: Victorian Soc Am 219 S 6th St Philadelphia PA 19106-3719

SNYDER, JULES, accountant, controller; b. Phila., May 24, 1937; s. Louis and Rose (Kimmel) S.; m. Carolyn Polsky, Nov. 15, 1958; children: Steven B., Andrea M. BS, Temple U., 1958. CPA, Pa., N.J. Staff acct. A.L. Diamond & Co., Phila., 1958-60; internal auditor Food Fair Stores, Inc., Phila., 1960-66; budget supr., contr. Rockower Bros. Inc. and subs., Phila., 1966-73; contr. Kay Automotive Warehouse, Phila., 1973-75, Todays Man, Moorestown, N.J., 1975-85, I. Goldberg Mgmt. Corp., Cinnaminson, N.J., 1985—. Scout leader Boy Scouts Am., Phila., 1968-80. Fellow N.J. Soc. CPAs; mem. Pa. Inst. CPAs. Republican. Jewish. Office: I Goldberg Mgmt Corp 2702 Cindel Dr Unit 3 Riverton NJ 08077-2099

SNYDER, LAWRENCE CLEMENT, chemistry educator; b. Ridley Park, Pa., Apr. 16, 1932; s. Lawrence Clement Snyder and Barbara Louise (Boyer) Miller; m. Anne Svedi, Jan. 6, 1958 (dec. Sept. 1987); children: Lenore, Evan, Leland; m. Lynn Ashley Mayer, Apr. 21, 1989; 1 step child, Justin. BS, U. Calif., Berkeley, 1953; MS, Carnegie-Mellon U., 1954, PhD, 1959. Mem. tech. staff Bell Telephone Labs., Murray Hill, N.J., 1959-84; prof. SUNY, Albany, 1980—; lectr. Robert A. Welch Found., 1971. Author: Molecular Wave Functions and Properties, 1972. Fellow AAAS, Am. Phys. Soc.; mem. Am. Chem. Soc. Office: SUNY 1400 Washington Ave Albany NY 12222-0001

SNYDER, MARK JEFFREY, financial consultant, actuary; b. Bklyn., May 16, 1947; s. Milton A. and June (Freed) S.; m. Gloria Carol Beskin, May 31, 1969; children: Chad Alan, Heather Lynn. B of Engring. Sci., SUNY, Stony Brook, 1969. CLU; chartered fin. cons.; registered fin. planner. Ins. agt. Mass. Mut. Life Ins., Holbrook, N.Y., 1971-79; dist. mgr. Guardian Life Ins. Co., Port Jefferson, N.Y., 1979-81; v.p. pensions Exec. Planners, Ronkonkoma, N.Y., 1981-84; pres. CAS Adv. Services, Inc., Patchogue, N.Y., 1984—; mng. exec. Integrated Resources Equity Corp., Patchogue, 1986-89, Royal Alliance Assocs., Inc., Patchogue, 1990—; pres. Snyder Fin. Svcs., Patchogue, 1986-91, Snyder Kresh Pension Svcs. Inc., Patchogue, 1989—, Snyder Kresh Fin. Svcs., Inc., Patchogue, 1990—; speaker in field. Moderator, host Moneywise, Brookhaven Cable TV, Port Jefferson Sta., N Y., 1987-88; host. WLIM Radio program; contbr. articles to profl. jours. Mem. South Setauket (N.Y.) Civic Assn., 1972—, Three Village Dem. Club, Setauket, 1984—; bd. dirs., pres. Suffolk Estate Planning Coun., 1991-92; chmn. planned giving com. Suffolk County coun. Boy Scouts Am., 1985-87, mem. exec. bd., 1985—, mem. trust com., 1989—. Mem. Internat. Assn. Fin. Planners, Am. Soc. Pension Actuaries (assoc.), Am. Soc. CLUs and Chartered Fin. Cons. (v.p. pub. rels. Suffolk chpt. 1986-89), Registered Fin. Planners L.I. (bd. dirs., pres. 1986-87), Pension Forum L.I. (bd. dirs., chmn. pub. rels. 1986-88), Rotary Internat., Lake Grove Unique Racquet Club, KP. Democrat. Jewish. Office: Royal Alliance Assocs Inc 1721 N Ocean Ave Ste D Medford NY 11763-2649

SNYDER, MARTHA JANE, educator; b. Brookline, Mass., Apr. 2, 1953; d. James Caldwell and Helen Rebecca (Magowan) Thompson; m. William I. Snyder, Dec. 28, 1983; 1 child, Rebecca Jane-Lee. BA, Maryville Coll., 1975; MEd, Boston State Coll., 1981; postgrad. Orton-Gillingham Tng. Program, Mass. Gen. Hosp., 1980. Cert. elem. tchr., reading specialist, Mass., Colo., N.H. Reading tutor Carroll Hall Sch. at Lesley Coll., Cambridge, Mass., 1979-80; reading tchr. Esma Lewis Elem. Sch., Rifle, Colo., 1980-85, 86-87; reading tutor Hopkinton (N.H.) Ind. Sch., 1988-89; pvt. practice Concord, N.H., 1989—. Mem. Orton Soc., Mass. Gen. Alumni Assn., Phi Delta Kappa. Home: Black Hall Rd RR 1 Box 302 Epsom NH 03234

SNYDER, ROBERT ORIN, recreation professional; b. Ossining, N.Y., Oct. 16, 1951; s. Robert Taney and Myra (McCormick) S.; m. Veronica Mary Degen, Apr. 14, 1989. BA, Cen. Iowa U., 1973; MA, Lehman Coll., 1985; cert., N.C. State U., 1990. Program coord. Town of Ossining, 1981-82, recreation supr., 1982-86, supt. recreation, 1986-87; supt. recreation Village of Dobbs Ferry, N.Y., 1987—; chmn. Inst. Coaches and Ofcls. Tng., 1988—; treas. Westchester Recreation and Parks Soc., 1990—. Roman Catholic. Office: Village of Dobbs Ferry 112 Main St Dobbs Ferry NY 10522-1698

SNYDER, SCOTT EDWARD, podiatrist; b. York, Pa., Feb. 17, 1963; s. Edwin Luther and Ann Elizabeth (Grove) S.; m. Sherri Lyn King, June 16, 1985. BS, Juniata Coll., 1985; D of Podiatric Medicine, Ill. Coll. Podiatry, 1989. Resident in podiatric medicine Norwegian Am. Hosp., Chgo., 1989-90; podiatrist Lion Foot and Ankle Ctr., Red Lion, Pa., 1990—, Glen Rock (Pa.) Foot and Ankle Ctr., 1991—; mem. med. staff York Hosp., Meml. Osteopathic Hosp., Apple Hill Surg. Ctr., Surg. Ctr. Volk, 1990—. Bd. dirs. Red Lion Youth Ctr. Pre-Sch., 1990, pres., 1991. Recipient Outstanding Leadership award Am. Legion, 1981; Nyman scholar Fund Podiatric Medicine, 1988. Mem. Am. Acad. Podiatric Sports Medicine (assoc.), Am. Podiatric Med. Assn., Red Lion Elks. Democrat. Roman Catholic. Home and Office: 426 S Main St Red Lion PA 17356-2413

SNYDER, STEVEN ELIOT, real estate developer, financier; b. N.Y.C., June 12, 1952; s. Lester M. and Selma (Sherman) S.; m. Janet Elaine Whitney, July 28, 1978; children: Barbara Lynn, Scott Howell. BS in Engring., Cornell U., 1974; MS in Engring., MIT, 1976; MBA, Yale U., 1978. Cons. Parsons, N.Y.C., 1971-72, URS Corp., N.Y.C., San Mateo, Calif., 1973-76; assoc. Donaldson, Lufkin & Jenrette, N.Y.C., 1978-79; sr. assoc. Wertheim & Co., N.Y.C., 1979-82; v.p. Spear, Leeds & Kellogg, N.Y.C., 1982-84; dir. Baring Bros. & Co., Inc., N.Y.C., 1986-88; pres. Windham Assocs., Westchester, N.Y., 1988—. Author: (report) Geometry Effects on Buoyant Convective Circulations in Cooling Pond Side Arms, 1976. Dist. leader Polit. Party, Westchester, 1991. Recipient Proclamation for Hist. Preservation, 1990. Mem. N.Y. Acad. Scis., Cornell Soc. Engrs., Yale Club N.Y.C., Yale Westchester Alumni Assn., Tau Beta Pi, Chi Epsilon. Office: Windham Assocs 104 Oregon Rd Cortlandt Manor NY 10566-1233

SNYDER, WILLIAM FORTUNE, broadcast executive; b. Scranton, Pa., June 24, 1941; s. Robert Fortune and Dorothy (Hutchings) S.; m. Patricia Di Benedetto, Dec. 29, 1962; children: George Fortune, William Severin, Richard Bennett. BA, SUNY, Albany, 1971. Radio and TV announcer Sta. WHEN Radio/TV, Syracuse, N.Y., 1960-65; program dir. Sta. WCNY-TV, Syracuse, 1965-66; journalist Herald Jour. Newspaper, Syracuse, 1966-67; TV journalist Sta. WRGB-TV, Schenectady, N.Y., 1968-77; press officer N.Y. Gov. Hugh L. Carey, Albany, 1977-81, dir. communications, 1981-82; media advisor N.Y. Gov. Mario M. Cuomo, Albany, 1983-85; exec. dir. N.Y. Network SUNYSAT, SUNY Crtl. Adminstrn., Albany, 1985—. Exec. producer: (news program) Education Newsbreak: NE, 1991, pub. TV series Soviet TV Tonight, 1990; various ofcl. N.Y. state programs, 1978—. Mem. NATAS (awards panel mem. N.Y. chpt.). Office: NY Network SUNYSAT PO Box 7012 12th Fl AESSOB Albany NY 12225

SO, LOUISA LEE, medical technologist; b. Manila, Santa Cruz, The Philippines, Feb. 12, 1947; d. Benito Kim Seng and Gavina (Lee) S.; m. Stanley Jay Buden, Nov. 4, 1979 (div. Oct. 1987). BS in Med. Tech., Far Eastern U., 1969; postgrad., Montgomery County Comm. Coll., 1976. Hematology technologist Norwalk (Conn.) Gen. Hosp., 1972-75; lab. technician Upjohn Clinical Lab., King of Prussia, Pa., 1975; blood bank technologist Phila. Coll. Osteo. Hosp., 1976-80; lab. technician St. Mary's Hosp., Langhorne, Pa., 1981-85, Rancocas (N.J.) Hosp. and Riverside (N.J.) Hosp., 1986-87; probationary supr. VA Hosp., Phila., 1987-88; blood bank technologist Mercy Cath. Med. Ctr., Phila., 1988—, acting supr., 1991. Contbr. poems to profl. publs. Mem. Am. Soc. Clin. Pathologists. Jewish Messianic.

SOARE, WARREN GORDON, college dean; b. Hackensack, N.J., Oct. 5, 1947; s. Irving Walker and Margaret (Whaley) S.; m. Mary Ann McSoley, July 15, 1978; children: Julia Ann, Thomas Warren, Andrew Gordon. BA, Miami U., Oxford, Ohio, 1970; MDiv, Princeton Theol. Sem., 1974; EdD, Columbia U., 1979. Asst. dean for residence life Rider Coll., Lawrenceville, N.J., 1974-76, asst. dean of students, coord. of housing, 1976-77, dir. housing, 1977-78; assoc. dean of students Lehigh U., Bethlehem, Pa., 1980-83; coord. student devel. C. W. Post Campus, L.I. U., Brookville, N.Y., 1984-90, assoc. dean of students, 1989-90, acting dean of students, 1990-91, dean of students, 1991—, adj. faculty mem. dept. curriculum and instrn. Elder, deacon, chair ch. growth and devel. com. Roslyn (N.Y.) Presbyn. Ch., 1987-91; mem. peace initiatives subcom. Coun. on Mission of Presbytery of L.I.; chair subcom. on coll. alcohol policies L.I. Alcohol Consortium, 1988-89. Mem. Nat. Assn. Student Pers. Adminstrs., Mid-Atlantic Assn. Coll. and Univ. Housing Officers (del.), L.I. Coun. Student Pers. Adminstrs. (conf. planning com., recognition award, Outstanding Orientation Program award 1987), Nat. Eagle Scout Assn., Sigma Lambda Rho, Omicron Delta Kappa, Phi Gamma Delta. Presbyterian. Home: PO Box 376 Greenvale NY 11548-0376 Office: LI U CW Post Campus Brookville NY 11548

SOARES, GREGORY LOUIS, health facility administrator, consultant; b. Fall River, Mass., Nov. 14, 1951; s. Louis Massa and Hilda (Enos) S.; m. Maria Fatima Fernandes, July 9, 1977 (div. 1982); m. Deborah Ann Smusz, Apr. 28, 1984. AA in Pre-profl. Studies, Bristol Community Coll., Fall River, Mass., 1971; BA in Psychology, Roger Williams Coll., 1973; MEd in Integrated Studies, Cambridge (Mass.) Coll., 1989. Spl. edn. tchr. St. Vincent's Home, Fall River, 1973-80, coord. vocat. edn. programs, 1980-83; family therapist Edgehill Newport, Newport, R.I., 1983-88, supr. family dept., 1988-90, dir. inpatient/outpatient rehab. svcs., 1991—; cons., New Eng. area, 1986—. Office: Edgehill Newport Newport RI 02840

SOBCZAK, MARK LESLIE, radiation oncology physician; b. Chgo., June 8, 1955; s. Frank Chester and Lorraine Elizabeth (Lewandowski) S.; m. Cindy Robin Trager, Nov. 9, 1980. BS in Oceanography, U.S. Naval Acad., 1977; MD, USHUS, 1987. Diplomate Nat. Bd. Med. Examiners, 1987. Commd. med. officer USN, 1977, advanced through grades to staff physician, 1991. Contbr. articles to profl. jours. Gov. coun. Mass. Med. Soc. Product Physician Sect., Waltham, 1989-91. CLin. Oncology fellow Am. Cancer Soc., 1990; Astronaut nominee USN, NASA, 1991. Mem. AMA, Am. Soc. Therapeutic Radiology & Oncology, Mass. Med. Soc. (exec. coun. 1990-91), USN Acad. Alumni Assn. Republican. Roman Catholic. Home: 10155 Castlewood Ln Oakton VA 22124 Office: Naval Hosp Dept Radiation Oncology Bethesda MD 20889-5000

SOBECKI, JOHN FRANCIS, management consultant; b. Bayonne, N.J., Feb. 25, 1948; s. Stanley Anthony and Lilia (Avogadri) S.; m. Virginia Ann Oliver, June 16, 1972; children: Lindsay Oliver Sobecki, Leigh Oliver Sobecki. BA, Fairleigh Dickinson U., 1970, MA, 1971; MA, Montclair State Coll., 1972. Cert. Mgmt. Cons., 1985. Tchr. Hillside (N.J.) High Sch., 1970-71, Stoneham (Mass.) High Sch., 1971-72; coord. counseling Montclair (N.J.) State Coll., 1972-80; pres. The Comwell Co., Flanders, N.J., 1984—; part time faculty Upsala Coll., Orange, N.J., 1984-90; exec. dir., co-founder WINGS (Christian Career Transition), Flanders, N.J., 1985—; editor Am. Civilization Inst., Morristown, N.J., 1970; cons. Future Studies, Fairleigh Dickinson U., 1976-80. Contbr. articles to profl. jours. Coach, v.p., Little League, Mountain Lakes, N.J., 1976-77. Moffet scholar Whitehall Found., 1970. Mem. World Future Soc., Inst. Mgmt. Cons., Future Careers Network. Democrat. Roman Catholic. Office: The Comwell Co Bartley Rd # 206 Flanders NJ 07836-9616

SOBEL, JAEL SABINA, biologist; b. Ramat-Gan, Israel, Nov. 29, 1935. BA, Cornell U., 1957; MA, Columbia U., 1961; PhD, U. Wis., 1966. Rsch. assoc. U. Calif., San Francisco, 1979; asst. prof. SUNY, Buffalo, 1979-86, assoc. prof., 1986—. Office: SUNY Dept Anatomy Buffalo NY 14214

SOBEL, JOSEPH PETER, meteorologist, consultant; b. Bklyn., Oct. 16, 1945; s. Henry I. and Lillian (Arum) S.; m. Jacqueline Beth Gerber, Aug. 31, 1969; children: Lynne, Kate. BS, U. Mich., 1967; MS, Pa. State U., 1970, PhD, 1976. Cert. weather observer, USAF. Rsch. asst. Univ. Mich., Ann Arbor, 1967; meterologist ESSA, U.S. Weather Bur., Garden City, N.Y., 1968-69; weather observer/forecaster Pa. Air N.G., 1969-76; TV meteorologist Pa. State Univ., University Park, 1970—; meteorologist ACCU-Weather, Inc., State College, Pa., 1971—; teaching asst. Pa. State Univ., 1969-76; dir. Forensic Meteorology, ACCU-Weather, Inc., 1978—. Capt. USAF, 1969-76. Mem. Am. Meteorol. Soc. (TV Seal of Approval 1973). Home: 458 E Fairmount Ave State College PA 16801-5710 Office: ACCU-Weather Inc 619 W College Ave State College PA 16801-3797

SOBEL, KENNETH MARK, electrical engineer, educator; b. Bklyn., Oct. 3, 1954; s. Seymour Phillip and Marilyn (Nanus) S. BSEE, CCNY, 1976; MEngring, Rensselaer Poly. Inst., 1978, PhD, 1980. Sr. rsch. specialist Lockheed Calif. Co., Burbank, 1980-87; assoc. prof. dept. elec. engring. CCNY, 1987—; adj. asst. prof. U. So. Calif., L.A., 1982-87; prin. investigator USAF, 1989, 91, mem. summer faculty fellowships, 1987, 88, 90; mem. exec. com. PhD program in engring. CUNY, 1989—. Contbr. articles to profl. jours., chpts. to books. Program vice-chmn. 1986 Am. Control Conf., Seattle. Recipient Prof. of Yr. award Beta Pi chpt. Eta Kappa Nu, 1991-92; PSC-CUNY rsch. grantee, 1988-90. Fellow AIAA (assoc.); mem. IEEE (sr., exhibits chmn. 23d conf. on decision and control 1984, registration chmn. 27th conf. on decision and control 1988, tech. assoc. editor Control Systems mag., 1986—), Am. Radio Relay League (life), Control System Soc. (bd. govs. 1990), Sigma Xi, Alpha Phi Omega. Office: CCNY Dept Elec Engring New York NY 10031

SOBEL, MARK ESAR, physician, researcher; b. N.Y.C., Apr. 14, 1949; s. Abraham David and Selma Etta (Spitzer) S. BA, Brandeis U., 1970; MD, Mt. Sinai Sch. Medicine, N.Y.C., 1975; PhD in Biomed. Scis., CUNY, 1975. Diplomate Nat. Bd. Med. Examiners. Med. intern, clin. fellow in pediatrics Children's Hosp. Med. Ctr./Harvard U. Med. Sch., Boston, 1975-76; rsch. assoc. NIH, Bethesda, Md., 1976-79, 80-83; sr. investigator Nat. Cancer Inst., Bethesda, 1983-92, chief molecular pathology sect., 1992—; vis. scientist Max Planck Inst. for Biochemistry, Martinsried bei Munchen, Germany, 1979-80; dir. Concepts in Molecular Biology course Am. Assn. Pathologists, Rockville, Md., 1987-92. Contbr. more than 60 articles to profl. jours.; patentee in field. Capt. USPHS, 1975—. Recipient Commendation medal USPHS, 1989, other awards. Mem. Am. Soc. for Biochemistry and Molecular Biology, Am. Assn. Pathologists, Am. Soc. for Cell Biology, Am. Soc. for Microbiology, Am. Assn. for Cancer Rsch., Phi Beta Kappa. Jewish. Office: Nat Cancer Inst Bldg 10 Rm 2A33 NIH Bethesda MD 20892

SOBERMAN, GLENN BARRY, psychotherapist, interfaith minister; b. Lakewood, N.J., June 18, 1952; s. Herbert J. Soberman and Lynn (Kinsberg) Refson; m. Andrea Barnes, Sept. 10, 1989. BA in Religion, Haverford Coll., 1974; MA in Psychology, New Sch. Social Rsch., 1978; MS, New Seminary, 1986. Caseworker Graham Windham, N.Y.C., 1985-86; behavior specialist United Cerebral Palsy, Bronx, N.Y., 1986-87, Assn. Children with Learning Disabilities, Alberton, N.Y., 1987-88; psychologist II Letinworth Coll, Thiells, N.Y., 1988-91; sr. behavior specialist Assn. Help Retardation, Campbell Hall, N.Y., 1991—; cons. Hudson Valley Community Svcs., Patterson, N.Y., 1988—, Assn. Citizens with Learning Disabilities, Orangeburg, N.Y., 1991—, Parent Resources Ctr., New Paltz, N.Y., 1991—; cons., therapist Orange County Dept. Mental Health. Mem. Rockland Coun. on Alcoholism, Psychosynthesis Collective. Home: 4 Lake Rd E Congers NY 10920-2320

SOBEY, DAVID F., food company executive; b. Stellarton, N.S., Can., Mar. 22, 1931; s. Frank Hoyse and Irene (MacDonald) S.; m. Faye B. Naugle, June 2, 1953; children—Paul David, Janis Irene Hames. D Commerce (hon.), St. Mary's U., 1991. With Sobeys Inc., Stellarton, N.S., Can., 1949—, store mgr., dir. merchandising and advt., v.p., exec. v.p., pres., dep. chmn., chief exec. officer, dir., 1981-85, chmn., dir., 1985—; bd. dirs. Empire Co. Ltd., Sobey Leased Properties Ltd., Atlantic Shopping Centres Ltd., Clover Group, Eastern Sign Print Ltd., Lumsden Bors. Ltd., Dominion Textile Inc., CHC Helicopter Corp., Evangeline Fin. Svcs. Corp., T.R.A. Foods Ltd., Univa Inc., Hannaford Bros Co., VS Svcs. Ltd., Horne & Pitfield Foods Ltd. Bd. dirs. Jr. Achievement Can., Retail Coun. of Can., Internat. Assn. Chain Stores, C.I.E.S., Food Mktg. Inst., Tim Horton Children's Found., Atlantic Salmon Fedn.; bd. govs. St. Mary's U.; mem. Halifax Bd. Trade. Clubs: Royal N.S. Yacht Squadron; Halifax; City (New Glasgow), Abercrombie Country. Office: Sobeys Inc 115 King St, Stellarton, NS Canada B0K 1S0

SOBIN, LESLIE HOWARD, pathologist, educator; b. N.Y.C., Feb. 10, 1934; s. Martin L. and Kitty N. Sobin; m. Margareta E.D. Ahlstrom, Dec. 21, 1962; 1 child, Annika D. BS, Union Coll., 1955; MD, SUNY, N.Y.C., 1959. Diplomate Am. Bd. Pathology. Instr. pathology Cornell U. Med. Coll., N.Y.C., 1962-65, asst. prof. pathology, 1965; WHO visiting prof. pathology Univ. Kabul, Afghanistan, 1965-68; assoc. prof. pathology Cornell U. Med. Coll., 1968-70; pathologist WHO, Geneva, 1970-81; prof. pathology Uniformed Svcs. Univ. Health Scis., Bethesda, Md., 1984—; head WHO collaborating ctr. tumor classification Armed Forces Inst. Pathology, Washington, 1983—, assoc. dir. sci. publs., 1987—, chief gastrointestinal pathology, 1991—; expert, panel on cancer WHO, Geneva, 1981—. Author: Pathology Primer in Verse, 1978; editor: International Histological Classification of Tumors, 1970—, TNM Classification of Tumors, 1987. Recipient Sr. Exec. Svc. award Dept. of Army, 1990, Meritorious Presdl. Rank award, 1991. Fellow Royal Coll. Pathologists; mem. Internat. Acad. Pathology (sec. 1982-88). Office: Armed Forces Inst Pathology Washington DC 20306

SOBKOWSKI, SHAWN, psychologist; b. Elmira, N.Y., Feb. 3, 1956; d. Edward John and Patricia Ann (Malnoski) S. BA in Psychology, SUNY, Cortland, 1978; MEd in Counseling Psychology, Rutgers U., 1980, EdD in Counseling Psychology, 1985. Lic. psychologist, N.J. Rsch. assoc. U. Medicine & Dentistry N.J., Piscataway, 1980-82; cons. Shore Mental Health Ctr., Lakewood, N.J., 1983-87; mental health clinician U. Medicine & Dentistry N.J., Piscataway, 1985-88; pvt. practice Highland Park, N.J., 1988—; psychotherapist, counselor Rutgers U., New Brunswick, N.J., 1983-84, supervising psychologist, 1989—. Co-author: The Broad Scope of Ego Function Assessment, 1984, Vocational Rehabilitation of Persons with Prolonged Psychiatric Disorders, 1988. Mem. Am. Psychol. Assn., N.J. Psychol. Assn. Office: 134 Raritan Ave Highland Park NJ 08904-2402

SOBOL, THOMAS, state education commissioner; b. Jan. 11, 1932; m. Harriet Sobol; three children. BA in English, Harvard U., 1953, grad., 1954; PhD, Columbia U., 1969. Head dept. English pub. sch. system Bedford, N.Y., 1961-65; dir. instrn., 1965-69; asst. supt. instrn. pub. sch. system Great Neck, N.Y., 1969-71; supt. sch. systems Scarsdale, N.Y., 1971-87; commr. N.Y. State edn. Albany, 1987—. Office: State Dept Edn 111 Edn Bldg Washington Ave Albany NY 12234 also: SUNY Regents Coll Degrees 1450 Western Ave Albany NY 12203

SOBOLEWSKI, TIMOTHY RICHARD, marketing executive; b. Buffalo, May 29, 1951; s. Richard Theodore and Gertrude Marie (Chudzik) S.; m. Melissa R. Thorburn, Apr. 13, 1985; 1 child, Richard. AB, Columbia U., 1972. Regional mgr. Universal Communicatons, Roanoke, Va., 1977-80; ptnr. Systems Planning Assocs., Braintree, Mass., 1980-81; v.p. Telecon, Inc., Boston, 1981-83; sr. mktg. cons. Telelogic, Inc., Cambridge, Mass., 1983-84; dist. mgr. Republic Telcom, Braintree, 1985; founder, pres., gen. mgr. Operaworld, Inc., Boston, 1985-89; v.p. Homisco, Inc., Melrose, Mass., 1989—; cons. Opera Con Brio, Brookline, Mass., 1986—. Mem. Puritan Club (Braintree). Democrat. Roman Catholic. Office: Homisco Inc 99 Washington St Melrose MA 02176-6024

SOCARIDES, CHARLES WILLIAM, psychiatrist, educator; b. Brockton, Mass., Jan. 24, 1922; s. James and Theodora (Cokas) S.; m. Veronica Rak (div.); children: Richard, Daphne; m. Barbara Bonner, Jan. 27, 1973 (div. Apr. 1987); children: Alexandra, Charles Jr.; m. Claire Alford, Oct. 19, 1988. Cert., Harvard Coll., Cambridge, Mass., 1945; MD, N.Y. Med. Coll., 1947; cert., Columiba, N.Y.C., 1952. Diplomate Am. Bd. Psychiatry and Neurology. Instr. in psychiatry Columbia U., N.Y.C., 1956-60, assoc. in psychiatry, 1960-62; clin. asst. prof. psychiatry SUNY, N.Y.C., 1955-58, clin. prof. psychiatry, 1976-78; assoc. attending psychiatrist Vanderbilt Clinic Coll. U., N.Y.C., 1960-62; assoc. clin. prof. psychiatry Albert Einstein Coll. Medicine, N.Y.C., 1969-76, clin. prof., 1976—; clin. prof. psychiatry Montefiore Med. Ctr., N.Y.C., 1978—; med. cons. Armed Svcs. Dept. Def., Washington, 1978—; tng. psychiat. residents Albert Einstein Coll. Medicine, 1968—. Author: The Overt Homosexual, 1968, Homosexuality, 1978, The Preoedipol Origin and Psychoanalytic Treatment of Sexual Perversion, 1988, Beyond Sexual Freedom, On Sexuality: Psychoanalytic Observations, 1979, The Homosexualities and the Therapeutic Process; contbr. articles to profl. jours.; numerous book reviews. Lt. USNR, 1952-54. Recipient Sigmund Freud award Am. Soc. Psychoanalytic Physicians, 1987, N.Y. Soc. for Psychoanalytic Tng., 1975. Fellow Am. Psychoanalytic Assn., Am. Psychiat. Assn., Am. Coll. Psychoanalysts, Am. Soc. Psychoanalytic Physicians (hon. fellow); mem. AMA, N.Y. County Med. Soc., Internat. Psychoanalytic Assn., Royal Soc. of Medicine London (affiliate), Coral Beach Club. Democrat. Greek Orthodox. Home and Office: 242 E 94th St New York NY 10128-3706

SOCH, HENRY JOHN, marketing professional; b. Chgo., Jan. 27, 1948; s. John Ted and Helen Wanda (Ambrozik) S.; m. Barbara Gwen Barsh, June 20, 1970. AS, Triton Jr. Coll., 1976. Cert. radiologic technologist. Music dir. St. Josaphat Ch., Chgo., 1963-70; clin. edn. dir. Resurrection Med. Ctr., Chgo., 1970-79; clin. specialist Philips Med. Systems, Chgo., 1979-81, mgr. applications, 1981-83, product mgr., 1983-85, internat. product mgr., 1985-87, mktg. mgr., 1987-89, dir. mktg., 1989—; cons. Acad. Ambulatory Cardiac Caths., Chgo., 1989-90; tchr. Triton Jr. Coll., Rivergrove, Ill., 1979-81, Coll. DuPage, Glen Ellyn, Ill., 1981-83. Contbr. articles to profl. jours. Mem. Save Our Stratford (polit. action com.), Conn., 1990-91. Mem. Am. Soc. Radiologic Technologists, Am. Hosp. Radiology Adminstrs., Am. Mgmt. Assn., Conn. Soc. Radiologic Technologists. Roman Catholic. Office: Philips Med Systems 710 Bridgeport Ave Shelton CT 06484-4708

SOCHET, MARY ALLEN, community organizer, psychotherapist, writer; b. Plattsburgh, N.Y., Feb. 10, 1938; d. Edwin Elisha and Mary Elizabeth (Thomson) Allen; m. Marvin J. Sochet, 1963; children: Melorra, David. BS in Childhood Edn., SUNY, Plattsburgh, 1958; MA in Human Rels., NYU, 1961, PhD in Human Devel., 1963. Tchr. kindergarten L.I. Pub. Schs., 1958-62; tchr. N.Y.C. Pub. Schs., 1962-64; prof. early childhood edn., child devel. and psychology Bklyn. Coll., 1964-71; program dir., acting exec. dir. Newark Pre-Sch. Coun., 1965-66; psychotherapist N.Y.C. Community Guidance Svc., 1966-78; staff cons. Human Resources Inst., 1966—; pvt. practice psychotherapy N.Y.C., 1966-87; writer, lectr., ednl. cons. and

editorial cons. in field. Author: (with Robert Allen) Toward a Caring Community, 1980; contbr. articles on edn., community orgns., peace and mental health to various jours. Founding mem. Community Loft, 1971-74, Neighbor's Network, 1979—; organizing mem. Childrne's Free Sch., 1969-81; co-chair Kids Meeting Kids Can Make a Difference, 1982—. NCCJ fellow, 1961-61; recipient Founder's Day award NYU, 1963. Mem. Am. Psychol. Assn., Soc. Psychol. Study Social Issues, Psychologists for Social Responsibility. Home and Office: 380 Riverside Dr New York NY 10025-1822

SOCOLOW, ARTHUR ABRAHAM, geologist; b. Bronx, N.Y., Mar. 23, 1921; s. Samuel and Yetta (Solomon) S.; m. Edith S. Blumenthal, Apr. 10, 1949; children: Carl, Roy. Jeff. B.S., Rutgers U., 1942; M.A., Columbia U., 1947, Ph.D., 1955. Photogrammetrist, U.S. Geol. Survey, 1942, 46; with Eagle Picher de Mexico, 1947; instr. geology So. Methodist U., 1948-50; dir. geology field camp Colo., 1948-50; asst. prof. Boston U., 1950-55; assoc. prof. U. Mass., 1955-57; econ. geologist Pa. Geol. Survey, 1957-61, dir., state geologist, 1961-86, cons. geologist, 1986—; geologist Def. Minerals Exploration Authority, Alaska, 1952; mem. Outer Continental Shelf Policy Com., 1974-88, Pa. rep., 1978-88; lectr. mineral conservation Pa. State U., 1959-75; mem. conf. earth sci. source materials NSF, 1959; chmn. ann. field conf. Pa. Geologists, 1961-86; past mem. U.S. Nat. Com. on Tunnelling Tech.; past mem. gov.'s adv. com. Nat. Coun. on Environ. Quality; past chmn. Pa. Water Resources Coordinating Com.; geol. advisor Boston Mus. Sci., 1955-57. Former editor Pa. Geology Bull.; author over 100 publs. and papers on environ. and econ. geology to profl. jours. Served with USAAF, 1942-46. Fellow Geol. Soc. Am. (sec.-treas. N.E. sect., past nat. councilor), Mineral. Soc. Am., AAAS (past pres. geography—geology sect.); mem. AAUP, Soc. Econ. Geologists, Phila. Geol. Soc. (past pres.), Am. Geol. Inst. (com. on manpower), Nat. Assn. Geology Tchrs. (past regional pres., Ralph Digman award for contbns. to geologic edn.1980), Pa. Acad. Sci., Am. Meteoritical Soc., Am. Assn. State Geologists (past pres., editor, compiler State Geological Surveys-A History 1988), Am. Geophys. Union, Am. Commn. Stratigraphic Nomenclature (past chmn.), Harrisburg Geol. Soc., Interstate Oil Compact Commn. (research com., environ. com.), Fgn. Policy Assn. (past chpt. pres.), Sigma Xi. Club: Internat. Torch (past pres. chpt.). Home and Office: 26 Salt Island Rd Gloucester MA 01930-1945

SODAK, JOHN JOSEPH, drug/alcohol abuse services professional; b. Scranton, Pa., Nov. 18, 1964; s. John George and Romaine Theresa (Talalai) S. BA in Sociology, Marywood Coll., 1988, MS in Secondary Ednl. Counseling, 1989. Cert. assoc. addictions counselor II. Treatment specialist Drug and Alcohol Treatment Svc., Scranton, 1989—; cons. in adolescent edn. Drug and Alcohol Treatment Svc., Scranton, 1989—. Grad. scholar Immaculate Heart of Mary Scholarship Found., 1990. Mem. AACD, Am. Sociol. Assn., Internat. Assn. for Addictions and Pub. Offenders, Chi Sigma Iota. Home: 1138 Austin St Old Forge PA 18518

SODARO, EDWARD RICHARD, psychiatrist; b. Glen Cove, N.Y., Oct. 3, 1947; s. Edward Richard and Mae Florence (Culp) S.; m. Denise Roberta Stetch; 2 children. BS, Siena Coll., Loudonville, N.Y., 1969; MD, Georgetown U., 1973; MA, Grad. Faculty of New Sch., N.Y.C., 1976. Diplomate Am. Bd. Psychiatry and Neurology; cert. addiction specialist Am. Soc. of Addiction Medicine; cert. geriatric psychiatry specialist. Resident in psychiatry L.I. Jewish Hosp., New Hyde Park, N.Y., 1973-76; staff psychiatrist N.Y. Hosp./Cornell Med. Ctr., White Plains, N.Y., 1979-81; faculty N.Y. Hosp./Cornell Med. Ctr., 1979-81; sr. psychiatrist South Oaks Hosp., Amityville, N.Y., 1981—; mem. exec. com. South Oaks Hosp., Amityville, 1991—. Mem. Am. Psychiatric Assn. (br. pres. 1990), N.Y. Psychiatric Assn. (legis. rep. 1987—). Democrat. Roman Catholic. Office: South Oaks Hosp 400 Sunrise Hwy Amityville NY 11701-2508

SODERBERG, DALE LEROY, English educator, drama director, producer; b. Warren, Pa., Apr. 24, 1929; s. Leroy Wilbur and Olive Hazel (Conboy) S.; m. Marjorie Ann Hamm, Aug. 19, 1951; children: David J., Valli K., W. Mark, Lisa T., Kathi L. BA, Gettysburg Coll., 1951; BD, Luth. Theol. Sem., Gettysburg, Pa., 1954. Cert. secondary English tchr., N.Y.; ordained mins. Luth. Ch., 1954. Pastor Grace Luth. Ch., Clarion, Pa., 1954-57; mission developer, 1st pastor Our Saviour's Luth. Ch., Horseheads, N.Y., 1957-60; dir. Ecclesia Tours (Luth. Fgn. Tours), Horseheads and North Syracuse, N.Y., 1958-67; mgr. Soderberg Travel Svc., Corning, N.Y., 1960-62; pastor St. John's Luth. Ch., Syracuse, N.Y., 1962-66; chapel preacher Wittenberg U., Ohio, 1966; tchr. English Ft. Myers (Fla.) High Sch., 1967-68; tchr. English, dir. drama Hamilton (N.Y.) Cen. Sch., 1968-92; retired, 1992; sermon and story writer Ecclesia Svcs., Hamilton, 1984—; lay preacher Upper N.Y. Synod Evang. Luth. Ch. Am., Syracuse, 1968—; advisor student tchrs. Colgate U., Hamilton, 1975-92. Author: (novel) Pawns, 1980. Dir. tours to Europe, the Holy Land and the Luth. mission fields in Brit. Guiana, East and West Africa and India. Named Picture of the Month HOLIDAY, 1960. Mem. N.Y. State United Tchrs., Hamilton Tchrs. Assn., Internat. Platform Assn., Dictionary of Internat. Biography. Republican. Home: RR 2 Box 99 Hamilton NY 13346-9522

SÖDERSTROM, CHRISTIAN EMANUEL, company executive, consultant; b. Stockholm, Feb. 23, 1938; came to U.S., 1971; s. Sture Emanuel and Gudrun (Casten Carlberg) S.; m. Bonita Kerry Boyd, Sept. 7, 1974; 1 child, Henric. Degree in civil engring., STI Stockholm, 1962. Bldg. insp. Stockholm Sch. Dist., 1962-64; supt. Widmark & Platzer, Stockholm, 1964-65; mgr. factory div. Skarne System Internat., Stockholm, 1965-71; prodn. mgr. Consyst/jespersen, Cleve. and Rochester, N.Y., 1971-73; pres. Skansyst & Stromtech, Inc., Rochester, 1973—; bd. dirs. Cornhill Property, Rochester; pres. Cornhill Waterfront Nav. Found. Inc., 1991—. Author: (book series of 9) Skarne Manuals, 1969-71; inventor heat treatment of concrete and paint for fresh concrete, 1969-70. Pres. Rochester Neighborhood Coalition, 1981; v.p. Cornhill, Rochester, 1989; trustee St. Paul's Episcopal Ch., Rochester, 1975-79, Landmark Soc. of Western N.Y., Rochester, 1980—. Res. officer Swedish Army Res. 1960-71. Home: 84 Adams St Rochester NY 14608-2212

SOFFRONOFF, PIERCE, physician; b. Phila., Jan. 14, 1949; s. Ernest Carl Gustave and Jane Kynett (Coggeshall) S.; m. Strachelle Barry, Jan. 1, 1976; children: Strachelle B., Alexandra J. Cesny P. BA in Biology, Baylor U., 1970; MD, U. Tex., 1974. Diplomate Am. Bd. Ob-Gyn. Resident in obsgyn U. Pitts., 1974-77; pvt. practice, attending physician Magee Womens Hosp., Pitts., 1978—; assoc. clin. prof. Dept. Ob-Gyn U. Pitts. Sch. Medicine, 1990—, asst. clin. prof., 1978-90. Fellow Am. Coll Ob-Gyn.; mem. AMA, Pitts. Ob-Gyn. Soc., Allegheny County Med. Soc., Pa. Med. Soc., Am. fertility Soc. Office: MaGee Womens Hosp 300 Halket St Pittsburgh PA 15213-3180

SOGBESAN-BENSON, ANTHONY OLU, mechanical engineer, design engineer; b. Lagos, Nigeria, June 2, 1957; came to U.S., 1980; s. Babatunde and Juliana (Pedro) Sogbesan; m. Alterry March, Nov. 10, 1981; children: Marcella, Victoria, Arthur. BS, St. Louis U., 1990; MS, U. New Haven, 1989. Aircraft mechanic So. Aero. Inc., Ozark, Ala., 1981-83; logistics engr. Sikorsky Aircraft div. United Tech., Stratford, Conn., 1986-88; mech. engr. Electric Boat div. Gen. Dynamics, Groton, Conn., 1988-90, Hutchens Industries, Inc., 1992—. Mem. ASME, AIAA, Soc. Automotive Engrs. Republican. Roman Catholic. Home: 1008-D E Villa Marie Springfield MO 65803

SOHN, BERTHA SCHOOLER, librarian; b. N.Y.C., Aug. 7, 1915; d. Jacob Mendel and Ida Sarah (Gatman) Schooler; m. Israel Gregory Sohn, June 8, 1941; children: Vivian Eden, Daniel. BA, CUNY, 1936; postgrad., U. Idaho, 1944-45, D.C. Tchr.'s Coll., 1955-58; MLS, Cath. U. Am., 1961; postgrad., Cath. U., 1965-66. Sec., translator Am. Jewish Joint Distbn. Com., N.Y.C., 1939-41; stenographer D.C. Social Security Bd., Washington, 1941-42; sec. German dept. U. Idaho, Moscow, 1944-45; tchr. D.C. Pub. Schs., Washington, 1958-60; libr., cataloger Smithsonian Instn. Librs., Washington, 1963-70, acting head cataloging div., 1970-73, sr. cataloger, 1973-87; freelance researcher and translator Washington, 1987—; vol. tchr., libr. Adas Israel Congregation, Washington, 1988—. Author: Oral History of An Immigrant Family, 1981; translator: Dankere, 1992, (manuscript) Kaminits-Podolsk Excerpts, 1990. Mem. Jewish Geneal. Soc. Greater Washington, Na'amat-Habira Club (life, co-pres. 1988-89), Kappa Delta Pi. Democrat. Home and Office: 3930 Livingston St NW Washington DC 20015-2922

SOHN, DAVID YOUNGWHAN, high technology business owner, publisher, engineer; b. Chung Nam, Korea, Feb. 8, 1942; came to U.S., 1968; s. Jun-Pal and Kum Ok (Park) S.; m. Kim Mokjah Kim, June 15, 1968; children: Gene Pyoung, Edward Genesuk. BSEE, Korean Mil. Acad., Seoul, 1963; postgrad., U.S. Army Signal Sch., Seoul, 1966-67; MSEE, Rutgers U., 1972, postgrad., 1978; OPM, Harvard U., 1991. Software project mgr. Varityper Word Processing Systems, Orange, N.J., 1972-75; sr. program analyst Lockheed Electronic Corp., Plainfield, N.J., 1975-79; prin. engr. Computer Sci. Corp., College Park, Md., 1979-80; software mgr. Planning Rsch. Corp., McLean, Va., 1980-81; owner, pres., chair, chief exec. officer Internat. Computer & Telecommunications, Inc., Rockville, Md., 1981—; chmn., founder Asian Pacific Coun., Inc., Rockville, Md., 1990; bd. dirs. ICT, Rockville, Mongtomery County High Tech. Coun., Rockville, Md., United Korean Lang. Sch. of Greater Washington. Pub. Korean-Am. Life Mag. Recipient Small Bus. Adminstr.'s award D.C. Office SBA, 1990, Econ. Excellence award State of Md., 1990, Republic of Korea Premiere's award, 1991. Mem. Pres.'s Assn., Korean Scientists and Engrs. Assn., Rockville C. of C., Chief Exec. Officers Club. Baptist. Office: Internat Computers Telecommunications Inc 15235 Shady Grove Rd # 303 Rockville MD 20850-3237

SOHN, ISRAEL GREGORY, micropaleontologist; b. Ukraine, Russia, Nov. 12, 1911; came to U.S., 1921; s. Moishe and Sarah (Shamus) S.; m. Bonnie Schooler, June 8, 1941; children: Vivian Eden, Daniel. BS, CCNY, 1935; AM, Columbia U., 1938; PhD, Hebrew U., Jerusalem, 1966. Technician paleontology and stratigraphy br. U.S. Geol. Survey, Washington, 1941-42; geologist mineral deposits br. U.S. Geol. Survey, Vt., 1942-43; geologist nonmetals br. Pacific N.W. U.S. Geol. Survey, 1943-45; geologist, nonmetals br. U.S. Geol. Survey, Ga.; geologist, minerals resources br. U.S. Geol. Survey, Washington, 1947-49, micropaleontologist, paleontology and stratigraphy br., 1949-85, 85-91; scientist emeritus U.S. Geol. Survey, 1991—; cons. Ostracoda, Petrobraz, Sao Paolo, Brazil, 1982; lectr. micropaleontology George Washington U., Washington, 1958-68, adj. prof., 1968-81; guest lectr. dept. geology Hebrew U., Jerusalem, Israel Geol. Survey, 1962-63; rsch. assoc. paleobiology Smithsonian Inst., Washington, 1968—; participant in numerous paleontol. confs., 1963—; mem. rev. panel Sci. Books, A Quar. Rev., 1965-74; mem. rev. panel coop. Smithsonian-Israel Rsch. Project, Smithsonian Inst., 1969. Assoc. editor Crustacea, Biol. Abstracts, 1957-83; editorial cons. BIOSIS, 1983—; contbr. articles to profl. jours. Mem. joint bd. sci. and engring. edn. Roosevelt Sr. High, Washington, 1955-86; mem. com. on edn. Jewish Community Coun., Washington, 1955-62. Grantee NSF, 1962-63. Fellow Geol. Soc. Am. (emeritus), Am. Assn. Petroleum Geologists (emeritus), Soc. Econ. Paleontologists and Mineralogists (rep. adv. bd. treatise on invertebrate paleontology 1979-82), Paleontol. Soc.; mem. Biol. Soc. Washington, Geol. Soc. Washington, Paleontol. Soc. Washington (ad hoc chmn. rsch. group on paleozoic ostracodes 1974-76, chmn. internat. rsch. group on paleozoic ostracodes 1976-79, pres. 1979-82, councilor 1982-85), Cosmos Club. Democrat. Jewish. Home: 3930 Livingston St NW Washington DC 20015-2922

SOHN, JEANNE, librarian; b. Milton, Pa.; d. Robert Wilson and Juliette Lightner (Hedenberg) Gift; m. Steven Neil Sohn, Nov. 23, 1962. BA, Temple U., 1966; MSLS, Drexel U., 1971. Lit. bibliographer Temple U., Phila., 1971-75, chief of collection devel., 1975-81; asst. dean for collection devel. U. N.Mex., Albuquerque, 1981-86, assoc. dean for libr. svcs., 1986-89; dir. libr. svcs. Cen. Conn. State U., New Britain, 1989—; cons. New Eng. Assn. Schs. and Colls., Winchester, Mass., 1991—. Mem. editorial bd. Collection Mgmt., 1984—; contbr. articles to profl. jours. Mem. ALA, New Eng. Libr. Assn., Conn. Libr. Assn., Assn. Coll. and Rsch. Librs., Beta Phi Mu. Home: 1820 Boulevard West Hartford CT 06107 Office: Elihu Burritt Libr Cen Conn State U New Britain CT 06050

SOHN, STEPHEN, international trade and finance consultant; b. N.Y.C., Mar. 9, 1941; s. Bert Max and Lillian (Bluth) S.; m. Suzanne Levine, Dec. 24, 1968; children: Michael, Daniell, Brittany. BS, Long Island U., 1963; MBA, Fordham U., 1972. Pvt. practice acctg. N.Y.C., 1961-65; internat. analyst TWA, Paris, 1965-67; auditor Dept. Def., N.Y.C., 1967-69; contr. Technicon Corp., Tarrytown, N.Y., 1969-73; v.p. Periphonics Corp., Bohemia, N.Y., 1973-75; treas. United Techs. Internat., Hartford, Conn., 1975-78; v.p. United Techs. Credit Corp., Hartford, 1978-84; pres. Bankers Trust Internat. Trading, N.Y.C., 1984-85, Internat. Mgmt. and Export Devel., Southport, Conn., 1985—, Schneider-Sohn & Assoc., Inc., Westport, Conn., 1986—. Contbr. articles to profl. jours. Mem. U.S. C. of C. (chmn. trade com.), Nat. Fgn. Trade Coun. Republican. Jewish. Clubs: U. (Washington), St. James's (London). Home: 485 Galloping Hill Rd Fairfield CT 06430-7123 Mailing Address: IMED PO Box 355 Southport CT 06490

SOJA, CLAIRE ELAINE, banker, portfolio manager; b. Fall River, Mass., May 2, 1946; d. Harold and Florence Molly (Popkin) Shapiro; m. Donald Thomas Soja, Dec. 6, 1970 (div. Dec. 1985). Student, Northeastern U., 1964-66; BA, Boston U., 1968. Registered rep. Kidder Peabody & Co., Boston, 1971-73; investment officer, asst. mgr. investments Brown Bros. Harriman & Co., Boston, 1974—; career cons. Boston U., 1983—. Jewish. Office: Brown Bros Harriman & Co 40 Water St Boston MA 02109-3661

SOKAL, MICHAEL MARK, historian, educator; b. Bklyn., Oct. 6, 1945; s. Martin and Adele (Wattenberg) S.; m. Charlene Marie Key, Aug. 18, 1968; children: Kathryn Olivia, Matthew Charles. BEngring., The Cooper Union, 1966; MA, Case Western Reserve U., 1968, PhD, 1972. Rsch. asst. Ctr. for History of Physics, N.Y.C., 1966; prof. history Worcester (Mass.) Poly. Inst., 1970—; exec. sec. History of Sci. Soc., Worcester, 1988-92; affiliate prof. Clark U., 1975-80; lecturer Coll. of the Holy Cross, 1982, 83. Editor: An Education in Psychology, 1981, A Guide to Manuscript Collections, 1982, Psychological Testing and American Society, 1987; contbr. articles to profl. jours. Visiting scholar Harvard U., 1981-82; nat. lecturer Sigma Xi, 1979-81; recipient rsch. grants Nat. Sci. Found. 1969, 76, 89, Nat. Endowment for the Humanities 1973, 84, 85, 90. Fellow AAAS; mem. Cheiron, Soc. for History of Tech. Unitarian. Office: Worcester Polytech Inst Dept of Humanities 100 Institute Rd Worcester MA 01609-3116

SOKOL, MAE SANDRA, psychiatrist, educator; b. N.Y.C., Apr. 11, 1951; d. Bernard Sokol and Ruth (Sher) Levitt; 1 child. BS in Biology cum laude, Bklyn. Coll., 1972; MD, U. Louvain, Belgium, 1980. Diplomate Am. Bd. Psychiatry. Resident physician L.I. Coll. Hosp., Bklyn., 1980-81; resident physician psychiatry NYU Med. Ctr., Bellevue Hosp., N.Y.C., 1981-84, resident physician child psychiatry, 1984-86; asst. dir. child inpatient unit N.Y. Hosp. Westchester div., White Plains, 1986—; teaching asst. NYU Med. Sch., 1982-84, clin. instr., 1984-86; instr. psychiatry Cornell U. Med. Coll., 1986-89, asst. prof., 1989—. Contbr. articles to profl. jours. Mem. Am. Acad. Child and Adolescent Psychiatry, Am. Psychiat. Assn. Office: NY Hosp Westchester Div 21 Bloomingdale Rd White Plains NY 10605-1596

SOKOLOFF, LOUIS, physiologist, neurochemist; b. Phila., Oct. 14, 1921; married; 2 children. BA, U. Pa., 1943, MD, 1946. Intern Phila. Gen. Hosp., 1946-47; rsch. fellow in physiology U. Pa. Grad. Sch. Medicine, 1949-51, instr., then assoc., 1951-56; assoc. chief, then chief sect. cerebral metabolism NIMH, Bethesda, Md., 1953-68; chief lab. cerebral metabolism NIMH, 1968—. Chief editor Jour. Neurochemistry, 1974-78. Served to capt. M.C. U.S. Army, 1947-49. Recipient F.O. Schmitt medal in neurosci., 1980, Albert Lasker clin. med. research award, 1981, Karl Spencer Lashley award Am. Philos. Soc., 1987, Disting. Grad. award U. Pa., 1987, Nat. Acad. Scis. award in Neurosci., 1988, Georg Charles de Hevesy Nuclear Medicine Pioneer award Soc. Nuclear Medicine, 1988, Mihara Cerebrovascular Disorder Rsch. Promotion award, 1988. Mem. Am. Physiol. Soc., Assn. Rsch. Nervous and Mental Diseases, Am. Biophys. Soc., Am. Acad. Neurology, Am. Neurol. Assn., Am. Soc. Biol. Chemists, Am. Soc. Neurochemistry, U.S. Nat. Acad. Scis. Office: NIMH Bldg 36 Rm 1A-05 Bethesda MD 20892

SOKOLOW, KENNETH, journalist; b. Balt., Mar. 24, 1955; s. Isadore and Betty (Oskie) S. BA, Johns Hopkins U., 1976. Polit. editor The City Paper, Baltimore, 1977-87; coordinator, fed. aid sect. Md. State Hwy. Adminstrn., Balt., 1979-83; agt., Land Acquisition Bur. Balt. County Gov., Towson, 1983—; contbg. writer Warfield's Mag., Balt., 1986-87. Contbg. editor Johns Hopkins Newsletter, 1975-76; contbr. articles, poetry to Baltimore Mag. and Warfield's Mag., 1983—; contbg. writer N.Y. Press, 1988—. Democrat. Clubs: Mt. Royal Dem., 1985—, Millard Fillmore Soc., 1984—. Home: 6807 Park Heights Ave Baltimore MD 21215-1645

SOKOLOW, LLOYD BRUCE, lawyer, psychotherapist; b. N.Y.C., Nov. 3, 1949; s. Edwin Jay and Harriet (Corman) S.; m. Christina Carol Smolinski, Jan. 27, 1979; children: Joshua, Jessica. BA, U. Buffalo, 1971, MS, 1974, JD, 1978, PhD, 1979. Bar: N.Y. 1979, U.S. Dist. Ct. (we. dist.) N.Y. 1979, U.S. Dist. Ct. (no. dist.) N.Y. 1982, Conn. 1985, U.S. Supreme Ct. 1985, U.S. Dist. Ct. Conn. 1986. Rsch. scientist Rsch. Inst. on Alcoholism, Buffalo, 1976-80; legal cons. N.Y. Gov.'s Task Force on Drinking and Driving, Albany, 1979-82; pvt. practice specializing in family, health and mcpl. law Schenectady, N.Y., 1980—; counsel, exec. dir. Conifer Park, Scotia, N.Y., 1981-83; counsel, dir. substance abuse svcs. Inst. of Living, Hartford, Conn., 1984-86; founder, exec. dir. Lifestart Health Svcs., 1986—; atty. Town of Knox, N.Y., 1980—. Bd. dirs., pres. Schenectady Community Svc. Bd., 1982-89; dir. addictions State of Md., 1988-89; mem. Surrogate Decision Making Commn., N.Y. Commn. on Quality of Care. Regent scholar NY State, 1967; Univ. fellow U. Buffalo, 1973, Baldy Law fellow, 1979. Mem. APA, ABA (task force on youth alcohol and drug abuse 1986), N.Y. State Bar Assn., Conn. Bar Assn. (chmn. lawyers impairment com. 1985-86), Albany County Bar Assn. Office: 1356 Union St Schenectady NY 12308-3036

SOKOLOWSKI, LINDA ROBINSON, artist, educator; b. Utica, N.Y., May 20, 1943; d. Walter Prentice and Doris Helene (Elwell) Robinson; m. Robert Louis Sokolowski, May 27, 1967; 1 child, Devin Sokolowski. BFA, R.I. Sch. Design, 1965; MA, U. Iowa, 1970, MFA, 1971. Assoc. prof. art Harpur Coll., SUNY, Binghamton, 1971—. Exhibited in one-person shows at Kraushaar Galleries, N.Y.C., 1976, 79, 82, 86, 89, 91; group shows at Pushkin Mus., Moscow, 1973, Mt. Holyoke Coll., 1974, Miami U., Oxford, Ohio, 1976, U. N.C., 1978, Emporia State U., 1979, Butler Inst. Am. Art, 1979, 80, 92, Nat. Mus. Art Smithsonian, 1981, Phila. Mus. Art Rental, 1983, Columbia (S.C.) Mus. Arts and Scis., 1984, NAD, 1986, Fed. Res. Bd., 1987, numerous others; represented in collections at IBM, Inc., Pepsico, Oak Ridge Art Ctr., Libr. Congress, others. Recipient Childe Hassam award Am. Acad. Arts and Letters, 1978; SUNY rsch. grantee, 1976, 90. Mem. United Univ. Professions. Democrat. Office: SUNY Dept Art and Art History Binghamton NY 13902-6000

SOLANCH, LARRY S., experimental psychologist, researcher, consultant; b. Bridgeport, Conn., June 27, 1947; s. Norman and Eleonore Lore (Ziegelstein) S.; m. Margaret Mary Philbin, July 18, 1987; stepchildren: Miriam Raphael Papp, Leah Sylvia Papp. BA in Math., U. Bridgeport, 1971; MA in Psychology, U. Bridgegport, 1974; PhD in Psychology, U. Miss., 1978. Math. instr. Engring. Drafting Coll., Lakewood, Colo., 1982-83; researcher and tech. writer Integrated Perceptual Info. for Designers Project Dept. of Psychology NYU, 1984-85; psychologist Colin Anderson Ctr., St. Marys, W.Va., 1985-86, Brandon (Vt.) Tng. Sch., 1986-87; assoc. psychologist Sunmount Devel. Disabilities Svcs. Office, Tupper Lake, N.Y., 1987-88, Potsdam, N.Y., 1988-89; fellow Ctr. for Ind. Scholars Associated Colls. of the St. Lawrence Valley, Potsdam, 1989—; adj. asst. prof. Dept. Psychology U. Vt., Burlington, 1987-88; NIH postdoctoral rsch. fellow Psychophysiology Dept. Nat. Asthma Ctr., Denver, 1978-79; instr. psychology Itawamba Jr. Coll., Tupelo, Miss., 1977; grad. tutor math. Learning Devel. Ctr. U. Miss., 1978; instr. Dept. Psychology U. Bridgeport, Conn., 1974, tutor Dept. Math., 1971; vol. sci. Sci.-By-Mail, Mus. of Sci., Boston, 1991-92; founder, proprietor Bunjin Bonsai, Potsdam, N.Y., 1991—. Mem. APA, Sigma Xi (assoc. 1980-90, chpt. v.p. 1990-92, chpt. pres. 1992—), Psi Chi. Home: 101 Market St Potsdam NY 13676-1770 Office: Assoc Colls St Lawrence Valley 116 Satterlee Hall SUNY Potsdam Potsdam NY 13676

SOLAND, RICHARD MARTIN, operations research specialist, educator; b. N.Y.C., July 27, 1940; s. Louis Soland and Flora Diana (Zelickson) Chale; m. Carol Vivian Lurie, June 9, 1963 (div. Apr. 1979); children: Valerie Lynn, Peter Alan; m. MyLinh Duong, July 4, 1979. BEE, Rensselaer Poly. Inst., 1961; PhD in Math., MIT, 1964. Registered profl. engr., D.C. Tech. staff Rsch. Analysis Corp., McLean, Va., 1964-71; assoc. prof. U. Tex., Austin, 1971-76, Ecole Poly., Montreal, Can., 1976-78; prof. ops. rsch. George Washington U., Washington, 1978—, chmn. dept. ops. rsch., 1989—; cons. Inst. Defense Analyses, Alexandria, Va., 1983-85, 90—; conf. chmn. 10th Triennial Conf. on Operational Rsch., 1984. Contbr. articles to profl. jours. NSF fellow, 1961-64; Fulbright Found. scholar, 1969-70. Fellow Wash. Acad. Scis.; mem. IEEE (sr.), Inst. Indsl. Engrs. (sr.), Ops. Rsch. Soc. Am., Canadian Operational Rsch. Soc., Wash. Ops. Rsch./Mgmt. Sci. Coun. (trustee 1989-91). Home: 5460 Fillmore Ave Alexandria VA 22311-1346 Office: George Washington Univ 707 Twenty second St NW Washington DC 20052

SOLANO, PAUL (LEONARD), finance educator; b. Somerville, Mass., Apr. 19, 1943; s. Edmund Joseph and Nora Mary (Di Pietro) S.; m. L. Linn Adams, Sept. 8, 1973; children: Amy, Alexis. BA, Northeastern U., 1966, MA, 1968; postgrad., U. Pa., 1968-70; PhD, U. Md., 1978. Ins. underwriter and rater Kemper Ins. Co., Boston, 1961-64; rsch. analyst Foreign Policy Rsch. Inst., Phila., 1970; rsch. cons. U.S. Agy. for Internat. Devel., Washington, 1972-73; budget analyst dept. budget and progamming Prince George's County, Md., 1974; instr. U. Md., College Park, 1974, 1976-77; asst. prof. U. Del., Newark, 1977-85, assoc. prof., 1985—; cons. State Agys. Del., 1977—; faculty Inter Univ. Ops. Rsch., U. Del., 1988—; ex officio economist State of Del. Commn. for Local Govt. Financing, 1987-88; mem. Pub. Mgmt. Program, U. Del., Newark, 1990—. Contbr. articles to profl. jours., chpts. to books. Home: 49 Shenandoah Dr Newark DE 19711-3772 Office: U Del Graham Hall Newark DE 19716

SOLANO, RONALD EDWARD, data security consultant, accountant; b. Bklyn., Nov. 11, 1948; s. Andrew E. and Rose Solano; m. Patricia Wynne, Oct., 1970 (div. June 1976); 1 child, Ronald J. (dec.); m. Bridget R. IcInerney, Sept. 9, 1978; children: Christopher, Matthew. AAS in Fin., Pace U., 1975; BBA in Fin., Hofstra U., 1979; postgrad., Dale Carnegie U., 1985. Acct. Am. Stock Exch., N.Y.C., 1970-72; fin. analyst Citgo Cities Svc. Co., N.Y.C., 1972-73; sr. acct. Am. Express Co., N.Y.C., 1973, project mgr., 1973-78; systems officer Citicorp, N.A., N.Y.C., 1978-80; EDP audit mgr. Conn. Nat. Bank, Hartford, 1981-83; sr. audit mgr. ITT-Hartford Ins. Group, 1983-86, systems cons., 1986-87, data security cons., 1987—; participant IBM Guide Security Project, Armonk, N.Y., 1990-91; speaker Vanguard Inc./IBM, Orange, Calif., 1992. Contbr. articles to profl. jours. Mem. Dem. Com., Tolland, Conn., 1988—; commr. Tolland Planning & Zoning Commn., 1988-92. Sgt. USAF, 1966-69. Mem. Assn. Systems Mgmt., EDP Auditors Assn. (sec. 1981-84, bd. dirs. 1983, Cert. of Appreciation 1986), K.C. Roman Catholic. Home: 79 High Ridge Dr Tolland CT 06084 Office: ITT Hartford Ins Hartford Pla Hartford CT 06115

SOLANTO, MARY VICTORIA, psychologist; b. N.Y.C., Sept. 8, 1951; d. Gregory Albert and Geraldine (Ricciardelli) S. BA, Princeton (N.J.) U., 1973; MS, Cornell U., 1977; PhD, SUNY, Buffalo, 1981. Lic. psychologist, N.Y. Post-doctoral fellow dept. psychiatry Albert Einstein Coll. Medicine, Bronx, 1981-83, asst. prof. dept. pediatrics, 1983-89, assoc. prof. dept pediatrics, 1989—; sr. psychologist Long Island Jewish Med. Ctr., New Hyde Park, N.Y., 1989—; guest reviewer various profl. publs. Contbr. articles on child psychopharmacology to profl. jours. Coord. com. children's sci. mus. Jr. League, Westchester-on-the-Sound, 1990; mem. Nat. Trust Historic Preservation. Grantee NIH, 1984, NIMH, 1986-89. Mem. Am. Psychol. Assn., Soc. for Pediatric Rsch., Soc. for Behavioral Pediatrics (nominations com. 1989-90), Soc. for Rsch. in Child and Adolescent Psychopathology, Princeton Club of N.Y. Roman Catholic. Office: Long Island Jewish Med Ctr Schneider Childrens Hosp New Hyde Park NY 11042

SOLARES, ANDRES JOSE, civil engineer, human rights advocate; b. Havana, Cuba, Jan. 28, 1946; came to U.S., 1968; s. Andres and Iluminada (Teseiro) S.; m. Adriana Chavez, May 5, 1967; children: Andres, Odette, Daniel. BSc, Sch. Civil Engring., Havana, 1968; diploma with distinction, U. Wales, Cardiff, Great Britain, 1970; diploma with excellence, Escuela Nacional Direccion Economia, Havana, 1980, Escuela Junta Nacional

Planificacion, Havana, 1980. Registered civil engr., Cuba. Civil engr. Ministry Constrn., Havana, 1968; lectr. sch. civil engring. U. Havana, 1967-72; PhD researcher dept. maritime transp. U. Wales, Cardiff, 1969-70, 71-72; v.p. Constrn. Enterprises, Havana, 1973-78; head dept. airport investment Ministry Transp., Havana, 1978-80; lectr. Ministry Higher Edn., Havana, 1980-81; project mgr. Calmaquip Engring. Corp., Miami, 1988—; radio commentator C.I.D. Radio Sta., Miami, 1989, Radio Voluntad Democratica, Voice of PRC-Autentico, 1991; realty assoc. Century 21 Bona Fide Realty. Author: Investigaciones de la Construccion, 1978; columnist: Actualidad Latinoamericana Revista Ahora mag., 1989; contbr. articles to newspapers and mags. in Cuba and U.S. Vice pres. Partido Revolucionario Cubano Autentico, Miami, 1988—; pres. Alianza de Presos Politicos Cubanos, Miami, 1989, Partido Revolucionario Cubano, Cuba, 1980-88; v.p. Comite Cubano de Derechor Humanos, Cuba, 1987-88; mem. Junta Patriotica Cubana, Miami, 1989—; del. Nat. Assembly of the Cuban Unity, 1991; founder first Dem. Polit. Party in Cuba after, 1959 (Partido Revolucionario Cubano) and polit. prisoner, 1981-88; mem. Directive Bd. Human Rights, 1990. UNESCO fellow, 1969-70, 71-72; named Prisoner of Month Amnesty Internat., 1987; named to Orden Jose Marti, 1989; recipient diploma for patriotic activities Ex Club, 1988, plaque Govt. of El Salvador for his efforts on behalf of democracy, 1991. Mem. Colegio de Ingenieros Cubanos en el Exilio. Roman Catholic. Office: Calmaquip Engring Corp 7240 NW 12th St Miami FL 33126-1968

SOLARZ, STEPHEN JOSHUA, congressman; b. N.Y.C., Sept. 12, 1940; s. Sanford and Ruth (Fertig) S.; m. Nina Koldin, Feb. 5, 1967; children: Randy, Lisa. B.A., Brandeis U., 1962; M.A., Columbia U., 1967. Mem. N.Y. State Assembly from 45th Dist., 1968-74; mem. 94th through 102nd Congresses from 13th Dist. N.Y., 1975—, Fgn. Affairs Com.; chmn. Fgn. affairs subcom. on Asian and Pacific affairs; mem. Merchant Marine and Fisheries Com., Joint Econ. Com., Permanent Select Com. on Intelligence; Congl. del. UN Gen. Assembly, 1983; past faculty Bklyn. Coll., City U. N.Y. Past nat. affairs editor: Newsfront; past asso. editor: Greater Philadelphia. Mem. Governing Council Am. Jewish Congress; trustee Brandeis U. Democrat. Office: US Ho of Reps 1536 Longworth House Office Bldg Washington DC 20515*

SOLBERT, PETER OMAR ABERNATHY, lawyer; b. Copenhagen, Mar. 9, 1919; (parents Am. citizens); s. Oscar N. and Elizabeth (Abernathy) S.; m. Deborah Kirk, Sept. 8, 1945. B.A., Yale U., 1941; J.D., Harvard U., 1948. Bar: N.Y. Assoc. Davis Polk & Wardwell, N.Y.C., 1948-57, ptnr., 1957-89, sr. counsel, 1989—; dep. asst. sec. for internat. security affairs U.S. Dept. Def., Washington, 1963-65. Bd. dirs., mem. Ctr. Am. Archaeology. Lt. comdr. USNR, 1941-45. Mem. Internat. Bar Assn., Internat. Law Assn., Am. Fgn. Law Assn., Am. Soc. Internat. Law, ABA, N.Y. State Bar, Assn. of Bar of City of N.Y., Union Internat. des Avocats, Am. Assn. for Internat. Commn. of Jurists (dir.). Home: 416 W Neck Rd Huntington NY 11743-1625 Office: Davis Polk & Wardwell 450 Lexington Ave New York NY 10017

SOLDON, NORBERT CARROLL, history educator; b. Nanticoke, Pa., Aug. 4, 1932; s. Stephen Paul and Leona Delores (Witkowski) S.; m. Alice Anne Eberle, Jan. 17, 1959; children: Shawn Alice, Sherry Lee, Sarah Eberle. BA, Pa. State U., 1954, MA, 1959; PhD, U. Del., 1969. Instr. history Brandywine High Sch., A.I. DuPont, Wilmington, Del., 1959-62; asst. prof. West Chester (Pa.) State Coll., 1963-64, assoc. prof., 1964-69, prof. history, 1969—; adj. prof. Pa. State U., State College, Pa., 1972-88; vis. prof. U. Del., Newark, 1990-91; reader Ednl. Testing Svc., Princeton, N.J., 1980-87; asst. chair history West Chester State Coll., 1976-86, chmn. history dept., 1990-91. Author: Women in British Trade Unions, 1978, John Wilkinson--Ironmaster, 1992; editor: World of Women's Trade Unions, 1985, Readings in British History: Variety of Views, 1991. 1st lt. USAF, 1954-57. Mem. Am. Hist. Assn., Soc. for Study of Labour History, N.E. Victorian Studies Assn., Penn State Blue and White Club, Phi Alpha Theta, Pi Gamma Mu. Episcopalian. Home: 957 Cloud Ln West Chester PA 19382-2113 Office: West Chester U West Chester PA 19380

SOLER, ARTHUR R., food products executive; b. Sliema, Malta, Feb. 12, 1944; arrived in Can., 1964; s. John and Helen (Parlato) S.; m. E. Elizabeth Baker, Aug. 8, 1970; children: Jonathon, Justine, Juliane. Degree in bus. adminstrn. with honours, Ryerson Polytech. Inst., Toronto, Ont., Can., 1967. Fin. planning supr., internal audit mgr. Proctor & Gamble, Toronto, 1964-70; fin. planning mgr. Warner Lambert, Toronto, 1970-73, product mgr., 1973-75; new product devel. mgr. Warner Lambert, London, 1975-76, Brussels, 1976-77; group product mgr. Warner Lambert, Toronto, 1977-80, mktg. dir., 1980-84, v.p. sales and mktg., 1984-90; pres. Neilson Cadbury Ltd., Toronto, 1990—. Mem. Confectionery Mfrs. Can. (bd. dirs. 1989—). Roman Catholic. Office: Neilson Cadbury Ltd, 277 Gladstone Ave, Toronto, ON Canada M6J 3L9

SOLER, TERRELL DIANE (DOMINIQUE RUSSELL), dramatic soprano, actress, real estate and marketing executive; b. South Bend, Ind., Apr. 26; d. Harold J. Metzler and Margaret Terrell (Whiteman) Metzler-Fogarty. BA, Ithaca Coll., 1960; diploma, Brown's Bus. Coll., Decatur, Ill., 1960; postgrad. in real estate sales, NYU, 1984. Lic. securities dealer, real estate salesperson. Exec. legal asst. Carb Luria Glassner Cook & Kufeld, N.Y.C., 1962-64; Exec. legal asst. Graubard Moskovitz McGoldrick Dannett & Horowitz, N.Y.C., 1964-79; opera and concert singer N.Y.C., 1964—; real estate salesperson Rosemary Edwards Realty, N.Y.C., 1985, Kenneth D. Laub & Co., Inc., N.Y.C., 1987-89, GSW Realty, Inc., N.Y.C., 1990-91, Kuzmuk Realty, Inc., 1992—; pres. Terrell Internat., Whiteman and Stewart Prodns., TS Assocs., TS Enterprises, DharMacduff Publs.; corr. sec., bd. dirs. Community Opera, Inc., N.Y.C., 1984—. Mem. internat. affairs com. and other coms. Women's Nat. Rep. Club, N.Y.C., 1968—; active Rep. County Vols., N.Y.C., 1976—; mem. nominating com. Ivy Rep. Club, N.Y.C., 1983-87; bd. dirs. Am. Landmark Festivals, 1986—. Named Female Singer of Yr., Internat. Beaux Arts, Inc., 1978-79, Princess Nightingale, Allied Indian Tribes N.Am. Continent-Cherokee Nation, 1985. Mem. Nat. Arts Club (music com. 1983-87), Wagner Internat. Instn. (dir. pub. rels. 1982-84), N.Y. Opera Club, Navy League U.S. (life, mem. N.Y. coun.), World Ship Soc., Assn. Former Intelligence Officers (assoc.), Friends of Spanish Opera (bd. dirs. 1982—), Finlandia Found., Inc. (life), World Ship Soc., Ziegfield Club, The Bohemians. Home: Apt 4J 2 Tudor City Pl S New York NY 10017-6800

SOLES, JAMES RALPH, political science educator, university administrator; b. Whiteville, N.C., June 23, 1935; s. Ralph Culbreath and Agnes (Langley) S.; m. Ada Leigh Wall, Aug. 1, 1959; children: Nancy Elizabeth, Catherine Winter. BS in History, Fla. State U., 1957, MS in Polit. Sci., 1961; PhD in Govt., U. Va., 1968. Lectr. U. Md., College Park, 1964-68; asst. prof. U. Del., Newark, 1968-71; asst. to pres. U. Conn., Storrs, 1971-72; assoc. prof. U. Del., 1972-84, prof. polit. sci., 1984—, chair, 1989—; cons. Greater Phila. Movement, 1972-74. Co-author: Government of Delaware, 1976. Vice chmn. Del. Dem. Party, 1978; chmn. Del. Heritage Com., 1989—; pres. First State Constn. Scholarship Corp., 1989—. Recipient Liberty Bell award Del. Bar Assn., 1987, Order of Excellence award State Bd. Edn., 1989, Disting. Svc. to Humanities award Del. Humanities Forum, 1991; fellow Am. Coun. Ednl., 1971-72, Salzburg Seminar, 1987. Mem. Am. Polit. Sci. Assn. Democrat. Home: 215 Vassar Dr Newark DE 19711-3158 Office: Univ Delaware Neward DE 19716

SOLETSKY, ALBERT, language educator; b. N.Y.C., Apr. 25, 1937; s. David and Della (Cherey) S. BA, Columbia U., 1958, MA, 1961, PhD, 1968. Lectr. Spanish Queens Coll., CUNY, N.Y.C., 1965-66; asst. prof. langs. Fairleigh Dickinson U., Teaneck, N.J., 1968-74, assoc. prof. langs., 1974—, acting chmn. lang. dept., 1972-74, chmn. lang. dept., 1979-80. Author: A Study of the Vocabulary of the Germania, 1968; contbr. articles to profl. jours. Dyckman Inst. scholar Columbia U., 1966-67. Mem. Modern Lang. Assn., AAUP. Home: 124 W 79th St New York NY 10024-6446 Office: Fairleigh Dickinson U 1000 River Rd Teaneck NJ 07666-1914

SOLLENBERGER, ROBERT NEIL, retired educator, retired naval officer; b. Birmingham, Ala., Dec. 2, 1929; s. Earl David Sollenberger and Harriet Mildred (Woodliff) Gombaskey; m. Marie Virginia Lawrence, Jan. 27,1 951; children: Cynthia, Theresa, Robert Neil Jr., Timothy, Christopher, Michael, Paul. BA, U. Akron, 1972; MS, East Conn. State U., 1982. Commd. ensign USN, 1960, advanced through grades to comdr., 1975, ret., 1977; tchr. math. Norwich (Conn.) Free Acad., 1978, Griswold High Sch., Jewett City, Conn., 1978-79, Wheeler High Sch., North Stonington, Conn., 1979-80; registrar Thames Valley State Tech. Coll., Norwich, 1982-84; tchr. math. Choate Rosemary Hall, Wallingford, Conn., 1985-90; adj. tchr. math. Mohegan Community Coll., Norwich, 1982-84, Thames Valley State Tech. Coll., 1982-84, City Colls., Groton, Conn., 1983-85, Mitchell Coll., New London, Conn., 1984-90. Mem. VFW, Nat. Coun. Tchrs. Math., Math. Assn. Am., Ret. Officers Assn., SAR, DAV, Am. Assn. Ret. Persons, Navy League, U.S. Naval Inst., Am. Legion, USS Nautilus Alumni Assn. Republican. Roman Catholic. Home and Office: 13 Kingswood Dr North Stonington CT 06359-1502

SOLLINS, SUSAN, curator art museums; m. Earle Brown. BA, Sarah Lawrence Coll.; postgrad., Columbia U. Dir. studio art program Barnard Coll., U. Columbia, N.Y.C., 1964-66; editor Harry N. Abrams, Inc., N.Y.C., 1967; curator of Edn. Nat. Mus. Am. Art, Smithsonian Inst., Washington, 1968-71; producer arts interviews Nat. Pub. Radio, 1972-74; exec. dir., co-founder, curator Independent Curators Inc., N.Y.C., 1974—; dir. Inner City Art Program, Collegiate Sch., N.Y.C., 1965; instr. in Art History, NYU, 1965-66; guest curator Balt. Mus. of Art, 1972-73; cons. Balt. Pub. Schs., 1972, San Francisco Mus. of Art, 1975, Am. Assn. of Mus., 1975, London (Ontario) Art Gallery, 1976, The Neuberger Mus., SUNY, 1976, The Denver Art Mus. 1976, Portland (Oreg.) Art Mus., 1977, Georgetown U., 1988 and numerous other museums, edn1 insts. and art galleries; curator contemporary art Art in Landscape, 1975, New Work, N.Y., 1977, Supershow!, 1979, New Sculpture: Icon and Environment, 1983, Points of View: Four Painters, 1985, Eternal Metaphors: New Art from Italy, 1988, Team Spirit, 1990. Author (tchr. instructional materials on art and art history) Great Ideas, 1976, The City-Project Ideas, 1977, The Decordova Lessons, 1979; (films) You're It, 1971, Learning to Look, 1977; contbr. articles to profl. jours., mags. and newspapers. Nat. Jury Awards in the Visual Arts, Southeastern Ctr. for Contemporary Art, 1988. Mem. Mass. Arts Coun., N.Y. State Arts Coun., Art Table, Inc. (bd. dirs. 1984-87), Ivy Labs. (bd. dirs., chmn. 1991—). Office: Independent Curators Inc 799 Broadway New York NY 10003-6811

SOLLON, PHILLIP BENEDICT, pharmacist, computer specialist; b. Canonsburg, Pa., Feb. 24, 1952; s. Louis Nicholas and Bernice D. (Bysick) S.; m. Margaret L. Sebelia, June 24, 1978; children: Elizabeth Ann, Phillip Louis. BS, Temple U., 1974; MS in Pharmacy, Duquesne U., 1978. Lic. pharmacist, Pa. Sales and promotion profl. Aero Nat., Inc., Washington, Pa., 1970-77; pharmacist Sollon Pharmacy, Canonsburg, 1979—; cons. Steel City Software, Pitts., 1984—; exec. v.p. Jetcraft, Inc., Washington, Pa., 1985—; gen. ptnr. Sollon Bros., Canonsburg, 1984—; adj. prof. pharmacy Duquesne U., Pitts., 1982—; health officer State of Pa., Canonsburg, 1986-90. Fellow Am. Soc. Cons. Pharmacists. Roman Catholic.

SOLO, ALAN JERE, medicinal chemistry educator, consultant; b. Phila., Nov. 7, 1933; s. David H. and Marion J. (Gottschall) S.; m. Elma Mardirosian, Oct. 5, 1963; children: David Matthew, Julia Ann. S.B., MIT, 1955; M.A., Columbia U., 1956, Ph.D., 1959. Research assoc. Rockefeller U., N.Y.C., 1958-62; asst. prof. med. chemistry SUNY-Buffalo, 1962-65, assoc. prof., 1965-70, dir. grad. studies med. chemistry, 1967-69, chmn. med. chemistry, 1969—, prof., chmn., 1970—; cons. Westwood Pharms. Inc., Buffalo, 1971—. Predoctoral fellow NSF, 1955-56; predoctoral fellow NIH, 1957-58. Mem. Am. Chem. Soc., N.Y. Acad. Sci., Sigma Xi. Office: SUNY-Buffalo Sch Pharmacy 439 Cooke Hall Buffalo NY 14260

SOLOMON, ANTHONY JOSEPH, state treasurer; b. Providence, Apr. 1, 1932; m. Sarah Symia; children: Michael A., Anthony E., Donna M., Sharon A. Student, Providence Coll., R.I. Coll. Pharmacy, 1956; LLD (hon.), U. New Eng. Coll. Osteopathic Medicine. Registered securities agt. Mem. R.I. Ho. of Reps. 11th Dist., 1967-76; state treas. State of R.I., 1977-84, 89—; chmn. R.I. Investment Commn.; mem. R.I. Unclassified Pay Bd.; registered securities agt. Alex Brown & Sons, 1985-88; chmn. R.I. State Employee's Retirement Bd., 1989—; vice chmn. Bd. Banking; with Alex Brown & Sons, 1985-88; chair R.I. Refunding Bond Authority, Coll. and Univ. Savs. Bond Program, R.I. Pub. Fin. Mgmt. Bd.; mem. R.I. Housing Mortgage and Fin. Corp. Past mem. Nat. Dem. Charter Commn., R.I. Dem. Charter Commn. Recipient Man of Yr. award Christian Bros. Boys Assn., LaSalle Acad., Providence, 1979. Mem. Nat. Assn. State Treas.'s (pres. 1980-81), R.I. Pharm. Assn., Lions, KC (4th degree). Roman Catholic. Office: Treasury Dept 102 State House Providence RI 02903

SOLOMON, BARBARA HOCHSTER, English educator, editor; b. Bklyn., Sept. 25, 1936; d. Lothar and Rose (Gruber) Hochster; m. Stanley J. Solomon, Jan. 26, 1958; children: Nancy, Jen. BA, Bklyn. Coll., 1958; MA, U. Kans., 1960; PhD, U. Pitts., 1968. Instr. English Doane Coll., Crete, Nebr., 1960-62, Temple U., Phila., 1965-67; asst. prof. Iona Coll., New Rochelle, N.Y., 1969-76, assoc. prof., 1976-80, prof. English, women's studies, 1980—. Editor: The Awakening and Selected Stories of Kate Chopin, 1976, The Experience of the American Woman: Thirty Stories, 1978, Short Fiction of Sarah Orne Jewett and Mary Wilkins Freeman, 1979, Ain't We Got Fun: Essays, Lyrics and Stories of the Twenties, 1980, American Wives: Thirty Stories by Women, 1986, American Families, 1989; co-editor: (with Paula Berggren) A Mary Wollstonecraft Reader, 1983, Other Voices, Other Vistas: Twenty-Five Non-Western Stories, 1992. Mem. MLA. Office: Iona Coll 715 North Ave New Rochelle NY 10801-1890

SOLOMON, GERALD BROOKS HUNT, congressman; b. Okeechobee, Fla., Aug. 14, 1930; s. Seymour and Rlee Eugenia (Hunt) S.; m. Freda Frances Parker, Feb. 5, 1955; children: Susan, Daniel, Robert, Linda, Jeffrey. Student, Siena Coll., Albany, N.Y., 1948-49, St. Lawrence U., Canton, N.Y., 1953-54. Town supr., chief exec. Queensbury, N.Y., 1967-72; legislator Warren County, N.Y., 1968-73; mem. N.Y. State Assembly, 1972-79, 96th-97th Congresses from 29th N.Y. dist., 1979-83, 98th-102nd Congresses from 24th N.Y. dist., 1983—; ambassador del. UN, 1985; house com. mem. Vets. Affairs Com., 1979-89, Pub. Wks. Com., 1979-83, Fgn. Affairs Com., 1983-89, Rules Com. (2d ranking rep. 1989—, ranking rep. 1991—); founding ptnr. Assoc. of Glens Falls (N.Y.) Inc. ins. agy., 1964—. Chmn. Warren County Social Service Com., 1968-72; active Eastern Adirondack Heart Assn., Adirondack Muscular Dystrophy Assn.; mem. Queensbury Cen. Vol. Fire Co., from 1967; bd. dirs. Adirondack Park Assn., Glens Falls Area Youth Ctr.; coun. Boy Scouts of Am.; mem. house rules com. U.S. Congress, 1989—, Task Force, Prisoner and Missing in S.E. Asia; amb. UN, N.Y., 1985. With USMC, 1951-52. Mem. Queensbury C. of C. (pres. 1972), Queensbury Jaycees (pres. 1964-65). Presbyterian. Lodges: Masons, Shriners, K.T, Elks, Kiwanis (bd. dir. Queensbury club 1965-69), Grange. Office: US Ho of Reps 2265 Rayburn House Office Bldg Washington DC 20515*

SOLOMON, JERRY LAWRENCE, sports marketing executive; b. N.Y.C., June 11, 1954; s. Edward David and Roberta Eleanor Madison; m. Kathryn Yanuck, June 15, 1986; 1 child, B. Clayton. Liaison men's/women's tennis tour Colgate Palmolive Co., N.Y.C., 1978-79; ProServ, Inc., Washington, 1980—; dir. tennis tour Volvo Grand Prix, N.Y.C., 1980-82; client mgr. Washington, 1982-84; v.p., tennis div. Proserv, Inc., Washington, 1984-85, sr. v.p., 1985-87, exec. v.p., chief oper. officer, 1987-90, pres., chief oper. officer, 1990—, also bd. dirs.; pres. Proserv Pub. Corp., 1990—. Founder, pub. Kidsports mag., 1989—. Founder Karch Kiraly Scholarship Fund to Benefit Jr. Volleyball; founder, pres. Kidsports Found. to Benefit Children through Sports, 1989—; donor U.S. Olympic Com.; mem. 2d generation co. Nat. Holocaust Mus. Named Agt. to Watch, World Tennis mag., 1987, one of Top 100 Most Powerful People in Sports, The Sporting News, 1992. Mem. Young Pres. Assn. Democrat. Jewish. Office: Proserv Inc 1101 Wilson Blvd Arlington VA 22209-2248

SOLOMON, JOEL MARTIN, professional society administrator; b. Malden, Mass., Dec. 25, 1932; m. Carol Natalie Levine, June 5, 1960 (div. 1983); children: Elaina Raquel, April Monique, Elissa Danielle; m. Eileen Mary Murphy, Feb. 24, 1984. BS, Boston Coll., 1953; SM, Johns Hopkins U., 1957; PhD, U. Wis., 1963. Dir. immunohematology Biologics Standards div. NIH, Bethesda, Md., 1957-60; rsch. fellow ARC, L.A., 1963-64; dir. lab. tng. ARC, Washington, 1964-67; blood bank dir. Bklyn.-Cumberland Med. Ctr., 1967-70; blood products mktg. dir. E. R. Squibb & Sons, Princeton, N.Y., 1970-73; dep. dir., dir. Blood & Blood Products div. FDA, Bethesda, 1974-81; various positions NIH, Bethesda, 1981-88; exec. dir. Am. Assn. Blood Banks, Bethesda, 1991—. Capt. USPHS, 1957-91. Democrat. Jewish. Home: 15714 Cherry Blossom Ln North Potomac MD 20878 Office: Am Assn Blood Banks 8101 Glenbrook Rd Bethesda MD 20814-2749

SOLOMON, MARTIN M., state senator; b. Jan. 24, 1950; BA magna cum laude, SUNY, Albany; LLB, N.Y. Law Sch. admitted to N.Y. bar, 1976; sole practice, Bklyn.; mem. N.Y. State Senate, 1978—, chmn. nat. conf. of ins. legislators com.-integrated fin. svcs., ranking mem. sen. ins. com., mem. finance, bank, judiciary coms. Mem. Oddfellows, KP. Office: NY State Senate State Capitol Albany NY 12224

SOLOMON, PAUL ROBERT, neuropsychologist, educator; b. Bklyn., Aug. 27, 1948; s. Maynard and Norma Harris (Ruben) S.; m. Suellen Zablow, Aug. 16, 1970; children: Todd, Jessica. BA in Psychology, SUNY, New Paltz, 1970, MA in Psychology, 1972; PhD in Psychology, U. Mass., 1972. lic. Psychologist, Mass. Prof. psychology and neuroscience Williams Coll, Williamstown, Mass., 1976—, neuroscience program chmn., 1990—; dir. memory disorders clinic S.W. Vt. Med. Ctr., Bennington, 1990—; bd. dirs. No. Bericshire Mental Health Assn., North Adams, Mass. Author: Scientific Writings, 1985, Memory, 1989, Psychology 3rd Ed., 1989; contbr. articles to profl. jours. Recipient Distinguished Teaching award U. Mass., Amherst, 1975; Rsch. grantee EPA, NIH, NSF, 1978—; Rsch. fellowships NIH, 1979, NSF, 1980. Fellow APA, Am. Psychol. Soc.; mem. AAAS, soc. for Neuroscience. Home: 130 Forest Rd Williamstown MA 01267-2029 Office: Williams Coll Dept of Psychology Williamstown MA 01262

SOLOMON, RICHARD LESTER, retired psychology educator; b. Boston, Oct. 2, 1918; s. Frank and Rose (Roud) S.; children by previous marriage—Janet Ellen, Elizabeth Grace. AB, Brown U., 1940, MSc, 1942, PhD, 1947, ScD (hon.), 1990. Instr. psychology Brown U., 1946; asst. prof. Harvard U., Cambridge, Mass., 1947-50, assoc. prof., 1950-57, prof. social psychology, 1957-60; prof. psychology U. Pa., Phila., 1960-74, James M. Skinner Univ. prof. sci., 1975-85, prof. emeritus, 1985—; staff OSRD, 1942-45. Mem. AAAS, NAS, Am. Psychol. Assn., Ea. Psychol. Assn. (pres.), Psychonomic Soc. (chmn. governing bd.), Am. Acad. Arts and Scis., Soc. Exptl. Psychologists, Phi Beta Kappa, Sigma Xi. Address: 72 Pollard St Conway NH 03818

SOLOMON, SEYMOUR, neurologist, consultant; b. Milw., May 27, 1924; s. Morris and Sylvia (Heifetz) S.; m. Ethel Marion Ross, Mar. 28, 1948; children: Robert, Debora. Student, Marquette U., 1942-44, MD, 1947. Diplomate Am. Bd. Psychiatry and Neurology. Intern Mt. Sinai Hosp., Milw., 1947-48, resident in internal medicine, 1948-50; resident in neurology Montefiore Hosp., N.Y.C., 1950-52; chief neurology Phila. Gen. Hosp., 1952-53; instr. neurology Temple U. Sch. Medicine, Phila., 1952-55, Woman's Med. Coll., Phila., 1952-55; attending neurologist Montefiore Hosp. and Med. Ctr., Bronx, N.Y., 1955—; dir. headache unit Montefiore Med. Ctr., Bronx, 1980—; asst. clin. prof. neurology Columbia U. Coll. Physicians and Surgeons, N.Y.C., 1958-64; assoc. prof. neurology Albert Einstein Coll. Medicine, Bronx, 1980-83, prof. neurology, 1983—. Author: The Headache Book, 1991; author 22 book chpts. and revs.; editor abstracts Jour. Headache, 1987—; editor Headache Rev., 1988—; contbr. 100 articles to profl. jours. Capt. USAF, 1953-55. Fellow Am. Acad. Neurology; mem. AMA, Am. Assn. for the Study of Headache (pres., sec.-treas. Am. Coun. of Headache Edn.), Am. Heart Assn., Internat. Assn. for the Study of Pain, Internat. Headache Soc., Assn. for Rsch. in Nervous and Mental Diseases. Office: Montefiore Med Ctr 111 E 210th St Bronx NY 10467-2490

SOLOMONS, MARK ELLIOTT, lawyer; b. Buffalo, Mar. 4, 1946; s. Alvin and Trude (Salant) S.; m. Jill E. Kent, Aug. 20, 1978. BA, U. Rochester, 1967; JD, U. Pa., 1970; LLM, George Washington U., 1973. Bar: N.Y. 1971, D.C. 1981. Staff atty. U.S. Dept. Labor, Washington, 1970-73, counsel coal miners benefits, 1973-77, legis. counsel, 1977-80; prin. Kilcullen Wilson & Kilcullen, Washington, 1980-86; ptnr. Arter and Hadden, Washington, 1986—, mem. exec. com., 1989—; guest lectr. law and history SUNY-Stony Brook, 1970-76, U. Mich., 1977-78, Hobart Coll., 1972-76. Contbr. articles to profl. jours. Mem. ABA (chair workers compensation and employers liability com. 1987-88, sr. vice chair 1988—), Fed. Bar Assn. (chair regulatory com. 1988—), D.C. Bar Assn., N.Y. State Bar Assn. (prin. coun. excellence in govt. 1990—), Am. Inn of Ct. (master 1991—), Coun. for Excellence in Govt. (prin. 1991—). Republican. Office: Arter & Hadden 1801 K St NW Washington DC 20006-1301

SOLOMON-SCHWARTZ, PHYLLIS, sculptor, artist; b. Phila., June 17, 1937; d. Louis and Mildred (Shatz) Solomon; m. Gordon Jay Schwartz, Dec. 23, 1956; children: Ronald, Joan, Lizanne, Arin. One woman show includes Keneseth Israel Reform Congregation, Temple Judea Mus., 1990; group exhibitions at Boise Bldg., Phila., 1985; permanent collections Old York Temple Beth Am., 1981, Phila. Geriatric Ctr., Levin Pavillion. Jewish. Home and Studio: PO Box 222 Cheltenham PA 19012

SOLOW, ROBERT MERTON, economist, educator; b. Bklyn., Aug. 23, 1924; s. Milton Henry and Hannah Gertrude (Sarney) S.; m. Barbara Lewis, Aug. 19, 1945; children: John Lewis, Andrew Robert, Katherine. BA, Harvard U., 1947, MA, 1949, PhD, 1951, DLitt (hon.), 1992; LLD (hon.), U. Chgo., 1967, Brown U., 1972, U. Warwick, 1976, Dartmouth Coll., 1990, Tulane U., 1983; DLitt (hon.), Williams Coll., 1974, Lehigh U., 1977, Wesleyan U., 1982, Boston Coll., 1986, Colgate U., 1990, Harvard U., Scotland, 1992, U. Glasgow, 1992; DSc (hon.), U. Paris, 1975, U. Geneva, 1982, Bryant Coll., 1988; D of Social Sci. (hon.), Yale U., 1976, U. Mass., Boston, 1989; D Social Sci. (hon.), U. Helsinki, 1990, SUNY, Albany, 1991; (hon), U. Glasgow, 1992. Mem. faculty MIT, 1949—, prof. econs., 1958—, Inst. prof., 1973—; sr. economist Coun. Econ. Advisers, 1961-62, cons., 1962-68; cons. RAND Corp., 1952-64; Marshall lectr., fellow commoner Peterhouse, Cambridge (Eng.) U., 1963-64; Eastman vis. prof. Oxford U., 1968-69; overseas fellow Churchhill Coll., Cambridge; sr. fellow Soc. Fellows, Harvard U., 1975-89; bd. dirs. Boston Red. Res. Bank, 1975-80, chmn., 1979-80; mem. President's Commn. on Income Maintenance, 1968-70, President's Com. on Tech., Automation and Econ. Progress, 1964-65, Carnegie Commn. Sci., Tech. and Govts., 1988—. Author: Linear Programming and Economic Analysis, 1958, Capital Theory and the Rate of Return, 1963, The Sources of Unemployment in the United States, 1964, Growth Theory, 1970, Price Expectations and the Behavior of the Price Level, 1970, (with M. Dertouzos, R. Lester) Made in America, 1989, The Labor Market as a Social Institution, 1990. Bd. dirs., mem. exec. com. Nat. Bur. Econ. Research; trustee Inst. for Advanced Study, Princeton U., 1972-78, Woods Hole Oceanographic Inst., 1988—. Served with AUS, 1942-45. Fellow Ctr. Advanced Study Behavioral Scis., 1957-58, trustee, 1982—, chmn., 1987—; recipient David A. Wells prize Harvard U., 1951, Seidman award in polit. economy, 1983, Nobel prize in Econs., 1987. Fellow Am. Acad. Arts and Scis., Brit Acad. (corr.); mem. AAAS (v.p. 1970), Am. Philos. Soc., Nat. Acad. Scis. (council 1977-80), Acad. dei Lincei, Am. Econ. Soc. (exec. com. 1964-66, John Bates Clark medal 1961, v.p. 1968, pres. 1979), Econometric Soc. (pres. 1964, mem. exec. com.). Home: 528 Lewis Wharf Boston MA 02110-3906 Office: MIT Dept Econs Cambridge MA 02139

SOLOWAY, SAUL, chemist, consultant; b. N.Y.C., Apr. 12, 1916; s. Philip and Bertha (Elkin) S.; m. Catharine M. Blumenthal, July 14, 1945; children: Susan, Daniel, Irene, Cathy. BS, CCNY, 1936; MA, Columbia U., 1938, PhD, 1942. Herscheim fellow Mt. Sinai Hosp., N.Y.C., 1940-41; rsch. chemist Nat. Def. Rsch. Com., Pitts., 1941-43, Panel Chem. Corp., N.Y.C., 1943-44, Grosvenor Labs., N.Y.C., 1944-47; mem. faculty CCNY, N.Y.C., 1947-72; pvt. practice cons. chemist N.Y.C. and New Rochelle, N.Y., 1950—. Contbr. articles to profl. publs.; patentee in field. Mem. Am. Chem. Soc., N.Y. Acad. Scis. Home and Office: 180 Broadview Ave New Rochelle NY 10804-4117

SOLSVIG, CURTIS GERHARDT, III, management consultant; b. Milw., Nov. 30, 1954; s. Curtis Gerhardt and Beverly Marie (Wyss) S.; m. Ginette Marie Elizabeth Norwood, Apr. 13, 1985; children: Catherine Norwood De Fiesque, Alexandra Elizabeth Norwood. BA, Harvard U., 1977, MBA, 1981. Mgr. Boston Cons. Group, 1981-86; mng. dir. Alvarez & Marsal, N.Y.C., 1986-91; pres. Gerhardt, Inc., Greenwich, Conn., 1991—. Home: 409 Stanwich Rd Greenwich CT 06830-3526

SOLT, PAUL ERVIN, engineering consultant; b. Allentown, Pa., Feb. 23, 1929; s. Jacob Charles and Lillian Mae (Walp) S.; m. Myrtle Mae Schmoyer, Apr. 1, 1950; children: Timothy Paul, Patricia Lynn. BSME, Lehigh U., 1950. Test engr. Fuller Co., Bethlehem, Pa., 1954-56; rsch. engr. Fuller Co., Bethlehem, 1962-72, mgr. rsch., 1972-84, chief engr., 1983-84; test engr. Mack Trucks, Allentown, Pa., 1956-59, project mgr., 1959-62; owner Pneumatic Conveying Cons., Allentown, 1984—; instr. Pa. State Extension, Allentown, 1954-72; course dir. Ctr. for Profl. Advancement, New Brunswick, 1972—. Cons. editor Powder and Bulk Engrng. Mag., 1989—; contbr. articles to profl. jours.; patentee in field. Supt. Sunday sch., Allentown, 1988—, tchr., 1954—; pres. Allentown Rescue Mission, 1956-70. With USAF, 1952-54. Mem. Am. Inst. of Chem. Engrs. (course dir. 1984—). Home: 529 S Berks St Allentown PA 18104-6647

SOLTANOFF, JACK, nutritionist, chiropractor; b. Newark, Apr. 24, 1915; s. Louis and Rose (Yomteff) S.; m. Esther Katcher, Sept. 29, 1959; children: Howard, Ruth C. Soltanoff Jacobs, Hillory Soltanoff Seaton. N.M.D. Mecca Coll. Chiropractic Medicine, 1928, U.S. Sch. Naturopathy and Allied Scis., 1951; D.Chiropractic, Chiropractic Inst. N.Y., 1956; postgrad. Atlantic States Chiropractic Inst., 1962-63, Nat. Coll. Chiropractic, 1964-65; PhD, diplomate in nutrition Fla. Natural Health Coll., 1982. Gen. practice chiropractic medicine, cons. in nutrition, N.Y.C., 1956-75, West Hurley, N.Y. and Singer Island, Fla., 1975—; lectr., cons. in field. Author: Natural Healing; pub. Warner Books; contbr. articles to profl. jours. Syndicated newspaper columnist. Fellow Internat. Coll. Naturopathic Physicians; mem. Am. Chiropractic Assn., Internat. Chiropractic Assn., Brit. Chiropractic Assn., N.Y. Acad. Scis., Am. Council on Diagnosis and Internal Disorders, Council on Nutrition, Ethical Culture Soc. Unitarian. Instrumental in instituting chiropractic care in union contracts for mems. of Teamsters Union. Home: Rte 28A PO Box 447 West Hurley NY 12491 also: Martinique II 4100 N Ocean Dr Singer Island FL 33404 Office: Rte 28 and Van Dale Rd West Hurley NY 12491

SOLTYS, MICHAEL JOSEPH, public relations executive; b. Willimantic, Conn., Dec. 31, 1959; s. Joseph and Elizabeth (Kearney) S.; m. Teresa Ann Gronda, Sept. 10, 1983; children: Katherine, Sean. BA, U. Conn., 1981; postgrad., U. Hartford. Communications asst. ESPN, Bristol, Conn., 1981-84; communications coord. ESPN, Bristol, 1984-87, mgr. program info., 1987-92, dir. communications, 1992—; mem. sports info. mktg. adv. bd. U. Hartford, 1990—. Mem. Basketball Writers Assn., Am. Football Writers Assn., Am. Nat. Sportscasters, Sportscasters Assn. Roman Catholic. Office: ESPN ESPN Pla Bristol CT 06010

SOLTZBERG, LEONARD JAY, chemistry educator; b. Wilmington, Del., July 10, 1944; s. Sol and Lillian (Woolf) S. BS, U. Del., 1965; MA, Brandeis U., 1967, PhD, 1968. Asst. prof. Simmons Coll., Boston, 1969-73, assoc. prof., 1973-80, prof. chemistry, 1980—, coord. acad. computing, 1976—, dir. adminstrv. computer svcs., 1980-85, Hazel Dick Leonard prof., 1985—; lectr. in chemistry Grad. Sch. Arts and Scis., Northeastern U., Boston, 1978-80; vis. assoc. prof. U. Nebr.-Lincoln, 1975-76. Author: Sing a Song of Software, 1984, Computer Strategies for Chemistry Students, 1987, (software) Computer-Assisted Blackboard, 1984. Mem. Am. Chem. Soc., Am. Crystallography Assn., Sigma Xi.

SOLUM, JOHN HENRY, flutist, educator, author; b. New Richmond, Wis., May 11, 1935; s. Irwin M. and Helen L. (Anderson) S.; m. Millicent Kemp Hunt, July 30, 1960; children: Eric, Andrew. AB, Princeton U., 1957. Concert flutist, 1957—; tchr. Ind. U., Bloomington, 1973, Vassar Coll., Poughkeepsie, N.Y., 1969-71, 77—, Oberlin (Ohio) Conservatory, 1976; co-dir. Bath (Eng.) Summer Sch. of Baroque Music, 1979-89; co-artistic dir. Conn. Early Music Festival, New London, 1982—; pres. N.Y. Flute Club, 1983-86; mem. music adv. panel NEA, 1990—. Compozer Cadenzas for Mozart's Flute Concertos, 1964; editor flute music; musci critic for Notes, Pro Musica, The Consort; author: The Early Flute, 1992; contbg. author: New Grove Dictionary of Musical Instruments, contbr. articles to Mus. Am., Flutist Quar., Hist. Performance Mag.; performing flutist throughout N. Am., 1957—, Asia, worldwide, 1962—, Russia, Europe, 1968—; rec. artist Arabesque, Cambridge, Chesky, Columbia, CRI, Decca Gold Label, EMI, RCA, Chesky, Smithsonian, others. Mem. Nat. Flute Assn. (bd. dirs., treas.), Dolmetsch Found. (bd. dirs.), Galpin Soc., Am. Musical Instrument Soc. Home: 10 Bobwhite Dr Westport CT 06880-1001

SOMACH, S. DENNIS, communications executive; b. Allentown, Pa., Sept. 30, 1952; s. Lawrence and Lillian Rose (Siegelbaum) S.; m. Kathleen Marie Levinsky, May 25, 1986; Theodore, Emily (twins), Reilly.. BA in English, Art, Moravian Coll., 1975. Announcer Sta. WSAN, Allentown, 1971-75, program dir., 1975; announcer, music dir. Sta. WYSP-FM, Phila., 1975-81; producer Evening/PM Mag., Phila., 1980-82; producer, pres. Denny Somach Prodns., Havertown, Pa., 1979—; pres. Cinema Records, Phila., 1986—, Voyager Records, Phila., 1986—. Producer: (radio shows) Psychedelic Psnack, 1985—, Ticket to Ride, 1985—, Legends of Rock, 1985—, Don Kirshner's History of Rock 'n' Roll, 1990, (TV shows) Hot Spots, USA Network, 1982-84, Rock 'n' Roll Show CBS-TV, 1982, John Debella Show, 1990; exec. producer: (albums) Dave Mason, 1987, Patrick Moraz, 1987, Johnny Winter, 1988, Eric Johnson, 1990; author: Ticket to Ride, 1989. Recipient Grammy award for best rock instrumental Eric Johnson's Cliffs of Dover, 1992. Office: 812 Darby Rd Havertown PA 19083

SOMAN, SHIRLEY CAMPER, writer, journalist, columnist, consultant, social worker; b. Boston; d. David and Fannie (Apteker) Isenberg; m. Frederic R. Camper (dec.); children: Frederic D., Frances A.; m. Robert D. Soman (dec.). BA, U. Wis.; M in Social Sci., Smith Coll. Sch. social worker Bur. Child Guidance N.Y.C. Bd. Edn.; assoc. editor My Baby mag., Shaws Market News, N.Y.C.; family life cons. Family Svc. Assn. Am., N.Y.C.; v.p., ptnr. Associated Film Cons., N.Y.C.; columnist Springfield (Mass.) Union-News, 1991—; pres., chief exec. officer, ptnr. Family Features Pub. Co., Inc., N.Y.C., 1991—; cons. White House Conf. Children and Youth, Washington, 1980, Child Welfare League Am., Washington, 1989; adj. prof. child advocacy and children's rights CUNY, 1976, 77. Author: How to Get Along With Your Child, Let's Stop Destroying Our Children, 1974, Preparing for Your New Baby, 1982; syndicated columnist; contbr. numerous articles to jours. and mags. Panelist 1st USA Conf. on Human Rights Amnesty Internat.; founder, chair Parents for Carter-Mondale, N.Y., 1976; bd. dirs. Pub. Action Coalition for Toys, N.Y., 1976-82, Creative Arts Rehab. Ctr., N.Y., 1977-82; chair First Nat. Child Advocacy Symposium, 1974; lectr. social and family issues numerous orgns. Recipient award Women in Communications, 1986. Mem. NATAS, Am. Soc. Journalists and Authors, Nat. Assn. Sci. Writers, Nat. Assn. Social Workers, Acad. Cert. Social Workers (cert. N.Y. State), N.Y. Bus. Press Editors, N.Y. Acad. Scis., Soc. Profl. Journalists, Authors Guild and League. Home and Office: 40 W 77th St New York NY 10094

SOMARY, JOHANNES FELIX, conductor; b. Zurich, Switzerland, Apr. 7, 1935; came to U.S., 1940; s. Felix and May (Demblin) S.; m. Anne Voorhees Van Zandt, July 20, 1963; children: Stephen, Geoffrey, Karen. BA magna cum laude, Yale U., 1957, MMus, 1959. Founder, music dir., conductor Amor Artis, N.Y.C., 1962—; chmn. arts and music dept. Horace Mann Sch., N.Y.C., 1971—; conductor Fairfield County Chorale, Westport, Conn., 1975—, Great Neck (L.I., N.Y.) Choral Soc., 1983—; conductor recordings English Chamber Orch., London, 1968-79; vis. prof. Yale Sch. Music, New Haven, 1983-84; choral dir. Madeira (Portugal) Bach Festival, 1984-86; guest conductor Dubrovnik (Yugoslavia) Music Festival, 1986, Sion (Switzerland) Music Festival, 1990; conductor for recordings Polish Radio Orch., Katowice, 1990; guest lectr., conductor U. Tex., Austin, 1973, U. B.C., Vancouver, 1987, U. Ala., Montevallo, 1985; program dir. UN Assn., Riverdale, N.Y., 1970-74. Conductor 54 recordings on CD, casettes, records including Handel oratorios, Schuetz and Bach passions, music by Vivaldi, Haydn, Tschaikowsky, Weill, others, onVanguard, Omega, Vox, Decca, Leonarda, Newport Classic, 1963—; composer liturgical music G.I.A., Galaxy, Collins, 1975—; composer oratorios and smaller works commissioned by various choral orgns.; guest conductor New Orleans Philharmonic, Milw. Chamber Orch., Royal Philharmonic, London, others; organist solo recitals. Recipient Record of Yr. awards Stereo-Rev., N.Y.C., 1969, 70, 75, 78; recipient Certs. of Merit Yale Sch. Music Alumni Assn., New Haven, 1982, U. Chgo., 1981, Choirmaster Cert., Am. Guild Organists, N.Y.C., 1959; French Baroque Music study grantee, 1982. Fellow Am. Guild Organists (bds. New Haven and N.Y. chpts.), Am. Symphony Orch. League, Assn. Musiciens Suisses, Yale Club N.Y.C., Riverdale Yacht Club; mem. Friendship Ambassadors, Inc. (bd. dirs. 1985—), N.Y. Archdiocesan Music Commn. Roman Catholic. Home: 620 W 254th St Bronx NY 10471-1252 Office: Amor Artis 620 W 254th St Bronx NY 10471-1252

SOMASUNDARAN, PONISSERIL, engineering and applied science educator, consultant, researcher; b. Pazhookara, Kerala, India, June 28, 1939; came to U.S., 1961; s. Kumara Moolayil and Lakshmikutty (Amma) Pillai; m. Usha N., May 25, 1966; 1 child, Tamara. BS, Kerala U., Trivandrum, India, 1958; BE, Indian Inst. Sci., Bangalore, 1961; MS, U. Calif., Berkeley, 1962, PhD, 1964. Rsch. engr. U. Calif., 1964; research engr. Internat. Minerals & Chem. Corp., Skokie, Ill., 1965-67; rsch. chemist R.J. Reynolds Industries, Inc., Winston-Salem, N.C., 1967-70; assoc. prof. Columbia U., N.Y.C., 1970-78, prof. mineral engrng., 1978-83, La Von Duddleson Krumb prof., 1983—; chmn. Henry Krumb Sch. Mines Columbia U., 1988—, dir. Langmuir Ctr. for Colloids and Interfaces, 1987—; cons. numerous agys., cos., including NIH, 1974, B.F. Goodrich, 1974, NSF, 1974, Alcan, 1981, UNESCO, 1982, Sohio, 1984-85, IBM, 1984, Am. Cyanamd, 1988-89, Duracell, 1988-89, DuPont, 1989, Canmet, 1990—, Unilever, 1991—, Engelhard, 1991—, UoP, 1991—, Alcoa, 1991—; mem. panel NRC; chmn. numerous internat. symposia and NSF workshops; mem. adv. panel Bur. Mines Generic Ctr., 1983—; keynote and plenary lectr. internat. meetings.; hon. prof. Cen. South U. Tech., China; Brahm Prakash chair in metallurgy and material sci. Indian Inst. Sci., Bangalore, 1990; hon. rsch. advisor Beijing Gen. Rsch. Inst., 1991—. Editor books, including Fine Particles Processing, 1980 (Publ. Bd. award 1980); editor-in-chief Colloids and Surfaces, 1980—; Henry Krumb lectr. AIME, 1988; contbr. numerous articles to profl. publs., patentee in field. Pres. Keralasamajam of Greater N.Y., N.Y.C., 1974-75; bd. dirs. Fedn. Indian Assocs., N.Y.C., 1974—, Vols. in Service to Edn. in India, Hartford, Conn., 1974—. Recipient Disting. Achievement in Engrng. award, AINA, 1980, Antoine M. Gaudin award Soc. Mining Engrs.-AIME, 1983, Achievements in Applied Sci. award 2d World Malayalam Conf., 1985, Robert H. Richards award, AIME, 1986, Arthur F. Taggart award Soc. Mining Engrs.-AIME, 1987, honor award Assn. Indian in Am., 1988, honor award AIA, 1988, VHP award of Excellence, Vishwa Hindu Parishad of Am., 1987, Ellis Island medal of Honor, 1990, Commendations citation State of N.J. Senate, 1991, SIAA award, 1992; named Mill Man of Distinction, Soc. Mining Engrs.-AIME, 1983, Disting. Alumnus award Indian Inst. Sci., Bangalore, 1989, Outstanding Contbns. and Achievement award CFI, 1991, Recognition award SIAA, 1992. Fellow Instn. Mining and Metallurgy (U.K.); mem. Soc. Mining Engrs. (bd. dirs. 1982-85, disting. mem., various awards), Engrng. Found. (chmn. conf. com. 1985-88, bd. exec. com. 1985-88, bd. dirs. 1991—, Frank Aplan award 1992), NAE, Am. Chem. Soc., N.Y. Acad. Scis., AICE, Soc. Petroleum Engrs., Internat. Assn. Colloid and Surface Scientists (councillor 1989—), Sigma Xi. Office: Columbia U 911 SW Mudd Bldg New York NY 10027

SOMERS, DAN MICHAEL, aeronautical engineer; b. Niles, Mich., Mar. 26, 1951; s. Kendall Lee and Madonna Maxine (Cutler) S. BS, Purdue U., 1974. Aeronautical engr. NASA Langley Rsch. Ctr., Hampton, Va., 1974-89; pres. Airfoils, Inc., State College, Pa., 1980—, Somers and Maughmer, Inc., State College, 1991—. Recipient R & D 100 award, 1991; Floyd L. Thompson fellow NASA Langley Rsch. Ctr., 1984-85. Mem. Soaring Soc. Am. (chmn. aerodynamics com., tech. bd. 1990—, Exceptional Svc. award 1991). Office: Airfoils Inc 601 Cricklewood Dr State College PA 16803-2111

SOMERS, GEORGE FREDRICK, emeritus biology educator; b. Garland, Utah, July 9, 1914; s. George Fredrick and Elizbuth (Sorenson) S.; m. Beulah Rich Morgan, June 24, 1939; children: Ralph M., Steven J., Gary F. B.S., Utah State U., 1935; B.A., Oxford U., 1938, B.Sc., 1939; Ph.D., Cornell U., 1942. Faculty Cornell U., 1941-51, asso. prof. biochemistry, 1949-51; plant physiologist U.S. Dept. Agr., 1944-51; faculty U. Del., Newark, 1951—; assoc. dir. Del. Agrl. Expt. Sta., 1951-59; assoc. dean Coll. Agr., 1954-59; chmn. dept. biol. scis. U. Del., 1959-71, H. Fletcher Brown prof. biology, 1962-81, emeritus prof., 1981—; vis. prof. U. Philippines, 1958-59. Author: (with J.B. Sumner) Chemistry and Methods of Enzymes, 3d edit, 1953, Laboratory Experiments in Biological Chemistry, 2d edit, 1949; also articles.; Editor: biochem. sect. Chem. Abstracts, 1968-75. Union Pacific scholar, 1930; Rhodes scholar, 1936; Henry Strong Denison fellow, 1939. H.C. fellow AAAS; mem. Am. Assn. Plant Physiology, Bot. Soc. Am., Sigma Xi, Phi Kappa Phi. Home: 22 Minquil Dr Newark DE 19713-1312

SOMERS, MARION, gerontologist, retirement specialist; b. N.Y.C.; d. John Joseph and Lottie (Kramer) Strahl; children: Lynne Caryl, Randy Mass, Craig Caryl; stepchildren: Carolyn Clark, Gail Sun, Matthew Somers. BA, CUNY, 1976; MS, Lehman Coll., 1980; PhD, The Fielding Inst., 1988. Lic. nursing home adminstr., N.Y. Activities dir. Wartburg Luth. Nursing Home, N.Y.C., 1980-82; prof. Lehman Coll., N.Y.C., 1982-84; pres. Marion Somers, Assoc., N.Y.C., 1985—; chief recreation therapist Kingsbrook Jewish Med. Ctr. and Rutland Nursing Home, 1989-91; adminstr. in tng. Hebrew Home for the Aging, Palisades Nursing Home, Riverdale, N.Y., 1991-92, Palisades Nursing Home, 1991—; grant reader HHS, Washington, 1980—; observer White House Conf. on Aging, 1982; bd. dirs. Sr. Action in Gray Environ., 1980-84. Author: Viewers Guide for ABC-TV prodn. of The Shell Seekers, Last Wish, The Home. Advisor Sen. A. D'Amato, N.Y., 1981-82. Recipient Profl. award Met. Recreation & Pk. Soc., N.Y.C., 1985. Mem. Gerontol. Soc. Am., Nat. Coun. on Aging, Nat. Recreation and Pk. Assn. (Presdl. award 1984), N.Y. State Therapeutic Recreation Soc. (chair 1983-84, pres. 1984-85), Am. Therapeutic Recreation Soc., Nat. Assn. Retirement Profls., Internat. Soc. Retirement Planning.

SOMERVILLE, WALTER RALEIGH, JR., government official; b. Macon, N.C., Feb. 17, 1930; s. Walter Raleigh and Bettie Lou (Hunt) S.; student Morgan State Coll., 1957-60; B.A. in Bus. Adminstrn., U. Md., 1970; m. Jean Renwick (Nava), Sept. 12, 1975; 1 child, Thomasine A. Walker Gilliam; 1 stepchild, Pamela Nava. Personnel staffing specialist FAA, Washington, 1962-65; personnel mgmt. specialist OEO, 1965-67; personnel mgmt. specialist Office Sec. Transp., 1967-70; chief civilian equal opportunity div. U.S. Coast Guard, Transp. Dept., 1970-83, dir. civil rights, 1983—, trainee Fed. Exec. Devel. Program, 1975-76. Chmn. fin. com. Christ United Meth. Ch., Washington, 1976-85, chmn. adminstrv. coun., 1985-86; mem. human relations edn. bd. Dept. Def., 1983-85; mem. Dept. of Def. Equal Opportunity Coun.; chmn. placement and counseling com. for industry cluster Paul Quinn Coll. With USAF, 1951-60. Recipient Outstanding Performance award, 1981, 82, 83, Proclamation award City Coun. of New Orleans, 1987. Mem. Am. Mgmt. Assn., NAACP (golden heritage life mem., Roy Wilkins meritorious service award, 1987), Sr. Execs. Assn., Washington Urban League (life), U. Md. Alumni Assn. (century club), Nat. Urban League (charter mem. Pres.'s Club, mem. black exec. exch. program, vis. prof. historically black colls. and univs.). Home: 1228 4th St SW Washington DC 20024-2302 Office: 2100 2nd St SW Washington DC 20593-0002

SOMERVILLE, WARREN THOMAS, management consultant; b. Balt., Oct. 28, 1942; s. Charles Arthur and Ruth Simpson (Bachtell) S.; m. Susan May Wittgrefe, Aug. 5, 1972; children: Stacey Michelle, Warren Thomas. BBA, Towson U., 1978. Electronics technician Towson Labs., Balt., 1963-64, Electronic Modules, Inc., Timonium, Md., 1964-65; specification writer Western Electric, Cockeysville, Md., 1965-67; bldgs. and support system engr. AT&T/Western Electric, Cockeysville, 1967-83; mgmt. cons., hot slide engrng. network cons. svcs. AT&T Network Svcs., Cockeysville, 1983—; pres. Jestage Investments, Shrewsbury, Pa., 1973—. Commr. Shrewsbury Water & Sewage Com., 1976—. Served with USN, 1961-63. Republican. Episcopalian. Home: 47 Crosswind Dr Shrewsbury PA 17361-1842 Office: AT&T Network Systems 225 Schilling Cir Cockeysville Hunt Valley MD 21031-1119

SOMMER, MIRIAM GOLDSTEIN, writer, photographer; b. Springfield, Mass., May 2, 1929; d. Nathan E. and Anna (Ginsberg) Goldstein; children: Babette, Anne. BA, Wells Coll., 1950; rsch. cert., London Sch. Econs., 1953; MS in Art History, So. Conn. State U., 1979. Music dept. adminstr. Yale U., 1963-83; free-lance travel writer, photographer New Haven, 1984—; mem. Creative Arts Workshop, New Haven, 1960—; mem. New Haven Arts Coun., 1970—, Met. Mus. Art/Springfield Mus. Yale U. Art Galleries; guest lectr. Journalism dept., So. Conn. State U., 1989—. Contbr. articles to profl. mags. including Colonial Homes Mag., Touring America mag., Travel Agent mag.; also newspapers including the Los Angeles Times. V.p. Decade Alumni Coun., Williston Northampton Sch., East Hampton, Mass., 1989, founder, panelist career day; bd. mem., co-dir. Assn. for Handicapped Artists, New Haven, 1989; co-founder Creative Arts Workshop course for handicapped artists. Mem. Soc. Profl. Journalists (Excellence in Journalism First Prize Winner 1991 for best mag. spl. supplement feature "Designing Woman, Conn. Mag.). Home: 603 Prospect St New Haven CT 06511

SON, MUN SHIG, education educator; b. Hwanggan, South Korea, Feb. 5, 1950; came to the U.S., 1978; s. Young Hee and Jeong Poon (Park) S.; m. Ock Jhee Kim, June 7, 1978; children: Jennifer, John. BA in Statistics, Sung Kyun Kwan U., Seoul, 1975; MS in Statistics, Okla. State U., 1982, MS in Econs., 1984, PhD in Statistics, 1984. Rsch. asst. Cen. Bank Korea, Seoul, 1975-78; lectr. Okla. State U., Stillwater, 1983-84; vis. asst. prof. U. Vt., Burlington, 1984-86, asst. prof., 1986-91, assoc. prof., 1991—; cons. Green Mountain Power, Burlington, 1987, Sugarbush Ski Planning Com., Waitsfield, Vt., 1987—. With Korean Army, 1976-77. NSF grantee, 1986-91, Pak-Doo Rsch. Found. grantee, 1989—. Mem. Inst. Math. Statistics, Am. Statis. Assn., Korean Scientists and Engrs. Assn. Am., KoreanAm. Univ. Profs. Assn. Home: 18 Prescott St Essex Junction VT 05452-2932 Office: U Vt 16 Colchester Ave Burlington VT 05405-0001

SONDHEIM, STEPHEN JOSHUA, composer, lyricist; b. N.Y.C., Mar. 22, 1930; s. Herbert and Janet (Fox) S. B.A., Williams Coll., 1950. vis. prof. contemporary theater Oxford U., England, 1990. Composer incidental music Girls of Summer, 1956, Invitation to a March, 1961, Twigs, 1971; lyrics West Side Story, 1957, Gypsy, 1959, Do I Hear A Waltz?, 1965; music and lyrics A Funny Thing Happened on the Way to The Forum, 1962, Anyone Can Whistle, 1964, Evening Primrose, 1966, Company, 1970 (Tony award 1971), Follies, 1971 (Tony award 1972), A Little Night Music, 1973 (Tony award 1973), The Frogs, 1974, Pacific Overtures, 1976, Sweeney Todd, 1979 (Tony award 1979), Merrily We Roll Along, 1981, Sunday in the Park with George, 1984 (Pulitzer prize 1985), Into the Woods, 1987 (Tony award 1988), Assassins, 1991; additional lyrics Candide, 1973; anthologies Side by Side by Sondheim, 1976, Marry Me a Little, 1981; film scores Stavisky, 1974, Reds, 1981; composer songs for film Dick Tracy, 1990 (Oscar award); co-author film The Last of Sheila, 1973. Recipient Poses Creative Arts medal Brandeis U., 1982; Grammy award, 1984, 86, 89. Mem. Am. Acad. and Inst. Arts and Letters.

SONENBERG, MARTIN, physician, biochemistry educator; b. N.Y.C., Dec. 1, 1920; s. Berl and Nellie (Gordon) S.; m. Dellie Madeleine Ellis, Jan. 17, 1956; children: Santha, Andrea. B.A., U. Pa., 1941; M.D., NYU, 1944, PhD in Chemistry, 1952. Mem. Sloan-Kettering Cancer Center, N.Y.C., 1950; faculty Cornell U., 1950—, prof. biochemistry, 1967—, prof. medicine, 1972—; chief endocrine div. Meml. Sloan-Kettering Cancer Ctr. Mem. editorial bd.: Endocrinology, 1967-75; contbr. articles to profl. jours. Mem. biomed. adv. com. Population Coun., 1960; mem. adv. com. Am. Cancer Soc., 1971; chmn. endocrinology study sect. NIH; mem. adv. com. div. rsch. grantes, NIH, 1989-91. Recipient Van Meter award Am. Thyroid Assn., 1952; Am. Cancer Soc. scholar, 1952-55; Guggenheim fellow, 1957-58; recipient Sloan award for cancer research, 1968. Mem. Am. Thyroid Assn., Am. Soc. Clin. Investigation, Am. Soc. Biol. Chemists, Endocrine Soc. Office: 1275 York Ave New York NY 10021-6094

SONENBERG, SUZY DALTON, foundation administrator; b. N.Y.C., Oct. 3, 1943; d. Ernest Roger Dalton and Edith Ruth (Loebl) Karel; m. Neil Stephen Sonenberg, Dec. 22, 1963 (dec. Oct. 1981); children: Nina Elise, Daniel Matthew. BA in English Lit., Queens Coll., 1965; M in Social Work, Adelphi U., 1976. Cert. social worker Acad. Cert. Social Workers. Resource assoc. Community Coun. Greater N.Y., N.Y.C., 1976, network cons., 1977, dir. info. svcs. project, 1978-79, dir. employment and tng. projects, 1979-81, dir. dept. info. svcs., 1981-82; caterer N.Y.C., 1982-83; program officer The N.Y. Found., N.Y.C., 1984-88; exec. dir. The L.I. Community Found., 1988—. Bd. dirs. Nassau Health and Welfare Coun., L.I., 1990—. Mem. L.I. Ctr. for Bus. and Profl. Women (Outstanding Achivement in Community Svc. award 1992), Nat. Soc. Fundraising Execs. (bd. dirs. L.I. chpt. 1989—), Nat. Assn. Mother's Ctrs. (interim bd. 1991—). Office: LI Community Found Elias Hicks House 1740 Old Jericho Tpke Jericho NY 11753

SONGER, ELENA MARGARITA, graphic designer; b. N.Y.C., Apr. 22, 1954; d. William Wendell and Dolores Geraldine S. BA, U. Interamericana, Puerto Rico, 1978; MS, Pratt Inst., 1990. Typesetter Parsons Sch. Design, N.Y.C., 1980-91; graphic artist Ogilvy & Mather, N.Y.C., 1983-91; pvt. practice N.Y.C., 1991—. Mem. Graphic Artists Guild, N.Y. MacUser's Group. Democrat. Adventist. Home and Office: PO Box 624 Corona-Elmhurst Queens NY 11373

SONGSTER, JOHN HUGH, legal administrator; b. Springfield, Pa., Mar. 20, 1934; s. James Thomas and Sarah Boyce (McMichael) S. BA, LaSalle Coll., Phila., 1956. Commd. ensign USN, 1956, advanced through grades to comdr., 1971, ret., 1976; asst. treas. Bradford Trust Co., N.Y.C., 1976-80; staff acct. Harcourt Brace Jovanovich, N.Y.C., 1980-83, Software Design Assocs., N.Y.C., 1983-87; legal adminstr. Gold Farrell & Marks, N.Y.C., 1988—. Mem. Assn. Legal Adminstrs. Republican. Roman Catholic. Office: Gold Farrell & Marks 41 Madison Ave New York NY 10010-2202

SONNEBORN, MARCENE SCHNELL, management consultant; b. Erie, Pa., Aug. 5, 1954; d. Albert John and Irene (Matusik) Schnell; m. James Lee Sonneborn. BA, Syracuse U., 1976, MPA, 1977, MBA, 1989. Adminstrv. resident Albany (N.Y.) Med. Ctr. Hosp., 1977-78; data and evaluation specialist Cen. N.Y. Hosp. Assn., Syracuse, N.Y., 1978-81; program adminstr. SUNY Health Sci. Ctr. Med. Sch., Syracuse, 1981-84; adminstrv. dir. nuclear magnetic resonance lab. Syracuse U., 1985-90; ind. mgmt. cons. Syracuse, 1985—; cons. New Methods Rsch., Inc., Syracuse, 1985—, Clean Room Technology, Syracuse, 1987-88, Nat. Employer's Coun., Inc., Syracuse, 1988-89, Knowledge Systems & Rsch., 1991—. Officer, Astride, Inc., Syracuse, 1981-86. Mem. Am. Mgmt. Assn., Beta Gamma Sigma. Republican. Office: Nuclear Magnetic Resonance 500 S Sauna St Syracuse NY 13202

SONNEMANN, GEORGE, insurance executive, consultant; b. Munich, Germany, Feb. 2, 1926; came to U.S., 1938; s. Leopold Lazarus and Emmy Edith (Markus) S. BAero Engring., NYU, 1947, MAero Engring., 1947; PhD in Engring. Mechanics, U. Mich., 1955. Registered profl. engr., N.Y., Pa. Westinghouse prof. mech. engring. U. Pitts., 1959-63; engring. mgr. United Tech., Hartford, Conn., 1964-69; project mgr. Raytheon, Boston, 1969-74; v.p. data processing Comml. Union Co., Boston, 1974-79; v.p. CIGNA, Hartford, 1979-80; v.p. MIS/strategic planning Nationwide Ins., Columbus, Ohio, 1980-86; pres., chief exec. officer I.F.T. Inc., Bala Cynwyd, Pa., 1986-90; mgmt. info. cons. Wynnewood, Pa., 1990—; sr. v.p., chief info. officer Robert Plan, Lynwood, N.Y. Contbr. articles to profl. jours.; inventor high speed pantagraph. Mem. Project Mgmt. Inst., Engrs. Club. Home and Office: 543 Montgomery School Ln Wynnewood PA 19096-1118

SONNENBLICK, CAROL ANNE, adult education educator; b. Bklyn.; d. Solomon and Lillian (Schwalberg) Feldman; children: Lissa, Jordan. BA, Barnard Coll., N.Y.C.; MS, Wagner Coll., S.I., N.Y., 1973; EdD, Rugers U., 1983. Cert. reading specialist. Founder, co-dir. Learning Inst., S.I., 1976—; dir. Creative Exchange, S.I., 1980—; dir. adult learning ctr. Coll. S.I., 1984-90, dir. adult edn., 1990—; cons. learning disabilities, 1983—, book series Famous Ams., 1980. Author: At-tack Pack, 1982; contbr. articles to lit. jours. Mem. Am. Psychol. Assn., Richmond County Psychol. Assn., S.I. Disabilities Coun., Am. Assn. Adult and Continuing Edn. Office: Coll S I 130 Stuyvesant Pl Staten Island NY 10301-1953

SONNENBLICK, HARVEY IRWIN, psychiatrist; b. N.Y.C., June 3, 1936; s. Paul and Adele (Newman) S.; children: Lissa, Jordan. BA, U. Va., 1958; MD, NYU, 1962. Diplomate Am. Bd. Psychiatry and Neurology. Intern Kings County Hosp., Bklyn., 1962-63, resident, 1963-65; resident, fellow S.I. (N.Y.) Mental Health Soc., 1965-67; attending psychiatrist S.I. Hosp., 1967—; staff psychiatrist Soc. for Seamen's Children, S.I., 1978—, Jewish Bd. Family & Children's Svcs., S.I., 1981—; pvt. practice psychiatry S.I., 1967—; vis. psychiatrist Sea View Hosp. and Home, S.I., 1966—. Maj. U.S.

Army, 1968-70. Mem. AMA, Am. Psychiatric Assn., Com. of Physicians of Vol. Child Care Agencies, Phi Beta Kappa. Office: 1361 Hylan Blvd Staten Island NY 10305-1902

SONNENFELD, MARION, linguist, educator; b. Berlin, Germany, Feb. 13, 1928; d. Kurt and Sibylla (Lemke) S. B.A. with high honors, Swarthmore Coll., 1950; M.A., Yale U., 1951, Ph.D., 1956. Instr., asst. prof. Smith Coll., Northampton, Mass., 1954-62; assoc. prof. Wells Coll., Aurora, N.Y., 1962-67, German chmn., dir. German sch., 1965-67; assoc. prof., prof. SUNY Coll., Fredonia, 1967-77, SUNY disting. teaching prof., 1977—, acting dean arts and humanities, 1980-81; mem. com. on learning assessment Fund for the Improvement of Post Secondary Edn., 1988-90, nat. screening com. for Fulbright grants, 1989-91. English translator of German books and plays. Yale U. Jr. Sterling fellow, 1951-53; NEH postdoctoral fellow Ind. U., 1977; SUNY faculty exchange scholar, 1984—. Mem. MLA, Am. Assn. Tchrs. German, AAUP, Hebbelgesellschaft. Office: SUNY Dept Fgn Langs and Lit Fredonia NY 14063

SONNICHSEN, GEORGE CARL, chemist; b. Chgo., Nov. 15, 1941; s. Carl Moritz and Eleanor Ann (Friese) S.; m. Marldel G. Burton, Dec. 19, 1970; children: Laura, Andrew. BA, DePauw U., 1963; PhD, Mich. State U., 1967. NSF fellow U. Calif., Berkeley, 1967-69; rsch. chemist DuPont, Wilmington, Del., 1969—. Patentee in field; contbr. articles to profl. jours. Mem. sch. bd. Brandywine Sch. Dist., Wilmington, 1988-90. Office: DuPont Experimental Sta Wilmington DE 19880

SONNICHSEN, HAROLD MARVIN, polymer chemist, consultant; b. Hancock, Minn., Apr. 4, 1912; s. Henry Matthew and Mary (Hults) S.; m. Thelma Ardath Lowenberg, Mar. 11, 1939; children: Susan Elizabeth Brown, H. Eric. BA, U. Tex., El Paso, 1934; MS, Harvard U., 1935, PhD, 1939. Chemist E.I. du Pont Electrochem Dept., Niagara Falls, N.Y., 1939-44; tech. svc. mgr. Indsl. Tape div. Johnson & Johnson, New Brunswick, N.J., 1944-48; asst. tech. dir. Permacel div. Johnson & Johnson, New Brunswick, N.J., 1948-56, v.p., rsch. dir., 1956-60; dir. fiber and saturant Rsch. W.R. Grace & Co., Cambridge, Mass., 1960-65; v.p. Precision Tech. Products, Perth Amboy, N.J., 1965-75; owner H.M. Sonnichsen & Assocs., Hudson, Mass., 1975—. Fellow Am. Inst. Chemists; mem. Am. Chem. Soc., Assn. Rsch. Dirs. (assoc.), Tech. Assn. of the Pulp and Paper Industry, Sigma Xi, Alpha Chi Sigma. Republican. Home: 37 Robin Hood Rd Arlington MA 02174-1240 Office: H M Sonnichsen & Assocs 6 Loring St Hudson MA 01749-2394

SONTAG, PETER MICHAEL, travel management company executive; b. Vienna, Austria, Apr. 25, 1943; came to U.S., 1960; s. Otto Schiedeck and Maria Katharina (Schmidt) Cigalle; m. Eleanor Ann Alexander, Jan. 24, 1971; children: Alicia Alexandra, Julie Katherine. Diploma in hotel mgmt., Schule fuer Gastgewerbe, Vienna, 1960; BS magna cum laude, West Liberty State Coll., 1969, LLD, 1991; MBA, Columbia U., 1971. Steel worker Weirton (W.Va.) Steel Co., 1965-69; fin. analyst Citicorp, N.Y.C., 1970-71; ops. staff exec. ITT, N.Y.C., 1971-73; asst. v.p. Sun Life Ins. Co. Am., Balt., 1974-75; exec. v.p. Travel Guide, Inc., Balt., 1975-76; pres. Travelwhirl, Inc., Balt., 1976-78; founder Gelco Travel Services, Mpls., 1978-83; chmn., chief exec. officer Sontag, Annis & Assocs., Washington, 1983-86, US Travel Systems, Inc., Washington, 1986—; prin. CORVES Cons., Inc., Rockville, Md., 1983-86; pub. Travel Bus. Mgr., 1983-86; speaker in field, 1983—. With Austrian Air Force, 1963-64. Named one of Twenty Five Most Influential Execs. in Travel Industry Travel Bus. News, 1985, 87, 88, 89; named Delta Sigma Pi scholar. Mem. Alpha Phi Sigma, Delta Mu Delta (charter), Lakewood Country Club. Republican. Office: US Travel Systems Inc 1401 Rockville Pike Ste 300 Rockville MD 20852-1445

SOOHOO, TONY GLEN, patent examiner; b. Silver Spring, Md., July 18, 1965; s. Quong Dick and Oi Ching (Chow) S. BS in Aerospace Engring., U. Md., 1990. Computer specialist U. Md. Dept. Aerospace Engring., College Park, 1989-90; patent examiner U.S. Patent & Trademark Office, Washington, 1990—. Mem. AIAA. Home: 8457 Early Bud Way Laurel MD 20723-1085 Office: US Patent & Trademark Group 240 Arlington VA 22202

SOPPELSA, GEORGE NICHOLAS, artist; b. Youngstown, Ohio, July 16, 1939; s. Joseph and Rose (Gaiarsa) S. BFA, Ohio State U., 1961. One-man shows include Mulvane Art Ctr., Washburn U., Topeka, 1985, John Szoke Gallery, N.Y.C., 1989, Homer Babbidge Libr., U. Conn., Storrs, 1990, Inter Art Galerie Reich, Cologne, Germany, 1990, The Gallery, St. Mary's Coll. of Md., St. Mary's City, 1991; exhibited in group shows at John Szoke Gallery, N.Y.C., 1989, Art at 100 Pearl, Hartford, Conn., 1989, Butler Inst. Am. Art, Youngstown, Ohio, 1990; represented in permanent collections at Mulvane Art Ctr., Topeka. Fellow Nat. Endowment for Arts, 1987, Vt. Studio Colony, 1988; grantee Conn. Commn. on Arts, 1991. Office: Brairton & Tubbs Art Agts 135 Central Ave East Hartford CT 06108-3103

SORA, SEBASTIAN ANTONY, business machines manufacturing executive, educator; b. N.Y.C., June 29, 1943; s. Joseph Louis and Angelina Maria (Maletta) S.; m. Janet Lee Dietz, Apr. 11, 1970 (dec. July 1972); 1 child, Joseph Walter; m. Mary Frances Elizabeth Boscketti, Oct. 12, 1974; children: Joseph Walter, Sebastian Nicholas, Frances Ann, Jenny Concetta. BS, Bklyn. Coll., 1964; MBA, Iona Coll., 1974, PMC, 1976; DPS, Pace U., 1989. Math. modeller Assoc. Univs. Inc., 1964-66; with U.S. Coast and Geodetic Survey, Washington, 1967-70; mgr. programming IBM, Yorktown, N.Y., 1966-67, 70-75, programmer, modeller, 1970-72; mgr. program system and design IBM, Fishkill, N.Y., 1971-77; analyst on market models IBM, Harrison, N.Y., 1977-81; sr. programmer IBM, Boeblingen, Fed. Republic Germany, 1981-82; mgr. rsch. staff 1st Josephson system IBM, Yorktown, 1982-84; program dir. Systems Rsch. Inst. IBM, N.Y.C., 1984-87; mgr. edn. program World Trade Corp. IBM, North Tarrytown, N.Y., 1989-90; mgr. promotional-artificial intelligence systems IBM, White Plains, N.Y., 1990—; assoc. prof. MIS Montclair State Coll., Upper Montclair, N.J., 1992—; assoc. prof. info. sci. Pace U., White Plains, N.Y., 1977—; asst. prof. telecommunications Iona Coll., New Rochelle, N.Y., 1986; asst. prof. mgmt. Manhattan Coll., Bronx, N.Y., 1988; cons. AID, Washington, 1989. Editor Jour. Value Based Mgmt., 1987—; contbr. articles to profl. jours.; patentee fluxless solder, also others. Mem. IEEE (technol. leadership com. 1986—, info. policy com. 1986—), Data Processing Mgmt. Assn. Roman Catholic. Home: Christie Ct Somers NY 10589 Office: IBM Mktg and Svcs Hdqrs 1133 Westchester Ave White Plains NY 10604-3599

SORDILL, PATRICIA ANNE, management/organizational development consultant; b. Passaic, N.J., Aug. 1, 1954; d. Michael and Ella Marie (Patterson); m. Jeffrey Ruurd Kenyon, Feb. 24, 1990. BSBA, Boston, 1987, EdM, 1990. Sec. Schering Pharm., Bloomfield, N.J., 1973-77; human resources sec. Arthur Anderson, Boston, 1977-79; adminstrv. sec. WR Grace & Co., Lexington, Mass., 1979-81; area adminstr. Apple Computer, Marlboro, Mass., 1981-85; pres., founder Sordill Cons., North Chelmsford, Mass., 1985—. Mem. ASTD, Marlboro C. of C. (bd. dirs. 1985-86), Acton C. of C. (bd. dirs. 1986-89, pres. 1988-89). Office: Sordill Cons 257 Wellman Ave North Chelmsford MA 01863-1362

SORDILLO, WILLIE, musician, record producer; b. Passaic, N.J., May 2, 1951; s. Michael and Ella Marie (Patterson) Sordill; m. Jenny Allen, Mar. 16, 1991. BA in Edn., Coll. William and Mary, 1973; MEd, U. N.D., 1974. Cert. elem. tchr., Va., N.D., Ind. Elem. tchr. Learning Ctr., Ft. Wayne, Ind., 1974-76; English and a Second Lang. tchr. Casa del Sol, Alianza Hispana, Boston, 1988-90; solo musician Cambridge, Mass., 1977-84; musician Flor de Caña, Cambridge, Mass., 1984—. Co-producer: Dancing on the Wall, 1991 (Billboard Top 10, 1992); producer: Feeding the Flame, 1990; record producer various artists; composer, lyricist numerous songs. Organizer Arts for a New Nicaragua, Brookline, Mass., 1984-88. Recipient Best Latin Act award Boston Music Awards, 1990, 92. Mem. Broadcast Music Inc., Am. Fedn. of Musicians (new dealcom.). Home and Office: Folkstream Music BMI 106 Hamilton St 19 Peters St #1 Cambridge MA 02139

SOREF, RICHARD ALLAN, electrical engineering researcher; b. Milw., June 26, 1936; s. Bernard and Rosalie (Stein) S.; m. Alice Rosen, June 7, 1969. BSEE, U. Wis., 1958, MSEE, 1959; PhD, Stanford U., 1964. Mem. tech. staff MIT Lincoln Lab., Lexington, Mass., 1964-65, Sperry Rsch. Ctr., Sudbury, Mass., 1965-83; rsch. scientist USAF Rome Lab., Hanscom AFB, Mass., 1983—; mem. program com. for confs., 1968—. Mem. editorial bd. Optical Engring., 1984-86; author 2 book chpts., 1970-75; contbr. articles to profl. jours. Recipient Cert. of Merit Air Force Systems Command, 1987, Charles E. Ryan Meml. award Rome Air Devel. Ctr., 1988, USAF Basic Rsch. award, 1991. Mem. IEEE (sr. chmn. Boston chpt. electron devices group 1969), Am. Phys. Soc., Optical Soc. Am., Soc. Photo Optical Instrument Engrs., Tau Beta Pi, Eta Kappa Nu. Home: 45 Westgate Rd Newton MA 02159-3133 Office: Rome Lab RL/ERO Hanscom AFB MA 01731

SOREGELOOS, KEITH RAYMOND, sales and marketing executive; b. Grosse Pointe, Mich., Apr. 22, 1952; s. Constant and Irene Marie (Van Rossen) S.; divorced, Jan. 1992; children: Scott and Rachel. BS in Mgmt., Oakland U., 1981. Various positions Dayton-Hudson Corp., Detroit, 1973-80, textile buyer, 1981-82; account mgr. J.P. Stevens, Dallas, 1983-84; regional sales mgr. J.P. Stevens, Chgo., 1984-88; bus. mgr. J.P. Stevens, N.Y.C., 1988-89; v.p. new brand devel. West Point Pepperell, N.Y.C., 1990, v.p. sales and mktg., 1990—. Recipient People of the Yr. award Home Furnishings Daily, 1991.

SORENSEN, MEREDITH JEAN, educator; b. Penn Yan, N.Y., May 23, 1940; d. Kenneth Edwin and Mary (Raiman) S. BA, Ottawa (Kans.) U., 1962; MA, No. Mich. U., 1976; postgrad., New Zealand Whole Lang. Mentorship Program, Hamilton, summer 1989. Cert. elem. tchr., elem. sch. prin. Tchr. Rochester (N.Y.) City Schs., 1962-63, Penfield (N.Y.) Cen. Sch., 1963-67, Marion (N.Y.) Cen. Sch., 1967—. Vol. (correctional facility) Industry (N.Y.) Sch., 1970-83, vis. dir., 1982—; bd. dirs. Ottawa U., 1970-74; mem. N.Y. State Legis. Adv. Com., Albany, 1977—; bd. dirs. Fairport Apts. for sr. citizens, 1981-83; founder Swinging Singles Western Sq. Dance Club, Rochester, 1967. Named one of Outstanding Young Women Am., 1971. Mem. Am. Fed. Tchrs., N.Y. State United Tchrs., Marion Tchrs. Assn. (treas., chair legis. com. social and sunshine com., negotiations com.), N.Y. State Reading Assn., Genesee Valley Devel. Learining Group, Danish Sisterhood (Penn Yan), Phi Delta Kappa. American Baptist. Office: Marion Cen Sch 3863 N Main St Marion NY 14505-9579

SORENSEN, RAYMOND ANDREW, physics educator; b. Pitts., Feb. 27, 1931; s. Andrew J. and Dora (Thuesen) S.; m. Audrey Nickols, Apr. 2, 1953; 1 dau., Lisa Kirsten. B.S., Carnegie Inst. Tech., 1953, M.S., 1955, Ph.D., 1958. Mem. faculty Columbia, 1959-61; asst. prof. Carnegie-Mellon U., Pitts., 1961-65, assoc. prof., 1965-68; prof. physics Carnegie-Mellon U., 1968—, chmn. dept., 1980-89. NSF sr. postdoctoral fellow, 1965-66. Mem. Am. Phys. Soc. Home: 1235 Murdoch Rd Pittsburgh PA 15217-1234

SORGENTI, HAROLD ANDREW, petroleum and chemical company executive; b. Bklyn., May 28, 1934; s. Louis J. and Lucille (Sisti) S.; m. Ann Rusnack, June 30, 1962; children: Elizabeth, Lucille. B.S.Ch.E., CCNY, 1956; M.S., Ohio State U., 1959. Research engr. Battelle Meml. Inst., Columbus, Ohio, 1956-59; with Atlantic Richfield Co., 1959-91, v.p. research and engring., products div., 1975-76; sr. v.p. chem. devel. Arco Chem. Co. subs. Atlantic Richfield Co., Phila., 1977-79, pres., 1979-87, pres., CEO, 1987-90, vice chmn. bd., 1991; ptnr. Freedom Group Partnership, Phila., 1991—; bd. dirs. Provident Mut. Life Ins. Co., Core States Fin. Corp., Crown Cork & Seal, O'Brien Environ. Energy Co. Bd. dirs. Phila. Orch. Assn., Phila. Acad. Fine Arts. Mem. Am. Chem. Soc., Am. Inst. Chem. Engrs., Soc. Chem. Industry, Ohio State U. Alumni Assn., CCNY Alumni Assn., Union League. Office: Freedom Group Partnership 1735 Market St Ste 3905 Philadelphia PA 19103-7501

SORIANO, BEVERLY ANN, accounting educator; b. Boston, Apr. 25, 1952; d. Patrick and Carmella (D'Amore) S.; m. Jeffrey M. Shabes, Aug. 8, 1982. B Bus. Edn., Bryant Coll., 1973; M Bus. Edn., Boston U., 1975; M Accountancy, Bentley Coll., 1980. Acct. Alan H. Newman, CPA, Framingham, Mass., 1984-85; pvt. practice acctg. Waltham, Mass., 1984-86; instr. Newbury Coll., Boston, 1973-80; vis. asst. prof. McGill U., Montreal, Que., Can., 1980-82, Wilfred Laurier U., Waterloo, Ont., Can., 1982-84; asst. prof. accountancy Framingham State Coll., 1984—; instr. Am. Coll. in Paris, summer, 1979, 80; grad. asst. Boston U., 1974-75. Mem. Am. Acctg. Assn., Nat. Bus. Edn. Assn., Mass. Bus. Edn. Assn., Boston Computer Soc., New Eng. Bus. Edn. Assn., Delta Pi Epsilon. Office: Framingham State Coll 100 State St Framingham MA 01701-2471

SORIO, CESARE, shipping transportation executive; b. Legnano, Lombardy, Italy, Jan. 29, 1936; came to U.S., 1975; s. Achille and Camilla (Cornolo) S.; m. Margherita Grassi, Mar. 2, 1959; children: Daniela, Marco, Stefano, Paolo. BA, Italian Merchant Marine Acad., 1955; MBA, Northwestern U., 1981. Master sea going vessels. From deck boy to master various shipping cos., Italy, U.S., 1956-67; supr. constrn. Exxon Internat., N.Y.C., 1967-70; chief insp. Amoco Internat., Chgo., 1970-75, supr. design and constrn., 1976-81; gen. mgr. ops. Ultramar Shipping Co., Mount Kisco, N.Y., 1981-83; v.p. ops. Ultramar Shipping Co., Tarrytown, N.Y., 1983-90, sr. v.p. ops., 1990—. Mem. Soc. Naval Architects and Marine Engrs., Am. Bur. Shipping, Inst. Marine Engrs. (assoc.), Liberian Shipowners Coun. (bd. dirs. 1988—), Labour Com. (chmn. 1991), Lions Club (v.p. 1987, 91). Republican. Roman Catholic. Home: 6 Old Wagon Rd Mount Kisco NY 10549 Office: Ultramar Shipping Co Inc 120 White Plains Rd Tarrytown NY 10591-5522

SOROBAY, ROMAN TARAS, librarian; b. N.Y.C., Feb. 27, 1958; s. Taras and Maria (Ostapiak) S. BA in Phys. and Econ. Geography, CCNY, 1980; MA in Resource Mgmt. and Urban Planning, SUNY, Albany, 1982; MLS, Columbia U., 1984. Info. specialist E.M. Warburg, Pincus & Co., Inc., N.Y.C., 1984-88; libr. svc. mgr. Wasserstein Perella & Co., N.Y.C., 1988—. Recipient scholarship Columbia U., 1983-84. Mem. ALA, Am. Soc. for Info. Sci., Spl. Libr. Assn. Office: Wasserstein Perella & Co 31 W 52d St New York NY 10019

SOROKA, JOHN MICHAEL, manufacturing executive; b. N.Y.C., July 8, 1956; s. John and Irene Mary (Dzurko) S. BEngring., SUNY, Stony Brook, 1978, BA, 1978; MBA, Duke U., 1985. Product line adminstr. Hazeltine Corp., Greenlawn, N.Y., 1979-80; program engr. Gen. Electric Corp., Pittsfield, Mass., 1980-84; project engr. Sperry Corp./Unisys Corp., Great Neck, N.Y., 1985-87; program mgr. Miltope Corp., Melville, N.Y., 1987—; pres. bd. dirs. Fardale Owners, Farmingdale, N.Y., 1991—. Home: 22-6B Ivy St Farmingdale NY 11735 Office: Miltope Corp 1770 Walt Whitman Rd Melville NY 11747

SOROURI, PARVIZ, gastroenterologist; b. Tehran, Iran, Feb. 14, 1929; s. Mohammad and Malekeh (Edalat) S.; m. Sally Elaine Simounet, June 22, 1957; children: Bijan, Kayvan, Andria. AB, Temple U., 1951; MS, U. Pa., 1953; MD, George Washington U., 1957. Intern Charity Hosp., New Orleans, 1958; resident in internal medicine Henry Ford Hosp., Detroit, 1961; resident in gastroenterology U. Pa. Grad. Hosp., Phila., 1962; prof. medicine Nat. U., Tehran, Iran, 1962-79, chmn. dept. medicine, 1970-79, chief div. gastroenterology, 1972-79, vice chancellor, 1977-79, dean sch. medicine, 1978-79; practice medicine specializing in gastroenterology Newark, Del., 1979—; chmn. research com. Med. Ctr. of Del., Wilmington, 1982-86; chmn. program and library com. St. Francis Hosp., Wilmington, 1987—; adv. to Minister of Health, Tehran, 1970-78, to Prime Minister, 1970-78. Author: (book) Gastrointestinal Cancer, 1983. Felsen fellow, U. Pa., 1952. Fellow Backus Internat. Soc. Gastroenterology; mem. AMA. Republican. Moslem. Club: Hercules Country (Wilmington). Lodges: Lions, Rotary (Wilmington). Home: 900 Hillside Rd Wilmington DE 19807-2212 Office: Darwin Profl Ctr 10 Darwin Dr Newark DE 19711-6658

SORRENTINO, JOHN ANTHONY, economics educator, consultant; b. Bklyn., Sept. 1, 1948; s. John Anthony and Monica Denise (Bissonnette) S.; m. Margaret Mary Johnson, Oct. 11, 1969 (div. Jan. 1981); children: Rachel Denise, Demian Andrew; m. Judith Ann King, July 14, 1986. BBA, Baruch Coll.-CUNY, 1969; MS, Purdue U., 1971, PhD, 1973. Instr. Purdue Univ., Lafayette, Ind., 1969-72; asst. prof. econs. Temple Univ., Phila., 1973-79, assoc. prof. econs., 1979—; consultant, Glenside, Pa., 1986—. Contbr. chpts. to books and articles to profl. procs. and jours. Mem. energy task force Consumer Coun. Phila., 1975; v.p. dir. Citizens Comm. on Environ. Control, Cheltenham, Pa., 1975-77; lectr. Am. Youth Hostels, Phila., 1978; mem. Energy Edn. Adv. Coun., Phila. Electric Co., 1987—. Recipient traineeship NSF, Purdue Univ., 1971-72, summer fellowships Nat. Aero. and Space Adminstrn., Huntsville, Ala., 1975, Energy R&D Adminstrn., Washington, 1976, Dept. Energy, Livermore, Calif., 1984. Mem. Am. Econ. Assn., Assn. Environ. and Res. Economists, Internat. Soc. for Ecol. Econs., Earthright. Office: Temple Univ Ambler 580 Meetinghouse Rd Ambler PA 19002-3989

SORROWS, HOWARD EARLE, executive, physicist; b. Hewitt, Tex., Aug. 10, 1918; s. George Jefferson and Lillian Nora (Gregory) S.; m. Martha Jane Summerville, Dec. 10, 1943; children: Mary Margaret Hughes, Carolyn Clare Stump, Joyce Jean Jimerson, Lynne Louise Moon, Bryan Bruce. BA in Physics and Math., Baylor U., 1940; postgrad. in elec. engring., George Washington U., 1944, MA in Physics, 1948; PhD in Physics, Math. and Civil Engring., Cath. U. Am., 1958. Tchr. math. and physics Sabinal (Tex.) Pub. High Sch., 1940-41; electronic scientist Nat. Bureau Standards, Washington, 1941-52; missile engr. U.S. Bur. Ordnance, Washington, 1952-54; sci. adminstr. U.S. Office Naval Rsch., Washington, 1954-59; dir. long range planning, tech. intelligence, new product Tex. Instruments, Inc., Dallas, 1959-62, mgr. space and environ. sci., 1962-65; sr. exec. Nat Bur. Standards, Gaithersburg, Md., 1965-87; pvt. practice Potomac, Md., 1987-88; staff dir. NRC, Washington, 1988—; adv. com. elec. engring. and applied sci. U. Pa., Phila., 1977-82; mem. adv. coun. La. Sea Grant Coll., Baton Rouge, 1979, '92; bd. regents, 1988—; founding mem. La. Partnership for Tech. and Innovation, 1989—; instr. Ministry Fed. Sci. and Tech., Lagos, Nigeria, 1981; adj. prof. Am. U., Washington, 1984-8%; Dept. of Commerce nat. tour speaker technol. forecasting. Pres. Standards Alumni Assn., Gaithersburg, Md., 1989; charter chmn. Fed. Profl. Assn. Nat, Bur. Standards chpt. Gaithersburg, 1963. Recipient Superior Performance award Dept. Commerce, Washington, 1966, 67, 74, 79, 84, 85. Fellow Washington Acad. Sci.; mem. IEEE (sr. mem., chmn. Dallas-Ft. Worth chpt. 1963-64, Outstanding Contbn. award 1958), AAAS (program com. Nat. Conf. for Advancement Sci. 1985-87), Masons, Sigma Pi Sigma (sr. mem.), Sigma Xi (pres. Nat. Bur. Standards chpt., Outstanding Contbn. award 1988). Home: 8820 Maxwell Dr Rockville MD 20854-3122 Office: Nat Rsch Coun 2101 Constitution Ave NW Washington DC 20418-0001

SORTER, BRUCE WILBUR, human resources specialist, organization development educator, consultant; b. Willoughby, Ohio, Sept. 1, 1931; s. Wilbur David and margaret Louise (Palmer) S.; m. Martha Ann Weirich, Sept. 2, 1960 (div. 1967); 1 child, David Robert. BA, U. Md., 1967; MCP, Howard U., 1969; PhD, U. Md., 1972. Cert. community developer. Commd. USAF, 1967, advanced through grades to lt. col., 1964; sr. planner, cons. Md. Nat. Capital Park and Planning Com., Greenbelt, 1968-71; instr. psychology, sociology Howard and P.G. Community Coll., Columbia and Largo, Md., 1971-72; community resource devel. specialist Md. Coop. Extension Svc., U. Md., College Park, Md., 1972—; adminstrv. coord. Md. Coop. Extension Svc., U. Md., College Park, 1989—, coord. rural info. ctr., 1989—; affiliate prof. U. Md., 1985—; extension advisor USDA Internat. Programs, Washington, 1991—; co-author, co-dir. U.S. Dept. Edn. Coun. Effectiveness Tng. Program, 1979-81; author First County Energy Conservation Plan, Prince George's County, 1978-85; presenter in field of human rels. and planning, 1972—. Author, co-author 12 books; contbr. articles to profl. publs., chpts. to books. Author Community Devel. Programs, 1972-92; cons. Fed. Power Commn. U.S., 1973-75, State Dept. Natural Resources, Md., 1978-79, Dept. Edn., Brazil, 1981-82, Nat. Grange U.A., 1987, Edn. Ext. Svcs., Poland, 1991—. With USAFR, 1964-89. Urban Planning fellow Howard U., 1968, Human Devel. fellow U. Md., 1970; recipient Meritorious Svc. award Dept. Def., 1983, Disting. Community Svc. award Md. Community Resource Devel. Assn., 1983, Citation for Outstanding Svc., Ptnrs. of Am., 1983, Excellence in Ednl. Programs award Am. Express, 1984. Mem. Internat. Community Devel. Soc. (bd. dirs., Achievement award for Outstanding Contbn. to Community Devel. 1985, Disting. Svc. award 1990), Md. Community Resource Devel. Assn. (sec./treas. 1979, pres. 1980, 88, 89), Md. Extension Specialists' Assn. (sec. 1984), Epsilon Sigma Phi (awards com.). Republican. Methodist. Office: MCES CRD Univ Md Symons Hall College Park MD 20742

SOSA, ERNEST, philosopher, educator; b. Cardenas, Cuba, June 17, 1940; s. Ernesto and Maria (Garriga) S.; m. Sara Mercedes, Dec. 21, 1961; children: E. David, Adrian J. BA, U. Miami, 1961; MA, U. Pitts., 1962, PhD, 1964. Instr. U. Western Ontario, London, Ontario, Can., 1963-64, U. Pitts., 1964; postdoctoral fellow Brown U., Providence, 1964-66; asst. prof. U. Western Ontario, London, Ontario, 1966-67; asst. prof. to full prof. Brown U., Providence, 1967-74, chmn. of philosophy, 1970-76, full prof., 1974—, Romeo Elton prof., 1981—; vis. prof. U. Miami, 1970, Nat. U. Mexico, 1979, 80, 81, Harvard U., Cambridge, Mass., 1982. Author: Knowledge in Perspective, 1991; gen. editor book series, Cambridge Univ. Pres., 1990—, Blackwell Publishers, 1991—; contbr. numerous articles to profl. jours. Grantee NSF, 1970-72, Exxon Ednl. Found., 1980-82; recipient Sr. fellowship NEH, 1988-89. Mem. Am. Philos. Assn. (sec.-treas. 1977-84, chair internat. corp. com. 1984-89), Am. coun. Learned Socs./Soviet Acad. Commn., Internat. Fedn. Philos. Soc. (steering com. mem. 1988-89, v.p. 1988-93). Office: Brown U Providence RI 02912

SOSA, HORACIO ALEJANDRO, mechanical engineering educator; b. La Plata, Buenos Aires, Argentina, Oct. 4, 1954; came to U.S., 1981; s. Justo Pastor and Nelida Edith (Dapia) S. BSME, Nat. U., La Plata, 1979; MSME, Stanford U., 1983, PhD, 1986. Lectr. math. and rational mechanics Nat. U., 1975-80; rsch. scientist Naval Svc. R & D, Buenos Aires, 1980-81; rsch. asst. Stanford (Calif.) U., 1984-86, postdoctoral resident affiliate, 1986-87; asst. prof. Drexel U., Phila., 1987—; reviewer articles and books NSF, Prentice Hall and sci. jours., 1987—. Contbr. articles on applied mechanics to profl. jours. Advanced Studies fellow Nat. Coun. Atomic Energy of Argentina, 1981-84; NSF Initiation grantee, 1989—. Mem. ASME, AAUP, Am. Acad. Mechanics. Home: 2108 Pine St # 2F Philadelphia PA 19103-6514

SOSLOW, ARNOLD, quality consulting company specialist; b. Phila., Nov. 13, 1938; s. Samuel and Betty (Goldfine) S.; m. Frances Isen, May 15, 1960; children: Michael Allan, Beverly Ruth Soslow Warner. AS in Bus. Adminstrn., Temple U., 1974, BBA in Ind. Mgmt., 1976. Design draftman Unisys, Blue Bell, Pa., 1959-66; process control/quality specialist Gen. Electric Co., Phila., 1966-69; mgr. ops. B & F Instruments, Cornwells Heights, Pa., 1969-75; quality engr. Ronson Corp., Bridgewater, N.J., 1976-78; quality assurance mgr. Kooltronics Inc., Hopewell, N.J., 1978-83; quality mgr. Electro-Sci. Labs., King of Prussia, Pa., 1983-90; pres., quality advisor The Quality Mgmt. Co., Phila., 1988—. Mem. Am. Soc. for Quality Control, Internat. Electronic Package Soc., Internat. Soc. for Hybrid Microelectronics (program chmn. joint symposium 1987-89, pres. Keystone chpt. 1989, gen. chmn. joint sympoosium 1990-92), Surface Mt. Tech. Assn. Republican. Jewish. Home and Office: The Quality Mgmt Co 8844 Manchester Ave Philadelphia PA 19152-1515

SOSNOW, PETER LEWIS, emergency medicine educator; b. N.Y.C., Oct. 15, 1951; m. Jeanne Munson, Apr. 21, 1985; children: Sara, Emily, Molly. BA, Amherst Coll., 1973; MD, Tulane U., 1977. Diplomate Am. Bd. Emergency Medicine, Am. Bd. Internal Medicine. Dir. emergency svcs. Wing Meml Hosp., Palmer, Mass., 1982-90; asst. prof. Medicine U. Mass. Med. Sch., Worcester, 1982—; dir. emergency & outpatient svcs. Albany (N.Y.) Meml. Hosp., 1990—; adj. asst. prof. emergency medicine Albany Med. Coll., Albany, 1990—; pres. Capital Region Emergency Medicine, Albany, 1991—. Author (book chpts.) Electrical Injuries in the Clinical Practice of Emergency Medicine, 1991, The Hypochondriacal Patient, 1992. Fellow Am. Coll. Emergency Physicians (bd. dirs. 1986-90). Office: Albany Meml Hosp 600 Northern Blvd Albany NY 12204

SOSTILIO, ROBERT FRANCIS, office equipment marketing executive; b. Boston, Nov. 17, 1942; s. Natale J. and Louise (Caruso) S.; m. Gail Marie McGuinness, Apr. 17, 1966. Student, U. Maine, 1960-61, Broward Jr. Coll., Ft. Lauderdale, 1967-70, Miami-Dade Jr. Coll., 1979. Product assurance engr. Saxon Copystatics, Miami, Fla., 1970-77; internat. svc. mgr. Saxon Export Corp., Miami, 1977-80; nat. svc. mgr. Cybernet Internat., Warren, N.J., 1980-81; mgr. nat. copier svc. Monroe Systems for Bus., Morris Plains, N.J., 1981-82; nat. OEM mgr. Panasonic Indsl. Co., Secaucus, N.J., 1982-86; assoc. dir. copier rsch. Dataquest, San Jose, Calif., 1987-90; mgr. product program Ricoh Corp., West Caldwell, N.J., 1986-87, dir. copier mktg.,

1990—. Editor newsletter Multifunctionality, 1987, Color Copiers, 1989. Block capt. Meadow Ridge Civic Assn., Basking Ridge, N.J., 1985-87; sgt.-at-arms UNICO Nat., San Jose, 1990. With USN, 1964-67. Roman Catholic. Office: Ricoh Corp 5 Dedrick Pl West Caldwell NJ 07006

SOTERIADES, MICHAEL COSMAS, civil engineering educator; b. Istambul, Turkey, Mar. 25, 1923; came to U.S., 1952; s. Cosmas S. and Evouli (Tsaoussoglu) S.; m. Rose Marie Rentroia, Nov. 30, 1928. Civil engring. diploma, Athens (Greece) Nat. Tech. U., 1948, D Engring., 1952; ScD, MIT, 1954. Registered profl. civil engr. Research asst. MIT, Cambridge, 1953-54; asst. engr. A. Woolf & Assocs., Boston, 1952-56; chief structural engr. Universal Engring. Corp., Boston, 1956-58; v.p., treas. Doxiadis Assocs., Washington and Athens, 1958-61; prof. civil engring. Cath. U. Am., Washington, 1961-90, chmn. dept., 1975-81, prof. emeritus, 1991—. Author: (in Greek) Aseismic Design-Construction, 1956. 2d lt. Greek Army, 1948-52. Fellow ASCE; mem. Am. Concrete Inst., Sigma Xi, Tau Beta Kappa. Home: 3380 Stephenson Pl NW Washington DC 20015-2452 Office: Cath U Am Washington DC 20064

SOTO, ELAINE, psychologist, artist; b. N.Y.C., Nov. 16, 1947; d. Jose Angel Soto and Alicia Ramirez Tomasulo; m. Herman Delgado, Sept. 16, 1981. BS, Baruch Coll., 1972; MEd, Harvard U., 1973; PhD, NYU, 1979; postgrad., Sch. Visual Arts, 1981-89. Psychologist Alcoholism Clin. Harlem Hosp., N.Y.C., 1977-79; psychologist, supr. South Bronx (N.Y.) Mental Health Council, 1979-81; psychologist, counselor Counseling Ctr. Baruch Coll., N.Y.C., 1983—; pvt. practice N.Y.C., 1981—; cons. Children's Aid Soc., N.Y.C., Office of Vocat. Rehab., N.Y.C., Community Guidance Svc., Concerned Parents Inc., Bklyn., Youth Action Programs; cons., art therapy Foundling Hosp. Contbr. articles to profl. jours. Active art therapy groups and parent workshops. Mem. Am. Psychol. Assn., Am. Soc. Group Psychotherapy and Psychodrama, Women's Caucus for Art, Coast to Coast Nat. Women Artists of Color, Vistas Latinas, Gala. Office: 184 Lexington Ave New York NY 10016-6839 Studio: 121 E 106th St New York City NY 10029

SOUCY, KEVIN ALBERT, banker; b. Farmington, Maine, Jan. 15, 1955; s. Albert Ernest and Adeline Mae (Meader) S.; m. Linda Jean Dolloff, June 20, 1981; children: Andrew Kevin, Brice Patrick. BS, Bates Coll., 1977. Sales rep., agy. mgr. Met. Ins. Co., Augusta and Lewiston, Maine, 1977-81; trust devel. officer Depositors Co., Augusta, 1981-82, asst. v.p., pension trust officer, 1982-85; v.p., trust officer Indian Head Nat. Bank (name now Fleet Bank-N.H.), Keene, N.H., 1985—; Contbr. articles to newspaper. Bd. dirs. Monadnock Area Pastoral Counseling, Keene, 1987—; pres. Cedarcrest Found., Inc., 1991; trustee Havenwood-Heritage Heights of United Ch. of Christ; mem. N.H. Employee Benefits Coun. Mem. Connecticut Valley Estate Planning Coun., Rotary. Republican. Baptist. Home: 43 Evans Cir Keene NH 03431-5244 Office: Fleet Bank-NH 20 Central Sq Keene NH 03431

SOUERWINE, ANDREW HARRY, management consultant; b. Slatington, Pa., Feb. 29, 1924; s. Harry Wilbur and Katie (Anthony) S.; m. Jane Dorell Day, Aug. 27, 1949; children: David Anthony, Andrew Day. BA, Ursinus Coll., Collegeville, Pa., 1947; MA, U. Pa., 1948; PhD, U. Conn., 1954. Lic. psychologist, Conn. Asst. dept. psychology U. Pa., Phila., 1947-49; asst. prof., acting chmn. dept. psychology Trinity Coll., Hartford, Conn., 1949-58; dir. career planning and devel. Travelers Corp., Hartford, 1958-67; dir. MBA prog. U. Conn., Hartford, 1967-77; prof. mgmt. and orgn. U. Conn., 1971-84, prof. emeritus, 1984—; pres., owner Career Planning Svcs., Wethersfield, Conn., 1980—; adj. faculty U. Hartford, 1959-61, Hartford Coll. for Women, 1960-62, U. Conn., 1963-67; cons. in field. Author: Career Strategies, 1978; contbr. articles to profl. jours.; mem. editorial adv. bd. Staff Care Rev. jour., 1989-90, Am. Soc. for Tng. and Devel. Jour., 1983-91. Bd. dir. Ch. Homes, Inc., 1986-89, chmn. pers. com., 1986-89; mem. adv. bd. Elliott Berv Assocs., 1989-90; bd. dirs. United Way of Hartford, 1975-77, Rsch. Ctr. of New Eng., 1977, Bristol Brass Corp., 1978-83, Community Coun. Greater Hartford, 1977-80. With U.S. Army, 1943-46, ETO. Mem. Am. Psychol. Assn., Am. Soc. Tng. and Devel., Pi Gamma Mu, Alpha Psi Omega, Beta Gamma Sigma, Tau Kappa Alpha. Congregationalist. Home and Office: 265 Dale Rd Wethersfield CT 06109-3250

SOUHAM, GÉRARD, communications executive; b. Paris, May 30, 1928; s. Lucien and Mary-Françoise (Husson) S.; m. Eliane Meyrat, June 23, 1951; children: Glenn (dec.), Yan, Philip. Diploma, Am. Community Sch., Paris, 1948; cert., Ecole Commerciale de Paris. Chargé de mission State Dept., Europe, 1950-52; pub. info. officer Allied Air Forces NATO, Fontainebleau, 1953-55; chmn. bd., chief exec. officer J. Walter Thompson, Paris, 1955-75; v.p. J. Walter Thompson, N.Y.C., 1970-75; prin. SC3 Gerard Souham Group Communication Cos., Paris and Lausanne, Switzerland, 1975—, N.Y.C., 1979—; bd. dirs. Am. Overseas Meml. Author: Général Souham Comte de l'Empire, 1964, Impressions sur..., 1970, Souham, 1989, Sur les Champs de Bataille de la Révolution et de l'Empire, 1990. Mem. pvt. sector internat., pub. rels. coms. USIA, 1984; mem. world bd. govs. USO, Washington, 1984, bd. dirs. Paris coun., 1971, chmn. fundraising com., 1989—. Decorated Knight of Legion of Honor (France); Officer Order of Leopold (Belgium), Knight of Belgian Crown. Mem. Internat. Advt. Assn. (v.p. pub. svc., bd. dirs.), Pub. Relations News Adv. Bd., Internat. Inst. Strategic Studies London, France, USA (bd. dirs.), Am. Overseas Meml. Assn. (bd. dirs. 1988—). Roman Catholic. Clubs: HM Guards Polo (Windsor, Eng.) (life); Polo de Bagatelle (Paris); N.Y. Athletic; Yacht of Monaco. Office: Souham Group Comm 500 5th Ave New York NY 10109-0995

SOULE, DAVID CONDER, urban planning executive; b. Washington, Dec. 31, 1946; s. George H. and Jean (Conder) S.; m. Rita Annette Godbout, June 24, 1968; children: Richard, Joseph, Amy Jeanne. BA, Trinity Coll., Hartford, Conn., 1968; postgrad., So. Conn. U., 1971-73, Northeastern U., Boston, 1990. Caseworker Conn. Dept. Pub. Welfare, Hartford, 1968-69; planner Conn. Dept. Community Affairs, Hartford, 1969-71; dep., planning dir. Capitol Region Coun. Govts., Hartford, 1971-80; exec. dir. Nashua (N.H.) Regional Planning Commn., 1980-86, Met. Area Planning Coun., Boston, 1986—; cons. N.E. Consulting Svcs., Inc., Manchester, N.H., 1985-86. Recipient Regional Leadership award New Eng. Regional Coun., 1985. Mem. Am. Planners Assn. (bd. dirs. N.H. chpt. 1983-84, Mass. chpt. 1989-92), Internat. City Mgmt. Assn.

SOULE, JEFFREY LYN, urban planner, consultant; b. Watertown, N.Y., Apr. 8, 1953; s. Robert William and Melva (Howe) S. BA cum laude, Colgate U., 1975; M in City and Regional Planning, Harvard U., 1978. Sr. resource planner N.Y. State Commn. on Tug Hill, Watertown, 1978-80; rural devel. specialist USDA, 1980-82; policy analyst office of rural devel. USDA, Washington, 1982-84, policy coord., 1984-86, employee devel. specialist, spl. projects mgr., 1986-87; dir., leadership coord. Ctr. for Rural Pa./Nat. Endowment Arts Design Div., Washington, 1987-92; phys. planning coord. Park Heights Community Corp., Balt., 1986-87; leader Planner Cert. Tng. Program, Washington, 1986; mem. faculty Mayor's Inst. for City Design, Washington, 1989; program dir. Your Town: Designing It's Future, 1990—; lectr. on urban design. Contbg. author: Design Competitions for Public Facilities, 1989; contbr. articles to profl. jours. Camp counselor, bd. dirs. United Meth. Ch. No. N.Y. Conf., 1974-80; alumni rep. Colgate U., 1976—; mem. Sandy Creek (N.Y.) Regional Planning Bd., 1978-80; mem. organizing com. Mid-Atlantic Planning Conf., Washington and Md., 1985, 87, 88. N.Y. State Regents scholar, 1971. Mem. Am. Inst. Cert. Planners, Am. Planning Assn. (profl. devel. officer Md. chpt. 1986-88, exec. bd., program com. chair 1990—), Beta Theta Pi (v.p. Balt. chpt.), Lambda Alpha. Office: Ctr for Rural Pa 212 Locust St Ste 408 Harrisburg PA 17101

SOURES, JOHN M., physicist, researcher; b. Galatz, Romania, Jan. 2, 1943; came to U.S., 1954; s. Michael Ioannis and Dia (Petrakis) S.; m. Diana Carrousos, June 29, 1969; children: Mandy M., Nicholas J., Eleni C., Alexander J., Sophia A. BS in Physics, U. Rochester, 1965, PhD in Mech. and Aerospace Scis., 1970. Rsch. assoc. Lab. for Laser Energetics, Rochester, N.Y., 1970-72, sr. scientist, 1972—, group leader, 1976-81, div. dir., 1979—, deputy dir., 1983—; cons. Oak Ridge (Tenn.) Nat. Lab., 1970-71, Lawrence Livermore (Calif.) Nat. Lab., 1988-90. Contbr. articles to profl. jours. Treas. Greek Orthodox Ch. of Annunciation, Rochester, 1990—. NASA trainee, 1967-69. Mem. Am. Physical Soc. (conf. chmn. 1986), Optical Soc. Am. (conf. organizer 1984-86). Republican. Orthodox. Home: 146 E Brook Rd Pittsford NY 14534 Office: Lab for Laser Energetics 250 E River Rd Rochester NY 14623

SOUSA, AUGUSTINE PEDRO, JR., paint company official; b. Providence, Aug. 2, 1949; s. Augustine Pedro and Lauretta V. (St. Laurent) S.; m. Elizabeth L. McCarthy, July 29, 1967 (div. 1975); children: Laurie, Dawn, Augustine Pedro III, Lisa Jean, Lisa Ann, Jennifer, Lori, Emilie, Katherine; m. Natalie Deady, Mar. 1, 1975 (div. Oct. 1981); m. Lorraine Ann Munroe, Oct. 13, 1989. Yacht paint foreman, marine coatings application insp. New Eng., Middletown, R.I.; AWL-Grip painter New Eng. Boat Works, 1991—. With U.S. Army, 1968-74, Vietnam. Decorated Bronze Star with oak leaf cluster; Cross of Gallantry (Vietnam). Roman Catholic. Home: 11 Pleasant St Bristol RI 02809-2108 Office: New Eng Boast Bend Boat Basin Middletown RI 02864

SOUSA, IRENE HELEN, guidance counselor; b. Somerville, Mass., Sept. 29, 1948; d. Clyde Johnson and Helen Mary (Roberts) Frost; m. Frank Ernest Sousa, Feb. 27, 1970; 1 child, Amy Christine. AS in Acctg., Newbury Coll., Boston, 1981; BS in Mgmt., Daniel Webster Coll., 1985; MEd in Counseling, Rivier Coll., 1988; PhD in Edn., Walden U., Mpls., 1991. Nat. cert. counselor; N.H. cert. guidance counselor. Fin. and acctg. staff Army Corp of Engrs., Waltham, Mass., 1968-73; adminstrv. asst. Wang Labs., Lowell, Mass., 1974-77; counselor Middlesex Regional Treatment Ctr., Waltham, Mass., 1983-84; credit specialist Allied Instrumentation Lab., Andover, Mass., 1985-86; guidance counselor Londonderry (N.H.) Sch. Dist., 1986-89; therapist/dir. Positive Pathways Counseling Svcs., Inc., Windham, N.H., 1988-89; guidance counselor Timberlane Sch. Dist., Sandown, N.H., 1989—. Mem. ASCD, Assn. for Counselor Edn. and Supervision, N.H. Assn. for Counseling and Devel., N.H. Sch. Counselors Assn. (inter-professions rels. chair 1990-91). Home: 9 Bowman Ln Pelham NH 03076 Office: Sandown Cen Sch 295 Main St Sandown NH 03873

SOUSA, JOAN ANN, elementary education educator; b. Providence, June 21, 1949; d. John Joseph and Jennie Evelyn (Colaluca) Cardi; m. John David Sousa, Nov. 18, 1973; children: Jonathan David, Darren Jerard. BA magna cum laude, Roger Williams Coll., 1971; MEd, Providence Coll., 1982; postgrad., Nova U., 1986—. Elem. tchr. Bristol (R.I.) Pub. Schs., 1971-80, coord. gifted and talented edn., 1980-87; prin. elem. East Greenwich (R.I.) Pub. Schs., 1987—; mem. adv. coun. young women in sci. R.I. State Dept. Edn., chair commr.'s adv. coun. on gifted and talented edn. City of Providence, 1983—, joint com. on sch./coll. articulation, Providence, 1983-86; cons. Ponnagansett Schs., 1986, Johnston (R.I.) Pub. Schs., 1989. Co-author: Characteristics and Identification of Gifted and Talented Students, 3d edit., 1988, Curriculum Design and Development for Gifted and Talented Students, 3d edit., 1988. Tour guide, vol. Women and Infants Hosp., Providence, 1987—; bd. trustees C.C.R.I., Warwick; judge Acad. Decathlon of R.I., 1985—; mem. edn. adv. com. Roger Williams Coll., 1990—; active Roger Williams Coll. Found., 1991—. Mem. Nat. Assn. Elem. Sch. Prins., R.I. Assn. Sch. Prins., State Advocates for Gifted Edn. (v.p. 1983-85). Roman Catholic. Home: 151 Catlin Ave Rumford RI 02916-2331 Office: East Greenwich Pub Schs Hanaford Sch 5 Lebaron Dr East Greenwich RI 02818-3031

SOUSER, ROSLYN COSKERY, plastic and reconstructive surgeon; b. Phila., Mar. 27, 1939; children: Kenneth, Eugene C. AB, Duke U., 1961; MD, Woman's Med. Coll. Pa., 1966; student, U. Munich, 1959-60. Lic. physician, Pa.; diplomate Nat. Bd. Med. Examiners, Am. Bd. Surgery, Am. Bd. Plastic Surgery. Intern in surgery Bryn Mawr (Pa.) Hosp., 1967-71, VA Hosp., Wilmington, Del., 1969-70; resident in plastic surgery Temple U. Hosp., 1971-72, Hosp. of U. Pa., 1972-73; pvt. practice West Chester, Pa., 1973—; sr. attending in plastic and reconstrv. surgery Bryn Mawr Hosp.; active staff Chester County Hosp., West Chester, Mercy-Haverford Hosp., Havertown, Pa.; instr. surgery U. Pa. Plastic Surgery Div., Phila.; lectr. in field. Contbr. numerous articles to profl. jours. Former bd. trustees Harcum Jr. Coll., Bryn Mawr, 1987-88. Fellow ACS, AMA, Coll. Physicians Phila.; mem. Montgomery County Med. Soc., Pa. Med. Soc., Am. Med. Women's Assn. (past chpt. pres.), Women's Med. Coll. Pa. Alumnae Assn. (sec. to exec. bd. 1975-76), Robert H. Ivy Soc., Am. Soc. Plastic and Reconstructive Surgeons, Am. Assn. for Hand Surgery, AAUW, Northeastern Soc. Plastic Surgeons (founding mem.), Internat. Soc. Clin. Plastic Surgeons. Home: 44 Haverford Rd Ardmore PA 19003-1021 Office: Westtown Bus Ctr 1558 Mcdaniel Dr West Chester PA 19380-7007

SOUTER, DAVID HACKETT, U.S. Supreme Court justice; b. Melrose, Mass., Sept. 17, 1939; s. Joseph Alexander and Helen Adams (Hackett) S. BA, Harvard U., 1961, LLB, 1966; Rhodes scholar, Oxford U., 1961-63, MA, 1989. Bar: N.H. Assoc. firm Orr & Reno, Concord, 1966-68; asst. atty. gen. N.H., 1968-71, dep. atty. gen., 1971-76, atty. gen., 1976-78; assoc. justice Superior Ct. N.H., 1978-83, N.H. Supreme Ct., 1983-90; judge U.S. Ct. Appeals (1st cir.) N.H., 1990; assoc. justice U.S. Supreme Ct., Washington, 1990—. Trustee Concord Hosp., 1973-85, pres. bd. trustees, 1978-84; bd. overseers Dartmouth Med. Sch., 1981-87. Mem. Am. Bar Assn., N.H. Bar Assn., N.H. Hist. Soc. (v.p. 1980-85, trustee 1976-85), Phi Beta Kappa. Republican. Episcopalian.

SOUTH, HUGH MILES, engineering executive; b. Houston, Nov. 10, 1947; s. Hugh Wilson and Lala (Miles) S.; m. Marilyn Maude Morrell, Oct. 1, 1976. BA in Elec. Engring., Rice U., 1971; PhD in Elec. Engring., Johns Hopkins U., 1981. Sr. engr. Johns Hopkins Applied Physics Lab., Laurel, Md., 1976-83; prin. engr. Johns Hopkins Applied Physics Lab., 1983—, supr. signal processing, 1985—, mgr. surveillance automation projects, 1991—; mem. edit. bd. APL Tech. Review, Laurel, 1989—. Contbr. articles to profl. jours. Mem. Acoustical Soc. Am., Inst. Electrical Electronics Engrs., Signal Processing Soc. (Underwater Acoustics Tech. Com.), European Assn. Signal Processing, Sigma Xi. Office: Applied Physics Lab Johns Hopkins Rd Laurel MD 20723-1140

SOUTHAM, CHESTER MILTON, physician; b. Salem, Mass., Oct. 4, 1919; s. Walter Aloysius and Elizabeth Effie (Furbish) S.; m. Anna Lenore Skow, Sept. 24, 1939 (div.); children: Lawrence Albert, Lenore Elizabeth, Arthur Milton; m. Gertrude Elizabeth Lundin, June 9, 1973. BS, U. Idaho, 1941, MS, 1943; MD, Columbia U., 1947. Intern Presbyn. Hosp., N.Y.C., 1947-48; rsch. fellow to full mem., chief divsn. virology/immunology Sloan-Kettering Inst. Cancer Rsch., N.Y.C., 1948-71; from clin. fellow to attending physician Meml. Hosp. for Cancer, N.Y.C., 1948-71; from instr. to assoc. prof. medicine Cornell U. Med. Ctr., N.Y.C., 1951-71; head Div. Med. Oncology Thomas Jefferson U. Med. Coll., Phila., 1971-79, prof. medicine, 1971—; attending physician Dept. Medicine Thomas Jefferson U. Hosp., Phila., 1971—. Contbr. articles to profl. jours. Trustee Leopold Shepp Found., N.Y.C., 1961-67, Strang Clinic and Preventive Medicine Inst., N.Y.C., 1963-68; adv. com. on rsch. and therapy cancer Am. Cancer Soc., N.Y.C., 1961-66; sci. adv. com. Damon Runyon Fund, N.Y.C., 1961-68; com. virology and immunology Internat. Union Against Cancer, Geneva, 1966-90; adv. com. tobacco and health rsch. AMA Edn. and Rsch. Found., Chgo., 1965-66; bd. dirs. Am. Assn. Cancer Rsch., 1966-70, pres., 1968-69. Capt. U.S. Army, 1953-55. Mem. Am. Soc. Clin. Oncologists. Home: 3705 Darby Rd Bryn Mawr PA 19010 Office: Thomas Jefferson Univ Hosp 111 S 11th St Ste G4110 Philadelphia PA 19107

SOUTHARD, DAVID GORDON, federal agency administrator; b. Burlington, Vt., Jan. 2, 1941; s. Guy Wendell and Iva Mae (Hull) S.; m. Elaine Florence Twiss, Feb. 22, 1964; children: David G. Jr., James Patrick, Sheryl Lyn. BA in Psychology, U. Vt., 1970; adv. mgmt. program, U. Va., 1972; postgrad., Am. U., 1981, Chapman U., 1990—. Cert. mgr., 1987. Mgmt. intern U.S. Postal Svc., Boston and Phil., 1970-73; asst. postmaster U.S. Postal Svc., Syracuse, N.Y., 1973-74; acting postmaster U.S. Postal Svc., Utica, N.Y., 1974-75; dir., fin. U.S. Postal Svc., Syracuse, 1975—; acting postmaster U.S. Postal Service, Arlington, Va., 1982, Oswego, N.Y., 1988-89. Moderator United Ch. of Christ in Bayberry, Liverpool, N.Y., 1989; mem. advocacy bd. Ctr. on Human Policy, Syracuse U., 1979—; bd. dirs. Syracuse Habitat for Humanity, 1988-90. Mem. Internat. Mgmt. Coun. (Cen. N.Y. chpt. pres. 1979-80, Excellence award, 1980), Postal Employee Toastmasters (pres. 1990), Bayberry Community Assn., Syracuse Toastmasters (pres. 1980). United Ch. of Christ. Home: 132 Riverdale Rd Liverpool NY 13090-2843 Office: US Postal Svc 5640 E Taft Rd Syracuse NY 13220-9998

SOUTHARD, PAUL RAYMOND, financial executive; b. Albany, N.Y., May 15, 1948; s. Harold G. and Frances L. (Shaylor) S.; BS, Rochester Inst. Tech., 1970. CPA, N.Y. Staff acct., Haskins & Sells, CPA's, Rochester, N.Y., 1969-70; sr. acct. Maurice F. Sammons & Co., CPAs, Rochester, 1970-73; fin. mgr. Radionics, Inc., Webster, N.Y., 1973-82, contr., 1982-87, Kitchen Concepts. Co., Fairport, N.Y., 1987-88, Spectra Svcs., Inc., Rochester, N.Y., 1989—. Mem. N.Y. State Soc. CPAs, Rochester C. of C. (mem. small bus. council), Indsl. Mgmt. Council Rochester. Lodge: Kiwanis. Home: 1096 Everwild Vw Webster NY 14580-8740 Office: Spectra Svcs Inc 1628 Dewey Ave Rochester NY 14615-3496

SOUTHERN, ARLEN DUANE, public relations executive; b. Liberal, Kans., Apr. 11, 1933; s. N. Leo and Lydia S.; student Panhandle State Coll., 1951-53; BA in Journalism, U. Okla., 1956, postgrad. in pub. rels. and advt., 1956; m. Beth Louise Rapp, Sept. 22, 1956; children: Randal David, Stanford Leo. With AP, Oklahoma City, 1954-56; editorial asst. Thompson Products, Cleve., 1956-57; mgr. communications Tapco Group, Cleve., 1959-63; asst. dir. pub. rels. and advt. TRW Inc., Cleve., 1964-68, dir. pub. rels. and advt., 1968-72; v.p. corp. affairs IU Internat. Corp., Phila., 1972-82; chmn. Shaeffer & Southern, Phila., 1982-83; pres. The Arlen Southern Co., Wayne and West Chester, Pa., 1983—; past officer, dir. Nat. Investor Rels. Inst., Washington; dir., past pres. Investor Rels. Assn., N.Y.C. Bd. dirs. Eastern Pa. Hugh O'Brian Youth Found. Served with U.S. Army, 1957-59. Named one of three most respected pub. rels. execs. in nationwide study, 1978; recipient Best-of-Industry award for corp. fin. advt., 1971, 72. Mem. Pub. Relations Soc. Am., Sigma Delta Chi, Omicron Delta Kappa. Republican. Writer, speaker profl., ednl., indsl. orgns. Home: 407 Chickadee Ln Westtown Twp West Chester PA 19382 Office: 407 Chickadee Ln West Chester PA 19382-7615

SOUTHWELL, WILLIAM JOSEPH, artist; b. Phila., Jan. 14, 1914; s. William Henry and Ellen Maria (Nolan) S.; m. Janet Keys Landy, Sept. 22, 1945; children: Richard Christopher, Michael Landy, William Joseph Jr. Student, Pa. Acad. Fine Arts, 1933-37; BFA, U. Pa., 1940, MA in Art, 1941; postgrad., Frudakis Acad. Sculptor, 1986-88. Visual artist Phila., 1946-52, 65-68; art dir. Smith Kline French Labs., Phila., 1952-57, Wyeth Pharm., Radnor, Pa., 1957-65; prof., art Northampton Coll., Bethlehem, Pa., 1968-74; instr. Art Inst. Phila., 1974-84. Executed murals Stockton (N.J.) Inn; represented in permanent collections Merkel Collection, Wanamaker, Pa., Hornberger Collection, Doylestown, Pa. Bd. dirs. Pa. Acad. Fine Arts Fellowship, 1989-91. With USN, 1943-46. Home: 1855 Edgehill Rd Abington PA 19001-1303

SOUTHWORTH, HAMILTON, internist, educator, consultant; b. N.Y.C., Apr. 7, 1907; s. Thomas Shepard and Jean Hamilton (Jene) S.; m. Katherine Jones, June 29, 1933; children: Hamilton, Jean, Thomas, Katharine. BA, Yale U., 1929; MD, Johns Hopkins U., 1933. Cert. internal medicine. Med. intern Presbyn. Hosp., N.Y.C., 1934-35, attending physician, 1960-72; asst. resident Johns Hopkins Hosp., Balt., 1936-37; from asst. prof. to prof. clin. medicine Presbyn. Hosp.-Coll. Physicians & Surgeons Columbia U., N.Y.C., 1952-72, emeritus prof., 1972—; cons. N.Y.C., 1972—; dir. Equitable Life Assurance Soc., 1973-79. Editor: two books on internal medicine; contbr. articles to profl. jours. Elder Madison Ave. Presbyn. Ch., N.Y.C., 1938-78; trustee Am. U. Beirut, 1967—; v.p. Concern for Dying. Lt. Col. USPHS, 1942-45. Named to Order Cedars Govt. of Lebanon, 1971. Mem. AMA, Am. Bd. Internal Medicine (examining bd. 1964-70, exec. com.), Am. Clin. & Climatological Assn. (v.p. 1969). Home: 200 E 66 St New York NY 10021

SOUTHWORTH, HORTON COE, education scholar; b. Monroe, Mich., Apr. 2, 1926; s. Frederick Osgood and Bertha Southworth; m. Jannene MacIntyre, Apr. 1971; children: Sueann, Nancy, Jim, Janet, Jaye, Bradford, Alexandra. BS, Mich. State U., East Lansing, 1950, MA, 1953, EdD, 1962. Cert. K-8 tchr., elem. prin., Mich. Mid. sch. tchr. Bellevue (Mich.) Pub. Schs., 1950-51, elem. prin., 1951-53, supervising prin., 1953-55; elem. prin. Pontiac (Mich.) Pub. Schs., 1955-59; coord. Macomb Tchr. Ctr. Mich. State U., Warren, 1959-67, asst. prof., 1962-64, assoc. prof., 1964-67; prof. edn., chmn. dept. U. Pitts., 1967-91; scholar-in-residence Duquesne U., Pitts., 1990—, cons., 1991-92; cons. Pa. Dept. Edn., Harrisburg, 1968-91; treas. Learning Tree Assocs. Pitts., 1974—. Chmn. Three Rivers dist. Boy Scouts Am., Pitts., 1980-90; pres. Univ. Childrens Sch., California, Pa., 1988—, mem. adv. coun. grad. program in Pa., Nova U., Harrisburg, 1989—. With USNR, 1944-46, PTO. Recipient Chancellor's Disting. Tchr. award U. Pitts., 1988, Prof. Emeritus award, 1991. Mem. ASCD, Assn. Tchrs. Educators (33 Yr. Mem. award 1991), Pa. Assn. Colls. and Tchr. Educators (exec. bd. 1985-91), Masons (life), Kappa Delta Pi (5 Yr. Chpt. Counselor award 1989), Phi Delta Kappa (25 Yr. Mem. award 1985), Theta Chi. Democrat. Presbyterian. Home: 619 S Linden Ave Pittsburgh PA 15208-2812 Office: Learning Tree Corp Penn West Bldg Pittsburgh PA 15221

SOVERN, MICHAEL IRA, university president, law educator; b. N.Y.C., Dec. 1, 1931; s. Julius and Lillian (Arnstein) S.; m. Lenore Goodman, Feb. 21, 1952 (div. Apr. 1963); children: Jeffrey Austin, Eilzabeth Ann, Douglas Todd; m. Eleanor Leen, Aug. 25, 1963 (div. Feb. 1974); 1 dau., Julie Danielle; m. Joan Wit, Mar. 9, 1974. AB summa cum laude, Columbia U., 1953, LLB (James Ordronaux prize), 1955, LLD (hon.), 1980, PhD (hon.), Tel Aviv U., 1982; LLD (hon.), U. So. Calif., 1989. Bar: N.Y. 1956, U.S. Supreme Ct. 1976. Asst. prof., then assoc. prof. law U. Minn. Law Sch., 1955-58; mem. faculty Columbia Law Sch., 1957—, prof. law, 1960—, Chancellor Kent prof., 1977—, dean Law Sch., 1970-79; chmn. exec. com. faculty Columbia U., 1968-69, provost, exec. v.p., 1979-80, univ. pres., 1980—; research dir. Legal Restraints on Racial Discrimination in Employment, Twentieth Century Fund, 1962-66; spl. counsel N.Y. State Joint Legis. Com. Indsl. and Labor Conditions, 1962-63; spl. counsel to gov. N.J., 1974-77; cons. Time mag., 1965-80; dir. Chem. Bank, AT&T, GNY Ins. Group., Orion Pictures Corp.; mem. N.J. Bd. Mediation Panel of Arbitrators; mem. panel arbitrators Fed. Mediation and Conciliation Service; bd. dirs. Asian Cultural Council, Shubert Orgn., Shubert Found., NAACP Legal Def. Fund; chmn. N.Y.C. Charter Revision Commn., 1982-83; co-chmn. 2d Circuit Commn. on Reduction of Burdens and Costs in Civil Litigation, 1977-80; chmn. Commn. on Integrity in Govt., 1986. Author: Legal Restraints on Racial Discrimination in Employment, 1966, Law and Poverty, 1969. Mem. Pulitzer Prize bd., 1980—, chmn. pro tem, 1986-87; pres. Italian Acad. for Advanced Studies in Am. Commendatore in the Order of Merit of the Republic of Italy, 1991. Fellow Am. Acad. Arts and Scis.; mem. ABA, Coun. Fgn. Rels., Assn. Bar City N.Y., Am. Arbitration Assn. (panel arbitrators), Am. Law Inst., Econ. Club, Nat. Acad. Arbitrators. Office: Columbia U 202 Low Libr New York NY 10027

SPACE, THEODORE MAXWELL, lawyer; b. Binghamton, N.Y., Apr. 3, 1938; s. Maxwell Evans and Dorothy Marie (Boone) S.; m. Susan Shultz, Aug. 18, 1962 (div. Apr. 1979); children: William Schuyler, Susanna; m. Martha Collins, Apr. 6, 1991. AB, Harvard U., 1960; LLB, Yale U., 1966. Bar: Conn., 1966. Assoc. Shipman & Goodwin, Hartford, Conn., 1966-71, ptnr., 1971—, mng. ptnr., 1984-87, adminstv. ptnr., 1988-91. Mem. Bloomfield (Conn.) Bd. Edn., 1973-85, chmn., 1975-85; treas. Citizens Scholarship Found., Bloomfield, 1971-73, bd. dirs., 1973-91; mem. Bloomfield Human Rels. Commn., 1973-75; mem. Bloomfield Town Dem. Com., 1976-83; corporator Hartford Pub. Libr., 1976—; libr. com. Conn. Hist. Soc., 1990—. Lt. (j.g.) USNR, 1960-63. Mem. ABA, Conn. Bar Assn. (exec. com. adminstrv. law sect. 1980—), Hartford County Bar Assn., Am. Law Inst., Nat. Health Lawyers Assn., Conn. Health Lawyers Assn., Swift's Inn, Hartford Club. Unitarian Universalist. Home: 59 Prospect St Bloomfield CT 06002-3038 Office: Shipman & Goodwin 1 American Row Hartford CT 06103-2833

SPAEDER, ROGER CAMPBELL, lawyer; b. Cleve., Dec. 20, 1943; s. Ferd N. and Luceil (Campbell) S.; m. Frances DeSales Sutherland, Sept. 7, 1968; children: Michael, Matthew. BS, Bowling Green U., 1965; JD with honors, George Washington U., 1970. Bar: D.C. 1971, U.S. Dist. Ct. D.C. 1971, U.S. Ct. Appeals (D.C. cir.) 1971, U.S. Supreme Ct. 1976, U.S. Ct. Claims 1979, U.S. Dist. Ct. Md. 1984, U.S. Ct. Appeals (2d and 4th cirs.) 1985. Asst. U.S. atty. D.C., Washington, 1971-76; ptnr. Zuckerman, Spaeder, Goldstein, Taylor & Kolker, Washington, 1976—; faculty Atty. Gen. Advocacy Inst., 1974-76, Nat. Inst. Trial Adv., 1978-79; adj. faculty Georgetown U. Law Ctr., 1979-80, Am. U. Ctr. Adminstrn. Justice, 1976-79; lectr. D.C. Bar Continuing Legal Edn. Programs, 1980—. Recipient Spl. Achievement

award Dept. Justice, 1971. Mem. ABA (co-chair com. on complex crimes litigation 1989—), Bar Assn. D.C. (lectr. Criminal Practice Inst. 1977-80), D.C. Bar (com. criminal jury instrns. 1972, div. courts, lawyers, adminstrn. of justice, 1976-78; adv. com. continuing legal edn. 1986), Def. Rsch. Inst., Assn. Trial Lawyers Am., Assn. Plaintiffs' Trial Attys., Nat. Assn. Criminal Def. Lawyers, Omicron Delta Kappa. Contbr. articles to profl. jours. and chpts. to books. Home: 7624 Georgetown Pike Mc Lean VA 22102-1412 Office: Zuckerman Spaeder Goldstein Taylor & Kolker 1201 Connecticut Ave NW 12th Fl Washington DC 20036

SPAETH, JAMES THOMAS, financial manager, controller; b. Neptune, N.J., Aug. 13, 1943; s. Edgar Vincent and Helen Louise (Schultz) S.; m. Eileen Patricia Donoghue, Sept. 10, 1966; children: Michael, Jennifer, Kevin. AB, Seton Hall U., 1965; MBA, Columbia U., 1967. Asst. contr. Alexander Inc., N.Y.C., 1967-76; v.p. Youth Centre Inc., Bloomfield, Conn., 1976-84; contr. Allied Stores Inc., N.y.C., 1984-88; asst. contr. Brooks Bros. Inc., N.y.C., 1988-91; contr. Met. Mus. Art, N.y.C., 1991—; instr. New Sch. Social Rsch., N.Y.C., 1977-79. Mem. Met. Retail Fin. Execs. Assn. Republican. Roman Catholic.

SPAETH, OTTO LUCIAN, JR. (TONY SPAETH), product and corporate identity consultant; b. St. Louis, Feb. 6, 1934; s. Otto Lucian and Eloise (O'Mara) S.; m. Ann Barringer, Apr. 18, 1960; children: Cahterine W., Jennifer M., Bridget B., Crispin C. BA, Princeton U., 1955; MBA, Harvard U., 1963. Identity cons. Lippincott & Margulies, N.Y.C., 1964-66; product mgr. Am. Home Products, N.Y.C., 1966-69; pres. Controlled Brand Mktg., N.Y.C., 1969-75; v.p. N.W. Ayer, N.Y.C., 1975-79, Citicorp, N.Y.C., 1979-84; prin. Anspach Grossman Portugal, N.Y.C., 1985-90, Identity, Rye, N.Y., 1990—; cons. The New Eng., Boston, 1990—, McGraw Hill/Primis, N.Y.C., 1990, Pfizer, Inc., N.Y.C., 1991—, Eastman Chem. Co., 1992—, Raytheon, 1992—. Contbr. articles to profl. jours. Recipient Cert. Excellence, Fed. Design Coun., 1975. Mem. Am. Inst. Graphic Arts (Cert. Excellence, 1972, com. mem., 1991—). Office: Identity 6 Kirby Ln N Rye NY 10580-4208

SPAGNA, ARNOLD JOSEPH, insurance company executive; b. N.Y.C., Jan. 5, 1952; s. Donato and Angelina (Ripollone) S.; children: Jill Marie, Gregory. BA, NYU, 1974. Lic. ins. broker, N.Y. Systems analyst Marsh & McLennan, Inc., N.Y.C., 1970-73, exec. compensation analyst, 1974-78, ins. rep., 1978-82, asst. v.p., 1980-89, v.p., sr. v.p., mng. dir., 1989—. Mem. Nat. Rep. Congrl. Com., Washington, 1981—. Mem. Am. Mgmt. Assn., Bus. Coun. of N.Y. State. Roman Catholic. Office: Marsh & McLennan Inc 1166 Ave Of The Americas New York NY 10036-2708

SPAGNA, RICHARD LEO, electrical engineer; b. Flushing, N.Y., Apr. 23, 1956; s. Leo Peter and Irene Theresa (Hubbs) S.; m. Lorraine Margaret Susino, May 4, 1980; children: Meghann Theresa, Patrick Thomas. SUNY, Farmingdale, 1976; BSEE, Rochester Inst. Tech., 1979; MSEE, Syracuse U., 1987. Elec. engr. IBM, Hopewell Junction, N.Y. Mem. Tau Beta Pi. Home: 27 Gold Rd Poughkeepsie NY 12603 Office: IBM Rte 52 Zip 3A1 Hopewell Junction NY 12599

SPAGNOLI, GINA GAIL, academic administrator, musicologist; b. Carbondale, Ill., Aug. 28, 1954; d. Joseph and Charlotte (Raubach) S. BME, Mich. State U., 1976, MA, 1979; PhD, Washington U., St. Louis, 1987. Dir. publs. St. Louis Symphony Orch., 1987-88; dir. grant support New England Conservatory, Boston, 1989-90; dir. found. and govt. rels. Carnegie Hall, N.Y.C., 1990-91; dir. Spencer fellowships, dir. devel. Woodrow Wilson Nat. Fellowship Found., Princeton, N.J., 1991-92; dir. spl. gifts Rider Coll. and Westminster Choir Coll., Lawrenceville, N.J., 1992—. Author: The Letters and Documents of Heinrich Schütz, 1656-1672: An Annotated Translation, 1990. Nussbaum fellow Washington U., 1984, Internat. Rsch. and Exchs. Bd. fellow, 1984, Deutscher Akademischer Austauschdienst fellow, 1984. Mem. Internat. Heinrich Schütz Soc. (newsletter editor 1985-87), Am. Mus. Soc. Home: 1 Halstead Pl Princeton NJ 08540-6320

SPAGNUOLA, FRANCIS MICHAEL, interior designer; b. Phila., Nov. 2, 1940; s. Michael and Marie (Vicchiarelli) S.; m. Janet Adelle Moretti, Nov. 23, 1963; children: Stephen, Carrie. BA, Phila. Coll. Art, 1972. Interior designer Rittenhouse Carpets, Phila., 1972-73, Sears, Roebuck & Co., Moorestown, N.J., 1973-76; pvt. practice interior design Phila., 1976—. Mem. Am. Soc. Interior Designers (bd.dirs. 1982-86), Nat. Trust Hist. Preservation (assoc. design), Sons Italy. Home: 2429 Locust St Apt 511 Philadelphia PA 19103-5559 Office: Locust Point 25th and Locust Philadelphia PA 19103

SPAHR, GREGORY GENE, educational coordinator, fencing coach; b. Apr. 7, 1955. BA in Music Theory, Indiana State U., Terre Haute, 1977; MA in Music History, Indiana State U., 1981; MS in Coll. Personnel, Indiana U., 1988. Lic. fencing instr., Ind. Area coord. Towson State U., Md., 1988—; fencing coach Goucher Coll., Towson, 1988—; internat. student adviser Peabody Inst., Johns Hopkins U., 1986-88. Mem. Nat. Assn. of Foreign Student Advisors, Am. Coll. Personnel Assn., U.S. Fencing Assn. (Md. chairperson 1989-91), U.S. Fencing Coaches Assn. Home: Towson State Univ Towson MD 21204

SPAK, GALE TENEN, college dean; b. Bklyn., Aug. 23, 1946; d. Alan R. and Florence (Hilsen) Tenen; m. Mark A. Spak, June 2, 1974; 1 child, Renya Starling. BA in Polit. Sci., CUNY, 1968; MPh in Polit. Sci., Yale U., 1971, PhD in Polit. Psychology, 1976. Dep. dir. Ctr. for Energy Policy and Rsch. N.Y. Inst. of Tech., Old Westbury, 1976-89, dean M.S. Energy Mgmt. degree program, 1982-87, dir. Ctr. for Energy Policy and Rsch., 1990—, dean Sch. Profl. and Continuing Edn., 1987—. Contbr. articles to profl. jours. Mem. Assn. of Energy Engrs. (Corp. Energy Mgr. award 1991), Assn. of Continuing Higher Edn., Phi Beta Kappa. Office: NY Inst Tech Old Westbury NY 11568

SPALDING, ROBERT GEORGE, manufacturing executive; b. Burton-on-Trent, Stafford, Eng., May 7, 1923; came to U.S., 1976; s. William and Mary Margaret (Cunningham) S.; m. Dorinne Patricia Christian, Dec. 20, 1944 (div. Oct. 1976); children: Ian Nicholas, Robert Neil; m. Diane Jane Harwood, Dec. 13, 1976; children: Julian, Zoe. BSME, Derby (Eng.) Coll. of Tech., 1944. Chartered engr., Eng. Tech. asst. Rolls Royce Ltd., Hucknall, Eng., 1944-46; asst. engr. Wayne Tank & Pump Co., Ltd., London, 1946-53, asst. chief engr., 1953-58; chief engr. Wayne Tank & Pump Co., Ltd., Bracknell, Eng., 1958-69; mng. dir. Wayne Tank & Pump Co Ltd. and Dresser Mfg., Bracknell, 1969-73; tech. dir. Dresser Industries Petroleum Equipment Group, Bracknell, 1973-76; v.p., tech. dir. Dresser Industries Petroleum Equipment Group, Houston, 1976-84, Dresser Industries, Wayne Ops., Salisbury, Md., 1984—; Bd. dirs. Wayne (West Africa) Ltd., Lagos, Nigeria, 1987—. Inventor: holds 14 Brit. and U.S. patents liquid fuel metering, dispensing and control, 1955-75; contbr. articles to profl. jours. Bd. dirs. Petrol Pump Mfrs. Assn., London, England, 1968-73, Bracknell Tech. Coll., 1968-75. Fellow Inst. Mech. Engrs.; mem. Greenhill Yacht and Country Club, Salisbury Kennel Club (treas. 1988-92, pres. 1992—), Mastiff Club Am., Mastiff Assn. England. Episcopalian. Home: 609 Fountain Rd Salisbury MD 21801-6703 Office: Dresser Industries Inc PO Box 1859 Salisbury MD 21802-1859

SPALTEHOLZ, ROBERT WILLIAM, real estate development executive; b. N.Y.C., Dec. 28, 1945; s. William P. and Edna (Cossens) S.; divorced; 1 child, Aimée L. BA, Bloomfield Coll., 1968. Acct., ops. foods div. The Connell Co., Westfield, N.J., 1970-81, mgr. real estate div., 1981-83; v.p., officer Connell Realty & Devel. Co., Westfield, N.J., 1983—. With U.S. Army, 1969-70, Vietnam. Lutheran. Home: 1123 Plainfield Ave Berkeley Heights NJ 07922 Office: The Connell Co 45 Cardinal Dr Westfield NJ 07090-1099

SPANDORF, LILY GABRIELLA, artist; b. Vienna, Austria; came to U.S., 1960; Student, Acad. Fine and Applied Arts, Vienna, hon. degree; student, St. Martin's Sch. Art, London. Contbg. artist Evening Star, Washington, Washington Post, Christian Sci. Monitor, Uptown Citizen, also others; speaker on slides of her paintings to various groups and schs. One-woman show Nat. Mus. Women in Arts, Washington, 1988, numerous others; exhibited in numerous group shows, London, Vienna, Rome, Palermo, Cagliari, Italy, Washington, N.Y.C., Pitts., Phila., Palm Beach, Fla.; participant D.C. Bicentennial Exhbn. in Mayor's Office-Gallery, 1991; author: Lily Spandorf's Washington Never More; subject of documentary A View from the Street--The Art of Lily Spandorf. Mem. Washington Water Color Assn. (hon.), Artists Equity Assn., Am. Art League, Internat. Platform Assn., Nat. Press Club, Am. News Women's Club, Arts Club of Washington (hon.). Home and Studio: 1603 19th St NW Washington DC 20009

SPANGLER, ARTHUR STEPHENSON, JR., mental health facility administrator; b. Boston, June 20, 1949; s. Arthur Stephenson and Barbara Louise (Fellows) S.; m. Deborah A. Kauders, Nov. 27, 1971; children—Heather Anita, Rebecca Haley. BS, Hobart Coll., 1971; MEd, Boston Coll., 1974; ScD, Boston U., 1985. Diplomate Am. Acad. Pain Mgmt.; bd. cert. counselor; lic. psychologist, Mass.; lic. clin. social worker, Mass. Mass. Counselor Met. State Hosp., Waltham, Mass., 1971-73; with J.T. Berry Rehab. Ctr., North Reading, Mass., 1974-75; program coord. Shore Collaborative, Medford, Mass., 1975-76; dir. instl. sch. programs So. Shore Collaborative, North Weymouth, Mass., 1976-79; dir. mental retardation program South Shore Mental Health Ctr., Quincy, Mass., 1979-85; coord. outpatient clinic Boston Pain Ctr., Spaulding Rehab. Hosp., Quincy, Mass., 1985-86; v.p., dir. behavioral medicine svcs. Mass. Bay Counseling, Quincy, Mass., 1985—; dir. indsl. disability mgmt. svcs., psychologist chronic pain program Miriam Hosp., Providence, Mass., 1987-88; pres. N.E. Indsl. Rehab. Assocs., Weston, Mass., 1988—; dir. functional restoration and pain ctr. Lake Shore Hosp., Manchester, N.H., 1989; adj. prof. Sargent Coll., Boston U., 1990—. Vol. counselor Multi-Svc. Ctr., Newton, Mass., 1973-75; bd. dirs. Newton-Wellesley-Weston-Needham Community Mental Health and Mental Retardation Ctr., Newton, 1976-80, pres. 1979-80; mem. Boston Symphony Assn. Vols. Recipient award Nat. Assn. Retarded Citizens, 1974. Mem. Am. Psychol. Assn. (assoc.), Nat. Rehab. Assn., Am. Assn. for Counseling and Devel., Coun. for Exceptional Children, Assn. for the Study of Pain, Soc. Behavioral Medicine, New Eng. Pain Assn. Episcopalian. Home: 88 Church St Weston MA 02193-2042 Office: 44 Billings Rd Quincy MA 02171

SPANGLER, MILLER BRANT, science and technology analyst, planner, consultant; b. Stoyestown, Pa., Sept. 1, 1923; s. Elbert Bruce and Raye Isabel (Brant) S.; m. Claire Labin Kussart, Sept. 20, 1947; children: Daryl Claire, Philip Miller, Coreen Sue. BS with honors, Carnegie-Mellon U., 1950; MA, U. Chgo., 1953, PhD, 1956. Chem. engr. Gulf Rsch. Corp., Harmarville, Pa., 1950-51; assoc. engr. rsch. corp. IBM, Yorktown Heights, N.Y., 1956-60; mgr., market rsch. fed. systems div. IBM, Rockville, Md., 1960-63; program economist U.S. Agy. for Internat. Devel., Turkey, India, 1963-66; dir. ctr. for techno-econ. studies Nat. Planning Assn., Washington, 1966-72; chief, cost benefit analysis br. U.S. Atomic Energy Commn., Washington, 1972-75; spl. asst. policy devel. U.S. Nuclear Regulatory Commn., Washington, 1975-89; pres. Techno-Planning, Inc., Bethesda, Md., 1989—; mem. adv. bd. NSF Sea Grant Program, Washington, 1969, Environ. Profl. Jour., L.A., 1981-88. Author: New Technology and the Supply of Petroleum, 1956, New Technology and Marine Resource Development, 1970, The Role of Research and Development in Water Resources Planning, 1972, U.S. Experience in Environmental Cost-Benefit Analysis, 1980; contbr. numerous articles and papers to profl. jours. Recipient Planning Rsch. award Program Edn. and Rsch. in Planning U. Chgo., 1953. Mem. N.Y. Acad. Scis., Am. Assn. for the Advancement Sci., Nat. Assn. Environ. Profls., Soc. for Risk Analysis, Internat. Assn. for Impact Assessment., Tau Beta Pi. Republican. Methodist. Home: 9115 Mcdonald Dr Bethesda MD 20817-1941

SPANGLER, RONALD LEROY, television executive, aircraft distributor; b. York, Pa., Mar. 5, 1937; s. Ivan L. and Sevilla (Senft) S.; children: Kathleen, Ronald, Beth Anne. Student U. Miami (Fla.), 1955-59. Radio announcer Sta. WSBA, York, 1955-57; TV producer-dir. Sta. WBAL-TV, Balt., 1959-65; pres., chmn. bd. LewRon Television, N.Y.C., 1965-74; now pres., chmn. bd. Spanair Inc., distbr. Rockwell Comdr. aircraft; owner Prancing Horse Farm. Mem. Video Tape Producers Assn. N.Y., Rolls Royce Owners Club, Ferrari Clubs Am. Avocation: racing Ferrari automobiles, collecting and dealing in vintage Ferrari automobiles. Home: 1210 E Macphail Rd Bel Air MD 21015-5666

SPANO, JOHN JOSEPH, journalist, public relations executive; b. N.Y.C., Sept. 10, 1919; s. John and Anna Spano; m. Lois Dorothy Heisinger, 1947; children: Martha Harris, John Joseph Jr., Susan. BJ, U. Mo., 1947; MA, Webster U., 1976. Reporter New Orleans States, 1947-50; reporter St. Louis Star-Times, 1950-51, Houston Press, 1951-53; asst. city editor St. Louis Globe-Democrat, 1953-59; div. dir. pub. relations/advt. Monsanto Co., St. Louis, 1959-85; chief Washington bur. St. Louis Globe-Democrat, 1986—; bd. dirs. St. Luke's House, Bethesda, md., 1988—. Author: Writing for the Press, 1969. Dir. Webster Groves (Mo.) Bd. Edn., 1970-76; mem. devel. adv. com. Montgomery County, Md., 1987-91. Lt. USNR, 1942-46, ETO. Mem. Pub. Relations Soc. Am. (pres. St. Louis chpt. 1974, accredited pub. relations, plaque, citation 1974), Soc. Profl. Journalists SDX, Nat. Press Club (chmn. freedom of the press com. 1988). Episcopalian. Home: 10700 Pine Haven Ter North Bethesda MD 20852-3441

SPANO, RINA GANGEMI, sociology educator; b. Jersey City, Aug. 22, 1948; d. Joseph and Rose (Calabria) Gangemi; m. Domenico Spano, Sept. 12, 1971; children: Elisabeth, Cristina. BA, Caldwell Coll., 1970; MA in Teaching, Montclair State Coll., 1975, MA in Sociology, 1982; PhD in Sociology, CUNY, 1991. Cert. tchr. English grades K-12, N.J. Tchr. St. Cecilia's Sch., Kearny, N.J., 1972-77; instr. sociology Caldwell (N.J.) Coll., 1979-82, asst. prof., 1982-92, assoc. prof., 1992—, chmn. dept., 1979—; presenter in field. Mem. West Caldwell (N.J.) Homeowners Assn.; vol. N.J. Div. on Aging Meals on Wheels, East Orange, N.J., 1987—. Mem. Am. Sociol. Assn., Ea. Sociol. Soc., N.J. Sociol. Soc., Nat. Orgn. Italian-Am. Women, Delta Epsilon Sigma, Kappa Gamma Pi, Pi Delta Epsilon. Roman Catholic. Home: 173 Forest Ave West Caldwell NJ 07006-7964 Office: Caldwell Coll Dept Sociol 9 Ryerson Ave Caldwell NJ 07006-6195

SPANOS, ELIAS, construction company executive; b. Athens, Greece, June 10, 1948; s. Dimitris and Maria S.; m. Anastasia Galiatsatos, Jan. 14, 1979; children: Dimitris, Petros, Marilia. PhD in Engring., Tech. U. Athens, Greece, 1974; MSC in Econs., Athens U., Greece, 1982. With project group Archirodom Constrn. Co., Athens, and Jeddah, Saudi Arabia, 1974-78, from purchasing mgr. to project mgr., 1978-84; project mgr. Middle East office Goulds Pumps, Athens, 1985-86; v.p. ops., engring. Goulds Pumps Worldwide, Ins., Seneca Falls, N.Y., 1987—. Author purchasing manual for constrn. cos., 1983. Mem. Soc. for Mktg. Profl. Svcs., Purchasing Inst. Greece. Greek Orthodox. Office: Goulds Pumps Worldwide Inc 240 Fall St Seneca Falls NY 13148

SPARACIO, ANNMARIE, training administrative manager. BS, Fashion Inst. of Tech., N.Y.C., 1986. Tng. adminstrv. mgr. Clarins USA Inc, N.Y.C. Mem. Meeting Planners Internat. Office: Clarins USA Inc 135 E 57th St New York NY 10022-2050

SPARK, MICHELLE, artist; b. Phila., July 25, 1951; d. Isadore and Geraldine (Milgram) S. BA, Carnegie Mellon U., 1973; BFA, U. Pa., 1975; MFA, Queens Coll., 1978; MA, NYU, 1981. Sr. creative arts therapist, supervising clinician St. Lukes-Roosevelt Hosp., N.Y.C., 1984—; prof. art therapy dept. NYU, 1984—; sr. supr., pvt. practice, N.Y.C., 1986—; art therapist, pvt. practice, N.Y.C., 1989—. One man shows include Ellen Sragow Gallery, N.Y.C., 1986, Susan Schreiber Gallery, N.Y.C., 1990, Va. Ctr. for Creative Arts, 1989, Carol Getz Gallery, Coconut Grove, 1989, 90, Windows, N.Y.C., 1991; exhibited in group shows at Lintas World Wide, N.Y.C., 1990, Traveling Group Show, Mpls., 1990-91. Mem. Am. Art Therapy Assn. (profl. mem.), Zen Mtn. Monastery.

SPARKOWSKI, EDWARD FRANK, financial executive; b. New Britian, Conn., Aug. 15, 1955; s. James Edmund and Elizabeth Rose (Ierna) S.; m. L. Maija Earl, May 28, 1989. BS, Bates Coll., 1979. Cert. fin. planner. Supr., mgr. Ayerst Labs, Inc., Rouses Point, N.Y., 1979-86; fin. counselor CIGNA Individual Fin. Svcs., Albany, N.Y., 1986-87; sales rep. to v.p. to co-owner Diversified Individual Brokerage Co., Glastonbury, Conn., 1987-90; v.p., co-founder Conn. Group Brokerage Corp., Glastonbury, 1989-90; pres., chief exec. officer Benefits Planning, Inc., Glastonbury, 1990—, also bd. dirs.; pres., chief exec. officer Benefits Planning, Inc., Syracuse, 1990—. Ranked top 100 in USA skiing, 1970's. Mem. Mason (master) Mensa. Republican. Office: Benefits Planning Inc 18 Westridge Dr Simsbury CT 06070-2916

SPARKS, LAURA JEAN, registration manager; b. N.Y.C., Aug. 16, 1962; d. William Henry and June Irma (Morrison) S.; m. Raymond Richard Rinfred, May 6, 1989. BS in Econs. and Bus., SUNY, Stony Brook, 1984. Registration mgr., asst. v.p. Oppenheimer & Co., Inc., N.Y.C., 1984—. Mem. Assn. Registration Mgmt. Office: Oppenheimer & Co Inc Oppenheimer Tower World Fin Ctr New York NY 10281

SPARKS-MACDIARMADA RUA, CASANDRA SESSA, educator; b. Detroit, May 25; d. George Russell and Mildred Anna (Christen) Sparks; m. Cormac Joseph Sean Sparks-MacDiarmadarua, Aug. 24, 1987. BS in Edn., Russell Sage Coll., 1965, MEd, 1980; CAS, SUNY, Albany, 1981; cert. in performing arts, Westham House, England, 1966. Cert. tchr., N.Y. Elem. tchr. Green Island, N.Y., 1966-76; adult reading educator Troy, N.Y., 1980-82; hist. researcher Albany, 1986-92; owner Sparks Svcs., Albany, 1980—. Contbr. articles and poems to jours. Office: Sparks Svcs PO Box 872 Troy NY 12181

SPATARO, FRANCIS CAJETAN, priest; b. N.Y.C., Feb. 5, 1936; s. Francis Anthony and Gilda (DeSimon) S.; m. Bokeeta Craft, Aug. 1, 1968; children: Francesca, Peter. MA, NYU, 1971; MS, St. John's U., 1984; Licentiate in Theology, Peoples' U., San Juan, 1976; DD, St. Ephrem's Inst., Solna, Sweden, 1982. Ordained priest Am. Orthodox Ch., 1976. Tchr. Oakland Acad., New Windsor, N.Y., 1962-65, John Adams High Sch., Ozone Park, N.Y., 1965-76; dir. The Vilatte Guild, Bellerose, L.I., 1976-85; priest Holy Orthodox Ch. in Am., Kingston, N.Y., 1985—; ednl. counselor The Remey Soc., Jamaica, N.Y., 1979-85. Author: Charles Mason Remey and the Bahai Faith, 1987; editor The Independent Catholic, 1976-85, The Remey Letter, 1979—. Mem. United Fedn. of Tchrs., N.Y., 1962-76, Knights of St. John of Jerusalem, Pa., 1980, Ind. Ednl. Cons. Assn., Mass., 1992. With U.S. Army, 1959-62. Named Knight of St. Volodimer Am. World Patrianchates, 1976; recipient 3d Prize for Poetry World Order of Narrative Poets, 1980. Mem. Soc. of Rosicrucians (treas. 1989—). Democrat.

SPATER-ZIMMERMAN, SUSAN, psychiatrist, educator; b. Brookline, Mass.; m. Seth Allan Zimmerman, Apr. 29, 1984. BA, U. Rochester, 1977; premed. cert., Columbia U., 1979; MD, Albert Einstein Coll. Medicine, 1983. Diplomate Nat. Bd. Med. Examiners. Intern in internal medicine Greenwich (Conn.) Hosp.-Yale U., 1983-84; resident in psychiatry N.Y. Med. Coll.-Westchester County Med. Ctr., Valhalla, 1984-87; pvt. practice, Garden City, N.Y., 1990-91, Manhasset, N.Y., 1991—; psychiatrist Madonna Heights Svcs. Residential Treatment Facility, Dix Hills, N.Y., 1990; cons., med. dir. outpatient svcs. Seafield Ctr., Mineola, N.Y., 1991—; mem. provisional attending staff North Shore Univ. Hosp.-Cornell U. Med. Coll. Manhasset, 1991—; clin. instr. psychiatry Cornell U. Med. Coll., N.Y.C., 1991—. Mem. Am. Psychiatr. Assn., Am. Med. Womens Assn. Office: Community Drive Med Ctr 444 Community Dr Ste 208 Manhasset NY 11030-3889

SPATT, ROBERT EDWARD, lawyer; b. Bklyn., Mar. 26, 1956; s. Milton E. and Blanche S. (Bakstansky) S.; m. Lisa B. Malkin, Aug. 11, 1979; 1 child, Mark Eric. AB, Brown U., 1977; JD magna cum laude, U. Mich., 1980. Bar: N.Y. 1981. Assoc. Simpson Thacher & Bartlett, N.Y.C., 1980-87, ptnr., 1987—. Mem. ABA, N.Y. State Bar Assn., Order of Coif, ACLU. Home: 286 West Trl Stamford CT 06903-2402 Office: Simpson Thacher & Bartlett 425 Lexington Ave New York NY 10017-3903

SPAULDING, MALCOLM L., ocean engineering educator; s. Marshall and Dorothy S.; divorced; 1 child, Allegra. BS in ME and Applied Mechanics, U. R.I., 1969, PhD in Engring. and Applied Mechanics, 1972; MSME, MIT, 1970. Registered profl. engr., R.I. Asst. prof. ocean engring. U. R.I., Kingston, 1973-77, assoc. prof., 1977-83, prof., 1983—; founder, project mgr. Applied Sci. Assocs., Narragansett, R.I., 1979—; founder, pres. Spaulding Environ. Assocs., Inc., Wakefield, R.I., 1991—; mem. phys. oceanogrpahy panel to review minerals mgmt. svc. environ. studies program, NRC, 1987-89. Contbr. articles to profl. jours. Apptd. to Mumford Cove Restoration com. by U.S. Dist. Ct., Conn. Environ. rsch. fellow NASA and Am. Soc. Engring. and Edn., 1974, 75; rsch. fellow Oak Ridge (Tenn.) Nat. Lab., 1978; sr. scientist vis. fellow Continental Shelf Inst., 1982-83. Mem. AAAS, ASME, ASCE, Am. Geophys. Union, Marine Tech. Soc., R.I. Soc. Profl. Engring., Sigma Xi, Pi Tau Sigma, Tau Beta Pi, Phi Kappa Phi. Office: U Rhode Island 208 Lippitt Hall Kingston RI 02881

SPAULDING, ROMEO ORLANDO, executive; b. Whiteville, N.C., Aug. 27, 1940; s. Ralph and Sarah (George) S.; m. Annette Richardson, Jan. 23, 1962; children: Valerie G., Bernardine E., Alva G., Karen R., Kevin R. Student, Howard U., 1962, U. Washington, 1970, U. Md., 1981. Procurement officer Columbia Hosp. Women, Washington, 1959-65; dir. community rels. Washington Fire & Emergency Svcs. Dept., 1965—; pres. Internat. Assn. Black Profl. Firefighters, Washington, 1988—; exec. mem. bd. dirs. Nat. Black Leadership Roundtable, Washington, 1981-90. Recipient Community Svc. award, Washington Govt., 1986, 87, Congressional commendation U.S. Congress, Washington, 1985; named Firefighter of Yr., Firehouse Mag., 1989, Nat. Sch. Vol. of Yr., 1989, Christian Man of Yr., Bethel Bible Ch., Camp Springs, Md., 1989. Baptist. Office: IABPFF 1025 Connecticut Ave NW # 610 Washington DC 20036

SPAULDING, SETH JOSEPH, education educator; b. Tucson, Dec. 17, 1928; s. Howard E. and Josephyne Seth (Harris) S.; m. Stephanie Granston Richards, Aug. 15, 1962; 1 child, Justin Seth. BA, U. Americas, Mex., 1948; MA, Ohio State U., 1950, PhD, 1953. Program specialist Orgn. Am. States, Washington, 1950-53; sr. advisor Ford Found., N.Y.C., 1953-60; chief of rsch. Title VII U.S. Office Edn., Washington, 1960-63; prof., dir. internat. programs U. Pitts., 1963-68, 73-83; dir. dept. of sch. & higher edn. UNESCO, Paris, 1968-73; dir. Internat. Bur. Edn., Geneva, Switzerland, 1983-86; prof. adminstrv. & policy studies U. Pitts., 1986—; cons. UN Develop. Program, N.Y.C., World Bank, Washington, Agy. for Internat. Devel., Washington, UNESCO, Paris, Govts. and Univs. Author: The World's Students in the US., 1977, Non-Formal Education in Tanzania, 1991, Research on Higher Education in Developing Countries, 1991, The Education System of Mongolia, 1992; contbr. articles to profl. jours. Bd. dirs. UN Assn. Pitts., World Federalists Pitts.; bd. trustees Am. U. of Paris, 1970-81. Mem. Am. Ednl. Rsch. Assn. (bd. dirs. internat. spl. interest group 1987—), Comparative & Internat. Edn. Soc. (chair edn. for all panels 1991), World Congress of Comparative Edn. (chair commn. on edn. and devel. 1992). Office: U Pitts Sch of Edn 5S38 Forbes Quad Pittsburgh PA 15260

SPAULDING, WILLIAM ROWE, investment consultant; b. Cambridge, Mass., Nov. 26, 1915; s. William Rowe and Jennie Jane (Gillam) S.; m. Gertrude Ellen Mowry, June 7, 1947; children: Edward Albert, William Mathews. BS, U. N.H., 1938; MBA, Harvard U., 1940. Trader Kidder Peabody & Co., N.Y.C., 1940-41; asst. exec. v.p. Mut. Savs. Cen. Fund, Inc., Boston, 1946-58; v.p. Vance Sanders & Co., Boston, 1959-63; trustee Century Shares Trust, Boston, 1963-71, mng. trustee, chmn., 1969-71; chmn. bd., chief exec. officer Wakefield Savs. Bank (Mass.), 1971-81, trustee, 1959-84; ind. dir., trustee Fidelity Group of Mut. Funds, Boston, 1972-87, active emeritus, 1988-89; ret., 1989; dir. Mass. Congl. Fund., 1970—. Trustee Melrose-Wakefield Hosp., 1973-84, Lakeside Cemetery, Wakefield, 1973—; dir., v.p. fin. com. Citizens Scholarship Found. Wakefield, 1962—; mem. nat. adv. bd. Citizens' Scholarship Fund. Am., 1989—; mem. fin. com., mem. ho. of dels. Mass. Easter Seal Soc., v.i.p. telethon, 1990—; trustee Laudholm Farm Trust, Wells Nat. Estuarine Rsch. Res., 1983—; exec. vol. Internat. Exec. Svc. Corps, Kingston, Jamaica, 1989; mem. Wakefield Hist. Commn., 1984-86. With AUS, 1942-45, MTO, ETO, lt. col. Mass. N.G., 1946-62. Decorated Bronze Star; Croix de Guerre (Belgium); named to Eagle Scout Boy Scouts Am., 1928. Mem. Pres.'s Coun. U. N.H., Fin. Analysts Fedn., Assn. Investment and Rsch., Boston Soc. Fin. Analysts Mgmt., Phi Kappa Phi. Congregationalist. Home and Office: 35 Outlook Rd Wakefield MA 01880-1430 also: Drakes Island PO Box 406 RR 4 Wells ME 04090

SPEAR, PAUL WILLIAM, physician, educator; b. Balt., Nov. 3, 1908; s. Sidney Paul and Edna (Lauer) S.; m. Belle Kazan, June 30, 1944 (dec. Dec.

1972); children: Susan, Margaret Ellen, Michael Lauer; m. Belle Ripps Kasofsky, Jan. 11, 1974. BA, Johns Hopkins U., 1930, MD, 1934. Diplomate Am. Bd. Internal Medicine. Intern medicine Sinai Hosp., Balt., 1934-35, asst. resident, 1935-36, chief resident, 1936-37; asst. chief and chief of medicine VA, Bklyn., 1947-63; dir. medicine Morrisania-Montefiore Affiliation, Bronx, N.Y., 1963-76; med. dir. Queens (N.Y) County Profl. Standards Rev. Orgn., 1977-85, Queens County div. Island Peer Rev. Orgn., 1984-86; attending physician Montefiore Hosp., Bronx, 1963—; prof. medicine emeritus Albert Einstein Coll. Medicine, Bronx, 1976—. Contbr. articles to profl. jours. Lt. col. U.S. Army, 1941-45. Fellow ACP; mem. Am. Soc. Hematology, N.Y. Acad. Medicine, Am. Fedn. for Clin. Rsch., N.Y. Soc. for the Study of Blood, Physicians Forum (pres. 1971-72), Phi Beta Kappa. Democrat. Jewish. Home: 55 Manhasset Woods Rd Manhasset NY 11030-2612

SPEAR, RUTH, writer; b. Phila.; d. Michael V. and Florence (Kligman) Abramson; m. Harvey M. Spear, June 27, 1965; children: Jessica, Elizabeth. BA, U. Pa., 1954. Author: Cooking Fish and Shellfish, 1980, Classic Vegetable Cookbook, 1985, The East Hampton Cookbook, 1988, What Can I Do With My Microwave, 1988, Low Fat and Loving It, 1991; contbr. articles to mags. and newspapers on food and womens health topics. Co-founder, former exec. dir. Nat. Alliance Breast Cancer Orgns., 1987—, editor NABCO News, 1992—. Mem. Authors Guild. Democrat. Address: 765 Park Ave New York NY 10021

SPEARS, HOWARD CALVIN KNOX, power plant design engineer; b. Denver, Colo., July 26, 1925; s. John Rankin and Edith Hall S.; m. Barbara Jeanne Johnson, July 11, 1946 (dec. 1986); children: Marjory, Ward, Michael, Elizabeth; m. Diane E. Crowell, June 21, 1987. BSME with honors, U. Colo., 1946, MSME with honors, 1948, BSEE with honors, 1948. Registered profl. engr., Mass. Turbine field engr. Gen Elec. Co., Omaha, Nebr., 1948-55; various turbine design positions Gen Elec. Co., Lynn, Mass., 1955-64; mgr. naval turbine design Gen Elec. Co., Lynn, 1964-68, mgr. propulsion systems engring., 1968-76, mgr. power systems engring., 1976-83, mgr. naval systems tech., 1983-86; cons. DARPA, Washington, 1988—. Moderator Town of Hamilton, Mass., 1974—. Lt. (j.g.) U.S. Navy, 1943-46 Atlantic. Mem. Soc. Naval Architects and Marine Engrs., Am. Soc. Naval Engrs., Naval Submarine League, Mass. Moderators' Soc. Republican. Congregationalist. Home: 47 Postgate Rd South Hamilton MA 01982-2421

SPEARS, JEROME JENNINGS, director, special education educator; b. Hutchinson, Kans., Apr. 8, 1943; s. Wilfred Jennings Spears and Arlean (Bourquin) Yetter; m. Marcia Elizabeth Neff, June, 1970 (div. Dec. 1986); children: Wesley, Jennifer. BA, Pa. State U., 1964; MA, U. Conn., 1971, PhD, 1982. Tchr. Baldwin-Whitehall Pub. Schs., Pitts., 1964-65; high sch. tchr. Concord (N.H.) Pub. Schs., 1967-70; tchr. spl. edn. Vernon (Conn.) Pub. Schs., 1971-72, Eastford (Conn.) Pub. Schs., 1972-73; adminstr. fed. grants U. Conn., Storrs, 1974-76; dir. pupil pers. Mansfield (Conn.) Pub. Schs., 1976—; adj. assoc. prof. U. Conn., 1986-91; bd. dirs. Conn. Parent Adv. Ctr., Norwich, 1985-88; cons. Conn. Dept. of Edn., Middletown, 1988-89; trainer Spl. Edn. Resource Ctr., Middletown, 1989; mem. Acad. Outcome Steering Com., Hartford, Conn., 1989-91. Author: (chpt.) Mainstreaming Emotionally Disturbed Children, 1977, (test manual) Raven Progressive Matrices, 1977; contbr. articles to profl. jours. Mem. standing com. on spl. edn. Conn. Legis., Hartford, 1981-91; mem. Planning and Zoning Commn., Mansfield, 1983-87, Dem. Town Com., Mansfield, 1981-90; mem. pres.'s adv. coun. Ea. Conn. State U., 1987-91. EPDA fellow U. Conn., 1972-74; U. Pitts. scholar, 1964. Mem. Coun. for Exceptional Children, Assn. for the Severely Handicapped, State Adv. Coun. on Spl. Edn. (chairperson 1989-91), Conn. Coun. Adminstrs. Spl. Edn. (pres. 1987-88), Phi Delta Kappa. Home: PO Box 237 Mansfield Center CT 06250-0237 Office: Mansfield Pub Schs 4 S Eagleville Rd Storrs Mansfield CT 06268-2599

SPEARS, R. WARREN, utility executive; b. Pitts., May 29, 1926; s. Ralph D. and Dorothea A. (Sewall) S.; m. Nadine M. Kildoo, May 31, 1948; children: Edwin Gerald, Lana Dorothea, David Warren. BA in Econs., Geneva Coll., 1950. Investigator Equifax Co., New Castle, Pa., 1950-51; sr. buyer Pa. Power Co., New Castle, 1951-71, asst. purchasing agent, 1971-73, gen. mgr. purchases and stores, 1973—. Pres. Jackson Knolls Homeowners Assn., New Castle, Pa., 1970; chmn. Beaver Twp. Zoning Bd., New Castle, 1982; comdr. Am. Legion Post 638, Bessemer, Pa., 1988; cubmaster Mt. Jackson (Pa.) Cub Pack, 1960; mem. YMCA. Mem. Purchasing Mgmt. Assn. Western Pa. (pres. 1972-73), Pa. Electric Assn. (chmn. purchasing sect. 1978-82), Nat. Assn. Purchasing Mgmt. (nat. dir. 1974-75), Edison Electric Inst. (Lifetime Cert. Purchasing Mgr. award 1984, purchasing com.). Republican. Presbyterian. Home: 18 Clark St New Castle PA 16102-1009 Office: Pa Power Co One E Washington St New Castle PA 16101

SPECHT, GORDON DEAN, retired petroleum executive; b. Garner, Iowa, June 3, 1927; s. Reuben William and Gladys (Leonard) S.; m. Cora Alice Emmert, May 24, 1952; children: Mary Ellen, Grant. BS in Chem. Engring., Iowa State U., 1950, MS in Chem. Engring., 1951; SM in Chem. Engring., MIT, 1954. Engr. Exxon Corp. Bayway Refinery, Linden, N.J., 1951-59, systemn services div. mgr., 1960-61, engring. services div. mgr., 1962-63, chem. coordinating div. mgr., 1964; mgr. systems dept. Exxon Corp.-Exxon Chem. Co., N.Y.C., 1965-70; sr. advisor communications and computer scis. dept. Exxon Corp., Florham Park, N.J., 1971-76, assoc. cons., 1977-85; retired, 1986. Patentee in field. Asst. scoutmaster Boy Scouts Am., Westfield, N.J., 1986—; sr. qualified observer Sperry Obs., Cranford, N.J., 1986—; celestial navigation instr. U.S. Power Squadrons, 1990—. With U.S. Army, 1945-46, 1st lt. C.E., 1952-53, Korea. Decorated Bronze Star. Mem. Am. Inst. Chem. Engrs., Amateur Astronomers, Inc., No. N.J. Power Squadron, MIT Club of No. N.J., Tau Beta Pi, Phi Lambda Upsilon, Phi Kappa Phi, Tau Kappa Epsilon. Republican. Methodist. Home: 15 Normandy Dr Westfield NJ 07090-3431

SPECHT, STEVEN MICHAEL, psychology educator; b. Utica, N.Y., May 6, 1959; s. William Alfred Specht and Marilyn Dolores (Schmidt) Mahanna. BS in Psychology, SUNY, Oswego, 1982; MA in Psychobiology, SUNY, Binghamton, 1987, PhD in Psychobiology, 1989. Rsch. asst. Colgate U., Hamilton, N.Y., 1983-84; rsch. fellow Duke U., Durham, N.C., 1989; asst. prof. Lebanon Valley Coll., Annville, Pa., 1989—; adj. instr. Mohawk Valley Community Coll., Utica, 1983-84; vis. asst. prof. Cornell U., Ithaca, summer 1990, 91, 92; co-dir. psychobiology program Lebanon Valley Coll., 1989—. Contbr. articles to profl. jours. NSF fellow (honorable mention), 1984, 85; Lebanon Valley Coll. grantee, 1990. Mem. Internat. Histamine Neurosci. Rsch. Group, Soc. for Neurosci., Soc. for the Study of Ingestive Behaviors, Ea. Psychol. Assn. (liaison to LVC). Home: 232 W Sheridan Ave # 3 Annville PA 17003-1240 Office: Lebanon Valley Coll 101 N College Ave Annville PA 17003-1400

SPECK, ROSS V., psychiatrist; b. St. Catharines, Ont., Can., Oct. 22, 1927; s. Victor E. and Evelyn C. (Fritshaw) S.; m. Joan L. Speck. MD, U. Toronto, 1951. Pvt. practice Phila.; clin. prof. dept. psychiatry Jefferson Med. Coll., Phila., 1980—. Co-author: The New Families, 1972, Family Networks, 1973; co-editor: Therapeutic Intervention, 1982. Capt. AUS, 1956-58. Fellow Royal Coll. Physicians, Am. Psychiatric Assn., Am. Assn. Marriage and Family Therapists, Am. Soc. Psychoanalytic Physicians. Home: 1350 Janet Dr Mount Joy PA 17552

SPECKER, ALEX JAMES, electrical engineer; b. N.Y.C., Feb. 3, 1955; s. Charles and Ethel (Fried) S.; m. Delora Ellen Howe; children: Eric James, Charles Jarrod. BSEE, CCNY, 1978. Design engr. TRW, L.A., 1978-80, Smith Corona, Cortland, N.Y., 1980-82; systems design engr. Hi-Speed Checkweigher, Ithaca, N.Y., 1983—. Inventor digital signal processing applied to weigh in motion sales, 1991. Mem. IEEE. Home: 9 E Miller Rd Ithaca NY 14850 Office: Hi Speed Checkweigher 5 Barr Rd Ithaca NY 14850

SPECKER, J. DAVID, company executive; b. San Francisco, Sept. 1, 1943; s. John and Elizabeth (Richardson) S.; m. Carol Griffiths, Aug. 27, 1966; children: Dana Lynn, Scott David. BS, Rider Coll., 1967. Mgr. catheter manufacturing Jelco Labs., Raritan, N.J., 1967-72; plant mgr. Burron Medical Products, Bethlehem, Pa., 1972-75; plant mgr. asst. Frito-Lay, Washington, 1975-76; dir. manufacturing Lehigh Packaging, Burlington, N.J., 1976-78; dir. orgnl. devel. Westwood Pharms., Buffalo, 1978-90; pres. PDC & Assocs., East Amherst, N.Y., 1990—. Pres. Ransom Oaks Community Corp., East Amherst, 1981, dir., 1979-80. Mem. Am. Soc. Tng. and Devel. (bd. dirs. 1991-92). Home: 30 Eveningwood Ln East Amherst NY 14051 Office: PDC & Assocs 30 Eveningwood Ln East Amherst NY 14051-1236

SPECTER, ARLEN, senator; b. Wichita, Kans., Feb. 12, 1930; s. Harry and Lillie (Shanin) S.; m. Joan L. Levy, June 14, 1953; children: Shanin, Stephen. Student, U. Okla., 1947-48; B.A., U. Pa., 1951; LL.B., Yale U., 1956. Asst. counsel Warren Commn., Washington, 1964; magisterial investigator Commn. of Pa., 1965; dist. atty. City of Phila., 1966-74; ptnr. Dechert Price & Rhoads, Phila., 1974-80; U.S. senator from Pa., 1981—; lectr. law Temple U., 1972-75, U. Pa., 1968-72. Contbr. articls to profl. jours. Served to 1st U.S. Army, 1951-53. Recipient Youth Svcs. award B'nai B'rith, 1966; recipient Sons of Italy award, 1968, Community Humanitarian award Bapt. Ch., 1969, man of Yr. award, Temple Beth Ami, 1971, N.E. Cath. High Sch. Outstanding Achievement award, 1973. Mem. Phi Beta Kappa. Republican. Jewish. Office: US Senate 303 Senate Hart Bldg Washington DC 20510*

SPECTOR, ADAM KEITH, podiatrist; b. Washington, Nov. 10, 1963; s. Israel and Regina (McLean) S.; m. Jennifer Lynn Ebstein, Aug. 15, 1987; 1 child, Sarah Emily. BS in Zoology, George Washington U., 1985; D Podiatric Medicine, Pa. Coll. Podiatric Medicine, 1989. Lic. podiatrist, Md. Resident in podiatric surgery Roseland (N.J.) Surg. Ctr., 1989-90; pvt. practice, Silver Spring, Md., 1990—. Lectr. ARC, sr. ctrs., YMCA's, also others; organizer shoe drive for homeless ARC; dir. Swim for Leukemia, 1986. Swimming scholar George Washington U., 1981-85. Mem. Am. Coll. Foot Surgeons, Am. Acad. Podiatric Sports Medicine, Am. Podiatric Med. Assn., Md. Podiatric Med. Assn. Republican. Jewish. Office: 1111 Spring St Silver Spring MD 20910-4003

SPECTOR, BRUCE DARWIN, college administrator, lawyer; b. East Islip, N.Y., Apr. 11, 1953; s. Moses Aaron and Ruth (Bondy) S. BA, U. Fla., 1975, JD, 1978. Dep., dir., atty. Legal Aid Soc. of Palm Beach County, West Palm Beach, Fla., 1978-81; assoc. counsel Sch. Bd. of Palm Beach County, West Palm Beach, 1981-85; assoc. Sutherland Assocs., Burlington, Vt., 1985-90; dir. community svc. learning program Trinity Coll. of Vt., Burlington, 1990—; hearing and rev. officer Vt. Dept. of Edn., Montpelier, 1985-91; adj. prof. polit. sci. Trinity Coll. of Vt., 1989—. Mem. exec. com. Alachua County Dems., Gainesville, Fla., 1972-76; campaign chair United Way/Trinity Coll. of Vt., 1990—; chmn. ombudsman com. Dist. IX Nursing Home, West Palm Beach, 1983; bd. dirs. Vt. Assn. for the Blind and Visually Impaired, Burlington, 1990—. Recipient Pres.'s award Palm Beach County Young Dems. Mem. Fla. Bar Assn., Vt. Bar Assn., Soc. for Preservation and Encouragement of Barbershop Quartet Singing in Am., Single Parent Edn. Assn. (bd. dirs. 1990—), Vermonters in Vol. Adminstrn., Vol. Coord. Network. Office: Trinity Coll of Vt 208 Colchester Ave Burlington VT 05401-1422

SPECTOR, CECILE CYRUL, speech and language pathologist; b. Bklyn.; d. Jack and Grace (Krinsky) Cyrul; m. Morton Spector, Dec. 18, 1955; children: Lauren Spector Morrissey, Jeffrey, Suzanne Spector Mlynarczyk. BA, CUNY, 1958, MA, 1960; PhD, NYU, 1977. Cert. speech pathologist. Pvt. practice Spring Valley, N.Y., 1960-80; speech pathologist North Rockland Schs., Thiells, N.Y., 1973—; dir. speech program L.I. Univ.-Rockland Campus, Orangeburg, N.Y., 1981—. Contbr. articles to profl. jours. Office: LI Univ-Rockland Campus RR 40 Orangeburg NY 10962

SPECTOR, HARVEY M., osteopathic physician; b. Phila., July 10, 1938; s. Philip and Sylvia (Rischall) S.; m. Rochelle Fleishman, June 16, 1963; children: Jill, Larry. DO, Phila. Coll. Osteo. Medicine, 1963. Osteopathic physician Phila., 1964—; preceptor Hershey (Pa.) Med. Sch., 1987—, Phila. Coll. Osteopathic Medicine, 1989—; assoc. prof. medicine Med. Coll. Pa., 1991—. Recipient Humanitarian award, Chapel of Four Chaplains, Phila., 1984. Mem. Am. Osteopathic Assn., Pa. Osteopathic Med. Assn., Am. Acad. Osteopathic Gen. Practitioners, Phila. County Osteopathic Med. Soc., Abington Dolphins Aquatic Club (pres. 1984-86), B'nai B'rith. Jewish. Office: 1220 Cottman Ave Philadelphia PA 19111-3694

SPECTOR, JUDITH ANN, dietician, consultant; b. New Brunswick, N.J., Dec. 16, 1958; d. Leon Joseph and Bernice Ruth (Galen) Scher; m. Marc Leon Spector, July 15, 1984; children: Elana Danielle, Marni Beth. BS, U. Md., 1981. Registered dietician, nationwide. Clin. dietician So. Md. Med. Ctr., Clinton, 1981-82, Newark Beth Israel Med. Ctr., 1982-86; nutrition cons. Profl. Nutritional Counseling, Millburn, N.J., 1986—; nutritional dir. The Gloria Rose Gourmet Long Life Cooking Schs., Springfield, N.J., 1986—; pres. Nutri-Choice, Inc., Millburn, N.J., 1990—. Mem. Am. Dietetic Assn., Consulting Nutritionists in Pvt. Practice, Sports and Cardiovascular Nutritionists. Office: Nutri-Choice 206 Main St Ste 22 Millburn NJ 07041-1158

SPECTOR, REYNOLD, medical scientist, science administrator; b. Stoneham, Mass., Nov. 3, 1940; m. Michiko; children: Regine, June. AB cum laude, harvard U., 1962; MD, Yale U., 1966. Intern, jr. and sr. resident internal medicine Peter Bent Brigham Hosp., Boston, 1966-68, 71; from instr. to assoc. prof. medicine Harvard Med. Sch., Peter Bent Brigham Hosp., Boston, 1971-78; prof. internal medicine and pharmacology U. Iowa Coll. Medicine, Iowa City, 1978-87; dir. divs. gen. internal medicine, clin. pharmacology Poison Control Ctr. & Clin. Rsch. Ctr U. Iowa Coll. Medicine, Iowa City, 1978-87; exec. dir. clin. scis. Merck Sharp & Dohme Rsch. Labs., Rahway, N.J., 1987-91, v.p. clin. pharmacology and endocrinology, 1991—. Author: The Scientific Basis of Clinical Pharmacology: Principles and Examples, 1986; contbr. numerous articles to profl. jours. Major U.S. Army, 1968-70. Fellow Am. Coll. Physicians; mem. Assn. Am. Physicians, Am. Soc. for Clin. Investigation, Internat. Soc. for Neurochemistry, Am. Soc. Pharmacology & Exptl. Therapeutics (Harry Gold award 1991), AAAS, Am. Fedn. for Clin. Rsch. Office: Merck Sharp & Dohme Rsch Labs 126 E Lincoln Ave Rahway NJ 07065-4687

SPEECE, JACK HOWARD, chemical engineer; b. Altoona, Pa., Jan. 8, 1947; s. Howard Herman and Audrey Naomi (Detwiler) S.; m. Vivian Diane Alwine, Aug. 16, 1969; children: Karen Diane, Ryan Howard. BS, Shippensburg U., 1968; postgrad., Ind. U., 1968-70. Educator Hollidaysburg (Pa.) High Sch., 1969-70; chemist Sitkin Smelting & Refining, Lewistown, Pa., 1970-73, Nat. Lead Co., Altoona, 1973-74; heat treating supr. Penn Jacobson Fasteners, Altoona, 1974-78; applications engr. Lee Industries, Philipsburg, Pa., 1978—. Author: Caves of Blair County, Pa., 1972, Caves of Huntingdon County, Pa., 1978; editor: 1984 Speleo Digest, 1984, Jour. Spelean History, 1979-88. Pres. PTO, Altoona, 1979-80; scoutmaster Boy Scouts Am., Altoona, 1980—. 1st class petty officer USCG, 1967-73. Named one of Outstanding Young Men Am., 1972. Fellow Nat. Speleological Soc. (chmn. 1965-67, History award 1979); mem. Masons (master 1983), Scottish Rite (comdr. 1986-89), DeMolay, Shriners, Knights Templer. Republican. Mormon. Home: 711 E Atlantic Ave Altoona PA 16602-5405

SPEELMAN, IRVING ARNOLD, medical/surgical products manufacturing executive; b. N.Y.C., July 20, 1919; s. Abraham and Esther (Linado) S.; m. Arline Jenny Fraenkel, Mar. 9, 1962; children: Alan, Patricia, Jill, Marsha, Jonathan. BChE, Cooper Union, 1951. Chief engring. Armed Svcs. Med. Procurement Agy., N.Y.C., 1946-54; exec. v.p. Propper Mfg. Co. Inc., N.Y.C., 1954—; bd. dirs. Propper Mfg. Co. Inc., 1961—; bd. dirs. Chance Propper, Birmingham, Eng. Patentee in U.S. and fgn. countries. 1st lt. CWS, U.S. Army, 1942-46. Mem. ASTM, Am. Assn. for Med. Instrumentation, N.Y. Acad. Scis. Home: 138 High St Williston Park NY 11596-1418 Office: Propper Mfg Co Inc 36 04 Skillman Ave Long Island City NY 11101

SPEICHER, EDWIN WALLER, machinery company executive, design engineer; b. Pitts., Mar. 12, 1931; s. Frank Samuel and Eleanor (Doersbacker) S.; m. Audrey Martha Sarver, May 9, 1953; children: Warren, Lynne, Laurie, Lisa. Grad. high sch., Pitts. With prodn. dept. M.E. Cunningham Co., Pitts., 1950-63, design engr., 1963-72; prodn. mgr. M.E. Cunningham Co., Pitts. and Ingomar, Pa., 1972-79; v.p. prodn. M.E. Cunningham Co., Ingomar, 1979—, chmn. bd., 1988—. Inventor single wheel billet marker, multiple movement marking machine, marking machine for forming variable size chair, marking pin for programmable machine, marker for accurate surfaces. Bd. dirs., v.p. Ingomar Vol. Fire Co., 1956—. Recipient award for 30 yrs. svc. as fireman Town of McCandless, 1988. Mem. Soc. Mfg. Engrs. (sr.), Masons, Shriners. Republican. Lutheran. Office: ME Cunningham Co Rochester Rd # 307 Ingomar PA 15127-9999

SPEIERL, CHARLES FRANK, JR., college administrator; b. N.Y.C., May 24, 1945; s. Charles and Julia (Papp) S. BA, Dowling Coll., 1969; MA, Adelphi U., 1971; EdD, Fairleigh Dickinson U., 1987. Asst. dir. student activities County Coll. of Morris, Dover, N.J., 1971-73; asst. dir. continuing edn. Somerset County Coll., Somerville, N.J., 1973-75, dir. evening programs, 1975-80; asst. dean community edn. Raritan Valley Community Coll., Somerville, 1980—; v.p. Somerset County Career Edn. Adv. Coun., Somerville, 1984-85, pres., 1985-88; pres. N.J. Community Coll. Continuing Edn. and Community Svc. Dirs., North Branch, 1987-89; 2d v.p. Co. Fifers & Drummers, 1978-79. Contbr. articles to profl. jours. Sgt. U.S. Army, 1963-66. Recipient Bronze Good Citizens award SAR, 1980, Cert. of Recognition for Hist. Rsch. and Preservation, Montgomery Meml. Observance, N.Y., 1975. Mem. Nat. Coun. on Community Svc. and Continuing Edn. (Region II Person of Yr. 1991), Assn. Higher Continuing Edn., Am. Hist. Assn., Orgn. Am. Historians, Civil War Round Table Ea. Pa., North-South Skirmish Assn., Brigade of Am. Revolution. Office: Raritan Valley Community Coll PO Box 3300 Somerville NJ 08876-1265

SPEIGHT, JEANETTE ALINE, government project executive; b. Lubbock, Tex., Jan. 28, 1946; d. Alfred Allen and Gertrude Naomi (Jalanivich) Medlock; m. Harvey Dempsey Speight, Jr., Aug. 27, 1966; children: Richard Allen, Shannon Cherie, Robert Chad. Student, Peckingston Jr. Coll., Miss., 1965, No. Va. Community Coll., 1989—. Owner, mgr. House of Ideas, Ocean Springs, Miss., 1973-74; office mgr. DD963 Project Office, Pascagoula, Miss., 1974-79; integrated logistics mgr. CG47 Project Office, Pascagoula, 1979-84; configuration mgr. Vertical Launching System, Washington, 1984-86; design specialist ship integration McDonnell Douglas Missile Systems Co., 1986-89; mgr. Tomahawk Fleet Logistics; comdr. naval air systems command cruise missiles project, mgr. Tomahawk fleet logistics Naval Air Systems Command (PDA14-C41), Washington, 1989—. Pres. St. Martin East Elem. Sch. PTA, Ocean Springs, 1980, St. Martin Jr. High Sch. PTA, 1981; Sunday sch. adult tchr. Word of Life Assembly of God Ch., Springfield, Va., 1985. Mem. Nat. Honor Soc., Internat. Toastmistress (sec. Dixie region 1979). Home: 8261 Hornbuckle Dr Springfield VA 22153-3535 Office: Naval Air Systems Command PEOCU-C41R4 Washington DC 20362

SPELKER, ARNOLD WILLIAM, banker; b. Newark, July 15, 1934; s. William M. and Helen F. (Wilhelm) S.; children: Mark, Scott, Matthew. BS in Acctg., Rutgers U., 1960; MBA, Fairleigh Dickinson U., 1978; postgrad., Harvard U., 1975. CPA, N.J. Sr. acct. KPMG Peat Marwick, N.Y.C., 1960-61; audit supr. Ernst & Young, N.Y.C., 1961-67; dir. op. auditing CBS, Inc., N.Y.C., 1967-70; v.p., asst. controller Chem. Bank, N.Y.C., 1970-81; sr. v.p., chief fin. officer U.S. Credit Suisse, N.Y.C., 1981—; sec., treas. Credit Suisse Investment Corp., Credit Suisse Capital Corp. Mem. parent's adv. coun. Dickinson Coll., 1981-85; mem. pres.'s alumni adv. coun. Fairleigh Dickinson U., 1985-86. Percy H. Johnston scholar Chem. Bank, 1978; recipient Anthony L. Gervino Outstanding Alumni award. Mem. AICPA, N.J. Soc. CPAs, Fin. Execs. Inst. (bd. dirs. 1982—, pres. N.Y.C. chpt. 1988-89, nat. membership com. 1987-88), Inst. Internat. Bankers (bd. trustees 1986-90), Fairleigh Dickinson U. Alumni Assn. (bd. govs. 1986-90). Home: 6050 Boulevard E West New York NJ 07093-3901 Office: Credit Suisse 100 Wall St New York NY 10005-3701

SPENCE, DONALD POND, psychologist, psychoanalyst; b. N.Y.C., Feb. 8, 1926; s. Ralph Beckett and Rita (Pond) S.; m. Mary Newbold Cross, June 2, 1951; children: Keith, Sarah, Laura, Katherine. AB, Harvard U., 1949; PhD, Columbia U., 1955. Lic. psychologist, N.Y., N.J. From rsch. asst. to prof. psychology NYU, 1954-74; prof. psychiatry Robert Wood Johnson Med. Sch., Piscataway, N.J., 1974—; vis. prof. psychology Stanford (Calif.) U., 1971-72, Princeton (N.J.) U., 1975—, Louvain-le-Neuve, Louvain, Belgium, 1980; mem. personality and cognition rsch. rev. com. NIMH, 1969-73 (recipient rsch. scientist award, 1968-72). Author: Narrative Truth and Historical Truth, 1982, The Freudian Metaphor, 1987; mem. editorial bd. Psychoanalysis and Contemporary Thought, Psychol. Inquiry, Theory and Psychology; contbr. articles to profl. jours. With U.S. Army, 1944-46, ETO. Mem. APA (pres.-elect theoretical and philos. div.), Am. Psychoanalytic Assn., N.Y. Acad. Sci., Sigma Xi. Democrat. Home: 9 Haslet Ave Princeton NJ 08540-4913 Office: Robert Wood Johnson Med Sch Piscataway NJ 08854

SPENCE, JANET BLAKE CONLEY (MRS. ALEXANDER PYOTT SPENCE), civic worker; b. Upper Montclair, N.J., Aug. 17, 1915; d. Walter Abbott and Ethel Maud (Blake) Conley; m. Alexander Pyott Spence, June 10, 1939; children: Janet Blake Spence Kerr, Robert Moray, Richard Taylor. Student, Vassar Coll., 1933-35; cert., Katharine Gibbs Sch., 1936. formerly active Jr. League, Neighborhood House, ARC, Girl Scouts U.S.A.; active various community drives; chmn. Darien (Conn.) Assembly, 1955-56; sec., chmn. Wilton Jr. Assembly, 1961-63; subscription chmn. Candlelight Concerts Wilton, Conn., 1963-65; rec. sec. Pub. Health Nursing Assn. Wilton Bd., 1964-67; corr., rec. sec. Royle Sch. Bd., Darien, 1952-55; fund raiser Vassar Class of 1937; mem. Washington Valley Community Assn.; mem. N.J. Symphony Orch. League, treas. Morris County br. 1978-83, corr. sec. 1982-83, pres. 1985-89, acting pres. 1989—, state coun. mem. 1985-89, acting pres. Morris br. 1989-90. Mem. Vassar Alumni Assn., Dobbs Alumni Assn., Jersey Hills Vassar Club, Wilton Garden Club, Washington Valley Community Assn. (life, corr. sec. 1977-82, pres. 1982-84, v.p. 1984-85, copres. 1985-86, treas. 1988—, chmn. membership com. 1987-89, mem. archives com. 1988—, budget com. 1990—), Washington Valley Home Econs. Club. Congregationalist. Home: Hilltop Washington Valley Rd Morristown NJ 07960 also: 8 Evergreen Ave Kennebunk ME 04043

SPENCE, ROBERT JAMES, plastic surgeon; b. Troy, N.Y., Mar. 9, 1947; s. James Robert and Ruth Elizabeth (Swanker) S.; m. Cressy Ann Starkweather, Aug. 14, 1971; children: Courtney Ann, Erin Elizabeth, Kevin Robert. BA, Johns Hopkins U., 1969, MD, 1972. Diplomate Am. Bd. Plastic Surgery, Am. Bd. Surgery. Asst. prof. plastic surgery U. Md., Balt., 1980-85, Johns Hopkins Med. Sch., Balt., 1985—; chief of plastic surgery Francis Scott Key Med. Ctr., Balt., 1985—; dir. Ctr. for Burn Reconstrn., Balt., 1990—; med. dir. Md. Tissue Bank, Balt., 1984—; co-dir. Balt. Regional Burn Ctr., 1985—. Patentee in field; contbg. author four books; contbr. articles to profl. jours. Bd. dirs., v.p. Transplant Resource Ctr. of Md., Balt., 1991-92; bd. dirs. Balt. Regional Burn CTr. Found., 1986—. Recipient Henry Strong Denison scholarship for med. rsch., 1970. Fellow ACS; mem. Am. Soc. Plastic and Reconstructive Surgeons, Northeastern Soc. Plastic Surgeons (bd. dirs. 1990-92), John Staige Davis Soc. Plastic Surgeons (sec. 1984-86, pres. 1991-92), Am. Assn. Tissue Banks, Am. Burn Assn. Office: Francis Scott Key Med Ctr 4940 Eastern Ave Baltimore MD 21224-2780

SPENCER, DAVID ROBERT, high technology executive; b. N.Y.C., Apr. 24, 1942; s. Alexander and Lillian Rose S.; m. Pamela Jeanne Katz, Sept. 21, 1968; children: Marc Douglas, Scott Eric. BS in Elec. Engring., MIT, 1964, MS in Elec. Engring., 1968. Electronic engr. EG&G, Inc., Wellesley, Mass., 1962-70, mgr. of engring., 1970-73; v.p. engring. Litton Industries, Melville, N.Y., 1973-77, div. pres., 1977-81; pres. N.A. Ops. Muirhead, Inc., Summit, N.J., 1982; chmn. Data Recording Systems, Inc., Melville, N.Y., 1983-88; mng. ptnr. Spencer & Assocs., Melville, N.Y., 1989—; dir. L.I. Venture Group, N.Y., 1988—, L.I. Forum for Tech., N.Y., 1978-81. Inventor various image data computer electrostatic recordings, 1968-86; contbr. articles to profl. jours. Pres. Tuxedo-Hills Civic Assn., Melville, N.Y., 1982-91. Mem. Inst. Elec. and Electronic Engrs. Office: Spencer & Assocs 3 Giffard Way Melville NY 11747-2310

SPENCER, DOMINA EBERLE, mathematics educator; b. New Castle, Pa., Sept. 26, 1920; d. Andrew Berger and Ina May (Eberle) S.; m. Parry Moon, Aug. 17, 1961; 1 child, Euclid Eberle Moon. SB, MIT, 1939, SM, 1940, PhD, 1942. Asst. prof. physics Am. U., Washington, 1942-43, Tufts Coll., Medford, Mass., 1943-47, Brown U., Providence, 1947-50; assoc. prof.

math. U. Conn., Storrs, 1950-60, prof. math., 1960—; cons. Sylvania, Salem, 1953-70, Ainsworth Lighting, L.I., 1943-53, Marlux Corp., Sommerville, Mass., 1948-61, Photo Rsch. Corp., Hollywood, Calif., 1945-58. Author: (with P. Moon) Lighting Design, 1947, Field Theory for Engineers, 1960, Field Theory Handbook, 1960, Foundations of Electrodynamics, 1960, Vectors, 1965, Partial Differential Equations, 1969, The Photic Field, 1981, Theory of Holors, 1986; co-inventor Aperture Lamp. Chmn. concert com. St. Paul's Ch., Brookline, 1988—; pres. Back Bay Manor Tenants Assn., Boston, 1985—. Recipient Disting. Alumna award Friends Select Sch., Phila. Fellow Illuminating Engring. Soc. (gold medal 1974), Optical Soc. Am.; mem. Am. Math. Soc., Math Assn. Am., Am. Phys. Soc., MIT Nautical Assn. Presbyterian. Home: 75 St Alphonsus St Apt 2101 Boston MA 02120-1676 Office: U Conn U-9 Storrs CT 06268

SPENCER, DONALD SPURGEON, historian, academic administrator; b. Anderson, Ind., Jan. 29, 1945; s. Thomas E. and Josephine (Litz) S.; m. Pamela Sue Roberts, June 19, 1965; 1 child, Jennifer Wynne. BA, Ill. Coll., 1967; PhD, U. Va., 1973. Asst. prof. history Westminster Coll., Fulton, Mo., 1973-76, Ohio U., Athens, 1976-77; from asst., assoc. to full prof., assoc. dean, asst. provost U. Mont., Missoula, 1977-90; provost SUNY, Geneseo, 1990—. Author: Louis Kossuth and Young America, 1978, The Carter Implosion: Jimmy Carter and the Amateur Style of Diplomacy,1989; contbr. articles to jours. in field. With U.S. Army, 1968-71, Korea. Woodrow Wilson Found. fellow, 1968; Danforth Found. univ. teaching fellow, 1971. Mem. Phi Beta Kappa. Republican. Congregationalist. Home: 36 Westview Cres Geneseo NY 14454-1012 Office: SUNY Office Provost Geneseo NY 14454

SPENCER, ERIC W., safety professional, consultant; b. N.Y.C., Apr. 1, 1930; s. Eric William and Bertha (Eyer) S.; m. Eleanor Bevilacqua, Mar. 2, 1957; children: Jo-Anne, John E., David, Gina M. BBA, Hofstra U., 1953; AM (hon.), Brown U., 1975. Supr. safety & tng. Am. Can Co., Bklyn., 1957-61; safety officer MIT Lincoln Lab., Lexington, Mass., 1961-65; dir. safety Brown U., Providence, R.I., 1965-77; safety cons. M&M Protection Cons., Boston, 1977-79; safety officer Woods Hole (Mass.) Oceanographic Inst., 1979—; bd. dirs. Mass. Safety Coun., Boston, 1981—; past pres. R.I. Safety Assn., Providence, 1970, '74, '75. Author: (with others) Handbook of Lab Safety, College and University Business Administration. Mem. Seekonk (Mass) Sch. Com., Sch. Bldg. Com.; trustee Seekonk Pub. Libr.; pres. Seekonk Citizens Scholarship Found.; Seekonk rep. Tri-County Regional Tech. Vocat., Franklin, Mass. Lt. USN, 1953-57. Named Man of Yr. R.I. Soc. to Prevent Blindness, Providence, 1970. Mem. Am. Soc. Safety Engrs. (chmn. admissions com., profl. paper awards com., mem. ethics review com., Tech. Paper award 1963), Health Physics Com. Soc. (plenary mem.), Nat. Protection Assn., Campus Safety Assn. (pres. 1972-73). Home: 1288 Newman Ave Seekonk MA 02771-2605 Office: Oceanographic Inst Water St Woods Hole MA 02543-1024

SPENCER, HAROLD EDWIN, retired art educator, art historian, painter; b. Corning, N.Y., Oct. 1, 1920; s. Clayton Judson Spencer and Hazel Leona (McCaslin) Foulkrod; m. Editha Mary Hayes, Sept. 13, 1947; children: David Hayes, Robert Alan, Eric James, Mark Edward. BA, U. Calif., Berkeley, 1948, MA, 1949; PhD, Harvard U., 1968. Teaching asst., vis. instr. U. Calif., Berkeley, 1949, 50; chmn. art dept. Blackburn Coll., Carlinville, Ill., 1949-62; assoc. prof. art dept., chmn. dept. Occidental Coll., L.A., 1962-68; assoc. prof. art U. Conn., Storrs, 1968-69, prof., 1969-88, adminstrv. assoc. to dept. head, 1972-73, assoc. dept. head, 1977-79, coord. art history, 1984-87, prof. emeritus, 1988—; guest curator William Benton Mus. Art, Storrs, 1979-80; mem. planning com. Weir Farm Heritage Trust, Branchville, Conn., 1988-89, bd. overseers, 1989—. Author: The Image Maker, 1975; editor: Readings in Art History, 2 vols., 1969, 3d rev. edit., 1983, American Art: Readings from the Colonial Era to the Present, 1980; contbr. numerous articles to profl. jours. With U.S. Mcht. Marine, 1942-46. Recipient various awards for art, 1941—; U. Calif. James Phelan scholar, 1948-49; Harvard U. Faculty Arts and Scis. fellow, 1960-61, Frank Knox Meml. fellow, 1964-65; U. Conn. Rsch. Found. grantee, 1969, 74-78. Mem. Coll. Art Assn., AAUP, Conn. Acad. Arts and Scis., Conn. Acad. Fine Arts, Phi Kappa Phi. Democrat. Home: 294 Mansfield Rd Ashford CT 06278-1414

SPENCER, JOYCE ANN, school counselor; b. Peckville, Pa., Sept. 24, 1942; m. Daniel H. Spencer, Aug. 10, 1963; children: Tom, Daniel H. Jr., Don, Mary, Kim. BS in Elem. Edn., East Stroudsburg (Pa.) U., 1964; MS in Counseling, Marywood Coll., Scranton, Pa., 1988. Elem. counselor Mountain View Sch. Dist., Kingsley, Pa., 1989—. Mem. AACD, N.E. Pa. Counselors Assn., Pa. Counseling Assn., Endless Mountains Counseling Assn., Nicholson Women's Club. Home: RR 1 Box 1057 Nicholson PA 18446-9801

SPENCER, PATRICIA LOUISE, flutist, artistic director; b. Niagara Falls, N.Y., June 28, 1943; d. Glenn Sherman and Charlotte Ellen (Donovan) S.; m. Thomas Arthur Osborn, Dec. 28, 1985. MusB, Oberlin Coll., 1965. Flutist Am. Symphony Orch., N.Y.C., 1966-67, Group for Contemporary Music, N.Y.C., 1969-85, Light Fantastic Players, N.Y.C., 1971-75, Da Capo Chamber Players, N.Y.C., 1970—, Am. Ballet Theatre, N.Y.C., 1971-76; artistic dir., flutist Aurora Musicale, Winnipeg, Man., Can., 1978—. Contbr. articles to mus. jour. Recipient rec. award for recs. of Sollberger and Tower, Am. Composers Alliance, 1976, Commissioning award Nat. Endowment for Arts Consortium, 1985. Mem. Nat. Flute Assn. (newly-published music com. 1984—, chair new music com. 1992—), N.Y. Consortium for New Music (pres.). Home: 215 W 90th St New York NY 10024-1221

SPENCER, RICHARD PAUL, biochemist, educator, physician; b. N.Y.C., June 7, 1929; s. David E. and Frances (Fried) S.; m. Gwendolyn Enid Williams, Apr. 7, 1956; children: Carolyn Roberts, Jennifer Holt, Priscilla James. AB, Dartmouth Coll., 1951; MD, U. So. Calif., 1954; MA (NSF fellow, Helen Hay Whitney fellow), Harvard U., 1958, PhD, 1961. Intern Beth Israel Hosp., Boston, 1954-55; practice medicine specializing in nuclear medicine; mem. faculty biophysics U. Buffalo, 1961-63; chief radioisotope service VA Hosp., Buffalo, 1961-63; assoc. prof. nuclear medicine Yale Sch. Medicine, 1963-68, prof., 1968-74; prof., chmn. dept. nuclear medicine U. Conn. Health Center, 1974—. Author: The Intestinal Tract, 1960, (with others) Biophysical Principles, 1965, Radionuclide Studies of the Spleen, 1975, Clinical Focus on Nuclear Medicine, 1977, Handbook of Nuclear Medicine, 1977, Therapy in Nuclear Medicine, 1978, Radiopharmaceuticals: Structure-Activity Relationships, 1981, Interventional Nuclear Medicine, 1984, New Procedures In Nuclear Medicine, 1988; contbr. (with others) articles to profl. jours. Mem. Am. Physiol. Soc., AAAS, Soc. Nuclear Medicine, Biophys. Soc. Office: U Conn Health Ctr Farmington CT 06030

SPENCER, SHERWOOD FREDRICK, home healthcare executive; b. N.Y.C., July 14, 1928; s. Abraham and Lillian (Lowenberg) S.; m. Renee Joyce Friedman, Mar. 8, 1958; children: Lauren Gail, Karen Anne. BA, U. Wis., 1948; MBA, Columbia U., 1952. Chief exec. officer A.C. Sears Co., N.Y.C., 1948-86, A Caring Hand Health Care Co., N.Y.C., 1986—; mem. com. Clinton Adv. Coun., N.Y.C., 1986—, Manhattan geriatric com., 1987—. Treas. Westchester Disabled on the Move, 1989—. Office: A Caring Hand Healthcare Co 267 5th Ave New York NY 10016-7503

SPENCER, SUSAN ELIZABETH, watercolor artist; b. Buffalo, Oct. 31, 1954; d. Charles Griffen and Elizabeth Jane (Pawlson) Fletcher; m. Michael Jeffrey Spencer, Sept. 6, 1975; children: Collin Micah, Ryan Christian. AAS, Sullivan County Community Coll, Loch Sheldrake, N.Y., 1974. workshop instr. and demonstrator Niagara Frontier Watercolor Soc., So. Tier Art Assn., Rome Art Assn., Centennial Art Assn., Utica Art Assn., North Country Art Assn., others; judge invitationals Tri-County Regional Art Exhbn., Syracuse Art Festival, SUNY Herkimer Regional Show, others. Selected exhbns. include Adirondack Nat. Exhbn. Am. Watercolors, Old Forge, N.Y., 1986-89, San Diego Watercolor Soc., Watercolor West, Miss. Watercolor Soc., Eudora Welty Libr., Jackson, Miss. Recipient Mary Garrison award Cooperstown Art Assn., 1987, best Adirondack Painting, Art Guild of Old Forge, 1990. Mem. Cen. N.Y. Watercolor Soc. (bd. dirs., sec. 1986-88), Nat. League of Am. Pen Women, Midwest Watercolor Soc. (assoc.), Pa. Watercolor Soc. Home: 306 Gordon Pky Syracuse NY 13219-1022

SPENCER-GREEN, GEORGE THOMAS, medical education educator; b. Lima, Ohio, Sept. 8, 1946; s. Ormond George and Elizabeth Ann (Thomas) Spencer-Green; m. Linda Ann Jonas, Oct. 31, 1980; 1 child, Elizabeth Ann. BA, Oberlin (Ohio) Coll., 1969; MD, Columbia U., 1974. Diplomate Am. Bd. Internal Medicine, Am. Bd. Rheumatology, Am. Bd. Allergy and Immunology (Diagnostic Lab. Immunology). Instr. in medicine Coll. of Medicine, U. Cin., 1980, asst. prof. medicine, pathology and lab. medicine, 1980-84; assoc. prof. medicine Dartmouth Med. Sch., Hanover, N.H., 1985—; assoc. med. dir. diagnostic immunology lab. U. Hosp., Cin., 1982-84; chief of immunology Vets. Hosp., Cin., 1982-84, White River Junction, Vt., 1985—. Author: (chpt.) Textbooks on Rheumatic Diseases, 1985—; contbr. articles to profl. jours. Mem. adv. bd. N.H. chpt. Arthritis Found., Concord, 1988—. Fellow ACP, Am. Coll. Rheumatology; mem. Am. Fedn. Clin. Rsch., N.Y. Acad. Sci. Home: RR 1 Box 522H Norwich VT 05055-9526 Office: Dartmouth-Hitchcock Med Ctr One Medical Center Dr Lebanon NH 03756

SPERAKIS, NICHOLAS GEORGE, artist; b. N.Y.C., June 8, 1943; s. George and Cathren (Cokatas) S.; m. Yolanda de Carmen Mesa, Feb. 1, 1983. Student, Pratt Inst., 1960, NAD, 1960-61, Art Students League N.Y., Pratt Graphic Art Center, 1961-63. Instr. Sumitt (N.J.) Art Center, 1971, New Sch. Social Research, N.Y.C., 1972—, Fashion Inst. Tech., N.Y.C., 1977—. Exhibited one-man shows at Paul Kessler Gallery, 1963, 64, Provincetown, Mass., Hinckley and Brohel Art Gallery, Washington, 1964, N.Y.C., 1965, Mari Galleries, Woodstock, N.Y., 1966, 67, 68, Larchmont, N.Y., 1967, Eric Schindler Galleries, 1965, Richmond (Va.) Art Gallery, N.Y. U. Student Loeb Center, 1969, L.I. U., 1971, Pratt Inst., 1971, Bienville Gallery, New Orleans, 1972, 74, Pace U., N.Y.C., 1972, Lerner-Heller Gallery, N.Y.C., 1975, 76, Daedal Gallery, Balt., 1976, Reading Mus. Art, (Pa.), 1977, Bklyn. Mus., 1977, Washington Irving Gallery, N.Y.C., 1982, Museo Universitario Del Chopo, Mexico City, 1984, Forum Gallery, N.Y.C., Mus. Contemporary Art, Bogota, The Atler Gallery, Munich, 1989, Galerieverein Blankenese, Hamburg, Fed. Republic Germany, 1988, Galeria Sextante, Bogota, 1989, La Francia, Centro de Arte, Medellin, Colombia, 1989, various woodcut exhbns., others; exhibited group shows, Mercy Hurst Coll., Erie, Pa., 1963, 64, Bklyn. Mus., 1964, 77, Jewish Mus., 1964, Chrysler Mus., 1964, 65, Assoc. Am. Artists Galleries, N.Y.C., 1965, Norfolk (Va.) Mus. Arts Scis., 1965, Long Beach (Calif.) Coll., 1969, Am. Acad. and Nat. Inst. Arts and Letters, 1969, 75, Mid West Mus-Am-Art, 1981, numerous others, print exhbns., France, Italy, Spain, other European Countries, Far East, 1970-71, Lerner-Heller Gallery, 1973, 76, Amherst Coll., 1974, Worcester (Mass.) Mus. Fine Art, 1977, Reading (Pa.) Mus. Art, 1977; represented in permanent collections Bklyn. Mus., Walter P. Chrysler Mus., Norfolk, Va., Norfolk Mus. Arts and Scis., N.Y.C. Public Library, Phila. Mus. Fine Arts, Worcester Mus. Fine Art, Flint (Mich.) Art Inst., Mus. Modern Art, N.Y.C., U. Conn., Storrs, Amherst Coll., Okla. Fine Arts Center Mus., Am. Acad. and Nat. Inst. Arts and Letters, Detroit Inst. Fine Art, Corcoran Gallery of Art, Midwest Mus. Am. Art, Exeter Acad., Conn., Mus. Modern Art, N.Y.C., print collections Nat. Mus. Am. Art Smithsonian Instn., DeHunter Mus. Art, Chattanooga, Libr. of Congress, Washington, High Mus. Art, Atlanta, Free Libr., Phila., Kunst Mus., Fine Arts Mus. Bern Switzerland, Australian Nat. Gallery, Canberra, Snite Mus. Art, U. Notre Dame, Ind., Bibliotheque Royale Albert/ER, Bruxelles, Belgium, Museo Rayo, Roldanillo, Colombia, Stedelijk Mus., Amsterdam, The Netherlands; organized (with others), Rhino Horn artist group, N.Y.C., 1970. Recipient First Prize Purchase award Mercy Hurst Coll., 1964; Lawrence and Hinda Rosenthal award Am. Acad. and Nat. Inst. Arts and Letters, 1969; Guggenheim graphics fellow, 1970; McDowell Colony summer residency, 1976. Mem. Soc. Am. Graphic Artists. Address: 245 W 29th St Floor 12A New York NY 10001

SPERBER, DANIEL, physicist; b. Vienna, Austria, May 8, 1930; came to U.S., 1955, naturalized, 1967; s. Emanuel and Nelly (Liberman) S.; m. Ora Yuval, Nov. 29, 1963; 1 son, Ron Emanuel. M.Sc., Hebrew U., 1954; Ph.D., Princeton U., 1960. Tng. and rsch. asst. Israel Inst. Tech., Haifa, 1954-55, Princeton U., 1955-60; sr. scientist, rsch. adviser Ill. Inst. Tech. Rsch. Inst., Chgo., 1960-67; assoc. prof. physics Ill. Inst. Tech. Rsch. Inst., 1964-67, Rensselaer Poly. Inst., Troy, N.Y., 1967-72; prof. Rensselaer Poly. Inst., 1972—; Nordita prof. Niels Bohr Inst., Copenhagen, 1973-74, NATO research fellow, vis., prof., 1974-77; vis. prof. G.S.I., Darmstadt, Fed. Republic Germany, 1981; sr. Fulbright research scholar, Saha Inst. Nuclear Physics, Calcutta, India, 1987-88. Contbr. 100 sci. papers to profl. jours. Served to capt. Israeli Army, 1950-52. Fellow Am. Phys. Soc.; mem. Israel Phys. Soc., N.Y. Acad. Scis., Sigma Xi. Jewish. Home: 1 Taylor Ln Troy NY 12180-7162 Office: Rensselaer Poly Inst Dept Physics Troy NY 12181

SPERBER, JAMES, human resources executive; b. N.Y.C., Mar. 27, 1929; s. Charles and Dorothy (Lansing) S.; m. Anne Dorward Nicol, Nov. 30, 1976; children by previous marriages: Lora E., James P.Q. BA, Yale U., 1952; MBA, U. Pa., 1956. Vice-pres. J.P. Morgan, N.Y.C., 1956-88, Nat. Exec. Svc. Corps., N.Y.C., 1990—. Trustee United Presbyn. Found., 1974-79; pres. Quogue (N.Y.) Libr., 1990—; bd. dirs. Quogue Assn., 1990—. 1st lt. inf. U.S. Army, 1951-53. Mem. AIME (chmn. N.Y.C. chpt. 1971-72), Am. Mining Congress (chmn. fin. adv. coun. 1973-74), Shinnecock Hills Golf Club (treas., chmn. fin. com. 1990—). Republican. Presbyterian. Home: 175 E Seventy Ninth St New York NY 10021 Office: Nat Exec Svc Corps 257 Park Ave S New York NY 10010-7304

SPERBER, ROBERT IRWIN, educational administrator, educator; b. N.Y.C., June 15, 1929; s. Jacob and Alice (Schwartz) S.; m. Edith Nancy Winter, Dec. 22, 1957; children: Matthew Winter, Laurence Todd, Beth Susan. BA, Western Reserve U., 1951; MA, Columbia U., 1952, EdD, 1957. Tchr. Levittown (N.Y.) Pub. Schs., 1952, 54-56; adminstrv. asst. to supt. Westfield (N.J.) Pub. Schs., 1956-59, Plainview-Old Bethpage Pub. Schs., Plainview, N.Y., 1959-61; asst. supt. for personnel Pitts. Pub. Schs., 1961-64; supt. Brookline (Mass.) Pub. Schs., 1964-82; exec. dir. Boston Higher Edn. Partnership, 1982—; spl. asst. to pres., prof. edn. Boston U., 1982—; pres. EWS Ednl. Assocs., Brookline, Mass., 1986—; mem. mgmt. team, Chelsea Project, Boston, 1989—. Founder Metco, 1965, Brookline (Mass.) Early Edn. Project, 1973; mem. Brookline Found., 1984-90; chmn. Brookline Deve. Com., 1989—. With U.S. Army, 1952-54. NEH grantee, 1975. Office: Boston Univ 147 Bay State Rd Boston MA 02215-1789

SPERLING, ALLAN GEORGE, lawyer; b. N.Y.C., Dec. 10, 1942; s. Saul Sperling and Gertrude (Lober) Sperling Bernstein; m. Susan Kelz, June 27, 1965; children: Matthew Laurence, Stuart Kelz, Jane Kendra. Bar: N.Y. 1969, U.S. Ct. Appeals (2d cir.) 1975. Law clk. to presiding justice U.S. Dist Ct., New Haven, 1967-68; assoc. Cleary, Gottlieb, Steen & Hamilton, N.Y.C., 1968-75, ptnr., 1976—. Editor Yale Law Jour. Vice chmn. bd. Merce Cunningham Dance Found., N.Y.C., 1985—; chmn. bd. Rye (N.Y.) Arts Ctr. Inc., 1985-88, bd. dirs., 1990—; bd. dirs. Friends of the Neuberger Mus., Purchase, N.Y., 1989—. Mem. N.Y. State Bar Assn., Order of Coif, Phi Beta Kappa. Home: Kirby Ln Rye NY 10580-4308 Office: Cleary Gottlieb Steen & Hamilton 1 Liberty Pla New York NY 10006

SPERLING, DANIEL LEE, import-export firm executive; b. N.Y.C., Dec. 22, 1949; s. Allen Aaron and Helen Miriam (Cohen) S. BA in Psychology, Duke U., 1971. Mktg. specialist C&P Telephone Co., Wheaton, Md., 1973-75; co-owner James Lee Co., Silver Spring, Md., 1975-76; feature writer USA Today, Arlington, Va., 1983-90; instr. Mt. Vernon Coll., Washington, 1990; pres. DSA Imports, Washington, 1990—. Author: A Spectator's Guide to Football, 1983, A Spectator's Guide to Baseball, 1983, A Spectator's Guide to Basketball, 1983; contbr. articles to newspapers and gen. interest mags.

SPERLING, MINDY TOBY, social sciences and bilingual education instructor; b. N.Y.C., Dec. 21, 1954; d. Albert and Jeanette (Klein) Goldweit; m. Jonathan Sperling, June 15, 1980; children: Joshua, Elliot Asher. BS, Cornell U., 1976; MA, New Sch. Social Rsch., 1978; PhD, Yeshiva U., 1989. Rsch. asst. Cornell U., Ithaca, N.Y., 1975; nursery sch. tchr. Women's and Children's Ctr., Pearl River, N.Y., 1976-77; instr. Cen. Colombo-Americano, Medellin, Colombia, 1979; translator Escuela Nacional de Salud Publica, Medellin, 1979; trilingual exec. sec. Bank Leumi Trust Co. N.Y., 1979-82; intern psychol. rsch. pediatrics unit Columbia Presbyn. Hosp., N.Y.C., 1983-84; adj. prof. Internat. Overseas Program, Coll. Edn. U. Ala., Tuscaloosa, 1984-85; instr. Yeshiva U., N.Y.C., 1985-89; program evaluation cons. multicultural edn. Office of Rsch. Evaluation and Assessment, Bklyn., 1990—, field cons. spl. rsch. div. study on effective svcs. to ltd. English proficient students in N.Y.C. Pub. Schs., 1990—; cons. N.Y.C. Bd. Edn., 1985, program evaluation cons. OREA, 1990, field cons. effective svc. study, 1990; adj. prof. Multicultural Ctr. Jersey City State Coll., summer 1990, bilingual/ESL program, dept. langs. and culture, William Paterson Coll., Wayne, N.J., 1990-91; presenter LLL of Md./Del./D.C. Area Conf., 1992; bilingual listed leader Columbia II La Leche League, 1992—; provider instructional svcs. to non-English speaking students, Elkridge (Md.) Elem. Sch., 1992—. Translator Further Studies on Family Formation Patterns and Health, 1981; reviewer in field. Storyteller, Queensboro Pub. Libr., 1987-88; leader La Leche League Cen.-Queens, N.Y., 1991-92, Columbia II La Leche League Md./Del./D.C., 1992—; mem. N.Y.C. Storytelling Ctr., 1987-88; bilingual project coord./parent liaison Dual Lang. Enrichment program Brook Ave. Sch., Bay Shore, N.Y., 1990-91. U.S. Dept. Edn. fellow, Yeshiva U., 1982-85. Mem. APA, AAAS, Psychology Soc. (chair 1977-78), Soc. Rsch. Child Devel., N.Y. Acad. Scis., Internat. Platform Assn., Nat. Assn. Bilingual Edn., Am. Acad. Polit. and Social Sci, Rockland Coun. for Young Children. Home: 9537 Sea Shadow Columbia MD 21046-2060 Office: Yeshiva U 1300 Morris Park Ave Bronx NY 10461-1924

SPERTELL, ALAYNE, personnel service executive; b. N.Y.C., Apr. 9, 1934; s. Irving and Lucy (Rubin) S.; m. Al Saltzman, Dec. 12, 1953; children: Mara, Robin, Michele. BA, Bklyn. Coll., 1954. Cert. personnel counselor. Counselor, pres. Smith Personnel Svc., N.Y.C., 1955—. Office: Smith Personnel 41 E 42nd St New York NY 10017-5202

SPETTER, BARRY HERBERT, principal; b. Newark, July 2, 1947; s. Donald and Lillian (Lefkowitz) S.; m. Patricia Burns, Dec. 20, 1970; children: Jackelyn, David. AA, Monmouth Coll., West Long Branch, N.J., 1968, BS, 1970; MA, Kean Coll., 1974. Cert. secondary tchr., N.J.; cert. prin./supr., N.J.; cert. sch. adminstr., N.J. Tchr. social studies Elizabeth (N.J.) Bd. Edn., 1970-71; tchr. social studies Morris Hills Regional Bd. Edn., Denville, N.J., 1971-75, adminstrv. asst., 1975-77, asst. prin., 1977-86, prin., 1986—; presenter Renaissance Edn. Found. throughout U.S., 1990—. Named one of Tchrs. Up Front, Newark Star Ledger, 1973, Outstanding Adminstr. of the Yr., N.J. Music Edn. Assn., 1991. Fellow Inst. for Devel. Ednl. Activities; mem. ASCD, Nat. Assn. Secondary Prins., N.J. Prins. and Suprs. Assn., Morris Hills Regional Dist. Adminstrs. Assn. (v.p. 1978-85). Office: Morris Hills High Sch 520 W Main St Rockaway NJ 07866-3799

SPEVACEK, JENNIFER JEANENE, newspaper reporter; b. Iowa City, Iowa, Dec. 9, 1961; d. John David and JoAnn Maxine (Cook) S. BA in English, U. Va., 1983. Va. bur. chief Washington Times, Washington, 1984-86, Capitol Hill reporter, 1986-89, Fairfax bur. chief, 1990—. Office: The Washington Times 3600 New York Ave NE Washington DC 20002-1996

SPEVAK, IRVING BERTRAM, real estate executive; b. Albany, N.Y., Dec. 10, 1917; s. Bernard and Bella (Belkin) S.; student Coll. City N.Y., 1936-37, U. Nebr., 1937-39, vet. edn. program Vassar Coll., 1948-49; m. Miriam Lillian Pols, Dec. 10, 1940; children: Elaine Sherry, Albert Bennet. Ins. agt. Poughkeepsie, 1946—; realtor, Poughkeepsie, 1955—. Vice pres. dir. Jewish Community Center, Poughkeepsie, 1953-56. Served with USN, 1943-46; PTO. Mem. Dutchess County Bd. Realtors (pres. 1968-70), Nat. Assn. Real Estate Bds. (exec. officers council 1959-65), Nat. Council of Exchangors (equity mktg. specialist, bd. dirs. Empire State Real Estate Exchange), Jewish War Vets. (comdr. 1952), N.Y. State Assn. Realtors (state dir., pres. comml. and investment div.), Am. Legion. Jewish. Lodge: Masons. (past master). Patentee collar stay, food container. Address: 287 New Hackensack Rd Poughkeepsie NY 12602

SPEZZANO, VINCENT EDWARD, newspaper publisher; b. Retsof, N.Y., Apr. 3, 1926; s. Frank and Lucy S.; m. Marjorie Elliott, Dec. 18, 1948; children: Steve, Judy, Mark, Christine (dec.). BA in Journalism, Syracuse (N.Y.) U., 1950. Reporter Livingston Republican, Geneseo, N.Y., 1950-51, Lynchburg (Va.) News, 1951-54, St. Louis Globe-Democrat, 1954-55; polit. writer, then dir. public service and research Rochester (N.Y.) Times Union, 1955-68; dir. public service, then dir. promotion and public service Gannett Co., Inc., 1968-75; pres., publisher Cape Publs., Inc., Cocoa, Fla., 1975-84; chmn. Cape Publs., Inc., 1984-91; asst., then v.p. Gannett/South, Gannett Co., Inc., 1977-79; pres. Gannett Southeast Newspaper Group, Gannett Co., Inc., 1979-82; exec. v.p. USA Today, 1982-83, pres., 1983; sr. v.p. communications Gannett Co., 1983-84, bd. dir.; pres., pub. Gannett Rochester Newspapers, 1984-90, chmn., 1990-91; pres. Gannett N.E. Div., 1984-86; past mem. journalism endowment adv. com. U. Fla.; bd. dirs. Marine Midland Bank. Editor handbook. Past trustee St. John Fisher Coll., Rochester; trustee Brevard Art Ctr. and Mus., Melbourne, Fla.; bd. dirs. United Way of Rochester, Rochester Mus. and Sci. Ctr., Cape Canaveral Hosp., 1991—, Fla. Inst. of Tech., 1991—, Astronauts Meml. Found., 1991—; past mem. adv. bd. U. Tex., Austin; bd. overseers Rochester Philharm. Orch., 1985—; vice chmn. Rochester Conv. Bur., 1986-91; mem. Founder's Com. The Rochesterians, 1986—; mem. adv. bd. Space Pioneers, Inc. With A.C., USNR, 1944-46. Recipient News Writing award Va. Press Assn., 1953, Citizen of Yr. award Citizens Club Rochester, 1960, Disting. Service award for non-members Kiwanis Club, 1960, Public Service Reporting award Am. Polit. Sci. Assn., 1963; named NE Kiwanis Citizen of Yr., 1987, Boss of Yr. Cocoa Beach chpt. Nat. Secretaries Assn., 1977, Rochester Communicator of Yr., 1987, Rochester Citizen of Yr., 1987. Mem. Internat. Newspaper Promotion Assn. (pres. 1970-71, Silver Shovel award 1975), Am. Newspapers Pubs. Assn., So. Newspaper Pubs. Assn. Found. (chmn.), Fla. Press Assn. (bd. dir., pres. 1984), N.Y. Newspaper Pubs. Assn. (bd. dirs.), Cocoa Beach Area C. of C., Rochester Area C. of C. (bd. dir. 1985—, chmn. bd. 1989-90). Roman Catholic. Home: 855 S Atlantic Ave Cocoa Beach FL 32931-2424 Office: 855 S Atlantic Ave Cocoa Beach FL 32931-2424 also: 1 Gannett Pla Melbourne FL 32940 Office: Cape Pubs Inc PO Box 363000 Melbourne FL 32936

SPHAR, LISA ANN, accountant; b. Charleroi, Pa., Oct. 20, 1967; d. Melvin Bruce and Barbara Ann (Biondi) S. BS, Carlow Coll., Pitts., 1989. CPA, Pa. Outpatient asst. The Rehab. Inst., Pitts., 1987-89; in-charge accts. Schneider, Downs & Co., Inc., Pitts., 1989—. Mem. Am. Soc. Women Accts. (bd. dirs. 1991—, chmn. membership 1991—). Office: Schneider Downs & Co Inc 1133 Penn Ave Pittsburgh PA 15222-4252

SPHAR, RAYMOND LESLIE, JR., physician, research administrator; b. Charleroi, Pa., July 27, 1934; s. Raymond Leslie and Alma Josephine (Massey) S.; m. Jean Frances Cusick, June 24, 1961 (div. 1976); 1 child, Christina Leslie. BS, Westminster Coll., 1956; MD, Jefferson Med. Coll., 1961; MPH, Yale U., 1972. Commd. lt. USN, 1961, advanced through grades to capt., 1975; resident in preventive medicine Yale U., New Haven, 1969-72; rsch. med. officer Naval Submarine Med. Rsch. Lab., Groton, Conn., 1972-73, comdg. officer, 1973-78; program mgr. med. rsch. Office of Naval Tech., 1978; dir. undersea and radiation medicine Bur. of Medicine and Surgery, Navy Dept., 1978-81; exec. officer Naval Med. Rsch. and Devel. Command, Bethesda, Md., 1981-83; comdg. officer Naval Med. Rsch. Inst., Bethesda, Md., 1983-86; asst. for med., life scis. rsch. Office of Sec. of Def., 1986-89; dir. R&D Bur. Medicine & Surgery, Washington, 1989-90; dir. med. rsch. svc. Dept. Vets. Affairs, Washington, 1991—; U.S. rep. to NATO panel, Brussels, 1986-89; DOD rep. Nat. Adv. Rsch. Resources Coun., NIH, 1986-89. Fellow Coll. of Physicians of Phila.; mem. Am. Coll. Preventive Medicine, Am. Coll. Occupational and Environ. Medicine (master), Army and Navy Club, English-Speaking Union, Yale Club. Presbyterian. Home: 2475 Virginia Ave NW Washington DC 20037-2639 Office: Dept Vets Affairs 810 Vermont Ave NW Washington DC 20420-0002

SPICER-BROOKS, MARIANNA CHASE, television producer; b. Denver, Nov. 23, 1951; d. William Sidney Jr. and Evelyn Lucille (Vogt) Spicer; m. Michael J. Brooks, Feb. 24, 1989. BA, Ohio Wesleyan U., 1973. Producer-dir. Sta. WJLA-TV, Washington, 1980-83; assoc. producer 60 Minutes, CBS Reports, CBS News, Washington, 1983-87; producer ABC News, Washington, 1987-89; show producer This Week With David Brinkley, ABC News, 1989-90; exec. producer Face the Nation, CBS News, Washington, 1990—. Producer: (documentaries) Getting There, 1983 (Emmy award), The Road Back Home, 1983 (Emmy award), The Newsmakers, 1984 (Emmy award), The Burger years, 1986 (Emmy award). Office: CBS News 2020 M St NW Washington DC 20036-3368

SPIEGEL, ALLEN D., medical educator, consultant; b. N.Y.C., June 11, 1927; s. Max and Betty (Silver) S.; m. Lila Spiegel, Apr. 16, 1958; children:

Merrill S., Marc B., Andrea M. AB, Bklyn. Coll., 1947; MPH, Columbia U., 1954; PhD, Brandeis U., 1969. Chief radio & TV unit N.Y.C. Health Dept., 1951-61; health edn. assoc. The Med. Found., Inc., Boston, 1961-69; prof. SUNY Health Sci. Ctr. at Bklyn., 1969—; cons. in field. Author, editor of numerous books including Strategic Health Planning, 1991, Home Health Care, 2d rev. edit., 1987; contbr. articles to profl. jours.; mem. editorial adv. bd. The Nation's Health. NEH fellow, 1979, WHO study/travel fellow, 1974, Nat. Ctr. for Health Svcs. Rsch. fellow, 1966-69; recipient of citations from govtl. and pub. agys; seminar leader Profl. Continuing Edn. Programs (overseas), 1988. Mem. Am. Pub. Health Assn. (com. chmn.), Internat. Union for Health Edn., Columbia U. Sch. of Pub. Health Alumni Assn., Community Agy. Pub. Rels. Assn., Coun. on Med. Television, Soc. of Pub. Health Educators, Health Edn. Media Assn., Consumer Commn. on the Accreditation of Health Svcs. Home: 47 Jensen Rd Sayreville NJ 08872-1969 Office: SUNY Health Sci Ctr 450 Clarkson Ave # 43 Brooklyn NY 11203-2098

SPIEGEL, JAYSON LESLIE, lawyer; b. N.Y.C., Mar. 1, 1959; s. Jack and Frieda Rhoda (Michaelson) S.; m. Deborah Marie Scott, Nov. 1, 1986; 1 child, Kyle Reid. AB, Georgetown U., 1980; JD, U. Va., 1983; postgrad., USMC Command and Staff Coll., 1991. Bar: Md. 1984, D.C. 1985, U.S. Ct. Appeals (D.C. cir.) 1986, U.S. Ct. Mil. Appeals 1987, U.S. Ct. Appeals (4th cir.) 1987, U.S. Supreme Ct. 1988, U.S. Ct. Claims 1990. Law clk. to assoc. judge Md. Ct. Appeals, Balt., 1983-84; assoc. Jordan, Coyne, Savits & Lopata, Washington, 1985-91, ptnr., 1991—; lectr. law and transfusion medicine NIH, 1989, 91. Contbr. articles to profl. jours. Mem. recreation adv. bd. Montgomery County, Md., 1989—. With USAR, 1981—, Desert Shield/Desert Storm, 1990-91. Mem. ABA (young lawyers mem. com. on law and nat. security, D.C. chmn. disaster legal assistance project 1989—, vice chair internat. criminal law com. 1991—), D.C. Bar Assn. (founder, chmn. com. on law and nat. security 1987—, Com. Chmn. of Yr. 1988, 91), Md. Bar Assn., Am. Def. Preparedness Assn., Nat. Security Indsl. Assn., Res. Officers Assn. (life), Army and Navy Club. Office: Jordan Coyne Savits & Lopata 1030 15th St NW Washington DC 20005-1503

SPIEGEL, STANLEY, psychologist; b. N.Y.C., Apr. 18, 1925; s. Samuel and Hermina (Manheim) S.; children: Joseph, Laura. BS in Psychology, Adelphi U., 1950; MS, CUNY, 1951; PhD in Psychology, U. Fla., 1957. Diplomate clin. psychology. Psychologist Highland Hosp., Asheville, N.C., 1951-53; researcher Health Ctr./U. Fla., Gainesville, 1956-57; chief psychologist Portsmouth (Va.) Guidance Ctr., 1957-62; pvt. practice N.Y.C. and Nyack, N.Y., 1962—; clin. prof. psychology Adelphi U., Garden City, N.Y., 1980—; supervising analyst W.A. White Inst., N.Y.C., 1986—. Author: An Interpersonal Approach to Child Therapy, 1989; contbr. articles to profl. jours. Exec. bd. dirs. faculty Adelphi U., 1985-89. With USAAF, 1943-46. Mem. W.A. White Soc. (bd. dirs. 1986-89, sec. 1977), Va. Psychol. Assn. (pres. 1961), Am. Psychol. Assn. (del. 1959). Home: 23 Hickory Hill Rd Tappan NY 10983-1803 Office: 48 Burd St Nyack NY 10960-3226

SPIEGELMAN, JAMES MICHAEL, presidential campaign official; b. Atlantic City, Aug. 13, 1958; s. William and Barbara (Cohen) S. BA in Polit. Sci., U. Pa., 1980; MA in Internat. Affairs, Am. U., 1984. Account exec. United Expn. Svc. Co., Inc., Washington, 1980-82; rsch. fellow Congl. Rsch. Svc., U.S. Libr. Congress, Washington, 1984; writer, editor Hudson Rsch. Internat., Paris, 1985; dir. rsch. and programs Ctr. for Internat. Bus. and Trade, Georgetown U., Washington, 1986-91; dep. policy dir. Bob Kerrey for Pres. Campaign, Washington, 1991—. Co-editor: Impediments to U.S.-Arab Economic Relations: Progress in the Midst of Crisis, 1989; editor-in-chief CIB&T Analyst, quar. newsletter, 1986-90; editor newsletter Bus. Opportunities in Eastern Europe, 1990; contbr. numerous articles on U.S. politics and trade policy to newspapers and profl. pubís. Mem. Ctr. for Study of the Presidency. Mem. Am. Polit. Sci. Assn., Assn. for Can. Studies in U.S., Nat. Geog. Soc., Ctr. Study of the Presidency, British-Am. Bus. Assn., French-Am. C. of C. Democrat.

SPIELHOLTZ, GERALD I., chemistry educator; b. Bronx, N.Y., Mar. 12, 1937; s. Murray and Joan (Kauders) S.; m. Susan Goldberg, Dec. 26, 1978; 1 child, Amy L. BS, CCNY, 1958; MS in Chemistry, U. Mich., 1960; PhD in Chemistry, Iowa State U., 1963. Postdoctoral assoc. Iowa State U., Ames, 1963; from instr. to asst. prof. Hunter Coll., CUNY, N.Y.C., 1963-68; from asst. prof. to prof. chemistry Lehman Coll., CUNY, 1968—. Contbr. articles to profl. publs. Mem. Am. Chem. Soc., Sigma Xi, Phi Lambda Upsilon. Office: Lehman Coll CUNY Dept Chemistry Bronx NY 10468

SPIELMAN, RICHARD SAUL, genetics educator; b. N.Y.C., Feb. 25, 1946; s. Ralph and Beatrice C. (Kramer) S.; m. Karen Sue Troutman, Oct. 25, 1969 (div. Jan. 1991). AB, Harvard Coll., 1967; PhD, U. Mich., 1971. Rsch. assoc. U. Mich., Ann Arbor, 1971-74; from asst. prof. to prof. U. Pa., Phila., 1974—. Office: U Pa Sch Medicine Dept Genetics 422 Curie Blvd Philadelphia PA 19104-6140

SPIELMANN, SOLVEIG BJORKE, international government relations consultant; b. Madison, Wis., Jan. 26, 1943; d. Hans and Marie Nellie (Landsness) Bjorke; m. Karl Frederick Spielmann, Dec. 24, 1968; children: Karl Hans, Nelson Landsness. BA, U. Wis., 1965; MA, Harvard U., 1968. V.p. Internat. Bus. Govt. Counsellors, Inc., Washington, sr. v.p., chmn., chief exec. officer, 1987—; bd. dirs. Gekeman-Am. Bus. Coun., Washington. Editor Washington Internat. Bus. Report; contbr. articles to profl. jours. Mem. Swedish Am. C. of C., Brazil Am. C. of C., Nat. Economists Club, Japan Am. Soc. Office: Internat Bus Govt Counselling 818 Connecticut Ave NW 1200 Washington DC 20018

SPIELVOGEL, CARL, marketing and advertising executive; b. N.Y.C., Dec. 27, 1928; s. Joseph and Sadie (Tellerman) S.; m. Barbaralee Diamonstein, Oct. 27, 1981; children: David Joseph, Rachel Fay, Paul Abram. BBA, CUNY, 1956, LLD (hon.), 1984. Reporter, columnist N.Y. Times, 1950-60; with McCann-Erickson, Inc., Interpublic Group of Cos., Inc., N.Y.C., 1960-74; vice chmn., chmn. exec. com., dir. Interpublic Group of Cos., Inc., 1974-80; chmn., chief exec. officer Backer & Spielvogel, Inc., 1980-87; chief exec. officer, chmn. bd. dirs. Backer Spielvogel Bates Worldwide, Inc., N.Y.C., 1987—; dir. Manhattan Industries, Franklin Corp. Chmn. Com. in the Public Interest, 1975-79, Tri-State United Way, 1984; pres. bd. trustees Baruch Coll. Fund, 1979; mem. Bus. Com. Arts; bd. dirs., mem. exec. com. Mt. Sinai Hosp., N.Y.C.; bd. dirs. N.Y. Council Humanities, N.Y. Philharmonic, 1987—, The Asia Soc., 1989—; bd. trustees The Lincoln Ctr. for the Performing Arts, 1987—; chmn. The Mayor's Com. for Pub.-Pvt. Partnerships; exec. com. Bus. Mktg. Corp., N.Y.C.; chmn. com. div. WNET-Public Broadcasting; bd. trustees, mem. exec. com., chmn. bus. com. Met. Mus. Art.; mem. internat. adv. bd. Bus. Coun. United Nations. With U.S. Army, 1953-55. Recipient Human Relations award Anti-Defamation League, 1972, Achievement award Sch. Bus. Alumni, CCNY, 1972, Citizens Union award, 1980, Disting. Alumni award for Outstanding Career Accomplishment Baruch Coll., 1990; named Marketer of Yr. N.Y. chpt. Am. Mktg. Assn., 1982, Outstanding Exec. Crain's N.Y. Bus., 1987. Mem. Mcpl. Art Soc. Clubs: Princeton (N.Y.C.), Yale. Office: Backer Spielvogel Bates Worldwide Inc/Chrysler Bldg 405 Lexington Ave New York NY 10174-0002

SPIES, WAYNE THOMAS, management consultant; b. Onawa, Iowa, Oct. 11, 1953; s. Leslie Merrill and Bettie Leola (Ericksen) S.; m. Nancy Ann Miller, Aug. 14, 1976; children: Dylan Wayne, Jonathan Miller, Claryn Ericka. BBA, Iowa State U., 1986; M in Pub. and Pvt. Mgmt., Yale U., 1990. Owner Am. Artists Mgmt., Ames, Iowa, 1975-83; owner, founder Music Master, West Des Moines, Iowa, 1976-84; cons. Rsch. Assocs., Ames, 1986-87; owner Spies & Co., New Haven, 1990—; bd. dirs. Eurobox Am., N.Y.C.; cons. Yale Computer Ctr., New Haven. Author: (column) Heebie Jeebie Ergo Sum, 1985—; editor: (newsletter) M-Pressions, 1985-87. Internat. del. Am. Fedn. Musicians, Boone, Iowa, 1978-83; corp. treas. Children's Svcs. of Cen. Iowa, Ames, 1985-86; fin. chair 1st United Meth. Ch., Ames, 1986-87. Recipient Spl. Recognition Muscular Dystrophy Assn., 1983. Mem. Inst. Mgmt. Sci., Acad. Mgmt., Yale Club of N.Y.C., ISU Ambassadors, Intertel, Scottish Rite (class orator 1986), Ancient Free & Accepted Masons, Mensa (life, nat. publs. officer 1989-90). Democrat. Home: 48 Dallas St Hamden CT 06514-3938 Office: DCSS 175 Whitney Ave New Haven CT 06511-3712

SPILHAUS, KARL HENRY, lawyer, trade association executive; b. N.Y.C., July 19, 1946; s. Athelstan Frederick and Mary (Atkins) S.; m. Constance DeLaMater, Dec. 30, 1989; stepchildren: Mary Alexis Welch, Antonia Morrow Welch. BA, U. Pa., 1971; JD, New Eng. Sch. Law, 1975. Bar: Mass. 1975. Staff atty. Legal Svcs., Cape Cod and the Islands, 1975-76; with No. Textile Assn., 1976—, pres., 1982—; exec. dir. Cashmere and Camel Hair Mfrs. Inst., 1984—; U.S. del. Internat. Labor Orgn. Textiles Com.; mem. adv. coun. U. Mass., Cartmouth, 1979—; arbitrator Am. Arbitration Assn., Boston. Trustee Mus. Am. Textile History; parish com. mem. Eliot Ch. of South Natick. Served with USMC, 1966-69, Vietnam. Mem. Lawyers Assn. Textile Industry, Mass. Bar Assn., Boston Bar Assn., Soc. King's Chapel, Phi Psi (hon.). Office: Northern Textile Assn 230 Congress St Boston MA 02110-2409

SPILLANE, STEPHEN ANDREW, special education educator; b. Boston, May 20, 1955; s. Timothy Joseph and Ruth Olivia (Hambelton) S.; m. Anne Elizabeth Fosnot, Aug. 11, 1984. BA, U. Mass., 1978; MA, U. Conn., 1983, PhD, 1991. Cert. spl. edn. educator, 1-12, Conn. Tchr. Charlestown High Sch., Boston, 1980-83; learning disabilities specialist Adelphi Univ., Garden City, N.Y., 1984; learning disabilities thcr. Eagle Hill Sch., Greenwich, Conn., 1984-86; doctoral fellow/grad. asst. U. Conn., Storrs, 1986-87, asst. coord., 1987-88; cons. Conn. Dept. High Edn., Hartford, 1990-91; ednl. cons. Brookfield, Conn., 1989—; adj. prof. U. Hartford, West Hartford, Conn., 1989-90; coord. svcs. for students with learning disabilities Norwalk Community Coll., 1991—. Co-author: (monograph) Teaching Dilemmas . . . 1991. Recipient Doctoral Rsch. fellowship U. Conn. Rsch. Found., Storrs, Conn., 1990, Leadership fellowship, U.S.O.E., Washington, 1986. Mem. AAUP, Conn. Assn. for Children with Learning Disabilities, Assn. On Handicapped Students Svc. Progs. in Postsecondary Edn. Home: 56 Village Walk Wilton CT 06897

SPILLER, HENRY ALFRED LAGRANDEUR, toxicologist; b. Asucion, Paraguay, Aug. 15, 1954; came to U.S., 1956; s. Jack Winslow and Mary Sibela (LaGrandeur) S.; m. Susan Joyce Essing, Aug. 25, 1984; children: Sarah Sybil Essing, Natalie Elizabeth. BA in English and Spanish, Rutgers U., 1977, BS in Nursing, 1983; MS in Epidemiology, Columbia Pacific U., 1988. Nurse trauma unit Univ. Hosp., Newark, 1983-84; poison specialist N.J. Poison Info. and Edn. System, Newark, 1984-86; clin. prof. Phila. Coll. Pharmacy, 1987—, Temple U. Sch. Pharmacy, Phila., 1991—; toxicologist Delaware Valley Regional Poison Ctr., Phila., 1986—. Mem. Am. Acad. Clin. Toxicology, Emergency Nurses Assn., Sigma Theta Tau.

SPILLMAN, MARJORIE ROSE, dancer; b. Norfork, Va., Jan. 5; d. William Bert and Rose Marjorie (Naperski) S.; m. David E. Marks, Apr. 4, 1985; children: F. Oscar Marks, Miranda Rose. AS, Mt. Ida Jr. Coll., 1974; CT, Northeastern U., 1975; BS in Nursing, U. Mass., 1977. RN, Mass. Charge nurse VA Med. Ctr., Northampton, Mass., 1977-82; dancer N.E. Am. Ballet, Northampton, 1982, Ballet Theater Sch., Springfield, Mass., 1982-84; sales rep. Winthrop Pharm., N.Y.C., 1982—; dancer Smith Coll., Northampton, 1984—; prin. dancer Project Opera, Northampton, 1984-86; dancer Polobulus East St. Dance, Hadley, Mass., 1985; dance and theatre reviewer Holyoke Trascript Telegram, 1991, producing dir., 1990-91. Dancer, creator part of Carmen in Carmen, 1985; dancer, choreographer A Victorian Evening, 1986; dancer Nutcracker Ballet Pioneer Valley Ballet, 1988; creator, producer The Halloween House at Sunnyside, 1990-91; author, actor play Mary P. Wells Smith Narrates, 1987. Democrat. Lutheran.

SPILMAN, RAYMOND, industrial designer; b. Wichita, Kans., Jan. 12, 1911; s. Robert Bruce and Willa (Wood) S.; m. Mary Jordan, May 15, 1937; children: Susan, Alden. Student, Kans. State U., 1933. Stylist Gen. Motors Corp., 1935-39; staff designer Walter Dorwin Teague, N.Y.C., 1940-42; chief designer Johnson Cushing & Nevell, N.Y.C., 1942-46; propr. Raymond Spilman Indsl. Design, N.Y.C., 1946, Stamford, Conn., 1963, Darien, Conn., 1983—; ednl. adviser, lectr. design and design curriculums, color applications in design. Mem. editorial bd., Color Research and Applications Quar., 1976-80; producer films on color and design. Recipient Elec. Mfg. Design award Gates Pub. Co., 1950, award U.S. Trade Fair Exhbns., Yugoslavia, 1955, Italy, 1957, Peru, 1959 and 63, Poland, 1964, Graphis award, Graphis mag. Italy, 1957, Internat. Triennale award Undicesima Triennale di Milano, Milan, Italy, 1957, Wescon award of merit West Cost Elec. Prodn. Mfg. Assn., 1959, Design USA award Indsl. Design Soc. Am., 1965, Product Engring. Master Dseign awards, 1959, 66, Housewares Design award, 1967, 68, citation for design in steel Am. Iron and Steel Inst., 1974, John Vassos award Indsl. Design Soc. Am., 1985; Endowment Arts design project fellow Nat. Endowment Arts, 1977; Design Advancement grantee Nat. Endowment Arts, 1989-90. Fellow Indsl. Design Soc. Am.; mem. Am. Soc. Indsl. Designers (pres. 1960-62, chmn. bd. 1963-64), Am. Inter-Soc. Color Council (dir. 1970-72, 76-77), Phi Delta Theta. Home and Office: Raymond Spilman Indsl Design One Althea Ln Darien CT 06820

SPILNER, MAGGIE L., editor; b. Elizabeth, N.J., June 6, 1952; d. Robert Walker and Dorothy Ann (Schoen) S.; m. Steven P. Schmitt, May 27, 1972 (div. Sept. 1981); children: Erice Spilner Schmitt, Robin Spilner Schmitt. BA, Cedar Crest Coll., 1974. Cert. elem. sch. tchr. Reader svc. corr. Rodale Press/Prevention Mag., Emmans, Pa., 1984, dir. reader svc. dept., 1984-86, exec. editor Walker's World newsletter, 1986—, sr. editor, walking editor, 1987—; speaker numerous orgns. Co-author: The Practical Encyclopedia of Walking for Health and Fitness, 1992; contbr. articles to mags. including Family Circle. Co-chair Interfaith Reflection Conf., Bethesda, Md., 1991; newsletter editor Parents Without Ptnrs., Allentown, Pa., 1990; bd. advisors Coalition to Make Am. More Walkable, 1992. Mem. Prevention Mag. Walking Club (bd. dirs. 1991—), Allentown Hiking Club (leader, co-founder 1988). Office: Rodale Press Inc 33 E Minor St Emmaus PA 18098

SPINDLER, HARRY KEELER, academic administrator; b. Grand Marsh, Wis., June 1, 1929; s. Harry O. and Mary E. (Keeler) S.; m. Eunice Marie Sheley, June 26, 1954; children: Laura, Brian, Stanley. BA, Hamline U., St. Paul, 1953; MPA, Syracuse U., 1954. Adminstrv. analyst Dept. Budget State of Wis., Madison, 1954-60, exec. sec. Mental Health Adv. Com., 1960-62, asst. dir. Coord. Coun. on Higher Edn., 1962-67; asst. vice chancellor SUNY System, Albany, 1967-72, vice chancellor fin. and bus., 1972-84; sr. vice chancellor SUNY, Albany, 1984—; trustee Coll. Retirement Equities Fund, N.Y.C., 1985—; evaluator Mid. States Assn. Colls. and Schs., Phila., 1972—. Mem. Natt. Assn. Coll. and Univ. Bus. Officers (com. chmn. 1984-86), Phi Beta Kappa. Home: 30 Longwood Dr Delmar NY 12054-3737 Office: SUNY State University Pla Albany NY 12246

SPINELLI, VINCENT JOHN, university administrator; b. Bklyn., Oct. 23, 1947; s. Salvatore Lawrence and Mary (Parascandola) S.; m. Eileen Regina Resch, Sept. 19, 1970; children: Robert, Maria. BA in English, St. Francis Coll., Bklyn., 1969. Asst. dir. United Hosp. Fund, N.Y.C., 1970-72, NYU Alumni Fedn., N.Y.C., 1972-75; devel. mgr. NYU, N.Y.C., 1975-77, assoc. dir. devel., 1977-79, dir. devel., 1979-81; dir. devel. N.Y. Hosp.-Cornell Med. Ctr., N.Y.C., 1981-86, Met. Opera, N.Y.C., 1986-91; exec. v.p. for institutional advancement Pace U., N.Y.C./Westchester, 1991—. Bd. dirs. St. Peter's Sch., Port Washington, N.Y., 1990—. Mem. Alpha Phi Delta. Roman Catholic. Office: Pace U 1 Pace Pla New York NY 10038

SPINGARN, CLIFFORD LEROY, internist, educator; b. Bklyn., May 8, 1912; s. Alexander and Eleanor (Trinz) S.; m. Eleanor Harrison, June 9, 1937; children: John Harrison, Alexandra. AB, Columbia U., 1933, MD, 1937. Diplomate Am. Bd. Internal Medicine. Intern Mt. Sinai Hosp., N.Y.C., 1937-40, asst. attending physician, 1946-63, assoc. attending physician, 1963—, chief parasitology clinic, 1956-80; attending physician Doctors Hosp., N.Y.C., 1968—, chmn. com. on continuing med. edn., 1976—; pvt. practice internal medicine N.Y.C., 1946—; instr. pharmacology Columbia, 1940-42; asst. clin. prof. preventive medicine NYU, 1956-68; assoc. clin. prof. medicine Mt. Sinai Sch. Medicine, 1966-83, lectr. in medicine, 1983—. Author numerous papers. Trustee Milton Helpern Libr. Legal Medicine, 1982—; bd. dirs. N.Y. Faculty Continuing Med. Edn., 1982-86. Lt. (j.g.) to lt. comdr. M.C., USNR, 1942-46; lt. comdr. ret. res. Recipient Disting. Svc. award Doctors Hosp., 1987. Fellow ACP, N.Y. Acad. Medicine; mem. AAAS, N.Y. Soc. Tropical Medicine, Am. Soc. Tropical Medicine and Hygiene, Am. Soc. Parasitologists, Am. Soc. Internal Medicine, Med. Soc. County N.Y. (chmn. grievance com. 1969-72, chmn. bd. censors 1978-80, pres. 1981, trustee 1982-87, Disting. Svc. award 1986), Gerontol. Soc. Am., Soc. Internal Medicine County New York (pres. 1965-67), N.Y. State Soc. Internal Medicine, N.Y. Cardiological Soc. (bd. dir. 1971-73), Phi Beta Kappa, Sigma Xi, Alpha Omega Alpha. Home: 201 E 79th St New York NY 10021-0830 Office: 66 E 80th St New York NY 10021-0223

SPINGARN, RICHARD ALAN, business owner; b. Newark, Mar. 20, 1951; s. Bernard J. and Rita (Marsa) S.; m. Penny Kay Andreas, Oct. 27, 1974; 1 child, Russell. BA, Syracuse (N.Y.) U., 1973, MS, 1974. Announcer Sta. KWMU U. Mo., St. Louis, 1975-77; writer Cornell U., Ithaca, 1978-80; reporter Ithaca Jour., 1980-81; owner Eagle Envelope Co., Trumansburg, N.Y., 1981—. Mem. Printing and Graphics Assn. of the Finger Lakes (pres. Ithaca chpt. 1988-89), Tompkins County Amateur Radio Club (pres.), Rotary. Home: 6067 Sirrine Rd Trumansburg NY 14886-9612 Office: PO Box 236 Ithaca NY 14851-0236

SPINK, FRANK HENRY, JR., association manager, urban planner; b. Chgo., Sept. 23, 1935; s. Frank Henry and Madeline Imogene (Ryan) S.; m. Barbara Jean Westbrook, June 30, 1962; children: Christina Jean, Suzan Josette. BArch, U. Ill., 1958; M of Urban Planning, U. Wash., 1963. Planner City of Bellevue, Wash., 1961-62, City of Fremont, Calif., 1963-66; planning dir. City of Pleasonton, Calif., 1966-67; community builders coun. dir. ULI-The Urban Land Inst., Washington, 1967-72; program div. dir. ULI-The Urban Land Inst., 1972-74, tech. publs. div. dir., 1974-75, publs. dir., 1976-80, publs. v.p., 1981—; founding mem. and trustee emeritus Partners for Liveable Places, Washington. Creator/pub.: (subscription svc.) Project Reference File, 1971—; creator (reference book series) Community Builders Handbook Series, 1975—; contbr. numerous books by ULI, 1975—. Lt. USNR, 1958-61. Mem. Am. Inst. of Cert. Planners, Va. Watercolor Soc. (founder artist), Sumi'e Soc. of Am. (gold medal 1990, Best of Show 1991), Potomac Valley Watercolorists (pres.), Fremont Artist Assn. (pres.), Soc. of Western Artists, Lambda Alpha Internat. (pres. George Washington chpt. 1990-91, v.p. East 1992-93). Republican. Episcopal. Home: 5158 Piedmont Pl Annandale VA 22003-5527 Office: ULI-The Urban Land Inst 625 Indiana Ave NW Washington DC 20004-2930

SPIRA, ROBERT S., gastroenterologist; b. N.Y.C., June 20, 1949; s. Bernhard and Molly (Linchitz) S.; m. Naomi Nutkis, Dec. 29, 1973; children: Daniele, Etan, Benjamin. BA, NYU, 1971, MD, 1975. Diplomate Nat. Bd. Med. Examiners, Am. Bd. Internal Medicine, Am. Bd. Gastroenterology. Resident in medicine NYU and N.Y. VA Med. Ctr., N.Y.C., 1975-79; fellow in gastroenterology N.Y. VA Med. Ctr., N.Y.C., 1979-81; clin. asst. prof. medicine N.J. Sch. Medicine, 1983—; assoc. prof. medicine Sch. Post Grad. Medicine, Seton Hall U., N.J., 1988—. Presenter in field, 1981—. Fellow Acad. Medicine N.J.; mem. N.J. Soc. Gastrointestinal Endoscopy (pres. 1990, 91), N.J. Soc. Gastroenterology (exec. bd. 1987—), Ileitis Colitis Found. (med. adv. bd. 1991—), Am. Coll. Physicians. Jewish. Office: 743 Northfield Ave West Orange NJ 07052

SPIRER, HERBERT FRED, statistician, information management educator, consultant; b. Phila., Oct. 8, 1925; s. Irvin E. and Rose (Rice) S.; m. Louise Ziegler, Feb. 3, 1950; children: Jeffrey David, Daniel Rice, Ellen Ruth. B Engring. Physics, Cornell U., 1951; MS, NYU, 1965, PhD, 1970. Dir. R&D CGS Labs., Stamford, Conn., 1954-60; pres. Engring. Info. Assocs., Stamford, 1960-62; mgr. servos AMF Rsch. Lab., Stamford, 1962-66; ops. mgr. Gen. Time Corp., Stamford, 1966-70; prof. MBA program U. Conn., Stamford, 1970—. Author: Business Statistics, 1975, (with others) Quantitative Analysis for Business, 1984, Misused Statistics, 1987; also articles. Vice pres. Inst. for Study of Genocide, John Jay Coll. Criminal Justice, 1988—. With USN, 1943-46, PTO. Mem. AAAS, Am. Statis. Assn. (chair sci. freedom and human rights com. 1989—). Democrat. Home: 71 Big Oak Rd Stamford CT 06903-4636 Office: U Conn Stamford CT 06903

SPIRITO, ANTHONY, clinical psychologist, psychiatry educator; b. Elizabeth, N.J., Mar. 25, 1953; s. Anthony L. and Ernestine (DeCabia) S.; m. Susan Gayle Baybutt, Aug. 20, 1977; children: Emilia, Evan. BA, Cornell U., 1975; PhD, Va. Commonwealth U., 1981; MA (hon.), Brown U., 1991. Staff psychologist Dana Farber Cancer Inst. Children's Hosp., Boston, 1982-84; assoc. prof. R.I. Hosp./Brown U., Providence, 1984-90; dir. psychology dept. R.I. Hosp., 1989—; assoc. dir. tng. Clin. Psychology Consortium, Brown U., Providence, 1991—. Contbr. articles to profl. jours., chpts. to books. Nat. Inst. Child Health and Human Devel. grantee, 1985-90, R.I. Dept. Health grantee, 1987-89. Mem. Am. Psychol. Assn., Assn. for Advancement of Behavior Therapy, Soc. Behavioral Medicine. Office: RI Hosp Psychiatry Dept 593 Eddy St Providence RI 02903-4923

SPIRO, JODY DONNA, educational manager; b. Queens, N.Y., Mar. 29, 1952. AB, Barnard Coll., 1974; EdD, Columbia U., 1989, MEd, 1986; MPA, NYU, 1979. Jr. tng. analyst Chase Manhattan Bank, N.A., N.Y.C., 1974-75, sr. tng. analyst, 1975-76, asst. treas., 1976-77, 2d v.p., 1977-79; mgmt. cons. N.Y.C. Bd. of Edn., Bklyn., 1979-80, dir. mgmt. and staff devel. high sch. div., 1980-84, exec. asst. to chancellor for planning and mgmt., 1984-88; planning officer L.I. U., Greenvale, N.Y., 1988-91; dir. of planning Soros Found., N.Y.C., 1991—; tchr. higher edn. CCNY, N.Y.C., 1981-82, Pace U., N.Y.C., 1987-88, L.I. U., Bklyn., 1988—, C.W. Post Coll., L.I. U., Greenvale, 1988-91, NYU, 1991—. Mem. Am. Assn. Higher Edn., Am. Coun. on Edn., N.Y. Organizational Devel. Network. Home: 115 E 34th St Apt 5A New York NY 10016-4616 Office: Soros Found 888 Seventh Ave Ste 1901 New York NY 10106

SPIRO, ROBERT GUNTER, biochemist, physician; b. Berlin, Germany, Jan. 5, 1929; s. Harry L. and Kate (Loewenstein) S.; m. Mary Jane Paisley, June 21, 1952; children: David Jonathan, Mark Douglas. A.B., Columbia Coll., 1951; M.D., SUNY, Syracuse, 1955; A.M. (hon.), Harvard U., 1975. Intern SUNY Upstate Med Center, Syracuse, 1955-56; research fellow in biol. chemistry Harvard Med. Sch., Boston, 1956-58; research fellow to assoc. in medicine Mass. Gen. Hosp., 1958-61; assoc., asst. prof., assoc. prof. Harvard Med. Sch., 1961-74, prof. biol. chemistry, 1974—; chief Lab. Complex Carbohydrates and Biomembranes, Joslin Diabetes Ctr.; sr. biochemist Peter Bent Brigham and Women's Hosp.; cons. Brigham and Women's Hosp. Editorial bd. Jour. Biol. Chemistry, Diabetologia. Contbr. articles to profl. jours. Recipient Lilly award Am. Diabetes Assn., 1968; Claude Bernard award European Diabetes Assn., 1975; Moses Barron award Twin Cities Assn. Diabetes, 1975; Disting. Alumnus award Syracuse Med. Alumni Assn., 1977. Mem. Am. Soc. Biol. Chemists, Am. Chem. Soc., Am. Diabetes Assn., Soc. Complex Carbohydrates (pres. 1978). Home: 19 Greylock Rd Allston MA 02134-2505 Office: 1 Joslin Pl Boston MA 02215-5397

SPIRO, THOMAS GEORGE, chemistry educator; b. Aruba, Netherlands Antilles, Nov. 7, 1935; s. Andor and Ilona S.; m. Helen Handin, Aug. 21, 1959; children—Peter, Michael. B.S., UCLA, 1956; Ph.D., M.I.T., 1960. Fulbright researcher U. Copenhagen, Denmark, 1960-61; NIH fellow Royal Inst. Tech., Stockholm, 1962-63; research chemist Calif. Research Corp., LaHabra, 1961-62; mem. faculty Princeton U., 1963—, prof. chemistry, 1974—, head dept., 1979-88, Eugene Higgins prof., 1981—. Author: (with William M. Stigliani) Environmental Issues in Chemical Perspective, 1980, Environmental Science in Perspective, 1980; contbr. articles to profl. jours. Recipient Bomem-Michelson award Bomem Corp., 1986; NATO sr. fellow, 1972, Guggenheim fellow, 1990. Fellow AAAS; mem. Am. Chem. Soc., Phi Beta Kappa, Sigma Xi. Office: Princeton U Dept Chemistry Princeton NJ 08544

SPITSBERG, VITALY LEV, biochemistry educator; b. Kazatin, USSR, July 27, 1938; came to U.S., 1975; s. Lev Israel and Anna Efim (Rubchinsky) S.; m. Margarita Bakaeva, Sept. 1960 (div. 1970); 1 child, Vladimir; m. Natalia Krasnova, Nov. 19, 1971. MD, Moscow 1st Med. Inst., 1961; PhD, Inst. Biophysics Acad. Sci., USSR, 1966. Jr. scientist Inst. Med. Chemistry, Moscow, 1961-62; sr. scientist Inst. Med. Biology Acad. USSR, Moscow, 1966-71, Inst. Devel. Biology Acad. USSR, Moscow, 1971-74; project assoc. Northwestern U., Chgo., 1975-76; rsch. assoc. U. Wis., Madison, 1976-78, Syracuse (N.Y.) U., 1978-79; sr. rsch. assoc. St. Louis U., 1979-82; vis. rsch. prof. U. Nebr., Lincoln, 1982-83; vis. prof. Cornell U., Ithaca, N.Y., 1983-86, sr. rsch. assoc., 1987-91. Contbr. articles to scholarly and profl. jours. Mem. Jewish World Congress, 1989. Grantee NSF, 1982, 84. Mem. Am.

Soc. Biol. Chemists, N.Y. Acad. Scis. Home: 124 Snyder Hill Rd Ithaca NY 14850-6320

SPITSBERGEN, JAMES C., chemist, consultant; b. Washington, Sept. 1, 1926; s. Henry Essing and Edith Lillian (Richter) S.; m. Margaret Ann Ableman, May 1957 (div. 1972); children: Glenn, Diane; m. Adelaide Mary Alvarez, June 28, 1980. BS, George Washington U., 1949; MS, U. Del., 1959, PhD, 1962. Chemist U.S. Army Engr. Corp, Ft. Belvior, Va., 1951; sr. chemist Electric Hose & Rubber, Wilmington, Del., 1951-61, DuPont, Wilmington, Del., 1962-68; project leader Witco Chem., Oakland, N.J., 1968-83; cons. Unitrode Corp., Watertown, Mass., 1983-85; mgr. Epoxy Cons., Franklin Lakes, N.J., 1985—. Contbr. articles to profl. jours.; patentee in field. With USN, 1944-46. Recipient Nat. Lead fellowship, 1961. Mem. IEEE, Internat. Electronics Packaging Soc., Internat. Soc. Hybrid Mfrs., Am. Chem. Soc., Soc. Plastics Engrs. (div. bd. dirs. 1990—), Surface Mount Tech. Assn. Republican. Home and Office: 696 Knollwood Rd Franklin Lakes NJ 07417-1710

SPITZ, CHARLES ALFRED, architect; b. N.Y.C., Aug. 4, 1945; s. Charles Herman and Ola Gladys (Monroe) S.; m. Margaret Anne Hundley, Oct. 31, 1970; children: Carla Kelly, Charles Andrew. BArch, U. Kans., 1972; M City and Regional Planning, Rutgers U., 1978. Registered architect, N.J., N.Y., Pa., S.C., Hawaii; cert. Nat. Coun. Archtl. Registration Bds.; lic. profl. planner, N.J. Project mgr. Anthony C. Covais, AIA, Middletown, N.J., 1972-74; prin. planner Monmouth County Planning Bd., Freehold, N.J., 1974-79; assoc. Tomaino & Tomaino Architects, Deal, N.J., 1979-83; prin., architect, planner Charles A. Spitz, AIA, West Long Branch, N.J., 1983—; coord., instr. Brookdale C.C., Lincroft, N.J., 1978-81; chmn. Monmouth County Constrn. Bd. Appeals, Freehold, 1976-80, alt., 1989-92; mem. Middletown Twp. Constrn. Bd. Appeals, 1977-82, chmn., 1982; chmn. Red Bank (N.J.) Constrn. Bd. Appeals,1 988-93; mem. pub. edn. adv. coun. N.J. Fire Safety Commn., 1985-92; commr. N.J. Bd. Architects, 1990—, v.p., 1991-92, pres., 1992-93. Contbr. articles to profl. publs. Past pres. Kahalu'u Bay Villas Condominium Assn.; v.p. Monmouth coun. Boy Scouts Am., 1990-93. Lt. comdr. USCGR. Recipient Disting. Eagle Scout award Nat. coun. Boy Scouts Am., 1991. Mem. AIA (bldg. performance & regulations com. 1987-92), N.J. Soc. Architects (bd. dirs. 1984-89, 90-92, pres. Jersey Shore chpt. 1987, bldg. performance & regulations com. 1981-92, com. chmn. 1982-91, award of merit 1981, honor award 1987), Nat. Acad. Bldg. Inspection Engrs., Constrn. Specifications Inst., Soc. Am. Mil. Engrs., Bldg. Ofcls. and Code Adminstrs. Internat. (nat. bldg. code change com. 1990-92), Internat. Conf. Bldg. Ofcls., So. Bldg. Code Congress Internat., Nat. Fire Protection Assn., Nat. Eagle Scout Assn. (life), Profl. Assn. Diving Instrs., Res. Officers Assn. (life), U.S. Navy League (life), U.S. Naval Inst. (life), Am. Philatelic Soc. (life), U. Kans. Alumni Assn. (life), Soc. of Sts. John, Molly Pitcher Camp Heroes of '76 (life), Red Bank Benevolent Assn. (past pres., life trustee), High Twelve Internat. (past pres., past state v.p.), Nat. Sojourners (life), Masons, K.T., Elks, Alpha Phi Omega (life). Lutheran. Home and Office: 51 Bampton Pl West Long Branch NJ 07764

SPITZ, HERMAN HEINRICH, retired psychologist; b. Paterson, N.J., Mar. 2, 1925; s. Benjamin and Ruth (Heinrich) S.; m. Ruth M. Goidel, May 13, 1952; children: Debra L., Kenneth A. BA, Lafayette Coll., Easton, Pa., 1948; PhD, NYU, 1955. Asst. psychologist Trenton (N.J.) State Hosp., 1951-55, sr. psychologist, 1955-57; rsch. assoc. E.R. Johnstone Tng. & Rsch. Ctr., Bordentown, N.J., 1957-62, dir. rsch., 1962-89; ret. Author: The Raising of Intelligence, 1986; contbr. articles to profl. jours. With U.S. Army, 1943-45. Recipient Founders Day award, NYU, 1956, Brian E. Tomlinson award, 1975, Profl. Accomplishment award, State of N.J., 1980. Fellow Am. Psychol. Assn.; mem. Am. Acad. on Mental Retardation. Home: 389 Terhune Rd Princeton NJ 08540-3637

SPITZ, ROBERT IRVING, educator; b. Lynn, Mass., Jan. 29, 1942; s. Abraham S. and Ethel (Bloom) S.; m. Mimi Deborah Lipman, June 16, 1963; children: Laurence M., Steven D., Amy R. AA, Boston U., 1961; BS in Edn., Salem State Coll., 1963; MS in Edn., CUNY, 1967; cert. in Jewish edn., Hebrew Union Coll., 1968; CAGS, Hofstra U., 1968; MEd, Columbia U., 1985; PhD, Pacific Western U., 1987. Tchr. Lynn Pub. Schs., 1963-64, Hempstead (N.Y.) Pub. Schs., 1964-65, Bellmore (N.Y.) Pub. Schs., 1965—; prin. East Northport (N.Y.) Jewish. Ctr., 1969-75, dir. edn., 1970-75; dir. edn. Old Westbury (N.Y.) Hebrew Congretation, 1987—; dir. edn. Merrick (N.Y.) Jewish Ctr., 1975-81, Temple Beth Torah, Dix Hills, N.Y., 1982-87; cons. Behrman House Books, N.Y.C., 1987; mem. cons. team USTEP Dept. Edn. United Synagogue, N.Y.C., 1991; mem. Bellmore Curriculum Devel. Com., 1989. Contbg. author Shofar Mag.; contbr. articles to mags. Sec.-treas. Elwood (N.Y.) Taxpayers Assn., 1980-81; mem. Jewish Educators Assembly. Mem. N.Y. State Tchrs. Retirement System (del. 1976—), N.Y. State United Tchrs., L.I. Prins. Assn. (v.p. 1985-89), Nat. Assn. Temple Edn., Fedn. Men's Clubs, East Northport Jewish Ctr. Men's Club (v.p., pres. 1988-90), Masons, Kappa Delta Phi. Home: 45 Verleye Ave East Northport NY 11731-5822 Office: Old Westbury Hebrew Cong 21 Old Westbury Rd Old Westbury NY 11568-1603

SPITZER, DAVID WILLIAM, instrumentation engineer, consultant, educator; b. N.Y.C., Apr. 30, 1951. BSEE, U. Conn., 1973; MSEE, U. Ill., 1975. Instrumentation engr. U.S. Steel Corp., Pitts., 1975-80; process control systems engr. Mobay Chem. Corp., Pitts., 1980-83; mgr. of utility, instrumentation engr. Nepera, Inc., Harriman, N.Y., 1983—; mem. adj. staff Instrument Soc. Am., Research Triangle Park, N.C., 1983—; instr. Assn. Energy Engrs., Atlanta, 1988—; cons. and educator in field, 1986—. Author: Industrial Flow Measurement, 1984, 2d edit., 1990, The Application of Variable Speed Drives, 1987, Variable Speed Drives-Principles and Applications for Energy Cost Savings, 1990; editor: Flow Measurement, 1991; contbr. articles to profl. jours. Mem. ASME (measurement of fluid flow in closed conduits com.), Assn. Energy Engrs., Instrument Soc. Am. (sr.). Home: 8 Perth Ave Chestnut Ridge NY 10977

SPITZER, ERIC RANDOLPH, healthcare utilization management executive; b. Malden, Mass., July 16, 1943; s. Richard and Sara (Bookman) S.; m. Suzanne Spitzer, July 2, 1966; children: James, Andre, Stephanie. BA, Colby Coll., 1965; MBA, Boston U., 1967. Supr. AT&T Long Lines, White Plains, N.Y., 1967-69; asst. to tech. dir. Perkin-Elmer Corp., Norwalk, Conn., 1969-70; comptroller ITT Corp., N.Y.C., 1970-86; dir. br. ops. Contel Bus. Systems, Dedham, Mass., 1986-88; pres., chief exec. officer Peer Review Analysis, Inc., Malden, Mass., 1988—. Pres. Temple Sinai, Warwick, R.I., 1983-86. Named to "Inc. 500" Inc. Mag., 1990. Mem. Pres.'s Assn. of Am. Mgmt. Assn., Inc. Coun. of Growing Cos., Fin. Execs. Inst. Home: 1255 High Hawk Rd East Greenwich RI 02818 Office: Peer Review Analysis 380 Pleasant St Malden MA 02148

SPIVACK, CHARLOTTE RUTH, English language educator, writer; b. Schoharie, N.Y., July 23, 1926; d. William Lewis and Laura (Snyder) Roscoe; m. Bernard Spivack, Oct. 17, 1956; children: Carla Naomi, Loren Adlai. BA, SUNY, Albany, 1947; MA, Cornell U., 1948; PhD, U. Mo., 1954. Instr. U. Mo., Columbia, 1952-54; asst. prof. Richmond (Va.) Profl. Inst., 1954-56; assoc. prof. Fisk U., Nashville, 1956-64; prof. English, U. Mass., Amherst, 1964—. Author: George Chapman, 1967, The Comedy of Evil on Shakespeare's Stage, 1978, Ursula K. Le Guin, 1984, Merlin's Daughters, 1987. AAUW fellow, 1959. Office: U Mass Amherst MA 01003

SPIVAK, JERRY LEPOW, physician, hematologist; b. N.Y.C., Jan. 5, 1938; s. Mitchell and Hilda (Lepow) S.; m. Wendy Ann Mulitz, Nov. 19, 1967; children: Laura, Adam. AB, Princeton U., 1960; MD, Cornell U., 1964. Cert. internal medicine, hematology. Intern Johns Hopkins Hosp., Balt., 1964-65, resident, 1965-66; resident N.Y. Hosp., 1968-69; clin. assoc. NIH, USPHS, 1966-68; fellow in hematology Johns Hopkins U., Balt., 1969-71; chief resident in medicine Johns Hopkins Hosp., Balt., 1971-72; asst. prof. medicine Johns Hopkins U., Balt., 1972-78, assoc. prof. medicine, 1978-88; prof. medicine Johns Hopkins Univ., Balt., 1988—, dir., hematology div., 1980, prof. oncology, 1991—; chmn. Erythropotin adv. bd. Ortho Biotech, Raritan, N.J., 1987—; cons. editor Johns Hopkins U. Press, Balt., 1986—. Co-author: Manual of Clinical Problems in Internal Medicine, 1990; editor: Yearbook of Hematology, 1987—, Fundamentals of Clinical Hematology, 1992; also over 100 articles. With USPHS, 1966-68. Fellow Am. Coll. Physicians; mem. Am. Soc. Hematology, Am. Clin. and Climatological Assn., So. Blood Club (pres. 1988), Phi Beta Kappa, Alpha Omega Alpha. Office: Johns Hopkins Univ Sch of Medicine 720 Rutland Ave Baltimore MD 21205-2109

SPIVAK, STEVEN MARK, textile and standards engineer, educator; b. N.Y.C., Oct. 11, 1942; s. Irving Samuel and Mollie (Epstein) S. BS in Textile Engring., Phila. Coll. Textiles, 1963; MS in Textiles, Ga. Inst. Tech., 1965; PhD in Fiber Sci., U. Manchester, United Kingdom, 1967. Asst. prof. Phila. Coll. Textiles and Sci., 1968-70; asst. prof. U. Md., College Park, 1970-74, assoc. prof., 1974-83, prof., 1983—; sr. standards analyst Nat. Inst. Standards and Tech., Gaithersburg, Md., 1974-75, 86-87; expert U.S.-Saudi Arabian Joint Commn. for Econ. Cooperation, Washington, 1985—, U.S. FTC, Washington, 1985—; chmn. ISO/COPOLCO consumer policy and internat. standards com., Geneva, 1991—; spl. asst. U.S. Gen. Svcs. Adminstrn., 1991—. Co-editor: A Sourcebook on Standards Information, 1991; contbr. articles to Textile Rsch. Jour., Textile Chemist and Colorist, ASTM Standardization News, Standards Engring. Fellow Textile Inst. (chartered textile tech. 1979), Standards Engring. Soc. (chmn. Washington sect. 1985-87), Am. Nat. Standards Inst. (bd. dirs. 1983-91), Fiber Soc. (pres. 1984). Home: 132 10th St NE Washington DC 20002-6212 Office: U Md Dept Textiles Consumer Econ College Park MD 20742-7531

SPLETE, ALLEN PETERJOHN, association executive, educator; b. Carthage, N.Y., June 24, 1938; s. Howard Henry and Minnie Bertha (Peterjohn) S.; m. Marilyn Lois Detweiler, June 18, 1966; children—Heidi, Michael. BA, St. Lawrence U., 1960; MA with distinction, Colgate U., 1962; PhD, Syracuse U., 1968; LHD, Campbellsville Coll., 1990; LLD, Davis and Elkins Coll., 1990. Adminstrv. asst. to v.p. acad. affairs Syracuse U., N.Y., 1965-68, assoc. dean, exec. asst. to provost, 1968-70; v.p. for acad. planning St. Lawrence U., Canton, N.Y., 1970-82; pres. Westminster Coll., New Wilmington, Pa., 1982-85, Council Ind. Colls., Washington, 1985-91; dir. Council for Understanding Tech. in Human Affairs, 1985-91; dir. Nat. Prepaid Tuition Plan, 1988-91; cons. York Coll., Pa., 1974; mem. planning and research com. N.Y. State Com. on Ind. Colls. and Univs., 1975-82; mem. statewide higher edn. adv. com. N.Y. State Senate Com. on Higher Edn., 1979-82; mem. nat. adv. bd. Flaming Rainbow U., 1989—; mem. adv. bd. Assn. Gov. Bds. Presdl. Search Consultation Svc., 1987—, Academic Search Consultation Svc., 1989—, New Pres. Inst., Harvard U., 1990-91; bd. dirs. Am. Coun. on Edn., 1991-92; mem. oversight and review com. leadership and orgnl. devel. program United Negro Coll. Fund, 1991—. Co-author: Frederic Remington-Selected Letters, 1988, A Good Place To Work: Sourcebook for the Academic Workplace, 1991; editor: (with others) Confs. on Adirondack Park, 1972-82, Can.-Am. Relations, 1974-75; contbr. articles to profl. jours. Chmn. planning bd. Village of Canton, 1974-81; elder Neelsville Presbyn. Ch., 1986-89; trustee Adirondack Conservancy, Wilsboro, N.Y., 1980-82. Served to 1st lt. U.S. Army, 1960-62. John Ben Snow Found. grantee, 1981. Mem. Pa. Assn. Colls and Univs. (govt. relations com. 1983-85), Middle States Assn. (team chmn. com. on higher edn. 1976-78, 81), Assn. Am. Colls. (project rev. cons. 1981-82), Soc. Educators and Scholars (bd. editors), Assn. Am. Colls. (pres. adv. com. 1977-78, reviewer Quill project 1978-79), St. Lawrence County Hist. Assn. (pres. 1977-82), Frederic Remington Mus. Assn., Beta Theta Pi (v.p. 1980-83). Republican. Home: 10821 Longmeadow Dr Damascus MD 20872-2240 Office: Coun Ind Colls 1 Dupont Cir NW Ste 320 Washington DC 20036-1172

SPODICK, DAVID HOWARD, cardiologist, educator; b. Hartford, Conn., Sept. 9, 1927; s. Frank and Esther Elizabeth (Sherry) S.; m. Gloria Varshbow, Sept. 2, 1951 (div. 1969); children: Marjory, Nancy; m. Carolyn Gosse, Aug. 9, 1969; children: John, Stephen. AB, Bard Coll., 1947, DSc (hon.), 1974; MD, N.Y. Med. Coll., 1950. Intern St. Francis Hosp., Hartford, 1950-51; resident Beth Israel Hosp., Boston, 1951-52, New Eng. Med. Ctr., Boston, 1952-53, 55-56; cardiology resident West Roxbury VA Hosp., Boston, 1956, Nat. Heart Inst. spl. postdoctoral fellow, 1956-57; cardiologist, chief of cardiology Lemuel Shattuck Hosp., Boston, 1962-76; from instr. to prof. medicine Tufts U. Sch. Medicine, Boston, 1957-76; dir. cardiology St. Vincent Hosp., Worcester, Mass., 1976-84, dir. cardiology, fellow, 1984—; prof. medicine U. Mass. Med. Sch., Worcester, 1976—. Editor-in-chief Am. Jour. Noninvasive Cardiology, 1986—, PRactical Cardiology. 1990-91; contbr. articles to profl. jours.; author, editor various books in field. Capt. USAF, 1953-55. Mem. ACP (Brower traveling scholar 1964), Am. Coll. Cardiology, Am. Coll. Chest Physicians (regent 1990—), Am. Heart Assn. (coun. on Endemiology 1972—). Democrat. Home: 17 Franklin Cir Northborough MA 01532-1212 Office: St Vincent Hosp Cardiology 25 Winthrop St Worcester MA 01604-4593

SPODICK, PEARL BLEGEN, medical psychotherapist; b. Mpls., June 4, 1927; d. Harry Cornelius and Vera Maude (Kidder) Blegen; m. Robert Casper Spodick, Nov. 1, 1955; children: Michael, Peter, Russell, Edward, Rebecca. BA, Albertus Magnus Coll., 1978; MA in Psychology and Art Therapy, Goddard Coll., 1980; postgrad., Simmon's Coll., 1977. Cert. med. psychotherapist, clin. mental health counselor. Cons., art psychotherapist Conn. D.C.Y.S., 1978—, Conn. Sexual Trauma Tratment Program, 1978-79, Arden House Long Term Care Facility, Hamden, Conn., 1979-82, Ctr. for Study of Normative Behavior, Hamden, 1982-85, Curtis Home Children's Residential Treatment Ctr., Meriden, Conn., 1982—; instr. psychology Albertus Magnus Coll., Hamden, 1988-90; med. psychotherapist, counselor The Psychotherapy Ctr., Woodbridge, Conn., 1980—, Art Psychotherapy and Counseling Ctr., Woodbridge, 1980—. Fellow Am. Bd. Med. Psychotherapists (diplomate); mem. ACA (cert.), Am. Art Therapy Assn. (ATR, legis. rep. 1983-89), Am. Assn. Study Mental Imagery, Am. Assn. Cert. Clin. Mental Health Counselors (cert.), Am. Bd. Behavioral Therapists (cert.), Am. Mental Health Counselors Assn. Democrat. Jewish. Office: The Psychotherapy Ctr 214 Amity Rd # 1 Woodbridge CT 06525-2237

SPOELSTRA, BETH E., nurse educator, consultant; b. Lake Worth, Fla., Jan. 10, 1961; d. Robert Chris and Lois Florence (Gjeltema) Guis; m. Frank Spoelstra, Sept. 6, 1989; children: Keith William, Lauren Aleida. Student, Calvin Coll., 1978-80; diploma in nursing, Blodgett Meml. Med. Ctr., 1982; BSN, William Paterson Coll., 1991. RN, N.J.; cert. in-patient obstets., childbirth and lactation edn. nurse. RN Worcester (Mass.) Meml. Hosp., 1982-83, Hackensack (N.J.) Med. Ctr., 1983-85, Orthopaedic Assocs., Paterson, N.J., 1985-86; coord. Olsten Health Care, South Hackensack, N.J., 1986-87; childbirth educator St. Joseph's Hosp. and Med. Ctr., Paterson, 1987—. Author: (pamphlet) Yes, You Can Breastfeed Your Premature Baby, 1990. Co-chair N.J. Task Force for Promotion of Breastfeeding, 1992—. Mem. Nat. League for Nursing, Internat. Childbirth Educators Assn., Internat. Lactation Cons. Assn., Nat. Assn. Ob-Gyn. and Neonatal Nursing, Le Leche League Internat., Am. Psychoprophylactic Orgn. Lamaze, Sigma Theta Tau (Iota Alpha chpt.). Home: 111 Fifth Ave Hawthorne NJ 07506 Office: St Josephs Hosp 703 Main St Paterson NJ 07503

SPOFFORD, SALLY HYSLOP, artist; b. N.Y.C., Aug. 20, 1929; d. George Hall and Esther (McNaull) Hyslop; m. Gavin Spofford, Mar. 11, 1950 (dec. Jan. 1976); children: Lizabeth Spofford Smith, Leslie Spofford Russell. Student, The China Inst., N.Y.C., 1949, The Art Students League, N.Y.C., 1950; BA with high honors, Swarthmore Coll., 1952. Instr. Somerset Art Assn., Peapack, N.J., 1978-85, Hunterdon Art Ctr., Clinton, N.J., 1985-88, chmn. Artists Adv. Coun. and bd. trustees; adv. bd., lectr. Apollo Muses, Inc., Gladstone, N.J.; bd. trustees Artshowcase, Inc. One-man show Riverside Studio, Pottersville, N.J., 1985, Morris Mus., Morristown, N.J. 1989, Schering-Plough Gallery, Madison, N.J., 1989, Phoenix Gallery, N.Y.C., 1990; exhibited in group shows at Hickory (N.C.) Mus., 1983, Purdue U., 1983, Monmouth (N.J.), 1984, Nabisco Brands Gallery, E. Hanover, N.J., 1985, 89, Hunterdon Art Ctr., Clinton, N.J., 1988, Schering-Plough Gallery, Madison, 1988, Morris Mus., Morristown, 1989, Robin Hutchins Gallery, Maplewood, N.J., 1992, Berlex Corp. Office, Wayne, N.J., 1992; represented in permanent collections N.J. State Mus., Trenton, Newark Mus. Painting residency fellow Vt. Studio Ctr., 1992. Mem. Assoc. Artists N.J. (pres. 1985-87), Allied Artists Am., N.J. Watercolor Soc., Federated Art Assns. of N.J. (panel mem. 1985, demonstrator 1991). Home: PO Box 443 Bernardsville NJ 07924-0443

SPOHN, WILLIAM GIDEON, JR., mathematician, musician; b. Lancaster, Pa., Mar. 8, 1923; s. William Gideon and Inza Mae (Huber) S.; m. Alice Liane Bailey, Sept. 13, 1946 (div.); children—Susan Jeannine Grochowina, Peter Jonathan, Kathleen Anne Precht, Mary Louise; m. 2d, Evelyn Walsh Moreland, June 15, 1963 (div. Oct. 1978); m. Claire Louise Burgstahler, Dec. 19, 1987. B.A., St. Johns Coll., 1947; M.A., U. Calif.-Berkeley, 1950; Ph.D., U. Pa., 1962. Instr. math. Temple U., Phila., 1952-54, U. Del., Newark, 1954-56; mathematician Aberdeen Proving Ground, Md., summer 1954-55; instr. math. Bowling Green State U., 1956-59; mathematician, sr. staff Johns Hopkins U. Applied Physics Lab., Laurel, Md., 1959-84; singer, producer Spohn Music Co., Columbia, Md., 1982—. Contbr. articles to profl. jours. Served to lt. USNR, 1943-46; PTO. Applied Physics Lab. Johns Hopkins U. fellow, 1966-67. Mem. Math. Assn. Am. Home: 5423 Stormdrift Columbia MD 21045-2436 Office: Spohn Music Co PO Box 1232 Columbia MD 21044-0232

SPOKONY, LAWRENCE, marketing executive; b. Newburgh, N.Y., Mar. 10, 1961; s. Morris Stanley and Rhoda Florence (Greenburg) S.; m. Danile Rose Rubinstein, Apr. 20, 1986. BEE, SUNY, Stony Brook, 1982; MS in Ops. Rsch., Columbia U., 1983, MBA in Fin., 1986. Systems engr. The Mitre Corp., McLean, Va., 1983-84; bus. cons. Am. Mgmt. Systems, N.Y.C., 1986; fin. mgr. Microband Corp., N.Y.C., 1987-88; planning mgr. Gen. Instrument-Corp., N.Y.C., 1988-90; v.p. mktg. Gen. Instrument-Jerrold, Hatboro, Pa., 1990—. Fellow Eta Kappa Nu. Home: 254 W Trenton Ave Morrisville PA 19067 Office: Jerrold Comm 2200 Byberry Rd Hatboro PA 19040

SPOONER, ROBERT BRUCE, physicist; b. Cleve., Aug. 7, 1920; s. Robert Henry and Elsie Irene (Colbrunn) S.; m. Gloria Muriel Hoffman, Jan. 2, 1945 (dec. Aug. 1985); children: Robert L., Holly R., Wendy A., Laura C. BA, Hiram Coll., 1941; PhD, Northwestern U., 1949. Bd. cert. clin. engr. Teaching asst. Northwestern U., Evanston, Ill., 1946-49; scientist, head thermodynamics analysis Nat. Adv. Com. Aeronautics, Cleve., 1949-53; dir. nuclear R&D Martin Co., Balt., 1953-55; mgr. assoc. researches Koppers Co., Pitts., 1955-62; coord. sci. and rsch. adv. group Regional Indsl. Devel. Corp., Pitts., 1963-65; pres. Impac Med. Instruments, Pitts., 1965-74; dir. med. instrumentation ctr. MPC Corp., Pitts., 1974-75; sr. project engr. Emergency Care Rsch. Inst., Plymouth Meeting, Pa., 1975—; chmn. Ann. Rsch. Conf. on Instrumentation Sci., Geneva, N.Y., 1970; del. Internat. Standards Com., 1982—; lectr. theoretical physics Case Tech./Nat. Adv. Com. Aeron., 1951-52; instr. biomed. instrumentation Bosphorus U., Istanbul, Turkey, 1983; bd. examiners Internat. Cert. Commn., 1991. Editor: Hospital Instrumentation, 1975, Hospital Electrical Safety, 1976; patentee in nuclear engring.; contbr. articles to profl. jours. Trustee Hiram Coll., 1963-69. Capt. U.S. Army, 1942-46, ETO. Mem. ASTM, IEEE (editor trans. 1968-72), Instrument Soc. Am., Am. Phys. Soc., Assn. Advancement Med. Instrumentation, Soc. Indsl. Electronics and Control Instrumentation (pres. 1972-74). Republican. Home: 534 Vista Rd Ambler PA 19002-2638 Office: Emergency Care Rsch Inst 5200 Butler Pike Plymouth Meeting PA 19462-1241

SPOOR, JOHN EDWARD, physician; b. Laurens, N.Y., Nov. 14, 1935; s. Elmer Eugene and Helen Blanche (Stanton) S.; m. Donna Lou Crandall; children: Kevin Chandler, Brian Stephen. MD, U. Buffalo, 1966. Diplomate Nat. Bd. Med. Examiners, Am. Bd. Emergency Medicine. Intern Lakeland (Fla.) Gen. Hosp., 1966-67; pvt. practice Laurens, N.Y., 1967-69; emergency physician Fox Hosp., Oneonta, N.Y., 1969-85; dir. health ctr. State U. Coll. Oneonta, 1977-81; dir. emergency dept. Park Ridge Hosp., Rochester, N.Y., 1978, Fox Hosp., Oneonta, 1981-85; dir. emergency svcs. M.I. Basstt Hosp., Cooperstown, N.Y., 1985—, chief emergency medicine, 1988—; cons. Schoharie County Community Hosp., Cobleskill, N.Y., 1985-90; med. dir. Susquehanna Adirondack EMS Program, Binghamton, N.Y.; mem. adv. com. Otsego County Emergency Health Svcs., 1974-76, 79—; mem. com. on emergency health svcs. Med. Soc. State N.Y., 1979—; mem. Adirondack Appalachian Regional EMS Coun., 1984—; mem. med. adv. com. N.Y. State EMS Devel. Office, 1987-89. Contbr. articles to profl. jours. Otsego County coroner, 1970-72; mem. bd. edn. Morris Central Sch., 1971-73; chpt. faculty Am. Heart Assn., Utica, N.Y., 1981—, bd. dirs., 1986-88; chmn. N.Y. State Emergency Med. Svcs. Coun., Albany, 1982; mem. Otsego County Econ. Devel. Coun., Oneonta, 1988. With USN, 1953-57. Recipient svc. award Otsego County Emergency Squad Assn., Cooperstown, 1979, award for outstanding community svc. Fox Hosp., Oneonta, 1981, First Aider of Yr. award Cen. N.Y. Emergency Squad Assn., Norwich, 1974, recognition of svc. award Otsego County CD, Cooperstown, 1982. Mem. Am. Coll. Emergency Physicians (com. emergency resources 1987—, chair sect. rural emergency medicine 1991-92), Am. Coll. Physician Execs., Nat. Rural Health Assn. (mem. spl. task force on rural EMS 1988-90, bd. dirs. 1992), N.Y. State Med. Soc., Otsego County Med. Soc., Am. Acad. Med. Dirs. Home: RR 1 Box 157 Laurens NY 13796-9780 Office: Mary Imogene Bassett Hosp 1 Atwell Rd Cooperstown NY 13326-1394

SPRADLIN, JOSEPH EDGAR, enzymologist, researcher; b. Cynthiana, Ind., Mar. 12, 1941; s. Chester Lenhart and Frances Mae (Lowe) S.; m. Nancy Ann Ennis, Aug. 18, 1963 (div. Mar. 1976); children: Jennifer, Emily; m. Nancy Naomi George, Sept. 4, 1976; 1 child, Suzanne. BS, Ind. U., 1963, PhD, 1969. Rsch. scientist Miles Labs., Elkhart, Ind., 1969-77; group leader Novo Labs., Wilton, Conn., 1977-79; prin. scientist Gen. Foods, Tarrytown, N.Y., 1979—; adj. prof. Pace Univ., Pleasantville, N.Y., 1986-87. Contbr. chpt. to The Enzymes Vol. 5, 3d edit., 1971, Biocatalysis in Agricultural Biotechnology, 1989; contbr. articles to profl. jours. V.p. YMCA, Elkhart, 1974-77; lay leader United Meth. Ch., Monroe, N.Y., 1987—; pres. Square Dancing Club, Orange County, N.Y., 1990—. Mem. N.Y. Acad. Sci., Sigma Xi. Home: 330 Lakes Blvd Monroe NY 10950-2615 Office: General Foods 555 S Broadway Tarrytown NY 10591-6399

SPRAFKIN, ROBERT PETER, psychologist, educator; b. N.Y.C., Dec. 18, 1940; s. Benjamin R. and Dora M. (Berman) S.; m. Barbara Marcus, July 19, 1964; children: Jeffrey P., Neal R., Noah M. AB, Dartmouth Coll., 1962; MA, Columbia U., 1964; PhD, Ohio State U., 1968. Lic. psychologist, N.Y. Asst. prof. psychology Syracuse (N.Y.) U., 1968-71, adj. assoc. prof., 1973-88, adj. prof., 1989—; chief day treatment ctr. VA Med. Ctr., Syracuse, 1971—, dir. psychology tng. program, 1983—; clin. assoc. prof. dept. psychiatry SUNY Health Sci. Ctr., Syracuse, 1973—; cons. psychologist Assn. for Retarded Citizens, Syracuse, 1983—. Co-author: Skilltraining for Community Living, 1976, Skillstreaming the Adolescent, 1980. Mem. Onondaga County Legis. Coun. on Disabled, Syracuse, 1982—,; mem. community svcs. bd. County Dept. Mental Health, 1987—. Mem. Am. Psychol. Assn., Assn. for Advancement Behavior Therapy, Soc. for Behavioral Medicine, Soc. for Clin. and Exptl. Hypnosis, Dartmouth Club (pres.). Office: VA Med Ctr 800 Irving Ave Syracuse NY 13210-2796

SPRAGUE, DAVID WAYNE, psychologist; b. Bklyn., May 5, 1958; s. Walter and Jennie A. (Sundberg) S.; m. Diane Patricia Roman, Jan. 5, 1985; 1 child, Brian Jason. AB in Psychology, Cornell U., 1983; PhD in Counseling Psychology, Penn State U., 1988. Lic. psychologist, N.Y. Assoc./staff psychologist Genesee County Mental Health Svcs., Batavia, N.Y., 1988-90; psychologist pvt. practice Batavia, 1991—; cons. psychologist Western N.Y. Inst. for the Psychotherapies, Amherst, N.Y., 1991—; cons. psychologist, clin. supr. Intensive Care Facility, Oakfield, N.Y., 1990—, Day Treatment Ctr., Elba, N.Y., 1990—. Regents scholar N.Y. State, 1976, Parents Assn. scholarship Bklyn. Tech. High Sch., 1976. Mem. APA, N.Y. State Psychol. Assn., Psychol. Assn. Western N.Y. Democrat. Baptist. Office: 113 Main St Batavia NY 14020-2110

SPRATT, ROBERT LEONARD, forensic photographer; b. Ft. Worth, Tex., Jan. 6, 1951; s. Oliver Leonard and Evelyn Lee (McClellan) S.; m. Shermaine Evans, Jan. 26, 1974; children: Robert Leonard II, Michael Phillip. AA, Prince George's Community Coll, Largo, Md., 1978; grad., Sch. Modern Photography, 1979, N.Y. Inst. Photography, 1990. Technician U.S. Capitol Police, Washington, 1974—, officer in charge of identification sect., 1980-86, officer in charge of photo devel. unit of spl. investigation, 1986—. Photography pub. various pubs. including Senate Sergeant at Arms Newsletter, Roll Call newspaper, Nat. Cath. Reporter, Jet Mag., Md. Ind., NYI Photoworld Newsletter, Peterson's Photographic Mag. Recipient Commendation Assoc. Photographers Internat., 1981, 1st place award Law and Order Mag., 1989, 91, 1st, 3d, 5th place martial arts Law Enforcement & Firefighter's Games, 1989, Commendation Metro Transit Police Dept., 1990, 91, 1st place award UN Internat. Photographic Coun., 1989, others. Mem. Internat. Assn. for Identification, World Hapkido Fedn. (2d deg.), Assoc. Photographers Internat. Home: 5111 Alfred Dr Waldorf MD 20601-3259 Office: US Capitol Police 119 D St NE Washington DC 20510-0001

SPRECHER, BARON WILLIAM GUNTHER, pianist, composer, conductor, diplomat; b. Saarbrucken, Germany, Jan. 20, 1924; came to U.S., 1952.; s. Wolf and Karoline (Jung) Sprecher; m. Blossom Tag, Aug. 6, 1952. Studied piano with Prof. Wittels, Tel Aviv; studied piano with Madame Vengerova, N.Y.C.; studied composition with Paul Ben-Haim, Tel Aviv, studied conducting with Georg Singer; hon. degree, Inst. of Vocal Arts, 1957; Dr. honoris causa in Philosophy of Music, World Univ. Roundtable, 1988; MusD (hon.), London Inst. Applied Rsch., 1991, Australian Inst. Coord. Rsch., 1991; diploma, Gran Premio Am., 1990, Paladino del Tricolore, 1990; D Musicology, Somerset U.; D Music (hon.), Atlantic Southeastern U.; Diploma, Acad. Argentina de Diplomacia. Korrepetitor Israel Folk Opera, Tel-Aviv, 1940-43; piano soloist Israel Philharm. Orch., Tel-Aviv, 1946-48; pres., music dir. Bronx Philharm., N.Y.C., 1971-83; music dir. Sta. WEVD, N.Y.C., 1969-85; asst. pianist accompanying Lotte Lenya, Richard Tucker, Jan Peerce, Itzhak Perlman, Jan Kiepura, Ilona Massey; prof. Inst. Hautes Edtudes Economiques et Sociales; rsch. prof. Alliance Universelle Paix Connaissance, Paris, 1991; prof. Haute Ecole de Recherche, Inst. des Hautes Etudes Economiques et Sociales; mem. coun. Inst. de Documentation et D'Etudes Europeennes; dep. mem., diplomat Internat. State Parliament. Composer: (Song Book) Yinglish, piano soloist 1st performance of Gershwin's Concerto in F in Israel; composer Piano Sonata, 1945, Jerusalem Concerto for Piano and Orch., 1967, (TV spl.) Great is Thy Faith, 1970; pianist-condr. 24 record albums; mem. The First Piano Quartet (Acad. award nomination, Peabody award). Consul Sovereign State Aeterna Lucina for State and City of N.Y. Named Noble Knight of Noble House of Amena, Knight, Order of Knight Templars of Jerusalem, 1991, Knight Comdr., Lofsensic Ursinius Order, 1991, Baron, Order of Bohemian Crown, 1992, Capt., Légion L'Aigle de Mar, 1992, Gran Mastre U.S.A., Cirulo Nobiliaro Caballeros Universlaes, 1992, Baron of Montsalvat, 1992. Fellow United Writers' Assn. India; mem. ASCAP, Maison Internat. des Intellectuels, Internat. Parliament for Safety and Peace, World Parliament Confederation of Chivalry, Bronx Philharm. Symphony Soc., Inc. (founder, pres.), Internat. Platform Assn., Am. Fedn. Musicians, Robert Stolz Soc. Great Britain, World Univ. Roundtable (trustee, founder), Internat. Cultural Correspondence Inst., Circulo Nobiliario de los Caballeros Universales (gran master U.S.), Royal Order Bohemian Crown (baron), Legion de L'Aigle de Mer (capt.). Home and Office: 2235 Cruger Ave Res Monsalvat 1 D Bronx NY 10467

SPRING, DEAN WILLIAM, municipal official; b. Rochester, N.Y., Jan. 13, 1951; s. LaVerne John and Maybelle Lucy (MacFadden) S.; m. Margo Kay Zegalia, Sept. 18, 1976; children: Michelle Lynn, Monica Ann. AB, Lafayette Coll., 1973; MBA, Rochester Inst. Tech., 1975. Asst. store mgr. F.W. Woolworth Co., Rochester, Geneva, N.Y., 1973-74; accounts receivable auditor Jones Chems. Inc., LeRoy, N.Y., 1976-77; asst. purchasing agt. Jones Chems. Inc., LeRoy, 1977-79; purchasing agt. City of Niagara Falls, N.Y., 1979—. City govt. chmn. United Way, Niagara Falls, 1982-89. Mem. Nat. Inst. Govtl. Purchasing, N.Y. State Assn. Mcpl. Purchasing Ofcls., Kiwanis Club (pres. 1985-86). Office: City of Niagara Falls City Hall 745 Main St Niagara Falls NY 14302-0069

SPRINGER, CAROLYN MAE, social psychologist, consultant, researcher; b. N.Y.C., Sept. 17, 1959; d. Oswald Leroy and Ruth Elaine (Miller) S. BA cum laude, Barnard Coll., 1981; M of Philosophy, Columbia U., N.Y.C., 1983; PhD, Columbia U., 1992. Assoc. mem. tech. staff, tech. assoc. Bell. Labs., Whippany, Piscataway, N.J., 1981-82; cons. S.I. Children's Mus., 1981-83; researcher, cons. Pub. Rels. Soc. Am., N.Y.C., 1984-85; cons. Urban League, N.Y.C., 1985-86; teaching asst. Tchrs. Coll., Columbia U., N.Y.C., 1982, 88; cons. Ednl. Video Ctr., N.Y.C., 1986-88, N.Y. Hosp.-Cornell U., N.Y.C., 1989—; teaching asst. Barnard Coll., Columbia U., N.Y.C., 1986—; cons. N.Y.C. Bd. Edn., Bklyn., 1986—; rsch. assoc. Ctr. for Policy Rsch., N.Y.C., 1988—; cons. Staten Island Children's Mus., 1981-83. Fellow Nat. Sci. Found., 1981-84, Kettering Found., 1985; named Outstanding Young Woman in Am., 1983. Mem. APA, Am. Psychol. Soc., Am. Sociol. Assn., Black Women in Higher Edn., Soc. for Psychol. Study of Social Issues, N.Y. Acad. Scis., N.Y. Coun. Family Rels., Soc. for Study of Social Problems. Democrat. Baptist. Home: 515 Clinton Ave Apt 20 Brooklyn NY 11238-2214 Office: Tchrs Coll Columbia U Box 6 525 W 120th St New York NY 10027

SPRINGER, ROBERT COLEMAN, III, advertising executive; b. Meridian, Miss., Nov. 13, 1945; s. Robert Jr. and Sudy Elizabeth (Tibbetts) S.; m. Anita Fay Hiatt, July 20, 1979; children: Aubrey Lyn, Robert Coleman IV. BS, Cen. Mo. State U., 1968. Regional mgr. BWA Advt., Boston, 1968-76; assoc. media dir. Cargill, Wilson and Acree, Inc., Atlanta, 1976-78; with RJR industries and subs. cos., 1978—; brand planning mgr. R.J. Reynolds Tobacco Co., Winston-Salem, N.C., 1978-80; mgr. advt. services Heublein, Inc., Farmington, Conn., 1980-82, dir. advt. services, 1985-86; v.p. mktg. and media services Stuart Ford, Inc., Richmond, Va., 1982-85; sr. dir. advt. svcs. Nabisco Brands USA, Parsippany, N.J., 1986—. Mem. Assn. Nat. Advertisers (mem. mag. com. 1985-88, mem. mgmt. com. 1989—), Am. Advt. Fedn., N.Y. Advt. Club, Worldwide Mktg. Leadership Coun. (bd. dirs. 1991—). Baptist. Home: 499 Drakestown Rd Long Valley NJ 07853-9017 Office: Nabisco Foods Group PO Box 311 Parsippany NJ 07054-0311

SPRINGER, TIMOTHY ALAN, health researcher, immunology educator; b. Ft. Benning, Ga., Feb. 23, 1948. BA in Biochemistry, U. Calif., Berkeley, 1971; PhD in Biochemistry & Molecular Biology, Harvard U., 1976. NIH rsch. fellow U. Cambridge (Eng.)/MRC Lab. Molecular Biology, 1976-77; asst. prof. Med. Sch., Harvard U., 1977-83, assoc. prof., 1983-89, Latham family prof., 1989—; chief lab. membrane immunochemistry Dana-Farber Cancer Inst., Boston, 1981-88; v.p. Ctr. for Blood Rsch., Boston, 1988—; organizer Juan March Found. Workshop, Madrid, 1991. Assoc. editor Jour. Immunology, 1981-85; adv. editor Jour. Exptl. Medicine, 1981—; mem. editorial bd. Hybridoma, 1981—, Regional Immunology, 1988—, Cellular Immunology, 1988—, Jour. Clin. Immunology, 1988—, Cell Regulation, 1989—, New Biologist, 1989—; contbr. numerous articles to profl. jours. NIH grantee, 1988. Mem. Am. Assn. Immunologists, Reticuloendothelial Soc. (membership chair 1986—, chair 1989), Am. Soc. Biol. Chemists, Am. Assn. Immunologists (block chmn. macrophages and natural killer cells 1985-86), Am. Assn. Pathologists, Phi Beta Kappa. Home: 28 Monadnock Rd Chestnut Hill MA 02167-1122

SPRINGETT, BRIAN EDWARD, physicist, electrophotography scientist; b. Chatham, Kent, Eng., Apr. 24, 1936; came to U.S., 1960; s. George Edward Thomas and Doris Gwendoline Olive (Crouch) S. BA, U. Cambridge, Eng., 1960, MA, 1964; MS, U. Chgo., 1963, PhD, 1966. R&D engr. Hoffman Semicondr., El Monte, Calif., 1960-61; rsch. asst., rsch. assoc. U. Chgo., 1961-67; asst. prof. U. Mich., Ann Arbor, 1967-72; vis. prof. U. Que., Trois Rivieres, Can., 1972-74, Oakland U., Rochester, Mich., 1973-74; tech. specialist Xerox Corp., Rochester, N.Y., 1974-77, mgr. tech. and strategy, 1977—; Contbr. articles to profl. jours; patentee in field. With Brit. Army Royal Armored Corps, 1955-57. Mem. AAAS, Am. Phys. Soc., Inst. Imaging Sci. and Tech. Office: Xerox Corp 800 Phillips Rd Webster NY 14580-9791

SPRINGOB, H. KARL, psychologist; b. Jersey City, May 23, 1930; s. Henry and Mary Hermine (Gossmann) S.; m. Helen Patricia Jemison, Apr. 18, 1964; children: Paul, Christine. BA, Am. U., 1950, MA, 1952; PhD, Columbia U., 1962; Profl. Dipl., Tchrs. Coll., Columbia U., 1962. Diplomate Am. Bd. Profl. Psychology; lic. psychologist, N.J.; cert. psychologist, N.Y. Field counselor Big Bros., Inc., N.Y.C., 1955-56; psychologist trainee VA, 1957-61; chief psychologist, dir. Counseling & Testing Svcs., YMCA of Greater N.Y., N.Y.C., 1961-67; asst. prof. Grad. Sch. Edn., CUNY, N.Y.C., 1967-68; instr., vis. assoc. prof. Tchrs. Coll., Columbia U., N.Y.C., 1963-73, 75-76; rsch. assoc. prof. Stevens Inst. Tech., Hoboken, N.J., 1969-82, mgr. counseling svcs., 1968-82, acting head dept. mgmt., 1986-88, dir., rsch. prof., 1982—; career devel. cons. The Travelers Ins. Co., 1975-77, Mut. Savs. Bank Assn., 1978-79; com. mem. Com. for Use of Human Subjects in Rsch., N.J. Coll. Dentistry, Jersey City, 1973-75. Co-author: Applied Psychology in Dentistry, 1972; contbr. articles to profl. jours.; author pamphlets. Bd. dirs. Cystic Fibrosis Found., 1970—; active Boy Scouts Am.; bd. trustees and pres. Stevens Acad., Hoboken, N.J., 1971-83; mem., pres. N.J. Chorale, Ridgefield, N.J., 1969-75. With U.S. Army, 1953-55. Recipient Breath of Life award Cystic Fibrosis Found., 1988, Silver Beaver Boy Scouts Am., 1984, Dist. Award of Merit, 1982, Nat. Pres.'s Scoutmaster Award of Merit, 1988. Mem. Am. Psychol. Assn., Am. Assn. Counseling & Devel., Nat. Career Devel. Assn., Am. Rehab. Counseling Assn., Assn. for Measurement and Evaluation in Counseling & Devel., Assn. for Interest Measurement, Am. Coll. Personnel Assn. Office: Lab of Psychol Studies Stevens Inst Tech Hoboken NJ 07030

SPRINGSTON, JAMES RAYMOND, college administrator, educator; b. Detroit, June 16, 1947; s. George Hatzel and Elizabeth Jane (Phelps) S.; m. Carol Sue Rhinehart, June 27, 1974 (div. Feb. 1984). BA, Mich. State U., 1971; MEd, Wayne State U., 1981. Cert. tchr. Mich. High sch. tchr., debate coach Wateford Sch. Dist., Pontiac, Mich., 1972-81; dir. debate, asst. prof. Marist Coll., Poughkeepsie, N.Y., 1985-91, dir. forensics, 1991-92; instr. speech, dir. of debate U. R.I., Kingston, 1992—; adj. prof. debate coach U. Mich., Flint, 1981-85; adj. faculty Wayne State U., Detroit, 1984-85, Henry Ford Community Coll., Dearborn, Mich., 1984-85; dir. Nat. Ceda Debate Inst., Poughkeepsie, 1991—, Boces Jr. High Debate Program, Poughkeepsie, 1988—. Author: (with others) Prima Facie, 1989, Championship Debates, 1991. Mem. communication com. Am. Heart Assn., Poughkeepsie, 1987—; vol. Trainer for United Way, Poughkeepsie, 1991—. Mem. Cross Examination Debate Assn. (rep. to nat. coun. 1991-93), Speech Communication Assn., Phi Kappa Delta. Bahai. Home: PO Box 38 Kingston RI 02881 Office: U RI 309 Independence Hall Kingston RI 02881

SPRINKLE, ROBERT MARSHALL, international educational exchange executive; b. Granite City, Ill., Dec. 12, 1936; s. Marshall Roseboro and Jean Pomeroy (Miller) S.; B.A., U. Colo., 1959; student N.Mex. State U., 1963-64, U. Mich., 1964-65; m. G(ladys) Sandra Fisher, Mar. 31, 1967; 1 dau., Lisa Jean McKee. Dir. pub. rels., editor, dir. Internat. Student Visitor Svc., USNSA/Ednl. Travel, Inc., N.Y.C., 1960-63; grad. asst., counselor N.Mex. State U. Guidance Ctr., 1963-64; program adv., adminstrv. coord. U. Mich. Internat. Ctr., 1964-67; exec. dir., sec., dir. Assn. Internat. Practical Tng., Columbia, Md., 1967—, mem. internat. IAESTE adv. com., 1978-81; v.p. Network for Internat. Exch., 1983-85; bd. dirs. Open Door Student Exch., 1987-89, Internat. Exch. Assn., 1985-89, Worldwise 2000, 1988-89; vice chmn., 1987-88; steering com. Liason Group for Internat. Edn. Exch., 1989-91, treas., 1989-91. Bd. dirs. Nat. Coun. for Community Svcs. to Internat. Visitors, 1969-73; mem. U.S. Nat. Commn. for UNESCO, Washington, 1969-75, 79-81, mem. exec. com., 1970-75, membership com. 1974-75, nominating com., 1974-75. Served to capt. AUS, 1959-60. Mem. Am. Assn. Higher Edn., Am. Fgn. Svc. Assn., Am. Soc. Engring. Edn., Am. Soc. Public Adminstrn., Am. Soc. Tng. and Devel. (exec. com. internat. div. 1982-83), Assn. Sandwich Edn. and Tng. (U.K.), Nat. Assn. Fgn. Student Affairs, Soc. Internat. Devel., Soc. Intercultural Edn., Tng. and Rsch., Railroadians of Am. Inc., South Street Seaport Mus. Inc. Republican. Baptist. Office: 10400 Little Patuxent Pky Columbia MD 21044-3510

SPRIZZO, JOHN EMILIO, federal judge; b. Bklyn., Dec. 23, 1934; s. Vincent James and Esther Nancy (Filosa) S.; children—Ann Esther, Johna Emily Sprizzo Bolka, Matthew John. BA summa cum laude, St. John's U., Jamaica, N.Y., 1956; LLB summa cum laude, St. John's U., 1959. Bar: N.Y. 1960. Atty. U.S. Dept. Justice, 1959-63; asst. U.S. atty. so. dist. N.Y. Dept. Justice, N.Y.C., 1963-68, chief appellate atty., 1965-66, asst. chief criminal div., 1966-68; assoc. prof. Fordham U. Law Sch., N.Y.C., 1968-72; ptnr. Curtis, Mallet-Prevost, N.Y.C., 1972-81; dist. judge U.S. Dist. Ct. (so. dist.) N.Y., N.Y.C., 1981—; cons. Nat. Com. for Reform of Criminal Laws, N.Y.C., 1971-72; mem. Knapp Commn., 1971-72; assoc. atty. Com. of Ct. on Judiciary, N.Y.C., 1971-72. Co-contbr. articles to profl. law revs. Mem. ABA, D.C. Bar Assn., Assn. of Bar of City of N.Y. Office: US Dist Ct US Courthouse Foley Sq New York NY 10007-1501

SPROUL, PHILIP TATE, retired electrical engineer, consultant; b. Des Moines, July 9, 1915; s. Philip Hussey and Helen (Tate) S.; m. Virginia Shivers, Aug. 26, 1938. BSEE, Iowa State U., 1937. Registered profl. engr., N.J. Mem. tech. staff, supr. AT&T Bell Labs., N.Y.C., Murray Hill, N.J., Whippany, N.J., 1937-80; pres. Sproul Engring., Inc., Chatham Township, N.J., 1982—. Co-inventor, patentee sweep frequency test circuit; inventor, patentee radar display. Chmn. Recreation Com., Chatham, N.J., 1952-55. Mem. IEEE (sr., ret., chmn. radio communication com. 1955-61, chmn. N.J. div. 1960), The Old Guard of Summit (N.J.), Fairmount Country Club, Masons (worshipful master 1966, past dist. dep. grand master 1980-82). Republican. Presbyterian. Home and Office: 11 Aberdeen Rd Chatham NJ 07928-1502

SPUDIC, THOMAS JOSEPH, clinical psychologist; b. Chgo., Nov. 24, 1946; s. John Thomas and Mary (Coccimiglio) S.; m. Linda Celeste Heuslein, June 28, 1969; children: Lisa, Michael. MA, So. Ill. U., 1974, PhD, 1978. Staff psychologist Mansfield (Conn.) Tng. Sch., 1978-80; dir. psychology, dept. mental retardation Seaside Regional Ctr., Waterford, Conn., 1980-87; psychologist Elmcrest Psychiat. Facility, Portland, Conn., 1987-89; pvt. practice Willimantic and Mansfield, Conn., 1987—. Sgt. U.S. Army, 1969-72. Mem. Am. Psychol. Assn., Assn. for Advancement Behavior Therapy, Am. Assn. on Mental Retardation, Conn. Psychol. Assn. Roman Catholic. Office: 196 Conantville Rd Mansfield Center CT 06250-1616

SPUNT, SHEPARD ARMIN, realty executive, management and financial consultant; b. Cambridge, Mass., Feb. 3, 1931; s. Harry and Naomi (Drooker) S.; B.S., U. Pa., 1952, M.B.A., 1956; m. Joan Murray Fooshee, Aug. 6, 1961 (dec. June 1969); children—Erica Frieda and Andrew Murray (twins). Owner, Colonial Realty Co., Brookline, Mass., 1953—, Cambridge, 1960—; sr. assoc. Gen. Solids Assocs., 1956—; chmn. bd. Gen. Solids Systems Corp., 1971-74; trustee Union Capital Trust, Boston; incorporator Liberty Bank & Trust Co., Boston; dir., clerk The Computer Co., Somerville, Mass., 1986—. Chmn., Com. for Fair Urban Renewal Laws, Mass., 1965—; treas. Ten Men of Mass., 1980. Pres., New Eng. Council of Young Republicans, 1964-67, 69-71; vice chmn. Young Rep. Nat. Fedn., 1967-69, dir. region 1, 1964-67, 69-71; mem. Brookline Republican Town Com., 1960—; del. Atlantic Conf. Young Polit. Leaders, Brussels, 1973; bd. dirs. Brookline Taxpayers Assn., 1964—, v.p., 1971-72, pres., 1972—. Registered profl. engr., Mass. Mem. Nat. Soc. Profl. Engrs., Rental Housing Assn., Greater Boston Real Estate Bd., Navy League, Boston Athenaeum, Copley Soc. Boston. Lodges: Masons, Shriners. Author: (with others) A Business Data Processing Service for Small Business Practitioners, 1956; A Business Data Processing Service for Medical Practitioners, 1956, rev. edit., 1959. Author, sponsor consumer protection and election law legislation Mass. Gen. Ct., 1969—. Patentee in field of automation, lasers, dielectric bonding. Home: 177 Reservoir Rd Chestnut Hill MA 02167-1426 Office: 21 Elmer St Cambridge MA 02238-0172

SQUADRA, JOHN HARLEY, artist, fine art restorer; b. N.Y.C., June 25, 1932; s. Enrico and Mary (Ludington) S.; m. Elizabeth Stachowiecka. BFA, R.I. Sch. Design, 1953. Artist Fine Art Restoration, Brooks, Maine, 1987—. Author: Dr. Miraculous, 1981; one-man shows include Mari Galleries, Mamaroneck, N.Y., 1983-84, Gallery Musee des Duncan, Paris, 1980, Miner's Gallery, Boulder, Colo., 1979, Nonson Gallery, Soho, N.Y.C., 1979, Bridgeport (Conn.) Mus. of Art, Sci. and Industry, 1978, Arts Coun. of Norwalk, Conn., 1984; group shows include Hudson River Mus., Yonkers, N.Y., Norfolk Mus., Fleming Mus., Burlington, Vt., The Herron Mus., Indpls., The Berkshire Mus., Pittsfield (Mass.) Mus., Gallery Sixty-Eight. Home: RR 2 Box 1440 Brooks ME 04921-9643

SQUASONI, DOUGLAS WADE, investment banking professional; b. Flushing, N.Y., Apr. 23, 1964; s. Harry Edward and Patricia Ann (Loscalzo) S.; m. Julie Ann Ordieres, June 23, 1990. BA in Econs., Boston Coll., 1986. Swap dealer Mfrs. Hanover Trust, N.Y.C., 1986-89, Allied Irish Bank, N.Y.C., 1989; options trader Long-Term Credit Bank of Japan, N.Y.C., 1990—. Mem. Math. Assn. Am.

SQUAZZO, MILDRED KATHERINE (MILDRED KATHERINE OETTING), corporate executive; b. Bklyn., Dec. 22; d. William John and Marie M. (Fromm) Oetting; student L.I. U. Sec.-treas., Stanley Engring., Inc. and v.p. Stanley Chems., Inc., 1960-68; founder, pres. Chem-Dynamics Corp., Scotch Plains, N.J., 1964-68; gen. adminstr., purchasing dir., Richardson Chem. Co., Metuchen, N.J., 1968-69; owner Berkeley Employment Agy. and Berkeley Temp. Help Service, Berkeley Heights, N.J., 1969-91, Berkeley Employment Agy., Morristown, N.J., 1982, Bridgewater, N.J., 1987-91; pres. M.K.S. Bus. Group, Inc., Berkeley Heights, 1980-91; mgmt. cons.; personnel fin.; lectr. Served with Nurse Corps, U.S. Army, 1946-47. Mem. Nat. Bus. and Profl. Women's Club. Home and Office: 16 Heather Ln Warren NJ 07059-5258

SQUIERS, CAROL, editor, writer; b. Oak Park, Ill., Dec. 25, 1948; d. Milorad Vukov and Mildred (Baco); m. John Squiers, Aug. 31, 1968 (div. 1983). BA in Art History, U. Ill., 1971. Photo critic The Village Voice, N.Y.C., 1982-83; adj. prof. Sch. Visual Arts Resources, N.Y.C., 1981-85; curator photography Pub. Sch. 1 The Inst. for Art & Urban Resources, Long Island City, N.Y., 1980-84; columnist Artforum Mag., N.Y.C., 1986—; assoc. editor Am. Photographer Mag., N.Y.C., 1986-89; sr. editor Am. Photo Mag., N.Y.C., 1989—. Editor: The Critical Image: Essays on Contemporary Photography, 1990; contbr. essays to Vanity Fair and other mags. Grantee Art Critics Fellowship Nat. Endowment for Arts, 1981.

SQUIRE, LAURIE RUBIN, media consultant; b. N.Y.C., Jan. 30, 1953; d. Daniel and Ruth Thelma (Deutsch) Rubin; m. Herbert E. Squire Jr., Aug. 6, 1975; children: Amy Ruth, Julie Wynn. BA cum laude (scholar), Finch Coll., 1974; MA, NYU, 1976; postgrad., Columbia U., 1977—. Actress TV commls., 1960-65; arts editor Finch/Metro newspaper, N.Y.C., 1970-74; co-editor Finch Alumnae mag., 1971-72; intern producer Sta. WBAI-FM, N.Y.C., 1973; music prodn. coord. Ballet Theatre spl. Sta. WNET-TV, 1973; coll. bd. writer Mademoiselle mag., 1973; intern asst. pub. affairs dir. N.Y. Cultural Ctr., 1974; mdse. coord. Sta. WOR-AM, N.Y.C., 1974-76, contbg. writer Bob and Ray's Mary Backstage serial, contbr. nostalgia features Joe Franklin Show, producer Jean Shepherd Show and sydicated markets, 1975-77, producer Bernard Meltzer What's Your Problem, 1977-80; broadcast stage mgr. Texaco Met. Opera, 1976—; dance critic Show Bus., theatre newspaper; bd. dir. publicity and advt. L.I. Playhouse, 1982—; press rep. Great Neck Pla.; writer Chanry Communications. Publicity cons. Nassau County Mus. Fine Art; v.p. pub. rels. United Community Fund. Recipient commendations for Leukemia Radiothons Peabody Broadcasting citation, 1983. Mem. Internat. Radio and TV Soc., Great Neck Hist. Soc. Home and Office: 892 Middle Neck Rd Great Neck NY 11024-1400

SQUIRE, WALTER CHARLES, lawyer; b. N.Y.C., Aug. 5, 1945; s. Sidney and Helen (Friedman) S.; m. Sara Jane Abramson; children: Harrison, Russell, Zachary, Andrew. BA, Yale U., 1967; JD, Columbia U., 1971. Bar: N.Y. 1971, U.S. Dist. Ct. (so. and ea. dists.) N.Y. 1975, U.S. Ct. Appeals (2d cir.) 1974, U.S. Supreme Ct. 1977. Ptnr. Jones Hirsch Connors & Bull, N.Y.C., 1986—. Mem. ABA, N.Y. State Bar Assn., Assn. of Bar of City of N.Y., Internat. Bar Assn., Licensing Execs. Soc., Am. Arbitration Assn. (arbitrator 1975—), Risk Ins. Mgmt. Soc. (lectr. 1983, 84). Office: Jones Hirsch Connors & Bull 101 E 52d St New York NY 10022

SQUIRES, PATRICIA EILEEN COLEMAN, free-lance journalist, writer; b. Beaver Falls, Pa., Jan. 28, 1927; d. John Wiley and Helen Marie (Barstow) Purtell; B.A. in Journalism, Ind. U., 1949; m. Mark B. Squires, Sr., June 30, 1951; children: Sally Regan, Mark B., Susan Barstow. Staff reporter LaPorte (Ind.) Herald-Argus, 1949-51, daily columnist, 1950-51, sect. editor, 1949-51; women's news and feature writer Muskegon (Mich.) bur. Grand Rapids Herald, 1956-57; editor suburban sect. North Shore Line, Chicagoland Mag., Chgo., 1967-69; staff writer Fairpress, Westport, Conn., 1972-73; regular contbr. New Canaan (Conn.) Advertiser, 1975-78, Bridgeport (Conn.) Sunday Post, 1976-78, Soundings, Essex, Conn., 1977-78, N.Y. Times, N.Y.C., 1976—; tchr. English, journalism, social studies jr. and sr. pub. high schs., Jackson, Mich., 1966-67, Niles Twp., Skokie, Ill., 1967-68; mem. Acad. Sr. Profls. Eckerd Coll.; vol. tutor Social Cultural Ednl. Enrichment Program, Protestant Community Ctr., 1979-86. Public rels., promotion dir. Ella Sharp Mus., Jackson, 1964-66; publicity chmn. New Canaan Soc. for Arts, 1977-78; bd. dirs. Centennial Celebration Com., Winnetka, Ill., 1968-69; Community Coun. New Canaan, 1972-75; New Canaan Bicentennial Com., 1975-76; publicity chmn. parent-tchr. coun. Frost Jr. High Sch., Jackson, 1963-64; active Girl Scouts Am. Mem. Soc. Profl. Journalists, AAUW, Ind. U. Alumni Assn. Presbyterian. Clubs: Cedar Point Yacht (Westport, Conn.); Lake Mohawk Golf (Sparta, N.J.). Home and Office: 688 W Shore Trl Sparta NJ 07871-1320 also: 6265 Sun Blvd 109 G Casa del Mar Saint Petersburg FL 33715-1011

SQUIRES, RICHARD FELT, research scientist; b. Sparta, Mich., Jan. 15, 1933; s. Monas Nathan and Dorothy Lois (Felt) S.; m. Else Saederup, 1 child, Iben. BS, Mich. State U., 1958; postgrad., Calif. Inst. Tech., 1961. Rsch. biochemist Pasadena Found. for Med. Rsch., 1961-62; chief biochemistry sect. rsch. dept. A/S Ferrosan Soeborg, Demark, 1963-78; neurochemistry group leader CNS Biology sect. Lederle Labs. div. Am. Cyanamid Co., Pearl River, N.Y., 1978-79; prin. rsch. scientist The Nathan S. Kline Inst. for Psychiat. Rsch., Orangeburg, N.Y., 1979—. Contbr. articles to profl. jours.; patentee in field. Nat. Inst. Neurol. and Communication Disorders and Stroke grantee, 1981-84. Mem. AAAS, Collegium Internationale Neuro-Psychopharmacologicum, Internat. Soc. Psychoneuroendocrinology, Soc. Neurosci., Internat. Soc. Neurochemistry, European Neurosci. Assn., Am. Soc. Neurochemistry, Am. Chem. Soc., Am. Soc. Biochemistry and Molecular Biology, Am. Soc. Pharmacology and Exptl. Therapeutics. Home: 10 Termakay Dr New City NY 10956-6434 Office: The Nathan S Kline Inst for Psychiat Rsch Orangeburg NY 10962

SREDY, JANET, biochemist; b. Monongahela, Pa., Aug. 10, 1954; d. Rudolph Matthew and Mildred (Kvocka) S.; m. Raul Oscar Chiesa, Mar. 7, 1986. BS, Pa. State U., 1976; PhD, Thomas Jefferson U., 1982. Postdoctoral researcher Columbia U., N.Y.C., 1981-84; fellow Nat. Eye Inst., NIH, Bethesda, Md., 1984-85; sr. scientist Wyeth-Ayerst Rsch., Princeton, N.J., 1985-87, rsch. scientist, 1987-90, prin. scientist, 1990—. Contbr. articles to profl. jours.; reviewer Metabolism jour. Mem. AAAS, Am. Soc. for Biochemistry and Molecular Biology, Am. Chem. Soc., Am. Diabetes Assn., Assn. for Rsch. in Vision and Ophthalmology, Internat. Diabetes Assn., N.Y. Acad. Scis. Home: 5900 Arlington Ave Apt 9E Bronx NY 10471-1310 Office: Wyeth Ayerst Rsch CN 8000 Princeton NJ 08543

SREEBNY, DANIEL, diplomat; b. Chgo., Dec. 19, 1955; s. Leo M. and Mathilda (Sternfeldt) S.; m. Diana Ruth Curtiss, July 24, 1982; children: Rachel Kay, Laura Curtiss. BA, Brandeis U., 1976; M in Internat. Affairs, Columbia U., 1978. Pub. affairs officer Am. Embassy, Muscat, Oman, 1982-84; info. officer Am. Consulate Gen., Hong Kong, 1986-88, asst. pub. affairs officer, 1988-90; fgn. svc. tng. coord. U.S. Info. Agy., Washington, 1990-91; chief of China svc. br. Voice of Am., Washington, 1992—. Contbr. articles to profl. jours. Recipient Meritorious Honor award Dept. of State, 1984, U.S Info. Agy., 1988. Jewish. Home: 2606 Stone Mountain Ct Herndon VA 22070-2883 Office: Voice of Am 330 Independence Ave SW Washington DC 20547

SREEDHAR, VIJAY, telecommunications executive; b. Bangalore, India; came to the U.S., 1977; m. C.S. Mamatha, Sept. 7, 1981; 1 child, Suhas. PhD, Johns Hopkins U. Rsch. physicist Case Western Res. U., Cleve., 1977-80; sr. scientist La. State U., Baton Rouge, 1980-84; mem. tech. staff AT&T Bell Labs., Holmdel, N.J., 1984—. Contbr. articles to profl. jours. Home: 23 Peachstone Rd Howell NJ 07731 Office: AT&T Bell Labs Crawfords Corner Rd Rm 2B628A Holmdel NJ 07733

SRERE, DAVID BENSON, advertising executive; b. N.Y.C., Apr. 11, 1958; s. Benson Mortimer and Betty Ann (Cerruti) S.; m. Linda Jean Forquignon, Sept. 10, 1983. BA cum laude, Williams Coll., 1980. With Ogilvy & Mather, Inc., N.Y.C., 1980-83; with Saatchi & Saatchi Advt., Inc., N.Y.C., 1983—, sr. v.p., mgmt. supr., 1988—. Home: 209 Osborne Ave Point Pleasant Beach NJ 08742-4633 Office: Saatchi & Saatchi Advt 375 Hudson St New York NY 10014-3658

SRINIDHI, BIN, accounting educator; b. Bangalore, Karnataka, India, Mar. 28, 1952; came to U.S., 1980; s. Narayana and Srirangamma (Iyengar) S.; m. Shreedevi Murthy, May 24, 1978; 1 child, Supriya. BTech in Electronics, Indian Inst. Tech., Madras, 1973; MBA, Indian Inst. Mgmt., Ahmedabad, India, 1975; MPhil in Acctg., Columbia U., 1982, PhD in Acctg., 1984. Account officer Bharat Heavy Elecs. Ltd., New Delhi, 1975-77; asst. commr. Govt. of India, Karnataka, 1977-80; asst. prof. Stern Sch. Bus. NYU, 1984-90; assoc. prof. Grad. Sch. Mgmt. Rutgers U., Newark, 1990—; cons. Deloitte & Touche, N.Y.C., 1989-90, Merrill Lynch, N.Y.C.,

1990, Alpha Wire Co., Elizabeth, N.J., 1990, Cybernetica Inc., N.Y.C., 1984-91. Contbr. articles to profl. jours. Grantee Peat Marwick Found., 1982, 85, 90, Coopers & Lybrand, 1986, Deloitte, Haskins & Sells, 1985, NYU, 1984-90; Hermes scholar Columbia U., 1981-82, Sriram Indsl. scholar Indian Inst. Mgmt. Mem. Nat. Assn. Acctg., Am. Acctg. Assn., Inst. of Mgmt. Scis., Beta Gamma Sigma (mem. Alpha chpt.). Home: 31 Bartman Rd East Brunswick NJ 08816-4635 Office: Rutgers U Grad Sch Mgmt 92 New St Newark NJ 07102-1818

SRINIVASAN, MANDAYAM PARAMEKANTHI, software services executive; b. Mysore City, India, July 1, 1940; s. Appalacharya Paramekanthi and Singamma Budugan; came to U.S., 1970; B.S., U. Mysore, 1959, B.E. in Mech. Engring., 1963; M.S. in Ops. Research, Poly. Inst. N.Y., 1974, M.S. in Computer Sci., 1983; m. Ranganayaki Srirangapatnam, June 18, 1967. Costing engr. Heavy Engring. Corp., Ranchi, Bihar, India, 1963-70; inventory analyst Ideal Corp., Bklyn., 1970-75; systems analyst Electronic Calculus, Inc., N.Y.C., 1975-76; cons. in software, project leader Computer Horizons Corp., N.Y.C., 1976-85; pres. Compmusic, Bellerose, N.Y., 1985—; tchr., cons. in-house tng. Founding mem. governing council Vishwa Hindu Parishad of U.S.A., 1973—, pres. N.Y. State chpt., 1977-86. Mem. Assn. for Computing Machinery, IEEE, Inst. Engrs. (India). Republican. Hindu. Office: Compmusic Inc 8229 251st St Jamaica NY 11426-2527

SROUJI, MAURICE NAKHLEH, pediatric surgeon; b. Nazareth, Palestine, June 13, 1928; came to U.S., 1965; s. Nakhleh Y. and Edma S. (Shomar) S.; m. Batishwa Badawi, June 25, 1966; children: Maureen G., Nadeem M. BA, Am. U. Beirut, 1948, MD, 1953; MA (hon.), U. Pa., 1974. Diplomate Am. Bd. Surgery (Gen. and Pediatric). Dir. surgery Holy Family Hosp., Nazareth, Israel, 1960-62; fellow in cardiovascular rsch. Rsch. Inst., Hosp. for Sick Children, Toronto, 1964-65; fellow in pediatric surg. rsch. Children's Hosp., Phila., 1965; rsch. assoc. in pediatric surgery Children's Hosp./U. Pa., Phila., 1966-67; chief pediatric surgery, attending surgeon Phila. Gen. Hosp./U. Pa., 1967-76; asst. surgeon Children's Hosp., Phila., 1967-71, assoc. surgeon, 1972-84; asst. prof. pediatric surgery U. Pa., Phila., 1968-74, assoc. prof., 1974—; vis. prof. surgery Am. U. Hosp., Beirut, 1984-85; vis. cons. in pediatric surgery Hamad Gen. Hosp., Ministry of Health, Doha, Qatar, 1986, King Fahd N.G. Hosp., Riyadh, Saudi Arabia, 1987; vis. pediatric surgeon Nazareth Hosp., 1987. Contbr. articles to profl. jours. Fellow ACS, Am. Acad. Pediatrics (surg. sect.), Am. Pediatric Surg. Assn.; mem. AMA, Pan Am. Med. Assn., Am. U. Beirut Alumni Surg. Soc. N.Am., AAUP. Roman Catholic. Home: 303 Penbree Cir Bala Cynwyd PA 19004-2332

SRUBAS, ROBERT CHARLES, engineering executive; b. N.Y.C., Feb. 22, 1953; s. Andrew Timothy and Helen Francis (Kuchta) S.; m. Darlene Marie Holmberg, Aug. 20, 1977; children: Allison Marie, Amanda Helen. BS in Chemistry, Rensselaer Poly. Inc., 1975; MS in Polymer Sci. Engring., U. Mass., 1980. Mgr., devel. Ensign Bickford Ind., Simsbury, Conn., 1978-84; mgr., prodn. Nelson Electric, Windsor Locks, Conn., 1984-87; v.p., engring. Specialty Cable Corp., Wallingford, Conn., 1987—. Mem. Soc. Mfg. Engrs. (sr.), Soc. Plastics Engrs. (sr.). Home: 10 Hampton Trl Wallingford CT 06492-2618 Office: Specialty Cable Corp 2 Tower Dr Wallingford CT 06492-1877

STABENAU, M. CATHERINE, engineering executive; b. Indpls., May 12, 1948; d. Charles Harold and Marie Catherine (Scharfenberger) Bishop; m. Walter Frank Stabenau, Nov. 20, 1971; children: Elizabeth Ann, Derek Walter. BA in Math., Spaulding Coll., 1970; BEE, U. Dayton, 1979. System programmer Air Force Logistics, WPAFB, Ohio, 1970-74; sr. engr. GE Heavy Mil. Equipment Div., Syracuse, N.Y., 1980-84; mgr. GE/Astrospace Div., King of Prussia, Pa., 1984-91, Princeton, N.J., 1991—. Recipient Women in Engring. Fellowship, NSF, 1979. Home: 1543 Silo Rd Morrisville PA 19067-4240 Office: GE ASD PO Box 800 Princeton NJ 08543-0800

STABENAU, WALTER FRANK, systems engineer; b. Cleve., Apr. 24, 1942; s. Walter Kurt and Helen (Koris) S.; m. Mary Catherine Bishop, Nov. 20, 1971; children: Elizabeth Ann, Derek Walter. BS in Physics, Case Inst. Tech., 1964; PhD in Nuclear Sci., Cornell U., 1969. Computer programmer Air Force Logistics Commd., Wright Patterson AFB, Ohio, 1970-74; navigation analyst Logicon, Inc., Dayton, Ohio, 1974-80; sonar engr. Gen. Electric, Syracuse, N.Y., 1980-84; prin. systems engr. RCA Corp., Moorestown, N.J., 1984-86, mgr. combat systems analysis, 1986-89, project mgr., 1989-91; cons. Sonalysts Inc., Willingboro, N.J., 1991—. Contbr. articles to profl. jours. Mem. Assn. Old Crows. Home: 1543 Silo Rd Morrisville PA 19067-4240 Office: Sonalysts Inc 624 Highland Dr 600 Highland Dr Mount Holly NJ 08060

STABY, JACK BRADFORD, cost engineer, retired; b. Mineola, N.Y., Mar. 20, 1926; s. Ernest John and Arlene Katherine (Kramer) S.; m. Dorothy Louise Sheffield; children: John Bradford, Robert Stanford, Mary Katherine. BS in Indsl. Mgmt., L.I. U., 1964; postgrad., Broome Community Coll., 1992—. With floor production dept. Grumman Aviation, Bethpage, N.Y., 1943-44; mfg. engr. Republic Aviation, Farmingdale, N.Y., 1947-64; mfg. engr. IBM, Endicott, N.Y., 1964-70, cost engr., 1970-90; retired, 1990. Author: (with others) Tooling for Aircraft and Missile Manufacture, 1964. Councilman Borough Coun., Little Meadows, Pa., 1970-74; trustee Fire Dept., Little Meadows, 1974-78; pres. Ch. Bd., Little Meadows, 1989—, mem. Amityville, 1958-62; bd. dirs. Montrose Area Sch. Bd. Susquehanna, Pa., 1975-89; active Boy Scouts Am.; vol. SCORE, Binghampton, N.Y. and Susquahanna. Republican. Methodist. Home: PO Box 475 Pa Ave # 410 Little Meadows PA 18830

STACEY, ROGER FOY, educator; b. Salem, Mass., Nov. 9, 1942; s. Joel Phillips and Vivian (Foy) S.; m. Nancy Clark Earle, Nov. 23, 1968 (dec. Dec. 1982); 1 child, Amanda Earle; m. Maureen M. Lynch, Oct. 12, 1986. AB, Hamilton Coll., 1965; postgrad., Oxford U., Eng., 1966, 74, Tufts U., 1967-70; MA in Teaching, Harvard U., 1967. Tchr., adminstr. Taft Sch., Watertown, Conn., 1970-83; tchr. Buckingham Browne and Nichols Sch., Cambridge, Mass., 1983—; bd. dirs. Boston Shakespeare Competition. Docent Cable Sta. Mus., Orleans, Mass., 1978—; propr. Boston Athenaeum Libr.; nat. patron English Speaking Union.; bd. dirs. E-SU, Boston Br. Mem. Eastward Ho Club, Harvard Faculty Club, Lansdowne Club (London). Episcopalian. Home: 59 Brewster St Cambridge MA 02138-2203 Office: BB&N Sch Gerrys Landing Rd Cambridge MA 02138-5512

STACHOWSKI, WILLIAM T., state senator; b. Buffalo, Feb. 14, 1949; s. Stanley J. and Pearl (Wojcik) S. BA in Polit. Sci., Coll. Holy Cross, 1972. Legislator Erie County Legislature, Buffalo, 1974-81; senator N.Y. State Legislature, Albany, 1981—; bd. dirs. U.S. Rte. 19 Assn., Western N.Y., 1982—, U.S. Rte. 62 Assn., Western N.Y., 1985—; mem. City of Buffalo Auditorium Task Force. Recipient Friend of Law Enforcement award N.Y. State Sheriffs, 1990. Mem. Erie County Dem. Party, 1967—. Roman Catholic. Home: 2030 Clinton St Buffalo NY 14206-3312 Office: NY State Senate State Capitol Legis Office Bldg Albany NY 12247

STACK, EDWARD WILLIAM, business management and foundation executive; b. Rockville Centre, N.Y., Feb. 1, 1935; s. Edward Henry and Helen Margaret (Leitner) S.; m. Christina Carol Hunt, Aug. 19, 1967; children: Amy Alison, Kimberly Anne, Suzanne Gail. BBA, Pace U., 1956; LLD (hon.), Hartwick Coll., 1982; LHD (hon.), Pace U., 1991. Sec., dir. Clark Estates, Inc., fin. and bus. mgmt., N.Y.C., 1956-90, pres., bd. dirs., 1990—; v.p., dir. Leatherstocking Corp., hotels and real estate, Cooperstown, N.Y., 1961-92; pres., bd. dir. Leatherstocking Corp., hotels and real estate, Cooperstown, 1992—; sec.-treas., dir. The New Republic, Inc., mag., Washington, 1974—. Sec., trustee N.Y. State Hist. Assn., Cooperstown, 1961—; vice chmn., trustee Mary Imogene Bassett Hosp., 1961—; sec. Nat. Baseball Hall of Fame and Mus., Inc., Cooperstown, 1961-77, pres., chmn. bd., 1977—; v.p. Farmers Mus., Inc., Cooperstown, 1964—; sec. Clark Found., N.Y.C., 1963-90, v.p., bd. dirs., 1990—; v.p., bd. dirs. Nourse Found., N.Y.C., 1976—; trustee, treas. Bethany Deaconess Soc., Bklyn.; trustee Park Ave. Meth. Ch. Trust Fund, Baseball Am. Found., Inc., others; bd. dirs. United Meth. City Soc. of Meth. Ch., N.Y.C. Mem. Downtown Assn. (N.Y.C.), Mohican Club (Cooperstown, N.Y.). Republican. Home: 25 Waverly St Glen Head NY 11545-1004 Office: 30 Wall St New York NY 10005-2201

STACK, ROBERT DOUGLAS, marketing communications executive; b. Las Vegas, Nev., Nov. 15, 1956; s. Benjamin J. and Doris J. (Rappaport) S. BS cum laude, Boston U., 1977. Salesman Stack's, N.Y.C., 1977-79; pres. Robert Stack Assocs., N.Y.C., 1979—; adj. faculty Mgmt. Inst. NYU, N.Y.C., 1987—. Mem. Pub. Rels. Soc. (accredited bd. dirs. N.Y. chpt. 1987—, nat. accreditation bd. 1988—), Am. Mktg. Assn., Nat. Acad. TV Arts and Scis., Internat. Radio and TV Soc., Sigma Delta Chi, Old Oaks Country Club. Office: 425 Madison Ave New York NY 10017-1110

STACKPOLE, KERRY CLIFFORD, association executive; b. Putnam, Conn., Feb. 24, 1955; s. Howard Thompson Stackpole and Shyrlee Gladys (Leazer) Burr; m. Miriam Weisberg, July 29, 1984. MEd, Cambridge Coll., 1983. Gen. mgr. E.J. Ardon Co., Boston, 1978-82; ops. mgr. Fotobeam/Brookside, Waltham, Mass., 1982-83; assoc. dir. Printing Industries of New Eng., Natick, Mass., 1983—; v.p. Printing Industries of New Eng., 1989-91; exec. dir. Smaller Bus. Assn. New Eng., Waltham, Mass., 1991—; dir. Graphic Arts Inst., Chgo., 1983-84, v.p. 1984-85, pres. 1985-88. Recipient HIRE Trust Fund award Graphic Arts Employers of Am., 1987. Mem. Am. Mgmt. Assn., Am. Soc. Assn. Execs., New Eng. Soc. Assn. Execs. (committeeman 1983-84, membership devel. com. 1989—, bd. dirs. 1991—, Ralph Louis Towne award 1986). Office: Smaller Bus Assn New Eng 69 Hickory Dr Waltham MA 02154-1006

STADNICKI, STANLEY WALTER, JR., health science association administrator; b. Norwich, Conn., Sept. 30, 1943; s. Stanley Walter Sr. and Beatrice Catherine (Dumais) S.; m. Jeanne Marie Couture, Sept. 6, 1965; children: Sandra, Scott, Steven, Robert. BA, Assumption Coll., Worcester, Mass., 1965; MA, Clark U., Worcester, 1970; PhD, Worcester Poly. Inst., 1976. Neurophysiologist Dept. Toxicology and Pharmacology, E.G. & G. Mason Research Inst., Worcester, 1967-70, sect. head, 1970-75, research scientist, 1975-76; toxicologist Drug Safety Evaluation, Pfizer, Inc., Groton, Conn., 1976-79, sr. toxicologist, 1979-81, project leader, 1981-85, mgr., 1985-86, asst. dir., 1986—; Contbr. articles to profl. jours. Leader Cub Scouts, East Lyme, Conn., 1978; mgr. East Lyme Little League Baseball, 1978-83; coach Babe Ruth Baseball, East Lyme, 1984-86; mem. Athletic Booster Club, East Lyme, 1984—. Clark U. grad. fellow, 1965-66. Mem. IEEE, Am. Soc. Pharmacology and Exptl. Therapeutics, Am. Coll. Toxicology, Soc. Toxicology (pres. N.E. chpt. 1990-92), Can. Soc. Toxicology. Roman Catholic. Home: 66 Quailcrest Rd East Lyme CT 06333-1328 Office: Pfizer Inc Drug Safety Evaluation Eastern Point Rd Groton CT 06340-4947

STAFF, DONALD ALBERT, chemical company owner; b. Totowa Boro, N.J., Mar. 20, 1935; s. Albert Thomas and Virginia Ida (Wageman) S.; m. Jacqueline Ann Draney, June 9, 1962 (dec. Dec. 1982); children: Donald A. Jr., Elizabeth A., Michael A. BS in Chemistry, St. Bonaventure U., 1957. Rsch. chemist Tenneco Chems. INc., Garfield, N.J., 1957-60; sales rep. Tenneco Chems. INc., N.Y.C., 1960-62, product mgr., 1962-66, distbn. mgr., 1966-69; industry mgr. Tenneco Chems. INc., Piscataway, N.J., 1969-71; dir. mktg. Givavdan Corp., Clifton, N.J., 1971-78; exec. v.p., co-owner Soca-Penn INc., Phila., 1978-80; eastern mgr. Great Lakes Chem. Corp., West Lafayette, Ind., 1980-86; pres., owner Chemstaff INc., Wyckoff, N.J., 1986—; N.J. region fundraiser Salve Regina U., Newport, R.I., 1990—. Contbr. articles to profl. jours. Ad hoc com. Wyckoff (N.J.) Bd. Edn., 1972. Sgt. U.S. Army, 1959-61. Mem. Am. Chem. Soc., Synthetic Organic Chem. Mfrs. Assn. (tech. com. rep. 1971-75), Sales Assn. Chem. Industry. Republican. Roman Catholic. Home: 441 Patton Pl Wyckoff NJ 07481-1511 Office: Chemstaff Inc PO Box 398 Wyckoff NJ 07481-0398

STAFFIER, PAMELA MOORMAN, psychologist; b. Passaic, N.J., Dec. 7, 1942; d. Wynant Clair and Jeannette Frances (Rentzsch) Moorman; B.A., Bucknell U., 1964; M.A. in Psychology, Assumption Coll., Worcester, Mass., 1970, C.A.G.S., 1977; Ph.D., Union Inst., 1978; m. John Staffier, Jr., Apr. 5, 1975; children—M. Anthony, C. Matthew. Psychologist, Westboro (Mass.) State Hosp., 1965, prin. psychologist, also asst. to supt., 1973-76; psychologist Moriarty Mental Health Clinic; psychiat. cons. local gen. hosp.; research psychologist Wrentham (Mass.) State Sch., 1966, Cushing Hosp., Framingham, Mass., 1967; prin. psychologist, also asst. to supt. Grafton (Mass.) State Hosp., 1967-72; dir. Staffier Psychol. Assocs., Inc., 1978—. Mem. Am. Psychol. Assn. (assoc.), Am. Psychol. Practitioners Assn. (founding mem.), Mass. Psychol. Assn., Nat. Register Health Service Providers in Psychology. Research, publs. on state hosp. closings, biochem. basis of Schizophrenia. Home: 68 Adams St PO Box 1103 Westboro MA 01581 Office: 57 E Main St Westborough MA 01581-1464

STAFFORD, DRUCILLE HUTCHINSON, principal; b. Washington, Dec. 2, 1938; d. Edward St. Clair Hutchinson and Eleise Velma (Murray) Moore; m. James L. Stafford, July 2, 1961 (div. Dec. 1980). BS, D.C. Tchrs., 1960; MS, U. Miami, 1969; EdD, U. Mass., 1986. Tchr. D.C. Pub. Schs., Washington, 1960-61, 62-63, Ft. Carson Schs., Fountain, Colo., 1961-62; tchr. Montgomery County Pub. Schs., Rockville, Md., 1963-68, spl. asst., supt., 1986-87, prin., 1969—; spl. asst., sec. Dept. of HEW, Washington, 1978-79; cons. Headstart Cpt. I/Dept. HEW, 1968-76; dep. dir. Dept. Edn., Washington, 1979-80; appointee intergovernmental Dept. of HEW, 1979. Bd. dirs. Secret Harbor Beach Owners Assn., St. Thomas, V.I., 1986—. Fellowship Dept. HEW, 1978-79, U. Miami, 1968-69. Mem. NAACP, Nat. Alliance of Black Sch. Educators Found. (chmn. 1991—, sec. 1987-91). Democrat. Methodist. Home: 2920 Toone St Baltimore MD 21224-4877 Office: Montgomery County Pub Schs 3301 Weller Rd Silver Spring MD 20906-4155

STAFFORD, FREDERICK E., lawyer; b. Jersey City, 1942. BS in Acctg., Rutgers U., 1972; MBA, Baruch Coll., N.Y.C., 1977; JD, Touro Coll., Huntington, N.Y., 1985. Bar: N.J. 1986, N.Y. 1986, D.C. 1986, U.S. Dist. Ct. (ea. and so. dists.) N.Y., U.S. Dist. Ct. N.J.; CPA, N.J. Asst. to tax mgr. Burns and Roe Inc., Oradell, N.J., 1969-72, Collins and Aikman Corp., N.Y.C., 1972-73; tax mgr. Essex Chemical Corp., Clifton, N.J., 1973-87; assoc. Cohn and Lifland, Saddle Brook, N.J., 1987; with AT&T, Morristown, N.J., 1987-88, M.S. Ackerman & Co., 1988-89, Equitable Life Ins. Soc., 1989-90. Mem. ABA, N.J. State Bar Assn., Bergen County Bar Assn., N.Y. State Bar Assn., N.J. Soc. CPAs, D.C. Bar Assn. Office: 808 Pascack Rd Paramus NJ 07652-4228

STAFFORD, MARY ELLEN, university administrator; b. Providence, July 1, 1933; d. Gordon Charles and Clarion Helen (Bachmann) Mackie; m. Rick Stafford, June 16, 1951; children: Charity, Felicity, Christopher. AB, Harvard U., 1971; MA, Met. U., Boston, 1976. Animal caretaker Mass. Gen. Hosp., Boston, 1950-53; clk. N.E. Credit Bur., Boston, 1957-59; dietician Franklin Park Childrens Zoo, Boston, 1961-65; sales clk. Lambert Co., Boston, 1967-69; mem. radiation safety staff Harvard Biology Labs., Cambridge, Mass., 1969-71; rsch. immunologist Boston U. Sch. Medicine, 1971-76, surgery office mgr., 1976-78, adminstrv. coord. surg. residency, 1978-83, adminstrv. coord. surg. edn., 1983—; owner Marrick Graphics, Allston, Mass.; co-owner Yankee Sarpint. Mem. Country Dance Soc. Boston Centre (pres. 1982), New Eng. Herpetol. Soc. (sec. 1989-90). Home: 26 Wadsworth St Allston MA 02134-1822 Office: Univ Hosp 88 E Newton St # 508D Roxbury MA 02118-2347

STAFFORD, SUSAN BUCHANAN, grants director; b. Cin., Nov. 17, 1948; d. Hubert Henry and June (Bauer) Huelsebusch; m. David F. Stafford, Sept. 1, 1982. BA, Ind. U., 1969; MA, U. Cin., 1970; PhD, NYU, 1980, cert. in careers in bus. studies, 1985. Program officer U.S. Dept. of State, Miami, Fla., 1980-81; program officer, (Office of Refugee Resettlement) U.S. Dept. Health and Human Svcs., Miami and N.Y.C., 1981, 82-83; exec. dir. Nat. Coalition for Haitian Refugees, N.Y.C., 1981-82; program mgr. U.S. Dept. of Justice, N.Y.C., 1983-87; asst. dir. grants and govt. rels. N.Y. Assn. for New Ams., N.Y.C., 1987-89; univ. dir. corp. found. and govt. grants L.I. U., Brookville, N.Y., 1990—. NDEA fellow NYU, 1971, Charles Kriser fellow, 1978. Mem. Am. Assn. Anthropologists, Nat. Assn. Practicing Anthropologists. Home: 47 Fleets Cove Rd Huntington NY 11743-1515 Office: LI U Grants Office Brookville NY 11548

STAGG, PAUL LYNWOOD, internist, hospital administrator; b. New Haven, Aug. 19, 1942; s. Paul Lynwood and Angeline (Nicola) S.; m. Lura Dean Winstead, June 3, 1967; children: Paul Lynwood, Carl Coltrane. BS, Tufts U., 1964; MD, Bowman Gray U., Winston-Salem, 1968. Diplomate Am. Bd. Internal Medicine. Chmn. ambulatory care Baystate Med. Ctr., Springfield, Mass., 1973-89; pres. Baystate Med. Edn. and Rsch. Found., Springfield, Mass., 1986-89; sr. v.p. med. affairs St. Vincent Health Ctr., Erie, Pa., 1989—. Mem. Am. Coll. Physician Execs. Home: 7210 Pinegate Rd Fairview PA 16415-1565 Office: St Vincent Health Ctr 232 W 25th St Erie PA 16502-2701

STAGLIANO, VITO ALEXANDER, federal official; b. Catanzaro, Calabria, Italy, May 13, 1942; came to U.S., 1956; s. Filippo and Maria Stagliano; m. Julie Ann Werth, Sept. 30, 1967; children: Jason Vito, Carlos Otobed. Program analyst U.S. Office Econ. Opportunity, Washington, 1968-69; exec. dir. Palau Community Devel. Agy., Micronesia, 1969-71; program officer U.S. Peace Corps, Ghana, Africa, 1971-73; dir. U.S. Peace Corps, Mauritania, Africa, 1973-74; dir. West Africa U.S. Peace Corps, Washington, 1974-77; counselor Interstate Commn. on Drought Control, Ouagadougou, Bourkina Faso, 1977-79; staff asst. Sec. of Energy, Washington, 1979-81; dir. River Basins Devel. Office, Dakar, Senegal, Africa, 1981-85; dir. Office of Energy Demands Policy Office of Energy Demand Policy, U.S. Dept. Energy, Washington, 1986-89, assoc. dep. undersec. of energy, 1990—. Contbr. articles to profl. jours. Founder Micronesia Legal Svcs. Program, 1991. Ampart fellow USIA, 1981; recipient Silver Medal for Meritorious Svc., U.S. Dept. Energy, Bronze medal for exceptional svc. Mem. NAACP (legal def. fund), Amnesty Internat. Home: 5916 Anniston Rd Bethesda MD 20817-3421

STAHL, BARBARA J., biologist, educator; b. Bklyn., Apr. 17, 1930; d. Samuel and Sophie (Kalison) Jaffe; m. David G. Stahl, July 7, 1951; children: Susan E. Hardy, Nancy R. Wilsker, Sarah A., John S. BA, Wellesley Coll., 1952; AM, Radcliffe Coll., 1953; PhD, Harvard U., 1965. Prof. biology St. Anselm Coll., Manchester, N.H., 1954—; instl. rev. bd. mem. Cath. Med. Ctr., Manchester, 1987—. Author: Vertebrate History: Problems in Evolution, 1974, 1985; contbr. articles to profl. jours. Trustee The Derryfield Sch., Manchester, 1965—. Mem. AAAS, AAUP, Am. Soc. Ichthyology and Herpetology, Nat. Assn. Advisors for Health Professions, Soc. Vertebrate Paleontology, Northeast Assn. Advisors for Health Professions (treas. 1981—), Sigma Xi. Office: Saint Anselm Coll Biol Dept 87 St Anselms Dr Manchester NH 03102-1310

STAHL, DAVID G., dentist; b. Manchester, N.H., Nov. 1, 1926; s. Samuel and Sadie (Flaxman) S.; m. Barbara Jaffe, July 7, 1951; children: Susan E. Hardy, Nancy R. Wilsker, Sarah A., John S. AB, Dartmouth Coll., 1947; DMD, Tufts U., 1951. Pvt. practice dentistry Manchester, 1951—; faculty mem. Boston U. Sch. Grad. Dentistry, Boston, 1958-73. Contbr. articles to profl. jours. Pres. N.H. Hist. Soc., Concord, 1990—, Greater Manchester Jewish Fedn., 1989-91. With USNR, 1945-46. Recipient MacRury award N.H. Dental Soc., 1986. Home: 100 Magnolia Rd Manchester NH 03104-1697 Office: 1361 Elm St Ste 204 Manchester NH 03101-1340

STAHL, LESLEY R., journalist; b. Lynn, Mass., Dec. 16, 1941; d. Louis and Dorothy J. (Tishler) S.; m. Aaron Latham; 1 dau. B.A. cum laude, Wheaton Coll., Norton, Mass., 1963. Asst. to speechwriter Mayor Lindsay's Office, N.Y.C., 1966-67; researcher N.Y. Election unit London-Huntley Brinkley Report, NBC News, 1967-69; producer, reporter WHDH-TV, Boston, 1970-72; news corr. CBS News, Washington, from 1972; moderator Face the Nation, 1983-91; co-editor, corr. CBS News, 60 Minutes, 1991—. Trustee Wheaton Coll. Recipient Tex. Headliners award, 1973. Office: CBS News 524 W 57th St New York NY 10019

STAHL, ROBERT ALAN, manufacturing executive, consultant; b. Bklyn., Dec. 27, 1942; s. William Leonard and Marion Teresa (Saunders) S.; m. Patricia Ann Loughery, Oct. 26, 1968; children: Robert Jr., Matthew. BS in Econs., Villanova U., 1966. Mgr. prodn. control Continental Can Co., Patterson, N.J., 1971-73; materials mgr. Schatz-Fed. Co., Poughkeepsie, N.Y., 1973-75, E.G.& G. Sealol, Inc., Warwick, R.I., 1975-81; prin. cons. Comserv Corp., Mnpls., 1981-82; pres. R.A. Stahl Co., Attleboro, Mass., 1982—; R.D. Garwood Assoc., 1988—. Contbr. articles to profl. jours.; speaker in field. Mgr. Attleboro Little League, 1977—, Seekonk (Mass.) Youth Hockey, 1975-79, Attleboro Babe Ruth League, 1981-85. Served to lt. USN, 1966-71, Vietnam. Mem. Ops. Mgmt. Assn., Am. Prodn. and Inventory Control Soc. (cert.). Roman Catholic. Lodge: KC. Home and Office: 6 Marlise Dr Attleboro MA 02703-6535

STAHLER, GERALD JAY, clincial psychologist; b. Harrisburg, Pa., Aug. 20, 1952; s. Abraham and Rose (Saxe) S.; m. Sheryl Levin, Oct. 9, 1983; children: David, Samuel, Eric Henry. BA, Clark U., 1974; MA, U. Toronto, 1976, Temple U., 1978; PhD, Temple U., 1982. Lic. psychologist, Md., Pa. Clin. psychologist Rappaport Assocs., Phila., 1982-83; v.p. rsch. Horizon Inst. Advanced Design, Rockville, Md., 1978-84; dir. program evaluation Nat. Ctr. Family Studies Cath. U., Washington, 1983-85; asst. vice provost Temple U., Phila., 1985-89, assoc. vice provost, 1989—; cons. psychologist Cooper Med. Ctr., Camden, N.J., 1982; sec., treas. Costar Indsl. Resource Ctr., Phila., 1988-91. Co-editor: Innovative Approaches to Mental Health Evaluation, 1982; contbr. articles to profl. jours. Grantee Nat. Inst. Mental Health, 1979-81, W.T. Grant Found, 1985-88, Dept. Commerce Pa., 1988-90, Nat. Inst. Alcohol Abuse & Alcoholism, 1990; fellow Harvard Med. Sch., 1980-81. Office: Temple U USB Broad and Oxford Sts Rm 406 Philadelphia PA 19122

STALBERG, ZACHARY, newspaper editor; b. Phila., Apr. 6, 1947; m. Helene Stalberg. Student polit. sci., Temple U., 1968. Reporter Bucks County Courier Times, Levittown, Pa., 1970-71; reporter Phila. Daily News, 1971-75, city editor, 1975-77, mng. editor, 1977-79, exec. editor, 1979-84, editor, 1984—. Served with U.S. Army, 1968-70. Mem. Am. Soc. Newspaper Editors. Home: 15 E Newfield Way Bala Cynwyd PA 19004-2321 Office: Phila Daily News 400 N Broad St Philadelphia PA 19130-4099*

STALEY, CHARLES EARL, economics educator; b. Wichita, Kans., Feb. 17, 1927; s. Clarence E. and Bernice (Russell) S.; m. Rhoda McCord, Aug. 19, 1954 (div. 1981); children: Duncan, Andrew, Jessica. BA, U. Kans., 1950; PhD, MIT, 1956. Instr. econs. U. Kans., Lawrence, 1953-57; asst. prof. econs. U. Kans., 1957-63, assoc. prof. econs., 1963-65; assoc. prof. econs. SUNY, Stony Brook, 1965—. Author: History of Economic Thought, 1989, paperback edit., 1991, International Economics, 1970; contbr. articles to profl. jours. With U.S. Army, 1945-46. Ford Found. faculty fellow, 1963. Fellow Royal Econ. Soc.; mem. Am. Econ. Assn., History of Econs. Soc. (mem. exec. bd. 1991—), Joseph A. Schumpeter Soc. Home: 19 Gnarled Hollow Rd East Setauket NY 11733-2926 Office: SUNY Dept Econs Stony Brook NY 11794

STALEY, DELBERT C., telecommunications executive; b. Hammond, Ind., Sept. 16, 1924; s. Eugene and Nellie (Downer) s.; m. Ingrid Andersen, Mar. 16, 1946; children—Crista Staley Ellis, Cynthia, Clifford, Corinn. Student, Rose Poly. Inst., Hammond, 1943-44; grad. advanced mgmt. program, Harvard U., 1962; D. Engring. (hon.), Rose Hulman Inst. Tech., 1981; LL.D. (hon.), Skidmore Coll., 1983. With Ill. Bell Telephone, 1946-76, v.p. ops., 1972-76; pres. Ind. Bell, 1976-78; v.p. residence mktg. AT&T, 1978-79; pres. N.Y. Telephone, 1979-83, chmn. bd., chief exec. officer, 1983; chmn. bd., chief exec. officer NYNEX Corp., White Plains, N.Y., 1983-89, chmn., dir. internat. mgmt. com., 1989-91; bd. dirs. Dean Foods, Franklin Park, Ill., Ball Corp., Muncie, Ind., Bank N.Y., N.Y.C., Allied-Signal Inc., John Hancock Mut. Life Ins. Co., Polaroid Corp. With U.S. Army, 1943-46; ETO. Recipient Puerto Rican Legal Def. and Edn. Fund award, 1981, Cleveland Dodge award YMCA Greater N.Y., 1983, New Yorker for N.Y. award Citizens Com. for N.Y., 1984, Leadership in Mgmt. award Pace U., 1988, Albert Schweitzer Leadership award Hugh O'Brian Youth Found., 1988, Hammond Achievement award The Hammond Hist. Soc., 1988, Gold Medal award USO, 1988, Am. Vocation Success award Pres. George Busch, 1989. Mem. Ind. Acad. (hon.), Telephone Pioneers Am. (pres. 1983-84), Westchester Country Club, Blind Brook Club, Exmoor Club, Royal Poinciana Club. Presbyterian. Home: 32 Polly Park Rd Rye NY 10580-1927 Office: Nynex Corp 335 Madison Ave New York NY 10017-4605

STALEY, FREDERICK SETON, executive and marketing professional; b. Cin., May 10, 1942; s. Frederick Seton and Madeleine (Ritter) S.; m. Nancy Jean Hodanish, Sept. 14, 1974; children: Frederick Seton III, Matthew Kyle. BBA, U. Cin., 1965. Brand supr., advt. and market rsch. Procter &

Gamble, Co., Cin., 1965-69; product mgr. to category dir. Consumer Health Products div. Warner-Lambert Co., Morris Plains, N.J., 1969-82; corp. v.p., mktg. and sales Entenmann's Bakeries div. Kraft Gen. Foods, U.S.A., Bay Shore and L.I., N.Y., 1982-87; owner F. Seton Staley and Assocs., Mendham, N.J., 1987—. Co-editor: (book) How to Develop New Products Better and Faster, 1984-85. Coach and fund raiser Randolph (N.J.) Youth Athletics, 1988—. Sgt. U.S. Army Res., 1966-72. Mem. Assn. Nat. Advertisers (com. chmn. 1981-86), Am. Mktg. Assn. (chpt. officer 1966-70). Republican. Roman Catholic. Home: Rd # 3 11 Cromwell Dr Mendham NJ 07945-2108 Office: F Seton Staley and Assocs Mktg and Mgmt Consulting PO Box 223 Chester NJ 07930-0223

STALLMAN, DONALD LEE, company executive; b. Rochester, N.Y., Feb. 20, 1930; s. William F. and Clara Elizabeth (Boulle) S.; m. Dolores Anita Putney, Nov. 8, 1958; stepchildren: Nancy, Terri, Jeff. Student, Hobart Coll., Geneva, N.Y., 1948-49, U. Rochester, 1953-54. V.p. Kolstad Assocs., Inc., Rochester, N.Y., 1954—; pres. Water Treatment Assocs., Latham, N.Y., 1975—, KB Fabrications, Latham, N.Y., 1977—; dir. Kolstad Assocs., Inc.; chmn. bd. Water Treatment Assocs.; vice chmn. bd. K.B. Fabrications; adv. bd., pres. Bruner Corp., Milw., 1982-83. Designer Chock-o-Lette Spl. Aircraft Wheel Chock, 1978, Water Treatment Skid for Oil Field Applications, 1980; inventor in field. Cons. Capital Dist. Planning Commn., Albany, 1980-81. With U.S. Army, 1951-53. Decorated Bronze Star medal, Purple Hearts (2). Mem. Am. Soc. Plumbing Engrs., Water Quality Assn., Quiet Birdman Soc., Latham Area C. of C. (mem. transport com. 1985—), Sigma Chi. Republican. Roman Catholic. Home: 16 Hillcrest Rd Latham NY 12110 Office: Water Treatment Assocs PO Box 367 Latham NY 12110-0367

STALZER, RICHARD FRANCIS, real estate developer; b. Joliet, Ill., Oct. 23, 1936; s. Joseph Albert and Charlotte Ann (Prznieslo) S.; m. Diane Mary Deitering, June 6, 1959; children:Richard Jr., Timothy, Elizabeth, Michael, Joseph. BCE, Catholic U. Am., 1958; postgrad., U. Wis., Madison. Vice pres. Sellergren, Inc., Park Ridge, Ill., 1965-68; v.p., pres. Aurora East Corp., St. Charles, Ill., 1965-68; chmn., pres. R.F. Stalzer & Assocs., Inc., Park Ridge, 1968-82; eastern regional v.p. Pub. Storage, Inc., Glendale, Calif., 1981-86; chief exec. officer Your Attic Properties, Inc., Troy, Mich., 1986-87, People's Storage, Marlton, N.J., 1987—; guest lectr. on urban planning. Coach, Park Ridge Mighty Mite Assn., 1969-78. Capt. USAF, 1959-63. Mem. Nat. Soc. Profl. Engrs., Soc. Mil. Engrs., Ill. Soc. Profl. Land Surveyors, Blue Key. Roman Catholic. Home: 1 Glen Lake Dr Medford NJ 08055-3101 Office: Peoples Storage 1317 Route 73 Mount Laurel NJ 08054-2202

STAMAS, THEODORE STEPHEN, lawyer; b. White Plains, N.Y., Aug. 6, 1960; s. Stephen and Elaine Heidi (Zervas) S. AB, Harvard U., 1982; MS in Fgn. Svc., Georgetown U., 1987, JD, 1987. Bar: N.Y. 1988, D.C. 1990. Assoc. Milbank, Tweed, Hadley & McCloy, N.Y.C., 1987—. Mem. ABA.

STAMBAUGH, JOHN EDGAR, oncologist, hematologist, pharmacologist, educator; b. Everett, Pa., Apr. 30, 1940; s. John Edgar and Rhoda Irene (Becker) S.; B.S. cum laude in Chemistry, Dickinson Coll., 1962; M.D., Jefferson Med. Coll., 1966, Ph.D., 1968; m. Shirley Louise Fultz, June 24, 1961; 4 children. Intern, Thomas Jefferson U. Hosp., Phila., 1968-69, resident, 1969-70, oncology fellow, 1970-72, instr. pharmacology, 1969-70, asst. prof., 1970-74, assoc. prof., 1974-82, prof., 1982—, asst. prof. medicine, 1976—; pvt. practice medical Oncology-Chronic Pain, Woodbury, N.J.; staff physician Thomas Jefferson Hosp., Phila., 1972—, Cooper Med. Center, Camden, N.J., 1972—, Underwood Meml. Hosp., Woodbury, 1972—, Garden State Hosp., Marlton, N.J., 1973—, Cherry Hill (N.J.) Med. Center, 1978—, West Jersey Hosp., Camden. Fellow Am. Coll. Clin. Pharmacology; mem. AMA, N.J. Med. Soc., Camden County Med. Soc., Am. Soc. for Pharmacology and Exptl. Therapeutics, Am. Soc. Clin. Oncology, Am. Assn. for Cancer Research, Internat. Assn. for Study of Pain, Am. Pain Soc., Am. Assn. Clin. Research, Sigma Xi. Contbr. articles to profl. jours.

STAMBAUGH, MERVIL RONALD, minister; b. South Mountain, Pa., May 21, 1939; s. Curvin Wilson and Lottie Ellen (Shaffer) S.; m. Terry Paulette Moss, Dec. 29, 1946. Diploma, Washington Bible Coll., 1964; BS in Bibl. Studies, Antietam Bible Coll., 1983; MA in Bibl. Studies, Antietam Bible Sem., 1987, D of Ministries, 1988. Ordained to ministry Ind. Bible Ch., 1966. Pastor Indian Springs (Md.) Bible Ch., 1964-70; pulpit supply/evangelistic work Chambersburg, Pa., 1971-87; pastor Pond Bank (Pa.) Ind. Ch., 1987—; asst. dean Camp Green Top, Thurmont, Md., 1964-66, Bread of Life Camp, Indian Springs, 1967-69; radio ministry WKSL Radio, Greencastle, Pa., 1980-81, dean evening coll. program Antietam Bible Coll., Hagerstown, Md., 1988—. Mem. Fellowship of Bible Churches (conf. sec. 1969-71). Republican. Home and Office: 1772 Orchard Rd Chambersburg PA 17201-9759

STAMBAUGH, PHILLIP FRANCIS, finance service executive; b. West Palm Beach, Fla., Sept. 26, 1944; s. William E. and Genevieve F. (Van Den Broecke) S.; m. Beverly Timbers, June 8, 1968; children: Allison, Carrie, P.J., Christopher. AB, Rockhurst Coll., 1966; postgrad., U. Wis., 1966-68. Mktg. mgr. IBM Corp., White Plains, N.Y., 1968-78; sr. v.p. State St. Bank, Boston, 1978-90, Fidelity Investments, Boston, 1990-91; pres. Stambaugh Mgmt. Svcs., Boston, 1991—; v.p. Scudder, Stevens & Clark, Boston, 1991—. Treas. Project Impact, Boston, 1983-86; pres. Boxford (Mass.) Athletic Assn., 1985. Home: 111 Herrick Rd Boxford MA 01921-1920

STAMBERG, SUSAN LEVITT, radio broadcaster; b. Newark, Sept. 7, 1938; d. Robert I. and Anne (Rosenberg) Levitt; m. Louis Collins Stamberg, Apr. 14, 1962; 1 child, Joshua Collins. BA, Barnard Coll, 1959; DHL (hon.), Gettysburg Coll., 1982, Dartmouth Coll., 1984, Knox Coll., U. N.H., SUNY, Brockport. Editorial asst. Daedalus, Cambridge, Mass., 1960-63; editorial asst. The New Republic, Washington, 1962-63; host, producer, mgr., program dir. Sta. WAMU-FM, Washington, 1963-69; host All Things Considered Washington, 1971-86; host Weekend Edition Nat Pub. Radio, Washington, 1987-89; spl. corr. Nat. Pub. Radio, 1990—; bd. dirs. AIA, Washington, 1983-85, PEN/Faulkner Fiction Award Found., 1985—. Author: Every Night at Five, 1982, The Wedding Cake in the Middle of the Road, 1992. Recipient Honor award Ohio U., 1977, Edward R. Murrow award Corp. for Pub. Broadcasting, 1980, Woman of Yr. award Barnard Coll., 1984; fellow Silliman Coll. Yale U., 1984—. Mem. Washington Ind. Writers (bd. dirs. 1984—), Sigma Delta Chi. Office: Nat Pub Radio 2025 M St NW Washington DC 20036-3309

STAMBONE, LISA MARIE, pharmacist; b. Scranton, Pa., June 22, 1964; d. Anthony Dominick and Therese Elaine (Motts) S. BS in Pharmacy, Temple U., 1987. Intern pharmacy Scranton State Gen. Hosp., 1985, Stephen's Pharmacy, Moscow, Pa., 1986, Rite Aid Pharmacy, Peckville, Pa., 1987; pharmacist mgr., computer tng. mgr. Rite Aid Pharmacy, Peckville, 1987—; cons. pharmacist drug therapy, blood pressure and glucose screenings, cholesterol screening, patient counseling and patient compliance follow-up, 1987—. Ch. lectr. St. Mary's Assumption Ch., Jessup, Pa., 1982-84. Mem. Am. Pharm. Assn., Pa. Pharm. Assn., Lackawanna Pharm. Assn., Rho Pi Phi. Democrat. Roman Catholic. Home: 706 Barrett St Jessup PA 18434-1424 Office: Rite Aid Pharmacy 1500 Main St Peckville PA 18452-2033

STAMPER, EUGENE, mechanical engineer; b. N.Y.C., Mar. 24, 1928; s. Morris and Diana (Gleberman) S.; m. Sally Goldfeder, Dec. 19, 1953; children: Marcy, Emily. BSME, CCNY, 1948; MME, NYU, 1952. Aero. rsch. scientist Nat. Adv. Com. for Aeros., Cleve., 1948-49; design engr. Seelye Stevenson Value & Knecht, N.Y.C., 1950-52; prof. mech. engring. N.J. Inst. Tech., Newark, 1952-88; sr. assoc. Joseph P. Loring & Assocs., N.Y.C., 1988-90; v.p. Arbitration, Mediation Svc., Hackensack, N.J., 1990—; cons. ASHRAE, Atlanta, 1969-73; vice chmn. Bldg. Thermal Envelope Coordinating Coun., Washington, 1982-86. Author: MEchanical Engineering for Professional Engineering Exams, 1971; editor: Handbook of Heating, Air Conditioning and Ventilation, 1979. Chmn. Zoning Bd. of Adjustment, Teaneck, N.J., 1986—. Fellow ASHRAE (Disting. Svc. award 1985); mem. ASME, Am. Soc. Engring. Edn. Home: 73 Cranford Pl Teaneck NJ 07666-4704

STAMPONE, JOHN RICHARD, SR., editorial cartoonist, author, illustrator; b. Balt., Sept. 29, 1918; s. Nicholas and Mary (Valentine) S.; m. Myrval D. Davies, Nov. 13, 1944 (dec. 1981); children: Janette, John Jr., Robert D.; m. Ethel M. Block, Aug. 13, 1983; 1 stepchild, Donald Brenner. Diploma, Balt. City Coll., 1936; student, Balt. U., 1936-38, Johns Hopkins U., 1938-40. Promotion artist Balt. Sun, 1936-38; freelance advt. Balt., 1938-40; cartoonist Office of Under-Sec. War, Washington, 1943-45, J. Walther Thompson Co., N.Y.C., 1960-63; editorial cartoonist Army Times Pub. Co., Washington, 1945-81. Author: (children's books) Little Liberty Belle, 1968, 898 Steps, 1975; author, patentee Little Liberty Belle doll, 1975. Served to tech. sgt. U.S. Army, 1940-45. Recipient award NCCJ, 1958, Pulitzer prize nomination, 1959, award Disabled Am. Vets, 1960, award Valley Forge Found., 1960, award Dept. Def., 1962. Mem. Assn. Am. Editorial Cartoonists (founder 1957, sec.-treas. 1957-64, pres. 1965-66), Ocean City Golf and Yacht Club. Roman Catholic. Home and Office: PO Box 744 Selbyville DE 19975

STANAWAY, ANNE, television producer, writer; b. Elkhart, Ind., Apr. 8, 1931; d. Alfred C. and Ersa S. (Flint) Arbogast; divorced; children: Susan, John, Robin, Sharon. BS, Northwestern U., 1952. Producer Sta. WITF-TV (PBS), Hershey, Pa., 1973-78; exec. producer Sta. WITF-TV, Hershey, Pa., 1978-80; owner, exec. producer Sunlight Prodns., Ltd., Lebanon, Pa., 1980—. Producer, writer documentaries Closing the Gap, 1976 (nat. Emmy nomination), Kids Today, 1982 (Am. Film Festival award), Alzheimer's Disease: You Are Not Alone, 1984 (Retirement Rsch. Found. nat. media award), Happiness and Longevity Club, 1987 (Cine Golden Eagle). Bd. dirs. Ctr. for Study First Ams., Oreg. State U., Corvallis; bd. dirs., pres., sec.-treas. Arbogast Found. NEH fellow U. Mich., 1978-79, Fulbright fellow Japan, 1985-86, Okinawa, 1991. Home and Office: 288 Tice Ln Lebanon PA 17042-9045

STANDISH, JOHN SPENCER, textile manufacturing company executive; b. Albany, N.Y., Apr. 17, 1925; s. John Carver and Florence (Spencer) S.; m. Elaine Joan Ritchie, Oct. 20, 1962 (div. 1984); children: John Carver, Christine Louise; m. Patricia Hunter, Nov. 9, 1985. BS, MIT, 1945. Asst. to prodn. mgr. Forstmann Woolen Co., Passaic, N.J., 1945-52; various positions Albany Internat. Corp., 1952-72, v.p., 1972-74, exec. v.p., 1974-76, vice chmn., 1976-84, chmn., 1984—; bd. dirs. Berkshire Life Ins. Co., Pittsfield, Mass. Bd. dirs. Albany chpt. ARC, 1966—, chpt. chmn., 1971-74; bd. govs. ARC, Washington, 1980-86; bd. dirs. United Way of Northeastern N.Y., Albany, 1980—, pres., 1984-85; trustee Albany Med. Coll. and Ctr., 1984—; trustee Sienna Coll., Loudonville, N.Y., 1987—; chmn. U. Albany Fund, 1982-87, 89—. Served to sgt. U.S. Army, 1945-46. Mem. Am. Mgmt. Assn., World Econ. Forum. Republican. Episcopalian. Clubs: Ft. Orange, Wolferts Roost Country (Albany); Schuyler Meadows Country (Loudonville). Home: 1 Schuyler Meadows Rd Loudonville NY 12211-1421 Office: Albany Internat Corp PO Box 1907 Albany NY 12201-1907

STANDISH, WILLIAM LLOYD, judge; b. Pitts., Feb. 16, 1930; s. William Lloyd and Eleanor (McCargo) S.; m. Marguerite Oliver, June 12, 1963; children: Baird M., N. Graham, James H., Constance S. Bar: Pa. 1957, U.S. Supreme Ct. 1967. Assoc. Reed, Smith, Shaw & McClay, Pitts., 1957-63, ptnr., 1963-80; judge Ct. Common Pleas of Allegheny County (Pa.), 1980-87; judge U.S. Dist. Ct., Pa. we. dist., 1987—; solicitor Edgeworth Borough Sch. Dist., 1963-66. Bd. dirs. Sewickley (Pa.) Community Ctr., 1981-83, Staunton Farm Found., mem, 1984—; corporator Sewickley Cemetery, 1971-87; trustee Mary and Alexander Laughlin Children's Ctr., 1972-90; trustee Leukemia Soc. Am., 1978-80, trustee western Pa. chpt., 1972-80, Western Pa. Sch. for the Deaf. Recipient Pres. award Leukemia Soc. Am., 1980. Mem. ABA, Pa. Bar Assn., Allegheny County Bar Assn., Am. Judicature Soc., Acad. Trial Lawyers Allegheny County (treas. 1977-78, bd. dirs. 1979-80). Office: US Dist Ct 911 US Courthouse Pittsburgh PA 15219

STANDLEY, RICHARD ALBERT, JR., civil engineer, consultant; b. Beverly, Mass., May 10, 1926; s. Richard Albert Sr. and Marjorie Rose (Green) S.; m. Adele Holt Brown, Sept, 17, 1949 (dec. June 1987); children: David Brown Standley, Dayle Marie Merchant. Student, U. Maine, 1946-49; cert. civil engr., Internat. Corr. Sch., 1958. Registered profl. engr., land surveyor, Maine. Engr.'s aide Maine State Hwy. Dept., Portland, 1948-49; engring. chemistry aide Maine State Hwy. Dept., Augusta, 1949-50, asst. project engr., 1950-58; enumerator U.S. Census Dept., Augusta, 1950; bituminous engr. So. region Maine Dept. Transp., Portland, 1958-66; engr. Office of Pavements Maine Dept. of Transp., Augusta, 1967-73; bituminous engr. Maine Dept. of Transp., Scarborough, 1973-86; materials engr. No. region L.M. Pike & Sons Co. Inc., Laconia, N.H., 1966-67; chief engr. Bituminous Materials Engring. Co., Portland, 1984—. Mem. ch. bd., Portland, 1975-80. With USAAF, 1944-45. Mem. NSPE (state pres. 1975-77, Office Rec. Pin 1976), Maine Assn. Engrs., Assn. Asphalt Paving Technologists, Am. Arbitration Assn. Baptist. Home and Office: 788 Brighton Ave Portland ME 04102-1016

STANFIELD, ROBERT EVERETT, sociologist; b. Bklyn., Dec. 28, 1934; s. Theophilus Bramwell and Winnie Mercer (Brown) S.; m. Joann Elizabeth Moulton, June 11, 1960; children: Kathleen, Cheryl, Paul. BA, CCNY, 1957; AM, Harvard U., 1961, PhD, 1963. Asst. prof. U. Mass., Amherst, 1963-69; assoc. prof. U. Vt., Burlington, 1969-75, prof., 1975—, exec. asst. to pres., 1975-90, univ. marshal, 1982-90; cons. Community Action Program, Providence, 1964-69, Vt. Dept. of Employment and Tng., Montpelier, 1974-75; mem. Rsch. Univs. Network, Washington, 1977-90. Contbr. articles to profl. jours. Bd. dirs., chmn. No. Vt. chpt. ARC, 1987-88; bd. dirs., chmn. Salvation Army, Burlington, 1985-87; trustee Pine Ridge Sch., Williston, Vt., 1974-89; vestryman St. Paul's Cathedral, Burlington, 1989-91. Episcopalian. Home: 107 Loomis St Burlington VT 05401-3356 Office: U Vt 31 S Prospect St Burlington VT 05405-0176

STANG, ROLF KRISTIAN, vocalist, teacher, writer, advertising executive; b. Rockford, Ill., Sept. 19, 1939; s. Trygve Ingvald and Kirsten (Anfinsen-Kristiansen) S. BA, Augustana Coll., 1961; MA, Columbia U., 1963; performance/repertoire cert., opera div., Musikhochschule, Hamburg, Fed. Republic of Germany, 1964. Vocal soloist Christoph-Weber-Barock Ensemble, Hamburg, 1965-67; German and music faculty Coll. of White Plains, N.Y., 1968-73; repertoire coach concerts and opera, 1968—; sec. Internat. Percy Grainger Soc., White Plains, N.Y., 1974-79, pres., 1979—; bd. dirs. Sibelius Soc., N.Y.; music critic Nordisk Tidende, N.Y.C., 1970—; advt. exec. The Frank Vos Co AS/VP, 1973-83; lectr. Translator Songs of Grieg, 1988; composoer "Backward Tracings" (for solo voice, chorus and orchestra)/commd. Tallahassee Sesquicentennial Assn., 1974, "Train Window Thoughts" (song cycle for soprano/15 stringed instruments), "Hymns in Praise of Night/Five Nietzschean Nocturnes" (for chorus/6 instruments), Lied/Romance and opera rep. (Danish, English, German, Norwegian, Swedish, 1968—); concert vocalist appearances 44 states, numerous countries in recital, 1963—, Esperanza Mgmt., N.Y.C., 1968—; contbr. articles to profl. jours. Vol. Cath. Ctr. for Deaf, N.Y.C., 1975-79, Children to the Beach prog., N.Y.C., 1978-83. Mem. Am. Choral Dirs. Assn. (life), Nordmanns Forbundet/Norsemen's Fedn. (hon., life), Delius Assn. of Fla. (life), Delius Soc. of Great Britain, Sons of Norway Internat., Delius Soc. of Phila. (life), Am.-Scandinavian Soc. of N.Y., Soc. for Advancement of Scandinavian Studies (life). Lutheran. Home: The Monks Cell 29 W 65th St New York NY 10023-6632

STANGER, ROBERT HENRY, psychiatrist, educator; b. N.Y.C., N.Y., May 19, 1937; s. Sidney and Mary (Strassner) S.; m. Andrea Rogin, Aug. 28, 1960; children: Lee Ann, David Neal. AB, Guilford Coll., 1959; MD, Emory U., 1964. Intern in internal medicine Wake Forest U., 1964-65; resident in gen. psychiatry U. Pitts., 1967-70; resident in psychiatry; pvt. practice Monroeville, Pa., 1970—; med. dir. Allegheny Valley Mental Health-Mental Retardation Ctr., New Kensington, Pa., 1970-76; dir. psychiat. svcs. Allegheny Valley Hosp., Natrona Heights, Pa., 1984—; chmn. dept. psychiatry and behavioral medicine Allegheny Valley Hosp., 1984—; clin. instr. psychiatry U. Pitts. Sch. Medicine, 1970-79, clin. asst. prof., 1980—; cons. Westinghouse Elec. Corp., East Pitts., 1977-87; mem. ethics com. human rsch. Allegheny Valley Hosp., 1976—; chmn. dept. psychiatry Citizens Gen. Hosp., 1978-88. Capt. M.C., U.S. Army, 1965-67, Vietnam. Mem. AMA, Am. Psychiat. Assn. (del. 1986-88), Pa. Psychiat. Soc. (councilor 1976-79, treas. 1979-80, sec. 1980-81, v.p. 1981-82, pres.-elect 1982-83, pres. 1983-84), Pitts. Psychiat. Soc. (councilor 1974-76, sec. 1977-78, pres.-elect 1978-79, pres. 1979-80), Allegheny County Med. Soc. Home and Office: 120 Daugherty Dr Monroeville PA 15146-2710 Office: Allegheny Valley Hosp 1301 Carlisle St Natrona Heights PA 15065

STANGO, JOSEPH, JR., financial consultant; b. Waterbury, Conn., Feb. 11, 1960; s. Joseph and Dora Rose (Stanco) S.; m. Maria B. Palmieri, June 29, 1985; children: Sarah Rose, Rachel Ann. BBA, Anna Maria Coll., 1982. Pres. The Boston Group, Waterbury, Conn., 1984-87; fin. cons. Shearson Lehman Bros., Waterbury, 1987-90, Merrill Lynch, Southbury, Conn., 1990—. Fin. columnist Waterbury-Rep.-Am., Northwestern Conn., 1988—; fin. commentator Stas. WATR, WWYZ, WSNG, 1989—; guest fin. commentator Sta. WVIT, 1991—. Vice chmn. Conn. Young Reps., 1982-84; candidate Conn. State Senate 16th Senatorial Dist., 1982; chmn. state reps. campaigns 72d dist., 1984-86; commr. City of Waterbury Pension Bd., 1991; bd. dirs., treas. Warner Theatre Torrington, 1991—, Family Svcs. Waterbury, 1989—; vice chmn. allocations com. United Way Waterbury, 1990—. Mem. Kiwanis (v.p. 1989-90). Office: Merrill Lynch Southbury Pla Southbury CT 06488

STANIAR, LINDA BURTON, insurance company executive; b. Glen Ridge, N.J., July 6, 1948; d. Harold Burton and Helen (Kintzing) Staniar; m. William Glasgow Bergh, Jan. 21, 1978; 1 child, Courtney Christian Bergh. BA, Briarcliff Coll., 1970; MA, NYU, 1974. Pub. rels. asst. N.Y. Life Ins. Co., N.Y.C., 1977-78, pub. rels. assoc., 1978-80, dir., 1981-84, asst. v.p., 1984-86, corp. v.p., 1986-88, v.p. pub. rels. and advt., 1988—. Mem. Advt. Women of N.Y. Office: NY Life Ins Co 51 Madison Ave New York NY 10010-1603

STANIG, GERALD JOSEPH, marketing manager; b. Jersey City, N.J., June 6, 1944; s. Mario Frank and Frances M. (Martinetto) S.; m. Lucy M. Aita, Apr. 3, 1971; children: Kara, Heather, Jeanette. BS in Mktg., St. Peters Coll., 1967; MBA in Mktg., cum laude, Fairleigh Dickinson U., 1971. Resident mktg. mgr. Sperry-Univac, Montclair, N.J., 1968-77; branch mgr. Datapoint Corp., Elmwood Pk., N.J., 1977-82; dist. mgr. WICAT Systems Inc., Paramus, N.J., 1982-86; mgr. Bell br. Stratus Computer Inc., Piscataway, N.J., 1986—. Named Salesman Yr. Sperry-Univac, 1976. Mem. Am. Mktg. Assn. (v.p. 1965-66), Delta Sigma Pi. Roman Catholic. Home: 11 Berkshire Rd Berardsville NJ 07924 Office: Stratus Computer Inc 371 Hoes Ln Piscataway NJ 08854-4143

STANISCI, THOMAS WILLIAM, lawyer; b. Bkln., Nov. 16, 1928; s. Vito and Angela Marie (Martino) S.; m. Catherine Ellen Cullen, June 4, 1955; children: Thomas, Marianne, Ellen, William, Peter. BA, St. John's Coll. Men, 1949, JD, 1953, postgrad., 1954. Bar: N.Y. 1953, U.S. Dist. Ct. (so. and ea. dist.) N.Y. 1956. Assoc. Diblasi Marasco & Simone, White Plains, N.Y., 1954-60; mem. Simone Brant & Stanisci, White Plains, 1960-66, Shayne Dachs Stanisci & Harwood, Mineola, N.Y., 1966-83; sr. mem. Shayne Dachs Stanisci & Corker, Mineola, 1983—; diplomate Am. Bd. Profl. Liability Attys., trustee; lectr. Practising Law Inst., 1975-79; instr., lectr. Am. Mgmt. Assn., 1976-77; guest instr. Adelphi U., Hofstra U., 1975-79; guest speaker, panelist network and local TV. Contbr. articles in field. Served with U.S. Army, 1950-52. Mem. Am. Arbitration Assn., Am. Bd. Trial Advs. (diplomate), Nassau Suffolk Trial Lawyers Assn. (bd. dirs. 1978-90, treas. 1991, sec. 1992), Nassau County Bar Assn. (lectr. acad. law), Assn. Trial Lawyers Am., Nassau County Med. Soc., Columbian Lawyers. Office: 250 Old Country Rd Mineola NY 11501-4253

STANKIEWICZ, RAYMOND, design engineer; b. Bklyn., Sept. 3, 1932; s. Benjimen and Stella (Baer) S.; m. Ann F. Carpenter, May 1, 1955; children: Michael Raymond, Stacy Ann, Raymond Thomas. Cert. tool design, SUNY, 1959; BS in Indsl. Engring., Allied Inst. Tech., 1967; MS in Engring. Tech., Am. Western U., 1982; D Design Engring., World U., 1991. Founder, owner Am. Engring. Model Co., Bohemia, L.I., N.Y., 1959-83; project engr., program mgr. Russell Plastice Tech. Inc., Lindenhurst, L.I., N.Y., 1983-86, tool design mgr., machine shop mgr., 1986; sr. devel. and methods mgr. Symbol Tech., Inc., Bohemia, L.I., N.Y., 1986-91; dir. ops. U.S. Air Tool Co., Inc., Ronkonkoma, N.Y., 1991—. Bd. dirs. Skills Unltd., Oakdale, N.Y., 1980-84, Gurrney's Inn, Montauk, N.Y., 1985, Suffolk County Spl. Olympics, 1985-86. Cpl. U.S. Army, 1951-54. Recipient Design Innovation award GE,. 1987, Cert. of Recognition, Rep. Nat. Com., 1991-92. Mem. Inst. Indsl. Engrs., Soc. Plastic Engrs., Soc. Mech. Engrs., Soc. Mfg. Engrs., Soc. Mil. Engrs., Res. Officers Assn. Roman Catholic. Office: US Air Tool Co Inc 60 Fleetwood Ct Ronkonkoma NY 11779

STANKO, ROBERT MICHAEL, manufacturing company executive, consultant; b. Stratford, Conn., Aug. 28, 1957; s. Arthur J. and Mary N. (Martino) S.; m. Lauren D. Hollister, Nov. 24, 1984. BS in Adminstrv. Sci. summa cum laude, Cen. Conn. State U., 1979; MBA, U. New Haven, 1986. Mgr. prodn. control Gen Data Comm Inc., Danbury, Conn., 1979-81; mgr. ops. materials Times Fiber Communications, Wallingford, Conn., 1981-84; materials mgr. Cramer Co., Old Saybrook, Conn., 1984-85; dir., exec. v.p. Optimum Electronics Inc., North Haven, Conn., 1986-87, chief exec. officer, pres., chmn., 1987—; dir., chief exec. officer, pres. VCS Inc. and subs., Carol Stream, Ill., 1988-90; cons. VMAC, New Haven, 1990—. Mem. AIAA, Info. Systems Security Assn., Lions Internat. Office: Optimum Electronics 425 Washington Ave North Haven CT 06473-1390

STANKOVIC, ALEKSANDAR M., electrical engineer; b. Zrenjanin, Vojvodina, Yugoslavia, May 10, 1960; came to U.S. 1987; s. Mihajlo A. and Miroslava B. (Belic) S. BS, U. Belgrade, Yugoslavia, 1982, MS, 1986; postgrad., MIT, 1988—. Jr. rsch. engr. to rsch. engr. Inst. Mihajlo Pupin, Belgrade, 1983, 84-85; teaching asst. U. Belgrade, 1987; rsch. asst. U. Ill., Urbana, 1987, MIT, Cambridge, Mass., 1988—. Co-author: Solution Manual for Principles of Power Electronics, 1991; contbr. articles to profl. jours. With Yugoslavian Army, 1986. Recipient Dragomir Suvakovic Found. award, 1982. Mem. IEEE (student mem.), Math. Assn. Am., Am. Math. Soc. Eastern Orthodox. Office: MIT 10-013 Cambridge MA 02139

STANKUS-SAULAITIS, MARIJA EDITA, English educator; b. Allenstein, E. Prussia, Germany, Feb. 28, 1941; came to U.S., 1949; d. Antanas Ksaveras and Ona Marija (Lichtenstein) Saulaitis; m. Algirdas Stankus, Dec. 6, 1976. BA, Annhurst Coll., 1965; MA, W. Conn. State U., 1974; PhD, U. Conn., 1981. Instr. English U. Md. European Div., Heidelburg, Fed. Republic Germany, 1978-79; asst. prof. U. Ill. at Chgo., 1979-84; instr. English U. Conn., Torrington, 1988—, Northwestern Conn. Community Coll., 1991—; instr. English West Conn. State U., Danbury, Sacred Heart U., Fairfield, Conn., Fairfield U., Post Coll., Waterbury, 1984-88. Author: (poetry books) Kai Mes Nutylam, 1967, And You, 1972, Viena Saule Danguje, 1972, Šeštoji Diena, 1974; contbr. articles, book reviews, poetry to mags. Grantee NEH, Chgo., 1983. Mem. Modern Lang. Assn. Home: 82 Old Colonial Rd Oakville CT 06779-1433

STANLEY, E. RICHARD, biomedical researcher; b. Sydney, N.S.W., Australia, Sept. 26, 1944; came to U.S. 1977; s. Neville Fenton and Muriel (MacDonald) S.; m. Pamela Mary Fetherstonhaugh, Feb. 6, 1970; children: Damian Alexander, Robert Fenton. BSc with honors, U. Western Australia, 1967; PhD, U. Melbourne, 1970. Lectr. Dept. Medicine and Biophysics, U. Toronto, 1972-73, asst. prof., 1973-77; mem. sr. scientific staff Ont. Cancer Inst., Toronto, 1972-77; asst. prof. Dept. Microbiology and Immunology, Cell Biology Albrt Einstein Coll. Medicine, Bronx, 1977-79, assoc. prof., 1979-84, prof., 1984-87; prof., chmn. Dept. Developmental Biology and Cancer Albrt Einstein Coll. Medicine, 1987—; cons. Cetus Corp., Emeryville, Calif., 1983—; sci. adv. bd. Internat. Coun. for Co-ord. Cancer Rsch., N.Y.C., 1989—. Contbr. over 120 articles to profl. jours. NIH Merit awardee, 1989, Soc. for Leukocyte Biology Rsch. award, 1989. Office: Albert Einstein Coll Med 1300 Morris Park Ave Bronx NY 10461-1924

STANLEY, HARRIETT LARI, financial advisor; b. Arlington County, Va., Mar. 30, 1950; d. E. L. and Mariana T. Stanley. AB, Coll. William and Mary, 1972; MS with honors, Boston U., 1974; MBA, Harvard U., 1982. NASD registered. Asst. to dir. Close-up Found., Washington, 1974-76; spokesman Boston Edison Co., 1976-79; asst. dir. Mass. Energy Office, Boston, 1979-80, Smith Barney, Harris Upham & Co., N.Y.C., 1983-87; v.p. Prudential-Bache Capital Funding, N.Y.C., 1987-90; mng. prin. The Hadley Group, Boston, 1990—. Mem. Town Dem. Com., Merrimac, Mass., 1989—;

mem. Town Fin. Com., Merrimac, 1990, vice chmn., 1990—, town treas., 1992—; mem. Essex County Advisors Coun., 1991—; trustee Boston Met. Dist., 1991—; bd. dirs. Coll. of William and Mary Soc. of Alumni, 1984—, treas., 1986-88, exec. com., 1988—, v.p., 1989. Mem. High Speed Rail Assn. (bd. dirs. 1987—), Publicity Club Boston (bd. dirs., pres. 1979-80, Bellringer award 1978). Office: The Hadley Group 11 Beacon St Boston MA 02108-3002

STANLEY, JULIAN CECIL, JR., psychology educator; b. Macon, Ga., July 9, 1918; s. Julian Cecil and Ethel (Cheney) S.; m. Rose Roberta Sanders, Aug. 18, 1946 (dec. Nov. 1978); 1 child, Susan Roberta Willhoft; m. Barbara Sprague Kerr, Jan. 1, 1980. B.S., Ga. So. U., 1937; Ed.M., Harvard U., 1946, Ed.D., 1950; D of Ednl. Excellence (hon.), U. North Tex., 1990. Tchr. Fulton and West Fulton high schs., Atlanta, 1937-42; instr. psychology Newton Jr. Coll., 1946-48; instr. edn. Harvard U., 1948-49; asso. prof. ednl. psychology George Peabody Coll. Tchrs., 1949-53; assoc. prof. edn., 1953-57, prof. edn., 1957-62, prof. ednl. psychology, 1962-67, chmn. dept., 1962-63; dir. lab. exptl. design U. Wis., Madison, 1961-67; prof. edn. and psychology Johns Hopkins U., 1967-71, prof. psychology, 1971—, dir. study mathematically precocious youth, 1971—; mem. research adv. council Coop. Research Br., U.S. Office Edn., 1962-64; mem. com. examiners for aptitude tests Coll. Entrance Exam. Bd., 1961-65, chmn., 1965-68; Fellow Social Sci. Research Council Inst. Math. for Social Scientists, U. Mich., summer 1955; postdoctoral fellow statistics U. Chgo., 1955-56; Fulbright research scholar U. Louvain, Belgium, 1958-59; Fulbright lectr., New Zealand and Australia, 1974; cons. U. Western Australia, 1980; fellow Center for Advanced Study in Behavioral Sci., 1965-67, vis. scholar, 1983; hon. prof. Shanghai (People's Republic of China) Tchrs. U.; disting. tchr. Commn. on Presdl. Scholars, 1987-92; disting. vis. prof. U. North Tex., 1990; mem. adv. bd. Tex. Acad. Maths. and Sci., 1988—; trustee Ctr. for Excellence in Edn., 1989—. Author: Measurement in Today's Schools, 4th edit, 1964, (with D.T. Campbell) Experimental and Quasi-Experimental Designs for Research, 1966, (with Gene V. Glass) Statistical Methods in Education and Psychology, 1970, (with K.D. and B. Hopkins) Educational and Psychological Measurement and Evaluation, 3d edit, 1990, (with K.D. Hopkins, G.H. Bracht) Perspectives in Educational and Psychological Measurement, 1972; Editor: Improving Experimental Design and Statistical Analysis, 1967, Preschool Programs for the Disadvantaged, 1972, Compensatory Education for Children, Ages 2-8, 1973, (with D.P. Keating, L.H. Fox) Mathematical Talent: Discovery, Description, and Development, 1974, (with W.C. George, C.H. Solano) The Gifted and the Creative: A Fifty-Year Perspective, 1977, Educational Programs and Intellectual Prodigies, 1978, (with W.C. George, S.J. Cohn) Educating the Gifted: Acceleration and Enrichment, 1979, (with C.P. Benbow) Academic Precocity: Aspects of Its Development, 1983; adv. editor jours. Served with USAAC, 1942-45. Recipient Thorndike award for disting. psychol. contbns. to edn., 1978, Mensa rsch. awards, 1985, 86, 91. Fellow APA (pres. div. ednl. psychology 1965-66, div. evaluation and measurement 1972-73, Thorndike award 1978), AAAS, Am. Statis. Assn., Am. Psychol. Soc.; mem. Nat. Council Measurement Edn. (pres. 1963-64), Am. Ednl. Research Assn. (pres. 1966-67, award for disting. contbns. to research in edn. 1980), Nat. Assn. for Gifted Children (2d v.p. 1977-79, Disting. Scholar award 1982), AAUP (past pres. chpt.), Psychometric Soc. (past dir.), AAUP (past chpt. pres.), Tenn. Psychol. Assn. (past pres.), Nat. Acad. Edn., Phi Beta Kappa (past chpt. pres.), Phi Beta Kappa Assocs., Sigma Xi, Phi Delta Kappa. Office: Johns Hopkins U SMPY 430 Gilman Hall Baltimore MD 21218

STANLEY, MARK JAMES, accountant; b. Binghamton, N.Y., May 23, 1955; s. James Leon and Marjorie Ann (Keefe) S.; m. Carole Anne Kaley, Aug. 4, 1979; children: Tricia Leigh, Corinne Kaley. Assoc. Applied Sci., Broome Community Coll., Binghamton, 1975; B. Profl. Studies, SUNY, Utica/Rome, 1977. CPA, N.Y. Jr. acct. Gruver & Hamelin, CPA, Oneonta, N.Y., 1978; acct. Johnson, Lauder, Savidge & Vieira, CPA, Binghamton, 1978-86; accounting mgr. Ken Wilson Chevrolet, Inc., Vestal, N.Y., 1986; pvt. practice accounting Greene, N.Y., 1987—; adj. instr. Broome Community Coll., 1990. Dir. Broome County Humane Soc., Binghamton, 1989. Mem. AICPA, N.Y. State Soc. CPAs, Nat. Assn. Accts. (chpt. pres. 1987-88), Lions (treas. Greene chpt. 1989—). Office: 62 Genesee St Greene NY 13778-1228

STANNARD, CARL ROY, JR., physicist; b. Syracuse, N.Y., July 24, 1935; s. Carl Roy and Ruth (McCloy) S.; m. L. Gay Hickox, Sept. 17, 1967; children: Kent Geoffrey, Ross McCloy. BS, Syracuse U., 1956; MS, Cornell U., 1960; PhD, Syracuse U., 1964. Lectr. physics Syracuse (N.Y.) U., 1961, vis. prof., 1965; asst. prof. physics SUNY, Binghamton, N.Y., 1964-70; dir. undergrad. physics program SUNY, Binghamton, 1970-78; dir. Harpur Coll., Broome C.C. Joint Degree Program, Binghamton, 1973-77; chair dept. physics SUNY, Binghamton, 1978-81, assoc. prof. physics, 1970—; co-dir. So. Tier Educators' Program for Understanding Physics, So. Tier, N.Y., 1988—; reviewer N.Y. State Dept. Edn., Albany, 1985; proposal reviewer NSF, 1975-84; proposal rev. panel Fund for Post-Secondary Edn., Washington, 1978. Contbr. articles to profl. jours. Mem. Local Adv. Com. to N.Y. State Div. Human Rights, Binghamton, 1980—. Recipient Tech. Physics grant NSF, 1971-75, Joint Degree Program grant Fund for Improvement Postsecondary Edn., 1973-77, Solar Energy Course grant NSF, 1979-81, Grants for Edn. K-12 Tchrs., N.Y. State Dept. Edn., 1988-89, 89-90, 90-91, Grant for K-12 Tchr. Network, 1991—, Statewide Tng. for Educators in the Phys. Scis. Leadership Program grant, NSF, 1992-95. Mem. AAUP, Am. Phys. Soc., Am. Assn. Physics Tchrs., Nat. Sci. Tchrs. Assn., Sigma Xi, Phi Beta Kappa, Sigma Pi Sigma, Phi Kappa Phi. Office: Binghamton U Physics Dept Vestal Pkwy E PO Box 6000 Binghamton NY 13902-6000

STANOJEV, JOHN EDWARD, financial services executive; b. Phila., Nov. 4, 1951; s. Edward Charles and Mildred Rosemary (Labov) S.; m. Patricia Marie Eppler, May 27, 1972; children: Michael Kenneth, Victoria Marie. Student, Taylor Sch. of Bus., Phila., 1970-71, Pierce Jr. Coll., Phila., 1971. Dispatcher, traffic mgr. Kale Equipment Rentals, Mt. Laurel, N.J., 1973-75; expeditor A. Christian and Sons, Feasterville, Pa., 1975-77; agt. Pa. Life Ins. Co., Allentown, 1971-78; gen. mgr. Am. Travellers LIfe Ins., Bensalem, Pa., 1978-80; exec. v.p. Karr Barth Assocs., Bala Cynwyd, Pa., 1981—; dist. mgr. Equitable Life Assurance Soc., Bala Cynwyd, 1985—. Bd. dirs. Lenape Valley Mental Health Found., Chalfont, Pa., 1986. Mem. Gen. Agts. and Mgrs. Assn. (Career Devel. award 1990), Million Dollar Round Table, Nat. Assn. Health Underwriters (Health Ins. Quality award 1985-88, 90, Nat. Quality award 1985-88, 90), Bucks County Estate Planning Coun., Lower Bucks County C. of C., Cen. Bucks County C. of C., VFW, Masons. Republican. Roman Catholic. Home: 29 Pheasant Rd Doylestown PA 18901-3108

STANTON, BARBARA HADLEY, researcher; b. N.Y.C., July 3, 1935; d. Morris and Katherine Cumnock (Blodgett) Hadley; m. Dixon La F. Stanton, June 16, 1955 (dec. Sept. 1987); children: Laura S. Bross, Linn H. BA, Vassar Coll., 1957; MSc in Urban Planning, Columbia U., 1964. Asst. planner A. Carl Stelling Assocs., N.Y.C., 1964-65; assoc. Project for Pub. Spaces, Inc., N.Y.C., 1979-80; assoc. mem. Ctr. for Human Environments Grad. Ctr. of CUNY, 1982—. Mem. & chair NAIS Trustee Com., Boston, 1979-85; bd. dirs. Correctional & Osborne Assns., N.Y.C., 1989—, Sex Info. and Edn. Coun. of U.S., N.Y.C., 1991—. Mem. Am. Planning Assn., Am. Psychol. Soc., Environ. Design Rsch. Assn., N.Y. Neuropsychol. Group, Phi Beta Kappa.

STANTON, BERNARD FREELAND, agricultural economics educator; b. Albany County, N.Y., Aug. 3, 1925; s. Rhodell Miller and Ethel (Kniffen) S.; m. Lara Stefania Kristjanson, June 25, 1955; children: Margaret, Karen, Randall. BS, Cornell U., 1949; MS, U. Minn., 1950, PhD, 1954; diploma agrl. econs., Oxford (U.K.) U., 1951. Instr. U. Minn., St. Paul, 1951-53; asst. prof. Cornell U., Ithaca, N.Y., 1953-56, assoc. prof., 1956-62, prof., 1962—, chmn. dept., 1968-76; Fulbright rsch. profl. U. Helsinki, 1965-66; vis. prof. Australian Nat. U., Canberra, 1976, Tami/Nadu Agrl. U., Coimbatore, India, 1976; sec., bd. dirs. Am. Agriculturist Found., Ithaca, 1982—; bd. dirs. Springfield (Mass.) Bank for Coops.; mem. faculty senate SUNY, Albany, 1978-84; bd. dirs. Fund for Internat. Conf. Agrl. Economists, 1970, pres., 1981—; mem. adv. com. U.S. Census Agr. Author: Production Costs for Cereals in European Community, 1977-84, 1986; contbg. author: Agricultural Economics and Rural Sociology, The Core Literature, 1991; also articles. Mem. Ithaca Planning Bd., 1977-85, Lansing (N.Y.) Cen. Sch. Bd., 1962-65. Fellow Am. Agrl. Econs. Assn. (bd. dirs. 1974-80, pres. 1979-80); mem. Internat. Assn. Agrl. Economists (v.p. 1988-91), N.E. Assn. Agrl. Economists (exec. com. 1970-76, Disting. Mem. award 1985). Lutheran. Home: 229 W 97th St Apt 7A New York NY 10025-5612 Office: Cornell U Dept Agrl Econs Ithaca NY 14853

STANTON, GREGORY HOWARD, lawyer, educator; b. Delta, Colo., June 25, 1946; s. Howard Earl and Alison May (White) S.; m. Mary Ellen Munsche, June 23, 1973; children: Elizabeth Chantana, Theodore Saroun. BA, Oberlin Coll., 1968; MA, U. Chgo., 1973, PhD, 1986; MTS, Harvard Div. Sch., 1974; JD, Yale U., 1982. Bar: Wis. 1982, U.S. Dist. Ct. (ea. and we. dists.) Wis. 1982, U.S. Ct. Appeals (9th cir.) 1982, Va. 1988. Legis. aide U.S. Senate, Washington, 1967; vol. U.S. Peace Corps, Abidjan, Ivory Coast, 1969-71; lect. U. Chgo., 1975; Fulbright fellow, dept. anthropology Abidjan, 1975-77; rsch. fellow Indian Law Inst., New Delhi, 1978-79; field dir. Ch. World Svc., Phnom Penh, Cambodia, 1980; law clk. U.S. Ct. Appeals (9th cir.), Portland, 1982-83; assoc. Foley & Lardner, Milw., 1983-85; asst. prof. law Washington & Lee U., Lexington, Va., 1985-91; asst. prof. justice, law and society Am. U., Washington, 1991—; cons. on law USIA, Rwanda, 1988-89; vis. prof. law U. Swaziland, 1989-90; legal advisor Rukh Kiev, Ukraine, 1990-91. Contbr. articles to profl. jours. Vice pres. Internat. Alert, London and L.A., 1988—; elder Lexington Presbyn. Ch., 1988-91. NSF fellow, 1975; Social Sci. Rsch. Coun. grantee, 1975; Woodrow Wilson fellow, 1968, Fulbright fellow, 1989. Fellow Am. Anthrop. Assn.; mem. Law and Society Assn., Am. Soc. Internat. Law. Office: Am U Sch Pub Affairs 4400 Massachusetts Ave NW Washington DC 20016-8001

STANTON, JOSEPH ROBERT, physician; b. Boston, Aug. 8, 1920; s. Joseph S. and Mary Elizabeth (Sullivan) S.; m. Mary Frances Gordon, May 10, 1950; children: Michael, Anne Marie, Joseph, John, Mark (dec.), Paul, William, Kathleen, Matthew, Luke, Thomas. AB, Boston Coll., 1942; MD, Yale U., 1945; LLD, St. Anselm Coll., 1973, Our Lady of Elms, 1974. Diplomate Am. Bd. Internal Medicine. Asst. surg. and medicine Boston U. Sch. Medicine, 1946-51; rsch. fellow Evans Meml. Hosp., 1946-51; instr. medicine Tufts Med. Sch., 1951-58, assoc. clin. prof. medicine, 1958-85; mem. attending staff Holy Ghost Hosp., Cambridge, Mass., 1948-55; attending physician Bethany Infirmary, Framingham, Mass., 1948-75; vis. physician St. Elizabeth's Hosp., Boston, 1952-85; del. White House Conf. on Aging, 1981; grant reviewer HHS, 1983; cons. Medico Moral Commn. Mass Cath. Conf., 1978-91. Author or co-author 30 papers on medicine. Founding mem., sec.-treas. Americans United for Life, Chgo., 1971-85; founding mem., dir. Value of Life Com., Boston, 1970-91; founding mem., dir., v.p. Mass. Citizens for Life, 1974-91. Recipient Alumni Sci. award Boston Coll., 1980, Poverello award U. Steubenville (Ohio), 1989, Pro Vita award Archdiocese Boston, 1991. Fellow AMA, ACP, Mass. Med. Soc.; mem. Boston Coll. Alumni Assn., Yale Med. Alumni Assn. Roman Catholic. Home: 760 Highland Ave Needham MA 02194-1635 Office: Value of Life Com 637 Cambridge St Brighton MA 02135-2899

STANTON, ROBERT ALAN, orthopaedic surgeon; b. N.Y.C., June 28, 1946; s. Jay and Shirley (Rader) S.; m. Debby Ellen Beach, June 16, 1973; 1 child, Jim. BA, Williams Coll., 1968; MD, Coll. Physicians and Surgeons, 1972. Intern Columbia-Presbyn. Med. Ctr., N.Y.C., 1972-73, resident in surgery, 1973-74; resident in orthopaedics Yale U., 1974-77; pres., dir. Orthopaedic Specialty Group, P.C., Fairfield, Conn., 1981—. Vice chmn. Alumni Fund of Williams Coll., Williamstown, Mass., 1988—; dir. Bridgeport Hosp. Found., 1988—. Edward John Noble Found. fellow Columbia U., 1969-70. Fellow ACS, Am. Acad. Orthopaedic Surgeons; mem. Am. Orthopaedic Soc. Sports Medicine, Arthrascopy Assn. N.Am., Am. Acad. Sports Physicians, Williams Club N.Y., Nantucket Yacht Club, Fairfield County Hunt Club (gov.). Office: Orthopaedic Specialty Group PC 325 Reef Rd Fairfield CT 06430

STANZIONE, KAYDON AL, aerospace industry executive, advisor; b. Phoenixville, Pa., Dec. 16, 1956; s. Dominic John and Katherine (Mitropolous) S.; m. Charlene Alane Bramble, Dec. 27, 1980; 1 child, Alyssa Marie. BSME, Rutgers U., 1978, MSME, 1979. Cert. comml. instrument pilot, multi-engine pilot. Chief engr. C.A. Tech., Oceanport, N.J., 1974-79; sr. engr. advanced design Boeing Vertol Co., Phila., 1979-84; chief engr. Korax Corp., Haddon Heights, N.J., 1984-86; chief exec. officer/chief engr. Praxis Techs. Corp., Woodbury, N.J., 1986—; expert advisor various domestic and internat. cos. including IBM, LTV Mil. Aircraft Div., Aerospatiale, Westland among others, 1986—, Inst. Def. Analyses, Alexandria, Va., 1987—; expert advisor/lectr. Coll. Engring. U. Md., College Park, 1986—, US Spl. Ops. Forces, 19990—. Author: Systems Approach to Helicopter Design and Technology Assesment, 1987, Aerospace Engineering Encyclopaedia Britannica, 1987, Helicopter Design, 1990; patentee in field; contbr. numerous articles to mags., newspapers and profl. jours. Mem. ASME, AIAA (chmn. students programs 1984-87, tech. V/STOL systems 1985—, tech. aircraft design 1987—, first place design award 1980, U.S. Space Shuttle Challenger award 1984), Am. Helicopter Soc. (design competition and edn. com. 1982—, bd. dirs., 1992—, Oustanding Mem. award. 1981), Aircraft Owners and Pilots Assn., U.S. Naval Inst, Washington C. of C., Rotary. Republican. Roman Catholic. Home: 105 St Regis Dr Woodbury NJ 08096-3902 Office: Praxis Techs Corp 17 S Broad St Ste 200 PO Box 247 Woodbury NJ 08096

STAPLES, JOHN ALBERT, public relations executive, editor; b. Haverhill, MA, Aug. 20, 1942; s. Paul LaPierre and Margaret Rhoda (Austin) S.; m. Marilyn Elizabeth Stone, July 5, 1965; 1 child, Jason Harland. BS, Boston U., 1966. Asst. headmaster Berwick Acad., South Berwick, Maine, 1973-81; assoc. dir. pub. rels. Culver (Ind.) Ednl. Found., 1981-85; dir. pub. rels. Maine Maritime Acad., Castine, 1985—. Editor Mariner mag., 1990—. Vol. Am. Cancer Soc., N.H. and Ind., 1975-85; bd. dirs. Culver C. of C., 1984-85, Castine Community Hosp., 1991—, Penobscot coun. U.S. Navy League, Bangor, Maine, 1986—; mem. Maine Pub. Rels. Coun., 1986—. Capt. USNG, 1981-85. Recipient George Washington Honor medal Freedoms Found. Valley Forge, Pa., 1979, cert. honor, 1985, Outstanding Svc. award U. N.H., Durham, 1988. Mem. Coun. Advancement and Support Edn., Masons (Gen. John Sullivan medal Grand Lodge N.H., Manchester 1981). Republican. Episcopalian. Office: Maine Maritime Acad Castine ME 04420

STAPLES, MARK ANDREW, biochemist; b. Norton, Kans., July 28, 1954; s. Austin Joyce and Virginia Lila (Gates) S.; m. Argie Inez Koons, Mar. 5, 1977. BA in Chemistry and Biochemistry with honors, U. Kans., 1975, BA in English, 1979, PhD in Biochemistry, 1979; MBA, Northeastern U., 1985. Postdoctoral fellow Med. Sch. Harvard U., Boston, 1979-80; chemist New Eng. Nuclear Div. E.I. DuPont deNemours Inc., Boston, 1980-82, prodn. supr., 1982-84; mgr. analytical biochemistry Seragen, Lexington, Mass., 1985-86; project mgr. Hopkinton, Mass., 1986-87; research scientist Immunogen, Cambridge, Mass., 1987-88; process scientist Biogen, Cambridge, 1988-89, sr. process scientist, 1989—. Contbr. articles to Jour. Am. Chem. Soc., Jour. Biol. Chemistry; contbr. articles to profl. jours. Fellow Am. Inst. Chemists; mem. Am. Chemistry Soc., AAAS, Internat. Interest Group in Biorecognition Tech., Parenteral Drug Assn., Beta Gamma Sigma. Home: 10 Rogers St Apt 906 Cambridge MA 02142-1251 Office: Biogen 14 Cambridge Ctr Cambridge MA 02142-1481

STAPLES, RICHARD BRUCE, mental health counselor; b. Lynn, Mass., Nov. 13, 1963; s. Bruce Allan Staples and Dorothy Louise (Coburn) Fazio. BS, Salem State Coll., 1986, MEd, 1989. Lic. mental health counselor; nat. cert. counselor; cert. guidance counselor, EMT. Head athletic trainer Reading (Mass.) Meml. High Sch., 1986-88; guidance aide Medford (Mass.) Vocat. Tech. High Sch., 1988; EMT-Ambulance Life Line Ambulance Svc., Wakefield, Mass., 1987-88; mental health worker McLean Hosp., Belmont, Mass., 1989; psychiat. counselor Melrose (Mass.)-Wakefield Hosp., 1990—; mental health coord. Community Human Svcs., Adolescent Day Treatment, Arlington, Mass., 1989-92; mental health counselor Brandon Residential Treatment Ctr., Framingham, Mass., 1992—. Advisor Order of DeMolay, Battle Green chpt., Lexington, 1976. Recipient Degree of Chevalier, Order of DeMolay, Lexington, 1985, Cross of Honor, 1991. Mem. AACD, Assn. Specialists in Group Work, Am. Mental Health Counselors Assn., Childrens Group Therapy Assn., Masons, Psi Chi. Roman Catholic. Home: 29 Spring St Wakefield MA 01880-4053 Office: Brandon Residential Treatment Ctr 569 Salem End Rd Framingham MA 01701

STAPLES, ROBERT EDWARD, teratologist, consultant; b. Cobourg, Ont., Can., Dec. 5, 1931; came to U.S., 1956; s. Edward Arnold and Helen Marguerite (Rorabeck) S.; m. Sandra Hay, June 15, 1957; children: Shannon Louise, Robert Timothy. BSA, U. Sask., Saskatoon, Can., 1954, MSc, 1956; PhD, Cornell U., 1961. Head endocrinology sect. William S. Merrell Co., Inc., Cin., 1961-63; staff scientist Worcester Found. for Exptl. Biology, Shrewsbury, Mass., 1963-67; head reprodn. and teratology, sr. rsch. fellow Merck Inst. Therapeutic Rsch., West Point, Pa., 1967-71; sect. head reprodn. and teratology Nat. Inst. Environ. Health Scis., NIH, Research Triangle Park, N.C., 1971-78; staff teratologist Haskell Lab. for Toxicology, Indsl. Med. E.I. Du Pont de Nemours & Co., Newark, Del., 1978—; U.S. rep. in teratology for U.S.-USSR Collaboration in Environ. Health, 1972-79; adj. assoc. prof. pharmacology U. N.C., Chapel Hill, 1974-78; adj. assoc. prof. anatomy Thomas Jefferson Med. Coll., Phila., 1980—; project dir. Environ. Teratology Info. Ctr., Research Triangle Park, Oak Ridge, Tenn., 1975-78; cons. Office Tech. Assessment, Congress of U.S., FDA, EPA, WHO, NIH, USSR Ministry Health, Inst. de la Vie, Pharm. Mfrs. Assn., Am. Petroleum Inst., Chem. Mfrs. Assn., Am. Indsl. Health Coun. Contbr. articles to sci. jours. Pres. Covered Bridge Farms Maintenance Corp., Newark, 1989-90. Rsch. grantee USPHS, 1964-67. Mem. Internat. Fedn. Teratology Socs. (chmn. 1983-85), Teratology Soc. (pres. 1983-84), Soc. Toxicology (pres. reproductive and devel. toxicology sect. 1991-92), Soc. for Study Reprodn. (charter), European Teratology Soc., Am. Coll. Toxicology, Neurotoxicology and Teratology Soc., Newark Rotary (club pres. 1981-82). Home: 18 Bridle Brook Ln Newark DE 19711-2061 Office: Haskell Lab PO Box 50 Newark DE 19714-0050

STAPLETON, DARWIN HEILMAN, historian, archival administrator; b. Lancaster, Pa., May 15, 1947; s. Martin Luther and Harriet Bernd (Heilman) S.; m. Donna Lee Heckman, June 12, 1971; children: Elizabeth R., Alice M. BA, Swarthmore Coll., 1969; MA, U. Del., 1970, PhD, 1975. Asst. editor Papers of Benjamin H. Latrobe, Balt., 1974-80; Mellon fellow Case Western Res. Univ., Cleve., 1976-77, asst. prof., 1977-83, assoc. prof., 1983-86; dir. Rockefeller Archive Ctr., North Tarrytown, N.Y., 1986—. Editor: Engineering Drawings of Benjamin Henry Latrobe, 1980, Establishing Foundation Archives, 1991; assoc. editor: Correspondence of Benjamin Henry Latrobe, 1984-88; author: Accounts of European Science, Technology and Medicine, 1985, History of Civil Engineering Since 1600: An Annotated Bibliography, 1986, The Transfer of Early Industrial Technologies to America, 1987 (John Frederick Lewis award 1987). Elder First Presbyn. Ch., Ossining, N.Y., 1988—. Recipient Hagley fellowship Univ. Del., Newark, 1969-74, Mellon fellowship Am. Philo. Soc., Phila., 1984. Mem. Am. Assn. for the History Medicine, Soc. Am. Archivists, Soc. for Indsl. Archeology, History Sci. Soc., Soc. for the History Tech. (exec. coun. 1984-86). Home: 25 Wolden Rd Ossining NY 10562-5124 Office: Rockefeller Archive Ctr 15 Dayton Ave Tarrytown NY 10591-1522

STAPLETON, THOMAS DAVID, physician; b. Auburn, N.Y., Dec. 10, 1912; s. John Edward and Anna (McDermott) S.; AB, Georgetown U., 1934, MD, 1938; m. Wilhelmina Eileen Meagher, Apr. 6, 1942; children: David, Sheila, Miriam, William. Intern Georgetown U. Hosp., Washington, 1938-40; practice gen. medicine, Auburn, N.Y., 1940-42; resident Bklyn. Eye and Ear Hosp., Bklyn., 1946-48; practice medicine specializing in ophthalmology Auburn, 1948-84; staff mem. Auburn Meml. Hosp., now hon. staff; staff mem. Mercy Hosp., Auburn, pres. staff, 1958. Bd. dirs. United Fund; bd. trustees Auburn Community Coll., 1958-75, vice chmn., 1965-75. Served from lt. (j.g.) to lt. comdr., USNR, 1942-46; med. officer 4th Marine Div., 1942-45; hon. mem. Marine Corps Cayuga Meml. Detachment. Decorated Bronze Star, Purple Heart, numerous others. Diplomate Nat. Bd. Med. Examiners. Mem. Pan-Am. Assn. Ophthalmology, N.Y. State Ophthal. Soc., Internat. Assn. Ocular Surgeons. Am. Acad. Ophthalmology, AMA, N.Y. State (Pres.'s Citizenship award 1985), Cayugo County med. socs., N.Y. Acad. Scis., Bklyn. Eye and Ear Hosp. Alumni Assn., Internat. Platform Assn., Central N.Y. Eye and Ear Assn., N.Y. Acad. Scis., N.Y. Pa. League (affiliated with Major Leagues, pres. Auburn community baseball orgn. 1959-62, chmn. bd. 1962—, v.p. 1962-80), Georgetown U. Alumni Assn. (bd. govs.), Auburn C. of C., Am. Legion, VFW. Roman Catholic. Clubs: Owasco Country. Lodges: KC, Elks (dir.). Home: 130 Walnut St Auburn NY 13021-4320

STAPLETON, WALTER KING, federal judge; b. Cuthbert, Ga., June 2, 1934; s. Theodore Newton and Elizabeth Grantland (King) S.; m. Georgianna Duross Stapleton; children: Russell K., Theodore N., Teryl J. B.A., Princeton, 1956; LL.B., Harvard, 1959; LL.M., U. Va., 1984. Bar: Del. Asso. mem. firm Morris, Nichols, Arsht & Tunnell, Wilmington, Del., 1959-65; partner Morris, Nichols, Arsht & Tunnell, 1966-70; judge U.S. Dist. Ct. Del., Wilmington, 1970-85; chief judge U.S. Dist. Ct. Del., 1983-85; judge U.S. Ct. Appeals (3d cir.), 1985—; Dep. atty. gen., Del., 1964; mem. Jud. Conf. U.S., 1984-85. Bd. dirs. Am. Bapt. Chs., U.S.A., 1978. Baptist. Office: US Ct Appeals 844 N King St Lockbox 33 Wilmington DE 19801-3587

STAPLEY, EDWARD OLLEY, microbiologist, research administrator; b. Bklyn., Sept. 25, 1927; s. Charles Olley and Helen Beulay (Mirrielees) S.; m. Helen Alberta Strang, July 2, 1949; children: Susan Jean, Robin Lynn, Janice Carol. BS, Rutgers U., 1950, MS, 1954, PhD, 1959. Microbiologist Merck & Co., Inc., Rahway, N.J., 1950-58; sr. rsch. microbiologist Merck Sharp & Dohme Rsch. Labs., Rahway, 1959-64, rsch. fellow in microbiology, 1965-68, asst. dir. microbiology, 1969-74, dir. microbiology, 1974-77, sr. dir. microbiology, 1978-83, exec. dir. microbiology, 1984—; vis. biologist program speaker Am. Inst. Biol. Scis., 1969-72. Mem. editorial bd. Jour. of Antibiotics, 1974—. Mem. Spotswood (N.J.) Bd. of Edn., 1965, pres., 1967-68. Named to Selman A. Wakeman Lectureship, Theobald Smith Soc., 1990. Fellow Am. Acad. Microbiology, Sigma Xi; mem. Soc. for Indsl. Microbiology (speaker's bur. 1968-71). Republican. Episcopalian. Home: 110 Highland Ave Metuchen NJ 08840-1913 Office: Merck Sharp & Dohme Rsch Labs 126 E Lincoln Ave Rahway NJ 07065-4687

STAPP, CAROL BUCHALTER, education educator, museum education consultant; b. N.Y.C., Feb. 27, 1946; d. Samuel and Doris Ida (Wahl) B.; m. William Francis Stapp, Aug. 27, 1967; 1 child, Rose Anna. BA, Tulane U., 1967; MA, U. Pa., 1970; PhD, George Washington U., 1990. Mus. tchr. Phila. Mus. Art., 1969-76; instr. edn. George Washington U., Washington, 1978-83, dir. mus. edn. program, 1983—, asst. prof. edn., 1990—; mus. educator Christopher Columbus Consortium, Washington, 1991-93. Editor, author issue Jour. Mus. Edn., 1990; editor issue Jour. Washington Acad. Scis., 1986. Recipient Bourse de France, French Govt., 1965-66; Woodrow Wilson fellow U. Pa., 1967-68, Ford Found. fellow, 1968-69. Mem. Mus. Edn. Roundtable (mem. editorial com. 1990—), Am. Assn. Mus., Am. Assn. for State and Local History, Nat. Trust for Historic Preservation, Visitor Studies Assn., Am. Studies Assn., Phi Beta Kappa. Office: George Washington U 2201 G St NW Washington DC 20052-0001

STARER, DAVID, electrical engineering educator; b. Bournemouth, England, Mar. 25, 1955; s. Benedict and Herculine Davyna (Kriel) S.; m. Marion Kay Harper; children: Briony Jennifer, Mark. BS, U. Cape Town, Republic of South Africa, 1980; M. Engring. cum laude, U. Pretoria, Pretoria, Republic of South Africa, 1983; MS, Yale U., 1985, M.Phil., 1986, PhD, 1990. Telecommunications technician Posts & Telecommunications Corp., Harare, Zimbabwe, 1972-77; rsch. engr. Siemens Communications Systems, Pretoria, 1980-84; sr. engr. Fuchs Electronics, Johannesburg, Republic of South Africa, 1984-87; teaching fellow Yale U., New Haven, 1987—; reviewer Internat. Fedn. Automatic Control, Oxford, England, 1987—. Contbr. articles on engring. to profl. jours. Fellow for advanced study Fuchs Electronics, 1984, Yale U. fellow, 1985. Mem. IEEE (reviewer 1987—), Sigma Xi. Office: Yale U Dept Elec Engring PO Box 2157 New Haven CT 06520-2157

STARK, CHARLES WERNER, mechanical engineer; b. Bklyn., Dec. 11, 1948; s. Thurston Werner and Elina Alexandra (Granholm) S.; m. Ruth Martha Engelsen, May 17, 1974. BME, CCNY, 1970; MCE, Manhattan Coll., 1978. Field engr. GE, Erie, Pa., 1970-78; asst. dir. engring. Met. Transp. Authority, N.Y.C., 1978-84; sr. v.p. Seelye Stevenson Value & Knecht, N.Y.C., 1984—. Republican. Lutheran. Home: 14 Dogwood Dr Annandale NJ 08801-3101

STARK, FRANCIS C., JR., horticulturist, educator; b. Drumright, Okla., Mar. 19, 1919; s. Francis C. and Maude Salena (Crowder) S.; m. Dorothy Lucille Moore, Sept. 14, 1941; children: Carolyn P. Stark Reich, Francis C. III. B.S., Okla. A&M Coll., 1940; M.S., U. Md., 1941, Ph.D., 1948. Asst. prof. horticulture U. Md., College Park, 1945-49; asso. prof. U. Md., 1949-51, prof., 1951-80, prof. emeritus, 1980—, head dept. horticulture, 1964-74, chmn. food sci. program, 1966-73, provost agr. and life scis., 1974-80, acting vice chancellor acad. affairs, 1981-82. Contbr. articles to profl. jours. Mem. Md. Gov.'s Commn. on Migratory Labor, 1959-79, chmn., 1963-76; bd. dirs. Capital Area Christian Ch., 1961-66, 89—, pres., 1963-66; bd. dirs. Christian Ch. Facilities for Aging, 1965—, pres., 1975-80; trustee Lynchburg (Va.) Coll., 1970-79. With USAAF, 1942-45. Recipient Hon. State Farmer award Md. Future Farmers Assn., 1966. Fellow Am. Soc. Hort. Sci., AAAS. Club: Rotary. Office: U Md Dept Horticulture College Park MD 20742

STARK, FREDERIC REMY, composer, singer; b. Indpls., Aug. 21, 1947; s. Harold Cleo and Mary Elizabeth (Remy) S.; m. Katherine Irving, Aug. 6, 1977; children: Christian Remy, Andrew Jordan. BS, Ball State U., 1969. Tchr. N.W. Consol. Sch. Dist., Shelby County, Ind., 1969-70; creative dir. Paul Lennon Advt., Indpls., 1970-72, Perception Records, Inc., N.Y.C., 1972-74; pres. Mainsail Music Ltd., South Salem, N.Y., 1974—. Recording artist Big Star, 1975; composer (musical plays) Rhythm Ranch, 1989, Sally Suicide, 1987, Empty Pleasures, 1990. Recipient Search For the New Sound winner Billboard Mag., 1970, Bicentennial Competition winner Am. Song Festival, 1975, Clio award, 1977. Mem. SAG, AFTRA, ASCAP, Am. Fedn. Musicians. Presbyterian.

STARK, MARTIN ALAN, strategic planner, telecommunications industry executive; b. Bklyn., May 4, 1956; s. Raymond Milton and Ella May (Sheiniuk) S.; m. Wendy Chesnov, Mar. 8, 1987 (div. May 1988). BS, SUNY, Stony Brook, 1977, MS, 1978. Tech. staff Bell Labs., Holmdel, N.J., 1978-83; competitive analysis mgr. AT&T Techs., Berkeley Heights, N.J., 1983-87; strategic planning mgr. AT&T Corp., Basking Ridge, N.J., 1987—; adj. instr. computer sci. Fairleigh Dickinson U., Ft. Monmouth, N.J., 1980-83, Union County Coll., Scotch Plains, N.J., 1985-86, Raritan Valley Community Coll., North Branch, N.J., 1989—; round table leader The Conf. Bd., N.Y.C., 1990; speaker COBA-Mid Conseil en Stratégie, Paris, 1991. Contbr. The Intelligent Corp., 1990. Mem. IEEE, Soc. Competitor Intelligence Profls. (founding mem., session leader Washington 1986, speaker San Antonio 1988), Am. Mktg. Assn., Assn. for Computing Machinery. Home: 205 Ten Eyck Rd Bridgewater NJ 08807 Office: AT&T Corp 17-3345 H1 295 N Maple Ave Basking Ridge NJ 07920

STARK, PAUL CALVERT HOLLISTER, communications company sales executive; b. Boston, Oct. 22, 1959; s. Paul Martin and Elaine (Seibert) S.; m. Jane Elizabeth Singleton, June 15, 1991. BA, U. N.H., 1983. Salesman Arrow Paper Co., Somerville, Mass., 1983-84; broker, salesman C.H. Robinson Co., Chelsea, Mass., 1984-86; salesman U.S. Sprint Communications, Somerville, 1986-87, Arlington, Va., 1988-89; salesman Nat. Telephone Svc., Rockville, Md., 1987; broker, salesman C.H. Robinson Co., Chelsea, Mass., 1984-86; mgr. sales Cleartel Communications, Washington, 1989-90, dir. sales, 1990-91, v.p. sales, 1991—. Republican. Episcopalian. Home: 1230 23d St NW Apt 811 Washington DC 20037 Office: Cleartel Comm 1232 22d St NW Washington DC 20037

STARK, RICHARD CLINTON, lawyer; b. Ann Arbor, Mich., May 23, 1948; s. Roscoe Clinton and Marion Jean (Aufderheide) S.; m. Getchen Elizabeth Rom, Feb. 4, 1978; 1 child, Elizabeth. BA, Vanderbilt U., 1970, JD, 1976. Assoc. Johnson & Gibbs, Dallas, 1976-81, ptnr., 1981-86; atty. Johnson & Gibbs, P.C., Washington, 1989—; asst. to commr. IRS, Washington, 1986-89. Mem. ABA (sect. of taxation 1978—), Order of Coif, Phi Beta Kappa. Office: Johnson & Gibbs PC 1301 K St NW Washington DC 20005-3307

STARK, STANLEY, architect, research facility designer, illustrator; b. N.Y.C., May 27, 1948; s. Bernard and Judith (Glasgow) S.; m. Deborah Lynn Faber, Jan. 25, 1985. BArch, Pratt Inst., 1970; MArch., Columbia U., 1975. Registered architect, N.Y., N.J.; cert. Nat. Coun. Archtl. Registration Bds. Archtl. planner Westermann Miller Assoc., P.C., N.Y.C., 1970-77, Mason DaSilva Assoc., N.Y.C., 1977-78; sr. facility planner Gruzen & Ptnrs., N.Y.C., 1978; project mgr. Prentice Chan Ohlhausen, N.Y.C., 1978; project mgr. Haines Lundberg Waehler, Architects & Engrs., N.Y.C., 1978-88, ptnr., 1988—; program dir., chief editor: Planning and Design and Academic Research Facilities: A Guidebook for the NSF; seminar speaker Soc. Rsch. Adminstrs., Tradelines, Orinda, Calif., 1984—; designer AIA sponsored regional urban design assistance team, Trenton, N.J., 1977. Artist: mag. illustrations, theatre and archtl. designs, drawings; profl dir., chief editor: Guidebook for the Planning and Design of Academic Research Facilities. Recipient citation for Research, Progressive Architecture, 1976. Mem. AIA (team leader Leadership Alliance Com. N.Y.C. chpt.), Archtl. League of N.Y., Soc. Coll. and Univ. Planners. Office: Haines Lundberg & Waehler 115 5th Ave New York NY 10003-1004

STARK, STEVEN, electrical engineer, systems architect; b. N.Y.C., Aug. 4, 1943; s. Herman and Betty (Lazar) S.; m. Rita Ellen Sussman, Sept. 5, 1966; children: Darlena Bari, Tiffany Allyson, Ilana Valerie. BS in Physics, Bklyn. Coll., 1965; MS in Physics, NYU, 1967. Lab. specialist Ridgewood Jr. High Sch., N.Y.C., 1965-66; physicist Naval Applied Sci. Lab., N.Y.C., 1966-73; elec. engr. Naval Underwater Systems Ctr., New London, Conn., 1973-76, Naval Air Devel. Ctr., Warminster, Pa., 1976-82; elec. engr. Grumman Corp., Bethpage, N.Y., 1982—, program mgr. computer integrated tech. environ., 1986-87; co-founder, mgr.integration program Computer Integrated Enterprise, 1988—; owner, mgr. Stark Software, Richboro, Pa., 1980-85; co-founder, mgr. systems integration program Integrated Systems Devel. Environ., 1990; founder corporate-wide bus. process modeling analysis methodology, process engring., 1991—. Author: (software program) Time-Table, 1981, Design A Diet, 1988; inventor computer aided engring. system Advanced Virtual Architecture, 1984. Profiled by Knowledgenare, Inc., 1990. Mem. Mensa, The One Percent Soc.

STARKE, CATHERINE JUANITA, English educator; b. Charlotte, N.C., Apr. 5, 1913; d. Joseph Thomas and Sadie Lee (Spencer) Gladden; m. William Campbell Starke, Oct. 28, 1939. BA, Hunter Coll., 1936; MA, Columbia U., 1937, EdD, 1963. Instr. St. Paul's Coll., Lawrenceville, Va., 1938-46; asst. prof. Morgan State U., Balt., 1947-56; prof. English Jersey City State Coll., 1957-78, prof. emeritus, 1978—. Author: Black Portraiture in American Literature, 1971. Mem. MLA, Pi Lambda Theta. Democrat. Episcopalian. Office: PO Box 135 Flushing NY 11365-0135

STARKEN, GEORGE MATHEW, program supervisor, educator; b. Tracy, Minn., Jan. 5, 1934; s. Mathew George and Cora Lee S.; m. Bernadine Marie Schnormeier, Dec. 29, 1953; children: Gail Robin, Timothy George, Thomas Phillip. BEE, S.D. State U., 1960; MS in Engring. Adminstrn., George Washington U., 1976; student, Cath. U. Am., 1977. Engr. GE, Pittsfield, Mass., 1960-66; assoc. engr. Johns Hopkins U. Applied Physics Lab. Ind. Rsch. and Devel., Laurel, Md., 1966-69, sr. engr., 1969-78, prin. profl. staff, 1978—, diagnostic reporting system program mgr., 1983-86, assoc. prof. Va. Poly. Inst. and State U., Blacksburg, 1983-87; lectr. Evening Coll., 1983-89; cons. Naval Sea Systems Comd., Arlington, Va., 1983-89; mem. Applied Physics Lab. Ind. Rsch. and Devle. com., 1983-89; exec. sec. Advanced Tech. Com., 1986-89; bd. dirs. Whiting Sch. Engring. Pkwy. Ctr. for continuing edn., 1989; program supr. pilot NATO Insensative Munitions Info. Ctr. Patentee digital side scan converter. Active Boy Scouts Am., 1943-78; treas. Friends of Library Montgomery County, 1983-87; treas. Library Bd. Merritt Island, Fla., 1964-67; pres. Silver Spring (Md.) Civic Assn., 1966-78. With USN, 1953-56. Fellow Am. Soc. Engring. Mgrs. (nat. pres. 1987, Sarchet award for svc. to soc.); mem. Marine Tech. Soc. (chpt. v.p. 1965-67), AAAS. Republican. Roman Catholic. Home: 3800 Lansdale Ct Burtonsville MD 20866-2101 Office: The Johns Hopkins U Applied Physics Lab Ind Rsch Devel Johns Hopkins Rd Laurel MD 20707

STARKES, DARNELL, JR., instrumental music director; b. Bermuda, Aug. 7, 1955; came to U.S., 1956; s. Darnell and Althea Marina (Douglas) S. BS, CUNY, 1984; MA, Lehman Coll., 1986. Cert. music educator, N.J. Music dir. West Side High Sch., Newark, 1987; music tchr. Camden Middle Sch., Newark, 1987-89, Maple Ave. Sch., Newark, 1987-89, Eighteenth Ave Sch., Newark, 1990—, Lafayette St. Sch., Newark, 1990—; percussion instr. Newark Drum and Bugle Corp., 1991—; substitute bass violin instr. Jazz Mobil Workshop, N.Y.C., 1984—, composer, arranger, 1990; third bassist Bronx (N.Y.) Symphony Orch., 1982-85; bassist, arranger Neo Bass Ensemble, Teaneck, N.J., 1983—; bassist Abdul Zahra's Ensemble, Saratoga, N.Y.; arranger, composer, co-leader Ja Ca Cla, N.Y.C., 1986-89. Composer numerous arrangements. Conductor All City Festival String Orch., Newark, 1991.

STARKS, WILLIAM EDWARD (SKIP), investment consultant; b. Pennsacola, Fla., Apr. 6, 1965; s. William Leroy and Sherry Lynne (Barkhau) S.; m. Susanne Badgett, Oct. 17, 1992. BA in Psychology and Fin., U. Conn., 1987. Asst. mgr. Stuart James & Co., Inc., Charlotte, N.C., 1987-89; mgr. Edward D. Jones & Co., Mystic, Conn., 1989—; prin. Edward D. Jones & Co., St. Louis, 1989—. Co-author newsletter: Individual Point of View, 1990. Phil Skalandunas Meml. scholar, Newtown (Conn.) Ednl. System, 1988. Mem. U. Conn. Alumni Assn., Southeastern C. of C., Mystic C. of C., Mystic Rotary (sec. 1990—), Zeta Psi (v.p. 1987, Ednl. scholar 1987). Office: Edward D Jones & Co 19 E Main St Mystic CT 06355

STARKWEATHER, CHARLES WOODRUFF, speech pathologist, educator; b. Newark, Sept. 20, 1938; s. William Cook and Elizabeth Bryant (Hawkins) S.; m. Vicki Ianucelli, June 5, 1961 (div. 1965); 1 child, Adam; m. Alexandra Lent, Sept. 29, 1985; 1 child, Brian Woodruff. BA, Hamilton Coll., Clinton, N.Y., 1961; PhD, So. Ill. U., 1970. Prodn. editor Prentice-Hall, Englewood Cliffs, N.J., 1961-65; head pubs. dept. Am. Speech & Hearing Assn., Bethesda, Md., 1965-66; assoc. prof. Hunter Coll., N.Y.C., 1969-76; prof. speech pathology Temple U., Phila., 1976—. Author: Speech and Language, 1983, Fluency and Stuttering, 1987, Stuttering Prevention, 1990; assoc. editor Jour. Speech & Hearing Rsch., 1983-86, Jour. Speech and Hearing Disorders, 1982-83. Fulbright fellow, 1987-88. Fellow Am. Speech-Hearing Assn. (pubs. bd. 1983-84); mem. Internat. Fluency Assn. (charter mem., sec. 1990—), Pa. Speech and Hearing Assn., Fulbright Assn. Jewish. Home: 457 Old Farm Rd Wyncote PA 19095-2033 Office: Temple Univ Philadelphia PA 19122

STARNES, EDWARD CLINTON, public relations executive; b. Marquette, Mich., Jan. 19, 1950; s. Edward Erwin and Florence Irene (Lemieux) S.; m. Claire Marie Brisebois, Apr. 12, 1973; children: Sean, Bryan. Student, Western Ill. U., 1968-69. Journalist, editor U.S. Army, Ft. Monroe, Va., 1969-72; spl. projects officer U.S. Continental Army Command, Ft. Monroe, 1972-73; pub. affairs intern U.S. Tng. and Doctrine Command, Ft. Monroe, 1973-75; dep. pub. affairs officer Air Defense Artillery Ctr. U.S. Army, Ft. Bliss, Tex., 1975-87; also pub. affairs officer to Gen. of the Army Omar N. Bradley, 1975-81; pub. affairs officer U.S. Army Ordnance Ctr. and Sch., Aberdeen Proving Ground, Md., 1987—; sec. pub. affairs council Fed. Exec. Bd., Balt., 1988—; pub. affairs cons. U.S. Interagency Task Force for Indo-China Refugees, Ft. Indiantown Gap, Pa., 1975. Contbr. articles to profl. publs. Exec. bd. El Paso County (Tex.) Hist. Soc., 1985-86; bd. dirs. Reach for a Star, El Paso, 1983-86; asst. varsity soccer coach Perryville High Sch., 1990—. Named Visitante Distinguido Presidente Municipal, Cuidad Juarez, Mexico, 1985, 87, Harford County Schs. Bus. Vol. of the Yr., 1990; recipient Cert. Appreciation Juvenile Ct. City of El Paso, 1985. Mem. Assn. of U.S. Army, Noncommd. Officer Assn., Air Defense Artillery Assn. (life), Nat. Soccer Coaches Assn. Am., Royal Neighbors Am. Episcopalian. Home: 548 Conowingo Rd Conowingo MD 21918-1314 Office: US Army Ordnance Ctr and Sch Pub Affairs Office Aberdeen Proving Ground MD 21005-5201

STAROBIN, HERMAN, economist; b. N.Y.C., Feb. 24, 1921; s. Harry and Elsie (Falkson) S.; m. Carol Fijan; 1 child, Christina. B.S., CUNY, 1941; M.A., NYU, 1969, Ph.D., 1969. Dir. research Harman Internat. Industries Inc., Lake Succes, N.Y., 1969-79; pres. Harman Kardon Inc., Plainview, N.Y., 1971-72, 78-79; dir. research Internat. Ladies Garment Workers' Union, N.Y.C., 1980—; advisor U.S. Govt. Textile Program. Co-author: The Death of a Democracy, 1967; editor: Stalinism in Prague, 1969. Recipient Founders' Day award NYU, 1969. Mem. Am. Econ. Assn., Am. Assn. Advancement Slavic Studies, Assn. Comparative Econs., Am. Statis. Assn., Coun. Fgn. Rels., Am. Polit. Sci. Assn., Indsl. Rels. Rsch. Assn. Home: 58 Rose Ave Great Neck NY 11021-1524 Office: Internat Ladies Garment Workers Union 1710 Broadway New York NY 11021

STARR, BARBARA SCHAAP, psychologist; b. Newark, Jan. 13, 1935; d. Louis George and Elsie (Dimond) Barron; B.A., Cornell U., 1956; M.Ed., Rutgers U., 1967, Ed.D., 1975; m. Robert M. Starr, Oct. 28, 1972; children: Renée Beth Levin, Michelle Anne Schaap. Psychologist, Glen Ridge (N.J.) Pub. Schs., 1971-80, Morris-Union Spl. Edn. Consortium, Passaic Twp., N.J., 1980-81; pvt. practice psychology, Livingston, N.J., 1977—; cons. psychologist Edn. Resource Ctr., 1984-87; adj. prof. Montclair State Coll., Upper Montclair, N.J., 1982. N.J. del. White House Conf. on Families, 1980; mem. nat. exec. com. Am. Jewish Congress, 1986—, nat. governing council, 1979—, co-chair, 1992—, Nat. v.p., 1988-92, v.p. state bd. N.J. region, 1979-87, sec., 1987—, nat. v.p., 1988—; trustee United Jewish Fedn. MetroWest, also chmn. task force on individual services, 1983-86; active Temple Emanu El, Livingston; mem. NOW, LWV, Nat. Council Jewish Women. Fellow N.J. Acad. Psychology (trustee 1983-88); mem. Am. Psychol. Assn. (divs. 17, 35, 37, 42), N.J. Psychol. Assn. (exec. bd. 1983-88, sec. 1987-88), Soc. Psychologists in Pvt. Practice (pres.-elect 1989, pres. 1990), N.J. Assn. for Advancement Psychology, N.J. Assn. Women Therapists, Phi Beta Kappa, Kappa Delta Pi, Pi Lambda Theta, Kappa Delta Epsilon. Contbr. articles to profl. publs.

STARR, DAVID, newspaper editor, publisher; b. N.Y.C., Aug. 1, 1922; s. Aaron and Helen (Simon) S.; m. Marjorie Giffen, Aug. 3, 1943; children: Pamela, Peter. B.A., Queens Coll., 1942. Reporter, rewriteman L.I. Daily Press, 1942-50; exec. editor Nassau Daily Rev. Star, 1950-53; asst. editor Newark Star-Ledger, 1954-56; asso. editor L.I. Press, 1953-54, 56-62, mng. editor, 1962-69, editor, 1969-77; sr. editor Newhouse Newspapers, 1971—; pub. Springfield Union-News, Sunday Republican, 1977—; mem. N.Y. State Fair Trial/Free Press Conf., 1969-77, vice-chmn., 1975-77; pres.Springfield Central, Inc., 1978-88, chmn. 1989—. Trustee Nassau Community Coll., SUNY, 1959-66; v.p. United Fund L.I., 1965-70; bd. dirs. Springfield Libr. and Mus. Assn., chmn., 1988-90; mem. Mass. Cultural Coun., 1980; bd. dirs. Am. Arts Alliance, chmn., 1989—. Mem. Am. Soc. Newspaper Editors, Am. Newspaper Pubs. Assn.

STARR, HAROLD PAGE, lawyer; b. Phila., June 17, 1932; s. Isaac and Edith Nelson (Page) S.; m. Emily W. Churchman, Sept. 3, 1960; children: Elizabeth Twells, Edith Nelson, Harold Page Jr., Alice Churchman, Isaac Barclay. BS, Yale U., 1954; LLB, Harvard U., 1961. Bar: Pa. 1962. Assoc. Pepper, Hamilton & Scheetz, Phila., 1961-69, ptnr., 1970-81; pvt. practice Phila., 1982—. Lt. (j.g.) USNR, 1955-58. Office: 320 Walnut St Ste 209 Philadelphia PA 19106-3821

STARR, JANICE DESOCIO, management consultant; b. Syracuse, N.Y., June 15, 1959; d. William Joseph and Jane Roberta (Pacheck) Desocio; m. Ira Starr, June 9, 1985; 1 child, Eric William. BS cum laude, U. Pa., 1981; MBA, Harvard U., 1985. Fin. intern Agway Corp., Syracuse, 1979; audit intern Deloitte, Haskins & Sells, N.Y.C., 1980; rsch. assoc. Booz, Allen & Hamilton, N.Y.C., 1981-83; asst. to pres. Chem. Bank, N.Y.C., 1984; assoc. Booz, Allen & Hamilton, N.Y.C., 1985-87, sr. assoc., 1987-91, staffing mgr., 1987-89; instr. Columbia Bus. Sch., N.Y.C., 1991—. Bd. dirs. 90 Riverside Corp., N.Y.C., 1989-91; active Republican County Com., N.Y.C., 1990—; vol. Collegiate Sch., N.Y.C., 1990-91. Mem. Beta Alpha Psi (alumnus, pres. 1980-81, award 1978). Roman Catholic.

STARR, JOYCE IVES, retired educator; b. Guilford, N.Y., Jan. 25, 1932; d. Paris Otto and Alta Lena (Wade) Ives; m. Leonard E. Cornell, July 7, 1956 (dec. Mar. 1973); children: Stephen, Lorrinda, Teresa Spycia, David; m. Donald Fay Starr, May 8, 1976 (dec. Apr. 1982); stepchildren: Donald Fay II, Matthew, Mark, Thor (dec. May 1986). Student, Rochester (N.Y.) Inst. of Tech., 1949-51; BS. in Edn., SUNY, New Paltz, 1955; student, Syracuse U., summers 1967-68. Art tchr. Oxford (N.Y.) Acad. and Cen. Sch., 1954-57; spl. edn. tchr. junior high sch. Liberty (N.Y.) Cen. Sch., 1966-67, spl. edn. tchr. primary grades, 1967-71; spl. edn. tchr. Del. Acad. and Cen. Sch., Delhi, N.Y., 1971-87; pres. Tchrs. Assn., Bd. Coop. Sch. Ednl. Services, Liberty, N.Y., 1970-71. Vol., coach Spl. Olympics, Liberty, Delhi, N.Y., 1958-87; chairperson Chenango County Environ. Mgmt. Coun., mem. Upper Catskill Community Coun. Arts; deacon Guilford Ctr. Presbyn. Ch., 1991-93. Mem. N.Y. State Tchrs. of Handicapped, Assn. Children with Learning Disabilities, Del. Acad. Faculty Assn. (regional polit. action com. 1982-83), Greens Party, Appalachian Mt. Club, Tri-Town Hikers.

STARZMANN, ELEANOR GLORIA, special education educator; b. Phila., Nov. 8, 1947; d. Raymond David Sr. and Eleanor (Leps) S. AAS, Community Coll. of Phila., 1969; BS in Edn., Temple U., 1971; MS in Edn., Trenton (N.J.) State Coll., 1976; MA in Human Svcs. and Counseling, Rider Coll., 1991. Cert. sch. psychologist. Substitute tchr. Mastbeam Vocat. High. Sch., Phila., 1971-73; tchr. self contained educable mentally retarded Morrison Elem. Sch., Phila., 1973-77; resource rm. tchr. Hackett Elem. Sch., Phila., 1977-79; ednl. evaluator Stevens Adminstrv. Ctr., Phila., 1979-80; instructional advisor Mayfair Sch., Phila., 1980-88; tchr. Webster Elem. Sch., Phila., 1988-89, Rush Mid. Sch., Phila., 1989—. William C. Jacobs scholar Sch. Dist. Phila., 1986, 88, 89, 91. Mem. AACD, APA, ASCD, Coun. for Exceptional Children, Coun. for Learning Disabilities, Internat. Reading Assn., Phi Delta Kappa. Home: 13032 Sewell Rd Philadelphia PA 19116-1338 Office: Rush Mid Sch Knights Rd Philadelphia PA 19154

STARZYK, RICHARD ALAN, secondary school educator; b. Poughkeepsie, N.Y., Nov. 16, 1964; s. Theodore Victor and Genevieve Julia (Smolenska) S. BS in Agrl. Edn., U. Wis., 1986; MS in Gen. Sci., SUNY, New Paltz, 1991. With Poughkeepsie Farm, Frank Bros. Farm Inc., 1976-82; high sch. agrl. tchr. Pine Plains (N.Y.) Cen. Sch., 1986—; advisor FFA Pine Plains chpt. 1986—; football coach Pine Plains Cen. Sch., 1986—. Mem. Assn. of Tchrs. of Agrl. in N.Y. (regional rep. 1987-89, pres.-elect 1990-91, pres. 1991-92), N.Y. State Occupational Edn. Assn., Am. Vocat. Assn., Nat. Vocat. Agrl. Tchrs. Assn. (Outstanding Young mem. in N.Y. 1989, 91). Roman Catholic. Home: RR1 Box 492 Clinton Corners NY 12514

STASKIEWICZ, BERNARD ALEXANDER, chemistry educator; b. Monessen, Pa., Aug. 20, 1924; s. Alexander S. and Veronica (Wojciehowski) S.; m. Phyllis J. Gauden, Sept. 1, 1949; children: Phyllis Gail, Catharine Ann, Thomas Bernard, Barbara Jean, Charles Alexander. BA, Washington & Jefferson Coll., 1947; MS, Carnegie Inst. Tech., 1951, PhD, 1954. Rsch. chemist Standard Oil of N.J., Linden, 1953-55, Rayonier Inc., Whippany, N.J., 1955-58; assoc. prof. Washington (Pa.) & Jefferson Coll., 1958-62, prof., 1962-69, chmn., 1969—; div. chmn. Washington & Jefferson Coll., 1989—. Roman Catholic. Home: 48 Old York Rd Washington PA 15301-6212 Office: Washington & Jefferson Coll Chemical Dept Washington PA 15301

STASZESKY, FRANCIS MYRON, consultant; b. Wilmington, Del., Apr. 16, 1918; s. Frank J. and Ruth (Jones) S.; m. Barbara F. Kearney, May 30, 1943; children—Francis Myron, John B., Barbara J., Faith A., Paul D. B.S. in Mech. Engring, Mass. Inst. Tech., 1943, M.S. in Mech. Engring, 1943. Mech. engr. Union Oil Co. Calif., Los Angeles, 1943-45; with E.I. duPont de Nemours Co., Wilmington, Del., 1946-48; joined Boston Edison Co., 1948, supervising engr. design and constrn., 1948-57, supt. engring. and constrn. dept., 1957-64, v.p., asst. to pres., 1964-67, exec. v.p., 1967-79, pres., chief operating officer, 1979-83; cons., 1983—; dir. Boston Edison Co., 1968-83. Fellow ASME (life); mem. IEEE (sr.), Nat. Acad. Engring., Engring. Soc. New Eng. (pres. 1961-62). Clubs: Algonquin (Boston); Brae Burn Country. Address: 144 Chestnut Circle Lincoln MA 01773

STASZEWSKI, HARRY, hematologist; b. Bronx, N.Y., Feb. 22, 1954; s. Morris and Tola (Kornbrot) S.; m. Sherrie Levine, Aug. 28, 1983; children: Risa, Cara, Alec. BA magna cum laude, Columbia Coll., 1974; MD, Yale U., 1978. Diplomate Am. Bd. Internal Medicine. Intern North Shore U. Hosp., Manhassett, N.Y., 1978-79, resident, 1979-81; fellow in hematol. oncology Meml. Sloan-Kettering Cancer Ctr., N.Y.C., 1981-83; fellow in hematology L.I. Jewish Med. Ctr., New Hyde Park, N.Y., 1983-84; dir. hematology svc. Winthrop Univ. Hosp., Mineola, N.Y., 1984—. Fellow Am. Coll. Physicians.

STATHIS, NICHOLAS JOHN, lawyer; b. Calchi, Dodecanese Islands, Greece, Feb. 27, 1924; s. John and Sylvia (Koutsonouris) S. Student Columbia U., 1942-43, 44-48, AB, 1946, JD, 1948. Bar: N.Y. 1949. Assoc. James Maxwell Fassett, N.Y.C., 1948-50; asst. counsel to spl. com. to investigate organized crime in interstate commerce U.S. Senate, Washington, 1951; trial atty. Fidelity & Casualty Co. N.Y., N.Y.C., 1952; law sec. to Harold R. Medina, judge U.S. Ct. Appeals 2d Cir., N.Y.C., 1952-54; spl. dep. atty. gen. N.Y. State Election Frauds Bur., Dept. Law, 1956; assoc. Watson, Leavenworth, Kelton & Taggart, N.Y.C., 1954-60, ptnr., N.Y.C., 1961-81; ptnr. Hopgood, Calimafde, Kalil, Blaustein & Judlowe, N.Y.C., 1981-84, Botein, Hays & Sklar, N.Y.C., 1984-89; of counsel White & Case, N.Y.C., 1989—; lectr. Practising Law Inst., 1968-69. Contbr. articles to profl. jours. on fed. civil litigation, patents, trademarks and copyrights. Pres., exec. dir., bd. dirs. Found. Classic Theatre and Acad., 1973—; bd. dirs. Concert Artists Guild, 1974-1991, Pirandello Soc., 1976—, Bklyn. Philharm. Orch., 1986-91, Orpheon, Inc., 1986—. Served with AUS, 1943-44. Mem. ABA, Assn. of Bar of City of N.Y., N.Y. State Bar Assn., Fed. Bar Coun., Am. Intellectual Property Law Assn., N.Y. Patent, Trademark and Copyright Law Assn. Democrat. Greek Orthodox. Home: 1885 Kennedy Blvd Jersey City NJ 07305 Office: 1155 Ave Of The Americas New York NY 10036-2711

STAUB, JACOB JOSEPH, rabbi, educator, dean; b. N.Y.C., May 4, 1951; s. Andrew Herbert Staub and Frieda (Yoselofsky) Cohen; m. Barbara C. Wechsler, Aug. 3, 1975; children: Leah, Andrew, Hana. BA, SUNY, Buffalo, 1972; PhD, Temple U., 1980. Ordained rabbi, 1977. Asst. prof. Lafayette Coll., Easton, Pa., 1977-82; Mellon Found. fellow Washington U., St. Louis, 1982-83; editor, reconstructionist Fedn. of Reconstructionist Congregations, Wyncote, Pa., 1983-89; prof. Reconstructionist Rabbinical Coll., Wyncote, 1983—, dean, 1989—; cons. Internat. Ctr. of Univ. Teaching of Judaism, Jerusalem, 1987; chair Acad. for Jewish Philosophy, Phila., 1988-90. Author: Creation According to Gersonides, 1982; co-author: Exploring Judaism, 1985; co-editor: Creative Jewish Education, 1985. Temple U. fellow, 1972-76, Nat. Found. for Jewish Culture fellow, 1977-78. Fellow Am. Acad. Jewish Philosophy; mem. Am. Acad. Religion, Assn. for Jewish Studies, Soc. for Medieval and Renaissance Philosophy, Reconstructionist Rabbinical Assn. (v.p. 1983-85, Levin award 1977), Medieval Acad. Am., Coalition for Advancement of Jewish Edn., Chevrah (steering com. N.Y.C.C. chpt. 1988—). Democrat. Office: Reconstructionist Rabbinical Coll Church Rd and Greenwood Ave Wyncote PA 19095

STAUDER, JACK RICHARD, social anthropology educator; b. Pueblo, Colo., Mar. 2, 1939; s. John Richard and Hilma Margaret (Johnson) S.; m. Wunderly Rich, Aug., 1963 (div. 1972); children: Samuel, Jeffrey. BA, Harvard U., 1962; PhD in Social Anthropology, Cambridge U., Eng., 1968. Instr. Harvard U., Cambridge, Mass., 1968-71; asst. prof. Northeastern U., Boston, 1971-73; prof. social anthropology U. Mass., Dartmouth, 1973—. Author: The Majangir, 1970; contbr. articles to profl. jours. Leader Harvard U. Strike, 1969. With USMC, 1958-59. Recipient Fulbright fellowship, Fulbright-Hays, Brazil, 1984. Fellow Am. Anthrop. Assn. Home: 180 Clinton St New Bedford MA 02740-3613 Office: U Mass at Dartmouth Dartmouth MA 02747

STAUFFER, DOUGLAS ANDREW, English educator; b. Ringtown, Pa., May 19, 1931; s. Arlene May (Stauffer) Gebhart; m. Everette Leila Gause, Aug. 18, 1956; children: Cathy Leila Stauffer McCorkel, William Allen. BS in Edn., Bloomsburg (Pa.) U., 1954; MS in Edn., Temple U., 1963; ArtsD in English, U. Mich., 1976. Tchr. English, chmn. dept. Fleetwood (Pa.) Joint Jr.-Sr. High Sch., 1954-55, 57-60, Lower Dauphin Joint Jr.-Sr. High Sch., Hummelstown, Pa., 1960-64; instr. Lebanon Valley Coll., Annville, Pa., 1964-66; sr. prof. Harrisburg (Pa.) Area Community Coll., 1966—. With inf. U.S. Army, 1955-57. Mem. Nat. Coun. Tchrs. English, Pa. Coun. Tchrs. English (v.p. 2-yr colls. 1981—), Moose, Phi Sigma Pi. Republican. Lutheran. Home: 349 William Dr Hershey PA 17033-1860 Office: Harrisburg Area Community Coll Humanities Dept 3300 N Cameron Street Rd Harrisburg PA 17110-2999

STAUFFER, RONALD EUGENE, lawyer; b. Hempstead, N.Y., Jan. 22, 1949; s. Hiram Eugene and Florence Marie (Heinz) S.; m. Vicki Lynn

Hartman, June 12, 1973; children: Eric Alan, Craig Aaron, Darren Adam. SB, MIT, 1970; JD magna cum laude, Harvard U., 1973. Bar: D.C. 1973, U.S. Ct. Mil. Appeals 1976, U.S. Tax Ct. 1979. Ptnr. Hogan & Hartson, Washington, 1977-87, Sonnenschein Nath & Rosenthal, Washington, 1988—. Contbr. articles to profl. publs. Capt. U.S. Army, 1970-77. Mem. ABA (chair TIPS Employee Benefits Com. 1977—), D.C. Bar Assn., Tau Beta Pi, Sigma Gamma Tau. Home: 10207 Woodvale Pond Dr Fairfax VA 22039-1658 Office: Sonnenschein Nath & Rosenthal 1301 K St NW Ste 600 Washington DC 20005-3307

STAVE, CARL EDWARD, obstetrician, gynecologist; b. Paterson, N.J., Jan. 30, 1942; s. Thomas Lewis and Sadye Marrion (Goldberg) S.; m. Norma Ann Weinberg, Aug. 22, 1964; children: Todd Michael, Nancy Tara. BA, Rutgers U., 1963; MD, Tufts U., 1967. Diplomate Am. Bd. Ob-Gyn, Am. Bd. Sexology. Intern Maimonides Hosp., Bklyn., 1967-68; resident in ob-gyn Pa. Hosp., Phila., 1968-71; pvt. practice, College Park, Md., 1973—; physician, surgeon Harrisburg (Pa.) Reproductive Health Svcs., 1976—, Prince Georges Reproductive Health Svcs., Adelphi, Md., 1975—, Germantown (Md.) Reprouductive Health Svcs., 1991—. Maj. M.C., USAF, 1971-73. Mem. AMA, Am. Fertility Soc., Md. Med. Soc., Prince Georges County Med. Soc., Am. Assn. Gynecol. Laparoscopists, Am. Assn. Sex Educators, Councilors and Therapists, Phi Delta Epsilon. Jewish. Office: 4700 Berwyn House Rd College Park MD 20740

STAVRIDIS, JACK, safety engineer, insurance company executive; b. N.Y.C., Oct. 23, 1949; s. Harry and Katherine (Economou) S.; m. Barbara Anne Taranowski, Feb. 11, 1972; children: Harry, Steven, Katherine. BSME, CCNY, 1972; MA, N.Y. U., 1980. Cert. nat. assoc. safety profl. Constrn. safety inst. N.Y. State Dept. Labor, Hempstead, N.Y., 1973-75; ins. agent Prudential Ins. Co., Long Island City, N.Y., 1975-76; sr. rep. Chubb and Son Inc., Carle Place, N.Y., 1976-86; cons. Hartford Ins. Co., Hauppauge, N.Y., 1986-87; sr. svc. cons. Home Ins. Co., N.Y.C., 1987-90; engring. mgr. Gerling Am. Ins. Co., N.Y.C., 1990—. Mem. Am. Soc. Safety Engrs., Soc. Fire Protection Engrs. Greek Orthodox. Office: Gerling Am Ins Co 717 5th Ave New York NY 10022-8101

STAYIN, RANDOLPH JOHN, lawyer; b. Cin., Oct. 30, 1942; s. Jack and Viola (Tomin) S.; children: Gregory S., Todd R., Elizabeth J. BA, Dartmouth Coll., 1964; JD, U. Cin., 1967. Bar: Ohio 1967, U.S. Dist. Ct. (so. dist.) Ohio 1968, U.S. Dist. Ct. D.C. 1977, U.S. Ct. Appeals (6th cir.) 1968, U.S. Ct. Appeals (fed. cir.) 1986, U.S. Supreme Ct. 1974, U.S. Ct. Appeals (D.C. cir.) 1976, U.S. Ct. Internat. Trade, 1985. Assoc. Frost & Jacobs, Cin., 1967-72; exec. asst., dir. of legislation U.S. Sen. Robert Taft, Jr., Washington, 1973-74, adminstrv. asst., dir. of legislation, 1975-76; assoc. Taft, Stettinius & Hollister, Washington, 1977, ptnr., 1978-88; ptnr. Barnes & Thornburg, Washington, 1988—; bd. dirs. W.J.S. Holdings Ltd., W.J.S. Inc.; mem. adv. coun. U.S. and FGN. Comml. Svc., U.S. Dept. Commerce. Active Ptnr. with Youth campaign YMCA, D.C.; chmn., mem. numerous coms., chmn., worker campaigns for local politicians Rep. Party state and local orgns.; mem. Citizens to Save WCET-TV, 1967-72, Fine Arts Fund, 1970-72, Cancer Soc., 1970-72; sec., dir. Serbian Am. Voters Alliance; chmn. agy. rels. com. Hamilton County Mental Health and Mental Retardation Bd., 1969-71, vice chmn., 1971, chmn., 1971-72; v.p. Recreation Commn., City of Cin., 1970-72; mem. funds mgmt. com. Westwood 1st Presbyn. Ch., 1968, v.p., 1969, pres., 1970, trustee, 1970, elder, 1971-72; bd. dirs. Evans Mill Pond Owners Assn., v.p., 1986, pres., 1987. Mem. ABA (sect. on internat. law and practice, vice chmn. com. on nat. legislation 1977-79, internat. sect., anti-trust sect.), Am. Soc. Assn. Execs. (legal sect., internat. sect.), Internat. Bar Assn., D.C. Bar Assn. (com. on internat. law). Office: Barnes & Thornburg 1815 H St NW # 800 Washington DC 20006-3692

STAYTON, JANET, artist; b. Natchez, Miss., Sept. 2; d. Willian David and Virginia (Stanley) S. BFA, Tex. Christian U., 1961; MFA, Tulane U., 1963. Contbr. of numerous solo exhibitions, group exhibitions and pub. collections. Home and Studio: 216 Lafayette St New York NY 10012 also: 19020 Battipagliano, Di Pignonte Italy

STAYTON, WILLIAM RALPH, psychologist, educator; b. Kelso, Wash., Dec. 25, 1933; s. Ralph Willard and Marguerite (Hunter) S.; m. Kathleen Boucher, Sept. 4, 1954; children: Mark, John, Cheryl, Paul. BA, U. Redlands, 1956; MDiv, Andover Newton Theol. Sem., 1960; ThD, Boston U., 1967. Ordained to ministry Am. Bapt. Ch., 1959. Assoc. min. 1st Bapt. Ch. in Newton, Mass., 1956-61; min. 1st Bapt. Ch., Gloucester, Mass., 1961-68; chaplain New Eng. Bapt. Hosp., Boston, 1968-71; asst. prof. U. Pa. Sch. Medicine, Phila., 1971-78, lectr., mem. faculty, 1982—; marriage and family therapist Wm R. Stayton & Assocs., Ltd., P.C., Phila., 1978—; mem. faculty La Salle U., Phila., 1983—. Editor spl. issue Topics in Clin. Nursing, 1980; contbr. articles to profl. jours., chpts. to books. Pres. Community Svcs. for Human Growth, Paoli, Pa., 1989-91. Named Man of Yr., B'nai B'rith, Gloucester, Mass., 1968; recipient Outstanding Svc. award Community Svcs. for Human Growth, 1990. Mem. APA, Am. Assn. Marriage and Family Therapists, Am. Assn. Sex Educators, Counselors and Therapists (bd. dirs.-at-large 1982-86, 88-90, chmn. dist. VI, 1982-86, Outstanding Svc. award 1978, 87), Sex. Info. and Edn. Coun. U.S. (pres. 1985-87, sec. 1990—), Soc. for Sci. Study SEx. (chmn. ann. meeting 1983), Pa. Assn. Marriage and Family Therapists (continuing edn. com. 1985-90). Democrat. Home: 188 Blackberry Ln Malvern PA 19355-9630 Office: 987 Old Eagle School Rd Ste 719 Wayne PA 19087-1708

STEARNS, PETER NATHANIEL, history educator; b. London, Mar. 3, 1936; (parents Am. citizens); s. Raymond P. and Elizabeth (Scott) S.; m. Nancy Driessel (div. 1976); children: Duncan, Deborah; m. Carol Zisowitz, Mar. 26, 1978; children: Clio Elizabeth, Cordelia Raymond. AB, Harvard U., 1957, MA, 1959, PhD, 1963. Instr. to assoc. prof. U. Chgo., 1962-65; prof., chmn. history dept. Rutgers U., New Brunswick, N.J., 1965-74; Heinz prof. history Carnegie Mellon U., Pitts., 1974—, chmn. dept. history, 1986-92, dean Coll. Humanities and Social Scis., 1992—; co-dir. Pitts. Ctr. for Social History, 1986-92; chmn. acad. adv. coun. N.Y.C. Coll. Bd., 1982-85. Author: European Society in Upheaval: Social History since 1800, 1967 (trans. Swedish), rev. edit., 1975, 3d edit., 1991, Priest and Revolutionary: Lamennais and the Dilemma of French Catholicism, 1967 (trans. Polish), Modern Europe, 1789-1914, 1969, Revolutionary Syndicalism and French Labor: a cause without rebels, 1971, (with Harvey Mitchell) Workers and Protest: The European Labor Movement, The Working Classes and the Rise of Socialism, 1890-1914, 1971, The European Experience since 1815, 1972, 1848: The Revolutionary Tide in Europe, 1974 (pub. in Eng. as The Revolutions of 1848), Lives of Labor: Work in Maturing Industrial Society, 1975 (trans. German), Old Age in European Society, 1977, Face of Europe, 1977, Paths to Authority: Toward the Formation of Middle Class Consciousness, 1978, Be A Man! Males in Modern Society, 1979, rev. edit., 1990, (with Linda Rosenzweig) Themes in Modern Social History, 1985, (with Carol Stearns) Anger: The Struggle for Emotional Control in America's History, 1986, World History: Patterns of Change and Continuity, 1987, (with others) Makers of Modern Europe, 1987 (with others) Readings in World History, Vol. 1: The Great Tradition and Vol. 2: The Modern Centuries, 1987, Expanding the Past: A Reader in Social History, 1988, Life and Society in the West, The Modern Centuries, 1988, World History: Traditions and New Directions, 1988, (with C. Stearns) Emotion and Social Change, Toward a New Psychohistory, 1988, (with Andrew Barnes) Social History and Issues in Consciousness and Cognition, 1989, Jealousy: Evolution of an Emotion in American History, 1989, Interpreting the Industrial Revolution, 1991, (with Michael Adas amd Stuart Schwartz) World Civilizations, 1991, Meaning Over Memory: The Humanities in Contemporary Society, 1992, Meaning Over Memory: Issues in the Humanities, 1992, The Industrial Revolution in World History, 1992; editor: Century for Debate, 1969, The Impact of the Industrial Revolution, 1972, (with Walkowitz) Workers in the Industrial Revolution, 1974, The Other Side of Western Civilization, 1979, rev. edit., 1984, 4th edit., 1991, The Rise of Modern Women, 1977, (with Michael Weber) The Spencers of Amberson Avenue: A Turn-of-the-Century Memoir, 1983, (with Van Tassel) Old Age in a Bureaucratic Society, 1986; editor in chief Jour. Social History, 1967—; editor: Garland Ency. of Social History; contbg. editor history of emotions series NYU Press; contbr. over 150 articles to profl. and popular jours. Guggenheim Found. fellow, 1973-74; NEH grantee, 1981-84, 86, 90, Rockefeller Found. grantee, 1982-83. Fellow Internat. Soc. for Rsch. on Emotion; mem. Am. Hist. Soc., World History Assn. Democrat. Home: 509 S Linden Ave Pittsburgh PA 15208-2846 Office: Carnegie Mellon U History Dept Pittsburgh PA 15213-3890

STEBBINGS, ROBERT YEO, lawyer; b. L.A., Feb. 11, 1942; s. Albion Edward Stebbings and Joan Vera (Bywater) Roark; 1 child, Matias. AB in History, Stanford U., 1963; postgrad., U. Paris, 1963-64; JD, Columbia U., 1967, MBA, 1968. Assoc. Davis Polk & Wardwell, N.Y.C., 1969-71; legal counsel Inst. Latin Am. Integration, Buenos Aires, 1971-74; internat. counsel Marcona Corp. and Utah Internat., San Francisco, 1974-78; sr. ptnr. Stebbings & Assocs., P.C., N.Y.C., 1978—; dir., gen. counsel Bus. Coun. Internat. Understanding, N.Y.C. Author: Pueblo Y Justicia, 1975; author Export Controls the Host Country Dilemna, Case Western Res. Jour. of Internat. Law, 1987. Mem. Am. Fgn. Law Assn. (bd. dirs., officer), Brazilian Am. C. of C. (bd. dirs.), Pan Am. Soc. U.S. (bd. dirs.), Venezuelan Am. Assn. of U.S. (pres., dir.), Soc. Internat. Devel. (N.Y. chpt. bd. dirs.). Office: Marks & Murase 399 Park Ave New York NY 10022-4689

STEBLAY, RAYMOND WILLIAM, immunopathologist, researcher; b. Chgo., Mar. 28, 1922; s. Joseph Bernard Jr. and Margaret (Kobadich) S. AB magna cum laude, Princeton U., 1947; MD, U. Chgo., 1952. Asst. prof. dept. ob-gyn. U. Chgo., 1959-67, asst. prof. depts. pathology and medicine, 1967-69; rsch. assoc prof. dept. pathology Albany (N.Y.) Med. Sch., 1969-72; rsch. physician N.Y. State Kidney Disease Inst., Albany, 1969-83. Contbr. articles to profl. jours. Recipient Disting. Svc. award U. Chgo., 1986. Mem. Am. Soc. Nephrology, Am. Assn. Pathologists, Am. Assn. Immunologists. Presbyterian. Home: 107 Heritage Rd Apt 11 Guilderland NY 12084-9662

STECKER, ELINOR HORWITZ, magazine editor; b. Rochester, N.Y., Feb. 6, 1928; d. Thomas Arthur and Selma Sylvia (Hollander) Horwitz; m. Arthur Stecker, Aug. 22, 1965 (dec. Nov. 1983); children: Lee Perrin, Janet Perrin. AB, U. Mich., 1949; MS, U. Pitts., 1953. Cert. clin. speech and lang. pathologist. Speech and lang. pathologist New Rochelle (N.Y.) Schs., 1970-75, United Cerebral Palsy of Westchester, Purchase, N.Y., 1975-82; sr. editor Photomethods, N.Y.C., 1982-85, Popular Photography, N.Y.C., 1985—; Freelance documentary filmmaker, photograher and slide-show producer. Author: Slide Showmanship, 1987, How to Create and Use High-contrast Images, 1982, Trick Photography, 1982, Master Handbook of Titling for Slides and Motion Pictures, 1979; audiovisual columnist Meetings and Conv. Mags.; contbr. articles to profl. jours. Mem. Westchester Photographic Soc. (v.p. 1987-90), Met. Motion Picture Club, Film Workshop of Westchester (treas. 1980-85). Home: 1013 The Colony Hartsdale NY 10530-1719 Office: Popular Photography 1633 Broadway New York NY 10019-6708

STECKER, FLOYD WILLIAM, astrophysicist; b. N.Y.C., Aug. 12, 1942; s. Norman and Helen Lillian (Stern) S.; m. Dorothy Ruth Bick, July 4, 1965; children: Benjamin, Jonathan. SB in Physics, MIT, 1963; AM in Astrophysics, Harvard U., 1965, PhD in Astrophysics, 1968. Rsch. asst. MIT Lab. for Nuclear Sci., Cambridge, 1962-63; physicist Harvard-Smithsonian Ctr. Astrophysics, Cambridge, 1963-67; postdoctoral rsch. assoc. NASA Goddard Space Flight Ctr., Greenbelt, Md., 1967-68, astrophysicist, 1968—; lectr. U. Md., College Park, 1985—. Author: Cosmic Gamma Rays, 1971; editor: Gamma Ray Astrophysics,s 1973, Structure of the Galaxy and Galactic Gamma Rays, 1976, Energetic Gamma Ray Telescope Science Symposium, 1990; contbr. over 150 articles to profl. jours. Recipient Medal for Exceptional Sci. Achievement, NASA, 1973. Fellow Am. Phys. Soc., Am. Astron. Soc., Internt. Astron. Union (galactic structure and cosmology commns.), Sigma Xi. Office: NASA Goddard Space Flight Ctr High Energy Astrophysics Lab Coe 660 Greenbelt MD 20771

STECKLER, PATRICIA, clinical psychologist; b. Mt. Vernon, N.Y., Dec. 4, 1951; d. Seymour Sidney Steckler and Jane Faggen; m. Phiroz Maneck Bhagat, Oct. 13, 1979; children: Kay Hannah, Sarah Maneck. BA, Brandeis U., 1973; MA, Case Western Res. U., 1976, PhD, 1980. Lic. clin. psychologist, N.Y., N.J. Intern Cleve. VA Hosp., 1976-77; intern Albert Einstein Coll. Medicine, Bronx, N.Y., 1977-78, faculty psychologist, 1980-81; pvt. practice Westfield, N.J., 1984—. Mem. APA, N.J. Assn. Women Therapists (v.p. 1986—, pres. 1988—), N.J. Psychol. Assn. (program chairperson 1987—, bd. dirs. 1990, pres.-elect 1991-92, pres. 1992-93). Office: 134 S Euclid Ave Westfield NJ 07090-2130

STEEG, JAMES HOWE, professional sports administrator; b. Boston, Nov. 29, 1950; s. Carl Worth and Janet (Johnson) S.; m. Sharon Smith; children: Bryce Evan, Darcy Lauren. BA, Miami U., 1972; MBA, Wake Forest U., 1975. Jr. acct. Jennings, Lindsey and Reimer, Hamilton, Ohio, 1972-73; acct., comptroller, bus. mgr. Miami Dolphins, Ltd., Miami, Fla., 1975-78; exec. dir. spl. events NFL, N.Y.C., 1979—; dir. Saddlebrook Resorts, Wesley Chapel, Fla., 1988—. Mem. Citizen's Advisory Task Force, Ramsey, N.J., 1987—. Mem. Internat. Assn. Auditorium Mgrs. Republican. Methodist. Home: 15 Farmington Ct Ramsey NJ 07446-2104 Office: NFL 410 Park Ave New York NY 10022-4407

STEELE, GEORGE PEABODY, marine transportation consultant; b. San Francisco, July 27, 1924; s. James Mortimer and Erma (Garrett) S.; m. Elizabeth Yates Fahrion, July 11, 1944 (div. May 1988); children: Jane Yates Steele Mitchell, James Fahrion; m. Betty McDonnell, May 20, 1988. BS, U.S. Naval Acad., 1944. Commd. ensign USN, 1944, advanced through grades to vice adm., 1973; service aboard submarines in Pacific World War II, 1973; comdr. U.S.S. Hardhead, 1955-56, comdr. nuclear powered U.S.S. Seadragon (made 1st NW passage under ice to North Pole), 1959-61, comdr. Polaris missile sub U.S.S. Daniel Boone, 1963-66; head politico-mil. policy div. Europe/NATO br. Office Chief Naval Ops., 1966-68, comdr. Naval Forces Korea, chief Naval adv. group, Korean Navy, comdr. Naval Component UN Command, 1968-70, comdr. Anti-Submarine Warfare Group 4, 1970-72; dep. asst. chief of staff Supreme Allied Comdr. SHAPE, Europe, SHAPE, Belgium, 1972-73; comdr. U.S. 7th Fleet, 1973-75, ret., 1975; exec. v.p. Interocean Mgmt. Corp., Phila., 1976-78, pres., 1978-81, chmn., chief exec. officer, 1981-89, dir., 1989—; chmn. bd. trustees Fgn. Policy Rsch. Inst., 1980-89, trustee, 1989—. Author: Seadragon, Northwest Under the Ice, 1962, (with H. Gimpel) Nuclear Submarine Skippers and What They Do, 1962, Vengeance in the Depths, 1963; contbr. articles to profl. publs. and newspapers. Decorated D.S.M., Legion of Merit with 4 gold stars, Navy Cross (Peru), Order of Rising Sun (Japan), Cloud and Banner (Republic China), Order Nat. Security of Merit (Republic Korea). Mem. Am. Bur. Shipping (mgmt. com. bd. mgrs. 1989-92), Am. Inst. Merchant Shipping (chmn. bd. dirs. 1986-87), U.S. Naval Inst. Episcopalian. Clubs: Univ., N.Y. Yacht; Union League (Phila.); Army-Navy, Army-Navy Country (Washington). Home: 6 Upland Rd Apt 2B Baltimore MD 21210-2254 Office: Interocean Mgmt Corp 3 Parkway Philadelphia PA 19102

STEELE, HOWARD LOUCKS, government official; b. Pitts., Jan. 27, 1929; s. Howard Bennington and Ruby Alberta (Loucks) S.; B.S., Washington and Lee U., 1950; M.S., Pa. State U., 1952; Ph.D., U. Ky., 1962; m. Sally E. Funk, June 6, 1952 (div. 1977); children: John F., David A., Patricia A.; m. 2d, Jane R. Cornelius, July 30, 1977; 1 dau., Jennifer L. Sales mgr. Greenville (Pa.) Dairy Co., 1952-56; owner H.L. Steele Bulk Milk Hauling, Greenville, Pa., 1955-60; asst. prof. Clemson (S.C.) U., 1956-57, asso. prof., 1957-64; assoc. prof. Ohio State U., Columbus, 1964-71; with Office Internat. Cooperation and Devel. U.S. Dept. Agr., Washington, 1971—, project mgr. AID, Guatemala, 1976-77, Bolivia, 1977-80, Honduras, 1980-82, Sri Lanka, 1982-84, Bur. Latin Am. and Caribbean AID, Washington, 1984-88, office of the dir. tech. assistance div., 1988-90, with external affairs Office of the Adminstr., 1990—; instr. U. Md., College Park, 1974-76; vis. prof. U. Sao Paulo, Piracicaba, Brazil, 1964-66; partner Kingwood Acres Farm, Rockwood, Pa., 1966—. Recipient Nat. Forensic Union award; named One of Outstanding Young Men in U.S., U.S. Jaycees, 1965; cert. of merit Dept. Agr., 1975, 1992. Mem. Am. Agrl. Econs. Assn., Internat. Assn. Agrl. Economists, Sons Am. Revolution, Gamma Sigma Delta, Sigma Nu. Lodges: Masons, Shriners. Author: Comercialização Agrícola; contbr. to Agriculture, Lincoln Library of Essential Information; contbr. articles to profl. jours. Home: 5204 Holden St Fairfax VA 22032-3418 Office: USDA/OICD 14th St and Independence Ave South Bldg Rm 3117 Washington DC 20250

STEELE, JOSEPH RICHARD, health educator, musician, producer; b. Washington, N.J., May 4, 1953; s. Edward and Edith Louise (Williams) S.; m. Lisa Phillips, Aug. 9, 1974 (div. 1986); m. Judith Lynn Bailey, Mar. 18, 1990; 1 stepchild, Quadidra Davis. Student in music theory, Fairleigh Dickinson U., 1972-74; student in music, Thomas Edison State Coll., 1989—. Community health educator Community Guidance Ctr. Mercer County, Princeton, N.J., 1987-88; program coord. L.I.F.T. Inc., Trenton, N.J., 1988-89, Union Indsl. Home for Children, Trenton, N.J., 1989-90; field coord. Area Health Edn. Ctr., Camden, N.J., 1989-92; owner LaHara Steele Prodns., Willingboro, N.J., 1988—; mem. LaHara Steele Ensemble, Willingboro, N.J., 1988—; adv., bd. dirs. African People Action Sch., Trenton, 1987-88, AIDS Task Force, Trenton, 1989-90; peer support facilitator Union Indsl. Homesm 1992—. Prodr., composer: (cassettes) The Aids Educator Song, 1990, No More Drugs, 1990, The Faces of Heroin, Mass Appeal, AIDS Rap; contbr. articles to profl. jour. Mem. Burlington City Block Bus. Profl. Orgn. (treas. 1991). Home: 705 Downing Ct Willingboro NJ 08046

STEELE, ROBERT STEVEN, psychology educator; b. Seattle, Nov. 20, 1946; s. Clifford W. and Georgia Rose (Wilson) S. BA magna cum laude, Whitman Coll., Walla Walla, Wash., 1968; PhD with distinction, Harvard U., 1973; MA, Wesleyan U., 1992. Asst. prof. Wesleyan U., Middletown, Conn., 1973-81, assoc. prof., 1982-90, prof. psychology, 1991—, chmn. dept. psychology, 1990—. Author: Freud and Jung, 1982. Photographer, Protectors of Animals, Colchester, Conn., 1989—. Rantoul fellow, Carnation Co., 1964-68. Mem. Phi Bta Kappa. Office: Wesleyan Univ Dept Psychology Middletown CT 06459-0408

STEEN, CAROL J., artist; b. Highland Park, Mich., Nov. 6, 1943; d. David and Jean (Cohen) S. B.A., Mich. State U., 1965; M.F.A., Cranbrook Acad. Art, 1971. Solo exhbns. include: Detroit Inst. Art, 1973, Hundred Acres Gallery, N.Y.C., 1975, Little Gallery, Birmingham, Mich., 1975, Gallery 7, Detroit, 1976, 55 Mercer, N.Y.C., 1978, 81, 82, 85, 87, 89, 91; Sill Gallery, Eastern Mich. U., 1979, Cade Gallery, Royal Oak, Mich., 1988; exhibited in group shows: DeCordova Mus., Lincoln, Mass., 1974, U. Mich. Alumni Mus., 1975, Willis Gallery, Detroit, 1976, Cranbrook Mus., 1976, Mus. Contemporary Crafts, Finch Coll., N.Y.C., 1975-77, Ctr. for Creative Studies, Detroit, 1977, The Detroit Inst. Art, 1977, 55 Mercer, 1978, Nobe Gallery, N.Y.C., 1978, Arte Fiore, Bologna, Italy, 1978, P.S. 1, L.I.C., 1979, Contemporary Art Mus., Chgo., 1981, Stonybrook Campus Gallery, 1981, A.I.R. Invitational, N.Y.C., 1982, 84, 85, 55 Mercer, 1983, Damon Brandt Gallery, N.Y.C., 1983, 84, City Gallery, N.Y.C., 1985, Galveston Art Ctr., Tex., 1985, Fed. Res. Bank, N.Y.C., 1986, Drew U., Madison, N.J., 1986, A.I.R. Gallery, N.Y.C., 1989, Brody's Gallery, N.Y.C., 1989, Cranbrook Acad. of Art, Bloomfield Hills, Mich., 1990, Phila. Mus. Art, 1990, B4A Gallery, N.Y.C., 1991; represented in permanent collections: Printmaking Workshop, N.Y.C., Detroit Inst. Art, Smithsonian Archives of Am. Art, Am. Craft Mus., N.Y.C., V.A.R.S., Slide File, N.Y.C.; dir. 55 Mercer, 1983. MacDowell Colony fellow, 1980; Printmaking Workshop guest artist, N.Y.C., 1983-85; vis. artist U. Mich., Ford Found., 1975; fellow N.Y. Found. for Arts, 1986-87, Materials For the Arts, 1987. Address: 163 Bowery New York NY 10002

STEER, ANNE EILEEN, bank executive; b. N.Y.C., Nov. 5, 1951; d. Charles Melvin and Catherine Mary (Quinn) Steer; m. Ralph Stephen Sheridan, May 18, 1985. BA, Mt. Holyoke Coll., 1974; MBA, U. Chgo., 1979. Mktg. rep. Continental Can Co., Stamford, Conn., 1979-80; sales rep. Continental Can Co., Wayne, N.J., 1980-87; asst. treas., v.p. State Street Bank, Boston, 1987—. Office: State Street Bank and Trust 225 Franklin St Boston MA 02110-2804

STEESY, WALTER WESLEY, publishing executive; b. San Diego, Nov. 15, 1940; s. Wesley J. and Marcella May (Walter) S.; m. Mary A. Cartwright, Aug. 25, 1962; children: Wendy, Scott, Shawn. AB in Human Rels., Salem (W.Va.) Coll., 1962. Cert. reunion planner; cert. cruise agt. Dist. scout exec. Boy Scouts Am., DuBois, Pa., 1962-65, L.A., 1965; dist. sales mgr. Growers Chem. Corp., Milan, Ohio, 1965-76; owner Circle B Feed Svc., Little Genesee, N.Y., 1965-70; dist. sales mgr. Todd Hybrid Corn Co., Abbottstown, Pa., 1965-74; owner, ptnr. Heart of the Lakes Pub., Interlaken, N.Y., 1976—, The Conf. Connection, Interlaken, 1990—, The Cruise Connection, Interlaken, 1991—; cons. on publs. numerous hist. socs., mil. and sch. reunion orgns. Author: Genealogy of Olmsted Family, 1970, 89; editor various genealogies and histories; contbr. articles to mil. reunion assn. newsletters. Dir. The Sampson History Project, Seneca County, N.Y., 1988—. Mem. Geneal. Conf. N.Y. (chmn. 1962-91). Office: Heart of the Lakes Pub PO Box 299 Interlaken NY 14847-0299

STEEVES, LYNNE MARY, accountant; b. Worcester, Mass., Aug. 14, 1922; d. Salim G. and Mary C. (Haddad) Ayik; m. Gerald N. Steeves, Dec. 29, 1953; children: Catherine L., Ruth E., Bette G. Student, Becker Jr. Coll., 1943, Worcester Jr. Coll., 1945-46. Pvt. practice Worcester, Mass., 1946—; ptnr., mgr. Steeves Ins. Agy., Inc., Worcester, 1953-87; justice of peace Commonwealth of Mass., Worcester, 1980—. Pres. welcome guild 1st Bapt. Ch., 1958-60, bd. deacons, 1984-87. Named Ky. Col., Gov. Ky., 1977. Mem. Altrusa Club (pres. 1982-84), Worcester Womans Club (bd. dirs. 1957-70), Altrusa Internat. (nominating com.), Blue and Gold Club (pres. 1943-46), Rep. Club, Womans golf League Worcester County, Eastern Star, Daughters of Mokanna. Baptist. Home: 10 Coventry Rd Worcester MA 01606-2133

STEEVES, ROBERT FRANCIS, federal agency administrator; b. Derby, Conn., Feb. 8, 1938; s. Robert Palmer and Catherine (Williams) S.; m. Doriene Melendy, Nov. 21, 1959; children: Kimberlee, Laura, Wendy. BS in Pharmacy, U. Conn., 1959; JD, Georgetown U., 1964, LLM, 1968. Bar: D.C. 1964, Va. 1964, U.S. Supreme Ct. 1972, U.S. Ct. Appeals (3d, 4th cirs.) 1973. Dir. legal div. Am. Pharm. Assn., Washington, 1964-69; v.p, gen. counsel Pharm. Card System, Inc., Phoenix, 1969-71; pvt. practice Washington, 1971-76; gen. counsel U.S. Office Consumer Affairs, Washington, 1976-77; dep. assoc. commr. legis. FDA, Washington, 1977-81; dep. dir. Office Spl. Adviser to Pres. for Consumer Affairs, Washington, 1981-89; staff adviser Office of Orphan Product Devel., Office of the Commr. FDA, Rockville, Md., 1989—. Columnist Am. Druggist Mag., Drug Topics, 1969-74. Active Soil and Erosion Control Rev. Bd., Fairfax County, Va., 1988—. Mem. ABA, Va. Bar Assn. Republican. Episcopalian. Home: 4657 Country Vale Ct Annandale VA 22003-4524 Office: FDA Office of Commr 5600 Fishers Ln Rockville MD 20857-0001

STEFANO, GEORGE B., neurobiologist, researcher; b. N.Y.C., Sept. 11, 1945; s. George and Agnes (Hendrickson) S.; m. Judith Mary Stefano, Aug. 24, 1968; 1 child, Michelle Laura. Ph.D., Fordham U., 1973. Mem. faculty N.Y.C. Community Coll., 1972-79, Medgar Evers Coll., CUNY, 1979-82; prof. cell biology, chmn. dept. biol. sci. SUNY, Old Westbury, 1982-86, asst. v.p. research, 1985-89, dir. Old Westbury Neurosci. Inst. and Gerontology Ctr., 1986—; pres., dir. East Coast Neurosci. Found., Dix Hills, N.Y., 1977-82; research coordinator dept. anesthesiology St. Joseph Hosp. and Med. Ctr., Paterson, N.J., 1979-82; disting. teaching prof. SUNY, 1991. Co-founder, mem. editorial bd. Molecular Cellular Neurobiology and Prog. Neuro Endcini Immunology; editor Advances in Neuroimmunology; contbr. over 1300 papers to sci. jours. Named CASE Prof. N.Y., 1991. Nat. Acad. Scis. grantee, 1978, 80; NIMH grantee, 1979—; NSF grantee, 1989—; project dir. ADAMHA-MARC, 1983—. Mem. AAAS, Soc. Neurosci. (pres. Old Westbury chpt.), Assn. Immuno-Neurobiologists (exec. pres. 1991—), N.Y. Acad. Sci., Gerontol. Soc. Am.

STEGEMAN, THOMAS ALBERT, lawyer; b. Quincy, Ill., Mar. 9, 1948; m. Cynthia J. Taylor, Aug. 11, 1973; 1 son, Corey A.T. A.B., U. Ill., 1970; J.D., Washington U., 1973. Bars: Mo. 1973, Ill. 1974, D.C. 1985. Assoc., James C. Moloney, Inc., Clayton, Mo., 1973-75, Thompson & Mitchell, St. Louis, 1975-79; v.p., gen. counsel Roosevelt Fed. Savs. & Loan Assn., St. Louis, 1979-84; atty. Akin, Gump, Strauss, Hauer & Feld, 1984-86; ptnr. Hazel Thomas Fiske Beckhorn & Hanes, P.C., Fairfax, Va., 1986-91; ptnr. Freer & Alagia, Washington, 1991—. Capt., Friends of Scouting, 1974. Mem. Ill. State Bar Assn., Mo. Bar Assn., ABA, Chgo. Bar Assn., St. Louis Bar Assn. (exec. com. 1979-80). Editor, Washington U. Law Quar., 1972-73. Home: 21 River Falls Ct Rockville MD 20854-3885 Office: Freer & Alagia 1000 Thomas Jefferson St NW Washington DC 20007-3835

STEGMAIER, SISTER ANNE MARIE, educator, counselor; b. Washington, Mar. 1, 1951; d. Robert Bernard and Mary Josephine (Muth) S. BA,

Immaculata Coll., 1978; MS in Pastoral Counseling, Neumann Coll., 1992. Cert. elem. and secondary social studies tchr., Pa. Tchr. Saint Bartholomew Sch., East Brunswick, N.J., 1972-75, Saint Gabriel Sch., Phila., 1975-76, Immaculate Conception Sch., Jim Thorpe, Pa., 1976-78, St. Pius Sch., Norfolk, Va., 1978-82, St. James Sch., Savannah, Ga., 1982-87, St. Louis Sch., Yeadon, Pa., 1987—. Mem. AACD, Nat. Cath. Edn. Assn., Am. Sch. Counselor Assn., Psi Chi.

STEHLE, EDWARD RAYMOND, educator; b. Pitts., May 30, 1942; s. Edward August and Mary Josephine (Veverka) S.; m. Alberta McConnell; 1 child, Christian Dollison. BA, U. Pitts., 1964; MA, Columbia U., 1966, doctoral student, 1966-68. Instr. European history C.W. Post Coll., Long Island U., Greenville, N.Y., 1967-68, Middlebury (Vt.) Coll., 1968-69; history master The Lawrenceville Sch., Lawrenceville, N.J., 1969—, dir. day students, 1978-83, asst. dir. coll. counseling, 1983-88, chmn. history dept., 1988—; asst. dir. The N.J. Scholars Program, Lawrenceville, 1981, dir., 1982-91; cons. U. Del. Sea Grant Coll., Newark, 1981-82; cons. on history of migrations Statue of Liberty-Ellis Island Found., N.Y.C., 1985-88; mem. selection com. Morris County (N.J.) Summer Opportunities for Tchrs. Program, Morristown, 1985-86; bd. mem. N.J. Scholars Program, Lawrenceville, 1988—; bd. trustees Craftsbury Chamber Players, Greensboro, Vt., 1985-89; chmn. Bd. N.J. Scholar Program, 1988—. Co-author: A Guide to Programming on Basic Plus, 1975; contbr. Harper's Encyclopedia of the Modern World, 1972. Vice pres. Assoc. Mems., Ch. of Christ, Greensboro, 1974-76, pres., 1976-78. Mem. Am. Hist. Assn., Common Cause, Nassau Club (Princeton, N.J.), Mountainview Country Club (Greensboro, Vt.). Democrat. Episcopalian. Home: 2810 Main St Trenton NJ 08648-1017 Office: The Lawrenceville Sch Main St Trenton NJ 08620-2310

STEHNO, JOSEPH JOHN, education educator, consultant, counselor; b. Chgo., Feb. 7, 1947; s. Joseph A. and Catherine M. (Davis) S.; m. Nancy L. Stehno, Dec. 11, 1987. BA, Loyola U., 1969, MRE, 1973; MEd with honors, De Paul U., 1978; postgrad., So. Ill. U., 1986—. Tchr. Immaculata High Sch., Chgo., 1969-73; counselor Viator High Sch., Arlington Heights, Ill., 1973-79; sr. instr. N.C. Outward Bound, Morganton, 1981—; program dir. So. Ill. U., Carbondale, 1981-84, conf. coord., 1984-88; corp. tng. coord. Amoskeag Bank Shares, Manchester, N.H., 1989-90; asst. prof. Franklin Pierce Coll., Concord, N.H., 1989—; cons., counselor Pembroke (N.H.) Acad., 1990—; cons. Sangamon State U., Springfield, Ill., 1983-87, Fed. Exec. Inst., Charlottesville, Va., 1990—; co-owner IMPACT Tng., Weare, N.H., 1990—; dir. CampFire, Inc., Manchester. Contbr. articles to profl. jours. Mem. New Eng. Assn. for Exptl. Edn. (pres. 1991—). Democrat. Home and Office: 145 Thorndike Rd Weare NH 03281-4530

STEIGER, DALE ARLEN, publishing executive; b. LaCrosse, Wis., May 14, 1928; s. Walter Elmer and Doris Adeline (Howe) S.; m. Alyce Ann Dyrdahl, Oct. 8, 1949; children: Christine Ann, Marta Louise. Student U. Wis., LaCrosse, 1945-46, 48-49; BA, Chgo. Acad. Fine Arts, 1951; postgrad. Drake U., 1958-62, Iona Coll., 1968. Art dir. Trane Co., LaCrosse, 1955, Look mag., Des Moines, 1956, promotions mgr. Cowles Subscription div., 1957-67, exec. v.p. Cowles Communications subdiv., 1960-71; v.p. mktg., asso. pub. Curtis Publs. Co., N.Y.C., 1971-72; pres. Dale Steiger Assocs., N.Y.C., 1972—, Blue Ribbon Reading Svc., Rye, N.Y., 1979, DASCO, Darien, Conn., 1991; pres., pub. Videofinder mag., 1981—, Pulling mag., 1981—; pres. SUBCO, 1986; chmn. Hair and Beauty Inc.; pub. Hair and Beauty News, 1988—; chief exec. officer Mktg. Group SMC Publs.; pres., chief exec. officer DASCO, Inc., Darien, Conn.; lectr. direct mail and mktg. Author: (with others) The Handbook of Circulation Management, 1980. Served with AUS, 1946-48. Recipient Industry Achievement award Fulfillment Mgmt. Assn., 1979; Lee C. Williams award for outstanding contbns. to periodical pub. field, 1982. Mem. Mag. Publs. Assn., Audit Bur. Circulations, Fulfillment Mgmt. Assn. (pres., chmn. bd.), Nat. Soc. Art Dirs., VFW, Am. Legion, Cornell Club, Westchester Country Club. Republican. Presbyterian (elder). Office: 488 Madison Ave New York NY 10022

STEIGER, FRED HAROLD, chemist; b. Cleve., May 11, 1929; s. Jacob and Helen (Gross) S.; m. Claire Geller, Sept. 7, 1952 (dec. Mar. 1985); children: Eden Steiger Fisher, Susan Steiger Baron; m. Estelle Dubin, Jan. 6, 1991. BA, U. Pa., 1951; MA, Temple U., 1956. Rsch. chemist Rohm and Haas Co., Phila., 1951-60; group leader Personal Products Co. Div. Johnson & Johnson, Milltown, N.J., 1960-62, sr. rsch. chemist, 1962-68, sr. rsch. scientist, 1968-74, sr. rsch. assoc., 1974-76, mgr. product devel., 1976-85, mgr. tech. assessment, 1985-88; pvt. practice East Brunswick, N.J., 1988—; v.p. N.J. Inst. Chemists, Mountainside, N.J., 1975-77. Editor: Chem. Abstracts, 1968—. Fellow Am. Inst. Chemists; mem. Am. Assn. Textile Chemists and Colorists (chmn. rsch. com. Lowell, Mass. 1958-60), Am. Chem. Soc., Phi Lambda Upsilon. Home: 10 Tompkins Rd East Brunswick NJ 08816-1709

STEIGER, HEIDI SCHWARZBAUER, investment executive; b. Boston, July 8, 1953; d. Wilhelm Frederick and Lucille Florence (Isabelle) Schwarzbauer; m. Kenneth Jay Brine, June 5, 1977 (div. 1982); m. Paul Ernest Steiger, Nov. 23, 1985; children: Erika, Laura, Isabelle, William. Cert., U. De Poitiers, La Rochelle, France, 1974; BA in English, Boston Coll., 1975; cert. in underwriting, Bryn Mawr (Pa.) Coll., 1979; MBA in Fin., Columbia U., 1985. Advt. and sales promotion specialist New England Life, Boston, 1975-77; product mgr. retail mktg. div. Fidelity Group, Boston, 1977-80, mgr. corp. comm., 1980-81, dir. mktg., 1981-83; sr. v.p. spl. products divsn. Herzfeld & Stern, N.Y.C., 1983-85; mng. dir. individual asset mgmt. Neuberger & Berman, N.Y.C., 1986—; mem. adv. bd. Fin. & Acctg. Audio Digest, Greenwich, Conn., 1988—. Contbr. articles to numerous profl. jours. Mem. fin. com. Ravitch for Mayor, N.Y.C.; chairperson assoc. bus. com. Met. Mus. Art, N.Y.C., 1989; bd. dirs., chairperson devel. com. Nat. Theatre of the Deaf, Chester, Conn., 1987—; bd. dirs. Fountain House. Mem. Boston Coll. Alumni Assn. (class corr. 1975—), Fin. Women's Assn. (pres. N.Y.C. chpt. 1988-89), Phi Beta Kappa. Republican. Episcopalian. Office: Neuberger & Berman 605 3d Ave New York NY 10158

STEIN, ALAN L., real estate executive; b. N.Y.C., Sept. 17, 1948; s. Ernest I. and Marsha (Putterman) S.; m. Susan Schuster; children: Matthew Benjamin, Joshua Ian. BS in Acctg., Lehman Coll., CUNY, 1970; JD, Bklyn. Law Sch., 1973. Bar: N.Y., U.S. Dist. Ct. (ea. and so. dist.) N.Y. Assoc. N.Y.C. Law Dept., 1973-75; real estate rep. Loews Corp., N.Y.C., 1975-77; assoc. Hess, Segall, Guterman Pelz & Steiner, N.Y.C., 1977-80; v.p. Rose Assocs., Inc., N.Y.C., 1980-87, Eichner Properties, N.Y.C., 1987; regional v.p. London & Leeds Devel. Corp., N.Y.C., 1988-91; v.p. mktg. Rockefeller Ctr. Mgmt. Corp., 1991—. Trustee, Temple Beth Israel, Port Washington, N.Y., 186—. With N.Y. State Army N.G., 1969-74. Mem. Real Estate Bd. of N.Y., Urban Land Inst., Nat. Assn. Corp. Real Estate Execs., N.Y. State Bar Assn., Young Men's and Women's Real Estate Assn. of N.Y. (gov. 1985-87). Home: 153 Soundview Dr Port Washington NY 11050-1748 Office: Rockefeller Ctr Mgmt Corp 1230 Ave of Americas New York NY 10020-1579

STEIN, BRUNO, economist; b. Vienna, Austria, July 19, 1930; s. Leo and Paula (Lindenbaum) S.; m. Judith A. Paris, Dec. 26, 1969; 1 child, Elizabeth P. AB, NYU, 1950, AM, 1952, PhD, 1959. Fellow NYU Ctr. for Internat. Studies, 1973-74; instr. NYU, 1956-59, asst. prof., 1959-63, assoc. prof., 1963-68, prof. econs. and dir. Inst. Labor Rels., 1968—; vis. fellow Policy Studies Inst., London; acad. visitor London Sch. Econs., 1972-73; lectr. Columbia U. Grad. Sch. Bus., summer 1958; vis. lectr. Cornell U., 1976; labor arbitrator, mediator; cons. in field; panel mem. Am. Arbitration Assn., Fed. Mediation and Conciliation Svc., others. Author: On Relief: The Economics of Poverty and Public Welfare, 1971, Work and Welfare in Britain and the USA, 1976, Social Security and the Private Pension System, 1979, Social Security and Pensions in Transition: Understanding the American Retirement System, 1980, 2d edit., 1983, Japanese edit., 1984; contbr. articles to profl. jours. Grantee, U.S. Dept. Labor, 1964-66, 66, 72-73, N.Y. C. Dept. Social Svcs., 1968, U.S. HEW, 1969-70, others. Mem. Am. Arbitration Assn., Am. Econ. Assn., History of Econs. Soc., Internat. Indsl. Rels. Assn., Indsl. Rels. Rsch. Assn. (N.Y.C. chpt. pres. 1980-81), Metro. Econ. Assn. N.Y.C. (sec. 1959-63, pres. 1976-77), Soc. of Profls. in Dispute Resolution, Soc. of Fed. Labor Rels. Profls., Nat. Acad. Social Ins. Office: New York Univ 269 Mercer St Fl 7 New York NY 10003-6633

STEIN, ELLEN COHEN, school administrator; b. N.Y.C., Oct. 22, 1947; d. Paul A. and Carol (Reichenbach) Cohen; m. David F. Stein, Sept. 6, 1973; children: Katharine, Nicholas; 1 stepchild, Jeremy. BA, U. Pa., 1969; MBA, Columbia U., 1972. Cert. elem. tchr., N.Y. Rsch. asst. Internat. Basic Economy Corp., N.Y.C., 1969-70; assoc. corp. fin. Donaldson, Lufkin & Jenrette, N.Y.C., 1972-74; tchr. The Brearley Sch., N.Y.C., 1974-78; dir. admissions Friends Sem., N.Y.C., 1979-85, dir. devel., 1985-89, vice prin., 1989—. Mem. Friends of Channel 13, N.Y.C., 1977-79, Parents League N.Y., 1978-79. Mem. Assn. Tchrs. in Ind. Schs., Ind. Sch. Admissions Assn. of Greater N.Y., Cosmopolitan Club. Home: 875 Park Ave New York NY 10021-0341

STEIN, JACOB, computer programmer, analyst; b. N.Y.C., Aug. 20, 1960; s. Lewis and Ann (Orth) Epple; m. Sara Wallach, Aug. 18, 1981. Student, Kazon Ish Rabbinical Inst., 1981-86; cert. programmer, Cope Inst., 1988. Programmer Eastern Systems, Bklyn., 1988-90, Presidential Life, N.Y.C., 1990—. Republican. Jewish. Home: 19 Homestead Ln Monsey NY 10952-3319 Office: Presidential Life 69 Lydecker St Nyack NY 10960-2199

STEIN, JANET LEE, molecular biology educator, researcher; b. Danville, Pa., Apr. 3, 1946; d. Mark Leroy and Arlene Amelia (Stehr) Swinehart; m. Gary Stephen Stein, Feb. 2, 1974. BS in Chemistry, Elizabethtown Coll., 1968; MA in Chemistry, Princeton U., 1971, PhD in Chemistry, 1975. Teaching asst. dept. chemistry Princeton (N.J.) U., 1968-69, NSF predoctoral trainee, 1969, NIH predoctoral fellow, 1969-73; vis. grad. student U. Fla. Coll. Medicine, Gainesville, 1971-74, rsch. assoc. dept. biochemistry and molecular biology, 1974-76, asst. prof. dept. immunology and med. microbiology, 1976-82, assoc. prof., 1982-86, prof., 1986-87; prof. dept. cell biology U. Mass. Med. Ctr., Worcester, 1987—; ad hoc grant reviewer NSF, 1982—; ad hoc mem. biomed. scis. study sect. NIH, Bethesda, Md., 1984-86, mem. physiol. chemistry study sect., 1985-90, chmn. 1988-90. Editor: Methods in Cell Biology Series, 1977-78, Recombinant DNA and Cell Proliferation, Histone Genes, 1984, Histones and Other Basic Nuclear Proteins, 1989, Critical Rev. Eukaryotic Gene Expression, 1990—; contbr. articles on molecular and cell biology to sci. jours. Recipient O.F. Stambaugh Chemistry Alumni award Elizabethtown Coll., 1980, Educate for Svc. through Profl. Achievement award, 1983. Mem. AAAS, Am. Soc. for Cell Biology, Am. Chem. Soc., Internat. Cell Cycle Soc., Am. Soc. for Microbiology, Am. Soc. Biochemistry and Molecular Biology. Home: 11 Rice St Shrewsbury MA 01545-5038 Office: U Mass Med Ctr 55 Lake Ave N Worcester MA 01655-0001

STEIN, MARK ANDREW, lawyer; b. Boston, Dec. 19, 1958; s. Samuel Wolf and Elaine Isabel (Shelnitz) S.; m. Alisa Andrea Harding. BA summa cum laude, Yale U., 1980; JD cum laude, Harvard U., 1984. Bar: Mass., U.S. Dist. Ct. Mass. Teaching asst. Harvard Law Sch., 1984; atty. Choate, Hall & Stewart, Boston, 1984-86; asst. counsel region I EPA, Boston, 1986—. Alumni advisor Harvard Law Sch., 1985—; alumni interviewer Yale Coll. Admissions Com., Hew Haven, 1984-89. Mem. Mass. Bar Assn., Essex County Group, Sierra Club, Phi Beta Kappa.

STEIN, MARSHA E., marketing and fashion merchandising educator; b. N.Y.C., Aug. 13, 1948; d. Abraham E. and Lillian I. (Gordon) Polonsky; m. Alan H. Stein, Feb. 1, 1969; 1 child, Audrey Beth. BA, Queens Coll., 1969; MA, NYU, 1972. Tchr. home econs. Parsons Jr. High Sch., Flushing, N.Y., 1969; asst. editor home econs. Macmillan Co., N.Y.C., 1969-71; mng. editor Fawcett Publs., N.Y.C., 1971-73, Simplicity Pattern Co., N.Y.C., 1973; ednl. coord. Stacy Fabrics Corp., N.Y.C., 1973-74; assoc. prof. Teikyo Post U., Waterbury, Conn., 1975—. Editor: Women's Day Knit and Stitch mag., 1971-73; contbr. Chavurah Community newspaper, 1980—. Bd. dirs. Waterbury Community Religious Sch., 1981-88, Waterbury High Sch. Hebrew Studies, 1988—; mem. Soviet Resettlement com. Jewish Fedn. Waterbury, 1978—. Mem. AAUP, Am. Mktg. Assn., Internat. Textile and Apparel Assn., Hadassah, Omicron Nu. Democrat. Home: 452 Farmington Ave Waterbury CT 06710-1228 Office: Teikyo Post U Box 2540 800 Country Club Rd Waterbury CT 06723-2540

STEIN, MARTIN ALEXANDER, marketing company executive; b. Kansas City, Mo., Dec. 13, 1951; s. Martin and Suzanne Marion (Heim) S.; m. Nancy Jane Taylor, June 5, 1982; children: Chelsea Elizabeth, Zachary Lane. BS, U. Dubuque, 1973. Salesman Current & Casual Men's Wear, New Rochelle, N.Y., 1973-75; v.p. Current & Casual Men's Wear, New Rochelle, 1975-80; account exec. Walter Karl Inc., Armonk, N.Y., 1980-82, v.p., 1982-85; ptnr., exec. v.p. RMI Direct Mktg. Inc., Hawthorne, N.Y., 1985—. Mem. Direct Mktg. Assn., Washington Direct Mktg. Assn., Midwest Direct Mktg. Assn., Club 101 (N.Y.C.), Trout Unltd. Republican. Unitarian.

STEIN, MELVIN A., accountant; b. N.Y.C., Sept. 7, 1932; s. William H. and Lillian (Goldberg) S.; m. Barbara Blumencranz, Dec. 17, 1955 (dec. Dec. 1988); children: Susan, Karen. BS, NYU, 1953. Pvt. practice acctg., Jericho, N.Y., 1961-75; pres. Stein & Stein, P.C., Hicksville, N.Y., 1975-81, Stein, Stein & Feit, P.C., Hicksville, 1982—. Bd. dirs. Stern Sch. Bus. NYU, 1990-91, 91-92, treas., 1991-92. Mem. AICPA, N.Y. State Soc. CPAs, N.J. Soc. CPAs, C.W. Post Tax Inst, NYU Club, Princeton Club. Jewish. Home: 7 Ingleside Ln White Plains NY 10605 Office: Stein Stein & Feit PC 1 Frederick Pl Hicksville NY 11801 also: Buccaneer Mall Saint Thomas VI 00801

STEIN, MICHAEL DAVID, psychologist; b. N.Y.C., Oct. 26, 1942; s. Barnet and Estelle A. (Fidell) S.; m. Cecile L. Gross, June 12, 1967; children: Peter, Nathanael. BS, CCNY, 1963, PhD, 1974. Lic. psychologist, N.Y. Supervising psychologist The Children's Village, Dobbs Ferry, N.Y., 1974-78; dir. psychology Hall-Brooke Hosp., Westport, Conn., 1979-81; chief psychologist Elmhurst (N.Y.) Hosp. Ctr., 1981-89; chief psychologist and chief psychiatry clinic Lenox Hill Hosp., N.Y.C., 1989—; pvt. practice N.Y.C and Hartsdale, 1975—. Author: (with others) Therapies for Adolescents, 1982. Mem. APA, Internat. Neuropsychol. Soc., N.Y. State Psychol. Assn. Office: 140 E Hartsdale Ave # 1D Hartsdale NY 10530-3305 also: 130 E 77th St # 327 New York NY 10021

STEIN, MILTON MICHAEL, lawyer, regulator; b. N.Y.C., Sept. 18, 1936; s. Isidore and Sadie (Lefkowitz) S.; m. Jacqueline Martin, June 17, 1962; children: April, Alicia. AB, Columbia U., 1958, LLB, 1961. Bar: N.Y. 1962, Pa. 1971, U.S. Supreme Ct. 1971. Asst. dist. atty. N.Y. County, 1962-67; sr. counsel Nat. Commn. for Reform of Fed. Criminal Law, Washington, 1967-70; asst. dist. atty., chief of appeals City of Phila., 1970-73; asst. dir. Nat. Wire Tapping Commn., Washington, 1973-75; dir. D.C. Law Revision, Washington, 1975-77; spl. asst. HUD, Washington, 1977-79; asst. gen. counsel U.S. Commodity Futures Trading Commn., Washington, 1979-83; v.p. N.Y. Futures Exch., N.Y.C., 1983-89, N.Y. Stock Exch., N.Y.C., 1989—. Mem. ABA, N.Y. State Bar Assn., Assn. of Bar of City of N.Y. Democrat. Jewish. Home: 3001 Henry Hudson Pky Bronx NY 10463-4717

STEIN, PAUL ARTHUR, financial services executive; b. St. Louis, Aug. 20, 1937; s. Harry Arthur and Julia (Vandivort) S.; m. Ann Garwood, Oct. 8, 1960; children: Valerie Suzanne, Paul Garwood. AB, Dartmouth U., 1959. From trainee to mktg. dir. nat. sales Merrill Lynch, N.Y.C. and Princeton, 1959—; dir., officer VPI, Inc. Mem. Beacon Hill Club (Summit, N.J.), N.J. Ctr. for Visual Arts (officer and trustee), Securities Industry Inst. (former trustee). Episcopalian.

STEIN, RALPH MICHAEL, law educator, lawyer, arbitrator, consultant; b. Far Rockaway, N.Y., July 14, 1943; s. Siegfried and Ruth (Spier) S.; m. Susan Heineman, Feb. 23, 1969 (div. Aug. 1982); m. Marla B. Rubin, Oct. 31, 1982; 1 child, Theodore Alan Rubin. BA, New Sch. Social Rsch., 1971; JD, Hofstra U., 1974. Assoc. Skadden, Arps, Slate, Meagher & Flom, N.Y.C., 1974-75; vis. prof. law Syracuse U., N.Y., 1975-76; prof. law Pace U. Sch. Law, White Plains, N.Y., 1976—; spl. counsel for med. malpractice legislation to lt. gov. N.Y. State, 1982-85; chief hearing officer Greenburgh Police Dept., N.Y., 1982—; cons. to hosps., nursing schs., 1975—. Co-author: Comparative Negligence, 1984; also law rev. articles on legal history, constl. law, torts, criminal law, historic preservation. Contbg. editor Real Estate Law Jour., 1984-91. Producer, moderator TV show: You and the Law, 1971-74. Investigator U.S. Senate Subcom. on Constl. Rights, Washington, 1970-71; mem. legal com. Anti-Defamation League, Westchester County, N.Y., 1984—, Westchester chpt. ACLU, 1984—. Served to capt. U.S. Army, 1965-68. Pace U. grantee, 1979, 81-83, 85, 87-88, 91-92. Mem. Soc. Am. Law Profs., Westchester County Med. Soc. (legal affairs com.), Am. Soc. Legal History, Am. Soc. Law and Medicine, Civil War Roundtable N.Y., Navy League of U.S., Am. Civil Liberties Union. Democrat. Avocations: books, Civil War, cooking, travel, classical music and opera. Office: Pace U Sch Law 78 N Broadway White Plains NY 10603-3796

STEIN, RICHARD JAMES, polymer chemist; b. Palmerton, Pa., Aug. 10, 1930; s. Luther Samuel and Olive Hilda (Handwerk) S.; m. Clare Mary Reardon, Sept. 7, 1953. BS, Pa. State U., 1958; MS, U. Akron, 1960, PhD, 1967. Lab. helper N.J. Zinc Co. Pa., Palmerton, 1952-54; chemist Goodyear Tire & Rubber Co., Akron, Ohio, 1960-63, sr. chemist, 1967-71; polymer specialist GE, Schenectady, 1971-88; chief chemist Insulating Materials, Inc., Schenectady, 1988—. Staff sgt. U.S. Army, 1948-52, Korea. Mem. AAAS, Am. Chem. Soc., Alpha Chi Sigma. Office: Insulating Materials Inc 1 Campbell Rd Schenectady NY 12306

STEIN, RICHARD JAY, consulting company executive; b. N.Y.C., Jan. 22, 1946; s. Murray and Bessie (Yarowitz) S. SB, Mass. Inst. Tech., 1967; MS, Poly. Inst. Bklyn., 1970, PhD, 1972. Scientist Nat. Bur. of Standards, Gaithersburg, Md., 1972-76; mem. tech. staff Tex. Instruments, Dallas, 1976-80; sr. scientist GTE Corp., Waltham, Mass., 1980-81; owner Stein Co., Stow, Mass., 1981-82; mgr., R & D Balzers Corp., Hudson, N.H., 1982-84; sr. scientist Perkin-Elmer Corp., Norwalk, Conn., 1984-86; owner R. J. Stein Assocs., West Redding, Conn., 1986—. Patentee in field; contbr. articles to profl. jours. Home: 61 Whortleberry Rd West Redding CT 06896-1302 Office: PO Box 252 West Redding CT 06896-0252

STEIN, ROBERT ELIHU, lawyer, educator; b. N.Y.C., Feb. 12, 1939; s. Joseph Max and Sadie (Spiritos) S.; m. Jane Jacobson, Sept. 6, 1965; children: Stephanie, Jeremy. BA, Brandeis U., 1960; LLB, Columbia U., 1963; diploma, Hague Acad. Internat. Law, Netherlands, 1964. Bar: N.Y. 1964, D.C. 1971. Atty. adviser U.S. Arms Control and Disarmament Agy., Washington, 1966-68, U.S. Dept. State, Washington, 1969-72; acting dir. studies Am. Soc. Internat. Law, Washington, 1972-74; dir. Internat. Inst. Environ. and Devel., Washington, 1974-78; pres. Environ. Mediation Internat., Washington, 1978-90; mem. Blicker Futterman & Stein, Attys. at Law, Washington, 1991—; adj. prof. law Georgetown U., Washington, 1984—; mem. group legal experts World Commn. on Environ. and Devel., Geneva, 1987. Co-author: Banking on the Biosphere, 1978; contbr. to legal and policy jours. Mem. AIDS com. Union of Hebrew Congregations, 1990—. Mem. ABA (AIDS com. 1990—), Am. Law Inst. Office: Blicker Futterman & Stein 1919 Pennsylvania Ave NW Ste 200 Washington DC 20006

STEIN, STEVEN ANDREW, commercial real estate agent; b. Phila., July 28, 1960; s. Norman Stein and Barbara Sandra (Sager) Lee. BA, San Francisco State U., 1981. Lic. real estate agt., Md., D.C. Mgr. Hyatt Hotels, San Francisco, L.A., 1979-85, Chart House Restaurants, San Diego, San Francisco, 1985-87; comml. acct. exec. Silver Carpet, Washington, 1987-89; assoc. Long & Foster Comml. Real Estate, Washington, 1989—. Contbr. articles to profl. jours. Patron Johns Hopkins Children's Hosp., Balt., 1989-91; vol. Help the Homeless Project, Washington, 1990-91, Spl. Olympics, Washington, 1991; patron Shakespeare Theatre at the Folger, Washington, 1990-91. Named Top Rookie Producer, Long & Foster Real Estate, 1990, Sectional Champion, Mid-Atlantic Tennis Assn., 1990. Mem. U.S. Tennis Assn., The Comml. Network, Mid-Atlantic Volleyball Assn., Nat. Capital YMCA. Office: Long & Foster Real Estate 1130 Connecticut Ave NW Ste 600 Washington DC 20036-3910

STEIN, STEVEN HAL, physician; b. Opelika, Ala., Apr. 20, 1956; s. Melvin and Joan (Sherrow) S.; m. Ann Candy, June 1, 1985; 1 child, David. BS, MIT, 1978; MD, U. Conn., 1982. Diplomate Am. Bd. Emergency Medicine, Am. Bd. Med. Examiners. Resident Med. Coll. Pa., Phila., 1982-85, clin. instr., 1988-89; physician Nat. Health Svc. Corp., Vt., 1985-86, Rutland (Vt.) Regional Med. Ctr., 1987-88, 1989—. Instr. advanced cardiac life support Am. Heart Assn., 1984—. Fellow Am. Coll. Emergency Physicians (pres. Vt. chpt. 1992, council rep. 1987). Home: Rte 1 PO Box 3995 Rutland Town VT 05701 Office: Rutland Regional Med Ctr Allen St Rutland VT 05701

STEIN, SUSAN ALYSON, museum exhibitions administrator; b. N.Y.C., Jan. 23, 1956; d. Alfred Eugene and Estelle (Joseph) Stein; m. Robert David Burwasser, June 2, 1985; 1 child, Alex Kyle Burwasser. Student, William Smith Coll., Geneva, N.Y., 1974-75; BA, SUNY, Binghamton, 1978, MA, 1980. Teaching asst. SUNY, Binghamton, N.Y., 1978-80; research asst. The Solomon R. Guggenheim Mus., N.Y.C., 1981; research asst. The Met. Mus., N.Y.C., 1981-85, research assoc., exhbn. coord., 1985-88, spl. exhbn. coord., 1988-89, spl. exhbns. assoc., 1989—; cons. in field; evaluator in field. Editor: Van Gogh: A Retrospective, 1986; co-editor: Album Amicorum Kenneth C. Lindsay Essays on Art and Literature, 1990; co-author: (mus. catalogues) Seurat, 1859-1891, 1991, Treasures from the Metropolitan Museum of Art: Aspects of French Art, 1989, From Delacroix to Matisse, 1988, Capolavori Impressionisti dei Musei Americani, 1986, others. Recipient Creative Work in the Fine Arts award, SUNY-Binghamton, 1978. Mem. Coll. Art Assn., Phi Beta Kappa. Home: 39 E 12th St New York NY 10003-4619 Office: The Metropolitan Mus of Art Fifth Ave and 82nd St New York NY 10028

STEINAU, LESLIE, lawyer; b. N.Y.C., May 27, 1943; s. Leslie Jr. and Edith (Mann) S.; m. Suzanne Joy Brooks, May 16, 1976; children: Andrew, James. BA, Cornell U., 1965; JD, Union U., Albany, N.Y., 1968; LLM in Taxation, NYU, 1969. Bar: N.Y. 1968. Mem. Parker Duryee Rosoff & Haft, P.C., N.Y.C., 1969—. Trustee YM-YWHA Mid-Westchester, Scarsdale, N.Y., 1983-88; bd. advisors MRA Coun., Washington, 1992—. Mem. ABA (com. on authors sect. patent, trademark and copyright law), Copyright Soc. U.S.A., Assn. of Bar of City of N.Y. (copyright and literary property com. 1984-87), Cornell Alumni Assn. Ambs. Network. Office: Parker Duryee Rosoff & Haft 529 Fifth Ave New York NY 10017

STEINBERG, ANDREW DAVID, business development executive; b. Morristown, N.J., July 1, 1957; s. Eliot and Judith (Silverstein) S. BBA, Coll. William and Mary, 1979. Account mgr. Master Design Corp., Morris Plains, N.J., 1981-82, NPS Automation Svcs., Morris Plains, 1982-83; nat. sales mgr. NPS Automation Svcs., 1983-85; v.p. mktg. and adminstrn. Nat. CADD Svcs., 1986-88; v.p. bus. devel. Nat. CADD Svcs., Secaucus, N.J., 1989-91; v.p. bus. devel. and adminstrn. East Coast Svcs., 1991—; cons. in field. Capt. U.S. Rugby Team, 1985, mem., 1989. Mem. Morris Rugby Club. (capt. 1985, 86). Jewish. Office: East Coast Svcs Group 14 Midvale Ave Lake Hiawatha NJ 07034-1011

STEINBERG, HERBERT JOSEPH, psychiatrist; b. N.Y.C., Dec. 7, 1929; s. Max and Rose (Dicker) S.; m. Mary Bugna, Oct. 8, 1955; children: Bruce, Stephen, Neil. AB, Columbia Coll., 1952; MD, NYU, 1956. Diplomate Am. Bd. Psychiatry and Neurology. Intern in medicine Kings County Hosp., Bklyn., 1956-57, resident in psychiatry, 1957-58; resident in psychiatry Hillside Hosp., Glen Oaks, N.Y., 1960-62, fellow in child psychiatry, 1962-64; candidate N.Y. Psychoanalytic Inst., N.Y.C., 1964-70; pvt. practice Great Neck, N.Y., 1962—; attending psych. cons. liaison svc. L.I. Jewish Hosp., New Hyde Park, N.Y., 1971—; staff North Shore Univ. Hosp., Glen Cove, N.Y., 1979—; asst. prof. clin. psychiatry Albert Einstein Coll. Medicine, 1989—. Contbr. articles to profl. jours. Capt. U.S. Army, 1958-60. Fellow Am. Psychiat. Assn., Nassau Acad. of Medicine; mem. Nassau Psychiatry Soc. (pres. 1982-83), Acad. of Psychosomatic Medicine, Am. Psychosomatic Soc., Nassau County Med. Assn., N.Y. State Med. Assn. Office: 17 Barstow Rd Great Neck NY 11021-2213

STEINBERG, JOSEPH, statistician, consultant; b. N.Y.C., Mar. 22, 1920; s. Solomon and Sophie (Sauer) S.; m. Ruth Mildred Cohen, Oct. 30, 1949; children: Steven L., Seth M. BS, CCNY, 1939. Statistician population div. Census Bur., Washington, 1940-42; sr. statistician statis. rsch. div. Census Bur., Suitland, Md., 1944-45, chief sampling br. population div., 1945-59, chief statis. methods div., 1959-63; prin. statistician Social Security Bd., Washington, 1942-44, chief math. statistician, 1963-72; asst. commr. Bur.

Labor Stats., Washington, 1972-75; pres. Survey Design, Inc., Silver Spring, Md., 1975—; instr. stats. USDA Grad. Sch., Washington, 1942-74; mem. Assembly of Behavioral and Social Scis. NAS/NRC, Washington, 1971-77, mem. Com. on Fed. Agy. EvaluationRsch., 1971-75, Com. on Energy Consumption Measurement, 1975-77, mem. Com. on Evaluation Rsch. Social Sci. Rsch. Coun., N.Y.C., 1977-80. Contbr. articles to profl. jours., chpts. to books. Recipient Meritorious Svc. award U.S. Dept. Commerce, 1955, Commr.'s citation Social Security Adminstrn., 1965, Disting. Svc. award HEW, 1968. Fellow AAAS, Am. Statis. Assn.; mem. Inst. Math. Stats., Phi Beta Kappa.

STEINBERG, LAURENCE, psychology educator; b. Long Branch, N.J., July 8, 1952; s. Irwin I. and Mollie (Deutsch) S.; m. Wendy Brodhead, Aug. 27, 1982; 1 child, Benjamin. AB, Vassar Coll., 1974; PhD, Cornell U., 1977. Asst. to assoc. prof. U. Calif., irvine, 1977-83; prof. U. Wis., Madison, 1983-88, Temple U., Phila., 1988—; cons. Carnegie Corp., N.Y.C., 1987—, W.T. Grant Found., N.Y.C., 1989—. Author: You and Your Adolescent, 1990, Adolescence, 1989, When Teenagers Work, 1985, Infancy, Childhood and Adolescence, 1991; contbr. articles to profl. jours. Faculty scholar W.T. Grant Found., 1983; recipient faculty excellence award U. Wis., 1988. Mem. Phi Beta Kappa. Office: Dept Psychology Temple U Philadelphia PA 19122

STEINBERG, LEO, art historian, educator; b. Moscow, July 9, 1920; came to U.S., 1945; s. Isaac N. and Anna (Esselson) S. Ph.D., NYU Inst Fine Arts, 1960; Ph.D. (hon.), Phila. Coll. Art, 1981, Parsons Sch. Design, 1986, Mass. Coll. Art, 1987. Assoc. prof. art history Hunter Coll., CUNY, N.Y.C., 1961-66, prof., 1966-75; prof. Grad. Ctr. CUNY, 1969-75; Benjamin Franklin prof. art. history U. Pa., Phila., 1975-91, prof. emeritus, 1991—. Author: Other Criteria, 1972, Michelangelo's Last Paintings, 1975, Borromini's San Carlo alle Quattro Fontane, 1977, The Sexuality of Christ in Renaissance Art and in Modern Oblivion, 1983. Recipient award in lit. Am. Acad. and Inst. Arts and Letters, 1983; fellow Am. Acad. Arts and Scis., 1978, Univ. Coll., London U., 1979, MacArthur Found., 1986; recipient Frank Jewett Mather award, 1956, 84. Mem. Coll. Art Assn. Am. Office: U Pa 3440 Market St Ste 560 Philadelphia PA 19104-6311

STEINBERG, MALCOLM SAUL, biologist, educator; b. New Brunswick, N.J., June 1, 1930; s. Morris and Esther (Lerner) S.; children—Jeffery, Julie, Eleanor, Catherine; m. Marjorie Campbell, 1983. B.A., Amherst Coll., 1952; M.A., U. Minn., 1954, Ph.D., 1956. Postdoctoral fellow dept. embryology Carnegie Instn., Washington, 1956-58; asst. prof. Johns Hopkins, Balt., 1958-64; assoc. prof. Johns Hopkins, 1964-66; prof. biology Princeton U., 1966-90, Henry Fairfield Osborn prof. biology, 1975—, prof. molecular biology, 1990—; instr.-in-charge embryology course Marine Biol. Lab., 1967-71, trustee, 1969-77; chmn. Gordon Research Conf. on Cell Contact and Adhesion, 1985; appointed to NAS/NRC Bd. on Biology, 1986-92. Mem. editorial bd. Bioscience, 1976-82; contbr. articles to profl. jours. Fellow AAAS; mem. AAUP, Am. Soc. Zoologists (program officer div. developmental biology 1966-69, chmn.-elect, then chmn. 1982-85), Am. Soc. Cell Biology, Internat. Soc. Developmental Biologists, Internat. Soc. Differentation, Soc. Developmental Biology (trustee, sec. 1970-73), Sigma Xi. Home: 86 Longview Dr Princeton NJ 08540-5642

STEINBERG, MELVIN ALLEN, lieutenant governor, lawyer; b. Balt., Oct. 4, 1933; s. Irvin and Julia (Levenson) S.; m. Anita Akman, 1958; children: Edward Bryan, Susan Renee, Barbara Ellen. AA, U. Balt., 1952, JD, 1955. Bar: Md. 1955. Ptnr. Steinberg Lichter Coleman & Rogers, Towson, Md., 1978-86, Levin Gann & Hankin, Towson, 1986—; mem. Md. State Senate, 1967-87, vice chmn. jud. process, 1975-79; chmn. fin. com., 1979-82, pres. of senate, 1983-87, lt. gov., Md., 1987—. Del. Dem. Nat. Conv., 1968. Mem. Am. Judicature Soc., ABA, Md. Bar Assn., Balt. Bar Assn., Nu Beta Epsilon. Democrat. Jewish. Lodges: B'nai B'rith, Masons. Home: 305 Chesapeake Ave Baltimore MD 21225-1863 Office: State House Office of Lt Gov Annapolis MD 21404*

STEINBERG, MICHAEL ALAN, meteorologist; b. N.Y.C., June 19, 1952; s. Ronald Theodore and Carolyn Ruth (Yellen) S.; m. Hilary Beth Gurner, Mar. 21, 1984; 1 child, Jordan Stephen. BS, Cornell U., 1974; MS, Pa. State U., 1976. Sr. chem. operator Alcolac, Inc., Ossining, N.Y., 1970-78; meteorologist Fleetweather, Inc., Hopewell Junction, N.Y., 1977-78; v.p. Accu-Weather, Inc., State College, Pa., 1978—, also bd. dirs. V.p., sec. Comar Bowling League, State College, 1982-85. Recipient Neuberger Award for Teaching Excellence, Pa. State U., 1976. Mem. Am. Meteorol. Soc. Office: Accu-Weather Inc 619 W College Ave State College PA 16801-3797

STEINBERG, PAUL JAY, psychiatrist; b. Norwalk, Conn., Mar. 5, 1948; s. Benjamin and Ethel (Friedman) S.; m. Helen Katz; children: Miritte, Arielle. BA, U. Pa., 1970; MD, SUNY, Bkyln., 1974. Diplomate Am. Bd. Psychiatry and Neurology. Intern U. Rochester, Rochester, N.Y., 1974-75; resident George Washington U., Washington, 1975-78; staff psychiatrist Psychiat. Inst. D.C., Washington, 1978-81; psychiatrist U. Md., College Park, 1981-89; asst. dir. counseling and psychiat. svc. Georgetown U., Washington, 1989—; coord. drug and alcohol treatment U. Md., College Park, 1981-89. Contbr. articles to profl. jours. Mem. Am. Psychiat. Assn., Am. Soc. Adolescent Psychiatry, Am. Coll. Health Assn., D.C. Med. Soc. Jewish. Office: Georgetown U Counseling and Psychiat Svc 37th and O Streets NW Washington DC 20007-3234

STEINBERG, SAUL PHILLIP, holding company executive; b. N.Y.C., Aug. 13, 1939; s. Julius and Anne (Cohen) S.; m. Barbara Herzog, May 28, 1961 (div. 1977); children: Laura, Jonothan, Nicholas; m. Laura Sconucchia, Dec. 21, 1978 (div. Dec. 1983); 1 child, Julian; m. Gayfryd McNabb, Jan. 22, 1984; children: Rayne, Holden. BS, Wharton Sch., U. Pa., 1959. Founder, chmn., chief exec. officer Reliance Group Holdings Inc., N.Y.C.; chmn. bd. dirs. Telemundo Group Inc.; chmn. exec. com. Frank B. Hall & C. Inc.; bd. dirs. Symbol Techs. Inc., Zenith Nat. Ins. Corp. Chmn. bd. overseers Wharton Sch. U. Pa.; mem. bd. overseers Cornell U. Med. Coll., N.Y.C.; trustee Jewish Med. Ctr., N.Y.C., U. Pa., N.Y. Pub. Libr. Jewish. Clubs: Glen Oaks, The Board Room (N.Y.C.). Home: 740 Park Ave New York NY 10021-4251 Office: Reliance Group Holdings Inc 55 E 52nd St New York NY 10055-0002

STEINBRENNER, GEORGE MICHAEL, III, professional baseball team executive, shipbuilding company executive; b. Rocky River, Ohio, July 4, 1930; s. Henry G. and Rita (Haley) S.; m. Elizabeth Joan Zieg, May 12, 1956; children: Henry G. III, Jennifer Lynn, Jessica Joan, Harold Zeig. BA, Williams Coll., 1952; postgrad., Ohio State U., 1954-55. Asst. football coach Northwestern U., 1955, Purdue U., 1956-67; treas. Kinsman Transit Co., Cleve., 1957-63; pres. Kinsman Marine Transit Co., Cleve., 1963-67, dir., 1965—; pres., chmn. bd. Am. Ship Bldg. Co., Cleve., 1967-78, chmn. bd., 1978—; prin. owner N.Y. Yankees, Bronx, 1973-90; limited ptnr. N.Y. Yankees, 1990—; owner Bay Harbor Inn, Tampa, Fla., 1988—; bd. dirs. Gt. Lakes Internat. Corp., Gt. Lakes Assocs., Cin. Sheet Metal & Roofing Co., Nashville Bridge Co., Nederlander-Steinbrenner Prodns. Mem. Cleve. Little Hoover Com., group chmn., 1966; chmn. Cleve. Urban Coalition; vice chmn. Greater Cleve. Growth Corp., Greater Cleve. Jr. Olympic Found. Served to 1st lt. USAF, 1952-54. Named Outstanding Young Man of Yr. Ohio Jr. C. of C., 1960, Cleve. Jr. C. of C., 1960; Chief Town Crier, Cleve., 1968; Man of Yr., Cleve. Press Club, 1968. Mem. Greater Cleve. Growth Assn. (bd. dirs.). Office: care NY Yankees Yankee Stadium Bronx NY 10451*

STEINBRICK, MARK GERARD, counselor; b. Newark, Nov. 8, 1958; s. Joseph Nicholas and Patricia (Burns) S.; m. Gay Agnes Filippone, Dec. 19, 1987. BS, U. Tampa, Fla., 1981; MS in Edn., Monmouth Coll., 1990; postgrad., Rutgers U., 1992—. Cert. tchr., N.J.; lic. counselor, N.J. Tchr. Manalapan (N.J.) High Sch., 1984-90, guidance counselor, 1990—. Mem. AACD, N.J. Assn. Counseling and Devel., Phi Delta Kappa, Pi Kappa Phi (Gold Lamp scholar 1980). Home: 21 Lakeview Ave West Long Branch NJ 07764-1315

STEINBROOK, RICHARD ALAN, anesthesiology educator; b. Phila., Mar. 20, 1951; s. Harry William and Elenore Esther (Hillerson) S.; m. Marcia Lois Weinstein, July 21, 1978; children: Hillary, Daniel. BA, U. Pa., 1972, MD, 1976. Diplomate Am. Bd. Anesthesiology. Clin. fellow Med. Sch., Harvard U., Boston, 1977-80, instr., 1980-84, asst. prof., 1984—. Mem. Am. Soc. Anesthesiologists, Am. Physiol. Soc., Internat. Anesthesia Rsch. Soc.

STEINDLER, WALTER G., lawyer; b. N.Y.C., Dec. 2, 1927; s. Mortimer B. and Ray (Feingold) S.; m. Carol A. Halpin, June 28, 1969; children: Michael, Morty, Melissa. BA, Queens Coll., 1950; JD, NYU, 1953. Bar: N.Y. 1953, U.S. Supreme Ct. 1965, U.S. Dist. Ct. (ea. dist.) N.Y. 1972, U.S. Dist. Ct. (so. dist.) 1974, U.S. Ct. Appeals (2d cir.) 1974. Ptnr. Borden Skidell Fleck & Steindler, Jamaica, N.Y., 1955-62; pvt. practice law Babylon, N.Y., 1962-67; town atty. Town of Babylon, 1967-69; asst. county atty. Suffolk County, N.Y., 1970-71; ptnr. Sarisohn, Sarisohn, Carner, Steindler, Lebow & Braun, Commack, N.Y., 1976—; capt., judge adv. 2d area command N.Y. Guard, N.Y.C., 1965-70. With U.S. Army, 1946-47. Mem. Free Sons Israel (pres. 1953), Masons. Office: Sarisohn Sarisohn Carner Steindler Lebow & Braun 350 Veterans Memorial Hwy Commack NY 11725-4330

STEINER, ANDREA LYNNE, mechanical engineer; b. Reidsville, N.C., Mar. 26, 1964; d. Herbert Carl and Patricia (Sobczyk) S. BSME, NYU, Buffalo, 1986; MSME, Rensselaer Polytech. Inst., 1988. Engr. Pratt and Whitney, East Hartford, Conn., 1986—. Mem. AIAA, Soc. Women Engrs. Roman Catholic. Home: 705 Tolland St East Hartford CT 06108-2746 Office: Pratt and Whitney 400 Main St East Hartford CT 06118-1873

STEINER, MICHAEL, sculptor; b. N.Y.C., May 12, 1945; s. Arthur and Eleanor (Perreira) S.; m. Phyllis I. Meshover, May 4, 1979. Student, Art Students League, 1964. One-man shows include Salander-O'Reilly Galleries, N.Y.C. and Berlin, Mus. of Art, Ft. Lauderdale, Fla., Mus. of Fine Arts, Boston, Andre Emmerich Gallery, N.Y.C., Meredith Long & Co., Houston, Hart House, Univ. Toronto, Norman Mackenzie Art Gallery, Regina, Sask., Galerie Wentzel, Hamburg, Germany, Dwan Gallery, N.Y.C., Fischbach Gallery, N.Y.C., numerous others; exhibited in group shows at Whitney Mus. Am. Art, N.Y.C., Univ. Mich. Mus. Art, Ann Arbor, Mus. Contemporary Art, Chgo., Grand Palais, Paris, Am. Embassy in Madrid, Inst. Contemporary Art, Phila., Larry Aldrich Mus. Contemporary Art, Ridgefield, Conn., Edmonton (Alta.) Art Gallery, Sonoma State Univ. Art Gallery, Rohnert Park, Calif., Lowe Art Gallery, Syracuse, N.Y., numerous others; represented in permanent collections including Mus. Modern Art, N.Y.C., Solomon R. Guggenheim Mus., N.Y.C., Hirshhorn Mus. and Sculpture Garden, Washington, Mus. Fine Arts, Boston, Mus. Fine Arts, Houston, Musee d'Art Moderne et d'Art Contemporain, Nice, France, Walker Art Ctr., Mpls., numerous others. Guggenheim fellow, 1971.

STEINER, MICHAEL STEVEN, real estate developer, teacher; b. N.Y.c., Apr. 3, 1950; s. Paul and Ellen Marie (Senter) S.; m. Ellen Gail Fader, Feb. l6, 1975 (div. 1980); m. Kristine Ann Williams, Oct. 16, 1986; 1 stepchild, Michael Sullivan. BA magna cum laude, Tufts U., 1972; MEd, Am. U., 1976. Cert. tchr., Md. Tchr. Fairmont Heights High Sch., Fairmont Park, Md., 1974-79; prin. real estate Va., 1979-8l, ea. region, 1981-84; real estate developer Banner Lodge Resort, Moodus, Conn., 1984—, Malleable Iron Foundry Waterfront Redevel., Branford, Conn., 1984—. Adviser yearbooks Fairmont Heights High Sch., 1974-79. Mem. Rep. Inner Circle, Washington, 1988—. Mem. Nat. Trust Hist. Preservation. Home: 10 Banner Rd # 370 Moodus CT 06469-1137 Office: Banner Lodge Resort Banner Rd Moodus CT 06469-1137

STEINER, PAUL, editor, columnist; b. Frankfurt, Germany; came to U.S., 1940; s. Otto and Bertha (Sulmann) S. BS, NYU, 1947. Editorial assoc. Esquire Inc., N.Y.C., 1947-52; syndicated columnist, corr. N.Am. Newspaper Alliance, 1955-78, Bell-McClure Syndicate, 1956-75, Women's News Svc., about 1965-72; columnist Models & Talent, 1982—, Theater Week, 1987—, Jewish Herald, 1988—, Call Back, 1989—, Car Pages mag., N.Y.C., 1990—, Big City Style, 1991—, Queens (N.Y.) Tribune, 1991—. Author 17 books, including: Israel Laughs, Humor from the Jewish State, 1950, Useless Information, 1962, Useless Facts of History, 1963, Little Known Facts About John F. Kennedy, 1964, 1001 Tips for Teens, 1967, Presidential Oddities, 1976; editor, author: The (Adlai) Stevenson Wit and Wisdom, 1965; contbg. editor Artspeak, 1979—, Show Illus., 1980-82, Jewish Jour., 1984-86, Metro Jewish LIfe, 1987—, N.Y.C. Bus. News, 1989—; contbr. articles to various publs., including Playbill, N.Y. Times Mag., N.Y. Mag., Stagebill, N.Y. Post, Parade, Family Weekly, N.Y. News (daily and Sunday edits.), People Weekly, Omni, USA Today, Met. Home, Star Mag., Reuters; columnist ASCAP Today, 1973-76, Big Apple Press, 1991—, Dramatics mag., 1991, LifeStyle, 1991—, Queens (N.Y.) Tribune, Greenwich Village Press, 1992—. With U.S. Army, 1943-45. Recipient Columnist award Beaux Arts Soc., 1969, Press award, 1970, Internat. Press award King Prodns., 1981, World Culture prize Italy Centro Studi Ricerche dell Nazione, 1985, Book Author award, 1991. Mem. Alpha Delta Sigma, Psi Chi Omega, Alpha Epsilon Pi. Office: 161 W 54th St Apt 402 New York NY 10019-5318

STEINER, ROBERT FRANK, biochemist; b. Manila, Philippines, Sept. 29, 1926; came to U.S., 1933; s. Frank and Clara Nell (Weems) S.; m. Ethel Mae Fisher, Nov. 3, 1956; children: Victoria, Laura. A.B., Princeton U., 1947; Ph.D., Harvard U., 1950. Chemist Naval Med. Research Inst., Bethesda, Md., 1950-70; chief lab. phys. biochemistry Naval Med. Research Inst., 1965-70; prof. chemistry U. Md., Balt., 1970—; chmn. dept. chemistry U. Md., 1974—, dir. grad. program in biochemistry, 1985; mem. biophysics study sect. NIH, 1976. Author: Life Chemistry, 1968, Excited States of Proteins and Nucleic Acids, 1971, The Chemistry of Living Systems, 1981, Excited States of Biopolymers, 1983; editor Jour. Biophys. Chemistry, 1972—, Jour. of Fluorescence, 1991; contbr. more than 150 artices to profl. jours. Served with AUS, 1945-47. Recipient Superior Civilian Achievement award Dept. Def., 1966; NSF rsch. grantee, 1971, NIH, 1973-89. Fellow Washington Acad. Sci., Japan Soc. for Promotion Sci.; mem. Am. Soc. Biol. Chemists. Club: Princeton (Washington). Home: 2609 Turf Valley Rd Ellicott City MD 21042-2021 Office: 5401 Wilkens Ave Baltimore MD 21228-5329

STEINER, ROGER JACOB, linguistics educator, author, researcher; b. South Byron, Wis., Mar. 27, 1924; s. Jakob Robert and Alice Mildred (Cowles) S.; m. Ida Kathryn Posey, Aug. 7, 1954 (dec. May 1992); children: David Posey, Andrew Posey. BA, Franklin & Marshall Coll., 1945; MDiv, Union Theol. Sem., 1947; MA, U. Pa., 1958, PhD, 1963. Ordained to ministry, Meth. Ch., 1947. Clergyman United Meth. Ch., N.Y., Wis., Pa., 1945—; lectr. U. Bordeaux, France, 1961-63; instr. dept. langs. & lit. U. Del., Newark, 1963-64, asst. prof., 1964-71, assoc. prof., 1971-80, prof., 1980-85; prof. dept. linguistics U. Del., Newark, 1985—; cons. Charles Scribner's Sons, N.Y.C., 1972-75, Larousse, N.Y.C., 1981-84, Houghton-Mifflin, Boston, 1981-84, Oxford U. Press, Eng., 1990; chmn. Herbert H. Lank Exchange Fellowship, U. Montreal, Can., 1973—. Author: Two Centuries of Spanish and English Bilingual Lexicography (1590-1800), 1970, New College French and English Dictionary, 1972, rev. 2nd edit. 1988; co-author: (with others) The History of Lexicography. Recipient fellowship Am. Philos. Soc., Phila., 1971, Lilly Found., Phila., 1979-81. Mem. Am. Assn. Tchrs. of French, Modern Lang. Assn. Am. (founder lexicography group, 1974-75, chmn. 1976, '77, '80, '85), Dictionary Soc. N. Am. (exec. bd.), Del. Coun. for Internat. Visitors (brochure chmn.), Phi Beta Kappa (pres. Alpha, Del. 1975-76). Republican. Office: U Del Dept Linguistics Newark DE 19716

STEINETZ, BERNARD GEORGE, JR., endocrinologist; b. Germantown, Pa., May 30, 1927; s. Bernard George Sr. and Hazel Scott (Jefferds) S.; m. Jane Rutledge Nash, June 17, 1949; children: Scott Jefferds, Ann Rutledge Steinetz Barton. AB, Princeton U., 1950; PhD, Rutgers U., 1954. Sr. scientist Warner-Chilcott Co., Morris Plains, N.J., 1954-58; sr. rsch. assoc. Warner-Lambert Rsch. Inst., Morris Plains, 1958-67; head reprod. endocrinology CIBA Pharm. Co., Summit, N.J., 1967-71; mgr. cartilage rsch. and endocrinology CIBA-Geigy Corp., Ardsley, N.Y., 1971-84; rsch. assoc. prof. NYU Med. Ctr. LEMSIP, Tuxedo, N.Y., 1984—, rsch. prof., 1991—; mem. conf. orgn. com. N.Y. Acad. Scis., N.Y.C., 1968-70. Contbr. more than 130 articles to profl. jours. Mem. Drug Utilization Rev. Coun. of the State of N.J., Trenton, 1977-86. Fellow CIBA Rsch. CIBA Pharm. Co., 1968; grantee March of Dimes, 1987-89, Morris Animal Found., 1987—. Mem. Endocrine Soc., Am. Physiol. Soc., Soc. for Study Reproduction, N.Y. Acad. Scis., Orthopaedic Rsch. Soc., Am. Diabetes Assn., Brookside Racket & Swim Club, Franklin Lakes Racket Club. Republican. Congregationalist. Home: 336 Long Bow Dr Franklin Lakes NJ 07417-2122 Office: NYU Med Ctr LEMSIP Long Meadow Rd Tuxedo Park NY 10987

STEINFELD, JEFFREY IRWIN, chemistry educator, consultant, author; b. Bklyn., July 2, 1940; s. Paul and Ann (Ravin) S. B.Sc., MIT, 1962; Ph.D., Harvard U., 1965. Postdoctoral fellow U. Sheffield, Yorkshire, Eng., 1965-66; asst. prof. chemistry MIT, Cambridge, 1966-70; assoc. prof. MIT, 1970-79, prof., 1980—; mem. sci. adv. bd. Lasertechnics, Inc., Albuquerque, 1982—. Author: Molecules & Radiation, 1974; co-author: Chemical Kinetics and Dynamics, 1989; editor: Laser and Coherence Spectroscopy, 1977, Laser-Induced Chemical Processes, 1981; co-editor: Spectrochimica Acta, 1983—; contbr. articles to profl. jours. Treas. Ward 2 Democratic Com., Cambridge, 1972-73. NSF fellow Harvard U., Cambridge, 1962-65; NSF fellow Sheffield U., 1965-66; Alfred P. Sloan Found. research fellow MIT, 1969-71; Guggenheim fellow, 1972-73. Fellow Am. Phys. Soc.; mem. AAAS, Fedn. Am. Scientists, Sigma Xi, Phi Lambda Upsilon. Jewish. Office: MIT Room 2-221 Cambridge MA 02139

STEINHARDT, NANCY SHATZMAN, art historian, educator; b. St. Louis, July 14, 1954; d. Ben and Miriam (Levin) Shatzman; m. Paul Joseph Steinhardt; children: Charles, Joseph, William. AB, Washington U., 1974; AM, Harvard U., 1975, PhD, 1981. Lectr. Bryn Mawr (Pa.) Coll., 1981-83; lectr. art history U. Pa., Phila., 1982-86, asst. prof., 1986-91, assoc. prof. Asian and Middle Eastern studies, 1991—. Author: Chinese Imperial City Planning, 1990, Chinese Traditional Architecture, 1984; contbr. articles to profl. jours. Grantee Am. Philos. Soc., 1992, Getty Sr. Fellowship, 1990, Am. Coun. Learned Socs., 1984, 89, Graham Found., 1989, NEH, 1983, Fulbright-Hays, 1976-77. Mem. Coll. Art Assn., Assn. Asian Studies, Soc. Archtl. Historians. Home: 1000 Cedargrove Rd Wynnewood PA 19096-2006 Office: Dept Asian & Middle Eastern Studies U Pa Philadelphia PA 19104-6305

STEINHAUER, GILLIAN, lawyer; b. Aylesbury, Bucks, Eng., Oct. 6, 1938; d. Eric Frederick and Maisie Kathleen (Yeates) Pearson; m. Bruce William Steinhauer, Jan. 2, 1960; children: Alison (Humphrey) Eric, John, Elspeth. AB cum laude, Bryn Mawr (Pa.) Coll., 1959; JD cum laude, U. Mich., 1976. Bar: Mich. 1976, U.S. Dist. Ct. (ea. dist.) Mich. 1976, U.S. Ct. Appeals (6th cir.), 1982. Assoc. Miller, Canfield, Paddock & Stone, Detroit, 1976-82, sr. ptnr., 1983-92; dir. Commonwealth of Mass. Workers' Compensation Def. Unit, Boston, 1992—. Chancellor Cath. Ch. St. Paul, Detroit, 1976-83, 91; pres. bd. trustees Cath. Community Svcs., Inc., 1989-92; bd. dirs. Spaulding for Children, 1991—. Fellow Mich. State Bar Found.; mem. ABA, State Bar of Mich., Fed. Bar Assn., Fed. Jud. Conf. 6th Cir. (life), Assn. Def. Trial Counsel, Women Lawyers Assn., Detroit Club, Bryn Mawr Club (pres. 1970-91). Home: 510 Hale St Prides Crossing MA 01965 Office: Miller Canfield Paddock and Stone 150 W Jefferson Ste # 2500 Detroit MI 48226

STEINHAUSEN, THEODORE BEHN, JR., manufacturing executive; b. Rochester, N.Y., Dec. 21, 1942; s. Theodore B. and Jane (Wolcott) S.; m. Mary Jo Lucas, July 14, 1965; children: Amy, Ted. BA, Hobart Coll., 1965; MBA, U. Pa., 1967. Market rsch. specialist profl. comml. and indsl. div. Eastman Kodak Co., Rochester, 1967-69, bus. rsch. specialist radiography markets div., 1969-70, market mgr. Washington radiography markets div., 1970-73, mktg. edn. specialist health scis. div., 1973-75, devel. assignment mgr. fin. and adminstrn. div., 1975-76, worldwide mktg. planner, 1981-83, mktg. planner for dental instruments, 1983-86, dir. dental markets, 1986—; program dir. mktg. edn. ctr. health scis. div. Eastman Kodak Co., London, 1976-77; med. and indsl. markets mktg. dir. health scis. div. Europe Eastman Kodak Co., 1977-82, U.S. div. planning dir. health scis. bus. unit, 1982-85, worldwide planning dir. health scis. bus. unit, 1985-89, dir. bus. devel. dental diagnostic bus. unit, 1989—. Bd. dirs. Hillside Children's Ctr., Rochester, 1987-88; advisor Boy Scouts Am., Rochester, 1987—; dir. Pittsford (N.Y.) Soccer Club, 1983—. Named Eagle Scout Boy Scouts Am., 1957. Mem. ADA, Am. Acad. Dental Radiology, Am. Mktg. Assn., ASTM. Republican. Presbyterian. Clubs: University; Ski Valley (Naples, N.Y.). Home: 6 Sugarwood Dr Pittsford NY 14534-3524 Office: Eastman Kodak Corp 343 State St Rochester NY 14650-0001

STEINHURST, WILLIAM, utilites executive, statistician; b. Boston, Nov. 15, 1947; s. Hyman J. and Josephine (Goldman) S.; m. Susan Elise Andersen, Dec. 28, 1968; children: Daniel, Sarah, Joshua, Benjamin. BA, Wesleyan U., 1970; MS, U. Vt., 1980, PhD, 1988. Dir. planning and rsch. Vt. Dept. Corrections, Waterbury, 1974-77; dir. planning and evaluation Vt. Dept. Social & Rehab. Svcs., Waterbury, 1977-79; dir. planning Vt. Agy. Human Svcs., Waterbury, 1979-81; econometrician Vt. Dept. Pub. Svc., Montpelier, 1981-86; dir. planning Vt. Dept. Pub. Svc., 1986—; statis. and energy cons.; stats. instr. U. Vt., Burlington, 1977-89, Adelphi U., L.I., 1980-88. Editor Internat. System Dynamics Soc. Bibliography, 1990—; contbg. editor Current Index to Stats., 1976-85. Sec. Vt. Girl Scout Coun., Essex Junction, Vt., 1989-92, sec., 1992—. Mem. Am. Statis. Assn., Internat. System Dynamics Soc., Tau Beta Pi. Office: Vt Dept Pub Svc 120 State St Montpelier VT 05620-0001

STEINLE, RUSSELL JOSEPH, marine engineering manager; b. N.Y.C., Nov. 23, 1950; s. Russell Logan and Estelle (Shannon) S.; m. Marie Turtora, July 8, 1978; children: Mark, Mia. BS in Aerospace Engring., Polytechic U., N.Y., 1971, MS in Applied Mechanics, 1975. Engring. supr. Gibbs & Cox, Inc., N.Y.C., 1972-81; project engr. Exxon Internat. Co., Florham Park, N.J., 1981-84; mgr. Westinghouse MTD, Pitts., 1984—. Mem. Soc. Naval Architects and Marine Engrs., Am. Soc. Naval Engrs. Unitarian Universalist. Office: Westinghouse MTD PO Box 18249 Pittsburgh PA 15236-0249

STEINMAN, GARY DAVID, physician; b. Detroit, June 1, 1941; s. Morris and Mildred Steinman; children: Jessica, Allegra, Ahuvah, Schuyler, Moriah, Jeremiah, Breana. BS, Mich. State U., 1963, MS, 1963; PhD, U. Calif., 1965; MD, U. Miami, 1973. Diplomate Nat. Bd. Med. Examiners, Am. Bd. Ob-Gyn. Resident in ob-gyn Dept. Ob-Gyn Albert Einstein Affiliated Hosps., N.Y.C., 1974-77; pvt. practice Astoria, N.Y., 1977—; pres. David Diagnostics, Inc., Astoria, 1984—. Scholar Elks Nat. Found., 1959-60, Disting. Alumni scholar, 1959-63, Wheeler Found., 1963-64, NSF, 1964-66. Fellowship NSF, 1964-66, Wheeler Found., 1963-64; Disting. Alumni scholarship 1959-63, Elks Nat. Found. scholarship 1959-60. Office: 4601 Broadway Long Island City NY 11103-1627

STEINMANN, DERICK OTIS, publisher; b. Colon, Panama, Dec. 3, 1943; s. Frederick S. and Viola (Otis) S.; B.A., Bowdoin Coll., 1964; M.S., Purdue U., 1967; Ph.D., Bowling Green State U., 1972; m. Marcia M. Bradley, 1966; children—David Barron, Victor Werner. Instr., Western Ill. State U., Macomb, 1966-67; research assoc. Inst. of Behavioral Sci., Boulder, Colo., 1972-74; research assoc. Met. Life, N.Y.C., 1974-76; chmn. bd. The Bond Buyer and American Banker, N.Y.C., 1976—; dir. Internat. Thomson Orgn., Inc. Mem. Am. Psychol. Assn., Young Presidents Orgn., Board Room. Office: Bond Buyer 1 State Street Pla New York NY 10004

STEINMETZ, PHILIP ROLF, membrane biologist; b. DeBilt, The Netherlands, June 10, 1927; came to U.S., 1955; s. Philip Christiaan and Johanna P. (Wagner) S.; m. Micheline Osmont, Apr. 14, 1955; children: Jan-Philip, Mark Christopher. BA, Rijnlands Lyceum, Wassenaar, The Netherlands, 1945; MD, Leiden U., The Netherlands, 1951, ScD, 1975. Cert. Nephrologist. Instr. medicine NYU Sch. Med., N.Y.C., 1961-65; from asst. prof. to assoc. prof. medicine Harvard Med. Sch., Boston, 1965-73; prof. medicine U. Iowa Sch. Medicine, Iowa City, 1973-81, U. Conn. Sch. Medicine, Farmington, 1981—; study sect. gen. medicine B mem. NIH, Bethesda, Md., 1977-81; rsch. oversight com. U. Conn. Sch. Medicine, Farmington, 1990—; mem. editorial bd. Jour. Gen. Physiology, N.Y.C., 1986-90. Author: (with others) H+ Transport in Model Epithelia, 1991—; lectr. in field. Pres. Netherlands-Am. Acad. Cir., Boston, 1970-71. Recipient Homer Smith award N.Y. Heart and Am. Soc. Nephrology, 1985, Career Devel. award NIH, 1964-73, Josiah Macy Faculty award, 1978-79; NIH grantee 1969—. Mem. Am. Soc. Clin. Inv., Soc. for Gen. Physiol., Assn. Am. Physicians. Home: 211 N Beacon St Hartford CT 06105-2246 Office: Univ Conn Health Ctr Dept Medicine Farmington CT 06030

STEINMEYER, CHARLES HENRY, clinical psychologist; b. Charleroi, Pa., Aug. 2, 1941; s. Wilmer Henry and Minnie Louise (Glennon) S.; m. Sarah M. Jamison, Apr. 21, 1968 (div. Dec. 1979); children: Randall Henry, Freya Margaret; m. Pauline Louise Demel, Feb. 14, 1981. BS in Physics, Carnegie Mellon U., 1963; PhD in Psychology, Ind. U., 1968. Lic.

psychologist, Pa. Asst. prof. psychology U. Iowa, Iowa City, 1970-72; staff psychologist Linn County Mental Health Ctr., Cedar Rapids, Iowa, 1972-77; dir. psychology dept. Warren (Pa.) State Hosp., 1977—; pvt. practice Warren, 1978—. Contbr. articles to profl. jours. Capt. U.S. Army, 1968-70. Fellow Pa. Psychol. Assn.; mem. Am. Psychol. Assn., Assn. for Advancement of Behavior Therapy, Soc. for Personality Assessment, Nat. Acad. Neuropsychology, Sigma Xi. Democrat. Home: 18 Prospect St Warren PA 16365-2751 Office: 805806 Pa Bank Warren PA 16365

STEINTHAL, THOMAS MICHAEL, programmer analyst; b. White Plains, N.Y., July 20, 1968; s. A. John and Jane (Gillespie) S. BA in Econs. cum laude, Georgetown U., 1990. Cons. Jones Instrument Corp., Stamford, Conn., 1984-90, Comml. Graphics Inc., N.Y.C., 1985-90; programmer analyst Software Creations Inc., East Falls Church, Va., 1988-89, Goldman Sachs & Co., N.Y.C., 1990—. Co-author: Swift Potomac's Lovely Daughter, 1990; co-founder a capella singing group The Phantom Singers, 1988. Co-chair Helping to Establish a Literate Population, Washington, 1989; mem. Dist. Action Project, Washington, 1988-89. Roman Catholic.

STEIR, PAT IRIS, artist; b. Newark, Apr. 10, 1940. Studies, Pratt Inst., 1956-58, 60-62; BFA, Boston U., 1961, studies, 1958-60; DFA (hon.), Pratt Inst., 1991. Art dir. Harper & Row, N.Y.C., 1968-69; tchr. Calif. Art Inst., 1973-75. One woman shows include Terry Dintenfass Gallery, N.Y., 1964, Bienville Gallery, N.Y., 1969, Graham Gallery, N.Y., 1971, Fourcade, Droll, Inc., N.Y., 1975, John Doyle Gallery, Paris, 1975, Galerie Farideh Cadot, Paris, 1976, 78, 79, 80, Morgan Thomas Gallery, Santa Monica, Calif., 1976, Otis Art Inst., L.A., 1976, Xavier Fourcade, Inc., N.Y., 1976, Carl Solway Gallery, Cin., 1977, Galeria Marilena Bonomo, Bari, Italy, 1978, Galerie d'Art Contemporain, Geneva, 1980, Art Mus. U. So. Fla., Tampa, 1990, Galerie Montenay, Paris, 1990, N.J. Ctr. for Visual Arts, Summit, 1990, Musée d'Art Contemporain, Lyon, France, Victoria Miro Gallery, London, 1990, Dennis Ochi Gallery, Sun Valley and Boise, Idaho, 1990, Robert Miller Gallery, N.Y.C., 1990, Linda Cathcart Gallery, Santa Monica, Calif., 1991, Galerie Franck & Schulte, Berlin, 1991, MacKenzie Art Gallery, Regina, Can., 1991, The Bklyn. Mus., 1992; group exhbns. include Ben Shahn Gallery William Patterson Coll., Wayne, N.J., 1990, Ecole Des Beaux Arts, Tourcoing, France, 1990, Mus. Art R.I. Sch. Design, 1990, Marc Richards Gallery, L.A., 1990, Louver Gallery, N.Y., 1990, Norah Haime Gallery, N.Y., 1990, Nat. Gallery of Art, Washington, 1990; represented in permanent collections including Kunstmuseum, Bern, Switzerland, Walker Art Ctr., Mpls., Bklyn. Mus., Musee d'art Contemporain, Lyons, France, Met. Mus. Art, N.Y., Mus. Modern Art, N.Y., Nat. Gallery, Washington, Nat. Mus. Am. Art, Washington, Whitney Mus. Am. Art, N.Y.

STEK, ROBERT JOSEPH, psychologist; b. Woodbridge, N.J., Oct. 23, 1948; s. Joseph and Ruth (Purkall) S.; m. Bonnie Eberle, July 27, 1991; children: Christopher, Ben, Ann. BS in Psychology, Rensselaer Poly. Inst., 1970; MS in Psychology, Ind. State U., 1972; PhD, U. Regina, Sask., 1978. Psychologist Wascana Hosp., Regina, 1973-74, Regina Mental Health Clinic, 1975-78; mgr. manpower and tng. Sask. Computer Utility Corp., Regina, 1978-80; psychologist PBS Assocs., Regina, 1980-84, Ctr. for Individual and Group Psychotherapy, Vernon, Conn., 1984—, Conn. Dept. Corrections, Somers, 1985-87; dir. mental health program devel. Conn. Dept. Corrections, Hartford, 1987—. Editor: An Electronic Holmes Companion, 1987. Mem. APA, Assn. for Transpersonal Psychology, Am. Soc. Psychical Rsch., Boston Computer Soc., Inst. Noetic Scis., Ancient Illuminated Seers of Bavaria. Home: 744 Shenipsit Lake Rd Tolland CT 06084

STELLAR, FREDERICK WILLIAM, career officer; b. Lodi, Ohio, Jan. 1, 1952; s. Chester Frank and Doreen (Line) S. BS, U.S. Mil. Acad., 1974; grad., U.S. Naval Test Pilot Sch., 1984; MS, Ga. Inst. Tech., 1990. Commd. 2nd lt. U.S. Army, 1974, advanced through grades to lt. col., 1991, platoon leader, 1975-76; aviator 501st Combat Aviation Bn. 501st Combat Aviation Bn. and 2d Armored Div. Forward, Germany, 1977-80; flight test engr. U.S. Army, Lancaster, Calif., 1981-83; exptl. test pilot U.S. Army, Edwards Air Force Base, Calif., 1985-88; assoc. prof. U.S. Mil. Acad., West Point, 1990—. Mem. AIAA, Am. Helicopter Soc., Soc. Exptl. Test Pilots, Soc. Flight Test Engrs., Am. Legion. Home: 53 Angola Rd Cornwall NY 12518-2125

STELMAK, DALTON ROY, engineering executive; b. Springfield, Mass., July 19, 1941; s. Severyn Valentine and Frances Mary (Wascowicz) S.; m. Burma Rose Greene, Aug. 29, 1964; children: Shawn Roy, Scott Christian. Draftsman/designer Electric Boat Co., Groton, Conn., 1964-66; mechanical engr. J.J. Henry Co., Phila., 1966-71; designer Combustion Engring., Windsor, Conn., 1971-72; mulitlayer product mgr. North Am. Printed Circuits, Stafford, Conn., 1972-76, engring. mgr., 1976-81; v.p. engr. Tyco Printed Circuit Group, Stafford, Conn., 1981—; coms. mem. The Inst. for Interconnecting and Packaging Electronic Circuits, Lincolnwood, Ill., 1978—; speaker N.E. Circuits Assn., 1989. Contbr. articles to profl. jours. and newspaper, mem. editorial review bd. PC Fab Magazine, 1988—. With USN, 1958-62. Mem. Stafford Fish and Game Club, Italian Benefit Soc., VFW Post 1990. Roman Catholic. Home: 71 Buckley Hwy Stafford Springs CT 06076-4410 Office: Tyco Printed Circuit Group PO Box 145 Old Monson Rd Stafford CT 06705

STELPSTRA, WILLIAM JOHN, minister; b. Paterson, N.J., Nov. 1, 1934; s. Duke and Nellie (Stapert) S.; m. Anna Rizkovsky, Sept. 6, 1958; 1 child, Linda Mae. BA, Alma White Coll., 1957; B. of Religion, Zarephath Bible Sem., 1958. Ordained to ministry Pillar of Fire Ch., 1954. Pastor Pillar of Fire Ch., Little Falls, N.J., 1956-60; evangelist Wesleyan Meth. Ch., 1960-64; founder, dir. Bethel Children's Home, Paterson, N.J., 1964-71, Bethel Ranch Rehab. for Men, West Milford, N.J., 1971—; founder, pres. World for Christ Crusade, Inc., N.J., Fla., 1960—; dir. fgn. missions World for Christ Crusade, Inc., Haiti, Ghana, India, 1980—; adminstr. Fellowship House, Bloomfield, N.J., 1979—, Bright Side Manor, Teaneck, N.J., 1978—. Mem. Ocean Grove C. of C. Republican. Wesleyan Ch. Home: 1005 Union Valley Rd West Milford NJ 07480 Office: World for Christ Crusade 1005 Union Valley Rd West Milford NJ 07480

STELZER, IRWIN MARK, economist; b. N.Y.C., May 22, 1932; s. Abraham and Fanny (Dolgins) S.; m. Marian Faris Stuntz, 1981. BA cum laude, NYU, 1951, MA, 1952; PhD, Cornell U., 1954. Fin. analyst Econometric Inst., 1952; teaching fellow Cornell U., 1953-54; instr. U. Conn., 1954-55; researcher Twentieth Century Fund, 1953-55; economist W.J. Levy, Inc., 1955-56; sr. cons., v.p. Boni, Watkins, Jason & Co., Inc., 1956-61; lectr. NYU, 1955-56, CCNY, 1957-58; researcher Brookings Instn., 1956-57; pres. Nat. Econ. Rsch. Assocs., Inc., 1961-85, I.M. Stelzer Assocs. Inc., 1986—; chmn. bd. Putnam, Hayes & Bartlett, Inc., N.Y.C., 1989-91; dir. regulatory policy studies Am. Enterprise Inst., 1990—; adv. coun. Electric Power Rsch. Inst.; adv. com. revision of rules of practice and proceudre FERC; chmn. com. on adequate power supply FPC. Author: Selected Antitrust Cases: Landmark Decisions; econ. columnist The Sunday Times, London, 1986—; columnist Boston Herald; contbr. articles in econs. field. Mem. Mayor's Energy Policy Adv. Group for N.Y.C.; adv. panel Pres.'s Nat. Commn. for Rev. of Antitrust Laws and Procedures; mem. Gov.'s Adv. Panel on Telecommunications, bd. governing trustees Am. Ballet Theatre; bd. dirs. U.S. Nat. Com., World Energy Conf.; mem. fin. adv. bd. Pitkin County (Colo). Mem. Am. Econ. Assn., Am. Statis. Assn., Nat. Assn. Bus. Economists, So. Econ. Assn., Japan Soc., Phi Beta Kappa. Home: PO Box 1008 Aspen CO 81612-1008 Office: Am Enterprise Inst 1150 17th St NW Washington DC 20036-4603

STEMMLER, EDWARD JOSEPH, physician, association executive, retired academic dean; b. Phila., Feb. 15, 1929; s. Edward C. and Josephine (Heitzmann) S.; m. Joan C. Koster, Dec. 27, 1958; children: Elizabeth, Margaret, Edward C., Catherine, Joan. B.A., La Salle Coll., Phila., 1950, Sc.D. (hon.), 1983; M.D., U. Pa., 1960; Sc.D. (hon.), Ursinus Coll., 1977, Phila. Coll. Pharmacy and Sci., 1989; L.H.D. (hon.), Rush U., 1986. Diplomate Am. Bd. Internal Medicine. Intern U. Pa. Hosp., 1960-61, med. resident, 1961-63, fellow in cardiology, 1963-64, chief med. resident, 1964-65, chief med. outpatient dept., 1966-67; chief of medicine U. Pa. Med. Svc., VA Hosp., Phila., 1967-73; mem. deans com. VA Hosp., 1974-88; instr. medicine Grad. Div. Medicine, U. Pa., 1964-66, NIH postdoctoral rsch. trainee, dept. physiology, 1965-67, assoc. in medicine, 1966-67; assoc. in physiology Grad. Div. Medicine, 1967-72, asst. prof. medicine, 1967-70, assoc. prof., 1970-74, prof., 1974—, Robert G. Dunlop prof., 1981-91, prof. emeritus, 1991—; assoc. dean Univ. Hosp. (Sch. Medicine), 1973, assoc. dean student affairs, 1973-75, acting dean, 1974-75, dean, 1975-88, dean emeritus, 1989—; exec. v.p. U. Pa. Med. Ctr., 1986-89, Assn. Am. Med. Colls., 1990—; mem. Nat. Bd. Med. Examiners, 1974-76, nominating and ad hoc governance coms., 1985, vice chmn., 1987-89, treas., 1989-91, chmn., 1991—, mem. exec. com.; mem. ednl. policy com. Nat. Fund for Med. edn., 1975-77; mem. deans com. VA Hosp., 1974-89; bd. dirs. Rhone-Poulenc Rorer, Inc.; trustee Dorothy Rider Pool Healthcare Trust, 1991—. Contbr. articles to med. jours. Chmn. Pa. Dean's Com., 1976-87; bd. govs. Mid-Eastern Regional Med. Libr. Svcs., 1977-81, chmn., 1978-81; bd. visitors U. Pitts. Sch. Medicine, 1980-85; mem. adv. com. dept. medicine U. Ala., Birmingham, 1985-89; vis. com. Tufts U. Sch. Medicine, 1986—, Case We. Res. U. Sch. Medicine, 1990—, Hershey Med. Ctr., 1992; trustee Ursinus Coll., 1991—. With Chem. Corps, U.S. Army, 1951-53. Decorated Commendation medal; recipient Frederick A. Packard award, 1960, Albert Einstein Med. Ctr. staff award, 1960, Roche award, 1960. Master ACP (treas., chmn. investment com. 1975-80, Laureate award Ea. Pa. region 1986); mem. AMA (health policy agenda), Phila. County Med. Soc., Am. Fedn. for Clin. Rsch., Am. Inst. Medicine NAS, Assn. Am. Med. Colls. (ad hoc external exam. rev. com. 1980—, exec. coun. 1980—, coun. of deans adminstrv. bd. 1980—, chmn. 1983-84, nat. chmn.-elect 1985-86, chmn. assembly 1986-87), Coll. of Physicians of Phila. (bd. censors 1979-85, coun. 1979-85, 90—), Am. Clin. and Climatological Soc., John Morgan Soc., Alpha Omega Alpha. Republican. Mem. Christian Ch. Home: 3540 Winfield Ln NW Washington DC 20007-2367 Office: Assn Am Med Colls 2450 N St NW Washington DC 20037-1167

STEMPEL, EDWARD, pharmacy educator; b. N.Y.C., Mar. 7, 1926; s. Herman and Clara (Sobel) S.; m. Rina Cheshes, Dec. 20, 1959; 1 child, Andrea Heidi. BS in Pharmacy, Bklyn. Coll. Pharmacy, 1949; MS, Columbia U., 1952, MA, 1955, EdD, 1956. Lic. pharmacist, Md., N.Y., N.J., Pa. Instr. Bklyn. Coll. Pharmacy, N.Y.C., 1949-54, asst. prof., 1954-58, assoc. prof., 1958-64, prof., chmn. pharmacy dept., 1964-78, prof., chmn. div. pharmaceutics, clin. & profl. practice, 1978-79; assoc. dean profl. programs Arnold & Marie Schwartz Coll. Pharmacy, N.Y.C., 1979-83, prof. pharmacy, 1983—. Author: (book chpts.) Long-Acting Medication, 1959, 66, 71, Marketing Generic Drugs, 1983; author: Community Pharmacy Externship Manual, 1977. Recipient Disting. Faculty award Arnold & Marie Schwartz Coll. Pharmacy, 1980; named Ptnr. in Edn. Clara Barton High Sch., 1980. Mem. Am. Pharm. Assn., AAUP, Bklyn. Coll. Pharmacy Alumni Assn., Columbia U. Coll. Pharmacy Alumni Assn., Rho Pi Phi Internat. Pharm. Frat. Home: 1817 E 29th St Brooklyn NY 11229-2518

STEMPLER, ALLAN IVAN, psychiatrist; b. N.Y.C., Dec. 11, 1942; s. Jack and Minerva (Rapoport) S.; m. Susan Koelling, May 30, 1970; children: Courtney, Preston. BA, U. Rochester, N.Y., 1963; MD, U. Miss., 1969. Intern Bklyn. Jewish Hosp., N.Y.C., 1969-70; resident in psychiatry Downstate Med. Ctr., N.Y.C., 1970-72, fellow in child psychiatry, 1972-74; staff psychiatrist L.I. Jewish Med. Ctr., New Hyde Park, N.Y., 1974-75, North Shore Child Guidance Ctr., Manhasset, N.Y., 1975-77, Queens Child Guidance Ctr., N.Y.C., 1977-80; cons. Nassau County (N.Y.) Dept. Mental Health, 1980—; pvt. practice Great Neck, N.Y., 1974—; cons. Cath. Guardian Soc., N.Y.C., 1974—. Fellow Am. Psychiat. Assn.; mem. Nassau Psychiat. Soc. (pres. 1987-88). Jewish. Office: 299 E Shore Rd Great Neck NY 11023-2429

STEN, CHRISTOPHER WILLIE, English educator; b. Mpls., Jan. 3, 1944; s. Willie John and Audrey Goldie (Wessel) S.; m. Janet Ann Rogers, July 26, 1969; children—Caroline, Elizabeth. B.A., Carleton Coll., 1966; M.A., Ind. U., 1968, Ph.D., 1971. Instr. English George Washington U., Washington, 1970, asst. prof., 1971-78, assoc. prof., 1978-84, dir. grad. studies, 1984-87, chmn. 1987-91; sr. Fulbright lectr. in Am. lit. Englische Inst. Universitaet Wuerzburg, W. Germany, 1975-76. Author: Savage Eye: Melville and The Visual Arts, 1992; contbr. articles to profl. jours. Mem. MLA, Fulbright Alumni Assn., Melville Soc. Home: 7406 Fairfax Rd Bethesda MD 20814-1241 Office: Dept English George Washington U Washington DC 20052

STENGER, JOHN ROBERT, artist, educator, farmer, naturalist, biologist; b. Clarksburg, W.Va., Oct. 17, 1926; s. Louis Jules and Zula Edra (Weaver) S.; m. Margaret Elizabeth Onestinghel, Jan. 28, 1949; children: John Louis, Cathy Ann Besche, Nancy Joan Tylecki, Robert Joseph. B., Salem Coll., 1950, M., U. Del., 1967; PhD, Kensington U., 1987. Cert. instr. of biology, gen. sci., earth sci., tchr. sci., dir. sci., supr. sci., Del. Glass cutter Am. Window Glass Co. of Am. Pittsburg Plate & Forco Glass Co, Clarksburg, W.Va., Okmulgee, Okla., 1944, 50-53; tchr., coach Cape Henlopen Sch. Dist., Nassau, Del., 1962-89; environmentalist, environ. litigant Warner Grant Lands, Cape Henlopen, Del., 1968-80; naturalist Cape Henlopen State Park, 1968-71; pres., founder Environ. Inst., Lewes, Del., 1970-75; farmer sheep and cattle West Milford, W.Va., Milton, Del., 1940—; artist Milton, 1989—; asst. prof. Marine Sci. Consortium, Millersville (Pa.) State Coll., 1972, 73; grant reviewer NSF, Washington, 1979; cons. West Fork Conservation Dist. Cartoonist for publs. Vol. worker Citizens for Biden, 1990; bd. dirs. Del. Conservation Edn. Assn., 1973-75; mem. utilization com. Cape Henlopen Edn. Assn. Pres. Rep., Lewes, Del.; pres. Cape Henlopen Edn. Assn., Lewes, Dover, Del., 1980-84; pres., founder Environ. Inst., Lewes, Milton, 1971; sta. mgr. asst. ARC Desert Storm, Washington,1991. Sgt. U.S. Army, 1945-47. Recipient Conservation award Am. Motors, 1971, William Baxter Conservation award Del. Wildlife Fedn., 1970, others; NSF grantee. Mem. NAACP, NEA (del. Detroit, L.A., 1980-84), Del. Acad. Sci., Rehoboth Art League, Nat. Assn. Ret. People, Am. Legion, Del. Edn. Assn. (del. convs., pres. coun.), Common Cause. Democrat. Home and Office: RR 3 Box 82 Milton DE 19968-9709

STENLAKE, RODNEY LEE, lawyer; b. Phillipsburg, N.J., Feb. 2, 1957; s. Harold William and Mae Rose (Flory) S.; 1 child, Katherine Anne. BA with high honors, Rutgers U., 1979, JD with high honors, 1985. Bar: N.J. 1986, N.Y. 1986, U.S. Dist. Ct. (so. dist.) N.Y. 1986, U.S. Dist. Ct. N.J. 1986, U.S. Ct. Appeals (3d cir.) 1986. Law clk. to judge U.S. Ct. Appeals (3d cir.) N.J., Newark, 1985-86; assoc. Cravath, Swaine & Moore, N.Y.C., 1986-88; assoc. Duker & Barrett, N.Y.C., 1988-89, ptnr., 1989—. Editor-in-chief Rutgers U. Law Rev., 1984-85. Tischler scholar Rutgers U., 1983. Mem. ABA, Phi Beta Kappa, Phi Alpha Theta. Democrat. Home: 155 W 70th St Apt 4phb New York NY 10023-4419 Office: Duker & Barrett 90 Broad St New York NY 10004-2205

STEPHAN, ROBERT CONRAD, bank executive; b. Lancaster, Pa., Feb. 2, 1952; s. Stanley Standish and Ethel Elizabeth (Heinaman) S.; m. Candace Carlyle: children: Kristen Ann, Haley Carlyle. BS, Bucknell U., 1974; MBA, The Wharton Sch., 1977. Cert. fin. analyst. Asst. mgr. Armstrong Cork Co., Lancaster, Pa., 1974-76; mgr. mktg. and planning Conn. Gen., Bloomfield, Conn., 1978-81; v.p. corp. devel. Fidelity Bank, Phila., 1982-84; pres. Corp. Investment Co., West Chester, Pa., 1984-85; v.p. mktg. Firstrust Savs. Bank, Phila., 1986—; speaker Am. Mktg. Assn., Washington, DISC Nat. Cash Mgmt., Kansas City, Kans., 1981. Mem. Bank Mktg. Assn., Main Line C. of C., Delta Mu Delta, Omicron Delta Kappa, Wharton Alumni Club, Bucknell Alumni Chpt. (pres. 1976-77). Republican. Lutheran. Home: 86 Thomas Rd Downingtown PA 19335-3338 Office: Firstrust Savs Bank Castor and Cottman Aves Philadelphia PA 19111

STEPHENS, EDWARD CARL, communications educator, writer; b. L.A., July 27, 1924; s. Carl Edward and Helen Mildred (Kerner) S.; children: Edward, Sarah, Matthew. AB, Occidental Coll., 1947; MS, Northwestern U., 1955. Advt. exec. Dancer-Fitzgerald-Sample Inc., N.Y.C., 1955-64; prof. Medill Sch. Journalism, Northwestern U., Evanston, Ill., 1964-76; prof., chmn. dept. advt. S.I. Newhouse Sch. Pub. Communications, Syracuse U., N.Y., 1976-80, dean, 1980-89; prof. communications S.I. Newhouse Sch. Pub. Communications Syracuse U., 1990—; cons. Foote, Cone & Belding Communications. Author: (novels) A Twist of Lemon, 1958, One More Summer, 1960, Blow Negative!, 1962, Roman Joy, 1965, A Turn in the Dark Wood, 1968, The Submariner, 1974. Mem. George Polk Awards Com. Capt. USN, 1943-46, PTO, USNR, 1946-68. Decorated Purple Heart. Mem. Am. Acad. Advt. (pres. 1976-77), Assn. Edn. Journalism and Mass Communication, Authors League, Century Club of Syracuse, Alpha Tau Omega. Episcopalian. Office: Syracuse U Newhouse Sch Pub Communications Syracuse NY 13210

STEPHENS, GEORGE ROBERT, scientist; b. Springfield, Mass., Nov. 10, 1929; s. George Robert and Edna Marie (Amundsen-Grant) S.; m. Irene Mary Hackett, Sept. 8, 1951; children: Timothy, Lynne, Ellen, Matthew, Charlotte, Mark, Kristina. BS, U. Mass., 1952; M. Forestry, Yale U., 1958, PhD, 1961. Rsch. asst. Conn. Agr. Exptl. Sta., New Haven, 1957-61, asst. scientist, 1961-65, assoc. scientist, 1965-75, scientist, 1975-80, chief scientist, 1980—; mem. State Tree Protection Exam. Bd., New Haven, 1962—, Conn. Acad. Sci. and Engring., Hartford, 1985—. Contbr. articles to profl. jours. Ordained permanent deacon Archdiocese of Hartford, 1981. 1st lt. U.S. Army, 1952-57. Mem. Soc. Am. Foresters. Roman Catholic. Office: Conn Agr Exptl Sta 123 Huntington St PO Box 1106 New Haven CT 06504

STEPHENS, JOHN FRANK, association executive, researcher; b. Malone, N.Y., Nov. 9, 1949; s. J. Frank and Marjorie (Drew) S.; m. Smaroula Georgina Paraskevoudakis, Sept. 1, 1989; 1 child, Georgina Elizabeth. B.A., Harpur Coll., 1971; M.A., SUNY-Binghamton, 1973, Ph.D., 1977. Research assoc. Fernand Braudel Ctr., SUNY-Binghamton, 1977; asst. to provost U. Md., College Park, 1978; vis. instr. St. Mary's Coll. Md., St. Mary's City, 1978-79; dir. Alexandria Regional Preservation Office, Va., 1980-83; exec. dir. Am. Studies Assn., College Park, Md., 1983—; cons. (in field); reviewer U.S. Dept. Interior, NEH, HEW, USIA, PBS, Washington, 1983—. Author: (with Immanuel Wallerstein) Libraries and Our Civilizations, 1978, (with others) Archaeology in Urban America: A Search for Pattern Process, 1982. Mem. exec. bd. Humanities Alliance, 1992—. Fulbright-Hays fellow, 1974-75; Spanish Govt. fellow, 1974-75. Mem. Am. Studies Assn., Fulbright Alumni Assn. Home: 7105 13th Ave Silver Spring MD 20912-7068 Office: Am Studies Assn 2101 S Campus Surge Bldg Univ Md College Park MD 20742-7711

STEPHENS, LAWRENCE JAMES, chemistry educator, program director; b. Chgo., Aug. 11, 1940; s. James Jenkyn and Mary Catherine (Caughlin) S.; m. Theresa Ann Duster, Aug. 8, 1964; children: Anne Marie, Mark, Susan. BS, Loyola U., 1963; PhD, U. Nebr., 1969. Postdoctoral rsch. assoc. Stanford (Calif.) U., 1968-69; asst. prof. chemistry Findlay (Ohio) Coll., 1969-73; asst. prof. chemistry Elmira (N.Y.) Coll., 1973-78, assoc. prof., 1978-83, prof., 1983—, chmn. div. math. and natural scis., 1977-86, 90—, dir. acad. advising, 1987—. Contbr. articles to ednl. jours. Pres. Chemung County Gen. Edn. Bd., Elmira, 1976-79. Mem. AAUP, Am. Chem. Soc. (sect. chair 1985-86), Nat. Acad. Advisors Assn., Nat. Sci. Tchrs. Assn., Ancient Order Hibernians (div. pres. 1988, 89). Republican. Roman Catholic. Home: 613 Moreland Ave Elmira NY 14904-1622 Office: Elmira Coll Elmira NY 14901

STEPHENS, RICHARD HARRY, chemical engineer; b. Bradford, Pa., Sept. 16, 1945; s. Maynard Moody and Muriel Ethylwen (Darrell) S.; m. Cynthia Sue Underwood, June 24, 1967 (div. June 1989); children: Brian Richard, Kevin Joseph; m. Carol Doris Chenard, Oct. 12, 1991. BSChemE, U. Tex., 1968; PhD, MIT, 1971. Registered profl. chem. engr., Mass., N.H. Prin. cons. engr. Arthur D. Little, Inc., Cambridge, Mass., 1971-76; mgr. energy systems Energy Resources Co., Cambridge, 1976-78; mgr. process R&D Polaroid Corp., Waltham, Mass., 1978-84; dir. R&D Markem Corp., Keene, N.H., 1984-90; v.p. engring. CIM Industries, Inc., Peterborough, N.H., 1990—; cons., Peterborough, N.Y., 1976—; sec., treas. C.C. Stephens & Co. Advt., Peterborough, N.H., 1992. Contbr. articles to profl. jours. Vice chmn. Acton (Mass.) Bd. Health, 1982-89; asst. scoutmaster Boy Scouts Am., Acton, 1986—. Mem. Am. Chem. Soc., Sigma Xi, Tau Beta Pi. Home: PO Box 652 Peterborough NH 03458 Office: CIM Industries Inc 94 Grove St Peterborough NH 03458

STEPHENS, ROBERT ALLAN, service agency executive; b. St. Louis County, Mo., Jan. 15, 1937; s. Charles Franklin and L. Pearl (Cales) Stephens; divorced; children: Shari Lee, Beth Ann. BA, Mo. Valley Coll., 1958; MS, Nova U., 1984. Claims supr. Gen. Am. Life Ins. Co., Pitts., 1958-61; underwriting mgr. Gen. Am. Life Ins. Co., St. Louis, 1961-67; dist. sales mgr. Gen. Am. Life Ins. Co., Oklahoma City and St. Louis, 1967-69, New Eng. Life, Dallas, 1969-71; exec. dir. Goodland Presbyn. Children's Home, Hugo, Okla., 1971-74, Beech Acres, Cin., 1974-89, New Eng. Home for Little Wanderers, Boston, 1989—. Mem. Hamilton County Juvenile Ct. Rev. Bd., 1975-83; Hamilton County Youth Services Adv. Bd., 1981-84; peer reviewer Coun. on Accreditation of Svcs. for Families and Children, 1987—; bd. dirs. Pro Kids, 1987-89; mem. planning com. Presbytery of Cin., 1984-86, chmn. stewardship and mission interpretation com. 1986-88; chmn. stewardship com. Presbytery of Boston, 1989—; mem. bd. deacons Presbyn. Ch. in Sudbury, 1990; moderator, 1991—; legis. bd. Southeastern Ecumenical Ministries Manor, 1976-81, bd. dirs., 1980-82; mem. Clermont County Mental Health Bd., 1980-86, vice chmn., 1981, chmn., 1982-85; mem. Clermont County Youth Svc. Coordinating Coun., 1980-83, Clermont County Juvenile Ct. Adv. Bd., 1980-81, Hamilton County Juvenile Ct. Adv. Bd., 1982-89. Named Nat. United Presbyn. Man of Mission, 1978, Anderson Twp. Citizen of Yr., 1988. Mem. Nat. Assn. Homes for Children (dir. 1975-80, accreditation commn. 1983-87, standards and ethics com. 1988-89, membership com. 1990—), Ohio Assn. Child Caring Agys. (bd. dirs. 1975-80, pres. 1978-79), Nat. Soc. Fund Raising Execs. (v.p. Cin. chpt. 1988), Family and Children's Execs. Greater Boston (vice chmn. 1990—), Boston Panel of Agy. Execs., Exchange Club (pres. 1980-81, Book of Golden Deeds award 1984, Exchangite of Yr. 1989). Home: 67 St Germain St Apt 11 Boston MA 02115-3219 Office: Home for Little Wanderers 20 Linden St Allston MA 02134-1737

STEPHENS, THOMAS MACK, foreign language educator; b. Spartanburg, S.C., Nov. 15, 1951; s. William Talmadge and Winifred Telewene (Whittle) S. BA, U. S.C., 1974, MA, 1976; PhD, U. Mich., 1984. Teaching asst. U. S.C., Columbia, 1974-76, U. Mich., Ann Arbor, 1976-81; adj. instr. Rutgers U., New Brunswick, N.J., 1981-84, asst. prof., 1984-90, assoc. prof., 1990—. Author: Dictionary of Latin American Racial and Ethnic Terminology, 1989 (Choice Outstanding Acad. Book 1990-91); editorial bd. Jour. of Hist. Linguistics and Philology, 1981—. NEH grantee, 1986; Fulbright Hays grantee, 1987. Mem. AAUP, MLA, Linguistic Soc. Am., Linguistic Assn. of Can. and U.S., Am. Assn. tchrs. of Spanish and Portuguese. Democrat. Baptist. Office: Rutgers Univ Dept Spanish & Portuguese New Brunswick NJ 08903-0270

STEPHENS, WILLIAM HENRY, software developer; b. Binghamton, N.Y., July 10, 1948; s. George Austin and Adelaide Frances (Coffey) S.; m. Patricia Gail Drop, June 3, 1972; children: Matthew, Thomas, Patrick. BS in Math., Indiana U. of Pa., 1970. Instr. Inst. Data Processing, Pitts., 1971-72; jr. systems programmer USAF, Washington, 1972-76; systems programmer Equibank, N.A., Pitts., 1976-78, Kinney Shoe Corp., Camp Hill, Pa., 1978-82, Hamilton Bank, N.A., Lancaster, Pa., 1982-83; lead systems programmer Beneficial Data Processing Corp., Peapack, N.J., 1983-85; mgr. VM systems AT&T Internat., Basking Ridge, N.J., 1985-86; rsch. and devel. programmer Computer Assocs. Internat., Inc., Princeton, N.J., 1986—. Sgt. USAF, 1972-76. Republican. Mem. Assembly of God Ch. Home: 423 Berkley St Easton PA 18042-3707

STEPHENSON, CYNDEE ANNE, counselor; b. Balt., May 6, 1948; d. Sydney and Melverne E. (Gresser) Havelock; m. Philip Stephenson, June 22, 1969; 1 child, James Havelock Stephenson. BS in Sociology, Towson (Md.) State U., 1979; MEd in Counseling, Loyola Coll., Balt., 1991. Cert. counselor, Md. Instructional asst. Howard County Pub. Schs., Ellicott, Md., 1980-91; guidance counselor elem. sch. Balt. County Pub. Schs., 1991—. Mem. AACD, Nat. Career Devel. Assn., Assn. for Humanistic Edn. and Devel., Am. Sch. Counselor Assn., Tchrs. Assn. Balt. County, Friends of Gettysburg Lacrosse, Assn. for Multicultural Counseling and Devel., Assn. for Specialists in Group Work, Pub. Offender Counselor Assn., Green Peace, Audubon Soc. Democrat. Home: 6133 Sinbad Pl Columbia MD 21045-4317

STEPHENSON, DAVID MERRILL, insurance company executive; b. Amityville, N.Y., Apr. 17, 1963; s. Ellsworth Ninde and Elizabeth (Merrill) S.; m. Michelle Susan Rague, Aug. 31, 1991. BS in Acctg., SUNY, Geneseo, 1985; MBA, Northeastern U., Boston, 1989. Auditor losses Liberty Mut. Ins. Co., Boston, 1985-87; sr. auditor Liberty Mut. Ins. Co., Weston, Mass., 1987-90; div. credit mgr. Liberty Mut. Ins. Co., Lynbrook, N.Y., 1990—. Profl. adviser Jr. Achievement New Eng., Boston, 1985; group capt. United Way, Lynbrook, 1991. Mem. Property and Casualty Surety Accts. Assn.

Republican. Methodist. Office: Liberty Mut Ins Co 444 Merrick Rd Lynbrook NY 11563

STEPHENSON, DONALD GRIER, JR., government educator; b. DeKalb County, Ga., Jan. 12, 1942; s. Donald Grier and Katherine Mason (Williams) S.; m. Ellen Claire Walker, Aug. 15, 1967; children: Todd Grier, Claire Walker. AB, Davidson Coll., N.C., 1964; MA, Princeton U., 1966, PhD, 1967. Research assoc. Nat. War Coll., Washington, 1968-70; asst. prof. govt. Franklin and Marshall Coll., Lancaster, Pa., 1970-73, assoc. prof. govt., 1973-81, prof. govt., 1981—, Charles A. Dana prof., 1989—; mem. adv. coun. to dean of the chapel Princeton U., 1974-85; Commonwealth lectr. Pa. Humanities Coun., Phila., 1987-88, 90, 92—. Co-author: American Constitutional Development, 1977, American Government, 1992; author: The Supreme Court and the American Republic, 1981, An Essential Safeguard, 1991; contbr. articles to profl. jours. Elder, mem. Session, First Presbyn. Ch., Lancaster, 1973-76; judge Pa. constl. competition Dickinson Coll., 1988—. Capt. U.S. Army, 1968-70. Woodrow Wilson fellow, 1964-65, 66-67; Nat. Endowment for Humanities grantee, 1972, 85-89. Mem. Am. Polit. Sci. Assn. (Corwin award com. 1978), Pa. Polit. Sci. Assn. (editorial bd. Polity 1972-78), Supreme Ct. Hist. Soc. (editorial award 1990). Presbyterian. Home: 62 Oak Ln Lancaster PA 17603-4762 Office: Franklin and Marshall Coll PO Box 3003 Lancaster PA 17604-3003

STEPTON, RICK, trombonist; b. Fitchburg, Mass., Feb. 28, 1942; s. Lawrence Edson Jr. and Beatrice Estelle (Teto) S. Trombone player Buddy Rich Big Band, 1968-70, 76-77, Woody Herman Orch., 1971-72, Maynard Ferguson Orch., 1975; tchr. Berklee Coll. Music, Boston, 1978-82; trombone player Buddy Rich, 1982, Gunther Schuller, Boston, 1988; tchr. jazz trombone New Eng. Conservatory, Boston, 1988—; freelance trombone player New Eng. area, 1977—. With U.S. Army, 1959-62. Home: 162 S Row Rd Lunenburg MA 01462

STERLING, ROBERT LEE, JR., investment company executive; b. Cleve., June 12, 1933; s. Robert Lee and Kathryn (Durell) S.; m. Deborah Platt, May 16, 1984; children: Robert Livingston, William Lee, Cameron Platt. Student, U. Edinburgh, Scotland, 1955; BA, Brown U., 1956; MBA, Columbia U., 1962. Corp. rsch. analyst Morgan Guaranty Trust, N.Y.C., 1962-63; asst. comptr. Western Hemisphere CPC Internat., N.Y.C., 1963-66; v.p. White, Weld & Co., Inc., N.Y.C., 1966-78, Merrill Lynch Asset Mgmt., 1978-80, Wood, Struthers & Winthrop Mgmt. Corp., N.Y.C., 1980-83; sr. v.p. Shearson/Am. Express Asset Mgmt., 1983-88; v.p., sr. portfolio mgr. Chase Manhattan Bank, 1988—. Bd. dirs. Nicholas Inst. Sports Medicine div. Lennox Hill Hosp.; mem. adv. bd. Mus. Modern Art, Oxford U., Eng. Lt. USNR, 1956-60. Mem. New Eng. Soc. (past pres., J.P. Morgan medal), Nat. Trust Scotland (Edinburgh), St. Andrews Soc., St. Nicholas Soc., Pilgrims, N.Y. State Soc. of Cin. (pres.), Squadron A (N.Y.), Round Hill Club (Conn.), Downtown Club, Univ. Club (N.Y.C.), Edgartown (Mass.) Yacht Club, Alpha Delta Phi, Alpha Kappa Psi. Home: 16 Pheasant Ln Greenwich CT 06830-3843 Office: 1211 Ave Of The Americas New York NY 10036-8701

STERN, ALAN ISAAC, education educator; b. Buffalo, N.Y., May 4, 1948; s. Harry and Lorraine (Lowe) S.; children: Alexander, Jacob. BA, SUNY, Buffalo, 1970, MA, 1972; MS, Canisius Coll., 1978. Cert. social studies educator, tchr. of deaf. Dir., adult learning Erie County Home and Infirmary, Alden, N.Y., 1973-74; tchr. homebound Buffalo Pub. Schs., 1974-77, tchr. of the deaf, 1978-80, mainstream facilitator, 1980-81, coord. fed. projects, 1981-83; tng. specialist Spl. Edn. Tng. and Resource Ctr., Buffalo, 1983-85; asst. N.Y. State Edn. Dept., Albany, 1985-86, assoc., 1986-92; supr. program devel. N.Y. State Edn. Dept., Albany, $D; lectr. Coll. of Saint Rose, Albany, N.Y., 1985—, SUNY, Buffalo, 1981-85; cons. Buffalo, 1980-85. Author: (poems) Voices in Poetry, 1989, edit., 1990. Albany Anthology, 1992, Voices on War and the Persian Gulf, 1991. Bd. dirs. Empire State Youth Orch., Albany, 1986—; mem. Mayor's Adv. Com. on Communicatively Impaired, Buffalo, 1981-85, Buffalo Philharmonic Orch. Hearing Electronic Arts Com., 1979-85; bd. dirs. Svcs. to Hearing Impaired, Buffalo, 1980-85. Mem. Hudson Valley Writers Guild (editor HVWG newsletter), Western N.Y. Registry of Interpretors for the Deaf (v.p. 1980-85), Adirondack Mountain Club. Republican. Jewish. Home: 276 Old London Rd Apt 1B Latham NY 12110-2954 Office: NY State Edn Dept Washington Avenue Ext Albany NY 12234-0001

STERN, ANNIE WARD, development executive; b. Jacksonville, Fla., Oct. 18, 1944; d. Peter Otey and Annie (Boyd) Ward; m. Edward J. Stern, Dec. 23, 1968; children: Robert W., Ward Preston. BA, Sweet Briar Coll., 1966; MS in Edn., U. Va., 1969. Tchr. pub. schs. Indpls., 1967-77; dir. community svcs. Ind. Repertory Theatre, Indpls., 1977; adminstrv. asst., then program dir. Young Audiences of Ind., Indpls., 1978-83; dir. pub. rels., alumnae dir. Oak Knoll Sch. of Holy Child, Summit, N.J., 1983-84; dir. devel. Oak Knoll Sch. of Holy Child, 1984—. Vol. pub. rels. and fundraising Indpls. Mus. Art, 1970-80, Ind. Repertory Theatre, 1970-80, St. John's Luth. Ch., Summit, 1985—. Mem. Nat. Soc. Fund Raising Execs. (bd. dirs. N.J. chpt., nat. recognition award 1989), N.J. Assn. Ind. Schs. (pres., v.p., devel. dirs. 1984-92), Coun. for Advancement and Support Edn., Ind. Sch. Mgmt. Assn., Maplewood Club, Spring Valley Hounds Hunt Club, Sweet Briar Coll. Club (v.p.). Office: Oak Knoll Sch Holy Child 44 Blackburn Rd Summit NJ 07901-2499

STERN, ARTHUR OGDEN, financial services company executive, lawyer; b. Roanoke, Va., Dec. 17, 1938; s. Arthur Harris Stern and Dorothy (Rhodes) May; m. Ellen Rothstein, May 13, 1989. BA in Econs., Cornell U., 1962; Cert. Prog. for Mgmt. Devel., Harvard U., 1970; J.D., Boston Coll., 1974. Exec. J.H. Filbert, Inc., Balt., 1964-71; lawyer Csaplar & Bok, Boston, 1974-78; v.p., investment counsel New Eng. Mutual Life Ins. Co., Boston, 1978-85; sr. v.p., gen. counsel Colonial Mgmt. Assocs., Inc., Boston, 1985—; instr. acctg. for lawyers Boston Coll. Law Sch., Boston, 1975-82; bd. govs. Investment Co. Inst., Washington, 1991—. Trustee Am. Mus. of Fly Fishing, Manchester, Vt., 1988—, Mus. Transp., Boston, 1991—. 1st lt. U.S. Army, 1962-64. Office: Colonial Mgmt Assocs Inc 1 Financial Ctr Boston MA 02111-2621

STERN, CELIA ELLEN, sales executive, consultant; b. Long Beach, N.Y., Apr. 26, 1954; d. Melvin and Helen (Einhorn) S. BA in Psychology, SUNY, Stony Brook, 1975; MSW, U. Md., 1978. Program adminstr. Balt. County CETA Adminstrn., 1978-81; employment, training mgr. Macy's, Balt., 1981-83; personnel mgr. Macy's, Wayne, N.J., 1983-84; sales support mgr. Info. Sci. Inc., Montvale, N.J., 1984-85; sr. human resource cons. Mgmt. Sci. Am., Paramus, N.J., 1985-88; sales exec. Dun & Bradstreet Software Svcs., Inc., Paramus, N.J., 1990—. Officer bd., sec., co-chmn. New Leadership Div., United Jewish Community, Bergen County, N.J., 1986—; bd. dirs. Jewish Nat. Fund, Balt., 1981-83. Mem. Human Resource System Profls., Am. Soc. Personnel Adminstrs. Democrat. Jewish. Office: Dun & Bradstreet Software Svcs Inc 61 S Paramus Rd Paramus NJ 07652-1236

STERN, HARVEY, physician, radiologist; b. N.Y.C., Dec. 14, 1946; s. Rudolph and Mary (Baron) S.; m. Ruth Green, Dec. 25, 1968; children: Neal, Seth. BA, Yeshiva U., 1967; MD, Albert Einstein Coll Medicine, 1971. Diplomate Am. Bd. Radiology. Intern Montefiore Med. Ctr., Bronx, N.Y., 1971-72; resident Einstein-Bronx Mcpl., Bronx, 1972-75; asst. radiologist Beth Israel Med. Ctr., N.Y.C., 1975-76; assoc. dir., attending radiologist Maimonides Med. Ctr., Bklyn., 1976-88, Bronx (N.Y.) Lebanon Med. Ctr., 1989—. Office: Bronx Lebanon Hosp Ctr 1650 Grand Concourse Bronx NY 10457-7697

STERN, JOHN, import-export toy executive; b. Hamburg, Fed. Republic of Germany, Apr. 28, 1926; s. James and Charlotte (Abel) S.; m. Alia Azancot, Sept. 4, 1957 (dec. Nov. 1987); 1 child, James. Sales VVE. James Stern, Tangier, Morocco, 1945-49; export asst. Pablo Adler, N.Y.C., 1949-51; prin. N.Y.C., 1953-55; mgr., prin. Tangier, Morocco, 1955-60; prin. N.Y.C., 1960-63; bus. mgr. Mediterraneal Ctr. N.Y. World's Fair, 1964-65; export mgr. Goldfarb Bros Inc., N.Y.C., 1965-66; office mgr. Dicker Internat. Inc., N.Y.C., 1968-74, exec. v.p., 1974—; exec. v.p. Ozen Sound Devices, Inc., N.Y.C., 1974—. Pres., trustee 'Aficomon" Am. Friends of the Jewish Communities of No. Moracco and Tangier, Rego Pk., N.Y., 1986—; trustee Rego Pk. Jewish Ctr.; mem. French Inst./Alliance Francaise, N.Y., 1967—. PFC U.S. Army, 1951-53. Guest of Honor Israel Bonds, 1987, Rego Pk. Jewish Ctr., 1989. Mem. N.Y. C. of C. and Industry, Am. Philatelic Soc., Bnai Brith. Democrat. Jewish.

STERN, JONATHAN MICHAEL, lawyer; b. Pitts., Nov. 22, 1959; s. Theodore and Elizabeth (Spier) S.; m. Joy Goldstein, Sept. 1, 1985. BS, Embry-Riddle Aero. U., 1981; JD magna cum laude, Am. U., 1986. Bar: Md. 1987, U.S. Dist. Ct. Md. 1987, U.S. Ct. Appeals (10th cir.) 1987, D.C. 1988, U.S. Dist. Ct. D.C. 1988, U.S. Ct. Appeals (4th cir.) 1989. Flight instr. Embry-Riddle Aero. U., Daytona, Fla., 1979-81; air traffic controller FAA, Washington, 1981-83; research analyst Phaneuf Assocs. Inc., Washington, 1984-86; trial atty. aviation torts U.S. Dept. Justice, Washington, 1986-87; assoc. Hughes Hubbard & Reed, Washington, 1987-89, Katten Muchin Zavis & Dombroff, Washington, 1989—. Author: Flying on Instruments with Flight Simulator, 1986. Mem. ABA. Office: Katten Muchin Zavis & Dombroff 1025 Thomas Jefferson St NW Washington DC 20007-5201

STERN, KALIKA EVELYN, artist; b. Bklyn., Jan. 19, 1941; d. Sylvan Phillip and Ethel May (Dashefsky) S. BFA, Pratt Inst., 1962; MA, NYU, 1975; MFA, Inst. Allende, 1975. TV producer Hoefen Dietrich & Brown, San Francisco, 1963-66; asst. art dir. Young & Rubicam, N.Y.C., 1966-68; mem. faculty Mercer County Coll., West Winsor, N.J., 1968-82; exec. dir. Soc. for Folk Arts Preservation, N.Y.C., 1977-89; designer, artist Kalika Design, N.Y.C., 1982—; cons. N.Y. State Dept. Edn., New Delhi, 1978, Thomas Edison Coll., Trenton, N.J., 1982-90. Artist, author: Impressions of India, 1985; one woman exhbn. N.J. State Mus., 1975; writer, designer, photographer A Sense of Beauty, 1975. Active artistic and spiritual projects SYDA Found. Recipient Art Dirs. award San Francisco Art Dirs. Club, San Francisco, 1965, Internat. Broadcasting award Hollywood Advt. Club, L.A., 1965; fellow NEH, Peoples Republic China, Japan, India, 1973-74. Mem. Ctr. for Book Arts (artist), Graphic Artists Guild. Jewish. Home and Office: Soc for Folk Arts Preservation 308 E 79th St New York NY 10021-0904

STERN, KATE MACOMBER, writer, educator; b. Iowa City, Iowa, Aug. 19, 1952; d. Richard Gustave and Ruth Gay (Clark) S.; m. Jeffrey Jay Baron, Dec. 27, 1980; children: Liza Cady, Alexander Macomber. BA in English, Washington U., St. Louis, 1973; MA in English, U. Iowa, 1976; PhD in English, Loyola U., Chgo., 1983. With sch. dept. Holt, Rinehart and Winston, N.Y.C., 1973-74; press sec. Congressman Clarence Long, Washington, 1979; legis. corr. Senate Fin. Com., Washington, 1980; lectr. Georgetown U., Washington, 1983-85. Author: Christina Stead's Heroine, 1989; contbr. book rev. to literary jours. Mem. MLA, Am. Assn. Australian Lit. Studies. Home: 5513 Mckinley St Bethesda MD 20817-3729

STERN, LOUISE, artist; b. New Haven, Apr. 24, 1921; d. Louis Michael and Bertha (Vorhaus) Gompertz; m. Siegfried Stern, June 30, 1945; children: Frederick, David. Student, Syracuse U., 1939-41; MusB, Boston U., 1943. One-woman shows include Ward-Nasse Gallery, N.Y.C., 1978, 80, Hudson River Mus., Yonkers, N.Y., 1982, Concordia Coll. Libr. Gallery, Bronxville, N.Y., 1987; exhibited in group shows Nat. Assn. Women Artists traveling shows, 1978-80, 81-83, 84-86, 89-90, Hudson River Mus., Ny Carlsberg Glyptokek Mus., Copenhagen, 1980, Fukuoka (Japan) Cultural Ctr., 1981, Bergen Community Mus., Paramus, N.J., 1983, Audubon Artists, N.Y.C., Prints Internat., 1990, 92, Gallery at Hastings, N.Y., 1992, Adelphi U. Manhattan Ctr., 1991, also others; represented in permanent collections Cabrini Med. Ctr., N.Y.C., Morani Art Gallery, Med. Coll. Pa., Gen. Foods, Tarrytown, N.Y., Simpson, Thacker, and Bartlett, N.Y.C., Genesis Hebrew Ctr., Tuckahoe, N.Y., also pvt. collections and cos. Recipient 1st in graphic award New Rochelle Art Assn., 1983, 2d award for graphics, 1985; 1st in graphics award Serge Hollerbach, 1989, Dr. and Mrs. I.C. Gayner award, 1990, also others. Mem. AAUW, Nat. assn. Women Artists (chmn. print jury 1988-90, chmn. nominating com. 1990-92, Morris J. Helman award 1984, Stelly Sterling Meml. award 1989), Silvermine Guild of Artists, Mamaroneck Artists Guild. Home and Studio: 120 Lakeshore Dr Eastchester NY 10707

STERN, MARIANNE, advertising agency owner and executive; b. Elizabeth, N.J., July 17, 1950; d. Arthur Leo and Anne (De Paola) Monaghan; m. Manfred Joseph Stern, July 11, 1970 (div.); children: Kathryn Anne, Manfred Joseph III. Student, Montclair (N.J.) State Coll., 1970; BA in English summa cum laude, Kean Coll. of N.J., 1978. Copywriter Patrick J. Gallagher Advt., Westfield, N.J., 1978-79; media dir. Rapp Advt., Springfield, N.J., 1979-85; account exec. Spectrum advt., Springfield, 1985; pres., account exec. Whitney A. Morgan Advt., Montclair, 1985—; cons. Monadel, Inc., Rahway, N.J., 1985—. Mem. publicity com. 200 Club of Union County, N.J., 1978; pub. chmn. Boy Scouts Am. Union County chpt., 1987. Mem. NAFE, Phi Kappa Phi, Lambda Alpha Sigma, Alpha Sigma Lambda. Office: Whitney A Morgan Advt 37 N Fullerton Ave Montclair NJ 07042-3446

STERN, MICHAEL LAWRENCE, psychologist; b. N.Y.C., July 3, 1948; s. Abraham Isaac and Etta (Silverberg) S.; m. Karen Beth Rivard, July 26, 1981; children: Joshua Ethan, Rachel Lynn. BA, Calif. State U., Long Beach, 1970; PhD, U. Wash., 1977. Diplomate Am. Bd. Med. Psychotherapists; cert. employee assistance profl., sex therapist. Instr. dept. psychology U. Wash., Seattle, 1975-77; rsch. assoc. dept. psychiatry U. Tenn. Med. Sch., Memphis, 1977-78; clin. dir. drug abuse program Fed. Correction Inst., Danbury, Conn., 1978-85, chief psychologist, 1985-86; dir. outpatient recovery ctr. Briarcliff Manor, N.Y., 1986-88; pvt. practice clin. psychology, 1981-86; cons. Addiction Recovery Corp, Westchester, 1987-88; adj. faculty Fairfield U., 1981-86. U. Tenn. postdoctoral fellow, 1977-78. Mem. Am. Psychol. Assn., Assn. Advancement Behavior Therapy, Am. Assn. Sex Educators, Counselor, and Therapists, Conn. Psychol. Assn. Cons. editor TSA News, 1977-78. Home: Saw Mill Ridge Rd Newtown CT 06470-1402 Office: Green Knoll Profl Ctr 60 Old New Milford Rd Brookfield CT 06804-2430

STERN, ROBERT, physician; b. Phila., May 4, 1932; s. Harry Frederick and Florence (Potamkin) S.; m. Roberta Yaffe, Nov. 11, 1960 (div. 1974); m. Mary Ellen Weber, May 17, 1987; children: Susan Lee, Leslie Belle, Diane Liz. AB, U. Pa., 1953; MD, Hahemann U., Phila., 1959. Internship Einstein Med. Ctr., Phila., 1956-60; resident NYU Bellevue, N.Y.C., 1960-64; attending MD U.S. Naval Hosp., Great Lakes, Ill., 1964-66; pvt. practice Mt. Holly, N.J., 1966—. Mem. AMA, Burlington County Med. Soc., Med. Soc. N.J., Am. Acad. Head and Neck Surgery. Office: 131 Madison Ave Mount Holly NJ 08060

STERN, WALTER PHILLIPS, investment executive; b. N.Y.C., Sept. 26, 1928; s. Leo and Marjorie (Phillips) S.; m. Elizabeth May, Feb. 12, 1958; children: Sarah May, William May, David May. AB, Williams Coll., 1950; MBA, Harvard U., 1952. With Lazard Freres & Co., N.Y.C., 1953-54; assoc. Burnham & Co., Inc. (now Drexel Burnham Lambert Group, Inc.), N.Y.C., 1954-60, ptnr., 1960-71, sr. exec. v.p., 1972-73; vice chmn., mng. dir. eastern ops. Capital Rsch. Co., 1973—; chmn. bd. New Perspective Fund, Inc., 1973—, Fundamental Investors Inc., 1978—; chmn. Capital Group Internat., Inc; vice chmn. Europacific Growth Fund, Inc., 1984—; chmn. bd. Emerging Markets Growth Fund; pres., dir. Income Fund Am., Inc., Growth Fund Am.; bd. dirs. Temple-Inland, Inc.; past mem. pub. bd. Mcpl. Securities Rulemaking Bd., 1984-87; trustee Fin. Analysts Rsch. Found.; chmn. bd. trustees Hudson Inst.; dir. Jewish Community Rels. Coun. of N.Y.; instr. in investment mgmt. and fin. NYU, 1956-62, 70-73. Contbr. articles to profl. jours. Chmn. fin. adv. com. Haddasah; trustee Am. Jewish Com., bd. dirs. Westchester chpt.; gov. Anti-Defamation League; bd. dirs. Am. Friends of Tel Aviv U.; trustee Tel Aviv U., Jaffee Inst. Strategic Studies, Tel Aviv; v.p., treas., exec. com. Washington Inst. Near East Policy; pres., bd. dirs. Rsch. Project on Energy and Econ. Policy; chmn. Am. steering com. Freedom Trade with Israel. Mem. N.Y. Soc. Security Analysts (bd. dir.), Fin. Analysts Fedn. (pres. 1971-72, bd. dirs.), Inst. Chartered Fin. Analysts (pres. 1976-77, bd. dirs.), Assn. Investment and Mgmt. Rsch. (bd. dirs., exec. com. 1990-91), Harvard Club, Williams Club, Econ. Club, Sunningdale Country Club, Calif. Club, Phi Beta Kappa. Mem. N.Y. Soc. Security Analysts (bd. dirs.), Fin. Analysts Fedn. (pres. 1971-72, bd. dirs.), Inst. Chartered Fin. Analysts (pres. 1976-77, bd. dirs.), Assn. Investment and Mgmt. Rsch. (bd. dirs., exec. com. 1990—), Harvard Club, Williams Club, Econ. Club, Sunningdale Country Club, Calif. Club, Phi Beta Kappa. Jewish. Home: 450 Fort Hill Rd Scarsdale NY 10583-2413 Office: Capital Group Inc 630 Fifth Ave Ste 36 New York NY 10111 also: Capital Group Inc 333 S Hope St Los Angeles CA 90071

STERNBERG, JUDI ANN, gifted and talented education coordinator; b. N.Y.C., Feb. 21, 1941; d. Theodore and Shirley (Raff) Weissman; m. Stanley R. Sternberg, Sept. 1, 1968. BS in Edn. magna cum laude, NYU, 1962; MS in Edn., Hunter Coll., 1967; postgrad., Greenburgh Inst., Hartsdale, N.Y., 1968—, Coll. New Rochelle, N.Y., 1976, 79, 81, 89—. Cert. elem. tchr., N.Y. Elem. tchr. Greenburgh Cen. Sch. Dist. No. 7, Hartsdale, 1962—, dist. gifted/talented tchr., 1980-89, 91; ednl. cons. Bd. Coop. Ednl. Svcs. So. Westchester, Ardsley, N.Y., 1982, 88, Nyack (N.Y.) Pub. Schs., 1984, Duchess County, Poughkeepsie, N.Y., 1986; workshop leader Ardsley, Elmsford, Greenburgh Tchr. Ctr., 1980, 81, 85, 86, 92; panelist N.Y. State Dept. Edn., 1985; presenter at profl. cons., 1981-92. Author: (with others) Creative Thinking Through Art, 1984. Trustee Woodlands High Sch. Scholarship Fund, Hartsdale, 1988-90; fundraiser Greenburgh Nature Ctr., Scarsdale, N.Y., 1987-89; mem. Westchester Coalition Legal Abortion, 1986—. Westchester Inst. Rsch. grantee, 1988. Mem. ASCD, Nat. Assn. for Gifted (bd. dirs. for advocacy for gifted and talented in N.Y. state 1991—), Coun. for Exceptional Children, N.Y. State United Tchrs., Pi Lambda Theta (curriculum innovation award 1986). Jewish. Office: Greenburgh CSD No 7 475 W Hartsdale Ave Hartsdale NY 10530-1359

STERNBERG, PHYLLIS, marketing executive; b. Bklyn., Oct. 18, 1960; d. Henry Russell and Elaine (Temple) S. BS in Psychology summa cum laude, Union Coll., Schenectady, N.Y., 1982. Account exec. Joseph Tardi Assocs., Albany, N.Y., 1984-86, v.p., 1986—. Mem. Am. Women in Radio and TV (Capital Dist. chpt. com. chair 1986-88, treas. 1988-90, pres. 1991-92), Sigma Xi, Phi Beta Kappa, Psi Chi. Office: Joseph Tardi Assocs 125 Wolf Rd # 108 Albany NY 12205-1262

STERNBERG, RICHARD IRA, psychologist; b. Bklyn.; s. Jay and Rae (Eisenberg) S.; m. Vivian Sternberg; children: Adam Joshua, Jared Scott, Brittany Lauren. B.A., Yeshiva U.; M.S., CCNY; Ph.D., Calif. Sch. Profl. Psychology. Lic. clin. psychologist; cert. forensic examiner. Grad. faculty CCNY, 1974-76; pvt. practice clin. psychology, Hartford, 1977—; instr. Eastern Mich. U., Ypsilanti, 1977-78; staff psychologist, then asst. dir. evaluation unit, exec. dir. Ctr. Forensic Psychiatry, Ann Arbor, Mich., 1976-79; chief psychologist, dir. diagnostic unit Whiting Forensic Inst., Middletown, Conn., 1976-79; cons. State Calif., 1977-78; cons. on sexual assaults HEW, 1977; cons. Child Murders Task Force, 1978-79; cons. career services CCNY, 1981-82; cons. youth services, Newington, Conn., 1982-84; vocat. disability expert examiner Social Security Adminstrn., 1982—, liaison Employee Assistance Program, 1986—; indsl. cons., 1985—; pres., clin. dir. Clin. Psychology Assocs. P.C., West Hartford, 1986—, EAP coord., 1985—; mem. probate judges ct. panel, 1983—; adj. prof. St. Joseph Coll., 1984-89; mem. grad. sch. faculty U. Hartford, 1986-87; chief cons. Rocky Hill Fire and Police Depts., 1983-85; mem. adv. bd. Police Athletic League, 1988—; cons. Police Dept., 1988—; acad. screening officer Calif. Sch. Profl. Psychology. Fellow Am. Bd. Vocat. Experts; mem. Am. Psychol. Assn. (editorial rev. bd. 1977), N.J. Psychol. Assn., Conn. Psychol. Assn., Nat. Migraine Found., Menninger Found., Alumni Assn. Yeshiva U., Alumni Assn. CCNY, Calif. Sch. Profl. Psychology Alumni Assn. Contbr. articles to profl. jours. Office: 836 Farmington Ave Ste 201 West Hartford CT 06119-1549

STERNE, LAWRENCE JON, economic consulting firm administrator; b. Cambridge, Mass., Sept. 28, 1949; s. Russell Justin and Dorothea (White) S.; m. Susan Mains, Apr. 17, 1976; children: Marjorie Mains, Caroline Adams. BA, Harvard U., 1972. V.p. Reynolds Rsch. Assocs. N.Y.C., 1976-77, ECOM Cons., Inc., N.Y.C., 1977-78; V.p. Reynolds Rsch. Assocs. Chem. Bank, N.Y.C., 1978-83, v.p., 1981—; sec. treas., dir. equity rsch. Econ. Analysis Assocs., Inc., Stowe, Vt., 1980—; pres. Paper and Forest Products Industry Analysts Group, N.Y.C., Vt., 1982-83. Mem. Stowe Sch. Bd., 1983-87, 89—. Mem. N.Y. Soc. Security Analysts, Assn. Investment Mgmt. and Rsch.

STERNFELD, LEON, health facility administrator; b. Bklyn., June 15, 1913; s. Solomon and Goldie (Levine) S.; m. Ruth Schwartz Sternfeld, Aug. 25, 1934; children: Kay, Barbara. BS, U. Chgo., 1932, MD, 1936, PhD, 1937; MSPH, Columbia U., 1943. Med. Diplomate in Pediatrics, Preventive Medicine. Asst. dist. health officer N.Y. State Dept. Health, Buffalo, N.Y., 1943-44; dir. Med. Rehab. N.Y. State Dept. Health, Albany, N.Y., 1944-50; asst. dir. Tuberculosis Control Mass. Dept. Pub. Health, Boston, 1950-52; dir. field training Harvard Sch. Pub. Health, Boston, 1952-53; active military duty U.S. Army Med. Corps., Korea, 1953-55; commr. Pub. Health City Cambridge, Mass., 1955-60; deputy commr. Mass. Dept. Pub. Health, Boston, 1960-70; cons. in med. care Fedn. Jewish Philanthropies, N.Y.C., 1970-71; med. dir. United Cerebral Palsy Assn., N.Y.C., 1971—; assoc. prof. Maternal and Child Health, Harvard Sch. Pub. Health, 1960-70; dir. Commn. Accreditation Rehab. Facilities, Tuscon, 1987-93, Accreditation Coun. Disabilities, Landover, Md., 1974-91. Contbr. articles to profl. jours. Col. U.S. Army, 1953-73, Korea. Recipient Disting. Svc. award Am. Acad. for Cerebral Palsy and Developmental Medicine, Louisville, Ky., 1991. Fellow Am. Pub. Health Assn., Am. Acad. Cerebral Palsy and Developmental Medicine. Jewish. Home: 1385 York Ave New York NY 10021 Office: United Cerebral Palsy Rsch 7 Penn Pla New York NY 10001-3900

STERNFELD, MARC HOWARD, investment banking executive; b. N.Y.C., July 12, 1947; s. Joseph and Jeane (Richstein) S.; m. Arleen Estelle Weinreb, Aug. 25, 1968; children: Joshua, Jonathan. BA, Queens Coll., 1968; MS, NYU, 1970; MBA, Columbia U., 1971. Spacecraft programmer Grumman Aero., 1968-70; fin. analyst CBS, N.Y.C., 1971-72; rsch. asst. Nat. Bur Econ. Rsch., 1970-71; sr. analyst N.Y.C. Police Dept., 1972-75; ptnr. Arthur Andersen & Co., 1975-88; prin. Morgan Stanley, 1985-87; mng. dir. Salomon Bros., 1988—; bd. dirs. Participant Trust Corp., N.Y.C.; active Fed. Res. Payment and Settlements Com., N.Y.C., 1990—. Treas. Vols. for Israel, Marlboro, N.J.; v.p. N.J. region United Synagogue of Am., pres.'s adv. com.; pres. Marlboro Jewish Ctr.; bd. dirs. Fedn. of Monmouth County, parents coun. exec. com., Washington U., St. Louis. Mem. Jazz Vt. (bd. dirs.). Home: 13 Evan Dr Morganville NJ 07751-1062

STERNS, HARVEY NELSON, education educator; b. Detroit, Feb. 25, 1924; s. Roy Andrew and Florence Edity (Gross) S.; children: Robin, Holly. BS, Wayne State U., 1950, MEd, 1955; PhD, U. Mich., 1968. Cert. tchr., Mich. Elem. tchr. Dependent Schs., Germany, 1952-57; art tchr. Oak Park (Mich.) Schs., 1957-62; elem. prin. L'Anse Creuse Schs., Mt. Clemens, Mich., 1962-66; asst. supt. Orchard Lake Schs., West Bloomfield, Mich., 1966-69; assoc. prof. Marshall U., Huntington, W.Va., 1969-72; from prof., assoc. dean to prof. edn. Lock Haven (Pa.) U., 1972-90, prof., chair, 1990-92. Contbr. chpt. to book, articles to profl. jours. With USAF, 1943-46. Mem. AAUP, ASCD, Phi Delta Kappa (historian 1988-90), Phi Kappa Phi.

STERNSON, LARRY ALLEN, pharmaceutical company executive; b. N.Y.C., Mar. 14, 1946; s. Henry and Mirri (Zimmerman) S.; m. Janet Mary Glasgow, May 21, 1977; children: Scott M., Thomas Q., Leslie A. BS, U. Ill., Chgo., 1968, PhD, 1970; postdoctoral study, U. Kans., 1970-72. Registered pharmacist. Asst. prof. U. Ga., Athens, 1972-75; prof. U. Kans., Lawrence, 1975-84; dir. ctr. for bioanalytical rsch. U. Kans., 1983-84; exec. dir. Smith Kline & French Labs., Phila., 1984-87; v.p. Sterling Drug-Kodak, Great Valley, Pa., 1987—; vis. scientist Soviet Acad. Scis., Moscow, 1979; vis. prof. Yrije U., Amsterdam, The Netherlands, 1980. Fellow Royal Soc. Chemistry, Am. Assn. Pharm. Scis.; mem. Am. Chem. Soc., Am. Soc. Pharmacology & Exptl. Therapeutics. Office: 9 Great Valley Pky Malvern PA 19355-1304

STERRER, NEIL E., real estate professional; b. Bklyn., Aug. 25, 1945; s. Abraham and Jennie (Miller) S.; m. Teri Marva Glass, Nov. 23, 1969 (div. Oct. 1982); 1 child, Andrew Ian; m. Camille Ann Ruggiero, June 16, 1986; 1 child, Joseph S. Catapano. BS, U. Wis., 1967; MA, George Washington U., 1970, Queens Coll., 1973; Advanced Real Estate Appraisal Diploma, Hofstra U., 1988. Cert. residential specialist. Tchr. Bd. of Edn., Bklyn., 1968-83, tchr. After/Sch. Learning Ctr., 1969-71; supr. remedial math Aux. Svcs. for High Schs., Bklyn., 1970-81; supr./coord. Nat. Leisure Systems/Pool Ventures, Queens, N.Y., 1974-81; assoc., broker/mgr. Panzarella Realty, Rosedale, N.Y., 1982-88; pres., owner, broker Sterrer Realty Inc., Long

Beach, N.Y., 1988—; real estate tchr. L.I. Bd. Realtors, Babylon, N.Y., 1989—; tax certiorari appraiser, Long Beach, 1988—; bd. dirs. L.I. Bd. Realtors, Babylon, Nassau South Shore Chpt., Merrick, N.Y. Editor (pamphlet) Children's Travel Book/Daytrips/New York City Metro Area, 1980; contbr. articles to profl. jours. Exec. coun. West End Civic Assn., Long Beach, 1984—; mem. Long Beach Hist. Soc., 1988—; sponsor Long Beach Summer Concert Series, 1990-91. Recipient field trip grants Bd. of Edn., Bklyn., 1976-81. Mem. N.Y. State Assn. Realtors, Nat. Assn. Realtors, N.Y. State Assn. Mortgage Brokers, L.I. Multiple Listing Svc., N.Y. State Soc. Real Estate Appraisers, Columbia Soc. Real Estate Appraisers, Nat. Assn. Real Estate Appraisers, RTC Contractor Appraisal Svcs., Grad. Realtor Inst., others. Office: Sterrer Realty Inc 966 W Beech St Long Beach NY 11561-1326

STETSON, EUGENE WILLIAM, III, film and television writer and producer; b. Norwalk, Conn., Mar. 31, 1951; s. Eugene William Jr. and Grace Stuart (Richardson) S. AB, Harvard U., 1982, postgrad. in Sch. Arts and Scis., 1986. Assoc. exec. dir. Conn. River Watershed Coun., Easthampton, Mass., 1978-81; v.p. Fairhill Oil & Gas Corp. (Fairhill Oil Ltd.-Can.), N.Y.C., Calgary, Alta., Can., 1981-84; pres. Fairhill Oil & Gas Corp. (Fairhill Oil Ltd.-Can.), N.Y.C., Calgary, 1984-92; film and TV writer and producer, 1991—; bd. dirs. Piedmont Fin. Co., Greensboro, N.C., 1978-80, Chisolm Mgmt. Corp., N.Y.C., 1983—; supr. Ottauquechee Conservation Dist., Woodstock, Vt., 1978-82; pres. Boatwright Found., N.Y.C., 1981—; exec. com. Westminster Sch., Simsbury, Conn., 1984-86; gov. Smith Richardson Found., N.Y., 1984—; trustee Proctor Acad., Andover, N.H., 1985—; co-founder River Watch Network, Montpelier, Vt., 1987—. Mem. Vt. Gov.'s Coun. of Environ. Advisers, 1992—. Mem. Harvard-Radcliffe Club Vt., Harvard Club N.Y.C., Hasty Pudding Club. Home: RR1 Box 167 Gully Rd Woodstock VT 05091

STETTNER, ENID BALLINGER, music institution director; b. N.Y.C., Feb. 1, 1933; d. Jack and Charlotte (Felder) Ballinger; m. Alfred M. Stettner, Apr. 27, 1960. BA, Barnard Coll., 1954; MA, Hunter Coll., 1960; MSW, SUNY, Albany, 1983. Founder, dir. Dorothy Taubman Inst., Medusa, N.Y., 1977—. Home and Office: Medusa NY 12120

STEUER, RICHARD MARC, lawyer; b. Bklyn., June 19, 1948; s. Harold and Gertrude (Vengar) S.; m. Audrey P. Forchheimer, Sept. 9, 1973; children: Hilary, Jeremy. BA, Hofstra U., 1970; JD, Columbia U., 1973. Bar: N.Y. 1974, U.S. Dist. Ct. (ea. and so. dists.) N.Y. 1974, U.S. Ct. Appeals (2nd cir.) 1974, U.S. Supreme Ct. 1979, U.S. Dist. Ct. (no. dist.) N.Y. 1984, U.S. Ct. Appeals (3rd cir.) 1987. Ptnr. Kaye, Scholer, Fierman, Hays & Handler, N.Y.C., 1973—; adj. assoc. prof. law NYU, 1985; lectr. various orgns. Author: A Guide to Marketing Law: Law and Business Inc., 1986; contbr. articles to profl. jours. Fellow Am. Bar Found.; mem. ABA (chmn. Sherman Act sect. 1 com. 1992—, chmn. spring meeting program com. 1991-92, vice-chmn. program com. 1988-91, chmn. monograph com. refusals to deal and exclusive distributorships 1983, various others, editorial bd. antitrust devel. volumn 1984-86, antitrust law sect., lectr. 1978, 85, 89), Assn. of Bar of City of N.Y. (antitrust and trade regulation, lectures and continuing edn. coms., lectr. 1983-92). Office: Kaye Scholer Fierman Hays & Handler 425 Park Ave New York NY 10022-3506

STEURER, STEPHEN JOSEPH, association executive; b. Chgo., Mar. 13, 1944; s. Stefan and Leone (May) S.; m. Judith Anne Friedman, Apr. 16, 1975; children: Aliza Anne, Erin Etefanie, Stephen Alexander. AB In History, Loyola U., Chgo., 1967; MS in Linguistics, Georgetown U., 1969; PhD in Edn., U. Md., 1975. Lic. tchr. reading, English, history, Italian. Tchr. mid. sch. Chgo. Pub. Schs., 1967; tchr. high sch. D.C. Pub. Schs., Washington, 1968-73; instr., project dir. U. Md., College Park, 1974-77; coord. chpt. I svcs. Md. State Dept. Edn., Balt., 1978-88, acad. coord. correctional edn., 1988—; exec. dir. Correctional Edn. Assn., Laurel, Md., 1986—. Guest editor Corrections Today mag., 1987; co-host nat. confs. PBS/Adult Learning Satellite System, 1989, 90; contbr. articles to profl. jours. Recipient Spl. Disting. Svc. awards Correctional Edn. Assn and Md. Adult Edn. Assn. Mem. Correctional Edn. Assn. (exec. dir. 1986—), Am. Correctional Assn. (del. assembly 1985—), Am. Vocat. Assn., Internat. Reading Assn., Md. Assn. Adult, Community and Continuing Edn. (pres., v.p., sec., regional dir. 1978—). Democrat. Home: 1303 Sarah Dr Silver Spring MD 20904-2149

STEVENS, ALBERT DAVID, educational coordinator; b. Burlington, Vt., Aug. 5, 1942; s. David Chynoweth and Dorothy Elizabeth (Gibson) S.; m. Barbara Ann Brothers, July 13, 1963; children: Mary, Nancy, Carolyn, Scott. BS in Dairy Sci., U. Vt., 1964; MS in Adminstrn., St. Michael's U., 1983. Owner, mgr. Sunset Hill Farm, Wells River, Vt., 1964-85; coord. coop. vocat. edn. Oxbow Vocat. Ctr., Bradford, Vt., 1984—; adult svcs. coord. Oxbow Vocat. Ctr., 1988—. exec. dir. lobbyist Common Cause Vt., Montpelier, 1985-88; chmn. Vt. State Libr. Bd., Montpelier, 1978-88, Evenstart Adv. Commn., Bradford, Vt., 1991—; mem. Vt. State Valuation Appeal Bd., Montpelier, 1979—; chmn., trustee Baldwin Meml. Libr., Wells River, Vt., 1972—; pres. Oxbow Sr. Independence Program, Newbury, Vt., 1988—; moderator Newbury Town, Wells River Village, 1991—; chmn. Selectmen of Newbury, 1972-78. Home: RR 1 Box 11 Wells River VT 05081 Office: Oxbow Vocat Ctr PO Box 618 Bradford VT 05033-0618

STEVENS, ALLYSSA ELIZABETH, retail executive; b. Townshend, Vt., Nov. 27, 1961; d. William Francis and Elizabeth Jane (Stevens) K.; m. Cedric Vaughn Stevens, Jan. 31, 1988. Student, Simmons Coll., 1979-80; cert. in purchasing, Bryant Coll., 1987. Sec., asst. to supt. Tehran (Iran) Am. Sch., summer 1979; asst. to pres., office mgr. Town & Country Furniture, S. Burlington, 1981-86; mgr. Center Store, Burlington, 1986-87; gen. mgr., contr. Novello Inc., Montpelier, Vt., 1988—; various towns, Vt.; ind. distbr. skin care and nutrition bus. Network Mktg., Skin Care and Nutrition, Hinesburg, Vt., 1991—; cons. Ctr. Store/Health Fun Inc., Burlington, 1987—; with Tehran Am. Sch., Iran, summer 1979. Forum mem. Govt. Commn. on Econ. Devel., Montpelier, 1989; pub. speaker Iran Hostage Crisis. Mem. Vt. Retail Assn. Roman Catholic. Office: Novello Inc Barre-Montpelier Rd PO Box 309 Montpelier VT 05601-0309

STEVENS, DANIEL DAVID DEAN, logistician, government official; b. Hickory, N.C., Mar. 3, 1935; s. George M. and Mattie Gladys (Richardson) S.; m. Janice C. Kilby, Mar. 26, 1958; children: Teresa Ann, Daniel Dean. AA in Bus. Adminstrn., Beaufort (S.C.) Tech. Coll., 1979; BA Human Resource Mgmt., Pepperdine U., 1979, MA Human Resource Mgmt., 1981; grad., Def. Systems Mgmt. Coll., Ft. Belvoir, Va., 1986. Enlisted man USMC, 1952, advanced through grades to master sgt., 1969; drill instr. USMC, Parris Island, S.C., 1964-67, Socialist Republic of Vietnam, 1968-69; ret., 1972; photographer Josten's Am. Yearbook Co., Parris Island, 1972-74; sales rep. Thomas Realty Co., Beaufort, S.C., 1974; plant account officer Marine Corps Recruit Depot, Parris Island, 1974-79; logistics mgmt. specialist Naval Air Systems Command, Washington, 1979-92, asst. program mgr. for logistics P-3 aircraft, 1981-84, asst. program mgr. for logistics H-46 helicopter, 1984-86, asst. program mgr. logistics Navy aircrew common ejection seat, 1986—. Treas. Rose Hill Bapt. Ch., Alexandria, Va. Mem. U.S. Navy League, Marine Corps League, Marine Corps Assn. (pres. Mt. Vernon Camp), Gideons Internat., Am. Legion, Fleet Res. Assoc., DSMC Alumni Assn. Republican. Home: 6106 Craft Rd Alexandria VA 22310 Office: Hdqrs Naval Air System Command Air-41042C Washington DC 20360

STEVENS, DANIEL JOSEPHUS, agricultural economist, educator; b. Leonardtown, Md., Apr. 18, 1946; s. Robert Alexander and Marion Virginia (Milstead) S.; m. Barbara Jean Nelson, June 29, 1968; children: Matthew Daniel, Philip Sean. AA, St. Mary's Coll. Md., 1966; BS, U. Md., 1968; MS, Tex. A&I U., 1972. Economist USDA, Washington, 1973—; instr. U. Md. Fire and Rescue Inst., College Park, 1982—; cons. Food and Agrl. Orgn., UN, Rome, 1988. Co-author: Tariff and Nontariff Barriers to World Tobacco Trade, 1973; contbr. numerous articles to profl. publs. Chief Waldorf (Md.) Vol. Fire Dept., 1988—; mem. Charles County Comprehensive Plan Task Force, 1988. Lt. USN, 1968-72. Named Fire Fighter of Yr., Waldorf Vol. Fire Dept., 1976, 90; recipient Tobacco Economist award Tobacco Mchts. Assn., 1989. Mem. U. Md. Alumni Assn., Alpha Zeta. Republican. Baptist. Home: SR 5 Box 490 La Plata MD 20646 Office: USDA FAS TC&S Div Rm 5932-S Washington DC 29250-1000

STEVENS, DONALD VERNET, JR., management consultant; b. Medford, Mass., Nov. 27, 1921; s. Donald V. and Louise Eulalia (Glidden) S.; m. Nancy Rosamond Jones, June 19, 1943; children: Joan Dorinda Stevens Anderson, Nancy Louise Stevens LaVallee. Student, R.I. Coll., 1990-92. Apprentice machinist Brown & Sharpe Mfg. Co., Providence, 1940-44, foreman, 1945-54, dept. mgr., 1954-59; cons., v.p. Vaule & Co., Inc., Providence and Wellesley, Mass., 1960-76; ptnr. Carlson & Stevens Mgmt. Cons., Rumford, R.I., 1976-77; staff cons. Bird Machine Co., Inc., South Walpole, Mass., 1977-82; prin. Donald V. Stevens, Rumford, 1982—. With U.S. Air Force, 1944-45. Mem. Inst. Mgmt. Cons. (cert., v.p. membership New Eng. chpt. 1985—), Providence Engrng. Soc. (life mem.), Am. Arbitration Assn. (panel of arbitrators 1980—). Republican.. Home and Office: 37 Beaumont St Rumford RI 02916-1909

STEVENS, ELISABETH GOSS (MRS. ROBERT SCHLEUSSNER, JR.), writer, journalist; b. Rome, N.Y., Aug. 11, 1929; d. George May and Elisabeth (Stryker) Stevens; m. Robert Schleussner, Jr., Mar. 12, 1966 (dec. 1977); 1 child, Laura Stevens. B.A., Wellesley Coll., 1951; M.A. with high honors, Columbia U., 1956. Editorial assoc. Art News Mag., 1964-65; art critic and reporter Washington Post, Washington, 1965-66; free-lance art critic and reporter Balt., 1966—; contbg. art critic Wall Street Jour., N.Y.C., 1969-72; art critic Trenton Times, N.J., 1974-77; art and architecture critic The Balt. Sun, 1978-86. Author: Elisabeth Stevens' Guide to Baltimore's Inner Harbor, 1981, Fire and Water: Six Short Stories, 1982, Children of Dust: Portraits and Preludes, 1985, Horse and Cart: Stories from the Country, 1990; contbr. articles, poetry and short stories to jours., nat. newspapers and popular mags. Recipient A.D. Emmart award for journalism, 1980, citation for critical writing Balt.-Washington Newspaper Guild, 1980; art critics' fellow Nat. Endowment Arts, 1973-74, fellow MacDowell Colony, 1981, Va. Ctr. for Creative Arts, 1982, 83, 84, 85, 88, 89, 90, Ragdale Found., 1984, 89, YADDO, 1991; work in Progress grantee for poetry Md. State Arts Coun., 1986, Creative Devel. grantee for short fiction collection Mayor's Com. on Art and Culture, Balt., 1986. Mem. Coll. Art Assn., Balt. Writers Alliance, Balt. Bibliophiles, Authors Guild, Am. Studies Assn. Home: 6604 Walnutwood Cir Baltimore MD 21212-1213

STEVENS, EUGENE STEVE, chemist, educator; b. Carnegie, Pa., Dec. 29, 1938; s. Wasyl and Anna (Makar) Pysh; m. Renate Theresa Weidner, Mar. 30, 1968; 1 child, Gregory Thomas. BS, Yale U., 1960; PhD, U. Chgo., 1965. Postdoctoral fellow Harvard U., Cambridge, Mass., 1965-66; from asst. prof. to prof. Brown U., Providence, 1966-77; prof. SUNY, Binghamton, 1977—. Contbr. over 90 articles to profl. jours. Regional chmn. N.Y. State Sci. Olympiad, Binghamton, 1990, 92. Rsch. grantee NSF, 1988-92. Mem. Am. Chem. Soc. (chmn. local sect. 1988), Am. Biophys. Soc. Office: SUNY Dept Chemistry PO Box 6000 Binghamton NY 13902-6000

STEVENS, FORD WOODS, JR., dentist; b. Balt., Mar. 2, 1942; s. Ford W. and Eleanor (Quinn) S.; m. Linie Westland, Dec. 4, 1971; children: Timothy Westland, Ford Woods III. BSc, Wheeling Coll., 1967; DMD, U. Pa., 1977. Pvt. practice gen. dentistry Phila., 1979-86, Drexel Hill, Pa., 1985-86, Clifton Heights, Pa., 1986—; ptnr. Delta Group, 1986; instr. gen. dentistry Suburban Gen. Hosp., 1983; founder Gerident, Inc., 1988; asst. prof. Sch. Dental Medicine, U. Pa., 1981-82. Mem. acad. adv. bd. Wheeling Coll., 1982; bd. dirs. Valley Forge Mil. Acad., 1982; mem. Presdl. Task Force, Washington, 1983-85; mem. Pa. Dental Polit. Action Com. Fellow Acad. Dentistry Internat.; mem. Pa. Acad. Gen. Dentistry (mem. long range planning com., ann. meeting com., constitution and by-laws com.). Republican. Roman Catholic. Home and Office: 400 Inskeep Ave Glenolden PA 19036

STEVENS, FRANK, utility official; b. Ashton-U-Lyne, Lancashire, Eng., Sept. 16, 1941; came to U.S., 1968; s. Clifford and Ellen (Sansom) S.; m. Barbara Hardman, June 24, 1961; 1 child, Alison J. EE, Oldham Coll., Lancashire, 1964. Engr. North Western Electric Bd., Lancashire, 1964-68, N.E. Utilities, Essex, Conn., 1968-71; operating supr. N.E. Utilities, Branford, Conn., 1971-72; dist. supt. N.E. Utilities, East Hampton, Conn., 1972-77; regional ops. engr. N.E. Utilities, Madison, Conn., 1977-84; mgr. standards N.E. Utilities, Meriden, Conn., 1984-91; mgr. tng. N.E. Utilities, Newington, Conn., 1991—; mem. C57/C37 com. Am. Nat. Standards Inst., 1984-89, chmn., 1989—. Mem. IEEE (chmn. PES transformer com. on distbn. transformers 1989—), Elec. Coun. New Eng. (standards and specifications com. 1984-87, chmn. 1987—). Office: NE Utilities PO Box 270 Hartford CT 06141-0270

STEVENS, HAROLD RAY, English educator; b. Macon, May 20, 1936; s. Manuel Eugene and Sudie (McManus) S.; m. Ruth Ann Wilson, June 20, 1959; children: David James, Joel Ray. BA summa cum laude, Western Md. Coll., 1958; PhD, U. Pa., 1964. Instr. English Butler U., Indpls., 1963-65, asst. prof, 1965-66; asst. prof Western Md. Coll., Westminster, 1966-70, assoc. prof., 1970-76, prof., 1976—. Co-editor: John Galsworthy Bibliography, 1980; contbr. articles to acad. jours. Chmn. Bd. Recreation and Parks, Carroll County, Md., 1979-85; bd. dirs. ARC, Carroll County, 1969-74. Grantee NEH, 1984-85. Mem. MLA (del. 1987-90), Byron Soc., Joseph Conrad Soc., Mencken Soc., Conf. on Christianity and Lit., Bibliog. Soc. Am., Folger Shakespeare Libr. Home: 1801 Bollinger Rd Westminster MD 21157-7218 Office: Western Md Coll 2 College Hl Westminster MD 21157-4303

STEVENS, ISAAC H., clothing executive; b. N.Y.C.; married; 2 children. Student, Queens Coll., 1971; grad., CUNY, 1975. Pres. Isaac H. Stevens Exec. Cons., N.Y.C., 1978—; cons. Associated Fabrics Corp., N.Y.C., 1980-82, dir. acctg., 1982-84, pres., 1984—. Pres., bd. dirs. The Yaron Found., 1982—. Office: Associated Fabrics Corp 104 E 25th St New York NY 10010-2917

STEVENS, JAMES WALTER, food equipment specialist; b. Albany, N.Y., Apr. 8, 1932; s. Geroge Walker and Alma Catherine (Sill) S.; m. Winifred Palmer, June 18, 1955; children: George, Deborah, Marc. AA, SUNY, Canton, 1956. Vice pres., sales mgr. Lewis Equipment Co., Albany, 1957-86; br. mgr. Plattsburg Supply, Albany, 1986-90; contract food equipment specialist Sysco Corp., Albany, 1990—; guest lectr. Rochester (N.Y.) Inst. Tech., 1985—. Author: Food Equipment Facts, 1981, Manual of Equipment and Design, 1989; columnist Restaurant Mgmt. mag., 1987-88; inventor food equipment. Sgt. USAF, 1950-54, Korea. Mem. Food Equipment Distbrs. Assn., K.C. (sec.-treas. 1975-77), Am. Legion. Republican. Roman Catholic. Home: 253 Hudson Ave Rensselaer NY 12144-3743 Office: Sysco Corp 77 Fuller Rd Albany NY 12205-5716

STEVENS, JOHN PAUL, U.S. Supreme Court justice; b. Chgo., Apr. 20, 1920; s. Ernest James and Elizabeth (Street) S.; m. Elizabeth Jane Sheeren, June 7, 1942; children: John Joseph, Kathryn Stevens Jedlicka, Elizabeth Jane Stevens Sesemann, Susan Roberta Stevens Mullen; m. Maryan Mulholland Simon, Dec. 1979. A.B., U. Chgo., 1941; J.D. magna cum laude, Northwestern U., 1947. Bar: Ill. 1949. Practiced in Chgo.; law clk. to U.S. Supreme Ct. Justice Wiley Rutledge, 1947-48; assoc. firm Poppenhusen, Johnston, Thompson & Raymond, 1948-52; asso. counsel sub-com. on study monopoly power, com. on judiciary U.S. Ho. of Reps., 1951; ptnr. firm Rothschild, Stevens, Barry & Myers, 1952-70; U.S. circuit judge, 1970-75; asso. justice U.S. Supreme Ct., 1975—; Lectr. anti-trust law Northwestern U. Sch. Law, 1953, U. Chgo. Law Sch., 1954-55; Mem. Atty. Gen.'s Nat. Com. to Study Anti-Trust Laws, 1953-55. Served with USNR, 1942-45. Decorated Bronze Star. Mem. Chgo. Bar Assn. (2d v.p. 1970), Am., Ill., Fed. bar assns., Am. Law Inst., Order of Coif, Phi Beta Kappa, Psi Upsilon, Phi Delta Phi. Office: US Supreme Ct 1 First St NE Washington DC 20543

STEVENS, JOSEPH JOHN, JR., federal agency administrator; b. Chgo., Oct. 20, 1949; s. Joseph John Sr. andAnn Mary (Vathokas) S.; m. Patti Jo Thomas, Sept. 15, 1973; children: Barcley Thomas, Tamarin Leigh. AA, Kendall Coll., 1972; BA, Lake Forest Coll., 1975; postgrad., U. Wis., 1976-77, SMSU, 1986-87. Tchr. Lake Mills (Wis.) Pub. Schs., 1976-80; radio broadcaster Sta. WTTN, Watertown, Wis., 1980, Sta. KCKW-KJNA, Jena, La., 1980-81; reading specialist Dept. Corrections State Tenn., Somerville, 1981-83; correctional officer Fed. Bur. Prisons, Memphis, 1983-85; reading specialist Fed. Bur. Prisons, Springfield, Mo., 1985-87; asst. supr. edn. Fed. Bur. Prisons, El Reno, Okla., 1987-88; supr. edn. Fed. Bur. Prisons, Pleasanton, Calif., 1988-89; edn. specialist Fed. Bur. Prisons, Washington, 1990—; nat. coord. Fed. Bur. Prisons Law Libraries, Washington, 1990—, Fed. Bur. Prisons Leisure Libraries, Washington, 1990—; nat. rep. Fed. Female Offenders Program, Washington, 1990—. Author: (short stories) Those You Remember Most, 1972; and editor Edn. Sentry Manual, 1991, Fed. Edn. Manual, 1991, Specialties Directory, 1990. Pres. Leeland Meadows Homeowners Assn., Shepherdstown, W.Va., 1990—; v.p. Affirmative Action Com., Modesto, Calif., 1989. With U.S. Army, 1969-71, Vietnam, 1990-91, Saudi Arabia. Mem. Am. Correctional Assn. (auditor 1986—), Correctional Edn. Assn., VFW. Home: RR 1 Box 3 Shepherdstown WV 25443-9701

STEVENS, MALCOLM PETER, chemistry educator; b. Birmingham, Eng., Apr. 3, 1934; came to U.S., 1948; s. Reginald Harold and Margaret Irene (Beresford) S. BS in Chemistry, San Jose (Calif.) State U., 1957; PhD in Organic Chemistry, Cornell U., 1961. Rsch. chemist Chevron Rsch. Co., Richmond, Calif., 1961-64; asst. prof. Robert Coll., Istanbul, Turkey, 1964-67; asst. prof., assoc. prof. Am. U. Beirut, 1968-71; asst. prof. chemistry U. Hartford, West Hartford, Conn., 1967-68, assoc. prof., 1971, prof., 1978—; vis. prof. U. Sussex, Falmer Brighton, Eng., 1976, Colo. State U., Ft. Collins, 1985. Author: Characterization and Analysis of Polymers by Gas Chromatography, 1969, Polymer Chemistry: An Introduction, 1975, 2d edit., 1990; co-author: Against the Devil's Current: Life and Times of Cyrus Hamlin, 1988, Fire: The Story of the Binghamton Clothing Company Fire of July 22, 1913, 1988; also numerous articles; patentee in field. With U.S. Army, 1953-55. Recipient Conn. Prof. of Yr. award Coun. for Advancement and Support Edn., 1989. Mem. AAUP, Am. Chem. Soc., Sigma Xi. Office: U Hartford Chemistry Dept 200 Bloomfield Ave West Hartford CT 06117-1500

STEVENS, MARK PAUL, insurance, risk management consultant, underwriter; b. Buffalo, Dec. 24, 1951; s. Harry C. and Natalie A. (Rakowski) S.; m. Kathleen Ann Kuestner, May 20, 1972; children: Michael Paul, Justin Matthew. BA in Polit. Sci., La Salle U., 1973. Chartered property and casualty underwriter, assoc. in risk mgmt. Mktg. rep. Royal Ins. Co., Phila., 1973-79; asst. v.p. McDowell Ins., Chambersburg, Pa., 1979-82; exec. v.p. Charles S. Gardner Assoc., Blue Ridge Summit, Pa., 1982-85; dir. security & risk mgmt. div. Am. Bankers Assn., Washington, 1985-86; cons. The Wyatt Co., Washington, 1986—; cons. MCI Communications, Washington, Suntrust Bank, Atlanta, AmSouth Bank, Birmingham, Ala., First Fidelity Bank, Newark, Carnegie Instn., Washington. Co-author: (book) Digest of Bank Insurance, 1987, 91; contbg. author: (book) Banker's Guide to Income Producing Insurance, 1990; contbr. profl. pubs.; speaker industry confs., seminars. Pres. Franklin County Ind. Ins. Agts. Assn., Pa., 1981; bd. dirs. St Maria Goretti High Sch. Athletic Assn., Hagerstown, Md., 1990—. Mem. Soc. Chartered Property and Casualty Underwriters. Democrat. Roman Catholic. Home: 10617 Carter Way Hagerstown MD 21742-9769 Office: The Wyatt Co 1500 K St NW Washington DC 20005-1209

STEVENS, RICHARD PAUL, human resources executive; b. Cleve., Mar. 11, 1944; s. Robert Paul and Elizabeth Naomi (Teeple) S.; m. Mary Kathleen Bohm, July 28, 1976; 1 child, Lisa. BBA in Indsl. Rels., Kent (Ohio) State U., 1972. Mgmt. trainee Eaton Corp., Cleve., 1973-74, employee rels. supr., 1974-76, employee rels. mgr., 1976-77; personnel mgr. Parker Hannifin Corp., Elyria, Ohio, 1978-79, Rockwell Internat. Corp., Wellington, Ohio, 1980-84; mgr. employee rels. Rockwell Internat. Corp., Astabula, Ohio, 1985-87; mgr. indsl. rels. Arcata Graphics, Buffalo, 1987—. Mem. Am. Mgmt. Assn., Am. Soc. for Pers. Adminstrn., Western N.Y. Ind. Rels. Rsch. Assn. Republican. Home: 17 Metzger Dr Orchard Park NY 14127-2018 Office: Arcata Graphics Tc Industrial Park Depew NY 14043-2015

STEVENS, ROGER LACEY, theatrical producer; b. Detroit, Mar. 12, 1910; s. Stanley and Florence (Jackson) S.; m. Christine Gesell, Jan. 1, 1938; 1 child, Christabel. Student, Choate Sch., 1928, U. Mich., 1928-30; DHL, U. Mich., 1964; HHD (hon.), Wayne State U., 1960; DHL, Tulane U., 1960; LLD, Amherst Coll., 1968; hon. degrees, Skidmore Coll., 1969, U. Ill., 1970, Boston U., 1970, Am. U., 1979, Boston U., 1979, Miami U., 1983, Phila. Coll. Art, 1986. Former real estate broker specializing in hotels and investment properties, 1934-60; spl. asst. to the Pres. on the arts, 1964-68; chmn. Nat. Coun. on the Arts, 1965-69, Nat. Endowment for the Arts, also trustee; pres. Nat. Inst. for Music Theater; chmn. Am. Film Inst., 1969-72; chmn. adv. com. Nat. Book Award, 1970-75, 1988-89; mem. Coun. for Arts, Mass. Inst. Tech.; chmn. Fund for New Am. Plays, 1986—; mem. Pres.'s Com. on Arts and Humanities, 1982—. Producing partner in more than 200 theatrical prodns. including Old Times, West Side Story, Cat on a Hot Tin Roof, Bus Stop, The Visit, Mary, Mary, A Man for all Seasons, The Best Man, Deathtrap, Death of a Salesman; Kennedy Ctr. prodns. include Annie, First Monday in October, On Your Toes, Mass, Jumpers, Night and Day, Wings, Texas Trilogy, Bedroom Farce, Cocktail Hour, Love Letters, Metamorphosis, A Few Good Men, Artist Descending a Staircase, Shadowlands. Chmn. fin. com. Dem. Party, 1956; Chmn. bd. trustees John F. Kennedy Center Performing Arts, 1961-88; trustee Am. Shakespeare Theater and Acad., Choate Sch., 1982—; bd. dirs. Met. Opera Assn., Ballet Theatre Found., Nat. Symphony Orch., Filene Center/Wolf Trap Farm Park for Performing Arts, Peabody Conservatory, 1979-82, Folger Library, Acad. Am. Poets. Decorated knight comdr. Brit. Empire; Royal Order of Vasa, Sweden; grand ufficiale Order of Merit Italy; comdr.'s cross Order of Merit Fed. Republic Germany; recipient award contbn. theatre Nat. Theater Conf., 1970, , Presdl. Medal of Freedom, 1988, Nat. Medal of Arts, 1988; Kennedy Ctr. honoree, 1988. Fellow Royal Soc. Arts; mem. ANTA (exec. com.), Phi Gamma Delta. Clubs: Bohemian (San Francisco); Racquet and Tennis (N.Y.C.), Century Assn. (N.Y.C.), Pilgrims (N.Y.C.). Office: John F Kennedy Ctr for Performing Arts Washington DC 20566

STEVENS, SHANE, novelist; b. N.Y.C., Oct. 8, 1951; s. John and Caroline (Royale) S. MA, Columbia U. mem. numerous writers confs. including Bread Loaf, Santa Barbara Writers Conf. Author: Go Down Dead, Way Uptown in Another World, Dead City, Rat Pack, By Reason of Insanity, The Anvil Chorus (as J.W. Rider) Jersey Tomatoes (Best Novel award), Hot Tickets, 1987; contbr. articles to many pubs. including N.Y. Times, Life, Washington Post; screenwriter: By Reason of Insanity, The Me Nobody Knows. Mem. Authors Guild, Writers Guild Am. Office: William Morris Agy 1350 Ave Americas New York NY 10019

STEVENS, WALTER JOSEPH, physicist; b. Atlantic City, Apr. 29, 1944; s. Walter Joseph and Marion Elizabeth (Evans) S.; m. Linda Ann Mescanti, Sept. 10, 1966; children: Marian Elizabeth, Walter Joseph. BS, Drexel U., Phila., 1967; PhD, Ind. U., 1971. Postdoctoral assoc. Argonne (Ill.) Nat. Lab., 1971-73; rsch. physicst Lawrence Livermore (Calif.) Lab., 1973-75, Nat. Bur. Stds., Boulder, Colo., 1975-77, Nat. Inst. Standards and Tech., Gaithersburg, Md., 1977—; assoc. dir. Ctr. for Adv. Rsch. in Biotech., Rockville, Md., 1988—. Contbr. over 75 articles to profl. jurs. Recipient Gold medal U.S. Dept. Commerce, 1990, Silver medal, 1984, Bronze medal Nat. Bur. Standards, 1979. Mem. Am. Chem. Soc., Am. Phys. Soc. Office: Ctr for Adv Rsch Biotech 9600 Gudelsky Dr Rockville MD 20850-3479

STEVENSON, A. BROCKIE, painter; b. Montgomery County, Pa., Sept. 24, 1919; s. Alfred Brockie and Caroline Lansdale (Sill) S.; m. Jane Merriman Mackenzie, Dec. 23, 1978. Student, Pa. Acad. Fine Arts, 1940-41, 46-50, Barnes Found., 1946-48, Skowhegan Sch., Maine, 1950. Instr. Sch. Fine Arts, Washington U., St. Louis, 1960-62; head dept. painting and drawing Corcoran Sch. Art, 1965-81, assoc. prof. to prof. design and watercolor, 1965—. One-man shows War Paintings, London and Salisbury, Eng., 1944, Instituto Cultural Peruano-Norteamericano, Lima, Peru, 1953, Art Center, Miraflores, Lima, 1958, 60, Association Cultural Peruano-Britanica, Lima, 1959, Mickelson Gallery, Washington, 1970, Pyramid Galleries Ltd., Washington, 1973, No. Va. Community Coll., 1974, Fendrick Gallery, Washington, 1978, 84, 88; group shows include, Nat. Gallery Art, London, 1944, Pa. Acad. Fine Arts, Phila., 1948, 49, 50, 51, Sociedad Bellas Artes del Peru, Lima, 1953, 54, 55, 56, SUNY at, Potsdam and Albany, 1971, Columbia (S.C.) Mus. Art, 1971, EXPO '74, Spokane, Wash., 1974, Corcoran Gallery, Washington, 1980; represented in permanent collections, including, Corcoran Gallery Art, Washington, Dept. Def., Washington, Nat. Mus. Am. Art, Washington, , Phillips Collection, Washington, Fed. Res. Bank Richmond, Va., Woodward Found., Washington, Ogunquit (Maine) Mus. Art. Served as artist correspondent U.S. Army, 1943-45, ETO. Home: 6106 Yale Ave Glen Echo MD 20812-1122 Office: Corcoran Sch Art 17 and New York Ave NW Washington DC 20006

STEVENSON, CHARLES ARTHUR, legislative assistant; b. Denver, May 18, 1942; s. Charles Francis and Harriet Amalia (Swanberg) S.; m. Andrea Zedalis, Aug. 4, 1979; children: Sarah, William. AB, Harvard U., 1963; MA, Tufts U., 1964; PhD, Harvard U., 1970. Legis. asst. U.S. Senator Harold Hughes, Washington, 1970-75, U.S. Senator John Culver, Washington, 1975-80, U.S. Senator Joseph Biden, Washington, 1980-85, U.S. Senator Lloyd Bentsen, Washington, 1985—. Fulbright grantee to U.K., 1964-65. Fulbright grante U.S. Govt., 1964-65. Mem. Coun. on Fgn. Rels., Internat. Inst. for Strategic Studies. Home: 23 Columbia Ave Takoma Park MD 20912 Office: Office of Senator Lloyd Bentsen US Senate Washington DC 20510

STEVENSON, IRONE EDMUND, JR., biochemist; b. Linthicum, Md., Apr. 21, 1930; s. Irone Edmund and Reba (Gustin) S.; m. Margaritia Hiroko Hasegawa, Aug. 20, 1960; children: David G., Richard H. BS, U. Md., 1953; PhD, U. Pa., 1961. Rsch. assoc. biology dept. Yale U., New Haven, 1960-63; chemist DuPont Cen. R&D, Wilmington, Del., 1963-72, sr. chemist, 1972-81; sr. chemist DuPont Agrl. Products, Wilmington, 1981-87, rsch. assoc., 1987—. Contbr. articles to profl. jours. District rep. Chatham Civic Assn., Wilmington, 1976-79, treas., 1979-82, com. chmn., 1982—. With U.S. Army, 1948-49. Mem. Am. Soc. Biol. Chemists. Roman Catholic. Home: 1218 Graylyn Rd Wilmington DE 19803-3349 Office: EI DuPont De Nemours Co Agrl Products Exptl Sta Wilmington DE 19880

STEVENSON, JOSIAH, IV, cultural arts administrator; b. Jamaica, N.Y., Oct. 4, 1935; s. Josiah and Ruth Lillian (Leech) S.; A.B., Dartmouth Coll., 1957; M.B.A., Amos Tuck Sch. Bus., 1958; m. Jane Margaret Kupfer, Sept. 1, 1957; children—Josiah V., Todd Sander. Instr., U. Md.-Far East, 1959-61; account supr. Benton & Bowles, Inc., N.Y.C., 1961-66; group product mgr., gen. mgr. Japan, Chesebrough-Pond's Inc., Greenwich, Conn., 1967-77; dir. devel. Dartmouth Coll., 1977-84; dir. devel. Boston Symphony Orch., 1984—; mng. ptnr. Dover Stevenson & Assocs., 1987—; chmn. bd. New Music Harvest, Boston, 1991—. With USAF, 1958-61. Mem. U.S. C. of C., Council for Advancement and Support of Edn., Nat. Soc. Fund Raising Execs. Republican. Presbyterian. Clubs: Dartmouth, Tokyo Lawn Tennis, Whippoorwill; Yale-Dartmouth (N.Y.C.), Badminton and Tennis (Boston). Home: Spring Pond Rd PO Box 422 Norwich VT 05055-0422 Office: Symphony Hall Boston MA 02115

STEVENSON, ROBERT LOUIS, writer, lecturer; b. Detroit, Sept. 30, 1952. Chief exec. officer Kahuna Enterprises, Greenwich, Conn., 1980—. Home and Office: 306 Orchard St Greenwich CT 06830-4009

STEVENSON, WILLIAM BOOTH, II, controller; b. Elgin, Ill., Mar. 22, 1952; s. William Bridge and Jean Scott (Goodie) S.; m. Anne Marie Hayes, Sept. 14, 1991. BA, Lawrence U., 1974; MBA, U. Mich., 1976; postgrad., 1989, 92. Fin. analyst Burroughs Corp. Internat. Group, Detroit, 1976-79, mgr. internat. fin., 1979-80; mgr. acctg. Burroughs Corp. Plymouth (Mich.) Plant, 1980-81; mgr. bus. planning Burroughs Corp., Detroit, 1981-82; corp. mgr. The Bendix Corp., Southfield, Mich., 1982-83; mgr. fin. analysis Allied Signal, Morristown, N.J., 1983-86; mgr. fin. Bendix Aerospace, Arlington, Va., 1986-91; asst. contr. ITT Avionics, Nutley, N.J., 1988-91; contr. ITT Electron Tech., Easton, Pa., 1991—. V.p. Windmill Pond Townhome Assn., Morristown, N.J., 1978—. Mem. Performance Measurement Assn., Lawrence Univ. Alumni Assn., Univ. Mich. Alumni Assn., Williams Club, Omicron Delta Epsilon. Republican. Episcopalian. Home: 18 Windmill Dr Morristown NJ 07960 Office: ITT Electron Technology PO Box 100 Easton PA 18042

STEVOVICH, ANDREW VLASTIMIR, artist; b. Salzburg, Austria, July 2, 1948; came to U.S., 1950; s. Vlastimir A. and Ella V. Stevovich; m. Pamela J. Ives, Apr. 28, 1977; 1 child, Alexander. BFA in Painting, R.I. Sch. Design, 1970; MFA in Painting, Mass. Coll. Art, 1980. One-man shows at Adelson Gallery, N.Y.C., 1992, Coe Kerr Gallery, N.Y.C., 1983, 85, 87, 90, Tatischeff Gallery, Santa Monica, Calif., 1989, others; group shows include Coe Kerr Gallery, N.Y.C., 1982, 84, 90, Galerie Kunst im Turm, Kleve, Germany, 1989, Fuller Art Mus., Brockton, Mass., 1989, Riverside (Calif.) Art Mus., 1990, others; represented in permanent collections Boston Athenaeum, Boston Mus. Fine Arts, Boston Pub. Libr., Danforth Mus., Framington, Mass., Fuller Art Mus., Brockton Mus., Portland (Oreg.) Mus. Art. Home and Office: 120 Sewall Ave Brookline MA 02146-5327

STEWART, ALBERT CLIFTON, college dean, marketing educator; b. Detroit, Nov. 25, 1919; s. Albert Queely and Jeanne Belle (Kaiser) S.; m. Colleen Moore Hyland, June 25, 1949. BS, U. Chgo., 1942, MS, 1948; PhD, St. Louis U., 1951. Chemist Sherwin Williams Paint Co., Chgo.; rsch. asst. dept. chemistry U. Chgo., 1947-48; instr. chemistry St. Louis U., 1949-51; exec. Union Carbide Corp., Danbury, Conn., 1951-84; prof. mktg. Western Conn. State U., Danbury, 1984—, dean Sch. of Bus., 1987-90; cons. Ford Found., 1963-69, Union Carbide Corp., 1984—; bd. dirs. Exec. Register, Inc., Danbury, 1985-90; assoc. Execom, Darien, Conn., 1986-90. Patentee in field. Bd. dirs. Am. Mus. Nat. History, N.Y.C., 1976-85, N.Y.C. Philharm., 1975-80; arbiter Am. Arbitration Assn., N.Y.C., Danbury; active Towm Council, Oak Bridge, Tenn., 1953-57. Recipient Cert. of Merit Soc. Chem. Professions, Cleve., 1962. Mem. Am. Mktg. Assn., Sigma Xi. Club: Rotary (Cleve., N.Y.C.). Home: 28 Hearthstone Dr Brookfield CT 06804-3006 Office: Western Conn State U 181 White St Danbury CT 06810-6885

STEWART, ARLENE JEAN GOLDEN, designer, stylist; b. Chgo., Nov. 26, 1943; d. Alexander Emerald and Nettie (Rosen) Golden; m. Randall Edward Stewart, Nov. 6, 1970; 1 child, Alexis Anne. BFA, Sch. of Art Inst. Chgo., 1966; postgrad., Ox Bow Summer Sch. Painting, Saugatuck, Mich., 1966. Designer, stylist Formica Corp., Cin., 1966-68; with Armstrong World Industries, Inc., Lancaster, Pa., 1968—, interior furnishings analyst, 1974-76, internat. staff project stylist, 1976-78, sr. stylist Corlon flooring, 1979-80, sr. exptl. project stylist, 1980-89, sr. project stylist residential DIY flooring floor div., 1989—. Exhibited textiles Art Inst. Chgo., 1966, Ox-Bow Gallery, Saugatuck, Mich., 1966. Home: 114 E Vine St Lancaster PA 17602-3550 Office: Armstrong Innovation Ctr 2500 Columbia Ave Lancaster PA 17603-4117

STEWART, ARTHUR IRVING, III (ART STEWART), communications executive; b. Plainfield, N.J., Aug. 1, 1958; s. Arthur Irving Jr. and Audree Claire (Rollerson) S. BS in Mass Communication, Emerson Coll., 1982. Intern Sta. KYW Newsradio/TV, Phila., 1977; free-lance announcer various cos., Boston, 1982-84; news anchorman, reporter Sta. WLBR-WUFM-FM, Lebanon, Pa., 1984; ops. mgr. Sta. WMSP-FM, Harrisburg, Pa., 1984-86; sr. account exec. mktg. and sales promotion Sta. WFCC-FM First Class Communications, Ltd., Chatham, Mass., 1987-88; account exec. Larson & Rosen Meeting Producers, Boston, 1988-89; account mgr. Vizwiz Film-Video, Inc., Brookline, Mass., 1989-90; pub. rels. account exec. The Interface Group, Needham, Mass., 1991—; dir. mktg. and pub. rels. Cape and Islands Chamber Music Festival, Cape Cod, Mass., 1988; asst. organist The United Parish, Brookline, 1982-84. Producer (radio) documentary on Daniel Pinkham, 1982, Retrospective on Career of E. Power Biggs, (with Margaret Power Biggs),1982, series on The Great Choral Works (with Ronald Arnatt), 1982, (concert broadcasts) Harrisburg Symphony Orch., 1984-86, documentary on U.S. debut tour of Westminster Cathedral Choir of London, 1985, investigative report on acid rain, 1985 (Excellence in Broadcasting award), documentary on Nat. Cathedral Washington, 1986 (Excellence in Broadcasting award). Communications coord. AIDS Support Com., Trinity Ch., Boston, 1989-91, editor OUTREACH newsletter, 1990—; co-chmn. pub. rels. IMMEDIAID -89; bd. dirs. Civic Symphony Boston, 1989-91. Recipient Excellence in Broadcasting award Pa. Assn. Broadcasters. Mem. Pub. Rels. Soc. Am., Internat. Assn. Bus. Communicators, Am. Mktg. Assn., Am. Guild Organists, Am. Symphony Orch. League. Episcopalian. Office: Interface Group Inc 300 1st Ave Needham MA 02194-2720

STEWART, BARBARA YOST, biology educator; b. Johnstown, Pa., Oct. 12, 1932; d. Russell Raymond and Ruth Elizabeth (Dorworth) Y.; m. Robert Ogden Stewart, July 24, 1954 (div. Aug. 1989); children: Russell R., Douglas W.; m. Robert Silmon Chase, June 28, 1991. BA, Swarthmore Coll., 1954; MA, Bryn Mawr Coll., 1972, PhD, 1975. Lectr. Swarthmore (Pa.) Coll., 1975-85, asst. prof., 1985-86, assoc. prof. biology, 1986—, assoc. chair dept. biology, 1985—; mem. editorial rev. bd. Jour. Coll. Sci. Teaching, 1990—; chair Pew Sci. Program, Princeton, N.J., 1991; speaker in field. Recipient Coll. Sci. Teaching award O'Haus-NSTA, 1987, Course Devel. award Sloan Found., 1988, Rsch. Collaboration award Pew Sci. Program, 1989. Mem. Nat. Sci. Tchrs. Assn., Sigma Xi. Office: Swarthmore Coll Dept Biology Swarthmore PA 19081

STEWART, BONNIE LOUISE, psychotherapist; b. Pittsfield, Mass., Nov. 9, 1952; d. Alan Perkins and Suzanne R. (Forster) S.; m. Allen Arthur Meyer, Sept. 13, 1975. BS, Springfield Coll., 1975; MEd, U. Pa., 1983, PhD, 1990. Asst. payroll mgr. G. Fox & Co., Hartford, Conn., 1973-77; territory mgr. Certain Teed Corp., Valley Forge, Pa., 1977-81; rsch. coord. U. Pa. Counseling Ctr., Phila., 1985-88, U. Pa. Ctr. for Cognitive Therapy, Phila., 1988-90; project coord. Dave Garroway Lab., Phila., 1990—; psychotherapist Comprehensive Psychol. Svcs., Havertown, Pa., 1990—. Contbr. articles to profl. jours. Mem. APA. Office: Dave Garroway Lab 111 N 49th St Philadelphia PA 19139-2718

STEWART, CAROL ANN, graphic arts professional; b. Cleve., Oct. 28, 1940; d. Joseph Chapman and Dorothy Jeanne (Page) Bronson; m. Claude Henry Wenner, Aug. 11, 1986 (dec.); m. Robert Ogden Stewart, Sept. 1, 1989. AA in Print Prodn. Mgmt., Graphic Arts Assn. of, Delaware Valley, Phila., 1973; BSBA cum laude, Villanova U., 1980, MBA, 1985. Film libr. Wyeth-Ayerst Labs., Radnor, Pa., 1963-67, prodn. asst., 1967-74, supr. promotion prodn., 1974-86, mgr. graphic arts, 1986—. Sec. Daylesford Hills Civic Assn., Berwyn, Pa., 1973-75; pres. Bear Creek Lakes Civic Assn., Jim Thorpe, Pa., 1985-87, bd. dirs., 1983-88. Recipient Capitol award Nat. Leadership Coun., 1991. Mem. NAFE, Execs. Club Graphic Arts (v.p. 1990-91, pres. 1991—). Republican. Home: 543 Marietta Ave Swarthmore PA 19081-2416 Office: Wyeth-Ayerst Labs PO Box 8299 Philadelphia PA 19101-8299

STEWART, CHARLES HAINES, political science educator; b. Winder, Ga., Mar. 31, 1958; s. Charlie Haines Stewart and Joan (Chastain) VanderBurg; m. Kathryn M. Hess, Sept. 10, 1983. BA, Emory U., 1979; AM, Stanford U., 1982, PhD, 1985. Asst. prof. MIT, Cambridge, Mass., 1985-89, assoc. prof. dept. polit. sci., 1989—; Cecil and Ida Green Career Devel. assoc. prof., nat. fellow Hoover Inst., Stanford, Calif., 1989-90. Author: Budget Reform Politics, 1989; columnist Toray World Confidential Report, Tokyo, 1988—; contbr. articles to profl. jours. Mem., sec. Commn. on the Status and Role of Women in the United Meth. Ch., Evanston, Ill., 1989-91. Mem. Am. Polit. Sci. Assn., Am. Econs. Assn., Midwest Polit. Sci. Assn., So. Polit. Sci. Assn. Democrat. Office: MIT Dept Polit Sci Cambridge MA 02139

STEWART, DIANE CAROL (DIDI STEWART), vocalist, musician; b. New Haven, Apr. 9, 1953; d. Herman Carl and Edith Bernice (Cohen) Schwartz. Vocalist, composer Didi Stewart and the Amplifiers, Boston, 1978-83, Girls' Night Out, Boston, 1983-87, Didi Stewart and Friends, Boston, 1987—. Composer, vocalist (albums) Begin Here, 1983, One True Heart, 1990. Named Best Female Vocalist, The Boston Music Awards, 1987, 90, Best Local Performer, Boston mag., 1986, 100 Women to Watch, Boston Woman mag., 1986, Female Cabaret Artist, Encore Cabaret Awards, 1988. Mem. Amnesty Internat. Office: Didi Stewart and Friends 25 Walnut St Somerville MA 02143

STEWART, DORIS MAE, biology educator; b. Sandsprings, Mont., Dec. 12, 1927; d. Virgil E. and Violet M. (Weaver) S.; m. Felix Loren Powell, Oct. 8, 1956; children: Leslie, Loren. BS, Coll. Puget Sound, 1948, MS, 1949; PhD, U. Wash., 1953. Instr. U. Mont., Missoula, 1954-56, asst. prof., 1956-57; asst. prof. U. Puget Sound, Tacoma, 1957-58; head sci. dept. Am. Kiz Lisesi, Istanbul, Turkey, 1958-62; rsch. asst. prof. U. Wash., Seattle, 1963-67, rsch. assoc. prof., 1967-68; assoc. prof. Cen. Mich. U., Mt. Pleasant, 1970-72; assoc. prof. U. Balt., 1973-81, prof., 1981—. Contbr. numerous articles to profl. jours. Mem. Am. Physiol. Soc., Sigma Xi. Home: 1103 Frederick Rd Baltimore MD 21228-5032

STEWART, EUGENE LAWRENCE, lawyer, trade association executive; b. Kansas City, Mo., Feb. 9, 1920; s. Edmund Dale and Mary Elizabeth (Raef) S.; m. Jeanne Ellen Powers, Oct. 19, 1945; children—Timothy, Terence, Brian. B.S., S.S., Georgetown U., 1947, J.D., 1951. Bar: D.C. 1951, U.S. Tax Ct. 1953, U.S. Ct. of Customs and Patent Appeals 1951-82, U.S. Ct. Appeals Fed. Circuit 1982, U.S. Ct. Appeals (3d cir.) 1985, U.S. Ct. Appeals (9th cir.) 1987, U.S. Ct. Appeals (11th cir.) 1988, U.S. Ct. Appeals (D.C. cir.) 1951, U.S. Ct. Internat. Trade 1958, U.S. Supreme Ct. 1967. Assoc. Steptoe & Johnson, Washington, 1951-56, ptnr., 1956-58; ptnr. Hume & Stewart, Washington, 1958-64; sole practice Law Offices of Eugene L. Stewart, Washington, 1964-69, 1978-83; ptnr. Lincoln & Stewart, Washington, 1969-73, Stewart & Ikenson, Washington, 1974-78; sr. ptnr. Stewart & Stewart, Inc., Washington, 1983—; adj. prof. law Georgetown U. Law Ctr., Washington, 1955-58; exec. sec. Trade Relations Council of U.S., Washington, 1962—. Contbr. articles to profl. publs. Pres., Sursum Corda, Inc. (low-income housing project), Washington, 1964-78. Served to lt. col. USAF, 1941-52; PTO. Recipient John Carroll award Georgetown U., 1966. Mem. ABA, D.C. Bar, Customs and Internat. Trade Bar Assn., Georgetown U. Alumni Assn. Inc. (pres. 1964-66). Republican. Roman Catholic. Office: Stewart & Stewart 808-17th St NW Washington DC 20006-3910

STEWART, HAROLD LEROY, physician, educator; b. Houtzdale, Pa., Aug. 6, 1899; s. Alexander and Lillie (Cox) S.; m. Cecelia Eleanor Finn, Sept. 30, 1929; children: Robert Campbell, Janet Eileen. Student, U. Pa., 1919-20, Dickinson Coll., 1921-22; M.D., Jefferson Med. Coll., 1926; grad., Army Med. Sch., Washington, 1929; research fellow, Jefferson Med. Coll., 1929-30, Harvard, 1937-39; Med. Sc.D. (hon.), Jefferson Med. Coll., 1964; D.Medicine and Surgery (hon.), U. Perugia, 1965, U. Turku, Finland, 1970; Doctor (hon.), Kagawa (Japan) Med. Sch., 1992. Diplomate Am. Bd. Pathology, Pan Am. Med. Assn. Intern Fitzimmons Gen. Hosp., Denver, 1926-27; instr. to asst. prof. pathology Jefferson Med. Coll., 1930-37; asst. pathologist Jefferson Med. Coll. Hosp., Phila. Gen. Hosp., 1929-37; pathologist Office Cancer Investigations Harvard, USPHS, 1937-39; chief lab. pathology Nat. Cancer Inst., USPHS, Bethesda, Md., 1939-69; chief pathologic anatomy dept. clin. ctr. NIH, 1954-69; organizer Registry Exptl. Cancers, 1970—, Sci. emeritus, 1976—; prin. investigator, head WHO Collaborating Centre for Rsch. on Tumors Lab. Animals, 1976—; clin. prof. pathology Georgetown U., 1965—; Cons. FDA, 1969-71, Nat. Cancer Inst., 1970-76, Armed Forces Inst. Pathology, 1950—; cons., mem. study groups WHO, 1957-81, mem. expert adv. panel cancer, 1957-81; Mem. subcom. oncology NRC, 1947-65, mem. com. pathology, 1958-66, com. cancer diagnosis and therapy, 1951-57, mem. com. animal models and genetic stocks, 1972-75, chmn. com. histologic classification Lab. Animal Tumors, 1975-79; chmn. subcom. classification rat liver tumors NRC (Lab. Animal Tumors), 1976-79; chmn. U.S.A. Com. Internat. Coun. Socs. Pathology, 1957-62, 69-75; chmn. U.S. nat. com. Internat. Union Against Cancer, 1953-59, U.S. del., 1952-74; Mem. adv. bd. Leonard Wood Meml., 1961-66; mem. com. to advance world-wide fight against cancer Am. Cancer Soc., 1963-76; mem. med. rsch. coun. Referees, New Zealand, 1987. Mem. editoral bd. Cancer Rsch., 1941-49, A.M.A. Archives of Pathology, 1957-62, Jour. Toxicology Pathology, 1988; editorial adviser Jour. Nat. Cancer Inst, 1947-56; contbr. articles to profl. jours. Trustee Thomas Jefferson U., Phila., 1969-72. Served as pvt. USMC, 1918-19; lt. M.C. U.S. Army, 1926-29; from maj. to lt. col. M.C. AUS, 1942-46. Recipient Lucy Wortham James award James Ewing Soc., 1967, Alumni Achievement award Jefferson Med. Coll., 1966, Disting. Svc. award HEW, 1966, Honors award NIH, The Directors award NIH, 1988; Dedication Jour. Exptl. Pathology, Vol. 1, No. 2, 1987; Harold L. Stewart Fund for Exptl. Pathology and Harold L. Stewart Lectureship established at Uniformed Svcs. U. of Health Scis., Bethesda, Md., 1986. Mem. Am. Soc. Clin. Pathologists (Ward Burdick award 1957), Am. Assn. Cancer Rsch. (pres. 1958-59), Am. Soc. Exptl. Pathology (hon.; pres. 1955), Am. Assn. Pathologists (Gold-headed Cane award 1978), Coll. Am. Pathologists, Md. Soc. Pathologists (pres. 1950-51), Washington Soc. Pathologists (sec.-treas. 1947-51), Internat. Acad. Pathology (pres. 1953-55, F.K. Mostofi award 1976), Internat. Union Against Cancer (exec. com. 1952-70, v.p. 1962), Mass. Med. Soc., Internat. Coun. Socs. Pathology (pres. 1962), Internat. Soc. Geog. Pathology, Colegio Anatomico Brasileiro (hon.), Societa Italiana di Cancerologia (hon.), Inst. Nacional de Cancerologia Mexico (hon.), Sociedad Columbiana de Patologia (hon.), Societe Belge d' Anatomie Pathologique (hon.), Sociedad Peruana Cancerologia (hon.), Soc. Cryobiology, Soc. Toxicologic Pathologists (hon.), Japanese Cancer Soc. (hon.), Purdy Stout Surg. Pathology Soc. (hon.), others. Home: 119 S Adams St Rockville MD 20850-2315 Office: NIH Nat Cancer Inst Registry Exptl Cancers Bethesda MD 20892

STEWART, HARRY EATON, geotechnical engineering educator, researcher; b. Elmira, N.Y., Sept. 9, 1951; s. Harry Eaton and Frances Jane (Conklin) S.; m. Kristin J. Culp, Aug. 7, 1982; children: Kim, Max. BS in Chemistry, SUNY, Brockport, 1973; BSCE, SUNY, Buffalo, 1978; MSCE, U. Mass., 1979, PhD, 1982. Registered profl. engr., N.Y., S.C. Rsch. asst. SUNY, Buffalo, 1978; rsch. asst. U. Mass., Amherst, 1978-82, vis. asst. prof., 1982-83; asst. prof. civil engring. U. S.C., Columbia, 1983-85; asst. prof. civil engring. Cornell U., Ithaca, N.Y., 1985-90, assoc. prof., 1990—; dir. Geotech. Lab. Takeo Mogami Geotech. Lab., Ithaca, N.Y., 1985—. Contbr. articles to profl. jours. Scholar Soc. Am. Mil. Engrs., 1977. Mem. ASCE, ASTM, Am. Ry. Engring. Assn., Earthquake Engring. Rsch. Inst., Transp. Rsch. Bd., Internat. Soc. for Soil Mechanics and Found. Engring. Office: Cornell U Sch Civil and Environ Engring 267 Hollister Hall Ithaca NY 14853-3501

STEWART, JACK, artist, educator, writer; b. Atlanta, Jan. 27, 1926; s. Jack Thomas and Lilly Ruth (Hemperley) S.; m. Margot S. Stewart (div.); 1 child, Brandon Burns; m. Regina Serniak, Dec. 10, 1976. BFA, Yale U., 1951; MA, NYU, 1975, PhD, 1989. Mem. faculty Columbia U. Grad. Sch. Art, N.Y.C., 1967-76; chmn. dept. art Cooper Union Sch. Art, N.Y.C., 1971-74; v.p., provost R.I. Sch. Design, Providence, 1976-77. Exhibited at George Binet Gallery, N.Y.C., 1950, Pa. Acad. Phila., 1953, Grippi and Waddell Gallery, N.Y.C., 1963-64, Collegeo Raffaello, Urbino, Italy, 1973, La Scuola di Teodora, Venice, Italy, 1976, Broome St. Gallery, N.Y.C., 1990-92; works include mosaic murals at Versaile Hotel, Miami Beach, Fla., Facade of Aruba (Netherlands Antilles) Carib Hotel, 1958, Cluett Shirt Group, Atlanta, 1990; editor: Modern Mosaic Techniques, 1967; author articles in encys. and mags; inventor laminated stained glass. Sgt. inf. U.S. Army, 1944-46, ETO. Mem. N.Y. Artists Equity Assn. (pres. 1987-89). Baptist. Home and Studio: Stewart Studio 31 E 7th St New York NY 10003

STEWART, JEANNIE CALDER, psychologist; b. Aberdeen, Scotland, Nov. 29, 1913; d. Jonathan and Isabella Jane (Calder) S. AB magna cum laude, Brown U., 1945; MA, U. Calif., 1945; postgrad., Stanford U., 1948-49, 50-51. Tchg. asst. U. Calif., Berkeley, 1944-45; research asst. Jackson Lab., Bar Harbor, Maine, 1946; research asst. to instr. Vassar Coll., Poughkeepsie, N.Y., 1946-48, 49-50; student house dir. Pembroke Coll. Brown U., Providence, 1954-61; sec. to physician Fitchburg, Mass., 1961-64; adv. Garland Jr. Coll., Boston, 1965-66, 70-71; sec. residence program Boston U., 1967-70; house dir. House in the Pines Sch., Norton, Mass., 1971-72; sec. Manpower Program, Boston, 1972-73; clerical worker Stone and Webster Engring. Corp., Boston, 1973-84; part time clerical worker Skill Bur., Boston, 1984-88, Jr. League of Boston, 1985—; del. Internat. Congress of Psychology, London, 1969, Brussels, 1992. Author: Ancient and Cherished Treasures of Scotland, 1982, Ancient Castles of Scotland, 1990. Mem. Nat. Trust for Hist. Preservation, Washington, 1986-88, Nat. Trust for Scotland, Edinburgh, Scottish Heritage U.S.A, 1977—. Margaret Floy Washburn fellow Vassar Coll., 1950, Miss Abbott's Sch. Alumnae fellow Brown U.; named Internat. Woman of Yr., Internat. Biog. Centre, 1991-92. Mem. APA (life), AAAS (emeritus), Ea. Psychol. Assn., Daus. of British Empire, Royal Overseas League, English Speaking Union (del. world mems. conf. 1977, 86, 89), Brit. Psychol. Soc., Internat. Biog. Assn. Conf. on Arts and Communications (del. 1979, 80, 92), Brit. Charitable Soc., Brown U. Club (Boston), Sigma Xi, Psi Chi. Republican. Presbyterian. Home: 3 Concord Ave Apt 3B Cambridge MA 02138-3616

STEWART, JOHN CAMERON, environmental protection specialist; b. Detroit, Oct. 2, 1943; s. Glenn Angus and Florence Ida (Cameron) S.; m. Maxine Helen Bohnet, June 20, 1980; 1 child, Ian Maximilian. BA, U. Miami, 1966; MA, Memphis State U., 1970. Urban planner Harland Bartholomew & Assocs., Memphis, 1968-70; sr. planner Jacksonville (Fla.) Area Planning Bd., 1970-73; prin. environ. planner Md. Nat. Capital Park and Planning Commn., Silver Spring, 1973-80; environ. protection specialist U.S. Dept. of Def., Alexandria, Va., 1980-81; rsch. scientist U.S. Nuclear Regulatory Commn., Washington, 1981-89; sr. envir. protection specialist Dept. Energy, Washington, 1989—. Author: The Application of Low Level Waste Siting Criteria to Geographic Information Systems, 1988, Politics and Planning for the Nuclear State, 1987, Geographic Guidelines for the Siting of Low-Level Disposal Sites, 1987; contbr. articles to profl. jours. 1st trombonist Rockville (Md.) Concert Band, 1987—. Mem. Am. Inst. Cert. Planners, St. Andrews Soc. of Washington (newsletter bus. mgr.), Clan Stewart Soc. of Am., Audubon Naturalist Soc. Episcopalian. Home: 3705 Dupont Ave Kensington MD 20895-2511 Office: US Dept Energy Washington DC 20585

STEWART, JOSEPH ALLEN, nuclear energy industry executive; b. Paris, Ill., Oct. 20, 1949; s. Herman Joseph and Marjorie Ann (Fitzgerald) S.; m. Rolene Carlson, June 23, 1949; children: Jeffrey Michael, Jennifer Lynn, Jolene Marie. Student, SUNY, Albany. Produce mgr. A&P Food Store, Wilmington, Ill., 1967-69; enlisted USN, 1969, advanced through grades to chief petty officer, 1978, resigned, 1982; prin. tng. specialist Gen. Physics Corp., Columbia, Md., 1982-90, radiation safety officer, 1988-90; supr. ops. tng. at Nuclear Tng. Ctr. Niagara Mohawk Power Corp., Oswego, N.Y., 1990—. Bd. dirs. Fulton (N.Y.) Consol. Sch. Dist., 1988-91. Mem. Fulton C. of C. (rep. 1988-91), The Health Physics Soc., Fulton Soccer Club, Masons, Order Easter Star (dist. lect. 1988-89). Republican. Lutheran. Office: Nuclear Tng Ctr RR 1 Box 148 Oswego NY 13126-9737

STEWART, MARK THOMAS, compressed gas company executive; b. Butler, Pa., June 9, 1948; s. Paul William and Donna Ruth (Wonderly) S.; m. Judith Lynne Christie, Aug. 12, 1967; children: Andrew Paul, Elizabeth Christie. BA, Indiana U. Pa., 1969; MAT, Duquesne U., 1972. Cert. tchr., Pa. Tchr. Butler (Pa.) Catholic Sch., 1970-74; acct. George F. Pott, CPA, Gibsonia, Pa., 1974-76; field rep. Republican State Com., Harrisburg, Pa., 1976; exec. dir. Harmony (Pa.) Mus., 1977-78; foreman Pullman Standard Co., Butler, 1978-82; mgr. P.W. Stewart Welding Supply, West Sunbury, Pa., 1982-84; v.p. Stewart & Stewart, Inc., West Sunbury, 1984-87, pres., 1987—; balloon design cons., dir. Stewart and Stewart, Inc., 1984—. Originator balloon art techniques. Mem. campaign staff, writer researcher various Rep. campaigns, Butler and Allegheny Counties, Pa., 1974-87; bd. dirs. Moniteau Sch. Dist., West Sunbury, 1982-85. Mem. Nat. Assn. Balloon Artists (cert. master balloon artist, 3d place award internat. design competition 1989), Nat. Fedn. Ind. Bus., Nat. Propane Gas Assn., Masons. Republican. Mem. Orthodox Ch. Home: RR 3 Box 937 Chicora PA 16025-9410 Office: RR 2 Box 2357 West Sunbury PA 16061-8816

STEWART, MARVIN LEWIS, human resources professional; b. Fairmont, W.Va., June 30, 1953; s. Charles T. and Edna W. (Jones) S.; m. Phyllis A. Mitchell, July 7, 1973; children: Autumn Nicole, Kristen Leighann, Danielle Denise, Matthew Lewis. BS in Bus. Adminstrn., Fairmont State U., 1976; MS in Econs., W.Va. U., 1984. Preload supr. United Parcel Svc., western Pa., 1974-76; pers. supr. United Parcel Svc., W.Va., 1976-82, packaging ctr. mgr., 1982-85, employment mgr., 1985-86; spl. assignment United Parcel Svc., Ky., 1987; employment mgr. United Parcel Svc., Phila., 1989; human resources div. mgr. United Parcel Svc., Air Dist., Pa., 1989—. Loaned exec. United Way, Phila., 1989, dist. coord., 1990; chmn. activity bd. dirs. Marion Parks and Recreation, Fairmont, 1983-84; mem. Leadership Marion, Fairmont, 1984-85. Baptist. Office: United Parcel Svc 1 Hog Island Rd Philadelphia PA 19153

STEWART, PAUL JAMES, JR., history educator; b. Chgo., 1929; s. Paul James and Kathryn (Baird) S.; m. Josephine Smania, 1960; children: Heather, Thomas. BA, U. Ill., 1950, PhD, 1961; MA, Columbia U., 1956. Grad. asst. U. Ill., Urbana, 1955-59, vis. lectr., 1967-68; asst. prof. U. Southwestern La., Lafayette, 1959-62, Lawrence U., Appleton, Wis., 1962-65, Wash. State U., Pullman, 1965-67; vis. asst. prof. U. Idaho, Moscow, 1966-67 summers; assoc. prof. U. Wis., Whitewater, 1968-70; vis. prof. U. New Haven, 1979; prof. history So. Conn. State U., New Haven, 1970—. Editor/translator (with Josephine Stewart): Vigil in Benicarlo, 1982; contbr. articles to profl. jours. Sr. warden Grace Episcopal Ch., Hamden, Conn., 1990. Cpl. AUS, 1952-53, Japan. Fulbright scholar, 1960-61. Mem. AAUP, Am. Hist. Assn., Conn. Acad. Arts and Scis., Am. Acad. of Rsch.

Historians of Medieval Spain, Soc. for Spanish and Portuguese Hist. Studies, Phi Alpha Theta, Sigma Delta Pi. Office: So Conn State Univ Dept History New Haven CT 06515

STEWART, ROBERT ALAN, lobbyist, lawyer; b. Woodbury, N.J., Oct. 4, 1943; s. Harry Francis and Helen (Data) S.; m. Judith Anne Malloy, July 20, 1968 (div. Sept. 1972); 1 child, Robert Scott Stewart; m. Martha Kay Anderson, May 18, 1984. BA, U. Dayton, 1965; JD, Rutgers Law Sch., 1968. Mcpl. judge Pennsville Twp., Salem City, Alloway Twp., Penns Grove, N.J., 1974-79; contract lobbyist The Stewart Agy., Penns Grove, Trenton, N.J., 1982—; atty. pvt. practice, Penns Grove, N.J., 1969—; cons. R.J. Reynolds, Proctor Gamble, Eastman Kodak, MCI, Coun. for Solid Waste Solutions, ANheuser Bush Co., FMC, E.I. DePont, Atlantic Electric, Trenton, N.J., 1982—. Mcpl. judge Salem Co., N.J., 1974-79; campaign chmn. N.J. Assembly Dist. 3, Salem, Gloucester Counties, N.J., 1971-72. Mem. N.J. State C. of C., N.J. Bus. and Industry Assn., N.J. Recycling Forum, N.J. Seed Soc. for Econ. Environ. Devel., The Stewart Agy. (v.p.), Statewide Pub. Affairs (v.p.). Office: 188 W Main St Penns Grove NJ 08069-1391

STEWART, SANDY BROWN, workforce empowerment consultant; b. Buffalo, May 15, 1938; d. Samuel LeRoy and Lula Mae (Gregory) Brown; m. John C. Stewart, Sept. 14, 1955 (div.); children: Gwendolyn, Dawn, A.J., Tracy. Student, Va. State U., 1957, Community Coll. of Balt., 1971-75; Cert. of Mgmt., U. Balt., 1978. Psychiat. nurse attendent Cen. State Hosp., Petersburg, Va., 1959-64; svc. rep. dist. office Social Security Administrn., Petersburg, 1964-69; social ins. claims examiner Social Security Administrn., Balt., 1969-74, social ins. specialist, 1974-81, social ins. mgr., 1981-83; founder, pres. LEADERS Internat., Inc., Balt., 1983—; cons. Dept. of Energy, Fed. Employee Women, New Orleans, 1987-88, Peoples Involvement Corp., Washington, 1987—, Md. State Mgmt. Devel. Ctr., Balt., 1986—, D.C. Dept. of Human Svcs., Washington, 1984-85, US. Dept. Health & Human Svcs. Author: Taking Control of Your Sandbox, 1988. Bd. dir. Nat Black Women's Health Project, Atlanta, 1988, WMAR-TV Citizen's Adv. Bd., Balt., 1983-88; commn. Balt. City Off-St. Parking, Balt., 1978-82; congrl.candidate 7th Congrl. Dist. of Md., Balt., 1987. Recipient Outstanding svc. Northwood Little League, 1976, Woman of Substance award Glover-Tillman Adult Literacy, 1988, Mayoral Cert. award New Orleans, 1988. Democrat. Office: PO Box 26813 Baltimore MD 21212-0813

STEWART, SHIRLEY ANNE, educator; b. Bridgeville, Del., June 8, 1957; d. James Elliott and Perline (Jacobs) S. BS in Spl. Edn., U. Del., 1979; MEd in Spl. Edn., Temple U., 1981. Cert. tchr., Del. Spl. edn. tchr. Caesar Rodney Sch. Dist., Camden, Del., 1979; spl. edn. tchr. Indian River Sch. Dist., Frankford, Del., 1980—, bldg. rep. grading com. and health and curriculm com., 1986-87, mem. Curriculum and Instrn. Com., 1987—; tchr. Frankford Elem. Sch., 1980-91, Sussex Cen. Mid. Sch., Millsboro, Del., 1991—; mem. Gov.'s Adv. Coun. for Exceptional Citizens, Dover, Del., 1986-91; mem. Coun. Exceptional Children, Dover, 1986—; mem. State-wide Multicultural Com., 1989-90; instr Del. Tchr. Ctr., 1990; mem. middle sch. adv. coun. State Del., 1990-91, adv. coun. on multicultural edn., 1991-92, Middle Sch. Reading Com., 1992, Indian River Sch. Dist. Recruitment/Critical Shortage Com., 1992. Mem. black recruitment com. U. Del., 1987; mem. Minority Action Com., Dover, 1985-87, chmn. Martin L. King Jr. Writing Contest, 1987-88, mem. exec. bd., 1988-89, chmn. black history com., 1986-87, sec. local minority action com., 1985-88; mem. attendance com. Indian River Sch. Dist., 1987-88, recruitment & retention com., 1992, mid. sch. reading com., 1992; chmn. Del. State Edn. Minority Action Com., 1989-90; mem. strategic planning com. Del. State Edn. Assn., 1989-90, issues for the 90's com., 1991; active Dept. Pub. Instrn. Multicultural Inst. Tng., 1989; mem. middle sch. com. State of Del., 1991; mem. Statewide Multicultural Adv. Com., 1991—. Recipient Instructional Profl. Devel. award Minority Action Com., 1987, Del. Tchr. Ctr. Svc. award, 1989, Instructional Profl. Devel. award Del. State Edn. Assn., 1990. Mem. NEA, Del. State Edn. Assn. (chairperson minority action com. 1988-91, Instructional Profl. Devel. award 1991), Indian River Edn. Assn. (treas. 1989-91, chairperson minority action com. 1990-92), Adults and Children with Learning Disabilities. Democrat. Pentacostal/Apostolic. Home: 5 Magnolia Dr Millsboro DE 19966

STEWART, TERESA MARIE, travel agent; b. Galion, Ohio, Nov. 25, 1957; d. Henry Malcolm and Grace Alma (Austin) S. Assoc., Bay State Jr. Coll., Boston, 1976. Cert. travel cons. Travel agt. Davidson Travel, Nashua, N.H., 1979-84; owner, mgr. Stewart Travel, Hudson, N.H., 1984—. Big Sister, Big Bros./Big Sisters, Nashua, 1984-92. Mem. Hudson Lioness Club (1st v.p. 1990-91, pres. 1991-92, Most Dedicated to Svc. award 1991). Republican.

STEWART, WANDA LEE, education educator; b. Johnstown, Pa., July 12, 1946; d. Charles Leslie and Marion Elaine (Callahan) Block-Pennel; m. Gary Dale Stewart, Aug. 15, 1970 (widowed Apr. 1990); children: Jennifer, Jill. Diploma, Moody Bible Inst., Chgo., 1968; Bs in Elem. Edn., Ill. State U., Normal, 1970; MA in Reading, Oakland U., Rochester, Mich., 1979; EdD, Ind. U. of Pa., 1990. Reading Specialist, Va., Pa., Elem. Edn. Montessori. 3rd grade tchr. L'Anse Creuse Pub. Schs., Mt. Clemens, Mich., 1970-74; reading clin. Warren Reading Clin., Warren, Mich., 1980-82; head tchr. Little Montessorian, Warren, Mich., 1980-82; tchr. Gratiot Christian Sch., Detroit, 1982; grad. asst. Ind. U. of Pa., Indiana, Pa., 1982-83; reading specialist Portsmouth City Schs., Portsmouth, Va., 1983-85; communication skills specialist Norfolk City Schs., Norfolk, Va., 1985-89; asst. prof. edn. Nyack Coll., Nyack, N.Y., 1989-91, Juniata Coll., Huntington, Pa., 1991—; seminar presenter Norfolk, Va., 1985-89, Albany, N.Y., 1989-91, Norwalk, Conn., 1991. Recipient School Bell award, Norfolk City Schs., Va., 1989; grantee Nyack Coll., N.Y., 1990. Mem. Internat. Reading Assn., Phi Delta Kappa. Republican. Baptist. Home: 1931 Moore St Huntingdon PA 16652-2122 Office: Juniata College Huntingdon PA 16652

STEWART, WILLIAM ROBERT, artist, educator; b. Plattsburgh, N.Y., June 21, 1941; s. William James and Ellen (Adams) S.; m. Bonita Mae Baker, June 27, 1964; children: Timothy, Gregory, Brad. BS, SUNY, Buffalo, 1963; MFA, Ohio U., 1966. Prof., chair art dept. SUNY, Brockport. Exhibited in group shows at Columbus (Ohio) Art Gallery, 1965, Everson Mus. Art, Syracuse, N.Y., 1967, 72, 80, Lee Nordness Gallery, N.Y.C., 1970, B.F.M. Gallery, N.Y.C., 1980; one-man shows include Schumann Gallery, Rochester, N.Y., 1971, Lee Nordness Galleries, N.Y.C., 1973, Oxford Gallery, Rochester, 1973, 83, Meml. Art Gallery, Rochester, 1974, Helen Drutt Gallery, Phila., 1975, Theo Portnoy Gallery, N.Y., 1976, Fendrick Gallery, Washington, 1976, Chautauqua (N.Y.) Art Gallery, 1982, Dawson Gallery, Rochester, 1991; created environ. sculpture for Rochester Internat. Airport, 1992. Recipient numerous awards. Mem. Nat. Coun. for the Edn. of Ceramic Arts. Home: 2489 Roosevelt Hwy Hamlin NY 14464-9329 Office: SUNY Dept Art Brockport NY 14420

STIBEL, GARY MARSHALL, consultant; b. Kansas City, Mo., June 19, 1946; s. Harry and Livie Lee (Halperin) S.; m. Elaine Marilyn Tucker, Aug. 10, 1968; children—Jeffrey Morgan, Bradley Aaron. B.S., U. So. Calif., 1968; M.B.A., Wharton Sch., U. Pa., 1970. Mktg. mgr. Procter & Gamble, Cin., 1970-76; cons. Glendinning Assocs., Westport, Conn., 1977-80; founder New Eng. Cons. Group, Westport, 1981—. Bd. dirs. Big Bros. and Big Sisters, 1972-81; founder One Plus, 1974-77; vol., bd. dirs. Cerebral Palsy Workshop; officer Young Leadership S.W. Conn. With U.S. Army, 1978. Mem. Beta Gamma Sigma, Omicron Delta Epsilon, Phi Kappa Phi, Phi Theta Kappa. Republican. Avocations: sports, stock market, reading, travel. Office: New Eng Cons 55 Greens Farms Rd Westport CT 06880

STICH, JUNE JEACOMA, psychotherapist; b. Mineola, N.Y., June 27, 1939; d. John Daniel and Mercedes (Serrano) Jeacoma; m. William Thomas Lloyd, Sept. 16, 1961 (div. 1967); m. Edward Stich, July 6, 1974; 1 child, Edward John. AA, Nassau Community Coll., 1967; BS, Empire State Coll., 1981; MSW, Adelphi U., 1990; postgrad., Hunter Coll., Manhattan, N.Y., 1986-87. Cert. social worker. Welfare examiner I Dept. Social Svcs., Mineola, N.Y., 1971-74; pres., founder Happy Marriage League, Long Beach, N.Y., 1974-81; asst. coord. St. Mary Roman Cath. Ch., Long Beach, N.Y., 1980-82; social worker, case mgr. Cath. Charities, Lynbrook, N.Y., 1985-87; social worker, counselor Peninsula Counseling Ctr., Woodmere, N.Y., 1988-89, Jewish Assn. of Svcs. to Aged, Long Beach, 1989-90; social worker, psychotherapist Winter Park (Fla.) Home Health Care, 1991-92, Margaret Tietz Nursing Home, Jamaica, N.Y., 1992—. Narrator, writer audio tape: Think Thin, 1985. Coord. retreats L.I. Charismatic Renewal, 1985, 86. Recipient Silberman award Scholarship Com. of Hunter Coll., 1986; recipient 4 vol. svc. awards VA, 1988-89. Mem. Am. Assn. for Counseling and Devel., Nat. Assn. Social Workers, N.Am. Assn. of Christians in Social Wk. Roman Catholic. Home: 61 Cromer Rd Elmont NY 11561

STICK, ALYCE CUSHING, information systems consultant; b. N.J., July 13, 1944; d. George William and Adele Margaret (Wilderotter) Cushing; m. James McAlpin Easter, July, 1970 (div. Aug. 1986); m. T. Howard F. Stick, June, 1989. AA, Colby-Sawyer Coll., 1964; student, Boston U., 1964-65, Johns Hopkins U., 1972-74; cert., Control Data Inst. and Life Office Mgmt. Assn., 1976. Claims investigator Continental Casualty Co., Phila., 1967-69; data processing coord. Chesapeake Life Ins. Co., Balt., 1970-72; sr. systems analyst Comml. Credit Computer Corp., Balt., 1972-80; v.p. Shawmut Computer Systems, Inc., Owings Mills, Md., 1980-85; pres. Computer Relevance, Inc., Gladwyne, Pa., 1985—; cons. Sinai Hosp., Balt., 1982-85, AT&T, Reading, Pa., 1987-88, Dun and Bradstreet, Allentown, Pa., 1988, Arco Chem. Co., Newtown Square, Pa., 1990-91. Designer/author: (computer software systems) Claim-Track, 1977, Property-Profiles, 1979, Stat-Model, 1989; co-designer/author: Patient-Profiles, 1983. Treas. Balt. Mus. Art, Sales and Rental Gallery, 1984; mem. exec. com. Springfield (Pa.) Twp. Concerned Citizens, 1989. Mem. Assn. for Systems Mgmt., Data Processing Mgmt. Assn., Ind. Computer Cons. Assn., Merion Cricket Club (Haverford, Pa.). Republican. Home: 1501 Monticello Dr Gladwyne PA 19035 Office: Computer Relevance Inc 1501 Monticello Dr Gladwyne PA 19035-1206

STICK, THOMAS HOWARD FITCHETT, architect, construction litigation consultant; b. Balt., Feb. 28, 1938; s. Gordon M.F. and Anne Howard (Fitchett) S.; m. Rosalie Wade Reynolds, 1959 (div. 1982); children: H. Edward M., Alexander W., David F.; m. Joyce Yeargin Carr, 1982 (div. 1989); m. Alyce C. Cushing, 1989. BA in Psychology, Yale U., 1960; postgrad. Md. Inst., 1962, U. Pa. Grad. Sch. Architecture, 1964. Registered architect, Pa., Md., Del., N.J., Va., Maine, N.Y., D.C., Mass., N.H., N.C., Vt., Tenn., Okla., Colo., Ind., Ga.; cert. recommendation Nat. Coun. Archtl. Registration Bds. Architect, Vincent G. Kling & Ptnrs., Phila., 1964-74, B.J. Hoffman & Assocs., Berwyn, Pa., 1974; ptnr. Grim & Stick, Ardmore, Pa., 1975-77; prin. Stick Assocs., Gladwyne, Pa., 1977-80; corp. architect Gino's Inc., King of Prussia, Pa., 1980-81; mgr. constrn. adminstrn. Ballinger Co., Phila., 1981-83; sr. constrn. claims cons. MDC Systems Corp., Phila., 1984-85; chief architect Day & Zimmermann Inc., Phila., 1985—, discipline mgr. 1987—; v.p. F-S Found., 1986—, also bd. dirs. Photographer in one-man show Eastern Camera Gallery, 1972. Mem. AIA, Pa. Soc. Architects, Bldg. Ofcls. and Code Adminstrs. Internat., Internat. Conf. Bldg. Officials, So. Bldg. Code Congress Internat., Constrn. Specifications Inst., Nat. Fire Protection Assn., Soc. War of 1812 (sec. 1977-82), Soc. of Cincinnati, Soc. Colonial Wars, SR, Descs. of Lords of the Md. Manors, Mil. Order of Loyal Legion of U.S., Huguenot Soc., Am. Clan Gregor Soc., St. Andrew's Soc. of Balt., St. George's Soc. of Balt., Zeta Psi., Merion Cricket Club (Haverford, Pa.), Yale Club, Sovereign Mil. of Temple of Jerusalem (comdr.), Sovereign Order of St. John of Jerusalem (Knight of Justice), Knights Malta. Republican. Episcopalian. Home: 1501 Monticello Dr Gladwyne PA 19035-1246 Office: Day & Zimmermann Inc 1818 Market St Philadelphia PA 19103-3717

STICKLER, DAVID BRUCE, research scientist; b. Taunton, Mass., Nov. 17, 1941; s. John George and Ruth Irene (Bryans) S.; m. Marjory Slade Bliss, July 18, 1964; children: Elizabeth, Eric, Karen. BS, MS, MIT, 1964, PhD, 1968. Asst. prof. MIT, Cambridge, 1966-73; sr. rsch. scientist Avco Everett (Mass.) Rsch. Lab. (now Textron Def. Systems), 1973-77, prin. rsch. scientist, 1977-78, chmn. aerophysics rsch., 1978-82, chief scientist Energy Tech. Office, 1982-92, dir. innovative rsch., 1987-91; exec. v.p. Aerodyne Rsch., Billerica, Mass., 1992—; cons. Textron Def. Systems, Everett, 1968-83, Arthur D. Little, Cambridge, 1991—; invited speaker in field. Patentee very high velocity entrained bed gasification of coal, subsonic velocity entrained-bed gasification of coal, solubilization of carbonaceous material, method and apparatus for heat processing of glass and glass forming material, method and apparatus for heat processing of glass and glass forming material, gas fired steel melting apparatus; reviewer profl. jours.; contbr. numerous articles to profl. jours. Fellow AIAA (assoc.); mem. Combustion Inst. Home: 15 Indian Hl Carlisle MA 01741-1746 Office: Aerodyne Rsch Inc 45 Manning Rd Billerica MA 01821-3976

STIEBER, SHARON JEWEL, singer, dancer; b. Bklyn., Sept. 29, 1953; d. Fred and Florence (Spector) S. Chef, Miss Farmers Sch. Cookery, 1973. Songwriter Woodstock, N.Y., 1979—; singer Winston Grennan Ska Rocks Inc., Woodstock, 1979—; dancer, singer AAA Flash-O-Grams Singing Telegrams, Austin, Tex., 1979—; cons. Winston Grennan Ska Rocks Inc., Woodstock, 1989—. Composer: Revelation, 1991, Jah Light, 1991, Clubhouse, 1991.

STIEFEL, EDWARD IRA, chemist, biochemist; b. Bklyn., Jan. 3, 1942; s. Harry and Blanche (Schneider) S.; m. Jeannette Marie Musco, June 7, 1964; 1 child, Karen. AB, NYU, 1963; MA, Columbia U., 1964, PhD, 1967. Asst. prof. chemistry SUNY, Stony Brook, 1967-74; from investigator to sr. investigator Charles F. Kettering Rsch. Lab., Yellow Springs, Ohio, 1974-80; cons. Exxon Rsch. & Engring Co., Linden, N.J., 1979-80, rsch. assoc. corp. rsch. lab., 1980-83; sr. rsch. assoc., group head bioinorganic and coordination chemistry Exxon Rsch. & Engring Co., Annandale, N.J., 1983-86, sr. rsch. assoc., group head molecular and biol. chemistry, 1986-89, sr. rsch. assoc., sci. area leader biol. and inorganic chemistry, 1989—; Cons. John Wiley & Sons, 1972, Manhattan Coll., 1973, Garnett-McKeen Corp., 1973-76, GTE, 1976-80, The Mitre Corp., 1977-80, photosynthesis and nitrogen fixation rsch. in the People's Republic China NAS, 1979-83; adj. prof. biolog. chemistry Wright State U. Sch. Medicine, Dayton, Ohio, 1978-80; vis. lectr. dept. chemistry Princeton (N.J.) U., 1983; vis. prof. chemistry Columbia U., N.Y.C., 1986; mem. adv. panel on nitrogen fixation USDA, 1983-84, mem. presdl. young investigators selection panel NSF, 1985, 1987, undergrad. edn. in chemistry panel, 1988, com. on scholarly communication with the People's Republic China, 1979-83, nat. organizing com. for Fourth Internat. Conf. Biorganic Chemistry, 1987-89, organizing com. for Soviet-Am. seminars on environmentally related catalysis, 1985-89, del., 1985; organizer mini symposium on biolog. nitrogen and sulfur cycles Fourth Internat. Conf. Bioinorganic Chemistry, Cambridge, Mass, 1989; co-organizer mini symposium transition metal sulfide chemistry and catalysis XXIV Internat. Conf. on Coordination Chemistry, Athens, Greece, 1986; vice chair Gordon Rsch. Conf. on Metals in Biology, 1992; mem. adv. panel on biotech. NSF, 1991; lectr., presenter in field. Assoc. editor Inorganic Chimica Acta Bioinorganic Chemistry Letters, 1983-88; adv. bd. Progress in Inorganic Chemistry, 1992—; contbr. over 100 articles to profl. jours. 1st. Lt. U.S. Army, 1968. Recipient tchr. scholar award Camille and Henry Dreyfuss Found., 1970-75, Sci. Citation Classic award, 1991; grantee NSF, 1977-80, 1978-80, USDA, 1979-80, NIH, 1989—. Mem. AAAS, Am. Chem. Soc. (chmn. bioinorganic subdivision 1991, Trenton sect. speaker of yr. 1987, nomination and symposium com. inorganic chemistry div. 1984-86, organizer symposium on catalytic chemistry of transition metal sulfide systems 1983, mem. adv. bd. petroleum rsch. fund 1992—, various lectures), Soc. Biol. Chemistry, N.Y. Acad. Scis., Phi Lambda Upsilon, Sigma Xi. Home: 3 Glen Eagles Dr Bridgewater NJ 08807-1339 Office: Exxon Rsch & Engring Co Clinton Twp Rte 22E Annandale NJ 08801

STIEGLITZ, PERRY JESSE, diplomat, journalist; b. Yonkers, N.Y., Apr. 18, 1920; s. Abraham Charles and Goldie (Klein) S.; m. Princess Moune Souvanna Phouma, Apr. 29, 1935; 1 child, Dara S.P. AB, NYU, 1941; postgrad., Harvard U., 1941-42, U. Lausanne, Switzerland, 1947-50. Asst. cultural attache Am. Embassy, Paris, 1963-67; cultural attache Am. Embassy, Vietiane, Laos, 1967-68; Am. consul Am. Consulate, Marseille, France, 1968-70; cultural attache Am. Embassy, Bangkok, Thailand, 1973-76, Brussels, 1976-80; Washington Bureau chief The Bangkok Post, Thailand, 1984-85; Am. rep. Thomson Found. of Eng., London, 1986-88; dir. Gibraltar Info. Bur., Washington, 1988—. Author: In A Little Kingdom, 1990. Lt. USN, 1942-46. Fulbright grantee, Laos, 1959-60; recipient meritorious award USIA, 1967. Mem. Cercle Royale Gaulois de Bruxelles, Dacor House, Internat. Club Washington, Atlantic Coun. Office: Gibraltar Info Bureau 1155 15th St NW Washington DC 20005-2706

STIELOW, FREDERICK JOSEPH, archivist, educator; b. May 28, 1946; s. Frederick B. and Eugenie (Terrebonne) S.; divorced; 1 child, Thane Scott. BA, Ind. U., South Bend, 1971; MA, Ind. U., 1972; MLS, U. R.I., 1980; PhD, Ind. U., 1977. Lectr. Grinnell (Iowa) Coll., 1977-79; records mgr. New England Libr. Bd., Augusta, Maine, 1980-81; head spl. collections U. Southwestern La., Lafayette, 1981-82; asst. prof. U. Md., Coll. Park, 1982-87; assoc. prof. Catholic U., Washington, 1987—; lectr. U. P.R., 1989, U. Suriname, 1990; cons. World Bank, Washington, 1989-90; investigator N.Y. Folklore Soc., Ithaca, 1990—; sr. archivist Afro Am. Newspapers Archives, Balt., 1987—. Author: Management of Oral History Sound Archive, 1986 (Leland and Custer award 1987); editor: Activism in American Libraries, 1987; contbr. articles to profl. jours. Mem. Intellectual Freedom Com., Chgo., 1989-91. With U.S. Army, 1967-70. Recipient Fulbright Lectureship, State Dept., Perugia, Italy, 1983; Ford Found. grantee Afro Am. Archives, 1989, Rockefeller Rsch. grantee Rockefeller Archives, N.Y., 1990, Academic Specialists award U.S. Info. Agency, Suriname and Curacoo, 1990. Mem. ALA (Winsor prize 1989), Mid Atlantic Archivists (parliamentarian 1989, Custer award 1987), Soc. Am. Archivists (Leland prize 1987), DC Archivists (chmn. 1986-87), Acad. Cert. Archivists, La. Soc., Soc. History in Fed. Govt. Office: Cath U Am Sch Libr and Info Sci Marist Hall Washington DC 20064

STIFEL, LAURENCE DAVIS, agricultural development administrator; b. Cleve., Aug. 29, 1930; s. Richard Ernest and Loretta Ann (Davis) S.; m. Dell C. Chenoweth, June 16, 1962; children: Laura Chenoweth, David Calvert. A.B. in Econs., Harvard U., 1952, M.B.A., 1954; LL.B., Cleve. Marshall Law Sch., 1960; Ph.D. in Econs., Western Res. U., 1962; L.H.D., Urbana Coll., 1976. Bar: Ohio 1960. Asst. prof. econs. Willamette U., Salem, Oreg., 1961-62; program economist AID, Rangoon, Burma, 1962-64; econ. adviser Nat. Econ. Devel. Bd., Bangkok, 1964-67; social sci. project leader Rockefeller Found. in Thailand, also vis. prof. econs. Thammasat U., Bangkok, 1967-74; vis. fellow Econ. Growth Center, Yale U., 1969-70; sec. Internat. Agrl. Devel. Service, N.Y.C., 1975-79, Rockefeller Found., N.Y.C., 1974-83; asso. dir. social scis. Rockefeller Found., 1977-78, v.p., 1977-85; dir. gen. Internat. Inst. Tropical Agr., Ibadan, Nigeria, 1985-90; vis. fellow Cornell Internat. Inst. Food, Agr. & Devel., Ithaca, N.Y., 1990—; trustee Gen. Edn. Bd., N.Y.C., 1974-85, Princeton-in-Asia, 1976-85, Thailand Devel. Research Inst., Bangkok, 1985—; mem. governing council, exec. com. Rockefeller Archive Center; chmn. mgmt. rev. of West Africa Rice Devel. Assn. for Consultative Group for Internat. Agrl. Research, 1983. Author: The Textile Industry-A Case Study of Industrial Development in the Philippines, 1963, Methodology for Preparation of the Second Economic and Social Development Plan of Thailand, 1967; also articles.; co-editor: Education and Training for Public Sector Management in the Developing Countries, 1977, Social Sciences and Public Policy in Developing Areas, 1982. Fulbright fellow Philippines, 1959-60. Mem. Asia Soc. (chmn. Thai council 1975-77), Siam Soc. (council 1969-72), Soc. Internat. Devel. (v.p., co-founder Bangkok chpt. 1968-70), Council Fgn. Relations, Am. Econs. Assn., Assn. Asian Studies. Club: Harvard, Century Assn. (N.Y.C.). Home: 701 Wyckoff Rd Ithaca NY 14850 Office: Cornell U PO Box 14 Ithaca NY 14853

STIFFLER, JACK JUSTIN, electrical engineer; b. Mitchellville, Iowa, May 22, 1934; s. John Justin and Helen Irene (Roorda) S.; m. Ardis Ann Ackerman, Aug. 21, 1955; 1 child, Julia Alise; m. Sally Voris Burns, Apr. 20, 1989. A.B. magna cum laude in Physics, Harvard U., 1956; M.S. in E.E, Calif. Inst. Tech., 1957, Ph.D., 1962; postgrad., U. Paris, 1957-58. Engr. Hughes Aircraft Corp., Culver City, Calif., 1956-57; mem. tech. staff Jet Propulsion Lab., Pasadena, Calif., 1959-67; cons. scientist Raytheon Corp., Sudbury, Mass., 1967-81; exec. v.p. Sequoia Systems, Inc., Marlborough, Mass., 1981—; lectr. Calif. Inst. Tech., U. So. Calif., UCLA, Northeastern U. Author: Theory of Synchronous Communications, 1971; contbr. chpts. to books, articles to profl. jours. Fellow IEEE; mem. Phi Beta Kappa, Sigma Xi. Office: Sequoia Systems Inc 400 Nickerson Rd Marlborough MA 01752

STIGLITZ, MARTIN RICHARD, electrical engineer; b. Vienna, Austria, Mar. 24, 1920; came to U.S., 1939, naturalized, 1942; s. Georg Adolph and Maria (Brun) S.; BS, Northeastern U., 1957, MS in Electronics Engring., 1959; MBA in Mgmt., Western New Eng. Coll., 1977; m. Lenna Schoenberg, Dec. 10, 1950 (dec. Apr. 1991); m. Sachiko Sakimura, May 1, 1990. Mech. engr. S.A. Woods Machine Co., Boston, 1939-51; electronics engr., rsch. scientist Air Force Cambridge Rsch. Labs., Hanscom AFB, Bedford, Mass., 1945-75; rsch. electronics scientist Rome Air Devel. Command electromagnetic scis. div. U.S. Air Force, Bedford, Mass., 1985-88; tech. editor Horizon House-Microwave, Inc., Norwood, Mass., 1985—; dir. Solar Energy Tech. Inc., Bedford. With U.S. Army, 1942-45. Mem. IEEE, N.Y. Acad. Scis., Sigma Xi. Patentee solid state devices, med. instruments; contbr. over 50 articles to sci. and profl. jours. Home: 30 Woodpark Cir Lexington MA 02173-7208

STIGWOOD, ROBERT COLIN, theater, movie, television and record producer; b. Adelaide, Australia, Apr. 16, 1934; came to Eng., 1956; s. Gordon and Gwendolyn (Burrows) S. Attended, Sacred Heart Coll., Adelaide. Worked as copywriter for advt. agy. Adelaide; held series of jobs, including mgr. provincial theater and halfway house for delinquents in Cambridge; opened talent agy. London, 1962; liquidated firm, 1965; became bus. mgr. for group Graham Bond Orgn.; became co-mng. dir. NEMS Enterprises, 1967; established own firm Robert Stigwood Orgn., 1967; formed RSO Records, 1973; became dir. of Polygram, 1976; co-founder (with Rupert Murdoch) R&R Films, 1979; founder Music for UNICEF. 1st ind. record producer in Eng. with release of single Johnny Remember Me; producer: films, including Jesus Christ Superstar, 1973, Bugsy Malone, Tommy, 1975, Survive, 1976, Saturday Night Fever, 1977, Grease I, 1978, Grease II, 1982, Moment By Moment, 1978, Sergeant Pepper's Lonely Hearts Club Band, The Fan, 1981, Times Square, 1980, Gallipoli, 1980, Staying Alive, 1983; stage musicals in Eng. and U.S., including, Hair, Oh! Calcutta, The Dirtiest Show in Town, Sweeney Todd, Pippin, Jesus Christ Superstar, Evita; TV producer in Eng. and U.S.; prodns. include The Entertainer (dramatic spl.); All in the Family (series), The Prime of Miss Jean Brodie (dramatic series). Bd. dirs. Police Athletic League, N.Y.C.; patron Australian Nat. Art Gallery. Recipient Tony award for best musical (Evita); named Internat. Producer of Yr. ABC Interstate Theatres, Inc., 1976, Knights of St. John of Jerusalem, Malta, 1985. Club: Royal Bermuda Yacht. Home: Barton Manor, Whippingham East Cowes, Isle of Wight PO32 6LB, Bermuda

STILES, ALVIN BARBER, chemical engineer; b. Springfield, Ohio, July 16, 1909; s. Paul Hocker and Lucille Luna (Barber) S.; m. Oct. 6, 1934; children: David, Cynthia, Jennifer. B Chem. Engring., Ohio State U., 1931, MS, 1933. Rsch. fellow Dupont Co., Wilmington, Del., 1931-74; rsch. prof. dept. chem. engring. U. Del., Newark, 1974—. Author: Catalyst Manufacture, 1983, Catalyst Supports and Supported Catalysts, 1987; contbr. articles to profl. jours., chpts. to books. Recipient Disting. Alumnus award Ohio State U., Outstanding Contbn. award Phila. Catalysis Club, 1979. Fellow Am. Inst. Chemists; mem. AAAS, Am. Chem. Soc., Am. Inst. Chem. Engrs., N.Y. Acad. Scis. Republican. Presbyterian. Home: 1301 Grayson Rd Wilmington DE 19803-4119 Office: U Del Newark DE 19716

STILES, KURT EDWARD, food company executive; b. Stamford, Conn., Feb. 10, 1963; s. Oliver Darwin and Diane Thia (Miller) S. AS, Mitchell Coll., 1985; B of Psychology, Assumption Coll., 1987; cert., Mohegan Coll., 1989. Restaurant mgr. JTK Mgmt. Co., Mystic, Conn., 1977-82; mgr. coll. food svc. Marriot Food Svc., New London, Conn., 1983-87; co-dist. mgr. Boston Concessions Group, New London, 1988-91; mktg. cons. Graphic Dimensions, New London, 1991; pres., cons., owner Stiles Foods Co., Mystic, 1990—. Inventor Moose Hopper!. Chmn. Incentive Community Enterprises, Gates Ferry, Conn., 1990—, bus. adv. bd.; state rep. Conn. Colls. at U.S. Senate subcom. hearing on budget for higher edn., Hartford, 1985; mem. chocolate challenge Easter Seals, 1990—. Recipient Cyrus G. Flanders Meritorious Svc. award State Conn., 1990. Mem. C. of C. Home: PO Box 567 Old Mystic CT 06372-0567

STILES, LYNN FEIBEL, JR., educator, consultant, researcher; b. Bklyn., July 4, 1942; s. Lynn F. and Gladys (Moore) S.; m. Sandra Larson, Aug. 12, 1967; children: Eric P., Jonathan N. BS in Physics, SUNY, Stony Brook, 1964; MS in Physics, Cornell U., 1967, PhD in Physics, 1990. Instr. physics Hobart & William Smith Coll., Geneva, N.Y., 1966-68; rsch. physicist E.I. du Pont de Nemours & Co., Wilmington, Del., 1969-73; rsch. scientist Univ.

Ill., 1981-83; prof. physics Stockton State Coll., Pomona, N.J., 1973-81, 1983—; vis. prof. Swarthmore Coll., Swarthmore, Pa., 1972; dir. of Tech. Assessment Atlantic County, Northfield, N.J., 1975-78; energy cons., 1979—; pres. Cape-Atlantic New Business Incubation, Pleasantville, N.J., 1988-90. Author: (book) Optics for Artists, 1975; contbr. numerous articles to profl. jours. V.P. Mainland Regional High Sch. Bd. Edn., Linwood, N.J., 1989—, mem. 1986—. Office: Stockton State Coll Pomona NJ 08240

STILL, JOHN C., III, insurance agent, state senator; b. Dover, Del., Oct. 27, 1952; s. John Clifton Jr. and Kathleen (Nichols) S.; m. Kathleen Heron, Mar. 6, 1982. AA, Wesley Coll., Dover, 1972; BS in Edn., U. Del., 1974. CLU, registered health underwriter, chartered fin. cons. Math. & sci. tchr. Newark (Del.) Sch., 1974-77; ins. agt. Dover, 1976—; senator State of N.J., 1988—. Recipient Pub. Svc. award March of Dimes, 1982, 83. Mem. Nat. Assn. Life Underwriters, Nat. Assn. Health Underwriters, Cen. Del. C. of C., Rotary. Republican. Methodist. Office: Still Ins Agy 872-C Walker Rd Dover DE 19901

STILLINGS, IRENE CORDINER, organization executive; b. Boston, Aug. 17, 1918; d. Matthew Wilson and Susan F. (Mason) Cordiner; m. Gordon A. Stillings, May 13, 1945; children: David Gordon, Susan Irene. Student, Radcliffe Coll., 1936-39; diploma, Burdett Coll., 1941. Sec., bookkeeper Boston Refrigerator Co., 1941-42; sec., tchr. Burdett Coll., 1942-44; sec., bookkeeper Gertrude Rittenburg, Boston, 1944-46. Town chmn. Heart Fund, Woodland, Maine, 1953-61; Brownie leader Girl Scouts U.S., 1954-58; pres. Woodland Woman's Club 1961-63; sec. PTA, 1961-62; chmn. Baileyville Superintending Sch. Com., 1962-64; chmn. women's activities Nat. Found., East Washington County, 1959-61; pres. Hosp. Aid, 1961-63; chmn. Newcomers Coll. group YWCA, 1965-66, chmn. theatre group, 1968-70, pres. Suburbanites, 1970-71; Stamford chmn. Expt. in Internat. Living, 1965-68; bd. dirs. YWCA of Stamford, chmn. devotion, 1970-92, ann. Antique Show benefit, 1970-77. Mem. Mass. Hort. Soc., St. Luke's Guild (treas. 1954-63), Radcliffe Club, Stamford Woman's Club (treas. 1975-79, program com., co-chmn. Am. home dept. 1974, 75, pres. 1981-83, bd. dir. 1985-87, 2d v.p. fin. 1983-85, 87-89, chmn. bldg. investment 1979-81, bd. dir. 1989—), Theta Alpha Chi, Stamford Women's Club. Episcopalian. Home: 277 W Hill Rd Stamford CT 06902-1708

STILLMAN, JOYCE L., artist, educator; b. N.Y.C., Jan. 19, 1943; d. Murray W. and Evelyn (Berger) Stillman. BA, NYU, 1964; MFA, L.I. U., 1975. Tchr. N.Y.C. Pub. Schs., 1964-71; artist Cen. Hall Gallery, Port Washington, N.Y., 1974-76, Louis K. Meisel Gallery, N.Y.C., 1975-84, Tolarno Gallery, Melbourne, Australia, 1976—, Allan Stone Gallery, N.Y.C., 1990—; visiting assoc. prof. Towson State U., 1982; tchr. Women in Art, Tompkins Cortland Community Coll., 1988; lectr. Cornell U., 1990. One-person shows include Cen. Hall Gallery, Port Washington, 1975, Tolarno Gallery, Melbourne, 1976, Louis K. Meisel Gallery, N.Y.C., 1977, 80, 81, 82, Heckscher Mus., Huntington, N.Y., 1980, Holtzman Gallery, Towson (Md.) State U., 1982, Roslyn Oxley Gallery, Sydney, 1976, 82, Tomasulo Gallery, Union College, N.J., 1983, Stages, Keuka Coll., Keuka Park, N.Y., 1985, New Visions, Ithaca, N.Y., 1989, Herr-Chambliss, Hot Springs, Ark., 1990; designer Mus. Modern Art Christmas Collection, 1978-81, Time-Life Poster, 1978; exhibited in over 50 group shows, corp. and mus. collections. Recipient Flower Painting award Artist's Mag., 1986, Art Dir.'s Club 58th Annual Distinctive Merit award, 1979, N.Y. State Creative Artist's Pub. Svc. grant, 1979. Mem. Nat. Assn. Women Artists, Allan Stone Gallery N.Y.C. Home and Studio: 5120 County Rd 4 Burdett NY 14818

STILLMAN, LUCILLE TERESE, artist; b. Chgo.; d. William A. and Lillian (Cooke) Knox; m. Richard N. Stillman, Feb. 14, 1946; children: Richard, Nancy, Robert. BA, Art Inst. Chgo.; MFA, Coll. Arts and Crafts, 1952. Executed mural Cath. Ch., Stamford, Conn., 1991; commd. portraits UNICEF, others. Recipient Creative Hands award. Mem. Hudson Valley Art Assn. (bd. dirs., historian 1989—), Am. Artist Profl. League (bd. dirs., treas. 1985-90), Pastel Soc. Am. (bd. dirs., editor, sec., charter mem.), Oil Pastel Soc. (master pastellist 1991), Nat. Arts Club (mem. exhbn. com.), Salmagundi Club (bd. dirs., sec., Kent Day Coes award 1991), Pen & Brush Club (bd. dirs., chmn. pastel sect. 1980-89, Best in Show 1991), Catharine Lorillard Wolfe Art Club (award of excellence 1991, exhbn. chmn. 1987—). Roman Catholic. Home and Studio: 8 Drum Ln Stamford CT 06902

STILLMAN, NORMAN ARTHUR, historian, educator; b. N.Y.C., July 6, 1945; s. Melvin and Joyce (Gidden) S.; m. Yedida Kalfon, June 25, 1967; children: Mia A., Enan E. BA in Oriental Studies magna cum laude, U. Pa., 1967, PhD in Oriental Studies, 1970; postdoctoral study, Jewish Theol. Seminary, N.Y.C., 1970-71. Asst. prof. NYU, N.Y.C., 1970-73; assoc. prof. SUNY, Binghamton, N.Y., 1973-85, prof. history and Arabic, 1985—; adv. com. mem. Geniza Rsch. Lab, Jerusalem, 1986—; cons. Social Sci. Rsch. Coun., N.Y.C., 1972-77. Editor AJS Rev., 1989—; author: The Jews of Arab Lands, 1979, The Language and Culture of the Jews of Sefrou, 1988, The Jews of Arab Lands in Modern Times, 1991. Recipient Chancellor's award for Excellence in Teaching, SUNY, Albany, 1986; Momigliano Lectr., Com. on Social Thought, U. Chgo., 1990. Mem. Am. Oriental Soc. (mem. com. 1975-83), Mid. East Studies Assn. (book rev. editor 1976-77), Assn. for Jewish Studies (bd. dirs. 1989—), Conf. on Jewish Social Studies, Soc. for Judeo-Arabic Studies, Phi Beta Kappa. Office: History Dept/SUNY PO Box 6000 Binghamton NY 13902-6000

STILLWAGON, JAMES GEORGE, maritime consultant, ship pilot; b. N.Y.C., Jan. 25, 1920; s. Walter J. and Sarah (McGrath) S.; m. Rosemary Gronachan, June 7, 1941; children: James M., John W., Eileen M. Diploma, St. Augustine High Sch. Tug capt. Russell Towing/Valentine Transp., N.Y.C., 1941-56; ship pilot, pres. Interport Pilots Agy., Inc., N.Y.C., 1956—; pres. Pilotage Cons., Inc., N.Y.C., 1980—; vice chmn. vessel traffic svc. adv. com. USCG, 1970—; mem. N.Y. Harbor Ops. Com., 1975—; lectr., expert witness in field. mem. Soc. Marine Cons. (exec. com.), Nautical Inst. London, Coun. Am. Master Mariners. Republican. Roman Catholic. Home: 46 Tenafly Dr New Hyde Park NY 11040-3610 Office: Pilotage Cons Inc PO Box 2046 New Hyde Park NY 11040-0701

STILLWAGON, WESLEY WILLIAM, corporate professional; b. Allentown, N.J., Sept. 16, 1940; s. Wesley L. and Catherine Cecilia (O'Malley) S.; children: Wesley William Jr., Matthew P., Beth Anne; m. Beverly D. Ross. AAS in Electronics Tech., USN Equivalency, 1961; BS in Psychology, Trenton State U., 1974. Cert. tchr., N.Y., N.J., cert. NASA instr., cert. signal corp instr. Quality control tech. RCA Astro, Princeton, N.J., 1962-68; tng. supr. RCA Astro, Princeton, 1968-74; mgr. skills tng. and quality control RCA G & CS, Camden, N.J., 1978-82; field engr. Research Cottrell, Somerville, N.J., 1975-76; mgr. skills tng. Loral Electronic Systems, Yonkers and Bronx, N.Y., 1976-78; mgr. sales tng. Honeywell MicroSwitch, Freeport, Ill., 1982-83; mgr. job devel. and tng. Mainstream Access, N.Y.C., 1983-85; generation tng. mgr. Penelec/GPU, Johnstown, Pa., 1985-90; co-owner Wes Stillwagon Cons., Bus. Svcs., North Plainfield, N.J., 1990—. Author: Human Factors Simulator Training Qualification, 1987, The Role of the Individual in Sound Process Control and Achieving Business Objectives, New Approach Speeds Simulator Design and Procurement, Improving the Competitive Edge through Human Performance Engineering. With USN, 1960-62. Mem. Pitts. Jung Soc., Mid-Atlantic Fossil Utility Trainers Assn. (bd. dirs. 1989-90). Democrat. Episcopalian. Home and Office: 80 Mali Dr North Plainfield NJ 07062

STILLWELL, RICHARD NEWHALL, chemist; b. Princeton, N.J., Nov. 22, 1935; s. Richard and Agnes Ellen (Newhall) S.; m. Wanda Sara Gardiner, Aug. 25, 1968. BA, Princeton U., 1957; PhD, Harvard U., 1964. Instr. Baylor Coll. Medicine, Houston, 1963-64, asst. prof., 1964-75, assoc. prof., 1975-84; pvt. practice cons. Bedford, Mass., 1984—; owner Sci. Computer Applications, Bedford, 1985—; co-prin. Sci. Instrument Svcs. Corp., Framingham, Mass., 1991. Contbr. articles to profl. publs. Mem. ACM, Am. Chem. Soc., Am. Soc. Mass Spectrometry, Sigma Xi. Home and Office: 10 Daniels Dr Bedford MA 01730-1202

STILLWELL, ROGER GEORGE, communication company, public relations executive; b. San Francisco, Oct. 13, 1939; s. George Victor and Veronica (Severini) S.; m. Bette Jane Kaplan, Nov. 1, 1969; children: David, Aaron, Matthew. BS, U. Wisc., 1964; MA, Am. U., 1972. Profl. writer varous publs., Washington, 1969-74; press sec. U.S. House Reps., Washington, 1974-85; co-pub., editor, owner Washington Pacific Reports, Washington, 1985-87; legis. dir. Wash. Office Commonwealth of No. Marianas Isles, Washington, 1987-89; pres. Stillwell Communications, Inc., Washington, 1989—; cons. Gov. Guam, 1985-87, Commonwealth No. Marianas, 1989-90, Federated States of Micronesia, 1990-92. Editor: (newsletters) Washington Pacific Reports, 1990, Micronesia Investment Quarterly, 1990—; writer, dir. 3 video documentaries, 1991. Precinct chmn. Dem. Party, Montgomery County, Md., 1986-92. Regipient Hon. Chamorro, 16th Guam Legis., 1986. Mem. Wash. Indep. Writers. Democrat. Home: 11400 Cephise Ct North Potomac MD 20878 Office: Stillwell Communications PO Box 3867 North Potomac MD 20855

STILWELL, RONALD EDWARD, manufacturing executive; b. Utica, N.Y., Feb. 20, 1948; s. Elmer Kenneth and Esther Irene (Hunziker) S.; m. Nancy Allyn Rademan, June 6, 1971; children: Carolyn Esther, Kathryn Alexa Rademan. BA in Polit. Sci., U. Rochester, 1970; MS in Adminstrn., Hartford Grad. Ctr., 1979. Field underwriter Mut. of N.Y. Ins., Rochester, 1970-71; credit/collection analyst Marine Midland Bank, Rochester, 1971-72; from credit trainee to v.p. mil. mktg. and adminstrn. Firearms div. Colt Industries, Hartford, Conn., 1972-90; exec. v.p., pres. Colt's Mfg. Co., Inc., Hartford, 1990—. Bd. dirs. Albano Ballet Co., Hartford, 1984—, Big Bros./Big Sisters, Hartford, 1978-85; pres. Waterfront Heights Assn., Coventry, Conn., 1979-81; treas. Oak Grove Assn., Coventry, 1973-80. Mem. Nat. Contract Mgmt. Assn. (pres. 1980-81), Am. Def. Preparedness Assn. (exec. bd. 1986-90, chair small arms 1987-89), Nat. Shooting Sports Found. (bd. dirs. 1990—), Am. Shooting Sports Coalition (bd. dirs. 1990—). Republican. Baptist. Office: Colts Mfg Co PO Box 1868 Hartford CT 06144-1868

STIMLER, MICHAEL KEVIN, home video manufacturing company executive; b. N.Y.C., Dec. 25, 1959; s. Irving and Norma (Raff) S. BA, U. Pa., 1982. Fin. cons. NFS Svcs. Inc., N.Y.C., 1982-87; video cons. Pvt. Screenings Inc., N.Y.C., 1987-88; sr. v.p. Water Bearer Films Inc., N.Y.C., 1988—; cons. Merrill Lynch, N.Y.C., 1983-84. Mem. Video Software Assn. Office: Water Bearer Films Inc 205 W End Ave New York NY 10023-4804

STINER, FREDERIC MATTHEW, JR., accounting educator, consultant, writer; b. Balt., Apr. 4, 1946; s. Frederic Matthew and Bertha Moulton (Kidd) S.; m. Martha Susan Scharper, June 21, 1969; children: Frederic Matthew, John Alexander, James Michael, Katherine Elizabeth. MS, U. Del., 1969; MBA, Marshall U., 1972; PhD, U. Nebr., 1976. CPA, W.Va. Staff acct. Goodman & Co., CPAs, Norfolk, Va., 1973-74; sr. acct. Snyder, Grant, Muehling, CPAs, Lincoln, Nebr., 1977-78; asst. prof. Iowa State U., Ames, 1978-79, U. Md., College Park, 1979-82; assoc. prof. acctg. U. Del., Newark, 1982—; cons. NSF, Washington, 1980-82. Contbr. articles to Jour. of Accountancy and other acad. and profl. jours.; editorial adv. bd. Jour. Accountancy, 1981-86. Mem. AAUP (bargaining team 1988, 90), AICPA, W.Va. Soc. CPAs. Home: 109 Autumn Horseshoe Bnd Newark DE 19702-2354 Office: U Del Coll Bus and Econs Newark DE 19716

STINSON, KATHERINE ANNE, public relations director; b. Summit, N.J., Jan. 29, 1949; d. Morton David and Irene Viola (Toabe) Fagen; m. William Stinson, Oct. 24, 1971 (dec. 1975); 1 child, Sasha Christine. BA in English summa cum laude, Brown U., 1971, BA in French summa cum laude, 1971. Editor Internat. Labour Orgn., Geneva, Switzerland, 1972-77; free-lance writer N.Y.C., 1977-87; pub. rels. mgr. AT&T, Short Hills, N.Y., 1977-87; pub. rels. dir. AT&T, Morristown, N.Y., 1990—; cons. in field. Ghost writer: Growth in Children, 1980, Starr Commonwealth, 1982. Mem. Am. Mgmt. Assn., Pub. Rels. Soc. Am., Internat. Assn. Bus. Communicators, Brown U. Club, South Am. Explorer's Club, Phi Beta Kappa. Home: 74 Fairmount Ave Chatham NJ 07928 Office: AT&T 475 South St Morristown NJ 07962

STINSON, PETER ANDREW, English language educator; b. Boston, Nov. 30, 1961; s. Richard Lyon and Anne Melanie (Freudenberg) S.; m. Dianne Kathleen Mount, Jan. 1, 1989. BA, Trinity Coll., 1984; MEd, George Mason U., 1987. Freelance writer Mt. Vernon, Va., 1984-86; acad. advisor George Mason U., Fairfax, Va., 1985-87; mem. faculty Wyo. Sem., Kingston, 1987—; sr. editor Word Master, Inc., Fairfax, 1988-90. Editor: The Coast Guard Reservist mag., 1985-87 (Letter of Commendation 1987); author poetry. With USCGR, 1980—. Fellow Washington Irving Soc.; mem. Nat. Coun. Tchrs. of English, Assn. for Asian Studies, Am. Assn. for Counseling and Devel. Episcopalian. Home: 201 N Sprague Ave Wilkes Barre PA 18704-3593 Office: Wyo Sem 201 N Sprague Ave Wilkes Barre PA 18704-3593

STIPANUK, MARTHA HARNEY, nutrition educator; b. Cynthiana, Ky., May 12, 1948; d. Arthur M. Jr. and Ruth (Ammerman) Harney; m. David M. Stipanuk, July 31, 1976; children: Peter, Rachel, Daniel. BS, U. Ky., 1970; MS, Cornell U., 1972; PhD, U. Wis., 1977. Instr. Auburn (Ala.) U., 1972-74; asst. prof. Cornell U., Ithaca, N.Y., 1977-83, assoc. prof. dept. nutritional scis., 1983—. Contbr. articles to profl. publs. Grantee Nutrition Found., 1979-80, NIH, 1980-89, USDA, 1982-85, 88—. Mem. Am. Inst. Nutrition, Am. Soc. Biochemistry and Molecular Biology, Sigma Xi, Phi Kappa Phi. Office: Cornell Univ Div Nutritional Scis 225 Savage Hall Ithaca NY 14853

STIRRAT, WILLIAM ALBERT, electronics engineer; b. Syracuse, N.Y., Nov. 5, 1919; s. Robert William and Doris (White) S.; m. Bernice Amelia Wilson, July 13, 1958; children: Valerie Lynne, Dorothy Grace, William Ellsworth. Student, Triuna (Yaddo) Arts of the Theater Sch., 1936; BS in Physics, Rensselaer Poly. Inst., 1942, postgrad., 1949-50; postgrad., Rutgers U., 1951-58, Fairleigh Dickinson U., 1971. With GE, Schenectady, N.Y., 1941-44; instr. physics Clarkson Coll. Tech., 1947-49; electronic engr. rsch. and devel. U.S. Army, Fort Monmouth, N.J., 1950-87; prin. engr. Eagle Tech., Inc., Eatontown, N.J., 1987-92; pres. Stirrat Arts & Scis., Freehold, N.J., 1992—. Author: (with Alex North) Unchained Melody, 1936 (Top song of Yr., Acad. award nomination 1955), Why 3? (Army award 1985); assoc. editor IEEE Transactions on Electromagnetic Compatability, 1970-76; contbr. articles to profl. jours.; patentee in field. Chmn. pub. rels. Battleground dist. Monmouth coun. Boy Scouts Am., 1970-77; mem. Rep. Congl. Leadership Coun. Mem. IEEE (sr. editor N.J. Coast sect. Scanner 1974-75), Internat. Platform Assn., Assn. of Old Crows, Cen. Jersey Natural Food Club (pres. 1970). Episcopalian. Home and Office: 218 Overbrook Dr Freehold NJ 07728-1525

STISHAN, PETER MICHAEL, restaurant executive; b. Warren, Ohio, Aug. 6, 1949; s. Peter Paul and Lona Belle (Casteel) S.; m. Hillary F. Mazer, Sept. 13, 1981; children: David Andrew Keith, Eric Scott. BS, Towson (Md.) State U., 1972. Asst. gen. mgr. The Kings Contrivance, Columbia, Md., 1975-77; chief adminstr. Fiori Restaurant, Reisterstown, Md., 1977-80; ptrn., chief fin. officer City Lights Restaurant, Balt., 1980—; ptnr., corp. pres. and sec. Pete's Pizza, Inc., Balt., 1980—, Kings Fare Inc., Balt., 1980—; ptnr. Internat. Foods, Inc., Washington, 1984—, Top Brass, Inc., Blat., 1980—; ptnr., corp. pres. Mamma Ilardo's of Pioneer Place, Portland, Oreg., 1990—, Columbia Fare, Inc., Columbia, Md., 1991—. With U.S. Army, 1972-75. Democrat. Methodist. Home: 7065 Montgomery Rd Baltimore MD 21227-5414 Office: City Lights 301 Light St Baltimore MD 21202-1037

STITT, DONALD MEREDITH, systems director; b. Middletown, Ohio, May 8, 1940; s. Arthur Brown and Dorothy Brewster (Moffat) S.; m. Mary Jane van Eyndhoven, Dec. 28, 1963 (div. Dec. 1968). AA, Kemper Mil. Sch., Booneville, Mo., 1960; BA, NYU, Bronx, 1962; MBA, Fordham U., 1975. Programmer, analyst Ameritrust, Cleve., 1966-68; systems programmer Citibank, N.A., N.Y.C., 1968-74, EDP audit mgr., 1974-84; EDP auditor Bloomingdale's, N.Y.C., 1982-84; corp. EDP audit mgr. Fischbach Corp., N.Y.C., 1984-88; sr. acct. St. Thomas Ch. Fifth Ave, N.Y.C., 1988-89, dir. systems and devel., 1989—; dir. Gallery Gift Shop, N.Y.C., 1985—. Fundraising chmn. bd. dirs. The Collegiate Chorale; treas. 102 W 75th St. Tenants' Com. 1st lt. U.S. Army, 1963-66. Mem. Am. Soc. of the Most Venerable Order of the Hosp. of St. John of Jerusalem (officer, bro.). Anglican. Home: 92 Betty Rd East Meadow NY 11554 Office: St Thomas Ch Fifth Ave One West Fifty-Third St New York NY 10019-5496

STITT, SUSAN, historical society executive; b. East Liverpool, Ohio, Jan. 1, 1942; d. Wilson Montgomery and Cora Blanche (Link) S. BA in American History, Coll. William and Mary, 1964; MA in American Civilization, U. Pa., 1966; postgrad. student, Wake Forest U., 1968, U. Del., 1970. Asst. to the dir. Historical Soc. Pa., Phila., 1966; first dir. Museum of the Albemarle, Elizabeth City, N.C., 1967-68; adminstr. Museum of Early Southern Decorative Arts, Winston-Salem, N.C., 1969-71; asst. to the dir. The Bklyn. Museum, 1971-72; project dir. Old Sturbridge (Mass.) Village, 1972-74; dir. The Museums at Stony Brook, N.Y., 1974-88; pres. Historical Soc. Pa., Phila., 1990—; mem. museum aid panel N.Y. State Coun. on the Arts, 1976-79; panelist and reviewer Nat. Endowment for the Humanities, Nat. Endowment for the Arts, Inst. Museum Svcs., 1975—. Mem. editorial bd. Museum Studies Jour., 1984-89; contbr. articles to profl. jours. Mem. advisory com. Long Island Community Found., 1986-88; mem. nonprofit subcom. advisory bd. SUNY, Stony Brook, 1987-88. Named N.C. Young Career Woman of Yr. Bus. and Profl. Womens Club, 1968, Woman of Yr. Village Times, Setauket, N.Y., 1979; recipient First Ann. Recognition award N.C. Mus. Coun., 1968, Katherine Coffey award Mid-Atlantic Assn. Museums, 1987, Ward Melville Community award Three Village Hist. Soc., 1988. Mem. Am. Assn. Museums (coun. mem. 1976-79, 1982-85, ethics com. mem. 1976-79, women's caucus mem. 1975-78, pres. 1977, v.p. 1985-86), Am. Assn. State and Local History (nat. steering com. 1987—), Mid Atlantic Assn. Museums (v.p. 1982-85), L.I. Museum Assn. (nominating com. 1977-79), Kappa Delta Pi, Chi Delta Phi, Theta Alpha Phi. Office: Historical Soc Pa 1300 Locust St Philadelphia PA 19107-5699

STIVALA, MICHAEL JOSEPH, futures trading company research analyst; b. Elizabeth, N.J., Aug. 20, 1966; s. Richard Anthony and Mary Patricia (McGovern) S. BA, Rutgers Coll., 1988; postgrad., Rutgers U., 1988—. Rsch. analyst Commodities Corp. (USA), Princeton, N.J., 1989—; chief fin. officer Raging Assets Investment Club, Union, N.J., 1990—. Home: 15 Locke Ct Trenton NJ 08628-2645

STIVER, WILLIAM EARL, retired government administrator; b. Madison, Ind., Mar. 30, 1921; s. John Virgil and Anna Lynne (Ryker) S.; student Hanover Coll., 1947-49; B.S., U. Calif. at Berkeley, 1951, M.B.A., 1952; m. Norma A. Cull, June 11, 1944; children—Vicki, Raymond, Gena, John. With Fed. Ser., Bur. Census, Commerce Dept., Suitland, Md., 1952-79, chief budget and finance div., 1963-73, dep. assoc. adminstr. Social and Econ. Stats. Adminstrn., 1973-75, spl. asst., assoc. dir. for adminstrn. and field ops. Bur. of Census, 1975-77, electronic data processing staff coordinator, 1977-78, ret., 1979. Served with AUS; 1942-43, 45-46. Recipient Silver medal Commerce Dept., 1969. Mem. Phi Beta Kappa, Beta Gamma Sigma. Home: 8104 Kerby Pky Ct Fort Washington MD 20744-4756

STIVISON, DAVID VAUGHN, lawyer; b. Logan, Ohio, Oct. 11, 1946; s. Robert Woodrow and Freda Mae (Smith) S.; m. Sandra Kay Geiger, July 12, 1985. BA in Philosophy, Ohio U., 1969, BS in Chemistry, 1969; JD, Harvard U., 1979. Bar: Ohio 1979, U.S. Dist. Ct. (so. dist.) Ohio 1980, U.S. Dist. Ct. (ea. dist.) Pa. 1990, Pa. 1983. Dir. commn. on poverty Ohio Council Churches, Columbus, 1975-76; assoc. firm Bricker and Eckler, Columbus, 1979-83, Morgan, Lewis and Bockius, Phila., 1983-85; pvt. practice, 1985—. Author: 1986 Public Utility Research Handbook, 1986, Anatomy of an Administrative Proceeding, 1986, Homosexuals and the Constitution, 1982, Public Utilities Law Anthology, vol. X, 1987; co-author: Pennsylvania Public Utility Law, 1990, The Bill of Rights: A Bicentennial View, 1991, The Bill of Rights: Securing the Blessings of Liberty, 1991, Discovering our Fundamental Freedoms, 1992; contbr. articles to legal publs. Pres. Ohio Housing Coalition, Columbus, 1973-75; chmn. bd. dirs. Hunger Task Force Ohio, Columbus, 1980-82; bd. dirs. Ohio State Legal Svcs. Assn., Columbus, 1980-83. Mem. ABA, Internat. Bar Assn., Fed. Bar Assn., Fed. Energy Bar Assn., Ohio Bar Assn. (chmn. com. 1983), Hist. Soc. U.S. Dist. Ct. Ea. Dist. (bd. dirs.), Pa. Bar Assn. (chmn. com. 1989-92, Pres.'s award 1991), Phila. Bar Assn. (com. chmn. 1986, 92), Selden Soc. (corr. sec. Ohio chpt. 1982-83, Pa. chpt. 1983—), Am. Chem. Soc., Am. Nuclear Soc., Am. Soc. for Legal History, Union League Phila., Engrs'. Club Phila., Harvard Club Phila., Phi Beta Kappa. Democrat. Mem. Met. Community Ch.

STOBBS, EMMETT EUGENE, JR., applied science engineer; b. Evanston, Ill., Oct. 9, 1946; s. Emmett Eugene Stobbs and Gladys Carlson Ritchie; m. Mary-jo Hall, July 19, 1975. BS in Engring., U.S. Mil. Acad., 1969; MS in Engring. Physics, U. Calif., Davis, 1977; MBA, L.I. U., 1981. Registered profl. engr., Va. Commd. 2d lt. U.S. Army, 1969, advanced through grades to col., 1991; platoon/co. comdr./S-3 78th Engr. BN, Karlsruhe, Germany, 1970-74; with S3 2nd Engr. Group, Seoul, Korea, 1974-75; assoc. prof. physics U.S. Mil. Acad., West Point, 1978-81; BN exec. officer 15th Engr. Bn., Div. Staff 9th ID, Comdr. I Corps, Ft. Lewis, Wash., 1981-84; contracting tech. mgr. Def. Nuclear Agy., Washington, 1984-87; bn. comdr. 589th Engr. BN, Ft. Leonardwood, Mo., 1987-89; stockpike chief JS Nuclear/Chem. Div. Pentagon, 1989-91; dep. dir. for shock physics Def. Nuclear Agy., Washington, 1992—. Mem. Engr. Regimental Assn., Delta Mu. Home: 7708 Gromwell Ct Springfield VA 22152-3134

STOBER, RICHARD PAUL, professional association executive; b. Lebanon, Pa., Dec. 30, 1942; s. Edward Harold and Violet Irene (Brubaker) S.; m. Karen Fay Schell, Aug. 1, 1965 (div. 1979); children: Crystal, Jennifer, Karick, Daniel; m. Judith A. Gerace, July 13, 1982. BS in Econs., Pa. State U., 1969; MS in Labor and Indsl. Rels., Mich. State U., 1971. Staff assoc. George Meany Ctr. for Labor Studies, Silver Spring, Md., 1972-76; asst. dir. Pa. Nurses Assn., Harrisburg, 1976-79, labor rep., 1979-81, edn. and rsch. dir., 1981-85, dir. Econ. and Gen. Welfare, 1985—; dir. Pa. Employees Benefit Trust Fund, Harrisburg, 1990—. Contbr. articles to profl. jours. With USN, 1960-63. Democrat. Lutheran. Office: Pa Nurses Assn 2578 Interstate Dr Harrisburg PA 17110-9601

STOCK, ANN MARIE, biochemistry educator, researcher; b. San Francisco, July 24, 1957; d. Lawerence Edward and Jean Frances (Ackerman) Maderis; m. Jeffry Benton Stock, June 20, 1982. AB, U. Calif., Berkeley, 1979, PhD, 1986. Damon Runyon-Walter Winchell postdoctoral fellow Princeton (N.J.) U., 1986-89; postdoctoral fellow Rosenstiel Ctr. Brandeis U., Waltham, Mass., 1990-91; asst. prof. biochemistry, Ctr. Advanced Biotech. & Medicine U. Medicine and Dentistry N.J., Piscataway, 1991—. Contbr. articles to profl. jours. Lucille P. Markey scholar Lucille P. Markey Charitable Trust, 1989—. Mem. Am. Soc. Microbiology, Am. Soc. Biochemistry and Molecular Biology, Phi Beta Kappa. Office: Ctr for Advanced Biotech and Medicine 679 Hoes Ln Piscataway NJ 08854-5638

STOCK, JEFFRY BENTON, molecular biology educator; b. L.A., Dec. 27, 1946; s. Gene and Jane S.; m. Ann Maderis. BA, Johns Hopkins U., 1967, PhD, 1975. Rsch. assoc. Johns Hopkins Univ., Balt., 1975-77; cystic fibrosis fellow Univ. Calif., Berkeley, 1977-79, rsch. assoc., 1979-82; assoc. mem., asst. prof. Princeton (N.J.) Univ., 1982-88, mem. molecular biophysiology, assoc. mem., assoc. prof., 1988—; lectr. Sigma Xi, 1979. Named Predoctoral fellow NIH, 1967-75; recipient fellowship Cystic Fibrosis, 1977-80, Wilson Coll. Faculty, 1986. Mem. AAAS, Am. Soc. for Biochemistry and Molecular Biology, Am. Soc. for Microbiology, Am. Chem. Soc., N.Y. Acad. Sci., Theabald Smith Soc. Office: Princeton Univ Dept Molecular Biology Princeton NJ 08544-1014

STOCKER, ERICH FRANZ, computer engineer; b. Hallein, Salzburg, Austria, Oct. 28, 1946; came to U.S., 1952; s. Otto Stocker and Erika Anna (Plattner) Hirschberg; m. Rose Mary White, Sept. 13, 1969; children: Anton Karl, Stephen Dean. BA in Classics, Ohio State U., 1969, MA in Ancient History, 1970; BS in Computer Sci., Armstrong State Coll., 1989. Teaching asst. Ohio State U., Columbus, 1970; asst. to pres., dir. devel. and pub. info. Armstrong State Coll., Savannah, Ga., 1976-83, asst. prof. history and computer sci., 1983-85; rsch. programmer analyst IIT Rsch. Inst., Annapolis, Md., 1985-87; prin. software engr., mgr. ST Systems Corp., Lanham, Md., 1987-91; supervisory computer engr. NASA/Goddard Space Flight Ctr., Greenbelt, Md., 1991—; computer cons. Inter Redec U.S.A. Inc., Savannah, 1983-87, Brimstone Sulphur Inc., Atlanta, 1989-91, various local firms, Annapolis, 1987—; classical radio announcer Sta. WSVH Pub. Radio, Savannah, 1983-85. Contbr. articles to profl. jours. Capt. U.S. Army, 1971-76. Fulbright scholar, 1970-71; NEH fellow, 1978. Mem. Assn. of Computing Machinery. Roman Catholic. Office: NASA/GSFC Code 423 Greenbelt MD 20771

STOCKMAL, HENRY F., JR., principal; b. Derby, Conn., Apr. 24, 1942; s. Henry F. and Helen T. (Filip) S.; m. Elizabeth G. Bachman, Apr. 22, 1967; children: Gregory F., Edward J. BS, So. Conn. State Coll., 1964; MA, Fairfield (Conn.) U., 1968; cert. adv. study (6th yr. cert.), Fairfield U., 1972. Tchr. Fairfield (Conn.) pub. schs., 1964-89; asst. prin. Greenwich (Conn.) pub. schs., 1989-91; prin. Andover (Conn.) Elem. Sch., 1991—; Conn. Dept. Edn. Assessor Beginning Educator Support Tng. Program and Trainer of State Assessors, 1988—. Adminstr. sr. div. Dist. 4 Little League Baseball, New Haven, 1984-89. Gen. Electric grantee, 1984, 85. Mem. NEA, ASCD, Nat. Assn. Elem. Sch. Prins., Elem. and Mid. Sch. Prins. Assn., Greenwich Orgn. Sch. Adminstrs., Fairfield Edn. Assn., Conn. Edn. Assn. (treas. 1975-78, bd. dirs.). Roman Catholic. Home: 112A Lake Rd Columbia CT 06237 Office: Andover Elem Sch 35 School Rd Andover CT 06232-1526

STOCKMAN, GERALD RICHARD, lawyer; b. Trenton, N.J., Mar. 31, 1935; s. Julius and Alice (Robinson) S.; m. Audrey Lenore; children—Maura, Melissa, Julie, Jeffrey, Richard, Monica, Chad. B.S., Holy Cross Coll., 1956; J.D., Villanova Law Sch., 1959. Bar: Pa., 1960, N.J., 1960. Clk. to chief judge U.S. Dist. Ct. (ea. dist.) Pa., 1961, to chief judge U.S. Dist. Ct. N.J.; assoc. Albridge C. Smith, Esquire, Princeton, N.J.; assoc., ptnr. George Y. Schoch, Trenton; now pres. Stockman & Gilman; state senator N.J., 1981-91, active numerous coms.; lectr. in law; participant various panels for Inst. for Continuing Legal Edn. Mem. N.J. Gen. Assembly, from 1978; mem. Mercer County Charter Study Commn., 1974; chmn. Del. River Joint Toll Bridge Commn., 1977-78; active Heart Fund, Am. Cancer Soc., Mercer County chpt. Big Bros.; mem. exec. bd. NAACP; chmn. Del. Valley United Way; advance gifts chmn. Hamilton Hosp. Expansion Fund Drive. Recipient Brotherhood award NCCJ, 1980, Polit. Action award NAACP, 1984, Community Devel. award Middlesex, Somerset and Mercer Regional Study Council, 1984. Fellow Am. Coll. Trial Lawyers; mem. Mercer County Bar Assn., N.J. Assn. on Corrections, N.J. State Bar Assn., Assn. Trial Lawyers Am. Democrat. Roman Catholic. Office: Stockman & Gilman 2211 White Horse-Mercerville Rd Trenton NJ 08619

STOCKMAYER, WALTER H(UGO), chemistry educator; b. Rutherford, N.J., Apr. 7, 1914; s. Hugo Paul and Dagmar (Bostroem) S.; m. Sylvia Kleist Bergen, Aug. 12, 1938; children—Ralph, Hugh,. S.B., MIT, 1935, Ph.D., 1940; B.Sc. (Rhodes scholar), Oxford U., 1937; D.Sc., U. Louis-Pasteur, Strasbourg, France, 1972; L.H.D., Dartmouth Coll., 1983. Instr. M.I.T., 1939-41, asst. prof., 1943-46, assoc. prof., 1946-52, prof., 1952-61; prof. chemistry Dartmouth, 1961-79, prof. emeritus, 1979—; instr. Columbia, 1941-43; cons. E.I. duPont de Nemours & Co., Inc., 1945—; vis. com. Nat. Bur. Standards, 1979-84. Contbr. articles on phys. and macromolecular chemistry to sci. jours. Recipient Nat. Medal of Sci., 1987, MCA Coll. Chemistry Tchr. award 1970, Internat. award Soc. Plastics Engrs., 1991; Guggenheim fellow, 1954-55, hon. fellow Jesus Coll., Oxford, Eng., 1976, Alexander von Humboldt fellow, 1978-79. Fellow Am. Acad. Arts and Scis., Am. Phys. Soc. (Polymer Physics prize 1975); mem. NAS, Am. Chem. Soc. (assoc. editor Macromolecules 1968-74, 76—, chmn. polymer chem. div. 1968, Polymer Chemistry award 1965, Peter Debye award 1974, T. W. Richards medal 1988, polymer div. award 1988), Soc. Polymer Sci. Japan (hon.), Soc. Plastics Engrs. (Internat. award 1991), Soc. Polymer Sci. Japan (hon. 1991). Club: Appalachian Mountain. Office: Dartmouth Coll Chemistry Dept Hanover NH 03755

STOCKTON, SCOTT, financial analyst, strategic planner; b. Pensacola, Fla., Aug. 15, 1954; s. Walter Scott and Marlene Jean (Brayack) S.; m. Linda Anne Luther. Nov. 25, 1989. BS, Ariz. State U., 1976, MBA, 1978; law student, Temple U., 1988-89. CPA, cert. mgmt. acct. Fin. analyst Motorola Semiconductors, Mesa, Ariz., 1978-83; internal auditor Motorola, Inc., Phoenix, 1983-85; asst. controller Jerrold Div. Gen. Instrument, Hatboro, Pa., 1985-89; mgr. strategic analysis Jerrold Div. Gen. Instrument, Hatboro, 1989—; software cons. pvt. practice, Phila., 1989-90. Mem. Soc. Competitive Intelligence Profls. Office: Gen Instrument 2200 Byberry Rd Hatboro PA 19040-3502

STODDARD, FORREST SHAFFER, aerospace engineer, educator; b. Eglin AFB, Fla., Nov. 4, 1944; s. Edward Forrest and Esther Grace (Shaffer) S.; SB, MIT, 1966, SM, 1968; PhD, U. Mass., 1979; m. Mary Anne Maher Matthews, June 16, 1979; children: Joshua Forrest, Nathan Edward. Partner, chief engr. U.S. Windpower Inc., Burlington, Mass., 1977-80 ; wind power engring. cons., Amherst, Mass., 1980—; cons. Wind Systems Test Center, U.S. Dept. Energy Solar Energy Rsch. Inst., Commonwealth of Mass.; asst. prof. mech. engring. U. Mass., 1982—; founder, pres. Pioneer Wind Power, Inc., 1982-87; cons., prin. investigator U.S. Dept. Energy, 1985-86; adj. rsch. prof. Alternative Energy Inst. West Tex. State U., 1987—; rsch. prof. West Tex. State U., 1986—. Served to capt. USAF, 1968-72. Co-author Wind Turbine Engineering Design, 1987. Mem. Am. Wind Energy Assn. (dir., sec.), Am. Helicopter Soc., AIAA, Am. Solar Energy Soc., Friends of Earth, Sigma Xi. Mem. United Ch. Christ. Acting editor Wind Tech. Jour., 1979-82. Home: 299 Amity St Amherst MA 01002-3810 also: 10 Cottonwood # 606 Amherst MA 01002 Office: AEI/WTSU PO Box 248 Canyon TX 79016-0002

STODDARD, PHILIP HENDRICK, foreign affairs analyst, writer; b. Iowa City, Apr. 30, 1929; s. George Dinsmore and Margaret (Trautwein) S.; m. Carol Cannon, Jan. 19, 1952 (div. 1959); children: Michele, Christopher, Eric; m. Doris Joyce Mills, Dec. 26, 1960; children: Leah, Evan. BA, U. Ill., 1950; MA, Princeton U., 1955, PhD, 1963. Asst. prof. SUNY New Paltz, 1958-60; analyst, 1963-80; with U.S. Dept. State, Washington, dep. asst. sec., 1980-83; exec. dir. Middle East Inst., Washington, 1983-87; cons. Nat. Intelligence Coun., Washington, 1988-90, dir., analytic group, 1990—. Editor: Change and the Muslim World, 1981; contbr. articles to profl. jours. Mem. com. Springfield Civic Assn., Bethesda, Md., 1966—. With USMC, 1951-53. Named Disting. Fed. Exec., U.S. Govt., 1982; recipient Nat. Disting. Intelligence medal Coun. of Fgn. Rels., N.Y.C., 1979-80. Mem. Middle East Inst., Am. Friends of Turkey, Middle East Studies Assn. Home: 6000 Springfield Dr Bethesda MD 20816-1232 Office: Nat Intelligence Council Washington DC 20550

STODDARD, WILLIAM BERT, JR., economist; b. Carbondale, Pa., Oct. 6, 1926; s. William Bert and Emily (Trautwein) S.; student Lafayette Coll., 1944-45; B.S., N.Y. U., 1950, A.M., 1952; m. Carol Marie Swartz, Feb. 28, 1970; 1 dau., Emily Coleman. Asst. chief accountant, budget dir. Hendrick Mfg. Co., Carbondale, Pa., 1952-54, asst. dir. prodn., 1956-68, also dir.; credit corr. U.S. Gypsum Co., N.Y.C., 1954-56; investment counselor, Carbondale, 1968-73, Ridgefield, Conn., 1973—; dir. First Nat. Bank Carbondale, 1968-73; bd. dirs. Lackawanna County Mfrs. Assn., Scranton, Pa., 1960-73. Treas., trustee Aldrich Museum Contemporary Art, Ridgefield, 1976-90; bd. dirs. Ridgefield Library and Hist. Assn., 1977-85, 87—; trustee Ridgefield Libr. Endowment Fund Trust, 1985—. Served with U.S. Army 1946-47. Mem. Nat. Assn. Accountants, Am. Def. Preparedness Assn., Phi Alpha Kappa, Phi Delta Theta. Republican. Methodist. Clubs: N.Y.U. (N.Y.C.), Waccabuc (N.Y.) Country, Princeton Club (N.Y.C.). Home: 59 Bridle Trl Ridgefield CT 06877-1401 Office: 23 Catoonah St Ridgefield CT 06877

STODDERT, SANDRA SMITH, media director; b. Easton, Pa., Mar. 12, 1942; d. Harry James and Agnes (Krueger) Smith; m. D. Dale Kleppinger, Aug. 22, 1964 (div. Sept. 1981); children: Eric David, Deborah Ellen; m. Dorwin W. Stoddert, July 15, 1983 (dec. Feb. 1987); stepchildren: Joel Thomas, Jennifer Lea. BS in Edn., Bloomsburg U., 1964; MEd, Lehigh U., 1967. Tchr. Bethlehem (Pa.) Sch. Dist., 1964-67; permanent substitute South Burlington (Vt.) Sch. Dist., 1978-79, media ctr. dir., 1979—. Mem. Nat. ASCD, LWV (pres. 1976-77), Nat. Coun. Social Studies (curriculum devel. com. mem. 1986-88, chmn. local standards bd. 1991—), Vt. Ednl. Media Assn., Vt. State Tech. Coun., South Burlington Educators Assn. (bldg. rep. 1984-86, pres. 1987-90, negotiating team mem. 1988-91, grievance chmn. 1991—). Republican. Lutheran. Office: Chamberlin Sch 262 White St South Burlington VT 05403-5900

STOEWSAND, GILBERT SAARI, toxicology educator; b. Chgo., Oct. 20, 1932; s. Frederick Byron and Esther (Saari) S.; m. Ellen Rhesa Bagby, June 7, 1957; children: Corrine, Cathryn. BS, U. Calif., Davis, 1954, MS, 1958; PhD, Cornell U., 1963. Rsch. assoc. Cornell U., Ithaca, N.Y., 1953-62; asst. prof. Cornell U., Geneva, N.Y., 1967-73, assoc. prof., 1973-79, prof., 1979—; rsch. nutritionist U.S. Army Labs., Natick, Mass., 1963-66; rsch. assoc. Albany (N.Y.) Med. Coll., 1966-67; cons. MUCIA, Gadja Mada U., Indonesia, 1988; mem. toxicology study sect. NIH, Washington, 1975-79; participant NSF Environ./Toxicology Conf., Taipei, Taiwan, 1985, others. Mem. editorial bd. Jour. Toxicology and Environ. Health, 1979—; contbr. articles to profl. jours. Cpl. U.S. Army, 1954-56. WHO travel fellow, Fed. Republic of Germany, Switzerland and Sweden, 1972. Mem. Soc. Toxicology, Am. Inst. Nutrition, AAAS, Inst. Food Technologists, Am. Soc. Enology Viticulture, Am. Kennel Club (del. 1982-91), Sigma Xi. Office: Cornell Univ NY State Agr Exptl Sta Geneva NY 14456

STOFFEL, KLAUS PETER, lawyer; b. Evergreen Park, Ill., Dec. 9, 1957; s. Karl and Ursula (Beckmann) S.; m. Cathy B. Wolff, Apr. 9, 1983; children: Lindsey Brooke, Michael Scott, Cali Blake. BSME, Bradley U., 1980; JD, Seton Hall U., 1984. Bar: N.Y. 1985, U.S. Patent and Trademark Office 1984, U.S. Dist. Ct. (so. dist.) N.Y. 1985, N.J. 1985, U.S. Dist. Ct. N.J. 1985. Engr. Okonite Co., Ramsey, N.J., 1980-81; assoc. Striker, Striker & Stenby, N.Y.C., 1984-85, Brumbaugh, Graves, Donohue & Raymond, N.Y.C., 1985-87, Cooper & Dunham, N.Y.C., 1987-88, Toren, McGeady & Assoc., P.C., N.Y.C., 1988—. Mem. ABA, N.Y. State Bar Assn., N.J. State Bar Assn. Home: 41 Cornell Dr Livingston NJ 07039-5505 Office: Toren McGeady & Assoc 521 5th Ave New York NY 10175-0003

STOFKO, KARL PETER, dentist; b. Bristol, Conn., Dec. 8, 1938; s. Charles Joseph and Isolde Louise (Jestinsky) S. BA, Gettysburg Coll., 1960; DDS, U. Mich., 1964. Gen. practice dentistry Moodus, Conn., 1965—. Author: (with Rachel I. Gibbs) A Brief History of East Haddam, Conn., 1977, A Survey of the Architectural and Historical Resources of East Haddam, Conn., Part II, 1980. Adviser, East Haddam (Conn.) Youth Recreation Coun., 1972; mem., chmn. East Haddam Hist. Dist. Commn., 1976—, clk., 1984—, bd. dirs., sec. East Haddam Pub. Health Nursing and Community Health Svc., 1974-79; East Haddam mcpl. historian; dir., treas. East Haddam Emergency Fuel Bank; deacon Congregational Ch., 1967-74, pres. Cemetery Assn., 1972—, supt., 1972—, treas., 1974-85, historian, 1984—. Mem. Middlesex County Dental Soc. (pres. 1971-72), Cappella Cantorum, East Haddam Hist. Soc. (v.p. 1974-77, chmn. rsch. com. 1978—). Home: 79 Orchard Rd East Haddam CT 06423-1373 Office: Wf Palmer Rd Moodus CT 06469

STOJILKOVIC, STANKO STAMEN, biologist; b. Karavukovo, Yugoslavia, Aug. 25, 1950; came to U.S., 1985; s. Stamen and Ana (Radojevic) S.; 1 child, Kosta. BSc in Biology, U. Novi Sad (Yugoslavia), 1974; MSc in Physiology, U. Belgrade (Yugoslavia), 1978; PhD in Endocrinology, U. Novi Sad, 1982. Rsch. asst. U. Novi Sad, 1975-83, asst. prof., 1983-87; vis. scientist NIH, Bethesda, Md., 1988—; assoc. prof. U. Belgrade, 1991—. Author: General Physiology, 1985; contbr. numerous articles to profl. jours. Mem. Am. Soc. for Biochemistry and Molecular Biology, Endocrine Soc., Yugoslav Soc. Biology (pres. 1983-85), Yugoslav Soc. Endocrinology, Yugoslav Soc. Physiology. Office: ERRB NIH 9000 Rockville Pike Bethesda MD 20892-0001

STOKELY, MARY CURRY, marketing specialist; b. San Francisco, Jan. 15, 1950; d. Patricia Irma Curry; m. Chesley Bernard Stokely Jr., Aug. 14, 1971; children: Brian Scott, Sharon Elizabeth. AA, Immaculata Coll., Washington, D.C., 1969. Lic. realtor. Claims processor Nat. Life Ins. Co. Vt., Washington, 1969-70; sec. Walker & Dunlop Inc., Washington, 1970-72, supr. word processing ctr., 1972-75; outreach worker Commn. on Aging, La Plata, Md., 1975-77, title III program dir., 1977-79; sales assoc. Long & Foster Real Estate Co., Waldorf, Md., 1979-80; adminstrv. asst. Raleigh Homes, Waldorf, 1980-82; mgr. new homes sales L. K. Farrall Ltd., Waldorf, 1982-88; dir. mktg. and mgmt. svcs. Mil-Mar & Sons Builders Inc., La Plata, Md., 1988-90; mktg. cons. L.K. Farrall, Ltd., La Plata, 1990-91, ReMax 100, Waldorf, Md., 1991—; Mem. Women's Coun. Realtors, Hughesville, Md., 1980-83, Strategic Planning Commn., Hughesville, 1987. Com. chmn. Bus. and Profl. Women's Club, Charles County, Md., 1978-80. Named Young Careerist Charles County Bus. and Profl. Women's Club, 1980. Mem. Nat. Assn. Realtors, Md. Assn. Realtors, So. Md. Assn. Realtors (bd. dirs. 1985-87), Suburban Md. Bldg. Industry Assn. (affiliate). Democrat. Roman Catholic. Office: ReMax 100 3211 Md 925 Waldorf MD 20602

STOKES, CHARLES SHANNON, educator; b. Berea, Ky., July 9, 1941; s. Burches and Emma (Queen) S.; m. Louise Carver; Children: Charles Shannon, John Coleman. BA, Georgetown Coll., 1964; MS, U. Ky., 1966, PhD, 1970. Asst. prof. U. Ga., 1968-73; from assoc. prof. to prof. and head Pa. State U., 1973—; visiting res. prof. Nat. Taiwan U., 1980-81. Co-editor Rural Developmentand Human Fertility, 1984; contbr. numerous articles to prof. jours. Mem. Population Assn. Am., Rural Social. Soc., Internat. Union for Scientific Study of Population, AM. Sociol. Assn., Am. Agrl. Econ. Assn. Office: Dept of AG EC & R SOC Penn State U 6 Weaver Bldg University Park PA 16802

STOLFI, ROBERT LOUIS, health research facility administrator; b. Bklyn., Sept. 16, 1938; s. Edward and Mollie (Friedman) S.; m. Leslie Mary Paterson, May 16, 1968. BS, Bklyn. Coll., 1960; PhD, U. Miami, Fla., 1967. Rsch. assoc. Howard Hughes Med. Inst., Miami, 1963-67, Variety Children Rsch. Found., Miami, 1967-69; from instr. to asst. prof. U. Miami, 1967-71; dir. immunology Cath. Med. Ctr., Woodhaven, N.Y., 1970-76, asst. dir., 1976—; cons. Hoffman LaRoche, Antley, N.J., 1988-90, Pro-Neuron, Rockville, Md., 1991—. Contbr. numerous articles to profl. jours. Mem. AAAS, Am. Assn. Cancer Rsch., Am. Assn. Immunologists, Am. Soc. Microbiology, Soc. Analytical Cytology, Am. Assn. Lab. Animal Sci., Sigma Xi.

STOLINE, ANNE MARIE, psychiatrist; b. Iowa City, May 22, 1961; d. Michael Ross and Marie Elmina (Thompson) S. BA, Kalamazoo (Mich.) Coll., 1983; MD, Johns Hopkins U., 1988. Intern in internal medicine Francis Scott Key Hosp., Balt., 1988-89; resident in psychiatry Johns Hopkins Hosp., Balt., 1989—. Author: (with others) The New Medical Marketplace, 1988. Mem. Am. Psychiat. Assn., Md. Psychiat. Soc., Phi Beta Kappa.

STOLLERY, DAVID PAUL, medical-scientific illustrator; b. Oxford, U.K., Jan. 1, 1954; came to U.S., 1986; Cert., John Hamden Sch., Thame, U.K., 1967, Wenman Sch., Thame, U.K., 1972; student, WOS, Aylesbudy, U.K., 1983. Med.-sci. illustrator Johns Hopkin's U., Balt., 1986—; cons. RER, Inc., Balt., 1986—. Illustrator (book) Transplantation Proceedings, 1986. Office: RER Med/Sci Illustrations 2833 Cross Country Ct Fallston MD 21047-1318

STOLLNITZ, FRED, psychologist; b. N.Y.C., Apr. 13, 1939; s. Henry Sande and Helen Cecile (Bessemer) S. m. Janet Louise Gabar, Aug. 6, 1961; children: Nancy Beth, Eric Joel. BA with high honors, Swarthmore Coll., 1959; MS, Brown U., 1961, PhD, 1963. Asst. prof. psychology Brown U., Providence, R.I., 1963-66, Cornell U., Ithaca, N.Y., 1966-71; asst. prog. dir. for psychobiology NSF, Washington, 1971-72, assoc. prog. dir., 1972-76, prog. dir. for psychobiology, 1976-88, prog. dir. for animal behavior, 1988—. Co-editor and contbg. author: (books) Behavior of Nonhuman Primates, 5 vols., 1965-74; contbr. articles to profl. jours. Recipient Crane prze Swarthmore (Pa.) Coll., 1958, predoctoral rsch. fellowship USPHS/Brown U., 1960-62, grad. fellowship NSF, 1962-63. Mem. Animal Behavior Soc., Psychonomic Soc., Am. Psychol. Assn., Am. Psychol. Soc., Internat. Primatol. Soc., Ea. Psychol. Assn., AAAS, Phi Beta Kappa, Sigma Xi. Office: NSF IBN Rm 321 Washington DC 20550

STOLOFF, NORMAN STANLEY, metallurgical engineering educator, researcher; b. Bklyn., Oct. 16, 1934; s. William F. and Lila (Dickman) S.; m. Helen Teresa Arcuri, May 15, 1971; children: Michael E., Linda M., David M., Stephen L. BMetE, NYU, 1955; MS, Columbia U., 1956, PhD, 1961. Metall. engr. Pratt & Whitney Aircraft, East Hartford, Conn., 1956-58; prin. rsch. scientist Ford Sci. Lab., Dearborn, Mich., 1961-65; asst. prof. materials engring. Rensselaer Polytechnic Inst., Troy, N.Y., 1965-68, assoc. prof., 1968-71, prof., 1971—; cons. Electric Boat Div. Gen. Dynamics, New London, Conn., 1987-89, Martin Marietta Rsch. Labs., Balt., 1990, Rockwell Internat., Thousand Oaks, Calif., 1989, Cummins Engine Co., Columbus, Ind., 1991—. Editor: (with others) High Temperature Ordered Intermetallic Alloys, 1985, Superalloys II, 1987, others; contbr. articles to profl. jours. Recipient Fulbright Rsch. award U.S. State Dept., 1968-69. Fellow Am. Soc. Materials Internat.; mem. AIME, ASTM, Materials Rsch. Soc. Office: Rensselaer Polytechnic Inst Materials Engring Dept Troy NY 12180-3590

STOLOVY, ALEXANDER, retired research physicist; b. Bklyn., Nov. 21, 1926; s. Isaac and Beatrice (Kahan) S.; m. Jan. 23, 1955; children: Gary, Sharon, Susan. BS, CUNY, 1948; MS, Calif. Inst. Tech., 1950; PhD, NYU, 1955. Rsch. asst. Brookhaven Nat. Lab., Upton, N.Y., 1953-55; rsch. physicist Naval Rsch. Lab., Washington, 1955-90; ret., 1990. Contbr. over 30 articles to sci. jours. With AUS, 1945-46. Mem. Am. Phys. Soc. Home: 14320 Yosemite Ct Rockville MD 20853-2374

STOLPE, NORMAN DEAN, presbyterian minister; b. Oakland, Calif., Sept. 30, 1946; s. L. Harold and H. Doris (Erikson) S.; m. Candace R. Miller, Jan. 25, 1969; children: Jon M., David P. Erik C. BA in English, Bethel Coll., 1969; student, Merritt Coll., 1964-67; MA in Christian Edn., Wheaton Coll., 1972. Cert. Christian educator, Presbyn. Ch., U.S. With pubs. Christian Svc. Brigade, Wheaton, Ill., 1969-74; asst. pastor Countryside Chapel, Glendale Heights, Ill., 1974-77; editorial and rsch. dir. Family Concern, Inc., Wheaton, 1974-80; min. of nurture First Presbyn. Ch., Mt. Holly, N.J., 1980—. Author: Coming Attractions, 1991, Genesis: The Beginning, 1991, What's Real and What's Not, 1991; contbr. articles to profl. jours. Mem. Assn. Presbyn. Ch. Educators, Greater Mt. Holly Clery Assn. (sec. 1983-85, pres. 1985-87). Home: 40 Glenwood Rd Mount Holly NJ 08060-3404 Office: First Presbyn Ch 125 Garden St Mount Holly NJ 08060-1841

STOLZ, ALAN J., youth camp executive; b. N.Y.C., May 7, 1931; s. Irving H. and Pearl (Maltz) S.; m. Sandra Stolz (div.); m. Gail C. Stolz; children: Maryann Stolz Ross, Gary M. AB, Wabash Coll., 1953; LHD (Hon), London Inst., 1973. Cert. camp dir. Outdoor Inst., state instr. emergency med. svc. Pres. Camp Cody for Boys, Freedom, N.H.; ptnr., prin. 72d St Assocs.; cons., profl. witness U.S. Senate and Ho. of Reps., White House, Washington; cons. youth camp health various govt. agys., Washington. Author: National Camp Directors Guide, 1990; contbr. articles to profl. jours. Primary instr. Emergency Med. Svcs., Westport, Conn., bd. dirs.; instr./trainer/cons. ARC, Conn. and N.H.; advisor explorer adv. coun. Boy Scouts Am.; justice of peace State of N.H., quorum mem.; vol. dist. coord. N.H. marine patrol Aux. State Dept. Safety, 1991—. Sgt. U.S. Army, 1955-57. Recipient Honor award Emergency Med. Svcs., 1989, numerous awards Boy Scouts Am.; named Conn. Vol. of Yr., Carosel Mag., 1990, Conn. Man of Yr., Spotlight Mag., 1991. Mem. Am. Camping Assn. (v.p, nat. legis. chmn., bd. dirs., numerous nat. awards), Am. Inst. Fgn. Study (sr. advisor, editor students handbook 1990), N.H. Camp Directors Assn. (pres., state sec.). Republican. Jewish. Home: 5 Lockwood Circle Westport CT 06880 Office: Ossipee Lake Rd Freedom NH 06836

STOLZBERG, MARK ELLIOTT, psychologist; b. N.Y.C., Apr. 30, 1944; s. Seymour and Ruth (Petesky) S.; B.A., Hofstra U., 1966; M.A. in Exptl. Psychology (Coll. fellow), C. W. Post Coll., 1970; postgrad. in clin. psychology (N.Y. State War Service scholar), SUNY-Albany, 1973; Ph.D., Hofstra U.; m. Marilyn Goldberg, Mar. 18, 1972; children—Susan Beth, David Jonathan, Daniel Jason. Intern in clin. psychology Maimonides Hosp., Bklyn., 1972-73; pres. Stolzberg Research Inc., Stony Brook, N.Y., 1976—; adj. lectr. Bklyn. Coll., 1973; mem. faculty Coll. Optometry, SUNY, 1985-86. Recipient Disting. Achievement award for Research N.Y. State Optometric Assn., 1983. Mem. Suffolk County Psychol. Assn., N.Y. Acad. Scis. Contbr. articles to profl. jours. Home and Office: 3 Seabrook Ct Stony Brook NY 11790-3305

STONE, ALAN JOHN, manufacturing company executive, real estate executive; b. Dansville, N.Y., Sept. 9, 1940; s. Guthrie Boyd and Doris Irene (Wolfanger) S.; m. Sandra Barber, Aug. 22, 1964; children: Teri, Timothy, Michael. B.S. in Mech. Engring., Rochester Inst. Tech., 1963; M.B.A., U. Pitts., 1964. Engring. aide Xerox Corp., Webster, N.Y., 1960-63; gen. mgr. plastic component div. Stone Conveyor Co., Inc., Honeoye, N.Y., 1964-67, v.p. sales, 1968; co-founder, chief exec. officer Stone Constrn. Equipment Inc., Honeoye, 1969-86, also cons., bd. dirs., 1969—; founder, pres. Canandaigua Apts. Inc., N.Y., 1968-83; pres. Wildtrak, Inc., 1983—; founder, mng. ptnr. Stone Properties, 1986—; v.p., co-founder, bd. dirs. Baker Rental Svc., Inc., 1973-76; mt. adv. bd. Chase Lincoln First Bank, 1981-84; co-founder, bd. dirs. Canandaigua Nat. Bank & Trust Co., F.F. Thompson Hosp. Patentee in field. Mem. Town of Richmond (N.Y.) Planning Bd., 1970-75, chmn., 1970-71; mem. Honeoye Central Sch. Bd. Edn., 1971-76, pres., 1973-74; com. chmn. pack 10 Boy Scouts Am., 1975-77; mem. Ontario County Overall Econ. Devel. Com., 1976-81. Mem. Honeoye C. of C. (chmn. indsl. com. 1974-82), Constrn. Industry Mfrs. Assn. (exec. mem. new bus. challenges coun. 1980-83), Honeoye Valley Assn. (dir. 1991—), Grand Slam Club, Safari Internat., Found N.Am. Wild Sheep. Methodist. Home and Office: 5170 County Rd 33 Honeoye NY 14471-9726

STONE, ALBERT MORDECAI, retired physicist; b. Boston, Dec. 24, 1913; s. Louis Gottlieb and Esther (Goldberg) S.; m. Louisa Van Wezel Schwartz, Aug. 24, 1941 (div. 1966); children: Antony Van Wezel, Katherine Van Wezel Stone Srennan, Daniel J.; m. Francesca Gobbi, Jan. 26, 1968. AB, Harvard U., 1934; PhD, MIT, 1938. From asst. to assoc. prof. Mont. State U., Bozeman, 1941-45; mem. staff MIT Radiation Lab., Cambridge, Mass., 1942-46; sci. liaison officer U.S. Embassy, London, Eng., 1946-48; cons. Dept. Def., Washington, 1948-49; asst. to dir. Applied Physics Lab. Johns Hopkins U., Laurel, Md., 1949-83, sr. fellow, 1983-88; mem. adv. bd. Fed. Emergency Mgmt. Agy., Washington, 1980—; bd. dirs. Selected Sectors Mut. Fund. Fellow AAAS, Am. Phy. Soc. Home: 4932 Sentinel Dr Bethesda MD 20816-3508

STONE, ALFRED WARD, educator; b. Meadville, Pa., Aug. 13, 1925; s. Clifford Alsworths and Freda (Bruehl) S.; m. Dolores Stone, Dec. 1, 1951 (div.); children: Clifford, John, Bonalyn, David; m. Mary L. Girardat, June 1, 1968; 1 child, 1 Scott. BA in Econs., Allegheny Coll., 1950, MEd, 1957; PhD in Psychology, U. Pitts., 1978; postgrad., U. So. Calif., L.A., 1979. Phys. boys sec. YMCA, Meadville, 1952-57; state sec. YMCA, Harrisburg, Pa., 1957-62; acting exec. sec. YMCA, Allentown, Pa., 1962-63; exec. dir. War on Poverty, C.A.P., Meadville, 1964-67; prof. psychology dept. Edinboro (Pa.) U., 1967—; host TV program Understanding People, 1970-92; pres. Regional Community Svcs., Inc. Edinboro U., coord. gerontology programs. Pres., mem. Prof. Assn. of Specialists of Aging, N.W. Pa., 1978-86. With U.S. Merchant Marine 1943-46, U.S. Army, 1950-52. Mem. APHA, Gerontol. Soc. Am., Am. Psychol. Assn.,. Home: 220 Meadville St Edinboro PA 16412-2558 Office: Edinboro U Dept Psychology Crompton Hall Edinboro PA 16444

STONE, ANDREW GROVER, lawyer; b. L.A., Oct. 2, 1942; s. Frank B. and Meryl (Pickering) S.; m. Sheila Flinn, June 3, 1972; 1 child, John Blair. BA, Yale U., 1965; JD, U. Mich., 1969. Bar: D.C. 1970, U.S. Dist. Ct. D.C. 1970, U.S. Ct. Appeals (D.C. cir.) 1972, Mass. 1981. Assoc. Rogers & Wells, Washington, 1969-71; atty. Bur. Competition, FTC, Washington, 1971-80; sr. atty. Digital Equipment Corp., Maynard, Mass., 1980-83, mgr. N.E. law group, 1983-86, mgr. sales law group, 1986-88; mgr. So. field law group and corp. counsel Digital Equipment Corp., Washington, 1988-90, corp. counsel, pub. sect. mktg., 1990-91; of counsel Thinking Machines Corp., Cambridge, Mass., 1992—. Corp. mem. Tenacre Country Day Sch., Wellesley, Mass., 1981-88. Mem. ABA (antitrust sect., pub. contracts sect., vice-chmn. comml. products and svcs. com. 1983-84). Office: Thinking Machines Corp 245 First St Cambridge MA 02142

STONE, ARTHUR JOSEPH, judge; b. St. Peters, N.S., Can., 1929; s. George and Charlotte S.; m. Anna M., 1956. B.A., St. Francis Xavier U., Antigonish, N.S., 1952; LL.B., Dalhousie Law Sch., 1955; LL.M., Harvard U., 1956. Assoc., Wright & McTaggart and successor firms, 1957-83; justice Fed. Ct. Appeal, Ottawa, Ont., Can., 1983—; lectr. faculty of law U. Toronto, Ont., 1971-76. Contbr. articles to profl. publs. Mem. N.S. Barristers Soc., Law Soc. of Upper Can., N.B. Barristers Soc., Law Soc. of B.C., Can. Bar Assn. (nat. exec. com. 1971-73), Can. Tax Found. (gov. 1977-79), Can. Maritime Law Assn. (pres.), Harvard U. Law Sch. Assn. Ont. (chmn.

law sch. fund). Club: Toronto Marine (pres. 1977-78). Office: Fed Ct, Kent & Wellington Sts, Ottawa, ON Canada K1A 0H9

STONE, DAN GILBERT, investment company executive, writer; b. N.Y.C., July 29, 1958; s. Thomas Elijah and Emilita (Rodriquez) S. BS, U. Pa., 1980, MBA, 1981. Instl. equity sales rep. Drexel, Burnham, Lambert, N.Y.C., 1981-84, v.p. instl. equity sales, 1984-89; exec. v.p., portfolio mgr. Steven Charles Capital, Centerport, N.Y., 1991—. Author: How To Invest in the Market, 1990, April Fools, 1990. Trustee Harborfields Pub. Libr.; v.p., bd. dirs. Huntington Freedom Ctr.

STONE, DAVID KENDALL, financial executive; b. Natick, Mass., Dec. 7, 1942; s. Harold Hamilton and Mary (Perkins) S.; m. Patricia Donahue, June 12, 1965; children: Jonathan, Andrew, Timothy. AB, Franklin & Marshall Coll., 1964. CPA, N.Y. Acct. Gilfoil & McNeal, Syracuse, N.Y., 1967-69, Ernst & Whinney, Cleve., 1969-83; sr. v.p., comptroller Fiduciary Trust Co. Internat., N.Y.C., 1983-87, sr. v.p. dir. ops., 1987—. Treas. Cerebral Palsy and Handicapped Children's Assn., Syracuse, N.Y., 1972-75. 1st lt. U.S. Army, 1964-67, Vietnam. Mem. AICPA, N.Y. State Soc. CPAs (com. on banking and savs. instns. 1983-87), Com. Banking Instns. on Taxation, N.Y. State Bankers Assn. (com. on trust ops.). Office: Fiduciary Trust Co Internat 2 World Trade Ctr New York NY 10048-0203

STONE, DIANE MARY, office technologies educator; b. Albany, N.Y.; d. Fred and Mary (Pulikowski) Patricelli; m. Edward G. Stone, June 12, 1971; children: Marilou, Brian. BS, SUNY, Albany, 1966; MEd, Kent (Ohio) State U., 1970. Instr. SUNY Agrl. and Tech. Coll., Cobleskill, N.Y., 1966-68; bus. edn. tchr. Loudonville (Ohio) High Sch., 1970-72, Frankfort (N.Y.) Schuyler High Sch., 1982-87; assoc. prof. Herkimer (N.Y.) County Community Coll., 1987—. Bd. dirs. Cancer Soc., Herkimer County, 1989—, Herkimer County Coll. Found., 1991—; mem. Munson Williams Proctor Inst., Utica, N.Y. Mem. Nat. Bus. Edn. Assn., N.Y. State Assn. of Two Yr. Colls., Office Technologists/Secondary Educators of CUNY/SUNY, Delta Kappa Gamma (Alpha Chi chpt.).

STONE, EDWARD LUKE, non-profit administrator; b. Englewood, N.J., Jan. 18, 1937; s. James and Anna (Druskin) S.; m. Cassandra Reeve, Mar. 15, 1969. BA, Yale U., 1958; postgrad., Cambridge U., Eng., 1959; MBA, Harvard U., 1966. Dir. fin. planning Yale U., New Haven, 1966-69; pres. HDC, Inc., Boston, 1969-77; ptnr. Dane, Falb, Stone, Boston, 1977-81; exec. dir. White House Preservation Fund, Washington, 1981-90; trustee Newport Art Mus., 1991—; cons. Booz Allen Hamilton, Bethesda, Md., 1987-88. Trustee Nat. Mus. of Women in the Arts, Washington, 1988-90, Tudor Pl. Found., Washington, 1988—, The Washington Home, 1988—. Mem. Newport Reading Rm., Somerset Club, F. Street Club, Elizabethan Club, Phi Beta Kappa. Home and office: Indian Spring Moorland Rd Newport RI 02840-4202

STONE, FRANCES, brokerage house executive, consultant, educator; b. N.Y.C., July 14, 1923; BA in Math. Stats., Hunter Coll., N.Y.C., 1943; MA in Econs., NYU, 1945; PhD, Columbia U., 1956. Researcher, portfolio analyst, valuating pvt. cos. Hallgarten and Co., N.Y.C., 1958-61; v.p. Merrill Lynch, Pierce, Fenner & Smith, N.Y.C., 1961—; cons. in fin. McGraw-Hill Pub. Co., also cons. editor; adj. prof. fin. and acctg. NYU, 1972—, Pace U., 1974-76, Baruch Coll., 1972; disting. vis. lectr. Rider Coll. Grad. Sch. Bus., 1983; dir. Internat. Schs. Services, Inc.; pres., bd. dirs. Coop. Cumberland House; speaker in field. Named one of 100 Top Exec. Women, Bus. Week, 1976; chartered fin. analyst. Mem. Am. Fin. Assn., Am. Econ. Assn., Internat. Fin. Analysts, Chartered Fin. Analysts (dir., sec. research and publs. com. 1968-72), Investor Relations Assn., N.Y. Soc. Security Analysts (bd. dirs.), Columbia U. Grad. Sch. Arts & Scis. Alumni (bd. dirs.). Cons. economist Image at the Top, 1983; cons. fin. McGraw-Hill; contbr. articles to profl. jours. Home: 30 E 62d St New York NY 10021 Office: 1 Liberty Pla New York NY 10080

STONE, FRANK ANDREWS, international education educator; b. Wilmington, Del., Jan. 12, 1929; s. Royal Amidon and Ruth Sherman (Andrews) S.; m. Barbara May Tinkham, June 15, 1957; children: David, Ruth, Beth, Priscilla. BA, Heidelberg Coll., 1949; MDiv, Oberlin (Ohio) Coll., 1952; DMin, Vanderbilt U., 1953; MA, Western Mich. U., 1960; EdD, Boston U., 1968. Cert. secondary English and social studies tchr., Mass.; ordained to ministry United Ch. of Christ, 1952. Tchr. Am. Sch., Tarsus, Turkey, 1953-66; dir. Am. Sch., Tarsus, 1963-66; from assoc. prof. to prof. U. Conn., Storrs, 1968—; Author six books; contbr. numerous articles to profl. jours. HEW grantee, 1974-79. Fellow Philosophy of Edn. Soc., Mid. East Studies Assn.; mem. World Edn. Fellowship (pres. 1982-86, gen. sec. U.S. sect. 1989—), Soc. for Ednl. Reconstrn. (editor jour. 1975-81), Turkish Studies Assn. (chairperson competition com. 1990). Democrat. Office: U Conn PO Box 93U Storrs Mansfield CT 06269-0001

STONE, FREDERIC SCOTT, salesman, writer, professional ice hockey referee; b. Winthrop, Mass., Apr. 20, 1959; s. Donald R. and Marilyn (Vaters) S.; m. Janet Marie Williams, Apr. 25, 1982; children: Shelley Reneé, Nancy Lynne, Joyce Marie. Grad. high sch., Wilmington, Pa. Comedian; sales rep. Gallagher Fluid Seals, Inc., King of Prussia, Pa., 1989-90. Writer (political commentary) The Sleeps Must Awaken, 1989—; profl. comedian appearances Perriwinkles, Providence, 1991, Stitches, Boston, 1991, Catcha Rising Star, Cambridge, Mass., 1991. Recipient Minuteman scholarship, Minuteman Co., Wilmington, Mass., 1977. Mem. Rotary Internat., Elks. Democrat. Office: Gallagher Fluid Seals Inc 44 Stedman St Lowell MA 01851-2734

STONE, FREDERICK JOSEPH, pathologist, educator; b. Chgo., Aug. 15, 1949; s. Charles and Dorothy (Halleck) S.; m. Lorraine C. Mandel, Aug. 14, 1977; children: Daniel, Philip, Jonathan, Hannah. BS in Med., Northwestern U., 1971, MD, 1973. Diplomate Am. Bd. of Pathology. Asst. prof. N.Y. Med. Coll., Valhalla, 1977-78; asst. pathologist Flower and Fifth Ave. Hosp., N.Y.C., 1977-78, Met. Hosp., N.Y.C., 1977-78; dep. med. examiner Middlesex County N.J., Perth Amboy, 1978—; clin. assoc. prof. Robert Wood Johnson Med. Ctr. Rutgers U., Piscataway, 1978—; sr. attending pathologist Raritan Bay Med. Ctr., Perth Amboy, 1978—. Contbr. articles to profl. jours. Pres. Congregation Bnai Israel, Rumson, N.J., 1987-89; co-chmn. Greater Red Bank (N.J.) United Jewish Appeal, 1986-87. Mem. Am. Thoracic Soc., Coll. Am. Pathologists, N.J. Soc. Pathologists, N.J. Thoracic Soc., Middlesex County N.J. Med. Socs. Democrat. Jewish. Home: 78 Black Point Rd Rumson NJ 07760-1742 Office: Raritan Bay Med Ctr 530 New Brunswick Ave Perth Amboy NJ 08861-3654

STONE, HARVEY H., civil engineer, executive; b. N.Y.C., Mar. 24, 1942; s. George and Sylvia (Stein) S.; m. Carol Lucia Piccirillo; children: Margarida Stone Kondak, Dan, Deborah, Jim, Marco. BCE, Rensselaer Polytech., 1963. Registered profl. engr., Vt., Pa.; registered surveyor, Pa. Engr. U.S. Army Corps of Engrs., N.Y.C., 1964-66; project engr. A.W. Cross & Co., Burlington, N.J., 1966-68, George Atkin Jr. Profl. Engr., Tidoute, Pa., 1968-69; v.p. engring. Northwest Engring. Inc., Tidoute, 1969-75, exec. v.p., 1975-79, pres., 1979—. Supr. Glade Twp. Warren County, Pa., 1983-88. Mem. Am. Consulting Engrs. Coun. (Outstanding Engring. Achievement, Pa. Coun., 1980, '82), Nat. Soc. Profl. Engrs. (pres. Buctails chpt. Pa. 1975-77), Am. Assn. State Highway Engrs. Office: Northwest Engring Inc RR 1 Tidioute PA 16351-9801

STONE, JAMES LESTER, mental health administrator; b. Syracuse, N.Y., May 31, 1940; s. Lester Herbert and Mary (Cowley) S.; BA, Syracuse U., 1962, MSW, 1964; m. Joan McDermott Borzelle, Aug. 5, 1967; children: Jeffrey Borzelle, Michael McDermott, Andrew Cowley. Dep. dir. Onondaga County detention care Syracuse, 1962-63; tchr. Fayetteville-Manlius (N.Y.) Schs., 1964-65; asst. dir. Edmond Fitzgerald Start Ctr., N.Y. State Div. Youth, Middletown, 1965-67; dir. Rochester (N.Y.) Urban Youth Home, 1967-73; asst. supt. N.Y. State Div. for Youth Tng. Sch., Industry, 1973-74, supt., 1974-78; dir. Livingston County Dept. Mental Health, Mt. Morris, N.Y., 1978-79; chief outpatient svcs. Willard Psychiat. Ctr., 1979-81; dir. community svcs. Rochester Psychiat. Ctr., 1981-82, chief treatment svc., 1982-88; dir. Monroe County Dept. Mental Health and Community Svcs., 1988—; lectr., Rochester Inst. Tech., 1968-71; cons. Community Svc.Bur. Upstate N.Y., 1968-71; field faculty Syracuse U., 1969-74, Colgate-Rochester Div. Sch., 1983-88; cons. Disability Determination N.Y. State Dept. of Social Svcs., 1982—; sr. social worker Family Counseling of Finger Lakes, 1980-89; mem. adv. com. Youth Residence Ctr. Greater Rochester; mem. youth svcs. system adv. com. Rochester-Monroe County Youth Bd.; chmn. tng. subcom. Monroe County Children's Detention Com.; exec. bd., chmn law com. Assn. for Community Transitional Svcs.; mem. adv. com. human svcs. dept. Monroe Community Coll., 1978—; mem. adv. com. Health Assn. DayBreak Alcoholism Treatment Ctr., 1986-88. With N.Y. Air N.G., 1962-68. Fellow Am. Orthopsychiat. Assn.; mem. Am. Assn. Mental Health Adminstrs., Am. Group Psychotherapy Assn., Nat. Assn. Social Workers, Acad. Cert. Social Workers. Home: 66 Yorktown Dr Webster NY 14580-2243 Office: Monroe County Dept Community Svcs 375 Westfall Rd Rochester NY 14620-4647

STONE, JEROME CARL, JR., controller; b. Scranton, Pa., Apr. 9, 1963; s. Jerome C. and Shirley J. (Royce) S.; m. Laurie L. Stone, Oct. 5, 1991. BS, Delaware Valley Coll., Doylestown, Pa., 1985; MS, Fairleigh Dickinson U., 1990. Supr. Merrill Lynch Pierce Fenner & Smith, Somerset, N.J., 1985-90, dept. controller, 1990—; owner New Dream Arabians, Hackettstown, N.J., 1989—. Author: Handbook of Financial Ratio's, 1990. Mem. AICPAs. Roman Catholic. Office: Merrill Lynch Pierce Fenner 500 Atrium Dr Somerset NJ 08873

STONE, JOE THOMAS, chemist; b. Miami, Okla., June 25, 1941; s. Jack Thomas and Reba Lorraine (Breeden) S.; m. Gail Ann Johnson, Dec. 28, 1963; children: Jason, Brandon. BS, Harvey Mudd Coll., 1963; PhD, U. Wash., 1967. Technician Narmco, San Diego, 1960-63; teaching asst., rsch. asst. U. Wash., Seattle, 1963-67; sr. rsch. chemist Eastman Kodak Co., Rochester, N.Y., 1968—. Inventor: Method of Silver Modification, 1991. Mem. Conservation Bd. Webster, N.Y., 1986—, Waterfront Utilization Study Com., Webster, 1989. Mem. Am. Chem. Soc., Royal Chem. Soc., N.Y. Acad. Scis. Home: 595 Drumm Rd Webster NY 14580 Office: Eastman Kodak Rochester NY 14650

STONE, L. MARK, banker; b. N.Y.C., Oct. 7, 1957. BS cum laude in Fin., SUNY, Albany, 1981; MS in Econs., London Sch. Econs., 1983. Prin. Autotechs East, Troy, N.Y., 1977-79; assoc. Henry Ansbacher, Inc., N.Y.C., 1984-86, v.p., 1986-88, exec. v.p., 1988-89; ptnr. AdMedia Corp. Advisors, Inc., N.Y.C., 1990—. Bd. dirs. Am. Friends of the London Sch. Econs., Washington, 1985—, treas., 1992—, chmn. N.Y.C. chpt. 1985-87. Office: AdMedia Corp Advisors Inc 780 Third Ave 14th Fl New York NY 10017

STONE, LINDA D., organizational development and human resources consultant; b. Keene, N.H., Dec. 18, 1947; d. Gordon D. and Sophie B. (Blacker) S. BA in English, Hartwick Coll., 1969; cert. in pers. mgmt., NYU, 1978; MA in Human Resources, New Sch. for Social Rsch., 1985. Adminstrv. asst. Arlans Dept. Store, N.Y.C., 1969-72; pers./office svcs. mgr. ABC Leisure Mags., N.Y.C., 1974-80; dir. pers. & adminstrn. Gruner and Jahr USA, N.Y.C., 1980-82; dir. human resources & adminstrn. Warren, Gorham and Lamont, N.Y.C., 1983; mgr. pers. adminstrn. John Wiley and Sons, Inc., N.Y.C., 1984-88; dir. staffing Simon & Schuster, N.Y.C., 1989-90; pres. Linda D. Stone Assocs., Inc., N.Y.C., 1990—; adj. prof. New Sch. for Social Rsch., N.Y.C., 1991—; adj. prof. NYU, N.Y.C., 1992—. Contbr. articles to profl. jours. Vol. N.Y.C. schs. Mem. AAUW, Applied Psychology (N.Y. chpt.), N.Y. Human Resource Planners, N.Y. Pers. Mgmt. Assn., Internat. Assn. Outplacement Profls., Assn. Psychol. Type, Soc. Human Resource Mgmt., Hartwick Coll. (alumni bd. 1983-91, class agt. 1984, founder N.Y.C. alumni chpt.). Office: Linda D Stone Assocs Inc 520 E 81st St New York NY 10028-7045

STONE, MELISSA MIDDLETON, management educator; b. Trenton, N.J., Feb. 4, 1948; d. Richard Vincent and Janet Smith (Bradley) Middleton; m. William Lewis Cook Jr., Nov. 18, 1978 (div. 1982); m. Paul Clois David Stone, June 24, 1989. BA, U. Pa., 1970; M Mgmt., Yale U., 1982, PhD, 1989. Founder, co-dir. Alaska Youth Advocates, Anchorage, 1973-76; founder, exec. dir. Family Connection, Anchorage, 1976-80; rsch. assoc., then assoc. dir. program on nonprofit orgns. Yale U., New Haven, 1985-88; asst. prof. mgmt. policy Boston U., 1988—; adv. coun. Ctr. on Philanthropy, Ind. U., 1990—; exec. com. pub. sector div. Acad. Mgmt., 1990—. Contbg. author: The Nonprofit Sector: A Research Handbook, 1987; dep. editor Nonprofit and Voluntary Sector Quar., 1988—; contbr. articles to profl. publs. Mem. Gov.'s Commn. on Adminstrn. of Justice, Alaska, 1976-80; chair Task Force on Foster Family Care, Alaska, 1976-77. John D. Rockefeller III fellow, 1983; grantee Yale-Lilly Endowment, 1990-91. Mem. Nat. Seminar on Trusteeship, Boston Mgmt. Consortium, Beta Gamma Sigma. Episcopalian. Office: Boston Univ 621 Commonwealth Ave Boston MA 02215-1609

STONE, MICHAEL P. W., federal official; b. London, June 2, 1925; married; 2 children. BA, Yale U., 1945; grad. law sch., NYU, 1949. Various positions Sterling Vineyards, Napa Valley, Calif., 1964-68, v.p., gen. mgr., dir., 1968-73, pres., dir., 1973-82; dir. U.S. Mission in Cairo, 1982-84; dir. Caribbean basin intitiative affairs AID, 1986-88; undersec. Dept. of the Army, Washington, 1988-89, sec., 1989—. Office: The Pentagon Dept Army Washington DC 20310-0101*

STONE, MORRIS DENOR, retired mechanical engineer; b. Cambridge, Mass., Dec. 2, 1902; s. Harry and Rose (Denor) S.; m. Marissa Gluckman, June 19, 1926; children: Richard Joseph, Elinore Eugenie Thomas, Philip Morris. BS in Mech. Engring. magna cum laude, Harvard U., 1923, MS in Mech. Engring., 1925; PhD in Applied Math., U. Pitts., 1934. Registered profl. engr., Pa. Rsch. engr. ASME, Cambridge, 1923-24; rsch. engr. Westinghouse Electric & Mfg. Co., East Pittsburgh, Pa., 1925-29, head mech. and elec. devel. power div., 1929-33; spl. engr. United Engring. and Foundry Co., Pitts., 1934-40, mgr. R&D, 1940-65, v.p. R&D, 1965-70, cons., 1970-72; engr. cons. Pitts., 1972-88; lectr., head advanced mech. design sch., 1926-32, 32-33; Lamme fellow Hochschule Charlottenburg, U. Berlin, 1930-31; bd. dirs. United Engring. and Foundry Co., 1968-70; materials adv. bd. Nat. Acad. Sci., 1956-63; indsl. advisor NATO, 1959. Contbr. articles to profl. jours.; patentee in field. Fellow ASME (mem. various coms.); mem. Assn. Iron and Steel Engrs. (life). Home: 1308 Macon Ave Pittsburgh PA 15218-1219

STONE, PAMELA ANNE, public relations manager; b. Waltham, Mass., Feb. 17, 1965; d. Robert E. and Jean (Tewksbury) S. BS in sport mgmt., U. Mass., 1988. Pub. rels. intern NBA, N.Y.C., 1988; media rels. coord. Spalding Sports Worldwide, Chicopee, Mass., 1988—. Office: Spalding Sports Worldwide 425 Meadow St Chicopee MA 01013-2201

STONE, PETER, playwright, scenarist; b. Los Angeles, Feb. 27, 1930; s. John and Hilda (Hess) S.; m. Mary O'Hanley, Feb. 17, 1961. BA, Bard Coll., 1951, DLitt, 1971; MFA, Yale U., 1953. Ind. stage and screen writer, 1961—. Author: (musical comedies) Kean, 1961, Skyscraper, 1965, 1776, 1969, Two by Two, 1970, Sugar, 1972, Woman of the Year, 1981, My One and Only, 1983, Grand Hotel, 1989, The Will Rogers Follies, 1991, (play) Full Circle, 1973, (films) Charade, 1963, Father Goose, 1964, Mirage, 1965, Arabesque, 1966, Secret War of Harry Frigg, 1968, Sweet Charity, 1969, Skin Game, 1971, 1776, 1972, Taking of Pelham 123, 1974, Silver Bears, 1977, Who is Killing the Great Chefs of Europe?, 1978, Why Would I Lie?, 1980, (TV scripts) Androcles and the Lion, (series) Adam's Rib and Ivan the Terrible, others. Recipient Acad. award, 1964, Emmy award, 1963, Mystery Writers award, 1964, Tony award, 1969, 81, N.Y. Drama Critics award, 1969, 91, Drama Desk award, 1969, Christopher award, 1973. Mem. Dramatists Guild (pres.), Authors League, Writers Guild Am. Home: 160 E 71st St New York NY 10021-5183 also: Stony Hill Rd Amagansett NY 11930

STONE, PETER HOWARD, cardiologist, educator; b. N.Y.C., Mar. 31, 1948; s. Harvey and Ronnie (Eilenberg) S.; m. Lisa Vosburgh, May 6, 1984; children: Emily, Michael, Benjamin. BA, Princeton U., 1970; MD, Cornell U., 1974. Intern in internal medicine San Francisco Gen. Hosp., 1974-75; resident in internal medicine U. Calif., San Francisco, 1975-77; cardiology fellow Pacific Med. Ctr., San Francisco, 1977-79; rsch. fellow in medicine Peter Bent Brigham Hosp., Boston, 1979-80; instr. in medicine Harvard Med. Sch., Boston, 1979-83, asst. prof. medicine, 1983-91; assoc. prof. medicine, 1991—; assoc. dir. Samuel A. Levine cardiac unit Brigham and Women's Hosp., Boston, 1982—; dir. clin. trials, cardiovascular div. Brigham and Women's Hosp., 1991—. Fellow Am. Coll. Cardiology, Am. Heart Assn. (coun. on clin. cardiology). Office: Brigham & Women's Hosp Cardiovascular Div 75 Francis St Boston MA 02115-6195

STONE, RALPH UPSON, research center official; b. Syracuse, N.Y., Nov. 23, 1958; s. Frederick Losee and Anne Louise (Upson) S. BA, Hamilton Coll., 1980; MA, Columbia U., 1986; postgrad., George Washington U. Vol. Peace Corps, Zaire, 1980-83; cons. Internat. Health Programs, Santa Cruz, Calif., 1987, Ctrs. for Disease Control, Atlanta, 1987--89, Delphi Rsch. Assocs., Waashington, 1987-89, UNICEF, Bujumbura, Burundi, 1988, Mgmt. Scis. for Health, Boston, 1988; project coord. Ctr. for Devel. and Population Activities, Washington, 1989-90, dep. dir. tng., 1990-92, dir. tng., 1992—. Co-founder Friends of Zaire, Washington, 1992—. Mem. Soc. for Internat. Devel. Republican. Methodist. Office: CEDPA 1717 Massachusetts Ave NW Washington DC 20036

STONE, ROBERT DELMAR, lawyer; b. Cleve., May 17, 1922; s. Charles D. and Marion P. (Schiffert) S.; m. Betty J. Bonnewell, Dec. 23, 1945; children: Carol S. Luckenbach, Judith A. Languish, Susan L. Schell. BA, Hamilton Coll., 1944; LLB, Columbia U., 1949, JD, 1970. Bar: N.Y. 1949, U.S. Dist. Ct. (no. dist.) N.Y. 1949, U.S. Dist. Ct. (we. dist.) N.Y. 1971, U.S. Dist. Ct. (ea. and so. dists.) N.Y. 1978, U.S. Ct. Appeals (2d cir.) 1980, U.S. Supreme Ct. 1980. Assoc. Pearis, Resseguie & McManus, Binghamton, N.Y., 1949-53, ptnr., 1953-59; exec. dept. Sec. of State N.Y. Dept. of State, Albany, 1959-60; dep. commr. gen. svcs. N.Y. Office Gen. Svcs., Albany, 1960-67; appointments officer to gov. Exec. Chamber State of N.Y., Albany, 1967; counsel, dep. commr. legal affairs N.Y. State Dept. of Edn., Albany, 1968-87, ret., 1987; lectr. N.Y. State Coun. Sch. Dist. Adminstrs., Albany, 1969-82, N.Y. State Sch. Bds. Assn., Albany, 1969-83, Mid-Hudson Sch. Study Coun., New Paltz, 1969-86, N.Y. State Bar Assn., 1969-82. Member adv. coun. N.Y. State D.A.R.E., Albany, 1991—; dir. Albany chpt. Salvation Army, 1985—; trustee Capital Dist. YMCA, Schenectady, N.Y., 1988—; co-chair Homes for the Homeless Program, Albany, 1990—. Mem. Normanside Country Club, Univ. Club of Albany (bd. dirs. 1983-89), Rotary (bd. dirs. Albany chpt. 1987-90). Republican. Presbyterian. Office: 198 Westchester Dr S Delmar NY 12054-4212

STONE, THOMAS RICHARDSON, arts council executive; b. Milw., Feb. 1, 1939; s. Thomas S. and Ann Louise (Taplin) S.; m. Cynthia White Hutchinson, July 20 1963; children: Sarah, Thomas. BS, U.S. Mil. Acad., 1961; MA, Rice U., 1971, PhD, 1974. Commd. 2d lt. field artillery U.S. Army, 1961, advanced through grades to col., 1988; v.p. medicare support svcs. Pa. Blue Shield, Camp Hill, 1988-90; dir. devel. and fin. Metro Arts of the Capital Region, Harrisburg, Pa., 1990—; dir. Susquehanna Cabinets, Hellam, Pa., 1989—. Author: The Second World War: Europe and the Mediterranean, Vol. II, 1980; contbr. articles to profl. publs. Deacon St. Paul's United Ch. Christ, Mechanicsburg, Pa., 1987-90, pres. of consistory, 1989-92, elder, 1990-92; Friends of the Pa. Historical and Museum Commn.; mem. Cumberland-Perry Assn. for Retarded Citizens, 1980—, bd. dirs., 1980-82, 86-89, 90—, pres., 1984-86. Decorated Bronze Star, Legion of Merit; grantee Rice U., 1971-72; recipient Community Service award, Am. Legion, Carlisle, Pa., 1987. Mem. Nat. Soc. Fund Raising Execs., Assn. U.S. Army, Capital Fedn. Cosmopolitan Interant. Club (Cosmo of Yr. award 1981-82, pres. 1980-82, lt. gov. 1983-86, gov. elect 1986-87, gov. 1987-88, found. dir. 1988-91,, internat. 2d v.p. 1991—). Home: 6319 Stephens Xing Mechanicsburg PA 17055-2347 Office: MetroArts of the Capital Region Harrisburg PA 17108

STONER, JEFFREY WAYNE, trucking company executive; b. Harrisburg, Pa., Jan. 1, 1953; s. Robert Elwood and Beatrice Louise (Angus) S.; M. Bonnie Denise Artz, Apr. 7, 1990; children from previous marriage: Daniel James, Amy Beth. Mgmt. trainee Haver Lockhart Lab., New Cumberland, Pa., 1970-72; svc. advisor Hoffman Ford Sales, Harrisburg, 1972-73; acctg. clk. Cen. Storage & Transfer Co., Harrisburg, 1973-77, programmer, 1977-78, mgr. data processing, 1978-83, dir. info. systems, 1983-85, gen. mgr. adminstrn., 1985, v.p. adminstrn., treas., 1985-92; v.p. Transcorps Enterprises Inc., Harrisburg, Pa., 1992; cons. transp., bus. pvt. practice, Harrisburg, Pa., 1992—. Mem. Nat. Acctg. and Fin. Coun., Am. Warehousing Assn., Cen. Pa. IBM Users Group, Harrisburg C. of C., Middletown Bottle Club (Pa., v.p. 1985-87). Republican. Methodist. Home and Office: Transcorps Enterprises 6111 Alleo Ln Harrisburg PA 17110

STONIER, TOM, author, educator; b. Hamburg, Fed. Republic Germany, Apr. 29, 1927; came to U.S., 1939; BA, Drew U., 1950; MS, Yale U., 1951, PhD, 1955. Jr. rsch. assoc. Brookhaven Nat. Lab., Upton, N.Y., 1952-54; postdoctoral fellow Rockefeller U., N.Y.C., 1954-57, rsch. assoc., 1957-62; assoc. prof. biology Manhattan Coll., N.Y.C., 1962-71, prof. biology, 1971-75; dir. Pacem/in Terris Inst., N.Y.C., 1971-75; prof., head sci. and soc. U. Bradford, U.K., 1975-90, prof. emeritus, 1990—; chmn. Valiant Tech., London, 1985—. Author: Nuclear Disaster, 1964, The Wealth of Information, 1983, The Three Cs: Children, Computers and Communication, 1985, Information and the Internal Structure of the Universe, 1990, Beyond Information, 1992; contbr. numerous articles to profl. jours. Sec. Fedn. of Am. Scientists, Washington, 1967-68, mem. coun., 1965-68. With USNR, 1945-46. H.D. Hooker fellowship Yale U., 1950-51, Damon Runyon Meml. fellowship Rockefeller U., 1956-57, postdoctoral fellowship NIH, Rockefeller U., 1954-56. Fellow Royal Soc. of Arts (life); mem. AAAS, N.Y. Acad. Scis., Phi Beta Kappa, Sigma Xi. Home: 838 East St Lenox MA 01240

STOOLMILLER, ALLEN CHARLES, science administrator; b. Battle Creek, Mich., Nov. 3, 1940; s. Charles Edward and Helen Marie (Taylor) S.; m. Laura Jean Liggett, Dec. 28, 1961 (div.); children: Scott Allen, Amy Lynn. BA, Western Reserve U., 1961; MA, U. Mich., 1964, PhD, 1966; postgrad., Brandeis U., 1964-66. Postdoctoral fellow U. Chgo., 1966-68, instr., 1968-69, asst. prof., 1969-76; assoc. biochemist E.K. Shriver Ctr., Waltham, Mass., 1976-79; exec. sec. div. rsch. grants NIH, Bethesda, Md., 1979-89; sci. rev. adminstr. Nat. Inst. Allergy and Infectious Diseases, NIH, Bethesda, 1989—, acting chief AIDS rev. sect., 1990-92; user's panel cons. file div. rsch. grants NIH, Bethesda, 1980, mem. merit pay com., 1980-81, mem. adv. com. referral and rev. br., 1986-89; mem. STEP com. NIH, Bethesda, 1985-88. Fellow Chgo. Heart Assn., 1966-68, Ill. Heart Assn., 1966-68. Prin. investigator State Ill. Dept. Mental Health, 1970-77, USDA, 1976-77. Mem. Am. Soc. Biochemistry and Molecular Biology, Am. Soc. for Neurochemistry, Am. Soc. Carbohydrate Chemistry, Sigma Xi. Presbyterian. Home: 13311 Grenoble Dr Rockville MD 20853-2821

STOOPLER, MARK BENJAMIN, physician; b. N.Y.C., Sept. 29, 1950; s. Alex and Blanche Sylvia (Kappel) S.; m. Lynn Sara Fruchter, Jan. 10, 1982; children: David Andrew, Emily Rachel, Jesse Bryan. BS, Tulane U., 1971; MD, Cornell U., 1975. Diplomate Am. Bd. Internal Medicine, Am. Bd. Oncology. Intern and resident in internal medicine North Shore U. Hosp., Manhasset, N.Y., 1975-78; intern and resident in internal medicine Meml. Sloan-Kettering Cancer Ctr., N.Y.C., 1975-78, asst. chief resident in medicine, 1978, fellow in med. oncology, 1978-80; asst. attending physician Presbyn. Hosp., N.Y.C., 1980—; asst. prof. of clin. medicine Columbia U. Coll. of Physicians and Surgeons, N.Y.C., 1980—. Contbr. articles to profl. jours. Recipient U. scholar Tulane U., 1970-71. Mem. ACP, Am. Soc. of Clin. Oncology, Am. Fedn. for Clin. Research, Internat. Assn. for the Study of Lung Cancer, Phi Beta Kappa. Office: Columbia-Presbyn Med Ctr 161 Ft Washington Ave New York NY 10032-3713

STOPHERD, JOHN RAYMOND, small business owner; b. Newark, N.J., Aug. 8, 1945; s. Edwin and Anna (Cadiz) S.; married; children: Stephene, Michelle, Christina, Renee. AA in Bus., Collegent Inst., 1969; BS in Mktg., Husson Coll., 1972. Pres. J.R.S. Machine & Tool Sales Corp. of Am., South Plainfield, N.J., G&A div. J.R.S. Machine & Tool Sales Corp. of Am., 1990—. Mem. N.J. Machine and Tool Assn., Am. Mktg. Assn., Kean Coll. Small Bus. Assn. (bd. dirs. 1992-93), N.J. Elks, KC. Republican. Roman Catholic. Office: J R S Machine & Tools 333 Hamilton Blvd South Plainfield NJ 07080-3339

STORCH, JOEL ABRAHAM, mathematician; b. N.Y.C., Nov. 11, 1949; s. Sidney and Hermione (Kaufman) S.; m. Therese Weiss, Dec. 25, 1981. BS, CCNY, 1971; MS, Columbia U., 1972; PhD, MIT, 1974. Numerical analyst Goddard Inst. for Space Studies, N.Y.C., 1972-76, Brookhaven Nat. Lab.,

Upton, N.Y., 1976-78; dynamicist Draper Lab., Cambridge, Mass., 1978-88, Jet Propulsion Lab., Pasadena, Calif., 1988-91, Draper Lab., Cambridge, 1991—; lectr. CCNY, 1974-76; adj. prof. Northeastern U., Boston, 1980-88. Contbr. articles to profl. jours. Recipient Citation, NASA, 1986. Mem. AIAA, Soc. Indsl. and Applied Math. Jewish. Home: 1809 Beacon St Brookline MA 02146-4206 Office: Draper Lab 555 Technology Sq Cambridge MA 02139-3563

STORCH, MARGARET MARY BRYCE, writer, consultant; b. Newcastle upon Tyne, Eng., Feb. 16, 1941; d. Stanley and May (Maughan) Bryce; m. Rudolf F. Storch, June 8, 1973; children: Vanessa Elizabeth, Nicholas Aidan. BA with honors, Durham (Eng.) U., 1962; Postgrad. Cert. in Edn., London U., 1963; PhD, McGill U., Montreal, Can., 1971. Lectr. English Newcastle Poly., Newcastle upon Tyne, 1964-67; lectr. English and Edn. St. Joseph's Tchrs.' Coll., McGill U. Faculty Edn., 1967-71; lectr. English Poly. of the South Bank, London, 1971-73; tutor Open U., London, 1974-75; lectr. English U. Mass., Boston, 1978-81; asst. prof. English Bentley Coll., Waltham, Mass., 1981-90; acting dir. New England Heritage Ctr., Waltham, 1989-90; writer on lit. and edn. policy; cons. Mass. Dept. Edn. Author (book) Sons and Adversaries: Women in William Blake and D.H. Lawrence, 1990; contbr. articles to profl. jours. Mem. MLA, Women in Politics and Govt., Nat. Coun. Tchrs. English, Women's Caucus for the Modern Langs., D.H. Lawrence Soc. N.Am., Friends of the Boston Psychoanalytic Soc. and Inst. Home: 330 Concord Ave Lexington MA 02173

STORCK, HERBERT EVAN, marketing professional; b. New Haven, Apr. 23, 1954; s. Herbert and Mary (Grove) S.; m. Susan Mary McConachie, Aug. 6, 1977; children: Christopher, Timothy, Kyle. BA, U. Bridgeport, 1976; MS, U. Wis., 1979. Asst. acct. exec. MRCA Info. Svcs., Stamford, Conn., 1980-81, acct. exec., 1981-82, group acct. mgr., 1983-84, dir. bus. devel., 1984-85, v.p. bus. devel., 1985-86, v.p., gen. mgr., 1986-90, sr. v.p., gen. mgr., 1990-92; pres. Advanced Mktg. Solutions, Trumbull, Conn., 1992—. Mem. Am. Mktg. Assn. Home: 12 Shelter Rock Rd Trumbull CT 06611-3325 Office: Advanced Mktg Solutions PO Box 1011-159 Trumbull CT 06611

STORER, DONALD E., corporate executive; b. Wilkinsburg, Pa., Jan. 1, 1939; s. John William and Nelle (Forsythe) S.; m. Yvonne E. Doney, June 8, 1958 (div. Nov. 1983); m. Joanne E., Aug. 29, 1985 (children: Douglas, Gerald, Mark. BA, Otterbein Coll., 1960; MA, Ohio State U., 1968. Tchr. Cleveland Schs./Wesley Coll., Dover, Del., 1960-66; sales rep. IBM Corp., Columbua, Ohio, 1966-69; dir. mktg. IBM Corp., Chgo., 1969-72; regional mgr. IBM Corp., Hershey, Pa., 1972-75; nat. sales mgr. CBS, Inc., L.A., 1975-80; v.p. sales ARA, Inc., Phila., 1980-83; v.p. mktg. Seiler Corp., Waltham, Mass., 1983-85, sr. v.p. mktg., 1985-87, pres. Dietary Div., 1987—. Office: The Seiler Corp 153 Second Ave Waltham MA 02254

STOREY, JAMES ROGER, public policy research analyst; b. Montgomery, Ala., Feb. 6, 1941; d; s. Roger William Jr. and Martha Eulene (Mulkey) S.; m. Elaine Shirley Amrozowicz, June 10, 1967; 1 child, Andrew James. BS in Physics/Math., U. Ala., 1963; MS in Indsl. Adminstrn., Carnegie-Mellon U., 1965. Budget analyst U.S. Bur. of the Budget, Washington, 1966-70; program analyst U.S. Dept. Health, Edn. and Welfare, Washington, 1971; sr. economist U.S. Joint Econ. Com., Washington, 1971-74; sr. rsch. analyst Inst. of Medicine, Washington, 1974-75; staff dir. human resources U.S. Senate Budget Com., Washington, 1975-77; rsch. ctr. dir. The Urban Inst., Washington, 1977-83; v.p. Chambers Assocs., Inc., Washington, 1983-87; specialist in social legislation U.S. Congrl. Rsch. Svc., Washington, 1987—. Contbr. articles to profl. jours. Mem. Ward One Civic Assn., Annapolis, Md., 1988—. Capt. USPHS, 1966-68. Booz, Allen & Hamilton fellowship Carnegie-Mellon U., 1964, W.L. Mellon fellowship, 1963. Mem. League of Am. Wheelmen, Annapolis Bicycle Club, Balt. Bicycle Club, Bike Centennial, Annapolis Striders, Chesapeake Bay Found., Phi Beta Kappa, Pi Mu Epsilon. Democrat. Methodist. Office: US Congrl Rsch Svc 1st St & Independence Ave SE Washington DC 20540

STORIN, MATTHEW VICTOR, newspaper editor; b. Springfield, Mass., Dec. 24, 1942; s. Harry Francis and Blanche Marie S.; m. Keiko Takita, Aug. 1, 1975; 1 child, Kenyatta; children by previous marriage: Karen, Aimee, Sean. BA, U. Notre Dame, 1964. Reporter Springfield Daily News, 1964-65, Griffin-Larrabee News Bur., Washington, 1965-69; Washington corr., city editor, Asian corr., nat. editor, asst. mng. editor, dep. mng. editor, mng. editor Boston Globe, 1969-85; dep. mng. editor U.S. News & World Report, Washington, 1985-86; editor, sr. v.p. Chgo. Sun-Times, 1986-87; editor The Maine Times, Topsham, 1988-89; mng. editor N.Y. Daily News, 1989-91, exec. editor, 1991-92; exec. editor Boston Globe, 1992—. Recipient Disting. Polit. Reporting award Am. Assn. Polit. Sci., 1969. Home: 201 W 70th St New York NY 10023-4301 Office: The Boston Globe 135 Morrissey Blvd Boston MA 02107

STORMONT, JONATHAN, engineering company executive; b. Malden, Mass., Mar. 11, 1955; s. Fred Joseph and Helen Susan (Maltby) S.; m. Maureen Hussey, Sept. 8, 1979; 1 child, Benjamin. BS cum laude, Tufts U., 1979. Asst. to pres. Hearthstone Corp., Morrisville, Vt., 1981-83; v.p., chief ops. officer, founder Internat. Mineral Resources Corp., Stone, Vt., 1983-87; gen. mgr. Twin Rivers Engring., Inc., Boothbay, Maine, 1987—, also bd. dirs.; treas. Mobius, Inc., Newcastle, Maine, 1988-90. Asst. cub scout leader Boy Scouts Am., Damtriscotta, Maine; vol. firefighter Waterbury Center (Vt.) Fire Dept., 1982-87. Home: RR 1 Box 488L Newcastle ME 04553-9700 Office: Twin Rivers/Rynel PO Box 298 Boothbay ME 04537-0298

STORRS, JAMES HOLLISTER, publishing executive, consultant; b. Savannah, Ga., Apr. 9, 1944; s. Gardner Hollister and Joan Elizabeth (Hile) S.; m. Jane Wise Montgomery, Dec. 28, 1968; children: Robert, Sarah. BS in Econs., Loyola U., Balt., 1968; MS in Fin. Adminstrn., George Washington U., 1972. Contr. Md. Health Maintenance Com., Balt., 1972-73; dir. strategic planning Comml. Credit Co., Balt., 1973-86; pub. Haras & Trebor, Inc., Gambrills, Md., 1987—. Editor Horizons newspaper, 1989, D.C. Mayor's award; pub. Horizons, 1990, D.C. Mayor's award. Coach Arden Recreation, Millersville, Md., 1982-88, Gambrills Athletic Club, 1989-90, Crownsville (Md.) Sports Assn., 1990-92. Republican. Methodist. Office: Haras & Trebor Inc PO Box 985 Gambrills MD 21054-0985

STORY, ANNE WINTHROP, psychologist, engineer; b. Havenhill, Mass., Jan. 12, 1914; d. John Winthrop and Anna Louise (Fennelly) S. Diplôme supérieure, Sorbonne, Paris, 1933; AB, Smith Coll., Northampton, Mass., 1934; PhD, U. Calif., Berkeley, 1957. Registered profl. engr., Mass. Rsch. psychologist USAF Flight Safety, San Bernardino, Calif., 1950; instr. Pa. State U., 1947-50; assoc. prof. U. Mass., Boston, 1972-74; engring. psychologist USAF, Bedford, Mass., 1958-66, NASA, Cambridge, Mass., 1966-70, U.S. Dept. Transp., Cambridge, 1970-77; pvt. practice cons., 1977—. Inventor, patentee flight safety devices.

STORY, CAROL M., education educator; b. Hanover, N.H., Oct. 21, 1947; d. Lee E. and Barbara B. (Graves) Story. BS in Elem. Edn., Johnson State Coll., 1969, MA in Edn., 1974; cert. advanced grad. study, U. Vt., 1981; PhD, U. Conn., 1984. Cert. early childhood edn. tchr. Tchr. Stowe Elem. Sch., Vt., 1969-71, Berkshire Elem. Sch., Vt., 1974-81; asst. prof. Boston U., 1985-87; prof. elem., early childhood and gifted edn. Johnson State Coll., Vt., 1987—. Contbr. articles to profl. jours. Recipient Hollingworth award; fellow Jessie B. Noyes Found. Mem. Nat. Assn. Gifted Children, Nat. Assn. for Edn. Young Children, Vt. Coun. Gifted Edn. (pres.), Phi Delta Kappa, Pi Lambda Theta. Office: Johnson State Coll Johnson VT 05656

STOTT, DONALD BISHOP, securities trader; b. N.Y.C., Jan. 18, 1939; s. Robert Leslie and Mary (Laase) S.; m. Joan Johnson, June 14, 1986; children: Christopher W. Quinn, Nicholas D. Quinn. AB, Princeton U., 1960; MBA, U. Pa., 1963. Gov. N.Y. Stock Exch., N.Y.C., 1975-80, sr. fl. gov., 1980, dir., 1980-83; dir. N.Y. Futures Exch., N.Y.C., 1982-87; chmn. specialist and floor ops. Securities Industry Assn. Exch., N.Y.C., 1980-81; ptnr., specialist, floor trader Wagner, Stott & Co., N.Y.C., 1963—, sr. ptnr., 1975—, chief exec. officer, 1980—; bd. advisors J.H. Foster & Co., N.Y.C., 1972—, Bus. Devel. Capital Co. I & II, N.Y.C., 1977—; pres. The Investment Assocs. of N.Y., 1973. Founding mem. Rep. Senatorial Trust, Washington, 1976—; chmn. ann dinner NCCJ, N.Y.C., 1979; trustee Taft Sch., Watertown, Conn., 1976-80. Staff sgt. USAF, 1962-68. Recipient Brotherhood award NCCJ, 1982. Mem. Wharton Bus. Sch. Club of N.Y. (dir. 1976-89), Canoe Brook Club, Cat Cay Assocs., The Everglades Club (Palm Beach, Fla.), Lost Tree Club, Bath and Tennis Club (Palm Beach). Republican. Presbyterian. Office: Wagner Stott & Co 20 Broad St Fl 9 New York NY 10005-2684

STOTT, JILL ANN, controller; b. Cohoes, N.Y., Nov. 21, 1959; d. William Henry and Mary Myrtle (Beaupre) S. AAS, Hudson Valley Community Coll., Troy, N.Y., 1979; BS, SUNY, New Paltz, 1983. From accounts payable acct. to contr. Royce W. Day Co., Voorheesville, N.Y., 1984-88; from corp. acct. to acctg. mgr. Insulating Materials Inc., Schenectady, N.Y., 1988-91; contr., sr. mgmt. operating com. Insulating Materials Inc., Schenectady, 1991—. Bd. dirs. Moh'oneson (N.Y.) Adv. Coun., 1992. Mem. Nat. Assn. Accts., Am. Mgmt. Assn. Office: Insulating Materials Inc 1 Campbell Rd Schenectady NY 12306

STOTT, PAUL EDWIN, chemist, research manager; b. Springfield, Mass., Jan. 18, 1948; s. Lyle Day and Shirley Ann (Fales) S.; m. Sharon Dowdle, Sept. 3, 1970; children: Melissa, Jason Allen, Gregory Robert. BS in Chemistry, Brigham Young U., 1971, PhD in Chemistry, 1979; MS in Chemistry, U. Mass., 1972. Gen. mgr. Parish Chem. Co., Orem, Utah, 1974-78; rsch. chemist Uniroyal Splty. Chems., Nagatuck, Conn., 1979-80, sr. group leader, 1980-82; rsch. mgr. Uniroyal Splty. Chems., Middlebury, Conn., 1985—; tech. dir. Lubritex, Inc., Houston, 1982-83; v.p. tech. Am. Texmark, Houston, 1982-85. 1st lt. USAF, 1972-74. Mem. Sigma Xi. Mem. LDS Ch. Home: 20 Clearview Dr Sandy Hook CT 06482-1334 Office: Uniroyal Splty Chems Benson Rd Waterbury CT 06749-0002

STOUDT, THOMAS HENRY, research microbiologist; b. Temple, Pa., Apr. 6, 1922; s. Thomas Lester and Edith (Yocum) S.; m. Kathryn H. Hendel, Dec. 31, 1943; children: Thomas H., Frank E., Carol A. BS, Albright Coll., 1943; MS, Rutgers U., 1944; PhD, Purdue U., 1949. Sr. microbiologist Merck & Co., Rahway, N.J., 1958-68; sect. head Merch Sharp & Dohme Rsch. Lab., Rahway, N.J., 1969-74; dir. Merck Sharp & Dohme Rsch. Lab., Rahway, N.J., 1975-76; sr. dir. Merck Sharpe & Dohme Rsch. Lab., Rahway, N.J., 1977-83, exec. dir., exec. tech. advisor, 1984—; pres. Stoudt Assocs., Westfield, N.J., 1982—. Mem. adv. bd. Health and Environment Union County, Elizabeth, N.J., 1988—; mcpl. chmn. Westfield Dem. Com., 1964-66. With USN, 1944-46. Mem. Am. Chem. Soc., Am. Soc. for Microbiology (pres. Theobald Smith Soc. 1964-65), N.Y. Acad. Scis. Home and Office: Stoudt Assocs 857 Village Grn Westfield NJ 07090-3515

STOUFFER, NANCY KATHLEEN, publishing company executive; b. Hershey, Pa., Feb. 14, 1951; d. William Lawrence Sweeny O'Brian and Edna Luttrell; m. David Joel Stouffer, July 19, 1980; children: Jennifer Belle, Vance David. Pres. Andé Pub. Co., Inc., Camp Hill, Pa., 1985-88; pres., chmn. B.C.I., Camp Hill, Pa., 1988-90; v.p. R&D E.S.P. Inc., N.Y.C., 1989—. Contbr. articles on dyslexia and learning disabilities to popular mags.; author children's books. Exec. researcher com. on advanced studies in learning disabilities Med. and Ednl. Profl., SPECTRA, devel. of the EZ read program. Republican. Office: 30 E 2d St Hummelstown PA 17036 Also: ESP Inc & SYN-Comm Group Penthouse 160 E 56th New York NY 10022 Studio: 30 E 2d St Hummelstown PA 17036

STOUT, DOUGLAS RICHARD, service company executive; b. Abington, Pa., Mar. 7, 1945; s. Frank Milton and Grace (Richards) S.; m. Linda Agnes Valentine, Aug. 30, 1965 (div. Jan. 1983); children: Laura, Tara, Thomas, Stephen; m. Nancy Anne Delmonte, Apr. 29, 1984. BS in Bus. Mgmt. and Econs., Shaw U., 1973. Field auditor A.C. Nielsen, various cities, 1969-76; salesman, svc. exec. Nielsen Clearing House, N.Y.C., 1976-79; account exec. Nielsen Clearing House, A.C. Nielsen, Hackensack, N.J., 1979-85, v.p., 1985-86; v.p. key accounts Dun & Bradstreet, Nielsen Clearing House, Hackensack, N.J., 1986-88; v.p., western sales mgr. Dun & Bradstreet, Nielsen Clearing House, Chgo., 1988-89; v.p. sales and mktg. L.M. Gordon, Inc., West Chester, Pa., 1989-91. Republican. Lutheran. Home: 1438 Old West Chester Pike West Chester PA 19382-6537

STOUT, FRANCIS JOSEPH, artist; b. Lynn, Mass., Feb. 17, 1926; s. Frank Joseph and Catherine (Horan) S.; m. Chaewoon Koh, July 27, 1959; 1 child, Mira. Student, Boston Mus. Sch., 1949-50, Marlboro Coll., 1985. Chmn. dept. arts, drawing, painting, sculpture Marlboro Coll., Vt., 1966-86; Solo exhibits include Landmark Gallery, N.Y., 1979-81, Mercer Price Landscape, Fleming Mus., Burlington, Vt., Nat. Acad. Design, N.Y., 1983, Vt. Skies, Brattleboro Mus., 1986; group shows at Springfield Mus., Mass., Wichita Art Mus., Sheldon Swope Art Gallery, Terre Haute, Ind., Vermont State House, Montpelier, U. Vt., Burlington, Am. Embassies, Peru, Brazil; commns. include mems. protrait Nat. Acad. Design, N.Y., 1979; portrait Ex-Gov. Emerson, Montpelier, Vt., 1980;. Monumental sculpture, Burlington, Vt., 1981, plaza fountain, Burlington. With USN, 1943-44. Recipient H.W. Ranger award Nat. Acad. Design, N.Y., 1982. Roman Catholic. Home: Butterfield Rd Marlboro VT 05344-9999

STOUT, JOHN WILSON, college administrator; b. Reading, Pa., Oct. 3, 1942; s. John Wellington and Helen Mary (Rothermel) S.; m. Helen Jean Hosty, July 30, 1977; 1 dau., Katie Irene; m. Jayne Frances Atherton, Mar. 25, 1967 (div. Dec. 1976); 1 son, John R. B.A., Dickinson Coll., 1964; M.A., Northeastern U., 1966; M.P.A., Nova U., 1980. Instr., R.I. Coll., Providence, 1971; mem. faculty Univ. Without Walls, Providence, 1972-74; asst. to pres. Roger Williams Coll., Bristol, R.I., 1974-75, dir. Open Div., 1974—; sr. lectr. Northeastern U., Boston, 1967—; cons. head start, model cities, Providence and Pawtucket, 1971-74; research coordinator Urban Observ. R.I., 1970-75. Mem. budget panel United Way Southwestern New Eng., Providence, 1972; mem. commn. Planning Project Post Secondary Edn., Providence, 1975. Recipient Achievement cert. Northeastern U., 1982, Disting. Teaching award Roger Williams Alumni Assn., 1974. Mem. Am. Soc. Public Adminstrn. (pres. 1979-80), NEA, Am. Acad. Polit. and Social Sci., Acad. Polit. Sci. Democrat. Mem. Ch. Christ. Home: 3 Nathaniel Rd Barrington RI 02806-3825 Office: Roger Williams Coll Bristol RI 02809

STOUT, MARK ROBERT, podiatric surgeon; b. Brick, N.J., Sept. 27, 1962. BA, Glassboro State Coll., 1984; D in Podiatric Medicine, N.Y. Coll. Podiatric Medicine, 1989. Resident physician St. Albans Hosp., N.Y.C., 1989-90, Bklyn. VA Med. Ctr., 1989-90; pvt. practice Brick, 1990—; mem. med. staff dept. orthopedics Community Med. Ctr., Toms River, N.J., 1990—. Mem. Am. Podiatric Med. Assn., Assn. Mil. Surgeons of U.S., N.J. Podiatric Med. Assn., Assn. Podiatric Physicians and Surgeons. Office: Yorktown Foot & Ankle Ctr 2860 Yorktowne Blvd Brick NJ 08723-7967

STOVER, CARL FREDERICK, foundation executive; b. Pasadena, Calif., Sept. 29, 1930; s. Carl Joseph and Margarete (Müller) S.; m. Catherine Swanson, Sept. 3, 1954; children: Matthew Joseph, Mary Margaret Stover Marker, Claire Ellen; m. Jacqueline Kast, Sept. 7, 1973. B.A. magna cum laude, Stanford U., 1951, M.A., 1954. Instr. polit. sci. Stanford U., 1953-55; fiscal mgmt. officer Office Sec. Dept. Agr., 1955-57; asso. dir. conf. program pub. affairs Brookings Instn., 1957-59, sr. staff mem. govtl. studies, 1960; fellow Center Study Democratic Instns., Santa Barbara, Calif., 1960-62; asst. to chmn. bd. editors Ency. Brit., 1960-62; sr. polit. scientist Stanford Research Inst., 1962-64; dir. pub. affairs fellowship program Stanford U., 1962-64; pres. Nat. Inst. Pub. Affairs, Washington, 1964-70, Nat. Com. U.S.-China Relations, 1971-72; pres., dir. Federalism Seventy-Six, 1972-74; dir. cultural resources devel. Nat. Endowment for Arts, 1974-78; pres. Cultural Resources, Inc., Washington, 1978-85; bd. dirs. H.E.A.R. Found., 1976-86, treas., 1976-80, pres., 1980-86; bd. dirs. Ctr. for World Lit., pres. 1987-90, chmn. 1990—; pvt. profl. cons., 1970—; scholar-in-residence Nat. Acad. Pub. Adminstrn., 1980-82; cons. to govt., 1953—. Author: The Government of Science, 1962, The Technological Order, 1963; Founding editor: Jour. Law and Edn., 1971-73; pub. Delos mag., 1987-92. Treas. Nat. Com. U.S.-China Rels., 1966-71, 82-87, 89—, bd. dirs., 1966-74, 79—, Coord. Coun. Lit. Mags., 1966-68; trustee Inst. of Nations, 1972-76, Nat. Inst. Pub. Affairs, 1967-71, Kinesis Ltd., 1972-78; vol. nat. Exec. Svc. Corps, 1984-89. Fellow AAAS; mem. Am. Soc. Pub. Adminstrn., Am. Com. on U.S.-Soviet Rels., Fedn. Am. Scientists, Soc. Internat. Devel., Jordan Soc. (dir. 1982-84), Nat. Acad. Pub. Adminstrn. (hon.), Md. U. Club, Internat. Soc. Panetics (pres., founding mem.), Phi Beta Kappa Assocs. (hon., lectr. 1972-87), Phi Beta Kappa. Democrat. Presbyterian. Home and Office: 4109 Metzerott Rd College Park MD 20740-2082

STOVER, MATTHEW JOSEPH, communications company executive; b. Palo Alto, Calif., May 5, 1955; s. Carl Frederick and Catherine (Swanson) S.; m. Elizabeth Biddle Richter, Apr. 27, 1985; 1 child, Katharine Elizabeth. BA, Yale U., 1976; postgrad., U. Va., 1987. Gen. mgr. K&S Assocs., Beltsville, Md., 1977-78; dir. outreach programs U.S. Office Personnel Mgmt., Washington, 1978-81; exec. asst. to chmn. Fed. Maritime Commn., Washington, 1981; exec. dir. STN Computer Services, Inc., Alexandria, Va., 1981-82; dir. corp. communications Norton Simon, Inc., N.Y.C., 1982-83; dist. mgr. corp. communications N.Y. Telephone Co., N.Y.C., 1983-86, dist. mgr. customer services, 1986-87; v.p. corp. communications Am. Express Co., N.Y.C., 1987-90, sr. v.p. communications, 1990; v.p. pub. affairs and corp. communications NYNEX Corp., White Plains, N.Y., 1990—; bd. dirs. Nat. Assn. Mfrs., Legal Aid Soc., N.Y. Editor, pub.: (lit. mag.) Buffalo Stamps, 1971-74. Mem. Internat. Assn. Bus. Communicators, Am. Mgmt. Assn., Nat. Com. U.S.-China Rels., Coun. for Excellence in Govt., Pub. Rels. Soc. Am., Nat. Advt. Rev. Bd. Conf. Bd. (coun. corp. communications execs.), Arthur W. Page, Soc., Yale Club (N.Y.C.). Office: NYNEX Corp 1113 Westchester Ave White Plains NY 10604-3510

STOWENS, DANIEL, pathologist; b. N.Y.C., Oct. 27, 1919; s. Oscar and Rose Lillian (Galkin) S.; m. Barbara Jean Hagmann, Sept. 28, 1944 (wid. May 1984); children: Daniel W., Christopher D.; m. Lamya Mary Shaheen, Mar. 20, 1985. AB, Columbia Coll., 1941; MD, Coll. Physicians and Surgeons, N.Y.C., 1943. Diplomate Am. Bd. Pediatrics, Pathology. Intern, resident Gorgas Hosp., Ancon, Canal Zone, 1944-45; instr., med. sch. Am. Univ., Beirut, 1947-48; fellow pediatrics Ochsner Clinic and Tulane Univ., New Orleans, 1948-51; resident, pathology Walter Reed Army Hosp., Washington, 1952-53; fellow, pathology Childrens Hosp., Boston, 1953-54; chief, pediatric pathology Armed Forces Inst. Pathology, Washington, 1954-58; dir. labs., assoc. prof. Childrens' Hosp./U. So. Calif. Med. Sch., L.A., 1958-60, Childrens' Hosp./U. Louisville, 1960-65; dir. labs. St. Luke's Meml. Hosp., Utica, N.Y., 1965-85; med. dir. MDS Labs, Rome, N.Y., 1985—. Author: Pediatric Pathology, 1959; contbr. articles to profl. jours. Maj. U.S. Army, 1945-47. Recipient 2nd prize Am. Soc. Gastroenterology, 1960. Mem. Am. Acad. Pediatrics, Am. Soc. Clin. Pathology (Gold medal 1955), N.Y. Acad. Sci., Am. Assn. Pathology, Internat. Acad. Pathology. Home and Office: RR 2 Clinton NY 13323-9802

STRAAT, KENT LEON, executive recruiter; b. Norwalk, Conn., Nov. 7, 1934; s. Kent Eggleston Straat and Margaret (Fish) Brecide; m. Donna Miller, Apr. 22, 1961; children: S. Hilary, T. Kent. BA in Indsl. Psychology, Lehigh U., 1959. Credit clk. Bethlehem Steel, Behlehem, Pa., 1960-61; salesman IBM, N.Y.C. and Washington, 1961-68; registered rep. McDonnell & Co., N.Y.C., 1968-69; v.p. Clark Dodge & Co., N.Y.C., 1969-73, William H. Clark & Assocs., N.Y.C., 1973-76; mng. dir. Paul Stafford Assocs., N.Y.C., 1976-84; pres. Straat Group Inc., Stamford, Conn., 1984-89; v.p. staffing Gartner Group, Inc., Stamford, 1989-91; ptnr. Object Resources Internat., Stamford, 1991—. Author: What Your Boss Can't Tell You, 1988. Dir. USO of Met. N.Y., N.Y.C., 1979—. With U.S. Army, 1954-57. Mem. Swedish Am. C. of C., St. Nicholas Soc. (pres. 1991—), Stamford Yacht Club (dir. 1978-84), SAR (pres. 1977-79), Univ. Club (N.Y.C.), Holland Soc. Home: 14 Cresthill Pl Stamford CT 06902-8038 Office: Object Resources Internat 14 Cresthill Pl Stamford CT 06902-8038

STRACHAN, GRAHAM, pharmaceutical company executive; b. Dundee, Scotland, Sept. 12, 1938; arrived in Can., 1968; s. Roualyn and Ellen Strachan. BSc, Glasgow U., 1961, MA, 1963. Registered patent and trade agt. Licensing officer Schering Inc., Switzerland, 1963-66; v.p. bus. devel. John Labatt Ltd., Can., 1967-82; pres., chief exec. officer Allelix Biopharms., Inc., Mississauga, Ont., Can., 1982—. Patentee in field. Fellow Patent and Trademark Inst. Can.; mem. Am. Chem. Soc., Licensing Execs. Soc., Indsl. Biotech. Assn. Can. (bd. dirs.), Assn. Biotech. Cos. (bd. dirs. 1985—, past pres.). Home: 118 W Deane Park Dr, Islington, ON Canada M9B2S3 Office: Allelix Biopharms, 6850 Goreway Dr, Mississauga, ON Canada L4V1P1

STRACHER, DOROTHY ALTMAN, education educator, consultant; b. N.Y.C., May 11, 1934; d. Joseph and Gussie (Newman) Altman; m. Alfred Stracher, July 4, 1954; children: Cameron Altman, Adam Reed, Erica Terri. BA, Bklyn. Coll., 1955; MA, Columbia U., 1957; postgrad., U. Copenhagen, 1958-59; acad. vis., Oxford (Eng.) U., 1973-74; PhD, Hofstra U., 1979. Cert. English and social sci. tchr., N.Y. Coordinator secondary reading Cen. Moriches (N.Y.) Sch. Dist., 1974-78; coordinator reading Ea. Williston (N.Y.) Sch. Dist., 1978-79; specialist reading and writing SUNY, Old Westbury, 1979-81; adj. prof. dept. reading Hofstra U., Hempstead, N.Y., 1979-82; asst. prof. edn. L.I. U., Bklyn., 1982-83, Coll. New Rochelle, N.Y., 1983-85; sr. learning diagnostic specialist child devel. div. L.I. Jewish Hosp., Bklyn., 1985-86; assoc. prof., dir. program for learning disabled coll. students Dowling Coll., Oakdale, N.Y., 1986—, acad. chair Sch. Edn., 1991—; cons. Johnson & Johnson, Inc., Princeton, N.J., 1982—, Sanford (Fla.) Sch. Dist., 1983, Lawrence (N.Y.) Sch. Dist., 1984, Sch. Dist. 7, N.Y.C., 1984—. Author: (with others) First the Fundamentals, 1980, What Do You Call a Well-Behaved Martian?, A Manual For Thinkers' Parents, 1981, Integrating Assessment, 1982; editor: Differentiated Curricula, 1986, A Literature Based Integrated Curriculum: Grades Pre-K-, 1989, Successful Strategies for Learning Disabled College Students: Reading, Writing and Reasoning, 1991; contbr. articles to profl. jours. Bd. dirs. Roslyn (N.Y.) Sch. Dist., 1975-84, v.p., 1980-82, pres., 1982-84; mem. adv. bd. Children's Sch. Sci., Woods Hole, Mass., 1976-82. Mem. Reading Forum Found., Orton Soc., Internat. Reading Assn., Nat. Assn. for Gifted Edn., League Women Voters (bd. dirs. 1961-70), NOW, Kappa Delta Pi. Home: 47 The Oaks Roslyn NY 11576-1704

STRAETZ, DONALD FREDERICK, trade association administrator; b. Mellen, Wis., July 11, 1938; s. Donald Barnabus and Marie Clara (Staedtler) Bulloch; m. Susan Marlborough Greco, Sept. 7, 1963; children: Robert Marshall, Nancy Marlborough. BS, U.S. Mil. Acad., 1960; MSME, N.Mex. State U., 1965; MS in Adminstrn., George Washington U., 1976. Registered profl. engr., Va. Commd. 2d lt. U.S. Army, 1960, advanced through grades to lt. col., 1982, ret., 1982; asst. exec. dir. N.Y. Gas Group, N.Y.C., 1982-86, exec. dir., 1986—. Mem. ASME. Republican. Lutheran. Office: NY Gas Group 500 Fifth Ave Ste 428 New York NY 10110

STRAHAN, LINDA CAROL, minister, educator, mental health professional; b. Council Bluffs, Iowa, Dec. 13, 1945; d. Charles Daniel and Helen Esther (Pedersen) S. AB, Stanford U., 1967; MA, U. Calif., Irvine, 1968; PhD, U. Calif., 1976; MDiv cum laude, Va. Theol. Sem., Alexandria, 1979. Lic. mental health counselor; cert. clin. mental health counselor Nat. Acad. Cert. Clin. Mental Health Counselors, master practitioner of neuro-linguistic programming New Eng. Inst. of Neuro-Linguistic Programming; ordained priest, Episcopal Ch., 1980. Teaching asst., instr. U. Calif., Irvine, 1968-72; english instr. Chapman Coll., Orange, Calif., 1972-73; seminarian St. Augustine Ch., Washington, 1974-76; chaplain intern Delaware State Hosp., New Castle, 1976; chaplain resident Meml. Hosp., Houston, 1977-78; asst. rector Ch. of the Redeemer, Chestnut Hill, Mass., 1979-83; assoc. rector St. Martin's Ch., Providence, 1983-85; interim rector St. Michael's Ch., Rumford, R.I., 1986, St. David's Episcopal Ch., Gales Ferry, Conn., 1987-88; dir., pres. Gateway Resources, Inc., Newport, R.I., 1988—, 1990—; chair Liturgy Study Com. (Diocese of R.I.) 1984—. Contbr. articles to various theol. pubs. Mem. Episcopal Clergy Assn., Nat. Assn. of Neuro-Linguistic Programming, AACD, Am. Mental Health Counselors Assn., Newport County C. of C., Newport Women's Network (bd. dirs.); assoc. Order of Holy Cross. Office: Gateway Resources Inc 111 Bellevue Ave Ste 140 Newport RI 02840-3268

STRAIGHT, BEATRICE WHITNEY, actress; b. Old Westbury, L.I., N.Y., Aug. 2, 1918; d. Willard and Dorothy (Whitney) Dickerman; m. Peter Cookson, June 2, 1949; children: Gary, Anthony. Studied with, Tamara Daykarhanova, with Michael Chekhov at Chekhov Theatre Sch. A founder Theatre, Inc. (producing orgn.), 1945. Appeared in Broadway plays including Bitter Oleander, 1935, The Possessed, 1939, Twelfth Night, 1941, Land of Fame, 1943, The Wanhope Bldg, 1947, Eastward in Eden, 1947, Macbeth, 1948, The Heiress, 1948, The Innocents, 1950, The Grand Tour, 1951, Heartbreak House, 1952, The Crucible, 1953 (Antoinette Perry award),

Sing Me No Lullaby, 1954, The River Line, 1957, Twelfth Night, King Lear, Phèdre, 1966, A Streetcar Named Desire, 1967, 69-70, Everything in the Garden, 1967, The Palace at 4 A.M, 1972, Ghosts, 1972, All My Sons, 1974; toured in: Broadway plays including The Right Honourable Gentleman, 1971; mem. Broadway plays including, L.I. Festival Repertory Co., 1968; film appearances include Phone Call for a Stranger, 1952, Patterns, 1956, The Silken Affair, 1957, The Nun's Story, 1959, The Young Lovers, 1964, Network, 1976 (Acad. award for best supporting actress), Bloodline, 1979, The Promise, 1979, The Formula, 1980, Poltergeist, The Power, 1986, Deceived, 1991; TV performances include The Magnificent Failure, 1952, The Borrowers, 1973, The Garden Party, 1974, Strangers in the Homeland, 1976; mini-series The Dain Curse, 1978; also guest roles on Lamp Unto My Feet; regular on: TV series Beacon Hill, 1975; operates, Young World Found.; producing: children's plays, including Who Am I?, 1971-73; conducted own radio program on, Sta. WMCA, N.Y.C., during World War II, appeared as Rose Kennedy in mini-series Robert Kennedy, His Life and Time, 1984, Run Till You Fall, 1989, People Like Us, 1990; founder Michael Chekov studio, Eng., U.S., reopened 1982—; co-founder Theatre Inc., 1946. Mem. Actors Equity, AFTRA, Screen Actors Guild. Home: 30 Norfolk Rd Southfield MA 01259 Office: care Mark Levy Mgmt 23826 Hartland St West Hills CA 91307-3022

STRAIN, GLADYS WITT, nutritionist, professor of medicine; b. Plymouth, Mich., Apr. 19, 1934; d. Elmer Milton and Iris Erleen (Palmer) Witt; m. James Joseph Strain, Sept. 3, 1956; children: Jay James, Jeffrey Witt, James Palmer. BS, Mich. State U., 1955; MS, Case Western Res. U., 1960, PhD, 1964. Diplomate Am. Bd. Nutrition. Dietetic intern Bronx VA, 1955-56; staff dietitian Harvard U., Cambridge, Mass., 1956-57; nutritionist Cleve. Welfare Fedn., 1958; pub. health trainee Case Western Res. U., Cleve., 1959-60; lectr. nutrition program Tchr.'s Coll. Columbia U., N.Y.C., 1974-75; nutrition cons. dept. medicine St. Luke's/Roosevelt Hosp. Ctr., 1975-85, rsch. assoc., 1985—; rsch. nutritionist clin. rsch. ctr. Montefiore Hosp. and Med. Ctr., 1977-81, rsch. assoc. oncology, 1980-81, rsch. nutritionist dept. medicine Beth Israel Med. Ctr., N.Y.C., 1981-91; rsch. nutritionist, assoc. prof. medicine Mt. Sinai Med. Ctr., 1991—. Mary Swartz Rose fellow; recipient Intern award Mich. Dietetic Assn., Hinman Donor award, Cleve. Found. award. Mem. Am. Dietetic Assn., Soc. for Nutrition Edn., Assn. for Women in Sci., AAAS, N.Y. Acad. Sci., A. Psychosomatic Soc., Am. Soc. for Clin. Nutrition, Am. Inst. Nutrition, Am. Pub. Health Assn., N.Am. Assn. for the Study of Obesity, Internat. Assn. for the Study of Obesity, Phi Kappa Phi, Omicron Nu. Office: Mt Sinai Med Ctr 1 Gustave L Levy Pl # 1055 New York NY 10029-6504

STRAIN, LUCILLE BREWTON, education educator, researcher; b. Florence, S.C.; d. William O. and Jurheutha (Gibbs) Brewton; m. Winston M. Strain (dec. 1984); 1 child, Rada Ruth Higgins. BA, Benedict Coll., 1943; MEd, Ohio State U., 1954, PhD, 1965. Cert. elem., secondary teaching, adminstrn., supervision. Tchr. Columbus (Ohio) Pub. Schs., 1950-62; prof. various U., 1965-79; policy analyst Nat. Ctr. Edn. Stats., Washington, 1979-83; from coord. to prof. and chmn. dept. edn. Bowie (Md.) State U., 1983-89, prof. edn., coord. grad. reading edn., 1989—; nat. policy fellow Inst. Edn. Leadership, Washington, 1979-80; mem. adv. coun. edn. stats. Nat. Ctr. Edn. Stats., Washington, 1982-85. Author: Accountability in Reading Instruction, 1976; contbr. articles to profl. jours. Recipient grant U.S. Dept. Edn., Washington, 1989, Bowie State U., 1989. Mem. Internat. Reading Assn. (tchrs. rsch. com. 1991—), Assn. Tchr. Educators (corp. by-laws com. 1990—), State of Md. Internat. Reading Assn. Coun. (chmn. internat. projects & activities com.). Home: 4701 Willard Ave Apt 1522 Chevy Chase MD 20815-4631

STRAIT, PEGGY TANG, mathematician, educator; b. Canton, China, Apr. 20, 1933; came to U.S., 1939; d. Paul and Doris (Chu) Tang; m. Roger Hadley Strait, June 10, 1955; children: Paul Stephen, David Samuel. BA, U. Calif., Berkeley, 1953; MS, MIT, 1957; PhD, NYU, 1965. Programmer U. Calif. Radiation Lab., Livermore, 1954-55, MIT Lincoln Lab., Lexington, 1955-57; rsch. assoc. G.C. Dewey Corp., N.Y.C., 1957-63; prof. math. Queens Coll., CUNY, Flushing, N.Y., 1964—. Author: A First Course in Probability and Statistics with Applications, 1983, 2d edit., 1988; contbr. papers to rsch. jours. Author: A First Course in Probability and Statistics with Applications, 1983, 2d edit., 1988; contbr. numerous rsch. papers to rsch. jours. NSF fellow, 1971-72. Mem. Am. Math. Soc., Math. Assn. Am. Office: Queens Coll Flushing NY 11367

STRANG, JOHN LAWRENCE, human services professional; b. Quincy, Mass., Jan. 31, 1951; s. Wilbur Hyler and Margaret Mary (Knaide) S.; m. Marjorie Frances Corey, Dec. 13, 1975; children: Erin Marie, Jessie Leah, Stacy Ann. AAS, Dutchess Community Coll., Poughkeepsie, N.Y., 1978; BS, Univ. Maine, 1981; MSW, U. Conn., 1986. Lic. clin. social worker. Dir. chem. dependency recovery prog. V.A. Adminstrn., Portland, Maine, 1987-89, Togus, Maine, 1989—; cons. Smith House, Portland, 1990—. With U.S. Army, 1971-74, Fed. Republic of Germany. Office: Togus VAMROC 116A2 Togus ME 04330

STRASSER, JOEL A., public relations executive, engineer; b. N.Y.C., Aug. 8, 1938; s. Albert Gerson and Nellie (Singer) S.; m. Isabel Gallant, Aug. 15, 1965; children: Alison Debra, Andria Jocelyn, Jon Fredric. BS, CCNY, 1961. News editor Electronic Design mag., N.Y.C., 1962; space electronics editor Electronics mag. McGraw-Hill, N.Y.C., 1963-65; account exec. Lescarboura Advt., Inc., Briarcliff Manor, N.Y., 1965-67; bur. chief Aerospace Tech. mag., N.Y.C., 1967-68; syndicated sci. columnist N.Am. Newspaper Alliance, N.Y.C., 1974-80; sr. v.p., founding dir. indsl. and sci. communications svcs. Hill & Knowlton, Inc., N.Y.C., 1968-83; exec. v.p. Thomas L. Richmond, Inc., N.Y.C., 1983-85; sr. v.p., mng. dir. Dorf & Stanton Tech. Communications, N.Y.C., 1985—; adj. asst. prof. NYU, 1988—; adj. instr. Marymount Coll., Tarrytown, N.Y., 1981—; course leader, guest lectr. Am. Mgmt. Assn., 1976—, Am. Med. Writers Assn., 1983—, Ecole Francais des Affaires Publique, 1988; speaker and program coord. in field. Transmitted 1st color photograph by communications satellite, 1963; conducted 1st press interview by communications satellite, 1963; regular columnist High-Tech Mktg., Atlantic Tech., O'Dwyer's PR Svcs. Report, The Counselor; contbr. numerous articles to profl. jours. V.p., Citizens of Ramapo, 1969-70, Jewish Temple, 1980-83. Fellow AIAA (assoc.); mem. IEEE (sr.), Pub. Rels. Soc. Am. (accredited, N.Y. chpt. pres., founding nat. chmn. tech. sect. 1985—, Silver Anvil award 1980, John W. Hill award 1989, Presdl. citations 1986, 87), Am. Astron. Soc., Chem. Communications Assn., Nat. Assn. Sci. Writers, Internat. Solar Energy Soc., Internat. Assn. Bus. Communicators, Am. Med. Writers Assn. (guest lectr. 1983—). Home: 119 Smith Hill Rd Suffern NY 10901-7791 Office: PO Box 203 Tallman NY 10982-0203 also: 111 Fifth Ave New York NY 10003

STRATIS, GEORGE, electronics company executive; b. N.Y.C., Oct. 10, 1947; s. James and Mary (Manias) S.; m. Tina Candiloros, June 21, 1970; children: Justin, Diana Christine. BSEE, Poly. Inst. Bklyn., 1969; MSEE, NYU, 1972, MBA, 1975. Devel. engr. def. activities div. Western Electric, Whippany, N.J., 1969-72; planning engr. engring. div. Western Electric, N.Y.C., 1972-75; dir. svc. costs AT&T, Basking Ridge, N.J., 1975-81, product mgr., 1981-84; dir. licensing Bellcore, Livingston, N.J., 1984-88, dir. market planning and analysis, 1988-90, dir. total quality mgmt. team bus. planning and benchmarking, 1990—. Comptroller Millington (N.J.) Bapt. Ch., 1983-84; ranger Boys Brigade Chatham, N.J., 1987—; facilities mgr. Long Hill Chapel Chatham, N.J., 1991—. Mem. Christian and Missionary Alliance, Planning Forum. Office: Bellcore 290 W Mount Pleasant Ave Livingston NJ 07039

STRATOUDAKIS, JAMES PETER, psychologist; b. Stamford, Conn., Feb. 21, 1949; s. James and Rose L. (Rotante) S.; m. Carol Jay Colello, Aug. 14, 1971; 1 child, Alexander Jay. BA, Fairfield U., 1971; MS, DePaul U., 1973; PhD, Mich. State U., 1976. Psychotherapist Battle Creek (Mich.) Sanitarium Hosp., 1975-77; coord. info., asst. prof. internat. rehab. and spl. edn. Mich. State U., East Lansing, 1976-78, asst. prof. urban devel. and met. studies, 1978-80; pvt. practice psychology East Lansing, 1977-80; dir. clin. svcs. Social Ctr. for Psychiat. Rehab., Alexandria, Va., 1980-82; dir. no. region Va. Dept. Mental Health, Richmond, 1982-84, community svcs. bd., facility liaison for mental health, mental retardation, substance abuse, 1984; dir. community planning, program dev. and tng., community support programs Del. div. Alcoholism Drug Abuse & Mental Health, New Castle, 1984-86; regional dir. Greater Wilmington/New Castle County Community Mental Health Program, New Castle, 1986-88, Mass. Dept. Mental Health, Taunton, 1988-90; dir. office mental health Fairfax Fall Church Community Svcs. Bd., Fairfax County, Va., 1990—; adj. prof. Va. Commonwealth U., 1984—, U. Del., 1986-88, 90, Bridgewater State Coll., George Washington U., U. Va., 1991—; cons. psychologist, Washington, 1980—; mem. nat. adv. coun. State Mental Health Planning, 1990—; mem. nat. adv. coun. Rehab. Rsch. and Tng. Ctr. for Persons with Psychiat. Disabilities, Albert Einstein Coll. Medicine, 1985-90. Sec. D.C. Psychology Polit. Action Com. Mem. APA (past chair community and state hosp. psychology sect.), Internat. Assn. Psycho-Social Rehab. Svcs., D.C. Psychol. Assn., Assn. Advancement Psychology, World Rehab. Assn. for Psychosocially Disabled (founding mem.), Nat. Assn. County Mental Health Dirs., Phi Kappa Theta. Office: Ofc of Mental Health Svcs 3340 Woodburn Rd Annandale VA 22003-1298

STRATTON, ELIZABETH MACY, psychologist; b. West Chester, Pa., Oct. 24, 1958; d. John Alfred Jr. and Katherine Macy (Stanton) S. BS in Individual Family Studies, Pa. State U., 1980; MA in Clin. Psychology, West Chester U., 1986. Lic. psychologist. Caseworker Kelsch Assocs., Inc., Lionville, Pa., 1980-81; creative arts therapist Haverford (Pa.) div. Sacred Heart Med. Ctr., Haverfod, Pa., 1981-86; therapist Hall Mercer of Pa. Hosp., Phila., 1986-89; prog. mgr., inpatient psychiat. svcs. Fitzgerald-Mercy Hosp., Darby, Pa., 1989-91, clin. dir. inpatient psychiat. svcs., 1991—; cons. psychotherapist Life Ctrs., Inc., Norristown, Pa., 1988-91. Mem. Pa. Psychol. Assn., Am. Psychol. Assn., Psi Chi. Mem. Soc. of Friends. Office: Fitzgerald-Mercy Hosp Dept of Psychiatry Lansdowne Avenue Rd Darby PA 19023-1214

STRATTON, RICHARD ALLEN, social worker, retired navy officer; b. Quincy, Mass., Oct. 14, 1931; s. Charles Arthur and Mary Lorretta (Hoar) S.; m. Alice Marie Robertson, Apr. 4, 1959; children: Patrick Thomas, Michael Francis, Charles Arthur. AB, Georgetown U., 1955; MA, Stanford U., 1964; MSW, R.I. Coll., 1988. Cert. social worker, chem. dependency profl., R.I. Commd. ensign USN, 1955, advanced through grades to capt., 1975, naval aviator, 1955-86; ret., 1986; clin. social worker South Shore Mental Health Ctr., Charlestown, R.I., 1988-91, Inst. for Human Devel., Charlestown, 1991—; cons. Stratton Leafs, Exeter, R.I., 1986—. Trustee Quincy Jr. Coll., 1980—, U.S. Naval Acad. Found.; mem. Exeter Rep. Town Com., 1988—; chmn. adv. com. on former prisoners of war Dept. Vets. Affairs, Washington, 1989—. Decorated Silver Star medal, Bronze Star medal, Legion of Merit, Purple Heart medal, Air Medal. Mem. NASW, Acad. Cert. Social Workers, VFW, DAV, AMVETS, Cath. War Vets., Am. Legion, Order Purple Heart. Home: 1163 Lita Ln Vista CA 92084-7236 Office: Inst for Human Devel PO Box 899 Charlestown RI 02813-0899

STRAUB, SYLVIA ANN, association executive; b. Dearborn, Mich., May 27, 1938; d. Thurman Andrew and Dorothy Inez (Pinnow) Clarke; m. Duane Gene Straub, July 27, 1960. BA with high distinction, Valparaiso U., 1960; MAT, Mich. State U., 1963; MA, Ind U., 1967, PhD, 1972. Cert. assn. exec. Instr. French Ohio U., Athens, 1963-65; dir. communications Agy. for Instructional Technol., Bloomington, Ind., 1974-82; publicity mgr. news dept. Nat. Pub. Radio, Washington, 1983-86; dir. info. and mktg. svcs. Am. Speech-Lang. Hearing Assn., Rockville, Md., 1986-89; exec. dir. Registry of Interpreters for the Deaf, Silver Spring, Md., 1989—; task force on instrnl. TV PBS, Washington, 1977-79; speaker mktg. seminar for instrnl. TV execs. Corp. for Pub. Broadcasting and U. of Lowell, Washington, 1987; writer, cons. Corp. Pub. Broadcasting, Washington, 1983. Bd. dirs. Valparaiso U. Alumni Assn., 1989—; ch. coun. mem. Luther Pl. Meml. Ch., Washington, 1985-87; task force job placement MLA, N.Y.C., 1977-78; pres. Brown County Humane Soc., Nashville, Ind., 1973-74. Recipient scholarship Valparaiso U., 1956. Mem. Am. Soc. Assn. Execs., Greater Washington Soc. of Assn. Execs., Women in Comms., Inc., Am. Assn. Tchrs. French, Am. Disabilities Found. and Channel. Office: Registry Interpreters Deaf 8719 Colesville Rd Ste 310 Silver Spring MD 20910-3919

STRAUSBAUGH, MELVIN ROY, academic dean; b. Orange, N.J., May 30, 1936; s. William Thomas and Emma Irene (Peters) S.; m. Rosanna Sweden, Dec. 29, 1961. BS, Millersville U., 1961; MA, Ind. U., 1966; PhD, Case Western Res. U., 1974. Prof. history Edinboro U. of Pa., 1966-83, assoc. v.p., 1983-85, dean continuing edn., 1985-87, dean acad. adminstrn., 1987—; pres. Edinboro Svcs. Inc., 1980—; mem. adv. bd. Marine Bank, Edinboro, 1979—. Pres., founder Flagship Niagara League, Erie, Pa., 1981-86; pres. Torch Club of Erie, 1985. With USN, 1954-58. Recipient Commendation award Senate, Commonwealth of Pa., 1986, Ho. Reps., Commonwealth of Pa., 1986, Pa. Hist. and Mus. Commn., 1986. Mem. Am. Assn. Higher Edn., Am. Assn. Collegiate Registrars and Admissions Officers, Erie Yacht Club (commodore 1986-87), Masons. Democrat. Lutheran. Office: Edinboro U Edinboro PA 16444

STRAUSS, CAROL KAHN, editor, consultant; b. N.Y.C., Sept. 21, 1944; d. Alfred and Lotte (Landau) K.; m. Peter Mathes, Dec. 1977 (div. 1980); m. Peter Strauss, June 1989. BS, Columbia U., 1970; MS, Hunter Coll., 1973. Asst. book editor Council on Fgn. Relations, N.Y.C., 1972-79; sr. editor, dir. pub. affairs Hudson Inst., Indpls., 1984-89; sr. editor, cons. 20th Century Fund, N.Y.C., 1990—; cons., writer, editor Ford Found., 20th Century Fund, Mayorial Task Forces, Kidder Peabody & Co., N.Y. Holocaust Commn. Editor: (books) The Coming Boom, 1982, Thinking About the Unthinkable in the 1980's, 1984; editor, co-author articles for profl. publs. Pres. Congregation Habonim, N.Y.C., 1984-92; trustee Self-Help, Inc., N.Y.C., 1986—, Leo Baeck Inst., N.Y.C., 1992—; v.p. Fedn. of Jews from Cen. Europe, 1990. Jewish. Club: Atrium (N.Y.C.). Home: 870 5th Ave New York NY 10021-4953 Office: 20th Century Fund 41 E 70th St New York NY 10021-4972

STRAUSS, DOROTHY BRANDFON, marital, family, and sex therapist; b. Bklyn.; d. Marcus and Beatrice (Wilson) Brandfon; widowed; 1 child, Josette Strauss Turner. BA, Bklyn. Coll., 1932; MA, NYU, 1937, PhD, 1963. Diplomate Am. Bd. Sexology. Instr. Hunter Coll. CUNY, 1960-63; prof. Kean Coll., Union, N.J., 1963-77; pvt. practice and clin. supervision Bklyn. and, N.J., 1970—; clin. assoc. prof. psychiatry Downstate Med. Ctr., SUNY, Bklyn., 1974—; assoc. dir. Ctr. for Human Sexuality, 1974-82. Contbr. articles on gerontology and sexual dysfunctions to profl. jours. Fellow Am. Assn. Clin. Sexologists (founding); mem. Am. Psychol. Assn., Am. Assn. for Marital and Family Therapy (clin. mem. 1971—, supr. 1981), Am. Assn. Sex Therapists, Counselors and Educators (chairperson task force on supervision 1984-86, chairperson supr. cert. com. 1986—, cert. steering com.), Kappa Delta Pi. Home and Office: 1401 Ocean Ave Brooklyn NY 11230-3917

STRAUSS, EDWARD ROBERT, carpet company executive; b. Jersey City, June 14, 1942; s. Abraham and Elsie Alice (Goldstein) S.; m. Martha Ann Patmore, Oct. 30, 1966; children: Jeffrey Aaron, Craig Michael. BSBA, Rutgers U., 1973. Dept. systems mgr. Port of N.Y. Authority, N.Y.C., 1961-68; account exec. Steiner Rouse & Co., N.Y.C., 1968-70; purchasing mgr. N.Y. State Urban Devel. Corp., N.Y.C., 1970-73; sales mgr. Siracco's, Staten Island, N.Y., 1973-76; carpet and TV buyer Hahnes Dept. Stores, Newark, 1976-80; sales mgr. Clodan Carpets, N.Y.C., 1980-83; regional mgr. Deans Carpets, Manchester, N.H., 1983-85; pres. Carpet Contractors Inc., N.Y.C., 1985—. Bd. dirs. Marlboro Little League, Marlboro, N.J., 1979—, Marlboro Pop Warner Football, 1979-83. Mem. Masons (Bayonne, N.J.) (past master Menorah lodge 1978), Free Sons of Israel (trustee, v.p.), Marlboro Mcpl. Swim Club (bd. dirs.). Hebrew. Office: Carpet Contractors Inc 3380 162nd St Flushing NY 11358-1327

STRAUSS, ELTON, orthopaedic surgeon; b. N.Y.C., Apr. 24, 1948; s. Carl and Shirley(Pinchuck) S.; m. Karen Louise Gustin, Jan. 2, 1971; children: Eric, Elisa. BA in Biology, C.W. Post Coll., 1970; MD, U. Autonoma, Guadalajara, Mexico, 1974. Intern Bronx-Lebanon Hosp., 1975-76, resident, 1976-79; pvt. practice N.Y.C., 1979—; chief orthopaedic trauma Mt. Sinai Sch. Medicine, N.Y.C., 1987—; assoc. dir. City Hosp. Ctr. at Elmhurst, Queens, N.Y., 1987—; orthopaedic cons. N.Y. Islanders Hockey Team, Uniondale, 1992—. Trustee Harlem Youth Devel. Found., N.Y. Geriatric scholar Mt. Sinai Sch. Medicine, 1992. Fellow Am. Bd. Orthopaedic Surgeons, Am. Coll. Surgeons; mem. Am. Foot Soc., Am. Fracture Soc., N.Y. Med. Soc. Office: Mt Sinai Sch Medicine 5 E 98th St Box 1188 New York NY 10029

STRAUSS, FRANK, communications executive; b. Stuttgart, Germany, May 31, 1935; came to U.S., 1936; s. Walter and Dorothy (Stanley) S.; m. Joan Fuld, Jan. 21, 1990; children from previous marrage: Mark, Karen, Stephen. BA in Polit. Svc., Antioch Coll., Yellow Springs, Ohio, 1957; postgrad., Boston U., 1957-58. Assoc. Antioch Coll. News Bur., 1958-59; prodn. asst. CBS, Hollywood, Calif., 1959-60; news dir. Sta. KSFE, Needles, Calif., 1960-61; editor Rockland Independent, Suffern, N.Y., 1961-65; exec. asst. Rockland County Bd. of Suprs., N.Y., 1965-67; dir. communications Met. Regional Coun., N.Y.C., 1967-76, Coun. Jewish Fedns., N.Y.C., 1976—; producer Jewish TV Mag., N.Y.C., 1985-88; dir. CJF Satellite Network, N.Y.C., 1988—. Councilman Town of Ramapo, Airmont, N.Y., 1967-68; committeeman Dem. Party, Rockland County, 1965-77; chmn. Rockland County Reapportionment com., 1966-67; sec. Rockland County Charter Commn., 1965-67. Recipient CAPE award N.J. Cable TV, 1987, 89. Mem. Internat. Teleconferency Assn., Soc. Satellite Profls. Internat., Pub. Rels. Soc. Am. Office: Coun Jewish Fedns 730 Broadway New York NY 10003-9511

STRAUSS, HERBERT ARTHUR, foundation administrator, history educator; b. Würzburg, Germany, June 1, 1918; came to U.S., 1946, naturalized, 1952; s. Benno and Magdalena (Hinterneder) S.; m. Lotte F. Schloss, Mar. 24, 1944; 1 child, Jane Helen. Grad., Hochsch Wissenschaft des Jüdentums, Berlin, 1942; PhD in European History summa cum laude, U. Berne, Switzerland, 1946; postgrad., Columbia U., 1949-51. Rsch. fellow Commn. European Jewish Reconstruction, 1946-48; tchr. religion sch. Congregation Habonim, 1946-48; lectr., instr. CUNY, 1948-54, asst., then assoc. prof. history dept., 1960-71, prof., 1971-82, prof. emeritus, 1982—; asst., then assoc. prof. acad. dept Juilliard Sch., N.Y.C., 1954-60; dir. Zentrum für Antisemitismusforschung, prof. Techmincke U., Berlin, 1982-90; mem. grad. faculty New Sch. for Social Rsch., N.Y.C., 1949-51; hon. mem. University, 1990. Editor: Jewish Immigrants of the Nazi Period in the U.S.A., 7 vols., 1978-92, A.F.J.C.E. Lerntag series; co-editor: Jubilee Volume Dedicated to Curt S. Silberman, 1969, Gegenwat im Rückblick: Festgabe für die Jüdische Gemeinde zu Berlin, 1970, International Biographical Dictionary of Central European Emigres, 1933-1945, 3 vols., 1980-83, Current Research on Autisemitism, 1987—, 4 vols.; contbr. numerous articles in field; appeared in Bavarian T.V. film Herbert Strauss, Flüchtling (Am. title We Were German Jews). Exec. v.p. Am. Fedn. Jews from Ctrl. Europe, N.Y.C., 1964-86; founder, sec., rsch. coord., dir. Rsch. Found. Jewish Immigration, 1972—; sec. Jewish Philanthropic Fund of 1933, 1970—; bd. dirs. N.Y. Found. Nursing Homes, 1975—, M. Tietz Ctr. Nursing Care, Selfhelp, Blue Card, United Help; mem. presidium Coun. Jews from Germany; rep. of Jewish refugees, Berne, 1944-46; alt. mem. Jewish del. to Flüchtlingsvertretung der Schweiz, 1945-46; mem. Swiss del. to conf. World Union for Progressive Judaism, London, 1946. Fellow and grantee Meml. Found. Jewish Culture, 1956, 60, 63, Am. Coun. Learned Socs., 1963, SOc. Sci. Rsch. Coun., 1963; fellow USPHS, 1949-51. Fellow Leo Baeck Inst. (bd. dirs. 1965-92); mem. AAUP, NAACP, Amnesty Internat., Am. Jewish Hist. Soc., Am. Hist. Assn. Conf. Group on German Politics, Am. Polit. Sci. Assn. Home: 90 La Salle St New York NY 10018

STRAUSS, JEROME FRANK, III, physician, educator, dean; b. Chgo., May 2, 1947; s. Jerome Frank Fr. and Josephine (Newberger) S.; m. Catherine Blumlein, June 20, 1970; children: Jordan L., Elizabeth J. BA, Brown U., 1969; MD, U. Pa., 1974, PhD, 1975. Asst. prof. Sch. of Medicine U. Pa., Phila., 1976-83, assoc. prof. Sch. of Medicine, 1983-85, prof. Sch. of Medicine, 1985—, assoc. chair Sch. of Medicine, 1987—, assoc. dean Sch. of Medicine, 1990—; mem. Biochem. Endocrinology study sect. NIH, 1983-87; mem., chair Population Rsch. Com. Nat. Inst. Child Health and Human Devel. Editor: Lipoprotein and Cholesterol Metabolism in Sterodogenic Tissues, 1985, Current Topics in Membrane Research, vol. 31, 1987; assoc. editor, mem. editorial bd. Jour. of Lipid Rsch., 1982-90; mem. editorial bd. Endocrinology, 1986-90, Biology of Reprodn., 1986-90. Mem. Am. Assn. Pathologists, Am. Physiol. Soc., Soc. Gynecologic Investigation, Endocrine Soc., Soc. for Study of Reprodn. (bd. dirs. 1989-91). Office: U Pa Dept Ob/Gyn 422 Curie Blvd Philadelphia PA 19104-6140

STRAUSS, RAYMOND BERNARD, otolaryngologist; b. N.Y.C., Mar. 25, 1930; s. Victor M. and Fannie (Price) S.; m. Lois Kelly, June 12, 1958; children: Steven Douglas, Keith Andrew. AB, Washington U., St. Louis, 1950, PhD, U. Fla., 1956; MD, Case-Western Res. U., 1958. Diplomate Am. Bd. Otolaryngology, Am. Bd. Cosmetic Plastic Surgery. Intern dept. medicine Univ. Hosps., Cleve., 1958-59, asst. resident surgery, 1959-60; resident otolaryngology Columbia-Presbyn. Med. Center, N.Y.C., 1960-63; practice medicine, specializing in otolaryngology and facial plastic surgery, Englewood, N.J., 1963—; attending otolaryngologist, chief otolaryngology Englewood Hosp.; assoc. attending otolaryngologist Vanderbilt Clinic and Presbyn. Hosp., N.Y.C.; past dir. facial plastic surgery clin.; assoc. prof. clin. otolaryngology Coll. Physicians and Surgeons, Columbia U.; dir., vice-chmn. bd. dirs. NVE Savs. Bank; past trustee Dwight-Englewood Sch.; bd. dirs. No. Valley chpt. ARC. Served to capt. M.C., AUS, 1964-66. Recipient Coakley Meml. prize in otolaryngology Columbia U., 1958; Marie and Henry Heiner fellow in otolaryngology, 1961-62; decorated Army Commendation medal. Fellow ACS, Internat. Coll. Surgeons, Am. Acad. Facial Plastic and Reconstructive Surgery, Am. Acad. Cosmetic Surgery, Am. Acad. Otolaryngology and Head and Neck Surgery; mem. AMA, Am. Speech and Hearing Assn. (cert. clin. competence in speech pathology and audiology), N.J. Med. Soc., Bergen County Med. Soc., N.Y. County Med. Soc., Bergen County Soc. Otolaryngologists, Head and Neck Surgeons (past pres.), N.Y. Laryngol. Soc. (past pres.), N.Y. Bronchoscopic Soc. (past pres.), N.Y. Otol. Soc. (past pres.), N.J. Soc. Cosmetic Surgery (trustee), N.J. Acad. Ophthalmology and Otolaryngology-Head and Neck Surgery (past pres.), Royal Soc. Medicine, First Presbyn. Ch. Mens Assn. (past pres.), Phi Beta Kappa, Alpha Omega Alpha, Nu Sigma Nu. Presbyterian (elder, past clk. of session, past pres. bd. trustees). Clubs: N.Y. Athletic; Englewood (past pres., Disting. Service award 1980), Knickerbocker Country. Lodge: Rotary (past pres.). Home: 436 Lewelen Cir Englewood NJ 07631-2021 Office: 216 Engle St Englewood NJ 07631-2428

STRAUSS, ROBERT PHILLIP, economics educator, director financial management; b. Cleve., May 11, 1944; s. Harry and Carrie Strauss; m. Celeste Gabrielle Meade, Jan. 11, 1980; children: Sarah Elizabeth, David Anthony, Elena Nicole. AB in Econs., U. Mich., 1966; MA, U. Wis., 1968, PhD in Econs., 1970. Asst. prof. U. N.C., 1969-73, assoc. prof., 1973-79; prof. econs. and pub. polity Carnegie Mellon U., Pitts., 1979—, assoc. dean Sch. Urban and Pub. Affairs, 1981-83, dir. ctr. for pub. fin. mgmt. Sch. Urban and Pub. Affairs, 1984-91. Author: (chpt.) Takeovers: Issues in Public and Corporate Policy, 1989. Member Pa. Local Tax Reform Commn., 1987, Revenue Estimating Adv. Com., 1989—; prin. advisor to chmn. House and Senate Fin. Com., W.Va. Legis., 1984-85; prin. researcher Wash. State Dept. of Revenue Study, 1986-87. Recipient Exceptional Svc. award U.S. Treasury, 1972, Disting. Svc. award Pitts. chpt. Tax Execs. Inst., 1987. Mem. Am. Acctg. Assn., Am. Econ. Assn., Am. Statis. Assn., Assn. Pub. Policy Analysis and Mgmt., Nat. Tax Assn., Econometric Soc., Cosmos Club. Office: Carnegie Mellon U Heinz Sch Pub Policy & Mgmt 5000 Forbes Ave Pittsburgh PA 15213-3816

STRAUSS, ULRICH PAUL, educator, chemist; b. Frankfurt, Germany, Jan. 10, 1920; s. Richard and Marianne (Seligmann) S.; m. Esther Lipetz, June 20, 1943 (dec. Sept. 1949); children—Dorothy, David; m. Elaine Greenbaum, Nov. 23, 1950; children—Elizabeth, Evelyn. A.B., Columbia U., 1941; Ph.D., Cornell U., 1944. Sterling fellow Yale U., 1946-48; faculty Rutgers U., New Brunswick, N.J., 1948—, prof. phys. chemistry, 1960-90, prof. emeritus, 1990—; also dir. Sch. Chemistry, 1965-71, chmn. dept. chemistry, 1974-80; prof. emeritus Rutgers U., 1990—. Mem. editorial adv. bd. Macromolecules, 1990—; contbr. articles to profl. jours. Recipient Sci. achievement award Johnson Wax Co., 1986; NSF sr. fellow Nat. Center Sci. Research, Strasbourg, France, 1961-62; Guggenheim fellow U. Oxford, Eng., 1971-72. Fellow N.Y. Acad. Scis.; mem. Am. Chem. Soc. (chmn. phys. chemistry group N.J. sect. 1956, councillor 1961-72, honored by 1-day symposium at nat. meeting N.Y.C. 1986). Home: 227 Lawrence Ave Highland Park NJ 08904-1837 Office: Dept Chemistry Rutgers U New Brunswick NJ 08903

STRAUSSNER, JOEL HARVEY, psychologist, psychotherapist; b. Bklyn., Apr. 7, 1947; s. William and Henrietta (Eddelson) S.; m. Shulamith L.

Ashenberg, Dec. 28, 1969; children: Adam, Sarika. PhD, Yeshiva U., 1982. Chief psychologist Queens (N.Y.) High Schs., 1986—; pvt. practice, N.Y.C., 1986—.

STRAZZELLA, JAMES ANTHONY, legal educator, lawyer; b. Hanover, Pa., May 18, 1939; s. Anthony F. and Teresa Ann (D'Alonzo) S.; m. Judith A. Coppola, Oct. 9, 1965; children: Jill M., Steven A., Tracy Ann, Michael P. AB Villanova U., 1961; JD, U. Pa., 1964. Bar: Pa. 1964, U.S. Ct. Appeals (3d cir.) 1964, D.C. 1965, U.S. Dist. Ct. D.C. 1965, U.S. Ct. Appeals (D.C. cir.) 1965, U.S. Dist Ct. (ea. and mid. dist.) Pa. 1969, U.S. Supreme Ct. 1969, U.S. Ct. Appeals (4th cir.) 1983. Law clk. to Hon. Samuel Roberts Pa. Supreme Ct., 1964-65; asst. U.S. atty. dept. chief appeals, spl. asst. to U.S. Atty., Washington, D.C., 1965-69; vice dean, asst. prof. law U. Pa., Phila., 1969-73; faculty Temple U., Phila., 1973—, James G. Schmidt Chair in law, 1989—, acting dean, 1987-89; chief counsel Kent State investigation Pres.'s Commn. Campus Unrest, 1970; chmn. Atty. Gen.'s Task Force on Family Violence, Pa., 1985-89; mem., chmn. justice ops. Mayor's Criminal Justice Coordinating Commn., Phila., 1983-85; Pa. Joint Council Criminal Justice, 1979-82; Com. to Study Pa.'s Unified Jud. System, 1980-82; Jud. Council Pa., 1972-82; chmn. criminal procedural rules com. Pa. Supreme Ct., 1972-85; mem. task force on prison overcrowding, 1983-85, rsch. adv. com. ,1988, Pa. Commn. on Crime and Delinquency; chmn. U.S. Magistrate Judge Merit Selection Com., U.S. Dist. Ct. (ea. dist.) Pa., 1989-91, mem., 1989-91; designate D.C. Com. on Adminstrv. Justice Under Emergency Conditions, 1968. Mem. adv. bd. dirs., past pres. A Better Chance in Lower Merion; dir. Hist. Fire Mus., Phila.; dir. Neighborhood Civic Assn. Bala-Cynwyd, Pa., 1984-87. Recipient Lindback Found. award for disting. teaching, 1983, Atty. Gen.'s Advancement of Justice award, 1989, Disting. Pub. Svc. award Assn. State and County Detectives, 1989, Spl. Merit award Pa. Assn. Police Chiefs, 1989. Fellow Am. Bar Found.; mem. Am. Law Inst., ABA (faculty appellate judges' seminars 1977-90, various coms.), Fed. Bar Assn. (Phila. Crim. Law com. adv. bd. 1988—, chmn. nat. law com. 1991—), Pa. Bar Assn. (commn. profl. standards 1981-84, chmn. criminal law sect., 1986-88, Spl. Merit award 1987), Phila. Bar Assn. (criminal justice sect., appellate cts. com., del. D.C. Jud. Conf. 1985), Order of the Coif (exec. bd. Pa.), St. Thomas More Soc. (pres., 1985-86, past dir. Phila. area). Roman Catholic. Contbr. articles to legal jours. Home and Office: 100 Maple Ave Bala Cynwyd PA 19004-3017 also: Temple U Law Sch 1719 N Broad St Philadelphia PA 19122

STREB, JACK MARTIN, photographic company executive; b. Rochester, N.Y., Aug. 14, 1931; s. Sylvester William and Cleo Winifred (Hungerford) S.; m. Natalie Harvey Kooker, June 12, 1954; children: William Bryan, Kendon Lee, Sheryl Ann. BS, Denison U., 1953; MS, Pa. State U., 1954; postgrad., U. N.C., 1954-55. Instr. U. N.C., Chapel Hill, 1954-55; with Eastman Kodak Co., Rochester, 1955-90, tech. editor, 1956-65, dir. pubs., 1965-69, product planning dir., 1970-79, mktg. dir., 1980-83, gen. mgr. mktg. and v.p. Electronic Photography div., 1984-90; founder, pres. Streb Enterprises, Consulting, 1990—; adj. prof. mktg. Rochester Inst. Tech., 1991. Editor photography sect. Grolier Book of Knowledge, 1976. Chmn. Scout Troop 127, Rochester; bd. dirs. West Irindequoit Found., Rochester, 1987-89; trustee, elder Summerville Presbyn. Ch., Rochester, 1969-75, 90-91; pres. Sixth and Seventh Lake Improvement Assn., Inc., 1990-92; dir. pub. rels. Flower City Habitat for Humanity, 1992. Mem. Photo Mktg. Assn. Internat., Internat. Teleconferencing Assn., Am. Antique Automobile Assn., (assoc.) Photographic Soc. Am. Mem. Am. Antique Automobile Assn. (assoc.), Photographic Soc. Am. Republican. Presbyterian. Home: 69 Lake Lea Rd Rochester NY 14617-1927 Office: Streb Enterprises 69 Lake Lea Rd Rochester NY 14617-1927 also: HC02 Box 365 Inlet NY 13360

STREET, JAMES STEWART, geology educator, consultant; b. Chgo., July 26, 1934; s. Frank William and Letha M. (Frost) S.; m. Sarah Cunningham, Sept. 3, 1957; children: James S. Jr., Anne F., David M. AA, Wright Coll., Chgo., 1955; BS, U. Ill., 1958; MS, Syracuse U., 1963, PhD, 1966. Geologist Texaco, Inc., New Orleans, 1965-66; dir., N.Y. State Tech. Svc. Program in Geology St. Lawrence U., Canton, N.Y., 1966-70, assoc. prof., 1972-78, prof., 1978—, dept. chmn., 1976-81, 87-88, 1991, dir. acad. summerterm, 1986-87, James Henry Chapin prof. geology, 1990—; vis. prof. geology U. S.C., Columbia, 1991—. Mem. Geol. Soc. Am., Internat. Assn. Quaternary Rsch., Am. Quaternary Assn., History of the Earth Scis. Soc., Empire State Pedologists Assn., Coun. on Undergrad. Rsch., Sigma Xi. Office: St Lawrence Univ Dept of Geology Canton NY 13617

STREET, PATRICIA LYNN, educator; b. Lillington, N.C., May 3, 1940; d. William Banks and Vandalia (McLean) S.; m. Col. Robert Gest, June 2, 1962 (div. 1985); children: Robert, Roblyn Renee. BS, Livingstone Coll., 1962; MEd, Salisbury State U., 1974; postgrad., various, 1968—. Tchr. Govt. of Guam Marianas Island, Agana, Guam, 1962-64; sec., typist USAF, Glasgow AFB, Mont., 1964-65, Syracuse (N.Y.) U. AeroSpace Engring., 1966-67; tchr. Syracuse (N.Y.) City Sch. System, 1967-69; lectr. U. of Md., Eastern Shore, Princess Anne, Md., 1970-72; tchr. Prince George's County Pub. Schs., Upper Marlboro, Md., 1973—; instr. U. Guam, Anderson AFB, 1963, U.S. Armed Forces Inst., Anderson AFB, 1963, Yorktowne Bus. Inst., Landover, Md., 1987-90, Cheseapeake Bus. Inst., Clinton, Md., 1983-89; asst. advisor student tchrs. U. Md. Ea. Shore, Princess Anne, 1972; adj. instr. Bowie State U., 1990—; conv. speaker. Mem. AAUW, NEA, ASCD, Am. Vocat. Assn., Md. Bus. Edn. Assn. (pres.-elect 1987-88, pres. 1988-89, Educator of Yr. 1989), Md. Vocat. Assn. (regional rep. 1986-89, audit chmn. 1987-89, Vocat.-Tech. Educator of Yr. 1989), Ea. Bus. Edn. Assn. (co-editor newsletter 1990-91, secondary exec. dir. 1991—), Md. State Tchrs. Assn., D.C. Bus. Edn. Assn., Nat. Bus. Edn. Assn., Data Processing Mgmt. Assn., Internat. Soc. for Bus. Edn., Md. Bus. Edn. Com., Prince George's County Edn. Assn., New Eng. Bus. Educators Assn., Balt. Coun. Fgn. Affairs. Democrat. Baptist. Home: 8922 Goldfield Pl Clinton MD 20735-2024 Office: Prince George's Pub Sch Upper Marlboro MD 20772

STREET, RONALD E., artist; b. San Anselmo, Calif., Sept. 27, 1950; s. Oscar Richard and Mary Theresa (Zaro) S. Student, U. Calif., Davis, 1969, Coll. of Marin, 1970, The Johnson Atelier Inst., 1978, Art Student League, N.Y., 1979. Tchr. ceramics and glass blowing Perth Tech. Coll., 1973-75; tchr. glassblowing and sculpture West Australian Inst. Tech., Perth, 1973-75; master glassblower Maslack Art Glass, Greenbra, Calif., 1975-78; projects coord. Modern Art Foundry, 1978-79; asst. to mgr. Alva Mus. Replicas, 1979-80; mgr. molding, devel. and rsch. Met. Mus. of Art, N.Y.C., 1980—; owner Chateau du Bateau Sculpture Svc., N.Y.C., 1986—; cons. Egyptian Antiquities Orgn., Cairo, 1989-90, Italian Nat. Restoration, Mussa Cannara, Italy, 1988-89; lectr. in field. Exhibited at group shows at LaPaix Gallery, Trenton, N.J., 1990, Quietude Gallery, Granberry, N.J., 1990, City Without Walls, Newark, N.J., 1990, St. Hubert's Giralda, Madison, N.J., 1991, Carrier Arts Found., Belle Mead, N.J., 1991; represented in permanent collections Mutual Benefits Life Ins., Nat. Gallery , Sydney, Asutralia, West Australian Mus., Perth. Home: 44 Oliver St Newark NJ 07105-1118

STREETEN, PAUL PATRICK, economist, educator; b. Vienna, Austria, July 18, 1917; came to U.S., 1976.; m. Ann Hilary Higgins, June 9, 1951; stepchild, Jay D. Palmer; children: Patricia D., Judith A. MA, Aberdeen (Scotland) U., 1943, LLD (hon.), 1980; BA, Oxford (Eng.) U., 1947, MA, 1952, DLitt, 1976. Fellow Balliol Coll. Oxford U., 1947-66, 68-78; prof. U. Sussex, Brighton, Eng., 1966-68; warden, dir. Queen Elizabeth House Inst. Commonwealth Studies, Oxford, 1968-78; spl. advisor World Bank, Washington, 1976-80; prof. Boston U., 1980—, dir. Asian Ctr., 1980-84, dir. World Devel. Inst., 1984-90; vis. prof. World Bank, Washington, 1984-86; dep. dir-gen. Ministry Overseas Devel., London, 1964-66; fellow dir. Inst. Devel. Studies, Brighton, 1966-68, vice chmn. governing body, 1968-76; mem. governing body Overseas Devel. Inst., Eng., 1970-79; chmn. edn. bd. dirs. World Devel., Oxford/U.S.; trustee Found. for Internat. Studies, U. Malta; mem. statutory commn. Royal U., Malta, 1972—; acad. advisor Overseas Devel. Coun., 1979-80; Raffaele Mattioli lectr., Milan, Italy, 1991; Jean Monnet prof. European Univ. Inst., Florence, 1991. Author: Economic Integration, 1961, Frontiers Development Studies, 1972, Development Perspectives, 1981, First Things First, 1981, What Price Food, 1987, Beyond Adjustment, 1988, Moblilizing Human Potential, 1989. Mem. Royal Commn. Environ. Pollution, 1974-76; bd. dirs. Commonwealth Devel. Corp., 1967-72. Served as sgt. Commandos, Brit. Army, 1941-43. Fellow Inst. Devel. Studies (hon.), 1980, Balliol Coll. (hon.), 1986; recipient Devel. prize Justus Liebig U., 1987. Mem. Royal Econ. Soc., Am. Econ. Assn., Soc. Internat. Devel. Council (pres. U.K.). Club: United Oxford and Cambridge Univ. (London). Home: PO Box 92 Spencertown NY 12165-0092

STREETER, BERNARD ALBRA, JR., medical facility foundation director; b. Keene, N.H., Feb. 6, 1935; s. Bernard A. Sr. and Isabella Cameron (Crane) S.; m. Janice Bowman, Aug. 30, 1958; children: Shannon Lea, Christopher Bowman, Stephanie Crane. BS, Boston U., 1957. Dir. pub. rels. Colby Sawyer Coll., New London, N.H., 1959-63, Am. Cancer Soc., Boston, 1963-66; dir. devel. Somerville (Mass.) Hosp., 1966-68; v.p. devel. St. John's Hosp., Lowell, Mass., 1968—, found. v.p., exec. dir., 1968—; exec. councilor State of N.H., Concord, 1969—; bd. dirs. The Plus Co. Dir. Am. Stage Festival, 1991—. Sgt. USAF Res., 1957-63. Recipient Outstanding Hosp. Pub. Rels. award Mass. Hosp. Assn., 1969, 71; named Outstanding Young Man of the Yr., N.H. Jaycees, 1966. Mem. Assn. for Health Care Philanthropy, Am. Hosp. Assn., Am. Hosp. Pub. Rels. and Mktg. Republican. Methodist. Home: 26 Indiana Dr Nashua NH 03060-5132 Office: St Johns Found PO Box 30 Lowell MA 01853-0030

STREHLE, GLENN PRESTON, university administrator; b. Schenectady, Mar. 22, 1936; s. Milton John and Ruth (Preston) S.; m. Katherine Conde Howe, June 29, 1963; children: Paul Conde, Andrew Preston, John Wilcox. BS, MIT, 1958, MS, 1960. CFA. Salesman Procter & Gamble Co., Boston, 1958-59; security analyst Colonial Mgmt. Assocs., Inc., Boston, 1962-68, v.p., 1968-75; treas. MIT, Cambridge, 1975-86, v.p., treas., 1986—; bd. dirs. SofTech, Waltham, Mass., BayBanks, Inc., Boston, Liberty Mut. Ins. Co., Boston. Trustee, chmn. The Common Fund for Non-Profit Orgns., Fairfield, Conn., 1977-88, 83-86; chmn. standing com. First Parish in Weston, Mass., 1981-83. 1st lt. U.S. Army, 1959. Recipient Bronze Beaver award, MIT Alumni Assn., 1974. Mem. Assn. for Investment Mgmt. and Rsch., Boston Security Analysts Soc. (pres. 1973-74), Boston Econ. Club (pres. 1978-79), Treas. Club of Boston. Home: 188 Country Dr Weston MA 02193-1136 Office: MIT 77 Massachusetts Ave # 4-204 Cambridge MA 02139-4307

STREIT, ALLAN LEE, chemist; b. N.Y.C., Aug. 1, 1950; s. Murray Aron and Ann (Fein) S.; m. Denise DiCorcia, Sept. 26, 1980; children: Nicole, Jessica. AAS in Chem. Tech., CUNY, 1972; BA in Chemistry, Jersey City State U., 1976; MA in Chemistry, Fairleigh Dickinson U., 1990. Project team leader Rickitt & Colman, Carlstadt, N.J., 1972-80; group leader L & F Products, Montvale, N.J., 1980—; mem. CSMA Task Force, Washington, 1990—, John Hopkins CAAT, Balt., 1990—. Patentee in field. Cpl. USMC, 1968-70. Home: 676 Cobh Rd River Vale NJ 07675 Office: L & F Products Tech Ctr 1 Philips Pky Montvale NJ 07645-1810

STREIT, FRANCES NORRIS, artist; b. Macy, Ind., May 22, 1918; d. Elmer Lee and Faye Hume (Hammond) Norris; m. George B. Streit, Aug. 1, 1943 (dec. 1988); children: Robert William, Kathryn Louise Streit Hyatt. BFA, John Herron Art Sch., 1940; MFA, State U. Iowa, 1942; postgrad., Ind. U., 1940-42, Adelphi U., 1966. Cert. tchr., N.Y. Portrait painter 1940—; art tchr. Nassau Community Coll., Garden City, N.Y., 1965-66, Valley Stream (N.Y.) Cen. High Sch., 1967-73. Exhibited prin. works in numerous exhbns. including 3d Ann. Nat. Exhbn. Am. Art N.Y.C., Art League Long Island, Allied Artists Am., Country Art Gallery, Merrick Art Gallery, South Huntington Libr., Fine Arts Mus. Long Island, Camberwell Libr. Collection, Corcoran Gallery, Washington, Smithsonian Art Inst. Gallery, Washington, Carnegie Inst., Pitts.; commd. for numerous portraits including Gen. David M. Shoup, Gov. George N. Craig, Dr. Robert H. Wyatt, Dr. J. Dan Hull, many others; hist. murals include Bellmores, N.Y., Farmingdale, N.Y., West Hempstead, N.Y., Milleridge Inn, Jericho, N.Y., Recreation Ctr. Freeport, Roslyn Savs. Bank. Mem. Nat. Soc. Mural Painters, Mus. Women in Arts, DAR. Home and Office: 301 Lincoln Blvd Merrick NY 11566

STRELKA, JOSEPH PETER, German educator; b. Weiner Neustadt, Austria, May 3, 1927; came to U.S., 1964; s. Joseph and Maria (Lisetz) S.; m. Brigitte Olga Vollmer, July 13, 1963; 1 child, Alexandra Claudia. PhD, U. Vienna, Austria, 1950. Head mcpl. cultural dept. City of Wiener Neustadt, 1950-51; chmn. sect. literary criticism Inst. fur Wissenschaft und Kunst, Vienna, 1952-57; freelance literary critic Austrian Broadcasting Corp., 1955-57; fellow Theodor Koerner Found., 1959-60; rsch. fellow Austrian Cultural Inst., Paris, 1961; assoc. prof. U. So. Calif., L.A., 1964-65; prof. German, Pa. State U., State College, 1966-71, SUNY, Albany, 1971—; vis. prof. Free U. Berlin, 1980, U. Augsburg, Fed. Republic Germany, 1981, U. Witwatersrand, Johannesburg, Republic South Africa, 1981, U. Parma, Italy, 1983. Author 16 books, 1957—; editor over 50 books, 1954—; mem. editorial bd. Collquia Germanica, 1972—, Modern Austrian Lit., 1972—, Mich. Germanic Studies, 1974—, Comparative Lit. Studies, 1987—. Decorated Cross of Honor for Arts Scis. 1st class (Austria); recipient award Theodor Körner Found., 1955, 56, 57, City of Vienna, 1959, medal of honor U. Parma, 1983; Festschrift in his honor, 1987. Mem. Am. Coun. for Study Austrian Lit. (v.p. 1981—), Humboldt Soc. (exec. bd. 1982—), Internat. Music Soc. (exec. bd. 1974—, v.p. 1992—), Internat. PEN Club. Home: 2131 Rice Rd Hope Falls Northville NY 12134 Office: SUNY 1400 Washington Ave Albany NY 12222-0001

STRIANO, JOHN A., insurance agency executive; b. Boston, Dec. 7, 1942; s. John Louis and Lucy Mary (Perrone) S.; m. Mary V. Rossetti, 1965; children: Linda A., Kathy A. BBA, U. Mass., 1965. Cert. ins. counselor; lic. ins. advisor, Mass. Mktg. rep. Atlantic Richfield Co., Phila., 1965-67; sales engr. Liquid Carbonic Corp., Tewksbury, Mass., 1967-73; dist. sales mgr. Allstate Ins. Co., Farmington, Conn., 1973-78; sales mgr. OBrion Russell Ins. Agy., Boston, 1978-83; v.p. Alexander & Alexander Ins. Brokers, Boston, 1983-84; pres., chief operating officer MacIntyre Fay & Thayer Ins. Agy., Newton, Mass., 1984—. Recipient awards for sales and managerial accomplishments in ins. industry. Mem. Cert. Ins. Counselors, Met. Yacht Club (Braintree, Mass.), Lambda Chi Alpha. Republican. Roman Catholic. Office: MacIntyre Fay & Thayer Ins 60 Wells Ave Newton MA 02159

STRICKLAND, CAROL COLCLOUGH, freelance writer; b. New Orleans, Oct. 7, 1946; d. John Ashby and Rebecca Ann (Prater) Colclough; m. Sidney Strickland, Apr. 11, 1968; children: Alison, Eliza. BA, Rhodes Coll., 1968; MA, U. Mich., 1969, PhD, 1973. Lectr. LaGuardia Community Coll., N.Y.C., 1974; asst. prof. Stevens Inst. Technology, Hoboken, N.J., 1974-81; editor/writer Courier mag., Geneva, 1986-87, Biotechnology Newsletter/SUNY, Stony Brook, 1990-91; freelance writer Setauket, N.Y., 1988—; adj. asst. prof. Rutgers U., Newark, 1974, L.I. U., Southampton, N.Y., 1983-84, SUNY, Stony Brook, 1984-86. Contbr. articles to New York Times, Wall Street Journal and various popular mags. Home and Office: 12 Coraway Rd East Setauket NY 11733-2266

STRICKLAND, STEPHEN PARKS, foundation executive; b. Birmingham, Ala., Nov. 25, 1933; s. Kelly Parks and Alice (Peeples) S.; m. Tamara Diana Gunsard, June 15, 1962. AB, Emory U., Atlanta, 1956; MA, Johns Hopkins U., Balt., 1966; PhD, Johns Hopkins U., 1971. Adminstrv. asst. Congressman George Huddleston, Jr., Washington, 1959-63; chief clk. and study dir. U.S. Ho. of Reps. Select Com. on Govt. Research, Washington, 1963-65; exec. sec. com. on sponsored research Am. Council on Edn., Washington, 1965-67; assoc. dir./acting dir. Pres. Comm. on White House Fellows, Washington, 1967-69; cons. on edn., 1969-71; founding faculty health policy program U. Calif., San Francisco, 1972-77; v.p. Aspen Inst., N.Y.C., 1977-84; sr. assoc. Kettering Found., Washington, 1984—; pres. Nat. Peace Found., Washington, 1988—. Author: Politics, Science and Dread Disease, 1972, Research on the Health of Americans, 1978, The Story of the NIH Grants Programs, 1989, U.S. Health Care: What's Right and What's Wrong, 1972; co-author: (with Douglass Cater) TV Violence and the Child, 1982, others; editor/co-author: Hugo Black and the Supreme Court, 1967, Sponsored Research in American Universities and Colleges, 1967. Bd. dirs. Washington Performing Arts Soc., 1985—, Friends of the Nat. Library of Medicine, Washington, 1985—; hon. trustee, former chmn. Choral Arts Soc. of Washington. Congl. Staff fellow, Am. Polit. Sci. Assn./Ford Found., 1965-66, others. Mem. Assn. of History of Medicine, Cosmos Club, Federal City Club. Home: 3010 32nd St NW Washington DC 20008-3417 Office: Nat Peace Found 1835 K St NW Washington DC 20006

STRICKLIN, CARL SPENCER, manufacturing company executive; b. Baconton, Ga., Nov. 23, 1917; s. Daniel Spencer and Alberta (Clarkson) S.; m. Constance Allen, Aug. 26, 1949; 1 child, Sandra Lee. BS in Bus. Adminstrn., cert. in fin., Boston U., 1950. Clk. stock control Eastern Air Lines, Miami, Fla., 1947; auditor Ernst & Ernst, Boston, 1950-54; asst. bus. mgr. Mass. Bible Soc., Boston, 1954-64, bus. mgr., 1964-74, dir., 1974-77, editor Comment, semi-monthly publ., 1974-77; v.p. fin., contr. Eastern Reprodn. Corp., Waltham, Mass., 1977-79; treas. Ivy Packet Co., Inc., Canton, Mass., 1980-84, pres., 1985-88, chief exec. officer, 1988—. Treas., trustee Daystar Found., Inc., non-profit retirement home, Needham, Mass. Served with Q.M.C., U.S. Army, 1942-46. Mem. Mass. Soc. CPAs, Mass. Assn. Pub. Accts., Nat. Soc. Pub. Accts., Aircraft Owners and Pilots Assn., Norwood Aviation Club, Young Man's Christian Union Camera Club (treas.), Masons, Shriners, Rotary (treas. Needham). Republican. Home and Office: 1019 Webster St Needham MA 02192-3216

STRIDER, MARJORIE VIRGINIA, artist, educator; b. Guthrie, Okla.; d. Clifford R. and Marjorie E. (Schley) S. BFA, Kansas City Art Inst., 1962. Mem. faculty Sch. Visual Arts, N.Y.C., 1970—; artist-in-residence City U. Grad. Center Mall, N.Y.C., 1976, Fabric Workshop, Phila., 1978, Grassi Palace, Venice, Italy, 1978. One-woman shows of sculpture, drawings and/or prints include, Nancy Hoffman Gallery, N.Y.C., 1973, 74, Weather Spoon Mus., U. N.C., Chapel Hill, 1974, City U. Grad. Center Mall, 1976, Clocktower, N.Y.C., 1976, Sculpture Center, N.Y.C., 1983, Steinbaum Gallery, N.Y.C., 1983, 84; exhibited in group shows The Sculpture Center, N.Y.C., 1981, Aldrich Mus., Ridgefield, Conn., 1981, New Mus., N.Y.C., 1981, Drawing Bienalle, Lisbon, 1981, C.W. Post Coll., L.I., N.Y., 1981, Useable Art travelling show, N.Y. State, 1981-82, Grey Art Gallery, N.Y.C., 1981; represented in permanent collections Guggenheim Mus., N.Y.C., U. Colo., Boulder, Albright-Knox Mus., Buffalo, Des Moines Art Center, Storm King (N.Y.) Art Center, Larry Aldrich Mus., Ridgefield, Conn., City U. Grad. Center, N.Y.C., Hirschhorn Mus. and Sculpture Garden, Washington, also pvt. collections. Nat. Endowment for Arts grantee, 1973, 80, Longview Found. grantee, 1974, Pollock-Krasner Found. grantee, 1990, Florsheim Art Fund grantee, 1991; Va. Ctr. for Creative Arts fellow, 1974.

STRIDSBERG, ALBERT BORDEN, advertising consultant, educator, editor; b. Wyoming, Ohio, July 22, 1929; s. Carl Alexander Herbert and Edith Vivian (Farley) S. BA with honors, Yale U., 1950; Diplome D'Etudes Franc., U. of Poitiers, Tours, France, 1951; postgrad., Am. U. Beirut, Lebanon, 1953-54; diploma, Direct Mktg. Inst., 1986. Copywriter Howard Swink Advt., Inc., Marion, Ohio, 1955-58; acct. supr. McCann-Erickson, Co., Brussels, 1958-60, J. Walter Thompson Co., Amsterdam, The Netherlands, 1960-63; asst. to internat. exec. v.p. J. Walter Thompson Co., N.Y.C., 1963-67, internat. cons. spl. projects, acquisitions and diversifications, 1969-73; cons., coord. Internat. Markets Advt. Agy., Inc., N.Y., London, 1967-69; editor-in-chief Advt. World mag., N.Y.C., 1975-77; lectr. in mktg. NYU, N.Y.C., 1978-84; lectr. in advt. Marist Coll., Poughkeepsie, N.Y., 1984—; U.S. features editor Media Internat. Mag., London, 1984-90; assoc. prof. NYU, 1966-78; ind. cons., freelance writer on advt. and mktg. issues, N.Y.C., 1972—; seminar leader, Lagos, Nigeria, 1991. Author: Effective Advertising Self-Regulation, 1974, Progress Toward Advertising Self Regulation, 1976, Controversy Advertising, 1977, Advertising Self-Regulation, 1980. With U.S. Army, 1951-53. Fulbright fellow U. Poitiers, 1950-51, Ford. Found. fellow Beirut U., 1953-54. Mem. Internat. Advt. Assn. (cons., project coord. 1974-80), Am. Mktg. Assn., Advt. Rsch. Found., Direct Mktg. Assn., Am. Acad. Advt., Yale Club N.y.C., Elizabethan Club New Haven. Democrat. Episcopalian. Home and Office: 28 S Clover St Poughkeepsie NY 12601-3005 Office: Lowell Thomas Communications Ctr Marist Coll Poughkeepsie NY 12601-1387

STRIEGEL, JEFFERY A., carpeting company executive; b. Balt., Mar. 13, 1958; s. John Francis and Ruth (Martin) S.; m. Doris Patricia Srtiegel (div. Feb. 1980); m. Rosemary Gloria Striegel, Feb. 21, 1986; children: Jeff A., Mike H., Nicky M. Gen. sales mgr. Carpet Fair Inc., Balt., 1975-85; v.p., CEO Elias Wilf Corp., Owings Mills, Md., 1985—; cons. Mannington Carpets, Dalton, Ga., 1990, BASF Fibers, Williamsburg, W.Va., 1990-91; trainer and speaker in field. Author: Wholesale Floorcover Sales Professional, 1991, Retail Sales Professional, 1991; pub./owner (catalog) Floorcovering Bits and Pieces, 1991-92. Mem. Am. Investor's Assn., Am. Floorcovering Assn., Nat. Assn. Floorcovering Distbrs. (Exec. of Yr. 1991), Mid-Atlantic Floorcovering Assn. (Man of Yr. 1991), Tae Kwondo Assn., Aikidio Assn. Am. Home: 44 Sandstone Baltimore MD 21236

STRIEGEL, LAWRENCE WILLIAM, editor; b. Monterey, Calif., June 18, 1957; s. Edward F. and Mary Elizabeth Striegel. BA in Communication Arts, Marist Coll., 1979; BA in Religious Studies, U. Dayton, 1984; MA in Journalism, Ohio State U., 1985. Asst. news editor, Part II Newsday, 1987—. Office: Newsday Long Island NY 11747

STRIER, MURRAY PAUL, chemist, consultant; b. N.Y.C., Oct. 19, 1923; s. Jack and Rose (Goldman) S.; m. Arlene Schimmel, Feb. 12, 1955; children: Sheri Jeanette, Karen Barbara, Robin Joy. BChemE, CCNY, 1944; MS, Emory U., 1947; PhD, U. Ky., 1952. Rsch. chemist Reaction Motors Inc. (named changed to Thiokol Co.), Denville, N.J., 1952-56; sect. head Air Reduction, Inc., Murray Hill, N.J., 1956-58; chief chmist Fulton-Irgan Corp. (now Inc. with Lithium Corp.), Lake Denmark, N.J., 1958-59; supr. Rayonier, Inc., Whippany, N.J., 1959-61; rsch. chemist McGraw Edison Co., West Orange, N.J., 1961-64; sr. rsch. scientist McDonnell Douglas Corp., Newport Beach, Calif., 1964-69; rsch. assoc. Hooker Rsch. Ctr., Grand Island, N.Y., 1969-71; phys. scientist EPA, Washington, 1972-86; cons. Rockville, Md., 1986—; instr. analytical chem. Upsala Coll., East Orange, N.J., 1963-64; cons. electroplating NSF, Washington, 1973-75. Contbr. articles to Jour. Am. Chem. Soc., Jour. Electrochem. Soc., Jour. Environ. Sci. & Tech. Commr. sci. and tech. commn. City of Rockville, 1985—; vol. office consumer affairs Montgomery County, Rockville, 1989-90, dept. environ. protection, 1989-90. With USNR, 1944-46. Recipient Gold medal EPA, Washington, 1979. Fellow Am. Inst. Chemists (cert.); mem. AAAS, ASTM, Am. Chem. Soc., Electrochem. Soc.

STRIKE, DONALD PETER, pharmaceutical research director, research chemist; b. Mt. Carmel, Pa., Oct. 24, 1936; s. Peter and Veronica (Dugan) S.; m. Sally Ann Cavanaugh, July 28, 1972; children: Brian, Samantha. BS in Chemistry, Phila. Coll. Pharmacy & Sci., 1958; MS, Iowa State U., 1960, PhD, 1963. Rsch. chemist Wyeth Labs., Radnor, Pa., 1965-69, group leader, 1969-77, mgr., 1977-87; assoc. dir. Wyeth-Ayerst Rsch., Princeton, N.J., 1987—. Contbr. articles to sci. jours.; author 53 patents in field. NIH postdoctoral rsch. fellow Southampton U., Eng., 1963-64. Mem. Am. Chem. Soc. (medicinal chemistry and organic chemistry sects.), Phila. Organic Chemist Club, Phi Delta Chi, Phi Lambda Upsilon. Democrat. Roman Catholic. Home: 445 Iven Ave Wayne PA 19087-4828 Office: Wyeth-Ayerst Rsch CN-8000 Princeton NJ 08543

STRINE, LINDA HULL, federal agency administrator; b. Hagerstown, Md., Jan. 18, 1953; d. James Floyd and Virginia (Messersmith) S. BS, Towson (Md.) State U., 1975; MPA, U. Balt., 1980. Sr. staff asst. to U.S. senator Charles McC. Mathias, Washington, 1975-86; rsch. analyst, spl. asst. Fed. Hwy. Adminstrn. U.S. Dept. Transp., 1986-87, dep. dir. program affairs Office of the Sec., 1987—. Member Rep. Women's Fed. Forum, Washington, 1987-90, Marian Martin Rep. Club, Washington, 1987-90, Jr. League of Balt., Inc., 1983-86; v.p., mem. Rep. Women of Capitol Hill, Washington, 1980-90. Mem. AIAA, Am. News Womens Club, Am. Astron. Soc., Am. Soc. Pub. Adminstrn. (bd. dirs., v.p. 1981-89, Pioneer of the Yr. award), Nat. Space Soc. (chair award com., conf. chmn., Pioneer of the Yr. award 1991), Women's Transp. Seminar, Women in Aerospace (pres. Springfield, Va. chpt. 1990—), Delta Nu Alpha (Appreciation award 1990). Methodist. Home: 1200 Braddock Pl Apt 808 Alexandria VA 22314-1667 Office: US Dept Transp Office of the Sec 400 7th St SW Washington DC 20590-0002

STRITTMATER, VICTORIA MOULTON, communications executive; b. Balt., May 27, 1954; d. William Guildea Sr. and Mary Eileen (Taylor) Moulton; m. Richard Christian Strittmater, Apr. 29, 1989. BA in Communications cum laude, Notre Dame of Md., Balt., 1980. Coord. publs. and spl. projects Mayor's Office, Balt., 1980-82; advt. coord. Md. Casualty Co., Balt., 1982-85; staff writer The Union Meml. Hosp., Balt., 1985-87; cons. The Forte Group, Alexandria, Va., 1987-89; dir. communications Am. Cancer Soc., Balt., 1989—, White Marsh, Md., 1990—. Mem. Md. Coalition on Smoking or Health, Balt., 1990—. Mem. Internat. Assn. Bus. Com-

municators (Balt. chpt., Print Communication award 1980, Design award 1985, Writing award 1985), Balt. Pub. Rels. Coun., Pub. Rels. Soc. Am. (Internal Communications award 1979). Democrat. Roman Catholic. Home: 2412 Madison Ave Baltimore MD 21217-4038 Office: Am Cancer Soc 8219 Town Center Dr PO Box 43026 Baltimore MD 21236-0026

STRITZINGER, JOHN LOUIS, data processing executive; b. Buffalo, Dec. 11, 1955; s. Edgar Debus and Rosemarie (Stein) S.; m. Alix Amar, Aug. 7, 1982; children: Zachary, Nathaniel. BS, U. Del., Newark, 1977. Programmer ICC, Ft. Washington, Pa., 1977-80, program mgr., 1980-83, project mgr., 1984-88, asst. v.p., 1989-90, v.p., 1991—. Developer CD-ROM software. Mem. ACM, IEEE. Home: 1008 Prospect Ave Philadelphia PA 19126-1205 Office: ICC 475 Virginia Dr Fort Washington PA 19034-2792

STRNISA, FRED, physicist; b. Cleve., Nov. 20, 1941; s. Fred and Josephine Strnisa; m. Diana Anderson; children: Jeanette, Jennifer, Jeannine. BS in Physics, Case Western Res. U., 1963; MS in Physics, John Carroll U., 1967; PhD in Physics, SUNY, Albany, 1972; MBA, Rensselaer Poly. Inst., 1990. Engr. lamp div. Gen. Electric, Cleve., 1963-67; physicist Gen. Electric Knolls Atomic Power Lab., Schenectady, N.Y., 1967-69; rsch. assoc. SUNY, Albany, 1969-73; sr. scientist N.Y. State Atomic Energy Coun., Albany, 1973-76; project mgr. N.Y. State Energy Office, Albany, 1976-77; dir. N.Y. State Energy R&D Authority, Albany, 1977—; mem. several nat. panels and adv. coms. concerning energy policy, issues and techs. Contbr. articles to profl. jours. Recipient Nat. Energy Innovation award U.S. Dept. Energy Innovation award U.S. Dept. Energy, 1984, Gov.'s award for mgmt. and productivity N.Y. State, 1989. Fellow Sunya Inst. for Study of Defects in Solids; mem. Internat. Dist. Heating and Cooling Assn. (Pub. Svc. Leadership award 1992), Sigma Pi Sigma. Home: RR 1 Box 389A Pattersonville NY 12137-9642 Office: NY State Energy R&D Author 2 Rockefeller Pla Albany NY 12223

STROBEL, RICHARD CHARLES, lawyer; b. Camden, N.J., Aug. 9, 1963; s. Frank Charles and Helen Dolores (Hoag) S. BA, St. Joseph's U., 1985; JD, Rutgers U., 1988. Legis. asst. Congressman H. James Saxton, Washington, 1985; law clk. Camden (N.J.) County Prosecutor's Office, 1986-87; summer assoc. Parker, McCay & Criscuolo, Marlton, N.J., 1987; clinic-in-law clk. U.S. Magistrate Jerome B. Simandle, Camden, N.J., 1987-88; assoc. Farr, Wolf & Lyons, Bellmawr, N.J., 1988-89; field dir. Edwards '89 Com., East Brunswick, N.J., 1989; counsel to the gov. N.J. Gov. Thomas H. Kean, Trenton, N.J., 1989-90; counsel County of Burlington, Mount Holly, N.J., 1990—; bd. govs. St. Josephs U. Mem. editorial bd. N.J. Lawyers Jour., 1990—. Chmn. Cinnaminson (N.J.) Rep. Orgn., 1988—, Cinnaminson Twp. Environ. Commn., 1987—; Cinnaminson Twp. Planning Bd., 1988—; county committeeman Burlington County Rep. Com., Mt. Holly, 1984—; mem. Burlington County Mil. Affairs Com., 1991—; platform com. N.J. Rep. Party, 1991. Named to Outstanding Young Men of Am., 1987; recipient Outstanding Citizen award Twp. of Cinnaminson, 1988. Mem. ABA, N.J. State Bar Assn. (mem. com. on profl. ethics 1990—, membership com. 1990—), Pa. Bar Assn., World Affairs Coun. Phila., N.J. Fedn. Planning Ofcls., Young Reps. (Pres. award 1989-90, parliamentarian 1989—, exec. bd. 1989—), PanAm. Assn. Phila., Rotary, KC, Alpha Sigma Nu, Pi Sigma Alpha, Omicron Delta Epsilon, Phi Alpha Delta. Roman Catholic. Republican. Home: 2306 Laurel Dr Cinnaminson NJ 08077-3827 Office: County of Burlington 1015 Woodlane Rd Mount Holly NJ 08060-3392

STROHL, TOM ASHLEY, counselor; b. Allentown, Pa., Nov. 29, 1954; s. Kenneth Elmer and Jean Leontine (Shaffer) S.; m. Elizabeth Sue Glenfield, June 9, 1979; children: Jonathan, David, Jenifer. BA in Psychology, U. Dayton, 1975; MEd in Counseling, Lehigh U., 1981; Cert. Adv. Grad. Study in Counseling, Coll. William and Mary, 1982. Nat. cert. counselor; cert. mental health counselor; cert. reality therapist; lic. psychologist, Pa. Counselor Wiley House, Bethlehem, Pa., 1976-81, Carrier Found., Belle Mead, N.J., 1982-83, Deveroux Found., Chester, N.J., 1983-84, St. Lukes Hosp, Bethlehem, 1984-86; pvt. practice counseling Allentown, Pa., 1986—; mem. faculty Inst. Reality Therapy, L.A., 1988—; cons. Big Bros./Big Sisters of Lehigh Valley, Allentown, 1989—. Contbg. author: Control Theory in the Practice of Reality Therapy (Naomi Glasser), 1989. Mem. APA, AACD, Am. Mental Health Counselors Assn., Inst. Reality Therapy. Office: 5000 W Tilghman St Bldg 147 Allentown PA 18104-9121

STROHLEIN, STEPHEN SANTO, physician; b. Bklyn., Apr. 7, 1953; s. James Michael and Carmella (LaSenna) S.; m. Annette Vazquez-Aran, June 8, 1985; children: Lisa Marie, Marissa Lynn. BA in Biology, Lafayete Coll., Easton, Pa., 1976; MD in Surgery, U. Rome (Italy), 1982. Diplomate Am. Bd. Internal Medicine and Gastroenterology. Intern, resident Interfaith Med. Ctr., Bklyn., 1982-84, chief resident in medicine, 1984-85, fellow in Gastroenterology, 1985-86; sr. fellow in Gastroenterology Tufts U., Boston, 1986-87; mem. staff in Gastroenterology Pocono Med. Ctr., East Stroudsburg, Pa., 1987—, dir. Endoscopy, 1988—. Fellow Am. Coll. Gastroenterology; mem. ACP, AMA, NRA, Am. Gastroenterological Assn. Office: Box 301 East Stroudsburg PA 18301

STROHM, ROBERT DEAN, publications executive; b. Chgo., Oct. 14, 1945; s. John Louis and Lillian Ann (Murphy) S.; m. Patricia Ann Quincannon, July 10, 1976; children: John Wilson, Charles Quincannon. BS, U. Ill., 1968. Assoc. editor Nat. Wildlife Fedn., Washington, 1968-73, mng. editor, 1973-81, exec. editor, 1981-88, editor-in-chief, 1989—, v.p. publs., 1989—. Mem. Am. Soc. Mag. Editors. Democrat. Roman Catholic. Office: Nat Wildlife Fedn 1400 16th St NW Washington DC 20036-2217

STROM, TERRY BARTON, physician, immunologist; b. Chgo., Nov. 30, 1941; s. David and Sylvia (Abelson) S.; m. Margot Stern, Aug. 2, 1964; children—Adam, Rachel. Student U. Ill.-Chgo./Urbana, 1959-62; M.D., U. Ill. Coll. Medicine, Chgo., 1966; MA (hon.) Harvard U., 1989; DSc (hon.) Hahnemann U., 1990. Diplomate Am. Bd. Internal Medicine. Intern/jr. resident U. Ill. Hosp., Chgo., 1966-68; sr. resident in internal medicine Beth Israel Hosp., Boston, 1970-71; research fellow in medicine Peter Bent Brigham Hosp. and Harvard Med. Sch., Boston, 1971-73; asst. prof. medicine Harvard Med. Sch., 1974-78, assoc. prof. medicine, 1978-88, prof. medicine, 1988—; med. dir. renal transplant service Peter Bent Brigham Hosp., 1973-83, assoc. dir. lab. immunogenetics and transplants, 1973-83; assoc. in medicine Beth Israel Hosp., 1981—, med. dir. renal transplant service, 1983—, dir. div. clin. immunology, 1983—; Lilly lectr. Royal Coll. Physicians, London, 1991. Author: 2 books, contbr. articles to profl. jours. Campaign worker polit. campaigns and peace orgns.; mem. U.S. Congl. Task Force on Transplantation, 1985-87, adv. panel for allergy and transplantation NIAID, 1988-91, NIH. Served to capt. USAF, 1968-70. Recipient Research Career Devel. award NIH, 1976-81; Acad. Honors Day award U. Ill., 1959-61. Mem. Internat. Soc. Nephrology (councillor), Assn. Am. Immunologists, Internat. Transplant Soc., Am. Soc. Clin. Investigation, Am. Soc. Transplant Physicians (pres. 1981), Assn. Am. Phys., Clin. Immunol. Soc. (pres. 1990). Democrat. Jewish. Office: Beth Israel Hosp 330 Brookline Ave Boston MA 02215-5491

STROMAN, CAROLYN A., academic program director, communications educator; b. Washington, July 23, 1945; d. John and Thelma Juanita (Williams) S. BA, Howard U., 1968; MLS, Syracuse U., 1970, PhD, 1978; MA, Atlanta U., 1973. Instr. Sch. Libr. Sci. Atlanta U., 1970-74; vis. lectr. African Am. studies U. N.C., Chapel Hill, 1978-80; rsch. assoc., asst. prof. Inst. Urban Affairs and Rsch. Howard U., Washington, 1980-86, assoc. prof. mass communications, dir. Ctr. Communications Rsch., 1986—, acting assoc. dean Sch. Communications, 1991—; rsch. cons. Nat. Rsch. Coun., Washington, 1987, L.A. Times, Washington, 1988. Contbr. articles to various publs. Mem. criminal justice subcom. D.C. Commn. on Women, 1983-85; active Coalition of 100 Black Women, Washington, 1986—, Friends of Syracuse, Washington, 1987—. Fellow Nat. Fellowships Fund, Ford Found., 1974-78; study grantee Am. Psychol. Assn., Washington, 1982. Mem. Assn. for Edn. in Journalism and Mass Communication (mem. adv. bd. 1988—, head minorities and communication div. 1989—), Delta Sigma Theta Alumnae (treas. Chapel Hill chpt. 1981-82). Democrat. Office: Howard U Ctr Comm 525 Bryant St NW Washington DC 20059-0001

STRONACH, FRANK, automobile parts manufacturing executive. Chmn., dir. Magna Internat. Inc., Markham, Ont., Can., 1971—. Office: Magna Internat Inc, 36 Apple Creek Blvd, Markham, ON Canada L3R 4Y4

STRONG, CHARMAINE RECKER, college dean; b. Pitts., July 12, 1952; d. Charles Regis and Veronica (Talbert) Recker. BS, Edinboro U. of Pa., 1974; MS in Edn., Duquesne U., 1977. Asst. dean students Duquesne U., Pitts., 1976-84; dean for student devel. Salem (W.Va.) Teikyo U., 1984-90; dean student svcs. Seton Hill Coll., Greensburg, Pa., 1990—. Mem. W.Va. Drug and Alcohol Consotrium; sec. Harrison County unit Am. Cancer Soc., Clarksburg, W.Va., 1988-90; co-chair Westmoreland County Food Dr., Greensburg, 1991; vol. Westmoreland County Am. Cancer Soc., Spl. Olympics; chair Boy Scouts Food Drive. Mem. Nat. Assn. Student Pers. Adminstrs., Lambda Sigma, Alpha Gamma Delta. Office: Seton Hill Coll Greensburg PA 15601

STRONG, ELIZABETH MAY, religious education professional; b. Cooperstown, N.Y., June 17, 1940; d. Ashley Walter and Marie Elizabeth (Miller) S.; divorced; children: David Franklin Taylor, Shari Lynne Taylor, Kathleen Elizabeth Taylor, Douglas Ashley Taylor. BA, Syracuse U., 1962; MS, Nazareth Coll., 1978; diploma, Unitarian Universalist Assn., Boston, 1983. Ordained to ministry, Unitarian Ch., 1983. Dir. religious edn. First Unitarian Ch., Rochester, N.Y., 1978-83, minister religious edn., 1983-88; minister religious edn. May Meml. Unitarian Soc., Syracuse, N.Y., 1988—; trustee Meadville/Lombard Theol. Sch., Chgo., 1989—; sec., trustee St. Lawrence Theol. Found., 1989—. Author curriculum materials. Corr. sec. Peace Child of Cen. N.Y., Syracuse, 1989—; bd. dirs., sec. Planned Parenthood Ctr. Syracuse, 1990—. Recipient Larry Axel Meml. Excellence in Teaching award Unitarian Universalist Assn., 1991. Mem. NOW, Liberal Religious Educators' Assn. (pres. 1988-90), Unitarian Universalist Ministers' Assn. (chpt. pres. 1986-89), Clergy for Choice, Religious Coalition for Abortion Rights. Democrat. Office: May Meml Unitarian Soc 3800 E Genesee St Syracuse NY 13214

STRONG, ELLIOT WILSON, surgeon, educator; b. Concord, Mass., Aug. 7, 1930; s. Lawrence Leroy and Helen Storey (Cole) S.; m. Marjorie Edith Linn, July 2, 1954; children: Scott Christian, Keith Raymond, Karen Linn. BS, Tufts U., 1952, MD, 1956. Diplomate Am. Bd. Surgery. Intern in surgery Hartford (Conn.) Hosp., 1956-57, resident in surgery, 1957-61; fellow in surg. oncology Meml. Sloan-Kettering Cancer Ctr., N.Y.C., 1961-63, clin. asst. surgeon, 1963-67, asst. attending, 1967-69, chief head and neck svc. dept. surgery, attending surgeon, 1969-92; prof. surgery Cornell U. Med. Coll., N.Y.C., 1976—; cons. Norwalk (Conn.) Hosp., 1975—, Temple U. Dental Sch., Phila., 1980-83. Contbr. numerous articles to med. jours., chpts. to books. Pres. bd. trustees Huguenot Meml. Ch., Pelham Manor, N.Y., 1976, ruling elder, 1977-83. Fellow ACS (bd. govs. 1989—); mem. Soc. Head and Neck Surgeons (sec. 1977, v.p. 1978, pres. 1979-80, Martin lectr. 1987), Am. Radium Soc. (v.p. 1975, sec. 1986-89, pres. 1989-90, Janeway lectr. 1983), N.Y. Head and Neck Soc. (pres. 1979-81), Phi Beta Kappa, Alpha Omega Alpha. Presbyterian. Office: Meml Sloan-Kettering Cancer Ctr 1275 York Ave New York NY 10021-6094

STRONG, LESLIE WALKER, artist, educator; b. Newport News, Va., Dec. 1, 1953; d. Henry Osborne and Jean (Walker) Strong; m. James Stewart Sutter, July 21, 1984; stepchildren: Jason Joel Sutter, Shannon Lyn Sutter. BS in Art, Skidmore Coll., 1976; MFA, Syracuse U., 1985. Art instr. Manor Plains Elem. Sch., Huntington, N.Y., 1977-78, Shendehowa Cen. Schs., Clifton Park, N.Y., 1978-81, Burnt Hills (N.Y.)-Ballston Lake Schs., 1981-83; instr. Skidmore Coll., Saratoga Springs, N.Y., 1981-88; gallery asst. St. Lawrence U., Canton, N.Y., 1986-87; instr. art Heuvelton (N.Y.) Cen. Sch., 1986-87, Potsdam (N.Y.) Cen. Sch., 1987—; in-house conservator Richard F. Brush Art Gallery, St. Lawrence U., 1985-86, cons., 1986-89. Exhibited sculpture in group shows at North Ga. Coll., 1989, Key Corp. Tower, Albany, N.Y., 1990, Delmar Coll., Corpus Christi, Tex., 1990, Munson Williams Proctor Inst., 1991, others. Recipient prize for sculpture Schoharie County Arts Coun., Cobleskill, N.Y., 1986, Best of Show award Massena Artists Assn., 1987, Roland Gibson award Potsdam Coll., 1988, 1st prize sculpture North Ga. Coll., 1990, others; grad. fellow Syracuse U., 1984-85. Home: 11 New St Norwood NY 13668-1005 Office: Potsdam Cen Sch 29 Leroy St Potsdam NY 13676-1798

STRONG, ROBERT THOMAS, middle school educator; b. N.Y.C., June 16, 1936; s. Joseph A. and Pauline R. (Manger) S.; m. Evelyn Ann Repasky, Aug. 23, 1958; children: Robyn, Robert Jr. BS, SUNY, Oswego, 1958; MLS, SUNY, Stony Brook, 1976. Social studies tchr. South Country Sch. Dist., Bellport, N.Y., 1958-66, asst. prin. middle sch., 1966-72, tchr., chmn. social studies dept., 1972-91; village trustee Port Jefferson Village, 1992—; student coun. adviser Bellport Middle Sch., 1968-91; prin. Infant Jesus Religious Sch., Port Jefferson, 1966-68. Trustee Village of Port Jefferson, 1991, code commr., 1991, chmn., mem. zoning bd. appeals, 1978-91; poll watcher Rep. Party, Port Jefferson Station, N.Y., 1964. Mem. N.Y. State Tchrs. Assn., Bellport Tchrs. Assn. (treas. 1974-76, bldg. rep. 1989-91), L.I. Coun. for Social Studies, Loyal Order of the House, Kiwanis, Moose. Roman Catholic. Home: 8 Shady Tree Ln Port Jefferson NY 11777

STRONGIN, BARBARA, management and development consultant; b. N.Y.C., Apr. 16, 1935; d. William and Edythe (Abramson) Spinrad; m. Alan Strongin, Mar. 28, 1956 (div. 1982); children: William, Stacey, Ronni, David; m. Gerhart Friedlander, Aug. 10, 1983. BA, Queens Coll., 1957. Field exec. Greater N.Y. Girl Scout Coun., Queens, N.Y., 1967-71; edn. dir. Suffolk County Girl Scout Coun., Long Island, N.Y., 1971-78; exec. dir. Planned Parenthood of Suffolk County, Long Island, 1978-86; cons. various non-profit orgns., Long Island, 1986—; bd. dirs. Nat. Exec. Dir. Coun. N.E. Region Planned Parenthood Fedn. of Am., 1980-84. Contbr. articles to profl. jours. and mags. Founding mem. Suffolk County Voluntary Action Ctr., 1976-78; pres. Suffolk Abortion Rights Coun., 1986-91; founder, treas. Suffolk Network on Adolescent Pregnancy, 1979-90; founder, pres., sec. Suffolk County Perinatal Coalition, 1984—; mem. County Exec. Adv. Com., AIDS, Women and AIDS Project; founding mem. Suffolk County Women's Dev. Caucus; chair Task Force on Equality of Women in Judaism; exec. com. N.Y. Fedn. of Reform Synagogues, 1977-84; active in many other civic groups. Recipient Margaret Sanger award Planned Parenthood of Suffolk County, Long Island, 1986, Outstanding Pvt. Citizen award Suffolk Network on Adolescent Pregnancy , Ann. award Suffolk Chpt. ACLU, 1989, Ann. award (with husband) Am. Jewish Congress Long Island, 1991. Mem. Nat. Soc. Fund Raising Execs. (bd. dirs. Long Island chpt. 1990—). Home and Office: 5 Lorraine Ct Smithtown NY 11787-1633

STROUD, PATRICIA TYSON, writer; b. Phila., Dec. 22, 1932; d. George Peterson and Jane (Chapman) Huber; m. Noel J. Tyson, Sept. 8, 1956 (dec. July 1982); children: John Tyson, Peter H. Tyson, Lisa Tyson Ennis; m. Morris Wistar Stroud III, Mar. 11, 1989 (dec. Apr. 1990); m. Alexander McCurdy III, Nov. 16, 1991. AB, Smith Coll., Northampton, Mass., 1955. Writer, pub. rels. releases First Pa. Bank, Phila., 1968-69; editor, Frontiers Acad. Natural Scis., Phila., 1979-82; writer pvt. practice, Phila., 1982—. Author: Thomas Say: New World Naturalist, 1992.

STROUP, ALICE, history educator; b. Hartford, Conn., Mar. 2, 1943; m. Timothy Stroup, June 2, 1962. BA, CCNY, 1965; diploma in history & philosophy of sci., Oxford (Eng.) U., 1970, DPhil., 1978. Asst. prof. history and sci. Harvard Univ., Cambridge, Mass., 1978-80; asst. prof. history Bard Coll., Annandale-on-Hudson, N.Y., 1980-85; assoc. prof. history Bard Coll., Annandale-on-Hudson, 1985-91, prof. history, 1991—. Author: Royal Funding, 1987, A Company of Scientists, 1990. Recipient fellowship for coll. tchrs. Nat. Endowment for the Humanities, 1984-85; named summer scholar NSF, 1989-91, rsch. scholar Fulbright Commn., Paris, 1991-92. Mem. Am. Hist. Assn., History Sci. Soc., Soc. for French Hist. Studies. Office: Bard Coll Annandale NY 12504

STROUP, ROLLAND EUGENE, safety specialist; b. Wells County, Ind., Apr. 9, 1943; s. Rolland Eugene and Norma Claudine (Gilbert) S.; m. Marlyd Tirado, Mar. 17, 1973; children: Alexander, Randolph, Jonathan. BA, Depauw U., 1966; postgrad., Ball State U., 1970; MS, Purdue U., 1979. Cert. safety profl. Office mgr. Overhead Door Co., Mishawaka, Ind., 1966-67; mgr. camera dept. Turnstyle Family Ctr., Indpls., 1971-72; mech. assembler Am. Monitor Corp., Indpls., 1972-73; letter carrier U.S. Postal Svc., Indpls., 1973-77; compliance officer Ind. area office OSHA U.S. Dept. Labor, Indpls., 1977-81; regional auditor Chgo. regional office OSHA U.S. Dept. Labor, 1981-83, sr. safety specialist Chgo. regional office OSHA, 1983-88; sr. safety specialist office field programs OSHA U.S. Dept. Labor, Washington, 1988-90; div. chief gen. industry safety abatement assistance OSHA U.S. Dept. Labor, 1990—. With U.S. Army, 1968-69.

STROUP, THOMAS ALLEN, trade association executive; b. Hazen, N.D., Mar. 18, 1954; s. Robert Lee and Lillian (Pridt) S.; m. Heather Pack, May 14, 1988. BS in Pub. Admnstrn., U. N.D., 1976; JD, Georgetown U., 1979. Bar: D.C., 1979. Assoc. Foley, Lardner, Hollabaugh and Jacobs, Washington, 1979-81, Schnader, Harrison, Segal and Lewis, Washington, 1981-85; mng. dir. paging div. Telocator, Washington, 1985-87, v.p., gen. counsel, 1987-90, pres., 1990—. Fellow Radio Club Am.; mem. Georgetown Club, Farmington Country Club. Office: Telocator 1019 19th St NW Washington DC 20036-5105

STROUSE, JOHN IRVIN, loss control manager; b. Reading, Pa., Feb. 9, 1946; s. Irvin Harold and Irene Isabella (Boone) S.; m. Peggi A. Hofmann, Oct. 7, 1975. AS, York Coll., 1966; BA, Slippery Rock State U., 1969; MS, U. Pa., 1985. News reporter Reading Eagle, 1969; pers. asst. Link Bolt/FMC Corp., Colmar, Pa., 1969-70; safety mgr. U. Pa., Phila., 1970-77; loss control supr. Atlantic Mut., Plymouth Meeting, Pa., 1977-88; loss control mgr. New Hampshire Group/AIG, Wayne, Pa., 1988-91; mgr. major accounts Regional Reporting, Inc., Mt. Laurel, N.J., 1991—. Editor (jour.) Flame Spread, 1989-91. Mem. Am. Soc. Safety Engrs., Cert. Safety Profls., Cert. Fire Protection Specialists (bd. govs., editor), Nat. Fire Protection Assn. Republican. Office: Regional Reporting Inc 1200 Church St Ste 11 Mount Laurel NJ 08054

STRUCK, NORMA JOHANSEN, artist; b. West Englewood, N.J., Feb. 17, 1929; d. Hans Christian and Amanda (Solberg) Johansen; m. H. Walter Struck, Aug. 21, 1955; children: Steven, Laurie. Student, N.Y. Phoenix Sch. Design, 1946-50; Art Students' League, N.Y.C., 1976-77. Staff artist Norcross, Inc., N.Y.C., 1950-60, free-lance artist, 1967-75; artist portraits, prints Scafa-Tornabene, Nyack, N.Y., 1976--; artist portraits, paintings U.S.N., U.S. Coast Guard, Washington, 1976--; com. bd. mem. Navy Art Coop. Liaison, N.Y.C., 1976-80, Coast Guard Art Program, N.Y.C., 1980--. One-man shows include Nabisco Co., Fairlawn, N.J., 1987; exhibited in group shows at Navy Hist. Mus., Washington, 1976, Navy Combat Art Gallery, Washington, World Trade Ctr., 1979, U.S. Coast Guard Aviation Art Exhibit, New Eng. Air Mus., Windsor Locks, Conn., 1984, Fed. Hall, N.Y.C., 1986, Salmagundi Club, N.Y.C., Officers Club, Governor's Island, Hudson Valley Show, White Plains, N.Y., Navy Combat Gallery, Washington; works in permanent collection at U.S. Pentagon, Washington. Recipient Louis E. Seley award, Navy Art Program, 1979; Grumbacher award, Catherine Lorillard Wolfe, Nat. Arts Club, N.Y.C., 1978; George Gray award Coast Guard Art Program, Governors Island, N.Y., 1983, 89. Mem. Art Students League (life), Hudson Valley Assn. (bd. mem. 1985-88, M. Dole award 1980), Salmagundi Club, Am. Artists Profl. League (President's award 1979). Home: 910 Midland Rd Oradell NJ 07649-1904

STRUCKHOFF, EUGENE CHARLES, foundation administrator, consultant; b. St. Louis, Nov. 14, 1920; s. Eugene C. and Elinor Mae (Cook) S.; m. Ruth Norma Brewer, Jan. 4, 1943; children: Eugene C. III, Laura Lee S. Cine. BA, Colby Coll., Waterville, ME, 1946; LLB, Harvard Law Sch., Cambridge, Mass., 1949; MA, Colby Coll., Waterville, ME, 1968. Ptnr. Orr and Reno Law Firm, Concord, N.H., 1949-71; exec. dir. Spaulding-Potter Charitable Trusts, Concord, N.H., 1960-71; v.p. Coun. on Found., Washington, 1971-78, pres., 1978-81; pres. Balt. Community Found., Balt., 1982-89; sr. cons. to coun. on found. Balt. Community Found. to Coun. on Found., Balt., 1981—; ind. cons. Strucks Consulting, Lutherville, Md., 1982—. Author: Handbook for Community Foundations, 1977, Ways to Grow, 1991; contbr. articles to profl. jours. Councilman at large City of Concrod, N.H., 1956-67; trustee U. N.H., Durham, 1967-71, Colby Coll., Waterville, Maine, 1966-69; chmn. emeritus Citizens Scholarship Found. of Am., St. Peter, Minn., 1968—. Recipient Award of Merit, City of Balt., 1990, Disting. Flying Cross, USAF, 1944. Home and office: 2243 Chapel Valley Ln Lutherville Timonium MD 21093-2963 Office: Baltimore Area Inc 2 E Read St Baltimore MD 21202-2470

STRUNK, ROBERT KEEN, II, banker; b. Lewisburg, Pa., Mar. 28, 1951; s. Robert Keen and Helen (Pfleegor) S.; m. Judith Moreau, July 19, 1975; children: Rebecca Lynn, Gretchen Lee. BA, Moravian Coll., Bethlehem, Pa., 1973; postgrad., Rutgers U., 1979, U. Okla., 1981, Northwestern U., 1989. With 1st Fidelity Bank, Newark, N.J., 1973—; v.p., group mgr. 1st Fidelity Bank, 1987—. Deacon Presbyn. Ch. on the Hill, Ocean, N.J., 1984-86, elder, 1988—, chmn. fin. and bldg. fund, 1989—, pres., 1990—; fundraiser Pop Warner Assn., 1990; coach Ocean Twp. Little League, 1990—; mem. Ocean Twp. Drug Alliance and Recreation. Mem. Masons. Republican. Home: 1216 Stewart Ave Asbury Park NJ 07712-4757 Office: 1st Fidelity Bank 550 Broad St Newark NJ 07102-4517

STRYKER, ALLAN KENT, plastic surgeon; b. Paterson, N.J., Sept. 15, 1946; s. Allan and Mildred Marie (Laycock) S.; m. Victoria Lynn tod, May 12, 1984; children: Danielle, Michelle. BA, U. Louisville, 1968, MD, 1972. Am. Bd. Plastic Surgery, 1981. Gen. surgery residency U. Louisville, 1972-76, plastic surgery residency, 1976-78; active staff Trover Clinic, Madisonville, Ky., 1978-86; clin. instr. U. Louisville Dept. Surgery, Madisonville, Ky., 1978-86; active staff Williamsport (Pa.) Hosp., 1986—, Divine Providence Hosp., Williamsport, Pa., 1986—. Contbr. articles to profl. jours. Recipient Physicians Recognition award AMA, 1984, 87, 90. Mem. AMA, Am. Soc. Plastic and Reconstructive Surgeons, Southeastern Soc. Plastic and Reconstructive Surgeons, Northeastern Soc. Plastic and Reconstructive Surgeons. Office: 425 Market St Williamsport PA 17701

STRYKER, TIMOTHY DEWEY, endocrinologist; b. Lubbock, Tex., June 6, 1952; s. Winfield and Lynda Ruth (Dewey) S. BS, Vanderbilt U., 1974, MD, 1979. Diplomate Am. Bd. Internal Medicine and Endocrinology. Intern, resident Vanderbilt Med. Ctr.; fellow Tufts New Eng. Med. Ctr., Boston; chief endocrinology New Eng. Meml. Hosp., Stoneham, Mass., 1991—. Contbr. articles to profl. jours. Mem. AMA, Am. Diabetes Assn., Endocrine Soc. Republican. Office: 106 Main St Stoneham MA 02180-3317

STUART, ALICE MELISSA, lawyer; b. N.Y.C., Apr. 7, 1957; d. John Marberger and Marjorie Louise (Browne) S. BA, Ohio State U., 1977; JD, U. Chgo., 1980; LLM, NYU, 1982. Bar: N.Y. 1981, Ohio 1982, N.Y. 1982, U.S. Dist. Ct. (so. dist.) Ohio 1983, U.S. Dist. Ct. (so. and ea. dists.) N.Y. 1985. Assoc. Schwartz, Shapiro, Kelm & Warren, Columbus, Ohio, 1982-84, Paul, Weiss, Rifkind, Wharton & Garrison, N.Y.C., 1984-85, Kassel, Neuwirth & Geiger, N.Y.C., 1985-86, Phillips, Nizer, Benjamin, Krim & Ballon, N.Y.C., 1987—. Surrogate Speakers' Bur. Reagan-Bush Campaign, N.Y.C., 1984; mem. Lawyers for Bush-Quayle Campaign, N.Y.C., 1988. Mem. ABA, N.Y. State Bar Assn., Winston Churchill Meml. Library Soc., Jr. League, Phi Beta Kappa, Phi Kappa Phi, Alpha Lambda Delta. Republican. Presbyterian. Club: Women's Nat. Rep. (N.Y.C.). Office: Phillips Nizer Benjamin Krim & Ballon 31 W 52d St New York NY 10010-4001

STUART, BARBARA LAWLOR, English educator; b. Pensacola, Fla., Nov. 6, 1951; d. Robert Lawlor and Rebecca Arlney (Berlin) Stuart; m. Louis Lohr Martz, May 5, 1990. BA, U. of the South, Sewanee, Tenn., 1973; MEd, U. S.C., 1974; MA, Ga. State U., 1982; PhD, Emory U., 1988. Tchr. Jesse Boyd Elem. Sch., Spartanburg, S.C., 1975, DeKalb County Schs., Atlanta, 1975-82; teaching asst. Emory U., Atlanta, 1984-87; instr. Auburn (Ala.) U., 1987-91; lectr. Yale U., New Haven, 1991—. Humanities fund of Auburn U. rsch. grantee, 1990, English speaking Union grantee, 1986, NEH Summer Inst. grantee, 1991; Emory U. dissertation fellow, 1987-88. Mem. MLA, Dickens Soc., Iris Murdoch Soc. Democrat. Episcopalian. Office: Yale U Dept English Box 3545 Yale Sta New Haven CT 06420

STUART, DONALD JAMES, management and marketing consultant; b. Springfield, Mass., Dec. 11, 1955; s. Donald Graham and Nancy Katherine (Topor) S.; m. Susan Browne Wolcott, June 27, 1981; children: Sally, Jennifer, Donald. BA, St. Lawrence U., 1977; MBA, Dartmouth Coll., 1979. Fin. analyst The Pillsbury Co., Mpls., 1979-80, asst. product mgr., 1980-82, product mgr., 1982-84, mktg. mgr., 1984-86, group mktg. mgr., 1986-89; sr. cons. Glendinning Assocs., Westport, Conn., 1989-90, v.p., 1991, v.p., group head, 1992—. Vol., tchr. Greenfield Hill Ch., Fairfield,

Conn., 1991/92. Mem. Omicron Delta Epsilon. Republican. Home: 192 Mulberry Hill Rd Fairfield CT 06430

STUART, DOUGLAS EARL, aerospace company executive; b. South Milwaukee, Wis., Mar. 6, 1938; s. Robert H. and Ruth A. (Orthmann) S.; m. Ruth A. McCauley, Aug. 13, 1960; children: James, Michael, Holly. BSME, Purdue U., 1960. Assembly supr. Grede Foundries, Milw., 1960-63; project engr. Hein Werner, Waukesha, Wis., 1963-68; staff mech. engr. Simmonds Precision, Vergennes, Vt., 1968-71, program mgr., 1971-73, system engr., 1973-76; engring. mgr. Simmonds Precision, Vergennes, 5, 1976-78, dir. indsl. engring., 1978-83, mktg. mgr., 1983-89, v.p. mktg., 1989—; mem. panel various confs. in field. Contbr. articles to profl. publs.; patentee in field. Mem. Lions (local pres. 1975). Home: RD 3 Box 3540 Vergennes VT 05491-0549 Office: Simmonds Presicion Panton Rd Vergennes VT 05491-1033

STUART, EVE LYNNE, elementary school educator; b. Atlantic City, N.J., Nov. 25, 1942; d. Berned Edward and Amelia Louise (Lieteau) Creswell; m. Henry E. Stuart, June 21, 1963 (div. Mar. 1978); children: Lisa Marie, Nanette Cecilia. Student, Cen. State U., Wilberforce, Ohio, 1960-63; BS, Glassboro State U., 1968. Cert. elem. tchr., N.J. Tchr. Head Start, Atlantic City, 1965-66, Atlantic City Pub. Schs., 1967—; tchr.-cons. N.J. Geog. Alliance, Montclair, N.J., 1990—; mentor tchr. project invest, multicultural tchr., trainer, 1992—; mem. leadership com. N.J. Geographic Alliance, 1992—. Founder, coord. Project Campsite/Summer Breeze, Atlantic City, 1989-90; mem. com. United Negro Coll. Fund, Atlantic City, 1988-89. Recipient Outstanding cert. Nat. Geog. Soc., 1990, Cape May (N.J.) Schs., 1991; Atlantic City Bd. Edn. grantee, 1989-90. Fellow Delta Sigma Theta; mem. NEA, NCCJ, N.J. Coun. for Social Studies (bd. dirs. 1991—), Atlantic City Edn. Assn. (officer 1984-88, award 1985, 86), A.C.C.E.A., A.C.E.A., Phi Delta Kappa (officer 1988-89). Democrat. Roman Catholic. Office: Atlantic City Pub Schs Indiana Ave Sch 117 N Indiana Ave Atlantic City NJ 08401-4209

STUART, KIEL, editor, publisher; b. N.Y.C., Nov. 20, 1951; m. Howard Austerlitz, June 20, 1978. Student, SUNY, Stony Brook, 1973-75. Editor Forum Sci. Fiction Writers Am., Stony Brook, 1985-88; exec. dir. The Writers Alliance, Stony Brook, 1982—, editor, pub., 1983—; cons. O-C-G, Farmingdale, N.Y., 1986-87, Marine Sci. Rsch. Ctr., Stony Brook, 1986-87, Steinetics, St. James, N.Y., 1985. Author: From Parts Unknown, 1991; editor (quarterly) Keystrokes, 1992, Island Women, 1984. Mem. Authors Guild, Sci. Fiction Writers Am. Office: PO Box 2014 Setauket NY 11733

STUART, LAURA JEAN, research executive; b. Ayer, Mass., July 15, 1961; d. James Allen and Lorraine Alma (Pote) S. BA in History & English, U. N.H., 1982. Rsch. analyst Internat. Data Corp., Framingham, Mass., 1980-83; sr. analyst, info. systems The Yankee Group, Boston, 1983-84, dir., small systems rsch., 1984-85, exec. dir., communications & info. systems rsch., 1985-86, mgr. dir., worldwide rsch., 1986; founder, chief exec. officer Stuart Rsch., Cambridge, Mass., 1987—. Office: Stuart Rsch 200 Msgr O'Brien Hwy Cambridge MA 02141

STUART, MARIAN RUTH, medical educator; b. Berlin, May 22, 1930; d. Martin Loewenberg and Margot (Jarislowsky) Alexander; m. August D. Stuart, Sept. 26, 1949 (div. Oct. 1976); children: Peter, Laura, Robert. BA summa cum laude, Kean Coll., Union, N.J., 1971; MS in Psychology, Rutgers U., 1973, PhD in Social and Personality Psychology, 1975. Lic. psychologist, N.J. Mental health clinician Rutgers Mental Health Ctr., Piscataway, N.J., 1972-75; staff psychologist St. Clare's Hosp., Denville, N.J., 1975-77; adj. asst., prof. psychiatry Rutgers Med. Sch., Piscataway, 1977-78; adj. asst., prof. dept. family medicine UMDNJ Rutgers Med. Sch., New Brunswick, N.J., 1978-86; clin. assoc. prof. family medicine, adj. asst. prof. psychiatry UMDNJ Robert Wood Johnson Med. Sch., New Brunswick, 1986—; pvt. practice clin. psychology, Morristown, N.J., 1976—. Sr. author: (textbook) The Fifteen Minute Hour, 1986, (chpt.) Family Dynamics, 1981; pub. The River Reporter, 1985—; contbr. articles to profl. jours. Mem. adv. com. Dept. on Aging, County of Morris, 1978-81. Grantee Morris County Dept. on Aging, 1976-77. Fellow Acad. of Medicine of N.J.; mem. APA, Soc. Tchrs. Family Medicine, Soc. Behavioral Medicine, Inst. for Advancement of Health, N.J. Psychol. Assn., Mensa. Home: 7 Harwich Rd Morristown NJ 07960-2639 Office: UMDNJ Robert Wood Johnson Med Sch Dept Family Medicine One Robert Wood Johnson Pl New Brunswick NJ 08903-0019

STUART, MARJORIE LOUISE, designer; b. St. Louis, Jan. 7, 1926; d. Herbert Judson and Vesta Jeannette (Winters) Browne; A.B., Fla. State U., 1947; m. John M. Stuart, Dec. 11, 1954; children: Jane Adkins, Alice Stuart, Richard Stuart. Designer of illusions, off Broadway magic show Make Me Disappear, 1969; designer of space stations, 1977—; lectr. on space architecture, 1977—. Mem. Nat. Space Soc., Internat. Brotherhood Magicians, Soc. Am. Magicians (life), Soc. Mayflower Descendants. Republican. Presbyterian. Author: (J. Marberger Stuart) You Don't Have to Slay A Dragon, 1975. Illustrator: Harbin on Magic, 1986. Home: 31 E Gate Blvd Manhasset NY 11030-1452

STUART, MARK FRANKLIN, computer specialist; b. Norwalk, Conn., Aug. 5, 1953; s. Arthur and Dorothy (Jacobson) S.; m. Andrea Faith Vaughan, Aug. 10, 1980. BA, U. Conn., 1975, MBA, 1979. Asst. treas. Conn. Bank and Trust, Hartford, 1979-81; pres. Omric Corp., Newington, Conn., 1981-83; computer cons. East Hartford, Conn., 1983-84; mgr. corp. accounts Enter Computer Group/Bkm Enterprises, East Hartford, 1984-88; mgr. Met. Life Ins. Co., Norwich, Conn., 1988-89; fin. svcs. supr. Travelers Ins. Co., Hartford, 1989-90; computer specialist St. Francis Hosp., Hartford, 1990—. Mem. Hebron Housing Partnership, 1989-90. Mem. Hebron Bus. and Profl. Assn. (pres. 1990), Masons (master Evergreen lodge 114 1992), Jaycees, Beta Gama Sigma, Phi Alpha Theta. Office: St Francis Hosp 114 Woodland St Hartford CT 06104

STUDDS, GERRY EASTMAN, congressman; b. Mineola, N.Y., May 12, 1937; s. Eastman and Beatrice (Murphy) S. B.A., Yale U., 1959, M.A.T., 1961. Fgn. service officer State Dept., Washington, 1961-63; exec. asst. to presdl. cons. for a nat. service corps White House, 1963; legis. asst. to Sen. Harrison Williams U.S. Senate, 1964; tchr. St. Paul's Sch., Concord, N.H., 1965-69; mem. 93d-97th Congresses from 12th Mass. dist., 1973-83, 98th-102nd Congresses from 10th Mass. dist., 1983—. Candidate for U.S. Congress from 12th Dist. Mass., 1970; del. Democratic Nat. Conv., 1968. Office: US Ho of Reps 237 Cannon House Office Bldg Washington DC 20515

STUDNESS, CHARLES MICHAEL, economist; b. Mpls., Nov. 2, 1935; s. Leo C. and Alma (Mehus) S.; m. Harriet Leah Katz, Oct. 27, 1968; children: Erica, Lisa, Roy. BA, U. Minn., 1957, MA, 1958; PhD in Econs., Columbia U., 1963. Lectr. CCNY, 1961-64, U. Minn., Mpls., 1964-65; economist Fed. Res. Bank N.Y., N.Y.C., 1965-67, N.Y. Stock Exchange, N.Y.C., 1967-68, Eastern Airlines, N.Y.C., 1968-70, Baker Weeks, N.Y.C., 1970-76, E.F. Hutton, N.Y.C., 1976-79; pres. Studness Rsch., Manhasset, N.Y., 1979—; lectr. Baruch Coll., N.Y.C., 1968-74; Contbg. editor Public Utilities Fortnightly, 1990—. Columnist, Pub. Utilities Fortnightly, 1979—.

STUKEY, VIRGINIA MARGARET, artist; b. N.Y.C.; d. Richard Charles and Madeline Theresa (Barton) Gramlich; m. John Henry Stukey, Nov. 12, 1949; children: Erin, John Henry, Richard Howe. Student, Columbia U., 1949-51. Tchr. painting various orgns., N.Y.C. and N.J., 1960-75; instr. Riverside Ch. Arts and Crafts Dept., N.Y.C., 1965-75; artist Keane Mason, N.Y.C., 1984-87, Salon des Artists Art Gallery, N.Y.C., 1987-89. Solo exhbns. include Rural Life Ctr., Hinton, N.C., 1967, 68, Pietrantonnio Gallery, N.Y.C., 1972; group shows include Studio 54, N.Y.C., 1982, N.Y. Acad. Scis., 1991, Interfaith Ctr., N.Y.C., 1989, Bergen Mus., 1985-90, Marbella Gallery, N.Y.C., 1989, 100 Years 100 Women, 1990-91, ARC Gallery, Chgo., 1992; represented in permanent collections including Riverside Ch., N.Y.C. Mem. Am. Soc. Contemporary Artists, Nat. Assn. Women Artists (1st v.p. 1991—), Painting Affiliates Art Ctr. N.J., N.Y. Artists Equity. Home: 87 Bennett Rd Teaneck NJ 07666-5532

STULL, FRANK WALTER, educator; b. Easton, Pa., June 4, 1935; s. George Washington and Minnie Elizabeth S.; m. Darlene Joy Hunsicker, Aug. 2, 1958; children: James, Ronald, Wendy. BS, East Stroudsburg State Coll., 1956; MEd, Lehigh U., 1966. Cert. tchr., N.J. Tchr. Howell Twp. Elem. Sch., Freehold, N.J., 1958-59, Holland Twp. Elem. Sch., Milford, N.J., 1959—. Bd. dirs., sec., treas., mgr. Hunterdon County Sch. Employes Fed. Credit Union, Phillipsburg, N.J., 1969-87; merit badge counselor Boy Scouts Am., 1970-84, cubmaster, 1971-72. With U.S. Army, 1956-58, Korea. Recipient Meritorious Svc. award N.J. Credit Union League, 1988, Tchr. Recognition award State N.J. Gov., 1987, Disting. Achievement award for rsch. and preservation of history of Holland Twp. and surrounding areas; named Outstanding Elem. Tchr. Am., 1972; Experienced Tchr. in Geography fellow Pa. State U., 1967. Mem. NEA, Nat. Coun. Social Studies, Holland Twp. Edn. Assn., Hunterdon County Edn. Assn., N.J. Edn. Assn., Phi Delta Kappa. Home and Office: 806 Rugby Rd Phillipsburg NJ 08865-2033

STULL, G. ALAN, university dean, health professions educator; b. Easton, Pa., Jan. 26, 1933; s. George Washington and Minnie Elizabeth (Walter) S.; m. Joan Carolyn Gittings, July 30, 1955 (div. 1981); children—Bobbi Ann, John David; m. Jeanine Joosten, Nov. 23, 1984. Student, Lafayette Coll., Easton, Pa., 1950-51; B.S., East Stroudsburg U., 1955; M.S., Pa. State U., 1957, Ed.D., 1961. From instr. to asst. prof. Pa. State U., State College, 1958-66; from assoc. prof. to prof. U. Md., College Park, 1966-72; prof., assoc. dean U. Ky., Lexington, 1972-77; prof., dir. U. Minn., Mpls., 1977-85; prof., dean Sch. Allied Health Professions U. Wis., Madison, 1985-88; prof., dean Sch. Health Related Professions SUNY, Buffalo, 1988—. Co-author: Statistical Principles and Procedures with Applications for Physical Education, 1975; editor: Ency. of Physical Education, Fitness, and Sports, 1980; contbr. articles to profl. jours. Served with U.S. Army, 1956-58. Recipient Alumni Disting. Service award East Stroudsburg U., 1974; recognition award Am. Corrective Therapy Assn., 1981. Fellow Am. Acad. Phys. Edn. (sec.-treas. 1982-84, pres. 1985-86), Am. Coll. Sports Medicine (chmn. position stands 1979-81); mem. AAHPERD (pres. rsch. consortium 1981-82, honor award 1981), Nat. Assn. Phys. Edn. in Higher Edn. (chmn. research com. 1976-77), Assn. for Research, Adminstrn., Profl. Couns. and Socs. (pres. 1976-77, honor award 1980), Assn. Schs. Allied Health Professions, Phi Epsilon Kappa. Republican. Methodist. Office: SUNY Sch Health Related Professions 435 Stockton Kimball Tower Buffalo NY 14214

STULTZ, JOHN ANTHONY, church official, counselor; b. Altoona, Pa., Feb. 24, 1963; s. John A. and Mary Ellen (Shaw) S.; m. Rebecca Ann Macesich, Aug. 23, 1986. MTh, Fairfax U., New Orleans, 1991; student, Cambria-Rowe Bus. Coll. Dir. edn., counseling, EYC Episcopal Youth Club - St. Mark's Episcopal Ch., Johnstown, Pa., 1988—; spiritual dir. St. Mark's Episcopal Ch., Johnstown, Pa., 1989—; v.p. bd. dirs. URT, Johnstown, 1990—; project dir. Vine Street Halfway House, Johnstown, 1990—. Author: Physio Dynamics, 1989. V.p. U. of PItts. at Johnstown Bd. Campus Ministry; bd. dirs. Assn. for Retarded Citizens, 1992; mentor Ext. Program, U. of the South; had instr. St. Mark's Lion Martial Arts Club. Mem. AACD. Democrat. Office: St Mark's Episcopal Ch 335 Locust St Johnstown PA 15901-1606

STUMBAUGH, KURT JOHN, accountant; b. Trenton, N.J., Dec. 9, 1957; s. William L. and Elizabeth F. (Prieth) S.; m. Katrine Marie Ashby, Sept. 4, 1989; 1 child, Ashley Rose. BS in Commerce, Rider Coll., 1980. CPA, N.J. Auditor State of N.J., Trenton, 1980-88; pvt. practice Mercerville, N.J., 1988—. Fellow N.J. Soc. CPA; mem. AICPA, Assn. of Govt. Accts., Nat. Assn. of Tax Profls. Office: 2382 Whitehorse Mercerville Rd Mercerville NJ 08619

STUMP, RICHARD CARL, environmental services administrator; b. Reading, Pa., Aug. 14, 1952; s. Richard Carl Stump and Jean Alice (Foose) Peters; m. Brenda Lee Roughton, Jan. 11, 1974; children: Richard, Nathan, Jonathan. Grad. high sch., Muhlenberg, Pa. Cert. radon testing specialist. Lab. dir. Suburban Water Testing Labs., Temple, Pa., 1978—. Mem. Am. Water Works Assn., Am. Assn. of Radon Scientists and Technologists, Pa. Assn. of Accreditation Environ. Labs. Office: Suburban Water Testing Labs 4600 Kutztown Rd Temple PA 19560-1548

STUMPF, CAROLYN JOAN, college program director, educator; b. Perth Amboy, N.J., Oct. 2, 1940; d. Walter John and Helen Bernice (Konkowitz) Gurka; m. Stephen Francis Stumpf Jr., July 6, 1963; children: Jon Stefan, David Mikhail. BS, Georgian Ct. Coll., 1962; EdM, Rutgers U., 1966, EdD, 1978. Edn.-mgmt. cons. Streit Cons., New Brunswick, N.J., 1978-80; dir. coop. edn. in bus. Georgian Ct. Coll., Lakewood, N.J., 1980—, assoc. prof. edn., 1989—; faculty cons., Ponsi cons. Thomas Edison State Coll., Trenton, N.J., 1985-91. Mem. AAUP (pres. chpt. 1990-91). Office: Georgian Ct Coll 900 Lakewood Ave Lakewood NJ 08701-2697

STUMPFF, ROBERT THOMAS, academic administrator; b. Lewistown, Pa., June 25, 1945; s. Harry Clarence and Marjorie Louise (Bossinger) S.; m. Sylvia Simmons, Apr. 22, 1972; children: Robert Dale, Cherie Lynn Stumpff Zimmer. BS, U. Md., 1968; cert., U. Ky., 1978. Adminstrv. asst. to dir. athletics U. Md., College Park, 1968-69, asst. dir. Md. student union, 1969-72, assoc. dir. Md. student union, 1973-80, acting dir. Md. student union, 1974-75, bus. mgr. athletics, 1980-81, asst. athletic dir., 1982-88, mgr. gen. svcs. phys. plant, 1988—; cons. U.S. Naval Acad. Athletic Assn., Annapolis, Md., 1984. Author, editor: Maryland Wrestling, 1964-65, 68-69 (Nation's Best award); asst. editor: Maryland Football Guide, 1965-69, Maryland Basketball, 1964-65, 68-69. Mem. ch. coun. Abiding Savior Lutheran Ch., Columbia, Md., 1986-87. Mem. Am. Pub. Works Assn., Solid Waste Assn. N.Am., Nat. Solid Wastes Mgmt. Assn., Assn. Phys. Plant Adminstrs., Md. Ednl. Found., Terrapin Club, U. Md. M Club Found., Inc. (life, bd. dirs. 1970—, Outstanding Wrestling Publ. 1967-68, Outstanding Awards Banquet Chmn. 1990), U. Md. Alumni Assn. (life), Omicron Delta Kappa (Sigma Circle, faculty advisor 1974—, sec.-treas. 1974-76). Home: 8206 Bubbling Spring Ct Laurel MD 20723-1079 Office: Univ Md Phys Plant Svc Bldg Annex (005) College Park MD 20742-6115

STUPIN, SUSAN LEE, investment banker; b. L.A., Sept. 14, 1954; d. Paul Alex and Elizabeth Lee (Williams) S.; m. Theodore Robert Gamble Jr., Mar. 3, 1984. AB cum laude, Princeton U., 1975; MBA, Harvard U., 1979. Rep. corp. bond sales Paine, Webber, Jackson & Curtis, N.Y.C., 1975-77; assoc. instl. fin. Eastdil Realty Inc., N.Y.C., 1979-83; assoc. real estate dept. Goldman, Sachs & Co., N.Y.C., 1983-85, v.p. real estate dept., 1985-88; prin. The Prescott Group Inc., N.Y.C., 1988—. Fellow Morgan Library; Bryant fellow Met. Mus. Art; exec. com., fund raiser Princeton Class of 1975. Mem. Urban Land Inst. (exec. group Comml. and Retail Devel. Council), Real Estate Bd. N.Y., Internat. Council Shopping Ctrs., Young Mortgage Bankers Assn., Doubles, N.Y. Jr. League, River Club, Harvard Club (N.Y.C., Boston). Republican. Episcopalian. Home: 860 United Nations Pla New York NY 10017 Office: The Prescott Group Inc 666 5th Ave New York NY 10103-0001

STUPP, EDWARD HENRY, physicist; b. Bklyn., Dec. 10, 1932; s. Samuel and Sarah (Reiss) S.; m. Roberta Hendelman, Aug. 28, 1954; children: Lori Allyson, Steven Elliott. BS, CCNY, 1954; MS, Syracuse U., 1958, PhD, 1960. Mem. tech. staff IBM Watson Rsch. Ctr., Yorktown, N.Y., 1959-62; mem. tech. staff Philips Labs., Briarcliff, N.Y., 1962-69, sr. program leader, 1969-81, dept. head, 1981—; cons. Philips Broadcast Equip. Corp., Montvale, N.J., 1973. Contbr. articles to profl. jours.; author 21 patents. Mem. IEEE, Soc. for Info. Display (chpt. sec. 1991—), Am. Phys. Soc., Phi Beta Kappa. Office: Philips Labs 345 Scarborough Rd Briarcliff Manor NY 10510-2099

STURDEVANT, EUGENE J., optical engineer; b. Newton, Kans., Dec. 27, 1930; s. Jesse Jackson and Lillian (David) S.; m. Ruth Jane Moore, Jan. 4, 1958 (dec. 1977); children: Eugene J. II, Tiffany Mark; m. Mollie Aline Boyd Lee, Aug. 10, 1985; children: Jennifer A. Lee, Michael W. Lee. BEE, U. Calif., Berkeley, 1963. Registered profl. engr., Del. Commd. 2d lt. USAF, 1952, advanced through grades to capt., 1959, ret., 1963; sr. design draftsman Lawrence Nat. Lab., Livermore, Calif., 1958-59; sr. rsch. tech. Lawrence Nat. Lab., Berkeley, 1960-63; sr. rsch. engr. E.I. DuPont Co., Wilmington, Del., 1963-68; sr. devel. engr. Holotron Corp., Newark, Del., 1968-71; pvt. practice Wilmington, 1971-77; sr. scientist Proctor div. SCM Corp., King of Prussia, Pa., 1977-83; pres., cons. scientist Sturdyco, Inc., Paoli, Pa., 1983—; sr. rsch. engr. Spitz, Inc., Chadds Ford, Pa., 1984—. Patentee heat transfer and electrohydrodynamics, photopolymer process, optical-electronic devices. Mem. Optical Soc. Am., Am. Inst. Physics, Planetary Soc., Del. Assn. Profl. Engrs. (registered 1971), AAAS. Home: 140 Biddle Rd Paoli PA 19301-1104 Office: Spitz Inc US Rt 1 Chadds Ford PA 19317

STURDIVANT, LINDA LEE, psychotherapist; b. Pitts., Dec. 19, 1949; d. Matthew Lewis and Doris (Richardson) S.; m. James D. Chandler, Dec. 19, 1980. BS in Psychology, U. Pitts., 1981, MEd, 1982. Cert. employee assistance profl. Addictions therapist St. Francis Med. Ctr., Pitts., 1978-80; adolescent therapist U. Pitts., 1980-82; counseling cons. USX Copr., Pitts., 1982-86; employee counselor U. Pitts. Med. Ctr., 1986—; cons. Sturdivant & Assocs., Pitts., 1990—; bd. dirs. Allegheny Valley Mental Health/Mental Retardation, New Kensington, Pa.; therapist Turtle Creek Mental Health/Mental Retardation, Pitts., 1986—. Bd. dirs. Pa. Orgn. Women in Early Recovery, Pitts., 1990—, United Way, Pitts., 1991—. Mem. Am. Soc. Training & Devel., Coalition for Addictive Diseases, Employee Assistance Profls. Assn. (pres. Pitts. chpt. 1989—). Democrat. Roman Catholic. Home: RR 2 Box 426 New Kensington PA 15068-9330 Office: Univ Pitts Med Ctr ECS DeSoto and O'Hara Sts Pittsburgh PA 15213

STURGE, MICHAEL DUDLEY, physicist; b. Bristol, Eng., May 25, 1931; came to U.S., 1961, naturalized 1991; s. Paul Dudley and Rachel (Graham) S.; m. Mary Balk, Aug. 21, 1956; children: David Mark, Thomas Graham, Peter Daniel, Benedict Paul. BA in Engring. and Physics, Gonville and Caius Coll., Cambridge, Eng., 1952; PhD in Physics, Cambridge U., Eng., 1957. Mem. staff Mullard Rsch. Lab. (now Philips), Redhill, Eng., 1956-58; sr. rsch. fellow Royal Radar Establishment, Malvern, Eng., 1958-61; mem. tech. staff Bell Labs., Murray Hill, N.J., 1961-83, Bellcore, Red Bank, N.J., 1984-86; prof. dept. physics Dartmouth Coll., Hanover, N.H., 1986—; rsch. assoc. Stanford U., 1965, U. B.C., Vancouver, Can., 1969; vis. prof. Technion, Haifa, Israel, 1972, 76, 81, 85, Williams Coll., Williamstown, Mass., 1982, 84, Trinity Coll., Dublin, 1989, U. Fourier, Grenoble, France, 1989, 91; exch. scientist Philips Rsch. Lab., Eindhoven, The Netherlands, 1973-74. Contbr. over 100 papers in solid state physics to profl. publs.; co-editor: Excitons, 1982; editor Jour. of Luminescence, 1984-90. Fellow Am. Phys. Soc. Office: Dartmouth Coll Dept Physics Wilder Lab Hanover NH 03755-3528

STURM, DOUGLAS EARL, religion and political science educator; b. Batavia, N.Y., Apr. 22, 1929; s. Fred William and Louise (Gillette) S.; m. Margie Jean Anderson, Sept. 13, 1953; children—Hans Martin, Rolf Anderson. A.B., Hiram Coll., 1950; D.B., U. Chgo., 1953, Ph.D., 1959; postgrad., Harvard, 1964-65. Exec. sec. Christian Action, N.Y.C., 1954-55; asst. prof. religion Bucknell U., Lewisburg, Pa., 1959-64; asso. prof. religion Bucknell U., 1964-67, asso. prof. religion and polit. sci., 1967-70, prof. religion and polit. sci., 1970—, Presdl. prof., 1974-80, dir. honors council, 1970-72; vis. prof. Perkins Sch. Theology, summer 1963; vis. tutor Grad. Inst. in Liberal Edn., St. John's Coll., Santa Fe, summer 1972; vis. prof. social ethics Andover Newton Theol. Sch., Newton Centre, Mass., 1972-73; vis. prof. ethics and soc. U. Chgo., 1976-77; adj. prof. religious studies U. Tenn., Knoxville, 1991-92. Author: Community and Alienation, 1988; cons. editor Bucknell Press, 1971-83; bd. cons. Jour. Religion, 1972-83; assoc. editor JRE Studies in Religious Ethics, 1974—; chmn. bd. dirs. Jour. Law and Religion, 1982-89; columnist Christianity and Crisis, 1983-85; contbr. articles to profl. jours., chpts. to books. Bd. dirs. Inst. Study of Human Values, 1966-67; bd. dirs. Susquehanna Valley Symphony Orch. Assn., 1977-82, pres., 1980-82. Recipient Lindback award for excellence in teaching, 1966; named Alumnus of Yr., U. Chgo. Div. Sch., 1988; fellow Am. Coun. Learned Socs., 1964-65, Soc. for Religion in Higher Edn., 1967-68, Inst. Advanced Study Religion, U. Chgo. Div. Sch., 1983-84. Mem. Am. Soc. Legal and Polit. Philosophy, Am. Polit. Sci. Assn., AAUP, Council on Religion and Law (bd. dirs. 1977—), Soc. Christian Ethics (dir. 1963-67, exec. sec. 1968-72, pres. 1980-81), Council Study Religion (exec. com. 1971-77, 80-81, vice chmn. 1974-76, chmn. 1976-77), Am. Acad. Religion, A.C.L.U., La Société Européenne de Culture. Home: 37 S Water St Lewisburg PA 17837-1935

STURNER, FRED, finance company executive; b. Bronx, May 24, 1932; s. Harry and Sally Sturner; m. Arlene Ann Kramer, June 18, 1955; children: Susan B., Michael R. BS, NYU, 1955. V.p. Merrill Lynch Asset Mgmt., Lawrenceville, N.J., 1978—. Author: What Did You Do as a Kid, 1973. Home: 17 Morton Ct Lawrenceville NJ 08648-2113

STURTEVANT, RICHARD PEARCE, insurance consultant; b. Phila., Apr. 26, 1943; s. Hazen Kimbell Sturtevant and Lois (Armstrong) Edgerly; m. Phyllis Lanier, Oct. 10, 1970 (div. Apr. 1984); children: Kristen K., Hazen P. Student, Newtown (Mass.) Jr. Coll., 1967. CLU; chartered fin. cons., Pa. Asst. to pres. KSW Controls, Inc., Fairfield, Conn., 1969-70; prin. R.P. Sturtevant and Assocs., Rocky Hill, Conn., 1970-81; mgr. mkt. devel. Phoenix Mut. Life Ins., Hartford, Conn., 1981-83; asst. v.p. Fin. Data Planning Corp., Miami, Fla., 1983-84; dir. large corp. mktg. Mass. Mut. Life Ins., Springfield, Mass., 1984-86; v.p. Brown Bridgman & Co., Hartford, 1986-89; dir., sr. v.p. Mouton Inc. dba Brown Bridgman Retiree Health Care Group, N.Y.C., 1989-90; dir., pres. BB Funding, Inc., Rocky Hill, Conn., 1989-90; pres., chief exec. officer Ultimate Benefits Corp., Cromwell, Conn., 1987—; pres. Retiree Benefits, Inc., Cromwell, 1990—. Chairperson Jaycee's Spl. Olympics, Newington, Conn., 1975. Served with USAF, 1961-65. Recipient Gov.'s Civic award State of Conn., 1975. Republican.

STURTZ, DONALD LEE, physician, naval officer; b. Coshocton, Ohio, Apr. 18, 1933; s. Walter Raymond and Helene Josephine (Kubic) S.; m. Alice Marie McGuire, June 11, 1955; children: Jimalee, Janel. BS, U.S. Navel Acad., Annapolis, Md., 1955; MD, U. Pa., 1965. Diplomate Am. Bd. Surgery. Surgical resident USN, Phila., 1965-70; ship's surgeon USN, 1970-71; staff surgeon Bethesda Naval Hosp., USN, 1971-80; chief of surgery San Diego Naval Hosp., USN, 1980-84; exec. officer Oakland (Calif.) Naval Hosp., USN, 1984-85; prof. clinical sugery USN, Bethesda, Md., 1985-87; commd. Naval Med. Command USN, 1987-88; fleet surgeon USN, Norfolk, Va., 1989-91; surgeon USUHS, Bethesda, Md., 1991—. Contbr. articles to profl. jours. Recipient B.D. Larrey award for Surgical Execellence, Surgical Dept. USUHS, Bethesda, 1988. Fellow ACS (gov. 1985-88); mem. Am. Assn. for Surgery of Trauma, Assn. Mil. Surgeons, USN Inst. Republican. Methodist. Office: USUHS Dept Surgery 4301 Jones Bridge Rd Bethesda MD 20814

STURTZ, GEORGE STEPHEN, pediatrician; b. Carthage, N.Y., May 14, 1924; s. Russell Edward and Martha Loretta (Foley) S.; B.S., St. Lawrence U., 1949; M.D., Georgetown U., 1953; M.S. in Pediatrics, U. Minn., 1957; m. Helen Dermady, Aug. 31, 1946; children—George Stephen, Gretchen Ann. Intern, Detroit Receiving Hosp., 1953-54; fellow in pediatrics Mayo Clinic, Rochester, Minn., 1954-57; practice medicine specializing in pediatrics; mem. staff Mercy Hosp., pres. staff, 1982—; mem. staff House of Good Samaritan, Watertown, N.Y.; asso. clin. prof. pediatrics Upstate Med. Center, Syracuse, N.Y., asst. clin. prof. family practice; ofcl. oral examiner, chmn. oral exam. com., bd. dirs., sec.-treas. Am. Bd. Pediatrics Found., also mem. recert. com., and del. to Am. Bd. Med. Spltys.; bd. dirs. Am. Bd. Family Practice, Am. Bd. Pediatrics Found. Chmn., Jefferson County Mental Health Bd., 1960-70; co-founder North Country Children's Clinic, 1971—; med. dir. North Country Children's Clinic, Jefferson County Head-start, Am. Diabetes Assn., Jefferson County; pediatric cons. Cath. Charities. Author: A Common Sense Guide to Growth and Nutrition. Served to 2d lt. USMC, 1942-46. Recipient Caritas Medal Catholic Charities, Ogdenburg, N.Y., 1982; St. Joachim Humanitarian award Mercy Hosp., 1982, Sol C. Feinstone award St. Lawrence U., 1990. Fellow Royal Soc. Health, Am. Acad. Pediatrics (chmn. N.Y. chpt. I); mem. Ambulatory Pediatric Assn., Irish and Am. Pediatric Soc., N.Y. State Med. Soc. (chmn. pediatric sect.), Jefferson County Med. Soc. (pres. 1984), Sigma Xi. Republican. Roman Catholic. Office: PO Box 6600 Outer Washington St Watertown NY 13601

STURTZ-DAVIS, SHIRLEY ZAMPELLI, arts educator, fashion archivist; b. Lewistown, Pa., Apr. 1, 1937; d. Frank Paul and Helen Larue (Barnes) Zampelli; m. William Sturtz (dec.); children: Kraig, Steffany; m. William D. Davis, Dec. 29, 1984; stepchildren: Kimberly, Bryan, Mark. BS, Pa. State U., 1959, MA, 1961. Instr. Frostburg (Md.) State U., 1961-62; instr. Penn State, University Park, 1962-76, cons., instr., 1962-86; dir. arts in edn. program Central Intermediate Unit 10, West Decatur, Pa., 1976-89; exec. dir. Pa. Alliance for Arts Edn., Shippensburg, Pa., 1988-89; dir. fashion archives,

adj. instr. art dept. Shippensburg U., 1990—. Author (handbook) Exploring My World, 1981; artist exhibits at mus. galleries, 1959—; contbr. articles to profl. jours. and pubs. Chairperson Central Pa. Festival of the Arts, State Coll., Pa., 1966-76; bd. chair for youth Palmer Mus. of Art, 1979-86. Mem. Nat. Art Edn. Assn. (nat. outstanding art educator for Pa. award, 1981), Pa. Art Edn. Assn. (Pa. outstanding art educator award, 1981), Theatre Assn. Pa., Kappa Delta Gamma, Phi Deta Kappa. Home: 265 Newville Rd Shippensburg PA 17257-9502 Office: Shippensburg U Fashion Archives Shippensburg PA 17257

STUTMAN, LEONARD JAY, research scientist, cardiologist; b. Boston, Apr. 8, 1928; s. Herbert Hyman and Nellie (Wiener) S.; BS, MIT, 1948; MA, Boston U., 1949; MD, U. Rochester, 1953; m. Jeanne Ann Soblen, Dec. 23, 1951; children: Peter, David, Marc, Robin. Intern, resident medicine Bellevue Hosp., 1953-57; chief, med. services br. WPAFB, Dayton, Ohio, 1957-59; spl. advanced research fellow NIH, Nat. Heart Inst. 1959-61; instr. in clin. medicine N.Y. U. Coll. Medicine, 1956-61, asst. prof. pathology, 1961-65; assoc. prof. clin. medicine N.Y. Med. Coll., 1980—; head coagulation research lab. St. Vincent's Hosp. and Med. Center, N.Y., 1965—; attending physician St. Vincent's Hosp.; sr. attending physician medicine, sr. cardiologist Nyack (N.Y.) Hosp.; med. dir. Presdl. Life Ins. Co., Nyack, Urbaine Life Reinsurance Co., Tarrytown, N.Y.; bd. dirs. Metriplex, Inc. Cambridge, Mass., 1992—. Contbr. articles to profl. jours. Dir. cardiac epidemiology study Ford Found. Vera Inst.; mem. Internat. Com. on Thrombosis and Hemostasis. Capt. USAF, 1957-59. Fellow Am. Coll. Cardiology, ACP, N.Y. Acad. Medicine; mem. Am. Soc. Hematology, N.Y. Med. Soc., Sigma Xi. Home: 250 Townline Rd West Nyack NY 10994-2824 Office: 153 W 11th St New York NY 10011

STUTZMAN, BYRON WILLIAM, software company executive; b. Spring Valley, Ill., Nov. 2, 1938; s. James Earl and Christina Louise (Steidinger) S.; m. Nancy Claire Stepan, Aug. 31, 1963. BSME, U. Ill., 1960; MSME, MIT, 1966; M in Liberal Arts, Harvard U., 1988. Registered profl. engr., Mass. System analyst PHI Computer Svcs., Arlington, Mass., 1966-69, project leader, 1969-72; software engr. Programart Corp., Cambridge, Mass., 1972-90, v.p. corp. devel., 1991—. Contbr. articles and revs. to profl. jours. Mem. ASME, Assn. Computing Machinery, Sigma Xi, Sigma Tau, Pi Tau Sigma. Office: Programart Corp 125 Mt Auburn St Cambridge MA 02138-5748

STUVEN, SUSAN KNAUF, engineer; b. Rochester, N.Y., Oct. 12, 1945; d. James Arthur and Ruth Blanche (Wacker) Knauf; m. Thomas Leo Hannan, Mar. 2, 1968 (div. Dec. 1980); m. Henry August Stuven, Jan. 29, 1982; children: Constance, James. BS in Physics, Nazareth Coll., 1967. Rsch. physicist Bausch & Lomb Optical Co., Rochester, N.Y., 1967-68; programmer Communications & Systems Inc., Falls Church, Va., 1968-69; software engr. Computing and Software Inc., Greenbelt, Md., 1969-70; mgr. software Computer Scis. Corp., Silver Spring, Md., 1970-79, GE, Lanham, Md., 1979-87; dir. systems Kodak Remote Sensing, Landover, Md., 1987-89; ops. mgr. Computer Scis. Corp., Calverton, Md., 1989—, deputy project mgr., 1991—. Tchr. Hands on Sci. Program, Prince Georges County, Md., 1989; v.p. PTA, Duval High Sch., Lanham, 1987. Regents scholar, N.Y. State, 1963, Full scholar, Nazareth Coll., 1963. Mem. AIAA. Democrat. Lutheran. Office: CSC 4600 Powder Mill Rd Beltsville MD 20705-2675

STUY, TIMOTHY OGDEN, industrial automation engineer; b. Teaneck, N.J., Feb. 22, 1962; s. Cornelius and Eunice (Shergur) S. B. Engring., Stevens Inst. Tech., 1984. Computer application engr. N.Am. Philips, South Plainfield, N.J., 1984-89; field application engr. Allen-Bradley Co., Parsippany, N.J., 1989—. Mem. N.Y., Susquehanna & Western Tech. & Hist. Soc. Inc. (pres. 1988—), United RR Hist. Soc. N.J. Inc. (bd. dirs. 1988—). Republican. Home: 56J Village Grn Budd Lake NJ 07828-1378 Office: Allen Bradley Co 400 Interpace Pky Bldg D Parsippany NJ 07054-1113

STYRON, WILLIAM, writer; b. Newport News, Va., June 11, 1925; s. William Clark and Pauline Margaret (Abraham) S.; m. Rose Burgunder, May 4, 1953; children: Susanna Margaret, Paola Clark, Thomas, Claire Alexandra. Student, Christchurch Sch., Davidson Coll.; Litt.D., Davidson Coll., 1986; A.B., Duke U., 1947, Litt.D., 1968. Fellow Am. Acad. Arts and Letters at Am. Acad. in Rome, 1953; fellow Silliman Coll., Yale, 1964—; hon. cons. Library of Congress.; jury pres. Cannes Film Festival, 1983. Author: novels Lie Down in Darkness, 1951, The Long March, 1953, Set This House on Fire, 1960, The Confessions of Nat Turner, 1967 (Pulitzer prize 1968, Howells medal Am. Acad. Arts and Letters 1970), Sophie's Choice, 1979 (Am. Book award 1980), In the Clap Shack, play, 1972, This Quiet Dust, 1982, Darkness Visible, 1990; also articles, essays, revs.; editor: Best Stories from the Paris Rev., 1959; adv. editor: Paris Rev., 1953—; mem. editorial bd. The Am. Scholar, 1970-76. Decorated Commandeur de l'Ordre des Arts et des Lettres, Commandeur Legion d'Honneur (France); recipient Duke U. Disting. Alumni award, 1984, Conn. Arts award, 1984, Prix Mondial del Duca, 1985, Elmer Holmes Bobst award for fiction, 1989, Edward MacDowell medal for excellence in the arts, 1988, Nat. Mag. award, 1990. Mem. Am. Acad. Arts and Scis., Am. Acad. Arts and Letters, Signet Soc., Harvard, Académie Goncourt, Phi Beta Kappa. Democrat.

SU, JEN-HOUNE HANNSEN, mechanical engineer; b. Taipei, Taiwan, China, Aug. 31, 1954; came to U.S. 1978; BS, Nat. Cen. U., Chung-Li, Taiwan, 1977; MS, Ohio State U., 1979, PhD, 1982. Rsch. asst. Ohio State U., Dept. Engring. Mechanics, Columbus, 1978-82; project engr. Structural Mechanics Consultants Corp., Warren, Mich., 1982-84; sr. rsch. engr. Goodyear Rsch. Div., Akron, Ohio, 1984-89; sr. rsch. engr., program mgr. Carderock div. Naval Surface Warfare Ctr., Bethesda, Md., 1989—. Contbr. articles to profl. jours. Pres. Taiwanese Assn. of Akron, 1988. Mem. AIAA (sr. mem.), ASME, SAE, Am. Soc. for Composites, Acoustical Soc. Am., Phi Kappa Phi. Home: 14123 Rock Canyon Dr Centreville VA 22020-3861 Office: Naval Surface Warfare Ctr Carderock Div Code 1941 Bethesda MD 20084-5000

SU, TEDDY TSAUH-AN, economist; b. Taiwan, Nov. 28, 1935; came to U.S., 1961; s. Long-Sea and Yen-Chu (Hsu) S.; m. Joyce Mei-Tzyy Lin, Sept. 4, 1965; children: Anthony, Catherine. BA, Nat. Taiwan U., 1959; PhD, Rutgers U., 1966. Teaching, rsch. asst. Rutgers U., New Brunswick, N.J., 1961-66; asst. prof. Atlanta (Ga.) U., 1966-67, U. S.C., Columbia, 1967-73; sr. economist Fed. Preparedness Agy., Washington, 1974-80, Dept. Energy, Washington, 1980-82; sr. staff scientist Sterling Systems Inc., McLean, Va., 1982-83; pres. Allied Bus. Investors Inc., L.A., 1983; sr. economist Fed. Emergency Mgmt. Agy., Washington, 1983-86, Dept. Interior, Washington, 1986—. Contbr. articles to profl. jours. Recipient Spl. Achievement award Bur. Land Mgmt., 1990, Outstanding Performance award GSA/FPA, 1979. Mem. Am. Econ. Assn. Office: Dept of the Interior 1849 C St NW Washington DC 20240-9996

SUBRAMANIAN, R. SHANKAR, chemical engineering educator; b. Madras, India, Aug. 10, 1947; arrived U.S., 1968, naturalized, 1977; s. R. K. Rama and Sita (Lakshmi) S.; m. Jane M. Gatta, Nov. 24, 1973; children: Laura S., Erin S. BTech. in Chem. Engring., U. Madras (India), 1968; MS, Clarkson U., 1969, PhD, 1972. Part-time instr. SUNY, Buffalo, 1972-73; asst. prof. chem. engring. Clarkson U., Potsdam, N.Y., 1973-79, assoc. prof., 1979-82, prof., 1982—, chmn. dept., 1986—; mem. tech. staff Jet Propulsion Lab. and vis. assoc. dept. chem. engring. Calif. Inst. Tech., Pasadena, 1979-80; assoc. dir. Inst. Colloid and Surface Sci., Clarkson U., 1981-87; prin. investigator NASA Space Shuttle Expts. on low gravity fluid mechanics. Editorial adv. bd. Jour. Colloid and Interface Sci., 1984-86; contbr. articles to profl., tech. jours. Recipient Graham Rsch. award Clarkson U., 1978, Dow Outstanding Young Faculty award, 1980; Disting. Teaching award Clarkson U. 1981. Fellow AAAS; mem. Am. Inst. Chem. Engrs., Am. Soc. Engring. Edn., Am. Ceramic Soc., Sigma Xi. Office: Clarkson U Potsdam NY 13699-5705

SUBRAMANYAM, MADAKASIRA, animal nutritionist; b. Donekal, India, Oct. 28, 1949; came to U.S., 1975; s. Srinivasa Murthy and Padmavathi (Donekal) M.; m. Sandhya Rani Mantravadi, May 22, 1983; 1 child, Srinivas Saran. BVSc, AP Agrl. U., Tirupati, India, 1971, MSc, 1974; PhD, Kans. State U., 1980. Cert. profl. animal scientist. Nutritionist Zeigler Bros., Inc., Gardners, Pa., 1980-83, dir. nutrition, 1983-86, dir. nutrition and rsch., 1986-89, v.p. nutrition/rsch., 1989—. Mem. Am. Soc. Animal Sci., Am. Dairy Sci. Assn., Inst. Food Technologists, Coun. for Agrl. Sci. and Tech., Am. Assn. Lab. Animal Sci., Gamma Sigma Delta, Alpha Chi Sigma. Hindu. Home: 1305 Windsor Ct Carlisle PA 17013-3562 Office: Zeigler Bros Inc PO Box 95 Gardners PA 17324-0095

SUCHAROW, LAWRENCE ALAN, lawyer; b. Bklyn., Sept. 18, 1949; s. Joseph Chaim and Bertha (Saposnick) S.; m. Frances Ann Sucharow, June 11, 1972. BBA cum laude, CUNY, 1971; JD cum laude, Bklyn. Law Sch., 1975. Bar: N.Y. 1976, N.J. 1980. Assoc. atty. Weinstein & Levinson, N.Y.C., 1975-77; atty. ptnr. Goodkind Labaton Rudoff & Sucharow, N.Y.C., 1977—. Mem. ABA, N.Y. State Bar Assn. (chair com. on class actions 1988—, comml. and fed. litigation sect.), N.Y. County Lawyers Assn. (exec. com. on the fed. ctrs. 1984—), Fed. Bar Coun., N.J. Bar Assn. Office: Goodkind Labaton Rudoff & Sucharow 122 E 42nd St New York NY 10168

SUCHODOLSKI, STANLEY EDWARD, JR., fire service instructor; b. Bristol, Conn., Aug. 2, 1949; s. Stanley Edward and Mary Ann (Sroka) S.; m. Alice Jean Boutieller, June 2, 1973. Assoc. in Applied Sci., Waterbury State Tech. Coll., 1971. Fire svc. instr. II, Nat. Profl. Qualifications Bd. for the Fire Svc. Sr. capt., drillmaster Bristol Fire Dept., Bristol, Conn., 1972—; assoc. dir. Mayor's Task Force on Hazardous Materials, Bristol, 1985-88; assoc. chmn. Local Emergency Planning Com., Bristol, 1988—. Author: Hazardous Materials Incident Manual, 1985, Harzardous Materials Response Plan, 1988. Fund raiser United Way of Bristol, Conn., 1982-87. With USNG, 1969-75. Recipient Disting. Svc. award Conn. State Firemen's Assn.; named Outstanding Young Fireman, Bristol Jaycees, 1983. Mem. Conn. Fire Dept. Instrs.' Assn., Internatl Soc. Fire Svc. Instrs. Republican. Roman Catholic. Home: 86 Rita Dr Bristol CT 06010-7842 Office: Bristol Fire Dept Co # 4 Vincent P Kelly Rd Bristol CT 06010-7446

SUCICH, DIANA CATHERINE, school psychologist, counselor; b. N.Y.C., Apr. 23, 1948; d. Nicholas and Mildred (Bobich) S. MEd, Springfield (Mass.) Coll., 1973, cert. counseling, 1974; PhD, U.S. Internat. U., 1975. Dean of women Anderson Sch., Staatsburg, N.Y., 1971; cons. human devel. dept. YMCA, San Diego, 1975-77; postdoctoral resident Navy Alcohol Rehab. and Tng. Ctr., San Diego, 1975-77; instr. Chapman Coll., Orange, Calif., 1977-79; pvt. practice cons.; cons., instr. Moreno Acad. Psychodrama, Beacon, N.Y., 1982-83; sch. psychologist Rhinebeck (N.Y.) Cen. Sch. Dist., 1984-86, Beacon City Sch. Dist., 1986-87, Wappingers Cen. Sch. Dist., Wappingers Falls, N.Y., 1987—. Mem. Am. Psychol. Assn., Psychologists in Marital and Family Therapy, Fedn. Trainers and Tng. Programs in Psychodrama, Am. Soc. Group Psychotherapy and Psychodrama, Am. Bd. Examiners Psychodramas, Psi Chi Psychol. Honor Soc. Home: Stony Brook Estate 237 Old Hopewell Rd Wappingers Falls NY 12590 Office: Meyers Corners Sch Meyers Corners Rd Wappingers Falls NY 12590

SUDAN, NALIN KUMAR, pediatric anesthesiologist; b. Jagadhari, Punjab, India, Sept. 19, 1951; came to U.S., 1975; s. Madan Lall and Sushila Devi (Sharma) S.; m. Cynthia Wilczewski, Oct. 22, 1983; children: Derek Nalin, Craig Kumar. MB, BS, Med. Coll. Rohtak, India, 1972. Diplomate Am. Bd. Pediatrics, Am. Bd. Anesthesiology, spl. qualification in critical care. Resident pediatrics Coll. Medicine and Dentistry N.J., Newark, 1975-77; chief resident pediatrics Children's Hosp. Newark, 1977-78; resident anesthesiology Yale New Haven Hosp., 1978-80, fellow pediatric anesthesia, 1980-81, chief div. pediatric anesthesia, 1981-83; fellow pediatric anesthesia Children's Hosp. Phila., 1981; chief div. pediatric anesthesia North Shore U. Hosp., Manhasset, N.Y., 1983—; clin. asst. prof. Cornell Med. Ctr., N.Y.C., 1985—. Fellow Am. Acad. Pediatrics; mem. Am. Soc. Anesthesiology, Internat. Anesthesia Rsch. Soc., Soc. Pediatric Anesthesia, Lake Naomi Country Club (Pocono Pines, Pa.), Plandome Country Club (Manhasset, N.Y.). Hindu. Office: North Shore U Hosp 300 Community Dr Manhasset NY 11030

SUFRIN, ERICA MARIE, clinical psychologist; b. Washington, Jan. 17, 1944; d. Sidney Charles and Grace (de Jong) S.; m. Edward Gustav Horn, June 18, 1976; children: Christopher Charles, Matthew Garrett. BS, Russell Sage Coll., 1965; cert. phys. therapy, Albany Med. Coll., 1965; MA, U. So. Calif., L.A., 1970, PhD, 1975. Lic. psychologist, N.Y. Clin. assoc. Suicide Prevention Ctr., L.A., 1970-72; clin. psychology intern L.A. County-U. So. Calif. Med. Ctr., 1971-72; chmn., dir. Sch. Phys. Therapy Russell Sage Coll./Albany (N.Y.) Med. Coll., 1972-77; mem. staff Sexual Function Clinic Albany Med. Coll., 1976-78; dir. Geriatric Day Hosp. Capital Dist. Psychiatric Ctr., Albany, 1977-78, chief Geriatric Svcs., 1978-80; clin. assoc. prof. Albany Med. Coll., 1980—; pvt. practice, 1980—; cons. psychologist St. Anne Inst., Albany, 1981-84; mem. N.Y. State Bd. Psychology, 1985—, vice chmn., 1991—. Author: (with Couture and Edelstein) Behavior Assessment of the Traumatically Brain Damaged, 1984. Mem. budget com. Voorheesville (N.Y.) Cen. Schs., 1991—, sci. club com.,1 991—, trustee bd. edn., 1992—. Grantee Rehab. Svcs. Adminstrn., Washington, 1964-65, 68-69, 69-71. Mem. APA, N.Y. State Psychol. Assn., Psychol. Assn. of Northeastern N.Y. (pres. 1982-83), Psi Chi. Office: Erica M Sufrin PhD 785 Delaware Ave Delmar NY 12054-9797

SUGAR, JACK, physicist; b. Balt., Dec. 22, 1929; s. Fredel and Bessie (Silverman) S.; m. Judith Blumberg, Aug. 12, 1956; children: Ross, Eve, Erica. BA, Johns Hopkins U., 1955, PhD, 1960. Physicist Nat. Inst. Standards and Tech., Gaithersburg, Md., 1960—. Book: Energy Levels of Iron-Period Elements, 1985; contbr. over 125 articles to profl. jours. Grantee Fulbright 1966, NATO 1990; recipient Silver medal U.S. Commerce Dept., 1971. Fellow Optical Soc. Am. (dir. 1976-78). Office: Nat Inst Standards Tech Bldg 221 Rm A167 Gaithersburg MD 20899

SUGIYAMA, KAZUNORI, music producer; b. Tokyo, Aug. 18, 1950; came to U.S., 1976; s. Hiroshi and Michiko (Maeda) S.; m. Emi Fukui, Aug. 11, 1981. BS, Waseda U., 1974, postgrad., 1974-75; MA, Boston U., 1977. Jr. adminstrv. officer Japanese Mission to UN, N.Y.C., 1978-88; rep. N.Y. Toshiba EMI Records, Jazz Div., Tokyo, 1990—; rep. U.S. U.S. D.I.W. Records, Tokyo, 1991—; corr. Jazz Life, Tokyo, 1980-88; columnist OCS News, N.Y.C., 1982-90. Recording engr. (album) Bud and Bird/Gil Evans, 1988 (Grammy); producer V/Ralph Paterson, 1990 (Jazz Album of Yr.); co-producer The Nurturer/Geri Allen, 1991 (2d pl. Jazz Album of Yr.); translator Autobiography of Miles Davis, 1989. Mem. Nat. Acad. Recording Arts and Scis. Office: 93 Mercer St 3W New York NY 10012

SUGIYAMA, TOKU MARY, school administrator; b. Sacramento, Sept. 6, 1921; d. Sakae and Kuniko (Kosaka) Koda; m. Yone J. Sugiyama, Apr. 5, 1952; m. George Y. Morishita, Mar. 23, 1942; (dec. Mar. 1949); children—Maeona, Carolyn, George. Jr. cert. U. Calif.-Berkeley, 1941; B.A., Towson State U., 1980, M.A., 1984. Tchr., Poston Relocation Ctr., Ariz., 1941-44; purchasing agt. U.S. Dept. Def., Tokyo Ordnance Depot, 1952-56; instr. Ikebana Sogetsu Sch., Tokyo, 1956-67, exec. dir. Sogetsu USA, sch. Japanese flower arrangement, 1967—. Recipient Mohan Sho, Sogetsu Sch., 1960, Sofu Sho, 1967, Flower Arranger of Yr. award Nat. Council State Garden Clubs, 1979, Sofu Teshigahara Meml. award, 1991, First Sofu Meml. award, 1991. Mem. Md. Fedn. Garden Clubs, Ikebana Internat. (charter), Balt.-Kawasaki Sitster City Cultural Com. Home: 959 Ellendale Dr Baltimore MD 21204-1511

SUGLIA, PATRICK VINCENT, company executive; b. Reading, Pa., Sept. 6, 1962; s. Vincent A. and Patricia F. (Straka) S. AA in Liberal Arts, Reading Area Community Coll., 1988, AA in Respiratory Care, 1992. Cert. EMT, PA. Nurse asst. Med. Pers. Pool, Reading, 1983—; driver trip report clk. Penske Truck Leasing Co., Reading, 1988-90; home health aide Berks Vis. Nurse Assn., Reading, 1985-86. Author: The Cross Reference Directory of the U.S.A., 1990; composer Songs to Live By, 1984. Coord. Reading Vol. Crime Watch, 1986; attendant Gov. Mifflin Area Ambulance Assn., Shillington, Pa.; capt. Berks County Fire Police Assn.; CPR instr. Am. Heart Assn. Recipient Paderewski Gold medal Nat. Guild Piano Tchrs., 1981. Mem. Am. Assn. for Respiratory Care.

SUH, BYUNGSE, internal medicine educator; b. Ansung, Korea, Mar. 6, 1941; came to U.S., 1964; s. Sang Keun and Chong Sang (Lee) S.; m. Youngjoo Lee, Dec. 21, 1974; children: Jason, Jessica, Janice. BS, Chungang U., Seoul, Korea, 1962; MA, U. Kans., 1967, PhD, 1969; MD, U. Miami, 1973. Diplomate Am. Bd. Internal Medicine; diplomate Am. Bd. Infectious Diseases. Asst. prof. medicine Temple U. Sch. Medicine, Phila., 1978-83, assoc. prof. medicine, 1983-90, prof. medicine, 1990—. Contbr. articles to profl. jours. Fellow Infectious Diseases Soc. Am., Am. Coll. Physicians, Coll. Physicians Phila., Am. Coll. Clin. Pharmacology; mem. Am. Soc. Microbiology. Office: Temple Univ Sch Medicine Sect Infectious Diseases Broad and Ontario Sts Philadelphia PA 19140

SUHOCKI, DONALD JAMES, consultant; b. Schenectady, N.Y., May 6, 1950; s. John and Sophie (Zywot) S.; m. Ann Marie Stalica, Mar. 7, 1989; 1 child, Mary Cathryn. BA, SUNY, Albany, 1972; MBA, Pace U., 1980. Cert. compensation profl. Sr. pers. adminstr. N.Y. Dept. of Correctional Svcs., Beacon, 1974-76; pers. mgr. Hosp. Bur., Inc., Pleasantville, N.Y., 1976-79; compensation and benefits mgr. Merrill Lynch & Co., White Plains, N.Y.C., N.Y., 1979-82; compensation cons. G. E. Capital Corp., Stamford, Conn., 1982-87; cons. prin. DJS Assocs., Pittsfield, Mass., 1987—; cons. N.J. Govs. Mgmt. Rev. Commn., Trenton, 1990-91. Contbr. chpt. to book. Mem. Am. Compensation Assn., Capital Region Human Resource Assn. Home: 65 Lexington Pky Pittsfield MA 01201-7329

SUHR, J. NICHOLAS, lawyer; b. N.Y.C., Nov. 14, 1942; s. Rev. Dr. Heinrich P. and Anna H. (Isenschmid) S.; m. Anne Aylett Stone, July 6, 1965; children: John Nicholas Jr., Erika Christl. BA, U. Va., 1964; JD, Am. U., 1967. Bar: N.Y. 1967, N.J. 1969, U.S. Supreme Ct. 1989. Assoc., ptnr. Topken & Farley, N.Y.C., 1967-73, Conboy, Hewitt, O'Brien & Boardman, N.Y.C., 1973-86; counsel Hunton & Williams, N.Y.C., 1986-87, Quinn, Cohen, Shields & Bock, N.Y.C., 1987-88; ptnr. Quinn & Suhr, White Plains, N.Y., 1988—; arbitrator U.S. Dist. Ct. N.J., Trenton, 1985—, Am. Arbitration Assn., N.Y.C., 1976—. Contbr. articles to profl. jours. Mem. ABA, N.Y. State Bar Assn., N.J. State Bar Assn., U.S. Supreme Ct. Bar, Internat. Law Soc., Consular Law Soc., Product Liability Advisory Coun., German Soc. of N.Y.C. (trustee 1976—), German-Am. Sch. Assn. (trustee 1986—), German Seamen's Mission N.Y. (pres., dir. 1972—). Lutheran. Office: Quinn & Suhr 170 Hamilton Ave White Plains NY 10601-1715

SUI, FRANK, telecommunications company marketing executive; b. Taipei, Taiwan, Oct. 28, 1962; came to U.S., 1963; s. Chin-Tang and Yen-Ching Sui; m. Bonnie Messing, Feb. 3, 1991. BS, Cornell U., 1983; MBA, Harvard U., 1987. Bus. cons. McKinsey and Co., N.Y.C., 1983-85; with and mktg. and bus. devel. dept. Lotus Devel. Corp., Cambridge, Mass., 1986; dir. mktg. and bus. devel. Integrated Network Corp., Bridgewater, N.J., 1988—; founding mem. FastConnect Point-of-Sale Svc. Steering Com., Atlanta, 1988—. Home: 142 Fairfield Dr Short Hills NJ 07078

SUJAN, MITA, marketing educator; b. Bombay, Sept. 24, 1953; came to U.S., 1979; d. Jadav and Meenal (Mangaldas) Chatterji; m. Harish Sujan, Dec. 6, 1976; children: Monisha Chatterji, Ayesha Chatterji, Susan. BA with honours, U. Delhi, India, 1973; MBA, U. Bombay, 1975; PhD, UCLA, 1983. Account planner Grant Advt., Bombay, 1975-77; market rsch. exec. Ogilvy, Benson & Mather, Bombay, 1977-79; rsch. and teaching asst. UCLA, 1979-83; asst. prof. mktg. Pa. State U., University Park, 1983-88, assoc. prof. mktg., 1988—. Contbr. articles to profl. jours. Merit scholar U. Delhi, 1971-73, U. Bombay, 1973-75; Chancellor's fellow UCLA, 1979-83. Mem. APA, Assn. for Consumer Rsch. Office: Pa State U 701 BAB University Park PA 16802

SUK, JIN HONG, pathologist; b. Seoul, Sept. 11, 1937; came to U.S., 1965; s. Il Keun and Soon Ae (Lee) S.; m. Soon Ja Lee, June 7, 1967; children: Peter, Mary. MD, Yonsei U., Seoul, 1962. Diplomate Am. Bd. Pathology. Staff pathologist Franklin (Pa.) Hosp., 1970-71; dir. lab. Grove City (Pa.) Hosp., 1971-75; staff pathologist N.W. Med. Ctr., Franklin, Pa., 1975—. Lt. USN, 1962-65. Mem. AMA, Am. Soc. Clin. Pathologist, Am. Soc. Cytology, Pa. Med. Soc., Internat. Acad. Pathology (U.S. and Can. div.). Democrat. Roman Catholic. Office: NW Med Ctr 1 Spruce St Franklin PA 16323

SULLIVAN, ANDREW RICHARD, financial consultant; b. Bryn Mawr, Pa., Nov. 14, 1956; s. John Francis and Ann Lee (Fitzhugh) S.; m. Lisa Christine Presson, Oct. 10, 1987. BA, Westminster Coll., 1978; MBA, St. Joseph's U., 1984. Asst. v.p. Continental Bank, Phila., 1978-88; pres. Sullivan Fairfax Corp., Wayne, Pa., 1988—; cons. CM Fin., Wayne. Dir. Hayes Manor, Phila. With Pa. NG, 1991—. Mem. Baronial Order Magna Carta (marshal), Penn Club, Union League Phila., Sons of Revolution (asst. sec.), Gavel Soc., First Troop Phila. City Cavalry, Soc. Colonial Wars Pa. Office: CM Fin 565 E Swedesford Rd Ste 100 Wayne PA 19085

SULLIVAN, ANNE DOROTHY HEVNER, artist; b. Boston, Mar. 17, 1929; m. James Leo Sullivan, Jan. 20, 1951; children: Maura, Mark, Lianne, Christopher. Student, Northeastern U., 1973-75; BA, U. Mass., Lowell, 1977; postgrad., De Cordova Mus., Lincoln, Mass., 1978-81. Art dir., instr. Whistler House Mus., Lowell, Mass., 1971-73; art instr., dir. alternatives for individual devel. program U. Mass., Lowell, 1976-84; incorporator Depot Square Artists Gallery, Lexington, Mass., 1981-84; dir., art cons. Abbey Art Gallery, Boston, 1987-88; juried artist Emerson Umbrella Ctr. for Arts, Concord, Mass., 1989—; assoc. artist Brush with History Gallery, 1990—; juror, lectr., demonstrator, tchr. to art groups and assns., 1971—. Exhibited in group shows at Fed. Res. Gallery, Boston, 1990, Brush with History Gallery, 1990, Lowell Urban Nat. Pk., 1990, Midwest Mus. of Am. Art, Elkhardt, Ind., 1991, Cahoon Mus., Cotuit, Mass., 1991; represented in collections at Neil Sulier Art Collection, Lexington, Ky., The New Eng. Bank, Shawmut Bank, Bay Banks, Concord Nat. Bank, Amoskeag Banks, N.H., 1st Capital Bank of Concord, N.H., Sheraton Corp., Boston, Calif., New Orleans. Bd. dirs. Human Svcs. Corp., Lowell, 1971-72; v.p. Whistler Mus. Art, 1972-73; chmn. Lowell Arts Coun., 1980-81; mem. Mass. Arts Advocacy Coun., Boston, 1982. Recipient hon. mention All New Eng. Competition, 1989, 2d prize Cahoon Mus., 1991. Mem. Nat. Assn. Women Artists (Martha Reed Meml. award 1988), New Eng. Watercolor Soc. (bd. dirs. 1984-92), Monotype Guild New Eng. (pres. 1992—), Nat. League Am. Penwomen (award of excellence 1990), Copley Soc. (Copley Artist award), Emerson Ctr. for Arts, Brush with History Gallery. Home: 28 Rindo Park Dr Lowell MA 01851-3413 Studio: Emerson Umbrella Ctr Arts 40 Stow St Concord MA 01742

SULLIVAN, ARTHUR PHILIP, psychologist; b. Jersey City, July 28, 1943; s. Arthur Philip and Margaret Rita (Griffin) S.; B.S., St. Peters Coll., 1967; M.S., Fordham U., 1974, Ph.D., 1978; m. Noreen Theresa Crowe, Aug. 3, 1968; children—Arthur, Stephen, Noreen, Meaghan, Mary, John, Gregory. Faculty CUNY, N.Y.C., 1973-78, 86—; prof. Hofstra U., Hempstead, N.Y., 1978-80; dir. ins. sales support systems Ednl. Instn., 1978-81; prof., sr. researcher on drug abuse Fordham U., N.Y.C., 1980-85; assoc. prof. psychology East Stroudsburg U., 1987—; prin. investigator N.Y.C. Substance Abuse Programs, 1985-88; cons. on religious edn. U.S. Mil. Acad., 1973; cons. on ednl. evaluation N.Y.C. Bd. Edn., 1978—; cons. on addiction research Daytop Village, Inc., 1982—; supr. mental health Sullivan County for Dupage Village, 1989—. Hon. bd. dirs. Birthright of Lower Westchester, 1975—; bd. dir. St. Jude's Christian Edn. Ctr., 1982—; elected mem. North Warren Regional Bd. Edn., 1987-89; pres. Blairstown Parent-Tchr. Group, 1982-85; evaluator Gov.'s Challenge Excellence grant Montclair State Coll. Sch. Fine and Performing Arts, 1987—; expert witness for mental health matters Superior Ct. N.J., 1987—. Co-recipient Nat. Inst. on Drug Abuse grant, 1980-83; recipient tchr. excellence award Hofstra U., 1980. Mem. Am. Psychol. Assn., Am. Ednl. Research Assn. Roman Catholic. Contbr. writings to profl. publs. Home and Office: 5 Ward Rd Blairstown NJ 07825-9636

SULLIVAN, CHARLES, university dean, educator, author; b. Boston, May 27, 1933; s. Charles Thomas and Marion Veronica (Donahue) S.; divorced; children: Charles Fulford, John Driscoll, Catherine Page. BA in English, Swarthmore Coll., 1955; MA, NYU, 1968, PhD in Social Psychology, 1973; MPA, Pa. State U., 1978. Ass't prof. Ursinus Coll., Collegeville, Pa., 1973-78; mgmt. cons., 1978-86; adj. prof. Pa. State U., Radnor, Pa., 1978-80; prof., dept. head Southeastern U., 1986-89; asst. dean Grad. Sch. Arts and Scis. Georgetown U., Washington, 1989-92, assoc. dean Grad. Sch. Arts and Scis., 1992—; exec. dir. Doylestown Found., Doylestown, Pa., 1958-73; mem. adj. faculty U. Coll. U. Md., 1984—; lectr., speaker on poetry and art Cooper-Hewitt Mus., N.Y., 1989, Nat. Soc. Arts and Letters, Washington,

1989, Martin Luther King Jr. Libr., Washington, 1989, 90, 91, 92, Met. Mus. Art, N.Y., 1989, 91, Smithsonian Instn., Washington, 1990, 91, 92, others. Author: Alphabet Animals, 1991, The Lover in Winter, 1991, Numbers at Play, 1992, Circus, 1992; ed.: America in Poetry, 1988, (2d edition) 1992, Imaginary Gardens, 1989, Ireland in Poetry, 1990, Children of Promise, 1991, Loving, 1992. predoctoral fellowship N.Y. U., 1964-68; postdoctoral fellowship Ednl. Testing Service, Princeton, N.J., 1973-74; univ. honors scholar N.Y. U. 1974; disting. prof. Southeastern U., Washington, 1987. Mem. Am. Poetry Soc., Nat. Soc. Arts and Letters, Folger Poetry Bd., Poetry Com. Greater Washington, Cosmos Club. Office: Georgetown U Grad Sch 302 Intercultural Ctr Washington DC 20057-1005

SULLIVAN, CHARLES IRVING, polymer chemist; b. Milw., Nov. 18, 1918; s. Charles Andrew and Bessie May (Blackwell) S.; m. Ruth Irene Wadsworth, Sept. 4, 1948; children: Charles Wadsworth, Janet Lynn. AB, Boston U., 1943; postgrad., MIT, 1943, 47, Northeastern U., 1945, 51. Chemist Union Bay State Chem. Co., Cambridge, Mass., 1943-46, head indsl. and shoe pect., 1946-54, group leader, 1954-59; mgr., rsch. and devel. Staley Chem. Div., A.E. Staley, Cambridge, 1959-67, rsch. assoc., 1967-69; sr. sci. Polaroid Corp., Cambridge, 1969-70, rsch. assoc., 1970-79, rsch. fellow, 1979-85, cons., 1985—; Patentee in field. Fellow Am. Inst. Chemists; mem. AAAS, Am. Chem. Soc., Beethoven Soc. (Melrose, Mass.). Home: 148 Bellevue Ave Melrose MA 02176-2818

SULLIVAN, DANIEL JOSEPH, orthopaedic surgeon; b. Cohasset, Mass., Oct. 8, 1949; s. Frederick L. and Marjorie (Figeriedo) S.; m. Arlene D. Alcasahas, May 22, 1983; 1 child, Daniel Joseph Jr. BS, U. Conn., 1972; MD, Georgetown U., 1982. Diplomate Am. Bd. Orthopaedic Surgeons. Intern in gen. surgery Georgetown U. Med. Ctr., 1982-83; resident Hosp. for Joint Diseases, 1983-87; orthopaedic surgeon USN Hosp., Charleston, S.C., 1987-88; dept. head USN Hosp., Yokosoka, Japan, 1988-91; head dept. spine surgery Buffalo (N.Y.) Gen. Hosp., 1991—. Recipient Simmons Spine fellowship Buffalo Gen. Hosp., 1992. Fellow Am. Acad. Orthopaedic Surgeons; mem. Alpha Omega Alpha. Home: 749 W Delavan Ave Buffalo NY 14222

SULLIVAN, DANIEL RICHARD, lawyer, anesthesiologist; b. Pitts., Sept. 8, 1951; s. Jeremiah B. and Marjorie Louraine (Eyles) S.; m. Kathleen Offner, Nov. 25, 1977; children: Ashleigh, Jared, Shannon, Caitlin, Brianne. BA magna cum laude, Holy Cross Coll., 1973; MD, Jefferson Med. Coll., 1976; JD cum laude, Duquesne U., 1984. Bar: Pa. 1984, U.S. Dist. Ct. (western dist.) Pa. 1984; diplomate Am. Bd. Anesthesiology. Residency U. Pa., Phila., 1977-79; physician Pitts. Anesthesia Assn., 1979—; assoc. Houston Harbaugh, Pitts., 1988—; pres., bd. dirs. Advanced Billing Concepts, Pitts.; cons. Med. Data Systems, Richmond, Va., 1988-91. Contbr. articles to profl. jours. Fellow Am. Bd. Anesthesia (examiner 1987—); mem. ABA, AMA, Western Pa. Soc. Anesthesiologists (pres. 1987-88), Pa. Bar Assn., Allegheny County Bar Assn. Republican. Roman Catholic. Office: Houston Harbough 2 Chatam Ctr 12th Fl Pittsburgh PA 15219

SULLIVAN, DENIS FRANCIS, JR., industrial technology educator, researcher; b. Boston, Oct. 11, 1944; s. Denis F. and Helen R. (Girard) S. BA, Tufts U., 1966; PhD, U. N.C., 1972; MLS, Cath. U., 1975. Librarian U. Coll. U. Md., College Park, 1976-78, asst. dean, 1978-79, asst. dean grad. studies, 1979-82; asst. prof. indsl. tech. U. Md., College Park, 1982-88, assoc. prof., 1988—. Author: Life of St. Nikon, 1987. Fellow Woodrow Wilson Ctr., 1969-70, Dumbarton Oaks, 1991—. Mem. Am. Philol. Assn. Office: U Md 3216 J M Patterson College Park MD 20742

SULLIVAN, DOROTHY LOUISE, nurse; b. Alton, Ill., July 20, 1938; d. Walter George William and Edna Louise (Poag) Huebner; m. Thomas L. Sullivan, Oct. 10, 1964 (div. 1989); children: Thomas L. Jr., Catherine L., Joseph D., Theresa E. RN, Alton Meml. Hosp., 1959; student, So. Ill. U., 1960, Ind. U., Bloomington, 1961-62, Community Coll. Allegheny Co., 1985, 87, Pa. State U., 1990. RN, Ill., Pa. Surgical nurse, operating room Alton (Ill.) Meml. Hosp., 1959-61; nurse, supr. Bloomington (Ind.) Hosp., 1961-63; surgical nursing, rehab. nursing Meth. Med. Ctr. of Ill., Peoria, 1963-65; operating room nurse St. Francis Med. Ctr., Peoria, 1965-66; staff nurse, inservice utilization Farmington (Ill.) Nursing Home, 1978-82, acting dir. nurses, instr. nurses aide, 1982; devel. and instr. nurses aide cert. program Spoon River Community Coll., Canton, Ill., 1981-82; surgical charge nurse, staff nurse St. Joseph Med. Ctr., Bloomington, Ill., 1982-84; day staff charge nurse, supr. Murray Manor Convalescent Ctr., Murrysville, Pa., 1984—. Med. chairperson Farmington PTA, 1980-81. Mem. Farmington Nurses Club (v.p. 1980-82). Republican. Roman Catholic. Home: 579 Carnival Dr Pittsburgh PA 15239-2626

SULLIVAN, DOROTHY RONA, state official; b. Boston, Jan. 7, 1941; d. Lewis Robert and Dorothy (Hopkins) S.; B.A., Boston U., 1963; M.Ed., State Coll. Boston, 1966; C.A.G.S., Boston U., 1972; postgrad. Northeastern U., 1970-71, Boston Coll., 1974-78, U. Mass., 1980. Rsch. asst. Boston Lying-in Hosp., 1963-64; employment counselor Mass. Div. Employment Security, Boston, 1964-66, sr. employment counselor, 1966-67, prin. employment counselor, 1967-70, employment office mgr., 1970-75, supr., 1975-78, chief rsch. dept., 1978-88, dir. def. employment analysis, 1985-87; chief rsch. dept. Mass. Dept. Employment and Tng., 1989—. Supr. community counselor interns and rehab. adminstrn. interns Northeastern U. Grad. Sch. Edn., 1968-74; supr. public adminstrn. interns Suffolk U., 1976; supr. econ. interns Boston U., 1979, Regis Coll., 1984. Recorder Gov.'s Conf. on Rehab., 1970, mem. Gov.'s Commn. Employment of Handicapped, 1972-78, Pres.'s Com. Employment of Handicapped, 1975-78; exec. bd. Greater Boston council Camp Fire Girls; R.S.V.P. adv. bd. Boston Commn. Affairs of the Elderly, 1977-78; mem. adv. com. equal employment opportunity practices Dept. Personnel Adminstrn., 1984-85. Mem. ACA (recorder), AACD, ASPA Mass. coun.), APGA (nat. redorder conf. 1968), Nat. Career Devel. Assn., Nat. Rehab. Assn. (Mass. sec. 1971-72, exec. bd. 1972-74, v.p. 1974-75, pres. 1976-77), Am. Fedn. State, County and Mcpl. Employees (exec. bd. local 164 1972-73, 74-76), Am. Acad. Polit. and Social Sci., Rockport Art Assn. (patron), Am. Econ. Assn., Am. Bus. Women's Assn. (del. nat. conv. 1980, 83, pres. Boston chpt. 1982, Woman of Yr., Boston chpt. 1983), Am. Soc. Pub. Adminstrn. (life, region I-II liaison, sect. women in pub. adminstrn. 1988-90, Mass. chtp. coun. mem., officer), Boston Ctr. for Internat. Visitors. Author: Boston Employment Service Guide, 1969, Careers and Training in the Allied Health Field, 1989; Massachusetts Cities and Towns, 1978-82; editor Mass. Trends, 1978-82; contbr. articles to profl. jours. Home: 33 Morey Rd Roslindale MA 02131-1037 Office: 19 Staniford St Charles F Hurley Bldg Boston MA 02114

SULLIVAN, EDMUND JOSEPH, educator, consultant; b. Cin., May 2, 1951; s. Edmund Joseph and Joan (Secco) S.; m. Joan Barbara Feldstein, Apr. 29, 1978; children: Alexandra Rachel, Ian Jeremy. BA, Columbia U., 1973, MA, 1981, MEd, 1985. Asst. dir. Student Ctr. Columbia U, N.Y.C., 1973-78; assoc. dir. Columbia Scholastic Press, N.Y.C., 1978-81, dir., 1981—; pres. Columbia Community Svcs., N.Y.C., 1989—; mem. adv. bd. U.-Nat. Coll. Monthly, Santa Monica, Calif., 1988—. Editor: Student Press Rev., 1984— (Editorial of Yr. award 1988). Bd. dirs. Student Press Law Ctr., Washington, 1983—. Mem. Am. Soc. Assn. Execs., Community Coll. Journalism Assn., Journalism Edn. Assn., Coll. Media Advisers. Office: Columbia U Central Mall Rm Box 11 New York NY 10025

SULLIVAN, GREGORY FRANCIS, cardiologist; b. Jersey City, Mar. 6, 1940; s. Francis Xavier and Lucy Agnes (Harmon) S.; m. Gene Marilyn Hejke, Sept. 24, 1966; children: Gregory Francis II, Brendan Jared, Alexandra, Tara, Natasha. BA, Georgetown U., 1962; postgrad., NYU, 1962-66, Cornell U., 1969-70. Diplomate Am. Bd. Internal Medicine, Am. Bd. Internal Medicine subsplty. Cardiovascular Disease. Intern in mixed medicine Montefiore Hosp. & Med. Ctr., Bronx, 1966-67; resident in cardiology NYU/Bellevue Med. Ctr., 1967-68; fellow in cardiology Cornell U./N.Y. Hosp. Med. Ctr., 1969-70, fellow in invasive cardiology, 1972-74; attending cardiologist Passaic (N.J.) Gen. Hosp., dir. Maj. U.S. Army, 1970-72, Korea. Fellow Am. Coll. Cardiology. Republican. Roman Catholic. Home: 257 Upper Mountain Ave Montclair NJ 07043-1015 Office: 202 Orient Way Rutherford NJ 07070-2498

SULLIVAN, JAMES ASH, visitor information service executive; b. Boston, July 25, 1946; s. Edward Joseph and Dorothea Mallon (Ash) S.; m. Alane Marie Karpinski, Oct. 7, 1979; children: Conor James, Casey Patrick. BA, U. Vt., 1968. Juvenile officer Burlington (Vt.) Police Dept., 1968-70; prin., ptnr. Tridel Constrn. Inc., Concord, N.H., 1970-72; owner, operator Ho-Tei Catamaran Cruises Inc., St. Thomas, Virgin Islands, 1972-78; tugboat operator Western Tug & Barge, Inc., San Francisco, 1978-82; founder, owner Here's Where Visitor Info. Svcs., Rye, N.H., 1983—. Mem. Vt. Gov.'s Crime Commn., Montpelier, 1969-70. Mem. Nat Assn. Profl. Brochure Distbrs., N.H. Hospitality Assn., N.H. Travel Coun., Seacoast Coun. on Tourism (v.p. 1984-85, pres. 1985-87), Hampton Beach C. of C., Portsmouth C. of C. Democrat. Roman Catholic. Home and Office: PO Box 592 619 Washington Rd Rye NH 03870

SULLIVAN, JOHN GERARD, surgeon; b. Boston, Mar. 2, 1941; s. Francis Gerard and Anna Maria (Maiorana) S.; m. Margaret B. McIntyre; children: Meghan, Erin, Caitlin. BS, Boston Coll., 1962; MD, Tufts U., 1966. Diplomate Am. Bd. Surgery. Intern St. Elizabeth's Hosp., Boston, 1966-67; asst. resident surgery St. Luke's Hosp., N.Y.C., 1969-72; chief surgical resident St. Luke's Med. Ctr., N.Y.C., 1972-73; gen. surgeon Brighton (Mass.) Surg. Assocs.; assoc. dir. surg. ICU, coord. surg. residency St. Elizabeth's Hosp., Boston, 1981-84, chmn. dept. surgery, 1984—; clin. instr. surgery Tufts U., 1973-77, asst. clin. prof. surgery, 1977-79, assoc. clin. prof. surgery, 1980-85, clin. prof. surgery, 1985—. Capt. U.S. Army, 1967-68, Vietnam. Mem. Mass. Med. Assn., Am. Coll. Surgeons (councilor Mass. chpt. 1982-85), Assn. Surg. Edn., Boston Surg. Soc., New Eng. Program Dirs. in Surgery, Assn. Program Dirs. in Surgery, New Eng. Surg. Soc., Boston Coll. Alumni Assn., Fides Club, 4th Inf. Div. Assn. Office: Brighton Surg Assocs 11 Nevins St Ste 201 Brighton MA 02135

SULLIVAN, JOSEPH PETER, insurance broker; b. Boston, Sept. 8, 1939; s. Joseph Francis and Mary Anna (Stokes) S.; m. Rachael Anne Cullen, Dec. 22, 1974; children: Philip, Sandra, Susan, Frederick. B Gen. Studies, U. Nebr., 1968; MA, U. No. Colo., 1973, Cen. Mich. U., 1976. Sr. acct. exec. Arkwright Ins., Greenwich, Conn., 1977-83; v.p. Frenkel & Co., N.Y.C., 1983-84; sr. account exec. Republic Hogg Robinson, N.Y.C., 1984-85; v.p. Alexander & Alexander, N.Y.C., 1985—; assoc. Miller-Heiman Internat., Walnut Creek, Calif., 1986—. Mem. membership com. Met. Rep. Club. With U.S. Army, 1956-77, ETO, Korea and Vietnam. Decorated Bronze Star. Mem. Soc. Human Resource Mgmt., Assn. Former Intelligence Officers (life), N.Y. C. of C. and Industry (membership com. 1992), Ret. Officers Assn. (bd. dirs. Knickerbocker chpt.), Soc. CPCUs, Am. Soc. CLUs, Toastmasters, N.Y. Athletic Club, Rotary, Masons. Republican. Roman Catholic. Home: 105 Oldfield Rd Fairfield CT 06430-6660 Office: Alexander & Alexander 1185 Ave Of The Americas New York NY 10036-2601

SULLIVAN, KEVIN MICHAEL, marketing professional; b. Detroit, Aug. 26, 1964; s. Michael P. and Carol (Schuyler) S. BA in Journalism, U. N.C. 1986. Asst. account exec. Biggs/Gilmore Advt., Hilton Head, S.C., 1986-87; sr. account exec. Doremus & Co., N.Y.C., 1987-89; mgr. pub. rels. Am. Express Travelers Cheques, N.Y.C., 1989-91; mgr. mktg. Am. Express, N.Y.C., 1990—; cons. M.P. Sullivan Assocs., Charlotte, N.C. Guest columnist Adweek, 1987; contbr. to profl. publ. Recipient Mercury award Mercury Communications, 1989. Mem. Pub. Rels. Soc. Am. (Silver Anvil award 1990), N.C. Soc. N.Y. Home: 84 Charles St New York NY 10014 Office: Am Express Co 100 Church St New York NY 10007-2601

SULLIVAN, LOUIS WADE, secretary of health and human services of U.S., physician; b. Atlanta, Nov. 3, 1933; s. Walter Wade and Lubirda Elizabeth (Priester) S.; m. Eve Williamson, Sept. 30, 1955; children: Paul, Shanta, Halsted. B.S. magna cum laude, Morehouse Coll., Atlanta, 1954; M.D. cum laude, Boston U., 1958. Diplomate: Am. Bd. Internal Medicine. Intern N.Y. Hosp.-Cornell Med. Ctr., N.Y.C., 1958-59, resident in internal medicine, 1959-60; fellow in pathology Mass. Gen. Hosp., Boston, 1960-61; rsch. fellow Thorndike Meml. Lab. Harvard Med. Sch., Boston, 1961-63; instr. medicine Harvard Med. Sch., 1963-64; asst. prof. medicine N.J. Coll. Medicine, 1964-66; co-dir. hematology Boston U. Med. Ctr., 1966; assoc. prof. medicine Boston U., 1968-74; dir. hematology Boston City Hosp., 1973-75; also prof. medicine and physiology Boston U., 1974-75; dean Sch. Medicine, Morehouse Coll., Atlanta, 1975-89, pres., until 1989; sec. Dept. of Health and Human Svcs., Washington, 1989—; mem. sickle cell anemia adv. com. NIH, 1974-75; ad hoc panel on blood diseases Nat. Heart, Lung Blood Disease Bur., 1973, Nat. Adv. Rsch. Coun., 1977; mem. med. adv. bd. Nat. Leukemia Assn., 1968-70, chmn., 1970; researcher suppression of hematopoiesis by ethanol, pernicious anemia in childhood, folates in human nutrition. John Hay Whitney Found. Opportunity fellow, 1960-61. Mem. Am. Soc. Hematology, Am. Soc. Clin. Investigation, Inst. Medicine, Phi Beta Kappa, Alpha Omega Alpha. Episcopalian. Office: Dept HHS Office of the Sec 200 Independence Ave SW Washington DC 20201*

SULLIVAN, PAUL JOSEPH, artist; b. Providence, May 19, 1947; s. Allyn Frederick and Isabel Marie (Moran) S.; m. Katheen A. Muldoon, Dec. 30, 1989; 1 child, Ryan Muldoon Sullivan. BS, Providence Coll., 1969. Computer programmer Olin Corp.-Winchester Western Div., New Haven, Conn., 1969-70; computer programmer/analyst Armstrong Rubber Co., New Haven, Conn., 1970-74, Gulf & Western Collyer Wire Div., Lincoln, R.I., 1974-76; computer specialist Office of Institutional Rsch. Brown U., Providence, 1976-82; pres. P. Sullivan & Co., Narragansett, R.I., 1982—. Creator design for over 140 coats of arms for Roman Catholic bishops, archbishops, cardinals etc., also for clubs, schs. etc. both in U.S. and abroad. Active in St. Thomas More Ch., Narragansett (liturgy com. 1985—, parish council 1988—); mem. liturgical commn. Roman Catholic Diocese of Providence 1987—. Mem. The Dunes Club. Roman Catholic. Home and Office: 34 Anawan Dr Narragansett RI 02882-1909

SULLIVAN, RALPH MICHAEL, space power systems engineer; b. Boston, July 6, 1934; s. Ralph Nutter and Mary Veronica (Carter) S.; m. June Elizabeth McAvoy, June 6, 1959; children: Kevin Joseph, Karen Ann Sullivan Smith. BS in Physics, Boston Coll., 1957; MS in Applied Sci., George Washington U., 1970. Aerospace technologist energy conversion Goddard Space Flight Ctr., NASA, Greenbelt, Md., 1961-65; power system engr. Applied Physics Lab., Johns Hopkins U., Laurel, Md., 1966-82; power system supr. Applied Physics Lab. JHU, Laurel, Md., 1982—; instr. Whiting Sch. Engring., Johns Hopkins U., Laurel, 1989—. Co-inventor battery charge control system, 1973; contbr. articles to profl. jours. Presentor of sci. show St. Catherine Labore, Metropolitan DC and other pub. grade schs., 1982-90; sci. fair judge St. Catherine Labore Elem. Sch., Wheaton, Md., 1989-90. With U.S. Army, 1957. Mem. AIAA (sr., aerospace power system tech. com. chmn. 1991—). Roman Catholic. Home: 13118 Greenmount Ave Beltsville MD 20705-3248 Office: JHU Applied Physics Lab 23-212 Johns Hopkins Rd Laurel MD 20705

SULLIVAN, RICHARD JOHN, public relations executive, consultant; b. Green Bay, Wis., May 9, 1949; s. John Brady and Jacqueline (Skellet) S.; m. Judith Helene Kimmel, Jan. 11, 1970; children: Josh, Katherine. AA, Canada Coll., 1970; BS, San Francisco State U., 1972. Newspaper reporter, editor San Mateo (Calif.) Times, 1973-79; newspaper stringer San Francisco Chronicle, 1979; press sec. Congressman Bill Royer, Washington, 1979-80; pub. rels. exec. Daniel J. Edelman Inc., Washington, 1980-82, A-K Assocs. Inc., Washington, 1982-85; exec. v.p. Fleishman-Hillard Inc., Washington, 1985—; guest lectr. Am. U., Washington, 1983; program cons. ABC News, N.Y.C., 1983; mem. Am. del. of USIA/Soviet Info. Talks, 1990. Assoc. editor Travelage West, 1974. Pub. rels. cons. Dem. Congl. Campaign Com., Washington, 1985. Mem. Pub. Rels. Soc. Am., The Nat. Press Club. Office: Fleishman Hillard Inc 1301 Connecticut Ave NW Washington DC 20036-1815

SULLIVAN, ROBERT MARTIN, academic administrator; b. Holyoke, Mass., Feb. 12, 1953; s. James John and Emily Mae (Belzarini) S. AB, St. Anselm Coll., 1975; EdM, Harvard U., 1986. Fundraiser Nat. Multiple Sclerosis Soc., N.Y.C., 1976-77; asst. to v.p. devel. St. Anselm Coll., Manchester, N.H., 1977-81, dir. ann. fund, 1981-85, asst. to pres., 1985-91; dir. of devel. St. Anselm Coll., Manchester, 1991—. vice chmn. allocations Greater Manchester United Way, 1988—; mem. People for The Am. Way, Manchester, 1985—, Common Cause, 1989—; campaign vol. N.H. Cath. Charities, Manchester, 1989-90. Mem. Nat. Soc. Fund Raising Execs. (v.p., sec. 1979-85), N.H. Coun. on Fund Raising (treas. 1984-86), Am. Assn. Higher Edn., Coun. Advancement and Support of Edn., Rotary. Democrat. Roman Catholic. Office: St Anselm Coll 87 St Anselms Dr Manchester NH 03102-1310

SULLIVAN, ROGER JOSEPH, university vice president; b. Waterbury, Conn., Dec. 12, 1947; s. John Thomas and Dorothy (Moss) S.; m. Susan D'Angelo, Aug. 24, 1968; children: Robert, Christopher. BA, Wesleyan U., 1970; MS, Hartford Grad. Ctr., 1983. Asst. dir. devel. Wesleyan U., Middletown, Conn., 1970-72; assoc. dir. devel. Wheaton Coll., Norton, Mass., 1972-74; dir. devel. and pub. rels. Cazenovia (N.Y.) Coll., 1974-75; dir. devel. and pub. affairs Child Welfare League, Stamford, Conn., 1975-83; dir. univ. relations U. New Eng., Biddeford, Maine, 1983-84, v.p., 1984—; mng. ptnr. Independents Inc., Hartford, 1980-84. Co-author book and lecture series: Marketing Mental Health, 1982. Pres. Wells (Maine) Pub. Libr., 1988—. Recipient Wells Pub. Schs. Bucklin award for community svc., 1990. Roman Catholic. Home: Quarry Rd Wells ME 04090 Office: Univ of New England Biddeford ME 04005

SULLIVAN, STEPHEN GENE, psychiatrist, pharmacologist, administrator; b. Manchester, N.H., Feb. 27, 1947. BS, Georgetown U., 1970; MS, NYU, 1976, PhD, 1977, MD, 1984. Assoc. research scientist NYU Sch. Med., 1978-81, rsch. asst. prof. pharmacology, 1981-82, adj. asst. prof. pharmacology, 1984-91; intern Beth Israel Med. Ctr., N.Y.C., 1984, resident in psychiatry, 1984-88, physician-in-charge Clin. Psychopharmacology Lab., 1988-90; sci. dir. The Corp. for Clin. Psychopharmacology Research, N.Y.C., 1988—; pvt. practice N.Y.C., 1986—; instr. psychiatry Mt. Sinai Sch. Med. CUNY, 1986-88, asst. clin. prof. psychiatry, 1988-90. Contbr. numerous articles to profl. jours. and author nine book chpts., 1976—. Med. scientist tng. program fellow NIH, 1970-76, 82-83, postdoctoral fellow, 1976-77. Mem. AAAS, AMA, Am. Psychiat. Assn., N.Y. Acad. Sciences. Office: Corp Clin Psychopharm Res 207 E 16th St Ste 4M New York NY 10003-3742

SULLIVAN, STEPHEN KELLY, biomedical research scientist; b. Kansas City, Mo., May 15, 1961; s. Herman Lin and Jo Anne (Larimer) S. BA summa cum laude, Drury Coll., 1983; PhD in Physiology (hons.), Kans. U., 1987. Postdoctoral fellow Columbia U., N.Y.C., 1987-90, assoc. rsch. scientist, 1990—. Contbr. articles to profl. jours. NIH grantee, 1987—. Mem. Am. Physiol. Soc., Soc. Gen. Physiologists, Harvey Soc., N.Y. Acad. Scis., Sigma Xi. Office: Columbia Univ 630 W 168th St 10-508 630 W 168th St P&S 10-508 New York NY 10032

SULLIVAN, SULLINS GRENFELL, surgeon, consultant; b. Stonewall, Okla., Oct. 6, 1912; s. Bedford Forrest and Jessie Eulalia (Lyles) S.; m. Alyce Idella Thomas, Oct. 6, 1937; 1 child, Thomas Joseph. BS in Medicine, U. Okla., 1933, MD, 1935. Diplomate Am. Bd. Surgery. Intern St. Joseph Hosp., Balt., 1935-36, resident in medicine, 1936-37, resident in surgery, 1937-39; chief resident in surgery Bon Secourse Hosp., —, 1939-40; chief of surgery Bon Secaurs Hosp., Balt., 1955-76, St. Joseph Hosp., Balt., 1976-83. With U.S. Army, 1942-46. Fellow ACS; mem. Med. Chirurg. Faculty of Md., (founder) Balt. Acad. of Surgery, Porsche Club Am. Home: 419 Oak Ln Baltimore MD 21204 Office: 1129 St Paul St Baltimore MD 21202

SULLIVAN, WILLIAM HALLISEY, JR., football league executive; b. Lowell, Mass., Sept. 13, 1915; s. William H. and Vera F. (Sullivan); m. Mary K. Malone, Dec. 29, 1941; children: Charles W., Kathleen Marie, Mary Jeannie, Nancie Vera, William Hallissey III, Patrick Jerome. A.B., Boston Coll., 1937, postgrad., 1938-39; postgrad., Harvard U. (summer 1938). Publicity dir. Boston Coll., 1938-40; spl. asst. to dir. athletics U. Notre Dame, 1941-42; dir. U.S. Naval Aviation Tng. Program, 1942-45; dir. pub. relations U.S. Naval Acad., 1946, Boston Braves, 1946-52; owner All Star Sports, Inc., 1952-55; asst. to pres. Met. Coal & Oil Co., Dorchester, Mass., 1955-56; v.p. Met. Coal & Oil Co., 1956-58, pres., 1958-76; group v.p. Met. Petroleum Co., 1977-84; owner New Eng. Patriots Football Club, 1975-88, pres., 1975—; pres. Am. Football League, 1963-69; chmn. TV com., merger com. of Nat. and Am. (football leagues); bd. dirs. Brynwood Ptnrs., Air Express Internat., Nat. Football League, Inc., Dana-Farber Inst.; chmn. bd. Nat. Football League Properties, Inc.; incorporator Union Savs. Bank. Chmn. Greater Boston Stadium Authority, 1962—; chmn. Christmas Seal campaign Mass. Tb Assn., 1963-64; bd. dirs. Catholic Counseling Service, Mass. Eye Research Corp., Stonehill Coll.; mem. Pres.'s Council Boston Coll. Served with USNR, 1942-46. Mem. New Eng. Fuel Dealers Assn., Knight of Malta. Clubs: Indian Creek Country, Hundred of Mass. (dir.), Algonquin (Boston), Woodland Golf, Vesper Country, Fort Hill, Oyster Harbors, Atlantis Country Club (Fla.). Office: care New England Patriots Sullivan Stadium RR 1 Foxboro MA 02035

SULLIVAN, WILLIAM PATRICK, construction executive; b. Bklyn., Jan. 1, 1952; s. William Joseph and Lorraine Patricia (Flynn) S.; m. Lynne Marie Chmurzynski; children. BSME, SUNY, Stony Brook, 1981. Engr. McCarthy Bros., St. Louis, 1981-82; gen. supt. Gilbane Bldg. Co., Providence, 1982-85, Lehrer/McGovern, N.Y.C., 1985-88; v.p. ops. Metcon Constrn. Corp., N.Y.C., 1988-89; prin., exec. v.p. DeJohn/Sullivan Co., Inc., N.Y.C., 1989—. Pres. Lawrance Farms Community Ass., Bay Shore, N.Y., 1988-89. Mem. ASME, Cement League N.Y. Office: DeJohn/Sullivan 19 Fulton St New York NY 10038-2100

SULT, JEFFERY SCOT, performing company executive, playwright, director; b. Washington, Dec. 29, 1956; s. Elmer Ray Sult and Elizabeth Bush (DeVary) Bocher. AA, Fla. Jr. Coll., Jacksonville, 1979; BFA, U. Fla., 1981; MA, NYU, 1982, cert. in film and video, 1990. Artistic dir. Acme Prodns., N.Y.C., 1983—. Writer, dir.: (plays) Relationship, 1983, Trialogue #1, 1983, Letter, 1984, Party, 1984, Trialogue #2, 1984, Marines, 1984, Thinking, 1984, Horseshoe, 1985, Anniversary, 1985, Trialogue #3, 1985, Wedding, 1985, Quagmire, 1985, Reunion, 1986, (teleplays) Call-In, 1987, Dialogue #1, 1988, Enigma, 1989, Maze, 1990, A Map of the City, 1991. Sgt. USMC, 1975-77. Mem. Authors League Am., Dramatists Guild (assoc.), Internat. Alliance Theatrical Stage Employees. Home: 4489 Broadway Apt 3G New York NY 10040-2406 Office: Acme Prodns PO Box 53 New York NY 10014-0053

SULTANOF, JEFFREY BRAD, composer, arranger, conductor, editor, lecturer; b. Jamaica, N.Y., July 24, 1954; s. Marc Louis and Sylvia (Weisberg) S. Studies with Lothar Perl, 1973-74, studies with Jerome Graff, 1973-78; BA in Music, CUNY, 1978. Freelance composer, condr., arranger, historian N.Y.C., Calif., 1978—; mng. editor Creative, 1990-91; editor Standard and Ednl. Music/Warner Bros. Pubs., Inc., N.Y.C., and Calif., 1978-82; chief editor Standard and Ednl. Music/Warner Bros. Pubs., Inc., N.Y.C., 1983; creative editor Warner Bros. Pubs., Inc., Secaucus, N.J., 1984-89; editorial dir. Warner Bros. Publs., Inc., Secaucus, N.J., 1991—; writer, lectr. Am. music and films, N.Y.C., Calif., 1972—; arranger, condr. for numerous club and cabaret artists, N.Y.C., Calif., 1974—. Editor (textbook) Arranged by Nelson Riddle, 1985; editor, annotator (4 hist. vols.) Gershwin Facsimile Edition, 1987; writer over 200 arrangements for various instrumental combinations and various pubs., 1984—. Mem. Internat. Assn. Jazz Record Collectors, Condrs. Guild, Am. Symphony Orch. League, Am. Fedn. Musicians, Robert Farnon Soc., Soc. for Animation Studies, Soc. for Preservation of Film Music. Democrat. Jewish. Office: Warner Bros Pubs Inc 265 Secaucus Rd Secaucus NJ 07094-2194

SULTZER, BARNET MARTIN, microbiology and immunology educator; b. Union City, N.J., Mar. 24, 1929; s. Moses Joseph and Florence Gertrude (Fischer) S.; m. Judith Ray Moreinis, Aug. 26, 1956; 1 child, Steven Bennett. BS, Rutgers U., 1950; MS, Mich. State U., 1951, PhD, 1958. Rsch. assoc. Princeton (N.J.) Labs., Inc., 1958-64; from asst. prof. to prof. microbiology SUNY, Bklyn., 1964—, interim chmn. dept. microbiology, 1980-82; vis. scientist Karolinska Inst., Stockholm, Sweden, 1971-72; vis. prof. Pasteur Inst., Paris, 1979-80. Assoc. editor Jour. of Immunology, 1983-86; contbr. book chpts. and 50 articles to profl. jours. on microbiology and immunology; mem. editorial bd. Infection and Immunity, 1980—. Pres. Tenants Assn. Gateway Pla., Manhattan, N.Y., 1990—; mem. Community Bd. # 1, Manhattan, 1989-93. 1st lt. USMC, 1952-55. Pres.'s fellow Am. Soc. Microbiology, 1957; grantee USPHS, NIH, Office of Naval Rsch., 1967-92. Mem. AAAS, Am. Soc. Microbiology, Am. Assn. Immunologists, N.Y. Acad. Sci., Harvey Soc., Internat. Endotoxin Soc., Reticuloendothelial Soc., Sigma Xi. Office: SUNY Health Sci Ctr 450 Clarkson Ave Brooklyn NY 11203-2098

SULYK, STEPHEN, archbishop; b. Balnycia, Western Ukraine, Oct. 2, 1924; s. Michael and Mary (Denys) S. Student, Ukrainian Cath. Sem. of Holy Spirit, Fed. Republic Germany, 1945-48, St. Josaphat's Sem., 1948-52; Licentia in Sacred Theology, Cath. U. Am., 1952. Ordained priest Ukrainian Cath. Ch., 1952. Assoc. pastor Omaha, 1952, Bklyn., 1953, Minersville, Pa., 1954, Youngstown, Ohio, 1955; pastor Ch. Sts. Peter and Paul, Phoenixville, Pa., 1955, St. Michael's Ch., Frackville, Pa., 1957-61, Assumption of Blessed Virgin Mary Ch., Perth Amboy, N.J., 1962-81; sec. Archeparchy Chancery, 1956-57; adminstr. St. Nicholas, Phila., 1961; archbishop Met. of Ukraine-Rite Catholics of Archeparchy, Phila., 1981—; vice chmn. Priests Senate, 1977-78; bd. dirs. Diocesan Adminstrn., 1972-79; pres. Ascension Manor, Inc.; archbishop Ukranian Rite Caths. Archeparchy Phila., Met. Ukranian-Rite Caths. U.S.A.; chmn. Priest's Senate; chmn. ad-hoc inter-rite com. Nat. Cath. Conf. Bishops/U.S. Cath. Conf., 1991. Mem. Providence Assn. Am. (Supreme Protector), Coll. Bishops of Roman Cath. Ch., Presidium of Synod of Ukranian Cath. Bishops (treas.). Office: 827 N Franklin St Philadelphia PA 19123-2097

SULZBERGER, ARTHUR OCHS, SR., newspaper executive; b. N.Y.C., Feb. 5, 1926; s. Arthur Hays and Iphigene (Ochs) S.; m. Barbara Grant, July 2, 1948 (div. 1956); children—Arthur Ochs, Karen Alden; m. Carol Fox, Dec. 19, 1956; 1 dau., Cynthia Fox; adopted dau., Cathy. B.A., Columbia, 1951; LL.D., Dartmouth, 1964, Bard Coll., 1967; L.H.D., Montclair State Coll., 1972, Tufts U.; LLD (hon.), U. Scranton; L.H.D., Columbia U., 1992. With N.Y. Times, N.Y.C., 1951—; asst. treas. N.Y. Times, 1958-63, pres., 1963-79, pub., 1963-92, chmn., chief exec. officer, 1992—, also bd. dirs.; dir. Times Printing Co., Chattanooga. Trustee emeritus Columbia U.; trustee Met. Mus. Art, chmn. bd. trustees, 1987—. Served to capt. USMCR, World War II. Mem. Bur. Newspaper Advt. (dir.), SAR, Overseas Press Club, Explorers Club, Met. Club (Washington). Office: NY Times Co 229 W 43rd St New York NY 10036-3913

SULZBERGER, ARTHUR OCHS, JR., newspaper publisher; b. Mt. Kisco, N.Y., Sept. 22, 1951; s. Arthur Ochs Sulzberger and Barbara Winslow Grant; m. Gail Gregg, May 24, 1975; children: Arthur Gregg, Ann Alden. BA, Tufts U., 1974; postgrad., Harvard U. Bus. Sch., 1985. Reporter The Raleigh (N.C.) Times, 1974-76; corr. AP, London, 1976-78; Washington corr. N.Y. Times, 1978-81, city hall reporter, 1981, asst. metro editor, 1981-82, group mgr. advt. dept., 1983-84, sr. analyst corp. planning, 1985, prodn. coordinator, 1985-87, asst. pub., 1987-88, dep. pub., 1988-92, pub., 1992—. Bd. dirs. N.C. Outward Bound Sch., Morganton, 1979, N.Y.C. Outward Bound Ctr., N.Y.C., 1988, Am. Press Inst., 1989; vice chmn. Task Force on Minorities in Newspaper Bus., 1989, chmn. 1992—. Office: The NY Times 229 W 43rd St New York NY 10036-3913

SULZER, DAVID LOUIS, neurobiologist; b. N.Y.C., Nov. 6, 1956; s. Edward Stanton and Beth (Weiner) Sulzer-Azaroff; m. Leslie Vosshall, June 20, 1987. BS, Mich. State U., 1979; MS, U. Fla., 1981; PhD, Columbia U., 1988. Rsch. scientist Columbia U., N.Y.C., 1988—. Recipient Young Investigator award Nat. Alliance for Rsch. in Schizophrenia and Depression, 1990-92, F.I.R.S.T. award NIMH, 1991-96. Mem. AAAS, N.Y. Acad. Sci., Soc. for Neuroscience. Home: 247 W Broadway New York NY 10013 Office: Columbia U Dept Psychiatry 722 W 168th St Box 62 New York NY 10032

SUMMERS, ANNE FAIRHURST, editor; b. Deniliquin, NSW, Australia, Mar. 12, 1945; came to U.S., 1986; d. Austin Henry Fairhurst and Eileen Frances (Hogan) Cooper; m. John Summers, Apr. 28, 1967. BA with honors, U. Adelaide, Australia, 1970; PhD, U. Sydney, Australia, 1979. Sr. writer Nat. Times, Sydney, 1975-78; fellow World Press Inst., St. Paul, 1978, now bd. dirs.; bur. chief Australian Fin. Review, Canberra, 1979-83; head Office of Status of Women Dept. of Prime Minister, Canberra, 1983-86; North Am. mgr. John Fairfax (U.S.) Ltd., N.Y.C., 1986-87; editor-in-chief Ms. Mag., N.Y.C., 1987-89, editor-at-large, 1990—; corr. Far Ea. Econ. Rev., Canberra, 1980-83, Le Monde, Canberra, 1983; bd. dirs. Matilda Publs., Inc., N.Y.C., 1988-89; mem. adv. bd. World Press Inst., 1989—. Author: Damned Whores and God's Police, 1975, Gamble for Power, 1983; co-author: Her Story: First Women in Print, 1979. Named to Order of Australia, Queen Elizabeth II, 1989; Young Writer's fellow Lit. Bd. Australia, 1974. Mem. Am. Soc. Mag. Editors. Home: 253 W 73d St New York NY 10023 Office: Lang Comm Inc 230 Park Ave New York NY 10169-0005

SUMMERS, DALE EDWARDS, school system administrator, education educator; b. Hershey, Pa., Oct. 19, 1949; s. Charles Edward and Phyllis Elaine (Risser) S.; m. Linda Louise Lashbrook, Sept. 12, 1950; children: Shannon Robert, Shelby Louise. BS, Ball State U., 1971, MA, 1973, EdD, 1977. Tchr. of emotionally disturbed Muncie (Ind.) Community Schs., 1971-76; asst. elem. prin. Derry Twp. Sch. Dist., Hershey, Pa., 1977-84, asst. high sch. prin., 1985-89; supr. secondary spl. edn. West Shore Sch. Dist., Lemoyne, Pa., 1989-90; prin. Highland Elem. Sch., Camp Hill, Pa., 1990—; asst. prof. edn. Lebanon Valley Coll., Annville, Pa., 1990—. Contbr. articles to profl. jours. Asst. coach Hershey (Pa.) Baseball Assn., 1987—; soccer coach Palmyra (Pa.) Recreation Assn., 1987—. Mem. Am. Assn. Secondary Sch. Prins. Republican. Methodist. Home: 24 S Center Ave Palmyra PA 17078-2001

SUMMERS, JOSEPH HOLMES, English language educator; b. Louisville, Feb. 9, 1920; s. Hollis Spurgeon and Hazel (Holmes) S.; m. U.T. Miller, Sept. 24, 1943; children—Mary Elliott, Hazel Lincoln, Joseph Holmes, Jr. A.B. magna cum laude, Harvard U., 1941, M.A., 1948, Ph.D. in English, 1950. Teaching fellow history and lit. Harvard U., 1945-48; instr. lit. Bard Coll., 1948-50; asst. prof. U. Conn., 1950-55, assoc. prof., 1955-59; prof. English Washington U., St. Louis, 1959-66; acting chmn. dept. Washington U., 1960-61, chmn., 1963-64; prof. Mich. State U., 1966-69, U. Rochester, N.Y., 1969-76; Roswell S. Burrows prof. English U. Rochester, 1976-85, Roswell S. Burrows prof. emeritus, 1985—; vis. prof. Amherst Coll., 1962-63, U. Kent, Canterbury, Eng., 1972. Author: George Herbert-His Religion and Art, 1954, The Muse's Method-An Introduction to Paradise Lost, 1962, The Heirs of Donne and Jonson, 1970, Dreams of Love and Power: On Shakespeare's Plays, 1984; Editor: Andrew Marvell-Selected Poems, 1961, The Lyric and Dramatic Milton, 1965, George Herbert-Selected Poetry, 1967; Bd. editors: George Herbert Jour., John Donne Jour., Studies in English Lit. Fund for Advancement Learning fellow Italy, 1952-53; Guggenheim fellow, 1957-58; Fulbright lectr Oxford U.; vis. fellow All Souls Coll., 1966-67; sr. fellow Folger Shakespeare Library, Washington, 1976; Nat. Endowment for Humanities-Huntington Library fellow, 1980-81; fellow Am. Acad. Arts and Scis., 1982. Mem. MLA, Internat. Assn. Univ. Profs. English, Milton Soc. Am. (pres. 1982), Guild of Scholars of Episc. Ch. (pres. 1985-86), Phi Beta Kappa. Episcopalian. Home: 179 Crosman Ter Rochester NY 14620-1829

SUMMERS, WILMA POOS, biochemist, biologist; b. Richmond, Ind., Dec. 8, 1937; d. Raymond Henry and Naomi Christina (Unger) Poos; m. William Cofield Summers, July 24, 1965; 1 child, Emily Alexandra. BS, Ohio U., 1959; PhD, U. Wis., 1966. Postdoctoral fellow U. Wis., Madison, 1966-67, Harvard U., Boston, 1967-68; postdoctoral fellow Yale U., New Haven, 1968-69, rsch. assoc., 1969-78, sr. rsch. assoc., 1978-83, rsch. scientist, 1983—. Contbr. articles to profl. jours. Mem. Am. Soc. for Virology, Am. Soc. for Biochemistry and Molecular Biology. Office: Yale U Sch Medicine 333 Cedar St New Haven CT 06510-3289

SUMMERSCALES, WILLIAM, educator; b. Silsden, Yorkshire, Eng., Aug. 5, 1921; came to U.S., 1953; s. Edmund and Margaret (Newns) S.; m. Ruth Bruere Sickler, Sept. 1945 (div. 1969); children: Marjorie Summerscales Hart, Stephen Tracy Summerscales (dec.); m. Elpida Tsonides, May 31, 1970. BA, BTh, Ea. Nazarene Coll., 1945; MDiv, San Francisco Theol. Sem., 1956; MA, U. Toronto, Can., 1965; PhD, Columbia U., 1969. Min. Presbyn. Ch., Calif., Can., 1945-60; study sec. hdqrs. staff Presbyn. Bd. of Christian Edn., Phila., 1960-67; adminstrv. assoc. Tchrs. Coll., Columbia U., N.Y.C., 1967-69, assoc. prof., 1970—, dir. placement, 1969-72, dir. devel., 1972-86. Author: Affirmation and Dissent, 1970, (with others) Jesus-Four Gospels in Modern English, 1974. Mem. San Mateo County Planning Commn., 1958-60. 1st lt. USAFA, 1958-60. Mem. Phi Delta Lambda. Democrat. Home: 400 W 119th St New York NY 10027-7125 Office: Tchrs Coll Columbia U PO Box 61 New York NY 10027-0061

SUMMERTON, JEFFREY EDWARD, clinical psychologist; b. Norwalk, Conn., Sept. 27, 1954; s. Edward Joseph and Marguerite (Farmer) S.; m. Susan Lynn Schwartz, Sept. 20, 1987; children: Jonathan Michael, Lauren Jane. BA, Boston U., 1976; MA, Temple U., 1980, PhD, 1986. Lic. psychologist, Pa. Ct. psychologist Superior Ct. N.J. Gloucester County, Woodbury, 1985-88; pvt. practice Phila., 1988—. Mem. Gloucester County Youth Svcs. Commn., Woodbury, 1985-86; chmn. subcom. Gloucester County Probation Adv. Bd., 1990—. Mem. Am. Psychol. Assn., Am. Psychology Law Soc., Phi Beta Kappa. Mem. Soc. Friends. Office: 1731 Delancey Pl Philadelphia PA 19103

SUMMERVILLE, DAVID, pediatrician, chemist. Pediatrician Children's Hosp., Boston. Office: Children's Hosp Boston MA 02202

SUMMONS-MCGUIRE, AGATHA BRYNA, state agency official; b. Suffolk, Mass., July 19, 1951; d. John Knowles and Agatha Valentine (MacIntosh) Summons;1 child, Lanisja N.; m. Sam McGuire, Nov. 21, 1989. AA, Roxbury Community Coll., 1979; BS, N.H. Coll., 1983; MEd, Cambridge Coll., 1984. Unit sec./mgr. Univ. Hosp., Boston, 1970-86; dir. employment Urban League of Ea. Mass., Boston, 1986-88; part-time vocat. and career counselor Madison Park Community Sch., Boston, 1986-88; asst. dir. affirmative action, EEO Met. Dist. Commn., Boston, 1988—; cons. Cambridge Coll., 1986-89. Mem. NAACP, Urban League of Ea. Mass., Employment Access Network, Joint Action in Community Svc., Lincoln Sudbury Regional High Parents Orgn., Cambridge Coll. Alumni Assn.

SUMNER, DAVID GEORGE, association executive; b. Norwich, Conn., Apr. 22, 1949; s. Raymond W. and Ruth M. (Crooks) S.; m. Linda Ann Churma, June 27, 1980; 1 child, Deryn Anne. MA in Polit. Sci., Mich. State U., 1970; MBA, U. Conn., 1979. Corr. Travelers Ins. Co., Hartford, Conn., 1971-72; asst. sec. Am. Radio Relay League, Newington, Conn., 1972-76, asst. gen. mgr., 1976-82, gen. mgr., 1982-85, exec. v.p., 1985—. Bd. dirs. Windham Regional Planning Agy., Willimantic, Conn., 1991—. Recipient Calcutta Key, Radio Soc. Gt. Britain, 1989, Region I award Internat. Amateur Radio Union, 1989; Radio Club Am. fellow, 1991. Mem. Newington C. of C. (bd. dirs. 1988-90). Democrat. Congregationalist. Office: Am Radio Relay League 225 Main St Newington CT 06111-1494

SUMNER, STEPHEN ISAAC, educator; b. Bronx, N.Y.; s. Charles S. and Mollie (Kaufman) S.; m. Ellen R. Rosenbaum, Apr. 22, 1967; children: Charles J., Randi Sue. BA, Brandeis U., 1964; MS in Edn., CUNY, 1968; EdD, Columbia U., 1974. V.p. Kaufman Iron Works, Bronx, 1964-68; tchr. N.Y.C., 1968-73; prin. Fletcher Sch., Jamestown, N.Y., 1973-77, Siwanoy Sch., Pelham, N.Y., 1977-80; v.p. Krell Software, St. James, N.Y., 1981-91; assoc. edn. support systems Whitcomb Assocs., 1991—. Editor, Logo Jour., 1982-87; sr. editor: Student Guide to the SAT; editor, contbr. to Connections, 1985, Nat. Tchr. Exam Prep., 1986, Scoring Higher Grade 1-9, 1987, LSAT-GMAT-GRE Prep, 1985-87. Mem. Am. Soc. Curriculum Devel., Am. Soc. Pers. Adminstrn., Brandeis U. Alumni Assn. (pres. Westchester chpt. 1987-89), Phi Delta Kappa. Home: 205 Carol Ave Pelham NY 10803-1803

SUMNER, WILLIAM THOMAS, metal products exeuctive, retail executive; b. Albany, N.Y., Oct. 16, 1954; s. James Thomas and Doris (Meron) S.; m. Barbara Jean Sumner, Aug. 14, 1976; children: Katie, Ellen. AS in Bus., Hudson Valley Community Coll., Troy, N.Y., 1974; BS in Mktg., Siena Coll., 1976. V.p. Arcadia Supply Inc., Albany, 1976—. 1st lt. U.S. Army, 1976-82. Home: 45 Voyage Dr Glenmont NY 12077 Office: Arcadia Supply Inc 60 Broadway Albany NY 12202

SUMSER, JOHN RAYMOND, electronics company executive, consultant; b. Tooele, Utah, Sept. 29, 1954; s. Raymond Joseph and Anne Carolyn (Miller) S.; m. Colleen Catherine Gildea, June 17, 1978; children: Bridget Moriah, Raymond Joseph, Catherine Cecilia. BA in Psychology/Philosophy, Cath. U. Am., 1978; postgrad., Johns Hopkins U., 1979-83, Loyola Coll., Balt., 1986-87. Cert. profl. logistician. Tech. writer Westinghouse Electric Corp., Balt., 1979-80, intercultural trainer, 1981, program mgr. ship design, 1982, program mgr. design, 1983-85, program mgr. AWACS, 1986-89, dir. bus. devel., 1990—; cons. on orgnl. devel. Sumser Enterpriss, Westminster, Md., 1987—. Contbr. articles to profl. jours. Home: 178 E Green St Westminster MD 21157 Office: Westinghouse Electric Corp PO Box 1898 MS 4310 Linthicum MD 21213

SUN, BENEDICT CHING-SAN, engineering educator, consultant; b. Nanking, People's Republic of China, Nov. 5, 1934; came to U.S., 1955; s. Kuang-Yu Sun and Ta (Chen) Chiang; m. Alice Kau-Hwa Mao, Sept. 18, 1965; children: Christina, David, Eileen. BSME, Nat. Taiwan U., Taipei, 1955; MSME, Kans. State Coll., 1959; PhD in Theoretical and Applied Mechs., U. Ill., 1967. Tool engr. Boeing Airplane Co., Renton, Wash., 1959-60; jr. engr. IBM, San Jose, Calif., 1960-63; asst. prof. mech. engring. N.J. Inst. Tech., Newark, 1967-70, assoc. prof., 1970-90, assoc. prof. engring. tech., 1990—; cons. Stone & Webster Engring., Inc., Boston, N.Y.C., 1970-73, 79-80; prin. engr., cons. Ebasco Svcs., Inc., N.Y.C., 1980—. Contbr. articles to profl. jours. Mem. ASME, Am. Soc. Engring. Edn. Roman Catholic. Home: 17 Sunset Dr Whippany NJ 07981-1626 Office: NJ Inst Tech 323 Martin Luther King Jr Blvd Newark NJ 07102-1824

SUN, CONGTING, mathematics educator; b. Pixian, Sichuan, People's Republic of China, Mar. 26, 1962; s. Dong Liang and Guiying (Feng) S. BS in Math., Sichuan U., Chengdu, 1983; Cert. in Eng. Lang., Sichuan U., 1985; MS in Math., U. Rochester (N.Y.), 1989. Instr. Dept. Math. Sichuan U., Chengdu, People's Rep. of China, 1983-86; instr. TV U., Chengdu, 1984-85, U. Rochester, 1989; lectr. math. dept. SUNY, Geneseo, N.Y., 1991-92. Bd. dirs. Am. Music Favroites, 1990, Chinese Solidarity Union, Rochester, 1989-92. Mem. Am. Math. Soc., Chinese Student and Scholar Assn. (bd. dirs. 1988-89), China Club, China Stamp Collecting Club, Commemorative Stamp Club. Office: U Rochester Dept Math Rochester NY 14627

SUN, EMILY M., economics educator; children: Patricia Viane, Caroline Marie, Diana Kate. MA, U. Mich., 1950, PhD, 1957. Prof. econs. Northland Coll., Ashland, Wis., 1957-64; assoc. prof. econs. Manhattan Coll., Riverdale, N.Y., 1964-79, prof. econs., 1979—; cons. Maritime Adminstrn., U.S. Dept. Commerce, 1969-70. Contbr. articles to profl. jours. Rosenthal grantee, 1980; recipient Trustees award, Manhattan Coll., 1987, Bonus et Fidelis medal, 1989. Mem. Am. Econ. Assn., Acad. Internat. Bus. Office: Manhattan Coll Manhattan College Pky Bronx NY 10471-3913

SUNBECK, DEBORAH TERESA, psychologist, author; b. Chgo., June 11, 1953; d. Edward Frank and Maggie Sue (Daniels) Kiereck. BS, Empire State Coll., 1976; MA, SUNY, Brockport, 1977; PhD, U. Rochester, N.Y., 1980. Lic. psychologist, N.Y. Asst. dir. Mt. Hope Family Therapy Ctr., Rochester, 1980-82; mem. clin. faculty U. Rochester, 1980-82; dir. The Nuholbe Ctr., Rochester, 1983—; pvt. practice Rochester, 1983—; dir. Rochester Peace Edn. Project, 1988-91. Author: Infinity Walk: Preparing Your Mind to Learn, 1991. Mem. APA, Assn. Humanistic Psychology, Applied Psychophysiology and Biofeedback, Soc. Clin. and Exptl. Hypnosis, Am. Soc. Clin. Hypnosis. Home: 1764 E River Rd Rochester NY 14623-1061

SUNDARAM, T. R., engineering company executive; b. Bangalore, India, June 18, 1937; came to U.S., 1960; s. T. N. and Vedavalli (Sampath) Rangaswamy; m. Judy Ann Chandler; children: (from former marriage) Meera, Kamala, Devin. B, U. Mysore, India, 1958; M, Indian Inst. Sci., India, 1960; PhD, Rensselaer Poly. Inst., 1965. Grad. asst. Rensselaer Poly. Inst., Troy, N.Y., 1961-65; prin. engr. Cornell Aero. Lab., Buffalo, 1965-71; dir. sci. dept. Hydronautics, Inc., Laurel, Md., 1971-78; pres. T.S. Assocs., Inc., Columbia, Md., 1979—, also bd. dirs. Contbr. numerous articles to profl. jours. Mem. AIAA, APS, AAAS, IEEE, Am. Assn. Artificial Intelligence. Hindu. Home: 11063 Iron Crown Ct Columbia MD 21044-2706 Office: TS Assocs Inc PO Box 1131 Columbia MD 21044-0131

SUNDARRAJAN, RAJ MATHCHAN, computer company executive; b. Palghat, Kerala, India, Nov. 12, 1956; came to U.S., 1978; s. Raju Narayana and Shantha Sundarrajan. BEE, U. Madras, Trichy, India, 1978; MSEE, U. Miss., 1982. Sr. design engr. Martin Marietta, New Orleans, 1981-83; sr. proposals engr. Harris/Farinon, San Carlos, Calif., 1984-86; applications engr. PCO, Inc., Chatsworth, Calif., 1986-87; sr. sales engr. Rockwell Internat., Westlake, Calif., 1987-88; founder, pres. Info Mart Enterprises, Stamford, Conn., 1989—; dir. Info Mart/Fenix Enterprises, Stamford, Conn., 1992—. Contbr. articles to profl. jours. Mem. World Affairs Forum, Stamford, 1992. Recipient First prize Indian Inst. Engr., Bangalore. Republican. Hindu. Office: Info Mart Enterprises 500 Summer St Ste 201 Stamford CT 06902

SUNDBERG, MARK WILLIAM, economist; b. Eugene, Oreg., Dec. 17, 1957; s. Norman Dale and Donna (Varner) S. BA, Yale U., 1981; PhD in Econs., Harvard U., 1991. Rsch. officer Nat. U. Singapore, Singapore, 1981-83; rsch. analyst Bus. Internat. Asia/Pacific, Singapore, 1983-84; project cons. Havard Inst. for Internat. Devel., Jakarta, Indonesia, 1986-87; teaching fellow Harvard U., Cambridge, Mass., 1987-88; economist World Bank, Washington, 1989—; Co-author: International Trade in Services: the ASEAN-Australian Experience, 1988; contbr. articles to profl. jours. Mem. Am. Econ. Assn. Office: World Bank 1818 H St NW Washington DC 20433-0002

SUNDER, SHYAM, economist, educator, researcher, accountant; b. Dankaur, India, July 10, 1944; came to U.S., 1970; s. Murari Lal and Yashoda (Devi) S.; m. Manjula Rastogi, Aug. 23, 1970; children: Richa, Neal Ranjan. Student, Indian Rwys. Sch., Jamalpur, India, 1963-66; MS, Carnegie Mellon U., 1972, PhD, 1974. Asst. mech. engr. Indian Rwys., Delhi, India, 1967-70; asst. prof. acctg. U. Chgo., 1973-77, 77-82; Honeywell prof. acctg. U. Minn., Mpls., 1983-88; Richard M. Cyert prof. mgmt. and econs. Carnegie-Mellon U., Pitts., 1988—; vis. prof. mgmt. Indian Inst. Ahmedabad, India, 1977, 81-82; vis. prof. bus. andecons. Calif. Inst. Tech., Pasadena, 1981; vis. prof. acctg. U. B.C., Vancouver, Can., 1982-83; vis. McClelland Centennial prof. acctg., fellow econ. sci. lab. U. Ariz., Tucson, 1986, mem. nat. adv. bd., 1986-90. Founding mem. editorial bd. Jour. Acctg. & Econs., 1978-88; mem. editorial bd. The Acctg. Rev., 1978-81, Jour. Acctg. Lit., 1986—, Auditing: A Journal of Theory and Practice, 1988—; mem. editorial bd. Rsch. in Govt. and Nonprofit Acctg., 1988—; contbr. numerous articles to profl. jours. Fellow Acctg. Researchers Internat. Assn.; mem. Am. Econ. Assn., Am. Acctg. Assn. (bd. dirs. rsch., exec. com. 1988-90), Am. Fin. Assn. (exec. com., head sect. on acctg., fin. and orgns.), Econ. Sci. Assn. (founding mem. exec. com.). Office: Carnegie-Mellon U Schenley Park Pittsburgh PA 15213-3830

SUNDLUN, BRUCE GEORGE, governor of Rhode Island; b. Providence, Jan. 19, 1920; s. Walter I. and Jane Z. (Colitz) S.; m. Marjorie G. Lee, Dec. 15, 1985; children: Mark Santelia, Kimberly Santelia; children by previous marriage: Tracy, Stuart, Peter. B.A., Williams Coll., 1942; LL.B., Harvard U., 1949; student, Air Command and Staff Sch., 1948; D.S.B.A. (hon.), Bryant Coll., 1980; D.B.A. (hon.), Roger Williams Coll., 1980. Bar: R.I. and D.C. 1949. Asst. U.S. atty., Washington, 1949-51; spl. asst. to U.S. atty. gen., Washington, 1951-54; ptnr. Amram, Hahn & Sundlun (and predecessor), Washington, 1954-72, Sundlun, Tirana & Scher, 1972-76; v.p., gen. counsel, dir. Outlet Co., Providence, 1960-76, pres., chief exec. officer, 1976-84, chmn. bd., chief exec. officer, 1984-88; gov. of R.I., 1990—; pres. Exec. Jet Aviation, Inc., Columbus, Ohio, 1970-76, chmn. bd., 1976-84; incorporator, bd. dirs. Communications Satellite Corp., 1962—; chmn. Round Hill Devel. Ltd., 1989-90; mem. Lloyd's. Mem. adv. group Nat. Aviation Goals, 1961; chmn. Inaugural Medal Com., Washington, 1961, 65; vice chmn. Inaugural Parade Com., 1961; bd. visitors USAF Acad., 1978-80; mem. R.I. Capital Center Commn., 1980, R.I. Legis. Pay Commn., 1980; vice chmn. Providence Rev. Com., 1981, chmn., 1982-85; mem. Providence Sch. Bd., 1985-90; mem. Providence Housing Authority, 1987, chmn. 1987-90; del. Dem. Nat. Conv. 1964, 68, 80, 88, R.I. Constl. Conv., 1985; Dem. candidate for gov. R.I., 1986, 88, elected, 1990; pres. Washington Internat. Horse Show, 1970-75, trustee, 1975-90; pres. Providence Performing Arts Ctr., 1978-90; bd. dirs. Touro Synagogue, Newport, R.I., 1979—, Miriam Hosp., 1985-90; bd. dirs. Temple Beth El, Providence, 1979-84, v.p., 1984-88, pres., 1988-91; bd. dirs. Trinity Sq. Repertory Theater, 1980-89, chmn., 1984-89; trustee R.I. Philharm. Orch., 1981-90; trustee Providence Preservation Soc., 1981-90, v.p., 1987-90; trustee Newport Art Mus., 1985, pres., 1987-91; pres. Providence Found., 1985-86; pres. R.I. C. of C. Fedn., 1981-84, bd. dirs., 1977-81; pres. Greater Providence C. of C., 1978-81, bd. dirs. 1976-85; bd. dirs. New Eng. Coun., 1978, vice chmn., 1980-81, chmn., 1981-83; trustee Bryant Coll., 1989—. Capt. USAAF, 1942-45; col. USAFR, ret., 1980. Decorated D.F.C., Air medal with oak leaf cluster, Purple Heart; chevalier Legion d'Honneur (France); Prime Minister's medal (Israel). Mem. Hope Club, Squantum Assn., University Club, Turks Head Club, Spouting Rock Beach Assn., Ida Lewis Club Yacht Club (R.I.), 1925 F Street Club (Washington), Middleburg Tennis Assn., Orange County Hunt Club (Va.), Saratoga Reading Room (N.Y.), Delta Upsilon. Home: 320 S Main St Providence RI 02903-2911 Office: Office of the Governor State House Providence RI 02903

SUNDSETH, CHRISTOPHER CARL, economist; b. Bellingham, Wash., June 25, 1954; s. Victor Olaf and Carolyn Travis (Brown) S.; m. Cynthia Marie Crooks, Jan. 4, 1980 (div. Nov. 1981); m. Naree Chaiyakam, Oct. 29, 1983; children: Israel Andrzej, Natalja Narissa. BA in Econs., U. Colo., 1980; BA in Polit. Sci. cum laude, Pepperdine U., 1979. Lic. pilot FAA. Dir. Coors PAC Adolph Coors Co., Golden, Colo., 1976-77, economist, 1979-83; field engr. Amecom div. Litton Industries, Mechernich, Fed. Republic Germany, 1977-78; staff asst. Office of Pub. Liaison The White House, Washington, 1983; asst. U.S. exec. dir. Inter-Am. Devel. Bank, Washington, 1983-85; economist I.O.P. Assocs., Washington, 1985-86; exec. dir. Contact Am. Radio Network, Washington, 1986-87; economist Legal Svcs. Corp., Washington, 1987—; instr. econs. Denver Community Coll., 1981, Leeward Community Coll., Honolulu, 1982. Co-author: Economic Impact of New Punitive Damages Legislation, 1990. Coord. Bush for Pres., Prince William County, Va., 1988; vice chmn. fin. Reagan for Pres., Colo., 1980; treas. Sam Zakhem for U.S. Senate, Colo., 1979-80. With USMC, 1972-76. Mem. Nat. Assn. Bus. Economists, Reagan Alumni Assn., Vietnam Vets. Am. Home: 2081 Mayflower Dr Lakeridge VA 22192-2337 Office: Legal Svcs Corp 750 1st St NE Washington DC 20002

SUNLEY, ROBERT M., social worker; b. Detroit, Mar. 27, 1917; children: Madeline, Christina. BA, New Sch. for Social Rsch., 1951; MSW, Adelphi U., 1953. Editor Prentice-Hall, Inc.; therapist, supr., chief social worker various psychiat. clinics, N.Y.C. and L.I., 1953-64; freelance writer, editor, 1939-50; assoc. dir. Family Svc. Assn. Nassau County, N.Y., 1964-83; cons., writer, 1985—; cons. to nat. and local community orgns.; pvt. practice psychotherapy, 1960-85; lectr., mem. adj. faculty several univs. Author: Advocating Today, 1984, Serving the Unemployed, 1987; also numerous articles, chpts. to books. Mem. numerous nat. and local bds. and coms. in social svc. field; pres. North Shore Unitarian Universalist Soc.; chmn. Veatch Bd. Govs.; del. to nat. and internat. orgns. With AUS, 1942-45. Home: 464 Main St Port Washington NY 11050-3137

SUNSHINE, NANCY JEAN, psychologist; b. Rahway, N.Y., May 2, 1935; d. Kenneth Hastings and Amy May (Colbeth) VanValkenburg; m. Robert Milton Sunshine, Dec. 16, 1965 (dec.); children: Winifred Sunshine-Hill, Christopher James (dec. 1988); m. Richard Harold Seroff, Jan. 2, 1978; 1 child, Barry Benjamin. BS, Cornell U., 1956; MA, Queens Coll., 1967; PhD, CUNY, 1971. Lic. psychologist, N.Y. Psychology clk. Manhattan State Hosp., Wards Island, N.Y., 1968-70; intern psychologist Kings County Hosp., Bklyn., 1970-71; pvt. practice Rego Park, N.Y., 1972—; fellow L.I. Consultation Ctr., Rego Park, 1971-73, staff supr., 1973—; cons. N.Y. Mental Health Svcs., Levittown, N.Y., 1989—. Mem. APA, N.Y. Soc. Clin. Psychologists, N.Y. Psychol. Assn. (sec.-treas. div. women's issues 1986-89), Nassau County Psychol. Assn. (chair spl. mktg. com. 1986-87), Queens County Psychol. Assn. Home and Office: 61-41 Saunders St B-39 Rego Park NY 11374

SUNUNU, JOHN H., federal official, former governor; b. Havana, Cuba, July 2, 1939; m. Nancy Hayes, 1958; children—Catherine, Elizabeth, Christina, John, Michael, James, Christopher, Peter. B.S., MIT, 1961, M.S., 1962, Ph.D., 1966. Founder, chief engr. Astro Dynamics, 1960-65; pres. J. H. S. Engring. Co. and Thermal Research Inc., Salem, N.H., 1965-82; assoc. prof. mech. engring. Tufts U., 1966-82; assoc. dean Coll. Engring., Tufts U., 1968-73; mem. N.H. Ho. of Reps., 1973-74, Gov.'s Energy Council, 1973-78;

chmn. Gov.'s Com. on N.H. Future, 1977-78; mem. Gov.'s Adv. Com. on Sci. and Tech., 1977-78; gov. State of N.H., Concord, 1983-89; chief of staff White House, Washington, 1989-91, counsellor to the President, 1991-92; co-host pub. affairs TV show Crossfire, CNN, 1992; cons.; pub. speaker. Chmn. Coalition of Northeastern Govs., 1985-86; vice chmn. Alliance for Acid Rain Control. Mem. Nat. Govs.' Assn. (vice chmn. 1986-87, chmn. task force on tech., task force on acid rain, chmn. 1987-88), Rep. Govs.' Assn. (chmn. 1985-86), New England Govs.' Assn. (chmn. 1984-85, vice chmn. adv. commn. on intergovtl. relations). Republican. Roman Catholic. Office: White House Office 1600 Pennsylvania Ave NW Washington DC 20500-0002*

SUP, STUART ALLEN See ALLEN, STUART

SURACI, RICHARD R., photographer; b. Newburgh, N.Y., Mar. 20, 1949; s. Anthony P. and Victoria Suraci. AA, Orange County Community Coll., 1969; BS, SUC Brockport, 1971; M Herbologist, Emerson Coll., Ont. Can., 1972. photographer MS Soc., Hawthorne, N.Y., Clearwater, Inc., Poughkeepsie, N.Y.; cons. location finder Fine Art Prodns., Newburgh, N.Y., film/videographer, camerman. Contbr. articles to profl. pubs.; inventor hand held 8M video/TV walkman. Mem. Hudson Valley Cavers, Hudson Valley Motion Picture, TV, Video, Still, Theatrical, Promotional Advt. Soc., Internat. Snake Charmers Assn., Internat. Bellydance Soc. Eclectic Rosicrucian, Urantian, Tantra Yoga, Theosophist. Home and Office: 67 Maple St Newburgh NY 12550-4034

SURDOVAL, LAWRENCE ANTHONY, JR., foundation administrator; b. Pitts., Sept. 10, 1930; s. Lawrence Anthony and Pearl (Elks) S.; m. Eileen Martha Bradford, July 10, 1950 (div. Sept. 1979); children: Nancy Jo, Robert James, Wayne Alan. BS in Acctg., Robert Morris Coll., 1954; BS in Econs., Duquesne U., 1962, MPF, 1972; MS, U. Pitts., 1974, postgrad., 1962. Acct. T. Mellon & Sons, Pitts., 1949-58; sec. Richard King Mellon Found., Pitts., 1959-71; treas. Alleghany Found., Pitts., 1972-78; adminstrv. officer, treas. Sarah Mellon Scaife Found., Pitts., 1971-76; pres. Philanthropic Cons., Inc., Farmington and Pitts., 1977—; pres. Nemacolin Inc., Farmington, 1979-81; lectr. in field. Bd. dirs., trustee Family and Children's Service, Pitts., 1965—; bd. visitors U. Pitts. Sch. Social Work, 1965—; bd. dirs. Pioneer Crafts Council, Uniontown, Pa., 1965—. Served with USMC, 1952-54. Republican. Clubs: Duquesne, Press (Pitts.). Home: RR 2 Box 463 Farmington PA 15437-9506

SURMAN, OWEN STANLEY, psychiatrist; b. Boston, Apr. 21, 1943; s. Aaron Harry and Edith Anne (Silver) S.; m. Lezlie Anne Humber, July 19, 1969; children: Craig Bruce Hackett, Kathleen Bridget Lezlie. BSc with honors, McGill U., 1964, MD, CM, 1968. Diplomate Am. Bd. Psychiatry and Neurology. Intern in internal medicine Balt. City Hosp., 1968-69; clin. fellow in medicine Johns Hopkins U., Balt., 1968-69; resident in psychiatry Mass. Gen. Hosp., Boston, 1969-72; clin. fellow in psychiatry Harvard Med. Sch., Boston, 1969-72; clin. asst. in psychiatry Mass. Gen. Hosp., Boston, 1975-76, asst. in psychiatry, 1977-80, asst. psychiatrist, 1980-86, assoc. psychiatrist, 1986-89, psychiatrist, 1990—; instr. psychiatry Harvard U. Med. Sch., Boston, 1975-80, asst. prof., 1980-90, assoc. prof., 1990—; mem., psychiat. cons. Boston Ctr. Heart Transplant; mem. ethics com. Boston Ctr. for Heart and Liver Transplant, 1988—; mem. subcom. Human Studies, Mass. Gen. Hosp., 1982—; mem. Inst. for Study of Smoking Behavior and Policy, John F. Kennedy Sch. Govt., 1982-89. Mem. editorial bd. Jour. Geriatric Psychiatry and Neurology, 1988—; contbr. articles, letters and book revs. to med. jours., chpts. to books. Bd. dirs. Unitarian-Universalist Area Ch., Sherborn, Mass., 1983-86; advancement officer troop 1 Boy Scouts Am., Sherborn, 1983-91. Lt. comdr. M.C., USNR, 1972-75. Milton Fund grantee, Upjohn Corp. grantee, Burroughs Wellcome Co. grantee, Eli Lily Corp. grantee, 1989. Fellow Am. Psychiat. Assn.; mem. AAAS, Mass. Med. Soc., N.Y. Acad. Scis., Am. Acad. Psychosomatic Medicine, Hastings Ctr. (assoc.), John Hopkins Med. Surg. Soc., Libr. of the Boston Athenaeum. Republican. Office: Mass Gen Hosp Wang All 815 15 Parkman St Belmont MA 02114

SURMELI, SUPHI, physician, director; b. Samandagi, Hatay, Turkey, Jan. 18, 1931; came to U.S., 1958; s. Saban and Munire (Bayaz) S.; m. Guner Erdal, June 13, 1965; children: Sahir, Sedat, Mina. BA, U. Istanbul, Turkey, 1951, MD, 1954. Diplomate Am. Bd. Psychiatry and Neurology. House staff physician Kingston (N.Y.) Gen. Hosp., 1966-67; sr. psychiatrist Harlem Valley State Hosp., Wingdale, N.Y., 1967-68; staff psychiatrist South Oaks Hosp., Amityville, N.Y., 1968-70, sr. psychiatrist, 1970-72, asst. clin. dir., 1972-86; clin. dir., 1986—; acting med. dir. S.E. Nassau Guidance Clinic, Seaford, N.Y., 1969-70; attending staff psychiatrist Brunswick Hosp. Ctr., Amityville, 1969-71, Mercy Hosp., Rockville Centre, N.Y., 1970-71; assoc. attending psychiatrist Good Samaritan Hosp., West Islip, N.Y., 1972—, cons. psychiatrist, 1986—; attending psychiatrist Lakeside Hosp., Copiague, N.Y., 1972-77; attending staff psychiatrist Cen. Gen. Hosp., Plainview, N.Y., 1981-83; asst. prof. clin. psychiatry SUNY, Stony Brook, 1975—. Capt. M.C., Turkish Army, 1954-56. Recipient Good Citizenship award Turkey Dept. Ministry and Edn., 1974; APA fellow, 1991. Mem. AMA, N.Y. State Med. Soc., Am. Psychiat. Assn., Nassau County Acad. Medicine, Suffolk County Neuropsychiat. Soc., Turkish Am. Neuropsychiat. Soc., Suffolk County Psychiat. Soc., Turkish Am. Physician's Assn. Office: GST Med Assocs PC 400 Sunrise Hwy Amityville NY 11701-2508

SURVING, NATALIE ANN BACON, sculptor; b. Wellsboro, Pa., Aug. 23, 1938; d. John S. and Harriet G. (Bunnell) Bacon; m. Richard A. Surving, June 14, 1959; children: Sabrina, Ilya Ryan. BFA, Art Ctr. Coll. Design, L.A., 1960. Art dir. Jewish Community Ctr., S.I., N.Y., 1963-68, Camp Kaufman, S.I., N.Y., 1963-68; owner, dir. Potter's Wheel, S.I., N.Y., 1969-79; prof. Coll. of S.I., CUNY, 1972-78; owner, dir. Millsburg Studios, Middletown, N.Y., 1979—; vis. artist Vasquez Taller, Dolores Hidalgo, Mex., 1987-90, Art Park, Lewistown, N.Y., 1979, Kohler, Sheboygan, Wis., 1978. Numerous one-woman shows, 1969-87. Founding bd. Ctr. for Creative Arts, S.I., 1967-68, S.I. Greenbelt Natural Area League, 1964. Recipient People Choice award Morristown Craft Show, 1985. Mem. Soc. and Animal Artists (3 ann. awards off excellence 1987-89), Pen and Brush Club (lectr., Solo award 1986), Am. Craft Coun. (exhibitor). Home and Studio: RR 4 Box 449 Middletown NY 10940-9804

SUSANN, PHILIP WILLIAM, surgeon; b. Troy, N.Y., Sept. 14, 1943; s. Philip John and Felicia Mary (Bluffline) S.; m. Carol Lee Drye, June 12, 1971; children: Philip, Stephen, Robert, Lisa. AB, Siena Coll., 1966; MD, Emory U., 1971. Intern Hartford (Conn.) Hosp., 1971-72; resident Emory U., Atlanta, 1972-76; staff surgeon USAH, Augsburg, Fed. Republic Germany, 1976-79, USAH-USMA-Keller Hosp., West Point, N.Y., 1979-81; surgery program dir. Hamot Med. Ctr., Erie, Pa., 1981-89, chief div. gen. surgery, 1989—; cosn. VAH, Shriner's Hosp. for Crippled Children, Erie, 1983—; clin. asst. prof. surgery Hahneman Med. Coll., Phila., 1982—. Editor: Cinical Nutrition Handbook for Surgical Research, 1986; contbr. articles to Mil. Medicine, Am. Surgeon, Human Pathology. Bd. dirs. Erie County Emergency Med. Svcs. Coun., 1985-91, White Swa Woods Home Owners Assn., Erie, 1985-91. Col. U.S. Army, 1976—, col. USAR, 1981—. Decorated Meritorious Svc. medal; recipient Cert. of Appreciation, Erie County Coun. for the Deaf, 1985. Fellow Soc. for Critical Care Medicine, Am. Coll. Surgeons (pres.-elect NW Pa. chpt. 1991); mem. N.Y. Acad. Scis., SAGES. Home: 720 Ridgeview Dr Erie PA 16505-1059 Office: 104 E 2d St Erie PA 16507

SUSKIE, LINDA ANNE, academic administrator; b. Doylestown, Pa., May 15, 1953; d. Edward Theodore and Emma Bertha (Staudte) Michaels; m. Stephen Raymond Suskie, Aug. 10, 1980; children: Melissa, Michael. BA, Johns Hopkins U., 1974; MA, U. Iowa, 1976. Rsch. assoc. instl. studies Stockton State Coll., Pomona, N.J., 1976-79; dir. instl. rsch. SUNY, Oswego, 1979-84; asst. to pres. for planning Millersville (Pa.) U., 1984—; presenter workshops numerous profl. confs., 1981—; cons. several local sch. dists., Pa., 1987—. Author: (monograph) Survey Research: What Works for the Institutional Researcher, 1988; contbr. articles to profl. jours. Active Girl Scouts USA, Oswego, 1983-84, Leadership Lancster, Pa., 1987; founder, chair Millersville U. Women's Coalition, 1986-89; trustee Rock Ford Found., Lancaster, 1988-91, Big Bros.-Big Sisters of Lancaster County, 1991—. Mem. Am. Ednl. Rsch. Assn., N.E. Assn. for Instl. Rsch. (conf. evaluator 1987-89, treas. 1988-91), Assn. for Instl. Rsch., Soc. for Coll. and Univ. Planning. Republican. Roman Catholic. Office: Millersville U Biemesderfer Exec Ctr Millersville PA 17551

SUSSKIND, HERBERT, biomedical engineer, educator; b. Ratibor, Germany, Mar. 23, 1929; came to U.S., 1938; s. Alex and Hertha (Loewy) S.; m. E. Suzanne Lieberman, June 18, 1961; children: Helen J., Alex M., David A. BChE cum laude, CCNY, 1950; MChE, NYU, 1961. Engr., sect. supr. Brookhaven Nat. Lab., Upton, N.Y., 1950-77, biomed. engr., 1977—; assoc. prof. medicine SUNY, Stony Brook, 1979—, asst. to the chmn. med. dept., 1989—. Co-inventor 3 patents in field. Co-founder, 1st pres. Huntington Twp. Jewish Forum, Huntington, N.Y., 1970-73; trustee Huntington Hebrew Congregation, 1970-78. Mem. Biomed. Engring. Soc., Soc. Nuclear Medicine, Am. Thoracic Soc., Am. Nuclear Soc. (exec. com., treas. L.I. Sect., 1979-83), Am. Inst. Chem. Engrs., CCNY Alumni Assn. (pres. 1982-84), CCNY Engring. & Architecture Alumni Assn., N.Y.C. (pres. 1963-65). Office: Brookhaven Nat Lab 30 Bell Ave Bldg 490 Upton NY 11973-9999

SUSSKIND, JACOB LOUIS, social studies educator; b. Newark, Sept. 24, 1933; s. Isadore and Frieda (Halpern) S.; m. Regina Von Allmen (dec. 1985); children: Lisa, Jeremy; m. Olivia Tucker Merrill, May 17, 1986. BA, Montclair State Coll., 1963; PhD, Vanderbilt U., 1969. Cert. tchr., N.J. Asst. prof. social studies Pa. State U., Middletown, 1969—; field liaison global edn. Pa. Dept. Edn., Harrisburg, 1980-81. Editor Social Studies Jour., 1987—; contbr. articles to profl. jours., chpts. to books. Mem. Middletown Sch. Bd., 1981-85. With USAF, 1952-56. NDEA fellow, 1966; grantee Am. Philos. Soc.; attendee summer seminar Fulbright Commn., India and Israel, 1977, 82; NEH felflow, 1989. Mem. AAUP, Am. Hist. Assn., Pa. Coun. Social Studies (pres. 1983-84), Nat. Coun. Social Studies (chair profl. ethics 1990-91), Phi Delta Kappa. Democrat. Unitarian. Office: Pa State Univ Middletown PA 17057-4898

SUSSMAN, GEORGE DAVID, educational association executive; b. Phila., Jan. 7, 1943; s. Sidney and Ann (Rosenberg) S.; m. Alexandra Kressel, Dec. 22, 1968; children: Michael Hugo, Jeremy Broder. AB, Amherst Coll., 1964; MA in History, Yale U., 1966, PhD in History, 1971. Instr. history Tuskegee (Ala.) Inst., 1966-67, C.W. Post Coll., L.I. U., Greenvale, N.Y., 1967-69; asst. prof. history Vanderbilt U., Nashville, 1971-78; asst. commr. N.Y. State Dept. Edn., Albany, 1978-83; dep. dir. Legis. Commn., Albany, 1983-87; exec. dir. Assn. Colls. and Univs. of State of N.Y., Albany, 1988—. Author: Selling Mothers' Milk, 1981; contbr. articles to ednl. publs. Mem. sch. bd. Bethlehem Cen. Schs., Delmar, N.Y., 1989—. Woodrow Wilson Found. felldow, 1964-65; fellowship Nat. Endowment Humanities, 1973, Nat. Libr. Medicine, 1975-77, Am. Coun. Learned Socs., 1975; recipient William Koren Jr. prize Soc. for French Hist. Studies, 1975. Home: 119 Dumbarton Dr Delmar NY 12054-4407 Office: Assn Colls/Univs State NY 100 State St Apt 939 Albany NY 12207-1810

SUSSMAN, GERALD, educator; b. Bronx, Jan. 5, 1927; s. Abraham and Lena (Richman) S.; m. Helen Caroline Webb, June 3, 1950; children: Webb, Cara, Sansi. BS, NYU, 1952, AM, 1954; PhD, Boston Coll., 1979. With Gimbel Bros.-N.Y., N.Y.C., 1947-66; pres. Hal's Domestics, Inc., N.Y.C., 1966-70; lectr. U. R.I., Kingston, 1970-71; asst. prof. Bryant Coll., Smithfield, R.I., 1971-75, Suffolk U., Boston, 1975-76, Babson Coll., Wellesley, Mass., 1976-77; assoc. prof. Northeastern U., Boston, 1977-82, Bentley Coll., Waltham, Mass., 1982-86; prof. Salem (Mass.) State Coll., 1986—; dir. Higher Edn. Strategic Planning Inst., Washington, 1983—, Hal's Domestics, Inc., N.Y.C., 1970—; cons. Am. Assn. of State Colls. and Univs., Washington, 1980-83. Contbr. articles to profl. jours.; editor R.I. Bus. Quar., 1970-71. Officer, trustee Peacock Farm Assn., Lexington, Mass., 1974-76, 86-88. With USN, 1945-46. Salem State Coll. faculty devel. grantee, 1987; Rauch Found. rsch. grantee, 1984, 85; Bentley Coll. and Northeastern U. grantee, 1979, 82, 83, 84; recipient Cert. of Merit, Mass. Press Assn., 1975. Mem. Am. Mktg. Assn., N.E. Bus. and Econs. Assn., Acad. Mktg. Sci., Atlantic Mktg. Assn. Home: 37 Peacock Farm Rd Lexington MA 02173-6341

SUSSMAN, LEONARD RICHARD, foundation executive; b. N.Y.C., Nov. 26, 1920; s. Jacob and Carrie (Marks) S.; m. Frances Rukeyser, May 9, 1942 (div. 1958); m. Marianne Rita Gutmann, May 28, 1958; children: Lynne, David William, Mark Jacob. A.B., NYU, 1940; M.S. in Journalism, Columbia U., 1941. Copy editor N.Y. Morning Telegraph, news editor radio sta. WQXR, 1941; cable editor San Juan (P.R.) World Jour., also corr. Business Week mag., 1941-42; editor fgn. broadcast intelligence svc. FCC, 1942; press sec. to Gov. of P.R., 1942-43; dir. info. in N.Y. for Govt. of P.R., 1946-49; regional dir., then nat. exec. dir. Am. Coun. Judaism, 1949-66; cons. pub. affairs cons. Nationwide Ins. Cos. (and indsl. subs.), 1955-57; mem. editorial com. Coun. Liberal Chs., 1956-59; exec. dir. Freedom House, 1967-88, sr. scholar in internat. communications, 1988—; evaluator Fulbright Program Bd. Fgn. Scholarships, 1990—; organizer, dir. Freedom House/Books USA, 1968-85; exec. dir. Willkie Meml., 1970-88; adj. prof. journalsim and mass communication NYU, N.Y.C., 1990—; organizer, dir. Freedom House/Books USA, 1968-85; editor Freedom at Issue, bimonthly, 1970-81; mem. U.S. Dels. to Conf. World Communicaiton Yr./83, 1982-83; organizer acad. confs.; participant Internat. Conf. on Press Freedom, Venice, Italy, 1976, 77, Cairo, 1978, Talloires, 1981, 83, San Jose, Costa Rica, Johannesburg, and Santiago Chile, 1987, also others; mem. panel competition in space Congl. Office Tech. Assessment, 1982-83. Author: American Press-Under Siege?, 1973, Mass News Media and the Third World Challenge, 1977, Glossary for International Communications: Warning of a Bloodless Dialect, 1983, Spanish version, 1987, Power, the Press and the Technology of Freedom: The Coming of Age of ISDN, 1990, The Culture of Freedom: The Small World of Fulbright Scholars, 1992; editor: Three Years at the East-West Divide, 1983, Today's American: How Free?, 1986; contbr. sects. to books, articles in profl. jours. and newspapers; project dir.: Big Story-How The American Press and Television Reported and Interpreted The Crisis of Tet-1968 in Vietnam and Washington, 1977; editor: textbook series, also quar. mag. Issues, 1953-66; editorial bd. Polit. Communication and Persuasion. Trustee Internat. Coun. on Future of Univ., 1973-84; bd. dirs. World Press Freedom Com., 1977—; chmn. Friends of Survey Mag. Charitable Trust, London, 1978-92; mem. U.S. Nat. Commn. for UNESCO, 1979-85, vice-chmn., 1983-85; mem. U.S. dels. to internat. conf. on space, African Aid, UNESCO, London Info. Forum. Decorated Legion of Merit. Mem. Internat. Inst. Communication, Century Club, Sigma Delta Chi (Annual First Amendment award N.Y. br. 1988). Home: 215 E 73d St New York NY 10021 Office: 800 3rd Ave New York NY 10022-7604

SUSSMAN, SUSAN KAMSKY, marketing executive; b. Washington, Jan. 8, 1951; d. Leonard and Sonya (Levien) Kamsky; m. Norman Sussman, Sept. 11, 1982; children: Rebecca Hope, Zachary Paul. BA with honors, Occidental Coll., L.A., 1972. Buyer J.W. Robinson's, L.A., 1972-78; product devel. mgr. Federated Dept. Stores, N.Y.C., 1978-82; mktg. mgr. Revlon Inc., N.Y.C., 1982-84; mktg. dir. Cosmair, N.Y.C., 1984-86, Parfums Nina Ricci, N.Y.C., 1986-88; v.p. Tiffany & Co., N.Y.C., 1988—. Recipient Best Package Design award for 1989, Drug & Cosmetic Ind. Jour., 1989, Fragrance Found. Best Fragrance Launch award 1989. Mem. The Fashion Group, Cosmetic Exec. Women, N.Y. State Jeweler's Assn. (adv. bd. 1990—), Fragrance Found. (application com. 1989—). Office: Tiffany & Co 727 5th Ave New York NY 10022-2503

SUSSNA, ROBERT EARL, architect; b. Lakewood, N.J., Mar. 21, 1939; s. Harry D. and Emma (Tarshish) S.; m. Deborah Sarah Beilin, Nov. 5, 1960; 1 child, Jeffrey Eric. BArch, Cornell U., 1963. Registered architect N.Y., N.J., Pa. Designer Holt, Morgan, Short & Agle, Princeton, N.J., 1966-68; architect Burton F. Weisbecker AIA, Princeton, 1968; prin. Weisbecker & Sussna AIA, Princeton, 1969-70, Robert Earl Sussna AIA, Princeton, 1970-90; pres. Sussna Architects PA, Princeton, 1990—. Prin. works include Chem. Bank, Princeton U., Bristol-Myers Squibb, Rhone-Poulenc Inc., Trenton State Coll.; numerous one-man shows for photography including Trenton State Mus., Newark Mus. and Jersey City Mus., 1974—. Mem. Hopewell (N.J.) Twp. Planning Bd., 1976. Grantee in photography N.J. Coun. on the Arts. Mem. AIA, N.J. Soc. Architects (pres.-elect cen. sect. 1991, Spl. award of merit 1988), Rotary (bd. dirs. Princeton Club), Nassau Club. Office: Sussna Architects PA 53 State Rd Princeton NJ 08540-1318

SUSTENDAL, DIANE MARIE, editor, consultant; b. New Orleans, Aug. 30, 1944; d. George and Mary (Anderson) S. Student, La. State U., 1963-64; cert., John McCrady Sch. Fine Arts, 1966. Asst. art critic Times-Picayune, New Orleans, 1966-68, fashion and beauty editor, 1970-82; asst. mng. editor spl. studies div. Frederick A. Praeger, N.Y.C., 1969; assoc. editor M & Men's Wear mags., Fairchild Publs., N.Y.C., 1982-83; cons. Men's Fashions of the Times, N.Y. Times, N.Y.C., 1983-86; fashion and interior design editor N.Y. Daily News, 1990-91; freelance writer, editor, stylist. Bd. dirs. New Orleans Ballet, 1971-73. Recipient award La. Press Anns., 1972, Aldo award Men's Fashion Assn. Am., 1985. Mem. Fashion Group N.Y. Republican.

SUSZCZYNSKI, LOUISE VERONICA, budget analyst; b. N.Y.C., Apr. 19, 1940; d. John and Lucy (DelGrosso) Buonocore; divorced; children: Peter, Mark. BS in Bus. Adminstrn., Mercy Coll., 1980. Tchr. N.Y. State Boces, Yorktown Hgts., N.Y., 1978-90; budget analyst F.D. Roosevelt VA Hosp., Montrose, N.Y., 1980—. Office: FDR VA Hosp Montrose NY 10548

SUTA, D. DEBORAH, secondary education educator; b. Jersey City, Dec. 27, 1946; d. James Clifford Gregory and Dorothy Eulalia (Donnelly) Conniff; m. Robert Wendell Suta, June 7, 1975; 1 child, John Gregory. BA, Caldwell (N.J.) Coll., 1968; MA, Montclair State Coll., 1990. Cert. elem. and secondary edn. tchr., N.J. Tchr. St. Joseph Sch., Lincoln Park, N.J., 1968-69, Sacred Heart Sch., Lyndhurst, N.J., 1969-76, St. Joseph Sch., Lodi, N.J., 1981-82; tchr., student assistance counselor St. Mary High Sch., Rutherford, N.J., 1982—; adj. prof. St. Peter Coll., Jersey City, 1977. Recipient Lilli Graham Leadership award Bergen County Alternatives to Domestic Violence, 1992. Mem. AACD. Roman Catholic. Office: St Mary High Sch 64 Chestnut St Rutherford NJ 07070-1783

SUTCLIFFE, MARION SHEA, writer; b. Washington, July 29, 1918; d. James William and Ida (Hewitt) Shea; m. James Montgomery Sutcliffe, Aug. 23, 1941; 1 child, Jill Marion. BMus, Boston Conservatory Music, 1956-60; EdM, Boston State Coll., 1969. Cert. music, English, psychology and reading tchr., Mass. Tchr. Milford (Mass.) Pub. Schs., 1966-70; tchr. music Worcester (Mass.) Pub. Schs., 1970-71; reading tchr. Natick (Mass.) Pub. Schs., 1971-73; real estate developer Sutcliffe Family Trust, South Dennis, Mass., 1969—; developer Delray Beach Club, Dennisport, Mass.; mfr. A&A Assocs., South Dennis, 1989—; dir., bd. mgrs. The Soundings Resort, Dennisport, Mass., 1990—. Songwriter Diablo, 1954. Founder, mgr. Boston Women's Symphony, 1962-66. Fuller grantee New England Conservatory, 1957, grantee State Mass., 1957. Mem. AAUW (bd. dirs. 1989—), Nat. Am. Theatre Organ Soc., Eastern Mass. Am. Theatre Organ Soc. (bd. dirs. 1989-92), Organ-Aires (v.p. 1991—). Episcopalian. Home: 145 Cove Rd South Dennis MA 02660-3515 Office: 60 Mac Arthur Rd Natick MA 01760-2938

SUTHERLAND, ANDREW VICTOR, II, software developer; b. Mountain Home AFB, Idaho, Nov. 3, 1966; s. Jeffrey Victor and Ellen Arline (Conan) S.; m. Amy Maureen Hegarty, Mar. 31, 1984; 1 child, Alexander James. SB, MIT, 1990, postgrad., 1990—. Sr. programmer analyst Mid-Continent Computer Svcs., Denver, 1984-86; sr. mem. sci. staff The Saddlebrook Corp., Cambridge, Mass., 1986-89; chief scientist, founder, dir. Escher Group Ltd., Cambridge, 1989—. NSF grad. fellow, Washington, 1990. Mem. Assn. Computing Machinery, Am. Math. Soc., Math. Assn. Am., Phi Beta Kappa. Home: 11 Crescent Hill Ave Lexington MA 02173 Office: Escher Group Ltd 238 Broadway Cambridge MA 02139-1926

SUTHERLAND, GEORGE LESLIE, retired chemical company executive; b. Dallas, Aug. 13, 1922; s. Leslie and Madge Alice (Henderson) S.; m. Mary Gail Hamilton, Sept. 9, 1961 (dec. Mar. 1984); children: Janet Leslie, Gail Irene, Elizabeth Hamilton; m. Carol Brenda Kaplan, Feb. 19, 1986. BA, U. Tex., Austin, 1943, MA, 1947, PhD, 1950. With Am. Cyanamid Co., various locations, 1951-87; asst. dir. research and devel. Princeton, N.J., 1969-70, dir. research and devel., agr. div., 1970-73; v.p. med. research and devel. Pearl River, N.Y., 1973-86, dir. med. research div., 1978-86, dir. chem. research div., 1980-81; v.p. corp. research tech. Pearl River, 1986-87. Served with USN, 1944-46. Mem. Assn. Research Dirs. (pres. 1975-76), AAAS, Am. Chem. Soc., Royal Soc. Chemistry. Home: 42 Sky Meadow Rd Suffern NY 10901-2519

SUTHERLAND, GREGG DAVID, environmental consultant; b. Casper, Wyo., June 3, 1959; s. David R. and Joan M. (Hurd) S.; m. Donna Maree Pilloud, Aug. 4, 1984; children: Donald Cody, Jackson Lewis. BSBA, U. Denver, 1981; MBA in Strategic Planning, Wharton U. Pa., Phila., 1983. Adj. prof. U. Denver, 1984-87; team leader Am. Mgmt. Systems, Denver, 1983-85; mgr. mktg. programs Data Gen. Corp., Denver, 1985-87; v.p. bus. devel. U.S. Recycling Industries, Denver, 1987-90; dir. Ea. region Resource Integration Systems, Ltd., Granby, Conn., 1990—. Author: (with others) Recycler's Handbook, 1992. Mem. Gov.'s Solid Waste Task Force, Denver, 1990. Office: Resource Integration Systems Ltd 1 Salmon Brook St Granby CT 06035

SUTHERLAND, ROBERT ALEC, computer consulting company executive; b. Milford, Mass., Oct. 1, 1945; s. Earl Palmer and Mable Weaver (Fenton) S.; m. Dawn Marie Fleming, May 11, 1968 (div. Feb. 1987); children: Meaghan Marie, Robert Alec Jr.; m. Diana Lynda Medeiros, July 24, 1987. AS in EDP, Northeastern U., 1976, BS in MIS, 1979. Programmer, analyst Arrow Automotive Industries, Framingham, Mass., 1969-72; sr. staff analyst Waters Assocs., Inc., Milford, Mass., 1972-76; mgr. data processing South Shore Pub. Co., Inc., Scituate, Mass., 1976-78; ptnr., v.p. SYS/3 Assocs., Inc., Scituate, 1978-80; regional mgr. Dynamic Control Corp., Norwell, Mass., 1980-82; ptnr., v.p. Andrea Data Systems, Norwell, 1982-83; owner, pres. Robert Sutherland Assocs., Inc., New Bedford, Mass., 1983-89; dir. MIS MacGray Co., Inc., Cambridge, Mass., 1989—. Mem. COMMON (treas. 1978-79, sec. 1979-80, v.p. 1980-86, pres. 1986-89, bd. dirs.), Internat. User Group Coun. Home: 2030 Phillips Rd New Bedford MA 02745-2143 Office: MacGray Co Inc 22 Water St Cambridge MA 02141-1228

SUTHERLAND, SCOTT MCKELLAN, insurance executive; b. Waterbury, Conn., Jan. 25, 1951; s. Robert C. and Jeanne (Scott) S.; m. Cynthia Gardner, Aug. 22, 1970; children: Christopher S., Ian Ashley, Kyle McKellan. BS in Bus., Monmouth Coll., 1974. Acct. exec. John M. Sutherland, Inc., Naugatuck, Conn., 1973-78; asst. sec.-treas. John M. Sutherland, Inc., Naugatuck, 1978-84, treas., 1984—; pres. The McKellan Group, Inc., Waterbury, 1984—. Trustee The Forman Sch., Inc., Litchfield, Conn., 1982—, v.p. bd. trustees, 1989-90, treas. bd. trustees 1991—; chmn. campaign United Way Naugatuck, 1978; corporator Waterbury Hosp., 1991—. Mem. Profl. Ins. Agts. Conn., Ind. Ins. Agts. Conn. (bd. dirs. 1979-80), Waterbury Assn. Ins. Agts. (pres. 1978-79), Rotary (pres. Naugatuck club 1982-83), Elks, Highfield Club (chmn. golf 1986—, v.p. 1991-93). Republican. Congregationalist. Office: The McKellan Group Inc 182 Grand St Ste 301 Waterbury CT 06702-1914

SUTNICK, ALTON IVAN, medical school dean, educator, researcher, physician; b. Trenton, N.J., July 6, 1928; s. Michael and Rose (Horwitz) S.; m. Mona Reidenberg, Aug. 17, 1958; children: Amy, Gary. A.B., U. Pa., 1950, M.D., 1954; postgrad. studies in biomed. math., Drexel Inst. Tech., 1961-62; postgrad. studies in biometrics, Temple U., 1969-70. Diplomate Am. Bd. Internal Medicine. Rotating intern Hosp. U. Pa., 1954-55, resident in anesthesiology, 1955-56, resident in medicine, 1956, USPHS postdoctoral research fellow, 1956-57; asst. instr. anesthesiology, then asst. instr. medicine U. Pa. Sch. Medicine, 1955-57; resident in medicine Wishard Meml. Hosp., Indpls., 1957-58; chief resident in medicine Wishard Meml. Hosp., 1960-61; resident instr. medicine Ind. U. Sch. Medicine, Indpls., 1957-58; USPHS postdoctoral research fellow Temple U. Hosp., 1961-63; instr., then asso. in medicine Temple U. Sch. Medicine, 1962-65; mem. faculty U. Pa. Sch. Medicine, 1965-75, assoc. prof. medicine, 1971-75; clin. asst. physician Pa. Hosp., 1966-71; research physician, then assoc. dir. Inst. Cancer Research, Phila., 1965-75; vis. prof. medicine Med. Coll. Pa., Phila., 1971-74; prof. medicine Med. Coll. Pa., 1975—, dean, 1975-89, sr. v.p., 1976-89; v.p. Ednl. Commn. Fgn. Med. Grads, 1989—; dir. clin. devel. Am. Oncologic Hosp., Phila., 1973-75; attending physician Phila. VA Hosp., 1967—, Hosp. Med. Coll. Pa., 1971—; cons. in field. Mem. U.S. nat. com. Internat. Union Against Cancer, 1969-72; mem. Nat. Conf. Cancer Prevention and Detection, 1973, Nat. Workshop Profl. Edn. in High Blood Pressure, 1973, Nat. Cancer Control Planning Conf., 1973; vice chmn. Gov. Pa. Task Force Cancer Control, 1974-76, chmn. com. cancer detection, 1974-76; mem. health

research adv. bd. State of Pa., 1976-78; mem. diagnostic research adv. group Nat. Cancer Inst., 1974-78; chmn. coordinating com., comprehensive cancer center program Fox Chase Cancer Center, U. Pa. Cancer Center, 1975; cons. WHO, Govt. of India, 1979, Govt. of Indonesia, 1980, entire S.E. Asia region, 1981, U. Zimbabwe, 1989, Ministry of Health of Poland, 1992; mem. Nat. Conf. on Med. Edn. Author numerous articles in field.; Asst. editor: Annals Internal Medicine, 1972-75; editorial bd. other med. jours. Bd. dirs. Phila. Coun. Internat. Visitors, 1972-77, Israel Cancer Rsch. Fund, 1975—, Am. Assocs. Ben Gurion U., 1986—, Internat. Med. Scholars Program, 1988-89, Sight Savers Internat., 1988-91; trustee Ednl. Commn. Fgn. Med. Grads., 1987-89; adv. commn. Internat. Participation Phila. '76, 1973-76. Capt. M.C. AUSA 1958-60. Recipient Arnold and Marie Schwartz award in medicine AMA, 1976, Torch of Learning award Am. Friends of Hebrew U., 1981, medal Ben Gurion U. of Negev, Israel, 1985, medal Université Catholique de Lille, France, 1987, medal U. Belgrade, Yugoslavia, 1988, Founder's award Med. Coll. Pa., 1989, Med. Coll. Pa., 1989, St. Thomas Aquinas award Santo Tomas U. Med. Alumni Assn., The Philippines, 1989, medal Kiev Med. Inst., Ukraine, 1991, Med. Coll. Pa., 1989. Fellow ACP, Coll. Physicians Phila. (censor 1977-86 , councillor 1977-86); mem. Am. Fedn. Clin. Research (pres. Temple U. chpt. 1964-65), Am. Assn. Cancer Research, Am. Soc. Clin. Oncology, Am. Dermatoglyphics Assn., Assn. Am. Cancer Insts., Assn. Am. Med. Colls., Northeast Consortium on Med. Edn. (treas. 1983-89, chmn. 1986-87), Council of Deans of Pvt. Free-Standing Med. Schs. (co-founder, nat. chmn. 1983-85), Pa. Council Deans (chmn. 1987-89), Am. Cancer Soc. (vice chmn. service com. Phila. div. 1974-76, bd. dirs. 1974-80, chmn. awards com. 1976), Am. Lung Assn., AMA, AAAS, Am. Heart Assn., Pan Am. Med. Assn., Phila. Coop. Cancer Assn., N.Y. Acad. Scis., Pa. Heart Assn., Heart Assn. Southeastern Pa., Pa. Med. Soc., Phila. County Med. Soc. (chmn. com. internat. med. affairs 1964-72), Pa. Lung Assn., Phila. Assn. for Clin. Trials (bd. dirs. 1980-81), Health Systems Agy. Southeastern Pa. (gov. bd., exec. com. 1983-87, sec. 1985-87), Am. Assn. Ben urion U. (bd. dirs. 1986—), Soc. des Medecins Militaires Français, Internat. Med. Sch. Affiliates Consortium (co-founder, vice chmn. 1985-87), Phi Beta Kappa, Sigma Xi, Alpha Omega Alpha (councillor 1963-65). Home: 2135 St James St Philadelphia PA 19103-4804

SUTPHIN, JAMES HOYNES, trade association administrator; b. Cleve., May 28, 1932; s. Albert C. and Mary H. (Hoynes) S.; m. Louise Dolence, Sept. 13, 1958; children: Mary Louise, James Jr., Ann Elizabeth, Susan Bernadette. B in Social Sci., John Carroll Coll., 1954. Sales mgr., v.p. Braden-Sutphin Ink, Cleve., 1964-67, pres., 1967-81, chmn. bd., 1981-85; pntr. Bus. Mgmt. Svcs., Akron, Ohio, 1987; asst. exec. dir. Nat. Assn. Printing Ink Mgrs., Harrison, N.Y., 1989-91; exec. dir. Nat. Assn. Printing Ink Mgrs., Hasbrouck Heights, N.J., 1991—. Republican. Roman Catholic. Office: Nat Assn Printing Ink Mfrs 777 Terrace Ave Hasbrouck Heights NJ 07604-3110

SUTTELL, PAUL ALLYN, associate justice; b. Providence, Jan. 10, 1949; s. Allyn Kingsley and Pauline Louise (Stickney) S.; m. Mary Wood Cissel, May 24, 1980; children: William Theodore Stickney, Grace Wood. BA, Northwestern U., 1971; JD, Suffolk U., 1976. Assoc. Beals & DiFiore, Providence, 1977-90; legal counsel R.I. Home Minority Leader, 1979-82; assoc. justice R.I. Family Ct., Providence, 1990—. Mem. Little Compton (R.I.) Rep. Town Commn., 1981-90; rep. R.I. Ho. of Reps., Providence, 1983-90; del. R.I. Rep. State Com., 1981-90, Rep. Nat. Conv., 1988. Mem. Sakonnet Preservation Assn. (bd. dirs. 1985), R.I. Agrl. Lands Preservation Com. Home: 515 W Main Rd Little Compton RI 02837-1129 Office: RI Family Ct One Dorrance Pla Providence RI 02857

SUTTER, JAMES STEWART, art educator, sculptor; b. Milw., Feb. 12, 1940; s. Joseph E. and Alberta (Biddison) S.; m. Georgia L. Kutnar, Mar. 11, 1965 (div. 1983); m. Leslie Walker Strong, July 21, 1984; children: Jason Joel, Shannon Lynn. BS, U. Wis., Mils., 1963; MA, U. Iowa, 1964; MFA, U. Mass., 1967. Prof. art SUNY, Potsdam, 1967—; artist-in-residence Skidmore Coll., Saratoga, N.Y., summers, 1979-88; guest lectr. N.Y. State Coun. Edn., Albany, 1981, SUNY, Oneonta, 1987, Cornell U., 1992, unis. throughout Eng., 1989-90. Exhibited in over 150 group shows; represented in numerous pub. and pvt. collections through U.S. and fgn. countries. Recipient over 25 best of show and 1st prizes for art; rsch. fellow SUNY, 1971, 76, fellow N.Y. State Found. for Arts, 1988; grantee SUNY, 1982. Home: 11 New St Norwood NY 13668-1005 Office: SUNY Art Dept Potsdam NY 13676

SUTTER, JAY LAURENCE, service company executive; b. S.I., N.Y., Mar. 25, 1927; s. Jacob George and Grace (Kline) S.; m. JoAnne L., June 12, 1965 (dec. Aug. 13, 1983). BA, BS, Wagner Coll., 1948. Regional mgr. Hooper-Holmes Bur., Inc., Basking Ridge, N.J., 1948-73; chief fin. officer Physicians for Gen. Practice, 1973-89; sec., treas. United Health Plan Inc., 1975-89; pres. Salem Svcs. Inc., Southwest Harbor, Maine, 1969—. Mem. Med. Mgrs. Assn., Denver, 1975-88; sec. Pitts. Claims Assn., 1878-80. Columbus Claims Assn., 1965-60. Sgt. U.S. Army, 1945-46. Mem. Am. Legion, Brookside Country Club. Republican. Lutheran. Home and Office: Phillips Ln PO Box 144 Southwest Harbor ME 04679-0144

SUTTON, CONSTANCE RITA, anthropologist, educator; b. Mpls., Jan. 29, 1926; d. Boris Peter and Vera (Constans) Woloshin; m. Alfonso Shimbel, Dec. 24, 1946 (div. June 1950); m. Samuel Sutton, Nov. 27, 1952 (dec. Mar. 1986); 1 child, David E. PhB, U. Chgo., 1947, MA, 1954; PhD, Columbia U., 1969. Lectr. CUNY, Queens and Hunter, 1959-60, N.Y. U., N.Y.C., 1960-61; instr. N.Y. U., 1961-68, asst. prof., 1968-71, anthropology dept. chair, 1971-73, assoc. prof., 1971—; assoc. Inst. of African Studies, Nigeria, 1977-79. Editor: (book) Caribbean Life in NYC, 1987, Anthropological Perspectives on Women's Collective Action. Pres. Internat. Women's Anthrop. Conf. 1980-86, exec. bd. mem., 1987—; co-chair Anthropology Sect. N.Y. Acad. of Scis., 1987-91; panel mem. Latin Am. & Caribbean-Am. Friends Svc. Com., Phila., 1984-90. Recipient Great Tchr.'s award NYU Alumni Found., 1988; Danforth Assoc. award, Iowa, 1974; rsch. grantee NSF, Soc. Sci. Rsch. Coun., Rsch. Inst. for the Study of Man, Ford Found., Population Coun.; Fulbright scholar U. Ibadan, India, 1977; vis. scholar U. Ilfe, Nigeria and U. Ibadan, 1977-79. Office: NYU Anthropology Dept New York NY 10003

SUTTON, EUGENE WILSON, computer software developer, computer consultant; b. Wilmington, Del., May 4, 1948; s. Wilson and Norma (Saulsbury) S.; m. Cynthia G. Marks, Mar. 25, 1978; children: Nathaniel M., Laura S. BA, Washington Coll., Chestertown, Md., 1970. Programmer, analyst Am. Mut. Ins. Co., Wakefield, Mass., 1971-73; project leader Codon Corp., Bedford, Mass., 1974-76; cons. Minicomputer Bus. Systems, Bedford, 1976-82; pres. Minicomputer Applications Corp., Sudbury, Mass., 1982—. Mem. Ind. Computer Cons. Assn. (bd. dirs. 1985—, past pres.). Office: Minicomputer Applications Corp 31 Meadowbrook Rd Sudbury MA 01776-2618

SUTTON, GARY WILLIAM, lawyer; b. Edmonton, Alta., Can., Feb. 12, 1944; s. Harold William and Mary Eugenie (Simpson) S.; m. Ellen McNair James, June 7, 1980; children: Holly Heath, Lindsay Anne. BA, U. Minn., 1966; JD, Harvard U., 1969; diploma in grad. legal studies, U. Stockholm, 1971. Bar: N.Y. 1972. Law clk. VISTA, New Orleans, 1969-70; assoc. Shearman & Sterling, N.Y.C., 1972-80; counsel U.S. Ho. of Reps. Juciciary Com.-Impeachment, Washington, 1974, Salomon Inc., N.Y.C., 1980-82; v.p., sen. assoc. counsel Chase Manhattan Bank, N.Y.C., 1983-84; v.p., dep. gen. counsel Conn. Nat. Bank, Hartford, 1984-87; sr. v.p., gen. counsel, sec. 1st Nat. Bank Md., Balt., 1987—. Scholar internat. law U. Stockholm, 1970. Mem. Am. Corp. Counsel Assn. Office: 1st Nat Bank Md 25 S Charles St Baltimore MD 21201-3330

SUTTON, H. SPENCE, III, interior designer; b. Memphis, Jan. 16, 1955; s. Herbert Spence Jr. and Mamie Rose (Smith) S. B of Interior Design, Auburn (Ala.) U.; postgrad., N.C. State U., 1977-79. Project design coord. Archtl. Graphics Assocs., New Canaan, Conn., 1979-81, Architectural Graphics Assn., Ft. Lauderdale, Fla., 1979-81; assoc. Charles Swerz & Associs., N.Y.C., 1981-82, 84-87; dir. environ. design Murth, DeSola, Finsilver, Fiore, N.Y.C., 1982-84; assoc. Linda Warren Assocs., N.Y.C., 1987-90, Tortola, Brit. V.I., 1987—. Featured in mags. including Interior Design, 1985, Forbes Mag. 1990, Connoisseur, 1990. Fund raiser AIDS Walk, N.Y.C., 1989—; vol. AIDS Resource Coun., N.Y.C., 1990—. Mem. Nat. Hist. Trust, Auburn U. Sch. Architecture Alumni. Home and Office: 251 W 19th St Apt 3C New York NY 10011-4044 Office: Linda Warren Assocs 260 5th Ave New York NY 10001-6408

SUTTON, JONATHAN FAIRBAIRN, sales executive; b. Newport, R.I., Dec. 8, 1954; s. Hoover Clark Sutton and Geraldine (Cass) Eastler. BA in Bus. and Econs., St. Anselm Coll., 1979. Salesperson Adpacs Inc., Manchester, N.H., 1979-89, N.E. Planning Assocs., Inc., Bedford, N.H., 1990—. Home: 1252 W Merrimack St Manchester NH 03101-2208 Office: Northeast Planning Assocs 18 Constitution Dr Bedford NH 03110-6000

SUTTON, WILLIAM JOSEPH, academic administrator; b. Duquque, Iowa, Jan. 27, 1945; s. Joseph A. and Myra J. (Fleege) S.; m. GenYvette Prudhomme Sutton, Sept. 3, 1966; children: Rachal, Suzanne, Annette, Natalie, Lucy. BS, U. Wis., Platteville, 1967; MA, No. Ill. U., 1971; post-grad., U. Okla., 1974-75. Ins. agt. State Farm Ins., Freeport, Ill., 1968-69; mem. faculty Seminole (Okla.) Jr. Coll., 1971-75, St. Mary of the Plains, Dodge City, Kans., 1975-76; dir. coll. rels. Benedictine Coll., Atchison, Kans., 1976-80; exec. dir. Kutztown (Pa.) U. Found., 1981-89; v.p. univ. advancement Kutztown U., 1989—. Mem. Kutztown C. of C. (bd. dirs. 1989—), Berks County C. of C. Republican. Roman Catholic. Office: Kutztown U Wiesenberger Alumni Ct Kutztown PA 19530

SUUBERG, ERIC MICHAEL, chemical engineering educator; b. N.Y.C., Nov. 23, 1951; s. Michael and Aino (Berg) S.; m. Ina Inara Vatvars, Apr. 26, 1987; 1 child, Alessandra Anna. BSChemE, MIT, 1974, MSChemE, 1974, BS in Bus. Mgmt., 1974, MS in Bus. Mgmt., 1976, ScD in Chem. Engring., 1978. Asst. prof. chem. engring. Carnegie-Mellon U., Pitts., 1977-81; asst. prof. engring. Brown U., Providence, 1981-84, assoc. prof. engring., 1984-90, prof. engring., 1990—; vis. scientist Centre National de la Recherche Scientifique, Mulhouse, France, 1988; invited lectr. Ministry Edn., Monbusho, Japan, 1991. Mem. internat. editorial bd. Fuel, 1988—; mem. editorial adv. bd. Energy and Fuels, 1990—; contbr. more than 40 articles to profl. jours. Elected mem. Estonian Am. Nat. Coun., N.Y.C., 1984—. Mem. Am. Inst. Chem. Engrs., Combustion Inst., Am. Chem. Soc. (chmn. div. fuel chemistry 1991). Office: Brown Univ Div Engring Box D Providence RI 02912

SVEDLOW, ANDREW JAY, museum administrator; b. Stamford, Conn., Dec. 9, 1955; s. Bernard Dave and Shirley (Bush) S.; m. Kim Bertrand (div. Dec. 1988); children: Aaron, David. Student, Dickinson Coll. and Chinese U., Hong Kong, 1973-74; BA, George Washington U., Washington, 1977; MS, Bank St. Coll., N.Y.C., 1982; PhD, Pa. State U., 1985. Instr. Pa. State U., University Park, 1983-85; vis. instr. Southeastern Mass. U., Dartmouth, 1985-86; assoc. prof. U. So. Miss., Hattiesburg, 1985; curator edn. Bruce Mus., Greenwich, Conn., 1978-80; coord. edn. Cooper Hewitt Mus., Smithsonian Inst., N.Y.C., 1980-83; exec. dir. Mulvane Art Mus., Topeka, 1986-89, Whistler House Mus. Art, Lowell, Mass., 1989-90; asst. dir. Mus. of City of N.Y., 1990—; grad. faculty NYU, N.Y.C., 1990—, Bank St. Coll. Edn., N.Y.C.; chmn. Kans. Youth Art mOnth, 1989. Author: Commuter Blues, 1983, Sacred Intimacies, 1989; one man shows various museums and galleris, 1975-89. State rep. Internat.Soc. Edn. through Art, 1988. Recipient award for exceptional svc. Smithsonian Instn., Washington, 1983. Mem. Am. Assn. Museums, Nat. Art Edn. Assn. (task force chmn. 1987-88), Kans. Mus. Assn. (N.E. rep. 1987-88, award of excellence 1987). Democrat. Jewish. Home: 22 Rolling Ridge Rd Stamford CT 06903-1318 Office: Mus of City of NY 103rd St and Fifth Ave New York NY 10029

SVENDSEN, IB ARNE, civil engineer; b. Copenhagen, July 19, 1937; came to U.S., 1987; m. Alice Marianne Zaber, Feb. 27, 1960; children: Kim Allan, Anne Marie. MSc, Tech. U., Denmark, 1960; PhD, Tech. U., 1974. Rsch. engr. Coastal Engring. Lab., Copenhagen, 1960-64; asst. prof., assoc. prof. Tech. U., Lyngby, Denmark, 1964-87; prof., chair civil engring. U. Del., Newark, 1987—, prof. marine studies, 1988—; mem. "Internat. Faculty" Danish Rsch. Acad., 1991—. Author 2 books 1976, 81; contbr. articles to profl. jours. Scholarship NSF Colo. State U. 1964, fellow NATO 1982; recipient Thos. B. Thrige travel award 1982, other travel awards 1972-87. Mem. ASCE, Internat. Assn. Hydraulic Rsch., Am. Soc. Engring. Edn., Am. Geophys. Union, Danish Inst. Civil Engrs., Danish Ctr. Applied Math. and Mechanics (sci. coun. 1979-87). Office: U Del Dept Civil Engring Newark DE 19716

SVENSSON, PAUL EDWARD, hospital executive; b. Cambridge, Mass., Aug. 26, 1953; s. Holger Svend and Eileen Winona (Parsons) S.; m. Providencia Rosa, Nov. 1, 1986; children: Erik Joseph, Sylvia Victoria. BA in Psychology, Coll. of the Holy Cross, 1976; MPH, U. Pitts., 1979. Asst. adminstr. U. Hosp., Stony Brook, N.Y., 1978-82; asst. dir. Montefiore Med. Ctr., Bronx, N.Y., 1982-87; chief exec. officer The Parkway Hosp., Forest Hills, N.Y., 1987—; adj. faculty Baruch Coll., N.Y.C., 1989—, Ithaca Coll., 1986—. Bd. dirs. Consumer Energy Coop., Beford Hills, N.Y., 1988-89; mem. Queens C. of C., 1989-91. Mem. Am. Hosp. Assn., Med. Group Practice Assn., Healthcare Fin. Mgmt. Assn., Healthcare Execs. Group, Met. Health Adminstrs. Assn. Office: Parkway Hosp 70-35 113th St Forest Hills NY 11375

SVIKLA, ALIUS JULIUS, pharmacist; b. Merbeck, Germany, Jan. 12, 1947; came to U.S., 1949; s. Julius and Brone (Maksimavich) S. BS in Pharmacy, Northeastern U., Boston, 1973. Pharmacist Osco Drug, Cambridge, Mass., 1973-75; profl. sales rep. Pfizer Labs., N.Y.C., 1976-77; pharmacist, mgr. CVS Pharmacy, South Dennis, Mass., 1977—; drug abuse cons. Healthcare Assn., Boston, First Group of Boston, 1979-87; liason Kaunas Med. Acad., Lithuania. Served with USMC, 1965-68. Decorated Purple Heart. Mem. Am. Pharm. Assn., Internat. Pharm. Fedn., Mass. Pub. Health Assn., Mass. State Pharm. Assn., Lithuanian Am. Pharm. Assn., Mil. Order of Purple Heart (life), Fleet Res. Assn. Republican. Roman Catholic. Home: 9 Seagrove Rd South Dennis MA 02660 Office: CVS Pharmacy PO Box 715 Rte 134 Patriots Sq South Dennis MA 02660

SVOBODA, JERRY JOSEPH, vascular surgeon; b. Cleve., Aug. 23, 1951; s. Jerry Frank and Janet (Texler) S.; m. Adelaide Elizabeth Jones, Apr. 16, 1977; children: Elizabeth, Mark. AB in Biology magna cum laude, St. Louis U., 1973; MD, Hahnemann Med. Coll., 1977. Diplomate Am. Bd. Surgery in surgery and vascular surgery. Intern Mercy Med. Ctr., Denver, 1977-78; surg. resident Guthrie Cilnic/Robert Packer Hosp., Sayre, Pa., 1978-82; vascular surgery fellow Englewood (N.J.) Hosp., 1982-83; staff surgeon Mercy Med. Ctr., Denver, 1983-84; attending surgeon St. Mary's and Park Ridge Hosps., Rochester, N.Y., 1984—; cons. surgeon Lakeside Meml. and Rochester Gen. Hosp., 1984—; clin. asst. prof. surgery U. Rochester Sch. Medicine and Dentistry, 1984—; mem. med. bd. St. Mary's Hosp., Rochester, 1989—, Park Ridge Hosp., Rochester, 1991-92. Contbr. articles to profl. jours. Sec. Christ Ch. Unity, Rochester, 1987-89. Recipient Physician Recognition award AMA, 1981-84, 84-87, 87-90, 90-93. Fellow ACS; mem. Soc. Clin. Vascular Surgery, Upstate N.Y. Vascular Soc., Ea. Vascular Soc., Monroe County Med. Soc. (asst. treas. 1990, sec. 1991-92), Rochester Vascular Soc. Home: 70 Brandywine Ln Rochester NY 14618 Office: Rochester Vascular Surgery Assocs 503 Beahan Rd Rochester NY 14624

SWAIM, ALICE MACKENZIE, poet; b. Craigdam, Scotland, June 5, 1911; d. Donald Campbell and Alice Annand (Murray) MacKenzie; m. William Thomas Swaim, Dec. 27, 1932; children: Elizabeth Anne, Kathleen MacKenzie. Student, Chatham Coll., Pitts., 1928-30; BA, Wilson Coll., 1932. Critic Nat. Writers' Club, 1951-53; columnist Cornucopia and Tejas, 1953-56, Carlisle (Pa.) Evening Sentinel, 1953-70; nat. cons. Poetry Therapy Assn.; contest judge; U.S. rep. 2nd World Congress of Poets. Book reviewer Am. Poetry League, 1966-68; author: Horizon Makrs, 1991, Beneath a Dancing Star, 1991, Children in Summer, 1983, Unicorn and Thistle, 1981, others; poetry and mktg. editor Soc. of N.Hampshire, 1975-82; contbr. articles to profl. jours. Sr. leader Girl Scouts U.S., Mt. Holly Springs, Pa., 1948-51; vol. ARC, Child Care Project, 1971-72. Recipient 1st prize Writer's Digest Contest, 1989, medals Poet Laureate of the Sonnet, 1960, many others. Mem. Poetry Soc. Am., Acad. Am. Poets, Poetry Therapy Assn., United Fedn. of State Poetry Socs., United Poets Laureate Internat. Presbyterian. Home and Office: 322 N Second St Apt 1606 Harrisburg PA 17101

SWAIN, KENNETH ROBERT, automobile company executive, consultant; b. Boston, Aug. 30, 1943; s. Fred Allen and Dorothy Helen (Lindsay) S.; m. Pamela Sue Cook, May 5, 1979; 1 child, Anthony. AA Speech Communication, Sierra Coll., Rocklin, Calif., 1966; BA in Bus. Adminstrn., Calif. State U., Chico, 1969. Warranty adminstr. Chevrolet Motor div. GM, L.A., 1971-73; traffic coord. Nissan Motor Corp. in USA, Gardena, Calif., 1973-75, transp. supr., 1975-81, adminstr. vehicle traffic, 1981-85, mgr. transp., 1985-87; nat. transp. mgr. Peugeot Motors Am., Lyndhurst, N.J., 1987-88, nat. distbn. mgr., 1988-89, nat. port ops. mgr., 1989-90; nat. mgr. logistics, traffic and customs BMW N.Am., Woodcliff Lake, N.J., 1990—; chmn. Port of Newark steering com. N.Y. and N.J. Port Authority, 1987-89. Author: Automotive Transportation and Damage Claims Handbook, 1974. With USN, 1969-70, Vietnam. Mem. Soc. Automotive Engrs., Automobile Importers Am. (chmn. vehicle com. 1987—), Assn. Internat. Automobile Mfrs. (sub-chmn. vehicle logistics). Republican. Office: BMW of N AM 300 Chestnut Ridge Rd Westwood NJ 07675-7731

SWAIN, MADELEINE TRAUBE, management consultant; b. N.Y.C., Jan. 15, 1938; d. Leonard and Marjorie (Bercovici) Traube; m. Robert Swain, Oct. 25, 1975; children: Lisa Swain Bienstock, Eric. AS, Endicott, Beverly, Mass, 1956; student, Hunter College, 1964. Franchise adminstr. Holiday Inns of America, N.Y.C., 1968-72; acct. mgr. and adminstr. Muir Weiss Inc., N.Y.C., 1972-75; mng. dir. Perfect Projects, N.Y.C., 1975-78; pres. and co-chmn. Swain & Swain Inc., N.Y.C., 1978—; pres. Outplacement Internat., Chgo., 1986-88; dir. Assn. of Outplacement Cons. Firms, Parsippany, N.J., 1981-84, Outplacement Internat., Chgo., 1986—. Co-author: Out the Organization, 1989, (reprint), 1992; contbr. newspaper articles to business jours. and mags. Vol. fundraiser Save the Children, Westport, Conn., 1990, 91, 92. Mem. Women's Campaign Fund, Women's Econ. Round Table, NAFE, PEER Group. Home: 420 E 72d St New York NY 10021 Office: Swain & Swain Inc 405 Lexington Ave New York NY 10174

SWAIN, PHILIP RAYMOND, publishing company executive; b. Meriden, Conn., Nov. 30, 1929; s. Raymond Francis and Angela Catherine (Maslow) S. AB cum laude, Harvard U., 1950; MBA, Boston U. Tchr. Latin, Greek, pvt. schs., Cambridge and Still River, Mass., 1950-55; editor Ravengate Press, Cambridge, 1955-65, pres., 1965—. Mem. bd. advisers St. Benedict Acad., Still River. Mem. Book Builders of Boston. Roman Catholic. Club: Harvard. Author (as Philip Douglas): Saint of Philadelphia, The Life of Bishop John Neumann, 1977. Home: 56 Carpenter Ave Meriden CT 06450-6196 Office: PO Box 103 Cambridge MA 02138

SWAIN, STEPHEN JAMES, banker; b. Ft. Sill, Okla., Apr. 20, 1949; s. Oren and Vera (Weber) S.; m. Jane Alison Charnley, July 19, 1986. BS, U.S. Mil. Acad., 1970; MBA, Harvard U., 1977. Commd. 2nd lt. U.S. Army, 1970, advanced through grades to capt.; assoc. Warburg, Paribas, Becker, N.Y.C., 1977-79; v.p. New Ct. Securities, N.Y.C., 1979-83; v.p., Dillon, Read & Co., N.Y.C., 1983-86; mng. dir. S.J. Conway & Co., N.Y.C., 1986-88; pres. S.J. Swain & Co., N.Y.C., 1988—; bd. dirs. Kron Chocolatier, Inc., N.Y.C., mem. bd. premiere mfg.; corp. sec. Bear-Bear, Inc., N.Y.C., 1987—, chief exec. officer mfg. Home and Office: SJ Swain & Co 400 E 52nd St Apt 11J New York NY 10022-6406

SWAIN, VIRGINIA MARY, human relations consultant; b. Buffalo, N.Y., June 8, 1943; d. Robert Burrough and Joan (Wood) S.; m. Thomas Edward Cone III, May 20, 1964 (div. 1974); 1 child, Thomas Edward Cone IV. AA, Colby Sawyer Coll., New London, N.H., 1963; postgrad., Lesley Coll., Cambridge, Mass. Tchr. U.S. Peace Corps, West Africa, 1964-66; personnel mgr. Pepperidge Farm Mail Order Co., Clinton, Conn., 1975-81; sales coord. Internat. Salt, Essex, Conn., 1981-84; dir. mktg. Mercy Ctr., Madison, Conn., 1984-86; dir. pub. rels., mktg. Wainwright House, Rye, N.Y., 1986; pres. Ginger Swain and Assoc., Old Lyme, Conn., 1986—; del. non-govtl. orgn. to UN, N.Y.C., 1991, Symphony for UN; mem. Comms. Coord. Com., Congress for a More Democratic UN, 1991; del. Earth Summit, UN Conf. on Environ. and Devel., Rio de Janeiro, 1992; bd. dirs. Symphony for UN. Co-author: The Gift of Peace, 1989. Facilitator, cons. Am. Cancer Soc., New London, Conn., 1991. Mem. Am. Assn. Counseling and Devel., Am. Assn. Specialists Group Work, Am. Assn. Religious/Value Issues in Counseling, Nat. Career Devel. Assn., UN Communications Non Govt. Agy. Episcopalian. Office: PO Box 921 Old Lyme CT 06371-0921

SWALLOM, DANIEL WARREN, mechanical engineer; b. Sioux Falls, S.D., Oct. 13, 1946; s. Maurice Leo and Mary Alice (Jacobs) S.; m. Elizabeth Ruth Pederson, June 7, 1969; children: Bradley Jay, Jeffrey Dean. BS in Mech. Engring., U. Iowa, 1969, MS in Mech. Engring., 1970, PhD, 1972. Research asst. U. Iowa, Iowa City, 1971-72; mech. engr. Argonne (Ill.) Nat. Lab., 1975-76; mgr. ops. Maxwell Labs., Inc., Woburn, Mass., 1976-78; pres. Odin Internat. Corp., 1978-79; dir. mil. power programs Textron Def. Systems (fomerly Avco Rsch. Lab. Textron), Everett, Mass., 1979—; mem. indsl. adv. panel Lincoln Coll., Northeastern U., Boston, 1980-83; bd. dirs. Symposium on Engring. Aspects Magnetohydrodynamics, Washington, 1988-92. Capt. USAF, 1972-75. U. Iowa Merit scholar, 1964. Mem. AIAA (assoc. fellow), Am. Phys. Soc., New. Eng. Iowa Club (bd. dirs., v.p. 1989—), Meadow Brook Golf Club, Sigma Xi, Tau Beta Pi, Pi Tau Sigma. Congregationalist. Club: Meadow Brook Golf (Reading, Mass.). Office: Textron Def Systems 2385 Revere Beach Pky Everett MA 02149-5900

SWAN, CHARLES E., state government administrator; b. Rochester, N.Y., May 11, 1935; s. Edwin M. and Florence E. (Doescher) S.; m. Mary Lawrence, June 17, 1961 (sep. 1984); children: Gregory C., Tracy A., Amy L. AB in Polit. Sci., U. Rochester, 1957, EdM in Adminstrn., 1963; cert. in urban policy, Brookings Instn., Washington, 1973. Purchasing agt. Rochester Germicide Co., 1957-60; dir. admissions Rochester Inst. Tech., 1960-63; U.S. sales mgr. C.H. Stuart & Co., Rochester, 1964; sales cons. Rochester, 1965-69; exec. dir. North East Area Devel., Rochester, 1969-71; research cons. Ford Found./U.S. Catholic Conf., Rochester, 1973-74; community program specialist N.Y. State Div. for Youth, Rochester, 1974—. Author: Careers in Business, 1963. Chmn. City Planning Commn., Rochester, 1970-73; vice chmn. City Charter Commn., Rochester, 1973; commr. Monroe County Planning Bd., Rochester, 1973, Regional Planning Bd., Rochester, 1973. Recipient Nat. citation Nat. Ctr./Vol. Action, Washington, 1973, County citation Monroe County Planning Coun., 1973, County award Wayne County, Lyons, N.Y., 1988, Dirs. award N.Y. State Div. for Youth, 1981. Republican. Office: NY State Div for Youth 109 S Union St Ste 302 Rochester NY 14607-1826

SWAN, JAMES ELLERY, medical editor; b. White Plains, N.Y., Oct. 6, 1937; s. Charles Elmer Jr. and Eleanor Gybbon (Spilsbury) S.; m. Lauren Cimarosa, May 18, 1968 (div. 1990); children: Jason Ellery, Andrew Patrick; m. Patricia Lesch, 1990. BA, Union Coll., 1959; MA, NYU, 1967. News reporter White Plains Reporter Dispatch, 1959-60, 65-66; supr. jours. Am. Inst. Physics, N.Y.C., 1969-75; mng. editor Soc. Nuclear Medicine, N.Y.C., 1975-78; editor Contemporary Ob/Gyn Mag. Contenporary Ob/Gyn Mag. Med. Econs. Pub., Montvale, N.J., 1978-90, editorial dir., 1990—. With U.S. Army, 1962-64. Woodrow Wilson Found. fellow, 1961. Mem. Am. Bus. Press (Jesse M. Neal award 1984, 87), Am. Med. Writers Assn. Home: 6 Craven Ln White Plains NY 10605-3312 Office: Med Econs Co Inc 680 Kinderkamack Rd Oradell NJ 07649-1601

SWAN, JOHN CHARLES, library director; b. Elkhorn, Wis., Apr. 12, 1945; s. John Clement and Winifred Jean (Sturtevant) S.; m. Susan Reynolds Crocker, May 1, 1971; children: Matthew Carey, Benjamin Charles. Student, Northwestern U., 1963-66; BA, Boston U., 1967; MA, Tufts U., 1969, PhD, 1975; MLS, Simmons Coll., 1979. Ref. libr. Wabash Coll., Crawfordsville, Ind., 1979-86; head libr. Bennington (Vt.) Coll., 1986—; part-time instr. English and Am. lit. U. Mass., Boston, Tufts U., Curry Coll., Massasoit Community Coll., U. Mass. Higher Edn. for Prisoners Program, 1970-79; learning librs. asst. lectureship NEH Boston Pub. Libr., 1975, lectureship, 1977. Editor: Music in Boston, 1978; co-author: The Triumph of Pierrot (Choice Outstanding Acad. 1986), 1986, The Freedom to Lie, 1989; contbr. articles to profl. jours. Bd. dirs. adult edn. The Tutorial Ctr., Bennington, 1989—; trustee McCullough Libr., North Bennington, Vt., 1991—; permanent trustee Bennington Free Libr., 1991—. Mem. ALA (chair intellectual freedom round table 1985-86, exec. bd. dirs. 1980—), ACLU (bd. dirs. Vt. chpt. 1990—), Vt. Libr. Assn. (chair intellectual freedom com.1987—), Ind. Libr. Assn. (chair intellectual freedom com.

1981-86), Granville Bantock Soc. (Ann. award 1983), Baker Street Breakfast Club. Democrat. Mem. Vedantist Ch. Home: Rte 2 Spg Rd Bennington VT 05201 Office: Bennington Coll Crossett Libr Rte 67A Bennington VT 05201

SWAN, RALPH EDWARD, secondary school educator; b. Harrisburg, Pa., May 2, 1946; s. Ralph C. and D. Grace (Cox) S.; m. Anne Marie Young. BS, Edinboro (Pa.) State Coll., 1969; MEd, Lehigh U., 1971. Cert. tchr., Pa. Tchr. Marple Newtown Sch. Dist., Newtown Square, Pa., 1969—; instr. U. Pa., Phila., 1984-89; adj. prof. Chestnut Hill Coll., Phila., 1987—. Mem. Phi Delta Kappa. Home: 165 Dowlin Forge Rd Downingtown PA 19335-1426 Office: Paxon Hollow Mid Sch Paxon Hollow Rd Broomall PA 19008

SWANGER, WILLIAM EARL, III, communications executive, writer; b. Wilkes-Barre, Pa., May 3, 1954; s. William Earl Jr. and Stella Mae (Walker) S.; m. Trudy Diane Benner, July 2, 1978; children: Nathan William, Rebecca Diane. BA in English, Susquehanna U., 1976. Newspaper writer Daily Item, Sunbury, Pa., 1972-76, newspaper writer, editor, 1976-78; pub. rels. specialist Tressler Luth. Svcs., Camp Hill, Pa., 1978-82, dir. pub. info., 1982-86; dir. communications Tressler Luth. Svcs., Mechanicsburg, Pa., 1986—. Writer Cen. Penn Bus. Jour., 1989—; contbr. articles to profl. jours. Recipient Capital award Internat. Assn. Bus. Communicators, 1988, 89, 91, Awards for Publ. Excellence award Communications Concepts, Inc., 1989, 90, 91. Mem. Pub. Rels. Soc. Am., Pa. Pub. Rels. Soc. Lutheran. Home: 22 Winding Hill Dr Mechanicsburg PA 17055-5642 Office: Tressler Luth Svcs PO Box 2001 Mechanicsburg PA 17055-0707

SWANICK, PATRICK JOSEPH, banker; b. Worcester, Mass., Oct. 8, 1957; s. Joseph A. and Catherine M. (McCall) S.; m. Diana Lynn Gilson, June 16, 1984. BS in Mktg., St. Joseph's U., Phila., 1979, MBA in Mgmt., 1982. Various executive positions Fidelity Bank, Phila., 1979-85, v.p., 1985-88; sr. v.p. First Fidelity Bancorp., Upper Darby, Pa., 1989—. Contbr. articles to bus. mags. and newspapers including Wall St. Jour., Fortune mag.; speaker at numerous banking seminars and customer service confs. Recipient Best Consumer Relations Effort award, Better Bus. Bur. Ea. Pa., Phila., 1988, Svc. Quality Mgmt. award Nat. Bank Mktg. Assn., Boston, 1990. Mem. Soc. Consumer Affairs Profls. in Bus. (Excellence in Consumer Response Techniques citation 1989), Internat. Customer Svc. Assn., Am. Soc. Quality Control, Lambda Chi Alpha. Office: First Fidelity Bancorp 100 Constitution Ave Upper Darby PA 19082-2295

SWANK, SCOTT TREGO, museum director; b. Lancaster, Pa., Jan. 5, 1941; s. Scott B. and Frances (Boyd) S.; m. Sylvia Eshleman, 1964 (div. 1976); children: Jennifer, Jonathan; m. Kathleen Bryer, 1977 (div. 1989); children: Lauren, Amanda. BA, Elizabethtown Coll., 1964; MA, U. Pa., 1966, PhD, 1970. Instr. Elizabethtown (Pa.) Coll., 1966-68, asst. prof., 1968-72, assoc. prof., 1972-74; head, edn. div. Winterthur (Del.) Mus. and Gardens, 1974-79, dep. dir. for interpretation, 1979-90; dir. Canterbury (N.H.) Shaker Village, 1990—. Author: Arts of the Pennsylvania Germans, 1983, The History Museum in The Museum: A Reference Guide, 1990; editor: Perspectives on American Folk Art, 1980; contbr. articles to profl. jours. Recipient Kent fellowship Danforth Found., St. Louis, 1966-68. Mem. Am. Assn. Mus. (coun. mem. 1988-91, chair Map adv. com. 1989-91, nat. task force on edn. 1990-91). Office: Shaker Village Inc 288 Shaker Rd Canterbury NH 03224-2728

SWANN, MADELINE BRUCE, chemist, consultant; b. Washington, July 24, 1951; d. Edwin Everette and Ruth Madeline (Rice) S. BA, Fisk U., 1973; PhD, Howard U., 1980. Teaching asst. dept. chemistry Howard U., Washington, 1973-74, teaching fellow dept. chemistry, 1974-80; rsch. chemist Res., Dev. and Engring. Ctr., Ft. Belvoir, Va., 1981-89, chemist, phys. scientist, 1989-90; chemist U.S. Army Materiel Command, Adelphi, Md., 1990—; cons. Tech. Applications Inc., Arlington, Va., 1981. Mem. Am. Chem. Soc., N.Y. Acad. Sci., Orgn. of Black Scientists, Beta Kappa Chi, Sigma Xi. Office: US Lab Command Attn AMSLC-TP-PS 2800 Powder Mill Rd Hyattsville MD 20783-1145

SWANSON, AUSTIN DELAIN, educational administration educator; b. Jamestown, N.Y., June 11, 1930; s. Manley Moris and Beulah Marjorie (Waite) S.; m. Marilyn Jean Peterson, Mar. 31, 1956; children: Paul Delain, Karin Lorine Swanson Daun. BS, Allegheny Coll., 1952; MS, Columbia U., 1955, EdD, 1960. Tchr. Ramapo Cen. High Sch., Suffern, N.Y., 1955-58; rsch. assoc. Tchrs. Coll. Columbia U., N.Y.C., 1958-63; prof. ednl. adminstrn. SUNY, Buffalo, 1963—, chair dept. ednl. orgn.. adminstrn. and policy, 1991—; vis. scholar Inst. Edn. U. London, 1979, Zold Inst., Israel, 1988. Author: Modernizing the Little Red Schoolhouse, 1979, School Finance, 1991, also monographs; contbr. articles to profl. jours. Mem. exec. bd. St. John Luth. Ch., Wiliamsville, N.Y., 1991. With U.S. Army, 1952-54. Fellow Stanford U., 1969-70; Fulbright scholar U. Melbourne, Australia, 1986. Mem. Am. Ednl. Rsch. Assn., Am. Edn. Fin. Assn., Am. Assn. Sch. Adminstrs., World Future Soc., Phi Delta Kappa. Republican. Lutheran. Office: SUNY Grad Sch Edn Buffalo NY 14260

SWANSON, DANE CRAIG, naval officer, pilot; b. Guam, Feb. 13, 1955; s. George Clair and Norma Francis (Brown) S. BS in Naval Architecture, U.S Naval Acad., 1977; MA, Webster U., 1980; grad., USAF Test Pilot Sch., 1985. Commd. ensign USN, 1977, advanced through grades to comdr., 1992; flight instr. USN, Kingsville, Tex., 1978-80; asst. ops. officer USS Eisenhower VF-142 USN, 1981-84; test pilot Air Test and Evaluation Air Test and Evaluation Squadron Four USN, Point Mugu, Calif., 1985-88; ops. officer USS Saratoga VF-103 USN, 1988-91; anti-air appraisal officer Naval Air System Command USN, Washington, 1991—. Decorated 4 Air medals. Mem. Soc. Exptl. Test Pilots, U.S. Naval Inst., Officers Christian Fellowship. Republican. Baptist. Home: 1801 Crystal Dr Apt 209 Arlington VA 22202-4413

SWANSON, DEAN EDWARD, foreign affairs officer; b. Alexandria, Minn., Apr. 29, 1949; s. Gordon Ira and Dorothy Evangeline (Hanson) S.; m. Patricia Ann Wenberg, Sept. 8, 1972; 1 child, Katharine Marie. BA magna cum laude, U. Minn., 1971; MA, Ohio State U., 1974, PhD, 1976. Grad. rsch. fellow Mershon Ctr., Columbus, Ohio, 1971-75; rsch. fellow Centre for Fgn. Policy Studies, Halifax, N.S., Can., 1975-78; fgn. affairs specialist Nat. Marine Fisheries Svc., Washington, 1978-81, fgn. affairs officer, 1981-89; chief internat. orgns. Nat. Marine Fisheries Svc., Silver Spring, Md., 1989—; assoc. Atlantic Opinion Rsch. Ctr., Halifax, 1978; data processing cons. Dalhousie U., Halifax, 1975-78. Contbr. articles to profl. jours., chpts. to books. Moderator Pilgrim Ch., Wheaton, Md., 1991—, chmn. worship bd., 1984-88. Recipient Outstanding Performance award Nat. Marine Fisheries Svc., 1980-90. Mem. Pi Sigma Alpha. Mem. United Ch. of Christ. Home: 1316 Sarah Dr Silver Spring MD 20904-2148 Office: Nat Marine Fisheries Svc 1335 East-West Hwy Silver Spring MD 20910

SWANSON, HARRY FREDERICK, artist; b. Hartford, Conn., June 5, 1931; s. Harry Bernard and Anna Maria (Glansholm) S.; m. Marion Louise Rydberg, Apr. 30, 1955; children: Alan Mark, Anne Louise. Cert., Art Instrn. Inc., Mpls., 1948-50; student, Hartford Art Sch., 1953, Practical Art Sch., Boston, 1955. Machinist, draftsman Pratt & Whitney Aircraft, East Hartford, Conn., 1950-55; draftsman MIT, Cambridge, Mass., 1955-56; tech. illustrator The Purnell Co., Boston, 1956-59; illustrator and graphics designer Itek Corp., Lexington, Mass., 1959-72; artist, illustrator Studio & Fine Art Gallery, Newbury, Mass., 1972-89. Exhibited in group shows inlcuding Nat. Exhibit Ellsworth Gallery, 1973; also pvt. collections. Recipient awards art assns. Mem. Copley Soc. Boston. Unitarian-Universalist. Home and Studio: Rte 1 PO Box 60 Lincolnville ME 04849

SWANSON, JUDITH ANN, political science educator; b. L.A., Nov. 4, 1957; d. Don Richard and Shirley Mae (Sollenberger) S.; m. David Raymond Mayhew, Nov. 20, 1987. BA magna cum laude, Colo. Coll., 1979; MSc with distinction, London Sch. Econs., 1980; PhD, U. Chgo., 1987. Teaching asst. U. Chgo., 1983-84; instr. Yale U., 1985-86; asst. prof. U. Ga., Athens, 1986-88; vis. fellow Yale U., New Haven, 1987; asst. prof. dept. polit. sci. Boston U., 1988—; systems analyst repeat offender unit Ill. State's Atty.'s Office, Chgo., 1984-85. Author: The Public and the Private in Aristotle's Political Philosophy, 1992; editorial asst. Ethics, U. Chgo. Press, 1982-83. Earhart Found. fellow, 1980-84, Josephine de Karman fellow Aerojet-Gen. Corp., 1983-84, NEH fellow for univ. tchrs., 1990-91. Mem. Am. Polit. Sci. Assn., Phi Beta Kappa. Office: Boston U Dept Polit Sci 232 Bay State Rd Boston MA 02215-1403

SWANSON, NORMA FRANCES, federal agency administrator; b. Blue Island, Ill., Oct. 24, 1923; d. Arnold Raymond and Bessie Oween (Bewley) Brown; m. George Clair Swanson, Mar. 18, 1948; 1 child, Dane Craig. AB, Asbury Coll., 1946; BS cum laude, Eastern Nazarene Coll., Wollaston, Mass., 1970; MA cum laude, Ind. Christian U., 1986. Confidential asst. dep. undersec. interagy. intergovt. affairs U.S. Dept. Edn., Washington, 1981—; pres. Window to the World, Schroon Lake, N.Y., 1985—; asst. dir. edn. Commn. Bicentennial U.S. Constn., Washington, 1987—; cons. Conf. Industrialized Nations, Williamsburg, Va., 1982, Nellie Thomas Inst. Learning, Monterey, Calif, 1981-82, N.T. Inst. Learning. Author: Dear Teenager, A Teen's Guide to Correct Social Behavior, 1987, A Constitution Is Born, A Teacher's Guide to Resource Materials, 1987, Sunlights and More; editor: (anthology) Horizon's Plus; developer ednl. materials Window to the World; theorem artist Early Am. Life mag., 1974. Bd. regents Ind. Christian U., 1986—. Republican. Baptist. Home: 3288 Page Ave Apt 1202 Virginia Beach VA 23451-1036

SWANTEK, JOHN EDWARD, III, public relations executive; b. Albany, N.Y., Jan. 9, 1947; s. John Edward and Dorothy Agnes (Caulfield) S.; m. Karen Leoni Coffey, Aug. 20, 1970; children: John Edward IV, Michael James. B, Syracuse U., 1975, MBA, 1987. Staff reporter Troy (N.Y.) Times-Record, 1970-72, polit. editor, 1972-75, state editor, 1975-80, mng. editor, 1980-82; pub. affairs officer Watervliet (N.Y.) Arsenal, 1982—; cons. Pub. Rels. Print Media; publisher World 21 Communications, Troy. Author: Moonlighter'sManual, 1980, Canters Bury Tales, 1990; contbr. articles to profl. jours.; inventor/patentee in field. Vol. Lit. Vols. Am., Troy, 1990, Boy Scouts Am., Troy, 1970—. With USN, 1966-70. Recipient George Washington medal Freedoms Found., 1976, Keith L. Ware award U.S. Army, 1980. Mem. Internat. Assn. Desktop Publishers, Nat. Assn. Govt. Communicators, Internat. Assn. Bus. Communicators, Am Legion, Legion of Moose , Loyal Order Moose. Home: 15 Hakes Rd Troy NY 12180

SWARE, RICHARD MICHAEL, JR., electric company executive; b. Phila., July 2, 1952; s. Richard Michael and Thelma Edna (Pressell) W.; Jean Marie Dischinger; children: Marc Avery Pitt, Matthew Michael. Student, Va. Polytech. Inst., 1970-73, Bucks County Community Coll., Newtown, Pa., 1973-74, Ursinus Coll., 1974-75; BS, York Coll., 1986. Substitute tchr. Centennial Sch. Dist., Warminster, Pa., 1973; from calculator to correspondent Prudential Ins. Co., Dresher, Pa., 1973-78; from jr. tech. asst. to compliance coord. Phila. Electric Co., Delta, Pa., 1978-91; supr. Phila. Electric Co., Delta, 1991—. Author weekly newsletter 1985-87. Dist. com. mem. Boy Scouts Am., Lancaster, Pa., 1989—, troop com. chmn. 1987-91, pack asst. cubmaster 1986, pack com. chmn. 1984-88. Recipient Dist. Merit award Boy Scouts Am., 1992. Mem. U.S. Volleyball Assn. (coach, regional referee), U.S. Golf Assn., Order of Arrow (Brotherhood mem.). Republican. Episcopalian. Home: 4 Kimberly Ct Lancaster PA 17602 Office: Phila Electric Co RR 1 Box 208 Delta PA 17314

SWARTZ, WILLIAM MICHAEL, physician; b. Detroit, May 26, 1946; s. Harry Louis and Helen Louise (Kiley) S.; m. Cynthia Bennett, 1978. BA, Johns Hopkins U., 1968; BM in Sci., Dartmouth Med. Sch., 1970; MD, U. N.W. Colo., 1972. Diplomate Am. Bd. Plastic Surgery. Intern Mary Hutchcock-Dartmouth Affil. Hosp., 1972, surgery resident, 1973; intern Dartmouth-Hitchcock Affiliate Hosps., 1972; resident in gen. surgery Dartmouth-Hitchcock Cook Hosp., 1973; resident in gen. surgery R.I. Hosp.-Brown U., 1974-75, resident in plastic surgery, 1976-78; asst. prof. surgery U. Pitts., 1980-86, clin. assoc. prof. surgery, 1992; assoc. prof. surgery Tulane U., New Orleans, 1986-89, prof. surgery, 1990; pvt. practice Pitts., 1990—. Author: Head and Neck Microsurgery, 1991. Lt. comdr. USNR, 1978-80. Mem. Am. Assn. Surgery of the Hand (treas. 1990-92), Am. Soc. Reconstructive Microsurgery (treas. 1992—), Am. Assn. Plastic Surgeons, Am. Soc. Plastic and Reconstructive Surgeons. Home: 5030 Castleman St Pittsburgh PA 15232-2107 Office: 580 S Aiken Ave Ste 100 Pittsburgh PA 15232

SWAYNE, LAWRENCE CALVIN, radiologist, consultant; b. Phila., Dec. 4, 1953; s. Calvin Vernon and Shirley Jane (Garwood) S.; m. Carol Sue Fesmire, Aug. 20, 1977; children: Beverly Carol, Brian Calvin. BS, Ursinus Coll., 1979; MD, Rutgers, 1979. Diplomate Am. Bd. Radiology. Diagnostic radiology resident Albert Einstein Med. Ctr., Phila., 1979-82, nuclear medicine fellow, 1982-83; attending radiologist Morristown (N.J.) Meml. Hosp., 1983—; asst. clin. prof. Columbia U., N.Y.C., 1988—; cons. Ctr. Molecular Medicine and Immunization, Newark, 1989—, Immunomedics, Warren, N.J., 1989—; adv. com. on nuclear medicine N.J. Dept. Environ. Protection, 1989. Contbr. articles to med. and sci. jours. Mem. AMA, Radiol. Soc. N.Am., N.Y. Acad. Scis., Soc. Nuclear Medicine. Office: Morristown Meml Hosp 100 Madison Ave Morristown NJ 07960-6095

SWEENEY, MICHAEL ANDREW, newspaper editor; b. York, Pa., Nov. 27, 1948; s. Felix William and Deuris C. (Ehehalt) S.; m. Linda Carol Gillam, Nov. 20, 1976; children: Barbara Catherine, Matthew Alan. BA in Communication Art, Seton Hall U., 1972; MA in Polit. Sci., Rutgers U., 1981. Reporter The Courier-News, Bridgwater, N.J., 1972-75, asst. night editor, 1975-77, night editor, 1977-78, nat. editor, 1978-79, asst. news editor, 1980-81; news editor The Advocate Southern Conn. Newspapers Inc., Stamford, Conn., 1981-83, exec. news editor, 1983-85, asst. mng. editor, 1985-88; editorial page editor Greenwich Time/So. Conn. Newspapers, Inc., 1988—, columnist, 1991—. Contbr. articles to profl. jours. Roman Catholic. Office: Greenwich Time 20 E Elm St Greenwich CT 06830-6573

SWEENEY, MICHAEL WILLIAM, investment banker; b. Phila., Nov. 13, 1962; s.Francis Joseph and Helen (Drueding) S. AB, Boston Coll., 1984; MBA, Cornell U., 1989. Trader Shearson Lehman Brothers, Phila., 1985-87; assoc. Chase Securities, N.Y.C., 1989-90; mng. dir. The Caserta Group, Roslyn, N.Y., 1991—. Co-author: Boston in Transition, 1984. Vol. Inner City, N.Y.C., 1990. Mem. The Cornell Club. Republican. Home: 252 E 61st St Apt 3F New York NY 10021-8558 Office: The Caserta Group 1615 Northern Blvd # 403 Manhasset NY 11030

SWEENEY, NED FRANCIS, editor; b. N.Y.C., Apr. 2, 1955; s. Ned Maurice and Nora May (Kitson) S. BA, Auburn U., 1983. Staff writer Columbus (Ga.) Ledger-Enquirer, 1984-85; state editor Opelika (Ala.) Auburn News, 1985-87; mng. editor Clay Today/Clay Countian, Orange Park, Fla., 1987-92; city editor Taunton (Mass.) Daily Gazette, 1992—. Mem. coun. St. Michael's Catholic Student Ctr., Auburn, Ala., 1977; bd. dirs. Crisis Ctr. East Ala., Auburn, 1982-83, Clay County Mental Health, Drug and Alcohol Svcs. With USMC, 1975-77. Republican. Roman Catholic. Home: 165 Winthrop St Apt 121 Taunton MA 02780

SWEENEY, SUSAN ELIZABETH, English educator; b. Hagerstown, Md., Mar. 7, 1958; d. Daniel Joseph and Dorothy Virginia (Daub) S.; m. Michael John Chapman, July 3, 1983. BA in English magna cum laude, Mt. Holyoke Coll., 1980; MA in English, Brown U., 1982, MFA in Writing, 1985, PhD in English, 1989. Teaching asst. Brown U., Providence, 1981-84; teaching fellow Brown U., 1985-86; instr. Holy Cross Coll., Worcester, Ma., 1986-88, asst. prof., 1988-92; assoc. prof. Holy Cross Coll., Worcester, 1992—. Judge NEMLA Award for Feminist Scholarship, 1990; com. chair Howe Award for Feminist Scholarship, 1991. Batchelor Summer fellow Holy Cross Coll., 1989, 91, Hazen fellow Mt. Holyoke Coll., 1981, 83, Univ. fellow Brown U., 1980; Salomon Incentive grantee Brown U., 1985, 86; recipient Poetry prize Acad. of Am. Poets, 1979. Mem. Vladimir Nabokov Soc. (v.p. 1987-89, pres. 1989-91), Edith Wharton Soc., Soc. Detective Fiction (exec. com.), MLA, N.E. MLA, Women's Caucus for the Modern Langs. (regional del. 1988-91). Democrat. Home: 295 N Main St North Brookfield MA 01535-2008 Office: Holy Cross Coll Dept of English Worcester MA 01610

SWEENY, BRADLEY PATTERSON, investment banker; b. N.Y.C., Mar. 24, 1940; s. Arthur Jr. and Bailey (Patterson) W.; m. Cynthia Morgan Davenport; children: Heather G., Hilary B. BS, Union Coll., 1962. Stockbroker Francis I. DuPont & Co., N.Y.C., 1964-70; ptnr. Bacon, Whipple & Co., N.Y.C., 1970-82; mng. dir. Tucker Anthony Inc., N.Y.C., 1983-90; sr. v.p. Dominick & Dominick Inc., N.Y.C., 1990—. Mem. Bond Club N.Y. (treas. 1986-87), Links Club, Union Club, Apawamis Club, Manursing Island Club. Republican. Episcopalian. Home: 20 Griswold Rd Rye NY 10580-1802

SWEENY, KENNETH S., graphic design consultant; b. Trenton, N.J., Aug. 8, 1948; s. Russell Lawrence and Elva Marion (Sibbitt) S.; m. Geraldine Ann Condemi, May 25, 1969 (div. Oct. 28, 1980). AA, Sch. Visual Arts, N.Y.C., 1970. Graphic artist Lasky Advt., Bloomfield, N.J., 1970-71; assoc. art dir. Ziff-Davis, N.Y.C., 1971-72, Warner Communications, N.Y.C., 1972-75; graphic designer NBC Network Mktg. Sales, N.Y.C., 1976-78; owner, creative dir. Sweeny Ink, Belleville, N.J., 1975-78; art dir. Al Paul Lefton Advt., N.Y.C., 1978-80, Corporations & Advt. Agencies, N.Y.C., Conn., N.J, 1978-80; graphic design cons. staff Loral Electronic Systems, Yonkers, N.Y., 1980-90; cons. in field; practitioner of letterforms through use of alphabets and typography; part-time substitute tchr. elem.-high sch., 1977-80. Designer INEWS Electronic Shield, 1985, N.J. Bankers Assn., 1972, Logo Designs and Trends, 1990, Graphics Jour. Com. chairperson Forum Employees Assn., Yonkers, 1983-84. Recipient DESI award Graphics: USA, 1978, 82, 84, 85, 88, 90, Bestsellers gold award Pub. Designers Assn., 1983, silver, gold and merit awards N.J. Art Dirs. Club, 1982, 84, 85, 88, 90. Mem. Nat. Computer Graphics Assn., Inter-Soc. Color Coun., Art Dirs. Club (merit award 1983), Type Dirs. Club, Advt. Club Westchester (silver, gold, copper awards 1984, 85, 86, 88), Advt. Club Fairfield (silver award 1986, 87, 88), Fairfield Advt. Club, N.J. Art Dirs. Club, Am. Irish Genealogists, Nat. Mgmt. Assn. (Achievement award 1982), Am. Mgmt. Assn. Republican. Roman Catholic. Home and Office: PO Box 1532 New Canaan CT 06840-1532

SWEENY, ROBERT JOSEPH, treasurer; b. Trenton, N.J., June 30, 1931; s. Edmund William and Margaret Veronica (Baur) S.; m. Dolores Mary Tindall, June 19, 1954; children: Robert Jr., Richard, Susan, Karen. BSBA, Rider Coll., 1962. Internal auditor CF&I Steel Corp., Roebling, N.J., 1966-67, budget adminstr., 1968-70; controller CF&I Steel Corp., Trenton, 1971-73; asst. controller CF&I Steel Corp., Roebling, 1973-74; v.p., controller Roebling Steel Corp., 1975-79; treas. Jarsco, Roebling, 1979-81; treas., chief fin. officer Royal Engring. Co., Trenton, 1982—. With USN, 1951-55. Mem. Inst. Mgmt. Accountants, Knights of Columbus, Elks. Republican. Roman Catholic. Home: 148 Soden Dr Yardville NJ 08620-2940 Office: Royal Engring Co 330 Pennington Ave Trenton NJ 08618-3698

SWEENY, STEPHEN JUDE, academic administrator; b. N.Y.C., Sept. 15, 1943; s. Herbert Vincent and Isabel Mary (Dolan) S.; m. Barbara Mary Stasz, Aug. 7, 1976. BA in Spanish, Cath. U., 1966; MA in Theology, Manhattan Coll., 1971, MA in Psychology, 1976; PhD, NYU, 1991. Prin. Incarnation Elem. and Jr. High Sch., N.Y.C., 1969-73; dir. campus ministry Manhattan Coll., N.Y.C., 1973-76; asst. to provost Coll. of New Rochelle, N.Y., 1976-78, mem. edn. dept., 1976—, exec. asst. to pres., 1978-80, v.p. for planning, 1980-81, sr. v.p., 1981—. Vice chair bd. dirs. The Home for the Aged, New Rochelle, 1988—; chair, bd. trustees Convent of the Sacred Heart, Greenwich, Conn., 1990—; mem. com. on goals Soc. of the Sacred Heart, St. Louis, 1990—. Mem. Nat. League Nurses (commn. on accreditation). Roman Catholic. Office: Coll New Rochelle 29 Castle Pl New Rochelle NY 10805-2308

SWEEPER, DEANN KAY, communications executive; b. Tucson, July 26, 1954; d. Millard Clarence Sweeper and Kay Frankey Blakeman. BS, Charter Oak Coll., 1986; MBA, U. New Haven, 1992. Lab. mgr. VA Med. Ctr., West Haven, Conn., 1985-88, Yale U. Sch. Med., New Haven, 1989; dir. mktg. Regent Controls Inc., Shelton, Conn., 1991; pres. Sweeper Communications Internat. Inc., Northford, Conn., 1991—. With USMC, 1978-80. Mem. Am. Mktg. Assn., Conn. World Trade Assn. (program chair 1991—), Conn. Bus. and Industry Assn. Office: Sweeper Communications Internat Inc 48 Alling Rd Northford CT 06472

SWEET, ROBERT WORKMAN, federal judge; b. Yonkers, N.Y., Oct. 15, 1922; s. James Allen and Delia (Workman) S.; m. Adele Hall, May 12, 1973; children by previous marriage—Robert, Deborah, Ames, Eliza. B.A., Yale U., 1944, LL.B., 1948. Bar: N.Y. 1949. Asso. firm Simpson, Thacher & Bartlett, 1948-53; asst. U.S. atty. So. Dist. N.Y., 1953-55; asso. firm Casey, Lane & Mittendorf, 1955-65, partner, 1957-65; counsel Interdepartmental Task Force on Youth and Juvenile Delinquency, 1958-78; dep. mayor City of N.Y., 1966-69; partner firm Skadden, Arps, Slate, Meagher & Flom, N.Y.C., 1970-77; mem. hearing office N.Y.C. Transit Authority, 1975-77; U.S. dist. judge So. Dist. N.Y., N.Y.C., 1978—; med. jud. conf. com. Adminstrn. of the Bankruptcy System; participant USIA Rule of Law Program in Albania, 1991; observer Albanian elections, 1992. Pres. Community Service Soc., 1961-78; trustee Sch. Mgmt. Urban Policy, 1970—, Taft Sch.; vestryman St. Georges Epis. Ch., 1958-63. Served to lt. (j.g.) USNR, 1943-46. Recipient Alumni citation of merit Taft Sch., 1985, various other awards, citations for service as dept mayor N.Y.C. Mem. ABA, Assn. of Bar of City of N.Y., N.Y. Law Inst., N.Y. County Lawyers Assn., State Bar Assn., Am. Legion (comdr. Willard Straight Post). Clubs: Quaker Hill Country, Century Assn., Merchants, Indian Harbor Yacht, Mid City Rep. Office: US Dist Ct US Courthouse 2202 Foley Sq New York NY 10007-1502

SWEETING, CHARLES HARVARD, columnist, film director; b. Derby, Eng.; s. Treleaven William and Josephine Harvard (Taylor) S. MA, U. Dublin, Ireland, 1959. Writer Associated British/Warner Bros., Elstree, Hertfordshire, Eng., 1954-55; film coord. theatre arts dept. Pa. State U., 1969-70; columnist Union Jack monthly, San Diego, 1984—; founder Brit. & Commonwealth Inst. N.Y., N.Y.C., 1979—. Author: A Film Course Manual, 1971; asst. film dir. Reach for the Sky, Anastasia, St. Joan, TV series including Robin Hood, The Invisible Man; 1st asst. dir. Freedom's Finest Hour. With RAF. Recipient George Washington Honor Gold medal Freedoms Found., 1965, Golden Eagle award Coun. on Internat. Nontheatrical Events, 1965. Mem. Assn. Cinematograph, TV and Allied Technicians, Australian Soc. N.Y., Can. Soc. N.Y. (life), St. David's Soc. N.Y. (life), St. George's Soc. N.Y., Dublin U. Grad. Assn. (life), Dublin U. Players (hon.), Dublin U. Philos. Soc. (hon.),Savage Club (life, London), TCD Dining Club London (life), London Press Club, Britannia Lodge (N.Y.C.). Office: Brit & Commonwealth Inst 71 W 23d St # 1006 New York NY 10010

SWEETMAN, JACK, historian, educator; b. Orlando, Fla., Jan. 5, 1940; s. Arthur J. and Bertha (Michael) S.; m. Gisela A. Tetzel., Apr. 19, 1962; 1 child, Jeanne Jacqueline. BA, Stetson U., 1961; MA, Emory U., 1970, PhD, 1973. V.p. Sweetman-Herb Constrn. & Realty, Inc., Orlando, 1964-68; vis. lectr. Ind. U., Bloomington, 1972-73; asst. to assoc. prof. history U.S. Naval Acad., Annapolis, Md., 1973—. Author: The Landing at Veracruz, 1914, 1968; The U.S. Naval Academy: An Illustrated History, 1979; American Naval History: An Illustrated Chronology of the U.S. Navy and Marine Corps, 1775—, 1984, 2nd edit., 1991; also articles and revs.; translator: Battleship Bismarck: A Survivor's Story, 1980, 2d edit., 1990; editor: Radm. Charles E. Clark, My Fifty Years in the Navy, 1984; series editor: Classics of Naval Literature, 1984—; co-editor: Changing Interpretations and New Sources of Naval History, 1980, New Interpretations in Naval History, 1991; cons. editor Naval History, 1987—. Lt. U.S. Army, 1962-63. Ford Found. fellow, 1968-72; recipient Alfred Thayer Mahan Lit. Achievement award, 1988. Mem. U.S. Naval Inst. (assoc. editor Procs. 1975-80), Orders and Medals Soc. Am. (bd. dirs. 1976-80), Soc. Mil. History, N.Am. Soc. Oceanic Historians, Marine Corps Hist. Found., U.S. Commn. Mil. History, German Studies Assn., Mil. Order of the World Wars, Officers and Faculty Club, Phi Beta Kappa. Republican. Episcopalian. Home: 884 Mallard Cir Arnold MD 21012-1508 Office: US Naval Acad Annapolis MD 21402

SWEETSER, RICHARD STUART, compressor technology research company executive; b. Norwalk, Conn., June 30, 1950; s. Donald Parker and Edythe Eleanor (Shephard) S.; m. Michele Lee Woods, July 29, 1972; children: Jennifer, Lindsay, Alison. BSME, Rose Hulman Inst. Tech., 1972; MBA, Pace U., 1978. Sales engr. York div. Borg-Warner Co., N.Y.C., 1972-77; mgr. spl. projects York div. Borg-Warner Co., York, Pa., 1977-79; mktg. mgr. oil and gas markets Elliott div. United Techs., Jeannette, Pa., 1979-83; v.p. SSCI, Norwalk, 1983—, also bd. dirs.; founder, exec. dir. Yankee Inst.

for Pub. Policy Studies, Norwalk, 1988-91; exec. dir. Yankee Inst. for Pub. Policy Studies, Norwalk, 1988—. Co-editor: The Best Solution for The Education of Our Children, 1989. Bd. dirs. Probe Found., Norwalk, 1984—; moderator New Eng. Ednl. Summit, Hartford, Conn., 1988; pub. policy expert Heritage Found., Washington, 1989, bd. trustees Conn. Policy and Econ. Coun., 1991—, Newtown Substance Avuse Task Force. Mem. ASHRAE (chmn. tech. com. 8.l, 1985-87), Phila. Soc. Republican. Mem. Independent Evangelical Ch. Home: Four Poorhouse Rd Newtown CT 06470 Office: SSCI/Probe Two Reynolds St E Norwalk CT 06855

SWELL, LILA, education educator; b. N.Y.C., Sept. 7, 1936; d. Isidore and Bessie (Abramson) S. BA in Psychology, NYU, 1956; MSW, U. Mich., 1956; EdD, Columbia U., 1964. Lectr. U. Mich. Sch. of Social Work, Ann Arbor, 1964-65; asst. prof. U. Chgo. Sch. Social Svcs. Adminstrn., 1965-68; vis. asst. prof. U. Ill., Chgo., 1969-70; assoc. prof. Queens Coll. CUNY, 1970—; caseworker Jackson (Mich.) Family Svc. Ctr., 1958-59, N.Y.C. Youth Consultation Svc., 1959-62; group leader interdepartmental Neighborhood Ctr., N.Y.C. summer project, 1961, N.Y.C. Jewish Guild for the Blind, 1961-63; sr. caseworker and supr. of students Salvation Army Family Svc., N.Y.C., 1962-64; dir., Dept. Psychiat. Social Svcs., N.Y. Clinic for Mental Health, 1962-64; exec. staff achievement motivation systems Stone-Brandel Ctr., Chgo., 1968-69; nat./internat. lectr. on motivation. Author: Success You Can Make It Happen, 1977, Self Esteem in the Classroom, 1991, Techniques for Teachers, Educating for Success: Theory Manual, Workbook and Leaders Guide, My Journal of Success (K-12) Teacher's Guide, 1992; also monographs, jour. articles, creative publs., audio and video tapes, films and revs.; 35 TV appearances in U.S and Australia; 51 radio appearances in U.S., Australia and New Zealand. Mem. Kappa Delta Pi, Pi Lambda Theta. Home: 130 E 67th St New York NY 10021-6136 Office: CUNY Queens Coll Dept Elem Early Child Edn 65-30 Kissena Blvd Flushing NY 11367-1575

SWENDSEN, ROBERT HAAKON, physicist, educator; b. N.Y.C., Apr. 4, 1943; s. Haakon August and Grace Louise (Trueg) S.; m. Carol Ann Formisano, July 11, 1971; children: Eric, David. BS, Yale U., 1964; MS, PhD, U. Pa., 1971. Postdoctoral fellow U. Cologne, Germany, 1971-73; researcher KFA Julich, Germany, 1973-76, Brookhaven Nat. Labs., Upton, N.Y., 1976-79, IBM Zurich Rsch. Labs., Rüschlikon, Switzerland, 1979-84; prof. physics Carnegie Mellon U., Pitts., 1984—. Contbr. numerous articles to profl. jours. NSF grantee, 1984—. Fellow Am. Phys. Soc. Office: Carnegie Mellon U 5000 Forbes Ave Pittsburgh PA 15213-3816

SWENSON, ERIC DAVID, environmental contorl superintendent, attorney; b. Glen Cove, N.Y., Oct. 27, 1954; s. Robert Fritz and Florence Betty (Bullard) S.; m. Deborah Catherine Johnston, Aug. 31, 1991. BA, SUNY, New Paltz, 1976; JD, St. John's Sch. Law, 1986; waste mgmt. student, SUNY, Stony Brook, 1990—. Bar: N.Y., Washington. Canvas field mgr. N.Y. Pub. Interest Rsch. Group, N.Y.C., 1978-79, project coord., 1979-81; legal file clerk Jessel Rothman, P.C., Mineola, N.Y., 1981-82; environ. control specialist trainee Town of Oyster Bay, Syosset, N.Y., 1982-83, enriron. control specialist, 1983-88, supt. environ. control, 1988—; bd. dirs. Long Island Regional Recycling Coop.; v.p. N.Y. Assn. for Solid Waste Mgmt., Albany, 1991-93; mem. Nat Environ. Leadership Coun., Washington, 1990—. Contbr. articles to profl. jours. 2d v.p. Locust Valley (N.Y.) Reps. Club, 1991-92; active Village of Sea Cliff (N.Y.) Recycling Task Force, 1991—; regional coord. Earth Day '80, Western N.Y., 1980. Mem. Kiwanis Club (Nassau East). Home: 31 Bay Ave Sea Cliff NY 11579 Office: Town of Oyster Bay 150 Miller Pl Syosset NY 11791

SWERGOLD, MARCELLE MIRIAM, sculptor; b. Antwerp, Belgium, Sept. 6, 1927; came to U.S., 1939, naturalized, 1947; d. Gillel and Sarah (Matuzewitz) Elfenbein; student NYU, Art Students League, Sculptors Workshop; m. Maurice Swergold, June 12, 1949; children—Diane Botnick, Henry, Gary Swergold, Paul Kogan, George Kogan. Sculptor, 1965—; one-woman exhbns. include: Studio 12, N.Y.C., 1980, 82, 86, Nat. Fedn. Temple Sisterhoods, 1984; group exhbns. include Farleigh Dickinson U., Teaneck, N.J., 1972, Audubon Artist Ann., N.Y.C., 1978-86, Internat. Treasury Fine Arts, Plainview, N.Y., 1979, New Britain (Conn.) Mus., 1980, also Cork Gallery, Lincoln Center, N.Y.C., Allied Artists Nat. Acad. Galleries, N.Y.C., U.S. Custom House, N.Y.C., others; represented in permanent collection New Britain Mus. Am. Art Yad Vashem Sculpture Garden, Holocaust Mus., Jerusalem; represented in pvt. collection of Master Moshe Castel, Israel. Recipient Best in Show award for Tetons, Women's Art Gallery, N.Y.C., 1977, 1st prize for sculpture Stanley Richter Assn. Arts, 1985, Vincent Glinski Meml. award Audubon Artists, 1986. Mem. N.Y. Soc. Women Artists (pres. 1979-81, exec. v.p. 1981—), Artists Equity, Contemporary Artists Guild. Home: 43 Paul St Danbury CT 06810-8365 Studio: 246 W 80th St New York NY 10024

SWETLAND, KENNETH L., seminary administrator, educator, counselor; b. Hastings, Nebr., Apr. 2, 1937; s. Lee Bernard and Frances Elizabeth (Ferguson) S.; m. Virginia Anne Montgomery, Aug. 22, 1959; children: Brock Walter, Reid Bernard. BA, Wheaton Coll., 1959, MA, 1962; MDiv, Gordon Div. Sch., South Hamilton, Mass., 1964; D of Ministry, Andover-Newton Theol. Sch., Newton Center, Mass., 1976. Ordained Bapt. Gen. Conf., 1964. Asst. to exec. dir. Nat. Assn. Evangelicals, Wheaton, Ill., 1959-62; pastor Pigeon Cove Chapel, Rockport, Mass., 1964-68, Calvary Bapt. Ch., State College, Pa., 1968-72; dir. alumni affairs Gordon-Gonwell Theol. Sem., South Hamilton, 1972-78, dir. pub. rels., 1976-78, dir. admissions, 1978-82, dir. field edn., 1982-88, assoc. dean, assoc. prof. of ministry, 1988—; chaplain Pa. State U., State College, 1968-72; ch. cons. Gordon-Conwell Theol. Sem., 1972—; pastoral counselor Health Integration Svcs., Peabody, Mass., 1979-82, Willowdale Ctr. Psychol. Svcs., South Hamilton, 1982-88; bd. dirs. N.E. Bapt. Conf. Rsch. grantee Gordon-Conwell Theol. Sem., 1990. Mem. Assn. for Case Teaching (exec. com. 1989—, jour. editor 1989—), Assn. Theol. Field Edn., Evang. Assn. Theol. Field Educators (chair 1987-88). Democrat. Office: Gordon-Conwell Theol Sem 130 Essex St South Hamilton MA 01982-2325

SWETT, RICHARD NELSON (DICK SWETT), congressman; b. Bryn Mawr, Pa., May 1, 1957; s. Philip Eugene Sr. and Ann (Parkhurst) S.; m. Yvonne Katrina Lantos, Aug. 29, 1980; children: Chelsea, Sebastian, Keaton, Chanteclaire, Kismet. BA in Architecture, Yale U., 1979. Lic. contractor, Calif.; lic. architect, Calif., N.H. Architect Skidmore Owings & Merrill, San Francisco, 1979-82; pres. Bastion Group, Inc., San Mateo, Calif., 1982-87; project mgr. Grosvenor Properties, San Francisco, 1986-87; pres. Veritas Group Inc., Gilford, N.H., 1987-90; mem. U.S. Congress from 2nd dist. N.H., 1990—; mem. pub. works and transp. com. U.S. Ho. of Reps., 1991—, mem. sci., space, and tech. com., 1991—, mem. select com. on aging, 1991—. Del. N.H. Dem. Conv., Henniker, 1988. Mem. AIA, Nat. Hist. Presentation Soc., Ind. Power Producers N.H. Assn., Yale Club N.H., Sierra Club. Office: US Ho of Reps 128 Cannon House Office Bldg Washington DC 20515 also: 18 N Main St Concord NH 03301 also: 5 Coliseum Ave Nashua NH 03063

SWETT, STEPHEN FREDERICK, JR., principal, educator; b. Englewood, N.J., Sept. 14, 1935; s. Stephen Frederick and Frances (Gulotta) S.; B.A., Montclair State Coll., 1959, M.A., 1965; Ed.D. in Ednl. Adminstrn., Rutgers U., 1976; m. Annette Palazzolo, Nov. 18, 1961; children—Susan, Kimberly Ann, Stephen Laurence. Tchr., Long Branch (N.J.) High Sch., 1961-62, Roselle Park (N.J.) High Sch., 1962-73; research asst. Rutgers U., New Brunswick, N.J., 1973-74; instructional supr. Elmwood Park (N.J.) Schs., 1974-76, Morris Hills Regional Schs., Denville, N.J., 1976-77; asst. prin. Lawrence High Sch., Lawrenceville, N.J., 1977-79; prin. Stafford Intermediate Sch., Manahawkin, N.J., 1979—; participant NSF Inst. in physics, chemistry and math. Seton Hall U., 1964, Newark Coll. Engring., 1965, Stevens Inst. Tech., summers 1966-68. Served with AUS, 1959-61. Mem. Roselle Park Edn. Assn. (pres. 1971-73). Nat. Soc. Study Edn., Am. Assn. Physics Tchrs., Am. Inst. Physics, Am., N.J. assns. sch. adminstrs., Nat. Assn. Elementary and Middle Sch. Adminstrs., N.J. Assn. Elementary and Middle Sch. Adminstrs., Nat. Assn. Secondary Sch. Prins., Phi Delta Kappa (sec. Rutgers chpt. 1977-80, v.p. 1980-82, pres. 1983-84). Research on sch. fin. Home: 12 Louis St Old Bridge NJ 08857-2235 Office: Stafford Intermediate Sch Mckinley Ave Manahawkin NJ 08050-2807

SWETZ, FRANK JOSEPH, mathematics and education educator, consultant; b. N.Y.C., July 30, 1937; s. Frank Leo and Helen Cecilia (Curtis) S.; m. Joan Patricia Flood, June 1, 1968; children: Laura, Mark, Steven. BA, Marist Coll., Poughkeepsie, N.Y., 1962; MA, Fordham U., N.Y.C., 1963; DEd, Columbia U., N.Y.C., 1972. Mech. designer Daystrom Electric Co., Poughkeepsie, 1957-58; electronic test engr. Ford Instrument Co., L.I., N.Y., 1958-60; grad. fellow Fordham U., N.Y.C., 1962-63; instr. math. Marist Coll., Poughkeepsie, 1963-64; tchr. math. U.S. Peace Corps, Malaysia, 1964-67; grad. asst. Columbia U., N.Y.C., 1967-69; instr. math. and edn. Pa. State U., Harrisburg, 1969-72, asst. prof., 1972-75, assoc. prof., 1975-80, prof., 1980—. Author: Mathematics Education in China, 1974, Was Pythagoras Chinese?, 1977 (merit award Nat. Coun. Tchrs. Math. 1977), Capitalism & Arithmetic, 1987; contbr. over 100 (3 award-winning) articles to profl. jours. Asean Rsch. fellow Fulbright Commn., Malaysia, 1985. Mem. Nat. Coun. Tchrs. Math. Office: Pa State U Middletown PA 17057

SWICK, JAMES ROBERT, lawyer; b. Easton, Pa., Mar. 17, 1950; s. Howard W. and Winifred (Dougherty) S.; m. Patricia A. Novak, May 25, 1974 (div. June 1984); children: Karen, Eileen. BA, U. Pa., 1971; JD, Villanova U., 1974. Bar: N.J. 1974. Ptnr., co-owner Swick & Swick, Esqs., Phillipsburg, N.J., 1974-86; sole owner Swick & Swick, Esqs., Phillipsburg, 1986-; mcpl. ct. judge, Phillipsburg, 1980-81; bd. dirs. Warren County Legal Svcs., Warren Hosp. Health Svcs. Corp. Freeholder Warren County, N.J., 1984-86; bd. dirs. United Way of Northampton (Pa.) and Warren Counties, 1987—, Warren County Community Coll. Found.; bd. mgrs. Am. Cancer Soc. of Warren County, 1990—. Capt. U.S. Army, 1974. Mem. Warren County Bar Assn. (v.p. 1987-88, pres. 1989—), Rotary (pres. Phillipsburg club, 1981-82). Democrat. Episcopalian. Home: 2805 Green Pond Rd Easton PA 18042-2503 Office: Swick & Swick Esqs 102 S Main St Phillipsburg NJ 08865-2898

SWIECICKI, MARTIN, neurosurgeon; b. Camden, N.J., June 29, 1934; s. Martin E. and Annetta Swiecicki; m. Gloria J. Whelpley; children: Diane, Annette, Karen, Sheryl, Marty. BA, Colgate U., 1956; MD, Hahnemann Med. Sch., 1960. Diplomate Am. Bd. Neurol. Surgery. Intern West Jersey Hosp., Camden, 1960-61; resident in neurological surgery Jefferson U., Phila., 1961-65; mem. staff in neurol. surgery West Jersey Hosp., Camden, Berlin, N.J., 1967—, chief Neurol. Surgery, 1967-89; clin. assoc prof. Neurol. Surgery Hahnemann Med. Coll., Phila., 1977—. Contbr. articles to profl. jours. Recipient N.J. Gov.'s award for Outstanding Svcs., 1970, 71, 72, 73, Award for Support and Svc. Boy Scouts Am., 1992. Fellow ACS; mem. AMA, Camden County Med. Soc., West Jersey Med. Soc., N.J. State Med. Soc., N.J. Neurosurg. Soc. (sec.-treas. 1978-79, pres.-elect 1980, pres. 1981, chmn. peer rev. com. 1983-89, mem. peer rev. com. 1989—), Camden County Med. Soc. (exec. com. 1977—), Soc. Air Force Clin. Surgeons, Am. Assn. Neurol. Surgeons. Office: Neurosurg Assocs NJ 2301 Evesham Rd Ste 406 Voorhees NJ 08043

SWIENTEK, FRANCIS MARTIN, naval officer; b. Waukegan, Ill., Sept. 21, 1944; s. Frank Joseph and Josephine Alice (Gielniak) S.; m. Diane Carol Silvey, June 17, 1972; children: Adam Benjamin, Heather Debra. BS in Naval Sci., U.S. Naval Acad., 1966; MSEE, U.S. Naval Postgrad., 1972. Ops. officer USS Fanning, San Diego, 1973-76; operational test dir. Comdr. Operational Test & Evaluation Force, Norfolk, Va., 1976-78; ops. officer USS La Salle, Manama, Bahran, 1978-79; ops. & plans officer Comdr. Amphibious Squadron Two, Norfolk, 1979-81; exec. officer USS Mount Whitney Group Two, Norfolk, 1981-83; ops. officer Comdr. Amphibious Group Two, Norfolk, 1983-85; commanding officer USS La Moure County, Little Creek, Va., 1986-87; exec. officer Fleet Combat Directions Systems Supportactivity, Dam Neck, Va., 1987-90; dir. Navy future force concepts Space & Naval Warfare Systems Command, Washington, 1990—. Lector Oceana Cath. Chapel, Virginia Beach, Va., 1981—. Mem. U.S. Naval Inst. Proceedings, Old Crows, U.S. Naval Acad. Alumni Assn., Army Navy Country Club, Canisius High Sch. Alumnus Assn. Republican. Roman Catholic. Home: 3837 Prince Andrew Ln Virginia Beach VA 23452-3912 Office: Space & Naval Warfare Systems Command Washington DC 20363

SWIERZAWSKI, TADEUSZ JERZY, fluid systems engineer; b. Zloczow, Poland, Sept. 14, 1925; came to U.S., 1972; s. Franciszek and Paulina (Winiarska) S. MSME, Wroclaw (Poland) Tech. U., 1950; grad., Moscow Energy Inst., 1958; MS in Nuclear Engring., MIT, 1962; ScD in Mech. Engring., Silesian Inst. Tech., Gliwice, Poland, 1963. Registered profl. engr., Mass. Sr. asst. Wroclaw Tech. U., 1949-52; head nuclear engring. Silesian Inst. Tech., Gliwice, 1952-68; assoc. prof. U. Mo., Columbia, 1968-70, 72-73; head nuclear power div. Inst. of Power, Warsaw, Poland, 1970-72; cons. Stone & Webster Engring. Corp., Boston, 1973—; sr. cons. engr. Advanced Engring. Assocs., Newton, Mass., 1990—; cons. Internat. Resources Group, Washington, 1991—; chmn. Stone & Webster Task Force on Fluid Systems Design Manual. Author 46 publs. including textbooks, manuals, etc. Recipient Best Paper award Stone & Webster, 1986. Home: 50 Chandler Rd Burlington MA 01803

SWIETEK, RICHARD MICHAEL, advertising executive; b. Hartford, Conn., Oct. 9, 1962; s. Frederick and Alice (Kufel) S.; m. Susan Louise Marino, Oct. 6, 1985; 1 child, Marina Louise. BA, Fairfield U., 1984. Jr. copywriter Keiler Advt., Farmington, Conn., 1985-87; copywriter Mintz and Hoke Advt., Boston, 1987—; dist. coord. nat. student advt. competition, 1990, 91, 92; mem. rev. com. Addy awards, 1990; mem. pub. rels. com. Jr. Achievement of Eastern Mass., 1990, 91. Recipient Merit award Hartford Advt. Club, 1985, Gold award, 1988, 90, 91, Silver award Conn. Art Dirs., 1987, 91, Best of Show award Hartford Advt. CLub, 1991, Merit award Hartford Bus. Profl. Am. Mktg. Assn., 1989, 91, Bell Ringer award, Publicity Club Boston, 1989, Silver award ADvt. Club of Greater AdEast Boston, 1991; named Rookie of Yr., AdEast mag., 1986. Mem. Advt. Club Greater Boston, Ad 2 Club of Boston (chmn. speaker events, creative com. 1988, pres. 1989, dist. coord. nat. student advt. competition 1990, 91, 92, Addy award rev. com. mem. 1990, pub. rels. com.), Jr. Achievement of Eastern Mass., Greater Hartford Clowns Am. (East Hartford). Democrat. Office: Mintz & Hoke Advt 1 Exeter Pla Boston MA 02116

SWIFT, GRAHAM, research chemist; b. Apr. 16, 1939; s. Joseph and Dorothy (Sutton) S.; m. Shirley May Sawers, Dec. 31, 1960; children: Christopher, Ian. BSc in Chemistry, U. London, 1961, PhD in Organic Chemistry, 1964. Rsch. scientist Imperial Chem. Industries, Eng., 1966-68; rsch. scientist Rohm & Haas Co., Phila., 1968-76, mgr. sch. sect., 1976-86, rsch. fellow, 1986—. Editor: Agricultural & Synthetic Polymers: Biodegradability & Utilization, 1990; numerous patents in coatings and polymers fields. Chmn. Whitpain (Pa.) Twp. Mcpl. Authority, 1976-88. Republican. Episcopalian. Office: Rohm & Haas Co Norristown Rd Spring House PA 19477

SWIFT, JANE MARIA, state senator; b. North Adams, Mass., Feb. 24, 1965; d. John Maynard and Jean Mary (Kent) S. BA in Am. Studies, Trinity Coll., Hartford, Conn., 1987. Exec. mgmt. trainee G. Fox. & Co., Hartford, 1987-88; adminstrv. aide Sen. Peter C. Webber, Boston, 1988-90; mem. Mass. State Senate, Boston, 1991—. Republican. Roman Catholic. Office: House of Senate Rm 407 State House Boston MA 02133

SWIFT, PAUL, editor; b. Spokane, Wash., June 29, 1942; s. Paul Lawrence and Kathleen (O'Reilly) S.; m. Mary McCall Nettles, May 18, 1976; children: Zachary Benner, Nicole Elizabeth. BA, Gonzaga U., 1968; MA, Boston Coll., 1973. Program officer, editor John D. Rockefeller 3rd, N.Y.C., 1970-72; ind. writer various orgns., N.Y.C., 1973-80; assoc. dir. Bard Coll. Ctr., Annandale-on-Hudson, N.Y., 1978-82; editor Pub. Relations Quarterly, Rhinebeck, N.Y., 1982—. Editor: Edward Bernays' The Later Years, 1987; Newsletter on Newsletters, N.Y., 1982—. Mem. Chamber Music Soc. (bd. dirs. 1984-85), Dollars For Scholars (bd. dirs. 1986—). Roman Catholic. Home: 12 Chestnut St Rhinebeck NY 12572-1502 Office: Newsletter on Newsletters 44 W Market St Rhinebeck NY 12572-1403

SWIFT, ROBERT FREDERIC, music educator; b. Ilion, N.Y., July 7, 1940; s. Frederic Fay and Ruth Eleanor (Ainslie) S.; m. Margot Sue Werme, Nov. 24, 1962; children: Jeffrey Robert, Jennifer Sue. BS, Hartwick Coll., 1962, MA, 1968; PhD, Eastman Sch. Music, Rochester, N.Y., 1970. Music instr. West Winfield (N.Y.) Cen. Sch., 1962-67, N.Y. State Music Camp, Oneonta, 1962—, Brighton High Sch., Rochester, 1970-71; asst. prof. music Eastman Sch. Music, Rochester, 1971-76; assoc. prof. music Memphis State U., 1976-79; prof. music, dept. chmn. Plymouth State Coll. of U. N.H., Plymouth, 1979—; music adjudicator, clinician U.S., Can., 1970—; choral conductor U.S., Can., Britain, Australia, New Zealand. Composer numerous musical compositions. Ch. musician Christian Sci., Presbyn., Bapt. chs. Nat. Def. Edn. Act Title IV fellow U. Rochester, 1967-70; recipient Disting. Teaching award, Memphis State U., 1979, Disting. Teaching award Sch. for Lifelong Learning of U. System of N.H., 1987. Mem. N.H. Music Edn. Assn., Music Educators Nat. Conf., Am. Choral Dirs. Assn., Coll. Music Soc., Royal Sch. Ch. Music., Phi Mu Alpha Sinfonia, Kappa Delta Pi. Republican. Mem. Christian Science Ch. Home: PO Box 125 Plymouth NH 03264-0125 Office: Plymouth State Coll Dept Music and Theatre Plymouth NH 03264

SWIFT, WAYNE BRADLEY, engineer; b. Lincoln, Nebr., May 9, 1927; s. Perry Clayton and Grace Sarah (Harrison) S.; m. Margaret Francine Morris, Oct. 15, 1977. BSEE, U. Nebr., 1949; MS, Kans. State U., 1950; PhD, U. Wis., 1955. Asst. prof., assoc. prof. U. Wis., Madison, 1951-61; div. dir., v.p. C-E-I-R, Washington, 1961-64, Boston, 1961-64; div. dir. Control Data Corp., Bloomington, Minn., 1964-65; sr. mem. adv. staff Computer Sci. Corp., Silver Spring, Md., 1965-72; pres. PSC, Falls Church, Va., 1972-76; gen. mgr. Adv. Tech. Svcs., Washington, 1976-79; div. dir. Exec. Resource Assocs. Inc., Arlington, Va., 1979-88; v.p. Digicon Corp., Bethesda, Md., 1988—. Kiekhofer Meml. award U. Wis., 1956. Mem. IEEE (chmn. Washington sect. 1964-65), BakerSt. Irregulars. Home: 4622 Morgan Dr Chevy Chase MD 20815

SWIFT, WILLIAM PORTER, psychologist, consultant; b. Albany, N.Y., Sept. 9, 1914; s. Cyrus Burgess and Georgia May (Fisher) S.; m. Jean S. MacPherson, June 19, 1943 (dec. 1978); children: Diane S., Neil Randolph, Frank Douglas; m. Jean Ruth Bennett, Aug. 18, 1979; stepchildren: Linda B. Simpson, Robert F. Snyder. AB, SUNY, Albany, 1936, MA, 1938; PhD, Cornell U., 1947. Lic. psychologist, N.Y., Pa.; lic. tchr., sch. psychologist, N.Y. Psychologist U.S. VA, Ithaca, N.Y., 1945-47, Syracuse (N.Y.) U., 1947-51; indsl. psychologist for various orgns. Phila., 1951-54; chair dept. psychology Ithaca Coll., 1954-59; cons. Hay Assocs., Phila., 1959-62; dir. psychol. svcs. Villanova (Pa.) U., 1962-64; clin. psychologist Broome County Mental Health Clinic, Binghamton, N.Y., 1965-75; prof., chair dept. psychology Broome Community Coll., Binghamton, 1965-83; pvt. practice N.Y., Pa., 1947-89; ret., 1989; cons. in field. Author 3 books.

SWINEY, WILLIE LEE, minister, educator; b. Bennestsville, S.C., July 16, 1948; s. Willie and Julia Mae (Monroe) S.; m. Cora Bell Suggs, Aug. 29, 1972 (div. July 1991); 1 child, Willie Terrell. BA, Livingstone Coll., 1970; MDiv, Hood Theol. Sem., 1973; postgrad., So. Calif. Grad. Sch. Theology, 1991. Lic. to ministry A.M.E. Zion Ch., 1966, ordained as deacon, 1971, as elder, 1973. Pastor St. Frances AME Zion Ch., Portchester, N.Y., 1973-74; assoc. min. Naomi AME Zion Ch., Bklyn., 1974-77, 82-85; pastor Sojourner Truth AME Zion Ch., St. Albans, N.Y., 1977-82; min., pastor Community Centralized, Bklyn., 1985-87; pastor, pres. Universal House of Prayer, Bklyn., 1987—; vol. chaplain N.Y.C. Police Dept., 1986—, N.Y.C. Housing Authority Police Dept., 1986—, Sea Gate Police Dept., Bklyn., 1988—, N.Y.C. Transit Police Dept., Bklyn., 1990—. Tchr. N.Y.C. Bd. Ed., Bklyn., 1986-87; office aide Dept. Social Svcs., N.Y.C., 1977-86; supr. Neighborhood Youth Corps, N.Y.C., summers 1970-75; aide summer work U.S. Naval Applied Sci. Lab., Bklyn., 1967; mem. Rep. Presdl. Task Force, 1989-92, Rep. Nat. Com.; mem. U.S. Senatorial Com.; State of N.Y. del. Dist. Presdl. Trust, 1992. Named Outstanding Community Leader Consol. Edison Co., Bklyn., 1988; recipient cert. merit Rep. Nat. Com., 1990, Presdl. Order Merit Nat. Rep. Senatorial Com., 1991, cert. recognition Pres. and Vice-Pres. U.S., 1991. Mem. United Fedn. Tchrs., Masons, Phi Beta Sigma. Home and Office: 2749 W 33 St # 6-A Brooklyn NY 11224-1638

SWING, ELIZABETH SHERMAN, education educator; b. Boston, June 29, 1927; d. James Beatty and Hilda (Ford) Sherman; m. Peter Gram Swing, May 27, 1948; children: Pamela, Bradford. AB cum laude, Harvard U., 1949, MA, 1952; PhD, U. Pa., 1979. Tchr. English Marple Newton High Sch., Newton Sq., 1966-73; rsch. asst. U. Pa., Phila., 1973-75; asst. prof. West Chester (Pa.) State U., 1975-77; asst. prof. St. Joseph's U., Phila., 1978-84, assoc. prof., 1984-89, prof. edn., 1989—. Author: Bilingualism and Linguistic Segregation in the Schools of Brussels, 1980; mem. editorial bd. European Edn., 1983—; contbr. articles to profl. jours. Mem. Collaborative Com. Phila. Schs. and Colls., 1983-90. Decorated knight Order of Crown (Belgium), 1989; recipient Legion of Honor award Chapel of Four Chaplains, 1984; grantee NEH Summer Seminar, 1981, U.S. Dept. Edn., 1984-87, Fulbright Found., 1989-90; vis. fellow U. London Inst. Edn., 1989-90. Mem. AAUP, Comparative Edn. Soc. Europe, Brit. Comparative and Internat. Edn. Soc., Comparative and Internat. Edn. Soc. (bd. dirs. 1988-91), Am. Ednl. Rsch. Assn., Am. Ednl. Studies Assn. Home: 614 Hillborn Ave Swarthmore PA 19081-1122 Office: St Joseph's U 5600 City Line Ave Philadelphia PA 19131-1308

SWISHER, RANDALL SCOTT, association executive; b. Oak Park, Ill., Jan. 19, 1947; s. Charles A. and Mary Anne (Fehrs) S.; m. Anne L. Simonsen, Aug. 31, 1968 (div. 1986); 1 child, Cena Colette. BA, U. Iowa, 1969; PhD, George Washington U., 1978. Rsch. dir. D.C. Pub. Interest Rsch. Group, Washington, 1973-76, exec. dir., 1976-77; adj. prof. Georgetown U. and Law Ctr., 1976-82; legis. asst. U.S. Rep. Robert Carr, Washington, 1979; energy project dir. Nat. Assn. Counties, Washington, 1980-84; legis. rep. Am. Pub. Power Assn., 1984-89; exec. dir. Am. Wind Energy Assn., 1989—; bd. dirs. Washington Ctr. for Study of Svcs., 1976—; treas. Export Coun. Renewable Energy, Washington, 1989—; vice-chmn. Coun. Renewable Energy Edn., Washington, 1989-91, chmn., 1991—; chmn. Frederick County Energy Futures Conf., Frederick, Md., 1982. Editor: Community Energy Strategies, 1984. Frederick County Dem. precinct chmn., 1983-85. Office: Am Wind Energy Assn 777 E Capitol St NE Ste 805 Washington DC 20002-4239

SWISTEL, ALEXANDER JULIAN, surgeon, researcher, educator; b. Munich, Fed. Republic of Germany, Jan. 18, 1949; came to U.S., 1950; s. George and Irene (Bohacka) S.; m. Patricia Lois Myskowski, July 31, 1976; children: Emily, Christopher. AB, Harvard U., 1971; M Med. Sci., Rutgers U., 1973; MD, Brown U., 1975. Diplomate Am. Bd. Surgery. From resident to chief resident St. Luke's-Roosevelt Hosp., N.Y.C., 1975-81; fellow in surg. oncology Meml. Sloan-Kettering Cancer Ctr., N.Y.C., 1981-83; attending staff, surgeon St. Luke's Roosevelt Hosp., N.Y.C., 1983—, Beth Israel Hosp., N.Y.C., 1984—; clin. instr. Columbia Coll. Physicians and Surgeons, N.Y.C., 1984—; bd. dirs. breast care program St. Luke's-Roosevelt Hosp., N.Y.C. Contbr. articles to profl. jours. Named Prin. Investigator Breast Screening Minority Population, N.Y. State, 1989—. Fellow Am. Coll. Surgeons (liaison physician cancer com. 1990—), Acad. Medicine N.Y.; mem. Am. Soc. Clin. Oncology, Soc. Head and Neck Surgeons, Assn. Acad. Surgeons, N.Y. Med. Soc., Metro. Breast Group. Office: 215 E 68th St New York NY 10021

SWITZ, THOMAS RICHARD, real estate broker; b. New London, Conn., Oct. 2, 1957; s. Alec Richard Jr. and Agnes Lillian (Quinlan) S. BS, Cen. Conn. State U., 1981; MBD, U. New Haven, 1992. Pres. Switz Real Estate Assocs., Mystic, Conn., 1981—; ptnr. Switz Ins. Agy., Mystic, 1981—; pres. Switz Ins. Assoc., Inc., Mystic, 1991—. Fin. chmn. Campaign to Reelect Sen. Spellman, Conn., 1989; bd. dirs. Mystic Community Ctr., 1989—, Stonington (Conn.) Community Credit Union, 1989—; campaign chmn. Mystic Art Assn. 80th Anniversary Campaign Dr. Mem. New London Bd. Realtors, Conn. Bd. Realtors, Ind. Ins. Agts. Southeastern Conn., Lions (pres. Mystic chpt. 1989—). Home: 25 Orchard St Stonington CT 06378-1359 Office: Switz Real Estate Assocs Victoria Park Profl Ctr Mystic CT 06355

SWOBODA, RICHARD ALLAN, foundation executive; b. Norfolk, Nebr., May 16, 1943; s. Forrest Allan and Iryl Laverne (Sandin) S.; m. Ronda Janice Johnson, May 28, 1969 (div. May 1975). Diploma, U. Paris Sorbonne, 1964; AB, Hamilton Coll., 1965; MS, U. Tex., 1968; postgrad., Grad. Sch. Ekistics, Athens, Greece, 1965-66. City planner City of Austin, Tex., 1967-69; asst. v.p. Rouse Co., Columbia, Md., 1969-74; dir. spl. projects Arlen Realty, Inc., N.Y.C., 1974-76; v.p. Am. Trade & Fin. Co., Arlington, Va., 1976-82; pres. Richard A. Swoboda, Inc., Washington,

1982—; co-founder, chmn., pres. Nat. Literacy Found., Inc., Washington, 1988—; bd. dirs. READ Inst., Washington, sec.-treas., 1991—; teaching fellow Athens (Greece) Coll., 1965-66. Author: Socioeconomic Implications of Urban Transportation, 1968, (poems) Eros-Ekos-Egos, 1990. Mem. C. of C. Com. of 100, Chattanooga, 1975. Mem. Am. Inst. of Planners, Am. Soc. Indsl. Security, Emerson Literary Soc., Near East Edn. Assn. Home: 1601 18th St NW Washington DC 20009-2529 Office: Nat Literacy Found Inc 655 15th St NW # 310 Washington DC 20005-5701

SWOPE, JOHN PETER, physician; b. Johnstown, Pa., June 19, 1935; s. Thomas Albert and Helen Marie (Sullivan) S.; m. Barbara Marie Heister, June 18, 1966; children: John Jr., Mary, Joseph, Margaret. BS, U.S. Naval Acad., 1958; MD, Georgetown U., 1966; MS, Case Western Res. U., 1970; postgrad., Indsl. Coll. of Armed Forces, Washington, 1981-82. Diplomate Am. Bd. Anesthesiology, Am. Bd. Quality Assurance and Utilization Review; cert. clin. engr. Commd. ensign USN, 1958, advanced through grades to capt., 1978, retired, 1986; prog. mgr. Fleet Hosp. Project, Washington, 1982-86; v.p. med. affairs Sacred Heart Hosp., Allentown, Pa., 1986; dir. grad. med. edn. George Wash. U., Washington, 1986-91; nat. med. dir. U.S. Postal Svc., Washington, 1991—; clin. asst. prof. Georgetown U., 1970-72, USPHS, Bethesda, Md., 1974-75; adj. assoc. prof. Georgetown U., 1986-91; cons. Quality Health Care Soc., Chgo., 1989-91. Contbg. books/publs. in field. Vice-chmn., bd. dirs. Nat. Fire Protection Assn., Quincy, Mass., 1988-92. Mem. IEEE, Am. Coll. Legal Medicine. Roman Catholic. Home: 5709 Foggy Ln Rockville MD 20855-1620 Office: US Postal Service 475 L Enfant Plz Rm 9301 Washington DC 20260

SWOPE, MARJORY MASON, association administrator; b. East Orange, N.J., June 5, 1940; d. Virgil Andrew and Edith Elizabeth (Rae) Mason; m. John Franklin Swope, June 9, 1962; children: Kristin, Kevin Andrew, John Gerard. BA, Mt. Holyoke Coll., 1962. Adminstrv. asst. Yale Law Sch. Capital Fund Dr, New Haven, 1962-63; office mgr. LWV N.H., Concord, 1975-81; state election supr. NBC News, N.Y.C., 1975-81; researcher Bur. Nat. Affairs, Washington, 1978-81, Legislex Assocs., Columbus, Ind., 1980-81; exec. dir. N.H. Assn. Conservation Commns., Concord, 1981—; mem. N.H. Current Use Bd., Concord, 1981—. Co-author: Guide to Designation of Prime Wetlands in New Hampshire, 1983; author: Handbook for Municipal Conservation Commissions in New Hampshire, 1988. Mem. Concord Sch. Bd., 1976-81, Downtown Concord Revitalization Corp., 1980-84; violinist N.H. Philharmonic Orch., Manchester, 1968—, treas., 1982-89. Mem. LWV (newsletter editor N.H. 1970-75), Concord Conservation Commn. (chmn. 1986—). Office: NH Assn Conservation Commns 54 Portsmouth St Concord NH 03301-5400

SWORTZEL, DOUGLAS SCOTT, food distribution group administrator; b. Waynesboro, Va., Dec. 27, 1962; s. Charles Edgar and Barbara Mae (Wiseman) S.; m. Denise Annette Jordan, May 18, 1991. BA, Va. Poly. Inst. and State U., 1986. Merchandising clk. Fleming Foods of Va., Waynesboro, 1986-87, retail pricing mgr., 1987-88, retail svcs. mgr., 1988-90, buyer, 1990-91; zone account mgr. Md. div. Wetterau Food Distbn. Group, Williamsport, Md., 1991—. Vice chmn. Staunton (Va.) Redevel. and Housing Authority, 1990—; commr. Staunton Youth Commn., 1992—. Mem. Staunton-Augusta Jaycees (state bd. dirs. 1991). Home: 1420 Aiken St Staunton VA 24401 Office: Wetterau Food Distbn Interstate Indsl Park Williamsport MD 21795

SWYGERT, H. PATRICK, law educator, university president; b. Phila., Mar. 17, 1943; s. LeRoy and Gustina (Rodgers) Huzzy; m. Sonja Branson, Aug. 22, 1969; children: Haywood Patrick, Michael Branson. AB in History, Howard U., 1965, JD cum laude, 1968. Bar: D.C. 1968, Pa. 1970, N.Y. 1970. Law clk. to presiding judge U.S. Ct. Appeals (3d cir.), Phila., 1968-69; assoc. Debevoise, Plimpton, Lyons & Gates, N.Y.C., 1969-70; adminstrv. asst. to Congressman Charles B. Rangel, N.Y., 1971-72; spl. asst. dist. atty., Phila., 1973; from asst. prof. to prof. law Temple U., 1972-90, v.p. adminstrn., 1982-88, exec. v.p., 1988-90; pres. SUNY, Albany, 1990—. Bd. dirs. New Community Devel. Corp., HUD, 1980-82; gov.'s rep. Southeastern Pa. Transp. Authority, 1987-91, also bd. dirs. Vice-chmn. Phila. Pub. Service Com., 1974-77, Sta. WHYY-TV, 1987-90; mem. exec. com. Pub. Law Ctr. Phila., 1980-88, N.Y. State Coun. on Humanities, 1991—; bd. dirs. Albany area chpt. ARC, 1991—. Mem. ABA, Middle States Assn Colls. and Schs. (commn. on higher edn. 1992—). Office: SUNY Albany Office of Pres 1400 Washington Ave Albany NY 12222-0001

SYCHTERZ, TERESA ANNE, educator; b. Reading, Pa., May 26, 1952; d. Chester F. and Dorothy (Andrejansky) S. BS in Elem. Edn., Kutztown (Pa.) U., 1974; cert. pastoral ministry, Allentown Coll. St. Francis, 1981; MS in Elem. Adminstrn., U. Scranton, 1991. Tchr. St. Catharine of Siena Sch., Reading, 1974—; facilitator Fatima Renewal Ctr., Dalton, Pa., 1980-91. Author: The Bible and Me, 1986; contbr. articles to profl. jours. Speaker at ch. groups, colls., schs., various cities in Pa., 1980-90; mem. adv. bd. Student Best program of Learning Mag.; mem. profl. devel. com. Diocese of Allentown. Named vol. of the yr. Our Lady of Fatima Ctr., Scranton, 1984; recipient cert. of participation in the tchr. in space program, NASA, Cape Canaveral, Fla., 1986. Mem. Sacred Dance Guild (pres. Ea. chpt. 1986-88), Nat. Cath. Edn. Assn. Roman Catholic. Office: St Catharine of Siena 2330 Perkiomen Ave Reading PA 19606-2098

SYDNOR, EDYTHE LOIS, retired administator, volunteer executive Bungoma Projects; b. Newark, Dec. 24, 1920; d. Samuel LeRoy and Sarah Lillian (Gaffney) S. Grad. high sch., Newark; cert. in engine repair, Casey Jones Sch. Aeronautics, 1942; student, NYU, 1956-57. Airplane engine mechanic U.S. Army Air Depot, Rome, N.Y., 1942-45; exec. sec. Neighborhood Ctr., Montclair, N.J., 1945-53; office mgr. pub. rels. div. Salvation Army, Newark, 1953-56; sec. to dir. fgn. ops. Morey Machinery Co., N.Y.C., 1956-58; adminstrv. supr. Essex County Div. Youth Svcs., Belleville, N.J., 1959-83, ret., 1983; founder, pres. Bungoma Projects, 1983. Contbr. articles to profl. jours. Participant, leader civil rights activities including March on Washington; mgr. hdqrs. for local and nat. polit. candidates, 1950-70; organizer of voter registration drives in Montclair, Essex County and N.J., 1950-70; 1st woman candidate for Town Commn. Election, Montclair, 1963. Named in proclamation N.J. State Senate, 1983; Edythe Sydnor Day in Essex County proclaimed by Essex County Executive, May 12, 1983; 1 of 15 finalists Salute Black Women Who Make It Happen Nat. Coun. Negro Women and Frito-Lay, 1987. Mem. Essex County League of Vol. Workers, Inc. (pres. 1958-82, 91—), NAACP. Democrat. Baptist. Office: Bungoma Projects Inc PO Box 1326 Montclair NJ 07042-1326

SYKES, DONALD JOSEPH, plastic company executive; b. Buffalo, Mar. 16, 1936; s. Joseph John and Josephine Mary (Zielinski) S.; m. Suzanne Kay Marble, May 28, 1960; children: Kathryn, Jeffrey. BS, Rochester (N.Y.) Inst. Tech., 1958. Dir. Cormac Chem. Corp., N.Y.C., 1959-63; from rsch. mgr. to sr. v.p. Hunt Chem. Co. (now Olin Hunt Specialty Co.), Palisades Park, N.J., 1963-83; dir., chief ops. officer Marpac Industries, Inc., Waldwick, N.J., 1983-88; chmn. of bd. Marpac Industries, Inc., Waldwick, 1988—. Contbr. articles and papers to field; patentee; holds over 20 U.S. patents. With U.S. Army Reserve, 1958-62. Mem. Am. Soc. Quality Control, Soc. Plastics Engrs., Am. Chem. Soc. Office: Marpac Industries Inc 164 Franklin Tpke Waldwick NJ 07463-1802

SYLK, LEONARD ALLEN, component built housing company executive, real estate developer; b. Phila., Feb. 25, 1941; s. Harry S. and Gertrude (Bardy) S.; m. Barbara Ann Lovenduski, Dec. 1, 1975; children: Tristan, Tyler, Galen. BS in Econs., U. Pa., 1963; MBA, Columbia U., 1965. Cert. comml. property builder. Founder, chmn. bd., chief exec. officer Shelter Systems Group Corp., Hainesport, N.J., 1965-91; bd. dirs. Hill Internat., Inc., Willingboro, N.J., Home Owners Warranty Corp., N.J., v.p., 1988—; presdl. advisor on housing trade with Soviet Union, 1990. Contbr. articles to industry publs. Chmn. ann. giving Friends Cen. Sch., Phila., 1983-86; co-chmn. ann. fundraiser Pa. Hosp., Phila., 1987, Inst. for Contemporary Art, Phila., 1988; chmn. ann. awards dinner Jewish Nat. Fund, Phila., 1987, v.p., bd. dirs.; bd. dirs. Phila. Orch. Assn., 1990—; N.J. chmn. Builders for Bush, 1988; bd. dirs. Acad. of Music, Phila., 1990—; bd. trustees Hahnemann U. and Hosp., 1991; bd. govs. Fgn. Policy Rsch. Inst., Middle East Coun., 1990—. Named Man of Yr., 1988. Mem. Nat. Assn. Homebuilders (com. chmn., nat. bd. dirs. 1984—, mem. exec. com. 1990—, fundraising chmn. 1991, Man of Yr. in Industrialized Housing 1990), Wood Truss Coun. Am. (bd. dirs. 1983—, pres. 1987, named to Hall of Fame 1990), Builders League South Jersey (v.p., bd. dirs. 1984—), N.J. Builders Assn. (bd. dirs., com. chmn., exec. com. 1990—), Locust Club, Le Club (N.Y.C.), Atlantic City Country Club, Masons. Republican. Home: 500 Delancey St Philadelphia PA 19106-4106 Office: Shelter Systems Group Corp Park Ave Hainesport NJ 08036-9999

SYLLA, RICHARD EUGENE, economics educator; b. Harvey, Ill., Jan. 16, 1940; s. Benedict Andrew and Mary Gladys (Curran) S.; m. Edith Anne Dudley, June 22, 1963; children: Anne Curran, Margaret Dudley. BA, Harvard U., 1962, MA, 1965, PhD, 1969. Prof. econs. and bus. N.C. State U., Raleigh, 1968-90; Henry Kaufman prof. history fin. insts. and markets NYU, N.Y.C., 1990—, prof. econs., 1990—; cons. Citibank NA, N.Y.C., 1979-82, Chase Manhattan Bank, N.Y.C., 1983-85; vis. prof. U. Pa., Phila., 1983, U. N.C., Chapel Hill, 1988. Author: The American Capital Market, 1975; co-author: A History of Interest Rates, 1991, Evolution of the American Economy, 1980; co-editor: Patterns of European Industrialization, 1991; editor Jour. Econ. History, 1978-84. Study fellow NEH, 1975-76; rsch. grantee NSF, 1985-91. Mem. Am. Econ. Assn., Econ. History Assn. (v.p. 1987-88, trustee 1978-88, Arthur H. Cole prize 1970), Am. Finance Assn., Bus. History Conf. (trustee 1991—), So. Econ. Assn. (v.p. 1981-82). Home: 110 Bleecker St Apt 23D New York NY 10012-2106 Office: NYU 90 Trinity Pl New York NY 10006-1806

SYLVESTER, JOHN VANCE, IV, lawyer, law educator, military officer; b. Schenectady, N.Y., July 22, 1954; s. John Vance III and Paula (Coveney) S.; m. Gina M. Maybury, Aug. 25, 1978. BA in English, Union Coll., Schenectady, 1976; JD, Union U., Albany, N.Y., 1979; postgrad. in bus. adminstrn., 1987, postgrad. in internat. rels., 1988; LLM, U. Va., 1989. Bar: N.Y. 1980, U.S. Dist. Ct. (so., ea. and no. dists.) N.Y. 1980, U.S. Army Ct. Mil. Rev. 1981, U.S. Ct. Mil. Appeals 1982. Instr. legal rsch. and writing Albany (N.Y.) Law Sch., Union U., 1978-79; assoc. Heidell, Pittoni & Moran, P.C., N.Y.C., 1979-80; chief prosecutor, chief legal svcs., mng. atty. claims, dep. legal advisor Joint Task Force Alaska Joint Task Force Alaska, Alaska, 1981-84; instr. U.S. Mil. Acad. U.S. Mil. Acad., West Point, N.Y., 1984-86; asst. prof. law U.S. Mil. Acad. West Point, N.Y., 1986-87; policy asst., counselor negotiations policy Office of Asst. Sec. Def. Internat. Security Policy U.S. Dept. Def., Washington, 1988; asst. corp. counsel City of Syracuse, N.Y., 1989—; adj. instr. in internat. law U.S. Army JAG Sch., Charlottesville, Va., 1987-91, assoc. with U.S. Army Ctr. Law and Military Ops., 1990; adj. internat. law atty., advisor Office of JAG, U.S. Dept. Army, Washington, 1991—. Mem. Alumni Coun. of Union Coll., 1989-92. Capt. JAGC, U.S. Army, 1982-87; maj. USAR, 1987—. Mem. N.Y. State Bar Assn., Army and Navy Club. Office: Office Corp Counsel 301 City Hall Syracuse NY 13202

SYLVESTER, LYNDA JOANN, product designer; b. Chgo., Apr. 30, 1950; d. Kenna (Gunderson) S. Student, U. Wis., Boston Mus. Fine Arts, Parsons Sch. of Design. Owner Kegonsa Gen. Store, Madison, 1969-75, Windward Specialties, Captiva Island, Fla., 1975-80, Lynda Sylvester Designs, N.Y.C., Sag Harbor, N.Y., 1980—; pres. C.L. Weekends (doing bus. as Sylvester & Co.), Sag Harbor, 1987—. patentee in field. Democrat. Home: PO Box 1192 Sag Harbor NY 11963-0039

SYME, DANIEL BAILEY, rabbi, institution executive; b. Sharon, Pa., Feb. 6, 1946; s. Monte Robert and Sonia (Hendin) S.; m. Deborah Shayne, Mar. 28, 1977; 1 child, Joshua. BA, U. Mich., Ann Arbor, 1967; BHL, MAHL, Hebrew Union Coll.-Jewish Inst. Religion, Cin., 1972; MEd, Columbia U., 1977, EdD, 1980. Ordained rabbi, 1972. Rabbi, Stamford Fellowship for Jewish Learning, Stamford, Conn., 1973-77; asst. dir. Nat. Fedn. Temple Youth, 1972-73; asst. nat. dir. edn. Union of Am. Hebrew Congregations, N.Y.C., 1973-77, dir., 1977—; asst. dir. Commn. Jewish Edn. for Reform Movement, N.Y.C., 1973-77, dir., 1977—; dir. Union Am. Hebrew Congregations TV Inst., N.Y.C., 1982-83, exec. asst. to pres., 1983-85, v.p., 1985-91, sr. v.p., 1991—; chmn. Coalition for Alternatives in Jewish Edn., N.Y.C., 1978-80; mem. Nat. Assn. Temple Educators, 1972-91, Commn. on Teaching of Israel and Zionism, World Zionist Orgn., 1980-84; dir. at large Jewish Nat. Fund; dir. at large internat. bd. Meml. Found. for Jewish Culture. Author: Finding God, My Body Is Something Special, Prayer Is Reaching, I'm Growing, I Learn About God, Books Are Treasures, Jewish Home, What Happens After I Die?, Why I Am a Reform Jew, Drugs, Sex and Integrity, The Jewish Wedding Book; exec. producer TV programs A Conversation with Menachem Begin, 1981, Choosing Judaism, 1981, To See the World Through Jewish Eyes, 1983, A Conversation with Yitzchak Navon, 1983, You Can Go Home Again, Jewish Youth and Cults, 1984; contbr. articles to religious publs. Mem. Rabbinic Adv. Coun., United Jewish Appeal, Nat. Religious Edn. Assn. (exec. bd.), Nat. Coun. for Jewish Edn. (exec. bd.). Office: Union Am Hebrew Congregations 838 5th Ave New York NY 10021-7064

SYPEK, JOSEPH PAUL, immunologist, researcher; b. Chicopee, Mass., Oct. 24, 1954; s. Stanley Paul and Mary Theresa (Baclawski) S. BS, Am. Internat. Coll., 1976; MS, U. R.I., 1979; PhD, William and Mary Coll., 1982. Postdoctoral rsch. fellow immunology program Sackler Sch. Tufts U., Boston, 1982-83, rsch. assoc., rsch. fellow div. geog. medicine, 1983-86, instr. New England Med. Ctr., 1986-87, asst. prof. medicine New England Med. Ctr., 1988—; staff scientist Infectious Disease Program, Genetics Inst., 1992—. Author: (with others) Contemporary Issues in Infectious Diseases Vol. 7, 1988, Vertebrate Blood Cells, 1988; contbr. articles to profl. jours. Recipient First award NIH, 1987-92. Mem. Am. Assn. Immunologists, Am. Soc. Microbiology, Am. Soc. Tropical Health and Hygiene, Internat. Soc. Devel. and Comparative Immunology, N.Y. Acad. Scis. Roman Catholic. Home: 29 Saint John St Jamaica Plain MA 02130 Office: Genetics Inst Preclinical Biology 87 Cambridge Park Dr Cambridge MA 02140

SYRACUSE, ROSS MICHAEL, priest; b. Buffalo, Sept. 27, 1950; s. Michael George and Patricia Ann (Maloney) S. BA in Philosophy, St. Hyacinth Coll., Granby, Mass., 1973; Lic. in Theology, U. Fribourg (Switzerland), 1978; MS in Counseling, Iona Coll., 1989. Ordained priest Roman Cath. Ch., 1978. Assoc. pastor St. Michael's Roman Cath. Ch., Birdgeport, Conn., 1978-79; assoc. dir. novices St. Joseph Cupertino Novitiate, Ellicott City, Md., 1979-82; assoc. pastor Most Holy Trinity Roman Cath. Ch., Bklyn., 1982-88, pastor, 1988—. Dir. Shelter for Homeless, Bklyn., 1982-84. Mem. AACD, Assn. Religious and Value Issues in Counseling, N.Y. Road Runners Club. Roman Catholic. Home and Office: Most Holy Trinity Ch 138 Montrose Ave Brooklyn NY 11206-2093

SYREK, RICHARD WILLIAM, consumer products company executive; b. Teaneck, N.J., Oct. 12, 1947; s. Stanley Steven and Mary (Turco) S.; m. Maryann Regina Sticco, Oct. 16, 1971. BS in Indsl. Engring., N.J. Inst. Tech., 1972; MBA, Pace U., 1979. Assoc. indsl. engr. Western Electric, Kearny, N.J., 1967-69, Westinghouse Electric, Relay Instrument div., Newark, 1969-71; indsl. engr. Am. Tack & Hardware Co., Inc., Monsey, N.Y., 1971-75, planning and systems mgr., 1975-79, v.p. ops., 1979-87, sr. v.p. ops., 1987—. Violinist, Ridgewood (N.J.) Symphony; mem. adv. bd. County of Rockland Office for the Aging; mem. mgmt. adv. com. Rockland Community Coll. Mem. Am. Prodn. and Inventory Control Soc. Home: 111 Kenilworth Rd Ridgewood NJ 07450-4604 Office: Am Tack & Hardware Co Inc 25 Robert Pitt Dr Monsey NY 10952-3392

SYWAK, MYRON, library educator; b. Bklyn., July 10, 1925; s. George and Mary (Litwin) S.; m. Esther Eisikoff, Mar. 31, 1951; children: Stephen, David. MS, L.I. U., 1966; PhD, N.Y. U., 1977. Prof. L.I.U., Brookville, N.Y., 1969-91; ret., 1992—. With U.S. Navy, 1944-46, ETO. Mem. Am. Libr. Assn., Am. Soc. for Info. Sci., N.Y. Libr. Assn. Office: Palmer Sch Libr & Info Sci LI Univ CW Post Campus Brookville NY 11854

SZABATURA, MICHAEL RAYMOND, dentist; b. Elmira, N.Y., Mar. 6, 1956; s. Raymond and Bertha (Barone) S.; m. Rosana Russo, July 9, 1988. BA, U. Rochester, 1978; DDS, Columbia U., 1982. Gen. resident Columbia-Presbyn. Hosp., N.Y.C., 1982-83; assoc. Kornbluh, Wilk & Szabatura, P.C., N.Y.C., 1983—; assoc. prof. Columbia U. Dental Sch., N.Y.C., 1983-90. Recipient Van Worrt award Columbia U., 1978-82. Mem. ADA, Acad. Gen. Dentistry (fellow 1990), St. Andrew's Golf Club. Republican. Roman Catholic. Office: Kornbluh Wilk & Szabatura PC 424 Madison Ave New York NY 10017-1106

SZABO, DENISE ZAROTNEY, insurance company executive; b. New Britain, Conn., Aug. 3, 1953; d. Henry and Jacquelyn (Frank) Zarotney; m. John Frederick Szabo, June 6, 1981. Student, Tunxis Community Coll., 1972-73. Office adminstr. Lenko Finishing Inc., Plainville, Conn., 1971-75; customer service rep. Aetna Life & Casualty Co., Hartford, Conn., 1975-76, sr. pension analyst, 1976—; consulting analyst, 1976—. Roman Catholic. Club: Tuesday Bowling (Plainville, Conn.) (v.p. 1985-86). Home: 421 Burritt St New Britain CT 06053-3614 Office: Aetna Life & Casualty Co 151 Farmington Ave Hartford CT 06156-0001

SZABO, JOSEPH GEORGE, publisher, journalist, cartoonist; b. Budapest, Feb. 4, 1950; came to U.S., 1981; s. József Imre and Erzsébet (Sólyom) S.; m. Flora Toth, July 19, 1975; children: Ágoston, Sylvester, Dominick, Veronica, Cecilia. BA, Hungarian Acad. Journalism, Budapest, 1974; cert., Sch. of Masters Typography, Budapest, 1969, Sch. of Commerce, 1978. Art dir. Nök Lapja Weekly mag., Budapest, 1975-78; mng. graphics editor Magyar Nemzet Daily Newspaper, Budapest, 1978-80; freelance cartoonist, 1980—; founder, editor-in-chief WittyWorld Internat. Cartoon Mag., North Wales, Pa., 1987—; pres. WittyWorld Books, North Wales, 1989—, Witty World Publs., North Wales, 1991—; mem. jury Montreal Internat. Salon of Cartoons, 1988; cons. United Media Syndicate, N.Y. and Budapest, 1989—; chmn. First Internat. Cartoon Festival, Budapest, 1990—. Editor Finest Internat. Polit. Cartoons of our Time, 1992, Was It Worth It?, 1992; editor, prodr. (cartoon series) Carrousel, 1992; contbr. articles to profl. jours. Mem. Nat. Cartoonists Soc., Assn. Am. Editorial Cartoonists. Office: WittyWorld Publs At 214 School St North Wales PA 19454-3121

SZALKAY, JOHN HARRO, engineer; b. Budapest, Hungary, Aug. 17, 1932; came to U.S. 1957; s. John Edward and Klara Renee (Milch) S.; m. Susan Gardos, Nov. 11, 1953 (div. 1959); children: Veronica J. Stevens-Jagusch; m. Simone Engler, Sept. 3, 1960. MA, Apaczai Csere Janos, Budapest, Hungary, 1954; BS in Engring., The Cooper Union Sch. Engring., 1969. Registered profl. engr. N.Y., Ohio, Ind., Pa., Fla. Calif., Vt. Secondry sch. tchr. various schs., Hungary, 1951-56; foreign accts. mgr. Mfg. Trust Co., N.Y.C., 1957-60; from draftsman, designer to associate, v.p. Meyer, Strong & Jones Consulting Engrs., N.Y.C., 1960-89; ptnr. Meyer, Strange & Jones Consulting Engrs., N.Y.C., 1989—. Mem. ASHRAE, Pi Tau Sigma. Office: Meyer Strong & Jones 11 Penn Plz New York NY 10001-2006

SZANTON, PETER LOEB, consultant; b. N.Y.C., Nov. 7, 1930; s. Jules and Carolyn (Loeb) S.; m. Eleanor Stokes, June 22, 1957; children: Nathan Stokes, Andrew Emlen, Sarah Loeb. BA, Harvard U., 1952, MA, 1955, LLB, 1958. Bar: N.Y. 1960. Law clk. to Judge O. Carter U.S. Dist. Ct., San Francisco, 1959; assoc. Solinger & Gordon, N.Y.C., 1960-62; mem. policy planning staff Office of Sec. of Def., Washington, 1962-64; sr. staff Bur. of Budget, Washington, 1965-67; pres. N.Y.C.-Rand Inst., 1967-71; rsch. dir. Nat. Commn. on Govt. Orgn., Washington, 1973-75; assoc. dir. Office of Mgmt. and Budget, Washington, 1977-79; v.p. Hamilton, Rabinovitz & Szanton, Washington, 1979-85; pres. Szanton Assocs., Washington, 1985—; cons. White House, Washington, 1977, Ford Found., N.Y.C., 1976-90, Bus. Roundtables, Boston, Honolulu, 1987-88, German Marshall Fund, Washington, 1989-91. Author: Not Well Advised, 1981; co-author: National Service: What Would It Mean?, 1986, Remaking Foreign Policy, 1976; editor: Federal Reorganization, 1981. Bd. pres. Youth Svc. Am., Washington, 1985-88; bd. dirs. Ptnrs. for Dem. Change, San Francisco, 1990—, Youthbuild USA, Belmont, Mass., 1991—; trustee Nat. Acad. Pub. Adminstrn., Washington, 1990—. Sgt. U.S. Army, 1952-54. Fellow Inst. of Politics, J.F. Kennedy Sch. of Govt., Harvard U., 1971-72, Nat. Acad. Pub. Adminstrn., 1983—. Mem. Coun. on Fgn. Rels., Cosmos Club. Democrat. Office: Szanton Assocs 1820 Jefferson Pl Washington DC 20036

SZCZYPINSKI, ADAM FRANCIS, surgeon; b. Balt., Mar. 17, 1931; s. Adam John and Frances Agnes (Brozozowski) S.; m. Susan Louise Boyer; children: Adam F. Jr., Keith, John, Jeffrey. AB, Johns Hopkins U., 1953, MD, 1957. Intern Johns Hopkins Hosp., Balt., 1957-58; resident Union Meml. Hosp., Balt., 1958-61, chief resident surgery, 1961-62; instr. surgery Emory U., Atlanta, 1964-65; instr. surgery U. Md., Balt., 1972-81, asst. prof. surgery, 1981—; cons. surgery Beufort (S.C.) Meml. Hosp., 1962-64; mem. med. and chirurgical faculty State of Md., 1958—. Chmn. Ambulatory Task Force of Md. Health and Planning Dept. Agy., Balt., 1980; pres. Am. Cancer Soc., Balt., 1971. Lt. comdr. USN, 1957-64. Fellow ACS, Southeastern Surg. Soc., Am. Coll. Chest Physicians, Am. Coll. Angiology, U. Surg. Soc.; mem. Balt. Acad. Surgeons (pres. 1974—). Office: 1422 E Joppa Rd Towson MD 21204

SZE, HEVEN, plant biology educator, researcher; b. The Hague, Netherlands, Oct. 22, 1947; d. Sung-Si and Mei-Fang (Fu) S.; m. Robert Tzyh-Chuan Su, July 10, 1974. BS in Botany, National Taiwan U., 1964-68; MS in Plant Physiology, U. Calif., Davis, 1968-70; PhD in Plant Physiology, Purdue U., 1971-75. Rsch. fellow Harvard Med. Sch., Boston, 1975-78; rsch. assoc. U. Kans., Lawrence, 1978-79, asst. prof., 1979-82; asst. prof. U. Md., College Park, 1982-85, assoc. prof., 1985-92; prof., 1992—. Author: Annual Review Plant Physiology, 1985. Office: Univ Maryland Dept Botany College Park MD 20742

SZE, KENNETH CHIACHE, surgeon; b. Peking, China, Jan. 6, 1918; came to U.S., 1939; s. Tsannyaen Phillip and Marian (Woo) S.; m. Denise, Oct. 1, 1949; 1 child, Gordon. AB, George Washington U., 1941, MD, 1943. Diplomate Am. Bd. Surgery, Am. Bd. Thoracic Surgery. Resident surgery Bellevue Hosp., NYU, N.Y.C., 1943-47; resident thoracic surgery Jersey City Med. Ctr., 1947-49; chief surgery Glenn Dale (Md.) Hosp., 1949-54; chief thoracic surgery VA Hosp., Bronx, N.Y., 1957-59; attending surgeon Beekman Downtown Hosp., N.Y.C., 1959-80; attending physician surgery N.Y. Infirmary Infirmary-Beekman Downtown Hosp., N.Y.C., 1981-91; assoc. attending thoracic surgeon Beth Israel Med. Ctr., N.Y.C., 1975-91; clin. asst. prof. surgery Albert Einstein Sch. Medicine, Bronx, 1959-62, N.Y. Med. Coll., N.Y.C., 1962-70; asst. prof. clin. surgery NYU Sch. Medicine, N.Y.C., 1970-76; lectr. Mt. Sinai Sch. Medicine, N.Y.C., 1977-91; cons. thoracic surgery U.S. Army, 1956-57. Contbr. articles to profl. jours. Trustee N.Y. Downtown Hosp., N.Y.C., 1991—. Maj., M.C. AUS, 1954-56. Recipient Svc. award VA, Bklyn., 1984, Commendation, VA Outpatient Clinic, Bklyn., 1989; named Alumni of the Yr. N.Y. Downtown Hosp. Alumni Assn., 1992. Fellow ACS; mem. Chinese Am. Med. Soc. (pres. 1969-70, dir. 1971-73), N.Y. Thoracic Surg. Soc., N.Y. County Med. Soc., N.Y. State Med. Soc. Home: 1150 Park Ave New York NY 10128-1244

SZEMES, ANITA READ, publisher; b. Brookline, Mass., Apr. 22, 1940; d. John Bertram and Anita Edith (Blacky) Read; m. Robert Stephens Szemes, Mar. 25, 1960; children: Susan Szemes McCann, Stephen Read, Stacey Ann. Student, Queens Coll., 1954-57, Hunter Coll., 1954-56, Columbia U., 1961-63, Union Coll., 1969-71. Cert. N.J. Press Assn. Buyer Mercantile Stores, N.Y.C., 1959-62; photo-journalist Summit (N.J.) Herald Newspapers; editor Chatham Press Summit Publs.; publisher Jour. Morris County, Morristown, N.J. Author (polit. booklet) When Coming in Second Isn't Good Enough, 1989 (Top Gop award 1990); pub. (jour. series) Investigative Reporting, 1990 (citations 1990-91). Bd. dirs. Union County (N.J.) Bar Assn., 1966-71; Union County Rep. Club, 1971—, New Providence (N.J.) Bd. Edn., 1976-79, Chatham (N.J.) C. of C., 1977-83, Morristown Christmas Com., 1989—; spl. dir. LWV, 1968-70; founder, bd. dirs. New Providence Care and Concern Found., 1979—; chmn. Union County Detention Ctr., Elizabeth, N.J., 1972-76; legis. aide Congressman Matthew Ranaldo, Union, N.J., 1972-76; polit. adv. Morris County Rep. Orgn., Morristown, 1979—; cons. Morris County Rep. Com., 1979—. Recipient First Media award N.J. Bar Assn., 1984, Community Rels. award Jewish War Vets., 1989, Resolution N.J. State Assembly and Senate, 1990, Outstanding Publisher award Morris County Retarded Citizens, 1991. Episcopalian. Home: 14 Vista Ln New Providence NJ 07974 Office: Jour Morris County 42 Court St Morristown NJ 07960

SZER, WLODZIMIERZ, biochemist, educator; b. Warsaw, Poland, June 3, 1924; came to U.S., 1968; s. Max and Chaia (Szapiro) S.; m. Felicja Kirsz, Oct. 1, 1946; children: Caroline, Ilona. M.S. in Chemistry, U. Lodz (Poland), 1950; Ph.D. in Biochemistry, Inst. Biochemistry and Biophysics, Polish Acad. Scis., 1959. Dozent Inst. Biochemistry and Biophysics, Warsaw, 1963-68; asst. prof., then assoc. prof. biochemistry Sch. Medicine, NYU, N.Y.C., 1968-73, prof., 1973—. Contbr. articles and revs. to profl. jours. Recipient Jacob K. Parnas Polish Biochem. Soc., 1964; recipient

Faculty Am. Cancer Soc., 1973; USPHS grantee, 1971—. Mem. Am. Soc. Biol. Chemists, Harvey Soc. Office: NYU Sch Medicine Dept Biochemistry 550 1st Ave New York NY 10016-6402

SZILAGYI, JOHN ALEX, federal agency administrator; b. N.Y.C., Feb. 6, 1940; s. John Michael and Elizabeth (Wesselenyi) S.; m. Mary Ann Mazzola, Sept. 7, 1963; 1 child, Sherry. BBA, Hofstra U., 1961. Tax auditor IRS, Bklyn., 1961-67; adminstrv. intern IRS, Washington, 1967-68, revenue agt., 1968-76, planning officer, 1976-79, chmn. deferred tax research programs, 1979—; drafted U.S. tax legislation requiring Social Security number of dependent to be listed on income tax returns; drafted U.S., tax legislation enacted in 1988 requiring taxpayer ID number of child care provider to be listed on income tax returns; interviewee for missing-children article, Forbes mag., 1990; interviewee for tax cheating on child care articles N.Y. Times, 1991; interviewee for Is the IRS After You? articles Working Mother mag., 1991. Author: (books): Energy Credit Limitations, 1983, Recapture of Deduction on HUD Housing, 1984, Monitoring Age 65 Exemptions, 1987, Improper Zero Bracket Amount Deductions, 1988, Where Have All the Dependents Gone?, 1989, Whatever Happened to Child Care in 1989?; editor (books): State Income Tax Refund Study, 1982, Stock Sales Disclosed by Dividends, 1983, Recapture of New Residence Credit, 1983, Monitoring Individual Noncash Contributions, 1988. Republican. Presbyterian. Office: IRS Rsch Div 1111 Constitution Ave NW Washington DC 20224-0002

SZILASSY, SANDOR, library director, educator; b. Magyarbarnag, Hungary, Apr. 9, 1921; came to U.S., 1957; s. Sandor Sr. and Jolan (Fenyves) S.; m. Clara Ida Varkonyi, July 21, 1951; children: Peter S., Thomas S., Paul A. D. LLD, U. Budapest, Hungary, 1944, Lawyer-Judge Dipl., 1949; MA, Ind. U., 1959. Practicing atty., pres. law firm Veszprém, Hungary, 1944-56; asst. libr. Anderson (Ind.) Coll. Libr., 1959-61; head div. sci. and tech. Auburn (Ala.) U. Libr., 1961-68; head libr., assoc. prof. Ind. State U., Evansville, 1968-69; dir. libr., prof. U. Tampa, Fla., 1969-72; dir. libs. Glassboro (N.J.) State Coll., 1972—; v.p. Ala. Acad. Sci., 1963-68; pres. Coun. N.J. Coll. and Univ. Librs., 1978-79, 89-90, Librs. Unltd., N.J., 1981-82, 88-89; lectr. Sta. WTEL, Phila., 1988—; cons. numerous orgns. Author: Revolutionary Hungary, 1971 (Arpad Acad. Gold medal 1972), Ein Amerikanischer Diplomat uber Ungarn, 1974, Hungary's Road to Trianon, 1988, numerous others; author book chpts.; mem. editorial bd. Ency. Hungarica, 1989—; contbr. essays, studies, articles to profl. jours. Bd. elders Presbyn. Ch., Lakeland, Fla., 1970-72. Recipient Legion of Honor award Chapel of Three Chaplains, 1981. Mem. N.J. Acad. Libr. Network (exec. bd. 1988—), Tri-State Coll. Libr. Coop. (pres. 1975-76), Johanniter Order Knights (Germany), Arpad Acad. (sect. pres. 1979—), Phi Alpha Theta. Mem. Reformed Ch. Home: 14 Polaris Rd Turnersville NJ 08012 Office: Glassboro State Coll Glassboro NJ 08028

SZPORN, RENEE MARLA, religious educator; b. N.Y.C., Sept. 6, 1956; d. Bernard and Charlotte Lee (Kustich) Siegal; m. Michael Szporn, Oct. 12, 1980; 1 child, Ari David. BA in Music with honors, CCNY, 1977; post-grad., Pa. State U., 1977-78, NYU, 1978-82. Cert. tchr. Credit analyst Lord & Taylor, N.Y.C., 1975-77; instr. Pa. State U., Univ. Park, 1977-78; estimator Medicus Communications, N.Y.C., 1978-80; fin. coord. Sudler & Hennessey, N.Y.C., 1980-87; tchr. Beth El Synagogue, 1988-90, Temple Beth Shalom, Manalapan, N.J., 1990—. Mem. Nat. C. of C. for Women, Am. Philatelic Soc., Soc. Israel Philatelists, CCNY Alumni Assn., Agudah Women Am. Republican.

SZUMLA, ROBERT JAMES, accountant; b. Balt., Sept. 26, 1961; s. Richard Joseph and Doris Wanda (Drury) S.; m. Theresa Elaine Bosley, May 11, 1985; children: Daniel Ryan, Lauren Marie. BA, Loyola Coll., Balt., 1983, MBA, 1991. CPA. Acctg. mgr. Seapac Svcs., Inc., Balt., 1983-84; asset control mgr. Kimmel Automotive, Inc., Balt., 1984-89; acctg. officer The Bank of Balt., 1989—. Model developer (software) Excess Servicing, 1990, Purchased Servicing, 1990. Bd. dirs. Judith S. Richey Youth Svcs. Bur., Balt., 1991—. Mem. Md. Assn. CPAs (mem. cooperation with fin. institutions com. 1991-93), Nat. Assn. of Accts. (dir. meetings 1991-92), Beta Gamma Sigma. Home: 2827 Hemlock Ave Baltimore MD 21214-1246

SZUSZ, PETER, mathematician, educator; b. Novi Sad, Yugoslavia, Nov. 11, 1924; came to U.S., 1965; s. Felix and Irma (Obersohn) S.; m. Margaret Wenner, Oct. 16, 1973. PhD, U. Budapest, 1951; DSc, Hungarian Acad. Sci., 1962. Rsch. fellow Hungarian Acad. Sci. Math. Dept., Budapest, 1950-65; prof. math. SUNY, Stony Brook, 1966—; vis. asst. prof. Pa. State U., State College, 1965-66. Contbr. articles to profl. jours. Home: 284 Hallock Rd Stony Brook NY 11790-3028 Office: Dept Math SUNY Stony Brook NY 11794

SZYCHER, LAWRENCE JOSEPH, artist educator; b. Bayonne, N.J., Mar. 5, 1950; s. Mitchell R. and Jeanette (Kowalak) S.; m. Theresa E. O'Loughlin, May 28, 1983. Student, U. Miami, 1967-70; AA, Newark Sch. Fine & Indsl. Art, 1970-73; BA, Jersey City State Coll., 1974; MFA magna cum laude, U. Md., 1976. Mgr. Cottage Gallery, Provincetown, Mass., 1979-82, Left Bank Gallery, Wellfleet, Mass., 1983; illustrator, designer Young Ideas Design Studio, N.Y.C., 1984-85; adj. prof. St. Peter's Coll., Jersey City, 1985-91, Jersey City State Coll., 1986-90, Kean Coll., Union, N.J., 1988-90; asst. prof. fine arts Caldwell (N.J.) Coll., 1990—. One-man shows include: Swansborough Gallery Mass., 1983, Customs House Gallery, Mass., 1985, Jersey City State Coll., 1989, Bayonne Jewish Community Ctr., 1990;represented in permanent collections Aetna Life and Casualty Co., Conn., Allegretti, Newitt, Witcoff & McAndrews, Chgo., Schiffenhause Industries, N.J., Seahawk Techs., Conn., United Techs., Conn., U. Md., U. Conn. Health Ctr., and numerous pvt. colls. throughout U.S. and Europe; exhbited in many group shows in EasternU.S. especially. Home: 873 Avenue C Bayonne NJ 07002-3030 Office: Caldwell Coll 9 Ryerson Ave Caldwell NJ 07006-6195

SZYDLOWSKI, THADDEUS RAYMOND, physician; b. Shenandoah, Pa., Aug. 31, 1947; s. Thaddeus Francis and Leona (Jurewicz) S.; m. Susan Marion Mathews, Apr. 14, 1973; children: Kristen, Ellen. BS, Albright Coll., 1968; MD, Jefferson Med. Coll., 1972. Diplomate Am. Bd. Internal Medicine and Gastroenterology. Intern in internal medicine Reading (Pa.) Hosp., 1972-73; resident in internal medicine Abington (Pa.) Hosp., 1973-75; fellow in hepatology N.J. Coll. Medicine, Newark, 1975-76; fellow in gastroenterology Lankenau Hosp., Phila., 1976-77; staff physician Naval Regional Med. Ctr., Portsmouth, Va., 1977-79; physician Lebanon (Pa.) Internal Medicine Specialist, 1979—. Lt. comdr. USNR, 1977-79. Fellow Am. Coll. Gastroenterology; mem. AMA, Am. Soc. Gastrointestinal Endoscopy, Am. Coll. Physicians, Pa. Soc. Gastroenterology, Am. Gastroent. Assn., Bocjus Alumni Internat. Soc. Gastroenterology. Home: 212 Spring Hill Ln Lebanon PA 17042 Office: Lebanon Internal Medicine 508 Oak St Lebanon PA 17042

SZYMANSKI, HERMAN VINCENT, psychiatrist; b. South Bend, Ind., Jan. 6, 1951; s. Herman Aloysius and Alice (Irene) S.; m. Anne Berst; children: Julie, Paul. BS, U. Notre Dame, Ind., 1972; MD, U. Rochester, N.Y., 1976. Diplomate Am. Bd. Psychiatry and Neurology. Intern, then resident in psychiatry Western Psychiat. Inst. U. Pitts., 1976-79, chief resident psychiat. and consultation, 1978-79; asst. prof. Western Psychiat. Inst. and Clinic VA Med. Ctr., Pitts., 1984-85; physician, cons. out-patient drug abuse program S.W. Community Mental Health Ctr./U. Pitts., 1978-79; Buswell rsch. fellow in schizophrenia Sch. Medicine SUNY, Buffalo, 1979-82, asst. prof., 1985—; rsch. asst. prof. VA Med. Ctr., Buffalo, 1979-84, staff psychiatrist, 1980—. Contbr. articles to profl. jours. Recipient Copin House award, 1987. Mem. Am. Psychiat. Assn., Soc. for Biol. Psychiatry, Western N.Y. Dist. Br. of Am. Psychiat. Assn. (program chmn. 1986-87, treas. 1987-88, sec. 1988-89, pres. elect, 1989-90, co-chairperson run for brain rsch. 1985-88). Office: VA Med Ctr Mental Health 3495 Bailey Ave Buffalo NY 14215-1129

SZYMANSKI, PATRICK JOSEPH, lawyer; b. Detroit, Jan. 18, 1949; s. Frank S. and Lillian F. (Mikula) S.; m. Margery E. Lieber, Apr. 10, 1983; children: Alyson Beth, Matthew Francis. Student, MIT, 1966-69; BA, Wayne State U., Detroit, 1973, JD, 1976. Bar: Mich. 1976, U.S. Ct. Appeals (D.C., 1st, 2d and 4th cirs.) 1977, U.S. Ct. Appeals (9th cir.) 1978, Calif. 1979, D.C. 1979, U.S. Dist. Ct. (no. dist.) Calif. 1979, U.S. Ct. Appeals (10th cir.) 1984, U.S. Supreme Ct. 1985, U.S. Dist. Ct. D.C. 1988, U.S. Dist. Ct. Md. 1988, U.S. Dist. Ct. Mich. (ea. dist.) 1991, U.S. Ct. Appeals (3d cir.) 1991. Atty. appellate ct. br. NLRB, Washington, 1976-78, 83-88; assoc. Beeson, Tayer, Silbert & Bodine, San Francisco, 1978-83; assoc. Baptiste & Wilder, P.C., Washington, 1988-89, ptnr., 1989—. Mem. editorial bd. Wayne State U. Law Rev., 1975-76. Mem. ABA (labor law sect. com. on practice and procedure before NLRB), Fed. Bar Assn., D.C. Bar Assn. (chair coun. on sects. 1988-89, co-chair labor law sect. 1984-90, cert. of appreciation 1989). Democrat. Roman Catholic. Office: Baptiste & Wilder PC 1919 Pennsylvania Ave NW #505 Washington DC 20006

SZYMKOWSKI, RICHARD WALTER, financial executive; b. Phila., Aug. 18, 1943; s. Sylvester V. and Cecelia (Wojciechowski) S.; m. Patricia Anne Reed, Oct. 28, 1967; children: Heidi W, Adam W. BS, Pa. State U., 1965; M Indsl. Adminstrn., Yale U., 1967. Cost analyst Office of Sec. Def., Washington, 1969-71; budget analyst Comptroller of Army, Washington, 1971-72; dir. Psychiat. Insts. Am., Washington, 1972-75; group leader JRB Assocs., McLean, Va., 1975-76; contr. Greenville (Pa.) Hosp., 1976-88; assoc. adminstr. Greenville Regional Hosp., 1988-89, v.p. fin., 1989-91; bd. dirs., v.p. Greenville Neurosensory Found., 1986—; treas. Greenville Health Systems Found., 1986—; presenter papers at profl. confs. Mem. Greenwood Twp. Planning Com., Geneva, Pa., 1985—, pres., 1988-90; v.p. Greenville Symphony Soc., 1985-91, pres., 1991-92; com. chmn. Greenville Econ. Devel. Corp., 1990—. Mem. Healthcare Fin. Mgmt. Assn. (pres. 1982-83, Pres.'s award 1983, Follmer award 1983, Reeves award 1987), Healthcare Mgmt. Systems Soc., Hosp. Assn. Pa. (com. mem.), Greenville Country Club, Lions Internat. (treas. Greenville chpt. 1985-87). Office: Greenville Regional Hosp 110 N Main St Greenville PA 16125-1726

SZYMONIK, PETER TED, computer systems coordinator; b. Boleslawiec, Jelena Gora, Jelena, Poland, Nov. 13, 1963; came to U.S., 1964; s. Jan and Genowefa (Bielak) S.; m. Stephanie Christine Sans, Feb. 14, 1991. BA, U. Conn., 1984, B Internat. Polit. Sci., 1988. Computer cons. Share, Greenwich, Conn., 1989; personel computer systems coord. Cummings & Lockwood, Hartford, 1989—; system operator GE Info. Network, Rockville, Md., 1986—; cons. Sacred Hoop of Am. Resource Exch., Greenwich, 1988-89. Editor and pub. mags. Simulations Online, 1991, GEnie Games RT NewsLetter, 1991. Republican. Home: 161 Woodbury Cir Middletown CT 06457-5650 Office: Cummings & Lockwood Cityplace I Hartford CT 06103

TABACHNICK, KENNETH ELIOT, lighting designer; b. N.Y.C., Nov. 20, 1955; s. Sol and Sheilah (Beck) T.; m. Yael Mandelstam, Mar. 12, 1983; 1 child, Guy Mandelstam. BA magna cum laude, SUNY, Buffalo, 1977. Pvt. practise N.Y.C., 1977—; lighting designer N.Y.C. Opera, 1986-89, Pitts. Opera, 1988-92, Roger Morgan Studios, N.Y.C., 1989-90, Greater Miami (Fla.) Opera, 1989-91, Bolshhoi Ballet and Opera, Moscow, 1989-91, Kirov (Maryinsky) Ballet and Opera, 1991-92; lighting dir. Live From Lincoln Ctr., N.Y.C., 1987-88; applicant judge Hemsley Internship, N.Y.C., 1987—. Contbr. articles to profl. jours. Recipient Drama Logue award, San Francisco, 1990. Mem. United Scenic Artists, U.S. Inst. Theatre Tech., Internat. Alliance Theatre and Stage Employees. Office: 73 Spring St Apt 401 New York NY 10012-5801

TABACHNICK, MILTON, biochemistry educator; b. N.Y.C., June 25, 1922; s. Harry and Sarah (Berman) T.; m. Elizabeth Swirnofsky, Feb. 7, 1952. BA, U. Calif., Berkeley, 1947, MA, 1949, PhD in Biochemistry, 1953. Am. Cancer Soc. fellow Dept. Biochemistry, Duke U., Durham, N.C., 1952-53; instr. Inst. of Indsl. Medicine, NYU Postgrad. Med. Sch., N.Y.C., 1953-55; vis. investigator Pub. Health Rsch. Inst., N.Y.C., 1955-57; rsch. assoc. Dept. Chemistry, Mt. Sinai Hosp., N.Y.C., 1957-59, N.Y. State Psychiat. Inst., N.Y.C., 1959-61; prof. biochemistry N.Y. Med. Coll., Valhalla, 1961—; dean grad. sch. N.Y. Med. Coll., 1971-79. With U.S. Army, 1942-46. NIH grantee, 1961-80, 83-86; NSF grantee, 1981-83. Mem. AAAS, Am. Thyroid Assn., Am. Soc. for Biochemistry and Molecular Biology, Endocrine Soc. Office: NY Med Coll Dept Biochemistry BSB Valhalla NY 10595

TABATABAI, MAHMOOD, anesthesiology educator; b. Kazeroon, Fars, Iran, Mar. 21, 1938; s. Seyyed Enayatollah and Behjat (Sharieh) T.; m. Mildred Fatemeh Hugonet, Dec. 9, 1967 (div. 1982); children: Hossein-Ali, Golnar, Leila. MD, Shiraz U., Shiraz, 1963; PhD in Physiology, U. Pa., 1969. Diplomate Am. Bd. Anesthesiologists. Intern Hahnemann U. Hosp., Phila., 1978-79; asst. prof. Physiology, chmn. dept. Physiology Shiraz U., Shiraz, 1969-74, assoc. prof. Physiology, chmn. dept. Physiology, 1974-77; resident in anesthesiology Yale U., New Haven, 1979-82; assist. prof. Anesthesiology U. Pitts., Pitts., 1983-89, assoc. prof. Anesthesiology, 1989—. Editor Iranian Jour. of Med. Scis., 1972-77. Mem. AAAS, Soc. for Experimental Biology and Medicine, Internat. Brain Rsch. Orgn., Internat. Soc. for Heart Rsch., Soc. for Devel. Neurosci., Am. Soc. of Anesthesiologists, Internat. Anesthesia Rsch. Soc., Assn. of Univ. Anesthesiologists. Home: 126 Morrison Dr Pittsburgh PA 15216 Office: VA Med Ctr Anesthesiology Svc University Dr C Pittsburgh PA 15240

TABER, DOUGLASS FLEMING, chemistry educator; b. Berkeley, Calif., Nov. 11, 1948; s. Richard Douglas and Barbara (Fleming) T.; m. Susan Buhler, Dec. 30, 1969; children: John, Alan, Emma, Christina, Abigail, Robert. BS, Stanford U., 1970; PhD, Columbia U., 1974. Postdoctoral fellow U. Wis., Madison, 1974-75; from instr. to asst. prof. dept. pharmacology Med. Sch., Vanderbilt U., Nashville, 1975-82; from asst. prof. to assoc. prof. chemistry and biochemistry U. Del., Newark, 1982—. NSF fellow, 1970-73. Mem. LDS Ch. Home: 717 Harvard Ln Newark DE 19711-3134 Office: U Del Dept Chemistry and Biochem Newark DE 19716

TABLER, KENNETH ALFRED, accountant; b. Ulm, Fed. Republic of Germany, Nov. 30, 1958; s. Kenneth Ted and Ann (Farber) T.; m. Ellen Blum, Sept. 18, 1982; 1 child, Russell Paul. BS, Loyola Coll., 1980. CPA, Md. Sr. tax mgr. Ernst & Young, Balt., 1980—; co-chmn. Advanced Tax Inst., Balt., 1989. Asst. scoutmaster Boy Scouts Am., Balt., 1983-89; bd. dirs. Pets on Wheels, Balt., 1986—. Mem. AICPA, Nat. Assn. Accts. (bd. dirs. 1986-88), Md. Assn. CPAs. Home: 209 Highmeadow Rd Baltimore MD 21136

TABNER, MARY FRANCES, educator; b. Rochester, N.Y., Dec. 11, 1918; d. William Herman and Mary Frances (Willenbacher) Arndt; m. James Gordon Tabner, June 27, 1942; 1 child, Barbara Jean. BA, SUNY, Albany, 1940, MA, 1959; postgrad., U. Rochester, N.Y., 1944, 45, Northwestern U. (John Hay fellow), 1963-64, U. Manchester (Eng.), 1971-72. Tchr. history pub. schs. Mattituck, N.Y., 1940-43, Gorham, N.Y., 1943-46; tchr. pub. schs. Waterford, N.Y., 1949-55; tchr. social studies Shaker High Sch., Latham, N.Y., 1959-83, also dir., 1959-83, ret., 1983; tchr. ch. history Our Lady of Assumption Ch., Latham. Author bibliographies on Russian history, also studies. Mem. Citizens Exch. Coun. N.Y. State Regents independent study grantee, 1966. Mem. Nat. Coun. Social Studies, N.Y. State United Tchrs. Assn., Advancement Slavic Studies, SUNY Albany Alumni Assn., Albany Inst. History and Art, Capital Dist. Coun. Social Studies, Shaker Heritage Soc. (trustee, guide, tchr.), Nat. Trust Historic Preservation, English Speaking Union, Am. Assn. Retired Persons. Republican. Roman Catholic. Home: 557 Columbia St Cohoes NY 12047-3807

TABOR, MARY LEEBA, oil trade association executive; b. Balt., Mar. 3, 1946; d. Gerson and Freda (Roseman) T.; m. Ardell Louis Persinger, Sept. 16, 1984; children: Benjamin George Hammerschlag, Sarah Esther Hammerschlag. BA with high honors, U. Md., 1966; MA in Teaching, Oberlin Coll., 1967; postgrad., U. Chgo., 1988. Tchr. Towson (Md.) High Sch., 1967-70; employment profl. Ctr. for Naval Analyses, Alexandria, Va., 1970-71; tchr. adult edn. Montgomery County (Md.) Bd. Edn., 1975-80; editor pub. affairs Am. Petroleum Inst., Washington, 1980-83, writer, editor-in-chief, 1983-86, mgr. environ., health and pub. affairs, 1986-89, dir. pub. affairs writing, 1989—; advisor on high sch. sci. curriculum reform NSTA, Washington, 1991—. Debate judge Nat. Cath. Forensic High Sch. League, Bethesda (Md.)-Chevy Chase High Sch., 1991. Mem. Nat. Press Club, Phi Beta Kappa, Phi Kappa Phi, Alpha Lambda Delta. Office: Am Petroleum Inst 1220 L St NW Washington DC 20005

TACKEL, IRA S., biomedical engineer, consultant; b. N.Y.C., Apr. 3, 1954; s. Herman William and Aida (Link) T.; m. Sherry Dee Melker, Aug. 28, 1977; children—Elana Rachael, Joshua Chad. B.S. in Biomed. Engring., Rensselaer Poly. Inst., 1976, M in Biomed. Engring., 1977; postgrad. in intensive and coronary care units George Washington U., 1978, Emergency Care Research Inst., 1979, Ind. U. Sch. Medicine, 1979. Mech. engr. Olin Corp., chem. div., Lake Charles, La., 1974; biomed. engr. Helen Hayes Hosp., West Haverstraw, N.Y., 1975, Vets. Hosp., Albany, N.Y., 1976-77; dir. dept. clin. engring. Hosp. of U. Pa., Phila., 1977-85; dir. dept. biomed. instrumentation Thomas Jefferson U. Hosp., Phila., 1985—; cons. Bisonics, Inc., Phila., 1982-86, Integrated Techs. Resource Corp., 1983—; adj. faculty Temple U., Phila., 1979—, Drexel U., Phila., 1981—. Mem. editorial bd. Emergency Care Research Inst.-Health Devices, 1982—. Contbr. articles to profl. jours. Mem. Assn. Advancement Med. Instrumentation (mem. bd. dirs.), IEEE (Engring. Medicine and Biology), Phila. Area Med. Instrumentation Assn. (pres. 1982), Am. Hosp. Assn., Am. Soc. Hosp. Engrs. Home: 1327 Barton Dr Fort Washington PA 19034-1654 Office: Thomas Jefferson U Hosp 129 S 9th St Philadelphia PA 19107

TADIO, SAMUEL WILLIAM, manufactured homes company executive; b. Buffalo, Apr. 30, 1937; s. William Michael and Marie Constance (Lo Bue) T.; divorced; children: William Joseph, Jennifer Marie. Grad. high sch., Buffalo. Pres. Sky Harbor Corp., Buffalo, 1962—. Chmn. Cheektowaga Econ. Devel. Corp., Buffalo, 1986-92; chmn. polit. action com. Good Govt. Club, Western, N.Y., 1982—, also bd. dirs. With N.G., 1955-61. Mem. N.Y. State Manufactured Homes Assn. (bd. dirs. 1972—). Republican. Roman Catholic. Office: Sky Harbor Corp 4959 Genesee St Buffalo NY 14225

TAESCHLER, DEBRA ANN, advertising executive; b. Jersey City, Jan. 7, 1953; d. Edward George and Marion Madeline (Naas) Miller; m. John Paul Taeschler, June 24, 1978. BA summa cum laude, Rutgers U., 1975. With mech. arts dept. Vornado, Inc., Garfield, N.J., 1975-76; asst. account exec. Clifton (N.J.) Graphix Assn., 1976-77; advt. mgr. Davis Printing Corp., Carlstadt, N.J., 1977-80; v.p. account mgr. Landmark Assocs., Whippany, N.J., 1980-85; account mgr. R.Z.A. Advt., Inc., Park Ridge, N.J., 1985-86; pres. Grafica, Inc., Chester, N.J., 1986—. Mem. Phi Beta Kappa. Roman Catholic. Office: Grafica Inc 50 Main St Chester NJ 07930-2535

TAFARES, ROBERT EDMOND, career officer; b. Bklyn., Aug. 28, 1941; s. OScar and Ivy M. (Taylor) T.; m. Hazel H. Chen Young, Sept. 4, 1962; children: David A., Tiffany R. BS in Earth Sci., Ind. State U., 1964; MA in Adminstrn. and Supr., Inter-Am. U., 1970. Commd. 2d lt. USAF, 1965, advanced through grades to col., 1986. Mem. AF COMAP, Washington. Mem. Air. Force Assn., Old Crows, Rotary, Omega Psi Phi. Roman Catholic. Office: Det 130 AFROTC Howard U Howard Univ Washington DC 20059

TAFFEL, ABRAM, romance language educator; b. Odessa, Russia, Jan. 26, 1906; s. Morris and Rachel (Smuckler) T.; m. Helen Hockfelder, June 26, 1949. AB, CCNY, 1934, MS in Edn., 1936; PhD, Columbia U., 1949. Reader Dept. Romance Lang., CCNY, 1934-37; asst. tchr. Townsend Harris High Sch., N.Y.C., 1937-41; fellow Dept. Romance Lang., CCNY, 1945-49, instr., 1949-53, asst. prof., 1953-57, assoc. prof., 1957-67, dept. chmn. and prof., 1967-70, prof. emeritus, 1975—. Author: The Prose Fiction and Dramatic Works of Henri Duvernois, 1951. With U.S. Army, 1942-45. Recipient Ward Medal in French, CCNY, 1934. Mem. MLA, Am. Soc. Geolinguistics (pres. 1982-83), Am. Assn. Tchrs. French.

TAFT, CHARLES KIRKLAND, mechanical engineering consultant; b. Cleve., July 24, 1928; s. Kingsley Arter and Louise (Dakin) T.; m. Carolyn Nancy Eggers, Aug. 25, 1951; children—Charles K., Fredrick D., Richard K. B.A., Amherst Coll., 1951; B.S. in Mech. Engring., MIT, 1953; M.S., Case Inst. Tech., 1956, Ph.D. (Charles W. Bingham fellow), 1960. Research engr. Warner and Swasey, Cleve., 1953-58; chief servo engr. Warner and Swasey, 1960-61; asst. prof. Case Inst. Tech., Cleve., 1961-64; asso. prof. Case Inst. Tech., 1964-67; prof. mech. engring. U. N.H., Durham, 1967-85, chmn. dept., 1985-91, prof. emeritus, 1991—; cons. Gen. Signal Co., Lord Mfg. Co., duPont Co., TRW, Parker Hannifin, McCord-Winn. Co-author: Introduction to Dynamic Systems; contbr. articles to publs.; patentee in field. Recipient Charles J. Stosacker Teaching award Case Inst. Tech., 1966, Nat. Fluid Power Assn. Achievement award, 1966; Outstanding Innovator award U. N.H., 1985. Mem. ASME (past chmn. No. New Eng. sect., Rail Transp. award 1980), IEEE (Best Transactions Paper award 1975), Instrument Soc. Am. (chmn. fluidics com.), Am. Soc. Engring. Educators (AT&T Outstanding Tchr. award New England sect. 1986-87), Sigma Xi, Pi Tau Sigma, Tau Beta Pi. Home: 9 Bucks Hill Rd Durham NH 03824-3202

TAFT, NATHANIEL BELMONT, lawyer; b. Tarrytown, N.Y., Aug. 12, 1919; s. Louis Eugene and Etta Minnie (Spivak) Topp; m. Norma Rosalind Pike, May 22, 1943; children: Charles Eliot, Stephen Pike. BS in Econs., Fordham U., 1940; JD, Harvard U., 1948. Bar: N.Y. 1949. Asst. to gen. counsel N.Y. State Ins. Dept., Albany, 1948-50; atty. law dept. N.Y. Life Ins. Co., N.Y.C., 1951-65; from asst. counsel to group v.p. N.Y. Life Ins. Co., 1965-84; sole practice law White Plains, N.Y., 1985—; chmn. group ins. com. Life Ins. Coun. N.Y., 1981-84; adviser Tex. State Bd. Ins., 1989-91. Contbr. articles to profl. jours.; author monographs on group ins. regulation. Chmn. W.P. Adult Edn. Coun., White Plains, 1960-62; trustee Jewish Community Ctr., White Plains, 1977-86, sec., treas., 1980-84; mem., bd. dirs. New Orch. of Westchester, 1991—. Mem. ABA, N.Y. State Bar Assn., Health Ins. Assn. Am. (chmn. N.Y. minimum standards com. 1981-83), Nat. Assn. Physians (sec.-treas. 1991—), Health Reins. Assn. Conn. (sec. 1975-85), Harvard Club. Republican. Jewish. Home and Office: 16 Sparrow Cir White Plains NY 10605-4624

TAGG, JANET MELODINI, elementary school counselor; b. Harrisburg, Pa., June 3, 1953; d. Americo Pasquale and Jean Claire (Lanza) Melodini; m. Stephen M. Tagg, Aug. 21, 1976; children: Rebecca Marie, Vanessa Michelle. B. Social Sci., Pa. State U., 1985; MEd, Shippensburg U., 1988. Nat. cert. counselor. Elem. sch. counselor Capital Area Intermediate Unit, Summerdale, Pa., 1988—; liaison Pa. Counseling Assn. and Keystone Counseling Assn. Exec. bd. mem. Children's Family Ctr., Mechanicsburg, Pa., 1987-90; juried mem. Yellow Breeches chpt. Pa. Guild Craftsmen, Grantham, Pa., 1988—; mem. Pa. Guild Craftsmen, Bushkill, Pa., 1989—. Mem. Keystone Couseling Assn., Pa. Counseling Assn., Pa. Sch. Counselors Assn., Am. Sch. Counselors Assn., AACD, Am. Psychol. Assn., Delta Tau Kappa (sec. 1985-86), Chi Sigma Iota (life). Home: 1210 McCormick Rd Mechanicsburg PA 17055 Office: Capital Area Intermediate 55 Miller St Unit 489 Summerdale PA 17093-9999

TAGGART, DAVID PETER, communications executive; b. Ithaca, N.Y., Apr. 8, 1954; s. Harry Arthur and Marion (Lieto) T. BS in Polit. Sci., SUNY, Brockport, 1975; MPA, George Washington U., 1979. Dir. communications svcs. The Media Inst., Washington, 1979—. Mem. Am. Mgmt. Assn. Republican. Roman Catholic. Office: The Media Inst 1000 Potomac St NW # 204 Washington DC 20007-3501

TAGGART, ROBERT ALEXANDER, JR., finance educator; b. Detroit, Aug. 13, 1946; s. Robert Alexander and Lillian Marie (Earley); m. Karen Kelly, June 1, 1974; children—Michael A., Alice C., Mary E. B.A., Amherst Coll., 1968; M.S., MIT, 1969, Ph.D., 1974. Asst. assoc. prof. fin. Northwestern U., Evanston, Ill., 1974-83; economist Fed. Res. Bank, Boston, 1976-77; vis. assoc. prof. Harvard Bus. Sch., Boston, 1982-84; prof. fin. Boston U., 1984-89, vis. prof. MIT, 1987-88; prof. fin. Boston Coll., 1989—. Editor, Fin. Mgmt. jour., 1984-87. Contbr. articles to fin. jours. Mem. Am. Fin. Assn., Fin. Mgmt. Assn., Am. Econ. Assn., Phi Beta Kappa. Office: Boston Coll Wallace E Carroll Sch Mgmt Chestnut Hill MA 02167

TAGLIABUE, PAUL JOHN, lawyer, professional football league commissioner; b. Jersey City, Nov. 24, 1940; s. Charles and Mary T.; m. Chandler M. Minter, Aug. 28, 1965; children: Drew, Emily. BA, Georgetown U., 1962; JD, NYU, 1965. Bar: NJ 1965, D.C. 1969. Atty. to sec. def. Dept. Def., Washington, 1966-69; assoc. Covington & Burling, Washington, 1969-74, ptnr., 1969-89; commissioner NFL, N.Y.C., 1989—. Contbr. articles to profl. jours. Mem. ABA (chmn. sports and entertainment industry com. antitrust section 1986—), D.C. Bar Assn. Office: NFL Commr's Office 410 Park Ave New York NY 10022-4407 also: Covington & Burling 1201 Pennsylvania Ave NW PO Box 7566 Washington DC 20044*

TAGLIAFERRI, LEE GENE, investment banker; b. Mahanoy City, Pa., Aug. 14, 1931; s. Charles and Adele (Cirilli) T.; B.S., U. Pa., 1957; M.B.A., U. Chgo., 1958; m. Maryellen Stanton, Apr. 29, 1962; children—Mark, John, Maryann. Div. comptroller Campbell Soup Co., Camden, N.J., 1958-60; securities analyst Merrill, Lynch, Pierce, Fenner & Smith, Inc., N.Y.C., 1960-62; asst. v.p. U.S. Trust Co. of N.Y., 1962-71; v.p. corporate finance div. Laidlaw & Co., Inc., N.Y.C., 1972-73; pres. Everest Corp., N.Y.C., 1973—; dir. Fairfield Communities Inc., UEC, Inc., LRA, Inc., Industrialized Bldg. Systems, Inc. Past pres. West Windsor Community Assn. Trustee Schuyler Hall, Columbia, Madison Sq. Boys Club. Served with AUS, 1953-55. K.C. Clubs: University of Pa., Princeton (N.Y.C.). Home: 77 Lillie St Princeton Junction NJ 08550-1307 Office: 1 Penn Plz New York NY 10119-0118

TAGLIERI, RICHARD JAMES, computer operator; b. Bklyn., Nov. 18, 1939; s. Joseph Albert and Mary Agnes (Leach) T.; m. Beverly Ann Grutadauria, June 24, 1967 (div. Aug. 1978); 1 child, Nicole; m. Mary Arma Smith, Apr. 21, 1984. AA in Elec. Engring., Wilmington Coll., 1959; BA in Langs., Bklyn. Coll., 1970; MA in Italian, Middlebury (Vt.) Coll., 1972; postgrad. in math, Italian, Nazareth Coll., Rochester, N.Y., 1975. Cert. tchr., math, Italian. Computer program compiler NIH, Bethesda, Md., 1963-65; passport adjudicator State Dept., Washington, 1965-68; tchr., tutor various schs., 1974-88; bilingual income maintenance examiner Monroe County Dept. Social Svcs., Rochester, N.Y., 1988-89; computer operator Monroe County Dental Social Svcs., Rochester, N.Y., 1989—; freelance translator/interpreter, 1972—. Editor, pub.: (newsletter) Rochester Guitar Bull.; translator (county publ.) Sr. Citizens Guide; interpreter People to People cruise. With USN, 1960-63. Mem. Am. Translator's Assn., Alliance Francaise, Am. Philatelic Soc. (translator 1980—).

TAGUE, BARRY ELWERT, securities trader; b. Phila., June 17, 1938; s. Edward James, Jr. and Eleanor May (Elwert) T.; m. Dorothy Elizabeth Beausang, May 14, 1960; children: Kimberly, Nancy, Barry Elwert, Edward James. Student, Bucknell U., 1956-59. Ptnr. E.J. Tague & Co., Phila., 1959-68, Barry E. Tague & Co., Phila., 1968—; exec. v.p., vice chmn. Raymond, James & Assocs., Inc., Phila., 1968-76; pres., dir. Tague Securities Corp., Phila., 1976—; chmn. bd. The Bryn Mawr Corp., 1977-88; pres., dir. The Bryn Mawr Group, 1977-88, BancAm. Options, Inc., 1983-88; mem. several investment partnerships and industry coms.; bd. govs. Phila. Stock Exch., 1967-77, 90—, vice chmn. bd., 1973-74, chmn. bd., 1974-76, 90-92, trustee, 1973-92, Options Clearing Corp., Chgo. Active Little League Baseball, 1961-65, 76-88, pres., 1978-86; pres. Ithan Sch. PTA, 1971-72, Radnor Twp. Sch. Authority, 1980—. With USMCR, 1959-65. Mem. Securities Industry Assn. (nat. market com.), Kappa Sigma. Republican. Episcopalian. Clubs: Waynesborough Country (Paoli, Pa.). Office: Tague Securities Corp 1900 Market St Ste 510 Philadelphia PA 19103-3712

TAIKEFF, STANLEY, playwright; b. Bklyn., Apr. 27, 1940; s. Irving and Lulu (Rosenberg) T.; m. Lenore Noval, Aug. 4, 1968. BA, CUNY, 1963, MA, 1971. playwright Joseph Jefferson Theatre Co., N.Y.C., 1977-79. Producer plays including Ah, Eurydice, 1978, Dolorosa Sanchez, 1984, Civilization and Its Malcontents, 1989. Recipient Best Play award Double Image Theatre, Samuel French, Inc., N.Y.C., 1989; fellow N.J. State Coun. on the Arts, 1989-90, Creative ARts Pub. Svc. awardee, 1981, Shubert Found., 1971; grantee John Golden award, N.Y., 1970. Mem. The Dramatists Guild, Inc. (assoc.).

TAITT, EARL PAUL, psychiatrist, army officer; b. L.A., Nov. 6, 1956; s. Earl and Mary (Freitas) T.; m. Puruca Estepa, May 11, 1985; children: Anamaria, Earl. AA, East L.A. Coll., 1976; BS, U. Calif., Irvine, 1978; MD, Northwestern U., Chgo., 1984. Commd. capt. U.S. Army, 1984, advanced through grades to maj., 1991; intern in psychiatry Tripler Army Med. Ctr., Honolulu, 1984-85; resident in psychiatry Eisenhower Army Med. Ctr., Ft. Gordon, Ga., 1985-88; staff psychiatrist Community Mental Health Ctr., Ft. Gordon, Ga., 1988; div. psychiatrist, chief mental health 10th Mountain Div., Ft. Drum, N.Y., 1988-90; staff psychiatrist Community Mental Health Ctr., Ft. Meade, Md., 1990—; chief resident in psychiatry U.S. Army Hosp., Ft. Gordon, Ga., 1988; cons. Army Drug and Alcohol Program, Ft. Drum, 1988-90, Installation Detention Facility, Ft. Meade, 1990—. Mem. San Gabriel (Calif.) Mission Parish Coun., 1975-76; pres. Medicai Soc., L.A., 1976. Mem. Assn. U.S. Army, Order of Green Key. Republican. Roman Catholic. Home: 6070 Granite Knls Columbia MD 21045-4017

TAKACS, MICHAEL JOSEPH, educator; b. N.Y.C., July 28, 1940; s. Michael and Elizabeth Agnes (Scharschmidt) T. AB in Sociology, Fordham U., 1964; MA in Sociology, St. John's U., 1968. Tchr. Bklyn. Prep. Sch., 1964-67, Turtle Hook Sch., Uniondale, N.Y., 1968-73, 74—, Nairobi U., 1971, Colegio San Ignacio, Rio Piedras, P.R. 1973-74; vis. scholar Robert Black Coll., Hong Kong U., 1975, Ramkamhang U., Bangkok, 1975. Vol. community outreach program Our Holy Redeemer Ch., Freeport, N.Y., L.I.. Assn. for AIDS Care, L.I. People with AIDS Coalition; advisor Nat. Jr. Honor Soc. Mem. Nat. Coun. for Social Studies, Mid. States Coun. for Social Studies, L.I. Coun. for Social Studies, N.Y. State Coun. for Social Studies. Roman Catholic. Home: 425 Newbridge Rd East Meadow NY 11554-4122 Office: Turtle Hook Sch Jerusalem Ave Uniondale NY 11553

TAKAHASHI, YASUO, psychiatrist; b. Sydney, Australia, Oct. 8, 1925; came to U.S., 1953; s. Goro and Chiyoko (Takekawa) T.; children: Nancy, Ken, Suzanne, Denise, Joy. Diploma, Shizuoka U., Japan, 1948; MD, Chiba U. Sch. of Medicine, Japan, 1952; postgrad., U. Pa. Diplomate Am. Bd. Psychiatry and Neurology 1960. Chief resident Dept. Psychiatry Med. Coll. of Va., Richmond, 1956-57; sr. psychiatrist Springfield Hosp. Ctr., Sykesville, Md., 1957-63; dir. Bur. Mental Health Prince Georges County Health Dept., Cheverly, Md., 1963-70; med. dir. Team C, Adult Mental Health Clinic Dept. Addictions, Mental Health Svcs., Montgomery County, Md., 1989-91; med. dir. Mental Health Clinic, Kent County, Md., 1991—; pvt. practice psychiatry, 1964-91. Mem. AMA, Am. Psychiat. Assn., Am. Soc. Clin. Hyponosis. Home: 483 Heron Point Chestertown MD 21620-1681

TAKETOMO, YASUHIKO, psychiatrist; b. Tokyo, July 30, 1921; came to U.S. 1950; s. Torao and Yoshi (Fujii) T.; m. Haruko Kishimoto, May 27, 1946; children: Masahiko, Toshihiko. BS, Daiichi Koto-Gakko, Tokyo, 1942; MD, Osaka U., Japan, 1945, PhD, 1949; Cert. in Psychoanalytic Medicine, Columbia U. Coll. Physicians and Surgeons, 1959; MD, SUNY Bd. Regents, 1981. Diplomate Am. Bd. Psychiatry & Neurology, Am. Acad. Psychoanalysis; lic. Japanese govt., 1945, N.Y., 1974, Conn., 1988. Rsch. fellow, asst. in biochemistry and neuropsychiatry Osaka U., 1945-50; resident in psychiatry Albany (N.Y.) Med. Coll., 1950-51, Worcester (Mass.) State Hosp., 1951-52; resident rsch. psychiatrist, sr. scientist rsch. facility Rockland State Hosp., Orangeburg, N.Y., 1952-64; rsch. asst., rsch. assoc. Columbia U. Coll. Physicians and Surgeons, N.Y.C., 1962-64; career scientist N.Y.C. Rsch. Coun. St. Vincent's Hosp. and N.Y. Med. Coll., N.Y.C., 1964-69; unit chief, assoc. dir. residency program Bronx Psychiat. Ctr., 1970-88; asst. prof./clin. prof. psychiatry Albert Einstein Coll. Medicine, 1970—; attending physician Montefiore Med. Ctr./The Jack D. Weiler Hosp., Bronx, 1976—, St. Vincent's Hosp./Med. Ctr. of N.Y., Westchester Facility, 1989—, The Regent Hosp., 1991; head transcultural psychaitry component Research Fellowship Prog., Dept. Psychiatry, Albert Einstein Coll. Medicine, 1988—. Contbg. author: The World Biennial of Psychiatry and Psychotherapy, 1970, Psychoanalysis and the Nuclear Threat: Clinical and Theoretical Studies, 1988; contbr. articles to profl. jours. Fellow Am. Psychiat. Assn., Am. Acad. Psychoanalysis (trustee 1990—); mem. Am. Psychoanalytic Assn., Assn. for Psychoanalytic Medicine, Internat. Psychoanalytic Assn., Japan Psycho-Analytic Assn. Democrat. Home: 1198 Post Rd Scarsdale NY 10583 Office: 950 Park Ave New York NY 10028

TAKIGUCHI, GENJI (GENE), medical equipment manufacturers executive; b. Osaka, Japan, Nov. 11, 1928; came to U.S., 1952; s. Noriyuki and Sode (Mikami) T.; m. Sumiko Sudo, June 21, 1961; children: Toshiyuki John, Kazuyuki Edward, Tomoyuki Robert. BS, Columbia U., 1956. Asst. engr. Hitachi, Ltd., N.Y.C., 1959-61; mgr. Hitachi, Ltd., San Francisco, 1962-72; dept. mgr. licensing dept. Hitachi, Ltd., Tokyo, 1973, dept. mgr. elevator sales dept., 1974-79; pres. Hitachi (Can.) Ltd., Toronto, Ont., 1980-83; gen. mgr. internat. div. Hitachi Med. Corp., Tokyo, 1984-87; pres. Hitachi Med. Corp. Am., Tarrytown, N.Y., 1988—; v.p., treas., pres. ultrasound div. Hitachi Med. Systems Am., Hudson, Ohio, 1989—; v.p., treas., sec. CT Scanner Mfg. Co., Concord, Mass., 1989—. Mem. Phi Lambda Epsilon. Office: Hitach Med Corp Am 50 Prospect Ave Tarrytown NY 10591

TAKMAN, BERTIL HERBERT, medicinal chemist, consultant; b. Stockholm, Aug. 15, 1921; came to U.S., 1958; s. Erling J. Takman and Dagmar (Fogelberg) von Schwerin; m. Margaretha S. Rabe, Apr. 30, 1944; children: Sven B., Lars E., Kerstin M., Elisabeth M., Ann M. BA, U. Stockholm, 1957, PhD, 1963. Instr. organic chemistry U. Stockholm, 1946-49, 54-58; mgr. sales, prodn. Cosmetics Inc., Stockholm, 1950-52; cons. Sabbatsberg Hosp., Stockholm, 1953; sr. scientist, head chem. sect. Astra Pharm. Products, Worcester, Framingham, Mass., 1958-75, internal cons., 1976-81; internal cons. Astra Pain Control, A.B., Södertälje, Sweden, 1982-91; pvt. practice cons. Boston, 1991—; rsch. assoc. Div. Endocrinol. and Metabolic Rsch., St. Vincent Hosp., Worcester, 1964-67; adj. prof. medicinal chmistry N.E. U., Boston, 1973-83; clin. instr. in anesthesia, rsch. assoc. pharmacology Harvard U. Sch. Medicine & Brigham Women's Hosp., Boston, 1982-85. Contbr. articles to profl. jours., author monographic chpts. in textbooks and handbooks of med. chemistry and pharmacology; patentee local anesthetics. Fellow Am. Inst. Chemists; mem. AAAS, Am. Chem. Soc., Am. Numismatic Soc., N.Y. Acad. Sci. Home and Office: 220 Boylston St Boston MA 02116-3916

TAKOOSHIAN, HAROLD, social psychology educator; b. N.Y.C., Nov. 21, 1949; s. Alfred C. and Dorothy H. T. BA, CCNY, 1971; PhD in Social Psychology, CUNY, 1979. Lic. psychologist, N.Y. Adj. faculty dept. psychology Bklyn. Coll., 1973-78; assoc. prof. div. social scis. Fordham U., N.Y.C., 1978—; vis. prof. U. Talca, Chile, 1983, U. Atacama, Copiapo, Chile, 1984, 85; Fulbright scholar USSR, 1987-88; cons. projects for indsl. and govtl. orgn., 1979—. Editor: Bull and Directory Armenian Behavioral Scientists, 1988—; Feminism Survey, 1990; Short-Form Scale of Attitudes toward Terrorism (with W.M. Verdi), 1989; contbr. articles to profl. jours. Founder Armenian Ch. Immigrant Counseling Svc., N.Y.C., 1974; nat. bd. dirs. Alliance Guardian Angels, 1982—; mentor Westinghouse Sci. Competition Student Researchers, 1986—. Recipient Apple Polisher award WOR-TV, N.Y.C., 1981, Denmark Faculty Adv. award Psi Chi, 1988, Kurt Lewin award N.Y. State Psychol. Assn., 1990. Fellow Am. Psychol. Assn.; mem. Soc. Psychol. Study Social Issues (chair N.Y.C. regional group PSSSI, 1991—), Am. Sociol. Assn., Soc. Indsl.-Orgnl. Psychology, Am. Psychology-Law Soc., Am. Evaluation Assn. (charter). Office: Div Social Sci Fordham Univ New York NY 10023

TAKYI, ISAAC KWAME, transportation analyst, researcher; b. Kumasi, Ashanti, Ghana; s. Kwame and Akua (Konadu) T.; m. Patience Adu, Aug. 10, 1983; children: Afua, Adwoa. BS summa cum laude, U. Sci. and Tech., Kumasi, 1979; M in City Planning, U. Pa., 1985, AM, 1991, PhD in City Planning, 1991. Teaching asst. Univ. Sci. and Tech., Kumasi, 1979-80; lectr., program dir. Auchi (Nigeria) Poly., 1981-84; rsch. coord. Translab, U. Pa., Phila., 1985-89; chief transp. planner Delaware County Planning Commn., Media, Pa., 1989-92; facilities analyst N.J. Transit Hqs., Newark, 1992—; cons., tech. svc. mgr. Davis and Co., Phila., 1987—; post-doctoral teaching fellow Dept. City Planning, U. Pa., 1992—; bd. dirs. Takach Systematics Ltd.; mem. regional tech. adv. com. transp., Phila., 1989—. Contbr. articles to tech. jours. Vol. Delaware County Paratransit Assn., 1989-92. Mem. Am. Planning Assn., Inst. Transp. Engrs., NRC (transp. rsch. bd.), Univ. Sci. and Tech. Alumni Assn. (pres. N.Am. chpt. 1989—). Office: Project Devel Planning NJ Transit Hqs 1 Penn Plaza E Newark NJ 07105

TALAMO, BARBARA LISANN, neuroscience educator; b. Washington, May 30, 1939; d. Isaac and Tessie (Silverman) Lisann; m. Richard C. Talamo, June 22, 1958 (dec. 1982); children: Jonathan H., David A., Anna B.; m. John S. Kauer, Feb. 2, 1985. AB, Radcliffe Coll., 1960; PhD, Harvard U., 1972. Postdoctoral fellow Med. Sch. Harvard U., Boston, 1972-74; asst. prof. Sch. Medicine Johns Hopkins U., Balt., 1974-80; asst. prof. Sch. Medicine Tufts U., Boston, 1980-83, assoc. prof., 1983—, dir. grad. program in neuroscis., 1983—; ad hoc reviewer Jour. Neurosci., Am. Jour. Physiology, 1980—; mem. various study sects. NIH, Bethesda, Md., 1979-83; ad hoc mem. study sects. NIH and NSF, Washington, 1983—. Grantee NIH, 1976—, NSF; Grass Found. fellow, 1973. Mem. Soc. for Neurosci., Am. Soc. Neurochemistry, Internat. Soc. Neurochemistry, Am. Soc. Chem. Senses. Office: Tufts U Sch Medicine 136 Harrison Ave Boston MA 02111-1800

TALAN, JAMIE LYNN, science journalist; b. N.Y.C, June 25, 1956; d. Jack Robert Talan and Suzanne Lois (Robinson) Habib; m. Richard Carl Firstman, Mar. 25, 1990; children: Amanda, Allison, Jordan. BA in Psychology, SUNY, Stony Brook, 1978. Freelance sci. writer, 1978-85; sci. reporter Newsday, Melville, N.Y., 1985—. Recipient Harvey Hypertension award Am. Med. Writers Assn., 1986, Journalism award Epilepsy Found., 1986, APA, 1988, Nat. Alliance for Mentally Ill, 1990. Mem. Mat. Assn. Sci. Writers. Office: Newsday 235 Pinelawn Rd Melville NY 11747

TALBOT, BERNARD, government medical research facility official, physician; b. N.Y.C., Oct. 6, 1937; s. Harry and Gertrude (Salkin) T.; m. Ane Katrine Larsen, June 2, 1963; children: Akia, Kamilla. B.A., Columbia U., 1958, M.D., 1962; Ph.D, MIT, 1967. NIH postdoctoral fellow MIT, 1962-69; NSF postdoctoral fellow U. Rome, 1969-70; commd. USPHS, 1975—, advanced through grades to med. dir.; med. officer Nat. Cancer Inst., Bethesda, Md., 1971-75; spl. asst. intramural affairs NIH, Bethesda, 1975-78; spl. asst. to dir. NIH, 1978-81; dep. dir. Nat. Inst. Allergy and Infectious Diseases, Bethesda, 1981-87, med. officer nat. ctr. for rsch. resources, 1987—. Contbr. articles on protein chemistry to profl. jours., chpts. on recombinant DNA guidelines to books. Recipient Commendation medal USPHS, 1977, Meritorious Service medal, 1984. Mem. Phi Beta Kappa. Office: NIH 9000 Rockville Pike Bethesda MD 20892-0001

TALBOT, FRANK HAMILTON, museum director, marine researcher; b. Pietermaritzburg, Natal, Republic of South Africa, Jan. 3, 1930; came to U.S., 1982; s. Ralph West and Willemina (Altmann) T.; m. Mabel Suzette Logeman, July 20, 1953; children: Helen Campbell, Richard Bill, Jonathan Charles, Neil Hamilton. BSc, U. Witwatersrand, South Africa, 1949; MSc, U. Cape Town, South Africa, 1951, PhD, 1959. Fisheries rsch. scientist Brit. Colonial Svc., Zanzibar, 1954-57; marine biologist South African Mus., Cape Town, 1958-59, asst. dir., 1960-63; curator fishes Australian Mus., Sydney, 1964-65, dir., 1965-74; prof. environ. studies MacQuarie U., Sydney, Australia, 1975-81; exec. dir. Calif. Acad. Scis., San Francisco, 1982-88; dir. Nat. Mus. Natural History, Smithsonian Inst., Washington, 1989—. Contbr. articles to sci. jours. Fellow AAAS, Calif. Acad. Sci., Royal Zool. Soc. (Australia); mem. Mus. Assn. Australia (pres. 1973-74), Australian Marine Scis. Assn. (pres. 1971-72), Explorers Club. Home: 2737 Devonshire Pl NW Apt 103 Washington DC 20008-3453 Office: Nat Mus Natural History Smithsonian Instn Washington DC 20560

TALBOT, JONATHAN, artist; b. N.Y.C., Nov. 14, 1939; s. Irwin and Helen (Talbot) Panken; m. Marsha Goldstein, Aug. 2, 1970; children: Loren, Garret. Student, The New Sch. for Social Rsch., N.Y.C., Brandeis U., 1958-59, San Francisco Acad. Art, 1970-71, Kean Coll., 1972. Artist various mediums (paintings, collages, etchings) Warwick, N.Y.; curator Conn. Collage, Hartford, 1989. Exhibited in shows at Bayly Art Mus. U. Va., N.Y. Acad. Art, Ulrich Mus. Art, Wichita, Kans., 1990, Palmer Mus. Pa. State U., 1988, U.S. Art in Embassies program, Manila, 1988, Squibb Gallery, Princeton, N.J., 1988, U. Hawaii, Hilo, 1988, Silvermine Gallery/Metro Ctr., Stamford, Conn., 1988, Brockton (Mass.) Art Mus., 1988, U. Wis., Kenosha, 1988, Hudson River Mus., Yonkers, N.Y., 1987, Ark. Art Ctr., Little Rock, 1986, Silvermine Ctr., New Canaan, Conn., 1983 (C.R. Gibson award 1983), NYU, 1983, National Arts Club, N.Y.C. (Audubon Artists award 1983), Brainerd Art Gallery State Univ. Coll. Arts and Sci., Potsdam, N.Y., 1983, Nat. Acad. Design, N.Y.C., 1982 (Ranger Fund award 1982), Trenton (N.J.) State Coll., 1982, De Cordova Mus., 1982, Atlanta Festival of the Arts, 1977 (award), Mus. Modern Art, N.Y.C., 1976; one-man shows include: Gimpel/Weitzenhoffer Gallery, N.Y.C., 1986, 87, 90, 92, Everhart Mus., Scranton, Pa., 1984, Collectors Gallery Columbus (Ohio) Mus. Art, 1984, Byer Mus. Arts, Evanston, Ill., 1984; also included in Smithsonian Instn. Traveling Exhbn. Svc., 1985-87; paintings, collages and etchings displayed in Smith Coll. Mus., Chase Manhattan Bank, Fairleigh Dickinson U., Drew U., others. Bd. mgrs. The Oakwood Sch., Poughkeepsie, 1990—; mem. Warwick (N.Y.) Dem. com. Mem. Soc. Friends. Home and Studio: 7 Amity Rd Warwick NY 10990

TALBOT, JOSEPH CHANEL, business executive; b. Hempstead, L.I., May 3, 1949; s. Joseph Appolinaine Chanel and Claudia Marie (LeBlanc) T.; m. Linda Marie Riberdy, July 9, 1972 (div. May 1983); m. Gail Jeanette Borrelli, Nov. 16, 1985; children: Jennifer Ann, Lori Lynn, Richard Borrelli. Grad. high sch., Dover, N.H. Asst. mgr. McDonald's, Salem, N.H., 1969-70; clk. Shaw's Supermarkets, Derry, N.H., 1970-72; trans. specialist Peter Fisher Inc., Lawrence, Mass., 1972-78; sales rep. Met. Ins. Co., Woburn, Mass., 1978-83, Arons Arcadia Ins. Agy., Peabody, Mass., 1983-88; pres. J. Chanel Assocs., Lawrence, 1988—, Courtesy Expressions, North Andover, Mass., 1990—. Pres. Smokers' Rights, Lawrence, Mass., 1991. Mem. Lions (sec. Lawrence breakfast 1984-85, pres. 1985-90). Roman Catholic. Home: 136 Hancock St Lawrence MA 01841-5028 Office: Courtesy Expressions Inc 707 Turnpike St North Andover MA 01845-6120

TALBOT, PHILLIPS, Asian affairs specialist; b. Pitts., June 7, 1915; s. Kenneth Hammet and Gertrude (Phillips) T.; m. Mildred Aleen Fisher, Aug. 18, 1943; children: Susan Talbot Jacox, Nancy, Bruce Kenneth. BA, U. Ill., 1936, BS in Journalism, 1936; student, London Sch. Oriental Studies, 1938-39, Aligarh Muslim U., India, 1939-40; Ph.D., U. Chgo., 1954; LL.D. (hon.), Mills Coll., 1963. Reporter, Chgo. Daily News, 1936-38; corr. Chgo. Daily News, India and Pakistan, 1946-48, 49-50; assoc. Inst. Current World Affairs, Eng. and India, 1938-41; part-time Inst. Current World Affairs, 1946-51; instr. U. Chgo., 1948-50; inst. Columbia U., N.Y.C., 1951; exec. dir. Am. Univs. Field Staff, 1951-61; asst. sec. Near Eastern and S. Asian affairs Dept. State, 1961-65; U.S. ambassador to Greece, 1965-69; pres. Asia Soc., N.Y.C., 1970-81; emeritus Asia Soc., 1981—; Phi Beta Kappa vis. scholar, 1973-74. Author: (with S.L. Poplai) India and America, 1958, India in the 1980s, 1983; editor: South Asia in the World Today, 1950. Trustee East Asian History of Sci., Inc., China Inst. in Am., U.S.-Japan Found.; elder Presbyn Ch. 2nd lt. cav. Officers Res. Corps., 1936; 1st lt. Ill. N.G., 1937-38; lt. comdr. USNR, 1941-46. Mem. Am. Acad. Diplomacy, Assn. Asian Studies, Coun. Fgn. Relations, Century Assn., Cosmos Club. Presbyterian (elder). Address: 200 E 66th St New York NY 10021

TALIAFERRO, JAMES HUBERT, JR., communications educator; b. Chattanooga, Feb. 21, 1924; s. James Hubert and Ida Estelle (Gilbert) T. Student, Davidson Coll., 1942-43; BS, U. Denver, 1948; MS, Columbia U., 1949; PhD, NYU, 1976. Advt. exec. McCann-Erickson Inc., N.Y.C., 1951-53, Grey Advt. Agy., N.Y.C., 1953-55, Kenyon & Eckhardt, Inc., N.Y.C., 1955-61, Sullivan Stauffer Colwell & Bayles, N.Y.C., 1961-68; instr. speech Bklyn. Coll., CUNY, N.Y.C., 1968-75, asst. prof., 1975-82, dep. chmn. dept. speech, 1980-82; prof. dept. communications Rutgers U., New Brunswick, N.J., 1982—; ptnr. Lifestory, Inc., 1985—; vis. prof. Fashion Inst. Tech., N.Y.C., 1987—; ptnr. Taliaferro/Grau & Assocs., Ltd.; cons. in field; assoc. producer New Am. Playwright Series, 1970; assoc. dir. Reading for Blind, Bklyn. Coll., 1976—; drama critic Housatonic Valley Pub. Co. newspapers, 1973-85. Author plays: Inside Out, 1963; Tour de Force, 1963; also articles, papers. Chmn., Found. for Mus. of Am. Theatre, 1974-80; trustee Rahway Landmarks Assn. (N.J.), 1983-85; bd. dirs. 320 E 57th St. Corp., 1982-86. Served with U.S. Army, 1943-45. Mem. Am. Soc. Theatre Rsch., Internat. Communication Assn., Speech Communication Assn., Eastern Communication Assn., Huguenot Soc. Am., SAR. Democrat. Episcopalian. Home: RR 1 Box 440 Rising Fawn GA 30738-9731 Office: Rutgers U Dept Comm Sch Comm Info Libr Sci New Brunswick NJ 08903

TALINGDAN, ARSENIO PREZA, health science administrator; b. Dolores, Abra, The Philippines, Mar. 30, 1930; came to U.S., 1973; s. Mariano T. and Candida (Tordil) Preza; m. Josefa Fernandez Biason. Apr. 21, 1954; children: Melda, Arsenio Jr., Jocelyn Almerick, Mario, Abe. AA, U. Philippines, 1951, AB, MPA, 1955; MAPA, The Am. U., 1956; BS, La Salle Extention U., Chgo., 1977; MBA, Century U., 1983, PhD, 1985. Cert. nursing home adminstr., life, health and securities underwriter. Job analyst, orgn. analyst, budget examiner Kroeger & Assocs. Project, Philippine Budget Commn., Manila, 1954-55; scholar, tech. asst., participant USA-ICA-NEC Program, 1955-56; supr. mgmt. analyst Philippine Budget Commn., Manila, 1957-59; asst. budget dir., IBM coordinator U. Philippines, Quezon City, 1959-65, mgmt. specialist, chief of studies, 1969-70; asst. v.p. for budget and mgmt. Sarmiento Enterprises, Inc., Makati, Rizal, Philippines, 1965-69; adminstr. Philippine Gen. Hosp., Manila, 1970-73; budget and facilities mgr. Hunter Coll., CUNY, N.Y.C., 1973-76; acctg. systems editor J.C. Penney Co., N.Y.C., 1977; regional med. care adminstr. N.Y. State Dept. Health, Office Health Systems Mgmt., N.Y.C., 1977-78, assoc. med. care adminstr., 1978—; asst. prof., chmn. social scis. dept. U.P. Coll., Manila, 1969-73; 1st Philippine tech. assistance fellow on orgn. and mgmt. U.S. Agy. for Internat. Devel., Washington, 1955-56; professorial lectr. U. Philippines, Manila, 1960-69. Co-author: Accounting, Auditing and Internal Auditing, 1964; author: Public Administration and Management, 1966, Management and Supervision, 1966, Work Simlification Handbook, 1957 and others; contbr. articles to profl. jours. Pres. Abra Varsitarians, Quezon City, 1949-53; founder, Dolores Young Men and Women's Assn., Manila, Abra, 1949-71; founder, pres. Philippine Execs. and Profls. Golf Assn., Quezon City, 1965-69, U. of the Philippines Alumni Assn. in Am., N.Y., N.J., 1980— and others. Major Res. Officer, Philippine Army, 1960-73. Recipient Hall of Nations award Am. U., 1956, Pub. Health Sci. award Del. Valley Assn. Philippines, 1980, Profl. award in Pub. Adminstrn. U. Philippines Alumni Assn. Am., 1991. Mem. Pub. Employees Fedn. Republican.

TALLENT, MARC ANDREW, clinical psychologist; b. Newport News, Va., Dec. 3, 1954; s. Norman and Shirley Dorothy (Rudman) T. BA, Columbia U., 1978; MA, Adelphi U., 1980, PhD, 1983. Lic. psychologist, N.Y. Pvt. practice N.Y.C., 1985—; psychoanalytic psychotherapist Ctr. for Modern Psychoanalytic Studies, N.Y.C., 1988—; supervising psychologist div. spl. edn. Bd. Edn. of N.Y.C., 1991—; cons. Big Bros./Big Sisters N.Y.C., 1988—, Task Force on AIDS N.Y. State Psychol. Assn., N.Y.C., 1989—. Editor: Modern Psychoanalysis, 1986—. Mem. APA, Nat. Assn. for Advancement of Psychoanalysis, N.Y. State Psychological Assn., Phi Beta Kappa. Office: Profl Ste B 51 5th Ave New York NY 10003-4320

TALLEY, DAN R., art gallery administrator; b. Hogansville, Ga., Jan. 6, 1951; s. Amos Grady and Mary (Baldwin) T. BFA, Atlanta Coll. Art, 1973; MFA, U. Hartford, 1976. Editor Art Papers, Atlanta, 1980-82; gallery dir. Atlanta Art Workers Coalition, 1977-80, Nexus Contemporary Art Ctr., Atlanta, 1987-89, Forum Gallery, Jamestown, N.Y., 1989—. Editor Arts Wire News, Seattle, 1990—; editor exhbn. catalogs. Mem. Coll. Art Assn. Democrat. Office: Forum Gallery 525 Falconer St Jamestown NY 14701-1999

TALLEY, EUGENE ALTON, retired chemist; b. Glen Allen, Va., June 5, 1911; s. James Crump and Minnie Lisette (Saxby) T.; m. Florence Elise Bowe, June 24, 1944; children: George Nelson, Carol Lynn. BS in Chemistry, Coll. William and Mary, 1936; MS, U. Richmond, 1938; PhD, Ohio State U., 1942. Asst. chemist carbohydrate div. ea. regional rsch. lab. USDA, Phila., 1942-44, sr. chemist plant products lab., 1953-80, emeritus chemist engring. lab., 1980-85; chemist agrl. and indsl. chemistry ERRL, Phila., 1944-53. Contbr. articles to profl. jours.; patentee in field. Mem. Am. Chem. Soc., Potato Assn. Am., Phi Beta Kappa, Phi Kappa Phi, Sigma Pi Sigma. Presbyterian. Home: 3100 Quarry Ln Lafayette Hill PA 19444-2006

TALLINI, FIORY ANTHONY, business systems analyst; b. Jamaica, N.Y., Sept. 23, 1962; s. Fiory Anthony and Barbara Ann (Picerno) T. BS, N.Y. Inst. Tech., 1986, MS in Computer Sci., 1992. Support analyst Blackbaud Microsystems, Huntington, N.Y., 1986-87; programmer analyst United Way, N.Y.C., 1987-88; bus. system analyst William Penn Life Ins., Garden City, N.Y., 1988-91; computer cons. Huntington Station, N.Y., 1991—. Republican. Roman Catholic. Home: 263 Cook St Huntington Station NY 11746-3525

TALWAR, DEVKI NANDAN, education educator; b. Gaziabad, India, Apr. 6, 1949; came to U.S., 1980; s. Jagdish M. and Shakuntla T.; married; children: Priyanka, Mayank. BS, Agra U., India, 1968, MS, 1970; PhD, Allahabad U., India, 1976. Prof. Tex. A&M U., Galveston, 1982-87, Indiana U. of Pennsylvania, Indiana, Pa., 1987—; vis. prof. U. Houston, 1980-82; vis.

scientist French Atomic Energy Commn., France, 1977-79. Recipient rsch. grant Rsch. Corp., 1989, NSF, 1990. Mem. Am. Phys. Soc., Material Rsch. Soc. Home: 977 Barclay Rd Indiana PA 15701-9776 Office: Weyandt Hall Indiana Univ of Pa Indiana PA 15705

TAMARELLI, ALAN WAYNE, chemical company executive; b. Wilkinsburg, Pa., Aug. 13, 1941; s. John Adam Tammarelli and Florence Eleanor (Heacock) T.; m. Carol Ann Crawford, Aug. 3, 1963; children: Robin Carol, Alan Wayne. BS, Carnegie Mellon U., 1963, MS, 1965, PhD, 1966; MBA, NYU, 1972. Engr. Exxon Corp., Linden, N.J., 1966, project leader, 1968-70; corp. planner Engelhard Minerals & Chem. Corp., Newark, 1970-71, asst. to exec. v.p., 1971-74, gen. mgr., 1974-77, v.p., 1977-79, group v.p., 1979-81; sr. v.p. Engelhard Corp., Iselin, N.J., 1981-83; chmn., chief exec. officer Dock Resins Corp, Linden, NJ, 1983—; mem. Gov.'s Econ. Task Force. Mem. exec. com. nat. adv. coun. for environ. policy and tech. U.S. Dept. Environment Protection, Gov's Econ. Task Force, N.J. Capt. U.S. Army, 1966-68. NSF fellow, 1963-66. Mem. Synthetic Organic Chems. Mfrs. Assn. (vice chmn., bd. govs.), Am. Chem. Soc., N.Y. Soc. Coatings Tech. (bd. dirs.), N.Y. Paint and Coatings Assn. (treas., bd. dirs.), Chem. Industry Coun. (chmn., bd. dir., exec. com.), N.J. Energy Rsch. Inst. (founding trustee), Am. Mgmt. Assn., N.Y. Acad. Scis., Scabbard and Blade, Rotary (pres. Linden club), Linden Indsl. Assn. (pres.), Sigma Xi, Tau Beta Pi, Phi Kappa Phi, Omicron Delta Kappa. Home: 49 Wexford Way Basking Ridge NJ 07920-2432 Office: Dock Resins Corp 1512 W Elizabeth Ave Linden NJ 07036-6323

TAMASI, RAYMOND VALENTINO, health care facility administrator; b. Princeton, N.J., Mar. 7, 1942; s. Domenico and Pearl Irene (Toto) T.; m. Barbara Anne Scheutz, Sept. 21, 1968; children: David Christopher, Christina Lynn. BA in Econs., Rutgers U., 1963; MEd in Counseling, Health Care Adminstrn, Cambridge (Mass.) Coll., 1982. Lic. cert. social worker, Mass. Rsch. exec. Market Dynamics, Inc., Princeton, N.J., 1963-69; sr. projects mgr. Chesebrough Ponds, Inc., N.Y.C., 1969-70; dir. Falmouth (Mass.) Ecumenical Program for Youth, 1971-73; counselor Cape Cod Alcoholism Unit, Pocasset, Mass., 1973-76, asst. dir., 1976-80; dir. Cape Cod Alcoholism Unit/Gosnold on Cape Cod, Falmouth, 1980-88, v.p., 1988—, pres., CEO, 1992—, also bd. dirs.; instr. Cape Cod C.C., Barnstable, Mass., 1982—, Cons. Advocates for Human Potential, Sudbury, Mass., 1990—. Originator, broadcaster weekly radio svc. Looking at You and Alcohol, 1980-85. Mem. substance abuse com. Cape Cod Baseball League, Hyannis, Mass., 1986; chmn. Human Svcs. Com., Dennis, Mass., 1989—; mem. Dennis-Yarmouth Substance Abuse Commn., 1989—; mem. Drug Free Campus Task Force, Hyannis, 1992. Mem. Mass. Assn. Detox Dirs. (pres. 1981), Samaritans of Cape Cod (v.p. 1984-86), Employee Assistance Profls. Assn., Cert. Alcoholism Counselors Assn. Home: 2 Farm Hill Rd Dennis MA 02638 Office: Gosnold on Cape Cod 200 Ter Heun Dr Falmouth MA 02540

TAMIR, THEODOR, electrophysics researcher, educator; b. Bucharest, Roumania, Sept. 17, 1927; came to U.S., 1958, naturalized, 1968; s. Martin and Helena (Hart) Berman; m. Hadassah Cohen, Oct. 5, 1949; children: Jonathan, Yael. B.S. Technion, Israel Inst. Tech., 1953, Dipl. Ingenieur, 1954, M.S., 1958; Ph.D., Poly. Inst. Bklyn., 1962. Instr. Technion Israel Inst. Tech., Haifa, 1956-58; research staff Poly. Inst. N.Y., 1958-62, mem. faculty, 1962—, prof. electrophysics, 1969-92, Univ. prof., 1992—, head dept. elec. engring., 1974-79; sci. and engring. cons. to indsl. and govtl. labs. Editor, author: Integrated Optics, 1975 (transl. into Russian and Chinese), Guided-Wave Optoelectronics, 1988; co-editor: Springer Series in Optical Sciences, 1979—; contbr. articles to profl. jours., chpts. to books. Served with Israeli Army, 1947-49. Awarded Instn. Premium, 1964, Electronics Premium, 1967, Instn. Elec. Engrs., London; citation for disting. research Polytechnic chpt. Sigma Xi, 1978. Fellow IEEE, Instn. Elec. Engrs. (London), Optical Soc. Am.; mem. Internat. Union Radio Sci., Sigma Xi. Home: 981 E Lawn Dr Teaneck NJ 07666-6604 Office: 333 Jay St Brooklyn NY 11201-2990

TAMIRAN, DAVID, publisher; b. July 27, 1951. BS in Bus., San Diego State U., 1977; postgrad., Western Coll. of Law, L.A., 1977. Copy writer/designer Internat. Creative Pubs., L.A., 1979-84; pres. Canine League Pubs., N.Y.C., 1984—. Author: Dogs Are Human Too!, 1991; pub. posters and postcards, 1985. Recipient T-shirt Design awards Impressions Mag., 1975, 76. Mem. Nat. Writers Club, Soc. Children's Book Writers, Pubs. Mktg. Assn., Com. sml. Mag. Editors and Pubs. Office: Canine Human Rights League 545 8th Ave Ste 401 New York NY 10018-4307

TAMISO, ROBERT M., executive, consultant; b. Hartford, Conn., Aug. 4, 1965; s. Harry Anthony and Rosemarie (Cappello) T. AA, DeVry Inst. of Technol., Columbus, Ohio, 1985; postgrad., Cen. Conn. State U., 1985—. Faculty assoc. DeVry Inst. of Technol., Columbus, Ohio, 1984-85; electronic technician Status Games, Newington, Conn., 1985; CAD/CAM systems technician Gerber Sci. Instruments, South Windsor, Conn., 1985-86; elec. mech. technician Windsor Mfg., Windsor, Conn., 1986-88; electronics instr. Data Inst. Bus. Sch., East Hartford, Conn., 1988-91; cons., pres. Electronics Tng. Cons. Group, East Hartford, Conn., 1991—; instr. electronics Tech. Careers Inst., Windsor, 1992—. Author: Electronics/Computer Repair Course, 1989. Mem. IEEE Cons. Network. Home and Office: 54 Wakefield Cir East Hartford CT 06118

TAMM, IGOR, biomedical scientist, educator; b. Tapa, Estonia, Apr. 27, 1922; s. Alexander and Olga Tamm; m. Olive Pitkin, May 9, 1953; children: Carol, Eric, Ellen. Student, Tartu U. Med. Faculty, Estonia, 1942-43; med. candid. exam., Karolinska Mediko-Kirurgiska Inst., Stockholm, 1945; MD cum laude, Yale U., 1947. Intern, asst. resident Grace-New Haven Community Hosp., 1947-49; asst. in medicine Yale U. Sch. Medicine, 1947-49; asst. and asst. physician The Rockefeller Inst., N.Y.C., 1949-53, assoc. and assoc. physician, 1953-56, assoc. prof., assoc. physician, 1956-58, assoc. prof. and physician, 1958-64; prof. and sr. physician The Rockefeller U., N.Y.C., 1964-86, Abby Rockefeller Mauzé prof. and sr. physician, 1986—; assoc. mem. Commn. on Acute Respiratory Diseases, Armed Forces Epidemiol. Bd., 1961-73; mem. virology and rickettsiology study sect. NIH, 1964-68; mem. bd. sci. cons. Sloan-Kettering Inst. Cancer Research, 1966-75, vice chmn., 1971-72, chmn., 1972-73; mem. study panel for allergy and infectious diseases Health Research Council of City of N.Y., 1968-75; mem. Am. Cancer Soc. adv. com. on virology and cell biology; gen. chmn. task force on virology Nat. Inst. Allergy and Infectious Diseases. Contbr. 248 sci. papers on biology of viruses and cells; assoc. editor: Jour. of Immunology, 1957-59, Procs. of Soc. for Exptl. Biology and Medicine, 1963-66; adv. editor: The Jour. of Exptl. Medicine, 1971-81; hon. editorial bd. Biochem. Pharmacology, 1974-84; mem. editorial bd. Jour. of Interferon Rsch., 1980-88; editor symposium on viruses Am. Jour. of Medicine, 1965; editor (with F.L. Horsfall) Viral and Rickettsial Infections of Man, 4th edit., 1965. Recipient Alfred Benzon prize, 1967; Centennial lectr. U. Ill., 1968. Fellow AAAS, N.Y. Acad. Scis. (Sarah L. Poiley award 1977); mem. NAS, Am. Soc. Microbiology, Am. Assn. Immunologists, Soc. for Exptl. Biology and Medicine, Am. Soc. Clin. Investigation, Am. Acad. Microbiology, Am. Soc. Cell Biology, Soc. Gen. Microbiology, Assn. Am. Physicians, Deutsche Gesellschaft für Hygiene und Mikrobiologie (corr.), Am. Soc. Virology, Internat. Cell Cycle Soc., Internat. Soc. Interferon Research, Harvey Soc., Alpha Omega Alpha. Office: Rockefeller Univ Dept of Virology 1230 York Ave New York NY 10021-6341

TAMM, MARY ANNE DECAMP, social services administrator; b. Oakland, Calif., June 30, 1949; d. Dwight E. and Jacklyn Margaret (Gordon) DeCamp; m. Quinn John Tamm Jr., May 29, 1971; 1 child, Quinn John III. BA, George Washington U., 1971; MA, U. Okla., 1974; postgrad., Temple U., 1975-77; MSW, Rutgers U., 1980. Instr. U.S. Army Edn. Ctr., Ft. Kobbe, Canal Zone, 1971-72, guidance counselor, 1972-73; social worker Norfolk (Va.) Social Svc. Bur., 1973-75; spl. asst. to regional commr. Office Edn., HEW, Phila., 1975-77; social worker State N.J., Div. Youth and Family Svcs., Camden, 1977-81, social work supr., 1981-82, asst. dist. office mgr., 1982-85, dist. office mgr., 1985—. Councilwoman Twp. of Cherry HIll, N.J., 1983-88; coun. liaison Local Assistance Bd., Youth Adv. Bd., Social Svc. Bd., Sr. Citizen Adv. Bd., Health Adv. Bd., Alcohol and Drug Abuse Adv. Bd., 1983-88; mem. Youth Svcs. Commn.; advisor YMCA; trustee Trinity Presbyn. Ch. Mem. Nat. Assn. Social Workers, Covered Bridge Swim Club. Republican. Home: 1251 Charleston Rd Cherry Hill NJ 08034-3129 Office: Youth and Family Svc Div 251 N Delsea Dr Ste 100 Woodbury NJ 08096-1907

TAMULEVICH, JOAN FRANCES, substance abuse therapist; b. Worcester, Mass., July 27, 1940; d. Anthony and Constance (Kucewicz) T. AS in Mech. Engring., Worcester Jr. Coll., 1978; BS, Worcester State Coll., 1989; MA, Framingham State Coll., 1990. Lic. mental health counselor. Mech. draftsperson Norton Co., Worcester, 1962-69, Morgan Constrn. Co., Worcester, 1973-87; substance abuse/intervention counselor Adcare Hosp., Worcester, 1987-88; substance abuse counselor Longwood Treatment Ctr., Jamaica Plain, Mass., 1989-90; word processor Fenwall Safety Systems, Marlboro, Mass., 1990; instr. driver alcohol edn. program G. B. Wells Human Svcs. Ctr., Southbridge, Mass., 1988—; group co-leader Women's Recovery Group, Framingham, 1990-91; with mech. drafting svcs. TBV Inc., Sutton, Mass., 1990-91; substance abuse therapist Together, Inc., Marlboro, 1990—. Candidate Selectman, Leicester, 1982; v.p. Belmont Home Community Assn., Worcester, 1990; cons., program dir. substance abuse Martha's Vineyard Community Svcs., Island Counseling, Vineyard Haven, Msss., 1992—. With WAC, 1959-62. Recipient scholarship to the New Eng. Inst. of Addiction Studies, The Commonwealth of Mass. Div. of Substance Abuse Svcs., Brown Univ., Providence, 1991. Mem. AACD, Mass. Mental Health Counselors Assn. Office: Together Inc 133 E Main St Marlborough MA 01752-1981

TAN, TJIAUW-LING, educator, psychiatrist; b. Pemalang, Java, Indonesia, June 2, 1935; came to U.S., 1967; naturalized, 1972; s. Ping-Hoey and Liep-Nio (Liem) T.; m. Esther Joyce Kho, June 2, 1961; children: Paul Budiman, Robert Yuling, Alice Ayling. BS, U. Indonesia Faculty Medicine, 1957, MD, 1961; postgrad. U. Indonesia, Jakarta, 1961-65, U. Calif. at L.A., 1967-71, Pa. State U., 1971-72. Diplomate Am. Bd. Psychiatry and Neurology, Am. Bd. Gen. Psychiatry, Am. Bd. Geriatric Psychiatry. Lectr. psychiatry U. Indonesia, Jakarta, 1965-67; psychiat. cons. Central Gen. Hosp., Jakarta, 1965-67; postdoctoral fellow U. Calif. at L.A. Brain Rsch. Inst., 1967-69; asst. rsch. psychiatrist, dept. psychiatry Neuropsychiat. Inst. U. Calif., L.A., 1969-70; asst. prof. psychiatry Pa. State U., 1972-87; assoc. prof. psychiatry Pa. State U., 1987—; chief inpatient psychiatry Univ. Hosp. Milton S. Hershey Med. Ctr., 1972—, dir. Behavioral Medicine Clinic, co-dir. Biofeedback Lab., 1975—; cons. psychiatry Family and Children's Svc. Lebanon County, Lebanon, Pa., 1971-79, Bd. dirs. Retarded Children's Assn. Dauphin County, Inc., 1971-73. Fellow Am. Psychiat. Assn.; mem. Pa. Psychiat. Soc., Central Pa. Psychiat. Soc., Pa. Med. Assn., Dauphin County Med. Soc., Assn. Advancement Behavior Therapy, Assn. Applied Psychophysiology and Biofeedback, Soc. Behavioral Medicine, N.Y. Acad. Scis., AAAS, Assn. Psychophysiol. Study of Sleep, Am. Acad. Sleep Disorder Medicine, Am. Assn. for Geriatric Psychiatry, Am. Geriatric Soc. Contbr. articles to profl. jours. Home: 1478 Bradley Ave Hummelstown PA 17036-9143 Office: Pa State U Coll Medicine Dept Psychiatry 500 University Dr Hershey PA 17033-2360

TANAKA, JOHN, educator; b. San Diego, June 18, 1924; s. Keinosuke and Tokuko (Shima) T.; m. Patricia Ellwein, Aug. 14, 1959; children: Peter, Paul. BA, UCLA, 1951; PhD, Iowa State U., 1956; doctorate, Paul Sabatier, Toulouse, France, 1983. Asst. prof. S.D. State U., Brookings, 1956-59; assoc. prof. S.D. State U., 1959-63; asst. prof. U. Conn., Storrs, 1965-68; assoc. prof. U. Conn., 1968-75, dir. honors program, 1974—, prof., 1975—. Mem. Am. Chem. Soc., IEEE (v.p. tech. 1981-83, v.p. adminstrn. 1983-85, pres. 1985-87, editor E.I. Mag. 1987—). Office: U Conn Chem Dept Storrs CT 06269-3060

TANAKA, MITSUYOSHI, physicist; b. Hamasaka City, Hyogo-ken, Japan, Nov. 7, 1944; came to U.S., 1970; s. Yoko and Kikue (Sugano) T.; m. Michiko Iwasaki, May 26, 1974; children: Hirohisa A., Amy M. BS, Rikkyo U., Tokyo, 1967, MS in Physics, 1969; MS in Physics, Carnegie-Mellon U., 1972, PhD in Physics, 1977. Postdoctoral fellow Carnegie-Mellon U., Pitts., 1977; rsch. assoc. Brookhaven Nat. Lab., Upton, N.Y., 1977-79, asst. physicist, 1979-81, assoc. physicist, 1981-84, physicist, 1984—; assoc. Ctr. for European Rsch. for Nuclear Physics, Geneva, 1983-85. Contbr. articles to profl. jours. Mem. Am. Phys. soc., Phys. Soc. of Japan, N.Y. Acad. of Sci. Episcopalian. Home: 69 Highland Down Shoreham NY 11786 Office: Brookhaven Nat Lab AGS Dept Upton NY 11973

TANDY, JESSICA, actress; b. London, Eng., June 7, 1909; d. Harry and Jessie Helen (Horspool) T.; m. Jack Hawkins, 1932 (div. 1942); 1 dau., Susan (Mrs. John Tettemer); m. Hume Cronyn, 1942; children: Christopher Hume, Tandy. Student, Dame Alice Owens Girls Sch., 1919-24, Ben Greet Acad. Acting, 1924-27; LL.D., U. Western Ont., 1974; LHD (hon.), Fordham U., 1985. Dramatic adviser Goddard Neighborhood Center, N.Y.C., 1948. First profl. acting role in: Manderson Girls; later appeared in: London debut in The Rumor, 1929; Comedy of Good and Evil, 1928, Alice Sit-By-The-Fire, 1928, Yellow Sands, 1929; other theatre appearances in Twelfth Night, 1930, Man Who Pays the Piper, Autumn Crocus, Port Said, 1931; various engagements, Old Vic, London, including Midsummer Night's Dream, Hamlet, King Lear, 1933-40; first stage appearance U.S., 1930; on Broadway in Time and Conways, 1938, White Steed, 1939, Yesterday's Magic, 1942, Streetcar Named Desire, 1947, Four Poster, 1951-53, Madame Will You Walk, 1953, The Honeys, 1955, A Day by the Sea, 1955, The Man in the Dog Suit, 1958, Five Finger Exercise, 1959, The Physicists, 1964, Noel Coward in Two Keys, 1974; played in Mpls. Hamlet, Three Sisters, Death of a Salesman, 1963; Foxfire; in The Glass Menagerie, summer theatre prodns. The Caucasian Chalk Circle, 1950-55; appeared: Triple Play, 1958-59, Big Fish, Little Fish, London, 1962; (with husband) reading tour U.S. Face to Face, 1954; A Delicate Balance, 1966-67, The Miser, 1968, Heartbreak House, Shaw Festival, 1968, Tchin-Tchin, Chgo., 1969, Camino Real, Lincoln Center, N.Y.C., 1970, Home, Morosco, N.Y., 1971, All Over, N.Y.C., 1971; (with husband) in) Samuel Beckett festival, Lincoln Center, N.Y.C., 1972, tour Promenade All, 1972-73, Not I, 1973; limited concert recital tour Many Faces of Love, 1974, 75, 76, also Seattle Repertory theatre; tour (with husband) Noel Coward in Two Keys, 1975; appeared in Eve, Stratford (Ont.) Festival, 1976; played Mary Tyrone in Long Day's Journey into Night, Theater London, Ont., Can., 1977; star of The Gin Game, at Long Wharf Theatre, New Haven, 1977, Golden Theatre, N.Y.C., 1978; on tour in U.S., Toronto, London, USSR, 1978-79, Rose, Cort Theater, N.Y.C., 1981; appeared (with husband) in Foxfire, Stratford Festival, Ont., 1980, The Guthrie Theatre, Mpls., 1981, Ahmanson Theatre, Los Angeles, 1985-86, Ethel Barrymore Theatre, N.Y.C., 1982-83; in The Glass Menagerie, Eugene O'Neill Theatre, N.Y.C., 1983-84; off-Broadway in Salonika, 1985; (with husband) in The Petition, Golden Theatre, N.Y.C., 1986; motion pictures include Valley of Decision, 1945, Green Years, 1946, Desert Fox, 1951, Light in the Forest, 1958, The Birds, 1962, Butley, 1973, Honky Tonk Freeway, 1980, Garp, 1981, Still of the Night, 1981, Best Friends, 1982, The Bostonians, 1983, Cocoon, 1984, Batteries Not Included, 1986, The House on Carroll Street, 1986, Cocoon: The Return, 1988, Driving Miss Daisy, 1989, Fried Green Tomatoes, 1991, Used People, 1991; TV prodns. Portrait of a Madonna, 1948, Christmas 'Till Closing, 1955, Marriage; series, 1954, The Fallen Idol, 1959, The Moon and Sixpence, 1959, Tennessee Williams' South, Many Faces of Love, 1977, The Gin Game, 1979, Foxfire, 1987, The Story Lady, 1991. Recipient Antoinette Perry award, Twelfth Night Club award for performance in Streetcar Named Desire, 1948, Delia Austria medal for Five Finger Exercise, 1960, bronze medallion (with husband) for performance in The Four Poster Comedia Matinee Club, 1952, Obie award for Not I, 1973, Drama Desk award for Happy Days and Not I, Creative Arts award Brandeis U., 1978, Antoinette Perry (Tony) award for The Gin Game, 1978, Drama Desk award, 1978, Los Angeles Critics award, 1979, Sarah Siddons award, 1979; named to Theatre Hall of Fame, 1979; recipient Antoinette Perry award for Foxfire, 1982, Common Wealth award, 1983, Alley Theatre award, 1987, Acad. Sci. Fiction, Fantasy and Horror Films award for Batteries Not Included, 1987, Franklin Haven Sargeant award Am. Acad. Dramatic Arts, 1988, Emmy award for Foxfire, 1988, Golden Globe award, Silver Bear award Berlin Film Festival, Baftra award, 1991, Nat. medal of Arts Pres. U.S., 1990; nominated for Tony award as best actress in The Petition, 1986; Acad. award for Driving Miss Daisy, 1990; honoree Kennedy Ctr. Honors, 1986. Office: 63-23 Carlton St Rego Park NY 11374*

TANENBAUM, JILL NANCY, graphic designer; b. Glen Cove, N.Y., Dec. 18, 1954; d. Joseph and Barbara Sally (Kosberg) W.; m. Alan Lloyd T. BA in Studio Arts, SUCO, Oneonta, 1976; MA in Publ. Design, U. Balt., 1981. Asst. art dir. John Wine Design, Washington, 1981-82; pres. art dir. Jill Tanenbaum Graphic Design, Inc., Bethesda, Md., 1982—. Work included in S.D. Warren Idea Exchange and Promotional Services Library. Recipient Cert. Excellence Strathmore Graphics Gallery, Westfield, Mass., 1984, Award of Excellence, Hopper Paper Co. Mem. Am. Inst. Graphic Artists, Women in Advt. and Design, Prodn. Club Greater Washington, Bethesda-Chevy Chase C. of C. Office: 4701 Sangamore Rd Bethesda MD 20816-2508

TANENBAUM, STUART WILLIAM, biotechnologist, educator; b. N.Y.C., July 15, 1924; s. Julius and Anna (Saphirstein) T.; m. Hannah Mehler, Feb. 18, 1962; children: Jonas, Stefanie. BS, CCNY, 1944; PhD, Columbia U., 1951. Prof. microbiology Columbia Univ., Coll. of Physicians and Surgeons, N.Y.C., 1953-73; dean, Sch. Biology, Chemistry and Ecology SUNY-Coll. of Environ. Sci. & Forestry, Syracuse, 1973-75, biotechnology prof., 1985—; program dir., biochemistry NSF, Washington, 1970-71; bd. dirs. Coll. Forestry Found., Syracuse, 1974-91. Editor: Cytochalasins, 1978; contbr. over 100 articles to profl. jours.; patentee in field. Vis. scientist Fedn. Am. Socs. for Exptl. Biology Minorities Instns. Program, 1989. With U.S. Army, 1944-46; ETO. Decorated Combat Infantry award, U.S. Army, 1944; recipient Sigma Xi Faculty Rsch. award 1986, SUNY's Best Teaching award 1990, United Univ. Professions Excellence award, 1991. Mem. Am. Chem. Soc., Am. Soc. Biol. Chemists, Soc. for Indsl. Microbiology, Soc. Am. Microbiologists. Home: 7472 Armstrong Rd Manlius NY 13104-1418 Office: Coll Environ Sci & Forestry 310 Baker Labs Syracuse NY 13205-1302

TANEY, J. CHARLES, advertising agency executive. Formerly sr. exec. v.p. FCB/Leber Katz Ptnrs., N.Y.C., now pres., chief operating officer. Office: FCB/Leber Katz Ptnrs GM Bldg 767 5th Ave New York NY 10153-0002*

TANG, ALBERT KWOK, environmental engineer; m. Phyllis M. Tang, 1969. MS, U. Birmingham, Eng., 1969. Registered profl. engr., Calif., Md.; chartered civil engr. and structural engr. Asst. engr. to chief engr. Water Authority, Hong Kong, 1963-88; sr. engr. Carson Mok Cons. Engrs., Silver Spring, Md., 1988-90, Greenhorne & O'Mara, Greenbelt, Md., 1990—. Mem. Am. Waterworks Assn., Instn. Civil Engrs. London (Bayliss prize 1963), Instn. Structural Engrs. London, Instn. Water and Environ. Mgmt. London. Baptist. Office: Greenhorne & O'Mara 9001 Edmonston Rd Greenbelt MD 20770

TANG, YU-SUN, consulting chemical engineer; b. Nanking, Kiang-su, China, Oct. 24, 1922; came to U.S., 1947; s. Chian-chung and Shier-Lan (Han) T.; m. Lillian Yu-Djang Mao, June 9, 1950; children: Paul C., Elaine Tang Lee, John C. BSME, Nat. Cen. U., Nanking, 1944; MSME, U. Wis., 1947; PhDChemE, U. Fla., 1952. Registered profl. engr., Pa. Sr. devel. engr. steam div. Westinghouse Co., Phila., 1956-59; prin. scientist Allison div. GM, Indpls., 1959-66; adv. engr. Westinghouse Astronaut. Lab., Large, Pa., 1966-71; adv. engr. advanced reactors div. Westinghouse Co., Madison, Pa., 1971-84; adj. assoc. prof. U. Pitts., 1984-86, adj. rsch. prof., 1987-90; cons. engr. Bethel Park, Pa., 1987—; vis. prof. Nanyang Tech. Inst., Singapore, 1985, Nat. Tsing-Hsu U., Hsinchu, Taiwan, 1986; cons. waste tech. div. Westinghouse, Madison, Pa., 1984-85. Co-author: Therman Analysis of Liquid Metal Fast Breeder Reactors, 1978, Radioactive Wast Management, 1990; also over 40 articles; patentee in heat removal apparatus field. Sec. Pitts. sect. Orgn. Chinese Ams., 1979. Fellow AAAS, Am. Inst. Chem. Engrs. (chmn. energy transfer rsch. com. 1976-82, nuclear energy com. 1988-91); mem. ASME (chmn. task force nuclear engring. div. high level nuclear waste mgmt. 1991), Am. Nuclear Soc. Republican. Methodist. Home and Office: 1552 Holly Hill Dr Bethel Park PA 15102-3508

TANGEN, ROY ALLAN, information scientist; b. Bklyn., Aug. 18, 1947; s. Harry Kristopher and Astrid Sophie (Hansen) T.; m. Elizabeth I. Thoms, June 29, 1968; 1 child, Dawn Elizabeth. B Bus., N.Y.C. Coll., 1968; Assoc. Animal Sci. and Math., Am. Sch. Animal Sci., 1974; BA, N.Y. Inst., 1975; MEd, MIT, 1979. Dir. pub. rels. Am. Guild Artists, N.Y.C., 1965; course developer N.Y. Telephone, N.Y.C., 1965-86; gen. mgr. Legend Data Systems, Holbrook, N.Y., 1987-90; MIS dir. Twin Labs., Ronkonkoma, N.Y., 1991—. Author employment mgmt. software, 1989, photographic software, 1986-91, bus. forcasting, 1990—. Merit badge counselor Boy Scouts Am., Suffolk County, N.Y., 1960—; coord. Suffolk County Aux. Police, 1990. With USN, 1965-69. Home: 3 Montauk Dr Bay Shore NY 11706-5402

TANGUAY, ANITA WALBURGA, real estate broker; b. Oberndorf, Fed. Republic of Germany, July 31, 1936; came to U.S., 1958, naturalized, 1968; d. Karl W. and Luise (Roescheisen) Ederle; m. Donald M. Tanguay, Jan. 21, 1958; children: Elizabeth Ivy, Aimee Marie. Student various schs., Oberndorf and Heidelberg, Fed. Republic of Germany; grad. in real estate, Middlesex (N.J.) Coll., 1981. Sales assoc. Lois Schneider Co., Summit, N.J., 1978-82; pres. Tanguay Assocs. Inc., Millburn, N.J., 1982—. Co-founder Hospice Overlook Hosp., Summit, 1978—, bd. dirs., 1980-84; mem. adv. bd. Summit Child Care Ctr; apptd. condemnation commr. Essex County Superior Ct., N.J., 1990; regent Nat. Fedn. Rep. Women. Recipient Women of Achievement award Greater Millburn (N.J.)/Short Hills (N.J.) Bus. and Profl. Women Inc., 1988. Mem. Bd. Realtors Maplewood Oranges (trustee), N.J. Assn. Realtors, Nat. Assn. Realtors, Indsl. Comml. Real Estate Women (exec. bd., treas. 1983—, past pres., indsl./comml. real estate women, N.J. del. nat. network), Nat. Comml. Network (nat. real estate women, N.J. del.). Republican. Roman Catholic. Avocations: gardening, classical music. Home: 11 Ferndale Rd Short Hills NJ 07078-2079 Office: 225 Millburn Ave Ste 101 Millburn NJ 07041

TANINGCO, CORA MARIE DE GUZMAN, medical-surgical nurse, researcher; b. Manila, Philippines, Mar. 13, 1959; came to U.S., 1984; d. Bernabe Carbonell and Felipa (De Guzman) T. BSN, Manuel V. Gallego Found. Coll., Philippines, 1980. RN, N.J., N.Y., Calif., Oreg. Staff nurse ICU U. Philippines-Philippine Gen. Hosp. Med. Ctr., 1981-84; charge nurse ICU Neil Gen. Hosp., N.Y.C., 1984-88; program rev. assoc. Island Peer Rev. Orgn., Flushing, N.Y., 1988-89; rev. coord. Axiom Rev., Milburn, N.J., 1989-90; rev. coord. quality assurance North Gen. Hosp., N.Y.C., 1990-91, Lenox Hill Hosp., N.Y.C., 1991—; charge nurse Rockefeller U. Hosp., N.Y.C., 1991—. Mem. AACN, Philippine Nurses Assn., Jaycees Toastmaster Club (asst. treas. 1991—), Philippine N.Y. Jaycees, Jaycees Internat., Toastmaster Internat. Home: 555 Sanderling Ct 27-07 Newtown Ave BR Astoria NY 11102 Office: Rockefeller U Hosp 1230 E York Ave New York NY 10021

TANKOOS, SANDRA MAXINE, court reporting services executive; b. Bklyn., Nov. 12, 1936; d. Samuel J. and Ethel (Seltzer) Rich; m. Kenneth Robert Tankoos, Mar. 17, 1957; children: Robert Ian, Gary Russell, Jenine Sheryl. AA, Stenotype Inst., 1957; BA, Queens Coll., 1969; MA, C.W. Post Coll., 1973. Cert. stenotype reporter, 1959. Ct. reporter free lance, N.Y.C., 1957-70; tchr. Spanish, various high schs., L.I., 1970-76; pres. Tankoos Reporting, N.Y.C., 1976—, Ar-Ti Recording, Mineola, N.Y., 1977—. Contbr. articles to profl. jours. Pres., bd. dirs. Temple Sinai, Roslyn Hts., N.Y., 1989—, Am. Jewish Acad., West Hempstead, 1984-91, LWV, Roslyn, 1969-75, NOW, Nassau County, 1975-77. Mem. Nat. Assn. Shorthand Reporters, Principal's Assn., Numismatic Club (pres. 1973-78). Avocations: writing, piano. Home: 77 Shepherd Ln Roslyn Heights NY 11577-2508 Office: Ar-Ti Recording Inc 286 Old Country Rd Mineola NY 11501-1606 also: Tankoos Reporting Co 11 John St New York NY 10038

TANNEHILL, NORMAN BRUCE, JR., information systems consultant, educator; b. Pitts., Aug. 22, 1950; s. Norman Bruce and Laura Maxine (Hart) T.; m. Marianne Witt, Sept. 22, 1979 (div. July, 1990); children: Andrea Emily, Norman Bruce III; m. Darcy Anita Bartins, Feb. 14, 1991. BBA, Robert Morris Coll., 1975, MS in computer info. systems, 1989. Cert. profl. cons. Instr. Robert Morris Coll., Pitts., 1989—; owner, chief exec. officer Tannehill Info. Systems, Coraopolis, Pa., 1989. Mem. Am. Cons. League, Mensa. Office: Tannehill Info Systems Ltd PO Box 528 Duquesne PA 15110-0531

TANNENBAUM, HARVEY, consultant defense technology; b. N.Y.C., June 26, 1923; s. Alfred and Ida (Kolbe) T.; m. Mildred Cohen, July 4, 1946; children: David Bruce, Mark Scott, Lynne Ellen. BS, NYU, 1946; postgrad., George Washington U., 1963-64. Chemist U.S. Army Chem. Research and

Devel. Ctr., Aberdeen Proving Ground, Md., 1949-62, chief remote sensing, 1962-79; prin. staff engr. Honeywell, Inc., Clearwater, Fla., 1979-84; cons., Reisterstown, Md., 1984-86; sr. program dir. SRI, Internat., 1986-88; cons. EPA, CIA, Arms Control and Disarmament Agy., USAF, 1962-79. Contbr. articles to profl. jours.; patentee in field. Served to cpl. USAF, 1942-45, ETO. Mem. Optical Soc. Am., Internat. Soc. Optical Engring., Infrared Symposia, Sigma Xi. Jewish. Avocations: bridge, photography. Home and Office: 12611 Mt Laurel Ct Reisterstown MD 21136-1801

TANNENBAUM, STEVEN ROBERT, toxicologist, chemist; b. N.Y.C., Feb. 23, 1937; m. Carol Eigen, Sept. 6, 1959; children: Lisa, Mark. B.S. in Food Tech, MIT, 1958, Ph.D. in Food Sci. and Tech, 1962. Asst. prof. dept. nutrition and food sci. MIT, Cambridge, Mass., 1964-69; assoc. prof. MIT, 1969-74, prof. food chemistry dept. nutrition and food sci., 1974-81, prof. toxicology and food chemistry, 1981-88, prof. chemistry and toxicology, registration and admissions officer, 1988—; vis. prof. Hebrew U. of Jerusalem Faculty of Agr., 1973-74; cons. Inst. of Nutrition for Central Am. and Panama, 1968; cons. protein adv. group UN, UN Devel. program, 1970-74; mem. com. on food standards and fortification policy Nat. Acad. Scis.-Nat. Research Council, 1970-73; cons. FDA, 1971-73, Am. Cancer Soc., 1977—, NCI-NIH, 1978-; mem. IFT Expert Panel on food safety and nutrition, 1971-73, co-chmn., 1976-77, chmn., 1977-78; mem. adv. com. on biochemistry and chem. carcinogensis Am. Cancer Soc., 1977-81; mem. adv. com. Frederick Cancer Rsch. Facility, Nat. Cancer Inst., mem. cancer spl. program adv. com., 1979-82; mem. peer rev. com. Nat. Toxicology Program, 1983-85; founder, bd. dirs. Vicam, Ltd. Partnership. Editor: (with R.I. Mateles) Single-Cell Protein, 1968, (with D.I.C. Wang) Single-Cell Protein II, 1975, (with others) The Economics, Marketing and Technology of Fish Protein Concentrate, 1974, (with J.R. Whitaker) Food Proteins, 1977, Nutritional Safety Aspects of Food Processing, 1979, (with others) Gastrointestinal Cancer: Endogenous Factors, 1981; (with R.A. Scanlan) N-Nitroso Compounds, 1981; Contbr. articles to profl. jours.; mem. editoral bd. Inst. Food Technologists Sci. Jours, 1970-73, Food Chemistry, 1977-85, Japanese Jour. Cancer Rsch., 1986—, Chem. Rsch. Toxicology, 1988—, Jour. Cancer Epidemiology, Prevention and Biomarkers, 1990—. Mem. AAAS, Am. Chem. Soc., Inst. Food Technologists (sect. councillor N.E. chpt. 1966-69, Samuel Cate Prescott Rsch. award 1970, Babcock Hart award 1980, editorial bd. sci. jours. 1970-73), Am. Inst. Nutrition, Am. Assn. Cancer Rsch., Am. Coll. Toxicology (councillor 1983-85), Sigma Xi. Office: MIT Dept Chemistry Cambridge MA 02139

TANNER, LAURENCE ARAM, hospital administrator; b. Chelsea, Mass., June 27, 1946; s. Sylvan and Doris (Liss) T.; m. Janis A. Piazza, Aug. 23, 1969; children: Rebecca, David, Sarah. BS in Mgmt., U. R.I., 1970; MPH, Yale U., 1972; postgrad., U. Indiana, 1974, Yale U., 1979. Resident in adminstrn. The Waterbury (Conn.) Hosp., 1972, asst. adminstr., 1972-76, assoc. adminstr., 1976-80; pres., chief exec. officer Bristol (Conn.) Hosp., 1980-87; pres. Greater Bristol Health Svcs. Corp., 1984-87, BHV, Inc., 1984-87, BMOB Corp., 1984-87, Bristol Hosp. Devel. Found., 1984-87; pres., chief exec. officer New Britain (Conn.) Gen. Hosp., 1987—; Preceptor dept. epidemiology and pub. health Yale U., 1974—, health care mgmt. U. Conn., 1978—; lectr. hosp. adminstrn. Yale U., 1980—; lectr. biostatistics The Hartford Grad. Ctr., 1977-78; bd. dirs. Burritt Internat. Fin. BanCorp, South Cen. Conn. Health Care Coalition, mem. Capital area health consortium mgmt. council, 1980—. Contbr. articles to profl. jours. Mem. health systems mgmt. adv. com. U. Conn., 1981—, adv. council U. Conn. Health Ctr., 1987—; bd. dirs. United Community Svcs., Inc., 1987—, Burritt Interfinancial Bancorp, 1990—; mem. adv. bd. United Bank and Trust Co., 1980-90, com. long range facilities Burlington Bd. Edn., 1986—; mem. adv. coun. to grad. program in health adminstrn. Western Conn. State U. Lt. USAF, 1967-70. James scholar, 1964. Mem. Am. Coll. Hosp. Adminstrs., Conn. Hosp. Assn., New Eng. Hosp. Assembly, Am. Hosp. Assn., Assn. for Advancement of Med. Instrumentation (v.p. health industry bd. dirs., mem. exec. com. 1983—), Yale U. Alumni Assn. in Mass. (pres.), Omicron Delta Epsilon, Phi Delta Phi. Home: 11 Two Buck Ring Burlington CT 06013-1407 Office: New Britain Gen Hosp 100 Grand St New Britain CT 06052-2000

TANTILLO, JOHN, marketing executive; b. N.Y.C., June 29, 1951; s. John and Angelina (Teta) T. BA, St. Francis Coll., Bklyn., 1973; MA, CUNY, 1976; PhD, Hofstra U., 1980. Asst. prof. Hofstra U., Hempstead, N.Y., 1979-82, St. John's U., Queens, N.Y., 1982-85, Manhattan Coll., Riverdale, N.Y., 1987-89; pres. Charles St. John Group, N.Y.C., 1985—. Contbr. articles to profl. jours. Named Outstanding Citizen of Yr. Ridgewood (N.Y.) Property Owners, 1980. Mem. Am. Mktg. Assn. (exec.), Psi Chi. Office: The Charles St John Group 224 W 35th St New York NY 10001

TANTILLO, JOSEPH GEORGE, JR., graphic design company executive, illustrator; b. Poughkeepsie, N.Y., July 22, 1952; s. Joseph George and Emma Rose (Moriello) T.; m. Maura D. Shaw, May 25, 1974; 1 child, Nicholas Joseph. BFA, Syracuse U., 1974. Graphic artist George Platt & Co., New Haven, 1974-75, Chronicle Printing Co., North Haven, Conn., 1975-76; graphic designer and illustrator Icon Graphics, Wallingford, Conn., 1975-76, Repich Group, North Branford, Conn., 1976-77, Paul Schiff Studio, Branford, Conn., 1977-79; creative dir., prin. Tantillo Design Group, Wappingers Falls, N.Y., 1979—. Author, illustrator: (juvenile) Amazeing Ancient America, 1983; illustrator: The New Haven Railroad: A Fond Look Back, 1978. Com. mem. So. Dutchess Inst. for Leadership Devel., Fishkill, N.Y., 1988. Recipient Bronze Target award Bus. and Profl. Advt. Assn., 1987, cert. of merit Healthcare Mktg. report, 1988-91, Best of Best award Mktg. IV, 1988, merit award Conn. chpt. Internat. Assn. Bus. Communicators, 1988, 90, Bronze Quill award, 1990. Mem. Hudson Valley Area Mktg. Assn. (treas. 1988-91), bd. dirs. 1988—, Bronze Eclat award 1988, 90, Silver Eclat award 1988, 90), Gold Eclat award, 1990, Greater So. Dutches C. of C. Democrat. Roman Catholic.

TANZI, ANTHONY, accountant, small business owner; b. Takoma Park, Md., Jan. 11, 1948; s. Luigi V. and Cecilia M. (Campanile) T.; m. Deborah Jean Houston, June 12, 1971; children: Brian Houston Tanzi, Alan Scott. BS in Acctg., Mt. St. Mary's Coll., Emmitsburg, Md., 1970. CPA, Md. Staff acct. Arthur Young & Co., Washington, 1970-76, audit mgr., 1976-80, prin., 1980-82; v.p. Jack Kent Cooke Inc., Middleburg, Va., 1982-83; audit mgr. Grossberg Co., Chevy Chase, Md., 1983-86; ptnr. Grossberg Co., Bethesda, Md., 1986—. Mem. Quince Orchard High Sch. Boosters, Darnestown, Md., 1990-91. Mem. AICPAs, D. C. Inst. CPAs (prins. com. 1991). Office: Grossberg Co 6707 Democracy Blvd Bethesda MD 20817-1129

TANZI, VITO, international organization administrator; b. Mola, Bari, Italy, Nov. 29, 1935; came to U.S., 1956; s. Luigi and Maria Tanzi; m. Madeleine S. Tanzi, July 25, 1965; children: Vito luigi, Alexandre Bruno, Giancarlo Olivier. BA, George Washington U., 1959, MA, 1961; MA, Harvard U., 1963, PhD, 1967. Sr. economist Orgn.-Am. States, Washington, 1965-67; prof. econs. Am. U., Washington, 1967-74, chmn. dept. econs., 1971-73; chief tax policy div. IMF, Washington, 1974-81, dir. fiscal affairs dept., 1981—. Author: Individual Income Tax and Economic Growth, 1969, Inflation & Personal Income Tax, 1980, Public Finance in Developing Countries, 1991, Fiscal Policies in Economies in Transition, 1992. Mem. Nat. Italian Am. Found., Internat. Inst. Pub. Fin. (pres. 1990—). Roman Catholic. Home: 5912 Walhonding Rd Bethesda MD 20816-2354 Office: IMF 700 19th St NW Washington DC 20431-0002

TAPELLA, GARY LOUIS, manufacturing company executive; b. Antioch, Calif., Sept. 1, 1943; s. Anthony M. and Mary (Lopez) T.; m. Karen Kent, June 24, 1967; children: Robert, Michael. BA in Internat. Rels., San Francisco State U., 1969. Staff asst. Rheem Mfg. Co., N.Y.C., 1969-71; plant mgr. Rheem Can., Vancouver, 1971-73; mktg. mgr. Rheem Can., Toronto, 1973-79; regional sales mgr. Rheem Mfg. Co., New Orleans, 1979-80; mng. dir. Rheem Far East, Singapore, 1980-85; gen. mgr. Rheem Can., Toronto, 1985-89; corp. v.p. internat. Rheem Mfg. Co., N.Y.C., 1989-90, chief oper. officer, 1990-91, pres., chief exec. officer, 1991—; dir. various Rheem Cos. With USN, 1961-63. Office: Rheem Mfg Co 405 Lexington Ave New York NY 10174-0002

TAPER, GERI, artist, educator; b. Pitts., Dec. 5, 1929; d. William and Fannye (Goldman) T.; children: Ronald, Richard, David. BS, U. Pitts., 1951; postgrad., Carnegie-Mellon U., Pitts., 1970-72. Art instr. Art Inst. Pitts., 1970-73, U. Pitts., 1970-71, Duquesne U., Pitts., 1970-71, Met. Mus. Art, N.Y.C., 1983-84; environ. artist N.Y.C. and Phila., 1980-89; tchr. Pitts. Pub. Schs., 1951-54; cons. Arts And The Handicappped, N.Y.C., 1983-85, environ. artist La Guardia Coll., N.Y.C., 1988-89. One-oman shows include Sculpted Paintings Accessible to the Blind and Visually-Impaired, N.Y.C., 1984, Transformation of Large Indsl. Bldgs. into Visual Experiences, N.Y.C., 1980-89; creator banner sculpture transit program Met. Transp. AUthority Arts, L.I., N.Y., 1989, Celebrating the Boroughs Van Project, Bronx Community Coll., N.Y.C., 1990; community mural project, Sunnyside Community Svcs. Early Childhood Ctr., N.Y.C., 1991. Mem. Arts and the Handicapped (charter), Found. for the Community of Artists, Artists Equity, Mus. Modern Art, New Mus. Contemporary Art, Whitney Mus. Art. Home and Studio: 458 Broome St New York NY 10013

TAPLEY, LANCE EDWIN, book publisher; b. Bar Harbor, Maine, Oct. 5, 1944; s. Lyman Holbrook and Barbara Ruth (Ferry) T.; m. Margaret Ann Libby; children: Isaac, Adam, Asa, Elias. AB, Dartmouth Coll., 1966; postgrad., U. Toulouse, France, 1966-67. Reporter Portland (Maine) Newspapers, 1967-68, Providence (R.I.) Jour., 1968-69; feature editor San Francisco Chronicle, 1970-71; free-lance writer Maine/N.Y., 1972-77; exec. dir. Maine Common Cause, Augusta, 1977-80; dept. dir. Maine Health Systems Agy., Augusta, 1980-81; editor Coping Mag., Augusta, 1982-85; pres. and pub. Lance Tapley Publ., Inc., Augusta, 1983-89, Yankee Books, Camden, Maine, 1989-91; prin. Lance Tapley & Assocs., Camden, 1991—; cons. writer U. Maine System, Portland, 1973-75; T.V. commentator Maine Pub. Broadcasting Network, Orono, 1974. Author: (books) Ski Touring in New England, 1973, Ski Touring in New England and New York, 1975; contbr. articles to popular jours. Founder, campaign coord. Friends of Bigelow Mountain, Wiscasset, Maine, 1974-76; mem. nat. governing bd. Common Cause, Washington, 1983-89; chmn. Maine Common Cause, Augusta, 1987-89; sec. Augusta Planning Bd., 1983-87. Recipient scholarship Dartmouth Coll., Hanover, N.H., 1962-66, gen. fellowship/Toulouse, France, 1966-67, French Govt. Teaching Assistantship (Fulbright), Montauban, France, 1966-67, writing residence grant Ossabaw Island (Ga.) Project, 1976. Home: 26 Sea St Camden ME 04843-1728 Office: 49 Bay View St Camden ME 04843

TAPP, LINDA MARIE (DENNISON), safety engineer; b. Phila., July 22, 1965; d. James A. Dennison and Phyllis Emma (Sharpe) Gable; m. Darren James Tapp, Dec. 28, 1990. BS, Drexel U., 1988; MS, Temple U., 1992. Toxicologist asst. ARCO Chem. Co., Newtown Square, Pa., 1985-87; sr. loss control rep. Fidelity Environ. Ins. Co., Princeton, N.J., 1988-91; safety coord. Elkins-Sinn Inc., Cherry Hill, N.J., 1991—. Author: Violations Handbook for Asbestos Abatement Contractors, 1990; editor N.J. Am. Indsl. Hygiene Assn. Newsletter, 1990—, Loss Control Bulletin, 1990; contbr. articles to profl. jours. Recipient Excellence Achievement award Environ. Control Group, 1990, ARCO Excel award, 1987. Mem. NAFE, Am. Soc. Safety Engrs., Am. Indsl. Hygiene Assn., Phila. High Sch. for Girls Alumnae Assn. (life), Women in Mgmt. Assn., Drexel U. Alumnae Assn. (planning bd.), Delta Zeta (alumna N.J. Ea. Pa. collegiate advisor 1988—, founder Ctrl. Phila. chpt., chmn. newsletter, collegiate rels., philantrophy, ways and means). Home: 21 Cobblestone Rd Cherry Hill NJ 08003 Office: Elkins Sinn Inc 2 Esterbrook Ln Cherry Hill NJ 08003-4096

TAPPAN, SANDRA HAZEN, choreographer, mental health counselor, hypnotherapist; b. Burlington, Vt., Sept. 25, 1940; d. Joseph and Elaine (Hazen) Rogow; m. Walter House Tappan II, Dec. 27, 1958; children: Suzanne E., Heidi L. BA, Trinity Coll., 1979; MS, U. Vt., 1983. Nat. cert. counselor Nat. Bd. Cert. Counselors; lic. cert. clin. mental health counselor. Cert. Clin. mental Health Counselors; cert. hypnotherapist. Tchr. pre-sch., Enosburg Falls, Vt., 1967; owner, choreographer, tchr. Sandra Tappan Profl. Sch. Dance, St. Albans, Vt., 1968—; counselor CRASH, 1977-79, Planned Parenthood of Vt., 1979-80, pvt. practice; tchr. Community Coll. Vt., 1982-84; cons. staff Northwestern Med. Ctr. Hosp., 1985—, speakers bur., mem. cancer com.; free lance writer newspaper St. Albans Messenger. Mem. Franklin County Planning Commn., 1974-76; exec. bd. United Way, 1984-85. Mem. Am. Assn. for Counseling and Devel, Am. Psychol. Assn. (assoc.). Republican. Avocations: scuba diving, downhill skiing, travel. Home: 22 Rugg St Saint Albans VT 05478-1713

TAPPÉ, ALBERT ANTHONY, architect; b. Pitts., Aug. 12, 1928; s. Albert Anthony and Martha Ann (McKee) T.; m. Jean Bates, June 27, 1963; children: Eliza Bruce, Albert Anthony III. Student, William and Mary Coll., 1947-48, Fontainebleau Fine Art and Music Sch., 1951; B.S., U. Va., 1952; M.Arch., MIT, 1958, M.City Planning. Designer, McLeod & Ferrara (Architects), Washington, 1954-55; planner Boston City Planning Bd., 1957-58; architect and planner Architects Collaborative, Cambridge, Mass., 1958-61; partner Huygens & Tappé, Inc. (architects and planners), Boston, 1962-80; pres. A. Anthony Tappé & Assocs., Inc., Boston, 1980—; instr. dept. city planning MIT, 1959-60; cons. architect Mass. Bur. Library Extension, 1965-76; chmn. bldg. commn., Brookline, Mass., 1977, mem. bd. examiners, Brookline; v.p. Guild Religious Architecture; mem. Back Bay Archtl. Commn.; bd. dirs. Boston Archtl. Center, 1980. Author: Guide to Planning a Library Building, 1967; important works include: Longy Concert Hall, Cambridge, Mass.; Campus N.H. Coll., Franklin Park Zoo, Boston, Lynn Inst. for Savs., Interfaith Religious Ctr., Columbia, Md., student housing W.Va. Wesleyan Coll., Hotel, Costa Smeralda, Sardinia, Newton Pub. Libr.; also residences in U.S., France, Switzerland, housing projects in New Eng. Served with AUS, 1946-47, 52-54. Recipient Progressive Architecture Design award, 1966, 1st place single family category Plywood Design Awards Program, 1973, award of Merit, 1974. Fellow AIA (mem. nat. urban planning and design com. 1975, citation, hon. mentions 1969, 1st honor award 1970, honor award New Eng. Regional Council 1976); mem. Mass. Assn. Architects (exec. com.), Boston Soc. Architects (dir., v.p. 1981-82, pres. 1982-83), Am. Inst. Planners, Am. Planning Assn., Am. Inst. Cons. Planners. Clubs: Union Boat (Boston); Eastern Point Yacht (Gloucester, Mass.). Home: 58 Euston St Brookline MA 02146-4045 Office: 132 Lincoln St Boston MA 02111-2522

TAPPEN, MARY LOU, school district staff development program supervisor; b. Lakewood, N.J.; d. Earl Leon and Zelda (Hulse) T. BA, Glassboro State Coll., 1967; MA, Georgian Ct. Coll., Lakewood, N.J., 1980. Classroom tchr. Toms River (N.J.) Regional Schs., 1967-75, remedial reading tchr., 1975-80, basic skills resource tchr., 1980-86, supr. of instrn., 1986-88, supr. staff devel. programs K-12, 1988—; adj. instr. grad. div. Georgian Ct. Coll., 1980-86. Mem. Internat. Reading Assn., Assn. for Supervision and Curriculum Devel., Nat. Staff Devel. Coun., N.J. Prins. and Suprs. Assn., N.J. Staff Devel. Coun. (founding), Alpha Delta Kappa (v.p. 1978-80, pres. 1980-82), Delta Kappa Gamma. Office: Toms River Regional Schs Superintendent's Office 54 Washington St Toms River NJ 08753-7693

TAPPER, DAVID ALFRED, producer, director, writer; b. N.Y.C., May 21, 1928; s. Edward M. and Deborah (Cohen) T.; children: Gwendolyn, Seth. BA, Hamilton Coll., 1948. Cameraman CBS, 1949-60; ind. producer, dir., writer Tapper Prodns., Inc., N.Y.C., 1960—. Producer, dir. (film) Street of the Flower Boxes, 1973 (Peabody award 1973); dir. (film) A Connecticut Yankee in King Arthur's Court, 1978 (Peabody award 1978); dir. numerous network documentaries; exec. producer of more than 105 half-hour documentary videos on social and religious topics. Served as sgt. U.S. Army, 1953-55. Recipient numerous Blue Ribbons Am. Film Festival, 1968-87, Gabriel award U.S. Cath. Conf., numerous other awards including CINE Golden Eagle, 1967—. Mem. Nat. Acad. TV Arts and Scis. (bd. govs. N.Y. chpt. 1984-86, numerous Emmy award nominations), Writers Guild Am., Dirs. Guild Am., Phi Beta Kappa. Office: Tapper Prodns Inc 133 W 17th St New York NY 10011-5423

TARABA, TIBOR, marketing communications executive; b. Gyömrö, Hungary; s. Tibor Sr. and Ilona (Becker) T.; m. Maria A. Wusterack, Apr. 16, 1955. BBA, Baruch Coll., 1963, MBA, 1965. Asst. advt. mgr. Sunshine Biscuits, Inc., L.I. City, N.Y., 1955-60; mktg. account exec. McCann-Erickson, N.Y.C., 1960-70; mgr. advt., sales promotion and pub. relations Reuben H. Donnelley Corp., N.Y.C., 1970-80; v.p. mktg. communication Reuben H. Donnelley Corp, Purchase, N.Y., 1980—. Editor Direct Line, Nationalink, Directory Record. With U.S. Army, 1953-55. Mem. Internat. Assn. Bus. Communicators, Am. Mktg. Assn., Sales & Mktg. Execs. Assn., Internat. Advt. Assn., Travelers Century Club. Office: The Reuben H Donnelley Corp 287 Bowman Ave Purchase NY 10577-2517

TARADASH, MERYL, artist, sculptor; b. Passaic, N.J., Jan. 25, 1953; d. Elliott and Gloria (Grossman) T.; m. Eric Koch, Dec. 16, 1979; 1 child, Jeffrey Dylan. MFA with honors, Pratt Inst., 1978. Teaching asst. Pratt Inst., Bklyn., 1976-78; seminar instr. Newark Mus., 1979—; vis. artist Montclair (N.J.) State Coll., 1988—; commd. by State of N.J. for Light Dance, Rutgers U. Med. Sch., 1984; pub. sculptures include Frozen Rain Series, David Bermant Found. for Conn., Hamden Plaza, Conn., 1988, Waves, ARA Svcs., Phila., 1989, Wind Dancing, David Bermant Found., 1992. Group faculty exhbn. Montclair (N.J.) Art Mus., 1978, Sounds of the Environment, Newark Mus., 1979, Noyes Mus., Oceanville, N.J., 1987, Hastings-on-Hudson Gallery, N.Y., 1990-91, New Mus. Contemporary Art, N.Y.C., 1986, Rutgers U., 1985, Elaine Benson Gallery, Bridgehampton, N.Y., 1989; solo exhbn. Gallery Henoch, N.Y.C., 1987. Exptl. arts panelist N.J. Art Coun., 1988. Grantee Ford Found., 1977-78, N.J. Arts Coun., 1985. Mem. Internat. Sculpture Ctr., Coll. Art Assn., Jimmy Ernst Art Alliance. Studio: 503 Broadway Rm 511 New York NY 10012

TARALLO, BARRY JOSEPH, actor, musician, songwriter; b. Pitts., Sept. 3; s. Lt. Col. G.J. and Mrs. M. Tarallo; m. Amy Lyn London, June 11, 1988; 1 child, Emily Elizabeth. Bachelors, Cath. U., Washington. actor t.v. commercials, nationwide, 1975--; backup vocalist various recording artists, N.Y.C., 1990--. Actor (Broadway mus.) Grease, 1974-78, Joseph and the Amazing Technicolor Dreamcoat, 1981-82, (pre-Broadway mus.) Elmer Gantry, 1988, 91; actor/musician Harry Chapin's Cotton Patch Nat. Tour, 1984-86, Woody Guthries American Song, 1990. Participant Flea Market Fundraise Equity Fights Aids, N.Y.C., 1989, 1990, solo performer Equity Fights Aids Benefit concert, N.Y.C., 1990. Mem. AFTRA, SAG, Actors Equity Assn.

TARANOW, GERDA, English educator, researcher, author; b. N.Y.C.; d. Samuel and Sabina (Ostro) T. B.A., NYU, 1952, M.A., 1955; Ph.D., Yale U., 1961, postdoctoral studies, 1962-63. Instr. English, U. Ky., Lexington, 1963-65, asst. prof., 1965-66, Syracuse U., N.Y., 1966-67; asst. prof. Conn. Coll., New London, 1967-70, assoc. prof., 1970-76, prof., 1976—; referee NEH, Washington, 1972—. Author: Sarah Bernhardt: The Art Within the Legend, 1972. Yale U. fellow, 1962-63, NEH fellow, 1980-81. Mem. MLA, Am. Soc. Theatre Research, Soc. for Theatre Research (England), Internat. Fedn. for Theatre Research, Société, d'Histoire du théâtre (France). Avocations: opera; theatre; ballet. Office: Conn Coll PO Box 5567 New London CT 06320-1799

TARANTINO, LOUIS GERALD, lawyer, business consultant; b. Bridgeport, Conn., Sept. 7, 1934; s. Louis Gerald and Mary Louise (Boyle) T. BA, U. Pa., 1955, LLB, 1958. Bar: Conn. 1958, N.Y. 1960. Assoc. Beekman & Bogue, 1959-76, ptnr., 1968-76; chmn. Berkeley Mgmt. Assocs., Inc., Sewickley, Pa., 1984—, also bd. dirs.; treas., dir. PERQ Systems Corp., Pitts.; bd.d irs. Beaver Valley Power Co., Beaver Falls, Pa.; mng. dir. Advanced Peptides, Sewickley, Pa., Wintzea Pharms., L.P., the Netherlands. Mem. Bar Assn. City N.Y., N.Y. Bar Assn., Conn. Bar Assn., SAR, Huguenot Soc. Pa., St. Anthony Hall, Knickerbocker Club, Broad St. Club, St. Anthony Club (Phila.), Duquesne Club (Pitts.). Home: 201 Grant St Sewickley PA 15143-1330

TARANTO, MARIA ANTOINETTE, psychology researcher and educator; b. Framingham, Mass., Dec. 28, 1941; d. Gaetano (Tom) Peter and Rose Marie (Busceme) T.; m. John Curtis Mahon, June 5, 1988. BA in Psychology, Bennington Coll., 1965; MA in Psychology, George Peabody Coll., 1968; M Philosophy in Psychology, Columbia U., 1981, PhD, 1985. Tchr. Head Start Pub Sch. System, Pitts., 1966-67; rsch. assoc. Hofstra U., Hempstead, N.Y., 1968-69; instr. Hofstra U., Hempstead, 1969-72; co-dir. Inst. for Piagetian Studies, Hempstead, 1972-76; instr. Nassau Community Coll., Garden City, N.Y., 1976-78; asst. prof. Nassau Community Coll., Garden City, 1978-85, assoc. prof. psychology, 1985—; jour. reviewer Baywood Pub. Co., Long Island, N.Y., 1989, Karger, Basel, Switzerland, 1989. Co-author: (monographs) A Study of Number..., 1972, Liquid Conservation, 1976; contbr. articles to profl. jours and govt. pubs. Mem. Union of Concerned Scientists, 1981—, Amnesty Internat., 1987—; sponsor Pearl S. Buck Found., 1984—. Recipient Mellon fellowship CUNY, N.Y.C., 1987. Mem. Am. Psychol. Assn., Jean Piaget Soc., Gerontol. Soc., New Eng. Psychol. Assn. Office: Nassau Community Coll Stewart Ave Garden City NY 11530-2200

TARBELL, ROBERTA KUPFRIAN, art history educator, curator; b. Mineola, N.Y., Jan. 6, 1944; d. Wilbur Joseph and Laura (Elliott) Kupfrian; m. James Verhoek Tarbell, Mar. 27, 1965; children: Karen Verhoek, Kristin Verhoek, Benjamin James Verhoek. BS, Cornell U., 1965; MA, U. Del., 1968, PhD, 1976. Asst. curator Sloan collections Del. Art Mus., Wilmington, 1966-68; instr. U. Del., Newark, 1967-69, adj. assoc. prof. art history, 1980-84, adj. assoc. prof. art conservation program, 1986—; guest curator for exhbns. Nat. Mus. Am. Art, Smithsonian Instn., Washington, 1972-80, Jewish mus., N.Y.C., Phila., 1977, 83, Rutgers U., New Brunswick, N.J., 1978-79, Whitney Mus. Am. Art, N.Y.C., 1979-80; asst. prof. art history Rutgers U., Camden, N.J., 1984-90, assoc. prof., 1990—; adj. assoc. prof. art history Winterthur (Del.) Mus., 1986—; sr. postdoctoral fellow Smithsonian Instn., 1989. Author: Marguerite Zorach, 1973, Hugo Robus, 1980; co-author: Peggy Bacon, 1975, Vanguard American Sculpture, 1979, The Figurative Tradition, 1980, Walt Whitman and the Visual Arts, 1992. Chmn. Citizens Adv. Coun. for Pub. Edn., Newcastle County, Del., 1977-80; del. Peninsula Conf. United Meth. Ch., 1983-92; coach Del. Team Nat. Sci. Olympiad, 1985-92. Unidel fellow, 1969-72, Smithsonian Instn. fellow, 1972-74; NEH grantee, 1985, Rutgers U. grantee, 1985-92. Mem. Coll. Art Assn., Soc. for Archtl. Historians, Women's Caucus for Art, Arts Club (N.Y.C.). Home: 628 Montgomery Woods Dr Hockessin DE 19707-9654 Office: Rutgers U 250 Fine Arts Bldg Camden NJ 08102

TARBOX, JUDITH ANN, naval officer; b. Ventura, Calif., Oct. 17, 1945; d. Lloyd Ralph Thomas and Bonnie (Ezell) McWayne; m. Thomas N. Tarbox, Apr. 4, 1974; children: Ward I., Tricia O. BA, Sacramento State Coll., 1970; MA, Calif. State U., Sacramento, 1972; student, Def. Intelligence Sch., Washington, 1976-77, Nat. War Coll., 1991-92. Commd. ensign USN, 1972, advanced through grades to comdr., 1988; tng. officer Naval Amphibious Sch. Coronado, San Diego, 1972-74; protocol officer Chief of Naval Ops., Washington, 1974-76; intelligence officer Commander in Chief Atlantic Forces, Norfolk, Va., 1977-79; ops. officer Joint Deployment Agency, MacDill AFB, Fla., 1979-82; communications officer Allied Forces No. Europe, Kolsas, Norway, 1982-85; exec. officer Naval Communication Station U.K., Thurso, Scotland, 1985-87; satellite communications officer Joint Staff Pentagon, Washington, 1987-89; comdg. officer Naval Communications Unit Cutler, East Machias, Maine, 1989-91; div. chief comm. directorate U.S. Spl. Ops. Command, MacDill AFB, Fla., 1992—. Mem. Washington County Bus. and Profl. Forum (sec. 1989-90, v.p. 1990-91), Women Officers Profl. Assn., Women in Internat. Security, Armed Forces Comm. Electronics Assn., Rotary Internat. (treas. Machias chpt. 1990-91), Sigma Kappa (v.p. Tampa chpt. 1981-82, sec. No. Va. chpt. 1991—). Republican. Home: 2315 S Ardson Pl Tampa FL 33629-6210 Office: US Spl Ops Command SOJ-6I Mac Dill A F B FL 33608

TARELLA, DOUGLAS FRANCIS, financial services executive; b. Poughkeepsie, N.Y., Oct. 26, 1952; s. Frank James and Virginia Catherine (Hoffman) T.; m. Kathleen Ann Motroni, June 21, 1975; children: Meghan Kathleen, Michael Douglas, Julianne Marie. BS, Stonehill Coll., North Easton, Mass., 1974; MBA, Northeastern U., 1981. Cert. fin. planner. Mktg. rep. Burroughs Wellcome Co., Research Triangle Park, N.C., 1974-77; industry liaison Pharm. Mfrs. Assn., Washington, 1977-81; pres., chief exec. officer Fin. Edn. Ctrs., Inc., Marlborough, Mass., 1981-84; sr. v.p. Pioneer Fin. Bank, Malden, Mass., 1984-90; prin. Tarella & Assocs. Bus. Devel. Cons., Hopedale, Mass., 1990—. Assoc. mem. Rep. Nat. Com., Washington, 1981—. Named Industry Spokesman of the Year, Pharm. Mfrs. Assn., 1979. Mem. Rotary. Roman Catholic. Home: 18 Bens Way Hopedale MA 01747-2008 Office: Waddell & Reed 33 Lyman St Westborough MA 01581

TARNEY, ROBERT E., research chemist; b. Hammond, Ind., Jan. 8, 1931; s. Edward Joseph and Rosella (Guinea) T.; m. Corlinda A. Maggitti, Nov. 20, 1966; children: Corlinda F., Robert J., Brian S. BS magna cum laude, Purdue U.; PhD, U. Wis. Sr. rsch. scientist E.I. duPont de Nemours & Co., Wilmington, Del., 1958—. Office: E I DuPont de Nemours & Co Tralee Pk Newark DE 19714-6098

TARPLEY, WILLIAM BEVERLY, JR., physics and chemistry consultant; b. Richmond, Va., Oct. 12, 1917; s. William B. and Sallie M. (Gatewood) T.; m. Nancy Tarpley, Aug. 10, 1948 (dec. Mar. 1980); 1 child, William B. III; m. Phyllis Malmquist, May 7, 1988. PhD, Columbia U., 1951. R & D chemist Schering Corp., Bloomfield, N.J., 1937-52; sr. phys. scientist U.S. Army Biol. Lab., Frederick, Md., 1952-55; v.p. R & D, Aeroprojects, Inc., West Chester, Pa., 1955-69; dir. materials dept. R & D Labs., Franklin Inst., Phila., 1969-71; v.p. R & D, Fluid Energy Equipment & Processing, Hatfield, N.J., 1971, Organic Recycling subs. UOP, West Chester, 1971-77, Energy & Minerals Rsch., Exton, Pa., 1977-85; ret., 1985; cons. in surface physics and chemistry, Downingtown, Pa., 1985—. Address: 29 Gunning Ln Woodmont North Downingtown PA 19335

TARPY, MARTIN LYSTER, beef wholesale executive; b. Central Falls, R.I., Aug. 22, 1913; s. Stephen and Mary Frances (Nolan) T.; m. Charlotte Joanna Hosfeld, Oct. 16, 1943; children: Peter, Susan. AB, Brown U., 1937. Pres. Tarpy's Inc., 1937—, West End Land Co, 1977—. Trustee Meml. Hosp., Pawtucket, R.I., 1962—, Hosp. Assn. R.I., Providence, 1985-91, Brown U., Providence, 1969—; bd. dirs. R.I. Renal Inst., Warwick, 1977—; corporator Delta Dental of R.I., Providence, 1974—; mem. Big Bros. Am. (Big Bro. of Yr.), Providence, Boys Club Am. (Keystone award), Pawtucket, R.I. Comdr. USN, 1942-46, PTO. Recipient Silver Beaver award Boy Scouts Am., 1953, Brown Bear award Brown U., 1991. Mem. New Eng. Wholesale Meat Dealers Assn. (bd. dirs. 1946—, pres. 1963). Roman Catholic. Home: 50 Pequot Rd Pawtucket RI 02861-3318 Office: Tarpy's 71 Dexter St Pawtucket RI 02860-1917

TARR, G. ALAN, political scientist, educator; b. Gloucester, Mass., Nov. 21, 1946; s. George Homer and Mary Ann (Krause) T.; m. Susan Jane Cote, Mar. 17, 1972; children: George Robert, Andrew Joseph. BA, Holy Cross Coll., 1968; MA, U. Chgo., 1970, PhD, 1976. Asst. prof. St. Olaf Coll., Northfield, Minn., 1975-78; asst. prof. Rutgers U., Camden, N.J., 1978-82, assoc. prof., 1982-88, prof., 1988—; cons. Nat. Independence Park, Phila., 1985-88, Ednl. Testing Svc., Princeton, N.J., 1989, Nat. Ctr.-State Cts., St. Paul, 1978-79, North Andover, Mass., 1979. Author: American Constitutional Law, 3d edit., 1991, State Supreme Courts in State and Nation, 1988. With U.S. Army, 1971-72. NEH fellow, 1986. Republican. Roman Catholic. Office: Rutgers U Camden NJ 08102

TARR, JOEL ARTHUR, history and public policy educator; b. Jersey City, May 8, 1934; s. Max Alfred and Florence (Levine) Tartalsky; m. Arlene Green, Sept. 2, 1956 (dec. June 1969); children: Michael Jay, Joanna Sue; m. Tova Brafman, Aug. 11, 1978; children: Maya Leah, Ilana Ariel. BS, Rutgers U., 1956, MA, 1957; PhD, Northwestern U., 1963. Asst. prof. Calif. State U., Long Beach, 1961-66; vis. prof. U. Calif., Santa Barbara, 1966-67; asst. prof. Carnegie Mellon U., Pitts., 1967-70, assoc. prof., 1969-72, prof. history and pub. policy, 1973-90, Richard S. Caliguiri prof. urban studies, 1990—, dir. program in tech. and soc., 1975-87, co-dir. program in applied history and social sci., 1978-86, acting dean Sch. Urban and Pub. Affairs, 1986, assoc. dean Coll. Humanities and Social Sci., 1988-91, acting dean Coll. Humanities and Social Sci., 1991-92. Author: A Study in Boss Politics, 1971; editor: Patterns of City Growth, 1974, Retrospective Technology Assessment, 1977, Transportation Innovation and Spatial Change in Pittsburgh, 1850-1934, 1978, Pittsburgh-Sheffield: Sister Cities, 1986, Technology and the Rise of the Networked City in Europe and America, 1988. Bd. dirs. Action Housing, Pitts., 1983. NEH fellow, 1969-70; grantee NSF, 1975-79, 78-80, 83-85, NOAA, 1982-84; recipient Robert Doherty Prize for contbns. to excellence in edn., 1992. Mem. AAAS, Pub. Works Hist. Soc. (pres. 1982-83, Abel Wolman prize 1989), Orgn. Am. Historians, Pub. History Assn. (nat. council), Am. Soc. Environ. History, Soc. for the History of Tech. Democrat. Jewish. Home: 5418 Normlee Pl Pittsburgh PA 15217-1116 Office: Carnegie-Mellon U Schneley Park Pittsburgh PA 15213

TARR, KENNETH J., investment company executive; b. N.Y.C., Mar. 1, 1945; s. Julius and Alice (Tamres) T.; 1 child, Alexandra Jennifer; m. Charlotte Kimball Kruesi, 1991. BA, U. Pa., 1967; MBA, Columbia U., 1971. With Chem. Bank, N.Y.C., 1971-72; asst. v.p. Standard and Poors/Inter Capital, N.Y.C., 1972-74; founder, mgr. S&P/Market Insights, N.Y.C., 1974-75; v.p. Kuhn Loeb and Co., N.Y.C., 1975-77; asst. v.p. Bessemer Trust Co., N.Y.C., 1977-80, v.p., 1980-82, sr. v.p., 1982-91, dir. rsch., 1984; pres., chief investment officer Credit Suisse Asset Mgmt., Inc., N.Y.C., 1991—. Mem. N.Y. Soc. Security Analysts. Clubs: N.Y. Yacht. Office: Credit Suisse Asset Mgmt Inc 12 E 49th St New York NY 10017

TARTAGLIA, ANTHONY PHILIP, dean, physician; b. Albany, N.Y., Sept. 14, 1932; s. Louis S. and Teresa (Vitale) T.; m. Jeanne Mochi; children: Robert, John, Catherine. BS, Union U., 1954; MD, Rochester (N.Y.) Med. Sch., 1958. Asst. resident Albany (N.Y.) Med. Ctr. Hosp., 1959-60, 1960-61, fellow in hematology, 1961-62, chief resident in medicine, 1962-63, asst. attending physician, asst. attending hematologist, 1963-70; chief hematologist Albany VA Hosp., 1970-75, attending physician, hematologist, 1975—, attending physician, 1963, cons. physician, 1970-75; cons. hematologist Children's Hosp., 1975—; chief of medicine St. Peter's Hosp., 1975-84; sr. v.p. patient and clin. affairs Albany Med. Ctr. Hosp., 1985, exec. v.p. patient care, 1985—, gen. dir., 1987-90; acting dean Albany Med. Coll., 1990, dean, 1990—; cons. hematologist Good Samaritan Hosp., 1975—. Contbr. numerous articles to profl. jours. Mem. State Bd. of Medicine, 1977-85; chmn. med. adv. com. blood program ARC, 1972-76, bd. dirs., 1976-82; chmn. med. adv. com. Leukemia Soc., Tri-Cities Cooley's Anemia Found., 1969-74; prin. investigator Nat. Polycythemia Vera Study Group; mem. task force on recredentialing and licensure N.Y. State Health Dept. and Bd. of Regents, 1986; mem. N.Y. State Coun. on Grad. Med. Edn., 1987—, chmn. subcom. on consortial devel., 1989—; mem. N.Y. State Hosp. Rev. and Planning Coun., 1990. Recipient Humanitarian of the Yr. award United Cerebral Palsy Ctr. for Disabled, 1982, Leone d'Oro award Sons of Italy in Am., 1989, Robert DeVillier's award Leukemia Soc. Am., 1989. Fellow ACP; mem. AMA, N.Y. State Med. Soc., Albany County Med. Soc. (sec. 1974-76, pres. 1978-80), Am. Soc. Hematology, Am. Fedn. Clin. Rsch., Northeastern Internal Med. Soc., Am. Internal Med. Soc., Phi Beta Kappa, Alpha Omega Alpha, Sigma Xi. Office: Albany Med Coll Ctr Hosp 43 New Scotland Ave Albany NY 12208-3478

TARTAGLIA, PAUL EDWARD, mechanical engineering educator; b. N.Y.C., Sept. 30, 1944; s. Anthony Joseph and Kathleen Agnes (Weiderkehr) T; children: David, Michael, Danielle. BSME, U. Detroit, 1967; MSME, Northwestern U., 1968; DEng, U. Detroit, 1970. Asst. prof. mech. engring. U. Mass., Amherst, 1970-75; project engr. Rodney Hunt Co., Orange, Mass., 1975-76; chief engr. Computerized Biomechanical Analysis, Amherst, 1976-77; from assoc. dean. engring. to dean engring. Norwich U., Northfield, Vt., 1980-91, prof. mech. engring., 1991—; cons. in field, 1970—. Recipient Ralph R. Teetor award Soc. Automotive Engrs., 1973. Mem. ASME, Am. Soc. Engring. Edn. Home: RD2-Box 3060 Northfield VT 05663 Office: Norwich U Dept Mech Engring Northfield VT 05663

TARTELL, ROBERT MORRIS, dentist; b. Bronx, N.Y., June 22, 1926; s. Julius and Ida (Saunders) T.; m. Lottie Haid Schachter, June 12, 1948; children: Ross Howard, Marc Sorrel, Adam Ethan. BA, N.Y.U., 1945, DDS, 1948. Lic. dentist, N.Y. V.p., dir. Medden, Inc., Valley Stream, N.Y., 1957-71; mng. ptnr. Profl. Investors, N.Y.C., 1957-91; pres., dir. Roberts Adv. Svc., Inc., N.Y.C., 1957-91; dir. postgrad. edn. Am. Soc. Study of Orthodontics, N.Y.C., 1971-72; mng. ptnr. RBT Co., Elmsford, N.Y., 1987—. Producer: Gilbert and Sullivan Light Opera Co., West Hempstead, N.Y., 1980—; co-copywrite: (Operetta) H.M.S. Pinafore in Yiddish, 1986. Pres. West Hempstead Sch. Commn. League, 1968-69; dir., founder West Hempstead Scholarship Fund, 1970-71. 1st lt. U.S. Army, 1952-54, Panama. Mem. Am. Dental Assn., 1st Dist. Dental Soc., Gen. Semantics Inst., ACLU, Mensa, Common Cause, Mason, Gallatin. Jewish. Home: 690 Hawthorne St West Hempstead NY 11552-3112 Office: 201 W Merrick Rd Valley Stream NY 11580-5595

TARTER, BARBARA JANE, entertainment executive; b. New Rochelle, N.Y., Nov. 27, 1946; d. Andrew Lewis and Dorothy (Bailey) Smith; m. Fred Barry Tarter, Apr. 12, 1969; children: Scott Andrew, Heather Michelle, Megan Elisabeth. V.p., owner Deerfield Communications, N.Y.C., 1973-85; v.p. The Rainbow Group, Ltd., N.Y.C., 1985—; v.p. Boardwalk Entertainment, N.Y.C., 1990—. Republican. Episcopalian. Office: The Rainbow Group Ltd 210 E 39th St New York NY 10016-0911

TARTER, FRED BARRY, advertising executive; b. Bklyn., Aug. 16, 1943; s. Irving and Edna (Kupferberg) T.; m. Barbara Jane Smith, Apr. 12, 1969; children: Scott Andrew, Heather, Megan. BS, CCNY, 1966. Pres. Jamie Publs. Hootenanny Enterprises, Inc., 1962-65; mdse. dir. Longines Symphonette Soc., 1965-67; with Universal Communications, Inc., N.Y.C., 1967—, pres., chief exec. officer, 1969-74; exec. v.p. Deerfield Communications, Inc., N.Y.C., 1974-87, pres., chief exec. officer, 1977-88; pres. Deerfield Books, Inc., N.Y.C., 1988-89; pub. S.E.W. mag., N.Y.C., 1977-88; pres. The Rainbow Group Ltd., N.Y.C., 1988—; bd. dirs. Caribbean Internat. News Corp., Screenvision, Inc., Lakeside Group, Inc., Boardwalk Entertainment, Ltd.; exec. producer Joanne Carson's VIP's, Miss Am. Teenager Pageant, 1972-73; pres. The Programme Exch., U.K. Ltd. Mem. Friars Club, The Reform Club (London). Home: 9 Davis Dr Armonk NY 10504-3006 Office: The Rainbow Group 210 E 39th St New York NY 10016-0911

TARZWELL, CLARENCE MATTHEW, aquatic biologist; b. Deckerville, Mich., Sept. 29, 1907; s. Matthew and Jessie J. (Wilson) T.; m. Vera V. Paiter, Sept. 3, 1938; children: Diane Kay Tarzwell Siegmund, Barbara Ann Tarzwell Fahey, Thomas Neil. Student, Eastern Mich. U., 1925-29; A.B., U. Mich., 1930, M.S., 1932, Ph.D., 1936; Sc. D. (hon.), Baldwin Wallace Coll., 1967. Inst. Fisheries Rsch. Mich. Dept. Conservation rsch. fellow U. Mich., Ann Arbor, 1930-33; doctorate problem trout steam improvement supr. Mich. Emergency Conservation Work Civilian Conservation Corps Stream Improvement, Lansing, 1933-34; asst. aquatic biologist, E. Coastal and Intermountain Region U.S. Fish and Wildlife Svcs., Stream Improvement, Salt Lake City, 1934; asst. range examiner Region 3 U.S. Forest Svcs., Lake and Stream Improvement, Albuquerque, 1935-38; asso. biologist, chief field sta. TVA, Decatur, Ala., 1938-43; chief biology sect. USPHS, Savannah, Ga., 1944-48; sci. dir., chief aquatic biology sect. R.A. Taft San. Engring. Center, Cin., 1948-65; founding dir. Nat. Marine Water Quality Lab., West Kingston, R.I., 1965-72, Nat. Fresh Water Quality Lab., Duluth, Minn., 1964-67; sr. rsch. adviser EPA, Nat. Environ. Rsch. Ctr., Corvallis, Oreg., 1972-75; adj. prof. Coll. Resource Devel., U. R.I., Kingston, 1966-75; vis. prof. Coll. Resource Devel., U. R.I., 1976-79; mem. aquatic life adv. com. Ohio River Valley San. Commn., 1952-68, Nat. Acad. Sci.-NRC Com. on Pest Control-Wildlife Relationships (subcom. on research), 1960-63; mem. expert adv. panel environ. health WHO, Geneva, 1962-64; mem. panel fisheries experts FAO, UN, 1962-63; mem. pesticide com. Internat. Assn. Game, Fish and Conservation Commrs., 1960-61; Am. del. 1st and 2d internat. meetings sci. research into water pollution OECD, Paris, 1961, 62, chmn. internat. com. on long-term effects toxicants on aquatic life, 1962-65; mem. adv. com. control stream temperatures Pa. San Water Bd., 1959-62; adv. com. water quality criteria project Calif. Water Pollution Control Bd., 1961-63; chmn. sec. interior's Nat. Tech. Adv. Com. on Water Quality Requirements for Fish, Other Aquatic Life and Wildlife, 1967-68; chmn., mem. water pollution com. Water Pollution Control Fedn., 1955-75; chmn. com. for devel. standard methods for bioassays, 1958-75, com. for methods of sampling and analysis, 1965-74; mem. N.Am. Game policy com., 1971-73; mem. com. on power plant siting Nat. Acad. Engring.-Nat. Acad. Scis., 1971-72; pollution abatement com. Am. Fisheries Soc., 1952-73; mem. regional task force, southeastern New Eng. water and related land resources study New Eng. River Basins Com., 1972-75; cons. Kuwait Inst. Sci. Research, 1975; mem. R.I. State Wide Planning Council, 1978-82, Ecology Action for R.I.; advisor Save the Bay, Bottle Bill Coalition. Author 125 publs. aquatic biology, water pollution, water quality criteria and standards, tocicity, studies, pesticides, malaria control, rodent ectoparasite and typhus control. Recipient Conservationist of Year award State of Ohio, 1961; Am. Motors Profl. Conservationist award, 1962; Aldo Leopold medal Wildlife Soc., 1963; Meritorious Service medal USPHS, 1964; Disting. Career award EPA, 1973; Bronze medal EPA, 1974. Mem. Am. Fisheries Soc. (hon. life., chmn. pollution com. 1950-51, 54-61, mem. 1962-73, award of excellence 1974), Am. Soc. Limnology and Oceanography (nat. adv. com. 1950-51, mem.-at-large 1959, bd. dirs. 1960-62), Societas Internationalis Limnologiae, Wildlife Soc. (hon. life), Am. Soc. Ichthyologists and Herpetologists (life), Am. Inst. Biol. Scis., USPHS Commd. Officers Assn. (pres. Cin. br. 1955-56), Stoic (pres. 1928), N.Am. Lake Mgmt. Soc., Phi Beta Kappa, Sigma Xi, Kappa Delta Pi, Phi Kappa Phi, Phi Sigma, Pi Kappa Delta. Home: 380B Post Rd Wakefield RI 02879-7508

TASH, STUART BARRY, accountant; b. Bklyn., Jan. 7, 1949; s. Irving and Ann (Schwartz) T.; m. Joyce Merrill Moss, Mar. 9, 1974; children: Allyson, Eric. BA in Polit. Sci., SUNY, Stony Brook, 1972. CPA. Revenue agt. IRS, N.Y.C., 1974-82; tax acct. Friedman Alpren and Green, N.Y.C., 1982-84, Konigsberg Wolf & Co., N.Y.C., 1984-85, Edward Isaacs and Co., N.Y.C., 1985-87; tax advisor Stollar & Assocs., Inc., N.Y.C., 1987—; cons. Nat. Commerce Exch., Inc., Jericho, N.Y., 1985—; instr. IRS, N.Y.C., 1978-80; fin. aid advisor Coll. Concerns, Inc., Baldwin, N.Y., 1991—. Vol. N.Y. State Soc. CPAs Accts. Hotline, N.Y.C., 1990—, Reading, Stony Brook, N.Y., 1970-73. Mem. N.Y. State Soc. CPA. Home: 2500 Enid Ct Baldwin NY 11510-3612 Office: 280 Park Ave S New York NY 10010-6121

TASHLICK, IRVING, financial research company executive, chemist; b. N.Y.C., July 5, 1928; s. Charles and Fanny (Uretzky) T.; m. Arlene Barsky, Nov. 22, 1950. BS, CCNY, 1949; MS, N.Y. Poly. U., 1953, PhD, 1958. Rsch. group leader Monsanto Co., Springfield, Mass., 1958-62; mgr. of rsch. InterPace Corp., Wharton, N.J., 1962-66; v.p. Wharton Industries, Inc., New Shrewsbury, N.J., 1966-72; pres. Alva-Tech Inc., Asbury Park, N.J., 1972-88; v.p. Bradley Rsch., Inc., West End, N.J., 1988—. Patentee in field. Mem. Am. Chem. Soc., Inst. Cert. Fin. Planners, Phi Beta Kappa. Home: 675 Ocean Ave # 7A Long Branch NJ 07740 Office: Bradley Rsch Inc 147 Brighton Ave PO Box 3194 West End NJ 07740

TASSINARI, SILVIO JOHN, nuclear chemist; b. N.Y.C., June 2, 1922; s. Ceasar and Adrean (Bacchiani) T.; B.S., St. Michael's Coll., 1943, M.S., 1947; Ph.D., Internat. U., Kansas City, Mo., 1949; m. Lorraine I. Murtha, Oct. 18, 1952; children—Patricia Jeanne, Barbara Lynne. Nuclear chemist Brookhaven Nat. Lab., Upton, N.Y., 1951-71, radiation safety officer and health physicist, 1952; nuclear chemist, tech. dir. nuclear medicine VA Hosp., Bklyn., 1971-72; nuclear chemist Sch. Nuclear Med. Tech., VA Hosp., Northport, N.Y., 1972-84; pres., dir. L.I. Labs., Inc.; cons. nuclear medicine, radiation protection, hazardous material mgmt., computers, office automation. Mem. Congl. Adv. Bd. Health, Energy and Edn. Vice pres. Smithtown Central Sch. Dist. Bd. Edn., 1954-67. Served with USN, 1942-45, USNR, 1946-70, as group comdr., 1966-70 (commendation Sec. Navy). Fellow Am Inst Chemists, Am. Soc. Radiologic Technologists; mem. Soc. Nuclear Medicine, Health Physics Soc., N.Y. Acad. Scis., Am. Men and Women in Sci., U.S. Naval Inst., Sigma Xi. Republican. Roman Catholic. Home: 47 Moriches Rd Nissequogue Saint James NY 11780 Office: LI Labs Inc PO Box 220 Saint James NY 11780-0601

TASSONE, BRUCE ANTHONY, chemical company executive; b. Phila., Sept. 8, 1960; s. Bruno Anthony and Julia A. (D'Alonzo) T. BSME, Univ. Pa., Phila., 1982; MBA with distinction, Univ. Pa., 1986. Asst. sales mgr. Gen. Electric, Schenectady, N.Y., 1982-84; dir., gen. mgr. Teleflex, King of Prussia, Pa., 1986—. Nominee, Entrepreneur of Year, Del. Valley, Phila., 1989. Mem. Soc. of Mech. Engrs., Beta Gamma. Republican. Roman Catholic. Home: 1722 Ridgeway Rd Upper Darby PA 19083-1614

TASSONE, GELSOMINA (GESSIE TASSONE), metal processing executive; b. N.Y.C., July 8, 1944; d. Enrico and A. Cira (Petriccione) Gargiulo; children: Ann Marie, Margaret, Theresa, Christine; m. Armando Tassone, Mar. 20, 1978. Student, Orange County Community Coll., 1975-79, Iona Coll., 1980—. Head bookkeeper Gargiulo Bros. Builders, N.Y.C., 1968-72; pres., owner A&T Iron Works, Inc., New Rochelle, N.Y., 1973—, Gessie Realty, New Rochelle, N.Y., 1980-86, Majestico Iron Works, Inc., 1980—, A&G Distbg. of West, New Rochelle, 1987—, A&T Contractors of Greater N.Y., 1987—. Recipient Profl. Image award Contractors Coun. Greater N.Y.C., 1986; named Businesswoman of Yr., Contractors Coun. Greater N.Y.C., 1985, N.Y. State Small Bus. Person of Yr., 1988, Entrepreneur of Yr. Inc. mag., 1990; company named a Successful Small Bus. Co. Westchester County C. of C./BSBA, 1986-88. Mem. Nat. Ornamental and Miscellaneous Metal Assn., Builders Inst. Westchester and Putnam County, Westchester Assn. Women Bus. Owners, Profl. Women in Constrn., Westchester C. of C. Office: A&T Iron Works Inc 25 Cliff St New Rochelle NY 10801-6803

TATE, JO OSBORNE, electronics engineer; b. Princeton, Ind.; d. Riley Frederick Jr. and Connie Ruby (Phillips) Osborne; m. Timothy Alan Tate, June 1, 1980; children: Jeffrey, Justine. BSEE, Purdue U., 1980; postgrad., U. Ariz., Air Force Inst. Tech., Wright-Patterson AFB. Cert. in EIT. Electronics engr. Emerson Electric, St. Louis, USAF Systems Command, Wright-Patterson AFB, U.S. Army Info. Systems Engring., Ft. Huachuca, Ariz.; computer specialist Office of Dir. Info. Systems for Command, Control, Communications and Computers Hdqrs. Dept. of the Army, 1989-91; supervisory electronics engr., chief engring. br. Ctr. for Info. Mgmt., Def. Info. Systems Agy., Arlington, Va., 1991—. Author: Local Area Network Specification for Army Minicomputer; editor Army OSI Implementation and Transition Plan, Army Minicomputer Menu Specification. Recipient Sustained Superior Performance award, 1985, Exceptional Performance award Hq. Dept. of Army, 1987, 90, 91, Quality Step Increase award, 1987, Spl. Act award, 1988. Mem. IEEE, Assn. Computing Machinery, Armed Forces Communications and Electronics Assn., Soc. Women Engrs. Republican. Baptist. Home: 3 Forester Ct Sterling VA 22170-6201 Office: HQDISA CIM/XINE 701 S Courthouse Rd Arlington VA 22204

TATE, LORETTA CLARA, health educator; b. Elberton, Ga., Mar. 6, 1948; d. Huit and Roberta (Edmond) T.; m. James Lucien Crump Jr., Oct. 16, 1980; chidlren: James Lucien III, Brendan Patrick. BS, St. Louis U., 1973; MS, SUNY, Buffalo, 1978; postgrad., Temple U., 1981, NYU, 1983. Staff radiographer Providence Hosp., Washington, 1968-69, Yonkers (N.Y.) Gen. Hosp., 1969, Mercy Hosp., Buffalo, 1970-73, Alexian Bros. Hosp., St. Louis, 1972-73; clin. instr. Thomas Jefferson U., Phila., 1974-76, instr., 1978-79, asst. prof., 1979-81, chmn. dept. radiation tech., 1981-85; dir. program and spl. projects Greater Phila. Health Action, Inc., 1985-87; health educator Educare, Phila., 1990—; cons. radiologic tech. texts F.A. Davis Pubs., Phila., 1982-83. Inventor health education game. Corr. sec. Ivy Leaf Parents Coun., Phila., 1990-92; mem. environ. edn. com. Awbury Arboretum Assn., Phila., 1990-92; asst. leader Boy Scouts Am., Cub Scout Pack 358, Phila., 1989-90. Recipient Mallinckrodt award Johns Hopkins Hosp., 1968. Mem. Phila. Soc. Radiologic Technologists (bd. chairperson, pres. elect., pres. 1980-84, cons. bd. dirs., 1990-92). Democrat. Baptist. Home: 1031 E Haines St Philadelphia PA 19138-1533

TATE, SHEILA BURKE, public relations executive; b. Washington, Mar. 3, 1942; d. Eugene L. and Mary J. (Doherty) Burke; m. William J. Tate, May 2, 1981; children: Hager Burke Patton, Courtney Paige Patton. BA in Journalism, Duquesne U., 1964; postgrad. in mass communications, U. Denver, 1975-76. Rsch. asst. Westinghouse Air Brake Co.; asst. account exec. Falhgren and Assos.; copywriter Ketchum, MacLeod and Grove, 1964-66; account exec. Burson-Marsteller Assocs., Pitts., 1967; sr. v.p. Burson-Marsteller Assocs., Washington, 1985-87; public rels. mgr. Colo. Nat. Bank, Denver, 1967-71; account exec. Hill and Knowlton, Inc., Houston, 1977-78; v.p. Hill and Knowlton, Inc., Washington, 1978-81; dep. to the chmn. Hill and Knowlton Inc., Washington, 1987-88; press sec. to First Lady White House, Washington, 1981-85; press sec. George Bush for Pres. Campaign, 1988; press sec. to Pres.-elect George Bush, 1988-89; vice chmn. Cassidy and Assocs. Pub. Affairs, Washington, 1989-91; pres. Powell Tate, Washington, 1991—; chmn. bd. dirs. Corp. for Pub. Broadcasting. Mem. Nat. Press Club, Nat. Press Found. (bd. dirs.). Republican. Clubs: Duquesne U. Century, F Street, Washington Golf and Country. Office: # 1000 700 13th St N W Washington DC 20005

TATELBAUM, SHELLEY GROD, grief counselor; b. Newark, Jan. 24, 1950; d. Irving Grod and Doris (Lewin) Welch; m. Ronald Jaye Tatelbaum, Jan. 16, 1977; children: Kara, Lisa. BS in Speech, Emerson Coll., 1972; MS in Counseling with highest honors, Iona Coll., 1990. Tchr. Arlington (Mass.) High Sch., 1972; med. asst. to pvt. practice physician Boston, 1972-77; dir. vol. and bereavement svcs. Hospice Dutchess County, Poughkeepsie, N.Y., 1989-90; pvt. practice grief counseling Poughkeepsie, 1990—; cons. Miller Funeral Home, Poughkeepsie, 1990—, Marist Coll. Counseling Ctr., Poughkeepsie, 1991, Vassar Hosp. Emergency, Poughkeepsie, 1991; presenter grief counseling support groups Jewish Community Ctr., YMCA, Poughkeepsie, 1990—; tchr. Dutchess Community Coll. Extension, 1990. Director visually handicapped rec. for blind Temple Beth El Sisterhood, Poughkeepsie, 1980-91; mem. Dutchess County Legis. Right to Die Com., Poughkeepsie, 1991, D.C. Legis. Med. Ethics Com.; active Vassar Hosp. Women's Aux., St. Francis Hosp. Women's Aux. Recipient Vol. Svc. award Temple Beth El Sisterhood, 1987. Mem. AACD, Assn. Death Edn. and Counseling, Elizabeth Kubler Ross Found., Am. Assn. Family and Marriage Counselors and Therapists, Hadassah, B'nai Brith Women. Jewish. Home: 147 Kingwood Park Poughkeepsie NY 12601-5452 Office: 39 Collegeview Ave Poughkeepsie NY 12603-2415

TATYREK, ALFRED FRANK, materials engineer, research chemist; b. Hillside, N.J., Jan. 23, 1930; s. Frank Peter and Frances (Luxa) T. BS, Seton Hall U., 1954; postgrad., Rutgers U., 1956-57. Rsch. chemist Bakelite div. Union Carbide, Bloomfield, N.J., 1953-58, U.S. Radium Corp., Morristown, N.J., 1959-62; analytical chemist insp. Chem. Procurement Dist. U.S. Army, N.Y.C., 1962-64; rsch. chemist Picatinny Arsenal U.S. Army, Dover, N.J., 1964-73; chem. materials engr. U.S. Army Armament Rsch., Devel. and Engring. Ctr., N.J., 1973—. Patentee chemiluminescent compounds and processes, crank case oil vacuum purification system for internal combustion engines; contbr. articles on mountaineering expdns. and adventures in the great mountain ranges of N.Am., S.Am., and Africa to mags.; contbr. over 25 sci. and tech. reports. First aid instr. ARC, Essex County, N.J., 1969-82; chief first aid Maplewood (N.J.) CD 1971—; patrol dir. Nat. Ski Patrol, Phoenicia, N.Y., 1978-84, sr. patroller So. N.Y. region, 1979—. Climbed Mt. Blanc, highest mountain peak in Europe; climbed to a summit of 19,730 on Mt. Kilimanjaro, highest mountain peak in Africa, 1972; also participated in numerous mountain expdns. in U.S. and Can., including 3 first ascents in No. Cascades of Wash. (the S.E. ridge of Mt. Goode, Aug. 1963, Peak 7732 via the Snow Chute, Aug. 1964, the East ridge of Bear Mt., Aug. 1964). Mem. Nat. Soc. Inventors, Magician's Round Table, Alpine Club of Can., Appalachian Mountain Club, Sierra Club, Sigma Xi (pres. Picatinny chpt. 1974-75, 79-80, 85-86). Roman Catholic. Home: 27 Orchard Rd Maplewood NJ 07040-1919 Office: US Army Armament Rsch Devel and Engring Ctr Dover NJ 07806-5000

TAUB, LARRY STEVEN, educator; b. N.Y.C., Dec. 28, 1952; s. Marvin and Blanche (Schweitzer) T. BA, Hofstra U., 1975; MA, NYU, 1976. Cert. social studies tchr., N.Y. Tchr. N.Y. Sch. for the Deaf, White Plains, N.Y., 1976—. Mem. Am. Deafness and Rehab. Assn., N.Y. State Educators of the Deaf, Bklyn. Assn. Deaf (athletic dir. 1971-74), Union League Assn., Fanwood Tchrs. Assn. (pres. 1989—). Office: NY Sch for the Deaf 555 Knollwood Rd White Plains NY 10603-1996

TAUBENFELD, HARRY SAMUEL, lawyer; b. Bklyn., June 27, 1929; s. Marcus Isaac and Anna (Engelhard) T.; m. Florence Spatz, June 17, 1956; children: Anne Gail Weisbrod, Stephen Marshall. BA, Bklyn. Coll., 1951; JD, Columbia U., 1954. Bar: N.Y. 1955, U.S. Supreme Ct. 1965, U.S. Dist. Ct. (so. and ea. dists.) N.Y. 1976. Assoc. Benjamin H. Schor, Bklyn., 1955-58; ptnr. Zuckerbrod & Taubenfeld, Cedarhurst (N.Y.), N.Y.C., 1958—; village atty. Village of Cedarhurst, 1977-88, trustee 1989—; legis. chmn., counsel Nassau County Village Ofcls., 1979-86, v.p., 1991—, mem. exec. com., 1989; mem. legis. com. N.Y. State Conf. Mayors, 1979-87; mem. exec. bd. Tri-County Village Ofcls.; arbitrator Am. Arbitration Assn. Dist. Ct. Nassau County, 1980—, Assessment Rev. Bd. Supreme Ct. Nassau County, 1981—; mem. Constl. Bicentennial Com., 1987-89. Assoc. chmn. Am. Zionist Fedn., 1985-87; pres. Herut Zionists Am., 1977-79; v.p. Hartman YMHA, 1983-87; del. World Zionist Congress, 1977, 82, 87; mem. Zionist Gen. coun., 1977-83; bd. govs. Jewish Agy., 1983—; mem. exec. com. World Zionist Orgn., 1983—; trustee United Jewish Appeal, 1986-91; bd. dirs.

United Israel Appeal, 1986—; hon. vice chmn., bd. dirs. Jewish Nat. Fund, Am. for a Safe Israel; hon. pres. World Coun. Herut Hatzoa, Jerusalem, Internat. Bd. Youthtowns of Israel. With USAR, 1948-56. Recipient Centenial award Jabotinsky Found. 1981, Betar Youth award World Betar 1982, award Internat. League for Repatriation of Russian Jews 1977, Youth Towns of Israel Leadership award 1973, Israel Bonds Leadership award 1976, Life Time Achievement award Israel Bonds 1991, Defender of Jerusalem award 1991. Mem. ABA, Nassau County Bar Assn. (mcpl. com. 1987, real property com. 1987), Internat. Assn. Jewish Lawyers and Jurists, B'nai B'rith, Nordau Circle Club, Cong. Beth Shalom (Lawrence, N.Y.). Home: 288 Leroy Ave Cedarhurst NY 11516-1424 Office: 575 Chestnut St PO Box 488 Cedarhurst NY 11516

TAUBER, DAVID MARK, emergency services professional; b. N.Y.C., Feb. 19, 1959; s. Walter Frank Tauber and Hanna Greenwood. Cert. paramedic, Springfield Tech. Community Co, 1979; MPH, U. Mass., 1985. Wilderness educator Experiment with Travel, Springfield, Mass., 1972-80; emergency med. technician Paramedic Ambulance, Springfield, 1972-80; dir. edn. Tauber Homestead Assocs., Northampton, Mass., 1980-86; paramedic City of Worchester, Mass., 1983-85; instr. paramedic tng. Vt. Paramedic Tng. Program, Battleboro, 1984-86; paramedic City of Hartford, Conn., 1986-89, dir. edn. and quality assurance, 1988-89; dir. edn. and advanced life support Stonehearth Open Living Opportunities, Conway, N.H., 1989—. Mem. Nat. Ski Patrol (instr.), Nat. Assn. Search and Rescue, Wilderness Med. Soc., AMA (program evaluator 1988—). Jewish. Office: Stonehearth Open Learning Opp RR 1 Box 163 Conway NH 03818-9512

TAUBER, GREGORY JOHN, priest; b. Whitehall, Pa., Oct. 23, 1951; s. Ferdinand Frank and Rose (Pramik) T. BA in Philosophy, Lateran, Rome, 1973; BA in Theology, Lateran, 1976; STL, Acad. Alfonianum, Rome, 1978. Ordained priest Roman Cath. Ch., 1977. Tchr., parish priest Reading (Pa.) Cen. Cath. High Sch., 1978-84, Pius X, Roseto, Pa., 1984-85; parish priest, assoc. pastor Sacred Heart, West Reading, Pa., 1985-91; assoc. pastor St. Francis of Assisi, Allentown, Pa., 1991—; asst. coord. Pro-Life Office, Allentown, Pa., 1988—; team leader Search Christian Maturity, 1978-82. Home and Office: St Francis of Assisi Rectory 801 N 11th St Allentown PA 18102-1387

TAUBMAN, MARTIN ARNOLD, immunologist; b. N.Y.C., July 10, 1940; s. Herman and Betty (Berger) T.; m. Joan Petra Mikelbank, May 30, 1965; children: Benjamin Abby, Joel David. B.S., Bklyn. Coll., 1961; D.D.S., Columbia U., 1965; Ph.D., SUNY, Buffalo, 1970. Asst. mem. staff Forsyth Dental Center, Boston, 1970—; head immunology dept. Forsyth Dental Center, 1972—, assoc. mem. staff, 1974-80, sr. staff mem., 1980—; asst. clin. prof. oral biology and pathophysiology Harvard U. Sch. Dental Medicine, 1976-79, assoc. clin. prof., 1979—; mem. oral biology and medicine study sect. NIH, 1980-84. Editor: (with J. Siots) Contemporary Microbiology and Immunology; contbr. articles to profl. jours, chpts. to books. Recipient Rsch. Career Devel. award, 1971-76, Fred Birnberg Alumni award for disting. dental research Columbia U. Assn. Dental Alumni, Disting. Faculty award Harvard Sch. Dental Medicine, 1990, Merit award NIH, 1991; fellow USPHS, 1962-63; postdoctoral fellow, 1966-70. Mem. Am. Soc. Microbiology, , Soc. Mucosal Immunology, Internat. Assn. Dental Research (Oral Biology award 1991), Am. Assn. Immunologists, Am. Assn. Dental Research (v.p. 1987—, pres. elect 1988, pres. 1989). Office: Forsyth Dental Ctr 140 Fenway Boston MA 02115

TAUKE, REGINA VOELKER, college dean; b. Phila., Oct. 19, 1938; d. Thomas A. and Madeline (McGlynn) Voelker; m. John D. Tauke, Dec. 26, 1964. BS in Physics, Chestnut Hill Coll., 1960; MS in Physics, Cath. U. of Am., 1964. Physicist Sun Oil Co., Newtown Square, Pa., 1960-62; grad. asst. Cath. U. of Am., Washington, 1962-64; rsch. physicist Naval Rsch. Lab., Washington, 1964-67; faculty mem. physics dept. Lafayette Coll., Easton, Pa., 1967; chair sci.-engrng.-physics, faculty electronics and physics Northampton Community Coll., Bethlehem, Pa., 1967-73, dean instructional svcs., 1973—. Contbr. over 30 sci. and ednl. papers in field. Home: 2579 Woods Edge Rd Bath PA 18014-1419 Office: Northampton Community Coll 3835 Green Pond Rd Bethlehem PA 18017-7599

TAURO, JOSEPH LOUIS, federal judge; b. Winchester, Mass., Sept. 26, 1931; s. G. Joseph and Helen Maria (Petrossi) T.; m. Elizabeth Mary Quinlan, Feb. 7, 1959 (dec. 1978); children—Joseph L., Elizabeth H., Christopher M.; m. Ann Lefavour Jones, July 12, 1980. AB, Brown U., 1953; LLB, Cornell U., 1956; JD (hon.), U. Mass., 1985; D.Laws (hon.), Suffolk U., 1986; JD (hon.), Northeastern U., 1990, New Eng. Sch. Law, 1992. Bar: Mass. 1956, D.C. 1960. Assoc. Tauro & Tauro, Lynn, Mass., 1958-59; asst. U.S. atty. Dept. Justice, Boston, 1959-60; ptnr. Jaffee & Tauro, Boston and Lynn, Mass., 1960-71; chief legal counsel Gov. of Mass., Boston, 1965-68; U.S. atty. Dept. Justice, Boston, 1972; judge U.S. Dist. Ct., Boston, 1972—; chief judge U.S. Dist. Ct., Mass., 1992—; exec. com. Cornell Law Assn., Ithaca, N.Y., 1968-71; adv. council Cornell Law Sch., Ithaca, 1975-80; dir. Security Nat. Bank, Lynn, 1961-72; adj. prof. of law Boston U. Law Sch., Boston, 1977—, judicial conf. of U.S.: Com. on the Operation of the Jury System, 1979-86, adv. com. on Codes of Conduct, 1988—; trustee Brown U., 1978—. Trustee Mass. Gen. Hosp., Boston, 1968-72, Children's Hosp. Med. Ctr., Boston, 1979—. 1st lt. U.S. Army, 1956-58. Named One of 10 Outstanding Young Men, Greater Boston Jaycees, 1966; recipient Disting. Alumnus award Cornell U. Law Sch., 1992. Fellow Am. Bar Found.; mem. ABA, Mass. Bar Assn., Boston Bar Assn. (coun. 1968-71), D.C. Bar Assn., Boston Yacht Club (Marblehead, Mass.). Republican. Roman Catholic. Office: US Dist Ct McCormack PO & Courthouse Rm 1615 Boston MA 02109

TAWA, NICHOLAS EDWARD, JR., surgical oncologist; b. Springfield, Mass., Feb. 14, 1956; s. Nicholas Edward and Michelina Maria (Siragusa) T.; m. Marianne Curran, Jan. 30, 1988. BA, U. Mass., 1977; PhD in Physiology, Harvard U., 1984; MD, Harvard Med. Sch., 1984. Cert. Am. Bd. Surgery, 1991. Assoc. surgeon Brigham and Women's Hosp., Boston, 1989-90, Beth Israel Hosp., Boston, 1991—; asst. prof. surgery, physiology Harvard Med. Sch., Boston, 1991—. Contbr. to books and articles to profl. jours. Warren-Whitman Alumni fellow, Harvard Med. Sch., 1990-91, Postdoctoral fellow, Am. Heart Assn., 1991—; NIH Nat. Rsch. Svc. award, 1991—. Fellow ACS (assoc.); mem. AAAS, Mass. Med. Soc., Assn. Acad. Surgery. Democrat. Office: Beth Israel Hosp Dept Surgery 330 Brookline Ave Boston MA 02215

TAX, RICHARD LOREN, ophthalmologist; b. N.Y.C., July 8, 1945; s. Anne Wolin, Aug. 18, 1968; children: Jason, Aaron. BA magna cum laude, Hofstra U., 1966; MD, Cornell U., 1970. Diplomate Nat. Bd. Med. Examiners. Intern Greenwich (Conn.) Hosp., 1970-71; flight surgeon USAF Malcolm Grow Med. Ctr., Andrews AFB, Md., 1971-73; resident Wills Eye Hosp., Phila., 1973-76; ophthalmologist Tri-County Eye Physicians and Surgeons, Southampton, Pa., 1976—. Contbr. articles to profl. jours. Capt. USAF, 1971-73. Fellow ACS, AAO; mem. AMA, Pa. Med. Soc., Bucks County Med. Soc., Del. Valley Ophthalmology Soc., Kerato Refractive Soc. Democrat. Office: Tri-County Eye Physicians and Surgeons 319 2d St Pike Southampton PA 18966

TAYLOR, BARBARA ALDEN, public relations executive; b. Dallas, Aug. 21, 1943; d. Harold Earl and Sally Alden (Howard) T.; BA, Smith Coll., 1965; MA, Antioch Coll., 1971. Vol., Peace Corps, India, 1966-68; tchr. Upper Merion Sch. Dist., King of Prussia, Pa., 1969-70; tchr. Cheltenham Sch. Dist., Elkins Park, Pa., 1970-74; pub. relations dir. Princess Hotels Internat., N.Y.C., 1974-75; chmn. Taylor & Hammond Ltd., N.Y.C., 1975-84; pres. Doremus/Marketshare, 1984-86; exec. v.p. Porter/Novelli, N.Y.C., 1986-90; sr. v.p. Hill and Knowlton, Inc., N.Y.C., 1990—. Bd. dirs. Madison Square Boys' and Girls' Club N.Y., 1978—, also mem. women's bd. Boys' Club N.Y. Named to Acad. of Women Achievers YWCA, 1985; bd. dirs. Up With People, Tucson, 1990—. Mem. Women in Communications, Pub. Relations Soc. Am. (counselors acad.), Soc. Am. Travel Writers, Advt. Women N.Y., Doubles Internat. Club, Smith Coll. Club N.Y., Lyford Cay Club, Jr. League City N.Y. Avocations: tennis, walking. Office: Hill and Knowlton Inc 420 Lexington Ave New York NY 10170-0002

TAYLOR, BARBARA ANN, psychologist, consultant; b. St. Croix Falls, Wis., Aug. 29, 1944; d. George Fallon and Helen Romelle (Olson) T.; divorced; children: Joseph Taylor Cerutti, Lara Jan Taylor Cerutti; m. Robert George Blaiklock, June 22, 1980. Student, U. Minn., 1962-64; BA, SUNY, Albany, 1966; MA, Montclair (N.J.) State Coll., 1977; PhD, Fordham U., 1985. Lic. psychologist, N.J., N.Y.; nationally cert. sch. psychologist, advanced level cognitive therapy. Cons. psychologist Straight & Narrow, Inc., Paterson, N.J., 1978-80; sch. psychologist Pascack Valley Bd. Edn., Hillsdale, N.J., 1979-83; rsch. cons. N.Y.C. Bd. Edn., 1985-87; cons. psychologist Lord Stirling Sch., Basking Ridge, N.J., 1984-91; pvt. practice, Cedar Grove, N.J., 1988—. Mem. Am. Psychol. Assn., N.J. Psychol. Assn., N.J. Assn. Sch. Psychology, Internat. Assn. Applied Psychology, Assn. Advancement Behavioral Therapy. Office: 466 Pompton Ave Cedar Grove NJ 07009-1812

TAYLOR, BARBARA JO ANNE HARRIS, government official, librarian, educator, civic and political worker; b. Providence, Sept. 9, 1936; d. Ross Cameron and Anita (Coia) Harris; m. Richard Powell Taylor, Dec. 19, 1959; 1 child, Douglas Howard. Student, Tex. Christian U., 1952, Salve Regina Coll., 1952-53; Student, Our Lady of the Lake Coll. and Convent, 1953-54, St. Mary's U., 1954, Incarnate Word Coll., 1954-55, Georgetown U., 1956-59, 62-63; BS cum laude, Georgetown U., 1963. Adminstrv. asst. profl. devel. and welfare NEA, Washington, 1956-59; asst. to dir. Georgetown U., Washington, 1956-59; exec. asst. All Am. Conf. to Combat Communism, Washington, 1960; spl. legis. asst. mil. affairs to chmn. mil. R & D subcom. U.S. Senate Armed Svcs. Com., 1971-72; U.S. nat. commr. UNESCO, 1982—, mem. exec. com. U.S. nat. commn., 1983—, sr. advisor 22d gen. conf., 1983. Del. numerous internat. confs.; U.S. commr. Nat. Commn. Librs. and Info. Sci., 1985—, mem. various coms.; gen. chmn. George Bush for Pres. Md. State Steering Com., 1987-88; co-chmn. Md. del. Rep. Nat. Conv., 1988, 92; dep. chmn. Md. Victory '88, Bush-Quayle Campaign; mem. Nat. Fin. Com. Reagan for Pres., 1980, Reagan-Bush, 1984; state fin. chmn. Md. Rep. Party, 1980; mem. Nat. Rep. Club; mem. exec. bd. Salvation Army Aux., Washington, 1967-75, chmn. membership com., 1969-70, chmn. fund-raising com., 1968-69, mem. exec. com. of exec. bd., 1970-75, treas., mem. fin. com., 1970-71, v.p., 1971-72, historian, 1972-73, editor newsletter, 1968-69, chmn. nominating com., 1974-75, spl. awards. for exceptional vol. svc., 1969, 72; mem. exec. bd. Welcome to Washington Internat., 1969-74, bd. advisers, 1969-74, dir. workshop, 1969-74; exec. bd. Am. Opera Sch. Soc., Washington, 1970—, v.p., 1974—; mem. Episc. Ch. Home for Aged Women's Aux., 1970-75, Episc. Ctr. for Emotionally Disturbed Children Women's Aux., 1970-75; exec. bd. St. David's Episc. Ch. Aux., 1970-72, 73-74; bd. dirs., treas. Spanish-Portuguese Study Group, 1970-72; mem. exec. bd. League Rep. Women D.C., 1964-67, 75-77, treas., 1964-67; mem. nat. coun. Women's Nat. Rep. Club, N.Y.C., 1969—, chmn. Washington-Md.-Va. legis. com., 1970-75; mem. Nat. Fedn. Rep. Women, 1964—; mem. nat. fin. com. Reagan for Pres., 1979-80; mem. governing bd. Capital Speakers Club, 1973-75, chmn. by-laws com., 1973-74; mem. exec. bd. Nat. Vols. in Action, 1975-77; mem. adv. com. Rock Creek Found. Mental Health, 1982-87; mem. 50th anniversary com. Save the Children; mem. fund-raising com. Washington Choral Arts Soc., 1982-84; state fin. chmn. Reagan-Bush campaign Md. Rep. Com., 1980; Md. coord. Nat. Inaugural Com., 1981, 85; trustee Crossnore Sch., Inc., N.C., 1983—, vice chmn. bd; trustee Kate Duncan Smith DAR Sch., Grant, Ala., 1983-86, Tamassee (S.C.) DAR Sch., 1983-86; adviser Bacone Am. Indian Coll., Inc., Muscogee, Okla., 1983-88. Mem. ALA, Spl. Librs. Assn., Coun. on Libr. Resources (commn. on preservation and access), Am. Libr. Trustees Assn., Libr. Adminstrn. and Mgmt. Assn., Assn. Coll. and Rsch. Librs., Am. Antiquarian Soc., Internat. Platform Assn., Spanish-Portuguese Study Group, Nat. Lawyers' Wives, Nat. Capital Law League, DAR (chmn. nat. resolutions com. 1980-83, chmn. nat. DAR sch. com. 1983-86; state historian 1978-80, mem. state bd. mgmt., 1973—, libr. gen., mem. exec. com. 1986-89, numerous other offices), Nat. Soc. Children Am. Revolution (sr. nat. asst. registrar 1978-80, mem. sr. nat. bd. mgmt. 1978-80, sr. nat. exec. com. 1978-80), Nat. Assn. Parliamentarians, World Affairs Council, League of Rep. Women, Md. Fedn. Rep. Women, WNRC, Nat. Fed. Rep. Women, Commn. on Preservation and Access, Lit. Vols. Am. (Washington Met. area affiliate), Exec. Women in Govt., Am. News Women's Club, Internat. Club, Capitol Hill Club, Washington Club, Congl. Country Club (Potomac, Md.).

TAYLOR, BARRY, museum director; b. Atlantic City, N.J., Nov. 6, 1945; s. E.H. and Dorothy (White) T.; m. E. Gay LeCleire, Sept. 26, 1976; children: Catherine, Sean. Student, U. So. Calif., L.A., 1963-64, Rutgers U., 1965-66; AS, Atlantic Community Coll., 1968. Asst. mgr. Town of Smithville, Absecon, N.J., 1964-70; bus. mgr. Wheaton Cultural Alliance, Millville, N.J., 1970-76; asst. dir. Wheaton Hist. Assoc., Millville, N.J., 1976-78, exec. dir., 1978-91; pres. Wheaton Cultural Alliance, Millville, N.J., 1991—; treas. Creative Glass Ctr. of Am., Millville, 1980—. Pres. Tuckahoe (N.J.) River Action Com. for Environment, 1988. Mem. Am. Assn. Mus., N.J. Mus. Coun., Mid-Atlantic Assn. Mus., Kiwanis (bd. dirs. Millville chpt. 1989—), Millville C. of C. (bd. dirs. 1982-84, 89—, v.p. 1984-85, pres. 1991). Office: Wheaton Cultural Alliance Wheaton Village Millville NJ 08232

TAYLOR, BARRY L., retail automotive executive; b. Richmond, Va., Sept. 27, 1948; s. Henry L. and Audrey (McMullen) T.; m. Sharon Amy Taylor, May 31, 1980; children: Heather, Bryan, Rachel. BBA, Marshall U., Huntington, W.Va., 1970. Div. mgr. Sears, Roebuck & Co., Richmond, Va., 1970-74; merchandise mgr. Sears, Roebuck & Co., Norfolk, Va., 1975-79; group buyer Sears, Roebuck & Co., Virginia Beach, Va., 1980-82; store ops. mgr. Sears, Roebuck & Co., Frackville, Pa., 1982-84; pres. David Ertley Leasing Corp., Kingston, Pa., 1984-87; v.p., gen. mgr. David Ertley Inc., Kingston, Pa., 1984-87; group v.p. ops. The Ertley Dealerships, Kingston, Pa., 1987-89; exec. v.p., chief fin. exec. The Ertley Dealerships, Wilkes-Barre, Pa., 1990—; bd. dirs. David Ertley, Inc., Wilkes-Barre. Participant Leadership Wilkes-Barre, 1988; fundraising com. mem. Com. for Econ. Growth, Wilkes-Barre, 1989. Mem. C. of C. (bd. dirs. 1989—), Kiwanis. Republican. Methodist.

TAYLOR, BRUCE RAYMOND, school system administrator; b. Brookville, Pa., Dec. 6, 1945; s. Bruce J. and Margaret (McVeigh) T.; m. M. Ann George, June 20, 1970; children: Dustin J., Erin C. BS, Slippery Rock U., 1969; MEd, Ind. U. of Pa., 1972; EdD, Temple U., 1988. Tchr. Norristown (Pa.) Area Sch. Dist., 1969-71; supr. spl. edn. Chester County Intermediate Unit, Coatesville, Pa., 1972-79, Capital Area Intermediate Unit, Harrisburg, Pa., 1979-84, Cen. Bucks Sch. Dist., Doylestown, Pa., 1984—; workshop dirs. Dept. Edn. Annual Conf., Shippensburg, Pa., 1989. Advocate Rights of Disabled Children, Bucks County, Pa., 1987. Mem. Coun. for Exceptional Children, Assn. for Children with Learning Disabilities, Assn. for Supervision and Curriculm Devel., Jaycees (v.p. Pa. chpt. 1979-80), Pa. Coun. for Exceptional Children (workshop dir. 1987). Democrat. Presbyterian. Home: 8202 Greyfriars Terr Chalfont PA 18914 Office: Cen Bucks Sch Dist 67 E Butler Ave Doylestown PA 18901-5271

TAYLOR, CHARLES GEORGE, arts educator, consultant; b. Cedar Rapids, Iowa, Aug. 16, 1917; s. Carson Lee and Phyllis Irene (Bruner) T.; m. Eleanor Custer Gitt, Apr. 19, 1941; children: Susan S. Taylor Menges, Carson G., Thomas G. AB, Amherst Coll., 1939; MEd, Rhode Island Coll., 1961; Diploma di Profitto, U. Florence, Italy, 1958; Diplôme d'Etudes Françaises, U. Poitiers, Tours, France, 1972. Advt. copywriter Carson, Pirie, Scott and Co., Chgo., 1939-40; asst. advt. mgr. Armstrong Cork Co., Lancaster, Pa., 1940-47; promotion mgr. CBS, Washington, 1947-48; owner, operator various radio stas., Providence, Worcester, Mass., and Albany, N.Y., 1948-58; tchr. langs., adminstr. Moses Brown Sch., 1960-71; tchr., adminstr. R.I. Sch. Design, Providence, 1972-75, asst. to pres., 1973-76, trustee, 1977—, sec. bd. trustees; dir. Hill Realty, Preservation Soc., Providence, 1977-90; cons. TV and radio stas., 1960-70. Pres. Meeting St. Sch., Providence, 1952; mem. Little Compton Sch. Com., 1967-71. Recipient Better Understanding award English Speaking Union, 1953; named Vol. of Yr., Providence Sch. Com., 1990. Mem. Providence Preservation Soc. (archtl. rev. com. 1972-85), Providence Art Club, Univ. Club, Hope Club, Sakonnet Golf, Sakonnet Yacht. Unitarian. Home: 92 Prospect St Providence RI 02906 Office: 21 Meeting St Providence RI 02903

TAYLOR, DAVID BROOKE, lawyer, banker; b. Salt Lake City, Oct. 14, 1942; s. Lee Neff and June (Bitner) T.; m. Carolyn Kaufholz, May 29, 1965; children: Stewart, Allison. BA, U. Utah, 1964; JD, Columbia U., 1967. Bar: N.Y. 1967. Ptnr. Wickes, Riddell, Bloomer, Jacobi & McGuire, N.Y.C., 1967-79, Morgan, Lewis & Bockius, N.Y.C., 1979-89; banker Chase Manhattan Bank, N.A., N.Y.C., 1989—. Mem. ABA, N.Y. State Bar Assn., Internat. Bar Assn. Home: 225 Loring Ave Pelham NY 10803-2254 Office: Chase Manhattan Bank NA 1 Chase Manhattan Plz New York NY 10081-0001

TAYLOR, DAVID COBB, chemistry educator, consultant; b. Portland, Maine, June 7, 1939; s. Wesley Ordway and Gertrude Harriman (Palmer) T.; m. Elaine Busch, May 28, 1971. AB, Bowdoin Coll., 1961; MA, Wesleyan U., 1963; PhD, U. Conn., 1970. Asst. prof. Slippery Rock (Pa.) State Coll., 1968-72, assoc. prof., 1972-83; prof. Slippery Rock U., 1983—; bd. dirs. Oil Well Automation Co., Inc., Oil City, Pa. Fellow Am. Inst. Chemists; mem. AAAS, Am. Chem. Soc. Office: Slippery Rock U Dept Chemistry Slippery Rock PA 16057-1326

TAYLOR, DAVID JOHN, real estate developer; b. Kansas City, Mo., Apr. 14, 1943; s. Harold Bertrum and Rose Mary (Casella) T.; children: Christie, Brett. AS, Mitchell Coll., 1963; BS, U. Hartford, 1965. Licensed real estate broker, Conn., Mass. Adminstr. Aetna Life & Casualty, Hartford, Conn., 1965-76; owner Taylor Assocs., Glastonbury, Conn., 1976—; pres. David J. Taylor, Inc., Glastonbury, 1980—; owner Hunters Run Stables, Glastonbury, 1983—; gen. ptnr. numerous ltd. partnerships, Glastonbury, 1977—. With USAR, 1965-71. Mem. U.S. Assn. Realtors, Conn. Assn. Realtors, Hartford Assn. Realtors, U.S. Tennis Assn. (Boston). Democrat. Roman Catholic. Home: 62 Hunter Ln Glastonbury CT 06033-1422 Office: Taylor Assocs 62 Hunter Ln Glastonbury CT 06033-1422

TAYLOR, DAVID KERR, international business educator, consultant; b. Oxford, N.C., Oct. 11, 1928; s. David Kerr and Myrtle Norman (Shamburger) T.; m. Isabel de Sousa Botelho de Albuquerque, Apr. 23, 1960; children: Anne de Albuquerque Taylor Grave, Katherine Rowena Taylor. BA, Duke U., 1947, JD, 1949. Bar: N.Y., N.C. Atty. Ins. Co. N.Am., N.Y.C., 1949-51, Milbank, Tweed, Hadley & McCloy, N.Y.C., 1954-55; internat. exec. Mobil Corp., N.Y.C., Washington, Can., Portugal, France, Angola, Indonesia, Tunisia, 1955-86; sr. fellow in internat. bus. diplomacy Georgetown U. Sch. Fgn. Svc., Washington, 1987—; mem. sr. adv. panel UN Sec. Gen. Panel on Iraq Oil Sales, N.Y.C.; pres. Luso-Am. Bus. Coun., 1987-89. 1st lt. U.S. Army, 1951-54, Germany. Mem. Am. Portuguese Soc. (bd. dirs. 1966—, pres. 1968-70, 76-80), Washington Export Coun., Nat. Economists Club, Washington Inst. Fgn. Affairs, Cosmos Club, Phi Beta Kappa. Home: 2737 Devonshire Pl NW Washington DC 20008 Office: Georgetown U Sch Fgn Ser Washington DC 20057

TAYLOR, DONALD ADAMS, lawyer; b. St. Louis, Mar. 25, 1943; s. Robert Lewis and Mary Ellen (McCord) T.; children: Sarah, Carrie, Seth. AB, Princeton U., 1965; JD, Cornell U., 1968. Systems analyst, mktg. rep. IBM Corp., N.Y.C., 1968-71; ct. planner Court System State of N.Y., Mineola, 1971-74; dir. edn. and tng. Office Ct. Adminstrn. State of N.Y., N.Y.C., 1974-87; ptnr. Taylor and Dalton Law Offices, Manhasset, N.Y., 1987-90; sole practice Manhasset, 1990—. Pres. The Ecology Group, Sea Cliff, N.Y., 1972. Mem. Nassau County Bar Assn., Manhasset C. of C. (pres. 1991), Kiwanis (pres. 1992-93). Republican. Office: 337 Plandome Rd Manhasset NY 11030-1940

TAYLOR, DOROTHY HARRIS, real estate broker; b. Richmond, Va., Nov. 3, 1931; d. Edgar Alan and Sadie (Wheeler) Harris; m. Gethsemane Jess Taylor (dec. Nov. 1964); children: Marlene J., Eric M., Andre E. Student, L.I. U., 1959, John J. Criminal Coll., 1974, Queen's Coll., 1983, 91—; diploma in Mgmt. of Residential Properties, Queen's Coll., 1987, postgrad., 1991; student, St. John's U., 1984, 86. Lic. real estate broker. Toll collector Port of N.Y. and N.J. Authority George Washington Bridge (formerly Port of N.Y. Authority), N.Y.C., 1967-80, tolls dispatcher, 1967; transp. driver George Washington Bridge/Port Authority of N.Y. & N.J., Ft. Lee, N.J., 1972-75, acting supervising toll collector, 1974-75; transp. driver Port of N.Y. and N.J. Authority George Washington Bridge (formerly Port of N.Y. Authority), Ft. Lee, N.J., 1972-75; acting supervising toll collector Port of N.Y. and N.J. Authority George Washington Bridge (formerly Port of N.Y. Authority), Ft. Lee, 1974-75; sales exec. Flushing Tribune, 1979; real estate salesperson Parkfield Realty, Queens Village, N.Y., 1982-83, Arro of Queens, 1983-84; real estate broker Arro of Queens, Queens Village, 1984-85; residential appraiser Arro of Queens, N.Y.C., 1986—. Active Nat. Arbor Day Found., North Shore Animal Shelter League; mem. com. for disabled children Queens Coll.; charter mem. Nat. Mus. Women in Arts; mem. Nat. Trust of Hist. Preservation, The Smithsonian Assocs., Am. Mus. Natural History, N.Y.C., ace program Queens Coll., Flushing N.Y.; contbr. Dem. Nat. Com.; mem. Sickle Cell Anemia Found. Greater N.Y.; contbr. The Lighthouse Vol. Cancer Fund Am., 1990; vol. community social work for children and sr. citizens, 1991. Named Hon. Citizen, City of Williamsburg, Va.; John F. Kennedy Libr. hon. fellow, Boston. Mem. NAFE (network dir. 1983-84), Am. Assn. Ret. Persons, Nat. Assn. Unknown Players for Film, TV and Print Modeling Arts, Nat. Geog. Soc., Am. Entrepreneurs' Assn., Dorcas Soc. (Bklyn. pres. 1957-58), Queens Coll. Women's Club, Nat. Audubon Soc., Order Ea. Star, Heroines of Jericho, Lady of Knights. Democrat.

TAYLOR, DOUGLAS NIALL, psychologist; b. Mt. Vernon, N.Y., May 13, 1957; s. Edwin Douglas and Lois Johnstone (O'Neill) T. BA, McGill U., 1979; MA, U. Hartford, 1983; PhD, CUNY, 1991; cert. in biofeedback tng., 1988. Rsch. asst. McGill U., 1979-81; rsch. asst. U. Hartford, 1982-83; instr. CUNY, 1985-87, 88-89; predoctoral rsch. fellow Narcotic & Drug Rsch., Inc., N.Y.C., 1988-91, postdoctoral rsch. fellow, 1991—; pvt. practice N.Y.C., 1988—. Contbr. numerous articles to profl. pubs.; has made many presentations on psychol. topics. Mem. Am. Psychol. Soc., Assn. for Applied Psychophysiology and Biofeedback, N.Y. Soc. for Clin. Hypnosis. Office: Narcotic & Drug Rsch Inc 11 Beach St New York NY 10013

TAYLOR, DUNCAN PAUL, research neuropharmacologist; b. Bremerton, Wash., Feb. 4, 1949; s. Alan Earl and Barbara Eleanor (Thiel) T.; m. Jeanne Louise Damgaard, Apr. 8, 1972; 1 child, Aubrey Elizabeth. BS in Chemistry, Calif. Inst. Tech., 1971; PhD in Biochemistry, Oreg. State U., 1977. Technician analytical svcs. Carnation Co. Rsch. Labs., Van Nuys, Calif., 1967-70; Peace Corps vol. Princess Margaret Secondary Sch., St. Johns, Antigua and Barbuda, 1971-73; grad. teaching and rsch. asst. biochemistry and biophysics Oreg. State U., Corvallis, 1973-77; rsch. assoc. sect. biochemistry and pharmacology NIMH, Bethesda, Md., 1977-79; scientist, neuropharmacologist, rsch. assoc. Pharm. div. Mead Johnson & Co., Evansville, Ind., 1979-80, sr. scientist, group leader, 1980-82; sr. scientist, group leader, neuropharmacologist Pharm. R & D div. Bristol-Myers Co., Evansville, 1982-83; sr. rsch. scientist, mgr. Pharm. R & D div. Bristol-Myers Co., 1983-85, rsch. fellow preclin. cen. nervous system rsch., 1985-89; sr. rsch. fellow preclin. cen. nervous system rsch. Pharm. R & D div. Bristol-Myers Squibb Co., Wallingford, Conn.; mem. external adv. bd. dept. chemistry U. So. Miss.; grant reviewer NSF, 1981, 2, Med. Rsch. Coun. Can., 1987, 88; frequent presenter to profl. confs. Contbr. numerous articles and abstracts to profl. jours. Bd. dirs. Posey County chpt. Am. Cancer Soc., 1983-85; mem. chancel choir 1st United Meth. Ch., Mt. Vernon, Ind., 1979-86, mem. adminstrv. bd., 1980-83, 84-86; mem. Tri-State Cursillo Community; mentor Horizons Leadership Acad., Evansville-Vanderburgh Sch. Corp., 1985; mem. adult choir South Congl. Ch., Middletown, Conn., 1986—, deacon, 1987-90, co-chmn., 1989-90, mem. coun., 1989-90, mem. task force on long-range planning, 1989-90; cons. Project Bus., Jr. Achievement, 1988. Scholar Carnation Co., 1967-70, Calif. State scholar, 1967-68, 70; rsch. fellow NSF, 1970, Cold Spring Harbor Labs., 1974. Fellow Am. Inst. Chemists; mem. AAAS, Am. Chem. Soc., Am. Soc. for Neurochemistry, Soc. for Exptl. Biology and Medicine, Am. Soc. for Pharmacology and Exptl. Therapeutics, Fedn. Am. Scientists, Soc. for Neurosci. (v.p. Conn. chpt. 1989—), Brit. Brain Rsch. Assn., European Brain and Behavior Soc., Fedn. Am. Socs. for Exptl. Biology, Internat. Brain Rsch. Orgn.-World Fedn. Neuroscientists, N.Y. Acad. Scis., Sigma Xi, Phi Lambda Upsilon. Democrat. Home: 49 Black Walnut Dr Middletown CT 06457-6130 Office: Bristol-Myers Squibb Co 5 Research Pky Wallingford CT 06492-1996

TAYLOR, EDMUND FREDERICK, investment banking executive; b. N.Y.C., Mar. 24, 1960; s. Douglas Frederick and Mary Fay (Midworth) T.; m. Diane Marie Copersino, Sept. 19, 1987; 1 child, Erica Fay. BA magna cum laude, Hamilton Coll., 1982; MBA, NYU, 1988. Analyst A. G. Becker,

N.Y.C., 1982-83; assoc. Goldman Sachs & Co., N.Y.C., 1983-84; corp. v.p. Drexel Burnham Lambert, N.Y.C., 1984-90; v.p. Daiwa Securities Am., Inc., N.Y.C., 1990—. Contbr. chpt. to book. Big bro. Cath. Big Bros. Am., Bklyn., 1983-85; tchr. Jr. Achievement Am., N.Y.C., 1983-84. Named Sybron Corp. scholar, Rochester, N.Y., 1981. Mem. N.Y. Rd. Runners Club, Delta Phi Nat. Fraternity (bd. govs. 1983—). Republican. Roman Catholic. Office: Daiwa Securities Am Inc 200 Liberty St New York NY 10281

TAYLOR, HAROLD ALLEN, JR., federal agency administrator; b. San Jose, Calif., June 27, 1936; s. Harold Allen and Marie Anna (Briody) T.; B.A., Brown U., 1958; M.A., U. Minn., 1968; m. Theresa Josephine Kustritz, Aug. 29, 1963; children: Harold A., III, Ruth F., Jonathan L.E. Project leader office Mineral Supply, U.S. Bur. Mines, Mpls., 1968-70, commodity specialist div. ferrous metals, Washington, 1970-74; commodity analyst U.S. Internat. Trade Commn., Washington, 1974-80; sr. commodity specialist br. indsl. minerals U.S. Bur. Mines, Washington, 1980—; chmn. subcom. on nomenclature Am. Soc. Testing Materials, 1987—, com. on dimension stone, 1989—. Coord. Furniture Bank, 1973-80; chmn. North Arlington Parish Council, 1976; precinct capt. Arlingtonians for a Better County, 1975, area chmn., 1976. Mem. AIME (sec. 1983-84, first vice chmn. 1984-85, chmn. 1985-86, exec. adv. bd. mineral econs. subsect. 1981-83, 87-91), Am. soc. Testing and Materials (sec. com. dimension stone 1990—), Soc. Govt. Economists (chmn. materials policy panels 1979-84), Toastmasters (sec. 1971, ednl. v.p. 1977, 85, pres. 1978, 81, 87, 91, asst. area gov. 1978-79, area gov. 1979-80, dep. div. lt. gov. 1989-90), Capitol Metals Forum (steering com. 1979-85), Nova Catholic Community (sec. 1975), Sigma Gamma Epsilon. Contbr. articles to profl. jours. and encys. Home: 6321 11th Rd N Arlington VA 22205-1717 Office: US Bur Mines 810 7th St NW Washington DC 20241-0001

TAYLOR, HAROLD EVANS, astrophysics educator; b. Phila., Sept. 13, 1939; s. Joseph Hooton and Sylvia (Evans) T.; m. Susan Tatum, Aug. 15, 1964 (div. Nov. 1983); children: Laura, Peter, Amy, Jeremy; m. Suzanne Rie Day, June 24, 1984; stepchildren: Bernard Day, Doren Day Tenerowitz. BA in Physics, Haverford (Pa.) Coll., 1961; MS in Meterology, MIT, 1962; PhD in Space Physics, U. Iowa, 1966. Rsch. assoc. U. Iowa, Iowa City, 1966, NASA/Goddard Space Flight Ctr., Greenbelt, Md., 1966-68, Princeton (N.J.) U., 1968-71; from asst. prof. to prof. Stockton State Coll., Pomona, N.J., 1971—; vis. prof. Princeton (N.J.) U., 1986-87. Contbr. articles to profl. jours. Bd. dirs. Atlantic County adv. bd., solid waste adv. coun., Mullica Twp. Zoning Bd., 1978-90. Mem. Am. Phys. Soc., IEEE, Am. Assn. Physics Tchrs., Am. Solar Energy Soc., Internat. Solar Energy Soc. Mem. Soc. of Friends. Home: Taylors Ln Riverside Homestead Farm Cinnaminson NJ 08077-1610 Office: Stockton State Coll NAMS Pomona NJ 08240

TAYLOR, HENRY ROTH, textiles company executive; b. Phila., Sept. 25, 1940; s. Henry and Helen Jacquelyn (Roth) T.; B.S., Millersville State Coll., 1962; postgrad., Pa. State U., 1963-65; MS, Temple U., 1966; postgrad., Queens Coll., Oxford U., summer 1973; m. Cynthia Mary DeMarco, Aug. 17, 1968; children: Christopher, Peter, Brett, Melissa. Mng. editor Montgomery Newspapers, Ft. Washington, Pa., 1962-66; news bur. dir. Drexel U., Phila., 1966-68, ann. fund dir., 1971-72; dir. pub. relations Ursinus Coll., Collegeville, Pa., 1968-71, Widener U., Chester, Pa., 1972-74; asst. v.p., dir. athletics Spring Garden Coll., Phila., 1974-87, lectr. mass media, 1979-87; exec. dir. Phila. sect. Profl. Golfers Assn., 1987-89; dir. Athletics, chmn. physical edn. Phila. Coll. Textiles and Sci., 1989-92; dir. hobby rels. Fleer Corp., Mt. Laurel, N.J., 1992—; mem. exec. com. Eastern Pa. Athletic Conf., 1982-86; pres. Eastern States Athletic Conf., 1985-87; part-time sportscaster, talk show host, announcer Sta. WIFI, Phila., 1965-70; with Ted Taylor Assocs., Abington, Pa., part-time 1965-74; part-time sportscaster and announcer WIBF Radio, Jenkintown, Pa., 1970-74, Sta. WNPV, Lansdale, Pa., 1983-88. Founding pres. Glenside Boys Athletic Club, 1958-63; commr. Keystone State Football Conf., 1959-62; dir. Pop Warner Found., 1963-65; pres. Warminster Youth 963-65; pres. Warminster Youth Activities Orgn., 1965-71; mem. Abington Twp. Spl. Police, 1974-81, sec., 1977-78; exec. com. Highland Sch. PTA, 1974-81; mem. Abington Twp. Police Rev. Bd., 1977-81; co-chmn. Phila. Baseball Card and Sports Memorabilia Shows, 1975-82, Ocean City (N.J.) Shows, 1981-84. Named Man of Yr., Hatboro Jr. C. of C., 1962, Suburban Bucks Jr. C. of C., 1967, Citizen of Yr., Southampton Kiwanis, 1972, One of 100 Outstanding Grads. in 100 Yrs., Cheltenham (Pa.) High Sch., 1984; recipient Ursinus Coll. Varsity Club award, 1970; Piece of the Walk civic award Ocean City, N.J., 1981. Mem. Council for Advancement and Support of Edn., Pa. Assn. Colls. and Univs., Phila. Pub. Relations Assn., Pub. Relations Soc. Am., Suburban Pub. Relations Club, Phila. Sportswriters Assn., Coll. Sports Info. Dirs. Am., Eastern Pa. Sports Collectors Club (pres. 1978-82). Republican. Presbyterian. Lodge: Rotary. Author: (with Robert E. Schmierer) Phillies Cheklist Book, 1979, World Series Baseball Cards, 1987, The Rookie Book, 1988, 300 All-Time Baseball Stars, 1988, Encyclopedia of Baseball Cards, 1988; assoc. editor Sports Collectors Bible, 1978; columnist Sports Collectors Digest, 1980-92, Phila. Daily News, 1991—; contbr. articles to profl. jours. Home: 1527 Edge Hill Rd Abington PA 19001 Office: Fleer Corp Exec Plz 1120 Rte 73 Mount Laurel NJ 08054

TAYLOR, HUMPHREY JOHN FAUSITT, information services executive; b. Meshed, Iran, Sept. 6, 1934; came to U.S., 1976; s. Geoffrey Fausitt and Frances Margaret (Kenyon) T.; m. Penelope Helen Taylor, Dec. 19, 1970; children: Zanthe, Helena. BA with honors, Cambridge (Eng.) U., 1958. Dist. officer Govt. of Tanganyika, 1959-62; mktg. and opinion researcher Nat. Opinion Poll, Eng., 1963-66; mng. dir. Opinion Rsch. Ctr., Eng., 1966-76; with Louis Harris and Assocs., N.Y.C., 1976-81; pres. Harris and Assocs., N.Y.C., 1981—, CEO, 1992—. Trustee U.S. com. UNICEF, N.Y.C., 1981-87, Overseas Devel. Coun., Washington, 1987—, Am. Health Found., 1988-91, chmn. 2d lt. Brit. Army, 1953-55. Office: Louis Harris & Assoc 630 5th Ave 11th Fl New York NY 10111

TAYLOR, JAMES DANIEL, consulting engineer; b. Tifton, Ga., June 30, 1941; s. Albert Lee and Josephine (Smith) T.; m. Rachel Zilber, Dec. 31, 1966. BSEE, Va. Mil. Inst., 1963; MSEE, Air Force Inst. Tech., 1977. Registered profl. engr., Mass. Commd. 2d lt. AUS, 1963, advanced through grades to capt., 1968; commd. capt. USAF, 1968, advanced through grades to lt. col., 1978; engring. officer Avionics Lab. USAF, Wright-Patterson AFB, Ohio, 1977-81; staff engr. electronic systems div. USAF, Hanscom AFB, Mass., 1981-91; retired USAF, 1991. Patentee, elec. pulse generator, variable geometry airship; author tech. papers, reports. Mem. IEEE, AIAA, Assn. Unmanned Vehicle Systems (Outstanding Contbr. award 1988), Assn. Old Crows. Home and Office: Apt 66 1643 Cambridge St Cambridge MA 02138

TAYLOR, JAMES HUGH, control systems engineer; b. San Jose, Calif., June 21, 1940; s. Harold Allen and Marie Anna (Briody) T.; m. Anne-Marie Caroline Rogozinski, June 15, 1963; children: Rachel C., Abigail M., Elisha R., Josiah J. BSEE, U. Rochester, 1962, MSEE, 1964; PhD in Engring. and Applied Sci., Yale U., 1969. Asst. prof. Indian Inst. Sci., Bangalore, India, 1969-72; mem. tech. staff The Analytic Scis. Corp., Reading, Mass., 1973-78; assoc. prof. Okla. State U., Stillwater, 1978-81; sr. R & D staff mem. GE Corp. R & D, Schenectady, N.Y., 1981-92; mgr. control and mfg. ORA Corp., Ithaca, N.Y., 1992—; adj. prof. Rensselaer Poly. Inst., Troy, N.Y., 1989-92. Mem. IEEE, IEEE Control Systems Soc. (bd. govs. 1992—), ASME (chmn. div. dynamic systems and control 1992), Am. Assn. for Artificial Intelligence. Home: 5080 Perry City Rd Trumansburg NY 14886 Office: ORA Corp 301 Dates Dr Ithaca NY 14850-1313

TAYLOR, JOHN ANDREW, flight test engineer; b. London, Nov. 22, 1953; came to U.S., 1982; s. John George and Joan (Gibson) T.; m. Christine Ann Hess, June 30, 1984; 1 child, Ann. BS in Aeronautics, Southahmpton U., Eng., 1976. Registered profl. engr., U.K. Flight test engr. Brit. Aerospace, Dunsfold, Surrey, Eng., 1972-82; program mgr. overseas div. Brit. Aerospace, Patuxent River, Md., 1982-84; project mgr. Veda, Inc., Lexington Park, Md., 1984—; pres. Lighter-Than-Air Techs., Leonardtown, Md., 1989—. Mem. AIAA (lighter than air tech. com. 1991—), Airship Assn. (coun. 1991—), Soc. Flight Test Engrs. (pres. Patuxent River chpt. 1989-90, tech. coun. 1986-91, Dirs. award 1992), Royal Aero. Soc. Home: Rt 3, 3 Breton Woods Ct Leonardtown MD 20650

TAYLOR, JUDITH ANNE, librarian; b. Bklyn., July 21, 1937; d. Edward S. and Ida (Osterland) Weber; m. Arnold H. Taylor, July 17, 1960; children: Beth Allison, Lynn Erica. BA, Barnard Coll., 1959; MS, Columbia U., 1960, postgrad., 1960-62; postgrad., L.I. U., 1970-72, U. Colo., 1980, 81. Cert. tchr., N.Y.; pub. libr., N.Y. Reference libr. CUNY, 1960-61; rsch. libr. Barnard Coll., N.Y.C., 1961-63; edn. libr. CUNY, Flushing, 1963-68; reference libr. Plainview (N.Y.)-Old Bethpage Pub. Libr., 1968-70, libr. media specialist, 1970-72; libr. media specialist Manhasset (N.Y.) Jr. High Sch., 1972—; bd. dirs. Tchr. Resource Ctr., Manhasset Schs. 1986-90. Author: Great Paperback Contest, 1980, newsletter Link Up, 1988-90; contbr. articles to profl. jours. Triviathon organizer, participant United Cerebral Palsy, Roosevelt, N.Y., 1989, 90; bd. trustees Internat. Brotherhood Elec. Workers Scholarship Alumnae, 1985—. Mem. N.Y. State United Tchrs., L.I. Sch. Media Assn., Nassau Sch. Libr. Assn. (rep. system coun. 1989—, cluster leader 1987—, liaison 1988—), Manhasset Edn. Assn., Barnard Coll. Alumnae Assn. (class corr. 1984-89, coun. mem. 1984-89). Jewish. Home: 90 Virginia Ave Plainview NY 11803-3626 Office: Manhasset Schs 200 Memorial Pl Manhasset NY 11030-2300

TAYLOR, KENDRA CLAIR, literary agent; b. Norfolk, Va., Dec. 16, 1963; d. Volney Maurice and Janise Clair (Jacobson) T. BA, U. Va., 1985; MA, Columbia U., 1988. Freelance writer Art News, Afterimage, Artweek, 1985—; reader The Paris Review, N.Y.C., 1990—; intern Corcoran Gallery of Art, Washington, summer 1985; staff writer Washington Tech., Vienna, Va., 1985-86, mng. editor, 1986-87; assoc. agt. Watkins/Loomis Agy., N.Y.C., 1988—. Contbr. articles to profl. jours. Lowe scholar Phi Mu, 1987-88; Echols scholar U. Va., 1981-85. Episcopalian.

TAYLOR, KENNETH DOUGLAS, finance and computer consultant, educator; b. Topeka, Nov. 21, 1942; s. Olin Orlando and Lola Louise (Conley) T.; AB, George Washington U., 1964, MS in Stats., 1966; MS in Computer Sci. SUNY, 1990, PhD in Math. Eurotech, 1992, (univ. fellow); postgrad., McGill U., 1974, Bowdoin Coll., U. Montreal; m. Joy Ellen Rice, May 25, 1973 (div. Nov. 1981). Sr. programmer C-E-I-R, Inc., 1963, 69; instr. Army Map Svc., 1964-65; student instr. McGill U., 1966-71; rsch. assoc. U. Va. Med. Sch., 1972; fin. and computer cons., Plymouth, N.Y., 1973-87; computer scientist USAF, 1989-90; sec. Richmond (Va.) Computer Club, 1977. Summer grantee NSF, Can. Research Council. Mem. ASTM, Am. Math. Soc. Author papers in field. Home and Office: PO Box 490 Chenango Bridge NY 13745

TAYLOR, KENNETH DOYLE, biomedical engineer; b. Hartford, Conn., Nov. 5, 1949; s. Frank Kenneth Taylor and Adelaide Pecaro (Tweedy) Jordan; m. M. Jane Dolphy, Aug. 25, 1972; 1 child, Jerome. BSEE, U. Conn., 1971, MSEE, 1974, PhD, 1981; MBA, Rensselaer Poly. Inst., 1988. Coord. rsch. lab. St. Francis Hosp. and Med. Ctr., Hartford, Conn., 1971-73; design engr. Picker Corp., Nuclear & Ultrasonics, Northford, Conn., 1973-74; mgr. rsch. lab. St. Francis Hosp. and Med. Ctr., Hartford, 1974-79; sr. project engr. United Techs. Rsch. Ctr., East Hartford, Conn., 1979-90; asst. dir. tech. assessment Pfizer Hosp. Products Group, N.Y.C., 1990—; lectr. U. Conn., Storrs, 1977-82; adj. prof. Trinity Coll., Hartford, 1988-90; adj. asst. prof., Hartford Grad. Ctr., 1980—. Corporator Newington (Conn.) Children's Hosp., 1989; bd. dirs. Channel 3 Country Camp, Hartford, 1989, Conn. Pre-Engring. Program, Hartford, 1989. Recipient Contbn. to Soc. award AIAA, 1985. Mem. IEEE (sr.), Sigma Xi, Tau Beta Pi, Eta Kappa Nu. Democrat. Methodist. Home: 17 Gorski Dr South Windsor CT 06074-2467 Office: Pfizer Hosp Products 235 E 42d St New York NY 10017

TAYLOR, KENT GREGORY, academic administrator; b. New London, Conn., Nov. 20, 1941; s. George Lackey and L. Faye (Sanborn) T.; m. Ruth Ann Sussman, June 14, 1969; 1 child, Joshua Eytan. BS, Bates Coll., 1964; MA, U. R.I., 1965; PhD, ABD, U. Wis., 1971. Caseworker I Brewer (Maine) Dept. Human Svcs., 1966-67; asst. prof. history Am. Coll., Jerusalem, Israel, 1971-77, dir. of admissions, 1975-77; asst. dir. continuing edn. dept. Westbrook Coll., Portland, Maine, 1978-80, dir. devel., 1980-86, v.p. for external affairs, 1987—; bd. dirs. So. Maine Cable TV Consortium, Portland, Portland Regional Transp. Cons. Portlant Pub. Library, 1983, Portland String Quartet, 1983, Portland YWCA, 1984, Portland Sch. Art, 1985, Temple Bet Ha'am, Portland, 1987. Hebrew U. Vis. Rsch. scholar, 1971-72. Mem. Coun. for Advancement and Support of Edn., So. Maine Devel. Officers Group. Office: Westbrook Coll Stevens Ave Portland ME 04102

TAYLOR, LEONARD BERNARD, lawyer; b. N.Y.C., Sept. 12, 1955; s. Emil and Olga Verna (Koval) Tychowsky; m. Edith Mae Thistle, June 1, 1985; children: Leonard Bernard, Christine Victoria. BS, Upsala Coll., 1978; JD, N.Y. Law Sch., 1986; LLM, Temple U., 1989. Bar: N.J. 1987, D.C. 1989. Programmer AT&T, Piscataway, N.J., 1979-81; programmer/analyst Chemical Bank, N.Y.C., 1981, ADP, N.Y.C., 1981-82; sr. programmer/analyst Johnson & Johnson, Raritan, N.J., 1982-83; pvt. practice Belle Mead, N.J., 1987—; pres. Intellidata Computer Svcs., Inc., Belle Mead, 1983—. Mem. ABA, D.C. Bar Assn., N.J. Bar Assn. Ukranian Catholic. Office: 33 2D St Raritan NJ 08869

TAYLOR, LOWELL, economics educator; b. Chattanooga, Nov. 30, 1958; s. Morris Lyle and Muriel Elaine (Myers) T.; m. Melissa Virginia Bush, Dec. 20, 1981; children: Evan James, Sarah Elaine. BA in Econs., Andrews U., 1980; MA in Econs., U. Mich., 1983, MA in Statistics, 1984, PhD in Econs., 1989. Instr. U. Tex., Austin, 1985-89; asst. prof. Carnegie Mellon U., Pitts., 1990—. Contbr. articles to profl. jours. Mem. Am. Econ. Assn., Population Assn. Am. Office: Carnegie Mellon U Sch Urban and Pub Affairs Pittsburgh PA 15213

TAYLOR, MARGARET TURNER, clothing designer, economist, writer, planner; b. Wilmington, N.C., May 7, 1944. A.B. in Econs., Smith Coll., 1966; M.A. in Econ. History, U. Pa., 1970, now Ph.D. candidate in City and Regional Planning. Tchr. Jefferson Jr. High Sch., New Orleans, 1966-69; instr. econs. U. Tex.-El Paso, 1974-75; adj. prof. econs., Salisbury State U., Md., 1976-78; prin. mgr., designer Margaret Norriss, women's clothing, Salisbury, Md., 1980—; planner at Wharton Ctr. Applied Research, Phila., 1985-86; planning cons., writer.

TAYLOR, MARYANN COURTNEY, elementary education educator; b. Lynn, Mass., May 6, 1948; d. Wilfred Rosario and Mary Evelyn (Brennan) LaFrance; m. Leonard Dwelley Taylor, Apr. 19, 1969; 1 child, Leonard Dwelley III. BS, Bridgewater State Coll., 1970, MEd, 1972; cert. in paralegal studies, Northeastern U., Boston, 1987; postgrad., New Eng. Sch. Law, 1987-88, Oxford (Eng.) U., 1989, Fairfield U., Boston U., Lesley Coll., Boston Archtl. Ctr., 1980—. Cert. tchr., Mass. Tchr. Plymouth (Mass.) Pub. Schs., 1970—; retail lumber sales Taylor Lumber Co., Inc., Marshfield, Mass., 1981—. Editor newsletter Cub Scout Pack 212, 1979-83. Vol. South Shore Sci. Ctr., Norwell, Mass., 1980-81, March of Dimes, Marshfield, 1982-85. Mem. NEA, Mass. Tchrs. Assn., Edn. Assn. Plymouth-Carver (union rep. 1989—), Better Bus. Bur. (vol.). Home: 124 Ferry St PO Box 1206 Marshfield MA 02050 Office: Plymouth Pub Sch System Lincoln St Plymouth MA 02360

TAYLOR, PATRICIA ELSIE, epidemiologist; b. Ayr, Queensland, Australia, Mar. 20, 1929; d. Ernest Howard and Mayzie Lucy (Kwong) Lee; m. Kenneth Douglas Taylor, Oct. 1, 1960; 1 child, Douglas Craig. BS, U. Queensland, 1952, postgrad., 1954; PhD, U. Calif., Berkeley, 1964; LLD (hon.), St. Francis Xavier U., N.S., Can., 1981. Mem. rsch. staff Queensland Inst. Med. Rsch., Brisbane, 1949-58; assoc. in epidemiology Sch. Pub. Health U. Calif., Berkeley, 1958-60; grad. rsch. fellow Inst. Nutrition for Cen. Am. and Panama, Guatemala, 1960-63; rsch. fellow Child Rsch. Ctr. of Mich., Detroit, 1965-66; sr. rsch. assoc. London Sch. Hygiene and Tropical Medicine, 1967-71; rsch. scientist Dept. Nat. Health and Welfare, Ottawa, Ont., Can., 1972-78; sr. cons. in virology and sci. rsch. Iranian Nat. Blood Transfusion Svc., Pasteur Inst., Tehran, 1978-80; epidemiologist Lindsley F. Kimball Rsch. Inst., N.Y. Blood Ctr., N.Y.C., 1981—; prin. dancer Queensland Ballet Theatre, 1956-58; solo dancer Guatemalan Nat. Ballet, 1960-63. Trustee Cathedral of St. John the Divine, N.Y., 1981. Named Woman of Yr., Can. Women's Club of N.Y., 1992; Paul Harris fellow, 1983, Internat. fellow AAUW, 1954-55; grantee Fulbright Found., 1954-55, Rockefeller Found., 1955. Mem. Royal Acad. Dancing, West Point Soc. N.Y. (hon.), Order of Can. (hon.). Home: 146 W 57th St # 61T New York NY 10019-3323 Office: Lindsley F Kimball Rsch Inst NY Blood Ctr 310 E 67th St New York NY 10021

TAYLOR, PAUL, art writer, art publisher; b. Melbourne, Australia, Sept. 10, 1958; came to U.S., 1984; BA with honors, Monash U., Melbourne, 1979. Tutor U. Tasmania, Hobart, Australia, 1980; pub., founding editor Art & Text Mag., Melbourne, 1981-84, pub., co-editor, 1984-89, co-pub., 1990—; freelance writer N.Y.C., 1984—; art critic Vanity Fair mag., N.Y.C., 1984-85. Editor: Anything Goes, 1984, Hysterical Tears, 1985, Impresario, 1988, Post-Pop Art, 1989; columnist, contbr. to Vogue, Connoisseur, Village Voice, The N.Y. Times, and others. Commr. Australia, 42d Biennale Venice, Italy, 1986; coord. chair Auction Partnership for the Homeless, Christie's N.Y., 1990.

TAYLOR, PAUL HOWARD, engineer, business executive; b. Chelsea, Mass., Aug. 29, 1916; s. George F. C. and Georganna G. (Pike) T.; B.S., N.C. State U., 1941; M.S. in Regional Planning, U. Mass., 1973; postgrad. Columbia U.,; m. Mildred Mundy, Oct. 4, 1941 (dec. 1976); children—Nancy D. Taylor Harrow, Paul H., William M., Mildred E.; m. 2d, Aline A. Poole, Mar. 22, 1980. With N.Y.C. Govt., 1943-66; mgr. loss prevention, naval reactors div. Combustion Engring. Co., Windsor, Conn., 1966-68; dir. corporate security United Nuclear Corp., New Haven, 1968-69; exec. v.p. ARMSAC, Wethersfield, Conn., 1969-72; pres. Paul H. Taylor Assos., Longmeadow, Mass., 1972—; dir. tng. OSHA div. Conn. Dept. Labor, 1974-75; v.p. Adrian Assos., importers, 1979—; partner, systems sales mgr. Protronics Systems Distbrs., 1982—; tchr. evening div. Springfield (Mass.) Tech. Community Coll., 1975-78; lectr. dept. criminal justice Westfield (Mass.) State Coll., 1972-74; dir. civil def. Town of Longmeadow (Mass.). Decorated Order of Merit (Italy); cert. protection profl.; cert. hazard control mgr. Mem. Am. Soc. Safety Engrs. (past pres. Connecticut Valley chpt.), Am. Soc. Indsl. Security (past chmn. Conn. chpt., chmn. Western Mass. chpt. 1984), Sons of Norway. Home and Office: 93 Edgewood Ave East Longmeadow MA 01106-1307

TAYLOR, RHODA EVANS, biology educator; b. Hartford City, Ind., Feb. 20, 1936; d. G. Harlowe and P. Joyce (Spalding) Evans; m. William R. Taylor, Sept. 14, 1957 (div. 1979); children: Diane, Richard; m. Vernon W. Mayer, May 5, 1981 (div. 1991). BA in Biology, Asbury Coll., 1957; MS, Purdue U., 1963, PhD in Physiology, 1965. Chemist Wyeth Labs., Skokie, Ill., 1957-58; lectr. biology Ind. U., Kokomo, 1963, asst. prof., 1965-67; assoc. prof. Slippery Rock (Pa.) U., 1967-80, prof., 1980—; congl. affairs specialist NOAA, Dept. Commerce, Washington, 1980-83. Contbr. articles to profl. jours. Grantee NSF, 1979, 80. Democrat. Episcopalian. Home: 923 Columbia Ave Grove City PA 16127-1307 Office: Slippery Rock U Dept Biology Slippery Rock PA 16057

TAYLOR, RICHARD POWELL, lawyer; b. Phila., Sept. 13, 1928; s. Earl Howard and Helen Moore (Martin) T.; m. Barbara Jo Anne Harris, Dec. 19, 1959; 1 child, Douglas Howard. BA, U. Va., 1950, JD, 1952. Bar: Va. 1952, D.C. 1956. Law clk. U.S. Ct. Appeals for 4th Circuit, 1951-52; assoc. Steptoe & Johnson, Washington, 1956-61, ptnr., 1962—, chmn. transp. dept., 1978—; sec., corp. counsel Slick Corp., 1963-69, asst. sec., 1969-72, also bd. dirs., 1965-68; sec., corp. counsel Slick Indsl. Co., 1963-72; sec., bd. dirs. Slick Indsl. Co. Can. Ltd, 1966-72; bd. dirs. Intercontinental Forwarders, Inc., 1969-72. Mem. Save the Children 50th Anniversary Com., 1982; gen. counsel Am. Opera Scholarship Soc., 1974—; mem. lawyer's com. Washington Performing Arts Soc., 1982—; mem. adv. com. Rock Creek Found. Mental Health, 1982—; mem. nat. adv. bd. DAR, 1980-83, chmn., 1983—; mem. men's com. Project Hope Ball, 1980—; nat. vice chmn. for fin. Reagan for Pres., 1979-80; mem. exec. fin. com. 1981 Presdl. Inauguration; mem. President's Adv. Com. for Arts, 1982—, Rep. Nat. Com., 1983—; Md. fin. chmn. Reagan-Bush '84, Bush-Quayle '88. Served to lt (j.g.), Air Intelligence USNR, 1952-56. Mem. ABA (co-chmn. aviation com. 1964-76, chmn. 1976-77), Fed. Bar Assn., D.C. Bar Assn., Va. Bar Assn., Fed. Energy Bar Assn., Am. Judicature Soc., Assn. Transp. Practitioners, Internat. Platform Assn., Raven Soc., Order of Coif. Episcopalian. Clubs: International, Capitol Hill, Nat. Aviation, Aero, Congl. Country (Washington); Potomac (Md.) Polo. Home: 14908 Spring Meadows Dr Germantown MD 20874-3444 Office: Steptoe & Johnson 1330 Connecticut Ave NW Washington DC 20036-1704

TAYLOR, ROBERT WAYNE, engineering educator; b. Taunton, Mass., Sept. 16, 1946; s. Arthur A. and Edna L. (Dion) T.; m. Linda Gregg, June 8, 1968 (div. 1978); m. Barbara M. Baum, Dec. 31, 1981. BSCE, Northeastern U., 1969; MS, MIT, 1973. 0. Lectr. math. Northeastern U., Boston, 1983-86, instr., lectr. civil engring., 1977-83, 86—. Recipient Outstanding Svc. award student chtp. ASCE, 1990, Desmond Fitzgerald award Boston Soc. of Civil Engrs., 1969. Mem. Phi Kappa Phi, Tau Beta Pi, Chi Epsilon (New Eng. Excellence in Teaching 1991), Sigma Xi. Home: 34 Mcbride St Jamaica Plain MA 02130-3227 Office: Northeastern U Dept Civil Engring Boston MA 02115

TAYLOR, ROSEMARY, artist; b. Joseph, Oreg.; d. Theodore and Sarah A. (Lambright) Resch; student Cleve. Inst. Art, 1937-40, NYU, 1947; m. Robert Hull Taylor; children—Barbara Taylor Ryalls, Robert H. Tchr. pottery Rahway (N.J.) Art Center, 1950-55; one-woman shows: Paterson (N.J.) Coll., 1964, Westchester (Pa.) Coll., 1970, Gallery 100, Princeton, N.J., 1967, George Jensen's, N.Y.C., 1972, Artisan Gallery, Princeton, 1974, Am. Crafts (Ohio), 1979-89, 92, Guild Gallery, 1986-91, Little Art Gallery, N.C., 1985-92, Olde Queens Gallery (N.J.), 1987, N.J. Designer Craftsmen, 1990 (bd. dirs. 1986-87); group shows include: Mus. Natural History, N.Y.C., Newark Mus., Trenton (N.J.) Mus., Montclair (N.J.) Mus., Phila. Art Alliance, Pa. Horticulture Soc., 1988, Nat. Design Center, N.Y.C.; represented in permanent collection Westchester Coll.; pottery cons. McCalls Mag., 1962-72. Bd. dirs. Solebury Community Sch.; mem. Fulbright award com., 1982, 83. Mem. LWV (pres. Plainfield, N.J. chpt.). Mem. Am. Craft Council, N.J. Designer-Craftsmen, Phila. Craft Group, Bucks County (Pa.) C. of C., Visual Artists and Galleries Assn., Nat. Assn. Am. Penwoman, Women in the Arts (charter). Democrat. Unitarian. Home: PO Box 46 Lumberville PA 18933-0046 Office: PO Box 282 Stockton NJ 08559-0282

TAYLOR, STEPHEN CRAIG, philosophy educator, researcher, lecturer; b. Salisbury, Md., May 12, 1954; s. Billy Brown and Bernetta Ann (Anderson) T.; m. Cynthia Joan Watto, May 24, 1975. Student, Salisbury State Coll., 1973-75; BA, U. Md., 1977, MA, 1979; postgrad., Bryn Mawr Coll., 1991—. Philosophy instr. Del. State Coll., Dover, 1981-85; philosophy asst. prof. Del. State Coll., 1985—; dir. Del. State Coll. Lecture Series, 1984-86; scholar Vis. Scholars Program Del. Humanities Forum, 1986—; lectr. ethical issues numerous orgns. and colls.; reviewer manuscripts St. Martins Press. Mem. Am. Philol. Assn. (reviewer, contbr. Newsletter on Teaching Philosophy), AAUP, Del. Humanities Forum (affiliate Nat. Endowment for the Humanities), Washington Philosophy Club. Office: Del State Coll Philosophy Dept N Du Pont Hwy Dover DE 19901

TAYLOR, VAN AARON, producer, songwriter; b. Buffalo, Apr. 25, 1956; s. Warner and V.A. (Hyche) T.; 1 child, Evelyn. Grad., Seneca Vocat. High Sch., Buffalo, 1974. Keyboardist Ace Tone's, Buffalo, 1968-73, Unique Sounds, Buffalo, 1973-75; keyboardist, producer Unique Sounds Topaze Concert Jazz Band, Buffalo, 1975-83; assembler Teledyne Hanva, Buffalo, 1975—; owner, mgr. Van Taylor Prodns., Buffalo, 1987—; TV producer Nite Time Entertainment City Rhythm, Buffalo, 1988; producer BCMK Studio, Buffalo, 1985—; keyboardist, producer Lance Diamond Band, Buffalo, 1985—, Taylor Made Jazz; owner AVT Prodns.; nat. talent coord. N.Y. State Gov. Challenge to Bus. and Youth, Buffalo, 1992; producer, talent coord. Rsch. for AIDS Benefit, Buffalo, 1992; producer, arranger Western N.Y. Fight Against Drugs and Alcohol, Buffalo, 1989. Procurer, composer: Keep Me Happy, 1980, Check It Out, 1980, Keep The Beat, 1981, We Will See, 1981, Father, 1987, A Nice Day, 1987. Talent coord. Jerry Lewis Telethon, Buffalo, 1985-86. Home: 67 Edgebrook ES # 6 Cheektowaga NY 14227 Office: AVT Prodns 67 Edgebrook Estates Apt 6 Buffalo NY 14227

TAYLOR, VOLNEY, marketing company executive; b. Portsmouth, Ohio, Dec. 6, 1939; s. Lafayette and Martha Louise (Frederick) T.; m. Kathleen Ann MacMahon, May 17, 1969; children—Lafayette, Lloyd MacMahon, Kerry Erin, Frederick Daly. B.S. in Indsl. Engring, Ohio State U., 1962; M.B.A., Harvard U., 1966. Asso. mem. McKinsey & Co., Inc. (mgmt. cons.), N.Y.C., 1966-72; exec. v.p., dir. Funk & Wagnalls, Inc., N.Y.C.,

1972-74; v.p. fin. Reuben H. Donnelley Co., N.Y.C., 1974-76; dir. corp. planning Dun & Bradstreet Corp., N.Y.C., 1976-77, v.p. corp. planning, 1977-78, corp. v.p., 1979-80, sr. v.p., 1980-82, exec. v.p., 1982—, also bd. dirs.; gen. mgr. Official Airline Guides, Oak Brook, Ill., 1978-79, also bd. dirs.; bd. dirs. Dun & Bradstreet Corp., Dun & Bradstreet, Inc., Dun & Bradstreet Europe, Dun & Bradstreet Internat., Dun's Mktg. Svcs., Inc., Moody's Investors Svc., Thomson Directories. Served to lt. (j.g.) USNR, 1962-64. Mem. Beta Theta Pi. Club: Harvard Bus. Sch. (N.Y.C.). Office: The Dun & Bradstreet Corp 299 Park Ave New York NY 10171-0002

TAYLOR, WARREN JUSTIN, thoracic surgeon; b. Boston, Nov. 2, 1921; s. William John and Virginia Stewart (Thompson) T.; m. Marjorie Marian Hutchins, Sept. 15, 1945; children: Wayne Jonathan, Leigh Whitham, Jane Stewart, Virginia Martha. AB, Dartmouth Coll., 1943; MD, Columbia U., 1945. Diplomate Am. Bd. Surgery, Am. Bd. Thoracic Surgery. Intern Mary Hitchcock Meml. Hosp., Hanover, N.H., 1945-46, resident anesthesia, 1948-49; resident surgery VA Hosp., White River Junction VA, Mary Hitchcock Meml. Hosp, 1949-52; chief surg. resident VA Hosp., White River Junction, 1952-53; surgeon VA Hosp., Rutland Heights, Mass., 1953-55; fellow thoracic surgery Malden (Mass.) Hosp., 1955-57, sr. surgeon, 1957-88, chief thoracic surgery, 1966-73, chief surgery, 1973-88; instr. surgery Harvard Med. Sch., 1961-68, clin. assoc. surgery, 1969-70, asst. clin. prof., 1970-74; clin. instr. Tufts Med. Sch., 1967—, assoc. clin. prof. surgery Boston U. Sch. Medicine, 1974-80, clin. prof., 1980—; mem. cons. staff numerous hosps. Contbr. articles to profl. jours. Mem. Winchester Bd. Health, 1963-75, 83-92. Maj., M.C., AUS, 1945-59. Fellow ACS, Am. Coll. Chest Physicians (treas. 1974-80), Am. Coll. Cardiology (pres.-elect 1975-76); mem. AMA, Mass. Med. Soc., Assn. Thoracic Surgeon, Soc. Thoracic Surgeons, Boston Surg. Soc. Home and Office: 209 Kinsman Franconia NH 03580-0623

TAYLOR, WILLIAM OSGOOD, newspaper executive; b. Boston, July 19, 1932; s. William Davis and Mary (Hammond) T.; m. Sally Coxe, June 20, 1959; children: William Davis II, Edmund C., Augustus R. B.A., Harvard U., 1954. With Globe Newspaper Co., Boston, 1956—; treas. Globe Newspaper Co., 1963—, bus. mgr., 1965-69, gen. mgr., 1969—, now chmn. bd., pub.; chmn. bd., dir. Affiliated Publs., Inc. Trustee Cotting Sch. for Handicapped Children, Kennedy Library Found., Wellesley Coll.; adv. coun. Trustees of Reservations. Served with U.S. Army, 1954-56. Office: Globe Newspaper Co 135 Morrissey Blvd Dorchester MA 02125-3338

TCHERTKOFF, VICTOR, pathologist; b. Lausanne, Switzerland, Aug. 7, 1919; s. Iekoussiel Gershon and Rose Schmuel (Dounaievsky) T.; m. Mildred Schwartz, June 25, 1942; children: Susan Antonelli, Adrienne Bonnie Glatzer. BS, CCNY, 1940; MD, N.Y. Med. Coll., 1943. Diplomate Am. Bd. Pathology. Intern N.Y. Beth Israel Hosp., Lincoln AFB, 1944-45; resident Met. Hosp., N.Y.C., 1946-48, fellow, 1948-49; acting chmn. pathology N.Y. Med. Coll., Valhalla, 1988-91; dir. labs. Met. Hosp., N.Y.C., 1961—, Luth. Hosp., Bklyn., 1965-70. Capt. USAAF, 1944-46. Fellow Am. Soc. Clin. Pathologists, Coll. Am. Pathologists, Internat. Acad. Pathologists; mem. AMA, N.Y. State Soc. Medicine, N.Y. County Med. Soc., Pathologists Club of N.Y. (pres. 1974-75). Office: Metro Hosp Ctr 1901 1st Ave New York NY 10029-7418

TEAGUE, BERNICE RITA, accountant; b. Lowell, Mass., Nov. 1, 1957; d. Francis Joseph and Agnes Lena (Laferriere) T. Grad. high sch., Lowell, Mass. Student aide Hanscom AFB, Bedford, Mass., 1974; sec. asst. Family Svcs. of Greater Lowell, 1975—, asst. bookkeeper, 1976-86, bookkeeper, 1986, asst. bus. mgr., 1987-88, prin. acct., 1988-89; bus. mgr., 1989—. Mem. Smithsonian Inst., Planetary Soc., Nat. Trust for Hist. Preservation, Am. Inst. Profl. Bookkeepers, NAFE. Democrat. Roman Catholic. Home: 163 A St Lowell MA 01851-4117 Office: Family Svc Greater Lowell 97 Central St Ste 400 Lowell MA 01852-1915

TEANEY, DALE THORPE, electronics executive; b. Monrovia, Calif., May 19, 1933; s. Victor Emmons and Virginia (Bauer) T.; m. Sigrid Flister, May 1970 (div. June 1977); children: Thorpe Burton, Derek Aloise, Kirsten Ursula. BA, Pomona Coll., 1955; PhD, U. Calif., Berkeley, 1960. Rsch. staff U.K. Atomic Energy Authority, Harwell, U.K., 1960-62; researcher IBM, Yorktown Hgts., N.Y., 1962-83; pres. SynchroVoice Inc., Harrison, N.J., 1983—; assoc. prof. elec. engring. (biomed.) N.J. Inst. Tech., 1983-91; staff scientist Nat. Acad. Scis., Washington, 1970-71; hon. fellow Univ. Coll. London, 1980-81; fellow Voice Found., N.Y.C., 1980-81. Contbr. over 60 articles to profl. jours.; patentee in field. Dir., creator non-profit housing Interfaith Coun. for Action, Ossining, N.Y., 1968-72. Fellow Am. Phys. Soc.; mem. N.Y. Acad. Scis. Orthodox. Office: SynchroVoice Inc 400 Harrison Ave Harrison NJ 07029

TEATOR, ROBERT HEMINGWAY, technology education educator; b. New Haven, Feb. 2, 1948; s. Harry Hemingway and Edna Madeline (Anderson) T.; m. Patricia Ann Maddaloni, June 21, 1972; children: Matthew H., Mark V., John P. BS, Cen. Conn. State U., 1969, MS, 1972. Tech. edn. educator B.F. Dodd Jr. High Sch., Cheshire, Conn., 1969—; adj. mem. faculty tech. edn. Cen. Conn. State U., New Britain, 1973—; mem. curriculum com. Cheshire Bd. of Edn., 1989-92. Treas. com. Boy Scouts Am. Troop 92, 1987—. Decorated Chevelier, Order of DeMolay; recipient Lord Baden Powell award Boy Scouts Am., 1990. Mem. NEA (life), Internat. Tech. Edn. Assn. (life), Conn. Tech. Assn. (life), Conn. Edn. Assn. (social chair summer workshops Hartford chpt. 1982-91), Edn. Assn. of Cheshire, New Eng. Tech. Tchr. Assn. (life), Conn. Ind. Arts Assn. (registration chair spring conv. Hartford chpt. 1970-72). Office: BF Dodd Jr High Sch 100 Park Pl Cheshire CT 06410-2100

TEC, LEON, psychiatrist; b. Baranovicze, Poland, June 1, 1919; came to U.S., 1952; s. Boris and Sarah (Limon) T.; m. Nechama Bawnik, May 15, 1931; children: Leora, Roland Boris. MD, St. Joseph U., Beirut, Lebanon, 1944. Diplomate Am. Bd. Psychiatry and Neurology, Am. Bd. Child Psychiatry. Intern Hadassah Hosp., Tel Aviv, Israel, 1943-44; resident psychiatry Bellevue Hosp., N.Y.C., 1952-55; fellow in child psychiatry Jewish Bd. Guardians, N.Y.C., 1955-57; faculty mem. Bellevue Coll. Medicine, NYU, N.Y.C., 1955-60, N.Y. Coll. Medicine, N.Y. Downstate U., N.Y.C., 1957-62; med. dir. Mid-Fairfield Child Guidance Ctr., Norwalk, Conn., 1959-86; pvt. practice psychiatry and child psychiatry Westport, Conn., 1959—; cons. staff mem. Norwalk Hosp., 1965—; radio host Sta. WEZN, Bridgeport, 1972-79; adv. bd. mem. Channel 5 TV Network, N.Y.C., 1987—. Author: The Fear of Success, 1976, Targets: How to Set Goals and Reach Them, 1980; contbr. articles to profl. jours. and The New York Times. Fellow Am. Orthopsychiat. Assn. (life), Am. Acad. Child Psychiatry (life), Royal Soc. Medicine (London, life), Am. Acad. Psychosomatic Medicine (life), Am. Group Psychotherapy Assn. (life), Am. Psychiat. Assn. (life, pres. Fairfield-Litchfield, Conn. chpt.); mem. Conn. Assn. Psychiat. Clinics for Children (v.p.), Conn. Group Psychotherapy Assn. (pres.), Internat. Coun. on Alcohol And Addictions (bd. dirs.), Internat. Assn. Child Psychiatry, World Mental Health Orgn., South Shore Music Club. Jewish. Home and Office: 11 Rockyfield Rd Westport CT 06880-2202

TEDESCHI, ROBERT JAMES, organic chemist; b. Woodside, N.Y., July 25, 1921; s. Romolo Valentine and Maria Antonetta (Prezzi) T.; m. Jean Lois Scruggs, June 21, 1953 (div. 1987); children: Marc, Lisa, Thomas. AB, Cornell U., 1944, MS, 1945, PhD, 1947. Sr. rsch. chemist Am. Cyanamid Co., Bound Brook, N.J., 1947-53; sect. head Air Reduction Co., Murray Hill, N.J., 1953-64; supr. Airco Chem. and Plastics Co., Piscataway, N.J., 1964-71; dir. rsch., assoc. dir. R&D Air Products and Chem., Piscataway, 1971-79; pres. Tedeschi Assocs., White House Station, 1979-88; cons. Tedeschi Assocs., Winslow, Maine, 1989—; cons. acetylene and gen. organic chemistry, corrosion inhibitors, surfactants, specialty monomers and polymers, Allentown, Pa., 1953-79, acetylenic chem. and derivatives, 1979-90; lectr. in field. Author: (with Marcel Dekker) Acetylene Based Chemicals from Coal and Other Natural Resources, 1983, Vitamins A, E, K, and Carotenes, 1991, (with others) Encyclopedia of Physical Science and Technology, 1988, 92; patentee in field; contbr. articles to profl. jours. Fellow Am. Inst. Chemists (accredited profl. chemist); mem. Am. Chem. Soc., Sigma Xi, Alpha Chi Sigma, Phi Kappa Tau. Congregationalist. Home and Office: 21 Court St Waterville ME 04901-7646

TEDESCO, ANNE CAVOLO, music educator, pianist; b. Valley Stream, N.Y., Oct. 5, 1951; d. Andrew and Elizabeth (St. Thomas) Cavolo; m. Carmine Tedesco, Aug. 15, 1976; children: Gregory, Louis. MusB cum laude, SUNY, Potsdam, 1973; MusM, Manhattan Sch. of Music, 1975. Tchr. piano Five Towns Music & Arts Found., Woodmere, N.Y., 1975-76, Stecher & Horowitz Sch. of Music, Cedarhurst, N.Y., 1976-80; adj. asst. prof. music St. John's U., Jamaica, N.Y., 1982—; lectr. on music history for various arts groups, Southshore of L.I., N.Y. Piano debut Carnegie Recital Hall, 1981. Manhattan Sch. of Music scholar, 1973-75. Mem. AAUP, Am. Keyboard Artists, N.Y. Music Tchrs. Assn., Woodmere Music Club. Home: 394 Cornwell Ave Malverne NY 11565-1532 Office: St Johns U Dept Fine Arts Music Div Utopia and Grand Central Pkwy Jamaica NY 11439

TEDESCO, LISA ANN, dental educator; b. Phillipsburg, N.J., July 4, 1950; d. Benjamin J. and Ann M. (DiGilio) T.; m. David William Kuehn, Sept. 3, 1980; children: Amelia Marie, Anna Louise. BS cum laude, U. Bridgeport, 1972; MEd, SUNY, Buffalo, 1975, PhD, 1981. Rsch. assoc. dept. edn1. psychology SUNY, Buffalo, 1978-79, rsch. assoc. dept. behavioral scis., 1979-81, contbg. investigator dept. oral biology, clin. periodontal, 1979—, from asst. to assoc. prof. dept. fixed prosthodontics, 1981—, assoc. dean for ednl. planning sch. dental medicine, 1989—; prin. investigator U.S. Dept. HHS, 1990—, Bur. Health Professions Edn., 1990—, Nat. Inst. Dental Rsch., 1986-89. Contbr. chpts. to books: Social and Applied Aspects of Perceiving Faces, 1988, Textbook of Preventive Dentistry, 1989, Foundations for Feminist Restructuring of the Academic Disciplines, 1990, Esthetic Need for Orthodontic Treatment, 1991. Mem. exec. bd. Ctr. for Behavioral and Social Aspects of Health, 1990—, Univ. Adv. Com. on Teaching Effectiveness, 1990—. Fellow Pew Nat. Dental Leadership Devel. Program, 1991, Health in Housing, A World Health Orgn. Collaborating Ctr., 1990—. Mem. Am. Assn. Dental Schs. (chairperson annual sessions program planning com. 1990—, spl. task force on curriculum reform 1990, ad hoc com. on outcomes assessment 1989-91), Am. Assn. for Dental Rsch. (various coms. and chairs 1986—), Am. Psychol. Assn. (div. 27 community psychology, div. 38 health psychology). Home: 552 Richmond Ave Buffalo NY 14222-1524 Office: SUNY Sch Dental Medicine 215 Squire Hall Buffalo NY 14214

TEDESKO, ANTON, consulting engineer; b. Gruenberg, Germany, May 25, 1903; came to U.S., 1927, naturalized, 1938; s. Victor and Alice (Weiss) T.; m. Sally Murray, June 16, 1938; children—Peter Alden, Suzanne Tedesko Affolter. C.E., Inst. Tech., Vienna, Austria, 1926, D.Sc., 1951; diploma engr., Berlin, 1930; D.Eng. (hon.), Lehigh U., 1966; D.Sc. (hon.), Technol. U., Vienna, 1978. Constrn. engr. Vienna, 1926; with Fairbanks-Morse Co., Chgo., 1927, Miss. Valley Structural Steel Co., Melrose Park, Ill., 1927-28; asst. prof. Inst. Tech., Vienna, 1929; designer dams, bridges, shells, indsl. structures Dyckerhoff & Widmann, Wiesbaden, Germany, 1930-32; with Roberts & Schaefer Co. (engrs.), Chgo., 1932-67; engring. mgr. Roberts & Schaefer Co., Washington, 1943-44; structural mgr. Roberts & Schaefer Co., Chgo., 1944-54; mgr. Roberts & Schaefer Co., N.Y.C., 1955; v.p. Roberts & Schaefer Co., 1956-67; pvt. cons. engring., 1967—, designer, supr. constrn. arenas, air terminals, bridges, toll roads, indsl. structures, ballistic missile and space rocket launching facilities, wide-span hangars, shell structures, evaluator structural failures, rehab. damaged structures; dir. Thompson-Starrett Co., 1960-61; arbitrator of engring. and constrn. disputes, structural engr. responsible for design rocket assembly and launch facilities for manned lunar landing program Kennedy Space Center, 1962-66; lectr. structural engring. numerous univs.; spl. work shell concrete structures of long span, prestressed concrete; cons. Hdqrs. USAF, 1955-70, to Chief Engr., C.E., U.S. Army, 1970-74, other govt. agys.; mem. various commns. and bds.; moderator engring. confs. Contbr. articles to profl jours. Recipient Alfred Lindau award in field long-span reinforced concrete structures, 1961, Engring. News Record citation, 1966. Fellow ASCE (hon. mem. award 1978); mem. Research Council Performance of Structures, Reinforced Concrete Research Council (exec. com. 1971—, Arthur J. Boase award 1978), Engrs. Joint Council (metric commn. 1973-80), Am. Concrete Inst. (dir. 1961-64, hon. mem., Henry C. Turner medal for applied innovation and profl. competence, 1987, Phil. M. Ferguson meml. lectr. 1992), Soc. Am. Mil. Engrs., Am. R.R. Engring. Assn., Internat. Assn. Bridge and Structural Engring. (U.S. del. permanent commn. 1965—, internat. award of merit in structural engring. 1978), Internat. Assn. Shell and Spatial Structures (Hon. Mem. award 1979), Nat. Acad. Engring. Address: 26 Brookside Circle Bronxville NY 10708

TEDOR, MICHAEL L., wholesale distribution executive; b. Allentown, Pa., Dec. 23, 1950; s. Nicholas and Ruth Ann (Henry) T.; m. Karen Marie Barlow, Jan. 8, 1972; children: Randolph, Bradley. BA, West Chester (Pa.) U., 1972. Dist. exec. Boy Scouts Am., West Chester, 1972-75; ops. mgr. Garrett Buchanan Co., Phila., 1975-77; sales mgr. Alling & Cory Co., Phila., 1977-80; v.p. Alling & Cory Co., Bensalem, Pa., 1980-88; pres. Cumberland Paper & Supply, Millville, N.J., 1988—. Mem. Internat. San. Supply Assn., Nat. Fedn. Ind. Bus., Baseball Umpires Assn. S. Jersey. Office: Cumberland Paper & Supply 201 N High St Millville NJ 08332-3833

TEETER, JAMES HERRING, surgeon; b. Taneytown, Md., Aug. 22, 1927; s. John Stuff and Margaret (Roop) T.; m. Mae McDaniel; children: Timothy, Paul, Jonathan, Mark. BA, Gettysburg Coll., 1950; MD, U. Md., 1954. Intern Mercy Hosp., Balt., 1954-55; resident Church Home Hosp., Balt., 1955-57, Franklin Sq. Hosp., Balt., 1957-59; attending surgeon Waynesboro (Pa.) Hosp., 1959—; clin. prof. surgery Hershey Med. Ctr., Pa. State U., 1988—; vol. World Med. Mission, Boone, N.C., 1963-92; attending surgeon Waynesboro Hosp., 1959-92. Mem. bd. World Med. Mission, 1978-92, United Brethren in Christ Missions, 1989-92. Fellow ACS (pres. Pa. chpt. 1988-89); mem. AMA, Christian Med. Soc., Pa. Med. Soc. Home: 11708 Country Club Rd Waynesboro PA 17268 Office: Surg Assocs 45 Roadside Ave Waynesboro PA 17268

TEEVAN, RICHARD COLLIER, psychology educator; b. Shelton, Conn., June 12, 1919; s. Daniel Joseph and Elizabeth (Halliwell) T.; m. Virginia Agnes Stehle, July 28, 1945; children—Jan Elizabeth, Kim Ellen, Clay Collier, Allison Tracy. B.A., Wesleyan U., Middletown, Conn., 1951; M.A., U. Mich., 1952, Ph.D., 1955. Rubber buffer Sponge Rubber Product Co., Derby, Conn., 1939-41; with U. Mich., 1951-57, teaching fellow, 1951-53, instr., 1953-57; asst. prof. Smith Coll., 1957-60; assoc. prof. Bucknell U., 1960-64, prof., 1964-69; chmn. psychology, prof. SUNY-Albany, 1969—; pres. Teevan Assocs., Cons., 1991—; cons. on coll. teaching, 1989—. Author: Reinforcement, 1961, Instinct, 1961, Color Vision, 1961, Measuring Human Motivation, 1962, Theories of Motivation in Learning, 1964, Theories of Motivation in Personality and Social Psychology, 1964, Motivation, 1967, Fear of Failure, 1969, Readings in Elementary Psychology, 1973; contbr. articles to sci. jours. Served to capt. AUS, 1941-47; prisoner of war 1943-45, Ger. Office Naval Research grantee, 1958-72; recipient Lindbach award Bucknell U., 1966. Mem. AAAS, AAUP, Am. Psychol. Assn. (Disting. visitor 1981-85), Eastern Psychol. Assn., Phi Beta Kappa, Sigma Xi. Home: 45 Pine St Delmar NY 12054-3413 Office: SUNY Dept Psychology 1400 Washington Ave Albany NY 12222-0001

TEICHER, ARTHUR MACE, personnel executive; b. N.Y.C., Dec. 17, 1946; s. Milton and Lilyan (Kaufman) T.; m. Marcia Fleschner, Nov. 23, 1974; 1 child, Craig Morgan. Student, U. Toledo, 1965-68, Long Island U., 1970-72. Mgmt. trainee Bank of N.Y., N.Y.C., 1970-72; agt. M & A Assocs., East Rutherford, N.J., 1972-73; sales rep. Fed. Express, N.Y.C., 1973-76; v.p., prin. Smith's 5th Ave., N.Y.C., 1976—. Asst. den leader Boy Scouts Am., Westchester, N.Y., 1987—, chmn. pack com., 1987-88, Weblos den leader, 1988-89, Troop 8 com. mem., Scarsdale, 1989—; mem. Edgemont Commn. on Developing Capable Young People, Westchester, 1986—, Fort Hill Assn., Westchester, 1980—. With USNG, 1969. Mem. Am. Mktg. Assn. (membership chmn. 1982-84), Assn. Personnel Cons. N.Y., Nat. Assn. Personnel Cons. Clubs: U.S. Power Squadron (lt. 1985—), Castaways Yacht. Office: Smiths Fifth Ave Agy Inc 17 E 45th St New York NY 10017-2415

TEICHER, MARTIN HERSCH, psychiatrist; b. Bklyn., May 17, 1951; s. James and Anna (Grassi) T.; m. Beverly Ann Willis, Aug. 4, 1973; children: Joseph Orrion, Emily Athena. BS, Rensselaer Poly. Inst., 1973; PhD highest distinctions, Johns Hopkins U., 1977; MD, Yale U., 1981. Diplomate Am. Bd. Med. Examiners, Am. Bd. Psychiatry and Neurology. Clin. rsch. fellow Harvard U. Med. Sch., Boston, 1981-85, DuPont Warren fellow, 1984-85; chief resident psychopharmacology McLean Hosp., Belmont, Mass., 1984-85; asst. prof. Harvard U. Med. Sch., Boston, 1985-90, assoc. prof., 1990—; assoc. chief neuropharmacology lab. Mailman Rsch. Ctr., Belmont, 1986-88; dir. outpatient psychopharmacology McLean Outpatient Clinic, Belmont, 1986-88; assoc. psychiatrist McLean Hosp., 1988—; chief devel. psychopharmacology lab. Mailman Rsch. Ctr., 1988--; dir. devel. biopsychiatry progrm. McLean Hosp., 1988--; cons., reviewer NSF, USAF Office Sci. Rsch., March of Dimes, 1980—; cons. psychoparmacology Bridgewater, Harry S. Solomon, Met. State Hosps., 1985-86; mem. com., chmn. NIHM rsch. com. on computers in mental health, 1984-86; mem. com. NIHM rsch. com. on neurobiology and psychopharmacology, 1988-92; rsch. com. neuropharmacology and neurochemistry NIMH, 1991—. Contbr. articles to profl. jours.; author (computer software) Apple-Ligand, Apple-Allfit, 1982, Cosifit, 1986; propsed relationship of fluoxetive to suicidal intention and violence. Recipient FIRST award. NIMH, 1988. Mem. Am. Psychiat. Assn., Soc. for Neurosci., Internat. Soc. Devel. Psychobiology, N.Y. Acad. Sci., Soc. Light Treatment and Biol. Rhythms. Office: McLean Hosp 115 Mill St Belmont MA 02178-1048

TEIRSTEIN, ALVIN STANLEY, physician; b. N.Y.C., Apr. 3, 1927. BA, Adelphi Coll., 1949; MD, SUNY, Bklyn., 1953. Intern Mt. Sinai Hosp., N.Y.C., 1953-54; resident Bronx VA Hosp., 1954-55; resident Mt. Sinai Hosp., 1955-56, chief resident, 1957, asst. attennding physician, 1958-66; attending cardio-pulmonary lab. Bronx VA Hosp., 1958-64; assoc. attending physician Mt. Sinai Hosp., 1966-74, attending physician, 1974, acting chief pulmonary div., 1974-75, dir. pulmonary div., 1975—; assoc. clin. prof. Mt. Sinai Sch. Medicine, 1968, clin. profl., 1974, prof. medicine, 1975, Florette and Ernst Rosenfeld and Joseph Solomon prof. medicine, 1977. Cardio-pulmonary lab. fellow Bronx VA Hosp., 1956, Mt. Sinai Hosp., 1958-59, Dazian fellow, 1959-61. Fellow Am. Coll. Chest Physicians, Am. Coll. Physicians; mem. Nat. Assn. Med. Dirs. of Respiratory Care, N.Y. State County Med. Socs., N.Y. Lung Assn., Assn. Pulmonary Program Dirs., Soc. Occupational Environ. Health. Office: Mt Sinai Pulmonary Assocs 5 E 98th St 10th fl Box 1232 New York NY 10029-6574

TEITEL, JEFFREY HALE, lawyer, environmentalist; b. Bklyn., Jan. 28, 1943; s. Milton Henry Teitel and Muriel Pearl (Cohen) Alper; m. Martha S. Teitel, Oct. 30, 1969 (div. Apr. 1980); children: Gregory Scott, Melissa Beth; m. Kathleen Breslin, Apr. 12, 1987. BA, Rutgers Coll., 1965; JD, Lewis & Clark Coll., 1973. Bar: Pa. 1974, Ky. 1982, U.S. Ct. Appeals (D.C. cir.) 1976. Atty. advisor EPA, Washington, 1973-74, OSHA Rev. Commn., Washington, 1974-75; environ. counsel Nat. Forest Products Assn., Washington, 1975-79; dir. regulatory affairs Conrail Corp., Phila., 1979-81; sr. atty. environ. and regulatory Ashland (Ky.) Oil, Inc., 1981-83; assoc. counsel GAF Corp., Wayne, N.J., 1983-84; sr. assoc. Hannoch, Weisman, Roseland, Roseland, N.J., 1984-85, Rivkin, Radler, Dunne & Bayh, Garden City, N.J., 1985-86; dir. environ. law Sequa Corp. (formerly Sun Chem. Corp.), N.Y.C., 1986—, 1990—; adj. prof. environ. law Lewis and Clark Law Sch., 1975-77, bd. visitors, 1991—, Washington Law Sch. Intern program, adminstrv. law judge Oreg. State Health Div., Portland, 1972; pub. health dir. Town of Agawam, Mass., 1966-68, 69-70. Contbg. author: The 1989 Environmental Yearbook. Pres. Upper Rock Creek Civic Assn., Derwood, Md., 1978-79. With U.S. Army, 1968-69, Vietnam. Mem. ABA, Ky. Bar Assn., Am. Corp. Counsel Assn. (chmn. environ. sect. N.Y.C. chpt. 1992—). Jewish. Office: Sequa Corp 200 Park Ave New York NY 10166-0005

TEITEL, SIMON, economist; b. Buenos Aires, Dec. 5, 1928; came to U.S., 1961; s. Gregorio and Regina (Tarnorudzka) T.; m. Raquel Schenkolewski, June 20, 1954; children: Rut Gabriela, Ariel Dan. BS in Indsl. Engring., U. Buenos Aires, 1956, MS in Indsl. Engring., 1963; PhD in Econs., Columbia U., 1969. Econ. affairs officer Ctr. for Indsl. Devel., UN, N.Y.C., 1963-67; sr. indsl. devel. officer policies and programming div. UN Indsl. Devel. Orgn., Vienna, Austria, 1967-68; sr. cons. Office Program Advisor to Pres., Inter-Am. Devel. Bank, Washington, 1968-76, sr. econ. advisor econ. and social devel. dept., 1976-89; sr. rsch. adv., 1989—; adj. assoc. prof. econs. Cath. U. Am., Washington, 1971-77, adj. prof., 1977-81, prof., 1981-88; adj. prof. Am. U., 1992; lectr. Georgetown U., Washington, 1976; vis. lectr. internat. econs. Yale U., New Haven, 1977-78; lectr. to numerous profl. assns. and univs.; occasional referee Econ. Devel. and Cultural Change, Jour. Devel. Econs., World Devel., Latin Am. Rsch. Rev.; mem. spl. internat. panel on appropriate techs. for developing countries Bd. on Sci. and Tech. for Internat. Devel., NAS-Nat. Acad. Engring., 1974-77. Editor: Política Económica en Centro y Periferia, 1976, Integracion Economica, 1977, Trade, Stability, Technology and Equity in Latin Am., 1982, Symposium on Technological Change and Industrial Development, 1984, Growth, Reform and Adjustment: Latin America's Trade and Macroeconomic Policies in the 1970s and 1980s, 1986, Handbook of Latin Am. Studies, Libr. of Congress, Economics: Argentina, 1989, Towards a New Development Strategy for Latin America, 1992; contbr. articles to profl. jours. Mem. Am. Econ. Assn. Jewish. Home: 3520 Albemarle St NW Washington DC 20008-4214 Office: Intern-Am Devel Bank 1300 New York Ave NW Washington DC 20577

TEITELBAUM, AARON, finance company executive, lawyer; b. Germany, Mar. 24, 1946; s. David and Bella (Weiser) T.; m. Sara Fraiman, Dec. 23, 1967; children: Elliot, Helene, Philip. BA, CCNY, 1969; JD, St. John's U., N.Y.C., 1973. Bar: U.S. Ct. Appeals (2d cir.) 1974, U.S. Dist. Ct. (so. and ea. dists.) M.Y. 1975, U.S. Supreme Ct. 1977. Asst. gen. counsel Bear Stearns & Co., N.Y.C., 1970-74; assoc. gen. counsel Oppenheimer Inc., N.Y.C., 1974-78; asst. v.p. Dean Witter Inc., N.Y.C., 1978-80; 1st v.p., br. mgr. Advest Inc., N.Y.C., 1980—. Office: Advest Inc 12 E 49th St New York NY 10017

TEITELBAUM, SEYMOUR, dentist; b. N.Y.C., Feb. 3, 1927; s. Charles and Ray (Nurick) T.; BS, 1950; DDS, NYU, 1955; postgrad. Bklyn. Coll., 1950; m. Lilian Ostrovsky, Jan. 7, 1960; children: Lizanne, Michael, Lorne. Intern Bronx-Lebanon Hosp. Center, 1955, then adj. attending; practice dentistry, specializing in preventive, restorative dentistry, N.Y.C., 1957-62, Briarcliff Manor, N.Y., 1963—; chief dental surgery Philps Meml. Hosp. Served with USAAF, 1944-46. Past chmn. United Jewish Appeal, Briarcliff Manor, Zionist Orgn. Am. Fellow Soc. Oral Physiology and Occlusion, Acad. Gen. Dentistry (master), Fedn. Prosthetic Orgns., Royal Soc. Health, Am. Prosthodontic Soc.; mem. AAAS, Ninth dist. dental socs., Am. Acad. Implant Dentistry, Acad. Osseointegration, Am. Analgesia, So. New Eng. Acad. Practice Adminstrn., Westchester Acad. Gen. Dentistry (past pres.), Am. Soc. Preventative Dentistry, Westchester Acad. Restorative Dentistry, Am. Dental Assn., Am. Assn. Hosp. Dentists, Western Westchester Dental Study Group, Westchester Acad. Practice Adminstrn., Fedn. Internat. Dentaire, Park Chester Rifle and Revolver Assn., Pleasantville Rifle Club, Briarcliff Manor Rotary Internat., Odd Fellows, B'nai B'rith. Home and Office: 1312 Pleasantville Rd Briarcliff Manor NY 10510-1691

TEITLER, RONALD FRED, colon and rectal surgeon; b. N.Y.C., Nov. 3, 1943; s. Simon and Esther (Blumenzweig) T.; m. Dana Lynn Kalish, June 27, 1968; children: Elizabeth, Katherine. BA, Hobart Coll., 1965; MD, SUNY, Buffalo, 1969. Diplomate Am. Bd. Surgery, Am. Bd. Colon & Rectal Surgeons, Am. Bd. Quality Assurance & Utilization Rev. Physicians. Gen. surgery resident Hartford (Conn.) Hosp., 1974; colorectal surgery fellow Ferguson Clinic, Grand Rapids, Mich., 1975-76; colorectal surgeon pvt. practice Buffalo, 1977—; clin. instr. surgery SUNY, Buffalo, 1979—; med. advisor Greater Buffalo Ostomy Assn., 1979—; chmn. utilization rev. Health Source P.P.O., Buffalo, 1988-91. Author: (book chpt.) Current Diagnosis, 1985; contbr. articles to profl. jours. Lt. comdr. USN, 1975-77. Fellow Am. Coll. Surgeons, Am. Soc. Colon & Rectal Surgeons; mem. Am. Soc. for Gastrointestinal Endoscopy, Soc. Am. Gastrointestinal Endoscopic Surgeons. Office: 1616 Kensington Ave Buffalo NY 14215-1433

TELESETSKY, WALTER, government official; b. Boston, Jan. 22, 1938; s. Keril and Nellie (Krelka) T.; m. Sharron-Dawn Lamp, July 15, 1961; children: Stephanie Ann, Anastasia Marie. BS in Mech. Engring., Northeastern U., 1960; MBA, U. Chgo., 1961. Mem. tech. staff The Mitre Corp., Bedford, Mass., 1962-68; sr. mem. tech. staff Data Dynamics, Inc., Washington, 1969; phys. scientist NOAA, Rockville, Md., 1970-71, U.S. Gate Project coord., 1972-74, dir. U.S. Global Weather Experiment Project Office, 1974, dir. Program Integration Office, 1975-77, dir. Programs and Tech. Devel. Office, 1977-79, dir. Programs and Internat. Activities Office, 1979-81; dep. assoc. dir. for tech. svcs., chief AFOS ops. div. Nat. Weather Svc., Silver Spring, Md., 1981-86, dir. Office of Systems Ops., 1986—; liaison to NAS coms. on

atmospheric scis., geophysics studies and internat. environ. programs, 1975-81; U.S. coord. U.S./Japan Coop. Program in Natural Resources, 1980-88; chmn. U.S.-Japan Marine Resources and Engring. Coordination Com., 1980-88; U.S. del. governing coun. UN Environ. Program and World Meteorol. Orgn.; mem. commn. for Basic Systems World Meteorol. Orgn., 1988—. Contbr. articles to profl. publs. Recipient Silver medal Dept. Commerce, 1975. Mem. AAAS, Am. Geophys. Union, Am. Meteorol. Soc. Home: 16 Eton Overlook Rockville MD 20850-3003 Office: 1325 E West Hwy Silver Spring MD 20910-3233

TELLEFSEN, GERALD, management consultant; b. Jersey City, Sept. 19, 1938; s. James and Anna (Freudenberg) T.; children: Eric, Jill, Lynn. BA, Columbia U., 1960. Programmer System Devel. Corp., Paramus, N.J., 1961-63; analyst Internat. Electric Co., Paramus, 1963-64, IBM, Poughkeepsie, N.Y., 1964-65; mgr. Western Union, Mahwah, N.J., 1965-67; sr. scientist Control Data Corp., N.Y.C., 1967-68; sr. v.p. Booz Allen & Hamilton, N.Y.C., 1968-84, Tellefsen Cons. Group, N.Y.C., 1984—; bd. dirs. Nat. Consumer Products Co., Atlanta, Delphi Ptnrs., Atlanta. Contbr. articles to profl. jours. Mem. Futures Industry Assn. Office: Tellefsen Cons Group 19 Rector St Ste 1708 New York NY 10006-2302

TELMER, FREDERICK HAROLD, fabricated steel products company executive; b. Edmonton, Alta., Can., Dec. 28, 1937; Ingar and Gertrude Bernice (Floen) T.; m. Margaret Goddard Hutchings, Oct. 30, 1959; children: Christopher, Kevin, Colin. BA in Econs., U. Alberta, 1961, MA in Econs., 1964. With Stelco, Inc., Hamilton, Ont., Can., 1963—, gen. mgr. corp. affairs and strategic planning, 1984-85, v.p. corp. affairs and strategic planning, 1985-87, dir., 1989, chmn., chief exec. officer, 1991—; vice chmn. representing employers Ont. Workers' Compensation Inst.; dir. Inco Ltd., CT Fin. Svcs., Inc.; founding dir. Japan Soc. Bd. govs. McMaster U., Hamilton; trustee Chedoke-McMaster Hosps., Hamilton. Mem. Toronto Club, Hamilton Club, Burlington Golf and Country Club, Delta Kappa Epsilon.. Office: Stelco Inc, PO Box 2030 100 King St W, Hamilton, ON Canada L8N 3T1

TELTSCHER, HERRY OTTO, psychologist, consultant; b. Vienna, Austria; came to U.S., 1939, naturalized, 1943; s. Oskar and Elsa (Feiler) T.; m. Betti Sternfield, June 26, 1962; children: John, Nina; children from a previous marriage: Elizabeth, Susan. M.A., N.Y. Sch. Social Research, 1954; Ph.D., Yeshiva U., N.Y.C., 1964. Pvt. practice psychology, N.Y.C., 1946—; lectr. Wayne U., Detroit, 1955; mem. faculty New Sch. Social Research, N.Y., 1976-83; cons. N.J. Dept. Human Services. Served with AUS, 1941-45. Recipient citation Mil. Intelligence War Dept., Cert. in Recognition of Disting. Contbns., 1986. Fellow Soc. Clin. and Exptl. Hypnosis; mem. Na. Register Health Svcs., Providers in Psychology, Am. Psychol. Assn., N.Y. State Psychol. Assn., N.Y. Soc. Clin. Psychology, Nat. Assn. Document Examines (Disting. Document Examiner of Yr. 1985). Author: Handwriting-An Introduction to Psycho-Graphology, 1942; Handwriting: Revelation of Self, 1970; contbr. articles to profl. jours. Address: 165 E 80th St New York NY 10021

TEMKIN, AARON, physicist; b. Morristown, N.J., Aug. 15, 1929; s. Maxwell M. and Mary C. (Feigelstein) T.; m. Miriam Hannah Schachter, Aug. 10, 1958; children: Philip H., Jean M. BS with highest honors, Rutgers U., 1951; PhD, MIT, 1956. Fulbright fellow Heidelberg (Fed. Republic Germany) U., 1956-57; physicist NAS NRC, Naval Rsch. Lab., Washington, 1957-58, Nat. Bur. Standards, Washington, 1958-60, NASA/Goddard Space Flight Ctr., Greenbelt, Md., 1960—. Editor, contbr.: Autoionization: Astrophysical, Theoretical Laboratory Experimental Aspects, 1966, Autoionization: Recent Developments and Applications, 1985. Goddard Study fellow, 1967. Fellow Am. Phys. Soc. (rep. of DAMOP to Com. on Internat. Freedom), Phi Beta Kappa. Office: NASA/Goddard Space Flight Ctr Greenbelt MD 20771

TEMKIN, KAREN KATZ, management consultant; b. Springfield, Mass., Aug. 1, 1963; d. David Bearg and Ruth (Cohen) K.; m. Bruce David Temkin, Dec. 29, 1990. BA, Mt. Holyoke Coll., South Hadley, Mass., 1985; MBA, MIT, 1989. Mgmt. trainee HP Hood, Boston, 1985-87; cons. Price Waterhouse, Boston, 1988; mng. assoc. CSC Index, Inc., Cambridge, Mass., 1989—. Office: CSC Index Inc 5 Cambridge Ctr Cambridge MA 02142-1493

TEMKIN, RICHARD JOEL, physicist, research scientist; b. Boston, Jan. 8, 1945; s. Max and Lillian (Giller) T.; m. Carol F. Temkin; children: Mark D., Daniel J., Jessica B. BA, Harvard Coll., 1966; PhD, MIT, 1971. Postdoctoral rsch. fellow Harvard U., Cambridge, Mass., 1971-74; project leader MIT Nat. Magnet Lab, Cambridge, 1974-79; staff mem. MIT Plasma Fusion Ctr., Cambridge, 1979-86, div. head, 1986—; sr. rsch. scientist MIT Physics Dept., Cambridge, 1985—. Editor: Conf. Digest, Internat. Conf. Infrared and Millimeter Waves, 1983, 85, 87-90; contbr. over 100 articles to profl. jours. Mem. IEEE (assoc. editor Transactions on Electron Devices 1986—, com. svc. 1983-87), Am. Phys. Soc. (program com. Plasma meeting 1991). Office: Plasma Fusion Ctr MIT Bldg NW 16 Cambridge MA 02139

TEMKIN, ROBERT HARVEY, accountant; b. Boston, Oct. 21, 1943; s. Max and Lillian (Giller) T.; m. Ellen Phyllis Band, Sept. 25, 1966; children—Aron, Rachel, Joshua. BBA, U. Mass., 1964. CPA, Mass., N.Y., Conn., Vt. With Ernst & Young (formerly Arthur Young & Co.), 1964-72, 73—; ptnr. Arthur Young & Co., CPA's, 1976-89, Ernst & Young, 1989—; nat. dir. auditing standards Arthur Young & Co., CPA's, 1980-88, assoc. regional dir. auditing, East, 1989-91; contr. SCA Svcs., Boston, 1972-73; assoc. prof. NYU, 1982. Mem. young leadership United Jewish Appeal, 1976-80; bd. dirs. Jewish Home for Elderly of Fairfield County, 1979—, pres., 1985-87; mem. Bd. Edn. Weston, Conn., 1983-87; v.p. United Synagogue Am., chmn. budget com.; mem. bus. adv. coun. U. Mass.; asst. sec. Jewish Community Ctrs. of Greater Boston; mem. exec. bd. N.E. region Anti-Defamation League; treas., mem. exec. com. Synagogue Coun. Mass. Recipient Acctg. Alumni award U. Mass., 1978, Alumnus Award Sch. Mgmt. U. Mass., 1986. Mem. AICPA (staff dir. commn. on auditors responsibilities 1976-78, mem. task force on auditor's report 1978-81, peer rev. com. 1982-84, auditing standards bd. 1984-88, chmn. internat. auditing task force), Mass. Soc. CPAs (Silver medal 1964, ethics com.), N.Y. State Soc. CPAs, Conn. Soc. CPAs, Greater Boston C. of C. (bd. dirs.), N.E.-Israel C. of C. (bd. dirs.), Bostonian Club (Boston), Belmont Country Club. Home: 1611 Commonwealth Ave Newton MA 02165-2800 Office: Ernst & Young 200 Clarendon St Boston MA 02116-5021

TEMKIN, SAMUEL, mechanical and aerospace engineering educator; b. Mexico City, Jan. 10, 1936; s. Tobias and Lea (Mericof) T.; m. Judith Celia Olchak, June 20, 1965; children: David, Michael. BSc, Nuevo Leon U., 1960; ScM, Brown U., 1964, PhD, 1966. Sr. scientist Bolt, Beranek & Newman, Inc., Cambridge, Mass., 1966-67; asst. prof. Rutgers U., New Brunswick, N.J., 1967-70, assoc. prof., 1970-73, prof. engring., 1980—, chmn. dept. mech. and aerospace engring., 1980-89; cons. Ballistic Rsch. Labs., Aberdeen, Md., 1972-74, Naval Rsch. Labs., Washington, 1986-89; Lady Davis vis. prof. Israel Inst. Tech., Haifa, 1974-75; vis. prof. Royal Inst. Tech., Stokholm, 1989, U. Twente, Enschede, The Netherlands, 1990. Author: Elements of Acoustics, 1981; contbr. articles to profl. publs. Recipient award Hasselblad Found., 1984. Fellow ASME; mem. Am. Phys. Soc., Acoustical Soc. Am. Office: Rutgers U Dept Engring PO Box 909 Piscataway NJ 08855-0909

TEMPESTA, MICHELE S., editor, consultant; b. Montclair, N.J., Dec. 29, 1946; d. Arthur A. and Mary (Galgano) T. BA, Wells Coll., 1968. Sr. editor Doubleday & Co., Inc., N.Y.C., 1969-91; ind. editorial cons. N.Y.C., 1991—. Mem. Acad. Club London, Tilling Soc. Eng., Mystery Writers Am. Home: 102 W 75th St Apt 78 New York NY 10023-1949

TEMPLE, CHARLES ADAMS, education educator, author; b. Rocky Mount, N.C., Apr. 21, 1947; s. Gray and Maria (Drane) T.; m. Frances Nolting, July 16, 1969; children: Anna Brooke, Jessica, Mary Tyler. BA in English, U. N.C., 1969; MEd, U. Va., 1975, PhD in Edn., 1978. Tchr. English Alston High Sch., Summerville, S.C., 1969-70; dir. remedial svcs. Powhatan (Va.) County Schs., 1970-75; asst. prof. U. Houston, Victoria, Tex., 1978-81; asst. then assoc. prof. Hobart and William Smith Colls., Geneva, N.Y., 1982—, dept. chair, 1984-88. Co-author: The Beginnings of Writing, 1982, Language Arts, 1984, 89, Stories and Readers, 1991; reviewer Young Children, 1985; mem. editorial bd. Lang. Arts, 1990—. Fulbright scholar Coun. Internat. Exchange Scholars, 1988. Mem. Internat. Reading Assn., Nat. Coun. Tchrs. English. Democrat. Episcopalian. Office: Hobart and William Smith Colls Geneva NY 14456

TEMPLE, DONALD EDWARD, association executive; b. N.Y.C., Nov. 28, 1946; s. James Edward and Helen Louise (Gannon) T.; m. Lucy Chirinos de Lorentzen, Feb. 23, 1974 (div. 1989); 1 child, Gail Marie. BBA, St. Francis Coll., Bklyn., 1968. Vol. U.S. Peace Corps, Lima, Peru, 1968-72; asst. to pres., gen. mgr. Barrons Ednl. Series, Inc., Woodbury, N.Y., 1973-78; dir. supply svc. Am. Lung Assn., N.Y.C., 1978-84; bus. mgr. Am. Rev. Respiratory Diseases, N.Y.C., 1985—, Am. Jour. Respiratory Cell and Molecular Biology, N.Y.C., 1989—; dir. bus. affairs Am. Lung Assn., N.Y.C., 1985-89; dep. mng. dir. bus. affairs Am. Lung Assn., N.Y.c., 1990—; mem. mailers tech. adv. com. U.S. Postal Svc., Washington, 1987—. Recipient merit award Soc. for Tech. Communication, 1990. Mem. Soc. Scholarly Pub., Dir. Mail Fundraisers Assn., Alliance Non-Profit Mailers (bd. dirs., chmn. tech. com. 1986—, v.p. 1990—), Pharm. Advt. Coun., Internat. Found. Employee Benefit Plans, Am. Soc. Assn. Execs. Roman Catholic. Home: 63 Vanderwater St Farmingdale NY 11735-5235 Office: Am Lung Assn 1740 Broadway New York NY 10019-4315

TEMPLIN, JOHN LEON, JR., healthcare consulting executive; b. New Brunswick, N.Y., Aug. 5, 1940; s. John Leon and Theresa Veronica (Revolinski) T.; m. Barbara Maria Ribley, Sept. 12, 1970; children: John, Joseph, Kevin, Nan, Danielle, Christopher. BS in Mgmt. Engring., Rensselaer Poly. Inst., 1962, MS in Mgmt., 1969. Mgr. customer svc. Norton Abrasives, Troy, N.Y., 1968-70; cons., sr. cons. Hosp. Assn. N.Y. State, Albany, 1970-79, dir. mgmt. svcs., 1979-80, sr. dir. mgmt. svc., 1981-83; dir. productivity improvement Applied Leadership Technologies, Inc., Greenfield Center, N.Y., 1983-84, v.p., productivity improvement div., 1984-85, pres., 1985-86; pres. Templin Mgmt. Assocs., Inc., Greenfield Center, 1987—. Editor. quar. jour. Healthcare Supr., 1983—; mem. editorial com. ann. Manual for Workload Recording, 1978—. Mem. budget com. Greater Saratoga Sch. Dist., Saratoga Springs, N.Y., 1978-79; mem. energy com. Blue Cross Assn., Chgo., 1978-81; mem. Gov.'s Task Force on Nursing, Albany, 1980; mem. parish coun. St. Joseph's Ch., Greenfield Center, 1981-87. Capt. U.S. Army, 1962-64. Fellow Am. Coll. Healthcare Execs., Healthcare Info. and Mgmt. Systems Soc. (liaison Coll. Am. Pathologists 1978-91); mem. Am. Hosp. Assn. (seminar speaker 1980—), Healthcare Fin. Mgmt. Assn., Clin. Lab. Mgmt. Assn. (bd. dirs. 1980-84), K.C. Republican. Roman Catholic. Home and Office: Templin Mgmt Assocs Inc 265 Locust Grove Rd Greenfield Center NY 12833-1501

TENENBAUM, BERNARD HIRSH, entrepreneur, educator; b. Long Beach, N.Y., Dec. 23, 1954; s. Abraham Benjamin and Helen Pearl (Wahrhaft) T. BA, Columbia Coll., 1976; postgrad., Stanford U., 1976-77; MBA, U. Pa., 1981. Mgr. Lido Beach (N.Y.) Hotel, 1976-77; gen. mgr. Sound Spectrum, Huntington, N.Y., 1977-78; dir. Small Bus. Ctr., Phila., 1980-84; asst. dir. Entre Ctr., Phila., 1984-85, assoc. dir., 1986-88; prof. entrepreneurial studies, dir. Fairleigh Dickinson U., Madison, N.J., 1988—; cons. Phila. Phillies, 1984-85; bd. dirs. Ogontz Ave. Redevel. Corp., West Phila. Ptnership; dir. Russ Berrie & Co. Del. Securities Exchange Commn. on Small Bus. Capital Formation, 1984-86; vice chmn. Small Bus. Devel. Ctr. adv. bd., Phila., 1983—; bd. dirs. Pvt. Industry Council, Phila., 1983—; chmn. Small Bus. Fair, Phila., 1983—. Mem. Phila. C. of C. (vice chmn. small bus. council, 1982-86, chmn. Small Bus. Council, 1986—), Venture Match of N.J., Inc., Venture Assn. N.J. (v.p.). Democrat. Jewish. Office: Fairleigh Dickinson U Rothman Inst Entrepreneurial Studies Madison NJ 07940

TENENBAUM, JEFFREY MARK, academic librarian; b. Phila., Apr. 10, 1945; s. Paul and Hansi (Barber) T. BA, Pa. State U., 1966; MLS, McGill U., 1968. Documents librarian, then reference librarian U. Toronto (Ont., Can.) Library, 1968-72; reference librarian U. Mass. Library, Amherst, 1973—. Mem. ALA, Assn. Can. Studies in U.S., Am. Coun. Que. Studies, Mid-Atlantic and New Eng. Conf. for Can. Studies, Pioneer Valley Assn., Acad. Librs. (pres. 1989-90), Assn. Coll. and Rsch. Librs., Beta Phi Mu, Phi Alpha Theta, Pi Gamma Mu. Jewish. Home: 48 Riverside Park Amherst MA 01002-1043 Office: U Mass Univ Libr Amherst MA 01003

TENEYCK, GREGORY ALDEN, communications executive; b. Albany, N.Y., Nov. 14, 1957; s. Alden Middlemore and Ida May (Burgess) T.; m. Carolyn Shipe, May 2, 1981; 1 child, Bess Burgess. AAS, SUNY, Morrisville, 1977; BS, U. Md., 1979. News aide Washington Post, 1978-79; asst. dir. pub. rels. Capital Ctr., Landover, Md., 1979-84; sr. acct. exec. Charles J. Brotman and Assoc., Washington, 1984-86; dir. pub. rels. Cardinal Industries Inc., Balt., 1986-88; dir. communications Interstate Gen. Co. L.P., St. Charles, Md., 1988—. Dir. Philip ministry Grace Brethren Ch., Waldorf, Md., 1991—; chmn. St. Charles 25th Anniversary Com., 1990. Mem. Suburban Md. Bldg. Industry Assn. (chmn. pub. rels. com. 1991), Pub. Rels. Soc. Am. (Best Pub. Rels. Program in Md. award 1987), Nat. Assn. Real Estate Editors (assoc.). Republican. Office: Interstate Gen Co LP 222 Smallwood Village Ctr Waldorf MD 20602-1840

TENGES, TOM ALAN, commercial insurance executive; b. Easton, Pa., Feb. 9, 1949; s. Harry Benjamin and Ethel Virginia (Amerman) T. BA, Moravian Coll., 1970. Advt. rep. The Easton Express, 1971-72; asst to v.p. Easton Nat. Bank, 1973-75; asst. dir. devel. Moravian Coll., Bethlehem, Pa., 1975-76, dir. devel., 1976-77, 77-84; v.p. devel. Moravian Coll., Bethlehem, 1984-88; acct. exec. Woodring-Roberts Corp., Bethlehem, 1990—. Pres., dir. Sun Inn Preservation Assn., Bethlehem, 1983; bd. dirs. Northampton Community Coll. Found., 1991—; dir. Burnside Plantation, 1990—; individuals chmn. United Way of Northampton and Warren Counties, 1991; mem. fin. devel. com. Bethlehem's 250th Anniversary, 1989—; mem. devel. com. Moravian Hall Sq., 1990—. Mem. Coun. Advancement and Support of Edn. (bd. dirs. Middle Atlantic dist. 1978), Bethlehem Area C. of C. (edn. com. 1987-88, bd. dirs. 1988—, chmn. Christmas city com. 1990), Moravian Coll. Alumni Assn. (bd. dirs. 1991—). Republican. Moravian. Club: Bethlehem. Home: 1118 N New St Bethlehem PA 18018-2718 Office: The Woodring-Roberts Corp 459 Main St Bethlehem PA 18018-5871

TENNER, EDWARD HARVEY, publishing executive, writer; b. Chgo., Aug. 1, 1944; s. Irving and Evelyn (Talmadge) T. AB, Princeton U., 1965; AM, U. Chgo., 1968, PhD, 1972. Jr. fellow Harvard Soc. Fellows, Cambridge, Mass., 1969-72; instr. Chgo. City Colls., 1972-73; research assoc. U. Chgo., 1973-74; editor Ctr. for Ill. Studies, Inc., Chgo., 1974-75; sci. editor Princeton (N.J.) U. Press, 1975-88, exec. editor phys. sci., 1988-91; visitor Sch. of Social Sci. Inst. for Advanced Study, Princeton, N.J., 1991—; cons. Exxon Edn. Found., N.Y.C., 1975-82, Charles A. Dana Found., N.Y.C., 1982-84; vis. lectr. Coun. of Humanities, Princeton U., 1990. Author: Tech Speak, 1986; contbg. editor Harvard Mag., 1988—; contbr. articles to periodicals. Mem. Friends of Princeton Pub. Libr., N.Y. Hist. Soc., Bucks County Hist. Soc., Princeton Hist. Soc. John Simon Guggenheim fellow, 1991; recipient Wadsworth prize Harvard mag., 1985. Mem. Am. Hist. Assn., Am. Geophys. Union, History Sci. Soc., Soc. for History Tech. Office: Inst Advanced Study Sch Social Sci Olden Ln Princeton NJ 08540-4920

TENNEY, CHARLES HENRY, federal judge; b. N.Y.C., Jan. 28, 1911; s. Daniel Gleason and Marguerite Sedgwick (Smith) T.; m. Joan Penfold Lusk, May 14, 1938; children: Patricia Lusk (Mrs. Bernard J. Ruggieri), Charles Henry, Joan Tenney Howard, Marguerite Sedgwick (Mrs. Talton R. Embry), Anne Gleason. Grad., Choate Sch., 1929; A.B., Yale U., 1933, LL.B., 1936. Bar: N.Y. 1937. With firm Breed, Abbott & Morgan, N.Y.C., 1936-51; mem. firm Breed, Abbott & Morgan, 1951-55; commr. investigation N.Y.C., 1955-58; corp. counsel, 1958-61, dep. mayor, city adminstr., 1961-64; U.S. dist. judge So. Dist. N.Y., 1964—, now sr. judge. Mem. N.Y.C. Bd. Ethics, 1960-61. Served to lt. comdr. USNR, 1942-45. Mem. Am., Fed., N.Y. County, N.Y. State bar assns., Assn. Bar City N.Y., Am. Judicature Soc., Phi Beta Kappa. Home: 340 E 72nd St New York NY 10021-4768 Office: US Dist Ct US Courthouse Foley Sq New York NY 10007-1501

TENNEY, FRANK PUTNAM, marketing executive; b. Orono, Maine, Oct. 6, 1937; s. Carl Bither and Velma May (Williamson) T.; m. Margaret Anne Seymour, Apr. 23, 1960; children: Jane Dossiere, Carl B., Janet M., Alan F., Janice M. With George D. Wetherrill, Phila., 1968-69; nat. sales mgr. Shaw & Tenney Oar & Paddle Co., Orono, 1958-68; with R.M. Flagg, Veazie, Maine, 1968-69; sales mgr. George D. Wetherill, Phila.; with Dubois Chem., Cin., 1969-75; Maine sales mgr. Rochester (N.Y.) Midland Co., 1976-82; with H.A. Manning Co., BellowsFalls, Vt., 1982-86; dist. sales mgr. U.S. West Mktg. Resources, Loveland, Colo., 1986-90; mgr. dist. sales City Directory, Inc., Belmond, Iowa, 1991—. Tech. sgt. Maine ANG, 1955-87. ret. Mem. Greater Bangor C. of C., Am. Legion, Golden Circle, KC (grant knight Pine Cone coun., 4th degree). Republican. Roman Catholic.

TENOPYR, MARY LOUISE WELSH (MRS. JOSEPH TENOPYR), psychologist; b. Youngstown, Ohio, Oct. 18, 1929; d. Roy Henry and Olive (Donegan) Welsh; AB, Ohio U., 1951, MA, 1951; PhD, U. So. Calif., 1966; m. Joseph Tenopyr, Oct. 30, 1955. Psychometrist, Ohio U., Athens, 1951-52, also housemother Sigma Kappa; personnel technician to research psychologist USAF, 1953-55, Dayton, Ohio, 1952-53, Hempstead, N.Y.; indsl. research analyst to mgr. employee evaluation N.Am. Rockwell Corp., El Segundo, Calif., 1956-70; asso. prof. Calif. State Coll.-Los Angeles, 1966-70; assoc. research educationist UCLA, 1970-71; program dir. U.S. CSC, 1971-72; dir. selection and testing AT&T, N.Y.C., 1972—; lectr. U. So. Calif., Los Angeles, 1967-70; vice chmn. research com. Tech. Adv. Com. on Testing, Fair Employment Practice Commn. Calif., 1966-70; adviser on testing Office Fed. Contract Compliance, U.S. Dept. Labor, Washington, 1967-73. Pres., ASPA Found., 1985-87; mem. Army Sci. Bd. Fellow Am. Psychol. Assn. (bd. profl. affairs, edn. and training bd., mem. council reps., pres. div. indsl. organizational psychology); mem. Eastern Psychol. Assn., Am. Soc. Personnel Adminstrn. (bd. dirs. 1984-87), Nat. Acad. Sci. (coms. on ability testing, math. and sci. edn., panel on secondary edn.), Soc. Indsl. and Organizational Psychology (Recipient Profl. Practices award 1984), Nat. Council Measurement in Edn., Psychometric Soc., Met. N.Y. Assn. Applied Psychology, Am. Ednl. Research Assn., Sigma Xi, Sigma Kappa, Psi Chi, Alpha Lambda Delta, Kappa Phi. Editorial bd. Jour. Applied Psychology, 1972-87, Jour. Vocat. Behavior; assoc. editor Am. Psychologist; contbr. chpts. to books and articles to profl. jours. Home: 557 Lyme Rock Rd Bridgewater NJ 08807-1604 Office: One Speedwell Ave Morristown NJ 07960

TENZER, RUDOLF KURT, physicist, consultant; b. Jena, Thuringen, Germany, Oct. 9, 1920; came to U.S., 1953, naturalized, 1959; s. Richard Konrad and Gertrud (Dworatzek) T.; m. Inge Elisabeth Hartmuth, Oct. 2, 1947; children: Kristina, Tomas, Mattias, Markus. Diploma in physics, J.W. von Goethe U., Frankfurt, Fed. Republic Germany, 1950, Dr.rer.nat., 1950. Tech. asst. Hartmann & Braun A.G., Frankfurt, 1948-53; scientist, sr. scientist Ind. Steel Products Co., Valparaiso, 1953-55, mgr. rsch., 1955-65; rsch. dir. Ind. Gen. Corp., Keasbey, N.J., 1965-76; tech. dir. Ind. Gen. div. EM&M Corp., Keasbey, 1976-84; owner, cons. Tenzer Assocs., Martinsville, N.J., 1984—; vol. exec. Internat. Exec. Svc. Corps., Sao Paulo, Brazil, 1986, Bhubaneswar, India, 1989-90, Tlalnepantla, Mex., 1990. Chmn. Princeton sect. Magnetics Soc., 1977. Mem. IEEE, Am. Ceramic Soc. Home and Office: Tenzer Assocs 1643 Brookdale Dr Martinsville NJ 08836-9733

TEPLY, KARLEEN INGRID, educational administrator; b. N.Y.C., Mar. 12, 1944; d. Karl Otto and E. Ingeborg (Schubert) Nie. BS in Mus. Edn., U. Vt., 1965, MEd, 1980. Cert. tchr., Vt. Music supr. South Burlington (Vt.) Sch. System, 1965—; condr. South Burlington Community Chorus, 1976—; instr. Trinity Coll., Burlington, Vt., 1976-86; music cons. Middlebury (Vt.) Coll., 1985-87. Author: A Music Handbook for Elementary Teachers, 1981. Mem. NEA, Vt. Educators Assn., Music Educators Nat. Conf., Am. Choral Dirs. Assn., Vt. Music Educators Assn. (co-chairperson Vt. All-State Music Festival Auditions 1988-91), USCG Aux. (vice-capt. Burlington 1976—), Shelburne Bay Boat Club (pres. 1980-82). Democrat. Lutheran. Home: 46 Martindale Rd Shelburne VT 05482-7281 Office: South Burlington Middle Sch 500 Dorset St South Burlington VT 05403-6274

TEPLY, LESTER J., nutritionist; b. Muccoda, Wis., Apr. 22, 1920; s. Joseph Francis and Helen Marie (Kubicek) T.; m. Nancy Sterling Winslow, June 24, 1950; children: Susan, Lee, Mark. BA, U. Wis., 1940, MS, 1944, PhD, 1945. Sec. Food Composition Com. Nat. Rsch. Coun., Washington, 1945; biochemist U.S. Pub. Health Svc., Bethesda, Md., 1945-46; rsch. assoc. Columbia U., N.Y.C., 1946-48; rsch. asst. Enzyme Inst. U. Wis. (Madison), 1948-51; project dir. Wis. Alumni Rsch. Found., Madison, 1951-60; sr. nutritionist UNICEF, N.Y.C., 1960-85; adj. prof. N.Y. Med. Coll., Valhalla, N.Y., 1986—; chmn. Internat. Vitamin A Consultative Group, 1980-85; pres. bd. League for Internat. Food Edn., 1985-88. Contbr. articles to profl. jours. Mem. Phi Beta Kappa, Inst. for Food Technologists, Am. Chemical Soc., Am. Pub. Health Assn. Home: 32 Colonial Ave Larchmont NY 10538-1621

TEPPER, BLOSSOM WEISS, psychologist; b. Bklyn., Oct. 15, 1921; d. Meyer and Anna (Lax) Weiss; m. Louis Tepper, Apr. 17, 1942 (dec. Aug. 1978); children: Irene Tepper Homa, Allan M. BA, Bklyn. Coll., 1942; MEd, Lehigh U., 1962, EdD in Clin. and Counseling Psychology, 1967. Lic. psychologist, Pa.; cert. sch. psychologist, Pa. Tchr. sci., guidance counselor Blue Mountain Sch. Dist., Schuylkill Haven, Pa., 1958-64; successively grad. asst., instr., asst. prof. Lehigh U., Bethlehem, Pa., 1964-71; dir. home and sch. visitor project Luzerne County Schs., Wilkes-Barre, Pa., 1968-71, also adj. prof. Wilkes Coll., Wilkes-Barre, 1969-71; clin. psychologist base service unit, dir. Schuylkill County Mental Health/Mental Retardation, Pottsville, Pa., 1971-72; clin. psychologist Northampton County Mental Health/Mental Retardation, Easton, Pa., 1972-75, clin. psychologist, specialist mental retardation and devel. disabilities, cons. community living program for mental retardation, Bethlehem and Easton, 1975—. Fellow Pa. Psychol. Assn.; mem. Am. Personnel and Guidance Assn., Pa. Personnel and Guidance Assn., Am. Psychol. Assn., Pa. Assn. Sch. Psychologists (charter), Nat. Register Mental Health Providers in Psychology, Am. Assn. Higher Edn. (charter, life), Hadassah (life). Developer exptl. program tng. sch. social workers. Home: Bridle Path Woods Bridle Path Rd Apt 12C Bethlehem PA 18017-3702 Office: Northampton County Dept Human Svcs Bethlehem Mental Health Treatment Unit 3rd Fl 44 E Broad St Bethlehem PA 18018

TERAMURA, ALAN HIROSHI, botany educator; b. L.A., Dec. 26, 1948; s. Kuniyoshi and Mineko (Nakamura) T.; m. Karen Lee McKnight, Sept. 10, 1974; 1 child. BA, Calif. State U., 1971, MA, 1973; PhD, Duke U., 1978. Asst. prof. botany U. Md., College Park, 1979-82, assoc. prof. botany, 1982-88, prof. botany, 1988—, chmn. botany dept., 1990—; guest prof. Botanishes Inst., Karlsruhe, Fed. Republic of Germany, 1982-83; chmn. sci. adv. bd. Ctr. Global Change, College Park, 1989—; cons. USDA, EPA, Nat. Acad. Sci., Washington, 1982—. Contbr. chpts. to 12 books and 80 articles to profl. jours. Grantee NSF, 1977, U.S. EPA, 1980-90, USDA, 1989—. Mem. Am. Soc. Plant Physiologists, Botanical Soc. Am., Ecol. Soc. Am., Sigma Xi. Office: U Md Dept Botany College Park MD 20742

TERASKIEWICZ, EDWARD ARNOLD, broker; b. Bklyn., June 9, 1946; s. Edward A. and Anna A. (Romeo) T.; m. Geraldine Lucchesi, May 7, 1966; children: Marie Elena, Lisa. Cert. Am. Inst. Banking, 1970. Money desk trader Citibank, N.Y.C., 1964-71; gen. ptnr. Mabon Nugent & Co., N.Y.C., 1971-84; chmn. Babcock, Fulton, Prebon U.S.A., Inc., N.Y.C., 1984—; vice chmn. Internat. City Holdings PLC 34-40 Ludgate Hill, London, 1986-87, c.e.o. Internat. City Holdings, 1989-91; c.e.o. Prebon Internat. Inc., 1991—. With U.S. Army, 1965-68. Home: 114 Tillman St Staten Island NY 10314-5632 Office: Babcock Fulton Prebon USA Inc 1 Exchange Plz New York NY 10006-3008

TERHES, JOYCE LYONS, advertising and public relations executive; b. Prince Frederick, Md., June 21, 1940; d. Arthur Gorman and Mildred G. (Ward) L. BA in History, Mary Washington Coll., 1962; postgrad., U. Md., 1966-69. Tchr. Prince Georges County Bd. Edn., Upper Marlboro, Md., 1962-84; campaign mgr. Williams for Congress, 1984; pres., cons. JLT Assocs., Prince Frederick, 1985—; v.p. Calvert County Bd. Commrs., Prince Frederick, 1986—. Co-author: U.S.S.R., 1979, The Middle East, 1980, Asia: China, India, Japan, 1980, Prince George's County, 1980, The United States, Book I, Exploration and Colonization, 1982, Book II, The Birth of a New Country, 1982; editor: $100,000 Reward, 1972; founding editor Goose Call. Former editor ch. bull. Jesus Good Shepherd Cath. Ch.; bd. dirs. Calvert County unit Am. Cancer Soc., 1984-86, South County Concert Assn., 1984-86, Calvert County Nursing Ctr., 1984-86; founding pres. Dunkirk Area Concerned Citizens Assn.; mem. Calvert County Rep. Cen. Com., 1984-86;

mem. Electoral Coll. Md., 1984, 88; chmn. voter registration Md. Rep. Com., also 1st vice chmn.; del. Rep. Nat. Conv., 1988; bd. dirs. Nat. Fedn. Rep. Women, chmn. 25th biennial con., 1989; chmn. Md. Rep. party. Mem. Ferry Landing Woods Civic Assn., Ferry Landing Woods Garden Club. Home: 10330 Three Doctors Rd Dunkirk MD 20754-9407 Office: Cal Exec Plz Ste 300 Prince Frederick MD 20678

TERMAN, MICHAEL, psychologist, chronobiologist; b. N.Y.C., Nov. 13, 1943; s. Isaiah and Daisy (Young) T.; m. Jiuan Su, July 14, 1966. AB, Columbia U., 1964; PhD, Brown U., 1968. Asst. prof. Brown U., Providence, 1968-69; prof. Northeastern U., Boston, 1969-84; rsch. scientist N.Y. State Psychiatric Inst., 1981—; assoc. prof. Coll. Physicians and Surgeons Columbia U., N.Y.C., 1984—; cons. Pub. Health Svc. Agy. for Health Care Policy and Rsch., Bethesda, Md, 1990-91; sr. sci. cons. Inst. for Circadian Physiology, Boston, 1991—. Contbr. articles to Sci., Ann. N.Y. Acad. Sci., Jour. Biol. Rhythms, Neuropsychopharm. Recipient Rsch. Sci. Devel. award NIMH, 1983, grantee, 1991. Fellow APA (Young Psychologist award 1969), Am. Psychol. Soc. (charter); mem. Soc. for Light Treatment and Biol. Rhythms (sec. 1988-90, bd. dirs. 1988—, pres. 1992), Soc. for Neurosci., Soc. for Rsch. in Biol. Rhythms. Office: Columbia U Dept Psychiatry 722 W 168th St # 50 New York NY 10032-2603

TERRELL, CHARLES RICHARD, federal agency administrator; b. Waltham, Mass., June 20, 1943; s. Warren Emerson and Viola (Rodenhiser) T.; m. Sandra Jean Sturtevant, Oct. 7, 1967; children: Julia Ann, Alicia Jean. BA in Biology, Boston U., 1965; MS in Marine Biology, Northeastern U., 1968. Biol. technician U.S. Marine Fisheries Svc. Biol. Lab., Boothbay Harbor, Maine, 1965-67; instr. biology dept. Salem (Mass.) State Coll., 1968-74; dir. State of Mass., Costal Rev. Ctr., Office Coastal Zone Mgmt., Boston, 1974-76; assoc. The Conservation Found., Washington, 1976-77; environ. scientist criteria and standards div. EPA, Washington, 1977-79, acting sect. chief dredge and fill sect., 1980; nat. water quality specialist Soil Conservation Svc., USDA, Washington, 1980—; chmn. plenary session various ecological confs., 1986-88; co-owner/operator Bed & Breakfast Inn, Cape Cod, Mass., 1989—. Co-author: Environmental Planning for Offshore Oil and Gas, 1978, Water Quality Indicators Guide, 1989; contbr. numerous articles to tech. jours. Legis. fellow Staff of U.S. Senator Charles McC. Mathias, Washington, 1985; mem. shellfish adv. commn. Town of Ipswich (Mass.), 1969-74, chmn., 1972-74. Mem. Fed. Water Quality Assn. (sec. 1989-91, v.p. 1991-92, pres.-elect 1992—), Am. Inst. Biol. Scis., Am. Water Resources Assn., Water Environ. Fedn. (nonpoint source coms. 1986—). Democrat. Office: Soil Conservation Svc Ecological Scis Div PO Box 2890 Washington DC 20013-2890

TERRIS, ALBERT, metal sculptor; b. N.Y.C., Nov. 10, 1916; s. Aaron and Fania (Rosenthal) Teraspulsky; children: Susan, Abby, David, Enoch. BSS, CCNY, 1939; postgrad., NYU Inst. Fine Arts, 1939-42. lectr. Met. Mus. Art, 1941-42; tchr. fine arts N.Y.C. High Sch. System, 1947-54; prof. emeritus Bklyn. Coll., 1947-86. Steel sculptures include Non-Fixed Relationship, 1948, Anti-Gravity, 1950, Giraffes, 1953, Short Art, 1953, Pro-Gravity Chains, 1956, Tools, 1956, Crushed Sculpture, 1956, Words, 1957, Plates of Charlemagne, 1975, Cycle of Life, 1977; one-man shows: Saidenberg, 1955, Duveen-Graham, 1958, Carnegie Internats., 1958, 62, Bklyn. Mus. Biennale (first prize), 1960, Allan Stone, 1962, Critics Choice, 1972, Artists Space, 1975, Gloria Cortella, 1977, (retrospective) Artist in the Civil Svc., Bklyn. Coll. Gallery, 1985; exhibited in group shows at Tanager Gallery, 1953-61, Stable anns., 1953-60, Mus. Modern Art, N.Y.C., 1962, others; represented in permanent collections: Stephen Paine, Boston, Arnold Maremont, Evanston, G. David Thompson Estate, NBC-TV, others. Served with 1st Allied Airborne, 1942-45. Home: 280 S Ocean Ave Freeport NY 11520-4939

TERRY, BRIAN R., counselor, academic administrator; b. Providence, June 8, 1961; s. Edwin R. and Mary W. (Ahern) T.; m. Stephanie A. Fogli; 1 child, Alexander Brian. AS, Community Coll. of R.I., 1982; BS, Bryant Coll., 1984; MA, R.I. Coll., 1990. Supr. Whitmarsh Corp., Providence, counselor; cottage mgr. tng. sch. for youth Dept. of Children, Youth, and Families, R.I. Acad. scholar Esterline Corp., acad. scholar City of Cranton, R.I., Tanner Meml. scholar. Am. Assn. for Counseling and Devel., Pub. Offender Counselor Assn., Nat. Ct. Appointed Spl. Advocate Assn., Am. Correctional Assn., Nat. Inst. for Reality Therapy (assoc., Northeast region), Community Leaders of Am., Phi Theta Kappa. Home: 115 E View Ave Cranston RI 02920-6505

TERRY, ELIZABETH HAYS, needlepoint designer; b. Bryn Mawr, Pa., July 29, 1935; d. James Franklin and Mary Ellen (Carmichael) Hays; m. Charles L. Terry, III, Feb. 8, 1958; children: Elizabeth Harllee Carmichael Terry Littlefield, Charles L. IV. AB, Smith Coll., 1957. Asst. to profs. Harvard U., Cambridge, Mass., 1957-58; art tchr. Exeter (N.H.) Day Sch., 1968-72; asst. editor Phillips Exeter Acad. Alumni Quarterly, 1972-75, dir. alumni records, 1975-85; owner Elizabeth Terry, Needlepoint Design, North Hampton, N.H., 1980—; tchr. needlepoint Guild of Strawbery Banke, Portsmouth, N.H., 1985—. Dir. for Town of Exeter-Save Our Shores, 1972. Mem. Smith Coll. Class of 1957 (class fund agt. 1972-77, alumni fund com. 1977-80, class bequest chair, 1982—, com. on deferred giving, 1990—), N.H. Colonial Dames (pres. 1989-92, nat. officer 1992—). Episcopalian. Home: 76 Exeter Rd North Hampton NH 03862-2004 Office: Nat Soc Colonial Dames Am Moffatt Ladd House 154 Market St Portsmouth NH 03801-3730

TERRY, FREDERICK H., management educator; b. Riverhead, N.Y., Oct. 7, 1944; s. Richard Collins and Sara Blanche (Hill) T.; m. Mary J. (div. 1977); m. Andrea M., Aug. 5, 1978; children: Ian, Sean, Daniel. AAS, SUNY, Farmingdale, 1964; BS, SUNY, Albany, 1966, MBA, 1968; MA, SUNY, Stony Brook, 1975. Pres. Terry Family Enterprises, Amagansett, N.Y., 1968—; prof. New Eng. Coll., Henniker, N.H., 1970; dept. chmn. restaurant mgmt. Nassau Coll., Garden City, N.Y., 1988-90, prof., 1971—. Mem. N.Y. State Restaurant Assn. (L.I. chpt., pres., 1989-90, bd. dirs. 1987—, chmn. for edn., 1987—).

TERRY, SARAH MEIKLEJOHN, political science educator; b. Newton, Mass., July 16, 1937; d. George Stewart Smith and Elizabeth Hollis (McCready) Meiklejohn; m. Robert Cushing Terry Jr., May 14, 1966. BA in Govt., Cornell U., 1959; MA in Soviet Studies, Harvard U., 1961, PhD in Polit. Sci., 1974. Assoc. dean, lectr. in polit. sci. Tufts U., Medford, Mass., 1976-78, asst. prof. polit. sci., 1978-84, assoc. prof. polit. sci., 1984—; vis. lectr. govt. Harvard U., Cambridge, Mass., 1977, 83; adj. assoc. prof. diplomacy Fletcher Sch. Law and Diplomacy, Tufts U., Medford, 1984-85; mem. program com. Internat. Rsch. and Exchs. Bd., Princeton, N.J., 1979-83; mem. com. on USSR and Ea. Europe NAS, Washington, 1986-89; bd. dirs. Coun. for Internat. Exch. of Scholars, Washington, 1987-91. Author: Poland's Place in Europe, 1983 (Am. Hist. Assns. prize for modern European Internat. Hist., 1983); co-author: Soviet Policy in Eastern Europe, 1984; contbr. articles to profl. jours. John M. Olin rsch. grantee Harvard Russian Rsch. Ctr., 1985-86, rsch. grantee NEH, 1979. Fellow Russian Rsch. Ctr.; mem. Coun. on Fgn. Rels., Am. Assn. for Advancement of Slavic Studies (bd. dirs., exec. com. 1983-86), Wilson Internat. Ctr. (mem. acad. adv. coun. East European Program 1988-91), Phi Beta Kappa, Phi Kappa Phi. Home: 396 Marsh St Belmont MA 02178-1108 Office: Tufts U Dept Polit Sci Medford MA 02155

TERZAKIS, JOHN ANTHONY, pathologist; b. Bridgeport, Conn., Sept. 13, 1935; s. Anthony and Magdalene (Zaffo) T.; m. Inger Alexandersson, July 29, 1961; children: Christina, Elizabeth, Eva. BA, Columbia Coll., 1957; MD, NYU, 1961. Diplomate Am. Bd. Pathology, anatomic pathology, dermatopathology, clin. pathology. Instr. in anatomy NYU Sch. of Medicine, N.Y.C., 1961-64, asst. prof., 1964-65; asst. prof. pathology Columbia U./Hosp. Div., N.Y.C., 1967-68; attending pathologist Lenox Hill Hosp., N.Y.C., 1968—, chief anatomic pathology, 1986—; clin. asst. prof. pathology Columbia U., N.Y.C., 1968-76; assoc. prof. pathology N.Y. Med. Coll., Valhalla, 1983-89; adj. assoc. prof. Columbia U., 1976—, N.Y. Med. Coll., Valhalla, 1989—; cons. Metpath, Inc., Teterboro, N.J., 1974—. Contbr. articles to profl. publs. Capt. U.S. Army Med. Corps, 1965-67. Fellow Coll. Am. Pathologists; mem. Am. Soc. Cell Biology, N.Y. Acad. Scis., N.Y. Soc. Electron Microscopists; Am. Soc. Dermatopathology, N.Y. Pathol. Soc., U.S. Acad. Pathologists, Can. Acad. Pathologists. Office: Lenox Hill Hosp 100 E 77th St New York NY 10021-1882

TERZIAN, PHILIP HENRY, journalist; b. Kensington, Md., July 5, 1950; s. L.A. and Louise (Anderson) T.; m. Grace Barrett Paine, Oct. 20, 1979; children: William Thomas Hillman, Grace Benedict Paine. BA, Villanova U., 1973; postgrad., Exeter Coll., Oxford, Eng., 1976. Desk editor Reuters, Washington, 1973, U.S. News & World Report, Washington, 1973-74; asst. editor The New Republic, Washington, 1974-78; mem. policy planning staff Dept. State, Washington, 1978-79; asst. editor Anniston (Ala.) Star, 1979-80; assoc. editor Lexington (Ky.) Herald, 1980-82; asst. editor of editorial pages L.A. Times, 1982-86; editor of editorial pages Providence Jour., 1986—. Contbr. articles to newspapers and jours. Dir. Providence Com. Fgn. Rels., 1989—. Recipient Edn. Writers award Edn. Writers Assn., 1981, Ida Lee Willis Svc. to Preservation award Ida Lee Willis Found., 1982; named finalist Pulitzer prize Disting. Commentary, 1991. Mem. Am. Soc. Newspaper Editors, Am. Coun. on Germany, Nat. Conf. Editorial Writers, St. Andrew's Soc. Washington, Nat. Press Club, Hope Club, Review Club. Republican. Episcopalian. Home: 10505 Adel Rd Oakton VA 22124 Office: Providence Jour 75 Fountain St Providence RI 02902

TESLIK, SARAH ANNA BALL, association executive, lawyer; b. Oberlin, Ohio, July 31, 1953; d. George Hudson and Nancy Ann (Cronon) Ball; m. Kennan Teslik, Aug. 21, 1976; children: Lee, William. BA, Whitman Coll., 1974; BA, MA, Oxford (Eng.) U., 1976; JD, Georgetown U., 1983. Bar: D.C. 1983. Assoc. Stroock and Stroock and Lavan, Washington, 1983-85, Wilkie, Farr and Gallagher, Washington, 1985-88; head of Washington office Hiscock and Barclay, N.Y.C., 1988-91; exec. dir. Coun. Instl. Investors, Washington, 1988—; pvt. practice law Washington, 1992—. Office: Coun Instl Investors 1616 P St NW Washington DC 20036-1434

TESORIERO, JOHN S., physician; b. Englewood, N.J., Jan. 22, 1953; s. John Albert and Mary A. (Tarace) T. Student, Washington and Jefferson Coll., 1970-72; BS, Manhattan Coll., 1974; European Cultural Diploma, Liceo Scientifico, Perugia, Italy, 1975. Faculty of medicine and chirurgia Univ. of Perugia, Italy, 1975-81; physician Ross U., N.Y.C., 1983-85. Hero in the rescue of Am. Gen. James Lee Dozier by Italian Red Brigade, 1981. Republican. Presbyterian. Home: 1150 Buckingham Rd Fort Lee NJ 07024-6442

TESSA, MARIAN LORRAINE, talk show host, writer, producer, educator; b. N.Y.C., Sept. 23, 1950; d. Sylvester Joseph and Emma Carol (Chimento) T. BA in English, SUNY, Cortland, 1972; postgrad., N.Y. Sch. Broadcasting, 1972-73. Writer CBS, N.Y.C., 1972-75; show host, producer, writer Manhattan Cable, N.Y.C., 1975—, S.I. Cable, 1988—; educator, 1991—. Spokesperson Miss Universe/Miss U.S.A. Beauty Pageants, 1976, promotion benefits; guest appearanced include David Susskind Show, 1978, ABC Wide World Spl., 1978, The Joe Franklin Show, 1980, The You Show, 1979, Natural Living Program, 1981; talk show host Kaleidoscope, 1983-85; voice over on cable TV, 1975—; performer Broadway in the Streets, 1969; photographic model Penzo Spagnoli Gallery, Florence, Italy, 1984, San Francisco, N.Y.C. and London, 1988. Com. mem. Am. Cancer Soc. Recipient Forensic award. Mem. NATAS, NAFE, Nat. Fedn. of Bus. and Profl. Women's Club Inc. Office: Tessa Prodns 10 Wagner St Staten Island NY 10305-2957

TESSLER, ARTHUR NED, physician; b. N.Y.C., Feb. 21, 1927; s. Isidore and Lillian (Josem) T.; m. Roslyn Chinitz, Feb. 14, 1953 (dec. May 1991); children: Daniel, Marc, Jonathan, Sara. AB, NYU, 1948, MD, 1952. Resident in urology NYU Med. Ctr., N.Y.C., 1956-59; prof. clin. urology NYU Sch. of Medicine, N.Y.C., 1975—, assoc. dir. dept. urology, 1975—. Feature editor: Urology jour., 1973—. Recipient med. award Kidney Disease Found., N.Y., N.J., 1984, Carl G. Hartman award Am. Soc. Study of Sterility and Ortho Rsch. Found., 1963. Fellow N.Y. Acad. Medicine (chmn. sect. urology 1977-78), Am. Coll. Surgeons; mem. AMA, N.Y. Sect. Am. Urol. Assn. (pres. 1983-84), Soc. Univ. Urologists, N.Y. Acad. Sci. Office: NYU Med Ctr 530 First Ave New York NY 10016

TESSLER, LISA BETH, career services director; b. Manhasset, N.Y., Apr. 2, 1957; d. Theodore and Eleanor F. (Licht) T. AB, Bowdoin Coll., 1979; EdM in Counseling & Cons. Psychology, Harvard Grad. Sch. Edn., 1981. Rsch. tech. Tufts U., Medford, Mass., 1979-80; project coord. Oxfam-America, Boston, 1979-81; univ. counselor Adelphi U., Garden City, N.Y., 1982; from career counselor to assoc. dir. placement N.Y. U. Sch. Law, 1982-89; assoc. dean student life Barnard Coll., N.Y.C., 1984-85; from asst. dir. career svcs. to dir. career svcs. Bowdoin Coll., Brunswick, Maine, 1989—. Membership chair Women's Counseling Project, Inc., N.Y.C., 1983-87; campus liaison United Way, Brunswick, 1990—; instr. Internat. Folk Dance Group, 1990—. Hon. Undergrad. fellow New Eng. Psychol. Assoc., 1978; Mgmt. Leadership Inst. scholar Coll. Placement Coun., Bethlehem, Pa., 1991; recipient 2 Profl. Achievement awards Nat. Assn. Law Placement, Washington, 1987. Mem. ASTD, Coll. Placement Coun., Ea. Coll. Personnel Officers, Phi Beta Kappa, N.E. Assn. Pre-Law Advs. Office: Bowdoin Coll Office of Career Svcs Brunswick ME 04011

TESSLER, MARTIN MELVYN, chemist, researcher; b. N.Y.C., Sept. 12, 1937; s. Herman and Charlotte (Kravitz) T.; m. Marilyn Ann Moskowitz, June 17, 1962; children: Jacqueline L., David M. BS in Chemistry, Bklyn. Coll., N.Y.C., 1958; PhD in Chemistry, U. Kans., 1962. Chemist Esso Rsch. & Engring. Co., Linden, N.J., 1965-68; project supr. Nat. Starch & Chem. Co., Plainfield, N.J., 1968-72; rsch. assoc. Nat. Starch & Chem. Co., Plainfield, 1972-81; sr. rsch. assoc. Nat. Starch & Chem. Co., Bridgewater, N.J., 1981-83; assoc. dir. rsch. Nat. Starch & Chem. Co., 1983-85, dir. natural polymer rsch., 1985—; mem. indsl. adv. bd. Food Sci. dept. Rutgers U., New Brunswick, N.J., 1989-91. Patentee in field. 1st lt. USAF, 1962-65. Mem. AAAS, Am. Assn. Cereal Chemists, Am. Chem. Soc. (sec. 1988-90, exec. sec. carbohydrate div. 1990—). Office: Nat Starch & Chem Co 10 Finderne Ave Bridgewater NJ 08807-3300

TESTER, LEONARD WAYNE, psychology educator; b. Nampa, Idaho, Aug. 21, 1933; s. Walter Vernon and Dora Dorothy (Peters) T. BTh, Kansas City Coll., Overland, Kansas, 1957; MA, Abilene Christian Coll. (now Abilene Christian U.), 1961; STB, Harvard U., 1969; EdM, Columbia U., 1971, EdD, 1976, M of Philosophy, 1979, PhD, 1981. Lic. psychologist, N.Y. Personnel mgr. Boston Safe Deposit & Trust Co., 1966-69; sr. counselor, prof. clin. counseling N.Y. Inst. Tech., Old Westbury, N.Y., 1971—; pvt. practice N.Y.C., 1983—; columnist Korea Times, N.Y.C., 1989-90; cons., grad. asst. Columbia U. Bus. Sch. and Tchrs. Coll., N.Y.C., 1977-81. Contbr. articles to profl. jours.; presenter workshops in field. Exec. dir. Ho. of te Carpenter, Boston, 1967-68; bd. dirs. Pierre (S.D.) Coun. of Arts; bd. dirs. Counseling Ctr. Episcopal Ch., Great Neck, N.Y., Tech. Sch. in N.Y.C. William Wayne Jackson Honors scholarship Harvard Div. Sch. Mem. Am. Psychol. Assn., N.Y. Soc. Clin. Psychologists, N.Y. Soc. Hypnosis and Psychotherapy and others. Home: PO Box 20107 New York NY 10023-1482 Office: NY Inst of Tech 1855 Broadway New York NY 10023-7692

TESTER, WILLIAM JOHN, oncologist; b. Aurora, Ill., July 2, 1950; s. William F. and Sylvia (Kish) T.; m. Linda M. Morante, July 30, 1972; children: Kristin, Marissa, Michael. BS, Rutgers Coll., 1972; MD, Hahnemann Coll., 1977. Diplomate Am. Bd. Hematology, Am. Bd. Med. Oncology, Am. Bd. Internal Medicine, Nat. Bd. Med. Examiners; lic. physician, Pa. Resident internal medicine Albert Einstein Med. Ctr., Bethesda, Md., 1977-80; chief med. resident Albert Einstein Med. Ctr., Phila., 1979-80, attending physician, 1983—; assoc. dir. Albert Einstein Med. Ctr., Bethesda, Md., 1991—; med. oncology fellow Nat. Cancer Inst., NIH, Bethesda, 1980-82; hematology fellow Georgetown U. Hosp., Washington, 1982-83. Editor Oncology in Practice; contbr. articles to profl. jours. Mem. profl. edn. com. Am. Cancer Soc. Mem. AMA (physicians recognition award), ACP, NIH Alumni Assn., Am. Soc. Clin. Oncology, Radiation Therapy Oncology Group, Nat. Surg. Adjuvant Breast Group, Ea. Coop. Oncology Group. Republican. Roman Catholic. Office: Albert Einstein Cancer Ctr Willowcrest Bldg 5501 Old York Rd Philadelphia PA 19141

TETELMAN, ALICE FRAN, non-profit organization executive; b. N.Y.C., Apr. 15, 1941; d. Harry and Leah (Markovitz) T.; m. Martin A. Wenick, Dec. 7, 1980. BA, Mt. Holyoke Coll., South Hadley, Mass., 1962. Rsch. and info. asst. Edn. and World Affairs, N.Y.C., 1963-67; legis. asst. U.S. Sen. Charles Goodell, Washington, 1968-70; land use and energy specialist Citizens Adv. Com. on Environ. Quality, Washington, 1973-74; sr. assoc. prog. mgr. Linton & Co., Washington, 1971-73, 75-76; pub policy cons. Washington, 1977-78; adminstrv. asst. U.S. Congressman Bill Green (N.Y.), Washington, 1978-81; cons. The Precious Legacy Project, Prague, Czechoslovakia, 1982-83; Rep. staff dir. Select Com. on Hunger, U.S. Ho. of Reps., Washington, 1984-85; dir. State of N.J. Washington Office, 1986-90; exec. dir. Coun. of Gov/'s Policy Advisors, Washington, 1991—. Bd. mem. Republican Women's Task Force, Nat. Women's Polit. Caucus, 1976-80. European Community grantee, 1975. Mem. Ripon Soc. (nat. exec. com. 1971-73). Republican.

TEUFEL, PARTRICIA ANN, actuary, consultant; b. Greenwich, Conn., Sept. 30, 1950; d. Robert Joseph and Virginia Adelaide (Hill) T.; m. Thomas Michael Driscoll, June 1, 1984; children: Sarah Elizabeth, Rachel Patricia. BA, Trinity Coll., 1972. Actuarial student Aetna Ins. Co., Hartford, Conn., 1972-79, actuary, 1979-82; v.p., nat. accts. CIGNA, Hartford, Conn., 1982-85; mktg. v.p. CIGNA, Springfield, Mass., 1985-86; regional v.p. CIGNA, Farmington, Conn., 1986-90; cons. actuary KPMG Peat Marwick, Hartford, Conn., 1990—. Pres., bd. dirs. Quaker Lane Coop. Nursery Sch., West Hartford, Conn., 1990-92. Fellow Casualty Actuarial Soc.; mem. Am. Acad. Actuaries, Casualty Actuaries New England. Office: KPMG Peat Marwick City Place II Hartford CT 06103

TEUTSCH, DAVID ALAN, rabbi, college administrator; b. Salt Lake City, Mar. 7, 1950; s. Eric F. and Hilda A. (Wormser) T.; m. Betsy P. Platkin, Dec. 27, 1973; children: Zachary, Nomi. BA, Harvard U., 1972; MA, Hebrew Union Coll., 1975, M Hebrew Letters, 1977; PhD, U. Pa., 1991. Ordained rabbi, 1977. Dir. program adminstrn. Ctr. for Learning and Leadership, N.Y.C., 1978-80; asst. dir. Fedn. of Reconstructionist Congregations, N.Y.C., 1980-82, exec. dir., 1982-86; dean of admissions Reconstructionist Rabbinical Coll., Wyncote, Pa., 1986-90, exec. v.p., 1990—; mem. editorial bd. Reconstructionist Mag., 1980—; mem. adv. bd. trustees Nat. Havurah Com., N.Y.C., 1979—; mem. edn. adv. bd. Hadassah, N.Y.C., 1979-84. Editor: Imagining the Jewish Future, 1992; editor-in-chief: (prayerbook series) Kil Haneshamah, Vol. I, 1989, Vol. II, 1991; contbr. articles to profl. publs. Mem. Reconstructionist Rabbinical Assn. (Prayerbook commn. 1981—), Cen. Conf. Am. Rabbis, Rabbinical Assembly, Conf. Jewish Communal Svc. Democrat. Office: Reconstructionist Rabbinical Coll Church Rd Philadelphia PA 19117-2206

TEUTSCH, JONATHAN, investment executive; b. Beer Sheba, Israel, Nov. 10, 1961; came to U.S., 1989; s. Walter and Sivia (Ruben) T. BA in Econs. and Mgmt., Tel-Aviv U., 1988; MBA, Ind. U., 1991. Asst. to the fin. mgr. Discount Investment Corp., Tel-Aviv, 1985-87; sales mgr., trader Ilanot-Discounts Mut. Fund Mgmt. Co. Ltd., Tel-Aviv, 1987-89; exec. investment assoc. Kidder, Peabody & Co. Inc., N.Y.C., 1991—. Pres. Internat. Bus. Soc., Ind. U. Sch. Bus., Bloomington, 1989-90; Ind. U. del. Can. Conf. of Bus. Schs., Toronto, Can., 1990. Capt. Israel Def. Force, 1980-84. Mem. Ind. U. Alumni Club of Metro N.Y. (bd. dirs. 1991—). Office: Kidder Peabody & Co Inc 200 Park Ave 30th Fl New York NY 10166

TEVAULT, DAVID EARL, chemist, researcher; b. Evansville, Ind., July 23, 1948; s. David Earl Tevault and Jo Ann (Jennings) Payne; m. Judy Louise Keith, May 19, 1973; children: Neil, Nancy. BA, U. Evansville, 1970; PhD, U. Va., 1974. Wehr postdoctoral fellow Marquette U., Milw., 1974-76; NRC postdoctoral fellow U.S. Naval Rsch. Lab., Washington, 1976-78, rsch. chemist, 1979-87; supervising rsch. chemist U.S. Army Chem. R&D Engring. Ctr., Aberdeen Proving Gound, Md., 1987—. Contbr. numerous articles to profl. jours. Mem. Am. Chem. Soc., Sigma Xi.

TEWI, THEA, sculptor; b. Berlin, Germany; came to U.S., 1938, naturalized, 1943; d. Jules and Claire (Kochmann) Wittner; m. Charles K. Schlachet; 1 son, Peter. Grad., Nat. Acad. Fine Arts, Berlin; student New Sch., Art Students League, N.Y.C., 1956-57. Pres. League of Present Day Artists, 1964-70; pres. Sculptors League, 1970-88. Exhibited in one-man shows at, Village Art Center, N.Y.C., 1961, La Boetie Gallery, N.Y.C., 1966, 68, 70, Sala Michelangelo, Carrara, Italy, 1969, Lehigh U., Bethlehem, Pa., 1970, U. Notre Dame, 1970, Hallway Gallery, Washington, 1976, 80, Randall Gallery, N.Y.C., 1977, 79, 81, 83, Vorpal Gallery, N.Y.C., 1985, 87, Bklyn. Bot. Garden, 1989, others; exhibited in numerous group shows; represented in permanent collections at, Smithsonian Instn., Washington, Cin. Art Mus., Norfolk (Va.) Mus. Arts and Scis., U. Notre Dame, Norton Simon Collection, Citicorp, N.Y., Fort Worth Nat. Bank, Parks Dept. City of N.Y.; also represented in pvt. collections in, U.S., France, Italy, Spain, Switzerland, Japan. Recipient numerous awards and purchase awards, including 1st prize Am. Soc. Contemporary Artists, 1971, 75, 76, 78, medal of merit Nat. Arts Club, 1974, Nawa Peabody award Nat. Acad., 1975, medal of merit Knickerbocker Artists, 1975. Mem. Nat. Assn. Women Artists (1st prize, medal of honor 1969), Am. Soc. Contemporary Artists, Sculptors League (founder, pres. 1971-88). Home: 10030 67th Dr Flushing NY 11375-3147

TEZEL, AHMET, finance educator; b. Istanbul, Turkey, Apr. 10, 1943; came to U.S., 1965; s. Sukru and Asiye Tezel; m. Tina Benig, Aug. 11, 1948; children: Philipa, Ayla, Lauren. BA, Acad. Commerce, Istanbul, 1964; MBA, U. Calif., Berkeley, 1968, PhD, 1973. Asst. prof. CCNY, N.Y.C., 1973-74; asst. prof. Kean Coll., N.J., 1974-75, Rutgers U. Camden, Camden, N.J., 1975-82; assoc. prof. Drexel U., Phila., 1982-85, St. Joseph's U., Phila., 1985—. Contbr. articles to profl. jours. Mem. Am. Fin. Assn., Ea. Fin. Assn., So. Fin. Assoc., Fin. Mgmt. Assn., Am. Acctg. Assn. Home: 15 Hanover Dr Medford NJ 08055 Office: St Joseph's U 5600 City Ave Philadelphia PA 19131-1376

THACKER, JAMES DOUGLAS, natural products chemist, manager; b. Palmerton, Pa., July 25, 1949; s. Charles Woodrow and Eleanor (Harcourt) T.; m. Cynthia Marie Schadlick, Mar. 4, 1972 (div. 1982); m. Emily Elizabeth Cameron, Mar. 7, 1984; 1 child, Cameron James. BS, N.C. State U., 1977, PhD, 1987. Pres Grainger Labs., Raleigh, N.C., 1982-85; cons. Cameron Thacker & Assocs., Raleigh, 1985-89; mgr. Wildlife Internat., Easton, Md., 1989—. Author: (with others) Plant Resistance to Insects, 1983; contbr. articles to profl. jours. Sgt. U.S. Army, 1969-75, Vietnam. Decorated Vietnam Cross of Gallantry, Bronze Star, Army Commendation medal; Allied Chem. Spl. Merit fellow, 1978, Keenan Rsch. fellow N.C. State U., 1979. Mem. AAAS, ASTM (com. biol. effects 1991—), Am. Chem. Soc., N.Y. Acad. Scis., Soc. Environ. Toxicology and Chemistry. Home: 100 Earle Ave Easton MD 21601-2811 Office: Wildlife Internat Ltd 305 Commerce Dr Easton MD 21601-9106

THACKRAY, ARNOLD WILFRID, historian, educator; b. Eng., July 30, 1939; came to U.S., 1967, naturalized, 1982; s. Wilfrid Cecil and Mary (Clarke) T.; children: Helen Mary, Gillian Winfrid, Timothy Arnold. B.Sc., Bristol (Eng.) U., 1960; M.A., Cambridge (Eng.) U., 1965, Ph.D., 1966. Research chemist Robert Dempster and Co., Yorkshire, Eng., 1960-61; research fellow Churchill Coll., Cambridge U., 1965-68; prof. history and sociology of sci. U. Pa., Phila., 1968-86, Joseph Priestley prof. history and sociology of sci., 1987—, chmn. dept., 1970-77, dir. Beckman Ctr. for History of Chemistry, 1982—; prof. history, prof. chemistry, dean grad. studies and research U. Md., 1985-86; exec. dir. dir. Chem. Heritage Found., 1987—; vis. lectr. Harvard U., 1967-68; vis. fellow All Souls Coll., Oxford, Eng., 1977-78; mem. Inst. Advanced Study, 1980. Editor: Isis, An Internat. Rev. of History of Sci. and its Cultural Influences, 1978-85, Osiris, 1985—, (with others) Science and Values, 1974, Toward A Metric of Science, 1978; author: Atoms and Powers, 1970, John Dalton, 1972, (with others) Gentlemen of Science, 1981-82, Chemistry in America, 1985; mem. editorial bd. Minerva, Victorian Studies, History of Science, The Scientist; contbr. articles to profl. jours. Recipient Gladstone Essay prize, also pub. speaking prize Churchill Coll., Cambridge U.; Guggenheim fellow, 1971-72, 85-86; Ctr. for Advanced Study in Behavioral Scis. fellow, 1973-74, 83-84. Fellow Am. Acad. Arts and Scis., Royal Hist. Soc., Royal Chem. Soc.; mem. Am. Chem. Soc. (Dexter award 1983), Am. Hist. Assn., Manchester Lit. and Philos. Soc. (corr.), History of Sci. Soc., Am. Council Learned Socs. (treas. 1985—), Soc. for Social Studies of Sci. (pres. 1981-83), Am. Council on Edn. (bd. dirs. 1987), Chemists Club (N.Y.C.), Cosmos Club (Washington). Episcopalian. Office: Univ Pa 215 S 34th St Philadelphia PA 19104-6310

THALER, RICHARD WINSTON, JR., investment banker; b. Boston, Apr. 9, 1951; s. Richard Winston and Victoria Louise (Sears) T.; m. Mary Alice

Gast, June 28, 1980; children: Julia Davis, Sarah Sears, Hannah Warren. BA in Am. Polit. History cum laude, Princeton U., 1973; MBA, Harvard U., 1978. Salesman Media Networks, N.Y.C., 1973-74; banker Bank of Boston, Rio De Janeiro, Brazil, 1975-77, Boston, 1978-80; investment banker Lehman Bros., N.Y.C., 1980—. Spl. Gifts Solicitor Princeton U. Annual Giving, N.Y.C., 1987-88, class agt. 1988—; trustee Daily Princetonian, 1989—. Mem. Princeton Alumni Schs. Com., Mass. Soc. Mayflower Descendants, Princeton Club, Siwanoy Country Club, University Cottage Club. Democrat. Episcopalian. Home: 44 Edgewood Ln Bronxville NY 10708-1943 Office: Lehman Bros Am Express Am Express Tower World Fin Ctr New York NY 10285

THALHEIM, JAY RICHARD, trade show producer; b. N.Y.C., Mar. 27, 1922; s. Sidney and Hannah (Platt) T.; m. Beth Tarshis, June 25, 1950; children: David, Amy, Neil. BS in Econs., U. Pa., 1943. Pres. Wearwell Shoe Co., N.Y.C., 1946-54; chmn. bd. Thalheim Expns., Manhasset, N.Y., 1955—. With U.S. Army, 1944-46. Mem. Nat. Premium Sales Execs., Major Am. Trade Show Organizers, Nat. Assn. Expn. Mgrs. (cert.), Friars Club, Fresh Meadow Country Club, Wharton Club L.I. Home: 264 Sparrow Dr Manhasset NY 11030-4007 Office: 42 Bayview Ave Manhasset NY 11030-1806

THALHEIMER, LOUIS B., diversified corporation executive; b. 1944. Grad., Amherst Coll., 1966; postgrad., NYU, 1969. With Cable McDaniel Bowie and Bond, 1970-80; With Am. Trading and Prodn. Corp., Balt., 1980—, previously pres., now CEO, chmn. bd. dirs. Office: Am Trading & Prodn Corp Blaustein Bldg PO Box 238 Baltimore MD 21203-0238

THALLER, KARL E., psychologist, educator; b. Manhatten, Kans., Nov. 7, 1936; s. Howard Iran and Hilda (Bryant) T.; m. Barbara Doyle, Jan. 31, 1968; children: David, John. BA, U. Conn., 1960, MA, 1962, PhD, 1967. Rsch. asst. dept. psychology U. Conn., Storrs, 1961-65; instr. U. Conn. Sch. Edn., Storrs, 1965-66; assoc. prof. dept. psychology SUNY, Potsdam, 1967-77, prof. dept. psychology, 1978-80, chmn. dept. psychology, 1976-88, prof. dept. psychology, 1988—. Editor: Sexuality and the Mentally Retarded; contbr. articles to profl. jours. Pres., chmn. Transitional Living, Watertown, N.Y. Recipient SUNY grant, 1969, 74, NSF grant, 1969-71. Mem. Am. Psychology Assn., Ea. Psychology Assn., Undergraduate Psychology Instrs. Office: SUNY Potsdam Coll Potsdam NY 13676

THARNEY, LEONARD JOHN, education educator; b. New Haven, Nov. 6, 1929; s. Lillian A. Batey; m. Denise A. Gauvin, June 20, 1981; children: Karen L., Linda L. BS, Trenton (N.J.) State Coll., 1954; MEd, Rutgers U., 1959; postgrad., Lehigh U., Bethlehem, Pa., Columbia U. Tchr. (elem. demonstration) Trenton State Coll., 1954-60; tchr. (Jr. High demonstration) Ewing Twp. (N.J.) Schs., 1960-63; cons., evaluator Am. Coun. on Edn. and Mid. States Assn., Washington, 1963—; prof. Trenton State Coll., 1963—, dept. chmn., 1988—. Co-author 7 manuals for uniform constrn. codes. Col. N.G., 1947-81. Recpient ACE Award ofOutstanding Svc. in Mil. Evaluations, 1987, Spl. Plaque award, others. Mem. ASCD, ATE, NCSS, AETS. Home: 20 Lawrenceville Penngtn Rd Lawrenceville NJ 08648

THARP, TWYLA, dancer, choreographer; b. Portland, Ind., July 1, 1941; 1 son, Jesse. Student, Pomona Coll.; grad., Barnard Coll.; D of Performing Arts (hon.), Calif. Inst. Arts, 1978, Brown U., 1981, Bard Coll., 1981; LHD, Ind. U., 1987; DFA, Pomona Coll., 1987; studies with, Richard Thomas, Merce Cunningham, Igor Schwezoff, Louis Mattox, Paul Taylor, Margaet Craske, Erick Hawkins. With Paul Taylor Dance Co., 1963-65; freelance choreographer with own modern dance troupe and various other cos. including Joffrey Ballet and Am. Ballet Theatre, 1965—; founder Twyla Tharp Dance Found., N.Y.C.; teaching residencies various colls. and univs. including U. Mass., Oberlin Coll., Walker Art Ctr., Boston U. Choreographer: Tank Dive, 1965, Re-Moves, 1966, Forevermore, 1967, Generation, 1968, Medley, 1969, Fugue, 1970, Eight Jelly Rolls, 1971, The Raggedy Dances, 1972, As Time Goes By, 1974, Sue's Leg, 1975, Push Comes to Shove, 1976, Once More Frank, 1976, Mud, 1977, Baker's Dozen, 1979, When We Were Very Young, 1980, Amadeus, 1984, White Nights, 1985, (film) Hair, 1979, (video spls.) Making Television Dance, 1977, CBS Cable Confessions of a Corner Maker, 1980, (Broadway shows) Sorrow Floats, 1985, Singin' In The Rain, 1985. Recipient Creative Arts award Brandeis U., 1972; Dance mag. award, 1981; Univ. Medal for Excellence, Columbia U., 1987. Office: Twyla Tharp Dance Found 170 W 74th St New York NY 10023 Office: Classical Artists Internat 61 Broadway Fl 18 New York NY 10006-2701*

THAYER, WILLIAM S., biochemist, educator; b. Plymouth, Ind., Sept. 23, 1948; s. William G. and Orefeise M. (Hudon) T. BS in Chemistry, Ind. U., 1970; PhD in Biochemistry, Cornell U., 1975. Nat. Cancer Inst. postdoctoral fellow U. Pa., Phila., 1975-77; asst. prof. biochemistry Sch. Medicine Hahnemann U., Phila., 1977-83, assoc. prof., 1983—. Contbr. articles to Jour. Biol. Chemistry, Biochimica Biophysica Acta, Biochem. Pharmacology, Annals N.Y. Acad. Scis., Ann. Rev. Nutrition. Grantee Nat. Inst. Child Health/Human Devel., 1981-84, Nat. Heart, Lung and Blood Inst., 1981-89, Am. Heart Assn., 1990-91; recipient Rsch. Scientist Devel. award Nat. Inst. Alcohol Abuse and Alcoholism, 1987-92. Mem. Am. Chem. Soc., Am. Soc. Biochemistry and Molecular Biology, Am. Assn. Pharm. Scientists, Oxygen Soc. Office: Hahnemann Univ Dept Biol Chemistry Philadelphia PA 19102

THEIS, BERNARD REGIS, investment company executive; b. Mckees Rocks, Pa., Aug. 3, 1957; s. John Regis and Mary D. (Hannigan) T.; m. Kathleen Marie Durinsky, Apr. 16, 1983; children: Michael (dec.), Daniel, David, Lauren. BSBA, Duquesne U., 1981. Regional rep. Federated Investors, Pitts., 1982-85; investment exec. Paine Webber, Inc., Pitts., 1985—. Mem. All Am. Team, Am. Funds Group, L.A., 1990, 91; bd. mem. Western Pa. affiliate SIDS Alliance, 1987—, vice chmn., 1991-92, chmn., 1992—; treas. Combined Health Appeal, 1992—. Mem. Dukes Ct. Orgn. (bd. dirs. 1990—). Roman Catholic. Office: Paine Webber Inc One Mellon Bank Ctr 46th Fl Pittsburgh PA 15219

THEIS, NANCY ELIZABETH, counselor, therapist; b. Springfield, Mass., July 16, 1948; d. Robert Louis and May (Bedell) Hazen; m. Philip Carl Theis, Sept. 22, 1973; children: Rachel Janette, Michelle May, Daniel Philip. BS in Bible, Lancaster Bible Coll., 1986; cert., Inst. Motivational Living, 1986; MA in Counseling, Liberty U.,, 1990. Behavioral cons. Approved Counseling Svcs., Lancaster, Pa., 1986—; counselor, therapist Hazen-Theis Counseling Svcs., Lancaster, 1989—. Mem. AACD, Assn. Religious and Value Issues in Counseling, Am. Mental Health Assn., Internat. Assn. Marriage and Family Counselors. Republican. Office: Hazen Theis Counseling Svcs 600 Eden Rd Lancaster PA 17601-4205

THEIS, PAUL ANTHONY, publishing executive; b. Ft. Wayne, Ind., Feb. 14, 1923; s. Albert Peter and Josephine Mary (Kinn) T.; m. Nancy Ann Wilbur, Aug. 21, 1971; children: Mitchell A. BA in Journalism, U. Notre Dame, Ind., 1948; BS in Fgn. Svc., Georgetown U., 1949; postgrad., Am U., 1949-52. Reporter Army Times & Fairchild Pubs., Washington, 1950-53; corres. Newsweek Mag., Washington, 1953-54; adminstrv. asst. to U.S. Congressman, Washington, 1955-57; radio-TV dir. Nat. Rep. Congl. Com., Washington, 1957-60; dir. pub. rels. Nat. Rep. Congl. Com., 1960-74; exec. editor to Pres. The White House, 1974-76; dep. undersec. Dept. Agr., Washington, 1976-77; staff cons. U.S. Ho. of Reps., Washington, 1977-81; pres. Headliner Editorial Svc., Washington, 1981—; pub. rels. officer Pres. Eisenhower's Inaugural, Washington, 1957; vice chmn. publicity Pres. Nixon's Inaugural Com., 1969. Co-author: All About Politics, 1972; co-inventor game Hat in the Ring, 1965; co-editor Who's Who in Am. Politics, 1965-75. Alt. del. Rep. Nat. Conv., Dallas, 1984, del., New Orleans, 1988; mem. D.C. Rep. Com., 1980—, exec. com. 1988—. Maj. USAF, 1943-46, ETO, USAFR Ret. Mem. Nat. Press Club, Capitol Hill Club. Republican. Roman Catholic. Home: 2903 Garfield St NW Washington DC 20008-3504 Office: Headliner Editorial Svc 2903 Garfield St NW Washington DC 20008-3504

THEIS, STEVEN THOMAS, company executive; b. Trenton, N.J., June 16, 1959; s. Thomas Donald and Pauline (Ciko) T.; m. Sharon Ann Marie DiChellis. BS, U. So. Calif., L.A., 1981; Cert. German Lang., Johann Wolfgang Goethe U., Frankfurt am Main, Germany, 1983; postgrad., Friedrich Alexander U., Erlangen, Germany, 1983-84. Cert. safety profl., EMT, N.J. With Henkels & McCoy, Inc., various locations, 1978—; constrn. coord. Henkels & McCoy, Inc., Phoenix, 1982; project mgr. Henkels & McCoy, Inc., Burlington, N.J., 1985-87; safety dir. N.J. div. Henkels & McCoy, Inc., Burlington, 1987-92; staff support coord. corp. office Henkels & McCoy, Blue Bell, Pa., 1992—; cert. safety profl., bd. certified safety profls., 1991—; safety and health instr. ARC, Woodbury, N.J., 1984—, safety and health instr. trainer, 1990—; basic instr. OSHA constrn. ind. stds. U.S. Dept. Labor, OSHA, Chgo., 1987—; chairperson safety and health com. Gloucester County ARC, Woodbury, 1991. Patentee in field. 1st lt. West Deptford Emergency Squad, Thorofare, N.J., 1987-88, capt., 1989-90, hon. mem. 1991—; vice chmn. West Deptford Twp. Bd. Health, 1989-90, v.p. West Deptford Vol. Fire and Ambulance Assn., 1989-90; emergency med. spl. coord. West Deptford Office Emergency Mtmg., 1989-90. Named Mem. of the Yr. West Deptford Emergency Squad, 1988; honorable mention Nat. Utility Contractors Assn. Mem. ASTM, Am. Soc. Safety Engrs., Am. Welding Soc., Nat. Safety Coun., World Safety Orgn., Am. Mgmt. Assn. Republican. Roman Catholic. Office: Henkels & McCoy Inc 985 Jolly Rd PO Box 950 Blue Bell PA 19422

THEISS, LOUIS LEONARD, JR., accountant; b. Hempstead, N.Y., May 21, 1925; s. Louis Leonard and Elizabeth Constance (Sheridan) T.; m. Vera McGlinchey, Dec. 27, 1947; children: Louis III, Betty, Sara, Jeanne Caroline. BS, Fordham U., 1950. CPA, N.Y. CPA, ptnr. Theiss &Theiss CPAs, Bayside, N.Y., 1948—, sr. ptnr.; chmn. Bayside (N.Y.) Fed. Savs. and Loan Assn., 1983-86, also dir. Commr. N.Y. State/Northeastern Queens Nature and Hist. Preserve Commn., Bayside, N.Y., 1983—; trustee Flushing Cemetery, 1983—; bd. dirs. Laura B. Vogler Found., Bayside, N.Y., 1962-87; pres. Queens Council Boy Scouts Am., 1985-88. Decorated Bronze Star. Mem. Am. Inst. CPAs, N.Y. State Soc. CPAs, Queens C. of C. (treas. 1989-91, pres.), Kiwanis (pres.-elect internat. found.). Office: Theiss & Theiss 214-11 Northern Blvd Bayside NY 11361

THELMAN, JOHN PATRICK, research chemist; b. Richmond Hill, N.Y., Dec. 25, 1942; s. Adolph and Helen (Forrest) T.; m. Barbara Ann Naim, Aug. 28, 1965; children: John S., James M., Jason D. BS in Chemistry, SUNY, Stony Brook, 1964; PhD in Organic Chemistry, SUNY, Buffalo, 1968. Sect. leader ITT Rayonier, Inc., Whippany, N.J., 1968-77; chief technologist Scott Paper Co., Phila., 1977—. Patentee in field. Mem. TAPPI. Republican. Roman Catholic. Home: 855 Old Horseshoe Pike Downingtown PA 19335-1364 Office: Scott Paper Co Scott Pla 3 Philadelphia PA 19113

THEODORE, EUSTACE D., alumni association executive, management consultant; b. Marietta, Ohio, Aug. 4, 1941; s. Demetrios E. and Nicoletta D. T.; m. Carol Nagy, June 13, 1964; children: Kyle James, Graham Clark. B.A., Yale U., 1963; M.A., Cornell U., 1965, Ph.D., 1967. Teaching fellow Cornell U., Ithaca, N.Y., 1965-67; faculty Hollins Coll., Roanoke, Va., 1967-71, Mt. Holyoke Coll., South Hadley, Mass., 1971-72; dean Calhoun Coll., Yale U., New Haven, 1972-81; exec. dir. Assn. Yale Alumni, 1981—; mgmt. cons., 1965—. Contbr. articles to jours. Recipient NSF-COSIP award, 1966. Mem. Am. Psychol. Assn., Am. Sociol. Assn. Office: Assn Yale Alumni Yale U 901 A Yale Sta New Haven CT 06520

THEODORE, LOUIS, chemical engineer, educator; b. N.Y.C., Apr. 19, 1934; s. George and Anna (Kourtakis) T.; m. Mary Kathleen Tonry, May 27, 1967; children: Georgeen, Molleen, Patrick. BSChemE, Cooper Union, N.Y.C., 1955; MSChemE, NYU, 1957, D in Engring. Sci., 1964. Asst. lab. instr. NYU, 1956-60; instr. Manhattan Coll., Bronx, N.Y., 1960-64, asst. prof., 1964-71, assoc. prof., 1971-78; prof. Manhattan Coll., Bronx, 5, 1978—; cons. Theodore Tutorials, East Williston, N.Y., 1990—, various industry and govt. orgns., 1973—. Author 24 books; contbr. 63 articles to profl. jours. Home: 5 Fairview Ave Williston Park NY 11596-2019

THEODORE, SAMUEL S., financial analyst; b. Bucharest, Rumania, Mar. 3, 1952; came to U.S., 1980; s. Mihai and Rodica (Edelstein) Theodoru; m. Sharon Mahni, Apr. 5, 1987; 1 child, Emily Rose. M World History, U. Bucharest, 1975; M Internat. Affairs, Columbia U., 1983. Editor Polit. Pub. Ho., Bucharest, 1975-80; credit analyst Bank Leumi Trust Co., N.Y.C., 1983-85; internat. banking officer, capital markets Marine Midland Bank, N.Y.C., 1985-87; sr. credit analyst Drexel Burnham Lambert, N.Y.C., 1987-88; asst. v.p., internat. bank analyst Moody's Investors Svc., N.Y.C., 1988—. Republican. Office: Moody's France, 22 Rue des Capucines, 75002 Paris France

THEODOROU, JERRY, insurance company executive; b. Kew Gardens, N.Y., Feb. 23, 1959; s. Chris and Maria (Manopoulou) T.; m. Alexis Niki Pateas, Oct. 12, 1991. AB, Cornell U., 1979; SM in Polit. Sci. and Pub. Policy, MIT, 1985. Rsch. scientist Tech. and Devel. Program, Cambridge, Mass., 1985-86; underwriter Chubb & Son, N.Y.C., 1986-89; underwriting mgr. Am. Internat. Group, N.Y.C., 1989—. Columnist (weekly newspaper) The Greek Am., 1986, also econs. editor; art editor BQE Mag., to 1990; contbg. editor Minerva Mag. Recipient Battalion First award Assn. U.S. Army, 1981. Mem. Assn. Polit. Risk Analysts (co-chmn. N.Y. chpt. 1987—, chmn. nat. conf. 1987-88, bd. dirs.), Hellenic Scientists Assn. Boston, Hellenic Am. Bankers Assn. (bd. dirs.), Greek Dem. Assn. N.Am., Greek Am. Behavioral Scis. Inst. (bd. dirs.), Chemists' Club. Greek Orthodox. Home: 31-62 29th St Apt 5M Astoria NY 11106

THERIAULT, NORMAND ADRIEN, metrologist; b. Lille, Maine, Sept. 9, 1938; s. Emile and Agnes (Paradis) T.; m. Roberta A. Wilson, May 21, 1960 (dec. 1974); children: Gregg, Gary, Jeff, Brian; m. Joan F. Lyons, July 29, 1976. Student, Wentworth Coll., 1960-64, Northeastern U., 1966-74. Machinist RCA, Burlington, Mass., 1958-61; technician MIT Instrument Lab., Cambridge, 1961-70, engring. asst., 1970-74; staff engr. Draper Lab., Cambridge, 1974-84, sect. head, 1984—; adv. bd. North Essex Community Coll., Haverhill, Mass., 1990—; pres. Quarter Century Club, Cambridge, 1990—. Developer laser coordinates measuring device; contbr. articles to profl. publs. Gen. chmn. United Way, Plainville, Mass., 1983, pres., 1984; pres. Plainville Lions Club, 1985; pres., sec. Plainville Planning Bd., 1988—. Mem. AIAA, Nat. Conf. Standards Labs. Roman Catholic. Office: Draper Lab 555 Technology Sq Cambridge MA 02139-3563

THERNSTROM, STEPHAN ALBERT, historian, educator; b. Port Huron, Mich., Nov. 5, 1934; s. Albert George and Bernadene (Robbins) T.; m. Abigail Mann, Jan. 3, 1959; children—Melanie Rachel, Samuel Altgeld. B.S., Northwestern U., 1956; A.M., Harvard, 1958, Ph.D., 1962. Instr. history Harvard U., Cambridge, Mass., 1962-66, asst. prof., 1966-67, prof., 1973-81, Winthrop prof., 1981—, chmn. com. on higher degrees in history of Am. civilization, 1985—; prof. Brandeis U., 1967-69, UCLA, 1969-73; Pitt. prof. Am. history and instns. Cambridge U., 1978-79; dir. Charles Warren Ctr. for Research in Am. History, 1980-83. Author: Poverty and Progress, 1964, Poverty, Planning and Politics in the New Boston, 1969, The Other Bostonians, 1973, History of the American People, 1983; editor: Harvard Ency. Am. Ethnic Groups; co-editor: Harvard Studies in Urban History; Cambridge Interdisciplinary Perspectives on Modern History Series. Recipient Bancroft prize, R. R. Hawkins award, Faculty prize Harvard U. Press, Waldo G. Leland prize; Guggenheim fellow; Am. Council Learned Socs. fellow. Office: Harvard U Robinson Hall Cambridge MA 02138

THEROUX, DENNIS ROBERT, engineering executive; b. New Haven, Conn., Aug. 17, 1951; s. Theogene Charles and Theresa Cecile (La Croix) T. BA, U. Conn., 1973; MS, U. Hawaii, Mamoa, 1975; cert. in occupational, safety, health, U. New Haven, 1986-88; postgrad., Columbia Pacific U. Cert. indsl. hygienist, safety profl. Pres. Hamden (Conn.) Pest Control Co., 1975-85; pres. and chief exec. officer Theroux Engring., Hamden, 1985—. Author (with others): Radon-The Invisible Threat, 1986. Sponsor St. Francis Home for Children, New Haven, 1986—; co-founder Profl. Coun. for Edn., Hadlyme, Conn., 1990. Mem. Am. Soc. Safety Engrs., Am. Industrial Hygiene Assn., Am. Mgmt. Assn. (pres. assoc. 1990—), Conn. Environ. Health Assn., Conn. Pest Control Assn. Roman Catholic. Home: 1 Ml Rd # 100 Hadlyme CT 06439-9999 Office: Theroux Engring PO Box 4096 Hamden CT 06514-0146

THERRIEN, WALLY C., protective services official, accountant; b. New Bedford, Mass., June 9, 1950; s. Leonard Francis and Irene (St. Pierre) T.; m. Linda Louise Elias, May 28, 1951; children: Crystal Dawn, Tiffany Michelle, Jeremy Scott, Timothy Michael. AS, Bristol Community Coll., Fall River, Mass., 1970; BS Fire Svc. Adminstrn., Empire State Coll., Saratoga Springs, N.Y., 1989; BS Acctg., Southeastern Mass. U., North Dartmouth, 1984; MBA, Southeastern Mass. U., 1988. Store mgr. Elliotts Home Furnishings, Wareham, Mass., 1974-75; gen. mgr. EMT-MAST Alert Ambulance Svc., Fairhaven, Mass., 1975-88; fire lt. Fairhaven Fire Dept., 1981—; pvt. practice acct. and tax practioner; pvt. practice acct. and tax practitioner; EMT-Ambulance instr. coord., Mass., examiner; instr. CPR Am. Heart Assn.; mem. adv. bd. Fire Sci. div. Bristol Community Coll. Recipient commendation, Fairhaven Fire Dept., 1985, 87. Mem. Profl. Firefighters Mass. Internat. Assn. Firefighters, Mass. Assn. EMT's, Assn. MBA Execs., Nat. Assn. EMT's, Nat. Corvette Owners Assn., Nat. Corvette Restorers Soc., Masons. Democrat. Home: 457 Washington St Fairhaven MA 02719-5125

THEXTON, PETER MASON, actuary; b. Ill., 1928; s. Arthur Louis and Mildred Aileen Thexton; married, 1949 (div. 1968); children: Arthur, Elspeth, Matthew, Bridget; m. Barbara Ahlers, Nov. 26, 1975. Student, Williams Coll., 1945-49. Actuarial student The Travelers Ins. Co., Hartford, Conn., 1950-51, Union Cen. Life Ins. Co., Cin., 1951-57; asst. group actuary Nationwide Ins., Columbus, Ohio, 1957-61; assoc. group actuary Mutual Benefit Life Ins. Co., Newark, N.J., 1961-75; actuary Health Ins. Assn., Washington, 1975-90; cons. actuary Walker & Assocs., Midvale, Utah, 1990-92; mng. actuary N.J. Ins. Dept., Trenton, 1992—. Active Dem. Party, 1954-64. Fellow Soc. Actuaries (coun. mem., treas. health sect. Chgo. 1981-84); mem. Am. Acad. Actuaries. Unitarian. Office: NJ Ins Dept CN 325 Trenton NJ 08625-0325

THIBADEAU, EUGENE FRANCIS, educator, consultant; b. N.Y.C., May 18, 1933; s. Eugene Servanis and Lillian (Archer) T.; m. Renee M. Pollock, Jan. 6, 1988; 1 child, Christine. BA, NYU, 1959, MA, 1967; MA, NYU, 1968, PhD, 1973. Instr. NYU, N.Y.C., 1968; lectr. in philosophy Dowling Coll., Oakdale, N.Y., 1968-70; prof. edn. Indiana U. of Pa., Indiana, Pa., 1970—; vis. assoc. prof. Adelphi U., Garden City, N.Y., 1974-75; vis. scholar NYU, N.Y.C., 1984-85; vis. prof. Hofstra U., Hempstead, N.Y., 1974, 75, 84, 86; cons. Central Bur. of Ednl. Visits, London, 1980-81, Commonwealth Speakers Bur., Harrisburg, Pa., 1983-85, U.S. Dept. Edn., Washington, 1983-85, Pa. Dept. Edn., Harrisburg, 1988—. Author: Opening Up Education-In Theory and Practice, 1976, Curriculum Theory, 1988, Existentialism in the Classroom, 1992; rev. editor Focus on Learning, 1973-77, editor, 1977-84; contbr. numerous articles and revs. to profl. jours. Active in United Way, Indiana, Pa., 1980—, NAACP, Indiana, 1985—, Red Cross, Indiana, 1985—. Fulbright sr. lectr. Thames Polytechnic, London, 1978-79, Janus Pannonius U., Peces, Hungary, 1990-91; foreign expert Shanghai (China) Tchrs. U., 1988; designated faculty rsch. assoc. Inst. for Applied Rsch. and Pub. Policy, Indiana U. of Pa., 1989; named Commonwealth Teaching fellow, Pa. State Colls. and Univ. Disting. Faculty Awards Com., 1976; recipient Founder's Day award, NYU, 1973. Fellow Am. Philosophy Edn. Soc.; mem. Am. Ednl. Studies Assn., AAUP, The S.W. Philosophy Edn. Soc., ASCD. Home: RR 1 Box 103 Penn Run PA 15765-9733 Office: Indiana Univ of Pa 133 Stouffer Hall Indiana PA 15701

THIBEAULT, GEORGE WALTER, lawyer; b. Cambridge, Mass., Sept. 21, 1941; s. George Walter and Josephine (Maraggia) T.; m. Antoinette Miller, June 30, 1963; children—Robin M., Holly Ann. B.S., Northeastern U., 1964; M.B.A., Boston Coll., 1966, J.D., 1969. Bar: Mass. 1969. Assoc. Gaston & Snow, Boston, 1969-73; ptnr. Testa, Hurwitz & Thibeault, Boston, 1973—. Mem. ABA, Mass. Bar Assn., Am. Arbitration Assn. Home: 181 Caterina Hts Concord MA 01742-4750 Office: Testa Hurwitz & Thibeault 53 State St Boston MA 02109-2809

THIBEAULT, JACK CLAUDE, research chemist; b. Lowell, Mass., June 23, 1946; s. Claude B. and Marjorie (Thompson) T.; m. Colette Lajoie, June 11, 1966 (div. 1988); 1 child, Patrick. BS, Lowell Technol. Inst., 1967; PhD, Calif. Inst. Tech., 1972. Postdoctoral fellow Cornell U., Ithaca, N.Y., 1972-74; sr. scientist Rohm and Haas Co., Spring House, Pa., 1974—. Contbr. articles to profl. jours. Mem. Am. Chem. Soc. Office: Rohm and Haas Co 727 Norristown Rd Spring House PA 19477

THIEL, JOHN E., religious studies educator; b. St. Albans, N.Y., July 28, 1951; s. Arthur Edwin and Louise Anita (Alagia) T.; m. Dorothea Cook; children: David, Benjamin. AB, Fairfield U., 1973; MA, McMaster U., Can., 1974, PhD, 1978. Prof. religious studies Fairfield (Conn.) U., 1977—. Author: Imagination and Authority: Theological Authorship in the Modern Tradition, 1991. Mem. AAUP, Am. Acad. Religion, Cath. Theol. Soc. Am. Home: 375 Westfield Ave Bridgeport CT 06606-4133 Office: Fairfield U N Benson Rd Fairfield CT 06430-5152

THIELE, ROBERT EDWARD, JR., water utility executive, civil engineer; b. N.Y.C., Dec. 7, 1948; s. Robert Edward and Norah Theresa (King) T.; m. Jacquelyn Ann Canonica, Nov. 14, 1970; children: Robert P., Cherilyn M., Kevin M. BSCE, Newark Coll. Engring., 1970. Registered profl. engr., N.J., N.Y. Engr. N.Y. Pub. Svc. Commn., N.Y.C., 1970-77; dir. ops. Spring Valley Water Co., West Nyack, N.Y., 1986-90; civil engr. Hackensack Water Co., Weehawken, N.J., 1977-78, supr. rate dept., 1978-79; mgr. rate devel. Hackensack Water Co., Harrington Park, N.J., 1979-83, dir. rate devel., 1984-86, project engr., 1990, dir. bus. devel., 1991—; expert witness various utility rate caes; speaker rate seminar Nat. Assn. Regulatory Utility Commrs., 1984. Treas. pack 139, Boy Scouts Am., Bergenfield, N.J., treas. troop 139, mem. exec. bd. Rockland County coun. Mem. Nat. Assn. Water Cos. (sec.-treas. N.J. chpt. 1985-86, vice chmn. 1986-87, chmn. 1987-88, speaker 1983), Am. Water Works Assn., Rotary (sec. Northern Valley 1984-86, pres. 1986-87). Republican. Roman Catholic. Home: 77 Clinton Park Dr Bergenfield NJ 07621-2452 Office: Hackensack Water Co 200 Old Hook Rd Harrington Park NJ 07640-1799

THIER, SAMUEL OSIAH, physician, educator; b. Bklyn., June 23, 1937; s. Sidney and May Henrietta (Kanner) T.; m. Paula Dell Finkelstein, June 28, 1958; children: Audrey Lauren, Stephanie Ellen, Sara Leslie. Student, Cornell U., 1953-56; MD, SUNY, Syracuse, 1960, DSc (hon.), 1987; DSc (hon.), Tufts U., 1988, George Washington U., 1988; LHD (hon.), Rush U., 1988. Diplomate: Am. Bd. Internal Medicine (dir. 1977-85, exec. com. 1981-85, chmn. 1984-85). Intern Mass. Gen. Hosp., Boston, 1960-61; asst. resident Mass. Gen. Hosp., 1961-62, sr. resident, 1964-65, clin. and research fellow, 1965, chief resident, 1966; clin. asso. Nat. Inst. Arthritis and Metabolic Diseases, 1962-64; from instr. to asst. prof. medicine Harvard U. Med. Sch., 1967-69; asst. in medicine, chief renal unit Mass. Gen. Hosp., Boston, 1967-69; asso. prof., then prof. medicine U. Pa. Med. Sch., 1969-72, vice chmn. dept., 1971-74; assoc. dir. med. svcs. Hosp. U. Pa., 1969-71; David Paige Smith prof. medicine Yale U. Sch. Medicine, 1978-81, Sterling prof. medicine, 1981-85, chmn. dept., 1975-85; pres. Inst. Medicine NAS, Washington, 1985-91, Brandeis U., Waltham, Mass., 1991—; chief medicine Yale-New Haven Hosp., 1975-85, trustee, 1978-85; bd. dirs. Conn. Hospice, Inc., 1976-82. Mem. editorial bd.: New Eng. Jour. Medicine, 1978-81; Contbr. articles to med. jours. Mem. adv. com. to the dir. NIH, 1980-85. Served with USPHS, 1962-64. Recipient Christian R. and Mary F. Lindback Found. Distinguished Teaching award, 1971. Fellow ACP (bd. regents 1982-85); mem. Assn. Am. Med. Colls. (adminstrv. bd. council acad. socs.), John Morgan Soc., Am. Fedn. Clin. Research (pres. 1976-77), Am. Soc. Nephrology, Am. Physiol. Soc., Inst. Medicine, Nat. Acad. Scis., Internat. Soc. Nephrology, Assn. Profs. Medicine, Assn. Am. Physicians, Interurban Clin. Club; Alpha Omega Alpha. Home: 1395 Commonwealth Ave West Newton MA 02165 Office: Brandeis U Office of Pres PO Box 9110 415 South St Waltham MA 02254-9110

THIERFELDER, WILLIAM RICHARD, III, humanities educator; b. Flushing, N.Y.; s. William Richard II and Wilma Hermine (Sondermann) T. BA cum laude, St. John's U., Jamaica, N.Y., 1973; MA cum laude, St. John's U., 1975, PhD summa cum laude, 1979; MA cum laude in Theology, Sem. Immaculate Conception, Huntington, N.Y., 1988. Adj. prof. English lit. and humanities St. John's U., 1979-87; adj. prof. NYU, 1980-89; asst. prof. Dowling Coll., Oakdale, N.Y., 1985—; lectr. on opera and musical theater, 1980—; composer in residence St. John's U., 1972-76. Contbr.

articles, poems to various jours. Mem. Alpha Psi Omega, Pi Delta Epsilon, Sigma Tau Delta. Roman Catholic.

THIERWECHTER, LESTER VALENTINE, JR., computer programmer; b. Rockville Centre, N.Y., Dec. 12, 1953; s. Lester Valentine and Dolores (Kosman) T.; m. Barbara Marie McMahon, May 19, 1984; 1 child, Elizabeth Ann. BA, Montclair State Coll., Upper Montclair, N.J., 1976. Programmer EBASCO Svcs., Inc., N.Y.C., 1976-78; from tech. programmer to lead software specialist Nat. Starch and Chem. Co., Bridgewater, N.J., 1978-87; mgr. system programming Baker & Taylor Books, Bridgewater, 1987—. Contbg. author: COBOL Programming, 1976. Mem. N.Y. Met. Local Users Burroughs Equipment (pres. 1985). Home: 208 Hockenbury Rd Neshanic Station NJ 08853-3228 Office: Baker & Taylor Books 652 E Main St Bridgewater NJ 08807-3384

THIMM, ALFRED LOUIS, management educator; b. Vienna, Austria, Dec. 10, 1923; came to U.S., 1939, naturalized, 1943; s. Hartwig H. and Olga F. (Felsner) T.; m. Patricia Mullen, Dec. 18, 1954; children: Alfred Louis, Peter H. B.A., NYU, 1948, M.A., 1949, Ph.D., 1959. Asst. prof. econs. St. Lawrence U., Canton, N.Y., 1953-55; research fellow NYU, 1955-56; assoc. prof. Clarkson Coll., Potsdam, N.Y., 1956-59; mem. faculty Union Coll., Schenectady, 1960-81, prof. econs. and indsl. adminstrn., 1968-81, dir. Inst. Adminstrn. and Mgmt., 1968-80, dir. Ph.D. program in adminstrn. and engring. systems, 1980-81; dean, dir. Sch. Bus. U. Vt., Burlington, 1981-85, prof. mgmt., 1981—; mgmt. cons., 1973-81; cons. in field; vis. prof. Wirtschafts U., Vienna, 1980, 85-86, 89, 92, Inst. Entscheidungs und Organisationsforschung, U. Munich, 1972, 74-75, 90. Author: Economists and Society: From Aquinas to Keynes, 1973, 81, Entscheidungstheorie, 1977, The False Promise of Codetermination, 1980, America's Stake in European Telecommuncation Policies, 1992; contbr. articles to profl. jours., monographs. Grantee NSF, 1951, 61; grantee Ford Found., summers 1960, 62; Fulbright research scholar Austria, 1967-68. Mem. Am. Econs. Assn., Am. Statis. Assn., Inst. Mgmt. Sci. Office: U Vt Sch Bus Burlington VT 05401

THOMAN, JAMES M., data processing consultant; b. Charleston, S.C., Sept. 16, 1955; s. James Harold Gillette and JoAnn (Collins) Thoman; m. Nicollette Smith, May 21, 1979 (div. Jan. 1989); children: Catina Ley, Galadriel Therese. AS in Data Processing/Computer Sci., Seminole Community Coll., Sanford, Fla., 1980. Programmer analyst Applied Computer Cons., Haddonfield, N.J., 1982-83, Brokers Mortgage Svc., Collingswood, N.J., 1983-86, Travelers Mortgage Svc., Cherry Hill, N.J., 1986-87; network adminstr. Legion Ins. Co., Phila., 1988-89; ind. cons. Marlton, N.J., 1989—. Co-founder Svcs. for the Missing, Woodbury, N.J., 1983—. With USAF, 1973-77. Home: 236 Fieldstone Ln Marlton NJ 08053-4111

THOMAN, JOSEPH KAROL, JR., educational administrator; b. Buffalo, Dec. 7, 1947; s. Joseph Karol and Edna Marie (Russ) T.; m. Nancy S., Aug. 16, 1969; children: Jennifer K., Jessica K., J. Kristopher. BS in Edn., St. U. Coll., Geneseo, N.Y., 1969; MS in Sec. Edn., St. U. Coll., Buffalo, 1973, cert. of advanced study, 1980. Cert. sec. math. tchr., sch. dist. adminstr., supr. Secondary math. tchr. Kenmore (N.Y.) Pub. Schs., 1969-70, Akron (N.Y.) Cen. Sch. Dist., 1970-79; sch. bus. intern Iroquois Cen. Sch. Dist., Elma, N.Y., 1979-80; sch. bus. adminstr. Penn Yan (N.Y.) Sch. Dist., 1980-84; asst. supt. bus. and pers. Niagara-Wheatfield Cen. Schs., Sanborn, N.Y., 1984—; adj. prof. L.I. U., 1990-91. Bd. trustees Penn Yan Presbyn. Ch., 1982-83. With USAR, 1971-80. Regents scholar N.Y. State Bd. Regents, 1965. Mem. Assn. Sch. Bus. Ofcls. Internat., N.Y. State Assn. Sch. Bus. Ofcls. (constn., appraisal and resolutions coms. 1984-89, bd. dirs. 1992—), Western N.Y. Assn. Sch. Bus. Ofcls. (v.p. 1989-90, pres. 1990-91), Buffalo Schola Cantorum, Kiwanis, Lions, Rotary, Niagara Cen. Club. Republican. Home: 3048 Krueger Rd North Tonawanda NY 14120-1445 Office: Niagara Wheatfield Cen Sch 2794 Saunders Settlement Rd Sanborn NY 14132-0309

THOMANN, J. DONALD, management training; b. N.Y.C., July 12, 1931; s. Charles James and Anne Colistus (Conway) T.; m. Ann M. Herron, July 13, 1956; children: Donald, Mark. BA, Kings Coll., 1953; BS in Fgn. Svc., Georgetown U., 1957. Internat. dept. liaison officer Chase Manhattan Bank, N.Y.C., 1957-60; mktg. mgr. Schering-Plough, Union, N.J., 1960-65; mil. sales mgr. Overseas Svc. Corp., N.Y.C., 1965-68; Ea. regional mktg. mgr. Marshall & Stevens, N.Y.C., 1968-72; mktg. officer AMA Planning Ctr., Hamilton, N.Y., 1972-78; dir. internat. bus. devel. AMA Internat. Div., N.Y.C., 1978-81; pres. Mktg. Svcs. Internat., Scotch Plains, N.J., 1981—; officer Planning Forum, Toronto, Can., 1982-83. Mem. Univ. Club of Toronto, Georgetown Univ. Club. Home: 206 Mountainview Ave Scotch Plains NJ 07076-1418 Office: Mktg Svcs Internat PO Box 273 Scotch Plains NJ 07076-0273

THOMAS, ALLEN LLOYD, lawyer; b. Orange, N.J., Sept. 15, 1939; s. Richard Lloyd and Dorothy (Carr) T.; m. Virginia Dehnert, June 24, 1961 (div. 1974); children: Sarah Ann, Anne Marjorie; m. Barbara Singer, Mar. 12, 1978; 1 child, Allen Lloyd Jr. BA, Wesleyan U., 1961; LLB, Yale U., 1964. Bar: N.Y. 1965, U.S. Ct. Appeals (D.C. cir.) 1981. Ptnr. Paul Weiss Rifkind Wharton & Garrison, N.Y.C., 1964—; resident ptnr. Hong Kong, 1983-87; bd. dirs. Mitsubishi Bank Trust Co. N.Y., N.Y.C., 1987—. Chmn. Urban Bus. Assis. Corp., N.Y.C., 1971-82; chmn. Hong Kong Ballet, 1985-87; co-chmn. Internat. Com., N.Y.C. Ballet, 1986-91; pres. Internat. Salzburg Assn. Am., 1987—; dir., mem. exec. com., gen. counsel Child Care Action Campaign. Fellow Am. Coll. Investment Counsel, Hartford, Conn. Mem. River Club, N.Y. Met. Club of Washington, Hong Kong Club, Royal Hong Kong Jockey Club, Coral Beach and Tennis Club, Lenox Club. Office: Paul Weiss Rifkind Wharton & Garrison 1285 Ave Of The Americas New York NY 10019-6028

THOMAS, ANDREW HOUSTON, computer company executive, consultant, educator; b. Colorado Springs, Colo., Dec. 31, 1935; s. Edward Gaskin and Margaret (Morris) T.; m. Nathalie Wendell, June 19, 1959; children: Emily Thomas Bates, Adrienne Thomas Conklin. AB, Dartmouth Coll., 1958; MBA, Babson Coll., 1973. Tech. sales rep. Atlas Chem. Industries, Wilmington, Del., 1959-62; contract adminstr. Ensign-Bickford, Simsbury, Conn., 1962-66; supr. fin. control Hamilton Standard, Windsor, Conn., 1966-69; dir. sales Honeywell Info. Systems, Newton, Mass., 1969-80; v.p. svc. Timeplex, Inc., Woodcliff Lake, N.J., 1980-81; prin. cons. Input Ltd., London, 1981-84; dir. mktg. Burroughs Corp., Detroit, 1984-85, Nynex, Burlington, Mass., 1985-88; mgr. cons. Digital Equipment Corp., Acton, Mass., 1988—; adj. prof. Nichols Coll., Dudley, Mass., 1987-89. Author: Manager's Guide to Systems, 1987 (Patton award 1988); contbr. articles to profl. publs. Pres. Simsbury (Conn.) Jaycees, 1965. 1st lt. U.S. Army, 1958-59. Mem. Assn. Field Svc. Mgrs. Internat. (pres. Boston chpt. 1986, nat. bd. dirs. 1987-89), Inst. Mgmt. Consultants, Dartmouth Coll. Alumni Assn. Ea. Mass. (pres. 1979), Wellesley Country Club (Mass.). Republican. Episcopalian. Home: 24 Marshall Rd Natick MA 01760-2945 Office: Digital Equipment Corp 2 Results Way Marlboro MA 01752

THOMAS, ANN EMERY, small business owner; b. Kingston, Pa., Aug. 5, 1924; d. John Francis and Miriam Olivia (Phillips) E.; m. William Samuel Thomas, Jan. 28, 1948; children: Miriam Addoms, Marcia. BS, Pa. State U., 1947. Tchr. Williamsport (Pa.) Jr. High Sch., 1947; libr. asst. Wilmington (Del.) Inst. Free Libr., 1968-72; pres. bd. dirs. Wilmington (Del). Inst. Free Libr., 1969-70; co-owner Hickory Swale Crafts and Antiques, Mountaintop, Pa., 1974—; owner Hickory Swale Creations by Ann, Mountaintop, 1987—. Patentee original designs. Active Brandywine Hundred Rep. Com., Wilmington, 1961-65, women's com. Wilmington Symphony, 1962-64; past-sec. Questers, chpt. 851, Wilkes-Barre, Pa., 1984-86; sec. Nuangola (Pa.) Libr. Bd., 1989—. Music scholar Washington U., 1943, Senatorial scholar Pa. Senate, 1943. Mem. Sr. Craftsmen Wyoming Valley (dir. 1983-89, bd. dirs., 1984—), Pa. Guild Craftsmen. Episcopalian. Home: 253 Heslop Rd Wilkes Barre PA 18707-9532

THOMAS, BARBARA YVONNE, counselor; b. Easton, Md., June 19, 1953; d. Leon W. and Eunice (Friend) T. BA, U. Del., Newark, 1975, MEd, 1989. Econ. developer Wilmington (Del.) Housing Authority, 1976; counselor Elwyn (Pa.) Inst., 1976-78; tchr./counselor Crockett Acad., Nashville, 1978-79; resident counselor Ind. Living, Inc., Wilmington, 1979-80, site supr., 1980-82, project dir., 1982-83, program mgr., 1983-84, program dir., 1984-85; counselor U. Del., Newark, 1986-91; dir. Upward Bound Del. Tech. and Community Coll., Wilmington, 1991—. Recipient Appreciation award Howard Career Ctr., 1987, Del. State Trio, 1991; named one of Outstanding Young Women of Am., 1987. Mem. Del. Coll. Personnel Assn., Nat. Assn. of Developmental Edn., Nat. Coun. of Equal Opportunity Assns., Assn. for Multicultural Counseling & Devel., Am. Assn. for Counseling and Devel., Mid-Eastern Assn. Equal Opportunity Program Personnel, Del. state Trio (treas. 1987-89, 91-92). Home: 107 N Connell St Wilmington DE 19805-3632 Office: U Del Counselor Newark DE 19711

THOMAS, BRIAN, college administrator; b. Bklyn., Nov. 8, 1955; s. Charles Robert and Winifred Arlene (Taylor) T.; m. Margaret Johanna Rogers, Dec. 10, 1988. BA in Philosophy, Cathedral Coll., 1977. Cert. fund raising exec. Guidance counselor Good Counsel Acad., White Plains, N.Y., 1977-78; sr. ops. mgr. Macy's N.Y., N.Y.C., 1978-81; staff mem. Parish Mission Team, Tappan, N.Y., 1981-83; exec. dir. Community Counseling Svc., N.Y.C., 1983-90; U.S. dir. devel. St. Patrick's Coll, Maynooth, N.Y.C., 1990—. Mem. Nat. Soc. Fund Raising Execs., Nat. Cath. Devel. Conf., Planned Giving Group Greater N.Y. Roman Catholic. Home: 1495 E 63d St Brooklyn NY 11234 Office: St Patricks Coll 315 E 47th St New York NY 10017-2301

THOMAS, CLARENCE, U.S. Supreme Court justice; b. Savannah, Ga., June 23, 1948. BA, Holy Cross Coll., 1971; JD, Yale U., 1974. Bar: Mo. Asst. atty. gen. State of Mo., Jefferson City, 1974-77; atty. Monsanto Co., St. Louis, 1977-79; legis. asst. to Sen. John C. Danforth, Washington, 1979-81; asst. sec. for civil rights Dept. Edn., Washington, 1981-82; chmn. U.S. EEOC, Washington, 1982-90; judge U.S. Ct. Appeals, Washington, 1990-91; assoc. justice U.S. Supreme Ct., Washington, 1991—. Office: US Supreme Court 1 First St NE Washington DC 20543*

THOMAS, DALE JOHN, telecommunications industry executive; b. Lansing, Mich., June 26, 1940; s. William Gentry and Ruth Agnes (Mattson) T.; m. Barbara Lee Andrews, July 6, 1963; children: Jennifer Lee, Christopher John. BA, Mich. State U., 1962, MBA, 1965. Traffic supr. N.Y. Telephone, N.Y.C., 1962-64; product planner Pitney Bowes, Inc., Stamford, Conn., 1965-70, asst. to chmn., 1970-71, project dir., 1971-78, dir. prodn. line mgmt., 1978-81, v.p., 1981-85; v.p. mktg. Nynex Internat. Co., White Plains, N.Y., 1985-89; v.p. acquisitions and devel. NYNEX Properties Co., N.Y.C., 1989-91, pres., 1991—; dir. PB, Japan, Tokyo, 1978-80, NY Focom Corp., Taipei, Taiwan, 1988-90; instr. Sacred Heart U., Fairfield, Conn., 1981-85. Editor, author: Marketing News, 1965-68; mem. editorial rev. bd. Jour. Indsl. Mktg. Mgmt., 1983—. Pres. Jaycees, Fairfield, 1967, Luth. Housing Corp., Bridgeport, Conn., 1975-85. With U.S. Army, 1966-68. Recipient Outstanding Svc. award Am. Mktg. Assn., 1969, 70. Mem. The Patterson Club. Republican. Lutheran. Home: 330 Winton Rd Fairfield CT 06430-3860 Office: Nynex Properties Co 21 Penn New York NY 10001-2003

THOMAS, DAVID ROBERT, lawyer; b. New Haven, Jan. 6, 1954; m. Sheila Deidre Norton, Oct. 18, 1975; children: Michael Patrick, Shawn Christopher. BA, U. New Haven, 1977; JD, George Mason U., 1980. Bar: Conn. 1981, U.S. Dist. Ct. Conn. 1981. Assoc. Groob & Ressler, P.C., New Haven, 1981, Tobin & Levine, New Haven, 1981-83; pvt. practice Wallingford, Conn., 1983-85, 92—; gen. counsel CMC Devel. Co., Inc., 1984-87; pres. Multitech New Eng., Inc., Wallingford, 1987-89; ptnr. Thomas & Flynn, Wallingford, 1990-92; pvt. practice Wallingford, 1992—; founder Housing Am., Inc., Home Am., Wallingford, 1990. Chmn. Community Nursery Sch., Guilford, Conn., 1989-90; coach Guilford Little League. Mem. ABA (devel. and fin. of condominium projects com. real property div. 1989), Conn. Bar Assn. (subcom. on residential practice 1988), Duck Island Yacht Club, Delta Theta Phi. Republican. Home: 146 Foxwood Rd S Guilford CT 06437-2238 Office: 130 N Main St Wallingford CT 06492-3732

THOMAS, DAVID TREVILLYAN, international business consultant; b. London, Mar. 28, 1921; came to U.S., 1949, naturalized citizen, 1964; s. Henry Trevillyan and Enriqueta (Brooking) T.; m. Ann Jean Davis, Aug. 9, 1952; children: Mark, Charlotte, Miranda, Tobias. Student, Marlborough Coll., 1932-38; Certificat d'Etudes, Grenoble (France) U., 1939; student, Cambridge (Eng.) U., 1939; MBA, Harvard U., 1954. Exec. Shell Petroleum Co. Ltd., San Francisco, Shanghai, London, 1945-49; v.p., dir. McCann Erickson Internat., N.Y.C., 1954-67; v.p. mktg. PepsiCo Internat., N.Y.C., 1967-70; gen. mgr. Far East STP Corp., Des Plaines, Ill., 1970-72; mgr. devel. of bus. Austiran Ltd., Sydney, Australia, 1972-79; mng. dir. Sibis Cons. Internat., Somerville, Mass., 1972—; fgn. investment advisor Gov.'s Internat. Trade Adv. Bd., Boston, 1992. Fundraiser Anti-Crime Communication, Somerville, 1990—. Lt. Royal Navy, 1940-46, ETO, MTO, PTO. Mem. Union Club Sydney (overseas mem.). Mem. Ch. of England. Home: Parterre Sq House 28 Maple Ave Somerville MA 02145 Office: Sibis Cons Internat 28 Maple Ave Somerville MA 02145-3805

THOMAS, DONALD JAMES, foreign language educator; b. Utica, N.Y., May 3, 1944; s. Lyle James and Lillian Mary (Trask) T. BA, Syracuse U., Utica, 1965; MA, Colgate U., 1969. Cert. secondary edn. french and spanish tchr., N.Y. Fgn. lang. tchr. Notre Dame High Sch., Utica, 1966-68, Oneida (N.Y.) Jr. High Sch., 1968-69, Herkimer (N.Y.) High Sch., 1969—. Author numerous newspaper editorials, poem. Mem. State Com, N.Y. State Right to Life, 25th Congl. Dist., 1985—, chmn. Oneida County, 1979—, candidate, 1982, 90; media coord. Louis Wein for Gov., Utica, 1990. Grantee N.Y. State Edn. Dept., Albany, 1975. Mem. Nocturnal Adoration Soc. Utica (pres. 1989-90). Roman Catholic. Home: 2704 Church Rd Sauquoit NY 13456 Office: Herkimer High Sch 801 W German St Herkimer NY 13350-2199

THOMAS, DUDLEY JEROME, logistics engineer, former naval officer; b. Allentown, Pa., Jan. 1, 1940; s. Harold Henry and Ruth (Wirtz) T.; m. Mary Louise Kaiser, Feb. 11, 1967; children: Karen Marie, Eric Matthew, Patrick Michael. BS, Pa. State U., 1961; MBA, Harvard U., 1969. Commd. ensign USN, 1961, advanced through grades to comdr., 1977; exec. officer Naval Publs. and Forms Ctr., Phila., 1980-82; ret., 1982; sr. systems analyst Advanced Tech., Inc., Reston, Va., 1982-85; logistics support coord. V-22 program Boeing Helicopters, Phila., 1985—; cons. ARA Svcs., Phila., 1982. Mem. Soc. Logistics Engrs. Roman Catholic. Home: 1507 Chalet Dr Cherry Hill NJ 08003 Office: Boeing Helicopters P24-34 Box 16858 Philadelphia PA 19142

THOMAS, FRANK JOSEPH, physician; b. Troy, N.Y., June 23, 1950; s. Frank Joseph Sr. and Marie (Graber) T.; m. Nancy E. O'Keeffe, Dec. 29, 1974. BS, Fordham U., 1972; MD, NYU, 1976. Diplomate Am. Bd. Radiology, Am. Bd. Radiation and Oncology. Intern Cin. Children's Hosp., 1976-77; resident U. Wis., Madison, 1977-80; fellow Cleve. Clinic, 1980, staff physician, 1981-83, chmn. radiation oncology, 1984-88; asst. prof. radiation oncology Case Western Res. U., Cleve., 1988-90; assoc. prof. Albany (N.Y.) Med. Coll., 1990—; med. dir. Ellis Hosp., Schenectady. N.Y., 1990—. Contbr. various articleto profl. jours. Mem. AMA, Am. Soc. Therapeutic Radiology and Oncology, Am. Coll. Radiology (com. on radiation theraphy tech.), Phi Beta Kappa. Office: Albany Med Coll 47 New Scotland Ave Albany NY 12208-3412

THOMAS, GARY L., academic administrator; b. Willows, Calif., May 12, 1937; s. Leonel Richard and Myrtle Blonch (Moncur) T.; m. Margaret Anderson, Aug. 11, 1960 (div. 1975); children: Katelin, Elizabeth Ann, Derek Alan. AA, Modesto Jr. Coll., 1958; BS in Elec. Engring., U. Calif., Berkeley, 1960, MA in Physics, 1962, PhD in Elec. and Computer Engring., 1967. Acting asst. prof. U. Calif., Berkeley, 1967; asst. prof. elec. engring. SUNY, Stony Brook, 1967-70, assoc. prof. elec. engring., 1970-73, assoc. dean grad. sch., 1973-74, chairperson, prof. elec. engring., 1975-79; congl. fellow A.A.A.S., Washington, 1974-75; provost, vp.p acad. affairs N.J. Inst. Tech., Newark, 1980—; student asst. bd. Dept. Higher Edn., N.J., 1980—; chairperson rsch. adv. bd. PSE & G, Newark, 1986-90, Regional Transp. Rsch. Bd., N.Y. and N.J., 1987-90; mem. Kessler Inst. for Rehab., West Orange, N.J., 1988—. Author, editor: Fundamentals of Electrical and Computer Engineering, 1983. State of Calif. scholar, 1960, Schunberger scholar, 1961; NSF grantee, 1973-79. Home: 209 Gregory Ave West Orange NJ 07052-4529 Office: NJ Inst Tech 323 High St Nutley NJ 07110-1434

THOMAS, GARY LYNN, financial executive; b. Port Vue, Pa., May 15, 1942; s. Willis L. and Luella M. (Rorabaugh) T.; m. Sharen A. Gibbons, May 13, 1967; children—Gregory Scott, Tara Elizabeth. B.S. in Bus. Adminstrn, Pa. State U., 1964; grad., Sch. Bank Adminstrn., U. Wis., 1973. CPA, Pa. Sr. auditor Arthur Andersen & Co., Los Angeles and Pitts., 1964-69; v.p. and dep. comptroller Pitts. Nat. Bank, 1969-77; v.p. and treas. Md. Nat. Corp., Balt., 1977-80; v.p., mgr. corp. fin. div. Md. Nat. Bank, Balt.; exec. v.p. adminstrn. Peterson, Howell & Heather, Hunt Valley, Md., 1980-82; v.p. fin. Am. TeleServices, Inc, a Metromedia co., Balt., 1983-85; chief fin. officer First Cellular Group, Inc., Balt., 1985-88, Schelle, Warner, Murray & Thomas, Inc., Balt., 1988—; mng. dir. Schelle Cellular Group, Inc., 1989—; pres. Ruxton Capital Group, Inc., 1989—; chief fin. officer Am. Personal Communications, Inc., Balt. and D.C., 1990—; adj. instr. Sch. Bank Adminstrn., U. Wis., 1975-80; speaker 14th ann. Bank Tax Inst., 1978. Mem. adv. bd., fin. com. St. Joseph Hosp., Balt.; bd. dirs. industry luncheon club Towson State U. Served with USAR, 1968. Mem. AICPA, Pa. Inst. CPAs, Md. Assn. CPAs (prior chmn. mems. in industry com.). Republican. Methodist. Home: 2211 Spring Lake Dr Lutherville Timonium MD 21093-3352 Office: 2212 Old Court Rd Baltimore MD 21208-3432

THOMAS, HAROLD STEPHEN, principal; b. Huntington, N.Y., Apr. 25, 1943; s. George Osborn Thomas and Evelyn May (Calyes) Krensavage; m. Kathleen Virginia Morgan, Apr. 17, 1971; children: Michael, Gregory, Jeffrey. BS, State U. Coll., Oswego, 1971, MS, 1981, Cert. Advanced Study in Ednl. Adminstrn., 1981. Tchr. Hannibal (N.Y.) Cen. Sch., 1971-81; adminstrv. intern Onondaga Madison Boces, Syracuse, N.Y., 1981-82, asst. prin., 1982-83; prin. OCM Boces Lakeside Campus, Syracuse, 1983-90; exec. prin. OCM Boces Lakeside and Thompson Campus, Syracuse, 1990—. Exec. sec. N.Y. State Vocat. Indsl. Clubs Am. Indsl. Adv. Coun., 1991—; vice chair N.Y. State Vocat. Indsl. Clubs Am. Bd. Trustees, 1989—; area II adminstr. N.Y. State Vocat. Indsl. Clubs Am., 1989—; exec. com. chair Boy Scout Am., Red Creek, N.Y. Staff sgt. USAF, 1963-68. Recipient Citizenship award DAR, Presdl. citation Pres. of U.S., 1962-63. Mem Am. Legion. Office: Onondaga Cortland Madison County BOCES 310 Lakeside Rd Syracuse NY 13209

THOMAS, HARRY DORRETT, insurance marketing professional; b. Balt., Sept. 22, 1944; s. Harry Dorrett and Clara Belle (Goldstraw) T.; m. Linda Carolyn Smith, 1968; 1 child, Kevin Dorrett. Student, Balt. City Coll., 1961-64. In various positions Selected Risks Ins. Co., Towson, Md., 1964-78; mktg. rep. Md. Casualty Ins. Co., Balt., 1978-80, Millers Mut. of Harrisburg, Pa., 1980-81, Northwestern Nat. Ins. Co., Towson, 1981-84; mktg. rep., mktg. mgr. Harleysville Ins. Cos., Columbia, Md., 1984—. Bd. officer PTA Pleasant Plains Elem. Sch., Baltimore County, 1977-83, PTA Loch Raven Middle Sch., Baltimore County, 1983-86; coach, mgr. Loch Raven Baseball League, 1979-88. Mem. Ins. Co. Reps. Md. (pres. 1981-82). Office: Harleysville Ins Cos 10025 Gov Warfield Pkwy Columbia MD 21044

THOMAS, HILARY BRYN, telecommunications executive; b. Brignorth, U.K., Jan. 31, 1943; came to U.S., 1985; parents, Kenneth Bryn and Nancy Barbara Tench (Cullum) T. BSc with honors, U. Wales, 1965. Instr. U. Victoria, B.C., Can., 1967-73; rsch. asst. Communications Studies Group Univ. Coll., London, 1975-76; cons. Communications Studies & Planning, Ltd., London, 1976-80; v.p. CSP Internat., Inc., London and N.Y.C., 1980-82, Aregon Internat., London and N.Y.C., 1982-85, Videodial, Inc., N.Y.C., 1985-88; pres. Minitel USA, Inc., N.Y.C., 1988-92; pres., bd. dirs. Minitel Holdings, Inc., Del.; chmn. bd. dirs. Minitel Svcs. Co., 1988-92; pres. Interactive Telecommunications Svcs. Inc., Mountain Lakes, N.J., 1992—; pres. bd. dirs. Minitel Holdings Inc., Del; chmn. bd. dirs. Minitel Svcs. Co., N.Y.C., 1988-92. Contbr. articles to industry publs. Mem. Interactive Svcs. Assn. (bd. dirs. 1985—, chmn. 1987-89; Disting. Svc. award 1989), Info. Industry Assn., Internat. Inst. Communications, World Inst. on Disability (bus. adv. coun.). Office: 420 The Boulevard Ste 101 Mountain Lakes NJ 07046

THOMAS, J. DARRELL, banker; b. Paterson, N.J., June 1, 1960; s. James and Elizabeth (Hollins) T.; m. Brenda Cornwell, May 24, 1986; 1 child, Bryan. BA in Econs., Tufts U., 1981; MBA in Fin., The Wharton Sch., 1984. Jr. acct. IBM, Franklin Lakes, N.J., 1980; traffic analyst Procter & Gamble, Cin., 1981-82; fin. analyst Am. Can Co., Greenwich, Conn., 1983; assoc. v.p. leasing Citicorp/Citibank, Harrison, N.Y., 1984-89; v.p. treasury Citicorp/Citibank, N.Y.C., 1989-92, v.p. corp. fin., 1992—. Treas., trustee First Bapt. Ch., Englewood, N.J., 1990—. Mem. Urban Bankers Coalition, Black MBA Assn. Home: 356 Liberty Rd Englewood NJ 07631-2110 Office: Citibank 4th Fl Zone 17 399 Park Avenue New York NY 10043

THOMAS, JAMES EDWARD, accountant; b. Darlington, S.C., Oct. 18, 1944; s. Willie Thomas and Cleola (Sawyer) T.; m. Joan Yvette Grant, Mar. 15, 1945; 1 child, James E. II. BS in Acctg., Johnson C. Smith Coll., Charlotte, N.C., 1966; MA in Fin., C.W. Post Coll., Greenvale, N.Y., 1980. Asst. mgr. Mfrs. Hanover Trust, N.Y.C., 1970-78, Met. Savs. Bank, N.Y.C., 1978-81; auditor N.Y. State Dept. Social Svcs., N.Y.C., 1981-83; acct. N.Y.C. Bd. Edn., 1983-86; acct., agt. IRS, N.Y.C., 1987—; instr. Katherine L. Gibbs, Inc., N.Y.C., 1987-89. Mem. Assn. MBA Execs., Am. Mgmt. Assn., Internat. Platform Assn., Sigma Rho Sigma. Home: 37-06 104th St #4C Flushing NY 11368

THOMAS, JOAB LANGSTON, academic administrator, biology educator; b. Holt, Ala., Feb. 14, 1933; s. Ralph Cage and Chamintney Elizabeth (Stovall) T.; m. Marly A. Dukes, Dec. 22, 1954; children: Catherine, David, Jennifer, Frances. AB, Harvard U., 1955, MA, 1957, PhD, 1959; DSc (hon.), U. Ala., 1981; LLD (hon.), Stillman Coll., 1987. Cytotaxonomist Arnold Aboretum, Harvard, 1959-61; faculty U. Ala., University, 1961-76, prof. biology, 1966-76, 88-91, asst. dean Coll. Arts and Scis., 1964-65, 69, dean for student devel. Coll., 1969-74, v.p., 1974-76, dir. Herbarium, 1961-76, dir. Arboretum, 1964-65, 66-69; pres. U. Ala., Tuscaloosa, 1981-88; chancellor N.C. State U., Raleigh, 1976-81; pres. Pa. State U., University Park, 1990—; dir. Blount, Inc., First Ala. Bank, Tuscaloosa; intern acad. adminstrn. Am. Coun. on Edn., 1971. Author: A Monographic Study of the Cyrillaceae, 1960, Wildflowers of Alabama and Adjoining States, 1973, The Rising South, 1976, Poisonous Plants and Venomous Animals of Alabama and Adjoining States, 1990. Bd. dirs. Internat. Potato Ctr., 1977-83, chmn. 1982-83; bd. dirs. Internat. Svc. for Nat. Agrl. Rsch., 1985-91. Named Outstanding Prof. U. Ala., 1964-65, Ala. Acad. Honor, 1983, Citizen of Yr., Tuscaloosa, 1987. Mem. Phi Beta Kappa, Sigma Xi, Omicron Delta Kappa, Phi Kappa Phi. Office: Pa State U 201 Old Main University Park PA 16802-1589

THOMAS, JOHN ROBERT, investments executive; b. Cleve., Oct. 7, 1939; s. William Kernahan and Dorothy Emma (Good) T.; m. Joyce Winter; children: Gregory, Darcy. BA, Ohio Weslyan U., 1961; MBA, U. Pa., 1963. Cert. fin. analyst. From security analyst to portfolio mgr. J.P. Morgan Investment Mgmt., Inc., N.Y.C., 1964-84, head mktg., 1984—, also bd. dirs. Mem. N.Y. Soc. Security Analysts, Fin. Analysts Fedn. Office: JP Morgan Investment Mgmt 522 5th Ave New York NY 10036-7601

THOMAS, JOHN WESLEY, psychiatrist; b. Birmingham, Ala., Feb. 13, 1932; s. James and Leila Mae (Berry) T.; m. Dorothy Thompson, 1955 (div. 1969); children: Courtland W., Stephen M. BA, Tenn. State U., 1953; MD, Meharry Med. Coll., Nashville, 1959. Intern McKeesport (Pa.) Hosp., 1959-60; resident Rollman Receiving Hosp. and Inst. of Psychiatry, Cin., 1960-61, Western Psychiat. Inst. and Clinic, Pitts., 1961-63; staff psychiatrist Mayview State Hosp., Bridgeville, Pa., 1963-66; med. dir. Adult Outpatient Svcs., St. Francis Mental Health Ctr., Pitts., 1971-89; supervising psychiatrist St. Francis Psychiatric Residency Prog., Pitts., 1982-89; field faculty dept. psychiatry Meharry Med. Coll., Nashville, 1980—; clin. instr. dept. psychiatry U. Pitts., 1963-89; pvt. practice psychiatry Pitts., 1963—; cons. in field. Fellow Am. Group Psychotherapy Assn.; mem. AMA, NAACP, Am. Psychiat. Assn., Nat. Med. Assn., Pa. Med. Soc., Pa. Psychiat. Soc., Tri-State Group Psychotherapy Soc., Alpha Phi Alpha, Chi Delta Mu. Office: 3708 Fifth Ave # 305 Pittsburgh PA 15213

THOMAS, JONATHAN WESLEY, physician; b. Enterprise, Ala., July 3, 1963; s. John Paul and Mary Glen (Cobb) T.; m. Meghan Mary Hawley, Sept. 1, 1990. BA, Huntingdon Coll., 1984; MD, U. Ala., 1988. Legis. asst. Lt. Gov.'s Office, State of Ala., Montgomery, 1981-83; intern St. Vincent's

Hosp. and Med. Ctr. of N.Y., N.Y.C., 1988-89, resident, 1989—; pres. house staff coun. St. Vincent's Hosp. and Med. Ctr., 1989—. Article reviewer Comprehensive Psychiatry, 1989—. Mem. AMA (pres. student sect. 1982-83), Am. Psychiat. Assn., Am. Assn. Community Psychiatrists. Republican. Methodist. Office: St Vincent's Hosp 153 W 11th St New York NY 10011-8397

THOMAS, JOYCE AUGUSTA, English educator; b. Annapolis, Md., Sept. 2, 1946; d. Carroll Rossiter and Gertrude (Nelson) T. BA, Shepherd Coll., Shepherdstown, W.Va., 1968; MA, W.Va. U., Morgantown, 1970; ArtsD, SUNY, 1978. English tchr. Albany Acad. for Girls, Albany, N.Y., 1977-80; adjunct instr. SUNY at Albany, Albany, N.Y., 1976-80; prof. of English Castleton State Coll., Castleton, Vt., 1980—; humanities scholar Vt. Coun. on Humanities, Montpelier, 1982-91. Author: Inside the Wolf's Belly: Aspects of the Fairy Tale, 1989, Introduction to The Broken Iris (poem), 1990; contbr. articles to profl. jours. Nominee Katherine Briggs Folklore award Folklore Soc., Eng., 1989, honorable mention Eve of St. Agnes Poetry Competition, 1987, 89. Mem. N.E. Modern Lang. Assn., Vt. Writers League. Home: PO Box 24 Castleton VT 05735-0024 Office: Castleton State Coll English Dept Castleton VT 05735

THOMAS, JUDITH A. WAUGH, education educator; b. New Kensington, Pa., Nov. 9, 1940; d. Charles Arthur and Violet (Stewart) Waugh; m. James Arthur Thomas, Aug. 16, 1969; children: Michelle Lynn, Bradley Arthur, Brian James. BS, Edinboro U. Pa., 1962; MEd, Duquesne U., 1967; EdD, U. Puget Sound, 1965. Tchr. English, Spanish and debate Highlands (Pa.) Sch. Dist., 1962-66, Penn Hills (Pa.) Sch. Dist., 1966-67; teaching fellow W.Va. U., Morgantown, 1967-70; asst. prof. speech Pa. State U., Uniontown, 1970-71, West Liberty (W.Va.) State Coll., 1971-74; assoc. prof. edn. Lincoln U., Lincoln University, Pa., 1974-79, chair, prof. edn., 1979—; vis. dean student affairs Phila. Coll. Textiles and Sci., 1987-88; vis. scholar Lock Haven (Pa.) U., 1987-88; mem. gov.'s task force for tchr. edn., 1979; appointee Profl. Standards and Practices Com., 1978-81; pres. Pa. Black Conf. on Higher Edn., 1980-83, Chester County Edn. Found., 1987-89. Danforth fellow, 1973. Mem. AAUP, Pa. Black Conf. Higher Edn., Jack and Jill Am., Assn. Rsch. and Supervision, Phi Delta Kappa, Delta Sigma Theta. Democrat. Baptist. Home: 867 Meadowcroft Rd West Chester PA 19382-8536

THOMAS, KENNETH ALFRED, JR., biochemist, researcher; b. Oklahoma City, Nov. 28, 1946; s. Kenneth Alfred and Nellymae (DeWitt) T.; m. Theresa Ellen Behrens, Dec. 1, 1973; children: Kenneth Auther, Christopher Alfred, Katharine Ann. BS in Chemistry, U. Del., 1969; PhD in Biochemistry, Duke U., 1974. Postdoctoral fellow Duke U., Durham, N.C., 1974-75, NIH, Bethesda, Md., 1975-77, Washington U., St. Louis, 1977-79; sr. rsch. scientist Merck Sharp & Dohme, Rahway, N.J., 1979-83, rsch. fellow, 1983-86, assoc. dir., 1986-88, dir., 1988—; corr. Trends in Biochem. Scis., 1988—; co-organizer Keystone (Colo.) Symposium (Fibroblast Growth Factors and Angiogenesis), 1991; speaker Heidelberg (Germany) U. 600th Anniversary Symposium, 1986, NIH 100th Anniversary Symposium, 1987; session chmn., speaker Max-Planck Inst., Munich, 1988. Mem. editorial bd. Jour. Biol. Chemistry, 1991—; contbr. articles to profl. jours.; patentee purification and characterization of fibroblast growth factor. Fellow NIH, 1975-77. Mem. AAAS, Am. Soc. Biol. Chemists, Protein Chemistry Soc., Am. Chem. Soc., N.Y. Acad. Scis., Sigma Xi. Office: Merck Sharp & Dohme Rsch Labs RM 80W-243 PO Box 2000 Rahway NJ 07065

THOMAS, LEE W., chemical engineer; b. Boswell, Pa., Oct. 31, 1926; s. Walter G. and Rhea M. (Cable) T.; m. Mary Jane Neuhof, Jan. 4, 1950; children: Sharon, Kathleen. BS in Chem. Engring., U. Pitts., 1949. Registered profl. engr., Del. Chemist, control lab analyst Jones & Laughlin, Pitts., 1949; instrument engr. Bethlehem Steel Co., Pitts., 1952; mem. R&D staff E. I. du Pont Co., Wilmington, Del., 1952-85; prin., cons. Cecon Group, Inc., Wilmington, 1985—. Contbr. articles to tech. jours.; patentee dispersion process, pigments in sythentic fiber polymers. Comml. pilot, comml. truck driver. Mem. Am. Inst. Chem. Engrs., Am. Chem. Soc., Am. Fedn. Paint Socs., Kiwanis (past pres.), Toastmasters (past pres.), Sigma Tau. Home: 230 Steeplechase Dr Wilmington DE 19808-1977 Office: Cencon Group Inc 242 N James St Ste 202 Wilmington DE 19804-3168

THOMAS, MARY ELIZABETH, publishing company executive; b. N.Y.C., Jan. 5, 1962; d. Lawrence Joseph and Jane Elizabeth (Stock) T. BA, Kenyon Coll., 1984; MA, U. Va., 1987. Editorial asst. PWS-Kent Pub. Co., Boston, 1987-88, asst. editor, 1988—. Mem. Quill and Scroll Soc. Home: 90 Highland Ave Apt 1 Somerville MA 02143-1814

THOMAS, MICHAEL RIDLEY, computer software scientist; b. Louisville, Oct. 29, 1948; s. James Ridley and Virginia Nell (Petty) T.; m. Paula Frances Cox, July 10, 1971; children: Brian Ridley, Geoffrey Paul. BA, U. Tex., 1973; MA, Wash. State U., 1976, PhD, 1978. Prin. rsch. scientist Sterling Software, Inc., Rome, N.Y., 1989—; co-founder TXS, Inc., San Antonio, 1984-89. Contbr. articles to profl. jours.; developer commercial software, text retrieval, natural language processing, artificial intelligence. Grantee Nat. Def. Fgn. Lang. Fellowship, Java, Indonesia, 1976. Mem. IEEE (chmn. Conf. on Tech. Transfer N.Y. 1993), Assn. for Computational Linguistics, Assn. for Computational Machines. Office: Sterling Software Beeches Tech Campus Rome NY 13440

THOMAS, PATRICK ROBERT MAXWELL, oncology educator, academic administrator; b. Exmouth, Devon, Eng., Feb. 23, 1943; came to U.S., 1976; s. Christopher Codrington and Aileen Daphne (Gordon) T.; m. Linda Sharon Rich, June 23, 1976 (dec. 1977). Diploma in biochemistry, London U., 1965, MB, BS, 1968. Lectr. Inst. Cancer Rsch., London, 1974-76; assoc. chief clinician Roswell Park Meml. Inst., Buffalo, 1976-79; asst. prof. Washington U., St. Louis, 1979-83, assoc. prof., 1983-89, prof., 1989-90; prof., chmn. Temple U., Phila., 1991—; extramural bd. PDQ, Bethesda, Md., 1989—; mem. in-svc. exam. com. Am. Coll. Radiology, Reston, Va., 1990—; examiner Am. Bd. Radiology, Louisville, 1990—. Fellow Am. Coll. Radiology, Royal Coll. Radiologists. Home: 106 Pier Five 7 N Delaware Philadelphia PA 19106 Office: Temple U 3401 N Broad St Philadelphia PA 19140-5189

THOMAS, RALPH C., III, trade association administrator, lawyer; b. Roanoke, Va., Apr. 10, 1949; s. Ralph C. Jr. and Dorothy (Easley) T. BA, U. Calif., Berkeley, 1975; JD, Harvard U., 1978. Assoc. Bergson, Borkland, Margolis & Adler, Washington, 1978-80; sr. ptnr. Thomas, John & Everett, Washington, 1980-85; clin. instr. in Law Sch. George Washington U., Washington, 1982-83; exec. dir. Nat. Assn. Minority Contractors, Washington, 1985—; adj. instr. U. Va., Charlottesville, 1989-91; mem. Chancellor's Adv. Com. on Constrn. Mgmt., Princess Anne, Md., 1986—. Contbr. articles to profl. jours. General counsel D.C. Statehood Constnl. Conv., Washington, 1982. Staff sgt. USAF, 1967-71, Vietnam. Mem. D.C. Bar Assn., Constrn. Writers Assn. Office: Nat Assn Minority Contractors 1333 F St NW # 500 Washington DC 20004-1191

THOMAS, RICHARD EMERY, federal government official; b. Laconia, N.H., Dec. 12, 1929; s. Emery Everett and Zera Mae (Bean) T.; m. Blythe Ann Jamieson, June 14, 1952; children—Karen, Douglas, Kathryn, Jeffrey. B.S., U. N.H., 1952, M.S., 1954; postgrad. U. Md., 1954-56; postgrad. Cornell U., 1961-63. Research scientist Pub. Health Service, Cin., 1957-67; sr. research scientist Fed. Water Quality Adminstrn., Ada, Okla., 1967-77; sr. program scientist EPA, Washington, 1977-82, program coordinator, 1983-86, environ. cons., 1987—. Editor, author design manual: Land Treatment of Municipal Wastewater, 1977, rev. edit., 1981, supplement, 1984. Contbr. articles to profl. jours., chpts. to books. Mem. troop com. Arbuchle council Boy Scouts Am., 1971-73, pack master, 1968-69. Recipient Cert. Appreciation, Boy Scouts Am., Ada, 1973; Bronze medal, EPA, 1975, Outstanding Performance award, 1984, Disting. Career award, 1986. Mem. Water Pollution Control Fedn., Irrigation Assn., Council for Agrl. Sci. and Tech. Republican. Methodist. Avocations: softball, bowling, swimming, hiking, golf.

THOMAS, ROBERT CHANLER BRYANT, real estate broker, executive; b. Stony Point, N.Y., Oct. 4, 1951; s. William Ruben Francis and Mildren Edna (Baptist) T., m. Judith Carol, July 15, 1978; children: Kristina Elizabeth, Kimberly Caitlin. AA, Rockland Community Coll., 1971; BS, SUNY, Cortland, 1973; MA, Fairfield U., 1978. Broker/owner/pres. Hudson House Real Estate, Ltd., Stony Point, N.Y.; profl. educator North Rockland Cen. Sch. Mem. Rockland Political Action Com.; warden Episc. Diocese of N.Y. Mem. Am. Fedn. Tchr., Nat. Assn. Realtors, Rockland County Bd. Realtors, Rockland County Tchrs. Assn., N.Y. State Congress Parents & Tchrs., N.Y. State United Tchrs. Del., North Rockland Tchrs. Assn. Home: 11 Franklin Dr Stony Point NY 10980-1507 Office: Hudson House Real Estate Lt 13 N Liberty Dr Stony Point NY 10980-1500

THOMAS, SAMUEL DEE, art educator; b. Sayre, Pa., Aug. 15, 1930; s. Edward Field and Martha Catharine (Wherry) T.; m. Bertha Lillian Miller, July 10, 1953; children: Mary Sue, Catharine Elizabeth. BS in Art Edn., Indiana U. Pa., 1952; MEd. in Art Edn., Pa. State U., 1959, postgrad., 1960, 62, 79; postgrad., Hofstra U., 1967. Cert. art tchr., Pa., N.Y. Art tchr., elem. supr. Chestnut Ridge St. Schs., Fishertown, Pa., 1952-53, 55-60; art tchr. high sch. Smithtown Cen. High, Smithtown, N.Y., 1960-61, USFD 3 Huntington High, Huntington, N.Y., 1961-68; coord., tchr. and insr. evening sch. classes in arts Hofstra U., Hempsted, N.Y., 1964-68; instr. evening sch. Elmira Coll., Elmira, N.Y., 1969-72; asst. prof. art Mansfield (Pa.) U., 1968—; dir., producer CE ES TA Puppets, Blossburg, Pa., 1974—. Painter exhibited in group shows and one-man shows. Bd. dirs. Williamson Rd. TV Corp., Blossburg, 1974—. Home: 119 N Williamson Rd Blossburg PA 16912-1206 Office: Mansfield U Dept Art Mansfield PA 16933 Studio: 107 Maple Hill Rd Blossburg PA 16912

THOMAS, STUART DENIS, international business consultant; b. Cheltenham, Gloucestershire, Eng., Aug. 15, 1938; s. Robert Morris and Rosamund Alice (Jervis) T.; m. Dayle Ellen Rado, Oct. 31, 1981; 1 child by previous marriage—Owen Leavitt; children—Derek Joseph, Samantha Kate. B.Sc., Bristol U., Eng., 1963; M.B.A., Harvard U., 1965, D.B.A., 1969. Staff engr. Westland Aircraft, East Cowes, Isle of Wight, Eng., 1956-62; instr. Harvard Bus. Sch., Boston, 1965-69; sr. lectr. London Bus. Sch, Eng., 1969-77; pres. Berol Corp., Danbury, Conn., 1977-91, chief exec. officer, 1988-91, vice chmn., 1991-92; pres. Empire Berol Corp., Danbury, 1987-88; dir. Ctr. for Mgmt. Devel., London. Contbr. articles to profl. jours. Mem. corp. coll. council Western Conn. State U., 1984-87; bd. dirs. Charles Ives Ctr. for the Arts., Danbury, 1985-86; chmn. No. Fairfield County council, Am. Heart Assn., Danbury, 1985-86. Mem. Writing Instruments Mfrs. Assn. (dir. Washington 1982-92, sec. 1985-87, v.p. 1987-89, pres. 1989-91, chmn. 1992), Fedn. Am. Writing Instrument Assns. (pres. 1991-92). Congregationalist.

THOMAS, SUSAN BARNES, university director; b. West Chester, Pa.; d. Harold and Hazel (Deery) Barnes. BSBA, Widener U., 1985, MS in Bus. Mgmt., 1988. Registered sch. bus. adminstr., Pa. Pers. asst. Schramm Inc., West Chester, 1971-75; acct. Wyeth Labs. Inc., West Chester, 1975-86; bus. mgr. Cen. Chester County Vocat. Tech. Sch., Coatesville, Pa., 1986-89; dir. bus. and fin. Great Valley campus Pa. State U., Malvern, 1989—. Mem. Assn. Sch. Bus. Ofcls., Pa. Assn. Sch. Bus. Ofcls., Delaware Valley Assn. Sch. Bus. Ofcls. Home: Beagle Club Rd RD 4 West Chester PA 19382 Office: Pa State U Great Valley 30 E Swedesford Rd Malvern PA 19355-1480

THOMAS, THALIA ANN, artist; b. Wilkes-Barre, Pa., Apr. 22, 1935; d. Thomas Charles and Alice (Thomas) T. BS, Coll. Misericordia, Dallas, Pa., 1956; MA, Columbia U., 1962; MFA, U. Guanajuato, Mex., 1976; MA, Marywood Coll., Scranton, Pa., 1987. Asst. prof. art Marywood Coll., 1962-85, bd. dirs. Inst. for Sr. Learners, 1991-92. One-woman shows include Galerie Internationale, N.Y.C., 1972, Marywood Coll., Scranton, Pa., 1975, Coll. Misericordia, Dallas, 1989. Mem. search com. Everhart Mus., Scranton, 1991; vol. Wyoming Valley Hist. Soc., 1991, St. Jude Hosp., Memphis, 1991, WVIA-TV/FM Phonathon, 1991. Recipient Cor Marieae Pro Fide et Cultura award Marywood Coll., 1991, Alumni Achievement award Coll. Misericordia, 1991; named Northeast Woman, Scranton Times, 1992. Mem. Am. Art Therapy Assn., Cath. Artists of 90's, Cath. Fine Arts Soc., Wyo. Hist. and Geol. Soc. Home: 18 Welles St Wilkes Barre PA 18704-4932

THOMAS, TOM, plastics company executive; b. Malang, Java, Indonesia, Feb. 15, 1932; arrived in Can., 1954; s. Ferdinand and Elfrieda Emma (Macht) T.; m. Jannie Chine Sneep, Jan. 19, 1956; children: Gregory John, Renée Sonja Elfrieda, Michael Grant, Thomas. Grad. high sch., The Hague, Holland. Jr. mgr. Lever Bros. Ltd., Toronto, Ont., Can., 1954-60; sr. mgr. Impac & Somerville Plastics, Toronto, Ont., Can., 1960-64; founder, C.E.O. Can. Cup Inc., Toronto, Ont., Can., 1964—, also bd. dirs., 1964—; Inventor in field. Trustee Frazer Inst., Vancouver, B.C., Can., 1977—; gov. Massey and Roy Thomson Hall, Toronto, 1991—; bd. dirs. Toronto Symphony, 1986—, mem. Maestro's Club, 1984, mem. pres.'s coun. Can. Opera Co., 1980. Office: Can Cup Div Headquarters, 137 Bentworth Ave, Toronto, ON Canada M6A 1P6

THOMAS, WENDY CATHERINE, special education educator; b. Manchester, N.H., Mar. 12, 1950; d. Walter and Emelia Ann (Twardy) Lacheta; m. William Eugene Thomas, Aug. 10, 1974; children: Amanda Marie, Bethany Ann. BEd, Keene State Coll., 1972; MEd, Notre Dame Coll., Manchester, 1981. Tchr. of English Cen. High Sch., Manchester, 1972-81, learning disabilities specialist, 1981-83; learning disabilities specialist Southside Jr. High Sch., Manchester, 1983—. Crisis worker YWCA, Manchester, 1991. Christa Macauliffe Sabbatical fellow, C.M. Sabbatical Trust, N.H., 1988. Mem. NEA (del. Phila. assembly 1983, Mpls. assembly 1984, exec. bd. N.H. chpt. 1985-90), Manchester Edn. Assn. Democrat. Polish National Catholic. Home: 6 Margate Dr Auburn NH 03032 Office: Southside Jr High Sch 140 S Jewett St Manchester NH 03103

THOMAS-ROMÁN, DELSEY IVETTE, office administrator; b. Aguadilla, P.R., June 8, 1954; d. Frank and Virginia (Román) T. AA, U. P.R., Aguadilla, 1974; BA, U. P.R., Mayagüez, 1981; MEd, U. Mass., 1990. Sec. San José Investors, Santurce, P.R., 1981-83, P.R. Found. for Med. Care, Inc., Hato Rey, 1983-84, U. Mass., Amherst, 1984—; asst. dir. summer program in Spain U. Mass., Amherst, 1988-89. Youth dir. Seventh Day Adventist Ch., Moca, P.R., 1980; bd. dirs. Casa Latina, Inc. Mem. Univ. Women Profl. Network. Office: U Mass Univ Health Svcs 127 Hills N Amherst MA 01003

THOMASSON, DAN KING, newspaper executive; b. Shelbyville, Ind., Dec. 22, 1933; s. Hubert Lee and Mary Margaret (King) T.; m. Laqueta Forducey, Sept. 7, 1958; children: Scot, Lisa, Sean, Patrick. BS, Ind. U., 1956; postgrad., Colo. U., 1959. Reporter, editor Indpls. Star, 1956; reporter Lawton (Okla.) Constitution, 1957-58, The Rocky Mountain News, Denver, 1959-64; corr. Scripps Howard Newspapers, Washington, 1964-74, asst. mng. editor, 1974-76; mng. editor Scripps Howard News Svc., Washington, 1976-80, editor, 1980—; v.p.news Scripps Howard Newspapers, Cin., 1986—. President Raymond Clapper Found., Washington, 1980—; bd. dirs. Scripps Howard Found., Cin., 1987—; trustee Franklin Coll., 1990—; mem. nat. adv. com. E.W. Scripps Sch. of Journalism, 1990, Ohio U., 1990, Nat. Pub. Affairs Coun., Ind. U., 1990—. With U.S. Army, 1956-58. Named Man of Yr., Shelbyville, Ind. C. of C., 1970. Mem. Am. Soc. Newspaper Editors, White House Corrs. Assn., Gridiron Club of Washington, Nat. Press Club, Univ. Club of Washington, Washington Golf and Country Club (Arlington, Va.), Sigma Delta Chi. Home: 3729 Morningside Dr Fairfax VA 22031-3317 Office: Scripps Howard 1090 Vermont Ave NW Washington DC 20005-4905

THOMKA-GAZDIK, JULIAN, lawyer, educator; b. Apatin, Hungary, Aug. 22, 1918; arrived in Can., 1947, U.S., 1989; s. Julian Thomka-Gazdik and Maria Michler; divorced 1985; children: Dorothy, Julian, Andrew. Bacalorea, Piarist Fathers, Budapest, Hungary, 1936; D in Polit. Sci., Queen Elizabeth U., Pech, Hungary, 1941, D of Law, 1942; M of Civil Law, McGill U., Montreal, Que., Can., 1949. Bar: Que. 1954; cert. queen's counsel Can.; Conseiller Juriduqie, Geneva, 1969. Prof. law McGill U., 1947-89; ptnr. Cutler Lacharel, Gazdik Advs., Montreal, 1954-57, McNaughton, Harvey, Michaud & Gazdik, Montreal, 1958-69; counsel Doheny, Day Advs., Montreal, 1970-89; pres. Tonga Corp., Washington, 1989—, Hatfield, Inc., Gloucester Estates, Inc.; asst. dir. gen. counsel Internat. Air Transp. Assn., Montreal, Geneva, 1969-79; counsel Soc. Internat. Telecommunication Aeron., Paris, 1980-85; chmn. maritime air law com. Can. Bar Assn., 1955; sec. Can. br. Internat. Law Assn., 1951-56. Contbr. articles to profl. jours. Officer, pilot RCAF, 1946-55. Mem. Univ. Club Montreal, Naval Mil. Club London, Cosmos Club Washington. Roman Catholic.

THOMPSON, ANNA-CHRISTINA, guidance counselor, vocational school educator; b. East Liverpool, Ohio, Sept. 23, 1937; d. Theodore and M. Louise (Gumbs) Cabral; m. William Carr Thompson, Apr. 20, 1963; children: William Christopher, Naomi Ruth. BS in Edn., Framingham State Coll., 1960; MEd in Counseling, Bridgewater State Coll., 1990. Registered dietitican, 1961; cert. tchr., Mass. Dietitian, instr. Burbank Hosp., Fitchburg, Mass., 1961-63; nutritionist Coun. of Elders, Roxbury, Mass., 1968-69; tchr. home econs. Medford (Mass.) Pub. Schs., 1973-84; tchr. home econs. Greater New Bedford (Mass.) Region Vocat. Tech. High Sch., 1984-90, guidance counselor, 1990—. Dem. Ward Commn., Medford, 1972; del. Dem. Conv., Miami, Fla., 1972; chmn. Coun. for Children, New Bedford, 1989—; coun. mem. March of Dimes, Middleboro, Mass., 1986—. Recipient Appreciation of Vol. Work award March of Dimes, Middleboro, 1990. Mem. Am. Home Econs. Assn., Mass. Vocat. Assn., Am. Vocat. Assn., Mass. Home Econs. Assn. (treas.), Mass. Sch. Guidance Assn., Southeastern Mass. Home Econs. Assn. (v.p.). Home: 17 Sandpiper Terr Wareham MA 02571

THOMPSON, BRIAN JOHN, university provost, optics educator; b. Glossop, Eng., June 10, 1932; came to U.S., 1962; s. Alexander William and Edna May (Gould) T.; m. Joyce Emily Cheshire, Mar. 31, 1956; children: Karen Joyce, Andrew Derrick. B of Sci. Tech., U. Manchester, Eng., 1955, PhD, 1959. Demonstrator in physics Dept. Tech., U. Manchester, 1955-56, asst. lectr., 1957-59; lectr. physics U. Leeds, Eng., 1959-62; sr. physicist Tech. Optics, Inc., Burlington, Mass., 1963-65, dir. dept. optics, 1966-67, mgr. tech. ops., Western tech. dir. Beckman & Whitley div., 1967-68; prof. Inst. Optics U. Rochester, N.Y., 1968—, dir. Inst. Optics, 1968-75, dean Coll. Engring. and Applied Scis., 1975-84, Wm. F. May prof. engring., 1982-85, provost, 1984—. Internat. editor: Optics and Laser Tech., 1969—; assoc. editor: Optical Engring., 1972-76, Optics Communications, 1978-86; Am. editor Optica Acta, 1981-85; editor: Optical Engring. Series, vol. 1-31, 1980—; mem. editorial adv. bd. Laser Focus, 1970—, Particle Characterization, 1984—, Optics and Lasers in Engring., 1985; chmn. adv. bd. Marquis Who's Who Directory Optical Scientists and Engrs., 1983-86; contbr. articles to profl. jours. Served with Brit. Army, 1950-52. Fellow Optical Soc. Am. (bd. dirs. 1969-72, exec. com. 1970-73, assoc. editor jour. 1966-77), Inst. Physics and Phys. Soc. (Gt. Britain 1955), Soc. Photo-Optical Instrumentation Engrs. (pres. 1974, 75-76, gen. editor series of selected papers 1983—, editor Optical Engring. jour. 1991—, Pres.'s award 1967, Pezzuto award 1978, Kingslake medal 1978, Gold medal 1986); mem. Am. Phys. Soc., AAAS. Mem. Ch. of Christ. Home: 692 Mt Hope Ave Rochester NY 14620 Office: U Rochester Provost Office Adminstrn Bldg 200 Rochester NY 14627

THOMPSON, DOUGLAS CARL, college dean; b. Torrance, Calif., July 26, 1940; s. Milbert Louis and Marjorie Eleanor (Reeve) T.; m. Elizabeth Dare Rust, June 21, 1969; children: Reeve, Courtland. BS, Swarthmore Coll., 1962. Physicist Bartol Rsch. Found., Swarthmore, Pa., 1962-66; assoc. dean admissions Swarthmore Coll., 1966-76; assoc. dir. admissions Brown U., Providence, 1976-80; dean admissions Hamilton Coll., Clinton, N.Y., 1980—; selection com. Nat. Merit Scholarship Corp., Evanston, Ill., 1987, 89, 90; mem. evaluation team Middle States Assn. Schs. and Colls., Phila., 1989; policy coun. test of English as a Fgn. Lang., Princeton, N.J., 1987-89; lectr. in field. Mem. Nat. assn. Coll. Admission Counselors (chmn. ad hoc com. 1988-91, sec.-treas. 1985-88), N.Y. State Assn. Coll. Admission Counselors (coll. del. 1991—), European Coun. of Internat. Schs. (chmn. coll. com., tour dir. 1982-83), Explorers Cub (chmn. Phila. chpt. 1973-76). Home: 3 Miller Rd Clinton NY 13323-1211 Office: Hamilton Coll 198 College Hill Rd Clinton NY 13323-1218

THOMPSON, EARL RYAN, materials scientist; b. Lenoir, N.C., Jan. 9, 1939; s. Roy E. and Bertha (Hincher) T.; m. Sylvia Ransdell, June 7, 1960; children: Ashley, Amy, Brian. BS, N.C. State U., 1960, MS, 1962; DSc, U. Va., 1966. Metallurg. engr. Reynolds Metals Co., Richmond, Va., 1961-62; instr. U. Va., Charlottesville, 1962-64; rsch. scientist United Techs. Rsch. Ctr., East Hartford, Conn., 1965-85, asst. dir. rsch., 1985—; vis. prof. Ecole Poly., Lausanne, Switzerland, 1973; mem. Nat. Materials Adv. Bd., Washington, 1990—; mem. adv. com. Oak Ridge (Tenn.) Nat. Lab., 1988-90; adv. coun. coll. engring. N.C. State U., Raleigh, 1989-91. Author: Yearbook of Science and Technology 1970; contbr. chpt. to Annual Rev. Materials Sci., 1982. Fellow Am. Soc. for Metals (Grossman Author's award 1970, Rockwell Meml. lectr. 1986), AIAA (assoc., chmn. materials tech. com. 1978); mem. AAAS, Am. Ceramic Soc., Conn. Acad. Sci. and Engring. Office: United Techs Rsch Ctr 400 Main St East Hartford CT 06118-1873

THOMPSON, EDMUND A(NDY), III, marketing professional; b. Bryn Mawr, Pa., Jan. 8, 1949; s. Edmund A. Jr. and Harriett T. (Thorpe) T.; m. Kathleen Frances Thompson, Aug. 15, 1970; children: Amy, Brian, Lindsay. BS, Fla. State U., 1970. Profl. golfer, 1971-73, profl. golfer PGA tour, 1974-76; sales rep. Morris-Walsh, Inc., Gaithersburg, Md., 1977-78; v.p. mktg. Am. Teleresponse Group Inc., Drexel Hill, Pa., 1978-83; mng. ptnr. Inter-Media Mktg., West Chester, Pa., 1983—. Contbr. articles to profl. jours. Mem. Phila. Direct Mktg. Assn. (bd. dirs. 1983-85), Direct Mktg. Assn., Overbrook Golf Club (bd. dirs. 1991-94). Republican. Episcopalian. Office: Inter Media Mktg 201 Carter Dr West Chester PA 19382-4998

THOMPSON, ELLEN KUBACKI, microbiologist, medical writer, consultant; b. Bethesda, Md., July 21, 1950; d. Edward Leonard and Ellen Angelina (Battaglia) Kubacki; AB, Miami U., Oxford, Ohio, 1972; m. Richard Kent Thompson, Jan. 25, 1975; 1 son, James Edward. Asst. microbiologist Hoffmann-La Roche Inc., Nutley, N.J., 1972-77, med. writer, 1977-79; freelance writer and cons., 1979-91; v.p. Princeton Trading Internat., Inc., 1991—. Elected Rep. committeewoman South Brunswick Twp. (dist. 3), 1983-89; pres. Chapin Sch. Parents' Assn., 1987-88; mem. Bd. Health South Brunswick Twp., 1985-90, vice chair, 1989-90, chair, 1990-91. Mem. Am. Soc. for Microbiology, Am. Med. Writers Assn., Theobald Smith Soc., Miami U. Alumni Assn. No. N.J. (trustee 1972—), Sigma Xi (treas. Roche research chpt. 1977, sec. 1978), Sigma Kappa. Home: 35 Fairfield Rd Princeton NJ 08540-9577

THOMPSON, GEORGE LEE, manufacturing company executive; b. Denver, June 12, 1933; s. George H. and Frances M. (Murphy) T.; m. Jean G. Meier, Aug. 25, 1957; children: Shannon, Tracy, Bradley. BS in Bus., U. Colo., 1957; postgrad. in advanced mgmt., NYU, 1969. With GTE Sylvania, Denvers, Mass., 1957-65, nat. sales mgr., 1965-67, mktg. mgr., 1967-68; v.p. sales entertainment products Batavia, N.Y., 1968-73; dir. corp. mktg. Stamford, Conn., 1973-74; v.p. mktg. Servomation Corp., N.Y.C., 1974-76, exec. v.p., 1976-78; exec. v.p. Singer Co., Edison, N.J., 1978-81, pres., 1981-83; pres. consumer products SCM Corp., N.Y.C., 1983-86; chmn., chief exec. officer Smith-Corona Corp., New Canaan, Conn., 1986-89, chmn., pres., chief executive officer, 1989—; bd. dirs. Smith Corona Ltd., U.K., Singapore, Can., Histacourt Corp., OSI. Bd. dirs. Internat. Tennis Hall of Fame, United Way of New Canaan, 1989; chmn. EC-92 Standards Com. U.S. Dept. of Commerce; mem. bus. alumni adv. coun., U. Colo., 1989—; mem. The Pres.'s Export Coun. Recipient Disting. Bus. Alumni award U. Colo., 1990. Mem. Computer and Bus. Equipment Mfg. Assn. (bd. dirs.), Industry Sector Adv. Coun., U.S. Dept. Commerce, Sales and Mktg. Execs. Internat. (trustee), St. John Assn. (bd. dirs., pres.), Atrium Villa Assn. (bd. dirs., treas.), New Canaan Field Club, Woodway Country Club, Seabright Lawn Tennis Club, Landmark Club, The Club at Seabrook Island, Wilton Riding Club (bd. govs. 1980-83), Navesink Country Club (bd. govs. 1981-83), Chi Psi. Episcopalian. Home: 98 South Ave New Canaan CT 06840-5721 Office: Smith Corona Corp 65 Locust Ave New Canaan CT 06840-4725

THOMPSON, GLENN HIRAM, JR., geology educator; b. Cherry Tree, Pa., Sept. 16, 1936; s. Glen H. and Mary A. (Auden) T.; m. Dayle Beverly, July 25, 1981. BS in Music Edn., Ind. U. of Pa., 1958; MEd in Earth Sci., Pa. State U., 1968. High sch. band dir. Sykersville (Pa.) Area Schs., 1958-62, Lewistown (Pa.) Area Schs., 1962-65; earth sci. tchr. Carlisle (Pa.) Area Schs., 1965-69; assoc. prof. earth sci. Elizabethtown (Pa.) Coll., 1969—. Author: Geomorphology of Lower Susquehanna River, 1990. Chmn. orgn. com. Strand/Capital Ctr. for Performing Arts, York, Pa., 1988—. Recipient

Citizen Svc. award Gov. Commonwealth of Pa., 1990. Mem. Geol. Soc. Am., Nat. Assn. Geology Tchrs., Nat. Speleological Soc., Nat. Theatre Orgn. Soc. Office: Elizabethtown Coll One Alpha Dr Elizabethtown PA 17022

THOMPSON, HERBERT WALTER, retired education educator, minister; b. Lincolnton, N.C., Sept. 22, 1915; s. John Wesley and Hester (Connor) T.; m. Elizabeth Gibbs; children: Betty Thompson Brown, James W., Linda K., Elaine Thompson Jones. BSc with honors, N.C. A&T State U., 1939, MS, 1953; EdD, Pa. State U., 1964. Cert. prin., N.C.; lic. minister Bapt. Ch., 1983; ordained to ministry Bapt. Ch., 1992. Prin., tchr. Tucker's Grove Sch., Lincolnton, 1935, Glen Alpine Sch., Burke County, N.C., 1942-43; mgr. labor camp USDA, N.C., Va., S.C., Fla., 1939-42, 44-46; tchr. USN, Bainbridge and Norfolk, Va., 1944-46; tchr. math. and social studies Catawba (N.C.) Rosenwald High Sch., 1947-54, prin., 1954-64; chmn. dept. edn. Livingstone Coll., Salisbury, N.C., 1964-68; prof. edn., chmn. dept. Del. State Coll., Dover, 1968-80; ret., 1980; assoc. pastor Eight St. Bapt. Ch., Dover, 1992—; mem. Del. Post Secondary Edn. Commn., Dover, 1968-80, Del. Long Range Planning Commn., 1968-80. Author book, monographs; contbr. articles to profl. jours. Mem. Dover Dem. Com., 1968-89; advisor Sunday Sch. Commn., Dover, 1968-80; v.p. West Dover Heights Assn., 1972; mem. Dem. Senatorial Com., Washington, 1987-89; With USNR, 1942-44. Mem. Black Educators Legis. Com., Pa. State U. Alumni Assn., NAACP, Kappa Delta Pi, Alpha Phi Alpha. Home: 16 Taylor Dr Dover DE 19901

THOMPSON, JACK LYLE, heliport developer; b. San Jose, Calif., Apr. 29, 1947; s. John Leslie and Margaret (Wilson) T.; separated; 1 child, Stephen Perry. BA in History, The Ohio State U., 1969; MS in Systems Mgmt., U. So. Calif., 1978. Cert. comml. pilot, instrument, multi-engine fixed wing & helicopter pilot. Aviation specialist Ohio Dept. of Transp., Div. of Aviation, Columbus, 1978-84; ops. analyst Systems Control Technology, Inc., Arlington, Va., 1984-91; dir. ops. Vertiport Systems, Inc., Washington, 1991—; dir. Helicopter Found. Internat., Alexandria, Va., 1989—. Co-author FAA tech. reports. Co-chmn. Brookside Woods Civic Assn., Worthington, Ohio, 1979. Capt. USMC, 1969-78. Recipient Cert. of Commendation FAA, 1983, 84. Mem. Helicopter Assn. Internat., Mid-Atlantic Helicopter Assn. (pres. 1984-88), Ohio Helicopter Pilots Assn., Am. Helicopter Soc., Nat. Fire Protection Assn. (sec. NFPA 418 1985-87), Marine Corps Aviations Assn., Vietnam Helicopter Pilots Assn. Republican. Home: 807 Duke St Alexandria VA 22314-3623 Office: Vertiport Systems Inc 200 G St NE Washington DC 20002-4328

THOMPSON, JEWEL TAYLOR, music educator; b. Kinsale, Va., Oct. 27, 1935; d. Waverly Edward and Ella Joyce (Holman) Taylor; m. Leon Everette Thompson, June 10, 1961 (dec. June 1983); children: Sonca Patrice, Miya Kateri. BS, Va. State U., 1956; MA, Eastman Sch. of Music, 1960, PhD, 1982. Asst. prof. Va. State U., Petersburg, 1960-62, W.Va. State Coll., Institute, 1967-68, W.Va. Inst. Tech., Montgomery, 1968-72; adj. asst. prof. Hunter Coll., CUNY, 1972-85, asst. prof., 1985-90, assoc. prof., 1990—; organist Abyssinian Bapt. Ch., N.Y.C., 1978-83, minister of music, choirmaster, 1983—. Author: Samuel Coleridge-Taylor, 1981; composer and arranger numerous compositions. Hattie M. Strong Found. fellow, 1959-60, Ford Found. fellow, 1974-77; Prince Hall Masons grantee, 1977-78; named Dame of Honour, Knights of Malta, 1982. Mem. ASCAP, Am. Women Composers, Inc., Music Theory Soc. N.Y. State, Links, Inc. (chair arts program), United Negro Coll. Fund (scholarship selection com.). Home: 1425 Lozier Pl Teaneck NJ 07666-5106 Office: CUNY Hunter Coll 695 Park Ave New York NY 10021-5085

THOMPSON, JOHN ROBERT, architect; b. Bethesda, Md., Sept. 8, 1955; s. James J. and Audrey (Grooms) T. BArch, U. Md., 1979. Architect Greenwell Goetz Architects, Washington, 1979-86, v.p., 1986-88; prin. John Thompson Architects, Washington, 1988—. Vol. Emmaus Svcs. for the Aging, Washington, 1986-87, D.C. Habitat for Humanity, Washington, 1991. Mem. AIA, Nat. Coun. Architects Registration Bds. Office: John Thomnpson Architects 4411 Q St NW Washington DC 20007-2016

THOMPSON, JOSEPH B., photography company owner; b. Camden, N.J., Sept. 22, 1937; s. Joseph B. Sr. and Carolyn (Magonigle) T.; m. Joyce C. Gard, Dec. 16, 1960; children: Pam, Joseph B. III. BS, Drexel U., 1964. V.p. Quaker Photo Svcs., Phila., 1958-65; group mfg. mgr. McGraw Hill, Inc., N.Y.C., 1965-70; pres., owner Berry & Homer, Inc., Phila., 1970—, Antonelli Insts., Phila., 1974—; coun. Pa. Adv. Coun., 1982-85. Trustee Winona, 1983—. Recipient Liberty Bell award Mayor of Phila., 1981, Valley Forge Gold Medal award Freedom Found. of Valley Forge, Pa., Citation, Commonwealth Pa., 1985, Phila. City Coun.; named U.S. Congl. Record, 1988. Mem. Prof. Photographers Am., Nat. Assn. Trade and Tech. Schs. (Outstanding Mem. award 1988), Exhibit Designers and Producers Assn., Pa. Assn. Pvt. Sch. Adminstrs., Inc., Soc. Comml. Photographers of Dela. Valley, Phila. C. of C. Office: Berry & Homer Inc 2035 Richmond St Philadelphia PA 19125-4388

THOMPSON, KAY FRANCIS, dentist; b. Pitts.; d. Lony C. and Betha E. (Porter) T.; m. Ralph P. Krichbaum, Jan. 10, 1959. BS, U. Pitts., 1951, DDS, 1953. Pvt. practice dentistry Pitts., 1953—; assoc. prof. U. Pitts., Behavioral Sci., Dentistry, Pitts., 1970-80, W.Va. U. Sch. Dentistry, Morgantown, 1980—; dentist for handicapped Robinson Devel. Ctr., McKees Rocks, Pa., 1976—; cons. Nat. Inst. Health, Washington, 1975—, VA Hosp., Pitts., 1978—; lectr. and educator various med. dental and psychol. assns. Contbr. articles to profl. jours. Chmn. Dental Legis. Fund Pa., Pitts., 1981-83; mem. World Affairs Coun., Pitts., 1980—, Pa. Dental Polit. Action Com., Harrisburg; bd. dirs. Am. Dental Polit. Action Com., Washington, 1985-90; trustee U. Pitts., 1988-91; mem. Amdental Assoc. Govt. Svcs., 1990—. Recipient Erickson award De Nederlands Vereniging voor Hypnotherapie, 1983, Bicentennial Medallion of Distinction, U. Pitts., 1988, Alumnae of the Yr., 1991. Fellow Am. Coll. Dentists, Internat. Coll. Dentists, Am. Soc. Clin. Hypnosis (pres. 1972-73, scientific 1970), Soc. Clin. and Exptl. Hypnosis (exec. bd. 1976-80), Pierre Fauchard Acad.; mem. Am. Assn. Women Dentists (trustee 1982—, Pres.'s award 1986), Pa. Dental Assn. (sec. 1984-88, pres. 1989-90), U. Pitts. Dental Alumni Assn. (pres. 1988-91). Lutheran. Office: PO Box 16141 Pittsburgh PA 15242-0141

THOMPSON, LARRY JAMES, journalist, editor, author; b. Allentown, Pa., Sept. 6, 1952; s. James Kent and Carol Ann (Sopper) T.; divorced; children: Dana Wynn, Julia Marie. BS in Biology, Kutztown U., 1976; MS in Molecular Biology, Lehigh U., 1982. Reporter The Morning Call, Allentown, 1976-78, med. editor, 1978-84; TV writer Med star Comm., Allentown, 1979-85; sci. and medicine editor San Jose (Calif.) Mercury News, 1982-84; asst. editor health The Washington Post, 1984-86, sci. editor health, 1986-92; Sci. Jour. panelist PBS, Washington, 1988-89. Contbr. articles to profl. jours. Dorothy Rider Pool fellow Yale U. Sch. Med., 1977-78. Mem. AAAS, Nat. Assn. Sci. Writers, D.C. Sci. Writers' Assn. (co-founder 1987, pres. 1989, bd. dirs.). Democrat. Roman Catholic. Home and Office: 6526 Elgin Ln Bethesda MD 20817

THOMPSON, LORAN TYSON, lawyer; b. N.Y.C., Dec. 23, 1947; s. Kenneth Webster and Mary (Tyson) T.; m. Meera Eleanora Agarwal, Apr. 2, 1976. BA magna cum laude, Amherst Coll., 1969; MA, Harvard U., 1970, JD, 1976. Bar: N.Y. 1977, U.S. Tax Ct. 1977, U.S. Claims Ct. 1977. Assoc. Breed, Abbott & Morgan, N.Y.C., 1976-83, ptnr., 1983—. Mem. ABA, N.Y. State Bar Assn. (exec. com., tax sect. 1991—, co-chmn. com. on non-qualified employee benefits 1991—), Phi Beta Kappa. Home: 79 W 12th St Apt 12G New York NY 10011-8510 Office: Breed Abbott & Morgan 153 East 53d St New York NY 10022

THOMPSON, LYNN POUCHER, artist; b. Plainfield, N.J., July 22, 1922; d. Ralph Irving and Margaret Morgan (Thomas) Poucher; m. David Duvall Thompson; children: David Duvall Jr., Richard Morgan, Catherine McKee, Peter Lynn. Student, Bennett Jr. Coll., 1939-40; BSc, Douglas Coll., 1943; MD, Cornell Med. Coll., 1946. Fellow Rockefeller Inst., N.Y.C., 1946-52; art chmn. N.Y. Hosp., N.Y.C., 1972-88; artist Khanbegian Gallery, Bar Harbor, Maine, 1979-85; dir. Mainescape Gallery, Bar Harbor, 1985—; art cons. Hosp. Audiences Inc., N.Y.C., 1982—; art dir. Child Life Ctr., N.Y. Hosp., N.Y.C., 1985—; co-dir. circulating Art Program, N.Y.C., 1977—; dir. N.Y. Hosp. Art Commn., 1966-74, 77-80, Child Life Ctr., N.Y.C., 1982—; instr. watercolor Sonogee, Bar Harbor, 1979—. One-person shows Bergen Mus., Paramus, N.J., 1974, El Molino, Spain, 1979, Federated Art Assn. N.J. State Mus., Trenton, 1975, N.Y. Physicians Art Assn. Ann., Union Carbide, 1976, N.Y. Physicians Art Exhbn., N.Y. Acad. Medicine, 1976-79; commd. George Moore, Sotogrande, Spain, 1980, Dr Eibl, Vienna, 1980, Drawing Rm., Pennsula, Ohio, 1981, N.Y. Hosp., 1983. Mem. Citizens Edn. Coun., Tenafly, N.J., 1975-77; pres. PTA, Tenafly, 1975. Recipient Vol. of Yr. award N.J. Assn. Health Care Facilities, 1983, Helen Hayes award Vol. Bur., N.J., 1986, prize Duncan Gallery, N.Y.C. and Paris, 1975, 1st and 2d awards N.Y. Physicians Art Assn. Ann., 1976-79, Bocour award Oran; Eastman Kodak grantee, Rochester, N.Y., 1991—. Mem. Am. Watercolor Soc. (assoc.), Allied Artists Am., Soc. Med. Art Adminstrs. (exec. com. 1990—), N.Y. Physicians Art Assn. (exec. com. 1976-81), Soc. Healtcare Adminstrs. (exec. com. 1991—), Salmagundi Club, Catherine Lorillard Wolfe Club, Bergen County Artists Guild. Episcopalian. Home: 11 Creston Ave Tenafly NJ 07670-2905 Office: Mainescape Gallery 54 West St Bar Harbor ME 04609-1858

THOMPSON, MICHAEL WILLIAM, aerospace engineer; b. Great Falls, Mont., Aug. 3, 1963; s. William John and Nancy (Hagglund) T.; m. Lisa Ann Sachs, Sept. 15, 1990; 1 child, Ryan Michael. BS in Aerospace Engring. summa cum laude, U. Notre Dame, 1985, MS in Aerospace Engring., 1986. Propulsion engr. applied physics lab. Johns Hopkins U., Laurel, Md., 1986—. Contbr. articles to profl. jours. Mem. AIAA. Republican. Roman Catholic. Office: Johns Hopkins U Applied Physics Lab Johns Hopkins Rd Laurel MD 20707

THOMPSON, MOZELLE WILLMONT, lawyer; b. Pitts., Dec. 11, 1954; s. Charles and Eiko (Suzaki) T. AB, Columbia U., 1976; M in Pub. Affairs, Princeton U., 1980; JD, Columbia U., 1981. Bar: N.Y. 1984, D.C. 1984, U.S. Dist. Ct. (ea. dist.) Mich. 1984, U.S. Dist. Ct. (so. and ea. dists.) N.Y. 1985, U.S. Ct. Appeals (11th cir.) 1986. Clk. to presiding judge U.S. Dist. Ct. (so. dist.) Fla., Miami, 1981-82; assoc. Skadden, Arps, Slate, Meagher & Flom, N.Y.C., 1982-90; spl. counsel to supr. Town of Babylon, N.Y., 1988-90; counsel and sec. N.Y. State Housing Fin. Agy., N.Y.C.; counsel, sec. N.Y. State Med. Care Facilities Fin. Agy., N.Y. State Affordable Housing Corp., N.Y. State Mcpl. Bond Bank Agy., N.Y. State Project Fin. Agy.; gen. counsel North Amityville Community Econ. Coun., Inc., 1989-90; pres. Greenwich Corp., 1987—; adj. assoc. prof. Bklyn. Law Sch., 1986; bd. dirs. ATT Prodns., N.Y.C. Mem. exec. bd. Practicing Attys. for Law Students, N.Y.C., 1986—. Mem. ABA (coms. litigation, tort and ins. practice 1984—), N.Y. State Bar Assn., N.Y. County Lawyers Assn. (com. on fed. cts. 1984-86), D.C. Bar Assn., Assn. of Bar of City of N.Y., Assn. Princeton Grad. Alumni, Assn. Black Princeton Alumni, Columbia Law Sch. Alumni Assn., Columbia Coll. Alumni Assn., Columbia Black and Latino Alumni Assn., Columbia Coll. Class 1976 (pres. 1986—). Home: 822 Greenwich St Apt 4A New York NY 10014-5166 Office: NYS Housing Fin Agy 3 Park Ave New York NY 10016-5902

THOMPSON, RICHARD LEON, pharmaceutical company executive, lawyer; b. Rochester, N.Y., Dec. 5, 1944; s. Leslie L. and Marion (Cosad) T.; m. Catherine Jean Terry, July 6, 1974; children: Kristin Anne, Catherine Elizabeth. AB cum laude, SUNY, Albany, 1966; MA, Syracuse U., 1967; JD, Cath. U., 1975. Staff dir., counsel U.S. Ho. of Reps., Washington, 1973-78; dir. Abbott Labs., Washington, 1978-83; v.p. Squibb Corp., Washington, 1983-89, Bristol-Myers Squibb Corp., Washington, 1989—; chmn. legis. adv. com. Proprietary Assn., Washington, 1984; bd. dirs. Bus. Govt. Rels. Coun. Mem. com. on changing enrollments Fairfax (Va.) County Pub. Sch., 1983-84, Supts. adv. com., 1984-85, mem., 1988—; chmn. legis com. P.R.-U.S.A. Found., 1985—; co-chair edn. in 2010; bd. dirs. D.C. Hospice, Bryce Harlow Found., 1990—. 1st lt. U.S. Army, 1968-69, Vietnam. Named one of Outstanding Young Men of Am., Jaycees, 1976. Mem. ABA, D.C. Bar Assn., Pharm. Mfrs. Assn. (chmn. Washington reps. com.1988), Congl. Country Club, Georgetown Club, City Club. Home: 1005 Woburn Ct Mc Lean VA 22102-2133 Office: Bristol-Myers Squibb Corp 655 15th St NW Ste 410 Washington DC 20005-5714

THOMPSON, ROBERT CLAY, government official; b. Cheverly, Md., June 16, 1949; s. Robert Bruce and Nancy (Whiteford) T.; m. Betty Ann Patrice Berling, Feb. 16, 1980; 1 child, Robert Clay Jr. BS magna cum laude, Am. U., Washington, 1975; MA, George Washington U., 1987. Spl. agt. Naval Investigative Service, Norfolk, Va., 1976-80; sr. spl. agt. Naval Investigative Service, Subic Bay, Philippines, 1980-84; desk officer Spl. Ops. div. Naval Investigative Service Hdqrs., Suitland, Md., 1984-85; dep. dir. counterintelligence and investigative program Dep. Undersec. Def. for Policy, Washington, 1986-90; asst. dep. dir. for counter-intelligence Naval Investigative Svc. Command Hdqrs., 1990—. Active Cub Scouts of Am., College Park, Md., 1954—, Boy Scouts of Am., Silver Spring, Md., 1959—, Explorer Scouts of Am., Silver Spring, 1964-67. Served as sgt. U.S. Army, 1969-72. Recipient Nat. Intelligence medal of achievement Dir. Cen. Intelligence, 1990. Mem. Fed. Criminal Investigator Assn., Phi Kappa Phi. Republican. Baptist. Home: 6853 Melrose Dr Mc Lean VA 22101-2808 Office: Naval Investigative Svc Command Hdqrs Bldg 111 Washington Navy Yard Washington DC 20388

THOMPSON, RONALD RUSSELL, involuntary mental patients rights activist; b. Dover, N.H., Oct. 14, 1942; s. Russell Earle and Georgianna (Andronopoulos) T.; m. Myrna Phyllis Tishler, June 2l, 1970 (div. 1979); m. Ariane Annick Espinasse, Dec. 2l, 1982. BA in History, Princeton U., 1964; JD, Georgetown U., 1975. Ins. adjuster Allstate Ins. Co., N.Y.C., 1967-68; with Bankers Trust Co., N.Y.C., 1968-69; pres., treas. Russ Thompson Motors, Inc., Dover, 1969-71; mem. patients rights com. Springfield State Hosp., Sykesville, Md., 1987—. Contbr. articles to profl. publs. Mem. adv. bd. Md. Protection and Advocacy Agy., Balt., 1987—, D.C. Protection and Advocacy Agy., 1988—; trustee Mental Health Law Project, Washington, 1991—. Mem. ACLU (bd. dirs. Montgomery County chpt. 1988—, Md. chpt. 1988—), D.C. Bar Assn., Nat. Assn. Psychiat. Survivors (bd. dirs., exec. bd. 1989—), Nat. Assn. Rights Prostection and Advocacy (bd. dirs. 1990—). Home and Office: 9807 Broad St Bethesda MD 20814

THOMPSON, SANDRA ROMAINE, corporate facility nurse; b. West Grove, Pa., Mar. 6, 1938; d. Thomas Walter and Florence Elizabeth (Mahan) T. Diploma in nursing, Del. Hosp., 1959. Cert. HIV infection and AIDS, N.Y. State Dept. Health, 1991, cert. HIV counselor, 1991. Staff nurse and charge nurse Mt. View Hosp., Lockport, N.Y., 1960-67; dir. nurses Newfane (N.Y.) Nursing Home, 1967-72; staff nurse Harrison Radiator Div., GM, Lockport, 1972—. Vol. AIDS Community Svcs., Buffalo, 1987, 88, 89, 90, 91, 92, 93, 94, Eastern Niagra County div. Am. Heart Assn., Buffalo, 1987, 90-94, bd. dirs, 1989-90, 91-92, 93-94, v.p. bd. dirs., 1991-92, 93-94, program com., 1989, 90, 91, 92, bd. dirs. western N.Y. region, 1991-92, pres. bd. dirs., 1992-94; active Niagra Falls chpt. Am. Cancer Soc., 1987, 90-94, bd. dirs., 1990-92; charter mem. Niagra County Healthy Heart program, 1988, 90, 91, 92, 93, 94, mem. task force on smoking cessation and obesity. Recipient Smoking Cessation Achievement award Lakeside Pharm. Co., Lockport, 1988, Program Award of Excellence Ea. Niagra County div. Am. Heart Assn., 1988, 89, 90, Program Vol. Yr. award Western N.Y. Region, 1991, Pub. Edn. Life Saver's award Niagra chpt. Am. Cancer Soc., 1988, Pub. Edn. award Am. Cancer Soc., 1989, Vol. award United Way, 1990, Community Svc. award Lockport Community Cable, 1991. Mem. Am. Assn. Occupational Health Nurses, Western N.Y. Assn. Occupational Health Nurses, N.Y. State Occupational Health Nurses, N.Y. State Am. Heart Assn. (profl. mem.). Liberal. Roman Catholic.

THOMPSON, TODD WILLIAM, insurance company executive, safety engineer; b. Harrisburg, Pa., Nov. 29, 1949. BS, Ind. U. Pa., 1971, MS, 1989. Loss control rep. Ins. Co. N.Am., Harrisburg, 1974-80, sr. loss control rep., 1980-82; mgr., mktg. support svcs. Glatfelter Ins. Group, York, Pa., 1982-88; asst. v.p., risk control svcs. Glatfelter Ins. Group, York, 1986-90, v.p., risk control svcs., 1990—; mem. York County Hwy. Safety Coun., 1988-90, chmn. 1990—; chmn. York County Safety Belt Adv. Coun., 1989—. With U.S. Army Reserve, 1971-77. Mem. Am. Soc. Safety Engrs. Home: 2339 Brandywine Ln York PA 17404-1309 Office: Glatfelter Ins Group 183 Leader Heights Rd York PA 17402

THOMPSON, WAYNE WRAY, historian; b. Wichita, Jan. 30, 1945; s. Clarence William and Elaine Maxine (Wray) T. m. Lillian Evelyn Hurlburt, June 28, 1969. BA, Union Coll., Schenectady, 1967; student, U. St. Andrews, Scotland, 1965-66; PhD, U. Calif., San Diego, 1975. Historian USAF, 1975—; historian Checkmate Air Campaign Planning Group, 1990-91; sr. hist. advisor Gulf War Air Power Survey, 1991—. Contbr. to Congress Investigates (Arthur M. Schlesinger, Jr. and Roger Bruns, editor), 1975; editor Air Leadership, 1986; contbr. War in the Pacific articles to newspapers, 1991. Served with AUS, 1971-72. Mem. Am. Hist. Assn., Orgn. Am. Historians, Air Force Hist. Found., Air Force Assn., Soc. Historians Am. Fgn. Rels., Soc. for Mil. History, U.S. Commn. on Mil. History, Inter-Univ. Seminar on Armed Forces and Soc., Assn. Asian Studies, Asia Soc., World History Assn., Phi Beta Kappa. Home: 9203 St Marks Pl Fairfax VA 22031-3045 Office: Hdqrs USAF History Bolling AFB DC 20332-6098

THOMPSON, WILLIAM, JR., engineering educator; b. Hyannis, Mass., Dec. 4, 1936; s. William and Dinella Helen (Szeliga) T.; m. Martha Marion Cate, July 4, 1959; children: Melanie A., Sharon E., Jennifer L., Keith W. SB, MIT, 1958; MS, Northeastern U., 1963; PhD, Pa. State U., 1971. Staff engr. Raytheon Co., Wayland, Mass., 1958-60; sr. engr. Cambridge (Mass.) Acoustical Assocs., 1960-66; research asst. Applied Research Lab., State College, Pa., 1966-72; asst. prof. engring. sci. Pa. State U., University Park, 1972-78, assoc. prof., 1978-85, prof., 1985—; head transducer group Applied Rsch. Lab., State College, 1971-80; sabbatic leave Naval Rsch. Lab., Orlando, Fla., 1988-89. Contbr. articles to profl. jours.; patentee in field. Bd. dirs., treas., past pres. Nittany Mountain chpt. Am. Diabetes Assn., State College, 1979—; bd. dirs., asst. treas., treas. Mid-Pa. affiliate Am. Diabetes Assn., Bethlehem, Pa., 1980-90. Recipient Disting. Svc. citation Mid-Pa. Affiliate Am. Diabetes Assn., 1981, and Affiliate Svc. award, 1988; Outstanding Teaching award Pa. State Engring. Soc., 1984. Fellow Acoustical Soc. Am. (patent reviewer of soc. jour. 1990—); mem. IEEE (sr.), Soc. Engring. Sci., Lions (pres. State Coll. 1981-82, 89-90, sec.-treas. 1984-88, 90—, dist. diabetes chmn. 1983-88, 91—, Melvin Jones fellow 1991). Republican. Home: 601 Glenn Rd State College PA 16803-3475 Office: Pa State U Dept of Engring Sci and Mechanics 230B Hammond Bldg University Park PA 16802

THOMPSON, WILLIAM GRANT, management executive; b. Westville, N.S., Can., June 27, 1925; s. Harvey Alden and Jessie (MacGregor) T.; m. Margaret Jean Mackenzie, Sept. 24, 1952; children: Heather, Anne, Andrew, Carole. Degree in bus. edns., Maritime Bus. Coll., Halifax, N.S., 1943. Chartered acct., N.S. Treas. Maritime Steel and Foundries, Ltd., New Glasgow, N.S., 1951-58; v.p, gen. mgr. EMI Elecs. Can., Ltd., Halifax, 1958-69; ptnr. Price Waterhouse, Ltd., Halifax, 1970-87, v.p., 1977-87; pres. Revenue Mgmt., Ltd., Halifax, 1987—; pres. MacCulloch & Co., Ltd., Halifax, 1983-87, Oakwood Investments, Halifax, 1983-87. Mem. Commn. Food Prices Rev. Bd., Ottawa, Ont., 1974-77; chmn. fin. com. Waterfront Devel. Corp., Halifax, 1977-81; chmn. Pine Hill Div. Hall, Halifax, 1974-79, Atlantic Sch. Theology, Halifax, 1982-85, Maritime Bd. Trustees, Sackville, N.B., 1982-88; treas., chmn. investment com. Fin. Svcs. Maritime Conf., 1988—; chmn. Windsor Elms Srs. Home, Windsor, N.S., 1983-87. Fellow Inst. Chartered Accts. N.S., Inst. Chartered Secs. and Adminstrs.; mem. Soc. Mgmt. Accts. N.S., Inst. Mgmt. Cons. Atlantic Can. Liberal. Mem. United Ch. Can. Clubs: Halifax, Saraguay. Home: 2184 Connaught Ave, Halifax, NS Canada B3L2Z3

THOMPSON, YAAKOV, rabbi; b. St. Mary's, Ohio, Dec. 2, 1954; s. Herbert and Carolyn Jean (Gallimore) T.; m. Sarah Jeffery, Dec. 30, 1982; children: Adina Michal, Benjamin Asher. BA, Ohio State U., 1977; MA, Jewish Theol. Sem. Am., 1983, DHL, 1988. Ordained rabbi, 1983. Asst. rabbi Jewish Ctr. Kew Gardens Hills, Flushing, N.Y., 1980-82; rabbi Uniondale Jewish Ctr., N.Y., 1982-84, Suburban Park Jewish Ctr., East Meadow, N.Y., 1984-88, Congregation Benai Israel of Fair Lawn, N.J., 1988—; bd. govs. L.I. Bd. Rabbis, 1985—; lectr. Jewish Welfare Bd. Lecture Bur., N.Y.C., 1986—; asst. prof. Bible Jewish Theol. Sem. Am., 1988—, Rabbinical Assembly, Nassau, Suffolk, L.I., N.Y., 1983—, com. chmn. 1986—; bd. dirs. Fair Lawn Mental Health Ctr. Contbr. articles to profl. jours. Bd. dirs. Fair Lawn Mental Health Ctr. Mem. East Meadow Interfraith Clergy Assn., N.Y. Bd. Rabbis, Soc. Bibl. Lit., Am. Acad. Religion, Assn. for Jewish Studies, Union for Traditional Conservative Judaism, Rotary Internat. Home: 28-02 Berkshire Rd Fair Lawn NJ 07410 Office: Congregation Benai Israel of Fair Lawn 30 St And Pine Ave Fair Lawn NJ 07410

THOMSEN, DONALD LAURENCE, JR., institute executive, mathematician; b. Stamford, Conn., Apr. 21, 1921; s. Donald Laurence and Linda (Comstock) T.; m. Linda Rollins Leach, June 14, 1958; children: Melinda Rollins, Katherine Long, Donald Laurence III. Grad., Phillips Exeter Acad., 1938; B.A. magna cum laude in Math., Amherst Coll., 1942; Ph.D., Mass. Inst. Tech., 1947. Teaching fellow Mass. Inst. Tech., 1942, instr., 1943-47; instr., then asst. prof. Haverford (Pa.) Coll., 1947-50; research fellow, then research engr. Jet Propulsion Lab., Calif. Inst. Tech., 1950-52; asst. prof. Pa. State U., 1952-54; with IBM Corp., 1954-72, spl. asst. to dir. edn., 1961-62, dir. profl. activities, 1963-66, corp. dir. engring. edn., 1967-72; pres. Societal Inst. of Math. Scis., New Canaan, Conn., 1972—, also bd. dirs.; mem. vis. com. Coll. Sci., Drexel Inst. Tech., 1969-71; mem. adv. com. for individualized sci. instructional system Coll. Edn., Fla. State U., 1973-75. Author: Higher Transcendental Functions, 3 vols; contbr. articles to profl. jours. Recipient spl. certificate Milw. Sch. Engring., 1969. Mem. AAAS, AAUW, Am. Math. Soc., Am. Statis. Assn., Math. Assn. Am. (chmn. com insts.), Soc. Indsl. and Applied Math. (pres. 1959, chmn. trustees 1960-72, Cert. of Merit, Inst. Math and Soc. 1983), Am. Fedn. Info. Processing Socs. (chmn. edn. com. 1965-66, chmn. U.S. com. IFIP Congress 1968, 66-69, bd. dirs. 1969-77, exec. com. 1975-77), Assn. Computing Machinery, Am. Ordnance Assn. (chmn. research div.), Internat. Fedn. Info. Processing (chmn. exhibits com. N.Y.C. Congress 1965), Conf. Bd. Math. Scis. (chmn. budget and fin. com.), Conn. Acad. Arts and Scis., Phi Beta Kappa, Sigma Xi, Delta Tau Delta. Presbyn. Clubs: Cosmos (Washington); The Princeton (N.Y.C.); Woodway Country (Darien, Conn.). Home and Office: Societal Inst Math Scis 97 Parish Rd S New Canaan CT 06840-4424

THOMSEN, JAMES M., risk management consultant; b. Albany, N.Y., Apr. 22, 1955; s. John Edward and Rose Marie (Winslow) T.; m. Kathryn S. Hansen, July 1, 1972 (div. 1989); children: James Jr., Allison. BS in Pub. Health, Empire State Coll., 1986. Chief exec. officer with bldg. svc. firm Profl. Svcs., Albany; fire fighter Town of Colonie, N.Y., paramedic; advanced med. instr. Regional Emergency Med. Orgn., Albany; profl. safety dir. Rensselaer County Red Cross, Troy, N.Y.; tng. cons. Guilderland, N.Y.; environ. specialist RCG Boces, Schodock, N.Y.; asbestos specialist City of Troy (N.Y.) Schs.; CEO, risk mgmt. cons. Failsafe Risk Mgmt. Alternatives, Inc., Albany. Author: Ideas Whose Time Have Not Yet Come, 1992; inventor. Tng. coord. Albany County Emergency Med. Svc. course, 1982; emergency med. svc. dir. Medico, Town of Colonie, 1984; program chmn. Spl. Olympics, Albany, 1989; seat belt seminar leaders, 1987; active Midway Fire Dept., Colonie Emergency Svcs., Albany County Emergency Med. Svc. Coun., West Albany Fire Dept.; treas. Regional Emergency Med. Svc. Coun.; disaster chmn. REMO, Albany, 1982-84, pub. info. officer, 1982-84. Mem. ASTM (task group chmn. 1984-89), Am. Heart Assn. (ECC chmn., recipient Outstanding Program 1984). Episcopalian. Office: Failsafe Risk Mgmt Alternatives 433 River St Bldg E Troy NY 12180

THOMSON, ALEXANDER BENNETT, JR., financial planner, tax and management consultant; b. Wyandotte, Mich., Sept. 1, 1954; s. Alexander Bennett and Norma Lee (Fields) T.; m. Rita Elizondo, May 8, 1982; 1 child, Luis Joaquin Elizondo. Student Eastern Mich. U., 1972-74, Kalamazoo Coll. 1975-77; MA, Antioch Sch. Law, 1983. Cert. fin. planner; chartered life underwriter, fin. cons.; registered rep., investment adviser, health underwriter. Pres. Thomson Mgmt. Group, Inc., Washington, 1977—; budget dir. The White House Conf. on Small Bus., 1979; asst. treas. Kennedy for Pres. Com. 1980, nat. scheduler, Geraldine A. Ferraro, 1984. Mem. ABA, Inst. Certified Fin. Planners, Internat. Assn. Fin. Planners, Am. Mgmt. Assn., Nat. Assn. Life Underwriters, Nat. Assn. Tax Practitioners, Nat. Assn. Security Dealers. Democrat.

THOMSON, ANGUS WILLIAM, immunologist, educator; b. Inverness, Scotland, Feb. 13, 1948; s. Angus and Jessie (MacDonald) T.; m. Robyn Gai Glover, Mar. 17, 1979; children: Andrew David, Natalie Helen, Emma Leanne. BSc with honors, U. Aberdeen, Scotland, 1970, PhD, 1974, DSc, 1986; MSc in Immunology, U. Birmingham, Eng., 1971. Rsch. fellow U.

Aberdeen, 1974-75, lectr. in pathology, 1975-81, sr. lectr. in pathology, 1982-87, reader in immunology, 1987-90; vis. fellow Kolling Rsch. Inst., Royal North Shore Hosp., Sydney, Australia, 1981-82; vis. prof. U. Pitts., 1990—; vis. prof. U. Pitts., 1990—; cons. Fisons Pharms., Loughborough, Eng., 1988—; mem. editorial bd. Transplantation, Immunology, 1989—; external examiner in immunology U. London, 1987, U. Strathclyde, Scotland, 1989—, U. Glasgow, Scotland, 1987—. Editor: Cyclosporin, 1989, The Cytokine Handbook, 1991, The Molecular Biologyh of Immunosuppression, 1992; guest editor Transplantation Procs., 1991, Immunology Letters, 1991; contbr. articles to profl. publs. Grantee Med. Rsch. Coun., 1984—, Cancer Rsch. Campaign, 1984—; Med. Rsch. Coun. travelling fellow, 1981-82. Fellow Inst. Biology, Royal Coll. Pathologists; mem. Brit. Soc. Immunology (com. mem. 1987-90), Brit. Transplantation Soc. (com. mem. 1987-90), Am. Assn. Immunologists. Mem. Ch. of Scotland. Home: 307 Cornwall Dr Pittsburgh PA 15238-2643 Office: U Pitts Dept Surgery Biomed Sci Tower Pittsburgh PA 15213

THOMSON, KEITH STEWART, science museum administrator; b. Heanor, Eng., July 29, 1938; s. Ronald William and Marian Adelaide (Coster) T.; m. Linda Gailbreath Price, Sept. 27, 1963; children: Jessica Adelaide, Elizabeth Rose. B.Sc. with honors, U. Birmingham, Eng., 1960; A.M., Harvard U., 1961, Ph.D. (NATO fellow), 1963. NATO postdoctoral fellow Univ. Coll., London U., 1963-65; asst. prof. to prof. biology Yale U., 1965-87; dean Yale U. (Grad. Sch.), 1979-87; dir. Peabody Mus. Natural History, 1976-79; pres. Acad. Natural Scis., Phila., 1987—; dir. Sears Found. Marine Research and Oceanographic History; hon. research fellow Australian Nat. U., 1967; trustee, mem. corp. Woods Hole Oceanographic Instn.; bd. dirs. Wistar Inst., Cen. Phila. Devel. Corp, Wetlands Inst.; researcher in vertebrate evolution. Mem. editorial bd. Paleobiology, Jour. Morphology, 1988, Aspects of Lower Vertebrate Evolution, 1968, Orgin of Terrestrial Vertebrates, 1968, Saltwater Fishes of Conn., 1971, 88, Priorities and Needs in Systematic Biology, 1981, Morphogenesis and Evolution, 1988, Living Fossil, 1991. Bd. dirs. Greater Phila. Cultural Alliance, Woods Hole Oceanographic Inst., Wiskar Inst. for Medicine, Wetlands Inst. Fellow Linnean Soc. London, Zool. Soc. London; mem. Soc. Vertebrate Palaeontology, Sigma Xi. Office: Acad Natural Scis 19th & Parkway Philadelphia PA 19103

THOMSON, TODD STUART, strategic planning consultant; b. Stanford, Calif., Jan. 30, 1961; s. Scott Dayton and Margaret Elaine (Guice) T.; m. Melissa Kay McKeithen, May 22, 1988. BA in Econs., Davidson Coll., 1983; MBA with distinction, U. Pa., 1987. Cons., sr. cons. Booz Allen & Hamilton, Bethesda, Md., 1983-85; cons., mgr. Bain & Co., Boston, 1986-91; sr. mgr. policy econs. group KPMG Peat Marwick, Washington, 1991—.

THONET, JOHN A., environmental consultant; b. Baldwin, N.Y., Aug. 4, 1950; s. John Chester and Grace W. (Keeling) T.; m. Kathi Lynn Blatt, May 1973; children: Hannah, Rebecca. BS in Forest Engring. cum laude, SUNY, Syracuse, 1972, MS, 1975. Registered profl. engr., Mass., N.J., Mich., W.Va., profl. planner, N.J.. Environ. engr. Power Authority of State of N.Y., N.Y.C., 1973-74; project mgr., civil engr. Tippetts Abbett McCarthy Stratton Engrs. & Architects, N.Y.C., 1974-79; assoc. Dresdner Assocs. Environ. Land Use Planning Cons., Summit, N.J., 1979-80; owner, prin. environ. cons. Thonet Assocs., Environ. Cons., Livingston, N.J., 1980—. Contbr. articles to profl. jours. Mem. ASCE, Soc. Am. Foresters, N.J. Soc. Profl. Engrs., Nat. Assn. Environ. Profls. Office: Thonet Assocs Environ Planning & Design Cons 14 S Orange Ave South Orange NJ 07079-1702

THOR, PAUL VIETS, personal computer specialist; b. Schenectady, N.Y., Mar. 10, 1946; s. Donald D. and Eleanor B. (Viets) T.; m. Barbara K. Nelson, Mar. 27, 1982. BSME, U. Denver, 1968; MS in Engring. Mgmt., UCLA, 1976; postgrad., George Mason U., 1990—. Engr. Martin Marietta Corp., Denver, 1968-69; commd. 2d lt. USAF, 1969, advanced through grades to maj., 1982; pilot trainee USAF-Williams AFB, Phoenix, Ariz., 1970-71; pilot C141A 15 MAS-Norton AFB, San Bernardino, Calif., 1971-75, pilot C141B, 1981-84; communications and computer officer 2044 CG-Pentagon, Washington, 1977-81; air field mgr. 18TFW-Kadena AB, Okinawa, Japan, 1984-86; pilot C12 1402 MAS-Andrews AFB, Washington, 1986-87; communications and computer officer 7 Communications Group-Pentagon, Washington, 1987-89; cons. George Mason U., Fairfax, Va., 1990—; wing flight examiner 63 MAW-Norton AFB, San Bernardino, 1981-84; acquisitions officer 7th Communications Group-Pentagon, 1987-89. Mem. Air Force Assn. (life), Ret. Officers Assn. Home and Office: 5435 Silver Dr Colorado Springs CO 80918

THORBECKE, WILLEM HENRY, international company executive, consultant; b. Paris, July 4, 1924; s. Willem Johan Rudolf and Madelaine (Salisbury) T.; m. Sonya Stokowski, June 8, 1946; children: Noel Evangeline, Johan Rudolf, Willem Leif, Christine Louise, BS in Engring., MIT, 1948, BS in Bus. Adminstrn., 1948. Exec., Royal Dutch Shell, N.Y.C., London, Tokyo, 1948-60, Mobil Corp., N.Y.C., 1960-69; cons. various cos., N.Y.C., Chgo., Houston, Tokyo, Taipei, Manila, Bangkok, Singapore, Paris, others, 1969-75; pres. Dravo Internat., Pitts., 1975-82, W.H. Thorbecke Assocs., Sewickley, Pa., 1982—; chmn., chief exec. officer Energy Support Svcs. Inc., Coraopolis, Pa., 1982-87, dir., 1987-90. Dir. World Affairs Council, Pitts., 1978—; chmn. MIT Enterprise Forum, Pitts., 1987-89. Flight lt. RAF, 1942-46, ETO. Decorated D.F.C., RAF; named tri-state area Entrepreneur of Yr. Venture Mag., 1987. Mem. Am. Mgmt. Assn. (internat. council 1977-83), Nat. Assn. Corp. Dirs. Republican. Episcopalian. Clubs: Duquesne (Pitts.), Haagse (The Netherlands). Home: Deer Haven Farm Stonedale Rd Sewickley PA 15143 Office: Energy Support Svcs Inc PO Box 26 Sewickley PA 15143-0026

THOREN, DANIEL EVAN, education educator; b. Worcester, Mass., Apr. 2, 1944; s. Sven Evan and Beatrice Maude (Putnam) T.; m. Beverly Alice Craft, Jan. 28, 1966; children: Caroline, Matthew, Christopher. BA in Polit. Sci., Heidelberg Coll., 1966; MPA, U. Detroit, 1970. Faculty Atlantic Community Coll., Mays Landing, N.J., 1970—; hon. vis. fellow York U., Eng., 1978-79; mid-career fellow Princeton (N.J.) U., 1986-87. Mayor Mullica Twp., Elwood, N.J., 1986-89, councilman, 1973-76. Mem. N.J. Bus. Adminstrs. Assn. (v.p. 1984-85). Democrat. Mem. Christian Ch. Home: PO Box 10 Egg Harbor City NJ 08215-0011 Office: Atlantic CC Black Hore Pike Mays Landing NJ 08330

THORNBURG, MARY LOU, physical education educator; b. Waukesha, Wis., June 19, 1937; d. William Howard and Eleanor (Sawyer) T. BS, U. Wis., LaCrosse, 1958; MS in Phys. Edn., U. N.C., Greensboro, 1963; PhD, U. Iowa, 1967. Cert. tchr., supr., adminstr., Mass. Tchr. Nicolet High Sch., Glendale, Wis., 1958-61; grad. asst. U. N.C., Greensboro, 1961-62; instr. U. Iowa, Iowa City, 1962-64; from instr. to prof. phys. edn. Bridgewater (Mass.) Coll., 1964—; program evaluator Mankato (Minn.) State U., 1980, Wooster Coll., Ohio, 1985, Seton Hall U., N.J., 1985; mem. Gov. Commn. for Fitness and Sport, Mass., 1973-76; dir. Suburban Hockey Day Camp, Dedham, Mass., 1973-84; mem. S.E. Regional Edn. Adv. Coun., Lakeville, Mass., 1979-91. Chair Mountain Lakes (N.H.) Recreation Com., 1990—; mem. Mountain Lakes Five Yr. Planning Com., 1988—. Recipient Honor award NAGWS, 1984. Mem. AAHPERD (bd. govs. 1984-86, 91—, Honor award 1989), NASPE (pres. 1984-85, rep. to bd. govs. 1991—), NCATE (mem. coun., bd. dirs. 1979-91), EAPECW (v.p. 1977-78), COPPE (chair 1987-88), Mass. Assn. Health Phys. Edn. Recreation and Dance (v.p., pres. 1970-73, Joseph McKenney award 1985, Honor award 1974), USFHA (umpire chair, adminstrv. coun. 1980-82). Home: 64 Carey Rd Needham MA 02194-1104 Office: Bridgewater State Coll Park Ave Bridgewater MA 02325-0001

THORNBURGH, DICK (RICHARD L. THORNBURGH), United Nations secretary, former U.S. attorney general, former governor; b. Pitts., July 16, 1932; s. Charles Garland and Alice (Sanborn) T.; m. Virginia Walton Judson, Oct. 12, 1963; children: John, David, Peter, William. B in Engring., Yale, 1954; LLB with high honors, U. Pitts., 1957; hon. degrees from 26 colls. and univs. Bar: Pa. 1958, U.S. Supreme Ct. 1965. Atty. Kirkpatrick & Lockhart, Pitts., 1959-69, 77-79, 87-88, 91-92; U.S. atty. for Western Pa. Pitts., 1969-75; asst. atty. gen. criminal div. Dept. Justice, Washington, 1975-77; gov. State of Pa., Harrisburg, 1979-87; dir. Inst. Politics, John F. Kennedy Sch. Govt., Harvard U., 1987-88; U.S. atty. gen. Washington, 1988-91; under-sec.-gen. dept. adminstrn. and mgmt. UN, N.Y.C., 1992—; del. Pa. Constl. Conv., 1967-68. Mem. Coun. on Fgn. Rels. Fellow Am. Bar Found.; mem. Am. Judicature Soc., Nat. Acad. Pub. Adminstrn. Republican. Office: UN Dept Adminstrn and Mgmt S-2700 New York NY 10017

THORNE, ELIZABETH, psychologist, psychoanalyst, lawyer; b. Evanston, Ill., Apr. 14, 1919; d. Clifford and Ruth (Latta) T. AB, Vassar Coll., 1940; JD, U. Mich., 1943; PhD, NYU, 1967. Lic. psychologist, N.Y. Lawyer Dewey, Ballantine, N.Y.C., 1943-52; pvt. practice N.Y.C., 1952—, psychoanalyst pvt. practice, 1963—, psychologist pvt. practice, 1969—. Editor: Psychoanalysis Today: A Case Book. Mem. Nat. Assn. Advancement Psychoanalysis (pres. 1985-87), Nat. Psychol. Assn. for Psychoanalysis (cert., pres. 1977-81, 87-89).

THORNE, GEORGE PAUL, JR., accountant; b. Washington, Oct. 13, 1946; s. George Thorne Sr. and Emma (Richards) Bennett; m. Sandra Jones, Jan. 15, 1965 (div. Oct. 13, 1972); 1 child, Bruce. BS in Acctg. & Fin., Roger Williams Coll., 1985; postgrad., U. Md., New Eng. Sch. of Law, 1991—. CPA, Mass. Sr. ptnr. DePaola Begg Assocs., P.C., Hyannis, Mass., 1974-84; ptnr. Hirschberg & Thorne, Hyannis, Mass., 1982-84; owner George P. Thorne Jr., CPA, Centerville, Mass., 1984—; treas. Cape Cod Contractors & Builders, Hyannis, 1978-88, Salisbury Jaycees, 1972-74. Treas. to elect Peter Morin State Rep., Centerville, 1985. Mem. AICPA, Mass. Soc. CPAs, Hyannis C. of C., Pres.'s Club Cape Code Hosp. Office: George P Thorne Jr CPA 889 Main St Centerville MA 02632-3312

THORNE, JOHN BENJAMIN, JR., human resources administrator; b. Rockville Center, N.Y., Mar. 17, 1939; s. John Benjamin and Ruth Marie (Mitchell) T.; m. Camela Theresa Di Marzio, May 16, 1975; 1 child, Kimberly Ann. BA, Center Coll., 1961; MBA, L.I. U., Greenvale, N.Y., 1985. Sales office mgr. Gelco, N.Y.C., 1965-72, mgr. sales and svc., 1972-77, mgr. communications, 1977-81, dir. human resources, 1981—. Mem. 21st Century com., chair occupational adv. coun. East Northport-Northport (N.Y.) Sch. Dist., 1990—; mem. adv. coun. Ctr. for Labor/Indsl. Rels., N.Y. Inst., 1989—; mem. adv. com. United Way, 1988—. Recipient United Cerebral Palsy Community Svc. award 1990, Community Svc. Citation Nassau County Exec. Mem. Pers. Soc. L.I. (pres. 1990-91). Office: Gelco 750 Woodbury Rd Woodbury NY 11797-2519

THORNE, SAMUEL, JR., investment company executive; b. N.Y.C., July 10, 1929; s. Samuel Sr. and Vera (Sokolova) T.; m. Elizabeth Jones; children: Susan Tierney, Samuel III, Guyton Boston. BA, Yale U., 1951. Portfolio mgr. Scudder Stevens & Clark, N.Y.C., 1955-65, gen. ptnr., 1965-85, mng. dir., 1985—; trustee Scudder Target Fund, N.Y.C., 1984-90. Trustee Greer Woodycrest Family Svcs., Millbrook, N.Y., 1975-90, Westminster Sch., Simsbury, Conn., 1985—, Leopold Schepp Found., N.Y.C., 1987—; mem. bd. overseers New Eng. Med. Ctr., Boston, 1992—. Home: 31 Harbor St Manchester MA 01944 Office: 175 Federal St Boston MA 02110-2210

THORNE, WILLIAM EDWARD, natural resource instruction; b. Milford, Conn., Oct. 5, 1954; s. William Edward and Rita Helen (O'Brien) T. BS, U. Conn., 1977, MS, 1983. Marine resources technician Nat. Marine Fisheries Svc., NOAA, Milford; agrl. apprentice Bavaria, Fed. Republic Germany; newspaper staff West Haven (Conn.) News, 1981; spl. edn. tchr. East Conn., Columbia; agrl. instr. E. O. Smith, Storrs, Conn., 1986. Mem. Planning and Zoning Commn., Town of Mansfield, Storrs, 1991. Democrat. Home: 123 Bundy Ln Storrs Mansfield CT 06268-1531 Office: E O Smith 1235 Storrs Rd Storrs Mansfield CT 06268-2287

THORNLEY, WENDY ANN, educator, sculptor; b. Bolton, Lancashire, Eng., Feb. 28, 1948; came to U.S., 1952; d. Ronald Thornley and Joan Gladys (Hancock) Green. BS, So. Conn. State U., 1970, MS, 1979; MA in LS, Wesleyan U., Middletown, Conn., 1991. Cert. tchr., Conn. Tchr. art New Canaan (Conn.) Pub. Schs., 1970-71, Bristol (Conn.) Pub. Schs., 1972—; bd. dirs. Artworks Gallery, Hartford, Conn., 1987-91. Exhibited in nat. and regional juried shows, 1978—, including tour Nat. Assn. Women Artists, 1989; commns. include wall relief Reichhold Chem. Co., 1987, Aetna Ins. Co., 1988, Bank of Boston, 1989, Law Offices Halloran, Sage, Pelon and Hagarty, 1990. Summer fellow Skidmore Coll., 1986. Mem. Nat. Art Edn. Assn., Conn. Art Edn. Assn., Nat. Assn. Women Artists, Soc. Conn. Craftsmen (bd. dirs. 1981-88, Best in Show award 1982, 84, 91, Best in Fiber award 1990), Conn. Women Artists (Binney & Smith award 1985), New Eng. Sculptors Assn. Home: 97 Summit Rd PO Box 7094 Prospect CT 06712

THORNTON, EDWARD RALPH, chemistry educator; b. Syracuse, N.Y., July 19, 1935; s. Ralph Olin and Edna Rosamund (Hettinger) T.; m. Elizabeth Dee Kaplan, Feb. 18, 1969; 1 dau., Cara Emily. B.A., Syracuse U., 1957; Ph.D. (NIH predoctoral fellow), M.I.T., 1959. NIH postdoctoral fellow MIT, 1959-60; NIH Postdoctoral fellow Harvard, 1960-61; asst. prof. chemistry U. Pa., Phila., 1961-65; assoc. prof. U. Pa., 1965-69, prof., 1969—. Author: Solvolysis Mechanisms, 1964. NIH, NSF, Petroleum Research Fund grantee. Mem. Am. Chem. Soc. (9th Phila. sect. award 1970), Fedn. Am. Scientists, Royal Soc. Chemistry (London), Am. Soc. Biochemistry and Molecular Biology, ACLU, Common Cause, Sierra Club, Phi Beta Kappa, Sigma Xi, Phi Kappa Phi, Phi Lambda Upsilon, Sigma Pi Sigma, Pi Mu Epsilon. Democrat. Home: 7 Swarthmore Pl Swarthmore PA 19081-1023

THORNTON, GEORGE FRED, physician, educator; b. Newton, Mass., Mar. 8, 1933; s. Fred Francis and Hilda Josephine (Valentine) T.; m. Roberta Yuskiewicz, May 18, 1964; children: Pamela M., G. Eric. AB, Harvard U., 1955; MD, Boston U., 1959. Diplomate Am. Bd. Internal Medicine, Am. Bd. Infectious Diseases. Intern Grace New Haven Hosp., 1959-60, resident, 1960-62; fellow Johns Hopkins U. Sch. Medicine, Allergy Infectious Disease, Balt., 1962-64; chief resident West Haven VA Hosp., 1964-65; instr. Yale U., New Haven, 1964-65, Johns Hopkins U., Balt., 1965-67; asst. prof. sch. medicine Yale U., New Haven, 1967-70, asst. clin. prof., 1970-71, assoc. clin. prof., 1971-78, clin. prof. medicine, 1978—; sr. investigator Johns Hopkins ICMRT Meningitis Rsch. Project, Calcutta, India, 1965-67; chief West Haven VA Hosp. Med. Svc. infectious disease sect., 1967-71, asst. chief Med. Svc., 1968-71, attending physician, 1971—; dir. div. medicine Waterbury Hosp., 1971—, attending physician, 1971—; assoc. clin. prof. medicine U. Conn., 1975-81, clin. prof. medicine, 1981—; cons. St. Mary's Hosp., 1971—, Yale-New Haven Hosp., 1971—, Danbury Hosp., 1972—, Charlotte Hungerford Hosp., 1972—, Milford Hosp., 1976—, Sharon Hosp., 1983—. Contbr. numerous articles and abstracts to profl. jours.; also book chpts. Surgeon USPHS, 1962-64. Fellow ACP (gov. Conn. chpt. 1989—), Infectious Disease Soc. Am. (chmn. clin. affairs 1985-89, coun. 1988-91); mem. AMA, Am. Soc. Microbiology, Am. Fedn. for Clin. Rsch., Conn. State Med. Soc., New Haven County Med. Soc., Waterbury Med. Soc., Nat. Assn. Program Dirs. Internal Medicine (coun. 1981-84), Conn. Infectious Disease Soc. (pres. 1985-87), Begg Soc., Leo F. Rettger Soc., Alpha Omega Alpha. Home: 191 Ford Rd Woodbridge CT 06525-1710 Office: Waterbury Hosp 64 Robbins St Waterbury CT 06708-2600

THORNTON, JAMES ALBERT, newspaper executive; b. Lewiston, Maine, Sept. 12, 1953; s. Frederick Joseph and Jacqueline (Fortin) T.; m. Cecile Muriel Desjardins, Oct. 18, 1975; children: Melissa, Andrea. A of Acctg., Bentley Coll., 1974, B of Mgmt., 1975; postgrad., N.H. Coll., 1991—. Acctg. mgr. Jos Kirschner Co. Inc., Augusta, Maine, 1976-82; controller Lewiston (Maine) Daily Sun, 1982-89, bus. mgr., 1989—; bd. dirs. Internat. Newspaper Fin. Execs., Reston, Va., 1989—. Mem. Lewiston C. of C., 1990—. Mem. Martindale Country Club. Office: Lewiston Daily Sun 104 Park St Lewiston ME 04240-0304

THORNTON, KATHLEEN MARY, nun, music educator; b. Worcester, Mass., Feb. 5, 1937; d. George Willis and Agnes Pearl (Carroll) T. BA, St. Joseph's Coll., 1971; affiliated tchr. & ext. faculty, Sherwood Music Sch., Chgo., 1977. Cert. elem. edn.; Sisters of Mercy, 1954—. Classroom tchr. Sacred Heart Sch., Portland, Maine, 1957-60; studio tchr., piano lessons Sisters of Mercy, Portland, 1967—. Composer Concerto in G Minor, 1990. Chorus singer Go Out Singing Co., Portland, 1980-84; chorus mem. Magic of Christmas, Portland, 1980-91; singer Embassy Theater, Portland, 1985-88; mem. Portland (Maine) Community Chorus, 1978—. Mem. Music Educators Nat. Conf. Home: 605 Stevens Ave Portland ME 04103-2691

THORNTON, NELLIE ARZELIA, university administrator; b. July 15, 1945; d. Albert and Fannie Strong; married. BA in Elem. Edn., Fisk U., Nashville, 1967; MS, CUNY, 1969, Adv. Cert. in Ednl. Adminstrn., 1971. Tchr. Robert Fulton Sch., Mt. Vernon, N.Y., 1967-71; project coord. Model Cities Program, Mt. Vernon, N.Y., 1971-74; prin. Washington Performing Arts Magnet Sch., Mt. Vernon, N.Y., 1974—; affirmative action officr Mt. Vernon Bd. Edn., 1988—; dir. Mercy Coll., Mt. Vernon, 1991—. Nat. pres. Jack and Jill of Am., Westchester County; organizer, pres. The Links, Inc., Greater Hudson Valley chpt.; active Interracial Round Table, PTA; chmn. Human Rights Commn., Mt. Vernon; participant Bedford Hills Prison Program; cons. for day care ctrs. Recipient Leadership award Westchester Woman's Cultural Experience, 1979, Spl. Award for Ednl. Accomplishments Key Women of Am., 1986; named Prin. of the Yr. 1987; named A Woman for All Years, Mt. Vernon Bd. Edn., 1989; inducted into Trailblazer Hall of Fame by Phalanx of African-Am. Men, 1989. Mem. Nat. Assn. Elem. Sch. prins., Nat. Assn. Black Bus. and Profl. Women, Nat. Coun. Negro Women, NAACP, Nat. Alliance of Black Sch. Educators, Alpha Kappa Alpha, Tau Gamma Delta. Home: 311 Hawthorne Ter Mount Vernon NY 10552-2405

THORPE, JAMES, III, publisher; b. Augusta, Ga., Sept. 10, 1942; s. James and Elizabeth (Daniells) T.; m. Diantha Chrystal, Oct. 18, 1969; 1 child, Elizabeth McLean. B.A., Swarthmore College, Pa., 1964; Ph.D., Yale U., 1968. Instr. dept. English Brandeis U., Waltham, Mass., 1968-69, Hunter Coll., N.Y.C., 1969-73; editor Shoe String Press, Hamden, Conn., 1974—, pres., 1980—, chmn. bd., 1982—. Fulbright Found. fellow, 1964-65; Woodrow Wilson fellow, 1964; Danforth Found. fellow, 1964-68. Office: Shoe String Press Inc 925 Sherman Ave PO Box 4327 Hamden CT 06514

THRALL, RICHARD CAMERON, JR., broadcasting executive; b. Delaware, Ohio, Nov. 13, 1929; s. Richard Cameron and Pauline (Taylor) T.; m. Nancy Burrows, June 7, 1952 (div. Jan. 1962); children: Vallerie E. Alm, Cynthia L. Graser; m. Shirley Annette, Oct. 6, 1962; children: Laurie Jo, James W. BA, Miami U., Oxford, Ohio, 1951. Producer, dir. Sta. WBNS-TV, Columbus, Ohio, 1951-57; producer, dir. Sta. KDKA-TV, Pitts., 1957-59, pub. affairs dir., 1959-63, asst. program dir., 1963-67; program mgr. Sta. WLWC, Columbus, 1967-68; mgr. corp. TV Avco Broadcasting, Cin., 1968-70, mgr. TV programming, 1970-76; v.p. programming Multimedia Broadcasting., Cin., 1976-82; sr. v.p. Multimedia Entertainment, Cin., 1982-84; sr. v.p., gen. mgr. Multimedia Entertainment of Tenn., Nashville, 1984-88; sr. v.p. ops. and adminstrn. Multimedia Entertainment, N.Y.C., 1988—. Writer numerous TV scripts and songs. Mem. Rep. Nat. Com. Served with USN, 1947-48. Recipient Outstanding Country Special award Music City News, Nashville, 1983-87; named to Hon. Order Ky. Cols. Mem. Nat. Assn. TV Program Execs. Internat., Country Music Assn., Acad. Country Music, Nashville Entertainment Assn. (pres. 1987-88), NATAS (pres. Columbus/Dayton/Cin. chpt. 1980-83, bd. dir. 85-87, chmn. nat. awards com. 1989—, winner regional Emmys and Emmy cert.), Nashville Talent Dirs. Assn. (sec. 1986-88). Congregationalist. Office: Multimedia Entertainment 75 Rockefeller Pla 22d Fl New York NY 10019

THRASHER, PAUL MCNEEL, III, accountant; b. Washington, Oct. 25, 1950; s. Paul McNeel Jr. and Vesta Harvey (Cassedy) T.; m. Ellen Mishkind, Dec. 22, 1974; children: Paul McNeel IV, Andrew Leland. BA in Econs., Georgetown U., 1976, MS in Acctg., 1978. CPA, D.C., Va. Supr. Coopers & Lybrand, Washington, 1978-83; mgr. acctg. Fed. Home Loan Mortgage Corp., Reston, Va., 1983-84; v.p., chief fin. officer Realty Ptnrs. Corp., Washington, 1984-86; ptnr. Halt, Jackson & Thrasher, Alexandria, Va., 1986—. Treas. Caribbean Hosp. Relief Fund, Washington, 1981-85; exec. advisor Jr. Achievement, Washington, 1984-85. Mem. Am. Inst. CPAs (apptd. cons. svcs. standards com. 1991—), D.C. Inst. CPAs (chmn. mgmt. adv. svcs. com. 1989-91, bd. govs. 1991—), Am. Showcase Theater (trustee, treas. 1990-91). Democrat. Roman Catholic. Home: 5059 Macarthur Blvd NW Washington DC 20016-3313 Office: Halt Jackson & Thrasher 99 Canal Center Plz Alexandria VA 22314-1588

THROCKMORTON, WILLIAM ROBERT, SR., sociologist; b. Washington, Feb. 28, 1923; s. Robert William and Katharine Eleanor (Crook) T.; m. Rosemary Anne Phillips, Sept. 11, 1943; children: William Robert, Nancy Elizabeth, Peter Joseph, Patricia Anne; m. Sharon Ann Jarrett, Aug. 18, 1961; children: Theresa Cecilia, Elizabeth Jean, Thomas Cleon. AB, George Washington U., 1954, postgrad., 1954-58. Br. mgr. Western Union Tel. Co., Washington and Alexandria Va., 1941-44, 46-48; libr. asst. Washington Pub. Libr., 1948-49; clk., stenographer So. Ry., Washington, 1949-50; spl. class tchr., pub. schs. Washington, 1954-56; probation officer Arlington County Juvenile Ct., 1957; rsch. asst., population rsch. project George Washington U., 1957; instr. Washington Sch. for Secs., 1958-60; asst. to counsel, office mgr. U.S. Senate, 1960-66; manpower analyst Dept. Labor, 1966-79; nat. coord. Fed. Bonding Program, 1980—; pvt. cons. in criminal justice, 1980—; asst. professorial lectr. sociology George Washington U., 1960-76. Mem Keyman, United Givers Fund, 1969-72; treas. Fairfax County Commn. for Women, 1977-81. With USAAF, 1944-46, Korea, Japan. Recipient Disting. Achievement award Dept. Labor, 1974. Mem. Lester F. Ward (treas. 1954), So. Sociol. Socs., D.C. Sociol. Soc., Am. Sociol. Assn., Am. Soc. Criminology, George Washington Univ. Faculty Club. Democrat. Roman Catholic.

THROWER, FREDERICK MITCHELL, III, advertising executive; b. N.Y.C., Jan. 16, 1968; s. Frederick Mitchell and Lori (Terhorst) T. BA, St. Lawrence Coll., 1990; SA, Yale U., 1989; student, Regent St. Diplomatic Acad., London, 1988. Cert. CPR. Counselor Open Line Counseling, Westport, Conn., 1985-86; promotions coord. WICC Radio, Bridgeport, Conn., 1986-87; intern Walt Disney World Prodns., Lake Buena Vista, Fla., 1987-88; author, rsch. staff Small Bus. Bur. Conservative Cen. Office, London, 1988-89; pres., chief exec. officer Coll. Connection, Inc., Westport, 1990—; cons., educator Staples High Sch., Westport, 1991—. Author: The Small Business Guide to Small Business Awards, 1989, The Passport-A Student's Best Resource Overseas, 1991. Chmn. and coord. UN Student Fellowship, 1991—; advisor Friends of the UN, 1991. Recipient Good Citizenship award DAR 1986, Jan Bruniczka Govt. award Bruniczka Found. 1986, Johanna Lambros award Lambros Found. 1984. Mem. Sigma Chi, Squadron A. Office: College Connection Inc Westport Castle 19 Newtown Turpike Westport CT 06880

THULSTRUP, ERIK WAABEN, chemist; b. Haderslev, Denmark, Oct. 14, 1941; came to U.S., 1989; s. Hans Waaben and Marie (Lange) Thulstrup; m. Lizzi Dencker Bargisen, May 6, 1966; children: Hans, Peter, Andreas. MS, Aarhus U., Denmark, 1967, PhD, 1969, Dr. Scient, 1979. Fulbright postdoctoral fellow U. Fla., Gainesville, 1968-69; assoc. prof. chemistry Aarhus U., 1972-81, chair dept., 1975-77; prof. Royal Danish S.E. Studies, Copenhagen, 1981-89; sr. specialist sci. and tech. World Bank, Washington, 1989—; vis. prof. U. Utah, Salt Lake City, 1974, 78, 81, 86, U. Fla., Gainesville, 1971, 74, 78, Bologna (Italy) U., 1985, U. Calif., Berkeley, 1985-86; chair sci. com. UNESCO Nat. Com., 1984-89. Author: Spectroscopy with Polarized Light, 1986, Elementary Polarization Spectroscopy, 1989, and 4 others; contbr. 150 scientific papers. Mem. Am. Chem. Soc., Danish Chem. Soc. Office: World Bank Rm S-6039 1818 H St NW Washington DC 20433

THUMMA, SAMUEL ANDERSON, lawyer; b. Emmetsburg, Iowa, May 2, 1962; s. H. Russell and Lanore Ava (Anderson) T. BS, Iowa State U., 1984; JD, U. Iowa, 1988. Bar: Iowa 1988, Ill. 1990, D.C. 1990. Broadcaster Sta. WOI-AM, Ames, Iowa, 1982-84; print journalist Iowa Dept. Agr., Des Moines, 1985; law clk. Commr. Seeley G. Lodwick, Washington, 1986; law clk. to hon. judge David R. Hansen, Cedar Rapids, Iowa, 1988-90; assoc. Arnold & Porter, Washington, 1990—. Contbr. articles to profl. jours. Bd. dirs. Gifts for the Homeless, Washington, 1990—. Harry S. Truman Found. scholar, 1982-87. Mem. ABA, Ill. Bar Assn., D.C. Bar Assn., Iowa Bar Assn., Order of Coif. Republican. Methodist. Office: Arnold & Porter 1200 New Hampshire Ave NW Washington DC 20036-6802

THUNMAN, NILS RONALD, academic administrator, former naval officer; b. Cleve., Feb. 26, 1932; s. Carl Erik and Julia (Lindblum) T.; m. Elizabeth Chase Caldwell, Sept. 6, 1954; children—Nils Ronald, Michael Erik. Student, U. Ill., 1950-51; BS, U.S. Naval Acad., 1954; grad., U.S. Naval Nuclear Power Sch., Vallejo, Calif., 1961, U.S. Nuclear Power Tng. Unit, Windsor, Conn., 1961; PhD in Pub. Svc. (hon.), U. West Fla., 1989;

PhD in Pub. Adminstrn. (hon.), Lincoln (Ill.) Coll., 1990. Commd. ensign U.S. Navy, 1954, advanced through grades to vice adm., 1981; engr. officer U.S.S. Shelton, 1954-57; comdg. officer U.S.S. Marysville, 1957-58; engr. officer U.S.S. Volador (submarine); instr. Nuclear Power Sch., Bainbridge, Md., 1962-63; engr. officer U.S.S. Robert E. Lee, 1963; exec. officer U.S.S. Snook, 1964-66; comdg. officer U.S.S. Plunger, 1968-71; staff billets Bur. Naval Personnel, Washington, 1966-68; staff Comdr. Submarine Force, U.S. Pacific Fleet, Pearl Harbor, Hawaii, 1971-72; sr. mem. Nuclear Propulsion Examining Bd., 1972-74; comdr. Submarine Squadron 15, Apra Harbor, Guam, Marianas Islands, 1974-76; flag officer, 1976; asst. chief naval personnel for officer devel. Bur. Naval Personnel, 1976-78; dir. mil. personnel and tng. div. Office Chief Naval Ops., Washington, 1978-79; comdr. submarine force U.S. Pacific Fleet, Pearl Harbor, 1979-81; dep. chief naval ops. for submarine warfare Washington, 1981-85; chief naval edn. and tng. Pensacola, Fla., 1985-88; ret., 1988; supt. Valley Forge Mil. Acad. and Jr. Coll., Wayne, Pa., 1990—. Trustee Lincoln Coll. Decorated Disting. Svc. medal with gold star, Legion of Merit with 3 gold stars, Navy Commendation medal with gold star, Navy Expeditionary medal, Navy Unit Commendation with Bronze Star, Meritorious Unit Commendation, Republic of Vietnam Meritorious Unit Citation. Mem. Naval Acad. Alumni Assn., Naval Submarine League, Assn. Naval Aviation, Abraham Lincoln Assn. (bd. dirs.), Phi Kappa Sigma. Home: 14 Fariston Rd Wayne PA 19087-3415 Office: Valley Forge Mil Acad & Jr Coll Wayne PA 19087

THURBER, WILLIAM BARTLETT, advertising executive; b. Boston, May 20, 1930; s. James Perry and Ruth (Burnett) T.; m. June Werchan; children: William B., Matthew C., James S.D.; m. Anne Hinderyckx; children: Pamela Ruth, Carla Marie. AB, Oberlin Coll., 1952. Account dir. J. Walter Thompson Co., Frankfurt, Germany, 1964-67; dir. J. Walter Thompson Co., Brussels, 1967-69, J. Walter Thompson Co. South Africa, Johannesburg, 1969-75; pres. Plymouth (Mass.) Air Svcs., 1977-85; pres., dir. Advt. Systems, Inc., Plymouth, 1986—; exec. v.p., dir. Parc-Ads Inc., Plymouth, 1989-92; with Advt. Systems, Inc., Plymouth, 1992—. Mem. Cape Cod Canal Region C. of C. (dir. 1989), Plymouth Aero Club. Office: Advtg Systems Inc 30 Winchester Ln Plymouth MA 02360

THUREAU, LANI CAROLE, speech-language pathologist, consultant; b. Jacksonville, Fla., Sept. 23, 1948; d. Samuel Howard and Joan (Miller) Zeigler; m. Donald Douglas Thureau, June 14, 1969. BA, U. Miami, 1970; MA, Kent State U., 1979. Cert. of clin. competence Am. Speech-Lang. Assn.; cert. tchr., Del. Speech therapist Vanguard Sch., Miami, Fla., 1970-71, Opa-Locka, Fla., 1971-73; speech-lang. pathologist Beechwood Sch., Wilmington, Del., 1979-80; speech-lang. pathologist, supr. Del. Curative Workshop, Wilmington, Del., 1980-86; speech-lang. pathologist Pilot Sch., Inc., Wilmington, Del., 1986—; cons. Del. Curative Workshop, 1986-88. Co-author, advisor (film) Del.: A Place to be Somebody, 1990. Exec. chmn. United Way, Wilmington, 1986-92. Recipient Adult Dance Silver, U.S. Figure Skating Assn., 1990, Sr. Improvement award Skating Club Del., 1988. Mem. Del. Speech Lang. Hearing Assn. (exec. coun., publicity, job bank), Skating Club of Wilmington (membership com., Level 10 Badge Improvement 1986), Delta Gamma. Home: 1605 Shipley Rd Wilmington DE 19803-3266

THURM, GIL, lawyer; b. Bklyn., Sept. 26, 1947; s. Isidore Leo and Rosalind (Greenstein) T.; m. Mary-Ellen Driscoll, Oct. 12, 1975; children: Michael Craig, Jennifer Leigh, Jeffrey Bryan. BA, Bklyn. Coll. of CUNY, 1969; JD, George Washington U., 1972, LLM in Taxation, 1974. Bar: D.C. 1973. Sr. tax staff Arthur Andersen & Co., Washington, 1972-75; v.p., chief of staff and legis. counsel Nat. Assn. Realtors, Washington, 1975-89; of counsel Arent Fox Kintner Plotkin & Kahn, Washington, 1989—; legal cons. Assn. of Global Real Estate Execs., Washington, 1989—; lectr. in field. Contbr. numerous articles to profl. jours.; contbg. editor: Jour. Real Estate Taxation "Washington Tax Watch" col., 1977—; editor Jour. Internat. Law and Econs., 1971-72; bd. advisors Housing and Devel. Reporter, 1977-88. Bd. dirs., pres. Fallswick Homeowners Assn., Potomac, Md., 1988-90; active various local, state and nat. polit. campaigns, 1975—. Recipient Outstanding Leadership award Ctrs. for Handicapped, Inc., 1988. Mem. ABA, Fed. Bar Assn. (officer tax sect. 1990—, vice chmn. 16th ann. tax law conf. 1992), D.C. Bldg. Industry Assn. (bd. dirs. 1990—), Assn. Global Real Estate Execs., Am. Soc. Assn. Execs. (coun. mem. govt. rels. section 1988-90, coun. mem. legal sect. 1991—), Greater Washington Bd. of Trade, D.C. Assn. Realtors, Greater Washington Soc. Assn. Execs., Exchequer Club of Washington. Home: 9409 Fox Hollow Dr Potomac MD 20854 Office: Arent Fox Kintner et al 1050 Connecticut Ave NW Washington DC 20036

THURSTON, DAVID E., lawyer, general counsel; b. Hartford, Conn., Apr. 16, 1957; s. Robert Charles and Carol Jean (Demson) T.; m. Gaye Winifred Hennemuth, Oct. 3, 1987; children: Perry Bishop, Demson Collin. BA, George Washington U., 1979; JD, Cath. U., 1982. Bar: Tex. 1982, Pa. 1984. Assoc. Johnson, Bromberg & Leeds, Dallas, 1982-84; assoc. Morgan, Lewis & Bockius, Phila., 1984-85, N.Y.C., 1985; assoc. Shea & Gould, N.Y.C., 1986-87; v.p., gen. counsel The Binswanger Co., Phila., 1987—. Recipient AmJur award in property Lawyers Co-op Pub. Co. Mem. ABA, Pa. Bar Assn., Tex. Bar Assn., Vesper Club. Republican. Office: Binswanger Co 1635 Market St 7 Penn Ctr Philadelphia PA 19103

THURUTHICKARA, JOHN CHANDY (T.C. JOHN THURUTHICKARA), systems engineer; b. Arakulam, Kerala, India, Oct. 9, 1955; came to U.S., 1980; s. Chandy Devasia Thuruthickara and Brigette (Joseph) Panackel; m. Apnanol Antony Thaliath, June 29, 1992. BSME, Coll. Engring., Trivandrum, Kerala, 1977; M in Tech. Indsl. Mgmt., Indian Inst. Tech., Madras, India, 1979; PhD in Indsl. Engring., Purudue U., 1984. Mantenance supr. Bhilai (India) Steel Plant, 1979-80; asst. prof. SIE dept. U. Ariz., Tucson, 1984-87; lead systems engr. AT&T Bell Labs., Middletown, N.J., 1987—; cons. in field. Contbr. articles to profl. jours. Mem. IEEE, Ops. Rsch. Soc., Mgmt. Sci., Inst. Indsl. Engrs. Roman Catholic. Home: 19 Inwood Terr Freehold NJ 07728 Office: AT&T Bell Labs 1A251 480 Red Will Rd Middletown NJ 07748

THYM, JÜRGEN, musicologist; b. Germany, July 2, 1943; came to U.S., 1969; s. Heinrich and Brunhilde (Kammbach) T.; m. Peggy Dettwiler, June 6, 1992. Diploma in Schulmusik, Berlin Hochschule für Musik, 1967; diploma in History, Berlin Free U., 1969; PhD in Musicology, Case Western Reserve U., 1974. Vis. instr. Oberlin (Ohio) Coll., 1973; instr. Eastman Sch. of Music, Rochester, N.Y., 1973-74; asst. prof. Eastman Sch. of Music, Rochester, 1974-80, assoc. prof., 1980-89, prof., 1989—, chmn. dept. musicology, 1982—; cons. Ednl. Testing Svc., Princeton, N.J., 1980-87. Co-translator: Kirnberger's Art of Composition, 1982 (ASCAP award 1983), Schenker's Counterpoint, 1987; editor: (scores) Schoenberg's Collected Works Vols. XIII and XIV, 100 Years of Eichendorff Songs, 1984. Mem. Am. Musicological Soc. (adv. coun. 1985-90, AMS '50 com. 1987-92). Unitarian. Office: Eastman Sch of Music 26 Gibbs St Rochester NY 14604

THYSEN, BENJAMIN, biochemist, health science facility administrator, researcher; b. N.Y.C., July 27, 1932; s. Bernard and Clara (Linietsky) Tissenbaum; m. Joan Albin; children: Julie Ann, Greg Eden. BS, CCNY, 1954; MS, U. Mo., 1963; PhD, St. Louis U., 1967. Instr. St. Louis U. Med. Sch., 1967-68; sr. research scientist Technicon Instrument Corp., Ardsly, N.Y., 1968-69; group leader Technicon Instrument Corp., Tarrytown, N.Y., 1969-70; asst. prof. lab., med., and ob-gyn depts. Albert Einstein Coll. Medicine, Bronx, N.Y., 1971-86, assoc. prof. lab. med. and ob-gyn depts., 1986—, dir. endocrine labs., 1971—; cons. Technicon Instrument Corp., Tarrytown, 1979-81, Albert Einstein Coll. of Medicine, Bronx, 1969-70. Contbr. articles to profl. jours. Served with U.S. Army, 1956-58. Recipient Cancer Research award St. Louis U., 1967-68; fellow NIH, 1963-67. Mem. AAAS, Assn. Clin. Scientists, Soc. Study of Reproduction, Endocrine Soc., Sigma Xi.

TIANGCO, ELITO, secondary education educator; b. Nueva Ecija, Philippines, Oct. 4, 1940; came to U.S. 1965; s. Isauro and Julita (Sapang) T.; m. Hermelina Tabing, Aug. 18, 1966; children: Elaine. BS, Cen. Luzon State U., Philippines, 1961; MS, Rutgers U., 1967, PhD, 1970. Research asst. Rutgers U., New Brunswick, 1965-69; genetics lectr. Ga. Ct. Coll., Lakewood, N.J., 1971; statistics lectr. Middlesex County Coll., Edison, N.J., 1977-85; chmn. dept. sci., tchr. New Brunswick High Sch., 1970—; lab mgr. Wasatch Computer Lab., New Brunswick, 1984—. Contbr. articles to profl. jours. Recipient N.J. Gov.'s Tchr. Recognition-Excellence in Teaching, 1989; N.J. Bus./Industry Sci. Edn. Consortium fellow, 1989. Mem. Am. Phytopathol. Soc., Sigma Xi. Roman Catholic. Home: 49 Hidden Lake Dr N Brunswick NJ 08902-1213 Office: New Brunswick High Sch 1125 Livingston Ave New Brunswick NJ 08901-3391

TICE, GEORGE ANDREW, photographer; b. Newark, Oct. 13, 1938; s. William S. and Margaret T. (Robertson) T.; m. Joanna Blaylock, 1958; m. Marie Tremmel, 1960; children: Christopher, Loretta, Lisa, Lynn, Jennifer. Instr. photography New Sch. Social Research, 1970—. One-man shows, Witkin Gallery, 1970, Met. Mus. Art, 1972, group shows include, Whitney Mus. Am. Art, 1974, Mus. Modern Art, 1979; represented in permanent collections, Mus. Modern Art, Met. Mus. Art, Art Inst. Chgo., Bibliothèque Nationale, Victoria and Albert Mus.; Books include Fields of Peace, 1970, Goodbye River, Goodbye, 1971, Paterson, 1972, Seacoast Maine, 1973, George A. Tice Photographs, 1953-73, 1975, Urban Landscapes, 1975, Artie Van Blarcum, 1977, Urban Romantic, 1982, Lincoln, 1984, Hometowns, 1988, Stone Walls, Grey Skies, 1991. Served with USN, 1956-59. Recipient Grand prix for best photography book of Year Arles, France, 1973; Guggenheim Found. fellow, 1973-74; Nat. Endowment for Arts fellow, 1973—; Nat. Mus. Photography and Bradford and Ilkley Community Coll. (Eng.) fellow, 1990-91. Address: 323 Gill Ln 9B Iselin NJ 08830

TICE, KIRK CLIFFORD, health care facility executive; b. Jersey City, July 3, 1954; s. Clifford Cromwell and Anneke Meta (Vanderveer) T.; m. Judith Elizabeth Sheppard, Oct. 15, 1988; 1 child, Brian Clifford. AAS, Bergen Community Coll., 1976; BA, New Sch. Social Rsch., 1987, M Profl. Svcs., 1987. Asst. dir. clin. svcs. Rahway (N.J.) Hosp., 1982-84, dir. clin. svcs., 1984-88, dir. bus. devel., 1987-88, v.p. clin. svcs., 1988—; bd. dirs., Rahway Geriatric Ctr. Com. mem. Union Juvenile Conf. Mem. Am. Hosp. Assn., N.J. Hosp. Assn., Sr. Healthcare Execs. N.J. (sec.-treas. 1991, v.p. 1991-92), Rahway Kiwanis (prse. 1991-92). Home: 580 Yorktown Rd Union NJ 07083-7842 Office: Rahway Hosp 865 Stone St Rahway NJ 07065-2797

TICKNER, JUDITH ANN, political science educator; b. London, Mar. 1, 1937; d. Frederick James and Lucy Winifred (James) T.; m. Hayward R. Alker Jr., June 3, 1961; children: Joan Christina, Heather Jane, Gwendolyn Ann. BA, London U., 1959; MA, Yale U., 1960; PhD, Brandeis U., 1983. Lectr. Boston U., 1979-82; asst. prof. polit. sci. Coll. of the Holy Cross, Worcester, Mass., 1984-90, assoc. prof. polit. sci., 1990—; rsch. assoc. Wellesley Coll., 1990-91; acad. visitor London Sch. Econs., 1989; vis. scholar Ctr. for Women Scholars, Uppsala U., Sweden, 1989. Author: Gender in International Relations, 1992, Self-Reliance Vs Power Politics, 1987. Mem. Am. Polit. Sci. Assn., Internat. Studies Assn. Home: 288 Mill St Newton MA 02160-2436 Office: Coll of the Holy Cross PO Box 121A Worcester MA 01610-0155

TIDD, RONALD ROBERT, accounting and taxation educator; b. Lincoln, Nebr., June 7, 1953; s. Robert Harvey Tidd and Nadine Marie (Legler) Munnelly; m. Doris Marie Hernandez, June 18, 1982. BS, Iowa State U., 1977; PhD, U. Minn., 1992. CPA. Auditor Peat, Marwick Mitchell & Co., Santa Fe, 1977-79; tax advisor, mgr. Peat, Marwick Mitchell & Co., Des Moines, 1980-82; fin. analyst Whittaker Corp., Jeddah, Saudi Arabia, 1980; tax advisor Fox & Co., Boise, Idaho, 1982-85; instr. U. Minn., Mpls., 1985-91; prof. Syracuse (N.Y.) U., 1991—; mem. adv. bd. Tax Inst., Syracuse U. Participant Boise C. of C., 1984; treas. Santa Fe Jaycees, 1978, Boise Kiwanis, 1983; med. dir. Idaho Mountain Search and Rescue, Boise, 1984. Mem. AICPAs, Am. Tax Assn., Phi Beta Kappa, Phi Kappa Phi, Beta Alpha Psi (faculty advisor). Republican. Office: Syracuse U 900 S Crouse Ave Syracuse NY 13244

TIDMARSH, KAREN MACAUSLAND, dean; b. Newton, Mass., May 19, 1949; d. Maurice William and Frances Lane (Green) T. AB, Bryn Mawr Coll., 1971; PhD, U. Va., 1988. Fellow U. Va., 1975-76, 76-77, teaching asst., 1976-77, 78-79; asst. dean Bryn Mawr (Pa.) Coll., 1979-80, 83-86, assoc. dir. admissions, 1980-83, assoc. dean, 1986-89, lectr. in English, 1988—, acting dean, 1989-90, dean undergrad. coll., 1990—. Trustee Baldwin Sch., Bryn Mawr, 1991—. Home: 519 Old Buck Ln Haverford PA 19041-1214 Office: Bryn Mawr Coll Bryn Mawr PA 19010

TIDWELL, MOODY R., federal judge; b. Kansas City, Mo., Feb. 15, 1939; s. Moody R., Jr. and Dorothy T.; m. Rena Alexandra, Jan. 28, 1966; children—Gregory, Jeremy. B.A., Ohio Wesleyan U., 1961; J.D., Am. U., 1964; LL.M., George Washington U., 1972. Bar: U.S. Ct. Appeals (D.C. cir.) 1964, U.S. Dist Ct. D.C. 1965, U.S. Ct. Claims 1972, U.S. Ct. Appeals (10th cir.) 1979. Assoc. solicitor gen. law div. Dept. Interior, Washington, 1972-75, assoc. solicitor Energy and Resources div., 1975-78; assoc. solicitor Mine Health and Safety div. Dept. Labor, Washington, 1978-80; deputy solicitor, counsellor to the sec. Dept. Interior, Washington, 1981-83; judge U.S. Claims Ct., Washington, 1983—; dir., corporate sec. Keco, Inc., Cin. Pres. Pine Lake Corp., Glengary, W.Va., 1975—. Recipient Disting. Service award Sec. of Interior, 1983, Meritorious Service award Sec. of Labor, 1979. Mem. ABA, Fed. Bar Assn., D.C. Bar Assn. Office: US Claims Ct 717 Madison Pl NW Washington DC 20005-1011

TIECK, WILLIAM ARTHUR, minister; b. Denver, June 5, 1908; s. Hugo and Edna Earle (Pique) T. BA, U. Redlands, 1930; BDiv, Drew U., 1942; MST, Union Theol. Sem., 1947; PhD, Columbia U., 1953; LittD (hon.), Manhattan Coll., 1973. Ordained to ministry, Meth. Ch., 1945. Pastor Cucamonga (Calif.) Meth. Ch., 1937-39, Red Hook (N.Y.) Meth. Ch., 1942-43, Wesley Meth. Ch., N.Y.C., 1943-46, St. Stephen's United Meth. Ch., N.Y.C., 1946-78, Edgehill Ch. at Spuyten Duyvil, N.Y.C., 1978—; ofcl. hist. Borough of The Bronx, N.Y.C., 1980—. Author: God's House and the Old Kingsbridge Road, 1948, Riverdale, Kingsbridge, Spuyten Duyvil: New York City, 1968, Schools and School Days in Riverdale, Kingsbridge, Spuyten Duyvil: New York City, 1971, America's Debt to John Peter Têtard, 1987, The Locale of Theodore Dreiser's Kingsbridge Experience, 1992. Home: 3930 Bailey Ave Bronx NY 10463-2701

TIEDEMAN, DONALD LOUIS, communications company executive; b. East Saint Louis, Ill., Oct. 1, 1936; s. Louis Edward and Lucille (Herman) T.; m. Sue Zan Keagle, June 6, 1959; children: Wendy Cawley, Kristin Calvert, Karyn Carr, Leslie Tiedeman. BS, U. Ill., 1958. Dist. data processing mgr. AT&T, Cin., 1970-72, dist. ops. mgr., 1972-74; div. engring. mgr. AT&T, Atlanta, 1974-75, so. region pers. dir., 1975-77; div. network svc. dir. AT&T, Bedminster, N.J., 1977-80, dir. acctg. ops., 1980-84, dir. network svcs., 1984-85; dir. systems arch. AT&T, Somerset, N.J., 1985-86; systems v.p. AT&T, Basking Ridge, N.J., 1986—. Campaign dir. United Way, Atlanta, 1975; mem. recycling com. City of Summit, N.J. Lt. USN, 1958-62.

TIEFENBRUN, SUSAN, lawyer; b. N.Y.C., Sept. 14, 1943; d. Jack and Adya (Avrutsky) Kissil; m. Jonathan Tiefenbrun; children: Michele, Jeremy, Gregory. BS, U. Wis., 1965, MA, 1966; PhD, Columbia U., 1971; JD, NYU, 1986. Bar: N.Y. 1987, Conn. 1987. Prof. French, Bklyn. Coll., 1967-71, Columbia U., N.Y.C., 1972-80; prof. French Sarah Lawrence Coll., Bronxville, N.Y., 1980-83; atty. Coudert Bros., N.Y.C., 1987-89; assoc. Holtzmann, Wise & Shepard, N.Y.C., 1989-91, of counsel, 1991-92; prof. law Hofstra Law Sch., 1991—. Author: Structural Analysis of La Princesse de Cleves, 1971 (Justin O'Brien award, Signs of the Hidden, 1980, A Classical Sign, 1983. Am. Counsel of Learned Societies grantee, 1971, 77, 83; Chamberlain fellow; recipient Nat. Counsel for Research award. Mem. ABA (exec. com. Soviet and Eastern European laws), Conn. Bar Assn., N.Y. State Bar Assn. (exec. com., Soviet law com.), Westchester Women's Bar Assn., Assn. Bar City N.Y. (exec. com. fgn. laws com.), Am. Arbitration Assn., French-Am. C. of C., Paris-Am. Club. Democrat. Jewish. Home: 62 Country Rd Mamaroneck NY 10543-1110 Office: 62 Country Rd Mamaroneck NY 10543

TIERNAN, BERNADETTE BRUNHUBER, human resources consultant; b. Rego Park, N.Y., Oct. 30, 1951; d. William Ernest and Mary Regina (Fitzpatrick) Brunhuber; m. William Clark Tiernan Jr., July 27, 1974; children: Katherine, Billy, Caroline. BA in Psychology, Merrimack Coll., 1973; Cert. in Human Factors Engring., U. Mich., 1976; MA in Indsl. Psychology, Fairleigh Dickinson U., 1979. Human factors engr. Long Lines div. AT&T, White Plains, N.Y., 1973-79, info. systems mgr. Data Svcs. div., 1979-81; dir. mgmt. devel. program Human Resources div. AT&T, Bedminster, N.Y., 1981-84; v.p. Human Resources Assocs., Englewood Cliffs, N.J., 1984-86; pres. Tiernan Assocs., Ridgewood, N.J., 1986—; instr. Bergen Community Coll., Paramus, N.J. Author: Segues: Smooth Transitions for the 90's, 1990. Publicist Valley Hosp. Auxiliary, Ridgewood, N.J., 1989-91, Coll. Club of Ridgewood, 1990-91. Mem. APA, Nat. Assn. Women Bus. Owners (program v.p. 1989-91), N.J. Assn. Women Bus. Owners (bd. dirs. 1986—, pres. 1991-93). Roman Catholic. Office: PO Box 1382 Ridgewood NJ 07451-1382

TIERNEY, ANITA RACHEL, project director; b. Fall River, Mass., Nov. 21, 1946; d. James Frances and Madeleine (Riley) T. BS, Columbia U., 1976, postgrad., 1971—. Rsch. asst. Bellevue Hosp., N.Y.C., 1975-76, Columbia P & S, N.Y.C., 1976-79; cons. Community Rsch. Initiative, N.Y.C., 1988-91; lab. technologist St. Luke's-Roosevelt Hosp. Ctr., N.Y.C., 1979-84, project coord., 1984-86, rsch. assoc., 1986-91, project dir., 1991—. Mem. AAAS, N.Y. Acad. Scis., Internat. AIDS Soc., Union Concerned Scientists. Office: St Lukes-Roosevelt Hosp GI Rsch/421 W 113th St New York NY 10025

TIERNEY, JAMES EDWARD, attorney general; b. Bklyn., Apr. 12, 1947; s. Charles J. and Agnes V. (Quinn) T.; m. Susan Webster, Jan. 26, 1969; children: Adam, Josie, Matthew, Daniel, Kate. B.A. with highest honors, U. Maine, 1969, J.D., 1974. Bar: Maine 1974. Tchr. civics high sch. Auburn, Maine, 1969-71; mem. Maine State Ho. Reps., 1972-80, majority leader, 1976-80; atty. gen. State of Maine, 1981-91; bd. dirs. People for the Am. Way, Topsham, Maine, 1991—; mem. bd. commentators Courtroom TV Network; bd. dirs. Ctr. for Nat. Policy. Office: PO 417 Topsham ME 04086

TIERNEY, JOHN MARK, non-profit organization administrator; b. Newark, Del., May 29, 1924; s. William Aloyious and Helen (O'Rouke) T.; m. Frances Stuart Rumfelt, July 12, 1952; children: Brenda Tierney Uyak, John Mark Jr., Maureen Tierney Donahue, Theresa Tierney Clark. BS, U.S. Naval Acad., 1945; BS in Aero. Engring., Naval Postgrad. Sch., 1954; MS in Engring., Princeton U., 1955; AM in Internat. Affairs, George Washington U., 1964. Commd. USN, 1945, advanced through grades to rear adm. (U.H.), 1972, ret., 1975; v.p. corp. devel. Luljian Assocs., Alexandria, Va., 1975-77; v.p. devel. St. Joseph's U., Phila., 1977-82; v.p. bus. devel. Lavino Shipping Co., Phila., 1982-86, mem. mgmt. bd., 1982—; v.p., gen. mgr. LSC Marine, Inc. subs. Lavino Shipping Co., Wilmington, Del., 1986-90; pres., chief exec. officer Cath. League for Religious & Civil Rights, Bala Cnywyd, Pa., 1990—; 1990-91; assoc. realtor Roach Bros., Gladwyne, Pa., 1991—; bd. dirs. XRT Inc., Wayne, Pa.; cons. Brown & Root, Houston, 1975-76; cons., study dir. Chief of Naval Personnel, Washington, 1976-77. Co-author: (text book) Aircraft Performance Testing, 1960. Pres. Holy Name Soc., Patuxent River, Md., 1959; active Cath. Philopatrian Lit. Inst., Phila. Decorated Bronze Star with combat V, D.F.C. with gold star, Legion of Merit with 2 gold stars, Air medal with silver star and 4 gold stars; fifth class medal Nat. Order of Vietnam Knight, Gallantry Cross (Republic of Vietnam); recipient Key to the City of San Diego, 1971; knighted Royal Rosarian, Portland, Oreg. Rose Festival, 1973. Mem. Navy League of U.S., Assn. Naval Aviation, Ret. Officers' Assn., St. Joseph's U. Pres.' Coun., U.S. Naval Acad. Alumni (chpt. pres. 1971-72), Union League Club (Phila.), Harbour League Club (Camden). Republican. Roman Catholic. Office: Roach Bros Realtors 956 Youngsford Rd 111 Presidential Blvd # 227 Gladwyne PA 19035

TIERNEY, MADELEINE HOOD, artist, stained glass company owner; b. Bronx, N.Y., July 30, 1937; d. Aubrey John and Dorita K. (Fischer) Hood; m. Joseph Leo Tierney III, June 23, 1962; children: Maureen J., Michael Joseph, Brian Paul, James Christopher. BS, SUNY, New Paltz, 1959. Cert. art edn. tchr., N.Y. Tchr. art Northport (N.Y.) Pub. Sch. System, 1959-63; owner Stained Glass Studio, Arnold, Md., 1980—; sales rep. Aurora Gallery, Annapolis, Md., 1985-91. Del. Creative Arts Coun., Md., Va. and D.C., 1984-86, treas., 1986-88, pres., 1988-90. Mem. Nat. Capitol Stained Glass Guild, Art Glass Alliance of Md. Republican. Roman Catholic. Home and Office: 250 Holly Ridge Cir Arnold MD 21012-2152

TIERNEY, WILLIAM GERARD, anthropogist, educator; b. Bklyn., Feb. 3, 1953; s. Paul Edward and Rosalie Gerard (Nolan) T. BA, Tufts U., 1975; MEd, Harvard U., 1978; MA, PhD, Stanford U., 1984. With Peace Corps, Morocco, 1975-77; acad. dean Fort Berthold Community Coll., New Town, S.D., 1978-80; sr. assoc. Nat. Ctr. for Higher Edn. Mgmt. Systems, Boulder, Colo., 1984-86; rsch. assoc. Pa. State U., University Park, 1986-89, sr. rsch. assoc., assoc. prof., 1989—. Author: The Web of Leadership: The Presidency in Higher Education, 1988, Curricular Landscapes, Democratic Vistas: Transformative Leadership in Higher Education, 1989, (with E. Chaffee) Collegiate Culture and Leadership Strategies, 1988; editor: Culture and Ideology in Higher Education: Advancing a Critical Agenda, 1991; mem. editorial bd. Rev. of Higher Edn., 1988—; contbr., editor numerous publs. Recipient Curriculum Change award Lilly Endowment, 1986, Native Ams. award Ford Found., 1988, Organizational Change award Fed. Govt., 1991. Mem. ACLU, Am. Anthrop. Assn., Am. Coun. on Edn. (nat. leadership group), Am. Ednl. Rsch. Assn. (program chmn. div. J 1991), Assn. for Study of Higher Edn. (co-chmn. rsch. papers 1990, adv. com. reader on orgns. and governance in higher edn. 1990, adv. com. reader on the curriculum 1990), Soc. Applied Anthropology, Amnesty Internat., Human Rights Campaign Fund. Democrat. Office: Pa State U Ctr Study Higher Edn 403 S Allen St Ste 104 University Park PA 16801-5252

TIERNO, PHILIP MARIO, JR., microbiologist, educator, researcher; b. Bklyn., June 5, 1943; s. Philip M. and Phyllis (Tringone) T.; m. Josephine Martinez, Apr. 2, 1967; children: Alexandra Lorraine, Meredith Anne. BS, Bklyn. Coll. Pharmacy/R.L. Conolly Coll., L.I. U., 1965; MS, NYU, 1974, PhD, 1977. Microbiologist, Luth. Med. Ctr., Bklyn., 1965-66; chief research microbiologist hemodialysis unit VA Hosp., Bronx, N.Y., 1966-70; dir. microbiology div. NYU Med. Ctr. Goldwater Meml. Hosp., F.D. Roosevelt Island, N.Y., 1970-81; assoc. and cons. microbiologist Maimonides Med. Ctr., Bklyn., 1970-79; dir. microbiology dept. Tisch-Univ. Hosp., NYU Med. Ctr., 1981—; adj. asst. prof. CUNY, 1974-76, Bloomfield (N.J.) Coll., 1975-82; assoc. prof. microbiology and pathology NYU Med. Sch., 1981—; cons. Office Atty. Gen. N.Y. State, NIH, and Dept. Health City of New York, 1981—. Pres., Flushing Taxpayers Assn., 1973-77; bd. dirs. Comprehensive Health Planning Agy. City N.Y., 1974-75, Norwood Bd. Adjustment, N.J., 1978-83, 86—, Norwood Bd. Edn., 1983-86; chmn. Norwood Environ. Commn., 1986—; co-founder, bd. dirs. Found. Sci. Research in Pub. Interest, S.I., N.Y., 1985—. Mem. AAAS, N.Y. Acad. Scis., Am. Acad. Microbiology, Am. Pub. Health Assn., Am. Soc. Microbiology, Phi Sigma, Alpha Epsilon Delta. Club: Optimists (v.p. Norwood 1978—). Lodge: Knights of Malta. Contbr. articles to profl. jours. and books. Home: 30 Carter St Norwood NJ 07648-1518

TIGANI, BRUCE WILLIAM, lawyer; b. Wilmington, Del., May 10, 1956; s. J. Vincent Jr. and Josephine C. (DeAngelis) T.; m. Janice Rowe, Sept. 25, 1982; children: Jessica Lynne, Bruce William Jr. Student, Georgetown U., 1974-75; BBS, U. Del., 1978; JD, Villanova U., 1981. Bar: Del. 1981, Pa. 1982, U.S. Dist. Ct. Del. 1982, U.S. Dist. Ct. (ea. dist.) Pa. 1982, U.S. Tax Ct. 1982. Assoc. Lord & Mulligan, Media, Pa., 1981-84; resident atty. Lord & Mulligan, Wilmington, 1984-87, ptnr., 1987-88; mng. mem. Werb, Tigani & Hood, Wilmington, 1988—; del. to IRS, Mid. Atlantic Regional liason. Active mem. Rep. Com. of State Del.; mem. parish coun. Immaculate Heart of Mary, Roman Cath. Ch. Mem. ABA, Del. State Bar Assn. (chmn. tax sect., real estate sect., trusts and estates sect., lectr. bus. and tax seminars), Wilmington Tax Group, Del. State C. of C. (commerce tax com.), Estate Planning Coun. of Del., Inc., Concord Country Club, Blue & Gold Club. Office: Werb Tigani & Hood 300 Delaware Ave PO Box 25046 Wilmington DE 19899

TIGGES, TIMOTHY JOHN, cellist; b. Dubuque, Iowa, Mar. 13, 1956; s. John Thomas and Kathryn Elizabeth (Johnson) T.; m. Bernadette Studelska, Jan. 26, 1976 (div. Aug. 1978); 1 child, Anthony Michael; m. Reiko Niiya, Apr. 23, 1982; 1 child, Koji Alexander. Student, U. Iowa, 1974-75, Carnegie-Mellon U., 1978-80. Assoc. prin. cello Symphony Orch. of Maracaibo, Venezuela, 1980-82; gen. mgr. Southwest Fla. Symphony, Ft. Myers, 1982-84; prin. cello Southwest Fla. Symphony, 1982-88; cellist Southwest

Fla. String Quartet, 1982-86; enlisted USAF, 1988; cellist USAF Concert Band, 1988—; piano trio Niiya-Otaki-Tigges, Raymond Weiss Artist Mgmt., N.Y.C., 1985-87; prodn. coord. USAF Band, Washington, 1989—; freelance musician/soloist/chamber musician Southwest Fla., 1982-88, Washington, 1988—. Asst. to producer (video tape) I Love America starring Robert Merrill, 1991, producer (spl. event) Roy Clark Robert Merrill Transcontinental Internat. Tours, 1 988—. Mem. Am. Fedn. Musicians, Washington Fedn. Musicians, Phi Mu Alpha, Sinfonia. Roman Catholic. Home: 7513 Republic Ct # 301 Alexandria VA 22306 Office: USAF Band Bolling AFB Washington DC 20332

TIGHE, THOMAS JAMES GASSON, JR., healthcare executive; b. Malden, Mass., July 11, 1946; s. Thomas J. G. and Barbara (Buckland) T.; m. Carolyn Payne, Mar. 29, 1969; children: Jessica, Chelsea, Alexandra. BA, Bates Coll., 1968; MSc, Columbia U., 1970; MPH, Johns Hopkins U., 1973. Adminstr. asst. Boston U. Med. Ctr. U. Hosp., 1970-71, asst. adminstr., 1971-72; asst. dir. Mary Imogene Bassett Hosp., Cooperstown, N.Y., 1973-80, Cen. Maine Med. Ctr., Lewiston, 1980-86; exec. v.p. Cen. Maine Healthcare Corp., Lewiston, 1986—; lectr. U. Maine, Augusta, 1987-88, St. Joseph's Coll., Windham, Maine, 1990—; corporator Androscoggin Savs. Bank, Lewiston, 1990—. Bd. dirs. Maine Acting Co., Lewiston, 1986-88, Auburn (Maine) Pub. Libr., 1987-90, LA Arts, Lewiston, 1988—. Fellow Am. Coll. Healthcare Execs. (coun. regents 1986—); mem. Am. Hosp. Assn., Soc. Healthcare Planning, Mktg., Maine Hosp. Assn. (bd. dirs. 1990—). Office: Cen Maine Healthcare Corp 364 Main St Lewiston ME 04240-7072

TILGHMAN, THOMAS SLOCUM, grain company executive; b. Norwood, Mass., Nov. 15, 1946; s. Henry Ashe and Olive Child (Pinney) T.; m. Jo-Ann Burt, Aug. 11, 1965; children: Henry, James, Edward. AB cum laude, Harvard Coll., 1968; MBA, Amos Tuck, 1970. Cons. Irwin Mgmt., Columbus, Ind., 1970-73; mgr. pers. rsch. Cumming Engine Co., Columbus, 1973-76; mgr. compensation Baxter Travenol, Deerfield, Ill., 1976-78; mgr. Arthur Young, N.Y.C., 1978-83, prin., 1983-87; dir. Arthur Young Ernst & Young, N.Y.C., 1987-90; asst. v.p. compensation Continental Grain, N.Y.C., 1990—. Author: Executive Compensation, 1987-90. Mem. com. Trustees of Reservation, Edgartown, Mass., 1990—. Amos Tuck scholar, 1969. Mem. Harvard Club N.Y. Republican. Episcopalian. Home: 58 Williams Rd Trumbull CT 06611-4338 Office: Continental Grain 277 Park Ave New York NY 10172-0003

TILLACK, ROBERT CHARLES, physician; b. Rochester, n.Y., June 11, 1952; s. Henry Philip and Elizabeth Jane (Helfer) T.; m. Diane Lynn Switlyk, Apr. 25, 1981; children: Lindsey Ann, Sandra Michelle. BS in Biology, Rensselaer Poly. Inst., 1976; MD, Albany Med. Coll., 1976. Diplomate Nat. Bd. Med. Examiners, Am. Bd. Emergency Medicine. Resident in gen. surgery Albany (N.Y.) Med. Ctr., 1976-77, resident in neurosurgery, 1977-78; attending physician Samaritan Hosp., Troy, N.Y., 1979-85, Columbia Meml. Hosp., Hudson, N.Y., 1979-85, Somerset (N.J.) Med. Ctr., 1985—; ptnr. Emergency Med. Assocs., Livingston, N.J., 1985—; instr. advanced cardiac life support Am. Heart Assn., 1988—. Fellow Am. Coll. Emergency Physicians. Republican. Lutheran. Office: Emergency Med Assocs 651 W Mt Pleasant Ave Livingston NJ 07039-1609

TILLEY, STEPHEN GEORGE, biology educator; b. Lima, Ohio, July 21, 1943; s. George Lewis and Ruth June (Whittington) T.; m. Mary Rand Lightner, June 6, 1965 (div. 1985); children: Jennifer Wayland, Christopher John. BS, Ohio State U., 1965; PhD, U. Mich., 1970. Asst. prof. dept. biol. scis. Smith Coll., Northampton, Mass., 1970-76, assoc. prof., 1976-82, prof., 1982—. Contbr. articles to profl. publs. Mem. AAAS, Am. Soc. Ichthyologists and Herpetologists, Soc. for Study Evolution, Soc. for Study Amphibians and Reptiles, Herpetologists' League (councilor 1990—). Office: Dept Biol Scis Smith Coll Northampton MA 01063

TILLIS, ALAN CASAL, orthopaedic surgeon; b. Newark, May 26, 1939; s. Herman Harold and Evelyn (Goldstein) T.; (div. Apr. 1981); children: Alyse Kassel, Kenneth, Peter (dec.), Stacey Kassel, Deborah; m. Sharon Dorflaufer, May 17, 1981. BA, Haverford Coll., 1961; MD, Georgetown U., 1965. Diplomate Am. Acad. Orthopaedic Surgeons, diplomate Am. Coll. Surgeons. Intern Hosp. for Joint Diseases, N.Y.C., 1965-66, resident, 1966-70; pvt. practice orthopaedic surgery Livingston, N.J., 1972—. Maj. U.S. Army, 1970-72. Fellow ACS, Am. Acad. Orthosurgeons; mem. AMA, N.Y. Med. Soc., N.J. Orthopaedic Soc., Essex County Med. Soc., B'nai B'rith. Jewish. Office: Orthopaedic and Joint Reconstrn Surg Assocs PA 22 Old Short Hills Rd Livingston NJ 07039-5605

TILLISTRAND, JOHN ANTHONY, insurance company executive; b. Amityville, N.Y., Jan. 15, 1956; s. Edward Joseph and Marie L. (Catale) T.; m. Ann Marie Hodson, Oct. 10, 1981; children: Laura Jeanne, Edward John. BS, U. Conn., 1978, MBA, 1990. Underwriting trainee Atlantic Mutual Ins. Co., Jericho, N.Y., 1978-80; staff underwriter Atlantic Mutual Ins. Co., N.Y.C., 1980-83; underwriting supr. Atlantic Mutual Ins. Co., Glastonbury, Conn., 1983-88, mgr. mktg. ctr., 1988—. Mem. Soc. CPCU. Democrat. Roman Catholic. Home: 70 Roberts Rd Marlborough CT 06447

TILLOTSON, KARIN RUTH MYERS, education educator; b. Greensburg, Pa., Sept. 16, 1942; d. Robert Eugene and Ruth Lois (Gardner) Myers; m. Clifford Eugene Tillotson, Feb. 14, 1976; 1 child, Elizabeth Gene. BS in Elem. Edn., Calif. State Tchrs. Coll., 1963; MS in Elem. Edn., U. Pitts., 1966; PhD in spl. Edn., Gifted, U. Ill., 1971. Cert. elem. edn., spl. edn., supervision. Tchr. Norwin Sch. Dist., Irwin, Pa., 1963-65; dir. ESEA math Norwin Sch. Dist., Irwin, 1966; gifted cons. Westmoreland County Schs., Greensburg, Pa., 1967-68; intern, dissemination Univ. Ill., Champaign, 1968-69; rsch. asst. Nat. Sch. Fin. Project, Champaign, 1969-70, Bur. Ednl. Rsch., Champaign, 1970-71; asst. prof. Ind. Univ., Bloomington, 1972-73; advisor of gifted Intermediate Unit #4, Greensburg, 1973-74; assoc. prof. Slippery Rock (Pa.) Univ., 1974—; mem. Mercer County Human Rights com., Hermitage, Pa., 1983—; edn. coord. Hickory United Meth. Ch., Heritage, 1985-91; mem. Mercer (Pa.) Sch. Dist. Long Range Planning Com., 1985—. Author: Class Acts, 1985; co-author: Today's Student-Tomorrows Teacher, 1979, Handbook for Student Teaching, 1985, Today's Student, 1986. Pres. Am. Bus. Women's Assn., Warren, Ohio, 1974-81; com. chair Sharon (Pa.) Coll. Club, 1981—. Mem. ASCD, Assn. Tchr. Educators, Pa. Assn. Gifted, Pa. Assn. Colls. and Tchr. Educators, Assn. Pa. State Coll. and Univ. Faculties, Phi Delta Kappa. Home: 50 Hazen Rd Sharpsville PA 16150-1623 Office: Slippery Rock Univ 116 Mckay Edn Slippery Rock PA 16057

TILLYARD, HELEN VIRGINIA, artist, art historian, writer; b. Bristol, Eng., July 2, 1954; came to U.S., 1983, naturalized 1991; d. Stephen and Margaret (Watson) T. MA in Art History, Cambridge (Eng.) U., 1978, Courtauld Inst., London, 1978. Copywriter, editor Sotheby's, London, 1978; researcher, asst. to Sir Niklaus Pevsner, Penguin Books, London, 1978-79; mus. asst., designer Well Arts Ctr., Wells-Next-the-Sea, Eng., 1979; researcher Diaghileff Ballet, Edvard Munch Exhbns., U. East Anglia, Norwich, Eng., 1979; arts adminstr. practical tng. scheme Arts Coun. Gt. Britain, London, Nottingham, Eng., N.Y.C., 1979-81; gallery curator, catalog compiler Brandt Dayton & Co., fine art, N.Y.C., 1983-85; art history writer and researcher, N.Y.C., 1985—. One-woman show Armoire Gallery, Ellsworth, Maine, 1989, Leger De Main Gallery, N.Y.C., 1991; contbr. art revs. to various publs. Organizer, spokesman La Plaza Def. League, N.Y.C., 1987—. Recipient Phyllis Tillyard prize Cambridge U., 1976; Hallam and Gurney travel scholar, 1972. Office: 630 E 9th St New York NY 10009-5235

TILSON, DOROTHY RUTH, word processing executive; b. Bloomsburg, Pa., Mar. 24, 1918; d. Roy Earl and Mary Etta (Masteller) Derr; m. Irving Tilson, Sept. 1949. BS, Bloomsburg U., 1940. Tchr. Madison Consol. Sch., Jerseytown, Pa., 1940-42; gage checker Phila. Ordinance Gage Lab., 1942-43; tabulating asst. Remington Rand, Phila., N.Y.C., 1943-46; copy writer Sears Roebuck, Phila., N.Y.C., 1946-48; statis. asst. Ford Internat., N.Y.C., 1949-56; word processing adminstrv. asst. Coopers & Lybrand, N.Y.C., 1956-91. Life mem. Rep. Senatorial Inner Circle, Washington, 1987—. Mem. Am. Movement for World Govt. (sec. 1991—), N.Y. Theosophical Soc. (libr. 1967—), Capitol Hill Club. Home: 435 W 119 St 9G New York NY 10027-7142 Office: Coopers & Lybrand 1301 Ave Of The Americas New York NY 10019-6022

TILSON, M. DAVID, surgeon; b. Texarkana, Tex., Aug. 25, 1941; s. M. David and Leta (Martin) T.; m. Joan E. Staneski, 1974; children: William Thomas, John Wainwright. BA, Rice U., 1963; MD, Yale U., 1967. Diplomate Am. Bd. Surgery, Nat. Bd. Med. Examiners. Asst. to assoc. prof. Yale U., New Haven, 1974-83, prof., 1983-89; prof. Columbia U., N.Y.C., 1989—; dir. surgery St. Lukes Roosvelt Hosp Ctr., N.Y.C., 1989—. Contbr. articles to profl. jours. Maj. USAF, 1972-74. Rsch. grantee NIH, 1983—. Mem. ACS, Soc. Univ. Surgeons, Am. Surg. Assn., Soc. Vascular Surgery, Internat. Soc. Cardiovascular Surgery, Halsted Soc., Med. Strollers. Office: St Lukes Roosevelt Hosp 428 W 59th St New York NY 10019-1105

TILTON, WEBSTER, JR., contractor; b. St. Louis, Sept. 11, 1922; s. Webster and Eleanor (Dozier) T.; student St. Marks Prep. Sch., 1936-40, Pawling Prep. Sch., 1940-42; master brewers degree, U.S. Brewers Acad., 1949; m. Grace Drew Wilson, Feb. 14, 1948 (div. Oct. 1959); 1 son, Webster III; m. 2d, Nancy McBlair Payne, Jan. 5, 1963. Asst. brewing technologist F&M Schaffer Brewing Co., Bklyn., 1948-52; factory sales rep. Cole Steel Equipment Co., N.Y.C., 1957-68; dist. sales mgr. Scantlin Electronics, Inc., Washington, 1968-70; sales rep. Comml. Washer & Dryer Sales Co., Washington, 1970-72; propr. Webster Tilton, Jr., contractor, Washington, 1972-86. Served from cadet to chief mate Mcht. Marine Res.-USNR, 1942-45. Episcopalian. Home: RD #2 Box 634 Cooperstown NY 13326

TILY, STEPHEN BROMLEY, III, banker; b. Phila., July 7, 1937; s. Stephen Bromley and Edith Helen (Straub) T.; m. Janet Anita Walz, July 10, 1965; children: Deborah Powell, Stephen Bromley, James Charles. B.A., Washington and Jefferson Coll., 1960; postgrad. Temple Sch. of Law, 1962-63. Trust officer Indsl. Valley Bank and Trust Co., Phila., 1968-71; v.p. Farmers Bank of the State of Del., Wilmington, 1971-77; exec. v.p., chief operating officer Del. Charter Guarantee and Trust Co., Wilmington, 1977-80, pres., chief executive officer, 1980-91; chmn., CEO,, 1992—;chmn. Declaration Holdings, Inc.; sec. Declaration Investment Advisors, Inc., 1990; pres., trustee Declaration Distbrs., Inc., 1990; tchr. Am. Inst. of Banking, Valley Forge chpt. Served in USAR, QMC, 1960-61. Mem. Fin. Analysts of Wilmington, Inc., Kimberton Fish and Game Assn., Ducks Unltd., Barnegat Light Yacht Club (Harvey Cedars, N.J.); Waynesbourgh Country Club (Paoli, Pa.); Union League Club (Phila.); University Club (Wilmington), Whist Club. Office: Del Charter Guarantee and Trust Co PO Box 8963 Wilmington DE 19899-8772

TIMBERS, WILLIAM HOMER, federal judge; b. Yonkers, N.Y., Sept. 5, 1915; s. Harley Homer and Florence (Birmingham) T.; m. Charlotte MacLachlan Tanner, June 21, 1941; children: John William, Nancy Joan, Dwight Edward, William Homer Jr. A.B. magna cum laude, Dartmouth Coll., 1937; LL.B., Yale U., 1940; LL.D. (hon.), Fairfield U., 1977. Bar: N.Y. 1940, U.S. Supreme Ct 1946, also other fed. cts 1946, Conn. 1948, D.C. 1954. Assoc. firm Davis, Polk, Wardwell, Sunderland & Kiendl, N.Y.C., 1940-48; mem. firm Cummings & Lockwood, Stamford, Conn., 1948-53; gen. counsel SEC, Washington, 1953-56; mem. firm Skadden, Arps, Slate & Timbers, N.Y.C., 1956-60; judge U.S. Dist. Ct., Dist. Conn., 1960-71, chief judge, 1964-71; judge U.S. Ct. Appeals, 2d Circuit, 1971—. Mem. alumni council Dartmouth Coll., 1967-71, pres., 1969-71, Yale Law Sch. Alumni Assn., 1953-61, sec. 1959-61, Pres.'s Adv. Com. on Fitness of Am. Youth, 1958-60. Mem. Phi Beta Kappa, Phi Kappa Psi. Presbyterian (elder, trustee). Clubs: Am. Kennel (dir. 1968-84, chmn. bd. 1982-84), Norwegian Elkhound Assn. Am. (pres. 1961-71, dir. 1961-71), Ox Ridge Kennel (pres. 1958-68, dir. 1958-85), Westminster Kennel. Home: RR 1 Box 109 Surry ME 04684-9710 also: 109 Newbury Neck Rd Surry ME 04684 Office: US Ct Appeals US Courthouse Foley Sq New York NY 10007-1501 also: US Courthouse 915 Lafayette Blvd Bridgeport CT 06604

TIMKO, FRANCIS MARTIN MICHAEL, probation officer; b. Yonkers, N.Y., Aug. 21, 1944; s. Frank Joseph and Mary Gemma (Musak) T.; m. Christine M. Duro, Oct. 24, 1975; children: Tara Nichole, April Ann, Jason Francis, Kelly Marie, Sara Leann. BA, Adams State Coll., 1967; MS, CCNY, 1972; PhD in Sociology, Fordham U., 1991. Instr. psychology Westchester Community Coll., Valhalla, N.Y., 1970-71; free-lance indsl. photographer, Technicon Corp., Tarrytown, N.Y., 1972-73; sr. group counselor Woodfield Detention Cottage, Valhalla, N.Y., 1973; probation officer Westchester County Dept. Probation, Mt. Vernon, N.Y., 1973-89; supervising probation officer Designated Assessment Svc. Westchester County, New Rochelle, N.Y., 1989-90, 3B Automated Mail Reporting System, 1990—. Contbr. articles to profl. jours. Mem. Apt. Owners' Adv. Council, Westchester County, N.Y., 1987-88; dist. leader (E.D. 21) Rep. Party of Yorktown, N.Y., 1987-88; mem. County Com. Rep. Party of Westchester County, 1987-88. With USAF, 1967-69. Recipient Disting. Service Key, Alpha Phi Omega, 1967. Mem. Am. Sociol. Assn., Am. Psychol. Assn., N.Y. Probation Officers Assn. (exec. bd. 1980—, regional v.p., chmn. standards and practices com. 1986—). Home: 1050 Barberry Rd Yorktown Heights NY 10598-2901 Office: 111 Grove St Fl 5 White Plains NY 10601-2592

TIMMERMAN, LEON BERNARD, pump industry consultant; b. Buffalo, Aug. 20, 1924; s. Leon D. and Julia (Schlau) T.; m. Kathryn Wagner, Feb. 26, 1924; children: Kathryn Timmerman Susak, Carol Timmerman Yorty. BSME, Purdue U., 1949; grad. bus. mgmt. program, Harvard U., 1970. Lic. profl. engr., N.Y. With Buffalo Pumps, 1949-87; engr., sales mgr. various locations, 1949-80; nat. sales and mktg. mgr. North Tonawanda, N.Y., 1981-87; pres., cons. to pump and related industries CP Cons. Svcs., Williamsville, N.Y., 1987—; com. chmn. Hydraulic Inst., 1961-78, v.p., 1978-79, pres., 1979-80, chmn. exec. com., 1980-81, Europump rep. 1978-81. Contbr. articles to profl. jours. With Signal Corps U.S. Army, 1943-45, PTO. Recipient numerous Salesman of Yr. awards Buffalo Pumps Inc. 1955-70. Mem. Tech. Assn. Pulp and Paper Industry, Scalp & Blade, Brookfield Country Club. Republican. Presbyterian. Office: CP Cons Svcs 41 Carriage Cir Buffalo NY 14221-2101

TIMMERMAN, ROBERT WILSON, engineer; b. Abington, Pa., July 27, 1944; s. Clarence Arthur and Mildred Wilson (Slack) T.; m. Nancy Jean Spinka, Sept. 28, 1974; children: Robert Jr., Elizabeth Jane. M in Engring., Cornell U., 1966, BS, 1965; postgrad., Northwestern U., Evanston, Ill., 1971-72, U. Pa., 1972-74. Project engr. Monsanto Co., Springfield, Mass., 1966-68; staff engr. Stone and Webster Engring. Corp., Boston, 1968-71, United Engrs. and Constructor, Boston, 1974-75; sr. engr. R.W. Beck and Assoc., Wellesley, Mass., 1975-77; prin. R.W. Timmerman and Assoc., Boston, 1977—. Patentee in field; contbr. articles to profl. jours. Mem. ASME (sect. chmn. 1979-89, nat. com. pub. affairs, 1981), ASHRAE, Mass. Engrs. Coun. (treas. 1984-86). Presbyterian. Home and Office: 25 Upton St Boston MA 02118-1609

TIMPANE, PHILIP MICHAEL, college administrator; b. Troy, N.Y., Nov. 27, 1934; s. Philip Thomas and Rita (Killeen) T.; m. Genevieve LaGrua, Nov. 30, 1957; children: Michael J., Joseph T., Paul J., David A. AB, Cath. U. Am., 1956, MA, 1964; MPA, Harvard U., 1970; LittD (hon.), Wagner Coll., 1986; LLD (hon.), Catholic U. Am., 1991. Historian Joint Chiefs of Staff Dept. Def., 1961-65; spl. asst. civil rights Office of Sec. Def., 1965-68; edn. policy planner HEW, 1968-72; sr. fellow Brookings Instn., 1972-74; dir. edn. policy ctr. Rand Corp., 1974-77; dep. dir. Nat. Inst. Edn., Washington, 1977-80; dir. Nat. Inst. Edn., 1980-81; prof. edn., dean Tchrs. Coll. Columbia U., N.Y.C., 1981-84, pres., 1984—; Aspen Inst. Edn. Program, 1974-77, 87—. Author: Corporate Interest in Public Education in the Cities, 1982; co-author: Youth Policy in Transition, 1976; co-editor: Planned Variation in Education, 1975, Work Incentives and Income Guarantees, 1975, Ethical and Legal Issues in Social Experimentation, 1975; editor: Federal Interest in Financing Schooling, 1978. Me. Arlington Sch. Bd., Va., 1972-76, chmn., 1973-74; bd. dirs. Am. Assn. for Higher Edn., 1985—, Synergos Inst., 1988—, Children's TV Workshop, 1989—, Am. Coun. Edn., 1991—. Mem. Century Assn., Cosmos Club. Democrat. Roman Catholic. Office: Columbia U Tchrs Coll Office of Pres PO Box 163 New York NY 10027-0163

TIMS, JODI LYNN, computer science educator; b. Johnstown, Pa., Nov. 1, 1958; d. Francis Clement and Joyce Evelyn (Stephens) Ruhe; m. Michael Lee Tims, Apr. 25, 1981; children: Stephen Michael, Christi Lynn. BS in Math./Computer Sci., U. Pitts., Johnstown, Pa., 1980; MS in Computer Sci., U. Pitts., 1987, postgrad., 1989—. Math learning ctr. supr. U. Pitts., Johnstown, 1981-82, instr., 1982-87, asst. prof., 1987—. Mem. Assn. for Computing Machinery, IEEE Computer Soc., Pa. Coun. of Tchrs. of Math., ACM Spl. Interest Group on Programming Langs. Office: U Pitts Johnstown PA 15904

TINARI, FRANK DALE, economics professor, consultant; b. N.Y.C., Apr. 19, 1943; s. Adelchi and Carmela (Neri) T.; m. Barbara Ann Nastro, June 8, 1968; children: April Erica, Alexandra Nicole, Christa Marie. BS, Fordham U., 1964, MA, 1966, PhD, 1976. Asst. prof. econs. Seton Hall U., South Orange, N.J., 1971-77, assoc. prof., 1977-82, prof., 1982—, dir. research sch. bus., 1980-82; lectr. Drew U., Madison, N.J., 1977-78; pres. Tinari Econs., Florham Park, N.J., 1979—; vis. scholar U. Internat. Bus. & Econs., Beijing, China, 1983, 85. Editorial referee Review of Social Economy, Milw., 1978—; editor, founder Mt. Carmel News, N.Y.C., 1966-68; author: Economics: The Options for Dealing with Scarcity, 1986; contbr. articles to profl. jours. Pres. Viri Literati Soc., N.Y.C., 1964-65; pres. Florham Park Jaycees, 1976-77, vice chmn. planning bd., 1979-88; v.p., pres. Madison-Chatham Adult Sch., 1987—. Capt. U.S. Army, 1968-70. Fellow Pace U., N.Y.C., 1967. Mem. Am. Econ. Assn., Assn. for Social Econs., Assn. for Forensic Econs., N.J. Assn. Bus. Economists. Roman Catholic. Office: Seton Hall U Dept Econs South Orange NJ 07079

TING, SAMUEL CHAO CHUNG, physicist, educator; b. Ann Arbor, Mich., Jan. 27, 1936; s. Kuan H. and Jeanne (Wong) T.; m. Susan Carol Marks, Apr. 28, 1985; children: Jeanne Min, Amy Min, Christopher M. BS in Engring, U. Mich., 1959, MS, 1960, PhD, 1962, ScD (hon.), 1978; ScD (hon.), Chinese U. Hong Kong, 1987, U. Bologna, Italy, 1988, Columbia U., 1990, Moscow State U., 1991. Ford Found. fellow CERN (European Orgn. Nuclear Research), Geneva, 1963; instr. physics Columbia U., 1964, asst. prof., 1965-67; group leader Deutsches Elektronen-Synchrotron, Hamburg, W.Ger., 1966; assoc. prof. physics MIT, Cambridge, 1967-68, prof., 1969—; Thomas Dudley Cabot Inst. prof. M.I.T., 1977—; program cons. Div. Particles and Fields, Am. Phys. Soc., 1970; hon. prof. Beijing Normal Coll., 1987, Jiatong U., Shanghai, 1987, U. Bologna, Italy, 1988. Assoc. editor: Nuclear Physics B, 1970; contbr. articles in field to profl. jours.; editorial bd.: Nuclear Instruments and Methods, Mathematical Modeling; advisor Jour. Modern Physics A. Recipient Nobel prize in Physics, 1976, De Gasperi prize in Sci., Italian Republic, 1988, Ernest Orlando Lawrence award U.S. Govt., 1976, Eringen medal Soc. Engring. Sci., 1977, Gold medal in Sci. City of Brescia, Italy, 1988, Golden Leopard award Town of Taormina, 1988; Am. Acad. Sci. and Arts fellow, 1975. Mem. NAS; fgn. mem. Pakistani Acad. Sci., Academia Sinica, Soviet Acad. Sci. USSR. Office: MIT Dept Physics 51 Vassar St Cambridge MA 02139-4308

TINGIR, RAFFI NURHAN, pediatrics educator; b. Istanbul, Turkey, Aug. 5, 1954; came to U.S., 1980; s. Nurhan Savars and Silla Sona (Dermarkarian) T.; m. Nadine Ani Guevrekian, May 31, 1981; children: Roxanne Ani, Nicole Arpi, Corinne Sona. BA, Robert Coll., Istanbul, 1973; MD summa cum laude, Istanbul U., 1979; postgrad., NYU, 1983, Cornell U., 1986. Diplomate Am. Bd. Pediatrics. Surg. resident Booth Meml. Med. Ctr., Flushing, N.Y., 1980-81, Beekman Downtown Hosp., N.Y.C., 1981-83, NYU Hosp., 1981-83, Bellevue Hosp., N.Y.C., 1981-83, N.Y. VA Hsop., N.Y.C., 1981-83; pediatric resident North Shore Univ. Hosp., Manhasset, N.Y., 1983-86; attending clin. instr. North Shore Univ. Hosp., Manhasset, 1986—; pediatric resident Sloan-Kettering Meml. Ctr., N.Y.C., 1983-86; attending Winthrop Univ. Hosp., Mineola, N.Y., 1986—; chief sch. physician, Manhasset Sch. Dist., 1986—, Roslyn (N.Y.) Sch. Dist., 1986—, Pt. Washington (N.Y.) Sch. Dist., 1986—, Armenian Parochial Sch., Bayside, N.Y., 1986—; clin. instr. pediatrics Cornell U. Med. Coll. Fellow Am. Acad. Pediatrics; mem. AMA, Med. Soc. State N.Y., Nassau County Med. Soc. Mem. Armenian Ch. Office: 1025 Northern Blvd Ste 210 Roslyn NY 11576-1506

TINGLEY, CHARLES ELBERT, transportation company executive; b. Braddock, Pa., Mar. 1, 1939; s. Elbert Roy and Catherine (DeMay) T.; children: Chad, Kristen. BA in Econs., U. Va., 1964. Various sales mgmt. positions Allied Chem., 1964-72, mgr. sales, div. chem., 1970-72; various exec. positions Itel Corp., 1972-79, v.p. North/South Am., 1977-79; v.p. North/South Am. Transamerica ICS, N.Y.C., 1979-80; exec. v.p. Transamerica ICS, 1980-81; pres. Transamerica Container Leasing, White Plains, N.Y., 1981-88, Transamerica Leasing, White Plains, 1988-89; pres., CEO Transamerica Leasing, 1989—; bd. dirs. Transamerica Fin. Corp., L.A., 1989—, Transamerica Leasing, White Plains, 1981—, Inst. Internat. Container Lessors, 1982—, former pres. Office: Transamerica Leasing Inc 711 Westchester Ave White Plains NY 10604-3504

TINKELMAN, JOSEPH, periodontist; b. N.Y.C., May 6, 1924; s. Charles and Freda (Glatzer) T.; m. Roslyn Edith Bernath, Apr. 29, 1945; children: Randall, Jeffrey, Steven. Student, Hobart Coll., Ohio State U.; DDS, U. Ill., Chgo., 1950. Cert. in periodontics, N.Y. Asst. prof. NYU, 1972-80; pvt. practice Poughkeepsie, N.Y., 1972—. Bus. editor Jour. of Acad. Oral Medicine, 1980-88. With Armed Forces, OSS, 1943-46. mem. ADA, Dental Soc. of N.Y., 9th Dist. Dentists of N.Y. (bd. dirs.), Dutchess County Dental Soc. (pres. 1978), Am. Acad. of Periodontology, N.Y. State Soc. Periodontists (pres. 1988-89), N.E. U.S. B'nai B'rith (dist. bd. dirs.). Office: 1 Field Ct Poughkeepsie NY 12601-5299

TINSLEY, PETER A., economist; b. Pikeville, Ky., Jan. 21, 1939; s. Benjamin W.H. and Evelyn (Ault) T.; children: Catherine, Margaret. BA, Hobart Coll., Geneva, N.Y., 1960; PhD, Princeton U., 1966. Econ. Fed. Res. Bd., Washington, 1965-70, sr. econ., 1970-71, chief, 1971-82, asst. dir., 1982-86, dep. assoc. dir., 1987—. Contbr. articles to profl. jours. Office: Fed Res Bd Div Res Statist 21st Constitution Ave NE Washington DC 20551-0001

TIPPETT, BRYAN KEITH, biology educator; b. Pitts., June 18, 1957; s. Joseph Calvin and Annie Mell (Woods) T. BS in Biology, Gannon U., 1979; MS in Biology, Duquesne U., 1982. Mental health technician Hamot Mental Health Ctr., Erie, Pa., 1979-80; clin. lab. tech. Allegheny Gen. Hosp., Pitts., 1982-88, clin. lab. supr., 1988-90; from assoc. prof. to prof. biology Community Coll. of Allegheny County, Pitts., 1990—. Author abstracts in field. Trustee Second Bapt. Ch., Homestead, Pa., 1983—, choir dir., 1984—; lectr. Steel Valley High Sch., Homestead, 1989—. Named to Outstanding Young Men of Am., 1988. Mem. Charles Givens Fin. Network, NAACP, Zool. Soc. Pitts., Beta Beta Beta. Democrat. Home: 105 Holmes Pl Pittsburgh PA 15213-4506

TIPTON, THOMAS WESLEY, flight engineer; b. Okmulgee, Okla., May 12, 1952; s. John Melvin and Norma Dean (Boyd) T.; m. Paula Jean Sumpter, Oct. 5, 1973 (div. June 1988); children: Samuel Lawrence, Stacy Lynn; m. Evelyn Marie Harzinski, Sept. 17, 1988; 1 child, Jonathan Clark. Student, William Penn Coll., Oskaloosa, Iowa, 1970-72. Enlisted U.S. Navy, 1972; div supr. Fighter Squadron 101, Naval Air Sta., Oceana, Va., 1973-76; quality assurance officer Naval Air Sta., Keflavik, Iceland, 1976-79; drill instr. Recruit Tng. Ctr., Great Lakes, Ill., 1980-83; flight engr., evaluator Patrol Squadron 26, Brunswick, Maine, 1983-89; flight engr., test and evaluation Force Warfare Naval Air Warfare Ctr. Aircraft Div., Patuxent River, Md., 1989—. Mem. Nat. Rifle Assn. (life), Smithsonian Air and Space Mus., Frinds of the Kennedy Ctr., Nat. Geographic Soc., Nat. Wildlife Fund. Home: 436 Council Bluffs Lusby MD 20657 Office: Force Warfare Directorate Naval Air Warfare Ctr Patuxent River MD 20670

TIRER, SAMUEL, physician; b. Haifa, Israel, Oct. 8, 1950; s. Morris and Sabina (Davidson) T.; m. Margaret Sheila Sullivan, Apr. 14, 1978; children: Alexandra, Daniel. BSc with honors, McGill, Montreal, Can., 1972, MD, CM, 1976. Intern Hosp. U. Pa., Phila., 1976-77; staff physician Mt. Sinai Hosp., Ste Agathe, Que., Can., 1977-78; resident Hosp. U. Pa., Phila., 1978-81; asst. prof. U. Pa., Phila., 1981-83; staff anesthesiologist Frankford Hosp., Phila., 1984-85; asst. prof. U. Pa., Phila., 1985-89, clin. asst. prof., 1989—; med. dir. Short Procedure Unit, Presbyn. Med. Ctr., Phila., 1990—. Contbr. articles to profl. jours. Mem. Town Watch, Lower Merion, Pa., 1991, Mus. Com. Wood Libr., Park Ridge, Ill., 1990—. Fellow Coll. Physicians Phila., 1989. Mem. McGill Soc. Phila. (pres. 1982—).

TIRINO, PHILIP JOSEPH, accountant; b. N.Y.C., Feb. 12, 1940; s. Philip Vincent and Louise Ann (Lanza) T.; m. Joan M. Marino, 1979; children: Philip Jr., Bart Scott, David. BBA in Bus. Acctg., Hofstra U., 1962. CPA, N.Y. Auditor N.Y. State Dept. Fin., N.Y.C., 1962-65; acct., auditor various publ. acctg. firms, N.Y.C., 1964-69; controller Berman Leasing Co., Englewood, N.J., 1969-73, Bank of Calif., Stanford, Conn., 1973-74, Chase Manhattan Bank, N.Y.C., 1975-78, Bankers Trust Co., N.Y.C., 1978-83; speaker Found. Acctg. Edn., N.Y.C., 1977—, Am. Assn. Equipment Lessors, Washington, 1977-82, World Trade Inst., 1980. Contbr. articles to profl. jours. Tax planner Taxpayer's Assn., Nanuet, N.Y., 1981; budget officer Clarkstown Suprs. Office, New City, N.Y., 1984. Mem. AICPA, N.Y. State Soc. CPAs (com. fin. leasing 1977-80, fin. acctg. standards com., 1980-83, 85-87). Republican. Roman Catholic. Home: 16 Maple Ave West Nyack NY 10994-1810 Office: NE Fin Systems 14 Maple Ave West Nyack NY 10994-1810

TIRNAUER, LAWRENCE THEODORE, psychologist, psychotherapist; b. N.Y.C., Apr. 15, 1933; s. Samuel and Rose Tirnauer; m. Sandra Smathers (div.); children: Jennifer, Karen, Diana, Eric. BA, Otterbein Coll., 1954; MS, Pa. State U., 1955, PhD, 1959. Lic. psychologist, Washington. Staff psychologist St. Elizabeth's Hosp., Washington, 1959-60; psychologist Child Guidance Clinic D.C. Health Dept., Washington, 1960-63, chief psychologist children's program area C, 1963-64, chief psychologist adolescent program area C, 1964-65; chief psychologist Bur. Infant and Maternal Care, Washington, 1965-68; pvt. practice psychology and psychotherapy Washington, 1968—; cons. McFarland Child Guidance Clinic, Washington, 1965-68, Washington Free Clinic, 1970-75, Pastoral Counseling Ctrs., 1965-85. Editorial bd. Voices: The Art and Sci. of Psychotherapy, 1977—; assoc. editor The Psychotherpay Patient, 1984—; contbr. articles on psychotherapy to profl. jours., chpts. to books. Mem. Am. Acad. Psychotherapists (pres. 1986-88), Am. Psychol. Assn., D.C. Psychol. Assn. Office: 5225 Connecticut Ave NW Washington DC 20015-1845

TIRONE, ROBERT J., insurance broker; b. Staten Island, N.Y., Apr. 12, 1945; s. Joseph L. and Madelyn (Garzone) T.; m. Stephanie M. Mura, Nov. 18, 1967; children: Kimberley, Christopher, Laura. BA in History, Marist Coll., 1966. Underwriter Associated Aviation Underwriters, N.Y.C., 1967-69; broker, mgr., staff v.p. Alexander & Alexander-Nat. Aviation & Areospace Div., N.Y.C., 1969-91; v.p. Nat. Aviation div. Sedgwick James Inc., Short Hills, N.J., 1991—. Contbr. articles to profl. jours. Pres. Staten Island Dem. Soc., 1975, mem. state com., 1974-77. Mem. Am. Inst. Aeronautics and Astronautics. Home: 4114 Central Ave Apt 317 4 Worthington Ct Sea Isle City NJ 08243 Office: Sedgwick James Inc Nat Aviation Div 830 Morris Turnpike Short Hills NJ 07078

TIRRELL, BRUCE KEVIN, hotel executive; b. Vineland, N.J., July 18, 1964; s. Walter Joseph and Yvonne Marie (Peteriet) T. Human resources rep. Claridge Casino Hotel, Atlantic City, 1984-87; compensation analyst Trump Pla. Hotel & Casino, Atlantic City, 1987-88, HR systems supr., 1988-89, compensation adminstr., 1989-90, compensation and benefits mgr., 1990—. Office: Trump Pla Hotel & Casino Mississippi Atlantic City NJ 08401-6662

TIRRELL, PEG HARRIET, association executive, round dance teacher; b. Hackensack, N.J., May 7, 1924; m. Robert W. Tirrell, Jr., June 16, 1948; children: Scott, Barbara, Gail. AA, Colby Jr. Coll., New London, N.H., 1943; BA in Edn., Glassboro (N.J.) State Coll., 1945; MA in Reading, Columbia U., 1948. Tchr. round dancing, N.J. area, 1949—; editor No. N.J. Square Dancers Assn., N.J. area, 1965-90; exec. sec. ROUNDALAB, 1984—; chmn. Legacy. Author short articles on square dance activity. Chmn. evening membership dept. Woman's Club of Tenafly, N.J.; active in scouting, Sunday Sch. Mem. No. N.J. Round Dance Leaders Coun. (treas.), Vt. Area Round Dance Leaders. Home and Office: PO Box 37 Lower Waterford VT 05848-0037

TISCH, LAURENCE ALAN, broadcast corporation executive; b. N.Y.C., Mar. 15, 1923; s. Al and Sadye (Brenner) T.; m. Wilma Stein, Oct. 31, 1948; children: Andrew, Daniel, James, Thomas. BSc cum laude, NYU, 1942; MA in Indsl. Engring, U. Pa., 1943; postgrad., Harvard Law Sch., 1946. Pres. Tisch Hotels, Inc., N.Y.C., 1946-74; chmn. bd., chief exec. officer Loews Corp., N.Y.C., 1960—, co-chief exec. officer, 1988—; pres., chief exec. officer CBS Inc., N.Y.C., 1987—, chmn., pres. chief exec. officer, 1990—, also bd. dirs.; chmn. bd. dirs. CNA Fin. Corp., Chgo.; bd. dirs. Bulova Corp. subs. Loews Corp., N.Y., Automatic Data Processing Corp., Petrie Stores Corp., R.H. Macy & Co. Bd. dirs. United Jewish Appeal-Fed.; chmn. bd. trustees NYU; trustee Met. Mus. Art, N.Y.C., N.Y. Pub. Libr., Carnegie Corp.; mem. Mayor's Com. for Pub.-Pvt. Partnerships, Coun. on Fgn. Rels. Home: Island Dr N Manursing Island Rye NY 10580 Office: CBS Inc 51 W 52nd St New York NY 10019-6101

TISCHER, CAROLYN LOIS, artist, designer; b. New Haven, Dec. 8, 1943; d. Walter Raymond and Lois Ruth (Polley) T.; m. Richard Cruthers Bartlett, Jr., Aug. 8, 1970; children: Richard Cruthers III, Raymond Walter. Grad. in bus. and acctg., Laurel Coll., 1961; student, Paier Sch. Art, Hamden, Conn., 1968. Freelance legal asst., researcher, portrait artist Meriden, Conn., 1962-70; pres. Timberlane Oil, Inc., Freehold, N.J., 1976-83; owner, mgr. Free Style Arts, Freehold, 1984-89, Tisch's Place, Farmingdale, N.J., 1988—; v.p. R.C.B. Trucking, Inc., Farmingdale, N.J., 1990—; promotional dir. Autumn Outdoor Art Exhibit, Wallingford, Conn., 1968; sem. dir. Ponal Studios, Farmingdale, 1985-87; mem. steering com. Monmouth County Arts Coun., 1992. Commd. artist Howell Hist. Soc., 1989; exhibited in group shows. Recipient best in show awards, 1985, 86, various other awards. Mem. Freehold Art Soc. (bd. dirs. 1985-89, pres. 1989-92, instr. 1988-92), Guild Creative Art, Art Alliance, Monmouth Arts Gallery, Farmingdale C. of C., N.J. Assn. Women Bus. Owners. Republican. Episcopalian. Office: Free Style Arts-Tisch's Pl 101 Main St PO Box 792 Farmingdale NJ 07727-1207

TISDALE, JOHN ROBERT, education educator; b. Cedar Rapids, Iowa, Dec. 10, 1932; s. Leslie Owen and Eleanor Grace (Clements) T.; m. Elizabeth Ann Snyder, June 8, 1954 (div. May 1973); m. Beverly Jean Luzietti, Feb. 27, 1975; children: Deborah, Paul, Scott, Erik. BA, Cornell Coll., 1954; MDiv, Boston U. Sch. Theology, 1958; PhD, Boston U., 1961. Asst. prof. psychology Cornell Coll., Mt. Vernon, Iowa, 1961-67; coll. counselor Cornell Coll., Mt. Vernon, 1964-67; rsch. assoc. Union Coll. Character Rsch. Project, Schenectady, N.Y., 1966-67; assoc. prof. psychology Cedar Crest Coll., Allentown, Pa., 1967-70; prof. psychology Cedar Crest Coll., Allentown, 1970—; pvt. practice psychotherapy self-employed, Coplay, Pa., 1973-78; rsch. coord. Pastoral Inst. Lehigh Valley, Allentown, 1967-72. Author: Growing Edges in Psychology of Religion, 1980; mem. adv. bd. Jour. Pastoral Counseling, 1990—; contbr. articles to profl. jours. Bd. dirs. Easter Pa. Emergency Med. Svcs. Coun., Allentown, 1978-84, Child Guidance Ctr. Lehigh Valley, Allentown, 1984-86, Edn. Ventures, Inc., Allentown, 1981-84, 1990—; trustee Cedar Crest Coll., 1976-80, 91—. Recipient NSF Coll. Tchr. Rsch. award, 1964-66, Outstanding Educators Am. award; named Lilly Pa. Fellow Lilly Found., 1980. Fellow: Lehigh Valley Psychol. Assn. (pres. 1970-71, 78-79); mem. APA, Div. 32 APA (pres. 1982-83), Div. 36 APA (sec. 1988-91, chmn. com. on div. rels. 1992—), Transpersonal Psychology Interest Group (pres. 1988-89), Nat. Register Health Svc. Providers Psychol., Soc. Sci. Study Religion, Phi Beta Kappa. Methodist. Home: 2983 Old Post Rd Slatington PA 18080-3103 Office: Cedar Crest Coll 100 College Dr Allentown PA 18104-6196

TISHLER, SIDNEY, communications and public relations executive; b. Balt., Aug. 14, 1937; s. Eli and Anna (Exler) T.; m. Marsha Leikach, Aug. 20, 1967; children: Julie Lynn, Alisa Lauren. BS, Towson State U., Balt., 1958; postgrad., Pasadena (Calif.) Playhouse, 1959; MLA, Johns Hopkins U., 1968. Tchr. elem. and secondary English Balt. Pub. Schs., 1958-65, producer, radio-TV specialist, 1965-69; apprentice, gen. mgr. Clinton (Conn.) Playhouse, 1956-58; gen. mgr. Southbury (Conn.) Playhouse, 1963; instructional TV specialist Md. State Dept. Edn., Owings MIlls, 1969-74; dir. telecommunications Md. Pub. TV, Owings Mills, 1974-86; cons. Tishler Communications, Balt., 1986-89; project dir. Md. State Bar Assn., Balt., 1989-90; dir. spl. projects The Chimes, Inc., Balt., 1990—; advisor/cons. Pub. Svc. Satellite Consortium, Washington, 1987-88. Home: 8219 Brattle Rd Baltimore MD 21208 Office: The Chimes Inc 3630 Milford Mill Rd Baltimore MD 21207

TISINGER, CATHERINE ANNE, college dean; b. Winchester, Va., Apr. 6, 1936; d. Richard Martin and Irma Regina (Ohl) T. BA, Coll. Wooster, 1958; MA, U. Pa., 1962, PhD, 1970; LLD (hon.), Coll. of Elms, 1985. Provost Callison Coll., U. of Pacific, Stockton, Calif., 1971-72; v.p. Met. State U., St. Paul, 1972-75; v.p. acad. affairs S.W. State U., Marshall, Minn., 1975-76, interim pres., 1976-77; dir. Ctr. for Econ. Edn., R.I. Coll., Providence, 1979-80; v.p. acad. affairs Cen. Mo. State U., Warrensburg, Mo., 1980-84; pres. North Adams State Coll., Mass., 1984-91; dean arts and scis. Shenandoah U., Winchester, Va., 1991—; cons. North Cen. Assn. Colls. and Schs., 1980-84, New Eng. Assn. Schs. and Colls., 1978-79, 85—, Minn. Acad. Family Physicians, 1973-77; mem. adv. bd. First Agrl. Bank, North Adams, 1985-91; pres. No. Berkshire Cooperating Colls., 1986-91; v.p. Coll. Consortium for Internat. Studies, 1989-90. V.p. Med. Simulation Found., 1986-88; bd. dirs. Williamstown Concerts, 1988-91, Shawnee coun. Girl Scouts U.S., 1992—. Mem. No. Berkshire C. of C. (bd. dirs. 1984-89, v.p. 1986-89). Avocations: fiber and textile arts, photography, choral and instrumental music. Office: Shenandoah U 1460 College Dr Winchester VA 22601

TITELMAN, RUSS, recording industry executive; b. L.A., Aug. 16, 1944; s. Herbert Titelman and Leonore (Greenburg) Hayman; m. Carol Ann Wikarska, May 10, 1978. Producer Warner Bros. Records, N.Y.C., 1971—. Record producer for albums Little Feat, 1970, Sail Away, Randy Newman, 1972, Paradise and Lunch, Ry Cooder, 1973, Good Old Boys, Randy Newman, 1974, Gorilla, James Taylor, 1975, In the Pocket, James Taylor, 1976, Little Criminals, Randy Newman, 1977, George Harrison, 1979, Rickie Lee Jones, 1979 (Grammy award Best New Artist), Pirates, Rickie Lee Jones, 1981, Hearts and Bones, Paul Simon, 1983, Ain't Nobody, Rufus with Chaka Khan, 1983 (Grammy award Best R&B Performance by Duo or Group with Vocal), 20/20, George Benson, 1985, Back in the High Life, Steve Winwood, 1986 (Grammy award Best Pop Vocal Male, Grammy nomination Album of Yr.), Sangoma, Mariam Makeba, 1988, Journey of Dreams, Ladysmith Black Mambazo, 1988, Journeyman, Eric Clapton, 1989, Higher Love, Steve Winwood (Grammy award Record of Yr., 1986), Bad Love, Eric Clapton, (Grammy award Best Rock Vocal Male, 1990). Jewish.

TITON, JEFF TODD, ethnomusicologist; b. Jersey City, Dec. 8, 1943; s. Milton Manuel and Edith Lee T.; m. Paula Winslow Protze, July 16, 1966; 1 child, Emily. BA in Am. Studies, Amherst Coll., 1965; MA in Am. Studies, U. Minn., 1967, MA in English, 1970, PhD in Am. Studies, 1971. Asst. prof. English Tufts U., Medford, Mass., 1971-77, assoc. prof., 1977-86; prof. music, ethnomusicology Brown U., Providence, 1986—; panelist Folk Arts program Nat. Endowment for Arts, 1981-84, 91-92; dir. Koetting Archive, Brown U., 1987—; bd. dirs. Main Folklife Ctr., U. Maine, Orono, 1989—. Author: Early Downhome Blues, 1977 (ASCAP award), Powerhouse for God, 1988; author, editor: Worlds of Music, 1984; co-dir. film Powerhouse for God, 1989. NEH fellow, 1977-78, 86; grantee Nat. Endowment for Arts, 1985; DuBois Inst. fellow Harvard U., 1986. Mem. Soc. Ethnomusicology (editor 1990—), Am. Folklore Soc., Am. Studies Assn., Appalachian Studies Assn., Sonneck Soc. Office: Brown Univ PO Box 1924 Providence RI 02912-1924

TITUS, CHARLES OTIS, health care medical director; b. Augusta, Maine, Jan. 26, 1927; s. Charles O. Titus and Effie M. Douphinelt; m. Joan M. Myles, Dec. 27, 1954; children: Donna, William, Elizabeth, Joseph, Mary, Melinda, Karen. BS, BA, U. Ottawa, Can., 1951, MD, 1956. Cert. Am. Bd. Ophthalmology. Intern Ottawa (Can.) Gen. Hosp., 1955-56; resident Northwestern Med. Ctr., Chgo., 1956-59; commd. 2d lt. USAF, 1959, advanced through grades to col., 1966; pvt. practice Washington, 1966-74; hosp. comdr. Air Nat. Guard, Washington, 1973-84; med. dir. Bausch & Lomb, Rochester, N.Y., 1974—. Fellow Am. Coll. Surgeons, Am. Acad. Ophthalmologists; mem. Contact Lens Assn. Ophthalmologists, Pan-Am. Med. Assn., Soc. Mil. Ophthalmologists. Home: 12 Niblick Ct Penfield NY 14526 Office: Bausch & Lomb 1400 N Goodman St Rochester NY 14692

TITUS, CURTIS VEST, lawyer; b. New Haven, Jan. 4, 1933; s. Curtis Turner and Margaret (Vest) T.; B.A., Williams Coll., 1954; LL.B., Harvard U. Law Sch., 1957; children from previous marriage: Curtis Elliot, Margaret Ann, Pamela Jane, Nancy Pogue, Laura Turner, Lavinia Resor Law; m. Janet B. Sweeney, 1987. Bar: Conn. 1957. Assoc. firm Pullman, Comley, Bradley & Reeves, Bridgeport, Conn., 1957-67; ptnr. firm Gager & Henry, Waterbury, Conn., 1967—; sec., dir. Middlebury (Conn.) Land Trust Inc., 1969—; sec., Risdon Mfg. Co., 1978-79. Dir. Easter Seal Rehab. Ctr., 1971-76, 79-86, v.p., 1981-82, pres., 1982-84; mem. Middlebury Planning and Zoning Commn., 1971-91, chmn., 1978-91; dir. Greater Waterbury Health Network, 1986—, Greater Waterbury Mgmt. Resources, Inc., 1991—; trustee Waterbury Hosp., 1981—, mem. exec. com., 1984—, sec., 1991; rep. Cen. Naugatuck Valley Regional Planning Agy., 1975-77; bd. dirs. Highfield, Inc., 1987-92, pres., 1992—, Mattatuck Community Coll. Found., Inc., 1981—, chmn., 1981-89. Mem. Greater Waterbury C. of C. (dir. 1976-84, chmn. Econ. Devel. Coun. 1980-84, vice chmn. econ. devel. 1981-84), ABA, Conn. Bar Assn., Waterbury Bar Assn. Republican. Congregationalist. Clubs: Highfield, Waterbury. Home: 201 Central Rd Middlebury CT 06762-2413 Office: One Exchange Place Waterbury CT 06722

TITUS, JAMES PAUL, university editor; b. Elmira, N.Y., Jan. 5, 1933; s. Paul Elwood and Anna (Kelly) T.; m. Jean Richardson, Nov. 23, 1963; children: Michael John, Daniel Leonard. Student, St. Vincent Coll., 1954-58, Duquesne U., 1958-59; BS, St. Vincent Coll., 1958. Intern in psychology Mayview (Pa.) State Hosp., 1958-60; editor Electronic Data Processing Weekly, Washington, 1963-66, pub., 1968-70; freelance writer Washington, 1966-68, Horseheads, N.Y., 1970-75; staff writer Cornell U., Ithaca, N.Y., 1975-79; sr. editor Cornell U., Ithaca, 1979—. Scout leader Cub Scouts, Erin, N.Y., 1975. Staff sgt. U.S. Army, 1952-53. Mem. Coun. for Advancement and Support of Edn., Soc. for Scholarly Pub. Democrat. Roman Catholic. Office: Cornell U 1150 Comstock Hall Ithaca NY 14853

TITUS, JOHN JOSEPH, fire engineering company executive; b. Ludlow, Mass., Dec. 21, 1945; s. John Joseph and Regina Rose (Pancotti) T.; m. Catherine Anne Wilcox; children: Erron, Andrea. BS, Poly. U. N.Y., 1967; postgrad., Worcester Poly. Inst., 1983-85. Registered profl. engr., Mass. Rsch. asst. Am. Inst. Physics, N.Y.C., 1967-70; design engr. Mawhinney Bros. Ltd., Vancouver, B.C., Can., 1971-82; project mgr. Vipond Corp. Ltd., Vancouver, 1982-83; cons. engr. MBS Fire Tech. Inc., Grafton, Mass., 1984-88, pres., 1989—; adj. instr. Worcester (Mass.) Poly. Inst., 1985—; invited lectr. FEMA Multi-Peril Design Inst., Emmitsburg, Md., 1987-88, SFPE Continuing Edn. courses. Author: (with others) Fire Protection Handbook, 1989. Regents scholar N.Y. State Bd. of Regents, 1963-67. Mem. ASME, Soc. Fire Protection Engrs. (dir. New Eng. chpt. 1988-90, course developer 1984—, publ. editor New Eng. chpt. 1985-90, edn. com. resource, A.L. Brown scholarship 1985), Nat. Fire Protection Assn. (mem. com. on hazards of contents and furnishings), Fire Protection Engrs. Honorary Soc. (pres. Gamma chpt. 1985-86). Office: MBS Fire Tech Inc PO Box 203 Grafton MA 01519

TITUS, ROBERT WAYNE, pharmaceutical executive; b. Buffalo, June 17, 1947; s. Robert Paul and Bertha (Wissman) T.; m. Judith Korte, June 16, 1972 (div. May 1976); m. Ann Louise Macnaughton, June 26, 1982; children: Jasper Paul, Amelia Ann. BA, Houghton Coll., 1969; BS in Chem. Engring., U. Rochester, 1969; MBA in Fin., U. New Haven, 1976. Prodn. engr. B.F. Goodrich Chem. Co., Louisville, 1969-70; devel. engr. B.F. Goodrich Plastics Co., Shelton, Conn., 1970-74; process engr. Stauffer Chem. Co., Newburgh, N.Y., 1974-76; asst. to pres. Lonza Inc., Fair Lawn, N.J., 1976-81; dir. bus. studies Engelhard Corp., Menlo Park, N.J., 1981-84; v.p. sales & mktg. Napp Chem. Co., Lodi, N.J., 1984-89; pres. Chorchem Noblemet Inc., Rochelle Park, N.J., 1989-91, Titus Chemical, 1992—; pres. N.Y. Chpt. Chem. Mktg. & Econs. Group, 1985-86. Mem. Comml. Devel. Assn., Chem. Mktg. Rsch. Assn., Soc. de Chemie. Prebyterian. Home and Office: 31 Chestnut St Mahwah NJ 07430-3104

TITUS-DILLON, PAULINE YVONNE, educator of medicine; b. Jamaica, W.I., Jan. 1, 1938; came to U.S., 1954; d. Ernest Hoddon Titus and Vera Imogene (Tate) Harvey; m. Owen Christopher Dillon, Nov. 29, 1963; children: Denyse, Paul. BS, Howard U., 1960, MD, 1964. Resident in internal medicine Freedmen's (now Howard U. Hosp.), Washington, 1967-68; fellow endocrinology Georgetown U. Hosp., Washington, 1968-69; asst. prof. Howard U. Coll. Medicine, Washington, 1971-77, assoc. prof., 1977-81, assoc. dean for acad. affairs, prof. internal medicine, 1980—; chief med. officer Howard U. Med. Svc., Washington, 1977-81. Contbr. articles to profl. jours. Recipient Nat. Rsch. Svcs. award Nat. Inst. Gen. Med. Scis., 1975-77. Fellow ACP; mem. AMA, Nat. Med. Assn., N.Y. Acad. Scis. (pres. br., 1992), Am. Med. Women's Assn. (v.p. br. I, 1991), Sigma Xi, Phi Beta Kappa, Betta Kappa Chi, Alpha Omega Alpha. Office: Howard U Coll Medicine 520 W Street NW Rm # 527 Washington DC 20059

TIZES, REUBEN, preventive health physician, educator; b. Ploesti, Romania, 1930; m. Carol Wiener, Nov. 27, 1959; children: Bruce R., Andrea C. Tizes-Feinberg, Simone M. MD, Hebrew U., Jerusalem, 1956; MPH, Columbia U., 1969. Diplomate Am. Bd. Preventive Medicine. Rotating intern Kaplan Hosp., Rehovoth, Israel, 1955-56, Samaritan Hosp., Troy, N.Y., 1959-60; resident in internal medicine Queens Gen. Hosp., Jamaica, N.Y., 1960-61; resident in internal medicine and pulmonary disease Kings County Hosp. Ctr., Bklyn., 1961-62, clin. asst., vis. physician, 1964-70, Tb coord., 1964-69; resident in renal and gastrointestinal disease Met. Hosp., N.Y.C., 1962-63; internal medicine staff South Nassau Community Hosp., Oceanside, N.Y., 1964—; dir. ambulatory care Newark Beth Isreal Med. Ctr., 1974; clin. asst. instr. SUNY, Bklyn., 1965-70, asst. prof. environ. medicine and community health, 1970-75, assoc. prof., 1975—; commr. health Orange County Dept. Health, Goshen, N.Y., 1972-73; physician-in-charge Williamsburg-Greenpoint Chest Clinic, N.Y.C., 1964-69; clinician Bur. Tb N.Y.C. Dept. Health, 1964-69; dir. respiratory diseases and Tb control program Nassau County Dept. Health, Mineola, N.Y., 1969-71; dir. ambulatory care svcs. and community medicine Kingsbrook Jewish Med. Ctr., Brklyn., 1974-77; dir. med. rehab. divsn. Peninsula Hosp. Ctr., Far Rockaway, N.Y., 1977-83. Maj. M.C. Israeli Army, 1957-59. Fellow ACP, APHA, Am. Coll. Angiology, Am. Coll. Chest Physicians, Am. Coll. Preventive Medicine; mem. Am. Thoracic Soc., Am. Soc. Internal Medicine. Address: Hewlett Bay Pk 49 Piermont Rd Hewlett NY 11557

TOBIAS, JUDY, university development executive; b. Pitts.; d. Saul Albert Landau and Bess (Previn) Kurzman; m. Seth Tobias (dec. May 1983); children: Stephen Frederic, Andrew Previn; m. Lewis F. Davis, 1990. Student Silvermine Artists Guild, 1951-55. Art cons. Westchester Mental Health Assn., White Plains, N.Y., 1968-69; cons. sch. social work NYU, 1973-74, devel. exec. 1976—; conf. coord. Today's Family: Implications for the Future, N.Y.C., 1974-75; cons. Playschools, Inc., N.Y.C., 1975; majority counsel mem. Emily & List, 1991—. Mem. Gov.'s Commn. on Continuing Edn., Albany, N.Y., 1968-70, Nat. Coun. on Children and Youth, Washington, 1974-75, Manhattan Inter-Hosp. Group on Child Abuse, 1975-76; chmn. N.Y. met. com. for UNICEF, 1976-77; mem. exec. com. Town Hall Found., N.Y.C., 1979—, vice chmn., 1986-90; founder, bd. dirs. N.Y. chpt. WAIF, Inc., 1961—, nat. pres., 1978-82, nat. bd. dirs. 1978—; bd. dirs. Citizen's Com. for Children, City of N.Y., 1975—, v.p., 1983-90; bd. dirs. Am. br. Internat. Social Svc., 1965-80; bd. dirs. Andrew Glover Youth Program, 1986-89, mem. adv. coun. 1989—; bd. dirs. Goddard Riverside Community Svcs., 1985—, Dance Mag. Found., 1986—, St. John's Place Family Ctr., 1987—, Capitol Hall Preservation Corp., 1989—. Recipient Nat. Humanitarian award WAIF, 1990. Mem. Child Study Assn. Am. (bd. dirs. 1963-71, pres. 1969-71, bd. dirs. Wel-Met Inc. 1972-85). Democrat.

TOBIAS, JULIUS, sculptor; b. N.Y.C., Aug. 27, 1915; s. Louis and Anna (Tabachnick) T.; m. Suzanne Tobias. Student, Atelier Fernand Leger, Paris, 1949-52. Pvt. tchr., 1950-63; tchr. Morris Davidson Sch. Modern Painting, 1947-48; instr. N.Y. Inst. Tech., 1966-70; lectr. Rutgers U., Queens Coll., N.Y.C., 1966-67, Ind. U., Bloomington, 1974. One-man shows include Esther Stuttman Gallery, 1959, Bleecker Gallery, 1961, Easthampton Gallery, 1962, 10 Downtown, 1968, Max Hutchinson Gallery, 1970, 71, 72, Alessandra Gallery, 1976, 55 Mercer St. Gallery, 1976, 77, 78, 80, all N.Y.C., Zriny-Hayes Gallery, Chgo., 1979, B4A Gallery, N.Y.C., 1991, The SUNY, Stony Brook, 1992, Artemisia Gallery, Chgo., 1992; group shows include, Provincetown (Mass.) Art Assn., 1946, Roko Gallery, N.Y.C., 1946, Camino Gallery, N.Y.C., 1957, Polari Gallery, Woodstock, N.Y., 1957, Art USA, Coliseum, N.Y.C., 1957, Brata Gallery, N.Y.C., 1957-59, Pa. Acad. Fine Arts, 1958, Gallery Creuze, Paris, 1958, Knoedler Gallery, N.Y.C., 1959, Mus. Modern Art, traveling exhbn. in Tokyo, 1959, New Eng. Exhbn., Silvermine, Conn., 1960, De Aenlle Gallery, N.Y.C., 1961, Bleecker Gallery, N.Y.C., 1962, Staten Island Mus., N.Y.C., 1962, Allan Stone Gallery, N.Y.C., 1962, Easthampton Gallery, N.Y.C., 1962-66, Windham Coll., Putney, Vt., 1963, Rutgers U., 1966, Park Pl. Gallery, N.Y.C., 1967, Tibor Dinagy Gallery, N.Y.C., 1968, Whitney Mus. Annual, N.Y.C., 1968, Parker St. 470, Boston, 1969, Everson Mus., Syracuse, N.Y., 1972, Hunter Gallery, N.Y.C., 1981, Art Park, Lewiston, N.Y., 1981, Jan Weiss Gallery, N.Y.C., 1990, numerous others; represented in numerous collections, Europe, N. and S.Am., also pvt. collections. Served to 1st lt. USAAF, 1942-45. Decorated D.F.C., Air medal with 3 oak leaf clusters; Guggenheim fellow, 1972-73, 78-79; N.Y. Found. for Arts fellow, 1985; Pollock-Krasner Found. fellow, 1986; grantee Nat. Endowment for Arts, 1975, 81; N.Y. Council Found., 1971-78; Adolf and Esther Gottlieb Found., 1980, The Penny McCall Found., 1988; recipient Oscar Williams and Gene Derwood award, 1989, award Adolph and Esther Gottlieb Found., 1991, The Pollock-Krasner Found., 1991, The Richard A. Florsheim Art Fund. Address: 9 Great Jones St New York NY 10012

TOBIAS, KAL, transportation executive; b. Bklyn., Feb. 1, 1946; m. Karen Liberty, Mar. 11, 1967; children: Kristopher, Kirk. BA, CUNY, Bklyn., 1967. Mgr. dealer devel. Volkswagon Can., Toronto, Ont., 1967-72; pres. cons. firm Toronto, Ont., Can., 1972-78; v.p. Burmah Oil Group, Toronto, Ont., Can., 1978-83; pres., C.E.O. DHL Internat. Express Ltd., Toronto, Ont., Can., 1983—, also bd. dirs., 1983—; bd. dirs DHL Customs Brokerage, Toronto, 1983—, Skyhawk Trans., Toronto, 1988—, Can. Courier Assn., pres., 1987—, C.E.O., 1987—. Office: DHL Internat Express Ltd, 6205 Airport Rd Ste 400, Mississauga, ON Canada L4V 1E1

TOBIAS, KEVIN RICHARD, zoning officer; b. Reading, Pa., Sept. 6, 1964; s. Frank Theodore and Stella Catherine (Kalinowski) T. Degree in Telecommunications, Pa. State U., 1986; postgrad., Kutztown U. Pa., 1989—. Communications intern Pa. State U., University Park, 1985-86; tax clk. City of Reading, 1988-90, zoning adminstr., sec. zoning hearing bd., 1990—. Mem. Berks County Dem. Com., Reading, 1988, Washington Fire Co., Reading, 1986. Recipient City of Reading Employee award Trinity Luth. Ch., 1988. Mem. ASPA, Am. Planning Assn. Democrat. Office: City of Reading 815 Washington St Rm 316A Reading PA 19601

TOBIAS, LESTER LEE, psychological consultant; b. Bklyn., Oct. 11, 1946; s. Nathan and Charlotte T.; m. Andrea Furmanek, July 10, 1977; children: Lauren A., Julia E. AB, Grinnell Coll., 1967; AM, U. Ill., 1971, PhD, 1972. Instr. dept. univ. extension U. Ill., Urbana, 1970-72, intern Psychol. and Counseling Ctr., 1970-71, clin. counselor, 1971-72; psychologist Jefferson County (Colo.) Mental Health Ctr., Denver, 1972-73, team leader, psychologist, 1973-74;; psychol. cons. to Denver OEO Colo. Dept. Social Svcs., 1973-74; instr. Denver Community Coll., 1973-74; cons. psychologist Nordli, Wilson Assocs., Westborough, Mass., 1974-81; ptnr., cons. psychologist, 1981—; pres. Psychol. Svcs. Internat., Inc., Westborough, 1983—. Author: Psychological Consulting to Management, 1990; contbr. articles to profl. and bus. publs. Bd. dirs. Worcester Big Bros., 1976, PMCS, 1983—. Meuhlstein Found. scholar, 1964-67; USPHS trainee, 1967-68. Mem. Nat. Psychol. Cons. to Mgmt., Am. Psychol. Assn., Mass. Psychol. Assn. Home: 6 John St Westborough MA 01581-2511 Office: Nordli Wilson Assocs 2000 W Park Dr PO Box 5000 Westborough MA 01581-5000

TOBIN, ALEXANDER, educational organization executive, consultant; b. Phila., Feb. 7, 1927; s. Louis and Katie (Nitkin) T.; m. Harriet Extein, Dec. 26, 1954 (div. Mar. 1979); children: Jay Lawrence, Barbara Ruth, Rhonda Joy; m. Susan Roslyn Wachtel, Apr. 8, 1979; 1 child, Allison Corson. BA, Temple U., 1949, MEd, 1953, EdD, 1974. Cert. secondary prin., math. supr., supt., Pa. Tchr. math., demonstration tchr., dept. head Sch. Dist. Phila., 1950-61, vice prin., 1961-62, prin., 1962-70, dir. math. edn., 1970-85, assoc. supt., 1982; exec. dir. Prime, Inc., Phila., 1985—; adj. prof. Beaver Coll., Glenside, Pa., 1974—, Temple U., Phila., 1974—; math. cons. Mifflin County

Sch. Dist., Lewistown, Pa., 1986, Tunkhannock (Pa.) Area Sch. Dist., 1986, CUNY, 1985, State College (Pa.) Area Sch. Dist., 1985. Author: Systemathix, 1972, Problem Solving, 1976, Think Metric, 1976, Mathematics for Today, 1979. With USNR, 1945-46. Recipient Man of Yr. award B'nai B'rith, Phila., 1975, John M. Patterson award Citizens Com. for Pub. Edn., Phila., 1980. Mem. Nat. Coun. Suprs. Math. (pres. 1975-77, Glenn Gilbert award 1984), Pa. Coun. Suprs. Math. (pres. 1989—), Pa. Coun. Tchrs. Math. (pres. 1978-80, Hall of Fame award 1989), Phila. Assn. Tchrs. Math. (pres. 1975-77, award 1989), Phila. Assn. Sch. Adminstrs. (v.p. 1976-85, award 1985). Democrat. Jewish. Home: 3256 Ayr Ln Fort Washington PA 19025-1636 Office: Prime Inc 1700 Walnut St Ste 1201 Philadelphia PA 19103

TOBIN, JAMES, economics educator; b. Champaign, Ill., Mar. 5, 1918; s. Louis Michael and Margaret (Edgerton) T.; m. Elizabeth Fay Ringo, Sept. 14, 1946; children: Margaret Ringo, Louis Michael, Hugh Ringo, Roger Gill. AB summa cum laude, Harvard U., 1939, MA, 1940, PhD, 1947; LLD (hon.), Syracuse U., 1967, U. Ill., 1969, Dartmouth Coll., 1970, Swarthmore Coll., 1980, New Sch. Social Research, 1982, NYU, 1982, Bates Coll., 1982, U. Hartford, 1984, Colgate U., 1984, Gustavus Adolphus Coll., 1986, Western Md. Coll., 1984, U. New Haven, 1986; D in Econs. (hon.), New U. Lisbon, 1980; D in Econs. (hon.), Athens U. Econ. & Bus., 1992; D in Econs. (hon.), Athens U. of Econ. and Bus., 1992; LHD (hon.), Hofstra U., 1983, Sacred Heart U., 1990; D in Social Scis. honoris causa, U. Helsinki, 1986. Assoc. economist OPA, WPB, Washington, 1941-42; teaching fellow econs. Harvard U., Cambridge, Mass., 1946-47, with Soc. Fellows, 1947-50; assoc. prof. econs. Yale U., New Haven, 1950-55, prof., 1955—, Sterling prof. econs., 1957-88, prof. emeritus, 1988—; mem. Council Econ. Advisers, 1961-62, Nat. Acad. Scis. Author: National Economic Policy, 1966, Essays in Economics-Macroeconomics, vol. 1, 1972, The New Economics One Decade Older, 1974, Consumption and Econometrics, vol. 2, 1975, Asset Accumulation and Economic Activity, 1980, Theory and Policy, Vol. 3, 1982, Policies for Prosperity, 1987; co-author: Two Revolutions in Economic Policy, 1988. Served to lt. USNR, 1942-46. Recipient Nobel prize in econs., 1981; Social Sci. Research Council faculty fellow, 1951-54; Grand cordon Order of the Sacred Treasure, Japan, 1988; Centennial medal Harvard Grad. Sch., 1989. Fellow Am. Acad. Arts and Scis., Econometric Soc. (pres. 1958), Am. Statis. Assn., Brit. Acad. (corr.); mem. Am. Philos. Soc., Am. Econ. Assn. (John Bates Clark medal 1955, v.p. 1964, pres. 1971), Acad. Scis. Portugal (fgn. assoc.), Phi Beta Kappa. Home: 117 Alden Ave New Haven CT 06515-2109 Office: Yale U Dept Econs PO Box 2125 New Haven CT 06520-2125

TOBIN, LOIS MOORE, home economist, educator; b. Johnstown, Pa., Oct. 8, 1928; d. William B. and Ida L. (Diehl) Moore; m. Warner E. Tobin, June 7, 1953; children: Brian W., Robert E. BS, Ind. (Pa.) State Tchrs. Coll., 1951; postgrad., U. Pitts., 1952, U. Colo., 1953; MEd, Pa. State U., 1967; postgrad., Ind. U. of Pa., 1977-85. Tchr. Allegheny Valley Joint Sch. Dist., Springdale, Pa., 1951-53, Kittanning (Pa.) Sch. Dist., 1953-55, Carlisle (Pa.) Joint Sch. Dist., 1964-66, State Coll. (Pa.) Sch. Dist., 1967-73; mem. faculty Dept. Food/Nut Ind. U. of Pa., 1974, 76-77, mem. faculty Home Econs. Edn., 1979-82, coord. Single Parent-Homemaker Svc. Ctr. Vocat. Pers. Prep., 1984—; mem. adv. com. Ind. Area Vocat.-Tech. Sch., 1981—; presenter Pa. Vocat. Edn. Conf., Seven Springs, 1985, Lancaster, 1991. Author: (booklet) Home Economics Education Bibliography on Special Needs, 1982, Teaching Special Needs Individuals in Home Economics, 1982; contbr. articles to profl. newsletters. Sec. Ind. County Human Svcs. Coun., 1990—; vol. Bloodmobile and Multiphasic Health, Ind., 1986—; pres. Calvary Ch. Women's Club, 1975-76, Ind. County Newcomer's Club, 1974, 75. Grantee Dept. Edn. Bur. of Vocat. Edn., 1980-82, 1986—, Human Svcs. Devel. Fund, 1989—. Mem. Am. Vocat. Assn., Am. Home Econ. Assn., Nat. Assn. Vocat. Edn. Spl. Needs Personnel, Pa. Assn. Vocat. Edn. Spl. Needs Personnel, Pa. Vocat. Assn., Pa. Assn. Home Econ. Educators (sec. 1990—), Pa. Home Econs. Assn. (treas. 1975-77), Pi Lambda Theta. Home: 896 White Farm Rd Indiana PA 15701-1254

TOBIN, NANCY RUTH, publishing executive, consultant; b. N.Y.C., Aug. 31, 1943; d. Robert and Sylvia (Moscowitz) T.; children: H. Jason Willig, Daniel Tobin Willig. BFA, Syracuse U., 1965. Asst. editor, dir. art Buffalo Mag., 1965-69, cons. dir. art, 1969-74; art critic Buffalo Courier Express, 1971-77, editor Sunday mag., 1977-81, dir. news art, 1981-82; editor graphics Buffalo News, 1983-85; asst. prof. Newhouse Sch. Syracuse (N.Y.) U., 1985-87; dir. design Asbury Pk. Press, Neptune, N.J., 1987-89; dir. publs. SUNY, Buffalo, 1989—; cons. Asbury Pk. Press, Neptune, 1983-87, Ann Arbor (Mich.) News, 1984-86, Watertown (N.Y.) Daily Times, 1985-86, Albany (N.Y.) Time Union, 1991—. Contbr. articles to popular newspapers and mags. Bd. dirs. Jewish Family Svcs. Buffalo and Erie County; mem. Erie County Cultural Resources Adv. Bd.; bd. dirs. CEPA. Recipient Writing, Criticism, Design award Am. Newspaper Guild, 1971-81, Design award N.J. Press Assn., 1987-89, CASE awards 1990, 91, 92, Edpress awards for publs., 1991, 92. Mem. Soc. Newspaper Design (1st v.p. 1991-92, Excellence award 1984). Home: 141 Mariner St Buffalo NY 14201-1412 Office: U at Buffalo 136 Crofts Hall Buffalo NY 14260

TOBIN, RICHARD GEORGE, automobile dealer; b. Utica, N.Y., June 3, 1943; s. Frank A. and Anne R. (Hargreaves) T.; m. Mary M. Seemann, Apr. 18, 1970; children: Colleen S., Kathleen A., Erin E. Sec.-treas. Tobin Oldsmobile Corp., Utica, 1969-71, N.J. Curri Oldsmobile, Inc., Marcy, N.Y., 1971-87; pres. Tobin Chrysler Plymouth Dodge Inc., Clinton, N.Y., 1988—. Treas., bd. dirs. Children's Mus., Utica, 1986—. Mem. KC, Elks. Office: Tobin Chrysler Plymouth 12 Franklin Ave Clinton NY 13323-1697

TOBIN, ROGER LEE, industrial engineer, educator; b. Grand Rapids, Mich., Oct. 11, 1940; s. Wendell R. and Marion L. (Kaechele) T.; m. Ilona L. Kotyuk, Aug. 22, 1966 (div. Dec. 1976); m. Barbara A. Payne, May 20, 1985; children: Anna, Thomas. BS in Indsl. Engring., U. Mich., 1964, MS in Indsl. Engring., 1969, MA in Math., 1972, PhD in Indsl. Engring., 1973. Indsl. engr. Hoover Ball and Bearing, Ann Arbor, Mich., 1964-66, sr. indsl. engr., process engr., 1966-68; assoc. sr. rsch. engr. GM Rsch. Labs., Warren, Mich., 1973-78, sr. rsch. engr., 1978-80; environ. systems engr. Argonne (Ill.) Nat. Lab., 1980-82, transp. systems analyst, 1982-85; prin. mem. tech. staff GTE Labs. Inc., Waltham, Mass., 1985—; adj. asst. prof. U. Pa., Phila., 1983-85, adj. assoc. prof., 1985-91. Co-editor spl. issue Intercity Freight Transp., 1983; assoc. editor Ops. Rsch., 1989—; mem. editorial adv. bd. Transp. Rsch., 1979—; contbr. over 35 articles to profl. jours. Mem. Am. Econ. Assn., Math. Programming Soc., Regional Sci. Assn., Inst. Mgmt. Scis., Ops. Rsch. Soc. Am., Phi Kappa Phi. Office: GTE Labs Inc 40 Sylvan Rd Waltham MA 02154-1168

TOBIN, THOMAS VINCENT, biology educator; b. Plymouth, Pa., Apr. 8, 1926; s. James Vincent and Mary (Evans) T.; m. Dolores Mary Chewey, Nov. 27, 1947; 1 child, Cynthia Joan. BS cum laude, King's Coll., 1951; MS in Biology, Boston Coll., 1953. Grad. asst. in biology Boston Coll., 1951-52; instr. biology King's Coll., Wilkes'Barre, Pa., 1952-54, asst. prof. biology, 1955-61, natural sci. div. chmn., 1971-77, chmn. dept. biology, 1985-91, assoc. prof. biology, 1962—, chief health professions advisor, 1989—; lectr. biology Pa. State U., University Park, 1972-77; lectr. biology Coll. Misericordia, Dallas, Pa., 1977-78. With USAAF, 1943-46. NSF sci. faculty fellow, 1960, summer sci. fellow, 1961; named O'Hara Disting. Svc. Prof. of Sci. King's Coll., 1984. Mem. Nat. Assn. Advisors for the Health Professions. Democrat. Roman Catholic. Home: 124 Forest Rd Wilkes Barre PA 18707-1320 Office: King's Coll Dept Biology Wilkes Barre PA 18711-0801

TOCCO, DOMINICK JOSEPH, pharmacologist, researcher; b. N.Y.C., Jan. 25, 1930; s. Frank Paul and Rose (D'Ambra) T.; m. Yvonne Victoria Cali, June 29, 1951; children: Donald, Gregory, Douglas, Brian. BS, St. John's U., N.Y.C., 1951, MS, 1953; PhD, Georgetown U., 1960. Sr. rsch. fellow Merck & Co., West Point, Pa., 1960—. Mem. Am. Soc. Pharmacology and Exptl. Therapeutics. Republican. Roman Catholic. Office: Merck Rsch Labs West Point PA 19486

TOCE, THOMAS CLIFFORD, actuary, lyricist; b. Hartford, Conn., Jan. 24, 1956; s. Joseph Paul and Catherine (Clifford) T.; m. Margaret Kaplan, Oct. 3, 1982; children: Hannah Kaplan, Julia Kaplan. BS, Yale U., 1978. Asst. mgr. Ins. Svcs. Office, N.Y.C., 1978-90, Milliman and Robertson, N.Y.C., 1990—. Lyricist: A Charles Dickens Christmas, 1988, Columbus, 1991. Mem. Casualty Actuarial Soc. (assoc.), Dramatists Guild (assoc.). Home: 201 W 92nd St # 2A New York NY 10025 Office: Milliman & Robertson 2 Penn Pla New York NY 10001

TODD, CHRISTINA ADRIAN TAMBURO, nurse, facility administrator; b. Balt., Apr. 11, 1943; d. Stephen John and Anna Elise (Reinhardt) Tamburo; m. Robert Franklin Todd Jr., Sept. 29, 1962; children: Diana Marie Todd Sansing, Aimée Elise. Student, Howard Community Coll., 1974-76. Office administr., head nurse Drs. Sigler, Roskes, Holden and Schuberth & Pediatric Cons., Lutherville, Md., 1961—; instr. breastfeeding and care of newborn babies Drs. Sigler, Roskes, Holden, Schuberth, Lutherville, Md., 1980—. Eucharistic minister St. Joseph's Ch., Sykesville, Md., 1985—. Mem. Am. Assn. Office Nurses, Kappa Sigma Theta. Democrat. Roman Catholic. Home: 6006 Snowdens Run Rd Sykesville MD 21784-6737 Office: Drs Sigler Roskes Holden & Schuberth 10807 Falls Rd Ste 200 Lutherville MD 21093-4595

TODD, EDWARD FRANCIS, JR., risk management consultant; b. Phila., Mar. 18, 1956; s. Edward Francis and Alberta (Meyer) T.; m. Catherine Theresa Mangino, Oct. 22, 1977; children: Edward Michael, Kristen Ann. BBA, Seton Hall U., N.Y.C., 1979; MBA, Seton Hall U., 1992. CPCU; assoc. risk mgmt. With Atlantic Mut., N.Y.C., 1972-79; sr. risk analyst Continental Ins. Co., N.Y.C., 1979-82; supervising underwriter Hartford Ins. Co., N.Y.C., 1982-84; staff cons. Blades & Macaulay, Union, N.J., 1984-88; cons. risk mgmt. Ernst & Young, Phila., 1988—. Mem. Am. Inst. CPCU's. Home: 23 Carter Rd East Brunswick NJ 08816-4603

TODD, NORMA JEAN ROSS, retired government official; b. Butler, Pa., Oct. 3, 1920; d. William Bryson and Doris Mae (Ferguson) Ross; m. Alden Frank Miller, Jr., Apr. 16, 1940 (dec. Feb. 1975); 1 child, Alden Frank III; m. Jack R. Todd, Dec. 23, 1977 (dec. Sept. 1990). Student, Pa. State U., 1944-46, Yale U., 1954-57. Exec. mgr. Donora (Pa.) C. of C., 1950-57, Donora Community Chest, 1950-57; office mgr. Donora Golden Jubilee, 1951; staff writer Herald-Am., Donora, 1957, city editor, 1957-70; assoc. editor Daily Herald, Donora, 1970-73; svc. rep. Pitts. Teleservice Ctr., Social Security Adminstrn., HHS, 1977-83. Mem. Mayor's Adv. Council, Donora, 1965-69, Citizens' Adv. Council, Donora, 1965-69; mem. Donora Bd. Edn., 1954-60, pres., 1960; mem. Donora Borough Council, 1970-72; bd. dirs. Mon Valley chpt. ARC, 1964—, sec. bd., 1966—; bd. dirs. Washington County Tourism Agy., 1970-90, sec., 1972-90; bd. dirs. Washington County History and Landmarks Found. 1971-80, 91—, sec., 1975-80, 91—; bd. dirs. Mon Valley council Camp Fire Girls, 1965-79, Mon Valley Drug and Alcoholism Council, 1971-78; hon. life mem. Pa. Congress PTAs; bd. dirs. United Way Mon Valley, 1973-82, chmn. pub. rels., 1973-74. Recipient Fine Arts Festival of Pa. Poetry first prize award Fedn. of Women's Clubs, 1987, 1st and 2nd pl. awards for photography Washington County Fine Arts Festival, County Fedn. of Women's Club, 1990. Mem. Pa. Soc. Newspaper Editors, Pitts. Press Club, Donora C. of C. (pres. 1971-72), DAR (regent Monongahela Valley chpt. 1974-77), Washington County Poetry Soc. (pres. 1967-69), Donora Hist. Soc. (curator 1990—), Family of Bruce Soc. (descendants of King Robert the Bruce of Scotland 1987—), Washington County Fedn. Women's Clubs (rec. sec. 1964-66, pub. rels. chmn. 1990—). Clubs: Order Ea. Star (worthy matron 1966-67, treas. 1986—), White Shrine of Jerusalem (high priestess 1973-74), Order of Amaranth (royal matron 1966, dist. dep. 3 times, grand rep. W.Va. 1979-80), Donora Forecast (pres. 1962-63), Donora Unidon (pres. 1965-66, 56-57). Avocation: genealogy. Home: Overlook Ter Donora PA 15033-2203 also: 1310 McKean Ave Donora PA 15033

TODD, RICHARD HENRY, retired physican, investor; b. Pottstown, Pa., Mar. 25, 1906; s. John Henry and Effie (Davis) T.; m. Lydia Carey Dick, Feb. 1, 1930; children: Richard Henry Jr., John Andrew. AB, Johns Hopkins U., 1929, MD, 1933. instr. Georgetown U. sect. Children's Hosp., Washington, 1961. Med. resident St. Lukes Hosp., N.Y.C., 1933-35; gen. practioner Hancock, Md., 1935-37, Middletown, Md., 1937-40; pediatric resident Children's Hosp., Washington, 1940-42; sch. physician St. Alban's Sch. for Boys, Washington, 1942-72; med. dir. Gallaudet Coll., Washington, 1942-72; pvt. practice Pediatric and Allergy Washington, 1942-80; clin. assoc. prof. Georgetown U. Med. Sch., Washington, 1942—. Co-author: Allergy in Relation to Pediatrics, 1951, The Allergic Child, 1963; contbr. articles to profl. jours. 2nd lt. inf. ROTC, 1929-39. Mem. AMA (life), Am. Assn. Pediatrics (life), Am. Assn. Allergies (life), D.C. Med. Soc. (life), Chevy Chase Country Club, Army and Navy Club. Home: 4000 Cathedral Ave NW # 304B Washington DC 20016-5249

TODOROFF, DAVIS STEVEN, podiatrist; b. Harrisburg, Pa., July 3, 1958; s. John Michael and Mary Elizabeth (Hepschmidt) T.; m. Cynthia Kihn, June 25, 1983; children: Stephanie, Melissa. BS, Lebanon Valley Coll., 1980; DPM, Pa. Coll. Podiatric Medicine, 1984. Resident VA Med. Ctr., Lebanon, Pa., 1984-85; pvt. practice Dr. Howard Schake, Harrisburg, Pa., 1985-90, Harrisburg, 1990—; assoc. prof. U. Osteopathic Medicine and Health Scis., Des Moines, 1990-91. Mem. Pa. Podiatric Medicine Assn.; assoc. Am. Coll. Foot Surgeons. Republican. Office: 2405 Linglestown Rd Harrisburg PA 17110-9429

TODREAS, TIMOTHY MICHAEL, legislative staff member; b. Washington, Mar. 29, 1961; s. Neil Emmanuel and Carol Sue (Schonberg) T. AB, Columbia U., 1983; MALD, Tufts. U., 1986. Assoc. McKinsey & Co., Inc., Boston, 1986-90; legis. asst. U.S. Senate John F. Kerry, Washington, 1990—; cons. Leader Assoc., Malden, Mass., 1986—. Home: 203 6th St NE Washington DC 20002-6009

TOENNIESSEN, GARY HERBERT, agricultural scientist, microbiologist; b. Lockport, N.Y., July 9, 1944; s. Clifford E. and Lois (Dale) T.; m. Janet Shelly, Jan. 28, 1967. MS in Microbiology, U. N.C., 1968, PhD in Microbiology, 1971. Program assoc. natural & environ. sci. The Rockefeller Found., N.Y.C., 1971-72, asst. dir., 1972-78, asst. dir. agrl. scis., 1978-84, assoc. dir. agrl. scis., 1984—; bd. dirs. N.Y. Bot. Garden, N.Y.C., 1986—, The Nature Conservancy, Mt. Kisco, N.Y., 1974-88. Editor: Rice Biotechnology, 1991, Salinity Tolerance in Plants: Strategies for Crop Improvement, 1984, Plant Disease Control: Resistance and Susceptibility, 1981. Home: 17 Fenimore Dr Harrison NY 10528-1412 Office: The Rockefeller Found 1133 Ave Of The Americas New York NY 10036-6710

TOFFLER, BARBARA LEY, management consultant; b. N.Y.C., Dec. 17, 1941; d. Theodore and Clarice Estelle (Weintraub) L.; m. Robert Benjamin Toffler, May 29, 1969 (div. 1981); children: Samuel Bruce, Aaron Michael, Judith Nell; m. Charles W. Powers, Apr. 17, 1982. BA, Columbia U., 1972; MA, Yale U., 1976, PhD, 1978. Producer Asbury Playhouse, Juno Prodns., Inc., Asbury Park, N.J., 1965-67; exec. dir. Ctr. for the Person in Transition, New Haven, 1972-73; rsch. asst. Dept. Adminstrv. Scis., Yale U., New Haven, 1974-75; project coord. Yale Ctr. for Study of Health Svcs., New Haven, 1975-76; teaching fellow Yale U., 1976-78; asst. prof. Boston U., 1978-80; asst. prof. Harvard Bus. Sch., Boston, 1980-87, lectr., 1987-88; lectr. Yale U., 1992—; co-founding prin. Resources for Responsible Mgmt., Boston, 1987—; story cons., on-camera narrator Bus. Ethics I, 1988, Bus. Ethics II, 1989; nat. fellow The Bus. Ent. Trust, 1989—; lectr. Tufts U. Sch. Dental Medicine, Boston, 1989—, Yale U., New Haven, 1992—; lectr. in field. Editorial adv. bd. Bus. Ethics Mag., 1989—; author: Tough Choices: Managers Talk Ethics, 1986; contbr. articles to profl. jours., chpts. to books. Fellow Soc. for Values in Higher Edn.; mem. Am. Psychol. Assn., Acad. Mgmt., Soc. for Psychol. Study of Social Issues. Democrat. Jewish. Office: Resources for Resp Mgmt 264 Beacon St Boston MA 02116-1236

TOFIAS, ALLAN, accountant; b. Boston, Apr. 13, 1930; s. George I. and Anna (Seidel) T.; m. Arlene Shube, Aug. 30, 1981; children: Bradley Neil, Laura Jean Silver. BA, Colgate U., 1951; MBA, Harvard U., 1956. CPA, Mass. Sr. acct. Peat, Marwick, Mitchell & Co., Boston, 1956-60; mng. ptnr. Tofias, Fleishman, Shapiro & Co., P.C., Boston, 1960—. Mem. town meeting Town of Brookline, Mass., 1970-77, mem. fin. adv. bd., 1975-81; mem. New Eng. Bapt. Health Care Corp., 1985—; bd. dirs. West Newton YMCA, 1986-89, Boston Aid for Blind, 1988—, v.p., mem. exec. com. Lt. (j.g.) USNR, 1951-54. Mem. AICPA, Mass. Soc. CPAs (v.p.), Nat. CPA Group (exec. com. 1983-88, vice chmn. 1985-88), Wightman Tennis Club (Weston, Mass., treas. 1974-76), Newton Squash and Tennis Club (bd. dirs. 1966—), BKR Internat. (World bd. dirs. 1988—), Moses Michael Hays. Home: 59 Monadnock Rd Wellesley MA 02181-1334 Office: Tofias Fleishman Shapiro & Co PC 205 Broadway Cambridge MA 02139-1901

TOKAR, BETTE LEWIS, economics educator; b. Phila, Mar. 26, 1935; d. Howard H. and Irma Rhodes (Pixton) Lewis; m. Jacob John Tokar, Oct. 1, 1955; children: Teresa, Bonnie, Michael, Robert. Student, Ursinus Coll., 1953-55; BA in Polit. Economy, Holy Family Coll., 1967, MA in Econs., Temple U., 1973, postgrad., 1980. Lectr. Holy Family Coll., Phila., 1972-75, instr., 1975-78, asst. prof., 1978-82, dept. chair, 1977-85, assoc. prof., 1982—; lectr. La Salle Coll., Phila., 1977, Community Coll. Phila., 1986—; assessor CLEO, Phila., 1979-85. Candidate for auditor, Lower Southampton Township, Bucks County, Pa., 1967, 69; Dem. committeewoman Lower Southampton Township, Bucks Co., 1968; treas. Dem. Club Lower Township, Bucks Co., 1968, bd. dirs. Pine Tree Farms Assoc., Feasterville, Pa., 1968. Mem. MENSA, Acad. Internat. Bus., Assn. social Econ., Nat. Bus. Edn. Assn., Am. Acctg. Assn., Am. Econ. Assn., Am. Management Assn., Internat. Trade & Fin. Assn., Delta Pi Epsilon, Pi Gamma Mu. Episcopalian. Home: 153 Pinehill Rd Langhorne PA 19053-7809 Office: Holy Family Coll Grant and Frankford Aves Philadelphia PA 19114

TOKOS, SYLVIA JURIGA, English and history educator; b. Johnson City, N.Y., July 21, 1940; d. John J. and Eve (Dohnalek) Juriga; m. J. H. Tokos, Aug. 4, 1962; children: Eve-Elizabeth, Paige-Jennifer, Courtney-Alyssa. BA in English and History, SUNY, Albany, 1961, MA in English and History, 1962. Cert. tchr., N.Y. Tchr. Vestal (N.Y.) Cen. Schs., 1962-68, 91—, Binghamton (N.Y.) City Schs., 1968-91. Docent Roberson Ctr. for Arts, Binghamton, 1965-80; asst. house mgr. Triple Cities Opera Co., Binghamton, 1986-90; vol. Anderson Ctr. for Arts, SUNY, Binghamton, 1985—, Binghamton Symphony, 1980—, B.C. Pops, Binghamton, 1980—. Mem. N.Y. State Coun. English, So. Tier Coun. for Social Studies, N.Y. State Coun. History, Substitutes United in Broome (bd. dirs. 1987—), N.Y. State United Tchrs. (labor negotiator, bd. dirs. Binghamton chpt. 1987-91). Republican. Home: 76 Grand Blvd Binghamton NY 13905-3326

TOLAND, PETER CHRISTOPHER, government official, lawyer; b. Boston, Nov. 29, 1942; s. Francis Paul and Frances (Smith) T.; m. Geraldine Mary Parent, Mar. 7, 1967; children: Alexandra, Jonathan. BSBA, Northeastern U., 1968; JD, Suffolk U., 1976; LLM, Boston U., 1983. Bar: Mass 1977. Foundry foreman Ford Motor Co., Dearborn, Mich., 1965-68; disability claims adjudicator VA, Boston, 1972-74; mgmt. analyst Social Security Adminstrn., Boston, 1974-77, chief pers. mgmt., 1977-80, asst. dist. mgr., 1980-83, dir. disability program, 1983-85, dist. mgr., 1986—. Founder Govt. Ctr. Child Care Corp., Boston, 1978; vol. Rosie's Place, homeless shelter, Boston, 1981; scoutmaster Boy Scouts Am., Boston, 1991. 1st lt. U.S. Army, 1969-72. Congl. fellow Am. Polit. Sci. Assn., 1985-86. Mem. Nat. Coun. Social Security Mgmt. Assns. (pres. 1990-91), New Eng. Social Security Mgmt. Assn. (pres. 1989-90). Home: 75 Milton Ave Hyde Park MA 02136-4009 Office: Social Security Adminstrn 10 Causeway St Rm 148 Boston MA 02222-1002

TOLES, THOMAS GREGORY, editorial cartoonist; b. Buffalo, Oct. 22, 1951; s. George Edward and Rose Elizabeth (Riehle) T.; m. Gretchen Amanda Saarnijoki, May 26, 1973; children: Amanda Laurel, Seth August. B.A. in English, SUNY-Buffalo, 1973. Artist Buffalo Courier-Express, 1973-80, cartoonist, 1980-82; cartoonist Buffalo News, 1982—, UPS, 1982—. Author: The Taxpayer's New Clothes, 1985, Mr. Gazoo: A Cartoon History of the Reagan Era, 1987, At Least Our Bombs Are Getting Smarter: A Cartoon Preview of the 1990's, 1991; creator (comic strip) Curious Avenue, 1992. Recipient John Fischetti Editorial Cartoon award Columbia Coll., Chgo., 1984, Pulitzer Prize for Editorial Cartooning, 1990. Mem. Am. Assn. Editorial Cartoonists. Home: 75 Central Ave Hamburg NY 14075-6219 Office: Buffalo News 1 News Plz Buffalo NY 14203-2994

TOLES-KENDALL, LOLITA, personnel case manager; b. Natchez, Miss., Aug. 15, 1949; d. Tom Toles and Vivian Elaine (Winston) Graham; m. Robert Kendall Jr., Mar. 25, 1972; children: Yolanda Y., Robert Kendall III. BA, Tex. So. U., 1971, MEd, 1973; postgrad., U. Md., 1974-91. Personnel analyst Prince George's County Govt., Upper Marlboro, Md., 1974-77; classification specialist Libr. of Congress, Washington, 1978; personnel analyst III Prince George's County Govt. Personnel, Upper Marlboro, 1974-82; chief assessment counseling Prince George's County Pvt. Industry Coun., Capitol Hgts., Md., 1982-84; assessment counselor Prince George's County Pvt. Industry Coun., Seat Pleasant, Md., 1986-89; case mgr. Prince George's County Pvt. Industry Coun., Landover, Md., 1986-91, support svcs. mgr., 1991-92, acting supr. case mgrs., 1991—; pres. Toles Enterprises Corp., 1983—; editor Family Reunion First, 1990; coord. Computer Analysis Data Program. Mem. Am. Assn. for Counseling and Devel., NAACP, JTPA Partnership. Democrat. Baptist. Home: 2309 Senator Ave District Heights MD 20747

TOLIA, BHUPENDRA MANILAL, urologist; b. Jamnagar, India, Dec. 21, 1936; came to U.S., 1967; s. Manilal Premji and Prabhavati Manilal (Mehta) T.; m. Chandrika J. Lakhani, Jan. 7, 1967; children: Nameeta B., Chirag B. MB BS, Med. Coll. Baroda, India, 1962; MS, Med. Coll. Baroda, 1966. Diplomate, Am. Bd. Urology. Resident in gen. surgery SSG Hosp., Baroda, India, 1962-66, Nazareth Hosp., Phila., 1967-68; resident in urology Thomas Jefferson U. Hosp., Phila., 1968-71; spl. fellow in urology Meml. Sloan-Kettering Cancer Ctr., N.Y.C., 1971-72; spl. trainee spinal cord injury svc. VA Hosp., Bronx, N.Y., 1972-73; dir. urology clinic Bronx Mcpl. Hosp. Ctr., 1973-80; attending urologist Albert Einstein Hosp., Bronx, 1973—; clin. instr. urology, then asst. prof. urology Albert Einstein Coll. Medicine, Bronx, 1973-80, assoc. prof. urology, 1980-91, assoc. clin. prof. urology, 1991—; cons. urologist, Dr. Martin Luther King Jr. Health Ctr., Bronx. Fellow ACS (Bronx chpt. treas. 1988-90, pres.-elect 1990-91, pres. 1991-92), N.Y. Acad. Medicine, Internat. Coll. Surgeons; mem. Am. Urol. Assn., Soc. Univ. Urologists, Societe Internat. d'Urologie. Republican. Jain. Office: 1695 Eastchester Rd Apt 306 Bronx NY 10461-2330

TOLIVER, MAXWELL DOEL, hypnotherapist; b. Staten Island, N.Y., Jan. 18, 1959; s. Russell and Estelle (Trower) T.; m. Janice M. Archibald-Toliver, Aug. 28, 1982; children: Ryan Eugene, Kyle Stewart. Student, Coll. Staten Island, 1977-80. Cert. profl. hypnotherapists, cert. behavioral therapists. Team leader Vols. of Am., N.Y.C., 1985—; pvt. practice hypnotherapist and behavioral therapist N.Y.C., 1988—; cons. John Stossel Show 20/20, N.Y.C., 1988, Ex-Mayor Ed Koch's Com. on the Homeless in the Subways, N.Y.C., 1989-90. Mem. The Black Polit. Action Com., S.I., 1990; bd. dirs. Crisis Pregnancy Ctr., S.I., 1991. Mem. Am. Assn. Behavioral Therapists, Am. Bd. Hypnotherapy, Am. Assn. Profl. Hypnotherapists, Internat. Hypnosis Network, Nat. Guild Hypnotists, Am. Inst. for Hypnotherapy and Psychotherapists. Democrat. Baptist. Home: 13602 N 44th St Apt 150 Phoenix AZ 85032-6343 Office: 1776 Broadway Ste 701 New York NY 10019-2002

TOLL, ALEXANDER ROBERT, education educator; b. Phila., Aug. 19, 1954; s. Edwin Richard and Beatrice Sylvia (Rockman) T.; m. Sharon Joy Forman, June 25, 1983. Student, Carnegie-Mellon U., 1972; BS, St. Joseph's Coll., 1976; MEd, Beaver Coll., 1980; EdD, Temple U., 1985. Cert. tchr., Pa., tchr., supr., N.J. Sales assoc. Gimbel Bros., Inc., Upper Darby, Pa., 1973-74, BASCO, Inc., Wayne, Pa., 1974-77; rsch. technician U. Pa. Sch. Medicine, Phila., 1977-78; tchr. Sch. Dist. Phila., 1978-80, Benchmark Sch., Media, Pa., 1979-80; adj. asst. prof. edn. Temple U., Phila., 1980-87; asst. prof. edn., K-12 clin. instrn. supr. grad. faculty Pa. State U., University Park, 1988—; edn. cons., Phila., 1985—. Patentee electronic apparatus for teaching math. Mem. ASCD, AAUP, Nat. Coun. Tchrs. English, Phila. Classical Guitar Soc., Fraternal Order Police, Phi Delta Kappa, Kappa Delta Pi, Alpha Epsilon Delta. Office: Coll Edn Pa State Univ 172 Chambers Bldg University Park PA 16802

TOLL, RICHARD JAY, construction executive; b. Phila., Apr. 27, 1954; s. Daniel Bruce and May (Task) T.; m. Karen Louise Lundberg, Apr. 26, 1981; children: Steven, Jaime. BA in History, Boston U., 1978. Mgmt. trainee Fidelity Bank of N.J., Pennsauken, 1979-81; pres., chief exec. officer Toll Constrn. Co., Marlton, N.J., 1981—. Asst. varsity football coach Sterling High Sch., Stratford, N.J., 1989-90; bd. dirs. March of Dimes South Jersey, Audubon, N.J., 1990—, Kennedy Meml. Hosp., Cherry Hill, N.J., 1990—, Capital Campaign Com.; chmn. bd. dirs. Daniel B. Toll Fund, Cherry Hill, 1990—. Mem. Woodcrest Country Club (chmn. rules com. 1990—). Home: 11 Nottingham Dr Medford NJ 08053 Office: Toll Constrn Co 111 Church Rd PO Box 1159 Marlton NJ 08055

TOLLER, WILLIAM ROBERT, chemical and oil company executive; b. Ft. Smith, Ark., Aug. 10, 1930; s. Audly Sr. and Martha (Anderson) T.; m. Jo Ella Perry, June 13, 1959; children: William R. Jr., Michelle D., Gregory A. BBA, U. Ark., 1956; postgrad., Stamford U., 1971. Various positions Conoco Inc., Okla., Tex. and Colo., 1955-77; v.p. fin. and adminstrn. Continental Carbon Co., Houston, 1977-81, pres., chief exec. officer, 1981-84; v.p., gen. mgr. Concarb div. Witco Corp., Houston, 1984-86; dir., chmn. bd., chief exec. officer Witco Corp., N.Y.C., 1990—. Mem. Rep. Nat. Com., Washington, 1988-92. Mem. Am. Chem. Soc., Am. Petroleum Inst., CMA Bd. Mem. Presbyterian. Home: 102 Windsor Cir Westwood NJ 07675-4363 Office: Witco Corp 520 Madison Ave New York NY 10022-4213

TOLLES, ROBERT ERVING, writer, editor; b. Norwalk, Conn., June 6, 1927; s. Wellington Erving and Marie (Sultan) T.; m. Barbara Ann Svec, Feb. 9, 1952; children: David Erving, Amanda Katherine. BA, Yale Coll., 1950; MA in Econs., New Sch. for Social Rsch., 1976. Reporter Norwalk (Conn.) Hour, 1950-60; staff writer Sikorsky Aircraft, Stratford, Conn., 1960-62; info. officer U.S. Info. Agy., Bogota, Colombia, 1962-65; staff writer, assoc. editor Radio Corp. of Am., N.Y.C., 1968-89; assoc. editor, dir. office of reports The Ford Found., N.Y.C., 1968-89; cons. New Canaan, Conn., 1989—; cons. Russell Sage Found., N.Y.C., 1989—, Nat. Exec. Svc. Corps, N.Y.C., 1991—, Phelps-Stokes Fund, N.Y.C., 1992, Seedco, N.Y.C., 1989—. Contbr. articles to booklets and jours. Exec. com. mem. Yale Club of New Canaan/Wilton, 1991—. Petty officer USN, 1945-46. Mem. Sr. Men's Club of New Canaan. Home: 91 Bickford Ln New Canaan CT 06840 Office: 134 Main St New Canaan CT 06840

TOLMIE, DAVID MCEACHERN, real estate executive; b. Evanston, Ill., June 12, 1955; s. Donald McEachern and Joann (Swanson) T.; m. Tracy Leigh Via, Apr. 7, 1984; children: Kelsey Via, Madeline Gilbert, Clayton MacEachern. BA in Econs., U. Va., 1977; MBA, Harvard U., 1980. Product mgr. Gen. Mills, Inc., Mpls., 1980-83; cons. McKinsey and Co., N.Y.C., 1983-85; corp. v.p. U.S. Health, Inc., Towson, Md., 1985-90; pres. Foundation Real Estate, Timonium, Md., 1990—; bd. dirs. The Found., Timonium. Pres. St. David's Lane Assn., Lutherville, Md., 1989-92; v.p. Faith Luth. Ch., Cockeysville, Md., 1991-92; active Baltimore County Leadership, Towson. Mem. Nat. Assn. Home Builders, Home Builders Assn. Md., Urban Land Inst. Home: 11639 Saint Davids Ln Lutherville MD 21093 Office: Foundation Real Estate 9690 Deereco Rd Ste 820 Timonium MD 21093

TOMAN, DONALD JOSEPH, electrical engineer; b. N.Y.C., Jan. 22, 1934; s. Joseph J. and Anna (Drgan) T.; m. Mathilde Shirley Trautner, July 4, 1959; children: Donna Jeanne, David John. BEE, Cooper Union, 1955; MSEE, NYU, 1964. Staff engr. ITT Fed. Telecommunication, Nutley, N.J., 1955-56; sr. staff engr. Gen. Precision Labs., Pleasantville, N.Y., 1956-69; chief systems engr. Tull Aviation Corp., Armonk, N.Y., 1969-78; sr. staff cons. Loral Electronic Systems, Yonkers, N.Y., 1978—. Contbr. chpts. to books; patentee in field. Mem. Assn. U.S. Army, Assn. Old Crows, Armed Forces Communications/Electronics Assn., Mensa. Home: 24 Old Farm Rd Pleasantville NY 10570-1506

TOMASI, THOMAS B., cell biologist, administrator; b. May 24, 1927; s. Thomas B. and Ivis (Ratazzi) T.; children—Barbara, Theodore, Anne. A.B., Dartmouth Coll., Hanover, N.H., 1950; M.D., U. Vt., Burlington, 1954; Ph.D., Rockefeller U., 1965. Intern, resident, chief resident Columbia Presbyn. Hosp., N.Y.C., 1954-58, instr. medicine, 1958-60; prof., chmn. div. exptl. medicine U. Vt., Burlington, 1960-65; prof. medicine, dir. immunology SUNY, Buffalo, 1965-73; prof., chmn. immunology dept. Mayo Med. Sch., Rochester, Minn., 1973-81; dir. Cancer Ctr., Disting. Univ. prof., chmn. dept. cell biology U. N. Mex., Albuquerque, 1981-86; dir. Roswell Park Cancer Inst., Buffalo, 1986—, chmn. dept. molecular medicine. Author: The Immune System of Secretions, 1976; contbr. over 200 articles to profl. jours. Served with USN, 1945-46. Mem. Am. Soc. Cell Biology, Am. Assn. Immunologists, Am. Assn. Cancer Research, Am. Soc. Clin. Investigation, Am. Fedn. Clin. Research, Assn. Am. Physicians. Roman Catholic. Home: 7980 E Quaker St Orchard Park NY 14127-2017 Office: Roswell Park Cancer Inst Elm and Carlton Sts Buffalo NY 14263

TOMASUOLO, VINCENT ANTHONY, physician; b. Bklyn., Jan. 27, 1958; s. Vincent Sr. and Madeline (Dinapoli) T.; m. Robin Lorraine Brienza, July 28, 1984; 1 child, Vincent III. BS in Biology, St. John's U., 1980; Cert. in Respiratory Therapy, NYU, 1982; MD, St. George's U., 1987. Diplomate Am. Coll. of Physicians. Resident in internal medicine St. Vincent's Med. Ctr., S.I., N.Y., 1987-90; fellow in critical care St. Micheal's Hosp., Newark, 1990-91; fellow U. Medicine and Dentistry of N.J., Robert Wood Johnson U., New Brunswick, N.J., 1991-92. Mem. Am. Coll. of Physicians, AMA. Roman Catholic.

TOMASZEK, THOMAS RICHARD, manufacturing executive; b. Blackstone, Mass., Jan. 12, 1952; s. Adolph Paul and Genevieve Barbara (Tycks) T.; m. Joyce Christine Lockwood, Dec. 18, 1952. BA, R.I. Coll., 1973; tech. cert., O'Keefe Tech., Framingham, Mass., 1979. Cert. sec. tchr., R.I. Technician, sales rep. Rockwell Internat., Charlotte, N.C., 1973-76; sales correspondent Nelmor Co., North Uxbridge, Mass., 1976-78, gen. sales mgr., 1979-87; sales mgr. Rapid Granulator Co., Rockford, Ill., 1978-79; sales, mktg. mgr. Eaglebrook East Plastics Corp., Middletown, N.Y., 1987-88; mgr. recycling ops. Plastics Again, Leominster, Mass., 1988-90; pres. N.Am. Plastics Recycling Corp., Ft. Edward, N.Y., 1990—; guest lectr. North Smithfield (R.I.) Hist. Soc., 1982-86, Plastics Recycling Retec, Charlotte, N.C., 1989. Inventor in field. Recipient Sen. Pell award, State of R.I., 1969, Appreciation award IML Tech., Inc., North Brook, N.J., 1986. Mem. ASTM, Soc. Plastics Engrs. (sr. mem., regional dir. recycling div., Appreciation awards Chgo., 1984, Phoenix, 1979), Assn. Post-Consumer Plastics Recyclers (founding mem.), Mass. Audubon Soc., Exch. Club. Republican. Roman Catholic. Home: 23 Blackstone St Blackstone MA 01504-1604 Office: N Am Plastics Recycling Corp Towpath Rd Fort Edward NY 12828

TOMB, MYRON HAY, lawyer; b. Indiana, Pa., Mar. 1, 1947; s. Myron Hay and Gertrude (Mangan) T.; m. Kathryn Bonach, June 21, 1986; children: Devin Elizabeth, Jordan Hay. BA in Econs., Indiana U. Pa., 1969; JD, U. Pitts., 1972. Bar: Pa., U.S. Supreme Ct. Assoc. Tomb & Tomb, Indiana, 1972-82; ptnr. Carmella & Tomb, Indiana, 1983—; instr. bus. law Ind. U. Pitts., 1975-76, instr. constitutional law, 1976-77. Author: (catalog) The Art of the Pattisons, 1987. Del. Dem. Nat. Conv., N.Y.C., 1980, rules com., 1984; chmn. Indiana County Com. to Elect Bob Casey Gov., 1986; bd. dirs., pres. Indiana U. Pa. Univ. Mus., 1989—; steering com. Found. for Indiana U. Pa., 1987—. Mem. Indiana county Bar Assn., Pa. Bar Assn., Assn. Trial Lawyers of Am., Nat. Sch. Bd. Assn., Coun. Sch. Attys. Home: 1536 Indian Springs Rd Indiana PA 15701-3223 Office: Carmella & Tomb 724 Church St Indiana PA 15701-2741

TOMEK, WILLIAM GOODRICH, agricultural economist; b. Table Rock, Nebr., Sept. 20, 1932; s. John and Ruth Genevieve (Goodrich) T. B.S., U. Nebr., 1956, M.A., 1957; Ph.D., U. Minn., 1961. Asst. prof. Cornell U., Ithaca, N.Y., 1961-66, NSF fellow, 1965, assoc. prof. agrl. econs., 1966-70, prof., 1970—, chmn. dept. agrl. econs., 1988—; vis. econ. USDA, 1978-79; vis. fellow Stanford U., 1968-69, U. New Eng., Australia, 1988. Author: Agricultural Product Prices, 1990; editor: Am. Jour. Agrl. Econs., 1975-77; mem. editorial bd. Jour. Futures Markets, 1992—; contbr. articles to profl. jours. Served with U.S. Army, 1953-55. Mem. Am. Agrl. Econs. Assn. (pres. 1985-86), Am. Econ. Assn., Econometric Soc., Northeastern Agrl. Econs. Assn., Am. Agrl. Econs. Assn. (awards 1981, 89, fellow), Gamma Sigma Delta. Democrat. Methodist. Office: Cornell U 102 Warren Hall Ithaca NY 14853-7801

TOMERA, JOHN FRANK, pharmacologist, scientist; b. Johnstown, Pa., May 7, 1952; s. Joseph Frank and Helen Victoria (Hebda) T.; m. Mona Jean Elensky, Oct. 22, 1977. BS, U. Pitts., 1974; PhD, Temple U., 1978. Postdoctoral fellow Sch. of Pub. Health Harvard U., Boston, 1978-80; postdoctoral assoc. MIT, Cambridge, Mass., 1980-82; instr. in anesthesiology Med. Sch. Harvard U., Mass. Gen. Hosp., Shriners Burns Inst., Boston, 1985-87; asst. prof. anesthesiology Med. Sch. Harvard U., Mass. Gen. Hosp., Boston, 1987—; asst. in neurosurgery Mass. Gen. Hosp., Boston, 1983-85; pharmacol. cons., Medfield, Mass., 1985-87; mem. rsch. coord. com. Shriners Burns Inst., Boston, 1989-90. Contbr. articles to profl. jours. Tableau mem. Rose Croix, Mt. Olivet chpt., Boston, 1987—; sr. warden St. John's Lodge Masons, Boston, 1987-91. Temple U. fellow, 1974-78; UpJohn Co. grantee, 1988, Am. Heart Assn. grantee, 1990, Shriner's Hosp. for Crippled Children grantee, 1991—. Mem. Am. Physiology Soc., Am Burn Assn., Arlington Masons. Democrat. Roman Catholic. Home: 354 South St Medfield MA 02052-3127 Office: Shriners Burn Inst Clin Pharmacol Lab Anesthesia Svcs 51 Blossom St Boston MA 02114

TOMKO, RONALD THOMAS, human resources executive; b. Wilkes-Barre, Pa., Sept. 12, 1966; s. Ronald Thomas Sr. and Jane Ellen (Hilbert) T. BS in Human Resources Mgmt., King's Coll., Wilkes-Barre, 1988, BA in Psychology, 1988. Pers. dir. Sheraton Crossgates, Wilkes-Barre, 1989-90; pers. adminstr. Document Automation Corp., Wilkes-Barre, 1990-91; asst. human resources dir. Hofmann Industries, Sinking Spring, Pa., 1991—. Mem. KC. Democrat. Roman Catholic. Office: Hofmann Industries Inc 3145 Shillington Rd Reading PA 19608-1606

TOMLIN, DONALD REID, investment manager, securities analyst; b. Greensboro, N.C., Aug. 8, 1933; s. Dock R. and Irene (Brown) T.; m. Sue Gormley, Apr. 2, 1959 (dec. Oct. 1959); m. Rose Moore, June 24, 1961; children: Donald Reid Jr., Jane Rose. BCE, N.C. State U., 1955; MBA, U. N.C., 1959. Chartered fin. analyst. V.p., mgr. securities dept. Liberty Life Ins., Greenville, S.C., 1961-68; v.p., dir. rsch. Goldman Sachs & Co., N.Y.C., 1968-72; pres. Tomlin, Zimmerman & Parmalee, N.Y.C., 1972-78; prin. Keinwort, Benson, McCowan, Inc., N.Y.C., 1978-80, McCowan Assocs., N.Y.C., 1980-82; mng. dir. Haven Capital Mgmt., Inc., N.Y.C., 1982-91, Tomlin Capital Mgmt., Charleston, S.C., 1991—; bd. dirs. Southeastern Thrift & Bank Fund, Inc., Atlanta. 1st lt. USAF, 1955-57. Mem. Atlanta Soc. Fin. Analysts, Fin. Analysts Fedn., N.Y. Yacht Club, Larchmont Yacht Club, Carolina Yacht Club. Republican. Home: 107 Cliff Ave Pelham NY 10803-2006 Office: Tomlin Capital Mgmt PO Box 1840 18 Broad St Charleston SC 29402

TOMLINSON, KENNETH Y., periodical editor in chief; b. Mt. Airy, N.C., Aug. 3, 1944; s. Young and Mattie (Wingate) T.; m. Rebecca Moore, Apr. 25, 1975; children: William Moore, Lucas Young. BA in History, Randolph Macon Coll., 1966. Reporter Richmond Times Dispatch, 1965-68; corr. Reader's Digest, Pleasantville, N.Y., 1968-81, editor, 1981-82, mng. editor, 1984-85, exec. editor, 1985-90, editor-in-chief, 1990—; dir. Voice of Am., 1982-84. Co-author: History of American Prisoners of War in Vietnam, 1975. Chmn. Nat. Commn. Librs. and Info. Sci., 1986-87; active Nat. Commn. Vol. Svc., 1981-83, U.S. Bd. Internat. Broadcasting, 1987—. Episcopalian. Office: Readers Digest Assn Inc Pleasantville NY 10570*

TOMPKINS, DANIEL REUBEN, horticulturist, researcher; b. N.Y.C., Oct. 2, 1931; s. Leo L. and Lillian O. (Korsakoff) T.; m. Linda Goff, Mar. 20, 1964; children: Laura, Carol. BS, U. Md., 1959, MS, 1962, PhD, 1963. Asst. horticulturist Wash. State U., Puyallup, 1962-68; assoc. prof. U. Ark., Fayetteville, 1969-74, prof., 1974-75; prin. horticulturist Coop. State Rsch. Svc., USDA, Washington, 1975—. Contbr. more than 50 articles to profl. jours. Staff sgt. U.S. Army, 1952-55, Korea. U. Md. fellow, 1959-62. Fellow Am. Soc. Hort. Sci. (v.p. rsch. 1987-88); mem. AAAS, Plant Growth Regulator Soc. Am., Sigma Xi (pres. Washington chpt. 1987-89). Office: USDA Coop State Rsch Svc Washington DC 20250

TOMPKINS, FRANCINE MARIA, administrative director; b. St. Louis, Sept. 23, 1947; d. William Leroy and Christina (Smith) T. BS in Acctg., Bklyn. Coll., 1991, MS in Guidance and Counseling, 1991; MS in Guidance and Counseling, 1991. Budget analyst Mfrs. Hanover Trust Co., N.Y.C., 1970-82; fiscal officer Social Concern Community Devel., Laurelton, N.Y., 1982-84; bus. instr. Am. Bus. Inst., Bklyn., 1984-89; administrv. dir. Horace E. Green Day Care Ctr., Bklyn., 1989-90; placement dir. Am. Bus. Inst., 19990—; acctg. cons. Dawn Star Systems Inc., N.Y.C., 1982-86, Bklyn. Teen Care, 1983-85. Singer in Broadway prodn. Gospel at Colonus, 1988. Acctg. cons. Ft. Green Community Outreach, Bklyn., 1980—, also bd. dirs.; bd. dirs., sec. Instl. Radio Choir, Bklyn., 1980—. Mem. Am. Bus. Women's Assn. (pres. N.Y.C. charter chpt. 1986-87, Woman of Yr. 1988), Delta Sigma Theta. Democrat. Mem. Pentecostal Ch. Home: 291 Clinton Ave Brooklyn NY 11205-4742

TOMPKINS, ROBERT CHARLES, physical scientist, researcher; b. Bucyrus, Ohio, Aug. 23, 1924; s. Ernest Rusler and Valeria Beatrice (Sames) T.; m. Elizabeth Lee Raynor, Aug. 31, 1957; children: Michael David, Stephen Charles, Joan Elizabeth Tompkins Lambert. BS, Ohio State U., 1944; postgrad., U. Chgo., 1946-48. Rsch. engr. Battelle Meml. Inst., Columbus, Ohio, 1946-48; phys. scientist U.S. Army Nuclear Def. Lab., Edgewood Arsenal, Md., 1949-71; phys. scientist U.S. Army Ballistic Rsch. Lab., Aberdeen Proving Ground, Md., 1971-86, ret., 1986; mem. Quadripartite Ad Hoc Working Group 62-5, London, 1963, DNA Fallout Working Group, Washington, 1965-71; mem. adv. com. on civil def. NAS-NRC, Washington, 1970-73; lectr. St. Mary's Sem. and U., Balt., 1975. Contbr. articles to Adv. Chem. Series, Jour. Chem. Physics. Mem. Am. Chem. Soc., Am. Phys. Soc., N.Y. Acad. Scis., Sigma Xi. Republican. Episcopalian. Home: 541 Valley View Rd Towson MD 21286

TONG, MARY POWDERLY, mathematician educator, retired; b. N.Y.C., May 24, 1924; d. William Joseph and Katherine Colwell Powderly; m. Hing Tong, Aug. 19, 1956; children: Christopher, Mary Elizabeth, William, Jane Frances, James. BA, St. Joseph's Coll., 1950; MA, Columbia U., 1951, PhD, 1969. Instr. math. St. Joseph's Coll., Bklyn., 1951-54, Columbia Univ., N.Y.C., 1954-60; asst. prof. math. Univ. Conn., Storrs, 1960-66; assoc. prof. math. Fairfield (Conn.) Univ., 1966-70; prof. math. William Paterson Coll., Wayne, N.J., 1970-81. Contbr. articles to profl. jours. Trustee South Bergen Mental Health Ctr., Lyndhurst, N.J., 1988—. Recipient fellowship NSF, Washington, 1959-60. Mem. Am. Math. Soc., Math. Assn. Am., Am. Phys. Soc., N.Y. Acad. Scis., Delta Epsilon Sigma. Roman Catholic. Home: 725 Cooper Ave Oradell NJ 07649-2334

TONI, EUGENE JOSEPH, government procurement official; b. Phila., Oct. 5, 1949; s. Joseph Anton and Anne Marie (McCullough) T.; m. Nancy Lee Wojtkowiak, Apr. 29, 1972; children: Rebecca, Emily, Sara. AS in Bus. Administrn., Camden County Community Coll., Blackwood, N.J., 1973; BS in Econs., U. Pa., 1975; MPA, George Washington U., Washington, 1992. Cert. profl. contract mgr. (fellow 1989). Contract specialist Naval Air Systems Command, Washington, 1976-82, prin. contracting officer, 1982-84; procurement analyst Air Force Systems Command, Andrews AFB, Md., 1984-86; command competition advocate Air Force Systems Command, Andrews AFB, 1986-87, chief competition mgmt. office hdqrs., 1987-88; dir acquisition policy, planning and cost estimating div. Space and Naval Warfare Systems Command, Washington, 1988-89, dir. info. mgmt., svc. and communications purchase div., 1989—. Editorial adv. bd. Contract Mgmt., 1987-90. With 101st Airborne, U.S. Army, 1969-71, Vietnam. Fellow Nat. Contracts Mgmt. Assn. (no. Va. chpt. v.p. projects 1987-89, nat. functional dir. for awards and honors 1989-90, 90-91, Spl. award 1987, 88); mem. Pi Alpha Alpha. Roman Catholic. Home: 3307 Carolina Pl Alexandria VA 22305-1707

TONKIN, HUMPHREY RICHARD, university president; b. Truro, Cornwall, Eng., Dec. 2, 1939; came to U.S., 1962; s. George Leslie and Lorna Winifred (Sandrey) T.; m. Sandra Julie Winberg, Mar. 9, 1968 (div. 1981); m. Jane Spencer Edwards, Oct. 1, 1983; 1 child, Sebastian George. BA, St. John's Coll., Cambridge, Eng., 1962, MA, 1966; AM, Harvard U., 1966, PhD, 1966. Asst. prof. English U. Pa., Phila., 1966-71, assoc. prof., 1971-80, prof., 1980-83, vice-provost undergrad. studies, 1971-75, coord. internat. programs, 1977-83, master Stouffer Coll. House, 1980-83; pres. State Univ. Coll., Potsdam, N.Y., 1983-88, U. Hartford, Conn., 1989—; vis. prof. English Columbia U., N.Y.C., 1980-81; dir. Ctr. Rsch. and Documentation on World Lang. Problems, Rotterdam and Hartford, 1974—; mem. editorial bd. Spenser Studies, Duquesne Studies in Lang. and Lit.; mng. editor Lang. Problems and Lang. Planning. Author: bibliography Sir Walter Raleigh, 1971; Spenser's Courteous Pastoral, 1972; bibliography Esperanto and International Language Problems, 4th edit., 1977; (with Jane Edwards) The World in the Curriculum, 1981; The Faerie Queene, 1989; (with Allison Keef) Language in Religion, 1989; contbr. articles, studies, revs. to profl. jours. Pres. Pa. Coun. Internat. Edn., 1980-81; bd. dirs. World Affairs Coun. Phila., 1979-83, Partnership for Service-Learning, 1985—, Am. Forum, 1985—, Zamenhof Found., 1987—, Hartford Symphony Orch., 1989—, World Affairs Coun. Conn., 1989—, Greater Hartford Arts Coun., 1989—; chmn. Coun. Internat. Exch. Scholars, 1991—, Esperantic Studies Found., 1991—. Recipient Lindback award for disting. teaching, 1970; Frank Knox fellow Harvard U., 1962-66; Guggenheim fellow, 1974. Fellow Acad. Esperanto; mem. Universal Esperanto Assn. (pres. 1974-80, 86-89; rep. to UN 1974—), Spenser Soc. (pres. 1983-84, former dir.), Renaissance Soc. Am. (former dir.), Esperanto Studies Assn. Am. (pres. 1977-90), Internat. Acad. Scis., San Marino, Conn. Acad. Arts and Scis., Cosmos, Hartford Golf Club, Hartford Club. Home: 85 Bloomfield Ave Hartford CT 06105 Office: U Hartford Office of Pres West Hartford CT 06117

TONN, VICTOR LUX, economics educator; b. Hualien, Taiwan, Oct. 10, 1943; came to U.S., 1972; s. Eugene Piang-Hsien Tong and Grace Tsen-Moi Chin. BA in Econs., Nat. Taiwan U., Taipei, 1961, BA in Fgn. Langs. and Lit., 1970; MA in Econs., Bklyn. Coll., 1980; PhD in Econs., Utah State U., 1984; MS in Math., U. R.I., 1988. Mgr. Fengkuang Shanghao Co., 1966-67; tchr. high sch., Taiwan, 1970-71; mem. faculty, chmn. dept. econs. Salve Regina U., Newport, R.I., 1981—; asst. prof. Salve Regina U., Newport, 1984-89, assoc. prof., 1989—; dir. grad. studies in internat. trade and fin. Salve Regina Coll., Newport, R.I., 1989-91. 2d lt. Taiwanese Army, 1965-66. Mem. Am. Econ. Assn., Western Econ. Assn. Internat., Chinese Econ. Assn. N.Am. Office: Salve Regina U Ochre Point Ave Newport RI 02840-6906

TOOGOOD, GRANVILLE NEWBOLD, executive communications consultant; b. Phila., May 31, 1943; s. Granville Ernest and Anne Coxe (Newbold) T.; m. Patricia Dale, May 4, 1968; children: Heather, Chase. BA, U. Pa., 1966. Asst. producer NFL Films, Phila., 1966; writer, reporter Life mag., N.Y.C., 1967-69, NBC News, N.Y.C., 1969-72; exec. dir. N.Y. Coun. Environ. Advisors, N.Y.C., 1972-73; editor ABC News, N.Y.C., 1973-74; writer Nat. Enquirer, Fla., 1975-79; v.p. Kingstree Group, Newport, R.I., 1979-82; pres. Granville Toogood Assocs., Darien, Conn., 1982—; nat. seminar speaker. Contbr. articles to mags. and newspapers. Mem. Pub. Rels. Soc. Am., Internat. Assn. Bus. Communicators, Nat. Assn. Corp. Speakers. Office: 5 Salem Straits Darien CT 06820-5924

TOOHEY, EDWARD JOSEPH, financial services company executive; b. Jersey City, Jan. 15, 1930; s. John Joseph and Estelle Anita (Hudson) T.; B.A., Yale U., 1953; m. Ruth Phyllis Scheidecker, Mar. 13, 1948; 1 dau., Phyllis Karen. With Merrill Lynch, Pierce, Fenner & Smith, Inc., N.Y.C., 1956—, mgmt. devel. program exec., 1966-68, v.p. resident mgr., N.Y.C., 1968-77, Washington, 1977-80, v.p., regional dir., N.Y.C., 1980-90, first v.p., 1990—; dir. Bunbury Co., N.Y.C. Trustee Windham Found., Grafton, Vt., 1978—; vice chmn. Peddie Sch., Hightstown, N.J., 1981—, trustee, 1976—; bd. dirs. N.Y.C. Ballet, 1983—. Served to maj. USMC, 1953-55. Clubs: Canoe Brook Country (Summit, N.J.); Yale, Sky, Univ. (N.Y.C.); Georgetown (Washington). Home: One Gracie Terr New York NY 10028 Office: 717 5th Ave New York NY 10022

TOOKER, ELISABETH JANE, anthropologist, educator; b. Bklyn., Aug. 2, 1927; d. Clyde and Amy (Luce) T. BA, Radcliffe Coll., 1949, PhD, 1958; MA, U. Ariz., 1953. Instr. anthropology U. Buffalo, 1957-60; asst. prof. Mt. Holyoke Coll., South Hadley, Mass., 1961-65; asst. prof. Temple U., Phila., 1965-67, assoc. prof., 1967-77, prof., 1977—. Author: An Ethnography of the Huron Indians, 1964, The Iroquois Ceremonial of Midwinter, 1970; editor: Native American Spirituality of the Eastern Woodlands, 1979, An Iroquois Source Book, 1985-86. NEH fellow, 1981-82, Smithsonian Instn. fellow, 1989-90; recipient Cornplanter medal Cayuea County Hist. Soc., 1986. Fellow AAAS, Am. Anthrop. Assn.; mem. Am. Soc. for Ethno History (pres. 1981-82), Am. Ethnol. Soc. (editor 1978-82). Home: 411 S Taney St Philadelphia PA 19146-1042 Office: Temple Univ Dept of Anthropology Philadelphia PA 19122

TOOLE, SISTER EILEEN MARIE, pastoral counselor; b. Wilkes-Barre, Pa., Oct. 20, 1940; d. Joseph Aloysius and Helen Marian (Conlon) T. BS in Elem. Edn., Coll. Misericordia, Dallas, Pa., 1963; MEd, Fordham U., 1971; PhD in Pastoral Counseling, Loyola Coll., Balt., 1991. Joined Sisters of Mercy, Roman Cath. Ch., 1958; cert. profl. counselor, md.; cert. Nat. Bd. Cert. Counselors. Elem. tchr. Diocese of Harrisburg and Altoona, Johnstown, Pa., 1963-74; elem. guidance counselor Lincoln Intermediate Unit # 12, New Oxford, Pa., 1974-76; pastoral asst. Diocese of Harrisburg, 1977-86; Vietnamese resettlement counselor Ft. Indiantown Gap, Annville, Pa., 1976; pastoral counselor Epoch Counseling Ctr., Catonville, Md., 1986-87, Citizens Against Spousal Assault, Columbia, Md., 1987-88, Cath. U. Am. Counseling Ctr., Washington, Md., 1988-89, Taylor Manor Hosp., Ellicott City, 1989-90, Centennial Counseling, Ellicott City, Md., 1990—, 1990—; practicum supr. Loyola Pastoral Counseling Program, Columbia, 1990—. Mem. AACD, Alpha Sigma Nu. Democrat. Home: Apt 101 3181 Pine Orchard Ln Ellicott City MD 21042 Office: Centennial Counseling 10320B Baltimore National Pike Ellicott City MD 21042-2128

TOOLE, JOHN EDWARD, accountant; b. Providence, Feb. 4, 1934; s. Harry Clement and Gertrude Mary (Deignan) T. BBA, Bryant Coll., 1953; postgrad., Ga. Inst. of Tech., 1960. CPA, D.C. Supervisory audit Fed. Power Commn., Washington, 1958-61; audit supr. Deloitte Haskins & Sells (formerly Niles & Niles), N.Y.C., 1961-66; br. acct. SEC, Washington, 1966-67; asst. chief, account regulations Civil Aeronautics Bd., Washington, 1967-69; mgr. Ernst & Whinney, Cleve., 1969-73; mgr. fed. program Ernst & Whinney, Washington, 1973-75, 1975-84, dir. fed. program, 1984-89; assoc. dir. govt. rels. Ernst & Young, Washington, 1989—; mem. D.C. Bd. Accountancy, 1991—, chmn., 1980-84. Bd. dirs. Art Barn Assn., Washington, 1984-86; trustee Corcoran Gallery of Art, Washington, 1986-88; pres. Friends of Corcoran, Washington, 1986-88. Mem. AICPA, D.C. Inst. CPAs, Assn. Govt. Accts. (nat. exec. com. 1985-88), Nat. Assn. State Bds. Accountancy (bd. dirs. 1982-84), Univ. Club, 1925 F St. Club. Roman Catholic. Home: 4600 Connecticut Ave NW Apt 713 Washington DC 20008-5706 Office: Ernst & Young 1200 19th St NW Ste 400 Washington DC 20036-2434

TOOLEY, LOWELL JAMES, city manager; b. Sauk County, Wis., July 21, 1923; m. Marceil Sprecher, July 9, 1949; children: David Son, Paul Wayne, Mary Lynn, Jeanne Louise. B.S. in Civil Engring., U. Wis., 1953. Registered profl. engr., N.Y., Wis. Engr., mgr. Shorewood Hills (Wis.), 1949-56; asst. mgr. Scarsdale (N.Y.), 1956-61, mgr., 1961—. Chmn. adv. council Inst. for Local Govt., Westchester Community Coll., 1965-85; mem. N.Y. Lt. Gov.'s Roundtable, 1983-84. Bd. dirs. Council on Mcpl. Performance, 1985-87; chmn. recycling adv. com. County of Westchester, 1988—; mem. Model Cities Charter Task Force, 1986-89. Recipient outstanding service award Scarsdale Village Bd., 1986; named Citizen of Yr., Scarsdale C. of C., 1992. Entered in Congressional Record, 1986. Mem. Internat. City Mgmt. Assn. (v.p. 1980-82, chmn. ethics com. 1982, 40 yr. service award 1989), N.Y. State Mcpl. Mgmt. Assn. (pres. 1964-65), Nat. Mcpl. League (council of advisors 1986-89), N.Y. State Conf. Mayors (legis. com. 1962—), Am. Soc. Pub. Administrn. (dir. 1980-83, named Man of Yr. Lower Hudson Valley chpt. 1979), Westchester County Village Ofcls. Assn. (exec. bd.), Nat. Soc. Profl. Engrs. (govt. adv. group 1982—), Am. Pub. Works Assn. (Edward P. Decher award N.Y.-N.J. Met. chpt. 1982), Am. Water Works Assn., Westchester County Assn., Westchester 2000 (chmn. intergovernmental relations com. 1987—, sec. adv. bd. for intergovtl. rels. 1988—), Nat. Council on Pub. Works Improvement (discussion participant), N.Y. State Soc. Profl. Engrs. (Westchester County chpt. sec. 1987-91, pres. 1991-92, Outstanding Engr. in Govt. Westchester County chpt. 1983). Office: Village of Scarsdale 1001 Post Rd Scarsdale NY 10583

TOOMBS, RUSS WILLIAM, laboratory director; b. Troy, N.Y., July 11, 1951; s. George John and Olive Catherine (Blodgett) T.; m. Patrice Ann De Paul, Aug. 19, 1972; children: David Christopher, Mark Patrick. BS, Cornell U., 1973. Environ. scientist Wapora, Inc., Washington, 1973-74; bacteriologist N.Y. State Dept. Health, Wadsworth Ctr. for Labs. and Rsch., Albany, N.Y., 1974-76, sr. bacteriologist, assoc. bacteriologist, 1976-78, assoc. bacteriologist, 1978-86, dir. ops., 1986-90, assoc. dir., 1990—. Contbr. articles to profl. jours. Mem. Saratoga Performing Arts Ctr., Am. Soc. for Microbiology. Roman Catholic. Home: 65 Huntleigh Dr Albany NY 12211-1175 Office: Wadsworth Ctr Labs and Rsch Empire State Pla Albany NY 12201-0509

TOOMER, CYNTHIA YVONNE, information manager; b. Camden, N.J., Nov. 9, 1947; d. Nathaniel and Dorothy (Hudson) T. BA, Brandeis U., 1969; MS, Simmons Coll., 1973. Reference librarian Boston U. Mugar Library, Boston, 1973-77; head reference dept. Harvard U. Lamont Library, Cambridge, Mass., 1977-84; sr. proposal writer CLSI, Inc., Newton, Mass., 1984-87; tech writer, analyst Index Tech., Cambridge, Mass., 1987; mgr. devel. info. systems Radcliffe Coll. Devel. Office, Cambridge, 1988—. Mem. Boston Computer Soc., Mensa. Independent. Home: 21 Wendell St Cambridge MA 02138-1850 Office: Radcliffe Coll Devel Office 10 Garden St Cambridge MA 02138-3600

TOOMEY, JEANNE ELIZABETH, animal activist; b. Manhattan, N.Y., Aug. 22, 1921; d. Edward Aloysius and Anna Margaret (O'Grady) Toomey; m. Peter Terranova, Sept. 28, 1951 (dec. 1968); children: Peter Terranova, Sheila Terranova Beasley. Student, Hofstra U., 1938-40, Fordham U., 1940-41; BA, Southampton Coll., 1976; postgrad., Monmouth Coll., 1978-79. Reporter, columnist Bklyn. Daily Eagle, 1943-52; with The Fitzgeralds, NBC Radio, N.Y.C., 1952-53; reporter, writer King Features Syndicate, N.Y.C., 1953-55; reporter, columnist N.Y. Jour.-Am., N.Y.C., 1955-61; newsman AP, N.Y.C., 1963-87; columnist New Tribune, Woodbridge, N.J.; editor community sect. Calexico (Calif.) Chronicle, 1987-88, Asbury Park (N.J.) Press, 1988; pres., dir. Last Post Animal Sanctuary, Falls Village, Conn., 1991—. Named Woman of the Yr. N.Y. Women's Press Club, 1960. Mem. Newswomen's Club of N.Y., Overseas Press Club, N.Y. Press Club, Siluri-ans. Roman Catholic. Home and Office: 95 Belden St Falls Village CT 06031

TOOMEY, LAURA CAROLYN, psychologist; b. Manchester, Conn., Mar. 29, 1929; d. David Clark and Olive (Hutchinson) T. BS, Bates Coll., 1950; MA, U. Conn., 1954, PhD, 1961. Lic. psychologist, Conn. Psychologist Community Child Guidance Clinic, Manchester, 1959-64; from psychologist to chief psychologist Springfield (Mass.) Hosp., 1964-73; with Conn. Valley Hosp., Middletown, 1973—, acting dir. psychol. svcs., 1986-87, dir. clin. internship tng., 1974-92, asst. chief of psychol. svcs., 1987-91. Co-author: Evaluation of Changes Associated with Psychiatric Treatment, 1959; contbr. chpts. in books and articles to profl. jours. Justice of the peace Town of Bolton, Conn., 1954-89; mem. Bolton Town Commn. on Aging, 1972-76; sec. Bolton Property Owners Assn., 1964-76. Mem. Am. Psychol. Assn. (treas. div. clin. psychology 1982-90), Conn. Psychol. Assn. (coun. bd. dirs. 1975-86). Republican. Home: 40 Steel Crossing Rd # 9486 Bolton CT 06043-7623 Office: Conn Valley Hosp Middletown CT 06457

TOPAZ, MURIEL, dance educator; b. Phila., May 7, 1932; d. Joseph Topaz and Rhea Rebecca Rosenbloom; m. Jacob Druckman, June 5, 1954; children: Karen Druckman, Daniel Druckman. Student, NYU, 1950-51; studies with Martha Graham, Antony Tudor, The Juilliard Sch., 1951-54; student, Dance Notation Bur., N.Y.C., 1954-56. Mem. faculty The Juilliard Sch., N.Y.C., 1959-70, dir. dance div., 1985-92; exec. dir. Dance Notation Bur., 1978-85; co-chmn. First Internat. Congress on Movement Notation Bur., Israel, 1984, 2d Internat. Congress, Hong Kong, 1990; chmn. artistic com. Dance Notation Bur.; adjudicator Reginal Dance/Am., Mid-States 1980, Pacific 1981, N.E. 1983. Author: Changes and New Developments in Labanotation, 1966, Intermediate Reading Studies, 1972, Intermediate Study Guide, 1972, Choreography and Dance: The Notation Issue, 1988; co-author (with Hackney & Manno) Elementary Study Guide, 1970, Elementary Reading Studies, 1970, (with Edelson) Readings in Modern Dance, 1972. Mem. May O'Donnell Hon. Com., 1979; chmn. dance panel N.Y. State Coun. on Arts, 1982-83; assessor Can. Coun., 1987; auditor NEA, 1989—. Recipient fgn. travel grant Inst. Internat. Edn., 1967. Fellow Internat. Coun. Kinetography Laban. Office: Juilliard Sch Dance Div Lincoln Ctr New York NY 10023

TOPCIK, BARRY, chemical engineer; b. Passaic, N.J., Apr. 7, 1924; s. Benjamin and Bess (Krug) T.; m. Marilyn Rothman, June 18, 1950. BSChemE, Cooper Union, 1952; MS, N.J. Inst. Tech., 1960. Draftsman Bell Telephone Labs., N.Y.C., 1941-44; sr. devel. engr. U.S. Rubber Co., Passaic, N.J., 1944-56; chief chemist Eberhard Faber Inc., Newark, 1956-62; lab. mgr. Cities Svc. Co., Columbian Div., Princeton, N.J., 1962-77; devel. mgr. Rhein-Chemie Inc., Trenton, N.J., 1977-83; cons. Union Carbide Co., Somerset, N.J., 1983-87, various cos., Somerset, N.J., 1987—. Author: (handbook) Pigment Handbook, 1973; contbr. numerous publs. to profl. jours.; 25 patents in field related to rubber, plastics & carbon black. Mem. N.Y. Rubber Group, Phila. Rubber Group, Am. Chem. Soc. Home and Office: 545 Spring Valley Dr Bridgewater NJ 08807-1948

TOPF, BARBARA MAY, nurse epidemiologist; b. N.Y.C., Mar. 1, 1944; d. Irving and Helen (Eidelheit) T.; m. Albert Uziel, June 29, 1980; children: Claire, Sarah. BSN, SUNY, Buffalo, 1965; MA in Nursing, NYU, 1976. RN, N.Y., Conn. Staff nurse N.Y. Hosp.-Cornell Med. Ctr., N.Y.C., 1965-69, nurse epidemiologist, 1971-81; nurse epidemiologist Bronx (N.Y.)-Lebanon Hosp., 1969-71; mgr. epidemiology and safety Griffin Hosp., Derby, Conn., 1981—; mem. speakers bur. AIDS program Conn. Dept. Health, Hartford, 1987—. Contbr. numerous articles to profl. jours. Mem. AIDS task force Lower Naugatuck Valley Health Dept., Shelton, Conn., 1985—; mem. New Haven County HIV Planning Project, New Haven, 1990-91; troop leader Girl Scouts U.S.A., Brookfield, Conn., 1990—. Mem. Assn. Practitioners in Infection Control (sec. Greater N.Y. chpt. 1977-79, membership dir. New England chpt. 1989-91), Sigma Theta Tau. Home: 93 Longmeadow Hill Rd Brookfield CT 06804-1340 Office: Griffin Hosp 130 Division St Derby CT 06418-1376

TOPF, MICHAEL DAVID, management consultant executive; b. Newark, Sept. 16, 1942; s. Ernest and Muriel (Laden) T.; m. Linda Noble, Sept. 9, 1979. BS in Biology and Chemistry, Upsala Coll., 1964; MS in Applied Psychology, U. Santa Monica, 1988. Cert. alcoholism/drug addiction counselor, N.J., Pa., teaching behavior modification, N.J. Asst. rsch. dir. Dept. Health State of N.J., 1964-65; rsch. asst. Med. Ctr. NYU, 1965-66; adminstrv. asst. Mt. Sinai Hosp. and Med. Ctr., N.Y.C., 1966-68, Montefiore Hosp., N.Y.C., 1968-69; asst. dir. Beth Israel Med. Ctr., N.Y.C., 1969; counselor alcohol and drug rehab. unit John E. Runnels Hosp., Berkeley Heights, N.J., 1974-76; primary alcohol counselor East Orange (N.J.) Gen. Hosp., 1976-78; dir. alcohol/drug counseling Suburban Counseling Ctr., Bryn Mawr, Pa., 1978-80; pres. Topf Orgn., Rosemont, Pa., 1980—. V.p., dir. Gulph Mills (Pa.) Civic Assn., 1990—. With U.S. Army Med. Res., 1964-67.

TOPOL, MARTIN THEODORE, marketing educator; b. Bklyn., May 20, 1952; s. Benjamin Carl and Esther (Abramowitz) T.; m. Melanie Susan Stilman, Dec. 12, 1981; 1 child, Jacqueline Gail. BA, Queens Coll., 1973; MBA, Mich. State U., 1975; M in Philosophy, CUNY, 1981, PhD, 1981. Lectr. Baruch Coll. CUNY, 1977-81, asst. prof., 1981-84; assoc. prof. Pace U., N.Y.C., 1984-87, prof., 1987—; bd. dirs. Am. Collegiate Retailing Assn., treas., 1986-90; assoc. rsch. dir. The Market Discovery Group, N.Y.C., 1982—; pres. Martin T. Topol & Assocs., Forest Hills, N.Y., 1987—. Mem. editorial rev. bd. Jour. Direct Mktg., 1987—, Jour. Direct Mktg. Rsch., 1987-88. Tandy Corp. grantee, Ft. Worth, 1986. Mem. Acad. Mktg. Sci. (Meritorious Paper award 1988), Direct Mktg. Assn., Am. Mktg. Assn. Jewish. Home: 9013 68th Ave Flushing NY 11375-5721 Office: Pace U Lubin Grad Sch Bus 1 Pace Pla New York NY 10038

TOPPER, BARBARA MACNEAL BLAKE, educator; b. Wilmington, Del., July 18, 1942; d. George Mitchell and Jean (Strickland) Blake; m. George Lee Topper, Aug. 7, 1964; children: Gordon Lee, Geoffrey Logan. MusB, Peabody Conservatory, 1964; MusM, Peabody Conservatory, Balt., 1968. Tchr. Prince George's County Schs., Upper Marlboro, Md., 1964-67; piano tchr. Peabody Prep. Sch., Balt., 1964-67; vocal music specialist Harford County Pub. Schs., Bel Air, Md., 1968-76; piano tchr., coord. continuing edn. Cecil Community Coll., North East, Md., 1977-82; vocal music specialist Cecil County Pub. Schs., Elkton, Md., 1981-86, Balt. County Pub. Schs., Towson, Md., 1986—; spl. lectr. music and music edn. Washington Coll., Chestertown, Md., 1970-74; choral adjudicator, guest conductor, clinician, supr. student tchrs., 1973; accompanist Md. Ctr. for the Arts. Developer ednl. curriculum; contbr. articles to profl. jours. Mem. NEA, Md. Music Educators Assn. (exec. bd., sec. 1974-88), Music Educators Nat. Conf., Johns Hopkins Alumni Assn. (steering com. 1987—), Phi Delta Kappa. Roman Catholic. Home: 3130 Berkshire Rd Baltimore MD 21214-3404 Office: Berkshire Elem Sch Poplar Ave Baltimore MD 21228

TOPPER, JOHN ABRAM, JR., social studies educator, coach, singer; b. Cumberland, Md., Dec. 20, 1943; s. John Abram and Mary Catherine (Barnes) T.; m. Cheryl Lee Miller, June 1965 (div. 1976); children: John III, Joby Martin; m. Ruth Libby Albert, July 1, 1978; 1 child, Jesse Wills. BA, Susquehanna U., 1965; MEd, Shippensburg U., 1972. Social studies tchr., football coach, wrestling coach Gov. Livingston Regional High Sch., Berkeley Heights, N.J., 1965-66, Bedford (Pa.) Area High Sch., 1966-91; social studies tchr. Hyndman (Pa.)-Londonderry Jr.-Sr. High Sch., 1991—; tchr. adult edn. class Bedford-Everett Vocat. Tech. Sch., 1992. Singer, songwriter (albums) God Walks These Hills, 1982, God Loves Cowboys, Too, 1984, New Edition Live, 1984, New Edition Live Again, 1985. Mem. Boy Scouts Am., Hyndman, 1950-61; sec. Hyndman Area Youth Ctr., 1992; chmn. evangelism Hyndman United Meth. Ch., 1980-92. Republican. Home: Box 176 Hyndman PA 15545 Office: Bedford Area Sch Dist John St Bedford PA 15522

TOPPER, LEONARD, consultant, chemical engineer; b. N.Y.C., Jan. 11, 1929; s. Jacob and Shirley (Gottlieb) T. BChemE, CCNY, 1948; MChemE, NYU, 1949; PhD, Cornell U., 1951. Asst. prof. chem. engring. Johns Hopkins U., Balt., 1953-55; chem. engr. ESSO Rsch. and Engring. Co., Linden, N.J., 1955-56; sr. rsch. scientist Columbia U., Heat Transfer Lab., N.Y.C., 1956-57; program mgr. U.S. AEC, Germantown, Md., 1957-73; program mgr., sr. policy analyst NSF, Washington, 1973-76; sr. policy analyst White House Office Sci. and Tech., Washington, 1976-77; asst. dir., Office of Commercialization Energy R&D Adminstrn., Washington, 1976-77; dir., Div. Rsch. Assessment U.S. Dept. Energy, Washington, 1977-79; cons. Washington, 1979—; cons. U.S. Dept. Energy, 1979—; bd. dirs. Washington Print Club. Co-editor: Statistical Theory of Turbulence, 1961; contbr. articles to profl. jours. Republican. Jewish. Home and Office: 2126 Connecticut Ave NW Washington DC 20008-1729

TOPPING, JOHN CARRUTHERS, JR., environmental organization administrator, lawyer; b. Wilkinsburg, Pa., Apr. 18, 1943; s. John Carruthers and Barbara Anne (Murray) T.; m. Linda Marie Thompson, Dec. 1, 1974; children: John Carruthers III, Elizabeth Barrett, Alexandra LaMotte. AB, Dartmouth Coll., 1964; JD, Yale U., 1967. Bar: Mass. 1967, D.C. 1968. Counsel Adv. Coun. for Minority Enterprise, Washington, 1970-73, staff dir., 1972-73; chief counsel office minority bus. enterprise U.S. Dept. Commerce, Washington, 1973-76; ptnr. Topping and Sherer, Washington, 1977-82; cons. U.S. EPA, Washington, 1982-83, staff dir. office air and radiation, 1983-86; ptnr. Topping & Swillinger, Washington, 1986-87; pres. Climate Inst., Washington, 1986—. Co-author: Southern Republicanism and the New South, 1966, Clean Air Handbook, 1987; editor: Preparing for Climate Change, 1988, Coping with Climate Change, 1989. Pres. Ripon Soc., Washington, 1978-80. Capt. USAF, 1968-70. Recipient Pres.'s award Nat. Bar Assn., 1976. Republican. Presbyterian. Home: 220 Maryland Ave NE Washington DC 20002-5704 Office: Climate Inst 324 4th St NE Washington DC 20002

TOPSACALIAN, HARUTIUN, electrical engineer, management consultant; b. Constantsa, Romania, Aug. 16, 1961; came to U.S., 1969; s. Atanaghine A. and Irma (Boyajian) T. BE, SUNY, Stony Brook, 1984; MBA, Baruch Coll., 1990. Project engr. L.I. Lighting Co., Hicksville, N.Y., 1985-87, mgmt. cons., 1988—; cons. Entek Devel. Corp., 1991—. Mem. U.S. com. Internat. Coun. on Monuments and Sites. Mem. IEEE, Assn. Internal Mgmt. Cons., Near East Found., Land and Culture Orgn. (bd. dir.1990—), Zoryan Inst., Stony Brook Alumni Assn. Mem. Armenian Apostolic Ch. Home: 39-65 52d St Apt 10P Flushing NY 11377

TORDJMAN, JEAN DANIEL, ambassador; b. Oran, Algeria, June 9, 1944; came to U.S., 1985; m. Nicole Bourgeat; 1 child, Nicolas. Student, Ecole Nationale d'Adminstrn., France; Polit. Sci. degree, Institut d"Etudes Politiques, Paris; Law degree, U. Paris. With Ministry of Fin., Paris, 1971-75; comml. attache French Embassy, Washington, 1975-76; head of office of indsl. policy Ministry of Fin., Paris, 1976-79; counselor internat. affairs Ministry of Research & Tech., Paris, 1979-82; dep. minister Ministry of Commerce and Tourism, Paris, 1982-85; minister for econ. and comml. affairs French Embassy, Washington, 1985-92, amb.-at-large, spl. rep. for internat. investment, 1992—; prof. internat. econ. Institut d'Etudes Politiques de Paris, 1971-75. Decorated Chevalier de la Legion D'Honneur. Office: French Embassy 4101 Reservoir Rd NW Washington DC 20007-2186

TOREN, MARK, state official, econometrician; b. Warsaw, Poland, Dec. 7, 1950; s. Jacob Toren and Assia (Hanukayeva) Merson; m. Tatiana G. Livshietz. Cert., U. Cologne, Fed. Republic Germany, 1974; AA, AAS, SUNY, Suffern, 1972; BA, SUNY, New Paltz, 1975; MA, SUNY, Albany, 1976; MS, Rensselaer Poly. Inst., 1983; PhD, Rensselaer Poly. Inst., 1992. Sr. statistician Triad Data Scis., Albany, N.Y., 1980-84; sr. economist N.Y. State Dept. Taxation and Fin., Albany, 1984-85; econometrician N.Y. State Dept. Social Svcs., Albany, 1985—. Served with U.S. Army, 1969-71. Mem. Am. Econ. Assn., Am. Statis. Assn., Health Econs. Rsch. Orgn., Micro-Computer Users Group, Internat. Platform Assn., Omicron Delta Epsilon. Office: NY State Dept Social Svcs Office Budget and Mgmt 40 N Pearl St Albany NY 12243-0001

TORINO, THOMAS MICHAEL, human resources administrator; b. Johnson City, N.Y., Apr. 27, 1947; s. Albert Augustus and Mary Kathleen (Comfort) T.; m. Kathleen T. Blanchfield, Mar. 20, 1970; children: Michael D., Susan M., Matthew T. BA, SUNY, Albany, 1970, MPA, 1981. Pers. adminstr. N.Y. State Dept. Transp., Albany, 1973-75; agy. labor rels. rep. N.Y. State Tchrs. Retirement System, Albany, 1975-80; assoc. pers. adminstr. N.Y. State Dept. Agr. and Markets, Albany, 1980-81; asst. dir. pers. N.Y. State Office Mental Retardation, Albany, 1981-85; dir. human resources mgmt. N.Y. State Div. Alcoholism and Alcohol Abuse, Albany, 1985—; cons. State of N.H., Concord, 1984, City of Rochester (N.Y.), 1987; co-chmn. N.Y. State Info. Resource Mgmt. Work Force Issues, 1992—. Bd. mem. Hazard Abatement Program, Ctr. for Women in Govt., Albany, 1988, 89. Mem. Internat. Pers. Mgmt. Assn., Assn. Mental Health Adminstrs., NY. State Pers. Coun. (exec. com. 1983—, chair 1986), N.Y. State Employee Rels. Adv. Coun. Office: NY State Div Alcoholism and Alcohol Abuse 194 Washington Ave Albany NY 12210-2314

TORMEY, TERRENCE O'BRIEN, pharmaceutical sales executive; b. Aliquippa, Pa., Nov. 29, 1954; s. James Michael and Theresa Eileen (Hallisey) T.; m. Donna Lee Campbell, 1974; children: Jason O'Brien, Justin Lee, Shannon Lee. BS in Biology, St. Vincent Coll., 1976; postgrad., Georgetown U., 1978, U. Pa., 1984. Pharm. sales rep. Johnson & Johnson Ortho Pharm., Washington, 1976-82; dist. mgr. Johnson & Johnson McNeil Cons. Prodn., Washington, 1982-84; dir. sales staff mgmt. Johnson & Johnson McNeil Cons. Prodn., Ft. Washington, Pa., 1984-85; asst. v.p. med. sales Am. Home Products, Whitehall Labs., N.Y.C., 1985-88; asst. v.p. hosp. sales Am. Home Products, Whitehall Labs., 1988-90; v.p. sales Profl. Detailing Network, N.Y.C., 1990—. Bd. dirs. Father's Assn. Holy Ghost Prep. Sch., 1989—; mem. Home & Sch. Assn. St. Ignatius, 1985—. Recipient Pa. State Senate award civic award, 1976, Outstanding Young Men Am. award U.S. Jaycees, 1982; named Man of Yr., Beaver County, Pa., 1976. Republican. Roman Catholic. Home: 844 Dekalb Dr Yardley PA 19067-4370 Office: Profl Detailing Network 41 Madison Ave Fl 29 New York NY 10010-2202

TORN, LAWRENCE, manufacturing executive; b. Bklyn., Mar. 31, 1926; s. William Ginsberg and Sadie (Garten) Torn; m. Rhoda Gould, Dec. 25, 1947; children: Marsha, David. BSEE, Pa. State U., 1947; MSEE, Polytech. Inst., 1950. Div. mgr. Airborne Inst. Labs., Deer Park, N.Y., 1947-60; v.p. Harman Kardon, Inc., Plainview, N.Y., 1960-64, Trygon Electronics, Roosevelt, N.Y., 1964-71; pres. 3 Dimensional Circuits, Plainview, 1971-72, Redyref-Sherron, Long Island City, N.Y., 1972—. Staff sgt. U.S. Army, 1945-47. Mem. Tau Beta Pi. Office: Redyref-Sherron 38-61 11th St Long Island City NY 11101

TORNETTA, FRANK JOSEPH, anesthesiologist, educator, consultant; b. Norristown, Pa., Jan. 22, 1916; s. Joseph F. and Maria (Ciaccio) T.; m. Edith Galullo, Nov. 21, 1941 (dec. 1952); m. Norma Zollers, July 16, 1957; children: Frank Jr., David A., Mark A. BS, Ursinus Coll., 1938; MA, U. Pa., 1940; PhD, NYU, 1943; MD, Hahnemann Med. Coll., 1946. Diplomate Am. Bd. Anesthesiology, 1953. Instr. U. Md., College Park, 1940, Hofstra Coll., Hempstead, N.Y., 1941; teaching fellow NYU, N.Y.C., 1941-43; asst. instr. Med. Sch. U. Pa., Phila., 1949-50; dir. dept. anesthesiology. dir. Sch. Anesthesia, founder Montgomery Hosp. Med. Ctr., Norristown, Pa., 1950-91; clin. assoc. prof. Sch. Medicine Temple U., Phila., 1985-91; lectr. Grad. Sch. St. Joseph's U., Phila., 1987-91. Contbr. articles to profl. jours. Chmn. task force Montgomery County Health Dept., Norristown, 1989-91; active Valley Forge chpt. Boy Scouts Am., Norristown, 1982. Lt. USN, 1943-50. Fellow Am. Coll. Chest Physicians, Am. Coll. Anesthesiologists, Coll. Physicians Phila.; mem. Pa. Soc. Anesthesiologists (pres. 1970), Montgomery County Med. Soc. (pres. 1969), Montgomery Hosp. Med. Staff Assn. (pres. 1960), Hahnemann Med. Coll. Alumni Assn. (v.p. 1982), KC. Republican. Roman Catholic. Home: 307 Anthony Dr Plymouth Meeting PA 19462-1109 Office: Montgomery Hosp Med Ctr 1300 Powell St Norristown PA 19401-3324

TORNEY-PURTA, JUDITH VOLLMAR, developmental psychologist; b. Oakland, Calif., Oct. 2, 1937; d. Ralph C. and Anne (Flournoy) Vollmar; m. E. Keith Torney, Sept. 10, 1960 (div. 1978); children: Elizabeth A., Katherine D.; m. Paul P. Purta, Oct. 18, 1980. AB in Psychology, Stanford U., 1959; postgrad., Harvard U., 1959-60; MA in Human Devel., U. Chgo., 1962, PhD in Human Devel., 1965. Asst. prof. psychology Ill. Inst. Tech., Chgo., 1967-69; asst. prof. edn. U. Ill., Chgo., 1969-70, assoc. prof. psychology and edn., 1970-77, prof., vice chmn. psychology dept., 1977-81; prof. human devel., asst. chmn. dept. U. Md., College Park, 1981—, affiliate prof. psychology dept., 1981—; vis. prof. Stanford (Calif.) U. Sch. Edn., 1988, 91; evaluator Internat. Communication Negotiations Simulation, College Park, 1983—; mem. bd. on internat. studies in edn. NRC, NAS, Washington, 1988—; mem. task force on youth devel. Carnegie Corp., N.Y.C., 1990—. Co-author: Development of Political Attitudes, 1967 (award NEA 1967), Civic Education in Ten Countries, 1975, Growth of Political Understanding, 1992; contbr. chpts. to books, articles to profl. jours. Mem. U.S. Nat. Commn. for UNESCO, Washington, 1976-82, 83-85; cons. on civil edn. Govt. of Can., Ottawa, 1990. Recipient career rsch. award Nat. Coun. for Social Studies, 1977, Global Apple award Am. Forum for Edn., 1988. Fellow APA, Am. Psychol. Soc.; mem. Am. Ednl. Rsch. assn. (chmn. book award com. 1991-92), Soc. for Rsch. in Child Devel. (chmn. internat. com. 1991-93), Comparative and Internat. Edn. Soc. (editorial bd. 1990-92), Internat. Assn. Evaluation Ednl. Achievement (civic edn. com. 1971-80, sci. and math. com. 1991—), Internat. Soc. for Polit. Psychology, Phi Beta Kappa, Sigma Xi. Office: U Md Dept Human Devel College Park MD 20742-1131

TOROSIAN, GEORGE, pharmaceutical chemist; b. Racine, Wis., Jan. 1, 1936; s. Azar and Manam (Zakian) T.; (div. June 1991); children: Gregory A., Michael J. BS, U. Wis., 1962, MS, 1964, PhD, 1966. Registered pharm. chemist, Wis., Fla. Instr. Coll. of Pharmacy U. Wis., Madison, 1966; sr. scientist Menly & James Div. Smith Kline Beecham, Phila., 1966-69; assoc. prof. Coll. of Pharmacy U. Fla., Gainesville, 1969-81; sr. rsch. supr. E.I. DuPont, Wilmington, Del., 1981-90; mgr. product and process tech. support DuPont/Merck Pharm. Co., Garden City, N.Y., 1991—; asst. prin. investigator Army Contract Devel., Gainesville, 1971-75; co-investigator Nat. Inst. for Child Health and Human Devel. Grants, Gainesville, 1980-82. Contbr. articles to profl. jours. With USNR, 1955-57. Named Tchr. of the Yr., U. Fla., 1978. Mem. Am. Pharm. Assn., Assn. Am. Pharm. Scientists, Sigma Xi, Rho Chi. Republican. Office: DuPont Merck Pharm Co 1000 Stewart Ave Garden City NY 11530-4888

TORPY, KATHLEEN ANN, educational association administrator; b. Wellsboro, Pa., July 17, 1950; d. Quentin Ward and Sophia Lucille (Tacka) T. AB, Wilson Coll., 1972; MBA, Shippensburg U., 1990. Mgr. The Naturalist, Exton/Plymouth Meeting, Pa., 1973; asst. mgr. Doubleday Bookstore, Bala Cynwyd, Pa., 1974-75; acctg. supt. and contracts adminstr. Ducon Fluid Transport Inc., King of Prussia, Pa., 1975-79; dir. budget and planning Wilson Coll., Chambersburg, Pa., 1979-88; assn. sec., bus. mgr. Middle States Assn. Colls. and Schs., Phila., 1988—; cons. Coll. Misericordia Alumnae Assn., Dallas, Pa., 1984, Cedar Crest Coll. Alumae Assn., Allentown, Pa., 1981. Mem. Nat. Assn. Coll. and Univ. Bus. Officers, Am. Soc. Assn. Execs., Nat. Women's Studies Assn., Greater Chambersburg C. of C. (sec. bd. dirs. 1984-85), NOW. Democrat. Home: Creek Dr Wayne PA 19087-5216

TORRANCE, KENNETH ERIC, engineering educator, researcher; b. Mpls., Aug. 23, 1940; s. Eric Maurice and Ellen Aili (Mattila) T.; m. Marcia Joy Greenfield, July 28, 1962; children: Charles Eric, Deborah Joy, Catherine Ellen. BS, U. Minn., 1961, MSME, 1964, PhD, 1966. Rsch. assoc. Nat. Bur. Standards, Gaithersburg, Md., 1966-68; asst. prof. engring. Cornell U., Ithaca, N.Y., 1968-74, assoc. prof., 1974-81, prof., 1981—, assoc. dean coll. engring., 1983-86; rsch. assoc. Nat. Ctr. for Atmospheric Rsch., Boulder, Colo., 1974-75. Author, contbr. articles to profl. jours. NSF grantee 1968—. Fellow AAAS, AIAA, ASME (best paper award 1982), Am. Phys. Soc., Combustion Inst. Home: 37 Deerhaven Dr Ithaca NY 14850-2910 Office: Cornell U Mech and Aerospace Engring Upson Hall Ithaca NY 14853

TORRES, MANUEL, aerospace engineer; b. Bklyn., Feb. 13, 1963; s. Manuel and Irma (Delgado) T.; m. Dorothy Eleanor Tallman, Apr. 25, 1987. BS in Aerospace Engring., Poly. Inst. N.Y., Bklyn., 1985; MS in Aerospace Engring., Boston U., 1990; postgrad., Pa. State U., 1991—. Wind tunnel tech. Grumman Aerospace Corp., Bethpage, N.Y., 1984-85; aerodynamic design engr. Textron Def. Sys., Wilmington, Mass., 1985-90, GE RESD, Phila., 1990—. Author, co-author various tech. reports. Mem. AIAA, ASME, Soc. Naval Architects & Marine Engrs., Soaring Soc. Am.

TORRES, PEDRO LUIS, educator; b. Guayanilla, P.R., Jan. 14, 1947; came to U.S., 1971; s. Pedro and Margarita (Santiago) T.; children: Pedro F., Ernesto J. BA, U. P.R., 1970; MA, NYU, 1983, postgrad., 1983—. Civil svc. instr. Commonwealth of P.R., N.Y.C., 1974-76, bilingual tchr. trainer, 1975-76, asst. dir., 1975-76, dir. bilingual edn., 1978; vocat. tng. coord. CUNY BMCC, N.Y.C., 1978-81; bilingual tchr. N.Y.C. Bd. Edn. CSD #9, 1981-85, 5th grade tchr., 1985-90; bilingual tchr. N.Y.C. Bd. Edn. CSD #4 P.S. 108, 1990—; Composer and song writer. Mem., organizer Expresion Creativa, N.Y.C., 1975—. Mem. N.Y. State Bilingual Edn., N.Y. State E.S.L. Tchrs. Assn. Office: NYC Bd Edn CSD #4 PS 108 1615 Madison Ave New York NY 10029-3513

TORRESE, DANTE MICHAEL, prosthodontist, educator; b. Yonkers, N.Y., Feb. 12, 1949; s. Dante Angelo and Matilda (Dal Lago) T.; m. Camille Patricia DiPaola, Aug. 7, 1982. BS in Biology, Manhattan Coll., 1971; DDS, Columbia U., 1975; prosthodontic cert. NYU, 1983. Resident in dentistry Presbyn. Hosp., N.Y.C., 1975-76; clin. instr. dentistry Columbia U., N.Y.C., 1976-78, asst. clin. prof. dentistry, 1978—; pvt. practice dentistry, Yonkers, N.Y., 1976—; attending dentist Presbyn. Hosp., N.Y.C., 1976-86; lectr. in field. Bd. dirs. United Way of Yonkers, 1981—. Recipient Am. Acad. Oral Pathology Grad. award, 1975; Densply Corp. award for removable prosthodontics, 1975; Psi Omega Scholastic Achievement award, 1975. Fellow Am. Coll. of Dentists, Royal Soc. Health; mem. NRA (life), Am. Coll. Prosthodontists, Yonkers Dental Soc., 9th Dist. State Dental Soc., Sherlock Holmes Wireless Soc., Yonkers Amateur Radio Club, Westchester Astronomy Club, Exch. Club (sec. 1979—), Three Garridebs of Westchester County Club, Priory Scholars of N.Y.C. Club, Montague Street Lodgers of Bklyn. Club, Omicron Kappa Upsilon. Office: 984 N Broadway Ste 503 Yonkers NY 10701-1308

TORRICELLI, ROBERT G., congressman; b. Paterson, N.J., Aug. 26, 1951; m. Susan King Holloway, 1980. B.A., Rutgers U., 1974, J.D., 1977; M.P.A., Harvard U., 1980. Bar: N.J. 1978. Dep. legis. counsel Office Gov. N.J., 1975-77; counsel to Vice Pres. Mondale, Washington, 1978-81; sole practice law Washington, 1981-82; mem. 98th-102nd Congresses from 9th Dist. N.J., 1983—. Bd. govs. Rutgers U., 1977-83. Mem. ABA, N.J. Bar Assn. Democrat. Office: US Ho of Reps 317 Cannon House Office Bldg Washington DC 20515

TORRINGTON, ARTHUR EDWARD, insurance and reinsurance executive; b. Oceanside, N.Y., May 12, 1940; s. Arthur Edward Torrington and Gertrude W. (Henning) Peters; m. Lois Diane Easty, Aug. 26, 1961; children: Arthur E. Jr., Laura E. BA summa cum laude, Hofstra U., 1974; M in Profl. Studies, L.I. U., 1976; cert. in casualty law, Am. Ednl. Inst., Basking Ridge, N.J, 1976; grad., Coll. Ins., N.Y.C., 1976. Cert. casualty claim law

assoc. Spl. agt. U.S. Army Intelligence, N.Y.C., 1963-66; sr. rep. Ins. Co. N.Am., Garden City, N.Y., 1966-75; exec. dir. Exec. Security & Intelligence Svcs., Smithtown, N.Y., 1971—; asst. v.p. Treaty Capacity, Inc., Huntington, N.Y., 1975-76; exec. v.p. Barrett Treaty Corp., Huntington, 1976-85; pres., chief exec. officer Oakside Mgmt. Corp., Commack, N.Y., 1985—; Bd. dirs. Concord (Calif.) Gen. Corp., Classic Fire and Marine Insur. Co., Des Moines. Editorial advisor Civil and Criminal Investigative Handbook, 1981. Bd. dirs. Luth. Ctr. for the Aging, Smithtown, N.Y., 1983—, Wartburg Luth. Svcs. of N.Y., Bklyn., 1987—. With U.S. Army, 1963-66. Recipient Outstanding Svc. award Hofstra U., Hempstead, N.Y., 1974. Mem. Am. Mgmt. Assn., Newcomen Soc. of Am., Assn. of Former Intelligence Officers, Nat. Counter-Intelligence Corps. Assn., Pres.'s Assn., Am. Legion, Phi Beta Kappa, Phi Alpha Theta. Office: Oakside Mgmt Corp 366 Vets Meml Hwy Commack NY 11725

TORRUELLA, JUAN R., federal judge; b. 1933. BS in Bus. and Fin., U. Pa., 1954; LLB, Boston U., 1957; LLM, U. Va., 1984; MPA, U. P.R., 1984. Judge U.S. Dist. Ct. P.R., San Juan, 1974-85, U.S. Ct. Appeals (1st cir.), San Juan, 1985—; mem. jud. conf. com. on the Adminstrn. of the Fed. Magistrate System. Mem. ABA, Fed. Bar Assn., Maritime Law Assn., Assn. Labor Relations Practitioners P.R. and V.I., D.C. Bar Assn., P.R. Bar Assn. Office: US Ct Appeals PO Box 3671 Bayamon PR 00958-0680 also: US Ct Appeals (1st cir) Boston MA 02109*

TORTO, RAYMOND GERALD, economist; b. Lynn, Mass., Dec. 16, 1941; s. Edward Dante and Lucy (Petrucci) T.; m. Elina Torto; children: Stephanie, Pamela. AB, Boston Coll., 1963, MA, 1967, PhD, 1969. Prof. econs. U. Mass., Boston, 1970—; spl. asst. to mayor for tax policy City of Boston, 1976-80, commr. assessing, 1980-82; pres. Torto Wheaton and Assocs., Boston, 1982-86; prin. CB Comml./Torto Wheaton Rsch., Boston, 1987—; sr. fellow, interim dir. McCormack Inst. U. Mass., Boston, 1984—; bd. dirs. Boston Mcpl. Rsch. Bur., Assoc. Ind. of Mass. Author: The Rich Get Richer and the Rest Pay Taxes, 1974, Money and Financial Institutions, 1981, Property Tax Reevaluation, 1983, Money and Banking, 1989. Chmn. fiscal issues study group Commonwealth of Mass., 1988—. Mem. Am. Soc. Real Estate Councilors, Am. Econ. Soc., Am. Real Estate Soc., Boston C. of C. (chmn. legis. com. 1986—), Corinthian Yacht Club. Home: 38 Foster St Marblehead MA 01945-3602 Office: CB Comml/Torto Wheaton Rsch 200 High St Boston MA 02110

TORTORELLA, ROBERT ANTHONY, political science and history educator; b. Bklyn., Oct. 24, 1939; s. Dominick Peter and Rose Ann (Russo) T. BA, L.I. U., 1964; MA, Fairleigh Dickinson U., 1967, New Sch. for Social Rsch., 1979. Instr. Fairleigh Dickinson U., Teaneck, N.J., 1973—, Montclair State Coll., Upper Montclair, N.J., 1986—. Mem. Leonia (N.J.) City Coun., 1981; police commr. City of Leonia, 1982; mem. Leonia Planning Commn., 1970.

TORTORELLI, ANN EICHORN, college educator, librarian and dean; b. Wilkes Barre, Pa.; d. Leo George and Mary Helen (Brennan) Eichorn; m. William Charles Tortorelli, Jan. 27, 1962; children: Marilee Tortorelli-Miller, Suzanne Tortorelli-Boyle. BS in Edn., Duquesne U., Pitts., 1962, MEd in Library Sci., 1969; advanced cert., U. Pitts., 1971, PhD, 1986. Elem. Edn. Tchr. 2nd grade Pitts. Pub. Schs., Pitts., 1962-63; tchr. Prince Georges Co., Balt., 1964-65; tchr. 6th grade Fort Cherry Schs., Washington County, Pa., 1965-66; libr., tchr. Pitts. Pub. Schs., Pitts., 1966-67; asst. libr. Community Coll. Allegheny County, Pitts., 1967-70; asst. dean, learning resources Community Coll. Alleghany County, Pitts., 1970-82, dean learning resources, 1977-83, dean bus. and math, 1983-90, dean acad. svcs., 1990—; bd. dirs., pres. Pitts. Regional Libr. Ctr., Pitts.; cons. Genesee Community Coll., 1981; evaluator Middle States Assn. Coll., 1975—. Author: Individualized Instruction, 1979, Computer Literacy in Pennsylvania Community Colleges, 1987; co-author: Status Media Centers in Higher Education, 1984. Adv. coun. Bethel Park High Sch., Pa., 1979-82; chair Reading Acad. Conf., 1979; mem. Allegheny County Commn. on the Future of Librs., 1991—; moderator, speaker Pa. Assn. Devel. Educators, 1982; presider Probe Conf., 1988. Recipient Merit award Community Coll., 1985. Mem. Pa. Libr. Assn., Pitts. Regional Libr. Ctr., Am. Assn. Dr. Coll., Nat. Coun. Instrnl. Adminstrs., Assn. Ednl. Comminications and tech. Office: Community Coll Allegheny Co County 1750 Clairton Rd West Mifflin PA 15122-3097

TORTORELLO, NICHOLAS JOHN, public opinion-market research company executive; b. Maspeth, N.Y., Dec. 1, 1948; s. John Anthony and Verla Jean (Odel) T.; m. Joan Elizabeth King, Jan. 13, 1973; children: Kerry Ann, Jennifer Joan. BA in Polit. Sci. with highest honors, Williams Coll., 1971; M Religious Studies, St. Joseph's Sem., Yonkers, N.Y., 1988. Vice pres. Louis Harris & Assocs., N.Y.C., 1971-73, sr. v.p., 1973-79; exec. v.p. DMT Inc., N.Y.C., 1979-83; pres. Tortorello Corp., Pearl River, N.Y., 1983-85; pres. Tortorello group Market Facts Inc.-N.Y., N.Y.C., 1985-86; v.p. Total Rsch. Corp., Princeton, N.J., 1986-88; chmn. Rsch. and Forecasts Inc., N.Y.C., 1989—. Editor, author Tortorello Trendline, 1983-85, Rsch. and Forecasts Trendline, 1989. Mem. Hosp. Chaplaincy Bd., 1991—; trustee Riverdale (N.Y.) Country Sch., 1982-90, v.p., 1986-89; trustee Marymount Manhattan Coll., N.Y.C., 1986-88; lectr., tchr. religion St. Anthony's Ch., Nanuet, N.Y., 1984-86. Recipient Disting. Alumnus of Yr. award Riverdale Country Sch., 1984. Mem. Am. Dirs. Inst. (trustee 1984-87), Williams Club. Democrat. Office: Rsch & Forecasts Inc 301 E 57th St New York NY 10022

TORTORICI, FRANK CHARLES, public relations manager; b. Bklyn., May 23, 1963; s. Charles and Marie (Puglisi) T.; m. Joy Ann Weber, Nov. 11, 1990. BA in Journalism, NYU, 1985. Intern Nichol & Co., N.Y.C., 1985; account exec. Lobsenz-Stevens Inc., N.Y.C., 1985-88; sr. account exec. Robert Marston Corp. Communications, N.Y.C., 1988-89; sr. account supr. Edelman Worldwide, N.Y.C., 1989-91; mgr. media rels. The Conf. Bd. Inc., N.Y.C., 1991—. Mem. Internat. Assn. Bus. Communicators, Phi Beta Kappa, Kappa Tau Alpha. Office: The Conf Bd Inc 845 3rd Ave New York NY 10022-6601

TOSCANO, FILIPPO-MARIA, foreign languages educator; b. Italy, Oct. 27, 1942; came to U.S., 1966.; Children: Nino, Franco. BA in Fgn. Lang., N.Mex. State U., 1969; MA in Spanish, U. Del., 1971; PhD in Romance Langs., Cath. U. of Am., 1988. Assoc. prof. fgn. lang. Del. State Coll., Dover, chmn. fgn. lang. dept., 1987-88, dir. ctr. for internat. advancement and rsch., 1990—; mem. gov.'s internat. trade coun., Del., 1989-90; vice-chmn. woman's studies, Del. State Coll., 1988-89, chmn. faculty affairs com. 1980, senator faculty senate, 1989, dir. ednl. studies abroad program. Translator: Una Biografia, 1981, I Tre Cavalieri Dalla Spagna, 1988; translator rsch. manuscripts, books and articles; contbr. articles to profl. jours. V.p. The Inst. for Global Perspective, 1983—. Named Hon. Citizen City of Las Cruces, 1969. Mem. N.E. MLA (chmn. Italian sect. 1991, sec. 1990). Home: RD 2 Box 342D-1 Dover DE 19901 Office: Del State Coll 1200 N duPont Hwy Dover DE 19901

TOTENBERG, NINA, journalist; b. N.Y.C., Jan. 14, 1944; d. Roman and Melanie (Shroder) T.; m. Floyd Haskell, Feb. 3, 1979. Student, Boston U. Reporter Boston Record Am., 1965, Peabody Times, 1967, Nat. Observer, 1968-71, Newtimes, 1973, Nat. Pub. Radio, Washington, 1974—. žontbr. articles to N.Y. Times Mag., Harvard Law Rev., Christian Sci. Monitor, N.Y. Mag., Parade. Office: Nat Pub Radio 2025 M St NW Washington DC 20036

TOTH, IMRE GERHARD, internist; b. Breslau, Germany, June 8, 1937; came to U.S., 1956; s. Laszlo Zoltan and Johanne Margarete (Boese) T.; m. Eleanor Mae Hodgins, May 15, 1965; children: Kimberly Michelle Genest, Randall Kenneth, Natalie Darlene. BA in Math., Harvard Coll., 1960; MD, NYU, 1964. Diplomate Am. Bd. Internal Medicine in internal medicine, gastroenterology, geriatrics. Intern Montefiore Hosp., Bronx; resident in medicine Boston VA Hosp., 1967-69, resident in gastroenterology, 1969-70, chief resident in hepatology, 1970-71; pvt. practice Hudson, Mass., 1971—; asst. med. dir., cons. Tufts Associated Health Plan, Waltham, Mass., 1986—; pres., founder Assabet Valley Ind. Practice Assn., Marlborough, Mass., 1983—; co-founder, chmn. New Health Enterprises, Inc., Marlborough, 1984—; pres. med. staff Marlborough Hosp., 1983-84. Pres. First Congl. Ch., Harvard, Mass., 1990—; coach Nashoba Regional High Sch. Chess Club, Bolton, Mass., 1980—. Master, postal chess U.S. Chess Fedn., 1989. Mem. Am. Gastroent. Assn., Am. Coll. Physician Execs., New Eng. Endoscopy Soc., Mass. Med. Soc. Unitarian-Universalist. Home: 37 Flanagan Rd Bolton MA 01740 Office: 101 Coolidge St Hudson MA 01749

TOTTA, PAUL ANTHONY, metallurgist; b. Middletown, N.Y., May 17, 1930; s. Anthony Vincent and Mary Anna (Vuolo) T.; m. Mary Ann Cashman, June 12, 1954; children: Mark P., Michael J. B in Metall. Engring., Rensselaer Poly. Inst., 1952. Metallurgist GM Rsch., Warren, Mich., 1952-53, GE, Ft. Wayne, Ind., 1954-58, Handy & Harman, Fairfield, Conn., 1958-59, IBM, Poughkeepsie, N.Y., 1959—; project mgr., thin film and interconnection specialist IBM, East Fishkill, N.Y., 1965—. Contbr. chpt. to book Microelectronics Packaging Handbook, 1989; patentee in field. Capt. USAF, 1953-58. Fellow IBM, 1987—. Fellow Am. Soc. Materials, Am. Vacuum Soc., Internat. Soc. Hybird Microelectronics (tech. achievement award 1984), Sigma Xi, Tau Beta Pi, Phi Lambda Upsilon. Home: 29 Sandi Dr Poughkeepsie NY 12603-6005 Office: IBM East Fishkill Facility MS 47B Hopewell Junction NY 12533

TOTTEY, ROBERT LESLIE, advertising and entertainment executive; b. Ithaca, N.Y., Dec. 16, 1945; s. Alfred George Sr. and Edna Lorraine (Willsey) T.; m. Julie Cleary, June 1, 1991. BA in History, Ithaca Coll., 1967. Tchr. Ithaca City Sch. Dist., 1969-72; owner Dugout-Sports Bar, Ithaca, 1973-78, Ithaca Stars Inc. Semi-Pro Hockey Team, Ithaca, 1974-79; sales rep. GM, Ithaca, 1980-85; pres. Rodentvelt Raceway, Inc., Ithaca, 1985—. Inventor Mighty Molars bar bellies, Rodentvelt Raceway. Board dirs. Ithaca Youth Bur., 1978-80. Mem. Am. Legion, Ithaca C. of C. Home and Office: 1402 W Danby Rd Newfield NY 14867-9214

TOUB, ALLAN HOWARD, podiatrist, composer; b. Paterson, N.J., Nov. 16, 1929; s. Abram Tavia and Margie (Lipkowitz) T.; m. Gwen H. Simon, Dec. 20, 1958; 1 son, David Blair. Student N.J. State Tchrs. Coll., 1947-49, Juilliard Sch. Music, 1975-80; DPM cum laude, Ill. Coll. Podiatric Medicine, 1953. Intern, Ill. Coll. Podiatric Medicine, 1954; pvt. practice podiatric medicine and surgery, Madison, N.J., 1956—; asst. prof. anatomy and clin. pathology Ill. Coll. Podiatric Medicine, 1952-54, chief podopediatric clinic, 1953-54; instr. natural sci. Chgo. YMCA, 1950-54; instr. Judaic studies Temple Sinai Religious Sch., Summit, N.J., 1990—; piano concerts in N.Y., N.J., Chgo.; composer 11 piano works and chamber music including: Piano Sonata, 1948; Toccata #1, 1948; The Kittatiny Mountains at Blairstown, 1969-70; Interplay for flute and piano, 1978; Toccata No. 2 for piano, 1978; Sketches for piano quartet, 1979; Sonata for Organ, 1979-80. Scoutmaster Boy Scouts Am., San Antonio, Irvington, N.J., Elizabeth, N.J., 1955-76, Hillside, N.J., 1976-85, Somerville, N.J., 1985-89; mem. Jewish relations com. and Cath. com. on scouting Watchung council, unit commr., 1961-62, recipient Dist. award of Merit, Arrowhead Tng. Honor, Scouters' Key, Order of Arrow, Wood Badge Tng. award, Silver Beaver award for disting. service to youth, 1984; chmn. United Jewish Appeal, Madison, 1956-57. Served with M.S.C., AUS, 1954-56. Recipient Podopediatrics award Ill. Coll. Podiatric Medicine, 1953; Shofar award for outstanding service to Jewish scouts and promoting understanding between Jewish and non-Jewish scouts, 1982; awards for scouting activities, Disting. Physician award Disting. Physicians Am., 1991. Diplomate Am. Bd. Podiatric Orthopedics. Fellow Am. Coll. Foot Orthopedists (sec.-treas. Eastern div. 1967-73), Royal Soc. Health; mem. N.J. Podiatric Med. Soc., Am. Podiatric Med. Assn., Mil. Assn. Podiatrists, Am. Podiatry Council, Zeta Delta Zeta. Jewish. Contbr. articles to scouting and profl. jours. Office: Madison Med Ctr 28 Walnut St Madison NJ 07940-1631

TOUBORG, MARGARET EARLEY BOWERS, non-profit executive; b. Rome, N.Y., Aug. 12, 1941; d. George Thomas and Margaret Earley (Brown) Bowers; m. Jens Touborg, Sept. 9, 1961 (div. 1985); children: Margaret Earley, Anne Monroe, Sarah Friis, Peter Nicolai. AB magna cum laude, Radcliffe Coll., 1965; MEd, Harvard U., 1984. Asst. to pres. Radcliffe Coll., Cambridge, Mass., 1984-86, exec. asst. to pres., 1986-87, dir. corp. and found. relations, 1988-89; pres. U. Cape Town Fund, Inc., N.Y.C., 1989—; sr. project dir. Open Soc. Scholars Fund, N.Y.C., 1989—. Trustee Bemis Lectr. Series, Lincoln, Mass., 1982-85; assoc. chmn. edn. div. United Way Mass., 1986; mem. S. African adv. com. New Eng. Bd. Higher Edn., 1987—; mem. Coun. on Competitiveness, Washington, 1987-89. Mem. Harvard Club N.Y.C., Phi Beta Kappa (chmn. com. hon. membership 1976—, mem. adv. bd. Schlesinger Library on History of Women in Am. 1989—). Episcopalian. Office: 441 Lexington Ave New York NY 10017 also: U Capetown Fund Inc 441 Lexington Ave New York NY 10017

TOUGER, JEROLD STEVEN, physics educator; b. Bklyn., Aug. 6, 1945; s. Morris P. and Freda (Sadowsky) T.; m. Hallie Elizabeth Ephron, May 11, 1969; children: Molly, Naomi. BA, Cornell U., 1966; PhD in Physics, CUNY, 1974. Asst. prof., assoc. prof., prof. physics Curry Coll., Milton, Mass., 1974—. Recipient Sears Roebuck Found. Teaching Excellence award Curry Coll., Milton, 1990. Mem. Am. Assn. Physics Tchrs. (v.p., pres.-elect, pres. New Eng. sect. 1984-87, chair Com. on Rsch. in Physics Edn. 1990-92). Office: Curry Coll Sci Div Milton MA 02186

TOURIN, RICHARD H(AROLD), physicist; b. N.Y.C., Dec. 4, 1922; s. Joseph Meyer and Rebecca (Greenberger) T.; m. Barbara Cotins, Aug. 29, 1948; children: Deirdre Beth, Emily Jean. BS in Physics, CUNY, 1947; MS in Physics, NYU, 1952. Div. mgr. Warner & Swasey Co., N.Y.C., 1948-71; mktg. dir. Klinger Sci. Corp., N.Y.C., 1972; program dir. N.Y. State Energy Rsch. & Devel. Authority, N.Y.C., 1973-77; mktg. mgr. Stone & Webster Engring., N.Y.C., 1978-80; devel. dir. Syska & Hennessy Engrs., N.Y.C., 1981-83; project mgr. Office of the Mayor City of N.Y., 1984-87; cons. Tourin Assocs., N.Y.C., 1988—; U.S. del. Internat. Flame Rsch. Found., IJmuiden, Holland, 1966-67. Author: Spectroscopic Gas Temperature Measurement, 1966, (with others) Advances in Energy Technology, 1978; contbr. over 50 articles to profl. jours. Sgt. U.S. Army, 1943-46, PTO. Fellow Optical Soc. Am.; mem. N.Y. Acad. Scis. (chmn. engring. sect. 1987-88, vice chair 1985-86, 89-91), Combustion Inst., Adirondack Mountain Club (gov. 1978-80, 86-88). Democrat. Home and Office: 195-10A 67th Ave Flushing NY 11365-3941

TOWE, KENNETH MCCARN, research geologist; b. Jacksonville, Fla., Jan. 31, 1935; s. Kenneth C. and Elizabeth (McCarn) T.; m. Margaret C. Jones, June 14, 1975; children: Brian M. Sebrell, Mary Ashton Sebrell. AB, Duke U., 1956; MSc, Brown U., 1958; PhD, U. Ill., 1961. Postdoctoral fellow Calif. Inst. Tech., Pasadena, 1962-64; sr. rsch. geologist dept. paleobiology Smithsonian Instn., Washington, 1964—; vis. prof. Utübingen (Fed. Republic Germany), 1973; dir. Precambrian paleobiology rsch. group UCLA, 1987-88. Editor in chief Jour. Foraminiferal Rsch., 1981-85, Clays and Clay Minerals, 1990-91; contbr. numerous articles to profl. jours. Bd. govs. St. Stephens and St. Agnes Sch., Alexandria, 1990—. Recipient Dirs.'s award Mus. Nat. History, Washington, 1986; Ford Found. Postdoctoral fellow Calif. Inst. Tech., Pasadena, 1963. Fellow AAAS (panel mem. Westinghouse Sci. Journalism award 1977-86), Geol. Soc. Am., Mineral. Soc. Am. (assoc. editor Am. Mineralogist 1976-81, fin. com. 1983-86, chair 1986); mem. Geol. Soc. Washington (pres. 1984, Best Paper award 1973), Paleontol. Soc. Washington (pres. 1968), Clay Minerals Soc. (treas. 1982—), Cushman Found. (pres. 1990). Home: 3720 Seminary Rd Alexandria VA 22304-5203 Office: Smithsonian Instn 10th Constitution Ave NE Washington DC 20560-0001

TOWELL, TIMOTHY LATHROP, foreign service officer; b. Cleve., Jan. 31, 1934; s. Bernard A. and Eleanor (Assmus) T.; m. Dane Anderson Nichols, Nov. 1, 1969; children: Timothy Nichols, Dane Billings. BA, Yale U., 1957; MA, Case-Western Res. U., 1962. Commd. fgn. svc. officer Dept. State; vice consul U.S. Consulate, Valencia, Spain, 1963-65; spl. asst. to ambassador Am. embassy, Madrid, 1965-66; U.S. Consul, Am. embassy, Asuncion, Paraguay, 1966-67; 1st sec. Am. Embassy, La Paz, Bolivia, 1967-68; Bolivian desk officer Dept. State, Washington, 1968-70, Spanish desk officer, 1970-72; U.S. consul U.S. Consulate, Porto Alegre, Brazil, 1972-75; 1st sec. Am. Embassy, Brussels, Belgium, 1975-79; dep. chief of mission, U.S. Mission, Havana, Cuba, 1979-80; congl. liaison officer Europe, Dept. State, Washington, 1980-83; dep. chief of protocol of U.S., Washington, 1983-88; ambassador to Paraguay, 1988-91; regional dir. Africa The Peace Corps, Washington, 1991—. Mem. Met. Club (Washington), Tavern Club (Cleve.). Office: The Peace Corps Washington DC 20526

TOWER, HORACE LINWOOD, III, consumer products company executive; b. New Haven, July 16, 1932; s. Horace Linwood, Jr. and Madeline Elizabeth (Davin) T.; m. Elizabeth Wright, Dec. 29, 1956; children: Cynthia, William, John. BA, Cornell U., 1955, MBA, 1960; DHL (hon.), Westfield (Mass.) State Coll., 1984. With Procter & Gamble Corp., Cin., 1960-62; mgmt. cons. Booz, Allen & Hamilton, N.Y.C., 1962-63; with Gen. Foods Corp., White Plains, N.Y., 1963-67, pres. Maxwell home divsn., 1963-78, pres., CEO, 1978-90; chmn. Stanhome Inc., Westfield, Mass., 1990—; bd. dirs. Stanhome Inc., Tambrands, Inc., Stanley Park. Mem. bd. visitors USAF Air U. Capt. USAF, 1956-59. Mem. Air Force Assn., Sabre Pilots Assn., Colony Club (Springfield, Mass.), Suffield (Conn.) Country Club, Suffield Paddle Club, Fox Hollow Club (Suffield), Thimble Island Sailing and Lit. Soc., Stoney Creek Boating Club, Pi Kappa Phi, Sigma Gamma Epsilon. Office: Stanhome Inc 333 Western Ave Westfield MA 01085-2560

TOWER, RONI BETH, psychologist; b. Akron, Ohio, Dec. 11, 1943; d. Arnold Edward Weinstein and Elva Hermoine (Gross) MacRae; m. Stuart James Lowenthal, June 2, 1983 (dec. 1984); m. M. Barry Schlosser, Jan. 1, 1989; children: Jennifer, Daniel. BA, Barnard Coll., N.Y.C., 1964; MS, Yale U., 1977, M in Philosphy, 1979, PhD, 1980. Lic. in clinical psychology, Conn., Diplomate Clinical Psychology Am. Bd. Professional Psychology. Psychologist Silver Hill Found., New Canaan, Conn., 1979-81; pvt. practice Westport, Conn., 1981—; co-founder, dir. rsch. Clarity Cons. Corp., Westport, 1990—; lectr. in psychology Yale U., New Haven, 1981-89, Am. Bd. Profl. Psychology seminar, Washington, 1990; cons. in field. Cons. editor Jour. of Imagination Cognition and Personality, 1983—; contbr. numerous articles to profl. jours. Recipient Traineeship award U.S. Pub. Health, 1979-80. Mem. Am. Assn. for Study of Mental Imagery (pres. 1988-89, conf. organizer New Haven 1988), Am. Psychol. Assn., Conn. Psychol. Assn., LWV (Westport chpt.), Sigma Xi. Office: Clarity Cons Corp 6 Signal Ln Westport CT 06880-6237

TOWEY, ANNE PATRICIA, nurse; b. Nassau County, N.Y., Apr. 10, 1945; d. Patrick Denis and Anne Marie (Quinn) T. RN, Mary Immaculate, Jamaica, N.Y., 1967; BSN, Molloy Coll., 1981; MSN, Adelphi U., 1987. RN, N.Y. Staff nurse Mercy Hosp., Rockville Centre, N.Y., 1967-71, asst. head nurse, 1971-75, head nurse, 1975-86, nursing supr., 1986-91; nurse mgr. Mercy Hosp., Rockville Centre, 1991—; accelerated care unit com. Mercy Hosp., pharmacy nursing com., com. and program for pilot project of primary care unit, selections com., skin care com., nursing audit com. Active Am. Heart Assn. (div. on stroke), Am. Cancer Soc.; vol. Internat. Genes for Disabled. Mem. Sigma Theta Tau. Democrat. Roman Catholic.

TOWIICZ, MICKY See **MIKUTOWICZ, MICHAEL ANTHONY**

TOWLE, LAIRD CHARLES, book publisher; b. Exeter, N.H., Sept. 13, 1933; s. Gerald Charles and Wilma Lois (Buzzell) T.; m. Marlene Ann Towne, Apr. 14, 1956; children: Karen Lee, Joel Andrew, Glenn Corbett, Leslie Kim. BS in Physics, U. N.H., 1955, MS in Physics, 1958; PhD, U. Va., 1962. Rsch. physicist AVCO Corp., Wilmington, Mass., 1962-63, Allis Chalmers Corp., West Allis, Wis., 1963-67; section head Naval Rsch. Lab., Washington, 1967-77, project mgr., 1977-81; pres., chief exec. officer Heritage Books, Inc., Bowie, Md., 1981—. Author: N.H. Genealogical Research Guide, 1973, The Descendants of William Brown and Isabella Kennedy, 1992; editor: Genealogical Periodical Annual Index, 1974—; contbr. articles to profl. jours. Pres. NRL Fed. Credit Union, Washington, 1970-71, treas., 1972-84; pres. Prince George's County General Soc., Bowie, 1970-71; mem. Bowie Adv. Planning Bd., 1987-91. Mem. Nat. Geneal. Soc., N.E. Historic Geneal. Soc., Prince George's County General Soc., Sigma Xi. Home: 3602 Maureen Ln Bowie MD 20715-2998 Office: Heritage Books Inc 1540 Pointer Ridge Pl Bowie MD 20716-1874

TOWNS, DONALD LIONEL, engineering executive; b. Sioux City, Iowa, Mar. 8, 1935; s. William Lionel and Violet V. (Robinson) T.; m. Joyce Harper, June 18, 1960; children: Jean Linda, Erik Donald. BChemE, Ga. Inst. Tech., 1957; PhD, U. Wis., 1962; cert. in bus. mgmt., Harvard U., 1985. Rsch. engr. FMC Corp., Princeton, N.J., 1962-73; team leader FMC Corp., Balt., 1973-74; operating supr. FMC Corp., Middleport, N.Y., 1974-80; project mgr. Herzog Hart Corp., Boston, 1980-85, 90—; engring. mgr. Carlson Process Co., Cochituate, Mass., 1985-88; mgr. engring. Facility Group, Framingham, Mass., 1988-90. 1st lt. U.S. Army, 1958. Mem. Am. Chem. Soc., Am. Inst. Chem. Engrs., Chem. Soc. London. Home: 2 Happy Hollow Rd Wayland MA 01778-3504 Office: Herzog Hart Corp 200 Berkeley St Boston MA 02116-5022

TOWNS, EDOLPHUS, congressman; b. Chadbourn, N.C., July 21, 1934; m. Gwendolyn Forbes, 1960; children: Darryl, Deidra. B.S., N.C. A & T State U., Greensboro, 1956; M.S.W., Adelphi U., Garden City, N.Y., 1973; PhD (hon.), N.C. A&T, Shaw U. Tchr. Medgar Evers Coll., Bklyn., N.Y.C. Pub. Schs.; dep. hosp. adminstr., 1965-71; dep. pres. Borough of Bklyn., 1976-82; mem. 98th-102nd Congresses from 11th Dist. N.Y., 1982—. Mem. adv. council Boy Scouts Am.; active Salvation Army. Served with U.S. Army, 1956-58. Named to Acad. of Distinction Adelphi U. Mem. Kiwanis, Phi Beta Sigma. Democrat. Office: US Ho of Reps 1726 Longworth House Office Bldg Washington DC 20515*

TOWNS, KATHRYN LOUISE, community psychology educator; b. Jamestown, N.Y., May 24, 1923; d. Ronald Earl and Ethel Louise (Peterson) T.; divorced; children: Michael, Kristin, Rhonda, Ann. BS in Edn., Miami (Ohio) U., 1944; MEd, Pa. State U., 1965, PhD, 1970. Cert. tchr., Ohio, Pa.; lic. psychologist, Pa. Statistician Scripps-Howard, Miami, 1943-44; mathematician Linde Air Corp., Buffalo, 1944; cost acct. Standard Brands, Terre Haute, Ind., 1952-64; tchr. Ohio and Pa. pub. schs., 1964—; prof. community psychology and women's studies Pa. State U., Harrisburg, 1990—; cons. Pa. sch. dists., 1970—, Danforth Found., Harrisburg, 1985-88; bd. dirs. Potential Reentry Opportunities in Bus. and Edn., Harrisburg. Bd. dirs. Pa. United Way, Harrisburg, 1985-88, Tri-County United Way, Harrisburg, 1984-87, Women's Agenda, Phila, 1984-90. With USN, 1944-45. Recipient 1st Service to Women award Pa. Commn. for Women, 1986. Mem. AAUW, Am. Ednl. Research Assn., Am. Psychol. Assn., Ea. Psychol. Assn., Assn. Woman Psychologists (membership file com. 1981-87), Nat. Women's Studies Assn. (co-convenor 1982-84). Office: Pa State U PROBE Middletown PA 17057

TOWNSEL, A. SYLVIANE, language educator; b. Moule, W.I., France, Dec. 3, 1943; d. Evariste G. and Fanny Yolande (Ferand) Griponne; m. Rdell Townsel, Oct. 23, 1978; 1 child, Timothy. BA, U. Madrid, Spain, 1975; MA, Atlanta U., 1977; PhD, Emory U., 1987. Teaching asst. Spanish Emory U., Atlanta, 1978-80; instr. French and Spanish Morehouse Coll., Atlanta, 1980-82; translator, sec. Atlanta Legal Aid, 1982-85; instr. Spanish Dekalb Coll., Atlanta, 1986-88; asst. prof. Spanish and French SUNY, Oswego, 1988—. Author: Donjuanism in Zorrilla and Valle-Inclan, 1987; (monograph) Negritude in French Caribbean Litgerature, 1991. Recipient French Prof. award French Govt., Strasbourg, 1990. Mem. Modern Lang. Assn., African Lit. Assn., Assn. Fgn. Lang. Tchrs. N.Y., Conseil Superieure Lang. Francaise. Roman Catholic. Office: SUNY Oswego NY 13126

TOWNSEND, ALAIR ANE, city official; b. Rochester, N.Y., Feb. 15, 1942; d. Harold Eugene and Dorothy (Sharpe) T.; m. Robert Harris, Dec. 31, 1970. BS, Elmira Coll., 1962; MS, U. Wis., 1964; postgrad. Columbia U., 1970-71. Assoc. dir. budget priorities Com. on Budget, U.S. Ho. of Reps., Washington, 1975-79; dep. asst. sec. for budget HEW, Washington, 1979-80, asst. sec. for mgmt. and budget, 1980-81; dir. N.Y.C. Office Mgmt. and Budget, 1981-85; dep. mayor for fin. and econ. devel. City of N.Y., 1985-89; pub. Crain's N.Y. Bus., N.Y.C., 1989—; former vice chmn., trustee Elmira Coll.; bd. dirs. Japan Soc.; mem. Coun. on Fgn. Rels.; chmn. Am. Woman's Econ. Devel. Corp. Mem. Women's Forum, Nat. Acad. Pub. Adminstrn., Fin. Women's Assn. N.Y., Advt. Women N.Y., N.Y.C. Partnership, N.Y. State Bus. Coun. (com. for econ. devel.), N.Y. C. of C. and Industry (bd. dirs.). Office: Crain's NY Bus 220 E 42d St New York NY 10017

TOWNSEND, HERBERT EARL, research engineering executive; b. Bristol, Pa., July 1, 1938; s. Herbert E. and Ruth Ann (Paules) T.; m. Carol Rose Costanzo, July 13, 1963; children: Anita, Lisa, Claressa. BSME, Drexel U., 1963; PhD in Math. Sci., U. Pa., 1967. Rsch. engr. Bethlehem (Pa.) Steel

Corp., 1967-72, rsch. supr., 1972-84, rsch. mgr., 1984-85, sr. rsch. fellow, 1985—. Author: (with others) Atmospheric Factors Affecting the Corrosion of Engineering Metals, 1978; contbr. articles to Jour. Electrochem. Soc., others; presenter to Soc. Automotive Eng., Nat. Assn. Corrosion Engrs., and others; patentee coating for cathodically protected structures, amorphous alloy, method of producing metal-filled organic coating, and others. Chmn. corrosion protection sect. of Metals Handbook Vol. on Corrosion, Am. Soc. Metals, 1985-87. Recipient Excellence in Oral Presentation award Soc. Automotive Engrs., 1990. Mem. Am. Iron and Steel Inst. (corrosion task force chmn. 1992—), Nat. Assn. Corrosion Engrs. (unit com. chmn. on automotive corrosion 1986-88). Office: Bethlehem Steel Corp Homer Rsch Labs Bethlehem PA 18016

TOWNSEND, IRENE FOGLEMAN, accountant, tax specialist; b. Birmingham, Ala., May 29, 1932; d. James Woods and Virginia (Martin) Fogleman; m. Kenneth Ross Townsend, Mar. 18, 1951; children: Marietta Irene, Martha Shapard, Kenneth Ross Jr., Elizabeth Buchanan. BSBA, East Carolina U., 1980. CPA, N.C., Va. Acct. Norwood P. Whitehurst & Assocs., Greenville, N.C., 1981-86; tax dir. Nat. Med. Enterprises, Inc., Washington, 1986—. Fellow AICPA, N.C. Assn. CPA's, D.C. Inst. CPA's; mem. DAR, N.C. Soc. Daughters of the Colonial Wars, Colonial Dames 17th Century. Democrat. Episcopalian (lay reader, chalice bearer). Home: 2521 Paxton St Lake Ridge VA 22192 Office: Nat Med Enterprises Inc 1010 Wisconsin Ave NW Ste 900 Washington DC 20007-3687

TOWNSEND, JANIS BARBARA LUBAWSKY, computer company executive, consultant; b. Bronx, N.J., Jan. 21, 1946; d. Paul Lubawsky and Sylvia Belkin; m. David J. Townsend, Sept. 8, 1968; children: Maya, Michael. BA, CCNY, 1966; MA, U. Mich., 1967; PhD, Wayne State U., 1977. Instr. Upsala Coll., East Orange, N.J., 1979-81, Rutgers U., Newark, 1981-82, N.J. Inst. Tech., Newark, 1982-84; pres. Janus Computing, Inc., Montclair, N.J., 1983—; cons. CES Tng., River Edge, N.J., 1984-86, Exec. Computer Network, Fairfield, N.J., 1985-88. Author: Am. Women Writers, 1980; co-author: The Teacher's Computer Book, 1985; author computer manuals. Recipient Best Essay on Lit. award AAUW, 1982. Mem. N.J. Computer Cons. Consortium (v.p. 1990—), N.J. Assn. Women Bus. Owners (sec. 1987—), Assn. Women in Computing. Office: Janus Computing Inc 159 Midland Ave Montclair NJ 07042-3035

TOWNSEND, JEREMY NOBLE, book publisher, editor; b. Norwalk, Conn., Mar. 18, 1957; d. Irving Joseph and Winifred Harriet (Thompson) T.; m. Nicholas Neal Orovich, Mar. 23, 1990. BA, Pepperdine U., Malibu, Calif., 1979. Asst. editor W.W. Norton & Co., N.Y.C., 1981-85; freelance editor W.W. Norton, St. Martin's, Crown, Upstart Pub., N.Y.C. and Dover, N.H., 1985—; pres. Ctr. for Wildlife, Cape Neddick, ME, 1991—; bd. mem. N.H. Writers and Pub., Concord, N.H., 1991—; pub. cons., 1989-91. Editor: Rainy Day Man, 1984; author, editor CFW News, 1990-91; contbr. articles to profl. jours. Tutor Lit. Vols., Exeter, N.H., 1990; adv. bd. Humane Soc. N.Y.C., 1988—. Mem. New England Booksellers Assn., Cosmep. Democrat. Home: 12 Greenleaf Dr Exeter NH 03833-4531 Office: JN Townsend Pub 12 Greenleaf Dr Exeter NH 03833-4531

TOWNSEND, JOHN MARSHALL, anthropology educator; b. Amarillo, Tex., Sept. 1, 1941; s. Tarlton Bird and Virgie Leona (McAlister) T.; m. Carolyn Marie Terkelson, July 2, 1967 (div. 1974); m. Kimberly Kay Menard, June 2, 1984; children: Virgie Liana, Kristin Elizabeth, Rebecca Nell. AB in Psychology, U. Calif., Berkeley, 1963; MA, U. Calif., Santa Barbara, 1967, PhD in Anthropology, 1972. Asst. prof. anthropology U. Mont., Missoula, 1972-73; asst. prof. anthropology Syracuse (N.Y.) U., 1973-77, assoc. prof., 1977—; adj. assoc. prof. SUNY, Coll. Medicine Health Sci. Ctr., Syracuse, 1990—. Author: Cultural Conceptions and Mental Illness; contbr. numerous articles to profl. jours. Fellow NIMH, 1968; grantee NEH, 1983-85. Office: Syracuse U Dept Anthropolog 308 Bowne Hall Syracuse NY 13244-1200

TOWNSEND, MARJORIE RHODES, aerospace engineer, business executive; b. Washington, Mar. 12, 1930; d. Lewis Boling and Marjorie Olive (Trees) Rhodes; m. Charles Eby Townsend, June 7, 1948; children: Charles Eby Jr., Lewis Rhodes, John Cunningham, Richard Leo. BEE, George Washington U., 1951. Registered profl. engr., D.C. Electronic scientist Naval Rsch. Lab., Washington, 1951-59; rsch. engr. to sect. head Goddard Space Flight Ctr.-NASA, Greenbelt, Md., 1959-65, tech. asst. to chief systems divsn., 1965-66, project mgr. small astronomy satellites, 1966-75, project mgr. applications explorer missions, 1975-76, mgr. preliminary systems design group, 1976-80; aerospace and electronics cons. Washington, 1980-83; v.p. systems devel. Space Am., 1983-84; aerospace cons. Washington, 1984-90; dir. space systems engring. BDM Internat., Inc., Washington, 1990-91; dir. space applications BDM ESC, Washington, 1991-92; sr. prin. staff mem. BDM Internat., Inc., Washington, 1992—. Patentee digital telemetry system. Decorated Knight Italian Republic Order, 1972; recipient Fed. Women's award, 1973, EUR Culture award, 1974, Engr. Alumni Achievement award George Washington, 1975, Gen. Alumni Achievement award George Washington U., 1976, Exceptional Svc. medal NASA, 1971, Eye-of-the-Needle award NASA, 1991, Outstanding Leadership medal NASA, 1980. Fellow IEEE (chmn. Washington sect. 1974-75), AIAA (assoc., chmn. nat. capitol sect. 1985), Washington Acad. Sci. (pres. 1980-81); mem. AAAS (coun. del. 1985-88), Internat. Acad. Astronautics, Am. Geophys. Union, Soc. Women Engrs., DAR, Daus. Colonial Wars, Mensa, Sigma Kappa. Republican. Episcopalian. Home: 3529 Tilden St NW Washington DC 20008-3194

TOWNSEND, PHILIP W., JR., library director; b. Phila., Aug. 14, 1949; s. Philip Walsh and Eleanor (Clay) T.; m. Mary Rasmussen, Aug., 1973; children: Grace, Philip, Erica. BA, U. Utah, 1973; MSLS, Villanova U., 1988. Libr. dir. Valley Forge Mil. Jr. Coll., Wayne, Pa., 1985—. Capt. U.S. Army Res., 1973-83. Office: Valley Forge Mil Jr Coll Office of Libr 1001 Eagle Rd Wayne PA 19087-3694

TOWNSEND, RUTH, secondary education educator; b. Ariz., Mar. 20, 1935; d. James Edward and Effie Fisher (Wester) Greene; m. Richard Edward Townsend, Sept. 1, 1955; children: Gavin Edward, Bryan Andrew. BA, UCLA, 1959; MA, Columbia U., 1966; postgrad., NYU, 1982, Northeastern U., 1985. Cert. tchr., N.Y. Tchr. English Yorktown High Sch., Yorktown Heights, N.Y., 1966—; cons. Putnam/Northern Westchester BOCES, Yorktown Heights, 1978—, Putnam/Northern Westchester Tchr. Ctr., South Salem, N.Y., 1989—, Effective Schs. Consortium, Albany, N.Y., 1990; tchr. trainer Bur. of English and Reading, State of N.Y., Albany, 1987—. Co-authhor: (textbooks) Language Works, 1991, English for the Disenchanted, 1992, (computer software programs) Persuasive Essay Series, Reading Doctor. Co-founder LWV, Mt. Kisco, N.Y., 1962; pres. Bedford (N.Y.) Christian Sch., 1984-88, Random Choristers, Bedford, 1990—, A-Home, Mt. Kisco, 1989. Bay Area Writing Project fellow, 1977. Fellow N.Y. State English Coun. (conf. chmn. 1989, 91, issues chmn. 1990, sec. 1991—, Tchr. of Excellence award 1985), Westchester Coun. English Educators (pres. 1986-87, program chmn. 1987—). Episcopalian. Home: 15 Courtmel Rd Mount Kisco NY 10549

TOWNSEND, TERRY, publishing executive; b. Camden, N.J., Dec. 14, 1920; d. Anthony and Rose DeMarco; BA, Duke U., 1942; LHD (hon.) Dowling Coll., 1991; m. Paul Brorstrom Townsend, Dec. 8, 1961; 1 son, Kim. Pub. rels. dir. North Shore Univ. Hosp., Manhasset, N.Y., 1955-68; pres. Theatre Soc. L.I., 1968-70; pres. Townsend Communications Bur., Ronkonkoma, N.Y., 1970—, L.I. Communicating Service, Ronkonkoma, 1977—; columnist, writer L.I./Bus., Ronkonkoma, 1970-75, pub., 1978—; pub. L.I. Bus. News, 1978—; v.p. Parr Meadows Racetrack, Yaphank, N.Y., 1977. Assoc. trustee North Shore U. Hosp., 1968—; bd. govs. Adelphi U. Friends Fin. Edn., 1978-85; chmn. ann. archtl. awards competition N.Y. Inst. Tech., 1970-83; trustee Dowling Coll., 1984—, L.I. Fine Arts Mus., 1984-85, pub. broadcasting Sta. WLIW TV, Garden City, L.I., N.Y., 1990—; bd. dirs. Family Svc. Assn. Nassau County, 1982—; dinner chmn. L.I. 400 Ball, 1987. Recipient Media award 110 Center Bus. and Profl. Women, 1977, Enterprise award Friends of Fin. Edn., 1981, L.I. Loves Bus. Showcase Salute, 1982, Community Svc. award N.Y. Diabetes Assn., 1983, Disting. Long Islander in Communications award L.I. United Epilepsy Assn., 1984, Spl. award Dowling Coll. Spring Tribute, 1989, Disting. Svc. award Episcopal Health Svcs., 1989, Disting. Citizen award Dowling Coll., 1991; named First Lady of L.I., L.I. Public Relations Assn., 1973, L.I. Woman of Yr. L.I. Assn. Action Com., 1989. Home: 26933V Grand Central Pky Floral Park NY 11005-1200 Office: LI Bus News 2150 Smithtown Ave Ronkonkoma NY 11779-7348

TOWNSEND, TERYL ARCHER, artist, educator; b. Coronado, Calif., May 9, 1938; d. Robert Lee and Elizabeth (Archer) T.; m. Arthur W. Viner; children: Shawn Elizabeth Speers, Don Philip Speers Jr. Studies with Chen Chi, Millard Sheets, Edgar Whitney, Carl Molno, Glen Bradshaw, Maubry Brown, Edward Betts, Robert E. Wood., 1971—. Free-lance tchr. Nantucket, Mass., Conn., 1974—. Designer book covers; exhibited at Veerhoff Gallery, Washington, James Hunt Barker Gallery, Palm Beach, Nantucket, Mass. Mem. community bd. Wavery House, New Canaan. Recipient Merit award Art League Houston, 1975, 77, 82, 3d place award Nat. Small Painting Show, 1976, Merit award So. Watercolor Soc., 1977. Mem. Am. Watercolor Soc., Nat. Watercolor Soc., Rocky Mountain Nat. Watermedia Soc. (Century award 1974, 77), Southwestern Watercolor Soc. (awards 1974-76, 78, 84), Nantucket Artists Assn. (bd. dirs., advisor, exec. com. 1986—, Merit award 1980, 82, 83, 86), Houston Watercolor Soc. (v.p., pres. 1974-75, advisor profl. standards 1976-82, various awards 1975-76, 82-83), Nantucket C. of C., Houston C. of C. (advisor cultural com. 1975-76). Episcopalian. Home: 109 Rosebrook Rd New Canaan CT 06840-3724 Studio: 16 Forest Ave New Canaan CT 06840

TOWNSLEY, MICHAEL K., college administrator; b. Logansport, Ind., Apr. 17, 1945; s. P. Keith and Helen M. (Hannagan) T.; m. Susanne V. Townsley, July 27, 1974; 1 child, Andrew Keith. BA, Purdue U., 1967; MA, U. Del., 1975; ABD, U. Pa., 1989. Planning assoc. Health Planning Coun., Dayton, Ohio, 1968-69; community rels. staff Assn. of Greater Wilmington (Del.) Neighborhood Assn., 1969-70; community specialist Appoquinimink Sch. Dist., Odessa, Del., 1971-73, asst. to supr., 1973-78; bus. mgr. Franklin (Ind.) Community Sch., 1978-81; bus. mgr. Wilmington Coll., New Castle, Del., 1981-86, v.p., 1987—. Contbr. articles to profl. jours. Advisor senate campaign, Del., 1988; treas. Am. Cancer Soc., Mid-Del. chpt., 1989—; bd. dirs. Community Agy., Mid-Del., 1972-78; advisor Bd. Campaign, 1990. U. Del. rsch. fellow, 1969-71; recipient U. Pa. Scholastic award, 1990. Republican. Roman Catholic. Home: 115 E Redding St Middletown DE 19709-1432 Office: Wilmington Coll PO Box 4596 Wilmington DE 19807-4596

TOY, ATALA DOROTHY, public relations executive, writer; b. Phila., Oct. 14, 1941; d. Irving Chester and Erma Jackson (McNeil) P.; children: Steven, Brian. BA, Swarthmore Coll., 1963. Dir. humanity publicity MIT, Cambridge, Mass., 1963-64; submissions editor Doubleday & Co., Inc., N.Y.C., 1964-65; freelance writer, publicist Croton, N.Y., 1965-78; dir. pub. rels. Sri Chinmoy Marathon Team, Jamaica, N.Y., 1977—; pres. Flame-Waves Pub. Rels., Jamaica, N.Y., 1978—; internat. lectr. on New Age philosophy; cons. internat. pub. rels. Sri Chinmoy Ctr., 1977—. Contbr. articles on New Age topics to mags. Home and Office: 16148 Normal Rd Jamaica NY 11432-3446

TOY, HERBERT JOHN, JR., sales executive; b. Springfield, Pa., June 23, 1936; s. Herbert John and Carolyn Arwilda (Newell) T.; m. Mary Frances Applegate, Oct. 1, 1960; children: Herbert John III, Timothy A. BS, Dickinson Coll., 1958; MA, Seton Hall U., 1963. Biology tchr., coach Middletown (N.J.) Twp. High Sch., 1958-64, vice prin., 1964-66; sales rep. Upjohn Co., Harrisburg, Pa., 1966-68; dir. field svc. Susquehanna Valley Regional Med. Program, Camp Hill, Pa., 1968-69; v.p. Hosp. Cen. Svcs. Inc., Allentown, Pa., 1969-74; pres., prin. Jack Toy Co., Bethlehem, Pa., 1974—. Mem. Mid Eastern Pa. Soc. Hosp. Pharmacists (chmn. membership com.), Am. Soc. Hosp. Materials Mgrs. (N.E. Pa. chpt.), Bethlehem Club, Silver Creek Country Club. Republican. Episcopalian. Home: 621 Main St Bethlehem PA 18018-3801 Home: 5858 Asbury Ave Ocean City NJ 08226-1267 Office: 717 Linden St Bethlehem PA 18018-4216

TOYE, RICHARD CHARLES, psychologist; b. Marion, Ohio, June 24, 1958; s. Robert James and Fenella LaFern (Fairall) T.; m. Mary Katherine Hogan, Oct. 5, 1985; children: Brian Andrew, James Edward. BA cum laude, Rice U., 1979; MSc, Brown U., 1980; PhD, U. Ill., Chgo., 1984. Diplomate Am. Bd. Profl. Psychology; lic. psychologist Mass., Maine, N.H. Sr. psychologist N.H. Hosp., Concord, 1985-88; pvt. practice Exeter, N.H., 1988—; cons. Head Injury Treatment Program, Dover, N.H., 1988—, Inst. Profl. Practice, N.H., 1987-89; trauma counselor Exeter Hosp., 1989—. Contbr. articles to profl. publs. Mem. consumer adv. coun. Vocat. Rehab., Nashua, N.H., 1990, sch. budget adv. coun., Exeter, 1989—. Recipient Excellence in Psychology award Houston Psychol. Assn., 1979; NSF fellow, 1979. Fellow N.H. Psychol. Orgn. (chair continuing edn. 1987-89, pres.-elect 1989-90, pres. 1990—); mem. Assn. Advancement Behavior Therapy, Soc. Personality Assessment, Am. Psychol. Assn., Nat. Eagle Scout Assn., Phi Kappa Phi. Office: 99 Water St Exeter NH 03833-2410

TRACHTENBERG, EDWARD NORMAN, chemistry educator; b. N.Y.C., Dec. 8, 1927; s. Jacob Mordecai and Eva (Adwokat) T.; m. Victoria Antoinette Gotsky, Aug. 21, 1954; children: Ellen, Judith, Richard. AB, NYU, 1949; AM, Harvard U., 1951, PhD, 1953. Instr. Columbia U., N.Y.C., 1953-58; asst. prof. Clark U., Worcester, Mass., 1958-61, assoc. prof., 1961-70, prof., 1970—; cons. Radiation Applications, Inc., L.I. City, 1956-61, E.F. Drew & Co., Inc., Boonton, N.J., 1958-61. Editor: Premedical Advisor's Reference Manual, 1990. Mem. Worcester Civil Liberties Union, 1968—, chair, 1982-85; mem. Mass. Dem. State Platform Com., Boston, 1972-76, Worcester Dem. Com., 1972-88; mem. exec. com. Citizens for Participation in Polit. Action, Boston, 1972—, chair, 1990-91. Cpl. USAAF, 1946-47. NSF fellow, 1967-68. Mem. AAUP, Am. Chem. Soc. (chair cen. Mass. chpt. 1965-66), Nat. Assn. Advisors for Health Professions (bd. dirs. 1986-88), Northeast Assn. Advisors for Health Professions (exec. com. 1983-89, pres. 1987-88), Chem. Soc. London, Phi Beta Kappa, Phi Lambda Upsilon, Sigma Xi. Home: 28 S Lenox St Worcester MA 01602-2502 Office: Clark U 950 Main St Worcester MA 01610-1473

TRACHTENBERG, MATTHEW J., bank holding company executive; b. N.Y.C., June 20, 1953; s. Mark Trachtenberg and Joanne Horne. BA magna cum laude, NYU, 1974; JD, Bklyn. Law Sch., 1977; MBA in Fin., Fordham U., 1982. Bar: N.Y. 1979. Mgmt. trainee Mfrs. Hanover Trust Co., N.Y.C., 1977-78, credit analyst, 1978-79, corp. banking rep., 1979-80, asst. sec., 1980-82, asst. v.p., 1982, v.p., 1982—, corp. sec., 1987—; v.p., corp. sec. Mfrs. Hanover Corp., N.Y.C., 1987—; v.p., sec. regional bd. Chem. Bank, N.Y.C., 1992—; v.p., dep. corp. sec. Chem. Banking Corp., N.Y.C., 1992—, Chem. Bank, 1992—; sec. Chem. Bank Regional Bd., 1992—; bd. dirs. Mfrs. Hanover Found., 1987—; v.p. Chem. Bank, 1992—, Chem. Banking Corp., 1992—; sec. Chem. Bank Regional bd., 1992—. Bd. dirs., treas. Nat. Orch. Assn.; bd. dirs. Joffrey Ballet, N.Y. Eye and Ear Infirmary, U.S.O. of Met. N.Y. N.Y. State Regents scholar. Mem. N.Y. State Bar Assn., Am. Soc. Corp. Secs., Phi Beta Kappa, Pi Sigma Alpha. Office: Chem Banking Corp 270 Park Ave New York NY 10017-2014

TRACHTENBERG, STEPHEN JOEL, university president; b. Bklyn., Dec. 14, 1937; s. Oscar M. and Shoshana G. (Weinstock) T.; m. Francine Zorn, June 24, 1971; children: Adam Maccabee, Ben-Lev. B.A., Columbia U., 1959; J.D., Yale U., 1962; M.Pub.Adminstrn., Harvard U., 1966; LHD (hon.), Trinity Coll., 1986; HHD (hon.), U. Hartford, 1989; LLD (hon.), Hanyang U., Seoul, Republic of Korea, 1990. Bar: N.Y. 1964, U.S. Supreme Ct. 1967. Atty. AEC, 1962-65; legis. asst. to Congressman John Brademas of Ind., Washington, 1965; tutor law Harvard Coll., also; teaching fellow edn. and pub. policy J.F. Kennedy Grad. Sch. Govt., Harvard U., 1965-66; spl. asst. to U.S. edn. commr. Office of Edn., HEW, Washington, 1966-68; asso. prof. polit. sci. Boston U., 1969-77, asso. dean, 1969-70, dean, 1970-74, asso. v.p., co-counsel, 1974-76, v.p. acad. services, 1976-77; pres., prof. law U. Hartford, Conn., 1977-88; pres., prof. mgmt. George Washington U., Washington, 1988—; mem. commn. on minorities in higher edn. Am. Coun. on Edn., also mem. adv. bd. Ednl. Record; bd. dirs. Consortium of Univs. Washington Met. Area; mem. coun. on competitiveness Fed. City Coun.; mem. pres. commn. NCAA; bd. dirs. Loctite Corp., MNC Fin., Inc., Security Trust Co. Contbr. articles to profl. jours. Bd. dirs. Urban League, Washington. Winston Churchill fellow Eng., 1969; named Outstanding Young Person, Boston Jr. C. of C., 1970, One of 100 Young Leaders, Acad. Am. Council Learning, 1978, Alumnus of Yr. James Madison High Sch., Bklyn., 1982, one of Fifty Outstanding Alumni Problem Solvers Harvard's John F. Kennedy Sch. Government; recipient Myrtle Wreath award Hadassah, 1982, Scopus award Am. Friends of Hebrew U., 1986, assoc. fellow Morse Coll. Yale U., 1980, Human Rels. award NCCJ, 1987, award NAACP, 1988, citation Conn. Bar Assn., 1988, Univ. medal of highest honor Kyung Hee U., Seoul, Korea, 1990, Martin Luther King, Jr. Internat. Salute award, 1992. Mem. Am. Assn. Univ. Adminstrs. (bd. dirs.), Internat. Assn. Univ. Pres. (N.Am. coun.), Sr. Soc. Sachems, Washington Urban League, Harvard Club (N.Y.C.), Tumblebrook Country Club (Bloomfield, Conn.), Cosmos Club (Washington), Univ. Club (Washington), Nineteen Twenty-five F St. Club, Inc. (Washington), Phi Beta Kappa. Office: George Washington U Washington DC 20052

TRACHTER, GARY DENNIS, pharmacy technician; b. Boston, July 3, 1948; s. Irving Trachter and Theodora Trachter Vernell; m. Mary Ellen Trachter, Nov. 24, 1973; 1 child, Jason. Student, Prospect Bus. Coll., Hollywood, Fla., 1981-82. With U.S. Postal Svc., Ft. Lauderdale, Fla., 1971-80; pharmacy tech. I Holy Cross Hosp., Ft. Lauderdale, Fla., 1980-82; mail clk. Grolier Inc., Danbury, Conn., 1982-83; pharmacy tech. II Stamford (Conn.) Hosp., 1983—. With USN, 1965-69. Mem. Assn. Pharmacy Technicians (dist. dir. 1990—), New Mass. Pharmacy Technicians Assn., Conn. Soc. Hosp. Pharmacists. Democrat. Jewish. Home: 39 Horton Hill Rd Naugatuck CT 06770-4861

TRACHTMAN, MICHAEL GLENN, lawyer; b. Phila., Oct. 31, 1949; s. Leonard and Esther (Pelta) T.; m. Jennifer Taber, Oct. 13, 1985; 1 child, Benjamin Taber. BA, Dickinson Coll., 1971; JD, Villanova U., 1974. Bar: Pa. 1974, U.S. Dist. Ct. (ea. dist.) Pa. 1974, U.S. Ct. Appeals (3d cir.) 1974, U.S. Supreme Ct. 1992. Assoc. Waters, Gallager, Collins & Masterson, Norristown, Pa., 1974-80; ptnr. Waters, Gallager & Trachtman, Norristown, 1981-85, Trachtman & Logan, Norristown, 1985-88, Powell, Trachtman, Logan & Carrle, King of Prussia, Pa., 1988—; del. 3d cir. Conf., Pitts., 1989; speaker in field. Author book and audio tapes: What Every Executive Better Know About the Law, 1987; contbr. articles to profl. publs. Mem. East Pikeland Twp. (Pa.) Planning Commn., 1977-80. Mem. Montgomery Bar Assn. (bd. dirs. 1984-87, chmn. com. 1990—), Order of Coif. Office: Powell Trachtman Logan & Carrle 367 S Gulph Rd King Of Prussia PA 19406

TRACKMAN, JAY H(AROLD), musician, educator; b. Orange, N.J., Aug. 24, 1929; s. William A. and Edith (Hersh) T.; m. Elaine Louise Roth, June 14, 1953; children: Andrew David, Karen Beth, Marc William. BS, Juilliard Sch. Music, 1951; MA, Columbia U., 1952. Band dir. Greenville (S.C.) Sr. High Sch., 1952-54; music tchr. Phila. Pub. Schs., 1954-56; music dir. Bordentown (N.J.) Pub. Schs., 1956-66, Burlington (N.J.) City Pub. Schs., 1966—; music instr. N.J. Div. Corrections, Bordentown, 1955-57. Mem. Kiwanis (pres. 1969-70), Temple Beth Abraham (pres. 1975-76). Home: 40 Vine Way Bordentown NJ 08505

TRACY, JOSEPH IGOE, clinical psychologist; b. Orange, N.J., Apr. 11, 1954; s. William Irwin and Virginia Mary (Igoe) T.; m. Carol Susan Busacca, May 29, 1982; children: Ryan, Lauren, Nicole. BA, Bowdoin Coll., 1976; MA, Columbia U., 1981; PhD, New Sch. Social Rsch., 1990. Rsch. assoc. Inst. for Health, Health Care Policy and Aging Rutgers U., New Brunswick, N.J., 1988-90; program dir. Carrier Found., Belle Meade, N.J., 1990-91; asst. prof. Med. Coll. Pa./E.P.P.I., Phila., 1991—; vis. asst. prof. Ctr. Alcohol Studies Rutgers U., Piscataway, N.J., 1990—. Recipient Alvin Johnson fellowship New Sch. for Social Rsch., 1987. Mem. APA (dissertaion rsch. award 1988), Am. Psychol. Soc., Internat. Neuropsychol. Soc., Soc. Psychologists in Addictive Behaviors, Ea. Psychol. Assn. Office: Med Coll Pa Dept Psychiatry 3200 Henry Ave Philadelphia PA 19129

TRACZ, WILLIAM JOSEPH, computer scientist, software engineer; b. Salamanca, N.Y., Sept. 8, 1950; s. Daniel Joseph and Lillian Josephine (Janowicz) T.; m. Sharon Ann Mitchell, May 27, 1972; children: Matthew, Nicholas, Megan. BA in Math., SUNY, Geneseo, 1972; MS in Computer Sci., Pa. State U., 1974; MS in Computer Engring., Syracuse U., 1979; postgrad., Stanford U., 1984—. Rsch. asst. SUNY-Geneseo, 1970-72; sr. programmer fed. systems co. IBM, Owego, N.Y., 1974—; vis. prof. Rochester (N.Y.) Inst. Tech., 1981-82; adj. prof. Syracuse (N.Y.) U., 1983-84. Editor: Software Reuse: Emerging Technology, 1988; contbg. author: Microprogramming Handbook, 1988; contbr. articles to profl. publs. Mem. IEEE (computer mag. editor 1991—), Assn. Computer Machinists (chair 1988-91, newsletter editor 1983-88, spl. interest group microprogramming). Democrat. Roman Catholic. Office: IBM Fed Systems Co MD0 210 Owego NY 13827-1298

TRAGESER, DEBRA ANNE, rehabilitation services professional; b. Mt. Lebanon, Pa., May 30, 1961; d. Raymond Mattern and Anne Marie (Kois) T. BS, U. Pitts., 1983, MEd, 1984; postgrad., Temple U., 1986, U. Pa., 1989. Cert. rehab. counselor. Stabilization counselor Guiffre Med. Ctr., Phila., 1985-86; vocat. counselor Coastal Assocs. Inc., Newtown Square, Pa., 1986-87; vocat. counselor Gen. Rehab. Svcs., Phila., 1987-89, rehab. supr., 1989-90; br. mgr. Gen. Rehab. Svcs., Fairfield, N.J., 1990—; supr., coord. The Bridge, Phila., 1988; cons. Juvenile Ct. System, Phila., 1988; witness for ins. industry, Phila., 1987—. Mem. Am. Assn. Counseling and Devel., Am. Rehab. Counseling Assn., Nat. Employment Counselors Assn. Democrat. Roman Catholic. Home: 2401 Sterling Rd Yardley PA 19067-7236 Office: Gen Rehab Svcs 30 Two Bridges Rd Ste 205 Fairfield NJ 07004-1530 Office: Gen Rehab Svcs 104 Interchange Plz Ste 3D Cranbury NJ 08512-9561

TRAGESER, RAYMOND MATTERN, JR., insurance company executive; b. Pitts., Sept. 30, 1934; s. Raymond Michael and Marcella Cecilia (Mattern) T.; m. Anne Marie Kois, June 4, 1960; 1 child, Debra Anne. Student, Duquesne U., 1952-54, U. Pitts., 1959-61. Underwriter Continental Ins., Pitts., 1957-58, sr. underwriter, 1958-59, asst. supt. casualty, 1959-63, supt. casualty, 1963-65; mgr. underwriting Transamerica Ins., Pitts., 1965-69, mgr. mktg., 1969-84, br. mgr., 1984-85; resident v.p., regional mgr. Transamerica Ins., Phila., 1985—; speaker, rep. Ins. Info. Inst., N.Y. Served with U.S. Army, 1955-57. Mem. Ins. Clubs Pitts., Casualty and Property Mgrs. Assn. Phila., Ins. Fedn. Pa., Casualty Assn. Pitts. (pres. 1965-67). Democrat. Roman Catholic. Clubs: Vesper, Urban (Phila.). Lodge: Rotary. Home: 338 Flint Rd Langhorne PA 19047-8206 Office: Transamerica Ins Group 2 Penn Center Plz Philadelphia PA 19102-1701

TRAINOR, BERNARD EDMUND, educator, journalist, retired marine corps officer; b. N.Y.C., Sept. 2, 1928; s. Joseph Patrick and Ann Veronica (Whalen) T.; m. Margaret Ann Hamilton, June 13, 1959; children: Kathleen Marie, Theresa Ann, Eileen Cecile, Claire Hamilton. B.S., Coll. of Holy Cross, 1951; M.A., U. Colo., 1963, postgrad., 1970—. Commd. 2d lt. USMC, 1951, advanced through grades to lt. gen., 1983; inf. comdr. Korea, 1952; assigned USS Columbus, 1953-55, staff Marine Corps Hdqrs., 1955-58, exchange office Royal Marine Commandos, 1958-59, inf. comdr. First Marine Div., 1959-61; asst. prof. naval sci. U. Colo., Boulder, 1961-64; assigned to Marine Corps Command and Staff Coll., 1964-65; adv. Republic of Vietnam, 1965-66; instr. Marine Corps Command and Staff Coll., 1966-69; student Air War Coll., Montgomery, Ala., 1969-70; bn. comdr. Vietnam, 1970-71; staff officer Hdqrs. Marine Corps, Washington, 1970-71; dir. First Marine Corps Dist., N.Y.C., 1974-76; asst. depot comdr. Marine Corps Recruit Depot, Parris Island, S.C., 1976-78; dir. Edn. Center, Quantico, Va., 1978-81; dep. chief of staff for plans, policies and ops. Hdqrs. Marine Corps, 1981-85; cons., 1985—; mil. corr. N.Y. Times, 1986-90; dir. nat. security program Kennedy Sch. Govt. Harvard U., Cambridge, Mass., 1990—; mem. adv. bd. Harvard Jour. Internat. Affairs. Author: History of the U.S. Marine Corps, 1968; mem. editorial bd. advisors Naval War Coll. Rev.; mem. editorial bd. Amphibious Warfare Rev.; columnist N.Y. Times News Svc.; contbr. articles to profl. jours. Mem. acad. adv. bd. U.S. Naval Acad.; adv. bd. to pres. of Naval War Coll.; mil. analyst ABC News; rsch. bd. dirs. Inst. for Fgn. Policy Analysis. Decorated D.S.M., Legion of Merit (2), Bronze Star, Navy Commendation medal (2), others; recipient Anderson Meml. award Air War Coll., 1970. Mem. Naval Inst., Marine Corps Assn., Coun. Fgn. Rels., Order of U.S., Army-Navy Club. Roman Catholic. Home: 1512 Hampton Hills Cir Mc Lean VA 22101-6017 Office: Harvard U Kennedy Sch Govt 79 Kennedy Rd Cambridge MA 02138-3352

TRAINOR, JEAN ANN, SR., dietitian, assistant director, consultant; b. Salem, Mass., Dec. 21, 1938; d. Raymond Joseph and Mary Elizabeth (Kingsley) T. BS in Food and Nutrition, Coll. St. Elizabeth, 1962; MS in

Food Sci. and Nutri, Colo. State U., 1974. Dietitian patient svcs. Hosp. St. Raphael, New Haven, 1964—; dietetic internship Yale-New Haven Med. Ctr., New Haven, 1964; mem. diabetes edn. com. Hosp. St. Raphael, 1967-89, outreach com., 1990—; instr. nutrition South Cen. Community Coll., New Haven, 1981; cons. Life Haven, New Haven, 1987-90; sec. Y-Me of New Eng. Breast Cancer Support Program, 1989-91. Vol. tutor Literacy Vols. of Greater New Haven, 1990—. U.S. Dept. Health Edn. and Welfare grantee, 1973-74. Mem. Am. Dietetic Assn., Conn. Dietetic Assn. Roman Catholic. Office: Hosp St Raphael 1450 Chapel St New Haven CT 06511-4405

TRAINOR, LILLIAN (MIDGE TRAINOR), elections official; b. Norma, N.J., Oct. 30, 1936; d. Loenell Lesley and Lillie Ara (Kenyon) Barber; m. Arthur James Trainor, Mar. 9, 1959; children: Michael, Arthur, Lynn Marie. Student pub. schs., Pleasantville, N.J. Chair Burlington County Bd. Elections, Mount Holly, N.J., 1978-81, commr. of registration, 1981-83, chair, 1983-90; dir. N.J. Div. Elections, 1990—. Vice chair, mem. exec. bd. Burlington County Dem. Com., 1977-90; chair Southampton Twp. Dem. County Com., 1976-79, Bd. County Convassers, Burlington County, 1978-90; v.p. Southeastern Dem. Coalition, 1977-87; mgr. Florio for Gov. Campaign, N.J., 1981, Carter for Pres. Campaign, Burlington County area, 1980; del. Dem. Nat. Conv., 1984, 88; coord. Women for Florio Gubanatorial campaign, 1989. Served with WAC, 1955-57. Mem. Nat. Assn. State Election Dirs., N.J. State Assn. Election Ofcls., VFW Aux. Club: Big Six (pres. 1973-79). Avocations: accordian, piano, birdwatching, reading. Home: PO Box 2266 Vincentown NJ 08088-2266 Office: NJ Div Elections 315 W State St Trenton NJ 08618-5703

TRAMMER, MONTE IRVIN, newspaper publisher; b. Birmingham, Ala., Nov. 11, 1951; s. Jimmie and Edwenia (Wilson) T.; m. Hilda Marie Hudson, May 20, 1972. Student, Ind. U., 1969-74. Reporter Indpls. Star, 1970-76, Balt. Sun, 1977-80; fin. writer Detroit Free Press, 1980-81, asst. city editor, 1981-82; dep. mng. editor USA Today, Washington, 1982-86; asst. to pub. Poughkeepsie (N.Y.) Jour., 1986; pres., pub. The Saratogian, Saratoga Springs, N.Y., 1986—; chmn. exec. com. multicultural mgmt. program U. Mo., Columbia, 1988. Vice pres. United Way N.E. N.Y., 1990—, bd. dirs. United Way N.Y. State, Sta. WMHT-TV, Schenectady, N.Y.; bd. dirs., trustee N.Y. State Pubs. Found., 1987—; mem. exec. com. Empire State Coll. Found. Bd., Saratoga Springs, 1990—. Ford Found. fellow, 1978. Mem. Soc. Profl. Journalists, Nat. Assn. Black Journalists (bd. dirs. 1977-82), Rotary (past bd. dirs.). Democrat. Methodist. Office: The Saratogian 20 Lake Ave Saratoga Springs NY 12866-2356

TRAN, DUNG PHUOC, psychiatrist; b. Hue, Vietnam, Oct. 20, 1949; came to U.S., 1981; s. Thanh P. and Luc-Ha T.; m. Minh-Quang Nguyen, Jan. 5, 1977; children: Duy, Dan. MD, Johannes Gutenberg U., Mainz, Fed. Republic Germany, 1977. Diplomate Am. Bd. Psychiatry and Neurology. Trainer trauma-surgery Aschaffenburg and Offenbach, Fed. Republic Germany, 1978-81; staff physician Moose Lake (Minn.) State Hosp., 1983-84; med. examiner Am. Paraprofl. System, Mpls., 1982-83; resident in psychiatry La. State U., New Orleans, 1984-88; chief-resident in psychiatry La. State U. Med. Ctr., New Orleans, 1987-88; staff psychiatrist Northampton County Mental Health, Bethlehem and Easton, Pa., 1988—; staff psychiatrist, med. staff Allentown (Pa.) State Hosp., Haven House Orgn., Allentown; former mental health cons. Vietnamese Assn., Phila. Mem. Am. Psychiat. Assn., Pa. Psychiat. Assn., Vietnamese Assn. (past officer Mpls. chpt., mem. adv. bd. Phila. chpt.).

TRAN, JOHN KIM-SON TAN, chemical senses executive, research administrator; b. Quang-Binh, Vietnam, Oct. 4, 1945; Came to U.S., 1975.; s. Dong Tan Tran and Chieu Thi Nguyen;m. Ann Xuyen Thi, July 30, 1972; children: Joseph Quoc-Bao Tan, Michael Quoc-Binh Tan, Regina Thuy-Quyen Tan, John Quoc-An Tan. Baccalaureate degree, Nat. Exam. Bd., Saigon, Vietnam, 1966; student, U. Saigon, 1966-70; grad., Republic of Vietnam Army Acad., 1971; BBA, U. Pa., 1976-80, postgrad., 1981-83; MS in Polit. Sci., So. Ill. U., Edwardsville, 1989. Journalist (TV, radio) Saigon bur. Tokyo Broadcasting System, 1968-75; tchr. English Cao-Nguyen Jr. Mil. Acad., Pleiku, Vietnam, 1971-75; bookkeeper, budget asst. U. Pa., Phila., 1976-81, bus. admins., 1981-84; bus. mgr., treas. Blackburn Coll., Carlinville, Ill., 1984-87; treas., adminstr. Monell Chem. Senses Ctr., Phila., 1987—, also sec. bd. dirs. Contbr. articles to profl. jours. Sec. gen. Young Christian Students Movement, Saigon, 1969-71; warrant officer, 1971-73; v.p. Vietnamese Cath. Community Archdiocese Phila., 1976-82; treas., bd. trustees Blackburn Coll., Carlinville, Ill., 1984-87. Lt. Republic of Vietnam Army (South), 1973-75. Mem. Nat. Coun. Univ. Rsch. Adminstrs., Inst. Mgmt. Accts., Soc. Rsch. Adminstrs., Assn. Ind. Rsch. Insts. Roman Catholic. Home: 1346 East Ave Abington PA 19001-2445 Office: Monell Chem Senses Ctr 3500 Market St Philadelphia PA 19104-3303

TRANCHITELLA, VINCENT EDWARD, psychologist, educator; b. Phila., Apr. 4, 1938; s. Vincent Nicholas and Josephine (Punk) T.; m. Hedwig Louise Kummer, Jan. 28, 1961; children: Hedy M., Vincent J., Theresa, Louis. AB, Temple U., 1963, MA, 1967. Lic. psychologist, Pa. Dir. admissions Spring Garden Coll., Phila., 1963-65, dean admissions and registrar, 1965-70, dean student personnel services, 1970-76, v.p. and dean acad. affairs, 1976-78, v.p. and dean student affairs, 1978—; cons. psychologist Catholic Social Services, Phila., 1965-68; pvt. practice cons. psychologist, Phila., 1965—. Committeeman Democratic Party, Phila., 1960; membership chmn. John F. Kennedy election campaign, Phila., 1960; appointed mem. planning commn. Buckingham Twp., Bucks County, Pa., 1987—. Served with U.S. Army, 1957-59. Mem. Assn. Coll. Personnel Adminstrs., Am. Assn. Counseling and Devel., Nat. Assn. Student Personnel Adminstrs., Nat. Assn. Inter-Collegiate Athletics (dist. 19 eligiblity chmn. 1982-84), Pa. Assn. Coll. Personnel Adminstrs., Pa. Assn. Student Personnel Adminstrs., Pa. Counseling Assn., Pa. Psychol. Assn. Republican. Roman Catholic. Home: 4127 Dunlin Ct Waldorf MD 20603-4648 Office: Spring Garden Coll 7500 Germantown Ave Philadelphia PA 19119-1651

TRAPP, PETER JARL RUDOLF, investment banker, farm owner; b. Darlington, Eng., Oct. 5, 1945; came to U.S., 1971; s. Jarl Rudolph and Olive Lindsay (Fairley) T.; m. Regina Antoinette Thomas, Sept. 6, 1969 (div. Dec. 1986); children: Sophia Antoinette, Alexander Rudolf, Olivia Henrietta Elizabeth. Mi Lic, Fribourg U., Switzerland, 1971; MBA, Columbia U., 1973. Vice pres. First Boston Corp., N.Y.C., 1973-78; v.p. Goldman Sachs & Co., N.Y.C., 1978-81; mng. dir. Dean Witter Reynolds Inc., N.Y.C., 1982-84; mng. dir., exec. officer Marine Midland Bank N.A., N.Y.C., 1985-88; bd. dirs. Marine Midland Securities Inc., N.Y.C., Marine Midland Capital Markets Ltd., London, Marine Midland Overseas Corp., N.Y.C.; sr. v.p. Gerard Klauer Mattison & Co., N.Y.C. Elder Presbyn. Ch. Pine Plains, N.Y. Cadet sgt. Swedish Army, 1968-69. Mem. The Leash and Doubles Club N.Y., Annabel's (London), Royal Windermere Yacht, Kandahar and Brit. Ski Clubs (Eng.), Coral Beach (Bermuda). Home: Bean Creek Farm Box 256 Pine Plains NY 12567 Office: 270 Madison Ave New York NY 10016-0601

TRASHER, VIRGINIA SNOW, mathematics educator; b. Ithaca, N.Y., Aug. 21, 1936; d. Richard Lamont and Winnifred (Palmer) Snow; m. Donald Watson Trasher, June 20, 1959; children: Laura, Diane, Steven, James. BA, Houghton Coll., 1958; MA, U. Buffalo, 1960. Asst. prof. SUNY, Buffalo, 1960-64; lectr. dept. math. SUNY, Geneseo, 1978—. Mem. York Cen. Sch. Bd., Retsof, N.Y., 1978-87, pres., 1979-82; mem. Livingston-Wyoming-Stueben Bd. Coop. Ednl. Svcs., Mt. Morris, N.Y., 1991—. Mem. Nat. Coun. Tchrs. Math., Assn. Math. Tchrs. N.Y. State, Math. Assn. Am., Sigma Xi, Pi Mu Epsilon. Republican. Baptist. Home: 183 Main St Leicester NY 14481-9761 Office: Dept Math SUNY Geneseo Geneseo NY 14454

TRASK, BETTY M., journalist; b. Laconia, N.H., Jan. 28, 1928; d. James Edwin and Clemency (Anstey) Burbank; m. Allison Keith Trask, June 28, 1947; children: Frank Edwin, Michael Thomas, Rory Scott, Allison Keith Jr. Women's editor Laconia Evening Citizen, 1966-70, county editor, 1970-89, life style editor, 1989—, travel columnist, 1981—; mem. adv. bd. N.H. Vocat.-Tech. Coll., Laconia, 1972-78; treas. N.H. Commn. on Status of Women, Concord, 1974-76; mem. state adv. bd. N.H. Vocat.-Tech. Coll. and Inst., Concord, 1981-84. Bd. dirs. Laconia Salvation Army, 1973-89, aux. 1984-90, Belknap Easter Seals, 1980-92; trustee Gilford Village Knolls, Inc., N.H., 1985-90; mem. task force on alcohol and drug abuse N.H. Gov.'s Commn. on Criminal Adminstrn. and Juvenile Delinquency, 1969-71; former mem. adv. bd. Lakes Region YMCA, Belknap County Unit Am. Cancer Soc., Lake Region Community Concert Assn., Child and Family Svcs., N.H. Orgn. for Drug Abuse Control, Belknap County Easter Seals, 1980-92. Recipient Recognition award Laconia Lions Club, 1977, Am. Legion Aux. (Recognition award), VFW Aux., Lakes Region Citizenship award N.H. Vocat. Tech. Coll., 1978. Mem. Laconia Altrusa Club (past pres., dist. pub. rels. chmn.), Laconia Bus. and Profl. Women's Club (past pres., dist. dir.), Sigma Delta Chi. Republican. Avocations: travel, photography. Home: 120 Liberty Hill Rd Gilford NH 03246 Office: PO Box 40 171 Fair St Laconia NH 03247

TRAUB, RICHARD KENNETH, lawyer; b. Lakewood, N.J., Aug. 4, 1950; s. Harold W. and Muriel N. (Zurlin) T.; m. Barbara Lynn Wright, July 9, 1972; children: Russell S., Melissa L. BBA, U. Miami, Coral Gables, Fla., 1972, JD cum laude, 1975. Bar: Fla. 1975, N.Y. 1976, N.J. 1976, U.S. Dist. Ct. N.J. 1976, U.S. Supreme Ct. 1979, U.S. Dist. Ct. (ea. & so. dists.) N.Y. 1981. Ptnr. Wilson, Elser, Moskowitz, Edelman & Dicker, N.Y.C., 1975—; lectr. Inst. for Internat Rsch., Washington, 1988, Engring. News Record Constrn. Claims Conf., 1991. Author: Legal and Professional Aspects of Construction Management, 1990; contbr. articles to profl. jours. Bd. dirs. Pop Warner Football Assn., Holmdel, N.J., 1989—. Mem. ABA (forum com. on constrn. industry 1989, tort and ins. practice sect. 1985—, computer litigation sect.), N.Y. State Bar Assn., N.J. Bar Assn., Fla. Bar Assn. Office: Wilson Elser Moskowitz Edelman & Dicker 150 E 42d St New York NY 10017-5639

TRAUB, ROBERT S., medical entomologist; b. N.Y.C., Oct. 26, 1916; s. Dezso S. and Jeannette (Moses) T.; m. Renée Charlotte Gluck, Aug. 18, 1939; children: Jeannette Roberta (dec.), Roger Dennis. BS, CCNY, 1938; MS, Cornell U., 1939; PhD, U. Ill., 1947. Commd. 1st lt. U.S. Army, 1942, advanced through grades to col.; entomologist U.S. Army and U.S. Typhus Commn., India, Burma, 1943-45; chief dept. entomology and parasitology Walter Reed Army Med. Ctr., Washington, 1945-55; field dir. U.S. Army Med. Rsch. Teams, Malaya, Korea, Borneo, 1948-53; commanding officer U.S. Army Med. Rsch. Unit, Kuala Lumpur, Malaya, 1955-59; interim chief preventive medicine br. Army Med. R&D Command, Washington, 1959-62; ret. U.S. Army, 1962; field dir. U. Md. Med. Rsch. Teams, Ethiopia, New Guinea, Pakistan, 1962-83; from prof. to prof. emeritus U. Md. Sch. Medicine, Balt., 1962—; mem. Armed Forces Epidemiological Bd. Commns. on Immunization, Hemorrhagic Fever and Rickettsial Diseases, Washington, 1948-73; cons. WHO, NIH, U.S. Army and Naval Med. Rsch. Units and R&D Commands, Washington and overseas, 1950—. Contbr. 160 tech. articles to profl. jours. Decorated Bronze Star, Army Commendation medal; recipient U.S.A. Typhus Commn. medal, Townsend Harris medal CCNY, 1990. Fellow Royal Soc. Tropical Medicine and Hygiene, Royal Entomol. Soc., Am. Soc. Tropical Medicine and Hygiene (Hoogstraal medal 1989), Washington Acad. Scis., Phi Beta Kappa, Sigma Xi. Home: 5702 Bradley Blvd Bethesda MD 20814-1026

TRAUM, RICHARD SCOT, entertainment company executive; b. N.Y.C., Oct. 7, 1940; s. Julius Artin and Silvia Marion (Fischel) T.; m. Deborah Joan Johnston, Jan. 4, 1978; 1 child, Alexandra Ariel. BS, NYU, 1967. Fin. adminstr. bus. affairs NBC TV Network, N.Y.C., 1974-75; gen. program exec. NBC Entertainment, N.Y.C., 1975-77, dir. late night programs, 1977-80; producer N.Y.C., 1980-82; dir. fin. control and adminstrn. NBC Enterprises, N.Y.C., 1982-83, dir. program devel. and prodn., 1983-85; producer N.Y.C. and L.A., 1985-89; v.p. fin. planning Radio City Music Hall Prodns., N.Y.C., 1989-90, sr. v.p., fin., 1990—. Recipient Emmy award NATAS, 1985, Cine Golden Eagle award Coun. on Northeatrical Events, Washington, 1985, Am. Spirit Honor medal Citizen's Com. for the Army, Navy, and Air Force, 1961. Office: Radio City Music Hall Prodns 1260 Ave Of The Americas New York NY 10020-1797

TRAVER, ROBERT WILLIAM, SR., management consultant, author, lecturer, engineer; b. Waterbury, Conn., Oct. 13, 1930; s. Alfred Matthew Sr. and Dorothy Viola (Thomson) T.; m. Eleanor Jean Finnemore (div. Feb. 1963); children: Robert William Jr., Jeffrey Matthew, Elizabeth; m. Valarie Jane Mason. B in Mech. Engring., Clarkson U., 1955; MBA, U. Mass., 1963. Registered profl. engr., N.Y. Quality control engr. Gen. Electric Co., Pittsfield, Mass., 1955-62; mgr. reliability and quality assurance Tansitor Electronics, Inc., Bennington, Vt., 1962-65; sr. cons. Rath & Strong, Inc., Lexington, Mass., 1965-70; regional mgr. TAC, Inc., Albany, N.Y., 1970-72; dist. mgr. IDS, Inc., Albany, 1972-81; v.p. Reddy, Traver & Woods, Inc., Lexington, 1981—; participant in ednl. exch. with Peoples Republic of China, 1985, Australia and New Zealand, 1986. Author: Industrial Problem Solving--Isolating The Key Variables; contbr. articles to profl. jours. Mem. Five Rivers Ltd., Delmar, N.Y., 1981—; chmn. lake com. Crooked Lake Improvement Assn., Averill Park, N.Y., 1973-74; v.p. Sand Lake (N.Y.) Businessmen's Assn., 1974-76. With U.S. Army, 1950. Fellow Am. Soc. for Quality Control; mem. Inst. Mgmt. Cons., Trout Unltd. Republican. Congregationalist. Home: Twin Lions on Crooked Lake Averill Park NY 12018 Office: Reddy Traver & Woods 2408 Massachusetts Ave Lexington MA 02173

TRAVERS, SCOTT ANDREW, numismatist; b. N.Y.C., Nov. 12, 1961; s. Harvey Charles and Barbara Joan (Goldman) T. BA in Politics, Brandeis U., 1983. Pres. Scott Travers Rare Coin Galleries, Inc., N.Y.C., 1979—; authenticator, grader Numismatic Guaranty Corp., 1987-90, grading standards cons., 1987—; bd. govs. Adelphi U. Inst. Numismatic and Philatelic Studies, 1980-86; state advisor U.S. Congl. Adv. Bd., 1983—; lectr. and mem. bd. overseers Numismatic Inst. of N.Am.; internat. writing competition coord. Numismatic Literary Guild; interviewed on various radio and TV programs. Author: The Coin Collector's Survival Manual, 1984 (Book of Yr.), 2d edit., 1988 (Investment and Consumer Protection award), Rare Coin Investment Strategy (Book of Yr.), The Investor's Guide to Coin Trading, 1989 (Investment Book Yr.), Travers' Rare Coin Investment Strategy, 1990, One Minute Coin Expert, 1991, The Guide to U.S. Coin Values, 1992; contbg. editor COINage mag.; author: (intro.) How to Grade U.S. Coins; author: (chpt.) Comprehensive U.S. Silver Dollar Encyclopedia; video host: The Future of The Rare Coin Marketplace; contbr. articles to profl. jours. Liquidator Bd. Gold Coins, El Salvador, 1989. Mem. Am. Numismatic Assn. (conv. speaker, consumer protection and edn. coms., Outstanding Young Numismatist, Adult Advisor of the Yr., Ray Byrne Lit. award), Numismatic Lit. Guild, Am. Israel Numismatic Assn., Cen. State Numismatic Soc., Mich. State Numismatic Soc., New Eng. Numismatic Assn., Fla. United Numismatists, Numismatics Internat., Internat. Assn. Fin. Planning, Coin Bullion Dealer Accreditation Program. Office: FDR Box 1711 New York NY 10150

TRAVERSE, ALFRED, educator, clergyman; b. Port Hill, P.E.I., Can., Sept. 7, 1925; s. Alfred Freeman and Pearle (Akerley) T.; m. Elizabeth Jane Insley, June 30, 1951; children: Paul, Martha, John, Celia. S.B., Harvard U., 1946, A.M., 1948, Ph.D., 1951; cert. in Botany, Kings Coll., Cambridge, Eng., 1947; M.Div., Episcopal Theol. Sem. S.W., 1965. Teaching fellow Harvard U., 1947-51; coal technologist U.S. Bur. Mines, Grand Forks, N.D., 1951-55; head Fuels Microscopy Lab., Denver, 1955; palynologist Shell Devel. Co., Houston, 1955-62; cons. palynologist Austin, Tex., 1962-65; asst. prof. geology U. Tex., Austin, 1965-66; assoc. prof. geology and biology Pa. State U., University Park, 1966-70; prof. palynology Pa. State U., 1970—; ordained to ministry Episcopal Ch., 1965; asst. priest St. Matthew's Ch., Austin, 1965-66, St. Paul's Ch., Philipsburg, Pa., 1966-75, Christuskirche (Old Cath.), Zurich, Switzerland, 1980-81; vicar St. John's Ch., Huntingdon, Pa., 1975-80; adj. prof. geobiology Juniata Coll., 1977—; guest prof. Geol. Inst., Swiss Fed. Tech. Inst., Zurich, 1980-81; councillor, Internat. Commn. Palynology, 1973-77, 80—, pres., 1977-80, archivist/historian, 1986—; on-bd. scientist Glomar Challenger, 1975; Fulbright prof. Senckenberg Rsch. Inst., Frankfurt, 1992. Author: Paleopalynology, 1988; mem. editorial bd. Catalog Fossil Spores and Pollen, 1957-66, editor-in-chief, 1966-76; palynological editor Palaeontographica, 1989—. Recipient Best Paper award Am. Assn. Stratigraphic Palynologists, 1973, Internat. prize Palaeobot. Soc. India, 1990-91; NSF rsch. grantee, 1966-87. Fellow Geol. Soc. Am., AAAS; mem. Bot. Soc. Am. (sec.-treas. paleobot. sect. 1957-60, chmn. sect. 1960-61), Internat. Assn. Plant Taxonomists (sec. com. fossil plants 1969—), Am. Assn. Stratigraphic Palynologists (sec.-treas. 1967-70, pres. 1970-71, chmn. type collections com. 1989-91). Club: Harvard of Cen. Pa. (mem. schs. com. 1966-77). Home: RR 2 Box 390 Huntingdon PA 16652-9209 Office: 435 Deike Bldg University Park PA 16802

TRAWICK, LAVERGNE, college administrator; b. Washington, Mar. 25, 1947; d. Lonnie Harper and Louise LaVergne (Hopson) T. BA in Latin Am. Area Studies, Barnard Coll., 1969; MA in Student Pers. Higher Edn., Columbia U., 1972, PhD in Ednl. Psychology, 1990. Spl. asst. to dir. Regional Opportunity Ctr. Ednl. and Vocat. Program, N.Y.C., 1969-71; counselor Hostos Community Coll., CUNY, Bronx, 1971-72; counselor LaGuardia Community Coll., CUNY, Long Island City, 1972-78, asst. to dean students, 1978—. Mem. Bd. Christian Social Concern, Abyssinian Bapt. Ch., N.Y.C., 1986—, vice-chairperson, 1990-91. Minority Group scholar Tchrs. Coll., Columbia U., N.Y.C., 1971-72, 80-81, Dissertation Yr. fellow Spencer Found., Princeton, 1988-89. Mem. AACD, Nat. Coun. on Black Am. Affairs (bd. dir. N.E. region 1986—, assoc. editor newsletter 1990—), Am. Ednl. Rsch. Assn., Park West Village Tenants Assn.

TRAWINSKI, DAVID LEE, aerospace engineer; b. Balt., Mar. 25, 1959; s. Leon Stanislaus and Mildred (Jarowcsyk) T.; m. Janice Diane Conigliaro, June 15, 1960. BS in Chemistry, Towson State U., 1982; M in Engring. Sci., Loyola Coll., Balt., 1985, exec. MBA fellow, 1990. Various engring. positions Martin Marietta, Balt., 1981-85, corp. tech. ops. intern, 1985-86, sr. group engr., 1986-87, mgr. material and process engrs., 1987—. Contbr. articles to profl. jours. Mem. AIAA, ASTM, Soc. Advanced Materials and Process Engrs. (chmn. Balt., Washington chpt. 1990—, vice chair 1989-90, tres. 1988-89, sec. 1987-88), Materials Engrs. Assocs. (pres. 1990—), Group Nine Videography (pres. 1990—). Republican. Roman Catholic. Home: 718 Fox Bow Dr Bel Air MD 21014-5210 Office: Martin Marietta 103 Chesapeake Pk Pl Bel Air MD 21014

TREACY, JAMES JOSEPH, JR., advertising executive; b. N.Y.C., Feb. 16, 1958; s. James Joseph Sr. and Catherine Lorraine (Campbell) T.; Nancy Barnes, May 6, 1989. BBA in Acctg., Siena Coll., 1980; MBA in Fin., St. John's U., Jamaica, N.Y., 1982. Internat. fin. analyst Texaco, Inc., Harrison, N.Y., 1981-84; mgr. corp. cash planning The Ogilvy Group, INc., N.Y.C., 1984-85, dir. fin. analysis and cash planning, 1985-86; v.p. The Ogilvy Group, Inc., N.Y.C., 1986-89; sr. v.p., chief fin. officer Euramerica, Inc. subs. Ogilvy Co., N.Y.C., 1988-89, also bd. dirs.; N. Am. treas., sr. v.p. WPP Group USA, Inc., N.Y.C., 1989—. Mem. editorial adv. bd. Business International Money Report, 1987-89. Corp. spokesman, liaison N.Y. Spl. Olym;ics, 1986—. Mem. N.Y. Corp. Treasury Assn. (vice chmn. 1985—), Omicron Delta Epsilon. Roman Catholic. Home: 117 Roosevelt Pl Palisades Park NJ 07650-1119 Office: WPP Group PLC Ltd 420 Lexington Ave New York NY 10170-0002

TREADWELL, CARLENE ROLLINS, counselor; b. Lincoln, Maine, Dec. 24, 1955; d. Carl Marvin and Yvonne (Wood) Rollins; m. Brian Earl Treadwell, Sept. 26, 1978; children: Erin Estelle, Jacob Brian. BS, U. Maine, 1978, MEd, 1988, CAS, 1991. Tchr. Orono (Maine) High Sch., 1978-79, Lee (Maine) Acad., 1979-85, Guy E. Rowe Sch., Norway, Maine, 1985-88; guidance counselor Oxford Hills Jr. High Sch., South Paris, Maine, 1988—. Mem. Maine Assn. Counselors in Group Work, Nat. Assn. Counseling and Devel., Am. Assn. Counseling and Devel., Maine Assn. Counseling and Devel., Delta Kappa Gamma (1st v.p. Zeta chpt. 1983—), Alpha Zeta. Home: 10 Boulder Ave South Paris ME 04281-1202 Office: Oxford Hills Jr High 100 Pine St South Paris ME 04281-1599

TREADWELL, KENNETH MYRON, mechanical engineer, consultant; b. Cleve., May 5, 1923; s. Herbert Eugene and Flora Mae Belle (Robinson) T.; m. Sally Ann Skeel, Aug. 8, 1951; 1 child, Karen Ann. BS, U.S. Naval Acad., 1948, BSME, 1954; MSME, MIT, 1955. Advanced through grades to lt. USN, 1942-54; sr. engr. Westinghouse (Bettis Lab.), West Mifflin, Pa., 1955-59, mgr. reactor design, 1959-64, mgr. reactor analysis, 1964-68, mgr. reactor engring., 1968-72, mgr. fuel element devel., 1972-77, mgr. fuel element devel. and statistics, 1977-82; pres. Treadwell Cons., Pitts., 1983—; sr. cons. SMC-O'Donnell Assoc., Pitts., 1986—. Inventor reactor safety system, 1975. Mem. Whitehall Pa. Zoning Hearing Bd., Pitts., 1985-90. Mem. ASME, South Hills Country Club, Sigma Xi. Home and Office: 4983 Parkvue Dr Pittsburgh PA 15236-2053

TREAT, ASHER EUGENE, retired biology educator; b. Antigo, Wis., July 6, 1907; s. Asher Robbins and Pearl Eugenia (Barnes) T.; m. Joy Gilder, Oct. 7, 1939 (dec. Sept. 1987); l child, Bryan G. PhD, Columbia U., 194l. Fellow dept. biology CUNY, 1930-31, tutor, 1931-41, instr., 1941-48, asst. prof., 1948-57, assoc. prof., 1957-64, prof., 1964-66, prof. emeritus, 1966—; rsch. assoc. Am. Mus. Natural History, N.Y.C., 1970-83. Author: Mites of Moths and Butterflies, 1975. With USAAF, 1942-46. Fellow AAAS; mem. ACLU, Entomol. Soc. Am., Acarological Soc. Am., N.Y. Entomol. Soc. Democrat. Home: Jerusalem Rd PO Box 393 Tyringham MA 01264-0393

TRECCAGNOLI, PHILIP DAVID, finance company executive; b. Bklyn., June 11, 1958; s. Alphonse and Theresa (Miglio) T.; m. Nancy Lee Olson, Oct. 25, 1986; children: Diana, Daniel. BS in Acctg., Manhattan Coll., 1980; MBA in Acctg., Adelphi U., 1986. Jr. acct. Merrill Lynch, Inc., N.Y.C., 1980; estimating specialist Fairchild Republic Co., Farmingdale, N.Y., 1980-82, sr. acct., 1982-85; controller Ames Indsl. Corp., Bohemia, N.Y., 1985; cost acctg. mgr. Marconi Cir. Tech., Inc., Farmingdale, 1985-89, contracts mgr., 1989-90; mgr. govt. contract svcs. Ernst & Young, Melville, N.Y., 1990—; sr. cons. T.A. Carlson and Co., Bohemia, N.Y., 1991—; v.p. TRP Assocs., Mt. Sinai, N.Y., 1989—. Chmn., Polit. Action Com., Farmingdale, 1979-82; fund raiser United Way, Farmingdale, 1983. Mem. Nat. Contract Mgmt. Assn. (workshop speaker presentation 1990), L.I. Forum Tech., Assn. Govt. Accts., Performance Mgmt. Assn., Amateur Softball Assn. (v.p., dep. commr. L.I. chpt. 1981—), Pen & Sword Honor Soc. Republican. Roman Catholic. Home: 3 Charlottsville Ct Coram NY 11727-1608 Office: Ernst & Young 395 Expressway Dr N Melville NY 11747

TRECKER, STAN MATTHEW, college president; b. Manning, Iowa, July 15, 1944; s. Joseph and Anetha (Graves) T.; m. Anne M. Rischberger, June 19, 1981; children: Dana Shawn, Heather Kindon, Amanda. BS, Miami U., Oxford, Ohio, 1966; MBA, Ind. U., 1968; MFA, Art Inst. Chgo., 1978. Asst. v.p. Continental Bank, Chgo., 1968-74; bus. mgr., curator Moming Dance and Art Ctr., Chgo., 1976-80; dir. Photog. Resource Ctr., Boston, 1980-90; pres. Art Inst. Boston, 1991—; cons. Horizons Camp for Teen Agers, Amherst, Mass., 1985. Cons., panelist Nat. Endowment for the Arts, Washington, 1981-90, Mass. Coun. on the Arts & Humanities, Boston, 1983—; adv. com. Art Inst. Boston, 1988. Sgt. U.S. Army, 1969-71. Recipient Grant Ill. Arts Coun., Chgo., 1979, The Artist Found., Boston, 1983; named finalist for Fellowship, The Artist Found., Boston, 1981. Mem. Soc. for Photog. Edn. (bd. dirs. 1983-87), Coll. Art Assn. Home: 6 Parkway Rd # 3 Brookline MA 02146-5461 Office: Art Inst Boston Office Pres 700 Beacon St Boston MA 02215-2598

TREFOUSSE, HANS LOUIS, history educator; b. Frankfurt, Ger., Dec. 18, 1921; came to U.S. 1936; s. George and Elizabeth (Albersheim) T.; m. Rashelle Friedlander, Jan. 26, 1947; 1 child, Roger Philip. BA, CCNY, 1942; MA, Columbia U., 1947, PhD, 1950. Instr. Adelphi Coll., Garden City, N.Y., 1949-50; from instr. to disting. prof. Bklyn. Coll., 1950—; assoc. prof. to disting. prof. history program Grad. Ctr., CUNY, 1961—. author: Andrew Johnson, 1989, Carl Schurz, 1982, Impeachment of a President, 1975, The Radical Republicans, 1969; editor: Twayne's Statesmen and Leaders of the World, 1967-77. Pvt. to lt. col. AUS, 1942-45, USAR, ret. Named Disting. Tchr. Bklyn. Coll., 1960; Guggenheim fellow, 1977; ACLS grantee, 1981. Mem. Am. Hist. Assn., Soc. Am. Historians, Orgn. Am. Historians, So. Hist. Assn. Democrat. Jewish. Home: 22 Shore Acres Rd Staten Island NY 10305-3912 Office: Dept History Bklyn Coll Brooklyn NY 11210

TREFTS, BYRON LEE, paper company executive; b. St. Louis, Aug. 15, 1938; s. Byron Gilbert Trefts and Florence (Lavelle) Gleason; m. Joyce Ellen Grigsby, June 29, 1963; children: Stacey Lee, Christopher Bradley. Student, Wash. U., St. Louis, 1957-59; BS, Butler U., 1961; postgrad., Ind. U., 1963-66; TEP, Dartmouth U., 1985. Bus. rep. Teamsters Union Local #135, Indpls., 1961-69; mgr. labor rels. Champion Internat. Corp., Hamilton, Ohio,

1969-79; dir. corp. labor rels. Champion Internat. Corp., Stamford, Conn., 1979-84; dir. corp. employee rels. Champion Internat. Corp., Stamford, 1984-86, v.p. corp. employee rels., 1986—; guest lectr. Cornell U. Sch. of Indsl. and Labor Rels., Ithaca, N.Y., 1980, N.C. State U., Raleigh, 1984, Butler U., Indpls., 1978. Polit. dir. Teamsters Union Local #135, 1964-68. With U.S. Army, 1956-57. Mem. Am. Paper Inst. (chmn. employee rels. com. 1988-89, vice-chair 1987-88, chmn. labor rels. com., 1987-88), Conn. Golf Club (chair membership com. 1990—, bd. govs. 1989—). Republican. Roman Catholic. Home: 38 Wells Hill Rd Weston CT 06883-2624 Office: Champion Internat Corp One Champion Pla Stamford CT 06921

TREFZ, LINDA MARIE, writer, editor video arts; b. Bridgeport, Conn., Mar. 13, 1959; d. Ernest Christian and Joan Marie (Frisk) T. BS in Mag. Journalism, Syracuse U., 1981. Editorial asst. McCall's Mag., McCall's Working Mother Mag., N.Y.C., 1979; asst. editor Millimeter Mag., N.Y.C., 1981-83; free-lance writer Millimeter, Back Stage, Am. Cinematographer, Cyber Edge Jour., others, 1983—. Mem. Soc. Profl. Journalists, Internat. Interactive Communications Soc., Internat. TV Assn., Artists Using Sci. & Tech.

TREGENZA, NORMAN HUGHSON, investment banker; b. Morristown, N.J., Feb. 1, 1937; s. Norman J. and Marion Esther (Hughson) T.; B.A., St. Lawrence U., 1959; M.B.A., N.Y. U., 1963; m. Alyce Virginia Bruene, Aug. 27, 1966; children—Norman Arthur, Suzanne Carol. Sr. investment officer Tchrs. Ins. & Annuity Assn., N.Y.C., 1960-71; sr. v.p. Republic Funding Corp., N.Y.C., 1971-82; pres. Convent Capital Corp., 1982—; dir. Patrick Media Group, Inc., N.Y.C.; chmn. Tellus, Inc., N.Y.C. Chmn. stewardship com. Presbyn. Ch., Morristown, N.J., 1978, ruling elder, 1979, pres. bd. trustees, 1982; trustee St. Lawrence U., Canton, N.Y., Gill/St. Bernards Sch. (hon.), The Morris Mus., Morristown, N.J. Mem. St. Lawrence U. Alumni Assn. N.J. (pres. 1970-72). Club: Baltusrol Golf. Home and Office: West Shore Dr Silver Lake NH 03875

TREHER, ELIZABETH NOAH, human resources executive, consultant; b. St. Louis, Apr. 5, 1947; d. Joseph William and Rita Jane Monteath (Roessel) Noah; m. Jack Nolan Treher, June 6, 1981. BA, Washington U., St. Louis, 1969, MA, 1971, PhD, 1976. Cert. tchr., Mo. Rsch. asst. Columbia Sch. Medicine, N.Y.C., 1967; tchr. Villa Duchesne Sch., St. Louis, 1971; Nat. Cancer Inst. postdoctoral fellow U. So. Calif., L.A., 1976-78; staff mem. Los Alamos (N.Mex.) Nat. Lab., 1978-83; rsch. group leader E. R. Squibb & Sons, New Brunswick, N.J., 1983-87; mgr. edn. and tng. E. R. Squibb & Sons, Princeton, N.J., 1987; dir. career and mgmt. devel. E. R. Squibb & Sons, Skillman, N.J., 1988-90; dir., Ctr. for Sci. Edn. Bristol-Myers Squibb, Princeton, N.J., 1990-91; v.p. Paris en Cuisine, Inc., 1983—; v.p. edn. and tng. The Learning Curve, Inc., Sergeantsville, N.J., 1991—; cons. SmithKline Beecham, Oticon, Ortho Diagnostics, Bristol-Myers Squibb, FMC Corp. and others; co-founder The Learning Curve Found., 1991; invited speaker Am. Chem. Soc., Soc. Nuclear Medicine, Women in Energy. Contbr. numerous articles to profl. jours.; patentee in radiopharmaceutical chemistry field. Mem. ASTD, Am. Chem. Soc., Assn. Psychol. Type, Princeton Area C. of C. (co-chair edn. com. 1990, 91). Office: The Learning Curve Inc Rt 523 & 604 Sergeantsville NJ 08557

TREICHLER, FRANCIS NORMAN, automotive engineer, consultant; b. Lockport, N.Y., June 11, 1928; s. John Clark and Eunice Olive (Longmate) T.; m. Ruth Keith Williams, July 15, 1950; children: David D., Barbara F. Treichler Huber, Scott E., Peter C. Student, Roosevelt Aviation Sch., Mineola, N.Y., 1947-48. Seaman UN, Brethren Svc. Commn., Norfolk, Va., 1946-47; aircraft mechanic Shawnee Flying Svc., North Tonawanda, N.Y., 1948-50; automobile mechanic D&E Motors Inc., Williamsville, N.Y., 1949-51, 55-61; automotive svc. mgr. Kirtland Motors, Inc., Lockport, 1961-62; dist. svc. engr. Ford Motor Co., Buffalo, 1962-90; ind. cons. Circle T, Tonawanda, N.Y., 1990—; tchr. automobile mechanics Buffalo Pub. Schs., 1957-62; mem. curriculum adv. bd. N.Y. Coll. Vocat. Studies, Alfred, 1980—. Co-author: Automotive Computer Systems and Circuits, 1988, Light and Heavy Truck Computer Systems and Circuit, 1989. Sgt. USAF, 1951-55. Home: 4005 Crescent Dr North Tonawanda NY 14120-1364

TREICHLER, RACHEL, reinsurance broker; b. Independence, Iowa, June 3, 1951; d. William Edmund and Martha (Rittenhouse) T. BA, Harvard U., 1973; JD, U. Tex., 1981. Bar: N.Y. 1982, U.S. Dist. Ct. (so. and ea. dists.) N.Y. 1982. Assoc. LeBoeuf, Lamb et al., N.Y.C., 1981-87, Debevoise & Plimpton, N.Y.C., 1987-89; pres. Manhattan Intermediaries, Inc., 1989—. Mem. Assn. of Bar City of N.Y. Home: 45 John St Ste 906 New York NY 10038 Office: 45 John St Ste 906 45 John St New York NY 10038-3706

TREICHLER, RAY, agricultural chemist; b. Rock Island, Ill., Sept. 10, 1907; s. Wallace and Pearl (Cushman) T.; B.S., M.S., Pa. State U., 1929; Ph.D., U. Ill., 1939; m. Kathryn Amelia Blakeley, June 13, 1942. Asst. state chemist Tex. Agrl. Expt. Sta., Tex. A&M Coll., College Station, 1929-40; chief, chemistry and biochemistry research Fish & Wildlife Service Labs., U.S. Dept. Interior, Laurel, Md., 1941-44; chief, biol. activities Office of Quartermaster Gen., U.S. Army, Washington, 1945-53; chief, toxic agents br. Rand D. Command, Army Chem. Center, Md., 1953-56, asst. to dir. med. research Chem. Warfare Labs., 1956-58; research adminstr. USAF, Bolling Field, Washington, 1958-68; tech. services mgr. H.D. Hudson Mfg. Co., Washington, 1968—. Fellow N.Y. Acad. Scis.; mem. Am. Chem. Soc., Entomol. Soc. Am., Am. Soc. Tropical Medicine and Hygiene, Am. Mosquito Assn., Am. Soc. Agrl. Engrs., ASTM, Sigma Xi, Gamma Sigma Delta. Club: Masons. Developed pesticide application equipment, prevention deterioration, chemistry and formulations pesticides, pesticide dissemination systems. Contbr. articles on vitamins, basal energy and endogenous nitrogen metabolism, nutrition, composition fishery products, toxic compounds, prevention material deterioration. Home: 4740 Connecticut Ave NW Washington DC 20008-5632 Office: HD Hudson Mfg Co 1130 17th St NW Ste 500 Washington DC 20036-4604

TREIMAN, SAM BARD, physics educator; b. Chgo., May 27, 1925; s. Abraham and Sarah (Bard) T.; m. Joan Little, Dec. 27, 1952; children—Rebecca, Katherine, Thomas. Student, Northwestern U., 1942-44; S.B., U. Chgo., 1948, S.M., 1949, Ph.D., 1952. Mem. faculty Princeton U., 1952—, instr., 1952-54, asst. prof., 1954-58, assoc. prof., 1958-63, prof. physics, 1963—, Eugene Higgins prof., 1976—, chmn. dept., 1981-87, chmn. univ. rsch. bd., 1988—. Author: (with M. Grossjean) Formal Scattering Theory, 1960, (with R. Jackiw and D.J. Gross) Current Algebra and Its Applications, 1972; Contbr. articles to profl. jours. Served with USNR, 1944-46. Recipient Oersted medal Am. Assn. Physics Tchrs. Mem. NAS, Am. Phys. Soc., Am. Acad. Arts and Scis. Home: 60 Mccosh Cir Princeton NJ 08540-5627

TREIRAT, EDUARD, marine engineer; b. Estonia, May 25, 1912; came to U.S., 1949, naturalized, 1955; marine engring. diploma Marine Coll. Tallinn (Estonia), 1942; student Baltic U., Hamburg, Germany, 1946-47; BS in Engring., Fairleigh Dickinson U., 1957; postgrad. Stevens Inst. Tech., 1957-59; m. Jenny Eugenia Hendriksson, Dec. 29, 1988. Asst. mgr. planning dept. Revaler Werft Tallinn Estonia, 1942-44; lectr. Nav. and Marine Engrs. Sch., Flensburg, Ger., 1946-49; toolmaker Bergenfield Devel. Co., Dumont, N.J., 1950-52; design engr. Star Kimble Electric Co., Bloomfield, N.J., 1952-56; design engr. Walter Kidde & Co., Belleville, N.J., 1956-61, engring. supr., 1961-71, chief design engr., 1971-76; sr. staff engr. advanced products devel. Valcor Engring. Corp., Springfield, N.J., 1976-83; dir. Gen. Valve Co., East Hanover, N.J.; also cons. Served with Estonian Army, 1931-32. Decorated Sharpshooters medal. Mem. Phi Omega Epsilon. Lutheran. Club: EÜS. Patentee in field; also articles. Office: 2 Lawrence Rd Springfield NJ 07081

TREISNER, GEORGE HENRY, JR., vocational educator, electrical constractor; b. N.Y.C., Feb. 26, 1936; s. George H. and Florence (Reade) T.; m. Darlene M. Merkle, Apr. 20, 1974; children: George H. III, Dorothy J., Rolf P. Student, Lehigh U., 1953-54, Am. Inst. Banking, 1954-62, Temple U., 1981-89, Northampton County Area Coll., 1970-72. Lic. elec. constrn. instr., Pa. Various positions Union Bank & Trust Co., Bethlehem, Pa., 1954-62; sales rep., gen. agt. Luth. Brotherhood Life Ins. Soc., Bethlehem, 1962-70; v.p. sales Mgmt. Assocs., Bethlehem, 1970-72; sales rep. Olivetti Corp. Am., Allentown, Pa., 1972-74, Pa. Water Works Co., Horsham, 1974-76; elec. contr. Treisner Elec., Bethlehem, 1972-81; tchr. Bethlehem Area Vocat. Tech. Sch., 1981—; coord., trainer Assoc. Bldg. Contrs. Apprenticeship, 1990—; adj. prof. elec. constrn. Northampton County Area Community Coll., 1984-87; chmn. spl. svcs. PSEA, Harrisburg, Pa., 1986—. Pres. Northampton City Coun. Educators, Easton, Pa., 1991; bible tchr., youth advisor Holy Cross Evang. Luth. Ch., Bethlehem, 1974—. Mem. Vocat. Indsl. Club Am., Nat. Assn. Vocat. Edn. Spl. Needs Pers., Pa. Assn. Vocat. Edn. Spl. Needs Pers., Am. Vocat. Assn., Pa. State Edn. Assn. (chmn. spl. svcs. 1986—), Pa. Vocat. Assn. (Vocat. Tchr. of the Yr. 1991, v.p. 1991), Bethlehem Area Vocat. Tech. Sch. Profl. Assn. (past v.p., treas., chief negotiator, pres. 1991—), Fraternal Ins. Counselors (past pres.). Democrat. Home: 236 E Ettwein St Bethlehem PA 18018-4137 Office: Bethlehem Area Vocat Tech 3300 Chester Ave Bethlehem PA 18017-2895

TREISTMAN, STEVEN N., neurobiologist, pharmacology educator; b. N.Y.C., May 3, 1945; s. Julius and Louise Treistman; m. Joanne Skidmore, Aug. 24, 1967; children: Ann, Ethan. BA, SUNY, Binghamton, 1967; PhD, U. N.C., 1972. Postdoctoral fellow Pub. Health Rsch. Inst., N.Y.C., 1972-75, Friedrich Miescher Inst., Basel, Switzerland, 1975-77; asst. prof. Bryn Mawr (Pa.) Coll., 1977-80; sr. scientist Worcester Found. for Exptl. Biology, Shrewsbury, Mass., 1980-91; prof. pharmacology U. Mass. Sch. Medicine, Worcester, 1982—; corp. mem. Marine Biol. Lab., Woods Hole, Mass., 1984—. Contbr. over 40 articles to sci. jours., chpts. to books. Rsch. grantee NIH, 1980—, Nat. Inst. on Alcoholism and Alcohol Abuse, 1982—. Mem. Soc. for Neurosci., Rsch. Soc. for Alcoholism, Biophys. Soc. Office: U Mass Sch Medicine Dept Pharmacology 55 Lake Ave N Worcester MA 01655-0001

TRELA, JAMES EDWARD, sociology educator; b. Adams, Mass., Aug. 23, 1943; s. Edward James and Janette (Fillion) T.; m. Carol Tristany, July 15, 1966; children: J. Eric, Thomas Tristany. BA, Am. Internat. Coll., 1965; postgrad., U. So. Calif., 1967; MA, Case Western Res. U., 1967, PhD, 1970. Rsch. asst. Case Western Res. U., Cleve., 1965-66, 1968, rsch. coord. Barton Ctr. Demonstration Project, 1967-69, rsch. coord. vocat. guidance and rehab. svcs., 1970-71, rsch. assoc. Inst. on Family in Bureaucratic Soc., 1970-72, rsch. dir. vocat. guidance and rehab. svcs., 1971-73; prof. social gerontology sociology U. Md. Baltimore County, Catonsville, Md., 1973—; cons. Cleve. Coll., Case Wetern Res. U. Programs on Aging, Yr. for Action Program, Kent State U., Vocat. Guidance and Rehab. Svcs., Cleve.; presentor papers on meetings and confs. Assoc. editor Case Western Res. Jour. Sociology, 1968-69. Fellow social gerontology Case Western Res. U., Cleve., 1960-67. Mem. Am. Sociol. Assn., Gerontol. Soc., North Cen. Sociol. Assn., Alpha Kappa Delta (v.p. 1968-69). Roman Catholic. Home: 5433 Patterson Rd Baldwin MD 21013-9358 Office: U Md Baltimore County 5401 Wilkens Ave Baltimore MD 21228-5329

TRELSTAD, ROBERT LAURENCE, pathology educator, cell biologist; b. Redding, Calif., June 16, 1940; s. Bertram Laurence and Dorothy (Axt) T.; m. Barbara Stanton Henken, Aug. 27, 1961; children: Derek, Graham, Brian, Jeremy. BA, Columbia U., 1961; MD, Harvard U., 1966. From asst. to assoc. prof. Harvard Med. Sch., Boston, 1972-81; chief pathology Shriners Burns Inst., Boston, 1975-81; staff pathologist Mass. Gen. Hosp., Boston, 1972-81; prof., chair pathology Robert Wood Johnson Med. Sch., Piscataway/New Brunswick, N.J., 1981—; mem. NIH Study Sect., Bethesda, Md., 1971-75, 86-90. Co-founder, editor-in-chief: Keyboard Publishing, Inc., 1990; past mem. editorial bd. various profl. jours. including Jour. Cell Biology, Am. Jour. Pathology. Lt. comdr. USPHS, 1967-69. Helen Hay Whitney Found. fellow, 1969-72; recipient Rsch. Faculty award Am. Cancer Soc., 1972-76. Mem. Am. Soc. Cell Biology (sec. 1982-88). Home: 35 Westcott Rd Princeton NJ 08540-3038 Office: Robert Wood Johnson Med Sch Dept of Pathology 675 Hoes Ln Piscataway NJ 08854-5635

TREMBLEY, HELEN REBECCA, personnel administrator; b. Ogdensburg, N.Y., Dec. 15, 1962; d. Gilbert Walker and Alberta Monique (Bouchard) Scott; m. Dan Trembley, July 22, 1983. BS, Cornell U., 1985. Pers. coord. Pers. Pool, INc., Syracuse, N.Y., 1986-88; pers. adminstr. Transistor Devices, Inc., Cedarknolls, N.J., 1988—. Advisor Children and Youth Svcs. of Monroe County, 1990—; social dept. chmn. Jr. Women's Club of Stroudsburg, 1988-89, sec., 1989-90, pres., 1990-91 (named Mem. of Yr. 1989-90). Mem. Indsl. Rels. Assn., Employers Adv. Coun. Office: Transistor Devices Inc PO Box H Delaware Water Gap PA 18327-0169

TREMEL, GERARD THOMAS, accountant; b. Pitts., Oct. 18, 1956; s. Anthony John and Josephine Agnes (Hergenroeder) T.; m. Joyce Ann Oliphant, Aug. 23, 1980; children: Andrew Thomas, Joshua James. BS in Bus. Adminstrn., Robert Morris Coll., 1978; MBA, Duquesne U., 1988. Cert. Mgmt. Acct. Controller Glenshaw (Pa.) Glass Co., 1979—. Roman Catholic. Office: Glenshaw Glass Co 1101 William Flynn Hwy Glenshaw PA 15116-2659

TRENK, LAWRENCE IRA, health care administrator; b. N.Y.C., Apr. 24, 1954; s. David and Pera Lee (Tumpeer) T.; m. Lora Joan Goldwater, June 17, 1979; 1 child, Diana Mollie. BA in History, George Washington U., 1976; MPA, U. So. Calif., L.A., 1981. Adminstrv. resident St. Barnabas Med. Ctr., Livingston, N.J., 1981; adminstrv. dir. MED/MARK, West Orange, 1982-84; exec. dir. SurgiCare Cen. Jersey, Inc., Watchung, N.J., 1984-86, Roseland Surg. Ctr., Roseland, N.J., 1986-91, Garden Acute Surgi-Ctr., 1991—; cons. Garden State Surgicenter, Jersey City, 1986-89, Day-Op Ctr. L.I., Mineola, N.Y., 1988-89, Mediplex Sur. Ctr., Edison, N.J., 1988; surveyor Assn. for Accreditation Ambulatory Health Care, 1990—. Mem. Federated Ambulatory Surg. Assn. Office: Roseland Surg Ctr 556 Eagle Rock Ave Roseland NJ 07068-1502

TRENNER, NELSON RICHARDS, JR., communications executive, writer; b. Plainfield, N.J., Aug. 3, 1948; s. Nelson Richards and Kathryn Theresa (Farrell) T.; m. Annabelle Clare Radcliffe, June 24, 1988; 1 child, Miles Richards Radcliffe. AB, Princeton U., 1970; MA, Rutgers U., 1978. Mng. editor Princeton (N.J.) Packet Newspapers, 1971-72; mgr. trade sales promotion Little, Brown & Co., Boston, 1972-73; assoc. curator New England Hist. Geneal. Soc., Boston, 1974-76; mng. editor Del. Valley News, Flemington, N.J., 1976-77; pres. Advanced Communication Tng., Princeton, 1981—; cons. AT&T Bell Labs., Murray Hill, N.J., 1981—; lectr. Princeton U., 1987-88, 91—. Author: The Bell Labs Writer, 1985; co-author: The Bell Labs Editor, 1986, The Bell Labs Style Guide, 1988 (internat. award for excellence 1989); co-author, editor: E. L. Doctorow, 1983; asst. editor Ontario Rev., 1980, 82-83. Campaign worker House and Senate Campaigns, N.J., Mass., 1974, 76, 78, 80, 82; com. chmn. Coalition for Nuclear Disarmament, N.J., 1980—; campaign staff writer Millicent Fenwick for U.S. Senate, N.J., 1981-82; admissions assoc. Princeton U., 1981-83; fellow Blue Mountain Ctr., Blue Mountain Lake, N.Y., 1983-87, Millay Colony for the Arts, Austerlitz, N.Y., 1985, Va. Ctr. for Creative Arts, Sweet Briar, 1986. Rutgers U. fellow, Columbia U. fellow; recipient Adirondack Fiction award Blueline Mag., 1986. Mem. ASTD. Democrat. Episcopalian. Home: 12 Park Pl Princeton NJ 08542-6919 Office: Advanced Communication Tng 350 Alexander St Princeton NJ 08540-7192

TRENT, BERTRAM JAMES, real estate executive; b. N.Y.C., Apr. 14, 1918; s. Gustave K. and Florence (Wertheimer) T.; m. Geraldine Eliza Jacobs, July 20, 1947; children: Bruce L., David P. (dec.), Michael S. Student, Yale U., 1939; BA, U. Va., 1940. Ptnr. Bert Mfg. Co., N.Y.C., 1940-57; v.p. Bert Mfg. Co., Inc., Irvington, N.Y., 1957-69, pres., 1969-72; pres. Bert Realty Co., Inc., Irvington, 1972—. Del. Rep. Nat. Conv., Kansas City, 1976; treas. Scarsdale (N.Y.) Rep. Town Com., 1957-74, chmn., 1974-77; asst. treas. Westchester County Rep. Com., White Plains, N.Y., 1976-78, del. nat. convs., 1960, 68, 72, 84; mem. various coms. Town Club Scarsdale, 1954—. Served with U.S. Army, 1943-46. Mem. Nat. Assn. Mfrs. (internat. rels. com. 1946-49), Yale Engring. Assn., Exch. Club (pres. 1975, 85), Scarsdale Golf Club, Breakers Golf Club, Yale Club N.Y.C., Colette Club. Republican. Office: Bert Realty Co Inc Trent Bldg Irvington NY 10533

TRENT, JAMES ALFRED, city official; b. Bklyn., May 25, 1946; s. Alfred and Helen (Vanasco) T. Assoc. deg. Applied Sci., SUNY, Farmingdale, 1966; B.Landscape Architecture, U. Ga., 1969. Lic. landscape architect, S.C. Jr. landscape architect Dept. Gen. Svcs., N.Y.C., 1969-70, asst. landscape architect, 1970-79, chief profl. contracts, 1979-84, asst. to dir. Bur. Bldg. Design, 1984-87, dep. chief profl. contracts mgmt. sect., 1987—. Art editor Civil Svc. Merit Coun. Inc., 1972-81, 86. Pres., Creedmoor Civic Assn. Inc., Bellerose, N.Y., 1970-80, v.p., 1980-84, exec. mem., 1984—, treas., 1989—; mem. ornamental hort. adv. commn. Occupational Edn. Adv. Coun., N.Y.C. Bd. Edn., 1973-85; founder, pres. Queens County Farm Mus., 1975—; pres. Profl. Svc. Ctrs. for the Handicapped, Inc., 1980-81; 1st v.p. Eastern Queens Civic Coun., 1975—; mem. Queens County Com. Rep. Party, 1968-85; v.p. Midland Rep. Club, N.Y. 23d Assembly Dist., 1970-80, pres., 1981—, grants disbursement judge Queens Coun. on Arts, 1982-86. Named Grad. of Yr., SUNY at Farmingdale Alumni Assn., 1966; Humanitarian of 1977, 105th Police Precinct Community Coun. Mem. Met. Hist. Structures Assn. (dir. 1982—), Poppenhusen Inst. (bd. dirs. 1991—). Roman Catholic. Home: 24233 90th Ave Bellerose NY 11426-1115 Office: Mcpl Bldg Rm 2141 New York NY 10007

TRENT, RICHARD LEE, education facility administrator; b. Kearny, N.J., July 6, 1937; s. Walter Russell and Roberta Trent; m. Anabel Curral, Aug. 1, 1965; children: Danielle, Jennifer. BS, Glassboro State Coll., 1960; MA, Columbia U., 1967. English tchr. River-Dell Jr. High Sch., River Edge, N.J., 1960-62; English/journalism tchr. Northern Valley Regional High Sch., Old Tappan, N.J., 1962-67; community rels. dir. Essex Community Coll., Balt., 1967—. Editor: (book) Public Relations in the Community College, 1981. Named one of Outstanding Young Men of Am., 1960. Mem. Coun. for Advancement and Support of Edn. Office: Essex CC 7201 Rossville Blvd Baltimore MD 21237-3855

TRETTER, JAMES RAY, pharmaceutical company executive; b. Boone, Iowa, June 7, 1933; s. Raymond J. and Freda E. (Ohge) T.; m. Neltje Van Loon; 1 child, Elsa. BS in Chemistry, Loras Coll., 1956; PhD in Chemistry, U. Calif., Berkeley, 1960. Chemist Pfizer, Inc., Groton, Conn., 1960-72, dir. med. chem. dept., 1972-74, dir. chem. process rsch., 1975-77, exec. dir. devel. rsch., 1977-80; v.p. R&D William H. Rorer, Inc., Ft. Washington, Pa., 1980-86; pres. Rorer Cen. Rsch. div. Rhone-Poulenc Rorer Cen. Rsch. (div. Rhone-Poulence Rorer), Ft. Washington, 1986—. Office: Rhone-Poulenc Rorer Cen Rsch 500 Arcola Rd Collegeville PA 19426-0107

TRETTER, STEVEN ALAN, electrical engineer, educator; b. Greenbelt, Md., May 28, 1940; s. George and Ruth (Bold) T.; m. Teresa Marie Whitaker, Sept. 8, 1968; 1 child, Anne Elizabeth. BSEE, U. Md., 1962; MA, Princeton U., 1964, PhD in Elec. Engring., 1966. Mem. tech. staff Hughes Aircraft Co., Culver City, Calif., 1965-66; asst. prof. elec. engring. U. Md., College Park, 1966-70, assoc. prof., 1970—; cons. to numerous pvt. and govt. orgns., Washington, Md., 1966—. Author: Introduction to Discrete Time Signal Processing, 1976; patentee in field; contbr. articles to profl. jours. Mem. IEEE (sr.). Home: 601 Hawkesbury Ter Silver Spring MD 20904-6311 Office: U Md Dept Elec Engring College Park MD 20742

TREVISAN, CAREY RALPH, JR., admissions and records director; b. Newark, N.J., May 29, 1948; s. Carey Ralph and Yolanda (Russo) T.; m. Adelia V. Beckent-Dawson (div. 1987); chldren: Jennifer Betite, Deborah Lizbeth. BA in Psychology and Sociology, Wilmington Coll., 1970; MEd, Seton Hall U., 1975; ABD, Rutgers U., 1981. Cert. child, adult, adloscent psychotherapy, N.Y., 1987. Claims investigation Liberty Mutual Ins. Co., East Orange, N.J., 1970-72; asst. dir. admissions Ocean County Coll., Toms River, N.J., 1973-75, assoc. dir. admissions, 1975-85, dir. admissions, 1985—; clin. counselor, instr. dept. community edn. Ocean County Coll., 1988—. Recipient N.J. Pub. Svc. award. Mem. Am. Assn. Collegiate Registrars and Officers Admissions, NAt. Assn. Student Personnel Adminstrs. (exec. bd.), N.J. Assn. Coll. Admissions Counselors (exec. bd.), Ocean County Personnel and Guidance Assn. Roman Catholic. Home: 79 P Fairway Villas Lakewood NJ 08701 Office: Ocean County Coll Dept Admissions/Records College Dr Toms River NJ 08753

TREVISANI, EDMUND THOMAS, JR., company executive, consultant; b. Utica, N.Y., Aug. 4, 1949; s. Edmund Thomas and Rose Mary (Graziano) T.; m. Jeri Lynn Trevisani, Sept. 6, 1986; children: Edmund, Marc. BS in Physics, Niagara U., 1971; MS in Engring. Physics, U. Va., 1973; postgrad., Wharton Sch., 1991—. Plant mgr. GE, 1981-83, project mgr., 1983-85, mgr. plant ops., 1985-89, mgr. employee tech. devel., 1989—; cons., pres. P. T. Internat., Ltd., Albany, N.Y. leader YMCA, N.Y.C.; asst. scoutmaster Boy Scouts Am., N.Y.C.; lectr., tchr. local ch. Mem. Am. Mgmt. Assn., Nat. Assn. Tng. and Devel., Am. Physics Assn., Am. Entreprenur Assn., Albany C. of C., Toastmasters (pres. 1984-86, speakers award 1986). Home: 309 Mountainview Dr Wayne PA 19087-5532

TREVITS, MICHAEL ANTHONY, geologist; b. Colorado Springs, Colo., June 10, 1953; s. Robert Alvin and Elsie (McEuen) T. BS in Geology, U. Pitts., 1975, MBA, 1989. Registered profl. geologist, N.C. Phys. sci. aid U.S. Bur. Mines, Pitts., 1974, phys. sci. technician, 1974-75, geologist, 1975-77, 79-82, geologist supr., 1982—; geologist U.S. Dept. Energy, Pitts., 1977-79; spl. cons. Am. Pub. Gas Assn., 1979-80. Contbr. articles to profl. jours.; co-patentee for method of enhancing the removal of methane gas and associated fluids from mine boreholes. Recipient Outstanding Paper award Nat. Symposium on Mining, Hydrology, Sedimentology, and Reclamation, 1986. Mem. Nat. Water Well Assn., Soc. for Mining, Metallurgy, and Exploration (bd. dirs. Pitts. chpt. 1991—), ASTM Coal Core Task Force. Roman Catholic. Office: US Bur of Mines PO Box 18070 Pittsburgh PA 15236-0070

TREVOR, BRONSON, economist; b. N.Y.C., Nov. 12, 1910; s. John Bond and Caroline Murray (Wilmerding) T.; A.B., Columbia Coll., 1931; m. Eleanor Darlington Fisher, Nov. 8, 1946; children—Eleanor, Bronson, Caroline. Own bus., 1931—; dir., asst. sec. Northwestern Terminal R.R., 1952-58; chmn. bd. Texinia Corp., 1959-92. Former dir. chmn. fin. com. Gen. Hosp. of Saranac Lake mem. Council for Agrl. and Chemurgic Research, Am. Forestry Assn. Mem. Republican County Com. of N.Y. County, 1937-39; leader in primary election campaigns N.Y. County, 1937, 38, 39 to free local Rep. party orgn. from leftwing affiliations. Served with U.S. Army, 1942, World War II. Mem. S.A.R., Soc. Colonial Wars. Clubs: Union, Knickerbocker, Racquet and Tennis, Piping Rock, Bath and Tennis. Author: (pamphlet) The United States Gold Purchase Program, 1941; also numerous articles on econ. subjects. Home: Paul Smiths NY 12970 Office: PO Box 182 Oyster Bay NY 11771-0182

TRIANTAFYLLOU, MICHAEL STAFANOS, educator; b. Athens, Greece, Oct. 27, 1951; came to U.S., 1974; s. Stefanos M. and Penelopi I. (Koutras) T.; m. Joan L. Kimball, Sept. 22, 1985; 1 child, Stefanos R. MS in Ocean Engring., MIT, 1977, MSME, 1977, ScD, 1979. Rsch. assoc. MIT, Cambridge, Mass., 1978-79, asst. prof., 1979-83, assoc. prof., 1983-86, tenured assoc. prof., 1986-90, prof., dir. ocean engring. testing tank, 1990—; vis. scientist Woods Hole (Mass.) Oceanographic Inst., 1990—. Contbr. articles to profl. jours. Rsch. grantee OFfice NAval Rsch., Office Naval Tech., NSF, Doherty Found. Dept. Commerce, 1979—. Mem. Internat. Soc. Offshore and Polar Engrs. (founding mem.), Soc. Naval Architects and Marine Engrs. (papers com., vice chmn. OC-2 com.). Office: MIT 77 Massachusetts Ave Rm 5-323 Cambridge MA 02139

TRIBBLE, JOHN ATWOOD, economics educator; b. Goffstown, N.H., Sept. 29, 1945; s. William Denis and Annette H. (Callan) T.; m. Annette H. (Callan) T.; m. Carol Jo Wockert, Mar. 1, 1974. BA in Econs., Boston Coll., Newton, Mass., 1967; MA in Econs., U. Maine, 1969; PhD in Econs., Utah State U., 1975. Rsch. fellow Utah State U., Logan, 1969; asst. prof. Newberry (S.C.) Coll., 1972-76; assoc. prof. econs. Russell Sage Coll., Troy, N.Y., 1976—, chmn. econs. and bus. dept., 1984—, dir. Ctr. for Econ. Edn., 1980—; Author: Study Guide for Introductory Economics, 1991. Sec. Boght Community Action Group, Colonie, N.Y., 1986-91; pres. Colonie Coalition Homeowners Assn., 1990-91. Mem. Am. Econ. Assn. Office: Russell Sage Coll Troy NY 12180

TRIBE, LAURENCE HENRY, lawyer, educator; b. Shanghai, Republic of China, Oct. 10, 1941; s. George Israel and Paulina (Diatlovitsky) T.; m. Carolyn Ricarda Kreye, June 20, 1965; children—Mark Alexander, Kerry Katrina. A.B. summa cum laude in Math. (Nat. scholar), Harvard U., 1962, J.D. magna cum laude, 1966; LL.D. (hon.), Gonzaga U., 1980, Pacific U., 1987, Am. U., 1987, Ill. Inst. Tech., 1988. Bar: Calif. 1966, U.S. Supreme Ct. 1966. Law clk. Calif. Supreme Ct., 1966-67, U.S. Supreme Ct., 1967-68; exec. dir. tech. assessment panel Nat. Acad. Scis., 1968-69; asst. prof. law

Harvard U., 1969-72, prof., 1972-82, Ralph S. Tyler, Jr. prof. constl. law, 1982—; chmn. Marshall Islands Jud. Service Commn., 1979-80; chief appellate counsel Calif. Nuclear Litigation, 1978-83; spl. dep. atty. gen. Hawaii, 1983-84; cons. NSF, Nat. Endowment Humanities, White House, others; cons. Marshall Islands for drafting new constitution, 1978-79. Author: American Constitutional Law, 1978 (recipient awards), 2d edit., 1988, Constitutional Choices, 1985, God Save this Honorable Court, 1985, Abortion: The Clash of Absolutes, 1990, (with Mike Dorf) On Reading the Constitution, 1991; contbr. articles to profl. jours. Recipient Triennial Coif award for the outstanding work of legal scholarship in U.S., 1978-80, Scribe award, 1980, Beale prize; 1966 Detur prize, 1969; nat. debate champion, 1961; NSF fellow, 1962-63. Fellow Am. Acad. Arts and Scis.; mem. ABA (Silver Gavel award 1991), ACLU, Phi Beta Kappa. Office: Harvard U Law Sch Griswold 307 Cambridge MA 02138

TRICE, MARTIN LOUIS, school administrator; b. Dover, Del., Jan. 11, 1957; s. Herman Noah and Margaret Louise (Lowman) T.; m. Beverly Smith, Oct. 9, 1982; children: Ian Louis, Andrew Noah. BA, Ea. Nazarene Coll., 1979, MA, 1983; postgrad., Boston U., 1990—. Cert. secondary sch. tchr., Mass. Tchr. Amego Sch., Quincy, Mass., 1978-80, Rockland (Mass.) Pub. High Sch., 1980-82; counselor R.W.H. and Assocs., Hingham, Mass., 1985-86; asst. dir. admissions Ea. Nazarene Coll., Quincy, 1982-86; dir. counseling Lexington (Mass.) Christian Acad., 1986—, dir. admissions and fin. aid, 1988—; dir. Armenia Edn. Project, 1992—; rsch. assoc. Ctr. for Advancement of Ethics & Character, Boston, 1992—; admissions cons., 1991—; workshop presenter F.A.N.E./A.C.S.I., Boston, 1986—; radio talk show guest Sta. WEZE, Boston, 1990—. Deacon, lay leader North Shore Community Bapt. Ch., Beverly Farms, Mass.; docent Steven Phillips Mus., Salem, Mass., 1990; instr. Well Yacht, Inc., Marblehead, Mass. Mem. ASCD, Nat. Assn. Ind. Schs., Ind. Sch. Assn. Mass., AACD, Phi Delta Kappa, Pi Lambda Theta. Republican. Home: 46 Bubier Rd Marblehead MA 01945 Office: Lexington Christian Acad 48 Bartlett Ave Lexington MA 02173-2699

TRICULES, HOMER GEORGE, minister, psychotherapist; b. Perth Amboy, N.J., Apr. 13, 1931; s. George and Eva (Vlahos) T.; m. Magdalene Sathmary, June 11, 1955; children: Evamarie, Nancy Susan, Lori. BS in Edn., Rutgers U., 1953; MDiv, New Brunswick Theol. Sem., 1958; MA, Fairleigh Dickinson U., 1975. Ordained to ministry Am. Bapt. Ch., 1958. Pastor Calvary Bapt. Ch., Carteret, N.J., 1956-61; tchr. Pt. Pleasant Beach (N.J.) High Sch., 1961-64; pastor First Bapt. Ch., Long Branch, N.J., 1962-73; missionary chaplain Race Track Chaplaincy of Am., N.J., 1973-82; pastor Scotch Plains (N.J.) Bapt. Ch., 1982-88; nat. exec. dir. Race Track Chaplaincy of Am., Long Branch, 1988—; founder, cons. Community Christian Counselling Ctr., First Bapt. Ch., Red Bank, N.J., 1976—; pres. Am. Bapt. Chs. of N.J., 1985. Author: (devotional book) Daily Oats. Mem. Long Branch Bd. Edn., 1990—. 2nd lt. U.S. Army, 1954. Mem. Am. Bapt. Mins. Coun. Home: 621 Westwood Ave Long Branch NJ 07740-5008 Office: Race Track Chaplaincy of Am 646 Broadway Long Branch NJ 07740-5444

TRIGOBOFF, DANIEL HOWARD, psychologist; b. Bklyn., Jan. 21, 1953; s. Philip and Eileen G. (Dubin) T.; m. Eileen Hazel Ruff, Mar. 30, 1985. BA, SUNY, 1974; MA, U. Iowa, 1978, PhD, 1980. Lic. clin. psychologist. Clin. psychologist VA, Buffalo, 1980-87; program dir. Buffalo Psychiat. Ctr., 1988-89; program coord. Buffalo Gen. Hosp., 1989-92; adj. prof. SUNY, Buffalo, 1984—; clin. psychologist pvt. practice Amherst, N.Y., 1982—; cons. Mid-Erie Mental Health Svcs., Buffalo, 1980-89. Mem. adv. bd. Langston Hughes Inst., Buffalo, 1986. Mem. Am. Psychol. Assn. Jewish.

TRILLI, JAMES VICTOR, podiatrist; b. Pitts., July 15, 1950; s. Giberto Luigi and Virginia Marie (Magone) T.; m. Suzanne Marie Walos, June 3, 1972; 1 child, Jonathan Christopher. BS in Bus. Mgmt., Point Park Coll., 1972; BS in Chemistry, Biology, California (Pa.) State U., 1978; D Podiatric Medicine, Ohio Coll. Podiatric Medicine, 1982. Diplomate Am. Bd. Podiatric Surgery. Sales mgr. Culligan Soft Water Svc., Star Junction, Pa., 1972-74; substitute tchr. Douglas Sch. Bus., Monessen, Pa., 1974-78; coal miner Consol. Coal, Library, Pa., 1974-78; resident Podiatry Hosp. Pitts., 1983-84; pvt. practice Monessen, 1984—; med. staff Podiatry Hosp. Pitts.; med. staff Monongahela Valley Hosp., mem. credentials com., laser com.; team podiatrist Mon-Valley Cath. High Sch. football team. Vol. Monessen March of Dimes, 1984-91; bd. dirs. Monongahela (Pa.) YMCA, 1988-92, Monessen United Way, 1991-92, Am. Diabetes Assn. Fellow Am. Coll. Foot Surgeons; mem. Am. Podiatric Med. Assn., Pa. Podiatric Med. Assn., Am. Running and Fitness. Democrat. Roman Catholic. Office: Eastgate Family Foot Care Eastgate 15 Ste 1-H Monessen PA 15062

TRIMBLE, BERNARD HENRY, trade association executive; b. McKeesport, Pa., Sept. 19, 1930; s. John Francis and Louise Esther (McKenna) T.; m. Jo McDonald, Nov. 26, 1959; children: Jeanne, Daniel Bernard. BA, St. Vincent COll., 1953; postgrad., Georgetown U., 1953-55, Sophia U., Tokyo, 1957. Dirs. staff FBI, Washington, 1953-55; asst. prof. U. Tex., Austin, 1958-60; market devel. mgr. Reuben H. Donnolley Corp., Washington, 1960-64; mktg. svcs. mgr. Nat. Elec. Contractors Assn., Washington, 1964-68, dirs. svcs., 1968-70, sec., treas., 1970-73; sec., mgr. Nat. Elec. Contractors Assn., Atlanta, 1973-78; exec. dir. Nat. Assn. Mfg., Washington, 1978—; pres. Product Design Inst., Austin, 1959-60, Constrn. Industry Found., Washington, 1968-70. Lt. USN, 1955-60. Acad. Elec. Contracting fellow, Wahsington, 1975. Mem. VFW, KC, Am. Legion, Order Moose.

TRIMBLE, GEORGE ROBERT, computer company executive; b. Elkton, Md.; s. George R. and Alice A. (Carson) T.; m. Helen Callie England, Feb. 11, 1950; children: Yvonne, Diane, David, Sharon, Steven, Phebe, Rebecca. BA, St. John's Coll., 1948; MA in Math., U. Del., 1951; postgrad., U. Md., 1951-52. Freelance mathematician Aberdeen, Md., 1949-52; sr. mathematician IBM, Endicott, N.Y., 1952-56; tech. dir. Computer Usage Co., N.Y.C., 1956-68; v.p. Penta Computer Assocs., N.Y.C., 1968-71; pres. T-Logic, Inc., Princeton, N.J., 1971—. Author: Development Workbook Guide, 1972, Digital PABX, 1983. Elder Westerly Road Ch., Princeton, 1975-91. Mem. Computer Soc. of IEEE. Republican. Home: Four Teak Ln Princeton NJ 08540 Office: T-Logic Inc 4 Teak Ln Princeton NJ 08540-4712

TRIMBLE, ROBERT BOGUE, research biologist; b. Balt., July 2, 1943; s. George Simpson and Janet Anna (Bogue) T.; m. Kathleen Marie Davis, May 17, 1969 (dec. Aug. 1988); 1 child, Alison. BS in Biology, Rensselaer Poly. Inst., 1965, PhD in Biology, 1969. Rsch. scientist Wadsworth Ctr. for Labs. and Rsch., N.Y. State Dept. Health, Albany, 1970-81, rsch. scientist V, 1981—; prof. biomed. sci. SUNY, Sch. Pub. Health, Albany, 1989—; mem. USPHS Study Sect., Bethesda, Md., 1985-89, Am. Cancer Soc. Personnel Rev. Group, Atlanta, 1991-95, USPHS Rev. Res. Panel, Bethesda, 1989-93. Mem. editorial bd. Jour. Biol. Chemistry, 1992—; contbr. 50 articles and revs. to profl. jours., chpts. to books. Grantee Nat. Inst. Aging, 1977-81, Nat. Inst. Gen. Med. Sci., 1977-91. Mem. Am. Soc. for Biochemistry and Molecular Biology, Soc. for Complex Carbohydrates, Am. Soc. for Microbiology, AAAS, Sigma Xi. Episcopalian. Office: NY State Dept Health Wadsworth Ctr E 524 Albany NY 12201-0509

TRINKLE, DAVID ALEXANDER, pharmaceutical company executive; b. Allentown, Pa., Nov. 12, 1964; s. Frank Edward and Theresa Helen (Szupper) T. BS in Chemistry and Psychology, Muhlenberg Coll., 1986. Med. rep. Lederle Labs. div. Am. Cyanamid, Bethlehem, Pa., 1986-88; diagnostic systems specialist Diagnostics div. Abbott Labs., Bklyn., 1988-90; account exec. Diagnostics div. Abbott Labs., N.Y.C., 1990—. Industry rep. Muhlenberg Coll. Career Counseling Ctr., Allentown, 1989—. Home: 5 Westover Ter West Orange NJ 07052-1612

TRIPODI, DANIEL, immunologist, consultant; b. Cliffside, N.J., Mar. 13, 1939; s. Charles and Carrie (Pitetti) T.; m. Sharon Hunsicker, June 22, 1963; children: D. Charles, Thomas. BS, U. Del., 1961, MS, 1963; PhD, Temple U., 1966. Dir. biotech. Johnson & Johnson, New Brunswick, N.J., 1981-88; v.p. rsch. and devel. Therakos div. Johnson & Johnson, West Chester, Pa., 1988-90; exec. v.p. Fibritech, Inc., Lebanon, N.J., 1990—; pres. Tricon Assocs., Lebanon, N.J., 1990—; adj. assoc. prof. Temple U., Phila., 1974-78, U. Pa., Phila., 1979-89; adj. prof. U. Del., Newark, 1989—. Patentee in field. Mem. Am. Assn. Immunologists. Home: 1 Burlinghoff Ln Lebanon NJ 08833

TRIPODI, TONY, social worker, educator; b. Sacramento, Calif., Nov. 30, 1932; s. Nicola and Christine Maria (Grandinetti) T.; m. Roni Roberts, Oct. 28, 1969 (div. 1986); children: Lee Anna, Anthony, David, Stephen. AB, U. Calif., Berkeley, 1954, MSW, 1958; D of Social Work, Columbia U., N.Y.C., 1963. Lic. social worker, Pa. Rsch. tech. Calif. Dept. Mental Hygiene, Sacramento, 1958-59; rsch. analyst Calif. Youth Authority, Sacramento, 1959-60; from rsch. asst. to asst. prof. Columbia U., N.Y.C., 1962-65; asst. prof. U. Calif., Berkeley, 1965-66; from assoc. prof. to prof. U. Mich. Sch. Social Work, Ann Arbor, 1966-87; assoc. dean prof. U. Pitts. Sch. Social Work, 1987—; rsch. assoc. Bklyn. Coll., 1963-65; editor in chief Social Work Rsch. and Abstracts, N.Y.C., 1980-84; interim assoc. dean U. Mich. Sch. Social Work, Ann Arbor, 1985, 1986, 1987; rsch. cons. Zancan Found., Padova, Italy, 1974--, NIMH, Silver Spring, Md., 1989--, Nat. Rsch. Adv. Com., Clinton, Mich., 1988--. Author: (with others) Clinical Social Judgement, 1966, numerous others; contbr. articles to profl. jours. Bd. dirs. Parental Stress Ctr., Pitts., 1990--. With USNR, 1954-56. Doctoral rsch. fellow Sage Found., N.Y.C., 1960-63; rsch. grantee NSF, 1965-66; Fulbright Hays scholar U.S. Govt., Italy, 1973-74; invited scholar Tilburg U., the Netherlands, 1977; vis. scholar U. Kent, Canterbury, Eng., 1980. Mem. Nat. Assn. Social Workers, Am. Psychol. Assn., Acad. Cert. Social Workers, Coun. Social Work Edn., Evaluation Rsch. Soc. Home: 100 Bryn Mawr Ct Apt 314 Pittsburgh PA 15221-3800

TRIPP, FREDERICK GERALD, investment advisor; b. Chgo., Oct. 1, 1936; s. Gerald F. and Kathryn Ann (Siebold) T.; m. Terry Anne Shull, Aug. 27, 1967. BS in Econs., Purdue U., 1958; MBA, Lehigh U., 1964; PhD, The Am. U., 1974. Sr. v.p. CRI, Inc., Rockville, Md., 1979-82, Security Pacific, Inc., Seattle, 1982-83; pres. Frederick G. Tripp & Assocs., Inc., Rockville, 1983—. Pres. Doctoral Assn., The Am. U., 1973. Maj. U.S. Army, 1958-67, Vietnam. Methodist. Office: Frederick G Tripp & Assocs 3200 Tower Oaks Blvd # 300 Rockville MD 20852-4216

TRIPP, SUSAN GERWE, museum director; b. Balt., Dec. 28, 1945; d. Earl Joseph and Maria Elizabeth (Wise) Gerwe; m. David Enders Tripp, June 9, 1977. BS, U. Md., 1967. Home econs. tchr. Balt. County Pub. Sch. Sys., 1967-74; curator of art Johns Hopkins U., Balt., 1974-76; curator of art, archivist Johns Hopkins U., 1976-78, instr. evening coll., 1978-84, dir. univ. collections, 1979—; supr., instr. art history Goucher Coll., Notre Dame U., Balt., 1977-86; dir. docent tng. Homewood Mus., Balt., 1987-89; dir. Homewood Restoration Adv. Com., 1983—, Evergreen Restoration Adv. Com., 1988—; lectr. in field. Co-author: The Garrett Collection of Japanese Art, 1990 (NEA Grant 1980); contbr. articles to profl. jours. Recipient Historic Preservation award, Balt. Heritage, Inc., 1988. Mem. Netsuke Kenkyokai Japanese Cir. of Art, Oriental Ceramic Soc., Balt. Mus. Art, Am. Assn. Mus., John Hopkins U. Faculty Club, Omicron Nu. Office: Johns Hopkins U 3400 N Charles St Baltimore MD 21218-2608

TRISCO, ROBERT FREDERICK, church historian, educator; b. Chgo., Nov. 11, 1929; s. Richard E. and Harriet Rose (Hardt) T. B.A., St. Mary of Lake Sem., Mundelein, Ill., 1951; S.T.L., Pontifical Gregorian U., Rome, 1955, Hist. Eccl.D., 1962. Ordained priest Roman Catholic Ch., 1954. Mem. faculty Cath. U. Am., Washington, 1959—; prof. ch. history Cath. U. Am., 1975—; editor Cath. Hist. Rev., 1963—; exec. sec. Am. Cath. Hist. Assn., 1961—, sec., treas., 1983—; expert 2d Vatican Coun., 1962-65; pres. Am. subcom. Internat. Commn. Comparative Ch. History, 1978-80; mem. subcoms. Nat. Conf. Cath. Bishops, 1966-76, 87—; assesseur (mem. bur.) Internat. Commn. for Comparative Ch. History, 1980—; mem. Pontifical Com. Hist. Scis., 1982—; hon. mem. Accademia di San Carlo (Milan), 1986—. Author: The Holy See and Nascent Church in the Middle Western U.S., 1826-1850, 1962, Bishops and Their Priests in the United States, 1988; co-author: A Guide to American Catholic History, 2d edit., 1982; editor: Catholics in Am., 1976; co-editor, contbr.: Studies in Catholic History in Honor of John Tracy Ellis, 1985; contbr. numerous articles to profl. publs. Mem. Am. Soc. Ch. History (council 1980-82). Office: Cath U Am Mullen Libr Rm 318 Washington DC 20064

TRISH, RITA KATHRYN, retired mathematics educator; b. Pa., Apr. 11, 1921; d. Harry Francis and Christina Margaret Ney; m. John Edward Trish, Dec. 2, 1944. BS, West Chester U., 1940; MS, Villanova U., 1965; MA, Pa. State U., 1970. Cert. guidance counselor. Tchr. math. Hanover (Pa.) Sr. High Sch., 1944-54; sec. Phila., 1955-61; tchr. math. Colonial Sch. Dist., Lafayette Hill, Pa., 1961-81; substitue tchr., tutor math. Lower Merion Sch. Dist., Ardmore, Pa., 1981-90. Mem. Del. county exec. com. Rep. Com. Orgn., Media, Pa., 1955-61. Mem. Bedlington Terrier Club Am. (sec.-treas. 1982-92), Pa. Valley Women's Club (treas. 1984-92). Home: 1206 Hartdale Ln Gladwyne PA 19035

TRITES, DONALD GEORGE, human service foundation executive; b. Boston, Sept. 26, 1941; s. George Herman and Ada Christena (Patten) T.; m. Ruth Ann Lewis, June 15, 1963 (div. 1987); children: Sarah Jeanne, Amy Bray; m. Beverly Jean Baker, Apr. 8, 1989; 1 child, Erica Christena. AB, Colgate U., 1963; EdM, Tufts U., 1964; PhD, Syracuse U., 1976. Thcr., then chair history dept. Hamilton (Mass.)-Wenham Regionial High Sch., 1964-70; instr. div. ednl. studies Emory U., Atlanta, 1973-76; asst. prof. ednl. studies Emory U., 1976-81, vis. faculty, 1981-86; exec. dir. Ga. Advocacy Office, Inc., Atlanta, 1981-86, Devel. Svcs. Strafford County, Inc., Dover, N.H., 1986—; cons. in human svc. mgmt. and evaluation, U.S. and Europe, 1978—. Editor, author: The College and A Human Future, 1986; contbr. articles to profl.publs. Deacon, First Bapt. Ch., Melrose, Mass., 1968-69, Syracuse, N.Y., 1972-73; deacon, Cen. Congl. Ch., Atlanta, 1984-86. Mem. Assn. for Persons with Severe Handicaps, Delta Upsilon. Democrat. Unitarian-Universalist. Home: RR 2 Box 1039 Wells ME 04090-9563 Office: Devel Svcs Strafford County 1 Forum Ct Dover NH 03820-4375

TRITTON, THOMAS RICHARD, pharmacology educator; b. Lakewood, Ohio, Dec. 20, 1947; s. William Frank and Margie Jean (Galbraith) T.; m. Louise Meschter Tritton; children: Lara, Christiana. BA, Ohio Wesleyan U., 1969; PhD, Boston U., 1973. Asst. prof. Yale Med. Sch., New Haven, Conn., 1975-80; assoc. prof. Yale U., New Haven, Conn., 1980-85; prof. U. Vt., Burlington, 1985—, vice provost, 1991—; mem. NIH Exptl. Therapeutics Study Sect., 1988—. Editor books; mem. editorial bd. 5 profl. jours.; contbr. numerous scientific papers to profl. jours. Rsch. grantee NIH, Am. Cancer Soc. Mem. Am. Assn. Cancer Rsch. (com. mem.), Am. Soc. Biol. Chemists. Mem. Soc. of Friends. Home: 28 Oakhill Rd Shelburne VT 05482-7279 Office: Univ of Vermont Med Sch Dept of Pharmacology Burlington VT 05405

TROEN, PHILIP, physician, educator; b. Portland, Maine, Nov. 24, 1925; s. Ben and Gertrude (Cope) T.; m. Betty Ann Zelig, Mar. 22, 1953 (dec.); children: Mark Lawrence, Bruce Robert, Gail Sheri. A.B., Harvard U., 1944, M.D., 1948. Diplomate: Nat. Bd. Med. Examiners, Am. Bd. Internal Medicine. Intern Boston City Hosp., 1948-49, asst. resident in medicine, 1949-50; resident in medicine Beth Israel Hosp., Boston, 1950, 52-53; chief resident Beth Israel Hosp., 1953-54, asst. in medicine, 1955-56, USPHS research fellow, 1955-56, assoc. in med. research, 1956-64, assoc. in medicine, 1956-58, asst. vis. physician, 1959-64; teaching fellow Harvard Med. Sch., 1952-53, asst. in medicine, 1953-54, research fellow, 1955-56, instr. medicine, 1956-59, asso. in medicine, 1959-60, asst. prof., 1960-64; prof. medicine U. Pitts. Sch. Medicine, 1964—, assoc. chmn. dept. medicine, 1969-79, vice chmn. dept. medicine, 1979-90, physician in chief Montefiore Univ. Hosp., 1964-90, physician in chief emeritus, 1990—; sci. counselor NIH, key cons. contraceptive devel. br., 1980; sci. counselor rev. Intramural Reproductive Biology Program, Nat. Inst. Child Health and Human Devel., 1977; cons. male fertility and infertility Nat. Inst. Occupational Safety and Health, 1977; mem. med. res. service merit rev. bd. in endocrinology VA, 1979-82; mem. contract rev. com. Nat. Inst. Child Health and Human Devel., 1975-84, chmn., 1976-89, reviewer intramural site visit devel. endocrinology br., 1983, 87; mem. endocrinologic and metabolic drugs adv. com. FDA, 1984-88, chmn. 1987-88; mem. expert advisor panel on occupational health, WHO, 1987—. Mem. editorial bd. Jour. Andrology, Jour. Clin. Endocrinology and Metabolism, Internat. Jour. Andrology, Andrologia; contbr. articles to profl. jours. Served to capt. M.C., AUS, 1950-52. Fellow in endocrinology and metabolism Mayo Clinic, Rochester, Minn., 1954-55; Kendall-Hench research fellow, 1955; Ziskind teaching fellow, 1956-59; Med. Found. Greater Boston research fellow, 1959-63; Guggenheim fellow Stockholm, 1960-61. Mem. AAAS, Assn. Am. Physicians, Am. Soc. Clin. Investigation, Am. Soc. for Biochemistry and Molecular Biology, Am. Fedn. Clin. Research, Am. Soc. Andrology (program and publs. com., exec. coun. 1977-79, v.p. 1979-80, pres. 1980-81, chmn. publ. com. 1990—, Disting. Andrologist award 1991), Internat. Soc. Andrology (sec. 1981-89, pres. 1989—), Endocrine Soc. (publ. com. 1984-90, chmn. 1987-90), N.Y. Acad. Scis., Central Soc. Clin. Research, Soc. Study of Reproduction. Office: U Pitts Sch Medicine Montefiore Univ Hosp 3459 Fifth Ave Pittsburgh PA 15213

TROILO, ARTHUR, III, lawyer; b. Frankfurt, Germany, Oct. 10, 1953; came to U.S., 1953; s. Arthur Charles Jr. and Nancy Ann (Sullivan) T.; m. S. Crystal Maldonado, Dec. 29, 1990. BFA, U. Tex., 1977; JD, U. Houston, 1984. Bar: Tex., 1985, D.C., 1991, U.S. Dist. Ct. (fed. dist.), U.S. Ct. Appeals (5th crct.), U.S. Ct. Claims, U.S. Supreme Ct. Assoc. Davidson, Troilo & Booth, San Antonio, 1984-90; assoc. dep. gen. counsel U.S. GSA, Washington, 1990—. Bd. dirs. Alamo Area Big Bors. and Big Sisters, 1989-90. With U.S. Army, 1990. Named one of Outstanding Young Men Am., 1988. Mem. ABA (D.C. chpt., sr. exec. svc.), San Antonio Bar Assn., The Coll. of State Bar of Tex., Phi Alpha Delta. Republican. Roman Catholic. Home: 3309 Wyndham Circle Alexandria VA 22302 Office: GSA 18th & F Sts NW Rm 4140 Washington DC 20405

TROLIO, WILLIAM MICHAEL, health care executive, educator; b. Amsterdam, N.Y., July 12, 1947; s. Morino Fiorello and Jeanne Estelle (Lawrence) T.; m. Judith Mary Starr, Sept. 27, 1969; children: Kristen Marie, Matthew Lawrence. A in Applied Sci., Hudson Valley Community Coll., Troy, N.Y., 1968; BS, SUNY, Albany, 1972; MBA, Northland U., Toronto, Ont., 1983. Lic. clin. lab. scientist. Med. technician Faxton Hosp., Utica, N.Y., 1968-69; mktg. devel. specialist GE, Milw., 1969-74; mktg. devel mgr. Bio Data Corp., Hatboro, Pa., 1974-79; lab. mgr. Cen. Maine Med. Ctr., Lewiston, 1979-80; gen. mgr. lab. svcs. Mary Imogene Basset Hosp. and Clinic, Cooperstown, N.Y., 1980—; adj. clin. prof. med. tech. Utica Coll., Syracuse U., 1980—; adj. clin. faculty Broome County Community Coll., Binghamton, N.Y., 1984—; officer advt. dir. Beaver Valley Music Festival, 1988-89; mem. N.Y. State com. on profl. and pers. standards Clin. Lab. Pers.; mem. mgmt. evaluation com. Nat. Cert. Aging for Clin. Labr. Pers., clin. lab. pers. N.Y. State Profession Pers. Standards Com., project exec. Bassett U. Health Edn. Consortium. Editor; Cen. N.Y. Clin. Lab. Assn. bull., 1984-88; contbr. articles to profl. jours. Asst. leader Webelos, Boy Scouts Am., 1988-90; bd. dirs. Cooperstown Baseball Fields Assn.; mem. bldg. and grounds com. St. Mary's Ch. 1st lt. Med. Svc. Corps, USAR. Fellow Bus. Adminstrn. Can. Sch. Mgmt., 1983. Mem. North Ea. N.Y. Hosp. Assn., Hosp. Assn. N.Y. (rep.), Clin. Lab. Mgmt. Assn. (chpt. pres. 1987-88, legis. liaison bd. 1984), Iroquois Hosp. Consortium (various coms. 1985—), Am. Soc. Clin. Pathologists (assoc.), Mid Atlantic Health Cong., N.Y. Acad. Sci., CSM Alumni Club. Republican. Roman Catholic. Home: RR 1 Box 23D Fly Creek NY 13337-9722 Office: Mary Imogene Basset Hosp One Atwell Rd Cooperstown NY 13326

TROLL, CHRISTIAN MICHAEL, financial executive; b. N.Y.C., July 10, 1954; s. Christian Clemens and Mary Jane (Michellini) T.; m. Diana Marie Wise, July 1, 1978; children: Michael, Christina, Melissa. AS in Bus. Adminstrn., SUNY-Farmingdale, 1980; BS cum laude, C.W. Post Ctr. of L.I. U., 1982; MBA, Adelphi U., Garden City, N.Y., 1985. Staff acct. Arnold Standard Rev. Corp., Rockville Center, N.Y., 1978; acctg. mgr. Gilbert Merrill Steel div. of Consolidated Goldfields Ltd., Syosset, N.Y., 1978-81, Amdax Corp., Bohemia, N.Y., 1981-82; treas., controller, mem. fin. com. AIAA, Washington, 1982-88; v.p. fin. W. Atlee Burpee Co., Warminster, Pa., 1989-90, pres., acting chief exec. officer, 1991-92, exec. v.p., 1992—. Treas. Boy Scouts of Am. Pack 8, Warminster, 1989-91; fin. com. Bucks County Coun., Doylestown, Pa., 1990—; exec. com., 1990—. Mem. Nat. Assn. Accts. Republican. Roman Catholic. Home: 2080 Buckingham Dr Jamison PA 18929-1537 Office: W Atlee Burpee & Co 300 Park Ave Warminster PA 18974-4818

TROMBINO, RAYMOND DAVID, retired air force officer, financial services professional; b. Bronx, Sept. 1, 1949; s. Sam S. and Elisa (Bosi) T.; m. Carole A. Polachowski, June 3, 1972; 1 child, Michelle Kierestin. BCE, Manhattan Coll., 1971; MSCE, Purdue U., 1977. Commd. 2d lt. U.S. Air Force, 1971—, advanced through grades to lt. col., 1988; programming engr. Plattsburg (N.Y.) AFB, 1971-75; site civil engr. Clear (Alaska) Air Force Sta., 1975-76; environ. planner Air Force Engring. and Svcs. Ctr., Tyndall AFB, Fla., 1977-80; asst. prof. aerospace studies N.C. State U., Raleigh, 1980-83; chief of ops. Rhein Main Air Base, Frankfurt, Germany, 1983-87; comdr. 10 CES RAF Alconbury, Huntingdon, U.K., 1987-90; chief readiness programs br. Nat. Guard Bur., Andrews AFB, Md., 1990-92—, ret., 1992; spl. agt., registered rep. Prudential Fin. Svcs., Bethesda, Md., 1992—. Mem. Soc. Am. Mil. Engrs. (chpt. pres. 1988-89), Air Force Assn., Am. Legion, Toastmasters (chpt. pres. 1979), Chi Epsilon. Baptist. Home: PO Box 532 3011 Constitution Dr Stafford VA 22554 Office: Prudential Fin Svcs 7200 Wisconsin Ave Ste 900 Bethesda MD 20814

TRONGONE, RICHARD JAMES, physician; b. N.Y.C., Mar. 26, 1953; s. Michael Anthony Sr. and Anne Marie (Capra) T.; m. Joann Alice De Santis, July 14, 1979; 1 child, Christina Marie. BS, Fordham U., 1975; MD, Mt. Sinai Sch. Medicine, 1981. Diplomate Am. Bd. Ob-gyn. Resident North Shore U. Hosp., Manhasset, N.Y., 1981-84, chief resident, 1984-85, attending staff, 1985—; clin. instr. Cornell Med. Coll., N.Y.C., 1985—. Mem. Am. Coll. Ob-gyn., Med. Soc. State of N.Y., Nassau County Med. Soc., Griffis Faculty Club, North Hempstead Country Club. Republican. Roman Catholic.

TRONOLONE, WILLIAM, educator; b. Newark, Feb. 10, 1936; s. Andrew F. and Bertha (Murray) T.; m. Joyce C. Bradel, May 28, 1960; children: William, Robert. BS in Music, Trenton State Coll., 1959, MA in Music, 1963, Cert. in Supervising, 1973; postgrad., Seton Hall Coll., 1989—. Tchr. music Hamilton Twp. Bd. Edn., N.J., 1959-63, dir. summer sch., 1960-63, chmn. music dept, 1961-63; tchr. music Scotch Plains-Fanwood (N.J.) Bd. Edn., 1963—; dir. summer session Scotch Plains-Farwood (N.J.) Bd. Edn., 1964-75, dist. coord. music, 1972-75; music dir. Green Laniers Bugle & Drum Corps, VFW, Ewing, N.J., 1958-63; music dir., conductor Bridgewater Recreation Concert Band, 1968-73. Mem. Planning Bd., Raritan, N.J., 1981-83; chmn. and mem. Assessment Commn., Raritan, 1985—; pres. and mem. Bridgewater-Raritan Bd. Edn., 1986—. Mem. NEA, N.J. Music Edn. Assn., Music Educators Nat. Conf., Am. String Tchrs. Assn., N.J. Sch. Bds. Assn., Nat. Sch. Bd. Assn., Somerset County Sch. Bd. Assn., N.J. Edn. Assn., Scotch Plains Farwood Edn. Assn. (pres. 1981-86). Home: 1006 Arnold Ave Raritan NJ 08869-1602

TROST, DONALD CRAIG, pharmaceutical company executive, epidemiologist; b. Creston, Iowa, Oct. 6, 1951; s. Donald Howard and Dorothy Mae (Selders) T.; m. Roberta Lee Reinert, May 22, 1976; children: Jason Reinert, Brian Christopher. BS, U. Iowa, 1974, MD, MS, 1978; PhD, U. N.C., 1988. Postdoctoral fellow U. N.C., Chapel Hill, 1978-81; resident in clin. pathology U. Fla., Gainesville, 1981-83, instr. pathology, 1983-84; dir. Pribor Systems, Inc., Nashville, 1984-85; div. v.p. Health Devel. Inc., Nashville, 1984-85, v.p., 1985-86; asst. dir. epidemiology E.R. Squibb & Sons, Princeton, N.J., 1986-87, dir., 1987-89; assoc. med. dir. DuPont Pharms., Wilmington, Del., 1989—. Office: DuPont Pharms BMP 26-2278 Wilmington DE 19880-0026

TROTTA, MARCIA MARIE, librarian, consultant, education educator; b. Meriden, Conn., Nov. 12, 1949; d. Salvatore Dominic and Teresa Stella (Fuda) Marando; m. Carmine Joseph Trotta, Oct. 23, 1971; 1 child, Christopher Michael. AB, Albertus Mangus Coll., 1971; MLS, So. Conn. State U., 1979. Tchr. St. Mary's Sch., Meriden, 1971-73; circulation libr. Meriden Pub. Libr., 1973-74, asst. children's libr., 1974-76, reference libr., 1976-81, dir. children's libr., 1981-91, asst. dir., 1992—; adj. prof. So. Conn. State U., New Haven, 1987—; cons. Pfizer Metall. Libr., Wallingford, Conn., 1987, Woodbridge Town Libr., 1987-89, Conn. Assocs. for Counseling, Wilton, 1988—. Editor: CDA Manual, Outreach Services for Children and Youth, 1992. Mem. coun. day care adv. com., Meriden, 1990—; mem. coun. Student Drug & Alcohol Abuse Prevention, Meriden, 1990—; pres. Conn. Jaycee Women, 1984-85. Named one of Outstanding Women of Am., U.S. Jaycee Women, 1983, recipient Steve Little award, 1986. Mem. ALA, Conn.

Libr. Assn. (pres. 1991—, Outstanding Libr. 1986), New Eng. Libr. Assn., Soroptimists Internat. (v.p. Meriden chpt. 1989). Democrat. Roman Catholic. Home: 28 Goffe St Meriden CT 06450-1808 Office: Meriden Pub Libr 105 Miller St Meriden CT 06450-4285

TROTTER-STEWART, AVA MARIE, educator; b. Baton Rouge, July 15, 1958; d. Albert and Julia (Harrell) Trotter; m. Polite Donald Stewart, Dec. 19, 1981. BS, So. U., Baton Rouge, 1979, MEd, 1984; MEd, Columbia U., 1987, EdD, 1989. Speech tchr. East Baton Rouge Parish Sch. Bd., 1980-81; teaching asst. So. U., Baton Rouge, 1983-84; tchr. English sci. and tech. enrichment program Columbia U., N.Y.C., 1986-88; adj. instr. Coll. of New Rochelle, N.Y., 1987-89, dir. English, 1989—. Mem. Nat. Coun. Tchrs. English, Kappa Delta Pi. Office: Coll New Rochelle Rosa Parks Campus 144 W 125th St New York NY 10027

TROUSDALE, MARION STELLING, English educator, researcher; b. Tacoma, Sept. 22, 1929; d. Herman John Jacob and Frances (Sconce) Stelling; m. William Brown Trousdale, July 23, 1953. BA, U. Mich., 1951; MA, U. Calif., Berkeley, 1955; PhD, U. London, 1975. Lectr. U. Md., College Park, 1970-75, asst. prof., 1975-78, assoc. prof., 1978-87, prof., 1987—. Author: Shakespeare and the Rhetoricians, 1982; editor: Texts and Pretexts in the English Renaissance, 1989, Shakespeare's Language, 1991. NEH fellow Huntington Libr., 1987-88, O.B. Hardison fellow Folger Shakespeare Libr., 1991—. Mem. Modern Lang. Assn., Internat. Shakespeare Assn., Soc. for Textual Studies, Internat. Assn. Univ. Profs. of English, Marlowe Assn. Am., Shakespeare Assn. Am., Malone Soc. Office: U Md Dept English College Park MD 20742

TROUTMAN, E. MAC, federal judge; b. Greenwood Township, Pa., Jan. 7, 1915; s. Emmett Theodore and Kathryn (Holman) T.; m. Margaret Petrick, Nov. 23, 1946; children—Jane A., Jean K. A.B., Dickinson Coll., 1934, LL.B., 1936. Bar: Pa. 1937. With Phila. and Reading Coal and Iron Co., 1937-58, gen. counsel, 1954-58; gen. atty. Phila. and Reading Corp., 1958-67; gen. counsel Reading Anthracita Co., 1958-61, Reserve Carbon Corp., 1961-66, So. Carbon Corp., 1966-67; solicitor Blue Mountain Sch. Dist., 1963-67, Blue Mountain Area Sch. Authority, 1963-67, Orwigsburg Municipal Authority, 1966-67, Am. Bank and Trust Co., Reading and Pottsville, Pa., 1957-67; exec. sec., gen. counsel Pa. Self-Insurers Assn., 1962-67; U.S. judge Eastern Dist. Pa., from 1967, now sr. judge. Bd. dirs. Greater Pottsville Indsl. Devel. Corp., 1963-67, Pa. C. of C., 1955-65, Greater Pottsville Area C. of C., 1961-64, Orwigsburg Community Meml. Assn., 1950-66, Schuylkill County Soc. Crippled Children, 1945-67; v.p., dir. Pottsville Hosp. and Warne Clinic, 1960-67. Served with AUS, World War II. Mem. ABA, Pa. Bar Assn., Schuylkill County Bar Assn. (vice chancellor 1955-57, chmn. jud. vacancies and unauthorized practice coms. 1960, chmn. medico-legal com. 1963-65). Lutheran (pres. coun. 1961—). Club: Lion (bd. dirs. Orwigsburg 1964). Home: Kimmel's Rd Orwigsburg PA 17961 Office: The Madison Bldg 400 Washington St Rm 517 Reading PA 19601-3908

TROXEL, DONALD EUGENE, electrical engineering educator; b. Trenton, N.J., Mar. 11, 1934; s. Shirley Monroe and Emma Ruth (Marvel) T.; m. Eileen Millicent Cronk, Aug. 23, 1963; children: Gregory, Jocelyn, Andrea. BS, Rutgers U., 1956; SM, MIT, 1960, PhD, 1962. Ford Found. postdoctoral fellow, asst. prof. MIT, Cambridge, Mass., 1962-64, asst. prof. dept. elec. engring., 1964-67, assoc. prof., 1967-85, prof. elec. engring., 1985—; asst. prof. Tufts U., Medford, Mass., 1963; bd. dirs. ECRM, Inc., Tewksbury, Mass. 1st lt. U.S. Army, 1956-58. Mem. IEEE (sr. mem., Leonard G. Abraham Prize Paper award 1971), Assn. for Computing Machinery, Sigma Xi, Tau Beta Pi, Eta Kappa Nu, Pi Mu Epsilon. Home: 4 Madison St Belmont MA 02178-3536 Office: MIT 36-287 77 Massachusetts Ave Cambridge MA 02139-4307

TROXELL, WILLIAM JAMES, association executive; b. Danville, Pa., Dec. 11, 1957; s. John Franklin and Ethyl Nancy (Geise) T. BS in Horticulture, Delaware Valley Coll., 1979; MS in Horticulture, Pa. State U., 1982. Greenhouse grower Dale Whitenight Farm Market, Danville, 1983-89; exec. sec. Pa. Vegetable Growers Assn., Northumberland, 1983—, Pa. Vegetable Mktg. and Rsch. Program, Harrisburg, 1989—; del. Pa. Hort. Trade Alliance, Harrisburg, 1988—, pres., 1992; mem. exec. com. Pa. Coun. Farm Orgns., Harrisburg, 1991—. Editor Pa. Vegetable Grower News, 1984—. Deacon Trinity Luth. Ch., 1984-88, 90—; supt. Trinity Union Sun. Sch., 1985—. Mem. Pa. Soc. Assn. Execs., Pa. Farmers Assn., Northumberland County Farmers Assn., Am. Soc. for Hort. Sci. Home and Office: RR 1 Box 392 Northumberland PA 17857-9723

TROYAN, JOHN ANTHONY, III, musician, graphic artist; b. Somerset, N.J., Dec. 28, 1968; s. John Anthony and Kathleen (Fetzko) T. AS, Raritan Valley Community Coll., Somerville, N.J., 1989; BS, Montclair State Coll., 1992. Database specialist Hoechst/Celanese Corp., Bridgewater, N.J., 1988-89; illustrator Ford Aerospace Corp., Sunnyvale, Calif., 1989-90; graphics mgr. The Montclarion, Upper Montclair, N.J., 1991—; co-owner, producer TroyDan Prodns., Hillsborough, N.J., 1989—; art dir. Class One Concerts, Upper Montclair, 1990—; freelance graphic artist. Rotary Found. scholar, 1987, Hancouski Found. scholar, 1991, SCORE scholar, 1991; recipient Gary L. Palumbo Found. award, 1991. Mem. RVCC Alumni Assn. Home: 5 Cranbrook Ave Hillsborough NJ 08876-4803

TROYER, THOMAS ALFRED, lawyer; b. Omaha, Aug. 15, 1933; s. Robert Raymond and Dorothy (Darlow) T.; m. Sally Jean Brown, June 28, 1958; children: Kenneth D., Robert C., Virginia D., Thomas C. BA, Harvard U., 1955; JD, U. Mich., 1958. Bar: Colo. 1958, U.S. Ct. Appeals (D.C. cir.) 1967. Assoc. Holme, Roberts, More & Owen, Denver, 1958-61; USAF, Denver, 1961-62; trial atty. U.S. Dept. Justice, Washington, 1962-64; mem. legal staff Asst. Sec. Treasury for Tax Policy, Washington, 1964-66; assoc. tax legis. counsel U.S. Dept. Treasury, Washington, 1966-67; mem. Caplin & Drysdale, Washington, 1967—; pres. Stern Fund, N.Y.C., 1985-86; bd. dirs., Children's Def. Fund, Washington, Mineral Policy Ctr., Washington, Am. Tax Policy Inst., Washington; mem. bd. trustees Natural Resources Def. Coun., N.Y.C., 1977—, Carnegie Corp., N.Y.C., 1983—. Contbr. numerous articles to profl. jours. Mem. Treasury Adv. Commn. on Pvt. Philanthropy and Pub. Needs, Washington, 1976-77; mem. adv. group to Commr. Internal Rev., Washington, 1978-80; mem. com. of visitors U. Mich. Law Sch., Ann Arbor, 1982—; mem. IRS Commr.'s Exempt Orgn. Adv. Group, Washington, 1987-90. Fellow Am. Coll. Tax Counsel; mem. Am. Law Inst., ABA (vice chmn. govt. rels. tax sect. 1989-91). Democrat. Home: 16 Primrose St Bethesda MD 20815-4229 Office: Caplin & Drysdale Chartered 1 Thomas Cir NW Washington DC 20005-5802

TRUDEAU, GARRY B., cartoonist; b. N.Y.C., 1948; m. Jane Pauley; children: 1 son, 1 dau. (twins). Grad., Yale U. and Yale U. Sch. Art and Architecture. Creator: comic strip Doonesbury; syndicated nationwide comic strip; author: Still a Few Bugs in the System, 1972, The President is a Lot Smarter Than You Think, 1973, But This War Had Such Promise, 1973, Call Me When You Find America, 1973, Guilty, Guilty, Guilty, 1974, The Doonesbury Chronicles, 1975, What Do We Have for the Witnesses, Johnnie?, 1975, Dare to Be Great, Ms. Caucus, 1975, Wouldn't A Gremlin Have Been More Sensible?, 1975, Speaking of Inalienable Rights, Amy..., 1976, You're Never Too Old for Nuts and Berries, 1976, An Especially Tricky People, 1977, As the Kid Goes For Broke, 1977, Stalking the Perfect Tan, 1978, Any Grooming Hints for Your Fans, Rollie?, 1978, Doonesbury's Greatest Hits, 1978, But The Pension Fund was Just Sitting There, 1979, We're Not Out of the Woods Yet, 1979, A Tad Overweight, but Violet Eyes to Die For, 1980, And That's My Final Offer!, 1980, The People's Doonesbury, 1981, He's Never Heard of You, Either, 1981, In Search of Reagan's Brain, 1981, Ask for May, Settle for June, 1982, Unfortunately, She Was Also Wired for Sound, 1982, The Wreck of the Rusty Nail, 1983, You Give Great Meeting, Sid, 1983, Doonesbury Dossier: The Reagan Years, 1984, Doonesbury: A Musical Comedy, 1984, Check Your Egos at the Door, 1986, That's Doctor Sinatra, You Little Bimbo, 1986, Death of a Party Animal, 1986, Doonesbury Deluxe: Selected Glances Askance, 1987, Downtown Doonesbury, 1987, Calling Dr. Whoopee, 1987, Talking Bout My G-G-Generation, 1988, We're Eating More Beets, 1988, Read My Lips, Make My Day, Eat Quiche & Die! A Doonesbury Collection, 1989, Recycled Doonesbury: Second Thoughts on a Gilded Age, 1990, You're Smokin' Now, Mr. Butts! A Doonesbury Book, 1990; contbr.: (with Nicholas von Hoffman) publs. including The People's Doonesbury; many others (recipient Pulitzer prize 1975); plays include: Doonesbury, 1983, Rapmaster Ronnie, A Partisan Review (with Elizabeth Swados), 1984. *

TRUDEAU, PIERRE ELLIOTT, lawyer, former Canadian prime minister; b. Montreal, Que., Can., Oct. 18, 1919; s. Charles-Emile and Grace (Elliott) T.; m. Margaret Sinclair, Mar. 4, 1971 (div.); children: Justin Pierre, Alexandre Emmanuel, Michel Charles-Emile. B.A., Jean de Brebeuf Coll., Montreal, 1940; LL.L., U. Montreal, 1943; M.A., Harvard U., 1945; student, Ecole des Sciences Politiques, Paris, London Sch. Econs.; LLD (hon.), U. Alta., 1968, Queen's U., Kingston, 1968, U. Ottawa, 1974, Duke U., 1974, U. Keio, Japan, 1976, St. Xavier U., N.S., 1982, Notre Dame U., 1982, Dalhousie U., 1983, McGill U., 1985, U. B.C., 1986, U. Montreal, 1987, U. East Asia, Macau, 1987, Mt. Alison U., 1989, U. Toronto, 1991; LittD (hon.), U. Moncton, 1969. Bar: Que. 1944, Ont. 1967; created Queen's counsel 1969. Practiced law in Montreal, 1952—; jr. economist staff Privy Council, Ottawa, Ont., Can., 1949; assoc. prof. law, mem. Inst. Pub. Law U. Montreal, 1961-65; former mem. Ho. of Commons, from 1965; parliamentary sec. to prime minister, 1966-67; minister justice, atty. gen. Can., 1967-68; leader Liberal party, from 1968; prime minister Can., 1968-79, 80-84; leader of opposition in parliment, 1979-80, mem. Privy Council,, from 1979; mem. Heenan Blaikie and predecessor firms, 1984—; co-founder Cité Libre (monthly rev.); del. France-Can. Interparliamentary Assn., 1966, UN, 1966. Author: Towards a Just Society: The Trudeau Years, 1990. Decorated Order of Companions of Honor (Gt. Britain). Recipient Ralston prize Faculty of Law Stanford U., Calif., 1990; Albert Einstein Internat. Peace prize, 1984; named Companion of Honour, 1984, Companion of the Order of Can., 1985, hon. dean Faculty of Law U. Poitiers, France, 1975; hon. fellow London Sch. Econs., 1968. Mem. Canadian Bar Assn., Montreal Civil Liberties Union, Royal Soc. Can. Liberal. Roman Catholic. Office: Heenan Blaikie y Assocs, 1001 de Maisonneuve, Montreal, PQ Canada H3A 3C8

TRUITT, DAVID CHARLES, music educator; b. Jamestown, N.Y., Nov. 15, 1951; s. David B. and Ann (Pierson) T.; m. Mary Lawn, June 1, 1974; children: Nathan, Martha, Timothy. B of Music Performance, U. Hartford, 1980; MA in Musicology, Marywood Coll., 1986. Mem. guitar faculty Barley Sch. of Music, Fairport, N.Y., 1974-75; lectr. in music Alfred (N.Y.) U., 1976; lectr. in music Marywood Coll., Scranton, Pa., 1980-83, 88—, assoc. in guitar, 1983-88; tchr., pvt. music lessons various, 1973—. Named to Outstanding Young Men of Am., 1984; recipient Melvin medal for Libr. Utilization, Marywood Coll., 1986. Mem. Am. Musicol. Soc. (presenter conf. 1986), Coll. Music Soc. (presenter conf. 1986), Am. String Tchrs. Assn., Guitar Found. of Am., Pi Kappa Lambda (pres. Zeta Epsilon chpt. 1987-88). Home: 123 College Ave PO Box 5 Factoryville PA 18419-0005 Office: Marywood Coll 2300 Adams Ave Scranton PA 18509-1598

TRUITT, GARY ARTHUR, pharmacologist; b. Boulder, Colo., Mar. 31, 1947; s. Arthur Leonard and Dorothy Velma (Reese) T.; m. Theresa Patricia-Ann Striegel, May 7, 1982; children: Kelley Catherine, Christian Alec. BA, Pitts. State U., Kans., 1970; PhD, U. Kans. Med. Ctr., 1975. Postdoctoral fellow Baylor Coll. Medicine, Houston, 1975-78; NSF fellow Nat. Naval Med. Ctr., Bethesda, Md., 1979-80; postdoctoral fellow Thomas Jefferson U., Phila., 1980-82; sr. scientist Hoffmann-La Roche, Inc., Nutley, N.J., 1982-87, rsch. investigator, 1987—. Contbr. articles to profl. jours.; patentee in field. Fellow Kelsey Leary Found., Houston, 1976-78. Mem. AAAS, Fedn. Am. Socs. for Exptl. Biology and Medicine, N.Y. Acad. Sci., Am.Assn. Immunology, Sigma Xi. Office: Hoffmann LaRoche Inc 340 Kingsland St Nutley NJ 07110

TRULUCK, PHILLIP NELSON, foundation administrator; b. Florence, S.C., June 18, 1947; s. Ray Nelson and Ethel Estelle (Mason) T.; m. Ann Barbara Wrobleski, Jan. 6, 1979; children, Mason Martha, Walker Edward, Sutton Arthur. BS, U. S.C., 1970. Rsch. asst. U.S. Senate, Washington, 1971-73; legis. asst. U.S. Ho. Reps., Washington, 1973-74, dep. dir. Rep. study com., 1974-77; dir. rsch. The Heritage Found., Washington, 1977-78, v.p., 1978-81, exec. v.p., chief operating officer, 1981—; chmn. Ctr. for Peace and Freedom, Washington, 1986—; founder, bd. dirs. Ctr. for Internat. Pvt. Enterprise, Washington, 1983-90. Editor: Balancing the Budget, 1978, Private Rights and Public Lands, 1980. Pub. mem. Adminstrv. Conf. of the U.S., Washington, 1986—; exec. com. Pres. Pvt. Sector Survey on Cost Control, Washington, 1982-83; mem. White Ho. Fellows Selection Com., Washington, 1985-86. Mem. Mont Pelerin Soc., Phila. Soc., U. Club, Capital Hill Club, Avenel Club. Office: The Heritage Found 214 Massachusetts Ave NE Washington DC 20002-4958

TRUMBORE, CONRAD NOBLE, chemistry educator; b. Denver, Feb. 17, 1931; s. Harry Andrew and Lola Virginia (Pusey) T.; m. Jean Isabel Foight, Aug. 19, 1955 (dec. Aug. 1990); children: Samuel Alan, Susan Elizabeth; m. Virginia Dunn Ahrens, Aug. 29, 1992. BS, Dickinson Coll., 1952; PhD, Pa. State U., 1955. Fulbright fellow Inst. for Nuclear Rsch., Amsterdam, Netherlands, 1955-56; postdoctoral chemist Argonne (Ill.) Nat. Lab., 1956-57; instr., chemistry Univ. Rochester, N.Y., 1957-60; asst. prof. Univ. Delaware, Newark, 1960-67, assoc. prof., 1967—, dir. grad. studies chemistry/biochemistry dept., 1990—, asst. chair chemistry/biochemistry dept., 1990—; U.S. Pub. Health fellow Inst. for Cancer Rsch., Sutton, Surrey, England, 1967-68. Patentee in field; contbr. articles to profl. jours. Chair Dem. Com. 23rd dist., Newark, 1970-73. Mem. Radiation Authority Delaware (chair 1980-82). Unitarian Universalist. Home: 113 Dallas Ave Newark DE 19711-5125 Office: Chemistry/Biochemistry Dept Univ of Delaware Newark DE 19716

TRUMP, BECKY ANN, hospital administrator; b. Lancaster, Pa., Oct. 28, 1955; d. John Raymond and Shirley Ann (Hess) Snyder; m. Peter Martin Trump, June 26, 1976 (div. Mar. 1984); children: Gretchen Marie, Savannah Lee. Diploma in nursing, St. Joseph Hosp., Lancaster, 1976; BS summa cum laude, Chapman Coll., Orange, Calif., 1981; MBA in Health Adminstrn., St. Joseph's U., Phila., 1989. RN. Mem. nursing staff Bass Meml. Bapt. Hosp., Enid, Okla., 1976-77, Columbus (Miss.) Hosp., Inc., 1982-83; supr. nursing Beverly Manor, Riverside, Calif., 1978-82; charge nurse Lancaster Gen. Hosp., 1984-85; from head nurse mental health to dir. clin. support svc. Ephrata (Pa.) Community Hosp., 1985-89, asst. v.p. for planning and ancillary svcs., 1989-91, aux. treas., 1990-91; adminstrv. dir. physical medicine and rehabilitation Lancaster (Pa.) Gen. Hosp., 1991—. Recipient Great Am. Family award Children and Youth Svcs. County of Lancaster, 1987. Mem. Am. Coll. Healthcare Execs. Republican. Lutheran. Home: 404 Hilton Dr Lancaster PA 17603-5706 Office: Lancaster Gen Hosp 555 N Duke St PO Box 3555 Lancaster PA 17603

TRUMP, DONALD JOHN, real estate developer; b. N.Y.C., 1946; s. Fred C. and Mary Trump; m. Ivana Zelnicek, 1977 (div. 1991); children: Donald Jr., Ivanka, Eric. Student, Fordham U.; BA, U. Pa., 1968. Pres. Trump Orgn., N.Y.C.; owner Trump Enterprises Inc., N.Y.C., The Trump Corp., N.Y.C., Trump Devel. Co., N.Y.C., Wembly Realty Inc., Park South Co., Land Corp. of Calif., Pla. Hotel, Trump Tower, Trump Pla., Trump Parc, Trump Palace, all N.Y.C.; chmn., owner Trump Shuttle (formerly Ea. Air Shuttle); owner Trump Pla., Trump Castle, Trump Taj Mahal, casinos, hotels, Atlantic City, Trump Pla. of the Palm Beaches, Fla., West Side Rail Yards to be devel. as Riverside South, N.Y.C., Trump Regency Hotel, Atlantic City. Author: The Art of the Deal, 1987, Surviving at the Top, 1990. Co-chmn. N.Y. Vietnam Vets. Meml. Fund; founding mem. constrn. com. Cathedral of St. John the Divine; mem. N.Y. Citizens Tax Coun., Fifth Ave Assn., Realty Found. of N.Y., Met. Mus. of Art's Real Estate Coun.; bd. dirs. Police Athletic League; mem. adv. bd. Lenox Hill Hosp., United Cerebral Palsy; spl. advisor to Pres.'s Coun. on Phys. Fitness and Sports; mem. N.Y. Sportsplex Commn.; bd. of overseers Wharton Sch.; mem. adv. bd. Wharton Real Estate Ctr.; bd. dirs. Fred C. Trump Found.; chmn. N.Y. citizens com. 78th Ann. NAACP Conv., 1987. Recipient Entrepreneur of Yr. award Wharton Entrepreneurial Club, 1984, Ellis Island Medal of Honor, 1986; inducted Wharton Hall of Fame. *

TRUOG, DEAN-DANIEL WESLEY, education educator, consultant; b. Denver, Apr. 1, 1938; s. George Calvin and Zelma Elizabeth (Bennett) T.; m. Dorothy Anne Harding, May 31, 1961; children: David Robert, Denise Dawn. BA in History, U. Colo., 1971; Diploma in Gen. Univ. Studies in French Civilization, U. Strasbourg, France, 1977; MA in Liberal Edn., St. John's Coll. Grad. Inst., 1986; M of Liberal Arts in History of Sci., Harvard U., 1987. Sr. resident adv. U. Colo., Boulder, 1964-65; rep. The Navigators, 1965—, rep. for greater Washington area, 1965-67; training asst. The Navigators, Colorado Springs, Colo., 1968; rep. at U. Colo. The Navigators, Boulder, 1968-70, No. Colo. dir., 1970-71; spl. adv. The Navigators, Birmingham, Eng., 1971-72; rep. at large The Navigators, Boulder, Colo., 1979-80; founding dir., pres. Les Navigators, France, 1972-84; v.p. Les Navigators, France, 1984-85, rep. to U. Strasbourg, 1973-79, rep. to U. Grenoble, 1980-85; sr. teaching fellow Harvard U., Cambridge, Mass., 1987-90; tutor North House, Harvard U., 1986-91; speaker, tchr. Profl. Confs.; designer, dir. leadership devel. programs Boston, Washington, Colo., Austria, France, Switzerland; pres. Cornerstone Inst., 1990—. With USN, 1958-59. Recipient Distinction in Teaching cert. Harvard U., 1990. Mem. History of Sci. Soc., Am. Sci. Affiliation, Soc. of Christian Philosophers, Assoc. for Religion and Intellectual Life, Inst. on Religion in an Age of Sci., Ctr. for Theology and the Natural Scis. Presbyterian. Home and Office: 15 Sheridan Rd Swampscott MA 01907

TRURAN, WILLIAM R., electrical engineer; b. Franklin, N.J., Feb. 14, 1951; s. Wilfred Hardy and Stella Eva (Hall) T.; m. Virginia Lynn Johnson, Aug. 18, 1979; children: Michael, Wendy. BSEE, U. Tenn., 1972; MBA, Fairleigh Dickinson U., 1981; postgrad., Columbia U., NYU. Registered profl. engr., N.J., N.Y., Pa., Calif.; registered profl. planner, N.J. Design engr. Gordos Corp., Bloomfield, N.J., 1972-73; project engr. Edwards Engring., Pompton Plains, N.J., 1973-78; sr. engr. Apollo Tech., Whippany, N.J., 1978-81; elec. product mgr. Dodge-Newark, Fairfield, N.J., 1981—; pres. Trupower Engring., Sparta, N.J., 1984—; pres. T.E.C. Corp. of N.J., Sparta; cons. in field. Contbr. articles to profl. jours. Active foster child orgn. Christian Children's Fund. Mem. Nat. Soc. Profl. Engrs. (legis. action network, minuteman), Nat. Assn. Environ. Profls., Wilderness Soc., Sierra (foster child program). Episcopalian. Home and Office: 37 Rainbow Trl Sparta NJ 07871-1724

TRUSSELLE, GAR DELANO, construction company executive; b. Albion, N.Y., Oct. 21, 1946; s. Kenneth Porter and Laurel Ann (Delano) T.; m. Janice Louise Passarell, Apr. 12, 1970; children: Jessica Anne, Martha Porter. Grad. pub. schs., Albion. Lic. master electrician. Pres. Suburban Electric Inc., Albion, 1969—. Chmn. Village of Albion Planning Bd., 1982—. Republican. Universalist. Lodge: Elks. Home: 223 S Clinton St Albion NY 14411-1505 Office: Suburban Electric Inc 225 E Bank St Albion NY 14411-1213

TRYON, GEORGIANA SHICK, psychologist; b. Glendale, Calif., Mar. 28, 1945; d. Norman Alton and Nancy Emily (Shaffer) Shick; m. Warren W. Tryon, July 31, 1970; 1 child, Elizabeth. B.A., Pa. State U., 1966; M.A., Kent State U., 1969, Ph.D., 1971. Lic. psychologist, N.Y. Psychologist to outpatients N.Y. Hosp., N.Y.C., 1971-72; dir. Counseling Ctr., Fordham U., N.Y.C., 1972-75, Bronx, N.Y., 1975—; pvt. practice psychology, Briarcliff Manor, N.Y., 1973—. Author, editor: The Professional Practice of Psychology, 1986. Contbr. articles to psychology jours. Mem. Am. Psychol. Assn., Assn. for Advancement Behavior Therapy, Nat. Assn. Women Deans, Counselors and Adminstrs., Eastern Psychol. Assn., N.Y. State Psychol. Assn. Office: Fordham U 226 Dealy Hall Bronx NY 10458

TRYON, WARREN WILLARD, psychologist, educator; b. Schenectady, N.Y., May 26, 1944; s. Warren Willard and Dorothy Elizabeth (Hill) T.; m. Georgiana Shick, July 31, 1970; 1 child, Elizabeth. BA, Ohio Northern U., 1966; MA, Kent State U., 1969, PhD, 1970. Diplomate Am. Bd. Profl. Psychology. Asst. prof. Fordham U., Bronx, N.Y., 1970-77, assoc. prof., 1977-83, prof., 1983—. Editor: Behavioral Assessment in Behavior Medicine, 1985, Ethics in Applied Dev. Psychology; author: Activity Measurement in Psychology and Medicine, 1991. Social Security grantee, 1988, NIH grantee, 1988, Nat. Multiple Sclerosis Soc. grantee, 1988. Mem. APA, N.Y. Psychological Assn., Assn. Advancement Behavior Therapy. Office: Fordham U Psychology Dept 338 Dealy Hall Bronx NY 10458-5198

TSAI, TONG-CHING, orthopedic surgeon; b. Yanli, Maili, Taiwan, May 1, 1934; came to U.S., 1963; s. Shu-Tau and A-Hei (Wang) T.; m. Tsuey-Ying Shih, Sept. 7, 1963; children: Melissa Pei-Wen, Albert Mu-Hong, Betsy Ching-Fen. MB, Nat. Taiwan U., 1960. Attending orthopedic surgeon Wayne (N.J.) Gen. Hosp., 1970—, Chilton Meml. Hosp., Pompton Plain, N.J., 1972—; pres. med. staff Wayne Gen. Hosp., 1984. Fellow, Am. Acad. Orthopedic Surgery, Am. Coll. Surgeons; mem. Passaic County Med. Soc., N.J. Med. Soc. Office: 220 Hamburg Tpk Wayne NJ 07470

TSE, MARY MO-YUNG, physician, obstetrician-gynecologist; b. Canton, Guangdong, China, Nov. 11, 1949; came to U.S., 1968; d. Chung Pun and Shai Kwan (Wong) T. BSc with distinction, Simmons Coll., Boston, 1972; MD, U. Mass., Worcester, 1977. Diplomate Am. Bd. Obstetrics and Gynecology. Legal sec. Samuel Bonaccorso, Esquire, Boston, 1968-69; lab. rsch. asst. Beth Israel Hosp. and Mass. Gen. Hosp., Boston, 1971-73; internship ob-gyn. Baystate Med. Ctr., Springfield, Mass., 1977-78; resident in ob-gyn. Baystate Med. Ctr., Springfield, 1978-81; physician Family Planning Clinic, Northampton, Mass., 1978-81; chief dept. of ob-gyn. Community Health Care Plan, Inc., New Haven, 1981-83; obstetrician-gynecologist Effie C. Chang M.D., P.C., New Haven, 1983-87; pvt. practice ob-gyn New Haven, 1987—; Emergency Med. Technician and examiner, Worcester, Mass., 1974-75; attending physician Yale New Haven Hosp. and Hosp. of St. Raphael, 1983—; clin. instr. Yale U. Sch. Medicine, 1981—. Staff mem. SAMPAN, Boston Bilingual Newsletter, 1971-72; student rep. search com. for dean U. Mass. Med. Sch., Worcester, 1975. Fellow Am. Coll. Ob-Gyn.; mem. New Haven County Med. Assn., New Eng. Ob-Gyn. Soc., New Haven Ob-Gyn. Soc., Conn. State Ob-Gyn, Conn. State Med. Soc. Roman Catholic. Office: 136 Sherman Ave New Haven CT 06511-5210

TSENG, AMELIE FAN-IN, public relations executive; b. Bklyn., Mar. 21, 1963; d. Charles Li-jen and Hua Chin (Chen) T. BA in Psychology, Vassar Coll., 1984. Adminstrv. asst. Benton & Bowles Advt., N.Y.C., 1984-85; asst. account exec. Manning, Selvage & Lee Pub. Rels., N.Y.C., 1985-87; account exec. pub. rels. Amy Alter Assocs., N.Y.C., 1987-88; pvt. practice N.Y.C., 1988; sr. account exec. Bender, Goldman & Helper Pub. Rels., N.Y.C., 1988-89; mgr. pub. rels. Group W Satellite Communications, N.Y.C., 1989—. Vol. The Lighthouse, 1989; alumna interviewer Vassar Coll., 1990; v.p. Class of '84/Vassar Coll., 1984-90. Mem. Cable TV Pub. Affairs Assn., Nat. Acad. Cable Programming, Cable TV Adminstrn. and Mktg. Soc., Nat. Acad. TV Arts and Scis., Internat. Ctr. Photography, Am. Film Inst., Nat. Cable TV Assn., Vassar Coll. Alumni Assn. (21st Century com. N.Y.C., 1988—). Office: Group W Comm 685 3d Ave New York NY 10017-4024

TSENG, KADIN, aeronautical research engineer; b. Haiphong, Vietnam, July 24, 1946; came to U.S., 1972; s. Tho-Dien and Tu-Phuong (Uong) T.; m. Chun-May Lam, Jan. 13, 1972; 1 child, Jane. BSME, Nat. Taiwan U., 1971; MS in Aerospace Engring., Boston U., 1980, PhD in Math., 1983. Rsch. assoc. Boston U., 1980-83; rsch. scientist, v.p. ACES, Inc., Boston, 1980-84; rsch. scientist Icarus, Boston, 1984-85; sr. rsch. engr. United Techs. Rsch. Ctr., East Hartford, Conn., 1985—; adj. asst. prof. Boston U., 1984-85; co-chmn. Internat. Symposium on Boundary Element Methods, East Hartford, 1989. Editor: Boundary Element Methods in Engineering, 1990; contbr. over 50 articles to profl. jours. Recipient citation Glastonbury (Conn.) Police Dept., 1987; rsch. grantee NASA, 1980-85. Mem. AIAA. Office: United Techs Rsch Ctr Silver Ln East Hartford CT 06118-1010

TSENG, LINDA, medical educator; b. Kiansu, People's Republic China, Sept. 29, 1936; came to U.S., 1963; d. Chia-yu Wang and Sin-pai Chiang; m. John K. Tseng, Dec. 23, 1936; 1 child, Angela. BS, Cheng Kung U., 1959; PhD, U. N.D., 1968. Asst. prof. U. Minn., Mpls., 1970-71, Mt. Sinai Sch. Medicine, CUNY, N.Y.C., 1971-76; assoc. prof. SUNY, Stony Brook, 1976-91, prof., 1991—. Author: (with others) Modern Pharmacology-Toxicology, Part I, Vol. 8, 1976, Endometrial Cancer, 1978, Obstetrics and Gynecology Annual, Vol. 8, 1979, Proceeding of 8th Brook Lodge on Problems of Reproductive Physiology, 1980, Serono Symposia Series, The Mechanism of Menstrual Bleeding, 1986, Consensus Development Conference on Progestogen, 1989; contbr. articles and abstracts to profl. jours. Recipient Irma T. Hirschl Rsch. Career Scientist award, 1976-80; grantee Biomed. Rsch. Grant, 1976-77, Community Ednl. Devel. Assn. Program, 1979-80, N.Y. Health Rsch. Coun., 1977-82, NIH Human Devel. Inst., 1977-81, 86-89, 89-92, Ciba-Geigy Pharm., 1982-84, Am. Cancer Soc. Prevention Therapeutic and

Drug Cancer Rsch., 1984-85, Lalor Found., 1985-87, NIH NRSA, 1987-91, WHO, 1991-92, Johnson-Johnson Orthopharm., 1991-92.

TSOUCALAS, NICHOLAS, federal judge; b. N.Y.C., Aug. 24, 1926; s. George Michael and Maria (Monogenis) T.; m. Catherine Aravantinos, Nov. 21, 1954; children: Stephanie, Georgia. BSBA, Kent State U., 1949; LLB, N.Y. Law Sch., 1951. Bar: N.Y. 1953. Sole practice, N.Y.C., 1953-55, 59-68; asst. U.S. atty. So. Dist. N.Y., 1955-59; judge Criminal Ct., City of N.Y., 1968-86; acting supreme ct. judge State of N.Y., N.Y.C., 1975-82; judge U.S. Ct. Internat. Trade, N.Y.C., 1986—. Dist. leader Republican Party N.Y. County, N.Y.C., 1961-68; mem. Rep. Exec. Com., N.Y.C., 1961-68. Served with USN, 1944-46, 51-52. Recipient Proficiency in Constl. Law award N.Y. Law Sch., N.Y.C., 1951, Man of Yr. award St. Paul Soc., N.Y.C., 1971. Mem. ABA, N.Y. County Lawyers Assn., Queens County Bar Assn., Fed. Bar Assn., Greek Am. Lawyers Assn., Am. Hellenic Ednl. Prog. Assn. Republican. Greek Orthodox. Lodges: Parthenon, Masons. Office: US Ct Internat Trade 1 Federal Pla New York NY 10007

TSUI, CHIA-CHI, electrical engineer, educator; b. Shanghai, Apr. 23, 1953; came to the U.S., 1979; s. Xue-Zhu and Zhao-Hui (Zhang) T. BS in Computer Sci., Concordia U., Montreal, 1979; MEE, SUNY, Stony Brook, 1980, PhD, 1983. Farmer Long River State Farm, Hei-Long-Jiang, Peoples Republic of China, 1969-75; asst. prof. dept. elec. engring. Northeastern U., Boston, 1983-88; assoc. prof. CUNY Coll. Staten Island, 1988—. Contbr. articles to profl. jours. Mem. IEEE (sr.). Home: 743 Clove Rd Staten Island NY 10310-2737 Office: CUNY Coll Staten Island Dept Applied Scis 130 Stuyvesant Pl Staten Island NY 10301-1953

TSUI, LAP-CHEE, molecular genetics educator; b. Shanghai, Republic of China, Dec. 21, 1950; arrived in Can., 1981; s. Jing Lue Hsue and Hui Ching Wang; m. Ellen Lan Fong, Feb. 11, 1977; children: Eugene, Felix. BS, The Chinese U. of Hong Kong, 1972, M of Philosophy, 1974; PhD, U. Pitts., 1979. Postdoctoral investigator Oak Ridge (Tenn.) Nat. Lab., 1979-80; postdoctoral fellow Hosp. for Sick Children, Toronto, Ont., Can., 1981-83; asst. prof. depts. genetics and med. genetics Hosp. for Sick Children and U. Toronto, 1983-88, assoc. prof., 1988-90, prof., 1990—; chmn. chromosome 7 subcom. Human Gene Mapping Workshop, 1988—; mem. Mammalian Genetics Study Sect. NIH, Bethesda, Md., 1988—; assoc. dir. Cystic Fibrosis Rsch. Ctr., Hosp. for Sick Children, 1989—; scientist Med. Rsch. Coun. Can, 1989—. Mem. editorial bd. Cytogenetics and Cell Genetics, 1988—, Am. Jour. Human Genetics, 1989—, Clin. Genetics, 1991—, PCR Methods and Application, 1991—; contbr. 95 articles to sci. publs.; co-discoverer of cystic fibrosis gene, 1989. Trustee Edn. Found., Fedn. Chinese Canadian Profls., Toronto, 1987—. Recipient Paul di Sant Agnese Disting. Achievement award Cystic Fibrosis Found., 1989, Gold medal of honor Pharm. Mfrs. Assn. Can., 1989, award of excellence Genetics Soc. Can., 1990, Gairdner Internat. award, 1990, Cresson medal Franklin Inst., 1992, E. Mead Johnson award, 1992; scholar Can. Cystic Fibrosis Found., 1984-86. Fellow Royal Soc. Can., Royal Soc. London; mem. Human Genome Orgn., Am. Soc. Human Genetics, Order of Can. (officer 1991). Office: Hosp for Sick Children, 555 University Ave, Toronto, ON Canada M5G 1XG

TU, LORING WULIANG, mathematics educator; b. Taipei, Taiwan, China, Aug. 17, 1952; came to U.S., 1965; s. Grant Tsuchih and Lillian Lichu Tu. AB, Princeton U., 1974; MA, Harvard U., 1976, PhD, 1979. Hildebrandt asst. prof. U. Mich., Ann Arbor, 1979-81, 82-83; mem. Inst. Advanced Study, Princeton, N.J., 1981-82; asst. prof. Johns Hopkins U., Balt., 1983-86; asst. prof. Tufts U., Medford, Mass., 1986-88, assoc. prof., 1988—; reviewer Math. Revs., Ann Arbor, 1984-89; referee numerous math. jours. and publs. Author: (with Raoul Bott) Differential Forms in Algebraic Topology, 1982. NSF grantee, 1980-82, Tufts U. faculty fellow, 1988. Mem. Am. Math. Soc., Phi Beta Kappa, Sigma Xi. Office: Tufts U Dept Math Medford MA 02155

TUAKLI-WILLIAMS, JULIETTE, pediatrician, researcher; b. London, Eng., Feb. 11, 1950; came to U.S., 1982; d. Latey and Catherine (Coker) Tuakli; div. Dec. 1988; children: Eyi and Yetsa Tuakli-Wosornu. BS, U. Zambia, Lusaka, Zambia, 1974, MB ChB, 1976; MPH, UCLA, 1979. Dir. pediatrics Martha Eliot Health Ctr., Boston, Mass., 1982-90; pvt. practice Dorchester, Mass.; cons. pediatrics Camille Cosbon Ctr., Judge Baker Guidance Ctr., Boston. Recipient Community Health Limitations Against Learning Disabilities award Jesse B. Cox Fund, 1988. Office: 512 Blue Hill Ave Dorchester MA 02121-3202 also: 400 Shawmut Ave South End MA 02115

TUBBS, GERALD PATRICK, human resources; b. Rochester, N.Y., Apr. 6, 1949; s. Donald James and Jean Eileen (Witherow) T.; m. Wanda Lorraine Sullivan, May 1, 1976. BS in Industrial Mgmt., Clarkson U., 1972. Plant mgr. Simplicity Machine & Mfging., Avon, N.Y., 1972-76; tool and die maker Kaddis Mfg., Rochester, N.Y., 1976-77, supr., 1977-78; tool maker Southco, Inc., Honeoye Falls, N.Y., 1978-79, 2nd shift supr., 1979-81, personnel svcs., 1981—; bd. mem. S.H.R.M. Genesee Valley Chpt., Rochester, N.Y., 1991-94. Vol. trainer ARC, Rochester. Mem. Soc. for Human resource Mgmt., Livingston Country Club, Austin Healy Club of Am. Republican. Roman Catholic. Home: 9029 Baker Rd Holcomb NY 14469-9523 Office: Southco Inc 250 East St Honeoye Falls NY 14472-1298

TUBBS, WILLIAM JOHNSTON, librarian; b. Phila., May 21, 1938; s. William Johnston Jr. and Frances Alverta (Williams) T.; m. Gail Thayer Lewis, July 1, 1961; children: Andrew, Sarah. BA, Davis & Elkins Coll., 1960; MDiv, Princeton (N.J.) Theol. Sem., 1963; MS, Columbia U., 1966. From cataloger to dept. head to asst. libr. Conn. Wesleyan U., Middletown, 1966-83; libr. Washington Coll., Chestertown, Md., 1983—; mem. Md. State Libr. Resources Ctrl. Adv. Commn., Balt., 1985-88, Md. Libr. Svcs. and Constrn. Act. Adv. Commn., Balt., 1985-90; mem. nominating com. Pa. Libr. Network, Phila., 1988, chair, 1992, mem. fin. com., 1990; mem. Md. Gov.'s Conf. on Librs. Resolutions Com., Balt., 1989-90. Member Friends of Kent County Pub. Libr., Chestertown, 1983—; mem., sec. Friends of Davison Art Ctr., Middletown, 1975-85. Mem. ALA, Assn. Coll. and Rsch. Librs. (New Eng. chpt.), Md. Libr. Assn., Acad. and Rsch. Librs. Div. Md. Assn. Coll. and Rsch. Librs. (v.p., pres. 1989-90), Md. Ind. Colls. and Univs. Assn. Librs. Round Table (pres. 1986-88), Congress Acad. Librs. Md. (sec., treas. 1984-86, mem. exec. bd. 1992—). Office: Washington Coll Miller Libr Washington Ave Chestertown MD 21620-1197

TUBLIN, IRA NATHAN, physician; b. Balt., Feb. 8, 1929; s. Morris and Rose (Cohen) T.; m. Marilyn Claire Scherlis, June 13, 1954; children: Marjorie Grossman, Robert, Gary, Eric. BS, U. Md., College Park, 1950; MD, U. Md., Balt., 1954. Intern D.C. Gen. Hosp., Washington, 1954-55, resident, 1957-59; fellow in nephrology VA Hosp., Washington, 1959-60; pvt. practice Silver Spring, Md., 1960—; clin. assoc. prof. medicine George Washington U. Med. Ctr., Washington, 1977—; cons. Montgomery Gen. Hosp., Olney, Md., 1970-87; bd. dirs. Nat. Kidney Found., D.C. Capt. AUS, 1955-57. Fellow Am. Coll. Physicians; mem. Montgomery County Med. Soc. (named Clinician of Yr. 1986), Am. Soc. Nephrology, Internat. Soc. Nephrology. Hebrew. Home: 1210 N Belgrade Rd Silver Spring MD 20902 Office: 8830 Cameron St Silver Spring MD 20910

TUCCERI, CLIVE KNOWLES, science writer, science educator, educational consultant; b. Bryn Mawr, Pa., Apr. 20, 1953; d. William Henry and Clive Ellis (Knowles) Hulick; m. Eugene Angelo Tucceri, Sept. 1, 1984 (div. Nov. 1991); 1 child, Clive Edna. BA in Geology, Williams Coll., 1975; MS in Coastal Geology, Boston Coll., 1982. Head sci. dept. Stuart Hall Sch., Staunton, Va., 1975-77; mem. sci. faculty William Penn Charter Sch., Phila., 1977-79, Tower Sch., Marblehead, Mass., 1982-86, Bentley Coll., Waltham, Mass., 1986-88; adminstrv. dir., co-founder Stout Aquatic Libr. Nat. Marine and Aquatic Edn. Resource Ctr., Wakefield, R.I., 1982-89; mem. sci. faculty Mabelle B. Avery Sch., Somers, Conn., 1989-90; mem. faculty MacDuffie Sch., Springfield, Mass., 1992—; cons. Longmeadow (Mass.) Pub. Schs., 1989—, Addison-Wesley Pub. Co., Menlo Park, Calif., 1986&; cons., freelance writer Prentice-Hall Inc., Needham, Mass., 1991—; mem. faculty The MacDuffie Sch., Springfield, Mass., 1992—. Bd. dirs. People against Rape, Staunton, 1976-77. Mem. AAUW (bd. dirs., br. pres.-elect 1975-77, v.p. 1985-86, sec. 1986-87), ASCD, Nat. Marine Edn. Assn. (sec. 1986-87, chpt. rep. 1987—), Mass. Marine Educators (pres. 1987-89, bd. dirs. 1983—), Cousteau Soc., Oceanic Soc., Woods Hole Oceanographic Inst., Internat. Oceanographic Found., Mass. Environ. Edn. Soc. (bd. dirs. 1985-88), Longmeadow Newcomers Club (bd. dirs. 1989—), Sigma Xi. Episcopalian. Home: 15 Berwick Ter Longmeadow MA 01106-2614

TUCCI, ALBERT WILLIAM, educator, school system administrator; b. Canastota, N.Y., Nov. 14, 1938; s. Samuel and Anna (Penna) T.; m. Mary Katherine Moseley, Mar. 25, 1961; children: Anne Elizabeth, Katherine Lynn. BS, St. Lawrence U., 1960; MS, Western Conn. U., 1971; PhD, U. Md., 1984. Advanced profl. certificate in math., pers. adminstrn. and supervision. Math. tchr. Long Beach, Huntington Beach (Calif.) Pub. Schs., 1960-63; supr. pers. Columbia Broadcasting System, N.Y.C., 1963-65; math. tchr. Chappaqua (N.Y.) Pub. Schs., 1965-71; from pers. asst. to mgr. human resources Howard County Pub. Schs., Ellicott City, Md., 1971—; cons., speaker colls. and univs., 1973—; assessor Md. Ctr. Progressive Assessments, Balt., 1974—. Author: Teacher Satisfaction, 1984, (manual) The Supervisor Interview, 1991; contbr. numerous articles to profl. publs. Mem. adv. bd. Johns Hopkins U., Balt., U. Md., College Park, 1985-92; fundraiser Am. Heart Assn.,1985, 86, United Way, 1980-83; coach, dir. Howard County Youth Program, Ellicott City, 1976-82. NDEA grantee, 1969; recipient rsch. award U. Md., 1985, award of excellence Nat. Assn. Secondary Sch. Prins., 1987. Mem. Middle Atlantic Assn. Schs., Colls. and Univs. (meritorious svc. award 1989), Mensa, Phi Delta Kappa. Roman Catholic. Home: 10124 Bell Inn Ln Ellicott City MD 21042

TUCCI, EDMOND R., chemical consultant; b. Pawtucket, R.I., May 31, 1933; s. Antonio and Caroline Tucci; m. Valerie Ann Karvey, Oct. 12, 1963. BS, R.I. Sch. Design, 1955; MS, St. Louis U., 1957; PhD, Duquesne U., 1961. Rsch. chemist Olin Mathieson Chem. Corp., Niagara Falls, N.Y., 1957-58; sr. rsch. chemist Gulf Rsch. & Devel. Co., Harmarville, Pa., 1961-73; rsch. supr. Engelhard Minerals & Chem. Co., Edison, N.J., 1973-75; mgr. comml. devel. Matthey Bishop, Inc., Malvern, Pa., 1976-80; pres., owner Catalysts & Catalytic Systems, Stockton, N.J., 1980—. Contbr. articles to profl. jours.; patentee in field. Mem. Comml. Devel. Assn. Home: 21 Sandy Ridge Rd Stockton NJ 08559-1605

TUCCI, GERALD FRANK, manufacturing company executive; b. N.Y.C., Sept. 9, 1926; s. Frank and Mary (Fattizzi) T.; student Dartmouth Coll., 1944; Sc.B. in Naval Sci., Brown U., 1946; Sc.B. In Mech. Engring., 1948; M.B.A. with distinction, Harvard U., 1950; m. Eva G. Gyllander, May 14, 1968; children—Francis Henrik, Michael Fredrik, Amy Christina. Mfg. trainee Am. Can Co., Jersey City, 1950-51; asst. v.p., plant mgr. Artcraft Hosiery Mills, Inc., Darby, Pa., 1951-53; v.p. Leach & Garner Co., Attleboro, Mass., 1953-63, Gen. Findings, Inc., Attleboro, 1953-63; pres. Micro Contacts Inc., Hicksville, N.Y., 1963—; v.p. Mold-A-Matic Corp., Oneota, N.Y., 1965—; chmn. bd., chief exec. officer Hallmark Findings, Inc., Warwick, R.I., 1965—; pres. Micro Pneumatic Logic, Inc., Ft. Lauderdale, Fla., 1975—. Served to lt. (s.g.) USNR, 1944-47. Mem. ASME, Am. Soc. Mfrs., Beta Theta Pi. Republican. Roman Catholic. Clubs: North Hempstead Country, Metropolitan (N.Y.), Harvard Bus. Sch. N.Y. Office: 62 Alpha Plz Hicksville NY 11801-2618

TUCCI, MARK ANTHONY, state agency administrator; b. Trenton, N.J., Dec. 14, 1950; s. William F. and Theresa M. (Miccio) T.; m. Carolyn J. Bilecki, July 10, 1971; children: Nicholas A., Anthony M., Vincent J. BS, Trenton State Coll., 1972, MEd, 1978. Cert. sch. adminstr., prin., supr., tchr. of deaf, tchr. of handicapped, N.J. Tchr. of deaf Katzenbach Sch. for the Deaf, West Trenton, N.J., 1972-82; spl. asst. to supt. Katzenbach Sch. for the Deaf, West Trenton, 1982-85; exec. asst. to asst. commr. edn. N.J. Dept. Edn., Trenton, 1985-87; chief of enterprise license bur. N.J. Casino Control Commn., Atlantic City, 1987-91, dir. organizational devel., 1991—. Mem. editorial bd. newsletter for Trenton chpt. Phi Delta Kappa; contbr. articles to pubs. Scout leader Trenton chpt. Boy Scouts Am., 1981-84; pres. Katzenbach (N.J.) chpt. N.J. State Employees' Assn., 1979; co-chairperson adv. coun. Mercer County Spl. Edn. Assn., 1984; mem. bus. adv. coun. Atlantic Community Coll., 1990. Mem. Am. Mgmt. Assn., Cert. Pub. Mgrs. Soc. of N.J., Phi Delta Kappa, Kappa Delta Pi. Roman Catholic. Home: 273 Neptune Dr Manahawkin NJ 08050-5026 Office: NJ Casino Control Commn Tennessee Ave Atlantic City NJ 08401-4602

TUCHMAN, MAURICE SIMON, library director; b. Bklyn., Sept. 14, 1936; s. William and Rose (Luria) T.; m. Helene Lillian Bodner, Aug. 30, 1959; children: Joel Aron, Miriam Auri. BA, CUNY, 1958; MLS, Columbia U., 1959; B Hebrew Lit., Jewish Theol. Sem., N.Y.C., 1964; D of Arts in LS, Simmons Coll., 1979. Cataloger. svcs. Buffalo and Erie County, 1959-60; asst. libr. N.Y. State Maritime Coll., Ft. Schuyler, 1962-64; libr. cons. Mid-Hudson Librs., Poughkeepsie, N.Y., 1964-66; libr. dir. Hebrew Coll., Brookline, Mass., 1966—; book appraiser, Auburndale, Mass., 1980—; book reviewer Libr. Jour., 1970—. With U.S. Army, 1960-62. N.Y. Regents scholar, 1959. Mem. ALA, Assn. Jewish Librs., Coun. Archives and Rsch. Librs. Jewish Studies, Ch. and Synagogue Libr. Assn. (pres. 1974-75), Fenway Libr. Consortium (coord. 1980-82, treas. 1990—). Home: 16 Dufferin Rd Newton MA 02166-1004 Office: Hebrew Coll 43 Hawes St Brookline MA 02146-5495

TUCHOLKE, BRIAN EDWARD, marine geologist, consultant; b. Hot Springs, S.D., Mar. 19, 1946; s. Adzit Edward and Lillian Mae (Odbert) T.; m. Anita Kaye Smith, Dec. 28, 1968; children: Dacia, Rachelle. BS in Geology, S.D. Sch. Mines and Tech., 1968; PhD in Oceanography, MIT-Woods Hole Oceanographic Instn., 1973. Postdoctoral fellow Lamont-Doherty Geol. Observatory Columbia U., Palisades, N.Y., 1973-74; rsch. assoc. Lamont-Doherty Geol. Observatory Columbia U., Palisades, 1974-78, sr. rsch. assoc., 1978-79; vis. sr. rsch. assoc. Lamont-Doherty Geol. Obs., Columbia U., Palisades, 1979-82, adj. sr. rsch. scientist, 1982—; assoc. scientist Woods Hole Oceanographic Instn. (Mass.), 1979-87, sr. scientist, 1987—; mem. planning com. Joint Oceanographic Instns. for Deep Earth Sampling, 1987-92, regional panels, 1981-87; interim U.S. sci. adv. com. Advanced Ocean Drilling Program, 1983. Editor: Initial Reports of the Deep Sea Drilling Project, vol. 43, 1979, The Geology of North America: The Western North Atlantic Region, 1986, An Angler's Guide to Trout Fishing in Massachusetts, 1988; assoc. editor: Geol. Soc. Am. Bulletin, 1985-88; editorial bd. mem. Geology, 1991-93; contbr. articles to profl. jours. Named Seward Johnson chair in oceanography Woods Hole Oceanographic Instn., 1986-88. Fellow AAAS, Geol. Assn. Can., Geol. Soc. Am.; mem. Am. Assn. Petroleum Geologists, Am. Geophys. Union, Trout Unltd. (pres. Cape Cod chpt. 1987-88, nat. bd. dirs. 1992—), Fedn. Fly Fishers, Citizens for Protection of Waquoit Bay (v.p. 1986-87), Theta Tau. Republican. Home: 40 Ambleside Dr West Falmouth MA 02574-0040 Office: Woods Hole Oceanographic Inst Woods Hole MA 02543

TUCK, MURRAY, accountant, insurance company executive; b. Bklyn., Nov. 12, 1920; s. Samuel and Rose (Green) T.; m. Leah Samuels, Aug. 6, 1971; 1 child, by previous marriage, Susan (Mrs. R. Greenbaum); stepchildren: Edward Schultz, Charlotte (Mrs. K. Hoek), Larry Schultz. Grad. with honors, Pace Inst., N.Y.C., 1945, student, 1949-50. Jr. acct. Morris Traum & Co., CPAs, Bklyn., 1938-39; jr. acct. Mathew Weiss & Co., CPAs, Bklyn., 1939-40, supervising sr. acct., 1940-45; asst. dept. head internal audit dept. United Mchts. and Mfrs., Inc., N.Y.C., 1945-52; comptr. TransRadio Press Svc., Inc., N.Y.C., 1952-57, Bus. Factors, Inc., N.Y.C., 1957-62; pvt. practice acctg. Farmingdale, N.Y., 1950—; prin. Murray Tuck, ins. broker, Farmingdale, 1950—; ins. cons. Assn. for Help of Retarded Children, Inc., Nassau, N.Y., 1965—, Suffolk, N.Y., 1967—; mem. C.W. Post Coll. Fin. Planning Inst., 1980, moderator tax practitioner forum, 1988—. Editor: ARC Lamplighter, 1965-69; contbr. numerous articles on ins. and taxes to various publs. Pres. Farmingdale Sr. High Sch. PTA, 1963-65; chmn. Farmingdale Community Scholarship Fund, 1962-67; sec., v.p. Group for Children's Welfare, Cen. Islip, N.Y., 1961-65; treas. Farmingdale Little League Assn., 1956—, Youth Coun., Inc., 1956—, 150th Anniversary Farmingdale R.R. Com., 1990; founder and donor Farmingdale Community award, 1962-65; co-committeeman Farmingdale Salvation Army, 1960-61; mem. Farmingdale Adult Edn. Adv. Com., 1955-60; mem. Farmingdale Police Aux., 1960-70; air raid warden, Farmingdale, 1944-50; Rep. committeeman, Farmingdale, 1966-76; bd. dirs. Advancement for Commerce & Industry, Inc., 1974-78, pres., 1971-73. Recipient Farmingdale Classroom Tchrs. Honor award 1963, cert. of appreciation Farmingdale CAP, 1964, Disting. Svc. plaque Advancement for Commerce and Industry, 1972, 74, cert. of svc. Farmingdale Youth Coun., 1964, cert. of merit N.Y. Gov. Rockefeller. 1961, Village of Farmingdale, 1981, Citizen of Yr. award Kiwanis-Lions-Rotary Club, 1981, Congress U.S. Proclamation, 1981, Oyster Bay citation, 1980, 81, numerous other awards for community svc.; accredited in accountancy and taxation Nat. Accreditation Coun.; enrolled to practice with U.S. Treasury Dept. Mem. Nat. Soc. Pub. Accts., Nat. Assn. Ins. Agts., Empire State Accts. Assn., C.W. Post Coll. Tax Practicioners Forum, Nat. Assn. Enrolled Agts. Jewish. Home and Office: 670 Conklin St Farmingdale NY 11735-3704

TUCKER, ALBERT WILLIAM, mathematician; b. Oshawa, Ont., Can., Nov. 28, 1905; s. William Benjamin and Florence Maude (Huff) T.; m. Alice Judson Curtiss, Dec. 17, 1938 (div. 1960); children: Alan C., Thomas W., Barbara J.; m. Mary Frances Shaw, Feb. 27, 1964. BA, U. Toronto, 1928, MA, 1929; PhD, Princeton U., 1932; DSc (hon.), Dartmouth Coll., 1961. Instr. dept. math. Princeton (N.J.) Univ., 1933-34, asst. prof., 1934-38, assoc. prof., 1938-46, prof., 1946-54, chmn. dept., 1953-63, Albert Baldwin Dod prof., 1954-74, Albert Baldwin Dod prof. emeritus, 1974—; assoc. dir. Fire Control Rsch. Group, Princeton, 1941-45; dir. Logistics Rsch. Project Office Naval Rsch., 1948-72; cons. Rand Corp., Santa Monica, Calif., 1949-63, IBM Rsch. Ctr., Yorktown Heights, N.Y., 1957-63; vis. prof. Stanford (Calif.) U., 1949-50, Dartmouth Coll., Hanover, N.H., 1963, Ariz. State U., Tempe, 1971, 77, U. West Australia, Nedlands, 1975, 78, 81; summer lectr. MIT, Cambridge, 1952, Bowdoin Coll., Brunswick, Maine, 1962, 65, 68; Philips visitor Haverford (Pa.) Coll., 1953, 58. Founding editor Princeton Math. Series, 1938-69; organizer Annals of Math. Studies, 1940-49; co-editor: Contributions to Theory of Games Vols. I-IV, 1950-58, Linear Inequalities and Related Systems, 1956; co-author Constructive Linear Algebra, 1974. Mem. phys. scis. com. Alfred P. Sloan Found., N.Y.C., 1955-59; lectr. Fulbright program, Australia, 1956; cons. OEEC, Paris, 1959; chmn. Conf. Bd. Math. Scis., Washington, 1961-62; mem. Pres. Com. on Nat. Medal Sci., Washington, 1962-66. Recipient British Assn. Advancement Sci. medal Univ. Toronto, 1928, J. von Neumann Theory prize Ops. Rsch. Soc. Am., Washington, 1980. Fellow AAAS (v.p. 1957, 66), N.Y. Acad. Sci., Am. Acad. Arts & Scis.; mem. Am. Math. Soc. (trustee 1964-68), Math. Assn. Am. (pres. 1961-62, award for disting. svc. to math. 1968), Can. Math. Soc. (sem. lectr. 1953, 57), Australian Math. Soc., Math. Programming Soc. (chmn. 1976-78). Home: 37 Lake Ln Princeton NJ 08540-7222

TUCKER, CHRISTOPHER SLOAN, plastics processing engineer; b. Berwyn, Pa., Mar. 19, 1963; s. William Hollingsworth and Marjory (Spencer) T. BSChemE, Syracuse U., 1984. Process engr. Welding Engrs., Inc., Blue Bell, Pa., 1985-88, product mgr., 1989, mgr. process tech., 1989—. Contbr. articles to profl. jours.; patentee in field. Mem. World Affairs Coun., Phila., 1991. Mem. Soc. Plastics Engrs., Polymer Processing Soc. Home: 47 Whistling Swan Ln Downingtown PA 19335-4506 Office: Welding Engrs Inc 1600 Union Meeting Rd Blue Bell PA 19422-1968

TUCKER, GARLAND SCOTT, III, investment banker; b. Raleigh, N.C., June 17, 1947; s. Garland Scott Jr. and Jean Smith (Barnes) T.; m. Greyson Conrad Shuff, Jan. 15, 1972; children—Greyson Carrington, Elizabeth Bradford. B.S. magna cum laude, Washington and Lee U., 1969; M.B.A., Harvard U., 1972. V.p. Tucker Furniture Co., Wilson, N.C., 1972-76; corp. fin. assoc. Investment Corp. of Va., Norfolk, 1976-78; v.p., to pres., chief exec. officer Carolina Securities Corp., Raleigh, N.C., 1978-88; v.p. corp. banking and fin. Chem. Bank, N.Y.C., 1988-90; pres. First Travelcorp., Inc., Raleigh, 1990—; mem. regional firms adv. com. N.Y. Stock Exchange, 1984-87. Dir. Raleigh Rescue Mission, 1980-83; vestry Christ Episcopal Ch., Raleigh, 1981-84; mem. N.C. Mus. Art Found., 1990—; bd. advisors NCO Investors, N.Y.C, 1991—; trustee Chatham Hall Sch. Mem. Carolina Securities Corp. (bd. dirs. 1979-88), Securities Industry Assn. (bd. dirs. Mid-Atlantic region 1981-82, 84-88, regional firms com. 1983-86), Raleigh C. of C. (bd. dirs. 1984-86), Phi Beta Kappa. Republican. Clubs: Capital City, Carolina Country (Raleigh); Harvard of N.Y.C., Roaring Gap Club. Home: 2327 Lake Dr Raleigh NC 27609-7667 Office: First Travelcorp Inc 4513 Creedmore Rd Raleigh NC 27612

TUCKER, JAMES ARTHUR, academic administrator; b. Saranac Lake, N.Y., Oct. 16, 1959; s. Donald Kenneth and Ruth Ann (Oliver) T.; m. Michele Anne Douglas, June 26, 1982; children: Lawrence James, Michael Robert. BA in History, SUNY, Potsdam, 1981; M in Edn. Adminstrn., Va. Tech. U., 1983. Dir. youth swim program Town of Brighton, Paul Smiths, N.Y., 1978-82; substitute tchr. pub. schs., N.Y., Va., 1981-84; asst. coach women's track and field Saranac Lake High Sch., 1982-87; guidance coord. Adirondack Ednl. Ctr., Saranac Lake, 1984-87; dir. Adirondack Bicycle Tours, Lake Placid, N.Y., 1986-87; dir. Higher Edn. Opportunity program Paul Smiths Coll., 1987—, Nordic ski coach, 1989-92; dir. Paul Smith's (N.Y.) Coll. Striders, 1987—. Cons. (book) Snowshoeing, numerous publs. and articles on snowshoeing. Organizer, head coach Brighton Youth Soccer, Paul Smiths, 1979-84; com. mem. Brighton Recreation, Paul Smiths, 1982—; scoutmaster troop 12 Boy Scouts Am., Gabriels, N.Y., 1982-88, com. chmn. 1988—; sec. Paul Smiths-Gabriels Vol. Fire Dept., 1987—; dir. N.Am. Snowshoe Classic, 1988—, Faster than a Thirsty Blackfly Biathlon, 1988-91, Tuberman Quadrathlon, 1989-91, St. Regis Invitational, 1990-91. Liberal. Roman Catholic. Home: Hobart Rd # 18 Gabriels NY 12939-9999 Office: Paul Smiths Coll Higher Edn Opportunity Program 211 Pickett Hall Paul Smiths NY 12970

TUCKER, JOHN AVERY, academic administrator, electrical engineer; b. Milton, Mass., Jan. 28, 1924; s. Seth Davenport and Ruth Lincoln (Avery) T. BSEE with honor, Northeastern U., 1949; M in Engring., Yale U., 1950. Registered profl. engr., Mass. Mem. tech. staff Bell Telephone Labs., Inc., N.Y.C., 1950; engr. New Eng. Tel & Tel. Co., Boston, 1951-56; instr. elec. engring., Lincoln Inst. Northeastern U., Boston, 1955; with dept. elec. engring. and computer sci. MIT, Cambridge, 1956—, first adminstrv. officer, 1963, dir. coop. (VI-A) program in elec. engring./computer sci., 1969—; spl. asst. to dept. head MIT, 1987—, emeritus dir. VI-A program, lectr., 1989—. Deacon Congregational Ch.; bd. dirs. Wellesley chpt. ARC, 1978. Sgt. Signal Corps, U.S. Army, 1943-46, PTO. Named hon. alumnus MIT, 1985. Mem. IEEE (life, sr. mem.), Am. Soc. Engring. Edn., Appalachian Mountain Club, Wellesley Hist. Soc., Tau Beta Pi (adv. bd. MIT chpt. 1956—), Eta Kappa Nu (founder Northeastern U. chpt. 1950, nat. bd. dirs. 1959-61). Home: 153 Brook St Wellesley MA 02181-6641 Office: MIT 77 Massachusetts Ave Rm 38473 Cambridge MA 02139-4307

TUCKER, JOSEPH, clergyman; b. Columbus, Ga., Mar. 5, 1920; s. John Joseph and Irene (Blakely) T.; m. Vivian Theodosia Hampton, Feb. 8, 1948; 1 child, Joy Celeste. BA, Fisk U., 1950; MDiv, Union Theol. Sem., 1953; MS in Libr. Svc., Columbia U., 1970; postgrad., Colgate Rochester Divinity Sch., 1987; DD (hon.), Va. Sem. and Coll., 1988. Asst. dean of men, basic coll. dir. Fisk U., Nashville, 1953-54; periodicals libr. Union Theol. Sem. Libr., N.Y.C., 1959-70; pastoral counselor Harlem Interfaith Counseling Svc., N.Y.C., 1967-68; reference libr. Hofstra U. Libr., Hempstead, N.Y., 1970-74; tchr. N.Y. Theol. Sem., N.Y.C., 1977; dean, tchr. Va. Sem. and Coll. N.Y. Extension, Queens Village, N.Y., 1988-91; founder, pastor Joyful Heart Bapt. Ch., Hempstead, 1969—. Mem. Bapt. Ministers' Conf. N.Y. and Vicinity (com. chmn. 1990—), Bapt. Ministers' Conf. Greater N.Y. and Vicinity. Home: 76 E Marshall St Hempstead NY 11550-7406 Office: Joyful Heart Bapt Ch 101 Greenwich St Hempstead NY 11550-5689

TUCKER, JO-VON, marketing executive; b. Dallas, Feb. 7, 1937; d. Worley Charles and Julia Allene (Mayo) Jones; m. George Richard Tucker, Mar. 1, 1958 (div. July 1977); 1 child, Tracy Lynn Tucker Rolsten. Student, Tex. U., 1955-58. Art asst. Bud Biggs Studio, Dallas, 1958-59; illustrator Ed Bearden Art Studio, Dallas, 1959-62; art dir. The Bloom Agy., Dallas, 1962-63, Glenn Advt., Dallas, 1963-66; pres. Unltd. Concepts, Dallas, 1966-73; v.p., creative dir. The Horchow Collection, Dallas, 1973-75; pres. JVT Direct Mktg., N.Y.C., 1975—; owner/chmn. Clambake Celebrations, Orleans, Mass., 1990—; internat. cons. P.J. Carroll & Co., Dublin, Ireland, 1988-90; direct mktg. cons. Walt Disney Co., Anaheim, Calif., 1986-87, Neiman-Marcus, Dallas, 1965-71; trustee Direct Mktg. Ednl. Found., N.Y.C., 1986—. Author, photographer: Perspectives, 1981; contbg. author: Successful Direct Marketing Methods, 1985, 87, 89, Ed Nash on Direct Marketing, 1987, 91; contbr. articles to profl. jours. Named Advt. Woman of Yr., Women in Communications, Dallas, 1978, Direct Marketer of Yr., Direct Mktg. Assn. North Tex., 1985, Direct Mktg. Woman of Yr., Women's Direct Response Group, N.Y.C., 1988; recipient graphic awards

nat. and internat. groups. Mem. Direct Mktg. Assn. (bd. mem. 1979-85, Echo award 1973, 75, 80, 83, 85), Direct Mktg. Ednl. Found. (trustee 1986—), Direct Mktg. Assn. (bd. sec., exec. com. 1984), Direct Mktg. Idea Exch. (bd. mem. 1980-90), Creative Guild. Republican. Office: Clambake Celebrations 5 Giddiah Hill Rd Orleans MA 02653-4000

TUCKER, JUDITH LYNNE, legal administrator, paralegal; b. Buffalo, Feb. 11, 1963; d. H. Pete Tucker and Joan Carolyn (Evans) Mescall. Diploma, Am. Inst. Paralegal Studies, Buffalo, 1986; student, SUNY, Buffalo, 1988—. Asst. to coord. continuing med. edn. Children's Hosp. of Buffalo, 1981-82; sec. Lawyers Title Ins. Corp., Colorado Springs, Colo., 1983-84; paralegal Moot & Sprague, Buffalo, 1984-86; paralegal Delaware North Cos., Inc., Buffalo, 1986-90, legal adminstr., 1990—; chmn. logistics com. Taste of Buffalo, Inc., 1991, 92. Co-chmn. signage com. Empire State Games, 1988-90; notary pub. Mem. Western N.Y. Paralegal Assn., Assn. Legal Adminstrs. Mem. Western N.Y. Paralegal Assn. Office: Delaware North Cos Inc 438 Main St Buffalo NY 14202

TUCKER, RAYMOND WILLIAM, JR., electrical engineer; b. N.Y.C., Mar. 26, 1951; s. Raymond William and Anna Marie (Holz) T.; m. Gail Susan Remsbecker, Nov., 1973; children: Raymond, Robert, Bethany. BEE with honors, Stevens Inst. Tech., Hoboken, N.J., 1973. Owner, operator Raytronics Electronic Systems, Ava, N.Y., 1967—; electronics engr. USAF-Rome Lab., Griffiss AFB, N.Y., 1974—. Contbr. articles to profl. jours. Trustee 1st Presbyn. Ch., Rome, 1991—, pres. Mem. IEEE, N.Y. State Divers Assn. (pres. 1988-91, treas. 1983—, Disting. Svc. award 1986), Underwater Soc. Am. (exec. v.p. 1991—, sec. 1987-92), Automatic Radio Frequency Technique Group (pres. 1985-87, treas. 1977-85, Disting. Svc. award 1987), Tau Beta Pi. Home: RR 1 Box 204A Ava NY 13303-9739 Office: Rome Lab RL/ERPT Griffiss AFB NY 13441-5700

TUCKER, RONALD EDWARD, paper company executive; b. Dublin, Ireland, May 19, 1955; came to U.S., 1991; s. William Reginald and Ida Phyllis (Orr) T.; m. Ruth Inger Margareta Sandell, Apr. 10, 1981; children: Sebastian Edward, Stephanie Siobhán. BS, Trinity Coll., Dublin, 1978; MBA, Stanford U., 1985. Sales rep. IBM (Ireland) Ltd., Dublin, 1979-80; asst. sales mgr. Finnpap, Helsinki, Finland, 1980-83, asst. dir., 1986-91; asst. to chief fin. officer Measurex Corp., Cupertino, Calif., 1984-85; sales mgr. The Madden Corp., San Francisco, 1985-86; sr. v.p. fin. and adminstrn., mem. bd. dirs. The Madden Corp., N.Y.C., 1991—. McKinsey Internat. fellow McKinsey & Co., Stanford U., 1984; Finnish Lang. and Culture scholar Min. of Edn. of Finland, 1980. Home: 71 Water's Edge Rye NY 10580-3256 Office: The Madden Corp 9 Rockefeller Pla New York NY 10020

TUDISCO, JASPER THOMAS, construction company executive; b. Astoria, N.Y., Jan. 21, 1917; s. Gaetano and Angelina T.; student public schs., Norwalk, Conn.; m. Annette Buzzeo, Dec. 14, 1942; children: Gaetano, Angela. With Tudisco & Diehl, Inc. and predecessors, constrn. co., Norwalk, 1935—, pres., ptnr., 1948-62, pres., owner, 1962—. With U.S. Army, 1942. Republican. Roman Catholic. Home and Office: 31 Summitt Ave Norwalk CT 06854-2035

TUDRYN, JOYCE MARIE, professional society administrator; b. Holyoke, Mass., July 27, 1959; d. Edward William and Frances Katherine (Bajor) T.; m. William Wallace Friberger III, Sept. 18, 1982. BS in Communications, Syracuse U., 1981. Asst. editor Nat. Assn. Broadcasters, Washington, 1981-83; dir. programs Internat. Radio and TV Soc., N.Y.C., 1983-87, assoc. exec. dir., 1988—; v.p. Corp. for Ednl. Radio and TV, N.Y.C., 1987—; speaker in field; pres. Joyscapes Photography, 1992—; nat. adv. bd. Alpha Epsilon Rho Broadcasting Soc., 1988-91. Editor-in-chief IRTS News, 1983—; columnist TV Facts, Figures and Film mag., 1983-88. Judge Comml. Excellence in Black Advt., N.Y.C., 1987; vice chmn. ann. awards luncheon Ctr. for Communication, 1985. Recipient Mass. Kodak Photography award, 1977; S.I. Newhouse scholar Syracuse U., 1980-81. Mem. Intercorp. Communications Group, N.Y. Women in Communications, Nat. Acad. TV Arts and Scis, Gamma Phi Beta. Home: 602 Bennington Dr Union NJ 07083-9104 Office: Internat Radio and TV Soc 420 Lexington Ave Ste 1714 Rm 1714 New York NY 10170

TUFARO, JUDITH BOETTGER, health facility administrator; b. Plainfield, N.J., June 7, 1939; d. John Ira and Jane (Danald) Boettger; m. Dominic Edward Tufaro, May 28, 1961 (div. 1983); children: Mark Edward, Scot-James, Todd Vincent. BA in Sociology, Western Md. U., 1961; cert., Newark State U., 1962; cert. elem. tchr., Kean Coll., 1961. Cert. alcoholism and addictions counselor, N.J.; nat. cert. addictions counselor level II; cert. relapse prevention specialist. Elem. sch. tchr. Parker Sch., Middlesex, N.J., 1961; alcoholism counselor Chem. Dependency Ctr., Summit, N.J., 1983-85; family program dir. Fair Oaks Hosp., Summit, 1985-89, clin. coord., 1989—. Contbr. chpt.: Dual Diagnosis in Substance Abuse, 1991. Active Bd. Edn., Watchung, N.J., 1983-87; mem. adv. bd. Watchung Hills High Sch., Warren, N.J., 1987-88. Mem. AACD, N.J. Assn. Alcoholism and Drug Abuse Counselors.

TUFTS, DAVID ALBERT, JR., securities company executive; b. Winchester, Mass., Sept. 9, 1945; s. David Albert and Florence Ida (Watters) T.; m. Jocelyne Maggiar-Nash, Aug. 21, 1971; children: Stephanie Elizabeth, Natalie Alexandra. BA, Hobart Coll., 1967. Dir. sales Kennedy Ctr. for Performing Arts, Washington, 1970-71; mgr. Merrill Lynch, Washington, 1971-81; asst. mgr. Oppenheimer & Co., N.Y.C., 1981-84, mng. dir., 1984—; mem. mgmt. com. Oppenheimer & Co., N.Y.C., 1986—. Bd. dirs. Brunswick Sch., Greenwich, Conn., 1986—, alumni council Hobart Coll., Geneva, N.Y., 1985—. Served to lt. USN, 1968, Vietnam. Mem. Kappa Alpha. Republican. Congregational. Clubs: Rocky Point (Greenwich); U. (Washington). Home: 37 Lockwood Dr Old Greenwich CT 06870-1912 Office: Oppenheimer & Co Inc World Fin Ctr New York NY 10081

TUFTS, DONNA LEE, interior designer, educator; b. Wareham, Mass., May 31, 1948; d. Arthur Clinton Thompson and Lillian Amelia (Clapp) Morse; m. Peter C. Tufts, June 4, 1970. BS in Edn., Bridgewater State, 1970. Cert. elem. edn., art edn. Tchr. Marion (Mass.) Pub. Sch. System, 1973-81; draftsman designer Saltonstall Assocs., Inc. Architects, Marion, Mass., 1982-87; prin. D.L. Tufts Interior Design, Marion, Mass., 1984—; tchr. Newbury Coll., New Bedford, Mass., 1991—; sec. Marion Assessment Capital Planning Com., 1987-89. Contbr. articles to mags. Mem. Am. Soc. Interior Design, Inst. Bus. Designers.

TUFTY, HAROLD GUILFORD, editor, publisher; b. Chgo., Sept. 1, 1922; s. Harold and Esther (Van Wagoner) T.; m. Barbara Jean Taeusch, Dec. 29, 1948; children: Christopher, Karen, Steven. BME, U. Va., 1949. Corr. Tufty News Svc., Washington, 1946-49; reporter Denver Post, 1949-51; European corr. Denver Post, Paris, 1951-52; pub. rels. Grant Advt., N.Y.C., 1953-55; info. officer U.S. Info. Agy., Madras, India, 1955-58, Bombay, India, 1958-59; pub. affairs officer, press attache U.S. Info. Agy., Conakry, Guinea, 1960, Abidjan, Ivory Coast, 1961-62; dir. French speaking African programs Peace Corps, Washington, 1963-64; pres. Tufty & Assoc., Washington, 1964—; bureau chief Tufty News Svc., Washington, 1984—; cons. U.S. Senate Com. Pub. Works, Washington, 1966-80; dir. The Ad Agy., Inc., Washington, 1970-78; pres. The Value Found., Washington, 1979—. Author: Compendium on Value Engineering, 1983; editor, pub. Value Engring. and Mgmt. Digest, 1972—; columnist Interactions, 1988—. Nat. v.p. Soc. Am. Value Engrs., Washington, 1970-72; bd. dirs. SAVE Nat. Capital, Washington, 1964—, chmn., 1973—, congl. receptions. Lt. USN, 1944-46. Fellow Soc. Am. Value Engrs., 1985; recipient Capital Honor award, SAVE, 1971, Disting. Svc. award SAVE, 1977-78. Mem. Soc. Am. Valve Engrs. (nat. pres. 1990—), Nat. Dem. Club. Home: 3812 Livingston St NW Washington DC 20015-2803 Office: Tufty Comm Co 1199 National Press Bldg Washington DC 20045

TUHY, PHILIP RADMIR, political science educator; b. Wilkes-Barre, Pa., Mar. 17, 1930; s. Stephan and Ludmilla (Lichner) T.; m. Fanny Meisner Krauss, Oct. 7, 1966 (dec. Oct. 1970); 1 child, Elena Viera. BA, Valparaiso U., 1952; M of Govtl. Adminstrn., U. Pa., 1954. Cert. planner. Asst. mgr. Borough of Downingtown, Pa., 1956-57; mem. staff Internat. City Mgrs.' Assn., Chgo., 1957-59; sr. planner Luzerne County Planning Commn., Wilkes-Barre, Pa., 1959-60; asst. prof. polit. sci. Wilkes U., Wilkes-Barre, 1960—, dir. Inst. Regional Affairs, 1985—. Pres. St. Matthew Evang. Luth. Ch., Wilkes-Barre, 1973-89; ambassador U.S. Jaycees, Tulsa, 1977; sec. Ecumenical Enterprises, Inc., Dallas, Pa., 1981—; vice chair Slovak Heritage Soc., Wilkes-Barre, 1987—; trustee Pa. Kiwanis Found., Inc. Harrisburg, 1987. With U.S. Army, 1954-56, Korea, Japan. Recipient Disting. Service award Wilkes Coll., 1980, Dr. Benjamin Rush award Luzerne County Med. Soc., 1984; Samuel S. Feis scholar U. Pa., 1952. Mem. Am. Inst. Planners (sect. chair 1974-75), Am. Inst. Parliamentarians, Am. Soc. Pub. Adminstrn. (chpt. pres. 1982—). Democrat. Lodge: Kiwanis (pres. Wilkes-Barre chpt. 1983-84, lt. gov. Pa. dist. 1987-88). Home: 34 S Main St Apt 209 Wilkes Barre PA 18701-1711 Office: Wilkes U Inst Regional Affairs Wilkes Barre PA 18766

TULL, WILLIS CLAYTON, JR., librarian; b. Crisfield, Md., Feb. 22, 1931; s. Willis Clayton and Agnes Virginia (Milbourne) T.; m. Taeko Itoi, Dec. 18, 1952. Student, U. Balt., 1948, Johns Hopkins U., 1956; BS, Towson (Md.) State Coll., 1957; MLS, Rutgers U., 1962; postgrad., Miami U., Oxford, Ohio, 1979. Editorial clk. 500th Mil. Intelligence Svc. Group, Tokyo, 1952-53; tchr. Hereford Jr.-Sr. High Sch., Parkton, Md., 1957-59; aide Enoch Pratt Free Libr., Balt., 1959-61, profl. asst., 1962-64; coord. adult svcs. Washington County Free Libr., Hagerstown, Md., 1964-67; asst. area libr. Eastern Shore Area Libr., Salisbury, Md., 1967; br. libr. Balt. County Pub. Libr., Pikesville, Md., 1968-71; asst. area br. libr. Balt. County Pub. Libr., Essex, Md., 1971-72; sr. info. specialist Balt. County Pub. Libr., Catonsville, Md., 1972-87; on-line supr. Balt. County Pub. Libr., Towson, Md., 1988-89; sr. info. specialist Balt. County Pub. Libr., Reisterstown, Md., 1989-90; exec. dir. Milbourne and Tull Rsch. Ctr., 1991—. Contbr. to profl. and geneal. jours. Mem. Rep. Cen. Com. Balt. County, 1971-72. With U.S. Army, 1949-52. Fellow Nat. Congress Patriotic Orgns. (founding); mem. Habitat for Humanity Internat., Internat. Rescue Com., Heritage Found., Inst. Religion and Democracy, Freedom to Read Found., Freedom House, Nat. Assn. Scholars, Nat. Ctr. for Neighborhood Enterprise, Md. Libr. Assn. (chmn. intellectual freedom com. 1969-70), Md. Assn. Adult Edn. (coord. Western Md. region 1965-67), Unitarian and Universalist Geneal. Soc. (founder, bd. dirs. 1971-87), Md. Geneal. Soc., Sons and Daus. of the Pilgrims, Soc. War of 1812, SAR, Md. Hist. Soc., St. George's Soc. Balt., Eastern Shore Soc. Balt. City, Balt. Coun. Fgn. Affairs, Star Spangled Banner Flag House Assn., Md. Coalition Against Crime, Woodrow Wilson Internat. Ctr. Scholars, English-Speaking Union U.S., Kappa Delta Pi. Home and Office: 10605 Lakespring Way Cockeysville Hunt Valley MD 21030-2818

TULLER, HARRY L., materials science and engineering educator. BS, Columbia U., 1966, MS, 1967, DSc in Engring., 1973. Rsch. assoc. physics Technion, Haifa, Israel, 1974-75; from asst. to assoc. prof. materials sci. and engring. MIT, Cambridge, 1975-81, prof. materials sci. and engring., 1981—, dir. Crystal Physics and Optical Electronics Lab., 1985—; vis. prof. U. Pierre et Marie Curie, Paris, 1990; faculty chair Sumitomo Electric Industries, 1992. Co-editor: High Temperature Superconductors, 1988, Electroceramics and Solid State Ionics, 1988, Science and Technology of Fast Ion Conductors, 1989, Sold State Ionics, 1992. Fulbright travel grantee, 1990. Fellow Am. Ceramic Soc. (N.E. chair 1983); mem. IEEE, Electrochem. Soc. (co-organizer 1st internat. symposium ionic and mixed conducting ceramics 1991), Materials Rsch. Soc., Am. Phys. Soc. Jewish. Office: MIT 77 Massachusetts Ave Cambridge MA 02139-4307

TULLIS, JAMES LUTHER LYMAN, investment banker, venture capitalist; b. Newton, Mass., Apr. 20, 1947; s. James Lyman and Marjorie (White) T.; m. Linda Altorfer, Aug. 22, 1970; children: John, Elisabeth, Sara. A.B., Stanford U., 1969; M.B.A., Harvard U., 1972. V.p., securities analyst Putnam Funds, Boston, 1972-74; prin. Morgan Stanley & Co., N.Y.C., 1974-83; sr. v.p. E.F. Hutton & Co., N.Y.C., 1983-86; ptnr., chmn. Tullis-Cook & Co., Inc., Greenwich, Conn., 1986—, Tullis Dickerson & Co., Inc., Greenwich, 1990—. Trustee Greenwich Hosp., 1984-91; elder 1st Presbyn. Ch., Greenwich, 1978-81. Named to 1st team All-Am. Securities Analysts, Institutional Investor, 1980, 81. Mem. Bond Club N.Y., Investment Assn. N.Y. (pres. 1983). Office: Tullis Dickerson & Co Inc 1 Green Ln Greenwich CT 06831-5101

TULLY, JUDD, newspaper correspondent, art critic; b. Chgo., Apr. 13, 1947; m. Donna Lucia Masini, June 28, 1986. BA in Polit. Sci., Am. Univ., 1969; postgrad., U. Oreg., 1971-72, Wright Inst., 1972. Oral historian Cultural Coun. Found., CETA Artists' Project, N.Y.C., 1978-80; sr. editor Art/World, N.Y.C., 1983-88; spl. correspondent Washington Post, Washington, 1985—; oral historian Archives Am. Art, N.Y.C., 1988—; contbg. editor New Art Examiner, 1989—; exhbn. curator, catalogue author Lost and Found at the Sculpture Ctr., 1991, Made in New York: Encounters with Contemporary Sculpture, 1989, The New Sculpture Group, A Look Back, 1957-62, 1988, Reuben Kadish Retrospective, 1986. Author: Red Grooms and Ruckus Manhattan, 1977, The Folk Art of Benny and George Andrews, 1990; U.S. corr. The Artnewsletter; contbg. editor: Art and Auction; contbr. articles to profl. jours. Mem. Internat. Assn. Art Critics, Authors' Guild. Office: PO Box 05 Prince St Sta New York NY 10012-0001

TULMAN, LORRAINE JOHNSON, nursing educator; b. Jacksonville, Fla., Nov. 19, 1950. BA, NYU, 1970; BS magna cum laude, SUNY, Bklyn., 1973; MS, Russell Sage Coll., 1977; DNSc, U. Pa., 1984. RN, Pa., N.J. Staff nurse NYU Med. Ctr., N.Y.C., 1973-74; asst. instr. Albany (N.Y.) Med. Ctr., 1974-75; instr. U. S. Fla., Tampa, 1977-78, asst. prof. nursing, 1978-79; asst. prof. nursing Villanova (Pa.) U., 1981-84; asst. prof. nursing U. Pa., Phila., 1984-91, assoc. prof., 1991—; sr. fellow Lonard Davis Inst. Health Econs., U. Pa., Phila. Contbr. articles to profl. jours.; mem. manuscript rev. panels: Nursing Rsch., 1986—, Advances in Nursing Scis., 1989—, Health Care for Women Internat., 1989—, Western Jour. Nursing Rsch., 1990—. Bd. dirs. Planned Parenthood of Greater Camden Area, 1983-89, 1990—. Nat. Orgn. Obstet., Gynecol. and Neonatal Nurses grantee, 1987-89; Rsrch. Found. of U. Pa. grantee, 1987-89; Am. Cancer Soc. grantee, 1989-91; NIH-Nat. Ctr. for Nursing Rsrch. grantee, 1990—. Mem. AAUP, Am. Nurses Assn., N.J. Nurses Assn., Am. Nurses Assn. Coun. of Nurse Researchers, Orgn. for Obstetric, Gynecologic and Neonatal Nursing, Am. Acad. Nursing, Sigma Theta Tau (rsch. rev. com. chair 1991—, collaterial reviewer 1989—). Office: Univ of Pa Sch Nursing 420 Guardian Dr Philadelphia PA 19104-6096

TULSKY, FREDRIC NEAL, journalist; b. Chgo., Sept. 30, 1950; s. George and Helen (Mailick) T.; m. Kim Rennard, June 20, 1971; children: Eric George, Elizabeth Rose. B.J., U. Mo., 1972; J.D. cum laude, Temple U., Phila., 1984. Bar: Pa. 1984. Reporter Saginaw News, Mich., 1973-74, Port Huron Times Herald, Mich., 1974-75, Jackson Clarion-Ledger, Miss., 1975-78, Los Angeles Herald Examiner, 1978-79, Phila. Inquirer, 1979—; adj. prof. urban studies U. Pa., 1990—. Recipient nat. awards including Robert F. Kennedy Found. award, 1979, Heywood Brown award Newspaper Guild, 1978, Disting. Svc. medal Sigma Delta Chi, 1978, Pub. Svc. award AP Mng. Editors, 1978, Silver Gavel award ABA, 1979, 87, Pulitzer prize for invetigative reporting, 1987, Pub. Svc. award Nat. Headliners Club, 1987; Nieman fellow Harvard U., 1989. Mem. Investigative Reporters and Editors (pres. 1988-91, chair 1991—), Reporters Com. for Freedom of Press, Kappa Tau Alpha. Office: Phila Inquirer 400 N Broad St Philadelphia PA 19130-4099

TUMARKIN, JOEL ELLIS, business consultant, educator; b. N.Y.C., Apr. 6, 1934; s. Herman and Cecelia (Ellis) T.; m. Sandra R. Pensak, Feb. 24, 1957; children: Jeffrey H., Lisa A. B in Mech. Engring., NYU, 1956, M in Indsl. Engring., 1963; DBA, George Washington U., 1968. Cons. Inst. for Def. Analyses, Alexandria, Va., 1965-69, 89—; dir. econ. studies U.S. Price Commn., Washington, 1971-72; asst. to chmn., dir. distbn. Peoples Drug Stores Inc., Washington, 1972-76; dean Sch. Bus. Adminstrn., Marymount U., Arlington, Va., 1976-83; pres. Solo Systems Inc., Potomac, Md., 1982—; adj. prof. U. Md., College Park, 1968—; mem. Nat. Coun. for Civil Engring. Rsch., Washington, 1990—; mem. bd. advisors Columbia Lighthouse for the Blind, Washington, 1985—. 1st lt. USAF, 1956-59. Home: 9461 Turnberry Dr Potomac MD 20854

TUNE, TOMMY (THOMAS JAMES TUNE), musical theater director, dancer, choreographer, actor; b. Wichita Falls, Tex., Feb. 28, 1939; s. Jim P. and Eva Mae (Clark) T. Student, Lon Morris Jr. Coll., 1958-59; BFA, U. Tex., 1962; postgrad., U. Houston, 1962-63. Dancer, choreographer, dir. various prodns., N.Y.C., 1963—. Dancer (Broadway prodns.): Baker Street, 1965, A Joyful Noise, 1966, How Now Dow Jones, 1967, Seesaw, 1974 (Tony award for best featured actor mus.), (films): Hello Dolly, 1968, The Boyfriend, 1971; dir., choreographer Broadway prodns.: The Best Little Whorehouse in Texas, 1978, A Day in Hollywood/A Night in the Ukraine, 1980 (Tony award for best choreographer), Nine, 1982 (Tony award for best dir. mus.), Grand Hotel, 1989 (Tony award for best dir. musical and best choreographer, 1990); dir., actor, choreographer My One and Only, 1983 (Tony awards for best actor mus. and best choreographer), The Will Rogers Follies, (Tony award bestdir. musical and best choreographer); dir. Broadway prodn.: Stepping Out, 1987; dir. Off-Broadway prodns.: The Club, 1976 (Obie award), Cloud 9, 1981 (Obie award); performed in the USSR, 1988. Recipient Drama Desk award, 1978, 80, 82, Dance mag. award, 1984. Mem. Dirs. Guild Am., Stage Soc. Dirs. and Choreographers, Actors Equity Assn. Office: care Internat Creative Mgmt 40 W 57th St New York NY 10019-4001*

TUNG, PO-NAN, architect; b. Taipei, Republic of China, Nov. 4, 1949; s. Chiu-Liang and Chin-Shu (Yuan) T.; m. Yunn-Chyn Lee, Sept. 1, 1976; children: E-Jan, EE-Lan. BArch, Tunghai U., Taichung, 1972; MArch, Yale U., 1976; M in Urban Design, CCNY, 1977. Registered architect, N.Y., N.J. Asst. designer Ting-I Architects Assn., Taipei, 1970-72; architect, urban designer Robert Lamb Hart, N.Y.C., 1976-79; architect I.M. Pei & Ptnrs., N.Y.C., 1979-83, assoc., 1983-90; sr. assoc. Pei Cobb Freed & Ptnrs., N.Y.C., 1990—. Editor: Architectural mag. Form and Environment, 1972-74. Mem. AIA, Chinese Am. Club S.I. (N.Y.C.) (exec. 1988-89), Yale Club. Clubs: Chinese Am. S.I. (N.Y.C.) (exec. 1988—), Yale. Home: 139 Grand Ave Staten Island NY 10301-4058 Office: Pei Cobb Freed & Ptnrs 600 Madison Ave New York NY 10022-1615

TUNNELL, DANIEL ROBINSON, trade association executive; b. Abington, Pa., Feb. 23, 1948; s. John Shroy and Mary Jane (Robinson) T.; m. M. Gail Allis, Mar. 30, 1968; children: Scott N., Matthew A. BA, U. Bridgeport, 1972. Mgmt. trainee Perkin-Elmer Corp., Norwalk, Conn., 1968-71; prodn. mgr. Casco Products Corp., Bridgeport, Conn., 1971-72; mng. editor Early American Life mag., Harrisburg, Pa., 1973-77; adminstrv. asst. U.S. Congressman Allen Ertel, Harrisburg, 1977-80; sr. v.p. Pa. C. of C., Harrisburg, 1980-87; pres. Pa. Gas Assn., Harrisburg, 1987—; chmn. bd. dirs. Keystone Svc. Systems, Inc., Harrisburg. Active Lower Dauphin Coun. Govts., Harrisburg, 1976; mem. Coun. Middletown (Pa.) Borough, 1976-77; chmn. Middletown Zoning Hearing Bd., 1977-80, Middletown Authority, 1980—. Mem. Am. Soc. Assn. Execs., Pa. Soc. Assn. Execs., Harrisburg Trade Assn. Execs. Democrat. Lutheran. Home: 50 Race St Middletown PA 17057-2238 Office: Pa Gas Assn 212 Locust St PO Box 805 Harrisburg PA 17108

TUNNICLIFFE, WILLIAM WARREN, graphics company executive; b. Washington, Apr. 22, 1922; s. Homer Warren and Christine (Hobbs) T.; m. Ruth Loretto Loftus, June 23, 1951; children: Peter Warren, Virginia Warren, Elizabeth Loftus, William Loftus. BEE, Worcester Poly., 1943; MA in Engring. Scis. and Applied Physics, Harvard U., 1951. Staff mem. MIT Radiation Lab., 1943-44; head electronics sect. Boston U. Optical Research Lab., 1946-51; electronics engr. Barkley & Dexter Labs. Inc., Fitchburg, Mass., 1953-55; mgr. Eastern engring. office Offner Electronics Inc., Somerville, Mass., 1955-56; systems engr., project mgr., program mgr. Raytheon Co., Wayland, Mass., 1956-63; v.p. Info. Dynamics Corp., Reading, Mass., 1963-65; program mgr. Courier Citizen Co., Lowell, Mass., 1965-68, v.p., 1969-72; nat. sales mgr. Graphic Services, an Am. Standard Co., Warren, Mich., 1972, pres., 1973-74; gen. mgr. Woodland Communications Co. subs. W.E. Andrews Co., Bedford, Mass., 1975; program dir. prepress systems Graphic Communications Computer Assn., Arlington, Va., 1976-77; v.p. Walter T. Armstrong, Phila., 1977-78; program mgr. Bobst Graphic Inc. (subs. Bobst SA, Lausanne, Switzerland), Bohemia, N.Y., 1979, dir. market research, 1979-80, dir. market mgmt. and research, 1980, mktg. mgr., 1980-81; mktg. mgr. Graphics Arts div. Imlac Corp. subs. Hazeltine, Needham, Mass., 1981; account exec. Altertext Inc., Boston, 1982-83; v.p. info. techs. Graphic Communications Assn., Arlington, 1983-85; pres. Tunnicliffe Assocs. Inc., Winchester, Mass., 1974—; cons. Raytheon Co., 1964-66, Courier-Citizen Co., 1972, Chrysler Corp., 1974, Bobst Graphic Inc., 1981, Printing Industries of Am. Inc., 1985-86, Aspen Systems Corp., 1986-87, Oak Ridge Nat. Lab., 1986-87, Xyvision Inc., 1987, Interleaf Inc., 1987-88, Sci. Typographers, Inc., 1990—; printing industry rep. concerning the Standard Generalized Markup Lang. (SGML) to Joint Industry-Dept. Def. Task Force on Computer-Aided Acquisitions & Logistic Support, 1983-85, the Internat. Orgn. for Standardization and corr. coms. of Am. Nat. Standards Inst./Computer & Bus. Equipment Mfrs. Assn., 1983-85 and The Assn. Am. Pubs., 1983-85. Bd. dirs. Horace L. and Florence E. Mayer Found. Inc., Balt.; organizing chmn. bd. dirs. Printing Research Inst. for New Techs. Inc., Washington, 1968-69, chmn. bd., pres., 1970-74. Served as lt. (j.g.) USNR, 1944-46, lt., 1951-53. Recipient Walter Sherman Gifford Jr. Trophy; also numerous industry awards related to SGML, including recognition award Printing Industries of Am. Inc., 1983, Gutenberg award Printing Industries of Am. Inc., 1984, Tekkie award Graphic Communications Assn., 1986. Mem. Am. Soc. Info. Scis., Armed Forces Communications and Electronics Assn., Assn. Computing Machinery, IEEE, Internat. Word Processing Assn., Nat. Micrographics Assn., Nat. Soc. Profl. Engrs., Soc. Info. Display, Soc. Motion Picture and TV Engrs., Soc. Scholarly Pub., Inst. Printing (London), Printing Industries Am., Graphic Communications Computer Assn. (chmn. character generation com. 1967-74, dir. 1970-74, v.p. 1973-74), Printing Industries New Eng. (co-chmn. computer conf. 1967), Nat. Composition Assn., Research and Engring. Council of Graphic Arts Industry, Am. Def. Preparedness Assn., Naval Res. Assn., Res. Officers Assn., Retired Officers Assn., Standard Generalized Markup Lang. Users' Group (hon. mem.), U.S. Naval Inst., Sci. Research Soc. Am., Sigma Xi. Club: Harvard (Boston). Home and Office: 39 Central St Winchester MA 01890-2629 also: 759 E Washington Rd Hillsborough NH 03244

TUPPER, DAVID EDWARD, neuropsychologist; b. Brockton, Mass., Sept. 17, 1955; s. John F. and Carol A. (Hammerquist) T.; m. Sharon Theresa Bateman, Sept. 3, 1977; children: Jonathan David, Ashley Michelle. BA in Psychology, Boston U., 1977; MA in Psychology, U. Hartford, 1979; PhD in Neuropsychology, U. Victoria, 1982. Diplomate Am. Bd. Profl. Disability Cons.; lic. psychologist, N.Y. Postdoctoral fellow Henry Ford Hosp., Detroit, 1982-83; sr. neuropsychologist Lifestyle Inst., John F. Kennedy Ctr., Edison, N.J., 1983-86; clin. care coord. The Head Injury Ctr. at Highgate, Troy, N.Y., 1986-88; dir. clin. svcs. New Medico Rehab. Ctr., Troy, 1988—. Editor: Soft Neurological Signs, 1987, The Neuropsychology of Everyday Life, Vol. I, 1990, Vol. II, 1991; co-author: Human Developmental Neuropsychology, 1984. Mem. Internat. Neuropsychol. Soc., Internat. Acad. for Rsch. in Learning Disabilities, Nat. Acad. Neuropsychology (mem. membership com. 1988—), Am. Psychol. Assn., Am. Congress Rehab. Medicine, N.Y. State Psychol. Assn., Soc. for Cognitive Rehab. (bd. dirs.), N.Y. State Head Injury Assn. (bd. dirs. 1990—), N.J. Head Injury Assn. (mem. adv. bd. 1985-86). Home: 18 Weston Dr Clifton Park NY 12065-6009 Office: New Medico Rehab Ctr 100 New Turnpike Rd Troy NY 12182-1499

TURBEVILLE, ROBERT MORRIS, engineering executive; b. Cleve., May 2, 1951; s. Wilfred and Patricia Alice (Lamb) T.; m. Lisa Edelman, Apr. 2, 1977; children: Adam, Dennis, Diana. Student, Drew U., London, 1971-72; BA in History, W. Va. Wesleyan, 1973. Mgmt. trainee U.S. Steel, Pitts., 1973-74, foreman, 1975-79; mgr. standard products Heyl & Patterson, Inc., Pitts., 1979-83, sales mgr. to gen. mgr., 1983-88, v.p., 1988-91, pres., 1991—; dir. Heyl & Patterson, Inc., Pitts., 1988—; chmn. Bridge & Crane Inspection, Inc., Pitts., 1990—. Asst. leader Cub Scouts Am., Pitts., 1991—; coach Mt. Lebanon Soccer Assn., Pitts., 1990—. Mem. Coal Prep. Adv. Bd. (co-chmn. 1985-89), AIME, Process Equipment Mfrs. Assn. Republican. Methodist. Office: Heyl & Patterson Inc Box 36 Pittsburgh PA 15230

TURBIDE, DAVID ANDREW, management consultant, educator; b. Newburyport, Mass., Mar. 5, 1949; s. Andrew Adelard and Alyce Bernadette (Plouff) T.; m. Deborah Anne Di Biase, Dec. 13, 1970; children: Danielle Amanda, Darcie Anne. BS, Rochester Inst. Tech., 1972. Cert. in prodn., inventory mgmt.; cert. mfg. engr. Engr., cons. ARINC Rsch., Annapolis, Md., 1976-78; cons. Salem Corp., Crofton, Md., 1978-83; pres. Salem Assocs. Ltd., Annapolis, Md., 1983-88, Prodn. Solutions, Inc., Beverly, Mass., 1988—; contbg. editor MAPICS mag., Atlanta, 1989—,

Partners, Atlanta, 1990, Systems 3X/400, Des Plaines, Ill., 1991—. Author: (book) Computers in Manufacturing, 1991; (home study course) Computer Integrated Manufacturing, 1991; contbr. articles to profl. jours., mags., 1987—. 1st lt. USAF, 1969-76. Mem. Am. Prodn. and Inventory Control Soc., Soc. Mfg. Engrs., Am. Soc. for Quality Control.

TURCO, LEWIS PUTNAM, language professional, educator; b. Buffalo, N.Y., May 2, 1934; s. Luigi and May Laura (Putnam) T.; m. Jean Cate Houdlette, May 29, 1934; children: Melora Ann, Christopher Cameron. BA, U. Conn., 1959; MA, U. Iowa, 1962. Instr. Cleve. State U., 1960-64; asst. prof. Hillsdale (Mich.) Coll., 1964-65; asst. prof. to full prof. SUNY, Oswego, 1965—; instr. English. U. Conn., 1959; editorial asst. Writer's Workshop, U. Iowa, 1959, 60; vis. prof. SUNY, Potsdam, 1968-69; Bingham Poet in Residence, U. Louisville, 1982; Writer in Residence, Ashland U., 1991; staff mem. various writers' confs., others. Author: First Poems, 1960, The Sketches of Lewis Turco and Livevil: A Mask, 1962, Awaken, Bells Fallings: Poems 1959-67, 1968, The Inhabitant, 1970, Pocoangelini: A Fantography & Other Poems, 1971, The Weed Garden, 1973, numerous other poetry books including A Family Album, 1990 and The Shifting Web: New and Selected Poems, 1989; author numerous non-fiction books including The Book of Forms: A Handbook of Poetics, 1968, The New Book of Forms, 1986, others; contbr. articles to jours. Sec. City of Oswego Charter Revision Commn., 1990-91; active Oswego Opera Theater Chorus, Oswego Festival Chorus, 1986—. With USN, 1952-56. Recipient fellowship Meriden Record-Jour. Pub. Co. Scholarship, U. Conn., 1957-58, 58-59, resident fellowships Yaddo Found., Saratoga Springs, N.Y., 1959, 1977, faculty fellowships Rsch. Found. of SUNY, 1966-67, 69, 71, 73, 78, grant-in-aid, 1969; others; numerous prizes in field. Mem. MLA, P.E.N. Am. Ctr., Poetry Soc. Am., N.E. MLA, Maine Writers' and Pubs. Alliance, Nat. Writers Unions. Home: PO Box 362 Oswego NY 13126-0362 Office: SUNY College 39A Swetman Hall Oswego NY 13126

TUREEN, PHYLLIS, speech pathology and audiology educator; b. N.Y.C., Dec. 27, 1932; m. Jack Tureen (dec. Dec. 1987). BA, Bklyn. Coll., 1951, MA, 1953; PhD, NYU, 1968. Lic. speech pathologist, N.Y. Tchr. speech improvement Bd. Edn., N.Y.C., 1952-59; instr. in edn. Hunter Coll., N.Y.C., 1960-62; prof. NYU, 1962—, program dir., 1984-89, chair, 1990—; adj. instr. in speech Bklyn. Coll., 1957-59; cons. Queens (N.Y.) Devel. Ctr., 1973-77, John Wiley and Sons, N.Y.C., 1977-87. Author: (with others) Childhood Exceptionality, 1986; contbr. articles to profl. jours. Mem. Malverne Oaks Civic Assn., West Hempstead, N.Y., 1980-88; senator Sch. Edn., Health, Nursing and Arts Professions NYU, 1985-89; elected faculty sec. NYU, 1989-92. Catholic U. summer fellow, 1967. Mem. Am. Speech and Hearing Assn. (cert. clin. competency), Am. Cleft Palate Assn., N.Y. State Speech and Hearing Assn. (sec. 1970-72, 80-82), L.I. Speech and Hearing Assn. (rsch. award 1988). Office: NYU 239 Greene St Rm 637 New York NY 10003-6601

TURESKY, SAMUEL, dentist, educator; b. Portland, Maine, Feb. 22, 1916; s. Philip and Gertrude (Perlin) T.; m. Barbara Proner, Nov. 23, 1952; children: Andrew, Jon, Robert, Philip, Lisa. AB, Harvard U., 1937; DMD, Tufts U., 1941. Resident in dentistry Mary Fletcher Hosp., Burlington, Vt., 1941-42; pvt. practice Dorchester, Mass., 1945-70, Brookline, Mass., 1970-92; rsch. asst. Tufts U. Dental Sch., Boston, 1946-50, assoc. rsch. prof., 1950-68, rsch. prof., 1968—; cons. dental rsch. oral hygiene div. Gillette Corp., Boston, 1987—. Contbr. articles to profl. jours. Capt. USAF, 1942-45. Mem. Internat. Assn. for Dental Rsch., Omicron Kappa Upsilon. Jewish. Home: 84 Wallis Rd Chestnut Hill MA 02167-3173

TURESKY, STANLEY F., communications consultant, trade association executive; b. Portland, Maine, June 18, 1947; s. Maurice and Alice (Silbert) T.; m. Geraldine M. Otremba, Oct. 26, 1975; 1 child, Sarah Catherine. BA, Clark U., 1969; PhD, Brown U., 1973. Dir. planning Nat. Endowment for the Humanities, Washington, 1973-82; profl. staffer U.S. Senate Commn. on Environment and Pub. Works, Washington, 1983-85; exec. dir. N.E.-Midwest Coalition, Washington, 1985-87; v.p. Van Dyk Assocs., Washington, 1987-89; ptnr. Potomac Ptrns., Washington, 1989—; dir. U.S.-New Zealand Coun., Washington, 1989—; Washington dir. Ctr. for Fgn. Policy Options, L.A., 1990—. Author: The Future of the Liberal Arts, 1979. Mem. adv. panel Nat. Acad. Scis., Washington, 1986-88, Duke Ellington Sch., Washington, 1987-89. Mem. Monterey Country Club. Home: Georgetown Washington DC 20007 Office: Potomac Ptnrs Ste # 600 1250 24th St NW Washington DC 22037

TURGEON, EDGAR LYNN, economics educator; b. Mitchell, S.D., Aug. 26, 1920; s. Edgar Franklin and Margie (Fellows) T.; m. Livia Racko, Oct. 13, 1950 (div. 1988); 1 child, Danielle Kim. AB, U. Calif., Berkeley, 1942, MA, 1948; PhD, Columbia U., 1959. With Rand Corp., Santa Monica, Calif., 1950-57; prof. econs. Hofstra U., Hempstead, N.Y., 1957-90, prof. emeritus, 1991—; Fulbright lectr. Moscow State U., 1978, Acad. for Fgn. Trade, Moscow, 1991. Author: The Contrasting Economies, 1963, The Advanced Capitalist System, 1980, State and Discrimination, 1989. Lt. USN, 1942-46, PTO. Home: 30 Duncan Rd Hempstead NY 11550-4616 Office: Hofstra U Dept Econs Hempstead NY 11550

TURILLO, MICHAEL JOSEPH, JR., management consultant; b. Hartford, Conn., Aug. 22, 1947; s. Michael Joseph and Alice (Vargas) T.; m. Deborah Sherburne; children: Stephanie, Christopher. BS, Providence Coll., 1969; MBA, Syracuse U., 1972; MS, U. Mass., 1973. Cons. Peat, Marwick, Mitchell & Co. (name changed to KPMG Peat Marwick), Boston, 1974-77, mgr., 1977-82, ptnr., 1982—, nat. cons. practice dir. for fin. svc. cos., 1985-91; chmn. Internat. Mgmt. Cons. Practice Com. on Banking and Fin., 1986—; nat. ptnr.-in-charge Fin. Svcs.- Specialized Cons., 1990—, Specialized Cons. Fin. Svc. Com. mem. United Way, Boston, 1981-83; trustee Elliot Montessori, South Natick, Mass., 1984-85; dir. Greater Boston coun. Boy Scouts Am., 1988—. Capt. U.S. Army, 1969-71, Vietnam. Decorated Bronze Star. Mem. Bank Mktg. Assn., Assn. Planning Execs., Assn. Corp. Planners, Beta Gamma Sigma. Roman Catholic. Home: 47 Stacey St Natick MA 01760-3710 Office: KPMG Peat Marwick 1 Boston Pl Boston MA 02108

TURINO, GERARD MICHAEL, physician, medical scientist, educator; b. N.Y.C., May 16, 1924; s. Michael and Lucy (Arciero) T.; m. Dorothy Estes, Aug. 25, 1951; children: Peter, Phillip, James. A.B., Princeton U., 1945; M.D., Columbia U., 1948. Diplomate: Am. Bd. Internal Medicine. Intern Columbia U., Bellevue Hosp., 1948-49, asst. resident in medicine, 1949-50; resident in medicine New Haven Hosp., 1950-51; chief resident in medicine Columbia U. div. Bellevue Hosp., 1953-54; sr. fellow N.Y. Heart Assn., 1956-60; career investigator Health Research Council City of N.Y., 1961-71; asst. prof. medicine Columbia U., 1960-67, assoc. prof., 1967-72, prof. medicine, 1973-83, John H. Keating prof. medicine, 1983—; mem. staff Presbyn. Hosp., N.Y.C., 1960—; attending physician Presbyn. Hosp., 1973—; dir. med. service St. Lukes-Roosevelt Hosp., N.Y.C.; cons. Nat. Heart, Lung, and Blood Inst., Am. Lung Assn., Am. Heart Assn., N.Y. Lung Assn., N.Y. Heart Assn.; mem. staff div. med. sci. Nat. Research Council, Washington; cons. VA Hosp., East Orange, N.J., 1962-67; cons. in medicine Englewood (N.J.) Hosp., Hackensack (N.J.) Hosp. Contbr. articles to med. jours. Mem. Bd. Edn., Alpine, N.J., 1960-67. Served to capt. USAF, 1951-53. Recipient Joseph Mather Smith prize Columbia U., 1965, Alumni medal, 1983; Silver medal Alumni Assn. Coll. Physicians and Surgeons Columbia U., 1979, gold medal, 1986. Fellow AAAS; mem. Assn. Am. Physicians, Am. Soc. Clin. Investigation, Harvey Soc., Am. Fedn. Clin. Rsch., Am. Physiol. Soc., Am. Heart Assn. (award of merit 1980, Disting. Achievement award 1989, bd. dirs.), N.Y. Heart Assn. (pres. 1981-83, dir.), N.Y. Lung Assn. (dir.), Am. Physiol. Soc. (chmn. steering com. respiration sect.), Am. Thoracic Soc. (pres. 1987-88), N.Y. Med.-Surg. Soc., N.Y. Clin. Soc. Clubs: Princeton (N.Y.C.); Maidstone, Devon Yacht, Century Assn. Home: 66 E 79th St New York NY 10021-0233 Office: St Lukes-Roosevelt Hosp W 114th St and Amsterdam Ave New York NY 10025

TURK, JESSIE ROSE, geography educator; b. Newark, N.J., June 27, 1920; d. George William and H. Mildred (Snyder) T. BA, Montclair (N.J.) State Coll., 1942; MA, Oberlin (Ohio) Coll., 1947; EdD, Columbia U., 1964. Grad. asst. Oberlin Coll., 1942-44; instr. Montclair State Coll., 1947-49; instr. to assoc. prof. Trenton (N.J.) State Coll., 1949-64, prof. geographer, 1964-82, prof. emeritus, 1983—. Bd. dirs. Unified Vailsburg Svcs. Orgn., Newark, 1986—; recording sec. Vailsburg Block Assn. Coun., Newark, 1984—. Mem. Nat. Coun. for Geog. Edn., Assn. Am. Geographers, NEA, Gamma Theta Upsilon, Delta Kappa Gamma, Pi Lambda Theta, Kappa Delta Pi. Home: 105 Stuyvesant Ave Newark NJ 07106-2502

TURKEVICH, JOHN, chemist, educator, clergyman; b. Mpls., Jan. 20, 1907; s. Metropolitan Leonty and Anna Olimph Turkevich; m. Ludmilla Buretoff, July 1934; children: Marina, Tamara. BSc, Dartmouth Coll., 1928, MSc, 1930; MA, Princeton U., 1932, PhD, 1934; DD (hon.), McMurray Coll.; DSc (hon.), Dartmouth Coll. Ordained priest Orthodox Ch. in Am., 1965. Instr. chemistry Dartmouth Coll., Hanover, N.H., 1928-31; prof. chemistry Princeton (N.J.) U., 1936-75, lectr. Russian, 1940-42, lectr. Woodrow Wilson Sch. Govt., 1963-66, Eugene Higgins prof. chemistry, 1955-75; prof. emeritus Woodrow Wilson Sch. Govt., 1975—; chaplain Princeton U.; cons. M.W. Kellogg Co., Jersey City, 1936-71, RCA Labs., Princeton, 1941-65, Union Carbide, N.Y.C., 1960-85, Dept. State, 1950, also U.S. AEC, Washington; vis. prof. Tokyo Inst. Tech., 1974, Lausanne (Switzerland) U., 1979; sci. attache U.S. Embassy, Moscow, 1962, U.S Embassy, Warsaw, Poland, 1962, Prague, Czechoslovakia, 1962. Author: Russian for Scientist. Named Outstanding Tchr., Mfg. Chemists Assn. Fellow AAAS; mem. Coun. on Fgn. Rels., Century Assn. Home: 109D Monroe Vlg Jamesburg NJ 08831-1913 Office: Princeton U Frick Chemisrty Lab Princeton NJ 08544

TURKO, JOHN WALTER, management information systems director; b. New Kensin, Pa., Nov. 14, 1944; s. John Turko and Joan Esther (Jasinski) Gutknecht; m. Linda Francis Ribich, Oct. 18, 1969; children: Christopher, Jessica. BS in Indsl. Adminstrn., Carnegie Mellon U., 1966; MBA, U. Pitts., 1969, MS in Indsl. Engring., 1976. Mgmt. trainee U.S.X., Braddock, Pa., 1966-68; ops. rsch. analyst Allegheny Ludlum Steel, Pitts., 1968-69; sr. system analyst Westinghouse Electric, Wilkens Twp., Pa., 1969-78; v.p., dir. MIS Kennametal Inc., Latrobe, Pa., 1978—. Recipient Achievement in Mng. Info. Tech. award Am. Mgmt. Systems and Carnegie Mellon U., 1991. Mem. Latrobe Country Club. Office: Kennametal PO Box 231 Latrobe PA 15650-0231

TURKOLY-JOCZIK, ROBERT LOUIS, military officer, educator; b. McKeesport, Pa., Aug. 5, 1931; s. Louis Alexander and Margaret (Stefan) Joczik; m. Kiyo Hamamoto, July 7, 1960; children: Beatrice Takemi, Joyce Kiyo, Gordon Nobunaga, Mark Tametomo. BS, Calif. U. of Pa., 1957; diploma, Def. Lang. Inst., Washington, 1966, U.S. Army Command and Gen. Staff Coll., Ft. Leavenworth, Mo., 1973; MA with honors, Duquesne U., 1983; PhD, U. of Wales, Great Britian, 1986. Commd. 2d lt. U.S. Army, 1952, advance through grade to lt. col., 1973; chief mission rels. U.S. Mil. Mission to Saudi Arabia, 1966-67; bn. comdr. U.S. Army Spl. Forces, Republic of Vietnam, 1970-71; chief ops. Unconventional Warfare div., U.S. Readiness Command, MacDill AFB, Fla., 1976-78; broker, owner Five Star Realty Co., Tampa, Fla., 1977-81; v.p. acdem. affairs Kemper Mil. Sch. & Coll., Boonville, Mo., 1986-88; observer, treaty and arms control specialist Multinat. Force and Observers, Sinai, Egypt, 1988—; adj. prof. U. Md., European div., Mediterranean, 1988—, Cen. Tex. Coll., European div., Mediterranean, 1989—. Contbr. articles to profl. jours. Decorated Bronze Star medal, Air medal, Gallentry Cross with Palm; recipient Gold Star award, Freedom Found. award Freedoms Found., Valley Forge, Pa., 1987; U.K. U. Chancellors Internat. scholar, Great Britain, 1983;. Fellow Royal Asiatic Soc.; mem. Internat. Inst. for Strategic Studies, Am. Polit. Sci. Assn., Am. Hist. Assn., Ret. Officers Assn., Spl. Forces Assn., Treaty Verification Observers Assn. (exec. coun. Sinai 1988—), Davis Island Yacht Club, Masons, Shriners. Republican. Episcopalian. Home: 24 Archdale St Charleston SC 29401-1961 Office: Multinat Force and Observers Civilian Observer Unit New York NY 09677-5000

TURNER, CAREN ZELDIE, lobbyist, lawyer; b. Bklyn., July 4, 1957; d. Bernard and Joyce (Stauber) T.; m. Henry James Fishman, Aug. 12, 1984; 1 child, Hallie Ann Turner Fishman. BA, Brandeis U., 1979; JD, Georgetown U., 1985. Atty. Cameron Hornbostel, Washington, 1985-87; v.p. Fleishman-Hillard, Washington, 1987—. Mem. ABA, D.C. Bar Assn., Women In Govt. Rels., Am. League Lobbyists. Office: Fleishman-Hillard 1301 Connecticut Ave NW Washington DC 20036-1815

TURNER, EDWIN ARNOLD, JR., occupational health physician; b. Plainfield, N.J., Nov. 29, 1937; s. Edwin Arnold and Ruth Alice (Carter) T.; m. Jean Marie Cooper, Dec. 27, 1964; children: Suzanne Marie, Scott Cooper. BS in Zoology, Wheaton Coll., 1959; MD, Cornell U. Med. Coll., 1963. Diplomate Am. Bd. Preventive Medicine/Occupational Medicine, Am. Bd. Med. Examiners; lic. N.J., N.Y. Resident, gen. surgery U.S.P.H.S. Hosps., Staten Island and Gallup, N.Mex., 1964-68; physician City of Plainfield, 1971—; corp. med. dir. Ethicon, Inc. (div. Johnson & Johnson), Somerville, N.J., 1969-75, Western Union, Upper Saddle River, N.J., 1975-85, Sterling Drug, Inc. (div. Eastman Kodak), N.Y.C., 1985-91; cons. Fair Oaks Hosp., Summit, N.J.; clin. asst. prof. Robert Wood Johnson Med. Sch., Univ. of Medicine and Dentistry of N.J., Piscataway, 1985—. Surgeon USPHS, 1967-69. Fellow Am. Coll. Occupational Medicine (bd. dirs. 1986-91), Am. Coll. Preventive Medicine; mem. Am. Soc. Legal and Indsl. Medicine (bd. govs. 1985—), Med. Execs. (exec. bd., pres. 1985-86), Nat. Soc. to Prevent Blindness (bd. dirs. 1985—, del. 1991), Med. Soc. N.J., AMA. Republican. Home: 1045 Oak Ln Plainfield NJ 07060-3429

TURNER, HARRY WOODRUFF, lawyer; b. Blairsville, Pa., May 2, 1939; s. James McKinnie and Dorothy Elizabeth (Tittle) T.; m. Mary Elizabeth Phelan, Dec. 30, 1972; children: James William, David Woodruff. AB, U. Pitts., 1961; JD, Harvard U., 1964. Bar: Pa., 1965, U.S. Supreme Ct., 1979. Assoc. Kirkpatrick & Lockhart, Pitts., 1964-71, ptnr., 1971—; bd. dirs., sec. Imperial Harbor Corp., Bonita Springs, Fla., 1968—, IH Utility Co., Bonita Springs, 1975—, IH Properties Co., Bonita Springs, 1980—. Trustee, sec. Wilson Coll., Chambersburg, Pa., 1978-89; pres. U. Pitts. Nat. Alumni Assn., 1990-91; alt. del. Rep. Nat. Conv., Miami, Fla., 1989, Houston, Tex., 1992; trustee, v.p. Torrance (Pa.) State Hosp., 1969-73; trustee ann. giving fund U. Pitts., 1982—; trustee, treas. Aspinwall Baseball Assn., 1985—. Mem. ABA, Pa. Bar Assn., Internat. Acad. Trial Lawyers, Allegheny County Bar Assn., Allegheny County Acad. Trial Lawyers, Fox Chapel Golf Club, Duquesne Club, Harvard-Yale-Princeton Club (Pitts.), Univ. Club. Presbyterian. Office: Kirkpatrick & Lockhart 1500 Oliver Pittsburgh PA 15222-2404

TURNER, HEATHER ANN, assistant director; b. Gallup, N.Mex., May 5, 1965; d. Norman S. Turner and Norma A. (Zounek) T. BA in Psychology, Russell Sage Coll., Troy, N.Y., 1988; MS in Student Personnel, SUNY, Buffalo, 1990. Residence hall dir. SUNY, Buffalo, 1988-90; residence hall dir. Boston Coll., Chestnut Hill, Mass., 1990-91, asst. dir. residential life, 1991—. Mem. Am. Coll. Personnel Assn., Boston Area Coll. Housing Assn., Nat. Assn. Women Deans, Adminstrs. and Counselors. Office: Office University Housing Boston Coll Chestnut Hill MA 02167

TURNER, HERBERT DAVID, international development consultant; b. N.Y.C., Feb. 24, 1923; s. Leo and Mollie (Dobrikin) T.; m. Edna Pauline Gluck, Sept. 11, 1948; children: Mark Ian, Steven Ives, Perry Adam. BSME, Case Inst. Tech., 1950; postgrad., U. Oxford, Eng., 1950-51. Chief productivity and tech. assistance U.S. Mission to Denmark, 1951-56; dir. interregional tech. coop. dir. U.S. Mission to OEEC, Europe, 1956-60; chief program devel. Office of Participant Tng. ICA, Washington, 1956-60; dep. exec. dir. pres.' task force on fgn. aid AID, Washington, 1961, dep. dir. analysis, sr. sci. rsch. adminstr., 1961-65, chief tech. assistance policy, 1965-69, chief program design and evaluation systems, 1969-80; chief of evaluation UN, N.Y.C., 1980-83; pvt. practice cons. Chevy Chase, Md., 1983—; lectr. vis. lectr. Woodrow Wilson Sch., Princeton U., 1985—. Author: AID Evaluation Handbook, 1979, United Nations Evaluation System, 1983, Integrated System for Programme Policy and Technical Assistance Management, 1986, The Design and Evaluation of Development Projects and Programs—Concepts, Methodologies and Techniques, 1992. Cpl. USAAF, 1942-46, ETO. Home and Office: 3419 Cummings Ln Chevy Chase MD 20815-3237

TURNER, JAMES THOMAS, judge; b. Clifton Forge, Va., Mar. 12, 1938; s. James Thomas and Ruth (Greene) T.; m. Patricia Sue Renfrow, July 8, 1962; 1 child, James Thomas. BA, Wake Forest Coll., 1960; JD, U. Va., 1965. Bars: Va. 1965, U.S. Ct. Appeals (4th and fed. cirs.), U.S. Supreme Ct. Assoc. firm Williams, Worrell, Kelly & Greer, Norfolk, Va., 1965, ptnr., 1971-79; U.S. magistrate U.S. Dist. Ct., Eastern Dist. Va., Norfolk, 1979-87. Mem. ABA, Va. Bar Assn., Norfolk and Portsmouth Bar Assn. (sec. 1975-79). Address: US Claims Ct 717 Madison Pl NW Washington DC 20005

TURNER, JANET SULLIVAN, painter; b. Gardiner, Maine, Nov. 15, 1935; d. Clayton Jefferson and Frances (Leighton) Sullivan; m. Terry Turner, Oct. 6, 1956; children: Lisa Turner Reid, Michael Ross, Jonathan Brett. BA cum laude, Mich. State U., 1956; Diploma in Painting, Haystack Mountain Sch. Arts and Crafts, Deer Isle, Maine, 1964. lectr. student cultural exch. program Pa. State U., Harrisburg, 1985; rep. Am. Women in Art, UN World Conf. on Women, Nairobi, Kenya, 1985. One-artist shows include San Diego Art Inst., 1971, Villanova (Pa.) U. Gallery, 1982, Pa. State U. Gallery, Middletown, 1985, Temple U. Gallery, 1986, Widener U. Art Mus., Chester, Pa., 1987, Suzanne Gross Gallery, Phila., 1986-89, Ariel Gallery Soho, N.Y.C., 1986-89, Trenton City Mus., 1990, Gloucester Coll., 1990; group shows include Del. Art Mus., Wilmington, 1978, Woodmere Art Mus., Phila., 1980, Port of History Museum, Phila., 1984, Allentown Art Mus., 1984, Trenton City Mus. Ellarslie Open VIII, Trenton, N.J., 1989, Gettysburg Coll., Ammo Gallery, Bklyn., 1989, Pa. State Mus., Harrisburg, 1990, 91, Galeria Mesa, Mesa, Ariz., 1991; represented in permanent collections Nat. Mus. Women in Arts, Washington, Mich. State U., East Lansing, ARA Services Inc., Phila., Blue Cross/Blue Shield, Phila, Am. Nat. Bank and Trust Co., Rockford, Ill., Burroughs Corp., Lisle, Ill.; contbg. writer and art critic Art Matters, Phila., 1987; artists of the 1990's series featured in Manhattan Arts mag., N.Y.C., 1990. Bd. dirs. Rittenhouse Sq. Fine Arts Ann., Phila., 1984-86. Recipient 2d pl. award San Diego Art Inst. 19th Ann. Exhbn., 1971, award of merit Pavilion Gallery, Mt. Holly, N.J., 1991, 3d pl. Art of State of Pa. Katonah Mus. of Art, N.Y., 1992. Mem. Artists' Equity (bd. dirs. 1985-86, 1st v.p. Phila. 1986-87, newsletter editor 1985-86, pres. 1987-88, honorable mention traveling exhbn. Stedman-Gallery 1985), Phila. Watercolor Club, Delta Phi Delta. Democrat. Roman Catholic. Home and Studio: 88 Cambridge Dr Glen Mills PA 19342

TURNER, JOHN ANDREW, economist; b. Chgo., July 9, 1949; s. Henry Andrew and Mary Margaret (Tilton) T.; m. Kathleen King Peery, June 21, 1975; 1 child, Sarah. BA, Pomona Coll., Claremont, Calif., 1971; MA, Stanford U., 1972; PhD, U. Chgo., 1977. Rsch. econ. SSA, Washington, 1976-80, U.S. Dept. Labor, Washington, 1980—; cons. Orgn. for Econ. Cooperation and Devel., Paris, 1989; conf. chair internat. pension conf. U.S. Dept. Labor, Washington, 1990. Editor: Trends in Pensions, 1989 (transl. into Japanese 1991), Pension Policy: An International Perspective, 1991, Trends in Health Benefits, 1992. Mem. Am. Econ. Assn. Methodist. Home: 3713 Chesapeake St NW Washington DC 20016-1813 Office: US Dept Labor 200 Constitution Ave NW Washington DC 20210-0002

TURNER, LEWIS THOMAS, environmental sanitarian; b. Alexandria, Va., July 4, 1947; s. Oscar Downey and Nancy Goode (Bland) T.; m. Sylvia Eileen Mott, Aug. 23, 1968; children: Eileen Lucille, Lewis Thomas, Joseph Daniel, Nancy Rose. BS in Biology, Wheaton (Ill.) Coll., 1969; MS in Food Sci., U. Md., 1984. Registered environ. sanitarian. Sanitarian Bur. Shellfish Sanitation, Richmond, Va., 1972-73; sanitarian Div. of Milk Control, Balt., 1973-85, environ. sanitarian, 1990—; quality control dir. East Greenwich (R.I.) Dairy, 1986-87; supply systems analyst R.I. Army Nat. Guard, Providence, 1987-90. Contbr. articles to profl. jours. Mem. Citizens Adv. Com. for West Warwick (R.I.) for Long Range Devel. Plan, 1989-90. 1st lt. Q.M.C., U.S. Army, 1970-72. Mem. Am. Daffodil Soc., Md. Assn. Sanitarians, Dairy Tech. Soc. Md. and D.C., Cen. Atlantic States Assn. Food and Drug Ofcls., Phi Kappa Phi. Baptist. Home: 4 Monocacy Ct Walkersville MD 21793 Office: Div Milk Control 4201 Patterson Baltimore MD 21793

TURNER, NORMAN HUNTINGTON, artist, educator; b. Storm Lake, Iowa, July 11, 1939; s. Thomas and Isabel (Lambly) T.; m. Patricia Mainardi (div. 1980); m. Joan Cherney, Apr. 12, 1987; 1 child, Hannah Alice. Student, U. Iowa, 1958-60; T, N.Y. Studio Sch., 1964-65; BA, Empire State Coll., Westbury, N.Y., 1981. Instr. Artists for Environ. Found., Wallpack, N.J., 1978-79, N.Y. Studio Sch., N.Y.C., 1982-84; adj. asst. prof. Queens Coll., CUNY, Flushing, 1982-90; dir. Caumsett Art, Huntington, N.Y., 1985-89; instr. New Sch. for Social Rsch., N.Y.C., 1991—; artist-in-residence Artists for Environ., 1978. Solo exhbns. include Ingber Gallery, 1977, Jersey City Mus., 1980, Bowery Gallery, N.Y.C., 1989, Coll. William and Mary, 1989; group shows include Blue Mountain, 1986, Bank St. Coll., 1986, Artists Choice Mus., 1982, L.I. U., 1975. Fellow N.J. Coun. on Arts, 1981. Mem. Bowery Gallery. Office: Bowery Gallery 121 Wooster St New York NY 10012-3857

TURNER, ROBERT HAL, telecommunications and computer executive; b. Kingsport, Tenn., July 12, 1948; s. Robert Harold Sr. and Mattie Louise (Gambrell) T.; m. Bonnie Carolotte Cromer, June 22, 1969; children: Robert H. III, Christopher Albert. BS in Mktg., U. S.C., 1972, MBA, 1973. Founder Bojangles Restaurants, Columbia, S.C., 1973-77; account exec. So. Bell Telephone, Columbia, 1977-80, industry mgr., 1980-81; tng. mgr. AT&T, Denver, 1981-82; area sales support mgr. AT&T, N.Y.C., 1983-85; region mgr. S. Cen. Bell Advanced System, New Orleans, 1985-87; v.p. Bell S. Communications Holdings, Inc., Atlanta, 1987; exec. v.p. Norlite Computer Systems, Kanata, Ont., Can., 1988; pres. Insightguide, N.Y.C., 1989-90; pres., chief exec. officer PTT Telecom Netherlands U.S., Inc., N.Y.C., 1991—. Lutheran.

TURNER, ROSS JAMES, investment corporation executive; b. Winnipeg, Man., Can., May 1, 1930; s. James Valentine and Gretta H. (Ross) T.; children: Ralph, Rick, Tracy. U. Man. Extension, 1951, Banff Sch. Advanced Mgmt., 1956. Various sr. operating and mgmt. positions Genstar Corp., San Francisco, 1961-76, chmn./pres., chief exec. officer, 1976-86, also bd. dirs.; chmn. Genstar Investment Corp., San Francisco, 1987—; dep. chmn., bd. dirs. Rio Algom Ltd.; bd. dirs. Gt. West Life Assurance Co., Fed. Industries Ltd., Western Corp. Enterprises, Blue Shield of Calif., Guy F. Atkinson Co. of Calif. Vice chmn. bd. dirs. YMCA, San Francisco. Fellow Soc. Mgmt. Accts. Can.; mem. Toronto Club, Vancouver Club, Pacific Union Club, Rancho Santa Fe Golf Club, Peninsula Golf and Country Club, Loxahatchee Club. Office: Genstar Investment Corp 801 Montgomery St Ste 500 San Francisco CA 94133-5151 also: Rio Algom Ltd, 120 Adelaide St W Ste 2600, Toronto, ON Canada M5H 1W5

TURNER, THOMAS EDWARD, company executive; b. Middletown, Conn., Apr. 18, 1948; s. Arthur Lincoln and Harriet (Raab) T.; m. Dianne Lucciano, Jan. 2, 1982 (div.); children: Chad Thomas, Crystal Joan. BSEE, Tufts U., 1970. Exec. dir. City of N.Y., 1972-74; exec. vp. Graphic Systems Inc., Hudson, N.H., 1974-78; dir. corp. mktg. Wang Labs., Lowell, Mass., 1978-81; dir. sales/mktg. Wang Australia Pty. Ltd., Sydney, 1981-83; dir. internat. mktg. Wang Labs., Lowell, 1983-86; pres. Wang Can. Ltd., Toronto, Ont., 1986-89; dir. N.Am. sales Wang Labs., Lowell, 1989-90; v.p. N.Am. Symbol Tech., Bohemia, N.Y., 1990-92; sr. v.p. Symbol Tech., Bohemia, 1992—.

TURNER, THOMAS MARSHALL, telecommunications executive, consultant; b. Cumberland, Md., Aug. 17, 1951; s. James Richard and Laura Roselie (Durst) T. BS in Indsl. Tech. and Mgmt., U. Md., 1973, MA in Indsl. Tech. and Mgmt., 1980. Grad. asst U. Md., College Park, 1975-76; sales assoc., gen. mgr. Equity Trades Reality, Riverdale, Md., 1976-83; account exec. RCA Corp., Greenbelt, Md., 1983; sr. telecommunications cons. CMC, Inc., Washington, 1984-86, ORS Assoc., McLean, Va., 1986-87; owner, pres. T-1 Communications, Silver Spring, Md., 1987—; cons. NASA, Washington, 1989—, Balt. County Govt., Towson, Md., 1989—, Marriott Corp., Rockville, Md., 1990, Group Health, Inc., N.Y.C., 1991—; grad. asst. instr. Dale Carnegie Inst., 1992. Contbr. articles to profl. jours. Vol. ARC, Riverdale, Md., 1977-80; instr. Jr. Achievement Bus. Co-op, Rockville, Md., 1979-82. Recipient Highest Achievment award Dale Carnegie Inst., 1989. Mem. Am. Soc. Tng. and Devel., Telecommunications Mgrs. Assn. of Capital Area, Toastmasters, Sigma Alpha Epsilon Alumni Assn.

TURNER, WELD WINSTON, industrial psychologist; b. St. Paul, July 25, 1931; s. Frank and Hazel Thirza (Weld) Prevratil; B.S. Commerce, Okla. State U., 1954; M.S., Purdue U., 1955, Ph.D., 1959; m. Helen Theo Kralicek,

June 12, 1953 (div. 1969); children: Jean Ann, Alan Weld. Personnel evaluation asso. Gen. Motors Inst., Flint, 1955-60; supr. personnel research B.F. Goodrich Co., Akron, 1960-67; sr. manpower adv. Mobil Oil Corp., N.Y.C., 1967—; lectr. adult edn. div. U. Akron, part-time. With U.S. Army, 1951-52. Mem. Am. Psychol. Assn., Am. Psychol. Soc., Sigma Xi, Phi Kappa Phi, Pi Gamma Mu. Home: 601 Rosery Rd E Apt 3905 Largo FL 34640-3829

TURNER, WILLIAM DONALD, retired psychologist; b. Heyworth, Ill., Dec. 1, 1904; s. Frank and Hariet Emma (Cogswell) T.; m. Pearl Elizabeth Paulson, Aug. 26, 1933 (dec. June 1977); children: Phyllis Alma, Frank Nelson, John Paulson, James Carlson. AA, Blackburn Coll., 1924; AB with highest honors, U. Ill., 1926; AM, PhD, Harvard U., 1929; postgrad., U. Vienna, Austria, 1929-30. Instr. in psychology Bryn Mawr (Pa.) Coll., 1931-35; rsch. psychologist Inst. Pa. Hosp., Phila., 1936-39, Cambridge (Mass.) Youth Study, 1939-42; instr. psychology MIT, Cambridge, 1942-43; mgmt. cons. Edward N. Hay and Assocs., Phila., 1944-48; prof., dean Sch. Social Work U. Pa., Phila., 1949-68; chmn. dept. behavioral sci. Widener Coll., Chester, Pa., 1969-72; pvt. inventor in electronic music Laurel, Md., 1972-87. Patentee electronic transfer organs; contbr. articles to profl. publs. LLD (hon.) Blackburn U., Carlinville, Ill., 1955. Home: 17320 Quaker Ln Sandy Spring MD 20860

TURNER, WILLIAM RUSSELL, broker; b. Gordon, Pa., July 27, 1911; s. William Robinson and Lena Christine (Russell) T.; m. Miriam Florence Toewe, Nov. 27, 1941 (dec. July 1962); children: Nancy Louise, Christine Emily, Susan Marie; m. Patricia Ann Nelson, Apr. 11, 1969; children: Charles A., Thomas W., Julia A. BS in Chemistry, U. Pa., 1942; postgrad., Pa. State U., 1962, Swarthmore (Pa.) Coll., 1963. Engring. draftsman Reading (Pa.) Co., 1929-32; with inventory control Am. St. Co., Phila., 1933-40; jr. chemist Atlantic Refining Co., Phila., 1940-42, asst. chemist, 1942-44, assoc. chemist, 1944-48; sr. rsch. scientist Atlantic Richfield Co., Phila., 1948-71; broker, dealer W.R. Turner Co., Ardmore, Pa., 1971—. Contbr. articles to profl. jours.; patentee in field. Mem. Am. Chem. Soc. (cons.), Phila. Securities Assn., Masons (Ivanhoe Royal Arch chpt.), St. Alban Commandery. Republican. Presbyterian. Home: 3050 Sulgrave Rd Ardmore PA 19003-1630

TURNES, GEORGE KEELER, environmental and safety specialist; b. Albany, N.Y., Jan. 22, 1947; s. George W. Jr. and Matilda (Keeler) T.; m. Kathleen Ruth Putman, Sept. 19, 1970; children: Gregory Keeler, Christine Marie, Karen Lynn, Mary Ellen. AS in Bus. Adminstrn., Schenectady (N.Y.) County Coll, 1978; AAS in Safety Tech., Community Coll. Air Force, 1985. Sr. engring. technician N.Y. State Dept. Transp., Albany, 1966-80; environ. specialist N.Y. State Thruway Authority, East Syracuse, 1980—. Mem. Salina (N.Y.) Planning Bd., 1987—; vice chmn. Salina Rep. Com., 1987—. Sgt. USAF, 1966-70, 90-91, Vietnam, Desert Shield/Desert Storm; mem. N.Y. Air N.G. Mem. Am. Soc. Safety Engrs., N.Y. State Planning Fedn., Cen. N.Y. Fed. Safety and Health Coun., Tactival Fighter Wing, VFW, Am. Legion. Roman Catholic. Home: 7415 Eastgate Cir Liverpool NY 13090-3158 Office: NY State Thruway Authority PO Box 308 East Syracuse NY 13057-0308

TURNQUIST, MARK ALAN, engineering management educator; b. Jamestown, N.D., July 26, 1949; s. Carl Eric and Alice Helen (Kost) T.; m. Lynn Karen Rutherford, June 19, 1971; children: Alan, Matthew. BS, Mich. State U., 1971; SM, MIT, 1972, PhD, 1975. Asst. prof. Northwestern U., Evanston, Ill., 1975-79; assoc. prof. Cornell U., Ithaca, N.Y., 1979-86, prof. engring. mgmt., 1986—, assoc. dean Coll. Engring., 1984-86; vis. prof. GM Rsch. Labs., Warren, Mich., 1986-87; cons. in field, 1984—. Co-editor jour. Transp. Sci., 1991; assoc. editor jour. Ops. Rsch., 1988-91; contbr. articles to profl. publs. Mem. Ops. Rsch. Soc. Am. (sect. chair 1990—), Inst. Mgmt. Scis., Transp. Rsch. Bd., Soc. Risk Analysis. Office: Cornell U Sch CEE 309 Hollister Hall Ithaca NY 14853

TUROFSKY, CHARLES SHELDON, landscape architect; b. Chgo., Oct. 1, 1942; s. Joseph and Lillian R. (Brownstein) T.; m. Diane Adrienne Haber, Aug. 22, 1971; children: Benjamin, Alexi, Nicole. BFA, U. Ill., 1964; M Landscape Architecture, U. Mich., 1966; student, Harvard Grad. Sch. Design, 1971. Registered landscape architect, N.Y., Conn., N.J., Mass., N.C. Assoc. landscape architect Sasaki Office, Watertown, Mass., 1966-71; prin. landscape architect Charles Turofsky, P.C., Great Neck, N.Y., 1971—; pres. Turlab Constrn. Corp., Scarsdale, N.Y., 1984—; prof. Rutgers U., 1975-76, Westchester Community Coll., Valhalla, N.Y., 1971-75, N.Y. Bot. Garden, Bronx, N.Y., 1975-81; tchr. Yonkers (N.Y.) Pub. Schs., 1973-85; teaching fellow U. Mich., Ann Arbor, 1965. Prin. works include Tarry Town Corp. Ctr., GE World Hdqrs., Fairfield, Conn., Rosecliff Condominiums, Briarcliff, N.Y., Tarry Elm Bus. Ctr., Elmsford, N.Y., Woodmere (N.Y.) Country Club, Hampshire Country Club, Mamaroneck, N.Y., adult handicapped playground Young Adult Inst., Tarrytown, N.Y., others. Recipient award Garden Clubs of Am., 1982, award N.Y. State Nurserymen Assn., 1987, 88. Mem. AIA, N.Y. State United Tchrs. (rep. 1983-85), Westchester-Putnam Builders Inst. (excellence in landscaping award 1986). Jewish. Office: 6 Bly Ct Great Neck NY 11023-1706

TUROW, JOSEPH GREGORY, communication educator; b. Bklyn., Apr. 5, 1950; s. Abraham and Danuta (Chaikin) T.; m. Judith Anne Forrest, June 17, 1979; children: Jonathan, Marissa, Rebecca. BA, U. Pa., 1971, MA, 1973, PhD, 1976. Asst. prof. Purdue U., W. Lafayette, Ind., 1976-86; assoc. full prof., prof. communications U. Pa., 1986—. Author: Entertainment, Education and the Hard Sell, 1981, Media Industries, 1984, Playing Doctor, 1989, Media Systems in Society, 1992. Div. head Speech Communication Assn., Fairfax, Va., 1987; active Internat. Communication Assn., Austin, Tex., 1990—. Recipient Russell Nye award Popular Culture Assn., Bowling Green, Ohio, 1982; Nat. Endowment for Humanities Stipend, Washington, 1986; Federal communications com. grantee Washington, 1978. Mem. Phi Beta Kappa. Jewish. Office: U Pa Annenberg Sch Philadelphia PA 19104

TURRELL, RICHARD HORTON, SR., banker; b. Kingston, Pa., Apr. 9, 1925; s. George Henry and Margaret (Clark) T.; m. Sally Wolfe, May 28, 1955; children: Richard H. Jr., David C., Douglas W. Student, Cornell U., 1943; BS in Commerce, Washington and Lee U., 1949. Rep. sales Del. Lackawanna and Western Coal Co., Phila., 1949-51; asst. to pres. N.Y.C., 1951-58; broker Auchincloss Parker & Redpath, N.Y.C., 1958-61; mgr. investments Fiduciary Trust Co. Internat., N.Y.C., 1961—, v.p., 1965, sr. v.p., 1968—, sec., 1971-84; asst. sec. Blue Coal Corp., N.Y.C., 1953-58; v.p., bd. dirs. Pine Raleigh (N.C.) Corp., 1966; bd. dirs. Lubke Enterprises Inc., Palm Coast, Fla. Trustee, overseer Simon's Rock of Bard Coll., Gt. Barrington, Mass., 1968—; trustee Monmouth Coll., West Long Branch, N.J., 1980—, chmn. bd. trustees, 1989-92; chmn. Millburn-Short Hills (N.J.) Rep. Com., 1973-78; trustee Children's Specialized Hosp. Found., Mountainside, N.J., 1989—. With Signal Corps, U.S. Army, , 1943-46, PTO. Named Disting. Alumnus, Washington and Lee U., 1986. Mem. Baltusrol Golf Club (Springfield, N.J., gov. 1977), Capitol Hill Club (Washington), Turtle Creek Club (Tequesta, Fla.), Masons, Irem Temple Aaonms, Phi Beta Kappa, Phi Eta Sigma, Alpha Kappa Psi, Omicron Delta Kappa (hon.), Beta Gamma Sigma, Phi Delta Theta. Presbyterian. Home: 26 Hobart Gap Rd Short Hills NJ 07078-1804 Office: Fiduciary Trust Co Internat 2 World Trade Ctr New York NY 10048-0203

TURRENTINE, HAYWOOD LYNWOOD, human resource executive, consultant; b. Bahama, N.C., Sept. 15, 1945; s. James Burnice and Jessie Mae (Rhodes) T.; m. Lelani Butler, Sept. 16, 1978; 1 child, James Lynwood. BA, N.C. Cen. U., 1967; MA, U. Cin., 1974; Cert. Completion, U. Md., 1988, U. Wis., 1966, 67. Vol. Peace Corps, Rajasthan, India, 1967-69; counseling coord. U. Cin., 1970-73; asst. dir. Ednl. Devel. Program, U. Cin., 1973-75, Laborers Internat. Union Tng., Washington, 1975-80; exec. dir. Laborers Tng. Trust Fund, Phila., 1980-85, Chester County OIC, West Chester, Pa., 1985—. Contbr. articles to profl. jours. Task force mem. Pa. Dept. Edn., Harrisburg, 1989—; mem. United Way Agy. Govt. Rels., Exton, Pa., 1990—; presiding elder 2nd Presbyn. Ch., West Chester, 1989—; organizer, devel. Edn. Coalition, Coatesville, 1990. Named Employee of the Yr., Chester County OIC, 1991; recipient Award of Excellence, Am. Soc. Tng. and Devel., Boston, 1981. Mem. Exec. Dirs. Assn. (regiona. convenor 1988-91, nat. sec. 1989-91), NAACP, The Network Group, Masons (sec. 1990), Rotary (vocat. trainer 1989). Republican. Presbyterian. Home: RR 7 Box 2200 Coatesville PA 19320-9807 Office: Chester County OIC 125 S Penn St West Chester PA 19382-3435

TURRIZIANI, VINCENT MICHAEL, transportation executive; b. Greensburg, Pa., Jan. 20, 1956; s. Archangel Anthony and Antoinette Rita (D'Itri) T.; m. Barbara Joann Kriek, May 5, 1984; 1 child, Jessica Catherine. BS, St. Vincent Coll., 1978. Asst. to pres. Romco Industries Corp., Greensburg, 1977-79; founder, pres., chief exec. officer Regency Limousine Svc., Inc., Greensburg, 1980—. Chmn. police dept. So. Greensburg Borough, 1982-85, coun. mem., 1982-85; mem. parish coun. mem. St. Bruno Cath. Ch., So. Greensburg, 1978-81, pres. parish coun., 1981-82, eucharistic minister, 1983—; mem. Better Bus. Bur., Dem. Club Westmoreland County. Mem. Nat. Fedn. Ind. Bus., Cen. Westmoreland C. of C. Democrat. Roman Catholic. Home: 1232 Ferree St Jeannette PA 15644-1562 Office: Regency Limousine Svc Regency Bldg 444 Steck St Greensburg PA 15601-4257

TURSO, VITO ANTHONY, public relations executive; b. N.Y.C., Jan. 3, 1948; s. Vito Anthony and Helen (Smanko) T.; m. MaryAnn Ponzo, July 12, 1980; children: Lisa Lynn, Laura Mae, Nicole Vita. Student, Queens Coll., Flushing, N.Y., 1965-69. Reporter, editor L.I. Press, Jamaica, N.Y., 1966-77; asst. editor The Trib, N.Y.C., 1977-78; dir. pub. affairs N.Y.C. Dept. Sanitation, 1978-90; dep. commr. for pub. affairs N.Y.C. Dept. Correction, 1990—; guest lectr. New Sch. for Social Rsch., N.Y.C., 1988, Pace U., 1990. Host pub. affairs shows on TV and radio, 1981, 88; contbr. articles to pop. mags. Bd. dirs. Ozone Tudor Civic Assn., Ozone Park, N.Y., 1982—. Recipient Bronze medal Internat. Film and TV Festival N.Y., 1985, Page One award N.Y. Newspaper Guild, 1976. Mem. Pub. Rels. Officers Soc. N.Y. (pres. 1983-85), Pub. Rels. Soc. Am. (bd. dirs. 1987-88), Am. Diabetes Assn. (bd. dirs. N.Y. chpt. 1989-91), Bklyn. Tech. High Sch. Alumni Assn. (bd. dirs. 1984—), Columbia Assn., N.Y. Press Club, Inc. (bd. dirs. 1978), Old Pucks Old Timers Ice Hockey Club, KC. Democrat. Roman Catholic. Home: 133-33 84th St Tudor Village NY 11417-1919 Office: NYC Dept Correction 60 Hudson St New York NY 10013-4393

TURTELL, NEAL TIMOTHY, librarian; b. N.Y.C., Nov. 1, 1949; s. Richard Roland and Ann Grace (Glover) T. AB, Fordham U., 1971; MLS, Pratt Inst., 1975. Cataloger-libr. Ford Found., N.Y.C., 1972-75, U.S. Dept. Transp., Washington, 1975-77; spl. projects libr. Smithsonian Instn., Washington, 1977-81, chief catalogue records, 1981-82; asst. dir. tech. svcs. U. Wis., Oshkosh, 1982-83, asst. prof. libr. sci., 1982-83; asst. chief libr. Nat. Gallery of Art, Washington, 1983-87, exec. libr., 1987—. Contbr. to book revs. Libr. Jour., 1972-75, exhbn. catalogue. Bd. trustees Pyramid Atlantic Ctr. for Printmaking and the Art of the Book, Riverdale, Md., 1988—, v.p. bd. trustees, 1991—. Mem. Art Librs. Soc. N. Am., Rsch. Librs. Group (steering com. for art and arch.a 1988-89). Home: 2301 Jeff Davis Hwy Arlington VA 22202 Office: Nat Gallery of Art 4th St & Constitution NW Washington DC 20565

TUSA, WAYNE KENENTH, environmental engineering executive; b. Plattsburgh, N.Y., Sept. 23, 1951; s. Eugene Kenneth and Florence Tusa. BS in Engring., Cornell U., 1973. Civil engr. Andrews & Clark, Inc., N.Y.C., 1973-75; environ. engr. Leonard S. Wegman Co., Inc., N.Y.C., 1975-77; mgr. N.Y. ops. Fred. C. Hart Assocs. Inc., N.Y.C., 1977-84; v.p. Dynamac Corp., Ft. Lee, N.J., 1985-90; pres. Environ. Risk and Loss Control, Inc., N.Y.C., 1991—. Contbr. numerous articles to profl. jours. Mem. ASCE (hazardous waste mgmt. com. 1982-83, solid waste mgmt. com. 1984, underground tank com. 1987-89, global environ. resource planning com. 1991—, chmn.), Air Pollution Control Assn., Water Pollution Control Fedn. Soc. for Risk Analysis, numerous environ. orgns. Home and Office: 309 E 90th St New York NY 10128-5244

TUTEIN, DAVID WARREN, English educator; b. Cambridge, Mass., Aug. 8, 1937; s. Warren and Maude Waddel (Flanagan) T. BA, Northeastern U., 1960; MA, U. Conn., 1962; postgrad., Boston U., 1962-68. Teaching fellow U. Conn., Storrs, 1960-62; lectr. English, New Eng. Sch. Law, Boston, 1962-67; adj. instr. Northeastern U., Boston, 1967-80, instr., sr. lectr., 1980—, mem. steering com. English dept., 1989—. Author: Joseph Conrad's Reading, 1990; editorial bd. Working Papers, 1985—. Sec. Friends of Muddy River, Inc., Brookline, Mass., 1980—. Mem. MLA, Nat. Coun. Tchrs. English, Amnesty Internat., Fellowship of Reconciliation, Fortune Soc. Democrat. Home: 190 Claflin St Belmont MA 02178-3220 Office: Northeastern U 360 Huntington Ave Boston MA 02115-5096

TUTINO, ROSALIE JACQUELINE, college administrator; b. Bklyn., Dec. 28, 1937; d. Peter Rocco and Rose (Oliva) T. BA, St. Joseph's Coll., 1959; MA, NYU, 1964. Licensed ins. broker, N.Y. Publ., annuity mgr. Equitable Life Assurance, N.Y.C., 1959-62; instr., dept. chmn. Our Lady Perpetual Help High Sch., Bklyn., 1962-70; dir. coll. relations St. Joseph's Coll., Bklyn., 1970-75, devel. and coll. rels. dirs., 1975-77, v.p. devel. and coll. rels., 1977—; pres. Rosalie Tutino Assocs., Hampton Bays, N.Y., 1980. Bd. dirs. Suffolk coun. Boy Scouts Am., 1988—, Suffolk Coun., 1988, Review bd. Town of Southampton. Mem. L.I. Coalition for Fair Broadcasting, Nat. Soc. Fundraising Execs., Pub. Rels. Soc. Am., L.I. Assn., CASE. Republican. Roman Catholic. Home: 49 Romana Dr Hampton Bays NY 11946-3718 Office: Saint Josephs Coll 155 W Roe Blvd Patchogue NY 11772-2399

TÜTSCH, HANS EMANUEL, newspaperman; b. Interlaken, Switzerland, Mar. 27, 1918; came to U.S., 1972; s. Henry and Lucie (Häsler) T.; m. Brida-Baronessa Palermo di Lazzarino, Dec. 18, 1952. Doctor iuris utriusque, U. Zurich, Switzerland, 1944. Fgn. editor, fgn. corr. Neue Zürcher Zeitung, Zurich, 1946—; vis. asst. prof. history Wayne State U., Detroit, 1954-55, vis. prof. history, 1961-62. Author: From Ankara to Marrakesh, 1963, Facets of Arab Nationalism, 1965; contbr. articles to profl. jours. Mem. Overseas Writers. Home: 4701 Willard Ave Chevy Chase MD 20815

TUTTLE, DAVID BAUMAN, data processing executive; b. N.Y.C., Oct. 25, 1948; s. John Bauman and Charlotte (Root) T.; m. Mildred Suzanne Lamb, May 5, 1973, (div. May 1978); m. Nancy Viola Caraber, Mar. 14, 1981; 1 child, Jason David. Student, MIT, 1966-69. Assoc., sr. assoc. programer IBM Cambridge (Mass.) Sci. Ctr., 1968-71; staff programmer IBM VM/370 Devel., Burlington, Mass., 1971-76; sr. prin. S/W engr. Digital Equipment Corp., Maynard, Mass., 1976-78; mgr. Cambridge Telecom/GTE Telenet, Burlington, 1978-81; sr. scientist GTE Telenet, Burlington, 1981-84, chief scientist, 1984-85; sr. tech. cons. Prime Computer, Inc., Framingham, Mass., 1985-86; prin. tech. cons. Prime Computer, Inc., Framingham, 1986-89; sr. rsch. engr. Ungermann-Bass Inc., Andover, Mass., 1990-91; chief engr. Ungermann-Bass, Inc., Andover, Mass., 1991—; strategy forum del. Corp. for Open Systems, McLean, Va., 1986-89, architecture com. mem., 1989, strategy forum nominating com., 1986-87; patent rev. com. Prime Computer, Inc., 1985-89. Co-author and editor: 3270 Display System Protocol, 1981, 83, Hotline BSC Access Method, 1970. Donor mem. Smithsonian Inst., Washington, 1980—. Mem. Assn. Computing Machinery, IEEE (computer soc.), Nat. Space Soc. (life mem.), The Cousteau Soc., USS Constitution Mus. Assn., Black and Blues of Killington (treas. 1986-89), Mandala Folk Dance Ensemble (dancer 1970-73). Republican. Presbyterian. Home: 27 Heather Dr Reading MA 01867-3961 Office: Ungermann-Bass Inc Andover Corporate Ctr 5 Corporate Dr Andover MA 01810-2442

TUTTLE, DOUGLAS FREEMAN, campus police administrator; b. Harrisburg, Pa., Oct. 3, 1950; s. Adelbert H. and Mary Louise (Kirkham) T.; m. Denise Alta Rothacker, Nov. 17, 1973; children: Jody Alta, David Douglas. BA in History, U. Del., 1976; grad., Nat. Crime Prevention Inst., Louisville, 1977, FBI Nat. Acad., Quantico, Va., 1984; MPA, U. Del., 1990. Patrol officer U. Del. Dept. Pub. Safety, Newark, 1972-73, corporal, 1973-74, investigator, 1974-77, lt., 1977-83, assoc. dir., 1983-85, dir., 1985—; cons. campus security Johns Hopkins U., Balt., Ramapo Coll., Mahwah, N.J., West Chester (Pa.) U., Goldey-Beacon Coll., Wilmington, Del., Md. Inst. Coll. Art, Balt., Lock Haven (Pa.) U., 1985—; conf. speaker in field, workshop instr. in field, 1982—. Author: Campus Security Act of 1990: Strategies for Compliance, 1991; contbr. articles to profl. jours. Faculty advisor U. Del. Sailing Team, Newark, 1990—; law enforcement torch run coord. Del. Spl. Olympics Summer Games, Newark, Dover, Del., 1986—. Mem. Fraternal Order Police # 7 (pres. 1982-84, John F. Schimmel Svc. award 1988), Assn. Campus Law Enforcement Adminstrs. of Del., Md., D.C., and Va. (chmn. 1990), Internat. Assn. Campus Law Enforcement Adminstrs. (regional dir. 1991-93, Pres.'s award 1990, 91), Internat. Assn. Chiefs of Police, Am. Soc. for Indsl. Security, Phi Kappa Phi, Pi Alpha Alpha. Office: U Delaware Dept Pub Safety Newark DE 19716

TUTTLE, GEORGE PALLISER, communication educator, entrepreneur; b. N.Y.C., Mar. 6, 1933; s. Miner Worthington and Margaret (Palliser) T.; m. Anne Temple, June 18, 1955; children: Grant Burlingame, Charles Palliser, Brian Temple, William Warner. BA, Middlebury (Vt.) Coll., 1956; MFA, Yale U., 1960; PhD in Theater History, Tufts U., 1972. Dir. theater Dartmouth Coll., Hanover, N.H., 1960-63; prof. theater, TV and speech communication Cape Cod Community Coll., West Barnstable, Mass., 1970—, chmn. dept. arts and oral communication, 1973-77; producer, dir. Sta. WGBH TV, Boston, 1963-64; chmn. dept. arts Wabash Coll., Crawfordsville, Ind., 1965-67; dir. summer arts program Cape Playhouse Sch. Theater, Dennis, Mass., 1970-75; pres. Tuttle Travel Svcs., Hyannis and Osterville, Mass., 1977—, TravelBooks, Hyannis, 1987—; bd. dirs. Community Broadcasting Boston, 1970-82, New Eng. TV Corp., Boston, 1982-86, Sta. WNEV-TV, Boston, 1982-86. Bd. dirs. Arts Found. Cape Cod, Hyannis, 1985—, dir. staging and prodn. Pops By The Sea, 1985—; active Barnstable (Mass.) Town Meeting, 1970-76; chmn., vice chmn. Barnstable Sch. Com., 1970-77; chmn. drug abuse com. Town of Barnstable, 1972, adv. com. cable TV, 1973-80, econ. devel. com., 1983-84. Lt. U.S. Army, 1956-60. Mem. Actors Equity, Met. Club, Beach Club. Republican. Episcopalian. Home: 483 Phinneys Ln Centerville MA 02632-2548 Office: Tuttle Travel Svcs 765 Falmouth Rd Hyannis MA 02601-2317

TUTTLE, HAROLD DOUGLAS, elementary school teacher, consultant; b. Bklyn., May 8, 1951; s. harold Douglas Tuttle Sr. and Lorraine Grace (Lehr) Doyon; m. Martha Ann Tarte, Oct. 13, 1979; children: Jon Richard, Thomas Michael. BS in Elem. Edn., Plymouth State Coll., 1973, MEd, 1989. Tchr. Bristol (N.H.) Elem. Sch., 1973-75, Blake Sch., Hill, N.H., 1975-77, Internat. Schule, Hamburg, West Germany, 1977-78, Atkinson (N.H.) Acad., 1978-80; head tchr. Franconia (N.H.) Elem. Sch., 1980--; resource coord. European Coun. Internat. Schs. Math. Conf., Hamburg Internat. Sch., 1977; adj. prof. Antioch U., Keene, N.H., 1987, 91; dir. N.H. Global Edn. Ctr., 1987-91; mem. bd. examiners Nat. Coun. for Accreditation of Tchr. Edn, 1989-92; contbr. to various other orgns. Editor: Games of the Word, 1987, Green Kids Book of Issues, 1991. Candidate Grafton County Sheriff, 1973; delegate N.H. Dem. Convention, 1980-82; pres. North Country Hockey League, 1983-85, Lafayette Skating Assn., 1980-85; bd. dirs. Tri County Community Action, 1989-91. Recipient State Presdl. award for Excellence in Math./Sci., 1991; named State of N.J. Environ. Educator of Yr., 1992; named candidate tchr. in space, 1985; NSF grantee, 1985-87, Critical Skills Inst. grantee, 1986, Govs. Inst. Gifted and Talented Edn. grantee, 1987. Mem. Nat. Edn. Assn. (various com. 1973—), Lafayette Regional Edn. Assn. (pres. 1984-91), Newfound Tchr. Assn. (pres. 1973-75), Nat. Mid. Level Sci. Tchrs. Assn. (state chair), Phi Delta Kappa. Home: 32 Magowan Hill Rd Franconia NH 03580-4710 Office: Lafayette Regional Sch Main St Franconia NH 03580-4813

TUTUNJIAN, JOHN PETER, marketing and computer software services executive; b. Bklyn. Aug. 1, 1936; s. George and Mary (Adjami) T.; m. Barbara Ann Bianco, Apr. 29, 1961 (div. 1992); children: Lisa, Andrea, John, Noelle. BS in Math., St. John's U., 1959; MBA in Adminstrv. Mgmt., L.I. U., 1966. Various positions IBM, NCR, S. Klein and EDS, 1959-68; v.p. Computer Guidance, 1968-70; v.p. human resources Bankers Trust Co., 1971-75; exec. v.p. Cornell Computer Corp., N.Y.C., 1976-87, chmn. 1987-89, pres., chief exec. officer, 1989-90; exec. dir. Aleppo Enterprises, 1990—; prin. CP Assocs., 1992—; speaker orgns. and univs.; mem. EDP Faculty Farmingdale Coll.; mem. curriculum adv. bd. Manhattan Community Coll.; cons. Am. Nat. Standards Inst.; mem. computer systems curriculum adv. com. SUNY; chmn. banking group Met. Info. Processing Conf.; nat. fundraising chmn. St. John's U., 1990-91, mem. exec. com. univ. coun., 1991—, mem. adv. bd. Bus. Coll., 1991—; bd. dirs. Cornell Holding Corp., Plainview, N.Y., Telesystems Software Exch. Inc., Huntington, N.Y., Crescent Computer Corp., Plainview, George Tut & Co., Bklyn. Editor: Computer Acronyms, 1991. Bd. dirs. L.I. Forum for Tech., 1990-91, TQM, 1991—. With Army NG, 1960-66. Fellow Georgetown U., 1959-60; cert. in data processing. Mem. Data Processing Mgmt. Assn., Assn. Computing Machinery, Long Island Assn. Office: PO Box 93 Jericho NY 11753-0093

TUTWILER, MARGARET ANN, agribusiness executive; b. Columbia, S.C., Jan. 23, 1958; d. William S. and Emily (Maroney) T.; m. Robert John Samors, Sept. 2, 1984; 1 child, Joshua Riley Samors. BA in Polit. Sci., Davidson Coll., 1980; M. in Pub. Policy, Harvard U., 1985. Publs. editor Group of Thirty, N.Y.C., 1981-83; program analyst World Bank, Washington, 1984; policy analyst Econ. Rsch. Svc., USDA, Washington, 1985-86, Nat. Ctr. for Food and Agrl. Policy, Washington, 1986-90; assoc. dir. Internat. Policy Coun. on Agr. and Trade, Washington, 1988-91; dir. agribus. policy Cen. Soya Co., Inc., Washington, 1991—; officer Internat. Policy Coun. on Agr. and Trade, Washington, 1990—. Editor: New Agrifood Systems, 1991, US Agriculture in a Global Setting, 1988. Mem. Am. Assn. Agrl. Economists, Internat. Assn. Agribus., Phi Beta Kappa, Omicron Delta Kappa. Home: 425 Greenbrier Dr Silver Spring MD 20960 Office: Cen Soya Co Inc 1722 I St NW Washington DC 20006

TWARDY, JOHN PHILIP, mechanical engineer, consultant; b. Hartford, Conn., Jan. 11, 1951; s. B. John and Beulah (Manning) T.; m. Donna Lee Dawson, Aug. 26, 1978; children: Rachel Lee, Nicole Marie. BSME, U. Hartford, 1973; MSME, U. Conn., 1978. Registered profl. engr., Conn. From assoc. engr. to design engr. Electric Boat, Groton, Conn., 1973-75; NSSS II engr. Combustion Engring., Windsor, Conn., 1975-78; sr. exptl. engr. Hamilton Standard, Windsor Locks, Conn., 1978-79; from engr. to sr. engr. Barnhart, Johnson, Francis and Wild, Inc., Avon, Conn., 1979-88, v.p., 1988—. Mem. ASHRAE, NSPE, ASME (assoc.), Nat. Fire Protection Assn. Home: 270 Barbourtown Rd Collinsville CT 06022-1705 Office: BJFW Inc 31 Ensign Dr Avon CT 06001-3700

TWEEDY, DAVID ALAN, management consultant, director; b. Providence, June 9, 1953; s. James Edward and Patricia Ann (Humphrey) T.; m. Laura Elizabeth Davidson, Sept. 20, 1980; children: Elizabeth, Matthew, Katharine. BS, U. Mass., 1975; MBA, U. R.I., 1984. Claims adjuster Liberty Mut. Ins. Co., Providence, 1977-79, claims supr., 1979-81; sr. systems analyst Liberty Mut. Ins. Co., Boston, 1982; cons. Betterley Risk Cons., Worcester, Mass., 1982-87, sr. cons., 1987—. Author: (chpt.) Risk Management Information Systems; editor: Betterley Risk Management Commentary; columnist: Bus. Ins. Mem. Beta Gamma Sigma. Republican. Reformed Presbyterian. Office: Betterley Risk Cons 1 Chestnut Pl Worcester MA 01608

TWEEDY, TIMOTHY THADDEUS, civil engineer; b. Mineola, N.Y., Mar. 7, 1964; s. James Edwin and Anne (Bracken) T.; m. Colleen Ann Breheny, Oct. 7, 1989. BCE, Cath. U. Am., 1987; MCE, N.Y. Poly. U., 1992. Pvt. practice Floral Park, N.Y., 1987-88; structural engr. Amman & Whitney, N.Y.C., 1988; resident engr. N.Y.C. Bd. of Edn., 1988-89; project officer N.Y. Sch. Constrn. Authority, 1989-90; sr. titled, cost and civil engr. Stone & Webster Engring. Corp., N.Y.C., 1990—. Assoc. editor Watch Your Step mag., 1989—; contbr. articles to profl. jours. Mem. 7th Precinct Community Coun., Bklyn., 1990-92; county committeeman Bklyn. Rep. Com., 1991. Mem. ASCE (constrn. group Met. sect. 1988—), N.Y. Athletic Club, Ancient Order Hibernians. Roman Catholic. Home: 351 92d Ave # D5 Brooklyn NY 11209-3594 Office: Stone & Webster Engring Corp 1 Penn Plz New York NY 10119-0118

TWEEL, NICHOLAS J., financial analyst; b. Huntington, W.Va., May 5, 1916; s. John William and Anna (Thabit) T.; m. Vivienne Joy Chapman, Sept. 13, 1942; children: Joyce Gail Tweel Lewis, Nina Lynn Tweel Wood. Grad. high sch., Huntington; student, Marshall U., 1934-36. Clk. U.S. Post Office Dept., Huntington, 1935-42; prin. Mayflower Distbrs., Huntington, 1946-49, Ceredo (W.Va.) Drive-In Theater, 1949-52, Waterford Park Race Track, Pitts., 1952-55; co-owner Tanforan Race Track, San Francisco, 1955-61; prin. Charlestown (W.Va.) Race Track, 1960-63; co-owner Holiday Inns, Huntington and Ft. Lauderdale, 1969-81; prin. River Downs Race Track, Cin., 1973-77; freelance fin. analyst N.Y.C., Ft. Lauderdale, Fla., 1961—; prin. Gen. Mgmt. Co, N.Y.C., Beverly Hills, Ft. Lauderdale, 1961; prin. motion picture industry Emprise Pictures Inc., Beverly Hills, Calif., 1988—. Patentee in field. Served to capt. US Army,

1942-46. Recipient hon. recognition awards Damon Runyon Cancer Fund, Am. Vets. Assn., Chriner's Crippled Children's Hosp. Mem. Am. Legion, Am. Vets. Assn., Phoenicians Internat., Thoroughbred Racing Assn., Horsemen's Benevolent and Protective Assn., Masons (32 degree), N.Y. Atletic Club. N.Y. Yacht Club, Army and Navy Club, Army Officers Club Le Club Internat., Coral Ridge Country Club, Lago Mar Beach Club, Mar Beach and Tennis Club. Democrat. Episcopalian. Clubs: Army & Navy; Army Officers; N.Y. Athletic; N.Y.A.C. Yacht; Coral Ridge Country; Lago Mar Beach & Tennis. Lodges: Knights of Malta, Elks, Masons, Shriners. Home and Office: 150 Central Park S New York NY 10019-1566

TWIETMEYER, DON HENRY, lawyer; b. Rochester, N.Y., June 4, 1954; s. Frederick Herman and Norma Frances (Porter) T.; m. Victoria Lynne Engleman, July 1, 1989; children: Laura Elizabeth, Jill Ann Cafarelli, Anthony R. Cafarelli. BA in Polit. Sci., Econs. with honors, SUNY, Buffalo, 1976; JD, Union U., 1979; LLM in Taxation, U. Miami, 1980; MBA in Acctg., Rochester Inst. Tech., 1983. Bar: N.Y. 1980, Fla. 1980, U.S. Dist. Ct. (we. dist.) N.Y. 1980, U.S. Dist. Ct. (so. dist.) Fla. 1980, U.S. Tax Ct. 1980, U.S. Ct. Appeals (5th and 11th cirs.) 1981; CPA, N.Y. Tax acct. Davie, Kaplan & Braverman, Rochester, 1980-82; assoc. DeHond-Stowe Law Office, Rochester, 1982-84, Lacy, Katzen, Ryen & Mittleman, Rochester, 1984-87; mng. atty. DeHond Law Office, Rochester, 1987-91, prin., 1991-92; assoc. Fix, Spindelman, Brovitz, Turk, Himelein & Shukoff, Rochester, 1992—; lectr. estate and gift taxes Found. Acctg. Edn., 1987—. V.p. coun. Hope Luth. Ch., 1989-91, active meml. fund com., 1990-91, bldg. use com., 1990-91; active Bethlehem Luth. Ch., 1991—. Mem. ABA (tax sect.), Fla. Bar Assn. (tax sect.), N.Y. State Bar Assn. (tax sect.), Monroe County Bar Assn. (tax sect. and trusts and estates section), N.Y. State Soc. CPAs, Am. Assn. Atty.-CPAs, Phi Beta Kappa, Phi Alpha Delta, Omicron Delta Epsilon, Phi Eta Sigma. Republican. Lutheran. Office: 2 State St Ste 500 Rochester NY 14614-1308

TWISTE, WALTER LEROY, insurance company executive; b. S.I., N.Y., Jan. 14, 1945; s. Walter Wesley and Mabel Ann (Guidi) T.; m. Marilyn Verrier, May 14, 1966 (div. 1990); children: Tracey Ann, Kerri Lynn. AAS, Union County Coll., 1991; BSBA, Thomas Edison State Coll., 1992. Real estate officer Chase Manhattan Bank, N.Y.C., 1966; security analyst Fiduciary Counsel, N.Y.C., 1967, F.I. DuPont, N.Y.C., 1968; v.p. Trainer Wortham & Co., Inc., N.Y.C., 1969-76; exec. v.p. Laidlaw Adams & Peck, N.Y.C., 1976-88; pres. Laidlaw Holdings, Inc., N.Y.C., 1988-90; vice chmn. Laidlaw Holdings Asset Mgmt., Inc., N.Y.C., 1988-90; sr. assoc. Spingarn Agy., Inc., Livingston, N.J., 1990—; pres. The Vest Sure Group, Inc., Livingston, N.J., 1991—. Office: The Vest Sure Group Inc 154 S Livingston Ave Ste 205 Livingston NJ 07039

TWIST-RUDOLPH, DONNA JOY, neurophysiology and psychology researcher; b. Cape May, N.J., Dec. 3, 1955; d. Donald and Mary Ann (Johnson) Twist; m. Daniel Jay Rudolph, Jan. 10, 1981; children: Andrew, Adam. BS, Boston U., 1978; MA, SUNY, Stony Brook, 1984; PhD, SUNY, 1986. Licensed phys. therapist, N.Y., Conn. Teaching asst., dept. phys. therapy N.Y. U., 1980; teaching asst., dept. psychology SUNY, Stony Brook, 1982-83, teaching asst., dept. grad. psychology, 1984; intern, dept. rehab. medicine N.Y. U. Med. Ctr., Rusk Inst. Rehab. Medicine, N.Y.C., 1984-86, postdoctoral fellow and rsch. scientist, 1986-87; dir. rsch. and edn., chief of phys. therapy Norwalk (Conn.) Hosp., 1987—; state bd. examiner N.Y. State Phys. Therapy Licensing Exam. Profl. Svcs., Albany, 1986—; adj. asst. prof. Mt. Sinai Sch. Med., N.Y.C., 1990—. Contbr. articles profl. jours. Named Outstanding Young Woman Am., 1981, 83; grantee Easter Seal Rsch. Found., 1985-87, Rehab. Svcs. Adminstr. Dept. Edn., 1991; recipient Therapeutic Techs. Ins. award, 1989. Mem. Am. Phys. Therapy Assn., Am. Congress Rehab. Medicine, N.Y. Acad. Scis. Home: 381 Hemlock Rd Fairfield CT 06430-1857 Office: Norwalk Hosp 24 Stevens St Norwalk CT 06850-3894

TWITCHELL, PAUL FRANCIS, JR., marketing executive; b. Boston, Aug. 1, 1960; s. Paul Francis and Eunice Anne (O'Brien) T. BS in Communication Studies, Emerson Coll., Boston, 1982. Sr. account svcs. rep. Bronner Slosberg Humphrey, Boston, 1984-86; promotions mgr. The Boston Phoenix, 1986-88; promotions dir. WFNX-FM, Boston, 1988-90; mktg. mgr. The Phoenix's NewPaper, Providence, 1990-91, Tele-Pub., Inc., Boston, 1990—.

TWOMEY, MARY REGINA, women's rights activist, writer; b. Trenton, N.J., Oct. 11, 1941; d. Anthony James and Mary Beatrice (Burns) Moran; div.; children: Moira, William III, Kathleen. Student, Trenton Jr. Coll., 1960, U. N.H., 1984, McIntosh Coll., Dover, N.H. Engrs.' asst. U.S. Govt., Burlington, Mass., 1961-62; ptnr. nursing home business various orgns., Mass., 1969—; tchr. Sacred Heart Sch., Amesbury, Mass., 1974-75; sports writer Rockingham County Newspapers, Hampton, N.H., 1986-88; exec. planning com. Women in Sports Conf., New Agenda/Northeast, 1987, 88, 89, 90; runner NOW/NAGWS Run for Equality, Washington to Phila., 1986. Cand. for N.H. State Legis., 1990; del. to Dem. Nat. Conv., 1984, 88; bd. dirs. Rockingham County Family Planning Program, 1988—; mem., lobbyist Epilepsy Found. Am., Landover, Md., 1970—. JFK Libr. fellow, 1989, 90; inducted into New Agenda/Northeast Sports Hall of Fame, 1990. Mem. NOW (past state and local v.p., N.H. pres., local publicity chmn., named 1st Woman of Yr. 1990), Dem. Alliance for Women in N.H. (founding mem.), N.H. Women's Lobby, Women's Sports Found. (lobbyist, N.H. chmn. Nat. Women's Sports Day 1989, 90), Assn. for Women in Sports Media, N.H. Common Cause (bd. dirs. 1991—). Democrat. Roman Catholic. Home: 7 Hedman Ave Hampton NH 03842-4022

TWOMEY, THOMAS ALOYSIUS, JR., lawyer; b. N.Y.C., Dec. 8, 1945; s. Thomas A. and Mary (Maloney) Elizabeth (Curtain) T.; m. Judith Hope Twomey, Dec. 15, 1979; stepchildren: Erling Hope, Nisse Hope. B.A., Manhattan Coll., 1967; postgrad. U. Va., 1967-68; J.D., Columbia U., 1970. Bar: N.Y. 1972, U.S. Tax Ct. 1974. Asst. town atty. Town of Southampton N.Y., 1973-74; spl. asst. dist. atty. Suffolk County, N.Y., 1973-74; pvt. practice law, Riverhead, N.Y., 1974-75; ptnr. Hubbard & Twomey, Riverhead, 1976-79, Twomey, Latham, Shea & Kelley, Riverhead, 1980—; mem. deans coun. Stonybrook Sch. Medicine, 1991—; adj. prof. environ. law Southampton Coll., 1977-78. Mem., bd. dirs. East End Arts Council, Riverhead, 1983; trustee L.I. Power Authority. Recipient Environ. award, U.S. EPA, 1980. Mem. ABA, Suffolk County Bar Assn., N.Y. State Energy Council, N.Y. State Fresh Water Wetlands Appeals Bd. Democrat. Home: 68 Oyster Shores Rd East Hampton NY 11937-1179 Office: Twomey Latham Shea & Kelley 33 W 2D St Riverhead NY 11901

TYLER, JOANNA ARMIGER, research and counseling psychologist; b. Balt., Jan. 23, 1943; d. William James Armiger and Marie Eileen (Edmonds) Lowery; AA, Coll. San Mateo, 1968; BA cum laude in Psychology, San Jose State U., 1971, MA in Psychology, 1973; PhD in Human Devel. Psychology (grad. fellow), U. Md., 1977; m. Richard Ridley (dec.); 1 son, Christopher Blair. Rsch. asst., instr. U. Md., 1973-77; adj. asst. prof. Catonsville (Md.) Community Coll., 1973-78; sr. rsch. analyst Teledyne Brown Engring., Rockville, Md., 1976-78; tech. mgr. Applied Mgmt. Scis., Silver Spring, Md., 1978-82; rsch. project mgr. Arbitron Co., Laurel, Md., 1982-83; pvt. practice psychology, Columbia, Md., 1978—; sr. rsch. analyst R.O.W. Scis., 1990—; conf. presenter; coord. rev. panel VA grant proposals rev. NIH, 1983—; coord./moderator psychology lecture series. Smithsonian Inst.; cons. Mem. Howard County Drug Abuse Adv. Coun., 1980-83, Howard County Mental Health Adv. Coun., 1983-85. Cert. community coll. tchr. and counselor, Calif.; lic. psychologist, Md. Mem. APA, Md. Psychol. Assn. (contbg. editor newsletter 1980-85), Phi Kappa Phi. Democrat. Contbr. articles to profl. jours. and newspapers. Office: Columbia Med Ctr 11055 Little Patutent Pkwy Suite 201 Columbia MD 21044

TYNAN, LAURIE FRANCINE, librarian; b. N. Tonawanda, N.Y., July 14, 1951; d. Bruce Homer and Marie Rosalie (De Ryck) T. AB, Bucknell U., 1973; MS, Columbia U., N.Y.C., 1975. Asst. dir. Meadville (Pa.) Pub. Library, 1975-80, Sussex County Library System, Newton, N.J., 1980-81; dir. Huntingdon (Pa.) County Library, 1982-87; dist. cons. Montgomery County-Norristown (Pa.) Pub. Library, 1987—; exec. dir. Montgomery County-Norristown Pub. Library, 1989—; chair Pa. Interlibrary Loan Adv. Coun., Harrisburg, Pa., 1987—. Treas. Women's Svcs., Inc., Meadville, 1979-80, Huntingdon House, Inc., 1985-87. Mem. ACLU, AAUW (pres. Huntingdon chpt. 1984-86, treas. Perkiomen chpt. 1988-91, co-chair 1991—), NOW, Am. Libr. Assn., Pa. Libr. Assn. (legis. day coord. 1989, chair Juniata-Conemaugh, Pa. chpt. 1985-86, chair pub. libr. div. 1992). Office: Montgomery County Libr 1001 Powell St Norristown PA 19401-3817

TYREE, MELVIN THOMAS, botany educator, forestry scientist; b. Santa Ana, Calif., Nov. 15, 1946; s. William Jensen and Marcella Laurena (Thomas) T.; m. Edmee Loeta Smith, Oct. 3, 1970; 1 child, Niki Corinna. BA, Pomona Coll., 1968; PhD, Cambridge (Eng.) U., 1972. Lectr. U. Toronto, Ont., Can., 1971-72, asst. prof., 1972-75, assoc. prof., 1975-77, prof., 1971-85; rsch. prof. botany U. Vt., Burlington, 1985-89, prof., 1989—; plant physiologist U.S. Forest Svc., Burlington, 1991—. Contbr. over 90 articles to sci. jours. Recipient Sci. Achievement award Internat. Union Forestry Rsch. Orgns., 1990; fellow Killam Found., 1980. Mem. Soc. for Exptl. Biology, Can. Soc. Plant Physiologists (C.D. Nelson award 1979), Am. Soc. Plant Physiologists, Scandinavian Soc. Plant Physiologists. Office: U Vt Botany Dept MLS Bldg Burlington VT 05405

TYRING, NELS ANDREW, manufacturing executive; b. Providence, June 11, 1931; s. Nels Andrew And Edith Hope (Cory) T.; m. Joan Elaine Blair, Feb. 20, 1954; children: Linda, Barbara Smith, Erica Leavitt, Kristen. Grad. high sch., Danielson, Conn. Sales engr. Grinell Co., Inc., Milw., 1955-63, Ladish Co., N.Y.C., 1963-65; dist. mgr. Worcester (Mass.) Controls, Inc., 1965-66; pres. Nels Tyring & Assoc., Inc., Hampton, N.H., 1966-73, Fire Systems, Inc., Hampton, 1972-75, The Valve Co., Hampton, 1975-81, TVC, Inc., Portsmouth, N.H., 1981—. Sgt. USMC, 1948-52, Korea. Mem. Soc. Mfg. Engrs., Instrument Soc. Am. (sr. v.p. 1979-81, 85-87, award recipient 1982). Home: 18 Peninsula Dr PO Box 328 Stratham NH 03885 Office: TVC Inc PO Box 900 Portsmouth NH 03802-0900

TYRRELL, ALBERT RAY, government liaison for industry; b. Indpls., Sept. 21, 1919; s. Laurence Ray and Nina Atherton (Mobley) T.; m. Sussie Fredrika Petersen, Oct. 4, 1954; children: Nina Fresanne, Robert Warren. AA, Reedley Jr. Coll., Calif., 1939; BA, Harvard U., 1948. With Lockheed Aircraft, Burbank, Calif., 1948-50; rep. Lockheed Aircraft, Dayton, Ohio, 1950-53; ops. mgr. Ind. Mil. Air Transport Assn., Washington, 1953-54; cons. Construciones Aeronauticas, Madrid, 1954-55; pres. Teleprompter of Washington, 1955-56; v.p. Teleprompter Corp., N.Y.C., 1956-57; v.p. mktg. Internat. Atlas Div. Atlas Corp., Oakland, Calif., 1958-63; chmn. mgmt. com. Global Assocs., Oakland, Calif., 1962-64; bd. dirs. Global Assocs., 1964-84; v.p. for congl. relations Atlas Corp., Washington; industry rep. Am. Mining Congress, Washington, 1964-84; founder joint venture Global Assocs., 1964-84. Apptd. mem. Def. Industry Adv. Coun., 1960. Col. USAF, 1940-50. Decorated DFC with 2 oak leaf clusters, Air medal with 3 oak leaf clusters, others. Mem. Harvard Club N.Y.C., Harvard Club Washington, Congl. Country Club, University Club, Masons, Quiet Birdmen. Baptist. Address: 3001 Veazey Ter NW #407 Washington DC 20008

TYSON, JULIAN FELL, chemistry educator; b. Glasgow, Scotland, Aug. 3, 1949; came to U.S., 1989; s. Geoffrey Howard and Mary Younger (Dickson) T.; m. Janet Aileen Logan, Aug. 3, 1972; children: John Alistair, Jennifer Anne. BS, Aberdeen U., Scotland, 1971; Diploma of Imperial Coll., London U., 1975, PhD, 1975. Chartered chemist. Lectr. U. Tech., Loughborough, Eng., 1976-85, sr. lectr., 1985-89; prof. chemistry U. Mass., Amherst, 1989—; assoc. editor The Analyst, Cambridge, Eng., 1990—; joint series editor Ellis Horwood Series in Analytical Chemistry, Chichester, Eng., 1989—. Author: Analysis What Analytical Chemists Do, 1988. Recipient Soc. Analytical Chemistry Silver medal Royal Soc. Chemistry, 1986, Disting. Svc. award Analytical Div. Rsch., 1989. Fellow Royal Soc. Chemistry; mem. Am. Chem. Soc., Soc. for Applied Spectroscopy, Assn. for Sci. Edn., Epee Club. Office: U Mass Dept of Chemistry Amherst MA 01003

TYSON, MARY (MRS. KENNETH W. THOMPSON), artist; b. Sewanee, Tenn., Nov. 2, 1909; d. Stuart L. and Katherine Tyson; student Grand Central Sch. Art, 1928-30, Eastport Sch. Art, 1928, New Sch. Social Research, 1975-76; m. Kenneth W. Thompson, Oct. 1, 1931; children: Kenneth Stuart, Loran Tyson. Exhibited one-man shows: Montross Gallery, N.Y.C., Bruce Mus., Greenwich, Conn., Present Day Club, Princeton, N.J., Pen and Brush Club, N.Y.C., Bodley Gallery, N.Y.C.; exhibited group shows: Balt. Water Color Club, Phila. Watercolor Club, Addison Gallery, Andover, Mass., Bklyn. Mus., Coll. Arts Assn., Morton Gallery, N.Y.C., St. Louis Mus. Contemporary Art, Government House, Nassau, Pen and Brush Club, N.Y.C. (23 awards), New Rochelle (N.Y.) Art Assn., Allied Artists, Knickerbocker Artists, Katherine Lorillard Wolfe, Nat. Arts Club, Lobster Pot Gallery, Nantucket, Am. Watercolor Soc., Easthampton Guild Hall (award), Nantucket Artists Assn.; represented in permanent collections: Guild Hall Mus., Easthampton, Monterey (Calif.) Peninsula Mus., Nantucket Artists Assn., Harrison Meml. Library, Carmel, Calif. Mem. Am. Watercolor Soc., Pen and Brush Club, Nat. Arts Club. Address: 20 W 11th St New York NY 10011

TZENG, KENNETH KAI-MING, electrical engineer, educator; b. Kaifeng, China, Aug. 6, 1937; came to the U.S., 1961; s. Chen-Hua and Meng-Hua (Hsiao) T.; m. Marjorie Kao, Aug. 6, 1961; children: Todd Ching-Tien, Ted Ching-Yu. BEE, Nat. Taiwan U., 1959; MEE, U. Ill., 1962, PhD in Elec. Engring., 1969. Jr. engr. IBM, Poughkeepsie, N.Y., 1962-63; rsch. engr. NCR, Dayton, Ohio, 1963-65; rsch. asst. U. Ill., Urbana, 1965-69; asst. prof. Lehigh U., Bethlehem, Pa., 1969-73, assoc. prof., 1973-77, prof., 1977—; instr. edn. program Bell Labs., Allentown, Pa., 1972-80, vis. scientist, Murray Hill, N.J., 1981-82, mem. tech. staff, Holmdel, N.J., 1969; vis. asst. prof. U. Ill., 1972; faculty fellow NASA Goddard Space Flight Ctr., Greenbelt, Md., 1976. Contbr. articles to profl. jours. NSF grantee, 1970-71, 73-79, 88—. Mem. IEEE (sr.). Office: Lehigh U Bethlehem PA 18015

TZIMOPOULOS, NICHOLAS D., science education specialist; b. Eptachorion, Greece, Feb. 19, 1941; came to U.S., 1956; s. Demetrius and Soultana (Davos) T. BA in Chemistry and Math., U. N.H., 1965; MS in Analytical Chemistry, Boston Coll., 1967, PhD in Phys. Chemistry, 1971. Dir. research So. N.H. Services, Manchester, 1978-80; prof. phys. chemistry U. Northern Fla., Jacksonville, 1981-82; chmn. math and sci. The Bartram Sch., Jacksonville, Fla., 1980-83; prof. chemistry Valencia Community Coll., Orlando, Fla., 1983-84; dir. sci. edn. Schs. of the Tarrytowns, North Tarrytown, N.Y., 1984-91; dir. sci., math. and tech. Lexington (Mass.) Pub. Schs., 1991—. Author: Modified Null-Point Potentiometry, 1967, Irreversible Processes, 1971, Mathematics-Science Curricula, 1982, Modern Chemistry, 1990, (with others) Life, Earth, Physical Sciences, 1987. N.H. rep. N.E. Metric Action Council, 1978-80; Tufts U. del. New Eng. Energy Congress, 1978; liaison Kiwanis Regional Sci. and Engring. Fair, Jacksonville, 1983; founder N.H. Legis. Acad. Sci. and Tech., Concord, 1980. Recipient Outstanding commendations in sci. achievement Internat. Sci. and Engring. Fair, 1986, CMA Catalyst award, 1987, N.Y. State Presdl. award for excellence in sci. and math., 1989. Mem. Am. Chem. Soc. (Fla. congl. del. 1984, treas. Fla. sect. 1983, 84, chmn. Jacksonville sect. 1982-83, dir. Westchester County, N.Y. sub-sect. 1986—, high sch. exams. com. 1982-86, Outstanding Chemistry Tchr. Fla. 1982, S.E. U.S. 1983, Nichols award 1986), N.Y. Acad. Sci., Fla. Acad. Sci., Nat. Sci. Tchrs. Assn., Greek Orthodox Youth Assn. (pres. Manchester, N.H. 1963-65), Sigma Xi. Democrat.

UBBEN, DONALD THOMAS, lawyer; b. Pekin, Ill., May 9, 1946; s. Wilbert Donald and Verna Lanelle (Ducker) U. BA, Furman U., 1968; MA, Baylor U., 1972; JD, U. Va., 1982. Bar: Pa. 1983, S.C. 1983, D.C. Ct. Appeals 1983, U.S. Dist. Ct. D.C. 1984, U.S. Dist. Ct. S.C. 1984, U.S. Ct. Appeals (D.C. cir.) 1984, U.S. Ct. Appeals (4th and fed. cirs.) 1984, U.S. Claims Ct. 1984, U.S. Tax. Ct. 1984, Va. 1991. Asst. to sec. for spl. programs HEW, Washington, 1973-75; legis. asst. U.S. Senate, Washington, 1975-77, 81-82; dir. exec. br. liaison U.S. C. of C., Washington, 1977-79; cons. Legal Svcs. Corp., acting dir. N.Y. regional office, 1984, acting dir. bar rels., 1985; atty. U.S. Dept. of Interior, 1988-91. Del. to county and state Rep. convs., S.C. and Va., 1968-87; alt. del. Rep. Nat. Conv., 1972, 84, del., 1976; mem. Albemarle County (Va.) Rep. Cen. Com., 1981-88, 91—; precinct capt. 1992—; bd. dirs. Opera Americana, 1990-92; bd. dirs. Alexandria Symphony, 1987-90, mem. exec. com., 1988-89, chmn. nominating com., 1988-89, chmn. govt. liaison com., 1989-90, mem. long range planning com., 1988-90. Mem. Va. Bar Assn. (com. on legal problems of elderly 1985—, chmn. 1988-90), Nat. Rep. Lawyers Assn., Conservative Network (counsel 1986-87), English Speaking Union, Albemarle County Geneal. Assn. Republican. Home: PO Box 171 Ivy VA 22945-0171

UBER, JOHN WILLIAM, therapist; b. Warwick, R.I., Mar. 17, 1955; s. William Joseph and Therese Julienne (Pinard) U.; m. Marta Ann Northcott, June 18, 1977; children: Marci Ann, Ian Chauncey, Vaughn Wick, Logan Otto, Kent Clayton, Isaac Nelson, Austin Orion, Wesley Zane. BS, Slippery Rock State Coll., 1988, MA, 1990. Therapist, counselor Irene Stacy CMHC, Butler, Pa., 1988-90; super. emergency svcs. Mercer County Mental Health/Mental Retardation, 1990—, acting mental health program specialist, 1991—. Mem. ACA, Assn. Mormon Counselors and Psychotherapists. Republican. Home: 113 Dale St Grove City PA 16127-1721

UCCELLINI, LOUIS WILLIAM, meteorologist; b. Mineola, N.Y., Apr. 16, 1949; s. Louis Dominic and Anna Margaret (Isemann) U.; m. Susan Eichman, June 10, 1971; children: Anthony Lloyd, Francesca Margot, Dominic Peter. BS, U. Wis., 1971, MS, 1972, PhD, 1977. Postdoctoral fellowship Space Sci. and Engring. Ctr., Madison, Wis., 1977-78; rsch. meteorologist NASA/Goddard Space Flight Ctr., Greenbelt, Md., 1978-89; div. chief Nat. Weather Svc./Nat. Meteorol. Ctr., Camp Springs, Md., 1989—; mem. nat. acad. sci. panel on mesoscale rsch. Nat. Rsch. Coun., Washington, 1984-88. Author: Snowstorms Along the Northeastern Coast of the United States, 1955 to 1985, 1990; contbr. articles to profl. jours. Recipient Disting. Young Scientist award Md. Acad. Scis., 1981, medal for exceptional sci. achievement NASA, 1985. Fellow Am. Meteorol. Soc. (co-chief editor Weather and Forecasting 1988-92, Clarence Leroyt Meisinger award 1985); mem. Nat. Weather Assn. (charter mem., counselor 1989-90). Office: Nat Meteorol Ctr 5200 Auth Rd Suitland MD 20746-4304

UDEL, GEORGE, film arts administrator; b. Greenwich, Conn., Sept. 6, 1930; s. Jacob and Rose Lee (Cohen) U.; m. Joan Erbe, May 21, 1956; children: Joan Randolph, Constance Carver, Jacob. Student, St. John's Coll., Annapolis, Md., 1948-50, Johns Hopkins U., 1951, NYU, 1954-55, New Sch. for Social Rsch., 1955. Photographer Udel Bros., Balt., 1945-57; film editor, cameraman Sta. WJZ-TV, Balt., 1957-60; claims rep., computer programmer, systems analyst Social Security Adminstrn., Balt., 1961-70; writer, producer, dir. G2 Svcs., Balt., 1970—; film programer Walters Art Gallery, 1992—; exec. dir. Balt. Film Forum, Balt., 1980-82; film reviewer Times/Messenger Newspapers, Balt., 1982-85; producer Balt. Film Factory, Sykesville, Md., 1990—; ptnr. R5/S8 Film Distbrs., Washington, 1984—; bd. dirs. Theatre Project, Balt., 1982—, chmn. bd. dirs., 1986-88; pres. bd. dirs. Balt. Film Forum, 1989-91. Writer, dir., producer (film) Plaster Casting, 1970 (3 Best of Fest awards 1970), New Architect in Town, 1971 (Columbia U. award 1972); writer (film series) Crime Prevention/Senior Citizens, 1980 (Nat. Mayor's award 1980); contbr. articles to profl. jours. Bd. dirs. Am. Visionary Art Mus., Balt., 1988—, Balt. Internat. Film Festival, 1971-91; co-founder Balt. Internat. Film Forum, Inc., 1974; mem. Md. State Arts Coun., 1982-88, vice chmn., 1986-88, mem. theater panel, 1988-89. With U.S. Army, 1951-53. Home: 103 Woodlawn Rd Baltimore MD 21210

UDELL, DANIEL ERLING, communications executive; b. Ossining, N.Y., Feb. 26, 1935; s. Carlton Granger and Martha Christine (Olson) U.; m. Patricia Ann Luby, June 30, 1955 (div. 1984); children: Seanne Elise Jersey, Brian Granger, Moira Ann Oliver, Kevin James; m. Mary Elizabeth Holtz, May 28, 1989; children: Laurie Schwartz, Heidi Luxemberg, Dana Luxenberg. BS in Physics, Rensselaer Poly. Inst., 1957. Engring. editor Westinghouse Engring., Pitts., 1957-59; with Fischer & Porter Co., Hatsboro, Pa., 1959-60; account exec. Molesworth Assocs., N.Y.C., 1961; engring. editor IBM Jour. of R & D, N.Y.C., 1961-63; sci. writer IBM T.J. Watson Rsch. ctr., Yorktown, N.Y., 1964-69; communications staff IBM DPD, White Plains, N.Y., 1969-70; program adminstrn. communications IBM, Armonk, N.Y., 1970-72; mgr. communications IBM TJ Watson Rsch. Div., Yorktown, N.Y., 1972-75; mgr. communications to dir. communications IBM, various locations, 1976-91; U.S. dir. communications IBM, Somers, N.Y., 1991—. Mem. Internat. Ctr. Photography. Democrat. Episcopalian. Home: 1 Strawberry Hill Ave Stamford CT 06902-2609 Office: IBM Rt 100 Somers NY 10589

UDEN, PETER CHRISTOPHER, chemistry educator; b. Lyndhurst, Hampshire, Eng., May 19, 1939; came to U.S., 1964; s. Henry Thomas and Winifred May (Gasking) U.; m. Janet Kopriva, Aug. 19, 1967; children: Michael, Andrew, David. BSc, U. Bristol, Eng., 1961, PhD, 1964. Rsch. fellow U. Ill., Champaign, 1964-65, instr., 1965-66; asst. lectr. U. Birmingham, Eng., 1966-67; lectr. U. Birmingham, 1967-70; asst. prof. U. Mass., Amherst, 1970-72, assoc. prof., 1972-78, prof. chemistry, 1978—; commn. chair Internat. Union of Pure and Applied Chemistry, Secretariat, Oxforduk, 1989-92; cons. UNESCO, Campinas, Brazil, 1982, World Bank, China, 1988-91. Contbr. articles to profl. jours. Mem. Am. Chem. Soc., Royal Soc. Chemistry (London), Chromatographic Soc., Sigma Xi. Office: U Mass Dept Chemistry Amherst MA 01003

UDO-INYANG, PHILIP DENIS, engineering educator; b. Ikot Abia, Akwa Ibom, Nigeria, June 6, 1960; came to U.S., 1985; s. Denis Saul and Patricia (Udoh) U. Assoc. diploma, Calabar (Nigeria) Poly., 1978; BSc with honors, Kurukshetra (India) U., 1984; MS, Okla. State U., 1986; PhD, U. Mo., 1989. Asst. tech. officer C.R.S. Water Corp., Calabar, 1978-79; computer user cons. U. Mo., Columbia, 1986-89; asst. prof. Temple U., Phila., 1989—; conf. planning and organizing com. Associated Schs. of Constrn., 1990-92. Grantee Flour Daniel, Inc., 1991, 92, Temple U., 1990, 91, Exxon Corp., 1988-89. Mem. ASCE (assoc. com. on constrn. equipment and techniques 1990-93), NSPE, Constrn. Specification Inst. Roman Catholic. Office: Temple U Civil Engring Dept 12th & Norris Sts Philadelphia PA 19122

UDOLF, ROY, psychology educator, lawyer; b. N.Y.C., Aug. 7, 1926; s. Barney and Esther (Kadis) U.; m. Marcelle Temkin, July 1, 1950; children—Bruce Lee, Penny Jill, Brad Robert, David William. B.E.E., NYU, 1950; J.D. cum laude, Bklyn. Law Sch., 1954; M.A., Hofstra Coll., 1963; Ph.D., Adelphi U., 1971. Bar: N.Y. 1954, U.S. Dist. Ct. (so. and ea. dists.) N.Y., 1954, U.S. Supreme Ct. 1958; diplomate Am. Bd. Forensic Psychology. Practice, East Meadow, N.Y., 1954-56; test engr. Arma Corp., Garden City, N.Y., 1956-63; asst. dept. head Gyrodyne Co., St. James, N.Y., 1963-67; prof. psychology New Coll. of Hofstra U., Hempstead, N.Y., 1967—. Author: Criminal Justice System and its Psychology, 1979; Handbook of Hypnosis, 1981; Forensic Hypnosis, 1983. Served with USMC, 1944-46, PTO. Home: 2777 Granz Ct East Meadow NY 11554-4302 Office: Weed Hall New Coll of Hofstra U Hempstead NY 11550

UDVARDY, JOHN WARREN, educator; b. Elyria, Ohio; s. Joseph Louis and Theresa (Hornyak) U.; m. Carolyn Lange, June 16, 1962; children: Jessica, Aaron, Chryssa, Shana. BFA, Cleve. Inst. Art, 1963; MFA, Yale U., 1965. Drawing instr. Cleve. Inst. Art, 1962-63; asst. printmaker Yale U., New Haven, 1964-65; asst. prof. art Brown U., Providence, R.I., 1965-73; assoc. prof. of design R.I. Sch. Design, Providence, 1973-86, prof. design, 1986—, dir./chmn. freshman found. div., 1973-85; dir. summer transfer program R.I. Sch. Design, 1973-85; advisor Inst. of Am. Indian Art, Santa Fe, 1974; adv. bd. R.I. State Coun. on the Arts, Providence, 1977-78; artist-in-residence Hopkins Ctr., Dartmouth Coll., Hanover, N.H., 1982; vis. critic Wellesley (Mass.) Coll., 1986. Prin. works include Newport (R.I.) Art Mus., 1989, Helander Gallery, Palm Beach, Fla., 1986, Shick Art Gallery, Skidmore Coll., 1984, Watson Gallery, Wheaton Coll., 1979. Advisor Bd. Edn. Town of Bristol, R.I., 1971-72; juror Providence Watercolor Soc., 1977; evaluator Dartmouth Coll. at Philips Exeter (N.H.) Acad., 1984. Named Disting. Alumnus Cleve. Inst. Art, 1970; recipient Silver medal, Tchr. of Yr. Alumni award R.I. Sch. Design, 1990, First Prize, Silver medal for Excellence Providence Art Club, 1980. Home: 900 Hope St Bristol RI 02809-1109 Office: RI Sch Design Freshman Found Div Two College St Providence RI 02903

UEHLEIN, EDWARD CARL, JR., lawyer; b. Boston, May 7, 1941; s. Edward Carl and Elizabeth (Thatcher) U.; m. Judith Taylor, June 16, 1962; children: Christine, Sara. Student, Bowdoin Coll., Brunswick, Maine, 1958-59; BA, Swarthmore Coll., 1962; LLB, Boston Coll., 1965. Bar: Mass. 1965, D.C. 1968. Atty. Nat. Labor Relations Bd., Atlanta, 1965-68; assoc. Morgan, Lewis & Bockius, Washington, 1968-71; exec. asst. to sec. U.S. Dept. Labor, Washington, 1971-73; ptnr. Morgan Lewis & Bockius, Wash-

ington, 1973—; sec.-treas. Carlou Corp., Wilmington, Del., 1969-71. Fellow Ford Found., 1961. Mem. ADA, D.C. Bar Assn., Fed. Bar Assn., Belehaven Country Club, Ballybunion Golf Club, Royal Dornoch Golf Club. Republican. Office: Morgan Lewis & Bockius 1800 M St NW Washington DC 20036-5802

UEHLING, JAMES HARVEY TOMB, entrepreneur, graphic designer; b. L.A., Apr. 4, 1935; s. Gordon A. and Alice B. (Tomb) U.; m. Colette M. Dubut, Aug. 20, 1968 (div.); children: Yvonne J. Loubiere, S. Gregory; m. Lindley Rapp Howat, Dec. 26, 1991. BFA, Pratt Inst., Bklyn., 1957. Instr. Pratt Inst., 1957-58; art dir. Alderman & Hogarth, N.Y.C., 1958-61; creative dir. FPS Prodns., N.Y.C., 1961-65; account exec. MPA, Inc., N.Y.C., 1965-68; design dir. Lippincott & Margulies, N.Y.C., 1968-69; prin. Mayo-Infurna Design, N.Y.C., 1969-74; sr. v.p. Siegel & Gale, N.Y.C., 1974-79; prin. Lefkowith Inc., N.Y.C., 1979-83; exec. v.p. Lippincott & Margulies, N.Y.C., 1983-87; prin. Kass Uehling Inc., N.Y.C., 1987—. Capt. U.S. Army, 1958-65. Home: 18 W 90th St New York NY 10024 Office: Kass Uehling 333 7th Ave New York NY 10001

UEK, ROBERT WILLIAM, accountant; b. Springfield, Mass., May 18, 1941; s. Robert T. and Norma F. (Marchant) U.; m. Mary Breen, Sept. 7, 1964; children: Barbara A., Robert J., Paul S. BS, Boston Coll., 1963; MS, U. Mass., 1964. CPA, Mass. With Coopers & Lybrand, Boston, 1964—, ptnr., 1974—; bd. dirs., pres. Internat. Instl. Svcs., Inc., N.Y.C. Trustee, pres. Norfolk Mental Health Assn., Inc., Cottage Norwood, Mass., 1980-86; trustee, gov., treas. New Eng. Acquarium, Boston, 1981—; trustee, treas. Anatolia Coll., Tessaloniki Pylaia, Greece, 1984—; selectman Town of Westwood (Mass.), 1986—. Mem. AICPAs, Mass. Soc. CPAs, Dennis (Mass.) Yacht Club (gov., treas. 1974-91). Home: 28 Old Carriage Rd Westwood MA 02090-2914

UFFNER, MICHAEL S., retail automotive executive; b. Phila., July 18, 1945; s. Ray and Shirley A. (Block) U.; m. Marilyn A. Ursomarso; 1 child, Lauren R. BA, MA, U. Pa., 1971. V.p. Union Park Pontiac, BMW, Honda, Wilmington, Del., 1972-82; pres. Del. Motor Sales Inc., Wilmington, 1982—; mem. manpower tng. adv. com. Gen. Motors Corp., pres. dealer adv. coun., 1985; mem. Gen. Motors Dealer policy bd., 1990-91. Bd. dirs. Del. chpt. Am. Heart Assn., 1981—, pres., 1985-86, chmn., 1986-87; bd. dirs. GM U. of Automotive Mgmt. Recipient various sales awards. Mem. Cadillac Motor Car div. Nat. Dealers Coun. (vice chmn. 1989—, chmn. 1990-91), Am. Heart Assn. (v.p., bd. dirs. Nat. Ctr. 1987-90), Am. Econ. Assn., Am. Mgmt. Assn., Better Bus. Bur. Del. (bd. dirs., exec. com. 1992—), Del. Automobile & Truck Dealers Assn. (bd. dirs.), Tavistock Civic Assn. (pres. 1976-77), U. Pa. Alumni Assn. (v.p. Del. chpt. 1978-80, pres. 1980-81), Del. State C. of C. (chmn. small bus. com. 1991—), Rodney Square Club, U. Club, Whist Club, U. Pa. Faculty Club, Concord County Club. Office: 1606 Pennsylvania Ave Wilmington DE 19806-4018

UHDE, THOMAS WHITLEY, psychiatrist; b. Louisville; s. George Irvin and Maurine (Whitley) U.; m. Marlene Ann Kraus, Oct. 26, 1977; children: Miles August, Katherine Kraus. BS, Duke U., 1971; MD, U. Louisville, 1975. Postdoctoral fellow Yale U., New Haven, 1975-79; rsch. fellow NIMH, 1979-81; chief resident clin. rsch. unit Yale U., 1979; asst. clin. prof. Uniformed Svcs. U. Health Scis., Bethesda, Md., 1982-85, assoc. clin. prof. uniformed svcs., 1985-91, clin. prof. of psychiatry, 1991—; clin. adminstr. sect. psychobiology BPB, NIMH, ADAMHA, Bethesda, 1979-80, chief unit on anxiety and affective disorders, 1982-89, chief 3-West clin. rsch. unit, 1980-90, chief sect. on anxiety and affective disorders, 1989—; cons. Primary Care Rsch. Program, ADAMHA, 1988—, Career Devel. Program Awards Com., VA, Washington, 1986—, Rsch. Scientist Devel. Rev. Com., HHS, ADAMHA, 1983—. Contbr. over 225 sci. articles to profl. publs.; editorial bd. Jour. Anxiety Disorders, Jour. Affective Disorders, Actualities Mediclaes Internationales en Psychiatrie. Capt. USPHS, 1979—. Recipient The Ackley award, 1975, Nat. Rsch. Svc. award, 1979; Am. Coll. Neurospcychopharmacology travel fellow, A.E. Bennett Neuropsychiat. Rsch. Found. award. Mem. AAAS, APA, Soc. Biol. Psychiatry, Internat. Soc. Psychoneuroendocrinology, Am. Coll. Neuropsychopharmacology, Sleep Rsch. Soc. Democrat. Home: 5120 Manning Dr Bethesda MD 20814-1227 Office: NIH 9000 Rockville Pike Bethesda MD 20892-0001

UHL, SCOTT MARK, state agency administrator; b. Balt., July 6, 1950; s. Edward George and Maurine Barbara (Keleher) U.; m. Charlene Hughins, Feb. 29, 1988. BA, Lehigh U., 1972. Community systems developer Md. Mental Hygiene Adminstrn., Balt., 1979-82, chief, housing and community support, 1982-88; adminstr., community programs, dep. secretariat pub. health Md. Health and Mental Hygiene, Balt., 1988—; cons. in field, 1983-85; mem. C.A.R.E. adv. bd. Md. Dept. Human Resources, Balt., 1987—; prin. staff Md. Gov.'s Task Force on Long Term Fin. Planning for Individuals with Disabilities, 1991-92. Gov.'s appointee State Adv. Coun. on Adminstrv. Hearings, 1990-93. Republican. Home: 4594 Kingscup Ct Ellicott City MD 21042-5986 Office: Md Health & Mental Hygiene 201 W Preston St Baltimore MD 21201

UHLER, WALTER CHARLES, government official; b. Lebanon, Pa., Feb. 23, 1948; s. Victor Cornelius and Barbara Jean (Malin) U.; m. Judy Ann Sherk, Aug. 7, 1967 (div. 1984); children: Terry Allen, Matthew David. BA Polit. Sci. cum laude, Pa. State U., 1973, BA in Russian cum laude, 1973, cert. Russian area, 1973, MPA, 1992. Teaching asst. Pa. State U., University Park, 1975-76; procurement agt. Naval Aviation Supply Office, Phila., 1976-80; contracts adminstr. GSA, Phila., 1980-81; contracting officer Def. Logistics Agy., Phila., 1981-86, corp. contracting officer, 1986—; regional cons. Def. Logistics Agy., L.A., 1985-86; nat. cons. Def. Logistics Agy., Cameron Station, Va., 1989-90; participant Air Force Intelligence Conf. on Soviet Affairs, Arlington, Va., 1988; speaker on contracts DOD Conf., Cleve., 1988; chmn. Ann. Nat. Conf. Contracting Officers and Auditors, 1987-91. Contbr. articles to profl. jours. Baseball coach Valley Athletic Assn., Bensalem, Pa., 1979-88, basketball coach, 1980-85, coord., 1981; tutor Ctr. for Literacy, Phila., 1991-92. With U.S. Army, 1966-71. Mem. Am. Assn. for Advancement Slavic Studies, Am. Def. Preparedness Assn., Acad. Polit. Sci., Phila. Writers Orgn., Am. Acad. of Polit. and Social Scis., Friends of the Free Libr. of Phila. Democrat. Office: DCASMA DCASR PHI-GAAC PO Box 7699 Philadelphia PA 19101-7699

UHLIG, JOHN RICHARD, real estate developer; b. Balt., Nov. 12, 1941; s. Earl Roosevelt and Jane (Rutt) U.; m. Susan Lewis Spickard, AUg. 16, 1969; children: John Davis, Robert Dunlap. BA, Washington and Lee U., 1963; MBA, Columbia U., 1968. Mktg. assoc. Am. Airlines, Dallas, 1968-71, N.Y.C., 1968-71; mktg. mgr. McCormick Properties Inc., Hunt Valley, Md., 1971-78, v.p., 1978-87; sr. v.p. The KMS Group Inc., Columbia, Md., 1987—; bd. dirs. Sandalwood Coop. Inc., Owings Mills, Md.; dir. McCormick Properties Inc., 1984-87, Huntington Realty Interests Inc., Hunt Valley, 1983-87, NACORE, West Palm Beach, Fla., 1980-83. Bd. dirs. Gilman Sch., Balt., 1984-89. Lt. comdr. USN, 1963-72. Mem. Nat. Assn. Corp. Real Estate Execs. (dir. 1980-83), L'Hirondelle (bd. govs. 1986-90). Republican. Presbyterian. Home: 2009 Ridgecrest Ct Baltimore MD 21204 Office: The KMS Group Inc 8808 Centre Park Dr Columbia MD 21045

UHRMAN, CELIA, artist, poet; b. New London, Conn., May 14, 1927; d. David Aaron and Pauline (Schwartz) U. BA, Bklyn. Coll., 1948, MA, 1953; PhD, U. Danzig, 1977; postgrad. Tchrs. Coll., Columbia U., 1961, CUNY, 1966, Bklyn. Mus. Art Sch., 1956-57, PhD (hon.), LittD, 1973; cert. Koret Living Library U. of San Francisco, 1982. One-woman shows: Leffert Jr. High Sch., Bklyn., 1958, Flatbush C. of C., N.Y.C., 1963, Conn. C. of C., New London, 1962; exhibited in group shows: Smithsonian Instn., Washington, 1958, Springfield (Mass.) Mus. Fine Arts, 1959, Bklyn. Mus., 1959, Old Mystic (Conn.) Art Center, 1959, Carnegie Endowment Internat. Center, N.Y.C., 1959, Lyman Allyn Mus., New London, 1960, Palacio de La Virrelna, Barcelona, Spain, 1961, YMCA, Bklyn., 1962, UFT Art Exhibit, N.Y.C., 1963, Soc. of 4 Arts, Palm Beach, Fla., 1964, Perspective 68, Monte-Carlo, Monaco, 1968, George W. Wingate High sch., Bklyn., 1967, Premier Salon Internat., Charleroi, Belgium, 1968, Palme d'or Beaux Arts, Monte-Carlo, 1970, 72, Dibuix-Joan Miro Premi Internacional, Barcelona, 1970; N.Y. Art Festival, 1970, Internat. Platform Assn. Art Show, Washington, 1971, 73, Ovar Mus., Portugal, 1974, others; represented in permanent collections: Bklyn. Coll., Ch. of Evangel, Bklyn.; tchr. N.Y.C. Sch. System, 1948-82; ptnr. Uhrman Studio, 1973-83; hon. rep. U.S., Centro Studi E Scambi Internazionali, Rome, mem. Internat. Com., 1969. Hon. life mem. World Poetry Day Com., Inc. and Nat. Poetry Day Com., 1977. Recipient award Freedoms Found., George Washington medal of honor, 1964, Diplome d'Honneur Palme d'Or des Beaux Arts Exhbn., Monaco, 1969, 72, Diploma and Gold medal, Centro Studi E Scambi Internazionali, 1972; decorated Order of Gandhi Award of Honour, Knight Grand Cross, 1972; personal poetry certificate WEFG Stereo, 1970; Gold Laurel award Esposizione Internazionale D'Art Contemporain, Paris, 1974; named Poetry Translator Laureate World Acad. Lang. and Lit., 1972, Poet of Mankind Acad. Philosophy, 1972; cert. of appreciation Bd. Edn. of N.Y.C., 1982. Fellow World Lit. Academy Eng.; mem. Internat. Arts Guild (comdr. 1966—), World Poetry Soc. Intercontinental (rep. at large 1969—), Internat. Acad. Poets (founding fellow). Author: Poetic Ponderances, 1969, A Pause for Poetry, 1970, Poetic Love Fancies, 1970, A Pause for Poetry for Children, 1973, The Chimps Are Coming, 1975, Love Fancies, 1987. Home: 1655 Flatbush Ave Apt 106C Brooklyn NY 11210-3271

UHRMAN, ESTHER, artist, writer, retired social worker; b. New London, Conn., July 7, 1921; d. David Aaron and Pauline (Schwartz) U. Grad. Traphagen Sch. Fashion, 1955; Diploma Di Benemerenza, Centro Studi E Scambi Internat., Rome, 1972, Diploma Academia Leonardo Da Vinci, 1980; A.A., N.Y.C. Community Coll., 1974; cert. in labor relations Cornell U., 1976, cert. unemployment ins. advocate, 1984; Ph.D., Danzig U., Poland, 1977; Ph.D. (hon.) World Acad. Langs. and Lit., 1977. Self-employed writer, artist, Bklyn., 1954—; social worker N.Y. State, Bklyn., N.Y.C., 1959-76; ptnr. Uhrman Studio, Bklyn., 1973-83. Author: Gypsy Logic, 1970, From Canarsie to Masada, 1978, Mitras II, 1988; (radio play) Holland 2067, 1971 (Golden Windmill award 1970); asst. editor: Inside Detective, 1977; contbr. articles to profl. jours.; two-man art shows include Ligoa Duncan Gallery, N.Y.C., 1960, New London C. of C., 1962, Flatbush C. of C., 1963, Uhrman Studio, 1973-83; exhibited in group shows at Traphagen Sch. Fashion, N.Y.C., 1954-55, Carnegie Endowment Internat. Ctr., N.Y.C., 1959, Exposcion De Obras, Palacio De La Virreina, Barcelona, Spain, 1961, Smithsonian Inst., Washington, 1962, Cape May (N.J.) County Lighthouse, 1965, N.Y. Art Festival, 1970, Premier Internacional Dibuix, Barcelona, 1970, Internat. Platform Assn., Washington, 1972-73. Recipient Civilian Service award U.S. Army, 1944, five N.Y. State awards, 1962-65, Silver medal Verso Mexico, 1968, cert. Stamp Designs, 1968, cert. Merit Rassegna Internazionale D'Arte Grafica, Ovar Mus., Portugal, 1974, cert. Merit 26th Exposition D'Arte Contemporain, Luxemborg, 1974. Fellow World Literary Acad., Internat. Acad. Poets (co-founder). Mem. AFL-CIO, Internat. Arts Guild (commandeur, Diplome D'Honneur award 1976), World Poetry Soc. Intercontinental, CSEA Retirees. Avocations: walking, theatre, anthropology. Home and Office: 1655 Flatbush Ave Apt 106C Brooklyn NY 11210-3271

UKHUEDUAN, MICHAEL EDD, account executive; b. Jos, Nigeria, Jan. 29, 1962; came to U.S., 1979; s. Festus Talle and Felicia (Oduah) U. BS, Jersey City State Coll., 1984. Salesman Morse Shoes, N.Y.C., 1980-8l; sales rep. Edison Bros., N.Y.C., 198l-83; mktg. rep. Tandy Corp.-Tandy Computers, N.Y.C., 1983-84; sr. account exec., ind. contractor Ebony Office Products, Inc., Long Island City, N.Y., 1984—. Bd. dirs., v.p., staff mem. United Youth Enterprise Inc., Hamden, Conn., 1989—; staff mem. Polished Acts, East Orange, N.J., 1989—. Recipient plaque Polished Acts, 1989. Mem Greater Newark C. of C. Home: 15l6 Schley St Apt 1 Hillside NJ 07205 Office: Ebony Office Products Inc 10-17 44th Ave Long Island City NY 11101

ULAN, MARTIN SYLVESTER, retired hospital administrator, health services consultant; b. Wilkes Barre, Pa., May 12, 1912; s. John Albert and Elizabeth (Marcinak) U.; m. Gladys Cecilia Olsen, Oct. 29, 1938; children: Martin Olsen, Mardys Cecilia Brooke Leeper. BS in Pharmacy, Phila. Coll. Pharmacy and Sci., 1934, MS in Biology, 1936; cert., Columbia U., 1950, U. Chgo., 1952. Diplomate Am. Bd. of Pharmacy. Pharmacology asst. Phila. Coll. Pharmacy and Sci., 1934-39; research asst. LaWall & Harrisson Lab., Phila., 1934-39; chief pharmacist White Haven (Pa.) Sanatorium, 1939; asst. prof., chmn. dept. pharmacology Rutgers U. Coll. Pharmacy, Newark, N.J., 1940-50; asst. adminstr. Hackensack (N.J.) Hosp., 1950-54, adminstr., 1954-72; adminstr. York (Maine) Hosp., 1972-78; private cons. York, Maine, 1978—; cons. drugs and chems. Bd. of Econ. Warfare, Washington, 1942-45; chmn. Pharmacy team Unitarian Svc. Com., Munich, 1949; lectr. Columbia U., N.Y., 1961-72; bd. dirs. Creative Work Systems Rehab. Ctr., Saco, Maine. Pres. York Health Found., 1981-84; vice chmn. Bd. Selectmen, York, 1986-89, 91—, chmn., 1988-89, 90; trustee York (Maine) Hosp.; mem. Pres. Com. on Mental Retardation, Washington, 1986—; mem. State of Maine Adv. Com. on Mental Retardation, 1989—; vol. Community Chest, Hackensack, Am. Cancer Soc., Hackensack, Hackensack area Girl Scouts U.S., Health Careers Programs, Hackensack. With Pa. N.G., 1935-38. Fellow Am. Coll. Health Care Execs., Am. Coll. Apothecaries; mem. Am. Pharm. Assn., Am. Hosp. Assn. (Ho. Dels. 1963-69), N.J. Pharm. Assn., Bergen County Pharm. Assn., Rho Chi. Republican. Roman Catholic. Home: 73 Agamenticus Ave Cape Neddick ME 03902-7110

ULAN, MICHAEL KENNETH, economist; b. Chester, Pa., Apr. 25, 1946; s. Martin and Dorothy Charlotte (Pomerantz) U. BA (magna cum laude), Lafayette Coll., 1967; student, London Sch. Econs., 1965-66; MA, U. Pa., 1971, PhD, 1974. Instr. econs. U. Pa., Phila., 1970-71; economist U.S. Dept. Labor, Washington, 1971-74, U.S. Dept. Commerce, Washington, 1974-79, U.S. Dept. State, Washington, 1979—. Editor: The Annals of the Am. Acad. Polit. and Social Sci., July 1991; contbr. articles to profl. jours. Mem. Phi Beta Kappa. Office: US Dept of State 2201 C St NW Washington DC 20520-9997

ULANOWICZ, ROBERT EDWARD, mathematical ecologist, educator; b. Balt., Sept. 17, 1943; s. Edward Stanislaus and Mary Isabel (Bielat) U.; m. Marie Antoinette Chmilewsky, July 1, 1967; children: Anastasia, Peter, Vera. B in Engrng. Sci., Johns Hopkins U., 1964, PhD, 1968. Rsch. asst. Martin Marietta Corp., Orlando, Fla., 1962-63; lab. asst. Inst. fuer Physikalische Chemie, Goettingen, Fed. Republic Germany, 1964; grad. asst. Johns Hopkins U., Balt., 1964-68; asst. prof. Cath. U. Am., Washington, 1968-69; prof. math. ecology U. Md., Solomons, 1970—; mem. sci. com. on oceanographic rsch. UNESCO, 1977-85; mem. panel NRC, Washington, 1987-88; Crafoord symposium speaker Royal Swedish Acad. Scis., Stockholm, 1987. Author: Growth and Development: Ecosystems Phenomenology, 1986; editor: Mathematical Models in Biological Oceanography, 1981, Ecosystem Theory for Biological Oceanography, 1985; contbr. articles to sci. jours. Bd. dirs. Am. Chestnut Land Trust, Port Republic, Md., 1988—; mem. adv. com. Battle Creek Cypress Swamp, Nature Conservancy, Prince Frederick, Md., 1980-84; mem. Pleasant Peninsula Planning Com., Prince Frederick, 1974; lector St. John Vianney Ch., Prince Frederick, 1975—. Recipient Frederick C. Hettinger Meml. award Md. sect. Am. Inst. Chem. Engrs., 1964, citation Gov. of Md., 1988. Mem. Atlantic Estuarine Rsch. Soc. (pres. 1980-81), Estuarine Rsch. Fedn. (exec. sec. 1986-87), Washington Evolutionary Systems Soc., Internat. Soc. for Ecol. Modelling, EcoGreen Global Soc. (mem. selection bd. 1990—), Phi Beta Kappa, Tau Beta Pi. Democrat. Roman Catholic. Office: Chesapeake Biol Lab 1 Williams St Solomons MD 20688

ULIN, PETER A., investment executive; b. Boston, Dec. 20, 1930; s. Benjamin and Rebecca (Cantarow) U.; m. Bonnie Handmaker, Aug. 24, 1958; children: Daniel, Jennifer. AB, Harvard U., 1953; postgrad., Columbia U., 1954. V.p. investment banking Hornblower-Weeks, Boston, 1964-67, F.I. du Pont Co., Boston, 1967-70; owner Peter Ulin Co., Boston, 1970-80; v.p., dir. corp. fin. E.F. Hutton Co., Boston, 1980-84; mng. dir. Ulin, Morton, Bradley & Welling, Inc., Boston, 1984-90; mgr. dir. Advest Inc., 1990-92; pres. Ulin and Holland, 1992—. Trustee Beth Israel Hosp., Boston, 1966—, Combined Jewish Philanthropies, Boston, 1966—, Harvard Hillel, Cambridge, Mass., 1976—. With U.S. Army, 1954-56. Office: Ulin & Holland 176 Federal St Boston MA 02110

ULIN, ROBERT CHARLES, anthropology educator; b. Phila., May 14, 1951; s. Alexander Wesley and Ruth (Brody) U.; m. Ingeborg Meffert, July 27, 1988. BA, Whittier Coll., 1973; PhD, New Sch. for Social Rsch., N.Y.C., 1980. Asst. prof. sociology and anthropology Allegheny Coll., Meadville, Pa., 1985—, assoc. prof., chair. Author: Understanding Cultures, 1984; contbr. articles to profl. jours. Rsch. grantee Wenner-Gren Found., 1983-84, 1989. Mem. AAUP (pres. Allegheny Coll. chpt. 1989-90), Am. Anthrop. Assn., Northeastern Anthrop. Assn., Soc. for Anthropology of Europe (exec. com. 1991-92). Office: Allegheny Coll. Meadville PA 16335

ULKE, ASIM, mechanical engineer; b. Kayseri, Turkey, Apr. 1, 1940; came to U.S., 1962; s. Ahmet and Ilmiye (Ozyilmaz) U.; children: Ayhan, Shener, Ersin, Taner. BSME, Mid. East Tech. U., Ankara, Turkey, 1962; MSME, U. N.D., 1964; PhD, Carnegie Mellon U., 1975. Rsch. engr. Westinghouse Sci. & Tech. Ctr., Pitts., 1969-86, Bettis Atomic Power Lab., Pitts., 1986—; instr. in mech. engring. U. N.D., Grand Forks, 1964; instr. Pa. State U., State College, 1965-66. Patentor super conducting magnet cooling system; contbr. articles to profl. jours. Lt. Turkish Army, 1967-69. Fulbright grantee, 1962. Office: Bettis Atomic Power Lab PO Box 79 West Mifflin PA 15122-0079

ULLMAN, HARLAN KENNETH, company executive; b. N.Y.C., Mar. 15, 1941; s. Gerald Howard and Sophia (Seltzer) U. BS, U.S. Naval Acad., 1963; MA, MALD, PhD, Tufts U., 1973. From ens. to comdr. USN, 1963-83; sr. fellow, sr. assoc. Ctr. for Strategic and Internat. Studies, Washington, 1983—; chmn. Killowen Group, Washington, 1987—; sr. fellow Ctr. for Naval Analysis, Alexandria, Va., 1989—; bd. dirs. Wall St. Fund, Korean Investment Fund, Commonwealth Enterprises, Polish Industries, Inc. Author: In Harm's Way: American Seapower and the 21st Century, 1991; editor various books; contbr. articles to profl. publs. Decorated Def. Disting. Service medal. Mem. Internat. Inst. for Strategic Studies, Atlantic Coun. (counsellor).

ULRICH, GEORGE HENRY, aerospace company executive; b. Allentown, Pa., June 23, 1947; s. Paul Theodore and Elizabeth Teal (Bender) U.; m. Margaret Renee Rodgers, Sept. 14, 1971 (div. 1979); children: Karl Brandon, Jennifer Tasca; m. Kimberly Kay Snyder, Apr. 15, 1989. BA in Math. and German, U. Tex., 1971; MS in Aero Systems, U. W. Fla., 1979; MBA, U. Houston, 1984, MA, 1991. Cert. space shuttle flight controller, cert. dive master, cert. rescue scuba diver, cert. airline transport pilot, flight engr. turbojet, flight engr. basic, many others. Space shuttle flight control Rockwell Internat., Houston, 1979-86, supr. space shuttle mission control, 1986-88; fleet marine force space ops. support Naval Space Command, Dahlgren, Va., 1990-91; tech. evaluator Synthesis Group, Nat. Space Coun., NASA, Washington, 1990-91; project mgr. space shuttle engring. integration Rockwell Internat., Washington, 1989—; tech. advisor Space Exploration Initiative, Washington, 1990-91; chmn. physiol. stds. AIAA, Washington, 1991; lectr. in field; conductor seminars in field. Editor: Systems Handbook, 1980-83, Orbit Pocket Checklist, 1986-88, Entry Pocket Checklist, 1986-88; author: Micro Gravity Effects, 1991; contbr. articles to profl. jours. Lt. col. USMC, 1970-78, 90-91. Recipient Nat. Def. Svc. award Dept. of Def., 1971, 91, Armed Forces Res. Medal, 1990. Mem. AIAA, Marine Corps Res. Officers Assn., Marine Corps Aviation Assn., Nat. Assn. Mgrs., Profl. Divers, Explorers Club, Smithsonian Resident Assn., Profl. Assn. Diving Instrs., Nat. Assn. Underwater Instrs., Nat. Geog. Soc., Aerospace Med. Assn. Presbyterian. Home: 7727 Jewelweed Ct Springfield VA 22152 Office: Rockwell Internat 600 Maryland Ave SW #450 Washington DC 20024

ULRICH, LAUREL THATCHER, historian, educator; b. Sugar City, Idaho, July 11, 1938; d. John Kenneth and Alice (Siddoway) Thatcher; m. Gael Dennis Ulrich, Sept. 22, 1958; children: Karl, Melinda, Nathan, Thatcher, Amy. BA in English, U. Utah, 1960; MA in English, Simmons Coll., 1971; PhD in History, U. N.H., 1980. Asst. prof. humanities U. N.H., Durham, 1980-84, asst. prof. history, 1985-88, assoc. prof. history, 1988-91, prof. history, 1991—; audiocourse cons. Annenberg Found.; cons., participating humanist numerous exhibits, pub. programs, other projects; project humanist Warner (N.H.) Women's Oral History Project; bd. editors William & Mary Quar., 1989-91, Winterthur Portfolio, 1991—. Author: Good Wives: Image and Reality in the Lives of Women in Northern New England, 1650-1750, 1982, A Midwife's Tale: The Life of Martha Ballard Based on Her Diary, 1785-1812, 1990; contbr. articles, abstracts, essays and revs. to profl. publs. Coun. mem. Inst. Early Am. History and Culture, 1989-91; trustee Strawbery Banke Mus., 1987—. John Simon Guggenheim fellow, 1991-92, NEH fellow, 1982, 84-85; women's studies rsch. grantee Woodrow Wilson Fellowship Found., 1979; co-recipient Best Book award Berkshire Conf. Women's Historians, 1990; recipient Best Book award Soc. for History of Early Republic, 1990, John S. Dunning prize and Joan Kelly Meml. prize Am. Hist. Assn., 1990, Bancroft Prize for Am. History, 1991, Pulitzer Prize for History, 1991. Mem. Orgn. Am. Historians (nominating com. 1992—, ABC-Clio award com. 1989), Am. Hist. Assn. Office: U NH History Dept Horton Social Sci Ctr Durham NH 03824

ULRICH, THEODORE ALBERT, lawyer; b. Spokane, Wash., Jan. 1, 1943; s. Herbert Roy and Martha (Hoffman) Ulrich; m. Nancy Allison, May 30, 1966; children: Donald Wayne, Frederick Albert. BS cum laude, U.S. Mcht. Marine Acad., 1965; JD cum laude, Fordham U., 1970; LLM, NYU, 1974. Bar: N.Y. 1971, U.S. Supreme Ct. 1974, U.S. Ct. Appeals (2nd cir.) 1971, U.S. Ct. Appeals (5th cir.) 1988, U.S. Dist. Ct. (so. and ea. dist.) N.Y. 1972, U.S. Ct. Claims 1977, U.S. Customs Ct. 1978, U.S. Ct. Internat. Trade 1981. Mng. clk. U.S. Dept. Justice, N.Y.C., 1968-69, law clk. to federal dist. judge, 1969-70; assoc. Cadwalader, Wickersham & Taft, N.Y.C., 1970-80, ptnr., 1980—. Author, editor Fordham Law Rev., 1969. Leader Boy Scouts Am., Nassau County, N.Y., 1984—. Capt. USCGR, 1965-86. Mem. ABA, Maritime Law Assn., Fed. Bar Coun., Am. Soc. Internat. Law, Soc. Naval Architects and Marine Engrs., U.S. Naval Inst., Am. Arbitration Assn., India-House Club. Office: Cadwalader Wickersham & Taft 100 Maiden Ln New York NY 10038-4818

ULTAN, LLOYD, historian; b. Bronx, N.Y., Feb. 16, 1938; s. Louis and Sophie U. BA cum laude, Hunter Coll., 1959; MA, Columbia U., 1960. Assoc. Edward Williams Coll. Fairleigh Dickinson U., Hackensack, N.J., 1964-74; asst. prof. history Edward Williams Coll. Fairleigh Dickinson U., Hackensack, 1974-75, assoc. prof. Edward Williams Coll., 1975-83, prof. Edward Williams Coll., 1983—; cons. in field. Editor Bronx County Hist. Soc. Jour., 1964—, Bronx County Hist. Soc. Press, 1981— ; author: The Beautiful Bronx, 1920-50, 1979, Legacy of the Revolution: The Valentine-Varian House, 1983, The Presidents of the United States, 1989; co-author: The Bronx in the Innocent Years, 1890-1925, 1985. Gen. sec. Bronx Civic League, 1964-67; v.p. bd. trustees Bronx County Hist. Soc., 1965-67, 77-84, curator, 1968-71, pres., 1971-76, historian, 1986—; founding mem., bd. dir. Bronx Coun. on Arts, 1968-71; chmn. Bronx County Bicentennial Commn., 1973-76, Bronx Borough Pres.'s Bicentennial Adv. Com., 1974-76; vice chmn. Commn. Celebrating 350 Yr. of the Bronx, 1989; program guidelines com. N.Y.C. Dept. Cultural Affairs, 1976-77; bd. dirs. Nat. Shrine Bill of Rights, Mt. Vernon, N.Y., 1983—; mem. N.Y.C. Com. on Cultural Concerns, 1982-88; bd. sponsors Historic Preservation com. St. Ann's Ch. Morrisania, 1987—; bd. dirs. 91 Van Cortlandt Owners Corp., 1986—. N.Y. State Regents Coll. Teaching fellow, 1959; elected to Hunter Coll. Alumni Hall of Fame, 1974; Fairleigh Dickinson U. Fifteen Yr. award, 1979, Twenty Yr. award, 1984, Twenty-five Yr. award, 1989. Mem. AAUP, Am. Hist. Assn., N.Y. Hist. Soc., Phi Alpha Theta, Alpha Chi Alpha, Sigma Lambda. Home and Office: 91 Van Cortlandt Ave W Bronx NY 10463-2712

UMAN, MYRON F., research administrator; b. Tampa, Fla., Oct. 13, 1939; s. Morrice S. and Edith (Brown) U.; m. Sandra Bloomberg, June 16, 1963; 1 child, Jennifer. BSEE, Princeton U., 1961; MS, U. Ill., 1962; PhD, Princeton U., 1968. Asst. prof. U. Calif., Davis, 1967-74; program officer NSF, Washington, 1974-75; from staff officer to asst. exec. officer Nat. Rsch. Coun. NAS, Washington, 1975—; lectr. George Mason U., Fairfax, Va., 1989—. Author: Introduction to Physics of Electronics, 1974; editor: Research and Development in the U.S. EPA, 1977, Causes and Effects of Stratospheric Ozone Reduction, 1982, Acid Deposition: Atmospheric Processes, 1983, Acid Deposition: Long Range Trends, 1986, The Nuclear Weapons Complex, 1990. Recipient resident fellow ASEE, East Fishkill, N.Y., 1972-73, Sloan resident fellow NAS, Washington, 1973-74, Pub. Svc. award NASA, Washington, 1989, Astronauts Achievement award NASA Corps of Astronauts, 1989. Mem. AAAS, Am. Phys. Soc., N.Y. Acad. Scis., Sigma Xi. Office: Nat Acad Scis 2101 Constitution Ave NW Washington DC 20418-0001

UMBREIT, GERALD ROSS, chemist; b. Mpls., June 17, 1930; s. William Arthur and Ruth Olive (Bodley) U.; m. Patricia Ruth Dahl, Feb. 6, 1953;

children: Kaytee Lea, Timothy Dwight, Steven Taylor. BA cum laude, Augustana Coll., Sioux Falls, S.D., 1954; PhD in Analytical Chemistry, Iowa State U., 1957. Rsch. asst. Ames (Iowa) Lab. U.S. AEC, 1954-58; rsch. assoc. Upjohn Co., Kalamazoo, Mich., 1958-63; rsch. scientist Lockheed Missiles & Space Co., Palo Alto, Calif., 1963-64; applications lab. mgr. F & M Sci. div. Hewlett-Packard Co., Avondale, Pa., 1964-66; chemist, owner Greenwood Labs., Kennett Square, Pa., 1966—. Contbr. articles to profl. publs., chpts. to books. Mem. East Marlboro Twp. Planning Commn., Pa., 1972-87; mem. East Marlboro Zoning Hearing Bd., 1981—. Cpl. U.S. Army, 1950-52. Mem. Am. Chem. Soc., Chromatography Forum of Delaware Valley (pres. 1970-71, 80-81, award 1985). Office: Greenwood Labs 903 E Baltimore Pike Kennett Square PA 19348-1854

UMBREIT, WAYNE WILLIAM, bacteriologist, educator; b. Markesan, Wis., May 1, 1913; s. William Traugott and Augusta (Abendroth) U.; m. Doris McQuade, July 31, 1937; children: Dorayne Loreda, Jay Nicholas, Thomas Hayden. B.A., U. Wis., 1934, M.S., 1936, Ph.D., 1939. Instr. soil microbiology Rutgers U., 1937-38; faculty U. Wis., Madison, 1938-44; asst. prof. bacteriology and chemistry U. Wis., 1941-44; faculty Cornell U., 1944-47, prof. bacteriology, 1946-47; head dept. enzyme chemistry Merck Inst., Rahway, N.J., 1947-58; asso. dir., 1958; chmn. dept. bacteriology Rutgers U., New Brunswick, N.J., 1958-75; prof. microbiology, dir. grad. programs Rutgers U., 1969-83, prof. emeritus microbiology, 1983—; dir. labs. So. Br. Watershed Assn., 1983-89. Author: (with Burris, Stauffer) Manometric Techniques, 1945, 5th edit., 1972, (with Oginsky) An Introduction to Bacterial Physiology, 1954, Metabolic Maps, 1960, Modern Microbiology, 1962, Essentials of Bacterial Physiology, 1976; Editor: Advances in Applied Microbiology, vols. 1-10, 1959-68; Contbr. articles to profl. jours. Recipient Biochem. Congress Symposium medal Paris, France, 1952. Fellow Am. Acad. Microbiology, N.Y. Acad. Sci., A.A.A.S.; mem. Am. Soc. for Microbiology (Eli Lilly award in bacteriology 1947, Carski Found. award for distinguished teaching 1968), Soc. Biol. Chemists, Am. Chem. Soc., Theobald Smith Soc. (Waksman award in microbiology 1957, past pres.), AAUP, Sigma Xi. Home: 18 Dogwood Dr Flemington NJ 08822-2708

UNCAPHER, MARK ELSON, communications executive, lawyer; b. Buffalo, Aug. 4, 1953; s. Mark Elson Uncapher Jr. and Joan (Willard) Gruen; m. Robin Nixon, Aug. 27, 1977; 1 child, Peter McLane. BA, George Washington U., 1975; JD, N.Y. Law Sch., 1978. Bar: N.Y., 1979. Asst. counsel Comptroller State of N.Y., N.Y.C., 1978-83; sales exec. Sta. WZFM-FM, Pleasantville, N.Y., 1983-86; sales exec. Sta. WPAT Park Communications, Inc., N.Y.C., 1986—; nat. pres. The Ripon Soc., Washington, 1987-90; chmn. Ripon Ednl. Fund, 1982-89, bd. dirs., 1982—; mng. dir. Signal Properties, Brooklyn Heights, N.Y., 1987—; ptnr. McLane Farms, LaPorte, Inc., 1980—; U.S. chmn. 5th Transatlantic Conf., London and Cambridge, Eng., 1988. Contbr. articles to profl. jours. including Broadcast Fin. Jour., Ripon Forum. Mem. Mark O. Hatfield Scholarship Com., Washington, 1985—; del. candidate for George Bush 14th Congl. Dist., Bklyn., 1980. Mem. ABA, N.Y. State Bar Assn., Fed. Communications Bar Assn., Bus. Exec. Nat. Security, Carnegie Coun. Internat. Affairs. Republican. Home: 99 State St Brooklyn NY 11201-5533 Office: WPAT Park Communications 675 3rd Ave New York NY 10017-5704

UNDERBERG, RITA POSNER, clinical psychologist, educator; b. N.Y.C., Nov. 16, 1926; d. Jacob Murray and Sophye (Horowitz) Posner; m. Stanley Underberg, Dec. 16, 1951; children: Leslie, Paul. BS, Queens Coll., 1948; MA, CCNY, 1949; PhD, U. Rochester, 1958. Lic. psychologist, N.Y. Sch. psychologist Rochester (N.Y.) City Schs., 1956-66; vis. psychologist Albion (N.Y.) Reformatory for Girls, 1958-71; cons. to bd. coop. svcs. Sch. Dist. 2, Rochester, 1966—; psychologist U. Rochester, 1974-84, clin. asst. prof. psychiatry and pediatrics, 1966-74, clin. assoc. prof. psychiatry, 1974-89, clin. prof. psychiatry, 1989—, dir. tng. in clin. psychology dept. psychiatry, 1986—; cons. Dist. II Bd. Coop. Ednl. Svcs., Rochester, 1965—, Greece (N.Y.) Youth Ctr., 1982—, Pediatric Hematology/Oncology Unit, Rochester, 1984-88, Pact Social Work Unit for mothers at risk for child abuse. Contbr. articles to various publs. Honoree Internat Women's Yr., United Way, Rochester, 1975. Mem. N.Y. State Psychol. Assn., Ea. Psychol. Assn., Genesee Valley Psychol. Assn. (Disting. Profl. Achievement award 1980), Rochester Area Assn. Clin. Psychology. Home: 95 Victoria Dr Rochester NY 14618-2755 Office: Univ Rochester Dept Psychiatry 300 Crittenden Blvd Rochester NY 14642-0001

UNDERHILL, JACK ARTHUR, federal agency administrator; b. Healdsburg, Calif., May 8, 1932; s. Harry Arthur and Lucile Marie (Kiesel) U.; m. Jane Sharon Russell, July 1961; children: Robert Arthur, Jeannie Lynn, Marie Suzanne. BA in Internat. Rels., U. Calif., Berkeley, 1954; MA in Pub. Law Govt., Columbia U., 1959; MPA, Harvard U., 1969. Program analyst Exec. Office of Pres. Office Emergency Planning, Washington, 1959-64; program devel. officer Open Space Program Dept. HUD, Washington, 1964-68, acting dep. dir. New Communities Div., 1968-69, dir. project devel. div. Office New Communities, 1970-71, spl. asst. to dir. Office New Communities, 1971-73, new towns specialist New Communities Devel., 1973-83, program analyst Office Program Analysis and Evaluation, 1983—. Author: Soviet New Towns, 1976, Paris Region New Towns, 1980; co-author: Planning New Towns: National Reports of the US & USSR, 1981, New Towns Management, 1986. Pres. PTA, Falls Ch. High Sch., Fairfax County, Va., 1987, Falls Ch. High Sch. Band Support Group, 1988; scoutmaster Boy Scouts Am., Troop 853, Fairfax County, 1978; bd. dirs. Fairfax County Fedn. of Civic Assns. Sgt. U.S. Army, 1954-57. Recipient Nat. Inst. Pub. Affairs scholarship Harvard U., 1967. Mem. ASPA, Phi Beta Kappa. Democrat. Methodist.

UNDERWEISER, IRWIN PHILIP, mining company executive, lawyer; b. N.Y.C., Jan. 3, 1929; s. Harry and Edith (Gladstein) U.; m. Beatrice J. Kortchmar, Aug. 17, 1959; children: Rosanne, Marian, Jeffrey. B.A., CCNY, 1950; LL.D., Fordham U., 1954; LL.M., NYU, 1961. Bar: N.Y. 1954. With firm Scribner & Miller, N.Y.C., 1951-54, 56-62; partner firm Feuerstein & Underweiser, 1962-73, Underweiser & Fuchs, 1973-77, Underweiser & Underweiser, 1977—; v.p., sec. Sunshine Mining Co., Kellogg, Idaho, 1965-70, chmn. bd., 1970-78, pres., 1971-74, 77, v.p., 1977-83; vice chmn., dir. Underwriters Bank and Trust Co., N.Y.C., 1969-73; dir. Anchor Post Products, Inc. Bd. dirs. Silver Inst. Inc.; gen. counsel, mem. bus. council Friends City Center Music and Drama, N.Y.C., 1966-67; pres. W. Quaker Ridge Assn., 1969-70; treas. Scarsdale Neighborhood Assn. Presidents, 1970-71. Served with AUS, 1954-56. Mem. Am., N.Y. State bar assns., Bar Assn. City N.Y., Phi Beta Kappa, Phi Alpha Theta. Home: 7 Rural Dr Scarsdale NY 10583-7701 Office: 405 Park Ave New York NY 10022-4405

UNDERWOOD, BARBARA ANN, biochemist, nutritionist; b. Santa Ana, Calif.. BA, Univ. Calif., Santa Barbara, 1956; MS, Cornell U., 1958; PhD, Columbia U., 1962. Rsch. assoc. dept. pediatrics and internat. medicine U. Md. Sch. of Medicine, Pakistan, 1962-64; asst. prof. nutrition, dir. Div. Nutrition, Internat. Ctr. U. Md. Sch. of Medicine, Lahore, Pakistan, 1964-66; rsch. assoc., asst. dir. USAID Spl. Tng. Course Inst. Human Nutrition/Columbia U., 1966-68, asst. prof. nutrition, 1968-72; assoc. prof. nutrition Pa. State U., 1972-78; various to asst. prof. nutrition MIT, Cambridge, Mass., 1977-82; lectr. dept. internat. health The Johns Hopkins U./Sch. Hygiene and Pub. Health, 1987—; spl. asst. to dir. for nutrition rsch. and internat. progs. Nat. Eye Inst./NIH, Bethesda, Md., 1982-89, asst. dir. internat. prog. activities, 1989—; resident coord. Internat. Food and Nutrition Policy Prog./UN Univ., 1977-80; cons. various orgns. in field including worldwide nutrition projects. Contbr. articles to profl. jours.; asst. editor Am. Jour. Clin. Nutrition, 1983-84, assoc. editor 1984—. Adv. bd. in Prevention of Blindness, Helen Keller Internat., Inc., N.Y., 1973-85, trustee, 1985-90, adv. com. on Tng. Aids and Materials, 1975-77; mem. malnutrition panel U.S.-Japan Cooperative Med. Sci. Prog./NIH, 1974-85, com. on Internat. Nutrition Progs., Food and Nutrition Bd./NAS, 1974-79; adv. bd. Child Care Project, Overseas Edn. Fund of the LVW, 1976-79, others. Recipient rsch. grants Cystic Fibrosis Found., 1967, 75-76, Nutrition Found., 1967-70, NIH, 1969-72, 73-76, 80-82, USDA 1978-80, 80-83, Hoffman-La Roche, 1979-80, Nestle Co., 1980-84; Whitehall Fellow, 1968-71. Mem. AAAS, Am. Inst. Nutrition, Am. Soc. Clin. Nutrition, Assn. for Rsch. in Vision Ophthalmology, Phi Kappa Phi, Sigma Xi, Omicron Nu, Phi Tau Sigma. Office: Nat Eye Inst Bldg 31 Rm 6A-17 Nat Insts of Health 9000 Rockville Pike Bethesda MD 20892

UNDERWOOD, BRENDA S., microbiologist, grants administrator; b. Oak Ridge, Tenn., Mar. 19, 1948; d. William Henry Hensley and Maudell (Walker) Townsend; m. Thomas L. Janiszewski, Feb. 14, 1984. BS, U. Tenn., 1970; MS, Hood Coll., 1980; MBA, Mt. St. Mary's Coll., 1992. Scientist I chem. carcinogenesis Frederick (Md.) Cancer Rsch. Ctr., 1977-84; microbiologist NCI/NIH, Bethesda, Md., 1984-86; sci. tech. writer Engrng. and Econs. Rsch., Germantown, Md., 1987-88; spl. asst. to assoc. dir., program dir. grants Divsn. Cancer Biology Diagnosis Ctrs., NCI/NIH, Bethesda, 1988-91; with Div. Extramural Activities, NCI/NIH, Bethesda, 1992—. Leader Riding for the Handicapped, Frederick, 1990-91; mem., recreational sec. Capital Hill Equestrian Soc., Washington, 1988. Mem. AAAS, Am. Soc. for Microbiology, Am. Assn. for Cancer Rsch., Women in Cancer Rsch., Federally Employed Women. Office: NCI/NIH Divsn Extramural Activities Bethesda MD 20892

UNGER, DONNA JEAN, data processing company executive; b. New Castle, Ind., Apr. 23, 1951; d. James Harley and Eva Ray (Loy) Means; m. John Keith Unger, Aug. 21, 1971; children: John Keith II, Tanya Shawn. BA, Purdue U., 1973. Cert. tchr., Mo., Ind. Tchr. Russelville (Mo.) Schs., 1978-80; systems, training analyst Modern Bus. Systems, Jefferson City, Mo., 1980-84; system trainer A-Copy Am., Glastonbury, Conn., 1984-86, mgr. data processing, 1986—; MIS trainer and coord. Alco Office Product Group div. Alco Standard Corp., 1990-91; mgr. MIS Alco Office Product Group div. Alco Standard Corp., Glastonbury, 1991—. Mem. NAFE, NEA, Conn. Citizen Action Group, Purdue Alumni Assn. Home: 26 Beaver Dam Trl Old Saybrook CT 06475-1025 Office: A-Copy Am 755 Winding Brook Dr Glastonbury CT 06033-4300

UNGER, HOWARD ALBERT, artist, photographer, educator; b. Mt. Vernon, N.Y., Oct. 13, 1944; s. Howard Albert and Florence A. (Peterson) U.; m. Anrita Abelow, Aug. 25, 1972; 1 son, Christopher Howard. Student, Art Students League, N.Y.C., 1960-61, Sch. Visual Arts, N.Y.C., 1975-76, N.Y. Inst. Holography, 1976; B.F.A., Kent State U., 1966, M.A., 1968; M.Ed., Columbia U., 1972, Ed.D., 1975. Cert. open water diver, 1988, advanced scuba diver, 1989. Grad. teaching fellow in photo-journalism Kent State U., 1966-67, instr. in art, 1966-67, grad. teaching fellow in art, 1967-68; head program in art, tchr. art Kew-Forest Prep. Sch., Kew Gardens, N.Y., 1968-69; technician TV sta. Tchrs. Coll., Columbia U., 1971-72, instr. art and edn., 1972-75, instr. curriculum and teaching, 1976-82, instr. dept. communication, computing and tech. in edn., 1982—; asst. prof. visual communications tech. dept. humanities Ocean County Coll., 1972-78, assoc. prof., 1979-82, prof., 1982—; gallery coordinator Fine Arts Ctr., Ocean County Coll., 1972—; instr. communications and edn. Sch. Edn. NYU, 1973-74; design and photograph coordination RCA Records, N.Y.C., 1969-70; freelance designer, 1965—. ExExhibitor photography in one-man shows, Photographis Societas Photographis, Columbia U., 1971, Ziegfeld Gallery, N.Y.C., 1972, group shows, Kent State U., 1965-68, Ocean County Coll., 1973-83, permanent collections, Internat. Ctr. Photography, N.Y.C., Mus. Holography, N.Y.C., Kent State U., Ocean County Coll., Tchrs. Coll., Columbia U., pvt. collections; lectr. in photography; co-author: (with William Maxwell) photog. illustrator Printmaking: A Beginner's Handbook, 1977; photog. illustrator: The Fourth R. Stewart Kranz, 1971; contbg. author: A Tour Through The Realm of Science Plus Art, 1974; photography critic: Village Voice, 1976-77; photography columnist Soho Weekly News, 1977-78. Recipient 1st place award Am. Greeting Card Competition, 1966; recipient honorarium dept. curriculum and teaching Tchrs. Coll., Columbia U., 1973. Mem. Soc. Photography Educators, NEA, Mus. Modern Art, N.J. Edn. Assn., Met. Mus. Art, Am. Mus. Natural History, Profl. Assn. Diving Instrs. (lic. advanced scuba diver), Nat. Assn. Underwater Instrs. (lic. advanced scuba diver). Republican. Lutheran. Home: 437 E 76th St New York NY 10021-2564 Office: Ocean County Coll College Dr Toms River NJ 08753-2102

UNGER, MARY ANN, artist, sculptor. BA magna cum laude, Mt. Holyoke Coll., 1967; postgrad., U. Calif.-Berkeley, 1968; MFA, Columbia U., 1975. One-woman shows: 10 Downtown, N.Y.C., 1977, CUNY Grad. Ctr., 1982, 88, 55 Mercer, N.Y.C., 1983, John Jay Coll., N.Y.C., 1984, Nassau County Mus. Fine Art, Roslyn, N.Y., 1985, Tweed Courthouse, N.Y.C., 1985, Sculpture Ctr., N.Y.C., 1986, Bellevue Sculpture Gardens, N.Y.C., 1988, Boulder (Colo.) Ctr. for the Visual Arts, 1990, Klarfeld Perry Gallery, 1992; group shows include: Aldrich Mus. Contemporary Art, Ridgefield, Conn., 1977, Boulder Arts Center, 1979, Hudson River Mus., Yonkers, N.Y., 1981; Bronx River Restoration Center, N.Y.C., 1983, Sculpture Center, N.Y.C., 1983, 85, 89, Newhouse Ctr. for Contemporary Art, S.I., N.Y., 1987, 89, Hillsborough Community Coll., Tampa, Fla., 1989, Socrates Sculpture Park, L.I., N.Y., 1989, L.I. U., Bklyn., 1989, DeCordova Mus. & Sculpture Garden, 1991; represented in permanent collections: E. F. Hutton, Inc., Best & Co., Columbia U., N.Y.C., Mt. Holyoke Coll., Printmaking Workshop, Mus. Internat. Art; also pvt. collections. Subject of profl. publs. Recipient funding award N.Y. State Coun. on the Arts, 1981, 1985, Betty Brazil Meml. Fund award, 1984, N.Y. State Coun. on the Arts award, 1985, Pollock-Krasner Found., Inc. award, 1989.

UNGER, PETER KENNETH, philosophy educator; b. N.Y.C., Apr. 25, 1942; s. Sidney and Naomi (Fein) U.; m. Susan Gill, June 2, 1977; 1 child, Andrew. BA, Swarthmore Coll., 1962 DPhil, Oxford U., Eng., 1966. Instr. U. Wis., Madison, 1965-66, asst. prof., 1966-70, assoc. prof., 1970-72; assoc. prof. philosophy NYU, N.Y.C., 1972-75, prof., 1975—. Author: Ignorance, 1975, Philosophical Relativity, 1984, Identity, Consciousness and Value, 1990; co-editor: Semantics and Philosophy, 1974; contbr. articles to profl. jours. Guggenheim fellow, 1974. Mem. Am. Philos. Assn., Oxfam Am., Phi Beta Kappa. Democrat. Home: 100 Bleecker St New York NY 10012-2202 Office: NYU Dept Philosophy 503 Main Bldg Washington Sq New York NY 10003

UNGER, RHODA KESLER, psychology educator; b. Bklyn., Feb. 22, 1939; d. Gustav and Ellen (Samuels) Kesler; m. Burton M. Unger, Apr. 11, 1966; children: Laurel, Rachel. BS, Bklyn. Coll., 1960; AM, Radcliffe Coll., 1964; PhD, Harvard U., 1966. Asst. prof. Hofstra U., Hempstead, N.Y., 1966-72; asst. prof., assoc. prof. psychology Montclair State Coll., Upper Montclair, N.J., 1972-81, prof., 1981—, dir. honors, 1985—; vis. prof. U. Haifa, Israel, 1988-89. Author: Female and Male, 1979; co-author: Women and Gender, 1992; editor: Representations, 1989; co-editor: Women, Gender and Social Psychology, 1985. Fulbright sr. prof., 1988-89. Fellow APA (pres. div. psychology of women 1980-81, mem. disting. leadership award com. for women in psychology 1991, 1st Carolyn Wood Sherif Meml award 1985), Am. Psychol. Soc., Soc. for Psychol. Study Social Issues (exec. com. 1980-86); mem. Assn. Women in Psychology (Disting. Publ. award 1984, 86), Nat. Women's Studies Assn. Jewish. Home: 11 Elston Rd Montclair NJ 07043-1955 Office: Montclair State Coll Honors Program Russ Hall Upper Montclair NJ 07043

UNGER, ROBERT MARTIN, lawyer, author, professional speaker, singer; b. N.Y.C., Jan. 26, 1954; s. Alex and Rose (Stuchinsky) U.; m. Phyllis Hollander; children: Adam Paul, Samantha Faye. BA magna cum laude, John Jay Coll., 1976; JD, Fordham U., 1979. Ptnr. Kupillas, Unger & Kupillas, Great Neck, N.Y., 1982—; counsel State Sen. Frank Padavan, Queens, 1985—; counsel Ins. Dept. Chgo. Tribune in N.Y., 1982—. Author: Tune In To Success: Strategies For Achieveing Your Greatest Potential; talk show host WMCA Radio N.Y.; spokesman for Hooked on Phonics. Pres. 25 A.D. Rep. Club, Queens, 1989—; bd. dirs. Anti-Defamation League-L.I. chpt., 1989—, Queens Farm Mus., 1988—, Playing It Safe, Pride of Judea. Mem. N.Y. State Trial Lawyers Assn., Queens County Bar Assn., Great Neck Village Assn., Nat. Speakers Assn., Great Neck C. of C., Rotary, KP. Republican. Jewish. Home: 38 Windsor Rd Great Neck NY 11021-2740 Office: Kupillas Unger & Kupillas 316 Great Neck Rd Great Neck NY 11021

UNGER, SHARON LOUISE (SHERRY LANE), artist; b. Chgo., Nov. 9, 1942; d. Arthur Eugene Unger and La Rayne (De Baun) Birk; m. Stuart Lanoff, Dec. 30, 1962 (div. Oct. 1965); 1 child, Lawrence. BFA, Hunter Coll., 1977. Caricaturist Star mag., N.Y.C., 1983-86; dir., curator Westbeth Gallery, N.Y.C., 1983-85. One-woman shows Westbeth Gallery, N.Y.C., 1983, Ward-Nasse Gallery, N.Y.C., 1987, 88; exhibited in group shows Westbeth Gallery, 1974-92, Micro V-Now Gallery, N.Y.C., 1986, Ward-Nasse Gallery, 1988, 89, Salmagundi Club, N.Y.C., 1988-92, Phase III Gallery, Tulsa, 1990, Sherry Lane Gallery, N.Y.C., 1992; contbr. to Contemporary Graphic Artists, Ency. Living Artists, Erotic Art by Living Artists. Mem. Salmagundi Club (entertainment com. 1987-89, chmn. entertainment co. 1991-93), Ward-Nasse Gallery, Graphic Artists Guild, N.Y. Artists Equity Assn., Found. for Community Artists, Caricaturists Collective (founder), N.Y. Visitors and Conv. Bur., Internat. Spl. Events Soc., Greenwich Village C. of C. Democrat. Home and Studio: 155 Bank St New York NY 10014

UNGER-SMITH, DAVID LLOYD, hospital administrator; b. Belle Fonte, Pa., Nov. 19, 1951; s. Robert Vernon and Mary Louise (Cheers) S.; divorced; children: Sarah Gene, Nathan Eli. BA, Pa. State U., 1973; MSPH, U. Mo., 1978. Detox counselor Fairmont Hosp., San Leandro, Calif., 1974-76, rehab. nursing asst., 1976-78; planning specialist Health Planning & Devel. Coun., Wooster, Ohio, 1978-80; adminstrv. asst. Alta Bates Hosp., Berkeley, Calif., 1980-82, dir. regulatory affairs, 1982-85; v.p. planning Franklin Sq. Hosp. Ctr., Balt., 1985-88, sr. v.p., 1988—. Contbr. articles to profl. jours. Pres., v.p. Rodgers Forge Elem. Sch. PTA, Balt., 1986-90. Mem. Am. Coll. Health Care Execs., Md. Soc. Health Planning and Mktg. (chairperson 1988-89, vice-chairperson 1987-88, treas. 1986-87), Soc. for Health Care Planning and Mktg. (Am Hosp. Assn.), MidAtlantic Planning Assn. (bd. mem. 1987-89, pres. 1990-91), Penn. State Club of Md. (bd. mem. 1987-89), Balt. County C. of C. (leadership com. 1985-89). Democrat. Office: Franklin Sq Hosp Ctr 9000 Franklin Square Dr Baltimore MD 21237-3901

UNRUH, JAMES ARLEN, business machines company executive; b. Goodrich, N.D., Mar. 22, 1941; m. Candice Leigh Voight, Apr. 28, 1984; children: Jeffrey A., Julie A. BSBA, Jamestown Coll., 1963; MBA, U. Denver, 1964. Dir. corp. planning and analysis Fairchild Camera & Instrument, Calif., 1974-76, v.p. treasury and corp. devel., 1976-79, v.p. fin., 1979-80; v.p. fin. Memorex Corp., Santa Clara, Calif., 1980-82; v.p. fin. Burroughs Corp. (now known as Unisys Corp.), Detroit, 1982-84, sr. v.p. fin., 1984-86, exec. v.p. fin., 1986, exec. v.p., 1986-89, pres., chief oper. officer, 1989-90, pres., chief exec. officer, 1990-91, chmn. bd. dirs., chief exec. officer, 1991—. Bd. dirs. Detroit Renaissance Ctr., U. Mich. vis. Com., Greater Phila. First Corp.; bd. trustees Jamestown Coll., N.D., Franklin Inst.; bd. overseers Wharton Sch. Bus., U. Pa. Mem. Greater Phila. C. of C. (exec. com.), Pa. Bus. Roundtable. Home: 208 Rose Ln Haverford PA 19041-1605 Office: Unisys Corp PO Box 500 Blue Bell PA 19424-0001

UNTERMEYER, WALTER, JR., investment consultant; b. N.Y.C., Sept. 19, 1924; s. Helne Edna (Mayer) U.; m. Patricia Finsterwald, Sept. 6, 1946 (div.); children: Michael Walter, Kathryn Patricia; m. Salle G. Podos, May 1, 1982. BA, Yale U., 1948. Head instnl. rsch. dept. Laird Bissel & Co., N.Y.C., 1962-70; money mgr. Henry Neuwirth & Co., N.Y.C., 1971-74, Fred Alger & Co., N.Y.C., 1974-77; rep. Mosely Securities, Inc., N.Y.C., 1977-88; investment advisor Josephthal Lyon & Ross, N.Y.C., 1988—. Author: (novel) Dark the Summer Dies, Evil Roots; contbr. articles to profl. mags. including New Yorker, Esquire, Barrons. Lt. (j.g.) USN, 1942-46, PTO. Mem. Yale Club N.Y. Jewish. Office: Knickerbocker Cons Inc 50 Vanderbilt Ave Box 45 New York NY 10017

UNVER, ERDAL ALI, research mechanical engineer; b. Nizip, Gaziantep, Turkey, Jan. 1, 1953; came to U.S., 1975; s. Ahmet Talat and Mukaddes (Seker) U.; m. Amira Victoria Margie Unver, Apr. 25, 1980; 1 child, Susan Ayse. BS, Tech. U. Istanbul, Turkey, 1975; MS, U. Calif., Berkeley, 1977; PhD, Lehigh U., 1981; MBA, George Washington U., 1991. Rsch. engr. U.S. Steel Rsch. Ctr., Monroeville, Pa., 1981-84, ENKA Constrn. Co. Rsch. Ctr., Istanbul, 1984-86; mech. engr. David Taylor Rsch. Ctr., Bethesda, Md., 1986-89; mem. tech. staff AT&T Bell Labs., Arlington, Va., 1989—. Contbr. articles to profl. jours. Mem. ASME, Acoustical Soc. Am. Home: 1515 Hugo Cir Silver Spring MD 20906 Office: AT&T Bell Labs 1919 S Eads St Ste 300 Arlington VA 22202

UPADHYAY, YOGENDRA NATH, physician, educator; b. Gorakhpur, India, Dec. 21, 1938; came to U.S., 1963; s. Murlidhar and Vansraji (Pande) U.; m. Cecile R. Yonish; children: Asha, Sameer, Sanjay. MB, BS, All India Inst. Med. Scis., New Delhi, 1962. Diplomate Am. Bd. Psychiatry and Neurology, Am. Bd. Pediatrics. Instr. in pediatrics Johns Hopkins U. Sch. Medicine, Balt., 1969-71; fellow in child psychiatry Johns Hopkins Hosp./Johns Hopkins U., Balt., 1971-72; resident, then sr. resident in psychiatry Albert Einstein Coll. Medicine/Bronx Mcpl. Hosp. Ctr., 1972-74, fellow in child psychiatry, 1974-75; chief, partial hosp. program for children, dept. psychiatry Brookdale Hosp., Bklyn., 1976-77; med. dir. West Nassau Mental Health Ctr., Franklin Sq., N.Y., 1977-80; asst. prof. clin. psychiatry SUNY, Stony Brook, 1978—; dir. child and adolescent psychiatry Nassau County Med. Ctr., East Meadow, N.Y., 1980-92; sr. psychiatrist South Oaks Hosp., Amityville, N.Y., 1992—. Fellow Am. Psychiatric Assn. (cons. task force treatments psychiatric disorders 1989—), Am. Acad. Child and Adolescent Psychiatry. Office: 400 Sunrise Hwy Amityville NY 11701

UPDIKE, JOHN HOYER, writer; b. Shillington, Pa., Mar. 18, 1932; s. Wesley R. and Linda G. (Hoyer) U.; m. Mary E. Pennington, June 26, 1953; children: Elizabeth, David, Michael, Miranda; m. Martha Bernhard, Sept. 30, 1977. AB, Harvard U., 1954; student, Ruskin Sch. Drawing and Fine Art, 1954-55. With New Yorker mag., N.Y.C., 1955-57. Author: (fiction) The Poorhouse Fair, 1959, The Same Door, 1959, Rabbit, Run, 1960, Pigeon Feathers, 1962, The Centaur, 1963 (Nat. Book award 1963), Of the Farm, 1965, Assorted Prose, 1965, The Music School, 1966, Couples, 1968, Bech: A Book, 1970, Rabbit Redux, 1971, Museums and Women, 1972, A Month of Sundays, 1975, Marry Me, 1976, The Coup, 1978, Problems, 1979, Rabbit is Rich, 1981 (Nat. Book Critics Circle award 1981, Pulitzer prize 1982, Am. Book award 1982), Bech is Back, 1982, The Witches of Eastwick, 1984, Roger's Version, 1986, Trust Me, 1987, S., 1988, Rabbit at Rest, 1990 (Pulitzer prize, 1991, Nat. Book Critics Circle award, 1991), Memories of the Ford Administration, 1992, (poetry) The Carpentered Hen, 1958, Telephone Poles, 1963, Assorted Prose, Midpoint, 1969, Tossing and Turning, 1977, Facing Nature, 1985, (play) Buchanan Dying, 1974, (non-fiction) Picked-Up Pieces, 1975, Hugging the Shore, 1983, Just Looking, 1989, Self-Consciousness, 1989, Odd Jobs, 1991; editor (with S. Ravenel) The Best American Short Stories 1984. Recipient Rosenthal award, 1960, O'Henry First Short Story award, 1966, 91, Macdowell medal, 1981, Nat. Medal of Arts, 1989. Mem. Am. Acad. Arts and Letters, Am. Acad. Arts. Democrat. Episcopalian. Address: Beverly Farms Beverly MA 01915

UPPER, DENNIS, clinical psychologist; b. Cleve., July 14, 1942; s. Robert Percy and Mary Ann (Muntean) U.; m. Nancy Carolyn Kock, Aug. 5, 1967; 1 child, Jason. BA, Yale U., 1964; MA, U. Cin., 1966; PhD, Case Western Res. U., 1969. Diplomate in clin. psychology. Coord. behavior therapy unit V.A. Med. Ctr., Brockton, Mass., 1969-82; dir. substance abuse treatment Lahey Clinic Med. Ctr., Burlington, Mass., 1982-91; dir. outpatient svcs. Northeast Psychiatric Assocs., Nashua, N.H., 1991—; dir. New Eng. Ctr. for Behavioral Modification, Boston, 1972-74; asst. prof. Harvard Med. Sch., Boston, 1976-82. Editor: 11 books on clin. psychology, 1970-85; contbr. chpts. to books and articles to profl. jours. Benefactor Boston (Mass.) Ballet Co., 1989-91. Recipient scholarship Yale Univ., New Haven, 1960-64. Mem. Assn. for Advancement of Behavior Therapy (bd. mem. 1973-76), Am. Psychol. Assn., Ea. Psychol. Assn., Mass. Psychol. Assn., Yale Club of Boston, Winchester Country Club. Home: 38 Amberwood Dr Winchester MA 01890-2233 Office: Northeast Psychiatric Assocs 14 Celina Ave Nashua NH 03063-1025

UPSON, JEANNINE MARTIN, university administrator; b. Woonsocket, R.I., Aug. 11, 1942; d. Leo Herve and Irene Florence (Dubois) Martin; m. Dean Blanchard Upson, Apr. 29, 1967; children: Ben Andrew and Jed Miles (twins). BA in History cum laude, Eastern Conn. State U., 1986; postgrad., U. Conn., 1991—. Asst. to v.p. for fin. and adminstrn. U. Conn., Storrs, 1979-87, asst. to pres. for adminstrn. affairs, 1987-92, interim dir. devel., 1992—. Editor: (book) Union Lands: A People's History, 1984; cons. (book) Lebanon, CT Town History, 1985. Founder, organizer, pres. Union Hist. Soc., Inc., Union, Conn., 1974—; mcpl. historian Union (Town of), 1990—. Grantee George Dudley Seymour Trust, 1984. Mem. Am. Mgmt. Assn., NAFE, Am. Assn. for Higher Edn. Office: Univ Conn 352 Mansfield Rd Storrs Mansfield CT 06268

UPSON, STUART BARNARD, advertising agency executive; b. Cin., Apr. 14, 1925; s. Mark and Alice (Barnard) U.; m. Barbara Jussen, Nov. 2, 1946;

children: Marguerite Nichols, Anne Marcus, Stuart Barnard. BS, Yale U., 1945. With Dancer, Fitzgerald, Sample, Inc., N.Y.C., 1946—, sr. v.p., 1963-66, exec. v.p., 1966-67, pres., 1967-74, chmn., 1974-86; chmn. DFS-Dorland, N.Y.C., 1986-87, Saatchi & Saatchi Advt. Inc., N.Y.C., 1987—; bd. dirs. Manhattan Life Ins. Co. Bd. dirs. Fresh Air Fund, N.Y., Advt. Coun. With USNR, 1943-46. Mem. St. Elmo Soc. Clubs: Wee Burn Country (Darien); Sky (N.Y.C.); Blind Brook, Pine Valley Golf. Home: 16 Wrenfield Ln Darien CT 06820-2201 Office: Saatchi & Saatchi Advt Inc 375 Hudson St New York NY 10014-3658

UPSON, THOMAS FISHER, state legislator, lawyer; b. Waterbury, Conn., Sept. 30, 1941; s. J. Warren and Grace (Fisher) U.; m. Barbara Secor (div. Jan. 1979); children: Secor, Chauncey Julius. BA in History, Washington and Jefferson Coll., 1963; LLB, U. Conn., 1968. Bar: Conn., 1969, U.S. Dist. Ct. (2d dist.), 1969. Lawyer Upson & Secor, Waterbury, 1969-70, 74-76; lawyer, spl. asst. U.S. Dept. Commerce, Washington, 1970-72; lawyer, spl. asst. to adminstr. GSA, Washington, 1973-74; dir. admissions St. Margaret's McTernan Sch., Waterbury, 1977-78; with div. spl. revenue State of Conn., Hartford, 1978-82; assoc. Moynahan & Ruskin, Waterbury, 1979-8l; pvt. practice, Waterbury, 198l—; mem. Conn. Senate, Hartford, 1985—. Moderator 1st Congl. Ch., Waterbury, 1986-91; bd. dirs. Easter Seals-United Way, Waterbury, 1984-88; mem. Conn. Rep. Cen. com., 1983-91. Mem. ABA, Conn. Bar Assn., Waterbury Bar Assn., SAR, Soc. Colonial Wars, Phi Gamma Delta. Republican. Congregationalist. Lodge: Kiwanis (former pres., lt. gov. SW New Eng. dist.), Elks. Home: Bldg 10 Unit 1 827 Oronoke Rd Waterbury CT 06708-3939 Office: Conn Senate Capitol Bldg Hartford CT 06106 also: 52 Holmes Ave Waterbury CT 06710

UPTON, CHARLES STANLEY, respiratory care practitioner; b. Lowell, Mass., Apr. 14, 1947; s. Charles and Maria (Ballas) U.; m. Kathleen O'Brien, Feb. 27, 1969; 1 child, Kristen M. Cert. respiratory care practitioner. Respiratory care dept. head St. Joseph's Hosp., Lowell, 1965-72; cardiopulmonary dept. head Hahnemann Hosp., Brighton, Mass., 1972-85; chief exec. officer The N.E.R.A. Group, Chelmsford, Mass., 1985—. Mem. profl. edn. com. Merrimack Valley Am. Cancer Soc., Tewksbury, Mass., 1986—; chmn. bd. Middlesex Resource Ctr., Inc., Lowell, 1986, mem. human rights com., 1987; mem. hospice adv. com. Lowell Vis. Nurses Assn., 1988. Mem. Am. Assn. for Respiratory Care, Mass. Soc. for Respiratory Care, Nat. Bd. for Respiratory Care, No. Middlesex C. of C. (bd. dirs. 1990). Home: 21 Thomas Dr Chelmsford MA 01824-2044 Office: The NERA Group 3 Courthouse Ln Chelmsford MA 01824-1722

UPTON, LARRY DEWAYNE, refrigeration engineer; b. Walnut Ridge, Ark., Dec. 29, 1949; s. Avon Ernest and Arizina Elizabeth (Evans) U.; m. Rhonda d. Frazier, Sept. 27, 1967 (div. Mar. 1976); children: Melony April Upton-Lewis, Alesha Raquel Upton-Rogers; m. Elizabeth Irene Garner, Mar. 27, 1976; 1 child, Jason Dewayne. Cert. refrigeration tech., Pulaski Vocat. Tech. Inst., 1985; student, Worcester Polytech., 1988, Am. Internat. Coll., 1989. Owner, operator North Shore Maintenance, Inc., North Little Rock, Ark., 1979-83; owner 12th St. Laundry & Cleaners, Little Rock, 1979-83; owner, real estate broker Larco Realty & Investments, North Little Rock, 1979-83; chief engr. Holiday Inn, Inc., Little Rock, 1983-86; plant engr. Arctic Ice & Cold Storage, Little Rock, 1986-87, Rathbone Precision Metals, Palmer, Mass., 1987-89; cen. engring. Monsanto Chem. Co., Indian Orchard, Mass., 1989—. Active North Little Rock Jaycees, 1977; pres. Benton (Ark.) Jaycees, 1982; head coach Suburban League Football, East Longmeadow, Mass., 1989-92; commn. mem. East Longmeadow Recreation Com., 1990-92; coach Suburban League Baseball, East Longmeadow, 1991. Recipient Ark. award for pub. svc. State Ark., Benton, 1982, Cert. Appreciation East Longmeadow Recreation Com., 1989-91. Fellow Nat. Youth Sports Coaches Assn., Pioneer Valley Yacht Club, Elks, Masons (bd. dirs., steward East Longmeadow 1990-91), Shriners. Home: 21 Allen St East Longmeadow MA 01028

UPTON, PETER DODDS, physician; b. Burlington, Vt., May 18, 1936; s. Hiram Eugene and Doris Atwater (Dodds) U.; m. Kathleen Ovitt; children: Michael Dodds, Timothy Ovitt, Louise Alice. AB, Dartmouth Coll., 1958; MS, U. Vt., 1961, MD, 1963. Cert. Am. Bd. Neurol. Surgery, 1972. Intern Colo. Gen. Hosp., Denver, 1963-64, resident neurology, 1964-65; resident neurosurgery Med. Ctr. Hosp. of Vt., Burlington, 1965-69; practice of neurosurgery Rutland (Vt.) Regional Med. Ctr., 1969—. Mem. Rutland Regional Med. Ctr., Rutland County Med. Soc., Vt. State Med. Soc., New England Neurosurgical Soc., Alpha Omega Alpha. Home: 34 S Main St Wallingford VT 05773 Office: 231 Mussey St Rutland VT 05701

URBACH, HERMAN B., mechanical engineer; b. N.Y.C., Jan. 19, 1923; s. Morris Eliezer and Bertha (Goldenberg) U.; m. Joan Patterson, Aug. 26, 1956; children: Jacqueline Mary, Jonathon Morris. AB in Chemistry cum laude, Ind. U., 1948; MS in Physical Chemistry, Columbia U., 1950; PhD in Physical Chemistry, Case Western Res. U., 1953; MS in Aerospace Engring., U. Md., 1987. Rsch. chemist Olin Mathieson Corp., Niagara Falls, N.Y., 1953-59; sr. rsch. scientist United Tech. Rsch. Lab., East Hartford, Conn., 1959-65; sci. staff asst. David Taylor Rsch. Lab., Annapolis, Md., 1965—; cons. Nat. Inst. Health, Washington, 1966-69; adj. prof. mech. engring. The Naval Acad., Annapolis, 1980-81. Contbr. articles to profl. jours. Mem. AIAA, N.Y. Acad. of Science, Electrochemical Soc., Am. Chem. Soc., Am. Soc. Mech. Engrs., Sigma Xi, Phi Beta Kappa. Jewish. Home: 1355 Tydings Dr Annapolis MD 21401-5738 Office: Carderock Divsn Naval Surface Weapons Ctr Annapolis MD 21402

URBAN, CATHLEEN ANDREA, software developer; b. Elizabeth, N.J., June 7, 1947; d. Emil Martin and Susan (Rahoche) Cupec; m. Walter Robert Urban, Nov. 5, 1966; children: Karen Louise, Kimberly Ann. Student, Rutgers U., 1965-66, 91—; AS in Computer Info. Systems, Raritan Valley Community Coll., North Branch, N.J., 1990, AAS in Computer Programming, 1990. Office mgr. K-Mart Corp., Somerville, N.J., 1987-90; software developer Bell Communications Rsch., Piscataway, N.J., 1990—. Leader Somerset County 4-H Program, Bridgewater, 1978-87. Mem. Phi Theta Kappa. Roman Catholic. Home: 570 Amwell Rd Neshanic Station NJ 08853-3404 Office: Bell Comm Rsch 444 Hoes Ln Piscataway NJ 08854-4104

URBAN, ERIN MARY, museum administrator, author; b. Teaneck, N.J., Feb. 4, 1948; d. John James and Mary Margaret (McCarthy) Kenefick; m. David Urban Jr., Sept. 13, 1969 (div. May. 1973); 1 child, Damon Alec; m. William James Murphy, Jan. 27, 1990; 1 child, Samuel Blaise. BA, Lake Forest (Ill.) Coll., 1969. Asst. dir. publs. and pub. info Wagner Coll., Staten Island, N.Y., 1980-83, dir. publs. and pub. info., 1983-84; curator Estate of John A. Noble., Staten Island, 1984-87; exec. dir. The John A. Noble Collection, Staten Island, 1987—. Author: John A. Noble: "The Rowboat Drawings", 1988; writer documentary Hulls and Hulks in the Tide of Time: A Portrait of John A. Noble, 1990 (CINE Golden Eagle award 1991). Panelist, Staten Island Coun. on the Arts Regrant Program, 1984, 85, 87. Mem. Am. Assn. Museums, Greenbelt Conservancy, Phi Beta Kappa. Episcopalian. Home: 29 Eadie Pl Staten Island NY 10301-1305 Office: The John A Noble Collection 270 Richmond Ter Staten Island NY 10301-1512

URCH, GEORGE E., educator, administrator; b. Oak Park, Ill., Dec. 4, 1930; s. George R. and Ida L. (Swedberg) U.; m. Dorothy M. Phillips, Aug. 1, 1958; children: George, Vanessa, Craig. BA, Western Mich. U., 1953, MA, 1959; PhD, U. Mich., 1967. Tchr. pub. schs. Mich. and Fed. Republic Germany, 1953-59; asst. prof. Ea. Mich. U., Ypsilanti, 1959-63; head dept. geography Kenyatta Coll., Nairobi, Kenya, 1964-66; instr. U. Mich., Ann Arbor, 1966-67; from asst. to assoc. U. Mass. Sch. Edn., Amherst, 1967-81, chairperson, div. edn. polit., rsch., evaluation, 1975-79, prof., 1981—, assoc. dean acad. affairs, 1986-87, 88—, acting dean, 1987-88. Author: Africanization of the Curriculum in Kenya, 1968, Ghana and Nonformal Education, 1983, Kenya: The Emergency of an Educated Elite, 1985, Reform in Tanzanian Education, 1989, Education in Sub-Saharan Africa, 1992. Fulbright grantee, 1974-75, Nat. Endowment Humanitites grantee, 1971-72. Mem. Am. Ednl. Studies Assn., Comparative Internat. Edn. Soc., Lions (pres. 1986-87), Phi Delta Kappa. Home: 18 Highland Cir Hadley MA 01035-9744 Office: U Mass Sch Edn Amherst MA 01003

URCIOLO, JOHN RAPHAEL, II, real estate developer, real estate and finance educator; b. Washington, July 29, 1947; s. Joseph John and Phillie Marie (Petrone) U.; m. Jean Marie Manning, Jan. 2, 1972 (dec. Jan. 1990). BBA, Am. U., 1969, MS in real estate, 1971. Cert. real estate broker, appraiser. Researcher Homer Hoyt Inst., Washington, 1967-69; economist Nat. Assn. Home Builders, Washington, 1971-75; lectr., assoc. prof. Montgomery Coll., Rockville, Md., 1971-72; assoc. prof. U. Md., College Park, 1972-79; property mgr. Urciolo Realty Co., Washington, 1976-79; adj. prof. Am. U., Washington, 1980—; comml. broker Urciolo & Urciolo, Washington, 1980-82; real estate developer Urciolo & Urciolo, Takoma Park, Md., 1982—; lectr., assoc. prof. Montgomery Coll., Rockville, Md., 1971-72; assoc. prof. U. Md., 1972-79, Am. U., Washington, 1980—; cons. Montgomery County Govt., Rockville, 1980-81, Nat. Ski Area Assn., Hartford, 1978-79; court expert Superior Ct. for D.C., Civil and Criminal divs.; lectr. to various organs. Author: Real Estate Manual, 1976; co-author: The White Book of Ski Areas (U.S. and Can.), 1977-79, Industry Edition-The White Book, 1978, The Housing Fact Book, 1976, Housing Component Costs, 1975, 2d edit., 1976, Material Usage in Housing, 1970; co-editor: Labor Wage Rate Bulletin, 1976. Fellow Urban Mass Transp. Assn., 1969, Am. U., 1970; Soc. Real Estate Appraisers scholar, 1968. Mem. Cert. Real Estate Appraisers, Am. Planning Assn., Am. Univ. Real Estate Assn. (charter mem., v.p. edn., v.p. award 1983), Ea. Ski Writers Assn. (com. mem.), Rho Epsilon (editor newsletter 1969). Republican. Roman Catholic. Office: Urciolo & Urciolo 6935 Laurel Ave Ste 100 Silver Spring MD 20912-4413

URICCHIO, WILLIAM ANDREW, biology educator; b. Hartford, Conn., Apr. 21, 1924; s. William and Mary (Donadio) U.; m. Velma Mathias, June 12, 1950; children: William, MaryLynn, Barbara, Robert, Michael. AB, Cath. U. Am., 1949, MS, 1951, PhD, 1953. Asst. prof. Carlow Coll., Pitts., 1953-57, assoc. prof., 1957-61, prof., 1961—, chair dept. biology, 1953-87, chair div. natural sci., 1987—; cons. edn. div. Xerox, Pitts., 1967-75; assoc. program dir. NSF, Washington, 1967-68. Author: Microbiology for Nurses, 1966, Independent Research in the Sciences, 1975; editor: Nat. Family Planning Proc., 1973, Pa. Acad. Sci. jour., 1963-67. Bd. dirs. Duquesne U., Pitts., 1973—, McGuire Meml., Pitts., 1972—, Human Life Found., Washington, 1968-80. With U.S. Army, 1943-46. Named Knight of St. Gregory, Pope Paul VI, 1967; recipient Pa. Sci. Edn. award Pa. Jr. Acad. Sci., 1976. Fellow AAAS; mem. Pa. Acad. Sci. (editor, pres. 1970-72), Am. Grad. and Profl. Com. (pres. 1970-74), Internat. Fedn. for Family Promotion (hon., bd. dirs. 1978—), Serra Club (pres. 1970-71), Delta Epsilon Sigma (nat. lectr. 1985, pres. 1960-82). Roman Catholic. Home: 1402 Murray Ave Pittsburgh PA 15217-1225 Office: Carlow Coll 3333 5th Ave Pittsburgh PA 15213-3165

URICHECK, MARYANNE, pharmacist; b. Phila., Sept. 23, 1960; d. Joseph Francis and Norma Joan (Miller) U. BS in Pharmacy, Phila. Coll. Pharmacy, 1983. Pharmacy tech. St. Francis Hosp., Wilmington, Del., 1980; pharmacy intern Wilmington Med. Ctr., 1980-83, Abbott Labs., Chgo., 1982; pharmacist-in-charge Rite Aid, Wilmington, 1983-88; staff pharmacist, cons. Happy Harry's Inst. Pharmacy, Newark, Del., 1988—. Mem. Am. Soc. Cons. Pharmacists, Am. Pharm. Assn., Nat. Coun. State Pharm. Assn. xecs., Am. Soc. Assn. Execs., Del. State Soc. Hosp. Pharmacists, Del. Pharm. Soc. (exec. dir. 1990—). Roman Catholic. Home: 169 E Green Valley Cir Newark DE 19711-6792 Office: Happy Harry's Inst Pharmacy 311 Ruthar Dr Newark DE 19711-8016

URIE, JOHN JAMES, lawyer, retired Canadian federal judge; b. Guelph, Ont., Can., Jan. 2, 1920; s. G. Norman and Jane A. U.; m. Dorothy Elizabeth James.; children: David, Janet, Alison. B.Commerce, Queen's U.; LL.B., Osgoode Hall Law Sch. Bar: Ont. 1948. Ptnr. firm Burke-Robertson, Urie, Weller & Chadwick, Ottawa, Ont., 1948-73; judge Fed. Ct. Can., Ottawa, 1973-90; counsel Scott and Aylen, Ottawa, 1991—; gen. counsel to Joint Com. of Senate and House of Commons on Consumer Credit; chmn. planning com. First Nat. Conf. on Law, Ottawa, 1972; judge Ct. Martial Appeal Ct., 1973-90. Past pres. County of Carleton Law Assn.; past v.p. Children's Aid Soc.; past pres. Eastern Profl. Hockey League. Served with Cameron Highlanders of Ottawa Can. Army, 1942-45. Mem. Royal Can. Mil. Inst., Phi Delta Phi. Mem. United Ch. of Canada. Clubs: Cameron Highlanders of Ottawa Assoc. (Ottawa), Ottawa Hunt and Golf (Ottawa), Rideau (Ottawa). Office: Scott and Aylen, 60 Queen St, Ottawa, ON Canada K1P 5Y7

URION, DAVID KIMBALL, pediatric neurologist, researcher, educator; b. Cin., Aug. 4, 1954; s. Phillip Allen and Lenore (Barrow) U.; m. Kerrie Eileen Flynn, Mar. 6, 1982 (div. Oct. 1986); 1 child, Kara Flynn; m. Deborah Choate, Sept. 27, 1987; 1 child, Rufus Walker Choate. AB, Dartmouth Coll., 1976; MD, Stanford U., 1980. Diplomate Am. Bd. Psychiatry and Neurology. Intern Peter Bent Brigham Hosp., Boston, 1980-81; resident, neurology Longwood Area Neurology Program, Boston, 1981-82; resident, pediatrics Children's Hosp., Boston, 1982-83; resident, child neurology Longwood Area Neurology Program, Boston, 1983-84, chief resident, child neurology, 1984-85; instr. neurology Med. Sch., Harvard U., Boston, 1985-87, asst. prof., 1987—; mem. faculty Sch. Edn. Harvard U., Cambridge, Mass., 1985—; asst. in neurology Children's Hosp., Boston, 1985-88; assoc. in neurology, 1988—; dir. learning disabilities-behavioral neurology program Children's Hosp., Boston, 1985—, dir. neurology clinics, 1987-91; treas. Children's Hosp. Neurology Found., 1986—, v.p., 1992—. Author: Pediatric Neurology for the House Officer, 1988; translator: The Brain Machine (Jeannerod), 1985; contbr. articles to med. jours., chpts. to books. Mem. Am. Acad. Neurology, Child Neurology Soc., AAAS, Am. Acad. Cerebral Palsy and Devel. Medicine, Am. Epilepsy Soc., Internat. Child Neurology Assn. Democratic Socialist. Roman Catholic. Office: Children's Hosp Neurology 300 Longwood Ave Boston MA 02115-5737

URLAUB, CHARLES JOSEPH, hospital administrator; b. Rochester, N.Y., Dec. 22, 1956; s. Warren Gerald and Elaine (Ringelstein) U.; m. Susan Lee Gorman, Sept. 12, 1981; children: Kaitlyn Marie, Morgan Lee. BS, Rensselaer Poly Tech. Inst., 1979, MBA, 1981. Project specialist St. Mary's Hosp., Rochester, N.Y., 1979-80; asst. v.p. St. Mary's Hosp., Rochester, 1981-84, v.p. ops., 1984-88; asst. v.p. Buffalo Gen. Hosp., 1988—. Bd. dirs. 19th Ward Community Orgn., Rochester, 1984-85; loaned exec. United Way Rochester, 1982, hosp. chmn. & liason, 1983-87, allocation com., Buffalo, 1990. Mem. Am. Hosp. Assn. Healthcare Info. & Mgmt. Systems Soc., Western N.Y. Healthcare Exec. Forum (chmn. membership com.) Western N.Y. Hosp. Assn. (com. mem.), Am. Soc. for Quality Control, Tripoly Rocketry, Canadaigua Emergency Squad (paramedic 1980-84), Tonawanda Sportsmens Club, Epsilon Delta Sigma, Phi Mu Delta (v.p. fin. 1978-79). Republican. Roman Catholic. Home: 255 Glen Oaks Dr East Amherst NY 14051-1252 Office: Buffalo Gen Hosp 100 High St Buffalo NY 14203-1154

URQUHART, STEPHEN E., lawyer; b. Quincy, Mass., Mar. 2, 1949; s. Raymond Miles and M. Eileen (MacDonald) U.; m. Katherine Driscoll, Mar. 15, 1970; 1 child, Stephen M. AB, Boston Coll., 1976, JD, 1979. Bar: Mass. 1979, U.S. Dist. Ct. Mass. 1980. Legis. aide Mass. Ho. of Reps., Boston, 1976; counsel B.C. Legal Assistance Bur., Waltham, Mass., 1976-79; assoc. Law Offices of Robert J. Ladd (formerly Law Offices of Roland I. Wood), North Andover, Mass., 1980-88, Law Offices Nicholas Macaronis, Lowell, Mass., 1988-91, Law Offices Ernest W. Piper, Jr., Boston, 1991—. Precinct capt. Edward M. Kennedy for Senator, Mass. 1979-80; campaign worker various Dem. candidates. Recipient cert. of merit United World Federalists, 1974. Mem. ABA, Mass. Bar Assn., Mass. Acad. Trial Attys., Am. Arbitration Assn., Internat. Platform Assn., Assn. Trial Lawyers Am., Phi Beta Kappa, Phi Delta Phi. Methodist. Club: Clan Urquhart (Va.). Home: PO Box 610 Danville NH 03819-0006 Office: 256 Friend St Boston MA 02114-1801

URSIAK, DAVID ALLEN, program manager; b. Ford City, Pa., Mar. 25, 1952; s. Nicholas and Josephine Sophia (Recny) U.; m. Judy M. Thiry, Aug. 18, 1973 (div. June 1989); children: Jennifer M., David A. Jr.; m. Roberta F. Mattioli, June 16, 1990. BS in Math., Ind. U. Pa., 1974, MS in Bus., 1977, MBA in Fin., 1979. Indsl. engr. McCreary Tire and Rubber CO., Indiana, Pa., 1975-80; mfg. engr. Fisher Scientific Co., Indiana, Pa., 1980-86; program mgr. Liberty Mirrir Co., Brackenridge, Pa., 1986—; instr. Ind. U. Pa., 1986-89. Mem. Am. Inst. Indsl. Engrs. Home: 1031 Terrace Ave Ford City PA 16226

URSO, JOSETTE MARIE, artist, educator; b. Tampa, Fla., June 5, 1959; d. Rosario and Connie Ann (Wood) U. BFA, U. South Fla., 1980, MFA, 1983. Art tchr. New Sch. for Visual Arts, Tampa, 1984-85, Hillsborough Community Coll., Tampa, 1984-85, Union County Coll., Cranford, N.J., 1986-88, The Chautauqua (N.Y.) Sch. Art, 1985-90, 92d St. YMHA, N.Y.C., 1985-90; art instr. to pvt. students, N.Y.C., 1990-92. Painting fellow Art Matters, Inc., N.Y.C., 1988, Div. Cultural Affairs, Tampa, 1986; art resident Va. Ctr. for Arts, Sweetbriar, 1990, Millay Colony for Arts, Austerlitz, N.Y., 1990, Camargo Found., Cassis, France, 1991.

URSPRUNG, ALEX WILLIAM, psychologist; b. N.Y.C., Feb. 12, 1952; s. Hans Felix and Ethel Marie (Oborne) U.; m. Susan Lee, Sept. 14, 1974. BA, Bates Coll., 1973; MA/CAGS, Assumption Coll., 1977; PhD, Syracuse U., 1983. Lic.psycholigist, Mass., Pa.; cert. rehab. counselor. Therapist Coop. Human Svcs., Worcester, Mass., 1977-79; prof. Pa. State U., State College, 1983-89; psychologist Dept. Mental Health Commonwealth Mass., Worcester, 1989-90; pvt. practice psychology Worcester, 1990—; dir. Ursprung Assocs., Holden, Mass., 1985—; cons. Social Security Adminstrn., Worcester, 1990—, Mass. Rehab. Commn., Worcester, 1990—; adj. prof. Assumption Coll., 1990—. Mem. Am. Psychol. Assn., Am. Assn. Counseling and Devel., Am. Rehab. Counseling Assn. Office: Ursprung Assocs 37 Fruit St Holden MA 01520-1014

URSTADT, CHARLES DEANE, real estate and publishing executive; b. N.Y.C., June 13, 1959; s. Charles Jordan and Elinor McClure (Funk) U. BA cum laude, NYU, 1982. News reporter Sta. WNYC-TV, N.Y.C., 1979-80; adminstrv. asst. Mayor's Press Office, N.Y.C., 1980-81; asst. v.p. Urstadt Property Co., Inc. (formerly Pearce, Urstadt, Mayer & Greer, Inc.), N.Y.C., 1981-84, v.p., mem. exec. com., 1984-86, sr. v.p., sec., 1986-91; exec. v.p. Urstadt Property Co., Inc., N.Y.C., 1991—, bd. dirs.; pub., editor-in-chief N.Y. Constrn. News, N.Y.C., 1984—; pub. Manhattan Real Estate Exch., N.Y.C., 1991—; bd. dirs. 61 E 86th St Owners Corp., 1987-89, 90—, sec., 1990—. Chmn. Young Reps. of Bronxville, 1984-85; Village Rep. campaign com., Bronxville, 1984-85, Young People for O'Rourke campaign, 1986; v.p. N.Y. Rep. State Com. Forum 500, 1989—; bd. dirs. The Ensemble Studio Theater, 1988-91, The Friends of Thirteen, Inc., 1992—; bd. dirs. East Side Assn., 1988—, v.p., 1990—; mem. adv. bd. HRE Properties, 1991—. Mem. N.Y. Bldg. Congress (bd. dirs. 1988—, treas. 1989-91). Office: 135 E 65th St New York NY 10021-7006 also: Office No 3 2 Park Pl Bronxville NY 10708

URY, JOAN LOUISE, human services manager; b. N.Y.C., July 23, 1944; d. Martin and Lorraine (Schantz) Simonson; m. Michael G. Ury, June 8, 1966; children: Elizabeth, Emily. BS, Cornell U., 1965; MA, Columbia U., 1966. Tchr. Cornell U., Ithaca, N.Y., 1966-70, teaching asst., 1970-71; rsch. asst. U. Md., College Pk., 1972-73; asst. dir. No. Va. Hotline, Arlington, 1973-79; dir. A Woman's Place, Rockville, Md., 1979-90; chairperson Ctr. for Divorcing Families, Bethesda, Md., 1990—; bd. dirs. Crittenton Svcs. of Washington, Silver Spring, Md., 1988—. Bd. dirs. Bannockburn Community Club, Bethesda, 1988. Recipient N.Y. Regents scholarship Cornell U., 1961-65, Extraordinary Performance award, 1984, 86, 88; named to Dean's List, Cornell U., 1961-65. Mem. Women's Polit. Caucus, NOW, Am. Assn. of Counseling. Home and Office: 6518 E Halbert Rd Bethesda MD 20817-5414

USSLER-TRUMBULL, CHRISTINE, architect, educator; b. Phila., Feb. 11, 1954; d. William and Josephine (Gravel) U. BA in Architecture summa cum laude, Lehigh U., 1981; MArch, Columbia U., 1984. Registered architect, Pa. Draftsman, designer The Archtl. Studio, Easton, Pa., 1984-86; owner, architect Artefact, Inc., Bethleham, Pa., 1986—; adj. asst. prof. Lehigh U., Bethlehem, 1984-88, vis. asst. prof., 1989—; hist. officer City of Bethlehem, 1988—; bd. dirs. South Bethlehem Hist. Soc., 1988-91. Mem. hist. survey rev. commn. Northampton County, Easton, Pa., 1989—. Grantee Pa. Coun. on Arts 1990. Mem. AAUW, Soc. Archtl. Hist. Archtl. League, Bethlehem C. of C., Phi Beta Kappa. Office: Artefact Inc 26 E 3rd St Bethlehem PA 18015-1304

UTERMOHLEN, HERBERT GEORG, dermatologist; b. Göttingen, Germany, Nov. 27, 1948; came to U.S., 1990; s. Paul Ernst and Gertrud (Quentin) U.; m. Miriam Berger, Dec. 13, 1989; children: Christian, Matthew. MD, U. Göttingen, 1976. Specialist in dermatology and allergy U. Hosps. Göttingen, 1980-84; pvt. practice Hamburg, Germany, 1986-89, Scarsdale, N.Y., 1990—. With German Armed Forces, 1977-79. Mem. AAAS, N.Y. Acad. Scis., Deutsche Gesellschaft Für Psychiat. and Nervenheilkunde, Deutsche Dermatology Gesellschaft. Home: 130 Garth Rd Ste 106 Scarsdale NY 10583

UTLEY, F. KNOWLTON, library director, educator; b. Northampton, Mass., May 4, 1935; s. Frederick K. and Florence E. (Moore) U.; m. Faith E. Green, July 2, 1960; children: Richard F., Stephen R., David E. BS, Castleton State Coll., 1960; MA, U. Conn., 1967; EdD, Boston U., 1979; MLS, U. Ala., 1983. Tchr. indsl. arts Montpelier (Vt.) High Sch., 1960-61, Southwick (Mass.) High Sch., 1961-63; tchr., drafting instr. Putnam (Conn.) High Sch., 1963-68; media specialist Cen. Conn. State U., New Britain, 1968-69, dir. media svcs., 1969-72; doctoral teaching fellow Boston U., 1972-73; dir. libr., media svcs. Manchester (Mass.) Pub. Schs., 1973-79; assoc. prof. libr. scis. U. Maine, Farmington, 1979-80; dir. grad. program libr. media Livingston (Ala.) U., 1980-83; dir. libr. media svcs. Am. Internat. Coll., Springfield, Mass., 1983—; pres. C/W Mars-Cen. and Western Mass. Auto. Res., 1987-88; chmn. bd. dirs. Cooperating Colls. of Great Springfield, 1988-89; vice chairman bd. dirs. Western Mass. Media Coun., 1990-91. Mem. ALA, Assn./Edn. Commun. and Tech. New England Edn. Media Assn., New England Libr. Assn., Mass. Assn. Edn. Media, Mass. Libr. Assn., Phi Delta Kappa. Home: 11 Canal Dr Belchertown MA 01007-9639 Office: Am Internat Coll 1000 State St Springfield MA 01109-3189

UTTER, CHARLES WILBAR, editor, publisher; b. Westerly, R.I., Dec. 6, 1917; s. Geroge B. and Katherine (Wilbar) U.; student Deerfield Acad., 1933-36, U. Vt., 1937-40; m. Annice N. Swertfeger, Feb. 6, 1943; children—George Benjamin III, Nicholas Charles, Christopher Oberly. With The Westerly (R.I.) Sun, 1945—, editor, 1955—, co-pub., 1967—; v.p., sec.-treas. The Utter Co., Westerly, 1955-91; ret. Moderator, Westerly Fire Dist., 1956-87; bd. dirs. Westerly and Pawcatuck Community Fund, 1957-70; bd. dirs. New Eng. Council, 1961-77, R.I. chmn., 1974-75; dir. AAA South Cen. New Eng., 1960-91, lifetime hon. dir., 1991—; dir. Narragansett council Boy Scouts Am., 1970—, Silver Beaver award, 1975; clk. vestry Christ Ch. Westerly, 1979-82, mem. vestry, 1982-84. Served from 2d lt. to capt., AUS and USAAF, 1940-45; ATO, ETO. Decorated D.F.C. with 4 oak leaf clusters, Air medal with 4 oak leaf clusters; accorded rank of col. Confederate Air Force; Eagle Scout, 1932. Mem. Am. Newspaper Pubs. Assn., N.E. Newspaper Assn., N.E. Soc. Newspaper Editors, Inter-Am. Press Assn., Nat. Press Photographers Assn. (life), 8th Air Force Assn., Air Force Assn., Navy League, 401st Bomb Group (H) Assn. (dir. 1982-86), AP, New Eng. AP News Execs. Assn., R.I. Press Assn. (pres. 1961-64), VFW, Am. Legion., R.I. News Photographers Assn., Greater Westerly-Pawcatuck Area C. of C. (pres. 1958-60), R.I. Tourist/Travel Assn. (v.p.), Sigma Delta Chi, Sigma Phi. Clubs: Masons, Soujourners (life), Westerly Yacht (life), Lions (Westerly, R.I.); Watch Hill (R.I.) Yacht; Mystic Seaport Pilot (Conn.); R.I. Commodores, Tenn. Squire, Ky. Col., Overseas Press. Home: 18 Happy Valley Rd Westerly RI 02891-3516

UTTERBACK, JOE, jazz pianist, composer; b. Hutchinson, Kans., Oct. 8, 1944; s. Joe and Betty (Greenstreet) U. MusB in Piano Performance, Wichita State U., 1968, MusM in Piano Performance, 1969; D.Mus.Arts, U. Kans., 1979. Freelance jazz pianist, 1962—; music faculty Stan Kenton Summer Jazz Camps, Kansas City, Mo., 1968-69, U. Iowa, Iowa City, 1969-70, U. Kans., Lawrence, 1975-78, San Francisco State U., 1981-83, Sacred Heart U., Stamford, Conn., 1992—; organist Rowayton (Conn.) United Meth. Ch., 1990—; pres. Jazzmuze Inc., Little Silver, N.J., 1991—. Composer (jazz-influenced classical works) Solace, Jazz Suite, Encounter, Transformation, Tuxedo Blues, Psalmsuite, Summer Pavan, Peace Prelude. Recipient ASCAP award, 1991-92. Mem. Nat. Jazz Svc. Orgn., Am. Music Ctr., Composer's Forum, Am. Guild of Organists. Home: 80 Crooked Trail 50 Crooked Trail Rowayton CT 06853

UVA, KENNETH J., corporate lawyer; b. Bklyn., Dec. 18, 1949; s. Joseph and Mildred (Marenghi) U.; m. Shelley Abramowitz, May 4, 1975; children: Diana, Katharine. BA, Adelphi U., Garden City, N.Y., 1970; JD, Fordham U., 1974; MA, NYU, 1980. Staff atty. CT Corp. System, N.Y.C., 1976-83,

atty., 1988—; exec. v.p. Trademark Svc. Corp., N.Y.C., 1983-88; adj. prof. Adelphi U., Garden City, 1987—. Author: U.S. in the Making, 1980; contbr. articles to profl. jours., book revs. to N.Y. Times. Mem. ABA, Am. Intellectual Property Law Assn., Fordham Law Alumni Assn.

UWUJAREN, GILBERT PATRICK, economist; b. Oza Agbor, Bendel, Nigeria, May 6, 1945; came to U.S., 1985; s. Jacob Aghahowa and Victoria (Lasila) Uwujaren; m. Ngozi Buzugbe, Aug. 25, 1973; children: Jane, Janice, Jacob, Jo-Anne, Joseph, Jarune. BSc, U. Ibadan, Nigeria, 1971; MA, Columbia U., 1975, MPhil, 1977, PhD, 1977. Asst. lectr. U. Ife, Ibadan, 1972-73; sr. lectr. U. Ife, Ile-Ife, Nigeria, 1977-85; economist World Bank, Washington, 1985-89, cons., 1989—. Contbr. articles to profl. jours. Recipient German Acad. award Govt. Fed. Republic Germany, Ibadan, 1970-71, Rockefeller award Rockefeller Found., Ibadan, 1971-73. Mem. Am. Econ. Assn. Home: 5801 Shana Pl Burke VA 22015-3663

UY, FELIPE RATUNIL, internist; b. Misamis Oriental, Philippines, Jan. 24, 1942; came to U.S., 1969; s. Ching Toh and Modesta (Ratunil) Uy; m. Ester Rodriquez Lambujon, May 22, 1971; children: Christine, Melanie, Vincent. AA, Cebu Inst. Tech., Philippines, 1962; MD, Southwestern U., Philippines, 1968. Cert. Am. Bd. Internal Medicine. Med. intern St. John Episcopal Hosp., Bklyn., 1969-70; med. resident Beekman Downtown Hosp., N.Y.C., 1970-72; anesthesia resident Kings County Hosp., Bklyn., 1972-74; fellow pulmonary medicine VA Hosp., East Orange, N.J., 1974-75; med. attending Charles Drew Health Ctr., Bklyn., 1975-77; med. specialist Kingsboro Psychiat. Hosp., Bklyn., 1977—; dir. emergency med. svc. Kingsboro Psychiat. Ctr., Bklyn., 1985—. Editor: (manual) Practical Guide on Advanced Cardiac Life Support,1987. Mem. Kingsboro Emergency Preparedness Com., Bklyn., 1992. Fellow Am. Coll. Anesthesiologists; mem. Am. Bd. Anesthesiology (diplomate). Roman Catholic. Home: 76-22 172d St Flushing NY 11366 Office: Kingsboro PC 681 Clarkson Ave Brooklyn NY 11366

UZAN, BERNARD FRANCK, artistic director; b. Tunis, Tunisia, Dec. 5, 1944; Arrived in Can., 1988; s. Henri and Elise Gabrielle (Pansieri) U.; m. Diana Soviero, Nov. 9, 1984. PhD, Paris U., 1968. Gen. & artistic dir. Théâtre français d'Amérique, Boston, 1973-83, Tulsa Opera, 1987-88, L'Opéra de Montreal, Que., Can., 1988—; adminstr., exec. dir. Alliance français de Boston, 1974-83; tchr. San Francisco Opera, Montreal Opera, U. Ill., Tulsa U., Middlebury Coll., Wellesley Coll. Author: Spoken French for Travelers, 1978. Office: L'Opéra de Montréal, 260 de Maisonneuve W, Montreal, PQ Canada H2X 1Y9

VAADIA, BOAZ, sculptor; b. Petah-Tiqva, Israel, Nov. 13, 1951; s. Nissim and Rivka Vaadia; m. Kim Turner, Sept. 10, 1989; 1 child, Rebecca Daniel-le. Student, Avni Inst. Fine Art, Tel Aviv, 1971. vis. artist Appalachian State U., Boone, N.C., 1982; resident Internat. Tel-Hai '80 Internat. Meeting, Israel, 1980. One-person shows include O.K. Harris Works of Art, N.Y.C., 1986, 88, 89, Birmingham, Mich., 1990, Phila. Mus. Judaica, 1987, Helander Gallery, Palm Beach, Fla., 1988, Jewish Mus., N.Y.C., 1988-89, Hokin Kaufman Gallery, Chgo., 1989, 90, others; exhibited in group shows at Helander Gallery, 1989, 90, Phyllis Rothman Gallery, Fairleigh Dickinson U., Madison, N.J., 1990, Margulies Taplin Gallery, Bar Harbor Islands, 1990, Utsukushi-ga-hara Open Air Mus., Japan, 1992, numerous others. Grantee NEA, 1988, Ariana Found. for Arts, 1986, Artists Space, 1983, Am.-Israel Cultural Found., 1975-76, Am. the Beautiful Fund, Palisades Internstate Park, 1977; Beeckman scholar, 1976-77. Home: 475 Broadway 7th Fl New York NY 10013 Studio: 104 Berry St Brooklyn NY 11211

VACCARO, MARTHA WALSH, secondary school educator; b. Centerville, Mass., July 26, 1930; d. Edwin Arnold and Anne (Molony) Walsh; m. Ralph Francis Vaccaro, Apr. 19, 1955; children: Christopher, Adelaide, John, Mark, Thomas (dec.), Peter. BS, Trinity Coll., Burlington, Vt., 1952; post-grad., Southeastern Mass. U., 1983, Bridgewater State U., 1987-88. Cert. math., sch., biology secondary tchr., Mass. Rsch. asst. Woods Hole (Mass.) Oceanographic Inst., 1952-58; substitute tchr. Falmouth (Mass.) Pub. Schs., 1981-87, math. tchr., 1987—; pvt. math. tutor, 1958-81. Mem. Falmouth Town Fin. Com., 1970-81; chmn. Falmouth Sewer Adv. Com., 1980-86; mem. Falmouth Human Svcs. Com., 1971-86; rep. Falmouth Town Meeting, 1981—. Recipient Marian medal Diocese of Fall River, 1971. Mem. NEA, Mass. Tchrs. Assn., Falmouth Educators Assn., Assn. Tchrs. of Math. Mass., Nat. Coun. Tchrs. Math., Cape Cod Math. Tchrs. Consortium, Birthright. Republican. Roman Catholic. Hme: Box 245 25 Hidden Village Rd West Falmouth MA 02574 Office: Lawrence Sch Lakeview Ave Falmouth MA 02540-2830

VACCARO, NICHOLAS CARMINE, English and media educator; b. Bklyn., July 16, 1942; s. Joseph Anthony Vaccaro and Carmela (Tallarico) Chicorelli; m. Jane Elizabeth Forgiel, July 7, 1973; children: Stephen Nicholas, Christopher Joseph. BA in English, St. John's U., 1964, MS in Edn., 1966, Profl. Diploma in Adminstrn., 1978. Tchr. English South Huntington (N.Y.) Schs., 1965-68, Elwood Schs., East Northport, N.Y., 1968-69; tchr. English and media Massapequa (N.Y.) Schs., 1969—; novelist Sterling Lord-Literistic Lit. Agy., N.Y.C., 1984—; screenwriter Sterlinglord-Literistic Literary Agy., N.Y.C., 1984—; curriculum rsch. & program devel. Massapequa Schs., 1971-72, 78, 82, 84, 88; drama club dir. Berner and Massapequa High Schs., 1970-73, 78-82, 91, creative writing advisor, 1982-91. Contbr. articles to profl. jours. Mgr. Little League Baseball, Northport, 1984-91, Youth Ctr. Soccer, 1989. Recipient Nat. Tchrs. award NBC and Carnegie Found. for Advancement of Teaching, 1990, NEH and Coun. for Basic Edn. fellow, 1991. Mem. Mensa, Nat. Coun. Tchrs. English, Massapequa Fedn. Tchrs., Phi Delta Kappa. Roman Catholic. Home: 208 Highland Ave Northport NY 11768-1657 Office: Massapequa High Sch 4925 Merrick Rd Massapequa NY 11758-6201

VACCARO, RICHARD FRANCIS, marketing executive; b. Phila., Apr. 9, 1949; s. Harold P. and Clara J. (Budell) V.; m. Joanne M. Rosa, Oct. 2, 1971 (div.); children: Jessica, Kelly. BS in Indsl. Mgmt., LaSalle U., Phila., 1971. Indsl. engr. Lenox China, Inc., Pomona, NJ, 1971-73; dist. sales rep. Airbourne Corp., Phila., 1973-74; gen. mgr. RGM Inc., Media, Pa., 1974-75; dir. of sales devel. Premier Indsl. Corp., Cleveland, 1975-79; field mktg. specialist GE, Waterford, N.Y., 1979-81; consumer mktg. mgr. GE, Waterford, 1981-83, mgr. mktg. devel., 1983-85, mgr. ventures and bus. devel., 1988—; v.p. mktg. Darworth Co., Avon, Conn., 1985-86; nat. sales, mktg. dir. Gordon & Lustre Corp., Boston, 1986-88; exec. v.p. SGI Mgmt. Cons., Torrington, Conn., 1990—; bd. dirs. Lustre, Inc. Mem. Greater Opportunity Alliance Lawrence. Recipient Gold & Silver Drum awards Building Supply & Home, 1986, Gold Drum award Ctr. Assn., 1984, Best of Industry award Point of Purchase Advt., 1982, 83. Office: SGI 265 E Elm St PO Box 1277 Torrington CT 06790

VADEHRA, DAVE KUMAR, advertising research company executive; b. New Delhi, Feb. 20, 1941; came to U.S., 1967; s. Faqir Chand Vadehra and Sushila Dhawan; m. Sally Colinvaux, Dec. 28, 1979; children: Emma, Geeta. BCom with honors, Delhi U., 1960; M Econs. Adminstrn., Delhi Sch. Econs., 1962; MSc in Econs., London Sch. Econs., 1964. Rsch. analyst J. Arthur Rank Orgn., London, 1964-66; asst. rsch. dir. MGM, N.Y.C., 1967-70; rsch. assoc. Lorilard/Daniel & Charles, N.Y.C., 1971-73; pres., founder Video Storyboard Tests, Inc., N.Y.C., 1975—; editor, pub. CommercialBreak newsletter. Columnist Ad Age, 1980-83, AdWeek, 1984-88. Mem. Advt. Rsch. Found., N.Y. Advt. Club. Office: Video Storyboard Tests Inc 107 E 31st St New York NY 10016

VADLAMUDI, SRI KRISHNA, immunologist, veterinarian; b. Moparru, Andhra Pradesh, India, Aug. 15, 1927; came to U.S., 1957; s. Venakta Ratnam and Pitchamma (Yelavarti) V.; m. Jamuna Bai Narra, Oct. 14, 1954; children: Anula Durga, Nagarjuna, Venkata Ratnam, Gautam Kishore. BVSc, Madras (India) U., 1952; PhD, U. Wis., 1959, MS, 1963. Cert. DVM, ECFVG. Vet. asst. surg. Andhra Pradesh State Govt., Hyderabad, 1952-55, rsch. vet. NDV labs. animal health dept., 1955-57; project asst. dept. vet. sci. U. Wis., Madison, 1957-62; sr. investigator Dept. Infectious Diseases, Waukegan, Ill., 1963-65; chief chemotherapy rsch. Microbiol. Assn. Inc., Bethesda, Md., 1965-74; chief immunology dept. HHS ODE/CDRH/FDA, Rockville, Md., 1975—, chief clin. chem. toxicology dept. HHS, 1981-85; cons. Smithsonian Sci. Info. Svc., Washington, 1974-86; mentor MS cands. Howard U., Washington, 1965-76, mentor PhD cands., Am. U., Washington, 1975, George Washington U., Washington, 1976, Madras U., 1988; presenter in field; invited speaker before many nat. and internat. sci. gatherings, representing FDA guidelines on tumor markers and other immunology devices; supervisory microbiologist DCLD/ODE/CDRH/FDA, 1991. Contbr. 50 articles to profl. jours. Pres. Greater Washington Telugu Cultural Soc., Silver Spring, Md., 1986-86, India Cultural Coordination Com., Silver Spring, 1989—; mem. Am. Assn. Cancer Rsch. Mem. Am. Vet. Med. Assn., Am. Soc. Microbiology, Fedn. Am. Socs. Exptl. Biology, Am. Assn. Pathology, Procs. Soc. Exptl. Biology and Medicine, Sigma Xi. Hindu. Home: 14625 Silverstone Dr Silver Spring MD 20905-7418 Office: ODE/DCLD/CDRH/FDA 1390 Piccard Dr Rockville MD 20850-4308

VADUS, GLORIA A., handwriting expert, graphologist; b. Forrestville, Pa.. Student, Cole Sch. Graphology, Calif., 1978; BA in Psychology Counseling, Columbia Pacific U., 1981, MA in Psychology, 1982; diploma from pvt. study, Edith Eisenberg, Bethesda, Md., 1991. Cert. Am. Acad. Graphology, Washington, 1978; cert. tchr. Coun. Graphological Socs. 1980; ct. qualified document examiner. Pres., owner Graphinc, Inc., 1976—; accredited instr. Montgomery County Schs., Md., 1978; instr. Psychogram Centre, 1978—; testifier superior and probate cts. Author numerous studies, papers, articles in field. Chmn. Letter of Hope for POW's; vol. Montgomery County, 1987-88. Recipient Gold Nib Analyst of Yr., 1982, Dancing Fan award Marine Tech. Soc. Japan, 1990; named Internat. Woman of Yr, 1991, 92. Mem. Am. Handwriting Analysis Found. (cert., pres. 1982-84, chmn. rsch. com. , adv. bd. 1981-86, chmn. nominations com. 1985-86, officiator 1986, mem. policy planning and ethics com. 1986-91, ethics chmn. 1989-91, chmn., past pres. adv. bd. 1989-91), Nat. Forensic Ctr., Nat. Assn. Document Examiners (ethics hearing bd. 1986, chmn. nominations com. 1987-88, elections chmn. 1988, parliamentarian 1988—), Internat. Platform Assn., Soc. Francaise de Graphologie, Nat. Writers Club, Meninnger Found., Soroptimist Interant. (v.p.), Nat. Capital Jaguars Club Am. (judge 1976-85), Henry Hicks Garden Club, Sierra Club. Home: 8500 Timber Hill Ln Potomac MD 20854

VAGELOS, PINDAROS ROY, pharmaceutical company executive; b. Westfield, N.J., Oct. 8, 1929; s. Roy John and Marianthi (Lambrinides) V.; m. Diana Touliatos, July 10, 1955; children: Randall, Cynthia, Andrew, Ellen. AB, U. Pa., 1950; MD, Columbia U., 1954; DSc (hon.), Washington U., 1980, Brown U., 1982, U. Medicine and Dentistry of N.J., 1984, NYU, 1989, Columbia U., 1990; LLD (hon.), Princeton U., 1990; LHD (hon.), Rutgers U., 1991. Intern medicine Mass. Gen. Hosp., 1954-55, asst. resident medicine, 1955-56; surgeon Lab. Cellular Physiology, NIH, 1956-59; surgeon Lab. Biochemistry, 1959-64, head sect. comparative biochemistry, 1964-66; prof. biochemistry, chmn. dept. biol. chemistry Washington U. Sch. Medicine, St. Louis, 1966-75; dir. div. biology and biomed. scis. Washington U. Sch. Medicine, 1973-75; sr. v.p. research Merck, Sharp & Dohme Research Labs., Rahway, N.J., 1975-76, pres., 1976-84; corp. sr. v.p. Merck & Co., Inc., Rahway, N.J., 1982-84, also bd. dirs., 1984—, exec. v.p., 1984-85, pres., chief exec. officer, 1985-86; chmn., pres., chief exec. officer Merck & Co., Inc., 1986—; mem. Inst. Medicine, NAS, 1974—; chmn. sci. adv. bd. Ctr. for Advanced Biotech. and Medicine, 1985—; bd. dirs. TRW, Inc., Prudential Ins. Co. Trustee U. Pa., 1988—, Rockefeller U., 1976—, Danforth Found., 1978—; mem. Bus. Coun., 1987—; bd. mng. dirs. Met. Opera Assn., Inc., 1989—; bd. dirs. N.J. Performing Arts Ctr., 1989—. Recipient N.J. Sci./Tech. medal R & D Coun. N.J., 1983. Mem. Am. Chem. Soc. (award enzyme chemistry 1967), Am. Soc. Biol. Chemists, Nat. Acad. Scis., Am. Acad. Arts and Scis., Bus. Roundtable (policy com. 1987—). Home: 82 Mosle Rd Far Hills NJ 07931 Office: Merck & Co Inc 126 E Lincoln Ave PO Box 2000 Rahway NJ 07065

VAHEY, HARRY MARTIN, educational administrator, psychologist; b. Phila., Jan. 30, 1936; s. Michael John and Sabina (Shevlin) V.; m. Regina Anne Grant, Dec. 23, 1972. BA, Mary Immaculate Coll., Northampton, Pa., 1960; MA, Rutgers U., 1966; MEd, Temple U., 1973, EdD, 1976. Lic. psychologist, N.J.; cert. sch. psychologist, prin., N.J. Tchr. St. Joseph's Coll. Prep, Princeton, N.J., 1963-66, dir. students, 1966-71; tchr. St. Thomas Moore High Sch., Phila., 1971-72; adminstrv. asst., adult edn. Camden (N.J.) Bd. Edn., 1972-73; dir., child study North Hanover (N.J.) Bd. Edn., 1974-77, Maple Shade (N.J.) Bd. Edn., 1977-91. Mem. APA, N.J. Assn. Sch. Psychologists, N.J. Psychol. Assn., Phi Delta Kappa. Home: 1 La Salle Dr Burlington NJ 08016-2905 Office: Maple Shade Bd of Edn Mshs Frederick & Clint St Maple Shade NJ 08052

VAIDMAN, ANNA, accountant; b. Odessa, Ukraine, USSR, June 29, 1948; came to U.S., 1976; d. Semyon and Polina Shkolnik) Margulis; m. Yuli Vaidman, Oct. 1, 1966; children: Gregory, Ely August. BA in English, Odessa State U., USSR; MBA in Acctg., Kean Coll., 1988. Cert. tax preparer, interpreter, notary pub. Office mgr. Silplan Textile Inc., N.Y.C., 1977-82; controller Mike Sell & Assoc., Newark, N.J., 1982-84; owner, prin. Vega Fin. Svcs., Clark, N.J., 1984—. Editor: Russian Monthly of Jewish Fedn. Cen. N.J., 1991—; contbr. articles to profl. jours. Bd. dirs. Jewish Family Svcs., Elisabeth, N.J., 1989—; treas. Temple Beth O'R, Clark, 1990. Mem. Nat. Soc. Tax Preparers, Bus. and Profl. Women. Republican. Home and Office: 73 White Pl Clark NJ 07066

VAIDYA, KIRIT RAMESHCHANDRA, physician, anesthesiologist; b. Sihor, India, Feb. 20, 1937; came to U.S., 1971; s. Rameshchandra Harilal Vaidya and Kanta Bachubhai Mulani; m. Rashmi Kirit Vaidya; children: Kaushal, Sujal. BSc, Gujrat U., India, 1959; MB BS, Karnatak U., India, 1965. Intern St. Joseph Hosp., Providence, 1971-72; resident in anesthesiology R.I. Hosp., Providence, 1973, Boston City Hosp., 1974-76; clin. instr. anesthesiology Boston U. Sch. Medicine, 1977-79; staff anesthesiologist Bridgeport (Conn.) Hosp., 1979—; asst. clin. prof. anesthesiology U. Conn. Med. Ctr., Farmington, 1987—. Mem. Am. Assn. Physicians from India, Conn. Assn. Physicians from India, Fairfield County Med. Assn., Conn. State Soc. Medicine, Conn. State Soc. Anesthesiologists, Am. Soc. Anesthesiologists, Internat. Anesthesiology Assn. Hindu. Home: 54 Quail Trl Trumbull CT 06611-5259 Office: Bridgeport Anesthesia Assocs 965 White Plains Rd Ste 301 Trumbull CT 06611-4566

VAIL, RICHARD T., public relations and development executive; b. Sayre, Pa., Oct. 26, 1938; s. James Francis and Ruth Alice (Reynolds) V.; m. Betty A. Harris, May 25, 1963; children: Amy, Brenda. BS, Mansfield (Pa.) U., 1963; MS, Elmira (N.Y.) Coll., 1968. Gov., econs. tchr. Tioga Ctr. (N.Y.) Cornell U., Ithaca, N.Y., 1963-68, asst. dir. admissions, 1968-72, dir. north cen. regional pub. affairs office, 1972-76, dir. met. N.Y. regional pub. affairs office, 1976-81; assoc. dean for inst. devel. and alumni affairs Sch. Medicine Case Western Reserve U., Cleve., 1981-88; v.p. devel. Brigham and Women's Hosp., Boston, 1988-91; exec. dir. Med. Alumni Assn./Found. U. Va. Sch. Medicine and U. Va. Med. Alumni Assn./Found., Charlottesville, 1992—, assoc. dean for med. sch. devel./alumni affairs, 1992—. Trustee Mansfield Found. Inc., Snee-Reinhardt Charitable Found. Home: 12 Meadowbrook Rd Dover MA 02030-2040

VAIL, VAN HORN, German educator; b. Buffalo, Dec. 23, 1934; s. Curtis Churchill and Faith Newbrook (Ely) V.; m. Michele Juliette Edelstein, May 5, 1969; 1 son, Mark Curtis. B.A., U. Wash., 1956; M.A., Princeton U., 1961, Ph.D., 1964. Instr. Princeton U., 1962-65, asst. prof., 1965-66; asst. prof. German Middlebury (Vt.) Coll., 1966-69, assoc. prof., 1969-75, prof., 1975—; chmn. dept. Middlebury Coll., Vt., 1970-73, 87-88; dir. studies Middlebury Grad. Sch. in Germany Middlebury Coll., 1967-68, 70-71, 74-75, 85-86, 88-89, 92—; mem. nat. screening com. Fulbright Scholarships, 1979-81. Author: German in Review, 1967, 2d edit., 1986, Der Weg zum Lesen, 1967, 3d edit., 1986, Modern German, 1971, 2d edit., 1978, 3d edit., 1992, Tonio Kroger als Weg zur Litertur, 1974, Workbook for Modern German, 1992. Served to 1st lt. M.I., U.S. Army, 1956-58. Fulbright scholar U. Heidelberg, 1958-59. Mem. MLA. Home: Cider Mill Rd Middlebury VT 05753 Office: Middlebury Coll Middlebury VT 05753

VAINIUS-NORMAN, MONIKA, graphic design company executive; b. Elmhurst, N.Y., Apr. 14, 1954; d. Kazimieras and Ellen Christa (Mocks) Vainius; m. Antanas Valys, Aug. 28, 1983 (div. Sept. 1990); 1 child, Alexander Vainius; m. David E. Norman, June 15, 1991. Student, Richmond Coll., 1972-74; BFA, Fla. Atlantic U., 1977. Asst. graphic designer Nina Design, Inc., N.Y.C., 1972-74; tech. illustrator Pratt Whitney Aircraft, West Palm Beach, Fla., 1977-78; freelance designer N.Y.C. and West Palm Beach, 1978-82; account exec. Impressions A.B.A. Industries, Roslyn Heights, N.Y., 1982-87; pres. Nika Design, Inc., Fairfield, Conn., 1987—; cons. Coun. for Adirondack Camps, Scarsdale, N.Y., 1988—. Mem. N.Y. Pub. Interest Rsch. Group, N.Y., 1988. Mem. NAFE, NOW, Fairfield Taxpayers Assn. Republican. Roman Catholic. Home: 65-16 Clinton Ave Maspeth NY 11378 Office: Nika Design Inc 287 Lakeside Dr Fairfield CT 06430-2909

VAJEEPRASEE THONGSAK, THOMAS, business planning executive; b. Udonthani, Thailand, Feb. 10, 1935; came to U.S., 1970; s. Chanmar and Pee Vajeeprasee; m. Somchit; 1 child, Rosarine. BS in Sociology, BA in Philosophy, Mahamakut U., Bangkok, 1968; MA in Edn., Kean Coll. of N.J., 1976; MA in Philosophy, NYU, 1989; PhD in Mgmt., AMA Mgmt. Inst., 1987. Tchr. Machimavas Sch., Udonthani, 1958-65; spl. instr. Chana Songkram Sch., Bangkok, 1965-68; tchrs. staff Thai Sripratoom U., Bangkok, 1968-70; salesman Met. Life of N.Y., 1974-76; rep. Mut. Life of N.Y., 1976-78; agt. Equitable Life Ins., N.Y.C., 1983-84; insp. IBI Security Svc. Inc., L.I., 1979-85; security police insp. Brandeis U., Waltham, Mass., 1985-86; chmn. Million Mut. Corp., Inc., Boston, N.Y.C., Fresno, Calif., 1987—; advisor Thai N.E. Assn., N.Y.C., 1980—, Rep. Nat. Com., Washingotn, 1980—; state advisor U.S. Congl. Adv., Washington, 1980; assoc. mem. Nat. Security Ctr., Citizen's Adv. Coun., Washington, 1989; pres., chief security agt. U.S. Bur. Security Agy., 1991; mem. Pres. Pvt. Sector Survey on Cost Control, Washington, 1989—; mem. Am. Security Coun. Adv. Bd., Washington, 1983-88. Mem. Nat. Rep. Senatorial Com., Washington; priest asst. U.S.A. Buddhayaram Temple, Bronx, 1970—; pres. S.E. Asia Found., 1970; mem. Citizens Against Govt. Waste, Washington; mem. U.S. Def. Com., Washington, 1982-86. Recipient Presdl. Seal, Rep. Orgn., 1983, 84. Mem. Internat. Assn. Chiefs of Police, President's Club, Senator's Club.

VAKIL, HASSAN CHARHARSOUGH, general and thoracic surgeon; b. Shiraz, Iran, Apr. 4, 1934; came to U.S., 1958; s. Mohammed Mehdi and Robab Vakil; m. Virgie M. Tshudy, Mar. 9, 1967; children—Jeffrey Jahan, Mark Mehdi. B.S., U. Tehran, 1954, M.D., 1958. Diplomate Am. Bd. Surgery, Am. Bd. Thoracic Surgery. Rotating intern Jersey City Med. Ctr., 1959; resident in gen. surgery Pa. Hosp. Phila., 1960-64; resident in thoracic surgery Allegheny Gen. Hosp., Pitts., 1964-66, Glen Dale Hosp., Md., 1964-66; sr. resident in thoracic surgery Emory U. Hosps., Atlanta, 1966-67; practice medicine specializing in gen. and thoracic surgery, Media, Pa., 1967—; mem. staff Riddle Meml. Hosp., chief div. surgery, 1981—; cons. in thoracic surgery Elwyn Inst. (Pa.), Fair Acres, Pa. Fellow ACS, Am. Coll. Chest Physicians; mem. AMA, Pa. Med. Soc., Delaware County Med. Soc., Am. Cancer Soc. (dir. Delaware County unit). Republican. Club: Springhaven (Wallingford, Pa.). Office: Riddle Meml Health Care Ctr I Ste 105 Media PA 19063

VALEGA, THOMAS MICHAEL, health science administrator; b. Linden, N.J., May 23, 1937; s. Paul and Anna (Bakalar) V.; m. Mary Margaret Orr, Aug. 30, 1958 (div. Mar. 15, 1988); children: Margaret, Thomas, Vinson, Catherine; m. Heidi Hughes, Mar. 15, 1988. BS, Rutgers U., 1959, PhD, 1963. Chemist USDA, Beltsville, Md., 1963-67; grants assoc. NIH, Bethesda, Md., 1968; health science adminstr. NIAMD-NIH, Bethesda, 1969-72, NIDR-NIH, Bethesda, 1972—; sec.-treas. Implantology Rsch. Group, IADR/AADR, Washington, 1985-91. Contbr. articles to profl. jours.; editor symposium proceedings, 1977. Mem. Soc. for Biomaterials (chmn. awards com. 1977, Spl. award 1984). Office: NIH-NIDR Westwood Bldg Rm 510 Bethesda MD 20892

VALENTI, CARL M., newspaper publisher. Pres., pub. Wall St. Jour., N.Y.C. Office: Dow Jones & Co Inc 200 Liberty St New York NY 10281*

VALENTINE, GEORGE EDWARD, dentist; b. Medford, Mass., Oct. 17, 1942; s. James Harold and Eleanor Alice (Newton) V.; 1 child, Adam Newton. BA in Microbiology, U. Mass., Boston, 1969; DDS, Georgetown U., 1973; MS in Health Care Mgmt., Hartford Grad. Ctr., 1980, MS in Corp. Mgmt., 1987. Lic. dentist, Conn. Sr. ptnr. Higganum/Middlesex Dental Assocs., Middletown, Conn., 1973-90; sr. attending surgery dept. Middlesex Meml. Hosp., Middletown, 1976—; pres., founder Biohazardous Environ. Cons., Middletown, 1988—; dental dir. New Eng. Cigna Employee Benefits. Cos. With USAF, 1960-64. Mem. ADA, Conn. Dental Assn., Middlesex County Dental Soc., Am. Mgmt. Assn., Acad. Gen. Dentistry, Exchange Club. Independent. Home: 126 Hopmeadow St Unit 7-G Simsbury CT 06089 Office: 1 Metro Ctr Box 297T Ste 1900 Hartford CT 06104

VALENZA, ANTOINETTE JOSEPHINE, health care executive; b. Boston, Jan. 14, 1923; d. Cesare and Antonina (BrunoGallo) V. Grad. high sch., Boston. Notary pub., Mass. Clk. Children's Hosp., Boston, 1943-45, bookkeeper, 1945-49, asst. office mgr., 1949-51, asst. treas., 1951-86, asst. sec. corp., 1951—, dir. investments, trusts, estates, ins., 1986—. Mem. Italian Home for Children, Boston, Don Orione Home for Elderly, East Boston. Mem. Exec. Women Internat. (pres. 1966-68, treas. 1989—), New Eng. Assn. for Healthcare Philanthropy, New Eng. Planned Giving Group of Nat. Com. on Planned Giving, Chatterbox Club (sec. 1952-54, pres. 1954-57, 90—, auditor 1988-90). Roman Catholic. Office: Children's Med Ctr 300 Longwood Ave Boston MA 02115-5737

VALERIO, MARK LUKE, automobile executive; b. N.Y.C., Jan. 7, 1954; s. Aronzo A. and Imelda Theresa (Bell) V. BA, Marquette U., 1976. Consumer relations rep. Chevrolet Motor div. GM, Tarrytown, N.Y., 1977-78, area service mgr., 1978-81; dist. sales mgr. GM, Phila., 1982-84; mgr. communication services CPC Group, GM, Detroit, 1985; asst. br. mgr. Motors Holding div. GM, Detroit and Denver, 1986; br. mgr. GM, Charlotte, N.C., 1986-89, L.A., 1989-91, N.Y.C., 1991—; bd. dirs. Motors Holding Investments, Conn., N.J., N.Y. Active with Statue of Liberty/Ellis Island Commn., N.Y.C., 1986. Roman Catholic. Club: Westchester Country (Rye, N.Y.). Office: GM Corp 2900 Westchester Ave 9 Sylvan Way Purchase NY 10577

VALETTE, JEAN PAUL, author; b. Paris, Oct. 21, 1937; s. Jean and Monique (Lavie) V.; m. Rebecca M. Valette, Aug. 6, 1959; children—Jean-Michael, Nathalie, Pierre. Baccalaureate, U. Poitiers (France), 1954. Diplome, Hautes Etudes Commerciales de Paris, 1959; Ph.D., U. Colo., 1962. Acct., Arthur Andersen, 1964-66; research economist Charles River Assocs., 1966-69. Author: Lisons, 1968, The Role of Transportation in Regional Economic Development, 1971, France, A Cultural Review Grammar, 1973, C'est comme ca, 1978, 86, Spanish for Mastery, 1980, 84, 88, Con. Mucho Gusto, 1980, 1984, 88, French for Mastery, 1975, 81, 86, 89, 90, Contacts: langue et culture francaises, 1976, 1981, 85, 89, French Fluency, 1985, Rencontres, 1985, Situaciones, 1988. Mem. Am. Assn. Tchrs. French, Am. Assn. Tchrs. Spanish and Portuguese. Address: 16 Mt Alvernia Rd Chestnut Hill MA 02167

VALGEMAE, MARDI, English educator; b. Viljandi, Estonia, Nov. 10, 1935; came to U.S., 1949; s. Parfeni and Ella (Peterson) V.; m. Mare M. Kivijarv, Dec. 28, 1957; children: Monika L., Sven M. BA, Rutgers U., 1957; PhD, UCLA, 1964. Asst. prof. English UCLA, L.A., 1964-68; assoc. prof. English Lehman Coll., CUNY, Bronx, 1968-74; prof. English Lehman Coll. CUNY, Bronx, 1975—; dir. city and humanities program Lehman Coll., CUNY, 1984-88, chmn. English dept., 1988—; vis. asst. profl. lectr., George Washington U., Washington, 1968. Author: Accelerated Grimace, 1972, Ikka Teatrist Moteldes, 1990; co-editor: Baltic Literature and Linguistics, 1973. 1st lt. U.S. Army. 1958-60. ACLS European Travel grantee, 1970, 81; Woodrow Wilson fellow, 1960. Mem. Modern Lang. Assn. Am., Assn. Advancement Baltic Studies, PEN. Office: CUNY Lehman Coll Dept English Bronx NY 10468

VALIMONT, SISTER ANASTASIA MARY, social services administrator; b. Karthaus, Pa., Dec. 3, 1920; d. Herman and Nellie (Fye) V. RN, St. Vincent's Sch. Nursing, Erie, Pa., 1943; BSN, Villa Maria Coll., 1950; MSN, Cath. U. Am., 1956. RN, Pa.; lic. nursing home adminstr., Pa. Dir. nursing edn. and nursing svc. Spencer Hosp., Meadville, Pa., 1958-74, hosp. adminstr., 1984-86; v.p. patient affairs St. Mary's Home of Erie, 1975-87, nursing home adminstr., 1987—; diocesan rep. Bishop's Call to Acting Meeting, Washington, 1979; in-svc. patient's rights and aging process Twinbrook, Alpine and Spencer Nursing Homes, Erie and Meadville, 1980; cons.

to SVD, Divine Word Residence, Techny, Ill., 1983, 87-90. Author: (publ.) Nursing Home Week, 1978; editor: (quar. newsletter) Coun. Nursing Home Nurses, 1982-84. Bd. dirs. Lake Area Health Edn. Ctr., sec., 1990, v.p., 1991; bd. dirs. Meadville Med. Ctr., 1991—. Recipient Outstanding Nursing award Crawford County Dist. Nurses, 1974, Erie County Dist. Nurses, 1980. Mem. ANA (talent bank), Exec. Coun. Nursing Homes, Erie Rotary, Sigma Theta Tau. Roman Catholic. Office: Saint Marys Home of Erie 607 E 26th St Erie PA 16504-2887

VALLONE, GERARD FRANK, philosopher, educator; b. Bronx, N.Y., Sept. 18, 1942; s. Frank and Ida (Marchesani) Vallone. BA, St. Joseph's Coll., Yonkers, N.Y., 1964; MA, Fordham U., 1967, PhD, 1979. Ordained to Interfaith Ministry, 1991. Instr. St. Joseph's Coll., Bklyn., 1967-69; prof. Pace U., White Plains, N.Y., 1969--. Contbr. articles to profl. jours. Mem. Am. Philos. Assn., Inst. Gen. Semantics, Inst. Advancement of Philosophy for Children (assoc. mem., cons. 1980--). Home: 1964 Lurting Ave Bronx NY 10461-1333 Office: Pace U North Broadway White Plains NY 10603

VALSAMAKIS, EMMANUEL ANTHONY, electrical engineer; b. Istanbul, Turkey, May 11, 1933; came to U.S., 1955; s. Andonios Dimitriou and Alexandra (Horianou) V.; m. Aliki Apostolides, Jan. 31, 1960; children: Andonios, Alexandra. BSEE, Robert Coll., 1955; MEE, Rensselaer Poly. Inst., 1958, PhD, 1963. Instr. Rensselaer Poly. Inst., Troy, N.Y., 1956-61, rsch. ast., 1961-62; rsch. scientist Grumman Aircraft, Bethpage, N.Y., 1962-67; staff, adv. physicist IBM, Hopewell Jct., N.Y., 1967-76; rsch. staff mem. IBM, Yorktown Heights, N.Y., 1976-80; adv. engr. IBM, Hopewell Junction, 1980-90, sr. engr., 1990—; lectr. elec. engring. dept. SUNY, New Paltz, 1985—. Mem. IEEE, Am. Phys. Soc., N.Y. Acad. Scis., Tau Beta Pi, Eta Kappa Nu, Sigma Xi. Office: IBM Corp Rte 52 Facility Z/40E Hopewell Junction NY 12533

VALSAMIS, MARIUS PETER, neuropathologist, educator; b. N.Y.C., Feb. 23, 1932; s. Peter Christ and Anna (Demetrokopoulous) V.; m. Nancy Weems, June 16, 1957; children: Helen Anna, Demetrios Peter, Ariadne Irene. AB, Columbia Coll., 1953; MD, SUNY, Bklyn., 1957. Intern Hosp. St. Raphael, New Haven, Conn., 1957-58; resident physician King's County Hosp., Bklyn., 1958-59; NIH tng. fellow SUNY Downstate Med. Ctr., Brklyn., 1959-63, clin. asst. prof. pathology, nueropathology, 1967-69; surgeon Off. Surg. Gen. PHS, Bethesda, Md., 1963-65; instr. Neurology, Pathology Jefferson Med. Coll., Phila., 1965-69; chief of labs. Bklyn. State Hosp., 1967-69; assoc. prof. Pathology (Neuropathology) Albert Einstein Med. Coll., The Bronx, N.Y., 1969-74; prof. pathology (neuropathology), dir pathophysiology course N.Y. Med. Coll., Valhalla, N.Y., 1974—; cons. Anatomic Pathology Cert. Nat. Cancer Inst., Bethesda, Md., 1964—, Clin. Ctr. Nat. Inst. Health, Bethesda, 1981—. Author (with others) AIDS (chapt. on neuropathology); contbr. articles sci. jours. Chmn. Med. Commn. U.S. Fencing Assn., Colo. Springs, Colo., 1972-84, 87—; mgr. Pan Am. Olympic Fencing Team, Colo. Springs, 1975, 1979, U.S. Olympic Fencing Team, 1976, 1980; mem. Commn. Medicale, Fed. Internat. d' Escrime, Paris, 1978—. Sr. surgeon USPHS, 1963-65. Fellow AAAS, N.Y. Acad. Scis., mem. Am. Assn. Neuropathologists (archivist), The Fencers' Club, (bd. dirs. N.Y. 1969—). Home: 375 Vanderbilt Ave Brooklyn NY 11238-1010 Office: NY Med Coll Valhalla NY 10595

VALTMAN, EDMUND, editorial cartoonist; b. Tallinn, Estonia, May 31, 1914; came to U.S., 1949, naturalized, 1959; s. Johannes and Pauline Elisabet (Kukk) V.; m. Helmi Grunberg, July 17, 1943. Student, Art and Applied Art Sch., Estonia, 1942-44, Hartford Art Sch. Conn., 1953-57. Freelance cartoonist and comml. artist Tallinn, 1936-42; editorial cartoonist Eesti Sona, Tallinn, 1942-44, Eesti Post, Geislingen, Germany, 1945-49, Hartford (Conn.) Times, 1951-75; freelance cartoonist, grapic artist Hartford, 1975—. Exhbns. include The Great Challange, Washington, London, Tokyo, 1958-59, Politics 1960, Columbia U., 1960, Internat. Salon Cartoons, Montreal, 1968-71, World Cartoon Festival, Belgium, 1971; exhibited paintings Wadworth Atheneum, Hartford, Silvermine Guild, Norwalk, New Britain Mus., Slater Meml. Mus., Norwich, Green Gallery, Guilford, Conn., Shepee Gallery, N.Y.C. Recipient Pulitzer prize for cartooning, 1962, Leadership medal Greater Hartford C. of C., 1962, Gannett Newspaper Frank Tripp award, 1963, Pub. Interest award Nat. Safety Coun., 1958, Graphic award Old Lyme Art Works, 1985. Mem. Assn. Am. Editorial Cartoonists, Nat. Cartoonists Soc. (Silver Plaque on T-Square 1962, graphic arts awards 1982, 84, painting award 1991), Conn. Acad. Fine Arts, Canton Artists Guild, West Hartford Art League.

VAN, PETER, lawyer; b. Boston, Sept. 7, 1936; s. Frank Lewis and Ruth (Spevack) V.; m. Faye Ann Zinck, 1991; children: Jami Lynne, Robert Charles. BA, Dartmouth, 1958; LLD, Boston Coll., 1961. Bar: Mass. 1962. Assoc. Brown, Rudnick, Freed and Gesmer, Boston, 1961-63; assoc. Fine and Ambrogne, Boston, 1963-65, prtnr., 1966-73, sr. ptnr., 1973—, mng. ptnr., chmn. exec. com., 1988-90; ptnr., mem. exec. com. Mintz, Levin, Cohn, Ferris, Glovsky and Popeo, P.C., Boston, 1990—. Mem. fin. com., trustee Beth Israel Hosp. Boston. Mem. Masons. Office: One Financial Ctr Boston MA 02111

VAN AGTMAEL, ANTOINE WILLEM, financial manager; b. Ryswyk, Netherlands, Nov. 7, 1944; came to U.S. 1968; s. Adriaan M.G. and Adriana (Verhulst) Van A.; m. Emily Barbara Kaufman, Aug. 12, 1948; children: Jenny, Peter. Ec.Candidatus, Erasmus U., Rotterdam, Holland, 1967; MA, Yale U., 1970; MBA, NYU, 1973. Adj. dir. NBBS, Leiden, Holland, 1967-68; v.p. Bankers Trust, N.Y.C., 1970-75; mng. dir. Thai Investment & Securities Co., Ltd., Bangkok, Thailand, 1975-79; sr. investment officer Internat. Fin. Corp., Washington, 1979-83; div. chief World Bank, Washington, 1984-85; dep. dir. Internat. Fin. Corp., Washington, 1986-87; pres. Emerging Mkts. Investors Corp., Washington, 1987—; mng. dir. Strategic Investment Mgmt., Washington, 1987—; bd. dirs. India Growth Fund, N.Y.C., 1988—, Emerging Markets Strategic Fund, Luxemburg, 1988—; adv. bd. Chile Investment Co., Santiago, 1988-90; capital markets com. Inter-Am. Investment Corp., Washington, 1990—. Author: Emerging Securities Markets, 1984, Practical Financial Management, 1979; co-editor: The World's Emerging Stock Markets, 1992. Office: Emerging Mkts Investors Corp 2000 K St NW Washington DC 20006-1809

VAN ANTWERPEN, FRANKLIN STUART, federal judge; b. Passaic, N.J., Oct. 23, 1941; s. Franklin John and Dorothy (Hoedemaker) Van A.; m. Kathleen Veronica O'Brien, Sept. 12, 1970; children: Joy, Franklin W., Virginia. BS in Engring. Physics, U. Maine, 1964; JD, Temple U., 1967; postgrad., Nat. Jud. Coll., 1980. Bar: Pa. 1969, U.S. Dist. Ct. (ea. dist.) Pa. 1971, U.S. Ct. Appeals (3d cir.) 1971, U.S. Supreme Ct. 1972. Corp. counsel Hazeltine, Corp., N.Y.C., 1967-70; chief counsel Northampton County Legal Aid Soc., Easton, Pa., 1970-71; assoc. Hemstreet & Smith, Easton, 1971-73; ptnr. Hemstreet & VanAntwerpen, Easton, 1973-79; judge Ct. Common Pleas of Northampton County (Pa.), 1979-87, U.S. Dist. Ct. (ea. dist.) Pa., Phila., 1987—; trial judge U.S. vs. Scarfo, 1988-89; adj. prof. Northampton County Area Community Coll., 1976-81; solicitor Palmer Twp., 1971-79; gen. counsel Fairview Savs. and Loan Assn., Easton, 1973-79. Recipient Booster award Bus. Indsl. and Profl. Assn., 1979, George Palmer award Palmer Twp., 1980, Man of Yr. award, 1981, Law Enforcement Commendation medal Nat. Soc. SAR, 1990; named an Alumnus Who Has Made a Difference in the World, U. Maine, 1991. Mem. ABA (com. on jud. edn.), Fed. Bar Assn. (hon.), Pa. Bar Assn., Northampton County Bar Assn., Am. Judicature Soc., Pomfret Club, Nat. Lawyers Club (Washington), Union League Club. Office: US Dist Ct 7614 US Courthouse Independence Mall W Philadelphia PA 19106

VANARSDALL, ROBERT LEE, JR., orthodontist, educator; b. Crewe, Va., Feb. 7, 1940; s. Robert Lee Sr. and Margie Mae (Jenkins) V.; m. Sandra E. Hoffman, Aug. 11, 1962; children: Robert Lee III, Lesley, Ashley. BA in Econs., Coll. William and Mary, 1962; DDS, Med. Coll. Va., 1970; cert. Orthodontics and Periodontics, U. Pa., 1973. Diplomate Am. Acad. Periodontology, Am. Bd. Orthodontics. Staff Children's Hosp., Phila., 1973—; chmn. dept. orthondontics U. Pa., Phila., 1981—; prof. dentistry Med. Coll. Pa., Phila., 1989—; bd. dirs. Nat. Dental Ins. Co., Denver. Editor: Internat. Jour. Adult Orthodontics and Orthognathic Surgery, 1986—; editorial bd. profl. jours.; contbr. articles to profl. jours. Bd. dirs. Phila. Soc. William and Mary Alumni Assn. Lt. USNR, 1962-65. Fellow Coll. Physicians of Phila. 1978, Am. Coll. Dentistry 1980. Mem. ADA, Am. Assn. Orthodontists, Stomatological Club Phila., Angle Soc. Orthodontists, Phila. Soc. Orthodontists (pres. 1989, chmn. sci. affairs coun. 1990—). Roman Catholic. Home: 208 Ashwood Rd Villanova PA 19085 Office: U Pa Sch Dental Medicine Hoth and Spruce Sts Philadelphia PA 19104

VANASSE, ROBERT BERNARD, management consultant; b. New Bedford, Mass., Feb. 20, 1962; s. Bernard Vincent and Gladys (Souza) V. BS, Boston Coll., 1985; postgrad., Georgetown U., 1986-91, Oxford U., 1988. Rsch. assoc. Temple, Barker & Sloane, Washington, 1986-88; policy analyst for sci. space and tech. Rep. Study Com., U.S. Ho. of Reps., Washington, 1988; asst. dir. Rep. Study Com., U.S. Ho. of Reps., 1988-89; analyst Naval Rsch. Lab., 1990; dir. microcomputer ctr. U.S. Naval Rsch. Lab., 1991; assoc. Samuels Internat. Assocs., 1991—; dir. U.S. Ho. of Reps. Legis. Assts. Assn., Washington, 1988-89. Co-chmn. Students for Reagan-Bush, Boston, 1984. Mem. Boston Coll. Club of Washington (chmn. career network 1991-92), Wamsutta Club (New Bedford, Mass.), Capitol Hill Club. Republican. Home: 3338 O St NW Washington DC 20007 Office: Samuels Internat Assocs 1912 Sunderland Pl NW Washington DC 20007

VAN BLARCUM, BARBARA HAPPE, corporate relations executive; b. Toronto, Can., Mar. 27, 1945; d. William Henry and Jane Hammond (Barnes) Happe. BA, Purdue U., 1968, MS in Edn., 1969. Dir. corp. info. Marriott Corp., Washington, 1972-80; dir. corp. rels. The Deltona Corp., Miami, Fla., 1980-82; sr. dir. investor rels. Wendy's Internat., Dublin, Ohio, 1982-85; v.p. corp. communications Dynalectron Corp., McLean, Va., 1986; dir. corp. and investor rels. Fedders Corp., Peapack, N.J., 1987—, v.p., 1992—; pvt. cons., 1979-87. NDEA fellow, 1968. Mem. Nat. Investor Rels. Inst., Pub. Rels. Soc. Am. (accredited, chmn. investors rels. sect. 1981, founding mem. Hall of Fame investor rels. sect. 1990). Episcopalian. Home: 12H Dorado Dr Morristown NJ 07960-6039 Office: Fedders Corp 158 Hwy 206 Peapack NJ 07977-0265

VAN BUREN, MAARTEN, consumer products company executive; b. The Netherlands, Feb. 27, 1941; came to U.S., 1963; m. Louise Visser, July 21, 1964; children: Erik, Alex, Kristin. BS in Chem. Engring., The Netherlands U., 1963; MBA in Fin., U. Chgo., 1970. Mgmt. positions with Abbott Labs., North Chgo., 1977; gen. mgr., corp. engring. Lever Bros. Co., N.Y.C., 1977-79, dir. mfg., 1980-82, v.p. mfg. and engring., 1982—, sr. v.p. mfg., engring., product and packaging devel., 1987—. Vice-pres. adv. bd. Juvenile Diabetes Found. Mem. Am. Inst. Chem. Engrs. Home: Hampton Ln New Canaan CT 06840-4141 Office: 390 Park Ave New York NY 10022-4613

VAN CAMPEN, DARRELL ROBERT, chemist; b. Trio Buttes, Colo., July 15, 1935; s. Robert Lewis and Pauline (Comer) Van C.; m. Orlene Crone, Sept. 8, 1958 (div. 1976); children: Anthony, Bryan; m. Judith Ann Gorsky, June 27, 1978; 1 child, John. BS, Colo. State U., 1957; MS, N.C. State U., 1960, PhD, 1962. Postdoctoral fellow Cornell U., Ithaca, N.Y., 1962-63; rsch. chemist USDA ARS, Ithaca, 1964-80, lab. dir., 1980—. Contbr. articles and revs. to profl. jours. and chpts. to books. NIH fellow, 1962. Mem. Sigma Xi, Alpha Zeta, Phi Kappa Phi. Home: 117 Simsbury Dr Ithaca NY 14850-1728 Office: USDA ARS Plant Soil & Nutrition Lab Tower Road Ithaca NY 14853

VAN CAMPEN, STEPHEN BERNARD, business executive, consultant; b. East Stroudsburg, Pa., Oct. 1, 1941; s. Bernard Allen and Marion (Van Whye) Van C.; m. Ellen Baars, July 22, 1989; children: Brendon, Regan, Meghan, Taylor, Hannah. BS in Sci. and Pre-Veterinary Med., Pa. State U., 1959-64; postgrad. in indsl. rels., George Washington U. Grad. Sch, 1965-68; law student, U. Balt., 1966-68. With FDA, Balt., Washington, 1964-66; indsl. rels. officer Joseph E. Seagrams & Sons, Balt., N.Y.C., San Francisco, 1966-72; worldwide dir. exec. staffing RCA/Hertz Corp., N.Y.C., 1972-74; dir. internat. indsl. rels. Revlon Internat., N.Y.C., 1974; pres./owner/cons. Gilbert & Van Campen Exec. Search, Internat. (subs.: J.B. Gilbert Assocs., Inc., Amtrade Assocs., Internat., GVC Fin. Svcs.), N.Y.C., 1974—; owner Lillagraved Hotel Corp., Ocean Grove, N.J., 1992—. Active Repub. fundraising, N.J. Repub. Gov.'s Club, N.J. State Fin. Com.; appointed Congressman Zimmer's Warren County N.J. Fed. Adv. Com., Warren County Econ. Adv. Coun., N.J. Gov.'s apointee and Chmn. of Fed. enacted Del. Water Gap Nat. Recreation Area Citizens Adv. Comm., Vice Chmn. Warren County Community Coll. Bd. Trustees; chmn. Warren County Community Coll. Found. Bd.; exec. bd. Tri-County Washington Coun. Boy Scouts of Am.; mem. First N.J. Trade Del. to Soviet Union. Mem. ASTD, Am. Mgmt Assns., Am. Coun. on Germany, U.S. C. of C., Nat. Fgn. Trade Coun., World Trade Inst., US-USSR Trade and Econ. Coun., N.Y. C. of C. and Industry, N.J. C. of C., Commerce and Industry Assn. N.J., Am. C. of C.s and U.S. Bus. Couns. Abroad, Soc. Human Resource Mgmt., Nat. Assn. of Corporate and Profl. Recruiters, Employment Mgmt. Assn., N.Y. Pers. Mgmt. Assn., Soc. Plastics Engrs., Soc. Cosmetic Chemists, Sm. Bus. Adv. Coun. Republican. Methodist. Home: 37 Petersburg Rd Hackettstown NJ 07840-4903 Office: Gilbert & Van Campen Intl 420 Lexington Ave Ste 1624 New York NY 10170-1624

VANCE, ANDREW PETER, lawyer; b. Detroit, Jan. 23, 1925; s. Peter Andrew and Anna (Maktos) V.; m. Olvia Cambourelis, Nov. 23, 1952; children: Peter, Cathy, Penny, Dorothy. BA, Harvard Coll., 1948; LLB, Harvard Law Sch., 1952. Trial atty. U.S. Dept. Justice, Washington, 1953-62; chief customs sect. U.S. Dept. Justice, N.Y.C., 1962-76; sr. ptnr. Barnes, Richardson & Colburn, N.Y.C., 1976—; mem. Adv. Com. to Ct. Appeals Fed. Cir., Washington, 1983—, chmn., 1992—; mem. Adv. Com. Ct. International. Trade, N.Y.C., 1987—. Contbr. articles to profl. jours. Trustee Greenwood Union Cemetary, Rye, N.Y., 1984—, St. Photios Found., St. Augustine, Fla., 1990—, Juanita Coll., Huntingdon, Pa., 1990—. Recipient St. Paul's medal Greek Orthodox Archdiocese N. Am. and S. Am., 1976. Mem. ABA (chmn. Standing Com. on Customs Law 1987-91), Customs & Internat. Trade Bar Assn. (pres. 1990—), Fed. Cir. Bar Assn. (pres. 1989-90), Order of St. Andrew. Greek Orthodox. Office: Barnes Richardson & Colburn 475 Park Ave S New York NY 10016

VANCE, CYRUS ROBERTS, lawyer, former government official; b. Clarksburg, W.Va., Mar. 27, 1917; s. John Carl and Amy (Roberts) V.; m. Grace Elsie Sloane, Feb. 15, 1947; children: Elsie Nicoll, Amy Sloane, Grace, Camilla, Cyrus Roberts. Student, Kent Sch.; B.A., Yale U., 1939, LL.B., 1942, LL.D. (hon.), 1968; LL.D. (hon.), Marshall U., 1963, Trinity Coll., 1968, W.Va. U., 1969, Bowling Green U., 1969, Salem Coll., 1970, Brandeis U., 1971, Amherst Coll., 1974, W.Va. Wesleyan U., 1974, Harvard U., 1981, Colgate U., 1981, Gen, Theol. Sem., 1981, Williams Coll., 1981, Notre Dame U., 1982, Mt. Holyoke Coll., 1982. Bar: N.Y. State 1947, U.S. Supreme Ct. 1970. Asst. to pres. Mead Corp., 1946-47; assoc. Simpson Thacher & Bartlett, N.Y.C., 1947-56; ptnr. Simpson Thacher & Bartlett, 1956-61, 67-77, 80—; gen. counsel Dept. Def., 1961-62; sec. of army, 1962-63, dep. sec. def., 1964-67; spl. rep. of Pres. Cyprus, 1967, Korea, 1968; U.S. negotiator Paris Peace Conf. on Vietnam, 1968-69; sec. state, 1977-80, personal envoy UN Sec. Gen. in Yugoslavia crisis, 1991—; spl. counsel preparedness investigating subcom. Senate Armed Services Com., 1957-60; cons. counsel Spl. Com. on Space and Astronautics, U.S. Senate, 1958; chmn. com. on adjudication of claims Adminstrv. Conf. U.S.; mem. Com. To Investigate Alleged Police Corruption in N.Y.C., 1970-72; chmn. UN Devel. Corp., 1976; mem. Ind. Com. on Disarmament and Security Issues, N.Y. State Commn. on Govt. Integrity, N.Y. State Jud. Commn. on Minorities in the Ct.; bd. dirs. Gen. Dynamics Corp., N.Y. Times; bd. dirs. Fed. Res. Bank of N.Y., chmn., 1989-91. Trustee Yale Corp., 1968-78, 80-87; trustee Rockefeller Found., 1970-77, 80-82, chmn., 1975-77; chmn. Am. Ditchley Found., 1981—. Lt. USNR, 1942-46. Recipient Medal of Freedom, 1969. Fellow Am. Coll. Trial Lawyers; mem. ABA, Assn. of Bar of City of N.Y. (pres. 1974-76), Council on Fgn. Relations (dir., vice chmn. 1985-87), Japan Soc. (chmn. 1985—). Office: Simpson Thacher & Bartlett 425 Lexington Ave New York NY 10017-3909

VANCE, DON KELVIN, baking company executive; b. Detroit, Jan. 3, 1935; s. George Paul and Marie Jo (Nichols) V.; children—James Delano, Sarah Elizabeth, David Paul. B.B.A., U. Mich., 1957, M.B.A., 1958. Various positions ITT Continental Baking Co., 1958-72; v.p. ITT Continental Baking Co., Rye, N.Y., 1972-83; sr. v.p., div. pres. Am. Bakeries Co., N.Y.C., 1983-86; cons. to baking industry; pres., chief oper. officer Country Home Bakers, Bridgeport, Conn., 1991—. Served with USAFR, 1958-64. Methodist. Club: WeeBurn Country (Darien, Conn.). Office: Country Home Bakers 1700 Barnum Ave Bridgeport CT 06610-3206

VANCE, JAMES HARRISON, computer science educator, consultant; b. Memphis, Jan. 15, 1941; s. James David and Fay Serepta (Harrison) V.; m. Maria Teresa Contreras, Dec. 29, 1960; children: Laura Marie, Deborah, Elaine. BS, Southeastern La. U., 1963; MS, U. Southwestern La.; 1966. Math modeler, programmer, engr. Apollo Program, Houston and Huntsville, Ala., 1966-71; instr. Wilkes Community Coll., Wilkesboro, N.C., 1971-73; high sch. tchr. Bellows Free Acad., Fairfax, Vt., 1973-74; prof. computer sci., math., computers for physics Wentworth Inst. Tech., Boston, 1974—; pvt. practice cons. New England area, 1978—. Author publs. on interstellar flight; devloped math. model and software for orbital heating analysis allowing 1st supercircular speed re-entry. Republican. Home: 4 Rocky Hill Rd Amherst NH 03031-2805 Office: Wentworth Inst Tech 550 Huntington Ave Boston MA 02115-5998

VANCE, WILLIAM LYNN NEWTON, writer, English educator; b. Dupree, S.D., Apr. 19, 1934; s. Earl Howard and Ruby Marie (Harmon) V. AB, Oberlin Coll., 1956; MA, U. Mich., 1957, PhD, 1962; LLD (hon.), U. S.D., 1992. Asst. prof. Boston U., 1962-69, assoc. prof., 1969-73, prof., 1973—, chmn. English dept., 1985-88, dir. Am. studies, 1988-90; cons. Giovanni Agnelli Found., Turin, Italy, 1991—. Author: America's Rome, vols. I-II, 1989 (Phi Beta Kappa Emerson award 1990, Assn. Am. Pub.'s award 1989); contbr. numerous articles to profl. jours. Recipient Metcalf Cup and prize for excellence in teaching Boston U., 1992; Guggenheim fellow, 1990-91. Democrat. Home: 255 Beacon St Boston MA 02116-1371 Office: Boston U 236 Bay State Rd Boston MA 02215-1403

VANCISIN, JOSEPH RICHARD, sports association executive; b. Bridgeport, Conn., June 14, 1922; s. Stephen and Susan V.; m. Elizabeth Ann Butler, Apr. 21, 1951; children—Richard, Susan. B.A., Dartmouth Coll., 1944; M.A., U. Minn., 1956. Supr. Joseph Seagram & Sons, Relay, Md., 1946-47; asst. basketball coach U. Mich., 1947-48; asst. coach basketball and baseball U. Minn., 1948-56; head basketball coach Yale U., 1956-75; exec. dir. Nat. Assn. Basketball Coachs U.S., Branford, Conn., 1975—; dir. Yale Golf Course, 1971-74; trustee Basketball Hall of Fame. Editor: Basketball Bull, 1975—. Chief of mission Intercontinental Cup.; assoc. fellow Morse Coll., Yale U.; mgr. 1976, 80 team Olympic Basketball. Cpl. USAF. Mem. U.S.A. Basketball Assn. (coun. 1979), Dartmouth Alumni Assn., Nat. Assn. Basketball Coaches (pres. 1973-74), Beta Theta Pi. Office: PO Box 307 Branford CT 06405-0307

VAN COVERDEN, THOMAS J., association executive; b. Detroit, Oct. 7, 1947; s. William and Virginia (Lawrence) Van C.; m. Nancy Ruth Siebert, Feb. 14, 1972; children: Erica, Rebecca, Deborah (dec.). MA-BA, U. Detroit, 1971. Congl. staff Honorable Martha Griffiths, Detroit, 1963-69; buyer comml. stationery J. L. Hudson Co., Detroit, 1970-72; dist. office mgr. Honorable Martha Griffiths, Detroit, 1972-73; legis. asst. Honorable Martha Griffiths, Washington, 1973-75; dir. policy analysis Nat. Assn. Community Health Ctrs., Washington, 1975-85, exec. dir., 1985—; pres. Nat. Primary Care Inst., Washington, 1988—, Nachc Ins. Consortium, Washington, 1988—, Community Health Ctr. Capital Corp., Washington, 1988—; bd. mem. Spl. Love, Inc., Front Royal, Va., 1990—. Co-author: Health Policy & Issue Guidebook, annually since 1978, Health Policy Seminar Series Guidebooks, annually since 1980; contbr. articles to profl. jours. With U.S. Army, 1971-75. Mem. Am. Soc. Assn. Execs., Am. Soc. for Pub. Adminstrn., Pi Kappa Delta, Pi Sigma Alpha, Am. Legion. Office: Nat Assn Community Health 1330 New Hampshire Ave #122 Washington DC 20036

VAN DAM, BRIAN MATHYS, SR., electronics executive; b. Pawtucket, R.I., Dec. 22, 1959; s. Mathys Jan and Pauline Eugenie (Dextraze) Van D.; m. Jane Ann Humes, Aug. 17, 1985; children: Brian Mathys Jr., Jenna Lea. BBA cum laude, Bryant Coll., 1981. Intern Arthur Young & Co., Providence, R.I., 1979-81; supervisory sr. auditor Arthur Young & Co., Providence, 1983-84; staff auditor Price Waterhouse, Providence, 1981-82, audit sr., 1982-83; sr. internal auditor Tyco Labs. Inc., Exeter, N.H., 1984-86; controller Atlantic Coast Electrnonics div. Tyco, Pompano Beach, Fla., 1986-87, N. Am. Printed Cirs. div. Tyco, Stafford, Conn., 1987-89; mgr. admninstrn. and fin. Tyco Backplane div. Tyco, Stafford Springs, Conn., 1989—; pres., treas. Stafford (Conn.) Water Power Co., 1989-90, bd. dirs.; patrolman Enfield Aux. Police, 1988-89, lt., 1990-91, capt., 1991—. Coach Cumberland (R.I.) Little Baseball League, 1980-81, Cumberland Pre-teen Football, 1980-81; bd. dirs. Rhode Island Youth Orgn., Providence, 1984. Mem. Delta Mu Delta. Republican. Episcopalian. Home: 7 Arrow St Enfield CT 06082-4609 Office: Tyco Backplanes 15 Industrial Rd Stafford CT 06075-9999

VANDEGRIFT, JOHN RAYMOND, priest, librarian; b. Wilmington, Del., Apr. 27, 1928; s. Ira Ambers and Florence (Metzler) V. AB in Chemistry, Princeton U., 1949; STB, Dominican House, 1959, STL/STLr, 1962; MLS, Columbia U., 1975. Ordained priest, Roman Cath. Ch., 1960. Lab. asst. Merck & Co., Inc., Rahway, N.J., 1949-52; instr. in theology Xaverian Coll., Silver Spring, Md., 1961-62, Aquinas Coll., Grand Rapids, Mich., 1962-65, Mercy Cen. Nursing Sch., Grand Rapids, 1963-65, Albertus Magnus Coll., New Haven, 1968-70; instr. in theology and philosophy St. Catharine (Ky.) Coll., 1965-68; dir. Dominican Coll. Libr., Washington, 1970—; instr. theology Aquinas Inst. for Religion, Grand Rapids, summers 1963-70; spiritual moderator Dominican Laity Chpt., McLean, Va., 1989—; chaplain Team of Our Lady, Arlington, Va., 1984—; preacher Sunday Eucharist, Washington, 1960—; confessor Shrine of Immaculate Conception, Washington, 1980—. Mem. ALA, D.C. Libr. Assn., Am. Theol. Libr. Assn., Washington Theol. Consortium (chmn. com. of librs. 1981), Cluster Periodical Ctr. (chmn. librs.). Home: 487 Michigan Ave NE Washington DC 20017-1584 Office: Dominican Coll Libr 487 Michigan Ave NE Washington DC 20017-1584

VANDEGRIFT, VAUGHN, chemistry educator, academic administrator; b. Jersey City, Dec. 7, 1946; s. Frederick M. and Marjorie A. (Frelond) V.; m. Suzanne Margaret Bouchoux, July 26, 1969; children: Beth Ann, David Vaughn, Mark Frederick. BA, Montclair State Coll., 1968, MA, 1970; PhD, Ohio U., 1974. Asst. prof. chemistry Ill. State U., Normal, 1974-76; asst. prof. Murray State U., Ky., 1976-79, assoc. prof., 1979-84, chmn. dept. chemistry, prof., 1982-88; dean, prof. chemistry sch. math. and natural sci. Montclair State U., 1988-91; vis. assoc. prof. So. Ill. U., Carbondale, 1980-81. Reviewer for pubs. Contbr. articles to profl. jours. Mem. edn. and tng. com. Rsch. and Devel. Coun. N.J. NDEA fellow, 1970-74; grantee Fats and Proteins Research Found., 1977-81, NSF, 1986-88. Mem. Am. Chem. Soc. (Ky. Lake sect.) (chmn. 1983-84, reviewer Jour. Chem. Edn., Jour. Agr. and Food Chemistry 1980—, alt. councillor North Jersey sect. 1990—), Sigma Xi (pres. Murray State U. chpt. 1980-81, southeast regional lectr. 1984—), Phi Kappa Phi, Omicron Delta Kappa (Outstanding Murray State U. Faculty mem. 1984). Home: 91 Birchwood Ter Wayne NJ 07470-3461 Office: Montclair State U Sch Math & Natural Sci Montclair NJ 07043

VANDEKIEFT, RUTH MARGUERITE, English literature educator; b. Holland, Mich., Sept. 12, 1925; d. John Martin and Cornelia (Bogard) Vande K. BA, Meredith Coll., 1946; MA, U. Mich., 1947, PhD, 1957. Instr. English Calvin Coll., Grand Rapids, Mich., 1947-50, Wellesley (Mass.) Coll., 1956-59; assoc. prof. English Fairleigh Dickinson U., Madison, N.J., 1959-60; asst. prof., assoc. prof., then prof. English lit. Queens Coll.-CUNY, 1961-90, prof. emeritus, 1990—. Author: Eudora Welty, 1962, 2d edit., 1988; editor: Thirteen Stories by Eudora Welty, 1965. Minnie Cummock Blodgett fellow AAUW, 1960-61. Mem. MLA, Soc. Study So. Lit. (pres. 1980-82). Democrat. Presbyterian. Home: 320 E 23d St Apt 16H New York NY 10010

VANDENBURG, MARY LOU, psychologist; b. Passaic, N.J., Dec. 18, 1943; d. Nicholas and Louise (Rosiello) Yacono; m. James Joseph Vandenburg, Jr., July 2, 1966; 1 child, James Joseph III. BA, William Paterson, 1965; MA, Montclair Coll., 1982; MS, Pace U., 1986, D of Psychology, 1988. Cert. tchr., sch. guidance counselor; lic. psychologist. Elem. tchr. various, 1966-67, 76-80; therapist Pequannock Valley Mental Health Ctr., 1985-90; sch. psychologist Andover Schs., 1988—; pvt. practice Butler, N.J.; lectr. ednl. enrichment programs, 1980—; psychotherapist various schs., clinics, hosps. Author children's books; contbr. articles to profl. jours. Recipient honor cert. Freedom Found., Valley Forge, Pa., Merit

Scholarship, Pace U. Mem. N.J. Assn. Sch. Psychologists, Nat. Assn. Sch. Psychologists, Am. Psychol. Assn., Sussex County Assn. of Sch. Psychologists. Home: RR 1 Box 462B Highland Lakes NJ 07422-9801 Office: 1395 State Route 23 Ste 4 Butler NJ 07405-1736

VAN DEN HAAG, ERNEST, psychology law and sociology educator; b. The Hague, Netherlands, Sept. 15, 1914; came to U.S., 1940, naturalized, 1947; s. Max and Flora (van den Haag) van den H. Student, U. Naples, Italy, 1937-38, U. Florence, Italy, 1937-38, Sorbonne U., Paris, 1938-40; M.A., State U. Iowa, 1942; Ph.D., NYU, 1952. Lectr., 1955-65, CCNY, Bklyn Coll., U. Minn., U. Colo., U. Calif.-Berkeley, Columbia U., Yale U., Harvard U.; adj. prof. social philosophy NYU, 1965-75; lectr. psychology and sociology New Sch. Social Research, N.Y.C., 1965-80; adj. prof. law N.Y. Law Sch., 1978-80; practice psychoanalysis N.Y.C., 1955-82; vis. Disting. prof. Queens Coll., CUNY, 1974-75; vis. prof. criminal justice SUNY-Albany, 1977-78; vis. prof. sociology Vassar Coll., 1969-70; John M. Olin prof. jurisprudence and pub. policy Fordham U., N.Y.C., 1982-88; Disting. scholar Heritage Found., 1981—; Freud Meml. lectr. Phila. Assn. Psychoanalysis, 1964. Author: The Fabric of Society, 1957, Education as an Industry, 1956, Passion and Social Constraint, 1963, The Jewish Mystique, 1969, Political Violence and Civil Disobedience, 1972, Punishing Criminals: Concerning a Very Old and Painful Question, 1975, Capitalism: Sources of Hostility, 1979, (with John P. Conrad) The Death Penalty: A Debate, 1983, (with John P. Conrad) The U.N.: In or Out?, 1987, (with Tom J. Farer) U.S. Ends and Means in Central America: A Debate, 1988; contbr. articles to profl. jours. Guggenheim fellow, 1967; NEH sr. fellow, 1973. Fellow Royal Econ. Soc., Am. Sociol. Assn.; mem. Mont. Pelerin Soc., Profl. Psychoanalytic Assn., Phila. Soc. (past pres.), Nat. News Council, Council on Fgn. relations. Home and Office: 118 W 79th St New York NY 10024-6445

VANDERBEEK, TONY MARTINUS, real estate broker; b. Queens, N.Y., May 2, 1967. BA, Rutgers U., 1989. Comml. real estate broker Fillmore Real Estate, Ltd., Bklyn., 1989—. Republican. Roman Catholic. Home: PO Box 2122 Livingston NJ 07039 Office: Fillmore Real Estate Ltd 1856 Flatbush Ave Brooklyn NY 11210

VANDERBILT, ALFRED GWYNNE, JR., public relations agency executive; b. N.Y.C., Dec. 20, 1949; s. Alfred Gwynne and Jeanne (Murray) V.; m. Alison Platten, Aug. 18, 1970; children: James Platten, Travis Murray. Assoc. Carl Byoir & Assocs, N.Y.C., 1981-86; v.p. Carl Byrne & Assocs., N.Y.C., 1986-88; sr. v.p., group dir. Hill & Knowlton, Inc., N.Y.C., 1988-90; pres., chief exec. officer The Vanderbilt Agy., N.Y.C., 1990—. Bd. dirs. Operation Sail, Inc., N.Y.C., 1990—, Goodwill Industries Greater N.Y., 1987—; com. mem. N.Y. '92, Dem. Conv., N.Y.C., 1992. Mem. Pub. Rels. Soc. Am. (Silver Anvil 1987), Nat. Acad. Recording Arts and Scis. (pres. 1979, nat. trustee 1978-82). Democrat. Office: The Vanderbilt Agy 11 E 47th St New York NY 10017

VANDERBILT, ARTHUR T., II, lawyer; b. Summit, N.J., Feb. 20, 1950; s. William Runyon and Jean (White) V. BA, Wesleyan U., Middletown, Conn., 1972; JD, U. Va., 1975. Bar: N.J. 1975, U.S. Dist. Ct. N.J. 1975, U.S. Supreme Ct. 1978. Jud. clk. to presiding justice N.J. Superior Ct., 1975-76, dep. atty. gen., 1976-78, asst. counsel to gov., 1978-79; ptnr. Carella, Byrne, Bain & Gilfillan, Roseland, N.J., 1979—. Author: Changing Law 1976, Jersey Justice, 1978, Law School, 1981, Treasure Wreck, 1986, Fortune's Children, 1989. Mem. ABA (Scribes award 1976), N.J. Bar Assn., Am. Judicature Soc., The Authors Guild, Inc. Republican. Presbyterian. Office: Carella Byrne Bain & Gilfillan 6 Becker Farm Rd Roseland NJ 07068-1735

VANDER DUSSEN, NEIL RICHARD, electronics company executive; b. Kansas City, Mo., Sept. 22, 1931; m. Geraldine Powers, Aug. 1953; children: Cathy, Carol. BSEE, Kans. State U., 1954; MS in Mgmt., MIT, 1970. With RCA Corp., N.Y.C., 1962-77, div. v.p., gen. mgr. broadcast systems, 1977-79, exec. v.p. diversified bus., 1979-81; pres. Sony Broadcast Products Co., Park Ridge, N.J., 1981-83; pres., chief exec. officer Sony U.S. Mktg. Co., Park Ridge, N.J., 1984-85, Sony Consumer Products Co., Park Ridge, N.J., 1984-85; pres., chief oper. officer Sony Corp. of Am., Park Ridge, N.J., 1985-91, vice chmn., 1991; ret.; bd. dirs. Sony Corp. of Am., N.Y.C. Served with U.S. Army 1954-56. Alfred P. Sloan fellow MIT, 1970; inductee Kans. State U. Coll. Engring. Hall of Fame, 1990. Mem. Soc. Motion Picture and TV Engrs., Electronic Industries Assn. (bd. govs. 1986—), Kans. State Alumni Assn., Kans. State Pres.'s Club, MIT Alumni Assn., Sigma Nu Alumni Assn. Clubs: Roxiticus Country, Mendham (N.J.) Country. Office: Sony Corp of Am Sony Dr Park Ridge NJ 07656-8001 also: Sony Corp of America 9 W 57th St New York NY 10019

VANDERHOOF-FORSCHNER, KAREN MACNEIL, foundation administrator; b. Montclair, N.J., July 25, 1951; d. Irwin and Ruth Vanderhoof; m. Thomas E. Forschner, Jan. 26, 1974; 1 child, James Thomas (dec. June 1991). BS, Muskingum Coll., 1974; MBA, U. Conn., 1982. CLU, Cert. chartered property and casualty underwriter, 1980. Corp. analyst State Auto Mutual, 1974-78; mgr. group casualty Hartford Ins. Group, 1978-80; pres., chair bd. Van-Fore Group, 1980-85; pres. Soc. of Ins. Rsch., 1987; chmn. Lyme Disease Found., Inc., Tolland, Conn., 1988—. Author: Group Automobile Insurance: A Developing Market, 1982, Entering the Group Personal Lines Market, 1983, Regulation of Group Automobile Ins., 1983; contbr. to jours. Office: Lyme Disease Found PO Box 462 Tolland CT 06084

VANDERHOST, LEONETTE LOUISE, psychologist; b. Phila., June 11, 1924; d. Charles and Pauline (McGhaney) V. BA, Hunter Coll., 1945; MA, NYU, 1949, PhD, 1968. Lic. psychologist, N.Y. Intern staff Lincoln (Ill.) State Sch., 1951-52; staff Evansville (Ind.) State Hosp., 1953-54, Children's Guidance Ctr., Dayton, Ohio, 1954-56; psychotherapist Hempstead (N.Y.) Consultation Services, 1963-66; staff, sr. psychologist Hillside Hosp., Glen Oaks, N.Y., 1957-69; sr. psychologist, chief West Nassau Mental Health Ctr., Franklin Sq., N.Y., 1959-63; pvt. practice psychologist N.Y.C., 1959—; cons. Big Sisters, N.Y., 1960-62, Health Ins. Planning, N.Y., 1962-64, Head Start, N.Y., 1967-73. Mem. Am. Psychol. Assn., Am. Orthopsychiatric Assn.

VANDER LINDE, ALBERT, educational administrator; b. Emery, S.D., Apr. 20, 1929; s. Albert and Frieda (Dittman) Vander L.; m. Odelphia Buchholz, Nov. 19, 1955 (dec. Oct. 1987); m. Roslyn Culp, Dec. 26, 1989; children: Karen Renee, Judith Ann, Mary Sue. BS, U. S.D., Springfield, 1958; MA, Colo. State U., 1962, PhD, 1971. Ednl. adminstr. secondary sch. S.D.; dir., pres. Mitchell (S.D.) Area Tech. Sch., 1967-73; dean No. Mont. Coll., Havre, 1973-78; dean, exec. dir. Sch. Vocat. Tech., Alfred State Coll., Wellsville, N.Y., 1978-91. County legislator Allegany County, N.Y., 1991—. Sgt. U.S. Army, 1952-55. Mem. Rotary (pres. sec. 1982-83, 89-91). Republican. Baptist. Home: 261 N Main St Wellsville NY 14895

VANDER NOOT, NORMAN CAREY, oil trade association administrator; b. Yonkers, N.Y., Oct. 10, 1935; s. Theodore John and Elinore Theresa (Cox) V.; m. Mary Morrison, Sept. 19, 1959; children: Matthew, Christopher, Jennifer, Stacy. BA, John Hopkins U., 1957; postgrad., Boston U., 1958-59. Asst. advt. mgr. Laconia (N.H.) Evening Citizen, 1961-64; gen. mgr. Hampton (N.H.) Union, 1964-67, Enfield (Conn.) Press, 1967-69; editor Laconia (N.H.) Evening Citizen, 1969-75; dir. energy office N.H. Gov. Meldrim Thomson, Concord, 1975-78; dir. tourism State of N.H., Concord, 1978-81; v.p. mktg. Mt. Washington Resort & Ski Area, Bretton Woods, N.H., 1981-82; dir. communications N.H. Gov. John H. Sununu, Concord, 1982-86; exec. dir. N.H. Petroleum Coun., Concord, 1986—. Editor: Live Free or Die, 1976. Trustee Ea. States Expn., Springfield, Mass., 1987—, Oil Disbursement Bd., Concord, 1988—, Air Resources Coun., Concord, 1987—; mem. Laconia Sch. Bd., 1972-78; vice chmn. Laconia Little League, 1971-75; chmn. Laconia Hwy. Safety Com., 1972-78; N.H. coord. N.E. Govs. Conf., 1982-89; chmn. Gov.'s Adv. Com. on Tourism, 1982-88, New Eng. Energy Dirs., 1977. Mem. N.H. Travel Coun. (trustee, Tourism Person of Yr. 1989), Lakes Region Assn. (pres. 1989—), Travel Industry of Am. (bd. dirs. 1979-81), Am. Bus. Assn. (bd. dirs. 1979-81), Elks. Home: RR 5 Box 161 Laconia NH 03246-9516 Office: NH Petroleum Coun 15 N Main St Concord NH 03301-4945

VANDER SCHRAAF, ANNA HENRIETTE, physician; b. Indonesia, May 22, 1928; d. Nicholas H. and Anna B.C. (Dumas) Altman; m. Eric E. Vander Schraaf; children: A. Marian, Dorine B. de Mena, Robert C., Walter D. MD, U. Amsterdam, The Netherlands, 1952. Cert. Am. Bd. Psychiatry and Neurology, child psychiatry. Pvt. practice child/adolescent & adult psychiatry Morristown, N.J., 1973—; attending dept. psychiatry Morristown Meml. Hosp., 1973—; clin. instr. Mt. Sinai Sch. Medicine, N.Y.C., 1973—; asst. psychiatrist Mt. Sinai Hosp., N.Y.C., 1973—; clin. asst. prof. Robert Wood Johnson Med. Sch. U. Medicine & Dentistry, Piscataway, N.J., 1973—; bd. dirs. Morris Somerset I.P.A., N.J.; cons. Morristown Sch. System, 1976-79. Co-author: Borderline Conditions in Children: Clinical Handbook of Child Psychiatry, 1979. Fellow Am. Acad. Child and Adolescent Psychiatry, Am. Soc. Adolescent Psychiatry; mem. AMA, Am. Psychiat. Assn., N.J. Coun. Child and Adolescent Psychiatry (past pres.). Office: 21 Perry St Morristown NJ 07960-5241

VANDERSTEEL, WILLIAM, transportation executive; b. Hilversum, The Netherlands, Mar. 21, 1919; s. Dionijs VanderSteel Schonegevel and Marion Scott Hamilton Martin; m. Betsey Stoddard, June 21, 1946 (div. Oct. 1963); children: Stoddard, Marion, William; m. Lee Benfield, Mar. 19, 1966; children: Ann, Tina. BS, MIT, 1940. Engr. Gen. Motors Corp., Detroit, 1941-42; chief engr. Cox and Stevens Aircraft Corp., Mineola, N.Y., 1945-48; pres., chief exec. officer Ampower Corp., North Bergen, N.J., 1948—, Tubexpress Systems Inc., North Bergen, N.J., 1982—; bd. dirs. Peacock Inc., Natural Park Systems, Inc. Patentee ship stabilizer, pneumatic capsule pipeline. Mem. Planning Bd., Alpine, N.J., 1982-90; bd. dirs. Citizens for a Sound Economy, Washington, Nat. Alliance for Constnl. Money, Washington. Capt. USAF, 1942-45. Mem. Exptl. Aircraft Assn., Phi Beta Epsilon. Club: Royal Scottish Automobile Soc., (Glasgow, Scotland). Home: Highwood Pl Alpine NJ 07620-9999

VAN DE WALLE, ETIENNE, demographer; b. Namur, Belgium, Apr. 29, 1932; came to U.S., 1961; s. Arnould and Yolande (Blommaert) Van De W.; m. Francine Robyns de Schneidauer, Aug. 24, 1955; children: Dominique, Nicolas, Jean-Francois, Patrice. Dr. in Law, U. Louvain, Belgium, 1956, MA in Econs., 1957, PhD in Demography, 1973. Researcher Irsac, Rwanda, Burundi, 1957-61; rsch. assoc. Princeton (N.J.) U., 1962-64, rsch. staff, 1964-67, rsch. demographer, 1967-72; vis. lectr. U. Calif., Berkeley, 1971-72; prof. U. Pa., Phila., 1972—; dir. Population Studies Ctr., U. Pa., 1976-82; sr. assoc. The Population Coun., Bamako, Mali, 1982. Author: The Female Population of France, 1974; co-author: The Demography of Tropical Africa, 1968. Fellowship Woodrow Wilson Ctr. for Scholars, 1976. Mem. Internat. Union for Scientific Study of Population, Population Assn. of Am. Home: 261 Sycamore Ave Merion Station PA 19066-1545 Office: Population Studies Ctr 3718 Locust Walk Philadelphia PA 19104-6298

VAN DE WATER, THOMAS ROGER, neuroscientist, educator; b. Oceanside, N.Y., Dec. 6, 1939; s. Lynn and Lenora (Winterson) Van De W.; m. Jeanette Adele Vilece, July 11, 1964; children: Ann Marie, Thomas Scott, Christopher Lynlee, Elizabeth Adele. AAS in Forestry, Paul Smith Coll., 1959; BS in Biology, Western Carolina U., 1961; MA in Biology, Hofstra U., 1965; PhD in Biology, NYU, 1976. Rsch. assoc. Med. Sch. Yale U., 1964-65; rsch. scientist Med. Sch. NYU, 1967-68; dir. devel. otobiology Albert Einstein Coll. Medicine, Bronx, N.Y., 1981—, prof. neurosci. and otolaryngology, 1987—, prof. otolaryngology, 1987—, dir. rsch., 1990—; lectr., author Nobel Symposium, 1985; acad. dir. ENT basic sci. course N.Y. Acad. Medicine Otolaryngology basic sci. course, 1988—. Editor: Biology & Change in Otobiology, 1986, Genetics of Hearing Impairment, 1990, Handbook of Auditory Research, Clinical Aspects; contbr. over 50 sci. publs. Eucharistic min. Holy Redeemer Ch., Freeport, N.Y. With U.S. Army Med. Corps, 1962. Mem. Assn. for Rsch. in Otolaryngology (sec./treas. 1990—), N.Y. Acad. Sci., Am. Otological Soc. (assoc.), Oto-Rhino-laryngologica Collegium Amitae Sacrum. Home: 262 Pennsylvania Ave Freeport NY 11520-1329 Office: Albert Einstein Coll Medicine 1410 Pelham Pky S Bronx NY 10461-1101

VAN DE WORKEEN, PRISCILLA TOWNSEND, small business owner and executive; b. Denver, July 9, 1946; d. Reginald and Ruth (Poor) Townsend; m. Melvin Charles Van de Workeen, Oct. 27, 1973; 1 stepchild, Scott Minot. BA in Chinese History, Wheaton Coll., Norton, Mass., 1968; postgrad., Cornell U., 1965. Asst. dir. Nat. Info. Bur., N.Y.C., 1969-73; dep. dir. Harkness Fellowships, N.Y.C. and London, 1973-83; owner, mgr. Vernalwood Enterprises, Splty. and Custom Crafts, Dudley, Mass., 1984—; co-owner, mgr. Vernalwood Bed & Breakfast, Dudley, 1989—, Folkstone/Cen. Mass. Bed & Breakfast Reservation Svc., Dudley, 1989—; co-founder, chairperson Vernalwood Conceptual Enhancements, Dudley, 1991—. Quilting and needlework tchr. Chester Corbin Libr., Webster, Mass.; bd. dirs. Hubbard Regional Hosp. Guild, Webster, 1986-91, Internat. Ctr., Worcester, Mass., 1989-90; coord. Nat. Coun. for Internat. Visitors, Washington, 1989-90; mem. Worcester County Conv. and Visitors Bus.; founder, chairperson The Concordia Found., Dudley, 1992—. Mem. Am. Bed and Breakfast Assn., Mass. Assn. Bed and Breakfast Reservation Svcs., Tri-Community Area C. of C., Webster-Dudley Garden Club. Democrat. Home and Office: Vernalwood RR 3 Box 375 Dudley MA 01571-9703

VAN DINE, ALAN CHARLES, advertising agency executive, writer; b. Ford City, Pa., Jan. 12, 1933; s. Albert and Helen (Remaley) Van D.; m. Joan Anne Hodges, Jan. 29, 1955 (div. Jan. 1971); children: Lynn, Mark, Barbara, Michael; m. Holly Long Shefler, Apr. 23, 1977. BA, Duquesne U., 1955; postgrad., U. Pitts., 1968-71. Editor Mt. Lebanon News, Pa., 1956-58; editorial dir. Pitts. Suburban Newspapers, 1958-61; writer and assoc. creative dir. Batten, Barton, Durstine & Osborne, Pitts., 1961-70; pres., creative dir. Van Dine, Horton, McNamara, Manges, Inc., Pitts., 1970-89; chmn. Van Dine, Humphrey, Inc., Pitts., 1989—; mem. adv. coun. Internat. Poetry Forum, Pitts., 1969-80. Author: Can You Imagine?, 1967, Unconventional Builders, 1977, (humor) The Encyclopedia of Advertising, 1987; columnist Pitts. mag., 1977-78, Pa. Illustrated, 1979-81; contbr. articles, essays, short stories, and poems to mags. 1st lt. USAR, 1956. Recipient numerous awards Art Dirs. Club N.Y., 1964—, Bus. and Profl. Advt. Assn., 1964—. Mem. Am. Assn. Advt. Agys., Pitts. Advt. Mgmt. Assn., Chartiers Country Club. Office: Van Dine Humphrey Inc 322 Blvd Of The Allies Pittsburgh PA 15222-1919

VAN DINE, C(HARLES) PETER, computer consultant; b. New Haven, Nov. 17, 1938; s. Charles Edward and Edith (Thorpe) Van D.; m. Elizabeth Ann Willard, Nov. 26, 1959; children: Mary Elizabeth, Jonathan Peter, Jennifer Ann, Heather Ann. BA, Yale U., 1960; MA, Trinity Coll., Hartford, Conn., 1963; postgrad., U. Conn., 1965-70. Programmer, analyst Gen. Dynamics, Elec. Boat, Groton, Conn., 1960-62; supr. engr. applications United Tech. Rsch. Ctr., E. Hartford, Conn., 1962-73; chief math. analysis United Tech. Rsch. Ctr., E. Hartford, 1973-78; mgr. CAD products Gerber Systems Tech., S. Windsor, Conn., 1978-81; mgr. mech. CAD products Prime Computer, Natick, Mass., 1981-84; prin. C. Peter Van Dine, Cons., Bolton, Conn., 1984—. Contbr. articles to profl. jours. Mem. IEEE, Ind. Computer Cons. Assn., Yale Sci. and Engring. Assn. (regional v.p. 1985—), Bolton Lake Sailing Club (vice commodore 1989—). Democrat. Roman Catholic. Home and Office: 81 Vernon Rd Bolton CT 06043-7324

VANDINE, DORA ELIZABETH, health and physical education educator; b. Muncy, Pa., Mar. 9, 1937; d. Walter Vandine and Lillian (Wagner) Manning. BS in Health and Phys. Edn., Lock Haven (Pa.) U., 1959; MA in Health and Phys. Edn., Iowa State U., 1964; PhD in Health and Phys. Edn., U. Ill., 1975. Tchr. health and phys. edn. Selinsgrove (Pa.) Area Jr./Sr. High Sch., 1959-60, Loyalsock Jr./Sr. High Sch., Williamsport, Pa., 1960-64; prof. Lock Haven (Pa.) U., 1964—. Co-author: (textbook) Teaching Tumbling, 1982. Recipient Outstanding Tchr. award Pa. Acad. for Profs. of Teaching, 1990. Mem. AAHPERD, Pa. Assn. health, Phys. Edn., Recreationa nd Dance (exec. bd. 1979-85, spl. projects com. 1987—, Honor award 1984), Phi Kappa Phi (past pres.). Lutheran. Office: Lock Haven U Zimmerli 109 Lock Haven PA 17745

VAN DONGEN, JAMES CHARLES, journalist; b. Hackensack, N.J., May 30, 1951; s. Henry and Grace (Smit) Van D.; m. Mary Frances McDermott, July 24, 1976 (div. 1979); m. Hendrika C. Hilbers, Dec. 31, 1982. BA, Thiel Coll., 1973; MA, Ohio U., 1974. Reporter, producer Sta. WQLN-FM-TV, Erie, Pa., 1975-83; reporter Sta. WCCK-FM, Erie, 1983-84; news dir. N.H. Pub. Radio, Concord, 1984-88; staff writer UPI, Concord, 1988-89, bur. chief, 1989-91; info. officer N.H. Ho. of Reps., Concord, 1991—; instr. broadcast newswriting New Eng. Coll., Henniker, N.H., 1986-88. Recipient Golden Mike award N.H. Assn. Broadcasters, 1986, 85. Home: 130 Borough Rd Concord NH 03303-1836 Office: NH Ho of Reps State House Concord NH 03301

VAN DOREN, RICHARD WITT, counseling psychologist, career consultant; b. Mpls., Mar. 27, 1946; s. William Ogden and Janet Jane (Pierce) Van D.; m. Nancy Whitman, June 8, 1968; children: Peter Davis, Katherine. BA, Macalester Coll., 1968; MA, Ball State U., 1972, EdD, 1975. Doctoral fellow Ball State U., Muncie, Ind., 1973-75; postdoctoral intern Counseling Ctr. Shippensburg (Pa.) State Coll., 1975-76; postdoctoral intern Elmcrest Psychiat. Inst., Portland, Conn., 1976-77; counseling assoc., adj. prof. Rider Coll., Lawrenceville, N.J., 1977-80; sr. cons., dir. interview tng. Mainstream Access, Inc., N.Y.C., 1981-87; regional dir. counseling svcs. Fuchs, Cuthrell and Co., N.Y.C., 1987-89; v.p. Minsuk, Macklin, Stein and Assocs., Princeton Junction, N.J., 1989—; speaker in field. Contbg. author: Career and Life Planning, 1975; author: Evaluation Interview Training Trainers Manual, 1987. Asst. cubmaster, troop com. Belle Mead (N.J.) area Boy Scouts Am., 1977-83; bd. dirs. Family Svc. Agy. Princeton, N.J., 1978-81; trustee Historic Morven, Inc., Princeton, 1986—. Capt. USAF, 1968-73. Mem. AACD, Assn. Counselor Edn. and Supervision, Assn. Application of Psychol. Type, Am. Psychol. Assn., Masons, Scottish Rite, Royal Order Scotland. Presbyterian. Home: 47 Jamestown Rd Belle Mead NJ 08502-5224 Office: 14 Washington Rd Princeton Junction NJ 08550-1028

VAN DUSEN, ALBERT CLARENCE, university official; b. Tampa, Fla., Aug. 30, 1915; s. Charles H. and Maude E. (Green) Van D.; m. Margaret Davis, Jan. 3, 1943; children: Margaret Anne (Mrs. Joseph J. Pysh), Jane Katherine , Sally Elizabeth (Mrs. Frank J. Matyskiela). B.S., U. Fla., 1937, A.M., 1938; Ph.D., Northwestern, 1942; Litt.D., U. Tampa, 1959; L.H.D., Duquesne U., 1967. Instr., asst. prof. dept. psychology U. Fla., 1938-41; asso. prof. psychology Northwestern U., 1946, dir. summer session, 1948-52, v.p. pub. relations, 1952-56; prof. psychology, bus. adminstrn. and edn. U. Pitts., 1956-85, asst. chancellor for planning and devel., 1956-59, vice chancellor the professions, 1959-67, vice chancellor program devel. and pub. affairs, 1967-71, vice chancellor, sec. univ., 1971-80, vice chancellor emeritus, spl. asst. for pub. affairs, 1980-85, vice chancellor emeritus, prof. emeritus psychology, bus. adminstrn. and edn., 1985—, ctr. assoc. univ. ctr. for internat. studies, 1986—; bd. dirs. Dollar Bank, Pitts. Editor: Proc. Am. Coll. Personnel Assn; contbr. articles to profl. jours. Bd. govs. Pinchot Inst. Conservation Studies; bd. dirs. World Affairs Coun. Pitts., vice chmn. bd. dirs. Duquesne U., acting chmn., 1987-88; bd. dirs. Pitts. YMCA, ACTION Housing, Inc., Assn. Am.'s Pub. TV Stas., QED Communications Inc., chmn. 1981-88; bd. dirs. Am. Japan Soc. Pitts.; mem. Pa. Pub. TV Network Commn.; vice chmn. bd. trustees Pitts. History and Landmarks Found.; pres. bd. trustees H.C. Frick Ednl. Commn., United Way Pa.; dir. South Hills Child Guidance Ctr.; chmn. selfcare study Health Edn. Ctr., Pitts., 1979-80. Lt. USNR, 1942-46. Fulbright sr. scholar Australian-Am. Ednl. Found., 1980. Fellow Am. Psychol. Assn., Am. Psychol. Soc., Pa. Psychol. Assn., Internat. Found. Social Econ. Deve.; mem. Internat. Assn. Schs. Insts. Adminstrn., C. of C. (dir. 1953-55), Am. Coll. Pub. Rels. Assn. (v.p. 1956-58), Assn. Deans and Dirs. Summer Sessions (sec. 1950-51), Profl. Schs. and World Affairs Com. (chmn. edn. and world affairs 1965-67), Am. Pers. and Guidance Assn., Midwest Psychol. Assn., Ea. Psychol. Assn., Pitts. Psychol. Assn., Internat. Assn. Applied Psychology, Western Pa. Coun. Econ. Edn., Internat. Assn. Schs. and Insts. Adminstrn., Friends of Art for Pitts. Schs. (charter mem.), Phi Beta Kappa, Sigma Xi, Beta Theta Pi, Beta Gamma Sigma. Clubs: Univ. (Pitts.), Duquesne (Pitts.). Home: 108 Blue Spruce Cir Pittsburgh PA 15243-1026

VAN DYKE, TERRY ANN, biological sciences educator; b. Wake Island, Hawaii, May 2, 1955; d. Harold Quinton and Betty Irene (Wolf) Van D.; m. Richard Jude Samulski, Aug. 14, 1982; children: Danielle, Richard. BS, U. Fla., 1977, PhD, 1981. Postdoctoral fellow Univ. Fla., Gainesville, 1981-82, SUNY, Stonybrook, N.Y., 1982-84; rsch. assoc. Princeton (N.J.) Univ., 1984-86; asst. prof. Univ. Pitts., Pa., 1986—; animal facilities chair Univ. Pitts., 1989-91, grad. student curriculum, 1990-91. Named Predoctoral trainee Nat. Inst. Health, 1978-81; postdoctoral fellow Am. Cancer Soc., 1982-84. Mem. AAAS, Am. Soc. for Microbiology, N.Y. Acad. Sci., Pitts. Cancer Inst. Office: Univ Pitts Fifth & Ruskin Pittsburgh PA 15260

VAN ESSEN, LASSE WILLEM, trade association executive; b. Ensenada, P.R., Dec. 28, 1953; came to U.S., 1959; s. Willem and Gertrude (Beigel) van E. BA, Harvard U., 1976. Programmer RAS svc. Nat. League of Cities, Washington, 1980-81; asst. dir. mktg. Nat. Assn. Home Builders, Washington, 1981-83, exec. dir. mktg., 1983-86, asst. staff v.p., 1987—; v.p. Nat. Inst. Bldg. Scis., Washington, 1986-87. Fulbright fellow DADD, 1977-78. Mem. Nat. Sales and Mktg. Coun. (Bill Molster award 1988), Greater Washington Soc. Assn. Execs., Dupont Circle Citizens Assn., Potomac Exec. Network, D.C. Road Runners Club, D.C. Front Runners. Home: Apt 804 1615 Q St NW Washington DC 20009 Office: Nat Assn Home Builders 1201 15th St NW Washington DC 20005

VAN GRAAFEILAND, ELLSWORTH ALFRED, federal judge; b. Rochester, N.Y., May 11, 1915; s. Ivan and Elsie (Gohr) VanG.; m. Rosemary Vaeth, May 26, 1945; children—Gary, Suzanne, Joan, John, Anne. A.B., U. Rochester, 1937; LL.B., Cornell U., 1940. Bar: N.Y. 1940. Practiced in Rochester; now sr. judge U.S. Ct. Appeals for 2d Cir. Fellow Am. Bar Found., N.Y. Bar Found.; mem. ABA (ho. dels. 1973-75), N.Y. State Bar Assn. (v.p. 1972-73, pres. 1973-74, chmn. negligence compensation and ins. sect. 1968-69), Monroe County Bar Assn. (past pres.), Am. Coll. Trial Lawyers., Masons, Kent Club, Oak Hill Country Club. Home: 76 Ramsey Park Rochester NY 14610-1333 Office: Fed Bldg 100 State St Ste 423 Rochester NY 14614-1369

VAN HARSSEL, JOHANNES HENRICUS, education educator; b. Etten-Leur, The Netherlands, June 15, 1954; came to U.S., 1976; s. Simon and Cornelia (Koevoets) Van H.; m. Linda Ann Siragusa, Oct. 30, 1976; children: Casey, Lindsay. BS, Markendael Coll., The Netherlands, 1976; MPS, The New Sch., N.Y.C., 1982; EdD, U. Vt., 1991. Mgr. Ziff-Davis, N.Y.C., 1976-81; prog. dir. Nat. Coll., Rapid City, S.D., 1981-85; prof. Champlain Coll., Burlington, Vt., 1985-88, Niagara Univ., Niagara Falls, N.Y., 1988—; cons. tourism industry, S.D., Vt., N.Y., 1981—, Am Ex, N.Y.C., 1991. Author: Tourism, An Exploration, 1986, Marketing in Higher Education, 1991, The Senior Traveler, 1991. Chmn. Main Street Econ. Devel., Niagara Falls, 1989-91. Democrat. Home: 589 Briarwood Ln Lewiston NY 14092-1473 Office: Niagara Univ Niagara Falls NY 14109

VAN HASTE, FRANK, plastics, chemicals executive; b. Paterson, N.J., Nov. 20, 1948; s. Frank Jr. and Dorothy (Peters) Van H.; m. Patricia Adshead, June 20, 1971; 1 child, Richard G. BS in Aero. Engring., NYU, 1970; MSME, Rensselaer Poly Inst., 1973, MBA, 1979. Design engr. Pratt & Whitney Aircraft, East Hartford, Conn., 1970-71, Electric Boat Div. Gen. Dynamics, Groton, Conn., 1971-79; bus. devel. specialist Gen. Dynamics, Groton, Conn., 1979-81; program mgr. Innotech Corp., Trumbull, Conn., 1981-84; prin. Van Haste Assocs., Inc., Trumbull, 1984—; mng. ptnr. Adept Group, Ltd., Shelton, Conn., 1986-89; gen. mgr. Novachem, Bridgeport, Conn., 1989—. Mem. Comml. Devel. Assn. Office: Novachem 955 Connecticut Ave Bridgeport CT 06607-1200

VAN HOVE, SCOTT JACOB, healthcare executive; b. Viborg, S.D., Apr. 19, 1957; s. Harvey Leonard and Norma Marie (Hovaldt) Van H. BA, Augustana Coll., Sioux Falls, S.D., 1979; JD, U. S.D., 1982. Bar: S.D. 1982, U.S. Dist. Ct. S.D. 1983, Pa. 1985, D.C. 1986; CPA, Md. Law clk. S.D. Supreme Ct., Pierre, 1982-83; tax atty. Arthur Andersen & Co., Washington, 1983-84; assoc. Epstein, Becker & Green, Washington, 1985-87; mgmt. intern Manor Care, Inc., Silver Spring, Md., 1987, regional dir., 1988-89, v.p. ops., 1989—; cons. various polit. campaigns, 1984—. Bd. mem. assocs. coun. George Washington U. Sch. Bus. and Pub. Mgmt. Mem. D.C. Inst. of CPAs. Office: Manor Care Inc 10770 Columbus Pike Silver Spring MD 20901

VANIM, GERALD ALVISE, education educator; b. Limeport, Pa., July 12, 1938; s. Marigo and Cecilia Edith (Gestl) V.; m. Margaret Marie Sycamore,

Aug. 10, 1963; children: Michael S., Jeanne M. BS, Pa. State U., 1960; MA, Villanova Univ., 1965; PhD, U. Md., 1985. Tchr. gen. sci./biology Rose Tree Media Schs., Media, Pa., 1960-71; counselor Delaware County Area Vocat.-Tech. Schs., Media, 1971-78, coord. guidance svcs., 1978-86; career counselor Delaware County Intermediate Unit, Media, 1986-88; adminstrv. asst. to prin. Upper Darby (Pa.) High Sch., 1988-90; edn. and tng. cons. Media, 1990—; mem. Pa. Coun. on Vocat. Edn., Harrisburg, 1980-86; program dir. CAEL, Phila., 1991; prin. trainer TRAC/USA Dusco Community Svcs., Lancaster, Pa., 1990—, Alexandria, Va., 1991—; porgram dir. Career Solutions Tng. Group, Inc., Paoli, Pa., 1991—; adj. faculty dept. edn. and human resources Villanova (Pa.) U., 1990—; appointee Bell Atlantic Tng. Adv. Bd., 1992; co-author MacArthur workshop Returning to Learning, 1992. Author: Films for Research and Development, 1980; co-author: (workshop) Returning to Learning, 1988. Pres. PTA, Springton Lake, Media, 1981-83, treas. PTA, Penncrest High, Media, 1987-89. Recipient fellowships U.S. Dept. Edn., U. Md., 1977-78, 79-80. Mem. Pa. Vocat. Assn. (life), ASCD, World Futures Soc., Coun. for Adult and Experiential Learning, Pa. Sch. Counselor's Assn., Kiwanis (pres. 1975), Iota Lambda Sigma, Phi Kappa Phi, Pi Lambda Phi. Home: 254 S Old Middletown Rd Media PA 19063-4831 Office: Career Solutions Tng Group 19 E Central Ave Paoli PA

VAN INWAGEN, PETER JAN, philosophy educator; b. Rochester, N.Y., Sept. 21, 1942; s. George Butler and Mildred Gloria (Knudson) van I; m. Margery Bedford Naylor, Mar. 31, 1967 (div. Apr. 1988); 1 child, Elizabeth Core; m. Elisabeth Marie Bolduc, June 3, 1989. B.S., Rensselaer Poly. Inst., 1965; Ph.D., U. Rochester, 1969. Vis. asst. prof. U. Rochester, N.Y., 1971-72; asst. prof. Syracuse U., N.Y., 1972-74, assoc. prof., 1974-80, prof. philosophy, 1980—; vis. prof. U. Ariz., Tucson, 1981. Author: An Essay on Free Will, 1983, Material Beings, 1990, Metaphysics, 1992; editor: Time and Cause, 1980, Alvin Plantinga, 1985; contbr. articles to profl. jours.; mem. editorial bd. Jour. Faith and Philosophy, Philos. Perspectives, Nous. Served to capt. U.S. Army, 1969-71. NEH grantee, 1983-84, 89-90. Mem. Am. Philos. Assn., Soc. Christian Philosophers, Creighton Club. Democrat. Episcopalian. Home: 517 Scott Ave Syracuse NY 13224-1909 Office: Syracuse U Dept Philosophy Syracuse NY 13244-1170

VAN KIRK, THOMAS L., lawyer; b. Pa., June 25; s. Theodore and Mary Jane (Young) Van K.; children: Thomas Jr., Christopher. BA, Bucknell U., 1967; JD cum laude, Dickinson U., 1970. Bar: Pa., U.S. Dist. Ct. (we. and ea. dists.) Pa. 1971, U.S. Ct. Appeals (3d cir.) 1972, U.S. Supreme Ct. 1976. Clk. Pa. Superior Ct., 1970-71; assoc. Buchanan Ingersoll, Pitts., 1971-77; with Allegheny County Ct., 1971; ptnr. Buchanan Ingersoll, Pitts., 1978—, chief oper. officer, 1985—; bd. dirs. Civic Light Opera, Western Div. of Pa. Economy League, Colony II Travel, Pitts. Chmn. Allegheny County Heart Assn. Walk, 1992. Mem. ABA, Allegheny County Bar Assn., Duquesne Club, Rivers Club, St. Clair Country Club, Racquet Club Phila. Democrat. Roman Catholic. Home: 1010 Osage Rd Pittsburgh PA 15243-1014 Office: Buchanan Ingersoll PC 600 Grant St 58th Fl Pittsburgh PA 15219-2701

VAN LAER, LEE EDWARD, import specialist; b. Yonkers, N.Y., Oct. 1, 1955; s. Nicholas and Helen Louise (Ruark) van L.; m. Kathy Dee Feldman, June 11, 1983; children: Rebecca, Adriaan. BA, St. Lawrence U., 1977. Artist N.Y.C., 1977-81; sales assoc. RH Macy & Co., N.Y.C., 1981-82, sales mgr., 1982-83; asst. buyer RH Macy & Co. Inc., N.Y.C., 1984-85, corp. buyer, 1985-86; dir. imports Sunweave Linens, N.Y.C., 1987-91; import specialist N.Y.C., 1991—; cons. Fashion Industries, Griffin, Ga., 1991, Fashion Pillow, Jackson, Ga., 1991. Democrat. Episcopalian. Home: 155 E 55th St Apt 12C New York NY 10022-4044

VAN LANDINGHAM, LEANDER SHELTON, JR., lawyer; b. Memphis, July 15, 1925; s. Leander Shelton Van L.; m. Henrietta Adena Stapf, July 5, 1959; children: Ann Henrietta, Leander Shelton III. B.S. in Chemistry, U. N.C., 1948, M.A. in Organic Chemistry, 1949; J.D., Georgetown U., 1955. Bar: D.C. 1955, Md. 1963, Va. 1976. Patent adviser Dept. Navy, Washington, 1953-55; sole practice comml. law and patent, trademark and copyright law, Washington met. area, 1955—. Served to lt. USNR, 1943-46, 51-53. Mem. Am. Chem. Soc., Sci. Assn., Fed. Bar Assn., ABA, D.C. Bar Assn., Va. Bar Assn., Md. Bar Assn., Am. Intellectual Property Law Assn., Am. Judicature Soc., Sigma Xi, Phi Alpha Delta. Home: 10726 Stanmore Dr Rockville MD 20854-1518 Office: 2001 Jefferson Davis Hwy Arlington VA 22202-3603

VAN LARE, BARRY LEE, association executive, consultant; b. Sodus, N.Y., Nov. 21, 1940; s. Roland Charles and Bertha Elizabeth (Elve) Van L.; m. Phyllis Grace Judd, June 16, 1962; children: Sherryl Jean Van Lare Arnold, Ian Judd, Susan Michelle Van Lare Bathras. BA, U. Rochester, 1962. Exec. deputy commnr. N.Y. State Dept. Social Svcs., Albany, 1971-72; dir. community svcs. Wash. State, Olympia, 1974-75; commr. Erie County N.Y. Dept. Social Svcs., Buffalo, 1976; assoc. commnr. Social Security Adminstrn., Washington, 1977-79; deputy asst. sec. for legislation U.S. Dept. Health and Human Svcs., Washington, 1980; special adminstr. for gasoline rationing U.S. Dept. Energy, Washington, 1980; dir. human resources Nat. Govs. Assn., Washington, 1981-85, dir. state svcs., 1985-89, deputy exec. dir., 1989—. Bd. dirs. Coalitionto Improve Mgmt. in State & Local Govmt., Pitts., 1989—; cons. Paralyzed Vets. of Am., Washington, 1990—. Mem. Am. Soc. Pub. Adminstrs. Protestant. Office: Nat Govs Assn 444 N Capitol St NW Washington DC 20001-1512

VANMARCKE, ERIK HECTOR, civil engineering educator; b. Menen, Belgium, Aug. 6, 1941; came to U.S., 1965, naturalized, 1976; m. Louis Eugene and Rachel Louisa (van Hollebeke) V.; m. Margaret Maria Delesie, May 25, 1965; children: Lieven, Ann, Kristien. BS, U. Louvain, Belgium, 1965; MS, U. Del., 1967; PhD in Civil Engring, MIT, 1970. From instr. to prof. civil engring. MIT, Cambridge, 1969-85; Gilbert W. Winslow Career Devel. prof. MIT, 1974-77, dir. civil engring. systems group, 1976-80; prof. civil engring. and ops. rsch. Princeton U., 1985—; cons. Office Sci. and Tech. Policy, 1978-80; vis. scholar in engring. Harvard U., 1984-85; Shimizu Corp. vis. prof. Stanford U., 1991; cons. various govt. agys. and engring. firms. Author: Random Fields: Analysis and Synthesis, 1983; editor Internat. Jour. Structural Safety, 1981-91. Recipient Sr. Scientist award for study in Japan, Japan Soc. for Promotion of Sci., 1991. Mem. ASCE (Raymond C. Reese research award 1975, Walter L. Huber research prize 1984), Am. Geophys. Union, Seismol. Soc. Am., Internat. Soc. Soil Mechanics and Found. Engring., Sigma Xi. Home: 50 Brooks Bnd Princeton NJ 08540-7530 Office: Room E311 Engring Quadrangle Princeton U Princeton NJ 08544

VAN METER, JAN RODDEN, public relations executive; b. Wilkes-Barre, Pa., May 29, 1941; s. William Rodden and Charlotte (Greenberg) Van M.; m. Marlene Stevens, Oct. 16, 1966 (div. Dec. 1987); m. Elena Maria Sansalone, Apr. 1988; 1 child, Benjamin Thayer. BA, Wesleyan U., Middletown, Ct., 1963; MA, SUNY, Stony Brook, 1968; PhD, SUNY, 1971. Asst. prof. U. Tex, Austin, 1970-74; account exec. Hill & Knowlton, Inc., N.Y.C., 1975-77, v.p., 1977-78, sr. v.p., 1978-81, exec. v.p., dep. dirs. N.Y. ops., 1982-87; exec. v.p. sr. ptnr. gen. mgr. Fleishman-Hillard, Inc., N.Y.C., 1987—. Served with USNR, 1965-71.

VANN, BOBB, artist; b. Phila., Apr. 27, 1939; s. Timothy and Eleanor (Ashford) V.; m. Patricia Hightower, Jan. 7, 1983; children: Karen, Robin, Michael. Student, Phila. Coll. of Art, 1959-62. Cert. artist, illustrator, lectr., tchr. Designer and illustrator Penn Emblem Co., Phila., 1964-66; illustrator J.B. Lippincott Book Pub., Phila., 1964-68; illustrator and designer Cawley Neff Assocs., Pennsauken, N.J., 1964-68, Mel Richman Advt., Phila., 1971-72; art dir. Hercules Inc., Wilmington, Del., 1973-80; freelance artist various advt. agys., 1980-87; artist, owner Vanngo Graphics, Phila., 1990—; asst. art dir. Black Am. Mag., Phila., 1970-71; illustrator Arrow Display Co., Phila., 1968-70; instr. Main Line Ctr. for the Arts, Haverford, Pa., 1988-89, Fleisher Art Meml., Phila., 1989, Phila. Art Inst., 1984-85; vis. lectr. Temple U. Children's Workshop, Phila., 1990; med. illustrator/designer Tate Advt. Agy., Malvern, Pa., 1989-91; instr./lectr. constructive art expression Phila. Mus. Art, 1987-88; courtroom artist Phila. City Cts., Channel 3 NBC Network, 1981-83, others. One man shows include Fed. Res. Bank, Phila., Hahnnemann U., Phila., Allens Ln. Art Ctr., Phila., Revsin Galleries, Phila.; group exhibits include Fleisher Art Meml., Phila., Ebel U.S. Pro Indoors Tennis in Art Exhibit, Phila., Port of History Mus., Phila., Cliveden Art Outdoor Exhibit, Phila., Rittenhouse Ann. Outdoor Exhibit, Phila., Hercules Country Club, Wilmington, Del., Hercules, Inc., Kenmore Galleries, Phila., Palmer Art Gallery, Phila.; works in pvt. and corp. collections. With U.S. Army, 1957-61. Recipient Platinum awards (2) 100 Black Women's Orgn., 1990, Croquis award Fleisher Art Meml., 1980; recipient Illustration of the Yr. award Fashionable Pubs., 1974. Home and Office: Vanngo Graphics 5306 Knox St Philadelphia PA 19144

VANN, JOHN DANIEL, III, university administrator, historian; b. Raleigh, N.C., June 14, 1935; s. John Daniel Jr. and Sybil Dean (Wilson) V.; m. Ellen Jane Rogers, June 21, 1969; children: John Daniel IV, Justin Fitz Patrick. BA with honors, U. N.C., 1957; MA, Yale U., 1959, PhD, 1965; M in Librarianship, Emory U., 1971; postgrad., Columbia U., 1962-63, Stanford U., 1977-78. Assoc. prof. history Campbell Coll., Buie's Creek, N.C., 1961-63; bibliographer European history and lit. Newberry Libr., Chgo., 1963-65, asst. reference librarian, 1963-65; prof. history Calif. Bapt. Coll., Riverside, 1965-66; dir. libr., prof. history Bapt. Coll. at Charleston, S.C., 1966-69; libr. Keuka Coll., Keuka Park, N.Y., 1969-71; chief libr., prof. libr., chmn. libr. dept. S.I. Community Coll. CUNY, 1971-76; prof. libr. Coll. S.I. CUNY, 1976-79; head libr. Lockwood Libr./SUNY, Buffalo, 1979-80; asst. dir. for planning, univ. librs. SUNY, Buffalo, 1980-81; exec. dir. librs. and learning resources, prof. U. Wis., Oshkosh, 1981-87; dir. libr. svcs. Bloomsburg U. Pa., 1987-89, dean libr. svcs., 1989—; resident planner, cons. on libr. bldgs. and collection devel. Contbr. chpts. to books, articles to profl. jours. Trustee Maplewood (N.J.) Meml. Libr., 1977-79, v.p., 1979; bd. dirs. Coun. Wis. Librs., 1983-86, Midwest Regional Multi-Dist. Short Term Internat. Youth Exch., 1987, Oshkosh (Wis.) Symphony Assn., 1986-87, United Cerebral Palsy of Winnebagoland, Oshkosh, 1986-87. Acad. Libr. Mgmt. intern Coun. on Libr. Resources Stanford U., 1977-78. Mem. ALA, Am. Hist. Assn., Archons of Colophon, Assn. for Libr. Collections and Tech. Svcs., Assn. Coll. and Rsch. Librs. (com. chmn., sec. chmn. 1977-78, editorial bd., bd. dirs. 1976-78), Bibliog. Soc. Am., Libr. Adminstrn. and Mgmt. Assn., Libr. and Info. Tech. Assn., Medieval Acad. Am., Pa. Libr. Assn. (sect. dir.), Bloomsburg Rotary Club, Beta Phi Mu, Phi Alpha Theta. Republican. Presbyterian. Home: 810 E Second St Bloomsburg PA 17815-8950 Office: Harvey A Andruss Libr Bloomsburg U Pa Bloomsburg PA 17815

VANN, JOSEPH MC ALPIN, nuclear engineer; b. Clinton, N.C., Dec. 30, 1937; s. Joseph Rose and Louise Myrtle (Beaver) V.; m. Edith Ausley, Apr. 1, 1961; 1 child, Natasha Vann Bottoms. BS in Math., N.C. State U., 1958; MEd in Math., U. N.C., Chapel Hill, 1961; M in Physics, East Carolina U., 1972; MS in Nuclear Engring., Va. Polytechnic Inst., 1973. Chmn. math. dept. Mt. Olive (N.C.) Coll., 1961-71; safety and licensing engr. Gen. Pub. Utility, Parsippany, N.J., 1973-76; nuclear engr. N.J. Dept. Environ. Protection, Trenton, 1976-81; sr. radiol. engr. Ebasco Co., N.Y.C., 1981-89; sr. engr. West Valley (N.Y.) Nuclear Svcs., 1990-92; emergency planner Princeton (N.J.) Plasma Physics Lab., 1992—. Contbr. articles to profl. jours. Mem. Am. Physical Soc., Sigma Xi, Sigma Pi Sigma, Pi Mu Epsilon. Home: 23 Hillview Ave Madison NJ 07940-1738 Office: Princeton Plasma Physics Lab Princeton NJ 28543

VAN NAME, FREDERICK WARREN, III, aerospace engineer; b. Torrington, Conn., Apr. 30, 1946; s. Frederick Warren Jr. and Barbara Francis (Leaper) Van N.; m. Judith A. Beyring, Aug. 8, 1970 (div. 1981). BME, U. Del., 1982, M of Mech. and Aerospace Engring., 1985. Registered profl. engr., Del. From engr. to staff engr. Morton Thiokol Inc., Elkton, Md., 1985-88; from engring. supr. to prin. engr. Thiokol Corp., Elkton, 1988-90, mgr. advanced tech., 1990-91; cons. Condux, Newark, 1991—. Mem. ASME, ASTM, AIAA, Soc. Advancement Material and Processing Engring., Soc. Mfg. Engrs. (Composites Group), Am. Soc. Composites. Home: 3276 Old Chisholm Rd Apt 1109B Florence AL 35630-1075 Office: Composites USA 3310 Wrangler Hill Rd Bear DE 19701

VANNASSE, DANA EDWARD, corporation executive; b. Boston, May 17, 1935; s. Edward Theophile and Anne (Barnes) V.; m. Susan Thomas, Sept. 2, 1983. BBA, Boston U., 1957. Pres. Beacon Hill Travel Svc. Inc., Boston, 1968—; v.p. Travel People Personnel, Boston, 1983—; adv. bd. mem. Alamo Rent A Car, Ft. Lauderdale, Fla., 1986-90, Hertz Rent A Car, Park Ridge, N.J., 1990—, Continental Airlines, Houston, 1990—, Pan Am. Airways, N.Y.C., 1985-88. Past pres. Beacon Hill Merchants Assn., Boston, 1970-73; dir. Friends of the Pub. Garden, Boston, 1984—. Mem. Skal Club of Boston (past pres. 1986-87), Am. Soc. Travel Agts. (past dir. 1983-84), Aero Club of New Eng. (past dir. 1986-89). Republican. Roman Catholic. Home: 103 Tyler Rd Weston MA 02193-1046 Office: Beacon Hill Travel Svc Inc 65 Beacon St Boston MA 02108-3594

VAN NESS, JOHN RALPH, college administrator; b. Columbus, Ohio, Oct. 22, 1939; s. Ralph Taylor and Norma Gertrude (Thorp) Van N.; m. Christine S. Moon, Dec. 19, 1964; children: Heather Thorp, Hilary Clark. BA, The Colo. Coll., Colo. Springs, 1965; MA, U. Pa., 1969, PhD, 1979. Instr. West Chester (Pa.) U., 1969-70, Knox Coll., Galesburg, Ill., 1970-73, Fort Lewis Coll., Durango, Colo., 1974-76; cons. fund raising pvt. practice Phila., 1977-79; dir., capital campaign consul. John F. Rich Co., Phila., 1979-84; v.p. for coll. relations, adjunct prof. Anthropology Ursinus Coll., Collegeville, Pa., 1984-89; exec. v.p., prof. Moore Coll. Art and Design, Phila., 1989-92, acting pres., 1990-91; bd. dirs. Ctr. for Land Grant Studies, Santa Fe, 1978—; editorial bd. Jour. of the West, Manhattan, Kans., 1980-88. Co-author: Canones: Values, Crisis and Survival in a Northern New Mexico Village, 1981; author: Hispanos in Northern New Mexico, 1991; co-editor: Spanish and Mexican Land Grants in New Mexico and Colorado, 1980, Land, Water and Culture, 1987; editor: New Mexico Land Grant Series, Vols. 1-5, 1983, 84, 87, 89, 92. Recipient Teaching Fellowship U. Pa.; grantee Ford Found., Nat. Sci. Found. Mem. Am. Anthrop. Assn., Coun. for Advance and Support of Edn., Nat. Soc. of Fund Raising Execs., Phila. Skating Club and Human Soc., Racquet Club of Phila., Pi Gamma Mu. Democrat.

VAN NESS, PAUL DUFFIELD, statistics educator; b. Jackson, Mich., Feb. 5, 1932; s. Paul Henry and Thelma (Tinkham) Van N.; m. Judith Lamb, Dec. 26, 1953 (div. 1974); children: Linda, Gretchen, Cynthia; m. Joan Duffield, June 23, 1979; step children: Adam, Gretchen. BA, U. Mich., 1953, MBA, 1958; MS in Statistics, Rochester Inst. Tech., 1979. Asst. prof. Agrl. & Tech. Coll. at Cobleskill, N.Y., 1963-66; assoc. prof. Rochester (N.Y.) Inst. Tech., 1966-91, ret., 1991. Author: (with others) Study Guide For Use With Understanding Business Statistics, 1991, Study Guide for Use With Management Science, 1989, Study Guide to Accompany Quantitative Methods for Management Decisions, 1985, Study Guide for Use With Production/Operations Management, 2d edit., 1986, 3d edit., 1990, Study Guide to Accompany Introductory Statistics for Management and Economics, 1st edit., 1981, 2d edit., 1984; contbr. articles to profl. jours. With U.S. Army, 1953-56. Home: 425 Rugby Ave Rochester NY 14619-1815 Office: Rochester Inst of Tech Coll of Business Rochester NY 14523-5671

VAN NIEVELT, M. C. AUGUSTUS, management consultant, educator; b. The Hague, Netherlands, Aug. 12, 1928; came to U.S., 1960; s. Willem F.H. and Seline K. (van Bennekom) van N.; m. Jacqueline E. Barrelet, Aug. 28, 1959; children: Alexander F.H., Caroline E. MSChemE and Biotech., Tech. U., Delft, Netherlands, 1956. Devel. engr. Siegfried Pharms., Zofingen, Switzerland, 1959-60; process devel. group leader Lederle Div. Am. Cyanamid, Pearl River, N.Y., 1960-65; mgr. mfg. Latin Am. Internat. Div. Am. Cyanamid, Wayne, N.J., 1965-68; dir. Tiger project Exxon-Nestlé Joint Venture, Marysville, Ohio, 1968-71; mgr. mfg. svcs. The Nestlé Co., White Plains, N.Y., 1971-74; gen. mgr. Nestlé Enterprises/USA, White Plains, N.Y., 1974-82; pres. VN Internat., Montvale, N.J., 1982—; trustee The Strategic Planning Inst., Cambridge, Mass., 1978-82; mem. adv. bd. Info. Strategy Jour., 1984—. Contbr. articles to profl. jours. 1st lt. Netherlands Army, 1956-58. Office: VN Internat 35 Hering Rd Montvale NJ 07645-1225

VAN NORTWICK, THOMAS H., radio broadcast executive; b. Syracuse, N.Y., Aug. 4, 1949; s. Howard J. and Virginia (Trost) Van N.; m. Linda Maccarone, Mar. 23, 1973; children: Melissa, Ryan, Jonathan. BS in Acctg., Canisius Coll., 1971. CPA, N.Y. Staff acct. Haskins and Sells, CPA, Buffalo, 1971-74; exec. dir. sub-bd. SUNY, Buffalo, 1974-78; contr. Sta. WBEN Algonquin Broadcasting Corp., Buffalo, 1978-84, v.p. fin. Sta. WBEN, 1984-90, exec. v.p., gen. mgr. Sta. WBEN, 1990—. Pres. Lancaster (N.Y.) Sch. Bd., 1990-91; bd. dirs. Jr. Achievement of Western N.Y., Buffalo, 1991—; town councilman, Lancaster, 1992—. Mem. AICPA, Nat. Assn. Broadcasters, N.Y. State Soc. CPAs, Rotary (dir. Buffalo chpt. 1991—). Home: 11 Shadyside Ln Lancaster NY 14086 Address: WBEN(AM) 2077 Elmwood Ave Buffalo NY 14207

VAN ORMAN, JEANNE, planning consultant, preservation executive; b. N.Y.C., Apr. 9, 1939; d. Wayne and Jean (O'Gara) Van O.; m. Robert F. Brown, May 25, 1963 (div. 1975); children: Frank Van Orman Brown, Virginia Corbin Brown. BA, Smith Coll., 1961; M in City Planning, Harvard U., 1974. Land use planner Mass. Exec. Office of Communities and Devel., Boston, 1979-83, mgr. planning grants program, 1984-85, dir. strategic planning program, 1985-87; prin. Van Orman & Assocs., Easton, Mass., 1987—. Contbr. articles to profl. jours. Mem. Easton Charter Commn., 1971-72, mem. fin. com., 1982-83, libr. com., 1984-86, selectman, 1973-75, Mass. DPW Privitization Com. 1991—; bd. overseers Moses Brown Sch., Providence. Mass. Housing Partnership grantee, 1987, NEA grantee, 1981; recipient Disting. Svc. award, Jaycees, 1973. Mem. Am. Planning Assn. (exec. bd. Mass. sect.), Westport (Mass.) Yacht Club. Mem. Soc. of Friends. Home: 479 Bay Rd South Easton MA 02375-1424 Office: Preservation Worcester 71 Pleasant St Worcester MA 01609

VANORSDALE, DAVID WILLIAM, JR., sales professional; b. Martinsburg, W.Va., Oct. 2, 1965; s. David William and Mary Elizabeth (Campbell) V.; m. Holly Darlene Cookus, July 10, 1988. BS, W.Va. U., 1988. Sales assoc. Long Fence Co., Inc., Ijamsville, Md., 1988—; porta panel sales mgr. Long Fence Co., Inc., 1989—. Mem. Associated Builders and Contractors, Frederick County Home Builders, Eastern Panhandle Home Builders (bd. dirs.). Democrat. Home: PO Box 461 Allensville Rd Hedgesville WV 25427 Office: Long Fence Co Inc 2520 Urbana Pike Ijamsville MD 21754-8624

VAN POZNAK, ALAN, anesthesiology and pharmacology educator; b. Newark, Dec. 30, 1927; s. Aaron and Florence (Danzis) Van P.; m. Dorothy Beatrice Lehmann, June 10, 1950; children: Christina, Theodore, John, Catherine. BA, Cornell U., 1948, MD, 1952. Diplomate Am. Bd. Anesthesiology. Prof. Med. Coll. Cornell U., N.Y.C., 1974—; adj. prof. N.Y. State Coll. Vet. Medicine, Ithaca, N.Y., 1981—; legal cons. various lawyers, 1975—. 1st lt. M.C., USAR, 1953-55. Mem. Am. Soc. Anesthesiologists, Assn. U. Anesthesiologists. Republican. Presbyterian. Home: 28 Northrop Ln Tenafly NJ 07670-2428 Office: NY Hosp/Cornell Med Ctr 525 E 68th St New York NY 10021-4873

VAN RAALTE, POLLY ANN, educator; b. N.Y.C., Sept. 22, 1951; d. Byron Emmanuel and Enid (Godnick) Van R.; student U. London, 1972; BA, Beaver Coll., 1973; MS in Edn., U. Pa., 1974, postgrad., 1975—, West Chester State Coll., 1975-77; student, Bank St. Coll.. Title I reading tchr. Oakview Sch., West Deptford Twp. Sch. Dist., Woodbury, N.J., 1974-75, Title I reading supr., summer 1975; lang. arts coord. Main Line Day Sch., Mitchell Sch., Haverford, Pa., 1975-76; reading supr. Salvation Army, Phila., summer 1976; reading Huntingdon Jr. High Sch., Abington (Pa.) Sch. Dist., 1976-78; reading specialist No. 2 Sch., Lawrence Pub. Sch., Inwood, N.Y., 1978-87, high sch. reading specialist, Cedarhurst, N.Y., 1988—, Lawrence (N.Y.) High Sch., 1988—; reading specialist Hewlett Elem. Sch., Hewlett-Woodmere Pub. Sch., Hewlett, N.Y., 1987-88; instr. reading and spl. edn. dept. Adelphi U., 1979—; columnist South Shore Record; bd. dirs., mem. exec. bd. Five Towns Community Ctr., 1991—, co-chmn ednl. youth svcs. edn. com., 1991—; cons. to sch. dists.; advisor Am. Biog. Inst., Inc.; speaker at reading convs. Coord., Five Towns Young Voter Registration, Hewlett, N.Y., summer, 1971; chmn. class fund Beaver Coll., also mem. internat. rels. com. U. Pa. scholar, 1977-78; mem. assoc. div. Jewish Guild for Blind; mem. N.Y. City Sprots Commn.; co-chair youth svcs. com., bd. dirs. Five Towns Community Ctr., mem. exec. bd. Mem. Internat. Reading Assn., Wis. Reading Assn., Nat. Council Tchrs. English, Nassau Reading Coun., N.Y. Reading Assn., Coun. Exceptional Children, Coun. for a Beautiful Israel, Nat. Assn. Gifted Children, Am. Assn. of the Gifted, Nat./State Leadership Tng. Inst. on the Gifted and Talented, Children's Lit. Assembly, N.Y. State English Coun., Assn. Curriculum Devel., Am. Israel Pub. Affairs Com., New Leadership com. of Jewish Nat. Fund, State of Israel Bonds New Leadership, Simon Wiesenthal New Leadership Soc., Nat. Polit. Action Com., Am. Friends of Hebrew U. (torch com.), Technion Soc., Am. Friends David Yellin Tchr's. Coll., Am. Friends Ben Gurion U., Am. Friends Israel Philharm., Am. Friends of Tel Aviv U., Am. Israel Cultural Found., Hadassah, Film Soc. Lincoln Ctr., U.S. Olympic Soc., Friends of N.Y.C. Sports Commn., Cooper-Hewitt Mus., Mus. Modern Art, Met. Mus. Art, Whitney Mus., Phila. Mus. Art, Smithsonian Inst., Friends of Carnegie Hall, Friends of Am. Ballet Theatre, Friends of Am. Theatre Wing, Women's Am. Orgn. for Rehab. Through Tng. (citi women div. N.Y.C.), U. Pa. Alumni Assn. N.Y.C., Dorot Soc., Human Rels. Club (sec.), Pi Lambda Theta, Kappa Delta Pi (sec.). Home: 26 Meadow Ln Lawrence NY 11559-1828 Office: Lawrence High Sch Reading Dept Reilly Rd Cedarhurst NY 11516-1002

VAN RIPER, ROBERT AUSTIN, public relations executive, writer; b. Mt. Vernon, N.Y., June 18, 1921; s. Austin Millard and Gladys Brownell Van R.; m. Barbara Jean Jacobs, Dec. 2, 1944; children: Alexandra, Tracy. BA, Oberlin Coll., 1943. Account exec. Edward L. Bernays Pub. Rels., N.Y.C., 1946-50, N.W. Ayer & Son, Inc., N.Y.C., 1950-54; account supr. N.W. Ayer & Son, Inc., Phila., 1954-61; v.p. N.W. Ayer & Son, Inc., N.Y.C., 1961-67, sr. v.p., 1967-73; pub. rels. counsel Fin. Acctg. Standards Bd., Norwalk, Conn., 1973-91, ret., 1991; cons. Gravure Tech. Assn., N.Y.C., 1950-55, Twp. of Springfield (Pa.), 1957-61. Author: (novels) A Really Sincere Guy, 1958, The Governor, 1970; contbr. articles to profl. jours. Bd. dirs. United Fund, Westchester County, N.Y., and Phila., 1956-61; trustee Lawrence Hosp., Westchester County, 1966-73, v.p., 1971-73. Lt. (j.g.) USN, 1943-46. Mem. Pub. Rels. Soc. Am. (pres. Phila. chpt. 1960-61), Fairfield County Pub. Rels. Assn. (bd. dirs. 1987-89), Holland Soc., Bronxville Field Club (N.Y.). Presbyterian. Home: 996 Sunset Rd Stamford CT 06903-2427

VAN ROSENDAAL, JOHN CORNELIUS GERARD MARIA, journalist; b. Steenbergen, The Netherlands, Nov. 18, 1962; came to U.S., 1989; s. Bas C. and Jo (Van Loenhout) Van R. LLM, Utrecht (Holland) U., 1989; MS in Journalism, Columbia U., 1990. Freelance reporter Holland, 1984-89; fin. journalist AP-Dow Jones, Dow Jones and Co., Inc., N.Y.C., 1990—. Coord. Amnesty Internat., Utrecht, 1986-87. Recipient Fulbright scholarship Dutch Fulbright Commn., 1989-90.

VAN RYN, TED MATTHEUS, electrical engineer; b. The Hague, The Netherlands, July 1, 1948; arrived in Can., 1952; came to U.S., 1990; s. Adrianus and Janna Christina (Keymel) van R.; m. Ricki Ann Kennedy, Mar. 23, 1976 (div. 1980); children: Michael Allan, Christopher Allan, Sandra Ann; m. Judith Mavis Seltzer, Nov. 25, 1981; 1 child, Saul Marlon. BASc, U. Waterloo, Ont., Can., 1976. Registered profl. engr., Ont. Engr. Toronto (Ont.) Lab., IBM, 1976-90; bus. analyst programming systems line-of-bus. IBM, Somers, N.Y., 1990—. Mem. Assn. Profl. Engrs. Province Ont. Office: IBM PO Box 100 Rte 100 Somers NY 10000

VAN SLOOTEN, RONALD HENRY JOSEPH, dentist; b. Paterson, N.J., July 12, 1937; s. Henry and Edythe (De Marco) Van S.; m. Joyce Elenor Mandel, 1962 (div. 1969); children: Ronald Henry Jr., Timothy Jay, Lauren; m. Barbara Rose Durante, July 1, 1979; children: Jonathon Henry, Brian Joseph. DDS, Farleigh Dickinson U., 1962; FAGD, Acad. Gen. Dentistry, 1986. Dentist pvt. practice, Paterson, N.J., 1965-76, Ridgewood, N.J., 1969-78, Ho Ho Kus, N.J., 1978—; staff mem. Bainert Meml. Hosp., Paterson, 1966-75, Ridgewood Valley Hosp., 1975—; assoc. prof. Fairleigh Dickinson Dental Sch., Hackensack, N.J., 1973-90; pres. Van Slooten Harbour Marina Inc., Port Henry, N.Y., 1989—; cons. N.J. Mfrs. Ins. Co., Trenton, 1966—. Lt. USN, Pres. Fairleigh DIckinson Sch. Dentistry Alumni Assn., 1976-77. Lt. USN, 1962-65. Fellow Acad. Gen. Dentistry, Acad. Dentistry Internat.; mem. Am. Dental Assn., Internat. Dental Health Found., N.J. Dental Soc., Bergen County Dental Soc. (Chmn. Nat. Dental Health Week citation 1970), Moriah C. of C. Republican. Roman Catholic. Office: Ho Ho Kus Profl Bldg 110 Warren Ave Ho Ho Kus NJ 07423

VAN SLYKE, RICHARD MAURICE, computer science educator, researcher; b. Manila, Aug. 17, 1937; came to U.S., 1937; s. Francis Allen and Dorothy Elizabeth (Quigley) Van S.; m. Irene Van Veen, Dec. 21, 1969. BS in Physics, Stanford U., 1959; PhD in Engring. Sci., U. Calif.,

Berkeley, 1965. Prof. U. Calif., Berkeley, 1965-69; sr. v.p. Network Analysis Corp., Glen Cove, N.Y., 1969-80; prof. Stevens Inst. Tech., Hoboken, N.J., 1980-83; chmn. rsch. ctr. N.Y. Poly. U., Bklyn., 1983-88, prof., 1988—. Office: Poly U 333 Jay St Brooklyn NY 11201-2990

VAN SON, L(EVINUS) GEORGE, speech pathology and audiology educator; b. West Palm Beach, Fla., June 15, 1934; s. Levinus and Grace Veronica (Ryan) Van S.; m. Helen Elizabeth Crane, Aug. 25, 1966; children: Elizabeth, Jeffrey, Catherine. BS, Boston U., EdM, BS, 1961, EdM, 1962, EdD, 1968. Cert. in clin. competence-speech lang. pathology. Instr. speech pathology and audiology Boston U., 1962-67; asst. prof. Temple U., Phila., 1968-69; assoc. prof. Ithaca (N.Y.) Coll., 1969—; advisor Sta. WRPI-TV Program Devel. George Jr. Republic, Freeville, N.Y., 1972—; specialist Finger Lakes Ind. Ctr., Ithaca, 1990—. Editor: (book) Video in Health, 1980. With AUS, 1957-59. Recipient Collaborative Rsch. award Ohio State U., 1985, 86. Mem. Am. Speech Lang. and Hearing Assn. Office: Ithaca Coll Ithaca NY 14850

VANSPLINTER, MICHAEL DENNIS, casino environmental services administrator; b. Paterson, N.J., May 28, 1939; s. Marinus and Eileen (Lowe) V.; m. Lozita Gatti, May 20, 1971 (div. 1969); 1 child, Mark Lewis; m. Norma Rowe Thomas, 1970 (div. 1978); m. Monica Mello, Jan. 21, 1979; children: Robin, Christopher, Mark, Karen, Shery. MBA, Southwestern U., 1983; AS+T, Hackensack (N.J.) Hosp. Dir. comm. Hackensack Hosp., until 1961; dir. environ. svcs. St. Raphael's Hosp., New Haven, 1961-64, Meriden (Conn.) Wal. Hosp., 1964-67, Mt. Sinai Hosp., Hartford, Conn., 1967-70, Union Truesdale Hosp., Fall River, Mass., 1970-78, Norwood (Mass.) Hosp., 1978-92; mgr. dept. interior Foxwoods Casino, Ledyard, Conn., 1991—; Pres. Anawon Solid Waste Com., Attleboro, Mass., 1987—; chmn. Solid Waste, Mansfield, Mass., 1988—. Patentee video system Dyno-Plexer, 1991; contbr. articles to profl. jours. Mem. Bd. Health, Mansfield, Mass., 1989—; mem. Anawan Region, Mass. Mem. ASHES (pres. 1986—, past pres. New Eng. chpt. 1988, Man. of Yr. 1989, Disting. Svc. award 1989), Am. Philatelic Soc., Croatian Stamp Soc. Home: 155 Gilbert St Mansfield MA 02048-2002 Office: Foxwood Casino Rte # 2 800 Washington St Ledyard CT 06339

VAN SWOL, NOEL WARREN, educator; b. N.Y.C., Dec. 30, 1941; s. Erwin Anton and Hildegard van S.; BA, Am. U., 1964; MA, Columbia U., 1967; MS, Syracuse U., 1972. Asst. underwriter Comml. Union Ins. Group Ltd., N.Y.C., 1964-66; tchr. social studies jr. high sch., Bklyn., 1966-67, Liberty (N.Y.) Cen. High Sch., 1967-69; instr. student personnel Sullivan County (N.Y.) Community Coll., 1969-70; tchr. social studies E. Syracuse-Minoa (N.Y.) High Sch., 1970—, coord. social studies, 1976—; adj. instr. polit. geography Columbia Coll. Residence Edn. Ctr., 1990—; adj. instr. pub. affairs Syracuse U., 1990—, adj. instr. econs., 1992—; cons. to trainer of tchr. trainers project Syracuse U., 1971-74. Contbr. articles to profl. jours. V.p. Fremont (N.Y.) Taxpayers and Civic Assn., 1971; mem. Town of Fremont Rep. Vacancy Com., 1967, 73, 74, 78, 80, 81, 83; mem. Task Force Against Nuclear Pollution, Inc.; bd. dirs. Project Legal, 1983-84; candidate Teacher in Space Project. Tchr. Leadership Devel. fellow, 1971, Freedoms Found. fellow, 1986, 87. Mem. Am. Hist. Assn., N.Y. State Hist. Assn., Am. Polit. Sci. Assn., Assn. Supervision and Curriculum Devel., Nat., N.Y. State, Cen. N.Y. Councils Social Studies, Social Studies Suprs. Assn., Orgn. Am. Historians, Soc. for History Edn., Upper Delaware Scenic River Assn., Upper Del. Coalition Concerned Citizens, Ind. Landholders Assn., Nat. Inholders Assn., Upper Del. Citizens Alliance, Western Sullivan County Taxpayers Assn., Planetary Soc., Nat. Space Soc., Phi Delta Kappa. Home: Route 97 Long Eddy NY 12760

VAN TASSEL, GARY WINTHROP, marine engineer, naval architect; b. Rockville Centre, N.Y., June 6, 1951; s. Robert Edwin and Dorothea Elizabeth (Hunt) V.; m. Bonita Kay Steele, Apr. 26, 1975; children—Deanna Michelle, Gary Winthrop II. B.S., U.S. Mcht. Marine Acad., 1973; M.E.-Ocean, Steven's Inst. Tech., 1980. Master ship Marine Sci. Consortium, Lewes, Del., 1973-77; project mgr. Marine Safety Internat., N.Y.C., 1977-80; sr. cryogenic engr. El Paso Marine Co., Solomons, Md., 1980-81; project engr. Levingston Marine Co., Annapolis, Md., 1981-82; mgr. marine engring. Giannotti & Assos., Annapolis, 1982-84; pres., owner Ocean Tech. Service, Solomons, Md., 1984—; pres., ptnr. Ocean Tech. Marine, Solomons, Md., 1985—; dir. cryogenic systems Argent Marine Ops., Inc., Solomons, 1991—. Served to lt. USNR, 1973-82. Mem. Soc. Naval Architects and Marine Engrs., Am. Boat and Yacht Council. Episcopalian. Club: So. Maryland Sailing Assn. (Solomons). Developer and patent holder innovative marine propulsion system, 1986; designer for Ocean Tech series of yachts. Home: 77F St Johns Creek Rd Lusby MD 20657 Office: Argent Marine Ops Inc PO Box 205 Solomons MD 20688

VAN TIENHOVEN, ARI, education educator; b. The Hague, The Netherlands, Apr. 22, 1922; came to U.S., 1949; s. Adrianus Baltus and Willemina Hendrika (Mulder) van T.; m. Annie van Haselen, Mar. 14, 1950; children: Richard Ari, Arianne Jeanette, Andrew Wijnand. Landbouwkundig Ingenieur, Agrl. U., Wageninen, The Netherlands, 1949; MS, U. Ill., 1951, PhD, 1953. Asst. prof. Miss. State Coll., Starkville, 1953-55; from asst. prof. to prof. emeritus Cornell U., Ithaca, N.Y., 1955—; assoc. edit. Poultry Sci., Urbana, Ill., 1964-67, 1980-83, Biology of Reproduction, Urbana, 1975-77, Gen. and Comparative Endocrinology, N.Y.C., 1968-74, veterinanry Quarterly, Utrecht, The Netherlands, 1980-87. Author: Physiology of Reproduction of Vertebrates, 1968, 83. Bd. dirs. Ithaca City Sch. Dist., 1968-71, pres. 1970-71; bd. dirs. Economic Opportunity Corp., Ithaca, 1969-70, 82-84, 86-89, v.p. 1980-89. Recipient Edgerton Career Teaching award Cornell U., Ithaca, 1985, Teacher of Merit award. Fellow AAAS, Poultry Sci. Assn., NSF. Democrat. Home: 9 Hudson Pl Ithaca NY 14850-5755 Office: Cornell U Avian and Poultry Sci Dept Rice Hall Ithaca NY 14853

VAN TRUMP, JAMES EDMOND, research chemist, renovator; b. Wood River, Nebr., Mar. 1, 1943; s. James Isaiah and June Alene (Spellman) Van T.; m. Betty Osborne, June 15, 1968; children: Nissa Rhea, James Christopher. BS, U. Wyo., 1964; MS, U. Calif., San Diego, 1973, PhD, 1975. Rsch. chemist Am. Potash, L.A., 1968-70, E.I. DuPont de Nemours & Co., Kingston, N.C., 1975-77; sr. rsch. chemist E.I. DuPont de Nemours & Co., Wilmington, Del., 1977-81, rsch. assoc., 1981—. Contbr. artilces to profl. jours. With U.S. Army, 1966-68. Mem. Soc. for Advancement of Material and Process Engring., Am. Chem. Soc. Republican. Office: DuPont Exptl Sta E302/313 Wilmington DE 19880-0302

VAN UMMERSEN, CLAIRE A(NN), chancellor, biologist, educator; b. Chelsea, Mass., July 28, 1935; d. George and Catherine (Courtovich); m. Frank Van Ummersen, June 7, 1958; children: Lynn, Scott. BS, Tufts U., 1957, MS, 1960, PhD, 1963; DSc (hon.), U. Mass., 1988, U. Maine, 1991. Rsch. asst. Tufts U., 1957-60, 60-67, grad. asst. in embryology, 1962, postdoctoral teaching asst., 1963-66, lectr. in biology, 1967-68; asst. prof. biology U. Mass., Boston, 1968-74; assoc. prof. U. Mass., 1974-86, assoc. dean acad. affairs, 1975-76, assoc. vice chancellor acad. affairs, 1976-78, chancellor, 1978-79, dir. Environ. Sci. Ctr., 1980-82; assoc. vice chancellor acad. affairs Mass. Bd. Regents for Higher Edn., 1982-85, vice chancellor for mgmt. systems and telecommunications, 1985-86; chancellor Univ. System N.H., Durham, 1986—; cons. Mass. Bd. Regents, 1981-82; asst. Lancaster Course in Ophthalmology, Mass. Eye and Ear Infirmary, 1962-69, lectr., 1970—, also coord.; reviewer HEW; mem. rsch. team which established safety standards for exposure to microwave radiation, 1958-65; participant Leadership Am. program, 1992. Mem. N.H. Ct. Systems Rev. Task Force, 1989-90; mem. New Eng. Bd. Higher Edn., 1986—, mem. exec. com., 1989—, N.H. Adv. Coun., 1990—; bd. dirs. N.H. Bus. and Ind. Assn., 1987-90, 90—; mem. steering com. N.H. Ptnrs. in Edn., 1991—; governing bd. N.H. Math. Coalition, 1991—; exec. com. 21st Century Learning Community, 1992—; state panelist N.H. Women in Higher Edn., 1986—, selected for leadership Am. program. Recipient Disting. Svc. medal U. Mass., 1979, Am. Cancer Soc. grantee Tufts U., 1960. Mem. AAAS, Am. Coun. on Edn. (com. on self-regulation 1987—), State Higher Exec. Officers (fed. rels. com., cost accountability task force, exec. com. 1990—), Nat. Assn. System Heads (exec. com. 1990—), Nat. Ctr. for Edn. Stats. (network adv. com. 1989—, chair accreditation teams 1988—), New Eng. Assn. Schs. and Colls. (comm. on higher edn. 1990—), Am. Soc. Zoologists, Soc. Devel. Biology, N.H. Coll. and Univ. Coun., Phi Beta Kappa, Sigma Xi. Office: NH U System Office of Chancellor Dunlap Ctr Durham NH 03824

VAN WAGENINGE, ROBERT, educator; b. Paterson, N.J., Mar. 11, 1953; s. Henry Clarence and Susan (Johnstone) Van W. Student, Juilliard Sch., 1973-75; BA, Kean Coll. N.J., 1977; MEd, William Paterson Coll., 1988. Cert. tchr., prin., N.J. Music tchr. Bernards Twp. Pub. Schs., Basking Rdige, N.J., 1977—. Mem. Assn. for Supervision and Curriculum Devel., Nat. Assn. Jazz Educators (bd. dirs. 1978-80), Music Educators Nat. Conf., N.J. Music Educators Assn. (bd. dirs. 1978-81), NEA, Kappa Delta Pi, Pi Lambda Theta. Baptist. Home: 11 Dubel Rd Wayne NJ 07470-2901

VAN WINKELEN, BARBARA, artist, art gallery director; d. Harold Dorr and Dorothy (Putnam) Hayes; m. Herbert van Winkelen, Aug. 13, 1966; children: Susan Putnam, Wendy Lesley. BFA, Yale U., 1943. Staff asst. Mus. Modern Art, N.Y.C., 1943-44; mem. World War II Clubmobile staff ARC, Eng., 1944-46; tchr. art Wadsworth Atheneum, Hartford, Conn., 1948-50; artist, tech. illustrator Hamilton Standard div. United Tech., Windsor Locks, Conn., 1953-72; owner, artist Spindrift Gallery, Nantucket, Mass., 1973-92; pres. Windsor Palette & Brush Assn., 1960-62. One woman shows include Invited Artists N.W. Pk., Windsor, Conn., 1990, Nantucket Artists Assn., 1991; group shows include N.Am. Open Show, Boston, 1990, Hudson Valley Art Assn., White Plains, N.Y., 1990, Conn. Women Artists, New Haven, Conn., 1990, 91, New Haven Paint and Clay Club, 1990, 91, N.E. Watercolor Ann., Boston, 1990, 91, 92, Conn. Watercolor Soc., New Haven, 1990,, 91, Acad. Artists Assn., 1990, 91, 92, Conn. Women Artists 63d Annual New Britain Mus. Am. Art, 1992. Author: Artists of New England, 1992. Recipient award Acad. Artists 37th Nat., 1987, Award for Excellence, New Eng. Watercolor N.Am. Open Show, 1988. award Nat. Watercolor Mems. Show, Colo., 1988. Juried-in mem. New Eng. Watercolor Soc., Conn. Acad. Fine Arts, Conn. Women Artist, Inc., Conn. Watercolor Soc.; mem. Nantucket Artists Assn., New Haven Paint & Clay Club, Inc., Acad. Artists Assn., Inc., Am. Watercolor Soc. (assoc.), Nat. Watercolor Soc. (assoc.). Home: 1864 Poquonock Ave Windsor CT 06095-1234 Office: Spindrift Gallery 11 Old South Wharf St Nantucket MA 02554-3834

VAN WOERT, JAMES WINSTON, guidance counselor; b. Freeport, N.Y., July 1, 1943; s. James Dutton and Esther Lippit (Steere) Van W.; m. Sandra Lee McMullen, Oct. 16, 1965; children: J. Scott, Jennifer L.. BS in Edn., SUNY, Oneonta, 1968; MS in Counseling, U. Scranton, 1991. Cert. tchr., sch. counselor. Tchr. Harpursville (N.Y.) Cen. Schs., 1967-88, sch. counselor, 1988—; park ranger Broome County Dept. of Parks, Binghamton, N.Y., 1971-85; mem. Com. for Drug Free Schs., Harpursville, 1990-91. Vice-pres. Citizens Found. of Am., Colesville, N.Y., 1988-91; emergency med. tech., Colesville Vol. Ambulance Corp., Harpursville, 1970-89; chmn. local troop Boy Scouts of Am., Harpursville, 1978-81. Mem. Rotary (pres. Colesville unit 1990-91, treas. 1986-90, chmn. Youth Exch., Harpursville, 1985-91), N.Y. State United Tchrs., Am. Fedn. of Tchrs., N.Y. State ASCD, Harpursville Tchrs. Assn. (pres. 1987-91). Republican. Home: Rte 2 Box 200A Chaffee Street Harpursville NY 13787-9542 Office: Harpursville High Sch Main St Harpursville NY 13787

VAN WYE, DAVID RODMAN, state agency administrator; b. Jersey City, June 15, 1947; s. Rodman Farley and Alice Adeline (August) Van W.; m. Elizabeth Joan Hayes, Feb. 1, 1969; children: Gretchen, Brian. BA, Lehigh U., 1969; MPA, Pa. State U., 1975. Asst. pers. dir. Pa. Bd. Probation and Parole, Harrisburg, 1971-81; mgr. employee benefits Pa. Dept. Labor and Industry, Harrisburg, 1981-83, mgr. employee devel. and safety, 1983—. Soccer coach Hampden Twp. Soccer Assn., Mechanicsburg, Pa., 1980-84; scoutmaster troop 49, Boy Scouts Am., Enola, Pa., 1985. Capt. U.S. Army, 1969-71, Vietnam. Mem. ASTD (dir. programs Cen. Pa. chpt. 1989, pres. 1990, past pres., bd. dirs. 1991, asst. regional dir. membership region 2, Outstanding Leadership and Pres. award 1990), Internat. Pers. Mgmt. Assn., Pi Alpha Alpha. Unitarian. Office: Pa Dept Labor and Industry 7th and Forster Sts Harrisburg PA 17120

VAN WYK, HELEN, artist; b. Fair Lawn, N.J., Apr. 22, 1930; d. Andrew and Alida (Stap) DeBoer; m. Herbert Rogoff, Feb. 17, 1984. Author: Basic Oil Painting the Van Wyk Way, Painting Flowers the Van Wyk Way, Portraits in Oil the Van Wyk Way, Welcome to my Studio, Color Mixing in Action; host Welcome to My Studio, PBS-TV. Home: 2 Briarstone Rd Rockport MA 01966-1904

VANYUR, JOHN MARTIN, psychologist; b. Phila., Jan. 14, 1956; s. John Martin and Louise Ann (Nessel) V.; m. Suzanne Howard Dawson, Sept. 17, 1983; children: Jennifer, Christen. BS summa cum laude, U. Scranton, 1977; MA, U. Md., 1980, PhD, 1985. Teaching asst. U. Md., College Park, 1977-79; statistician U.S. Bur. Census, Suitland, Md., 1979; research asst. U. Md., College Park, 1980-81; research analyst Fed. Bur. Prisons, Washington, 1980-82, chief personnel program analysis, 1982-86; asst. to warden Fed. Bur. Prisons, Terminal Island, Calif., 1986-87; chief career devel. Fed. Bur. Prisons, Washington, 1987-88, personnel dir., 1988-91, dep. asst. dir., 1991—. Asst. scoutmaster Boy Scouts Am., Phila., 1974-76. Recipient Asst. Dir. award Fed. Bur. Prisons, 1985. Mem. Am. Psychol. Assn., Am. Statis. Assn., Am. Correctional Assn., Personnel Testing Council Met. Washington. Republican. Roman Catholic. Clubs: Toastmasters (Washington) (pres. 1985-86). Office: Fed Bur Prisons 320 1st St NW Washington DC 20534-0001

VAN ZANDT, TINA LOUISE, entrepreneur; b. Gloversville, N.Y., July 14, 1960; d. Lester Sanford Van Zandt and Carol Ester Tibbles; m. Del Michael Cook, Aug. 3, 1978 (div. 1986); 1 child, Morgan Van Zandt. Student, Mountain Bell Tng. Ctr., 1981, Mountain Bell Tng. Ctr., 1982. Cable maintenance adminstr. Mountain Bell, Casper, Wyo., 1980-82; freelance musician and audio engr. Speculator, N.Y., 1982-84; optician Am. Vision, Chgo., 1984-85; owner, speculator Van Zandt Designs, Warrensburg, Queensbury, N.Y., 1985—; emergency operator N.Y. Telephone, Glens Falls, 1990—; freelance musician, 1982—; freelance astrological cons., Warrensburg, 1981—.

VAN ZILE, PHILIP TAYLOR, III, lawyer, educator; b. Detroit, Feb. 17, 1945; s. Philip Taylor II and Ruth (Butzel) Van Z.; m. Susan Jones, Sept. 12, 1981; children: Caroline Sage, Philip Taylor IV. BA, Oberlin Coll., 1968; MDiv, Union Theol. Sem., 1971; JD, Detroit U., 1975. Bar: Mich. 1976, D.C. 1976, U.S. Dist. Ct. (ea. dist.) Mich. 1976, U.S. Ct. Appeals (6th cir.) 1976, U.S. Supreme Ct. 1977, Pa. 1981. Law clk. Mich. Ct. Appeals, Detroit, 1976-78, Mich. Supreme Ct., Detroit and Lansing, Mich., 1978-80; asst. corp. counsel Office of Corp. Counsel, Washington, 1980-87; assoc. Killian & Gephart, Harrisburg, Pa., 1987-89; prin. Law Office of Philip T. Van Zile, Harrisburg, 1989-91; assoc. coun. Office Chief Coun. Pa. Dept. Environ. Resources, Harrisburg, 1991—; teaching fellow Detroit Coll. Law, 1976-80; teaching asst. Detroit Gen. Hosp., 1978-80; teaching assoc. Acad. Med. Arts and Bus., Harrisburg, 1990-91. Contbr. articles to profl. jours. Mem. ABA, Kenwood Club (Chevy Chase, Md.). Office: Pa Dept Environ Resources Office Chief Counsel 301 Chestnut St Harrisburg PA 17101-2755

VARAS, BARBARA GUADALUPE, features editor; b. Valparaiso, Chile, Nov. 23, 1953; came to U.S., 1976; d. Jose Alejandro and Teresa Adela (Parra) V. Student, Santa Maria U., Valparaiso, 1973-76, N.Y. Sch. Social Rsch., 1977, NYU, 1979, Ctr. for the Media Arts, 1982. Audio visual specialist Philip Morris, Inc., N.Y.C., SONY Corp., N.J., Minolta Corp., N.Y.C., Channel 4, N.Y.C., United Artists Communications, East Meadow, N.Y., Canon U.S.A., Inc., N.Y., Audio Visual Workshop, N.Y.C.; features editor Amusement Features Syndicate, N.Y.C. and Bklyn., 1986—. Dir., editor: Spanish film The Bitter Honey, 1986, Broadway's Magic Carpet, 1986; editor: Playing with Fire, 1988. Roman Catholic.

VARET, MICHAEL A., lawyer; b. N.Y.C., Mar. 9, 1942; s. Guster V. and Frances B. (Goldberg) V.; m. Elizabeth R. Varet, June 3, 1973; 3 children. BS in Econs., U. Pa., 1962; LLB, Yale U., 1965. Bar: N.Y. 1966, U.S. Supreme Ct. 1975, U.S. Dist. Ct. (ea. and so. dists.) N.Y. 1975, U.S. Tax Ct. 1975, U.S. Claims Ct. 1975, U.S. Ct. Appeals (2d cir.) 1975. Mem. Milgrim Thomajan & Lee P.C., N.Y.C., 1982—. Trustee Montefiore Med. Ctr., Bronx, N.Y., 1980-92; bd. dirs. Sem. Libr. Corp. Jewish Theol. Sem., N.Y.C., 1983-87, United Jewish Appeal-Fedn. Jewish Philanthropies of Greater N.Y., Inc., 1979-86, Mosholu Preservation Corp., Bronx, 1982-88; bd. overseers Jewish Theol. Sem., 1982-90, Jewish Publ. Soc. of Am., 1986—, exec. com., 1989—; mem. exec. com. Montefiore Med. Ctr., 1985-92, Yale Law Sch. Assn., 1990—; mem. coun. of overseers United Jewish Appeal Fedn. of Jewish Philanthropies of Greater N.Y., Inc., 1986—. Mem. ABA, N.Y. State Bar Assn., Assn. of Bar of City of N.Y. (bd. dirs., exec. com. 1971-75), Internat. Fiscal Assn., Internat. Tax Planning Assn., Yale Club, (N.Y.C.), Lotos Club (N.Y.C.). Democrat. Office: Milgrim Thomajan & Lee PC 53 Wall St New York NY 10005-2834

VARGAS, JOSEPHINE, illustrator, painter; b. N.Y.C., July 31, 1946; d. Jose and Jennie (Concepcion) V. Student, Fasion Inst. Tech., 1964-65, Sch. Visual ARts, 1978-79. Artist Allied Stores Corp., N.Y.C., 1966-69, Simplicity Pattern Co., N.Y.C., 1969-73, McCall Pattern Co., N.Y.C., 1973-79, Masters Inc., Westbury, N.Y., 1981—; freelance artist various pattern and pub. cos., N.Y.C., 1979-80. One-woman show at Mallette Gallery, Garden City, 1989; exhibited in group shows at Nassau County Mus. Fine Art, Roslyn, N.Y., 1987, Chelsea Mansion, Muttontown, N.Y., 1988 (Merit award), Salmagundi Club, N.Y.C., 1989, Jacob Javits Fed. Plaza, N.Y.C., 1989, 90, 91, Pt. Washington (N.Y.) Libr., 1991, Visual Art Alliance of L.I. (Peacock Showcase award 1991), Am. Watercolor Soc. 125th Ann. Internat. Exhbn. Monitor watercolor alumni program Sch. Visual Art, 1982-84. Mem. Nat. Art League (trustee 1986—, 1st Place Watercolor award 1991, Bronze medal 1987), Nat. Assn. Women Artists, Thirty Artists. Roman Catholic. Home: 83-40 Austin St Kew Gardens NY 11415

VARLEY, ROBERT CHRISTOPHER GOUGH, management consultant, economist; b. Perth, Scotland, Dec. 11, 1949; came to U.S., 1990; s. Rowland Michael Gough and Elizabeth Joan (Asher) V.; m. Widayati Ambarkahi Supangat, Sept. 4, 1986; children: Krishna, Harold. BSc in Econ., London U., 1971, MSc in Econ., 1973; cert. edn., Inst. Edn., London, 1975; MPPM, Yale U., 1992. Econs. lectr. Polytech. of South Bank, London, 1973-75; researcher U.K., Fiji, 1975-77; sr. economist Hunting Tech. Svcs., Elstree, U.K., 1977-85; cons., project assoc. Harvard Inst. for Internat. Devel., Cambridge, Mass., 1985-91; cons. New Haven, 1991—. Author: Tourism in Fiji, 1978, (monograph) Irrigation Policy, 1989; contbr. articles to profl. jours. Home and Office: 110 Livingston St # B3 New Haven CT 06511

VARMA, RANBIR, economics educator; b. Nov. 29, 1928. BA, Patna U., 1949; MA, Columbia U., 1952; PhD, New Sch. for Social Rsch., 1957. Lectr. Columbia U., 1955-57; asst. prof. L.I. U., 1959-63, assoc. prof., 1963-66, prof. econs., 1966—, chmn. econs. dept., 1963-76, 85—; bd. dirs. L.I. U.-Chung-and U. Program, 1963-64; chmn. commn. I, Bklyn. Ctr., 1964, chmn. dean's selection com., 1969-70; assoc. Columbia U. Faculty Seminar; cons. USIA, 1953-66; session chairperson devel. funds vs. needs, 8th World Conf., Soc. for Internat. Devel., 1966; session chairperson Montclair State Coll., 1977; conf. chairperson Eastern Econ. Assn., Washington, 1978. Author: (with others) Contemporary India, 1964, Goals Priorities and Dollars-The Next Decade, 1966, The Yearbook of the American Philosophical Society, 1968; contbr. articles to profl. jours; mem. editorial bd. Internat. Jour. of Devel. Planning Literature. Sidney Hillman fellowship, 1953-54; grantee Am. Philos. Soc., 1968. Mem. Am. Econ. Assn., Met. Econ. Assn., Soc. for Internat. Devel. Home: 565 W End Ave New York NY 10024-2705 Office: Long Island U Dept Econs University Pla Brooklyn NY 11201

VARRENTI, ADAM, JR., financial executive; b. Phila., Apr. 9, 1949; s. Adam Sr. and Yolanda (Messina) V.; m. Diane Maria Squillace; children: Jocelyn, Adam III, Melissa, Andrew. BS in Acctg., Villanova U., 1971; cert. CLU, Am. Coll., 1981, cert. chartered fin. cons., 1985. Pres. Diversified Fin. Group, West Chester, Pa., 1981—; mng. ptnr. Adam Varrenti, Jr. and Assocs., West Chester, 1989—; bd. dirs. Equipment Leasing Corp. Am., Bala Cynwyd, Pa., Guthrie Landscaping Co., Inc., Elwyn, Pa., DMSV, Inc., West Chester, Pa., Guthrie Landscape Nursery, Inc., Glenmoore, Pa., Pa. Long Distance, Inc. Guest columnist The Daily Local newspaper, 1988—. Bd. dirs. Pa. Assn. for the Blind Chester County div. Named Man of Yr. Phila. Gen. Agts. and Mgrs. Assn., 1978. Mem. Nat. Assn. Security Dealers (registered rep.), Am. Soc. CLUs, Am. Soc. Chartered Fin. Cons., Chester County Estate Planning Coun., Nat. Assn. Life Underwriters (Nat. Quality award 1991), Pa. Assn. Life Underwriters (regional v.p. 1990—), Chester County Life Underwriters (past pres., nat. committeeman 1989—), Nat. Soc. Pub. Accts., Million Dollar Round Table (life and qualifying), Lions (past pres. Brandywine Club, Pa.).

VARRONE, CRESCENT RICHARD, management consultant; b. Queens, N.Y., Mar. 23, 1964; s. Crescent Michael and Camille Marie (Zaino) V. BA in Polit. Sci., Williams Coll., 1985; student, U. Oslo, Norway, 1986; MA/BA in Econs., Cambridge (Eng.) U., 1988. Assoc. McKinsey & Co., N.Y.C., 1988-90, engagement mgr., 1991—; bd. dirs. Louis August Jonas Found., Rhinebeck, N.Y., 1991—; selection-com. Herchel Smith Scholarship com. Williams Coll., 1989—. Herchel Smith scholarship H. Smith Fund, Williams Coll., 1985, Fulbright scholarship 1985, Tyng scholarship, Williams Coll., 1981, Regis scholarship, 1977. Office: McKinsey & Co 55 E 52nd St New York NY 10022-5905

VARS, ADDISON FOSTER, III, lawyer; b. Washington, May 3, 1945; s. Addison Foster Vars Jr. and Nancy (Kincaid) Breslin; m. Barbara Ruth Vars, Sept. 1, 1974; 1 child, Lesley Foster. BA, U. N.C., 1967; JD, Syracuse U., 1971. Bar: N.Y. 1972. Ptnr. O'Hara, O'Hara, and Vars, Liverpool, N.Y., 1974-78, Conboy, McKay, Bachman, and Kendall, Watertown, N.Y., 1978—; bd. dirs. H.M. Quackenbush, Inc., Herkimer, N.Y., Empire Cruise Lines, Ltd., Alexandria Bay, N.Y. Chmn. Jefferson County chpt. ARC, Watertown, 1984-86, Antique Boat Mus., Clayton, 1988-90, trustee, 1983—. Mem. ABA, N.Y. State Bar Assn., Jefferson County Bar Assn. (dir. 1988). Republican. Office: Conboy McKay Bachman and Kendall 407 Sherman St Watertown NY 13601

VARY, THOMAS CRISPIN, physiologist; b. Fountain Hill, Pa., Sept. 15, 1954; s. George Crispin and Clairebette (Folk) V.; m. Kathleen Ann O'Neal, May 3, 1991; 1 child, Katherine Ann; stepchildren: Jennifer Taverna, Charles Taverna. BA, Johns Hopkins U., 1976; MS, Lehigh U., 1978; PhD, Pa. State U., 1982. Postdoctoral fellow Pa. State U. Coll. Medicine, Hershey, 1982; British-Am. rsch. fellow Nuffield dept. clin. biochemistry U. Oxford, England, 1982-83; asst. prof. Md. Shock Trauma Ctr., Balt., 1983-88; asst. prof. dept. cells and molecular physiology Pa. State U., 1988-90, assoc. prof., 1990—. Contbr. articles to profl. jours. and chpts. to books. Coach Hampden Area (Pa.) Youth Soccer, 1990—, Hampden Area Little League, 1990—. NIH grantee, 1989—, Career Devel. award, 1990—. Mem. Shock Soc., Internat. Soc. for Heart Rsch., Am. Physiol. Soc. (editorial bd. 1990—), Am. Soc. Biol. Chemists, Hershey Country Club. Republican. Episcopalian. Office: Pa State U Coll Medicine Dept Cellular Molecular Physiology Hershey PA 17033

VASAS, MARY TERESA MARWOOD, emergency nurse; b. Norristown, Pa., Apr. 16, 1958; d. Charles Joseph and Mary Teresa (Burns) M.; m. Steven G. Vasas. Assoc. of Nursing, Gwynedd-Merey Coll., 1978, B of Nursing, 1980. Cert. emergency nurse. Staff nurse Sacred Heart Hosp. and Rehab. Ctr., Norristown, 1978-81, nurse spl. care unit, 1981-83, staff nurse emergency dept., 1983—, preceptor emergency dept., 1984-91, acting nurse mgr. emergency dept., 1991, staff mem. emergency dept., 1991—. Mem. Emergency Nurse's Assn. (pres. 1990), Sigma Theta Tau.

VASELLA, DANIEL LUCIUS, pharmaceutical marketing executive; b. Fribourg, Switzerland, Aug. 15, 1953; came to U.S., 1988; s. Oskar Emil and Ursulina Isabella (Vieli) V.; m. Anne-Laurence Moret, May 12, 1978; children: Emilia Anna, Mauro Giovanni, Flavio Bernardo Placi. Swiss fed. physician diploma, U. Berne, Switzerland, 1979, MD, 1980; postgrad., Harvard U., 1989. Resident in pathology U. Berne, 1980-81, psychoanalyst, 1983-88; resident in internal medicine Inselspital, Berne, 1982-83, attending physician, 1984-88; resident in internal medicine Waid-Spital, Zurich, Switzerland, 1983-84; mgr. spl. projects Sandoz Pharms. Corp., East Hanover, N.J., 1988-90, product mgr., 1990-91, dir. mktg., 1991-92; asst. to COO Sandoz Pharms. AG, Basel, Switzerland, 1992—; lectr. U. Fribourg, Berne and Fribourg, 1985-88. Author: (with others) Psychosomatische Medizin, 1986; contbr. articles to profl. jours. Speaker various orgns., U.S.A. and Switzerland, 1985-92. Recipient Patron award U. Mich., 1992. Mem. Am. Mgmt. Assn., Swiss Med. Assn. (bd. cert. for internal medicine 1985), Swiss Soc. for Geriatrics, Swiss Psychosomatic Assn., Swiss Psychoanalytical Assn. (candidate), Deutsches Kollegium fuer Psychosomatik. Office: Sandoz Pharms Assn 59 Rt 10 East Hanover NJ 07936

VASEY, ANN L., education educator; b. Cleve., May 3, 1949; d. Albert and Norma (Miller) Ringler; m. Graham C. Vasey, Feb. 20, 1972; children: Rachel N., Corinne E. BS in Elem. Edn. and Early Childhood, Boston U., 1972; MEd in Counseling Psychology, Northeastern U., 1974. Nat. cert. clin. mental health counselor, nat. cert. counselor; lic. mental health counselor, Mass.; lic. marriage and family therapist, Mass. Adolescent and family therapist SHARE, Lowell, Mass.; instr. Framingham (Mass.) State Coll., Cambridge Ctr. for Adult Edn., Framingham, Cen. Mass. Job Tng., Worcester; dir. The Learning Experience Elem. Sch., Marlborough, Mass.; instr. Quinsigamond Community Coll., Worcester; psychol. cons. Quinsigamond Community Coll., Childcare Lab. Sch., Worcester, Mass.; ednl. and psychol. cons. Chpt. author tchr. guide by The Network, Inc. Mem. Am. Assn. for Counseling and Devel. Home: 83 Woodland Rd Ashland MA 01721-1411

VASSALLE, MARIO, physiologist; b. Viareggio, Lucca, Italy, May 26, 1928; came to U.S., 1958; s. Giuseppe and Antonietta (Vassalle) V.; m. Anna Maria Petrucci; children: Andrew G., Alessandra A., Massimo B., Roberto M., Francesca A. MD cum laude, U. Pisa, Italy, 1953, specialization in cardiology cum laude, 1955; doctorate honoris causa, U. Ferrara, Italy, 1990. Med. diplomate. Intern Istituto di Medicine and Cardiology U. Pisa, 1953-55, asst. Istituto di Patologia Medica, 1956-58; acting chief resident in medicine French Hosp., N.Y.C., 1958-59; trainee cardiovascular rsch. & tng. program dept. physiology Med. Coll. Ga., Augusta, 1959-60; postdoctoral fellow dept. physiology SUNY-Downstate Med. Ctr., Bklyn., 1960-61, N.Y. Heart Assn. fellow dept. physiology, 1961-62, instr., 1962, vis. asst. prof., 1964-65, asst. prof., 1965-66, assoc. prof., 1966-71, prof., 1971—; NIH fellow Physiologisches Institut U. Bern, Switzerland, 1962-64; vis. prof. U. Ferrara, 1971, U. Vt., Burlington, 1978, Cath. Univ. Gemelli, Rome, 1984-85; assoc. editor Am. Jour. Physiology: Heart and Circulatory Physiology, 1976-80; mem. editorial bd. Circulation Rsch., 1974-80, European Jour. Pharmacology, 1985-90, Jour. Electrocardiology, 1985—; mem. editorial bd. New Trends in Arrhythmias, 1985—, assoc. editor, 1991—; editorial cons. Am. Jour. Physiology, Circulation, Science, Jour. Gen. Physiology, Pflügers Archiv; NIH cons.; mem. NIH Cardiopulmonary Study Sect., 1981-85, ad hoc mem., 1988; invited participant numerous confs., symposiums and workshops. Author, editor: Research in Physiology, 1971, Cardiac Physiology for the Clinician, 1976, translated into Chinese, 1978, Excitation and Neural Control of the Heart, 1982; author, co-author 140 papers; editor: Chandler McCuskey Brooks: The Scientist and the Man, 1990; contbr. 42 revs. and chpts., 122 abstracts to books and profl. jours. Fulbright travel grantee, 1958-62; recipient A. and A. Sinsheimer Fund award, 1966-71, N.Y. Health Rsch. Coun. award, 1972-75. Mem. AAAS, Am. Physiol. Soc., Am. Heart Assn. (coun. on basic scis. 1969—), N.Y. Heart Assn. (bd. dirs. 1978-84), N.Y. Acad. Scis., Cardiac Muscle Soc., Cardiac Electrophysiol. Group (pres. 1972-73), Internat. Study Group for Rsch. in Cardiac Metabolism, Harvey Soc., Mex. Soc. Cardiology (hon.), Sigma Xi (pres. Downstate Med. Ctr. chpt. 1984). Roman Catholic. Home: 104 Huntington Rd Port Washington NY 11050-3511 Office: SUNY Health Sci Ctr 450 Clarkson Ave Brooklyn NY 11203-2098

VASSALLO, HOLLY, group home director. BA, So. Conn. State U., 1981, MS, 1990. Psychiat. tech. Waterbury (Conn.) Hosp., 1983-87, community liaison, case mgr. for homeless mentally ill, 1987-89, sr. mental health clinician, 1989-90; dir. group home St. Vincent DePaul Soc., Waterbury, 1990—; pvt. therapist.

VASSAR, JOHN DIXIE, JR., management, financial and technical consultant; b. Portsmouth, Va., Dec. 10, 1953; s. John Dixie and Hazell Marrie (Barr) V.; m. Karen Patricia Schad, May 6, 1990; 1 child, Kathryn Schad. BS in Biology/Nuclear Sci., Va. Tech., 1976, postgrad., 1981-83; postgrad., Johns Hopkins U., 1987-89; MA in Mgmt., U.S. Army Command & Gen. Staff Coll., 1991. Radiol. technician Va. Power, Surry, 1976; asst. reactor supr. Va. Tech., Blacksburg, Va., 1982-83; project mgr. Westinghouse, Columbia, Md., 1983-87; liaison officer, cons. to gen. staff, aviator, capt. CWO USAR, Ft. Meade, Md., 1987—; prin. cons. Edison Enterprises, Columbia, Md., 1987—; indsl. advisor Va. Tech. Nuclear Sci. Engring. Program, Blacksburg, Va., 1983-84; fin. planner, registered rep. Waddell and Reed Fin. Svcs., Columbia, Md., 1992—. Contbr. articles to profl. jours. Mem. Sound Money Assn., Cocoa Beach, Fla., 1981—, Mt. Zion United Meth. Ch.; pastoral cons. South Columbia Bapt. Ch. Capt. USAFR, 1976-88. Mem. Am. Nuclear Soc. (sec. Va. Tech. chpt. 1982-83), Health Physics Soc. (v.p. Va. Tech. chpt. 1975-76), Am. Assn. Fin. Profls., Nat. Assn. Securities Dealers, Va. Tech. Alumni and Athletic Assns., Highty Tightly Alumni Assn., Va. Tech. Corps of Cadets Alumni Assn., Sierra Club, Masons. Republican. Baptist. Home: 6026 Tree Swallow Ct Columbia MD 21044-5607 Office: Edison Enterprises 6026 Tree Swallow Columbia MD 21044

VASTA, VINCENT JOSEPH, JR., lawyer; b. N.Y.C., Jan. 15, 1944; s. Vincent Joseph and Frances (Monetta) V.; m. Virginia Eileen Kiesel, July 24, 1965; children: Jeffrey Scott, Russell Todd. BS in Chem. Engring., Manhattan Coll., 1965; MS in Chem. Engring., N.J. Inst. Tech., 1968; JD, Fordham U., 1972. Bar: N.Y. 1972, Conn. 1988; registered patent atty. Project engr. Exxon Research and Devel. Co., Florham Park, N.J., 1965-68, Hoffman-LaRoche Co., Nutley, N.J., 1968-72; assoc. Pennie & Edmonds, N.Y.C., 1972-77; sr. assoc. Morgan, Finnegan, Pine, Foley & Lee, N.Y.C., 1977-80; participating sr. assoc. Bryan & Bollo, Stamford, Conn., 1980-81; sole practice N.Y.C., 1981-83; internat. patent counsel Gen. Electric Co., N.Y.C., 1983-86; div. patent counsel Union Carbide Corp., Danbury, Conn., 1986-89, UOP, Tarrytown, N.Y., 1989-90; ptnr. Sprung, Horn, Kramer & Woods, N.Y.C. and Terrytown, N.Y., 1990—; pres. Vincent J. Vasta Jr. P.C., N.Y.C., 1981-90; bd. dirs., gen. counsel Calif. Taste, Inc., Santa Monica, 1982-88. Contbr. articles to profl. jours. Bd. dirs. student support com. Manhatten Ctr. High Sch., 1985-86; mentor Manhattan Ctr. High Sch. Mentor Program, 1985-86; bd. dirs., treas. ELFUN, N.Y.C., 1985-86. Mem. ABA, N.Y. Bar Assn., Assn. Bar City N.Y., Am. Patent Law Assn., N.Y. Patent, Trademark and Copyright Law Assn. Republican. Roman Catholic. Club: N.Y. Patent.

VATNE, DIANE CECELIA, museum administrator, art historian, photographer; b. Springfield, Vt., Jan. 19, 1956; d. Magnor and Jeanne (Gamlin) V.; m. Martin George Yates, June 25, 1983; children: Alexander Robert, Emily Jeanne. AB, Smith Coll., 1978; MFA, Ind. U., 1981, MA, 1984, PhD, 1990. Assoc. instr. Ind. U., Bloomington, 1980, grad. asst., 1980-83, 86, assoc. instr., 1983-86; asst. prof. Valparaiso (Ind.) U., 1982; instr. Colby Coll., Waterville, Maine, 1986-87; asst. prof. U. Maine, Orono, 1987; exec. dir. Bangor (Maine) Hist. Soc., 1987—. Author catalog entries. Ex-officio com. mem. Isaac Farrar Mansion Com., Bangor, 1989—; ex-officio mem. pub. rels. com. C. of C., Bangor, 1991. Lilly fellow, Florence, Italy, 1985-86; Ind. U. grantee, 1980, 81, 85; Ford Found. fellow, 1978-79, other grants. Mem. Maine Assn. Museums (founding coun. mem. 1988-90, editor-in-chief newsletter 1989-90, v.p. 1992-93), New Eng. Mus. Assn., Am. Assn. Museums, Am. Assn. for State and Local History, Coll. Art Assn., Friends of Photography, N.E. Hist. Film. Methodist. Office: Bangor Hist Soc 159 Union St Bangor ME 04401-6147

VATTILANA, JOSEPH WILLIAM, chief state safety inspector; b. Wilmington, Del., Mar. 22, 1928; s. Andrew and Elizabeth (Castiglione) V.; (div. 1974); children: Joseph W., Joy Ann; m. Gladys Mary Spence, Nov. 18, 1978. Student, Del. Tech. Community Coll., 1966-70, 89—, Pa. State U., 1976-80. Cert. Field Instr., Instr. for Radiation Control, Work Zone Safety Supr., Dir. Fleet Maintenance. Heavy equipment mechanic Dept. Hwys. and Transp., Bear, Del., 1963-70; equipment supt. Dept. Hwys. and Transp., Bear, 1970-79, hwy. safety engr., 1979-84, chief safety inspector, 1984—; speaker and instr. in field. Author: Safety Manual Pass the Word, 1987, Equipment Certification Manuel, 1987. Dep. chief, asst. chief-chief driver, bd. dirs., capt. of rescue, sec. Talleyville (Del.) Vol. Fire Co., 1946—; instr. ARC Del. chpt., Wilmington, 1956—; hon. life mem. Wilmington Manor Vol. Fire Co., 1985—. Recipient State Del. Disting. Svc. award Gov. State of Del. 1986, Lammot duPont Jr. Meml. award ARC Del. Chpt. 1989, Nat. Safety award Am. Traffic Safety Svcs. 1992. Mem. New Castle County Fire Chiefs Assn. (pres. 1985-86), New Castle County Vol. Firemans Assn. (pres. 1986-87), Del. State Fire Chiefs Assn., Del. Hwy. Engrs. (1st and 2nd v.p. 1987-89), Soc. Hwy. Engrs. (pres. 1st state chpt. 1988-90), Del. State Fire Police Assn. (hon. life.), Del. Safety Engrs. (pres. 1986-87), Am. Legion, VFW. Roman Catholic. Home: 3333 Silverside Rd Wilmington DE 19810-3306 Office: State of Del Div Hwys RR 7 Box 8 Bear DE 19701-9807

VAUGHAN, ALDEN TRUE, history educator; b. Providence, Jan. 23, 1929; s. Dana Prescott and Muriel Louise (True) V.; m. Lauraine A. Freethy, June 1, 1956 (div. 1981); children: Jeffrey Alden, Lynn Elizabeth; m. Virginia Mason Carr, July 16, 1983. BA, Amherst Coll., 1950; MEd, Columbia U., 1956, MA in History, 1958, PhD, 1964. Tchr. Hackley Sch., Tarrytown, N.Y., 1950-51, A.B. Davis High Sch., Mt. Vernon, N.Y., 1956-60; From history instr. to prof. Columbia U., N.Y.C., 1961—; editor Polit. Sci. Quar., N.Y., 1970-71; gen. editor Early Am. Indian Documents, Univ. Pubs. of Am., 1977—; assoc. editor Ency. of the N.Am. Colonies, Scribners, N.Y., 1990—; vis. adj. prof. CUNY, Lehman, Coll., N.Y.C., 1971; vis. prof. Clark U., Worcester, Mass., 1987. Author: New England Frontier, 1965, rev. edit., 1979, American Genesis, 1975, Shakespeare's Caliban, 1991; contbr. articles to Am. Heritage, Am. Hist. Rev., New Eng. Quar., and others. Lt. (j.g.) USNR, 1951-55. Recipient fellowship Guggenheim Found., 1973, Sr. fellowship Folger Shakespeare Libr., 1977, 89, Sr. fellowship Am. Antiquarian Soc., 1983. Mem. Am. Antiquarian Soc. (sr. fellowship), Am. Hist. Assn., Soc. Am. Historians (exec. sec., treas. 1965-70), Orgn. Am. Historians (program chmn. 1976), Inst. Early Am. History and Culture (coun. mem. 1985-87), Colonial Soc. Mass. Home: 50 Howland Ter Worcester MA 01602-2631 Office: Columbia U New York NY 10027

VAUGHAN, HERBERT WILEY, lawyer; b. Brookline, Mass., June 1, 1920; s. David D. and Elzie G. (Wiley) V.; m. Ann Graustein, June 28, 1941. Student, U. Chgo., 1937-38; SB cum laude, Harvard U., 1941, LLB, 1948. Bar: Mass. 1948. Assoc. Hale and Dorr, Boston, 1948-54, jr. ptnr., 1954-56, sr. ptnr., 1956-82, co-mng. ptnr., 1976-80; pres. Herbert W. Vaughan, P.C., sr. ptnr. Hale and Dorr, 1982-89, of counsel, 1990—. Chmn. The Trustees of Reservations; mem. bd. trustees, Am. Friends of New Coll. (Oxford Univ.). Fellow Am. Bar Found. (life); mem. ABA, Chesterton Soc. (internat. com.), Mass. Bar Assn., Boston Bar Assn., Internat. Bar Assn., Am. Law Inst., Am. Coll. Mortgage Attys., Am. Coll. Real Estate Lawyers, Bay, Badminton and Tennis Club, Union Club (Boston), Boston Econ. Club, Longwood Cricket Club (Brookline, Mass.).

VAUGHAN, JONATHAN, psychologist; b. New Haven, June 10, 1944; s. Victor Clarence and Deborah (Cloud) V.; m. Virginia Gray, July 2, 1968; children: Joseph, Alexander. BA, Swarthmore Coll., 1966; MA, Brown U., 1968, PhD, 1970. Prof. Hamilton Coll., Clinton, N.Y., 1971—; vis. scholar Univ. Oregon, 1981-83, Univ. Mass., 1987—; computing psychology dir. Carnegie Mellon Univ., 1990-91. Predoctoral fellow NSF, Brown Univ., 1967-70; Rsch. grantee NIMH, Hamilton Coll., 1974, 76-80; recipient Rsch. Svc. award NIMH, Univ. Oreg., 1981-83, Rsch. Opportunity award NSF, Univ. Mass., 1988—. Mem. Soc. for Computers in Psychology (pres. 1990-91). Office: Hamilton Coll Psychology Dept Clinton NY 13323

VAUGHAN, OLIVE ELIZABETH, marketing and industrial specialist, educator; b. Bridgeport, Conn., Oct. 23, 1925; d. Joseph Jackson and Olive Elizabeth (Sears) V. BA, Mt. Holyoke Coll., 1947, MA, 1949; PhD in Econs., Columbia U., 1973. Price economist U.S. Bur. Labor Stats., N.Y.C., 1949-50; econ. researcher, chief price sect. The Conf. Bd., N.Y.C., 1951-58; research analyst Gen. Electric Co., N.Y.C., 1958-66; asst. prof. C.W. Post Coll., Greenvale, N.Y., 1967-73, Fordham U., Bronx, N.Y., 1973-76; staff specialist, planning So. New Eng. Telephone, New Haven, Conn., 1977-89; planning cons. Gen. Electric Co. N.Y.C., 1973-74. Contbr. articles to bus. publs. Mem. Nat. Assn. Bus. Economists, Am. Econ. Assn., Am. Mktg. Assn., Am. Statis. Assn. Home: 153 Bull Hill Ln West Haven CT 06516-3928

VAUGHAN, WAYLAND EDWARD, marketing educator; b. Boston, July 18, 1934; s. Wayland Farries and Clara (Colton) V.; m. Barbara Ann Badoian, Apr. 26, 1959; children: Wayland Edward, Richard Martin, Robert Peter, John Michael. BA, Brown U., 1955; MBA, Rutgers U., 1969; postgrad., Kent State U., 1977-90. Midwest sales rep. Nashua (N.H.) Corp., 1957-59; eastern sales and mktg mgr. Daniels Mfg. Co., Rhinelander, Wis., 1959-69; regional sales mgr. Metal Edge Industries, Barrington, N.J., 1969-71; owner, pres. Village Ice Cream Shoppe, Edinboro, Pa., 1971-84; asst. prof. Westminster Coll., New Wilmington, Pa., 1978-79; adj. assoc. prof. Alliance Coll., Cambridge Springs, Pa., 1984-86; asst. prof. Slippery Rock (Pa.) U., 1979—, rsch. supr. grad. sch., 1986—; adj. prof. Dahlkemper Sch. Bus., Gannon U., Erie, Pa., 1989—; instr. Edinboro U., 1974-76, Kent State U., Ohio, 1977-78; mktg. cons. IBM Corp. Reviewer manuscripts Merrill Pub. Co., Columbus, Ohio, 1987; contbr. articles to profl. jours. Youth hockey coach Princeton, N.J., Crawford County, Meadville, Pa., 1965-84; ice hockey coach Slippery Rock U., 1979—; commr. Dist. 1 Pa. Big League Baseball, 1990—. Mem. Am. Mktg. Assn. (Outstanding Svc. award 1987), East Econ. Assn., Am. Hockey Coaches Assn., Delta Upsilon. Republican. Baptist. Lodge: Lions (treas. 1974-76). Home: 117 S Skytop Rd Edinboro PA 16412-2414 Office: Slippery Rock U 313 Eisenberg St Slippery Rock PA 16057

VAUGHN, JAMES LLOYD, microbiologist, researcher; b. Marshfield, Wis., Mar. 2, 1934; s. Lloyd Robert and Irene (Tague) V.; m. Jeanette Darlene Lustig, June 11, 1955 (div. 1988); children: Susan, Katherine, Michael, David.; m. Carol Schiller, June 23, 1989. BS, U. Wis., 1957, MS, 1959, PhD, 1962. Rsch. officer Insect Pathology Inst., Sault Ste. Marie, Ont., Can., 1962-65; rsch. microbiologist Agrl. Rsch. Svc. USDA, Beltsville, Md., 1965-79, rsch. leader, 1979—; adv. bd. Agr. Rsch. Svc. USDA. Mem. AAAS, Am. Soc. Microbiology, Tissue Culture Assn. (bd. dirs.), Soc. Invertebrate Pathology. Office: Insect Biocontrol Lab Bldg 011A Rm 214 BARC-West Beltsville MD 20705-2350

VAUGHN, JAMES T., former state police officer, state senator; b. Cheswold, Del., Apr. 12, 1925; s. Charles Townsend and Ada (Van Pelt) V.; m. Sylvia Harris, Nov. 12, 1947; children—James T., Robert G., Judith A. Student schs. Smyrna, Del. Policeman, Del. State Police, 1946-66; with Vaughn Law Office, Dover, Del., 1966-76; commr. Dept. Corrections, Del., 1976-79; chief police dept. Smyrna, 1980; mem. Del. Senate, 1980—. Mgr., coach Smyrna-Clayton Little League, 1957-91; mem. Bd. Edn., Smyrna, 1966-81. Served with USMC, 1943-46. Mem. F.B.I. Nat. Acad., Del. Assn. Chiefs of Police, Am. Legion, VFW. Democrat. Methodist. Lodge: Masons. Office: Del State Senate Legis Hall Dover DE 19901

VAUGHN, ROSELLA HARRIS, human relations professional; b. Statesville, N.C., May 4, 1934; d. Richard James and Mary Jane (Smith) Harris; m. Henry P. Pierce, Sept. 25, 1956 (dec. July 1978); children: Dyrel Pierce, Ledra P. Mesta, Phillip Oji Pierce; m. James Earl Vaughn, Sept. 20, 1983 (dec.); stepchildren: Sarah, Shirley, James E. Jr., Patricia. BA in Edn., Livingstone Coll., 1955; MA in gen. studies., George Washington U., 1975, postgrad., 1977-78. Card punch operator Nat. Security Agy., Washington, 1956-57, Dept. Motor Vehicles, Sacramento, 1957-59; substitute tchr. Calif. Pub. Schs., Sacramento, 1959-60; elm. sch. tchr. D.C. Pub. Schs., Washington, 1960-83; dir. employment tng. program YWCA, Lancaster, Pa., 1983-85; program coord. Lancaster Employment/Tng. Agy., 1985-87; human rels. rep. Lancaster County Human Rels. Commn., Lancaster, 1988—, mem. employment com., 1988—; mem. employment adv. coun. Lancaster County Office of the Aging, 1989—. Bd. dirs. Lancaster Literacy Coun., 1987-88; active ptnrs. in edn. Sch. Dist. of Lancaster, 1991—, Cultural Coun. Lancaster County, 1990-91. Mem. Crispus Attucks Community Ctr. (pres. bd. dirs. 1985-87, outstanding svc. plaque 1989). Office: 1445 Harris St Statesville NC 28677

VAUGHT, JEFFRY LYNN, pharmaceutical researcher; b. China Lake, Calif., Sept. 28, 1950; s. P. William and H. Evelyn (Reynolds) V.; m. Christine A. Wheeler, July 7, 1973; children: Amanda Shannon, Morgan Noelle. BA in Chemistry and German, Ind. State U., 1974; PhD in Pharmacology and Biochemistry, U. Minn., 1979. Quality control lab. technician Pfizer, Inc., Terre Haute, Ind., 1970-75; asst. prof. Sch. Pharmacy, Rutgers U., Piscataway, N.J., 1979-82; sr. scientist McNeil Pharm. Co. div. Johnson & Johnson, Springhouse, Pa., 1982-83; Janssen Rsch. Found. div. Johnson & Johnson McNeil Pharm. Co. div. J & J, Springhouse, Pa., 1983-87; sect. head Janssen Rsch. Found. div. J & J, Springhouse, 1987-90; asst. dir. R.W. Johnson Pharm. Rsch. Inst. div. Johnson & Johnson, Springhouse, 1990-91; v.p. rsch Cephalon, Inc., West Chester, Pa., 1991—; adj. asst. prof. pharmacology Rutgers U., 1982—; adj. assoc. prof. pharmacology Temple U., Phila., 1987—; mem. editorial staff Life Scis. Jour., Tucson, 1990—. Contbr. articles to profl. publs. Mem. Perkasie (Pa.) Zoning/Hearing Bd., 1985-87; mem. Perkasie Planning Commn., 1986-88; mem. Perkasie Borough Coun., 1988—; leader Girl Scouts U.S.A., Perkasie, 1991—. Mem. AAAS, Soc. Exptl. Biology and Medicine, Am. Soc. Pharmacology and Exptl. Therapeutics, Am. Pain Soc., Soc. Neurosci., Internat. Assn. for Study of Pain. Office: Cephalon Inc 145 Brandywine Pky West Chester PA 19380-4245

VAUL, FRANCIS MICHAEL, health care facility administrator, financial manager; b. Ridley Park, Pa., Sept. 9, 1957; s. Francis Anthony and Irene (Ramos) V.; m. Joanne Helen Gentzler, Oct. 17, 1981; 1 child, Lyndsy. BS, Widener U., 1979, MBA, 1988. Dir. housekeeping Servicemaster Inc., Valley Forge, Pa., 1980-85; tng. devel. mgr. Geriatric and Med., Phila., 1985-87; sr. acct. West Jersey Health System, Camden, N.J., 1987-89; asst. v.p. fin. Kimball Med. Ctr., Lakewood, N.J., 1989—. Mem. baptismal team St. Catherine's/St. Margaret's, Spring Lake, N.J., 1991. Mem. Health Care Fin. Mgmt. Assn. Roman Catholic. Home: 3045 Governors Xing Wall NJ 07719-4542

VAUX, RICHARD, artist, educator; b. Greensburg, Pa., Sept. 15, 1940; s. H. Kenneth and Lois (Shoup) V.; m. Sandra Benny, Sept. 6, 1969; 1 child, Joseph. BFA, Miami U., Oxford, Ohio, 1963; MFA, No. Ill. U., 1969. Prof. art Adelphi U., Garden City, N.Y., 1969—. Exhbns. in group shows James Yu Gallery, N.Y.C., 1976, Heckscher Mus. of Art, 1977, Hudson River Mus., 1978, Rijks Centrum, Belgium, 1979, Silvermine Guild, 1980, Dubins Gallery, L.A., 1989, Jain Marunouchi Gallery, N.Y.C., 1992, Elaine Benson Gallery, Bridgehampton, N.Y., 1992. With U.S. Army, 1965-67. Recipient award Guild Hall Mus., 1974, Heckscher Mus. of Art, 1988. Home and Studio: 4 Lloyd Ln Huntington NY 11743-9758

VAZ, JOSEPH, propulsion systems engineer; b. Hackensack, N.J., Dec. 17, 1958; s. Jack and Rose Provedence (Cracolicie) V.; m. Lisa Michelle Austerman, May 18, 1986. BS in Aerospace Engring., Ind. Inst. Tech., 1980. Design engr. Martin Marietta Aerospace Co., New Orleans, 1980-83; propulsion engr. Astro Space div. GE, Princeton, N.J., 1983—. Design team leader world's first dual mode satellite propulsion system, 1990. Mem. AIAA (liquid propulsion tech. com. 1990—). Office: GE Astro Space Div PO Box 800 Princeton NJ 08543-0800

VAZIRI, FAKHRI FAY, financial consultant, insurance broker; b. Teheran, Iran, July 4, 1929; came to U.S., 1947; d. Abass and Hamiyat (Monif) V.; divorced; 1 child, Kew. BA in Drama, Hofstra U., 1953; M in Dramatic Art, Columbia U., 1955. Actress Bombay Film Co., 1942-47; film reporter by correspondence Iranian Dept. Info. and Radio, 1947-50; radio MC Voice of Am., N.Y.C., 1952-54; scriptwriter, announcer featured as "Star of the East" Voice of Am., Washington, 1954-61; agent Reserve Life Ins. Co., Dallas, 1962-81; fin. cons., ins. broker Vaziri Ins. Agy., Bethesda, Md., 1982—. Actress in numerous Persian films, including Shirin-Farhad, one of first Persian films made. Fellow Life Underwriters Tng. Coun.; named Woman of the Yr. Reserve Life Ins. Co., 1966, named to All-Star Honor Roll issue of Insurance mag., 1967; one of few women to be named a charter member for Nat. Sales Achievement award, Nat. Assn. Life Underwriters, 1966; named Agent of Yr. Atlantic Terr. Pruduential Ins. Co. Am., 1980; recipient Human Rights award UN Assn., 1990; numerous other awards from ins. industry, also subject of articles for industry publs. Mem. NOW, Women Leaders Roundtable of Nat. Assn. Life Underwriters, D.C. Life Underwriters Assn., Bus. and Profl. Women's Assn. (pres. Washington chpt. 1987, Woman of the Yr. 1987), Muslim Women Assn. Washington (co-founder, chairwoman postgrad. scholarship for Muslim girls 1985). Office: 5317 Sangamore Rd Bethesda MD 20816-2323

VÁZQUEZ, JOSÉ ANTONIO, education educator; b. San Germ(á)n, P.R., Nov. 30, 1936; came to U.S., 1957; s. Jos(é) and Montserrate (Faria) V. BA, Inter-Am. U., P.R., 1956; MA, Columbia U., 1959. Bilingual tchr. in sch. and community rels. N.Y.C. Bd. Edn., 1957-65, supr., bilingual tchrs. in sch. and community rels., 1965-68, dir., bilingual tchrs. in sch. and community rels., 1968-71; prof. CUNY (Hunter Coll.), 1971—; div. dir. Project BEST, Hunter Coll. component of N.Y.C. Consortium for Bilingual Edn., 1971-75; chief, bilingual/multicultural div. Nat. Inst. Edn., Washington, 1976-77; dir. Hunter-C.W. Post Bilingual Edn. Svc. Ctr., N.Y.C., 1981-83; prin. investigator Significant Bilingual Instrn. Features Study, 1981-83; dir. N.Y.C. Bilingual Edn. Multifunctional Support Ctr., 1983-86; co-dir. Ford Found. Dropout Prevention Collaboratives Program, 1986-87; dir. N.Y.C. Multifunctional Resource Ctr., 1987—. Author: El Espanol: Eslabon Cultural, 1978. Mem. N.Y. State Commr. of Edn.'s Adv. Coun. on Bilingual Edn., 1971— (chair, 1971-74); chmn. Fed. Task Force on the Assessment of Ednl. Needs of Puerto Rican Children and Youth in N.Y. State (HEW), 1972-73. Recipient Cuban Nat. Planning Coun. award, 1986, Gladys Correa Meml. award N.Y. State Assn. for Bilingual Edn., 1982, Am. Heritage award John F. Kennedy Lib. for Minorities, 1974. Mem. Nat. Assn. Bilingual Edn., Am. Ednl. Rsch. Assn., N.Y. State Assn. for Bilingual Edn., Tchrs. of English to Speakers of Other Languages. Office: CUNY Hunter Coll 695 Park Ave Rm 925W New York NY 10021-5085

VEACH, STEPHEN READ, oncologist, researcher; b. Alpine, Tex., Apr. 24, 1943; s. Stanley and Jessie Alice (Nooney) V.; m. Arlene Portney; children: Darren, Justin, Alexander, Merideth. BA, So. Ill. U., 1965; MD, U. Ill., 1970. Intern Rush/Presbyn. St. Luke's Hosp., Chgo., 1970-71; commd. ensign USN, 1971; advanced through grades to capt., 1991; head internal medicine Dept. haval Hosp., Oakland, Calif., 1988-91, dir. med. svcs., 1989-91, med. dir., 1990-91; assoc. prof. medicine Uniformed Svcs. U. Health Scis., Bethesda, Md., 1991, mem. student interview com., 1982-91; adj. clin. staff Nat. Cancer Inst., Bethesda, 1983-88; mem. nat. cancer adv. bd. Dept. of Def., 1986-88; cons. in field. Contbr. to book chpts. and articles to profl. jours. Recipient Presdl. Meritorious Svc. Med. award, 1988, 91. Mem. AMA, AAAS, ACP, Am. Soc. Clin. Oncology, Am. Coll. Physician Execs., Soc. U.S. Naval Flight Surgeons. Home: 1352 Michael Rd Jenkintown PA 19045-2525 Office: US Biosci 100 Front St 1 Tower Bridge West Conshohocken PA 19428

VEBLEN, THOMAS CLAYTON, management consultant; b. Hallock, Minn., Dec. 17, 1929; s. Edgar R. and Hattie (Lundgren) V.; m. Susan Alma Beaver, Sept. 1, 1950 (div. 1971); children: Kari Christen, Erik Rodli, Mark Andrew, Sara Catherine; m. Linda Joyce Eaton, Aug. 30, 1975; 1 child, Kristen Kirby. Student, U. Calif., Santa Barbara, 1950-51; BS, Calif. Poly. U., 1953; MS, Oreg. State U., 1955. Corp. v.p. Cargill, Inc., Wayzata, Minn., 1955-75; spl. asst. Sec. Interior, Washington, 1965; dir. food and agr. SRI Internat., Menlo Park, Calif., 1975-80; pres. Food System Assocs., Inc., Washington, 1980—, also bd. dirs.; mng. dir. Enterprise Cons., Inc., Washington, 1990—; mem. CMC Inst. Mgmt. Cons., 1988—, pres. Washington chpt., 1991—. Author: The U.S. Food System, 1978 (with M. Abel) Creating a Superior National Food System, 1992; editor Food System Update, 1986—. Treas., bd. dirs. White House Fellows Assn., Washington, 1985; trustee Freedom from Hunger Found., Davis, Calif., 1980—, chmn. 1986-89; bd. dirs. Patterson Sch., U. Ky., Lexington, Pax World Found. Recipient Presdl. Appointment White House Fellows Commn., Washington, 1965. Mem. Inst. Food Technologists, The Nature Conservancy, Coun. on Fgn. Rels. Episcopalian. Office: Enterprise Cons Inc PO Box 32273 Washington DC 20007-0573

VECCHIARELLI, PANFILO GUIDO, communications executive; b. Poughkeepsie, N.Y., Jan. 5, 1937; s. Loreto and Lucrezia (DeBellis) V.; m. Lillian Delgado, June 25, 1966; children: Michelle, Nicole. BS in Mech. Engring., Clarkson U., 1958; MBA cum laude, U. Miami, 1978. Mgr., field project ITT World Communications, San Juan, P.R., 1958-60; dir. ops. V.I. Telephone Co., St. Thomas, 1960-67; regional dir. P.R. Telephone Co., San Juan, 1967-69; dir. purchasing ITT Latin Am., Buenos Aires, 1970-72; dir. materials mgmt. ITT Latin Am., Coral Gables, Fla., 1973-75, dir. ops., 1976-80; dir. capital assets and expenditures ITT Europe, Brussels, 1980-83, dir. bus. ops., 1983-87; pres., chief ops. officer Terraplexer Corp. of Am., N.Y.C., 1987—, The Inteleplex Corp., N.Y.C., 1988—; pres., chief ops. officer, bd. dirs. Autosafe Internat. Inc.; bd. dirs. Terraplexer Corp., the Inteleplex Corp., 1990—. Mem. Rye (N.Y.) Hist. Soc., N.Y. Philharmonic Soc., N.Y.

Met. Mus. Art; sponsor Christian Children's Fund. Republican. Roman Catholic. Home: 32 Cayuga St Rye NY 10580-1702

VEDERMAN, RON KEITH, sports association executive, coach; b. Phila., May 12, 1950; s. Joseph Fels and Blanche Gertrude (Weinberg) V.; m. Helen Elaine Stevens, Jan. 6, 1973; children: Elizabeth, Aaron. BS, Kent State U., 1972; MS, U. Iowa, 1974; EdD, Temple U., 1990. Dir. recreation Warrensville (Ohio) Ctr., 1975-76; program dir. Hiram House, Inc., Chagrin Falls, Ohio, 1976-79; instr. Centenary Coll., Hackettstown, N.J., 1979-81; dir. recreation svc. Tng. Sch., Vineland, N.J., 1981-87; assoc. dir. N.J. Spl. Olympics, Cherry Hill, 1988—; adj. instr. Cleve. State U., 1977-78, Glassboro (N.J.) State U., 1990-91. Mem. Am. Assn. on Mental Retardation (regional chair 1989—), Mid-Atlantic Region Spl. Olympics Internat. (named outstanding coach 1987), N.J. Spl. Olympics (named outstanding coach 1987). Jewish. Office: NJ Spl Olympics 1060 Kings Hwy N Ste 111 Cherry Hill NJ 08034-1910

VEILLEUX, GÉRARD, broadcasting executive; b. East Broughton, Que., Can., May 8, 1942; m. Céline Bisson; 1 child, Elaine. B Commerce, Laval U., Que., 1963; MPA, Carleton U., Can., 1968; D Adminstrn. (hon.), U. Ottawa, 1990. With Man. (Can.) Dept. Fin., Winnipeg, 1963-65; with Can. Dept. Fin., Ottawa, Ont., 1966-70, worked in fields of social policy and manpower, 1973-76, dir. gen. tax policy and fed.-provincial rels. br., 1977-79; dir. gen. fed.-provincial rels. Que. Dept. Intergovtl. Affairs, 1970; asst. sec. Can. Treasury Bd. Secretariat, 1971-73; asst. dep. min. Can. Dept. Nat. Health and Welfare, 1976; asst. dep. min. fed.-provincial rels. and social policy, 1979; assoc. dep. min. Can. Ministry of State for Econ. Devel., 1980-82; sec. to Cabinet for Fed.-Provincial Rels.; dep. clk. Privy Coun., 1982-86; sec. Treasury Bd., 1986-89; pres., chief exec. officer Can. Broadcasting Corp., Ottawa, 1989—. Author: Les relations intergouvernementales, 1971; also articles. Mem. nat. adv. com. Banff Sch. Mgmt., 1988—, adv. bd. faculty adminstrn. U. Ottawa, 1988—; ex officio mem. bd. dirs. Nat. Arts Centre; mem. bd. Inst. for Rsch. on Pub. Policy, 1987-89; trustee Civic Hosp. Ottawa, 1990. Recipient Outstanding Achievement award Pub. Svc. Can., 1990, Prix Hermeé Laval U., 1991; Can. John's Manville scholar, 1960, Royal Trust scholar, 1961. Roman Catholic. Office: Can Broadcasting Corp, PO Box 8478, Ottawa, ON Canada K1G 3J5

VEILLEUX, KIMBERLEY ANNE, nurse; b. Waterville, Maine, Mar. 13, 1958; d. Lee Worthington and Chelsea (Silva Bans) Smith; m. Jeffrey Donald Veilleux, Aug. 26, 1978; 1 child, Nicholas Jon. BSN, U. Maine, 1980. RN, Maine. Staff nurse, med.-surgical Mercy Hosp., Portland, Maine, 1980-81; staff nurse, med. Maine Med. Ctr., Portland, 1982-83; charge nurse, med.-surgical Park View Meml. Hosp., Brunswick, Maine, 1983-87; relief charge nurse, ICU Bath (Maine) Meml. Hosp., 1987—. Team mem. sch. dist. health team, Topsham, Maine, 1986—. Mem. AACCN, Maine Br. Assn. Critical Care Nurses, Women's Fitness. Republican. Office: Bath Meml Hosp 1356 Washington St Bath ME 04530-2897 Home: 15 Goldeneye Dr Topsham ME 04086-1505

VEITCH, BOYER LEWIS, printing company executive; b. Phila., Oct. 20, 1930; s. Samuel Lewis and Agnes May (Bell) V.; A.B., Lafayette Coll., 1953; postgrad. Wharton Evening Sch. Acctg. and Fin., U. Pa., 1957-59; m. Emmeline Barbara Smith, Nov. 22, 1952; children—William S., Nancy B., Thomas C. Advt. dir. Ware Bros. Co., Phila., 1956-62, v.p., 1962-69; salesman Zabel Bros. Co., Phila., 1969-75; chmn., pres. Veitch Printing Corp., Lancaster, Pa., 1975—. Trustee Lafayette Coll., Easton, Pa., 1981-86, 87—; vice chmn. coll. rels. com., chmn. ann. fund, 1982-86, mem. fin. com., 1987—; bd. dirs., Boys and Girls Club, Lancaster, 1980—, pres., 1990-92; dir. Boy's Club Lancaster Found., 1989—, Gt. Valley Civic Assn., 1969-79; trustee Fulton Opera House Found., 1985-91, treas., 1987-89; chmn. citizens for Schulze Com., Pa. 5th Congressional Dist., 1972-78; vestryman, sr. Warden St. Peter's Ch. of Gt. Valley, 1972-78. Served with CIC, U.S. Army, 1954-56. Recipient Bronze Hope Chest award Nat. Multiple Sclerosis Soc., 1982, Nat. Svc. to Youth award Boys and Girls Clubs Am., 1992; named Small Bus. Person of Yr. Lancaster Co., 1991. Mem. SAR, NAM, Printing Industries Am., Graphic Arts Assn. (dir. 1980—, chmn. 1990—), Lancaster Assn. Commerce and Industry (dir. 1990—), Aircraft Owners and Pilots Assn., Lafayette Coll. Alumni Assn. (dir. 1974-78, pres. 1978-80), Pa. Economy League, Nat. Fedn. Ind. Bus., Phi Kappa Psi (past pres. and dir. chpt. alumni assn.). Republican. Episcopalian. Lodge: Rotary (Paul Harris fellow). Clubs: Hamilton, Wash Day, Lancaster Country, Dawtaw Country, Avalon Yacht, Lancaster Aero., Susquehanna Litho (dir. 1976-80, pres. 1979-80). Home: 264 Little Creek Rd Lancaster PA 17601-5514 also: 65 E 17th St Avalon NJ 08202 Office: Veitch Printing Corp 1740 Hempstead Rd Lancaster PA 17601-5889

VELASCO-MILLS, JOHN ANTHONY, publishing company executive; b. Rugby, Eng., July 19, 1945; came to U.S., 1985; s. Robert Victor and Brenda Mona (Velasco) Mills; m. Fiona Davis, Aug. 16, 1984; children: Jack, Adam, Christian. Student photography, Sch. Art, Coventry, Eng., 1963. Dir. Canopy Music, London, 1965-68, Edwin H. Morris Ltd., London, 1968-71; mng. dir. United Artists Ltd., London, 1971-74, Pure Cream Entertainment Ltd., London, 1974-77, Interworld Ltd., London, 1977-80, Audio Visual Media Ltd., London, 1980-83, Cherry Lane Ltd., London, 1983-85; v.p. CBS Songs Inc., N.Y.C., 1985-87; pres. Music Pub. Internat. Inc., N.Y.C., 1987—, North Am. Entertainment Ltd., N.Y.C.; mgr. Randy Edelman, L.A., 1983—, Joe Raposo, N.Y.C., 1986-89, Jimmy Webb, N.Y.C., 1988—; cons. Those Characters from Cleveland, Phil Ramone, D.L. Toffner; exec. producer Sesame St. Record Series, 1988, audio series Batman, Superman, Spiderman, Capt. Am., Archie, 1990; producer Osibisa in India. Recipient achievement award Nat. Assn. Boys Clubs, London, 1983. Mem. Performing Rights Soc., Royal Automobile Club (London), Leewood Golf Club, Variety Club Internat. Office: Music Pub Internat Inc 881 7th Ave Ste 906 New York NY 10019-3264

VELCEK, DAMIR, urologist; b. Zagreb, Croatia, Oct. 10, 1944; came to U.S., 1971; s. Kajetan and Nela (Ferk) V.; m. Francisca Tolete, July 3, 1971; children: John, Jennifer. MD, Med. Sch., Zagreb, 1968. Diplomate Am. Bd. Urology. Pvt. practice urology N.Y.C., 1979—; internship St Clare's Hosp., N.Y.C., 1971-72; residency surgery St Clare's Hosp., 1972-73; medical residency N.Y. Hosp., 1973-77, rsch. fellow, 1977-79. Author essay (2nd prize Ferdinand C. Valentine Fell award 1978-79); contbr. articles to profl. jours. Lt. comdr. U.S. Army, 1991, Desert Storm. Fellow Am. Coll. Surgeons, Am. Coll. Internat. Physicians (treas. 1989—); mem. Am. Urol. Assn., Assn. Mil. Surgeons U.S., N.Y. Acad. Medicine, Internat. Soc. Impotence Rsch., N.Y. State Med. Soc. Republican. Roman Catholic. Office: 965 5th Ave New York NY 10021

VELDER, ELI, education educator; b. Balt., Nov. 9, 1925; s. Abraham and Rose (Nissel) V.; m. Jane Carol Kasper, Dec. 21, 1952 (dec.. Mar. 1970); m. Zahava Brand Pearl, May 26, 1977; children: Ruth N. Corobow, David M. BA, Johns Hopkins U., 1948, PhD, 1952. Asst. prof., assoc. prof. edn. Balt. Hebrew Coll., 1952-63; from lectr. to assoc. prof. Goucher Coll., Balt., 1958-71; prof., Goucher Coll., Balt., 1971—; prof. Goucher Coll., Towson, Md., dir. grad. program in edn., 1972-75, 91—, chmn. dept., 1983-90, Dean Van Meter prof., 1985; tchr. English, Agrl. Secondary Sch., Israel, 1954-55; lectr. Johns Hopkins U. Evening Coll., Balt., 1960-81. With AUS, 1944-46, ETO. Recipient Outstanding Teaching award Goucher Coll., 1979, svc. award, 1986. Mem. AAUP, History Edn. Soc., Md. Assn. Small Tchr. Edn. Programs (chmn. 1985-88), Md. Assn. Colls. for Tchr. Edn. (treas. 1987-88). Democrat. Jewish. Home: 2119 Sulgrave Ave Baltimore MD 21209-4409 Office: Goucher Coll Dept Edn 1021 Dulaney Valley Rd Baltimore MD 21204-2753

VELEZ, MIGUEL, information systems specialist; b. Mayaguez, P.R., Apr. 13, 1949; s. Miguel Angel and Nereida (Beauchamp) V.; m. Anna H. Rawlins; children: Rebecca Victoria, Michael Berkley. BE in Indsl. Engring./Ops. Rsch., NYU, 1972; MBA, Pace U., 1982. Pres. Informatix Corp. of Am., Summit, N.J., 1987—; cons. Econ. Devel. Coun. of N.Y.C., Inc., 1976-77. Del. Dem. Nat. Conv., Miami, Fla., 1972; candidate N.Y. State Assembly, N.Y.C., 1976; mem. Rep. Nat. Hispanic Assembly, N.Y., 1991—. Democrat. Roman Catholic.

VELIGDAN, ROBERT GEORGE, dentist; b. Rochester, Pa., Mar. 3, 1949; s. George and Mary (Vinc) V. BS, U. Pitts., 1971, DMD, 1975; postgrad., U. Pa., Phila. Chemistry lab. asst. St. Margaret's Hosp., Pitts., 1971-72; asst. autopsies Montifiore Hosp., Pitts., 1972-74; pvt. practice dentistry N.Y.C., 1975—; clin. instr. Columbia U. Dental Sch., N.Y.C., 1976-82, asst. clin. prof., 1982—; advisor cons. Queens, N.Y. Pub. Schs., 1977-79; lectr. dental esthetics U.S. and abroad, 1984—; asst. attending dentist Presbyn. Hosp., N.Y.C., 1986—; self-help seminars given to vol. working for homeless men, N.Y.C., 1989, 90. Author, producer, dir. (videos) Esthetics and Etched Porcelain Veneers, 1985; contbr. articles to profl. jours. Recipient Recognoition award Greater N.Y. Dental Meeting, N.Y.C., 1985. Mem. Am. Dental Assn., Acad. Gen. Dentistry, Acad. Oral Rehab., Internal Conf. Oral Implantology, Acad. Esthetic Dentistry, I Franklin Miller Study Club. Home: 25 Central Park W #3-D New York NY 10023 Office: 30 Central Park S Ste 7A New York NY 10019-1628

VENA, H. DANTE, artist, educator; b. Castrolibero, Calibria, Italy, Nov. 12, 1930; came to U.S., 1940; s. Frank M. and Josephine (Maria) V.; m. Phyllis Strauss (div.); 1 child, Michael Dante; m. Amy Jane Himmelspach; children: Sarah Megan, Lauren Kerry. BS, U. Wis., 1957, MS, 1960; PhD, U. Iowa, 1976. Cert. art educator, K-12. Chairperson Nazareth Coll., Bardstown, Ky., 1960-61; art dir. Bellarmine Coll., Louisville, 1961-65; exch. tchr. Collage & Sch. of Art, England, 1966; art dir. Bellarmine Coll., Louisville, 1966-67; chairperson Ohio U., Portsmouth, 1967-69; teaching asst. U. Iowa, Iowa City, 1969-72; chairperson U. Mass. (formerly Southeastern Mass. U.), 1972-91, U. Mass., Dartmouth, 1991—; vis. fellow Edith Cowan U., Perth, Australia; rsch. fellowship Western Australian Coll. of Advanced Edn., 1991; coord. Boston Globe Scholastic Art awards, 1984-86; speaker and presenter in field. Editor: Integrated Arts in The Elem. Classroom, 1990. Mem. Bd. Edn., Fairhaven, Mass., 1984—. Recipient Fulbright scholarship State Dept., 1965-66; rsch. grant, 1978, found. grant, 1987, art grant Fairhaven Arts Coun., 1991; SMU Found. grantee, 1977, 91. Mem. Nat. Art Edn. Assn., Mass. Assn. Sch. Com., Mass. Art Edn. Assn. Democrat. Roman Catholic. Home: 241 Green St Fairhaven MA 02719-3285 Office: U Mass-Dartmouth North Dartmouth MA 02747

VENDETTI, RANDALL PETER, mechanical engineer; b. Glen Ridge, N.J., Jan. 29, 1953; s. Ronald and Anna N. (Miscia) V.; m. Judith Anne Krietz, June 5, 1977; 1 child, Jonathan Randall. BSME magna cum laude, Fairleigh Dickinson U., 1975. Registered profl. engr., N.J. Engr. Midland-Ross Corp., Somerset, N.J., 1975-76; sr. devel. engr. Becton-Dickinson Corp., Lincoln Park, N.J., 1976-80; rsch. engr. Engelhard Corp., Edison, N.J., 1980-82; sr. systems engr. Werner & Pfleiderer Corp., Ramsey, N.J., 1982-86; mgr. engring., dist. sales mgr. APV Chem. Machinery, Inc. (formerly Baker Perkins, Inc.), South Plainfield, N.J., 1986-89; mgr. engring. Vibra Screw, Inc., Totowa, N.J., 1989-91; product mgr. Mikropul Environ. Systems, Morris Plains, N.J., 1991—; adj. instr. County Coll. Morris, Randolph, N.J., 1985-86; speaker on creativity. Inventor suction canister with unitary shut-off valve and filter features. Mem. NSPE, Phi Omega Epsilon. Republican. Home: 1100 Sioux Ave Lake Hiawatha NJ 07034-2833 Office: Mikropul Environ Systems 102 American Rd Morris Plains NJ 07950-2447

VENETO, A. JOSEPH, insurance company executive; b. Boston, Nov. 11, 1941; s. Joseph Angelo and Amalia Rose (Gabardi) V.; m. Janet Louise Hatcher, Sept. 19, 1963; 1 child, Michael Scott. BS in Bus. Mgmt., Northeastern U., Boston, 1968. Cert. hazard control cons. Joint Bd. Indsl. Hygiene and Cert. Safety Profls. Ops. and project mgr. Constrn. Industry, Boston, 1963-74; safety cons. Comml. Union Ins. Co., Boston, 1974-78; branch mgr. of loss prevention Comml. Union Ins. Co., Braintree, Mass., 1978-82; field mgr. constrn. tech. Comml. Union Ins. Co., Quincy, Mass., 1982-86; area regional mgr. risk control Comml. Union Ins. Co., Foxboro, Mass., 1986—; constrn. safety cons. Pub. Svc. Power Co., Seabrook Station, N.H., 1975-86; course instr. Comml. Union Ins. Co., Wenham, Mass., 1982-84; seminar chmn. C.U. Producer Adv. Coun., Norwood, Mass., 1987-88; accident prevention com. Automobile Insurers Bur. Mass., 1991—. Mem. Am. Soc. Safety Engrs. (prof.), Hingham Hist. Soc. Roman Catholic. Home: Three Rocky Run Hingham MA 02043 Office: Comml Union Ins Co 1 Constitution Way Foxboro MA 02035

VENIT, MARK LOUIS, management consultant, author, lecturer; b. Phila., Dec. 5, 1948; s. Irving Gordon Venit and Mildred F. (Schnoll) Klugman; div.; children: Kyle, Gabriel. BA, Temple U., 1970, MPA, 1973, MBA, 1976. Pres. U.S. Advt. Corp., Broomall, Pa., 1974-83, Empire Specialty Printing Corp., Yeadon, Pa., 1976-82; v.p. Plymouth Mills Inc., N.Y.C., 1983-84; pres., chief exec. officer Roundtable Mgmt. Systems Ltd., U.S., Can., Ger., 1985—; pres. The Mktg. Dept. Inc., Ocean City, Md., 1990-92; exec. v.p. Talbot Street Pier Devel. Corp., Ocean City, Md., 1992—; cons. in field. Co-author: Textile Business, 1981; contbr. articles to profl. jours. Mem. Rep. City Exec. Com., Phila., 1970-72; mem. Del. County Rep. Exec. Com., 1975-90; treas. Del. County Libr. System, Media, 1978-85, Del. County chmn. Dole for Pres., 1988. Recipient Svc. to Industry award Gralla Pubs., Dallas, 1983-88. Mem. Screen Printing Anns. Internat. (Magnus award 1982), Apparel Decorators Assn. Internat. (pres. 1991), Am. Soc. Assn. Execs., Rotary (Haverford Twp. dir. 1982-84, Man of the Yr. 1984, Internat. Svc. award 1990), Masons (chmn. Masonic Edn. 1982-83), B'nai B'rith Youth Orgn. (Leadership award 1976), Variety Club (Award of Merit 1991, fund raising co-chair 1991). Home: 58 Boston Dr Ocean Pines MD 21811

VENKATESAN, SHARON (LYNNE), writer, small business owner; b. Endicott, N.Y., July 5, 1946; d. Robert Edward and Alberta (Jones) Lee; m. Shane Venkatesan, Oct. 11, 1969; children: Jody, Joeal, Sani, Mali, Keri, Beni. Grad. high sch., Am. Sch., Chgo. Prin. Sharrie Lynne Constrn. Co., Endicott, N.Y.; owner Sharrie Lynne Coll. Funds, Endicott, 1991—; part owner The Am. Dream Homes, Greenbelt, Md., 1991—; tutor, pvt. practice, Endicott, N.Y., 1976-83. Author: (story) In God's Backyard, 1966; (poem) Reagan, 1990 (Pub.'s Choice award, 1990); (book): The Licensed Butcher. Young Republican worker, Endicott, 1960's; spokesperson For Better Edn., Endicott, 1982. Mem. Ch. of Christ. Home and Office: Sharrie Lynne Constrn Co 2620 Magnolia St RD #3 Endicott NY 13760

VENNAT, MICHEL, corporate executive, lawyer; b. Sept. 17, 1941; m. Marie-Anne Tawil; children: Catherine, Charles-Alexandre, Frédéric, Michèle. B.A. magna cum laude, Coll. Jean-de-Brébeuf, Montreal, Que., Can., 1960; LL.L., U. Montreal, 1963; M.A., Oxford U., Eng., 1965. Bar: Que. 1966; apptd. Queen's Counsel 1983. Fgn. affairs officer Dept. External Affairs, Ottawa, Ont., Can., 1965; spl. asst. to Min. Fin., 1966-68; spl. asst. to Hon. Pierre E. Trudeau, Prime Min. of Can., 1968-70, spl. counsel, 1977; chmn. Can. Film Devel. Corp., Montreal, 1976-81; sr. ptnr. Stikeman, Elliott, Montreal, 1970-90; pres. Dumez Investments Inc., 1986-87, Westburne Internat. Industries Ltd., 1987; vice chmn. United Westburne Inc., 1990, vice chmn., CEO, 1991—, also bd. dirs.; pres. Bastos du Canada Limitée, 1987—, also bd. dirs.; lectr. in constl. law U. Montreal, 1970; bd. dirs. Atlas-Gest Inc., Dumez N.Am. Inc., Nat. Bank of Greece (Can.), Sidbec-Dosco Inc. Rhodes scholar, 1963-65. Mem. Barreau du Que., Montreal C. of C., France-Can. C. of C., Montreal Badminton and Squash Club, Mt.-Bruno Country Club, Hillside Tennis Club, Mt.-Royal Club, Hermitage Club. Home: 22 Claude Champagne, Outremont, PQ Canada H2V 2X1 Office: United Westburne Inc, 6333 Decarie Blvd, Montreal, PQ Canada H3W 3E1

VENTOLA, DEAN SAMUEL, architect, architectural company executive; b. Montclair, N.J., Aug. 20, 1958; s. Nicholas Samuel and Josephine (Caputo) V. BArch, U. Md., 1982, BA with honors, 1983. Draftsman Associated Designers, Snow Hill, Md., 1981-82; draftsman designer Solar Design Group, Silver Spring, Md., 1982-83; draftsman, designer Osman & Assocs., Reston, Va., 1983-85; draftsman/designer Grimm & Parker, Greenbelt, Md., 1985, project mgr., 1985-86; archtl. designer Milliner Constrn., Frederick, Md., 1986, dir. design, 1986-88, registered architect, 1987, v.p., 1988-90; pres. Dean Ventola Architects, Gaithersburg, Md., 1990—; pvt. design cons., Gaithersburg, Md., 1983-87; officer equal employment opportunity HUD, Frederick, 1986—. Prin. designs include Quad Home, 1985, New Market Shopping Ctr., 1987, Englar Office Condominiums, 1988, Dearbrought Exec. Complex, 1989, Westminster Self Storage, 1990, Copper Oaks Urban Design Guidelines, 1991; author articles Builder/Architect Jour., The Concept of Contextualism, 1987, NAHB Working with the Architect, 1989. Recipient 1st pl. winner award of excellence in custom home design, 1989, 90, Thesis award, 1983, Nat. Deans List, 1982. Mem. AIA, Am. Art Deco Soc., Nat. Bldg. Mus., Bldg. Ofcls. and Code Adminstrs. Assn. Republican. Office: Dean Ventola Architects 9853 Lake Shore Dr Gaithersburg MD 20879-2241

VENTRES, ROMEO JOHN, manufacturing company executive; b. Boston, Nov. 2, 1924; s. Christy and Marzia (Giammarco) V.; m. Norma Louise Chapman, July 10, 1948; children: Judith, Jane, Mary, Patricia, Katherine, Michael, Peter. BSChemE, Worcester Poly. Inst., 1948; DSc (hon.), Mercy Coll., 1989. Lic. profl. engr., Mass. Jr. engr. Atlantic Refining Co., Phila., 1948-55, group leader, 1955; oil indsl. engr. Govt. Refineries Adminstrn., Baghdad, Iraq, 1955-57; asst. chief engr. Borden Chem. Div. Borden Inc., Leominster, Mass., 1957, chief engr., 1958, ops. mgr., 1961, gen. mgr., 1966, div. v.p., 1968-72, group v.p., 1972-74; exec. v.p. Haven Industries, Phila., 1974-79; group v.p. Borden Chem. div. Borden Inc., Columbus, Ohio, 1979-83, div. pres., 1983-85; pres. Borden Inc., N.Y.C., 1985-90, chief exec. officer, 1986-91, chmn., 1987-92; chmn. exec. com. Borden, Inc., N.Y.C., 1992—; bd. dirs. Borden-Banc One Corp., Marsh & McLennan Cos., Inc., Schering-Plough Corp. Trustee St. Clare's Hosp., N.Y.C. With USN, 1944-46, PTO. Republican. Roman Catholic. Office: Borden Inc 903 Park Ave Apt 18 New York NY 10021-0362

VENTRY, CATHERINE VALERIE, lawyer; b. Bronxville, N.Y., Feb. 19, 1949; d. Victor and Catherine Regina (Dillon) V. AB in Logic and Philosophy, Vassar Coll., 1971; postgrad., Boston U., 1972; JD, N.Y. Law Sch., 1978. Bar: N.Y. 1979, U.S. Dist. Ct. (so. and ea. dists.) N.Y. 1979. Adj. asst. prof. John Jay Coll. of Criminal Justice, N.Y.C., 1978-80; adj. asst. prof. bus. law Coll. Mount St. Vincent Lehman Coll., N.Y.C., 1978-82; staff atty. City of N.Y. Dept. Housing Preservation and Devel. Litigation Bureau, N.Y.C., 1981-84; pvt. practice N.Y., 1984—; Tax editor Prentice-Hall Pub. Co., Englewood Cliffs, N.J., 1980-81. Mem. N.Y. State Bar, Rockland County Women's Bar, Rockland County Bar Assn., MENSA. Office: 873 Union Ave New Windsor NY 12553-5034

VENTRY, PAUL GUERIN, physician, government official; b. Ossining, N.Y., Sept. 1, 1934; s. Victor and Catherine (Dillon) V.; B.S., Manhattan Coll., 1957; M.D., Syracuse U., 1962; m. Betty Anne Baildon, Aug. 20, 1960. Diplomate Am. Bd. Profl. Disability Cons. Commd. 1st lt. M.C., U.S. Army, 1962, advanced through grades to lt. col., 1971; intern Walter Reed Gen. Hosp., 1962-63, resident in internal medicine, 1963-66, fellow in immunology, 1966, fellow in allergy, 1967, chief med. outpatient clinic, 1971, allergy cons. to Surgeon Gen., Europe, 1967-70, ret., 1971; chief adult services Montgomery County Health Dept. (Md.), 1972; med. dir. Goddard Space Flight Ctr., NASA, 1973; ptnr. Med. Assocs. D.C., Washington, 1974; med. dir. Civilian Employees Health Service, Dept. Def., Washington, also med. dir. Pentagon Drug and Alcohol Program and dir. Dept. Def. Blood Donor Program, 1975-83; prin. med. cons. to Office Hearings and Appeals, Social Security Adminstrn., Arlington, Va., 1983—; asst. clin. prof. medicine George Washington U., 1973-79; chief med. cons. Social Security Adminstrn., 1983—; med. dir. Nat. Coun. Social Security Adminstrn. OHA, 1991, Am. Fedn. Govt. Employees # 3615, 1991—. Fellow Am. Occupational Med. Assn., Am. Coll. Occupational and Environ. Medicine, Am. Acad. Disability Evaluating Physicians; mem. ACP, Fed. Physicians Assn. (treas.), Am. Pub. Health Assn., Am. Acad. Allergy, Royal Soc. Medicine, Brit. Allergy Soc., Am. Acad. Civil Service Physicians (treas.), Potomac C. of C., Washington Performing Arts Soc., D.C. Med. Soc., Montgomery County Med. Soc., Alpha Kappa Kappa. Contbr. articles to med. jours. Home: 7813 Masters Dr Rockville MD 20854-3860

VENTURA, ANTHONY P., artist, fine art educator; b. Southampton, N.Y., Jan. 24, 1927; s. Salvatore and Lillian (Morgan) V.; m. Barbara Jean Height, Apr. 9, 1961 (dec. May 1990); children: Tina, Mark, Paul. Student, Acad. of Arts, 1947-51, Pratt Inst., 1952-53, Art Students League, 1954-55. Tchr. Anthony Ventura Studio, Neptune, N.J., 1961—; mem. traveling exhbns. Am. Watercolor Soc., N.Y.C., 1983; demonstrator Noyes Mus., Oceanville, N.J., 1988; mem. workshops Allendale (N.J.) Art Assn., 1990. Represented in permanent collections Winsor-Newton Co., 1975, Ft. Schyler Maritime Mus., 1986. With USN, 1945-46, PTO. Recipient Wells Stroud award Am. Artist Profl. League, 1987. Mem. Guild Creative Art (adv. com. Shrewsbury, N.J. chpt. 1980-84), N.J. Watercolor Soc. (exhbn. com. 1980-84, 2d v.p. 1982-84, 1st v.p. 1984-86, pres. 1987-88, jury of selection 1984-88, 91—), Knickerbocker Artists (Knickerbocker Artist award 1985), Garden State Watercolor Soc. (jury of selection and awards Princeton, N.J. chpt. 1984-88, Warga award 1986), North Shore Art Assn., Hudson Valley Art Assn. (Transparent Watercolor award 1988), Salmagundi Club (Jane Impastato award 1990). Roman Catholic. Home and Office: 3430 Hwy # 66 Neptune NJ 07753

VENTURI, ROBERT, architect; b. Phila., June 25, 1925; s. Robert C. and Vanna (Lanzetta) V.; m. Denise (Lakofski) Scott Brown, July 23, 1967; 1 child, James Charles. Grad., Episcopal Acad., 1943; A.B. summa cum laude, Princeton U., 1947, M.F.A., 1950, D.F.A. (hon.), 1983; D.F.A. (hon.), Oberlin Coll., 1977, Yale U., 1979, U. Pa., 1980, Phila. Coll. Art, 1985; LHD (hon.), N.J. Inst. Tech., 1984. Designer firms of Oskar Stonorov, Eero Saarinen and Assos., Louis I. Kahn, 1950-58; partner firm Venturi, Cope & Lippincott, Phila., 1958-61, Venturi and Short, Phila., 1961-64, Venturi and Rauch, Phila., 1964-80; ptnr. firm Venturi, Rauch & Scott Brown, Phila., 1980-89, Venturi, Scott, Brown and Assocs., Inc., 1989—; from asst. to asso. prof. architecture U. Pa., 1957-65; Charlotte Shepherd Davenport prof. architecture Yale, 1966-70. Author: Complexity and Contradiction in Architecture, 1966, 2d edit., 1977; also articles.; author: (with Denise Scott Brown and Steven Izenour) Learning from Las Vegas, 1972, 2d edit., 1977, (with Denise Scott Brown) A View from the Campidoglio, Selected Essays, 1953-84; others; Prin. works include Vanna Venturi House, Phila., 1961, Guild House, Phila., 1961, Humanities Bldg, SUNY, 1972, Franklin Ct., Phila., 1972, addition to Allen Meml. Art Mus., Oberlin Coll., 1973, Inst. for Sci. Info. Corp. Hdqrts., Phila., 1978, Gordon Wu Hall, Princeton U., 1980, Seattle Art Mus., 1984, The Nat. Gallery, Sainsbury Wing, London, 1986, Fisher and Bendheim Halls, Princeton U., 1986, Gordon and Virginia MacDonald Med. Rsch. Labs. (with Payette Assocs.), UCLA, 1986, Orch. Hall, Phila., 1987. Trustee Am. Acad. Rome, 1966-71. Recipient Pritzker Architecture prize, 1991; Rome Prize fellow Am. Acad. in Rome, 1954-56. Fellow AIA (awards 1974, 77, 78), Am. Acad. in Rome, Am. Acad. and Inst. Arts and Letters, Am. Acad. Arts and Scis., Royal Incorp. Architects of Scotland (hon.), Accademia Nazionale di San Luca; mem. Phi Beta Kappa. Office: 4236 Main St Philadelphia PA 19127-1696

VENUTO, MICHAEL FRANCIS, educational administrator; b. Washington, Dec. 4, 1946; s. Samuel John and Martha (Holden) V.; m. Jeannine Anne Carroll, June 15, 1965 (div. 1976); children: Christopher John, Michele Teresa, Gregory; m. Gail Evelyn Carreau, Dec. 30, 1986; children: Virginia Macintosh Venuto, Nathaniel Holden Venuto. BA, Am. U., 1967, MA, 1973. Ins. agt. Venuto Inc., McLean, Va., 1976-81; internal auditor Vets. Affairs Dept. of U.S., Washington, 1974-76; adminstr. Newtown (Conn.) Bd. Edn., 1989—; dir. Wescon, Bethel, Conn., 1989—; cons. CASBO, 1989—, Ventana Corp., Bethel, 1987—. Contbr. articles to profl. jours., poetry anthology, Angels Beyond the Hill, 1970. Account exec. Com. to Re-Elect the Pres., Washington, 1971, other polit. campaigns in past. With U.S. Army, 1963-69. Decorated Army Commendation medal; recipient Service award, Humboldt County Youth Svc. Assn., 1980, DAV, 1988, U.S. Dept. Vets. Affairs, 1988, Performance award, Pres.'s Coun. on Mgmt. Improvement, 1986. Mem. Conn. Assn. Sch. Bus. Ofcls., Assn. Sch. Bus. Ofcls. Internat., YMCA, Triathelon Fedn. USA, World Wildlife Fedn., Am. Med. Assn. Aux., Western Conn. Bus. Adminstrs. Assn. (dir. 1989—), Am. Legion (vice comdr. 1987-89). Democrat. Roman Catholic. Home and Office: PO Box 99 Union ME 04862-0099

VERBA, SIDNEY, political scientist, educator; b. Bklyn., May 26, 1932; s. Morris Harold and Recci (Salman) V.; m. E. Cynthia Winston, June 17, 1955; children—Margaret Lynn, Ericka Kim, Martina Claire. B.A., Harvard U., 1953; M.A., Princeton U., 1955, Ph.D., 1959. Asst. prof. polit. sci. Princeton U., 1960-63, asso. prof., 1963-64; prof. Stanford U., 1964-68, U. Chgo., 1968-72; prof. govt. Harvard U., 1972—, now Carl H. Pforzheimer prof., dir. univ. library, chmn. dept. govt., 1976-80, assn. dean Faculty Arts and Scis., 1981—; dir. Harvard U. Library; chmn. bd. dirs. Harvard U. Press, 1991—; chmn. policy com. Social Sci. Rsch. Coun., 1980-86; mem. Commn. on Behavioral and Social Scis., NRC, 1986-91; Commn. on

Preservation and Access. chair com. on internat. conflict and cooperation, NRC, 1991—; vis. com. MIT Polit. Sci. Dept., Stanford U. Libr. Author: Small Groups and Political Behavior, 1961, The Civic Culture, 1963, Caste, Race and Politics, 1969, Participation in America, 1972, Vietnam and the Silent Majority, 1972, The Changing American Voter, 1976, Participation and Political Equality, 1978, Injury to Insult, 1979, Introduction to American Government, 1983, Equality in America, 1985, Elites and the Idea of Equality, 1987. Guggenheim fellow, 1980-81. Fellow Am. Acad. Arts and Scis.; mem. Am. Polit. Sci. Assn., Nat. Acad. Scis., Am. Polit. Sci. Assn. (Gladys Kammerer award 1972, Woodrow Wilson Found. award 1976, exec. council 1971-74, v.p. 1979-81), Internat. Studies Assn. (v.p. 1971-72). Jewish. Home: 142 Summit Ave Brookline MA 02146-2358 Office: Harvard U Libr Cambridge MA 02138

VERBURG, EDWIN ARNOLD, federal agency administrator; b. Lakehurst, N.J., Oct. 6, 1945; s. Edwin Donald Verburg and Dorothy (Orrell) Hoodless; m. Joyce Elaine Majack, Sept. 14, 1968; children: Adelle Kristine, Wendi Elizabeth. BS, Calif. Polytech. U., 1968; M in City Planning, U. Calif., Berkeley, 1970; D in Pub. Adminstrn., George Washington U., 1975. Asst. planner City of Inglewood (Calif.), 1970-71; planner City of Glendale (Calif.), 1971-72; grad. assoc. U.S. Army Corps Engrs., Washington, 1974-75; mgr. fiscal analysis Met. Washington Council Govts., 1975-77; sr. program analyst U.S. Fish and Wildlife Service, Washington, 1977-79, asst. div. chief, 1979-80, div. chief, 1980-82, asst. dir. planning and budget, 1982-86, dep. asst. dir. policy budget and adminstrn., 1986-87; dir. office of fin. U.S. Dept. Treas., Washington, 1987-88; dir. fin. svcs. directorate, 1988-91, dir. fin. svcs. directorate, dep. chief fin. officer, 1991—. Author: Local State and Federal Fiscal Flows, 5 Vols., 1976; contbr. articles to fed. jours. Mem. Am. Inst. Cert. Planners, Am. Planning Assn. (Merit award Calif. chpt. 1973, First award Nat. Capital area chpt. 1980, Peer award for pub. svc. Dept. of Treasury 1990, sec.'s cert. appreciation 1991, Pres.'s Meritorious Svc. award 1991.). Home: 538 N Oakland St Arlington VA 22203-2219

VERDESCA, ARTHUR SALVATORE, internist, corporate medical director; b. Cliffside Park, N.J., May 25, 1930; s. Cosimo Theodore and Giulia Elvira (DeLipsis) V.; m. Ann Edith Copping, June 24, 1961; children: Stephen, Julia, Edith. AB, Columbia U., 1951, MD, 1955. Diplomate Am. Bd. Internal Medicine. Intern St. Luke's Hosp., N.Y.C., 1955-56, resident, 1956-57, 59-60, fellow Nat. Heart Inst., 1960-61; staff physician Western Electric, N.Y.C., 1961-63, assoc. hdqrs. med. dir., 1963-65, hdqrs. med. dir., 1965-85; corp. med. dir. Am. Internat. Group, N.Y.C., 1985—. Author: Live, Work and Be Healthy, 1980. Capt. USAF, 1957-59. Fellow ACP, Am. Acad. Occupational Medicine; mem. N.Y. Occupational Med. Assn. (pres. 1979-80). Roman Catholic. Home: 19 Randolph Dr Morristown NJ 07960-5319 Office: Am Internat Group Inc 70 Pine St New York NY 10270-0199

VERDIER, PETER HOWARD, research chemist; b. Pasadena, Calif., Dec. 16, 1931; s. Albert Russell and Margaret Blossom (Buck) V.; m. Marilyn Jean Cornelius, 1953; 1 child, Geoffrey Stephen. BS, Calif. Inst. Tech., 1952; PhD, Harvard U., 1957. Rsch. assoc. in chemistry MIT, Cambridge, 1957-58; rsch. fellow Harvard U., Cambridge, 1958-59; rsch. chemist Union Carbide Rsch. Inst., Tarrytown, N.Y., 1959-64; staff cons. Union Carbide Corp., N.Y.C., 1964-65; rsch. chemist Nat. Bur. Standards, Gaithersburg, Md., 1965-70, chief molecular characterization sect., 1970-75; rsch. chemist Nat. Inst. Standards Tech., Gaithersburg, Md., 1975—. Contbr. articles to profl. jours. Fellow Am. Physical Soc.; mem. Folklore Soc. Greater Washington, West River Sailing Club. Office: Nat Inst Standards Tech Gaithersburg MD 20899

VERDON, JOHN JOSEPH, JR., psychiatrist; b. N.Y.C., Dec. 8, 1939; s. John Joseph and Hazel (Pindar) V.; m. Kathleen Breslin, Dec. 28, 1963 (div. Mar. 16, 1989); children: John J. III, Amy M., Kathleen, Michael, Renee. BA, Holy Cross, 1961; MD, Georgetown U., 1965. Diplomate Am. Bd. Psychiatry and Neurology. Intern Albany (N.Y.) Med. Ctr., 1965-66; psychiat. resident Strong Meml. Hosp. U. Rochester (N.Y.) Med. Sch., 1966-69; psychiatrist pvt. practice, Tinton Falls, N.J., 1971—; dir. psychiat. residency tng. Monmouth Med. Coll., Long Branch, N.J., 1971-74; asst. prof. psychiatry Hahnemann Med. Coll., Phila., 1971-85; clin. asst. psychiatry, clin. assoc. Robert Wood Johnson Med. Sch., 1972-75, 75—; cons. in field; dir. Mental Health Program for Jersey Shore Med. Ctr. at Monmouth County Correctional Institution, Freehold, N.J., 1974-81, Alcoholism Treatment Ctr., Monmouth Med. Ctr., Long Branch, N.J., 1971-79, addictive disorders com. N.J. Psychiatr. Assn., 1984—. Lt. commdr. USN, 1969-71. Fellow Am. Psychiat. Assn., Am. Acad. Psychiatry and Law; mem. Am. Soc. Addiction Medicine (cert. expert 1986), N.J. Med. Soc., N.J. Psychiat. Assn., Monmouth County Med. Soc., Am. Acad. Psychiatrists in Alcoholism and Addictions, Nat. Coun. of Alcoholism (bd. trustees). Republican. Roman Catholic. Home: G-2 Twin Lights Ct Highlands NJ 07732 Office: John J Verdon 712 Sycamore Ave Red Bank NJ 07701-4991

VERDON, JOSEPH MICHAEL, engineering manager, researcher; b. N.Y.C., July 4, 1941; s. James Patrick and Anna (Delahunty) V.; m. Margaret Rose Furey, July 6, 1963; children: Mary, Joseph, Carolyn. BS in Engring., Webb Inst. Naval Architecture, 1963; MS in Engring. Sci., U. Notre Dame, 1965, PhD in Engring. Sci., 1967. Rsch. engr. aeroelasticity United Aircraft Rsch. Labs., East Hartford, Conn., 1967-68; asst. prof. mech. engring. U. Conn., Storrs, 1968-72; cons. Pratt & Whitney Aircraft, East Hartford, 1970-71; sr. rsch. engr. computational fluid dynamics United Techs. Rsch. Ctr., East Hartford, 1972-81, prin. scientist, 1981-88, mgr. theoretical and computational fluid dynamics, 1988—; vis. rsch. fellow NASA Lewis Rsch. Ctr., Cleve., 1985-88; prin. investigator or co-investigator over 20 U.S. Govt. rsch. contracts. Contbr. articles to profl. jours. Coach youth sports. Schmitt fellow U. Notre Dame, 1963-64, NASA fellow, 1971-72; recipient Spl. award for rsch. in unsteady aerodynamics United Techs. Rsch. Ctr., 1988. Fellow AIAA (assoc. editor jours. 1988-91); mem. ASME, Soc. Indsl. and Applied Math., Sigma Xi. Home: 19 Briarwood Ln Vernon Rockville CT 06066-5905 Office: United Techs Rsch Ctr Silver Lane East Hartford CT 06108

VEREB, MICHAEL JOSEPH, pharmaceutical and cosmetic executive; b. Leechburg, Pa., Apr. 1, 1931; s. Michael Andrew and Mary Elizabeth (Chernay) V.; m. Joanne Maria Helms, Oct. 9, 1955; children: Kenneth Michael, Wayne William. BS in Indsl. Mgmt., Carnegie Mellon U., 1953; postgrad., U. Pitts., 1955-56, U. So. Ill., 1959. Registered profl. engr., Calif. Methods engr. Schenley (Pa.) Distillers, 1955-57; cons. EnServCo, Pitts., 1957-58; sr. indsl. engr. Olin Industries, Alton, Ill., 1958-59; mgr. indsl. engr. Ormet Aluminum subs. Olin Industries, Bucks Bottom, Ohio, 1959-66; resource mgr. Olin Aluminum, N.Y.C., 1966-67; dir. engring. Squibb Corp., New Brunswick, N.J., 1967-78; dir. facilities planning Squibb Corp., Lawrenceville, N.J., 1978-84; v.p. facilities planning Charles of Ritz Group, Ltd. div. Squibb Corp., Holmdel, N.J., 1984-87; div. mgr. pharms. Fluor Daniel, Inc., Marlton, N.J., 1988—; cons. EnServCo, Pitts., 1957-58, Pitman Moore div. of IMC, Washington Crossing, N.J.; rsch. coord. Lehigh U., Bethlehem, Pa., 1984-86. Inventor disposable containers. Coord. fund drives Carnegie Mellon U., Lawrenceville, N.J., 1973-83; 1st v.p. Raritan Valley Regional Chpt. C. of C., 1976-78. With U.S. Army, 1953-55. Mem. Am. Inst. Indsl. Engring., Assn. Info. and Image Mgmt., Soc. Mfg. Engrs., Elks (v.p. 1960-66), Pi Kappa Alpha (v.p. 1952-53). Home: 5 Arncliffe Rise Medford NJ 08055-3337

VEREBEY, KARL GEZA, toxicologist, educator; b. Budapest, Hungary, Mar. 12, 1938; came to U.S., 1956; s. Karoly and Etelka (Szabo) V.; m. Debra Adler, Feb. 22, 1962; children: Rita, Todd, Marc. AA, Eotvos J. Gimnazium, Budapest, Hungary, 1956; BA, Hunter Coll., 1965; MA, CUNY, 1968; PhD, Cornell U. Med. Coll., 1972. Diplomate Am. Bd. Forensic Toxicology; cert. clin. lab. dir. Am. Bd. Bioanalysis; lic. clin. lab. dir., N.Y., N.J., Ill., Md., Vt. Dir. clin. pharmacology State of N.Y., N.Y.C., 1973-88; dir. clin. lab. Psychiat. Diagnostic Lab. Am., South Plainfield, N.J., 1988-89; chief toxicologist City of N.Y., 1989—; assoc. prof. SUNY Health Sci. Ctr., 1978; mem. exec. com. Drug Abuse Adv. Bd., N.Y. State Dept. Health, Nat. Forensic Ctr.; advisor Nat. Found. Addictive Diseases. Mem. editorial bd. Jour. Addictive Diseases, 1981; contbr. numerous articles to sci. jours. With U.S. Army, 1961-63. USPHS rsch. fellow, 1968-73; grantee Cornell U. Med. Coll., 1974-77, Narcotic and Drug Rsch., Inc., 1974-76, 79-81, DuPont Pharm., 1985. Mem. Am. Acad. Forensic Sci., N.Y. Acad. Sci., Am. Soc. Pharmacology and Exptl. Therapeutics. Home: 638 Debchar Ct River Vale NJ 07675-6409

VERMA, RAM SAGAR, geneticist, educator, author, administrator; b. Barabanki, India, Mar. 3, 1946; came to the U.S., 1972; s. Gaya Prasad and Late Moonga (Devi) V.; m. Shakuntala Devi, May 4, 1962; children: Harendra K., Narendra K. BSc, Agra U., India, 1965, MSc in Quantitative Genetics, 1967; PhD in Cytogenetics, U. Western Ont., London, Ont., Can., 1972; diploma clinical cytogenetics, The Royal Coll. Pathologists, London, 1984. Diplomate The Royal Coll of Pathologists, London; lic. dir. clin. Cytogenetics, N.Y.C. and N.Y. state. Rsch. and teaching asst. dept. plant scis. U. Western London, Ont., Can., 1967-73; postdoctoral rsch. assoc. cytogenetics U. Colo. Dept. of Pediatrics, Denver, 1973-76; instr. to prof. human cytogenetics dept. of medicine Health Sci. Ctr. SUNY, Bklyn., 1976—, prof. dept. anatomy and cell biology, 1988—; chief cytogenetics div. hematology and cytogenetics Interfaith Med. Ctr. (formerly Jewish Hosp. and Med. Ctr. Bklyn.), 1980-86; chief div. genetics L.I. Coll. Hosp., Bklyn., 1986—; cons. WHO, Switzerland, 1982, Nat. Geog. Soc., Washington, 1982, Phototake, 1982-87; mem. cytogenetic adv. com. Prenatal Diagnosis Lab. N.Y.C. Dept. Health, 1978-90, Genetic Task Force N.Y. State, N.Y.C., 1976—; reviewer grants Nat. and Internat. Health Agys. and Socs.; lectr. colls., univs. and profl. assns. Author: Heterochromatin: Molecular and Structural Aspects, 1988, The Genome, 1990, (with A. Babu) Human Chromosomes: Manual of Basic Techniques, 1989; editor-in-chief: Advances in Genome Biology, 1989; contbr. of over 200 abstracts and presentations and over 250 articles to profl. publs. including Am. Jour. Ob.-Gyn., Blood, Jour. Med. Genetics, Japanese Jour. Human Genetics, Onclogy, Cytobios, Am. Jour. Human Genetics, Am. Jour. Clin. Oncology, Internat. Jour. Cancer, Chromosoma, Cytogenetics. Apptd. to Adv. Coun. to Asst. Commr. City of N.Y. Dept. Health, Bur. Lab. Svcs., 1988. Nat. Merit scholar Gov. India, 1964-67, 1965-67; rsch. scholar Nat. Rsch. Coun. Can. and U. Western Ont., 1967-72, also teaching assistantship, 1972-73; rsch. grantee N.Y. State Dept. Health, Albany, 1985, 85-86, Cancer Treatment Fund, Cornell Med. Coll., 1985-86, United Leukemia Fund, Cornell Med. Coll., 1985-86, 86-87, Nat. Cancer Inst. of Health, Md., 1985-86, 86-87, 97-88, 88-90, Nat. Cancer Inst., 1976-77, 77-78, 78-80. Fellow AAAS, Assn. Clin. Scientists, The Inst. of Biology, N.Y. Acad. Scis., N.Y. Acad. Medicine (assoc.); mem. Am. Assn. Clin. Rsch., Am. Fedn. Clin. Rsch., Am. Genetic Assn. (life), Am. Soc. Cell Biology, Am. Soc. Human Genetics (life), European Soc. Human Genetics, Fedn. Am. Scientists, Genetic Soc. Am., Genetic Soc. Can., Genetic Toxicology Assn., Internat. Assn. Human Biologists, Indian Soc. Human Genetics (life), Soc. Exptl. Biology and Medicine, The Royal Coll. of Pathologists, London. Home: 45-38 Springfield Blvd Bayside NY 11361 Office: The L I Coll Hosp Div of Genetics Brooklyn NY 11201

VERMEER, MAUREEN DOROTHY, sales executive; b. Bronxville, N.Y., Mar. 21, 1945; d. Albert Casey and Helen (Valentine Casey) Vermeer; m. John R. Fassnacht, Feb. 11, 1966 (div. 1975); m. George M. Dallas Peltz IV, Oct. 26, 1985. Grad., NYU Real Estate Inst., 1976. Lic. real estate broker, notary pub., N.Y. Personnel mgr. Douglas Elliman, N.Y.C., 1965-74, mgmt. supr., 1974-78, v.p., 1978-83; real estate broker Rachmani Corp., N.Y.C., 1983-84; v.p. sales and mktg. Carol Mgmt. Corp., N.Y.C., 1984-90; v.p. mktg. The Sunshine Group, N.Y.C., 1990; v.p. sales and mktg., sec. H.J. Kalikow & Co., Inc., N.Y.C., 1991—; bd. dirs. Ascot Owners, Inc., N.Y.C.; speaker in field. Mem. Real Estate Bd. N.Y., Assn. Real Estate Women, Sales and Mktg. Coun. Republican. Presbyterian. Home: 206 County Rd Demarest NJ 07627-2202 Office: H J Kalikow & Co Inc 101 Park Ave New York NY 10178

VERMILLION, STEPHEN DORSEY, III, foundation executive; b. Washington, June 19, 1960; s. Stephen Dorsey Jr. and Alice Catherine (Cleary) V. BA, Loyola Coll., Balt., 1982; cert. Latin Am. studies, U. Fla., 1980; MA, U. Miami, 1985. Asst. to dir. Inter Am. Studies Inst., U. Miami, Fla., 1984-86; rsch. asst. Nat. Ctr. for State Ctrs., Washington, 1986; dir. communications Rep. Study Com., Washington, 1986-87; legis. asst. to Congressman F. James Sensenbrenner of Wis., U.S. Ho. of Reps., Washington, 1987-89; dir. congl. rels. Cuban-Am. Nat. Found., Washington, 1989—; assoc. editor Capitol Hill Pub., Inc., 1991—; cons. Valladares Human Rights Found., Washington, 1989—; cons. Cuban Exodus Relief Fund; U.S. observer delegation 1990 Guatemalan Presdl. Elections. Assoc. editor Capitol Hill Publs., 1991—; contbr. to various newspapers. Mem. Rep. Communications Assn., Jefferson Polit. Soc., Jefferson Ale Club (founder), U.S. Rowing Assn., Capitol Rowing Club (bd. dirs.), Phi Alpha Theta. Roman Catholic. Home: 3295 Arcadia Pl NW Washington DC 20015-2329 Office: Cuban-Am Nat Found 1000 T Jefferson St NW Washington DC 20007

VERMUND, STEN HALVOR, government official; b. Mpls., Jan. 31, 1954; s. Halvor and Karen (Bergfjord) V.; m. Pilar Vargas, Apr. 8, 1978; children: Julian, Gabriel. BA, Stanford U., 1974; MD, Albert Einstein Coll. Medicine, 1977; MSc, London Sch. Hygiene and Tropical Medicine, 1981; PhD, Columbia U., 1990. Diplomate Am. Bd. Pediatrics, Am. Bd. Preventive Medicine, Nat. Bd. Med. Examiners. Intern Presbyn. Hosp., N.Y.C., 1977-78, resident in pediatrics, 1979-80; asst. prof. Columbia U., N.Y.C., 1982-85; asst. prof. Albert Einstein Coll. Medicine, Bronx, N.Y., 1985-88, assoc. clin. prof., 1989—; chief epidemiology br. div. AIDS Nat. Inst. Allergy and Infectious Diseases, Bethesda, Md., 1988-92; chief vaccine trials and epidemiology br. div. AIDS Nat. Inst. Allergy and Infectious Diseases, Bethesda, 1992—; cons. N.Y.C. Dept. Environ. Protection, 1986-88, Med. Bd. Nat. Coun. Chs., N.Y.C., 1984-85, Ctrs. for Disease Control, Atlanta, 1989—, FDA, Rockville, Md., 1991—. Contbg. author: Annual Review of Aids Research, Vol. 1, 1991, Reproductive and Perinatal Epidemiology, 1991; contbr. articles to profl. jours. Mem. adv. bd. health rsch. tng. program N.Y.C. Dept. Health, 1986-88. Recipient Curnan award Babies Hosp., N.Y.C., 1980, Lalcaca medal U. London, 1981, Commnrs. Spl. Svc. award N.Y.C. Dept. Health, 1988, Merit award USPHS, Bethesda, 1989; med. rsch. grantee Ctrs. for Disease Control, Nat. Cancer Inst., others, 1986-88. Fellow Am. Acad. Pediatrics (sec., founding mem. regional com. on homeless children 1986-88), Am. Coll. Epidemiology, Soc. Adolescent Medicine, Royal Soc. Tropical Medicine and Hygiene; mem. APHA, Internat. AIDS Soc., Internat. Epidemiologic Assn. Office: Div of AIDS NIH 6003 Executive Blvd Bethesda MD 20892

VERNA, MARIO, surgeon; b. Buenos Aires, May 12, 1937; came to U.S., 1963; s. Carmelo and Raquel P. (Vitale) V.; m. Ana E. Blanc, June 9, 1963; children: Mario F., Paul, Matias A. MD, U. Buenos Aires, 1961. Diplomate, Am. Bd. Surgery. Asst. instr. microbiology and parasitology U. Buenos Aires Med. Sch., 1959-60; intern Hackensack (N.J.) Hosp., 1963-64, resident in surgery, 1964-68; pvt. practice Hackensack; mem. med. staff Hackensack Med. Ctr., chief oncology sect., dept. surgery, 1990—, chmn. cancer com. and tumor bd., 1978&, pres. gen. active staff, 1989, chmn. med. bd., 1990; dir. surg. edn. Policlinico Ferroviario, Mendoza, Argentina, 1972-76; chief instr. surgery U. Cuyo, Argentina, 1974-75; clin. asst. prof. surgery Coll. Medicine and Dentistry N.J./M.J. Med. Sch., 1980—; lectr. at profl. meetings. Contbr. to med. publs. Fellow ACS, Argentine Assn. Surgery; mem. Bergen County Med. Soc., N.J. Med. Soc., No. N.J. Surg. Soc., Mendoza Med. Soc. Roman Catholic. Home: 10 Depeyster Ave Tenafly NJ 07670-2208 Office: 211 Essex St Hackensack NJ 07601-3231

VERNARELLI, MICHAEL JOSEPH, economics educator, consultant; b. Rochester, N.Y., Nov. 24, 1948; s. S. John and Angelica Dolores (Morabito) V.; m. Joan Ann Taylor, Oct. 4, 1975; children: Jacqueline Andrea, Laurel Aileen. BA in Econs., U. Mich., 1970; MA in Econs., SUNY, Binghamton, 1974, PhD in Econs., 1978. Account analyst Travelers Ins. Co., Rochester, 1970-71; prof. econs. Rochester Inst. Tech., 1976—, chmn. dept., 1987—; econs. cons. Rochester Downtown Devel. Corp., 1980; rsch. economist div. housing rsch. HUD, Washington, 1980-81, vis. scholar, 1980; pres., forensic economist Rochester Econ. Cons., 1983—. Contbg. author: Federal Housing Policy and Desegregation, 1986. Mem. Brighton (N.Y.) Bd. Archtl. Rev., 1990-91, mem. planning bd., 1991—. Recipient Eisenhart award Rochester Inst. Tech., 1987; grantee SUNY, Binghamton, 1974. Mem. Am. Econ. Assn., Nat. Assn. Forensic Economists, Ea. Econ. Assn., Greater Rochester C. of C. (panel mem. bus. trends com. 1987—), Omicron Delta Epsilon. Roman Catholic. Home: 133 Esplanade Dr Rochester NY 14610-3325 Office: Rochester Inst Tech PO Box 9887 Rochester NY 14623-0887

VERNEY, RICHARD GREVILLE, paper company executive; b. Providence, Aug. 24, 1946; s. Gilbert and Virginia Ruth (Piggott) V.; m. Dorothy Howard, Aug. 26, 1967; children: Virginia F., Elizabeth I., Heather B., Eric G. AB, Brown U., 1968. Mgmt. trainee Monadnock Paper Mills, Bennington, N.H., 1969-70, asst. gen. mgr., 1970, exec. v.p., 1970-76, pres., 1977-85, chmn., chief exec. officer, 1978—. Mem. exec. com. Crotched Mt. Found., Greenfield, N.H., 1974-87, trustee, 1974—; trustee St. George's Sch., Newport, R.I., 1978—, chmn., 1985-89. Mem. Am. Paper Inst. (bd. dirs. 1991—, chmn. splty. packaging and indsl. div. 1984-85, chmn. exec. bd. API-pulp consumers div. 1980-82, chmn. cover and text exec. com. 1989-91), Bus. Industry Assn. N.H. (bd. dirs. 1991—), Sales Assn. Paper Industry, Boston Paper Trade Assn. (pres. 1985-86), Algonquin Club (Boston), Nantucket Yacht Club (Mass.), N.Y. Yacht Club (N.Y.C.). Republican. Episcopalian. Home: The Verney Farm Bennington NH 03442 Office: Monadnock Paper Mills Inc Antrim Rd Bennington NH 03442-4206

VERNON, MCCAY, psychologist, educator; b. Washington, Oct. 14, 1928; s. Percy McCay and Octavia Preble (Hall) V.; m. Edith Goldston, June 8, 1955 (dec. 1988); 1 child, Eve Edith Vernon Peters. BA, U. Fla., 1951; MS in Edn., PhD (hon.), Gallandet U., 1954, 1979; MA, Fla. State U., 1958; PhD, Claremont U., 1966. Cert. and lic. psychologist, Md., D.C. Tchr., coach Fla. Sch. for Deaf & Blind, St. Augustine, 1951-54, Tex. Sch. for Deaf, Austin, 1955-56, Colo. Sch. for Deaf, Colorado Springs, 1957-58; psychologist, tchr. Calif. Sch. for Deaf, Riverside, 1959-64; rsch. assoc. U. Ill., Champaign-Urbana, 1964-65, Depaul U., Chgo., 1965-66; rsch. psychologist Michael Reese Hosp., Chgo., 1966-69; prof. psychology Western Md. Coll., Westminster, 1969-90; pvt. practice, Md., Ill., and Calif., 1958—; researcher and cons. in field. Author: Etiological Factors in Deafness: Medical, Psychological and Educational Sequelae, 1969, The Language Arts Handbook, 1978, They Grow in Silence, 1971, rev. edit., 1987, Ushers Syndrome, 1988, Success for Hard of Hearing People: The Randy Inskip Story, 1988; Psychology of Deafness: Understanding Deaf and Hard of Hearing People, 1990; editor jour. Am. Annals of Deaf, 1969-90; contbr. articles to profl. jours. Sec. psychology sect. World Fedn. of Deaf, Italy, 1972. Recipient Human Svc. award Nat. Assn. of Deaf, Silver Spring, Md., 1970, Medal of Honor, British Deaf Assn., Eng., 1972. Fellow APA, Md. Psychol. Assn.; mem. Coun. Exceptional Children (governing bd. 1970-73), Convention Am. Inst. Deaf, Order of Merit (Italy), Claremont Gard Sch. Alumni (Alumnus of Yr. 1985). Home and Office: 37 Ridge Rd Westminster MD 21157-4458

VERNON, WESTON, III (WES VERNON), journalist; b. N.Y.C., Aug. 23, 1931; s. Weston, Jr. and Adelaide (Neilson) V.; m. Alida Steinvoort, Oct. 5, 1951; children: Rosanne, Weston IV, Diane, John Randall. Student, Utah State U., 1949-50, Brigham Young U., 1953-54. Reporter, producer KBUH, Brigham City, Utah, 1950-51, KVRS, Rock Springs, Wyo., 1952, KOVO, Provo, Utah, 1952-54, Intermountain Network, Salt Lake City, 1954, KLO, Ogden, Utah, 1954, KBMY, Billings, Mont., 1954-63; news dir.-polit. specialist KSL Radio-TV, Salt Lake City, 1963-68; bur. chief Bonneville Internat. Corp., Washington, 1968-72; corr. CBS Radio Stas. News Service, CBS Radio, Washington, 1972—; bd. dirs. Am. Zephyr, Inc. Columnist The High Green, The Timetable; contbr. to Passenger Train jour. Bd. dirs. Winding-Orchard Citizens Assn., Wheaton-Glenmont, Md., 1974-77, 86—, pres., 1975-76. Served with AUS, 1951-52. Recipient Journalism awards Mont. A.P. Press Stas., 1960, Journalism awards Utah Bar Assn., 1965, Journalism awards Utah Broadcasters Assn., 1965-66. Mem. Radio-TV Corrs. Assn., Am. Legion (comdr. Yellowstone Post 4 1962-63), Railroad Enthusiasts (bd. dirs. Chesapeake div.). Office: CBS Radio Stas News Svc 2020 M St NW Washington DC 20036-3368

VERRET, JOSEPH MARC, psychiatrist; b. Port au Prince, Haiti, Sept. 2, 1953; came to U.S., 1981; s. Louis C. and Mrie Therese (Martelly) V.; m. Nicole Desir, Mar. 29, 1980; children: Mrie Christine, Joseph Marc Jr. BS, Petit Seminaire Coll., Haiti, 1972; MD, State U. Haiti, 1978; MPH, Columbia U., 1983. Rotating intern State U. Haiti Hosp., Port-au-Prince, 1977-78; resident in internal medicine State U. Haiti Hosp., 1978-81; resident in psychiatry Harlem Hosp./Columbia U., N.Y.C., 1983-87; attending physician, psychiatrist St. Joseph Hosp. and Med. Ctr., Paterson, N.J., 1987—; chief outpatient dept., psychiat. emergency room St. Joseph Hosp. and Med. Ctr., 1989-90; med. chief substance abuse svcs. Elizabeth (N.J.) Gen. Med. Ctr., 1990—; attending psychiatrist St. Joseph Hosp. and Med. Ctr., 1990—; cons. Office of Minority of Mental Health, Washington, 1989—. Fellow Acad. Medicine N.J.; mem. AMA, Am. Psychiat. Assn., Am. Pub. Health Assn., Am. Geriatric Soc. Office: Elizabeth Gen Med Ctr Substance Abuse Svcs East Bldg 655 E Jersey St Elizabeth NJ 07206

VERRETTE, JAMES FRANCIS, creative director; b. Syracuse, N.Y., Apr. 7, 1956; s. Charles Roy and Lorraine Frances (Grala) Dewolf; m. Marion Lee Garfinkel, Sept. 27, 1980; children: Kate Sarah, Callie Renee (twins). AA, Onondaga Community Coll., 1976; BA, SUNY, Oswego, 1978. Graphic artist Tri-Kolor Printing, Syracuse, 1978-83, art dir., 1983-88, creative dir., 1988—. Recipient Design and Printing award Internat. Assn. Printing House Craftsmen, 1987. Mem. Three Rivers Bassmasters (treas. 1987-88), N.Y. State Cert. Football Ofcls. Roman Catholic. Home: 4155 Torrey Ln Liverpool NY 13090-1623 Office: Tri-Kolor Printing 1035 Montgomery St Syracuse NY 13202-3521

VERRILL, CHARLES OWEN, JR., lawyer; b. Biddeford, Maine, Sept. 30, 1937; s. Charles Owen and Elizabeth (Handy) V.; m. Mary Ann Blanchard, Aug. 13, 1960 (dec.); children: Martha Anne, Edward Blanchard, Ethan Christopher, Elizabeth Handy, Matthew Lawton, Peter Goldthwait. AB, Tufts U., 1959; LLB, Duke U., 1962. Bar: D.C. 1962. Assoc. Weaver & Glassie, 1962-64; assoc. Barco, Cook, Patton & Blow, 1964-66, ptnr., 1967; ptnr. Patton, Boggs & Blow, 1967-84, Wiley, Rein & Fielding, Washington, 1984—; lectr. law sch. Duke U., 1970-73; adj. prof. internat. trade law, Georgetown U. Law Ctr., Washington, 1978—; conf. chmn. The Future of the Internat. Steel Industry, Bellagio, Italy, 1984, The U.S. Agenda for the Uruguay Round, Airlie House, Warenton, Va., 1986, The Polish Joint Venture Law, Cracow, Poland, 1987, Internat. Steel Industry II, Bellagio, 1987, Bulgaria and the GATT, Washington, 1988. Local dir. Tufts U. Ann. Fund, 1965-69; mem. Duke Law Alumni Coun., 1972-75; trustee Internat. Law Inst., 1981—, chmn. bd. trustees, 1983-87; trustee Bulgarian Am. Friendship Soc., 1992—. Mem. ABA, Internat. Bar Assn., D.C. Bar Assn., Order of Coif, Theta Delta Chi, Phi Delta Phi, Met. Club (Washington), Chevy Chase Club (Md.), Tarratine Club (Dark Harbor, Maine). Home: 1624 29th St NW Washington DC 20007-2901 Office: 1776 K St NW Washington DC 20006-2304

VERVILLE, ANNE-LEE, electronics company executive; b. Concord, N.H., June 9, 1945; d. Homer Anthony and Anne Mary (McCready) V. BA, Smith Coll., 1967. With IBM, Purchase, N.Y., 1967-77, revenue planning mgr., mgr. copier pricing, 1977-80, mgr. fin. analysis, 1980-81, controller data processing div., 1981-83, v.p. plans and controls, mktg. div., 1983-85, group dir. adminstrn. and fin., 1985-86, gen. mgr. gen. and pub. sectors, 1986-87, dir. info. and telecommunications systems, 1987-88, asst. gen. mgr. fin. and planning, 1988-90; pres. gen. sector div. IBM Corp., Purchase, 1991—; bd. dirs. Stanhome Corp., Westfield, Mass.; bd. visitors Fuqua Bus. Sch. Duke U. Office: IBM Corp 472 Wheelers Farms Rd 2000 Purchase St Milford CT 06460

VESELL, ELLIOT SAUL, pharmacologist, educator; b. N.Y.C., Dec. 24, 1933; s. Harry and Evelyn (Jaffe) V.; m. Kristen Paige Peery, Mar. 24, 1968; children: Liane Clark, Hilary Peery. AB, Harvard U., 1955, MD, 1959; DSc (hon.), Phila. Coll. Pharmacy & Sci., 1988. Intern, children's med. svc. Mass. Gen. Hosp., Boston, 1959-60; rsch. assoc. Rockefeller U., N.Y.C., 1960-62; resident in medicine Peter Bent Brigham Hosp., Boston, 1962-63; clin. assoc. Nat. Inst. Arthritis and Metabolic Diseases, NIH, Bethesda, Md., 1963-65; head sect. pharmacogenetics Nat. Heart Inst., NIH, Bethesda, 1965-68; Evan Pugh prof. pharmacology Pa. State U., Hershey, 1968—; 1968—; asst. dean grad. edn. Pa. State U., Hershey, 1973—; Frohlich vis. prof. Royal Soc. Medicine, 1985, Pfizer vis. prof., Burroughs Wellcome vis. prof. Editor: The Life and Works of Thomas Cole, 1964, Progress in Basic and Clinical Pharmacology, 1990, numerous others; contbr. more than 250 articles to profl. jours. Von Humboldt fellow, 1988. Fellow AAAS; mem. Assn. Am. Physicians, Am. Soc. for Clin. Investigation, Am. Soc. Pharmacology and Exptl. Therapeutics (awrad for exptl. therapeutics 1971,

Harry Gold award in clin. pharmacology 1985), Am. Coll. Clin. Pharmacology (pres. 1980-82), Assn. for Med. Sch. Pharmacology (pres. 1980-82), Am. Soc. Clin. Pharmacoloty and Therapeutics (Oscar B. Hunter meml. award 1991). Office: Pa State U Coll Medicine Dept Pharmacology PO Box 850 Hershey PA 17033-0850

VESKI, ERIK, lawyer, choral conductor, real estate developer; b. N.Y.C., Nov. 19, 1952; s. Edgar and Malle (Lonkovits) V.; m. Katrin Maria Kuuskne, Dec. 25, 1976; children: Kristen Alexis, Kristjan Erik. MusB, Syracuse U., 1974; MusM, Manhattan Sch. Music, 1978; JD, N.Y. Law Sch., 1982. Bar: N.Y. State 1982. Assoc. Goldberg, Weprin & Ustin, N.Y.C., 1980—. Condr. N.Y. Estonian Male Chorus, N.Y.C., 1978—, ESTO, Toronto, 1984, prin. choral dir. ESTO '92, N.Y.C., 1992. N.Y. State Coun. on Arts grantee, 1973, Am. the Beautiful Fund grantee, 1973, IBM grantee, 1973. Office: Goldberg Weprin & Ustin 1501 Broadway New York NY 10036

VESLER, IGOR, information systems designer; b. Kiev, USSR, Oct. 31, 1949; came to U.S., 1990.; s. Yuri and Liya (Braginskaya) V.; m. Inna Gresko, May 6, 1989. BSEE, Polytech U., Kiev, 1971. Sr. researcher Inst. Scientific & Tech. Info., Kiev, 1973-89; analyst AIAA Tech. Info. System, N.Y.C., 1990—; cons. in field. Translator (book) U.S. Immigration Made Easy, 1991. Mem. AIAA, Am. Assn. for the Advancement of Slavic Studies, Bally's Health and Tennis Corp. Home: 868 46th St # 2R Brooklyn NY 11220-1621 Office: AIAA TIS 555 W 57th St Ste 1200 New York NY 10019-2925

VESPO, JO ELLEN, psychology educator; b. Queens, N.Y., Dec. 12, 1956; d. Charles John and Josephine Marie (Mahoney) Hofmann; m. Joseph Jude Vespo, Nov. 22, 1980. BA, SUNY, Stony Brook, 1978, PhD, 1985; MA, U. Md., Baltimore County, 1980. Instr. SUNY, Stony Brook, 1983-84, vis. asst. prof., 1985-87; assoc. prof. psychology and psychology-child life Utica (N.Y.) Coll. of Syracuse U., 1987—, sec. coll. coun., 1988-89; presenter Nat. Issues Forum: Daycare Dilemma, Utica, 1989; conf. presenter, 1983—. Contbr. articles to profl. jours., chpt. to book. Bd. dirs. Mid York Child Care Coordinating Coun., Utica, 1987—; chmn. children's health Herkimer-Oneida County Health Promotion Coalition, Utica, 1987-90; mem. Herkimer-Oneida County Adv. Com. on Child Care, 1987-88; presenter State Tchr.'s Ctr. and Neighborhood Ctr., Utica, 1987-89. Grantee SUNY, Stony Brook, 1985, Utica Coll. of Syracuse U., 1989. Mem. Am. Psychol. Soc., Soc. for Rsch. in Child Devel., Internat. Network Analysis Soc., Assn. for Care of Children's Health, Child Life Coun., Cen. N.Y. Psychol. Assn., Iowa Network on Personal Relationships, Phi Beta Kappa, Sigma Xi (grantee 1982, 84). Office: Utica Coll of Syracuse U Burrstone Rd Utica NY 13502-5406

VEST, CHARLES MARSTILLER, university president; b. Morgantown, W.Va., Sept. 9, 1941; s. Marvin Lewis and Winifred Louise (Buzzard) V.; m. Rebecca Ann McCue, June 8, 1963; children—Ann Kemper, John Andrew. BSME, W.Va. U., 1963; MS in Engring., U. Mich., 1964, PhD, 1967. Asst. prof., then assoc. prof. U. Mich., Ann Arbor, 1968-77, prof. mech. engring., 1977-90, assoc. dean acad. affairs Coll. Engring., 1981-86, dean Coll. Engring., 1986-89, provost, v.p. acad. affairs, 1989-90; pres. MIT, Cambridge, 1990—; vis. assoc. prof. Stanford U., Calif., 1974-75. Author: Holographic Interferometry, 1979; assoc. editor Jour. Optical Soc. Am., 1982-83; contbr. articles to profl. jours. Trustee Environ. Rsch. Inst. Mich., WGBH, Boston Mus. Sci., Woods Hole Oceanographic Inst., New Eng. Aquarium; mem. exec. com. Coun. on Competitiveness. Recipient Excellence in Research award U. Mich., 1980, Disting. Service award, 1972, Disting. Visitor award U. La Plata, Argentina, 1978. Fellow AAAS, Am. Acad. Arts and Sci., Optical Soc. Am.; mem. ASME, Sigma Xi, Tau Beta Pi, Pi Tau Sigma. Presbyterian. Home: 111 Memorial Dr Cambridge MA 02142-1348 Office: MIT Office of President Cambridge MA 02139

VETTER, BETTY MCGEE, commissioner; b. Center, Colo., Oct. 25, 1924; d. William Allen and Bonnie Hunsaker McGee; m. Richard C. Vetter, Sept. 4, 1951; children: David Bruce, Richard Dean, Robert Alan. BA, U. Colo., 1944; MA, Stanford U., 1948; LLD (hon.), Ill. Wesleyan U., 1992. Chemist Shell Devel. Co., Emeryville, Calif., 1944-45; instr. Fresno State Coll., 1948-50, Far Eastern div. U. Calif., 1950-51; adj. prof. Am. U., Washington, 1952-64; part-time U. Va., Arlington, 1952-64, U. Md. Ext. div., College Park, 1960-61; exec. dir. Commn. on Profls. in Sci. and Tech. (formerly Sci. Manpower Commn.), Washington, 1964—. Editor: Sci., Engring., Tech. Manpower Comments, 1965—. Served with U.S. Naval Women's Res., 1944-45. Recipient Disting. Svc. award U. Colo. 1990. Mem. AAUW, AAAS, Women in Engring. Program Advocates Network (treas. 1992). Home: 4779 N 33d St Arlington VA 22207 Office: 1500 Massachusetts Ave NW Suite 831 Washington DC 20005

VEUM, JONATHAN ROGER, economist; b. San Bernardino, Calif., Oct. 5, 1963; s. Roger Dean and Grace Rhoda (Mathre) V. BA, U. Calif., Santa Barbara, 1985; PhD, U. N.C., 1990. Analyst Hughes Aircraft Co., Pt. Mugu, Calif., 1984; rsch. asst. U. N.C., Chapel Hill, 1985-89; lectr. U. N.C., Greensboro, 1989, Elon Coll., Elon Coll., N.C., 1989-90; sr. economist Dept. Labor, Bur. Labor Stats., Washington D.C., 1990—; asst. dir. Nat. Longitudinal Surveys, Washington D.C., 1990—. Contbr. articles to profl. jours. U. Calif. Regent's scholar, 1981, Mortimer Andron Grad. scholar, 1985; Dissertation fellowship, U. N.C., 1989. Mem. Am. Econ. Assn., So. Econ. Assn. Lutheran. Home: 1530 Key Blvd Apt 205 Arlington VA 22209-1533 Office: Dept Labor/Bur Labor Stats 441 G St NW Washington DC 20212-0001

VEVERS, TONY, artist, educator; b. London, May 20, 1926; came to U.S., 1940; s. Geoffrey Marr and Laura Mary (Bowman) V.; m. Elspeth Colette Halvorsen, Sept. 23, 1953; children: Stephanie, Tabitha. BA, Yale U., 1950; postgrad., Accademia Di Belle Arti, Florence, Italy, 1950-51, Hans Hofmann Sch., 1952-53. lectr. Univ. N.C., Greensboro, 1963-64; creative arts prof. Purdue Univ., West Lafayette, 1964-88; cons. Fine Arts Work Ctr., Provincetown, 1970-73; vis. artistUniv. Ga., 1979, 84, Am. Univ., Washington, 1981; pres. Long Point Gallery, 1979—. One man shows include over 40 exhbns. in N.Y., Chgo., Washington, Indpls. and others; retrospective exhbns. include Greater Lafayette (Ind.) Art Mus., 1986,a Provincetown (Mass.) Art Assn., 1986; exhibited in over 175 group shows in U.S. and Europe; author: (catalog text) Alvin Ross: Retrospective, 1980, The Sun Gallery, 1981, Founders, 1990, H.C. Smith: Paintings, 1991. Com. chmn. Truro (Mass.) Ctr. for the Arts, 1990, 91. Sgt. U.S. Infantry, 1944-46, ETO. Recipient grant Nat. Coun. on Arts & Humanities, Washington, 1967, Purdue Univ., West Lafayette, 1970, New Eng. Painting & Sculpture, Provincetown, Boston, 1971. Mem. Provincetown (Mass.) Art Assn. & Mus. (officer 1960-91, com. chmn. 1990, 91), Coll. Art Assn., Archives of Am. Art. Home: 250 Bradford St Provincetown MA 02657-1745

VEZERIDIS, MICHAEL PANAGIOTIS, surgeon, researcher, educator; b. Thessaloniki, Greece, Dec. 16, 1943; came to U.S., 1974; s. Panagiotis and Sofia (Avramidis) V.; m. Therese Mary Statz; children: Peter Statz, Alexander Michael. MD, U. Athens, 1967; MA (hon) ad eundem, Brown U., 1989. Diplomate Am. Bd. Surgery. Fellow surg. rsch. Harvard Med. Sch./Mass. Gen. Hosp., Boston, 1974-77; resident U. Mass., Worcester, 1977-80; fellow in surg. oncology Roswell Park Meml. Inst., Buffalo, 1980-81, Attending surgeon, 1981-82; staff surgeon VA Med. Ctr., Providence, 1982-84; asst. prof. surgery Brown U., Providence, 1982-88; chief surg. oncology VA Med. Ctr., Providence, 1984—, assoc. chief surgery, 1986—; cons. in surgery R.I. Hosp., Providence, 1987—; surg. oncologist Roger Williams Med. Ctr., Providence, 1989—; assoc. dir. div. surg. oncology Brown U., Providence, 1989—, assoc. prof. surgery, 1988—; chmn. profl. edn. com. R.I. div. Am. Cancer Soc., Providence, 1987-89, bd. dirs., 1987—, pres.-elect. 1989-91, pres., 1991—; vis. prof. U. Patras (Greece) Med. Sch., 1988; mem. sci. adv. com. Clin. Rsch. Ctr., Brown U., Providence, 1989-91. Contbr. articles to profl. jours. and chpts. in med. books. Mem. parish coun. Ch. of Annunciation, Cranston, R.I., 1985-91; v.p. Hellenic Cultural Soc. Southeastern New Eng., Providence, 1987-89. Merit Review Cancer Research grantee Vets. Adminstr., 1983-89; named Profl. Fed. Employee of Yr., R.I. Fed. Exec. Coun., 1987; decorated Commendation medal USN. Fellow ACS; mem. Soc. Surg. Oncology, Assn. for Acad. Surgery, Am. Soc. Clin. Oncology, N.Y. Acad. Scis. (life), Soc. for Surgery of the Alimentary Tract, Am. Assn. for Cancer Rsch., Collegium Internat. Chirurgiae Digestivae, New Eng. Cancer Soc., Quidnessett Country Club. Greek Orthodox. Home: 50 Limerock Dr East Greenwich RI 02818-1643 Office: Roger Williams Med Ctr 825 Chalkstone Ave Providence RI 02908-4728

VEZINA, MONIQUE, Canadian government official; b. Rimouski, Que., Canada, July 13; 4 children. Mem. cabinet, minister external relations, mem. Parliament, Govt. of Canada, Ottawa, Ont., 1984-86, minister supply and services and receiver gen., 1986-87; minister of state for transport Govt. of Canada, 1987-88, minister of state for employment and immigration, minister of state for srs., 1988—. Chmn. parents com. Lower St. Lawrence Sch. Bd., 1964-77; bd. dirs., pres. Assoc. Family Orgns., Que., Can., 1974-81; nat. pres. Dames Helene de Champlain, 1976-79; pres. Fedn. des Caisses populaires Desjardins du Bas St-Laurent, 1976-84, Girardin-Vaillancourt Found., 1976-84; bd. dirs. Confedn. des Caisses populaires et d'economies Desjardins du Québec 1977-84, Societe immobiliere du Que., 1984; mem. Conseil a superieur de l'education du Que., 1978-82, chmn. secondary sch. bd., 1978-82; dep. bd. chmn. Régie de l'assurance automobile du Que., 1978-81; chmn. bd. dirs. Institut cooperatif desjarding, 1981-84.78-81. Office: House of Commons, Parliament Bldgs, Ottawa, ON Canada K1A 0A6

VIACAVA, LILLIAN D., librarian; b. Bklyn.; d. Frank and Camille (Raffetto) V. B.A., Coll. New Rochelle, 1951; M.S. in Library Service, Columbia U., 1954. Reference librarian Iona Coll., New Rochelle, 1954-59, asst. librarian, 1960-75, assoc. librarian, 1976—. Mem. ALA, AAUP, Cath. Library Assn. Westchester Library Assn. (chair coll. sect. 1978-79). Office: Iona Coll Ryan Library New Rochelle NY 10801

VICE, LAVONNA LEE, lawyer; b. Lexington, Ky., May 27, 1952; d. Keith Romould and Helen (Singer) V. BA summa cum laude, U. Balt., 1980, JD, 1983. Bar: Md. 1983, U.S. Ct. Appeals (4th cir.) 1987, U.S. Dist. Ct. Md. 1988, D.C. 1989, U.S. Supreme Ct. 1989. Trial atty. Ellin & Baker, Balt., 1983—; writer, researcher med., surg. and hosp. standards of care. Home: 2222 Tufton Ridge Rd Reisterstown MD 21136-5522 Office: Ellin & Baker 1101 St Paul St Baltimore MD 21202-2640

VICK, GERALD KEITH, chemistry educator; b. Dixon, Ill., Mar. 6, 1930; s. Arthur F. and Fannie Mae Vick; m. Patricia A. Kenney, June 11, 1950; children: Roger K., Kathryn A., Christopher A. BS in Chemistry, U. Ill., 1952; PhD in Organic Chemistry, U. Rochester, 1956. Rsch. chemist Exxon Rsch. & Engring. Co., Linden, N.J., 1955-58, group head, 1958-62, sect. head, 1962-66, dir. lubes and specialties lab., 1967-75; sr. staff advisor Exxon Rsch. & Engring. Co., Florahm Park, N.J., 1976-86, Exxon Corp., N.Y.C., 1975-76; adj. instr. Bucks County Community Coll., Newtown, Pa., 1988—. Contbr. articles on coal liquefaction and coal gasification, various motor oils, synthesis of pleiadiene and acepleiadylene. Fellow Am. Inst. Chemists; mem. AAAS, Am. Chem. Soc., Soc. Auto. Engrs.,. Home: 3 Devon Dr New Hope PA 18938-9210

VICKERMAN, JOHN CLIFFORD, association executive, publisher; b. Canton, S.D., Nov. 7, 1937; s. Clifford Earl and Eva Margaret (Carlson) V.; m. Diana Dornan, June 22, 1963; children: Kari Ann, Mark J., Kristen G., Peter C. B in Journalism, U. Mo., 1959. Editor Sioux Valley News, Canton, 1964-68; asst. adminstr. mgmt. Small Bus. Adminstrn., Washington, 1969-72; dir. bus. and trade assn. liaison The White House, Washington, 1973-77; dir. pub. affairs Am. Soc. Assn. Execs., Washington, 1977-81; pres. Internat. Conf. Industry Assn., Washington, 1981-85; exec. dir. Assn. Bus. Products Mfrs., Washington, 1985—. Pub. Association Meeting Directory, 1987, 88, 89, 90, 92. Lt. USNR, 1960-63. Mem. Found. for Internat. Meetings (pres. 1986-88). Republican. Episcopalian. Office: Assn Bus Products Mfrs 1001 Connecticut Ave NW Ste 1035 Washington DC 20036

VICKERS, TIREY KENNETH, air traffic control consultant; b. St. Louis, Mar. 31, 1915; s. Arthur Kenneth and Elgie (Hollingsworth) V.; m. Lora Beck, July 25, 1940; children: Nancy Ann, Betty Jean, Virginia Sue. Student, Harris Tchrs. Coll., St. Louis, 1931-32, Parks Air Coll., East St. Louis, Ill., 1932-33. Air traffic controller CAA, St. Louis, Washington, 1937-42; chief airport traffic controller CAA, Louisville, Cleve., 1942-50; chief air traffic controller specialist Tech. Devel. Ctr. CAA, Indpls., 1950-59; engring. leader Hazeltine Corp., Indpls., Little Neck, Ind, N.Y., 1959-65; dir. air traffic controller adv. unit Decca Navigator Systems, Washington, 1965-70; dir. air traffic controller planning Airways Engring. Corp., Washington, 1970-79, 81-84; helicopter cons. Vitro Labs., Silver Spring, Md., 1979-81; air traffic contr. cons., Adelphi, Md., 1985—. Author: Increasing Airport Capacity, 1988, Introduction to MLS, Introduction to TCAS; editor Jour. Air Traffic Control, 1967—; also articles; inventor air traffic control simulator, procedure for simultaneous approaches. Home and Office: 1906 Wooded Ct Hyattsville MD 20783-1343

VICKERY, BRICE ELWOOD, chiropractor, consultant; b. Bronx, N.Y., July 16, 1928; s. Ralph Jefferson and Linda (Yarvote) V.; divorced; children: Jeffrey, Randall, Brett, Laura, Valerie; m. Marilyn Avis, July 4, 1975; stepchildren: Wendy, Melanie, David Wade. D in Chiropractic, Lincoln Chiropractic Coll., Indpls., 1951; postgrad., Internat. Coll. Applied Kinesiology, 1976. Chiropractor Redding and Norwalk, Conn., 1952—; tchr., cons. Vickery Seminar Cons., Conn., 1985—. Author: The Pocket T.S. Line Manual, 1984, The Vickery Method of Chiropractic and Osteopathy, 1991, (video) The Confirmatory Challenge Test, 1990. With USN, 1945-47. Grantee Med. Tech. Inc., 1986. Mem. Flying Chiropractors. Republican. Episcopalian. Home: 727 Redding Rd West Redding CT 06896-1222 Office: Conn Holistic Chiropractic Office Redding CT 06896

VICO, PAUL, social worker; b. Englewood, N.J., July 18, 1946; s. Paolo and Carmella Anne (Bartillo) V.; m. Marian; children: Gregory, Stefanie. BA in Elem. Edn., Jersey City State Coll., 1973; MA/Student Personnel Svc., Montclair State Coll., 1977. Cert. prin., supr., tchr. of handicapped, sch. social worker, dir. student personnel svcs., elem. sch. tchr., N.J. Elem. edn. tchr. Ridgefield Park (N.J.) Sch., 1973-79, supplemental instr., 1979-81, sch. social worker, 1979—; camp counselor Region VI Handicapped Program, Leonia, N.J., 1986—; Saddlebrook Jess Counselor, Paramus (N.J.) Mental Health, 1980; instr. GED adult sch., Saddlebrook (N.J.), 1979-81. Writer: Special Svcs. Newsletter for the Handicapped, 1979—. Asst. Sunday Sch. dir. Saint Athanasio's Greek Orthodox Ch., Paramus, 1987-89; baseball and soccer coach, Saddlebrook Little League, 1984—. With U.S. Army, 1969-71, Vietnam. Named to Hackensack Sports Hall of Fame, Hackensack High Sch., 1974; nominated Tchr. of Yr., Roosevelt Sch. PTA, Ridgefield Park, 1977; recipient N.J. Tchr. Directed Mini-Grant, Gov. N.J., Trenton, 1988, Vietnam Svc. medal, 1970. Mem. Am. Legion, VFW. Democrat. Home: 14 John Ochs Ct Rochelle Park NJ 07662-5003 Office: Ridgefield Park Bd Edn 98 Cen Ave Ridgefield Park NJ

VICTOR, JAMES STUART, III, federal agency administrator; b. Frankfort, Ky., June 6, 1961; s. James Stuart Jr. and Agnes (Rowan) V. BA in History, U. Ky., 1984, BA in Polit. Sci., 1984. Dir. vol., dep. dir. coalitions Bush/Quayle Victory 88 Campaign, Lexington, Ky., 1988; pers. polit. affairs asst. to dir. vol. Bicentennial Presdl. Inaugural Commn., Washington, 1988-89; staff asst. to spl. asst. to dep. sec. Dept. of Interior, Washington, 1989-90; staff asst. to spl. advisor to dep. undersec. Ctr. for Choice, U.S. Dept. Edn., Washington, 1990—; asst. to mgr. local theaters, Chevy Chase, Md. and Brighton Park. Vol. Reagan/Bush Campaign, Lexington, 1980-84, Policy Innovation Polit. Action Com., Washington, 1989, Pres.'s Dinner, Washington, 1989, 90, 91, Nat. Victory Celebration, Washington, 1991; asst. vol., asst. to art dir. Nat. Bush/Quayle Com. Primary, 1992. mem. Ky. Soc., Schedule Soc. Bush-Quayle, Ky. Reps., Nat. Geog. Soc. Home: 5021 Seminary Rd Apt 1425 Alexandria VA 22311-1941 Office: Ctr for Choice US Dept Edn 400 Maryland Ave SW Washington DC 20202-0002

VICTOR, RONALD JOSEPH, JR., systems specialist; b. Sewickley, Pa., Oct. 30, 1964; s. Ronald Joseph Sr. and Nancy Carol (Kniess) V. BSBA, Robert Morris Coll., Pitts., 1987. Remittance processing operator Mellon Bank, N.A., Pitts., 1983-84, mini-computer operator, 1984-85, sr. mini-computer operator, 1985-87, systems specialist, 1987—; project leader Profl. Mgmt. Svcs., Carnegie, Pa., 1986-87. Fireman Fleming Park Vol. Fire Dept., Stowe Twp., Pa., 1979. Recipient Cert. of Attainment, ARC, 1984, Am. Heart Assn., 1984. Mem. Stallions Hockey Team, Penn Hills Hockey League. Democrat. Roman Catholic. Home: 21 Downs Dr Coraopolis PA 15108-3607 Office: Mellon Bank 3 Mellon Bank Ctr Pittsburgh PA 15259-0001

VICTORIN, STEVEN ROBERT, bank executive; b. Englewood, N.J., Feb. 3, 1961; s. Robert Raymond and Janet (Wilbourn) V. BA in History and Econs., Skidmore Coll., 1983. Assoc. Leveraged Capital div. Citibank, N.A., N.Y.C., 1983-85; account officer Leveraged Capital div. Citibank, N.A., L.A., 1985-87; asst. v.p. Leveraged Capital div. Citibank, N.A., Harrison, N.Y., 1987-89; v.p. Citicorp Venture Capital Ltd. div. Citibank, N.Y.C., 1989—. Mem. Skidmore Coll. Alumni Assn. (sec. bd. dirs. 1984-88, admissions corr. 1985-87). Home: The Albert 23 E 10th St New York NY 10003-6118 Office: Citicorp Venture Capital Ltd 399 Park Ave Fl 6 New York NY 10043-0001

VIDAL, EDUARDO R., lawyer; b. Cruces, Cuba, Apr. 20, 1957; came to U.S., 1966; s. Aldo and Lourdes (Capiro) V.; m. Katrina Lofgren, Apr. 10, 1981; children: Ingrid Amelia, Charles Edward. BA, U. Chgo., 1978, JD, 1981. Bar: N.Y., Ill. Assoc. Chapman & Cutler, Chgo., 1981-86, Skadden, Arps, Slate, Meagher & Flom, N.Y.C., 1986-90; ptnr. Skadden, Arps, Slate, Meagher & Flom, 1990—. Mem. ABA (aircraft fin. subcom.), Am. Coll. Investment Counsel. Republican. Episcopalian. Home: 32 Crane Rd Scarsdale NY 10583-4248 Office: Skadden Arps Slate Meagher & Flom 919 3rd Ave New York NY 10022-3903

VIDAL, EVALENA SHARP, advertising manager; b. Bridgeton, N.J., Jan. 26, 1927; d. Charles Edward and Eva M. (Robbins) Sharp; m. Joseph Vidal, Oct., 1957 (div. 1970); children: Charles Henry Lawrence, Victoria Eva. BA in Polit. Economy, Sweet Briar Coll., 1948; MA in Polit. Sci., Wellesley, 1950; diploma in internat. law, Acad. of Internat. Law, The Hague, Netherlands, 1951; LLD in Internat. Law, Faculté de Droit, U. Paris, 1952. Intelligence officer CIA, Washington, 1953-79, ret., 1979; patent and trademark mgr. Durand Internat., Millville, N.J., 1982-88, advt. mgr., 1988—. Elected ofcl. Commercial Twp., Cumberland County, N.J., 1982-85; pres. Commercial Twp. Rep. Club, 1983—; bd trustees Clyde A. Phillips Schooner Project, Commercial Twp., 1991—. Mem. Am. Soc. Internat. Law, Nat. Trust for Historic Preservation, Mauricetown Hist. Soc., Cumberland County Hist. Soc., Rotary (pres. Port Norris, N.J. chpt. 1990-91). Home: PO Box 153 High St Mauricetown NJ 08329-9998 Office: Durand Internat Wade Blvd Millville NJ 08332-2202

VIECHNICKI, DENNIS JOHN, ceramic engineer; b. Passaic, N.J., Dec. 25, 1940; s. John Victor and Emily (Serafin) V.; m. Barbara Austin Bradshaw, Sept. 11, 1965; children: John, Peter, Josef, Katherine. BS in Ceramic Sci., Rutgers U., 1962; PhD in Ceramic Sci., Pa. State U., 1966. Sr. scientist Westinghouse R & D Labs., Churchillboro, Pa., 1966; project officer U.S. Army Materials Tech. Lab., Watertown, Mass., 1966-68, rsch. ceramic engr., 1968-72, supervisory rsch. ceramic engr., 1973-87, chief ceramics rsch. br., 1987-92, acting dir. emerging materials divsn., 1992—; exch. scientist Ctr. d'Etudes Chimie Metallurgique, Vitry-Sur-Seine, France, 1972-73; program dir. 37th Sagamore Army Materials Rsch. Conf., Plymouth, Mass., 1990. Contbr. articles to profl. publs. Fellow Am. Ceramic Soc. (treas. New Eng. sect. 1970-71, chmn.-elect 1972-73, chmn. 1974); mem. Chatham Yacht Club. Roman Catholic.

VIEGAS, LOUIS PAUL, postmaster; b. Bklyn., Aug. 24, 1940; s. Jack and Antoinette (Cappiello) V.; m. Charlotte Sonia Storey, May 28, 1967; children: Cindy, Tracy. A.A.S. in Bus., N.Y. Inst. Tech., 1978, BS in Bus., 1979; postgrad., St. John's U., Queens, N.Y., 1987. Traffic asst. Berkshire Chem. Corp., N.Y.C., 1956-59; engring. aide Bd. Higher Edn., N.Y.C., 1959-61; letter carrier U.S. Postal Svc., Bklyn., 1961-68; supr. U.S. Postal Svc., 1968-79, area mgr., 1979-82, mgr., deliveries & collections, 1982-85, dir. city ops., 1985-87; postmaster U.S. Postal Svc., Staten Island, N.Y., 1987—; mem. Northeast Region Speakers Bur., N.Y., N.J., New Eng., 1985—. Mem. Assn. for the Help Retarded Children, Nassau County, N.Y., 1974-89, Valley Stream Civilian Patrol, Valley Stream, N.Y., 1984-86, Nassau County Foster Parents Assn., 1982-87. Named Man of Yr. Holy Name Soc. Bklyn., 1986, Christopher Columbus Assn., Bklyn., Staten Island, 1987, Bklyn. Jewish Postal Workers Welfare League, 1989. Mem. Nat. League Postmasters of U.S., Nat. Assn. Postal Suprs., Sons of Italy. Republican. Roman Catholic. Office: US Postal Svc 550 Manor Rd Staten Island NY 10314-9998

VIEIRA, SHER JANET, small business owner; b. New Haven, Conn., Jan. 6, 1962. BA cum laude, Smith Coll., 1990. Direct care advocate Community Homes for Children, Easthampton, Mass., 1984-85; owner, mgr. Cleaning Business, Northampton, Mass., 1985—. Vol. AIDS Allies, Springfield, Mass.; mem. Hampshire County Civil Rights Advisory Bd., Northampton, 1986-90, Soc. Orgnized Against Racism, Northampton, 1987-90, Northampton Com. for Multi-racial Unity, 1986-87. Mem. NAACP, Phi Beta Kappa. Democrat.

VIERECK, PETER, educator, poet, historian; b. N.Y.C., Aug. 5, 1916; s. George S. and Margaret (Hein) V.; m. Anya de Markov, June 1945 (div. May 1970); children—John-Alexis, Valerie Edwina (Mrs. John Gibbs); m. Betty Martin Falkenberg, Aug. 30, 1972. B.S. summa cum laude, Harvard, 1937, M.A., 1939, Ph.D., 1942; Henry fellow, Christ Ch., Oxford U., Eng., 1937-38; L.H.D. (hon.), Olivet Coll., 1959. Teaching asst. Harvard, 1941-42, instr. German lit., tutor history and lit. dept., 1946-47; instr. history U.S. Army U., Florence, Italy, 1945; asst. prof. history Smith Coll., 1947-48, vis. lectr. Russian history, 1948-49; assoc. prof. Modern European, Russian history Mt. Holyoke Coll., 1948-55, prof., 1955—; vis. lectr. Am. Culture Oxford U., 1953; Whittal lectr. in poetry Library of Congress, 1954, 63, 79; Fulbright prof. Am. poetry and civilization U. Florence, Italy, 1954-56; Elliston chair poetry lectr. U. Cin., 1956; vis. lectr. U. Calif. at, Berkeley, 1957; Disting. William R. Kenan prof. Mt. Holyoke Coll., 1979—; Charter mem. Council Basic Edn.; vis. poet Russian-Am. cultural exchange program Dept. State, USSR, 1961; vis. research scholar 20th Century Fund, USSR, 1962-63; vis. scholar Rockefeller Study Center at Bellagio, Italy, 1977; vis. artist and scholar Am. Acad. in, Rome, 1949-50, 78; dir. poetry workshop N.Y. Writers Conf., 1965-67; research fellow Huntington Library, San Marino, Calif., 1978. Author: Metapolitics—From the Romantics to Hitler, 1941 (Swedish edit., 1942, Italian, 1948), Terror and Decorum, poems, 1948, reprinted, 1972, Who Killed the Universe, novelette included in anthology New Directions Ten, 1948, Conservatism Revisited-The Revolt Against Revolt 1815-1949, 1949 (English edit, 1950), Strike Through the Mask, New Lyrical Poems, 1950, reprinted, 1972, The First Morning: New Poems, 1952, reprinted, 1972, Shame and Glory of the Intellectuals, 1953, rev. edit., 1965, reprinted 1978, Dream and Responsibility, The Tension Between Poetry and Society, 1953, The Unadjusted Man; a New Hero for Americans, 1956, reprinted, 1973, Conservatism: From John Adams to Churchill, 1956, reprinted, 1978, The Persimmon Tree, poems, 1956, Inner Liberty, The Stubborn Grit in the Machine, 1957, The Tree Witch: A Verse Drama, 1961, reprinted, 1973, Meta-politics, The Roots of the Nazi Mind, 1961, rev. expanded edit. 1965, Conservatism Revisited and The New Conservatives: What Went Wrong; rev. paperback edits., 1962, 65, reprinted hardcover, 1978, New and Selected Poems, 1932-67, 1967, Archer in the Marrow: The Applewood Poetry Cycles of 1967-87, 1987; also author of selections in symposium books Towards a World Community, 1950, Midcentury American Poets, 1950, Arts in Renewal, 1951, The New American Right, 1955, Education in a Free Society, 1958, The Radical Right, 1962, Soviet Policy Making, 1967, Outside Looking In, 1972, A Question of Quality, 1976, The Southern California Anthology, 1987, rev. edits., 1987, 89, Decade: New Letters Anthology of the 80s, 1990; contbr. essays, poems to popular mags., and profl. jours., monograph on Conservatism in Ency. Brit., 1974. Sgt. U.S. Army, 1943-45, Africa and Italy. Decorated 2 battle stars; awarded Tietjens prize for poetry, 1948, Pulitzer prize for poetry, 1949; recipient Most Disting. Alumnus award Horace Mann School for Boys, 1958, Poetry Translation award Translation Center, Columbia U., 1978, Sadin poetry prize N.Y. Quar., 1977, Golden Rose award New Eng. Poetry Club, 1981, Varoujan prize, 1983; Guggenheim fellow Rome, 1949-50; Rockefeller Found. researcher in history Germany, summer 1958; NEH sr. rsch. fellow USSR, 1969; Mass. Artists Found. fellow, 1978. Mem. Am. Hist. Assn., Oxford Soc., Poetry Soc. Am., P.E.N., Phi Beta Kappa. Clubs: Harvard (N.Y.C. and London); Bryce (Oxford, Eng.). Home: 12 Silver St South Hadley MA 01075-1616

VIESER, RICHARD WILLIAM, electrical manufacturing company executive; b. Newark, Nov. 14, 1927; s. William L. and Viola S. (Coltorti) V.; m. Lois Barbara Johnson, Sept. 8, 1951; children: Richard, Cheryl Vieser Kleckner, Cynthia, William, Jaime. A.B., Lafayette Coll., 1951. Mgmt. trainee Western Electric Co., N.Y.C., 1951-52; sales mgr. to div. mgr. Chatham Electronics Corp./Tung Sol Electric, Livingston, N.J., 1954-66; div. gen. mgr. Wagner Electric Corp., Livingston, 1966-70, v.p., 1970, group v.p., 1971-73, pres., 1973-74, chief exec. officer, 1974-79; exec. v.p. Studebaker Worthington, 1979, McGraw-Edison Co., 1979-84; pres., chief operating officer McGraw-Edison Co. (now Cooper Industries), 1984-85; chmn., chief exec. officer FL Industries, Inc., 1985-89, Midland Ross Corp., N.J., 1986-89; chmn., pres., chief exec. officer Lear Siegler Diversified Holdings Corp., Livingston, N.J., 1987-89; bd. dirs. Varian Assocs., Control Data Corp., Dresser Industries, FL Industries, Midland-Ross, Lear Siegler. With U.S. Army, 1946-48, Korea. Mem. Automotive Pres. Coun., Soc. Automotive Engrs., Motor Equipment Mfrs. Assn. (chmn.), Theta Delta Chi, Baltusrol Golf Club, Pine Valley (N.J.) Golf Club, Morris County Golf Club. Office: 147 Columbia Tpke Ste 304 Florham Park NJ 07932-2102

VIETS, HERMANN, college president, consultant; b. Quedlinburg, Fed. Republic Germany, Jan. 28, 1943; came to U.S., 1949, naturalized, 1961; s. Hans and Herta (Heik) V.; m. Pamela Deane, June 30, 1968; children: Danielle, Deane, Hans, Hillary. BS, Polytech. U., 1965, MS, 1966, PhD, 1970. Postdoctoral fellow von Karman Inst., Brussels, 1969-70; group leader Wright-Patterson AFB, Dayton, Ohio, 1970-76; prof. Wright State U., Dayton, Ohio, 1976-81; assoc. dean W.Va. U., Morgantown, 1981-83; dean U. R.I., Kingston, 1983-91; pres. Milw. Sch. Engring., 1991—; chmn. bd., dir. Precision Stampings, Inc., Beaumont, Calif.; bd. dirs. Astro-Med, Inc., West Warwick, R.I., Promptus Communications Inc., Portsmouth, R.I.; cons. U.S. Air Force Aero Propulsion Lab., Dayton, 1976-80, Covington & Burling, Washington, 1976-77; cons. several cos. and govt. agys. Patentee in aero. field; contbr. numerous articles to tech. publs. Recipient Tech. Achievement award U.S. Air Force, 1974, Sci. Achievement award, 1975, Gov.'s Sci. and Tech. award State of R.I., 1987, Goodrich Pub. Svc. award, 1990, Citation R.I. Legislature, 1987, 90, 91; postdoctoral fellow NATO, 1969-70, NASA, 1965-69. Fellow AIAA (assoc., best tech. paper award Allegheny-Pitts. sect. 1982); mem. Deutsche Gesellschaft für Luft und Raumfahrt, Am. Soc. Engring. Edn., Soc. Mfg. Engrs., Phi Kappa Phi, Sigma Xi, Tau Beta Pi, Sigma Gamma Tau. Home: 4216 N Lake Dr Shorewood WI 53211 Office: Milw Sch Engring 1025 N Broadway Milwaukee WI 53202-3109

VIGDOR, MARTIN GEORGE, psychologist; b. Bronx, N.Y., Jan. 14, 1939; s. Leo and Ida (Rosenblatt) V.; m. Lorraine Louise Retta, Mar. 31, 1971; 1 child, Neil Andrew. BA, CCNY, 1959; PhD, NYU, 1971. Lic. psychologist, N.Y., Conn. Psychologist intern VA, Bklyn., 1965-70; clin. psychologist Family Ct., N.Y.C., 1971-72; staff psychologist Cath. Charities Guidance Inst., Bronx, 1973-78, Jewish Child Care Assoc., N.Y., 1973-78, Pleasantville (N.Y.) Diagnostic Ctr., 1978-81; clin. psychologist Putnam Community Svcs., Inc., Carmel, N.Y., 1982-84; clin. dir. Green Chimneys Children's Svcs. Inc., Brewster, N.Y., 1981—; adj. prof. The Union Grad. Sch., Cin., 1987—; cons. Northeast Counseling Ctr., Katonah, N.Y., 1984—. Contbr. articles to profl. jours. Pres. Temple Beth Elohim, Brewster, 1985-87; v.p. Jewish Fedn., Danbury, Conn., 1990-92, pres., 1992—. Mem. APA, N.Y. Psychol. Assn., Conn. Psychol. Assn., Residential Treatment Facilty Coalition N.Y. (bd. dirs. 1988—), Com. Psychologists of Voluntary Child Care Agys., Rotary (pres. Brewster club 1988-89, dist. gov. rep. 1986-87, asst. to dist. gov. 1989-90, Paul Harris fellow 1989, Dean of coll. of pres. 1990-92). Jewish. Office: Green Chimneys Childrens Svcs Inc Putnam Lake Rd Brewster NY 10509-1113

VIGLIATORE, LEONARD JAMES, physical therapist; b. Glen Cove, N.Y., Aug. 14, 1954; s. Cosimo and Louise (Nudo) V.; m. Kathleen Ricciardi; children: Christopher, Jonathan, Kathleen Jessica. BS, Columbia U., 1976. Cert. hypnotherapist; cert. therapist in spinal disorders; cert. orthopedic specialist. Staff physical therapist Suffolk Developmental Ctr., Melville, N.Y., 1976-77; sr. physical therapist Saint Johns Hosp., Smithtown, N.Y., 1977-80; asst. chief physical therapy Mid Island Hosp., Bethpage, N.Y., 1980-83; owner Physical Therapy & Rehab. Ctr., Bay Shore, N.Y., 1983—; guest lectr. Mid Island Hosp., Bethpage, 1981-84; cons. Smithtown (N.Y.) Parkinsons Ctr., 1977-82, Ross Nursing Home, Brentwood, N.Y., 1977-80, Smithtown Gen. Hosp., 1984—. Author: (booklet) Low Back Pain-A New Approach, 1982. Founder Thanksgiving Food for Families, Port Jefferson and Bay Shore, N.Y., 1983—; vol. Saint Patrick's Soup Kitchen, Bay Shore, 1986-89, Leukemia Soc. Am., Farmingdale, N.Y., 1980-83; sponsor Christian Childrens Fund, Indonesia, 1984—. Recipient First Degree Black Belt, World Tae Kwon Do Fedn., Korea, 1980, Ranking of 98 in USA, U.S., 1980, Cert. Appreciation, Saint Lukes Soup Kitchen, N.Y., 1985. Mem. Am. Physical Therapy Assn., State Soc. Physical Therapists, Harbor Hills Country Club. Republican. Roman Catholic. Office: 1855 Union Blvd Bay Shore NY 11706-7949

VIGNOLA, CHAD ALEXANDER, lawyer; b. Cleve., Mar. 13, 1958; s. Leonard and Dorothea Maude (Costello) V. BS, U. Pa., Phila., 1979, JD, 1982. Law clk. U.S. Dist. Judge, N.Y.C., 1982-84; asst. corp. counsel City of N.Y. Law Dept., N.Y.C., 1984-87; asst. U.S. atty. So. Dist. N.Y. Dept. Justice, N.Y.C., 1987—; lead atty. in 60 defendant civil racketeering trial involving Longshoremen's Union, Mafia and employers on the waterfront, N.Y.C., 1988—. Home: 255 E 10th St Apt 5C New York NY 10009-4852 Office: US Atty 1 St Andrews Plz New York NY 10007-1703

VIKNER, DAVID WALTER, educational administrator; b. Berkeley, Calif., Dec. 24, 1944; s. David Luther and Louise (Lindbeck) V.; m. Lin Ma, Apr. 25, 1987; 1 child, Louisa Ma. BA, Upsala Coll., 1966; MDiv, Yale Div. Sch., 1973; EdD, Columbia U., 1987. Tchr. Luth. Middle Sch., Hong Kong, 1966-69; instr. Nat. Taiwan U., Taipei, 1973-77; headmaster Luth. Middle Sch., Hong Kong, 1977-81; instr. Cen. China Normal U., Wuhan, 1981-82; cons. Luth. World Fedn., Geneva, 1984-86; v.p. United Bd. for Christian Higher Edn. in Asia, N.Y.C., 1987-89, pres., 1989—. Trustee Harvard-Yenching Inst., Cambridge, Mass., 1989—, Partnership for Svc. Learning, N.Y.C., 1990—. Office: UBCHEA 475 Riverside Dr #1221 New York NY 10115

VILLA, JUAN FRANCISCO, chemistry educator; b. Matanzas, Cuba, Sept. 23, 1941; came to U.S. 1961; s. Urbano and Eulalia M. (Graciaa) V.; m. Elena M. Baez, Feb. 4, 1967; children: John F., Ellen M., Paul A., Irene L. BS, U. Miami, 1965, MS, 1967, PhD, 1969. Postdoctoral assoc. U. N.C., Chapel Hill, 1969-71; from asst. to assoc. prof. Lehman Coll. of CUNY, Bronx, 1971-77, acting dean of natural and social scis., 1980-81, prof. chemistry, 1977—; team mem. Middle Atlantic Accreditation Assn., Phila., 1989—. Referee Jour. Chem. Edn., 1978—; contbr. articles to profl. jours. Bd. dirs. Hal Block Ramapo Soccer League, Rockland County, N.Y., 1981—, treas., 1981-90; bd. dirs. Spring Valley Little League, 1980-82. Am. Chem. Soc. rsch. grantee, 1971-73, CUNY rsch. grantee, 1972, 74-75, U.S. Dept. Edn. grantee, 1991—; Fulbright-Hays fellow, 1979-81. Mem. Am. Chem. Soc., Sigma Xi. Republican. Roman Catholic. Home: 378 Blauvelt Rd Pearl River NY 10965-2009 Office: Lehman Coll of CUNY Bedford Park Blvd W Bronx NY 10468-1539

VILLAMIL, RICHARD J., botany educator; b. Warwick, N.Y., July 31, 1942; s. Richard James and Helen (Hayden) V.; m. Beverly Ann Schmitt, Aug. 26, 1968; children: Kathryn, Richard J. BA in Botany, Drew U., Madison, N.J., 1964; MS in Ecology, Rutgers U., New Brunswick, N.J., 1967; PhD in Plant/Soil Sci., U. Vt., Burlington, 1976. Instr. Ulster County Community Coll., Stone Ridge, N.Y., 1967-68; horticulturist/adj. U. Vt., Burlington, 1979-88; adj. prof. Sterling Coll., Craftsbury, Vt., 1979-85, St. Michaels Prof., Winooski, Vt., 1985-88; prof. natural sci. Trinity Coll. of Vt., Burlington, 1974—; mtg. chmn., sci. advisor Vt. Acad. Arts & Scis., Burlington, 1987, 89. Contbr. articles to profl. jours. Trustee Chittenden Solid Waste Dist.; chmn. bd. dirs. Vt. Whey Pollution Abatement Authority, 1985-89, Winooski Valley Park Dist., 1979-87. With USN, 1968-72. Mem. Botany and Bird Clubs of Vt., Ecol. Soc. Am., Vt. Natural Resources Council (advisor), Am. Isnt. Biol. Scis., Malletts Bay Boat Club (commodore 1988—), Lite n Lens Camera Club, Sigma Xi. Home: 18 North St Essex Junction VT 05452-3129 Office: Trinity Coll of Vt 208 Colchester Ave Burlington VT 05401-1422

VILLANI, FRANK JOHN, research chemist retired; b. Bklyn., May 9, 1921; s. Anthony Nicolas and Christine (Ferranto) V.; m. Florence J. Brykowski, Dec. 1, 1951; children: Frank John Jr., Marianne Ella, Thomas S., John Robert. BS, Bklyn. Coll., 1941; MS, Fordham U., 1943, PhD, 1946. Tchr. Holy Trinity High Sch., Hackensack, N.J., 1942-43; teaching fellow Fordham U., Bronx, N.Y., 1943-46; sr. chemist Schering Corp., Bloomfield, N.J., 1946-48; sr. medicinal chemist Schering Corp., Bloomfield, 1948-58; fellow medicinal chemist Schering Corp., Bloomfield, N.J., 1964-83. Contbr. over 45 publs. to profl. jours.; patentee in field. Mem. Am. Chem. Soc., AAAS, N.Y. Acad. Sci. Home: 22 Oakland Ter Fairfield NJ 07004-3827 Office: Schering Plough Bloomfield NJ 07003

VILLAR, CECILIA Y., actuary; b. Guayaquil, Ecuador, Nov. 1, 1960; came to U.S., 1962; d. Francisco Elias and Olga Beatriz (Eljuri) V. BA in Math., Fordham U., 1982; postgrad., Soc. of Actuaries, N.Y.C., 1982-92. Enrolled actuary Joint Bd. Enrollment of Actuaries. With The Segal Co. (formerly Martin E. Segal Co.), N.Y.C., 1992—; asst. actuary The Segal Co. (formerly Martin E. Segal Co.), 1992—. Mem. Am. Acad. Actuaries. Office: Segal Co 1 Park Ave New York NY 10016

VILLAR, ISABEL ELSA, language educator; b. Havana, Cuba, Sept. 23, 1948; came to U.S., 1966; BA, Manhattanville Coll., Purchase, N.Y., 1972; MA, NYU, 1975; profl. diploma, Iona Coll., New Rochelle, N.Y., 1986; postgrad., L.I. U., 1987. Lic. guidance counselor. Bilingual tchr. Benjamin Franklin Middle Sch., South Norwalk, Conn., 1972-78; counselor Brien McMahon High Sch., South Norwalk, 1978—; founder, dir. Centro Hispano, White Plains, N.Y., 1974—. Adv. mem. Community Devel. Adv. Com., White Plains, 1979—; bd. dirs. Western Hispanic Adv. Bd., Westchester County, 1984—; v.p. Western Hispanic Coalition, White Plains, 1974—; trustee St. Bernard's Ch., White Plains, 1986—; bd. dirs. Human Rights Commn., White Plains, 1979—, Am. Cancer Soc., Westchester County, 1985—. Recipient Excellence in Teaching award U. Conn., 1986, Conn. Assn. Latin Ams. in Higher Edn. award, 1987, Educator of Yr. award Phi Delta Kappa, Iona Coll.; named in Mayoral Proclamation City of White Plains, 1980. Office: Brien McMahon High Sch Highlands White Plains NY 10605-1248

VILLARI, ROBERT, sales executive; b. Phila., June 12, 1932; s. Leo and Ethel (Saritz) V.; m. Rhoda Stillman, May 29, 1955; children: Marla, Beth. Grad. high sch., Phila. Asst. buyer Strawbridge & Clother, Phila., 1951-53, Lit Bros., Phila., 1955-56; mgr. order dept. His Nibs Shirt, Souderton Pa., 1956-59; div. head Wldon Paj, N.Y.C., 1959-63; v.p. Solveg Corp., N.Y.C., 1964-70; v.p. sales PCA Apparel Industries, Inc., N.Y.C., 1971—; bd. dirs. Licensing Industry Merchandisers Assn., N.Y.C. Cpl. U.S. Army, 1952-54. Office: PCA Apparel Industries Inc 16E W 34th St New York NY 10016-4328

VILLEMONTEIX, JEAN-CLAUDE, personnel officer, management educator; b. Saint-Junien, France, Aug. 1, 1957; came to U.S., 1990; s. Adolphe and Michelle (Pascaux) V.; m. Minna Mari Ylitalo, July 5, 1986. BA in Econ., U. Limoges (France), 1978, MA in Econ., 1980, MPhil, 1985; BA in Mgmt., Limoges Inst. Tech., 1981; B of Law, Inst. Nat. des Techniques Economiques et Comptables, Paris, 1981; M of Labor Law, U. Poitiers, France, 1989, D of Law, 1991; cert. advanced studies in internat. bus. adminstrn., Inst. de Commerce Internat., Paris, 1988; cert. advanced studies in pers. mgmt., ISFOGEP/ESSEC Grad. Sch. Mgmt., 1989. Cons. B. Mansoux Cons., Limoges, France, 1981-87, Alcan France Inc., Toulouse, France, 1987-88; vis. prof. Essec Grad. Sch., Limoges, 1989—; pers. officer IMF, Washington, 1990—. Mem. AACD, French Assn. Human Resource Profls., Soc. Human Resource Mgmt., Assn. Human Resource Profls. Quebec, European Inst. Pers. Lawyers. Office: IMF 700 19th St NW Rm 6518 Washington DC 20431-0002

VILLEREAL, GARY LYNN, social work educator; b. Pontiac, Mich., Mar. 29, 1949; s. Jesse and Mary (Felix) V.; m. Catherine Hovey Robinson, Aug. 6, 1977. BA, Oakland U., 1975, MA, 1977; PhD, U. Pitts., 1991. Lic. cert. social worker, W.Va.; nationally cert. employee assistance profl. Assembly Pontiac (Mich.) Motors Div., 1968-74; parking lot attendant Bloomfield Hills (Mich.) Sch. Dist., 1975-77; gen. supr. Weirton (W.Va.) Steel Corp., 1977-90; asst. prof. Marywood Coll., Scranton, Pa., 1991—; bd. dirs. Family Svc. Assn., Steubenville, Ohio, 1978-91, Instl. Rev. Bd., Scranton, 1991—. Author: Veterans Diagnostic Scale, 1991. Vol. therapist Vet. Ctr., Pitts., 1985-91, Scranton, 1991—. With U.S. Army, 1968-70. Named Bd. Mem. of Yr., Family Svc. Assn., 1989, Outstanding vol. Vet. Ctr., 1991. Mem. NASW, Disable Am. Vets., Vietnam Vets. Inc., AmVet, Coun. on Social Work Edn., Employee Assistance Profl. Assn., Employee Assistance Soc. of North Am. Republican. Roman Catholic. Office: Marywood Coll 2300 Adams Ave Scranton PA 18509

VILLINSKI, PAUL STEPHEN, artist; b. York, Maine, May 28, 1960; s. Paul Bernard and Jacqueline L. (Whalen) V. Student, Mass. Coll. Art, 1980-82; BFA, Cooper Union, 1984. adj. lectr. art history LaGuardia Community Coll., CUNY, Long Island City, 1990—. Solo exhbns. include St. Peter's Ch. at Citicorp Ctr., N.Y.C., 1987, Midtown Galleries, N.Y.C., 1989, Queens Mus. Art at Bulova Corp. Ctr., Jackson Heights, N.Y., 1990; group shows include Ridge St. Gallery, N.Y.C., 1986, 87, Queens Mus. Art, Flushing, N.Y., 1987, Studio K Gallery, L.I., N.Y., 1987, 88, Midtown Galleries, N.Y.C., 1988, 89, The Barn Gallery, Ogunquit, Maine, 1990, PS Gallery, Ogunquit, 1991, DMB&B, N.Y.C., 1991, Cooper Union, N.Y.C., 1992, Nat. Acad. Design, N.Y.C., 1992, Paine Webber Art Gallery, N.Y.C., 1992; represented in permanent collections. Resident Millay Colony for Arts, Austerlitz, N.Y., 1987; grantee Nat. Endowment Arts, 1987; Agnes Bourne fellow in painting Djerassi Found., Woodside, Calif., 1988, fellow Montalvo Ctr. for the Arts, Saratoga, Calif., 1991, fellow Ucross Found., 1992. Home: 9-01 44th Dr Long Island City NY 11101

VINCENT, FRANCIS THOMAS, JR., sports executive; b. Waterbury, Conn., May 29, 1938; s. Francis Thomas and Alice (Lynch) V.; m. Valerie McMahon, July 3, 1965; children: Anne, William, Edward. BA cum laude, Williams Coll., 1960; LLB, Yale U., 1963. Bar: Conn. 1963, N.Y. 1964, D.C. 1969. Assoc. Whitman & Ransom, N.Y.C., 1963-68; ptnr. Caplin & Drysdale, Washington, 1968-78; assoc. dir. div. corp. fin. SEC, Washington, 1978; pres., chief exec. officer Columbia Pictures Industries, Inc., N.Y.C., 1978-83, chmn., chief exec. officer, 1983-87; pres., chief exec. officer entertainment bus. sect. The Coca-Cola Co., N.Y.C., 1987; dep. commr., chief oper. officer Major League Baseball, New York, 1989, commr., 1989-92. Trustee Williams Coll., 1970-88, Hotchkiss Sch., 1975—, Carleton Coll., 1988—. Mem. N.Y. Athletic Club, Belle Haven Club, Phi Beta Kappa. Roman Catholic. Clubs: University, Belle Haven. *

VINCENT, JAMES SIDNEY, university educator, chemist; b. Redlands, Calif., Sept. 19, 1935; s. Rex Oliver and Sara (Wood) V.; m. Ruth Lewin, May 31, 1964 (div. June 1966); m. Margot Uppman, Mar. 23, 1969; children: Jennifer, Jonathan. BS, U. Redlands (Calif.), 1957; PhD, Harvard U., 1963. Rsch. fellow Harvard U., Cambridge, Mass., 1963-64, Calif. Inst. Tech., Pasadina, 1964-65; asst. prof. chemistry U. Calif., Davis, 1965-71; assoc. prof. chemistry U. Md. Baltimore County, Catonsville, 1971—. Recipient Sr. Rsch. Svc. award NIH, 1984. Home: 10124 Spring Pools Ln Columbia MD 21044-1709 Office: UMBC 5401 Wilkens Ave Baltimore MD 21228-5329

VINCENT, MARY LILLIAN CARTER, librarian; b. Sandersville, Ga., Nov. 30, 1931; d. Virgil and Mamie (Etheridge) Carter; m. Timothy Vincent, Jan. 29, 1965; 1 stepchild, Renee. BA, Fordham U., 1977; MS, Pratt Inst., 1986, MLS, 1988. Owner, operator Pin & Curl Beauty Salon, Bklyn., 1959-72; data processing supr., operator Statis. Tabulating Corp., N.Y.C., 1957-75; dir. Bethel at Weeksville, Child Devel. Ctr., Bklyn., 1975-80; media technician Pratt Inst., Bklyn., 1981-88, asst. dir. multi media svcs., 1988-89, dir., 1989—. Author manual, 1980. Trustee Weeksville Soc., Bklyn., 1978-91, treas. bd. trustees, 1980-91. Mem. AAUW, Assn. for Edn. Comm. and Tech.-Minorities in Media, African Am. Mus. Assn., Black Alumni of Pratt. Office: Pratt Inst 200 Willoughby Ave Brooklyn NY 11205-3899

VINCENT, MICHAEL THOR, food products executive, communications executive; b. Syracuse, N.Y.; s. James Roswell and Barbara Marie (Sessions) V. AAS, Onondaga Community Coll., Syracuse, 1983; BS, Syracuse U., 1986, MBA, 1991. Terminal mgr. Arnolds Thrift, Syracuse, 1980-82; distbn. mgr. Arnolds, Syracuse, 1982-86, dir. mktg. and advt., 1989-91; also bd. dirs. BMJ Arnolds Internat. Inc. (formerly Arnolds Thrift), Syracuse, 1991—; media researcher Syracuse U., 1987-89; pres. Thor Communications Inc., Syracuse, 1988—, also bd. dirs. Mem. Alpha Epsilon Rho. Home: 3757 Watervale Rd #2 Manlius NY 13104-9523 Office: BMJ Arnolds Internat Inc 2792 Erie Blvd E Syracuse NY 13224

VINCENT, SCOTT GARRISON, entertainment company executive, consultant; b. White Plains, N.Y., Sept. 3, 1958; s. Scott and Anne (Cassell) V.; m. Marisa Moncada, June 2, 1990. BA, Lafayette Coll., 1980. Intern Sta. WFMZ-TV, Allentown, Pa., 1979-80; DA, assignment editor Sta. WABC-TV, N.Y.C., 1980-81; field producer "Nightline" ABC News, N.Y.C., 1981-84; bur. chief "84 Olympics" ABC News, L.A. and Long Beach, Calif., 1984; producer ABC News, L.A., 1984-85, Harvard U., Reeves Co., N.Y.C., 1985; project cons. Statue of Peace Project, N.Y.C., 1985-86; program producer Turner Broadcasting, N.Y.C., 1987; pres. Blue Sword Entertainment Inc., N.Y.C., 1988—; cons. UN, N.Y.C., 1986, Theosophical Soc., Wheaton, Ill., 1987-89, Legion Good Will, N.Y.C. and Brazil, 1989. Cons. Rep. Nat. Com., Washington, 1991. Mem. Colonial Soc. Pa., Loyal Legion N.Y. Commandery, Swedish Colonial Soc., Welcome Soc., Zeta Psi. Episcopalian. Office: Blue Sword Entertainment 799 Wilmot Rd # 355H Scarsdale NY 10583-6528

VINCENTI, JOHN RICHARD, educational coordinator; b. Nanticoke, Pa., Jan. 3, 1946; s. Celeste Thomas and Olga (Ottaviani) V.; m. Cynthia Barger; 1 child, Lisa. BS, Mansfield U., 1967; MEd, Penn State U., 1974. Research aide Pa. State U., University Park, Pa., 1965-67; instr., staff Pa. State U., University Park, 1979-83, summer course instr., 1985-88, researcher, 1986-88, dir., 1987—, program mgr., 1989—, coord. edn. program nuclear engring. dept., 1990—; sr. high sch. tchr. State College Area Sch., State College, Pa., 1981-82, alt. sch. tchr., 1982-83, jr. high sch. tchr., 1967-81; project. dir. ENTER 2000 Conf., 1986-91, SEE The Future, 1991; exec. sec. ACURI Assn. Inc., 1989—; cons. UNC Industries, Washington, 1986, West Penn Power Co., Greensburg, Pa., 1978-91. Contbr. to Energy: Issues, Impacts and Investigation, LLRW: A Media Handbook on Low-Level Radioactive Waste, Citizen's Handbook: Low Level Radioactive Waste Disposal and Management Issues, Management of Radioactive Waste, Training Manual: Right-to-Know-Chemicals in the Workplace; reviewer EPA pamphlet, Lead in Drinking Water. Bd. dirs. Neighborhood Civic Assn., State College, Pa., 1989—; township supt. Ferguson Township Bd., Centre County, Pa., 1979-83; commr. Pa. Dept. of Edn., Harrisburg, 1979-83; mem., grad. Pa. Leadership, Pa. Chamber of Bus. and Industry, 1991—. Named Outstanding Educator, U.S. Jaycees and State Coll., 19811, Region III Honorable Mention, Nat. U. Continuing Edn. Assn., N.Y., 1987. Mem. Am. Soc. Engring. Edn., Am. Nuclear Soc., Pa. Coun. for the Social Studies, Pa. Sci. Tchrs. Assn., Phi Delta Kappa. Home: 1344 Curtin St State College PA 16803-3017 Office: Pa State U Barbara Bldg University Park PA 16802

VINCENTI, WILLIAM GENE, college program director; b. Elizabeth, N.J., Jan. 26, 1934; s. Charles and Lucy (Diange) V.; m. Marilyn A. Mueller, Apr. 14, 1956; children: Anne Karen Vincenti-Lambert, William George. BS in Edn., Kean Coll. N.J., 1960, MA in Adminstrn. and Supervision, 1964. Cert. tchr. K-12, prin., and supr., N.J. Tchr. Kawameeh Jr. High Sch., Union, N.J., 1960-67; acad. advisor Kean Coll. N.J., Union, 1967-80, coord. profl. svcs., 1980-88, dir. computer rsch. and tng. inst., 1983—, dir. profl. svcs., 1988—; cons. Nat. Assn. Coll. Admissions Counselors, Chgo., 1970-74, N.J. Dept. Higher Edn., Trenton, 1970-74, N.J. Ind. Coll. Assn., Union, 1972-74. Author, editor: (manual) Veterans Benefits, 1973, (newsletter) Vector, 1972-74. Mem., com. chairman Clark (N.J.) Bd. Edn., 1972-74. With U.S. Army, 1953-56. Grantee U.S. Office of Edn., 1972-73, IBM, 1990-91. Mem. N.J. Edn. Activiites Task Force, Arbitration Assn. Presbyterian. Home: 69 Emerson Rd Clark NJ 07066 Office: Kean Coll NJ Morris Ave Union NJ 07083

VINCENZI, HARRY, psychologist; b. New Haven, Oct. 14, 1950; s. Henry and Rose (Martino) V. BA, Franklin Pierce Coll., 1973; MS, So. Conn. State Coll., 1974; EdD, Temple U., 1982. Lic. psychologist, Pa.; cert. rational emotive therapy. Rsch. intern Office Rsch. and Evaluation, Phila. Sch. Dist., 1974-77, rsch. asst., 1977-87, dist. rsch. specialist, 1987—; psychologist Pa. Assocs., Phila., 1988—; cons. Counseling Ctr., Hall Mercer, Pa. Hosp., Phila., 1989—. Bd. dirs. Phila. Citizens for Children and Youth, 1988—; committeeman Dem. party, Phila., 1980—. Mem. Am. Psychol. Assn. Office: Pa Assocs 829 Spruce St Ste 400 Philadelphia PA 19107-5752

VINING, MICHAEL PAUL, banker; b. Salina, Kans., Nov. 9, 1949; s. Joe Alvin and Lucy (Carig) V.; m. Donna Maria Boles, June 2, 1973. BS, U.S. Naval Acad., 1971. Salesperson Procter & Gamble, Harrisburg, Pa., 1977-78; mktg. adv. Control Data Corp., N.Y.C., 1978-83; bank officer Chemical Bank, N.Y.C., 1983—; mem., speaker Decision Support Conf., Stamford, Conn., 1986—; speaker Internat. Info. Assn., N.Y.C., 1987. Mem. Harrisburg (Pa.) Jaycees, 1977-78. Lt. USN, 1971-78. Mem. Chatham (N.J.) C. of C.

VINSON, BERNARD L., temporary personnel services executive; b. N.Y.C., May 31, 1919; s. I. Edward and Eva (Levin) V.; m. Gloria Ann Konowitch, Oct. 17, 1948; children: Marsha Lynn, Edward B. BA, U. Mich., 1940, MA, 1941. Asst. to v.p. sales M. Lowenstein & Sons, N.Y.C., 1946-48; chmn. The Original Tempo Svcs. Corp., East Meadow, N.Y., 1949—. Pres. Nassau County Conv. & Visitors Bur., Mineola, N.Y., 1978, chmn., 1979; mem. adv. bd. Hofstra U., 1975—. Lt. comdr. USN, 1941-46. Mem. L.I.-Mid Suffolk Bus. Assn. (pres. 1986—), Nassau County Indsl. Devel. Agy., Bailli de L.I. Confrerie de la Chaine des Rotisseurs, Conseiller, L'Ordre Mondial, Chmn.'s Club Mineola, Princeton Club, U. Mich. Club, Govs. Club, Hofstra U. Club, Masons, Shriners, Elks. Republican. Jewish. Home: 500 Northern Blvd Great Neck NY 11021-5104 Office: The Original Tempo Svcs Corp 1900 Hempstead Tpke East Meadow NY 11554-1702

VINSON, WILLIAM LLOYD, accountant; b. Coaldale, Pa., May 22, 1959; s. Donald Ralph and Ruth (Bennett) V.; m. Cynthia Ann Berdis, May 23, 1987; 1 child, Timothy Bennett. BS in Acctg., Pa. State U., 1989. CPA, Pa. Store sales mgr. Mace Electronics, Erie, Pa., 1983-87; acctg. asst. ENGX, Inc., North East, Pa., 1989; staff acct. Vincent & Voss CPAs, Erie, Pa., 1989—. Recipient Alexander E. Loeb Silver Medal, Pa. Inst. CPAs, 1990, Elijah Watt Sells Cert., AICPA, 1990, Award for Excellence in Acctg. Studies, Nat. Assn. Accts., 1990. Republican. Methodist. Home: 2922 Myrtle St Erie PA 16508-1841 Office: Vincent & Voss CPAs 554 W 10th St Erie PA 16502-1352

VIOLA, ALFRED, chemistry educator; b. Vienna, Austria, July 8, 1928; s. Isidore and Greta (Broch) V.; m. Joy Darlene Winkie, Oct. 19, 1963. BS in Chemistry, Johns Hopkins U., 1949, MS in Chemistry, 1950; PhD in Chemistry, U. Md., 1955. Postdoctoral rsch. fellow U. Md., College Park, summers 1957-58; rsch. assoc. Boston U., 1955-57; asst. prof. Northeastern U., Boston, 1957-62, assoc. prof., 1962-68, prof. organic chemistry, 1968—; vis. instr. biochemistry Boston U., 1956-57; vis. prof. U. Munich, 1977, Monash U., Melbourne, Australia, 1984, Wellesley Coll., 1991-92. Contbr. articles to profl. jours. Recipient Excellence in Teaching award Northeastern U., 1991. Mem. Am. Chem. Soc. (councilor N.E. sect. 1963-68, 86-89, 90-91, 92-94, Norris award selection com. 1979-86, chmn. 1981, 95), Sigma Xi. Home: 14 Glover Rd Wayland MA 01778-2305 Office: Dept Chemistry Northeastern U Boston MA 02115

VIOLENUS, AGNES A., vice principal; b. N.Y.C.; d. Antonio and Constance Violenus. BA, Hunter Coll., 1952; MA, Columbia U., 1958; EdD, Nova U., 1990. Tchr. N.Y. State Day Care, N.Y.C., 1952-53, N.Y.C. Bd. Edn., 1953-66; asst. prin. N.Y.C. Elem. and Jr. High Sch., 1966—; adj. instr. computer dept. continuing edn. div. York Coll., N.Y.C., 1985-88; adj. instr. tchr. mentor program grad. edn. div. CCNY, 1990-91; reviewer ednl. and instructional films. Co-author: LOGO: K-12, 1980; contbr. articles to profl. jours. Life mem. Girl Scouts U.S., N.Y.C. Recipient Dedicated Svc. award Coun. Suprs. and Adminstrs. Mem. N.Y. Acad. Scis., Nat. Assn. Negro Bus. and Profl. Women's Clubs (scholarship com. 1989—), Nat. Black Child Devel. Inst. (bd. dir. 1991—, pub. policy com. 1991—), Pub. Edn. Assn. (mem. good schs. exch. com.), Schomburg Ctr. Rsch. in Black Culture (bd.

trustee, co-chair corp. task force on African-Am. in math., sci., and tech. 1992—), Doctorate Assn. N.Y. Educators, N.Y. Alliance Black Sch. Educators, Bank St. Alumni Coun. Greater N.Y. (asst. sec. 1991—), Wistarians Alumni Hunter Coll. (pres. 1990—). Democrat. Roman Catholic. Office: PO Box # 85 Canal St Sta 350 Canal St New York NY 10013

VISCO, FERDINAND JOSEPH, cardiologist, educator; b. Bklyn., July 8, 1941; s. Joseph Thomas and Susan (Baratta) V.; m. Laurie Judith Glass, Sept. 18, 1983; 1 child, Melissa; children by previous marriage, Ruth, Joseph, Jennifer. BS in Biology, Fairfield U., 1963; MD, U. Padua, Italy, 1969. Diplomate Am. Bd. Internal Medicine, specialty cardiovascular disease; lic. physician and surgeon, N.Y. Intern medicine Flushing (N.Y.) Hosp., 1969-70; jr. and sr. resident medicine Cath. Med. Ctr., Queens Hosp. Ctr., Jamaica, N.Y., 1970-72; fellow cardiology Nassau County Med. Ctr., East Meadow, N.Y., 1972-74; dir. medicine Freeport (N.Y.) Hosp., 1975; instr. medicine SUNY, Stony Brook, 1973-75; instr. medicine Albert Einstein Coll. Medicine, Bronx, N.Y., 1975-78, asst. prof. medicine, 1978—; assoc. cardiologist Bronx Lebanon Hosp., 1975—, attending physician, 1978—, dir. noninvasive cardiology lab., 1975—. Fellow Am. Coll. Cardiology; mem. ACP. Office: Bronx Lebanon Hosp 1650 Grand Concourse Bronx NY 10457

VISCONTI, JOAN MARIE, payroll manager; b. Boston, Jan. 11, 1935; d. Henry Sylvester and Catherine Irene (Shea) Caine; m. Emery John Visconti, Jan. 23, 1955; children: James J., Dennis E. Grad., Mass. Bay Community Coll., 1991. Acctg. clk. Bank of Boston, Mass., 1952-54, U.S. Govt., Watertown, Mass., 1954-55; accounts receivable clk. Wells Jewelry, Attleboro, Mass., 1968-70; acctg. adminstr. Drake Bakery, Mansfield, Mass., 1970-77; payroll adminstr. Becton Dickinson, Sharon, Mass., 1977-80; payroll supr. Gulf & Western Casket, Wellesley, Mass., 1980-83; payroll mgr. The Interface Group, Needham, Mass., 1983—. Mem. M.I.T. Women's League, Cambridge, Mass., Right to Life, Boston. Mem. Am. Payroll Assn., Control Data Users Group. Democrat. Roman Catholic.

VISWANATHAN, GAURI, English educator, scholar; b. Calcutta, India, Nov. 5, 1950; came to U.S., 1982; d. T. Venkatesan and Subbalakshmi Viswanathan. BA, U. Delhi, 1971, MA, 1973; PhD, Columbia U., 1985. Lectr. in English U. Delhi, Delhi, India, 1978-85, Barnard Coll., N.Y.C., 1985-86; lectr. in English, Mellon fellow Columbia U., N.Y.C., 1986-88; asst. prof. English U. Mass., Amherst, 1988-89; asst. prof. English and comparative lit. Columbia U., N.Y.C., 1989—; editorial cons. Harper Collins (World Reader), N.Y.C., 1991-92; cons. Social Sci. Rsch. Coun. (South Asian Humanities Project), N.Y.C., 1991. Author: Masks of Conquest, 1989; contbr. articles to profl. jours. Andrew W. Mellon Found. fellow, 1986-88, NEH summer fellow, 1990, Guggenheim Meml. Found. fellow, 1990-91, Am. Inst. Indian Studies sr. fellow, 1991. Mem. Modern Lang. Assn., Assn. Asian Studies. Home: 601 W 113th St Apt 7E New York NY 10025-7943 Office: Columbia Univ 602 Philosophy Hall New York NY 10027

VITAGLIANO, KENNETH JOHN, cultural event producer; b. Everett, Mass., July 28, 1954; s. Albert and Evelyn Vitagliano; m. Nancy McCann, July 23, 1988; 1 child, Hallie Ann. BS in Pub. Adminstrn. cum laude, Suffolk U., 1979. Cert. meeting profl. Dir. spl. events unit Commonwealth of Mass., Boston, 1983-90; dir. event svcs./show dir. The Interface Group, Needham, 1990-91; pres. ProEvents, Boston, 1988—; instr. Bentley Coll., Waltham, Mass., 1991—; speaker in field. Exec. producer performing arts series at the Hatch Shell, Commonwealth of Mass./Met. Dist. Commn., Boston, 1984-90. Regional campaign mgr. Geary for Lt. Gov., Boston, 1982; del. Dem. Conv., Springfield, Mass., 1986; advanceman U.S. Presdl. Campaign, Boston, 1987-88; vol. various not-for-profit orgns.; cons. U.S. Olympic Torch Row, 1992. Recipient Pride in Performance award Gov. Mass., 1987, Top Event Program award Nat. Recreation and Pks. Assn., Hartford, Conn., 1988. Mem. Internat. Spl. Events Soc. (chpt. pres. 1988-90, v.p. internat. 1989, bd. govs. 1987-89, 92—, Ann. award 1991), Internat. Festival Assn., Nat. Assn. Exhibit Mgrs., Am. Soc. Assn. Execs., Meeting Planning Internat. Roman Catholic. Office: ProEvents 46 Turner St Brighton MA 02135-2507

VITALE, FREDERICK R., safety professional; b. Kenilworth, N.J., Sept. 2, 1941; s. Ferdinand Paul and Rita Patricia (Moretti) V.; B.S., Rutgers U., 1967; Ph.D., N.Y.U., 1978; m. Anna M. Franchak, May 7, 1961; children—F. Richard, J. Steven, J. Christopher. Regional indsl. hygienist Nat. Loss Control Service Corp., Summit, N.J., 1969-74; supr. indsl. hygiene and safety Occupational Safety and Health Adminstrn., Belle Meade, N.J., 1974-76; mgr. safety and environ. affairs Ciba-Geigy, Summit, N.J., 1976-79; dir. safety and environ. affairs Revlon, Inc., N.Y.C., 1979-86; v.p. Enviro Scis., Inc., Rockaway, N.J., 1986-87, dir. safety and environ. affairs Sterling Drug Co., 1987—; v.p. Travel World, 1989—; pres. Vitran, Inc., 1975—; ptnr. Hampton Mgmt., Mount Holly, N.J. Real estate devel., 1970—; constrn. and zoning officer North Hanover Twp. (N.J.), 1970-74, safety officer, 1974-76, health officer, 1973-75. Served with USAF, 1960-64. Cert. safety profl., hazard control mgr. Mem. Am. Indsl. Hygiene Assn., Am. Soc. Safety Engrs., N.J. Safety Council, N.Y. Safety Execs., N.A.M., Pharm. Safety Group. Club: Masons.

VITALE, MAGDA, artist; b. N.Y.C., July 20, 1939; d. John and Tomasita (Couso) Reyes; m. Robert James Vitale, Dec. 23, 1957 (dec. Sept. 1990); children: Pamela, Robert, John. BFA, Moore Coll. Art, Phila., 1980; student, Barnes Found., Merion, Pa., Skowhegan (Maine) Sch. Painting and Sculpture. One-woman shows include Nexus Gallery, Phila., 1982, 84, St. Joseph's U., Phila., 1983, U. Pitts. Gallery, 1987, Camden County Coll., Blackwood, N.J., 1988, Becton Hall Gallery, Fairleigh Dickinson U., Rutherford, N.J., 1991, No. Ind. Arts Assn. William J. Bachman Gallery, Munster, Ind., 1992, Henri Gallery, Washington, 1991; exhibited in group shows the most recent being Schomarie County Arts Gallery, Cobleskill, N.Y., 1990, Nexus Gallery, 1990, Zepher Gallery, Louisville, 1990, Henri Gallery, Washington, 1991, Zoller Gallery, Pa. State U., 1991; works represented in permanent collections including Best Products, Inc., 1838 Investment Advisers, N.J. Power and Light, Carnegie Ctr. Recipient Purchase prize Delaware County Community Coll., 1976, Scholarship Skowehegan (Maine) Sch. Paintng and Sculpture, 1979, Expo V award Northport (N.Y.) Galleries, 1986. Home: 12 Springton Lake Rd Media PA 19063-1824

VITALE, TAMAAM (TAMMY VITALE), sound engineering executive non-profit consultant; b. Washington, Mar. 22, 1948; d. Samuel George and Edith Belle (Kinard) Tehaan; m. Shawn William Vitale, Feb. 14, 1985; children: Jessie Carlyn, John Samuel. BA in Bus., Trinity Coll., 1989. Prodn. typist Allen Wayne Ltd., Arlington, Va., 1967-68; sec. to v.p. Strayer Coll., Washington, 1969; supr. prodn. Am. Bank Stationery, Ft. Lauderdale, Fla., 1972-74; sales adminstr. Modular Computer Systems, Ft. Lauderdale, 1974-76; dir. adminstrn. Aqualux Water Processing, Ft. Lauderdale, 1977-79; contract adminstr. GTE Telenet, Reston, Va., 1979-85; pres. Gussound, Forrestville, Md., 1985—; exec. dir. Betterment for United Seniors, 1989-91; cons. to non-profit orgns. Forestville, Md., 1991—. Mem. Greenpeace; chair Washington Area Tng. Ctr.; v.p. Longfields Elem. PTA; rep. County Coun. of PTAs. Mem. NOW, Am. Home Bus. Assn.

VITARELLI, ROBERT FRANCIS, company owner; b. Waterbury, Conn., Sept. 21, 1940; s. Romeo Anthony and Eva Cynthia (Cicchetti) V.; (div. 1976); children: Douglas, Jonathan, Gregory. BA, Clark U., 1962; postgrad., U. Hartford, 1962-72. Tchr. various elem. and secondary schs., Conn., Mass., 1962-65; editor to mng. editor Am. Edn. Publ., Conn. and, Great Britain, 1965-72; freelance writer Conn., 1972-77; sr. editor McGraw-Hill Publ., N.Y.C., 1977-78; agt. B. Davis Agy., N.Y.C., 1978-81; owner, pres. Curriculum Targets, Inc., Woodbridge, Conn., 1981—. Author of about 100 children's books. Roman Catholic. Home: 33-C Harbor Village Branford CT 06405-4408 Office: Curriculum Targets Inc New Haven CT 06525-2210

VITELLO, STANLEY JOHN, law educator; b. Phila., Jan. 13, 1944; s. Orazio and Beatrice (Chaiken) V.; children: Emily, David. PhD, U. Conn., 1972; MS in Law, Yale U., 1983. Asst. prof. Pa. State U., State College, 1972-77; prof. spl. edn. Rutgers U., New Brunswick, N.J., 1977—; Congl fellow U.S. Senate, Washington, 1990-91. Author: Mental Retardation: Social and Legal Context, 1985; contbr. articles to profl. jours. Recipient award Rehab. Internat., 1985, U.S. Dept. Edn., 1989. Home: 39 Columbia Ave Hopewell NJ 08525-2027 Office: Rutgers U 10 Seminary Pl New Brunswick NJ 08901-1183

VITKOWSKY, VINCENT JOSEPH, lawyer; b. Newark, Oct. 3, 1955; s. Boniface and Rosemary (Ofack) V.; m. Mary Gunzburg, May 16, 1981; children: Vincent Jr., Victoria. BA, Northwestern U., 1977; JD, Cornell U., 1980. Bar: N.Y. 1981, N.Y. Dist. Ct. (so. and ea. dists.) N.Y. 1981. Assoc. Hart and Hume, N.Y.C., 1980-84, Kroll & Tract, N.Y.C., 1984-87; of counsel Nixon, Hargrave, Devans & Doyle, N.Y.C., 1988-89; ptnr. Buchalter, Nemer, Fields & Younger, N.Y.C., 1990—; lectr. industry and bar groups. Contbr. articles to profl. jours. Mem. ABA, Assn. Bar City of N.Y., Internat. Bar Assn., Lawyers Alliance for World Security (spl. counsel to pres., steering com. N.Y. chpt., chair non-profliferation com., nat. bd. dirs. 1990—), Am. Arbitration Assn., Am. Soc. Internat. Law, Acad. Polit. Sci., Cornell Club. Democrat. Home: 24 Radio Pl Stamford CT 06906-2219 Office: Buchalter Nemer Fields & Younger 150 E 52d St New York NY 10022

VITT, SAM B., communications media services executive; b. Greensboro, N.C., Oct. 23, 1926; s. Bruno Caesar and Gray (Bradshaw) V.; m. Marie Foster, Oct. 30, 1955; children: Joanne Louise, Michael Bradshaw, Mark Thomas. A.B., Dartmouth Coll., 1950. Exec. asst. TV film CBS, N.Y.C., 1950-52; broadcast media buyer Benton & Bowles, Inc., N.Y.C., 1952-54; broadcast media buyer Biow Co., N.Y.C., 1954-55, assoc. account exec., 1955-56; broadcast media buyer Doherty, Clifford, Steers & Shenfield, Inc., N.Y.C., 1956-57, media supr., 1958-59, v.p. media supr., 1960, v.p., assoc. media dir., 1960, v.p., media dir., 1960-63, v.p. in charge media and broadcast programming, 1963-64; v.p., exec. dir. media-program dept. Ted Bates & Co., Inc., N.Y.C., 1964-66, sr. v.p., exec. dir. media-program dept., 1966-69; dir. Advt. Info. Services, Inc., 1964-65; founder, pres. Vitt Media Internat., Inc., N.Y.C., 1969-81, chmn., chief exec. officer, 1982-91, chmn. emeritus, 1991—; advt. dir. Banking Law Jour., 1955-69; lectr. in field, 1967—; lectr. advt. media NYU, 1973, 74, Am. Mgmt. Assn., 1974, 75, Assn. Nat. Advertisers, 1967, 69, 70, Advt. Age Media Workshop, 1975. Media columnist: Madison Ave, 1963-68; editorial cons.: Media/Scope, 1968-69; contbg. editor: Handbook of Advertising Management, 1970; contbr. to: Advertising Procedure, 1969, rev. edit., 1973, 5th, 6th, 7th edits., 1977, Exploring Advertising, 1970; contbr. editor to Nation's Bus., Broadcasting, Variety, Anny, TV/Radio Age, Sponsor, Printer's Ink; producer rec. album The Body in the Seine; cover story guest editor: Media Decisions, 1967. Mem. com. Nat. UN Day Com., 1973, vice chmn., 1974, assoc. chmn. 1975, co-chmn., 1976-77; bd. dirs. UN Assn. Am., 1977; bd. dirs., chmn. Rsch. Inst. Hearing and Balance Disorders Ltd., 1979—; mem. Pres. Reagan's Joint Presdl. Congl. Steering Com., 1982; mem. Bush Presdl. Roundtable, 1990—; mem. advd. adv. com. The Acting Com., 1984; chmn. radio-TV reps. div. Greater N.Y. Fund, 1962, chmn. consumer pub. div., 1963. Served to Lt. (j.g.) USN, 1944-46. Recipient Media award sta. WRAP, Norfolk, Va., 1962, award of Merit Greater N.Y. Fund, 1963, Gold Key Advt. Leadership award Sta. Reps. Assn., 1967, ann. honors Ad Daily, 1967, certificate of merit Media/Scope, 1967, 1969 Creative Pub. Statement Concerning Advt. award; named one of 10 Best Dressed Men in Advt. Community Gentlemen's Quar., 1979. Mem. Am. Assn. Advt. Agys. (broadcast media com. dir. corr. 1958-63, media operating com. on consumer mags. 1964-65), Internat. Radio and TV Soc. (timebuying and selling seminar com. dir. 1961-62), Internat. Radio and TV Found. (faculty seminar 1974), Nat. Acad. Arts Sci. (mem. com. dir.), Media Dirs. Council, Sigma Alpha Epsilon. Presbyterian. Clubs: Manor Park Beach (Larchmont, N.Y.); N.Y. Athletic (N.Y.C.); Roxbury Run (Denver, N.Y.). Home: 3 Roosevelt Ave Larchmont NY 10538-2912 Office: Vitt Media Internat Inc 1114 Ave Of The Americas New York NY 10036-7703

VITTEK, JOZEF, dentist, educator, researcher; b. Bukova, Czechoslovakia, May 14, 1934; came to U.S., 1970; s. Jaromir and Elizabet (Kaffana) V.; m. Vilma Silesova, Dec. 19, 1959. MD, Komensky U., Bratislava, Czecho-Slovak Federative Republic, 1959; PhD, Slovak Acad. Sci., Bratislava, Czecho-Slovak Federative Republic, 1966; DDS, SUNY, Albany, N.Y., 1974. Diplomate in Dentistry, CSFR. Asst. prof. stomatology Komensky U., Bratislava, CSFR, 1959-70; vis. asst. prof. biochemistry N.Y. Med. Coll., N.Y.C., 1969-70, instr. medicine, 1970-73, asst. prof. med. dentistry, 1973-79, assoc. prof., 1980-83, prof. med. dentistry, 1984—; lectr. medicine Mt. Sinai Sch. Medicine CUNY, N.Y.C., 1980—; mem. peer rev. panel for grants NIH, NIDR, Washington, 1983—; sr. investigator Ctr. for Aging and Human Devel., N.Y. Med. Coll., 1984—; dir. dentistry dept. Westchester Inst. Human Devel., Valhalla, N.Y., New York Med. Coll., 1989—. Author: 3 books; co-author: book chpts.; contbr. over 100 articles to profl. jours. Grantee, NIH, NIDR, Grants, 1975—. Mem. Internat. Assn. Dental Rsch., Fed. Dentaire Internat., N.Y. Acad. Scis., Apimondia (exec. com.). Office: NY Med Coll Cedarwood Hall Valhalla NY 10595

VITTI, LOUIS PETER, lawyer; b. Pitts., Dec. 27, 1940; s. Peter J. and Flora (Napolitano) V.; m. Joan Ganley, Aug. 6, 1967 (div. Aug. 1982); children: Lois Marie, Monica; m. Elizabeth Mary Quinlan, Aug. 30, 1986. BA, Duquesne U., 1963, JD, 1968. Bar: Pa. 1969, U.S. Dist. Ct. (we. dist.) Pa. 1969, U.S. Tax Ct. 1984, U.S. Ct. of Appeals (3d cir.) 1977. Assoc. Ryan & Bowser, Pitts., 1974-76; ptnr. Markovitz & Vitti, Pitts., 1976-86; pres. Louis P. Vitti and Assocs., Pitts., 1986—; gen. counsel Associated Trades & Crafts Nat. Union; instr. bus. law Bradford Sch. of Bus., 1969-71; mem. Fed. Ct. Criminal Justice panel, Allegheny County Indigent Divorce panel, Lawyer Referral Svc. vol. panel. Candidate for state legis., Penn Hills, 1980; Dem. candidate for committeeman, 1972. Sgt. USMCR, 1966, lt. USNR, 1972-83. Named Man of the Yr., Italian Am. Radio and Press Assn. Phila., 1974; recipient Outstanding Achievement award Italian Am. Radio and Press Assn. Phila., 1976. Mem. Am. Arbitration Assn., Am. Trial Lawyers, Pa. State Bar Assn., Criminal Trial Lawyers Assn., Allegheny County Bar Assn., Pitts. Zool. Soc., Am. Legion, Sons of Columbus Am., Kingsley Assn., Res. Officer's Assn., Phi Kappa Thata. Home: 4827 Tremont Dr Allison Park PA 15101-1034 Office: 1031 Fifth Ave Pittsburgh PA 15219

VITTONE, BERNARD JOHN, psychiatrist, researcher; b. Latrobe, Pa., Oct. 5, 1951; s. Felix Edward and Jessie (Mosso) V.; 1 child, Matthew. BS in Psychology, Georgetown U., 1969-73, DMS, 1973-77. Diplomate Am. Bd. Psychiatry and Neurology. Intern in flexible medicine, then resident in psychiatry St. Vincent's Hosp and Med. Ctr., N.Y.C., 1977-82; resident in ophthalmology Wills Eye Hosp., Phila., 1978-79; staff psychiatrist Phila. State Hosp., Phila., 1979; med. staff fellow NIMH, Bethesda, Md., 1982-84; dir. Nat. Ctr. for Treatment of Phobias, Anxiety, and Depression, Washington, 1985—; cons. Roundhouse Square Psychiat. Ctr., Alexandria, Va., 1984-85; guest researcher NIMH, 1984—; mem. tng. com. St. Vincent's Hosp. and Med. Ctr., N.Y.C., 1980-81; attending staff Dominion Hosp., 1991—. Contbg. author to profl. jours. and books. Mem. instnl. rev. bd. Inst. for Behavior and Health, Rockville, Md., 1988-91; dir. adv. bd. Am. Against Drugs, 1990—. Recipient Outstanding achievement award in microbiology, Georgetown Univ., 1976. Mem. AMA, Am. Psychiat. Assn., Washington Psychiat. Soc., D.C. Mental Health Counselors Assn., Anxiety Disorders Assn. of Am., Alpha Omega Alpha. Office: NCTPAD 1755 S St NW Washington DC 20009-6199

VITTORIO, SALVATORE ANTHONY, technical editor; b. N.Y.C., Dec. 14, 1952; s. Giovanni and Concetta (DiPaola) V. BA in Math., Pace U., 1975. Tech. indexer AIAA Tech. Info. Svc., N.Y.C., 1975-78, index copy editor, 1978-80, chief indexer, 1980—. Mem. AIAA (assoc.), N.Y. Road Runners Club. Office: Am Inst Aeronautics/Astron 555 W 57th St # 1200 New York NY 10019-2925

VIVELO, JACQUELINE JEAN, author, English educator; b. Lumberton, Miss., Jan. 23, 1943; d. Jack and Virginia Olivia (Bond) Jones; m. Frank Robert Vivelo, June 19, 1965; 1 child, Alexandra J. BA, U. Tenn., Knoxville, 1965, MA, 1970. Caseworker N.Y.C. Dept. Welfare, 1965-66; instr. reading Knoxville Coll., 1968-70; instr. English Middlesex County Coll., Edison, N.J., 1970-72, U. Mo., Rolla, 1975-77, Middlesex County Coll., Edison, 1978-80, Lebanon Valley Coll., Annville, Pa., 1981-87, 1987-91; vis. author West. Chester (Pa.) U., 1988. Author: Super Sleuth, 1985 (Best Book award), Beagle in Trouble, 1986, A Trick of the Light, 1987, Super Sleuth and the Bare Bones, 1988; editor: College Education Achievement Project's Handbook for College Reading Teachers, 1969; co-editor: American Indian Prose and Poetry, 1974; contbr. articles and short stories to various publs. Recipient Best Book award Nat. Child Study Assn., 1985, Pa. Coun. of the Arts Fellowship award for Lit., 1992; NIMH grantee, 1969-70. Mem. Children's Lit. Coun. Pa. (v.p. 1991), Soc. Children's Book Writers, Sigma Tau Delta (sponsor Omicron Omicron chpt.). Home: 8620 New Haven Rd Columbia MO 65201

VIVERA, ARSENIO BONDOC, allergist; b. Cebu City, Philippines, Oct. 29, 1931; s. Arsenio R. and Ramona del Mar (Bondoc) V.; A.A., Cebu Coll., U. Philippines, 1950, M.D., 1954. Intern, Philippines Gen. Hosp., 1954-55; resident in medicine Beekman-Downtown Hosp., N.Y.C., 1955-57, Detroit Meml. Hosp., 1957-58; resident in allergy Robert A. Cooke Inst. Allergy, Roosevelt Hosp., N.Y.C., 1958-59, fellow in allergy, 1959-61; sr. cons. scientist Philippines Nat. Inst. Sci. and Tech., Manila, 1961-62; practice medicine specializing in allergy, N.Y.C.; chief allergy dept. attending physician N.Y. Polyclinic Med. Sch. and Health Center, 1972-77, adj. prof., 1972-77; clin. attending physician Robert A. Cooke Inst. Allergy, 1969—; asst. attending physician N.Y. Infirmary, N.Y.C., 1969—; chief allergy, attending St. Vincent's Hosp. and Med. Center, N.Y.C., 1977—. Diplomate Am. Bd. Allergy and Immunology. Fellow Am. Acad. Allergy, Am. Coll. Allergists, Am. Assn. Clin. Immunology and Allergy; mem. N.Y. Allergy Soc., AMA, Am. Assn. Cert. Allergists, N.Y. Acad. Scis., N.Y. Acad. Medicine, Am. Geriatric Soc., N.Y. State Med. Soc., N.Y. County Med. Socs. Office: 681 Lexington Ave Fl 5 New York NY 10022-2607

VIVIAN, JAMES ROBERT, educational administrator; b. Clovis, N.Mex., Dec. 3, 1946; s. James Robert and Mildred Christine (Day) V. BA, Yale Coll., 1968; MA, Yale U., 1974, MPhil, 1975. Exec. asst. Edn. Assocs., Inc., Washington, 1968-69; edn. program specialist U.S. Office Edn., Washington, 1969; legis. asst. U.S. Congress, Washington, 1970; curator edn. Nat. Portrait Gallery, Washington, 1970-72; instr. Yale U., New Haven, 1975; dir. Yale-New Haven History Edn. Project, 1974-77, Yale-New Haven Tchrs. Inst., 1978—; cons. U.S. Office Edn., Washington and Boston, 1974-81; dir. U.S. Grant Found., New Haven, 1974—; past pres. Conn. Coord. Com. for Promotion History; past chmn. Clinton (Conn.) Historic Dist. Commn. Mem. Yale Club N.Y.C. Office: Yale U 53 Wall St New Haven CT 06520

VIVONA, JOHN ANTHONY, educator; b. Bklyn., July 16, 1952; s. Anthony and Rosalie Vivona; m. Ronelle Maher, July 22, 1957. BS, Wagner Coll., 1974, MS, 1975. Cert. elem. tchr. High sch. math. tchr. Charlotte County Bd. Edn., Punta Gorda, Fla., 1975-78; math. tchr., dept. chmn. Eatontown (N.J.) Bd. Edn., 1978—; computer cons.; pvt. instr. in field. Math. cons.: Reading Skills for Math, 1981.

VIZARD, FRANK JOSEPH, journalist; b. N.Y.C., July 7, 1955; s. Matthew Joseph and Anne (Tierney) V.; m. Mary McAleer, Apr. 28, 1984. BA, NYU, 1977. News editor Paper Trade Jour., N.Y.C., 1977-78; mng. editor Paperboard Packaging, N.Y.C., 1978-80; editor Autosound & Communications, N.Y.C., 1980-84; freelance writer N.Y.C., 1984-90; electronics and photography editor Popular Mechanics mag., N.Y.C., 1990—. Office: Popular Mechanics Mag 224 W 57th St New York NY 10019-3203

VIZNER, NIKOLA, art gallery director, consultant, art historian; b. Bezdan, Yugoslavia, Nov. 9, 1945; came to U.S., 1974; s. Mavro and Nella (Lazibat) V.; married, 1970 (div. 1990); children: Vladimir, Julius. BA, Belgrade (Yugoslavia) U., 1970, MA, 1974. Curator Jewish Hist. Mus., Belgrade, 1970-74; art critic Umetnost Art Mag., Belgrade, 1970-74; art reviewer 3d program Radio Belgrade, 1970-74; translator, instr. Berlitz Sch. Langs., Pitts., 1974-77; pvt. art dealer N.Y.C., 1977-84; dir. Wiesner Gallery, N.Y.C., 1984—. Editor-in-chief Belgrade Bull., 1983-86; mem. editorial bd., sec. Jewish Studies, 1971-74; mem. editorial bd. Cross-Cultural Communications, 1985—. Bd. dirs. Student Cultural Ctr., Belgrade, 1970-74. Office: Wiesner Gallery 730 57th St Brooklyn NY 11220-3560

VIZY, KALMAN NICHOLAS, research physicist; b. Gyor, Hungary, July 7, 1940; came to U.S., 1954, naturalized, 1962; s. Joseph and Helen Julianna (Meleg) V.; m. Mary Anne Smith, Aug. 31, 1968; children: Anne Katharine, Edward Kalman. BEngring. Sci., Cleve. State U., 1964; MS, John Carroll U., 1967; PhD, Walden U., 1990. Registered profl. engr., N.Y. Apprentice design engr. Warner & Swasey, Cleve., 1959-64; tchr. and dept. head scis. Byzantine Ednl. Ctr., Parma, Ohio, 1964-67; rsch. physicist Eastman Kodak Rsch. Labs., Rochester, N.Y., 1967-79, corp. tech. and sci. adv., 1980-91; worldwide tech. lectr., 1980—; asst. dir. acad. div. and faculty Rochester Inst. Tech., 1968—; adj. asst. prof. radiology U. Rochester Med. Ctr., 1990—. Mem. Rochester-Rennes Sister Cities Com., 1977—; mem. Ogden (N.Y.) Republican Com., 1974—. Recipient Excellence in Teaching award Rochester Inst. Tech., 1980. Mem. Am. Soc. Photogrammetry (cert. photogrammetrist; autometric award 1975), Nat., N.Y. State socs. profl. engrs., ASME, Am. Assn. Physics Tchrs., Am. Assn. Physicists in Medicine, Optical Soc. Am. (house chmn. 1975), Soc. Photog. Scientists and Engrs. (inter-soc. rep. 1975-79), Soc. Info. Displays, Am. Coll. Radiology. Inventor in field. Home: 16 Clearview Dr Spencerport NY 14559-1118 Office: Rochester Inst Tech Rochester NY 14614-1274

VLAD, VIOREL GEORGE, software engineer; b. Pucioasa, Romania, Apr. 4, 1946; came to U.S., 1982; s. Vasile and Maria (Popa) V.; m. Carmen Doina Vasilescu, June 30, 1979. MS in Computer Sci., Poly. U. N.Y., 1987. Software engr. AT&T Computer Systems, N.Y.C., 1982—; asst. prof. William Paterson Coll. N.J., 1986—. Author: Europe, 1975-80, William Paterson College, 1990.

VLADUTIU, ADRIAN O., clinical pathologist, pathology educator; b. Bucharest, Romania, Aug. 5, 1940; came to U.S., 1969, naturalized 1974; s. Octavian and Veturia (Chirescu) V.; m. Georgirene D. Therrien; children: Christina Lynn, Catherine Joy. MD, Sch. Medicine, Bucharest, 1962; PhD, Sch. Medicine, Jassy, Romania, 1968. Diplomate Am. Bd. Pathology. Asst. prof. physiopathology Sch. Medicine, Bucharest, 1968-71; assoc. prof. pathology SUNY Sch. Medicine, Buffalo, 1978-81, prof. pathology, 1981—; pathologist Buffalo Gen. Hosp., 1974—, dir. clin. labs., 1982—, prof. microbiology, 1982—, prof. medicine, 1985—; cons. Niagara Falls (N.Y.) Meml. Hosp., 1976-82, Tri-County Hosp., Gowanda, N.Y., 1991—; acting head dept. pathology Buffalo Gen. Hosp., 1985-86. Author: Pleural Effusions, 1986; co-author: Molecular Immunology, 1984, Progress in Autoimmunity, 1990, Encyclopedia of Human Biology, 1991; contbr. over 135 articles to sci. jours. Med. Rsch. Coun. fellow, 1968, Buswell fellow, 1969; recipient rsch. award NIH, 1985. Fellow Am. Coll. Physicians; mem. Am. Soc. Immunologists, Am. Assn. Pathologists, N.Y. Acad. Scis. Home: 80 Oakview Dr Buffalo NY 14221-1420

VLADUTIU, GEORGIRENE DIETRICH, biochemical geneticist; b. Bremerton, Wash., Dec. 21, 1944; m. Adrian O. Vladutiu, Sept. 4, 1971; children: Christina Lynn, Catherine Joy. BS in Bacteriology, Syracuse U., 1966; postgrad., U. N.C., 1967-68; MA in Microbiology and Immunology, SUNY, Buffalo, 1970, PhD in Microbiology and Immunology, 1973. Rsch. asst. Duke U. Sch. Medicine, Durham, N.C., 1966-67; postdoctoral fellow Children's Hosp.-SUNY, Buffalo, 1974-76, rsch. instr., asst. prof., 1976-81, rsch. assoc. prof., 1981-84, assoc. prof. pediatrics, 1984—, dir. Biochem. Genetics Lab., 1984—, acting dir. div. human genetics, 1986-89; vis. scientist Minority Instns. FASEB, 1987—; mentor basic scis. Empire State Coll., 1983-85; coord. screening program Tay-Sachs Disease Carriers, 1984—; researcher metabolic myopathies. Reviewer: Pediatrics, Jour. Biol. Chemistry, New Eng. Jour. of Medicine; contbr. articles to profl. jours. Recipient Rsch. Career Devel. award NIH, 1980-85; grantee NSF, 1977-80, NIH, 1979-82, Cystic Fibrosis Found., 1981-82 and others. Mem. Am. Soc. Human Genetics, Am. Soc. Biol. Chemists, Am. Soc. Cell Biology, Soc. for Pediatric Rsch., Biochem. Soc. of Gt. Britain, Soc. Inherited Metabolic Disorders. Office: Children's Hosp of Buffalo 936 Delaware Ave Buffalo NY 14209-1887

VLAOVIC, MILAN STEPHEN, pathologist; b. Novi Sad, Yugoslavia, Feb. 1, 1936; came to U.S., 1970; s. Stevan and Olga (Kantardzic) V.; m. Sharon Helen Rabatich, July 24, 1969; children: Stevan Alexander, Sofija Ann, Peter Michael. DVM, U. Belgrade, Yugoslavia, 1961; MS, U. Sask., Saskatoon, Can., 1970; postgrad., Wash. State U., 1970-71; PhD, U. Mo., 1974. Veterinarian Prosina, Beli Manastir, Yugoslavia, 1961-63; head technologist

Banatski Karlovac (Yugoslavia) Meat Plant, 1963-65; pvt. practice vet. medicine various cities, Fed. Republic Germany, 1965-67; insp. various meat plants, Winnipeg, Man., Can., 1967-68; mgr. Frederick (Md.) Cancer Rsch. Ctr., 1974-77; toxicologic pathologist Indsl. Bio-Test, Decatur, Ill., 1977-78; mgr. toxicology support Eastman Kodak Co., Rochester, N.Y., 1978—. Mem. Soc. Toxicologic Pathologists, Soc. Vet. Immunologists. Serbian Orthodox. Home: 7 Dixon Woods Honeoye Falls NY 14472-9322 Office: Eastman Kodak Co 1100 Ridgeway Ave # 320B Rochester NY 14652-0001

VLAVIANOS, JOHN G., federal agency administrator; b. Athens, Greece, Oct. 10, 1933; came to U.S., 1951; s. George and Maria (Rudolph) V.; m. Lina T. Skucas. Bachelor Mech. Engring., NYU, 1956. Cert. engr., U.K. Marine applications engr. Worthington Pump Co., Inc., Harrison, N.J., 1956-60; supt. engr. Hellenic Lines, Ltd., N.Y.C., 1960-63; sr. supr. planning dept., electric boat div. Gen. Dynamics Corp., Groton, Conn., 1963-68; mgr., European marine div. Worthington Pump Co., Inc., Hamburg, Germany, 1968-72; v.p., Europe, Africa, Middle East Worthington Pump Co., Inc., London, 1972-77; v.p. internat. Balt. Aircoil Co., Inc., Jessup, Md., 1977-80; dir. exports devel. office U.S. Dept. Commerce, Washington, 1980-86, dir. trade events div., 1986-91; U.S. and fgn. comml. svc. dir. ops. western hemisphere U.S. Dept. Commerce, 1991—. Mem. Soc. Naval Architects and Marine Engrs. Home: 478 Old Orchard Cir Millersville MD 21108-2009

VOCIA, PHOENIX (JOY VOCIA), entrepreneur, loan officer mortgage company; b. Phila., May 17, 1956; d. Anthony Christinzio and Anna (DeJohn) Christie; m. Robert J. Furgione, June 26, 1984 (div.). AA, Atlantic Community Coll., Mayslanding, N.J., 1983. Cert. paralegal, Am. Inst. for Paralegal Studies, Inc. Owner, mgr. Nature's Finest Restaurant, Atlantic City, N.J., 1976-77; various positions Resorts Internat. Hotel Casino, Atlantic City, 1978-83; exec. sec. Chelsea Title & Guaranty Co., Northfield, 1983-84; inventory specialist B&R Equipment and Auto Suppy, Atlantic City, 1984; pres. Harmony Mark, Inc., Ventnor, N.J., 1986—; owner, ptnr. B&R Auto Supply, Ocean City, 1987-90; mortgage agt. UFMC, Cherry Hill, N.J., 1990-91; loan officer Am. Residential Mortgage Corp., Cherry Hill, 1991; mortgage agt. Atlantic Coast Mortgage, 1991—. Designer: (poster) Lady Luck, 1978; author: Bizzare Ways to Quit Smoking, 1986, Letter Perfect, 1988; (comic strip) Seemore on Health, 1986. Vol. Rep. mayoral campaign, Atlantic City, 1986; vol. coord. freeholder campaign, 1988—; events coord. mayoral campaign, 1990; founder Say Nope to Dope Assn. (name now Living Life, Be A Life Lover), Ventnor, 1989—. Recipient Am. Legion award, Brigantine, N.J., 1970, Equal Opportunity award Atlantic Community Coll., Mayslanding, 1976. Mem. Rosicrucians.

VOGEL, BRUCE SANDOR, clinical psychologist; b. N.Y.C., May 19, 1937; s. David T. and Bettie (Levine) V.; m. Roberta Burrage, Apr. 4, 1964 (div. Sept. 1991); children: Darrell, Duane, Shoshana. BA, Bklyn. Coll., 1959; MA, Mich. State U., 1964, PhD, 1968. Diplomate Am. Bd. Sexology; lic. psychologist, N.Y. Chief psychologist Lansing (Mich.) Boys Tng. Sch., Mich., 1966-68; asst. prof. psychology CUNY, 1968—; pvt. practice, 1969—; dir. tng. N.Y. Ctr. for Sexual Therapy, N.Y.C., 1972—. Mem. Am. Psychology Assn., N.Y. Soc. Clin. Psychologists. Home: 115 Oxford Pl Staten Island NY 10301-3016 Office: 993 Park Ave New York NY 10028-0809

VOGEL, CHARLES ORVILLE, history and mathematics educator; b. Chelsea, Mass., Dec. 2, 1948; s. Allen W. Sr. and Harriet (Cosmopoulos) V.; m. Gloria Jean Hilts, Oct. 6, 1973; children: Mark Robert, Amanda Jean. BA, U. Mass., 1972; MEd in History, Fitchburg State Coll., 1978. Cert. secondary tchr., Mass. Math. tchr. Salem (N.H.) Pub. Schs., 1972-73; math. and history tchr. Westford (Mass.) Pub. Schs., 1973—; lectr. on Am. art various New Eng. hist. socs., 1973—. Co-author: The Boston Art Club Exhibition Record 1873-1909, 1991; author exhbn. catalogues. Mem. North Middlesex Regional Sch. Com., Townsend, Mass., 1987-90, chmn., 1989-90; mem. North Middlesex Bldg. Com., Townsend, 1988-92, vice-chmn., 1989-92. Mem. NEA, Mass. Edn. Assn., N.H. Hist. Soc., Mt. Washington Valley Arts Assn., Nat. Trust Historic Preservation. Home: 3 Sycamore Dr Townsend MA 01469 Office: Westford Pub Schs Westford MA 01886

VOGEL, H. VICTORIA, psychotherapist, educator. B.A., U. Md., 1968; M.A., NYU, 1970, 75; M.Ed., Tchrs. Coll. Columbia U., 1982, postgrad., 1982—; cert., Am. Projective Drawing Inst., 1983. Art Therapist Childville, Bklyn., 1962-64; tchr., Montgomery County (Md.) Jr. High Sch., 1968-69; with High Sch. div. N.Y.C. Bd. Edn., 1970—, tchr., guidance counselor, psychotherapist in pvt. practice; counseling cons. psychodiagnosis and devel. studies, 1984—; art/play therapist Hosp. Ctr. for Neuromuscular Disease and Devel. Disorders, 1987—; employment counselor-adminstr. N.Y. State Dept. Labor Concentrated Employment Program, 1971-72; intern psychotherapy and psychoanalysis psychiat. div. Cen. Islip Hosp., 1973-75; with Calif. Grad. Inst., L.A.; Columbia U. Tchrs. coll., N.Y. intern psychol. counseling and rehab. N.J. Coll. Medicine, Newark, 1979. Mem. com. for spl. events NYU, 1989; participant clin. and artistic perspectives Am. Acad. Psychoanalysis Conf., 1990. Mem. APA, AAAS, Am. Psychol. Soc., Am. Orthopsychiat. Assn., Am. Soc. Group Psychotherapy & Psychodrama (publs. com. 1984—), Am. Counseling Assn., N.Y.C. Art Tchrs. Assn., Art/Play Therapy, Assn. Humanistic Psychology (exec. sec. 1981), Tchrs. Coll. Adminstrv. Women in Edn., Phi Delta Kappa (editor chpt. newsletter 1981-84, exec. sec. Columbia U. chpt. 1984—, chmn. nominating com. for chpt. officers 1986—, nominating com. 1991, pub. rels. exec. bd. dirs. 1991, rsch. rep. 1986—), Kappa Delta Pi. Author: The Never Ending Story of Alcohol, Drugs and Other Substance Abuse, 1992, Variant Sexual Behavior and the Aesthetic Modern Nudes, 1992.

VOGEL, HOWARD STANLEY, lawyer; b. N.Y.C., Jan. 21, 1934; s. Moe and Sylvia (Miller) V.; m. Judith Anne Gelb, June 30, 1962; 1 son, Michael S. B.A., Bklyn. Coll., 1954; J.D., Columbia U., 1957; LL.M. in Corp. Law, NYU, 1969. Bar: N.Y. 1957, U.S. Supreme Ct. 1964. Assoc. Whitman & Ransom, N.Y.C., 1961-66; with Texaco Inc., 1966—, gen. atty., 1970-73, assoc. gen. counsel, 1973-81, gen. counsel Texaco Philanthropic Found. Inc., 1979-82, gen. counsel Jefferson Chem. Co., Texaco Chems. Can. Inc., 1973-82, assoc. gen. tax counsel, White Plains, N.Y., 1981—. Pres., dir. 169 E. 69th Corp., 1981—. Served to 1st lt. JAGC, U.S. Army, 1958-60. Mem. ABA, Assn. Bar City N.Y., Fed. Bar Council, Assn. Ex-Mems. of Squadron A (N.Y.C.). Club: Princeton (N.Y.C.). Home: 169 E 69th St Apt 9D New York NY 10021-5163 Office: 2000 Westchester Ave White Plains NY 10650-0001

VOGEL, JOHN WALTER, lawyer; b. Dansville, N.Y., Sept. 19, 1948; s. Walter Earl and Betty (Elston) V.; m. Pamela Hill; children: Michael John, Jennifer Alexandra. BA, SUNY, Albany, 1970; JD, Syracuse U., 1976. Bar: N.Y. 1976, U.S. Dist. Ct. (we. dist.) N.Y. 1979, U.S. Tax Ct. 1980, U.S. Supreme Ct., 1980, U.S. Dist. Ct. (no. dist.) N.Y. 1985, U.S. Ct. Appeals (2d cir.) 1985. Assoc. Edward J. Degnan Law Offices, Caniesteo, N.Y., 1976-77; atty. N.Y. State Dept. Agrl. & Markets, Albany, 1977-78; sole practice law Dansville, 1978—; v.p., legal counsel Dansville Econ. Devel. Corp., 1983—; closing atty. Farmers Home Adminstrn., Dansville, 1982—. Dir. Livingston County (N.Y.) Drug Abuse Prevention Council, 1981-82. Served with U.S. Army, 1970-73. Mem. N.Y. State Bar Assn., Livingston County Bar Assn. (sec., treas. 1980-82, v.p. 1984-85, pres. 1985-86), Assn. Trial Lawyers Am., N.Y. State Trial Lawyers Assn., Dansville C. of C. (bd. dirs. 1985—). Republican. Presbyterian. Home: 261 Main St Dansville NY 14437-1111 Office: 125 Main St Dansville NY 14437-1611

VOGEL, MICHAEL N., journalist, writer, historian; b. Buffalo, May 26, 1947; s. Ralph John and Florence Helen (Pohlmann) V.; m. Stasia Zoladz, Aug. 28, 1971; children: Charity Ann, Rebecca Marie, Alex Christian. BA in English, Canisius Coll., 1969; MA in English, So. Ill. U., 1970. Journalist Buffalo News, 1970—; assoc. prof. journalism Buffalo State U. Coll., 1979-80. Author: Maritime Buffalo, 1990, Echoes in the Mist, 1991. Pres. Buffalo Lighthouse Assn., Inc., 1985—; co-founder St. Michael's Sch. at Greycliff, Derby, N.Y., 1987; bd. dirs. Landmark Soc. Niagara Frontier, 1990-91. 1st lt. U.S. Army, 1971-73. Recipient numerous awards including One to One Media award, 1978, 79, Newspaper Editorial Workshop award, 1979-80, N.Y. State AP award, 1982-90, Am. Planning Assn. award, 1987. Mem. AAAS, U.S. Lighthouse Soc., Nat. Assn. Sci. Writers, Gt. Lakes Hist. Soc., Gt. Lakes Lighthouse Keepers Assn., Buffalo & Erie County Hist. Soc. (Augspurger award 1989, Niederlander award 1990), Buffalo Mus. Sci. Roman Catholic. Home: 6540 Lake Shore Rd Derby NY 14047 Office: Buffalo News PO Box 100 Buffalo NY 14240

VOGEL, ROBERT ALAN, cardiologist; b. N.Y.C., May 7, 1943. BA, Columbia U., 1963; MD, Yale U., 1967. Diplomate Am. Bd. Cardiology. Intern U. Colo., Denver, 1967-68, resident, 1968-71, asst. prof. Medicine, 1975-79; assoc. prof. Medicine U. Mich., Ann Arbor, 1980-85, prof. Medicine, 1986-87; prof. Medicine U. Md., Balt., 1987—; head div. Cardiology U. Md., Balt., 1987. Office: U Md Hosp 22 S Greene St Baltimore MD 21201

VOGEL, VIRGINIA REYNOLDS, educational consultant; b. N.Y.C., Dec. 10, 1946; d. Robert Dwight and Louise Helen (Persina) Reynolds; m. John Henry Vogel, June 27, 1970; children: Christopher John, Melissa Louise. BA, Mary Baldwin Coll., 1968; MA, NYU, 1969; EdS, George Washington U., 1976. Admissions counselor NYU Grad. Sch. of Bus., N.Y.C., 1969-71; edml. counselor George Washington Univ., Coll. of Gen. Studies, Washington, 1971-73; dir. guidance and coll. counseling Georgetown Visitation Preparatory Sch., Washington, 1973-83; dir. Ednl. Guidance Svc., Chevy Chase, Md., 1983—. Editorial bd.: Coll. Bound., Evanston, Ill., 1985—. Mem. AACD, Nat. Assn. Coll. Admissions Counselors, Ind. Ednl. Cons. Assn. (treas. 1990-91, bd. dirs. 1989-91), Washington Ind. Svcs. for Ednl. Resources (membership dir. 1984-85), Secondary Sch. Admissions Bd., Jr. League of Washington. Episcopalian. Office: Ednl Guidance Svcs 6405 Offutt Rd Bethesda MD 20815-5361

VOGLER, THERESA MARY, accounting firm executive; b. Plattsburgh, N.Y., Nov. 7, 1957; d. Edward Walter and June (Roff) V. AB, Vassar Coll., 1979; AM, Brown U., 1980; JD, George Washington U., 1983; M. Laws in Taxation, Georgetown U., 1986. Atty., advisor U.S. Dept. Commerce, Washington, 1983-84; tax law specialist IRS, Washington, 1984-86; assoc. Kelley Drye & Warren, N.Y.C., 1986-88, Dow, Lohnes & Albertson, N.Y.C., 1988-90; mgr. Arthur Andersen & Co., Washington, 1990—. Mem. Vassar Club of Washington (steering com. mem., career devel. com.), U.S. C. of C. (com. on employee benefits), A Network of Profls. Working in Employee Benefits. Office: Arthur Andersen & Co 1666 K St NW Washington DC 20006

VOGT, ROBERT LAWRENCE, engine company manager, engineering consultant; b. St. Louis, Aug. 30, 1942; s. Alfred Paul and Elsie Gertrude (Marx) V.; m. Nancy Whitney, Sept. 10, 1966; children: Robert Lawrence, James, Jon, Joseph. BS in Engring. Sci., Long Island U., 1974; MS in Mech. Engring., Poly. U., Bklyn., 1976. Registered profl. engr., N.Y.; cert. in energy policy. Designer McDonnell Aircraft Co., St. Louis, 1961-66; engr. Grumman Aerospace Corp., Bethpage, N.Y., 1966-76; mgr. combustion Gen. Electric Co., Schenectady, N.Y., 1976-79; mgr. bus. devel. Sulzer Bros. Inc., N.Y.C., 1980-85; mgr. engines Gen. Electric Co., Lynn, Mass., 1985-88; mgr. engine program Textron Lycoming, Stratford, Conn., 1988—. Contbr. articles to profl. jours.; patentee in field. Mem. AIAA (sr.; chmn. air breath propulsion 1991—), ASME. Home: 150 Sasco River Ln Southport CT 06490-1047 Office: Textron Lycoming 550 Main St Stratford CT 06497-7593

VOGT, SUE, songwriter, lyricist; b. Rochester, N.Y., 1953; d. Ozzie and Lucille I. (Powers) V.; m. Nov. 25, 1971; 2 children. Grad., Monroe High Sch., Rochester, 1970. Bank teller Lincoln Rochester Bank, Canandaigua, N.Y., 1970-72; quality control technician Voplex, Canandaigua, N.Y., 1972-80; homemaker Canandaigua, N.Y., 1980—, freelance songwriter, lyricist, 1986—; speaker Canandaigua Elem. Sch., 1989—; cons. Gavett Sec. Svcs., Canandaigua, 1990. Author (lyrics) I'm Not Afraid to Die, 1988, In a Hurry, 1990, A Man Doesn't Marry Himself, 1990. Bd. dirs. Pets Anonymous Humane Soc., Canandaigua, 1977-84; vol. Canandaigua Elem. Sch., 1990—. Mem. ASCAP, Cheshire Coop (newsletter coord. 1989—), Ontario County Arts Coun. Home: RD 3 Canandaigua NY 14424-9352

VOIGHT, JERRY D., lawyer; b. Bozeman, Mont., Aug. 21, 1937; children: Janet, Jason. BS in Chem. Engring., Mont. State U., 1959; JD with hons., George Washington U., 1965. Bar: D.C. 1966, U.S. Supreme Ct. 1969, U.S. Ct. Appeals (Fed. cir.) 1982. Ptnr. Finnegan, Henderson, Farabow, Garrett & Dunner, Washington, 1972—. Contbr. articles to profl. jours. Mem. ABA, D.C. Bar Assn., Am. Intellectual Property Law Assn. Office: Finnegan Henderson Farabow Garrett & Dunner 1300 I St NW Washington DC 20005-3314

VOIGT, HERBERT FREDERICK, biomedical engineer, educator, auditory neurophysiologist; b. N.Y.C., Oct. 27, 1952; s. Herbert Frederick and Simona (Communali) V.; m. Ronit Gunst, Apr. 5, 1975; children: Justin David, Emily Talia. BEE, CUNY, 1974; PhD, Johns Hopkins U., 1979, postgrad., 1979-80. Asst. prof. biomed. engring. Boston U. Coll. Engring., 1981-89, assoc. prof., 1989—, dir. grad. program, 1982-92, dept. chmn., 1992—, dir. auditory neurophysiobioloby lab., 1985—; asst. rsch. prof. otolaryngology Boston U. Med. Sch., 1981-90, assoc. rsch. prof., 1990—; reviewer NSF, Washington, 1985—. Contbr. articles to profl. jours. Grantee NIH, 1987-91, 88—, 91—. Mem. AAAS, IEEE, Acoustical Soc. Am. (reviewer), Assn. Rsch. Otolaryngology, Internat. Brain Rsch. Orgn. World Fedn. Neuroscientists, Soc. Neurosci., Tan Beta Pi. Home: 223 Churchills Ln Milton MA 02186-4015 Office: Boston U Dept Biomed Engring 44 Cummington St Boston MA 02215-2407

VOIGT, JOHN JACOB, telecommunications executive; b. Atlantic City, Apr. 2, 1942; s. Jacob Joseph and Mary Margret (Camp) V.; grad. Lawrenceville Sch., 1960; student U. Pitts., 1960-61; BS in Econs., U. Pa., 1963, postgrad., 1964; m. Glenna Fitzsimons, Sept. 22, 1961; children: Bridget Glenna, John Jacob Jr. Pres., Nat. Accessories Co., Phila., 1970—; chmn. ICCI, ICCI Europe Ltd., Brussels, The Dynoptics Corp., Lausanne, Switzerland, 1984—, also bd. dirs.; pres., treas., dir. The Inteleplex Corp.; pres. Howard Butcher Trading Corp., Phila., 1976— ; chmn. IMS Corp., Geneva, Switzerland, 1987—; dir. Atlantic Metal Finishing Co., Butcher Foods Inc., Cont. Quality Industries, IHESA, San Pedro Sula, Honduras, Sterling Group Ltd., London, Torreya Fin. Corp., Palm Beach, Fla., Metea Trading & Fin. Internat., Geneva, Switzerland, Euro-Am. Money Fund, Sea Consult Ltd., Pan Am. Casuality & Liability Ins. Co.; cons. Compagnie Generale d'Electricite, Paris, Matra Group, Paris; bd. dirs. Howell, Dreyden & Dolan. Bd. govs. Betty Bacharach Hosp., 1976—, European Econ. Inst.; mem. vestry, sr. warden Ch. of Epiphany, Ventnor, N.J., 1975—. Republican. Mem. European Econ. Inst. (Liechtenstein). Clubs: Union League Phila., Princeton N.Y.C., Atlantic City Country, Seaview Country, Ocean City Yacht, U. Pa. (N.Y.C.), Phi Gamma Delta. Lodges: Order of St. John Jerusalem, Knights of Malta. Home: 2215 Burroughs Ave Linwood NJ 08221-1330

VOLDMAN, STEVEN HOWARD, electrical engineer; b. Rochester, N.Y., Sept. 8, 1957; s. Carl Jerome and Blossom (Passer) V.; m. Annie Curry Brown, July 1986; children: Aaron Samuel, Rachel Pesha. BS, U. Buffalo, 1979; MS, MIT, 1981, EE, 1982; MS in Engring. Physics, U. Vt., 1986, PhD, 1991; postgrad. resident study, IBM, 1988-91. Engring. asst. R.E. Ginna Nuclear plant Rochester Gas & Electric, N.Y., 1977, 78; rsch. assoc. MIT, Boston, 1979-81, rsch. assoc. high voltage rsch. lab., 1981-82; staff level engr. IBM, Burlington, Vt., 1982—, mem. 4-Mb DRAM devel. staff, 1985-88, mem. 16-Mb DRAM devel. staff, 1991—. Contbr. articles to profl. jours. Elected bd. govs. Ohavi Zedek Synagogue, 1987-91, chmn. social action, 1989—; active Soviet Resettlement Com., Burlington, Vt., United Jewish Appeal; chmn., mem. fundraising Burlington Jewish Community Coun. Soviet Resettlement; mem. Am. Israel Pub. Affairs com., U.S. Holocaust Mus. Mem. IEEE, AAAS, Am. Assn. Ethiopian Jewry, Sigma Xi, Phi Eta Sigma, Tau Beta Pi. Democrat.

VOLICER, LADISLAV, physician, educator; b. Prague, Czechoslovakia, May 21, 1935; came to U.S., 1969, naturalized, 1977; s. Ladislav and Vilma (Molnarova) V.; m. Olga Holeckova, July 14, 1959 (div. 1970); children: Irena, Katerina; m. Beverly J. Beers, May 20, 1972; children: Zuzka, Marika, Nadine. MD, Charles U., Prague, 1959; PhD in Pharmacology, Czechoslovak Acad. Scis., Prague, 1964. Research assoc. Czechoslovak Acad. Sci., Prague, 1966-68; research asst. prof. U. Munich, Fed. Republic Germany, 1968-69; from asst. to assoc. prof. pharmacology Boston U. Sch. Medicine, 1969-77, asst. prof. medicine, 1975—, prof. pharmacology, 1977—, prof. psychiatry, 1985—, mem. inst. rev. bd., 1975-78; clin. pharmacologist E.N. Rogers Meml. Vets. Hosp., Bedford, Mass., 1980-87, dep. dir. Geriatric Research Edn. Clin. Ctr., 1987—; mem. drug formulary com. State Mass., Boston, 1977-83; mem. inst. rev. bd. McLean Hosp., Belmont, Mass., 1980—. Editor: Clinical Aspects of Cyclic Nucleotides, 1977, Clinical Management of Alzheimer's Disease, 1988; contbr. papers to profl. publs. Grantee Nat. Inst. Aging, 1986—, Nat. Inst. Alcoholism and Alcohol Abuse, 1972-79, Nat. Inst. Drug Abuse, 1973-78, Merck, Sharp & Dohme, 1971; recipient Alcoholism Research award VA, 1979-85. Mem. Soc. for Neurosci., Am. Soc. Pharmacology Exptl. Therapeutics, Gerontol. Soc. Democrat. Unitarian. Home: 11 Beverly Rd Bedford MA 01730-1136 Office: EN Rogers Meml Vets Hosp 200 Springs Rd Bedford MA 01730-1114

VOLK, CHRISTINE SUZANNE, accountant; b. Kingston, N.Y., Dec. 1, 1969; d. Raymond Guy and Diane Lynn (Sheldon) Merwin; m. Zarren Robert Volk, Dec. 24, 1987. AS in Bus. Adminstrn., Jefferson Community Coll., Watertown, N.Y., 1988; BS in Pub. Acctg., Syracuse U., 1990. Staff acct. DiMarco, Abiusi, Pascarella & Firnstein, CPAs, Syracuse, 1991—. Regents scholarship N.Y. State Bd. Regents, 1987, Frederick Killian scholarship Syracuse U., 1990. Office: DiMarco Abiusi Pascarella & Firnstein CPAs 4 Clinton Square Ste # 104 Syracuse NY 13202-1074

VOLK, NORMAN HANS, financial executive; b. N.Y.C., Jan. 10, 1935; s. Hans and Mary (Zurl) V.; m. Karlyn Schram, Aug. 17, 1959; children: Kari, Heidi, Jenny. BA, Valparaiso (Ind.) U., 1957; MA, Marquette U., Milw., 1959. Dir. pub. rels. Wagner Coll., N.Y.C., 1961-62; asst. to owner Alan M. Wood, N.Y.C., 1962-72; sr. v.p. Bessemer Trust Co., N.Y.C., 1972-85; pres. Chamberlain & Steward, N.Y.C., 1985—. Trustee John Hartford Found., N.Y.C., 1979—. With U.S. Army, 1959-61. Mem. Univ. Club, Univ. Glee Club of N.Y.C., Doubles Club. Lutheran. Home: 400 Park Maplewood NJ 07040-1119 Office: 717 5th Ave New York NY 10022-8101

VOLKER, DALE MARTIN, state senator, lawyer; b. Lancaster, N.Y., Aug. 2, 1940; s. Julius J. and Loretta (O'Neill) V.; m. Carol A. Suchyna, Nov. 28, 1970; children: Martin Andrew, Mark Dale, Meredith Ann. BA, Canisius Coll., 1963; JD, SUNY-Buffalo, 1966. Bar: N.Y. 1967. Police officer Village of Depew, N.Y., 1966-72; assemblyman State Assembly, Albany, N.Y., 1972-74; mem. N.Y. State Senate, Albany, 1975—; sole practice law, Lancaster. Mem. Erie County Bar Assn., Elks, Moose, Eagles. Republican. Roman Catholic. Home: 92 Center Dr Depew NY 14043-1706 Office: NY State Senate State Capitol Albany NY 12224

VOLKMAN, DAVID J., immunology educator; b. Bklyn., Jan. 11, 1945; s. Clarence and Ruth (Fox) V.; m. Pamela Marian Bickerman, Jan. 29, 1967; children: Eric, Aaron Jon. BS in Math., Union Coll., 1966; PhD in Biochemistry, U. Rochester, 1971, MD with distinction, 1976. Diplomate Am. Bd. Internal Medicine, Am. Bd. Allergy and Immunology, Am. Bd. Diagnostic Lab. Immunology. Intern, 1976-77, resident internal medicine, 1977-78; rsch. assoc. Sloan-Kettering Inst., N.Y.C., 1971-72; resident medicine U. Pitts., 1976-78; clin. assoc. Nat. Inst. Allergy/Infectious Diseases, Bethesda, Md., 1978-82; sr. investigator NIAID, NIH, Bethesda, 1983-85; assoc. prof. medicine SUNY, Stony Brook, 1985—; mem. immunological scis. study sect. NIH, Bethesda, 1987-91; mem. sci. com. III Internat. AIDS Conf., Washington, 1987. Assoc. editor Jour. of Immunology, 1984-91; editorial bd. Clin. Immunology and Immunopathology, 1991—; contbr. articles to profl. jours. Sr. surgeon USPHS, 1978-85. Fellow Am. Coll. Physicians, Am. Acad. Allergy & Immunology. Jewish. Home: 15 James Neck Rd Saint James NY 11780-9738 Office: SUNY Dept of Allergy Health Scis Ctr. T-16040 Stony Brook NY 11794

VOLL, SARAH POTTS, state agency administrator; b. Wilmington, Del., Nov. 13, 1942; d. Robert Curtis and Dorothy Ruth (Counahan) Potts; m. John Obert Voll, June 12, 1965; children: Sarah Layla, Michael Obert. BA, Goucher Coll., Towson, Md., 1964; AM, Harvard U., 1966; PhD, U. N.H., 1977. Exec. sec. N.H. Council on World Affairs, Durham, 1966-68; mem. N.H. Ho. of Reps., Concord, 1977-78; ind. econ. cons. U.S. Agy. Internat. Devel., Ford Found., Middle East Adv. Group, Cairo, Egypt, 1978-79; dist. mgr. U.S. Census Bur. 1st Congl. Dist. N.H., Portsmouth, 1979-80; asst. budget dir. Office of Gov., Concord, N.H., 1980-81; chief economist N.H. Pub. Utilities Commn., Concord, 1981—; lectr. regulatory studies program Nat. Rsch. Inst., 1987-91, mem. rsch. adv. com., 1988-92, chair, 1990-92; mem. Durham Town Coun., 1988—; treas. United Campus Ministry to the U. N.H. Author: Plough in Field Arable, 1980, N.H. Regulatory Handbook for Small Scale Electric Producers; co-author: The Sudan: Unity & Diversity, 1985; contbr. articles to profl. jours. Mem. Durham Budget Com., 1975-78, 87-88; co-chmn. Pres. Jimmy Carter Primary campaign for Towns of Durham, Lee and Madbury, 1975-76; sec. Strafford County Dems., 1977-78; chmn. bd. stewards Community Ch. of Durham, 1984-86; mem. staff sub-com. on econs. and fin., task forces on electric cost allocation, rate design and least cost planning Nat. Assn. Regulatory Utility Commrs. Harvard U. fellow, 1964-65, Nat. Def. for Language fellow Harvard U., 1965-66. Mem. Internat. Assn. Energy Economists, Am. Econs. Assn. (transp. and pub. utilities group), Mid East Studies Assn., Sudan Studies Assn. (co-exec. dir., treas.), DAR (chpt. regent 1976-80, state sec. 1980-83, 92—, state treas. 1983-86), State Officers Club (v.p. 1988-90, pres. 1990-92), Phi Beta Kappa. Democrat. Mem. United Ch. of Christ. Home: 4 Croghan Ln Durham NH 03824-3027 Office: NH Pub Utilities Commn 8 Old Suncook Rd Concord NH 03301-7320

VOLLBRECHT, EDWARD ALAN, school superintendent; b. Freeport, N.Y., July 22, 1941; s. Edward Chester and Lillian Elizabeth (Heinecke) V.; m. Catherine Ann Salgado, Dec. 2, 1977; 1 child, Matthew Grayson. BS, SUNY, New Paltz, 1963; MS, Hofstra U., 1968; PhD, Walden U., Naples, Fla., 1973. Adminstrv. asst. Pearl River (N.Y.) Sch. Dist., 1968-70, asst. prin., 1970-71; prin. Mark Twain Mid. Sch., Yonkers, N.Y., 1971-73; asst. dir. mid. schs. Yonkers Pub. Schs., 1973-74, dir. secondary edn., 1974-75; asst. supt. Bethlehem (Pa.) Area Sch. Dist., 1975-78; supt. schs. South Williamsport (Pa.) Area Sch. Dist., 1978-84, N.W. Area Sch. Dist., Shickshinny, Pa., 1984-88, Everett (Pa.) Area Sch. Dist., 1988—; cons. New Eng. Sch. Devel. Coun., Boston, 1973-75; adj. prof. Manhattan Coll., N.Y.C., 1975-76, Lehigh U., Bethlehem, 1978-79. Mem. Everett Area Indsl. Devel. Corp., 1988—, West Providence Indsl. Devel. Authority. Recipient Jenkins Meml. award Yonkers PTA, 1974, Svc. for Youth award YMCA, Yonkers, 1975. Mem. ASCD, Am. Assn. Sch. Adminstrs., Pa. Assn. Sch. Adminstrs., Pa. Sch. Bds. Assn., Bedford County Endl. Found., Lions, Rotary, Naurashank, Phi Delta Kappa. Republican. Roman Catholic. Home: 415 Locust Ct Dr Everett PA 15537 Office: Everett Area Sch Dist 15 South St Extension Everett PA 15537

VOLLMANN, JOHN JACOB, JR., cosmetic packaging executive; b. Elizabeth, N.J., Apr. 10, 1938; s. John Jacob and Marie Louise (Sirois) V.; m. Marian Ethel Snetsinger, May 29, 1976; children: Andrea Leah, John Jacob III. BA, Queen's U., Kingston, Ont., 1973, BA with honor, 1976; postgrad., Rutgers U., 1977; PhD, Walden U., Naples, Fla., 1991. Cert. hypnotherapist; criminal justice instr., Fla. V.p. No. Trading Co., Inc., Madawaska, Maine, 1976—, also bd. dirs.; instr. Sch. of Justice and Safety Adminstrn., Miami-Dade Community Coll., 1978—; bd. dirs. Edward Sagarin Inst. for Study of Deviance and Social Issues. Contbr. articles to profl. jours. Vice chmn. Police & Fire Pension Bd., Dania, Fla., 1984; chmn. Unsafe Structures Bd., Dania, 1984, Code Enforcement Bd., Dania, 1984; adv. dep. Broward County Sheriff, Ft. Lauderdale, Fla., 1986—. Mem. NRA, Am. Correctional Assn., Am. Soc. Criminology (life), Acad. Criminal Justice Scis. (life), Am. Jail Assn., Am. Probation and Parole Assn., Northeastern Criminal Justice Assn. (life), Fla. Criminal Justice Educators (pres. 1984-88), Southern Assn. Criminal Justice (bd. dirs. 1981-90). Home: 411 SE 3D Pl Dania FL 33004 Office: No Trading Co Inc 190202 E Main St Madawaska ME 04756-1510

VOLLUM, ROBERT BOONE, management consultant; b. Abington, Pa., Sept. 13, 1933; s. Charles Milton and Marion (Yocum) V.; m. Gayle Lorraine Timmerman, July 8, 1956; children: Robert Boone III, Jeffrey Charles. BS in Engring. and Sci., U.S. Naval Acad., 1955. Sr. cons., group leader Stevenson, Jordan & Harrison, Inc., N.Y.C., 1959-65; asst. to pres., plant supt., sales engr. W.L. Gore & Assocs., Inc., Newark, Del., 1965-69; gen. mgr. Philmont Pressed Steel subs. Gulf & Western Industries, Inc.,

Bethayres, Pa., 1969-72, Air Shields div. Narco Sci. Industries, Inc., Hatboro, Pa., 1972-75; pres. Advanced Airflow Tech., Inc., Warminster, Pa., 1975-76, R.B. Vollum & Assocs., Huntingdon Valley, Pa., 1986—; prin. mfg. cons. Sperry Corp., Blue Bell, Pa., 1976-84; dir. cons. Creative Output, Inc., Milford, Conn., 1984-86; speaker in field. Contbr. articles to profl. jours. Bd. dirs. Upper Moreland Little League, 1965-76. Served to lt. USN, 1955-59. Fellow Am. Prodn. and Inventory Control Soc. (chpt. pres. 1984-85); mem. soc. Mfg. Engrs (sr. mem.), Computer and Automated Systems Assn. (sr. mem.). Republican. Episcopalian. Home: 2045 Overlook Ave Willow Grove PA 19090-2818 Office: PO Box 206 Huntingdon Valley PA 19006-0206

VOLOSHIN, ARKADY, mechanical engineering and mechanics educator; b. Kishinev, USSR, Aug. 7, 1946; came to U.S., 1979; s. Saul and Ita (Nazimok) V.; m. Ilana Gitelman, Nov. 26, 1972; children: Ron, Dan. MS, Leningrad (USSR) Poly. Inst., 1969; PhD, Tel-Aviv U., 1978. Rsch. engr. Inst. for Non-destructive Evaluation, Kishinev, USSR, 1969-70; rsch. asst. Tel-Aviv U., 1973-78, post-doctoral fellow, 1978-79; asst. prof. Iowa State U., Ames, 1979-89; assoc. prof. Lehigh U., Bethlehem, Pa., 1987-91, prof., 1991—. Assoc. editor: Experimental Mechanics, 1992—; contbr. articles to profl. jours.; presenter in field. Recipient M. Hetenyi award Exptl. Mechanics, Sept. 1983. Jewish. Office: Lehigh U 354 Packard Lab #19 Bethlehem PA 18015

VOLOVNIK, PATRICIA ANN, elementary educator; b. Phila., May 31, 1947; d. Joseph A. and Elizabeth M. (Radvonsky) Lashinger; m. William Volovnik, Apr. 11, 1970; children: Beth A., William J. BS, West Chester State U., 1969; MEd, Temple U., 1979. Editor TV Guide Mag., Radnor, Pa., 1969-71; English tchr. St. Helena Sch., Whitpain, Pa., 1971-74; reading specialist Montgomery County Intermediate Unit, Erdenheim, Pa., 1974—; children's book reviewer Montgomery County-Norristown (Pa.) Pub. Libr., 1989—; mem. Action Plan Com., Colonial Sch. Dist., Pa., 1992—. Mem. Internat. Reading Assn., Keystone State Reading Assn., Del. Valley Reading Assn., Am. Assn. Sch. Counselors. Republican. Roman Catholic.

VOLPE, JUDITH ANN, pathologist, medicolegal consultant; b. Paterson, N.J., May 4, 1955; d. Dominick Frank and Gaetana Maria (Mauiri) V. BS with highest honors, Rutgers U., 1978; MD, U. Medicine & Dentistry N.J., 1985. Diplomate Am. Bd. Pathology (Anatomic/Clinical Pathology). Intern, resident anatomic pathology Johns Hopkins Hosp., Balt., 1985-88; resident clin. pathology Beth Israel Med. Ctr., N.Y.C., 1988-90; pathologist The Washington (Pa.) Hosp., 1990—; med. investigator Chief Med. Examiners Office, N.Y.C., 1988-90; gen. med. practice Pvt. Physicians' Office Complex, N.Y.C., 1988-90; medicolegal cons. various legal firms, N.Y.C., Pitts., Phila., 1988—; cytopathology cons. various comml. labs., Pitts., 1991—; assoc. staff Washington Hosp. Med. Staff, 1991—. Contbr. articles to profl. jours. Mem. AMA, Coll. Am. Pathologists (jr. mem.), Am. Soc. Clin. Pathology, Pa. Med. Soc., Washington County Med. Soc., Pitts. Pathol. Soc. Republican. Office: Pathology Assocs Washington 155 Wilson Ave Washington PA 15301-3398

VOLPE, KENNETH RALPH, accountant; b. Millville, N.J., Feb. 17, 1945; s. James Romeo and Angeline (DelBuono) V.; m. Rita Mary Badame, May 16, 1970; 1 child, Jamie Marie. BS in Econs., Villanova U., 1967. CPA, Pa., N.J. Sr. acct. Haskins & Sells, CPAs, Phila., 1967-70, Cherry Hill, N.J., 1970-76; pvt. practice Vineland, N.J., 1976—; v.p. fin. Friedrich & Dimmock, Inc., Millville, N.J., 1991—. Pres. Jaycees, Newfield, N.J., 1975. Mem. AICPA, Nat. Model Railroad Assn., Pa. Inst. CPAs, N.J. Soc. CPAs. Office: 2630 E Chestnut Ave Vineland NJ 08360

VOLPE, RALPH PASQUALE, insurance company executive; b. Souderton, Pa., Sept. 20, 1936; s. Pasquale S. and Katie M. (Hartzell) V.; m. Marie F. Romano, Feb. 6, 1965; children: William, Anthony, Lynda. BA in Polit. Sci., Pa. State U., University Park, 1963. Claim cons. comml. ins. div. Aetna Life & Casualty Co., Phila., 1964—. Mem. Upper Merion Twp. Bd. Suprs., 1974-79, 82-87, chmn., 1984, 86, 87, vice chmn., 1985; mem. Upper Merion Govt. Study Commn., 1974; chmn. Upper Merion Dems., 1980-81, Montgomery County Dem. Campaign, 1975. Served with U.S. Army, 1959-61. Recipient Good Govt. award Upper Merion Jaycees, 1977. Mem. Chapel Four Chaplains, Legion Hon. Mem., Optimists, Valley Forge Order Sons of Italy in Am. #1776. Republican. Roman Catholic. Home: 240 Strawberry Ln King Of Prussia PA 19406-2217

VOLPÉ, ROBERT, endocrinologist; b. Toronto, Ont., Can., Mar. 6, 1926; s. Aaron G. and Esther (Shulman) V.; m. Ruth Vera Pullan, Sept. 5, 1949; children: Catherine, Elizabeth, Peter, Edward, Rose Ellen. MD, U. Toronto, 1950. Intern U. Toronto, 1950-51, resident in medicine, 1951-52, 53-55, fellow in endocrinology, 1952-53, 55-57, sr. rsch. fellow dept. medicine, 1957-62, McPhedran fellow, 1957-65, asst. prof., 1962-68, assoc. prof., 1968-72, prof., 1972-92, prof. emeritus, 1992—, dir. div. endocrinology and metabolism, 1987-92, chmn. Centennial Com., 1987-88; attending staff St. Joseph's Hosp., Toronto, 1957-66; active staff Wellesley Hosp., Toronto, 1966—; dir. endocrinology rsch. lab. Wellesley Hosp., 1968—, physician-in-chief, 1974-87; trans-Atlantic vis. prof. Caledonia Endocrine Soc., 1985. Author: Systematic Endocrinology, 1973, 2d edit., 1979, Thyrotoxicosis, 1978, Autoimmunity and Endocrine Disease, 1985, Thyroid Function and Disease, 1989, Autoimmunity in Endocrine Disease, 1990; also over 250 rsch. articles, especially on immunology of thyroid disease; editorial bd. Endocrine Pathology; past editorial bd. Jour. Clin. Endocrinology and Metabolism, Clin. Medicine, Clin. Endocrinology, Annals Internal Medicine. Served with Royal Can. Naval Vol. Res., 1943-45. Recipient Goldie medal for med. rsch. U. Toronto, 1971, Novo-Nordisk prize Irish Endocrine Soc., 1990; Med. Rsch. Coun. Can. grantee, 1955—. Fellow Royal Coll. Physicians Can. (coun. 1988—, chmn. annual meetings com. 1988—, sci. program com. 1988—, chmn. rsch. com. 1990—), Royal Coll. Physicians Edinburgh, Royal Soc. Medicine, ACP (gov. for Ont. 1978-83); mem. AAAS, Can. Soc. Endocrinology and Metabolism (past pres., Sandoz prize lectr. 1985, disting. svc. award 1990), Toronto Soc. Clin. Rsch. (Baxter prize lectr. 1984), Can. Soc. Clin. Investigation, Am. Thyroid Assn. (pres. 1980-81, disting. scientist award 1991), Assn. Am. Physicians, Endocrine Soc., Am. Fedn. Clin. Rsch., Can. Soc. Nuclear Medicine (Jamieson prize lectr. 1980), Can. Inst. Acad. Medicine, N.Y. Acad. Sci., European Thyroid Assn. (corr.), Latin Am. Thyroid Assn. (corr.), Soc. Endocrinology and Metabolism of Chile (hon.), Japan Endocrine Soc. (hon., gold medal 1986), Donalda Club, Alpine Ski Club (bd. dirs. 1987-89), U. Toronto Faculty Club. Home: 3 Daleberry Pl, Don Mills, ON Canada M3B 2A5 Office: Wellesley Hosp, Toronto, ON Canada M4Y 1J3

VOLTZ, RAMON JOHN, mathematics educator; b. Butler, Pa., Dec. 8, 1938; s. Leo James and Jane C. (Boyle) V.; m. Carolyn E. Huemmrich, Nov. 23, 1963; children: Ramon Jr., Rebecca, Paul, Stephen, Renee, Joel, Rachel, Marla, Elisabeth, Jesse. BS in Edn., Indiana U. of Pa., 1961; MEd in Math., Pa. State U., 1966; PhD, U. Pitts., 1970. Math.-physics tchr. Etna (Pa.) Sch. Dist., 1961-64, York (Pa.) Suburban Sch. Dist., 1964-65; instr. math. Pa. State U., Monaca, 1966-71; prof. math. Grove City (Pa.) Coll., 1971—; programs evaluator Pa. Dept. Edn., Harrisburg, 1967-74. Author: Student Directed Curriculum, 1971. Advisor Eagle Scouts, Mercer, Pa., 1980-82; bd. dirs. Billy Graham Films, Grove City, 1976-82. Mem. Nat. Coun. Tchrs. Math. (life), Math Assn. Am., Pa. Coun. Suprs. Math, Pa. Coun. Tchrs. Math., Math. Coun. Western Pa., Math. Tchrs. Northwestern Pa. (organizational com. 1990). Republican. Home: 825 Centertown Rd Grove City PA 16127-8352 Office: Grove City Coll Memorial Ave Grove City PA 16127-2106

VOLUCK, ALLAN S., packaging company executive; b. Phila.; m. Sondra Ritter; children: Philip Ritter Voluck, Lisa Sue Voluck Jurick. BS, St. Joseph Coll., Phila., 1947; student, N.C. State U., 1942-43. Account exec. United Container Co., Phila., 1948-50; asst. sales mgr. United Container Co., 1950-55, gen. sales mgr., 1955-62, v.p. sales, 1962-74, exec. v.p., gen. mgr., chief operating officer, 1974-83, pres., chief exec. officer, 1983-86, pres., owner, 1986-88; pres. Visy Board Packaging Sales, Bala Cynwyd, Pa., 1988-91; exec. v.p. Kardon Industries, Phila., 1983-86. Contbr. articles to profl. jours. Bd. dirs. Children's Hosp. of Phila., Oncology div., Phila., 1976—; trustee Ronald McDonald House, Phila., 1976—; chmn., pres. bd. trustees Eagles Fly for Leukemia, 1975—, pres., 1990—. Lt. col. USAF, 1943-46. Recipient Merit award, Continental Bank N.A., Phila., 1987; Negav award, State of Israel, 1983. Mem. Am. Mgmt. Assn., Assoc. Ind. Corrugated Converters, Green Valley Country Club (pres. 1982-83, bd. govs. 1960—), Locust Club. Office: Mour So Container Corp 215 Presidential Blvd Bala Cynwyd PA 19004-1201

VONA EVANS, GAIL MARGARET, educator; b. Kenmore, N.Y., Aug. 10, 1954; d. Michael Robert and Janette Shirley (Ver Hague) Vona; m. John Mark Evans, Feb. 5, 1977; children: Michael John, Zachary Mark. BS, SUNY, Buffalo, 1976; MS, Nazareth Coll., 1980; EdD, U. Rochester, 1990. Cert. tchr., N.Y. Tchr. Wayne Cen. Sch. Dist., Ontario Center, N.Y., 1977—; mem. adj. faculty Nazareth Coll., 1989—, U. Rochester, 1991—; dir. day camp Ontario (N.Y.) Recreation Dept., 1978-81. Mem. Assn. for Learning Disabilities (bd. dirs. 1983-85), Assn. for Supervision and Curriculum Devel., Coun. Exceptional Children, Kappa Delta Pi. Episcopalian. Home: 3523 Atlantic Ave Penfield NY 14526 Office: Wayne Cen Sch Dist 6209 Ontario Center Rd Ontario Center NY 14520-9999

VON ARX, JEFFREY PAUL, history educator; b. Bellefont, Pa., May 12, 1947; s. Eugene Francis and Margaret Elizabeth (Entwistle) von A. AB, Princeton U., 1969; MA, Yale U., 1973, MPhil, 1974, PhD, 1980. Asst. prof. dept. history Georgetown U., Washington, 1982-88, assoc. prof., 1988—, chmn. dept. history, 1991—; vis. fellow Australian Nat. U., Canberra, 1990. Author: Progress and Pessimism, 1985; contbr. articles to profl. jours. Mem. Jesuits. Home: Jesuit Community Georgetown U Washington DC 20057 Office: Georgetown U Dept History 37th O St NW Washington DC 20057-0001

VON BAUMGART-PSAYLA, ROMEO LEOPOLD, journalist; b. Fleur-de-lys, Birkirkara, Malta, June 11, 1916; m. Adele Baumgart, June 23, 1952; children: Cornelius Ludwig Wolfgang Hildebrand, Helga Marie Louise. Photographer No. 1 Photographic Reconnaissance Unit, Royal Air Force Vols., Egypt, Palestine, Syria, Lebanon, Sicily, Italy, Malta; founder Malta Overseas Press News Svc.; editor, pub. Malta Times, The Times Advertiser, The Maltese Cross and Forum Melitense; U.S. corr. Allied Newspapers, Ltd., The Times, The Sunday Times of Malta; chmn. Com. for Maltese-Am. Publs.; editor, pub. Maltese lit. competitions. Co-founder Malta Prospective Emigrants Orgn., 1945; founder The Inst. Maltese-Am. Affairs and fgn. subs., The Inst. Maltese-Can. Affairs, Toronto, The Inst. Maltese-Swedish Affairs, Stockholm. Decorated Defence medal, Africa Star, War medal, Italy Star, Star of 1939-45; apptd. Vice-chancellor Maltese-Am. Affairs div., 1969; recipient Cavaliere Gran Croce di Giustizia, Militare Ordine del Collare di Sant'Agata dei Paterno, 1969, citation Time mag. Mem. Sovereign Order St. John of Jerusalem, Knights of Malta (editorial bd., supreme coun., head pub. rels. dept.), Internat. Platform Assn., Ancient and Honourable Order Contemporary Historians, Fgn. Press Assn. Home: Malta House Cooper Ave # 36 Dumont NJ 07628

VON BERG, HORST RÜDIGER, computer company executive; b. Gotenhafen, Germany, Nov. 20, 1941; came to U.S., 1988; s. Alexander Nicolai and Kira (Tahv) von B.; m. Montserrat R. Torres, May 9, 1968 (div. Sept. 1987); children: Nathalie, Alexandre; m. Micheline T. Verhaegen, Mar. 19, 1988. Lic. in linguistics, U. Antwerp, 1967; postgrad., Inst. Catholique Hautes Études Commerciales, Brussels, 1970. Freelance translator Brussels, 1967-69; with Redirack, Nivelles, Belgium, 1969-70; sales mgr. Desmed & Meynaert, Brussels, 1970-71, Metal Profil, Liege, Belgium, 1972-73; br. mgr. Applicon Inc., Brussels and Paris, 1973-81; mktg. exec. Computervision Corp., Hayes, Eng., 1981-83; mng. dir. Computervision Corp., Brussels, 1983-87; v.p. internat. sales Prime Computer Corp. div. Computervision Corp., Bedford, Mass., 1988-89, v.p. European ops., 1989—. Mem. Am. Mgmt. Assn., Mgmt. Ctr. Europe. Office: Prime Computer Corp 100 Crosby Dr Bedford MA 01730

VON BUN, FRIEDRICH OTTO, physicist, consultant; b. Vienna, Austria, June 22, 1925; came to U.S., 1953; s. Franz Josef and Frieda (Gernert) von B.; m. Maria Leopoldine Seidl, Aug. 30, 1953; children: Friedrich J., Elisabeth C. MS, Tech. U., Vienna, 1952; PhD, Tech. U., Graz, Austria, 1956. Chief molecular beam sect. U.S. Army Signal Corps, Ft. Monmouth, N.J., 1953-60; chief systems analysis office NASA Goddard Space Flight Ctr., Greenbelt, Md., 1960-72, asst. dir. for applications, 1972-83, asst. dir. for space sta. planning, 1983-88; dir. systems analysis Applied Rsch. Corp., Landover, Md., 1988—, also bd. dirs. Contbr. numerous articles to profl. jours.; patentee in field. Recipient Exceptional Sci. Achievement award NASA, 1975, also others, 1960-88. Fellow AIAA (assoc.); mem. Am. Geophys. Union. Home: 12506 White Dr Silver Spring MD 20904 Office: Applied Rsch Corp 8201 Corporate Dr Landover MD 20785

VON FLOTOW, ANDREAS HUBERTUS, university educator, consultant; b. St. Thomas, Ontario, Can., Dec. 18, 1955; came to U.S., 1980; s. Andreas Hans and Hildegard (Keunecke) Von F.; m. Lucia Laura Alviano, Sept. 2, 1984; children: Andreas Luigi, Friedrich Leopold, Claudia Maria, Maurizio Auguste. BA in Sci., U. Toronto, 1977, MA in Sci., 1979; PhD, Stanford U., 1984. Rsch. scientist Univ. Toronto, 1979-80, Standord Univ., 1984, Deutshe Forshungs und Versuchs Anstalt Für Luft und Raumfahrt, Munich, 1984-85; prof. MIT, Cambridge, Mass., 1985—; pres. Flowtow and Assocs., Somerville, Mass., 1989—; v.p. Mide Tech. Corp., Cambridge, Mass., 1991—. Patentee in field; contbr. numberous tech. articles to profl. jours. and books. With Can. Army, 1973-74. Recipient NATO Post Doctoral fellowship, Germany, 1984-85; Alexander Von Humboldt fellowship A.V. Humboldt Found., Germany, 1984-85. Mem. AIAA, ASME. Office: MIT 37-335 Cambridge MA 02139

VON GLASERSFELD, ERNST C., educational researcher; b. Munich, Germany, Mar. 8, 1917; s. Leopold and Helen (Kommenda) Von G.; m. Isabel Davis, June 15, 1939 (dec. 1969); 1 child, Sandra; m. Charlotte Anker, Mar. 31, 1970. Student, U. Zurich, 1936-37, U. Vienna, 1937-38. Farmer County Wicklow, Ireland, 1938-45; editor Der Standpunkt, Merano, Italy, 1950-55; correspondent Die Weltwoche, Zürich, Switzerland, 1952-64; rsch. assoc. Ctr. for Cybernetics, Milan, Italy, 1959-62; rsch. dir. Ga. Inst. for Rsch., Athens, 1966-69; asst. prof. U. Ga. dept. psychology, Athens, 1970-75, assoc. prof., 1975-79, prof. psychology, 1979-87, prof. emeritus, 1987—; adj. prof. U. Mass., Amherst, 1987—; rsch. assoc. Sci. Reasoning Rsch. Inst. U. Mass., Amherst, 1987—. Author: The Construction of Knowledge, 1987, Language and Communication, Italy, 1989; editor: Constructivism in Mathematics Education, 1991, Knowledge, Language, Reality, Fed. Republic of Germany, 1987. Recipient U. Ga. Rsch. medal, 1983, Chris Janer award U. Ga., 1984; grantee AFOSR, NICH, NSF, 1971-88. Mem. Am. Soc. Cybernetics (trustee 1986—, W. S. McCulloch award 1991), Jean Piaget Soc. Home: 37 Long Plain Rd # 3 Amherst MA 01002-9523

VON HAKE, MARGARET JOAN, librarian; b. Santa Monica, Calif., Oct. 27, 1933; d. Carl August and Inez Garnet (Johnson) von Hake;. BA, La Sierra U., 1955; MS in Library Sci., U. So. Calif., 1963. Tchr., librarian Newbury Park (Calif.) Acad., 1955-60; librarian Columbia Union Coll., Takoma Park, Md., 1962-67, library dir., 1967—. Mem. ALA, Md. Library Assn., Assn. Seventh Day Adventist Librarians (newsletter editor 1982, 83, pres. 1989-90), Sligo Federated Music Club (pres. 1988-89), Paul Hill Chorale. Republican. Office: Columbia Union Coll 7600 Flower Ave Silver Spring MD 20912-7796

VON HOELLE, JOHN JACOB, publisher, commercial developer; b. Miami, Fla., Sept. 21, 1940; s. John Charles and Susan Ann (Lewis) von H.; m. Jenice Behringer, Oct. 7, 1961; children: Eric, Chris, Tim, Andy, Ellen. BA, U. Cambridge, Eng., 1963; MBA, Harvard U., 1981. V.p. Del. Dry Goods Co., Wilmington, 1965-79, McCall's Pattern Co., N.Y.C., 1979-81; pres. Dyne-Am. Publs., Wilmington, 1981—; cons. Smithsonian Instn., Washington, 1983—; speaker internat. antique conventions, 1980—. Author: Collector's Encyclopedia, 1983, 84, 86, Sound and Glory, 1990, various other books in history, biography and sewing collectibles. Pres. Kiwanis, Wilmington, 1973, Internat. Soc. Digitabilis, Phila., 1986. Lt. col. USAF, 1958-62, USAFR, 1964-91. Recipient N.Y. award Scholarship and Rsch. Collector's Internat., 1986. Office: Dyne-Am Publs 2070 Naaman's Rd Ste 103 Wilmington DE 19810

VON HOFFMAN, NICHOLAS, writer, former journalist; b. N.Y.C., Oct. 16, 1929; s. Carl and Anna (Bruenn) von H.; m. Ann Byrne, 1950 (div.); children: Alexander, Aristodemos, Constantine; m. Patricia Bennett, 1979 (div.). Grad., Fordham Prep. Sch., 1948. Assoc. dir. Indsl. Area Found., Chgo., 1954-63; mem. staff Chgo. Daily News, 1963-66, Washington Post, 1966-76. Author: Mississippi Notebook, 1964, Multiversity, 1966, We Are The People Our Parents Warned Us Against, 1968, Two, Three, Many More, 1969, Left at The Post, 1970, (with Garry Trudeau) Fireside Watergate, 1973, Tales From the Margaret Mead Taproom, 1976, Make-Believe Presidents: Illusions of Power from McKinley to Carter, 1978, Organized Crimes, 1984, Citizen Cohn, 1988, Capitalist Fools, 1992; also articles.

VON HOLDEN, MARTIN HARVEY, psychologist; b. Bronx, N.Y., May 29, 1942; s. Leon and Gertrude (Fishbein) Von H.; m. Virginia T. Brown, Dec. 17, 1971; 1 child, Mark Walter; children by previous marriage—Sandi Gwen, David Lawrence; 1 stepchild, Theresa Ann Brilli-Rogers. B.A., NYU, 1964; M.A., U. Toledo, 1965; D.P.A., NYU, 1981. Sr. psychologist N.Y. State Dept. Mental Hygiene, Rockland State Hosp., Orangeberg, 1966-67, team leader, 1970-71, dir. interdisciplinary tng. team, 1971-73; chief of service Metro Unit Harlem Valley Psychiat. Ctr., Wingdale, N.Y., 1973-74, dep. dir. programs, 1974-75; dep. dir. treatment services Pilgrim Psychiat. Ctr., West Brentwood, N.Y., 1975-76; dir. Matteawan State Hosp., Beacon, N.Y., 1977, Central N.Y. Psychiat. Ctr., Marcy, N.Y., 1977-82; exec. dir. Rochester Psychiat. Ctr., Rochester, N.Y., 1982—; assoc. dir. Inst. for Motivation Rsch., Croton-on-Hudson, N.Y., 1965-73; dir. Martin H. Von Holden Assocs., motivation rsch., Fairlawn, N.J., 1970-74; cons. psychologist, group therapist Green Haven Correctional Facility, Stormville, N.Y., 1970-77; cons. psychologist, group therapist Auburn Correctional Facility, N.Y., 1977—; clin. assoc. prof. dept. psychiatry Sch. Medicine, U. Rochester, 1983—; speaker nat. and internat. profl. confs. including 2d World Congress on Prison Health Care, 1983. Contbr. articles to profl. jours. Mem. adv. coun. N.Y. State Commn. Quality Care to Mentally Disabled, 1989—. Capt. MSC, U.S. Army, 1967-70. Recipient James Gordan Bennett prize NYU, 1964. Fellow Am. Assn. Mental Health Adminstrs. (cert. mental health adminstr.); mem. Am. Psychol. Assn., Am. Correctional Assn., Am. Assn. Correctional Psychologists, Assn. Facility Dirs. N.Y. State Office Mental Health (pres. 1984-85), Order of Arrow, Psi Chi. Democrat. Jewish. Home: 1900 South Ave Rochester NY 14620 Office: Rochester Psychiat Ctr 1600 S Ave Rochester NY 14620

VON KEVICZKY, COLMAN STEPHEN, military research scientist, lecturer; b. Ruttka, Hungary, Aug. 21, 1909; came to U.S., 1952; s. Kalman and Caroline (Musza) vonK.; m. Eva Yon Takach, Sept., 1938 (dec. 1958); 1 child, Attila; m. Yolanda Mackay, June 23, 1960. M in Mil. Sci. and Engring., Royal Hungarian Mil. Acad., 1932. Registered profl. engr., N.Y. Founder, dir. Intercontinental U.F.O. Galactic Spacecraft Rsch. and Analytic Network, Jackson Heights, N.Y., 1966, researcher, 1966—. Maj. Royal Hungarian Armed Forces, 1927-45. Recipient Pope Paul Meml. medal UN, 1963, Comdr. cross European Confederation of Ancient Combattants, 1986, Meml. cross 1st class, World Fedn. of Hungarian Vets., 1987, Arpad award NAS in Exile, 1980. Mem. AIAA, Hermann Oberth Rocket Soc. (bd. dirs.). Republican. Roman Catholic. Home: 35-40 75th St A4G Jackson Heights NY 11372

VON KUNES, KAREN ZDENKA JESSICA, Czech studies educator; b. Prague, Bohemia, Czechoslovakia, Mar. 21, 1949; came to U.S., 1980; d. Franz Josef and Anna (Strnadova) von Kunesch; m. Robert R. Newton, June 4, 1983; children: Ryan IV, Alexis Victoria. AB, Prague Inst., 1968; BA (summa cum laude), McGill U., Montreal, Canada, 1974; PhD, McGill U., 1980; MBA Cert., U. Tex., 1982. Prof. Boston Coll., 1980-81, The U. Tex., Austin, 1981-82, Harvard U., Cambridge, Mass., 1984—; fellow Russian Rsch. Ctr., Harvard U., 1987-91; vis. lectr. Tufts U., Boston U., 1982-84. Mem. editorial bd. Jour. of Czechoslovak and Cen. European Studies, 1992; contbr. articles on Czech Lit. to various profl. jours., book revs. and short stories to various mags.; author: (book/tape) Fast & Easy Czech, 1992. Adviser Masaryk Club, Boston, 1985-91; dir., adviser Internat. Inst. of Boston, 1983-84. Grantee Am. Coun. Learned Socs., 1991, 92; named for Innovation in Teaching, Ivy League Consortium, 1989-91, IREX, Charles U., Prague, 1992—; Quebec Postdoctoral fellow, 1980, Can. Coun. Doctoral fellow, 1975-78, J.W. McConnell Meml. fellow McGill U., 1976; Fulbright scholar, Czechoslovakia, 1992—. em. Am. Assn. Tchrs. of Czech (co-founder, mem. exec. com. 1992), Am. Assn. Tchrs. Slavic and East European Langs. (chmn. panels 1985-91), Am. Assn. for Advancement of Slavic Studies (organizer panels 1986-89). Roman Catholic. Home: 71 Commonwealth Ave Chestnut Hill MA 02167-1003 Office: Harvard U Dept Slavic Langs & Lits Cambridge MA 02138

VON KUTZLEBEN, SIEGFRIED EDWIN, engineering consultant; b. Veckerhagen, Germany, May 19, 1920; s. Erich Melchior and Katherina Helene (Klotz) von K.; m. Ursula Herta, July 21, 1915; children: Bernd E., Roy E., Werner E. BS, NYU, 1951. Naval disarmament control officer U.S./Brit. Mil. Govt. Germany, 1945-47; plant engr. Colgate-Palmolive-Peet, Jersey City, 1951; sr. sales engr. C.E. Lummus Nederland, The Hague, The Netherlands, 1951-58, mng. dir., 1958-71; exec. v.p. C.E. Lummus Co., Bloomfield, N.J., 1971-74; pres. C.E. Constrn. Internat., Bloomfield, 1974-81; group v.p. C.E. Lummus Group, Bloomfield, 1974-81; dir. Fluor Europe Ltd., London, 1981-82; mng. dir. Fluor Nederland B.V., Haarlem, The Netherlands, 1982-85; dir. Kaefer Techs., Houston, 1985-90, Bremtex Corp., Houston, 1990—; cons. to industry. Bd. deacons Am. Protestant Ch. The Hague, 1964-68; trustee N.J. Independent Colls., 1974-75, Suomi Coll., Hancock, Mich., 1978-81; pres. Am. C. of C. The Netherlands, 1970-71, 83-85. Decorated Officer Order Oranje-Nassau (Netherlands), 1971, Comdr. Order Lion of Finland (Finland), 1973. Mem. Am. Inst. Chem. Engrs. Lutheran.

VONNEGUT, KURT, JR., writer; b. Indpls., Nov. 11, 1922; s. Kurt and Edith (Lieber) V.; m. Jane Marie Cox, Sept. 1, 1945 (div. 1979); children: Mark, Edith, Nanette; adopted nephews: James, Steven and Kurt Adams; m. Jill Krementz, 1979, 1 child, Lily. Student, Cornell U., 1940-42, U. Chgo., 1945-47; MA in Anthropology, U. Chgo., 1971. Reporter Chgo. City News Bur., 1946; pub. relations with Gen. Electric Co., 1947-50; free-lance writer N.Y.C., 1950-65, 74—; lectr. writers workshop U. Iowa, Iowa City, 1965-67; lectr. in English Harvard U., Cambridge, Mass., 1970; disting. prof. CCNY, 1973-74. Author: (novels) Player Piano, 1951, Sirens of Titan, 1959, Mother Night, 1961, Cat's Cradle, 1963, God Bless You, Mr. Rosewater, 1964, Slaughterhouse-Five, 1969, Breakfast of Champions, 1973, Slapstick, or Lonesome No More, 1976, Jailbird, 1979, Deadeye Dick, 1982, Galápagos, 1985, Bluebeard, 1987, Hocus Pocus, 1990; (collected stories) Welcome to the Monkey House, 1968; (play) Happy Birthday, Wanda June, 1970; (TV script) Between Time and Timbuktu or Prometheus-5, 1972; (essays) Wampeters, Foma and Granfalloons, 1974; (Christmas Story with illustrations by Ivan Chermayeff) Sun Moon Star, 1980; (autobiographical collage) Palm Sunday, 1981, (collection of speeches and essays) Fates Worse Than Death, 1991; also short stories, articles, revs. Served with inf. AUS, 1942-45. Guggenheim fellow, 1967-68. Mem. Nat. Inst. Arts and Letters (recipient Lit. award 1970). Office: care Donald C Farber 99 Park 25th Ave New York NY 10016-1503

VON ROSENSTIEL, MARTHA ELIZABETH, lawyer; b. Hackensack, N.J., Aug. 25, 1950; d. Werner and Marion (Ahrens) Von R.; m. Elliot R. Borgman, Aug. 12, 1978; children: Skyler Timothy, Nolan. BA, U. Pa., 1972; JD with hons., Rutgers U., Camden, 1988. Bar: N.J. 1988, Pa. 1988. Paralegal W. H. Von Rosenstiel, Phila., 1971-88; ptnr. Werner H. Von Rosenstiel & Assocs., Phila., 1988-89; pvt. practice Phila., 1989—. Block capt. 4800 Hazel Ave. Assn., Phila., 1976—. Recipient Don F. D'Agui Meml. award, Rutgers U., 1988, others. Mem. Phila. Bar Assn., Nat. Assn. Women Lawyers (Oustanding Woman Law Grad. 1988). Democrat. Office: 21 S 12th St # 720 Philadelphia PA 19107-3607

VOOK, RICHARD WERNER, physics educator; b. Milw., Aug. 2, 1929; s. Fred Ludwig and Hedwig Anna (Werner) V.; m. Julia Deskins, Sept. 7, 1957; children: Katherine, Elizabeth, Richard S., Frederick W. BA, Carleton Coll., 1951; MS, U. Ill., 1952, PhD, 1957. Staff physicist IBM Rsch. Lab., Yorktown Heights, N.Y., 1957-61; sr. rsch. physicist Franklin Inst. Rsch. Labs., Phila., 1961-65; assoc. prof. of metallurgy Syracuse (N.Y.) U., 1965-70, prof. of materials sci., 1970-84, prof. of physics, 1984—, dir. solid state sci. and tech., 1984-87, 90-91; physicist/chemist U. Calif., Lawrence Livermore Nat. Lab., summers 1977-81; summer faculty mem. Sandia Nat.

Lab., Albuquerque, 1983, 84; bd. editors Thin Solid Films, 1985—. Contbr. articles to profl. publs., chpts. to books. Recipient L. B. Pfeil medal and prize Metals Soc. of Great Britain, 1983. Mem. Am. Phys. Soc., Am. Vacuum Soc., Electron Microscope Soc. Am., Materials Rsch. Soc., Phi Beta Kappa, Sigma Xi, Pi Mu Epsilon. Lutheran. Office: Syracuse U 201 Physics Bldg Syracuse NY 13244-1130

VOORHEES, WILLIAM WOLVERTON, JR., lawyer; b. Bridgeport, Conn., Aug. 2, 1946; s. William Wolverton Sr. and Eleanor (Lawrence) V.; m. Iris Barnes, Oct. 10, 1986. BA, Seton Hall U., 1968; JD, Rutgers U., 1973. Assoc. Jung & Howard, Chatham, N.J., 1973-77; ptnr. Jung, Wilson & Voorhees, Chatham, 1977-79, Voorhees, McGuire & Wilson, Morristown, N.J., 1979-84, Voorhees & Acciavatti, Morristown, 1985—. Pres. United Cerebral Palsy of N.J., Trenton, 1984-86; me. Legal Ethics Com., Morristown, 1985-89. Mem. N.J. Bar Assn., N.J. Def. Assn., Def. Rsch. Inst., Morris County Bar Assn. (trustee 1988-91, treas. 1992—), Worrall F. Mountain Inn of Ct. (master of the bench 1989). Office: Voorhees & Acciavatti PO Box 1236 Morristown NJ 07962-1236

VORCHHEIMER, NORMAN, chemist; b. Thüngen, Germany, Sept. 10, 1935; s. Siegbert and Kathe (Weinberg) V.; m. Mary Lou Townsley, May 6, 1967; children: Jonathan Joshua, Eric Seth, Katherine Anne. BS cum laude, Bklyn. Coll., 1957; PhD, Poly. Inst. Bklyn., 1962. Rsch. chemist E.I. du-Pont de Nemours & Co., Wilmington, Del., 1962-67; sr. rsch. chemist Betz Labs., Inc., Trevose, Pa., 1967-70, 1971-73, group leader, 1973-77, supr., 1977-80, sect. head, 1980-82, mgr., 1982-86, rsch. fellow, 1986—; exec. v.p. Shasta Fund, Mountchanin, Del., 1970-71. Patentee in field; contbr. to book: Synthetic Polyelectrolytes for Water and Waste Water Treatment, 1981; contbr. Ency. of Polymer Sci. and Engring., 1988. Mem. Am. Chem. Soc., Royal Soc. of Chemistry. Home: PO Box 403 Buckingham PA 18912 Office: Betz Labs Inc 4636 Somerton Rd Trevose PA 19053

VORNLE VON HAAGENFELS, JOHN P., financial services executive; b. N.Y.C., July 22, 1958; s. Paul M. and Rita K. (Szigetter) V.; m. Beatrice Jacqueline Riga, Aug. 28, 1982; children: Stephanie, Nicholas, Marina, Alexandra. Diploma, Aiglon Coll., Chesières, Switzerland, 1976; student, Heidelberg U., Fed. Republic Germany, 1978; BA, Colgate U., 1980; MBA, NYU, 1985. Asst. sec., loan rev. officer European Am. Bank, N.Y.C., 1980-83; fin. mgr. tax exempt bonds Continental Ins., N.Y.C., 1985; asst. v.p. Continental Guaranty & Credit/Continental Ins., N.Y.C., 1985-86, v.p. credit enhancement structured financing products, 1986-90, v.p. mktg. specialized liability ins. products, 1990—; bd. dirs. IDBI Mgrs., Inc., N.Y.C., 1989—; speaker, lectr., instr. in field. Com. mem. Petrouska Charity, N.Y., 1983; mem. Aiglon Coll. Adv. Com., N.Y., 1986—; bus. advisor INROADS, N.Y., 1986—; mem. trustee/bond insurer task force Am. Bankers Assn., N.Y.C., 1987-89. Mem. NYU Finance Club (program com. 1990), Nat. Rifle Assn., Longshore Club. Republican. Roman Catholic. Home: 2 Mystic Ln Westport CT 06880-2223 Office: Continental Ins 180 Maiden Ln New York NY 10038-4925

VOROS, JOSEPH PAUL, jewelry firm executive, composer; b. Pitts., Feb. 5, 1961; s. Joseph Paul and Rita Elizabeth (Santarone) V. BA in Communication Arts, Villanova U., 1983. Musician, songwriter World One Music, Phila., 1983—; jeweler, designer Specialty Gems, Jenkintown, Pa., 1989—; mus. performer Troubador Folk Club, Churchville, Pa., 1992; actor, musician Temple U. Grad Sch. film project "The Move", Phila., 1992; founder, owner Health Enhancement, Sunrider Internat., Creative Leather Design Co., Exec. Estates; VCEO Voros Holdings. Songwriter: J. Paul Voros Songbook Vols. I, II, 1991; producer "Folksongs of America" show, Phila., 1992; pasteled abstract art. Mem. ASCAP, BMI, Songwriters Guild Am., Musicians Artist Poets and Performers, Phila. Music Alliance, Com. for Progressive Radio, Pa. Jeweler's Assn., Jeweler's of Am. Office: Specialty Gems World One Music PO Box 2204 Jenkintown PA 19046

VOROSMARTI, JAMES, physician; b. Palmerton, Pa., Oct. 18, 1935; s. James and Ruth Smith (Mohler) V.; m. Carol Ann Schoch, June 1959; children: James III, Richard Stefan, Erika Lynn. AB, Lafayette Coll., 1957; MD, Jefferson Coll., 1961. Diplomate Am. Bd. Preventive Medicine. Sr. med. officer USN submarine base, Pearl Harbor, Hawaii, 1964-66; med. officer Submergence Project, San Diego, 1966-70; post-doctoral fellow physiology dept. SUNY, Buffalo, 1970-72; exchange med. officer Inst. Naval Medicine, Gosport, Eng., 1972-75; exec. officer Naval Med. Research Inst., Bethesda, Md., 1975-78, comdg. officer, 1980-83; program mgr. Naval Med. Research, Devel. Command, Bethesda, 1978-80; med., life scis. asst. Sec. Def., Washington, 1983-86; cons. occupational medicine Rockville, Md., 1986—. Editor: Undersea Biomedical Research, 1978-82. Recipient Def. Superior Svc. medal Sec. of Def., 1986. Fellow Am. Coll. Preventive Medicine, Am. Coll. Physicians, Am. Acad. Occupational Medicine, Am. Acad. Family Physicians; mem. Am. Physiol. Soc., Underseas Hyperbaric Med. Soc. (Shilling award 1987). Home and Office: 16 Orchard Way S Rockville MD 20854-6130

VOS, ALVIN PAUL, English educator; b. Pella, Iowa, Aug. 13, 1943; s. Peter Gerrit and Edith (DeVries) Vos; m. Joyce E. VanZee, Aug. 1967; children: Miriam, Sarah. BA, Calvin Coll., 1965; MA, U. Chgo., 1967, PhD, 1971. Asst. prof. SUNY, Binghamton, 1970-77, assoc. prof. English, 1977—; chair Faculty Senate, 1990-91. Author: Letters of Roger Ascham, 1990; contbr. articles to scholarly publs. Chmn. bd. dirs. Probe, Binghamton, 1971-73. Mem. MLA, Nat. Coun. Tchrs. English, Am. Acad. Religions. Office: Dept English SUNY Binghamton PO Box 6000 Binghamton NY 13902-2422

VOS-FITZSIMMONS, NANCY ELLEN, public relations and public affairs professional; b. Plainfield, N.J., Feb. 20, 1954; d. Joseph Alfred and Marilyn Patricia (Bloom) Vos; m. John Joseph Fitzsimmons, Nov. 10, 1990. Assocs., Lab. Inst. Merchandising, N.Y.C., 1976; BA, NYU, 1991. From asst. buyer to pub. rels. mgr. Abraham & Straus, Bklyn., 1976-80; mgr. pub. rels. Springs Mills, N.Y.C., 1980-81; from account exec. to v.p. and accounts supr. Burson Marsteller, N.Y.C., 1981-89; dir. mktg. com. Warner-Lambert Co., Morris Plains, N.J., 1989-90; dir. issues and media Warner-Lambert Co., Morris Plains, 1990—. Chair spl. events United Way, Morris County, N.J., 1992. Mem. Pharm. Ad Coun., Healthcare Bus. Womens Assn., Food and Drug Law Inst. Conf. Bd. Office: Warner-Lambert Co 201 Tabor Rd Morris Plains NJ 07950

VOSHALL, ROY EDWARD, electrical engineering educator, consultant; b. Beacon, N.Y., May 29, 1933; s. Leroy Brodbeck Voshall and Mabel Jeannette (Johnson) Brown; m. Marilyn Eloise Van Voorhis, June 2, 1956; children: Lindamarie, Robert Edward. BSEE, Carnegie Inst. Tech., 1956, MS, 1957, PhD, 1961. Assoc. engr. Westinghouse Electric Co., Pitts., 1958; engr. Westinghouse Rsch. Labs., Pitts., 1959-63, rsch. engr., fellow, 1963-89; instr. Carnegie Inst. Tech., Pitts., 1957-61, asst. prof., 1961-63, night lectr., 1963-69; prof. Gannon U., Erie, Pa., 1989—. Co-author: Circuit Interruption, Theory & Application, 1985; patentor 11 patents in field of circuit breakers and circuit interrupters. Supporter Greenpeace, Sierra, Audubon Soc. Mem. IEEE (sr.), Am. Phys. Soc., Sigma Xi, Eta Kappa Nu. Mem. Christian Ch. Office: Gannon U University Sq Erie PA 16541

VOSS, PAUL JOSEPH, physicist; b. Chgo., Mar. 10, 1943; s. Paul Joseph and Irene Ester (Bergman) V.; divorced; children: Kalila Laurel Mage, Lisa Jean Voss. BS, Syracuse U., 1969; MS, Johns Hopkins U., Balt., 1972. From assoc. physicist to sr. physicist Johns Hopkins U. Aplied Physics Lab., Laurel, Md., 1969—; facility mgr. guidance system evaluation lab. Johns Hopkins U. Applied Physics Lab., Laurel, Md., 1981—; chmn. AEGIS Scenario Cert. Com., Washington, 1987—. Home: 5635B Harpers Farm Rd Columbia MD 21044-2002 Office: Applied Physics Lab John Hopkins Univ Johns Hopkins Rd Laurel MD 20723-1140

VOSSLER, JOHN ALBERT, civil engineer; b. Newburgh, N.Y., Oct. 9, 1925; s. Vernon Martense and Frieda (Bachmann) V.; m. Betiejean Sleight Erts, Sept. 4, 1948; children: Karen Ann, Susan Jean. BS in Structural Engring., U. Mich., 1951. Registered profl. engr., N.Y., Conn. Structural engr. Marine div. Maxon Constrn. Co., Tell City, Ind., 1953-56; staff engr. Systems Mfg. div. IBM, Poughkeepsie, N.Y., 1956-68; project mgr. Real Estate & Constrn. div. IBM, Stamford, Conn., 1968-88; adv. engr. Gen. Systems div. IBM, Hopewell Junction, N.Y., 1988-89; dir. devel. Getter, Segner & Gironda, P.E., P.C., Valhalla, N.Y., 1989—; prin. John A. Vossler Assocs., Danbury, Conn., 1988—. Bd. dirs. Lake Pl. Condo Assn., 1989—.With U.S. Army, 1944-46; PTO; 1st lt. USAF, 1951-53. Mem. ASCE, NSPE, Conn. Soc. Profl. Engrs., Conn. Engrs. in Pvt. Practice, Am. Radio Relay League. Home: 12-147 Boulevard Dr Danbury CT 06810 Office: John A Vossler Assocs 12-147 Boulevard Dr Danbury CT 06810

VOSTI, STEPHEN ANTHONY, economist; b. Salinas, Calif., Feb. 26, 1955; s. Angelo Vosti and Beverly (Macklin) Wertz; m. Yvonne Ramelli, Jan. 18, 1986; children: Daniela, Lia. BA, Whitman Coll., 1977; PhD, U. Pa., 1984. Postdoctoral fellow Rockefeller Found., Belo Horizonto, Brazil, 1985-86; rsch. fellow Internat. Food Policy Rsch. Inst., Washington, 1987—. Mem. Am. Econ. Assn., Am. Agrl. Econs. Assn., Population Assn. Am. Office: Internat Food Policy Rsch Inst 1776 Massachusetts Ave NW Washington DC 20036-1904

VOURNAKIS, JOHN NICHOLAS, biophysicist, biotechnology company executive; b. Cambridge, Ohio, Dec. 1, 1939; s. Nicholas John and Pota (Andritsakis) V.; m. Karen Ann Munro, Sept. 9, 1961; 1 child, Christopher. BS, Albion Coll., 1961; PhD, Cornell U., 1968. Rsch. fellow MIT, Cambridge, 1969-72, Harvard U., Cambridge, 1972-73; from asst. prof. to full prof. Syracuse (N.Y.) U., 1973-85; prof. Dartmouth Coll., Hanover, N.H., 1985-87; v.p. sci. Verax Corp., Lebanon, N.H., 1988-90; sr. v.p. Genmap, Inc., Boston, 1990—; cons. Bristol Myers, Syracuse, 1980-83, Bayer A.G., West Haven, Conn., 1986-88, Nat. Biotech. Co. of Greece, Athens, 1983—; affiliated mem. Inst. Biology and Biotechnal, Crete, Greece, 1986—. Editor several biochem. and biotech. jours.; contbr. over 100 articles to profl. jours. and chpts. to books. Rsch. grantee NIH, NSF, Am. Chem. Soc., 1968—. Mem. AAAS, Am. Soc. Microbiology, Sigma Xi. Home: 6 Carriage Ln Lyme NH 03768-4700

VOWELL, JEFF D., consulting company executive; b. Hobbs, N.Mex., Apr. 19, 1952; s. Jeff D. and Dolly Jo (White) V.; m. Carol Ann Setaro, Mar. 17, 1974; children: Daniel Patrick, Christopher Brian. BS, SUNY, Albany, 1976; MBA, Pacific Western U., 1987. Data base cons. variou orgns., 1976-79; data base adminstr. Greyhound Corp., Phoenix, 1979-80; sr. systems engr. Amdahl Corp., Tempe, Ariz., 1980-82; mgr. systems quality Avco-Lycoming, Stratford, Conn., 1982-83; engr. account systems IBM, Boston, 1983-84; mgr. systems Litton Itek Optical Systems, Lexington, Mass., 1984-85; pres. Vowell Systems Group, Middletown, N.J., 1985—. Author: Implementation and Usage of DB2, 1987; developer Relationally Integrated Design Devel. and Control System software; contbr. articles to profl. jours. Pres. Sierra Vista Jaycees, Ariz., 1975-76; regional dir. Minn. Jaycees, 1977-78; v.p. Ariz. Jaycees, 1979-81; cubmaster pack 242 Boy Scouts Am., Middletown, N.J., 1986-91. With U.S. Army, 1970-76. Recipient Outstanding Performance in EDP award Am. Soc. Mil. Compts., 1975, Keyman award U.S. Jaycees, 1976; named one of 3 Outstanding Young Men of Ariz., Ariz. Jaycees, 1976. Mem. Jaycees (v.p. Mass. chpt. 1984-85, mgmt. v.p. N.J. chpt. 1988-89, JCI senator). Home: 22 Stoney Brook Rd Holmdel NJ 07733 Home: 22 Sutton Pl Middletown NJ 07748-3260

VOYAGER, ALYN See WARDEN, GARY RUSSELL

VOYTKO, JAMES EMERY, electrical engineer; b. Windber, Pa., Jan. 30, 1933; s. Joseph and Mary (Adeline) V.; m. Mary Elizabeth Weis, June 4, 1955; children: Wayne Edward, David Allan, Karen Louise Turner. BSEE with honors, Johns Hopkins U., 1964; MS in Materials Scis., Lehigh U., 1966; postgrad., Ohio State U., 1966-68. Sr. engr. Western Electric Co., Columbus, Ohio, 1956-67; v.p. engring. Swift Ohio Corp., Kenton, 1967-69; sr. staff engr. Western Electric/AT&T, Atlanta, 1969-84, AT&T Techs., Omaha, 1984-86; dept. mgr., sr. mem. tech. staff Sandia Nat. Labs., Albuquerque, 1986-90; tech. cons U.S. Dept. Energy, Washington, 1990—; cons. in electroplating and surface finishing and tech. transfer. Inventor connector manufacture. Recipient AESF Leadership and Svc. award, 1984. Fellow Inst. of Metal Finishing; mem. Am. Electroplaters and Surface Finishers Soc. (pres. 1980-81, bd. dirs. 1973-78, cert. electroplater, finisher), Am. Soc. for Metals, Soc. Mfg. Engrs. Republican. Roman Catholic. Home: 11804 Riding Loop Ter Gaithersburg MD 20878-3880

VREELAND, RUSSELL GLENN, accountant, consultant; b. Princeton, N.J., Apr. 27, 1960; s. Glenn Earl and Barbara Ann (Jungels) V.; m. Traci Ann Harbold, Dec. 17, 1988; 1 child, Hans Russell. BSBA, Bloomsburg (Pa.) U., 1982. CPA, Pa., Md. Sr. acct. Louis H. Linowitz & Co., Trenton, N.J., 1982-85; tax supr. Horty & Horty, P.A., Wilmington, Del., 1985-87; tax mgr. Stewart Waddell & Co., P.A., Columbia, Md., 1988—; speaker in field. Contbr. articles to profl. jours. Chmn. fin. com. Woodland Village Condominium Assn., 1989-90. Mem. AICPAs (tax div.), Md. Assn. CPAs (fed. taxation com. 1990-91), D.C. Inst. CPAs, Howard County C. of C., Columbia Bus. Exch. Republican. Lutheran. Office: 9881 Broken Land Pky # 300 Columbia MD 21046-1173

VRIS, THOMAS W., surgeon; b. Elkins, W.Va., Apr. 27, 1951; s. Thomas and Barbara (Johns) V.; m. Donna Merrill, Oct. 6, 1973; children: Tracy, Courtney. BA, Columbia U., 1973; MD with honors, NYU, 1979. Diplomate Am. Bd. Otolaryngology. Resident Harvard Sch. Medicine, Boston, 1979-81, Yale U., New Haven, Conn., 1982-85; attending surgeon Norwalk (Conn.) Hosp., 1985—; sec. med. staff Norwalk Hosp., 1991—. Mem. Norwalk Med. Soc. (treas. 1991—), The Riding Club Wilton (Conn.), Yale Club. Republican. Episcopalian. Office: Norwalk Hosp 10 Mott Ave Norwalk CT 06850

VUCKOVICH, CAROL YETSO (MRS. MICHAEL VUCKOVICH), librarian; b. East Liverpool, Ohio, Sept. 23, 1940; d. Stephen A. and Louise (Sever) Yetso; m. Michael Vuckovich, Sept. 24, 1970. BS, Geneva Coll., 1966; MLS, U. Pitts., 1968. Computation analyst Crucible Steel div. Colt Industries, Midland, Pa., 1958-62; library dir. Community Coll. Beaver County, Monaca, Pa., 1968—, instr. human anatomy and physiology, 1970—. Mem. Am. Library Assn., Pa. Library Assn., Spl. Libraries Assn., Am. Inst. Biol. Scis., Am. Anti-Vivisection Soc., Nat. Wildlife Fedn., Coll. and Research Libraries. Home: 21 Elm St Midland PA 15059-1615

VUILLEMIN, JEAN-CLAUDE, foreign language educator; b. Rodez, Aveyron, France, Mar. 24, 1954; came to U.S. 1979; s. Jacques and Genevieve (Cayssials) V.; m. Guada Marti-Pena, June 18, 1987. Licence d'Anglais, U. Paul Valery, Montpellier, France, 1977, Licence de Lettres, 1978, Maitrise de Lettres, 1979; PhD in French Lit., Mich. State U., 1986. Mem. faculty dept. French, Dept. French, Pa. State U., University Park. Editor: Esthétique baroque et imagination créatrice, Mont-de-Marsan, Editions Inter Universitaires, 1993; author: Théâtralité dans le Texte dramatique de Jean Rotrou, 1993; contbr. articles to profl. jours. Mem. MLA, Am. Assn. Tchrs. French, Am. Translators Assn., N. Am. Soc. for Seventeenth Century French Lit., Societe d'Etude du Theatre, Societe d'Etude du XVIIeme siecle. Office: Pa State Univ Dept French University Park PA 16802

VULIS, DIMITRI LVOVICH, computer consultancy executive; b. Leningrad, Russia, Dec. 29, 1964; came to U.S., 1979; s. Lev Klyukvin and Inna Vulis; m. Maryam Inzel, Mar. 30, 1988; 1 child, Daniel Benjamin. BA in Math. cum laude, CUNY, 1985, MA in Math., 1989, postgrad., 1989—. Pres. D&M Consulting Svcs., Inc., Forest Hills, N.Y., 1990—; cons. in math. Fordham U., N.Y.C., 1989—, Cornerstone Asset Mgmt., N.Y.C., 1989—, Possev-USA, N.Y.C., 1990—. Author: (computer program) Russian TeX, 1989. Mem. Am. Math. Soc., TeX Users' Group. Republican. Office: D&M Cons Svc Inc 67-67 Burns St Forest Hills NY 11375

VURGAROPULOS, FOTINI, sculptor, educator; b. Arta, Greece, Oct. 31, 1961; came to U.S., 1962; d. Christopher Charles and Penelope (Rangos) V. BFA, R.I. Sch. Design, 1984; cert. in Art Edn., Coll. of Art, Boston, 1985; MFA, Parsons Sch. Design, 1990. Cert. art tchr., Mass., N.Y., R.I. Instr. Wheeler Sch., Providence, 1984, Mass. Migrant Edn. Program, Boston, 1985-86, Coll. of Art, Boston, 1984; artist-in-residence Keefe Tech. Sch., Framingham, Mass., 1985-87; assistantship in sculpture Parsons Sch. Design, N.Y.C., 1989-90; art tchr. Lorge Sch., N.Y.C., 1990-92, Fantis Sch., N.Y.C., 1990-92. One-woman shows include Club Cafe, Boston, 1985, James Whistler House Mus., Lowell, Mass., 1987, Flamingo East, N.Y.C., 1991, Indsl. Design Ctr., N.Y.C., 1992; exhibited in group shows at David Bernstein Gallery, Boston, 1986, Atwood Gallery, Worcester, Mass., 1987, Lannon Gallery, Boston 1987, Fine Arts Gallery, N.Y.C., 1989, 90, Parsons Exhibition Ctr., N.Y.C., 1990, Colubmia U., N.Y.C., 1990, Woods Gerry Gallery, Providence, 1990, Belanthi Gallery, Bklyn., 1991, A.I.R. Gallery, N.Y.C., 1991. Recipient scholarship grant Vera List, 1989, grant DeMoulas Found., 1988 Advanced Standing Honors award R.I. Sch. Design, 1983. Mem. NOW, Coll. Art Assn., Women's Caucus for Art, Internat. Sculpture Ctr., N.Y. R.I. Sch. Design Alumni Assn. (exec. com.). Home and Studio: 324 Pearl St 5C New York NY 10038

VYSE, STUART ARTHUR, psychology educator; b. Evanston, Ill., Nov. 18, 1950; s. Arthur F. Vyse III and Norma M. Richards; m. Judith Chick, Aug. 4, 1979; 1 child, Graham Chick Vyse. BA in English, So. Ill. U., 1972, MA in English, 1974; MA in Psychology, U. R.I., 1984, PhD in Psychology, 1987. Behavioral cons. Psychology Assocs., Fall River, Mass., 1982; spl. instr. U. R.I., 1984; spl. lectr. Providence Coll., 1985; assoc. psychologist R.I. Youth Guidance Ctr., Pawtucket, 1985-86; vis. instr. Conn. Coll., New London, 1986-87, asst. prof., 1987-92, assoc. prof., 1992—; vis. scholar Harvard U., Cambridge, Mass., 1990; presenter in field. Author: (with others) Ecobehavioral Analysis and Developmental Disabilities: The Twenty-First Century, 1990; contbr. articles to profl. jours.; guest reviewer Applied Rsh. in Mental Retardation, Behavioral Assessment, Human Orgn., Jour. Asian Studies, Psychol. Record. Mem. APA, Assn. for Behavior Analysis, Am. Pscyhol. Soc., Ea. Psychol. Assn., Psychonomic Soc. Office: Conn Coll 270 Mohegan Ave New London CT 06320-4112

WABECK, CHARLES JOHN, poultry science educator; b. Montague, Mass., July 16, 1938; s. John Donald Wabeck and Laura Samorajski; m. Sandra Marie Borowski, June 6, 1964; children: John Edward, Karen Marie. BS, U. Mass., 1962; MS, U. N.H., 1964; PhD, Purdue U., 1966. Rsch. assoc. Armour & Co., Oak Brook, Ill., 1966-69; dir. rsch. and quality Ocoma Foods, Omaha, 1969; prof. poultry sci. U. Md., Princess Anne, 1969—, mem. extension faculty senate, chmn. legis. com., 1989—; chmn. Nat. Poultry and Egg Conf., Louisville, 1990-91; chmn. nat. acceptable quality leval Joint USDA-Industry, Washington, 1973-89; mem. Delmarva Poulty Industry Processor Commn., 1969—, chmn., 1977-83; mem. Nat. P-3 Standards Commn., 1969-75. Recipient cert. of appreciation USDA, 1974, Medal of Achievement, Delmarva Poultry Industry, 1977, Agr. Degree, Md. Future Farmers Am., 1988, Excellence in Extension award Washington-Balt. chpt. Gamma Sigma Delta, 1990. Mem. Poultry Sci. Assn. (careers com. 1982-86, membership com. 1987—), Inst. Food Technologists, Am. Poultry Assn. (chmn. judges licensing com. 1962—). Republican. Roman Catholic. Office: U Md LESREC RR 2 Box 229A Princess Anne MD 21853

WACHS, SAUL PHILIP, Jewish education educator; b. Phila., Dec. 24, 1931; s. Abraham and Annette (Schaller) W.; m. Barbara Ruth Eidelman, Jan. 27, 1957; children: Sharona Rachel, Hillel Eliezer, Devorah Leah, Aviva Marcia. Hebrew tchr. diploma, Gratz Coll., 1951; BS in Edn., Temple U., 1953; BRE, Jewish Theol. Sem., 1956, B in Sacred Music, 1959, D Pedagogy (hon.), 1989; MA, Ohio State U., 1966, PhD, 1970. Dir. edn. Congregation Tifereth Israel, Columbus, Ohio, 1960-70, Park Ave Synagogue, N.Y.C., 1970-72; asst. prof., dir. Jewish edn. program Brandeis U., Waltham, Mass., 1972-75; dean Gratz Coll., Phila., 1975-80, Rosaline B. Feinstein prof. of Jewish edn., chair dept., 1980—; bd. dirs. Jewish Edn. Assembly, N.Y.C., 1965-70, Akiba, Merion, Pa., 1975—, Beth Hillel-Beth El, Wynnewood, Pa., 1984-88, Coun. for Jewish Edn., N.Y.C., 1970-74; vis. lectr. Hebrew U., 1986-89, tutor, 1988-89, vis. rschr., 1985; vis. professorial lectr. Am. U.-George Washington U.; vis. prof. Jewish Theol. Sem. Am.; vis. instr. Coll. of Jewish Studies, Cleve., 1965-69. Co-author texts: Judaism, 1979, Jewish Education, 1991, also curriculum materials; contbr. articles to religious publs. Mem. Soviet Jewry com. Phila Jewish Community Rels. Coun.; bd. dirs. Akiba Hebrew Acad. Recipient Aaron Zacks award Am. Assn. for Jewish Edn., 1969. Mem. Coalition for Jewish Edn., ASCD, Assn. for Jewish Studies, Phi Delta Kappa. Home: 107 Maple Ave Bala Cynwyd PA 19004 Office: Gratz Coll Melrose Avenue Rd Philadelphia PA 19126-1905

WACHSTEIN, JOAN MARTHA, dental hygienist; b. Phila., Nov. 12, 1941; d. Milton and Mabel Louise (Friedman) Hertzfeld; m. Mortimer Berwyn Wachstein, July 14, 1962 (dec. 1989); children: Lisa Beth, Esther Lynn. RDH, Temple U., Phila., 1961. Registered dental hygienist. Dental hygienist Dr. M.B. Wachstein, Newark, Del., 1970-89. Mem. allocations panel & mem. planning coms. United Way, Wilmington, Del., 1986-92; bd. dirs. Jewish Family Svcs., Del., 1983—, rec. sec., 1984-86, 88-91, pres., 1992—, treas. 1989-91; bd. dirs. Milton and Hattie Kutz Home, Inc., 1987—, v.p., 1988—; pres. Aux. Milton and Hattie Kutz Home, Inc., 1985-87; bd. dirs. Jewish Fedn. Del., 1983-89, 91-92, mem. exec. com., 1992—; bd. dirs. Mid-Atlantic Coun. Union Am. Hewbrew Congregations, 1981—, vice chair biennial program com., 1990-92; mem. Nat. Fedn. Temple Sisterhood, 1975—, v.p. 1987-89, 89-91, 91—; pres. Beth Emeth Sisterhood, 1968-70. Recipient Community Builder award NCCJ, 1985. Mem. Am. Dental Hygienist Assn., Del. Dental Hygiene Assn., Aux. of ADA, Nat. Coun. Jewish Women, Orgn. for Rehab. and Tng., Temple U. Dental Hygiene Alumni Assn., B'nai B'rith, Hadassah. Jewish. Home: 3331 Silverside Rd Wilmington DE 19810-3306

WACHTER, SUSAN MELINDA, finance educator, consultant; b. Newark, June 22, 1943; d. Nathaniel and Edith (Dubow) Jaffe; m. Michael Lawrence Wachter, June 23, 1968; children—Jessica, Jonathan. B.A., Radcliffe Coll., 1965; Ph.D., Boston Coll. Grad. Sch. Arts and Sci., 1974; M.A. (hon.), U. Pa., 1978. Lectr., Bryn Mawr Coll. (Pa.), 1969-72; lectr. Wharton Sch., U. Pa., Phila., 1972-74, asst. prof. fin., 1974-78, assoc. prof., 1978—; bd. dirs. Beneficial Corp., Beneficial Mortgage Corp.; mem. adv. bd. Office Housing Policy Rsch., 1989—; Fed. Nat. Mortgage Assn., 1989—. Author: Latin American Inflation: The Structuralist-Monetarist Debate, 1976, Inflation and Pensions, 1987; co-author: Redlining and Public Policy, 1980; editor: Social Security and Private Pensions: Planning for the 21st Century, 1988; co-editor: Towards a New U.S. Industrial Policy?, 1981; Removing Obstacles to Economic Growth, 1984; Savings and Capital Formation: The Policy Options; bd. editors: Jour Real Estate Research, Jour. Am. Real Estate and Urban Econs., Jour. Housing Econs., Jour. Real Estate Lit., Jour. Real Estate Fin. and Econs. Recipient Lindbach award for disting. teaching Lindbach Soc., U. Pa., 1974-75; Wharton Grad. Anvil award for teaching excellence Wharton Sch., U. Pa., 1973-74; research fellow Ctr. for Internat. Affairs, Harvard U., 1966. Mem. Am. Econ. Assn., Am. Fin. Assn., Econometric Soc., Am. Real Estate and Urban Econs. Assn. (bd. dirs. 1984-91, pres. 1988), Lambda Alpha. Home: 355 Margo Ln Berwyn PA 19312-1453 Office: U Pa Finance Dept Philadelphia PA 19104

WACK, HENRY PAUL, design and planning company executive; b. Hatfield, Pa., Mar. 4, 1934; s. Paul Mittham and Elizabeth Ruth W.; m. Charlotte Anne Booz, Oct. 1, 1955; 1 child, Andrew Paul. Degree in archtl. tech., Temple U., 1961. Designer Am. Olean, Lansdale, Pa., 1960-62; constrn. engr. Am. Olean, Lansdale, 1963-65, adminstrv. engr., 1966-71, mgr. engring., 1972-83, facilities engr., 1984-85; dir. ops. Happy Viking Interiors, Hathied, Pa., 1986-87; pres., owner Unique Design & Planning, Inc., Souderton, Pa., 1987—. Pres., bd. trustees Indian Valley Pub. Libr., Telford, Pa., 1979—. Named Trustee of Yr., Pa. Libr. Assn., Harrisburg, 1989. Fellow Souderton Telford (sec. 1976-84); mem. Rotary Club (pres. 1986-87). Office: Unique Design & Planning PO Box 482 Souderton PA 18964

WADDEN, THOMAS ANTONY, psychology educator; b. Richmond, Va., Sept. 3, 1952; s. Thomas Antony Jr. and Mary Lloyd (Cradock) W.; m. Jan Robin Linowitz, Nov. 11, 1984; children: David Joseph, Michael James. AB magna cum laude, Brown U., 1975; PhD, U. N.C., 1981. Psychology intern Boston VA Med. Ctr., 1980-81; instr. in psychology U. Pa. Sch. Medicine, Phila., 1981-82, asst. prof. psychology, 1982-87, assoc. prof. psychology, 1987-91; prof. psychology, dir. clin. tng. Syracuse (N.Y.) U., 1992—; clin. dir. Obesity Rsch. Group, U. Pa., Phila., 1983-91; dir. Ctr. for Health and Behavior, Syracuse U., 1992—. Assoc. editor Annals of Behavioral Medicine, 1990—, mem. editorial bd. Internat. Jour. Obesity, 1986—, Health Psychology, 1989—; editor: (with T.B. VanItallie) Treatment of the Seriously Obese Patient, 1992, (with A.J. Stunkard) Obesity: Theory and Therapy, 1992; contbr. chpts. to books; writer numerous sci. papers. Recipient Nat. Rsch. Svc. award Nat. Inst. Mental Health, 1983-85, Rsch. Scientist Devel.

award, 1987—. Mem. APA, Soc. Behavioral Medicine (bd. dirs. 1987-90), Assn. for Advancement of Behavior Therapy (New Rschr. award 1986), Acad. Behavioral Medicine, N.Y. Acad. Scis., Phi Beta Kappa, Sigma Xi. Democrat. Home: 8304 Glen Eagle Dr Manlius NY 13104 Office: Syracuse U 503 Huntington Hall Syracuse NY 13244

WADLEIGH, RICHARD STANLEY, college safety official; b. Kansas City, Mo., June 24, 1944; s. Stanley Thoburn Wadleigh and Corrinne Ester (Meece) Anderson; m. Elaine K. Donner-Lawrence, May 18, 1982; children: Kandi, Marci, Keith, Kenneth, Meegan. BA, U. Nebr., 1973. Protection mgr. Montgomery Ward, Omaha, 1974-76; plant supt. Midlands Mall, Council Bluffs, Iowa, 1976-78; asst. security dir. U. Nebr. Med. Ctr., Omaha, 1978-79; assoc. dir. pub. safety Creighton U., Omaha, 1979-88; safety dir. Glassboro (N.J.) State Coll., 1988—; lectr. Omaha Safety & Health Coun., 1988. Author: (with others) NACUBO: Washington, D.C., 1987. Mem. Iowa Air N.G., Sioux City, 1978-88; vol. instr. ARC, Omaha and Woodbury, N.J., 1981—. With U.S. Army, 1962-72, Vietnam. Recipient cert. of safety excellence Safety Coun. Nebr., 1982. Mem. Am. Soc. Safety Engrs., Am. Soc. Indsl. Security (treas. Omaha chpt. 1985-86, sec. Omaha chpt. 1986-87), Internat. Assn. Campus Law Enforcement Adminstrs., Internat. Assn. Bomb Technicians and Investigators, VFW. Republican. Methodist. Office: Glassboro State Coll Safety Office Linden Hall Glassboro NJ 08028

WAEHNER, RALPH LIVINGSTON, business forms company executive, consultant; b. Bay City, Mich., Nov. 21, 1935; s. Ralph Otto W.; m. Donna Jean Kennie, Feb. 1, 1958; children: Eric R., Julie K., Jill A. BSME, U. Mich., 1959; MBA, Northwestern U., 1964. Devel. engr. Sikorsky Aircraft, Stratford, Conn., 1959-60, Chgo. Rawhide Mfg. Co., 1960-62; with Moore Bus. Forms & Systems, 1962—, mfg. staff, Park Ridge, Ill., 1962-68, plant supt., Charleston, Ill., 1968-70, plant mgr., Albany, Ga., 1970-76, prodn. mgr., Niagara Falls, N.Y., 1976-78, dir. mfg., Glenview, Ill., 1978-83, v.p. mfg., 1983-88, also bd. dirs.; pres. Moore Bus. Forms & Systems, Ltd., Toronto, Ont., Can., 1988-91; v.p. Moore-N.Am. Procurement, Lake Forest, Ill., 1991—; chmn. bd. Command Records, Toronto, 1988-91. With Mich. N.G., 1955-58. Mem. Can. U.S. Bus. Assn. (bd. dirs. 1989), Ivanhoe Country Club. Republican. Roman Catholic. Office: Moore-NAm Procurement 275 N Field Dr Lake Forest IL 60045-2592

WAELDE, GAIL PATRICIA, recreation aid, music educator; b. Teaneck, N.J., July 14, 1953; d. Clinton Brewster and Eileen Florence (Kennedy) W. BA in Music Edn., Glassboro State Coll., 1976. Cert. educator, N.J. Music dir. Music Found. for Visually Handicapped, Ridgewood, N.J., 1982-87, v.p., 1990—; receptionist U.S. Customs, N.Y.C., 1979-81; recreation aid Bergen County Adult Day Care Ctr., Paramus, N.J., 1978-79, 81—. Author: (pamphlet) Word Pictures, (novella) In His Time; composer of 26 songs. Mem. Christian Overcomers. Democrat. Home: 153 Garden Ave Paramus NJ 07652-1918

WAGEMAN, JAMES CARTER, art director and designer; b. Lake Forest, Ill., May 7, 1935; s. George Edward and Joyous Eco (White) W.; m. Lynette Jagbandhansingh, June 7, 1960 (div. 1968); m. Virginia Carter Farley, Apr. 28, 1968; children: Melissa, Robinson, Sarah. BA, Park Coll., 1958; MA, U. Hawaii, 1964. Asst. dir. and designer U. Hawaii Press, Honolulu, 1964-68; chief designer Johns Hopkins U. Press., Balt., 1968-70; designer Princeton (N.J.) U. Press., 1970-71; sr. designer Mus. Modern Art, N.Y.C., 1971-74, dir. design, 1987-88; prin. James Wageman Graphic Design, Princeton and Washington, 1974-84; art dir. Abbeville Press, N.Y.C., 1984-87, 1988-89; dir. art and design Stewart, Tabori & Chang, N.Y.C., 1989—; design cons., designer The Art Museum, Princeton U., Princeton, 1971-81, Libr. of Congress Publishing Office, Washington, 1982-84. Author: (with others) graphic arts manual; designer: numerous award winning books, including In A Desert Land, 1987 (Leipzig Gold medal 1989). With U.S. Army, 1959-62. Mem. Am. Inst. Graphic Arts (juror book show 1988), Type Dirs. Club (juror ann. competition 1990). Home: 360 Ridgeview Rd Princeton NJ 08540-7667 Office: 575 Broadway New York NY 10012-3230

WAGENFUEHRER, CARL MITCHELL, financial analyst; b. Balt., July 8, 1947; s. Carl Siegfried and Bessie Adele (Ensor) W. BA, Am. U., 1969. Fin. analyst Goddard Space Flight Ctr., NASA, Greenbelt, Md., 1969-79, bus. mgr., 1980-87, fin. mgr., 1987-90; program fin. analyst hdqrs. NASA, Washington, 1990—. Editor: (manual) Technical Manager's Handbook, 1988. With U.S. Navy, 1971-74. Republican. Lutheran. Home: 10110 Treetop Ln Seabrook MD 20706 Office: NASA Box RB Washington DC 20546

WAGLEY, JOHN RAIBLE, political consultant; b. Cleve., Aug. 12, 1931; s. Ernest Norman Wagley and Mary Elizabeth (Raible) Evans; m. Elizabeth Symington Landreth, Jan. 1, 1968 (div. Sept. 1975); children: Elizabeth, John Jr.; m. Polly Lavinia King, Oct. 1982; children: Louisa Caroline, Isabella. AB, Harvard U., 1955; postgrad., Sorbonne, Paris, 1956; postgrad. sch. govt., Georgetown U. Staff mem. U.S. Senate Commerce Com., Washington, 1965-67; state liaison officer EEOC, Washington, 1967-68; ptnr. Washington Info. Assocs., 1969-76; Congl. liaison officer AID, Washington, 1976-81; treas. Congl. Agenda: 80's, Washington, 1981—; pres. TransAm. Assocs., Washington, 1981—; chmn. Bingham Investigative Reporting Prize, Washington, 1967—. Commr. Georgetown Adv. Neighborhood Commn., Washington, 1984—. Recipient Beautification award D.C. Fedn. Citizens Assn., 1977,. Mem. Am. Assn. Polit. Cons. Democrat. Episcopalian. Clubs: Pacific, Nantucket (Mass.) Yacht; University (Washington). Home: 314812 O St NW Washington DC 20007-3116 Office: Congl Agenda 80's 3148 O St NW Washington DC 20007-3116

WAGMAN, GERALD HOWARD, library administrator; b. Newark, Mar. 4, 1926; s. David and Sophie (Milinsky) W.; B.S., Lehigh U., 1946; M.S., Va. Poly. Inst. and State U., 1947; m. Rhoda Kirschner, Dec. 9, 1948; children: Jan Donald, Neil Mark. Tech. research asst. Squibb Inst. for Med. Research, New Brunswick, N.J., 1947-49, research asst., 1954-57; mgr. Yankee Radio Corp., N.Y.C., 1950-54; assoc. biochemist Schering Corp. (now Schering-Plough Rsch. Inst.), Bloomfield, N.J., 1957-58, biochemist, 1958-65, sr. biochemist, 1966-68, sect. leader, 1969-70, mgr. antibiotics dept., 1970-74, assoc. dir. microbiol. scis.-antibiotics, 1974-76, assoc. dir. microbiol. scis. and head screening lab., 1977-78, dir. microbiol. strain lab., 1979-84, antibiotics isolation, 1984-85, dir. microbial products chem. screening, 1985-87, prin. scientist, 1987-89, mgr. libr. info. ctr., 1989—; mem. adv. bd. Nat. Cert. Commn. in Chemistry and Chem. Engring., 1985-88. Coun. mem. Troop 23 Boy Scouts Am., 1964-66; communications officer East Brunswick Civil Def. and Disaster Control, 1966-71; mem. sci. adv. com. East Brunswick Bd. Edn., 1960-68; bd. dirs. Tamarack N. Homeowners Assn., 1983-84, 89—, pres., 1989—. Recipient Public Svc. award Am. Radio Relay League, 1965. Cert. profl. chemist; chartered chemist, Gt. Britain. Fellow Am. Inst. Chemists; mem. AAAS, ALA, Spl. Librs. Assn., Am. Chem. Soc., Am. Soc. Microbiology, Am. Inst. Biol. Scis., Soc. Indsl. Microbiology, N.Y. Acad. Sci., Soc. Applied Bacteriology (Gt. Britain), Royal Soc. Chemistry, Sigma Xi, Tau Delta Phi. Author: Chromatography of Antibiotics, 1973, rev. edit., 1984; mem. editorial bd. Antimicrobial Agents and Chemotherapy, 1971-74; co-editor: Isolation, Separation and Purification of Antibiotics, 1978, Natural Products Isolation, 1989; contbr. articles to profl. jours. and books. Patentee in field. Home: 17 Crommelin Ct East Brunswick NJ 08816-2406 Office: 60 Orange St Bloomfield NJ 07003-4795

WAGNER, ALAN CYRIL, television and film producer; b. N.Y.C., Oct. 1, 1931; s. Joseph and Isabelle (Chanson) W.; m. Martha Celia Dreyfus, Mar. 11, 1956; children: David Mark, Susan Jill, Elizabeth Celia. BA, Columbia U., 1951, MA in English, 1952. Mgr. network programs Benton & Bowles, Inc., N.Y.C., 1957-61; dir. program devel. CBS, N.Y.C., 1961-68; v.p. program devel. CBS, Hollywood, Calif., 1968-73; v.p. program planning and devel. CBS, N.Y.C., 1973-75, v.p. nighttime programs, 1975-78, v.p. programs, 1978-82; pres., chief exec. officer The Disney Channel, N.Y.C., 1982-83, Alan Wagner Prodns., Inc., N.Y.C., 1983—; exec. v.p. feature and TV devel. and prodn. Grosso-Jacobson Entertainment Corp., N.Y.C., 1985-90; pres. Boardwalk Entertainment, N.Y.C., 1990—; mem. N.Y.C. Mayor's Adv. Coun. Motion Pictures, Radio and TV. Producer, dir., host: program Living Opera, Stas. WNYC/WNYC-FM, N.Y.C., 1958-68; host radio broadcasts, N.Y.C. Opera Co., 1978-80; exec. producer (film) Reunion at Fairborough, 1985; producer (TV pilot) We're Puttin'on the Ritz, 1986; author: Prima Donnas and Other Wild Beasts, 1961; exec. cons. The Gunfighters, Diamonds; supervising producer Cop Talk: Behind the Shield, 1988, 89, True Blue, TV movie and series, 1989, A Family for Joe, TV movie and series, 1989-90; TV series Counterstrike, 1990—, Top Cops, 1990—. Lt. (j.g.) USNR, 1953-57. Recipient Evelyn Burkey Meml. award Writers Guild Am., 1983. Mem. Am. Arbitration Assn., NATAS (bd. govs. N.Y. chpt.), Internat. Radio and TV Soc., Acad. of Cable Programming, Columbia Coll. Alumni Assn., Columbia Coll. Grad. Faculty Alumni Assn. Office: Boardwalk Entertainment 210 E 39th St New York NY 10016-0911

WAGNER, ALLAN RAY, psychology educator, experimental psychologist; b. Springfield, Ill., Jan. 6, 1934; s. Raymond August and Grace (Johnson) W.; m. Barbara Rae Meland, Nov. 21, 1959; children: Krystn Rae, Kathryn Rae. B.A., U. Iowa, 1956, M.A., 1958, Ph.D., 1959; M.A. hon., Yale U., 1970. Asst. prof. psychology Yale U., New Haven, 1959-64, assoc. prof., 1964-69, prof., 1970-89, chmn. psychology dept., 1983-89, James Rowland Angell prof. psychology, 1990—, chmn. philosophy dept., 1991—; cons. NIMH, 1968-71; mem. Pres. Biomed. Research Panel, 1975-76; adv. bd. Cambridge Ctr. Behavioral Studies, 1982—; mem. psychobiology panel NSF, 1984-85, com. on basic research in behavioral and social scis. NRC, 1984-87. Author: Reward and Punishment, 1965; assoc. editor: Learning and Motivation, 1969-74, Animal Learning and Behavior, 1972-74; editor: Jour. Exptl. Psychology, 1974-81, Quantitative Analyses of Behavior, Vol. 3, 1982, Vol. 4, 1983, Vol. 7, 1988. Fellow NSF, 1958 (grantee 1960—, recipient NIMH, 1963. Fellow Am. Psychol. Assn., AAAS (mem. council 1988-91); mem. Soc. Exptl. Psychologists, Am. Psychol. Soc., Psychonomic Soc., So. Quantitative Analysis of Behavior (sec. 1983—), Eastern Psychol. Assn. (bd. dirs. 1985-88), Sigma Xi. Club: New Haven Lawn. Home: 1405 Ridge Rd North Haven CT 06473-3051 Office: Yale U Psychology Dept New Haven CT 06520

WAGNER, CECILIA LOUISE, finance educator, consultant, researcher; b. Agana, Guam, Feb. 5, 1958; d. Carl M. and Gabrielle E. (Blong) W. BA in Polit. Sci., SUNY, Brockport, 1979; MBA in Fin., Seton Hall U., 1983; PhD in Internat. Bus., U. Internat. Bus. and Econs., Beijing, 1988. Acct. Congoleum Corp., Kearny, N.J., 1981; instr. fin. Seton Hall U., South Orange, N.J., 1984-85, asst. prof., 1985-91, assoc. prof., 1991—; cons. on microcomputers and fin. to AT&T, World Trade Inst., PSE&G, N.J. Soc. CPA's, also others, 1983—; presenter in field; vis. prof. U. Internat. Bus. and Econs., 1986, 87-88. Contbr. articles to profl. jours. Vol. St. Barnabas Med. Ctr., Livingston, N.J., 1989—. Grantee Ctr. for Internat. Bus. Edn. and Rsch., U. So. Calif., 1991. Mem. Internat. Trade and Fin. Assn., Assn. for Third World Studies, Fin. Mgmt. Assn., Acad. Internat. Bus., Assn. for Internat. Bus. Risk Mgmt., Assn. for Conflict Mgmt. Democrat. Office: Seton Hall U Fin Dept South Orange NJ 07079

WAGNER, DAVID, social scientist; b. Bklyn., Jan. 31, 1950; s. Sam and Sylvia (Goldberg) W.; m. Marcia B. Cohen, Aug. 5, 1980. BA, Columbia U., 1972, MS in Social Work, 1976; MA in Labor Studies, U. Mass., 1980; PhD in Sociology, CUNY, 1988. Lectr., asst. dir. field work Columbia U. Sch. Social Work, N.Y.C., 1985-88; asst. prof. social welfare U. So. Maine, Portland, 1988—. Author: The Quest for a Radical Profession: Social Service Careers and Political Ideology, 1990; contbr. articles to profl. jours. Mem. Am. Sociol.Assn., Soc. for the Study of Social Problems, NASW, Coun. on Social Work Edn., Bertha Capen Reynolds Soc. Home: 14 Clinton St Portland ME 04103-3206 Office: U So Maine 96 Falmouth St Portland ME 04103-4899

WAGNER, DENNIS LARRY, engineering project management professional; b. Ft. Dodge, Iowa, Aug. 8, 1940; s. Walter and Dorothy Althea (Oleson) W.; m. Nancy Mae Szeluga, Aug. 11, 1962; children: Jeffrey Todd, Christopher Jon, Lori Carol. BS in Physics, BA in Math., U. Kans., 1965; postgrad., U. Idaho, Idaho Falls, 1970-71. Cert. project management professional. Enlisted USN, 1958, commd. ensign, 1965, advanced through grades to lt. comdr., 1974; mgr. tng. nuclear power tng. unit Idaho Falls, 1970-72; submarine engr. officer New London, Conn., 1973-76; material officer submarine div. Yokosuka, Japan, 1976-78; ret. USN, 1978; asst. project mgr. Stone & Webster Engring. Corp., Boston, 1978-80, asst. div. mgr., 1981-83, div. mgr., 1984-88, project mgr., 1988—. Vestry mem., with fund raising, planning coms., mem. choir Ch. of the Good Shepherd, Reading, Mass., 1980—; loaned exec. United Way, 1989. Mem. Project Mgmt. Inst. (bd. dirs. local chpt. 1986, panel mem. jour. 1987). Republican. Episcopalian. Club: Quannopowitt Yacht (Wakefield, Mass.) (rear commodore 1985). Home: 192 Woburn St Reading MA 01867-3560 Office: Stone & Webster Engring Corp 245 Summer St Boston MA 02210-1116

WAGNER, ERIC GERHARDT, mathematician, researcher; b. Ossining, N.Y., Oct. 1, 1931; s. Gerdt August and Charlotte (Candee) W.; m. Miriam Elizabeth Linnevold, June 3, 1960; children: Benjamin, Matthew, Elizabeth. BA, Harvard U., 1953; MA, Columbia U., 1959, PhD, 1963. Assoc. engr. IBM, Poughkeepsie, N.Y., 1953-61; mem. rsch. staff IBM Rsch., Yorktown Heights, N.Y., 1961—; adj. asst. prof. NYU, N.Y.C., 1965-66; sr. vis. rsch. fellow U. London, 1973-74; vis. scholar U. Sydney, Australia, 1991. Mem. editorial bd. Math. Structures in Computer Sci., 1989; also articles and chpt. to book; patentee in field. Committeeman Putnam County (N.Y.) Dem. Com., 1967-71; scoutmaster troop 4, Boy Scouts Am., Garrison, N.Y., 1979—; chmn. Garrison Art Ctr., 1983—. With U.S. Army, 1954-56. Mem. Am. Math. Soc., Assn. for Symbolic Logic, Assn. for Computing Machinery. Home: Old Albany Post Rd Garrison NY 10524 Office: IBM Rsch PO Box 218 Yorktown Heights NY 10598-0218

WAGNER, HERMAN LEON, chemist consultant; b. N.Y.C., Mar. 21, 1921; s. Max and Regina (Hahn) W.; m. Jean, June 20, 1954 (dec. 1976); 1 child, Nancy; m. Elaine Janet Feinberg, Sept. 14, 1986. BS, CCNY, 1942; MS, Bklyn. Poly., 1946; PhD, Cornell U., 1950. Rsch. chemist E.I. du Pont, Phila., 1951-55, MW Kellogg Co., Jersey City, 1955-57, Celanese Corp., Summit, N.J., 1957-68, Nat. Bur. Standards, Gaithersburg, Md., 1968-87, Atlantic Rsch. Corp., Alexandria, Va., 1987-91. Contbr. articles to Jour. Phys. and Colloid Chemistry, Jour. Am. Chem. Soc., SPE Transactions, Makromol. Chem., Jour. Applied Polymer Sci., Jour. Macromolecular Sci. Physics, Jour. Polymer Sci., Jour. Rsch. NBS; author: (with others) Polymer Molecular Weight Methods, 1973. Mem. Am. Chem. Soc., Phi Beta Kappa, Sigma Xi. Home: 12038 Gatewater Dr Rockville MD 20854-2876

WAGNER, MARK TODD, psychologist, researcher; b. Evanston, Ill., Feb. 26, 1953; s. Charles Kay and Margie (Elias) W.; m. Carol Lynn Cusson, Sept. 8, 1990. BA, Met. State Coll., 1976; MA, U. of the Pacific, 1980; PhD, Memphis State U., 1985. Lic. psychologist, N.Y. Teaching fellow Boston U., 1986; sr. instr. U. Rochester, N.Y., 1986-87, asst. prof., 1987—; neuropsychologist Monroe Community Hosp., Rochester, 1986—. Contbr. articles on brain functions to profl. jours. and chpts. to books. Program dir. Stroke Support Group, Rochester, 1988—. Mem. Am. Psychol. Assn., Internat. Neuropsychol. Soc., Nat. Acad. Neuropshychologists, Am. Congress Rehab. Medicine. Office: Monroe Community Hosp Rehab Unit 435 E Henrietta Rd Rochester NY 14620-4684

WAGNER, NORBERT, water utility executive; b. Bklyn., May 20, 1935; s. Nicholas and Elsa (Stutz) W.; m. Carol Jean Klauer, July 7, 1962; children: Elizabeth, Catherine, Margaret. BA, Columbia U., 1957, BSCE, 1958. Registered profl. engr., N.J. Staff engr. Bklyn. Union Gas, 1961-63, Elizabethtown Water, Elizabeth, N.J., 1963-66; supt. Elizabethtown Water, Plainfield, N.J., 1966-70, dir. T & D, 1970-78, chief engr. ops., 1978-87, v.p. ops., 1987—; bd. dirs. N.J. One Number to Call. Lt. USN, 1958-61. Mem. NSPE (Union County chpt. pres. 1975-76), Am. Water Works Assn., N.J. Water Resources Assn. (pres. 1977-78), North Jersey Water Conf. (pres. 1974-75), Rotary (Plainfield club pres. 1976-77). Office: Elizabethtown Water Co 1341 North Ave Plainfield NJ 07062-1781

WAGNER, PETER EWING, academic administrator; b. Ann Arbor, Mich., July 4, 1929; s. Paul Clark and Charlotta Josephine (Ewing) W.; m. Caryl Jean Veon, June 23, 1951; children—Ann Frances, Stephen Charles. Student, Occidental Coll., 1946-48; A.B. (with honors), U. Calif. at Berkeley, 1950; Ph.D., U. Calif., Berkeley, 1956. Teaching, research asst. U. Calif., 1950-56; research physicist Westinghouse Research Labs., Pitts., 1956-59; asso. prof. elec. engring. Johns Hopkins, 1960-65, prof., 1965-73; dir. U. Md. Center for Environ. and Estuarine Studies, 1973-80, prof., 1973-81; vis. prof. physics U. Ala., Huntsville, 1980-81, prof., 1981; vice chancellor for acad. affairs, prof. physics U. Miss., 1981-84; provost, prof. physics and elec. engring. Utah State U., 1984-89; v.p. acad. affairs, provost, prof. physics and elec. engring. SUNY, Binghamton, 1989—; spl. projects engr., State of Md., 1971-72; mem. Gov.'s Sci. Adv. Council, 1973-77, Md. Power Plant Siting Advisory Com., 1972-80; cons. in field. Contbr. articles to profl. jours. Trustee Chesapeake Research Consortium, 1974-80, chmn. bd. trustees, 1979-80. Guggenheim fellow Oxford U., 1966-67. Mem. Nat. Assn. State Univs. and Land Grant Colls. (coun. acad. affairs, affirmative action com. 1986-89, chmn. nominating com. 1988-89, chmn. libr. commn. 1989—), Ctr. Rsch. Librs. (bd. dirs. 1991—, budget and fin. com. 1991—), Cosmos Club, Blue Key, Gold Key, Phi Beta Kappa Assocs., Sigma Xi, Phi Kappa Phi, Sigma Alpha Epsilon. Home: 705 Marian Dr Johnson City NY 13790-9621

WAGNER, ROBIN L., science research executive; b. Pitts., Apr. 4, 1959; d. John Oliver and Dolores Jean (Stepp) W. BS in Biology, Westminster Coll., 1982. Rsch. technician dept. otolaryngology Eye and Ear Hosp., Pitts., 1982-83, rsch. asst., 1983-86; rsch. coor. Eye and Ear Inst. of Pitts., 1986-91, rsch. mgr., 1991—. Author: (with others) chpts. in profl. books; contbr. articles to profl. jours.; lectr. in field. Mem. AAAS, Am. Diopter and Decibel Soc. (adminstrv. coord 1990—), Otolaryngology Alumni Assn. (adminstrv. coord. 1985—). Office: Eye and Ear Inst Dept of Otolaryngology 203 Lothrop St Pittsburgh PA 15213-2588

WAGNER, ROBIN SAMUEL ANTON, stage and set designer; b. San Francisco, Aug. 31, 1933; s. Jens Otto and Phyllis Edna (Smith-Spurgeon) W.; children: Kurt, Leslie, Christie. Student, Calif. Sch. Fine Arts, 1953-54. Pres. Scarab Prodns., Inc., 1975-92; prof. theatre arts Columbia U., 1988-92; sr. v.p. The Design Edge, 1989-92. Designer on Broadway, including Crazy for You, Jelly's Last Jam, City of Angels, Jerome Robbins's Broadway, Teddy and Alice, Chess, Song and Dance, Merlin, Dreamgirls, 42nd Street, A Chorus Line, On the Twentieth Century, Ballroom, Mack and Mabel, Seesaw, Sugar, Jesus Christ Superstar, The Great White Hope, Promises, Promises, Lenny, Inner City, Hair; designer off Broadway, including: Hamlet 90, In White America, View from the Bridge, Mahogony, The Prodigal, Between Two Thieves, Cages; designer regional theatres including Pub Theatre, N.Y., Arena Stage, Washington, Actor's Workshop, San Francisco, Met Opera, San Francisco Ballet, Am. Ballet Theatre, Am. Shakespeare Festival, Eliot Feld Ballet, N.Y. Shakespeare Festival, Ensemble Studio Theater, N.Y., N.Y.C. Ballet, Vienna State Opera, Hamburg State Opera, Royal Opera, Covent Garden, Rolling Stones Tour of Ams., 1975, (London prodns.) Chess, 42d Street, A Chorus Line, Promises, Promises, Hair. Mem. adv. bd. Nat. Corp. Theatre Fund, Theatre Adv. Coun. for City of N.Y.; mem. art adv. com. N.Y. Internat. Festival of the Arts; bd. trustees N.Y. Shakespeare Festival. Recipient Antoinette Perry (Tony) award for On the Twentieth Century, 1978, City of Angels, 1990, also numerous nominations; Drama Desk award, 1971, 78, 82, 90, Theatre World award, 1975, Outer Circle Critics award, 1978, 90, 92, Maharam award, 1973, 75, 82, Lumen award, 1975, Dramalogue award, 1980, Boston Critics Circle award, 1983, L.A. Drama Critics Circle award, 1974, 92, award for excellence in theatre Ensemble Studio Theatre, 1990. Mem. United Scenic Artists. Office: Robin Wagner Studio 890 Broadway New York NY 10003-1211

WAGNER, RONALD FRANCIS VINCENT, interior designer; b. Buffalo, June 8, 1952; s. Stephen Stanley and Florence Helen (Buczkowski) W. BFA in Environ. Design, Pratt Inst., Bklyn., 1975; student, SUNY, Buffalo, 1970-72. Jr. designer Johnson, Hehr, Nehin, Inc., Buffalo, 1975-76; project designer Swanke, Hayden, Connell, N.Y.C., 1976-79; sr. designer GN Assocs., Inc., N.Y.C., 1979-83; prin. Ron Wagner Design, N.Y.C., 1983—; assoc. prof. Pratt Inst., Bklyn., 1984-90; guest critic Parsons Sch. Design, 1985. Contbr. articles to profl. jours. Sec. Hamilton Heights Homeowners Assn., 1987. Mem. Am. Soc. Interior Designers (profl. mem.), Nat. Trust for Hist. Preservation, Mcpl. Art Soc. N.Y., Soc. Archtl. Historians. Democrat. Home: 471 W 143d St New York NY 10031 Office: 853 Broadway Ste 606 New York NY 10003-4703

WAGNER, STERLING ROBACKER, forest products company executive; b. Pocono Lake, Pa., Dec. 2, 1904; s. George Edward and Eva (Robacker) W.; m. Alice Vernoy Roberts, June 30, 1930. BS, Syracuse U., 1927, M.Landscape Engring., 1930. Instr. N.Y. State Coll. Forestry, Syracuse U., Syracuse, N.Y., 1929-36; landscape architect U.S. Dept. Agr., Resettlement Adminstrn., New Haven, 1937; asst. prof. N.Y. State Coll. Forestry, 1938-40; mgr. Wagners Tree Farm, Pocono Lake, Pa., 1941-47; pres. Wagners Forest Products, Inc., Pocono Lake, 1947—; adv. bd. Franklin First Fed. Savs. and Loan Assn. Stroudsburg, Pa., 1969-87. Chmn. Tobyhanna Twp. Planning Commn., Pocono Pines, 1964-86; mem. Monroe County Planning Commn., Stroudsburg, 1980-84. Mem. Pocono Forestry Assn., Pa. Forestry Assn., Soc. Am. Foresters, Lions. Democrat. Home and Office: Star Rte Box 107 Pocono Lake PA 18347

WAGNER, SUSAN JANE, communications executive; b. Englewood, N.J., Aug. 11; d. Jules A. and Florence I. (Froeba) W.; m. Mark E. McKenna, May 4, 1984. MusB with honors, Syracuse U., 1974; MPA with honors, Fairleigh Dickinson U., 1983. Dir. music, theater dependant sch. U.S. Dept. Def., Fed. Republic Germany, 1976-82; grad. asst. Fairleigh Dickinson U., Rutherford, N.J., 1982-83; account exec. Katz Radio/Katz Communications, Inc., N.Y.C., 1983-85; account mgr. network Katz Radio Group, N.Y.C., 1985-87, v.p., dir. mktg., 1987-90, sr. v.p. dir.mktg., 1990-91; v.p. corp. mktg. Katz Communications, Inc., N.Y.C., 1992—. Mem. Am. Women in Radio and TV, Electronic Media Mktg. Assn., Am. Mktg. Assn., Promotion Mktg. Assn. Am., Broadcast Promotion Mktg. Execs., Sigma Alpha Iota, Gamma Phi Beta. Office: Katz Comm Inc 125 W 55th St New York NY 10019-5366

WAGNER, WAYNE ELWELL, small business owner; b. Brockport, N.Y., Oct. 12, 1938; s. Anthony and Edythe W.; m. Linda Paap; children: Belinda, Wendy, Nancy, Patricia, Susan. BA, U. Pa., 1960. Bd. officer Marine Midland, Buffalo, 1960-68; exec. officer Schenectady (N.Y.) Trust, 1968-75; pres., chief exec. officer Galesi Group, Albany, N.Y., 1976-86; owner various small bus., Scotia, N.Y., 1986—; bd. dirs. numerous corps. Bd. dirs. SUNY, Albany, 1971-81; Rep. candidate for U.S. Cong. Served to capt. U.S. Army, 1960-61. Methodist. Clubs: The Mohawk, The Buffalo.

WAGSTAFF, MARK CLELAND, educational association administrator; b. Lexington, N.C., Feb. 26, 1959; s. Lewis Jackson and Kay (Beatty) W. BS in Parks and Recreation Adminstrn., N.C. State U., 1981, MS, 1988. Guide, river mgr. Wildwater Ltd., Long Creek, S.C., 1981-83, 87; instr. Outward Bound, Morganton, N.C., 1988, 89; exec. dir. Wilderness Edn. Assn., Saranac Lake, N.Y., 1989—; curriculum adviser recreation dept. Slippery Rock (Pa.) U., 1990—; bd. dirs. Augsburg Inst., Potsdam, N.Y.; outdoor edn. cons. Am. Mus. Natural History, N.Y.C., 1991, 92. Contbr. to profl. publs. Mem. Phi Kappa Phi. Office: Wilderness Edn Assn 20 Winona St Box 89 Saranac Lake NY 12983

WAHBY, VICTOR SAMUEL, physician, educator, researcher; b. Alexandria, Egypt, July 8, 1945; came to U.S, 1976; s. Samuel Hobby and Angela Linda (Chafik) W.; m. Susan Todd Nash, Dec. 4, 1984 (div. Mar. 1989); 1 child, William Samuel. MB, ChB, Alexandria Med. Sch., 1966, Med. Dip., 1970; PhD in Biochemistry, Am. U., Beirut, Lebanon, 1976. Cert. med. dr. Intern Alexandria U. Hosp., Egypt, 1967; resident, fellow in endocrinology Mayo Clinic, Rochester, Minn., 1977-80; asst. prof. Yale Med. Sch., New Haven, 1981-85; assoc. dir. of psychoendocrine lab. VA Med. Ctr., West Haven, Conn., 1981-85; assoc. chief of staff VA Med. Ctr., North Chicago, Ill., 1985-89, dir. psychoendocrine and obesity rsch. lab., 1989-91; assoc. prof. Chgo. Med. Sch., North Chicago, Ill., 1985-91; prof. Chgo. Med. Sch., North Chicago, 1992—; dep. dir. med. and dental edn. VA Cen. Office, Washington, 1989-92; assoc. prof. George Washington Med. Sch., Washington, 1989-92; cons. Am. Assn. World Health, Washington, 1991; lect. various profl. assns. Contbr. articles to profl. jours. Program dir. Dept. Veterans Affairs Benefit for Homeless Veterans, 1990-91. Recipient award of distinction U.S. Mission to UN, N.Y.C., 1984, rsch. award, 1983, Dairy Bur. Can., 1985-89, spl. recognition award Office Nat. Svc., White House, Washington, 1991. Mem. Soc. Neurosci., Endocrine Soc., Am. Coll. Physicians, Am. Diabetes Assn., Am. Fedn. Clin. Rsch., Internat. Soc. Psychoneuroendocrinolgy, Soc. Biol. Psychiatry, N.Am. Soc. for Study of Obesity, Am. U. Beirut Alumni Assn., Mayo Alumni Assn.

WAHL, KEITH ANDREW, national sales trainer; b. Buffalo, May 27, 1959; s. Richard C. and Shirley J. (Riedel) W.; m. Sara Jean Willoughby, June 13, 1987; children: Holly Christine, Kyle David. Pres. Hein-Wahl Woodworking, Bowmansville, N.Y., 1975-78, Advanced Security Systems, Amherst, N.Y., 1978-80, Excellence Through Sales, Columbia, Md., 1980—; seminar speaker Excellence Through Sales, Columbia, 1980—. Author: Sales Survival in the 90s. Mem. Meth. Ch., Savage, Md., 1991. Republican. Home: 9308 Spring Water Path Jessup MD 20794 Office: Excellence Through Sales 9308 Spring Water Path Jessup MD 20794

WAHL, SHARON MARIE, immunologist; b. Mt. Vernon, Wash., Mar. 16, 1945; d. Leonard A. and Clara Marie (Soine) Knudson; m. Larry Marion Wahl, Dec. 26, 1971; children: Allison Marie, Christopher Loren. BS, Pacific Luth. U., 1967; PhD, U. Wash., 1971. Postdoctoral fellow dept. pathology U. Wash., Seattle, 1971-72; postdoctoral fellow lab. micro and immunology NIDR NIH, Bethesda, 1972-74, staff fellow, 1974-76, sr. staff fellow, 1974-76, rsch. microbiologist humoral immunology, 1976-83, chief cellular immunology, 1983—; project officer George Washington U. NIH, Bethesda, 1991—. Contbr. chpts. to books and articles to profl. jours.; mem. editorial bd.: Jour. Immunology, 1983-87. Recipient Holley Rsch. prize in Rheumatology U. Ala., 1990, Dirs. award NIH, 1985, USPHS Superior Svc. award, 1992; grantee NIH, 1989-90, Seragen, Hopkinton, Mass., 1989-90, Upjohn, Kalamazoo, 1991. Mem. AAAS, Am. Assn. Immunologists, Am. Fedn. for Clin. Rsch. Lutheran. Office: Cellular Immunology NIDR Bldg 30 Rm 331 Bethesda MD 20892

WAHL, STEVEN ALAN, podiatric physician and surgeon; b. Jersey City, Mar. 27, 1953; s. Harold Irving and Libby Rose (Stiskin) W.; 1 child, Meredith Hope; m. Jordanna Kyle Lenter, Feb. 2, 1990. BS in Biology, Upsala Coll., 1975; BS in Podiatry, Ill. Coll. Podiatric Medicine, 1979, D Podiatric Medicine, 1979. Diplomate Nat. Bd. Podiatry Examiners; lic. podiatrist, N.J., Pa. With Ill. Coll. Podiatric Medicine Clinic, Chgo., 1976-78, 78; podiatrist Mt. Sinai Hosp., Englewood Health Ctr., Henrotin Hosp., Chgo., 1978—; asst. chief resident dept. surgery div. podiatry Coney Island Hosp., Bklyn., 1979-80; pvt. practice, Paterson, N.J., 1980-81, Englewood, N.J., 1980-81, Millburn, N.J., 1981—; clin. instr., attending podiatry staff, asst. chief dept. St. Michael's Med. Ctr., Newark, 1987—; mem. adj. clin. faculty Pa. Coll. Podiatric Medicine, Phila.; mem. exec. com. div. podiatry West Essex Gen. Hosp., Livingston, N.J., 1983-88; attending podiatry staff Roseland (N.J.) Surg. Ctr.; former attending Irvington Gen., South Bergen, No. Community, Bergen Pines, Barnet hosps.; former editorial cons. Current Podiatry; former cons. Wood Crest Ctr. Nursing Home, Camp Nejeda. Podiatric screener Health Fair, Millburn and Maplewood Twps., 1981—. Fellow Am. Soc. Podiatric Medicine, Am. Acad. Podiatric Microsurgery (charter), Am. Assn. Hosp. Podiatrists; mem. APHA, Am. Podiatric Med. Assn., Am. Coll. Podopediatrics (assoc.), Am. Acad. Podiatric Sports Medicine (assoc.), N.J. Podiatric Med. Soc. (ho. of dels. ea. div. 1982-85, pres. 1984-85), N.J. Pub. Health Assn., Am. Physicians Fellowship for Medicine in Israel, N.Y. Acad. Scis., Ill. Coll. Podiatric Medicine Alumni Assn., Upsala Coll. Alumni Assn., Nat. Honor Soc., Beta Beta Beta. Office: 120 Millburn Ave Ste 205 Millburn NJ 07041-1935

WAHL, WILLIAM JOSEPH, JR., informatin systems specialist; b. Pottsville, Pa., Jan. 19, 1947; s. William Joseph and Edith (Adams) W.; m. Mary Ellen Trautman, Oct. 17, 1964; children: Patricia Marie, William Joseph III, Monica Marie, Michael Anthony. MS in Bus. Policy, Columbia U., 1983. Mgr. bus. systems planning IBM Gen. Bus. Group Internat., White Plains, N.Y., 1977-78, dir. info systems, 1979-81; dir. info. systems programs IBM Corp. Hdqrs., White Plains, N.Y., 1982; dir. info. systems IBM Systems Products Div., White Plains, N.Y., 1983, IBM Info. Systems and Communications Group, White Plains, N.Y., 1984; group dir. mgmt. control systems IBM Info. Systems and Tech. Group, Harrison, N.Y., 1985-87; group dir. info. systems and telecommunications IBM Enterprise Systems, Somers, N.Y., 1988-92; group dir. info. architecture IBM Personal Systems, Somers, N.Y., 1992—; rsch. affiliate NYU Stern Sch. Bus., N.Y.C., 1991—; ops. mgmt. advisor Columbia Grad. Sch. Bus., N.Y.C., 1988-90. Mem. Beta Gamma Sigma. Home: 36 Pleasant Hill Rd Hopewell Junction NY 12533 Office: IBM PO Box 100 Rte 100 Somers NY 10589

WAHLBERG, ALLEN HENRY, construction executive; b. Stockholm, Sweden, May 12, 1933; s. Allan H. and Oda J. Wahlberg; m. Barbara Bogert, June 16, 1962; children: Susan, Andrew. BS, MIT, 1956. Cost engr. Turner Constrn. Co., N.Y.C., 1966-69, chief cost engr., 1969-70, asst. treas., 1970-73, controller, 1973—, v.p., 1980-91, chief fin. officer, 1985-91, sr. v.p. and chief fin. officer, 1991—; pres., treas. The Turner Constrn. Co. Found., N.Y.C., 1980—. Mem. City Council and Planning Bd., Ho-Ho-Kus, N.J. Served with U.S. Army C.E., 1957-59. Mem. Fin. Execs. Inst., Am. Mgmt. Assn., The Conf. Bd., Nat. Assn. Accts., MIT Alumni Ctr. N.Y., Econ. Club N.Y. Republican. Clubs: Barnegat Light Yacht (Harvey Cedars, N.J.) (commodore 1987-88); Ridgewood (N.J.) Country. Office: The Turner Corp 375 Hudson St New York NY 10014-3658

WAHMAN, THOMAS WALTER, foundation director; b. St. Paul, Feb. 1, 1938; s. Walton Egin Samuel and Helen Margaret (Johnson) W.; m. Susan Pillsbury Tabor, Sept. 8, 1962; children: Jessica, Gwendolyn. BA, Dartmouth Coll., 1960; MDiv, Union Theol. Sem., 1964. Coord. religious and civil rights activities NYU, 1964-66; asst. dir. N.Y. Found., 1966-68; program assoc. Rockefeller Bros. Fund, N.Y.C., 1968-79; pres. Tabor-Wahman, Ltd., N.Y.C., 1979-90; pres., mng. dir. Resources Devel. Found., N.Y.C., 1989—; bd. dirs. Biomass Users Network, Washington, 1987—, Internat. Svc. for Agri-Biotech Acquisitions and Applications, Ithaca, N.Y., 1991—. Mem. Dartmouth Club. Office: Resources Devel Found 8 W 40th St Rm 1105 New York NY 10018

WAHRAHAFTIG, PAUL, mediator. AB with honors in Polit. Sci., Stanford U., 1960; JD, U. Calif., Berkeley, 1963. Bar: Calif. 1964, Pa. 1970. Atty. McKee, Tasheira & Wahrhaftig, Oakland, Calif., 1964-65; vol. Am. Friends Svc. Com., 1965; program sec. Am. Friends Svc. Com., Pitts., 1969-80; assoc. field sec. Ga. Coun. on Human Rels., Atlanta, 1966-68; asst. dir. Anti-Defamation League of B'nai B'rith, Atlanta and Houston, 1968-69; ptnr. Divorce and Separation Mediation Ctr., Pitts., 1981—; pres. Conflict Resolution Ctr., Internat., Pitts., 1981—; guest lectr. U. Pitts., 1986—; lectr. in field. Author: (with Hizkias Assefa) Extremist Groups and Conflict Resolution: The MOVE Crisis in Philadelphia, 1988; editor: Conflict Resolution Notes, 1981; contbr. articles to profl. jours. Bd. dirs. Pitts. Mediation Ctr., 1981-90, Nat. Conf. on Peacemaking and Conflict Resolution, 1989—, chair, 1991—; mem. Commn. on Qualifications of Soc. of Profls. in Dispute Resolution, 1988-89; pres. Family Mediation Coun. of Western Pa., 1988-89. Mem. Acad. Family Mediators (practitioner membership status, bd. dirs. 1989-91), Pa. Coun. Mediators (co-chair 1988-90), Nat. Assn. Community Justice (bd. dirs. 1985-89). Office: 7514 Kensington St Pittsburgh PA 15221

WAINGER, ALLEN JAY, civil engineering company executive, consultant; b. Bloomsburg, Pa., Nov. 22, 1953; s. Pierson Weldon and Gertrude Bessie (Sherman) W.; m. Sherry Mim Poskanzer, Aug. 17, 1980; children: Robert James, Jeffrey Mark. BS, Lehigh U., 1975; MS, U. Md., 1981. Registered profl. engr., Va. Project engr. Michael Baker Jr. Inc., Harrisburg, Pa., 1975-77; project engr. Greenhorne & O'Mara Inc., Greenbelt, Md., 1977-79, sr. project engr., 1979-81, sr. earth scientist, 1981-84, dept. head computer aided design and drafting, 1984-89, mgr. computer engring. systems, 1989-90; div. mgr. GIS/Mapping, Greenbelt, Md., 1990—; cons. Howard County Community Coll., Columbia, Md., 1987-89. Co-recipient Engring. Excellence award for Md., Am. Cons. Engrs. Coun., 1987. Mem. Mid-Atlantic Region Intergraph Users Group (vice chmn. 1986-88, chmn. 1988-90, residential archtl. com. 1989—), Balt. Garden Club, Culinary Connection. Republican. Jewish. Home: 6033 Watch Chain Way Columbia MD 21044-4714 Office: Greenhorne & O'Mara Inc 9001 Edmonston Rd Greenbelt MD 20770

WAISMAN, JERRY, pathologist, educator; b. Borger, Tex., Sept. 14, 1934; s. Sammie and Lillie W.; m. Jane B. Atkins, June 15, 1958 (div. 1985); children: Eric A., Nina A. A., John C.; m. Lenore V. Gale, Mar. 24, 1990. BA, U. Tex., 1956; MD, U. Tex., Galveston, 1960. Diplomate Am. Bd. Pathology. Intern medicine SUNY, Bklyn., 1960-61; resident pathology U. Utah, Salt Lake City, 1961-62, fellow pathology, 1964-66, instr. pathology, 1967-68; asst. prof. to prof. pathology UCLA, L.A., 1968-81; prof. pathology NYU, N.Y.C., 1981—. Contbr. chpts. to books and articles to profl. jours. Capt. USAF, 1962-64. Mem. Am. Soc. Clin. Pathology, Am. Assn. Pathologists, Am. Soc. Cytology, Electron Microscopy Soc. Am., N.Y. Pathol. Soc. (v.p. 1991), N.Y. State Bd. Profl. Med. Conduct, Coll. Anatomical Pathology. Office: NYU Med Ctr Dept Pathology 560 1st Ave New York NY 10016

WAIT, CAROL GRACE COX, organization administrator; b. L.A., Dec. 20, 1942; d. Earl George Atkinson Sr. and Virginia Rose (Clanton) Boggs; m. David L. Edwards (div. 1974); children: Nicole Rose Smith, Alexandra Edwards; m. Gary G. Cox, Jan. 25, 1975 (div. 1982); m. Robert Atwood Wait, July 4, 1991. AA in Pre Law, Cerritos Coll., 1966; AB in History, Whittier Coll., 1969. Probation counselor Los Angeles County Probation Dept., Downey, Calif., 1967-69; corp. sec., mgr. Dennis and Dennis Personnel, Santa Ana, Calif., 1969-71; owner, pres. Cox Edwards & Assocs., Santa Ana, 1971-73; adminstrv. services officer County of Santa Cruz (Calif.), 1973-74; cons. State of Calif., Sacramento, 1974-75; project dir. Nat. Assn. Counties, Washington, 1975-77; legis. dir. U.S. Senate Com. on the Budget, Washington, 1977-81; pres. Com. for a Responsible Budget, Washington, 1981—, Carol Cox & Assocs., Washington, 1984—; cons. to bus. and other orgns. on the fed. budget, the budget process and other econ. issues; writer and speaker on the budget and budget process. Am. participant USIS/Brazilian Senate Symposium on Budget Process, Brazilia, Brazil, 1985—, Ampart speaker on 1990 budget agreement France, Ger., 1990. Named one of 150 Who Make a Difference Nat. Jour., 1986; recipient Nat. Disting. Svc. award Am. Assn. Budget and Program Analysis. Mem. Washington Women's Forum. Republican. Episcopalian. Office: Com for Responsible Fed Budget 22012 E St NE Washington DC 20002-4923

WAIT, CHARLES VALENTINE, banker; b. Albany, N.Y., May 28, 1951; s. Newman Edward Jr. and Jane Caroline (Adams) W.; m. Candace Ellin Hollar, May 27, 1978; children: Charles Valentine Jr., Christopher David, Alexandra Dallas Wait. BA, Cornell U., 1973; cert. in banking, Rutgers U., 1981. Asst. v.p. The Adirondack Trust Co., Saratoga Springs, N.Y., 1974, treas., 1978-81, sec., treas., 1981-84, pres., 1984—, also bd. dirs.; trustee N.Y. State Bankers Retirement System, 1987—, vice chmn., 1990. Trustee Skidmore Coll., Saratoga Springs, 1984—, Nat. Mus. Dance, Saratoga Springs, 1987—, N.Y. Racing Assn., Nat. Mus. Racing, 1988-91, v.p., 1989-91;trustee Chrles R. Wood Found., 1991—; chmn. Saratoga Springs City Ctr. Authority, 1983-89; treas. Saratoga Performing Arts Ctr., 1987, chmn., 1989—. Named Outstanding New Yorker, N.Y. State Jaycees, 1984; recipient Pvt. Sector Initiative award Pres. Ronald Reagan. Mem. Ind. Bankers Assn. of N.Y. State (bd. dirs., sec. 1986-87), N.Y. State Bankers Assn. (bd. dirs. 1987), N.Y. State Bankers Retirement System (trustee 1987—, vice chmn.), Am. Inst. Banking (Counsel of Yr. 1976), Greater Saratoga C. of C., Pillar Soc., Rotary (hon.), Elks. Republican. Home: 658 N Broadway Saratoga Springs NY 12866-1624 Office: The Adirondack Trust Co 473 Broadway Saratoga Springs NY 12866-2251

WAITE, PETER ARTHUR, literacy educator, educational consultant; b. San Mateo, Calif., Jan. 8, 1951; s. James Bishop and Beverly Jane (Petrich) W.; m. Lauren Chapman Singer, Sept. 10, 1977; children: Hillary, Christopher, Hannah. BA, U. Vt., 1973, MEd, 1976; EdD, Seattle U., 1986. Cert. tchr. Tchr. Winooski (Vt.) High Sch., 1972-73; program developer NEA, Washington, 1973-74; coord. Ctr. for Svc. Learning, Burlington, Vt., 1974-76; instr. Champlain Coll., Burlington, 1975-76; exec. dir. Winooski Youth Commn., 1976-79, Wash. Literacy, Inc., Seattle, 1979-82, Laubach Literacy Action, Syracuse, N.Y., 1982—; sr. policy advisor Bus. Coun. for Effective Literacy, N.Y.C., 1982—; bd. dirs. Literacy Network, Mpls., 1987—; mem. exec. com. Nat. Coalition for Literacy, Chgo., 1989—. Author: Handbook for Industry-Literacy, 1986. Del. Seattle Dem. Com., 1981; bd. dirs. Friends of VISTA, Washington, 1986—; founder Concerned Citizens Skaneateles (N.Y.), 1987—. Named Ky. col. State of Ky., 1985, hon. citizen City of Memphis, 1986, San Diego County, 1988; recipient state achievement award State of Okla., 1988. Mem. Assn. for Adult and Continuing Edn., Am. Literacy Assn., Community Edn. Assn., Ind. Sector. Democrat. Episcopalian. Office: Laubach Literacy Internat 1320 Jamesville Ave Syracuse NY 13210

WAITHE, FITZ STEVEN, music company executive; b. Bklyn., July 28, 1966; s. F.H. and Edith (DeLois) W. Grad., Grover Cleveland High Sch., Queens, N.Y., 1984. Pres. Kool Internat. Inc., Bklyn., 1987-88, chairman, chief exec. officer, 1985—; owner Kool Steve Music Pub. Co., Bklyn., 1985—; CEO New Found. Records, Inc., Bklyn., 1985—. With U.S. Army, 1985-88. Democrat. Office: Kool Internat Inc 755 Washington Ave Ste 408 Brooklyn NY 11238-4504

WAITZKIN, STELLA PUMPKIN, artist; b. Bklyn., Nov. 17, 1920; children: Fred, Bill. Student, Salem (N.C.) Coll., 1935, Alfred (N.Y.) U., 1936, NYU, 1937, Columbia U., 1949. Exhibited in group shows at Va. Mus. of Fine Arts, Richmond, 1973, Bronx Mus. of the Arts, 1976, Renwick Gallery of Nat. Mus. of Am. Art, 1977, Dayton (Ohio) Art Inst., 1979, Cleve. Mus. of Art, Jewish Mus., N.Y.C., 1986, Ft. Wayne (Ind.) Mus. of Art, 1988, Barbara Fendrick Gallery, Soho, N.Y., 1990, Peter M. David Gallery, Mpls., 1990, Anita Shapolsky Gallery, Soho, 1990, Book Arts Ctr., N.Y.C., 1990, Le Chateau de Vascoeuil, France, 1990, U.S. Exhbn. Agy., Africa, 1990—, Witkin Gallery, Soho; one-woman shows include James Yu Gallery, N.Y., 1974, 75, Lowenstein Libr. of Fordham U., N.Y.C., 1975, Donnell Libr., N.Y., 1976, Everson Mus. of Art, Syracuse, N.Y., 1983, Creiger Sesen Gallery, Boston, 1984, Galerie Caroline Corre, Paris, 1987; represented in pub. collections Walker Art Ctr., Mpls., N.Y. Pub. Libr., Israel Mus., Jewish Mus., Nat. Mus. Am. Art Smithsonian Instn., Washington, Everson Mus. Fine Art, Va. Mus., Richmond; represented in corp. collections including Phillip Morris, Bectin Dickenson, Dow Jones; commn. by N.Y. Post Office. Mem. N.Y. Artists Equity, Ctr. for Book Arts. Home: Chelsea Hotel 222 W 23d St New York NY 10011 Studio: Music St West Tisbury MA 24575

WAIXEL, VIVIAN, journalist; b. Norfolk, Va., July 22, 1946; d. Julius and Julia (Heimann) W.; m. Steven E. Scharbach, Aug. 24, 1969. BS in Communication, Simmons Coll., 1967; MA in Communication, U. Wis., 1971. Teaching asst. U. Wis., Madison, 1967-69; reporter Wis. State Jour., Madison, 1969-72, The Record, Hackensack, N.J., 1972-74; bus. editor The Record, Hackensack, 1974-76, assignment editor, 1976-86, sports editor, 1986-88, chief news editor, 1988—. Recipient Tribute to Women and Industry award, YWCA, 1976. Jewish. Home: 76 Wilson St Hackensack NJ 07601-2911 Office: The Record 150 River St Hackensack NJ 07601-7110

WAKE, ROBERT ALAN, lawyer; b. Ft. Belvoir, Va.; s. Robert Warner and Esther Jeannette (Schreiber) W.; m. Marcia Greenbaum, July 17, 1977; children: Benjamin Ehren, Koren Alison. BS, MIT, 1974; PhD, Brown U., 1979; JD, Harvard U., 1988. Bar: Maine 1988. Lectr. U. Wis., Milw., 1979-81; asst. prof. U. Maine, Orono, 1981-82, U. Calif., Santa Cruz, 1982-85; law clk. to chief justice Vincent L. McKusick Portland, Maine, 1988-89; asst. atty. gen. State of Maine, Augusta, 1989—. Author poems. Mem. Common Cause, 1980—; vice-chair Maine Dem. Party Rules com. Mem. ABA, Maine Bar Assn., Am. Math. Soc., ACLU, Am. Contract Bridge League. Democrat. Home: 1 Covered Bridge Rd Windham ME 04062-4609 Office: State of Maine Atty Gen State House Sta 6 Augusta ME 04333

WAKEFIELD, JANET RUTH, clinical psychologist; b. Derby, Conn., Nov. 29, 1926; d. George Alexander and Ruth Anna (Hall) W.; m. Donald Gabriel Forgays, Dec. 18, 1948 (div. July 1979); children: Janice Anne, Gabrielle, Ian Wakefield, Donal Hall. BA, Conn. Coll. for Women, New London, 1948; MEd, U. Vt., 1967, PhD, 1979. Lic. psychologist, Vt.; cert. psychologist, N.H. Rsch. asst. dept. psychology McGill U., Montreal, Can., 1949-50, Western Mich. U., Kalamazoo, 1950-51, Cornell U., Ithaca, N.Y., 1953-54; asst. survey dir. dept. interdisciplinary studies Rutgers U., New Brunswick, N.J., 1954-56; psychol. counselor U. Vt., Burlington, 1966-78, rschr. dept. psychiatry, 1979-80; psychologist Psychol. Assoc. Vt., Burlington, 1979-81; chief psychologist No. N.H. Mental Health and Devel. Svcs., Littleton, 1981—; rschr., cons. Weiss Assoc., Montpelier, Vt., 1979; Morrison Nursing Home, Whitefield, N.H., 1988—, Country Village Helath Care Ctr., Lancaster, N.H., 1988—; employee assistance program mem. McKerley's Health Care Ctr., Franconia, N.H., 1988—. Sec. Sugar Hill (N.H.) Improvement Assn., 1984—; civic planting com. White Mt. Garden Club, Sugar Hill, 1989—. Nat. Found. for Infantile Paralysis grantee, 1954. Mem. APA, N.H. Psychol. Orgn. (ethics com. 1981—), Profile Club, Inc., North Country Psychologists Jour. Club (founder). Home: Sugar Hill NH 03585 Office: Whte Mt Mental Health and Devel Svcs 16 Maple St Littleton NH 03561-1108

WAKEFIELD, ROGER EMERSON, electrical engineer; b. Worcester, Mass., Mar. 31, 1948; s. Frederick Wendall and Adelaide (Gerrish) W.; m. Elizabeth Dunbar; children: Carolyn Dunbar, Seth Emerson. BSEE, Brown U., 1971, BA in Econs., 1971; MSEE, Northeastern U., Boston, 1988. Sales engr. Unitrode Corp., Watertown, Mass., 1972-74; design engr. Bendix Corp., Teterboro, N.J., 1974-76; sr. design engr. GE, Wilmington, Mass., 1976-80; sr. prin. engr. Sanders Assn., Nahua, N.H., 1980-86; group leader MITRE Corp., Bedford, Mass., 1986—. Author: Radar Clutter Analysis, 1986, Radar Testing Analysis, 1989. Mem. Parent Tchr. Group. Office: MITRE Burlington Rd Bedford MA 01730

WAKEMAN, OLIVIA VAN HORN, professional society administrator; b. Starkville, Miss.; d. Thomas Oliver and Mary Jeanne (Walker) W. BA in Mgmt., Eckerd Coll., St. Petersburg, Fla., 1980; MIM in Mktg./Advt., Am. Grad. Sch. Internat. Mgmt., 1982. Bus. analyst Dun & Bradstreet, Tampa, Fla., 1980; mgmt. cons. Cardinal Mgmt. Assocs., L.A., 1982-83; asst. account exec. McCann-Erickson, N.Y.C., 1984-86; account exec. Hearst Mag., N.Y.C., 1986-87, Ribaudo & Schaefer, N.Y.C., 1987-88; dir. pub. affairs/bus. soc. and ethics program Carnegie Coun. on Ethics and Internat. Affairs, N.Y.C., 1989—; adult edn. mktg. prof. Touro Coll., N.Y.C., 1989. Reading vol. Vol. Svcs. for Children, N.Y.C., 1991; vol. Habitat for Humanity, N.Y.C., 1991. Episcopalian. Office: Carnegie Coun on Ethics 170 E 64th St New York NY 10021-7496

WALBRIDGE, WILLIAM MARK, accountant; b. Schenectady, N.Y., June 28, 1957; s. LeRoy T. and Claire (Tracy) W.; m. Lisa Ann Traver, Feb. 14, 1981; children: Bradley, Rachael. BS in Acctg., Ithaca Coll., 1980; MBA in Fin., Russell Sage U., 1991. Ops. auditor, budget analyst Smith Corona Corp., Cortland, N.Y., 1980-82; asst. contr. St. Mary's Hosp., Amsterdam, N.Y., 1982-86; asst. bus. adminstr. Saratoga Springs (N.Y.) City Schs., 1986-89; mgr. acctg. Glens Falls (N.Y.) Hosp., 1989—. Mem. Rotary, Saratoga County C. of C. (amb. 1990—), HFMA (membership com. 1991-92). Republican. Roman Catholic. Home: 19 Conver Dr Saratoga Springs NY 12866 Office: Glens Falls Hosp 100 Park St Glens Falls NY 12801

WALD, BARBARA ANN, computer software consultant, retired; b. Council Bluffs, Iowa, Mar. 9, 1935; d. Leon Shevah and Mildred Gertrude (Meyerson) Frankel; m. Martin Wald, Aug. 3, 1958; children: Leah Wald Zollman, Marcie Sue, Adam David. AB, U. Chgo., 1957. Advt. copywriter Brandeis Dept. Store, Omaha, 1953; tchr. White Plains (N.Y.) Pub. Sch. System, 1957-58, West Allyce (Wis.) Pub. Sch. System, 1958-59, Akiba Jewish Day Sch., Chgo., 1961-64; writing tchr. Drexel U., Phila., 1971-72; owner, cons. Software Supporters, Merion, Pa., 1983-89. Author: Achieving Patient Power: One Family Masters the Medical Maze, 1992; contbr. articles to profl. pubs. Com. chmn. Religious Sch. Main Line Reform Temple, Wynnewood, Pa., 1974-77; active patroler Lower Merion Community Watch, Ardmore, Pa., 1978-87; del. Fedn. Civic Assn., Lower Merion, 1984-91; v.p. Merion Civic Assn., 1984-88; bd. dirs. Smart Family Found., Inc., 1991—. Mem. Ind. Computer Cons., Main Line Women's Bus. Network (charter), Home Based Bus. Profls. (pres. 1987-88), Nat. Better Bus. Bur. (arbitrator 1988—).

WALD, BERNARD JOSEPH, lawyer; b. Bklyn., Sept. 14, 1932; s. Max and Ruth (Mencher) W.; m. Francine Joy Weintraub, Feb. 2, 1964; children—David Evan, Kevin Mitchell. B.B.A. magna cum laude, CCNY; J.D. cum laude, NYU, 1955. Bar: N.Y. 1955, U.S. Dist. Ct. (so. dist.) N.Y. 1960, U.S. Dist. Ct. (ea. dist.) N.Y. 1960, U.S. Ct. Appeals (2d cir.) 1960, U.S. Supreme Ct. 1971. Mem. Herzfeld & Rubin, P.C. and predecessor firms, N.Y.C., 1955—. Mem. ABA, N.Y. State Bar Assn., Assn. Bar City N.Y., N.Y. County Lawyers Assn. Office: 40 Wall St New York NY 10005-1303

WALD, FRANCINE JOY WEINTRAUB (MRS. BERNARD J. WALD), physicist; b. Bklyn., Jan. 13, 1938; d. Irving and Minnie (Reisig) Weintraub; student Bklyn. Coll., 1955-57; B.E.E., CCNY, 1960; M.S., Poly. Inst. Bklyn., 1962, Ph.D., 1969; m. Bernard J. Wald, Feb. 2, 1964; children—David Evan, Kevin Mitchell. Engr., Remington Rand Univac div. Sperry Rand Corp., Phila., 1960; instr. Poly. Inst. Bklyn., 1962-64, adj. research asso., 1969-70; lectr. N.Y. Community Coll., Bklyn., 1969, 70; instr. sci. Friends Sem., N.Y.C., 1975-76, chmn. dept. sci., 1976—. NDEA fellow, 1962-64. Mem. Am. Phys. Soc., Am. Assn. Physics Tchrs., Assn. Tchrs. in Ind. Schs., N.Y. Acad. Scis., Nat. Sci. Tchrs. Assn., AAAS, Sigma Xi, Tau Beta Pi, Eta Kappa Nu.

WALD, MARY S., risk management and personal finance educator; b. Baker, Oreg., June 17, 1943; d. Paul H. and Mary Elsie (Bartshe) Stoner; m. Lance Albert Wald, June 22, 1968. BA in English, Coll. of Idaho, Caldwell, 1966; MBA in Fin., Temple U., 1984. Tchr. Salt Lake City Bd. Edn., 1967-74; office mgr. Montgomery County Homemaker-Home Health Aide Svc., Inc., Blue Bell, Pa., 1975-82; adj. lectr. risk mgmt. and personal fin. Temple U., Phila., 1984—. Co-author: Controlling Your Money, Step By Step, 1987. Named Outstanding Tchr. of Yr., Salt Lake City Bd. Edn., 1973-74. Mem. Am. Risk and Ins. Assn., Gamma Iota Sigma. Republican. Office: Temple U Ambler Campus 580 Meetinghouse Rd Ambler PA 19002-3989

WALD, PATRICIA MCGOWAN, federal judge; b. Torrington, Conn., Sept. 16, 1928; d. Joseph F. and Margaret (O'Keefe) McGowan; m. Robert L. Wald, June 22, 1952; children—Sarah, Douglas, Johanna, Frederica, Thomas. BA, Conn. Coll., 1948; LLB, Yale U., 1951; HHD (hon.), Mt. Vernon Jr. Coll., 1980; LLD (hon.), George Washington Law Sch., 1983, CUNY, 1984, Notre Dame U., John Jay Sch. Criminal Justice, Mt. Holyoke Coll., 1985, Georgetown U., 1987, Villanova U. Law Sch., Amherst Coll., N.Y. Law Sch., 1988, Colgate U., 1989, Hofstra Law Sch., 1991, New Eng. Coll., 1991, Hoffstra U., 1991. Bar: D.C. 1952. Clk. to judge Jerome Frank U.S. Ct. Appeals, 1951-52; asso. firm Arnold, Fortas & Porter, Washington, 1952-53; mem. D.C. Crime Commn., 1964-65; atty. Office of Criminal Justice, 1967-68, Neighborhood Legal Svc., Washington, 1968-70; co-dir. Ford Found. Project on Drug Abuse, 1970, Ctr. for Law and Social Policy, 1971-72, Mental Health Law Project, 1972-77; asst. atty. gen. for legis. affairs U.S. Dept. Justice, Washington, 1977-79; judge U.S. Ct. Appeals (D.C. cir.), 1979—, chief judge, 1986-91. Author: Law and Poverty, 1965; co-author: Bail in the United States, 1964, Dealing with Drug Abuse, 1973; contbr. articles on legal topics. Trustee Ford Found., 1972-77, Phillips Exeter Acad., 1975-77, Agnes Meyer Found., 1976-77, Conn. Coll., 1976-77; mem. Carnegie Council on Children, 1972-77. Mem. ABA (bd. editors ABA Jour. 1978-84), Am. Law Inst. (coun. 1979—, exec. com. 1985—, 2d v.p. 1988—), Inst. Medicine, Am. Acad. Arts and Scis., Phi Beta Kappa. Office: US Ct Appeals US Courthouse 3rd & Constitution Ave NW Washington DC 20001

WALDAU, HELEN FRANCES, educator; b. Torrington, Conn., Mar. 21, 1925; d. Teofil and Michaelena (Plaga) Budney; B.A., U. Conn., 1953, 6th yr. certificate, 1968; M.A., U. Hartford; divorced; children—Geoffrey, Christopher, Peter, Sandra. Mem. faculty Hopewell Sch., Glastonbury, Conn., 1966-91, Naubac Sch., 1991; tchr. academically talented, Glastonbury, 1982-85; dir. Apple Computer Project, 1984; supr. U. Conn. open edn. interns, 1971-75. Fellow U. Conn., 1967-68. Mem. NEA, Conn., Glastonbury edn. assns., Greater Conn. Council for Open Edn. (charter), Glastonbury Task Force for Gifted Edn., Conn. Tchrs. Center for Humanistic Edn., Psi Upsilon Omicron. Home: 1808 Main St Glastonbury CT 06033-2944

WALDBILLIG, GERALD WILLIAM, construction company executive; b. Albany, N.Y., Aug. 6, 1905; s. John B. and Katherine M. (Monman) W.; m. Frances D. McDonough, July 13, 1932; children: Susanna, Michael, Gretchen, Kirsten, Stephen. BSCE, Rensselaer Poly. Inst., 1925. Registered profl. engr., N.Y. State. Jr. engr. Horter Barrows Middlebrok, Boston, 1925-26, Conn. Middlebrook, Albany, N.Y., 1926-28; constrn. mgr. Duplex Constrn., Glens Falls, N.Y., 1928-29; engr.-in-charge Wells Bros., Chgo., 1929-30; pres. Waldbillig Constrn. Corp., Albany, 1930—; trustee Home Savs. Bank, Albany, 1950-85. Trustee Oliver Dist. Sch., Slingerlands, N.Y., 1937, St. Mary's Roman Cath. Ch., albany, 1980—. Fellow ASCE; mem. Albany

Bldrs. Exchange (pres. 1940), Bldg. Industry Employers Assn. N.Y. State (pres. 1953), Univ. Club, Ft. Orange Club (pres. 1956), Albany Country Club, Lake Placid Club, Knights of Malta. Roman Catholic. Home: RD 4 Normanskill Rd Slingerlands NY 12159 Office: Waldbillig Constrn Corp 423 First St Albany NY 12206

WALDMAN, JAY CARL, judge; b. Pitts., Nov. 16, 1944; s. Milton and Dorothy (Florence) W.; m. Roberta Tex Landy, Aug. 28, 1969. B.S., U. Wis., 1966; J.D., U. Pa., 1969. Bar: Pa. 1970, D.C. 1976, U.S. Supreme Ct. 1976. Assoc., Rose, Schmidt, Dixon & Hasley, Pitts., 1970-71; asst. U.S. atty. western dist. Pa., Pitts., 1971-75; dep. asst. U.S. Atty. Gen., Washington, 1975-77; counsel Gov. of Pa., Harrisburg, 1978-86; sr. ptnr., Dilworth, Paxson, Kalish & Kauffman, Phila., 1986-88; judge U.S. Dist. Ct. (ea. dist.) Pa., 1988—. Dir. Thornburgh for Gov. campaign., Pa., 1977-78; commr. Pa. Convention Ctr. Authority, 1986-88. Fellow Am. Bar Found.; mem. ABA, Fed. Bar Assn., Union League Phila. Republican. Office: US Dist Ct Pa 5918 US Courthouse 601 Market St Philadelphia PA 19106-1510*

WALDMAN, MYRON RICHARD, electronics company executive; b. Providence, July 8, 1940; s. Edmund I. and Janet L. (Fain) W.; ed. Worcester Poly. Inst., 1959-62; children: Sherry, Alexis, Joshua, Jenna. Civil engr. Collins & Kronstadt, Md., 1962-64; engring. mgr. Walco Electric Co., Providence, 1965-70; with WST Power Electronics, Inc., Providence, 1971—, pres., 1982—; cons. in field. Mem. Wire Assn. Internat., Wire Industry Suppliers Assn. (sec.-treas.), Am. Technion Soc. (dir. 1980-82), Soc. Plastics Engrs., Wire Assn., Instrument Soc. Am., Small Bus. Assn. N.Eng. (exec. com.). Patentee in field. Office: WST Power Electronics Inc 25 Acorn St Providence RI 02903-1087

WALDMAN, PAUL, artist; b. Erie, Pa., 1936. Student, Bklyn. Mus. Art Sch., 1955, Pratt Inst., 1956. Instr. painting Greenwich (Conn.) Art Ctr., 1963, N.Y. Community Coll., 1963-64, Bklyn. Mus. Art Sch., 1963-67, Sch. Visual Arts, N.Y.C., 1966—; vis. prof. U. Calif., Davis, 1966; vis. artist Ohio State U., 1966; artist-in-residence The Clayworks Studio Workshop, N.Y., 1982. One man shows include Allan Stone Gallery, N.Y., 1963, 65, Albright Gallery of Art, Hax Art Ctr., St. Joseph, Mo., 1966, Leo Castelli Gallery, N.Y.C., 1973, 75, 78, 81, 84, 88, 91, Blum-Helman Gallery, N.Y.C., 1978, Kunsthalle Tranegarden, Copenhagen, 1981, Norblyllands Kunstmuseum, Aalborg, Denmark, 1981, Castelli Graphics, N.Y.C., 1984, Fariden Cadot Gallery, Paris, 1987, 88, 91, Phyllis Kind Gallery, Chgo., 1988; exhibited in group shows include Allan Stone Gallery, 1961, Louis Alexander Gallery, N.Y.C., 1962, Gallery of Modern Art, Washington, 1963, 64, Wadworth Atheneum, Hartford, Conn., 1964, Rutgers U., New Brunswick, N.J., 1964, Knoedler Gallery, 1965, Visual Arts Gallery, The Sch. of Visual Arts, N.Y.C., 1965, 68, 83, Art Mus., U. of Ind., Bloomington, 1965, Richard Feigen Gallery, Chgo., 1965, Ark. Arts Ctr., Little Rock, 1966, Ithaca Coll. Mus. Art, N.Y., 1967, Smithsonian Inst., 1967-68, Kansas City Art Inst., Mo., 1967, Newark Mus., 1968, Leo Castelli Gallery, 1974, 77, 79, 80, 83, Castelli Graphics, 1976, 82, 84, Phila. Coll. Art., 1976, Guggenheim Mus., 1977, 79, 84, La Jolla Mus. Art, 1982, Jan van Eyck Acad., Maastricht, Germany, 1985, Cooper-Hewitt Mus., N.Y.C., 1987; represented in permanent collections Mus. Modern Art, Newark Mus., Bklyn. Mus., L.A. County Mus. Art, NYU, Hirshhorn Mus. and Sculpture Garden, Smithsonian Inst., Des Moines Mus., Guggenheim Mus., Mus. Fine Arts, Houston, Balt. Mus. Art, Carnegie Mus., Dallas Mus. Fine Arts. Grantee Ford Foundation, 1965.

WALDMANN, THOMAS ALEXANDER, medical research scientist, physician; b. N.Y.C., Sept. 21, 1930; s. Charles Elizabeth (Sipos) W.; m. Katharine Emory Spreng, Mar. 29, 1958; children—Richard Allen, Robert James, Carol Ann. A.B., U. Chgo., 1951; M.D., Harvard U., 1955. Diplomate Am. Bd. Allergy and Immunology. Intern Mass. Gen. Hosp., Boston, 1955-56; clin. assoc. Nat. Cancer Inst. NIH, Bethesda, Md., 1956-58, sr. investigator, 1958-68, head immunophysiology sect., 1968-73, chief metabolism br., 1971—; cons. WHO, 1975, 78; bd. dirs. Found. for Advanced Edn. in Scis., Bethesda, 1980—, treas., 1988-90, v.p., 1990—; William Dameshek vis. prof. Tufts U., 1983; Burroughs Welcome vis. prof. U. Calif., Irvine, 1984; mem. med. adv. bd. Howard Hughes Med. Inst., 1986-92. Author: Plasma Protein Metabolism, 1970; contbr. over 500 articles to profl. jours. Discoverer diseases intestinal lymphangiectasia and allergic enteropathy. Served with USPHS, 1956-58, 59-63, 75—. Recipient Henry M. Stratton medal Am. Hemotology Soc., 1977; named Man of Yr. Am. Leukemia Soc., 1980; recipient G. Burroughs Mider award NIH, 1980; Disting. Service medal Dept. Health and Human Services, 1983. Fellow Am. Acad. Allergy (Bela Schick award 1974, John M. Shelton award 1984, Lila Gruber prize 1986, Simon Shubitz prize 1987, CIBA-GEIGY Drew award 1987, Milken Family Med. Found. Disting. Basic Scientist prize, Artois Latour Internat. Rsch. prize 1991, Bristol-Myer Cancer prize 1992); mem. NAS (Artois-Ballet-Latour prize), Am. Acad. Arts and Scis., Assn. Am. Physicians, Am. Soc. Clin. Investigation (mem. editorial bd. 1978-80, 83—), Clin. Immunology Soc. (pres. 1988), Plasma Protein Study Group (sec. treas. 1974-77), NIH Camera Club (pres. 1972-73). Home: 3910 Rickover Rd Silver Spring MD 20902-2329 Office: Nat Cancer Inst NIH Bethesda MD 20892

WALDO, ROBERT CARL, JR., electrical engineer; b. Stamford, Conn., Nov. 17, 1954; s. Robert Carl and Dawn Patricia (Hough) W.; m. Linne Marie Perrotti, Oct. 24, 1981; children: Victoria Linne, Jessica Marie. Assoc. in Sci., Charter Oak, 1978, BA, 1979; MSD (hon.), U.L. Ch., 1990. Cert. telecommunications engr. Electronic tech. Kantek Rsch., Norwalk, Conn., 1976-77, Gen. DataComm, Inc., Danbury, Conn., 1977-78; supr. Gen. DataComm, Inc., Middlebury, Conn., 1978-84, configuration engr., 1984-87, mgr. systems engring., 1987-90, applications engr., 1990-91; instr. Brookfield Continuing Adult Edn., 1990-91; database adminstr. DataComm Svc. Corp., Middlebury, Conn., 1991—. Author: More Lines From Cornelius Waldo, 1992, (with others) Moses Family in America, 1987. Mem. com. ARC, Danbury, 1985—. Mem. IEEE Computer Soc., Nat. Assn. Radio and Telecommunications Engrs., Nat. Geneal. Soc., Candlewood Auto Racers, New Eng. Hist. Geneal. Soc., Conn. Soc. Genealogists, Conn. Ancestry Soc., Geneal. Soc. Ct., Internat. Soc. for Brit. Genealogy and Family History, Bethel Ednl. Radio Soc., Nat. Assn. Rocketry. Republican. Roman Catholic. Office: DCS Park Rd Ext Middlebury CT 06762

WALDO, SUZANNE TRACEY, health facility supervisor; b. Phila., Oct. 28, 1953; d. J. Joseph and M. Catherine (Stahl) T.; m. William D. Granieri, Dec. 2, 1972 (div.); children: Christina, William D. Jr.; m. Mark Waldo, Feb. 11, 1979 (div. May 1984). Practical Nursing, St. Mary's Hosp., 1972; cert. in intensive coronary care, Rolling Hill Hosp., Elkins Park, Pa., 1975; student, Montgomery County Community, 1989—. LPN, Pa. Staff nurse emergency rm. St. Mary's Hosp., Phila., 1972-73; charge nurse Township Manor Nursing Ctr., Elkins Park, 1973-74; charge nurse emergency rm. Rolling Hill Hosp., Elkins Park, 1974-79; LGPN/supr. Township Manor Nursing Ctr., Elkins Park, 1981-89, LGPN supr., 1981-89, supr. Alzheimers unit, 1989—; co-dir. ARC Landsdale (Pa.) chpt., 1973-74, instr., 1st aide Phila. chpt., 1972-75. Vol. Burholme Ambulance, Phila., 1971-73; mem. 2d Alarmers-Rescue Squad, Willow Grove, Pa., 1971-74; youth leader, puppet dir. 1st Brethren Ch., Phila., 1983-87. Republican. Presbyterian. Home: 2931 Madison Ave Abington PA 19001-4011

WALDRON, ANTHONY JAMES, writer, engineer, consultant, expert witness; b. Jersey City, Mar. 25, 1924; s. Anthony J. and Bridget Mary (Burke) W.; m. Helen Jean McDevitt, May 28, 1948; children: Daniel, Maura, Elaine, Brian. Student, Carnegie Inst. Tech., 1949-51. Test engr. M.W. Kellogg Co., Jersey City, 1946-48; instrument engr. Blaw Knox Co., Pitts., 1948-51; div. engr. Catalytic Constrn. Co., Phila., 1951-59; prin. engr. Stromberg Carlson Corp., Rochester, N.Y., 1959-60; cons. Mauchly Assocs., Ambler, Pa., 1960-61; cons., forensic scheduling expert, provider tng. courses Haddonfield, N.J., 1961—. Author: Fundamentals of Project Planning and Control, Applied Principles of Project Planning and Control, Project Scheduling and Construction Claims; contbr. articles to profl. jours. Elector N.J. Conservative Party, 1958; sec., bd. dirs. Hideaway Beach Assn., Marco Islnd, Fla. Mem. Soc. Critical Path Cons. (charter mem.), Am. Arbitration Assn. (arbitrator), Hideaway Beach Assn. (sec., bd. dirs. Marco Island chpt.), Tavistock Club (N.J.), Eagle Creek (Naples, Fla.), Army Navy Club (Washington). Roman Catholic. Home and Office: 371 Kings Hwy W Haddonfield NJ 08033-2103

WALDRON, ROBERT JAMES, bank officer, lawyer; b. Augusta, Maine, July 19, 1928; s. James Neal and Alice Louise (Rideout) W.; m. Janet Lois Dorrer, Dec. 14, 1957; children: Roger, James, Scott, Barbara. BA cum laude, Bowdoin Coll., 1949; JD cum laude, Harvard U., 1952. Bar: Maine 1952, Mass. 1952, U.S. Dist. Ct. Mass. 1953. Legal assoc. L. B. Newman Law Office, Boston, 1953-58; trust officer No. Nat. Bank, Presque Isle, Maine, 1958-60; v.p. and trust officer No. Nat. Bank, Presque Isle, 1960-84; v.p. Casco No. Corp., Portland, Maine, 1972-80; v.p. and trust officer Casco No. Corp., Portland and Presque Isle, 1980-85; pvt. practice law Presque Isle, 1984-86; v.p. and trust officer Bank of N.H., Manchester, 1986—, Strafford Nat. Bank, Dover, N.H., 1990—; cons. Casco. No. Bank, Presque Isle, 1984-85; pres. Aroostook County Bar, Houlton, Maine, 1979-80, Corp. Fiduciaries Maine, Augusta, 1963-65. Mem. sch. bd. Presque Isle, 1981-86; Maine Rep. del., Portland, 1984-86; pres. Gould Meml. Hosp., Presque Isle, 1965-67, N.E. dist. YMCA, Aroostook County, 1967-70, Found. of U. Maine, Presque Isle, 1975-85. Capt. USAF, 1952-53. Mem. IAFP N.H. (dir. 1988-89), N.H. Estate Planning Coun., Harvard Alumni Club, Bowdoin Alumni Club, Dover Rotary Club. Home: 23 Mountain West Wolfeboro NH 03894 Office: Strafford Nat Bank Central Ave Dover NH 03820-4020

WALDRON, SHARON ELAINE, real estate broker; b. Boston, Nov. 8, 1941; d. Winston Cushman and Evelyn (Murphy) Lawson; m. James E. Waldron, Oct. 15, 1961 (div. Apr. 1987); children: Peter M., Kathleen M. AA, Massasoit Community Coll., 1984; grad., Realtors Inst., 1987. Cert. residential specialist. Staff asst. student activities office Massasoit Community Coll., Brockton, Mass., 1983—; assoc. broker Anderson Real Estate, Inc., East Bridgewater, Mass., 1984—. Den mother Cub Scouts Boy Scouts Am., East Bridgewater, 1972-76, den leader, coach, 1976-78; mem. com., 1978-79. Mem. Am. Soc. Notaries (life), Nat. Assn. Realtors, Mass. Assn. Realtors, Nat. Assn. Cert. Residential Specialists, Mass. Assn. Cert. Residential Specialists, Green Key Soc. Roman Catholic. Home: 1725 Washington St East Bridgewater MA 02333-2219 Office: Anderson Real Estate Inc 324 N Bedford St East Bridgewater MA 02333-1146

WALDSMITH, DINAH LEIGH, charitable contributions program executive; b. Muskegon, Mich., Oct. 21, 1958; d. Richard Weldon Waldsmith and Barbara Kent (Funchess) Sheldon. BS, Grand Valley State Coll., 1980; MBA, Boston U., 1988. Ops. engr. WGVC-TV, Grand Rapids, Mich., 1978-82, asst. prodn. mgr., 1982-86; asst. to exec. dir. Mass. Cultural Alliance, Boston, 1986-88; rsch. assoc. Tech. Devel. Corp., Boston, 1988; contbns. mgr. Shawmut Nat. Corp., Boston, 1988—; treas. Child Care Initiative-Capital Investment Fund, Boston, 1990—; adv. com. Maternal and Infant Health Project, Boston, 1991—. Vol. Income Tax Assistance program vol. IRS, Boston, 1991, 92; mem. pub. policy com. Assn. Grantmakers Mass. Mem. Women in Philanthropy, Coun. on Founds. (site visit subcom., 1990). Office: Shawmut National Corp One Federal St Boston MA 02211

WALGRAN, CRAIG CHANCE, health services executive, consultant; b. Phila., May 6, 1953; s. Robert Eugene and Martha Jeanne (Chance) W.; div.; children: Justin Chance, Ethan Tyler. Student, Susquehanna U., 1971-73. Pvt. practice constrn. Lewisburg, Pa., 1972-73, pvt. practice antiques, 1973-74; retail salesman Stero House, Lewisburg, Pa., 1974-75; dir. sales, mktg. Beyer & Fortner, Inc., Lewisburg, Pa., 1975-78; regional sales dir. Warmth, Inc., Danville, Pa., 1978-80, Kero-Sun Inc., Kent, Conn., 1980-83; sales dir. Pharm. Group Svcs., Mifflinburg, Pa., 1983-85; v.p. sales PGS, Inc., Mifflinburg, Pa., 1985-88, Cost Containment Corp. Inc., Mifflinburg, Pa., 1988—; bd. dirs. Cost Containment Corp., Mifflinburg, Susquehanna Mgmt. Assn., Mifflinburg. Mem. Internat. Found. Employee Benefit Plans, Pitts. Club, Bucknell Golf Club. Republican. Methodist.

WALINSKY, MICHAEL DAVID, podiatrist, educator; b. Phila., Apr. 23, 1945; s. Benjamin and Bertha (Feierstein) W.; m. Bernice Vivian Sursky, Nov. 23, 1969; children: Andrew Eric, Marc Lawrence, Stacy Meredith. BSc in Pharmacy, Temple U., 1967; MBA in Mgmt., Widener U., 1973; D of Podiatric Medicine, Pa. Coll. Podiatric Medicine, 1987. Pharmacy intern Peoples Drug Store, Cheverly, Md., 1967; asst. mgr. Peoples Drug Store, Chaverly, Md., 1967-68; assoc. dir. pharm. cen. svcs. Crozer-Chester (Pa.) Med. Ctr., 1968-73; dir. dept. pharmacy Albert Einstein Med. Ctr., Phila., 1973-76; pres., chief exec. officer And-Mar Drug Corp., Phila., 1976—; resident in podiatric orthopedics J.C. Giuffre Med. Ctr., Phila., 1987-88; podiatrist Narberth, Pa., 1988—; instr. Pa. Coll. Podiatric Medicine, Phila., 1989—; clin. affiliate Temple U. Sch. Pharmacy, Phila., 1977—. Contbr. articles to profl. jours. Bd. dirs. Narberth Civic Assn., 1990. Fellow Am. Coll. Foot orthopoedists (assoc.); mem. Am. Soc. Podiatric Medicine (diplomate), Am. Podiatric Med. Assn., Am. Diabetes Assn., Phila. Assn. Retail Druggists (bd. dirs.). Home: 726 Yale Rd Bala Cynwyd PA 19004-2116

WALINSKY, PAUL, cardiology educator; b. Phila., June 21, 1940; s. Aaron and Bess (Kleiman) W.; m. Stephanie Sosenko, Nov. 27, 1971; children: Shira, Daniel. BA, Temple U., 1961; MD, U. Pa., 1965. Cert. Nat. Bd. Med. Examiners, Am. Bd. Internal Medicine Cardiovascular. Instr. medicine Thomas Jefferson U., Phila., 1973-75, asst. prof. medicine, 1975-79, assoc. prof. medicine, 1979-82, prof. medicine, 1982—; cons. EP Technologies, Mountain View, Calif., 1991—, Baxter Edwards, Irving, Calif., 1988-91. Contbr. articles to profl. jours.; inventor method for high frequency ablation, percutaneous microwave catheter angioplasty. Capt. USAF, 1967-69. Fellow Am. Coll. Cardiology, ACP; mem. AMA, Pa. Med. Soc., Phila. County Med. Assn. Office: Thomas Jefferson U 111 S 11th St Philadelphia PA 19107

WALISH, GERALYN ROSE, business consultant/analyst; b. Bryn Mawr, Pa., Jan. 9, 1956; d. George Martin and Carolyn Rose (O'Neill) W.; m. John Francis Aigeltinger, June 24, 1978 (div. 1983); m. Robert Kenneth Cole, June 25, 1989. AA in Psychology, Barry U., Miami Shores, Fla., 1975; student, Villanova U., 1986—. Systems mgr. Nat. Liberty Corp., Frazer, Pa., 1978-85; project mgr. Reliance Life Cos., Phila., 1985-86; cons. Fidelity Mut. Life Ins. Co., Radnor, Pa., 1986-89; sr. bus. analyst Aon, Trevose, Pa., 1989—. Chmn. Moonlighting Soc., Multiple Sclerosis Soc., Phila, 1986-88; mem. Super Cities Walk Adv. Com., Devel. Com., Multiple Sclerosis Soc., Phila., 1989; trustee Greater Del. Valley Multiple Sclerosis Soc., 1990—. Mem. Life Office Mgmt. Assn., Am. Bus. Women's Assn. (treas. Frazer, Pa. 1980-82). Home: 232 Josephs Way Malvern PA 19355-1672 Office: AON 4850 Street Rd Langhorne PA 19049-0002

WALKER, ARTHUR CARLETON, wholesale company executive, accountant; b. Montclair, N.J., July 14, 1943; s. Ralph Carleton and Dorothy (Riker) W.; m. Patricia Cooper, Apr. 24, 1966; children—Barbara, Arthur. B.S. in Acctg., Fairleigh/Dickinson U., 1967; M.B.A. in Fin., Seton Hall U., 1978. C.P.A., N.J. Acct., Arthur Andersen & Co., N.Y.C., 1968-73; contr. Panasote, Inc., Passaic, N.J., 1973-81; v.p. fin., treas. JSL Video Svc., Inc., N.Y.C., 1981-88, also bd. dirs.; chief fin. officer L&R Distbrs., Inc., Bklyn., 1988—; pvt. acctg., fin. cons. svc. Various offices Jaycees, Bloomfield, N.J., 1973-78; pres., various offices Home and School Assn., Bloomfield, N.J., 1978—. Served to sgt. USAR, 1960-68. Mem. Clifton N.J. C. of C. (bd. dirs., treas. 1980-81), Nat. Assn. Acctg. (bd. dirs. 1973), N.J. Soc. C.P.A.s, Am. Inst. C.P.A.s. Home: 47 Perry Rd Bloomfield NJ 07003-4421 Office: L&R Distbrs Inc 9301 Avenue D Brooklyn NY 11236-1899

WALKER, BARBARA HILLS, secondary education educator; b. Pitts., Apr. 7, 1946; d. Wesley E. and Anne Margaret (Baker) Hills; m. George William Walker, Dec. 22, 1967; children: Kelley, George, Joshua, Zachary. BA, U. Mich., 1968. Cert. biology, gen. sci. secondary tchr., N.Y. Tchr. Batavia (N.Y.) High Sch., 1988; biology tutor Genesee (N.Y.) Community Coll. Mem. Leonard Nimoy Fan Club (founder, v.p. 1983-86, pres. 1985—). Republican. Presbyterian. Home: 17 Gateway Dr Batavia NY 14020-1027

WALKER, CHARLOTTE ZOE, English educator, fiction writer; b. New Orleans, July 13, 1935; d. Charles Henry and Helen Corinne (Reynolds) Walker; m. J. Ignacio Mendez, 1957 (div. 1966); children: David Ignacio, Rebecca Helen, Rachel Susanna Gabriela; m. Roland Greefkes, 1988. BA in Psychology, San Diego State U., 1957; MA, Syracuse U., 1967, PhD in English Lit., 1972. Prof. English SUNY, Oneonta, 1970—. Author: Condor and Hummingbird, 1986, Touching Earth; author short stories, contbr. The Very Pinapple to Prize Stories, 1991, Goat's Milk to Ms. mag., 1992; co-editor Phoebe--An Interdisciplinary Jour. of Feminist Scholarship, Theory and Aesthetics, 1988-91. Nat. Endowment for Arts fellow, 1987. Mem. Poets and Writers Inc. Office: SUNY-Oneonta English Dept Oneonta NY 13820

WALKER, CLARENCE, marriage and family therapist, minister; b. Washington, Mar. 5, 1951; s. Clarence and Eva Mae W.; m. Ja'Ola Ruth McNeil, June 20, 1976; 1 child, Justin Christopher. BA, Eastern Coll., St. Davids, Pa., 1975; MSW, Temple U., 1978; postgrad. cert., Marriage Coun., Phila., 1986; PhD, Trinity Theol. Sem., 1987. Ordained to ministry. Recreation counselor/play st. City of Phila., 1969; Youth for Christ counselor Dimension, Phila., 1970-71; community evangelism worker Southside Ctr., Phila., 1971-72; neighborhood svc. counselor United Meth. Ch., Phila., 1972-74, br. coord., 1974-75, program dir., 1975-80; community liaison City of Phila.-YSCO, 1980-86; sr. family therapist Caaft Counseling Svc., Phila., 1986—; pres. Clarence Walker Ministries, P.E.A.C.E. Ministries; founding elder New Covenant Ch. Author: Ethiopian Chariot, 1992; author video series: So, What do You Want, 1989; author audio cassette series: The Black Family, 1986—; exec. producer music: Honorable Marriage, 1991. Ministerial mem. Coalition for Traditional Values, Washington, 1991—; mem. Black Ams. for Life, 1990—; bd. dirs. United Meth. Neighborhood Svcs., Phila., 1984-86; com. mem. Concerned REsidents/800 Block Wynnewood Rd., Phila., 1980—. Recipient Plaque for Christian Educator of the Yr., Nat. Christian Edn. Conf., Chgo., 1990, City Citation Marriage and Family Enrichment, Mayor B. Moyer, 1990, others. Mem. Am. Assn. for Counseling and Devel., Nat. Assn. Mental Health Counselors, Nat. Assn. Social Workers, Nat. Coun. on Family Rels., Christian Assn. for Psychol. Studies, United Assn. Christian Counselors Internat., Am. Assn. Marriage and Family Therapists. Home: 2471 N 54th St Ste 231 Philadelphia PA 19131-1447 Office: Clarence Walker Ministries 2471 N 54th St # 231 Philadelphia PA 19131-1447

WALKER, CRAIG MICHAEL, lawyer; b. Hardwick, Vt., Mar. 16, 1947; m. Patricia A. Magruder; 2 children. BA, Williams Coll., 1969; JD, Cornell U., 1972. Bar: N.Y. 1973, U.S. Dist. Ct. (so. dist.) N.Y. 1975, U.S. Ct. Appeals (2d cir) 1975, U.S. Supreme Ct 1976. Assoc. Alexander & Green, N.Y.C., 1972-80, ptnr., 1980-86, chmn. litigation dept., 1985-86; ptnr. Walter, Conston, Alexander & Green P.C., N.Y.C., 1987-89, Rogers & Wells, N.Y.C., 1990—. Contbr. articles to profl. jours. Fellow Am. Bar Found.; mem. ABA, N.Y. State Bar Assn., Def. Rsch. Inst., Fed. Bar Coun. (sustaining mem.). Democrat. Home: New York NY 10010

WALKER, GEORGE THEOPHILUS, JR., composer, pianist, music educator; b. Washington, June 27, 1922; s. George Theophilus Sr. and Rosa (King) W.; m. Helen Siemens; children: Gregory, Ian. MusB, Oberlin Coll., 1941; Artist Diploma, Curtis Inst. music, 1945; D of Mus. Arts, U. Rochester, 1957; DFA (hon.), Lafayette Coll., 1982; MusD (hon.), Oberlin Coll., 1983. Instr. Dillard U., New Orleans, 1953-54; instr. Dalcroze Sch. Music, N.Y.C., 1960-61, New Sch. Social Research, N.Y.C., 1961; instr. to assoc. prof. Smith Coll., Northampton, Mass., 1961-68; assoc. prof. U. Colo., Boulder, 1968-69; prof. music Rutgers U., Newark, 1969-76, disting. prof., 1976—; concert pianist Nat. Concert Artists, N.Y.C., 1950-53, Columbia Artists, N.Y.C., 1959-60; adj. prof. Peabody Inst. Johns Hopkins U., Balt., 1973-76; disting. prof. U. Del., Newark, 1975-76. Composer: Sonata for 2 Pianos (Harvey Gaul prize 1963), numerous sonatas, cantatas and concertos, Concerto for Cello and Orch., 1982. Bd. dirs. Am. Bach Found., 1988. Recipient award Am. Acad. and Inst. Arts and Letters, 1982, Koussevitsky award, 1988; grantee Smith Coll., U. Colo., Rutgers U. Rsch. Coun., NEA, N.J. State Coun. for Arts; Fulbright fellow, 1957; John Hay Whitney fellow, 1958; Guggenheim fellow, 1971, 75. Mem. ASCAP, Am. Bach Found. (bd. dirs. 1988), Am. Symphony League. Democrat. Home: 323 Grove St Montclair NJ 07042-4223 Office: Rutgers U Newark NJ 07102

WALKER, JAMES GEORGE, pharmacist; b. Washington, Feb. 15, 1958; s. James and Matilda Roumania (Peters) W. BS in Zoology, Howard U., 1979, BS in Pharmacy, 1982, JD, 1985. Registered pharmacist. Pres. Walker Pharmacy, Inc., Silver Spring, Md., 1983—. Mem. Nat. Pharm. Assn., Am. Pharm. Assn. Nat. Assn. Retail Druggists, D.C. Pharm. Assn. (chmn. resolution com.), Md. Pharm. Assn., Commonwealth of Pa. Bar., Chi Delta Mu. Roman Catholic. Home: 1412 Whittier Pl NW Washington DC 20012-2846

WALKER, JANE ANN, communications executive; b. Elizabeth, N.J.; d. Gordon Charles and Irma (Ellison) W. BA, Pa. State U., 1972. Advt. assoc. Harper & Row Pubs., Hagerstown, Md., 1973-74; mktg. communications mgr. Air Products & Chems., Allentown, Pa., 1974-82; v.p. Advt. Ctr., Inc., Ft. Myers, Fla., 1982-83; mktg. communications mgr. Great Lakes Chem. Corp., Lafayette, Ind., 1983-86; mktg. mgr. Medigroup (subs. Blue Cross/Blue Shield), Newark, 1986-87; corp. communications mgr. Medco Containment Svcs., Inc., Fair Lawn, N.J., 1987—.

WALKER, JOHN ALFRED, physician; b. Mt. Vernon, Oct. 6, 1950; s. Alfred Jr. and Elsa Elizabeth (Johnson) W.; m. Victoria Cronin, May 8, 1976; 1 child, Emily Brennan. BA summa cum laude, L.I. U., 1972; MD, SUNY, Bklyn., 1976. Diplomate Am. Bd. Internal Medicine, Am. Bd. Nephrology, Nat. Bd. Med. Examiners. Resident in medicine Bridgeport (Conn.) Hosp., 1976-79; fellow in nephrology Montefiore Hosp. and Med. Ctr., N.Y.C., 1979-81; asst. prof. medicine UMDNJ Robert Wood Johnson Med. Sch., New Brunswick, 1981-87, assoc. prof. of clin. medicine, 1987—; attending physician R.W. Johnson U. Hosp., New Brunswick, 1981—; cons. physician St. Peter's Med. Ctr., New Brunswick, 1985—. Assoc. editor Seminars in Dialysis; contbr. articles to profl. jours. Fellow ACP; mem. Am. Soc. Nephrology, Internat. Soc. of Nephrology, N.Y. Acad. Scis., Nephrology Soc. of N.J. (v.p. 1982-84, pres. 1985-86). Office: UMDNJ RW Johnson Med Sch Dept Medicine CN-19 New Brunswick NJ 08903-0019

WALKER, KENNETH ADLEY, aluminum fabricating company executive; b. Hartford, Conn., May 16, 1949; s. George Gould and Elizabeth Mae (Parcher) W.; m. Ruth Ann Danowski; children: Kenneth, Gregory, Daniel. BSME with honors, Cornell U., 1971; M in Adminstrv. Sci., Johns Hopkins U., 1978; M in Fin., Loyola Coll., Balt., 1981; postgrad., U. Md., 1990—. Test engr. Koppers Co. Inc., Balt., 1971-72, project engr., 1973; mgr. accessory equipment Environ. Elements Corp., Balt., 1974-76, mgr. scrubber/ filter products, 1976-82, gen. mgr. water treatment systems, 1983-88; v.p. ops. Washington Aluminum Co., Balt., 1988—; bd. dirs., 1990—; bd. dirs. Md. Healthcorp, Inc., Dovco Indsl. Fabricators, Inc., TriFab, Inc.; pvt. industry rep. Gov.'s Com. Study Anticipated Sewage Treatment Needs, State of Md., 1986-88. Patentee method and system cleansing a filter bed. Bd. dirs. Greater Balt. Med. Ctr., 1986—, mem. fin. and bldg. coms., 1986—; bd. dirs. Towson (Md.) Presbyn. Kindergarten, 1986-89, v.p. 1987-89. Mem. Am. Waterworks Assn., Am. Welding Soc., Cornell Soc. Engrs., Quill and Dagger Soc., Balt. Road Runners, Autocrossers, Inc., Adirondack Mountain Club, Porsche club Am., Sports Car Club Am., Appalachian Mtn. Club, Tau Beta Pi, Delta Chi. Republican. Office: Washington Aluminum Co Knecht Ave Baltimore MD 21229-5513

WALKER, LISA J., journalism association executive; b. Buffalo, N.Y., Dec. 30, 1945; d. Ellis A. and Eugenia (Houck) W.; m. Christopher Barron Bedford, Oct. 13, 1990. AB in Polit. Sci., Syracuse U., 1967; MA in Polit. Sci., U. Rochester, 1970. Profl. staff mem. U.S. Senate Labor & Human Resources Com., Washington, 1971-78; v.p., program dir. Inst. for Ednl. Leadership, Washington, 1978-81, v.p., 1981-86; exec. dir. Edn. Writers Assn., Washington, 1986—. Co-author: Financing Special Education: A Guide for Policymakers, 1993, Working in Urban Schools, 1988. Mem. Maxwell Alumni Assn. (pres. 1989-90). Office: Edn Writers Assn 1001 Connecticut Ave NW Washington DC 20036-5504

WALKER, LUCILLE YOST, accountant; b. Allentown, Pa., Mar. 1, 1933; d. Frank and Minnie (Kuder) Yost; m. Robert Edwin Walker, Sept. 19, 1952; children: R. Mark, Theresa, Janet, Pauline, Rodger, Ryan. Assoc., Cen. City Bus. Coll., Syracuse, N.Y., 1952. Acct. Straightline Svc. Corp., Syracuse, 1976-85; pvt. practice acctg. Syracuse, 1985—. Writer, dir. TV program, 1988. Dir., organizer Syracuse Community Band, 1976—; in-

terviewer Oral History Program, Syracuse, 1983; dir., organizer Betts Book Discussion, Syracuse, 1977—; pianist St. James Folk Choir, Syracuse, 1987—. Mem. Syracuse Bus. and Profl. Club (sec. 1989-91), Southside Businessmen's Orgn. Roman Catholic.

WALKER, MARTIN ALAN, journalist; b. Durham, England, July 23, 1947; came to U.S., 1978; s. Tom and Dorothy (McNeill) W.; m. Julia Watson, 1978; children: Kate, Fanny. MA, U. Oxford, 1966-69; student, Harvard U., 1969-71. Journalist, bur. chief The Guardian, Washington, 1988—. Author: The National Front, 1978, Power of the Press, 1982, The Walking Giant, 1986, Martin Walker's Russia, 1988. Named Reporter of Yr., U.K. Press, 1986, 87, Fgn. Journalist of Yr. Krokodil, Moscow, 1988; Brackenbury scholar U. Oxford, 1966-69; Harkness fellow Harvard U., 1969-71, Am. Polit. Sci. Assn. fellow, 1971-72. Mem. White House Press Assn. Home: 7055 Old Chester Rd Bethesda MD 20817-6162 Office: The Guardian 2025 M St NW Washington DC 20036-3309

WALKER, MELVIN DUANE, academic administrator, ministry consultant; b. Meshoppen, Pa., Apr. 26, 1954; s. James A. and Louise (Holenbeck) W.; m. Peggy Lou Bartling, Aug. 13, 1976; children: Kristi Marie, Todd Marcus, Travis Alan. AA, Bapt. Bible Coll., 1974, BRE, 1976; postgrad., Iowa State U., 1985-86, Faith Bapt. Sem., 1986-89, Bapt. Bible Sem., 1989-92. Youth pastor Calvary Bapt. Ch., Ypsilanti, Mich., 1976-82, interim pastor, 1982-83; dean of men Faith Bapt. Bible Coll., Ankeny, Iowa, 1983-84, prof., 1984-89; dir. alumni Bapt. Bible Coll., Clarks Summit, Pa., 1989—; chmn. Vision for Youth, Brownsburg, Ind., 1986—; pres. Next Generation Ministries, Des Moines, 1983—; coord. Nat. Youth Fest-Gen. Assn. of Regular Bapt. Chs., 1985—. Contbr. articles to profl. publs. Mem. adult edn. bd. Ankeny Pub. Schs., 1982-83; mem. Gov.'s Youth com. State of Iowa, Des Moines, 1980-83. Office: Bapt Bible Coll & Sem 538 Venard Rd Clarks Summit PA 18411-1297

WALKER, RICHARD WILLARD, writer, consultant; b. Cheverly, Md., Nov. 7, 1946; s. Richard Lee and Cynthia (Willard) W.; m. Cynthia Ann Collins, 1981. BA in Philosophy, U. Md., 1972. Editor, writer various newspapers and mags., 1974-79; sr. editor Antiques World mag., N.Y.C., 1979-82; editor The ARTnewsletter, N.Y.C., 1982-88; staff writer ARTnews mag., N.Y.C., 1982-88; editor at large The ARTnewsletter, N.Y.C., 1988--; contbg. editor ARTnews mag., N.Y.C., 1988--. Contbr. articles on various aspects of the art market and art investment to gen. and profl. publs. Mem. Nat. Press Club, Univ. Club Balt. Home and Office: 3100 St Paul St Apt 110 Baltimore MD 21218-3860

WALKER, ROBERT SMITH, congressman; b. Bradford, Pa., Dec. 23, 1942; s. Joseph Eddman and Rachael Viola (Smith) W.; m. Sue Ellen Albertson, Apr. 13, 1968. BS, Millersville (Pa.) U., 1964; MA in Polit. Sci, U. Del., 1968. Tchr. Penn Manor High Sch., Lancaster, Pa., 1964-67; legis. asst. to Congressman Edwin D. Eshleman, 1967-74, adminstrv. asst., 1974-76; mem. 95th-102d Congresses from 16th Pa. dist., 1977—. Co-author: Congress-The Pennsylvania Dutch Representatives, 1774-1974. Can You Afford This House, 1978, House of Ill Repute, 1987; contbr. articles to profl. jours. Served with Pa. NG, 1967-73. Republican. Office: US Ho of Reps 2369 Rayburn House Office Bldg Washington DC 20515

WALKER, RONALD R., writer, newspaper editor, government official; b. Newport News, Va., Sept. 2, 1934; s. William R. and Jean Marie (King) W.; m. O. Diane Mawson, Apr. 16, 1961; children—Mark Jonathan, Steven Christopher. B.S., Pa. State U., 1956; postgrad. (Nieman fellow) Harvard U., 1970-71. Reporter, news editor, sr. editor, editorial page editor, mng. editor San Juan Star (P.R.), 1962-73, Washington columnist, 1982-84, city editor, 1984-87; instr. journalism Pa. State U., State College, 1973-74; asst. prof. Columbia U. Grad. Sch. Journalism, N.Y.C., 1974-76; editor The Daily News, V.I., 1976-77; press sec. Gov. V.I., 1978-79; adminstrv. asst. Rep. James H. Scheuer, U.S. Congress, 1980-82, special asst., chief of staff, Resident Commr. Jaime B. Fuster, U.S. Congress, 1987-92, spl. asst. Resident Commr. Antonio J. Colorado, 1992—. Served with U.S. Army, 1957-59. Mem. Soc. Nieman Fellows., Harvard Club of Washington. Contbr. articles to nat. mags. and jours. Address: 5500 Friendship Blvd Apt 1522N Bethesda MD 20815 Office: 427 Cannon Bldg Washington DC 20515

WALKER, STANLEY P., publishing executive; b. Arkham, Mass., May 23, 1955; s. Gerald Jeffrey and Rebecca (Chamberlain) W.; m. Faith Darwin, Aug. 17, 1977; children: Erin, Emily, Amy. BA in English, Oberlin Coll., 1977; MFA in Creative Writing, Western Mich. U., 1979; MA in English Lit., Columbia U., 1982, PhD in English Lit., 1983. Sr. editor Farrar Straus Giroux, N.Y.C., 1980-83; assoc. prof. creative writing, early English lit. Columbia U., N.Y.C., 1983-87; pres., editor-in-chief Walker Press, N.Y.C., 1987-90; pres. Walker/Sturgeon Publs., Inc., New Providence, N.J., 1990—; vis. assoc. prof. Grinnell (Iowa) Coll., 1985-86; adj. prof. CUNY, 1987-90; cons. Farrar Straus Giroux, N.Y.C., 1990—. Author: (short story collections) I Think We Smoked It, 1987, The Rudeness of Youth, 1989, Life in the Sour Patch, 1991; co-author: (with L.Q. Sturgeon) Succeeding in Small-Scale Publishing, 1991; book reviewer numerous publs., N.Y.C., 1987—; contbr. articles to profl. jours. Trustee Grinnell Coll., 1990—; soccer coach, referee Am. Youth Soccer League, New Providence, 1990—. Mem. Writers Guild, Mensa, Ragnarok Lumberjacks, Phi Beta Kappa. Office: 121 Chanlon Rd New Providence NJ 07974

WALKER, TIMOTHY CRAIG, transportation executive; b. Huntington, W.Va., Jan. 16, 1945; s. John Paul and Marjorie Frances (Withers) W. BA, Northwestern U., 1967; B of Fgn. Trade, Am. Grad. Sch. Internat. Mgmt., 1968. Mgmt. trainee to dir. OIM/internat. mktg. ops. NCR Corp., Dayton, Ohio, 1968-79; v.p. mktg. Do-Ray Lamp Co., Inc., Colorado City, Colo., 1979-87; v.p. mktg. Truck-Lite Co., Inc., Jamestown, N.Y., 1984-90; pres., chief oper. officer Truck-Lite Internat., Inc., 1990—, also bd. dirs.; recruiter Am. Grad. Sch. Internat. Mgmt., 1971—. Bd. dirs. Valley Human Resources, United Way Agy., 1980-84, Goodwill Industries of Pueblo, Colo., 1983-84; mem. Working Group for U.S. Dept. Commerce MOSS Talks. Recipient Pres.'s award 1st alumnus Am. Grad. Sch. Internat. Mgmt., 1976, award for excellence in internat. advt., 1968; named to Automotive Hall of Fame. Mem. Transp. Safety Equipment Inst. N.Am. (chmn. mktg. and statis. com. 1980-82), European Transport Maintenance Coun. (bd. dirs. 1991—), Heavy Duty Bus. Forum, Heavy Duty Mfrs. Assn. (bd. govs. 1987—, sec. 1990-91), Pueblo Area C. of C. (transp. com. 1981-84), Coun. Fleet Specialists (mfrs. liaison com. 1989-91), 500 Automotive Execs. Club. Republican. Presbyterian. Home: PO Box 1263 Jamestown NY 14702-1263 Office: Truck-Lite Co PO Box 387 Jamestown NY 14702-0387

WALKER, WALLACE EARL, public policy educator, army officer; b. Decatur, Ill., Feb. 28, 1944; s. Harry Dale and Evelyn (Starkey) W.; m. Susan Porter, June 5, 1968; children: Allen D., Kathryn M. BS with distinction, U.S. Mil. Acad., 1967; MS, MIT, 1973, PhD, 1980; grad. with distinction, Command and Gen. Staff Coll., 1979. Commd. 2d lt. U.S. Army, 1967, advanced through grades to col., 1990; platoon leader, adj. 2d Squadron, 2d Armored Cav., Bamberg, Germany, 1968-69; troop comdr. 3d Squadron, 5th Armored Cavalry, Dong Ha, Vietnam, 1969-70; co. comdr., ops. officer 2d Armored Div., Ft. Hood, Tex., 1973-75; prof. pub. policy U.S. Mil. Acad., West Point, N.Y., 1975—; White House fellow U.S. Dept. of Energy and White House, Washington, 1980-81; fellow Nat. War Coll., Washington, 1984-85; rsch. fellow NATO, Brussels, 1989-90; dir. debate coun. and forum U.S. Mil. Acad., 1981-84, 91—, chmn. humanities and pub. affairs rsch. com., 1990—, mem. admissions com., 1981-84, 90—. Author: Changing Organizational Culture, 1986 (award Choice mag. 1987), Reserve Forces and the British Territorial Army, 1990; co-editor: National Security and the U.S. Constitution, 1988; contbr. articles to profl. publs. Lay reader St. Michael's Ch., West Point, 1982—, sr. warden, 1991—. Fellow Interuniv. Seminar on Armed Forces and Soc.; mem. Am. Polit. Sci. Assn., West Point Assn. of Grads., Assn. of U.S. Army, White House Fellows Assn. (pres. 1986-87, bd. dirs. Found. 1986-87). Episcopalian. Home: 42 Wilson Rd # B West Point NY 10996-1912 Office: US Mil Acad Dept Social Sci West Point NY 10996

WALKER, WARREN FRANKLIN, JR., biology educator; b. Malden, Mass., Sept. 27, 1918; s. Warren Franklin and Alda (Miner) W.; m. Hortense Ballantine Allen, June 24, 1944; children: Edward A., Henry A., Susan Gay, Carol Ann. SB, Harvard Coll., 1941; PhD, Harvard U., 1946. Teaching fellow Harvard U., Cambridge, Mass., 1941-45; instr. Boston U. Med. Sch., 1945-47; instr. Oberlin (Ohio) Coll., 1947, asst. prof., 1949-52, assoc. prof., 1953-56, prof., 1957-66, dept. chmn., 1967-74, acting provost, 1974-75, prof. emeritus, 1985—. Author: Anatomy of Fetal Pig, 4th edit., 1988, Functional Anatomy of Vertebrates, 1987, Zoology, 1991, Vertebrate Dissection, 1992. Fellow AAAS, Appalachian Mtn. Club, Water Village Community Ch. (moderator 1990); mem. Am. Soc. Zoologists (divisional chmn. 1965-66), Ohio Acad. Scis., Soc. Ichthyologists and Herpetologists, Am. Assn. Anatomists. Democrat. Baptist. Home and Office: PO Box 436 Ossipee NH 03864

WALKER, WILLIAM JOHN, education educator; b. Bennington, Vt., Aug. 17, 1930; s. Donald John and Cecelia Helena (Liberty) W.; m. Barbara Irene Watt, Feb. 27, 1954; children—Steven Andrew, William John, James Donald. A.B., Syracuse U., 1952, M.A., 1956, Ed.D., 1964. Tchr. various schs. Calif., N.Y., 1956-61; prin., supt. Mexico Central Schs., N.Y., 1964-67; prof. edn. Alfred U., N.Y., 1967—, chmn. dept., 1970-81; dir. Alfred Area Sch. Study Coun. and Sch. Bds. Inst., 1974—. Contbr. articles to profl. jours. Pres. Andover Bd. Edn., 1970-75; chmn. Andover Republican Com., 1975-78; bd. dirs., past pres. Rural Health and Human Services, Belmont, N.Y., 1974-84. Served to lt. comdr. USNR, 1952-56. Grad. fellow Syracuse U., 1961; U.S. Dept. Edn. grantee, 1962, 70. Mem. NEA (life), Assn. Supervision and Curriculum Devel., Phi Delta Kappa, Phi Kappa Phi. Unitarian. Lodges: Lions, Masons. Avocations: hiking; camping; gardening; pottery. Home: 57 S Main St Alfred NY 14802-1322 Office: Alfred U Div Edn Alfred NY 14802

WALKOWSKI, KEVIN MICHAEL, lawyer; b. Springfield, Mass., Aug. 15, 1964; s. James Anthony Jr. and Sandra Lois Ann (Chmura) W. BA in Econs., Wesleyan U., 1986; JD, Harvard U., 1991. Bar: Mass., Conn. Dir. corp. tng. Sounds Great, Inc., Albany, N.Y., 1983-86; group sales mgr. G. Fox and Co., Hartford, Conn., 1986-87; dir. law adminstrn. Mass. Mut. Life Ins. Co., Springfield, 1987-88; pres. and chief exec. officer Reunions, Inc., West Springfield, Mass., 1988—; mem. staff Hebb & Gitlin, P.C., Hartford, 1989; dep. sheriff Law Enforcement Div. Hampden County Sheriff's Dept., Springfield, 1989-91; mem. staff Ivins, Phillips & Barker, Washington, 1990; law clk. Hon. Frank H. Freedman, Chief U.S. Dist. Judge, Springfield, 1991—; teaching fellow dept. econs. Harvard U., Cambridge, Mass., 1989-91; trustee, treas. Doverbrook Estates, Chicopee, Mass., 1992—; dep. clk. ct. U.S. Dist. Ct., Springfield, 1992—. Author: Expropriation Law: A Conceptual Analysis, 1991. Mem. Phi Beta Kappa. Republican. Roman Catholic.

WALL, ERVING HENRY, JR., sales agency executive, state senator; b. Plymouth, Mass., Sept. 27, 1934; s. Erving Henry Sr. and Madeline Blanche (Northrup) W.; m. Harriett Florence Marr, July 6, 1959; children: Deborah, Carol, Harriett, Susan. Grad. high sch., Plymouth. Lic. real estate broker, Mass. Electronics technician Raytheon, Waltham, North Dighton, and Quincy, Mass., 1957-65; tech. rep. Mt. Hope Machinery, Taunton, Mass., 1965-68, Beckman Instruments, Palo Alto, Calif., 1968-70; sales rep. Louis Batson Co., Greenville, S.C., 1970-73, Marshall & Williams Co., Providence, 1973-76, W.R. Grace and Co., Lexington, Mass., 1976-78; owner, operator Wall Machinery Inc., Taunton, 1978—; mem. Mass. State Senate, 1991—. Mem. Mass. Rep. Senate Com., Corp. Morton Hosp. Chief petty officer USN, 1953-57, with USNR, 1964-82. Mem. Am. Assn. Textile Colorists, Nat. Rep. Legis. Assn., Mass. Archeol. Soc., Inc., Korean War Vets., Tin Can Sailors, Segregansett Country Club. Baptist. Home: 128 Winthrop St Taunton MA 02780 Office: House of Senate State House Rm 314 Boston MA 02133

WALL, TIMOTHY LEE, writer, community organizer; b. Bayside, N.Y., Jan. 26, 1950; s. Gaylord N. and Marie Ruth (Fast) W. BA, Antioch Coll., 1973. Asst. editor The Andean Times, Bogota, Columbia, 1970; organizer Eastern Farm Workers Assn., Suffolk, N.Y., 1973-75; ops. mgr. Ea. Svc. Workers Assn., New Brunswick, N.J., 1975-80; assoc. editor N.J. Living, Princeton, 1981-84, Action, N.Y.C., 1985-86; publ. dir. Local 32B-32J Svc. Employees Union, N.Y.C.; asst. dir. pub. info. Citizens Com. for N.Y.C., 1988—; editor, writer Community Publ., Princeton, N.J., 1983-85; columnist Garden State Home and Garden, Morganville, N.J., 1987-88; cons. writer UN Pub. Info., N.Y.C., 1989—; reviewer ART News, N.Y.C., 1989-90. Author: Two-Time Loser, 1983; The UN and Crime Prevention, 1990, African Alternative Framework, 1990; editor: An Alternative School for Pregnant and Parenting Students, 1991. Founder, dir. Prisoner Support Group, Yellow Springs, Ohio, 1971, L.I. Equal Justice Assn. Suffolk County, N.Y., 1972; state coord. Com. In Solidarity with the People of El Salvador, N.J., 1985. Mem. Nat. Writers Union. Home: 149 Welton St Apt K New Brunswick NJ 08901 Office: Citizens Committee for NYC 3 W 29 St New York NY 10001

WALLACE, BARBARA J., bank executive; b. Newport News, Va., Feb. 25, 1944; d. Joseph T. and Muriel E. (Ponder) Jenkins; m. John Shepardson Wallace, June 10, 1967; children: Alison P., Joseph H. BA, Emory U., 1966, postgrad., 1966-67; MBA, U. Mass., 1986. Tchr. Tenn. A&I State U., Nashville, 1967-68; tchr. Pioneer Valley Coll., Edwards, Calif., 1968-70, Wilmington, N.C., 1976-78, Longmeadow, Mass., 1982-83; asst. v.p. Bank of Boston, Boston and Springfield, Mass., 1986-89; v.p. Bank of Western Mass., Springfield, 1989—. Mem. fin. com. Springfield Libr. & Mus. Assn., 1990—; mem. capital planning com. Town of Longmeadow, 1990-92; treas., bd. dirs. Springfield Theatre Arts Assn., 1990—. NDEA fellow Emory U., 1967. Mem. Phi Beta Kappa. Episcopalian. Home: 48 Hillcrest Ave Longmeadow MA 01106 Office: Bank of Western Mass 29 State St PO Box 4950 Springfield MA 01106

WALLACE, CAROL ANN, public relations executive; b. Pittsfield, Mass., Mar. 17, 1962; d. Philip Victor George and Ann Elizabeth (Moran) W. BA in English and Writing, Fairfield U., 1984. Pub. rels. coord. Kraft, Inc., West Haven, Conn., 1985-88; mgr. communications Colgate-Palmolive, N.Y.C., 1988-89; sr. account exec. Ketchum Pub. Rels., N.Y.C., 1989-92; account supr. Creamer Dickson Basford, N.Y.C., 1992—. Tutor with Literacy Vols., West Haven, 1987-88. Office: CDB 1633 Broadway New York NY 10019

WALLACE, DAVID WILLIAM, corporate executive; b. N.Y.C., Feb. 23, 1924; s. Fergus Ferguson and Isabelle Taylor (Wilson) W.; m. Jean Ives McLean, June 20, 1953; children: Mary H., Anne S. BS, Yale U., 1948; JD, Harvard U., 1951. Bar: N.Y. 1952, U.S. Supreme Ct. 1976. Assoc. White & Case, N.Y.C., 1951-54; gen. counsel Alleghany Corp., 1954, sec.-treas., 1954-56, v.p., 1956-58, exec. v.p., 1958-59; exec. v.p. chmn. exec. com. United Brands Corp., until 1967; dir., pres. Bangor Punta Corp., 1967-84, chief exec. officer, 1969-84, chmn. bd., 1973-84; chmn. bd., chief exec. officer Todd Shipyards Corp., Seattle, Wash., 1987-91; chmn. bd. Nat. Securities & Rsch. Corp., 1988—; mem. Lloyds of London, 1975—; chmn. bd. FECO Engring. Systems; bd. dirs. Aitken Hume Internat.; bd. dirs., mem. exec. com., chmn. and chief exec. officer Lone Star Industries, Inc.; bd. dirs. Emigrant Savs. Bank, BV Capital Corp., UMC Electronics Co., Zurn Industries, Putnam Trust Co. Pres. trustee Robert R. Young Found.; bd. govs. N.Y. Hosp.; bd. trustees Smith Coll. 1st lt. U.S. Army, 1943-46. Mem. St. Andrew's Soc. N.Y., Brook, Yale Club, Econ. Club, Greenwich Country Club, Sky Club. Presbyterian. Home: Deer Park Greenwich CT 06830-3803 Office: 2 Greenwich Pla Ste 100 Greenwich CT 06830

WALLACE, GEORGE F., publishing executive; b. Jersey City, Oct. 24, 1938; m. Mary Jane Wallace (div.); children: Jessica, David.; m. Nessa Wallace, Mar. 2, 1985; 1 child, Brendan. BA in Classics, Fordham U., 1962, MS in Edn., 1965. Sr. editor Croft Ednl. Svcs., Inc., New London, Conn., 1970-73; pub., editor in chief Gregg div. McGraw Hill Book Co., N.Y.C., 1973-76, pub. Webster div., 1976-80, v.p., gen. mgr., 1985-90; v.p., editorial dir. McGraw Hill Internat. Book Co., N.Y.C., 1980-81; group v.p. Europe, Middle East & Africa div. McGraw Hill Internat. Book Co., Maidenhead, Berkshire, Eng., 1983-85; v.p., mng. dir. McGraw Hill Book (U.K.) Ltd., Maidenhead, 1981-83; v.p., splty. practice Lawyers Coop. Pub., Rochester, N.Y., 1990; pres., chief exec. officer Clark Boardman Callaghan, Rochester, 1991—. Office: Clark Boardman Callaghan 50 Broad St E Rochester NY 14694

WALLACE, GEORGE FRANCIS, podiatrist; b. Elizabeth, N.J., Jan. 31, 1954; s. Francis and Joyce (Scheele) W.; m. Ann Marie Dziewiatek, June 14, 1981; 1 child, Kelly. BS, Seton Hall U., 1976; D of Podiatric Medicine, Pa. Coll. Podiatric Medicine, 1981. Diplomate Am. Bd. Podiatric Surgery, Am. Bd. Podiatric Orthopedics. Jr. resident Northlake (Ill.) Community Hosp., 1981-82; sr. resident Cen. Community Hosp., Chgo., 1982-83; podiatrist pvt. practice Hasbrouck Hgts., N.J., 1983—; cons. Medigroup HMO, Newark, 1986—; clin. instr. dept. of surgery Univ. Medicine and Dentistry of N.J., 1990—; chief podiatric surgery Holy Name Hosp., Teaneck, N.J., 1987—. Editor: Clinics in Podiatric Medicine and Surgery, 1991; co-author: (book chpt.) Podiatric Surgery, 1989; contbr. articles to profl. jours. Mem. Kiwanis, Hasbrouck Hgts., 1984—; com. mem. Boy Scouts Am., River Edge, N.J., 1990—. Recipient Eagle Scout award, 1968, Cert. of Merit, N.J. Podiatric Med. Soc., 1990, 91. Fellow Am. Coll. Foot Surgeons, Am. Coll. Foot Orthopedics. Office: 440 Boulevard Hasbrouck Heights NJ 07604-1518

WALLACE, JAMES MICHAEL, English educator; b. Wilkes-Barre, Pa., Dec. 19, 1958; s. James Francis and Louise (Krissinger) W.; m. Anna Maria Smacchi, July 12, 1986. BA, Wilkes Coll., 1980; MA, Lehigh U., 1986, PhD, 1989. Teaching fellow Lehigh U., Bethlehem, Pa., 1981-88; asst. prof. King's Coll., Wilkes-Barre, 1988—. Contbr. numerous articles to profl. jours. Member Lehigh-Pocono Com. of Concern, Bethlehem, 1991—, Wyoming Valley Peace Com., Wilkes-Barre, 1991—. Mem. Modern Lang. Assn., Delta Epsilon Sigma, Sigma Tau Delta. Democrat. Roman Catholic. Home: 606 Wildflower Dr Wilkes Barre PA 18702-7928 Office: Kings Coll Dept English Wilkes Barre PA 18711

WALLACE, JANE HOUSE, geologist; b. Ft. Worth, Aug. 12, 1926; d. Fred Leroy and Helen Gould (Kixmiller) Wallace; A.B., Smith Coll., 1947, M.A., 1949; postgrad. Bryn Mawr Coll., 1949-52. Geologist, U.S. Geol. Survey, 1952—, chief Pub. Inquiries Offices, Washington, 1964-72, spl. asst. to dir., 1974—, dep. bur. ethics counselor, 1975—, Washington liaison Office of Dir., 1978—. Recipient Meritorious Service award Dept. Interior, 1971, Disting. Svc. award, 1976, Sec.'s Commendation, 1988, Smith Coll. medal, 1992. Fellow Geol. Socs. Am., Washington (treas. 1963-67); mem. Sigma Xi (asso.). Home: 3003 Van Ness St NW Washington DC 20008-4701 Office: Interior Bldg 19th and C Sts NW Washington DC Address: US Geol Survey 103 National Ctr Reston VA 22092

WALLACE, JOHN DOUGLAS, automotive professional; b. Glen Ridge, N.J., Apr. 29, 1951; s. John William Wallace and Edith (Clark) Griesenbeck; m. Catherine Elizabeth Wolff, May 20, 1972; 1 child, Andrew Douglas. Student, Ocean County Coll., 1969-71. Technician East Dover Marina, Toms River, N.J., 1967-69, Silverton Marine Corp., Toms River, 1969-70; svc. mgr. Somerville (N.J.) Dodge Inc., 1971-77; svc. and parts dir. Warnock Dodge Inc., East Hanover, N.J., 1977—. Fireman, West Caldwell (N.J.) Fire Dept., 1980—. With AUS, 1970-77. Mem. Svc. and Parts Mgrs. Guild, Masons. Republican. Methodist. Home: 9 Piermont Pl West Caldwell NJ 07006-8227 Office: Warnock Dodge Inc 175 State Route 10 East Hanover NJ 07936-2185

WALLACE, MARK EDWARD, psychiatrist; b. Louisville, Oct. 16, 1955; s. Lyle Gay and Emily Jean (Hardesty) W. BA in Chemistry, 1977; DMS, MD, U. Louisville, 1981. Intern Cook County Hosp., Chgo., 1981-82; with nat. health svc. corps City of Chgo. Bd. Health, 1982-85; resident St. Vincent's Hosp., N.Y.C., 1985-87; fellow St. Vincent's Hosp., 1987-89; rsch. attending psychiatrist NYU Med. Ctr.-Bellevue Hosp., N.Y.C., 1989—; chief fellow St. Vincent's Hosp., N.Y.C., 1988-89. Co-author: Mental Retardation and Delinquency, 1989. Vol. Catholic Corps. Vols., 1976-78. Mem. Am. Psychiat. Assn., AMA, Am. Acad. Child and Adolescent Psychiatry, Delta Epsilon Sigma (pres. Louisville chpt. 1976-77). Democrat. Roman Catholic.

WALLACE, MARK I., religion educator; b. Covina, Calif., June 26, 1956; s. H. Homer and Shirley (Hastings) W.; m. Ellen Marie Ross, Sept. 11, 1983. BA, U. Calif., Santa Barbara, 1978; MDiv, Princeton Theol. Sem., 1982; PhD, U. Chgo., 1986. Ordained to ministry Presbyn. Ch., 1990. Asst. prof. Ga. State U., 1987-89, Swarthmore (Pa.) Coll., 1989—. Author: The Second Naiveté. Summer grantee Nat. Endowment for the Humanities, 1989. Fellow Soc. for Values in Higher Edn.; mem. Am. Acad. Religion. Democrat. Home: 318 N Chester Rd Swarthmore PA 19081-1107 Office: Swarthmore Coll Religion Swarthmore PA 19081

WALLACE, MIKE, television interviewer and reporter; b. Brookline, Mass., May 9, 1918; s. Frank and Zina (Sharfman) W.; m. Lorraine Perigord, July 21, 1955 (div. 1985); children: Peter (dec.), Christopher; m. Mary Yates, June 28, 1986. AB, U. Mich., 1935-39, hon. degree, 1987; hon. degree, U. Mass., 1978, U. Pa., 1989. Associated with radio, 1939—, TV, 1946—; commentator, CBS-TV, 1951-54, TV interviewer, reporter, 1951—, CBS news corr., 1963—; co-editor: 60 Minutes, CBS; Author: Mike Wallace Asks, 1958, Close Encounters, 1984. Recipient Robert Sherwood award, 1971, 72, 73; recipient 13 ATVAS Emmy awards; George Foster Peabody awards, 1963-71; DuPont Columbia Journalism award, 1972, 83; Carr Van Anda award, 1977; Thomas Hart Benton award, 1978. Mem. Century Assocs., Sigma Delta Chi. Office: CBS News 524 W 57th St New York NY 10019-2902

WALLACE, RALPH, superintendent; b. Halifax, Nova Scotia; s. Ralph and Alberta (Warren) W.; m. Haunani Wallace, Aug. 1, 1980; children: Lianne, Travis. BEd, U. British Columbia, 1968, MEd, 1976; postgrad., U. Conn., 1986; CAGS, Boston U., 1987, EdD, 1992. Cert. supt., int. adminstr., Conn. Asst. supt. West Vancouver (B.C.) Bd. Edn.; prin. Granby (Conn.) Bd. Edn., Farmington (Conn.) Bd. Edn.; supt. Granby (Conn.) Bd. Edn.; apptd. Pres. Nat. Excellence Panel. Contbr. articles to profl. jours. Dir. Gov.'s Sch., Conn. State U. Recipient Nat. Excellence award U.S. Dept. Edn.; named Conn. Supt. of Yr., 1992. Mem. Conn. Transp. Commn. (hon.), AASA/CASA (legis.), AERA, ERS, ASCD. Home: 40 Dorset Ln Farmington CT 06032-2330

WALLACE, RAYMOND HOWARD, JR., hydrologist; b. Columbus, Ga., July 29, 1936; s. Raymond Howard Sr. and Fannie Serrelle (Rutland) W.; m. Katharine Frances Ritter, Apr. 4, 1958; children: Raymond Howard III, Mary Haviland. BS, Fla. State U., 1960; MS, La. State U., 1966. Geologist U.S. Geol. Survey WRD, Baton Rouge, 1966-69; hydrologist U.S. Geol. Survey WRD, St. Louis, 1969-71; hydrologist U.S. Geol. Survey WRD, Bay St. Louis, Miss., 1971-73, rsch. project chief, 1973-83; geothermal liaison U.S. Geol. Survey GD, Washington, 1984-87; liaison high-level radioactive waste mgmt. U.S. Geol. Survey WRD, Washington, 1987—; geothermal program mgr. U.S. Dept. Energy, Washington, 1984-87; geologist trainee Gulf Oil Corp., New Orleans, 1964; rsch. assoc. La. Water Resources Rsch. Inst., Baton Rouge, 1965-66; mem. supply-tech. adv. task force Fed. Energy Regulatory Commn., Washington, 1975-78. Contbr. articles to profl. jours. Capt. USMCR, 1960-63. Recipient Superior Svc. award Dept. Interior, 1982. Mem. Geol. Soc. Am., Am. Assn. Petroleum Geologists, Am. Legion, Sigma Xi. Methodist. Home: 6663 Tennyson Dr Mc Lean VA 22101-5716 Office: Dept Energy RW-22 1000 Independence Ave SW Washington DC 20585-0001

WALLACE, RON, city official; b. Halifax, N.S., Can.; m. Patricia McColough; six children. Ed. Dalhousie U.; grad. Royal Rds. Naval Coll. Mem. Legis. Assembly N.S. Legislature, 1970-78; mayor of Halifax, 1980—. Exec. officer Can. Navy. Office: Office of the Mayor, City Hall, Halifax, NS Canada B3T 3A5

WALLACE, RONALD DEREK, sales executive; b. Darlington, Durham, England, Oct. 11, 1943; came to U.S., 1983; s. Henry and Margot (Plaut) W.; m. Sally Ann Sassienie, Mar. 10, 1968; children: Nicola Samantha, James Mark. Export sales exec. G.A. Harvey & Son Ltd., London, 1964-68; gen. mgr. Bernard Wald Ltd., London, 1968-71; adminstrn. mgr. Chinacraft Ltd., London, 1971-75; dye-house mgr. Roscol Ltd., London, 1975-78; sales mgr. Europe Belding Hausman Fabrics, N.Y.C., 1977-78; dir. C.M. Offray & Son Ltd., London, 1978-83; v.p. C.M. Offray & Son Inc., Chester, N.J., 1983—; ptnr. The Dorset Bye, Morristown, N.J., 1991—. Chmn. Reform Synagogues in Gt. Britain Youth Orgns., 1970-75; youth leader Temple Shalom, Succasunna, N.J., 1983-90 (Man of Yr. 1985-86). Jewish. Home: 8 Dorset Rd Long Valley NJ 07853-9717 Office: CM Offray & Son Inc Rte # 24 Box # 601 Chester NJ 07930-0601

WALLACE, RUTH E., development officer; b. Silver Spring, Md., Oct. 1, 1965; d. David Windsor and Sara Rebecca (Sakoff) Harris; m. Jonathan Marc Wallace, Oct. 27, 1991. BA cum laude, Washington U., St. Louis, 1987. Program asst. Am. Chem. Soc., Washington, 1987-88, staff asst., devel. scvs., 1988, coord. devel. svcs., 1989, devel. officer, 1990—. Contbr. articles to Am. Chem. Soc. membership publs. Mem. Am. Prospect Rsch. Assn. Office: Am Chem Soc 3075 Taylor Way Costa Mesa CA 92626-2831

WALLACE, THOMAS EDWARD, JR., public transportation executive; b. N.Y.C., Dec. 10, 1948; s. Thomas Edward Sr. and Antoinette Dolores (Sabattie) W.; m. Ranulfa Subiel, Jan 29, 1982; children: Vanessa, Antoinette, Thomas Jr. AS, Cuyohoga Community Coll., Cleve., 1971; BSBA, Lake Erie Coll., 1977, MBA in Systems Mgmt., 1984. Gen. mgr. McDonald's Systems, Cleve., 1977-78; br. mgr. Canteen Corp., Mentor, Ohio, 1979-82; project dir. Bus. Devel. Ctr., Office of Mayor City of Cleve., 1982-86; dir. disadvantaged bus. enterprises div. N.Y.C. Transit Authority, Bklyn., 1986—. Bd. dirs. Harlem Restoration Project, Inc., N.Y.C., 1990—. Recipient Most Outstanding Bus. Devel. Ctr. Nat. award for City of Cleve., U.S. Dept. Commerce, 1984. Mem. Am. Mgmt. Assn., Omega Psi Phi. Democrat.

WALLACE, WILLIAM SHELDON, editor; b. Oakland, Calif., Mar. 17, 1915; s. Alfred Franklin and Hattie May (Wicker) W.; m. Marcia Cutler Vickery, Jan. 8, 1954 (dec. Aug. 1985); children: James Derby, David Cutler, Kate Anne Wallace Rogers. BA, U. Calif., Berkeley, 1938; MA, U. Ala., 1948. Editor pub. rels. dept. Am. Express Co., N.Y.C., 1948-50; asst. dir. pub. rels. French Govt. Tourist Office, N.Y.C., 1950-55; account exec. pub. rels. J. Walter Thompson Co., N.Y.C., 1955-64; dir. pub. rels. Kelly, Nason, Inc., N.Y.C., 1964-66; v.p. mktg. div. Rockresorts, Inc., N.Y.C., 1966-68; exec. v.p., co-owner Jacobson/Wallace, Inc., N.Y.C., 1968-83; freelance writer and editor N.Y.C., 1983-86; editor Merrill Lynch, N.Y.C., 1986—. Author: (play) Beer, Said the Privates, 1949; (novel) The Lightning on Telegraph Hill, 1989; author poems and short stories. Sgt. U.S. Army, 1942-45, PTO. Mem. Dickens Fellowship of N.Y., Soc. Am. Baseball Researchers, Nat. Assn. Travel Orgns. (pub. rels. chmn., nat. chmn. 1956-60), Soc. Am. Travel Writers (assoc. mems. chmn., nat. chmn. 1957-62), U. Calif. Alumni Assn. Democrat. Episcopalian. Home: 307 E 93d St Apt 4W New York NY 10128-1761

WALLACH, DAVID LEE, physicist; b. Cleve., Aug. 21, 1940; s. Edward Isaac and Dorothy Rachel (Lee) W.; m. Carole Ann Gerstacker, June 16, 1962; children: Elizabeth, Daniel, Deborah. Student, Rensselaer Poly. Inst., 1958-60; BS in Physics, Case Inst. of Tech., 1962; MS in Physics, Carnegie Inst. Tech., 1966; PhD in Planetary Sci., U. Pitts., 1979. Assoc. scientist Bettis Atomic Power Lab., West Mifflin, Pa., 1962-67; asst. prof. of physics Pa. State U., McKeesport, 1967—; owner Wallco Sci. Co., Bridgeville, Pa., 1977—; v.p. Hoyt West 6th St. Co., Inc., Cleve., 1962-77, Buckeye E. 119th St. Co., Inc., Cleve., 1962-82. Author: Outlines of Selected Topics in Technical Physics, 1975; inventor Spectacle lenses, scruler; contbr. articles to profl. jours. Bd. dirs. Rodef Shalom Jr. Congregation, Pitts., 1967-76, pres., 1971; bd. dirs. Peters Twp. Sch. Dist., McMurray, Pa., 1979-89, v.p., 1984, 86, pres., 1985. Mem. Am. Assn. Physics Tchrs., Nat. Sci. Tchrs. Assn. Home: 2809 Old Washington Rd Bridgeville PA 15017-1751 Office: Pa State U McKeesport Campus Mckeesport PA 15132

WALLACH, HANS GERT PETER, political science educator; b. N.Y.C., Nov. 16, 1938; s. Gert Max Klaus and Gerda Wilhemina (Lewenz) W.; m. Martha Hess, June 19, 1971. AB, Kenyon Coll., 1961; MA, U. Conn., 1964, PhD, 1973; postgrad., U. Mich., 1967. Instr., then asst. prof. U. Wis., Green Bay, 1970-77, acad. coordinator, urban consortium, 1977-78; asst. prof., then assoc. prof. Cen. Conn. State U., New Britain, 1978-90, chmn. German Studies Coun., 1985—, prof., 1990—; dir. Conn. Inst. for European and Am. Studies; head survey unit Inst. Practical Politics, New Britain, 1986—; organizer New England Conf. on Germany, New Britain, 1989; vis. faculty fellow Mellon Found., Yale U., 1981-82. Author handbook: Teaching Am. Dem. Debated, 1981, United Germany, 1992; editor: West German Politics in Mid-80's, 1985; contbr. articles to profl. publs. Bd. dirs. Fairfield County (Conn.) YMCA, 1986—; rsch. dir. campaign Congressman Cornell, Green Bay, 1974-78. Grantee, Ford Found., 1974-76, NEH, 1976, Volkswagen Found., 1988. Mem. Internat. Polit. Sci. Assn., Am. Polit. Sci. Assn., German-Am. Law Assn., Law and Soc. Assn., Conf. Group on German Politics, ACLU (pres. New Haven chpt. 1987-), Conn. Civil Liberties Union and Found. (bd. dirs. 1983-). Democrat. Office: Cen Conn State U New Britain CT 06050

WALLACH, JACQUES BURTON, pathologist, educator; b. N.Y.C., Jan. 25, 1926; s. Joseph Irving and Rose Gertrude (Bernstein) W.; m. Doris Foss, Sept. 5, 1953; children: Kim, Lisa, Tracy. Student, NYU, 1941-43; MD, L.I. Coll. Medicine, SUNY, 1947. Diplomate Am. Bd. Pathology. Instr. pathology Albert Einstein Coll. Medicine, Bronx, N.Y., 1954-55, asst. prof. pathology, 1955-59, vis. asst. prof. pathology, 1959-69; clin. assoc. prof. pathology Rutgers Med. Sch., Piscataway, N.J., 1971—; clin. prof. pathology SUNY, Bklyn., 1979—; cons. in clin. pathology N.Y. Zool. Soc., Bronx (N.Y.) Zoo, 1954-84. Author: Rheumatic Heart Disease, 1962, Interpretation of Diagnostic Tests, 1970, 5th ed., 1991, Interpretation of Pediatric Tests, 1983. With USNR, 1944-45. Named Hon. Prof. of Pathology, Univ. Ica, Peru, 1981. Fellow Am. Coll. Physicians, Am. Soc. Clin. Pathologists, Coll. Am. Pathologists, N.Y. Acad. Medicine. Home and Office: 18 Dartmouth Rd Cranford NJ 07016-1609

WALLACH, JANET LEE, writer; b. N.Y.C., May 4, 1942; d. George and Sylvia (Weil); m. John Paul Wallach, June 9, 1974; children: David, Michael. BA, NYU, 1965. Fashion designer Herman Geist, N.Y.C., 1970-74, Garfinckel's, Washington, 1976-80; fashion coord. Woodward & Lothrop, Washington, 1975-76. Author: Working Wardrobe, 1981, Looks That Work, 1985, Still Small Voices, 1989, Arafat: In the Eyes of the Beholder, 1990; contbg. editor Dossier Mag., Washington Post Mag. Mem. Washington Ind. Writers. Home: 102 E Lenox St Bethesda MD 20815

WALLACH, JOHN PAUL, newspaper editor; b. N.Y.C., Jan. 18, 1943; s. Paul and Edith (Putzel) W.; m. Janet Lee Weil, June 9, 1974; children: David, Michael. BA, Middlebury Coll., 1964; MA, New Sch. for Social Research, 1966. Corr. state dept. Hearst Newspapers, Washington, 1968-74, corr. white house, 1974-76, fgn. editor, 1976—. Author: Still Small Voices: The Human Story Benind the Intifada, 1989, Arafat: In the Eyes of the Beholder, 1990; contbg. editor Washingtonian mag., 1984—. Dir. Chautauqua (N.Y.) Conf. U.S.-Soviet Relations, 1983-87; mem. nat. adv. bd. Am. U., Washington. Recipient Raymond Clapper award Standing Com. Corrs., 1979, Edward Weintal prize Georgetown U., 1980, Overseas Press Club award, 1980, 83; named Adj. Prof. of Yr. Am. U., 1985. Mem. Overseas Writers Club (pres. 1991-92). Office: Hearst Newspapers 1701 Pennsylvania Ave NW Washington DC 20006-5805

WALLE, GERALD YVON, electronics executive; b. Marseille, France, Apr. 17, 1953; came to U.S., 1981; s. Emile and Germaine (Grossemy) W.; m. Laurie Laird, June 9, 1978; children: Georgia, Remy, Spencer, Juliette. Diploma in engring., Ecole Poly., 1976; MBA, Harvard U., 1978. Cons. Boston Cons. Group, Paris, 1978-79; sr. cons. Mars & Co., Paris, 1979-81; mgr., internat. bus. devel. Bendix (Allied-Signal), N.Y.C., 1981-83; internat. mktg. mgr. Instrumentation Lab. (Allied Signal), Lexington, Mass., 1983-87; v.p., gen. mgr., microelectronics Millipore, Bedford, Mass., 1987—. Ensign French Navy, 1973-76. Office: Millipore 80 Ashby Rd Bedford MA 01730-2271

WALLENDER, MICHAEL TODD, lawyer; b. Schenectady, N.Y., Apr. 8, 1950; s. Kenneth Clark and Martha Lee (Getty) W.; m. Joyce Ann Mushaw, June 3, 1978; children: Kristina Lee, Michael David. BA, Colgate U., 1972; JD, Harvard U., 1975. Law asst. N.Y. State Supreme Ct. Appellate Div., Albany, 1975-76; assoc. DeGraff, Foy, Conway, Holt-Harris & Mealey, Albany, 1976-80, ptnr., 1981-90; counsel N.Y. State Assn. Realtors, Albany, 1981—, Albany County Bd. Realtors, 1985—, Capital Region Multiple Listing Svc., Albany, 1986—. Author: Realtors and the Law of Agency, 1988. counsel Tercentenary Fund, Schenectady, 1978, Step 6 Citizens Against Child Sexual Abuse, Schenectady, 1985. Mem. Am. Trial Lawyers Assn., ABA, N.Y. State Bar Assn., Albany County Bar Assn., Ft. Orange Club, Mohawk Golf Club, Colgate Club (capital dist. chpt., Albany), Saratoga Reading Rm. Home: 28 Cheshire Pl Niskayuna NY 12309-4939 Office: 100 State St Ste 800 Albany NY 12207-1809

WALLER, ROBERT BRADFORD, JR., trade association executive; b. S.I., May 20, 1960; s. Robert Bradford and Corrine (Simon) W.; m. Susan Cohen, Sept. 1, 1990. BS, Castleton State Coll., 1982. Resident dir. Castleton (Vt.) State Coll., 1981-82; staff mgr. ASTM, Phila., 1982-85; v.p. Words Unlimited, Rutland, Vt., 1985; mortgage broker D. C. Reilly Assocs., Middletown, N.J., 1985-87; v.p. Assn. Hdqrs., Marlton, N.J., 1987—; exec. dir. Juvenile Products Mfrs. Assn., Marlton, 1987—. Mem. Nat. Assn. Exposition Mgrs., N.J. Soc. Assn. Execs. (program chmn. 1991, vice chmn. 1992), Inst. for Orgn. Mgmt. (class adviser 1991, 92). Office: Juvenile Products Mfrs Assn 2 Greentree Ctr Ste 225 Marlton NJ 08053-3102

WALLERSTEIN, HARRY, retired hematologist; b. N.Y.C., Dec. 11, 1906; s. Jacob Mordecai and Lena (Goldberg) W.; m. Gussie Arnold, June 29, 1926; children: Sally W. Sedler, Caryl W. Sands. AB, George Washington U., 1927, MD, 1930. Intern Sydenham Hosp., N.Y.C., 1930-31; assoc. pathologist to dir. rsch. Jewish Meml. Hosp., 1964-83; from dir. blood bank to vis. pathologist Bronx Mcpl. Hosp. Ctr., 1956-83; cons. in hematology St. Elizabeth Hosp., 1954—, Fordham City Hosp., 1951—, Morrisania City Hosp., 1948—, St. Clare's Hosp. and Health Ctr., 1971—; lectr. pathology Albert Einstein Coll. Medicine, 1956-59, vis. asst. prof. pathology, 1959-76; dir. labs., pathologist Jewish Meml. Hosp., 1933-37, assoc. hematologist, 1937-50; assoc vis. pathologist Bronx Mcpl. Hosp., 1956-58; asst./assoc. vis. pathologist Queens Cen. Hosp., 1942-56; assoc. pathologist Sea View Hosp., 1933. Contbr. articles to profl. jours. Mem. Blood Bank and Transfusion Adv. Bd. to Dept. Health, N.Y.C., 1967—. Recipient Hon. Mention Med. Soc. State N.Y., 1948, 3d award for Meritorious Individual Investigation, 1948, 1st award for Sci. Rsch., 1964; grantee Dept. HEW. Fellow N.Y. Acad. Medicine, N.Y. Acad. Sci., AMA, Am. Soc. Clin. Pathologists, Internat. Soc. Hematology (founder); mem. AAAS, Am. Assn. Blood Banks, Blood Bank Assn. N.Y. State, Internat. Soc. Blood Transfusions, Am. Soc. Hematology, N.Y. Pathol. Soc. (life), Am. Soc. Human Genetics, N.Y. Acad. Scis. (life), N.Y. Soc. for Study of Blood, N.Y. State Soc. Pathologists, Am. Eugenics Soc., Am. Assn. Cancer Rsch., Albert Gallatin Assocs. of NYU (life), Luther Rice Soc. George Washington U. (life).

WALLERSTEIN, LEIBERT BENET, economist; b. Bklyn., July 5, 1922; s. William Mark and Ray Leah (Goldberg) W.; m. Alice Stehle, Oct. 10, 1929; stepchildren: Nora Odendahl, Steven Odendahl. 1947-50; BA, U. N.Mex., 1950, MA in Econs., 1951; postgrad., U. Minn., 1951-53; MA in Econs., U. N.Mex., 1951; postgrad., U.S. Mcht. Marine Acad., 1977. With U.S. Corps of Engrs. and Army Air Corps Matl. Command, Washington, 1943-46, AUS, 1945-47, U.S. Navy Bur. ORD, 1954-55, U.S. Dept. Labor, 1956-67, HUD, 1967-69, U.S. DOT, 1961-80; faculty U. Minn., U. Md., U. New Mex., Pentagon, Georgetown U., Ben Franklin U., Montgomery Coll., Montgomery County Adult Edn. Ctr.; cons. economist 1980—. Contbr. articles to profl. jours. Vol. Shepard's Table, Washington, 1985—, Chevy Chase (Md.) grade schs., 1986; v.p. Univ. Young Dems. U. N.Mex., Albuquerque, 1947-50, NAACP, 1947-50. Mem. Atlantic Econ. Soc., Am. Econ. Assn., Economists Club Washington (charter), Sr. Club (chmn. 1983—), Disabled Am. Vets., Am. Legion. Jewish. Home and Office: 3505 Thornapple St Bethesda MD 20815-4014

WALLERSTEIN, SETH MICHAEL, dentist; b. Newark, Feb. 6, 1960; s. Sheldon Melvin Wallerstein and Jeanne Alice (Rothenberger) Kushinsky; m. Lisa Mary Calvani, June 21, 1986; 1 child, Genna Marie. BA, Haverford (Pa.) Coll., 1982; DMD, U. Pa., 1986. Resident in dentistry John F. Kennedy Meml. Hosp., Edison, N.J., 1986-87; gen. practice dentistry Edison, 1987—; mem. staff dental dept. John F. Kennedy Meml. Hosp., 1987—. Mem. ADA, Acad. Gen. Dentistry, Alpha Omega. Jewish. Home: 33 Tower Rd Edison NJ 08820-3513

WALLERSTEIN, SHELDON M., mortgage company executive; b. Newark, Dec. 17, 1931; s. Solomon Wallerstein and Gussie (Cohen) Wallach; m. Jeanne A. Rothenberger, May 9, 1959 (div. Aug. 1978); children: Seth M., Gail E. Wallerstein Melichar; m. Loretta Myles Allen, Nov. 24, 1979; stepchildren: Thomas W. Allen, Tammy J. Allen. BA, Seton Hall U., 1955. Lic. real estate broker, N.J. Advt. mgr. Union (N.J.) Leader, 1957-62; salesman Maidenform, N.Y.C. and L.A., 1962-65, George Wolf Real Estate, Jersey City, 1965-67; v.p. Stern Mgmt. & Constrn., N.Y.C., 1967-68; pres. Sheldon Constrn. & Affiliate Cos., Summit, N.J., 1968-75; v.p. real estate sales Martin Witzburg & Son, Union, 1975-76, Leo Rutenberg, Kearny, N.J., 1976-77; dir. real estate The Money Store & Affiliated Cos., Springfield, N.J., 1977-86; v.p. The Money Store Investment Corp., Union, 1986—; trustee residuary trust R.C. Leibowitz, Lanoka Harbor, N.J., 1986—. Cons. Mayor's R.R. Sta. Com., Summit, 1986-87. 1st lt. U.S. Army, 1955-57. Fellow Order of the Cross and Crescent, Seton Hall U., 1955. Mem. DAV, AMVETS, Nat. Assn. Atomic Vets., Seton Hall U. Alumni Assn. Jewish. Office: Money Store Investment Corp 2840 Morris Ave Union NJ 07083-4809

WALLIE, WILLIAM JACK, savings executive; b. Stroudsburg, Pa., Jan. 26, 1940; s. William Jack and Esther (Cowling) W.; m. Edith Kathleen Caretta, May 14, 1960; children: Susan Randall, Bryan, Jennifer. Grad., Churchman Bus. Coll., 1959; grad. Pa. Bankers Sch., Bucknell U., 1962; grad. Bank Adminstrn. Inst., U. Wis., 1968; grad. Nat. Comml. Lending Sch., U. Okla., 1980. Note teller East Stroudsburg (Pa.) Nat. Bank, 1959-62, auditor, 1962-66, asst. cashier, 1966-67, asst. v.p., comptr., 1967-68, v.p. comptr., 1968-70; v.p. comptr. Pocono Bank, 1970-71; v.p. Northeastern Bank Pa., 1971-78, v.p., mgr. East Stroudsburg office, 1978-83; pres., chief exec. officer East Stroudsburg Savs. Assn., 1983—; instr. Am. Inst. Banking; bd. dirs. Lehigh Valley League of Savings Instns. Auditor, councilman Borough of East Stroudsburg; mem. Monroe County Planning Commn.; lay leader, Sunday sch. tchr., adminstrv. bd. East Stroudsburg United Meth. Ch.; treas., exec. com. United Way of Monroe County; chmn. East Stroudsburg Civil Svc. Commn., Pocono Raceway Ambassadors; bd. mem. Pocono Med. Ctr., Pocono Med. Ctr. Found., Pocono Mountains C. of C., Pocono Mountain Industries, Pocono Mountain Ctr. for the Performing Arts, Monroe County Indsl. Devel. Authority and others. Recipient Businessman of the Yr. award Pocono Mountains C. of C., 1987. Mem. Optimist Club of the Stroudsburgs, Gideons Internat. Republican. Office: East Stroudsburg Savs Box L 744 Main St Stroudsburg PA 18360-2029

WALLIN, FREDERICK E., real estate developer, consultant; b. Chgo., Dec. 17, 1943; s. Roy Gordon and Margaret Helen (Lundquist) W.; m. Dorothy Jean Drummond, July 3, 1964; children: Margaret Anne, Julia Alice. BA, Am. U., 1966; cert., Quality Coll.-Crosby, 1990. Copywriter Feldman & Kahn, Pitts., 1967-69; pres. Frederick E. Wallin Inc., Pitts., 1969-76; exec. v.p. Kahn & Wallin, Pitts., 1976-79; acct. supr. Marc & Co., Pitts., 1979-81; v.p. Ketchum Advt., Pitts., 1981-84; dir. mktg. com. Glass Group Industries, Pitts., 1984-86, dir. mktg., 1986-90; pres. Consolidated Glass & Mirror, Galax, Va., 1990-91; bus. cons. Pitts., 1991—. Bd. dirs. We. Pa. Leukemia Soc., Pitts., 1982-85, Support Ctr. for Cancer, 1989-90. Named Advt. Exec. of Yr. Bus. Profl. Advt. Assn., 1985. Mem. Nat. Assn. of Mirror Mfrs. (bd. dirs. 1990-91), Valley Brook Country Club. Republican. Methodist. Home: 116 Woodside Dr McMurray PA 15317

WALLIN, JUDITH KERSTIN, pediatrician, educator; b. Paris, Apr. 23, 1938; came to U.S., 1938; d. Theodore Bror and Ella Charlotte (Butler) Wallin. BS in Chemistry, Elizabethtown (Pa.) Coll., 1960; MD, Temple U., 1964. Diplomate Am. Bd. Pediatrics. Intern Bellevue Hosp., N.Y.C., 1964-65, resident specializing in pediatrics, 1965-67, attending pediatrician, 1967—; instr. pediatrics, NYU, 1967-71, asst. prof. clin. pediatrics, 1971-74, assoc. prof., 1974—. Trustee Elizabethtown Coll., 1988—. Recipient Educate for Service through Profl. Achievement award, O.F. Stambaugh Alumni award Elizabethtown Coll., 1978. Home: 300 E 33d St New York NY 10016 Office: Bellevue Hosp Dept Pediatrics 27th St and 1st Ave New York NY 10016

WALLIN, LELAND DEAN, artist, educator; b. Sioux Falls, S.D., Oct. 14, 1942; s. Clarence Forrest and Leona Mae (McInnis) W.; m. Meredith Maria Hawkins, Mar. 26, 1977; 1 child, Jessica Hawkins. Student, Columbus Coll. Art and Design, 1961-62; BFA in Painting, Kansas City (Mo.) Art Inst., 1965; MFA in Painting, U. Cin. and Cin. Art Acad., 1967. Prof., coord. drawing St. Cloud (Minn.) State U., 1967-86; prof. Queens Coll., CUNY, Flushing, 1983-84; prof., coord. MFA painting Marywood Coll., Scranton, Pa., 1985-90; MFA artist-instr. Vt. Coll., Norwich U., Montpelier, 1991—; lectr. Carnegie-Mellon U., Pitts., 1988; juror Belin Arts Grant Com., Waverly, Pa., 1989; curator Philip Pearlstein Retrospective Exhibit, Scranton, 1988. One man shows include Mpls. Coll. Art and Design, 1978, Harold Reed Gallery, 1983, Gallery Henoch, N.Y.C., 1991, also others; group shows at Harold Reed Gallery, 1979, The Bklyn. Mus., 1979, Greenville County Mus. of Art, 1983, Weatherspoon Gallery, U. N.C., 1981, Mpls. Coll. of Art and Design, 1985, Kutztown U., 1990, Gallery Henoch, 1990; contbr. articles to profl. jours. Mem. Coll. Art Assn. Am., Pa. Soc. Watercolor Painters. Home and Studio: Grouse Hill RD 1 Box 376 Dalton PA 18414

WALLING, CHEVES T., chemistry educator; b. Evanston, Ill., Feb. 28, 1916; s. Willoughby George and Frederika Christina (Haskell) W.; m. Jane Ann Wilson, Sept. 17, 1940; children—Hazel, Rosalind, Cheves, Janie, Barbara. A.B., Harvard, 1937; Ph.D., U. Chgo., 1939. Research chemist E. I. dePont de Nemours, 1939-43; research chemist U.S. Rubber Co., 1943-49; tech. aide Office Sci. Research, Washington, 1945; sr. research assoc. Lever Bros. Co., 1949-52; prof. chemistry Columbia U., N.Y.C., 1952-69; Disting. prof. chemistry U. Utah, Salt Lake City, 1970-91, prof. chemistry emeritus, 1991—. Author: Free Radicals in Solution, 1957; also numerous articles. Fellow AAAS; mem. Nat. Acad. Scis., Am. Acad. Arts and Scis., Am. Chem. Soc. (editor jour. 1975-81, James Flack Norris award 1970, Lubrizol award 1984). Home: Box 537 Jaffrey NH 03452

WALLIS, JAMES STEPHEN, sales and marketing executive; b. South East Cleveland, Ohio, Oct. 25, 1951; s. Stephen A. and Celia Anne (Skony) W.; m. Jeanne L. Morris Gush, May 10, 1975; 1 child, Laura Anne. AA in Chem. Engring., BA, Cleve. State U., 1969; MBA, John Carroll U., 1985. Sales engr. Rohm & Haas Corp., Phila., 1969-72; tech. specialist Beta Labs. Inc., Trevose, Pa., 1972-73; regional mgr., internat. dir., v.p. sales and mktg. Dexter Corp., Windsor Locks, Conn., 1973-89; v.p. sales and mktg. NDM Corp., Phila., 1989—; dir. Sales and Mktg. Execs. Internat., Cleve., 1987-88; cons. Taylor Techs. Inc., 1988—. Big Bro., Cath. Big Bros., Cleve., 1985, 86, 87. Mem. Delaware Valley Mktg. Assn., Doylestown Country Club, Ocean Creek Myrtle Beach S.C. Home: 64 Country Club Dr Warrington PA 18976-1218 Office: NDM Corp 2190 Hornig Rd Philadelphia PA 19116-4296 also: GH 41 Ocean Creek North Myrtle Beach SC 29582

WALLIS, LILA AMDURSKA, medicine educator; b. Grodno, Poland, June 21, 1921; came to U.S., 1946; d. Samuel and Barbara (Hoffman) Amdurski; m. Benedict Lawrence Wallis, Apr. 5, 1941; children: James B., B. Jeffrey. BA summa cum laude, Barnard Coll., 1947; MD, Columbia U., 1951. Diplomate Nat. Bd. Examiners, Am. Bd. Internal Medicine, Subspeciality Bd. Hematology and Subspeciality Bd. Endocrinology and Metabolism. Intern to asst. resident physician and asst. in medicine Cornell/N.Y. Hosp. Med. Ctr., 1951-53, fellow in hematology, asst. physician to outpatients, 1953-54, resident physician to outpatients and instr. medicine, 1954-55, instr. in medicine and physician to outpatients, 1955-62, clin. asst. prof. of medicine, asst. attending physician, 1962-76, clin. assoc. prof. medicine, assoc. attending physician, 1976-84, clin. prof. medicine, attending physician, 1984—; organizer many workshops; lectr. in field. Contbr. numerous articles to profl. jours. Fellow ACP, N.Y. Acad. Medicine (sec. com. on admission 1977-80), N.Y. Acad. Scis.; mem. Internat. Soc. Hematology, Am. Soc. Hematology, N.Y. Soc. Study of Blood, N.Y. State Med. Soc., N.Y. County Med. Soc. (com. CME 1981-84, com. med. econs. 1985-86, com. pub. rels. 1986-89, chair task force women physicians 1987—), Am. Med. Women's Assn. (pres. 1988-90, numerous coms., Elizabeth Blackwell medal 1990, Calcium/Nutrition award 1989, Women of Yr. 1981), Alpha Omega Alpha.

WALLIS, SANDRA RHODES, educator; b. Bel Air, Md., Nov. 16, 1945; d. Lawrence Edgar and Alverta (Kohler) Rhodes; m. W. Robert Wallis, June 25, 1977; children by previous marriage: John Robert, David Matthew. BA in Secondary Edn., U. Md., 1967; MEd in Reading, Towson U., 1974. Cert. tchr., Md. Tchr. Harford County Pub. Schs., Bel Air, 1968-89; reading specialist Harford County Pub. Schs., 1972-89, supr. reading, 1989—; tchr. cons., Md. Writing Project, Towson, 1988—. Mem. Harford County Reading Coun. (pres. 1986-87), State of Md. Internat. Reading Assn. (chair newspaper in edn. com. 1987-90), Assn. Supervision and Currriculum Devel., Md. Coun. Tchrs. English and Lang. arts, NCTE, Internat. Reading Assn., Alpha Delta Kappa (pres. Chi chpt. 1987-90). Democrat. Methodist. Home: 309 Glenville Rd Churchville MD 21028-1416 Office: Harford County Pub Schs 45 E Gordon St Bel Air MD 21014-2915

WALLIS, WILLIAM ROBERT, editor; b. Bel Air, Md., Oct. 18, 1931; s. William Stanley and Flossie Marie (Hayden) W.; Sandra Rhodes, June 25, 1977; children: Don, Doug, Debbie, Pat, Phillip, David. AA, U. Balt., 1965. Reporter The Harford Gazette, Bel Air, Md., 1949-50; adminstrv. clk. Aberdeen (Md.) Proving Ground, 1950-51; staff writer Army Chem. Ctr., Edgewood, Md., 1951-52; reporter, sports editor, news editor, editor The Aegis, Bel Air, Md., 1953-90; owner, pres. The 324 Corp., 1986—. Pres. Harford League amateur baseball league, Bel Air, 1954-59; mem. Food Market Authority, Balt., 1969-75; mem., vice-chmn. Md. Censor Bd., Balt., 1976-80; chmn. Md. Home Improvement Commn., Balt., 1980-85; mem. Md. Stadium Authority, Balt., 1987—; mem., bd. dirs. Fallston (Md.) Gen. Hosp., 1978-87, Franklin Sq. Hosp., Rosedale, Md., 1987—. Recipient numerous awards Md. Press Assn., Del. Press Assn., D.C. Press Assn., 1960—. Mem. Kiwanis (charter mem., bd. trustees 1988—), Sigma Delta Chi. Democrat. Roman Catholic. Home: PO Box 324 Bel Air MD 21014-0324 Office: 522 Rock Spring Ave Bel Air MD 21014

WALLIS, W(ILSON) ALLEN, economist, educator, statistician; b. Phila., Nov. 5, 1912; s. Wilson Dallam and Grace Steele (Allen) W.; m. Anne Armstrong, Oct. 5, 1935; children: Nancy Wallis Ingling, Virginia Wallis Cates. AB, U. Minn., 1932, postgrad., 1932-33; postgrad. fellow, U. Chgo., 1933-35, Columbia U., 1935-36; DSc, Hobart and William Smith Colls., 1973; LLD, Roberts Wesleyan Coll., 1973, U. Rochester, 1984; LHD, Grove City Coll., 1975. Economist Nat. Resources Com., 1935-37; instr. econs. Yale U., 1937-38; asst. to assoc. prof. econs. Stanford U., 1938-46; Carnegie rsch. assoc. Nat. Bur. Econ. Rsch., 1939-40, 41; dir. war rsch. Stats. Rsch. Group Columbia U., 1942-46; prof. stats. and econs. U. Chgo., 1946-62, chmn. dept. stats., 1949-57, dean Grad. Sch. Bus., 1956-62; pres. (title later chancellor) U. Rochester, N.Y., 1962-82; under sec. for econ. affairs U.S. Dept. State, Washington, 1982-89; resident scholar Am. Enterprise Inst., Washington, 1989—; staff Ford Found., 1953-54; fellow Ctr. for Advanced Study in Behavioral Scis., 1956-57. mem. math. div. NRC, 1958-60; bd. dir. Nat. Bur. Econ. Rsch., 1953-74; spl. asst. Pres. Eisenhower, 1959-61; pres. Nat. Commn. Study of Nursing and Nursing Edn., 1967-70; chmn. Commn. Presdl. Scholars, 1969-78; mem. Pres.'s Commn. on All-Vol. Armed Force, 1969-70; chmn. Pres.'s Commn. Fed. Stats., 1970-71; mem. Nat. Coun. Ednl. Rsch., 1973-75; chmn. Adv. Coun. Social Security, 1974-75; bd. dirs. Corp. Pub. Broadcasting, 1975-78, chmn., 1977-78. Author: (with others) Consumer Expenditures in the United States, 1939, A Significance Test for Time Series and Other Ordered Observations, 1941, Sequential Analysis of Statistical Data: Applications, 1945, Techniques of Statistical Analysis, 1947, Sampling Inspection, 1948, Acceptance Sampling, 1950, Statistics: A New Approach, 1956, The Nature of Statistics, 1962, Welfare Programs: An Economic Appraisal, 1968; An Overgoverned Society, 1976; co-compiler: The Ethics of Competition and Other Essays by Frank H. Knight, 1935; chmn. editorial adv. bd.: Internat. Ency. Social Scis., 1960-68; contbr. articles to profl. jours. Trustee Tax Found., 1961-82, chmn. bd., 1972-75, chmn. exec. com., 1975-78; bd. overseers Hoover Instn. War, Revolution and Peace, 1972-78; trustee Eisenhower Coll., 1969-79, Nat. Opinion Rsch. Ctr., 1957-62, 64-68, Com. Econ. Devel., 1965-71, Colgate Rochester Div. Sch., 1963-82, Ctr. Govtl. Rsch., Inc., 1962-82, Internat. Mus. Photography at George Eastman House, 1963-82, Robert A. Taft Inst. Govt., 1973-77, Ethics and Pub. Policy Ctr., 1980-82, 89—; mem. Com. on the Present Danger, 1980-82, 1989—; chmn. bd. overseers Ctr. Naval Analyses, 1967-82. Recipient Sec.'s Disting. Svc. award Dept. of State, Washington, 1988. Fellow Am. Soc. Quality Control, Inst. Math. Stats., Am. Statis. Assn. (editor Jour. 1950-59, pres. 1965), Am. Acad. Arts and Scis.; mem. Am. Econ. Assn. (exec. com. 1962-64), Rochester C. of C. (trustee 1963-68, 70-75), Mont Pelerin Soc. (treas. 1949-54), Washington Inst. of Fgn. Affairs, Phi Beta Kappa, Chi Phi, Beta Gamma Sigma. Clubs: Cosmos (Washington); Bohemian (San

Francisco). Office: Am Enterprise Inst 1150 17th St NW Washington DC 20036-4603

WALLISON, FRIEDA K., lawyer; b. N.Y.C., Jan. 15, 1943; d. Ruvin H. and Edith (Landes) Koslow; m. Peter J. Wallison, Nov. 24, 1966; children: Ethan S., Jeremy L., Rebecca K. AB, Smith Coll., 1963; LLB, Harvard U., 1966. Bar: N.Y. 1967, DC 1982. Assoc. Carter, Ledyard & Milburn, N.Y.C., 1966-75; spl. counsel, div. market regulation Securities & Exchange Commn., Washington, 1975; exec. dir., gen. counsel Mcpl. Securities Rulemaking Bd., Washington, 1975-78; ptnr. Rogers & Wells, N.Y.C. and Washington, 1978-83, Jones, Day, Reavis & Pogue, Washington, 1983—; mem. Govtl. Acctg. Standards Adv. Council, Washington, Nat. Council on Pub. Works Improvement, Washington; vice chair environ. fin. adv. bd. EPA. Fellow Am. Bar Found.; mem. Nat. Council Govtl. Acctg., Nat. Assn. Bond Lawyers, Fed. Bar Assn., ABA, N.Y.C. Bar Assn. Contbr. articles to profl. jours. Office: Jones Day Reavis & Pogue Ste 600 1450 G St NW Washington DC 20005-2088

WALLMAN, RAYMOND LOUIS, computer company executive, consultant; b. Port Jefferson, N.Y., June 28, 1953; s. Raymond Louis and Ellen (Moe) W.; m. Lynn Francis Facini, Mar. 18, 1978; children: Elizabeth, Raymond. BS in Engring., U. Mich., 1976; MS, N.Y. Poly., 1977. Owner Computer Cons. of L.I., Bohemia, N.Y., 1979—. Mem. Assn. Computing Machinery, Ind. Computer Cons. Assn. Office: Computer Cons LI Atrium Exec Ctr 80 Orville Dr Bohemia NY 11716-2505

WALLOT, JEAN-PIERRE, archivist, historian; b. Valleyfield, Que., Can., May 22, 1935; s. Albert and Adrienne (Thibodeau) W.; m. Denyse Caron; children: Normand, Robert, Sylvie. B.A., Coll. Valleyfield, 1954; lic. es lettres, U. Montreal, 1957, M.A. in History, 1957, Ph.D. in History, 1965; D (hon.), U. Rennes, France, 1987. Reporter Le Progres de Valleyfield, 1954-61; lectr. U. Montreal, 1961-65, asst. prof., 1965-66, prof. dept. history, 1973-85, chmn. dept., 1973-75, vice dean studies faculty arts and scis., 1975-78, vice dean research Faculty Arts and Scis, 1979-82, academic v.p., 1982-85; nat. archivist, Can., 1985—; historian Nat. Mus. Man, Ottawa, Ont., 1966-69, assoc. prof. U. Toronto, 1969-71; prof. Concordia U., Montreal, Que., 1971-73; dir. Etude Associé Ecole Pratique des Hautes Etudes en Sciences Sociales, Paris, 1975, 79, 81, 83, 85, 87, 89. Author: Intrigues françaises et americaines au Canada, 1965, (with John Hare) Les Imprimés dans le Bas-Canada, 1967, Confrontations, 1971, (with G. Paquet) Patronage et Pouvoir dans le Bas-Canada, 1973, Un Quebec qui bougeait, 1973; Editor: (with R. Girard) Memoires de J.E. McComber, bourgeois de Montréal, 1981; (with J. Goy) Evolution et eclatement du monde rural, 1986. Decorated officer Order Arts et Lettres (France), 1987; officer Order of Can., 1991; recipient Marie Tremaine medal, 1973, Tyrrell medal, 1982. Fellow Royal Soc. Can. (sect. pres. 1985-87); mem. Am. Antiquarian Soc., Acad. Can. Française, Inst. d'Histoire l'Amerique Française (pres. 1973-77), Can. Hist. Assn. (v.p. 1981, pres. 1982), Assn. Can.-Française l'Avancement Scis. (pres. 1982-83), Assn. Archivists Que., Assn. Can. Archivists, Internat. Coun. on Archives (v.p. 1988—). Roman Catholic. Office: Nat Archives, 395 Wellington St, Ottawa, ON Canada K1A 0N3

WALMAN, JEROME, publisher, psychotherapist, consultant, restaurant and entertainment critic; b. Charleston, W.Va., June 19, 1937; s. Joe and Madeline Minnie (Levy) W.; m. Mary Joan Granara, Sept. 5, 1960. Student, U. W.Va.; student, Boston U., Berkley Sch. Music, Boston. Producer, composer, writer mus. compositions Carnegie Hall, Broadway Theatre, 1962, 63; pvt. practice psychotherapy in spl. hypnosis and music therapy, 1964—; designer Jerome Walman Systems Applied Hypnosis, 1969; travel-restaurant-wine-entertainment critic Sta. WNCN-FM Radio; marriage and family counselor; lectr., dir. tng. programs in memory improvement and speed reading; cons. personal image, wine and food Dept. Def., NYU; cons., dir. Cooking for Relaxation and Weight Control; restaurant publicist; condr. courses in wine appreciation and food; restaurant, wine and food critic Sta. WNCN-GAF FM Radio. Dir., producer syndicated TV show Enterprises Unltd., 1978—; producer, composer I Murdered Mary, N.Y.C., 1976, Last Call, N.Y.C., 1977, TV Mag., 1978; lectr. East-West Ctr., N.Y.C., 1978, Actors Tng. and Acting Therapy Ctr. Am., Westwinds Learning Ctr., The Learning Exchange, 1986; editor Punch In Internat. Electronic Travel, Wine and Restaurant mag.; pub. Wine On Line mag., The Computer User's Survival Newsletter and Syndicated Column; originator facimile news svc. Fax It To Me; Author papers on hypnosis, psychic phenomena and memory, music therapy, biofeedback and meditation application; featured in various publs. including Fortune, Gentleman's Quar., Cosmopolitan, Leaders mag., Mademoiselle; editor Punch in Internat. Wine, Restaurant and Travel Electronic mag.; reviewer Wine-on-Line Internat. Wire Svc., The Computer User's Survival Newsletter; contbr. The Official Airline Guides Electronic Edition. Mem. Music Therapy Internat., Meditation and Mental Devel. Ctr. N.Y., Memory Improvement and Concentration Ctr. Am., Delphi-Gen. Videotex Svc.-Nynex Info-Logic. Address: 400 E 59th Sr Apt 9F New York NY 10022

WALSH, CHARLES RICHARD, banker; b. Bklyn., Jan. 30, 1939; s. Charles John and Anna Ellen Walsh; m. Marie Anne Goulden, June 24, 1961; children: Kevin C., Brian R., Gregory M. BS, Fordham U., 1960; MBA, St. John's U., 1966, D of Comml. Scis. (hon.), 1985. V.p. Mfrs. Hanover Trust Co., Hicksville, N.Y., 1974-80, sr. v.p., 1980-86, exec. v.p., 1986-90, group exec., mem. mgmt. com., 1990—; bd. dir., former chmn. bd. dirs. Eastern States Monetary Svcs., Lake Success, N.Y., 1978-88; pres., chief exec. officer, bd. dir. The Bankcard Assn., Hicksville, 1988—. Sustaining mem. Rep. Nat. Com., 1978—; vice chmn. adv. bd. St. John's U., 1982—. With USAR, 1960, 61-62. Mem. N.Y. State Bankers Assn. (former bd. dir., mem. gov. coun., chmn. consumer banking div.), Am. Bankers Assn. (chmn. bank card div., mem. exec. com., former mem. communications coun. and chmn. edn. com.), Am. Mgmt. Assn., N.Y. Credit and Fin. Mgmt. Assn., Soc. Cert. Consumer Credit Execs. (cert.), Beta Gamma Sigma, Omicron Delta Epsilon, Forest Estates Club (Oyster Bay, N.Y.). Republican. Home: 9 Blueberry Ln Oyster Bay NY 11771-3901 Office: 100 Duffy Ave Hicksville NY 11801-3639

WALSH, EDWARD NELSON, chemist, consultant; b. Chgo., Nov. 22, 1925; s. Edward John and Edna Catherine (Nelson) W.; m. Mary Catherine O'Leary, May 27, 1950; children: Edward Patrick, Kathleen Mary Duarte. BS, Ill. Inst. Tech., Chgo., 1948, PhD, 1965; MSc, DePaul U., Chgo., 1952. Mgr. organic rsch. Victor Chem. Wks., Chicago Hts., Ill., 1958-63, mgr. chem. dept., 1963-65; mgr. chem. sect. Stauffer Chem. Co., Dobbs Ferry, N.Y., 1965-69, mgr. organic rsch., 1969-76, mgr. chem. dept., 1976-84, sr. scientist, 1984-86; asst. prof. St. Peter's Coll., Jersey City, 1986-89; chem. cons. Edward N. Walsh, Cons., New City, N.Y., 1986—; cons. in field. Co-author: Phosphorus Chemistry in Everyday Living, 1988; co-editor: Phosphorus Chemistry, 1992; patentee in field. Recipient Disting. Svc. award Rockland Chem. Soc., 1981, Inventors award Stauffer Chem. Co., 1984. Mem. AAAS, Am. Chem. Soc. (Outstanding Svc. award 1985, chmn. N.Y. sect. 1982), Sigma Xi, Phi Lambda Upsilon, Alpha Chi Sigma. Home: 33 Concord Dr New City NY 10956-4038

WALSH, HOLLY ANN, sales manager; b. White Plains, N.Y., Dec. 22, 1963; d. William David and Rosaleen (McGowan) W. BA, Wheaton Coll., 1985. Prin., sales mgr. JSA Corp., N.Y.C., 1985-90; mgr. sales and customer svc. depts. Edward Jacobson, Inc., Boston, 1990—. Mitsubishi Corp./Japan scholar, 1981-82, Kardon Found. Acad. scholar, 1982-85. Mem. Jr. League. Roman Catholic. Home: 48 Phillips St Boston MA 02114

WALSH, JAMES PAUL, engineering executive; b. Fall River, Mass., Apr. 3, 1917; s. James Patrick and Cecilia (Lowe) W.; m. Joan Edwards, Apr. 11, 1942; children: Joanne, James Jr., William. BSME, Stevens Inst. Tech., 1938, DEng., 1958; MS, U. Md., 1950. Registered profl. engr., D.C. Project engr. Bikini Bomb Tests, 1946-52; project mgr. First Nuclear Submarine, Washington, 1952-56; dep. dir. First Earth Satellite Program, Washington, 1956-60; pres. Matrix Corp., Alexandria, Va., 1960-68; supt. Naval Rsch. Lab., Washington, 1968-78; cons. engr. J. Paul Walsh & Assocs., Annapolis, Md., 1978—. Mem. Annapolis Yacht Club. Home: 946 Clumber Hill Sherwood Forest MD 21405 Office: PO Box 946 Annapolis MD 21405

WALSH, JAMES THOMAS, congressman; b. Syracuse, N.Y., June 19, 1947. BA, St. Bonaventure U., 1970. Agrl. extension agt. Peace Corps, 1970-72; mktg. exec. telecommunications co., 1974-88; exec.-in-residence telecommunications inst. Coll. Tech. SUNY, Utica, Rome, N.Y., 1986-87; common councilor City of Syracuse, 1977-85, pres. common coun., 1986-88; mem. 101st-102nd Congresses from 27th N.Y. dist., 1989—. Republican. Office: US Ho of Reps 1238 Longworth House Office Bldg Washington DC 20515 also: 1269 Federal Bldg Syracuse NY 13261

WALSH, JENI LEE, nursing administrator; b. Alva, Okla., Mar. 2, 1944; d. Russell L. and Virginia L. (Norris) Kilmer; m. Willard K. Walsh, May 29, 1971. RN, Joseph Lawrence Sch. Nursing, New London, Conn., 1974; BS in Profl. Arts., St. Joseph's Coll., North Windham, Maine, 1982, postgrad., 1990—; MBA, Rensselaer Poly. Inst., 1991. Nursing supr. Norwich (Conn.) Hosp.; asst. dir. nursing Whiting Forensic Inst., Middletown, Conn., dir. nursing. Mem. Am. Nurses Assn., Conn. Nurses Assn., Nat. League Nursing.

WALSH, J(OHN) B(RONSON), lawyer; b. Buffalo, Feb. 20, 1927; s. John A. and Alice (Condon) W.; m. Barbara Ashford, May 20, 1966; 1 child, Martha. AB, Canisius Coll., 1950; JD, Georgetown U., 1952. Bar: N.Y. 1953, U.S. Supreme Ct. 1958, U.S. Ct. Internat. Trade 1969, U.S. Ct. Customs and Patent Appeals 1973. Trial atty. Garvey & Conway, N.Y.C., 1953-54; vol. atty. Nativity Mission, N.Y.C., 1953-54; ptnr. Jaeckle, Fleischmann, Kelly, Swart & Augspurger, Buffalo, 1955-60; pvt. practice Buffalo, 1960-75, 84—; ptnr. Jaeckle, Fleischmann & Mugel, Buffalo, 1976-80, Walsh & Cleary, P.C., Buffalo, 1980-84; pvt. practice, 1984—; spl. counsel Ecology and Environment, Inc., Lancaster, N.Y., 1980-84; trial counsel antitrust div. Dept. Justice, Washington, 1960-61; spl. counsel on disciplinary procedures N.Y. Supreme Ct., 1960-76; appointee legal disciplinary coordinating com. State of N.Y., 1971; legis. counsel, spl. counsel to mayor Buffalo, 1969-75; counsel to sheriff Erie County, 1969-72; legis counsel Niagara Frontier Transp. Authority; cons. Norfolk So. R.R., Ecology and Environment on Govtl. Affairs; guest lectr. univs. and profl. groups. Author: (TV series) The Law and You (Freedom Found. award, ABA award, Internat. Police Assn. award). Past pres. Ashford Hollow Found. Visual and Performing Arts; past trustee Dollar Bills, Inc.; past co-producer Grand Island Playhouse and Players. With U.S. Army, 1945-46. Recipient Gold Key Buffalo Jr. C. of C., 1962, award Freedom Found., 1966. Fellow Am. Bar Found.; mem. ABA (del. internat. conf. Brussels 1963, Mexico City 1964, Lausanne, Switzerland 1964, merit award com. 1961-68, crime prevention and control com. 1968-70), N.Y. Trial Lawyers Assn., Am. Immigration Lawyers Assn., Am. Judicature Soc., N.Y. State Bar Assn. (past sec.), Buffalo Bar Assn., Nat. Pub. Employer Labor Relations Assn., Am. League, Capital Hill Club of Buffalo, Am. Assn. Airport Execs., N.Y. State Bus. Council (environ. law subcom., chmn. subcom.), Erie County Bar Assn., Buffalo Irish Club (bd. dirs.), Buffalo Athletic Club (past bd. dirs., past v.p.), Buffalo Canoe Club, Buffalo City Club, Ft. Orange of Albany Club, KC, Knights of Equity, Leoknights. Roman Catholic. Home: 193 Depew Ave Buffalo NY 14214-1619 Office: 368 Pleasant View Dr Lancaster NY 14086-1397 also: Ecology & Environ Inc 368 Pleasantview Dr Lancaster NY 14086

WALSH, JOHN FLEWELLEN, realtor; b. White Plains, N.Y., May 15, 1928; s. John and Edith (Flewellen) W.; children: John Richard, Matthew William. Student, NYU, 1950,54. Dir. Nat. Broadcasting Co., N.Y.C., 1949-79; mgr. AT&T, Washington, 1980-91; realtor Village Realty, Gaithersburg, Md., 1991—. Chmn. bd., pres. D.C. chpt., Nat. Hemophilia Found., 1969-79. With U.S. Army, 1950-52. Mem. C. of C. Republican. Home: 20668 Highland Hall Dr Gaithersburg MD 20879-4022

WALSH, KEITH KEELER (KEELER), composer, musician; b. San Diego, June 3, 1952; s. William Thomas Jr. and Elizabeth Bernice (Brack) W. Owner Great Orm Prodns., N.Y.C., 1987—. Composer, performer cassette albums including Planet of Lovers, 1984, Legerdemain, 1986, Outward Signs, 1988, compact discs including Autofocus, 1988, The Present Link, 1990, Playing Field, 1992, The Age of the Inventor, 1992; compilations include Deux Lapins, Underground Prodns., 1988, The Electronic Cottage Internat. Compilation Cassette Series, Vol. 2, 1991; video/film Terminal Art, Media-M-Prodns., 1986, Outside the Window, Video One/Presbyn. Ch. U.S.A., 1987. Recipient Silver Angel award for outstanding nat. religious broadcast drama, 1987. Mem. Internat. Soc. Cryptozoology, Internat. Fortean Orgn., Broadcast Music, Inc., World Ship Soc. Office: Great Orm Prodns 496-A Hudson St Ste D-35 New York NY 10014

WALSH, KEVIN KANE, psychologist, consultant, researcher; b. Phila., Feb. 28, 1950; s. George F. and Dora Louise (Galbiati) W.; m. Janet Ellen Calovi, Oct. 30, 1971; children: Amanda, Douglas, Edward, Elizabeth. BS in Psychology, Mt. St. Mary's Coll., Emmitsburg, Md., 1972; MA in Psychology, U. Akron, 1978, PhD in Psychology, 1982. Grad. rsch. asst. U. Akron, Ohio, 1975-80; assoc. staff psychologist Broome Svcs.-State of N.Y., Binghamton, 1980-81; dir. residential svcs. The Tng. Sch. at Vineland, N.J., 1981-83, dir. psychology/habilitation, 1984-86, asst. exec. dir., 1988-91; cons. psychologist Vineland, 1991—; dir. rsch. Devel. Disabilities Ctr. of Morristown (N.J.) Meml. Hosp., 1992—; mem. long-term planning com. N.J. Div. devel. Disabilities, Trenton, 1989-92. Author: (with others) Role of Institutions in Community Services, 1987, Developmentally Disabled People Grow-Up, 1991; editor: Threads of Change: Historical Readings, 1988; contbr. numerous articles to profl. jours. Sec. bd. trustees Ellison Sch., Vineland, 1983-85; bd. dirs. Citizens Investments, Vineland, 1990—, Cumberland unit Assn. for Retarded Citizens, 1992—. Named Intern in Community Svc., State of N.J., 1970; DeGraff scholar, Akron, 1979-80. Mem. APA, Am. Assn. Mental Retardation (chair region psychol. div. 1985-90, region chair 1992). Home: 2490 Vine Rd Vineland NJ 08360-2520

WALSH, MARIANNE LYDA, social services administrator; b. Cambridge, Mass., Sept. 26, 1942; d. Robert and Marie Annette (Remillard) Wilson; m. John Joseph Walsh Jr., Oct. 26, 1963 (dec. 1981); 1 child, John Joseph III. Student, Franklin Pierce Coll., 1986-87. Bookkeeper Commd. Officers Mess, Charlestown, Mass., 1959-63, 71-73; expediter Internat. Equipment Co., Needham, Mass., 1963-69; acct. Clark and Shaunessey, Milford, Mass., 1974-78; staff acct. Craftsmen, Medway, Mass., 1979-80, Alpha-Omega, Salem, N.H., 1981-83; bus. mgr., dir. adminstrv. services Region Ten Community Support Services, Atkinson, N.H., 1983—; treas. H.E.A.R.T. System, Atkinson, 1987—. Legis. adv. com. Grante State Assn. Human Services, Concord, N.H., 1988. Mem. Nat. Assn. Reimbursement Officers, Am. Assn. Mental Retardation, Assn. Severe Handicap. Roman Catholic. Home: 16 Mt Vernon St Reading MA 01867-2535 Office: Region Ten Community Support Svcs Inc 8 Commerce Dr Atkinson NH 03811-2173

WALSH, MARTHA BOSSE, conservationist; d. Leon and Lenore (Carter) Bosse; m. Leo S. Walsh, Sept. 30, 1972 (div. Oct. 1982). Student, U. Mo., 1966, Baker U., 1966-67, Marymount-Manhattan, 1980-82. Flight attendant TWA, N.Y.C., 1967-78; pres. Island Conservation Effort, 1988—; trustee Rare Ctr. for Tropical Bird Conservation, Phila., 1987-91. Ptnr. in conservation World Wildlife Fund, Washington, 1986—; assoc. World Resources Inst., Washington, 1987—; mem. St. Croix (V.I.) Landmarks Soc., 1985—, Sherman (Conn.) Hist. Soc., 1986, Sherman Libr. Assn., 1986. St. Croix Environ. Assn., 1987—; mem. Saba Conservation Found. Nature Conservancy. Mem. Caribbean Conservation Assn., St. Lucia Naturalists Soc., Cedam Internat., Soc. Caribbean Ornithology, Friends of Abaco Parrot. Republican. Home: 2 Wagon Wheel Rd Sherman CT 06784 also: Windwardside PO Box 6784, Saba The Netherlands

WALSH, MICHIYO SHIOTA, accounting secretary; b. Kōchi, Koch, Japan, May 18, 1953; d. Sadaki and Yoshiko (Inui) Shiota. Student, Osaka (Japan) Hukushima, Japan, 1971, World Lang., Osaka, 1973; Abacus, Master, Osaka Abacus, 1969; Cooking Master, Tsuji Cooking, Osaka, 1973. Acctg. sec. Morishita Chem. Co., Ltd., Osaka, 1971-72, Yamaichi Securities Co., Ltd., Osaka, 1972-78, Daiyoshi Drugstore Co., Ltd., Nara, Japan, 1979-80, Biwall Co., Ltd., Osaka, 1980-81, Japanese Embassy, Washington, 1987—; master bookkeeping, 1972, master bus., 1973. Master flower arrangement, 1973, tea ceremony, 1974, dressmaking, 1974. Master flower arrangement, 1973, tea ceremony, 1974. Buddhist. Home: 501 N Armistead St Apt 203 Alexandria VA 22312-2870 Office: Japanese Embassy 2520 Massachusetts Ave NW Washington DC 20008-2869

WALSH, PETER JOSEPH, physics educator; b. N.Y.C., Aug. 21, 1929; s. Peter and Mary Ellen (Kelly) W.; m. Rosemarie Imundo, May 13, 1952; children: Kathleen, Mary Ellen, Susan, Carole, Karen. B.S., Fordham U., 1951; M.S., N.Y.U., 1953, Ph.D., 1960. Research physicist Westinghouse Elec. Co., Bloomfield, N.J., 1951-60; supervisory physicist Am. Standard, Piscattaway, N.J., 1960-62; prof. physics and elec. engring. Fairleigh Dickinson U., 1962—; vis. rsch. scientist MIT, 1977; vis. prof. electronics and elec. engring. U. Sheffield, 1978-79; NASA fellow U. Santa Clara, 1980; Am. Soc. Engring. Edn. Navy fellow Naval Rsch. Labs., 1981, 82, 86, NASA Langley, 1987, Air Force fellow Hanscom AFB, 1988, Kirtland AFB, 1990; vis. prof. U. Genoa, 1984; vis. scholar Stanford U., 1984-85, cons. physics to 20 labs., 1963—. Author: Dark Side of Knowledge, articles in field. Mem. Am. Phys. Soc., AAAS, N.J. Acad. Sci., Sigma Xi (sec. 1969). Home: 40 St Josephs Dr Stirling NJ 07980-1224 Office: Fairleigh Dickinson U Teaneck NJ 07666

WALSH, SUSAN LINDA, arts administrator, video producer; b. Jamaica, N.Y., Jan. 26, 1957; d. George Frederick and Joyce (Salla) W.; m. Frederick Alan Simon, July 30, 1982; children: Mira Simon, Benjamin Simon. Student, Boston State Coll., 1974-76; BA, Mass. Coll. Art, 1980. Ptnr. Fred Simon Prodns., Norfolk, Mass., 1981—; exec. dir. Newton (Mass.) TV Found., 1983—. Prodn. asst.: (video prodn.) Frank: A Vietnam Veteran, 1981 (Nat. PBS broadcast 1981); co-producer: (video prodn.) Men and Women, 1984 (Nat. PBS broadcast 1984); assoc. producer: (video prodn.) There Was A Child, 1991 (Documentary of Yr., Nat. Hospice Orgn., 1991, Outstanding Documentary award New Eng. Film Festival). Bd. mem. Norfolk (Mass.) Arts Coun., 1984-86, Norfolk (Mass.) Cable TV Corp., 1984-86; pres. Friends of the Norfolk (Mass.) Libr., 1991-92. Mem. Boston Film/Video Found., Women in Film and Video. Office: Newton TV Found 1608 Beacon St Newton MA 02168-1532

WALSH, THOMAS JOSEPH, neuro-ophthalmologist; b. N.Y.C., Sept. 18, 1931; s. Thomas Joseph and Virginia (Hughes) W.; m. Sally Ann Maust, June 21, 1958; children—Thomas Raymond, Sara Ann, Mary Kelly, Kathleen Meghan. BA, Coll. Fordham, 1954; MD, Bowman Gray Med. Sch., 1958. Intern St. Vincent's Hosp., N.Y.C., 1958-59; resident ophthalmology Bowman Gray Med. Sch., Winston-Salem, N.C., 1961-64; fellow neuro-ophthalmology Bascom Palmer Eye Inst., Miami, Fla., 1964-65; practice medicine specializing in neuro-ophthalmology Stamford, Conn., 1965—; dir. neuro-ophthalmology service, asst. prof. ophthalmology and neurology Yale Sch. Medicine, New Haven, 1965-74; assoc. prof. Yale Sch. Medicine, 1974-79, prof., 1979—, also bd. permanent officers; dir. ophthalmology Stamford Hosp., 1978-83; mem. staff St. Joseph Hosp., Yale New Haven Hosp.; cons. to surgeon gen. army in neuro-ophthalmology Walter Reed Hosp., Washington, 1966—, VA Hosp., West Haven, 1965—, Silver Hill Found., New Canaan, Conn., 1974—; frequent lectr. various univs. Contbr. articles to various publs. Mem. adv. bd. Stamford Salvation Army, 1972—; mem. med. bd. Darien Nurses Assn., Conn., 1972—; surgeon Darien Fire Dept., 1969—. With AUS, 1959-61. Decorated Knight of Malta, 1983; Centennial fellow Johns Hopkins, 1976. Mem. AMA, Conn., Fairfield County med. socs., Acad. Ophthalmology, Oxford Ophthal. Congress, Acad. Neurology, Am. Assn. Neurol. Surgeons, Internat. Neuro-Ophthalmology Soc., Soc. Med. Cons. to Armed Forces, Cosmos Club (Washington), Darien County Club, Yale Club (N.Y.C.), Lions, Army-Navy Club. Office: 1100 Bedford St Stamford CT 06905-5301

WALT, CATHY LYNN, consultant; b. Akron, Ohio, Aug. 17, 1957; d. Bernard and Barbara (Wolverton) Greenberg; m. Bryan M. Walt, Oct. 7, 1990; 1 child, Elisabeth Oriana. BA, BS, Livingston Coll., 1978; MS, Rutgers U., 1980, PhD, 1990. Instr. Rutgers U., New Brunswick, N.J., 1979-91; asst. v.p. internat. banking Meridian Bank, Phila., 1986-90; cons. CSC Ptnrs., Phila., 1990—. Author: The Secret of Making JAD Successful, 1992; also articles. Fellow NIMH, 1979-80. Mem. Decus (fin. subcom. 1991).

WALTER, CAROLYN AMBLER, clinical social worker, educator; b. Phila., Jan. 29, 1945; d. Joseph Penrose and Betty (Alles) Ambler; m. John Wallace Walter, Aug. 19, 1967; children: Kimberly, Brian. BA, Juniata Coll., Huntingdon, Pa., 1966; MS, Bryn Mawr (Pa.) Coll., 1968, PhD, 1984. Lic. social worker, Pa. Family counselor Family Svc. Phila., 1968-69; psychiat. social worker Cen. Montgomery County Mental Health Ctr., Norristown, Pa., 1969-71; clin. social worker, field instr. Crozer Chester (Pa.) Community Mental Health Ctr., 1974-75; program dir., family counselor Family Svc. Montgomery County, 1975-84; asst. prof. sch. social work U. Md., Balt., 1984-86; vis. lectr. grad. sch. social work Bryn Mawr Coll., 1986-87; assoc. prof. Widener U. Ctr. for Social Work Edn., Chester, 1987—; dir. baccalaureate social work program Widener U., 1991—; adj. instr. Great Lakes Coll. Assn., Phila., 1983-84; pvt. practice, Swarthmore, Pa., 1982—. Author: The Timing of Motherhood, 1986; co-author: Breast Cancer in the Life Course, 1991; contbr. articles to profl. jours. Bd. dirs. Sr. Community Svcs., Folsom, Pa., 1990—, Youth Advocates, Media, Pa., 1973-75. Grantee Widener U., 1989-90, 90-91, 92—, Tirlawyn Bd. Dirs., 1989. Mem. Pa. Assn. Undergrad. Social Work Educators (sec. 1988-90), Pa. Soc. for Clin. Social Work, NASW, ACSW, Baccalaureate Program Dirs., Coun. Social Work Edn., Nat. Registry Health Care Providers in Clin. Social Work (diplomate 1988). Home: 500 N Chester Rd Swarthmore PA 19081-1109 Office: Widener U Ctr for Social Work Edn Chester PA 19013

WALTER, ERIC G., podiatrist; b. Long Island City, N.Y., Feb. 16, 1964; s. Gerd Emil and Aloisia Maria (Knaus) W.; m. Daphne Frances Reinhardt, Nov. 24, 1990. BS in Biology, Boston Coll., 1986; DPM, N.Y. Coll. Podiatric Medicine, 1990. Podiatric med. resident postgrad. program N.Y. Coll. Podiatric Medicine, N.Y.C., 1990-91, podiatric surg. resident postgrad. program, 1991—; cons. podiatrist Running Sch. Inc., Dix Hills, N.Y., 1990, 91. Mem. Am. Podiatric Med. Assn., N.Y. State Podiatric Med. Assn. Roman Catholic. Home: 25 Elizabeth St Apt 1K Farmingdale NY 11735-1932

WALTER, HENRY ALEXANDER, research chemist; b. Muehlhausen, Thur, Germany, Jan. 8, 1912; came to U.S., 1939; s. Heinrich Paul Ernst and Marie Walter; m. Nellie Peters Rucker, May 15, 1939; children: Henry Alexander Jr., Lamar Cobb, Peter R., Nita M. Student, Goetingen Coll., Germany, 1933, Lund U., Sweden, 1933-34; diploma chemistry, Breslav U., Germany, 1936, Heidelberg (Germany) U., 1939. Rsch. chemist Plaskon Libey Ownes, Toledo, Ohio, 1939-41; asst. prof. U. Mo., Columbia, 1941-44; rsch. specialist Monsanto Plastics, Springfield, Mass., 1945-62; sr. scientist Plastic Coating, Holyoke, Mass., 1962-75; researcher Scott Paper, 1975; cons. Scott Paper, James River Graphics, 1982. Patentee in field. Mem. AAAS, Am. Chem. Soc., Acad. Sci. N.Y. Home: 11 Scotch House Cove Rd Cataumet MA 02534-9999

WALTER, J. JACKSON, educational organization executive; b. Abington, Pa., Nov. 6, 1940; s. Joseph Horace and Edith Wilson (Jackson) W.; m. Susan Draude, Feb. 3, 1978; 1 child, Allison K. Mabe. A.B., Amherst Coll., Mass., 1962; LL.B., Yale U., New Haven, 1966. Sec. Fla. Dept. Bus. Regulation, Tallahassee, 1976-79; dir. U.S. Office Govt. Ethics, Washington, 1979-82; pres. Nat. Acad. Pub. Adminstrn., Washington, 1982-84, Nat. Trust Historic Preservation, Washington, 1984-92. Co-author: America's Unelected Government, 1983. Contbr. articles to profl. jours. Dir., Sabre Found., Boston, 1983—. Mem. Nat. Acad. Pub. Adminstrn., ABA, Yale (N.Y.C.) Club, Met. (Washington) Club.

WALTER, JOHN FENNER, college president; b. Far Rockaway, N.Y., Apr. 22, 1934; s. Leroy Lockwood and Helen (Fenner) W.; m. Nancy May Fosdick, Dec. 19, 1959 (div. June 1979); children: Pamela, Suzanne; m. Barbara McGeorge DeWire, Feb. 19, 1983. ScB, Brown U., 1955; MA, Columbia U., 1959; PhD, NYU, 1969. Tchr. Uxbridge (Mass.) High Sch., 1955-57, Mamaroneck (N.Y.) High Sch., 1957-61; prof. Nassau County Community Coll., Garden City, N.Y., 1961-69; dean of college Columbia-Greene Community Coll., Hudson, N.Y., 1969-79; v.p. Lake Mich. Coll., Benton Harbor, Mich., 1979-81; pres. Sullivan County Community Coll., Loch Sheldrake, N.Y., 1981—; chair bd. dirs. Columbia Meml. Hosp. Sch. Nursing, Hudson, N.Y., 1977-79; mem. N.Y. State Planning Bd., Albany, 1974-76. Author: Basic Facts of Advanced Algebra, 1965, Arithmetic, Dosages and Solutions, 1967. Sec. Indsl. Devel. Agy., Sullivan County, N.Y., 1988—; chmn. United Way, Sullivan County, 1990. Recipient Chancellor's award for excellence SUNY, 1977, Myrtle Wreath award Lower, N.Y., Region of Hadassah, 1991, Community Svc. award Nova-len

dist. Boy Scouts Am., 1991; named man of yr. Mem. Am. Coun. Edn. (mem. commn. on internat. edn. 1991—), N.Y. State Math. Assn. 2 Yr. Coll. (pres. 1971-72), Sullivan County C. of C. (bd. dirs. 1986—), Rotary (pres. Monticello chpt. 1990-91). Office: Sullivan County CC Loch Sheldrake NY 12759

WALTER, JOHN FITLER, physicist; b. Yeadon, Pa., Mar. 19, 1943; s. John F. and Ruth T. (Martindell) W.; m. Gail Konhaus, Mar. 16, 1968; children: John, Andrew, Katharine. BSEE, Drexel U., 1966, MS, 1968, PhD, 1970. Engr. Collins Radio Co., Cedar Rapids, Iowa, 1966-67; physicist applied physics lab. Johns Hopkins U., Laurel, Md., 1970—; chmn. Inter-Agy. Laser Gyro Coordination Com., Washington, 1972-74. Inventor high performance ring laser gyro with magneto-optic bias. Mem. AIAA, Am. Defense Preparedness Assn. Office: Johns Hopkins U Applied Physics Lab Laurel MD 20723

WALTER, KENNETH GAINES, library director; b. Atlanta, Mar. 14, 1932; s. Gaines Winningham and Freddie Lou (Thigpen) W.; m. Eva Lou McClelland, June 10, 1965; children: Regina Eileen, Kevin Michael. BA, Emory U., 1954, MS, 1958; postgrad., U. Vienna, Austria, 1962; MSLS, U. N.C., Chapel Hill, 1966; ABD, U. Ga., 1984. Asst. cataloging libr. Ohio U., Athens, 1961-65, head cataloging libr., 1965-68; asst. dir. librs. U. S.C., Columbia, 1968-75; dir. librs. Ga. So. U., Statesboro, 1975-84; dir. libr. svcs. So. Conn. State U., New Haven, 1985—, faculty rep. Bapt. Student Union, 1985-88; cons. libr. tech. svcs., evaluation of book collections; faculty advisor Delta Tau Delta, Statesboro, 1976-83; book reviewer Libr. Jour., 1970-78. Contbr. articles to profl. jours. Mem. Interagy. Libr. Planning Coun., Hartford, Conn., 1986-89; mem. cataloging bd. New Haven Colony Hist. Soc., 1987—; mem. Statesboro-Ga. So. Community Chorus, 1980-84; bd. suprs. CORE Credit Union, Statesboro, 1978-81. Staff sgt. U.S. Army, 1956-57. Recipient scholarship Emory U., 1950-53; Fulbright scholar, 1961-62. Mem. ALA (life), Assn. Coll. and Rsch. Librs., Libr. Adminstrn. and Mgmt. Assn., Libr. and Info. Tech. Assn., Southeastern Libr. Assn., Ga. Libr. Assn., Conn. Libr. Assn., Cen. Ga. Assoc. Librs. (pres. 1980-82), East. Ga. Libr. Triangle (pres. 1976-83), Ga. Acad. Sci., Rotary (New Haven), Sigma Gamma Epsilon, Beta Phi Mu, Phi Delta Kappa, Delta Tau Delta. Baptist. Home: 512 Wallingford Rd Cheshire CT 06410-2844 Office: So Conn State U Buley Libr 501 Crescent St New Haven CT 06515-1355

WALTER, TIMOTHY HAROLD, marketing professional; b. Huron, S.D., Nov. 6, 1957; s. Harold Emil and Betty Lou (Losing) W. BSME, S.D. Sch. Mines & Tech., 1980; MBA, Rensselaer Poly., 1984. Engr., Remington Arms div. DuPont, Ilion, N.Y., 1980-82; engr. DuPont, Glasgow, Del., 1982-84; recruiter DuPont, Newark, 1984-85; mktg. analyst DuPont, Wilmington, Del., 1985-86; devel. rep. DuPont, Wilmington, 1986-89, mgr., devel. programs, 1989-90; dir. polymer mktg. Mitsui Petrochemicals (Am.) Ltd., N.Y.C., 1990—. Co-inventer, patentee in field. Youth leader Red Lion (Del.) Evangelical Assn., 1985-86; bd. assocs. S.D. Sch. of Mines & Tech. Alumni Found., Rapid City, 1991. Mem. Soc. Plastic Engrs., Footwear Inst. Am. (corp. mem., bottoms task force 1990). Republican. Evangelical. Office: Mitsui Petrochemicals Ltd 250 Park Ave Rm 950 New York NY 10177-0056

WALTERS, ALLAN N., forensic chemist; b. Salina, Kans., Dec. 27, 1944; m. Barbara A. Walters, Sept. 20, 1969. BS, U. Rochester, 1967; MS, S.D. Sch. of Mines and Tech., Rapid City, 1972. Forensic chemist Monroe Coutny Pub. Safety Lab., Rochester, N.Y., 1977-88, Bur. Alcohol, Tobacco and Firearms, Rockville, Md., 1988-92; sr. forensic chemist U.S. Postal Svc. Forensic Lab., Washington, 1992—. 1st lt. USAF, 1969-72. Mem. Washington Chromatography Discussion Group, Isaac Walton League of Am., Alpha Chi Sigma (pres. Washington chpt. 1991—). Home: PO Box 10825 Rockville MD 20850 Office: Div Forensic & Tech Svcs 475 L'Enfant Plaza SW 1401 Research Blvd Washington DC 20260

WALTERS, CHARLES JOSEPH, real estate developer; b. Phila., Mar. 11, 1945; s. Vincent William and Gertrude Clare Walters; children: Charles J., Timothy M., Kristen A., Kathleen M., Lindsay E., Ryan M.; m. Sharleen Sandler, Dec. 1, 1984. BS, Drexel U., 1968; MBA, U. Pa., 1972. Project mgr. Griffith Services, Inc., Jacksonville, Fla., 1967-69; asst. to pres. Valley Forge (Pa.) Corp., 1972-74; v.p. Pureland Indsl. Complex, Bridgeport, Pa., 1976—; bd. dirs. Ctr. Sq. Real Estate Devel. Co., Inc., Ctr. Sq. Builders. Bd. dirs. South Jersey Devel. Coun., South Jersey Tech. Consortium, Gloucester Cty. Col. HRD. Decorated Silver Star with oak leaf cluster, Bronze Star with Valor device, Purple Heart with oak leaf cluster, Air medal. Mem. Nat. Assn. Office and Indsl. Parks, Soc. Indsl. Realtors, Soc. for Advancement Mgmt., So. N.J. C. of C. (bd. dirs.), Raquet Club, Wharton Club. Home: Frog Spring Farm PO Box 5347 Chadds Ford PA 19317-0602 Office: Pureland Indsl Complex 510 Heron Dr Bridgeport NJ 08014

WALTERS, DONALD LEE, education educator; b. Roachdale, Ind., Feb. 13, 1937; s. Lee and Beryl (Douglas) W.; m. Nina Walters, June 10, 1972; 1 child, Mark R. BS, Ind. U., 1959, MS, 1960; EdD, U. Miami, 1966. Math. tchr. Kokomo (Ind.)-Ctr. Twp. Schs., 1961-63; asst. to bus. mgr. Dade County Sch. Dist., Miami, Fla., 1964-65; prof. Temple Univ., Phila., 1966—; cons. on sch. fiscal adminstrn.; speaker in field. Contbr. articles to profl. jours. Cert. lay speaker, United Meth. Ch. Capt. USAR, 1959-66. Mem. Am. Ednl. Fin. Assn., Am. Edn. Rsch. Assn., Am. Fedn. Tchrs., Assn. Sch. Bus. Ofcls. Internat. (sch. acctg. rsch. com., panel of rev. for cert. of excellence in fin. reporting), NEA, Phi Eta Sigma, Phi Kappa Phi, Phi Delta Kappa. Office: Temple U ELPS 003-00 Philadelphia PA 19122

WALTERS, ERNEST EDWARD, artist, writer; b. Elizabethtown, Ky., Nov. 11, 1927; s. William Paul and Iva Jane (Jones) W.; m. Dorothy Gene, Aug. 5, 1961; children: Judith Rika, Kristina Elizabeth, Marcella Virginia. Student, U. Louisville, 1949-52, U. Miami, 1952-53, Studio Art Schs., Paris, 1953-54, Towson (Md.) U., 1963. Tchr. Balt. Pub. Schs., 1963-66; co-owner Daedal Art Pubs., 1985—. Sgt. USAF, 1947-48. Mem. Md. Printmakers (treas. 1989—), Erewhon Art Publs. (bd. dirs., chief exec. officer 1955-58), Md. Country Club. Home: 257 Foster Knolls Dr Joppa MD 21085-4756 Office: Daedal Art Pubs The Fallston Mall Fallston MD 21047

WALTERS, HEATHER MACLEAN, biology educator; b. Stamford, Conn., Aug. 16; d. David Cameron and Cynthia Frances (Maynard) MacLean; m. Robert Alan Walters, June 11, 1983. BS, Cornell U., 1981; MEd, U. Lowell, 1987, MS, 1988. Rsch. asst. Cornell U., Ithaca, N.Y., 1981-83; staff mem. Billerica (Mass.) Bd. Health, 1988-90; adj. faculty mem. Middlesex Community Coll., Bedford, Mass., 1988-90, Bentley Coll., Waltham, Mass., 1989-90, Raritan Valley Community Coll., North Branch, N.J., 1990—; USDA fellow in food sci. and nutrition Rutgers U., New Brunswick, N.J., 1991—; mem. DuPont Biosafety Com., Billerica, Mass., 1990—. Editor NSBE News, 1983; author lab. manual Biology: The Study of Life, 1989. Chmn. com. Cornell U. Alumni Ambassabor Network, 1987. Recipient Citizenship award N.Y. Bd. Realtors. Mem. Inst. Food Technologists.

WALTERS, JAMES MICHAEL, security company executive; b. Phila., July 18, 1947; s. James Jacob and Theresa Chromczak W.; m. Martha Christine Kenty; children: Elizabeth, Evelyn. BA in Anthropology, U. Pa., 1971, MS in Social Psychiatry, 1978; PhD in Social Sci., Med. Coll. of Pa., 1979. Police officer Phila. Police Dept., 1971-75; staff anthropologist Med. Coll. of Pa., Phila., 1976-78; sr. researcher Sci. Ctr. U. City, Phila., 1978-83, dir. social scis. Sci. Ctr., 1980-83; dir. Citizen's Crime Commn., Phila., 1983-87; v.p. quality assurance and tng. SpectaGuard, Inc., Phila., 1987—. Editor: (contbr.) Life With Heroin, 1981; co-author: (with others) Private Policing, 1987, Buzzin': PCP in Philadelphia, 1978, Workin' the Corner, 1976; contbr. articles to profl. jours. Mem. Chestnut Hill Civic Assn., Pa., 1987—, Citizens Crime Commn., Phila., 1985—, Safe Schs./Safe Soc. Ctr., Phila., 1987—, N.W. Victim Svcs., 1988—. Govs. Coun. fellow, Pa., 1974-76. Fellow Soc. for Applied Anthropology; mem. Issue Mgmt. Assn., Am. Anthropological Assn., Nat. Assn. Ethnography and Social Policy (2d v.p. 1980—), Am. Soc. Tng. and Devel., Am. Soc. Quality Control, Nat. Soc. for Performance Instrn. Democrat. Unitarian. Office: SpectaGuard Inc 1 E Wynnewood Rd Wynnewood PA 19096-1918

WALTERS, JERRY WILLARD, intelligence officer; b. Paducah, Ky., Aug. 26, 1936; s. Rex Willard and Dorothy Maureen (Smith) W.; m. Rita Anne Middledorf, Oct. 10, 1960; children: Rex Robert, Wade Alan, Stacy Lee. BA, U. Md., 1959. Fingerprint specialist FBI, Washington, 1955-57; commd. ensign USN, 1960; served as intelligence officer U.S. Naval Security Group, The Philippines and Ala., 1960-70; intelligence analyst Nat. Security Agy., Washington, 1966-69; advanced through grades to lt. USN, 1970; human intelligence case officer U.S. Naval Intelligence, Japan, 1973-77; intelligence analyst Bur. Alcohol, Tobacco & Firearms, Washington, 1978-88; mgr. customs intelligence officer U.S. Customs Svc., Washington, 1988—. Mem. Internat. Assn. Law Enforcement Intelligence Analysts (charter, bd. dirs. 1980-90, pres. 1986-89, Achievement Cert. 1987). Republican. Home: Bull Run Mountain Haymarket VA 22069

WALTERS, JESSE CHANDLER, city official; b. Fountain Hill, Pa., Feb. 4, 1956; s. Richard Dennis and Madelyne Bertha (Freund) W. Student, St. Joseph's U., 1974-79. Counselor Delaware County, Media, Pa., 1979-81; food & beverage mgr. Holiday Inn, Phila., 1981-83; dir. catering Hotel Bethlehem, Pa., 1983-85; dir. catering MHM Inc., Scranton, Pa., Niagara Falls, N.Y., 1985-88; dir. sales Howard Johnson Hotel, Phila., 1988-89; sr. sales rep. Penn Pub., Phila., 1989-90; dir. membership Phila. Conv. and Visitors Bur., 1990—. Bd. dirs. Washington Square West Civic Assn., Phila.; bd. dirs., sec. Washington Square West Polit. Actioon Com.; trustee Parkers, Phila., 1991; mem. Chestnut Street Assn., Phila., 1990—; committeeman Rep. City Com., Phila., 1989—; active St. Paul's Ch. Mem. Hotel Sales and Mktg. Assn. (newsletter editor 1989-90, bd. dirs., program chmn. 1990-91), Lower Bucks County C. of C. (conv. and visitors com. 1988-91), St. Joseph's U. Basketball Club, City of Brotherly Love Softball League. Roman Catholic. Home: 416 S Iseminger St Philadelphia PA 19147-1114

WALTERS, LAWRENCE JAMES, career naval officer; b. Greensboro, N.C., Sept. 2, 1948; s. Floyd Perry and Lucy Parker (Vaughan) W.; m. Fay Lorraine Griesemer, July 24, 1976; children: Kristina Dawn, Meghan Gail. BS cum laude, U. N.C., Greensboro, 1973; MHA, Duke U., 1976. With USCG, 1967-71, USCGR, 1971-73; commd. ensign USN, 1974, advanced through grades to comdr., 1974—; dir. logistics div. Bur. Medicine and Surgery USN, Washington, 1991-92, deputy asst. chief, 1992—; with Wesley Long Community Hosp., Greensboro, N.C., 1973-74; lectr. bus. adminstrn. Durham (N.C.) County Community Coll., 1974-76; adj. prof. hosp. adminstrn. Golden Gate U., Tidewater, Va. Campus, 1977-84; navy mem. Health Industry Fed. Adv. Coun., 1991-92. Fellow Am. Coll. Healthcare Execs. (regent advisor for mil. affiliates). Home: 9813 Mainsail Dr Gaithersburg MD 20879-1139 Office: USN Bur of Medicine and Surgery 23rd and E Sts Washington DC 20372

WALTERS, MARC ANTON, chemistry educator; b. N.Y.C., July 18, 1952; s. William and Ida (Francis) W. BS, CCNY, 1976; PhD, Princeton U., 1981. Asst. prof. NYU, N.Y.C., 1985—. Contbr. articles to profl. jours.

WALTERS, THOMAS JOSEPH, automotive company executive; b. New Brunswick, N.J., Mar. 12, 1930; s. Robert Leonard and Mary Theresa (Sehulster) W.; m. Estelle Dorothy Diorio, Feb. 14, 1953; children: Thomas J. Jr., Joseph J., Janet E., Michael J., James E. Comptroller City Garage Inc., North Brunswick, N.J., 1953-61, Mid State Oil Heating Corp., North Brunswick, 1961-70, Perrine's Pontiac, Jamesburg, N.J., 1970-73; instr. Wassel Automotive Sch., Livingston, N.J., 1973-75; comptroller DeAngelis Buick, New Brunswick, N.J., 1975-81, Volvo of Princeton (N.J.), 1981—. V.p. North Brusnwick C. of C., 1970; pres. Midd. County Fuel Dealers Assn., 1968; pres. Sacred Heart Holy Name Soc., New Brunswick, 1965. Mem. KC. Roman Catholic. Office: Volvo of Princeton 2931 Brunswick Ave Lawrenceville NJ 08648-2403

WALTERS, TIMOTHY EDWARD, software developer; b. Altadena, Calif., Sept. 11, 1949; s. Jackson Kent and Julia (Marugg) W.; m. Susanne Maria Prokscha, Oct. 21, 1984. BS in Math., Mich. State U., 1971. Programmer U. Rochester, N.Y., 1973-74, Mass. Gen. Hosp., Boston, 1974-79; cons. Computer Factory, Cambridge, Mass., 1979; programmer Datacrown, Inc., Wellesley, Mass., 1979-81; sr. programmer Software Arts, Wellesley, 1981-84; dir. Info. Resources Inc., Waltham, Mass., 1984-86; mem. tech. staff Interleaf, Inc., Cambridge, Mass., 1986-88, Munich, Fed. Republic of Germany, 1988-90; fellow Interleaf, Inc., Waltham, 1991—; cons. Pompidou Ctr., Paris, 1981. Mem. Phi Beta Kappa. Office: Interleaf Inc Prospect Hill Park 9 Hillside Ave Waltham MA 02154-7556

WALTERS, WILLIAM BEN, chemistry educator; b. Highland, Kans., Apr. 26, 1938; s. Ben Guthrie and Dolly Varden (Shaw) W.; m. Barbara Lulu Sternaman, Aug. 5, 1962; children: Katharine, David. AS, Highland Coll., 1957; BS, Kans. State U., 1960; PhD, U. Ill., 1964. Asst. prof. MIT, Cambridge, 1965-70; assoc. prof. chemistry U. Md., College Park, 1970-77, prof., 1977—, assoc. chmn. dept., 1982-86; vis. prof. U. Louvain, Belgium, 1978. Guggenheim fellow Oxford U., 1986-87. Mem. Am. Phys. Soc., European Phys. Soc., Am. Chem. Soc. (chmn. div. nuclear chemistry 1986), Rotary (bd. dirs. College Park 1990-91). Office: U Md Dept Chemistry College Park MD 20742

WALTKING, ARTHUR ERNEST, food scientist, chemist; b. N.Y.C., Nov. 7, 1937; s. Ernest Conrad and Jennie Violet (Gilles)W.; m. Kathryn Martha Schraut, June 4, 1961; children: Claire Virginia, Adrienne Rosa. BS, Lehigh U., 1959. Tech. asst. Durkee Foods, Bethlehem, Pa., 1957; assoc. chemist Best Foods div. CPC Internat., Bayonne, N.J., 1959-64, chemist, 1964-66, group leader, 1966-67; sect. head Best Foods div. CPC Internat., Union, N.J., 1967-79, assoc. rsch. scientist, 1979-84, prin. materials scientist, 1984—. Contbr. articles to profl. jours.; patentee in field. Mem. ch. coun. Good Shepherd Luth. Ch., Glen Rock, N.J., 1979-82. Recipient Golden Peanut award Nat. Peanut Coun., 1971. Fellow Assn. Ofcl. Analytical Chemists (N.Y.-N.J. regional sect. pres. 1988-90, mem. com. foods 1979-88); mem. Am. Oil Chemists Soc. (chmn. phys. methods com. 1988—), Internat. Union of Pure and Applied Chemists (U.S. nat. rep. commn. on oils, fats, derivitatives 1978-91). Republican. Lutheran. Office: Best Foods Rsch & Engring 1120 Commerce Ave Union NJ 07083-5088

WALTON, AMANDA LORETTA, educator; b. Millen, Ga., Sept. 16, 1941; d. Willie and Gussia (Wilson) Jones; m. Van L. Walton, July 3, 1966; children: Myshiel Massa, Van Lawrence Walton Jr. AA in Liberal Arts, Manhatten Community Coll., 1975; BA in Polit. Sci., York Coll., 1980; M, City Coll. of N.Y., 1983, postgrad., 1985. Teacher asst. Pub. Sch. 200, Manhatten, 1970-73; aux. trainer Pub. Sch. 132, N.Y.C., 1974-81; tchr. Pub. Sch. 274, Bkyln., 1981—; ednl. cons., Queens, N.Y., 1981—; developer grant N.Y. Bd. Edn., 1989-90; adaptor grant N.Y. Bd. Edn., 1989-90 Calif. Books Across Am., 1991-92. Mem. legisl. adv. com., Albany, N.Y., 1981, Queens Village Bellrose Dems., Queens Village, 1983. Grantee Am. Heart Assn., Am. Cancer Soc., Cool Cats Don't Smoke, 1989-90, Nat. Diffusion Network, 1991-92. Mem. NAFE, Internat. Reading Assn., Manhattan Reading Coun. Democrat. Roman Catholic. Home: 22139 112th Ave Jamaica NY 11429-2510

WALTON, MARK ALAN, manufacturing company executive; b. Houlton, Maine, Sept. 9, 1955; s. Alan H. and Edith (Varney) W.; m. Roxanne Jean Rattray, Apr. 8, 1978; children: Mikala, Brooke, Travis. Student, U. Maine, Presque Isle, 1973-77. With Cianbro Corp., Presque Isle, 1978; with pers. and safety dept. Cianbro Corp., Pittsfield, Maine, 1978; concrete plant mgr. Cianbro Corp., Brunswick, Maine, 1979, Lewiston, Maine, 1980-81; packing and shipping supt. Cianbro Corp., Thomaston, Maine, 1981-83; quarry supt. Dragon Products Inc., Thomaston, 1983-84, maintenance mgr., 1984-85; plant mgr. Dragon Products Inc., Presque Isle, 1985-88, Thomaston, 1988—; presenter Inst. Electronics Engrs., 1989. Recipient Citizens Bravery award Maine State Legis., 1986. Mem. Am. Concrete Inst. (New England chpt.), Portland Cement Assn. (mem. gen. tech. com.), Warren Mining Commn., Presque Isle C. of C. (bd. dirs. 1986-87, Citizens Bravery award 1986), Thomaston C. of C. (bd. dirs. 1989), Rotary (bd. dirs. Presque Isle chpt., v.p. Rockland chpt. 1992, Paul Harris fellow 1992), Quoggy Joe Ski Club Presque Isle (bd. dirs.). Office: Dragon Products Corp US Rte 1 Thomaston ME 04861

WALTON, ROBERT MARTIN, electrical engineer; b. Center, Tex., Feb. 9, 1964; s. Billy Mac and Lenora (Batts) W. BSEE, U. Tex., 1986; postgra., Long Island U., Dobbs Ferry, N.Y., 1990—. Supervisory gen. engr. VA Med. Ctr., Marlin, Tex., 1987-90, FDR VA Hosp., Montrose, N.Y., 1990-91, VA Med. Ctr., Bronx, N.Y., 1991—. Mem. Am. Soc. Hosp. Engrs., NSPE, IEEE. Home: 43 S Highland Ave Apt 1 Ossining NY 10562-5217 Office: VA Med Ctr 130 W Kingsbridge Rd Bronx NY 10468

WALTZ, JOSEPH MCKENDREE, neurosurgeon, educator; b. Detroit, July 23, 1931; s. Ralph McKinley and Bertha (Seelye) W.; m. Janet Maureen Journey, June 26, 1954; children: Jeffrey McKinley, Mary Elaine, David Seelye, Stephen McKendree; m. Marilyn Liska, June 5, 1967; 1 child, Tristana McKendree. Student, U. Mich., 1950; B.S., U. Oreg., 1954, M.D., 1956. Diplomate Am. Bd. Neurol. Surgery. Surg. intern U. Mich. Hosp., 1956-57, gen. surg. resident, 1957-58, clin. instr. neurosurgery, 1960-63; neurosurg. assoc. St. Barnabas Hosp., N.Y.C., 1963—; assoc. dir. Inst. Neurosci., 1974—, dir. dept. neurol. surgery, 1977—; assoc. cons. in neurosurgery Englewood (N.J.) Hosp., 1964—; assoc. prof. neurosurgery NYU Med. Ctr., 1974—; asst. prof. dept. surgery (neurosurgery) N.Y. Coll. Osteo. Medicine, 1989—; bd. dirs. Neurol. Surgery Rsch. Found., 1978. Author papers on functional neurosurg. treatment of abnormal movement disorders cerebral palsy, others; cryothalamectomy-cryopulvinectomy and implantation brain pacemakers; chpt. in book on cryogenic surgery; contbr. chpts. to Cryogenic Surgery, Neurology, 1982, Advances in Neurology, 1983. Patentee 4-electrode quadrapolar computerized spinal cord stimulator. Mem. sci. adv. bd. Dystonia Med. Research Found., 1980—; trustee St. Barnabas Hosp., 1980—. Served to capt. M.C. AUS, 1958-60. Recipient bronze award Am. Congress Rehab. Medicine, 1967. Mem. Am. Paralysis Assn., World Soc. Stereotactic and Functional Neurosurgery, Congress Neurol. Surgeons, Nat. Ski Patrol, Soc. for Cryobiology, AMA, N.Y. State, Bronx County med. socs., N.Y. State Neurosurg. Soc., Phi Beta Pi. Home: Four B Island South 720 Milton Rd Rye NY 10580-3258 Office: St Barnabas Hosp 4422 3d Ave Bronx NY 10457

WALTZ, MARK EDWARD, dentist; b. Altoona, Pa., Mar. 9, 1932; s. Benjamin Franklin and Mary Elizabeth (Myers) W.; m. Kathryn Baur, May 14, 1955; children: Mark (dec.), Sharon, Stephen, Debra. BA, Temple U., 1955, DDS, 1959. Lic. dental surgeon, Pa. Pres. Montgomery-Bucks Dental Assn., Pa., 1973-74; chmn. self assessment Acad. of Gen. Dentistry, Chgo., 1979-80, nat. bd. dirs., 1984-90, chmn. nat. com. on jour. publs., 1985-86; pres. L.D. Pankey Inst. Alumni Assn., Key Biscayne, Fla., 1985-87, Acad. Gen. Dentistry Found., Chgo., 1989—; cons. ADA Inst. Sponsorship Program, 1979-80, FDA, Bur. of Radiol. Health, 1980; bd. dirs. L.D. Pankey Inst.; asst. prof. Temple U. Dental Sch., 1961-72. Contbg. author: Denture Prosthesis: Polished Surface, 1973, 78; contbr. articles to profl. jours. Capt. U.S. Army, 1959-61. Recipient Legion of Honor award Chapel of Four Chaplains, 1981. Fellow Am. Coll. Dentistry, Internat. Coll. Dentistry; mem. Acad. Gen. Dentistry (master), Pearre Fauchard Acad., Old York Rd. Study Club, Am. Equilibration Soc., Am. Prosthodontic Soc., Acad. of Practice Adminstrn., Delaware Valley L.D. Pankey Study Club (pres. 1991—), PSI Omega, Omicron Kappa Upsilon. Republican. Mem. Ch. of the Brethren. Home: 1503 Valley View Rd Gwynedd Valley PA 19437

WALUK, STANLEY PETER, corporate engineering official; b. Palmer, Mass., July 29, 1943; s. Stanley John and Bertha Rose (Mozden) W.; A.S. in E.E., Northeast Inst., 1963; B.S. in Indsl. Engring., Western New Eng. Coll., 1973; postgrad. in forensic engring. and patent law Brown U., 1983; postgrad. in product liability law Providence Coll., 1981; m. Mary Ann Mechonski, June 6, 1964; 1 dau., Angela Kim. Quality control mgr., chief engr. Gavitt Wire and Cable Co., Brookfield, Mass., 1963-71; spl. project engr. TRW-Holyoke Wire and Cable Co., South Hadley, Mass., 1971-74; plant mgr. Standard Wire and Cable Co., Attleboro, Mass., 1974-75; v.p., gen. mgr. Lyall Electric, Kendallville, Ind., 1975; tech. dir. Miller Electric Co. (Carol Cable Co.), Woonsocket, R.I., 1976-83; engring. mgr. Judd Wire Inc. div. High Voltage Engring., 1983-90; corp. mgr. quality and standards Judd Wire, Inc., 1990—; cons. wire and cable engring., 1975—; mem. tech. adv. panel Underwriters Lab., also rep. Industry Adv. Conf. Aux. staff officer USCG; mfg. insp. rep. FAA, 1985—. Mem. ASTM, Nat. Fire Protection Assn., Stat. Process Control Soc., Internat. Electrotech. Comm. (mem. com.), Am. Inst. Indsl. Engrs., Wire Assn., Am. Soc. Quality Control, Soc. Automotive Engrs., Am. Mgmt. Soc. (affiliate), Providence Engring. Soc. (affiliate), U.S. Coast Guard Aux. (staff officer), U.S. Yacht Racing Union. Expert in elec. engring. and consumer elec. products. Home: 7 Oak Knolls Dr South Deerfield MA 01373-9736 Office: Turnpike Rd Turners Falls MA 01376

WALWORTH, EDWARD ZINSSER, surgeon; b. Washington, Jan. 30, 1945; s. Edward Henry and Nancy Knowlton (Zinsser) W.; m. Candace Wentworth Cooper, Dec. 27, 1969; children: Elizabeth Zinsser, Nancy Cooper. AB, Princeton U., 1966; MD, Columbia U., 1970. Diplomate Am. Bd. Surgery. Pvt. practice Lewiston, Maine; mem. active med. staff St. Mary's Regional Med. Ctr., Lewiston, Maine, 1977—, pres. med. staff, 1989—; mem. active med. staff Cen. Maine Med. Ctr., Lewiston, 1983—. Mem. bd. LA Arts, Lewiston-Auburn, Maine, 1991—. Lt. comdr. USN, 1975-77. Fellow ACS (pres. Maine chpt. 1988-89, gov. Maine 1991-94); mem. AMA, New Eng. Surg. Soc., Maine Med. Assn., County Med. Assn. (pres. 1982). Democrat. Congregationalist. Office: Androscoggin Clin Assocs 710 Main St Lewiston ME 04240

WALZER, ANN WERLIN, radiologist; b. Houston, June 13, 1945; d. Sam and Marcelle (Maier) W.; m. Robert Steven Walzer, Aug. 8, 1968; children: Steven, Eric. AB, Radcliffe Coll., 1967; MD, NYU, 1971. Diplomate Am. Bd. Radiology, Nat. Bd. Med. Examiners. Asst. clin. prof. Albert Einstein Coll. Medicine, N.Y.C., 1975-88; ptnr. New Milford (Conn.) Radiol. Assocs., 1980—. Contbr. articles to profl. jours. Mem. N.Y. Roentgen Soc., Radiol. Soc. North Am. Office: New Milford Hosp 21 Elm St New Milford CT 06776

WAMESTER, WILLIAM DAVID, public health sanitarian; b. Buffalo, Oct. 3, 1945; s. Merrill Bancroft and Ruth (Reed) W.; m. Norma Ruth Schilke, June 16, 1968; children: Sarah, Tadd. BA, Cen. Conn. State U., New Britain, 1967; MPH, Yale U., 1992. Registered sanitarian. Tchr. Regional Dist. 13, Durham, Conn., 1968-73; pub. health sanitarian City of Middletown, Conn., 1973—; adj. instr. Middlesex Community Coll., Middletown, 1972-73; sr. scientist Bermuda Biol. Sta., St. Georges, 1970-73; pres. Middconn Mcpl. Fed. Credit Union, 1984-88. Mem. Planning and Zoning Commn., Clinton, 1985-88; mem. bd. Edn., Clinton, 1991-92; pres. Clinton Beach Assn., 1984-88; active Girl Scouts U.S., 1987-91. Mem. NEA (life), London Vintage Taxi Assn. Republican. Lutheran. Home: 152 Shore Rd Clinton CT 06413

WAMPLER, DONALD EUGENE, biochemist; b. Luanfu, Shanxi, China, July 24, 1935; arrived in U.S., 1940; s. Ernest M. and Elizabeth (Baker) W.; m. E. Theresa Shaft, June 17, 1961; children: Susan M., Stanley S., Pamela J. BA, Bridgewater Coll., 1959; MS, Mich. State U., 1961, PhD, 1965. Asst. prof. Sch. Medicine, U. Conn., Farmington, 1968-75; rsch. specialist Mich. State U., East Lansing, 1976-77; sr. rsch. fellow Merck & Co., Inc., West Point, Pa., 1977—. Contbr. articles to profl. publs.; patentee in field. Office: Merck & Co Inc West Point PA 19486

WAMSER, CHRISTIAN ALBERT, retired chemist; b. L.I., N.Y, July 15, 1913; s. Christian Ludwig and Margaret (Fuchner) W.; m. Madeline Grace Miller, May 30, 1940; children: Carl C., Christina A. Trautman. BSChemE, Cooper Union Inst. Tech., 1934. Analytical chemist Jelenko & Co., N.Y.C., 1934-41; supr. analytical chem. div. Gen. Chem. Co., Laurel Hill, N.Y., 1941-48; rsch. chemist Vitro Corp. (fomerly Kellex), West Orange, N.J., 1948-62; rsch. chemist Allied Chem. Corp., Morristown, N.J., 1962-69; rsch. chemist Allied Chem. Corp., Syracuse, N.Y., 1969-78, ret., 1978; cons. Allied Chem. Corp., Syracuse, 1978-82, Buffalo, N.Y., 1986-87. Contbr. articles to profl. jours.; patentee in field. Mem. Am. Chem. Soc. Home: 207 Rebhahn Dr Camillus NY 13031-1919

WAN, SHAO-HONG, business executive; b. Chongqing, Sichuan, China, Jan. 6, 1946; s. Dingguo and Juanru (Shen) W.; m. Hua-Hua Xie, Aug. 15, 1976; 1 child, Qifu. BS, Tsinghua U., Beijing, 1968; MS, Stanford U., 1983, PhD, 1988. Engr. Weifun (China) Computer Co., 1968-76, Rsch. Inst.

Automation, Beijing, 1976-80, Systems Control Inc., Palo Alto, Calif., 1981-87; v.p. Nampac Inc., Montreal, Que., Can., 1988—; pres. Xenexi Group Investments Ltd., Montreal, 1986—; advisor China Venturetech Investment Corp., Beijing, 1986-88. Contbr. articles to profl. jours. Mem. Ops. Rsch. Soc. Am. Office: Nampac Inc, 5165 Sherbrooke W Ste 300, Montreal, PQ Canada H4A 1T6

WANAT, STANLEY FRANK, chemist, research executive; b. Nanticoke, Pa., Dec. 31, 1939; s. Stanley John and Irene Rita (Sobolewski) W.; m. Joy M. Edmonds, July 25, 1964; children: Brian S., Jill D. AB, Rutgers U., 1963; MS, Seton Hall U., 1969, PhD, 1971. Chemistry inst. Union County Tech. Inst., Berkeley Hts., N.J., 1971-73; sr. rsch. chemist Hoechst Celanese Corp., Branchburg, N.J., 1973-79, group leader, 1979-84; rsch. mgr. Hoechst Celanesr Corp., Branchburg, N.J., 1984-88, process devel. mgr., 1988—. Contbr. articles to profl. jours; patentee in field. With USARNG, 1957-65. Mem. Am. Chem. Soc. Home: 3 Frances Ln Scotch Plains NJ 07076-2534 Office: Hoechst Celanese Corp 51 Meister Ave Somerville NJ 08876-3434

WANDASIEWICZ, STEFANIA, mathematics and economics educator; b. Szczecin, Poland, Nov. 14, 1948; arrived in England, 1973; d. Janusz and Wanda (Martynionska) Biskupski; m. George James Wandasiewicz, Aug. 17, 1973; children: Edward, Nelson, Anna. MA in Math., The Adam Mickiewicz U., Poznan, Poland, 1971; MA in Econs., U. Essex, Colchester, England, 1987, postgrad., 1987—. Cert. postgrad. tech. educator, 1973. Asst. Gdansk (Poland) Polytechnic, 1971-73; lectr. U.S. Internat. U.-Europe, London, 1981-84, European Div. U. Md., Heidelberg, West Germany, 1984—. Mem. Am. Econ. Assn., Soc. for Indsl. and Applied Math. Roman Catholic. Home: Box 1175 APO AE 09405-5000

WANDEL, WILLIAM ROBERT, medical malpractice consultant; b. Camden, N.J., Sept. 5, 1951; William and Evelyn (Hendrickson) W.; m. Marietta Gail Eubanks, Apr, 28, 1973; children: Brian M., Jason A., Kathleen J. BSE, Okla. Christian U., 1973; MBA, Coll. Ins., 1986; car. Supr. Argonaut, Cranford, N.J., 1974-79; dir. Cigna, N.Y.C., 1979-85; v.p. Albany Atlas Group, N.Y.C., 1985-86; sr. v.p. Continental Ins. Group, N.Y.C., 1986—. Active sch. bd., Tinton Falls, N.J., 1981-83; ch. deacon, 1980—. Mem. Phi Alpha Theta. Mem. Church of Christ. Office: Continental Ins Healthcare Group 180 Maiden Ln New York NY 10038

WANG, BOSCO SHANG, immunologist; b. Shang Hai, China, Aug. 30, 1947; came to U.S., 1970; s. Tai-Yung and Sun-Sen (Ho) W.; m. Helen Ku, Dec. 4, 1972; children: Burkon, Tammy. MS, Mich. State U., 1973; PhD, Boston U., 1976. Postdoctoral fellow Harvard U. Med. Sch., Boston, 1976-77, instr., 1977-79, asst. prof., 1979-81; sr. scientist Lederle Labs., Pearl River, N.Y., 1981-88; prin. scientist Am. Cyanamid Co., Princeton, N.J., 1988—. Contbr. to over 100 sci. pubis. Recipient Wilson S. Stone Meml. award M.D. Anderson Hosp. and Tumor Inst., 1977, Milton Fund award Harvard U., 1981, Cyanamid's Sci. Achievement award Cyanamid Co., 1985. Mem.Am. Assn. Immunologists, Am. Assn. Cancer Rsch. Office: Am Cyanamid Co PO Box 400 Princeton NJ 08543-0400

WANG, CHIA PING, physicist, educator; (parents Chinese citizens); came to U.S., 1963, naturalized; s. Guan Can and Tah (Lin) W. BS, U. London, 1950; MS, U. Malaya, 1951; PhD in Physics, U. Malaya and U. Cambridge, 1953; DSc in Physics, U. Singapore, 1972. Asst. lectr. U. Malaya, 1951-53; mem. faculty Nankai U., Tientsin, 1954-58, prof. physics, 1956-58, head electron physics div., 1955-58, mem. steering com. nuclear physics div., 1956-58; head electron physics Lanchow Atomic Project, 1958; mem. faculty Hong Kong U.; mem. faculty Chinese U., Hong Kong, 1958-63, prof. physics, 1959-63, acting head physics, math. depts., 1959; rsch. assoc. lab. nuclear studies Cornell U., Ithaca, N.Y., 1963-64; assoc. prof. space sci. and applied physics Cath. U. Am., Washington, 1964-68; assoc. prof. physics Case Inst. Tech. Case Western Res. U., Cleve., 1966-70; vis. scientist, vis. prof. U. Cambridge (Eng.), U. Leuven (Belgium), U.S. Naval Rsch. Labs., U. Md., MIT, 1970-75; rsch. physicist radiation lab. U.S. Army Natick (Mass.) R & D Command, 1975—; pioneer in fields of nuclear sub-structure (now often referred to as parton), nucleon sub-unit structure, multiparticle prodn., cosmic radiation, picosecond time to pulse-height conversion, thermal physics, lasers, microwaves. Contbg. author: Atomic Structure and Interactions of Ionizing Radiations with Matter in Preservation of Food by Ionizing Radiation, 1982; contbr. numerous articles to profl. jours. Recipient Outstanding Performance award Dept. Army, 1980, Quality Increase award, 1980. Mem. Am. Phys. Soc., Inst. Physics London, N.Y. Acad. Scis., AAAS, Sigma Xi. Home: 28 Hallett Hill Rd Weston MA 02193-1753 Office: US Army Natick Rsch and Devel Ctr Natick MA 01760

WANG, EDWIN JAMES, investment banker; b. Waltham, Mass., July 16, 1962; s. Chih-Wong and Amy Chi-Wen (Liang) W. AB, Columbia U., 1984. Vis. fellow MIT, 1985; asst. v.p. Constn. Capital Mgmt., Boston, 1985-86; v.p. Shearson Lehman Bros., N.Y.C., 1986-90, Prudential Securities, N.Y.C., 1990-91. Mem. Purchase Country Club. Republican. Episcopalian. Office: First Boston Corp Park Avenue Pla New York NY 10055

WANG, HSUEH-HWA, pharmacology educator, physician; b. Peking, People's Republic of China, July 10, 1923; came to U.S., 1946; d. Shih Chieh and Teh-Hwa (Hsiao) W.; m. Shih-hsun Ngai, Nov. 6, 1948; children: Mae, Janet, John. MD, Nat. Cen. U., Nanking, China, 1946. Intern Univ. Hosp., Nat. Cen. U. Med. Sch., Chengtu, China, 1945-46; med. resident Hackensack (N.J.) Hosp., 1948-50; pharmacology instr. Columbia U., N.Y.C., 1958-61, assoc., 1961-64, asst. prof., 1964-69; assoc. prof., 1969-80; prof. Columbia U., N.Y.C., 1980-90, prof. emeritus, 1990—. Named Outstanding Woman award Met. chpt. Am. Women in Sci., 1991. Mem. Am. Soc. Pharmacology, Am. Physiol. Soc. Home: 281 Edgewood Ave Teaneck NJ 07666-3023 Office: Columbia U Dept Pharmacology 630 W 168th St New York NY 10032-3702

WANG, JAMES CHUO, biochemistry and molecular biology educator; b. Kiangsu, China, Nov. 18, 1936; came to U.S., 1960; s. Chin and H.-L. (Shih) W.; m. Sophia Shu-lan Hwang, Dec. 23, 1961; children: Janice S., Jessica A. BS, Nat. Taiwan U., 1959; MA, U. S.D., 1961; PhD, U. Mo. Coll. Arts and Sci., 1964. Asst. instr. Nat. Taiwan U., Taipei, 1959-60; rsch. fellow in chemistry Calif. Inst. Tech., Pasadena, 1964-66; asst. prof. chemistry U. Calif. at Berkeley, 1966-69, assoc. prof., 1969-74, prof., 1974-77; prof. biochemistry and molecular biology Harvard U., Cambridge, Mass., 1977-88, Mallinckrodt prof. biochemistry and molecular biology, 1988—; Chancellor's Disting. lectr. U. Calif., Berkeley, 1984; mem. molecular biology study sect. NIH, 1988-91, chair, 1990-91; disting. faculty lectr. U. Tex., M.D. Anderson Cancer Ctr., 1989. Mem. editorial bd. Quar. Rev. Biophysics, 1988—. Guggenheim fellow Guggenheim Found., 1986-87; recipient Disting. Alumnus award U. Mo. Coll. Arts and Scis., 1991. Fellow Am. Acad. Arts and Scis.; mem. NAS (molecular biology award 1983), Third World Acad. Scis., Academia Sinica (Taipei). Office: Harvard U Dept Biochemistry & Molecular Biology 7 Divinity Ave Cambridge MA 02138-2092

WANG, XIAOLU, mathematics educator; b. Changsha, Hunan, People's Republic of China, Apr. 25, 1954; came to U.S., 1980; parents Xian Rong and Yong Cai (Tan) W. Student, Hunan U., Changsha, 1978, Academia Sinica, Beijing, 1978-79; MA in Math., Wayne State U., 1981; PhD in Math., U. Calif., Berkeley, 1985. Artist, technician mech. engring. lab. Hunan U., Changsha, 1973-74, engr. elec. engring. lab., 1974-75, with civil engring. lab., 1975-77; instr. U. Chgo., 1985-87; asst. prof. math. U. Md., College Park, 1987-91, assoc. prof., 1992—. Author: On the Deformation of the Main Shafts of Lathes, 1974, On the C*-Algebras of Foliations of the Plane, 1988, On the C*-Algebras of a Family of Solvable Lie Groups, 1989; co-author (with others) The Statistical Methods in Civil Engineering, 1975; contbr. articles to profl. jours. Acadamia Sinica fellow, 1978, U. Calif.-Berkeley regents fellow, 1982-83, Wilson and Albert Flagg fellow, U. Calif., 1983-84; NSF rsch. grantee, 1985-92. Mem. Am. Math. Soc. Office: U Md Dept Math College Park MD 20742

WANGEL, LANCE HEYWOOD, customs brokerage house executive; b. Bklyn., July 11, 1960; s. Monroe Walter and Brenda Susan (Weinberger) W.; m. Nicola Farman, Sept. 16, 1990. BA in Polit. Sci., Pace U., 1991; postgrad., NYU. Lic. custom house broker. Mgr. C.F. Ocean Svc. Inc., N.Y.C., 1985-86; v.p. Rohde and Liesenfield, Inc., N.Y.C., 1986-87; pvt. practice Queens, N.Y., 1987-91; v.p. J.H. Bachmann, Inc., N.Y.C., 1991—; cons. D.H.L. Airways, Queens, 1988, Ryder Internat., Queens, 1988-90. Editor, author: (manual) Customs Entry Made Simpler, 1990. Tutor Star Learning Ctr., N.Y.C., 1990-91; mem. Neighborhood Civic Assn., N.Y.C., 1990-91. Mem. Pi Gamma Mu.

WANKEL, CHARLES BERNHARD, educator; b. N.Y.C., Feb. 23, 1948; s. Carl Bernhard and Dorothy Margaret (Quinn) W.; m. Laura Louise Avitabile, June 4, 1988; children: Kathryn Elizebeth, Bret Avery. BBA, Iona Coll., 1969; MBA, NYU, 1971, PhD, 1990. V.p. Wankel Harware Corp., N.Y.C.; researcher Prentice-Hall, Englewood Cliffs, N.J., 1976-77; asst. dean, instr. Forham U., N.Y.C., 1977-85; asst. prof. mgmt. U. New Haven, West Haven, Conn., 1985-89; assoc. prof. St. John's U., Jamaica, N.Y., 1990—; cons. IBM, Briarcliff, N.Y., 1985, McDonald's, Oak Grove, Ill., 1985. Author: Anticommunist Students and The Polish Renewel, 1992; co-author: Management, 1986. Mem. Acad. Mgmt., Strategic Mgmt. Soc., Beta Gamma Sigma. Roman Catholic. Home: 12 Pilgrim Dr Greenwich CT 06831 Office: St John s U Bent Hall 3 Jamaica NY 11439

WANNALL, WALTER RAYMOND, III, computer software company executive; b. Darby, Pa., Aug. 10, 1944; s. Walter Raymond and Gertrude Lillian (Crane) W.; m. Marianne Elise Sanguinetti, Jan. 29, 1966 (div. Oct. 1978); children: Douglas Keith, Steven Howison; m. Doris Lynne Strong, Sept. 1, 1979. AA, Montgomery Coll., 1972; BA, U. Md., 1974. Corp. recruiter Data Tech. Industries, Riverdale, Md., 1979-80; programmer-analyst Balt. Software, 1980-81, Spentech, Beltsville, Md., 1981-82; pres. Basic Software Corp., Balt., 1982—. Author: Basic Job Costing software program, 1983, Return to Continue, 1987, Best of the Basic Advisor, 1991; co-author: Basic Quick Bid Software Package, 1988; contbr. monthly column to Basic Advisor, 1985-90. Served as sgt. U.S. Army, 1963-67. Home: 5203 Powhatan Ave Baltimore MD 21207-6519 Office: Basic Software Corp 5201 Powhatan Ave Baltimore MD 21207-6519

WANTZ, GEORGE EDWARD, surgeon; b. Charlevoix, Mich., Apr. 14, 1923; s. George Edward and Dorothy Alice (Armstrong) W.; m. Mary Jane Dyble, 1947 (dec. 1961); m. Diana Dilworth, Sept. 30, 1965; children: David DeWeese Hoguet, Diana Logan Hoguet. MD, U. Mich., 1946. Diplomate Am. Bd. Surgery. Intern Wesley Meml. Hosp., Chgo., 1947, Presbyn. Hosp., Chgo., 1948; asst. resident Presbyn. Hosp., 1949; intern in surgery The N.Y. Hosp., N.Y.C., 1949-50, asst. resident, 1950-52, 1954-55, resident, 1955-56, attending physician, 1956—; assoc. prof. Cornell U., N.Y.C., 1956-90, prof., 1990—. Author: Atlas of Hernia Surgery, 1991; editor: Problems in Surgery, 1961. Served to capt. USMC, 1952-54. Fellow ACS; mem. Am. Geriatric Soc., N.Y. Acad. of Medicine, Soc. Internat. de Chirurgie, Soc. Surgery of the Alimentary Tract, Century Assn., The Leash, Anglers Club N.Y. Republican. Office: 517 E 71st St New York NY 10021-4871

WARCHOL, KENNETH J., learning technologies specialist, consultant; b. Greenfield, Mass., June 18, 1943; s. Frank and Celia Warchol. EdM, Boston U., 1971; cert., U. Hawaii, Honolulu, 1972. Tchr. Middleboro (Mass.) Bd. of Edn., 1965-69, Old Saybrook (Conn.) Bd. of Edn., 1969-70; media specialist Norwalk (Conn.) Bd. of Edn., 1972—; evaluator New Eng. Assn. Secondary Schs., Milford; contbr., cons., presenter Conn. Inst. Teaching & Learning, Norwalk, 1990; cons., forum mgr. Channel 13 Tchr. Tng. Inst., N.Y.C., 1991-92. Recipient awards Conn. Dept. Edn. and So. N.E. Telecommunications, 1990, cert. excellence Sta. WNET and Texaco, 1991. Mem. Conn. Ednl. Media Assn., Conn. Ednl. Computer Assn. Office: c/o Norwalk High Sch County St Norwalk CT 06851

WARD, ANTHONY THOMAS, physical chemistry researcher; b. London, Mar. 9, 1941; came to U.S., 1962; s. Percy John and May Mary Grace (Blumfield) W.; m. Sandra Lee Elliott, Oct. 22, 1966; children: Teresa, Stephanie. BSc with honors, Imperial Coll., London, 1962; MS, Rensselaer Poly. Inst., 1964, PhD in Phys. Chemistry, 1966. From assoc. to sr. scientist Xerox Corp., Webster, N.Y., 1966-77, prin. scientist, 1977—. Contbr. articles to profl. jours.; patentee in field. Mem. Soc. for Imaging Sci. and Tech., Sigma Xi, Phi Lambda Upsilon. Office: Xerox Corp 800 Phillips Rd Webster NY 14580-9791

WARD, DEBORA ELLIOTT, psychologist; b. Malone, N.Y., Mar. 24, 1954; d. Donald Joseph and Marion Pearl (Briggs) Elliott; m. Bernard Daniel Ward, Sept. 26, 1987; 1 child, Daniel Elliott. BA in Psychology, SUNY, Binghamton, 1976; MS in Clin. Psychology, Syracuse U., 1978, PhD in Clin. Psychology, 1983. Lic. in psychology, Maine. Psychol. asst. Neuropsychology Lab., Hutchings Psychiatric Ctr., Syracuse, N.Y., 1978-79, Syracuse U. Counseling Ctr., 1979-80; psychology assoc. West Haven (Conn.) VA Med. Ctr., 1980-81; rsch. asst. Syracuse U., 1981-82; psychology trainee Syracuse VA Med. Ctr., 1982; staff psychologist Bangor (Maine) Mental Health Inst., 1983-91. Contbr. articles to profl. jours. USPHS fellow, 1976-78. Mem. APA, Maine Psychol. Assn., Phi Beta Kappa. Home: RR 2 Box 265 Carmel ME 04419-9622

WARD, DORIS ELIZABETH, career counselor, biologist, educator; b. Charlotte, N.C., Jan. 11, 1935; d. James Hopkins and Florie Kathryn Cofield; m. Eddie Eugene Ward, Sept. 18, 1954; children: Eddie Eugene, Tanya Devonne, Tracia Lynnore, Tamara Elizabeth. BS, Howard U., 1966, postgrad., 1967-70; MEd in Guidance and Counseling, Bowie State U., 1985; EdS, George Washington U., 1987, EdD, 1990. Cert. sci. tchr. and guidance counselor, Md.; nat. cert. counselor. Med. technician U.S. Dept. Agr., Washington, 1958-64; biol. lab. technician U.S. Dept. Agr., Bethesda, Md., 1964-65; histologic tech. lab. instr. Howard U., Washington, 1966-67; biologist (histopathology) NIH, Bethesda, 1969-71; tchr. Our Lady Queen of Peace Sch., Washington, 1972-74; program analyst/mgmt. analysis HHS, Washington, 1974-82; career counselor Prince Georges Community Coll., Largo, Md., 1985—; asst. prof. counseling and psychology Grad. Sch. Arts and Scis., Marywood Coll., Scranton, Pa., 1990-91; doctoral intern in counseling Career Devel. Ctr., U. Md., College Park, 1988-89; asst. prof. counseling and psychology Marywood Coll., Scranton, Pa., 1990-91. Hospice vol.; developer, facilitator bereavement support ministry St. Joseph's Ch., Landover, Md., 1984; cons./vol., career counselor for transition and spl. needs populations Cerebral Palsy Assn. Prince Georges County, 1986. Mem. AACD, Am. Soc. Clin. Pathologists (assoc. mem.). Democrat. Roman Catholic. Home: 13003 Keverton Dr Upper Marlboro MD 20772-1839

WARD, DOUGLAS ALFRED, writer, cruise industry executive; b. Birmingham, Eng., Nov. 15, 1945; came to U.S., 1979; s. Thomas Alfred and Gwendoline (Bird) W.; m. Georgia Louise Wolkowick (div. June 1989). Band leader various cruise lines, worldwide, 1965-79; cruise dir. Cunard Line, worldwide, 1979-82; pres. Internat. Cruise Passengers Assn., N.Y.C., 1982—; cons. cruise industry, 1990—. Author: Berlitz Complete Guide to Cruising and Cruise Ships, 1985, rev. edit. 1990, 92; editor: World Cruise Industry Review, 1991-92; pub.: Cruise Digest Reports, 1982—. Anglican. Office: International Cruise Passengers Assn 1521 Alton Rd Ste 350 Miami Beach FL 33139

WARD, HASKELL GEORGE, economic development and human resource consultant; b. Griffin, Ga., Mar. 13, 1940; s. George Allen Ward and Margaret (Poe) Dumas; m. Jennifer Claudette Baswick, Mar. 17, 1968 (div. 1975); m. Kathryn Russo Lecube, June 14, 1980; children: Alexandra, Michelle Lecube. BA, Clark Coll., 1963; MA, UCLA, 1967. Vol. U.S. Peace Corps; instr. Haile Selassie U., Ethiopia, 1963-65; dir. recruitment and selection Ops. Crossroads Africa, N.Y.C., 1967-69; asst. program officer Ford Found., N.Y.C., 1969-72, program officer Office for Middle East and Africa, 1972-75; asst. rep. Office for Middle East and Africa Ford Found., Lagos, Nigeria, 1975-77; specialist Africa, mem. policy planning staff U.S. Dept. State, Washington, 1977-78; commr. Community Devel. Agy. City of N.Y., 1978, dep. mayor human services, 1979, chmn. health and hosps. corp., 1979; pres. Haskell G. Ward Assocs., N.Y.C., 1980—; participant Aspen Inst., 1973-87, speakers program U.S. Info. Service, Washington, 1981-85; lectr., cons. in field. Author: A Matter of Vision: Community and Economic Development in the Philadelphia Area, 1987, African Development Reconsidered: New Perspectives from the Continent, 1989; author, narrator TV mini-series In Search of the Dream, 1990 (Award for Cable Excellence 1991), re-telecast Jan. 1991, Feb. 1991; contbr. articles tprofl. jours. Mem. adv. commn. to Gov. Mario Coumo World Trade Council, N.Y., 1984; mem. Trilateral Commn., 1980-87; bd. dirs. N.Y. City Partnership, 1982-86, N.Y.C. Housing Partnership, 1982-86, Am. Council on Germany, 1985—. John Hay Whitney fellow, 1965-66, hon. Woodrow Wilson fellow, 1965-66; recipient Disting. Service award Clark Coll., 1982; Haskell G. Ward Day proclaimed by City of Griffin, 1979. Democrat. Club: Mid Atlantic (N.Y.C.). Home and Office: 444 E 57th St New York NY 10022-3063

WARD, J(OHN) LEROY, director university goverment contracts program; b. New Haven, Nov. 9, 1949; s. LeRoy James and Rita (Musico) W.; m. Patricia Fahey, Feb. 28, 1976; children: Erin, Caroline. BS, So. Conn. State U., 1973, MS, 1975; MS, Am. U., 1984. Cartographer U.S. Geol. Survey, Reston, Va., 1975-81; project mgr. U.S. Dept. Interior, Washington, 1981-85; dir. ADP U.S. Bur. Indian Affairs, Washington, 1985-89; with U.S. Gen. Svcs. Adminstrn., Washington, 1989-91; dir. govt. contracts program George Washington U., 1991—; cons. in field; instr. George Washington U., 1987—; adj. prof. Am. U., Washington, 1984-86. Author: ADP Contracting, 1988. Commr. Reston (Va.) Soccer Assn., 1990-91, equipment mgr., 1991; vice chair St. John Neuman Social Action, Reston, 1990-91. Mem. Nat. Contract Mgmt. Assn. (chair directory com. 1991), ABA, Project Mgmt. Inst. Roman Catholic. Home: 2417 Myrtle Ln Reston VA 22091-3911

WARD, JOHN THOMAS, newspaper columnist; b. Chgo., Apr. 29, 1925; s. Martin Joseph and Catherine (Collins) W.; m. Marie Elizabeth Mauro, Apr. 26, 1952; children: Clare Ann, Catherine, Eileen Mary, Christine, Stephen John. BA, Rugers U., 1956; MA, Seton Hall U., 1962. Cert. secondary English and math. tchr. Mathematician Army Signal Corps Labs., Ft. Monmouth, N.J., 1955-59; tchr., coach Union Beach (N.J.) Bd. Edn., 1957-62, Long Branch (N.J.) Bd. Edn., 1962-86; columnist Shannon News Svc., Long Branch, 1984—. Contbr. weekly gen. interest column One Man's Opinion to local newspaper and topical reports as investigative reporter. Sgt. USMC, 1943-49. Recipient awards N.J. Working Press Assn., 1990, North Jersey Press Club, 1991. Mem. NEA, Nat. Sports Ofcls. Assn., N.J. Edn. Assn., N.J. Ret. Educators Assn., Shore Athletic Club, N.J., Knights Columbus, Long Branch, Ancient Order Hibernians, Long Branch and Chgo., Am. Legion. Democrat. Roman Catholic. Home: 208 Norwood Ave West Long Branch NJ 02764

WARD, JOHN WHITELEY, financial executive; b. Birmingham, U.K., Feb. 20, 1943; came to U.S., 1978; s. Hedley John and Beryl Margaret (Sims) W.; m. Hilary Jane Proffitt, Apr. 26, 1969; children: Simon Mark, Nicholas James. MA with honors, Oxford U., 1962-66; Diploma in Bus. Adminstrn. with honors, Manchester Bus. Sch., U.K., 1968. V.p. Citibank, N.A., N.Y.C., 1970-81; chmn. Merrill Lynch Internat. Banking Group, N.Y.C., 1981-87; chief exec. officer Midland Montague U.S. Group, N.Y.C., 1987-90; chmn. 3i Corp., Boston, 1991—; owner, dir. ExecuTrain of Westchester, Tarrytown, N.Y., 1991—. With British Air Force, 1962-66. Mem. British Am. C. of C. (bd. dirs. 1989—), Coun. on Fgn. Rels., Econ. Club of N.Y. Office: 3i Corp 99 High St Boston MA 02110

WARD, ROBERT JOSEPH, federal judge; b. N.Y.C., Jan. 31, 1926; s. Joseph G. and Honor V. (Hess) W.; m. Florence C. Maisel, Apr. 15, 1951; children—Laura Alice, Carolyn. S.B., Harvard, 1945, LL.B., 1949. Bar: N.Y. State bar 1949. Practiced in N.Y.C., 1949-51, 61-72; asst. dist. atty. N.Y. County, 1951-55; asst. U.S. atty. So. Dist. N.Y., 1956-61; judge U.S. Dist. Ct. (so. dist.) N.Y., 1972—. Served with USNR, 1944-46. Mem. Am., N.Y. State bar assns., Assn. of the Bar of City of N.Y. Office: US Dist Ct US Courthouse Foley Sq New York NY 10007-1501

WARD, RUSSELL, publisher; b. N.Y.C., July 20, 1924; s. Sam and Lilly M. (Kaye) W.; m. Lyla Blake, Mar. 8, 1951; children: Regina Blake, Belinda Frances. BA, Syracuse U., 1947; MBA, U. Conn., Stamford, 1972. Advt. rep. Fairchild Publs., N.Y.C., 1947-66; advt. mgr. Esquire Mag., N.Y.C., 1966-76; owner Nat. Rep. Co., Stamford, Conn., 1976-85; publisher Party and Paper Retailer, Stamford, 1985—. Pres., PTA, Stamford, 1965-67. Second lt. USAF, 1942-46, 51-52, Korea. Decorated Bronze Star. Mem. Party Retailers Orgn. (pres. 1988-90), Nat. Assn. Publishing Reps. (pres. 1984-85). Office: Party and Paper Retailer 70 New Canaan Ave Norwalk CT 06850

WARD, SETH CRAWFORD, sports management executive; b. Beverly, Mass., Apr. 28, 1961; s. Hugh Campbell and Diana (Goss) W. BA in Polit. Sci., Yale U., 1983; MBA, Harvard U., 1988. Client account exec. Internat. Mgmt. Group, Cleve., 1983-86; intern Russell Reynolds Assocs., N.Y.C., summer 1987; dir. internat. div. Advantage Internat., London, 1988-90; dir. golf div. Advantage Internat., Washington, 1990—. Republican. Episcopalian. Home: 412 Prince St #1 Alexandria VA 22314 Office: Advantage Internat 1025 Thomas Jefferson St NW Washington DC 20007

WARD, TERESA JOANNE, college official; b. Rock Island, Ill., May 20, 1960; d. Martin Thomas Ward and Nancy Jane (Garrett) Vess;. BS, Western Ill. U., 1982, MS, 1988. Resident dir., asst. dir. student activities U. Ark., Monticello, 1985-88; complex dir. Ohio U., Athens, 1988-90; asst. dir. student life Roger Williams Coll., Bristol, R.I., 1990—. Mem. Am. Coll. Pers. Assn., Coll. Pers. Assn. R.I. (at-large).

WARD, THOMAS FRANCIS, construction company executive; b. Brookline, Mass., May 11, 1934; s. Thomas Francis and Pauline (Zeiger) W.; m. Elizabeth Marino, Feb. 9, 1957; children: Monica, Paula-Marie, Thomas Francis III. BSBA, Drexel U., 1956, MBA, 1966; postgrad., Temple U., 1970-71. Acct. GE, Phila., 1956-57; treas. Joseph R. Farrell, Inc., Phila., 1957-83; owner, chief fin. officer, chmn. Counsel Constrn. Co., Inc., Conshohocken, Pa., 1983—, also bd. dirs.; bd. dirs. Capital Devel. Corp., Conshohocken, Michael J. Walsh & Assocs., Inc., Lansdale, Pa. Mem. Joint Party U.S. Congl. Adv. Bd., Boston, Va., 1983—, Conshohocken Rev. Bd., 1990—; vice chmn. Plymouth Twp. (Pa.) Planning Agy., 1984—. Mem. Constrn. Fin. Mgrs. Assn., Plymouth Country Club. Republican. Roman Catholic.

WARD, THOMAS JOSEPH, association executive, researcher, writer; b. Pitts., Oct. 18, 1948; s. Thomas James and Mary (Conroy) W.; m. Julia Alexandra Fish, July 1, 1982; children: Alexander, Masjo Hamilton, Rebecca, Roosevelt Fish. BA, Notre Dame U., 1970; MA, Calif. State U., Dominguez Hills, 1985; EdD, De La Salle U., Manila, Phillipines, 1988. Trainee internat. dept. Equibank, Pitts., 1970-71; credit analyst Bank of Am., Lyons, France, 1972-73; dir. Internat. One World Crusade, U.S., Japan, Korea, 1973-76; dir. Spanish lang. ministries Unification Ch. of N.Y., 1977-79; dir. Causa Internat., U.S., Latin Am., 1980-86; exec. dir. Am. Leadership Conf., N.Y.C., 1986—. Co-author: Cause Lecture Manual, 1985; translator: A Guide to Pension in the EEC, 1991; contbr. articles to profl. publs. Advisor Am. Constn. Com., Washington, 1987-92. Mem. Phi Beta Kappa. Republican. Office: Am Leadership Conf 401 5th Ave New York NY 10016

WARD, THOMAS JULIAN, chemical engineering educator; b. Amsterdam, N.Y., Aug. 14, 1930; s. Julian Thomas and Helen (Brown) W.; m. Florence Jessie, July 15, 1967; children: Peter, Amy. BSChemE, Clarkson U., 1952; MS in Chem. Engring., U. Tex., 1956; PhD in Chem. Engring., Rensselaer Poly. Inst., 1959. Reactor engr. Oak Ridge (Tenn.) Sch. Reactor Tech., 1952-53; design engr. E.I. duPont de Nemours & Co., Wilmington, Del., 1953; rsch. assoc. E.J. Weiss (Shell Devel. Co.), Austin, Tex., 1953-55; Ill. prodn. rsch. fellow U. Tex., Austin, 1954-55; rsch. asst. Rensselaer Poly. Inst., Troy, N.Y., 1955-58; asst. prof. Clarkson U., Potsdam, N.Y., 1958-61, assoc. prof., 1961-82, prof. chem. engring., 1982—; dir. undergrad. rsch. program Clarkson U., Potsdam, 1960-66, dir. Nuclear Sci. Inst., 1964-66; oral test examiner N.Y. State Dept. Civil Svc., Albany, 1985—; cons. Contbr. articles to profl. jours. and encys. Mem. Bd. Assessment Rev., Colton, N.Y., 1974—. Fellow Am. Inst. Chemists; mem. Am. Inst. Chem. Engrs., Instrument Soc. Am. Home: PO Box 178 Colton NY 13625-0178 Office: Clarkson U Chem Engring Dept Potsdam NY 13699-5705

WARD, WILLIAM WEAVER, electrical engineer; b. Dallas, Feb. 19, 1924; s. Carroll Ross Ward and Dorothy Jane (Weaver) O'Rourke; m. Lydia Maeve McPeek, June 4, 1955; children: Geoffrey William, Christopher Andrew. BSEE, Tex. A & M Coll., 1948; MSEE, Calif. Inst. Tech., 1949, PhD in Elec. Engring., 1952. Registered profl. elec. engr., Mass. Engr. Texaco Geophys. Lab., Bellaire, Tex., summer 1948, Hughes Aircraft Co., Culver

City, Calif., summer 1949, 50; teaching asst. Calif. Inst. Tech., Pasadena, 1949-52; staff mem. to group leader to mgr. satellite ops. Lincoln Lab., MIT, Lexington, 1952—; cons. on various tech. matters, U.S. and Can. Govts.; presenter, lectr. in field. Vestryman, treas. local ch., Newton Highlands, Mass. With U.S. Army, 1943-46, PTO. Mem. IEEE (reviewer, named regional outstanding lectr. 1974), AIAA (disting. lectr. 1986-87), Nat. Soc. Profl. Engrs., Mass. Soc. Profl. Engrs., Dalhousie Lodge, Masons, Sigma Xi, Tau Beta Pi. Democrat. Episcopalian. Home: 22 Carver Rd Newton MA 02161-1008 Office: Lincoln Lab MIT 244 Wood St Lexington MA 02173-6499

WARDELL, JOE RUSSELL, JR., pharmacologist; b. Omaha, Nov. 11, 1929; s. Joe Russell and Marie Hamilton (Waugh) W.; m. Leta Harris, July 14, 1952 (div. Oct. 1981); children: Michael R., Susan E., John D.; m. Doris Erway, Aug. 27, 1983. BS in Pharmacy, Creighton U., 1951; MS in Pharmacology, U. Nebr., Omaha, 1959, PhD in Pharmacology, 1962. Lic. pharmacist Nebr. Pharmacist Osco Drug, Waterloo, Iowa, 1953-56; grad. asst. Coll. of Medicine U. Nebr., Omaha, 1956-62; sr. pharmacologist Smith Kline & French Labs., Phila., 1962-64, advanced to assoc. dir. biol. rsch., 1974-78; dir. R & D compound acquistions R&D, 1978-86; pres. Wardell Assocs., Beaver, Pa., 1986—. Author: more than 40 articles in profl. pubs.; inventor/co-inventor 4 patents respiratory and cardiovascular drugs. Asst. scoutmaster, Boy Scouts of Am., N.J., 1969-75. Recipient Merck Award Creighton U., 1951. Mem. Soc. of Parmacology & Experiemental Therapeutics, Am. Acad. of Pharmaceutical Scis., Am. Chem. Soc., Licensing Exec. Soc., Exptl. Aircraft Assn. Home and Office: Wardell Assocs 105 Oak St Beaver PA 15009-2406

WARDEN, GARY RUSSELL (ALYN VOYAGER), municipal official, author, sculptor; b. Camden, N.J., Mar. 2, 1950; s. Russell James Jr. and Harriet May (Tupper) W. BA with honors, U. Calif., San Diego, 1972; postgrad., U. Calif., Irvine, 1973, Calif. State U., Fullerton, 1975-79. Cert. tchr., Calif., N.J., Mass. Exec. asst. State of Calif., Costa Mesa, 1973-76; staff aide Orange County, Santa Ana, Calif., 1978-79; tchr. N.J. Pub. Schs., 1979-84; sr. budget examiner City of Camden, 1984—. Author: A Proposal to Revise The Voting Procedures Of The U.N. General Assembly, 1984, What Record High and Low Temperature Data Reveal About Global Atmospheric Warming, 1991, (poems) Here On Your Planet, 1981; works of sculpture include Life Form #1, 1987, Carved In Stone, 1987, Petrified Tree, 1988, Cryptocrystalline Man, 1988. Mem. Am. Assn. for Budget and Program Analysis, Pa. Poetry Soc., Acad. Natural Scis., ARTWORKS, Greenpeace, The Nature Conservancy. Home: 216 Atlantic Ave SW Magnolia NJ 08049-1716 Office: City of Camden City Hall Rm 430 Camden NJ 08101

WARDLAW, ANDREW BOWIE, JR., aerospace engineer; b. Washington, Sept. 1, 1944; s. Andrew Bowie and Frances (Blakeslee) W.; div. Feb. 17, 1986; children: Dawn Elizabeth, Andrew Bowie III; m. Katharine Elizabeth Snell, Apr. 16, 1988. BS in Mech. Engring., Bucknell U., 1967; MS in Mech. Engring., U. Pa., 1968, PhD, 1971. Registered profl. engr., Md. Aerospace engr. Naval Surface Warfare Ctr., Silver Springs, Md., 1972-77; project leader Naval Surface Warfare Ctr., Silver Springs, 1978—; staff mem. Lincoln Lab., Lexington, Mass., 1977-78; lectr. George Washington U., Washington, 1982, U. Md., College Park, 1986-87; guest lectr. Von Kerman Inst., Brussels, 1976, '77, '87. Author: (computer software) SWINT, 1981, ZEUS, 1986; author: (with others) Technical Missile Aerodynamics; contbr. articles to profl. jours. tech. papers to meeting and sci. confs. Recipient Sci. and Tech. award Naval Surface Warfare Ctr., 1988, Meritorious Civilian Scientist award, 1989. Fellow AIAA (assoc.). Home: 10410 Green Mountain Cir Columbia MD 21044-2456 Office: Naval Surface Warfare Ctr New Hampshire Ave Silver Spring MD 20903-3408

WARE, ROBERT, business executive; b. Albuquerque, Apr. 3, 1958; s. Robert and Thelma L. (Francis) W.; m. Marie-Pierre Sanseverina, Feb. 23, 1981; 1 child, Marie-Antoinette. BA, Harvard U., 1980; MS, MIT, 1985. Mktg. and internat. mgmt. analyst The Gillette Co., Boston, 1980-82; forecaster Brown & Williamson, Louisville, 1982-83; mktg. asst. Johnson & Johnson, Milltown, N.J., 1983, 84; project mgr. Reuters N.A., N.Y.C., 1985-87; sales exec. Reuters Info. Svcs., Boston, 1987-88; bus. mgr. Reuters Korea, Seoul, 1988-89; prin. DRI/McGraw-Hill, Lexington, Mass., 1990-91; area mktg. mgr. Brown & Williamson (Europe) S.A., Brussels, 1992—. Recipient Johnson & Johnson Leadership award, 1983. Home: 9 Clos de Rivoli, 1410 Waterloo Belgium

WARE, SANDRA COLE, town and state official; b. Bangor, Maine, Mar. 16, 1935; d. Gerald Albert and Edwyna E. (Cohlan) Cole; children: Candace, Bill, Timothy. AA, Green Mt. Coll., 1955. Cert. tax collector, Maine. Sec. RCA, Cape Canaveral, Fla., 1956-57; asst. to dir. Student Union U. Maine, Orono, 1957-61; rep. Avon Products, Rye, N.Y., 1966-71; tax collector Town of Alfred, Maine, 1975—; mcpl. agt. Motor Vehicle Div., Augusta, Maine, 1980—; agt. Dept. Inland Fisheries, Augusta, 1985—. Sec., Rep. Com., Alfred, 1985-87; delgate Rep. State Conv.; bd. dirs. Mass. and Maine Girl Scout Councils; riding cons. Nat. Girl Scout Ctr. West, 1969, co-founder The Singles Network, Portland, Maine, 1982. Mem. Beta Sigma Phi (Woman of Yr. award 1988). Republican. Home: Rural Route 202 Box Pobox153 Alfred ME 04002-9802 Office: Alfred Town Hall Village Gree Alfred ME 04002

WARGA, DAVID, controller; b. N.Y.C., Jan. 22, 1932; s. Kenneth and Evelyn (Bocknek) W.; m. Renee Gurin, July 3, 1960; children: Michael, Adam. BS, U. Scranton, 1954; MBA, NYU, 1964. CPA, N.Y. Mgr. computer audit Coopers & Lybrand, N.Y.C., 1975-81; dir. internal audit Frank B. Hall & Co., Inc., Briarcliff Manor, N.Y., 1981-87; litigation support auditor, 1989-90; controller/cons. various, N.Y.C., 1987-92; mem. adj. faculty Pace U., 1971-81. Com. chmn. Interlaken Owners Assn., Eastchester, N.Y., 1989-90; treas. Young Israel of New Rochelle, N.Y., 1976-79. With USN, 1955-57. Mem. AICPA (com. mem. 1978-81), N.Y. State Soc. CPAs (com. chmn.), Masons (trustee). Home: 1277 California Rd Eastchester NY 10709-1003

WARGA, JACK, mathematician, educator; b. Warsaw, Poland, Dec. 5, 1922; came to U.S., 1943, naturalized, 1944; s. Herman and Czarna (Lichtenstein) W.; m. Faye Kleinman, Feb. 27, 1949; children—Charna Ruth, Arthur David. Student, Brussels (Belgium) U., 1939-40; B.A., Carleton Coll., 1944; Ph.D., N.Y. U., 1950. Assoc. mathematician Reeves Instrument Corp., N.Y.C., 1951-52; Chief engring. computing sect. Republic Aviation Corp., Farmingdale, N.Y., 1952-53; head math dept. Burroughs Corp., Pasadena, Cal., 1954-56; mgr., math dept. Avco Research and Devel., Wilmington, Mass., 1957-66; prof. math. Northeastern U., Boston, 1966—. Author: Optimal Control of Differential and Functional Equations, 1972, expanded Russian transl., 1977; contbr. articles to profl. jours. Served with AUS, 1944-46. Weizmann Meml. fellow, 1956-57. Fellow AAAS; mem. Am. Math. Soc., Soc. Indsl. and Applied Math. (editor Jour. on Control and Optimization 1963-89). Home: 233 Clark Rd Brookline MA 02146-5823 Office: Northeastern U Dept Math Boston MA 02115

WARMBRAND, MARTIN JOSEPH, university administrator; b. N.Y.C., Jan. 29, 1926; s. Meyer B. and Celia (Lester) W.; m. Arlyne Beverly Agin, Mar. 30, 1958 (div. Apr. 1985); 1 child, Myra Nass; m. Evelyn Ann Rosenblum, May 14, 1985; 1 child, Allison Taggart. BA, CUNY, 1954; MA, Grad. Faculty New Sch., N.Y.C., 1972. Corr. World Union Press, 1958—; gen. mgr. Marshall Bus. Svcs., N.Y.C., 1954-62; account exec. Triton Assocs., N.Y.C., 1966-68; estate mgmt., 1963-65; mng. editor Leader Observer, 1965-66; exec. dir. The Brotherhood Synagogue, N.Y.C., 1968-70, The Suburban Temple, Wantagh, N.Y., 1970-72, East N.Y. Devel. Corp., Bklyn., 1972-79; sec., trustee CUNY, N.Y.C., 1979—; adj. prof. CUNY, 1972-79; cons. East N.Y. Devel. Corp., 1979—. Contbr. articles to mags. Mem. Liberal Party County Com., N.Y., 1990; pres. Am. Pro-Falasha Com., N.Y.; chmn. Reading is Fundamental, Bklyn., 1974; comdr. Corp Sydney Rosenberg Post, Bklyn.; dir. 11th Congl. Dist. Commn. on Edn., 1989—; mem. Friends of A. Philip Randolph High Sch., 1987—, City Univ. Acad. for the Humanities and Scis., 1991—. Named Disting. Citizen, Rosetta Gadsen Polit. Assn., 1981; named to Hall of Fame, Minority Educators Coun., 1982; recipient Inspiration and Professionalism award United Men and Women of Coulour, 1982. Mem. AACD, Am. Sociol. Assn., Am. Jewish Pub. Rels. Soc. (v.p. 1989-91), N.Y. Soc. Assn. Execs., Am. Assn. Ethiopian Jews (exec. com. 1982). Home: 365 W 25th St Apt 19B New York NY 10001-5824 Office: CUNY 535 E 80th St New York NY 10021-0767

WARNER, ADOLPHE JOSEPH, economist, financial analyst; b. Frankfurt, Germany, May 22, 1917; came to U.S., 1936; s. Moritz and Ella (Plaut) W.; m. Ursula Wolter; children: Joan, Theodore M. MA in Econs., U. Ill., 1945. V.p., ptnr. Model Roland & Co., N.Y.C., 1954-68; v.p. Smith Barney & Co., Inc., N.Y.C., 1968-73; sr. v.p. Warburg Paribas Becker, N.Y.C., 1974-77; v.p. Salomon Bros., Inc., N.Y.C., 1978-80; chmn. Global Asset Mgmt. Assocs., Inc., N.Y.C., 1981—; sr. advisor Deutsche Bank Capital Corp., N.Y.C., 1984-92; spl. advisor The Germany Fund, Inc., N.Y.C., 1988-92, The New Germany Fund, 1989-92, The Future Germany Fund, 1990-92, U.S. Dept. Def., Washington, 1961-62, UN Environ. Program, N.Y.C., Nairobi, 1981-82. Assoc. editor Fin. Analysts Jour., 1967-87. Capt. U.S. Army, 1943-46, USAR, ETO. Mem. Am. Econ. Assn., U.S. Coun. on Germany, Assn. for Investment Mgmt. and Rsch. (chmn. internat. analysts rels. com. 1967-77), N.Y. Soc. Security Analysts (program com.), Analysts Club (chmn. N.Y.C. 1985-86), India House.

WARNER, ALICE SIZER, information systems specialist, consultant; b. New Haven, Conn., Dec. 8, 1929; d. Theodore and Caroline (Foster) S.; m. Caleb Warner, July 1, 1950; children: Langdon, Anne, Alice, Caleb Nicholas. AB, Harvard U., 1950; MLS, Simmons Coll., 1973. Field dir. ARC, Del., 1950-52; vol. libr. Pub. Schs., Lexington and Boston, Mass., 1957-72; pres. Warner-Eddison Assocs., Inc., Cambridge, Mass., 1973-80; owner Info. Guild, Lexington, 1980—; instr. libr. and info. sci. Simmons Coll., Syracuse U., U. N.C., U. Mich., U. Hawaii, 1981—. Author: Making Money, 1989, Mind Your Own Business, 1987, Volunteers in Libraries, 1985, Owning Your Numbers, 1992. Pres. Five Fields, Inc., Lexington, 1977. Recipient Disting. Alumni award Simmons Coll., 1986. Mem. ALA, Spl. Librs. Assn., Am. Soc. for Info. Sci., Assn. for Ind. Info. Profls., Smaller Bus. Assn. of New Eng. (com. chair 1973—), Phi Beta Kappa (pres. Iota chpt. 1972), Beta Phi Mu. Democrat. Unitarian. Home: 546 Concord Ave Lexington MA 02173-8036 Office: Info Guild PO Box 254 Lexington MA 02173-0003

WARNER, DONALD FRANCIS, financial executive; b. Blasdell, N.Y., Dec. 3, 1931; s. Eldred Joseph and Eileen Geraldine (Heary) W.; BBA, Canisius Coll., Buffalo, 1953; MBA, SUNY, Buffalo, 1967; cert. with honors, Grad. Sch. Savs. Banking, Brown U., 1975; m. Deborah Jean Lane, Sept. 8, 1984; 1 child, David; children by previous marriage: Michael, Linda, Elizabeth, Thomas, Mark, Colleen. Office mgr. Beals McCarthy and Rogers Inc., Buffalo, 1955-61; asst. planning and control Union Carbide Corp., Tonawanda, N.Y., 1962-68; fin. analyst, mgr. budget dept. Hoffman LaRoche Inc., Nutley, N.J., 1968-71; contr. Howard Savs. Bank, Newark, 1971-77, v.p., treas., Livingston, N.J., 1978-82; v.p. fin. Lincoln Ctr. Performing Arts, N.Y.C., 1982-88; contr. Dist. Coun. 37, Am. Fedn. State, County and Mcpl. Employees, AFL-CIO, 1988—; part-time instr. M.B.A. program Fairleigh Dickinson U., Rutherford, N.J., 1980-83; mem. Bank Adminstrn. Inst., 1974-82. Trustee, Cen. Essex Health Plan, 1975-79, W. Essex Gen. Hosp., Livingston, 1980-87; adv. com. Essex coun. Boy Scouts Am., 1980-84; co-chmn. edn. in human sexuality program Roman Cath. Archdiocese Newark, 1976-78. With U.S. Army, 1953-55. CPA, N.J. Mem. AICPA, Fin. Execs. Inst. (past pres. N.J.), Assn. Systems Mgmt. (sec. N.Y. chpt. 1980-81), N.J. Soc. CPAs, Mensa. Author articles in field.

WARNER, DOUGLAS ALEXANDER, III, banker; b. Cin., June 9, 1946; s. Douglas Alexander Jr. and Eleanor (Wright) W.; m. Patricia Grant, May 13, 1977; children: Alexander, Katherine, Michael. BA, Yale U., 1968. Officer's asst. Morgan Guaranty Trust Co., N.Y.C., 1968-70, asst. treas., 1970-72, asst. v.p., 1972-75, v.p., 1975-85; sr. v.p. Morgan Guaranty Trust Co., London, 1983-87; exec. v.p. Morgan Guaranty Trust Co., N.Y.C., 1987-89, mng. dir., 1989-90, pres., 1990—, also bd. dirs.; bd. dirs. Anheuser-Busch Cos., Inc.; bd. overseers Meml. Sloan-Kettering Cancer Ctr., N.Y.C. Trustee Pierpont Morgan Libr., Cold Spring Harbor Lab. Mem. Assn. Res. City Bankers, Fgn. Policy Assn. (gov.), Links River Club, Meadowbrook Club (L.I.). Home: 520 Chicken Valley Rd Locust Valley NY 11560 Office: J P Morgan & Co Inc 60 Wall St New York NY 10260-0001

WARNER, ROBERT ANIO, corporate executive, entrepreneur; b. New Haven, Aug. 9, 1966; s. Robert Edwin Jr. and Beverly Ida (Galdenzi) W.; m. Anne Mary Cozzolino, Mar. 19, 1988; 1 child, Robert Anio II. BA in Econs., U. R.I., 1989, postgrad. Legal intern U.S. Dist. Ct., Dist. of R.I., Providence, 1988-89; researcher Yale Law Sch., 1991; pres., chmn. of bd. Warner Svcs. Inc., Kingston, R.I., 1988—; pres. Warner Allaire Holdings, Inc., 1990—; chmn. Orgn. of Economists, Kingston, 1987-89. Trustee, Rep. Presdl. Task Force, 1989—; mem. Westerly Bd. Edn., 1990; mem. Westerly adv. Charter Revision Commn., 1988-91; tutor Literacy Vol. Am., 1989. With USMC Res. 1984-90. Recipient Medal of Merit. Mem. Internat. Inst. Pub. Fin., Am. Forestry Assn., Natural Resources Def. Coun., Environ. Def. Fund, Sierra Club, Nature Conservancy, Nat. Economists Club, U.S. Chess Fedn., Sigma Phi Epsilon (bd. dirs. R.I. Beta Corp.). Office: Warner Svcs Inc PO Box 1631 Kingston RI 02881-0489

WARNER, W. DAVID, controller; b. Rochester, N.Y., Mar. 31, 1931; s. William James and Matilda Eva (Ehmann) W.; m. Patricia Adele Slee, Aug. 6, 1955; children: David, Stephen, Amy, Michael, Sally, Judith. BS, Georgetown U., 1953, Georgetown U., 1959. CPA, D.C. Staff acct. Erig G. Jansson & Co., Washington, 1955-60, ptnr., 1961-81; ptnr. Cunningham, Warner & Co., Washington, 1982-83, Thomas Havey & Co., Washington, 1983-88; contr. Internat. Union of Operating Engrs., Washington, 1988—. With U.S. Army, 1953-55. Roman Catholic. Home: 14007 Shippers Ln Rockville MD 20853-2666 Office: Internat Union Op Engrs 1125 17th St NW Washington DC 20036-4707

WARNICK, JORDAN EDWARD, pharmacologist; b. Boston, Mar. 21, 1942; s. Samuel William and Ruth Barbara (Hite) W.; m. Hazel Augusta Cohen, Aug. 16, 1970; 1 child, Meredith Nicole. BS in Pharmacy, Mass. Coll. Pharmacy, 1963; PhD in Pharmacology, Purdue U., 1968. Registered pharmacist, Mass. Grad. teaching asst. Purdue U., West Lafayette, Ind., 1963-65; grad. rsch. asst. Purdue U., West Lafayette, 1965-68; post-doctoral fellow SUNY, Buffalo, 1968-70, NIH spl. awardee, 1970-71, asst. prof. Sch. of Pharmacy, 1971-74; asst. prof. U. Md. Sch. Medicine, Balt., 1974-80, assoc. prof., 1980—; dir. short term rsch. tng. programs U. Md. Sch. Medicine, Balt., 1983—. Contbr. numerous articles, abstracts to profl. jours., chpts. to books. Chmn. Balt.-Rotterdam Sister City Com., 1991—. Grantee Nat. Sci Found., 1987-92, Am. Heart Assn., 1989-92, NIH, 1985-95, 1991-96. Mem. Am. Soc. for Pharmacology and Exptl. Therapeutics, Soc. for Neurosci. Office: U Md Sch Medicine Dept Pharm & Exptl Therap 655 W Baltimore St Baltimore MD 21201

WARRACK, MARIA PERINI, psychotherapist; b. N.Y.C., June 2, 1931; d. Yoso and Concetta (Sano) Perini; m. James Thomas Warrack, June 10, 1956; children: Thomas, John. BEd, CCNY, 1954; MS in Social Work, Columbia U., 1956. Diplomate Am. Bd. Clin. Social Work. Clin. social worker N.Y. VA Hosp., N.Y.C., 1956-62; psychotherapist L.I. Consultation Ctr., N.Y.C., 1964-69; staff psychotherapist Pederson-Krag Ctr. for Psychotherapy, South Huntington, N.Y., 1969-72, psychotheraphy supr., 1972-85, dir. social work internship program, 1985—; pvt. practice psychotherapy Plainview, N.Y., 1966—; mem. faculty, supr. Pederson-Krag Inst. for Psychotherapy, South Huntington, 1985—; adj. asst. prof. Adelphia U. Sch. Social Wk., 1990—. Mem. NASW, N.Y. State Soc. Clin. Social Work Psychotherapists (diplomate; pres. Nassau chpt. 1981-83, v.p. 1983-85, bd. dirs. 1991—), Am. Group Psychotherapy Assn. (faculty mem. 1986), Eastern Group Psychotherapy Assn. (bd. dirs. 1988—). Home and Office: 29 Shelter Hill Rd Plainview NY 11803-4813

WARREN, ALBERT, publishing executive; b. Warren, Ohio, May 18, 1920; s. David and Clara W.; m. Margaret Virginia Yeomans, Jan. 9, 1947; children: Ellen, Paul, Claire, Daniel, Thomas, Joan. BA in Journalism, Ohio State U., 1942. Assoc. editor TV Digest, Washington, 1945-50, sr. editor, 1950-58, chief Washington Bur., 1958-61; pres., editor, pub. Warren Pub., Inc., Washington, 1961—; lectr. Columbia Grad. Sch. Journalism, N.Y.C., 1962-75; mem. alumni adv. coun. Ohio State U., Columbus, 1982-88. Contbr. articles to profl. jours. With USNR, 1942-45, PTO. Mem. Ind. Newsletter Assn. (co-founder 1963, pres. 1965-66), Newsletter Pubs. Assn. (Pub. of Yr.), Broadcast Pioneers, Cable TV Pioneers, Internat. Radio and TV Soc. Pubs., Mus. of Broadcasting, White House Corr. Assn., U.S. Congress Periodical Gallery, Soc. Profl. Journalists (Hall of Fame 1991). Home: 26 W Kirke St Chevy Chase MD 20815 Office: Warren Pub Inc 2115 Ward Ct NW Washington DC 20037-1209

WARREN, CALEB THOMAS, money manager; b. Hartford, Conn., Oct. 22, 1950; s. George Upson and Dorothy Harvey (Davis) W.; m. Patricia Robinson, Sept. 27, 1974; children: Otis, Silas, Grace, Mercy. BA, Harvard U., 1973. Registered investment advisor. Tchr. Friendship Sch., Brewster, Mass., 1974-76; tchr. and asst. prin. Cape Cod Acad., Osterville, Mass., 1976-81; tchr. Tabor Acad., Marion, Mass., 1982-84; stockbroker Prudential-Bache, Dean Witter, Hyannis, Mass., 1984-91; investment advisor Warren Asset Mgmt, West Barnstable, Mass., 1991—. Contbr. articles to newspapers. Mem. Spee Club, Barnstable Yacht Club (tennis champ 1991), Am. Softball Assn. (MVP 1986).

WARREN, JESSE FRANCIS, mechanical engineer; b. N.Y.C., Aug. 29, 1944; s. Francis Joel and Elinor (Furlano) W.; m. Anna May Cronin, Jan. 12, 1965 (div. Jan. 1986); children: Jesse, Michael, Christopher, Vittoria. AA, Suffolk County Coll., 1962; BSME, Columbia U., 1967; postgrad., Rutgers U., 1986. Project mgr. Treadwell Corp., N.Y.C., 1966-73, Courter and Co. Inc., N.Y.C., 1973-88; mgr. Durr Mech. Constrn. Inc., N.Y.C., 1988—; cons. Frank Briscoe Co., Inc., Roseland, N.J., 1977-87, Morton R. Galane, Profl. Corp., Las Vegas, Nev., 1980-87. Served to sgt. U.S. Army, 1962-65, Vietnam. Republican. Roman Catholic. Home: 2 Old Oscaleta Rd Ridgefield CT 06877-2908 Office: Durr Mech Constrn Inc 80 8th Ave New York NY 10011-5126

WARREN, JONATHAN TURNER, immunologist; b. Portsmouth, Va., Sept. 20, 1950; s. Robert Warren and Janice Tyre von Trapp; m. Elizabeth Huber, June 16, 1973 (div. 1988); m. Heather Hanson, Aug. 24, 1990; stepchildren: Matthew Aaron Napier, Sarah Jane Napier. BS, Baldwin-Wallace Coll., 1973; postgrad., Johns Hopkins U., 1988; MS, Hood Coll., Frederick, Md., 1980; PhD, U. Pa., 1985. Cert. med. lab. technologist. Med. lab. technologist Lorain (Ohio) Community Hosp., 1975; med. lab. rsch. specialist U.S. Army, USAMRIID, Frederick, Md., 1976-80; profl. musician (violinist) Frederick, Md., 1976—; rsch. scientist, fellow Nat. Cancer Inst.-FCRDC, Frederick, Md., 1988-90; immunologist AIDS Vaccine Devel. Network The Emmes Corp., Potomac, Md., 1990—; co-founder, pres., pers. dir. Frederick Symphony Orch., 1976—. Contbr. articles to profl. jours., chpts. to books. NIH fellow, 1980-85, 86-88. Mem. AAAS, Union of Concerned Scientists, Am. Soc. Clin. Pathologists, Am. String Tchrs. Assn., N.Y. Acad. Scis., Clin. Immunology Soc., Johns Hopkins Immunology Coun. Home: 2047 Fire Tower Ln Ijamsville MD 21754 Office: The Emmes Corp 11325 Seven Locks Rd #214 Potomac MD 20854

WARREN, PETER, advertising executive; b. Iran, Sept. 9, 1943; s. Paul and Heda (Adler) W.; m. Carla Ringler, Aug. 26, 1967; children: Jill, Paul. BS, NYU, 1965; MBA, Pace U., 1986. Promotion rsch. analyst Look Mag., N.Y.C., 1965; from media planner to account supr. Ogilvy & Mather, N.Y.C., 1966-72; exec. v.p. Tromson Monroe, N.Y.C., 1972-74; founder, pres. Warren/Kremer Advt., Inc., N.Y.C., 1974—. Contbr. articles to travel mags. Judge Andy and Addy awards; mem. Marlboro (N.J.) Twp. Zoning Bd. Adjustment; mem. Freehold Regional High Sch.; advisor United Jewish Appeal, Marlboro Bd. Edn., Monmouth County Dem. and Rep. Coms. Recipient Effie award Am. Mktg. Assn., 1978. Mem. Hotel Sales and Mktg. Assn. (co-chmn. mktg. adv. com., numerous gold, silver and bronze awards 1976-92), Travel and Tourism Rsch. Assn., Caribbean Tourism Orgn. (treas. N.Y.C. chpt., 3 Best of Show awards internat. competition, 1982, 83, 85), Advt. Club N.Y. (Addy awards 1982, 83), Mktg. Adv. Bd. (treas. N.Y. chpt.), Alpha Delta Sigma. Jewish. Office: Warren/Kremer/CMP Advt Inc 2 Park Ave Ste 2201 2 Park Ave Ste 1804 New York NY 10016-9393

WARREN, WILLIAM CLEMENTS, lawyer, educator; b. Paris, Tex., Feb. 3, 1909; s. Archibald Levy and Elma (Clements) W.; m. Diana June Peel Willock, Jan. 13, 1945; children—Robert Peel, Larissa Eve, William Liversidge. A.B., U. Tex., 1930, A.M., 1931; LL.B., Harvard U., 1935; LL.D. (hon.), L.I. U., 1955, Columbia U., 1981; Dr. rer. pol., U. Basle, 1965. Bar: Ohio 1937, N.Y. 1952, D.C. 1959. Assoc. Davis, Polk & Wardwell, N.Y.C., 1935-37; assoc. Holiday, Grossman & McAfee, Cleve., 1937-42; assoc. Milbank, Tweed, Hadley & McCloy, N.Y.C., 1942-47; prof. law Western Res. U., Cleve., 1937-42; mem. faculty Columbia Law Sch., N.Y.C., 1946-82, Kent prof. law, 1959-77, Kent prof. emeritus, 1977—, dean, 1952-70, dean emeritus, 1970—; of counsel Roberts & Holland, N.Y.C., 1952; bd. dirs. Guardian Life Ins. Co. Am., Sterling Nat. Bank & Trust Co. N.Y.C., Barnwell Industries, Inc., Sterling Bancorp, CSS Industries, Aston-Martin LaGonda Group, Aladan Corp., Columbia Yeast, Inc.; hon. chmn. bd. dirs. Sandoz U.S.; mem. N.Am. adv. bd. Swissair. Served as lt. col. U.S. Army, 1943-46. Decorated Bronze Star (2), Legion of Merit; comdr. Order of the Crown (Italy); recipient Medal for excellence Columbia Law Sch. Alumni Assn., 1969. Mem. ABA, Am. Judicature Soc., Am. Law Inst., Assn. of Bar of City of N.Y., N.Y. County Lawyers Assn., N.Y. State Bar Assn., Inst. Internat. Edn. (trustee), Order Moral Scis. (fgn. corr.), Accademia delle Scienze dell' Instituto di Bologna (fgn. corr. mem.; Order Moral Scis. 1971). Presbyterian. Clubs: Broad Street, Century Assn., Cosmos, Links, Metropolitan, Univ. Co-author: U.S. Income Taxation of Foreign Corporations and Nonresident Aliens, 1966; Cases and Materials on Accounting and the Law, 1978; Cases and Materials on Federal Wealth Transfer Taxation, 1982; Cases and Materials on Federal Income Taxation, Vol. I, 1972, supplement, 1983, Vol. II, 1980; pres., dir. Columbia Law Rev. Office: Roberts & Holland 30 Rockefeller Pla New York NY 10112

WARSAWER, HAROLD NEWTON, real estate appraiser and consultant; b. N.Y.C.; s. Sidney L. and Alice (Frachtman) W.; m. Sally Kingsbury; children: Alice Cooper, Nancy Arkuss, Carole Greenblatt. BA, U. Mo.; MBA, Harvard U. Acct. Warner Bros. Pictures, N.Y.C.; property mgr. and real estate broker Sidney L. Warsawer & Son, N.Y.C.; appraiser Atlantic Appraisal Co., Inc., N.Y.C., 1960—; pres. Atlantic Appraisal Co., Inc., N.Y.C., 1960—, Consolidated Capital, N.Y.C., 1962-68; dir. Contemporary Enterprises, N.Y.C., 1974-76. Mem. editorial bd. The Appraisal Jour., 1970-85. Candidate Teaneck N.J. Sch. Bd., Teaneck N.J. Coun.; chmn. bldg. com. Temple Emeth, Teaneck, 1954-64. Mem. Am. Inst. Real Estte Appraisers (pres. N.Y. chpt. 1977, bd. dirs. 1970-80, 90—, gov. counsellor 1978), Nat. Assn. Rev. Appraisers, Real Estate Bd. N.Y., Nat. Realty Club (pres. 1992, bd. dirs.), Am. Arbitration Assn., Haworth Golf Club. Home: 430 Rutland Ave Teaneck NJ 07666-2823 Office: 60 E 42d St New York NY 10165

WARSH, LEWIS DAVID, poet, educator; b. Bronx, N.Y., Nov. 9, 1944; s. Harry and Ray (Bienhacker) W.; m. Bernadette Mayer, Nov. 1, 1975 (div. Aug. 1985); children: Marie, Sophia, Max. BA, CCNY, 1966, MA, 1975. Instr. New England Coll., Henniker, N.H., 1979-80, Queens (N.Y.) Coll., 1985-87, Yeshiva U., N.Y.C., 1986-87, Fairleigh Dickinson U., Teaneck, N.J., 1987-89, La Guardia Community Coll., Queens, 1989-90; adj. assoc. prof. L.I. U., Bklyn., 1985—, instr. The Poetry Project, 1991—; publ., editor Angel Hair Books, N.Y.C., 1966-75, United Artists Books, N.Y.C., 1977—. Author: Dreaming As One, 1971, Agnes and Sally, 1984, The Corset, 1987, A Free Man, 1991; editor Boston Eagle, 1972-74, United Artists mag., 1977-83. Grantee N.Y. Found. Arts, 1988, Coord. Coun. on Lit. Mags., 1982, CAPS Found., 1977; NEA fellow, 1980. Home: 701 President St Brooklyn NY 11215-1270

WARSTADT, GARY MICHAEL, psychiatrist; b. N.Y.C., Jan. 21, 1959; s. Jack and Flora Rosalyn (Freilicher) W.; m. Anne Sydney Weiner, May 20, 1984. BA, MD, Boston U., 1983; cert. in psychiatry, U. Calif., San Diego, 1987. Diplomate Am. Bd. Psychiatry and Neurology. Staff physician Westwood (Mass.) Lodge Hosp., 1987-89; pvt. practice Dorchester, 1987—; attending physician Carney Hosp., Dorchester, 1989—; psychiat. cons. Carney Hosp., 1989—. Mem. Mass. Med. Soc., Am. Psychiat. Assn., Mass. Psychiat. Soc. Democrat. Jewish. Office: Carney Hosp 2100 Dorchester Ave Dorchester MA 02124-5666

WARTH, JAMES ARTHUR, physician, researcher; b. N.Y.C., Apr. 30, 1942; s. Peter and Anne (Furgang) W.; m. Maria Archer Russell, May 3, 1969; children: David M., Andrew A. BS, Tufts U., 1963, MD, 1967. Diplomate Am. Bd. Internal Medicine, Am. Bd. Hematology, Am. Bd.

Oncology. Hematologist Harvard Health Svcs. Harvard U., Cambridge, Mass., 1976-77, officer, 1976-77; attending hematologist Harper-Grace Hosps., Detroit, 1977-84; asst. prof. medicine Wayne State U., Detroit, 1977-84; rsch. scientist New Eng. Med. Ctr., Boston, 1984-86; attending hematologist-oncologist The Faulkner Hosp., Boston, 1986—; asst. prof. medicine Tufts U. Sch. Medicine, Boston, 1986—; cons. NIH, Bethesda, Md., 1987, 1980-83, Mass. Profl. Rev. Orgn., Waltham, 1991—; vis. prof. Yale U., New Haven, 1986; faculty advisor Tufts U. Sch. Medicine, 1991-92; appearance on NBC affiliate TV news program, Detroit, 1980; rsch. lectr. NIH, Tarrytown, N.Y., 1986. Contbg. author: Hematologic Disorders in Maternal-Fetal Medicine, 1990; reviewer Am. Jour. Hematology, 1986, Andrology, 1991-92; contbr. articles to profl. jours. Maj. U.S. Army, 1969-71. Rsch. grantee NIH, 1980-83, 83-86, spl. fellowship, 1974-76. Fellow Am. Coll. Physicians; mem. Am. Soc. Hematology, Am. Fedn. Clin. Rsch., Biomembranes in Sickle Cell Rsch. Group. Office: Faulkner Hosp 1153 Centre St Rm 5950 Boston MA 02130

WARYE, RICHARD JONATHAN, theater arts educator; b. Columbus, Ohio, Mar. 4, 1929; s. John Elton and Alma Barbara (Sanger) W.; m. Verna Elizabeth Beckler, Aug. 21, 1964; 1 stepchild, Pamela Moulton Wilson. BS in Edn., Ohio State U., 1951, MA, 1952, PhD, 1966. Cert. tchr., Mass. Tchr. Claridon Local Sch., Marion County, Ohio, 1953, West High Sch., Columbus, 1957-60; instr., then asst. prof. speech Bates Coll., Lewiston, Maine, 1960-68; prof. theater arts Bridgewater (Mass.) State Coll., 1968—. Dist. dir. Northeast Dist. Unitarian Universalist Ch., Maine, 1962-68; preparer, presenter religious svcs.; bd. mgrs. Universalist-Unitarian Ch., Brockton, Mass. Lt. (j.g.) USNR, 1953-56. Mem. Assn. Theatre in Higher Edn., New Engl. Theatre Conf. Democrat. Office: Bridgewater State Coll Rondileau Campus Ctr Bridgewater MA 02325

WASHBURN, A. MICHAEL, management consultant; b. Chgo., Feb. 26, 1940; s. Abbott McConnell and Mary (Brennan) W.; m. Linda Fisher, May 5, 1963 (div. 1981); children: Mara Hope, Kate Fisher. BA magna cum laude, Harvard U., 1962; MA, Princeton U., 1967. Account exec. Dancer-Fitzgerld-Sample, N.Y.C., 1962-65; program assoc. Internat. Inst. Ednl. Planning, Paris, 1966; exec. dir. Fund for Peace, N.Y.C., 1967-70; exec. v.p. World Policy Inst., N.Y.C., 1970-76; pres. Michael Washburn & Assocs., N.Y.C., 1976-88, Caesar & Washburn, Inc., N.Y.C., 1988—; cons. Nat. Endowment for Arts, Washington, 1979-81, Warner Communications, N.Y.C., 1982-84, Rockefeller Found., N.Y.C., 1985. Co-author: Creating the Future, 1973, Peace and World Order Studies, 1975; contbr. articles to profl. jours. V.p. The Writers Community, N.Y.C., 1980-86; bd. dirs. Dome Project, N.Y.C., 1980-91; treas. Ctr. for Arts Info., N.Y.C., 1982-88, West Side Y Ctr. for ARts, N.Y.C., 1987-91. Home: 166 E 96th St New York NY 10128-2565 Office: Caesar & Washburn Inc 1841 Broadway New York NY 10023-7603

WASHBURN, STEWART ALEXANDER, management consultant; b. Boston, June 14, 1923; s. Charles Parker and Mary Ethel (Stewart) W. AB, St. John's Coll., Annapolis, Md., 1951. Cert. mgmt. cons. Sr. engr. to asst. dir. indsl. hygiene Nat. Safety Council, Chgo., 1951-54; mng. dir. Stewart A. Washburn & Co., Inc., N.Y.C., 1954-62; ptnr. Porter Henry & Co., Inc., N.Y.C., 1962-77; pvt. practice cons. Lakeville, Mass., 1977—; dir. Entrepreneur's Forum of Mass. Author: Measuring Sales Effectiveness and Productivity, 1983, Successful Pricing, 1985, Finding and Launching Successful New Products, 1985, Managing the Market Functions, 1988; co-founder, practice devel. editor: Jour. Mgmt. Cons., 1982—. Active various mcpl. offices and coms.; pub. mem. Seed Corp With U.S. Army, 1943-46. Recipient Silver medal Internat. Film Festival, 1968, 69. Mem. Inst. Mgmt. Cons. (founding mem., chpt. pres. 1984-87), Am. Arbitration Assn. (mem. comml. panel). Home and Office: Off Old Maine St E Lakeville MA 02347-1601

WASHBURN, STEWART PUTNAM, management consultant; b. Claremont, N.H., Apr. 6, 1929; s. Walter Henry and Josephine (Dana) W.; m. Josephine F. Foster, Aug. 20, 1960 (dec. 1980); children: Patricia, Alice. BS in Commerce and Econs., U. Vt., 1951; MBA, Harvard U., 1953. Cert. comml. lender. V.p. Worcester County Nat. Bank, Worcester, Mass., 1955-74; v.p., sr. loan officer First Nat. Bank, New Bedford, Mass., 1974-77; sr. v.p., sr. loan officer Durfee Attleboro Bank, Fall River, Mass., 1977-90; mgmt. cons. in comml. lending Fall River, Mass., 1990—. Chmn. Bristol Regional Employment Bd., Fall River, 1987—; pres. Southeastern Econ. Devel. Corp., Taunton, Mass., 1991—; dir. Jobs for Fall River, 1981—. With U.S. Army, 1953-55. Mem. Inst. Mgmt. Cons., Robert Morris Assocs. (bd. govs. N.E. chpt. 1973-75, chmn. credit policy roundtable 1989, Spl. Svc. award 1989). Home: 5 Middle St South Dartmouth MA 02748-3427 Office: PO Box 643 Fall River MA 02722-0643

WASHCO, CHRISTOPHER JOHN, banker; b. Newark, Oct. 16, 1957; s. Gerard George and Jean Marie (Cummisky) W.; m. Laurie Rae Cohen, Apr. 21, 1985. BA in Acctg., Upsala Coll., 197. CPA, N.J. Internal auditor Llewellyn-Edison Savs., West Orange, N.J., 1980-85; sr. acct. Health Learning Systems, Lyndhurst, N.Y., 1985-87; v.p., treas. Llewellyn Edison Savs. Bank, SLA, West Orange, N.J., 1987—. Mem. AICPA, N.J. Soc. CPAs, Fin. Mgrs. Soc., Alpha Kappa Psi. Office: Llewellyn-Edison Savs Bank 474 Prospect Ave West Orange NJ 07052-4196

WASHIC, THOMAS EUGENE, controller; b. Philipsburg, Pa., Aug. 16, 1950; s. Michael Andrew and Helen (Thomas) W.; m. Elizabeth Lenker, June 29, 1985. BBA, Pa. State U., 1985. Adminstv. asst. Sen. George Gekas/Sen. of Pa., Harrisburg, 1979; controller County of Dauphin, Harrisburg, 1980—. Mem. Govt. Fin. Officers Assn. (pres. Harrisburg chpt. 1990-91), Pa. State Assn. County Controllers (pres. 1991-92), Lions (treas. Susquehanna Twp. 1988-91, 3d v.p. 1991—), Kappa Kappa (treas. 1984). Republican. Office: County of Dauphin 1 S Front St Harrisburg PA 17101-2007

WASHINGTON, CLARENCE EDWARD, JR., insurance company executive; b. New Orleans, Nov. 20, 1953; s. Clarence Edward and Alice Mildred (Jones) W.; m. Denise Sandra Agard, June 29, 1985. BS cum laude, Xavier U., 1983. Mgr. Time Saver, Inc., New Orleans, 1972-79; budget, fin. analyst Equitable Life Assurance, N.Y.C., 1983-84; actuarial asst. Prudential Life Assurance, Newark, 1984-87; pension mgr. Am. Internat. Life, N.Y.C., 1987—. Democrat. Roman Catholic. Office: Am Internat Life 80 Pine St # 13 New York NY 10005

WASHINGTON, GARY, music educator; b. Mineola, N.Y., Aug. 13, 1953; s. George Joseph and Elaine W.; m. Mindy Hope Goldstein, July 16, 1978. BA magna cum laude, L.I. U., 1974, MA, 1976. Lectr., adminstr. C.W. Post campus L.I. U., Greenvale, N.Y., 1976-86; prof. music L.I. U., Southampton, N.Y., 1987—; guest conductor Suffolk County Music Educators Assn., Jamesport, N.Y., 1989. Composer approx. 100 works of chamber music and 6 recordings of music for synthesizer, 1974—; contbr. articles to profl. jours. Pres. Kagyu Ozamling Kunchab, Manhattan, 1980-84. Recipient Excellence in Sound Design, Am. Coll. Theatre Festival, 1986, Faculty award Omicron Delta Kappa, 1986; Meet the Composer Program grantee, L.I.U., 1982. Mem. Coll. Music Soc., Soc. Composrs, Inc., Am. Music Ctr. Office: LI U Southampton Campus Southampton NY 11968

WASHINGTON, JUSTINE GLORIA-MAE, singer, composer; b. Bamberg, S.C., Oct. 13, 1941; d. Cleveland and Wilhelmina (Moody) W.; divorced; 1 child, Lancey W. Baskett. Student, Hills Bus. U., Oklahoma City, 1961-62; diploma exec. sec. speedwriting, Monroe Bus. Inst., Bronx, N.Y., 1976; diploma med. sec., The Laural Sch., Phoenix, 1985. Singer, writer Baton Records, N.Y.C., 1956, J & S Records, N.Y.C., 1957, Neptune Records, Newark, 1960, Sue Records, N.Y.C., 1962-67, Veep, United Artist Records, N.Y.C., 1968, Cotillion, Atlantic Records, N.Y.C., 1969, Chess Records, Chgo., 1971, Master 5 Records, Teaneck, N.J., 1973-75, 88, AVI Records, Calif., 1978-79, Lawton Records, Teaneck, N.J., 1981, 90-92; song writer Broadcast Music, Inc., 1956—, WindSwept Pacific Entertainment Co., 1991—. Author: (song lyrics) The Time, 1959 (Cashbox award 1959), Rock On Volume I Singles, 1942-88, Show Time at the Apollo, 1983, Soul Survivor Magazine, 1988-89. Chmn. Robert J. Magnum State Com. for Human Rights, 1967, Don't Let Them Starve, 1985, Apollo Theatre, 1992; mem. capital stewardship program Canaan Bapt. Ch., 1988—. Recipient Rhythm and Blues award, Washington, 1982. Fellow For the Love of Rock 'N Roll, Rhythm N Blues Found.

WASHINGTON, TIA DENISE, educational consultant; b. Austin, Tex., Feb. 23, 1955; d. A.T. and Bette Jo (McKenzie) W. BS in Psychology, U. Md., 1976; MA in Edn., George Washington U., 1981. Tchr. Compu-Tech Ednl. Svcs., Garden City, N.Y., 1983-86, Prince George's County Pub. Schs., Upper Marlboro, Md., 1987; ednl. cons. Jostens Learning Corp., Phoenix, 1987—. Author staff devel. modules-course workshop Making Life Skills Come Alive Teaching Employability, 1991. Com. mem., fundraiser, singer, soloist St. Margaret's Ch., Seat Pleasant, Md., 1990—. Mem. AACD, Am. Mental Health Counselors Assn., Am. Sch. Counselor Assn. Roman Catholic. Office: Jostens Learning Corp 300 I St NE Ste 4 Washington DC 20002-4389

WASIELE, HARRY W., JR., diversified electrical manufacturing company executive; b. Chgo., June 29, 1926; s. Harry W. and Antoinette (Tuleja) W.; m. Loretta K. Anderson, Jan. 3, 1948; children: Kathleen Ann Wasiele Bach, Brian David, Larry Scott, Mark Thomas. Grad. high sch. Asst. sales mgr. Drake Mfg. Co., Chgo., 1950-55; sales engr. AMP, Inc., Chgo., 1955, Detroit, 1956-57; product mgr. AMP, Inc., Harrisburg, Pa., 1958-61; industry mgr. AMP, Inc., 1961-67, dir. marketing, 1967-68; div. gen. mgr. Brand-Rex div. Am. Enka Corp., Willimantic, Conn., 1968-70; pres. Brand-Rex Co., subs. Akzona Inc., 1970-83; chmn. Brand-Rex Ltd., Glenrothes, Scotland, 1974-83; v.p. sales and corp. devel. Cablec Corp., New City, N.Y., 1985—; dir. Berkel Inc.; chmn., pres. Tarpon Springs (Fla.) Internat. Tannery, Inc., 1990—. Bd. dirs. Eastern Conn. State Coll. Found., 1972-83; trustee Windham Community Hosp., Willimantic, 1969-83, trustee emeritus, 1983—, pres. bd. trustees, 1981-83. With USNR, 1944-46. Mem. Nat. Elec. Mfrs. Assn. (chmn. wire and cable div., bd. govs. 1982-84), Conn. Bus. and Industry Assn. (emeritus dir.), New Seabury Country Club, Mariner Sands Country Club. Republican. Roman Catholic. Home (summer): 53 Shore Dr W PO Box 826 New Seabury MA 02649 Home (winter): Mariner Sands 6755 Barrington Dr Stuart FL 34997

WASIUTYNSKI, WOJCIECH JOSEPH, journalist, columnist; b. Warsaw, Poland, Sept. 8, 1910; s. Bohdan Szczepan Ksawery and Maria Jadwiga (Buchbinder) W.; m. Halina g. Janecka, Jan. 14, 1946; children: Joanna, Bohdan. D of Law, U. Warsaw, 1936. Editor Akademik Polski, Warsaw, 1929-32, ABC Daily, Warsaw, 1933-34, Wieczor Warszawski, Warsaw, 1935-39; editor underground newpapers France, 1940-42; editor I/CM Polish Thought, London, 1947-58; asst. chief Polish desk Radio Free Europe, N.Y.C., 1958-73; editor in chief New World, N.Y.C., 1973-75; freelance writer, 1976—. Author 16 books. Pres. Roman Dmowski Inst., N.Y.C., 1961-92. Lt. Polish Army, 1942-47, Europe. Decorated Silver Cross with Swords Polish Army in West, 1945, Croix de Guerre L'Orde de Brigade, 1945; recipient lit. award Veritas Found., 1944, lit. award Polish Journalists Union, 1969, lit. award Kultura Monthly, 1990. Mem. Internat. Broadcasters. Roman Catholic.

WASMER, CARMENIA ANN, English language educator, librarian; b. White Plains, N.J., Sept. 23, 1934; d. Peter and Catherine (Chioma) Medure; m. John David Wasmer, Apr. 12, 1958; children: Michael, Christopher. BA with honors, Douglass Coll., 1956; MLS, Rutgers U., 1966; MA, William Paterson Coll., 1982. Cert. ESL tchr., reading specialist, ednl. media specialist, profl. libr., N.J.; cert. braillist ARC. Tchr. Spanish and French Bergenfield (N.J.) High Sch., 1956-61, River Dell Jr.-Sr. High Sch., Oradell, N.J., 1961-62; sch. libr. Holdrum Sch., Rivervale, N.J., 1964-67; part-time libr. Ridgewood (N.J.) Libr., 1971—; ESL tchr. Westwood (N.J.) Regional Schs., 1980—; adj. instr. ESL, Bergen Community Coll., Paramus, N.J., 1988—; coord. ESL tchr. intern program Fairleigh Dickinson U., Teaneck, N.J., 1991. Active ARC, Ridgewood, N.J., 1973-76; chmn. PTO, Paramus, 1975-78; leader Cub Scouts, Paramus, 1975-77; vol. Cath. Charities, Paramus, 1975-76. Leopold Schepp Found. scholar, N.Y.C., 1953, 54, 55. Mem. NEA, N.J. Edn. Assn., Bergen County Edn. Assn., Westwood Edn. Assn., N.J. Bilingual/ESL Tchrs. Assn., Beta Phi Mu, Kappa Delta Pi, Pi Lambda Theta. Home: 271 Wilson Ave Paramus NJ 07652-4755

WASON, ROBERT WESLEY, music theory educator; b. Bridgeport, Conn., July 25, 1945; s. David Fairchild and Esther Milton (Barnes) W.; m. Elizabeth Watson, June 1965 (div. 1975); 1 child, Abigail; m. Barbara Clare McIver, Mar. 27, 1977; children: Julia, Oliver. MusB, U. Hartford, 1967, MusM, 1969; MPhil, Yale U., 1978, PhD, 1981. Instr. Hartt Coll. Music, 1970-76, 77-79; lectr. Clark U., Worcester, Mass., 1980; asst. prof. North Tex. State U., Denton, 1981-83; asst. prof. Eastman Sch. Music, Rochester, N.Y., 1983-86, assoc. prof., 1986—; vis. prof. U. Basel, Switzerland, 1991, U. B.C., Vancouver, 1992. Author: Viennese Harmonic Theory, 1985; composer: Theme and Variations of Guitar, 1974 (Bronze medal Radio France 1975). Fulbright fellow, 1979, NEH fellow, Washington, 1989, Guggenheim Found. Fellow, N.Y.C., 1990. Mem. Soc. Music Theory (chair publs. com. 1988-91, mem. exec. bd. 1991—). Office: Eastman Sch Music 26 Gibbs St Rochester NY 14604

WASSELL, WILLIAM JOHN, communications executive, consultant; b. New Phila., July 24, 1934; s. William Charles and Mary Alice (Fergel) W.; m. Eleanor Kirsten Hansen, July 1, 1961; children: Peter W., Kristen Elizabeth Wassell Chevalier. BA in Journalism, Pa. State U., 1960; MA in Communications, Fairfield (Conn.) U., 1982. Advt./pub. rels. trainee Gen. Electric Co., N.Y.C., 1960-70; advt. mgr. Gen. Electric Co., Bloomington, Ill., 1965-70; communications mgr. Gen. Electric Co., Harrison, N.Y., 1970-75; mgr. mgmt. communications Gen. Electric Co., Bridgeport, Conn., 1975-80, Norwalk, Conn., 1980-82; corp. communications mgr. Gen. Electric Co., Fairfield, 1982-88; pres., chief exec. officer Sudden Impact Corp., Westport, Conn., 1988-90; prin., ptnr. Sudden Impact Corp., 1991—. Author booklet Thoughts on Communicat's, 1987; contbr. articles to publs. Community cons. ECLIPSE, Weston, 1980—, Keep Weston Rural, 1987-89, writer, organizer, 1988. With U.S. Army, 1953-56. Mem. Assn. Multi Image Internat. Democrat. Roman Catholic. Home: 40 Old Orchard Dr Weston CT 06883-1309 Office: Sudden Impact Corp 49 Richmondville Ave Westport CT 06880-2004

WASSER, ALAN CHARLES, theatrical manager; b. Portland, Oreg., Dec. 28, 1948; s. Earl Stanley and Rosemary (Geneste) W. BA, Columbia U., 1971. Assoc. mgr. Circle in the Square, N.Y.C., 1973-77; co. mgr. Calif. Suite, on tour, 1977-78; gen. mgr. Sugar Babies, on tour, 1979-86, John F. Kennedy Ctr. for the Performing Arts, Washington, 1985-87, Legends, on tour, 1986-87, Les Miserables, N.Y.C., 1987—, The Phantom of the Opera, N.Y.C., 1988—, Miss Saigon, N.Y.C., 1991—; owner, pres. Alan Wasser Assocs., N.Y.C., 1981—. Mem. League Am. Theatres and Producers, Am. Assn. Theatrical Press Agts. and Mgrs. Office: Alan Wasser Assocs 1650 Broadway Ste 800 New York NY 10019-6865

WASSERMAN, BERNARD, engineering executive; b. Hamilton, Ont., Can., June 12, 1925; came to U.S., 1947; m. Joan B. Baucum, Dec. 28, 1973; children: Katherine, Deborah, Henry, Jan, Kyle. B of Applied Sci., U. Toronto, Can., 1947; MS, MIT, 1949. Instr. U. Wis., Madison, 1949-51; sr. engr. Sylvania Inc., Buffalo, 1952-56; program mgr. Bell Aero Systems, Buffalo, 1956-61; chief engr. Epsco Inc., Westwood, Mass., 1961-64; program mgr. Avco Systems Div., Wilmington, Mass., 1964-68; program dir. Avco Everett Research Labs., Everett, Mass., 1968-75; mgr. systems engring. Am. Sci. and Engring., Cambridge, Mass., 1975-77; program dir. Dynatrend Inc., Woburn, Mass., 1977-83; v.p. engring. Textron Def. Systems, Wilmington, 1983—. Inventor in field. Mem. Wayland (Mass.) Conservation Commn., 1966; mem. industry task force Cen. New Eng. Coll., 1986-88; mem. Rep. Presdl. Task Force. Mem. IEEE (sr.), Am. Assn. Individual Investors, Assn. of the U.S. Army, Am. Mgmt. Assn., Am. Def. Preparedness Assn., Nat. Wildlife Fedn., Profl. Engrs. Ont., Sigma Xi (assoc.), Eta Kappa Nu. Republican. Jewish. Home: 37 Moonpenny Dr Boxford MA 01921-2736 also: Sint Maarten Netherlands Antilles Office: Textron Def Systems 201 Lowell St Wilmington MA 01887-2969

WASSERMAN, CHARLES, banker; b. Guayaquil, Ecuador, Aug. 31, 1929; came to U.S., 1948, naturalized, 1960; s. Mendel and Mary Wasserman; m. Jacqueline Royer, Oct. 4, 1960; children: Roger, Mark. BA, Farleigh Dickinson U., 1949; MBA, U. Havana, 1956. Trainee internat. dept. Chase Manhattan Bank, N.Y., 1958-60, Swiss Bank Corp., N.Y., 1960-64; area sr. credit analyst Am. Express Bank, N.Y., 1965-66; exec. v.p. Republic Nat. Bank, N.Y., 1967—, cons. to World Bank, 1989; chmn., pres. Republic Internat. Bank N.Y., L.A., 1988-89. Mem. Internat. Exec. Svc. Corps. Home: 224 Nassau Ave Manhasset NY 11030-2440 Office: 127 E 59th St Rm 222 New York NY 10022

WASSERMAN, EUGENE M., pediatrician; b. Bklyn., Mar. 2, 1931; s. Jacob and Lena (Kartell) W.; m. Nancy C. Ziluck, Sept. 1, 1959; children—Brett D., A. Michael, Julie B. A.B., Columbia U., 1952; M.D., Chgo. Med. Sch., 1956. Rotating intern Kings County Hosp. Med. Ctr., Bklyn., 1956-57; resident in pediatrics, Mt. Sinai Hosp., N.Y.C., 1957-59; practice medicine specializing in pediatrics, Mamaroneck, N.Y., 1961—; chmn. pediatrics United Hosp., Port Chester, N.Y., 1975-80; asst. attending in pediatrics St. Agnes Hosp., White Plains, N.Y., 1975—; pediatric cons. Rye Psychiat. Hosp., N.Y., 1975—. Chmn. doctors' com. Village of Mamaroneck, 1975—. Served as capt. M.C., U.S. Army, 1959-61. Mem. Med. Soc. N.Y. Jewish. Avocation: cabinet making. Office: 701 Palmer Ct PO Box 186 Mamaroneck NY 10543-0186

WASSERMAN, JEFFREY ANDREW, artist; b. Mt. Vernon, N.Y., July 21, 1946; s. Arthur Jay and Lenore (Robinson) W.; m. Anne Colby Newburg, Jan. 2, 1990. BFA, Temple U., 1968; postgrad., Royal Coll. Art, London, 1968-69. Sr. lectr. painting Phila. Coll. Arts, 1988. Solo exhbns. include Mcpl. Theatre, Caen, France, 1980, Red Bar, N.Y.C., 1982, Virtual Garrison, N.Y.C., 1984, Daniel Newburg Gallery, N.Y.C., Philippe Briet Gallery, N.Y.C., 1988, Nina Freudenheim Gallery, Buffalo, 1991; group shows include Charles More Gallery, Phila., 1984, Ted Greenwald Gallery, N.Y.C., 1985, Rosa Esman Gallery, N.Y.C., 1986, Daniel Newburg Gallery, 1987, Scott Hanson Gallery, N.Y.C., 1988, 89, 90, Fay Gold Gallery, Atlanta, 1991; represented in permanent collections.

WASSERMAN, KRYSTYNA, librarian, art historian; b. Lodz, Poland, Aug. 10, 1937; came to U.S., 1971; d. Henryk and Polina (Volk) Ostrowski; m. Paul Wasserman, Apr. 14, 1972. M in Journalism, U. Warsaw, Poland, 1963; MLS, Pratt Inst., Bklyn., 1972; MA, U. Md., 1981. Reporter Ekran-The Screen Mag., Warsaw, Poland, 1960-62; sec. edn. com. Inst. Sci., Tech. and Econ. Info., Warsaw, Poland and Internat. Fedn. for Documentation, The Hague, Netherlands, 1962-71; pvt. practice reference book editing College Park, Md., 1972-82; librarian Nat. Mus. Women in Arts, Washington, 1982—. Contbr. articles to profl. jours; editor: A Guide to the World Training Facilities in Documentation and Information Work, 1965. ASTEF fellow Govt. of France, 1967. Mem. Art Libraries Soc. North Am. Home: 4940 Sentinel Dr Apt 401 Bethesda MD 20816-3554 Office: Nat Mus Women in Arts 1250 New York Ave NW Washington DC 20005-3920

WASSERMAN, MANUÈLE D., financial planner; b. Alexandria, Egypt, Apr. 13, 1950; d. Edward Daniel and J. Andree (Menache) Delbourgo; m. Richard Leo Wasserman, May 13, 1973; children: Alexander Edward, Lauren Elise. BA, Vassar Coll., 1970; MA in History, Columbia U., 1971, PhD in History, 1977. Cert. fin. planner. Asst. prof. European history U. Md., College Park, 1978-81; fin. advisor Prudential Securities, Balt., 1983—; active Women's Fin. Network, Balt., 1990—; lectr. in field. Treas., bd. dirs. Cen. Scholarship Bur., Balt., 1987—; steering com. career div. Nat. Coun. Jewish Women, Balt., 1984—; active Associated Jewish Charitable Bus. and Profl. Women, Balt., 1986—. Herbert Lehman fellow, 1977; named Matthew Vassar scholar, 1970. Mem. Suburban Club Balt., Vassar Club Md., Phi Beta Kappa. Democrat. Office: Prudential Securities 250 W Pratt St Baltimore MD 21201

WASSERMAN, MYRON BEAU, artist, designer; b. Phila., Mar. 11, 1947; s. Milton and Elsie (Tissian)W. Grad. high sch., Phila. Graphic designer Goodway Pub., Phila., 1965-66, N.Am. Pub., Phila., 1966; art dir. Met. mag., Phila., 1966-68, Listen mag., Phila., 1966-68, Progressive Grocer mag., Phila., 1966-68, Popular Dog mag., Phila., 1968-69; art. dir., illustrator Lionel Leisure, Inc., Phila., 1969-70, Elkman Advt., Bala Cynwd, Pa., 1970-72, Shaefer Advt., Bala Cynwd, 1972-74; freelance artist Bala Cynwd, 1974—; owner Myron Wasserman's Graphics Design Group, Old City Phila., 1974-86; fine artist, 1986—. Cpl. USMC, 1965-69. Mem. Graphic Artists Guild (pres. Phila. chpt. 1990—). Office: Wassermans Studio 1817 N 5th St # Lr Philadelphia PA 19122-2199

WASSERMAN, WALTER LEONARD, magnetics company executive; b. N.Y.C., Sept. 16, 1936; s. Soloman J. and Esther (Honigman) W.; m. Barbara Koenig, June 15, 1957 (div. 1973); children: Beth, Greg, Eli. BSEE, CUNY, 1957; MSEE, U. Pa., 1961, PhD in Bio Engring., 1964. Engring. supr. Hevey Mil. Electric GE, Syracuse, N.Y., 1958-60; engring. mgr. Philco Corp., Phila., 1960-65; v.p. bioengring. Hoffman-LaRoche, Nutley, N.J., 1965-67; pres. Health Tech. Corp., Moorestown, N.J., 1967-70; gen. mgr. Med. Data Systems, Dublin, Ireland, 1971-77; dir. mktg. El Scint (Israel), Inc., London, 1978-81; v.p. R&D Electro Biology, Inc., Parsippany, N.J., 1982-85; chief exec. officer Meditron Corp., Spring valley, N.Y., 1985-90, Modular Magnetics, New City, N.Y., 1990—; bd. dirs. Interpore Internat., Inc., Irvine, Calif., Theradyne, Inc., Salt Lake City, TriDyne, Inc., Salt Lake City. Contbr. articles to profl. jours.; patentee in field. Mem. Pres.'s Commn. for Handicapped, 1964. Capt. USAF, 1964-66, Vietnam. Recipient Gold medal Am. Assn. Rehab. Medicine, 1964. Democrat. Jewish. Office: Modular Magnetics Inc PO Box 119 New City NY 10956

WASSERMAN, ZELDA RAKOWITZ, computational chemist; b. N.Y.C., July 19, 1935; d. Samuel and Florence (Weisberg) Rakowitz; m. Edel Wasserman, Jan. 29, 1955; children: Stephen Rak, Diane C.W. Feldman. AB, Radcliffe Coll., 1956; MS, Rutgers U., 1965. Computational asst. MIT, Cambridge, 1956-57; with tech. staff Bell Labs., Murray Hill, N.J., 1965-81; prin. investigator E.I. DuPont de Nemours and Co., Wilmington, Del., 1981-90, The DuPont Merck Pharm. Co., Wilmington, 1991—. Mem. Am. Chem. Soc., Assn. for Computing Machinery. Home: 1904 Academy Pl Wilmington DE 19806-2135 Office: DuPont Merck Pharm Co Experimental Station Wilmington DE 19880-0228

WASSERMANN, HERBERT EDWARD, ophthalmologist, oculoplastic surgeon; b. Mannheim, Germany, Nov. 30, 1936; came to U.S., 1946; s. Emil and Edith (Linz) W.; m. Runa Sleipnaes, Nov. 16, 1969; children: Jessica, Jonathan. Student, Rutgers U., 1955-57; BSc, Ohio State U., 1959; MD, U. Chgo., 1964. Diplomate Am. Bd. Ophthalmology. Intern Barnes Hosp.-Washington U., St. Louis, 1964-65; resident in ophthalmology Cornell U.-N.Y. Hosp., N.Y.C., 1967-71; fellow in oculoplastics Manhattan Eye and Ear Hosp., N.Y.C., 1971-72; ophthalmologist Project Hope, Natal, Brazil, 1972; pvt. practice, West Hartford, Conn., 1972—; sr. attending physician Hartford (Conn.) Hosp., 1972—, Mt. Sinai Hosp., Hartford, 1972—; assoc. attending physician U. Conn. Med. Sch., Farmington, 1972—. Lt. M.C., USNR, 1965-67. NIH fellow U. Chgo., 1959-60. Fellow ACS, Internat. Coll. Surgeons, Am. Acad. Ophthalmology; mem. AMA, New Eng. Ophthal. Soc., Conn. Med. Soc., Hartford County Med. Soc. Office: Affiliated Eye Cons 8 Ellsworth Rd West Hartford CT 06107

WASSERSTEIN, WENDY, playwright; b. Bklyn., Oct. 18, 1950; d. Morris and Lola W. BA, Mt. Holyoke Coll.; MA, CCNY; MFA, Yale Drama Sch., 1976. Adapted John Cheever's The Sorrows of Gin for PBS TV series Great Performances, also Uncommon Women and Others; author: (plays) Any Woman Can't, Montpelier Pazazz, When Dinah Shore Ruled the Earth, Uncommon Women and Others, Isn't It Romantic, The Heidi Chronicles, (Recipient Pulitzer prize for drama, 1989, Outer Critics Circle award for best Broadway play, 1989, Antoinette Perry award, 1989, Susan Smith Blackburn prize, 1989), (screenplay, with Christopher Durang) The House of Husbands, (essays) Bachelor Girls, 1990. Mem. British Am. Arts Assn., Found. of the Dramatists Guild.

WASYLYK, JOHN STANLEY, glass technology consultant; b. Passaic, N.J., Feb. 15, 1942; s. Stanley and Emma (Decker) W.; m. Deborah Lee Smith, Nov. 8, 1969; children: Wendy Jean, Rebecca Lynn. BA, Rutgers U., 1964, BS, 1964, PhD, 1969. Chief glass technologist AGR Internat. Inc., Butler, Pa., 1976-87; dir. rsch. AGR Informational, Inc., Butler, Pa., 1987-89, dir. internat. cons. svcs., 1989-91; ind. cons. John S. Wasylyk, PhD., Cons. in Glass Tech., 1991—. Contbr. tech. papers to profl. jours.; patentee in field. Mem. Am. Ceramic Soc., German Glass Tech. Soc., British Glass

Tech. Soc., Am. Soc. for Testing and Materials, Internat. Commn. Glass, Internat. Standards Orgn. Home and Office: 107 Beverly Rd Butler PA 16001-1948

WATANABE, RUTH TAIKO, music historian, library science educator; b. Los Angeles, May 12, 1916; d. Kohei and Iwa (Watanabe) W. B.Mus., U. So. Calif., 1937, A.B., 1939, A.M., 1941, M.Mus., 1942; postgrad., Eastman Sch. Music, Rochester, N.Y., 1942-46, Columbia U., 1947; Ph.D., U. Rochester, 1952. Dir. Sibley Music Library Eastman Sch. of Music, Rochester, N.Y., 1947-84; prof. music bibliography Eastman Sch. of Music, 1978-85, historian, archivist, 1984—; adj. prof. Sch. Library Sci. State U. Coll. at Geneseo, 1975-83; coordinator adult edn. program Rochester Civic Music Assn., 1963-75; mem. adv. com. Hochstein Music Sch.; lectr. on music, book reviewer, 1966—; program annotater Rochester Philharmonic Orch., 1959—. Author: Introduction to Music Research, 1967, Madrigali-II Verso, 1978; editor: Scribners New Music Library, vols. 2, 5, 8, 1973, Treasury of Four Hand Piano Music, 1979; contbr. articles to profl. jours., contbr. symphony orchs. of U.S., 1986, internat. music jours.; modern music librarianship, 1989; contbr. to Festschrift for Carleton Sprague Smith, 1989, DeMúsica Hispana et aliis, 1990. Mem. overseers vis. com. Baxter Sch. Library Sci., Case Western Res. U., 1979-85, Alderman Book Com., 1986-89. Mem. ALA, AAUW (Pa.-Del. fellowship. 1949-50, 1st v.p. Rochester 1964-65, mem. N.Y. state bd. 1965-66, mem. nat. com. on soc.'s reflection on arts 1967-69, nat. com. Am. fellowships awards 1969-74, br. pres. 1969-71, hon. co-chair Capital Fund Drive, 1986-88, Woman of Yr. award 1990), Internat. Assn. Music Libraries (2d v.p. commn. on conservatory libraries, commn. research libraries), Am. Musicol. Soc., Music Library Assn. (v.p. 1968-70, citation 1986, mem. editorial bd. 1967—, pres. 1979-81), Music Library Assn./Internat. Assn. Music Libraries (joint com., 1986-87), Civic Music Assn. Rochester, Riemenscheider Bach Inst. (hon.), Hanson Inst. Am. Music (bd. mem. 1981—), Univ. Club, Century Club, Phi Beta Kappa (pres. Iota chpt. of N.Y. 1969-71), Phi Kappa Phi, Mu Phi Epsilon (gen. chmn. nat. conv. 1956, nat. librarian 1958-60, recipient citation 1977, Ora Ashley Lambke award 1989), Pi Kappa Lambda (sec. 1978—, treas. 1980—), Delta Phi Alpha, Epsilon Phi, Delta Kappa Gamma (parliamentarian 1986-88). Home: 111 East Ave Apt 610 Rochester NY 14604-2539 Office: Eastman Sch Music Rochester NY 14604

WATERHOUSE, STEPHEN LEE, management consultant; b. Sanford, Maine, Mar. 31, 1943; s. James William and Evelyn Anita (Johnson) W.; m. Linda Sue Lenge, July 3, 1967; children: Melinda Harwood, James Stephen. AB in Chemistry, Dartmouth Coll., 1965, MBA in Mktg., 1967. Mfg. exec. Procter and Gamble, Boston, Chgo., N.Y.C., 1967-73; cons. to pres. Avon Products, N.Y.C., 1973-75; head European ops. London, 1976-77; sr. exec. officer jewelry div. N.Y.C., 1978-80; v.p. European ops. Revlon, Paris, 1981-82; v.p. U.S. div. Thomas Tilling Ltd., N.Y.C. and London, 1983; chmn., sr. ptnr. Hanover (N.H.) Ptnrs. Ltd., N.Y.C., London, Zurich and Lugano, Switzerland, 1983—; pres. Waterhouse and Assocs., N.Y.C., 1981—. Mem. Dartmouth Coll. Alumni Council, Hanover, N.H., 1979-82; bd. dirs. Internat. Festival of Statue of Liberty Celebration, N.Y.C., 1986, 87. Served with USAR, 1967-73. Mem. Global Exec. Search Profl. Assn., U.K. Inst. Dirs., Friends of Templeton Coll., Oxford U., London Sch. Econs. Club. also: 870 Bradford Ave Westfield NJ 07090

WATERMAN, DANIEL, mathematician, educator; b. Bklyn., Oct. 24, 1927; s. Samuel and Anna (Robson) W.; m. Mudite Upesleja, Nov. 4, 1960; children—Erica, Susan, Scott. B.A., Bklyn. Coll., 1947; M.A., Johns Hopkins U., 1948; Ph.D., U. Chgo., 1954. Research assoc. Cowles Commn. Research in Econs., Chgo., 1951-52; instr. Purdue U., West Lafayette, Ind., 1953-55, asst. prof., 1955-59; asst. prof. U. Wis.-Milw., 1959-61; prof. Wayne State U., Detroit, 1961-69; prof. Syracuse (N.Y.) U., 1969—, chmn. math dept., 1988—; cons. Martin-Marietta, Denver, 1960-61; researcher in real and Fourier analysis. Editor: Classical Real Analysis, 1985: contbr. articles to profl. jours. Fulbright fellow U. Vienna, 1952-53. Mem. Math. Assn. Am., Am. Math. Soc. (council mem.-at-large 1975-78), Sigma Xi. Home: 116 Donridge Dr Syracuse NY 13214-2344 Office: Syracuse U Dept Math Syracuse NY 13244-1150

WATERS, GREGORY LEO, academic affairs executive; b. Newark, N.J., Jan. 23, 1948; s. Thomas E. and Marie (Daly) W.; m. Theresa Mary Zeiss, Apr. 4, 1971; children: Gregory, Deirdre. AB, Georgetown U., Washington, 1969; MA, Rutgers U., 1972, PhD, 1974. From asst. prof. English to dir. grad. and special programs U. Mich., 1974-84; prof. English, dep. provost, assoc. v.p. acad. affairs Montclair State Coll., 1984—; bd. dirs. Am. Assn. Univ. Adminstrs., Washington, 1989—; chmn. N.J. Com. Humanities, New Brunswick, N.J., 1988-90. Contbr. numerous articles to profl. jours. Bd. dirs. Black Achievers of N.J., Newark, N.J., 1989—, Family Svcs. Agy, Flint, Mich., 1982-84. Rutgers U. English Dept. fellow, 1969-70. Mem. Phi Beta Kappa, Phi Kappa Phi. Home: 10 Garden St Montclair NJ 07042-4116 Office: Montclair State Coll Upper Montclair NJ 07043

WATERS, JOHN, film director, writer, actor; b. Balt., Apr. 22, 1946; s. John Samuel and Patricia Ann (Whitaker) W. Student, NYU, 1966. Speaker various colls., comedy clubs, U.S., Europe, Australia, 1968—. Writer, dir. films Roman Candles, 1966, Eat Your Makeup, 1968, Mondo Trasho, 1969, Multiple Maniacs, 1970, Pink Flamingos, 1972, Female Trouble, 1974, Desperate Living, 1977, Polyester, 1981, Cry-Baby, 1990; writer, dir., actor film Hairspray, 1987; actor Something Wild, 1988, Homer and Eddie, 1990, (TV show) 21 Jump Street, 1990; author: Shock Value, 1981, Crackpot, 1986, Trash Trio, 1988; contbr. articles to N.Y. Times, Am. Film, other mags. Fund raiser AIDS Action Balt.; spokesperson Anti-Violence Campaign, N.Y.C., 1991. John Waters Day named in his honor State of Md., 1985; John Waters Week named in his honor City of Balt., 1988. Mem. AFTRA, SAG, Dirs. Guild Am., Writers Guild Am., Acad. Motion Picture Arts and Scis.

WATERS, MICHAEL ROBERT, insurance management executive; b. Johnson City, N.Y., Jan. 31, 1955; s. Robert C. and Ruth A. (Grogan) W.; m. Ann R. Crompton, June 25, 1977; children: Laura, Robert. AAS, Monroe C.C., Rochester, N.Y., 1975; BS, U. Md., 1978; postgrad., Pa. State U., 1979-81. Engring. aide DOD, NAVSEC USN, Washington, 1977-78; field rep. ISO Comml. Risk Svcs., Phila., 1979-80, asst. mgr., 1980-86; br. mgr ISO Comml. Risk Svcs., Bklyn., 1986-88; regional dir. ISO Comml. Risk Svcs., Marlton, N.J., 1988—. Vice-chmn. indsl. comm. Twp. of Jackson (N.J.), 1990, chmn., 1991—. Mem. KC. Roman Catholic. Office: ISO Comml Risk Svcs Inc 4 B Eves Dr Ste 200 Marlton NJ 08053

WATERS-SAVANT, MARC EDWARD, opera singer; b. Newark, May 31, 1966; s. Matthew Theodore II and Malissa Marie (Collins) Waters. Student, Westminster Choir Coll., 1986-88, Salzburg (Austria) Coll., 1987-89, Akademie Mozarteum, Salzburg, 1987. Diplomate voice Akademie Mozarteum. Adolescent mental health specialist Community Mental Health Ctr., U. Medicine/Dentistry N.J., Piscataway, N.J., 1985—; lectr. voice pvt. studios, Piscataway, 1987—; tchr. The Learning Inst., Piscataway, 1989-90; pres., artistic dir. Savant Prodns. Mgmt., U.S.A., Piscataway and London, 1989—; lectr. theatre arts for the disabled Vey Spl. Arts N.J., North Brunswick, N.J., 1991-92. Lyricist: (song cycle) Le Voyages de L'Etudiant Pauvre, 1990-91.; author: (analysis) Handel's Messiah, 1988, Aaron Copland: His America, 1988. Mem. Piscataway Mayoral Cultural Arts Adv. Commn., 1989-91; adjucator NAACP Arts and Scis. Competition, Red Bank, N.J., 1992; co-founder Coalition of Women and Men Against Violence, New Brunswick, 1992. Home and Office: Savant Prodns. Mgmt. USA 21 Redbud Rd Piscataway NJ 08854-5926

WATHNE, CARL NORMAN, hospital administrator; b. Johnstown, Mass., Oct. 16, 1930; s. Odd and Alice (Anderson) W.; m. Alice Adele Tucker, Jan. 25, 1958; children: John M., Carl K. BS, U. Pitts., 1952; MS, Columbia U., 1958. Asst. adminstr. Bayonne (N.J.) Hosp., 1958-60; assoc. adminstr. Binghamton (N.Y.) Gen. Hosp., 1960-63; chief exec. officer Putnam Community Hosp., Carmel, N.Y., 1963-65; v.p. A.J.J. Rourke, Inc., New Rochelle, N.Y., 1965-72; exec. dir. Lahey Clinic, Boston, 1972-79; pres., chief exec. officer Leonard Morse Health System, Natick, Mass., 1980-85, Leominster (Mass.) Health System, 1985—; pres. Wathne Health Strategists, 1992—; adj. asst. prof. Boston U., 1981—; pres. Cen. New. Eng. PHO, Leominster, 1991—; hosp. cons. Contbr. articles to profl. jours. Mem. Mass. Hosp. Assn. (pres. 1987-88), New Eng. Hosp. Supts. Club (pres. 1986-88), North Cen. Mass. C. of C. (dir. 1988-91), Harvard Club. Home: 6 Colony Rd Lexington MA 02173-2004 Office: Leominster Health System Hospital Dr Leominster MA 01453

WATKINS, DAVID, information systems consultant; b. Manhattan, N.Y., May 22, 1966; s. Henry Charles and Jacqueline (Slevens) W.; m. Lillian M. Valls, June 22, 1991. BBA in Fin., U. Mass., 1988. Analyst, cons. Andersen Cons., Boston, 1988-90; sr. cons. Ernst & Young, Boston, 1990—. Mem. Lions (exec. bd. 1989—). Home: 85 E India Row Boston MA 02110-3320 Office: Ernst & Young 200 Clarendon St Boston MA 02116-5021

WATKINS, EUGENE LEONARD, surgeon, educator; b. Worcester, Mass., Jan. 4, 1918; s. George Joseph and Marcella Katherine (Akels) W.; A.B. with honors in biology, Clark U., 1940; M.D. (Hood scholar), Harvard U., 1943; m. Victoria Peake, Sept. 23, 1944; children—Roswell Peake, Priscilla Avery. Intern, Roosevelt Hosp., N.Y.C., 1944; resident in surgery, 1944-46, sr. asst. resident in surgery, 1948-49, resident surgery, 1949-50; fellow in surgery, clin. research fellow, Mass. Gen. Hosp., Boston, 1947-48; practice medicine specializing in surgery, N.Y.C., 1950-56, Morristown, N.J., 1950—, Denville, N.J., 1956-85, Boonton, N.J., 1961-85; mem. staff Morristown Meml. Hosp., 1950, vice chmn. dept. surgery, 1974-77, chmn., 1959-61, mem. corp.; cons. surgeon St. Clare's Hosp., Denville, N.J., Riverside Hosp., Boonton, N.J., Community Med. Center, Morristown; courtesy surg. staff St. Luke's-Roosevelt Hosp. Center, N.Y.C.; asst. clin. prof. surgery Rutgers U. Coll. Medicine and Dentistry, New Brunswick, N.J., 1972-85; asst. clin. prof. surgery Columbia Coll. Phys. and Surg., 1985—; v.p. chmn. fin. com. Morristown Bd. Health, 1954-56. Served to 1st lt., AUS, 1946. Diplomate Am. Bd. Surgery. Fellow ACS (chmn. N.J. Adv. Com. 1965-77, chmn. N.J. State com. Trauma, 1960); mem. N.J., Morris County med. socs., AMA, Soc. Surgeons N.J. (1st v.p. 1982, pres. 1983), Am. Thoracic Soc., AAAS, Harvard Med. Soc. N.Y. (pres. 1960-61), West Side Med. Soc., Roosevelt Hosp. Alumni Assn. Republican. Presbyterian. Clubs: Harvard (N.Y.C.), Morristown, Morristown Field. Development spring-loop surg. suture holder. Home: 1062 Soldier Creek Rd Wolf WY 82844

WATKINS, GILBERT KIM, accountant; b. Norwalk, Conn., July 29, 1952; s. Gilbert Harold and Monica Ann (Parker) W.; m. Anne Martin, Apr. 26, 1975; children: Gregory Gilbert, Sarah Martin, Geoffrey Robert. BS, Fairfield (Conn.) U., 1974. CPA, Conn. Acct. Arthur Young & Co., Stamford, Conn., 1974-78; sr. acct. H.M. Green & Co., Norwalk, 1978-79; ptnr. Schwartz & Hofflich, Norwalk, 1979—; sec., bd. dirs. Community Acctg. Aid and Services, Inc., Hartford, Conn., 1982-85. Treas. Community House, Inc., Norwalk, 1985-88, Grace Episcopal Ch., Norwalk, 1987—. Mem. AICPA, Conn. Soc. CPA's, Rotary (pres. Norwalk 1989-90, bd. dirs. 1984-91). Republican. Episcopalian. Home: 12 Kreiner Ln Norwalk CT 06850-1525 Office: Schwartz & Hofflich 37 North Ave Norwalk CT 06851-3827

WATKINS, JAMES DAVID, government official, naval officer; b. Alhambra, Calif., Mar. 7, 1927; s. Edward Francis and Louise Whipple (Ward) W.; m. Sheila Jo McKinney, Aug. 19, 1950; children: Katherine Marie, Laura Jo, Charles Lancaster, Susan Elizabeth, James David, Edward Francis. BS, U.S. Naval Acad., 1949; MS, Naval Postgrad. Sch., 1958; LHD (hon.), Marymount Coll., 1982, N.Y. Med. Coll., 1988; DSc (hon.), Dowling Coll., 1983, U. Ala., 1991; LLD (hon.), Cath. U., 1985. Commd. ensign USN, 1949, advanced through grades to adm., 1979, comdg. officer U.S.S. Snook, 1964-66, exec. officer U.S.S. Long Beach, 1967-69; head submarine/nuclear power distbn. control br. Bur. Naval Pers., Dept. Navy, Washington, 1969-71, dir. enlisted pers. div., 1971-72; asst. chief of naval pers. for enlisted pers. control Bur. Naval Personnel, Dept. Navy, Washington, 1972-73; comdr. Cruiser-Destroyer Group 1 USN, 1973-75; dep. chief naval ops. manpower Navy Dept., Washington, 1975-78, chief of naval pers., 1975-78, chief Bur. Naval Pers., 1975-78; comdr. U.S. Sixth Fleet USN, 1978-79; vice chief naval ops. Navy Dept., 1979-81, comdr.-in-chief U.S. Pacific Fleet, 1981-82, chief naval ops., 1982-86; chmn. Presdl. Commn. on Human Immunodeficiency Virus Epidemic, 1987-88; sec. Dept. of Energy, Washington, 1989—. Decorated D.S.M. with 1 gold star, Legion of Merit with 2 gold stars, Bronze Star medal with Combat V; recipient Disting. Alumni award Naval Postgrad. Sch., 1958. Mem. U.S. Naval Acad. Alumni Assn. Roman Catholic. Lodge: Knights of Malta. Office: Dept Energy 1000 Independence Ave SE Washington DC 20585-0001

WATKINS, OLIVER TIMBERLAKE, sales and marketing administrator; b. Wilmington, N.C., Aug. 30, 1928; s. Edison Lee and Maysie Carlton (Gunter) W.; m. Edna Mae Harrell, July 1, 1952 (div. Feb. 1980); m. Kathleen Ann Coole, Aug. 3, 1980; children: Lynsie Annabel, William Woolfolk, Oliver Timberlake Jr., Douglas Lee. BSBA, U. N.C., 1952. From account exec. to retail advt. mgr. Hawaii Star Bull. & Hawaii Newspaper Agy., Honolulu, 1960-65; advt. promotion mgr. Detroit Free Press, 1965-68; market mgr. and account exec. Story & Kelly-Smith, Inc., N.Y.C., 1968-75, v.p. rsch. and sales devel., 1975-76; N.Y. regional mgr. Gannett Newspaper Advt. Sales, N.Y.C., 1976-77, v.p. sales and N.Y. regional mgr., 1977-81; pres. Newspaper Coop Advt., Westport, Conn., 1981-83; dir. of advt. The Washington Times, 1984-90, dir. of corp. sales and mktg., 1990-92, dir. community & corp. rels., 1992—; participant Advt. Age Creative Workshop, Chgo., 1965; mem. nat. adv. seminar AP Inst., Reston, Va., 1978. Mem. Greater Washington Bd. of Trade, 1990-92, D.C. C. of C., Washington, 1990-92, Fairfax (Va.) County C. of C., 1990-92, Leadership of Fairfax Class of 91, 1991-92. With U.S. Army, 1946-48, ETO. Mem. Am. Mktg. Assn. (local bd. dirs. 1985-87), Internat. Newspaper Advt. and Mktg. Execs., Sales and Mktg. Execs. of D.C., Washington Advt. Club. Republican. Episcopalian. Home: 13902 Marblestone Dr Clifton VA 22024 Office: The Washington Times Corp 3600 New York Ave NE Washington DC 20002

WATKINS, ROBERT WAYNE, pharmacologist; b. Norfolk, Va., Dec. 19, 1949; s. Robert Vaden and Marjorie Anne (Stakes) W.; m. Carmella Jane Blades, Aug. 30; children: Christine Virginia, Jeffrey Ryland. BS in Chemistry, Old Dominion U., 1973; PhD in Pharmacology, Wake Forest U., 1977. Cert. in physiology. Cardiovascular trainee, postdoctoral fellow in pharmacology U. Miami Sch. Medicine, 1977-78, Fla. Heart Assn. postdoctoral fellow, 1978-79; sr. scientist in cardiovascular pharmacology Schering-Plough, Bloomfield, N.J., 1979-83, prin. scientist, 1983-88, sr. prin. scientist, 1988—; guest lectr. in cardiovascular physiology Fairleigh Dickinson U., 1981-85, adj. assoc. prof. human physiology Coll. Dental Medicine, 1986-89. Contbr. articles to profl. jours. Mem. exec. com. Independence Vol. First Aid Squad, 1986-88, treas., 1986-871 mem. Jane Billows Meml. Scholarship Com., 1988—. Recipient fellowships and awards. Mem. AAAS, Am. Soc. for Hypertension, Am. Chem. Soc. (medicinal chemistry div.), Am. Heart Assn., N.Y. Acad. Scis., Phila. Physiol. Soc., Cardiovascular Discussion Group, Appaloosa Horse Club Am. Republican. Home: RR 1 Box 510B Great Meadows NJ 07838 Office: Schering-Plough Rsch Inst 60 Orange St B-5-2 # 87 Bloomfield NJ 07003

WATLINGTON-COX, ADRIAN DENISE, jewelry expeditor; b. Bklyn., Mar. 10, 1954; d. Armond Roosevelt and Geneva Gladys (Bigelow) W.; m. Philip LeMar Cox, June 30, 1984; 1 child, Philip L. II. BA, Hofstra U., 1976. Asst. to clothing buyer Saks Fifth Ave., N.Y.C., 1976-80; prodn. mgr. Charles Turi, Inc., N.Y.C., 1980-82; expeditor Class Jewelry, N.Y.C., 1982-87, Austern & Paul, Inc., N.Y.C., 1987-91; customer svc. rep. Samuel Aaron Inc., Long Island City, N.Y.C., 1991—. Bd. dirs., 2d v.p. Rochdale Village, Jamaica, N.Y., 1985—. Mem. NAFE, Nat. Coun. Negro Women, Alpha Kappa Alpha. Democrat. Mem. African Methodist Episcopal Ch. Home: 17210 133rd Ave Apt 9B Jamaica NY 11434-3920 Office: Austern & Paul Inc 34-00 47th Ave Long Island NY

WATRAL, DAVID MICHAEL, psychologist, consultant; b. McKeesport, Pa., Oct. 19, 1948; s. Michael and Anna (Kraynak) W.; m. Louise Anne Cressman, Dec. 31, 1976; children: Daniel, Nicole, Marc, Anna, Edward, Michael. BA, Indiana U. of Pa., 1970, MA, 1972; PhD, Temple U., 1979. Diplomate Am. Bd. Med. Psychotherapy. Rsch. coord. C.O.R.A. Svcs., Phila., 1975-77; psychologist Atlantic Mental Health Ctr., McKee City, N.J., 1977-83; sr. psychologist Betty Bacharach Rehab. Hosp., Pomona, N.J., 1983-85, dir. psychology, 1985-88; pvt. practice Hammonton, N.J., 1988—. Capt. USARNG, 1972-78. Mem. APA, N.J. Head Injury Assn. (adv. bd. 1987-90), N.J. Biofeedback Soc. (exec. bd. 1987-89), N.J. Psychol. Assn., N.Y. Acad. Scis., Phila. Neuropsychologic Group. Democrat. Episcopalian.

WATREL, WARREN GEORGE, pharmaceutical company executive; b. N.Y.C., Jan. 5, 1935; s. John and Julia (Rock) W.; children: Marc, Justin, Stephen. BS, Syracuse U., 1957, MS, 1958, postgrad., 1958; postgrad., Columbia U. Gen. sales mgr. Pharmacia AB Sweden, Piscataway, N.J., 1964-65, dir. mktg. and sales, gen. mgr., 1965-72; v.p., gen. mgr. Damon Corp., Vineland, N.J., 1972-74; ops. and mktg. exec. Pharmachem Corp., Bethlehem, Pa., 1974-75; exec. v.p., chief operating officer Newton (N.J.) Industry Inc., 1976-79; v.p. Seton Co., Newark, N.J., 1980-84, George Warren Assocs., Hasbrouck Heights, N.J., 1984—; bd. dirs. Newton Industries, 1976-79; cons. ITT, Paramus, N.J., 1971-72, Jay Holland-Moritz Inc., Hillside, N.Y., 1975, Xonics Inc., L.A., 1975; instr. bacteriology Syracuse (N.Y.) U., 1958. Author: Encyclopedia of Chemistry, 3d edition., 1971. Capt. U.S. Army, 1959-60. Mem. Am. Chem. Soc., AAAS, Am. Soc. Microbiology, N.Y. Acad. Scis., Inst. Chemists. Home: 506 Collins Ave Hasbrouck Heights NJ 07604-2232

WATROUS, PHILIP JORDAN, financial executive; b. Chgo., Apr. 16, 1933; s. Robert Morgan and Blanche (Greene) W.; m. Ann Elizabeth Merchant, Sept. 30, 1955 (div. Jan. 1965); children: Deborah Greene, Wendy Watrous Smith; m. Linda Louise Lenz, Jan. 2, 1982. BS, Yale U., 1958. V.p., sec., treas. Kenton Corp., N.Y.C., 1969-79; pres. P.J. Watrous & Co., Inc., N.Y.C., 1979—; v.p., sec., treas. Internat. Inst. for Med. Scis., N.Y.C., 1980-82, Medizone Internat., Inc., N.Y.C., 1986—; v.p., sec. Trans-Resources, Inc., N.Y.C., 1986—. Trustee Episcopal Diocese of N.Y., 1990—. Cpl. U.S. Army, 1953-55. Mem. Yale Club of N.Y.C. Republican. Episcopalian. Home: 20 W 84th St New York NY 10024-4790 Office: PJ Watrous & Co Inc 685 5th Ave Fl 14 New York NY 10022-4242

WATROUS, ROBERT THOMAS, academic director; b. Cleve., Apr. 20, 1952; s. Frank Thomas and Marie Anne (Kmeicik) W.; m. Robin Joyce Braun, Mar. 14, 1981; 1 child, Michael Francis. BS, U. Dayton, 1974, MS, 1977. Dir. student ctr. for off campus community rels. Univ. Dayton, Ohio, 1974-76; resident dir. Univ. Dayton, 1976-78; dir. of housing St. Bonaventure Univ., Olean, N.Y., 1978-81; asst. dean of student life/housing Kutztown (Pa.) Univ. of Pa., 1981-86, dir. commuter and jud. affairs, 1986—; faculty senate Kutztown (Pa.) Univ., 1986-89; mem. Pa. Task Force on Intergroup Behavior in Higher Edn., 1991—; trainer Pa. Interagency Task Force on Civil Tension, Harrisburg, Pa., 1989—; exec. coun. Adult Learners Consortium, Bloomsburg, Pa., 1990-91. Bd. mgr. Tri Valley YMCA, Fleetwood, Pa., 1983—; adv. bd. Crossroads, Kutztown, 1989—; bd. dirs. Jr. Achievement of Berks County, Reading, Pa., 1990, Reading and Berks Coun. YMCA, 1992—, mem. Leadership Berks, Reading, 1990. mem. Nat. Assn. Student Pers. Adminstrs. (profl. affiliate), Hawk Mt. Coun. Boy Scouts Am. (sustaining mem.). Office: Kutztown Univ Box 37 Kutztown PA 19530

WATSON, ARTHUR RICHARD, retail executive; b. Cleve., June 25, 1915; s. George Henry and Martha Helen (Rathensperger) W.; m. Ruth Eleanor Garland, Nov. 1939 (div. 1955); 1 child, Lois Ruth Watson Ferber; m. Marybeth Wiemer Anderson, Nov. 2, 1967. Student, Case Western Res. U., 1935-47. Asst. to dir. Cleve. Zoo, 1942-48; dir. Balt. Zoo, 1948-80; pres., owner Zoo Animals Inc., Balt., 1980—; mem. collecting safaris to Africa for gorillas, 1954, for giraffes, 1966. Editor zoo sect. Parks And Recreation mag., 1952-53; host (TV shows) This is Your Zoo, 1949-59, 71-72, (radio show) The Balt. Zoo, 1966-76. Recipient Unsung Pub. Service award McCormick Spice Co., Balt., 1949, Hats Off award Order of DeMolay, Balt., 1956, commendation Am. Legion, Balt., 1958, citation U.S. Hall of Fame Soc., 1968, Pub. Service award Boy Scouts Am., Balt., 1976. Mem. Am. Assn. Zool. Parks and Aquariums, Advt. and Profl. Club of Balt. (Notable Svc. award 1954), St. Georges Soc. of Balt., English Speaking Union. Democrat. Unitarian. Home: 2519 Pickwick Rd Baltimore MD 21207-6637 Office: Harbor Place 201 E Pratt St Baltimore MD 21202-1039

WATSON, BERNARD CHARLES, foundation administrator; m. Lois Lathan, July 1, 1961; children: Barbra, Bernard Jr. BS in History and Polit. Sci., Ind. U., 1951; MEd in Guidance and Ednl. Adminstrn., U. Ill., 1955; PhD in Ednl. Adminstrn. and Sociology, U. Chgo., 1967; postdoctoral in advanced adminstrn., Harvard U., 1968; LHD (hon.), Allen U., 1981, LaSalle U., 1987, Spring Garden Coll., Elizabethtown Coll., Beaver Coll., 1988, Harris-Stowe State Coll., Morris Brown Coll., 1989, Millersville U., 1991; LLD (hon.), Lincoln U., 1974, Fla. Meml. Coll., 1984, Temple U., 1986, Med. Coll. Pa., 1986, Tuskegee U., 1991, Millersville U., 1991, Lincoln U., 1992; HHD (hon.), Wilberforce U., 1979; LLD (hon.), Millersville U., 1991; HHD (hon.), Tuskegee U., 1991; DFA, Univ. of the Arts, 1992; D of Pedagogy, Drexel U., 1992. Tchr., counselor, dir. guidance Roosevelt Jr.-Sr. High Sch., Gary, Ind., 1955-59; prin. Roosevelt Jr. High Sch., Gary, 1960-62; asst. prin. Roosevelt High Sch., Gary, 1962-65; staff assoc. Midwest Adminstrn. Ctr. U. Chgo., 1965-67, chmn. continuing seminar on ednl. adminstrn. Grad. Dept. Edn., 1966-67; dir. innovative programs Office of Planning Sch. Dist. Phila., 1967, assoc. supt. for innovative programs, 1967-68, dep. supt. for planning, 1968-70; prof., chmn. dept. urban edn. Temple U., Phila., 1970-75, also prof. social foundations Coll. Edn. and prof. urban studies Coll. Liberal Arts, 1970-75, v.p. acad. adminstrn., 1976-81; pres.-designate William Penn Found., Phila., 1981, pres., chief exec. officer, 1982—; bd. dirs. Comcast Inc., Comcast Cablevision Phila. Inc., First Fidelity Bancorp., Fidelity Bank, Keystone AAA Club, Keystone Ins. Co., Phila. Contributionship ; mem. vis. com. Grad. Sch. Edn. Bd. Overseers Harvard Coll., Cambridge, Mass., 1981-87, mem. vis. com. dept. Afro-Am. Studies Bd. Overseers, 1974-78, assoc. in edn. Grad. Sch. Edn., 1970-72; mem. fed. judiciary nominating commn. Pa., 1981-89; mem. Nat. Council on Ednl. Research, 1980-82; mem. nat. adv. com. Curriculum Innovations Inc., Chgo., 1969-74; lectr. various univs. Author: In Spite of the System: The Individual and Educational Reform, 1974; editor in chief Cross Reference: A Jour. Pub. Policy and Multi-Cultural Edn., 1976-79; contbr. numerous articles to profl. jours., chpts. to books. Mem. William T. Grant Found. Commn. on Work, Family and Citizenship; vice chmn. Pa. Council on Arts; vice chmn. bd. dirs. Pa. Conv. Ctr. Authority; sr. vice chmn. bd. trustees Nat. Urban League, 1983—; mem. steering com., exec. com. Nat. Urban Coalition, Washington, 1973-89; bd. mgrs. St. Christopher's Hosp. for Children, Phila., 1978-81; trustee Lincoln (Pa.) U., 1975-78, Cheyney State Coll., Pa., 1975-77, Edn. Law Ctr. Inc. Rutgers U., N.J., 1973-76; mem. adv. bd. Ctr. for Urban and Minority Affairs Tchrs. Coll. Columbia U., N.Y.C., 1973-77; bd. dirs., mem. exec. com. Greater Phila. Partnership, 1977-83, co-chmn., 1975-77; Univ. City Sci. Ctr./Inst., 1980-81; bd. dirs. World Affairs Council Phila., 1980-81, Phila. Council for Community Advancement, 1977-81, Pub. Interest Law Ctr. Phila., 1975-81. Served to 1st lt. USAF, 1951-54. Recipient Benjamin Hooks award NAACP Life Membership Com., Outstanding Educator award Nat. Assn. Black Sch. Educators, Cecil B. Moore Community Service award Barristers Assn. Phila., Horace Mann award Antioch U., Achievement award Nat. Assn. Black Accountants, City of Phila Bowl award, 1981, Legion of Merit award Chapel of Four Chaplains, 1982, Achievement award Nat. Black MBA Assn., 1983, citation Gov. Commonwealth of Pa., Community Service award Frontiers Internat. Inc., Ednl. Leadership award U. Pa. Grad. Sch. Edn., 1984, Hobart C. Jackson award Phila. Inter-Alumni Council United Negro Coll. Fund Inc., 1985, Disting. Nat. Leadership award Nat. Urban Coalition, 1986, Whitney M. Young Jr. Leadership award Urban League Phila., 1986, Torch of Liberty award Phila. Soc. Fellows Anti-Defamation League, 1987, Drum Major award for Beloved Community Phila. Martin Luer King Jr. Ctr. for Nonviolence, 1989, George Washington Carver award Acad. Natural Scis., 1991, Crystal award: Man of the Decade, Afro-Am. Hist. and Cultural Mus., 1991, Phila. Bowl award, 1991, A. Philip Randolph award Nat. Urban Coalition, 1991, Judge William H. Hastie award NAACP Legal Def. Fund, 1991, Nat. Leadership award Children's Def. Fund, 1992, Russell H. Conwell award Temple U., 1992; Bernard C. Watson Seminar Room and Scholarships named in his honor, Temple U., Phila., 1981. Mem. Am. Philos. Soc., Am. Acad. Polit. and Social Sci., N.J. Acad. for Aquatic Scis. (bd. dirs., sec. 1988—), Phi Delta Kappa, Kappa Delta Pi. Office: William Penn Found 1630 Locust St Philadelphia PA 19103-6305

WATSON, CHARLOTTE BUSHNELL, import/export consultant, wholesale company executive; b. Phila., Nov. 24, 1943; d. George Smith Watson and Helen Elise (Wilmer) Hilbert; 1 child, Edward Giulian Pecelli. BS, John Hopkins U., 1969; MPhil in Philosophy, Grad. Ctr. CUNY, 1980, D of Polit. Sci., 1985; cert. in internat. trade, NYU, 1989. Cert. Italian lang. tchr. Grad. asst. Bklyn. Coll., 1972-76; adj. lectr. Hunter Coll., N.Y.C., 1976-80; pres. TMS Imports, N.Y.C. and Irvington, Va., 1985-90, Bushnell Assocs., N.Y.C., 1990—; adj. asst. prof. mgmt. NYU, 1990—;

cons. ind. Italian Mfgrs., 1982—. Author: The Politics of Agrarian Assistance in Italy, 1985. Mem. Am. Polit. Sci. Assn. Office: Bushnell Assocs 24 Strong Pl Brooklyn NY 11231-3757

WATSON, CLARISSA ALDEN, author, consultant, gallery owner and director; b. Ashland, Wis.; d. Arthur John Hanson and Berenice (Miars) Waterson; m. Edward Louis Watson; children: Robin Picarle, Alden Wentworth. BA, Milw. Downer Coll. art advisor Adelphi U., Garden City, N.Y., 1971-73; trustee Nassau Mus. Fine Art, Roslyn, N.Y., 1980-84, Heckscher Mus., Huntington, N.Y., 1984-87. Author: The Sensuous Carrot, 1975, The Fourth Stage Gainsborough Brown, 1976, Bishop in the Back Seat, 1980, Runaway, 1985, Last Plane from Nice, 1987, Somebody Killed the Messenger, 1988. Mem. Mystery Writers Am. Republican. Episcopalian.

WATSON, EDWARD DONALD, elementary school educator; b. Trenton, N.J., Feb. 14, 1932; s. Alfred Breece and Jennie (Smith) W.; m. Joyce Leslie Stockton, Oct. 4, 1980; 1 child, Michelle; divorced; children: Diane, Donna, David. BS in Elem. Edn., Kutztown U., 1952; MEd in Elem. Edn., Pa. State U., State College, 1956; EdD in Tchr. Edn., Rutgers U., 1962. Cert. elem. edn., Pa. Tchr. Neshaminy Sch. Dist., Pa., 1952-57; from demonstration tchr. to prof. elem. edn. Trenton (N.J.) State Coll., 1957—. Conducted numours workshop programs, 1985-87. Contbr. articles to profl. jours. With U.S. Army, 1952-54. Recipient Alumni Citation award Kutztown U., 1964. Mem. NEA, N.J. Edn. Assn., N.J. Coun. Edn., Internat. Coun. for Computers Edn., Phi Delta Kappa. Home: 10 Shelly Ln Morrisville PA 19067-7320 Office: Trenton State Coll Trenton NJ 08625

WATSON, GEORGE ELDER, III, ornithologist; b. N.Y.C., Aug. 13, 1931; s. George Elder, Jr. and Forsyth (Patterson) W.; m. Louisa Carter Johnson, Dec. 10, 1966; children: Elisabeth Carter, George Elder IV. BA, Yale U., 1953; postgrad., Am. Sch. Classical Studies, Athens, 1953-54, 58-60; MS, Yale U., 1961, PhD, 1964. Asst. curator Nat. Mus. Nat. History, Smithsonian Instn., Washington, 1962-64, assoc. curator, 1964-65, curator of birds, 1966-85, chmn. dept. of vertebrate zoology, 1967-72; ornithological cons., 1985—. Author: Birds of the Tropical Atlantic Ocean, 1966, Birds of the Antarctic and Sub-Antarctic, 1975; co-author: Birds of the World, Vol. 11, 1986, Preliminary Field Guide to the Birds of the Indian Ocean, 1963, Antarctic Mapo Folio 14, Birds of the Antarctic and Sub-Antarctic, 1971; contbr. bird articles to Ency. Americana, Ency. Britannica; contbr. articles to profl. jours. Recipient rsch. grants and contracts NSF, Office of Naval Rsch., Army Rsch. Office. Fellow Am. Ornithologist's Union (sec. 1973-77, coun. 1977-80, v.p. 1984-85); mem. AAAS, Cooper Ornithol. Soc., Wilson Ornithol. Soc., Brit. Ornithol. Union, Deutsche Ornithologen Gesellschaft (corres. mem.), Washington Biologists Field Club (pres. 1981-84), Cosmos Club (governing bd. 1981-84), Nat. Geographic Soc. (mem. com. on rsch. and exploration 1975—). Home: 4323 Cathedral Ave NW Washington DC 20016-3560

WATSON, JAMES LOPEZ, federal judge; b. N.Y.C., May 21, 1922; s. James S. and Violet (Lopez) W.; m. D'Jaris Hinton Watson, July 14, 1956 (dec. Nov. 1989); children: Norman, Karen, Kris. B.A. in Govt, N.Y. U., 1947; LL.B., Bklyn. Law Sch., 1951. Bar: N.Y. bar 1951. Mem. N.Y. Senate from 21st Senatorial Dist., 1954-63; judge Civil Ct. N.Y., 1964-66; acting judge N.Y. State Supreme Ct., 1965; judge U.S. Customs Ct., 1966-80, U.S. Ct. Internat. Trade, 1980—. Bd. dirs. N.Y.C. Police Athletic League. Served with inf. AUS, World War II, ETO. Decorated Purple Heart, Combat Inf. badge. Mem. ABA, N.Y. State Bar Assn., Fed. Bar Council, World Peace Through Law. Home: 676 Riverside Dr New York NY 10031-5529 Office: US Ct Internat Trade 1 Federal Pla New York NY 10007

WATSON, JERRY CARROLL, advertising executive; b. Greenville, Ala., Aug. 22, 1943; s. William J. and Georgia Katherine (Mixon) W.; m. Judith Zeigler Brooks, Sept. 16, 1988. BS, U. Ala., Tuscaloosa, 1967. Staff writer Phillips, Eindhoven, The Netherlands, 1967-68; mgr. mktg. Fuller & Dees Mktg., Montgomery, Ala., 1968-70; v.p. Univ. Programs, Washington, 1970-73; pres. Coll. & Univ. Press, Washington, 1973-80; ptnr. Watson & Hughey Co., Alexandria, Va., 1981—; bd. dirs. Foxhall Corp., The Art Co., The Mustigue Co. Founding mem. Am. Inst. Cancer Rsch. Mem. Direct Mktg. Assn., Non-Profit Mailer Fedn., Promotional Mktg. Assn., Assn. Direct Response Fund Raising Coun., Am. Forestry Assn., Nature Conservancy, Sierra Club, Falls Church (Va.) C. of C. (bd. dirs.), Phi Kappa Psi. Home: 850 Dolley Madison Blvd Mc Lean VA 22101-1821 Office: Watson & Hughey Co 510 King St Ste 515 Alexandria VA 22314-3183

WATSON, KATHARINE JOHNSON, art museum director, art historian; b. Providence, Nov. 11, 1942; d. William Randolph and Katharine Johnson (Badger) W.; m. Paul Luther Nyhus, Dec. 17, 1983; stepchildren: Kristina Victoria, Karen Ida, Katharine Ellen. BA, Duke U., 1964; MA, U. Pa., 1967, PhD, 1973. Teaching asst. U. Pa., 1966-67; instr., curator exhbns. U. Pitts., 1969-70; curator of art before 1800 Allen Meml. Art Mus., Oberlin, Ohio, 1973-77; lectr. Oberlin Coll., 1973-77; dir. Peary-MacMillan Artic Mus. Bowdoin Coll., Brunswick, Maine, 1977-83, dir. Mus. of Art, 1977—; trustee Mus. Art of Ogonquit, 1977-89, Regional Art Conservation Lab., Williamstown, 1977-90, Surf Point Found., York, Maine; mem. Smithsonian Coun. Author: Pietro Tacca, 1983; author text for exhbn. catalogues; co-editor: Allen Meml. Art Mus. Bull, 1974-77; contbr. articles to profl. jours. Mem. profl. adv. com. Victoria Soc. Maine; mem. adv. coun. Archives of Am. Art, 1982-90. Kress Found. fellow, 1967-68, Chester Dale Fellow, 1970-71, Am. Coun. Learned Socs. fellow, 1977-78, Villa I Tatti fellow, 1977-78. Mem. Am. Assn. Art Mus. Dirs., Am. Assn. Museums, Coll. Art Assn. Office: Bowdoin Coll Mus Art Walker Art Bldg Brunswick ME 04011

WATSON, MARK CHRISTOPHER, educator; b. Honesdale, Pa., Dec. 17, 1968; s. Marvin Herman and Gertrude (Bartenbach) W. AA, Williamsport Area Community Co, 1989; BS, Pa. State U., 1992. Mechanic Watson Bros. Garage, White Mills, Pa., 1984—; tchr. Wallenpaupack Area Sch. Dist., Hawley, Pa., 1991—. Mem. Am. Vocat. Assn., Vocat. Indsl. Clubs of Am. (advisor 1991-92, pres. 1989-90, Leader of the Yr. 1990), Golden Key. Home: Box 59 White Mills PA 18473 Office: Wallenpaupack Area Sch Dist HC 6 Box 6075 Hawley PA 18428

WATSON, RALPH EVANS, management consultant; b. Englewood, N.J., Jan. 16, 1940; s. Thomas S. and Nancy Evans Watson; m. Sheila Valtz, Nov. 26, 1966 (dec. Mar. 1977); children: Lucas, Nicole; m. Deirdre Stillman Marsters, Aug. 18, 1978; children: Jamie McCleary, Kate McCleary. BA, Brown U., 1962. Mgr. mktg., advt. and pub. rels. Chase Manhattan Bank, N.Y.C., 1963-69; div. pres. Decision Tech., Cambridge, Mass., 1969-71; pres., chief exec. officer Powerbase Systems, N.Y.C., 1971-84; v.p., bus. mgr. Citibank, N.Y.C., 1984-86; div. exec., gen. mgr. Ashton Tate, East Hartford, Conn., 1986-88; mng. ptnr. Mktg. Corp. Am., Westport, Conn., 1988—. Advance man Nixon for Pres. campaign, 1968. Mem. Country Club of New Canaan, Sakonnet Golf Club, Sakonnet Yacht Club. Republican. Episcopalian. Home: 81 Canoe Hill Rd New Canaan CT 06840-3702

WATSON, ROBERT JAY, university dean; b. New Castle, Pa., Jan. 26, 1949; s. John A. and G. Irene (Hockenberry) W.; m. Karen McKeag, June 1, 1974; children: Katherine I., Laura J., Emily E. BS, Slippery Rock (Pa.) U., 1970; MEd, Johns Hopkins U., 1972; PhD, U. Pitts., 1979. Cert. secondary biology tchr., Md. Tchr. Anne Arundel County Schs., Annapolis, Md., 1970-72; asst. dean men, asst. registrar Slippery Rock U., 1972-79, asst. dean grad. and spl. acad. programs, 1979-82, assoc. dean spl. acad. programs, 1982-85, dean acad. svcs., 1985—; chmn. Pa./Am. Coll. Testing, Albany, N.Y., 1988—; dean Jumonville Family Week Coun., Hopwood, Pa., 1988-91. Author: Slippery Rock State College: The Legend behind the Name, 1981. Lay leader United Meth. Ch., Slippery Rock, 1983-86, chmn. adminstrv. bd., 1984-86, counselor univ. student group, 1985-91, counselor youth group, 1991—. Recipient Outstanding Alumnus award State Coll. Alumni Assn., 1990. Mem. Slippery Rock U. Alumni Assn. (bd. dirs. 1976-90, pres. 1989-90, Outstanding Alumnus award 1981), Ruffed Grouse Soc. (pres. 1986-87), Masons. Republican. Home: RR 5 Box 9100 Slippery Rock PA 16057-9102 Office: Slippery Rock U Lowry Ctr Slippery Rock PA 16057

WATSON, ROBERT JONES, state government executive; b. Corvallis, Oreg., Sept. 27, 1929; s. Harry and Ella (Fleming) Jones; m. Patricia Lois Spaulding, May 22, 1946. BA, Willamette U., 1957. Adminstr. Oreg. Corrections Div., Salem, 1976-85; commnr. Del. Dept. Correction, Smyrna, 1987—; nat. chmn. Commn. on Accreditation, Rockville, Md., 1979-81. Mem. Assn. State Correctional Adminstrs. (nat. pres. 1981-82), Am. Correctional Assn., (bd. govs. 1985, E.R. Cass Achievement award 1989). Home: 31 S Delaware St Smyrna DE 19977-1356

WATSON, ROYCE ANDREW, retired federal official; b. N.Y.C., Mar. 8, 1932; s. Robert Dealing and Kristen Marie (Johansen) W.; m. Edith Christine Luik, Aug. 29, 1964; children: Paul Andrew, Gayle Ellen, Jeanne Marie. BS, U. Miami, Coral Gables, Fla., 1954; MT, U. Miami, 1956; BBA, U. Miami, Coral Gables, Fla., 1967, MBA, 1968; PhD, Fla. State U., 1971. Lic. lab. dir., Fla.; ordained to ministry Luth. Ch. as deacon, 1985. Dir. clin. anatomical and blood bank Dept. of Hosps., Miami, Fla., 1957-68; dir. health svcs. planning and state programs Gov.'s Office, Tallahassee, 1968-72; project officer Nat. Ctr. Health Svcs. Rsch., Washington, 1972-78, br. chief, 1978-81; chief advisor Office Asst. Sec. for Health and Surgeon Gen. HHS, Washington, 1981-90, ret., 1990; pres. Watson & Assocs., Gaithersburg, Md., 1985—. Author: Foundations in Relation to Their Partial Involvment in the Financing of the Health Field, 1971; co-author: Medical Education in Florida: Examination of the Issues, 1964, and others. Deacon Good Shepherd Luth. Ch., Gaithersburg, 1985—; bd. dirs. Nat. Chamber Orch., Washington, 1986-92; pres. Bethesda chpt. 445 Nat. Soujourers, Bethesda, 1991—. 1st lt. USMC, 1950-60. Fellow Royal Soc. Health; mem. Am. Soc. for Med. Tech. (pres. Fla. div. 1970-72, Mem. of Yr. award 1972, 86, numerous leadership positions on local, state and nat. levels), Md. Soc. Med. Tech. (pres. 1981-86, Mem. of Yr. award 1983, 84), Montgomery County Agrl. Fair (life), Fla. Edn. Found. (life), Alpha Mu Tau, Alpha Kappa Psi, Masons (past master R.W., active youth orgns., Rainbow Girls, Jobs Daughters, Master Mason of Yr. 1984, Lamb award 1980, Chevalier award 1985, Cross of Colors, recipient other nat. awards). Republican. Lutheran. Home: 16728 Shea Ln Gaithersburg MD 20877

WATSON, STEVEN CHRISTOPHER, computer executive; b. N.Y.C., June 18, 1949; s. Francis Xavier and Olga Johanna (Olsen) W.; m. Marjorie Augenbraum, July 14, 1985 (div. Feb. 1989). BS, Worcester Poly. Inst., 1971; MBA, Harvard U., 1977, MPA, 1991. Controller Digital Equipment Corp., Geneva, Switzerland, 1977-82; regional mktg. mgr. Digital Equipment Corp., Maynard, Mass., 1982-83; compensation mgr. Bank of Boston, 1983-84; pres. Euro-Software Svcs., Inc., Boston, 1984-87; v.p. Computerland Corp., Oakland, Calif., 1987-88; pres. Go Technologies Inc., Incline Village, Nev., 1988; mng. dir. SW Assocs., Boston, 1988-91; v.p. internat. Software Developers Co., Inc., Hingham, Mass., 1991—. Com. mem. Citizens Democracy Corps., Washington, 1991—, WPI Master Plan, Worcester, Mass., 1991—. Office: Software Developers Co Inc 90 Industrial Park Rd Hingham MA 02093

WATSON, WARREN EDWARD, library administrator; b. Quincy, Mass., Apr. 5, 1925; s. Eimer Loring and Alice Loretta (Campbell) Watson; m. Elizabeth Mary Paul. AB, Boston Coll., 1948, MA, 1950; MLS, Simmons Coll., 1962. Broadcast news editor various radio stas., Mass., R.I., 1950-53; news editor Sta. WJAR-TV, Providence, 1953-55, spl. news assignments, 1958-59; spl. fgn. corr. on Operation Deepfreeze I CBS, Internat. News Svc., 1955-56; tech. writer Lincoln Lab., Lexington, Mass., 1956-58; libr. asst. Boston Pub. Libr., 1959-60, Boston Coll. Lib., 1960-61; asst. dir. Framingham (Mass.) Pub. Libr., 1961-64, dir., 1964-68; dir. librs. Thomas Crane Pub. Libr., Quincy, 1968—; pres. Old Colony Libr. Network, Canton, Mass., 1984-86, Simmons Coll. Grad. Sch. of Libr. and Info. Sci. Alumni Bd., Boston, 1988-89. Contrb. articles to publs. Mem. U.S. Power Squadrons, Raleigh, N.C., 1964—, Quincy (Mass.) Hist. Soc. Aviation Cadet US Army Air Corps, 1943-44. Mem. Mass. Libr. Assn. (pres. 1971), ALA, New England Libr. Assn. Democrat. Home: 7 Dorchester St # 3 Quincy MA 02171-1152 Office: Thomas Crane Pub Libr 40 Washington St Quincy MA 02169-5346

WATSON, WILLIAM CALVIN, JR., architect; b. Shawnee, Okla., Feb. 6, 1938; s. William Calvin and Grace Margaret (Bridges) W.; m. Betty Lou Holt, July 21, 1955; children: Vicki Lynn Watson Gilly, Cynthia Gayle Watson Bubba, Shelly Dianne. BArch, Okla. State U., 1961. Registered architect, Pa., N.J., Md., Del., N.C. Designer Coston-Frankfurt-Short, Oklahoma City, 1961-63, chief designer, Bethlehem, Pa., 1963-67; assoc. Coston-Wallace, Bethlehem, 1967-70; ptnr. Coston-Wallace-Watson, Bethlehem, 1970-73; prin. Wallace & Watson Assocs., Bethlehem, 1973-79, prin., sec.-treas., 1979-88; pres., chief exec. officer, 1988—; adj. prof. Lehigh U., Bethlehem, 1979. Bd. dirs. Lehigh Valley Indsl. Park, Bethlehem, 1979-86, 1991—, Baum Sch. of Art; chmn. bd. dirs. Easter Seal Soc., Lehigh Valley, Pa.; mem. adv. bd. dirs. Northhampton County Area Community Coll., Bethlehem; mem. found. bd. Northampton Community Coll., 1990—. Mem. Pa. Soc. Architects, AIA (pres. eastern Pa. chpt. 1976). Democrat. Moravian. Club: Bethlehem (bd. dirs. 1981-84). Club: Lehigh Country. Lodge: Kiwanis (pres. 1975-76). Avocations: sailing; models. Home: 41 E Wall St Bethlehem PA 18018-6012 Office: Wallace & Watson Assocs 609 Hamilton Mall Ste 200 Allentown PA 18101-2189

WATT, CHARLES VANCE, development, marketing and public relations; b. Wilmington, Del., Aug. 7, 1934; s. Henry Vance and Nancy Paule (Beck) W.; m. Diana Mae Bates, Apr. 3, 1964; children: Steven Vance, Kristin Marie. AA, St. Petersburg (Fla.) Jr. Coll., 1957; BS, U. Fla., 1959; postgrad., Case Western Res. U., 1959-60. Mgr. lab. contract dept. Am. Hosp. Supply corp., Edison, N.J., 1960-69; dir. sales and mktg. Alberene Stone div. Ga. Marble, Schuyler, Va., 1969-72; pres. Watt Assocs., Charlotte, N.C., 1972-79; dir. planned giving Open Doors With Bro. Andrew, Greensboro, N.C., 1979-82, The Salvation Army, Oklahoma City, 1982-84; pres. Devel. Resource Group, Edmond, Okla., 1984-86; pres. devel. and mktg. Elyria (Ohio) United Meth. Home, 1986-89; dir. devel. and pub. rels. Masonic Homes of Grand Lodge F.& A.M. Pa., Elizabethtown, 1989-92; pres. Cardinal Assocs., Ltd., Elizabethtown, 1992—; bd. dirs. Reconciliation Ministries, Inc., Elyria, 1986—. Cons. United Cerebral Palsy, Oklahoma City, 1984-86, Edmond Youth Coun., 1985-86, Drug Rehab. Program, Oklahoma City, 1985-86; pres. Edmond Crimestoppers Assn., 1985-86; chmn. bd. Labor/Mgmt. Prayer Ministry, Elyria, 1987-89; bd. dirs. Lorain County Arts Coun., Elyria, 1988-89; mem. adv. bd. Salvation Army, Elyria, 1988-89. With USN, 1952-55. Named to Hon. Order Ky. Cols., 1982. Mem. Nat. Soc. Fund Raising Execs. (pres. Okla. chpt. 1985-86), Assn. for Healthcare Philanthropy, Internat. Platform Assn., Pa. Assn. Non-Profit Homes for the Aging, Nat. Planned Giving Assn. (chartered), Christian Legal Soc. (assoc.), Elizabethtown Cen. Bus. Dist. Commn. (vice. chmn.), Elizabethtown C. of C. (pres.), Cosmopolitan Internat., Rotary. Office: Cardinal Assocs Ltd 4943 Bossler Rd Elizabethtown PA 17022-9452

WATT, WILLIAM BUELL, air transportation safety executive; b. Portland, Oreg., Jan. 13, 1919; s. William G. and Florence R. (Nelson) W.; m. Barbara L. Pfaender, June 28, 1942; children: William B., Linda K., Pamela J. McBride. LLB, U. Akron, 1958. Cert. airline transport pilot. Trainee US Bancorp, Portland, Oreg., 1936-41; flight dept. mgr. ITT, N.Y.C., 1945-54, Hoover Co., North Canton, Ohio, 1954-61, AT&T, N.Y.C., 1961-68; exec. v.p. Exec. Air Fleet, Teterboro, N.J., 1968-86; pres. Aviation Consulting Inc., Teterboro, 1986-90, Fleet Safety Internat., Franklin Lakes, N.J., 1988—; lectr. Am. Mgmt. Assn., N.Y.C., 1982—. Contbr. articles to profl. jours. Scout leader Boy Scouts Am., Canton, 1956-60; treas. Nat. Air Transp. Assn., Arlington, Va., 1985-88. Capt. USAF, 1942-46, NATOUSA. Mem. Nat. Bus. Aircraft Assn. (bd. dirs. 1970—, Doswell award 1989), Flight Safety Found. (bd. dirs. 1971—), Wings Club (N.Y.C.), Aero Club (Washington), Quiet Birdmen (N.Y.C.). Home and office: 829 Aztec Trl Franklin Lakes NJ 07417-2101

WATTEL, HAROLD LOUIS, economics educator; b. Bklyn., Sept. 30, 1921; s. David Max and Carolyn (Abrams) W.; m. Sara Gordon, Sept. 1, 1946; children: Karen, Jill. B.A., Queens Coll., 1942; M.A., Columbia U., 1947; Ph.D. magna cum laude, New Sch. Social Research, 1954. Jr. economist WPB, 1942; economist Dept. Agr., 1946; econ. cons. Boni, Watkins & Mounteer, 1952; economist Bur. Bus. and Community Research, Hofstra U., 1954, 57, dir., 1957-58; prof. econs. Bur. Bus. and Community Rsch., Hofstra U., 1957-86, prof. emeritus, 1986—, chmn. dept. econs., 1957-61, chmn. div. bus., 1961—, dean Sch. Bus., 1965-73; econ. cons. to consumer counsel, staff Gov. N.Y., 1956-58; cons. N.Y. State Moreland Commn. on Alcoholic Beverage Control Law, 1963-64, Legislative Reference Bur., U. Hawaii, 1966, Schenley Industries, 1967—, Ralston Purina Co., 1967—, Am. Can Co., 1965—; econ. cons. Nat. Millinery Planning Bd., 1959-70; ednl. cons. U.S. Mcht. Marine Acad., Kings Point, 1972, Bulova Watch Co., 1975-82. Author ann. publ.: The Millinery Industry; Editor: Planning in Higher Education, 1975, Chief Executive Officer Compensation, 1978, The Gross Personal Income Tax, 1981; Contbr. chpts. to books, encys., dictionaries, also reports.; Editor, contbr.: L.I. Bus, 1954-59. Mem. Comprehensive Health Planning Coun., 1970-75; bd. dirs., v. p., N.Y. State unit Am. Lung Assn.; pres. Nassau-Suffolk unit; bd. dirs. Comprehensive Health Planning Coun., Nassau-Suffolk, N.Y., N.Y. State Citizen Coun., Consumer Farmer Found., Regional Med. Program Nassau-Suffolk, consumer rep., bd. dirs. Island Peer Rev. Orgn. , 1990. Lt. USNR, 1942-46. Edn. fellow, 1949; Hazen Found. fellow, 1952; Ford Found. regional fellow, 1960. Mem. Middle Atlantic Assn. Colls. Bus. Adminstrn. (pres. 1970-71), Am., Met. econs. assns., Am. Assn. U. Profs. (chpt. pres. 1953), N.Y. State Environ. Health Assn. (v.p.), Coop. Extension Assn. Nassau County (pres. 1984-85), Island Peer Rev. Orgn. (consumer/AARP rep. 1990—), Pi Gamma Mu, Omicron Chi Epsilon, Beta Gamma Sigma (hon. asso.). Home: 181 Shepherd Ln Roslyn Heights NY 11577-2525 Office: Hofstra U Hempstead NY 11550

WATTENBERG, FRANK ARVEY, mathematician; b. N.Y.C., May 16, 1943; s. William W. and Jean A. W.; m. Julie Cheryl Miles Wattenberg, Sept. 1, 1964; children: Martin, Alina. BS, Wayne State U., Detroit, 1964; MS, U. Wis., Madison, 1965, PhD, 1968. Asst. prof. Harvard U., Cambridge, Mass., 1968-71; prof. U. Mass., Amherst, 1971-. Mem. Am. Math. Soc. Office: Univ of Mass Math Dept Amherst MA 01003

WATTENMAKER, RICHARD JOEL, director archives, art scholar; b. Phila., Feb. 22, 1941; s. Nathan H. and Frances (Rynes) W.; m. Eva Augusta Oscarsson, June 25, 1968; children: Adrian Ezra, Barnaby Leo. B.A., U. Pa., 1963; postgrad., The Barnes Found., 1959-66; M.A., NYU Inst Fine Arts, 1965; Ph.D., NYU Inst Arts, 1972. Dir. Rutgers U. Art Gallery, New Brunswick, N.J., 1966-69; chief curator Art Gallery Ont., Toronto, Can., 1972-78; dir. Chrysler Mus., Norfolk, Va., 1979-80, Flint (Mich.) Inst. Arts, 1980-88, Archives of Am. Art, Smithsonian Instn., Washington, 1990—; lectr. Barnes Found., 1991—. Author: The Art of Charles Prendergast, 1968, The Art of Jean Hugo, 1973, Puvis de Chavannes and The Modern Tradition, 1975. Trustee Intermus. Conservation Lab., Oberlin, Ohio, 1982-88; trustee Samuel Yellin Found., Phila., 1983—. Recipient Founders Day award NYU, 1972. Office: Smithsonian Instn Archives of Am Art Washington DC 20560

WATTERS, CHRISTOPHER DEFFNER, biology educator; b. Ironton, Ohio, Dec. 7, 1939; s. Joseph Lawrence and Anna Mae (Lyneman) W.; m. Cynthia Merritt Comb, Aug. 12, 1967; children: Alexander, David, Martin. BS, Notre Dame U., 1961; MS, Princeton U., 1964, PhD, 1966. Instr. Princeton (N.J.) U., 1965-66; rsch. assoc. U. Minn., St. Paul, 1966-68; asst. prf. Middlebury (Vt.) Coll., 1968-73; vis. scientist physiol. lab. Cambridge (Eng.) U., 1973-74; assoc. prof. Middlebury Coll., 1973-78, prof., 1978—, Irene Heinz & John Laporte Given prof. premed. scis., 1983—; vis. prof. dept. physiology U. Colo. Med. Sch., Denver, 1980-81; vis. scientist dept. biochemistry Hannah Rsch. Inst., Ayr, Scotland, 1986-87; mem. rev. panel NSF, Washington, 1986. Commr. CIHE-NEASC, Burlington, Mass., 1976-80; mem. com. examiners Grad. Record Exam.-Biology/Ednl. Testing Svc., Princeton, N.J., 1980—; mem. fellowship rev. Vt. Heart Assn., Burlington, 1977-85; co-chair United Way/Middlebury Coll., 1990—; mem. swim team adv. bd. Middlebury Recreation Dept., 1987—; treas. Champlain Valley Swim League, Burlington, 1991—. Office: Middlebury Coll Dept Biology Middlebury VT 05753

WATTS, JOHN MORTON, JR., fire safety consultant; b. Mineola, N.Y., June 3, 1941; s. John Morton and Mary Morton (Phelps) W.; m. Judith Ann Geisler, Sept. 3, 1966; children: Robert Judson, Alexis Smith. BS, U. Md., 1966; MS, U. Mass., 1973, PhD, 1978. Engr. N.Y. Fire Ins. Rating Orgn., Syracuse, 1961-65; supr. N.Y. Fire Ins. Rating Orgn., N.Y.C., 1966-67; systems analyst Great Am. Ins. Co., N.Y.C., 1967-68; asst. prof. U. Md., College Park, 1973-81; dir. Fire Safety Inst., Middlebury, Vt., 1981—; dep. chief Amherst (Mass.) Fire Dept., 1970-73; systems analyst Ctr. for Fire Rsch., Gaithersburg, Md., 1975-76; vis. academic U. Edinburgh, Scotland, 1979-80. Author: Industrial Fire Hazards Handbook, 1989, Handbook of Fire Protection Engineering, 1989, Fire Protection Handbook, 1991; contbr. articles to profl. jours. Auditor Town of Cornwall, Vt., 1982-87; dir. Vt. Conf. United Ch. of Christ, Burlington, 1988-90; campaign chmn. United Way, Addison County, Vt., 1990. Recipient Air Force ROTC Siver medal Chgo. Tribune, 1963; grantee Nat. Bur. Standards, 1976, Nat. Fire Prevention and Control Adminstrn., 1977. Mem. ASTM (chmn. subcom. 1989—), Nat. Fire Protection Assn. (editor Fire Tech. 1983—), Soc. Fire Protection Engrs. (editorial bd. Jour. Fire Protection Engring. 1989—), Inst. Indsl. Engrs. Office: Fire Safety Inst PO Box 674 Middlebury VT 05753-0674

WATTS, MARY ANN, retired educator; b. Harrisburg, Pa., Sept. 13, 1927; d. Major Allan and Ellana Susan (Robinson) Brown; m. Spencer R. Watts, June 23, 1951; children: Shelley Lynn, Allison Dee, Howard Allan. BS, Cheyney U., 1949; student, Temple U., 1965-67, Pa. State U., 1969-72. Tchr. Harrisburg Sch. Dist., 1949-51, 59-69, Balt. Sch. Dist., 1951-57, tchr. Reading (Pa.) Sch. Dist., 1969-89, mem. sch. dist. dress and discipline code com., 1977-79; corr. Hamburg Item, West Berks Crier. Mem. Bernville Borough Council, 1976—, v.p., 1988—; sec., treas. Berks County Boroughs Assn., 1977—. Mem. NAACP, LWV, Pa. Elected Women's Assn., Pa. Assn. Sch. Retirees, Berks County Assn. Sch. Retiress, Delta Sigma Theta. Democrat. Mem. United Ch. Christ. Clubs: Bernville Woman's (pres. 1978-80, 86-88, Woman of Yr. 1985, Grange Community Svc. award 1988), GNO of Harrisburg.

WATTS, ROSS LESLIE, accounting educator, consultant; b. Hamilton, Australia, Nov. 10, 1942; came to U.S., 1966; s. Leslie R. and Elsie B. (Horadam) W. m. Helen Clare Firkin, Jan. 15, 1966; children: Andrew David, James Michael. B. Commerce with honors (Commonwealth Govt. scholar 1960-65), U. Newcastle (Australia), 1966; MBA (Ford Found. fellow 1967-68), U. Chgo., 1968, PhD, 1971. Audit clk. Forsythe & Co., Newcastle, Australia, 1960-64, acct., 1964-66; instr. Grad. Sch. Bus., U. Chgo., 1969-70; asst. prof. Simon Sch. Mgmt., U. Rochester (N.Y.), 1971-78, assoc. prof., 1978-84, prof., 1984-86; prof. Rochester Telephone Corp., 1986—; prof. commerce U. Newcastle, 1974-76; cons. to bus. firms, 1972—. Contbr. articles on acctg. rsch. to profl. jours.; asso. editor Jour. Acctg. Rsch., 1972-78, Jour. Fin. Econs., 1974-89, Australian Jour. Mgmt., 1976-81; co-editor Jour. Acctg. and Econs., 1979—; mem. adv. bd. Midland Corp. Fin. Jour., 1983-88, Continental Bank Jour. of Applied Corp. Fin., 1988—; mem. editorial bd. Contemporary Acctg. Rsch., 1983-85. Recipient Notable Contbn. award AICPA, 1979, 80, award Alpha Kappa Psi Found., 1985. Mem. Am. Acctg. Assn., Am. Fin. Assn., Inst. Chartered Accts. in Australia. Home: 17 Burncoat Way Pittsford NY 14534-2215 Office: U Rochester Simon Sch Mgmt Wilson Blvd Rochester NY 14620-2241

WATTS, STACY CHYLA, compliance specialist; b. Washington, May 30, 1963; d. Richard Chylon and Dolores Louvenia (Frye) W. BA in Am. Govt., U. Va., 1985; MPA, George Washington U., 1989. Outbound telemktg. rep. Xerox Corp., Arlington, Va., 1985-87, adminstrv. asst., contract trainee, 1987-88; cost acctg. analyst, fin. adminstr. Xerox Corp., McLean, Va., 1988-91, fin. compliance specialist, 1991—. Co-chmn. membership diversification com. Jr. League Washington, 1991. Mem. Am. Soc. Pub. Adminstrs., Am. Bus. Womens Assn., Delta Sigma Theta. Democrat. Methodist. Home: 1407 Juniper St NW Washington DC 20012 Office: Xerox Corp 7900 Westpark Dr Ste 400 Mc Lean VA 22102

WAUGH, RICHARD EARL, banker; b. Winnipeg, Manitoba, Can., Dec. 23, 1947; came to U.S., 1985; s. Earl F. and Francis M. (Richardson) W.; m. Lynne Zenone, Apr. 1974; children: David, Stephen, Christopher. B Commerce with honors, U. Manitoba, Can., 1970; MBA, York U., York, Can., 1974. Corp. rsch. analyst Bank Nova Scotia, Toronto, Can., 1970-72; div. head corp. rsch. Bank Nova Scotia, 1972-73, asst. supr. corp. rsch., 1973-74, supr. equity/rsch., 1974-77, ass.t gen. mgr. Can. corp. banking, 1977-79,

asst. gen. mgr., mgr. Toronto br., 1979-81, asst. gen. mgr. corp. banking, 1981-83, gen. mgr. N. Am. corp. banking, 1983-84; sr. v.p. N.Am. corp. banking, Toronto Bank Nova Scotia, N.Y.C., 1984-85; exec. v.p. Bank Nova Scotia, 1985-91, Bank of Nova Scotia, 1991—; pres., bd. dirs. Bank Nova Scotia Trust Co., N.Y.C., 1988—. Mem. Nat. Club (Toronto), Granite Club (Toronto), Can. Club N.Y., Met. Club. Office: The Bank of Nova Scotia 1 Liberty Pla 165 Broadway New York NY 10006

WAURISHUK, JAMES M., JR., military officer; b. Port Chester, N.Y., Dec. 24, 1954; s. James M. Sr. and Dorothy M. (Gleason) W.; m. Deborah Ann Cathell, Sept. 10, 1983. BA in Behavioral Sci., Nichols Coll., Dudley, Mass., 1977; MS in Internat. Relations, Troy (Ala.) State U., 1986. Enlisted USAF, 1979, advanced through grades to capt.; exec. officer 3372 Tech. Squadron 3372 Sch. Squadron, Chanute AFB, Ill., 1980-81; comdr. Hdqtrs. 3345 Consol. Maintenance Squadron, Chanute AFB, 1981-83; exec. officer 16th Spl. Ops. Squadron, Hurlburt Field, Fla., 1983, 1723 Combat Control Squadron, Hurlburt Field, 1983-84; dep. chief, chief intelligence ops. 1st Spl. Ops. Wing Intelligence Div., Hurlburt Field, 1984-86, chief, 1986; chief contingency support team Hdqtrs. U.S. So. Command Quarry Heights, Republic of Panama, 1986-87; chief Nicaragua Analysis Sect. USAF, 1987-89; asst. chief of staff for intelligence, duty dir. intelligence, dep. chief Latin Am. div., The Pentagon USAF, Washington, 1990-91; asst. to the President, nat. security advisor Nat. Security Coun., The White House, Washington, 1991—. Contbr. articles to mags. Mem. Air Force Assn., Air Commando Assn., Nat. Mil. Intelligence Assn., Nat. Rifle Assn., Council for Inter-Am. Security, Spectre Assn. Republican. Roman Catholic. Office: Hdqtrs US So Command, Quarry Heights Panama 34003

WAWROSE, FREDERICK EUGENE, psychiatrist; b. Binghamton, N.Y., Jan. 23, 1929; s. John Joseph and Marie Johanna (Anton) W.; m. Dorothy Jean Stewart, Sept. ll, 1954; children: John, David, Susan, Stephen, Dorothy. AB cum laude, U. Colo., l950; MD, U. Pa., 1954. Diplomate Am. Bd. Psychiatry and Neurology, Am. Bd. Child Psychiatry. Dir. pre-sch. unit Child Study Ctr., Phila., 1963-64, dir. Ctr., 1964-70; psychiatrist J.C. Blair Hosp., Huntingdon, Pa., 1970—, dir., 1986—; intern Univ. Pa. Hosp., 1954-55; resident in adult psychiatry Inst. of the Pa. Hosp., 1958-61; resident in child psychiatry Child Study Ctr. Phila., 1961-63; psychiatrist State Correctional Inst., Huntington, 197l—, Juniata Valley Mental Health-Mental Retardation Program, Huntington, 970—. Capt. M.C., U.S. Army, l955-57. Fellow Am. Acad. Child Psychiatry; mem. AMA (physicians recognition award l988), Am. Psychiat. Assn., Am. Cad. Psychiatry and Law. Office: JC Blair Hosp Warm Springs Ave Huntingdon PA 16652-2451

WAX, EDWARD L., advertising executive; b. 1937; 2 children: Elizabeth, Alex. BS, Northeastern U., 1959; MBA, U. Pa., 1961. With E.I. DuPont de Nemours, 1955-63; account exec. Compton Advertising, N.Y.C., 1963-68; gen. mgr. Ace Compton Manila, Philippines, 1968-72; sr. v.p. Compton Advertising, N.Y.C., 1972-77; pres. Saatchi & Saatchi Compton Inc. (now Saatchi & Saatchi Advt.), N.Y.C., 1983-88, chief exec. officer, 1983-87, 1988-89, co-chief exec. officer, 1987-88, chmn., 1988-89; pres., chief exec. officer Saatchi & Saatchi Advt. Inc., N.Y.C., 1989—, also bd. dirs.; pres., chief operating officer Richard K. Manoff Inc., later Geers Gross Advertising, 1977-81; exec. v.p. Wells Rich Greene, Inc., 1981-82. Served to capt. signal corps U.S. Army, 1965-67. Office: Saatchi & Saatchi Advt Worldwide 375 Hudson St New York NY 10014-3658

WAX, MICHAEL JAY, chemist; b. Bronx, N.Y., June 12, 1957; s. Marvin and Sandra Barbara (Choda) W.; m. Sandra Mary Waters, Aug. 26, 1988. SB, MIT, 1979; PhD, U. Calif., Berkeley, 1983. Postdoctoral rsch. assoc. Nat. Bus. Stds., Gaithersburg, Md., 1983-85; sr. rsch. chemist W.R. Grace & Co., Columbia, Md., 1985-92; dep. dir. Inst. of Clear Air Cos., Washington, 1992—. Contbr. articles to profl. jours. Patentee in field. Mem. Am. Chem. Soc., Am. Vacuum Soc. Home: 5515 Northfield Rd Bethesda MD 20817 Office: Inst of Clean Air Cos 7379 Rt 32 1707 L St NW Washington DC 20036

WAXENBERG, ALAN M., publisher; b. Davenport, Iowa, Mar. 1, 1935; s. George and Rose Waxenberg; m. Suzanne C. Ecker, Oct. 26, 1958; children: Robin Lynn, Scott Stephen. BA, U. Iowa, 1956. Cen. advt. dir. Look mag., Detroit, 1958-71; mgr. Petersen Pub. Co., Detroit, 1971-72; v.p. nat. advt. dir. Petersen Pub. Co., N.Y.C., 1972-76; pub. Motor, N.Y.C., 1976-79; v.p., pub. Sports Afield, N.Y.C., 1979-82, Good Housekeeping, Hearst Pub. Co., N.Y.C., 1988—, Redbook mag., N.Y.C., 1992—. Active United Jewish Appeal Fedn., Anti-Defamation League, Jr. Achievement, United /fund; bd. dirs. adv. coun. Am. Health Found. Served with U.S. Army, 1956-58. Mem. Am. Advt. Fedn. (bd. dirs.), Mag. Pubs. Assn., Adcraft Club Detroit, U. Iowa Alumni Assn. Clubs: Franklin Hills Country (Franklin, Mich.), Metropolis Country (White Plains N.Y.); University (N.Y.). Office: Good Housekeeping Mag Hearst Mags 959 8th Ave New York NY 10019-3737

WAXLER, ROBERT PHILLIP, educator, consultant; b. Cambridge, Mass., Dec. 16, 1944; s. Felix Benjamin and Helen Ruth (Fonfara) W.; m. Linda Davida Lassoff, June 25, 1967; children: Jonathan Blake, Jeremy Regan. BA, Brown U., 1967; MA, Boston Coll., 1969; PhD, SUNY, Stony Brook, 1976. Instr. Whitman Coll., Walla Walla, Wash., 1974-75; asst. prof. U. Mass., Dartmouth, 1975-80; assoc. prof. Southeastern Mass. U., North Dartmouth, 1980-86, prof. lit., 1986—, asst. dean, 1987-88, assoc. dean, 1988-89; co-dir. Ctr. for Jewish Culture, North Dartmouth, 1981—; ptnr. Communication Mgmt. Co., Inc., South Dartmouth, 1981-85; communication cons. Tricom, Inc., South Dartmouth, 1981-90; chmn. Judaic Studies U. Mass., Dartmouth, 1984—; vis. fellow NEH Princeton U., summer 1983; participant 12th ann. acad seminar Am. Jewish Com., Israel, 1981. Contbg. editor Compass Mag., 1981-85; contbr. lit. and communcation articles to profl. jours. Founding mem. Jewish Student Svc. Ctr., North Dartmouth, 1978-85; mem. steering com. Labor Edn. Ctr., North Dartmouth, 1981—; mem. bd. of regents Mass. Task Force on Undergrad. Experience, Boston, 1988; bd. dirs. Tifereth Israel Synagogue, New Bedford, Mass., 1976-80, Jewish Fedn., New Bedford, 1980-81; co-chmn. Azorean Synagogue Restoration Com., 1989—. NEH summer grantee UCLA, 1978; grantee So. Mass. U. Found. 1984; recipient Eisner Citizenship award Boy Scouts Am., 1987, Richard M. Fontera award Labor Edn. Ctr., 1988, Hon. medal U. of the Azores, 1989. Mem. Mass. Speech Communication Assn. (exec. com. 1984-85). Home: 25 Strathmore Rd North Dartmouth MA 02747-3113 Office: U Mass-Dartmouth Old Westport Rd North Dartmouth MA 02747-2512

WAXMAN, HENRY ALAN, recycling executive; b. Bklyn., May 28, 1945; s. Alfred Irving and Bernice Julie (Sommerfield) W.; m. Gail Shumate, May 3, 1970; children: Francine, David. BA, Bklyn. Coll., 1967. Sales adminstr. Aluminum Co. Am., N.Y.C., 1968-69; industry sales asst. Aluminum Co. Am., Pitts., 1969-73; sales specialist Aluminum Co. Am., L.A., 1973-75; mktg. com. mgr. Aluminum Co. Am., Pitts., 1975-76; mgr. distbr. sales Aluminum Co. Am., Richmond, Ind., 1976-83; pres. Met. Mining Co., Inc., Maspeth, N.Y., 1983—; dir. Met. Mining Co. Maspeth, N.Y., 1983—. Mem. W. Maspeth (N.Y.) Devel. Assn., 1990, Queens (N.Y.), 1991. Recipient Handicapped Employment award N.Y.C., 1984, 85; named Leading Work Release Participant, Town of Hempstead, N.Y., 1990, N.Y. Entrepreneur of Yr., Ernst & Young, Merrill Lynch, Inc., N.Y.C., 1991; Recycling Rsch. grantee, N.Y.C., 1991. Mem. N.Y. State Food Mchts. Assn., Nat. Soft Drink Assn., Assn. Past Consumer Plastic Recyclers (bd. dirs. 1992). Jewish. Home: 12 Hawthorne Rd Larchmont NY 10538-3225 Office: Metropolitan Mining Co Inc 58-30 57th St Maspeth NY 11378

WAXMAN, HERBERT SUMNER, medical educator; b. Boston, Sept. 1, 1936; s. Samuel David and Martha (Jacobs) W.; m. Paula Mae Sagoff, June 26, 1960; children: Matthew, Marcy, Eric. BS in Food Tech., MIT, 1958; MD magna cum laude, Harvard U., 1962. Diplomate Am. Bd. Internal Medicine. Intern in medicine Mass. Gen. Hosp., Boston, 1962-63, asst. resident, 1963-64, resident, 1966-67; rsch. assoc. NIH, Bethesda, Md., 1964-66; fellow in hematology Wash. U. Sch. Medicine, St. Louis, 1967-68; faculty to prof. Temple U. Sch. Medicine, Phila., 1968-77, prof. medicine, dep. chmn. dept. medicine, 1979—; chmn. dept. of medicine Baystate Med. Ctr., Springfield, Mass., 1977-79; prof. medicine Tufts U. Sch. Medicine, 1977-79; chmn. dept. medicine Albert Einstein Med. Ctr., Phila., 1979—; cons. Am. Bd. Internal Medicine, 1989, Nat. Bd. Med. Examiners, 1986—. Editor Medical Knowledge Self-Assessment Program, 1989—; contbr. articles to profl. jours. Advisor Franklin Inst., Phila., 1988; adv. coun. Greater Phila. Health Corps, Phila., 1988-90. With USPHS, 1964-66. Advanced clin. fellowship Am. Cancer Soc., 1968-71. Fellow ACP, Coll. Physicians of Phila.; mem. Am. Fedn. for Clin. Rsch., Am. Soc. Hematology, Solis-Cohen Med. Lit. Soc., Am. Soc. Med. Informatics, Assn. Program Dirs. Internal Medicine (councillor 1989-92, pres.-elect 1992—), Pa. Soc. Hematology and Oncology (sec.-treas. 1987—), Phi Lambda Upsilon, Alpha Omega Alpha. Office: Albert Einstein Med Ctr 5501 Old York Rd Philadelphia PA 19141-3098

WAYMAN, DONALD PAUL, insurance company executive; b. Webster, Mass., Apr. 14, 1957; s. Donald Alan and Teresa Margaret (Drake) W.; m. Donna Marie Hall, Aug. 21, 1982; children: Sarah Ann, Amy Elizabeth. AB in Polit. Sci., Coll. of the Holy Cross, Worcester, Mass., 1979. Underwriter State Mut. Life, Worcester, 1979-81, sr. underwriter, 1981-84, chief underwriter, 1984-87, mgr., 1987-88, dir., 1988—. Apptd. mem. Indsl. Fin. and Devel. Com., Dudley, Mass., 1987, Home Rule Study Com., Dudley, 1989; elected mem. Charter Commn., Dudley, 1990; vice chmn. Rep. Town Com., Dudley, 1988—. Mem. Life Office Mgmt. Assn. (group pension investment products com. 1990—). Roman Catholic. Home: 29 G&S Dr Dudley MA 01571 Office: State Mut Life 440 Lincoln St Worcester MA 01605

WAYNE, BOBBIE JOAN, musician, composer; b. Astoria, N.Y., Jan. 15, 1947; d. Robert Fredrick and Joan Virginia (Mears) W. BA in Music, Juniata Coll., 1969; MFA in Painting, Md. Inst. Art, 1976. Music therapist Pennhurst State Sch. & Hosp., Spring City, Pa., 1969-72, Morristown (Pa.) State Hosp., 1972-74; dir. music therapy Embreeville State Hosp., Coatesville, Pa., 1974-75; dir. activities Dulaney Towson (Md.) Nursing Home, 1975-76; artist N.Y.C., 1976-83, performer, 1983—; tchr. songwriting Westchester Community Coll., Valhalla, N.Y., 1989; artist-in-residence Holy Cross Monastery, West Park, 1991. Creator collage Going Home the Hard Way, 1976 (Balt. biennial); composer, performer, arranger: (mus. recording) Coenties Slip, 1989. Organizer Concert for Hunger, St. Bartholomew's Ch., N.Y.C., 1984, Concert for Friends of Paul, Nyack, N.Y., 1991; performer Benefit for Holy Cross Monastery, West Park, N.Y., 1992. Recipient 2d pl. award Scottish Harp Soc., Alexandria, Va., 1989. Mem. ASCAP, Nashville Songwriters Assn. Internat., Scottish Harp Assn., Hudson River Sloop Clearwater.

WAYNER, PETER CHARLES, JR., chemical engineering educator, consultant; b. Taunton, Mass., Aug. 18, 1934; s. Peter Charles and Stella (Koc) W.; m. Donna Shpikula, Jan. 26, 1963; children—Peter Charles III, Taras, Elizabeth. B.S.Ch.E., Rensselaer Poly. Inst., 1956; S.M.Ch.E., MIT, 1960, Chem. Engr., 1961; Ph.D. in Chem. Enging., Northwestern U., 1963. Research scientist United Aircraft Research Lab., East Hartford, Conn., 1963-65, from asst. prof. to assoc. prof. chem. enging. Rensselaer Poly. Inst., Troy, 1965-76, prof., 1976—; cons. editor Chem. Enging. Progress, 1986-88. Contbr. numerous articles on heat transfer to profl. publs. Served from ensign to lt. (j.g.) USN, 1956-58. Fellow Am. Inst. Chem. Engrs. (chmn. heat transfer and energy conversion div. 1985); mem. ASME, Am. Chem. Soc. Office: Rensselaer Poly Inst Troy NY 12180-3590

WAYNIK, CYRIL, psychiatrist; b. Cape Town, South Africa, May 3, 1928; came to U.S., 1963; s. Louis and Leah (Yuter) W.; m. Loraine Katz; children: Mark, Melanie. MB ChB, U. Cape Town, 1950. Diplomate, Am. Bd. Psychiatry and Neurology. Pvt. practice Fairfield, Conn.; dir. out-patient clinic, Bridgeport (Conn.) Hosp., 1966, 67; chmn. psychiatry, Park City Hosp., Bridgeport, 1970-79. Fellow Am. Psychiat. Assn.; mem. Conn. Psychiat. Soc. (pres. 1979-80). Office: 52 Beach Rd Fairfield CT 06430-6017

WDOWIAK, JOHN S., public relations executive; b. Pitts., Feb. 5, 1963; s. Leo and Sylvia (Kmieciak) W.; m. Corinne Marie Manns, Sept. 15, 1984; children: Sarah Marie, Kelly Ann. BA in Journalism, Duquesne U., 1985. Sportswriter The Pittsburgh Press, 1981-85; asst. dir., pub. rels. Duquesne U., Pitts., 1985-87; dir. devel., pub. rels. St. Peter's Child Devel. Ctrs., Pitts., 1987-90; dir. devel. and pub. rels. Divine Providence Hosp., Pitts., 1990—. Recipient Matrix - Hon. Mention Women in Communcations, Pitts., 1985, Hon. Mention West Pa. Printers Assn., 1987; named Marketer of the Yr., Non-Profit Orgn., Am. Mktg. Assn., Pitts. 1988. Mem. Nat. Soc. Fund Raising Execs., North Side C. of C. Office: Divine Providence Hosp 1004 Arch St Pittsburgh PA 15212-5294

WEARY, THOMAS SQUIRES, lawyer; b. Junction City, Kans., Feb. 15, 1925; s. Ulysses S. and Ina Belle (Kirkpatrick) W.; m. Helen Stephenson, Sept. 25, 1967. A.B. cum laude, Harvard U., 1946, J.D., 1950. Bar: Pa. 1951, U.S. Supreme Ct. 1963. ptnr. Saul, Ewing, Remick & Saul, Phila., 1967—; chief exec. officer Invisible Fence Co., Inc., Wayne, Pa., 1979—; arbitrator Am. Arbitration Assn. Bd. dirs., v.p., gen. counsel Acad. Vocal Arts, Phila.; bd. dirs. World Affairs Council Phila., mem. exec. com., treas.; bd. dirs. Diversified Community Services, Phila. Served to lt. (j.g.) USNR, 1943-49. Recipient Legion of Honor award Chapel of Four Chaplains, Phila., 1982. Mem. Interlex Group (founding ptnr.), Phila. Bar Assn., Pa. Bar Assn., Internat. Law Office Assn., ABA. Presbyterian. Clubs: Racquet, Harvard (dir.) (Phila.); Merion Cricket (Haverford, Pa.); Edgemere (Pike County, Pa.). Office: 3800 Centre Sq W Philadelphia PA 19102-2174

WEAVER, CAROLYN LESLIE, economist, public policy researcher; b. Washington, Jan. 20, 1952; d. Kenneth Faulkner and Margaret Mae (Taylor) Weaver; m. Robert John Mackay, Aug. 12, 1980; children: Taylor Cotesworth, Bennett Faulkner. BA, Mary Washington Coll., 1973; PhD in Econs., Va. Polytech. Inst. & State U., 1977. From instr. to asst. prof. econs. Tulane U., New Orleans, 1976-78; from asst. prof. to assoc. prof. and rsch. assoc. Ctr. for Pub. Choice, Va. Poly. Inst. and State U., Blacksburg, 1978-83; chief profl. staff mem. on social security U.S. Senate Com. on Fin., Washington, 1981-84; sr. rsch. fellow Hoover Instn., Stanford (Calif.) U., Calif., 1984-86; resident scholar, dir. social security & pension project Am. Enterprise Inst., Washington, 1987—; sr. advisor Nat. Commn. on Social Security Reform, 1982-83; cons. U.S. Senate Fin. Com., 1984, Social Security Adminstrn., 1984-85; mem. U.S. Disability Adv. Coun., 1987-88, U.S. Social Security Commrs. Disability Adv. Com., 1989, Social Security Pub. Trustees Working Group on Trust Fund Solvency, 1989-90, Acad. Bd. Avisors Americans for Generational Equity, 1986—, Ind. Inst., 1986—, Retirement Policy Inst., 1989—; founding mem. Nat. Acad. Social Insur., 1988—. Author: The Sources and Dimensions of Crisis in Social Security: A First Step Toward Meaningful Reform, 1981, Crisis in Social Security: Economic and Political Origins, 1982; editor: Social Security's Looming Surpluses: Prospects and Implications, 1990, Disability and Work, 1991; contbr. numerous articles to profl. jours., editorials to bus. pubs. Domestic policy advisor Dole-for-President campaign, 1988; mem. Mt. Vernon Womens Rep. Club, 1988—, Va. Fiscal Alternatives Commn., 1989—. Recipient Grad. fellowship, The Scaife Found., 1973-75, Grad. fellowship, the Earhart Found., 1975-76, Rsch. grant NSF, Washington, 1979-81. Mem. Am. Econs. Assn., Nat. Acad. Social Ins. (founding mem.). Episcopalian. Office: Am Enterprise Inst 1150 17th St NW Washington DC 20036-4603

WEAVER, DONALD WESLEY, investment counsellor; b. Gap, Pa., May 25, 1933; s. Warren Wesley and Bertha A. (Amnon) W.; m. Nancy Verlaine Johnson, Aug. 10, 1957; children: Susan Jill, Scott Wesley. BA, Ohio Wesleyan U., 1959; MBA, U. Pa., 1960. Asst. to pres. Doylestown (Pa.) Trust Co., 1960-61; trust officer Indsl. Valley Bank, Phila., 1961-62; investment counsellor T. Rowe Price & Assocs., Balt., 1962-63; pres. Arthur E. Spellissy & Assocs., Wayne, Pa., 1963—. Mem. Investment Counsel Assn. of Am. (bd. govs. 1990—), Fin. Analysts Soc. of Phila., Racquet Club of Phila. Home: 114 Jaffrey Rd Malvern PA 19355-3419 Office: Arthur E Spellissy & Assocs 308 W Lancaster Ave Wayne PA 19087-3905

WEAVER, ERIC JAMES, educational administrator; b. Purley, Surrey, Eng., May 14, 1938; came to U.S., 1947, naturalized, 1963; s. Edward Arthur and Amelia Cecily (Ealden) W.; m. Joyce Lynn McKean, Aug. 19, 1973; children: Stephanie Lynn, Heather Elizabeth, Jonathan Eric, Christopher James. AB, Princeton U., 1958; STB, Gen. Theol. Sem., 1961, MDiv, 1972; MS, CCNY, 1968; profl. diploma Hofstra U., 1973, EdD, 1980. Rsch. assoc. Meadow Brook Nat. Bank, West Hempstead, N.Y., 1957-61; dir. Christian edn. and youth work Ch. of Holy Cross, Bklyn., 1958-61; vicar Ch. of Messiah, Central Islip, N.Y. and St. Michael and All Angel's Ch., Gordon Heights, N.Y., 1961-63; tchr. spl. edn. Nassau County Vocat. Edn. and Extension Bd., N.Y., 1963-67; supr. cen. adminstrn. Nassau Bd. Coop. Ednl. Svcs., 1967-70; asst. prin. Rosemary Kennedy Sch. for Trainable Mentally Retarded, Wantagh, N.Y., 1970-73; dir. spl. edn. Middle County Schs., Suffolk County, N.Y., 1973-81, dir. spl. ednl. svcs., 1981—; vice chmn. Project EQUALS, 1983-86; ednl. cons., instr. Spl. Edn. Tng. Resource Ctr., 1986—; impartial hearing officer State of N.Y., 1982—; dir. presch. and child care com. Middle County Schs., 1990—; mem. Spl. Edn. Adminstrv. Leadership Tng. Acad., 1989—; adj. asst. prof. spl. edn. C.W. Post Coll., 1979-80. Capt. Aux. Police, County of Suffolk, N.Y., 1962-69; bd. dirs. Traffic Safety Bd., County of Nassau, N.Y., 1969-71, Robin Park Civic Assn., Huntington, N.Y., 1963-66; trustee Police Hall of Fame; hon. mem. steering com. ann. art auction Lake Grove (N.Y.) Sch., 1985—; asst. to rector Grace Ch., Huntington Sta., N.Y. 1963-66, Trinity Episc. Ch., Northport, N.Y., 1966—. Fellow Am. Assn. Mental Deficiency; mem. Interagy. Coun. on Recreation for Handicapped (dir. 1970-73), Coun. Exceptional Children (pres. 1973-74), Coun. Adminstrs. Spl. Edn. (treas. 1985—), Internat. Assn. Sci. Study Mental Deficiency, L.I. Assn. Spl. Edn. Adminstrn. (sec. 1975-76, v.p. 1976-77, pres. 1977-78, exec. com. 1978—), Assn. to Help Retarded Children, Am. Ednl. Rsch. Assn., Am. Assn. Sch. Adminstrs., Sch. Adminstrs. Assn. N.Y. State, Phi Delta Kappa. Republican. Episcopalian. Author monographs: The Sources of the First Gospel, 1958, Rudolf Bultman and Entmythologisierung, 1961, Ocular, Manual, and Podiatric Dominance in a Severely Retarded Older Adolescent Population, 1968, Efforts of Special Education Administrators to Meet the Needs of Special Education Teachers by Inservice Training, 1980. Home: 8 Oceanside Ct Northport NY 11768-1301 Office: 11 Unity Dr Centereach NY 11720

WEAVER, ROSETTA LORAINE, fashion designer, inventor; b. Phila., Mar. 23, 1935; d. Raymond Lorenza and Rebecca Ina (Tyler) W.; m. Sekayi Loraine Weaver-Nixon. Dipoma fine arts, fashion design, Moore Coll. Art, 1957. Wardrobe asst. Mr. Blackwell, L.A., 1958-59; U.S. rep. to 7th Congress Architects, Havana, Cuba, 1960; pvt. practice designer Accra, Ghanna, 1964-66; asst. designer Mr. Friend-Mi Lady Fashions, Phila., 1967-68; artistic cons. Opportunities Industrialization Ctr., Phila., 1970-72; pvt. practice inventor Phila., 1981—; Inventor: Baby Carrier, 1981. Affiliate Phila. (Pa.) Congress of the Nat. Polit. Congress of Black Women, 1985-91; mem. Women's Caucus for Art, Moore Coll. Art, 1991. Mem. Women's Enterprise Resource Ctr. (affiliate). Democrat. Universalist.

WEBB, ALEXANDER DWIGHT, photographer; b. San Francisco, May 5, 1952; s. Dwight Willson and Nancy (McIvor) W.; m. Susan Jacqueline O'Connor, Sept. 23, 1991; 1 child, Maxwell Thomas Sura. BA, Harvard U., 1974. Freelance photographer, N.Y.C., 1974—; photographer Magnum Photos, N.Y.C. and Paris, 1976—, v.p., 1985-86, 91. Author: Hot Light/Half-Made Worlds, 1986, Under a Grudging Sun, 1989 (Photojournalism Book of Yr., Maine Photog. Workshop 1989), (catalog) From the Tropics, 1989; exhibited in group shows Fogg Art Mus., Cambridge, Mass., 1980, Walker Art Mus., Mpls., 1986, Mus. Photog. Arts, San Diego, 1987, 89, Mus. Contemporary Photography, Chgo., 1987, Whitney Mus. Am. Art, N.Y.C., 1991, numerous others. Recipient award Overseas Press Club, 1980, Leopold Godowsky color photography award Photog. Resource Ctr., 1988; grantee N.Y. Found. for Arts, 1986, Nat. Endowment for Arts, 1990, W. Eugene Smith Found., 1990. Office: Magnum Photos 72 Spring St New York NY 10012-4019

WEBB, FRANCIS HUBERT, painter, educator; b. Pitts., Sept. 14, 1927; s. Francis Hubert and Margaret Pauline (Berkoben) W.; m. Barbara Anne Smith, Sept. 10, 1949; children: Christopher, Wendy, Rebecca. Diploma, Art Inst. Pitts. Pres. Phillips Studio, Pitts., 1960-80; self employed painter Pitts., 1980—; dir. Pitts. Ctr. for the Arts, 1974-78, Cheap Joe's Art Stuff, Boone, N.C., 1991—; guest instr., juror Art Assns. world wide, 1980—. Author: Watercolor Energies, 1983, Webb on Watercolor, 1990; contbr. articles to profl. jours.; subject: (movie-video) Contemporary Watercolor Master, 1989. With USNR, 1945-46, 50-52. Recipient Sisek award Butler Inst. Am. Art, Youngstown, Ohio, 1973, First award La. Watercolor Soc., New Orleans, 1976, Nat. Arts Club, N.Y.C., 1983, Dana award Phila. Watercolor Club, 1988; Dolphin fellow, 1989—. Mem. Am. Watercolor Soc. (nat. v.p. 1989-91, Walser Greathouse medal 1989), Allied Artists of Am. (award of distinction 1978), Rocky Mountain Nat. Watermedia Assn. (Watermedia award 1975), Pitts. Watercolor Soc. (pres. 1974-77, numerous awards), Audubon Artists (Winsor and Newton medal 1977), Knickerbocker Artists (Myers medal 1989), Midwest Watercolor Soc. (nat. dir. 1981-82), Southwestern Watercolor Soc. (hon.). Lutheran. Home and Studio: 108 Washington St Pittsburgh PA 15218

WEBB, JOHN GIBBON, III, lawyer; b. Flint, Mich., June 1, 1944; s. John Gibbon Jr. and Martha Elizabeth (Sweet) W.; m. Fain Murphey, July 6, 1968; children: Jennifer, Philip, Andrew, Matthew. AB, Davidson Coll., 1966; JD, Vanderbilt U., 1970. Bar: N.Y. 1971, N.J. 1981. Assoc. Curtis, Mallet, Prevost, Colt & Mosle, N.Y.C., 1970-80; gen. counsel, sec. J.M. Huber Corp., Rumson, N.J., 1980—, v.p., 1991—. Lay eucharistic min. Episcopal chs., S.I., N.Y., Milburn, N.J., Rumson, 1972-80, 89-90; trustee Lunch Break, Red Bank, N.J., 1986-89, pres., 1988-89. Named Vol. of Yr., Jr. League of Monmouth County, Red Bank, 1990.

WEBB, KATHARINE, counselor; b. Bklyn., Sept. 13, 1931; d. Joseph Norris and Thelma (Black) Norris Sharpton; m. John James Webb, May 25, 1956 (div. Aug. 1971); children—John, Tyra, Lori. B.S. in Home Econs., Hunter Coll., 1954, M.S. in Home Econs., 1957; M.S. in Guidance and Counseling, Western Mich. U., 1969; Ph.D. in Guidance and Psychol. Services, Ind. State U., 1972. Tchr. home econs. N.Y.C. Bd. Edn., Bklyn., 1954-65, counselor, 1965-68; counselor Ind. State U., Terre Haute, 1970-72; assoc. prof. counselor edn. SUNY-Brockport, 1972-79; commr. N.Y. State Commn.of Correction, Albany, 1979-85; dir. guidance and counseling N.Y. State Dept. Correctional Services, 1985—; mediator, arbitrator Community Dispute Ctr., Rochester, N.Y., 1973-79; mediator, fact-finder N.Y. State Pub. Employees Relations Bd., Albany, 1975-79. Pres. bd. dirs. Brockport Childcare Ctr. (N.Y.), 1973-74, Nat. Migrant Found., Inc., Albany, 1983-84; bd. dirs. YWCA of Rochester (N.Y.), 1975-77, YWCA of Albany, 1985-92, Albany Catholic Family and Community Svcs., 1991—, St.Casimir's Regional Sch., 1991—. Recipient cert. recognition YWCA of Rochester, 1975, cert. disting. svc. Urban League Rochester, 1976, award for disting. spl. programs SUNY Office Spl. Programs, Albany, 1978, award for support and contbns. Rochester Ednl. Opportunity Ctr., 1978, award for svc. Mental Health Assn. Rochester, 1979, Disting. Alumni award Ind. State U., 1986, Albany Humanitarian award, 1988. Mem. Am. Correctional Assn., N.Y. State Minorities in Corrections, N.Y. State Personnel and Guidance Assn. (v.p. for profl. svcs. 1979-80), Am. Assn. Counseling and Devel., Pub. Offender Counselor Assn., Assn. for Non-White Concerns, 100 Black Women, Delta Kappa Gamma Soc., Delta Sigma Theta. Democrat. Roman Catholic.

WEBB, PATRICIA HOLLAND, playwright; b. Cleve., Aug. 1, 1957; d. Frank H. and Virginia Florence (Fries) H.; m. Robert Mark Webb, Oct. 10, 1981; children: William Robertson, Arielle Ann. BS in Nursing, Ohio State U., 1979; BA in English Writing with honors, U. Pitts., 1988. Lic. R.N. Staff nurse cardiac ICU Ohio State U. Hosps., Columbus, 1979-81; nurse case mgr. Kimberly Home Health Care Svcs., Pitts., 1985-87; copy editor Horty, Springer & Mattern, P.C., Pitts., 1986-88; legal writer, editor Patient Care Law Action-Kit Publs., Pitts., 1988-91; freelance tech. writer Pitts., 1992—, playwright, poet, 1986—; ensemble mem. Ascension Players, Pitts., 1987-88; participant Manchester Playwrights, Pitts., 1989-91. Author: (2-act play) Kings, 1990; poet: Woman Over Thirty, 1991, After The Law, 1991. Mem. The Dramatists' Guild, Christians in Theatre Arts (honorable mention in nat. new script competition 1991). Episcopalian.

WEBB, RICHARD STEPHEN, manufacturing executive; b. Nottingham, Eng., Aug. 3, 1944; came to U.S., 1988; s. Sydney and Kathleen Florence (Day) W.; m. Pamela Anne Fowlds, Sept. 3, 1966 (dec. July 1976); children: Jane, Simon, Elizabeth; m. Anne Hessel, Aug. 19, 1978; children: Clare, Penelope. BSc, U. Sheffield, Eng., 1966, PhD, 1970. Rsch. scientist U. Sheffield, 1966-69; tech. asst. C.E. Ramsden & Co. Ltd., Stoke-on-Trent, Eng., 1969-74; mktg. exec. Magnesium Elektron Ltd., Manchester, Eng., 1974-80, mktg. mgr., 1980-84; bus. devel. mgr. Alcan Aluminium, Mont., Can., 1984-88; bus. mgr. Alanx Products L.P., Newark, Del., 1988-91, pres., 1991—. Contbr. articles to profl. jours. Fellow Inst. Ceramics U.K.; mem.

Am. Ceramic Soc., Can. Ceramic Soc., Am. Chem. Soc. Office: Alanx Products LP 101 Lake Dr Newark DE 19702-3318

WEBB, ROBERT MARK, psychiatrist; b. Ft. Leonardwood, Mo., Sept. 1, 1953; s. Robert O. and Betty Jo (Griffin) W.; m. Patricia Holland, Oct. 10, 1981; 2 children. BS in Microbiology, Ohio State U., 1975, MD, 1980. Intern U. Pitts. Hosp./Western Psychiat. Inst. and Clinic, 1981; resident in psychiatry Western Psychiat. Inst. and Clinic, Pitts., 1981-84; fellow in consultation and liaison psychiatry Western Psychiat. Inst. and Clinic, 1985; instr. psychiatry Western Psychiat. Inst. and Clinic, Pitts., 1985, asst. prof. psychiatry, 1986-89; neuropsychiatrist Allegheny Neuropsychiat. Inst., Oakdale, Pa., 1989-90; pvt. practice, 1990—; psychiat. cons. East Liberty Family Health Care Ctr., Pitts., 1983-84; cons. neurology clinic, U. Pitts., 1984-85, Montefiore Hosp., Pitts., 1986-87, memory clinic Alzheimer Disease Rsch. Ctr., Pitts., 1986-89; presenter in field. R.T. Lewis scholar, 1971-75, Kellogg scholar, 1975-80. Mem. Am. Psychiat. Assn., Pa. Psychiat. Assn. Episcopalian. Office: 230 N Craig St Pittsburgh PA 15213-1565

WEBB, SAMUEL BLATCHLEY, JR., academic administrator; b. N.Y.C., Jan. 7, 1939; s. Samuel Blatchley and Elizabeth Fisk (Johnson) W.; m. Julia Wheeler Dempsey, Dec. 27, 1965 (div. 1984); children: Samuel Watson, Edward Wheeler, William Vanderbilt; m. Marshall Marian Borwn, Sept. 6, 1986; 1 child, Marshall Samantha Havemeyer Webb. BA, Yale U., 1961, MPH, 1963; PhD, UCLA, 1970. Adminstrv. resident Montefiore Hosp., N.Y.C., 1962-64; med. care specialist HEW, Washington, 1964-66; prof. Med. Sch., Yale U., New Haven, 1968-81, dir. hosp. adminstrn. program, 1977-81; pres. Shelburne (Vt.) Mus., 1977-88; asst. to the pres. U. Vt., Burlington, 1991—; cons. NIH, Washington, 1970-82, Nat. Spinal Injuries Ctrl., Stoke Mandville, Eng., 1976-78. Author: Emergency Medical Services, 1977; contbr. articles to profl. jours. Mem. Health Adv. Com., Guilford, Conn., 1970-80; bd. dirs. Kingsley Trust Assn., pres., 1972-73. Lt. comdr. USPHS, 1964-66. Fellow APHA; mem. ACS (sec., treas. com. trauma New Haven chpt. 1970-82), Spinal Cord Injury Assn., Atlantic Salmon Assn. (bd. dirs. 1986—), S.C. Plantation Soc., Brook Club of N.Y.C., Bath and Tennis CLub Palm Beach (Fla.), Piping Rock Club (Locust Valley, N.Y.), Southampton (N.Y.) Club, Okeetee Club (bd. dirs. Ridgeland S.C.), Racquet and Tennis Club (N.Y.). Republican. Episcopalian. Home: Southern Acres Farm Harbor Rd Shelburne VT 05482 Office: U Vt 411 Main St Burlington VT 05401

WEBB, WILLIAM HESS, lawyer; b. Scottdale, Pa., Sept. 10, 1905; s. Austin Allison and Gertrude (Hess) W.; m. Marian Elizabeth Wellings, Nov. 26, 1931; children: John M., Patricia Ann (Mrs. Terence S. Small). BS, U. Pitts, 1926, LLB, 1929. Bar: Pa. 1929. Since practiced in Pitts.; sr. ptnr. Webb, Burden, Ziesenheim & Webb (and predecessor firm), Pitts., 1948—. Bd. dirs., v.p., treas. Pitts. Opera, Inc.; mem. Pitts. Symphony Soc. Served to 1st lt. U.S. Army Res., 1926-34. Mem. ABA (ho. of dels. 1961-65), Am. Intellectual Property Law Assn. (bd. mgrs. 1953-62, pres. 1959-60), Pa. Bar Assn., Inter-Am. Bar Assn., Allegheny County Bar Assn., Am. Law Inst., Licensing Execs. Soc., Internat. Assn. Protection Indsl. Property, Delta Theta Phi, Theta Chi, Duquesne Club, Univ. Club (Pitts.), Edgeworth Club (Sewickley, Pa.), Allegheny Country Club. Home: 201 Grant St Apt 305 Sewickley PA 15143-1337 Office: 700 Koppers Bldg 436 Seventh Ave Pittsburgh PA 15219

WEBB, WILLIAM JOHN, public relations counsel; b. Chgo., Jan. 9, 1922; s. Archibald Roy and Nina Spencer (Brown) W.; m. Madeline Betty Calkins, Oct. 24, 1989. BA, U. Calif., L.A., 1947; MA in Polit. Sci. and Pub. Adminstrn., Am. U., 1976. Spl. projects, plans and policy staff officer CIA, Washington, 1951-58; press sec., spl. asst. Senator William Knowland of Calif., Washington, 1958-59; spl. asst. pub. info. Army Chief R & D, 1959-63; spl. asst. Senator John Tower of Tex., Washington, 1963-64; spl. asst. to asst. dir. inspections and spl. projects OEO, 1965, spl. asst. regional rels., sr. pub. affairs officer, 1973-74; spl. asst. pub. affairs, chief public info. Navy Seabees Naval Facilities Engrng. Command, Washington, 1966-69; dir. spl. projects Maritime Adminstrn., 1969-70; spl. asst. regional liaison-coordination Office of Sec. Dept. Transp., 1970-71; dir. congl. and pub. affairs Nat. Reading Ctr., 1972-73; spl. asst. communication liaison-coordination White House, Washington, 1974; regional and intergovtl. liaison officer Office of Adminstr. EPA, 1975; staff specialist in indsl. rels. communication Fed. Energy Adminstrn., Washington, 1976; sr. public affairs officer, dir. Pubs. Health Care Financing Adminstrn. HHS, 1976-79; sr. staff officer intergovt. and regional affairs Office of Sec. Dept. Energy, 1980-81; dep. spl. asst. public affairs to Sec. of Labor, 1981. Mem. Pub. Rels. Soc. Am. (Nat. Capital chpt. bd. dirs. 1963, 65-67, 69-70, 72, 74, 76-77, 79, Silver Anvil award 1968), Nat. Assn. Govt. Communicators (bd. dirs. 1977-78, pres. Nat. Capital chpt. 1977-78, Blue Pencil awards), Mensa, Nat. Press Club, Am. Legion, Kappa Sigma. Home: 2124 Powhatan St Falls Church VA 22043-1910

WEBER, CLARENCE ADAM, education educator, author; b. Winfield, Kans., May 2, 1903; s. William J. and Pearl L. (Hunter) W.; m. Mary E. Beaty, Aug. 7, 1925; children: Jane Weber Ruck, Betty L. (Mrs. Charles A. Dewey). AB, Ill. Coll., 1924; MA, U. Ill., 1929; PhD, Northwestern U., 1943. Head dept. math. and coach Oakland Twp. High Sch., Ill., 1924-27; supt. schs. Hume, Galva, Cicero, Ill., 1927-44; assoc. prof. edn. U. Conn., Storrs, 1945-46, dir. Fort Trumbull br., 1946-50, prof. edn., 1950-66, prof. emeritus, 1967—, chmn. dept. sch. adminstrn., 1966, dean Sch. Edn., 1960-61. Author: Organization and Administration of Public Education in Connecticut, 1951, Personnel Problems of School Administrators, 1954, Fundamentals of Education Leadership, 1955, Industrial Leadership, 1956, Leadership in Personnel Management, 1970, Roots of Rebellion, 1970, What the People Ought to Know about School Administration, 1971, Welcome to the Rotary Club, 1971, Mary E. Weber, a biography, 1977, Diamonds in the Driveway, 1979, Songs of Cajean, 1979, Let's Cut the Cost of College Education, Double Trouble (an autobiography), 1980. Corporator Windham Meml. Hosp., Willimantic, Conn., 1966—. Mem. Am. Assn. Sch. Adminstrs., Phi Delta Kappa, Masons, Rotary (dist. gov. 1965-66). Home: Whitney Commons #110 1204 Whitney Ave Hamden CT 06517-2847

WEBER, DEANE FAY, microbiologist, retired; b. Aberdeen, S.D., May 17, 1925; s. Lowell Henry and Grace Manzer (Wyckoff) W.; m. Rosemary Bozak, Dec. 23, 1950; children: Myles Deane, Kevin Lee, Kent Jonathan. BS in Biology, Jamestown Coll., 1950; MS in Bacteriology, Kans. State U., 1952, PhD in Soil Microbiology, 1959. Lab. technician Quain and Ramstad Clinic, Bismarck, N.D., 1952-55; soil scientist Agrl. Rsch. Svc., USDA, Prosser, Wash., 1958-64; microbiologist IRI Rsch. Inst., Campinas, Brazil, 1964-66, ARS, USDA, Beltsville, Md., 1967-90; acting lab. dir. ARS, USDA, Beltsville, 1984-86. Author: (chpt.) Soybeans, 1973. With USN, 1944-46. D.F. Weber scholarship in soil microbiology at Kans. State U. established in his honor, 1981. Fellow AAAS. Republican. Home: 14972 Belle Ami Dr Laurel MD 20707-3655

WEBER, RICHARD EARLE, economics and finance educator, consultant; b. Upper Darby, Pa., Jan. 20, 1931; s. Harold E. and Edna L. (MacKannan) W.; m. Nancy L. King, Sept. 17, 1950; children: Richard E., Lorena S. BA in Econs., Rutgers U., 1969, MA in Econs., 1973, PhD in Econs., 1974. Lab. asst. Johns-Manville (N.J.) Rsch. Ctr., 1949-50; electronic engr. Signal Corps Engrng. Lab., Ft. Monmouth, N.J., 1950-53; product sales mgr. Weston Elec. Instrument, Newark, 1953-56; field sales engr. Kearfott Co., Clifton, N.J., 1956-57; mfr.'s rep. R.E. Weber Co., East Brunswick, N.J., 1957-63; gen. mgr. Weber & Sons, Freehold, N.J., 1963-67; teaching and rsch. asst., instr. Rutgers U., New Brunswick, N.J., 1967-72, exec. dir. human resources devel. feasibility study, 1978-79; asst. prof. econs. Montclair State Coll., Upper Montclair, N.J., 1972—; prof. Monmouth Coll., West Long Branch, N.J., 1979—; rsch. economist N.J. Labor and Industry Dept., Trenton, 1972-76; sr. econ. analyst PSE&G Co., Newark, 1976-78; pres. Raritan Container Corp., Milltown, N.J., 1965-68; econ. cons. AFIPS, Montvale, N.J., 1971-73; cons. on analysis coll. and univ. fin. activities, 1981—; expert witness in field. Contbr. numerous articles and monographs to profl. publs. With USN, 1948-49. Recipient merit award for svc. Monmouth Coll., 1981-84, 86; fellow NSF, 1970; rsch. grantee Montclair Coll., 1973-75, 86. Mem. AAUP, Ea. Econ. Assn., Ea. Fin. Assn., N.J. Assn. Bus. Economists. Home: 10 Moline Rd East Brunswick NJ 08816-4118

WEBER, ROSE MINNA, financial management executive; b. Bklyn., Feb. 20, 1955; d. Meyer and Esther (Glushien) W. BA, U. Pa., 1975. Sr. research evaluator West Phila. Mental Health Consortium, 1976-78; co-dir. Women's Resources, Inc., Phila., 1979-81; exec. dir. Ars Femina, Inc., Phila., 1981-89; chief exec. officer Affiliated Mgmt. Svcs. Inc., Williamstown, N.J., 1989—; bd. dirs. MultiData Corp., Phila. Recipient Benjamin Franklin scholarship U. Pa., 1972. Jewish. Office: Affiliated Mgmt Svcs Inc 598 N Black Horse Pike Williamstown NJ 08094-1043

WEBER, TERRENCE EMIL, sales executive; b. Dayton, Ohio, June 18, 1958; s. Vernon Emil and Beverly Jo (Neiman) W.; m. Suzanne Marie Asman, Aug. 30, 1980; 1 child, Kathryn Elizabeth. BA, Union Coll., Schenectady, N.Y., 1980. Salesman Albany Valve & Fitting Co., Schenectady, 1980-83; sales mgr. Swagelok Co., Solon, Ohio, 1983-90; v.p. sales Hoke Inc., Cresskill, N.J., 1990—. Mem. ASME. Republican. Roman Catholic. Home: 19 Cottonwood Randolph NJ 07869 Office: Hoke Inc 1 Tenakill Pk Cresskill NJ 07626

WEBSTER, DAVID CLARK, finance executive; b. Chester, Pa., Sept. 17, 1927; s. Maurice L. and Elsie M. (Bagenstose) W.; BS in Econs., Wharton Sch., U. Pa., 1952; MBA in Acctg., N.Y. U., 1961; m. Helen Landa, June 1, 1952; children: Elise, Leslie, Michael, Mort, Jeremy. Contr., treas. F. & M. Schaefer Corp., N.Y.C., 1960-73; v.p., treas., sec. Cadbury Schweppes U.S.A. Inc., Stamford, Conn., 1973-75; dir. fin. Alexander Proudfoot Co., Chgo., 1975-80; prin. Webster Mgmt. Systems, Stamford, 1980-88; treas., chief fin. officer E.T. Wright & Co., Inc., 1988-90; prin. Impact Mgmt. Cons. Ltd., 1990—. Creator productivity measurements for industry; contbr. articles to fin. publs. Served with USN, 1945-47. Mem. Fin. Execs. Inst., Planning Execs. Inst. (pres. N.Y. chpt. 1967-68), Inst. Mgmt. Accts., Am. Mgmt. Assn. (course leader, contbr. acctg. and fin.), Beta Gamma Sigma. Home: 23 Drummer Ln West Redding CT 06896-1414

WEBSTER, PETER JOHN, meteorology educator; b. Cheshire, U.K., May 30, 1942; s. James Robert and Olive W.; children: Benjamin, David. BS, Royal Melbourne Inst. Technol., Australia, 1965; PhD, MIT, 1971. Meteorologist Commn. Bur. Meteorology, 1961-67; postdoctoral fellow UCLA, 1972-73; asst. prof. U. Wash., Seattle, 1973-77; rsch. scientist CSIRO, Melbourne, Australia, 1977-83; adj. prof. Monash U., Melbourne, Australia, 1979-83; prof. Penn State U., University Pk., 1983—; chmn. TOGA Sci. Steering Group, 1986-90, TOGA COARE panel, 1989—; co-chmn. TOGA COARE Sci. Working Group, 1988—. Recipient Wilson Rsch. award Penn State U., 1989, Jule G. Charney award Am. Meterol. Soc., 1990, Creativity award NSF, 1990, Alexander von Humboldt Found. award, 1991. Fellow Am. Meteorol. Soc. Office: Pa State U 518 Walker Bldg University Park PA 16802

WEBSTER, SALLY BEYER, art historian, educator; b. Hammond, Ind., May 24, 1938; d. James Edward Beyer and Robin (Hopkins) Wright; m. Albert K. Webster; children: Albert V.B., Katherine Lee. BA, Barnard Coll., 1959; cert. in bus. adminstrn., Harvard-Radcliffe, 1960; MA, U. Cin., 1974; PhD, CUNY, 1985. Art critic, editor Cin. Post, 1973-74; mem. edn. and publicity staff Taft Mus., Cin., 1974-75; dir. A.I.R. Gallery, N.Y.C., 1979-81; lectr. Coll. S.I., N.Y.C., 1983; assoc. prof. CUNY, N.Y.C., 1985—; vis. fellow Smithsonian Instn., Washington, 1990. Author: William Morris Hunt, 1991. Pres. Lehmann Coll. Art Gallery, 1989—. Office: CUNY Lehman Coll Art Dept Bronx NY 10468

WEBSTER, SHARON B., economist; b. Wildwood, Fla., Aug. 23, 1937; d. James McWilliams and Marion (Hallbrook) Boen; BA in Polit. Sci., Econs. and Psychology, U. Fla., 1959; postgrad. (vis. doctoral fellow), Princeton U., 1964-65; PhD, U. Va., 1965. . Asst. prof. No. Mich. U., Marquette, 1962-64, U. Md., 1964-66, Hollins Coll., Roanoke, Va., 1966-71; prof. Fed. Exec. Inst., Charlottesville, Va., 1971-72; internat. program mgr. Dept. Treasury, Washington, 1972-74; economist Econs., Statistics and Coop. Svc., U.S. Dept. Agr., Washington, 1974-79; mem. Presdl. Commn. for Exec. Exchange, 1979-80; dir. internat. econs. Occidental Petroleum Corp., L.A., 1980-83; investment banker, account exec. Johnston, Lemon and Co., Inc., Washington, 1983-88; fin. cons. Shearson Lehman Hutton, 1988—. Mem. adv. bd. Pres.'s Carribbean Basin Initiative, 1982; chmn. bd. dirs. NATA, Inc.; bd. dirs. GENTA, Inc., NABE; pres., chief exec. officer A.A. Global; bd. advisors Sintal Communications USA, Inc., Internat. Trade Council, Patterson Sch. Diplomacy and Internat. Commerce, U. Ky., Consumer Health and Svcs. of Am., Inc. Contbr. articles to profl. jours. Recipient Presdl. award Pvt. Sector Initiative, 1982; NDEA fellow. Mem. AAUP, Internat. Policy Inst. (v.p. 1977—), Internat. Assn. Energy Economists, Am. Assn. Agrl. Economists, Am. Polit. Sci. Assn., Nat. Assn. Bus. Economists, Internat. Studies Assn., Soc. Internat. Devel., Nat. Council Career Women, Washington Soc. Money Mgrs., Assn. Polit. Risk Analysts, Pres.'s Exec. Exchange Assn., Fed. Exec. Inst. Alumni Assn., Capital Speakers Club, Army Navy Club, Internat. Club. Home: The Winthrop # 602 1727 Massachusetts Ave NW Washington DC 20036-2153 Office: AA Global 9039 Furrow Ave Ellicott City MD 21042-1841

WECHMAN, ROBERT JOSEPH, economist, educator; b. N.Y.C., Sept. 23, 1939; s. David Samuel and Blanche (Udell) W.; B.A., City U. N.Y., 1961, M.A., 1964; M.A., Columbia, 1966; Ph.D., Syracuse U., 1970; postdoctoral U. Pa., 1974; C.B.M., Am. Mgmt. Assn. Inst., 1980, C.M.M., 1981, C.F.M., 1982; m. Stephanie Helene Kellman, June 18, 1967; children: Craig Samuel, Evan Mitchell, Darren Max. Tchr. history and econs., N.Y.C., 1961-63, Dobbs Ferry (N.Y.) High Sch., 1963-66; instr. history and econs. Elmira (N.Y.) Coll., 1966-70; vis. lectr. history and econs. SUNY, Corning, summers 1967, 70—; asst. prof. social sci., coordinator urban studies Hartwick Coll., Oneonta, N.Y., 1970-74; asst. v.p. Beavertown Mills, 1976-80, v.p., 1980-90; pres. Robert J. Wechman, Cons., 1984-90, Verdin Assocs., Inc., 1982-88; pres. Robert J. Wechman Assocs., Inc., 1990—; adj. prof. social sci. and bus. adminstrn. New Sch. for Social Research, also SUNY, Rockland Community Coll., 1974-80, Empire State Coll., 1974—, Bergen Community Coll., 1976-80, Berkeley Coll., 1979; adj. assoc. prof. mktg. Pace U., 1980-86; adj. prof. econs. and bus. adminstrn. and econs. St. Thomas Aquinas Coll., 1981—, Dominican Coll., summer 1981; adj. assoc. prof. bus. mgmt. City U. N.Y., 1981—; cons. urban affairs SUNY, Corning, 1969-70; cons. Choice Jour., 1972—. Mem. Oneonta Bd. Ethics, 1971-74, Oneonta Anti-Pollution Commn., 1972-74; committeeman and dist. chmn. Rockland County Republican Com., 1978—, Heritage Found. Served with U.S. Army, 1959, USAR, 1959-65. Recipient Marcus award for disting. teaching, 1972, Outstanding Educators Am. award, 1972, President's Appreciation award, 1989, 90. Mem. Phi Alpha Theta, Delta Tau Kappa, Delta Pi Epsilon. Republican. Club: K.P. Author: The Eager Immigrants, 1972, The Economic Development of the Italian-American, 1983, Encountering Management, 1987, Essentials of American Business, 1990; editor: Critical Issues in Modern American Life, 1968; The Crisis in Population, 1969, Urban America: A Guide to the Literature, 1971. Reviewer for social sci. and bus. jours. Home: 9 Verdin Dr New City NY 10956-3707

WECHSLER, GIL, lighting designer; b. N.Y.C., Feb. 5, 1942; s. Arnold J. and Miriam (Steinberg) W. Student Rensselaer Poly. Inst., 1958-61; BS, NYU, 1964; MFA, Yale U., 1967. Lighting designer Harkness Ballet, N.Y.C., 1967-69, Pa. Ballet, Phila., 1969-70, Stratford Shakespeare Festival, Ont., Can., 1969-78, Guthrie Theatre, Mpls., 1971, Lyric Opera Chgo., 1972-76, Met. Opera, N.Y.C., 1976—; guest lectr. Teatro Colon, Buenos Aires, Argentina, 1985, Yale U., New Haven, 1980; guest lighting designer Am. Ballet Theatre, N.Y.C., 1980, Paris Opera, 1983, Chatelet Theatre, Paris, 1991. Cons. editor Opera Quar., 1983-90. Recipient Emmy award nominations. Mem. U.S. Inst. for Theatre Tech., Illuminating Engring. Soc., United Scenic Artists. Avocations: collecting ocean liner memorabilia, gardening, painting. Home: 1 Lincoln Pla New York NY 10023 Office: Met Opera Lincoln Ctr New York NY 10023

WECHTER, IRA MARTIN, financial planner; b. Bkyn., June 26, 1947; s. Nathan Harris and Mollie (Bauer) W.; m. Myrna Ellen Rosenbaum, Dec. 22, 1968; 1 child, Megan Jill. BA, CCNY, 1969; MPA, Bernard Baruch Coll., 1973. Cert. fin. planner, tax profl.; registered investment advisor. Dir. adminstrv. svcs. N.Y.C. Dept. City Planning, 1971-77; dep. asst. budget dir. N.Y. N.Y.C. Office Mgmt. and Budget, 1977-81; dep. commr. N.Y.C. Dept. Environ. Protection, 1981-84; pres. Wechter Fin. Svcs., Inc., Morris Plains, N.J., 1984—. Mem. Community Bd. No. 1 S.I., 1973-76, 1st v.p., 1976-77; treas. S.I. Coun. on Arts, 1974-75. Recipient Outstanding Citizenship award Borough Pres. of S.I., 1977. Mem. Nat. Soc. Enrolled Agts., Inst. Cert. Fin. Planners, Nat. Assn. Tax Practitioners. Republican. Jewish. Office: Wechter Fin Svcs Inc 20 Walsh Way Morris Plains NJ 07950-1942

WECHTER, VIVIENNE THAUL, artist, poet, educator; b. N.Y.C.; d. Samuel Joshua and Hilda (Thaul) Rosenthal; m. Nathan Wechter; 1 dau., Robyrta Joan Wechter Rapoport. B. Pedagogy, Jamaica Tchrs. Coll.; postgrad., Columbia U., N.Y. U., New Sch. for Social Research, Art Students League, Sculpture Center, Pratt Inst. Graphic Center; Ph.D. in Interarts and Psychology of Creativity, Union Grad. Sch. artist in residence Fordham U., 1964—, asst. prof. art and esthetics, 1964, now prof. interdisciplinary creative arts, chmn. acquisitions and exhbns.; vis. poet-artist Kansas City Art Inst., 1975, Md. Inst. Coll. Art, 1975, New Sch., N.Y.C., 1976, Marist Coll., Poughkeepsie, N.Y., 1977; vis. prof. New Sch. for Social Research, spring 1986; past chmn. coll. liaison div. Bronx Council on Arts. Moderator: weekly radio broadcast Today's World, WFUV, 1951—, created 6 programs in South Pacific, 1986-87; illustrator: (Alfeo Marzi) book cover Park of Jonas, 1965; author: A View from the Ark, 1973; contbr. articles to profl. jours.; one-woman shows Castellane Gallery, East Hampton Gallery, N.Y.C., Cornell U., Ithaca, N.Y., Neville Pub. Mus., Green Bay, Wis., Nashville Fine Arts Ctr., Fairleigh Dickinson U., Rutgers U., Waterloo (Iowa) Mcpl. Galleries, Bodley Gallery, Gloria Cortella Gallery, N.Y.C., Manhattan Coll., N.Y.C., Kouros Gallery, N.Y.C., Everson Mus. Art, Syracuse, N.Y., CCNY, B.R. Kornblatt Gallery, Balt., New Sch. Social Research, N.Y.C., also Paris, Rejik, Yugoslavia, multimedia show, Everson Mus. Fine Art, Syracuse, 1979, Dyansen Gallery, N.Y.C., 1981, L.I. U., 1986, Schiller-Wapner, N.Y.C., Shapolsky Gallery, N.Y.C., 1989; solo shows and poetry readings New Sch., N.Y.C., Arts Interaction, N.Y.C., L.I. U., 1988; represented in permanent collections Corcoran Gallery, Washington, Houston Mus. Fine Arts, Jewish Mus. N.Y.C., Fordham U., N.Y.C., Univ. Art Museum Berkeley, Calif., Museum Art and Sci., Norfolk, Va., N.Y. U., Mus. of Fine Arts, Moscow, Russia, Mus. of Fine Art, Newark, Ohio State U., Phoenix Mus. Fine Arts, Fairleigh Dickinson U., Madison, N.J., UN, Internat. Culture Ctr., Jerusalem, Mus. Modern Art Warsaw, Poland, Mus. Fine Arts Moscow, N.J. State Mus., Trenton, others; monumental outdoor sculpture The Emerging Sun commd. for Manhattan Psychiat. Ctr., Ward's Island, N.Y.C.; permanent sculpture installed George Meany Internat. Ctr. Labor Studies, Washington, 1981, Simple Justice on Columbus Ave. nr. Lincoln Ctr., N.Y.C., 1989; logo sculpture Miami Jewish Home & Hosp. for Aged; developer, curator, 1st Biennial of Outdoor Sculpture, Fordham U. Rose Hill Campus, 1983. Author: Art, Where Are We Today and Why?, 1985; solo exbn. and video presentation New Sch. for Social Research, Mar. and Apr., 1986, Wagner-Schiller Galleries, Sept., 1986; solo painting, sculpture, video presentation and poetry reading, Nov. Dec., 1986; sole exhbn. and poetry reading, The Silver Dream, Provincetown Art Assn. and Mus., July, 1987; chair, moderator Influences in Art (Italian Am. Roundtable Art & Lit., 1988, video on RAI TV, Rome, 1989; panelist St. Bartholomew's, N.Y.C., 1987; rep., exhbns. Leister Fine Arts, Ltd., London. Bd. dirs. Urban Arts Corps; founder, trustee, past pres. Bronx Mus. Art; v.p. U.S. Com. IAA-UNESCO; trustee Bronx Soc. Arts and Letters, 1988—. Recipient awards Am. Acad. Arts and Letters, awards Am. Soc. Contemporary Art. Mem. Am. Abstract Artists, Univ. Council of Art Educators, Urban League Center Greater N.Y. (dir., mem. advisory bd. 1952—), United World Federalists (1st chmn.), Fedn. Modern Painters and Sculptors (v.p.), Alpha Mu Gamma, Kappa Pi.

WECKER, STUART, computer science educator, consultant; b. N.Y.C., July 1, 1944; s. Frank and Sue (Levin) W.; m. Ellen Zellner, Dec. 22, 1968 (div. May 1991); children: Jessica, Amy. BS, Rensselaer Polytech. Inst., 1966; MS, SUNY, Stony Brook, 1970. Systems architect SUNY, Stony Brook, 1968-72; network architect Digital Equipment Corp., Maynard, Mass., 1972-81; pres. Tech. Concepts Inc., Sudbury, Mass., 1981-87; prof. Northeastern U., Boston, 1989—; cons. in field; architect DECnet. Mem. IEEE (Koji Kobayashi Computers and Communications award 1988), Assn. Computing Machinery. Home: 14 Babe Ruth Dr Sudbury MA 01776-1942

WECKER, WILLIAM A., preventive medicine physician, neuropsychiatrist; b. N.Y.C., Mar. 14, 1923; s. Philip and Ruth (Frumkin) W. BA, NYU, 1943, MD, 1946; MPH, Harvard U., 1950. Lic. physician, surgeon, N.Y. Intern Bellevue Hosp., N.Y.C., 1946, Bayonne Gen. Hosp., 1946-47; health officer N.Y.C. Health Dept., 1948-50; dist. health officer N.Y. State Health Dept., Albany, 1950-52; pvt. practice medicine N.Y.C., 1954-59; resident in psychiatry U.S. VA Hosp., N.Y.C., 1959-62, psychiatrist, 1962-64; psychiatrist Riverside Hosp., N.Y.C. Hosp. Dept., 1964-65, Postgrad. Ctr. for Mental Health, N.Y.C., 1964-65; pvt. practice preventive medicine, neuropsychiatry N.Y.C., 1948—; advisor Pan Am. Med. Assn., N.Y.C., 1952-55; cons. World Med. Assn., N.Y.C., 1954-61; staff physician Meml. Hosp., Queens, N.Y., 1955-64, Springfield (Mass.) Hosp., 1970-71; advisor, charter mem. Acad. Religion and Mental Health, N.Y.C., 1959-62; psychiatrist Youth House, N.Y.C., 1963-71; psychiat. cons. Mahoney Health Ctr., N.Y.C. Dept. Health, Bklyn., 1964-71. Author: 3d World Economics, 1981, Psychecology for Everybody, 1983, Comprehensive Psychenomics, 1983, American Confetti, 1990. Cons. Allen Haus, Zurich, 1990-91; advisor English Gentelmen's Club, Zurich, 1982-87, Centro Cultural, Honduras, 1978-82; corr. Harry Schultz Newsletter, Switzerland and Monaco, 1983-91. 2d lt. U.S. Army, 1943-45, capt. USAF, 1952-54. Fellow Nat. Poliomyelitis Found., 1949-50, U.S. VA, 1960-61. Mem. Acad. Medicine Bklyn. (life), N.Y. State Med. Soc. (life), Kings County Med. Soc. (life), Royal Soc. Health (London). Home and Office: 52 Macdougal St New York NY 10012-2937

WECKESSER, PAUL MAURICE, civil and traffic engineer; b. Rochester, N.Y., June 20, 1933; s. Joseph Louis and Marie Margaret W.; m. Mildred Jacqueline Schreiber, Sept. 13, 1958; children: Gerard, Wendy M., Melissa A., Paul M. Jr. BSCE, U. Detroit, 1956; MSCE, Purdue U., 1958. Sr. traffic engr. City of Rochester, N.Y., 1958-59; traffic engr. N.J. Turnpike Authority, New Brunswick, 1959-76, dir. ops., 1976-83, chief engr., 1983-90; v.p. hwy. systems Deleuw Cather & Co., Boston, 1990—. Registered profl. engr., N.J., Calif. Fellow Inst. Transp. Engrs.; mem. ASCE, Nat. Soc. Profl. Engrs., Am. Assn. Hwy. and Transp. Ofcls., Internat. Bridge Tunnel and Turnpike Assn. (bd. dirs.). Roman Catholic. Home: 186 Rick Rd Milford NJ 08848-2112 Office: 101 Huntington Ave 22d Fl Boston MA 02199

WEDDINGTON, LIZ GARDNER (LIZ GARDNER), actress, editor; b. N.Y.C., Oct. 13, 1932; d. A. Adolph and Anne Mary (Gardner) Blank; m. George Lee Weddington, Jr., Oct. 23, 1965; 1 child, Georgiana Marie. Actress TV, radio, telephone, N.Y./Calif, 1957—; editor comml. scripts N.Y., 1969—; freelance writer N.Y. City Tribune, various other publs., N.Y., nat., 1984—. Columnist polit. commentary, 1984—; appeared in over 300 TV commls., also TV and radio voice-overs. Mem. County Com., Conservative Party, N.Y.C., 1988-90, 17th Precinct Community Coun., N.Y.C., 1974—; rep. Yorkville Area Cath. Coun., N.Y.C., 1986—. Recipient Mayor's Vol. Action Ctr. award, N.Y.C., 1981-82, Cert. Recognition N.Y.C. Dept. Police Dep. Commr. Community Affairs, 1981. Mem. Screen Actors Guild, Am. Fedn. Radio and TV artists, Nat. League Am. Pen Women, Internat. Platform assn., Nat. Soc. Children of Am. Revolution - Fraunces Tavern Soc. (sr. pres. 1985-89), N.Y. State Soc. Children Am. Revolution (sr. historian 1988-90, sr. 2d v.p. 1990-92), Nat. Soc. DAR (chmn. com. Mary Washington Colonial chpt., corr. sec. 1992—), Nat. Soc. U.S. Daughters of 1812 (organizing pres. Pres. James Madison Chpt. 360 1988—), N.Y. State Soc. Daughters 1812, N.Y. State Soc. Dames of Ct. of Honor (pres. 1984-88), United Daughters of Confederacy (pres. N.Y. div. 1988-90, nat. chmn. revision of gen. bylaws com. 1989-91, McMath Scholarship gen. com. 1991-92), Daus. Colonial Wars (N.Y. State chpt.), Nat. Geneal. Soc., Internat. Platform Assn., and others. Conservative. Roman Catholic. Home and Office: 401 E 74th St Apt 6D New York NY 10021-3931

WEDEEN, MARVIN MEYER, hospital executive; b. Perth Amboy, N.J., Jan. 3, 1926; s. Nathan and Gertrude (Rappaport) W.; m. Hannah Haas; children: Rachel, Miriam. BS, Cornell U., 1949; MSc in Hosp. Adminstrn., Columbia U., 1971. Rsch. asst. Sealtest div. Kraft Foods, Schenectady, N.Y., 1949-55, dir. work simplification, 1955-59; pers. mgr. Dellwood Foods, Yonkers, N.Y., 1959-63; asst. v.p. Dellwood Foods, Yonkers, 1964-69; cons. pers. N.Y. Infirmary, N.Y.C., 1971; asst. adminstr. Sewickley Valley Hosp., Sewickley, Pa., 1971-80; v.p. Sewickley Valley Hosp., Sewickley, 1980-90; spl.

advisor to pres. Sewickley (Pa.) Valley Hosp., 1991; ret., 1992; cons. Exec. Svc. Corp., 1992—; bd. dirs. Valley Care Assn., Sewickley, 1979—; mem. Human Resources Com., Hosp. Coun. Western Pa., 1987-89; cons. Sr. Med. Cons., N.Y.C., 1971. Chmn. oper. com. Health Systems Agy., Pitts.; class fund rep. Cornell U. Alumni Fund, 1967-72; bd. dirs. United Jewish Fedn. Bd., 1991—. Named Man of the Yr., Sewickley Hist. Soc. and Gateway Press, 1980. Fellow, Am. Coll. Health Care Execs.; mem. Am. Pub. Health Assn., Am. Hosp. Assn., Hosp. Assn. (planning and mktg. section, 1984—), Edgeworth Club. Home: RR #4 Sewickley PA 15143-9806

WEDEEN, RICHARD PETER, physician; b. Bklyn., Jan. 19, 1934; s. Marcus D. and Dorothy Mason; m. Roberta Rubien, June 28, 1957; 1 child, Timothy Douglas. AB, Harvard Coll., 1955; MD, NYU, 1959. Diplomate Am. Bd. Internal Medicine, Am. Bd. Nephrology. Intern Beth Israel Hosp., N.Y.C., 1959-60, med. resident, 1960-61; med. resident Mt. Sinai Hosp., N.Y.C., 1963-64, rsch. fellow in medicine, NIH trainee, 1961-63, rsch. asst., 1961-65, rsch. assoc., 1965-66, Polechek Found. Fellow, 1967-68; various hosp. appointments to dir., dept. medicine Jersey City Med. Ctr., 1976-78; assoc., chief of staff for rsch. and devel. VA Med. Ctr., East Orange, N.J., 1978—; staff physician Univ. Hosp., Newark, 1990—; various univ. positions including prof. preventive medicine, dir. Div. Occupation and Environ. Medicine, 1990—, prof. of medicine, 1976—, others; vis. lectr. Harvard Med. Sch., Boston, 1968-69; vis. prof. Univ. Antwerp, Edegem, Belgium, 1985; others. Author: Poison in the Pot: The Legacy of Lead, 1984; contbg. editor: Am. Jour. Indsl. Medicine, 1987—; cons. editor: Archives of Environ. Health, 1986—; asst. editor: Mt. Sinai Jour. Medicine, 1990—; contbr. articles to profl. jours. Active N.J. State Working Group on Occupational Health Clinic Network, 1989—, Lead Paint Working Group/Legal Svcs. Of N.J., 1989—, Operation Crossroads Africa, 1964-76, others. Recipient rsch. grants NIH, 1964-77, VA Merit Rev., 1978-88, others. Fellow Am. Coll. Physicians, Collegium Ramazzini, Am. Physiol. Soc., Am. Fedn. Clin. Rsch. Med. Hist. Soc. N.J. (v.p. 1986-87, pres. 1988-89); mem. Am. Soc. Clin. Investigation (emeritus). Office: VA Medical Ctr East Orange NJ 07018-1095

WEDGWOOD, RUTH, law educator; b. N.Y.C.; d. Morris P. and Anne (Williams) Glushien; m. Josiah Francis Wedgwood; May 29, 1982. BA magna cum laude, Harvard U., 1972; fellow, London Sch. Econs., 1972-73; JD, Yale U., 1976. Bar: D.C., N.Y. Law clk. to judge Henry Friendly U.S. Ct. Appeals (2d cir.), N.Y.C., 1976-77; law clk. to justice Harry Blackmun U.S. Supreme Ct., Washington, 1977-78; spl. asst. to asst. atty. gen. criminal div. U.S. Dept. Justice, Washington, 1978-80; asst. U.S. atty. U.S. Dist. Ct. (so. dist.) N.Y., N.Y.C., 1980-86; assoc. prof. law Yale U., New Haven, 1986—, faculty fellow Inst. for Social and Policy Studies, 1989—, faculty fellow Berkeley Coll., 1989—. Exec. editor Yale Law Jour., 1975-76. Prin. rapporteur U.S. Atty. Gen.'s Guidelines on FBI Undercover Ops., Informant Use and Racketeering and Gen. Crime Investigations, 1980; bd. dirs. Lawyers Com. for Human Rights, N.Y.C., 1988—. Mem. ABA, Am. Soc. Internat. Law, Internat. Law Assn. (program chmn. Am. br. 1992), Assn. Bar City N.Y. (arms control and internat. security affairs com., chmn. 1989-92, chmn. internat. affairs coun. 1992—), Coun. on Fgn. Rels., Elizabethan Club, Yale Club (N.Y.C.), Mchts. Club (N.Y.C.). Office: Yale U Sch Law PO Box 401A New Haven CT 06520-7397

WEEDER, RICHARD STOCKTON, surgeon; b. Phila., Sept. 2, 1936; s. Stephen Dana and Caroline Denny (Nixon) W.; m. Areta Oebel Parle, May 17, 1987; children by previous marriage: Erica Crispin, Megan Alexandra; 1 stepchild, Annika Oebel. BA, Princeton U., 1958; MD, U. Pa., 1962. Diplomate Am. Bd. Surgery. Intern Germantown Hosp., Phila., 1962-63; surg. resident Geisinger Med. Ctr., Danville, Pa., 1963-67; gen. surgeon Hunterdon Med. Ctr., Flemington, N.J., 1969—. Author: Surgeon: The View From Behind the Mask, 1988, 91. Trustee Princeton Day Sch., 1982-85; founding trustee Princeton Friends Sch., 1987-91. Fellow ACS. Mem. Soc. Friends. Home: 45 Green Ave Lawrenceville NJ 08648 Office: Hunterdon Med Ctr Dept Surgery Flemington NJ 08822

WEEKS, ANN ARMSTRONG, university administrator; b. N.Y.C., Jan. 5, 1935; d. Spencer and Milda Olga (Martin) Armstrong; m. William Thomas Weeks, June 27, 1954; children: Linda Susan Weeks Balduyck, James Spencer, Donald William (dec.). AAS, Dutchess Community Coll., Poughkeepsie, N.Y., 1977; BA, U. Mich., 1956; MS, SUNY, New Paltz, 1974; EdD, Columbia U., 1985. Cert. tchr. math., N.Y. State; RN, N.Y. Math. instr. Hudson Valley Opportunities Indsl. Ctr., Poughkeepsie, 1977-78; math. lectr. Dutchess Community Coll., Poughkeepsie, 1977-78, asst. registrar, 1978-83, math. instr., 1981-82, dir. instl. rsch., 1983-87; assoc. v.p. computing, asst. to pres. Inst. Rsch. & Planning, SUNY, Old Westbury, N.Y., 1987—; cons. Sch. New Resources, Coll. New Rochelle, N.Y., 1986. Contbr. articles to profl. jours. Vol. United Way allocations rev. process, Melville, N.Y., 1991—, prospect rsch. com., 1991—. Mem. Am. Assn. for Higher Edn., Assn. for Instl. Rsch., Assn. for Instl. Rsch. and Planning Officers, N.E. Assn. for Instl. Rsch., Phi Delta Kappa, Kappa Delta Pi. Home: 19 Innsbruck Blvd Hopewell Junction NY 12533-5301 Office: SUNY PO Box 210 Old Westbury NY 11568-0210

WEEKS, CHRISTOPHER HENRY CLARK, writer, historian; b. Schenectady, N.Y., May 4, 1950; s. Maurice Harold and June King (Clark) W. BA, U. Va., 1972, MA, 1976. Cons. The Nat. Trust, Gloucestershire, U.K., 1973-74; writer, editor Md. Hist. Trust, Annapolis, Md., 1976-85; adj. lectr. U. Md., College Pk., 1978—; curator, cons. Centro Internazionale A. Palladio, Vicenza, Italy, 1976-80; lectr. Goucher Coll., Towson, Md., 1979; trustee Balt. Mus. of Art, 1985-90; cons. com. Ladew Topiary Gardens, Monkton, 1985—; dir., v.p. Ctr. for Palladian Studies, Richmond, Va., 1980—; speakers' com. Md. Hist. Soc., Balt., 1978-84. Author: Architectural History of Westminster, 1978, Where Land and Water Intertwine, 1985, Between the Nanticoke and Choptank, 1985, AIA Guide to Washington, D.C., 1992; co-author: W.L. Bottomley in Richmond, 1986, Clues to American Gardens, 1988; author: Gardens of the Chesapeake, 1993; contbr. numerous articles to profl. jours. Named Knight of St. John., Episcopal Ch., 1989. Mem. Hist. Soc. of Hartford County (dir. 1988—), Liriodendron Found. (dir. 1979—). Republican. Episcopalian. Home and Office: 3615A Hess Rd Monkton MD 21111

WEEKS, WILLIAM THOMAS, software engineer; b. Port Chester, N.Y., Mar. 28, 1932; s. William Henry and Mae (Taylor) W.; m. Ann Armstrong, June 27, 1954; children: Linda Susan Weeks Balduyck, James Spenser. BA, Williams Coll., 1954; MS, U. Mich., 1956, PhD, 1960. Engr. IBM Corp., Poughkeepsie, N.Y., 1960-68; sr. engr. IBM Corp., Hopewell, N.Y., 1968-84, sr. tech. staff mem., 1984—. Contbr. articles to profl. publs.; inventor in field. Mem. Phi Beta Kappa, Sigma Xi. Home: 19 Innsbruck Blvd Hopewell Junction NY 12533-5301

WEEMS, CLARA C., educator, counselor, consultant; b. N.Y.C., June 15, 1933; d. Joseph and Itala (Nerone) Carbonara; m. Clarence Norwood Weems, Dec. 28, 1954; children: Nancy M., Clarence N. BA in Chemistry, Hunter Coll., 1954; postgrad. in law, NYU, 1954-55, Franklin Pierce Coll., 1969-72. Cert. med. lab. technologist. Instr. chemistry lab. Fairleigh Dickinson U., Rutherford, N.J., 1956-57; tchr. med. techniques Mandl Sch., N.Y.C., 1962-64; chmn. sci. dept. Holy Trinity High Sch., Westfield, N.J., 1973-76; med. lab. tchr. Advanced Career Tng., N.Y.C., 1976-78; med. lab. tchr., placement dir. Allen Sch. for Physicians Aides, Jamaica, N.Y., 1978—; dir. placement, cons.; dir., organizer Clara Barton Sch., Nutley, N.J., 1986-87. Mem. AAUW, Am. Assn. Med. Assts., Faculty Wives of Franklin Pierce Coll. (pres. 1970-72). Roman Catholic. Home: 14 Donna Ct Nutley NJ 07110-3116 Office: Allen Sch Physician Aides 188 Montague St Brooklyn NY 11201-3609

WEGENER, PETER PAUL, educator, author; b. Berlin, Aug. 29, 1917; came to U.S., 1946; naturalized, 1953.; m. Annette Schleiermacher, Aug. 14, 1961; children: Paul, Christopher, Philip. Dr rer. nat., U. Berlin, 1943; MA (priv.), Yale U., 1960; Dr. Ing. (E.h.) (hon.), U. Karlsruhe, Germany, 1979. Researcher supersonic wind tunnels Kochel, Germany, 1943-45; researcher gasdynamics, hypersonic wind tunnels U.S. Naval Ordnance Lab., 1946-53, Jet Propulsion Lab. Calif. Inst. Tech., 1953-60; prof. applied sci. Yale U., New Haven, 1960-72, Harold Hodgkinson prof. engring. and applied sci., 1972—, chmn. dept. engring, applied sci., 1966-71, prof. emeritus, 1987—; sr. Am. scientist Humboldt Found., 1979;. Researcher and contbr. articles on hypersonics, condensation metastable state, chem. kinetics, flow systems real gases, bubbles to profl. jours. Inst. Advanced Study fellow, 1986. Fellow Am. Phys. Soc., Conn. Acad. Sci. & Engring. (charter). Home: 29 Montgomery Pkwy Branford CT 06405 Office: Yale U PO Box 2159 New Haven CT 06520-2159

WEHE, DAVID CARL, construction company executive; b. Urbana, Ill., June 29, 1949; s. Robert Louis Sr. and Marjorie Louise (McComb) W.; m. Maryam Tashakori; children: Kevin Michael, Christopher Mehdi. BCE, Cornell U., 1972, MCE, 1975. Project mgr. Stone & Webster Engrs., Boston, 1972-74, LeMessurier Assoc. Structural Engrs., Cambridge, Mass., 1975-77, Martin & Cagley Engrs., Bethesda, Md., 1977-78, Hyman Constrn. Co., Bethesda, 1978-80; pres. WDC Devel. Co., Bethesda, 1980-82, Met. Constrn. and Design, Rosslyn, Va., 1986-91; sr. estimator Tiber Constrn Co., Fairfax, Va., 1982-84; sr. project mgr. McDevitt & Street Co., Rockville, Md., 1984-86; pres. Timeline Constr. Inc., Rosslyn, Va., 1991—. Mem. Nat. Assn. Indsl. and Office Parks (No. Va. chpt.), D.C. Bldg. Indsl. Assn., Md. Assoc. Builders and Contractors. Republican. Presbyterian. Office: Timeline Constrn Inc 6701 Democracy Blvd Ste 300 Bethesda MD 20817-2405

WEHRHAHN, ALLEN LONG, financial services executive; b. Kinston, N.C., Mar. 26, 1959; s. Albert and Jacqueline Leigh (Allen) W.; m. Maureen Patricia Tregoning, Apr. 25, 1987; children: Michael Albert, Matthew Thomas. BSBA in Acctg., Bucknell U., 1981; MBA in Fin., Fairleigh Dickinson U., 1986. Cert. mgmt. acct. Fin. mgmt. trainee Beneficial Mgmt. Corp., Peapack, N.J., 1981-82; acctg. fin. analyst Beneficial Mgmt. Corp., Peapack, 1982-83, fin. systems analyst, 1983-86, dir., loan office planning, 1986-87, asst. v.p., planning and budgeting, 1987-89, asst. v.p., ops. planning and reporting, 1989-90, v.p., acquisitions, 1990—. Vestry mem. St. James Episcopal Ch., Hackettstown, N.J., 1990. Mem. Inst. Mgmt. Accts., Nat. Second Mortgage Assn. Republican. Office: Beneficial Mgmt Corp Am 200 Beneficial Ctr Peapack NJ 07977-9999

WEI, FU-SHANG (JOHN WEI), mechanical engineer; b. Nanking, China, June 21, 1948; came to U.S., 1975; s. Jo-Chen and Yu-Yuan (Cheng) W.; m. Daisy Li-Ren Sun, Jan. 20, 1954; children: John C., Paul H. BSME, Nat. Cheng-Kung U., Taiwan, 1970; MSME, Nat. Cheng-Kung U., 1972; PhD in Mech. Engring., Washington U., St. Louis, 1978. Registered profl. engr., Conn. Rsch. engr. specialist Kamen Aerospace Corp., Bloomfield, Conn., 1978-81; engr. specialist Bell Helicopter Textron, Ft. Worth, 1981-83; group leader structure and performance group test and devel. dept. Kaman Aerospace Corp., Bloomfield, 1983—; pres. Wei Engring., Inc., Windsor, Conn., 1984-87; v.p. New Eng. Tech., West Hartford, Conn., 1986-88. Contbr. articles to profl. jours. Chmn. Conn. Com. for Chinese Dem. Movement, Hartford, 1989; pres. Chinese Culture Ctr., Hartford, 1985-91. Mem. Am. helicopter Soc. (tech. dir. 1984-87). Office: Kaman Aerospace Corp Old Windsor Rd Bloomfield CT 06002-1312

WEIANT, ELIZABETH ABBOTT, retired biology educator; b. New Britain, Conn., July 4, 1913; d. William Armstrong and Flora (Abbott) W. BS, MS, Tufts U., 1943; MA, Radcliffe Coll., 1952; EdD, Boston U., 1970. Instr. biology Tufts Coll., Medford, Mass., 1943-56, asst. prof., 1957-61; asst. prof. biology Simmons Coll., Boston, 1961-71, assoc. prof., 1972-79, chmn. dept., 1977-79, ret., 1979; corr. Evening Citizen, Laconia, N.H., 1987—; researcher OSRD, USPHS, NSF, 1943-61; sr. rsch. fellow Max-Planck Inst., Seewiesen, Fed. Republic Germany, 1958; physiologist for product validation Cordis Corp., Miami, Fla., 1970;. Contbr. articles to profl. jours. Mem. Hist. Dist. Commn., Sanbornton, N.H., 1979-83; sec., mem. Sanbornton Conservation Commn., 1979-83, Trustees of Trust Fund, Sanbornton, 1985—; bd. dirs., sec. N.H. affiliate Am. Heart Assn., Manchester, 1981-85; bd. dirs., mem. coms. Franklin (N.H.) Regional Hosp., 1984-91; pres. Sanbornton Hist. Soc., 1980-82; publicity chmn. Friends N.H. Music Festival. Recipient Distng. Svc. award Tufts U., 1970, Tower award Westbrook Coll., Portland, Maine, 1974, Woman of Yr. award Tilton=Northfield Bus and Profl. Women, 1980, Heart of Gold award Am. Heart Assn., 1986, award for Pub. Svc., Belknap County Pomona Grange, 1990. Mem. Am. Inst. Biol. Scis., Sigma Xi (sec. 1947-59), Grange. Republican. Home: PO Box 11 Sanbornton NH 03269-0001

WEICKER, LOWELL PALMER, JR., governor of Connecticut; b. Paris, May 16, 1931; s. Lowell Palmer and Mary (Bickford) Paulsen; m. Claudia Testa Ingram, Dec. 21, 1984; children by previous marriage—Scot, Gray, Brian, Sonny, Mason Ingram, Lowell Palmer III, Andrew Ingram. Grad., Lawrenceville Sch., 1949; B.A. in Polit. Sci. Yale, 1953; LL.B., U. Va., 1958. Bar: Conn. 1960. Mem. Conn. Gen. Assembly, 1963-69; 1st selectmen Greenwich, Conn., 1964-68; mem. 91st Congress, 4th Dist. Conn., 1969-71; U.S. senator from Conn., 1971-89; mem. Com. on Energy and Natural Resources, Com. on Appropriations, Com. on Labor and Human Resources; ranking mem. Com. on Small Bus., Labor and Human Resources subcom. on Handicapped, Appropriations subcom. of Labor, Health and Human Resources; pres., chief exec. officer Research!America, Alexandria, Va., from 1989; gov. State of Conn., 1991—. Served with US Army, 1953-55. Republican. Episcopalian. Office: Office of Governor 210 Capitol Ave Hartford CT 06106-1568*

WEIDEMANN, CELIA JEAN, social scientist, international business development consultant; b. Denver, Dec. 6, 1942; d. John Clement and Hazel (Van Tuyl) Kirlin; m. Wesley Clark Weidemann, July 1, 1972; 1 child, Stephanie Jean. BS, Iowa State U., 1964; MS, U. Wis.-Madison, 1970, PhD, 1973; postgrad. U. So. Calif., 1983. Advisor, UN Food & Agr. Orgn., Ibadan, Nigeria, 1973-77; ind. researcher, Asia and Near East, 1977-78; program coord., asst. prof., rsch. assoc. U. Wis., Madison, 1979-81; chief institutional and human resources U.S. Agy. for Internat. Devel., Washington, 1982-85, team leader, cons., Sumatra, Indonesia, 1984; dir. fed. econs. program Midwest Rsch. Inst., Washington, 1985-86; pres. Weidemann Associates, Arlington, Va., 1986—; cons. U.S. Congress, Aspen Inst., Ford Found., World Bank, Nigeria, Gambia, Pakistan, Indonesia, AID, Kenya, Jordan, Egypt, Finnish Internat. Devel. Agy., Namibia, Internat. Ctr. Rsch. on Women, Zaire, UN Food and Agriculture Orgn., Ghana, Internat. Statis. Inst., The Netherlands, Global Exchange, 1986-87. Author: Planning Home Economics Curriculum for Social and Economic Development, Agricultural Extension for Women Farmers in Africa, 1990, Financial Services for Women, 1991; contbr. chpts. to books and articles to profl. jours. Am. Home Econs. Assn. fellow, 1969-73 (recipient research grant Ford Found. 1987-89). Mem. Soc. Internat. Devel., Am. Sociol. Assn., U.S. Dirs. of Internat. Agrl. Programs, Assn. for Women in Devel. (pres. 1989, founder, bd. dirs.), Internat. Devel. Conf. (bd. dirs., exec. com.), Am. Home Econs. Assn. (Wis. internat. chmn. 1980-81), Internat. Fedn. Home Econs., Internat. Platform Assn., Pi Lambda Theta, Omicron Nu. Roman Catholic. Avocations: mountain trekking, piano/pipe organ, canoeing, photography, poetry. Home and Office: 2607 24th St N Arlington VA 22207-4908

WEIDEMANN, JULIA CLARK, principal, educator; b. Batavia, N.Y., May 21, 1937; d. Edward Thomas and Grace Eloise (Kenna) Clark; m. Rudolph John Weidemann, July 9, 1960; 1 child, Michael John. BA in English, Daemen Coll., 1958; MS in Edn., SUNY, Buffalo, 1961, MEd in Reading Edn., 1973. Remedial reading tchr. West Seneca (N.Y.) Cen. Sch. Dist., 1972-79, coord. chpt. I reading program, 1974-79, reading coord., 1980-87; prin. Parkdale Elem. Sch./East Aurora (N.Y.) Union Free Sch., 1987—; adj. prof. edn. Canisius Coll.; tchr. cons. Scott Foresman Lang. Arts Textbooks. Mem. West Seneca Dist. Computer Adv. Com., 1980-87. Scholar Rosary Hill Coll., 1954, N.Y. State Regents, 1954; recipient Reading award Niagara Frontier Reading Coun., 1986. Mem. AAUW (life, Buffalo br., exec. bd. dir.), Assn. Compensatory Edn. (pres. 1984-85, exec. bd. mem. Region VI 1983-87 1982-87, conf. chmn. Region VI 1985-87), Internat. Reading Assn. (acting chmn. 3d eastern regional reading conf. 1980), Niagara Frontier Reading Assn. (pres. 1979-80, fin. com. chmn., bd. dir. 1973—), Daemen Coll. Alumni Assn. (bd. govs. 1987-87, chmn. alumni reunion weekend, chmn. sr. reception), Assn. Supervision and Devel., Assn. Tchr. Educators, Roycrofters (East Aurora 1989—), Delta Kappa Gamma (pres., Ruth Fraser scholar 1986), Beta Zeta (pres.), Phi Delta Kappa (Buffalo-South chpt. 1989). Democrat. Roman Catholic. Home: 50 Boxwood Cir Hamburg NY 14075-4212 Office: Parkdale Elem Sch 80 Parkdale Ave East Aurora NY 14052-1615

WEIDENFELD, EDWARD LEE, lawyer; b. Akron, Ohio, July 15, 1943; s. Sam and Beatrice (Cooper) W.; m. Sheila Rabb, Aug. 11, 1968; children: Nicholas, Daniel. BS, U. Wis., 1965; JD, Columbia U., 1968. Bar: N.Y. 1968, U.S. Supreme Ct. 1972, D.C. 1973. Pvt. practice N.Y.C., 1969-71, 73-82, Washington, 1982—; counsel, dir. energy staff Com. on Interior and Insular Affairs, U.S. Ho. of Reps., 1971-73; mem. faculty Am. Law Inst.-Am. Bar Assn. Continuing Legal Edn. Programs; mem. internat. del. to observe Philippine Election, 1986, internat. del. to observe Republic Korea Election, 1987, Pakistan Election, 1988, Chilean Election, 1989; lectr. to profl. groups; spl. cons. N.Y.C. Dept. Bldgs., 1967. Editor in chief Atomic Energy Law Jour., 1975-76. Mem. Pres.'s Commn. on White House Fellowships, 1977; nat. chmn. Lawyers for Reagan/Bush, 1980; chief dep. counsel Reagan/Bush Campaign, 1980; chmn. Reagan/Bush '84 Legal Adv. Bd., 1984; vice chmn. D.C. Rep. Com., 1984-88; mem. Coun. Adminstrv. Conf. of U.S., 1981-92, D.C. Rep. Com., 1988—; trustee Danny & Sylvia Fine Kaye Found., 1992—. Mem. ABA, D.C. Bar Assn., Fed. Communications Bar Assn., Internat. Bar Assn., Am. Law Inst., Assn. Bar City N.Y., Internat. Human Rights Law Group (vice chmn. bd. dirs.). Club: Met. (Washington). Home: 3059 Q St NW Washington DC 20007-3081

WEIDLINGER, PAUL, civil engineer; b. Budapest, Hungary, Dec. 22, 1914; came to U.S., 1944; s. Andrew and Juliete W.; m. Solveig Hojberg, Dec. 24, 1964; children—Thomas, Pauline, Jonathan. B.S., Tech. Inst., Brno, Czechoslovakia, 1934; M.S., Swiss Poly. Inst., Zurich, 1937. Registered profl. engr. 17 states. Chief engr. Atlas Aircraft Products, N.Y.C., 1944-46; chief tech. cons., dir. Nat. Housing Agy., Industrialization Program Div., Washington, 1946-47; dir. engring. div. United Indsl. Assocs., Washington, 1947-48; sr. ptnr. Weidlinger Assocs., cons. engrs., N.Y.C., 1948—; mem. seismic loads com. Am. Nat. Standards Inst., 1978-80; chmn. Nat. Acad. Scis. Evaluation Panel, Nat. Bur. Standards, 1978-80; mem. sci. adv. bd. to chief staff USAF, 1957-58; vis. lectr. Harvard U., 1955-64, MIT, 1952-64. Author: Aluminum in Modern Architecture, Vol. II, 1956; contbr. articles to profl. jours. Recipient award Engring. News-Record, 1966. Fellow ASCE (Ernest E. Howard award 1985, Moisseiff award 1975, J. James R. Croes medal 1963), Hudson Inst., Franklin Inst. (Frank P. Brown medal 1987); mem. Am. Concrete Inst., Nat. Acad. Engring., Earthquake Engring. Research Inst., AIAA, Internat. Assn. Bridge and Structural Engrs., N.Y. Acad. Scis. (bd. dirs nat. bldg. mus. 1982-88). Office: Weidlinger Assocs 333 7th Ave New York NY 10001-5004

WEIDMAN, JAMES EDWARD, jazz pianist; b. Youngstown, Ohio, July 23, 1953; s. James E. Sr. and Gertrude T. (Fagan) W. MusB in Piano, MusB in Edn., Youngstown State U., 1976. Pianist Abbey Lincoln, N.Y.C., 1982-91; pianist keyboards Steve Coleman, N.Y.C., 1987-92; pianist Cassandra Wilson, N.Y.C., 1990—; co-leader quartet, saxophonist Talib Kibwe, N.Y.C., 1991—. Home: 38 Cumberland St # 2C Brooklyn NY 11205

WEIDMAN, JOHN CARL, II, education educator, consultant; b. Ephrata, Pa., Oct. 3, 1945; s. John Carl and Mary Elizabeth (Grube) W.; m. Carla Sue Fassnacht, Aug. 6, 1967; children: Jonathan Scott, Rebecca Mary. AB in Sociology cum laude, Princeton U., 1967; AM, U. Chgo., 1968, PhD, 1974. Acting asst. prof. edn. U. Minn., Mpls., 1970-74, asst. prof. edn., sociology and Am. studies, 1974-77; sr. rsch. assoc. Bur. Social Sci. Rsch., Inc., Washington, 1977-78; assoc. prof. edn. and sociology U. Pitts., 1979-86, prof. edn. and sociology, 1986—, chmn. dept. adminstrv. and policy studies, 1986—; cons. Nat. Ctr. Adminstrv. Justice, Youthwork, Inc., Upper Midwest Tri-Racial Gen. Assistance Ctr. Mem. editorial bd. Jour. Higher Edn., 1989—, Rev. of Higher Edn., 1984-88, Am. Ednl. Rsch. Jour., 1990—; contbr. chts. to books, articles to profl. jours. Bd. dirs. Sch. Vol. Assn. Pitts., 1982-90, pres., 1984-87. Grantee U.S. Office Edn., 1971-73, Spencer Found., 1973-76, Nat. Inst. Edn., 1976-79; Fulbright scholar U. Augsburg, Germany, 1986-87; NEH grantee, 1985-86. Mem. Am. Ednl. Rsch. Assn. (sec. postsecondary div. 1987-89), Am. Sociol. Assn., Assn. Study Higher Edn., Am. Evaluation Assn., Comp. and Internat. Edn. Soc. Office: U Pitts 5S40 Forbes Quadrangle 230 S Bouquet St Pittsburgh PA 15260-0001

WEIDNER, JAMES HENRY, publishing executive; b. Carlisle, Pa., Nov. 27, 1940; s. Chester Walter and Marion B. (Henry) W.; m. Patricia Ann Tropp, Dec. 31, 1962 (div. June 1983); children: James David, Jeffrey Walter, Timothy Allen; m. Regina Marie Stuart, Aug. 4, 1991. BS, U. Pa., 1962; postgrad., Glassboro State. Pres., chief exec. officer Weidner Assocs., Inc., Riverton, N.J., 1967—; v.p. Foris Publs., Dordrecht, Holland, 1971-81; pres. Tycooly Pub., Oxford, England, 1982-89; editor W.B. Saunders Co., Phila., 1966-68; dept. chair No. Burlington County Regional High Sch., Columbus, 1962—; pres. Weidner & Sons, Pub., Cinnaminson, N.J., 1990—; cons. and lectr. in field. Author: Rusky, 1980; co-editor: Woodpeckers of the World, 1982; contbg. author: Helpbook, 1985. Mem. Cinnaminson Zoning Bd. Adjustment, 1985; committeeman Burlington County Dem. Orgn., 1983-85; sec. Merchantville (N.J.) Bd. Health, 1990—; trustee Joseph A. Sakach Meml. Scholarship Fund. Named Master Tchr. of Yr.; recipient Community Svc. award, Mayor's Recognition award. Mem. NEA, N.J. Edn. Assn. (del. to assembly), Burlington County Edn. Assn. (exec. com.), Am. Radio Relay League, Dredge Harbor Yacht Basin, BASS, Quill and Scroll, Nat. Hon. Soc. (hon.). Democrat. Home: 114 Woodbine Ave Merchantville NJ 08109-1854 Office: Weidner & Sons Pub PO Box 2178 Riverton NJ 08077-5178

WEIERMAN, ROBERT JOSEPH, orthopedic surgeon; b. Neptune, N.J., July 31, 1942; s. Albert F. and Dorothy V. W.; B.A., St. Peter's Coll., 1964; M.D., Georgetown U., 1968; m. Claire A. Boyle, Apr. 12, 1969; children—Christine, Robert Joseph, Thomas. Intern, Jersey Shore Med. Center, Neptune, 1968-69, resident in gen. surgery, 1969-70; resident orthopedic surgery N.J. Coll. Medicine and Dentistry, Newark, 1970-73, N.J. Orthopedic Hosp., Orange, 1970-73; practice medicine specializing in orthopedic surgery, Irvington, N.J., 1973—, South Orange, N.J., 1984—; clin. asso. prof. surgery U. Medicine and Dentistry N.J., 1973—; dir. Spine Center, Hosp. Center at Orange, 1979—, chmn. dept., 1981-90, pres.-elect, 1990—. Diplomate Am. Bd. Orthopedics. Fellow Am. Acad. Orthopedic Surgery, A.C.S.; mem. AMA (hosp. med. staff section governing coun. 1988—), Essex County Med. Soc., N.J. Orthopedic Soc., Acad. Medicine N.J., Am. Acad. Cerebral Palsy and Developmental Medicine, Eastern Orthopaedic Scoliosis Research Soc. Roman Catholic. Office: 519 S Orange Ave South Orange NJ 07079-2636

WEIGEL, ELSIE DIVEN, publishing executive, writer, editor; b. Phila., May 31, 1948; d. William Bleakley Diven and Elsie May (Betts) Darling; m. John C. Weigel, Dec. 19, 1970 (div. 1979); 1 Child, Kimberly Joy. BA, Am. U., 1970. Editorial asst. Water Pollution Control Fedn., Alexandria, Va., 1970-72; asst. dir. publs. Am. Speech, Hearing, and Lang. Assn., Rockville, Md., 1972-78; editor-in-chief Potato Chip/Snack Food Assn., Alexandria, 1978-79; dir. publs. Nat. Soc. Pub. Accts., Alexandria, 1979-80; editorial project dir. Energy Info. Adminstrn. U.S. Dept Energy, Washington, 1980-91; editorial project dir. NASA, Washington, 1991—. Editor newsletter Rittenhouse Family Assn.; contbr. articles to profl. jours. Mem. Life Skills Ctr. (bd. dirs. 1987—) Washington. Mem. Nat. Assn. Govt. Communicators (Blue Pencil award), Nat. Assn Female Execs., Sigma Delta Chi. Home: 11317 River Rd Lorton VA 22079-4221 Office: NASA 400 Maryland Ave SW Washington DC 20546-0001

WEIGLEY, RUSSELL FRANK, history educator; b. Reading, Pa., July 2, 1930; s. Frank Francis and Meta Beulah (Rohrbach) W.; m. Emma Eleanor Seifrit, July 27, 1963; children: Jared Francis Guldin, Catherine Emma Rohrbach. BA, Albright Coll., 1952; MA, U. Pa., 1953, PhD, 1956; HLD (hon.), Albright Coll., 1978. Instr. history U. Pa., Phila., 1956-58; asst. prof. Drexel Inst. Tech., Phila., 1958-60, assoc. prof., 1960-62; assoc. prof. Temple U., Phila., 1962-64, prof. history, 1964-85, Disting. Univ. prof., 1985—; vis. prof. Dartmouth Coll., Hanover, N.H., 1967-68; U.S. Army vis. prof. mil. history rsch. U.S. Army War Coll., 1973-74; U.S. Army Mil. History Rsch. Collection, Carlisle Barrakcs, Pa., 1973-74; pres. Am. Mil. Inst., Washington, 1975-76. Author: Quartermaster General of the Union Army: A Biography of M.C. Meigs, 1959, Towards an American Army: Military Thought from Washington to Marshall, 1962, History of the United States Army, 1967, 84, The Partisan War: The South Carolina Campaign of 1780-82, 1970, The American Way of War, 1973, Eisenhower's Lieutenants, 1981 (Athenaeum of Phila. Spl. award for Nonfiction by a Phila. Author, 1983), The Age of Battles: The Quest for Decisive Warfare from Breitenfeld to Waterloo, 1991; editor: The American Military: Readings in the History of the Military in

American Society, 1969, New Dimensions in Military History, 1976, Philadelphia: A 300-Year History, 1982. Mem. Dept. of the Army Hist. Adv. Commn., Washington, 1976-79, 88—, Pa. Hist. Records Adv. Com., Harrisburg, 1977-79; bd. dirs. Masonic Libr., Mus. of Pa., The Grand Lodge F & A.M. of Pa., Phila., 1990—. Penrose Fund grantee Am. Philos. Soc., 1958; fellow John Simon Guggenheim Meml. Found., 1969-70; recipient Samuel Eliot Morison prize Am. Mil. Inst., 1989. Mem. Hist. Soc. Pa. (vice chmn. 1989—, councilor 1983-89), Pa. Hist. Assn. (pres. 1975-78, v.p. 1967-75, coun. 1967—, editor jour. 1962-67), Am. Hist. Assn., Orgn. Am. Historians, Soc. Mil. Hist. (Disting. Book award 1992), So. Hist. Assn. Soc. Am. Historians Inc., Interuniv. Seminar on Armed Forces and Soc. Democrat. Unitarian. Home: 327 S Smedley St Philadelphia PA 19103-6717 Office: Temple U Dept History Philadelphia PA 19122

WEIHS, ERIKA, painter, illustrator; b. Vienna, Austria, Nov. 4, 1917; came to U.S., 1940; d. Arthur S. and Vilma (Friedman) Foster; m. Kurt Weihs, June, 1942; children: Tom (dec. 1985), John. Grad., Graphische Lehr und Versuchsanstalt, Vienna, 1937. Painter, illustrator N.Y.C. Illus. Don't Sing Before Breakfast, 1988, Menorahs, Mezuzas and Other Jewish Symbols, 1990, Cakes and Miracles, 1991, Days of Awe, 1991; 12 one-person shows, 1950-91. Mem. Nat. Assn. Women Artists (1st v.p. 1981, 2d v.p. 1983-84, Charles Horman Meml. prize 1982, Mr. and Mrs. Charles H. Levitt prize 1983, Charlotte Winston Meml. prize 1984, Elizabeth Stanton Blake Meml. award 1987), Audubon Artists (exhbn. chair, coord. 1984—), Am. Soc. Contemporary Artists, N.Y. Artists Equity. Studio: 41 Union Sq W # 1526 New York NY 10003

WEIK, CHARLES, chemistry educator. Prof. chemistry Union Coll., Schenectady, N.Y. Office: Union Coll Dept Chemistry Schenectady NY 12308

WEIKART, LYNNE ALKIRE, state agency administrator; b. Barberton, Ohio, Jan. 29, 1943; d. Leo and Lodran (Moore) Alkire; m. James Weikart, Aug. 19, 1965; children: Eric, Jeanne. BA, Case Western Res. U., 1964; PhD, Columbia U., 1983. Chief adminstr. fin. and mgmt. N.Y.C. Bd. Edn., 1980-84; coord. mgmt. info. systems Literacy Assistance Ctr., N.Y.C., 1984-88; dep. coord. youth svcs. Office of Youth Svcs., N.Y.C., 1986-88; asst. commr. adminstrn. N.Y. State Div. Human Rights, N.Y.C., 1988—. Bd. dirs. Cities in Schs., Inc., N.Y.C., 1988-89; pres. bd. Support for Tng. and Edn. in Programs, N.Y.C., 1988-89. Ford Found. fellow, 1978-80. Mem. Am. Polit. Sci. Assn., Am. Edn. Rsch. Assn., Am. Soc. Pub. Adminstrn. Democrat. Home: 536 W 111th St Apt 5 New York NY 10025-1954 Office: NY State Div Human Rights 55 W 125th St New York NY 10027-4512

WEIL, JAMES BEVERLY, insurance executive; b. Corpus Christi, Tx, Aug. 31, 1944; s. Charles B. and Dorothy Spinks; m. Pamela Martinek, Sept. 2, 1970; children: Heather Ashley, Allison Brooke. Student, Centre Coll., Danville, Ky., 1962-64; BA in Econ., U. New Mexico, 1966. Regional dir. Travelers Ins., San Francisco, 1966-70; regional dir. Metropolitan Life, N.Y.C., 1971-74, nat. dir. mktg., 1974-75, 1975-79, v.p. mktg., 1975-83, v.p. sr. svc., 1984--; . Contbr. articles to profl. jours. Chmn. Hospice, Norwalk, Ct. 1987-88, bd. dir.1985-88; chmn. Bus. Forum on Aging,San Francisco, 1986--; bd. advisors Healthways Foundations, Iselin, NJ., 1989--;Nat. Advisory councilman Robert Wood Johnson Foundation, Princeton, NJ. 1985-88. Mem. Am. Soc. Aging (bd. dirs. San Francisco chpt. 1985—), Nat. Leadership award 1990). Home: 90 Turkey Hill Rd S Westport CT 06880-6311 Office: Metropolitan Life One Madison Ave New York NY 10010

WEIL, LISL, artist; b. Vienna, Austria; came to U.S., 1939; Art dir. specialty store, N.Y.C.; writer, artist NBC-TV; freelance writer, illustrator N.Y.C. Performer children's concerts Little Orch. Soc., visual music Carnegie Hall and Avery Fisher Hall; performances with Mayor Philharmonic Orchestra's Around the U.S.; dancer, illustrator: Like Firebird, Carnival of the Animals; written and illus. 139 children's books. Home: 25 Central Park W New York NY 10023 also: 349 West End Ave New York NY 10024

WEIL, ROLF, educator; b. Neunkirchen, Germany, Aug. 5, 1926; came to U.S., 1940, naturalized, 1947; s. Julius Nathan and Jane (Heymann) W. B.S., Carnegie-Mellon U., 1946, M.S., 1949; Ph.D., Pa. State U., 1951; M. Engring. (hon.), Stevens Inst. Tech., 1967. Metallurgist, Am. Metal Co., Pitts., 1946-48; assoc. metallurgist Argonne Nat. Lab., Ill., 1951-54; mem. faculty Stevens Inst. Tech., Hoboken, N.J., 1956-91, prof. emeritus materials sci. and engring. Contbr. articles to profl. jours. Cons. govt. agys., pvt. cos. With AUS, 1954-56. Fellow Electrochem. Soc. (Electrodep. Div. Rsch. award 1980); mem. AIME, ASTM, Am. Electroplaters Soc. (Sci. Achievement award 1981), Inst. Metal Finishing, Sigma Xi, Tau Beta Pi, Phi Kappa Phi, Pi Lambda Upsilon. Home: 47 Carteret St West Orange NJ 07052-3402 Office: Castle Point Sta Hoboken NJ 07030-5907

WEILAND, JULIETTE MARIE, public relations executive, freelance writer and photographer; b. St. Cloud, Minn., Oct. 5, 1944; d. Raymond Henry and Marie Julie (Fradette) Peterson; m. James Edward Weiland, Sept. 18, 1965; children: James Edward Jr., Timothy Paul, Kristin Juliette, Stephanie Marie. BS, U. Minn., 1967; student, U. Calif., Berkeley, 1978-83, Silvermine Sch. Art, New Canaan, Conn., 1987. Cert. English tchr. English tchr. Anoka Hennepin Sch. Dist., Coon Rapids, Minn., 1968-71; ESL tutor Anoka Hennepin Sch. Dist., Anoka, Minn., 1971-73, Cherry Creek Sch. Dist., Englewood, Colo., 1975-76; ESL pvt. tutor Bethel, Conn., 1976-78; ptnr., owner, author Pamphleteers & Co., Wilton, Conn., 1986—; pub. rels. dir. Nursing & Home Care, Wilton, Conn., 1988—; owner Breathe Easy Environ. Assocs., Wilton, Conn., 1991—; freelance writer, Acton. Mass., 1982-84. Author (short story) Somewhere There's A Child Waiting For Me, 1984; newspaper columnist on polit. govt. issues, 1987-89; photographer various newspapers, mags., reports; contbr. numerous articles to profl. jours. Co-chmn. Open Door Soc. for Adoptive Parents, Acton, 1980-83; pub. rels. dir. League of Women Voters of Conn., Hamden, 1986-88, communications cons., 1988-89; publicity dir. Crop Walk for the Hungry, Wilton, 1987-88. Mem. Internat. Freelance Photographers Orgn., Nat. Fedn. Press Women, Pub. Rels. Soc. Am., Women in Communications Inc., Fairfield County Pub. Rels. Assn., Inc., Conn. Press Club (3d prize external ann. report for non-profits 1990, 2d prize 1991, 3d prize news photo 1991). Democrat. Roman Catholic. Home: 67 Signal Hill Rd Wilton CT 06897-1930 Office: Nursing & Home Care 180 School Rd Wilton CT 06897-2520

WEILBURG, DONALD KARL, orthodontist; b. N.Y.C., Apr. 12, 1936; s. John and Esther Edith (Alexandre) W.; m. Sally Rae Curwood, Sept. 5, 1937; children: Heidi Maria, Burkley Curwood, Lindsay Alexandre. AB, Dartmouth Coll., 1958; DMD, U. Pa., Phila., 1967, orthodontic cert., 1968. Clin. instr. oral medicine U. Pa. Sch. Dental Medicine, Phila., 1967; clin. instr. oral hygiene U. R.I. Sch. Oral Medicine, Kingstown, 1969; pvt. practice orthodontics Westerly, R.I., 1969—. Del. Dem. Nat. Conv., Miami, Fla., 1972, mem. rules com., Washington, 1972; mem. exec. com. Westerly Dem. Town Com., 1972-85, R.I. Dem. Com., Providence, 1972-84; bd. dirs. Trinity Square Reperatory Theater, Providence, 1976-82. With USPHS, 1966. Mem. Am. Assn. Orthodontics, ADA, Fedn. Dentaire Internat., R.I. Dental Assn., South County Dist. Dental Soc. (pres. 1974-75), Watch Hill (R.I.) Yacht Club (bd. dirs. 1975-80), Westerly Yacht Club, Omicron Kappa Upsilon. Democrat. Unitarian. Home: 13 Timothy Dr Westerly RI 02891-3200 Office: 5 Crestview Dr Westerly RI 02891

WEILER, HENRY RUTTER, JR., county clerk; b. Holtwood, Pa., Apr. 7, 1928; s. Henry Rutter and Anna May (Beckstedt) W.; m. Rita Elaine Keeney, Feb. 10, 1952; children: Robin Kay Nehls, Greta Ann (dec.), Scott William. BS in Chemistry, Pa. State U., 1951. Analytical chemist, R & D div. Babcock & Wilson Co., Alliance, Ohio, 1951-57; sr. rsch. engr., Carborundum Metals div. Carborundum Co., Akron, N.Y., 1957-65; sr. rsch. engr Carborundum Co., Falconer, N.Y., 1965-72; manpower program coord. Chautauqua Opportunities Inc., Mayville, N.Y., 1972-73; exec. dir. United Way S. Chaut Co., Jamestown, N.Y., 1973-85; procurement coord. N.Y. State Agrl. and Markets Dept., Albany, N.Y., 1985; county clk. County of Chautauqua, Mayville, 1986—. Inventor in field. Bd. mem. Akron (N.Y.) Cen. Sch. Bd., 1962-67, Chautauqua Bd. Health, Mayville, 1978-91; pres. Chautauqua County Hist. Soc., 1988-91, trustee, 1991—, life mem. With U.S. Army, 1946-47, Korea. Mem. Lakewood Kiwanis Club, Westfield Fish & Game Club, Free & Accepted Masons and Related Bodies, Pa. State Alumni Assn. (life mem.). Democrat. Methodist. Home: 14 Webster St Lakewood NY 14750-1059 Office: County Chautauqua Chautauqua at Erie Sts Mayville NY 14757

WEILL, GEORGES GUSTAVE, mathematics educator; b. Strasbourg, France, Apr. 9, 1926; came to U.S., 1956; s. Edmond and Germaine (Falck) W. Ed., Ecole Polytechnique, Paris, 1950; E.N.S., Telecom., Paris, 1952; Licence de Mathematiques, U. Paris, France, 1954, D.Sc. in Physics, 1955; Ph.D. in Math, U. Calif. at Los Angeles, 1960. Research scientist Compagnie Generale de Telegraphie Sans Fil, France, 1952-56; research fellow dept. elec. engring. Calif. Inst. Tech., Pasadena, 1956-59; teaching asso. math. U. Calif. at Los Angeles, 1959-60; research fellow math. Harvard, 1960-62; lectr., research asso. Yale, 1962-64; vis. asst. prof. Belfer Grad. Sch. Sci., Yeshiva U., 1964-65; assoc. prof. math. Poly. U., Bklyn., 1964-65, prof., 1966—. Mem. Am. Math. Soc., Societe Mathematique de France, IEEE (sr. mem.), Sigma Xi, Pi Mu Epsilon. Office: Polytechnic Univ 333 Jay St Brooklyn NY 11201-2990

WEIMER, DOUGLAS REID, lawyer; b. Somerset, Pa., Apr. 10, 1953; s. Reid A. and Thelma L. (Lint) W. Student, U. Pa., 1975; BA summa cum laude, U. Pitts., 1975; JD, U. Notre Dame, 1978. Bar: Pa. 1978, D.C. 1986, U.S. Supreme Ct. 1986. Law clkt. to atty. gen. Pa. Dept. of Justice, Harrisburg, Pa., 1974; fed. intern USDA, Washington, 1975, instr., 1991; law clk. to chief judge U.S. Army JAG Corps, Washington, 1976; law clk. U.S. Dept. Edn., Washington, 1977; atty. U.S. Securities & Exch. Commn., Washington, 1978-79; legis. atty. Congl. Rsch. Svc. Libr. of Congress, Washington, 1979—; teaching asst. law sch. U. Notre Dame, Ind., 1976-78; atty. Office of Tech. Assessment, U.S. Congress, Washington, 1988-90; mem. U.S. Del. to Berne Conv., Geneva, 1992; cons. in field. Contbr. articles to profl. jours. Recipient Svc. award Fed. Bar Assn., 1986. Mem. Fed. Bar Assn. (bd. dirs. Younger Lawyers div. 1983-86, Svc. award 1986), D.C. Bar Assn., Pa. Bar Assn., Soc. of Cincinnati (Pa.), Soc. of Pilgrims St. Mary's (sec. 1990—), Order of Founders and Patriots of Am. (states atty. 1988—), SAR (libr. 1986-91), Sons of the Revolution (asst. sec. 1985—), Soc. of Colonial Wars (asst. sec. 1985—), Soc. of the War of 1812 (historian 1987—), Racquet Club Phila., Phi Eta Sigma (sec. 1973-74), Lambda Iota Tau, Alpha Mu Gamma, Pi Gamma Mu, Phi Alpha Delta (v.p. 1977-78). Lutheran. Home: 3016 Tilden St NW Washington DC 20008 Office: Congrl Rsch Svc Libr Congress LMM 227 ALD Libr Washington DC 20540

WEINBAUM, GEORGE, medical educator; b. Bklyn., July 27, 1932; s. Hyman Al and Sarah Ruth (Kaplan) W.; m. Carol Miriam Rosenblatt, June 19, 1963; children: Eve, Cindy, Laura, Elliot. BA in Chemistry, U. Pa., 1953; MS in Biochemistry, Pa. State U., 1955, PhD in Biochemistry, 1957. Vis. researcher Marine Biol. Labs., Woods Hole, Mass., 1970-80; rsch. assoc. prof. microbiology Temple U., Phila., 1973-81, rsch. prof. microbiology, 1981—; rsch. assoc. prof. medicine U. Pa. Sch. Medicine, Phila., 1983-88, rsch. prof. medicine, 1988—; asst. chmn. for rsch., dir. rsch. div. dept. medicine The Grad. Hosp., Phila., 1982—; dir. rsch. div. dept. medicine Albert Einstein Med. Ctr., Phila., 1980-82, full mem., 1969-82; dir. biochem. sect. dept. pathology Geisinger Med. Ctr., Danville, Pa., 1957-61; lectr. in field. Contbr. articles to profl. jours. Grantee Nat. Heart, Lung and Blood Inst., 1972-91. Mem. Am. Soc. Biochemistry and Molecular Biology, Am. Assn. Pathologists, Am. Soc. for Microbiology, Am. Thoracic Soc. (bd. dirs. 1986-89), Sigma Xi, Gamma Sigma Delta, Phi Lambda Upsilon. Jewish. Home: 6532 N 12th St Philadelphia PA 19126-3640 Office: The Grad Hosp 415 S 19th St Philadelphia PA 19146-1464

WEINBAUM, MARTIN PAUL, insurance company executive; b. Bklyn., June 13, 1947; s. Ira and Betty (Diamond) W.; m. Susan Joye Eckhause, June 7, 1970; children: Ronald, Scott. AAS, Kingsborough Community Coll., Bklyn., 1967; BBA, Pace Coll., 1970. Acct. Met. Life Ins., N.Y.C., 1970-72; asst. treas. GEICO, Woodbury, N.Y., 1973-78; controller Continental Ins. Co., N.Y.C., 1978-86; v.p., chief fin. officer Assoc. Aviation Underwriters, Short Hills, N.J., 1986—. Cub pack treas. Boy Scouts Am., Mt. Sinai, N.Y., 1984-86; treas. North Shore Jewish Ctr., Port Jefferson, 1983-85; bd. dirs. White Meadow Temple. Mem. Am. Mgmt. Assn., Ins. Acctg. and Statis. Assn., Am. Payroll Assn., Soc. Ins. Accts., White Mead Jewish Ctr. Mens Club (v.p.), Lions (bd. dirs.). Democrat. Jewish. Office: Associated Aviation 51 John F Kennedy Pky Short Hills NJ 07078-2702

WEINBERG, GARY L., direct mail advertising executive; b. Hastings-On-Hudson, N.Y., June 22, 1962. BS in Mktg., MIS, Syracuse U., 1984. With Quality Letter Svc., N.Y.C., 1984—; Chmn. Pro-Mail User Group. Chmn. Stopirg Funding, Syracuse, N.Y., 1982-84; bd. dirs. Direct Mail Fundraisers of N.Y., 1990—. Mem. Mail Advt. Svcs. Assn. (bd. dirs.), Nat. Soc. Fundraising Execs. Office: Quality Letter Svc 22 W 32nd St New York NY 10001-3807

WEINBERG, JOHN LIVINGSTON, investment banker; b. N.Y.C., Jan. 5, 1925; s. Sidney James and Helen (Livingston) W.; m. Sue Ann Gotshal, Dec. 6, 1952; children: Ann K. (dec.), John, Jean. A.B. cum laude, Princeton U., 1948; M.B.A., Harvard U., 1950. With Goldman, Sachs & Co., N.Y.C., 1950—, ptnr., 1956-76, sr. ptnr., 1976-90, co-chmn. mgmt. com., 1976-84, chmn. mgmt. com., 1984-90; sr. chmn. Goldman, Sachs & Co., 1990—; bd. dirs. B.F. Goodrich Co., Knight-Ridder, Inc., Seagram Co. Ltd., Capital Holding Corp., E.I. du Pont de Nemours & Co., Champion Internat. Corp.; mem. Conf. Bd. Bd. govs., mem. exec. com. N.Y. Hosp.-Cornell Med. Ctr.; charter trustee Princeton U. 2d lt. USMCR, 1942-46; capt. 1951-52. Mem. Coun. on Fgn. Rels., The Bus. Coun., Japan Soc. (bd. dirs.), Blind Brook Club, Century Country Club. Clubs: Blind Brook, Century Country. Office: Goldman Sachs & Co 85 Broad St Fl 22 New York NY 10004-2434

WEINBERG, MARC BERNARD, management consultant; b. Olten, Switzerland, Aug. 22, 1954; came to U.S., 1961; s. Don and Paula (Troller) W. BS in Acctg., SUNY, Binghamton, 1976; MBA in Fin., Baruch Coll., 1981. CPA, Ga. Sr. acct. Macmillan, Inc., N.Y.C., 1978-80; mgr. planning & budgeting Simmons Internat., Ltd., Atlanta, 1981-86; treas. Anorad Corp., Hauppauge, N.Y., 1987-90; cons., prin. Marc Weinberg, CMA, CPA, Westbury, N.Y., 1991—. Mem. AICPA, N.Y. Soc. CPAs, Inst. Mgmt. Accts. (cert., dir. cert. mgmt. acct. programs 1989—), Soc. Cost Estimating and Analysis, Toastmasters (competent toastmaster 1991). Home: 121 E Cabot Ln Westbury NY 11590-6433

WEINBERG, SAMUEL, pediatric dermatologist; b. N.Y.C., Jan. 12, 1926; s. Harry and Rose (Stecher) W.; m. Pearl Oksner, Dec. 12, 1948; children: Ronald Andrew, Robin Ann. MB, Chgo. Med. Sch., 1947, MD, 1948. Clin. asst. prof. dermatology to prof. dermatology Med. Ctr. NYU, N.Y.C., 1961—. Author: Color Atlas of Pediatric Dermatology, 1975, 2d rev. edit., 1990. Capt. USAF, 1951-53. Fellow Am. Acad. Pediatrics, ACP, Am. Acad. Dermatology (chmn. pediatric dermatology sect. 1978-81, com. dermatolog. subspecialties 1984-86, task force pediatric dermatology 1981-84); mem. Soc. Pediatric Dermatology (charter, pres. 1980-81). Office: NYU Med Ctr 530 1st Ave New York NY 10016-6402

WEINBERGER, CASPAR WILLARD, former secretary of defense; b. San Francisco, Aug. 18, 1917; s. Herman and Cerise Carpenter (Hampson) W.; m. Jane Dalton, Aug. 16, 1942; children: Arlin Cerise, Caspar Willard. A.B. magna cum laude, Harvard, 1938, LL.B., 1941; LLD (hon.), U. Leeds, England, 1989. Bar: Calif. Law clk. U.S. Judge William E. Orr, 1945-47; with firm Heller, Ehrman, White & McAuliffe, 1947-69, ptnr., 1959-69; mem. Calif. Legislature from 21st Dist., 1952-58; vice chmn. Calif. Rep. Cen. Com., 1960-62, chmn., 1962-64; chmn. Com. Calif. Govt. Orgn. and Econs., 1967-68; dir. fin. Calif., 1968-69; chmn. FTC, 1970; dep. dir. Office Mgmt. and Budget, 1970-72, dir., 1972-73; counsellor to the Pres., 1973; sec. HEW, 1973-75; gen. counsel, v.p., dir. Bechtel Power Corp., San Francisco, 1975-80, Bechtel, Inc., 1975-80, Bechtel Corp., 1975-80; sec. Dept. Def., Washington, 1981-87; counsel Law Firm of Rogers & Wells, Washington, N.Y.C., 1988—; pub. Forbes Magazine, New York, 1989—; formerly staff book reviewer San Francisco Chronicle; moderator weekly TV program Profile, Bay Area, sta. KQED, San Francisco, 1959-68; Frank Nelson Doubleday lectr., 1974. Writer column on Calif. govt., 1959-68; author: Fighting for Peace: Seven Critical Years in the Pentagon, 1990. Chmn. Pres.'s Com. on Mental Retardation, 1973-75; former mem. Trilateral Commn.; former mem. adv. council Am. Ditchley Found.; former bd. dirs. Yosemite Inst.; former trustee St. Luke's Hosp., San Francisco, Mechanics Inst.; former chmn. nat. bd. trustees Nat. Symphony, Washington; former bd. govs. San Francisco Symphony; chmn. bd. USA-ROC Econ. Coun., 1991—; co-chair Winston Churchill Travelling Fellowships Found., 1989—. Served from pvt. to capt., inf. AUS, 1941-45, PTO. Decorated Bronze Star, Grand Cordon of Order of the Rising Sun (Japan), Hon. Knight Grand Cross Civil Div. Order of Brit. Empire; recipient Presdl. medal Freedom with distinction, 1987, George Catlet Marshall medal, 1988, Civil award Hilal-i-Pakistan, 1989. Mem. ABA, State Bar Calif., Century Club (N.Y.), Bohemian Club (San Francisco), Pacific Union Club (San Francisco), Harvard Club (Washington). Episcopalian (former treas. Diocese of Calif.). Office: Forbes Mag 60 5th Ave New York NY 10011-8865

WEINBERGER, STEVEN ELLIOTT, internist; b. Phila., Jan. 28, 1949; s. Leon and Ruth (Shoemaker) W.; m. Janet Harrison Brauer, June 14, 1970; children: Eric, Mark. AB, Princeton U., 1969; MD, Harvard U., 1973. Diplomate Am. Bd. Internal Medicine, Am. Bd. Pulmonary Disease, Am. Bd. Critical Care Medicine. Intern, then resident U. Calif. Med. Ctr., San Francisco, 1973-75; intern U. Calif. Med. Ctr., San Francisco, Md., 1973-74; resident U. Calif. Med. Ctr., San Francisco, 1974-75; fellow Nat. Heart Lung and Blood Inst., NIH, 1975-78; attending physician Beth Israel Hosp., Boston, 1978—, clin. dir. pulmonary and critical care div., 1986—; instr. Harvard Med. Sch., Boston, 1978-80, asst. prof. medicine, 1980-89, assoc. prof., 1989—;. Author: Principles of Pulmonary Medicine, 1986, 2d edit., 1992. Fellow ACP, Am. Coll. Chest Physicians. Office: Beth Israel Hosp 330 Brookline Ave Boston MA 02215-5491

WEINBLATT, SEYMOUR SOLOMON, lawyer; b. Bklyn., May 6, 1922; s. David and Lillian (Kantor) W.; m. Dorothy Robinovitz, June 29, 1922 (div. May 1973); children: Jeffrey Howard, Jan Robin; m. Elizabeth Jean King Shelton, June 23, 1939; children: Eric H. Waser, Mark S. Waser (dec.). BA in Zoology, Ind. U., 1947; JD with honors, Rutgers U., 1950, postgrad., 1950-53. Bar: N.J. 1951, U.S. Dist. Ct. N.J. 1951, U.S. Supreme Ct. 1957, U.S. Ct. Appeals (3d cir.) 1975. Atty. City of Manville, N.J., 1962-64, atty. bd. edn., 1962-66; ptnr. Strauss & Tauriello, Flemington, N.J., 1984—. Mem. bd. edn. Twp. of Bethlehem, 1977-80, pres. bd. edn., 1979. Mem. ABA, Hunterdon County (N.J.) Bar Assn. Jewish. Home: 15011 Punta Rassa Rd Apt 503 Fort Myers FL 33908-2738 Office: Strauss & Tauriello 63 Main St Flemington NJ 08822-1452

WEINER, CLAIRE MURIEL, freelance writer; b. Bronx, N.Y., Dec. 18, 1951; d. David and Norma (Berry) W. BA, U. Miami, Coral Gables, Fla., 1973; MA, U. Md., 1980. Pub. rels. specialist Hialeah Recreation Div., Hialeah, Fla., 1974-77; freelance writer North Miami Beach, 1977-78, Germantown, Md., 1989—, Montgomery County, Md., 1981—; govt. affairs liaison for new ednl. data base co. being formed, Montgomery County, 1982—. Contbr. articles to local newspapers; contbr. travel articles to profl. jours, mags. Active membership com. newsletter Greater Miami Jewish Fedn., 1974-77; charter mem. Women for Today chpt. B'nai B'rith Women, Washington, 1985-89. Mem. NAFE, Pub. Rels. Soc. Am., Internat. Platform Assn. Jewish. Home: 18828 Sky Blue Cir Germantown MD 20874-5398

WEINER, EARL DAVID, lawyer; b. Balt., Aug. 21, 1939; s. Jacob Joseph and Sophia Gertrude (Rachanow) W.; m. Gina Helen Priestley Ingoglia, Mar. 30, 1962; children: Melissa Danis Balmain, John Barlow. A.B., Dickinson Coll., 1960; LL.B., Yale U., 1968. Bar: N.Y. 1969. Assoc. Sullivan & Cromwell, N.Y.C., 1968-76, ptnr., 1976—; adj. prof. Rutgers U. Sch. Law, 1987-88; bd. dirs. The Acting Co., 1988—, v.p. 1991—. Gov. Brooklyn Heights Assn., 1980-87, pres., 1985-87, adv. com., 1987—; gov. The Heights Casino, 1979-84, pres., 1981-84; trustee Bklyn. Bot. Garden, 1985—, vice chmn., 1989—; trustee Green-Wood Cemetery, 1986—, vice chmn., 1991—; bd. advisers Dickinson Coll., Carlisle, Pa., 1986-90, chmn., 1988-90, trustee, 1988—; mem. adv. com. East Rock Inst., 1988—. Lt. USN, 1961-65. Mem. ABA, N.Y. State Bar Assn., Assn. of Bar of City of N.Y. Office: Sullivan & Cromwell 125 Broad St New York NY 10004-2400

WEINER, EDWARD, civil engineer, federal agency official; b. Bklyn., Mar. 31, 1941; s. Abe C. and Elsie (Botwinick) W.; m. Joanne Jessen, Sept. 9, 1967 (div. Mar. 1988); children: Jennifer Lynn, Michael Andrew. BA, NYU, 1963, BCE, 1963; MS in Civil Engring., Purdue U., 1964; M in Pub. Adminstrn., U. So. Calif., 1978. Registered profl. engr. Hwy. research engr. Bur. of Pub. Rds., then Fed. Hwy. Adminstrn., Washington, 1964-70; mgr. urban analysis program Office Sec. of Transp., Washington, 1970-77, sr. policy analyst, 1978—; sec. Task Force on Pub. Transp., Transp. Research Bd., 1971-72, mem. adv. com. Transit Performance Standards, 1973-75, mem. Com. on Travel Behavior and Values, Oct. 1973—; mem. subcom. on Evaluation of Urban Transp. Alternatives, 1977-78, mem. com. Econ. Devel. of Land and Transp. Systems, 1983-86; mem. group 1 council, transp. systems planning and adminstrn., 1984—; mem. com. Internat. Relations and Policy Process; guest lectr. George Washington U., U. Va., Portland State U., U. Wis. Co-editor: Emerging Transportation Planning Methods, 1978; author, co-author: Urban Transportation Planning in the U.S., 1987, 3d edit., 1988; (monographs) Role of Taxicabs in Urban Transportation, Glossary of Urban Public Transportation Terms, Modal Split, 1966; co-editor Internat. Assn. for Travel Behavior newsletter, 1985—; contbr. over 50 articles to profl. jours. Mem. editorial adv. bd. Transp., 1978-80. Asst. troop leader Girl Scouts Am., Silver Spring, Md., 1981-82; v.p. Unitarian Universalist Ch. of Silver Spring, 1984, pres., 1985-86. Edn. for Public Mgmt. fellow U.S. Dept. Transp., 1978; recipient Bronze medal Dept. Transp., 1981, Spl Achievement awad, 1990. Mem. ASCE, Transp. Research Bd. Home: 12915 Buccaneer Rd Silver Spring MD 20904-3311 Office: US Dept Transp P-30 400 7th St SW Washington DC 20590-0002

WEINER, HERBERT BERGER, financial consultant; b. Boston, Apr. 23, 1949; m. Leslie N. Weiner, Aug. 27, 1972. BA in Econs., U. Mass., 1971; MBA, Cornell U., 1973. CPA, Mass. In-charge auditor Price Waterhouse, Boston, 1973-76; dir. acctg. Computervision Corp., Bedford, Mass., 1976-85; v.p. fin., treas. Denning Mobile Robotics, Wilmington, Mass., 1985-89; pres. Weiner Assocs., Wellesley Hills, Mass., 1989—. Mem. AICPAs, Mass. Soc. CPAs, Treas. Club of Boston, B'nai B'rith (treas. 1977—). Home: 56 Clifton Rd Newton MA 02159-3147 Office: Weiner Assocs 70 Walnut St Wellesley MA 02181-2100

WEINER, JONATHAN, management consultant; b. N.Y.C., May 27, 1943; s. David and Paula Ganzer W.; divorced; 1 child, Joanna. BA, Harvard U., 1964. Asst. budget dir. City of N.Y., 1967-74; staff dir. N.Y. State Moreland Art Commn., N.Y.C., 1974-76; prin. McKinsey & Co. Inc., N.Y.C., 1976-91; dir. APM, Inc., N.Y.C., 1991—. Trustee Interfaith Med. Ctr., Bklyn., 1989-90, Citizens Budget Commn., N.Y.C., 1990—. Home: 393 W End Ave New York NY 10019 Office: APM Inc 810 7th Ave New York NY 10019-5818

WEINER, LESLIE J., trade association administrator; b. Boston, Nov. 28, 1958; d. Loretta M. (Rimer) DeStefano. BS, Gulford Coll., 1981; MA, Ind. State U., 1986; postgrad., U. Md., 1991—. Project adminstr. Nat. Conf. Christ & Jews Inc., Greensboro, N.C., 1978-79; adminstr. Ctr. Energy Policy Inc., Boston, 1981; sci. technician Nat. Climatic Ctr., Asheville, N.C., 1992—; social rsch. asst. Rsch. Triangle Inst., Rsch. Triangle Park, N.C., 1985; curriculum evaluation coord. U. N.C. Sch. Medicine, Chapel Hill, 1985-88; assoc. dir. mem. svcs. Am. Seed Trade Assn., Washington, 1989—; cons. Looking Glass Rock Film & TV, Asheville, 1991; pres. Concepts Unlimited Internat., Bethesda, Md., 1991. Contbr. articles to profl. jours. Mem. leadership doner com. WAMU Pub. Radio, 1989—; feed the homeless, Joshua House, 1989—; tutor Melrose (Mass.) Pub. Sch. and Asheville Pub. Sch., 1983-89; teen counselor Teen Outreach Ctr., 1977-78. Dana scholar, Guilford Coll., 1980, 81. Mem. Assn. for Women in Sci., Amnesty Internat., Sierra Club (vice chmn. exec. com. Rock Creek chpt., co-chmn. edn. com.), Nature Conservancy, Greenpeace, Theta Gamma Epsilon, Pi Gamma Mu. Democrat. Jewish. Home: 313 Elm Ave Silver Spring MD 20912-5437

WEINER, LYNN JOY, technical writer; b. Bklyn., Jan. 22, 1959; d. Herman and Shirley (Campi) W. AA, Nassau Community Coll., Garden City, N.Y., 1980; BA, L.I. U., 1982, MPA, 1983. Systems control asst. Standard Chartered Bank, N.Y.C., 1983-84, asst adminstr. internat. cash mgmt., 1984-86, tech. documentation officer, 1986; officer's asst. for spl. projects Chem. Bank, N.Y.C., 1986-87; mgr. med. office Dr. Harvey H. Jay,

N.Y.C., 1987-88; tech. writer Seaman Furniture Co., Inc., Uniondale, N.Y., 1988-91; sr. tech. writer, mgr. ICM Electronic Banking Svcs., Great Neck, N.Y., 1991—; tech. cons. Kaplan Theatres, Bronx, N.Y., 1988. Co-editor: (newsletter) The Living Society. Vol. Syosset (N.Y.) Sr. Day Care Ctr., 1982-83; bd. dirs. Congregation Peace and Brotherhood of Monastir, Inc. Recipient vol. award Syosset Sr. Day Care Ctr., 1982. Mem. NAFE. Home: 2941 Carlyle Rd Wantagh NY 11793-1708 Office: ICM Electronic Banking Svcs 60 Cuttermill Rd Great Neck NY 11021-3104

WEINER, MERVYN, mergers and acquisitions executive; b. Boston, Aug. 21, 1935; s. Samuel and Celia Sophia (Weiner) W.; m. Marjorie J. Kapelsohn, June 1962 (div. May 1978): children: Joshua, Michael. BS, U. Mass., 1957; MS, Tufts U., 1962; MBA with honors, Boston U., 1967. Group leader New England Nuclear, Boston, 1962-68; mgr. mktg. Hoffmann-LaRoche, Nutley, N.J., 1968-75; mgr. corp. strategic planning Pfizer, Inc., N.Y.C., 1975-77; v.p. mktg. Nichols Inst., San Pedro, Calif., 1977-78; cons. Marina del Rey, Calif., 1978-80; dir. corp. devel. Bristol-Myers Squibb Co., N.Y.C., 1980-92, v.p. health care group, 1992—; adj. prof. Calif. State U., Long Beach, 1978-80. Contbr. articles to profl. jours. Chmn. bd. dirs. Co Dance Co., N.Y.C., 1985. Tufts U. rsch. fellow, 1962. Mem. AAAS, Am. Chem. Soc., Am. Assn. Advancement Med. Instrumentation, N.Y. Acad. Scis., Biomedical Mktg. Assn. Home: 245 E 54th St New York NY 10022-4707

WEINER, MURRAY, structural engineer; b. Phila., Nov. 2, 1934; s. Albert and Sally (Weiss) W.; m. Corinne Borden (div.); children: Stuart Howard, Stanton David; m. Marcia Karen Toth, Oct. 23, 1976; 1 child, Adam Robert. BSCE, Tri-State Coll., 1962; MCE, Villanova U., 1969. Registered profl. engr., Pa., Md. Draftsman, engr., sr. assoc. Schulcz & Padlasky, Phila., 1957-70; mgr. engring. Lamprecht Cons., Balt., 1970-74; asst. dir. engring. RTKL, Balt., 1974-75; sr. structural engr., mgr. engring. Mass Transit Adminstrn., —, 1975-82; prin. LPJ, Inc., —, 1982—; fallout shelter analyst for fed. govt., 1969. Mem. ASCE, Nat. Soc. Civil Engrs., Precst Concrete Inst., Md. Soc. Profl. Engrs., Md. Homebuilders Assn., NRA. Office: LPJ Inc 16 W 25th St Baltimore MD 21218

WEINER, RICHARD ALAN, clinical psychologist; b. Phila., Nov. 12, 1952; s. Alvin Martin and Elaine (Lotman) W. AB, Franklin and Marshall Coll., 1975; MA in Counseling Psychology, Long Island U., 1978, MS in Clin. Psychology, 1981, PhD in Clin. Psychology, 1988. Lic. psychologist. Psychology intern Roosevelt Hosp., N.Y.C., 1980-81; staff psychology resident Bronx (N.Y.) Psychiatric Hosp., 1981-88; pvt. practice Bala Cynwyd, Pa., 1990-; supervising psychologist Bustleton Guidance Ctr., Phila., 1988-; presenter Ea. Psychol. Assn. Conv., Boston, 1989. Contbr. articles to profl. jours. Recipient rsch. grant NSF, N.Y.C., 1979. Mem. Am. Psychol. Assn., Pa. Psychol. Assn., Phila. Soc. Clin. Psychologists, N.Y. Soc. Clin. Psychologists, Nat. Sculpture Soc. Jewish. Office: Belmont and City Line Aves Ste 304 GSB Bldg Bala Cynwyd PA 19004

WEINER, ROBERT STEPHEN, federal agency administrator; b. Paterson, N.J., Apr. 3, 1947; s. Jess Joseph Weiner and Dorothea Violet (Slavin) Tabor. BA, Oberlin Coll., 1969; MA, U. Mass., 1974. Student coord. Hampshire County, dir. telephone bank Kennedy for U.S. Senate, Amherst, Mass., 1970; dir. nat. voter registration Young Dems. Am., Washington, 1971-72; dir. voter registration, media dir. get out the vote Dem. Nat. Com., Washington, 1972; legis. asst. Congressman Edward Koch, Washington, 1974-75; staff dir. subcom. health and long-term care U.S. Ho. of Reps., Washington, 1975-76, staff dir. com. aging, 1976-80, media dir., press sec. com. narcotics, 1987-90, press sec./communications dir. Com. on Govt. Ops., 1990—; nat. campaign aide Kennedy for Pres., Washington, 1980; sr. assoc. Mgmt. Recruiters Internat., Springfield, Mass., 1981-83; dir. Robert Weiner Assocs., Amherst, 1983-86; dir. gen. press room Dem. Nat. Convention, Atlanta, 1988; cons. Carter-Mondale Transition, Washington, 1976-77, Congressman Claude Pepper, Washington, 1984. Represented in permanent exhbns. Nat. Mus. Am. History, Smithsonian Instn., Washington; contbr. numerous articles to profl. jours. Dem. nominee for U.S. Congress, Mass., 1986; chmn. Road Runners Am. Nat. 10 Mile Championship, Amherst, 1984; vice chmn. Dem. Town Com., Amherst, 1984-87; legis. chmn. Pioneer Valley Gray Panthers, Amherst, 1981-87. Named Communicator of Yr. Washington Crime News Svcs., 1988, 89, 90. Mem. Assn. House Dem. Press Assts., Congl. Staff Club, Nat. Dem. Club, Sugarloaf Mountain Athletic Club (pres. 1984-86), Potomac Valley Sr. Track Club, Capitol Hill Runners (pres. 1991—). Home: 1104 Sanford Ln Accokeek MD 20607-2324 Office: US Ho of Reps Com on Govt Ops 2157 Rayburn House Ofc Bldg Washington DC 20515

WEINER, SEYMOUR SIDNEY, French educator; b. N.Y.C., Sept. 4, 1917; s. Morris and Jennie (Ostashinski) W.; m. Bobbie West; children: Anthony (dec.), Marc, Paula. BA, CCNY, 1940; MA, U. Calif., Berkeley, 1941; PhD, Columbia U., 1950, MSLS, 1952. Bibliographer U. Ill. Libr., Champaign, 1952-53; asst. to assoc. prof. U. Wash., Seattle, 1953-63; assoc. prof. French SUNY, Stony Brook, 1963-64; prof. French U. Mass., Amherst, 1964-89, dir. grad. studies, 1965-75, prof. emeritus, 1989—. Mng. editor French Rev., 1965-68; editor-in-chief Critical Bibliography of French Literature, 1965-75; author: Francis Carco, 1952; contbr. 50 articles to profl. jours. U. Wash. grantee, 1954-62; Knight, Order of Merit of the Acad. Palms, France, 1970; recipient medallion Cath. U. of the West, Angers, France, 1987. Mem. ALA, MLA, Am. Assn. Tchrs. French (exec. coun. 1965-68, chpt. pres. 1984-85), Societe des Lettres, Sciences et Beaux Arts de l' Aveyron, Societe des Professeurs Francais et Francophones en Amerique. Democrat. Jewish. Home: 38 Echo Hill Rd Amherst MA 01002-1633 Office: U Mass Dept French/Italian Amherst MA 01003

WEINERT, HENRY M., biomedical business executive; b. Nordhausen, Kassel, Fed. Republic Germany, May 31, 1940; s. Heinrich V. Nennenstiehl and Martha H. Weinert; m. Helen Koopmans, Feb. 14, 1966 (div. June 1982); children: Jason C., Brian T.; m. Kerri V. Keaton, Sept. 25, 1989. BA in Sci., Columbia Coll., 1962; MBA, Harvard Grad. Sch. Bus., 1970. Med. rsch. assoc. Columbia Univ., N.Y.C., 1964-65; exec. v.p., founder Clin. Diagnostic Lab., New Haven, Conn., 1966-68; dir. planning, bus. devel. Lederle Labs./Am. Cyan., Pearl River, N.Y., 1970-73, mktg. dir., 1973-74; bus. devel. mgr. Corning (N.Y.) Glass Works, 1974-77; pres., founder Boston Biomed. Cons., Waltham, Mass., 1977—; spl. ltd. ptnr. MedVenture Assocs., San Francisco, 1965—, Interwest Ptnrs., San Francisco, 1989; presenter, lectr. in field. Patentee laser fabrication of microsuture needles; contbr. articles to profl. jours. Pres. Svc. Soc., Columbia Coll., 1959; chmn. Student Union Com., Columbia Coll., 1961; treas. Class 1962, Columbia Coll., 1962-64; others. Recipient Alumni Achievement award Columbia Coll., 1962; grantee NIH, 1964-66. Mem. Biomed. Mktg. Assn. (bd. dirs. 1978-86, Recognition award 1986), Am. Assn. Clin. Chemistry. Lutheran. Home: 86 Myles Standish Rd Weston MA 02193-2124 Office: Boston Biomed Cons 100 5th Ave Waltham MA 02154-8703

WEINHOLD, JOHN R., medical oncologist; b. North Kingstown, R.I., Nov. 19, 1956; s. John R. and Carol A. (Rourke) W.; m. Diane M. Trippany, May 24, 1978; 1 child, John Lincoln. BS magna cum laude, St. Lawrence U., 1978; MD, Tel Aviv U., 1982. Intern internal medicine Mt. Sinai Svcs., City Hosp. Ctr. at Elmhurst (N.Y.), 1982-83, resident internal medicine, 1983-85; clin. fellow hematology Mt. Sinai Hosp., N.Y.C., 1985-86; rsch. fellow med. oncology Roswell Park Cancer Inst., N.Y. State Dept. Health, Buffalo, 1986-88; physician, active staff TriCounty Meml. Hosp., Gowanda, N.Y., 1988-90; physician, cons. staff Gowanda Psychiat. Ctr., Helmuth, N.Y., 1988-90; active staff Corning (N.Y.) Hosp., 1990—; assoc. hematology med. oncology Guthrie Med. Group, Corning, 1990—; assoc. staff St. Joseph's Hosp., Elmira, N.Y., 1991—; cons. staff Schuyler Hosp., Montour Falls, N.Y., 1992—. Mem. Ch. in the World com. 1st Presbyn. Ch., Corning, 1992, elder, 1989—. Mem. ACP, AMA, Med. Soc. State of N.Y., Med. Soc. County of Steuben, Irving Bachelier Soc., Phi Beta Kappa, Beta Beta Beta. Republican. Home: 118 W Hill Terr Painted Post NY 14870 Office: Guthrie Med Group PC 130 Centerway Corning NY 14830

WEININGER, ROBERT S., lawyer; b. Washington, Apr. 12, 1950; s. Arthur David and Annette (Shore) W.; m. Nancy Fitzgerald, Aug. 12, 1978; children: Andrew, Lauren. BA, U. Wis., 1973; JD, Washington U., St. Louis, 1979. Law clk. to judge Harlington Wood Jr. U.S. Ct. of Appeals 7th cir., Chgo., 1979-80; assoc. Kirkland & Ellis, Chgo., 1981-83, Paul, Weiss, Rifkind, Wharton & Garrison, N.Y.C., 1983-87; pvt. practice, 1987-90; ptnr. Hochfelder & Weininger, White Plains, N.Y., 1990—. Editor-in-chief Washington U. Law Quar., 1978-79. Mem. ABA, N.Y. State Bar Assn., Westchester County Bar Assn. Republican. Home: 11 Highfield Rd Harrison NY 10528-2201 Office: Hochfelder & Weininger 81 Main St White Plains NY 10601-1711

WEININGER, STEPHEN JOEL, chemistry educator; b. N.Y.C., Mar. 28, 1937; s. Isadore and Ruth (Hochman) W.; m. Jennifer Lynn Barkham, Oct. 15, 1961; children: Elliot B., David G. BA, CUNY, 1957; PhD, U. Pa., 1964. Sr. demonstrator U. Durham, Eng., 1964-65; asst. prof. Worcester (Mass.) Poly. Inst., 1965-70, assoc. prof., 1970-77, prof., 1977—; vis. assoc. prof. Colo. State U., Fort Collins, 1977-78; cons. U.S. Army, Rsch., Devel. & Engring. Ctr., Natick, 1979-90. Author: Comtemporary Organic Chemistry, 1972; co-author: Organic Chemistry, 1984. Mem. Worcester Commn. Fgn. Rels., 1978—. Faculty Sci. fellow NSF, Colo. State U., 1976-77, Mellon fellow Mellon Found., MIT, 1987. Mem. Am. Chem. Soc., Soc. for Lit. and Sci. (v.p., pres. 1985-89), History of Sci. Soc., Soc. Hist. Chemistry and Alchemy. Jewish. Home: 18 Chiltern Hill Dr Worcester MA 01602-1415 Office: Worcester Poly Inst Dept Chemistry Worcester MA 01609

WEINMAN, JOEL B., optometrist; b. Bklyn., Jan. 8, 1937; s. Frank and Rose (Sobel) W.; student U. Pitts., 1954-56; B.S., O.D., Pa. Coll. Optometry, 1960; m. Gretchen FonDersmith, Sept. 20, 1970; children by previous marriage-Jay, Michael, Richard. Practice optometry, Kutztown, Pa., 1960—; pres. Kutztown Optical, Inc.; instr. Reading Area Community Coll.; cons., lectr. rehab. of partially sighted children Kutztown State Coll.; mem. council sports and vision Bausch & Lomb. Mem. Gov.'s Council to Study Health Trend in State of Pa., 1970; mem. opticianary sci. adv. com. Reading Area Community Coll.; bd. dirs. N.E. chpt. Cystic Fibrosis, 1989—. Diplomate Nat. Bd. Optometric Examiners. Fellow Am. Acad. Optometry; mem. Am. (charter mem. sect. contact lenses), Pa. (vision screening chmn. 1966-67, chmn. practice mgmt. 1967-68, 73-—) optometric assns., Berks County Optometric Soc. (pres. 1968-69), Berkeleigh Optometric Profl. Assn. (pres. 1970—), Vision Conservation Inst., Am. Optometric Found., Am. Assn. Ethical Hypnosis, Beta Sigma Kappa. Jewish (dir. temple 1967-69). Clubs: Lions, Rotary. Home: PO Box 268 Kutztown PA 19530-0268

WEINMANN, BERT MILLICENT LANDES, artist; b. N.Y.C., July 20, 1924; d. Harry and Esther (Lurie) Landes; student Hunter Coll., 1941-43, Queens Coll., 1958-59, Bklyn. Mus. Art Sch., 1959. New Sch. for Social Research, 1963; grad. Fashion Inst. Tech., 1943; also pvt. student art; m. Richard A. Weinmann, Dec. 26, 1944; children—Harriet, Elaine. Fashion illustrator, designer with Mainbocher, Maurice Rentner, Tabin Picker, others, 1942-50; exhibited one-woman shows Six Trees Gallery, Edgartown, Mass., 1971, Kron Gallery, Mattituck, N.Y., 1972, Firehouse Gallery, Garden City, N.Y., 1975, Unicorn Gallery, N.Y.C., 1974, Gallery 33, N.Y.C., 1976, The Galery, N.Y.C., 1982; exhibited in group shows at Palazzo Vecchio, Florence, Italy, 1972, Nat. Acad. Art, 1969, 72, 73. Hecksher Mus., Huntington, N.Y., 1971, Salvator Rosa, Naples, Italy, 1972, Port Washington (N.Y.) Public Library, 1972, Fairfield (Conn.) U., 1973, Royal Acad., Stockholm, 1978, Sindin Gallery, N.Y.C., 1981, Suziki Gallery, N.Y.C., 1986, Discovery Gallery, 1987, Jehangar Art Gallery, Bombay, 1989, Sansker Kendra Mus., Ahmedebed, India, 1989, Fine Arts Mus. of the South, Mobile, Ala., 1989, Sabbeth Art Gallery, Glencove, N.Y., 1990, also numerous art galleries; works represented in numerous pvt. and corp. collections; tchr. drawing and painting North Shore Community Arts Center, Great Neck, N.Y., 1973-81, AIA, Great Neck, 1981-84. Recipient awards from numerous juried art exhbns., purchase award Nassau Coll. Assn., 1973. Mem. Nat. Assn. Women Artists (co-chmn. fgn. exhbns. com. 1973-74, Ziuta G. and Joseph James Akston prize 1972), Women in Arts, Profl. Artists Guild, Artists in Am. Home and Studio: 61 Franklin Pl Great Neck NY 11023

WEINMANN, JOHN GIFFEN, lawyer, diplomat; b. New Orleans, Aug. 29, 1928; S. Rudolph John and Mary Victoria (Mills) W.; m. Virginia Lee Eason, June 11, 1955; children: Winston Eason, Robert St. George Tucker, John Giffen Jr., Mary Virginia Lewis, George Gustaf. BA, Tulane U., 1950, JD, 1952. Bar: La. 1952. Pvt. practice law Phelps Dunbar and predecessor firm, New Orleans; ptnr. Phelps Dunbar and predecessor firm, 1955-80, of counsel, 1981-83, 85-89, 92—; gen. counsel Times-Picayune Pub. Corp., 1968-80; pres., dir. Waverly Oil Corp., 1981-89; amb. to Finland Am. Embassy, Helsinki, 1989-91; chief of protocol of White House Dept. of State, Washington, 1991—; lectr. bills and notes New Orleans chpt. Am. Inst. Banking, 1958-59; bd. dir. Eason Oil Co., 1961-81, chmn., 1977; bd. dir. 1st Nat. Bank of Oklahoma City, 1978-84, Am. Life Ins. Co. of N.Y., 1981-88, Allied Investment Corp., 1985-88; asst. sec. Am. Bar Endowment, 1971-74, bd. dirs., sec., 1975-80. Mem. adv. bd.: Tulane Law Rev. Bd. govs. Tulane Med. Ctr., 1968-81; bd. adminstrs. Tulane Ednl. Fund, 1981-91, emeritus bd. mem., 1992—, chmn. devel. com., 1985-89, co-chmn. Tulane Parents Fund, 1980-81; nat. chmn. ann. giving Campaign for Tulane, 1983-85; bd. dirs. Coun. for Better La., 1987-89, Tulane Children's Ctr., 1981-84, WYES Ednl. TV Sta., 1981-82; trustee S.W. Legal Found., 1978-80, Metairie Park Country Day Sch., v.p., 1976-77, pres., 1978-80, U.S. commr. gen. for 1984 La. World Expn., 1983-85; U.S. del. Bur. Internat. Expositions, Paris, 1984-85, chmn. del., 1985; state fin. chmn. George Bush for Pres., and Victory La. '88, 1987-88; mem. Pres.'s Nat. Adv. Bd. Personnel, 1988-89. Named Outstanding Law Alumnus, Tulane U., 1985. Mem. ABA (chmn. jr. bar conf. 1963-64, mem. ho. dels. 1964-66, 70, 72-76, sec. com. ethics evaluation 1965, rep. to conv. Union des Jeunes Avocats de France 1964, chmn. sect. bar activities 1969-70), La. Bar Assn. (sec. treas. 1965-67, Outstanding Young Lawyer award), La. Soc. Colonial Wars (gov. 1976), Phi Beta Kappa, Order of Coif, Delta Kappa Epsilon, Omicron Delta Kappa. Episcopalian. Home: 611 Hector Ave Metairie LA 70005-4415 Office: Office of Chief of Protocol Rm 1232 Dept of State Washington DC 20520-2317

WEINREB, MICHAEL PHILIP, physicist; b. Lakewood, N.J., Feb. 2, 1939; s. Sol and Lillian (Bolotsky) W.; m. Alice Kogan, Aug. 28, 1966; children: Jenya, Elizabeth. BA, U. Pa., 1960; MA, Brandeis U., 1963, PhD, 1966. Physicist NASA, Cambridge, Mass., 1965-70, U.S. Dept. Transp., Cambridge, 1970, Nat. Oceanic and Atmospheric Adminstrn., Washington, 1970—; adj. prof. math. Am. U., Washington, 1984-85. Contbr. articles to profl. jours. Mem. Optical Soc. Am., Am. Meteorol. Soc., Am. Geophys. Union, Phi Beta Kappa. Office: NOAA NESDIS World Weather Bldg Rm 810 Washington DC 20233

WEINRIB, CAROL ELLEN, health care executive; b. N.Y.C., Dec. 19, 1949; d. Murray Weinrib and Hilda (Erdheim) Katz; m. Richard Guiney, May 30, 1981. BA, Carnegie-Mellon U., 1971; MHS, Johns Hopkins U., 1975. Planning analyst Children's Hosp., Boston, 1974-78; dir. emergency svcs. Boston (Mass.) City Hosp., 1978; v.p. Health Systems, Inc., 1978-85, Children's Hosp., 1985—; co-chair med. svcs. Mass. Pub. Health Assn., Boston, 1979-81; bd. mem. fin. com. Community Family Svcs., Everett, Mass., 1985-86; chair Regional Emergency Med. Svcs. Adv. Circle, Brulington, Mass., 1990-92. Mem. Mass. Pub. Health Assn., Women in Health Care Mgmt. Office: Childrens Hosp 300 Longwood Ave Boston MA 02115-5737

WEINRICH, BRIAN ERWIN, mathematics educator; b. Passaic, N.J., Jan. 8, 1952; s. Erwin H. and Ann E. (Gall) W. BS, Pa. State U., 1974, MA, 1978; MS, Shippensburg (Pa.) U., 1983. Mathematician U.S. Dept. Agr., SEA-ARS, N.E. Watershed Rsch. Ctr., University Park, Pa., 1974-80; instr. math and computer sci. Shippensburg U., 1980-84; assoc. prof. maths. and computer sci. California U. of Pa., 1984—; cons. in field; mem. Wall St. Jour. Panel, 1990—. Author: (with A. S. Rogowski) Water Movement and Quality on Strip-Mined Lands: A Compilation of Computer Programs, 1984; (with others) Surface Mining, 1990; contbr. articles to profl. jours. Mem. Missions Bd. Calvary Bapt. Ch., State College, Pa., 1975-80; visitation team Prince St. United Brethren Ch., Shippensburg, 1982-84; Bible study leader, asst. Sunday sch. tchr., Libr. Bapt. Ch., 1986—. U.S. Dept. Age, grantee, 1982—. Mem. Computer Soc. of IEEE, Am. Biog. Inst. (bd. advisors 1989—), Math. Assn. Am., Assn. Computing Machinery. Republican. Home: 448 Rear Carson St Monongahela PA 15063 Office: California U of Pa Dept Math and Computer Sci California PA 15419

WEINRICH, MARCEL, physics educator; b. Jerdzejow, Kielce, Poland, July 23, 1927; came to U.S., 1942; s. Golda R. Weinrich; m. Eleanor A. Tulman, Aug. 30, 1958 (div. Jan. 1965); 1 child, Mason. BS magna cum laude, Bethany Coll., 1946; MS, W. Va. U., 1949; PhD, Columbia U., 1958. Instr. W.Va. U., Morgantown, 1946-49; tech. asst. Columbia U., N.Y.C., 1949-50, rsch. assoc., 1951-57; physicist GE Rsch. Lab., Schenectady, N.Y., 1957-69; prof. physics Jersey City State Coll., 1969—, chmn. dept. physics, 1969-73. Dir. Citizen's League, Schenectady, 1965-69; v.p. Schenectady Ednl. Rsch. Coun., 1965-69; mem. Human Rights Commn., Schenectady, 1967-69. Fellow AAAS; mem. Am. Physics Soc., Am. Assn. Physics Tchrs. (pres. N.J. chpt. 1970-72), N.Y. Acad. Scis. Home: 6 Broadman Pky Jersey City NJ 07305-1519 Office: Physics Dept Jersey City State Coll Jersey City NJ 07305

WEINSAFT, PAUL PHINEAS, physician; b. Zbaraz, Austria, July 18, 1908; came to U.S., 1941; s. Lipa and Basia (Landesberg) W.; m. Rachel Rosenfeld, Mar. 24, 1934. BS, Sorbonne, Paris, 1931; MD, U. Paris Faculty of Medicine, 1935. Diplomate Am. Bd. Internal Medicine. Asst. surgeon Soldiers' Home, Chelsea, Mass., 1941-45; physician pvt. practice Winthrop, Mass., 1945-51; staff physician VA Hosp., Martinsburg, Va., 1952-55; asst. dir. profl. svc. VA Hosp., N.Y.C., 1955-61; med. dir. Bklyn. Hebrew Home & Hosp., 1961-64; chief geriatric sect. Coney Island Hosp., Bklyn., 1964-67; med. dir. Met. Jewish Geriatric Ctr., Bklyn., 1967-79; ret., 1979—; cons. in field. Sci. and Med. editor, The Jewish Forward, N.Y.C.; contbr. numerous articles to profl. jours. Fellow Am. Coll. Physicians, N.Y. Acad. Medicine; mem. N.Y. State and County Med. Soc., Mass. Med. Soc., Am. Coll. Cardiology, N.Y. Acad. Scis. Democrat. Jewish. Home: 205 W 54th St New York NY 10019-5518

WEINSCHEL, BRUNO OSCAR, engineer, physicist; b. Stuttgart, Federal Republic of Germany, May 26, 1919; came to U.S., 1939; m. Shirley Kittredge; 6 children. BA in Physics, Technische Hochschule, Stuttgart, 1938; Dr. Engring., Technische Hochschule, Munich, Fed. Republic of Germany, 1966; DSc (hon.), Capitol Inst. Tech., 1984. Registered profl. engr., Md., D.C. Sr. engr. Western Electric, 1943-44; chief engr. Indsl. Instruments Co., Jersey City, 1944-48; group leader, rsch. scientist Nat. Bur. of Standards, 1949-52; chief engr., pres. Weinschel Engring. Co., Inc., Gaithersburg, Md., 1952-86, cons., 1987-88; pres., chief engr. Weinschel Rsch. Found., Gaithersburg, Md., 1987—; chief engr. Weinschel Assocs., Gaithersburg, 1988—; cons. Weinschel Engring. Co., Inc., 1987-89. Contbr. over 50 articles to profl. jours.; inventor and co-inventor with 20 patents. Mem. Pres. Reagan's Com. Medal of Sci., 1986-87. Recipient William A. Wildhack award Nat. Conf. of Standards Labs., 1985. Fellow IEEE (pres. 1986, Richard M. Emberson award 1992), Instn. Elec. Engrs.-U.K.; mem. Annapolis Yacht Club, Cosmos Club, Internat. Club. Republican.

WEINSHALL, PHYLLIS ANN, financial executive; b. Bklyn., Apr. 15, 1963; d. Leon Paul Weinshall and Carol Rose Cooper. BS in Mgmt., SUNY, Binghamton, 1985; postgrad., Pace U., 1990—. CPA, N.Y. Acctg. supr. Marks Shron & Co., Great Neck, N.Y., 1985-89; mgr., corp. fin. Volt Info. Scis., Inc., N.Y.C., 1989—. Mem. AICPA, N.Y. Soc. CPA (fin. planning com. 1991—). Office: Volt Info Scis 1133 6th Ave New York NY 10036-6710

WEINSTEIN, AARON MEYER, accountant, insurance broker; b. Middle Village, N.Y., May 4, 1924; s. Sam and Rose S. (Holtzman) W.; m. Cecily L. Schoen, Sept. 18, 1949; children: Ronnee, Donna, Robert, Leonard. BBA, Pace U., 1951. Lic. pub. acct., N.Y. Jr. acct. F.W. Greenfield, N.Y.C., 1951-53; sr. acct. Goldwasser Co., N.Y.C., 1954-57, Schneider, Glickman, N.Y.C., 1958-64; pub. acct. pvt. practice, Queens, N.Y., 1964—. Pres. Franklin Sq. (N.Y.) Men's Club, 1971, Franklin Sq. Jewish Ctr., 1972-74. Sgt. US Air Force, 1942-45, ETO. Jewish War Vets. Jewish. Office: Aarons Agy Co 75-34 Metropolitan Ave Middle Village NY 11379

WEINSTEIN, ALFRED BERNARD, psychotherapist, psychoanalyst; b. N.Y.C., Nov. 6, 1917; s. Morris and Mamie; B.A. in English, Bklyn. Coll., 1941; M.A. in Teaching English, Columbia U., 1947; Ed.D. in Secondary Sch. Adminstrn., 1951; postdoctoral fellow in clin. psychology New Sch. for Social Research; cert. in individual psychotherapy Alfred Adler Inst., 1977, in group psychotherapy, 1979; m. Muriel Band, Dec. 25, 1975; 1 son by previous marriage, Bruce. Asst. prin. Pub. Sch. 144, Bklyn., 1956-57; prin. Pub. Sch. 56, Bklyn., 1957-59, Pub. Sch. 144, Queens, 1959-64, Col. David Marcus Jr. High Sch., Bklyn., 1964-70; head unit 2 Bd. Examiners, N.Y.C. Bd. Edn., 1970-71; prin. Myra S. Barnes Intermediate Sch., S.I., N.Y., 1971-78; dir. edn. Maimonides Sch., Maimonides Inst., Far Rockaway, N.Y., 1978—; reading clinician, instr. reading Hofstra Coll., 1954-57; instr. reading Queens Coll., 1957-60; adj. instr. dept. edn. grad. div. Bklyn. Coll., 1965-69; psychotherapist Alfred Adler Mental Hygiene Clinic, N.Y.C.; reading clinician, instr. Hofstra Coll., 1957-60; instr. reading dept. Queens Coll., 1960-70; instr., coll. advisor grad. edn. div. Bklyn Coll., CUNY, 1962-70; instr. Alfred Adler Inst., N.Y.C., 1977—; practice individual and group psychotherapy, hypnotherapy and marriage counseling, West Hempstead, N.Y.C., 1977—; field cons. Superctr.; writer, cons. N.Y.C. Bd. Edn. Task Force of Mid. Sch. Mem. exec. bd., former v.p. council suprs. and adminstrs., former dir. public relations Local 1 AFL-CIO, N.Y.C., 1974-78. Served with USAAF, 1941-45, ETO. Decorated Air medal with 3 oak leaf clusters, 2 presdl. commendations; lic. prin. day high schs. Mem. Doctorate Assn. of N.Y. Educators, Jr. High Sch. Prins. Assn. (pres. 1969-71), N.Y. Assn. Exptl. Study of Edn., N.Y. Acad. Pub. Edn., Assn. Supervision and Curriculum Devel., Bklyn. Coll. Alumni Assn. (dir.), Nat. Assn. for Advancement Psychoanalysis, Am. Bds. Accreditation and Cert., Individual Psychology Assn. (dir.), Internat. Reading Assn., Phi Delta Kappa, Kappa Delta Pi. Clubs: Bnai Brith (pres. Schoolman's lodge 1969-71). Author: (with William Elfert) Achieving Reading Skills, 1958; (with Sidney Rauch) Mastery of College Reading Skills, 1968; (with Sidney Rauch and Muriel Weinstein) World of Vocabulary series, 1976-82; (with others) Dilemma computer reading software program, others (with Howard Hurwitz, Toby Kurzband and Simpson Sasserath) High Points, 1968-71; columnist (with Muriel Weinstein) Hot Line; contbr. short stories to New Voices-American Writing Today (C.I. Glicksberg), 1958, The Nassau Rev. and The Zayda. Home: 644 Pauley Dr West Hempstead NY 11552-2225

WEINSTEIN, ARNOLD K., education educator; b. Newark, Nov. 4, 1937; s. Harry B. and Sally (Krich) W.; m. Judith C. Weinstein, Aug. 22, 1965; children: Stephanie, Jennifer. BS in Mgmt., U. Pa., 1959; MBA in Mktg., Columbia U., 1962, PhD in Internat. Bus., 1973. Lectr. U. New South Wales, Sydney, Australia, 1965-68; asst. prof. U. Western (London) Ont., Can., 1968-70; prof. bus. adminstrn. IMEDE Mgmt. Devel. Inst., Lausanne, Switzerland, 1975-76; assoc. prof. Boston Coll., 1973-80; chief exec. officer, dean Arthur D. Little Mgmt. Edn. Inst., Boston, 1980-84; dean U. Mass., Boston, 1984-90, prof., 1990—. Author two books; contbr. articles to profl. jours. Home: 67 Prentice Rd Newton MA 02159-1325 Office: U Mass Coll Mgmt Harbor Campus Boston MA 02125

WEINSTEIN, BERNARD ALLEN, physics educator, researcher; b. Bridgeport, Conn., Nov. 15, 1946; s. Jacob and Gertrude (Shapiro) W.; m. Helen S. Rosenbloom, July 19, 1970; children: Michael Abraham, Seth Adam. BS, U. Rochester, 1968; PhD, Brown U., 1974. Doctorand Max-Planck Inst. Festkorperforschung, Stuttgart, Germany, 1972-74; postdoctoral assoc. Nat. Bur. Standards, Washington, 1974-75; asst. prof. Purdue U., Lafayette, Ind., 1975-77; rsch. scientist Xerox Webster Rsch. Ctr., Rochester, N.Y., 1977-87; prof. physics SUNY, Buffalo, 1987—; researcher in condensed matter physics. Contbr. over 70 articles to profl. jours. Alfred P. Sloan fellow, 1976. Mem. AAAS, Am. Phys. Soc., Assn. Internat. Rsch. in Advanced High Pressure Tech. Jewish. Office: SUNY Physics Dept 239 Fronczak Hall Buffalo NY 14260

WEINSTEIN, CAROL WENDY, psychiatrist; b. N.Y.C., Dec. 7, 1958. BS, Cornell U., 1980; MD, SUNY, Buffalo, 1984. Diplomate Am. Bd. Psychiatry and Neurology, Nat. Bd. Med. Examiners. Resident in psychiatry Westchester div. Cornell U.-N.Y. Hosp., White Plains, 1984-88; clin. affiliate Cornell U.-N.Y. Hosp., N.Y.C., 1988-91; staff psychiatrist for chem. dependency Four Winds Hosp., Katonah, N.Y., 1988-89; med. dir. treatment-resistant young adult unit Four Winds Hosp., Katonah, 1989-91; co-med. dir. acute adolescent unit Four Winds Hosp., Katonah, N.Y., 1992; with emergency rm. and schizophrenia rsch. clinic Montefiore Med. Ctr., 1992—; clin. instr.

Cornell U. Med. Coll., N.Y.C., 1988-91. Mem. Am. Psychiat. Assn., Cornell U.-N.Y. Hosp. Alumni Assn. (Alumni award 1988). Office: Four Winds Hosp 800 Cross River Rd Katonah NY 10536-9694

WEINSTEIN, GRACE WOHLNER, writer, consultant; b. N.Y.C.; d. David and Esther (Lobel) Wohlner; m. Stephen D. Weinstein; children: Lawrence, Janet. BA, Cornell U. Cons. editor Star-Ledger N.J. Investor, Newark, 1986—; columnist Good Housekeeping Mag., N.Y.C., 1979-87, columnist, fin. editor, 1990—; cons. Am. Express, N.Y.C., 1990—. Author: Children and Money, 1975, 85, Life Plans: Looking Forward to Retirement, 1979, Men, Women and Money: New Roles, New Rules, 1986, The Lifetime Book of Money Management, 1984, 87, The Bottom Line: Inside Accounting Today, 1987; columnist Universal Press Syndicate, 1987-89. Recipient Nat. Media award Am. Psychol. Found., 1975, Sci. Writer award Am. Dental Assn., 1979. Mem. Am. Soc. Journalists and Authors (v.p. 1977-78, pres. 1978-79, 79-80), Authors Guild. Office: Sanford Greenburger Assocs 55 Fifth Ave New York NY 10003

WEINSTEIN, HAREL, physiologist, biophysicist, educator; b. Romania, June 5, 1945; came to U.S., 1973; s. Adolf and Klara (Brief) W.; m. Barbara Manski, June 9, 1967; 1 child, Elhav. BS, Technion-Israel Inst. Tech., Haifa, 1966, MS, 1968, DSc, 1971. Lectr. Technion-Israel Inst. Tech., 1971-73; rsch. assoc. chemistry Johns Hopkins U., Balt., 1973-74; asst. prof. pharmacology Mount Sinai Sch. Medicine, N.Y.C., 1974-76, assoc. prof., 1976-79, prof., 1979—, chmn., prof. physiology and biophysics, 1985—; cons. Merck, Sharp & Dohme, Rahway, N.J., 1979-81; mem. study sect. Nat. Inst. Drug Abuse, Bethesda, Md., 1979-83, 90—; mem. health & environ. rsch. adv. com. U.S. Dept. Energy, Washington, 1986—. Editor: Quantum Chemistry in Biomedical Sciences, Computational Approaches to Enzyme Structure and Function; contbr. over 135 articles to profl. jours. Recipient Irma T. Hirschl Career Scientist award, 1978-82, Alcohol, Drug Abuse & Mental Health Assn. Rsch. Scientist Devel. award, 1979-89, award Outstanding Contbns. Internat. Soc. Quantum Biology, 1988, Rsch. Scientist award Nat. Inst. Drug Abuse, 1990—; named Park-Davis Disting. lectr. U. Mich., 1988. Mem. Assn. Chmn. Depts. Physiology (councillor 1989-91, pres.-elect 1991—); Internat. Soc. Quantum Biology and Pharmacology (pres. 1989), N.Y. Acad. Scis. (chair. biophysics sect. 1992). Office: CUNY Mt Sinai Sch Medicine 1 Gustave L Levy Pl Box 1218 New York NY 10029-6574

WEINSTEIN, HARRIS, lawyer; b. Providence; s. Joseph and Gertrude (Rusitzky) W.; m. Rosa Grunberg, June 3, 1956; children: Teme Feldman, Joshua, Jacob. BS in Math., MIT, 1956, MS in Math., 1958; LLB, Columbia U., 1961. Bar: D.C. 1962. Law clk. to Judge Wm. H. Hastie U.S. Ct. Appeals (3rd cir.), Phila., 1961-62; with Covington & Burling, Washington, 1962-67, 69-90; chief counsel Office of Thrift Supervision U.S. Dept. of Treasury, Washington, 1990—; pub. mem. Adminstrv. Conf. of U.S., 1982-90. Mem. MIT Corp. Home: 1836 Randolph St NW Washington DC 20011-5340 Office: US Dept Treasury Office Thrift Supervision 1700 G St NW Washington DC 20552-0001

WEINSTEIN, HERBERT, chemical engineer, educator; b. Bklyn., Mar. 10, 1933; s. Abraham and Pauline (Feldman) W.; m. Judith Cooper, Apr. 6, 1957; children: Michael Howard, Edward Marc, Ellen Rachel. B.Engring. in Chem. Engring, Coll. City N.Y., 1955; M.S. in Chem. Engring, Purdue U., 1957; Ph.D., Case Inst. Tech., 1963. Staff mem. Los Alamos Sci. Lab., 1956-58; research engr. NASA Lewis Research Center, Cleve., 1959-63; asst. prof. chem. engring. Ill. Inst. Tech., 1963-66, assoc. prof., 1966-72, prof., 1972-77; dir. Center for Biomed. Engring., 1973-77; prof. CUNY, 1977—; Herbert G. Kayser prof. of chem. engring., 1987—; vis. rsch. assoc., mem. Med. Rsch. Inst. Michael Reese Hosp. and Med. Ctr., Chgo., 1965-77; vis. prof. mech. engring. Technion-Israel Inst. Tech., 1972-73; vis. prof. biomed. engring. Rush Med. Coll., Chgo., 1973-76; summer prof. Exxon Rsch. and Engring. Co., annually, 1981-92; Lady Davis vis. prof. Technion-Israel Inst. Tech., 1985; cons. to industry, rsch. labs. Mem. Am. Inst. Chem. Engrs., Sigma Xi. Jewish. Office: CUNY Dept Chem Engring New York NY 10031

WEINSTEIN, JEROME WILLIAM, economist; b. Bklyn., Feb. 3, 1942; s. Sydney and Dorothy (Ripstein) W.; m. Etarae Blatt, June 13, 1965; 1 child, Barak Reuben. B.A., Fla. So. Coll., 1970; M.A., La. State U., 1972; grad. Indls. Coll. Armed Forces, 1990. Rsch. analyst Nat. Security Agy., Ft. Meade, Md., 1964-70; economist Def. Intelligence Agy., Washington, 1973-79, chief, indsl. econs. sect. strategic def. econs. br., 1979-86, sr. economist Soviet/Warsaw pact div., 1986-89, spl. asst. for strategic planning, 1990—; Contbr. to govtl. publs. Bd. dirs. Columbia Religious Facilities Corp., Columbia, Md., 1979-85; pres. Jewish Council Howard County, Columbia, 1976-78, treas., 1986-87; trustee Temple Beth Shalom, Columbia, 1974-83, pres., 1975-76, 78-79; adminstrv. v.p. Congregation Oseh Shalom, Laurel, Md., 1990—. With USAF, 1959-63. Recipient Israel Leadership award, 1978, Meritorious Civilian Svc. medal Def. Intelligence Agy., 1984. Mem. Am. Econ. Assn., So. Econ. Assn., Assn. for Comparative Econ. Study, Delta Sigma Pi. Democrat. Lodge: B'nai B'rith (v.p. 1975-76).-76). Home: 6964 Sunfleck Row Columbia MD 21045-4622 Office: Def Intelligence Agy Washington DC 20340-6100

WEINSTEIN, LARRY PHILIP, plastic surgeon; b. Bklyn., Oct. 11, 1953; s. Morris and Edith (Kreeger) W.; m. Beverly Zagofsky; children: Joshua Z., Melanie Z. BS, Syracuse U., 1976; MD, U. Guadalajara, Mex., 1979. Fifth pathway Mt. Sinai Sch. Medicine/Elmhurst Gen. Hosp., 1979-80; resident in gen. surgery Univ. Hosp., Newark, 1980-82, Morristown (N.J.) Meml. Hosp./Columbia U., 1982-84; resident in surg. oncology Meml. Sloan-Kettering Cancer Ctr./Cornell U., N.Y.C., 1983, 84-85; plastic surgery rsch. fellow U. Pitts., 1985-86; resident in plastic surgery, clin. asst. instr. SUNY-Bklyn. Health Sci. Ctr., 1986-88; pvt. practice Chester and Chatham, N.J. Contbr. chpts. to books, articles to profl. jours. Grantee Surgitek Corp., 1985-87, Allegheny-Singer Corp., 1986-87, SUNY-Bklyn., 1987-88. Fellow Acad. Medicine N.J.; mem. ACS (pres. Somerset County chpt.). Office: Chester Woods Profl Park 500 State Route 24 Chester NJ 07930-2903 also: 338 Main St Chatham NJ 07928

WEINSTEIN, MICHAEL MAGEN, economics journalist, educator; b. Phila., Sept. 7, 1948; s. Matthew B. and Rosalie (Magen) W.; m. Frances Schwartz, Nov. 22, 1974; children: Zachary, Lev. BA with great distinction, Stanford U., 1970; student, U. Chgo., 1970-71; PhD, MIT, 1979. Mem. faculty Haverford (Pa.) Coll., 1975-89, chmn. dept., 1981-89; pres. M.B.W. Mgmt. Corp., Narberth, Pa., 1986—; pres., founder W.A.D. Fin. Counseling Inc., Narberth, 1989—; mem. editorial bd. New York Times, 1989—; cons. in field. Author: Recovery and Redistribution Under the NIRA, 1980; also articles. NSF fellow U. Chgo., 1970-71, MIT, 1971-74. Mem. Am. Econs. Assn., Econ. History Assn., Phi Beta Kappa. Office: NY Times 229 W 43d St New York NY 10036

WEINSTEIN, PAUL ALLEN, economics educator; b. Bklyn., Jan. 20, 1933; s. George and Anna (Flam) W.; m. Alice Elizabeth Goldsmith, June 24, 1956; children: Matthew George Edward, Beth Miriam. BA, Coll. William and Mary, 1954; MA, Northwestern U., 1958, PhD, 1961. Asst. prof. Columbia U., N.Y.C., 1962-65; assoc. prof. U. Md., College Park, 1965—, dir. Indsl. Rels. Labor Studies Ctr., 1983-91; exec. asst. to Gov. Exec. Dept. Md., Annapolis, 1968-70; dir. rsch. Md. Dept. Econs. and Community Devel., Annapolis, 1971; cons. World Bank, Washington, OAS, Washington; neutral designate mem. Pub. Employment Rels. Bd., Prince George County, Md.; chmn. Pub. Sector Labor Rels. Conf. Bd.; mem. Indsl. Rels. Rsch. Assn. Stats. Commn., Pers. Appeals Bd., U.S. Gen. Acctg. Office, 1987—, vice chmn., 1990—. Author: Impact to Fringe Benefits on Collective Bargaining, 1977, (monograph) Strategic Forces in Construction, 1986; contbr. articles to profl. jours. Grantee Ford Found., 1963, German Marshall Fund U.S., 1979, 89, Urban Observatory, 1974, Md. Dept. Employment Tng., 1985, Joint Spain U.S. Com. Cultural Ednl. Exchange, The Tinker Found., 1987-89. Mem. Am. Arbitration Assn. (cert. Fed. Mediation Conciliation Svc. arbitrator), Ind. Rels. Rsch. Assn. (chmn. stats. com. 1985—, 1st v.p. Md. chpt. 1986-87), Am. Econs. Assn., Soc. Profls. Dispute Resolution. Democrat. Jewish. Home: 11105 Hurdle Hill Dr Rockville MD 20854-2527 Office: U Md Dept Econs College Park MD 20742

WEINSTEIN, PHILIP MEYER, English educator, literary critic; b. Memphis, July 8, 1940; s. Jacob and Rose (Wahl) W.; m. Elizabeth Pendleton Ogden, June 7, 1963; children: Elizabeth, Katherine. BA, Princeton U., 1962; MA, Harvard U., 1966, PhD, 1968. Asst. prof. dept. English Harvard U., Cambridge, Mass., 1968-71; asst. prof. dept. English Swarthmore (Pa.) Coll., 1971-74, assoc. prof., 1974-81, prof. English, 1981—; assoc. prof. Ecole Normale Superieure, Paris, 1983; disting. vis. prof. Rhodes Coll., Memphis, 1987. Author: Henry James and Requirements of Imagination, 1971, The Semantics of Desire, 1984, A Cosmos No One Owns, 1992. Fellow NEH, 1974-75, 82-83, Mellon Found., 1978-79; ACLS, 1987-88. Mem. MLA, Faulkner Soc. Democrat. Office: Dept English Swarthmore Coll Swarthmore PA 19081

WEINSTEIN, STEVEN PHILIP, journalist, consultant; b. El Paso, Tex., July 30, 1958; s. Philip Weinstein Jr. and Dorothy (Oshlag) Weinstein Friedman. BA, Tufts U., 1980. Journalist AP, Jackson, Miss., 1980, Richmond, Va., 1980, Atlanta, 1980-81, N.Y.C., 1981-83; journalist Reuters Ltd., N.Y.C., 1983-86, database mgr. N.Am., 1986-89; info. tech. mgr. Reuters Ltd., London, 1989-91; cons. N.Y.C., 1991—. Contbr. articles to profl. publs. Home and Office: 67 Park Ave New York NY 10016-2557

WEINSTEIN, SYDNEY S., software company executive; b. Phila., Oct. 20, 1955; s. Horace Edwin and Deborah Joyce (Lauter) W.; m. Michele Lynn Goldman, Nov. 11, 1984; children: Joseph Jacob, Eric Alan. BSEE (cum laude), Lehigh U., 1977; MS Elec. and Computer Engring., U. Mass., 1978. Tech. staff United Computing Svcs., Kansas City, Mo., 1978-79; software engr. Fischer & Porter Co., Horsham, Pa., 1979-83; pres. Datacom Systems Inc., Huntingdon Valley, Pa., 1977—; coord. Elm Devel. Group, 1988—; adj. assoc. prof. elec. engring. dept. Villanova U. Contbg. author: Unix Programmers Reference Manual, 1990; co-editor Ars Ceramica, 1988—; editor Users Jour., 1990—. Bd. dirs. Warminster (Pa.) Ambulance Corps, 1984-85, chmn. of bd., 1985. Mem. IEEE, Assn. for Computing Machinery, Assn. Inst. for Cert. Computer Profls., N.Y. Soc. Wedgwood, English Ceramics Study Group. Office: Datacomp Systems Inc 3837 Byron Rd Huntingdon Valley PA 19006-2320

WEINSTOCK, ANNE MARIE, career consultant; b. Providence, Oct. 24, 1948; d. Charles Cornelius and Esther (Ahlquist) Murphy; m. Kenneth L. MacNaught, June 6, 1970 (div. 1976); 1 child, Heather Joy; m. Thomas Alan Weinstock, Dec. 9, 1978. BA, Simmons Coll., 1970; MA, U. R.I., 1977. Tchr. Seekonk (Mass.) High Sch., 1972-73; freelance editor Providence, 1973-75; tng. mgr. Indsl. Nat. Bank, Providence, 1975-78; sr. tng. advisor Mobil Oil Corp., N.Y.C., 1978-80, corp. tng. and devel. specialist, 1980-83, corp. employee info. coord., 1983-84, mgr. profl. recruiting, 1984-86; v.p. Drake Beam Morin, Inc., Stamford, Conn., 1986—; mem. Eastern Coll. Placement Coun., N.Y.C., 1984-86; bd. dirs. Coll. Rels. Coun., N.Y.C., 1984-86. Dir. Project 91-Youth Coun., Wilton, Conn., 1985-91. Mem. Women in Mgmt. (bd. dirs. 1980—), Simmons Club of Fairfield County (bd. dirs. 1980—).

WEINSTOCK, GEORGE DAVID, financial services company executive; b. Vienna, Austria, Jan. 31, 1937; came to U.S., 1940; s. Paul and Ernestine Esther (Stark) W.; m. Lorna Smith, July 17, 1965; children: Pamela Ellen, Andrea Joan. AB, Columbia U., 1958, BSEE, 1959, MS, 1962; cert., Coll. for Fin. Planning, Denver, 1985. cert. fin. planner. Sr. engr. ITT, Nutley, N.J., 1959-61; sr. mem. tech. staff RCA, N.Y.C., 1961-65; project dir. Computer Scis. Co., Paramus, N.J., 1965-69; v.p., dir., sec. Ultimacc Systems, Inc., Maywood, N.J., 1969-78; v.p. Satnick Devel. Group, Hoboken, N.J., 1978-84; sr. v.p. Knitwaves, Inc., Moonachie, N.J., 1984-85; chmn. bd. Bancroft Group, Inc., Paramus, 1985-88; securities coord. Equico Securities, Inc., Paramus, 1989—; pres. Atrium Adv. Group, Inc., Paramus, 1990—; faculty Fairleigh Dickinson U. Author: System 360/DOS Operation, 1971. Com. mem. United Jewish Community Bergen County, 1988. Mem. IEEE, Inst. for Cert. Fin. Planners, Nat. Assn. Accts., N.J. Estate Planning Coun. (v.p.). Jewish. Home: 64 Ellsworth Ter Glen Rock NJ 07452-3706 Office: Atrium Adv Group Inc East 80 Rte 4 PO Box 15 Paramus NJ 07653-0015

WEINSTOCK, MARK ROBERT, podiatrist; b. Bklyn., May 15, 1961; s. Stephen and Harriet (Teitelbaum) W. BA cum laude, Boston U., 1983; DPM, N.Y. Coll. Podiatric Medicine, 1989. Resident in surgery N.Y. Coll. Podiatric Medicine affiliated Hosps., N.Y.C., 1989-90; podiatrist Community Foot Care Ctr., Bklyn., 1990—; attending physician Interfaith Med. Ctr., Bklyn., 1991—, Bklyn. Jewish Hosp., 1991—, St. John's Hosp., Bklyn., 1991—. Mem. com. Boston U. Alumni Schs., 1987—; mem. B'nai B'rith, N.Y.C., 1992—. Mem. Am. Coll. Foot Surgeons (assoc.), Am. Podiatric Med. Assn., N.Y. State Podiatric Med. Assn., N.Y. Coll. Podiatric Medicine Alumni Assn., Nat. Assn. of the Professions. Home: 2445 E 71st St Brooklyn NY 11234-6513

WEINTRAUB, DANIEL RALPH, social welfare administrator; b. N.Y.C., Apr. 23, 1939; s. Benjamin Zion and Ida (Barman) W.; B.A. in Biology, N.Y. U., 1959; D.D.S., Columbia U., 1963; certificate pub. health U. Wash., 1963; m. Sally Ann Franco, Mar. 16, 1968; children—David Arlo, Jeremy Michael. Rural community devel. adviser AID, Dominican Republic, 1966-68, population and pub. health adviser, 1968-69; asso. planning dir. Alan Guttmacher Inst. (formerly Center for Family Planning Program Devel.), N.Y.C., 1969-74; dep. dir. Family Planning Internat. Assistance, N.Y.C., 1974-76, chief operating officer, 1977-92; v.p. internat. programs Planned Parenthood Fedn. Am., N.Y.C., 1978—, mem. speaker's bur., 1982—; vol. leader, coordinator U.S. Peace Corps, Bolivia, 1964-65; cons. HEW, 1971-74, Nat. Center Health Statistics, 1974. Mem. Am. Mus. Natural History. Recipient Certificate of Honor, Dominican Republic, 1969; commendation Dept. Interior, Cochabamba, Bolivia, 1965. Mem. Population Assn. Am., Nat. Geog. Soc. Author books and manuals on community devel. theory and practice, plans for area-wide family planning programs in met. areas, family planning tech. assistance in developing nations, nat. studies including Need for Subsidized Family Planning Services: United States, Each State and County, 1971. Home: 8 Dock Ln Port Washington NY 11050-1732 Office: 810 7th Ave New York NY 10019

WEINTRAUB, LESTER, chemist consultant; b. N.Y.C., Feb. 1, 1924; s. Morris and Clara (Richman) W.; m. Harriet Mollen, Aug. 26, 1950; children: Beverly, Mitchell. BS, CCNY, 1946; MS, Fordham U., 1949; PhD, NYU, 1954. Group leader Columbia U., N.Y.C., 1953-58, NYU, N.Y.C., 1958-59; sr. chemist Air Reduction Co. Inc., Murray Hill, N.J., 1959-71; mgr. R & D Pantasote, Inc., Passaic, N.J., 1971-86; chem. cons. self-employed, Mt. Laurel, N.J., 1986—. Contbr. articles to profl. jours.; patentee in field. Pvt. U.S. Army, 1944-46, Germany. Mem. Am. Chem. Soc., Soc. Plastics Engrs., Sigma Xi. Jewish. Home and Office: 10 Pardee Ct Mount Laurel NJ 08054-3044

WEINTZ, CAROLINE GILES, advertising executive, travel writer; b. Columbia, Tenn., Dec. 8, 1952; d. Raymond Clark Jr. and Caroline Higdon (Wagstaff) Giles; m. Walter Louis Weintz; children: Alexander Harwood, Elizabeth Pettus. AB, Princeton U., 1974; postgrad. diploma, U. London, 1976. Dir. advt. and promotion E.P. Dutton Pubs., N.Y.C., 1977-86; advt. cons. Assn. Jr. Leagues Internat., N.Y.C., 1986-91, advt. mgr., 1992—. Author: The Discount Guide for Travelers over 55, 4th edit., 1988. Vol. researcher St. Paul's Nat. Hist. Site and Bill of Rights Mus., Westchester, N.Y., 1986—; treas. Soc. Nat. Shrine of The Bill of Rights; mem. Jr. League, Pelham, N.Y. Mem. Authors Guild, Nat. Soc. Colonial Dames, Huguenot Soc. Am., Daus. Cin., Mensa. Episcopalian. Home: 444 Wolfs Ln Pelham NY 10803-2127

WEIR, THOMAS EDWARD, JR., archivist; b. Newport, R.I., Nov. 7, 1949; s. Thomas Edward and Rebekah Kennedy (Turner) W.; m. Constance Potter, May 27, 1984. BA in History, U. Md., 1971, MA, 1977. Cert. archivist. Archivist, reference staff Nat. Archives, Washington, 1978-84, archives specialist, rsch. and evaluation staff, 1984—; tech. advisor Orgn. for Econ. Cooperation and Devel., Paris, 1988—. Author tape cartridges for archival use; contbr. articles to profl. jours. Mem. Soc. Am. Archivists (com. on archival info. exch. 1987-90, standards bd. 1990—), Am. Soc. Info. Sci. Office: Archival Rsch/Evaluation Nat Archives and Record Adminstrn Washington DC 20408

WEIS, MONICA ROSEMARY, English educator; b. Rochester, N.Y., Nov. 9, 1942; d. Raymond Peter and Josephine Marie (McGrath) W. BA, Nazareth Coll. Rochester, 1965; MA, Bread Loaf Sch. English, 1973; postgrad., Oxford (Eng.) U., 1976; PhD, U. Va., 1985. Joined Sisters of St. Joseph, Roman Cath. Ch., 1961; cert. English tchr. grades 7-12, N.Y. Tchr. Our Lady of Lourdes Sch., Brighton, N.Y., 1964-72, vice prin., 1970-71; tchr. St. Lawrence Sch., Greece, N.Y., 1972-74; prof. English Nazareth Coll. Rochester (N.Y.), 1974—; writing cons. U. Cen. Fla., Orlando, 1988-91; coord. English/edn. Nazareth Coll., Rochester, 1982—. Contbr. articles to profl. jours. Rsch. grantee Nazareth Coll., Grasmere, Eng., 1986, Nazareth Coll. Rochester, 1991. Mem. Coll. English Assn. (bd. dirs. 1990-93), MLA, Nat. Coun. Tchrs. English, Conf. on Coll. Composition/Communication, Conf. on English Edn. Home: 55 Chestnut Ridge Rd Rochester NY 14624-3845 Office: Nazareth Coll Rochester PO Box 18950 Rochester NY 14618-3790

WEIS, RANDALL DAVID, small business owner; b. Hamilton, Ohio, Oct. 16, 1950; s. Ralph D. and Joan E. (Ertle) W.; divorced; children: Kimberly A., Stephanie L., Randall D. II. BS in Logistics, U. Cin., 1974. Dir. logistics Drackett Co., Cin., 1970-80; dir. ops. Clairol Inc., Stamford, Conn., 1980-85; dir. adminstrv. svcs. Bristol-Myers Squibb, N.Y.C., 1985-87, dir. human resources and adminstrn., 1987-89; pres. RD Weis & Co. Inc., Port Chester, N.Y., 1989—. Mem. Assn. ICC Practitioners (founder, pres. 1975-80, Nat. Assn. Corp. Real Estate Execs. (treas. 1986-88), Nat. Coun. Phys. Distbn. Mgmt. (pres. 1982-85). Office: 108 Midland Ave Port Chester NY 10573-4900

WEISBARD, JAMES JOSEPH, psychiatrist, educator; b. Elmhurst, N.Y., Oct. 25, 1953; s. Pincus and Cecilia (Adler) W. AA, Sullivan C.C., Loch Sheldrake, N.Y., 1973; BA in Polit. Sci., SUNY, Albany, 1976; MD, U. Noreste, Tampico, Mex., 1983. Diplomate Am. Bd. Psychiatry and Neurology, Am. Bd. Gen. Psychiatry, Am. Bd. Geriatric Psychiatry. Intern L.I. Coll. Hosp., Bklyn., 1984-85; resident in psychiatry N.Y. Med. Coll., 1985-88; attending psychiatrist St. Joseph's Med. Ctr., Yonkers, N.Y., 1988-89, Dutchess County Dept. Mental Hygiene, Poughkeepsie, N.Y., 1989-92; fellow in clin. geriatric psychiatry Westchester divsn. N.Y. Hosp.-Cornell Med. Ctr., White Plains, 1992—; instr. psychiatry Cornell U. Med. Coll., 1992—; clin. instr. psychiatry N.Y. Med. Coll., Valhalla, 1988-90. Mem. AMA, Am. Psychiat. Assn. (editorial cons. Jour. Hosp. and Community Psychiatry 1988—). Office: NY Hosp-Cornell Med Ctr 21 Bloomingdale Rd White Plains NY 10605

WEISBECKER, HENRY BEZALEL, electrical engineer, consultant; b. Kassel, Fed. Republic Germany, July 20, 1925; came to U.S., 1937; s. Willi and Rose (Ackermann) W.; m. Barbara Schilling, June 5, 1972; children: Miriam, Henry. BEE, Pratt Inst., 1945; MEE, N.Y. U., 1948; DEng, Munich Tech. U., 1957. Sr. engr. A.B. Dumont Corp., Passaic, N.J., 1948-51, Warner, Inc., N.Y.C., 1951-53, W. L. Maxson Corp., N.Y.C., 1953-55; project engr. Simmonds Aerosociates, Tarrytown, N.Y., 1955-58; head lab. Loral, Inc., Bronx, N.Y., 1958-60; sr. profl. engr. Litton Industries, Pleasantville, N.Y., 1960-66; assoc. prof. elec. engring. N.J. Inst. Tech., Newark, 1966-72; cons. Union City, N.J., 1972—; translator German-Eng., Union City, 1972—. Author: The Calculus Problem Solver, 1974; co-author: Solid State Devices and Integrated Circuits, 1978; contbr. articles to profl. jours. Home and Office: 712 10th St Union City NJ 07087-5540

WEISBERG, JOSEPH SIMPSON, college dean; b. Jersey City, June 7, 1937; s. Samuel and Augusta (Biel) W.; m. Gloria Helen Weisberg, June 21, 1964; children: Debra Susan, David Jeffrey. BA, Jersey City State Coll., 1960; MA, Montclair State Coll., 1964; EdD, Columbia U., N.Y.C., 1969. Tchr. earth sci. Wayne (N.J.) Pub. Schs., 1960-64; prof. geosci. Jersey City State Coll., 1964—, chmn. geosci., 1973-83, dean arts and scis., 1983-92; cons. JSW Assocs., Parsippany, N.J., 1966—; cons. in field. Author: Oceanography, 1979, Meteorology, 1981; co-author: Science Investiguides, 1967, Earth Science, 1970; reviewer, author various encys., pubrs. Advisor environ. Mayor's Office, Jersey City, 1967—, Parsippany, 1975—; v.p. Bd. of Edn., Parsippany, 1979-88; mem. and pres. Town Coun., Parsippany, 1987—. Jewish. Home: 4 Camelot Way Parsippany NJ 07054-1408 Office: Jersey City State Coll 2039 Kennedy Blvd Jersey City NJ 07305

WEISBERG, LYNNE WILLING, psychiatrist, consultant; b. N.Y.C., Apr. 11, 1948; d. Stanley S. and Pearl R. Willing; m. David E. Weisberg, Jan. 6, 1970. BA, Barnard Coll., 1969; PhD, U. Mich., 1974; MD, SUNY, Downstate, 1978. Diplomate Am. Bd. Psychiatry and Neurology. Intern NYU Med. Ctr., 1978-79; resident in adult psychiatry Mt. Sinai Hosp., N.Y.C., 1979-81; fellow in child psychiatry Columbia Med. Ctr., 1981-83; staff psychiatrist Fair Oaks Hosp., Summit, N.J., 1983-85, asst. dir. child and adolescent psychiatry, 1985—, assoc. dir. child and adolescent psychiatry, 1988—; dir. child and adolescent outpatient psychiat. svcs. Psychiat. Assocs. N.J. at Fair Oaks Hosp., 1992—; cons. Bonnie Brae Sch., Millington, N.J., 1984-92. Author: When Acting Out Isn't Acting, 1991. Mem. AMA, Am. Psychiat. Assn. Office: Fair Oaks Hosp 1 Prospect St Summit NJ 07901-2442

WEISBROD, CARL BARRY, lawyer, public official; b. N.Y.C., Oct. 5, 1944; s. Walter and Hilda (Pelzer) W.; m. Jody Adams, Jan. 21, 1979; 1 child, William. BS, Cornell U., 1965; JD, NYU, 1968. Bar: N.Y., 1968; U.S. Dist. Ct. (so. dist.) N.Y., 1969. Asst. commr. N.Y.C. Housing Dept., 1970-72; counsel, chief exec. officer Wildcat Svc. Corp., N.Y.C., 1972-77; gen. counsel Manpower Demonstration Rsch. Corp., N.Y.C., 1977-78; dir. Mayor's Office of Midtown Enforcement, N.Y.C., 1978-84; exec. dir. City Vol. Corps, N.Y.C., 1984-86, N.Y.C. Planning Commn., 1986-87; pres. 42d St. Devel. Project, N.Y.C., 1987-90; pres., chief exec. officer N.Y.C. Econ. Devel. Corp., 1990—; chmn. N.Y.C. Loft Bd., 1982-84. Contbr. articles to profl. jours. Office: NYC Econ Devel Corp 110 William St New York NY 10038

WEISBROD, ROBERTA ELLEN, state agency executive; b. Bklyn., July 15, 1943; d. Nathan Weisbrod and Martha Honig Scharf; m. David Gershon Trager, May 2, 1972; children: Mara Emet, Josiah Samuel, Naomi Gabrielle. BS in Chemistry, Bklyn. Coll., 1964; PhD in Biochemistry, Cornell U., 1971. Postdoctoral fellow N.Y. Blood Ctr., N.Y.C., 1970-72, Rockefeller U., N.Y.C., 1972-75; adj. lectr. Columbia Coll., N.Y.C., 1975-78; asst. prof. Yeshiva U., N.Y.C., 1978-80; adj. lectr. Columbia Coll., N.Y.C., 1980-81; environ. cons. Anne Simon, others, N.Y.C., 1981-85; spl. asst. to the commr. N.Y.State Dept. Environ. Cons., N.Y.C., 1985—. Contbr. articles to profl. jours. Trustee Bklyn. Botanic Garden; adv. bd. Am. Littoral Soc., Sandy Hook, N.J., 1989—. NIH postdoctoral fellow, 1972-75. Mem. N.Y. Acad. Sci. (chair environ. sci. sect. 1987-89, 91—), Am. Chem. Soc. (chair environ. chemistry com. L.I. chpt. 1984-87). Jewish.

WEISBROTH, STEVEN HARRIS, laboratory director; b. N.Y.C., Sept. 2, 1934; s. Samual W. and Rose (Schrenell) W.; m. Stephanie P. Philip, June 15, 1956; children: Nina A. Weisbroth Culleen, Spencer W., Stacy P. BS, Cornell U., 1958; MS, Wash. State U., 1960, DVM, 1964. Diplomate Am. Coll. Lab. Animal Medicine. Asst. prof., dir. Rockefeller U., N.Y.C., 1966-69; assoc. prof., dir. Health Scis. Ctr. SUNY, Stony Brook, 1969-78; pres. Anmed/Biosafe, Inc., Rockville, Md., 1978—. Author, editor: The Biology of the Laboratory Rabbit, 1978, The Laboratory Rat, 1985. Mem. Am. Assn. Accreditation Lab. Animal Care (mem. coun. 1975-83, trustee 1988—), Am. Vet. Med. Assn., Am. Assn. Lab. Animal Sci. (rsch. award 1974, Griffin award 1990). Home: 10800 S Glen Rd Rockville MD 20854-1839 Office: Anmed/Biosafe inc 7642 Standish Pl Rockville MD 20855-2701

WEISBURGER, ELIZABETH KREISER, retired chemist, editor; b. Greenlane, Pa., Apr. 9, 1924; d. Raymond Samuel and Amy Elizabeth (Snavely) Kreiser; m. John H. Weisburger, Apr. 7, 1947 (div. May 1974); children: William Raymond, Diane Susan, Andrew John. BS, Lebanon Valley Coll., Annville, Pa., 1944, DSc (hon.), 1989; PhD, U. Cin., 1947, DSc (hon.), 1981. Rsch. assoc. U. Cin., 1947-49; col. USPHS, 1951-89; postdoctoral fellow Nat. Cancer Inst., Bethesda, Md., 1949-51, chemist, 1951-73, chief carcinogen metabolism and toxicology br., 1972-75, chief Lab. Carcinogen Metabolism, 1975-81, asst. dir. chem. carcinogenesis, 1981-89, ret.; cons. in field; lectr. Found. for Advanced Edn. in Scis., Bethesda, 1980—; adj. prof. Am. U., Washington, 1982—. Asst. editor-in-chief Jour. Nat. Cancer Inst., 1971-87; contbr. articles to profl. jours. Trustee Lebanon Valley Coll., 1970—, pres. bd. trustees, 1985-89. Recipient Meritorious Service medal USPHS, 1973, Disting. Service medal, 1985; Hillebrand prize Chem. Soc. Washington, 1981. Fellow AAAS (nominating com. 1978-81);

mem. Am. Chem. Soc. (Garvan medal 1981), Am. Assn. Cancer Research, Soc. Toxicology, Am. Soc. Biochem. and Molecular Biology, Royal Soc. Chemistry, Am. Conf. Govtl. Indsl. Hygienists, Grad. Women in Sci. (hon.), Iota Sigma Pi (hon.). Lutheran.

WEISCHADLE, DAVID EMMANUEL, education educator; b. Sayreville, N.J., Oct. 4, 1941; s. Richard G. and Christina (Dailey) W.; m. Mary Ann Piscopo, June 22, 1968; children: David E. II, Douglas E. BS, Rutgers U., 1963, EdM, 1964, EdD, 1970. Cert. tchr., supr., prin., supt., N.J. Tchr. Edison (N.J.) Pub. Schs., 1964-65, 67-69; program specialist N.J. Urban Sch. Devel. Coun., Trenton, 1969-70; dir. planning Trenton Pub. Schs., 1970-73; prof. Montclair State Coll., Upper Montclair, N.J., 1973—; vis. fellow Woodrow Wilson Sch. of Pub. and Internat. Affairs, Princeton (N.J.) U., 1989-90; cons. Commn. to Study Programs and Svcs. for the Hearing-Impaired, Trenton, 1989-90, N.J. Dept. Edn., 1973-90; presenter in field. Contbr. articles to profl. jours. Capt. U.S. Army, 1965-67, Republic of Vietnam. Recipient Outstanding Achievement for Vietnam Vet award, Pres. of U.S., 1979, Achievement award Assessment and Devel. Ctr., N.J., 1989-90, Individual Achievement award, ASTD, 1988. Mem. ASTD (award 1988), ASCD, Ednl. Adminstrn. Profs. N.J. (pres. 1987-89), N.J. Staff Devel. Coun., N.J. Vietnam Vets. Meml. Commn., others. Home: 6 Ribsam St Trenton NJ 08619-3605 Office: Montclair State Coll Normal Ave Montclair NJ 07043-1607

WEISE, W. JEFFREY, textile company executive; b. Paterson, N.J., July 3, 1942; s. William and Maude (Hoffman) W.; m. Carol A. Romanski, Oct. 3, 1964; children: Kerri A., Robin B. BA in Psychology, Clark U., 1964, MBA, 1973. Fundraiser Easter Seal Soc., Worcester, Mass., 1964-66; from MIS project leader to mktg. mgr. Dennison Mfg. Co., Framingham, Mass., 1966-82; corp. purchasing dir. Malden Mills Industries Inc., Lawrence, Mass., 1982-84; purchasing dir. Data Checker DTS, Maynard, Mass., 1985; prodn. mgr. Malden Mills Industries Inc., Lawrence, 1986-88, corp. purchasing dir., 1988—. Fin. com. mem. Town of Holliston, Mass., 1079-81. Mem. Purchasing Mgmt. Assn. Boston (bd. dirs. 1979-81, cert. purchasing mgr. 1985). Republican. Episcopalian. Home: 60 Bonney Dr Holliston MA 01746-1010 Office: Malden Mills Industries Inc 46 Stafford St Lawrence MA 01841-2422

WEISENBERGER, SCOTT, therapist, newspaper editor; b. Phila., Dec. 16, 1955; s. George A. and Gertrude (Anderson) W. BA, U. Va., Charlottesville, 1977; MA in Counseling Psychology, Beaver Coll., 1991. Stringer Time mag., Atlanta, 1976-77; editor Counselor mag., Trevose, Pa., 1978; editor, reporter Montgomery Newspapers, Ft. Washington, Pa., 1978-86; editor Montgomery County Record, Horsham, Pa., 1986-88; project editor The Reporter, Lansdale, Pa., 1988-89, city editor, 1989-91; clin. supr. Advantage Recovery Network, Phila., 1991—; student therapist Harbison Recovery Ctr., Phila., 1990-91. Founder Pa. chpt. Sibling Bond, Lansdale, 1986; bd. mem. Montgomery County chpt. Families United for Mental Health, Oreland, Pa., 1985-86. Recipient Best News Story award Phila. chpt. Sigma Delta Chi, 1984, Best Media Reporting award Nat. Newspaper Assn., 1985, Best Feature Series award PNPA, Harrisburg, 1985. Democrat. Roman Catholic. Office: Advantage Recovery Network 7901 Bustleton Ave Philadelphia PA 19152-3302

WEISER, NORMAN SIDNEY, publishing executive; b. Mpls., Oct. 1, 1919; s. Simon and Rosa (Davidson) W.; m. Ruth Miller, Mar. 23, 1943 (dec. July 1986); children: Judith Ann, Richard Alan. BA, Northwestern U., 1939. Reporter Radio Daily, 1938-42; reporter, editor Billboard Mag., 1947-52; pub. Down Beat Mag., 1952-59; v.p. United Artists, 1959-62, 64-68, 20th Century Fox, 1962-64; v.p., dir. European ops. Paramount Music Div., 1968-69; v.p., gen. mgr. Chappell Music Co., N.Y.C., 1969-73; pres. Chappell Music Co., 1973-77; sr. v.p., dir. Polygram Corp. U.S.; mem. mgmt. com., v.p. Internat. Polygram Pub. Div.; pres. Sesac, Inc., 1978-81; v.p., gen. mgr. Largo Music Corp., 1981-85; chmn. bd., chief exec. officer WMC Entertainment Corp., 1985—; chmn. Am. Acad. of Comedy Hall of Fame, N.Y.C., 1987—. Author: Writers' Radio Theater, 1940, Writers' Radio-TV Theater, 1942, Under The Big Top, 1947, History AAF, World War II, 1947; lyricist 40 songs. Bd. dirs. Parkinson Found.; mem. corp., bd. dirs. UNICEF. Capt. USAAF, 1943-47. Decorated Purple Heart, Commendation medal Sec. War; recipient Ben Gurion award, 1975. Mem. ASCAP (dir.), Nat. Music Pubs'. Assn. (v.p., dir.), Country Music Assn. (chmn. bd.). Club: Friars. Lodge: B'nai Brith. Home and Office: 58 W 58th St Apt 14E New York NY 10019-2508

WEISERT, KENT ALBERT FREDERICK, lawyer; b. Passaic, N.J., Sept. 9, 1949; s. Frederick William and Waleska Anna Sophia (Bischoff) W.; m. Deborah Jean Searing, Mar. 12, 1983; 1 child, Christianna Lillian. BA magna cum laude, Rutgers U., 1971, JD, 1974. Bar: N.J. 1974, U.S. Dist. Ct. N.J. 1974, U.S. Tax Ct. 1975, U.S. Ct. Appeals (3d cir.) 1978, U.S. Supreme Ct. 1987. Adminstrv. asst. trust dept. Howard Savs. Bank, Newark, 1973-74; ptnr. Schwartz, Tobia & Stanziale, Montclair, N.J., 1975—; arbitrator U.S. Dist. Ct., Newark, 1985—. Contbr. chpt. to book New Jersey Transaction Guide, 1987. Pres. ch. coun. Holy Trinity Luth. Ch., Nutley, N.J., 1982-83; mem. Greater N.J. Estate Planning Coun. Mem. ABA, Fed. Bar Assn., N.J. State Bar Assn., Essex County Bar Assn., Rutgers Law Sch. Alumni Assn., Nat. Trust Hist. Preservation, N.J. Hist. Soc., Phi Beta Kappa, Phi Alpha Theta, Pi Delta Epsilon. Republican. Lutheran. Home: 51 Fairway St Bloomfield NJ 07003-5515 Office: Schwartz Tobia & Stanziale 22 Crestmont Rd Verona NJ 07044-2902

WEISGOLD, MYRA IRENE (MARCI WEISGOLD), sculptor; b. Phila., Apr. 10, 1939; d. Samuel Wolfe and Mae Hannah (Kaufman) Chernoff; m. Arnold Stanley Weisgold, June 14, 1959; children: Dean Eric, Richard Craig, Melissa Jill. BA, U. Pa., 1961. Sculptures include (Bronze Bust) D. Walter Cohen, 1981, (Bronze Bas Reliefs) Memorial: Robert Ravdin, 1982, Memorial: J. George Coslet, 1985, (Bronze compositions) Stepping Stones, 1989, Testing the Waters, 1992. Recipient Pietro and Alfreda Montana Meml. award Allied Artists of Am., 1982, Edwin and Theresa Richard Meml. award, 1987, Excalbur Bronze Sculpture Foundry award Pen and Brush, 1990, Helen G. Oehler Meml. award Am. Artists Profl. League, 1991. Mem. Nat. Sculpture Soc., Catherine L. Wolfe Art Club, Am. Artists Profl. League, Allied Artists Am. (assoc.), Pen and Brush Inc., Knickerbocker Artists (assoc.), Artists Equity, Internat. Sculpture Ctr., Phi Beta Kappa. Home: 150 Summit Ln Bala Cynwyd PA 19004 Office: Mill Artists Studio 123 Leverington Ave Philadelphia PA 19127

WEISIGER, KATHLEEN WENDELL, resource consultant; b. N.Y.C., Apr. 20, 1949; d. James Richard and Elisabeth Patricia (O'Brien) W.; m. Kaarle Koivula; children: Mikael Kristian, Lindsey Elisabeth. Student, Montgomery Coll., 1967-74; AA in Human Svcs., Anne Arundel Community Coll., Arnold, Md., 1985. Group counselor Nat. Children's Rehab. Ctr., Leesburg, Va., 1969-70; psychiat. technician Montgomery Gen. Hosp., Olney, Md., 1972; adminstrv. asst. Manna House Group Homes, Sunshine, Md., 1973-74; counselor Youth Sanctuary, Pasadena, Md., 1975-77, Arundel Lodge, Annapolis, Md., 1977-80; juvenile counselor Juvenile Svcs. Adminstrn., Annapolis, 1980-81; counselor Psychol. Health Svcs., Annapolis, 1983-84; intensive counselor Juvenile Svcs. Adminstrn., Annapolis, 1984-85; juvenile counselor Juvenile Svcs. Agy., Annapolis, 1985—; bd. dirs. Teen Age Crisis Intervention, Annapolis, 1971-74, Sex Offense Crisis Ctr., Annapolis, 1976-79; chair Children's Coun., Annapolis; bd. dirs. children and youth Coun. Community Svcs., Annapolis. Vol. Mental Health Assn., Kensington, Md., 1970-74; bd. dirs., pub. info. chair Alcoholics Anonymous, Annapolis, 1978-81; co-founder Bache Meml. Free Clinic, Bethesda, Md., 1970; rep. Coun. on Adolescents, Montgomery County, Md., 1971-74. Mem. Md. Conf. on Social Concern, Mensa. Methodist. Home: 3260 Kitty Duvall Dr Annapolis MD 21403-4625 Office: Dept Juvenile Svcs 1623 Forest Ave Annapolis MD 21403

WEISKERGER, RENEE ANN, accountant; b. Buffalo, Aug. 27, 1967; d. Roy Charles and Sandra Lee (Palmer) W. BS in Bus. Adminstrn., Duquesne U., 1989. CPA, Pa. Asst. acct. KPMG Peat Marwick, Pitts., 1989-90, staff acct., 1990-91; sr. acct. KPMG Peat Marwick, 1991—.

WEISMAN, BART LOUIS, personnel placement executive; b. Washington, Aug. 25, 1958; s. David Bruce and Morelyn (Levy) W.; m. Amy Susan Heller, Oct. 30, 1987. AA in Music, Montgomery Coll., 1983; BS in Tech. and Mgmt., U. Md., 1984. Programmer GTE Corp. Telenet, McLean, Va., 1980-81; project mgr. Booz, Allen & Hamilton, Bethesda, Md., 1981-85; dir. Source Svcs. Corp., Washington, 1985-89; owner Bart Weisman Assocs., Silver Spring, Md., 1989—. Musician USAF Band, Washington, 1978-83; prin. Perform Music for Sr. Citizens, Washington, 1978—. Sgt. USAF, 1978-83. Recipient several civic awards for music performance Montgomery County, Md., 1978—. Mem. Md. Assn. Profl. Placement Cons. (assoc.). Office: Bart Weisman Assoc 1010 Wayne Ave Silver Spring MD 20910

WEISMAN, HARLAN FREDERICK, biopharmaceutical company executive; b. Bklyn., July 17, 1952; s. Herman Muni and Margaret Madelin (Cohen) W.; m. Sally Harowitz, June 7, 1981; children: Sara Rachel, Daniel Michael. BA, U. Md., 1975, MD, 1979. Cert. Nat. Bd. Med. Examiners, Am. Bd. Internal Medicine-Cardiovascular Disease. Resident internal medicine Mt. Sinai Hosp., N.Y.C., 1979-82; fellow cardiology Johns Hopkins Hosp., Balt., 1982-84; asst. in medicine Johns Hopkins Sch. Medicine, Balt., 1984-85, asst. prof. medicine, 1985-90; guest researcher Gerontology Rsch. Ctr., NIH, Balt., 1985-90; dir. cardiology Centocor, Inc., Malvern, Pa., 1990—; cons. cardiologist Johns Hopkins Hosp., Balt., 1985-90. Guest reviewer Circulation, 1983—, Jour. of the Am. Coll. Cardiology, 1988—; contbr. articles to profl. jours. Samuel J. Katcef Meml. fellow Am. Heart Assn., 1989-90. Fellow Am. Coll. Cardiology, Am. Coll. Chest Physicians, Coun. on Clin. Cardiology Am. Heart Assn.; mem. Internat. Soc. for Thrombosis and Hemostasis, Internat. Soc. for Heart Rsch., Am. Fedn. for Clin. Rsch., Phi Beta Kappa, Alpha Omega Alpha. Home: 759 Applegate Ln Rosemont PA 19010 Office: Centocor Inc 200 Great Valley Pkwy Malvern PA 19355

WEISMAN, JOHN, journalist; b. N.Y.C., Aug. 1, 1942; s. Abner I. Weisman and Syde (Lubowe) Kremer; m. Susan Lee Povenmire, Feb. 12, 1983. AB, Bard Coll., 1964. Mng. editor Coast mag., Los Angeles, 1969-70; staff writer Rolling Stone, San Francisco, 1971, Detroit Free Press, 1971-73; assoc. editor TV Guide, Radnor, Pa., 1973-77; bur. chief TV Guide, Washington, 1977-89; sr. fellow Annenberg Washington program Northwestern U., Washington, 1989-91; bd. dirs. Va. Writing mag. Author: (nonfiction) Guerrilla Theatre, 1973, Shadow Warrior, 1989, Rogue Warrior, 1992 (novels) Evidence, 1980, Watchdogs, 1983, Blood Cries, 1987. Mem. White House Corrs. Assn., Bard Coll. Alumni Assn. (bd. govs. 1975-81, pres. 1981-83). Club: Army and Navy (Washington). Home: 5522 Trent St Bethesda MD 20815-5512

WEISMAN, MAXWELL NAPIER, psychiatrist, educator; b. N.Y.C., July 9, 1912; s. Morris and Pauline (Malevatsky) W. BS, CCNY, 1930, MA, 1931, PhD, 1936; MD, U. Amsterdam, The Netherlands, 1958. Dir. house plan CCNY, N.Y.C., 1935-41; prof. U. P.R., Rio Piedras, 1946-49; acting dir. vets. edn. P.R. Dept. Instrn., San Juan, 1949-51; dir. community psychiatry Md. Dept. Mental Health, Balt., 1962-68; dir. alcoholism control Md. Dept. Health, Balt., 1968-80, ret., 1980; cons. FAA, Washington, 1975—; cons. Westinghouse Corp., Pitts., 1975—. Co-author: Relapse/Slips, 1983. Fellow Am. Psychiat. Assn. (life); emm. Am. Pub. Health Assn., Md. Med. and Chirurgical Soc., ACLU, Nat. Coun. on Alcoholism. Democrat.

WEISS, ALLEN, freelance writer and editor, accountant; b. N.Y.C., July 11, 1918; s. Jacob and Lillian (Comick) W.; m. Florence Golub, July 20, 1941 (dec. Sept. 1955); children: Susan Louise, Robert Irwin; m. Enid Suzanne Marks, Feb. 21, 1957. BS cum laude, CCNY, 1937; MBA, NYU, 1939. CPA, N.Y. Cons. Social Security Bd., Washington, 1941-42; various positions Lever Bros. Co., N.Y.C., 1949-58; contr. Kickerbocker Biols. Inc., N.Y.C., 1958-61; treas.-contr. Her Majesty, Inc., Greenville, S.C., 1961-62; mgr. mgmt. svcs. Anchin, Block & Anchin, N.Y.C., 1963-66; dir. communications, mgmt. cons. svcs. Coopers & Lybrand (Nat.), N.Y.C., 1966-69; dir. communications Laventhol & Horwath, N.Y.C., 1970-74; mng. editor CPA Jour. N.Y. State Soc. CPA's, N.Y.C., 1974; freelance writer and editor books and courses Upper Montclair, N.J., 1975—; speaker, lectr. to univs. and profl. assns., 1967—. Author: The Organization Guerrilla, 1975, Write What You Mean, 1977, Writing Reports That Work, rev. edit., 1980; (cassette course) Writing Sense, 1981; editor: Einstein: Successful Personnel Selection, 1982; contbr. articles to profl. jours. Co-chmn. Montclair '76 United, 1975-76; campaign treas. state and county candidates; sec. Montclair Housing Adv. Com., 1976-80; mem. fin. com. Montclair chpt. ARC, 1980-90; vol. tutor VISTE Program, 1991-92; mem. exec. com. Good Govt. Dems., Montclair, 1965-75; active Essex County Dem. Com., 1965-79. Lt. USCG, 1942-46. Mem. AICPA (con. editor Mgmt. Svcs. 1966-70), Authors Guild, Writers League Am., N.Y. State Soc. CPAs (com. chmn. 1971-72), Am. Mgmt. Assn. (contbg. editor Supervisory Mgmt. 1979-81), Amnesty Internat. (contbr. to Policy Forum 1992), Inst. for Critical Thinking (contbr. to Inquiry 1992), Phi Beta Kappa (pres. No. N.J. Alumni Assn. 1973-75). Jewish. Home: 8 Tuers Pl Montclair NJ 07043-2520

WEISS, ALLEN CHARLES, psychiatrist; b. N.Y.C., Sept. 27, 1945; s. Sidney H. and Ida (Perlstein) W. BS, U. Ga., 1967; MD, Universidad Central Deleste, Dominican Republic, 1980. Intern Trenton (N.J.) Affiliated Hosps., 1982-83; resident in radiation oncology Beth Israel Med. Ctr., N.Y.C., 1983-84; resident in psychiatry Norwich (Conn.) Hosp., 1984-87; pvt. practice Milford, Del., 1987—; cons. Kent Sussex County Mental Health, Stokely Ctr. Hosp.; med. dir. Peoples Pl. Counseling Ctr. Mem. Am. Psychiat. Assn., Del. Psychiat. Assn. Office: PO Box 782 Milford DE 19963-0782

WEISS, ALVIN HARVEY, chemical engineering educator, catalysis researcher and consultant; b. Phila., Apr. 28, 1928; s. Louis and Helen F. (Wilinsky) W.; children: Linda S., Louis B.; m. Devorah Schwartz, June 10, 1979. BSChemE, U. Pa., 1949, PhD in Phys. Chemistry, 1965; MSChemE, Newark Coll. Engring., 1955. Registered profl. engr., Mass., Del. Chem. engr. Fiber Chem. Corp., Cliffwood, N.J., 1949-51, Colgate-Palmolive Co., Jersey City, 1953-55, Houdry Process and Chems. Co., Linwood, Pa., 1956-63; research assoc., lectr. U. Pa., Phila., 1963-66; prof. chem. engring. Worcester Poly. Inst., Mass., 1966—; NASA-ASEE summer faculty fellow Stanford U., Ames Research Ctr., 1967, 68; affiliate scientist Worcester Found. Exptl. Biology, 1972-74; Fulbright-Hays sr. faculty fellow to dept. chem. engring. Ben-Gurion U. of Negev, Beersheva, Israel, 1973-74, vis. prof. chem. engring., 1974; U.S. coord. U.S.-USSR Coop. Sci. Program in Chem. Catalysis, Topic IV, 1973-76, prin. investigator (with M.M. Sakharov), 1976-78; prin. investigator (with K.I. Ione) U.S.-USSR Coop. Sci. Program in Chem. Catalysis, Topic III, 1978-80; Fulbright-Hays vis. lectr. dept. chem. engring. Middle East Tech. U., Ankara, Turkey, 1974, vis. prof., 1991; vis. research scientist dept. organic chemistry Weizmann Inst., Rehovoth, Israel, 1974; vis. lectr. Inst. Isotopes and Central Inst. Chemistry, Hungarian Acad. Scis., Budapest, 1976; vis. prof. Inst. Cultural Relations and Inst. Isotopes, Hungarian Acad. Scis., 1978, 80; UNIDO chief tech. advisor to Petrochem. Complex of Bahia Blanca, Argentina, 1980; sr. research fellow chem. systems lab. Army Chem. Ctr., Md., 1981; UNIDO expert in chem. process devel. Rsch. Inst. for Chem. Industry, Beijing, Peoples Republic of China, 1982; UNIDO expert in catalysis to YARPET Petrochemical Complex, Yarimca, Turkey, 1986-87; bd. dirs. U.S. com. for sci. coop. with Vietnam; vis. lectr. Nat. Ctr. for Sci. Rshc., Inst. of Indsl. Chemistry, 1986. translator: (with M. Delleo, G. Dembinski and J. Happel) Catalyis by Non-Metals (O.V. Krylov), 1970; contbr. articles to profl. jours.; patentee in field. With U.S. Army, 1951-53. Named Outstanding Researcher and Creative Scholar, Worcester Poly. Inst., 1984; recipient Sci. Achievement award Worcester Engring. Soc., 1984; research grantee NSF, PRF, NASA, DOD, DOE. Fellow Am. Inst. Chem. Engrs. (rsch. com. 1968-80, symposia chmn. 1973-84); mem.AAUP, ACS, Am. Inst. Chem. Engrs., Catalysis Soc. (bd. dirs., sec. 1968-88), Catalysis Soc. New England (founding pres. 1967-68, bd. dirs. 1968—), Am. Chem. Soc. (New England petroleum div. rep. 1970-88, session chmn. 1973—), Deutsche Gesellschaft für Chemische Apparatwesen. Office: Worcester Poly Inst 100 Institute Rd Worcester MA 01609-2276

WEISS, ANDRE, psychiatrist; b. Mar. 31, 1926; s. Melchior and Magda (Sziklas) W.; m. Renee Veit, 1952; children: Madeleine Eve Fagan, Stephen Philip. BS, U. Geneva, 1950, MD, 1954. Intern Sewickley Valley (Pa.) Hosp., 1955-56; resident Cen. Islip (N.Y.) State Hosp., 1956; pvt. practice in gen. medicine Aberdeen, Md., 1957-64; resident in psychiatry Sheppard Pratt Hosp., Balt., 1964-67; psychiatrist out patient dept., instr. psychiatry John Hopkins Med. Sch., Balt., 1966-67; med. officer WHO, Geneva, 1968-76; staff psychiatrist Sheppard Pratt Hosp., Balt., 1977-78, Taylor Manor Hosp., Ellicott City, Md., 1984-92, Balt. County Community Mental Health Ctr., Catonsville, Md., 1991—; pvt. practice Geneva, 1978-84. Author: Typhus in Concentration Camps, 1954 (Brit. Imperial War Mus. recognition); exhibitor stamp collection (Grand award), 1964. Mem. Am. Psychiat. Assn., Md. Psychiat. Soc., Am. Numismatic Soc.

WEISS, ANDREW MURRAY, economics educator; b. Jan. 2, 1947; s. Daniel I. and Gloria (Nestel) W.; m. Bonnie Klinger, Dec. 23, 1979; children: Danielle, Kara, Judith. BA, Williams Coll., 1968; MA, Stanford U., 1974, PhD, 1976. Mem. tech. staff Bell Labs., Murray Hill, N.J., 1976-83; mem. tech. staff Bell Communications Rsch., Morristown, N.J., 1983-86; assoc. prof. Columbia U., N.Y.C., 1983-85; prof. Boston U., 1986—; Woodrow Wilson fellow vis. prof. Tel Aviv U., 1991, 92. Author: Efficiency Wages, 1990; contbr. articles profl. jours. Mem. panel on drug use in the work place NAS. Fellow Econometric Soc. Jewish. Home: 46 Abbottsford Rd Brookline MA 02146-3106 Office: Boston U 270 Bay State Rd Boston MA 02176-1426

WEISS, ANN, filmmaker, editor, writer, photographer, information specialist, consultant; b. Modena, Italy, July 17, 1949; came to U.S., 1951, naturalized, 1959; d. Leo and Athalie Weiss; children: Julia Emily, Rebecca Lauren. BA magna cum laude in English Lit. and Edn., U. Rochester, 1971; MA in Info. Sci. summa cum laude, Drexel U., 1973; doctoral studies edn., culture and soc., U. Pa., 1989-92, postgrad. in edn., 1992—. Editor, chief cons. monographs, articles, freelance photographer, 1974—; cataloguer Drexel U., Phila., 1971-73; libr. Akiba Lower Sch., Merion, Pa., 1973; head children's dept. Tredyffrin Pub. Libr., Strafford, Pa., 1973-79, co-head reference dept., 1979-87; cons. in edn. and librs. Gulf Arab States Edn. and Rsch. Ctr., UNESCO, 1974—; cons. Rabbi Zalman Schachter-Shalomi, P'nai Or Fellowhsip, 1987-88; photojournalist in Ea. Europe, mainly Poland and Czechoslovakia, 1987—; mem. editorial bd. Studies of the Shoah, 1991—; mem. Holocaust rsch. team U. Pa., 1989—;. Dir. producer (video documentary and archive creation) oral history project Inst. Pa. Hosp., (video documentary) The Institute: An Intimate History, 1992; dir., producer, writer, narrator, photographer (video documentary) Eyes From The Ashes, Archival Photographs from Auschwitz, 1989-90; dir., producer, writer, narrator, photographer (with D. Rosenberg, co-produced with sta. WPBT) Auschwitz documentary Lighting Six Candles, 1992—; author, lyricist (with Thaddeus Lorentz/musical), Zosia: An Immigrant's Story; chief editorial cons. Puppetry and the Art of Story Creation, 1981, Puppetry in Early Childhood Education, 1982, Puppetry, Language and the Special Child: Discovering Alternative Language, 1984, Humanizing the Enemy...and Ourselves, 1986, Imagination, 1987, Celebrate! Holidays, Puppetry and Creative Dramatics, 1987; one-person photographic shows throughout U.S., Europe, Israel; represented in permanent collections including Martyr's Meml. Mus./Yad Vashem, Simon Wiesenthal Ctr./Mus. Tolerance. Active So. Poverty Law Ctr., Common Cause, advocacy and fundraising for Ethiopian Jews, promoting dialogue and understanding between Jews and Arabs, Jews and Poles; active Coun. for Soviet Jews, Internat. Network Children Holocaust Survivors; photographer Bob Edgar's Campaign U.S. Senate, 1985-86, David Landau's Congl. Campaign, 1986. Mem. ACLU, NOW, SANE, Free Wallenberg Alliance, Union Concerned Scientists, Physicians for Social Responsibility, Amnesty Internat., New Israel Fund, Sierra Club. Office: PO Box 1133 Bryn Mawr PA 19010

WEISS, BERNARD, toxicology educator; b. N.Y.C., May 27, 1925; s. Max and Sadie (Albert) W.; m. Ann Bartlett, Oct. 10, 1950 (div. 1972); children: Wendy, Thomas; m. Susan Edelman, Dec. 16, 1978. BA, NYU, 1949; PhD, U. Rochester, 1953. Exptl. psychologist USAF Sch. Aviation Medicine, San Antonio, Tex., 1954-56; asst. prof. Johns Hopkins Med. Sch., Balt., 1956-65; prof. U. Rochester (N.Y.) Med. Sch., 1965—; mem. Sci. Adv. Bd., EPA, Washington, 1981—, Toxicology Study Sect., NIH, Bethesda, Md., 1982-86, Bd. Sci. Counselors Nat. Inst. Environ. Health Sci., Research Triangle Park, N.C., 1986-90, Nat. Acad. Scis. Com. on Neurotoxicology, Washington, 1986-91; Burroughs Wellcome vis. prof. U. Miss., 1986. Editor: Digital Computers in the Behavioral Laboratory, 1973, Behavioral Toxicology, 1975; contbr. 160 articles to profl. jours. Sgt. USAF, 1944-46, PTO. Recipient Stokinger award Am Conf. Govt., Indsl. Hygienists, 1990; named Scientist of Yr., Assn. Children with Learning Disabilities. Fellow AAAS, Amer. Psychol. Assn. (pres. div. 28 1961-62); mem. Behavioral Toxicology Soc., (pres. 1984-86), Soc. Toxicology (neurology spl. sect. pres. 1990-91). Office: U Rochester Med Ctr Box EHSC Rochester NY 14642

WEISS, BRIAN, lawyer; b. Bklyn., Aug. 16, 1945; s. Morris and Ruth (Schimelman) W.; m. Susan Rae Klarreich, July 3, 1983. BA cum laude, CUNY, 1965, MA, 1968, PhD, 1974; JD, Columbia U., 1978. Bar: N.Y. 1979. Instr. Eng. SUNY, Geneseo, 1968-72; adj. asst. prof. CUNY, Baruch, 1974-75; editorial cons. N.Y.C., 1974-75; staff rserecher ABA, N.Y.C., 1979-80; pvt. practice Queens, N.Y., 1980-81; chief of appeals F. Lee Bailey & Aaron J. Broder Firm, N.Y.C., 1981-82; pvt. practice N.Y.C., 1982—. Editor The Broder N.Y. Tort Reporter. Adminstr. Harry Bermack Pro Bono Litigation Panel, B'nai B'rith, 1986—. NDEA fellow, 1965. Mem. N.Y. County Lawyers Assn. (legal assistance com.), Assn. of Bar of City of N.Y., N.Y. Trial Lawyers Assn., N.Y. Criminal Bar Assn., Columbia Law Sch. Alumni Assn., Am. Mensa, MLA, N.Y. Lawyers Unit, B'nai B'rith (v.p. 1983—), Phi Beta Kappa (gamma chpt.). Democrat. Office: 11 Park Pl New York NY 10007-2801

WEISS, DAVID ALAN, international economist; b. Washington, June 22, 1953; s. Leonard and Mary Louise (Barker) W.; m. Mamie Kresses, June 2, 1991. BA, Hamilton Coll., 1975; MS in Fgn. Svc., Georgetown U., 1978. Staff asst. Office of Senator Thomas F. Eagleton, Washington, 1970-71; rsch. fellow Carnegie Endowment for Internat. Peace, Washington, 1975-76; spl. asst. to dir. Peace Corps, Washington, 1978-80; fgn. svc. officer U.S. Dept of State, Washington, 1980-90; with econ. office Am. Embassy, Port-au-Prince, Haiti, 1981-83; with secretariat staff Office of Sec. of State, 1983-84; sr. spl. asst. to dep. sec. of state U.S. Dept. of State, 1985-87; dir. European Community high tech and east-west trade policy Office of European Affairs, U.S. Trade Rep., Washington, 1987-89; exec. dir. for policy coordination Exec. Office of The Pres., U.S. Trade Rep., Washington, 1989-92; dep. asst. U.S. Trade Rep. for North Am. Affairs, 1992—. Mem. Am. Fgn. Svc. Assn., Diplomatic and Consular Officers Ret. Home: 1816 New Hampshire Ave NW Washington DC 20009 Office: US Trade Rep 600 17th St NW Washington DC 20506

WEISS, EDWARD, food products executive; b. Phila., May 7, 1929; s. Stephen and Minerva (Gerson) W.; m. Eleanor Bunny Hersh, June 5, 1954; children: Samuel D., Kenneth T., Cynthia J. BS, Temple U., 1951. Plant mgr. Quaker Salad Co., Inc., Phila., 1953-56, corp. sec., 1956-73, pres., 1973-85; chmn. Luzerne Enterprises, Inc., Phila., 1979-82; pres. Phila. div. Orval Kent Food Co., 1985—. Contbr. articles to profl. jours. Bd. dirs. Congregation Beth Chaim, Feasterville, Pa., 1969-75, pres. men's club, 1970-71. Served with U.S. Army, 1951-53. Mem. Mensa. Democrat. Jewish. Lodge: B'Nai Brith. Home: 144 Forge Ln Langhorne PA 19053 Office: Phila div Orval Kent Food Co 3901 Old York Rd Philadelphia PA 19140-2098

WEISS, ELAINE LANDSBERG, community development management official; b. N.Y.C.; d. Louis and Sadie Blossum (Schoenfeld); divorced. BA in Philosophy and Polit. Sci., Bklyn. Coll., 1960; postgrad., NYU Law Sch., 1960-62; MA in Sociology, Hunter Coll., N.Y.C., 1969. Social investigator N.Y.C. Dept. Social Services, 1963-64; intern, fellow Eleanor Roosevelt Meml. Found., Nat. Assn. Intergroup Relations Ofcls., 1964-65; asst. dir. housing and asst. project dir. Operation Equality, Nat. Urban League, 1965-67; program assoc. housing div. ch. missions Am. Bapt. Home Mission Socs., 1967-70; pres. E.L. Weiss Assocs., 1970-76; exec. dir. Suffolk Community Devel. Corp., Coram, N.Y., 1976-89, E.L. Weiss Assocs., East Quoque, N.Y., 1990—, Grenadier Realty Corp., 1990—; mem. citizens adv. com. N.Y.C. Dept. Housing Preservation and Devel.; exec. com. L.I. Community Devel. Orgn.; past 2d v.p. Suffolk Housing Task Force; chmn. Suffolk County Citizens Adv. Com., 1981-82. Recipient cert. of commendation L.I. Council Chs., 1981. Mem. Nat. Assn. Housing Ofcls., N.Y. State Assn. Housing and Redevel. Ofcls., Am. Contract Bridge League (life master). Home: PO Box 1532 East Quogue NY 11942-1333

WEISS, EVE, foundation executive; b. N.Y.C., May 15, 1930; d. Irving David and Beatrice (Krauthamer) Sapir; m. Gustave Weiss, Mar. 18, 1951;

children: Jonathan Ben, Robin Sue, Ricky Alison. BA, NYU, 1949, JD, 1952. Dir. vols. Albert Einstein Med. Ctr., Bronx, 1966-68; regional dir. Am. Jewish Congress, N.Y.C., 1968-70; nat. w.d. dir. Nat. United Jewish Appeal, N.Y.C., 1970-77, asst. exec. vice chmn., 1977-81; fin. dir. Dem. Nat. Com., Washington, 1981-82; dir. devel. Beth Israel Med. Ctr., N.Y.C., 1982-84; exec. dir. Hasbro Children's Found., N.Y.C., 1984—; dir. Futures for Children, Albuquerque, 1965—; cons. Green Chimneys, Putnam Valley, N.Y., 1988—, Happiness is Camping, Wayne, N.J., 1989—, N.Y. State Coun. on Alcoholism, Albany, N.Y., 1991. Mem. Queens County Com., 1967. Fellow Inst. for Contemporary Jewery. Home: 220 Madison Ave New York NY 10016-3416 Office: Hasbro Childrens Found 32 W 23d St New York NY 10010

WEISS, GEORGE ARTHUR, orthodontist; b. Bklyn., Feb. 1, 1921; s. Nathan L. and Ida (Rosenthal) W.; m. Jacqueline Hellermann, Jan. 28, 1945; children: Ellen Joy Weiss Finberg, Leslie Donna Weiss Schoenfeld. BA, Bklyn. Coll., 1941; DDS, Columbia U., 1944, cert. Orthodontics, 1954. Diplomate Am. Bd. of Orthodontics. Dir. dentistry Dental Clinic Southen Japan, Kobe, 1946; chief dentistry Olmstead AFB, Middleburg, Pa., 1947; pvt. practice Orthodontics Bayside, N.Y., 1947—; chief orthodontics Community Svc. Soc., N.Y.C., 1954-57; dir. orthodontics Jamaica (N.Y.) Hosp., 1977—; cons. State Aid Orthodontic Program for Handicapped Children, Suffolk County, N.Y., 1987—. Founder, Oakland Gardens Jewish Ctr., Bayside, N.Y., 1949; Bayside Oaks Jewish Ctr., Bayside, 1954. Major U.S. Army, 1944-48, Japan. Recipient Chemistry award, Am. Inst. Chem., N.Y.C., 1941. Fellow Am. Coll. Dentistry; mem. Am. Bd. Orthodontists, Am. Assn. Orthodontists, Northeastern Soc. Orthodontists, Dental Soc. State of N.Y. (bd. govs. 1976-86, mem. coun. on ins. 1965-75), Queens County Dental Soc. (trustee 1960—, chief adminstr. retirement fund, 1964-72, pres. 1975, Disting. Svc. award, 1988), Old Westbury Golf and Country Club, Alpha Omega Dental Soc. Home and Office: 5901 Springfield Blvd Flushing NY 11364-1996

WEISS, GEORGE HERBERT, mathematician, consultant; b. N.Y.C., Feb. 19, 1930; s. Morris and Violet (Mayer) W.; m. Delia Esther Orgel, Dec. 20, 1961; children: Miriam Judith, Alan Keith, Daniel Mordechai. BA, Columbia U., 1951; MA, U. Md., 1953, PhD, 1958. Physicist USN, White Oak, Md., 1951-61; asst. prof. U. Md., College Park, 1959-63; fellow Rockefeller U., N.Y.C., 1963-64, Weizmann Inst., Rehovot, Israel, 1958-59; mathematician NIH, Bethesda, Md., 1964—; cons. GM, IBM, GE. Author: Lattice Dynamics in the Harmonic Approximation, 1963, 2d edit., 1971, The Master Equation in Chemical Physics, 1977. With U.S. Army, 1954-56. Recipient Disting. Svc. in Math. award Washington Acad. Sci., 1967, Disting. Svc. award NIH, 1970. Office: NIH Bethesda MD 20892

WEISS, HARLAN LEE, lawyer; b. Washington, Dec. 6, 1941; s. Richard Stanley and Ethel (Shulman) W.; m. Elaine Sharon Schooler, Feb. 14, 1971; children: Rachel Shayna, Brian Adam. BA, U. Md.-College Park, 1963; JD with honors, U. Md.-Balt., 1966. Bar: Md. 1967, D.C. 1967, U.S. Dist. Ct. Md., 1967, U.S. Dist. Ct. D.C., 1967, U.S. Ct. Appeals (D.C. cir.) 1968, U.S. Ct. Appeals (4th cir.) 1977, U.S. Supreme Ct. 1970. Law clk. Ct. Appeals of Md., 1966-67; assoc. Surrey & Morse and predecessors, Washington, 1967-72; assoc. Sachs, Greenebaum & Tayler, Washington, 1972-76, ptnr., 1976-90, Kivitz & Liptz, Washington, 1990; mem. Jud. Conf. D.C., 1978-79; arbitrator Am. Arbitration Assn. Mem. D.C. Bar, ABA, Md. State Bar Assn., Montgomery County Bar Assn. Home: 12017 Cheyenne Rd Gaithersburg MD 20878-2011 Office: 5225 Wisconsin Ave NW Washington DC 20015-2014

WEISS, HARVEY JEROME, physician; b. N.Y.C., June 30, 1929; s. Sidney and Henrietta (Horowitz) W.; m. Thirell Marilyn Lipsey, Apr. 28, 1957; children: Deborah Marion, Adrienne Elizabeth. AB, Harvard U., 1951, MD, 1955. Instr. medicine NYU Sch. Medicine, 1962-64; asst. prof. medicine Mt. Sinai Sch. Medicine, 1966-69; dir. hematology/oncology Roosevelt Hosp., N.Y.C., 1969—; assoc. prof. medicine Columbia U., N.Y.C., 1972-75, prof. medicine, 1975—; cons. Walter Reed Inst. Rsch., Washington, 1965-70, NIH, Bethesda, Md., 1975—, Am. Bd. Internal Medicine, Phila., 1980-86. Author: Platelets: Pathophysiology and Anti-Platelet Therapy, 1982; contbr. articles to profl. jours. Capt. M.C. U.S. Army, 1959-62. Recipient Career Scientist award Health Rsch. N.Y.C., 1969-72; grantee NIH, 1970—. Fellow Am. Coll. Physicians; mem. Assn. Am. Physicians, Am. Soc. Clin. Investigation, Am. Physiol. Soc. Office: Saint Lukes-Roosevelt Hosp 428 W 59th St New York NY 10019-1105

WEISS, HARVEY RICHARD, physiology and biophysics educator, researcher; b. Bklyn., May 13, 1943; s. Edgar D. and Frances (Warshavsky) w.; m. Sandra Levy, Aug. 13, 1966; children: Johanna, Andrew. BS, CUNY, 1965; PhD, Duke U., 1969. Postdoctoral fellow Warner-Lambert Rsch. Inst. Columbia U., N.Y.C., 1969-71; mem. grad. program Rutgers U., 1972; from asst. prof. to asst. chmn. U. Medicine and Dentistry of (Piscataway) N.J., 1971-86, prof., dir. heart and brain lab., 1982, acting chair, 1986—; joint adv. com. Robert Wood Johnson Med. Sch., 1972-75, adv. 1st yr. med. students, 1972—, com. of review, 1976-79, curriculum com., co-chmn., 1977-83, radiation safety com., 1980-87, grant review com., 1984-88; seminar com. Rutgers U., 1974,75, exec. com. Physiology Program, 1974-80, 89—; reviewer Nat. Heart Lung and Blood Inst., NIH, Am. Jour. Physiology, Basic Rsch. in Cardiology, Canadian Jour. Physiology and Pharmacology, Cardiovascular Rsch., Circulation Rsch., and others. Grantee NIH, AHA. Office: U of Medicine Dentistry Robert Wood Johnson Med Sch 675 Hoes Ln Piscataway NJ 08854-5635

WEISS, JANET LOIS, assistant editor; b. N.Y.C., Sept. 13, 1946; d. Marvin and Ruth Pearl (Schumacher) W. Grad. high sch., New Providence, N.J. Clk. Kemper Ins. Co., Summit, N.J., 1965-69; mail deposit clk. Summit Trust Co., 1969-72; CRT terminal operator Martindale-Hubbell, Inc., New Providence, 1973-90; asst. editor ISBN Agt., R.R. Bowker, New Providence, 1991—. Trustee Summit Recycling, 1982-84; bd. dirs. Edison (N.J.) Hollow Condominium Assn., 1986-89. Jewish. Office: Martindale-Hubbell/RR Bowker 121 Chanlon Rd New Providence NJ 07974-1544

WEISS, JOEL ALEXANDER, aerospace industry executive; b. Washington; s. Jack Lawrence and Margaret (Siegel) W.; m. Sandra Jean Spaulding, July 6, 1969; children: Martin, Robert, Eric, Amy. B of Engring. Sci., Johns Hopkins U., 1969; AM, Harvard U., 1970, PhD, 1975. Rsch. physicist U.S. Naval Rsch. Lab., Washington, 1966-75; program mgr. U.S. Dept. Energy, Washington, 1975-78, exec. asst., 1978-80; mgr. Washington ops. Acurex Corp., Mtn. View, Calif., 1980-84; dir. tactical warfare Gould Inc., Glen Burnie, Md., 1984-87; mgr. rsch. & technology Martin Marietta Aero & Naval Systems, Balt., 1987-90; v.p. bus. devel. Marietta Tech. Svcs. Inc., Bethesda, Md., 1990—; cons. Micro Power Systems, Sunnyvale, Calif., 1983-84; chmn. govt. rels. com. Solar Energy Industries Assn., Washington, 1983-84. Patentee in field. Pres. Fair Oaks Community Assn., Severna Park, Md., 1988, Kings Pk. West Civic Assn., Fairfax, Va., 1978, Lakepointe Community Coun., Burke, Va., 1973. Mem. IEEE, Sigma Xi. Unitarian. Home: 210 Arundel Beach Rd Severna Park MD 21146-3115 Office: Martin Marietta Tech Svcs 6801 Rockledge Dr Bethesda MD 20817-1836

WEISS, JOSEPH FRANCIS, biochemist; b. Taylor, Pa., Jan. 26, 1940; s. Joseph Patrick and Clare Rita (Sekelsky) W.; m. Elvira S. deCastro, Sept. 7, 1968; children: Joseph M., Michael I. BS in Chemistry, U. Scranton, 1961; MS in Physiol. Chemistry, Ohio State U., 1963, PhD in Physiol. Chemistry, 1966. Postdoctoral fellow Inst. of Pharmacology U. Milan, Italy, 1966-68; from instr. to asst. prof. neurosurgery NYU Med. Ctr., 1968-74; from rsch. chemist to project mgr. Biochemistry Dept. Armed Forces Radiobiology Rsch. Inst., Bethesda, Md., 1974-91, adminstr. rsch. requirements, 1991—; vis. prof. U. Cagliari (Italy) Med. Sch., 1987-88, U. Pisa (Italy) Med. Sch., 1989-90. Editor: Perspectives in Radioprotection, 1988, Treatment of Radiation Injuries, 1990; mem. editorial bd. Internat. Jour. Radiation Biology, London, 1991—; contbr. articles to profl. jours. Commnr. Community Ministry of Montgomery County, Rockville, Md.; mem. local adv. coun. for vocat. and tech. edn. Montgomery County Pub. Schs. and Montgomery Coll., Rockville, 1990—. Mem. Am. Chem. Soc., Am. Assn. Cancer Rsch., Am. Soc. Clin. Oncology, Radiation Rsch. Soc., European Soc. for Radiation Biology, Oxygen Club Greater Washington. Roman Catholic. Office: Armed Forces Radiobiology Rsch Inst Bethesda MD 20889-5145

WEISS, L. LEONARD, pathologist, biophysicist; b. London, June 15, 1928; came to U.S., 1964; m. Maureen A. Weiss, Feb. 23, 1951; children: Gregory, Simon, Emma. MB, BChir, Cambridge U., 1953, MD, 1958, PhD, 1963, ScD, 1971. Lic. in N.Y. State, U.K. Hon. registrar Westminster Hosp., London, 1954-58; scientist Nat. Inst. Med. Rsch., London, 1958-60; cell physiologist Strangeways Rsch. Lab., Cambridge, U.K., 1960-64; dir. dept. exptl. pathology N.Y. State Health Dept. Roswell Pk. Meml. Inst., Buffalo, 1964—; prof. biophysics, interdisciplinary scis. SUNY, Buffalo, 1965—. Author: Metastasis, 1965-91, Watchmaking in England. 1760-1820, 1982. Maj. RAMC, 1960-64, U.K. Fellow Royal Coll. Pathologists, Coll. Am. Pathologists; mem. Youngstown Yacht Club. Office: Roswell Pk Cancer Inst Buffalo NY 14263-0001

WEISS, LOUIS ALAN, accounting administrator; b. N.Y.C., Dec. 29, 1948; s. Benjamin and Edith (Kiviat) W. BS, L.I. U., 1970, MS in Taxes, 1975. Acct. Abex Corp., N.Y.C., 1972-77; tax acct. Babcock & Wilcox, N.Y.C., 1977-79, Mfrs. Hanover & Trust, N.Y.C., 1979-81; corp. dir. taxes Handy & Harman, N.Y.C., 1981—. Mem. Tax Execs. Inst. Democrat. Jewish. Home: 161 W 16th St Apt 6G New York NY 10011-6203 Office: Handy & Harman 850 3rd Ave New York NY 10022-6222

WEISS, MARVIN, lawyer; b. Jersey City, Oct. 11, 1929; s. William and Malvina (Weinstock) W.; m. S. Henriette, Dec. 19, 1959; children: Stacey Debra Tollin, Mitchell William. BS, NYU, 1951, JD, 1954. Bar: N.Y. 1954, U.S. Dist. Ct. (so. and ea. dists.) N.Y. 1960, U.S. Ct. Appeals (2d cir.) 1962, U.S. Tax. Ct. 1965, U.S. Supreme Ct. 1990. Assoc. Rosling & Eisenberg, Bklyn., 1956-60; ptnr. Eisenberg & Weiss, Bklyn., 1960-77, Moses & Singer, N.Y.C., 1977-79, Olnick, Boxer, Blumberg, Lane & Troy, N.Y.C., 1979-87, Stroock, Stroock & Lavan, N.Y.C., 1987-89, Wilson, Elser, Moskowitz, Edelman & Dicker, N.Y.C., 1989—. Served with U.S. Army, 1954-56. Mem. ABA, N.Y. State Bar Assn., Bklyn. Bar Assn., Nassau County Bar Assn., N.Y. County Lawyers Assn. Home: 883 Cranford Ave Valley Stream NY 11581-3115 Office: Wilson Elser Moskowitz Edelman & Dicker 150 E 42d St New York NY 10017

WEISS, MICHAEL DAVID, mathematical economist; b. Chgo., Nov. 12, 1942; s. Harry Edward and Gertrude (Plotkin) W. BA, Brandeis U., 1964; PhD, Brown U., 1970; MA, U. Md., 1984. Asst. prof. math. Wayne State U., Detroit, 1969-74; ops. research analyst Ketron, Inc., Arlington, Va., 1974-76; math. statistician USDA, Washington, 1976-85, agrl. economist, 1985—. Author: (U.S. Govt. rsch. monographs) Conceptual Foundations of Risk Theory, 1987, The Automated Weather/Yield System, 1983; contbr. rsch. publs. to jours., books, others. Mem. Am. Math. Soc., Soc. for Indsl. and Applied Math., Econometric Soc., Soc. for Risk Analysis, Sigma Xi. Home: 7797 Heatherton Ln Potomac MD 20854-3264 Office: Econ Research Svc USDA 1301 New York Ave NW Washington DC 20005-4718

WEISS, MONTE EUGINE, advertising manager; b. N.Y.C.; s. Harry E. and Florenel (Jabin) W.; divorced; children: Gregory, David. BS, U. Miami, 1951. Nat. sales mgr., prodn. mgr. Issac B. Cohen Sons Co., N.Y.C., 1973-80; supr. R. H. Donnely, N.Y.C., 1980-84, Robb Report, N.Y.C., 1984-86; classified advt. mgr. Westsider & Chelsea Clinton News, N.Y.C., 1986-87, Noticias Del Mundo, N.Y.C., 1987-88, Downtown Express, N.Y.C., 1990—; nat. advt. mgr. India Abroad, N.Y.C., 1989-90. Home: 300 E 40th St Apt 8M New York NY 10016-2153

WEISS, RAYMOND OTTO, JR., public relations executive; b. Balt., June 5, 1952; s. Raymond O. Sr. and Mary M. (Willinger) W.; m. Joanne E. Gischlar, Apr. 9, 1983; children: Laura Elizabeth, Michael Patrick. BA, Loyola Coll., 1974. Clk. Office of Md. Atty. Gen., Balt., 1974-77; pub. info. dir. Md. Energy Policy Office, Balt., 1977-79; pub. rels. coord. U. Md., Balt., 1979-81; asst. dir. pub. info. Peabody Inst. Johns Hopkins U., Balt., 1981-83; dir. communications, dep. dir. Washington/Balt. Regional Assn., Balt., 1983-89; dir. mktg. and communications Frank, Bernstein, Conaway & Goldman, Balt., 1989—; cons. Stanton Communications, 1990—. Contbr. articles to profl. jours. Counselor Loyola Coll. Alumni Adv. Network, Balt. Recipient Merit award for publs. So. Indsl. Devel. Coun., 1988. Mem. Pub. Rels. Soc. Am., Am. Econ. Devel. Coun., Balt. Pub. Rels. Coun., Md. Indsl. Devel. Assn., Nat. Assn. Law Firm Mktg. Adminstrs. Democrat. Roman Catholic. Office: Frank Bernstein Conaway & Goldman 300 E Lombard St Baltimore MD 21202-3219

WEISS, RICHARD JEROME, physics educator; b. N.Y.C., Dec. 14, 1923; s. Morris and Anna (Harper) W.; m. Daphne Patricia Watson, Aug. 31, 1960; children: Catharine, Randi, Christopher. BS, CCNY, 1944; MA, U. Calif., Berkeley, 1947; PhD, NYU, 1950. Physicist Materials Lab., Watertown, Mass., 1949-79; prof. physics King's Coll., London, 1979—; cons. Harwell Atomic Energy Establishment, 1980—; prof. U. Surrey, Guildford, Eng., 1981-84; mem. staff Brookhaven Nat. Lab., 1948-52, Cavendish Labs., Cambridge, 1956-57, Imperial Coll., London, 1962-63, AEC, Harwell, Eng., 1959, U. Helsinki, Finland, 1976, U. Munich, 1985. Author: Solid State Physics for Metallurgists, 1962, X-ray Determinatin of Electron Distributions, 1966, (with others) X-ray Diffraction, 1972, (with others) Compton Effect, 1976, The Magic of Physics, 1987, Physics of Materials, 1989, Leonardo to Oppenheimer, 500 Light Years, 1990; editor Internat. Jour. Optoelectronics, 1985—, Artech Series on Optoelectronics, 1988—; contbg. editor Lasers and Optronics, 1980—; contbr. articles to profl. publs.; author, narrator, dir. TV programs. Lt. USN, 1943-46, PTO. Recipient Rockefeller award Princeton U., 1956. Home: 4 Lawson St Avon MA 02322-1708

WEISS, ROBERT FRANKLIN, podiatrist; b. Bridgeport, Conn., May 2, 1946; s. Murray Harold and Sara (Kramer) W.; m. Kathy Barbara Herstein, June 6, 1971; children: Lauren Jennifer, Scott Heath. Student, Norwalk (Conn.) Community Coll., 1965-67, U. Bridgeport, 1967; DPM, Ohio Coll. Podiatric Medicine, 1971. Resident James C. Giuffré Med. Ctr., Phila., 1971-72; chief dept. podiatry St. Joseph Med. Ctr., Stamford, Conn., 1985—; mem. dept. podiatry Stamford Hosp., 1987—, Norwalk Hosp., 1987—; police surgeon Conn. State Police, Meriden, 1985-91; sports medicine cons. IBM, White Plains, N.Y., 1985-91. Author: Archives of Podiatric Medicine & Foot Surgery, 1978, 2d edit., 1979; mem. editorial bd. Conn. Runner mag., 1991—; syndicated columnist Sports Medicine & Health, 1980-91; inventor foot support walking and running systems. Sustaining mem. Rep. Nat. Com., Washington, 1986-91; mem. trial adv. com. U.S. Olympic Marathon, Buffalo, 1984, Liberty Park, N.J., 1988. Fellow Am. Acad. Podiatric Sports Medicine (chmn. credentials and exam. com. 1985-87, Robert Barnes Disting. Svc. award 1988); mem. Am. Coll. Ft. Surgeons (assoc.), Am. Coll. Sports Medicine, Am. Med. Athletic Assn., Am. Podiatric Med. Assn., Conn. Podiatric Med. Assn. (peer rev. com. 1984-86), Fairfield County Podiatric Med. Assn. Home: 350 Barrack Hill Rd Ridgefield CT 06877-3031 Office: Running Doctor Inc 800 Post Rd Darien CT 06820-4622

WEISS, ROBERT HOWARD, English educator; b. Phila., Aug. 3, 1938; s. Jesse Joseph and Sara Blanche (Yankowitz) W.; 1 child, Molly. AB in Creative Writing, U. Pa., 1960; MA in English, Temple U., 1964, PhD, 1968. English instr. U. of the Arts, Phila., 1963, U. Toledo, Ohio, 1964-66, Akiba Acad., Merion, Pa., 1966-67; asst. prof. English to prof. English West Chester (Pa.) U., 1967—; nat. adv. bd. Nat. Writing Project, Berkeley, Calif., 1983—; cons. Pa. Dept. Edn., Harrisburg, 1981—; cons. NEH, Washington, 1978-84. Co-author: Cases for Composition, 2d edit., 1984; contbr. articles to profl. jours. Mem. literacy badge com. Phila. Boy Scout Coun., 1990—. Recipient Disting. Faculty award, Commonwealth of Pa., 1982; writing project grants, Pa. Dept. Edn., 1989, Nat. Endowment for Arts, 1987-88, Arco Found., 1984-86, William Penn Found., 1980-82, State System Higher Edn., 1989-90. Mem. MLA, Nat. Coun. Tchrs. English (nominating com. 1980-81), Coll. English Assn. (bd. dirs. 1985-88, membership chmn. 1985-88). Jewish. Office: English Dept West Chester Univ West Chester PA 19383

WEISS, ROBERT M., urologist, educator; b. N.Y.C., Jan. 13, 1936; s. David and Laura W.; m. Ilana Shemer, May 20, 1973; children—Erik Daniel, Dana Alexandra. B.S. magna cum laude, Franklin and Marshall Coll., Lancaster, Pa., 1957; M.D., SUNY, Bklyn., 1960; M.A. (hon.), Yale U., 1976. Diplomate: Am. Bd. Urology, Nat. Bd. Med. Examiners. Intern Cornell Med. Div., Bellevue Hosp., N.Y.C., 1960-61; resident in gen. surgery Beth Israel Hosp., N.Y.C., 1961-62; resident in urology Squier Urol. Clinic, Presbyn. Hosp., N.Y.C., 1963-64, 65-67; vs. fellow Columbia U. Coll. Physicians and Surgeons, N.Y.C., 1964-65, adj. assoc. prof. pharmacology, 1975-77, adj. prof. pharmacology, 1977—; mem. faculty Yale U. M,ed. Sch., New Haven, 1967—, prof. urology, 1976-88, prof., chief sect. of urology, 1988—; attending urology Yale-New Haven Hosp., New Haven, 1967-88, head sect. of urology, 1988—; cons. West Haven VA Hosp., Waterbury (Conn.) Hosp. Contbr. articles to med. publs. Served with USAR, 1962-63. Fellow ACS, Am. Acad. Pediatrics; mem. Am. Assn. Genito-Urinary Surgeons, Am. Physiol. Soc., Soc. Gen. Physiologists, Assn. Univ. Urologists, Soc. Pediatric Urology, Am. Urol. Assn., Am. Soc. Clin. Pharmacology and Therapeutics, Internat. Urodynamics Soc., AAAS, N.Y. Acad. Scis., Internat. Soc. Dynamics of Upper Urinary Tract, Clin. Soc. Genito-Urinary Surgeons, Phi Beta Kappa, Sigma Xi. Office: 333 Cedar St New Haven CT 06510-3289

WEISS, ROBERT MICHAEL, dentist; b. Bklyn., June 5, 1940; s. Henry and Rena (Bluth) W.; (Trustees scholar) L.I. U., 1958-61; DDS, N.Y.U., 1965; postdoctoral cert. LD Pankey Inst. for Advanced Dental Edn., 1979; m. Irene Marilyn Sternick, June 30, 1962; children—Lori Ann, Julie Lynn, Karen Michelle. Pvt. practice dentistry, Avon, Conn., 1967—, pres. Avon Dental Group, P.C., 1972—; nat. cons. Conn. Gen. Ins. Co. for ins. coverage for Gen. Electric Co., 1980—; cons. CNA Ins. Co., 1988—; bd. dirs. Sentinel Bank. Chmn. Children's Dental Health Week, Hartford County, 1971; chmn. Jewish Adult Edn., West Hartford, Conn., 1986-87; trustee Temple Beth Israel, 1983—. Served to capt. USAF, 1965-67. Fellow Acad. Gen. Dentistry; mem. Am. Soc. Preventive Dentistry (pres. Conn. chpt.), Am. Dental Assn., Hartford Dental Soc., So. New Eng. Assn. Practice Adminstrn., Starnard Beach Assn. (pres. 1984-86). Avon Jr. C. of C. (pres. 1971-72), Alpha Omega, Sigma Alpha Mu. Mason. Home: 74 Ferncliff Dr West Hartford CT 06117-1014 Office: 20 W Avon Rd Avon CT 06001

WEISS, RONALD PHILLIP, lawyer; b. Springfield, Mass., Apr. 28, 1947; s. Kermit Paul and Fay Roslyn (Robinovitz) W.; m. Janet Faye Landon, June 15, 1969; children: Emily, Katherine. BA, Dartmouth Coll., 1968; JD, U. Pa., 1972. Bar: Mass. 1972, U.S. Dist. Ct. Mass. 1975, U.S. Tax Ct. 1979. Assoc. Bulkley, Richardson and Gelinas, Springfield, Mass., 1972-78, ptnr., 1978—; pres. Estate Planning Coun. Hampden County, 1979-81; trustee Mass. Continuing Legal Edn. Inc., 1978-81. Author: (with others) Drafting Wills and Trusts in Massachusetts, 1990; editor: (with others) Massachusetts Corporate Tax Manual, 1986. Trustee Springfield Orch. Assn., 1986—, v.p. 1988-89, pres. 1989-91, chmn. 1991—; trustee Springfield Jewish Fedn., 1986-90; mem. appropriations com. Town of Longmeadow, Mass., 1990—, chmn. 1991-92. Mem. ABA, Mass. Bar Assn. (chmn. taxation sect. 1978-81, bd. dels. 1979-81), Mass. Bar Found., Hampden County Bar Assn., Rotary. Office: 1500 Main St Ste 2700 Springfield MA 01115-0001

WEISS, SAMUEL ABRAHAM, psychologist, psychoanalyst; b. N.Y.C., May 13, 1923; s. Kasiel and Sophie (Schachter) W.; m. Alice Langer, May 20, 1958; children: Benjamin Z., Naomi E., Susan J. BA, Yeshiva U., 1944; MA, NYU, 1948, PhD, 1957. Diplomate Am. Bd. Profl. Psychology, Nat. Register of Health Svcs.; cert. in psychoanalytic psychotherapy. Intern Bellevue Psychiat. Hosp., N.Y.C., 1955-56; assoc. rsch. scientist NYU Med. Ctr., N.Y.C., 1956-59, rsch. scientist, 1959-68, assoc. dir. amputee psychology rsch., 1958-66; assoc. prof. psychology Yeshiva U., N.Y.C., 1961-71; psychol. cons. Stern Coll. for Women, Yeshiva U., N.Y.C., 1960-71; psychologist/psychotherapist in pvt. practice N.Y.C.; cons. N.Y. State Div. Vocat. Rehab., 1958-73. Contbr. articles to profl. jours. Fellow AAAS (Rosette award 1991), APA (editorial cons. rehab. psychology 1972-80). Jewish. Home: 80-40 Lefferts Blvd Kew Garden NY 11415 Office: 7 Park Ave Ste 66 New York NY 10016-4330

WEISS, STANLEY ALAN, mining, chemicals, refractory company executive; b. Phila., Dec. 21, 1926; s. Walter Joseph and Anne Betty (Lubin) W.; m. Lisa Popper, May 23, 1958; children: Lori Christina, Anthony Walter. Student, Georgetown U., 1950-51; fellow, Ctr. for Internat. Affairs, Cambridge, Mass., 1977-78. Founder Minera La Mundial, SA, San Luis Potosi, Mexico, 1954-56, Manganeso Mexicano SA, Mexico City, 1957-61, Mercurio Internacional SA, Mexico City, 1957-61; founder Flux, SA, Mexico City, 1960-82, Sao Paulo, Brazil, 1964-74; founder, chmn. bd., chief exec. officer Am. Minerals, Inc., El Paso, Tex., 1960-91; chmn. bd. Am. Premier, Inc., Washington, 1991—; co-founder, exec. v.p. Ralstan Trading & Devel. Corp., 1968-91, chmn. bd. dirs., 1991; chmn. bd. dirs. Am. Premier, Inc., King of Prussia, Pa., 1991—. Author: Manganese: The Other Uses, 1976; contbr. articles on nat. security issues. Founder, chmn. Bus. Execs. for Nat. Security, Washington, 1982—; bd. dirs. New Am. Schs. Devel. Corp., Washington. With U.S. Army, 1944-46, ATO. Mem. Am. Bus. Conf., Am. Ditchley Found., Internat. Inst. Strategic Studies (Eng.), World Econ. Forum (Switzerland), Garrick Club, Queens Club (London), The Royal Instn. of G.B. (London). Jewish. Home: 2126 Connecticut Ave NW # 5 Washington DC 20008-1729 Office: American Premier Inc 601 Pennsylvania Ave NW Ste 700 Washington DC 20004-2602

WEISS, STEPHEN JOEL, lawyer; b. N.Y.C., Sept. 12, 1938; s. Morris and Frances (Dinkin) W.; m. Madeline Adler, Aug. 12, 1962; children: Lowell Andrew, Valerie Elizabeth, Bradley Lawrence. B.S., Queens Coll., 1959; LL.B., Cornell U., 1962; LL.M., Georgetown U., 1966. Bar: N.Y. 1963, D.C. 1966, U.S. Supreme Ct. 1975. Atty. SEC, Washington, 1962-65; assoc. firm Arent, Fox, Kintner, Plotkin & Kahn, Washington, 1965-70; partner Arent, Fox, Kintner, Plotkin & Kahn, 1971—; lectr. securities and corporate law Am. Law Inst., Am., Fed. bar assns., Practicing Law Inst., Bur. Nat. Affairs, Exec. Enterprises, Orgn. Mgmt., Inc.; confs. Am. Land Devel. Assn. Mem. adv. bd.: Securities Regulation and Law Report, Bur. Nat. Affairs, 1980—; contbr. articles on securities and corp. law to legal jours. Mem. nat. com. Cornell Law Sch. Fund, 1987-88. Mem. ABA (fed. regulation securities com. 1970—, chmn. Rule 10b-5 subcom. 1976-78, chmn. civil liabilities subcom. 1978-81, chmn. ad hoc com. fgn. payments legislation 1976-77, devels. in bus. financing com. 1982—), Fed. Bar Assn. (chmn. securities law com. 1966-70, mem. exec. com. of securities law com. 1971—, chmn. council on financing and taxation 1971-72, chmn. publs. bd. 1977-78, nat. council 1972-80, Leadership commendation 1973, Distinguished Service award 1970), D.C. Bar Assn., Am. Law Inst., Cornell Law Assn. (exec. com. 1981-84). Club: Cornell Law (Washington) (pres. 1971-79). Office: Arent Fox Kintner Plotkin & Kahn 1050 Connecticut Ave NW Washington DC 20036-5303

WEISS, THEODORE S., congressman; b. Hungary, Sept. 17, 1927; came to U.S., 1938, naturalized, 1953; s. Joseph and Pearl (Weiss) W.; m. Sonya M. Hoover; children: Thomas D., Stephen R. B.A., Syracuse U., 1951, LL.B., 1952. Bar: N.Y. 1953. Asst. dist. atty. for N.Y. county, 1955-59; mem. 95th-102nd Congresses from 17th N.Y. Dist., 1977—; mem. edn. and labor com. 95th-101st Congresses from 17th N.Y. Dist., 1977-83, mem. govt. ops. com., 1977—, mem. fgn. affairs com., mem. com. on children, youth and families, 1983—, chmn. subcom. on human resources and intergovtl. relations, 1983—, mem. banking fin. and urban affairs com., 1990—; chmn. congl. arts caucus U.S. Ho. of Reps., Washington, 1991—; sec. N.Y. State Cong. Delegation, 1987—. Served with AUS, 1946-47. Mem. NAACP, ABA, ACLU, Ams. for Dem. Action (pres. 1986-89), New Dem. Coalition, N.Y. County Lawyers Assn. Jewish. Office: US Ho of Reps 2467 Rayburn House Office Bldg Washington DC 20515

WEISS, WILLIAM, retired pulmonary medicine-epidemiology educator; b. Phila., July 30, 1919; s. William and Anna (Grossman) W.; m. Esther E. Sabul, June 22, 1941; children: Winifred A., Seth S., Deborah E. BA, U. Pa., 1940, MD, 1944. Clin. dir. pulmonary disease svc. Phila. Gen. Hosp., 1950-74; chest cons. Norristown (Pa.) State Hosp., 1951-60; dir. Pulmonary Neoplasm Rsch. Project, Phila., 1957-67; faculty U. Pa. Grad. Sch. Medicine, Phila., 1952-66, Med. Coll. Pa., Phila., 1952-86; from assoc. prof. to prof. pulmonary disease-epidemiology Hahnemann U. Med. Coll., Phila., 1966-84, prof. emeritus, 1984—; cons. to various indsl. cos., Pa., N.J., 1962—. Editor Phila. Medicine, 1976—; contbr. over 200 articles to profl. jours., 17 chpts. to books. Bd. dirs. Am. Cancer Soc., Phila., 1980-86; cons. on asbestos Bd. Edn., Phila., 1983—; mem. EPA Sci. Review Panel for Health Rsch., Washington, 1980-81, Toxics/Health Effects adv. com. Pa. Dept. Health, 1985-87. Capt. USAF, 1953-55. Recipient Annual Sci. award Am. Cancer Soc., 1979, Cristol award Phila. County Med. Soc., 1989; picture on cover Cancer Rsch., Mar. 1, 1990 for lung cancer rsch. Fellow ACP,

Coll. Physicians Phila., Am. Coll. Occupational Medicine (merit in authorhip award 1974, 85); mem. AMA, Laennec Soc. Phila. (pres. 1970), Phila. Occupational Med. Assn. (pres. 1980-81), Am. Thoracic Soc., Pa. Med. Soc., Philadelphia County Med. Soc. (Strittmatter award 1991). Home: 3912 Netherfield Rd Philadelphia PA 19129-1014

WEISSBACH, HERBERT, biochemist; b. N.Y.C., Mar. 16, 1932; s. Louis and Vivian (Ruhalter) W.; m. Renee Kohl, Dec. 27, 1953; children—Lawrence, Nancy, Marjorie, Robert. B.S., CUNY, 1953; M.S., George Washington U., 1955, Ph.D., 1957. Chemist Nat. Heart Inst., Bethesda, Md., 1953-68; acting chief NIH, Bethesda, Md., 1968-69; assoc. dir. Roche Inst. Molecular Biology, Nutley, N.J., 1969-83, dir., 1983—; v.p. Hoffmann-La Roche, Nutley, N.J., 1983—; Adj. prof. George Washington U., 1964-69, Columbia U., 1969-85, U. Medicine and Dentistry N.J., Newark, 1981—, Princeton U., 1984-85. Editor: Molecular Mechanisms of Protein Biosynthesis, 1977, Archives of Biochemistry and Biophysics; contbr. articles to profl. jours. Recipient Superior Service award HEW, 1968; Enzyme award Am. Chem. Soc., 1970. Mem. Am. Soc. Biol. Chemists, Am. Soc. Pharmacology and Exptl. Therapeutics, Nat. Acad. Scis., AAAS. Home: 5 Blackfoot Circle Wayne NJ 07470 Office: Roche Inst Molecular Biology 340 Kingsland St Nutley NJ 07110-1199

WEISSBARD, SAMUEL HELD, lawyer; b. N.Y.C., Mar. 3, 1947; children: Andrew Joshua, David S. BA, Case Western Res. U., 1967; JD with highest honors, George Washington U., 1970. Bar: D.C. 1970, U.S. Supreme Ct. 1974. Assoc. Fried, Frank, Harris, Shriver & Kampelman, 1970-73, Arent, Fox, Kintner, Plotkin & Kahn, 1973-78; prin. Weissbard & Fields, P.C., 1978-83; shareholder, v.p. Wilkes, Artis, Hedrick & Lane, Washington, 1983-86; ptnr. Foley & Lardner, Washington, 1986—; co-chair creditors' rights Workout and Bankruptcy Group. Editor in chief George Washington U. Law Rev., 1969-70. Bd. dirs. Luther Rice Soc. George Washington U., 1985-87; chmn. steering com. of Lawyers' Alliance for Nat. Learning Ctr. and Capital Children's Mus., 1989-90. Recipient John Bell Larner medal, 1970. Mem. ABA, D.C. Bar Assn., Order of Coif. Office: Foley & Lardner 1775 Pennsylvania Ave NW Washington DC 20006-4680

WEISSMAN, ROBERT EVAN, publisher, financial information company executive; b. New Haven, May 22, 1940; s. Samuel and Lillian (Warren) W.; m. Janet Johl, Aug. 27, 1960; children—Gregory, Christopher, Michael. B.S. in Bus. Adminstrn., Babson Coll., Wellesley, Mass., 1964. Exec. v.p. Redifusion Inc., Saugus, Mass, 1972-73; dir. corp. devel. Nat. CSS, Wilton, Conn., 1973-74, chmn., 1975-81; exec. v.p. Dun & Bradstreet Corp., N.Y.C., 1981-84, pres., chief operating officer, 1985—; bd. dirs. State St. Boston Corp. Trustee Babson Coll. Mem. IEEE, Info. Tech. Assn. Am., Inst. Mgmt. Accts., Soc. Mfg. Engrs. (sr.). Office: Dun & Bradstreet Corp 299 Park Ave New York NY 10171-0002

WEISSMAN, SUSAN, social services professional; b. N.Y.C., Feb. 11, 1938; d. Samuel and Anne (Kunis) Miller; m. Irwin Weissman, June 2, 1957; children: Debra, Emily. BS, Queens Coll., 1976; MSW, Columbia U., 1978; postgrad., CUNY, 1988—. Lic. social worker, N.Y.; cert. elem. tchr. Pvt. practice clin. social worker N.Y.C., 1978-81; social worker L.I. (N.Y.) Jewish Hosp., 1978-80, psychoednl. therapist, 1979-80; founder, exec. dir. Park Ctr. Preschs. (4), N.Y.C., 1981-91; with Child Care Cons. Corp., N.Y.C., 1991—; pvt. corp. child care cons., N.Y.C., 1985—; lectr. Learning Annex, N.Y.C., 1986—, Borough Manhattan Community Coll., N.Y.C., 1987—; bd. dirs. Child Care, Inc., N.Y.C., 1986-88; pres. Child Care Cons. Corp. div. HRA. Author: Parents Guide to DayCare, 1986; contbr. articles to Parent's Mag., Working Woman, Parent Guide, others. Mem. NAFE, Nat. Assn. Edn. Young Children, Early Childhood Edn. Soc., Nat. Assn. Child Care Mgmt., Nat. Assn. Social Workers. Home: 250 E 40th St New York NY 10016-1721 Office: Child Care Cons Corp 52 Duane St New York NY 10007-1207

WEISSMANN, HEIDI SEITELBLUM, radiologist, educator; b. N.Y.C., Feb. 4, 1951; d. Louis and June (Joseph) Seitel Bloom; m. Murray H. Weissmann, June 16, 1973; 1 dau., Lauren Erica. BS in Chemistry magna cum laude, Bklyn. Coll., CUNY, 1970; MD, Mt. Sinai Sch. Medicine, N.Y.C., 1974. Diplomate Nat. Bd. Med. Examiners. Intern Montefiore Med. Ctr. Bronx, N.Y., 1974-75, resident in diagnostic radiology, 1975-78; fellow in computerized transaxial tomography and ultrasonography N.Y. Hosp.-Cornell U. Med. Ctr., N.Y.C., N.Y., 1978-79; instr. in radiology and nuclear medicine Albert Einstein Coll. Medicine, Montefiore Med. Ctr., Bronx, N.Y., 1979-80; asst. prof. radiology and nuclear medicine Albert Einstein Coll. Medicine and Montefiore Med. Ctr., Bronx, N.Y., 1980-84, assoc. prof. nuclear medicine, 1984—, assoc. prof. radiology, 1986—; adj. attending physician Montefiore Med. Ctr., 1979-87; chmn. Nuclear Medicine Grand Rounds: Greater N.Y., 1980-87; physician coord. Nuclear Medicine Technologist In-Service Tng. Program, 1982-86; cons. NIH, 1984-86, NIH Diagnostic Radiology, 1985-86. Assoc. editor Nuclear Medicine Ann., 5 vols., 1979-84, editor, 5 vols., 1985—; contbr. chpts. to books, articles to jours.; reviewer Jour. of Radiology, 1981—, mem. editorial adv. bd., 1985-86, assoc. editor, 1986—; reviewer. Jour. of Nuclear Medicine, 1981—, Am. Jour. of Roentgenology, 1986—, Gastroenterology, 1986—, Western Jour. of Medicine, 1985—; contbr. audiovisual programs and films. Recipient Saul Horowitz, Jr., Meml. award (Disting. Alumnus award), Mt. Sinai Sch. Medicine, 1980, Pres.' award, Am. Roentgen Ray Soc., 1979, Berta Rubinstein, M.D., Resident award, 1978, others. Mem. Radiol. Soc. N.Am. (mem. subcom. for nuclear medicine of program com., 1981, 82, 83, chmn. 1984, 85, 86), Soc. Nuclear Medicine (trustee 1983-87, 88—, sec.-treas. Correlative Imaging Council 1979-82, exec. bd. 1982-84, pres. 1984-86, exec. bd. 1986—, mem. acad. council 1980—, task force on interrelationship between nuclear medicine and nuclear magnetic resonance 1983-85 , gov. Greater N.Y. chpt. 1983-85, treas., 1985-86, 86-87, 2d ann. Tetalman award of Edn. and Research Found. 1982, mem., vice chmn. coms. and subcoms.), Soc. Gastrointestinal Radiologists, Am. Inst. Ultrasound in Medicine, N.Y. Acad. Scis., Assoc. Alumni Mt. Sinai Med. Ctr., Nuclear Radiology Club (chmn. 1983—). Phi Beta Kappa.

WEISWASSER, STEPHEN ANTHONY, lawyer, broadcast executive; b. Detroit, Nov. 21, 1940; s. Avery and Eleanor (Sherman) W.; m. July 3, 1962 (div. 1985); children: Jonathan, Gayle; m. Andrea Timko, Apr. 19, 1986; children: Anne, Emily. BA, Wayne State U., 1962; student, Johns Hopkins U., 1962-63; JD, Harvard U., 1966. Bar: D.C. 1967, U.S. Supreme Ct. 1970. Law clk. to chief judge U.S. Ct. Appeals, Washington, 1966-67; assoc. Wilmer, Cutler and Pickering, Washington, 1967-74, ptnr., 1974-86; sr. v.p., gen. counsel Capital Cities/ABC, Inc., N.Y.C., 1986-91, sr. v.p., exec. v.p. ABC-TV network group, 1991—; sr. v.p. CC/ABC, Inc., 1991—; exec. v.p. ABC News, N.Y.C., 1991—; bd. dirs. Ctr. for Communications, Inc., 1990—. Trustee Arena Stage, Washington, 1982-86, Nat. Capital Region NCCJ, Washington, 1984-86. Mem. ABA, Fed. Comm. Bar Assn., ITRS (bd. govs. 1992—). Jewish. Home: 2 Quincy St Chevy Chase MD 20815-4227 Office: Capital Cities/ABC Inc 47 W 66th St New York NY 10023-6290

WEISZ, HELEN, ceramics educator; b. Phila., Nov. 26, 1947. BFA in Sculpture, Phila. Coll. Art, 1969; MFA in Ceramics, Temple U., 1972. Prof. ceramics, dept. coord. Bucks County Community Coll., Newtown, Pa., 1975—. Works included in group exhbns. at 46th Internat. Ceramic Art Exhbn. Faenza (Italy) Internat. Ceramics Mus., 1989 (Purchase prize Assn. Provinciale Turismo di Ravenna), Artist's Soc. Internat., San Francisco, 1987 (Art Achievement award finalist), Craft Concepts '85, Margate, N.J. (2d prize), Am. Clay Artists: Phila. '85, (1st prize best of show), many others. Mem. Nat. Coun. on Edn. for the Ceramic Arts, Am. Crafts Coun. (visual documentation on file at slide libr.). Home and studio: 1775 Hillside Rd Southampton PA 18966

WEISZ, IVAN EHRLICH, executive; b. Budapest, Hungary, May 1, 1946; came to U.S., 1956; s. Laszlo and Katalin (Fried) W.; m. Djerizza Cruz, Sept. 26, 1981; children: Mark, Melissa. BS, Manhattan U., 1972. V.p. Fehr Bros. Inc., N.Y.C., 1969-91; pres. Weisz & Co. Inc., Randolph, N.J., 1991—; dir. Prestressed Concrete Inst., Chgo., 1978-82. With U.S. Army, 1964-66. Republican. Baptist. Home: 113 Dover Chester Rd Randolph NJ 07869 Office: Weisz & Co Inc 540 Rt 10 W Randolph NJ 07869

WEISZ, PAUL B(URG), engineer, scientist; b. Pilsen, Czechoslovakia, July 2, 1919; naturalized, 1946; s. Alexander and Amalia (Sulc) W.; m. Rhoda A.M. Burg, Sept. 4, 1943; children: Ingrid B., P. Randall. Student, Tech. U. Berlin, 1938-39; BS, Auburn U., 1940; ScD, Swiss Fed. Inst. Tech., Zurich, 1965, ScD (hon.), 1980. Research physicist Bartol Research Found., Swarthmore, Pa., 1940-46; Research physicist Mobil Oil Corp. (formerly Socony Mobil Oil Corp.), 1958-61, sr. scientist, 1961-69, mgr. process research sect., 1967-69; mgr. Central Research Lab. Mobil Research & Devel. Corp., Princeton, N.J., 1969-82, sr. scientist and sci. adv., 1982-84; Disting. prof. chem. and bio-engrng. sci. U. Pa., 1984-90, prof. emeritus, 1990—; adj. prof. Pa. State U., 1992—; cons. rsch. and tech. strategy, 1984—; vis. prof. Princeton U., 1974-76, mem. adv. council dept. chem. engrng., 1973-78; mem. adv. and resource council Princeton U. Sch. Engrng., 1974-78; chmn. center policy bd. Center for Catalytic Sci. and Tech., U. Del., 1977-81; mem. energy research adv. bd. U.S. Dept. Energy, 1985-90. Editor: Advances in Catalysis, 1956—; editorial bd.: Jour. Catalysis, 1962-83, Chem. Engrng. Communications, 1972-78; contbr. monthly column The Science of the Possible, Chemtech, 1980-84; contbr. numerous articles to sci. jours.; holder 78 patents. Recipient ann. award Catalysis Club Phila., 1973, Lavoisier medal Société Chimique de France, 1983. Fellow Am. Phys. Soc., Am. Inst. Chemists (Chem. Pioneer award 1974); mem. Am. Chem. Soc. (sci. award South Jersey sect. 1963, E.V. Murphree award 1972, Leo Friend award 1977, chemistry of contemporary tech. problems award 1986, Carothers award 1987), Am. Inst. Chem. Engrs. (R.H. Wilhelm award 1978), N.Y. Acad. Scis., Nat. Acad. Engrng., Soc. Chem. Industry (Perkin medal 1986, Nat. medal of tech. 1992), Nassau Club (Princeton), Cosmos Club (Washington). Quaker. Office: Univ Pa Dept Chem Engring Philadelphia PA 19104

WEISZMANN, ANDREI, physics educator; b. Satu-Mare, Romania, Sept. 30, 1923; came to the U.S., 1973; s. Elemer and Kato (Heimovics) W.; m. Edith Neumann, Oct. 1, 1949; children: Kathy Weiszmann Scher, Juliette Weiszmann Samson. BS in Physics and Math., U. Bolyai, Cluj, Romania, 1949, MS, 1950; PhD, U. Bucharest, 1965. Asst. prof. U. Bolyai, 1949-59, assoc. prof., 1959-62; assoc. prof. U. Babes-Bolyai, 1962-69; vis. prof. NYU, 1969-70; prof. physics Coll. of S.I., CUNY, 1973—; assoc. prof. Poly. Inst., Cluj, 1950-55; div. mgr. Times Mag., 1963-70; vis. scholar Summer Sch. Physics, Varena, Italy, 1967; vis. researcher Weizmann Inst., Rehovot, Israel, 1982-83; cons. Hi-Tech Cons., Fort Lee, N.J., 1983-84, Acad. Sci., Bucharest, 1959-65. Author: The 4th Dimension, 1958, The Psi Function, 1960; also over 80 articles. Mem. Am. Phys. Soc., Acad. Humanities and Scis., Concerned Scientists. Republican. Jewish. Office: CUNY Coll SI 130 Stuyvesant Pl Staten Island NY 10301-1953

WEITZEN, EDWIN HYLAN, retired radiologist; b. Balt., Sept. 12, 1917; s. Jacob and Rose (Kramer) W. BA, George Washington U., 1941, MD, 1943. Diplomate Am. Bd. Radiology. Assoc. radiologist Sibley Meml. Hosp., Washington, 1951-58; pvt. practice Silver Spring, Md., 1958-85, ret., 1985. Mem. AMA, Am. Coll. Radiology, N.Y. Acad. Sci., Royal Soc. Medicine. Home: 1005 Dale Dr Silver Spring MD 20910

WEITZENHOFFER, AARON MAX, JR., theatrical producer; b. Oklahoma City, Oct. 30, 1939; s. Aaron Max and Clara Irene (Rosenthal) W. BFA, U. Okla., 1961. Co. mgr. La Jolla (Calif.) Playhouse, 1963-64; dir. David B. Findlay Gallery, N.Y., 1965-69; pres. Weitzenhoffer Prodns., Ltd., N.Y.C. and London, 1965—; pres., chief exec. officer, chmn. Seminole Mfg. Co., Kalamazoo; adj. prof. drama U. Okla.; chief pub. rels. Okla. Health Dept., 1964-65. Trustee Am. Acad. Dramatic Arts; chmn. Circle Repertory Co.; bd. dirs. New Dramatists, Drama League, Theatreworks, Theatre Investment Fund, London. Recipient Tony award, 1978, 91, Disting. Svc. citation U. Okla., 1988. Mem. Am. League Theatres and Producers (bd. govs.), Players Club (bd. dir.), Century Assn., Delta Kappa Epsilon. Republican. Home: 70 E 77th St New York NY 10021-1811 Office: 350 Park Ave New York NY 10022-6022 also: Cambridge Theatre, Earlham St, London WC2, England

WEITZMAN, ARTHUR JOSHUA, educator; b. Newark, Sept. 13, 1933; s. Louis I. and Cecele W.; m. Catherine Ezell, Aug. 8, 1982; children: Peter A., Anne E. B.A., U. Chgo., 1956, M.A., 1957; Ph.D., NYU, 1964. Instr. English, Bklyn. Coll., 1960-63; asst. prof. Temple U., Phila., 1963-69; assoc. prof. Northeastern U., Boston, 1969-72; prof. Northeastern U., 1972—; field editor G.K. Hall Pub. Co. Editor: Letters Writ by a Turkish Spy (G.P. Marana), 1970; founder, co-editor: The Scriblerian, 1968—; co-editor: Milton and the Romantics, 1980-81; contbr.: revs. and articles to profl. jours. and newspapers including Los Angeles Times, Boston Globe, Miami Herald. NEH fellow, 1972-73; Mellon fellow, 1976; research grantee Temple U.; research grantee Northeastern U. Mem. MLA, Am. Soc. 18th Century Studies, Conf. Editors Learned Jours. Jewish. Home: 4 Bellis Ct Cambridge MA 02140-3240 Office: Northeastern U Dept English E Mail 406 Holmes Boston MA 02115

WELBER, DAVID ALAN, accountant; b. York, Pa., Oct. 14, 1949; s. Harry and Julia Welber. BS in Acctg., York Coll., 1975. CPA, Pa.; cert. fin. planner, Coll. for Fin. Planners. Acct. Einhorn, Butler, Gingerich & Co., York, 1974-82; ptnr. Bergdoll & Martin, York, 1984-86; prin. David A. Welber, CPA, York, 1982-84, 86—. Mem. coun. Colony Park Homeowners Assn., York, 1982-84; bd. dirs. Exch. Club Ctr. for Prevention of Child Abuse, Harrisburg, Pa., 1979-87, Rehab. and Indsl. Tng. Ctr., York, 1987-90, Bell Socialization Svcs., 1991—; co-chmn. Ohev Sholom Bd. Edn., York, 1987-90. Mem. Pa. Inst. CPAs (mem. personal fin. planning com. 1987—, Edn. award 1973), Exch. Club York (treas. 1984-90, pres. 1991-92). Republican. Jewish. Office: 212 E Market St York PA 17403-2013

WELCH, CHARLES DAVID, U.S. diplomat; b. Munich, Germany, Dec. 25, 1953; s. Donald Mansel and Jackie (Brown) W.; m. Gretchen Anne Gerwe, May 14, 1983; children: Emma Frances, Margaret Elizabeth. Student, London Sch. Econs., 1973-74; BS in Fgn. Svc., Georgetown U., 1975; MA in Law and Diplomacy, MA, Tufts U., 1977. Staff asst. office of undersecretary U.S. State Dept. Security Assistance, Washington, 1977-79; polit. officer U.S. Embassy, Islamabad, Pakistan, 1979-81; country officer Syria desk U.S. State Dept. Bur. of Near Ea. and South Asian Affairs, Washington, 1981-82, country officer Lebanon desk, 1982-83; polit. sect. chief U.S. Embassy, Damascus, Syria, 1984-86; polit. counselor U.S. Embassy, Amman, Jordan, 1986-88; mem. sr. seminar fgn. policy U.S. State Dept. Fgn. Svc. Inst., Washington, 1988-89; dir. near Ea. and South Asian affairs Nat. Security Coun., White House, Washington, 1989-91; exec. asst. to undersec. for polit. affairs Dept. of State, Washington, 1991—. Mem. Am. Fgn. Svc. Assn., Phi Beta Kappa, Phi Alpha Theta. Presbyterian. Home: 3355 Quesada St NW Washington DC 20015-1664 Office: Under Sec of State for Polit Affairs Dept of State Washington DC 20520

WELCH, CHARLES DEFOREST, artist; b. Kearney, Nebr., Oct. 5, 1948; s. Roland Benjamin and Elaine Francis (DeForest) W.; m. Cathryn Louise Holzrichter, Aug. 10, 1974; 1 child, Lauryn Elayne. BA in Art Edn., Kearney State Coll., 1970, MS in Art Edn., 1974; MFA in Studio Art, Tufts Univ., 1987. Art instr. Bellevue (Nebr.) West High Sch., 1974-84, art dept. chmn., 1980-84; grad. asst. Boston Mus. Sch./Tufts Univ., 1984-87; printmaking instr. Ava Gallery, Lebanon, N.H., 1988—; dir. Crackerjack Kid Eternal Network Mail Art Archive, Lebanon, 1978—. Author: Material Metamorphosis, 1980, Networking Currents, 1985; contbr. articles to profl. jours.; exhbns. include Palmer House Hotel, Chgo./Internat. Philatelic Exhbn., 1987, Tokyo Met. Mus., 1985, Ogimachi Mus. Square, Osaka, Japan, 1985, Kyoto Mus., Japan, 1985, Peace Park, Hiroshima, Japan, 1985, Acad. Art Coll., San Francisco, 1984, NEA Hdqrs. Lobby, Washington, 1980, AVA Gallery, Hanover, 1990, others. Sgt. U.S. Army, 1970-71, Vietnam. Recipient Fulbright-Hayes scholarship, Belgium, Netherlands, Luxembourg, 1976, Hilda Maehling fellowship, NEA, Bellevue, 1980, Spl. Artistic Excellence award 17th Internat. Contemporary Art Exhibit, Tokyo Met. Art Mus., 1990, medal in Mixed Media, Metro Art's Internat. Art Competition, Art 54 Gallery, SoHo, N.Y.C., 1987, Merit award nat. Juried Exhbn. of Xerox Art, Ga. State U., Atlanta, 1980. Home: PO Box 978 Hanover NH 03755-0978

WELCH, DAVID OTIS, materials scientist; b. Richmond, Va., Mar. 9, 1938; s. Otis Washington and Sarah Edith (Alexander) W.; m. Katherine Kertesz, 1961 (div. 1975); children: Wendy Margaret, Alison Edith; m. Sharon Doyle, 1978. BS, U. Tenn., 1960; SM, MIT, 1962; PHD, U. Pa., 1964. NATO postdoctoral fellow U.K. Atomic Energy Rsch. Establishment Harwell, Didcot, Eng., 1964-65; asst. prof. Princeton (N.J.) U., 1966-72; assoc. physicist Brookhaven Nat. Lab., Upton, N.Y., 1972-75, physicist, 1975-90, asst. div. head, 1982-90, div. head, 1990-91, sr. physicist, 1990—; vis. prof. materials sci. U. São Paulo, Brazil, 1970, U. Campinas, Brazil, 1988; adj. prof. materials sci. SUNY, Stony Brook, 1979—. Author: (with L.A. Girifalco) Point Defects and Diffusion in Strained Metals, 1967; contbr. articles to profl. jours. Mem. AAAS, Am. Phys. Soc., Materials Rsch. Soc., Sigma Xi. Home: 12 Dogwood Dr Stony Brook NY 11790-2116 Office: Brookhaven Nat Lab Bldg 480 Upton NY 11973

WELCH, J(OAN) KATHLEEN, entrepreneur; b. Pensacola, Fla., Jan. 28, 1950; d. Leslie Peter and Frances Louise (Hughes) Morales. Salesperson with Arthur Murray Dance Studio, Colo., Fla., Pa. and N.J., 1970-81; sales rep. Warner-Lambert Co., Morris Plains, N.J., 1981-83; supr., mgr. Dance Club Internat., Chatham, N.J., 1983-90; dist. rep. Nat. Fedn. Ind. Bus., 1990—; developer sales program adapted nationwide Dance Club Internat.; judge Nat. Dance Coun. Am., 1977-90; dance coach U.S. Ballroom Championships, 1975-90, coach competition winners hustle divsn., 1978, choreographer, 1971-90, competitor, 1972-81. Co-producer, promoter, talent scout for TV program Astrology Today, 1989—; performed on nat. TV with leading personalities including George Raft, Donald O'Connor and Mike Douglas. Recipient awards Arthur Murray Studio, 1971-81, 1st place counselor award Arthur Murray All Star Tournament, 1977, 1st place Supr. award Dance Club Internat., 1st place Registrar award Dance Club Internat. in the Tournament of Champions, 1984; ranked #1 rep. in the Profls. Corner, N.Y. div. Nat. Fedn. Ind. Bus., 1991. Mem. Imperial Soc. Tchrs. of Dancing (assoc. Ballroom br., Latin-Am. br.), Am. Dence Tchrs. Assn. Mem. Unity Ch. Home and Office: 117 E Westfield Ave Roselle Park NJ 07204-2052

WELCH, JOHN FRANCIS, JR., electrical manufacturing company executive; b. Peabody, Mass., Nov. 19, 1935; s. John Francis and Grace (Andrews) W.; m. Carolyn B. Osburn, Nov. 1959 (div. 1987); children: Katherine, John, Anne, Mark; m. Jane Beasley, Apr. 1989. B.S. in Chem. Engring, U. Mass., 1957; M.S., U. Ill., 1958, Ph.D., 1960. With Gen. Electric Co., Fairfield, Conn., 1960—, v.p., 1972, v.p., group exec. components and materials group, 1973-77, sr. v.p., sector exec., consumer products and services sector, 1977-79, vice chmn., exec. officer, 1979-81, chmn., chief exec. officer, 1981—; also dir. Gen. Electric Fin. Services. Patentee in field. Mem. NAE, Bus. Coun. (chmn.), Bus. Roundtable. Office: GE 3135 Easton Tpke Fairfield CT 06431-0001

WELCH, MARY-SCOTT (STEWART WELCH), writer; b. Chgo., Dec. 14 1919; d. William Scott and Myrtle (Ferrin) Stewart; A.B., U. Ill., 1940; m. Barrett Farley Welch (dec.); children: Farley, Laurie, Margaret, Mary Barrett. Newsstand promotion mgr. Esquire-Coronet, Chgo., 1940-42; West Coast editor Esquire, Hollywood, Calif., 1943-45; assoc. editor Pageant mag., N.Y.C., 1947-50; entertainment editor Look mag., N.Y.C., 1950-52; food editor Glamour mag., N.Y.C., 1953-55; columnist Seventeen, N.Y.C., 1960-63, Vogue mag., McCall's, 1974-76, Exec. Female, 1981-82; editor-in-chief Homemaker's Digest, 1971-72; tchr. mag. writing Womanschool and Ethical Culture Soc., N.Y.C., 1975-77. Coord. rape prevention com. NOW, N.Y.C., 1972-74; mem. adv. bd. Inst. for Women and Work, Cornell U.; former mem. adv. bd. Working Women, Nat. Assn. Office Workers; mem. Nat. Abortion Rights Action League, Planned Parenthood, People For, environ. orgns. Ensign USNR, 1942-43. Mem. ACLU, NOW (bd. dirs. N.Y.C. chpt. 1973-75, adv. bd. N.Y.C. chpt. 1982), N.Y. Civil Liberties Union., Authors Guild, Authors League, Women in Communications (named one of 60 outstanding mems. 1984), Nat. Women's Polit. Caucus, Manhattan Women's Polit. Caucus, Phi Beta Kappa, Kappa Kappa Gamma. Author: Networking: The Great New Way for Women to Get Ahead, 1980; The Family Wilderness Handbook, 1973; (with Ronnie Welch) Esquire Party Book, 1970; Seventeen Guide to Travel, 1970; Esquire Etiquette, 1958; What Every Young Man Should Know, 1970; Handbook for Hosts, 1950; Your First Hundred Meals, 1947, Children: Pets, Paris, others; contbr. articles various mags. including Redbook, McCall's, Ladies Home Jour., Woman's Day, Working Woman, Mademoiselle, Ms., Seventeen, Modern Maturity, Glamour, Vogue, others. Home and Office: 30 Waterside Plz Apt 2K New York NY 10010-2624

WELCH, NOBLE, real estate broker; b. New Haven, June 1, 1930; s. G. Harold and Harriet (Hitchcock) W.; m. Suzanne H. Holmes, Oct. 28, 1961 (div.); children: Alison B., S. Whitney, Hilary H., Phoebe A. BA, Yale U., 1953. V.p. Chem. Bank, N.Y., 1957-81; exec. v.p. New England Land Co., Greenwich, Conn., 1981-86; v.p. Pearce, Urstadt, Mayer & Greer, Greenwich, 1986-88; sr. v.p. Urstadt Property Co., Inc., Greenwich, 1988-91; pvt. practice Greenwich, 1991—. Lt. USN, 1953-56. Mem. Yale Alumni Assn. Greenwich (bd. dirs. 1987—), Oquossoc Angling Assn., Round Hill Club (bd. dirs. 1968-71), Indian Harbor Yacht Club. Republican. Episcopalian. Home: 1465 E Putnam Ave Unit 106 Old Greenwich CT 06870 Office: 3 Pickwick Plz Ste 300 Greenwich CT 06830-5526

WELCH, NORMAN ALPHONSUS, JR., career officer; b. Cambridge, Mass., May 1, 1945; s. Norman Alphonsus and Katherine Mary (Hayes) W.; m. Patricia Ann McCarthy, June 20, 1970 (div. Dec. 1989); children: Meridith, Heather Maria; m. Linda Louise Wheeler Mallers, DEc. 16, 1989; 1 child Brandon Curtis. BA in Polit. Sci., Boston Coll., 1970; MBA in Logistics, Mktg., Babson Coll., 1986; grad., Staff Coll., 1979, U.S. Army War Coll, 1992. Cert. mil. logistician. Commd. 2d lt. U.S. Army, 1967, advanced through grades to col., 1991; ptnr. Archt. Assocs., Boston, 1975—. Contbr. articles to profl. jours. Mem. exec. bd. Young Ams. for Freedom, Mass., 1965-66; sec. Young Reps., Mass., 1963-66. Decorated Bronze Star. Mem. Nat. Guard Assn. U.S., Nat. Guard Assn. Mass. (exec. councillor), Amvets, DAV. Republican. Roman Catholic. Home: PO Box 222 Sagamore Beach MA 02562 Office: Hdqrs 26th Infantry Div Camp Edwards MA 02542

WELCH, OLIVER WENDELL, pharmaceutical executive; b. Jacksonville, Tex., Jan. 9, 1930; s. Jackson Andrew and Annie Laura (Trapp) W.; m. Wanda Virginia Urrey, Nov. 14, 1948. BA, Tex. Tech U., 1952; MA, Columbia U., 1958. Pharm. rep., supr. mktg. rsch., manpower devel. Warner Lambert Co., Morris Plains, N.J., 1962-72; mgr. corp. devel. Boehringer Mannheim Corp., N.Y.C., 1972-75; v.p. Biomed. Data Co., N.Y.C., 1975-77; assoc. dir., dep. dir. regulatory affairs Sterling Winthrop Inc., N.Y.C., 1977—. Mem. Regulatory Affairs Profls. Soc., Drug Info. Assn. Republican. Episcopalian.

WELCH, STELLA REGINA, college dean; d. Charles Edward and Ann marie (Temmerman) W. BA, Nazareth Coll., Rochester, N.Y.; MA, Cath. U., Washington; postgrad., Cornell U., NYU, Fordham U. Vice prin. Mt. Crmel High Sch., Auburn, N.Y.; dir. admissions Nazareth Coll., Rochester, N.Y., dean freshmen, fgn. student advisor. Contbr. articles to profl. jours. Pres. Cath. Guidance Coun. of Western N.Y.; advisor Aspira, Rochester. Mem. Am. Assn. Counseling and Devel., Am. Personnel and Guidance Assn., nat. Assn. Fgn. Student Advisors, N.Y. State Assn. for Counseling and Devel. Office: Nazareth Coll PO Box 18950 Rochester NY 14618-0950

WELCHER, WILLIAM ALEXANDER, pension fund executive; b. Roanoke, Va., Mar. 6, 1947; s. William Alexander Sr. and Gladys Etruia (Gray) W.; m. LaMorn Linda Hill, Oct. 9, 1971; children: William Alexander III, Gernell Andrea, Arif Lamont. BA, Howard U., 1970; MBA, Rutgers U., 1976; diploma in real estate, NYU, 1978; grad., Command and Gen. Staff Coll., 1984. Group svc. asst. Tchrs. Ins. and Annuity Assn./Coll. Retirement Equities Fund, N.Y.C., 1971-74, group svc. adminstr., 1974-77, asst. mortgage analyst, 1977-80, mortgage loan adminstr., 1980-83, asst. mortgage officer, 1983-87, investment officer, 1987-89, asst. v.p., 1989-90, dir., 1990—. Trustee, treas. Polished Acts, Inc., East Orange, N.J., 1985—. 1st lt. U.S. Army, 1970-71, USAR. Fellow Life Mgmt. Inst.; mem. Res. Officers Assn. (life), Assn. Mil. Surgeons (life), Am. Legion, Minority Interchange, Inc. Home: 80 Kenwood Pl East Orange NJ 07018-1104 Office: TIAA/CREF 730 3rd Ave New York NY 10017-3206

WELCOME, LINDA PAAR, interior designer; b. South Bend, Ind., June 12, 1949; d. Robert Steven and Dolores (Arndt) Paar; m. Thomas Wayne Welcome, Sept. 14, 1975 (div. 1979); m. Robert Edward Ingram, Apr. 27, 1988; children: James William Adams, Jason Robert Ingram. BS in Fine Arts/Art Edn., Ind. Univ., 1975; MS in Interior Design, Ind. State Univ.,

1979. Cert. interior design/art educator, K-12. Instr., interior design Purdue-Ind. Univ., Indpls., 1976; instr., in-residence artist Indpls. Art League, 1978-79; graphic art designer State of Ind., Indpls., 1977-78; owner/pres. Welcome Interiors, Kensington, Md., 1980—; radio personality The Welcome Interior Design Show, Silver Spring, Md., 1987-88; interior designer Embassy of Kuwait, Washington, 1985-86; interior design cons. Embassy Iraq, Washington, 1987-89; designer Nat. Symphony Decorator Show House, Potomac, Md., 1987, 88, Design for Living Show, Washington, 1989—. Designer various layouts in profl./popular mags. Mem. Nat. Mus. Women of the Arts, Kensington Hist. Soc., Nat. Trust for Hist. Preservation. Office: Welcome Interiors 3707 Farragut Ave Kensington MD 20895-2109

WELD, WILLIAM FLOYD, governor of Massachusetts, lawyer; b. Smithtown, N.Y., July 31, 1945; s. David and Mary Blake (Nichols) W.; m. Susan Roosevelt, June 7, 1975; children: David Minot, Ethel Derby, Mary Blake, Quentin Roosevelt, Frances Wylie. A.B. summa cum laude, Harvard U., 1966, J.D. cum laude, 1970; diploma with distinction, Oxford (Eng.) U., 1967. Bar: Mass. 1970. Law clk. to Hon. R.A. Cutter, Supreme Jud. Ct. Mass., 1970-71; ptnr. firm Hill & Barlow, Boston, 1971-81; assoc. minority counsel U.S. Ho. of Reps. Judiciary Com. Impeachment Inquiry, 1973-74; U.S. atty. for the Dist. of Mass., 1981-86; asst. atty. gen., criminal div. U.S. Justice Dept., Washington, 1986-88; sr. ptnr. Hale & Dorr, Boston, Washington, 1988-90; gov. Commonwealth of Mass., 1990—. Republican nominee for atty. gen., Mass., 1978. Mem. Am. Law Inst., Boston Bar Assn., Am. Bar Assn. Republican. Office: State House Office of Gov Boston MA 02133

WELDEN, DANIEL WILLIAM, small business owner, art educator; s. William and Rita C. (Schwinger) W.; m. Shirley Ann Pedersen (div. 1988); children: Carl William, Jeffrey Peder. BA in Art Edn., Adelphi U., 1964, MA in Art Edn., 1967; postgrad., Acad. of Fine Art, Munich, Germany, 1969-71. Tenured art tchr. Lindenhurst/Massapequa and Smithtown High Schs., 1964-77; stone litographer Universal Ltd. Art Editions, 1972; owner, dir. Hampton Editions Ltd., 1972—; asst. prof. SUNY, Stony Brook, 1977-85; artist-in-residence Cen. Conn. State U., 1986-87, asst. prof., 1987-88; lectr. in field; drawing asst. Asa Wright Nature Ctr. Trinidad, W.I., 1976; juror ann. student exhbn. SUNY, Purchase, 1981; juror Gallery North, Setauket, N.Y., 1979, Nassau Community Coll., 1982, East End Arts Coun., Riverhead, N.Y., 1980, 85; master printer Kilchess Press, Canon Beach, Oreg., 1982, 84; vis. artist Master Workshop in Art, Southampton Coll.; adj. faculty Suffolk Community Coll., Riverhead, 1987—; adj. assoc. prof. L.I. U., Southampton Coll. Displayed in 35 solo exhbns., 100 group shows; represented in pvt. collections including Benton Gallery, Guild Hall Mus., Alice Baber Meml., Greater Art Mus., Lafayette, Ind., Rijkscentrum Frans Masereel, Kunsthochschule, Chase Manhattan Bank. Grantee Ministry Dutch Culture, 1979, 81, SUNY, 1982, Nat. Endowment Arts, 1985. Mem. Soc. Am. Graphic Artists (v.p. 1982-88, pres. 1988-89, Print award 1979). Home: PO Box 520 Sag Harbor NY 11963-0024

WELDON, DANIEL PATRICK, psychologist; b. Lansing, Mich., Mar. 18, 1950; s. William James and Marie Helen (Kremer) W.; B.A. in Psychology, Temple U., 1973; M.A., Rider Coll., 1979; Ed.D. in Counseling, Lehigh U., 1983; m. Monica Rose Ferris, May 22, 1977; children: Matthew, Benjamin. Social worker N.J. Div. Youth and Family Services, Burlington County, 1973-74; group living dir. St. Francis Vocat. Sch., Bensalem, Pa., 1974-79; group home supr., houseparent, Chalfont, Pa., 1979-82; grad. asst. Lehigh U. Counseling Service, 1981-83; adj. counselor Family Life Service, Lutheran Home for Children, Topton, Pa., 1982-87; dir. psychology Children's Rehab. Hosp. Phila., 1985—; mem. faculty Thomas Jefferson U. Hosp., Phila., 1985—; pvt. practice psychology, 1982—; cons. Weaversville Intensive Treatment Unit, 1983-87; leader workshops. Tchr. Confraternity for Christian Doctrine; active Nat. Conf. Catholic Charities. Mem. Am. Psychol. Assn., Pa. Psychol. Assn. (pres. pub. sector div. 1990-91, treas. 1991—), Am. Personnel and Guidance Assn., Assn. Specialists in Group Work, Am. Mental Health Counselors Assn., Pa. Personnel and Guidance Assn., Pa. Assn. Counselor Edn. and Supervision, Pa. Assn. Specialists in Group Work (pres. 1982-83). Roman Catholic. Home: 17 Stacey Dr Doylestown PA 18901-3339 Office: 25 E State St Doylestown PA 18901-6301

WELDON, EARL WILLIAM, advertising agency art director; b. Chester, Pa., Sept. 8, 1956; s. Harry Charles and Mary Katherine (Henning) W.; m. Linda Ann Taylor, July 15, 1978; children: William David, Matthew Brian, Jonathan Taylor, Heidi Elizabeth. BA in Art, Bob Jones U., 1981. Staff artist Brunetti Art Studios, Greenville, S.C., 1981, Bi-Lo Supermarkets, Mauldin, S.C., 1981-82; art/advt. dir. Wholesale Furniture Distbrs., Phila., 1983-87; art dir. USI Advt., Phila., 1987-88; free-lance art dir./illustrator Phila., 1988-90; art dir. Roska Direct Mktg., North Wales, Pa., 1990—; free-lance artist Roska Direct Mktg., North Wales, Springhouse (Pa.) Corp., Scharfberg Assocs., Jenkintown, Pa., Munroe Design Group, Phila., 1988-90. One-man show at Bob Jones U., Greenville, 1980. Sunday sch. tchr. Overbrook Gospel Chapel, Greenville, 1979-82; Sunday sch. tchr., supt. Olney Gospel Hall, Phila., 1983—. Republican. Office: Roska Direct Mktg 1364 Welsh Rd North Wales PA 19454-1913

WELDON, JOSEPH PATRICK, psychologist, consultant; b. Phila., Sept. 27, 1955; s. Thomas Anthony and Clare Mary (Dorsey) W.; married, 1978; 1 child, Michael Joseph Patrick. BA in Psychology and Edn., La Salle Coll., 1977; MS in Counseling Psychology, Villanova U., 1979. Cert. secondary schs. counselor, Pa., cert. practitioner Rubenfeld Synergy Method, cert. Gestalt therapist, cert. in family systems; lic. psychologist, Pa. Psychology tchr. Archbishop Ryan High Sch., Phila., 1976; counselor Cora Svcs., Pa., 1977-80; faculty mem., group leader psychology dept. Trenton State Coll., N.J., 1981-83; psychotherapist, cons. Huntington Valley (Pa.) Counseling Svcs., 1983-87; psychodramatist, cons. Eugenia Hosp., 1987-90; psychotherapist, cons. Karen Goodman and Assocs., 1987—; dir., co-founder Manaaz Assocs., 1985—; pvt. practice psychologist Pa., 1982—; faculty mem. grad. counseling dept. Villanova Univ., 1979; psychotherapist, group leader Shalom, Inc., Phila., 1980-84; faculty mem., leader Esalen Inst., Calif., 1984; co-facilitator, guest lectr. grad. psychology dept. L.I. Univ., 1985; faculty mem., trainer grad. sch. of counseling, Gestalt Inst., L.I. Univ., 1985; faculty mem., cons. Rubenfeld Tng. Inst., N.Y.C., 1983—. Named Outstanding Young Men of Am., Montgomery, Ala., 1983, 84, 85. Mem. AACD, Assn. for Humanistic Psychology, Rubenfeld Synergy Assn. (chair ethics com. 1989—), Am. Humanistic Psychology Somatics Community, Kappa Delta Pi. Office: 21 S 5th St Fl 592 Philadelphia PA 19106-2519

WELDON, LINDA JEAN, psychology educator; b. Cape Girardeau, Mo., Oct. 2, 1949; d. Cecil Elza and Ida (Zimmerman) W. AA, Coll. San Mateo, Calif., 1969; BA, Calif. State U., Chico, 1971, MA, 1974; PhD, U. Md., 1980. Rsch. psychologist Johns Hopkins U., Balt., 1978-80, ARRO, Washington, 1980-84; rsch. scientist U. Md., College Park, 1984-90; asst. prof. psychology Essex Community Coll., Balt., 1986-90, assoc. prof. psychology, 1990—. Contbr. articles to profl. jours. Democrat. Home: 2515 K St NW Space 202 Washington DC 20037-2052 Office: Essex Community Coll 7201 Rossville Blvd Baltimore MD 21237-3855

WELDON, W(AYNE) CURTIS, congressman; b. Marcus Hook, Pa., July 22, 1947; m. Mary Gallagher; children: Karen, Kristin, Kimberly, Curt, Andrew. BA in Humanities, West Chester State Coll., 1969; AAS in Fire Sci., Del. County Community Coll., Media, Pa., 1972; state instrn. cert., Cheyney State Coll.; postgrad., Cabrini Coll., Temple U., St. Joseph's U. Lic. tchr. Pa. From tchr. to head tchr. Walnut St. Sch., Darby-Colwyn-William Penn Sch. Dist., Pa., 1972-76; dir. tng. and manpower CIGNA (INA Corp.), Del. County, 1976-87; mayor City of Marcus Hook, 1977-81; councilman Del. County Council, 1981-87, vice chmn. then chmn., 1984-87; mem. 100th-102nd Congresses from 7th Pa. dist., 1987—; former chmn. Del. Valley Regional Planning Commn.; asst. dir. Elem. Secondary Edn. Act Title I Program, 1972-76; environ. specialist Project KARE, 1972-76; mem. Armed Svcs. Com., Merchant Marine and Fisheries Com., Select Com. on Children, Youth, and Family; chmn. Congl. Fire Svcs. Caucus. Served in various capacities with Sacred Heart Med. Ctr., Neumann Call., Del. County Econ. Devel. Ctr., Del. County Indsl. Devel. Authority, Del. County Community Action Agy., Del. County Hero Scholarship Fund, Marcus Hook Community Devel. Corp., Boy Scouts Am., United Way SE Pa., Del. County Fire Acad., Darby-Colwyn-William Penn Sch. Dist. Edn. Assn., Media ARC. Named Man of Yr. Del. County Irish-Am. Assn., 1984, Man of Yr. Chester Bus. and Profl. Assn., 1984, Most Effective Freshman Legislator Am. Security Coun., Citizen of the Yr. Del. County C. of C., Clean Air Champion Sierra Club, Man of Yr. Internat. Soc. Fire Protection Engrs., 1988; recipient Outstanding Govt. Leadership award Nat. Recycling Coalition, Golden Apple award, Del. County C. of C., Fed. Legis. award Pa. Dirs. Assn. Community Action Agys., Spirit of Enterprise award U.S. C. of C., etc. Office: US Ho of Reps Office House Mems 316 Cannon Washington DC 20515*

WELIKSON, JEFFREY ALAN, lawyer; b. Bklyn., Jan. 8, 1957; s. Bennet Joseph and Cynthia Ann Welikson; m. Laura Sanders, Aug. 19, 1979; children: Gregory Andrew, Joshua Stuart. BS, U. Pa., 1976, MBA, 1977; JD, Harvard U., 1980. CPA, N.Y.; bar: N.Y. 1981. Assoc. Shearman & Sterling, N.Y.C., 1980-83; staff counsel Reliance Group Holdings Inc., N.Y.C., 1983-84, dir. legal dept., 1984-85, asst. v.p. corp. counsel, 1985-88, v.p., asst. gen. counsel, asst. sec., 1988—. Contbg. editor Harvard U. Internat. Law Jour., 1979-80. Mem. ABA, N.Y. State Bar Assn., Am. Inst. CPAs. Office: Reliance Group Holdings Inc Park Ave Pl New York NY 10055-0198

WELKOWITZ, WALTER, biomedical engineer, educator; b. Bklyn., Aug. 3, 1926; s. Samuel and Shirley (Rosenblum) W.; m. Joan Horowitz, June 17, 1951; children: David, Lawrence, Julie. BS, The Cooper Union, N.Y.C., 1948; MS, U. Ill., 1949, PhD, 1954. Profl. engr., N.J. Rsch. assoc. U. Ill., Urbana, 1948-54, Columbia U., N.Y.C., 1954-55; asst. to pres., gen. mgr. Gulton Industries, Inc., Metuchen, N.J., 1955-64; prof., chmn. elec. engring. Rutgers U., Piscataway, N.J., 1964-86, prof. biomed. engring., 1986—, chmn. biomedical engring., 1986-90; cons. Gulton Industries, Metuchen, N.J., 1964-74. Author: (book) Engineering Hemodynamics: Application to Cardiac Assist Devices, 1977, 2d edit. 1987; co-author: (book) Biomedical Instruments: Theory and Design, 1976; author of numerous chpts. in books; contbr. over 50 articles in profl. jours. With U.S. Navy, 1944-46. Rutgers U. Rsch. Coun. fellow, 1974-75; recipient Centennial medal IEEE, 1984, Excellence in Rsch. award Rutgers Bd. Trustees, 1985, IEEE Career Achievement award Soc. Engring. Med. Biology, 1991; Llewellyn Thomas vis. prof. U. Toronto, Can., 1989. Fellow Am. Inst. of Med. and Biological Engring., IEEE (engring. in medicine and biological soc. career achievement award 1991). Home: 138 Highland Ave Metuchen NJ 08840-1942 Office: Rutgers U Biomed Engring PO Box 909 Piscataway NJ 08855-0909

WELLER, SOL WILLIAM, chemical engineering educator; b. Detroit, July 27, 1918; s. Ira and Bessie (Wieselthier) W.; m. Miriam Damick, June 11, 1943; children—Judith, Susan, Robert, Ira. B.S., Wayne State U., 1938; Ph.D., U. Chgo., 1941. Asst. chief coal hydrogenation U.S. Bur. Mines, Pitts., 1945-50; head fundamental rsch. Houdry Process Corp., Linwood, Pa., 1950-58; mgr. propulsion rsch. Ford Aeronutronic Co., Newport Beach, Calif., 1958-61; dir. chem. lab. and materials rsch. lab. Philco-Ford Co., Newport Beach, 1961-65; prof. chem. engring. SUNY-Buffalo, 1965—, C.C. Furnas prof., 1983—; vis. fellow Oxford U., 1989. Author numerous sci. papers, book chpts., ency. entries. Fulbright lectr. Madrid, 1975, Istanbul, 1980. Mem. Am. Chem. Soc. (chmn. Orange County sect. 1964, H.H. Storch award 1981, E.V. Murphree award 1982, Schoellkopf medal 1984, Dean's award 1991), ASTM (founder com. D32 on catalysts, cert. of appreciation 1978), Am. Inst. Chem. Engrs. (chmn. catalysis subcom. 1972-73). Office: SUNY Buffalo 305 Furnas Hall Buffalo NY 14260

WELLER, THOMAS HUCKLE, physician, emeritus educator; b. Ann Arbor, Mich., June 15, 1915; s. Carl V. and Elsie A. (Huckle) W.; m. Kathleen R. Fahey, Aug. 18, 1945; children: Peter Fahey, Nancy Kathleen, Robert Andrew, Janet Louise. A.B., U. Mich., 1936; M.S., 1937, LL.D. (hon.), 1956; M.D., Harvard, 1940; Sc.D., Gustavus Adolphus U., 1975, U. Mass., 1985; L.H.D., Lowell U., 1977. Diplomate Am. Bd. Pediatrics. Teaching fellow bacteriology Harvard Med. Sch., 1940-41, research fellow tropical medicine, pediatrics, 1947-48, instr. comparative pathology, tropical medicine, 1948-49, asst. prof. tropical pub. health Sch. Pub. Health, 1949-50, assoc. prof., 1950-54, Richard Pearson Strong prof. tropical pub. health, 1954-85, prof. emeritus, 1985—, head dept., 1954-81; intern bacteriology and pathology Children's Hosp., Boston, 1941; intern medicine Children's Hosp., 1942, asst. resident medicine, 1946, asst. dir. research div. infectious diseases, 1949-55; mem. commn. parasitic diseases Armed Forces Epidemiol. Bd., 1953-72, dir., 1953-59; charge parasitology, bacteriology, virology sections Antilles Dept. Med. Lab., P.R. Author sci. papers. Served to maj. M.C. AUS, 1942-46. Recipient E. Mead Johnson award for devel. tissue culture procedures in study virus diseases Am. Acad. Pediatrics, 1953; Kimble Methodology award, 1954; Nobel prize in physiology and medicine, 1954; George Ledlie prize, 1963; Weinstein Cerebral Palsy award, 1973; Stern Symposium honoree, 1972; Bristol award Infectious Diseases Soc. Am., 1980; Gold medal and diploma of honor U. Costa Rica, 1984. Fellow Am. Acad. Arts and Scis.; mem. Harvey Soc., AMA, Am. Soc. Parasitologists, Am., Royal socs. tropical medicine and hygiene, Am. Pub. Health Assn., AAAS, Am. Epidemiological Soc., Nat. Acad. Scis., Am. Pediatric Soc., Assn. Am. Physicians, Soc. Exptl. Biology and Medicine, Am. Assn. Immunologists. Soc. Pediatric Research, Phi Beta Kappa., Sigma Xi, Alpha Omega Alpha. Home and Office: 56 Winding River Rd Needham MA 02192-1025

WELLES, ERNEST I., chemical company executive; b. N.Y.C., Aug. 5, 1925; s. Henry and Lena (Halberg) W.; B.S. cum laude, Coll. City N.Y., 1946, B.S., Sch. Edn., 1949, M.S., 1953; Sc.D. (hon), London Inst., 1973 . Chemist, Lucius Pitkin, Inc., N.Y.C., 1944-45; research chemist Nuodex Products Co., Elizabeth, N.J., 1946-50; group leader Foster D. Snell, Inc., N.Y.C., 1950-51; asst. tech. dir. Permatex, Inc., Bklyn., 1951-52; chief chemist Dexter Chem. Corp., N.Y.C., 1952-67; product mgr. textile chem. sales Quaker Chem. Corp., Conshohocken, Pa., 1967-74; dir. mktg., textile chem. sales Hart Products Corp., Jersey City, 1974; mktg. dir. Leatex Chem. Co., Phila., 1974-78; v.p. mktg. Eaton Labs., Inc., 1978-85; mgr. sales div. Pure-Kem, Inc., Paterson, N.J., 1985—. Fellow Am. Inst. Chemists; mem. Am. Chem. Soc. (sr.), Am. Assn. Textile Chemists and Colorists. Club: Masons. Patentee in field. Home: PO Box 1140 Bryn Mawr PA 19010-7140 Office: 295 Governor St Paterson NJ 07501-1320

WELLES, VIRGINIA CHRISMAN, land use planner; b. Denver, June 17, 1954; d. John Galt and Barbara Lee (Chrisman) W.; m. Dwight Lyman Gertz, Oct. 9, 1982. Student, Hampshire Coll., 1972-74; BA in Polit. & Econ. Systems, Yale Coll., 1976; M in City Planning, MIT, 1981. Planning cons. Sugarloaf Mountain Corp., Carrabassett Valley, Maine, 1982-84; regional dir. EIP/Northeast, Boston, 1984-85; project mgr. MetroWest Growth Mgmt. Com., Natick, Mass., 1985-88; planner & environ. analyst Exec. Office of Transp. and Costr. State Mass., 1988-89, Cen. Transp. Planning Staff, Boston, 1989-91; gen. ptnr. Welles Farms Partnership, 1991—. Chair Loon Preservation Com., 1991—; trustee Squam Lakes Assn., 1988-91, Squam Lakes Conservation Trust, 1988—, Audubon Soc. N.H., 1988—. Named Public Policy Fellow MIT, 1979-81. Mem. Women in Transp. Seminars, Am. Planning Assn. (officer New Eng. chpt. 1987-89). Democrat.

WELLIKOFF, ALAN GABRIEL, journalist; b. N.Y.C., May 14, 1946; s. Joseph Leon and Anne (Frimer) W. BA, George Washington U., 1968. Supt. New Windsor (N.Y.) Cantonment State Hist. Site, 1968-74; pres. WTG Energy Systems, Buffalo, 1975-78, dir., 1976; freelance journalist PRNDL Editorial Svc., Balt., 1979—; field faculty Goddard Coll., Plainfield, Vt., 1978. Author: American Historical Supply Catalogue, 1984, rev. edit., 1986, Modern Man's Guide to Life, 1987; contbr. articles to popular mags. Mem. Washington Automotive Press Assn., Assn. Living History Farms and Mus., Internat. Motor Press Assn.

WELLISCH, HANS HERBERT, library science educator; b. Vienna, Austria, Apr. 25, 1920; came to U.S., 1969; s. Fritz and Marianne (Fischer) W.; m. Shulamith B. Oberlander, Feb. 5, 1946; children: Tamar, Ilana, Yuval. MLS, U. Md., 1972, PhD, 1975. Head documentation ctr. Tahal Cons. Engrs., Tel Aviv, 1956-69; head libr. svcs. Ctr. of Scientific & Technol. Info., Tel Aviv, 1966-67; vis. lectr. Coll. of Libr. & Info. Svcs., U. Md., College Park, 1969-75, prof., 1976-87, prof. emeritus, 1988—; bd. dirs. U.S. Info. Ctr. for the Universal Decimal Classification, College Park. Author: The Conversion of Scripts, 1978 (award 1979), Abstracting and Indexing: An International Bibliography, 1980, 84, Indexing From A to Z, 1991; contbr. articles to profl. jours. Mem. Am. Soc. Indexers (pres. 1984-85), Nat. Info. Standards Orgn. (mem. several coms.), Israel Soc. of Spl. Librs. and Info. Ctrs. (founding mem.). Jewish. Home: 5015 Berwyn Rd College Park MD 20740 Office: Coll of Libr and Info Svcs Univ Md College Park MD 20742

WELLMAN, ANTHONY DONALD EMERSON, advertising executive; b. Phila., Nov. 22, 1955; s. Walter Edwin and Hazel May (Holmes) W. BS, Syracuse U., 1978. Asst. producer Ogilvy & Mather Advt., N.Y.C., 1978-80; owner Anthony Wellman Prodns., N.Y.C., 1980—; cons. radio advt. The Mercantile Libr., N.Y.C., 1985. Writer, producer, dir. (film) Audio Archive, 1981; producer (album) Over There, 1981; exec. producer (album) Dostoyevsky, Poe & Co., 1987; assoc. producer, music pub. (album) Mallets in Wonderland; contbr. articles to profl. jours; producer, dir. various radio commls., 1979—; editor, pub. various newsletters; actor, narrator short films, commls. Recipient 3 Gold awards Internat. Radio Festival of N.Y., 1985, ADDY award Am. Advt. Fedn., 1986. Mem. SAG, AFTRA, Sons. of the Revolution (pub. affairs dir., bd. mgrs. 1986-89, N.Y. chpt.), Soc. Colonial Wars (editor The Bull. 1986-90, N.Y. chpt.), Dutch Treat Club (N.Y.C.). Republican. Home: 315 E 73d St New York NY 10021

WELLMAN, DAVID ALLAN, computer science and systems educator, consultant; b. Frankfort, Ind., Sept. 27, 1947; s. Charles R. and Mary Eileen (Etienne) W.; m. Debora Ann Sites, Apr. 24, 1976; children: Matthew, Kevin, Andrew, Stephen. BS in Physics, Ind. State U., Terre Haute, 1969; MBA in Info. Systems, George Washington U., 1974. Commd. 2d lt. U.S. Marine Corps, 1969, advanced through grades to lt. col., 1985, ret., 1989; asst. prof. Wilson Coll., Chambersburg, Pa., 1989—; computer mgr. Mt. Alto Campus Pa. State U., Mt. Alto, 1991—; adj. faculty George Washington U., Washington, 1987-89; cons. Confidential Data Systems, Chambersburg, 1989—, Tng. Svcs. div. CAE-Link, Washington, 1989-90, OC Inc., Washington, 1990—. Author: A Chip in the Curtain, 1989; co-author: Joint Doctrine Compendium, 1990; editor, reviewer: A First Book of ANSI C, 1992. Coach various youth sports, 1984—; judge High Sch. Sci. Fair, Chambersburg, 1990—; vol., event coord. State Regional Sci. Olympiad, Wilson Coll., 1990—; instr. various youth and spl. edn. computer courses, 1990—. Nat. Def. U. fellow, 1986-88. Mem. IEEE Computer Soc., Ret. Officers Assn. (v.p. chpt. 1991—), Pa. Sci. Tchrs. Assn. Office: Wilson Coll 1015 Philadelphia Ave Chambersburg PA 17201-1285

WELLMAN, HOWARD STOLTE, chemical company executive; b. Brattleboro, Vt., Nov. 7, 1939; s. Henry D. and Ellen (Weaver) W.; m. Regina Regan, Oct. 6, 1961 (div. Aug. 1987); children: Lisa A., Stephen M., Julie M.; m. Debra Ann Fasti, Oct. 23, 1987 (div. Mar. 1992); m. Eileen Thompson, Mar. 14, 1992. BS, Tufts U., 1961. Research chemist E.I. DuPont De Nemours & Co., Flint, Mich., 1961-66; research supr. E.I. Du-Pont De Nemours & Co., Phila., 1967-69, research mgr., 1970-72; mktg. mgr. E.I. DuPont De Nemours & Co., Wilmington, Del., 1973-77; bus. mgr. E.I. Du Pont De Nemours & Co., Wilmington, Del., 1982-84, new bus. mgr., 1985—; lab. dir. E.I. Du Pont De Nemours & Co., Troy, Mich., 1978-81; adv. bd. Tech. Transfer Conf. Mem. Comml. Devel. Assn., Product Mgmt. & Devel. Assn. Office: E I Du Pont Nemours 1007 N Market St Wilmington DE 19898-0001

WELLMAN, MARY MARGARET, psychologist; b. Bklyn., May 20, 1946; d. John F. and Anna H. Haunss; m. Robert J. Wellman. BS, SUNY, Geneseo, 1967; MA, SUNY, Stony Brook, 1970; PhD, U. Conn., 1980. Lic. psychologist, Mass., R.I. Tchr. elem. sch. Kings Park (N.Y.) Schs., 1967-74; reading cons. Thompson (Conn.) Pub. Schs., 1974-81; asst. prof. R.I. Coll., Providence, 1981-87, dir. Sch. Psychology, 1984-89, assoc. prof., 1987—; adj. instr. psychology Anna Maria Coll., Paxton, Mass., 1980-82, Worcester (Mass.) State Coll., 1982-84; pvt. practice, Charlton, Mass., 1985-88, Uxbridge, Mass., 1988—; cons. psychologist Comprehensive Mental Health Svc., Waban, Mass., 1983-85; asst. attending child psychologist McLean Hosp., Belmont, Mass., 1986-88; ednl. psychology cons. Ednl. Testing Svc., Princeton, N.J., 1989. Contbr. articles to profl. jours. Pres. Charlton Hist. Soc., 1977-79; vol. librarian and grant writer AIDS Project, Worcester. 1987-90. Recipient Disting. Svc. award Southbridge (Mass.) C. of C., 1980, Outstanding Vol. award APW, 1988. Mem. Am. Psychol. Assn., R.I. Psychol. Assn., R.I. Sch. Psychologists Assn. (bd. dirs. 1985-89). Office: RI Coll Adams Libr 115 Providence RI 02908

WELLNER, ROBERT FRANCIS, civil engineer; b. St. Clair, Pa., July 28, 1928; s. Leo Francis and Marcella Frances (Monahan) W.; m. Mary Elizabeth Scanlan, Dec. 27, 1952; children: Teresa M., Mary Louise, Robert L., Maureen E. BSCE, U. S.C., 1951. Registered profl. engr., Pa., N.C., S.C., Fla. Design engr. Bethlehem (Pa.) Steel Corp., 1954-59, devel. engr., 1959-60, sales engr., 1960-67, dist. coord., 1967-69, mgr. constrn. mktg., 1969-83; v.p. Figg Engring. Group, Alexandria, Va., 1983-88, sr. v.p., 1988—. Bd. dirs. YMCA, Bethlehem, 1975-81, chmn. bldg. com., 1981-82. Lt. USN, 1951-54. Mem. ASCE (sect. pres. 1972-73), Engring. Soc. West Pa., Am. Road and Transp. Builders Assn. (pres. material svc. div. 1974-75, bd. dirs. 1974-77, dir. planning and design div. 1988—), Saucon Valley Country Club, Pinehurst Country Club. Republican. Roman Catholic. Home: 2645 Belaire Rd Bethlehem PA 18017-3501 Office: Figg Engring Group PO Box 1620 Bethlehem PA 18016-1620

WELLS, BARRY LEIGHTON, college administrator; b. Bklyn., July 19, 1951; s. Isaac Lee and Louise (Henderson) W.; m. Claudette Patricia McGowan, May 23, 1987. BA, St. John's U., 1973; postgrad., Cornell U., 1973-75. Profl. tutor Ithaca (N.Y.) Coll., 1975; coord. for minority affairs Syracuse (N.Y.) U., 1976-79, asst. dir. for minority affairs, 1979, assoc. dir. admissions and fin. aid, 1979-80; dir. acad. advising and counseling svcs. Syracuse U., Coll. of Arts and Scis., 1980-85, asst. dean, 1985—; bd. dirs. Community-Dist. Intercommunications Group, Syracuse City Sch. Dist., 1992; mem. Cen. N.Y. Regional Adv. Coun. of N.Y. State Div. Human Rights, 1983-85, City Sch. Dist. Community Edn. Adv. Coun., 1983-85; bd. dirs. City of N.Y. Enterprises, Inc., Liverpool, N.Y., 1982-83. Editor: A Handbook of Financial Aid, 1978; contbr. articles to profl. jours. Bd. dirs., treas Cen. City Fed. Credit Union, Syracuse, 1990-91; bd. dirs. Minority Econ. Devel. Coun. of Syracuse Inc., 1984-86; mem. Cen. N.Y. Campaign Commn. of United Negro Coll. Fund., Syracuse, 1988-91; pres. The Dunbar Assn. Inc., Syracuse, 1978-85, 82-85. Named Outstanding Young Man of Am., U.S. Jaycees, 1979; recipient Meritorious Achievement award Syracuse U. Office of Minority Affairs, 1980, Cert. of Appreciation,1 985, Dedicated Svc. award Dunbar Assn. Inc., 1986, Black Positive Image award for Outstanding Svc., 1989. Mem. Am. Assn. Higher Edn., Black and Latino Faculty and Profl. Staff Assn. (v.p. 1987-89), Assn. for Multicultural Counseling & Devel., Syracuse Challenge Steering Com. (co-chair 1987-89). Democrat. Roman Catholic. Office: Syracuse U Coll of Arts & Scis 329 Hall of Languages Syracuse NY 13244-1170

WELLS, BRYAN MICHAEL, jazz pianist, composer, conductor, arranger; b. Detroit, Apr. 19, 1943; s. Samuel Oliver and Pearl (Levine) Weltman. BA in English, Detroit Inst. Tech., 1966. Staff composer Motown Record Corp., Detroit, 1966-70; condr. Bette Midler, N.Y.C., 1971; v.p., music dir. No Soap Prodns., N.Y.C., 1972-82; condr. Karen Akers, N.Y.C., 1973, Donna McKechnie/Wayside Theatre, Middletown, Va., 1973, Easter Seals Telethon, N.Y.C., 1978; pres. Brywell Prodns., N.Y.C., 1983—. Composer/arranger songs recorded by Stevie Wonder, Tempations, Glen Campbell, Diana Ross, Dionne Warwick, Engelbert Humperdinck, others; composer/ arranger advt. music for Sears, K-Mart, Dentyne, Exxon, Burger King, Mercedes-Benz, Miller Beer, Am. Express, Nat. Car Rental, Macy's, Saks Fifth Ave., Dior Perfume, Woolite, Gillette, Welch's, Norelco, numerous others. Recipient Clio awards, 1975, 76, 78, 80, 2 Gold Records, 1966, 69. Mem. ASCAP.

WELLS, CHARLES JOSEPH, public administrator, author; b. Balt., July 19, 1948; s. Charles Laban and Emma (Branchetti) W.; m. Geraldina L. Blades, May 16, 1987. BS, Towson State U., 1974; MPA, George Mason U., 1988. Statis. researcher Firestone Tire and Rubber Co., Albany, Ga., 1971-72; research analyst Defense Intelligence Agy., Washington, 1974-82; adviser U.S. del. to Mut. and Balanced Force Reduction Talks, Vienna, Austria, 1983; advisor U.S. Del. to the Conf. on Disarmament, Geneva, 1983-84; policy analyst Defense Intelligence Agy., Washington, 1984-88; Congl. fellow U.S. Congress, Washington, 1988—; leg. liaison Defense Intelligence Agy., Washington, 1990-92. Author: Maryland and D.C. Volunteers in the Mexican War, 1991; contbr. article to Jour. Mgmt. Sci. and Policy Analysis, 1988. Treas. Oakmont Spl. Taxing Dist., 1989-91 (chmn. 1991-92). With USMC, 1966-70, Vietnam. Fgn. Affairs fellow Am. Polit. Sci. Assn.,

1988. Fellow Am. Polit. Sci. Assn. (Congl. fellow 1989); mem. Am. Polit. Sci. Assn., Am. Soc. for Pub. Adminstrn., Md. Hist. Soc. Home: 5526 Oakmont Ave Bethesda MD 20817-3528

WELLS, CLYDE KIRBY, Canadian provincial government official; b. Buchans Junction, Newfoundland, Nov. 9, 1937; s. Ralph and Maude (Kirby) W. B.A. in polit. sci., Meml. U., 1959; LL.B., Dalhousie U. Law Sch., 1962. Bar: N.S. 1963, Nfld. 1964. Pvt. practice, 1964-66; rep. dist. Humber East Nfld. Ho. of Assembly, 1966; mem. cabinet Premier Joseph R. Smallwood, 1966-68; pvt. practice, 1968-77; rep. from Nfld. Can. Bar Assn. com. constitutional changes, 1977-79; counsel to fed. govt. and Nfld. Supreme Ct., 1979-87; elected leader Liberal Party of Nfld. and Labrador, 1987; mem. Ho. of Assembly for dist. Windsor-Buchans, 1987; premier Nfld. and Labrador, 1987—; mem. Bay of Islands, 1989—. Liberal. Office: Office of Premier, Confederation Bldg 8th Fl, Saint John's, NF Canada A1B 4J6

WELLS, DAVID JOHN, university official, mechanical engineer; b. Ithaca, N.Y., Jan. 4, 1949; s. Arthur John and Dorothy Helen (Edwards) W.; m. Jane Baran, July 10, 1971; children: Jacob David, Abbe Grace, Anastasia Catherine. BS in Interdisciplinary Engring. and Mgmt., Clarkson U., 1972, MSME, 1980, PhD in Engring. Sci., 1985. Planning engr. Newport News (Va.) Shipbuilding, 1973-76, Stone & Webster Engring., Boston, 1976-78; instr., counselor Clarkson U., Potsdam, N.Y., 1978-81, dir., 1986—86; project mgr., mgr. Combustion Engring., Windsor, Conn., 1981-86; dir. engring. and mgmt. program, mem. adminstrv. coun. Clarkson U., Potsdam, N.Y., 1986—, mem. exec. com., 1986—; cons. in field; cons. Excellence in Edn. Action Plan, Potsdam Pub. Schs. Contbr. articles to profl. jours. Bd. dirs. Windsor Pub. Schs., 1985-86. Mem. ASME, IEEE, Engring. Mgmt. Soc., Reliability Soc. of IEEE, Am. Mgmt. Soc., 21st Century Ltd. (edn. com.). Home: Rte 1 Bagdad Rd Box 368A Potsdam NY 13676 Office: Clarkson U Engring and Mgmt Program Potsdam NY 13699

WELLS, GLENN ALBERT, real estate manager; b. Pitts., Mar. 16, 1943; s. Albert John and Sophia (Staub) W.; m. Nancy Louise Treskot, May 18, 1968; children: Christian, Nicole, Lynn, Glenn II. BS in Met. Engring., Lettigh U., 1967, BSBA, 1967. Lic. real estate agt.,Pa. Metallurgist U.S. Steel Corp., Duquesne, Pa., 1967-68; owner, mgr. Wells Properties, Mt. Lebanon, Pa., 1968—; real estate sales Frontier Realty, McMurray, Pa., 1985, Vacca Realty, Darmont, Pa., 1988, Albrook Realty, Mt. Lebanon, 1991. Mem. Greater Pitts. Bd. Realtors, Apr. Owners Assn. Pitts. Republican. Presbyterian. Home: 146 Longue Vue Dr Pittsburgh PA 15228

WELLS, LINDA MAY, property manager; b. Little Washington, Pa., Dec. 19, 1953; d. Charles E. and Violet (McBurnie) Boyd; m. Randall Bush, July 4, 1976 (div. 1979); m. Raymond B. Wells; 1 child, Alexander. AA, No. Va. Community Coll., Annandale, 1973. Account exec. NRI, Falls Church, Va., 1976-82; asst. project mgr. Fidicorp, Washington, 1982-84; property mgr. Condominium Venture, Greenbelt, Md., 1984-86, Zalco Realty, Silver Spring, Md., 1986-87; v.p., property mgr. Williams & Wells Realty, Inc., Upper Marlboro, Md., 1987—; speaker in field. Mem. NOW, Women Bus. Owners, Exec. Women in Bus., Property Mgmt. Assn., Community Assocs. Inst., Md. Condo and Homeowner Assn. (sponsor). Republican. Methodist. Office: Williams & Wells Realty Inc 9520 Pennsylvania Ave # 103 Upper Marlboro MD 20772

WELLS, MARK HOWARD, data processing executive; b. Austin, Minn., July 7, 1951; s. Wayne Alwin and Marilyn Jeanette (Hanks) W.; m. Joan Michele Clifford (div. 1981); 1 child, Alison Michele; m. Penelope Susan Grabiec, June 7, 1987. BS in Computer Sci./Math., Mankato State U., Minn., 1973; postgrad., U. Colo., 1981-85. Programmer Trojan Seed Co., Olivia, Minn., 1974-75; programmer/analyst Gelco Inc., Eden Prairie, Minn., 1975-78, Fairway Foods, Inc., Northfield, Minn., 1978-79; systems supr. Current, Inc., Colorado Springs, 1979-85; project mgr. Keane, Inc., Lexington, Mass., 1985—. Mem. Mensa, The Nature Conservancy, Pentax Owners Club. Presbyterian. Home: 1 Minton Rd Billerica MA 01821-5263 Office: Keane Inc 430 Bedford St Lexington MA 02173-1548

WELLS, RAYMOND, college administrator; b. Kingston, N.Y., Jan. 26, 1950; s. Ralph Chester and Jean Louise (Kelly) W.; m. M. Linda Munson, July 8, 1973. BA, Hope Coll., Holland, Mich., 1971; EdS, SUNY, Albany, 1975. Dir. acad. counseling and career devel. Upsala Coll., East Orange, N.J., 1976-79; dir. career devel. and field experience Marist Coll., Poughkeepsie, N.Y., 1979-89; dir. career svcs. Culinary Inst. Am., Hyde Park, N.Y., 1989—. Ch. sch. supt. Port Ewen (N.Y.) Reformed Ch., 1984-89, mem. consistory, 1982-88, 91—; classis rep. Mid-Hudson Classis of Reformed Ch. in Am. Mem. Eastern Coll. Pers. Officers (v.p. coll. rels. 1986-88, pres.-elect 1989, pres. 1989-90, exec. bd.), Mid-Hudson Career Consortium, Blue Key Honor Soc. Office: Culinary Inst Am 651 Albany Post Rd Hyde Park NY 12538-1501

WELLS, RONALD AUSTIN, foundation administrator; b. Richmond Hill, N.Y., Aug. 7, 1933; s. Clarence Eugene and Marion (Bird) W.; m. Karen K. Jambeck, Apr. 11, 1986; children: Aileen, Christine, Diana, Per. AB, Queens Coll., 1955; MA in English, U. Conn., 1961, PhD in English and Linguistics, 1966. Commd. ensign USCG, 1955, advanced through grades to capt., 1976; prof., head dept. humanities USCG Acad., New London, 1969-79; exec. dir. Conn. Humanities Coun., Middletown, Conn., 1979-82; v.p. program devel. Phelps-Stokes Fund, N.Y.C., 1983-88, exec. v.p., 1989—, also bd. dirs.; exec. editor Phelps-Stokes Inst. Publications, 1985—; Fulbright lectr. U. Oulu, Finland, 1968-69; mem. accreditation teams New Eng. Assn. Schs. and Colls., Wellesley, Mass., 1975; mem. Gov.'s Task Force on Higher Edn., Hartford, Conn., 1975; panelist, seminar leader NEH, Washington, 1981-83; cons. U.S. Internat. Communication Agy., Washington, 1982, Non-Profit Sector Rsch. Fund, Aspen Inst., 1991. Author: Dictionaries and The Authoritarian Tradition, 1973; contbr. articles to profl. jours. Sr. advisor, bd. dirs. Am. Indian Coll. Fund. Sr. Fulbright lectr., 1968. Fellow Salzburg Seminar; mem. N.Y. Regional Assn. Grantmakers (bd. dirs. 1989—), Fulbright Assn. (pres. 1981-82, bd. dirs. 1978-82). Home: 12 Olcott Way Ridgefield CT 06877-3924 Office: Phelps-Stokes Fund 10 E 87th St New York NY 10128-0501

WELLS, SAMUEL FOGLE, JR., research center administrator; b. Mullins, S.C., Sept. 13, 1935; s. Samuel Fogle and Mildred Inez (Meeks) W.; m. Novella R. Cloninger, June 15, 1957 (div. 1969); children: Lauren, Anthony (dec.), Jeffrey (dec.); m. Sherrill Perkins Brown, June 7, 1969; 1 child, Christopher Wentworth. AB, U. N.C., 1957; MA, Harvard U., 1961, PhD, 1967. Instr. Wellesley (Mass.) Coll., 1963-65; asst. prof. U. N.C., Chapel Hill, 1965-70, assoc. prof., 1970-78; dir. internat. security studies program Woodrow Wilson Ctr., Washington, 1977-87, assoc. dir., 1985-88, dep. dir., 1988—; cons. Office of Sec. of Def., Washington, 1974-77; trustee Z. Smith Reynolds Found., Winston-Salem, 1977-83. Author: The Challenges of Power: American Diplomacy, 1900-1921, 1990; editor and contbr. books: Economics and World Power: An Assessment of American Diplomacy Since 1789, 1984, Limiting Nuclear Proliferation, 1985, Strategic Defenses and Soviet-American Relations, 1987, Security in the Middle East: Regional Change and Great Power Strategies, 1987, Superpower Competition and Security in the Third World, 1988, The Helsinki Process and the Future of Europe, 1990; contbr. articles to profl. jours. Capt. USMC, 1957-60. Woodrow Wilson fellow, 1957, Danforth Found. fellow, 1957, Peace fellow Hoover Instn., 1972-73, Woodrow Wilson Internat. Ctr. for Scholars fellow, 1976-77. Mem. Am. Hist. Assn., Internat. Inst. for Strategic Studies, Orgn. Am. Historians, Soc. for Historians of Am. Fgn. Rels., Internat. Studies Assn., Coun. on Fgn. Rels. Home: 1509 Woodacre Dr McLean VA 22101-2538 Office: Woodrow Wilson Internat Ctr 1000 Jefferson Dr SW Washington DC 20560

WELLWARTH, GEORGE E., writer, educator; b. Vienna, Austria, June 6, 1932; came to U.S., 1946; s. Erwin and Martha (Sobotka) W.; m. Pamela W. Hean, May 13, 1978. BA, NYU, 1953; MA, Columbia U., 1954; PhD, U. Chgo., 1957. Asst. to assoc. prof. CUNY, 1960-64, Pa. State U., State College, 1964-70; prof. SUNY, Binghamton, 1970—. Author: The Theatre of Protest and Paradox, 1964, Brit. edit., 1964, Spanish edit., 1965, 2nd revised edit., 1971, 2nd. revised Spanish edit., 1974, Spanish Underground Drama, 1972, Modern Drama and the Death of God, 1986; editor: The New Wave Spanish Drama, 1972, German Drama Between the Wars, 1972, Themes of Drama, 1972, Three Catalan Dramatists, 1976, New Generation Spanish Drama, 1976; co-editor: Modern Spanish Theatre, 1968; co-editor, translator Post War German Theatre, 1967, Brit. edit., 1968, Modern French Theatre, 1964, Brit. edit., 1964; translator: Concise Encyclopedia of the Modern Drama, 1964; co-founder, editor Modern Internat. Drama Mag., 1967—; contbr. articles to profl. jours. Home: 16 Murray St Binghamton NY 13905-4503 Office: SUNY Theatre Dept PO Box 6000 Binghamton NY 13902

WELSH, GREG JON, information systems educator; b. Milw., July 6, 1951; s. Robert William and Beverly Claire (Chapman) W. BA in Humanities, U. Chgo., 1977; MS in Tech. Mgmt., Am. U., 1988, postgrad., 1991—. Mem. media and publs. staff Library of Congress, Washington, 1982-83; asst. dir. publs. Am. U., Washington, 1983-85; pres., chmn. Oasis Group, Inc., Fairfax, Va., 1985-91; v.p. Broadcast Investment Analysts, Washington, 1987-89; mem. faculty computer sci. and info. systems dept. The Am. U., Washington, 1989—. Co-author: Radio Acquisition Handbook, 1988; editor hardware revs. Jour. Microcomputer Systems Mgmt. Danforth Found. fellow, 1968. Mem. IEEE, Data Processing Mgmt. Assn. (exec. v.p. 1989), Assn. Computing Machinery, Info. Resources Mgmt. Assn. Office: Am U Clark Hall 117 4400 Massachusetts Ave NW Washington DC 20016

WELSH, HARRY EDWARD, librarian; b. Westernport, Md., July 19, 1939; s. Harry Edward Sr. and Elizabeth (Veach) W. BA, W.Va. U., 1962; MS, Drexel U., 1968; MPA, Wayne State U., 1975. Ref. libr. Wayne State U., Detroit, 1970-75; head govt. docs. U. Wash., Seattle, 1975-79; libr. dir. Sch. Mines S.D. Univ., Rapid City, 1979-83; libr. dir. Manhattan Coll., N.Y.C., 1983—; vice-chair Westchester Acad. Librs. Dirs. Orgn., Westchester County, 1986-88. Mem. editorial bd. Environ. Impact Statements Key, 1979—. Democrat. Roman Catholic. Home: 315 W 23rd St New York NY 10011-2247 Office: Manhattan Coll Manhattan College Pky Bronx NY 10471-3913

WELSH, MICHAEL L., soft drink bottling company administrator; b. Clayton, Ga., June 14, 1959; s. John F. and Mary Ann (Casimes) W.; m. Susie Googe, June 5, 1982; children: Sarah Alex, Daniel. BBA magna cum laude, U. Ga., 1981, MACC, 1986. Consolidation acct. Tex. Instruments, Dallas, 1981-82, fin. analyst, 1982-84; v.p. cons. MISA, Atlanta, 1986-87; consolidation analyst Coca-Cola Enterprise, Atlanta, 1987-88; mid-Atlantic supr., mgr. Coca-Cola Bottling Co., Columbia, Md., 1988-90; div. mgr. Coca-Cola Enterprises-North, Columbia, 1990—; acctg. and system implementation cons., Dallas and Athens, Ga., 1982-86. Youth leader Ascension Ch., Dallas, 1982-83, St. Michael's Ch., Stone Mountain, Ga., 1986-88, St. John's Episc. Ch., Ellicott City, Md., 1988-91. Mem. U. Ga. Alumni Soc. (pres. Dallas chpt. 1983-84), Blue Key, Phi Kappa Phi, Beta Gamma Sigma, Phi Eta Sigma, Beta Alpha Psi. Home: 4265 Burleigh Dr Tucker GA 30084-7906 Office: Coca-Cola Enterprises-North 9770 Patuxent Woods Dr Columbia MD 21045

WELT, HENRY, lawyer; b. Vienna, Austria, Oct. 16, 1946; s. Abraham Joseph and Rose (Eisen) W.; m. Cheryl Alice Hedaya, June 9, 1968; children: Daniel Stephen, Michael David, William Joseph. AB, Columbia Coll., 1968, JD, 1972. Bar: N.Y 1973. Assoc. Proskauer, Rose, Goetz & Mendelsohn, N.Y.C., 1972-74, Shereff, Friedman, Hoffman & Goodman, N.Y.C., 1974-76; ptnr. Schoeman, Marsh, Updike & Welt, N.Y.C., 1977-89, Kronish, Lieb, Weiner & Hellman, N.Y.C., 1990—; instr. Real Estate Inst., NYU. Vice chmn., bd. dirs., trustee, chmn. devel. com. The Bklyn. Mus., 1985—; mem. Am. Jewish Com.; trustee Roundtable Polit. Action Com., M.I. Polit. Action Com. Guttman fellow, 1966, Carnegie fellow, 1967. Mem. ABA (corp. law sect., art law com.), N.Y.C. Bar Assn. (mem. real property law com.), N.Y. County Lawyers Assn. (mem. securities regulation com.), Internat. Bar Assn., Internat. Fiscal Assn., The Drawing Soc. (trustee 1988—), The Harlem Sch. of the Arts (trustee 1988—), Am Art Forum (trustee 1987—), Century Assn., Union League, Phi Beta Kappa. Office: Kronish Lieb Weiner & Hellman 1345 Ave Of The Americas New York NY 10105-0099

WELTE, A. THEODORE, chamber of commerce executive; b. Mankato, Minn., Feb. 11, 1944; s. Arthur William and Bernice (Town) M.; m. Kathleen P. Browne, May 3, 1969; 1 child, Jason N. BA in Sociology, Psychology, Mankato State U., 1966, MA in Econs., 1972; cert., U. Notre Dame, 1987; cert. mgmt., Stonehill Coll., 1990. Program officer, br. officer Peace Corp, Washington, 1968-69; rsch. dir. Tech. Found., W.Va. Tech., Montgomery, 1969-70; project dir. Self-Help, Inc., Brockton, Mass., 1972-73; regional planner, planning supr. Old Colony Planning Coun., Brockton, 1974-81; pres., chief exec. officer Metro South C. of C., Brockton, 1981-90, MetroWest C. of C., Framingham, Mass., 1990—; trustee Brockton Regional Econ. Devel. Corp., 1982-90; treas. Brockton Area Pvt. Industry Coun., 1987-89. Cubmaster pack 68 Boy Scouts Am., Easton, Mass., 1989-90, boy scout troop 87, 1991—, bd. dirs. Algonquin coun., 1991—. Mem. New Eng. Assn. C. of C. Execs. (sec. 1990-92, 2d v.p. 1992—), Mass. Assn. C. of C. Execs. (pres. 1988-89), Rotary (sec. Brockton chpt. 1988-90, v.p. Framingham chpt. 1991-92, pres.-elect. 1992—). Presbyterian. Office: MetroWest C of C 1671 Worcester Rd Ste 201 Framingham MA 01701-5404

WELTERS, LINDA MARIE, textiles educator, academic administrator; b. St. Paul, May 7, 1949; d. Herman Anthony and Marie Welters; m. Nicholas Georgiades, Dec. 27, 1986. BA, St. Catherine's Coll., 1971; MA, Colo. State U., 1973; PhD, U. Minn., 1981. Instr. U. Wyo., Laramie, 1973-77; asst. prof. U. R.I., Kingston, 1979-86, assoc. prof., 1986—, chairperson textiles, fashion merchandising and design dept., 1989; rsch. assoc. Peloponnesian Folklore Found., Nafplion, Greece, 1983—. Author: Women's Costume in Greece, 1988; contbr. articles to profl. jours. Grantee NEH, Philos. Soc., State of R.I., Earthwatch, Pasold Rsch. Fund; recipient Merit award U. R.I., 1986, 87, 88, 89. Mem. Assn. Textile Chemists and Colorists, Textile Soc. Am., Costume Soc. Am. (bd. dirs. 1986—, pres. region I 1988-90), Internat. Textile and Apparel Assn., Centre Internationale Etudes Textiles Anciens, Phi Kappa Phi. Democrat. Roman Catholic. Office: U RI Quinn Hall # 303 Kingston RI 02881

WELTMAN, MICK GENE, non-profit organization administrator; b. St. Louis, July 13, 1952; s. Albert Bernard and Joyce Toby (Lieberman) W. BA in Gen. Studies, U. Kans., 1975; MA in Polit. Sci., Lindenwood Coll., 1982; MA in Internat. Devel. Mgmt., Sch. for Internat. Tng., 1984; MBA in Fin., Southeastern U., 1989. Ter. mktg. rep. 3M Cen. Micrographics, St. Louis, 1976-79, Numeridex, Wheeling, Ill., 1979-81, Sycom, St. Louis, 1981-82; dep. dir. Tech. Transfer div. Boles World Trade Corp., Washington, 1984-85; assoc. dir. Intersupply A/S, Copenhagen, Denmark, 1985-87; dir. Inst. for Transp. and Devel. Policy, Washington, 1989-91; cons. TransCentury Corp., Washington, 1987, Horizon Trading Co., Washington, 1987-88, Yugo Trade Ltd., Washington, 1988, Pvt. Agys. Collaborating Together, Washington, 1988, The Washington Ctr., 1988-89, mktg. and mgmt., 1992—. Bd. dirs. Ethical Soc., St. Louis, 1981-82, ACLU, 1980-82. Mem. Soc. for Internat. Devel., Soc. for Intercultural Edn., Tng. and Rsch., Soc. of Profls. in Dispute Resolution, Toastmasters Internat. (Toastmaster of Yr. 1979). Democrat. Home and Office: PO Box 387 Brattleboro VT 05302

WELU, JAMES A., art museum director; b. Dubuque, Iowa, Dec. 15, 1943; s. Andrew L. and Anna E. (Riley) W. BA, Loras Coll., 1966; MA, U. Notre Dame, 1967, MFA, 1968; PhD, Boston U., 1977. Instr. St. Mary-of-the-Woods (Ind.) Coll., 1968-70; asst. curator Worcester (Mass.) Art Mus., 1974-76, assoc. curator, 1976-80, instr., 1977-78, 80-81, chief curator, 1980-86, dir., 1986—; instr. Clark U., Worcester, 1980. Panelist Mass. Coun. on Arts and Humanities, Boston, 1981-82, 90, Utilization of Mus. Resources Nat. Endowment for the Arts, 1988; trustee Williamstown Regional Art Conservation Lab., Inc., Mass., 1981-86; mem. panel Utilization Mus. Resources, NEA, 1988. Boston U. grantee, 1973, NEA Mus.' Profl. grantee, 1976-81; Samuel H. Kress Found. fellow, 1973; recipient Netherland-Am. Found. award Netherland Found., 1973, Disting. Alumni award Boston U. Grad. Sch., 1986. Mem. Assn. Art Mus. Dirs., Coll. Art Assn. Am., Am. Assn. Museums, New Eng. Mus. Assn., Historians of Netherlandish Art. Home: 16 Rutland Ter Worcester MA 01609-1664 Office: Worcester Art Mus 55 Salisbury St Worcester MA 01609-3196

WENCK, EDWIN O., lawyer; b. Balt., July 29, 1936; s. Millard F. III and Doris Margaret (Addison) W.; m. Mary Elizabeth Long (div. 1985); m. Patricia Ann Kelly; children: Edwin O., Erick Andrew. AB, Catawba Coll., 1958; BD, Lancaster Theol. Seminary, 1961; JD, U. Balt. Law Sch., 1973. Bar: Md., U.S. Dist. Ct. Md. Pastor Trinity Reformed Ch., Berlin, Pa., 1961-63, Faith United Ch. of Christ, Frederick, Md., 1963-70; asst. state's atty. Balt. City State's Atty. Office, 1973—. Bd. dirs. German Soc. of Md., 1989, Chesapeake Ctr., Balt. County, 1989, Community Svcs. of Md., Inc., 1985—. Mem. Md. Bar Assn., Balt. City Bar Assn. Home: 230 Stony Run Ln # Sa Baltimore MD 21210-3035 Office: Baltimore City State's Atty Court House Baltimore MD 21202

WENCK, WILLIAM ARISTÉ, marketing data analyst; b. New Orleans, Apr. 20, 1947; s. William Aristé and Esther Hardy (Bragg) W.; m. Marian Gould Ruggles, May 28, 1983; 1 child, Alexander Ruggles. BS in Indsl. Engring., Cornell U., 1969; MEd, Columbia U., 1975, PhD in Social Psychology, 1981. Owner Wenck Capital Ventures, Essex, Conn., 1982-92, William A. Wenck and Assocs., Old Lyme, Conn., 1992—. Chmn. Old Lyme (Conn.) Repub. Town Com., 1989—; commr. Old Lyme Harbor Mgmt. Commn., 1989—. Mem. Am. Psychol. Assn., A.K. Rice Inst., N.Y. Yacht Club. Home: 110 Mile Creek Rd Old Lyme CT 06371-1716

WENDEL, CHRISTOPHER MARK, exhibition designer; b. Mpls., Mar. 29, 1954; s. Adolph Henry and Cordelia Marie (Ruthenbeck) W.; m. Catherine Mary Boe, Sept. 13, 1975; children: Amy, Adam. BS in Design, U. Minn., 1979; postgrad., Robert Morris Coll., 1988-90, Seton Hall U., 1992. Designer Polivka-Logan Designers, Wayzata, Minn., 1975-79, Lakeside Ltd., Mpls., 1979-80, Omnicon Ltd., Chgo., 1981-82; design dir. CEI, Chgo., 1982-86; sr. designer Giltspur, Pitts., 1986-90; v.p., creative dir. Exhibitgroup N.Y., Edison, 1990—. Mem. Indsl. Designers Soc. Am., Harley Owners Group. Republican. Lutheran. Office: Exhibitgroup NY 201 Mill Rd Edison NJ 08837-3801

WENDEL, WENDEL R., industrial engineer; b. N.Y.C., Sept. 18, 1946; s. Walter and Betty (Carroll) W. BS in Indsl. Engring. cum laude, Hofstra U., 1969. Pres., founder Space Structures Internat. Inc., STAR*FLITE Airships, Inc., STAR*NET Structures, Inc., West Babylon, N.Y.; chmn. bd. dirs. STAR*TECH Engring.; lectr. in field; mem. panel Office of Tech. Assessment, U.S. Congress, 1984; mem. workshop on measurement tech. Nat. Bur. Standards, 1985; appeared on radio program WCBS, 1986. Author: Spaceframe Basics, a Handbook for Spaceframe Design and Engineering; patentee in field. Recipient 1st Place award Plastic in Bldg. Tech., Plastic World Mag., 1979, Excellence in Design award Design News Mag., 1981. Mem. AIAA, Am. Astronaut. Soc., Lighter-than-Air Soc., Assn. Balloon and Airship Constructors, Airship Assn., Airship Explorers Club. Office: Starnet Structures 106 Bell St West Babylon NY 11704-1004

WENDELL, CHARLES WARNER, French and humanities educator; b. Schenectady, N.Y., Feb. 11, 1930; s. Simpson Barney and Anna Elizabeth (Maue) W.; m. Frana Maria Summa, Oct. 17, 1955 (dec. 1982); 1 child, Melissa Anne. BA, Cath. U., 1951, MA, 1952; PhD, Yale U., 1963. Instr. St. John's U., Jamaica, N.Y., 1960-66; asst. prof. Rutgers Coll., New Brunswick, N.J., 1966-69; assoc. prof. Kean Coll. of N.J., Union, 1969—. Recording sec., 1st v.p., bd. dirs. King's Daughters Day Sch., Plainfield, N.J., 1985—. With U.S. Army, 1952-55. Mem. Modern Lang. Assn., Am. Comparative Lit. Assn., Am. Soc. for 18th Cemtury Studies, N.Y. Hist. Soc., The New Netherlands Project, The Holland Soc., Yale Club N.Y. Democrat. Roman Catholic. Home: 205 W 9th St Plainfield NJ 07060 Office: Kean Coll of NJ Morris Ave Union NJ 07083

WENDT, HENRY, III, pharmaceutical company executive; b. Neptune City, N.J., July 19, 1933; s. Henry II and Rachel L. (Wood) W.; m. Holly Peterson, June 23, 1956; children: Henry IV, Laura. AB, Princeton U., 1955. With Smith Kline & French Labs, Phila., 1955-70, v.p. mktg., gen. mgr., 1970-71; pres., chief operating officer Smith Kline Corp., Phila., 1971-76, also bd. dirs.; chief exec. officer SmithKline Beckman Corp., Phila., 1982-87, pres., 1982, chmn., from 1987; now chmn. SmithKline Beecham, Phila.; bd. dirs. Atlantic Richfield Co., Allergan, Inc., Beckman Industries, Inc., Wiggins, Teape & Appleton. Contbr. articles to profl. jours. Member adv. coun. dept. East Asian studies Princeton U. Mme. Japan Soc., U.S.-Japan Bus. Coun. (chmn.). Office: SmithKline Beecham One Franklin Pla Philadelphia PA 19102

WENGER, DENNIS EUGENE, business affairs director, accounting educator; b. Chambersburg, Pa., Oct. 13, 1951; s. Charles Leroy and Ruth (Oberholser) W.; m. Rebecca Groff, July 24, 1976; children: Brian Michael, Christopher Matthew. Student, Case Western Res. U., 1969-70; BA, Messiah Coll., 1972; MBA, Shippensburg U., 1977. Asst. mgr. K-Mart, York, Pa., 1973; acct. Messiah Coll., Grantham, Pa., 1973-77; instr. Ea. Mennonite Coll., Harrisonburg, Va., 1977-78; fiscal mgr. Franklin County CETA, Chambersburg, Pa., 1978-81; asst. contr. Wilson Coll., Chambersburg, Pa., 1981-82; contr. Wilson Coll., Chambersburg, 1982-84, bus. mgr., 1984—. Bd. dirs. Cumberland Valley Sch. Music, Chambersburg, 1990—, Christian Resdl. Opportunities and Social Svcs., Chambersburg, 1990—, pres., 1992; sec. New Guilford Ch., Chambersburg, 1988-89, treas., 1985-88; treas. Water Wheel Child Care Ctr., Chambersburg, 1989. Mem. Rotary (Chambersburg). Republican. Mem. Brethren in Christ Ch. Home: 229 S 6th St Chambersburg PA 17201-2617 Office: Wilson Coll 1015 Philadelphia Ave Chambersburg PA 17201-1285

WENGER, VICKI, interior designer; b. Indpls., Aug. 30, 1928. Ed., U. Nebr., Internat. Inst. Interior Design, Parsons in Paris. Pres. Vicki Wenger Interiors, Bethesda, Md., 1963-71, Washington, 1982—; pres. Beautiful Spaces Inc., Washington, 1982—; chief designer Creative Design, Capitol Heights, Md., 1969-84; lectr. Nat. Assn. Home Builders, 1983-88; mem. programs com. D.C. Assn. Home Builders, 1983-88. Author-host: (patented TV interior design show) Beautiful Spaces 1984; producer, host (cable TV show) Design Edition, 1988—. Designer Gourmet Gala, March of Dimes, Washington, 1986-88; decorator showhouse Nat. Symphony Orch., Washington, 1983-88, Am. Cancer Soc., Washington, 1983, Alexandria Community YWCA, 1990. Mem. Am. Soc. Interior Designers (profl. mem. 1973—, mem. nat. bd. 1973-75, nat. examining com. 1977-78, pres. Md. chpt. 1976, bd. dirs. D.C. chpt. 1989-91, mem. pres.'s barrier free com. 1980), Nat. Trust Hist. Preservation, Smithsonian Instn. (sponsor), Nat. Symphony Orch. (D.C. chmn. women's com. 1991—), Pisces Club (Washington). Democrat. Presbyterian. Office: Vicki Wenger Interiors 2801 New Mexico Ave NW Washington DC 20007-3921

WENICK, MARTIN ARTHUR, cultural organization administrator; b. Jersey City, N.J., May 15, 1939; s. Joseph and Dorothy (Greenberg) W.; m. Alice Tetelman, Dec. 7, 1980. AB, Brown U., 1961. Fgn. svc. officer U.S. Dept. of State, Washington, 1962-89; exec. dir. Nat. Conf. on Soviet Jewry, 1989-92; exec. v.p. Hebrew Immigrant Aid Soc., N.Y.C., 1992—. Mem. nat. adv. coun. Am. Jewish Com. Mem. Am. Fgn. Svc. Assn., Atlantic Coun. Home: 3919 Watson Pl NW Washington DC 20016 Office: 333 7th Ave New York NY 10001

WENIS, EDWARD, chemist; b. Linden, N.J., May 21, 1919; s. William and Susie (Dzuboy) W.; m. Helene M. Zinnel, Nov. 26, 1942; children: Michael Edward, Karen H. BSChemE with honors, N.J. Inst. Tech., 1940; MSChemE, Stevens Inst. Tech., 1941. Registered profl. engr., N.J. Chemist USDA, Phillipsburg, N.J., 1937-38; foreman USDA, Trenton, N.J., 1938-39; supr. Dutch Elm disease project USDA, Paoli, Pa., 1939-40; county field supr. USDA, Alexandria, Va., 1940-41; asst. chemist Hoffman La Roche, Inc., Nutley, N.J., 1941-45, assoc. chemist, 1945-47, personal asst. to rsch. v.p., 1957-60, mgr. rsch. svcs. thin layer labs., 1960-80; ret. Hoffman La Roche, Inc., Nutley, 1980; minority corp. dir. Phoenix Labs., East Orange, 1950-70. Patentee in field; contbr. articles to profl. jours. Scoutmaster Boy Scouts Am., Leonia, N.J., 1951-56; mem. county com. Rep. Party, Hackensack, N.J., 1956-62. Fellow Am. Inst. Chemists; mem. Am. Chem. Soc. (life). Home: 104 Hillcrest Ave Leonia NJ 07605-1531

WENNBERG, HANS-ERIK, communications educator; b. Mineola, N.Y., Feb. 13, 1946; s. Hans Jacob and Edith (Junker) W.; m. Linda Wright, Apr. 21, 1979; children: Steven Michael, Melissa Ann. BS in Edn., SUNY, Geneseo, 1969; MEd, Temple U., 1973; PhD, U. Conn., 1986. Cert. secondary math. tchr., N.Y. Jr. high sch. math. tchr. Rush Henrietta (N.Y.) Cen. Sch., 1969-72; asst. dir. audio-visual dept. R.I. Coll., Providence, 1973-84; dir. instnl. svcs. Elizabethtown (Pa.) Coll., 1984-90, asst. prof. communica-

tions, 1984-92, assoc. prof. communications, 1992—; presenter workshop in field. Producer multi-image presentation Spectrum award, 1988-91. pres. Edn. Communications Found., Washington, 1992—. Mem. Am. Assn. Higher Edn., Assn. Ednl. Communications and Tech., Assn. for Multi-Image Internat., Internat. Assn. Bus. Communicators, Pa. Assn. Ednl. Communications and Tech. Office: Elizabethtown Coll Communications Dept 1 Alpha Dr Elizabethtown PA 17022-2699

WENNER, JANN SIMON, editor, publisher; b. N.Y.C., Jan. 7, 1946; s. Edward and Ruth N. (Simmons) W.; m. Jane Ellen Schindelhiem, July 1, 1968; children: Alexander Jann, Theodore Simon, Edward Augustus. Student, U. Calif.-Berkeley, 1964-66. Editor, pub. Rolling Stone mag., N.Y.C., 1967—, Record, N.Y.C., 1981-86, Look mag., N.Y.C., 1979, Men's Jour., 1992—; editor in chief Outside Mag., San Francisco, 1977-78, US Mag., N.Y.C., 1985—, Men's Jour., 1992—; exec. v.p. Rock & Roll Hall of Fame. Author: Lennon Remembers, 1971, Garcia, 1972. Bd. dirs. Robinhood Found. Recipient Disting. Achievement award U. So. Calif. Sch. Journalism and Alumni Assn., 1976, Nat. Mag. award, 1970, 77, 86, 87, 88, 89. Mem. Am. Soc. Mag. Editors. Office: Straight Arrow Publs Inc 1290 Ave of the Americas New York NY 10104

WENTE, VAN ARTHUR, consultant, retired government official; b. Johnston City, Ill., Jan. 11, 1925; s. Edward H. and Pauline Lucille (Barham) W.; m. Jane Van Derveer Updike, Sept. 22, 1962; children: Gretchen Jane, Robert Edward. BSChemE, Washington U., St. Louis, 1945. Chem. engr. Firestone Tire & Rubber Co., Pottstown, Pa., 1945-50, USN Research Lab., Washington, 1950-56; info. officer U.S. Atomic Energy Agy., Germantown, Md., 1956-59, sci. advisor, 1959-61; documentation head NASA, Washington, 1961-64, systems head, 1965-80, sci. and tech. info. dir., 1981-89; mem. adv. group on aerospace R & D info. NATO, 1983-89. Contbr. articles to profl. jours., chpts. to books. Fellow Nat. Fedn. Abstracting and Info. Svcs. (hon., bd. dirs. 1986-88); mem. Am. Inst. Chem. Engrs., Am. Soc. for Info. Scis., Chem. Engrs. Washington (treas. 1958-59), Kenwood Golf and Country Club, Mil. Officers Club. Home and Office: 5919 Gloster Rd Bethesda MD 20816-1144

WEPNER, SHELLEY BETH, education educator, software developer; b. Phila., Oct. 23, 1951; d. Bernard and Carole Frances (Abramson) Markovitz; m. Roy Henry Wepner, Aug. 3, 1974; children: Leslie Marcia and Meredith Susan (twins). BS magna cum laude, U. Pitts., 1972; MS, U. Pa., 1973, EdD, 1980. Cert. reading specialist, prin., supr., elem. tchr., N.J. Reading tchr. West Deptford (N.J.) Sch. Dist., 1973-74; reading resource tchr. Middletown (N.J.) Sch. Dist., 1974-75, Title I tchr., 1975-76; reading specialist Marlboro (N.J.) Sch. Dist., 1976-78, curriculum cons., 1978-80, supr. curriculum and instrn., 1980-82; asst. prof. edn. William Paterson Coll., Wayne, N.J., 1989, chair dept. curriculum and instrn., 1991—; cons. Tchr. Support Software, Gainesville, Fla., 1988—, East Brunswick (N.J.) Sch., 1989. Co-author: Using Computers in the Teaching of Reading, 1987; co-editor: The Administration and Supervision of Reading Programs, 1989, Process Reading and Writing: A Literature Based Approach; author software Read-A-Logo, 1987, Reading Realities, 1989 (Top Five award), Reading Realities Elem. Series, 1990 (Top 36 award). Chmn. gifted and talented Coles Sch. PTA, Scotch Plains, N.J., 1989-90. Mem. Nat. Reading Conf., Coll. Reading Assn., Internat. Soc. for Tech. in Edn., Internat. Reading Assn., N.J. Reading Assn. (bd. dirs. 1982-85), Phi Delta Kappa. Home: 3 Hacklorn Ln Scotch Plains NJ 07076-2836 Office: William Paterson Coll 300 Pompton Rd Wayne NJ 07470-2103

WEPPLER, JAY ROBERT, banking executive; b. Montclair, N.J., May 16, 1943; s. George Robert and Cornelia (Menard) W.; m. Cynthia Anne Stone, June 21, 1969 (div. Jan. 1982); children: Ashley Menard, George Reid Willcutt; m. Pauline Ann Kelly, Sept. 27, 1983. Student, U. Conn., 1961-64; BS, Johnson Coll., 1966. Asst. sec. Chem. Bank, N.Y.C., 1972-74; asst. v.p. Chem. Bank, San Francisco, 1974-77; v.p., gen. mgr. Chem. Bank, Sydney, New South Wales, Australia, 1978-80, Hong Kong, 1980-82; v.p., regional mgr. Chem. Bank, London, 1982-85; v.p. Chem. Bank, Wilmington, Del., 1985-86; v.p., group head Chem. Bank, N.Y.C., 1987-88; sr. v.p., mgr. corp. fin. GE Capital, Stamford, Conn., 1988—. Served to lt. USNR, 1968-71. Mem. Hurlingham Club, Univ. Club, Royal Hong Kong Jockey Club. Republican. Home: 934 S Pine Creek Rd Fairfield CT 06430-6348 Office: GE Capital 292 Long Ridge Rd Stamford CT 06902-1695

WERBITT, WARREN, gastroenterologist; b. Phila., Jan. 29, 1939; s. Saull Boris and Pearl (Weiner) W,; m. Drue Natalie Engman Werbitt, Aug. 30, 1964; children: Julie Michele, Jeffrey Brian. BS in Pharmacy, Temple U., 1960; D in Osteopathy, Coll. Osteopathic Medicine, Des Moines, 1966; MD, Med. Coll. Pa., 1973. Diplomate Am. Osteopathic Bd. Internal Medicine, 1974, 76, Am.Osteopathic Bd. Internal Medicine Subspecialty Gastroenterology, 1978, 81. Internship Doctor's Hosp., Columbus, Ohio, 1966-67; residency in internal medicine Doctor's Hosp., Columbus, 1967-68, Cherry Hill (N.J.) Med. Ctr., 1968-69, Mercy Catholic Med. Ctr., Phila., 1969-70; residency in internal medicine Med. Coll. Pa. Hosp., Phila., 1971-72, fellow, 1970-74; instr. Med. Coll. Pa., Phila., 1971—; instr. Phila. Coll. Osteopathic Medicine, 1975-77, chmn. div. gastroenterology, 1977—; clin. assoc. prof. medicine N.J. Coll. Medicine and Dentistry, 1977—; attending physician and cons. in gastroenterology Med. Coll. Pa., Phila., 1974—, Vet. Adminstrn. Hosp., Phila., 1972-75; chmn. Div. Gastroenterology, Dept. Medicine Phila. Coll. Osteopathic Medicine, 1975-77; chmn. Dept. Medicine Kennedy Meml. Hosp. U. Med. Ctr., Cherry Hill, 1979-81, chmn. subsect. Gastroenterology, 1979-87. Contbg. editor The N.J. Jour. for Ostepathic Physicians and Surgeons, 1980—; mem. scientific adv. com. Phila. chpt. Nat. Found. Ileitis & Colitis, Inc., 1982—; contbr. articles to profl. jours. Recipient Profl. Svc. award Med. Soc. N.J., 1991. Fellow Am. Coll. Physicians, Am. Coll. Gastroenterology, Acad. Med. N.J.; mem. AMA, Am. Soc. Gastrointestinal Endoscopy, Am. Gastroenterology Assn., Am. Soc. Parenteral and Enteric Nutrition, Am. Inst. Ultrasound in Medicine, Phila. Gastrointestinal Rsch. Forum, State Med. Soc. N.J., Camden County Med. Soc., N.J. Endoscopic Soc., Del. Valley Soc. for Gastrointestinal Endoscopy, South Jersey Gastroenterological Soc., Am. Osteopathic Assn., N.J. Soc. Osteopathic Physicians and Surgeons, Am. Coll. Osteopathic Internists, Camden County Osteopathic Assn., Am. Cancer Soc. (bd. dirs. N.J. chpt.), Pres.'s Circle Am. U., N.Y. Acad. Scis., John Sherman Myers Soc., Lambda Omicron Gamma. Office: Profl Gastroenterology Assn 1939 Rt 70 E Ste 250 Cherry Hill NJ 08003

WERFELMAN, WILLIAM H., JR., public relations executive; b. Bridgeport, Conn., July 11, 1953; s. William H. and Helen D. (Rainier) W.; m. Patricia Aileen Maytrott, Aug. 28, 1977; 1 child, Lauren Aileen. BA in English, St. Bonaventure U., 1975; postgrad., Georgetown U., 1975-76. Staff writer Post-Telegram newspapers, Bridgeport, 1976-79; product publicity specialist Dictaphone Corp., Rye, N.Y., 1979-81; supr. press relations Gen. Electric Co., Fairfield, Conn., 1981-84; mgr. corp. pub. relations Olin Corp., Stamford, Conn., 1984-90; dir. pub. rels., 1990—. Mem., chmn. Zoning Bd. Appeals, Redding, Conn., 1977-89; mem., recruitment chmn. Rep. Town Com., Redding, 1976-90. Mem. Internat. Assn. Bus. Communicators (Best Pub. Rels. results 1982), Pub. Rels. Soc. Am., Nat. Assn. Investors (Best Ann. Report 1988, 90), Fairfield County Pub. Rels. Assn. Republican. Roman Catholic. Home: Picketts Ridge Rd West Redding CT 06896-1008 Office: Olin Corp 120 Long Ridge Rd Stamford CT 06902-1839

WERKMAN, ROSEMARIE ANNE, past public relations professional, civic worker; b. Washingtonville, N.Y., Apr. 21, 1926; d. Alexander and Michelina (Russo) Di Benedetto; m. Henry J. Werkman, June 29, 1947; children: Elizabeth, Kristine, Hendrik. Student, U. Miami, Fla. Billing clk. Stern's Dept. Store, N.Y.C., 1945; clk., typist Doubleday-Doran Book Pub., N.Y.C., 1945-46; receptionist Moser & Cotins Advt. Agy., Utica, N.Y., 1947-48, Washingtonville Sch., N.Y., 1960-75. Author: (biography/autobiography) Love, War and Remembrance, 1992, short stories, poems. Dem. com. person, Blooming Grove; trustee Theatre of the Hudson Highlands, Orange County, N.Y.; bd. dirs. Blooming Grove Hist. Assn.; com. mem. Update: Blooming Grove Master Plan.; mem. Orange County Council of Disabled. Named Poet of Merit, Am. Poetry Assn., 1989. Mem. Blooming Grove C. of C. (v.p.). Democrat. Roman Catholic.

WERNER, ANDREW JOSEPH, physician, endocrinologist, musicologist; b. Budapest, Hungary, June 5, 1936; came to U.S., 1956; s. Steven and Clara (Gutfreund) W.; m. Elaine Audrey Friedenn; 1 child, Andrea Lisa. MD, Med. Coll. of Va., 1962. Intern Kings County Hosp. Downstate Med. Ctr., Bklyn., 1962-63; resident in internal medicine N.Y. Med. Coll. Flower and 5th Ave. Hosps., N.Y.C., 1963-65; NIH fellow in endocrinology Mt. Sinai Hosp., N.Y.C., 1965-66; attending physician Mt. Sinai Med. Ctr., N.Y.C., 1966—; mem. professorial faculty Mt. Sinai Sch. of Medicine, N.Y.C., 1966—; cons. in endocrinology Hosp. for Joint Diseases-Orthopedic Inst., N.Y.C., 1979—. Author: Wolfgang Amadeus Mozart, Summa Summarum, 1990; co-author: Malignant Tumors of the Thyroid: Current Concept and Controversies, 1992. Patron Met. Opera Assn. Recipient Festung Medallion State of Salsburg, Austria, 1989. Fellow N.Y. Acad. Medicine; mem. Am. Diabetes Assn., Endocrine Soc., N.Y. Acad. Scis., Am. Assn. Clin. Endocrinologists, The Philharmonic-Symphony Soc. of N.Y., Am. Inst. for Verdi Studies, Internat. Stiftung Mozarteum-Salzburg (Austria), Internat. Salzburg Assn. (pres. N.Y.C. and Salzburg 1989—). Office: 1112 Park Ave New York NY 10128-1235

WERNER, DAVID WILLIAM, psychologist; b. Pitts., Mar. 18, 1952; s. Roy H. and Mable (Clift) W.; m. Maryfrances Gitto, June 6, 1987. BA, Amherst Coll., 1975; EdM, Boston U., 1977; D of Psychology, Mass. Sch. Profl. Psychology, 1983. Psychotherapist Counseling Clinic Inc., Middletown, R.I., 1977-79; faculty R.I. Jr. Coll., Cranston, 1977-78; exec. dir. Counseling Self-Help Inc., Walpole, Mass., 1982-86; adj. faculty Mass. Sch. Profl. Psychology, Dedham, Mass., 1984-87; cons. Mass. Dept. Mental Health, Boston, 1984—; staff psychologist Cutler Counseling Ctr., Norwood, Mass., 1983-85; assoc. med. staff Medfield (Mass.) State Hosp., 1988—; owner Dedham Psychotherapy, 1988—; cons. in field; human rights bd. Norfolk Mental Health. Chair Save Our Swamp, Millis, Mass., 1990-91. Grantee Amherst Coll., 1973. Mem. APA, Mass. Psychol. Assn. Office: Dedham Psychotherapy Assoc 10 Pearl St Dedham MA 02026-4345

WERNER, JOSEPH, secondary education educator, administrator; b. Jersey City, Sept. 7, 1925; s. Jerome and Catherine (Daniels) W.; m. Madeline Margaret Hopke, Feb. 7, 1960. BBA, Hofstra U., 1959; MS, C.W. Post Coll., 1969. Cert secondary sch. educator, adminstr., guidance counselor. Educator Mid. Country Cen. Sch. Dist. No. 11, Centereach, N.Y., 1964-90; ind. researcher; creator of term Silent Majority, 1969; conducted 10 ann. (Aug. 13) all-day, lone vigils at Berlin Wall, 1981-90, 1 all-night, lone vigil, Christmas, 1988, 1 all-day lone vigil, Christmas, 1989; designator of Black Flag as Symbol of Sorrow for Germans held behind Berlin Wall, 1982, gave away 1,000 small Black Flags at each vigil; established Johanna Hoppe award (recipient selections based on outstanding aid to Berlin or Berliners), 1986. Author: (poetry) Berlin Wall Trilogy: 1) Berlin Wall Prayer, 2) Those We Should Never Forget, 3) Music of the Berlin Wall, 1985-90, Why Can They Not Be Free?, 1985, Berlin Airlift (Peace Warriors' Eternal Echo), 1988, (tribute to fallen Am. mil. heroes), The One Who Will Never Be, 1984, (pamphlets) Good Government and You, 1969; creator Berlin Wall Calendar, 1989; writer and contbr. hist. materials to spl. collections dept. SUNY Libr., Stony Brook, 1972. Organizer nat. campaign Appreciate Am. Day (Jan. 1), 1969-74, internat. campaign Berlin Wall Demise, 1981-90. With USMC, 1943-46, PTO, China. Named Hon. Citizen, Mayor Stuart Krienbrook, 1986, Press Agt. for Am., Port Jefferson Record, 1972; declared Hon. Mem. Berlin Airlift Assn., 1992; recipient Patriotic award KC, 1971; invited to photographic ceremony with Berlin mayor, Heinrich Lummer, 1985. Home: 7 High Gate Dr Setauket NY 11733

WERNER, PATRICE (PATRICIA ANN WERNER), college dean; b. Jersey City, May 31, 1937; d. Louis and Ella Blanche (Smith) W. BA in French, Caldwell Coll., 1966; MA in French, McGill U., 1970; PhD in French, NYU, 1976; postgrad. Inst. Ednl. Mgmt., Harvard U., 1991. Joined Dominican Sisters of Caldwell, 1954. Sch. tchr. Archdiocesan Sch. Systems, N.J., Ala., 1954-62; tchr. French, Latin Jersey City, Caldwell, N.J., 1962-72; instr. French Caldwell Coll., 1973-76; dir. continuing edn. Caldwell Coll., Caldwell, 1976-79, chair dept. fgn. langs., assoc. prof. French, 1979-85, acad. dean, prof. French, 1985—; cons. Dept. of Higher Edn. Grant Program, 1986; bd. trustees Caldwell Coll. Mem. Am. Assn. Tchrs. French, Am. Assn. Higher Edn., Ea. Assn. Coll. Deans and Advisors of Students, Am. Conf. Acad. Deans, Assn. Ind. Colls. and Univs. N.J. (acad. affairs com.), N.J. Assn. Affirmative Action in Higher Edn. Office: Caldwell Coll 9 Ryerson Ave Caldwell NJ 07006-6195

WERNER, ROBERT GEORGE, ecology educator; b. Plymouth, Ind., Mar. 6, 1936; s. Robert Hampton and Selma Naomi (Dunn) W.; m. Norma Jo Hite, June 7, 1958; children: Kitty Ann, Kurt Robert. BS, Purdue U., 1958; MA, UCLA, 1963; PhD, Ind. U., 1966. Asst. prof. ecology SUNY, Syracuse, 1966-69, assoc. prof., 1970-76, prof., 1976—; rsch. assoc. Cornell U., Ithaca, N.Y., 1969-70; vis. scientist Scottish Marine Biol., Oban, Argyll, Eng., 1978; co-dir. Great Lakes Rsch. Consortium, Syracuse, 1986—; cons. Argentina/Paraguay River Devel., Yacirete, Argentina, 1988. Author: (book) Freshwater Fishes of New York, 1980; contbr. articles to profl. publs. 1st lt. USMC, 1958-61. Recipient spl. recognition N.Y. chpt. Am. Fish Soc., 1972; Fulbright fellow, 1988-89. Fellow Am. Inst. Fishery, Rsch. Biologists; mem. Am. Fisheries Soc. (exec. com. 1988-90, pres. Early Life History sect. 1988-90), Ecol. Soc. Am., Am. Soc. Limnology and Oceanography. Home: 8 Tracy Dr Skaneateles NY 13152-8918 Office: SUNY Coll Environ Sci & Forestry 1 Forestry Dr Syracuse NY 13210-2778

WERNER, RONALD CORNELIUS, mental health executive; b. Peublo, Colo., Oct. 30, 1935; s. Clarence Alfred and Myrtle Jane (Wright) W.; m. Margaret Jachetta, Aug. 29, 1955 (div.); children: Ronald Jr., Paul; m. Judith Carse, May 28, 1988; children: Sarah, Joan. AB, Colo. State Coll., 1957; MA, U. Ill., 1959; BD, Colgate-Rochester Div. Sch., 1966; STM, Andover Theol. Sch., 1969; PhD, Boston Coll., 1976. Lic. psychologist Mass.; ordained to ministry Bapt. Ch. Min. 1st Bapt. Ch., Mansfield, Mass., 1966-69; assoc. dir. Attleboro (Mass.) Mental Health Ctr., 1969-71; deputy area dir. Mass. Dept. Mental Health, Taunton, 1971-75; exec. dir. West Cen. Mental Health Ctr., Canon City, Colo., 1975-79; area dir. Mass. Dept. Mental Health, Milford, 1979-81; pres. Ctr. Human Potential, Whitinsville, Mass., 1981-84; min. Cen. Bapt. Ch., Tiverton, R.I., 1984-87; v.p. Am. Geriatric Svcs., Rockland, Mass., 1987—; adj. faculty Mass. Sch. Profl. Psychology, Dedham, 1991; cons. Am. Bapt. Chs. R.I., Providence, 1984-90, Waters Assocs., Milford, 1974-76. Author: Obra and Mental Health, 1990. Mem., officer ARC, Pueblo, 1950-79; mem. Rep. Town Com., Mansfield, 1973-75; deacon 1st Bapt. Ch. Christ, Sandwich, Mass., 1990—. Commdr. U.S. Coast Guard Aux., 1982-84. Mem. Am. Psychol. Assn., Mass. Psychol. Assn. Office: Am Geriatric Svcs 800 Hingham St Rockland MA 02370-1067

WERNER, STUART LLOYD, computer services company executive; b. N.Y.C., June 2, 1932; s. Leroy Louis and Frances Werner; m. Davideen Price, Jan. 6, 1990; children by previous marriage: Joan Leslie, Susan Lyn, Richard Wayne. BArch, Rensselaer Poly. Inst., 1954. Ptnr. in charge architecture Werner-Dyer & Assos., Washington, 1959-68; v.p. Rentex Corp., Phila., 1968-70; pres. Werner & Assos., Inc., Washington, 1970-81; v.p. spl. projects ARA Services, Inc.; v.p. ARA, 1981-83; chmn. STN Computer Services, Inc., Falls Church, Va., 1983—; pres. Werner & Monk, Inc., 1984-87; mem. indsl. engring. terminology U.S. Standards Inst. Bd. dirs. Watergate South, Opera Soc., Friends of the Corcoran Gallery, Washington. With AUS, 1955-57. Mem. AIA, Am. Inst. Indsl. Engrs., Marinette Yacht Club, Masons,Tau Beta Pi. Republican. Contbr. articles to tech. jours. Home: 700 New Hampshire Ave NW Washington DC 20037-2406 Office: STN Inc 5113 Leesburg Pike Falls Church VA 22041-3204

WERNICK, JUSTIN, podiatrist, educator; b. N.Y.C., Feb. 26, 1936; s. Charles and Ethel (Crown) W.; m. Susan Schoenfeld, Oct. 16, 1960; children: Elissa, Peter. D Podiatric Medicine, N.Y. Coll. Podiatric Medicine, N.Y.C., 1959. Diplomate Am. Bd. Podiatric Orthopedics. Pvt. practice Seaford, N.Y., 1960-78; co-founder, exec. v.p. Langer Biomechanics Group, Inc., Deer Park, N.Y., 1969—; prof. orthopedics N.Y. Coll. Podiatric Medicine, 1969—; mem. adv. bd. Rockport Shoe Co., Marlboro, Mass., 1988—. Co-author: A Practical Manual for a Basic Approach to Biomechanics, 1972; guest editor Jour. Current Podiatric Medicine, 1989; editorial adv. Podiatry Tracts. Fellow Am. Coll. Foot Orthopedics, Am. Acad. Podiatric Sports Medicine; mem. Am. Podiatric Med. Assn., N.Y. State Podiatric Med. Assn. (Podiatrist of Yr. award 1976), Nat. Acad. Practice in Podiatry (Disting. Practitioner award 1985). Republican. Jewish. Home: 96 5th Ave Apt 6J New York NY 10011-7611 Office: Langer Biomechanics Group 2l E Industry Ct Deer Park NY 11729

WERNICKI, M. CHRIS, electrical engineering educator; b. Warsaw, Poland, Aug. 22, 1945; came to U.S., 1970; s. Paul and Daria (Kondratoff) W.; m. Anna Wernicki, Mar. 8, 1969; children: Monica Christina, Elizabeth Irene. AS in Elec. Engring., Warsaw Telecommunication Inst., 1965; BSEE summa cum laude, Kiev (USSR) Poly., 1969; MEE, NYU, 1972, PhD in Elec. Engring., 1976. Lectr. NYU, 1971-73; instr. N.Y. Poly. Inst., N.Y.C., 1973-76; asst. prof. Manhattan Coll., N.Y.C., 1976-82; assoc. prof. SUNY, N.Y.C., 1981-92, N.Y. Inst. Tech., N.Y.C., 1985—; pres. M.C.W. Cons., Palisades, N.Y., 1981—. Contbr. articles to profl. jours. USN fellow, 1980, U.S. Army fellow, 1984; NASA grantee, 1985, 86, 91, 92, Naval Underwater Systems Ctr. grantee, 1990. Mem. IEEE, , N.Y. Acad. Sci., Am. Soc. Engring. Edn., Lasers and Electro-Optics Soc., Optical Soc. Am., Quantum Electronics Soc., Solid-State Cirs. Soc., Sigma Xi, Tau Beta Pi, Eta Kappa Nu. Republican. Home: PO Box 179 Palisades NY 10964-0179 Office: NY Inst Tech Dept Elec Engring 1856 Broadway New York NY 10023-7608

WERT, JONATHAN MAXWELL, II, management consultant; b. Port Royal, Pa., Nov. 8, 1939; s. Jonathan Maxwell I and Helen Leona (Leonard) W.; m. Monica Kay Manbeck; children: Jonathan Maxwell III, Kimberly Dee, Jon Adam, Justin Tyler, Amanda Elizabeth. B.S. in Biology, Austin Peay State U., 1966, M.S. in Biology, 1968; Ph.D. in Adminstrn., U. Ala., 1974. Park supt., chief interpretive services Bur. State Parks Pa. Dept. Environ. Resources, Harrisburg, 1968-69; chief naturalist Bays Mountain Park Environ. Edn. Ctr., Kingsport, Tenn., 1969-71; environ. and energy edn. specialist TVA, Knoxville, 1971-75; cons. energy, environment, conservation U. Tenn., Knoxville, 1975; sr. assoc.-energy Energy Extension Svc., Coop. Extension Svc., Pa. State U., 1977-80; pres. Energy-Environ. Consultants, Port Royal, Pa., 1981-83, Energy and Environ. Cons., Inc., Port Royal, Pa., 1983-85, Mgmt. Diagnostics. Cons. to Mgmt., Port Royal, 1985—; mem. environ. adv. com. U.S. Dept. Energy. Author: Writing Environmental Education Grant Proposals, 1974, Environmental Education Study Projects for High School Students, 1974, Environmental Education Study Projects for College Students, 1974, Developing Environmental Study Areas, 1974, Developing Environmental Education Curriculum Material, 1974, Finding Solutions to Environmental Problems . . . A Process Guide, 1975, Assessing an Issue in Relation to Environmental, Economic, and Social Impact . . . A Process Guide, 1976, Energy Conservation Measures for Mobile Home Dwellers, 1978, Selected Energy Conservation Options for the Home, 1978, Selected Energy Management Options for Small Business and Local Government, 1978, Life Lines: A Book of Poetry, Prose, and Axioms, 1983, Survivorship and Growth in Employment: A Question and Answer Guide, 1983; mem. adv. bd.: Environ. Edn. Report, 1974—; cons. editor: Jour. Environ. Edn, 1975; contbr. articles to profl. jours. Counselor Boy Scouts Am., 1975. Served with USMC, 1958-61. Recipient Conservation award Am. Motors Co., 1976. Mem. Am. Soc. Environ. Edn., Conservation Edn. Assn., Phi Delta Kappa. Lutheran. Office: Mgmt Diagnostics PO Box 194 Port Royal PA 17082-0194

WERT, ROBERT CLIFTON, lawyer; b. Pleasantville, N.J., Jan. 8, 1944; s. Clifton Robert and Anna Louise (McLarren) W.; m. Grace Elizabeth Dunbar, Dec. 16, 1967; children: Andrew, Amy, Bethany, Laura. BS in Acctg., Temple U., 1965, JD, 1868. Bar: Pa. 1968, U.S. Dist. Ct. (ea. dist.) Pa. 1968, U.S. Ct. Mil. Appeals 1969, US. Supreme Ct. 1981. Commd. 2d lt. mil. police USAR, 1965, advanced through ranks to lt. col., 1984, ret., 1990; mil. judge U.S. Army, Okinawa, Japan, 1970-73, chief trial counsel, 1973; staff judge adv. Valley Forge Army Hosp. U.S. Army, 1973-74; chief trial counsel U.S. Army, Fort Dix, N.J., 1974-76; chief legal asst. and claims U.S. Army, 1976-77, ret., 1990; chief staff counsel Southeastern Penn Transp. Authority, Phila., 1977-78, acting chief counsel, 1978-80, gen. counsel, 1980-84, dept. gen. mgr., 1984-86; exec. dir. Blank Rome Comisky & McCauley, Phila., 1986—; owner Insulco, King of Prussia, Pa., 1972-79; pres., co-owner Master Page Inc., Malvern, Pa., 1985—. Bd. dirs. Evang. Assn. for Promotion of Edn., St. David's, Pa., Eastern Coll., 1988—, Crime Prevention Assn., Phila., 1988—, Crime Prevention Assn. Charitable Giving, Phila., 1991—, Charlestown Townwatch; coord. Twp. Emergency; deacon Sunday Sch. Supt., mem. bldg. com., chmn. property com. Ch. of the Savior, Wayne, Pa.; bd. dirs., asst. treas. Adv. Meth. Ch., Phila. Decorated Meritorious Svc. medal, Army Achievement medal, Overseas Svc. medal, Nat. Def. Svc. medal, various Res. decorations; recipient Pa. Gov.'s award, 1989. Mem. ABA (vice-chmn. com. on utilization of support staff), Assn. Trial Lawyers Am., Phila. Bar Assn., Chester County Bar Assn., Pa. Def. Inst., Phila. Assn. Def. Counsel, Masons. Office: Blank Rome Comisky & McCauley 4 Penn Plz Philadelphia PA 19103

WERTHEIMER, FRANC, retired corporate executive; b. Nuremberg, Germany, Sept. 26, 1927; came to U.S., 1938; s. Erich Z. and Sophie (Prager) W.; m. Sidelle Shaiken, Sept. 2, 1951; children: Laura S., David F. BA summa cum laude, Bklyn. Coll., 1950; MA, Columbia U., 1951. Head dept. systems analysis Vitro Labs., West Orange, N.J., 1952-68; pres., chief exec. officer ManTech Internat. Corp., Alexandria, Va., 1968-91; vice chmn. Forensic Techs. Internat. Corp., Annapolis, Md., 1968-92; adj. prof. math. Bklyn. Coll., 1951-53, Fairleigh Dickinson U., Rutherford, N.J., 1954-58, Kean Coll., Union, N.J., 1968-72; trustee Stevens Inst. Tech., Hoboken, N.J., 1989—; trustee, v.p. Nat. Security Indsl. Assn., Washington, 1985-91. Contbr. over 500 reports, monographs, position papers, concept documents pub. and submitted to U.S. Govt. and pvt. sector clients, articles to profl. jours.; guest editor Technical Jour., 1969; session chmn. tech. seminar, 1980. Pres. D.C. chpt. Bklyn. Coll. Alumni Assn., 1989; bd. dirs. Washington Urban League, 1978-84; bd. dirs., v.p., sec. Sumner Village Condominium, Bethesda, Md., 1988—; mem. Com. on Coms., Montgomery County, Md., 1991—; docent Nat. ARchives and Record Adminstrn., Phillips Collection, 1991—, instr. math. Project Apply, AAAS, 1991—. With U.S. Army, 1950-51. Grad. scholar Columbia U., 1950. Mem. Ops. Rsch. Soc. Am., Navy League U.S. (life), Cosmos Club. B'nai Brith, Phi Beta Kappa, Pi Mu Epsilon. Home: 4956 Sentinel Dr Bethesda MD 20816-3512

WERTHEIMER, LINDA, broadcaster. Grad. with distinction, Wellesley Coll., 1965. Congl. corr. Nat. Pub. Radio, Washington, 1971-76, polit. corr., 1976-89, host All Things Considered newsmag., 1989—. Recipient Alfred I. duPond-Columbia U. spl. citation, 1978, Corp. Pub. Broadcasting award, 1988. Office: Nat Pub Radio 2025 M St NW Washington DC 20036-3309*

WERTHEIMER, MARC JOEL, internist; b. Phila., July 15, 1949; m. Judy Okin; children: Joshua, Sarah. BA, Swarthmore Coll., 197l; MD, Jefferson Med. Coll., 1975. Diplomate Am. Bd. Internal Medicine. Intern Laukenau Hosp., Phila., 1975-76, resident in internal medicine, 1976-78; pvt. practice Media, Pa.; mem. staff Riddle Meml. Hosp.; mem. staff Riddle Meml. Hosp.; med. cons. A Better Chance, Swarthmore, Pa., Crozer-Chester Med. Ctr., 1987—. Mem. Pa. Med. Soc., Delaware County Med. Soc., Phi Beta Kappa, Alpha Omega Alpha. Office: Internal Medicine Assocs Chesley Dr Media PA 19063-1763

WERTLIEB, DONALD LAWRENCE, psychologist, educator; b. Washington, Feb. 22, 1952; s. Norman N. and Helen (Rubin) W.; m. Lorre Beth Polinger, Aug. 12, 1973; children: Joshua Michael, Mollie Rebecca, Miriam Tamar. BS in Psychology summa cum laude, Tufts U., 1974, MA in Child Study, 1975; MA in Psychology, Boston U., PhD in Clin. and Community Psychology, 1979. Instr. psychology Harvard U. Med. Sch., Boston, 1978-81, also staff psychologist Judge Baker Guidance Ctr., Boston, 1978-81; asst. prof. Eliot-Pearson dept. child study Tufts U., Medford, Mass., 1981-86, assoc. prof., 1986-89, chmn., 1989—, chmn. dept. edn. interim, 1990—; sr. rsch. assoc. Harvard U. Community Health Plan, Boston, 1981-87; mem. faculty Inst. for Health Rsch., Harvard Sch. Pub. Health, 1983-87; lectr. dept. social medicine and health policy, Harvard Med. Sch., 1984-89; cons. mental health svcs. Mem. editorial bd. Profl. Psychology, 1979-82, Jour. Applied Devel. Psychology, 1981—, Jour. Clin. Child Psychology, 1981—, Jour. Pediatric Psychology, 1986—. Carmichael prize scholar, 1973; NIMH tng. fellow, 1974-76; NIMH rsch. grantee, 1977-81, 83-86; Office Spl. Edn. tng. grantee, 1981-83; NIH Biomed. Rsch. grantee, 1982; W.T. Grant Found. grantee, 1982-86; lic. psychologist, Mass. Fellow Am. Orthopsychiat. Assn. Mem. Am. Psychol. Assn., Assn. Advancement Psychology, New Eng. Psychol. Assn., Mass. Psychol. Assn., Am. Psychol. Soc. (charter),

Boston Inst. Devel. Infants and Parents, Soc. Psychol. Study of Social Issues, Soc. Rsch. in Child Devel., Phi Beta Kappa, Psi Chi.

WESCHLER, ANITA, sculptor, painter; b. N.Y.C.; d. J. Charles and Hulda Eva (Mayer) W.; married. Exhibited Met. Mus., Mus. Modern Art, Art Inst. Chgo., Phila. Mus. Internat., Am. Acad., Inst. Arts and Letters, Bklyn. Mus., Newark Mus., Hofstra Mus., U. Conn., Carnegie Inst. Internat., Whitney Mus. Annuals, Storm King Art Ctr., mus. and galleries, throughout U.S.; represented in permanent collections U. Pa., Michael Wolfson Found., Miami, Fla., Met. Mus. Art, Syracuse U., Butler Art Inst., Whitney Mus., Norfolk Mus., Brandeis U., Amherst Coll., Yale U., Wichita State Mus., SUNY Binghamton, U. Iowa, U. Nebr., La Salle U., Pa. Acad. Fine Arts, U. Pa. Insts. for Achievement of Human Potential in Pa., Italy and Brazil, Art Students League; 3 one-man shows Stover Mill Gallery, Erwinna, Pa.; 13 one-man shows in N.Y.C., 12 group traveling shows, 30 one-man shows nationwide, 1964—; one-man shows include Birmingham (Ala.) Mus. Art, Main Library, Winston-Salem, N.C., U. Wis., Milw., del., U.S. Com. of Internat. Assn. Art, Fine Arts Fedn. N.Y., Miami Beach (Fla.) Art Ctr., Tel Fair Acad., Savanna, Ga., Columbia (S.C.) Mus., U. N.C., Chapel Hill, Suffolk Art Mus., Stony Brook, N.Y.; creator plastic resins and fiberglas as sculpture medium (bonded bronze), plastic resins and synthetic glazes as painting media; author: poetry book Nightshade, A Sculptors Summary. Recipient prizes Corcoran Gallery, San Francisco Mus., Am. Fedn. Arts Traveling Show, Montclair Art Mus.; fellow MacDowell Colony, Yaddo. Mem. Archtl. League, Sculptors Guild (past bd. dirs., treas.), Nat. Assn. Women Artists, Internat. Inst. Arts and Letters, Artist Craftsmen N.Y., Fedn. Modern Painters and Sculptors. Address: 136 Waverly Pl New York NY 10014

WESELOH, RONALD MACK, entomologist, researcher; b. L.A., June 30, 1944; s. Helmut and Ruth (Whitney) W.; m. Eleanor I. Helgert, Feb. 2, 1974. BS magna cum laude, Brigham Young U., 1966; PhD, U. Calif., Riverside, 1970. Asst. entomologist Conn. Agrl. Experiment Sta., New Haven, 1970-75, assoc. entomologist, 1975-81, entomologist, 1981—. Contbr. numerous articles to profl. jours. NSF fellow U. Calif., 1966-70; Magnum-Lewis scholar, 1962-66. Mem. Internat. Orgn. Biol. Control, Entomol. Soc. Am. (chmn. sect. C. 1981-82), Can. Entomol. Soc., Ecol. Soc. Am., Sigma Xi. Office: Conn Agrl Experiment Sta 123 Huntington St New Haven CT 06511-2000

WESELY, YOLANDA THEREZA, retired sociologist, marketing professional, researcher; b. São Paulo, Brazil, Nov. 9, 1927; came to U.S., 1946; d. Richard Milton and Etelvina (Pacheco E Silva) Pyles; m. Edwin Joseph Wesely, July 1, 1950; children: Marissa C., Adrienne Lee. BA in Math., Barnard Coll., 1950; MA in Sociology, Columbia U., 1968, PhD in Sociology with honors, 1975. CLU, 1984. With The Equitable, N.Y.C., 1974-76, dir. spl. studies, 1976-78, exec. asst. to chmn. and vice chmn. of the bd., 1978-79, dir. market research, 1979-84, asst. v.p. market rsch., 1984-88, ret.; cofounder Sociologists in Bus. Bd. dirs. Westchester Older Women's League, 1985—; vice chairperson bd. dirs. Union Theol. Sem., N.Y.C., 1980-88; bd. dirs. John Milton Soc. for the Blind, N.Y.C., 1986—; trustee Scarsdale Congl. Ch., 1989-91; dir. Westchester Civil Liberties Union, 1991. Mem. Am. Sociol. Assn., Older Women's League, Phi Beta Kappa. Democrat. Congregationalist. Home: Scarsdale Chateaux Scarsdale NY 10583

WESLAGER, CLINTON ALFRED, historian, writer; b. Pitts., Apr. 30, 1909; s. Fred H. and Alice (Lowe) W.; m. Ruth G. Hurst, June 9, 1934; children: Ruth Ann (Mrs. George G. Tatnall), Clinton Alfred, Thomas Hurst. B.A., U. Pitts., 1933; L.H.D. (hon.), Widener U., 1986. Vis. prof. Am. history Wesley Coll., 1969, U. Del., 1971-73; vis. prof. Am. history Brandywine Coll., 1970-82, prof. emeritus, 1983—; pres. Archeol. Soc. Del., 1942-48, Eastern States Archeol. Fedn., 1954-58. Author: Delaware's Forgotten Folk, 1943, Delaware's Buried Past, 1944, Delaware's Forgotten River, 1947, The Nanticoke Indians, 1948, Brandywine Springs, 1949, Indian Place-Names in Delaware, 1950, Red Men on the Brandywine, 1953, Richardsons of Delaware, 1957, Dutch Explorers, Traders and Settlers, 1961, Garrett Snuff Fortune, 1965, English on the Delaware, 1967, Log Cabin in America, 1969, The Delaware Indians, A History, 1972, Magic Medicines of the Indians, 1973, The Stamp Act Congress, 1976, The Delaware Indian Westward Migration, 1978, The Delawares, A Critical Bibliography, 1978, The Nanticoke Indians, Past and Present, 1983, Swedes and Dutch at New Castle, 1987, New Sweden on the Delaware, 1988, A Man and His Ship: Peter Minuit and the Kalmar Nyckel, 1990; editor: Historic Red Clay Valley, Inc, 1961-69. Pres. trustees Richardson Park Sch., 1953-57. Recipient Merit award Am. Assn. State and Local History, 1965, '68, Christian Lindback award for teaching excellence, 1977, Archibald Crozier award, Archeo. Soc. Del., 1978, Trustee award, Hist. Soc. Del., 1987, medal of Distinction, U. Del., 1988, History medal DAR, 1990, del Tufo award Del. Humanities Forum, 1991. Fellow Archeol. Soc. N.J., Holland Soc. N.Y.; mem. AAUP, Hist. Soc. Pa., Soc. Pa. Archaeology, Am. Name Soc., Dupont Country Club, Sigma Delta Chi. Lodge: Masons. Home: 859 Old Public Rd Hockessin DE 19707-9631

WESOLOWSKI, ANDRZEJ WITOLD, refrigeration engineer, consultant, researcher; b. Hrubieszow, Poland, July 14, 1942; came to U.S., 1988; s. Witold and Leokadia (Kowalska) W.; m. Maria Irene Kojtka, Sept. 22, 1967; children: Monika Barbara, Agnieszka Alicja. MSc, Tech. U., Poland, 1969; BS, U. Torun, Poland, 1986; doctoral student, Tech. U., Warsaw. Registered profl. engr. Chief engr. Factory of Refrigerating Equip., Bydgoszcz, Poland, 1969-74; cheif engr. Rsch. and Devel. Ctr. for Refrigeration Catering Equipment, Bydgoszcz, Poland, 1974-82; lectr., sci. researcher Acad. Tech. and Agr., Bydgoszcz, Poland, 1983; asst. prof., div. head Rsch. and Devel. Ctr. Refrigeration and Catering Equipment, Bydgoszcz, Poland, 1984-88; chief engr. Jade Refrigeration Inc., Vernon, Calif., 1989, Foster Refrigeration Corp., Hudson, N.Y., 1989-91; sr. engr. Carrier Corp., Syracuse, N.Y., 1991—; cons. engr. Assn. Sci. and Tech., Bydgoszcz, 1969—; refrigeration systems cons. United Nation Indsl. Devel. Org., Vienna, Austria, 1990—. Author: Refrigerating and Cryogenic Machines and Their Heat Testing, 1980, Automatic Regulation of Refrigerating Equipment, 1984; author 13 papers, 35 articles; 27 patents in field. Pres. Assn. Sci. and Tech. Refrigeration and Heat Transfer Section, Bydgoszcz, 1978-87. Mem. Orgn. Tech. Engring., Am. Soc. Heating Refrigerating and Air Conditioning Engrs. Inc. (corres. mem., tech. com.). Roman Catholic. Office: Carrier Corp Carrier Pkwy PO Box 4808 Syracuse NY 13221

WESOLOWSKI, CINDY LEE, financial executive; b. Balt., Oct. 5, 1960; d. Stanley Clifford and Anna Mae (Parlett) Thomas; m. Randall Michael Wesolowski, June 24, 1978. BBA summa cum laude, Loyola Coll., 1986. CPA, Md. Acct., clk. Genstar Stone Products Co., Hunt Valley, Md., 1978-84, acctg. supr., 1984-87; controller Am. Stone Mix, Inc., Towson, Md., 1987; controller, chief fin. officer Omega Acquisition Corp., Hampstead, Md., 1989-91, v.p., 1991—. Mem. Am. Legion Aux., Perry Hall, Md., 1981—. Mem. AICPAs, Md. Assn. CPAs (Vol. Svc. award 1990, 91), Alpha Sigma Nu. Republican. Office: Omega Acquisition Corp PO Box 2078 Westminster MD 21158

WESOLOWSKI, PAUL G., publisher; b. Phila., Oct. 2, 1956; s. Leonard V. and Valerie W.;. BS, St. Joseph's U., Phila., 1978; MBA, Temple U., 1980; D. Letters, SUNY, Fredonia, 1990. CPA, Pa. Controller Fredonia Gazette, Drexel Hill, Pa., 1978-84, editor-in-chief, 1980-84; pubr. Fredonia Gazette, New Hope, Pa., 1984—; bd. dirs. Marx Bros. Study Unit, New Hope, Pa. Cons. documentary film: Marx Bros. in a Nutshell, 1978; researcher books: Groucho, 1980, Growing Up with Chico, 1980. Recipient Neal E. Gorman award The Design Inst., 1982. Mem. Marx Brotherhood (hon. mem.). Republican. Roman Catholic. Office: Marx Bros Study Unit Darien 28 New Hope PA 18938

WESOLOWSKI, SYLVIA MOLENDA, counselor; b. Checktowaga, N.Y., Jan. 19, 1948; d. Constantine Stanley and Florence Mary (Homa) Molenda; m. Thomas Lockwood Rumsey, June, 1969 (div. Jan. 1977); m. Richard James Wesolowski, July 31, 1976; children: Michael, Kenneth, Daniel. BS, SUNY, Buffalo, 1970; MS, SUNY Coll., Buffalo, 1976; MEd, SUNY Coll., Brockport, 1989. Occupational therapist Children's Rehab. Ctr., Buffalo, 1970-71; chief occupational therapist United Cerebral Palsy Assn., Buffalo, 1972-73; asst. prof. health scis. SUNY, Buffalo, 1974-77; occupational therapy cons. Bd. Coop. Edn., Leicester, N.Y., 1977; occupational therapist United Cerebral Palsy Assn., Rochester, N.Y., 1978-79; counselor Cath. Family Ctr., Rochester, 1989-90; project supr. Rochester Rehab. Ctr., 1989-92, coord. employment svcs., 1992—; supr. Rochester Rehab. Ctr., 1989—; cons. Cayuga Heights Elem. Sch., Depew, N.Y., 1975, West Seneca (N.Y.) Devel. Ctr., 1977, Child Find, Bd. Coop. Ednl. Svcs., Leicester, 1978-79. Co-founder, mem. Fairport (N.Y.) Coun. on the Disabled, 1985-86; sch. bd. liaison AAUW, Fairport, 1986-87; mem. adv. bd. Rochester Brain Injury Assn. Mem. AACD, Am. Rehab. Counseling Assn., N.Y.S. Assn. Counseling and Devel., N.Y. Rehab. Counselors Assn., N.Y. State Mental Health Counselor Assn. Roman Catholic. Home: 24 Meadow Cove Rd Pittsford NY 14534-3351 Office: Rochester Rehab Ctr 46 Mt Hope Ave Rochester NY 14620-1015

WESOLY, LORRIE PAULETTE, vocalist, composer; b. L.I., N.Y., Sept. 19, 1954; d. Paul John and Marion Marcella (Schultz) W. BA in Music and Drama, Marymount Coll., 1976; cert. alcohol and drug counseling, No. Essex Community Coll., 1991. Bookstore mgr. Follett Coll. Bookstores, Westborough, Mass., 1985-89; chem. dependency counselor Community Health Svcs., Hartford, Conn., 1991; support svcs. coord. Hartford region YWCA, 1991—; vocalist, composer Night Vision Prodns., Inc., Southington, Conn., 1987—; benefit performer AIDS Project Worcester, Mass., 1989-90, Take Back the Night, Manchester, N.H., Worcester, 1989-90, AIDS Project Hartford, AIDS Response to the Seacoast, Portsmouth, N.H., AIDS Action Com., Boston, 1990-91, Touch of Love, West Hartford, Conn., 1991-92. Vocalist: (cassette-album) WES, 1988; composer, vocalist: (cassette) Tidal Waves/Touch of Love, 1989; vocalist, performer (cassette-album) WES-Live at Nicks, 1991; producer, composer, performer: (ednl. AIDS music video) Tidal Waves, 1992. Vice pres. programming Sober in the Sun, 1991-92; bd. dirs. touch of Love/Pediatric AIDS Orgn., Conn., 1991-92; adv. bd. Women's Recovery Network, 1990-92. Recipient Certs. of Achievement, Billboard Songs-2d Ann., Tulsa, 1989, Billboard Songs-3d Ann., Tulsa, 1990, AIDS Action Com., Boston, 1990, Spl. Svc. award Women in Touch, Nashua, N.H., 1990. Democrat. Home: 158 Meriden Ave Southington CT 06489 Office: Night Vision Prodns Inc PO Box 383 Southington CT 06489

WESSEL, THOMAS MARK, human resources executive; b. Pitts., Aug. 23, 1956; s. Thomas Edward and Helen Rosalyn (Yurinko) W. BS, Drexel U., 1980; MA, New Sch. Rsch., 1988. Analyst Hay Assocs., Phila., 1977-79, UGI Corp., Phila., 1980-81, Sperry Corp., N.Y.C., 1982-84; mgr. compensation Standard and Poor's, N.Y.C., 1984-89; dir. compensation John Wiley and Sons, Inc., N.Y.C., 1989—. Mem. Am. Compensation Assn. Republican. Roman Catholic. Home: PO Box 1195 New York NY 10011 Office: John Wiley and Sons Inc 605 Third Ave New York NY 10158

WESSER, YVONNE DOREEN, artist; b. London, Eng., Jan. 28, 1935; m. David R. Wesser (div.); children: Marius Charles Sebastian, Pavelle Garance Alethia. BA in Religion, CUNY, 1991. One-woman shows include Main St. Gallery, Brewster, N.Y., 1975, Little Carnegie Art Gallery, N.Y.C., 1980, 34th St. Theatre Gallery, N.Y.C., 1980, Lida Gallery, N.Y.C., 1982, Gallery 84, N.Y.C., 1984, 85, Discovery Art Gallery, Glen Cove, N.Y., 1987, Plaza Gallery, City Hall Bldg., Binghampton, N.Y., 1987, Stehle-Rd. Gallery, Midland, Tex., 1987, Pleiades Gallery, N.Y.C., 1991; exhibited in group shows at Galeria Mesa, Ariz., 1988, Schoharie County Arts Coun., Cobbleskill, N.Y., Cen. Mo. State Univ. Art Ctr. Gallery, Warrensburg, 1989, Viridian Gallery, N.Y.C., 1990, Columbus (Ohio) Art Gallery, 1991, Jacob Javits Fed. Bldg., N.Y.C., 1991, Multi Media Gallery, N.Y.C., 1991, The Corner Gallery, N.Y.C., 1991, Broadway Mall Gallery, N.Y.C., 1991; represented in permanent collections including Barky Hosp., Saigon, Vietnam, Art Students League, N.Y.C., Nat. Art Mus. of Sport U. New Haven, West Haven, Conn.; commns. include for Barsky Hosp., John Disiere, Larry Freed. Mem. Whitney Mus., Mus. Modern Art, Burr Artists. Recipient Elmer Perkin award Mus. Modern Art, N.Y.C., 1986, Juror's Merit award Alexandria Mus., N.Y.C., 1986, 2d prize Mus. of Contemporary Art, L.A., 1989, 1st prize Whitney Mus., N.Y.C., 1987. Mem. Nat. Assn. Women's Pen League, Visual Individualists United, N.Y. Acad. Sci. Roman Catholic. Home: 12 E 86th St Apt 1631 New York NY 10028-0517

WESSON, ROBERT MICHAEL, company executive, consultant; b. Lynn, Mass., Jan. 13, 1935; s. Charles Henry and Helen (Hogan) W.; m. Michelle Long, Feb. 20, 1982; children: Robert MichaelJr. , Kerry Ann. B.A., Merrimack Coll., 1956, LL.D., 1980; M.A., Villanova U., 1961; M.A., Augustinian Coll., 1962. Asst. prof. Merrimack Coll., North Andover, Mass., 1962-68, Villanova U., Pa., 1968-79; v.p., pres. The Augustinians, Villanova, 1971-81; pres. Pandick SE, Inc., Arlington, Va., 1981-90; CEO, sr. v.p. Bowne of D.C., Washington, 1990—. Trustee Biscayne Coll., 1975-81, Villanova U., 1977-81, Merrimack Coll., 1975-81. Named Outstanding Man of Yr., Jr. C. of C., 1970. Mem. Westwood Country Club (pres. Vienna chpt.). Democrat. Roman Catholic. Lodge: KC (Arlington, Va.). Avocations: American history, politics, sports, reading. Home: 1631 Montmorency Dr Vienna VA 22182-2022 Office: 1341 G St Washington DC 20005

WEST, ALAN IRVING, business manager; b. Lawrence, Mass., Jan. 10, 1948; s. Howard A. and Mildred J. (Lee) W.; m. Katherine S. Shick, Sept. 11, 1981; 1 child, Zachary M. BS, Brown U., 1970; MS, Tufts U., 1978. Metallurgist Pratt & Whitney, Hartford, Mass., 1970-72; tchr. Shelburne (Vt.) Mid. Sch., 1972-75, Andover (Mass.) High Sch., 1975-77; project engr. Codman, Randolph, Mass., 1978-80; product mgr. Advanced Mech. Tech., Newton, Mass., 1980-82; v.p. rsch. and devel. Boston Sci., Watertown, Mass., 1982-90; bus. mgr. Vision Scis., Natick, Mass., 1990—; chmn. SPIE Conf., L.A., 1988-90; teaching fellow Tufts U., Medford, Mass., 1976-78. Editor Microsensors and Imaging, 1988-90; contbr. articles to profl. jours. Mem. Sigma Xi. Home: 223 Winter St Hopkinton MA 01748-2005 Office: Vision Scis 6 Strathmore Rd Natick MA 01760-2419

WEST, DOE, civil rights activist; b. Tucson, July 14, 1951; d. George Oliver and Dorothy Marie (Watson) W.; m. Bruce Malcolm Gale, Feb. 1, 1980. AA with honors, Dutchess Community Coll., 1975; BS magna cum laude, SUNY, New Paltz, 1977; BA, Logos Bible Coll., 1986; MS, Boston U., 1980; postgrad., Northeastern U., 1990—. Ordained minister. Dir. 504, compliance officer dept. health and hosps. City of Boston, 1979-81, commr. handicap affairs, 1981-84; pres. Myth Breakers, Inc., 1984—; writer, photographer, 1982—; author, pub. speaker, pvt. psychotherapist; lectr. Northeastern U., Mass. Bay Community Coll.; dir. chaplaincy svcs. Quincy (Mass.) Hosp., 1991-92; chief of staff State House Boston, 1992—.

WEST, JOHN H(ENRY), III, clergyman, educator; b. Moorestown, N.J., 1954; s. John Henry Jr. and Gwendolyn (Clark) W.; m. Patricia Lynn Murray. BA in History, Lincoln (Pa.) U., 1976; MDiv, Pitts. Theol. Sem., 1979. Assoc. pastor Martin Luther King Jr. Meml. Bapt. Ch., Pitts., 1977-78, Cornerstone Bapt. Ch., Pitts., 1978-79; chaplain, intern John J. Kane Hosp., Pitts., 1978-79; chaplain Lincoln U., 1979—, instr. religion, 1981-84, asst. prof., 1984—, chair dept. religion, 1984—; pres. West Inspirational Network, Lincoln Univ., 1988—. Bd. dirs. Downtown (Pa.) Indsl. and Agrl. Sch., 1989; bd. dirs., v.p. Lincoln Community Assn. Mem. Am. Bapt. Chs., U.S.A., Nat. Bapt. Chs., U.S.A., Inc., Oxford Area Ministerium, Ministeries to Blacks in Higher Edn., Soc. Bibl. Lit., So. Chester County NAACP. Democrat. Home: PO Box 59 Lincoln University PA 19352-0059 Office: Lincoln U Campus Box 44 Lincoln University PA 19352

WEST, LEONARD J., retired education educator, consultant, writer; b. N.Y.C., Apr. 29, 1921; m. Doris L. Kaplan, July 29, 1948; children: Kenneth D., Erica A., Nicole E. BBA, CCNY, 1941; MA, Columbia U., 1948, PhD, 1953. Tchr. N.Y.C. High Schs., 1946-52; rsch. psychologist Air Force Pers. and Tng. Rsch. Ctr., Chanute AFB, Ill., 1953-57; assoc. prof. So. Ill. U., Carbondale, 1957-64; rsch. asst. div. tchr. edn. CUNY, 1950-52, prof. edn. rsch., 1964-74, prof. edn. Baruch Coll., 1974-90; ret., 1990; adj. prof. Tchrs. Coll., Columbia U., N.Y.C., 1964-70; cons. Perceptual Devel. Labs., St. Louis, 1960-62, Ill. Bell Telephone Co., Chgo., 1964, N.Y.-New Eng. Bell Telephone and AT&T, N.Y.C., Boston, 1969-77. Author: Acquisition of Typewriting Skills, 1969, 2d edit., 1983, Modern College Typewriting, 1979, Keyboarding/Typewriting: Employment Applications, 1990; cons. editor Jour. Edn. for Bus., 1980—; also numerous articles. Sgt. U.S. Army, 1942-46. Recipient John Robert Gregg award McGraw-Hill Book Co., 1987. Mem. APA, Am. Ednl. Rsch. Assn., Nat. Bus. Edn. Assn., Phi Delta Kappa, Delta Pi Epsilon. Home: 89 Sandy Hollow Rd Port Washington NY 11050-2532

WEST, MARVIN LEON, sports editor; b. Knoxville, May 1, 1934; s. Alvin Leon and Alma Oneta (Bishop) W.; m. Sarah Jane Blackburn, July 24, 1954; children: Michael, Gary, Jayne, Donna. BA in Journalism, U. Tenn., 1955. Sports writer Knoxville News-Sentinel, Tenn., 1955-80, sports editor, 1980-83, mng. editor, 1983-85; nat. sports editor Scripps Howard News Service, Washington, 1985—. Named Sportswriter of Yr., Tenn. Nat. Broadcasters and Sports Writers Assn., Salisbury, N.C., 1967, 1974. Mem. U.S. Basketball Writers Assn. (pres. 1983-84). Presbyterian. Home: PO Box 327 Mount Vernon VA 22121-0327 Office: Scripps Howard News Svc 1090 Vermont Ave NW Washington DC 20005-4905

WEST, MARYANNE, psychologist; b. Boston; d. Kenneth Paul and Mary (Gately) W. AB, Boston Coll., MEd; EdD, Boston U., 1989. Cert. sch. psychologist; cert. elem. sch. prin., supr., spl. edn. tchr., elem. tchr.; lic. cert. social worker, Mass. Psychologist Boston Sch. System, 1976-91; asst. dir. psychol. svcs. Boston Pub. Schs., 1991—. Mem. World Affairs Coun., Boston. Mem. Am. Psychol. Assn., Nat. Assn. of Sch. Psychologists, Mass. Speech and Hearing Found., Oyster Harbors Club, Phi Delta Kappa, Pi Lambda Theta. Roman Catholic. Home: 25 Greycliff Rd Brighton MA 02135-3103 Office: Boston Pub Schs 26 Court St Boston MA 02108-2505

WEST, MICHAEL GORDON, industry analyst; b. San Francisco, Nov. 10, 1947; s. Gordon Hill and Lucille Claire (O'Sullivan) W.; m. Cynthia Sue Woods, Aug. 28, 1982; 1 child, Christopher Patrick. AB in Polit. Sci., Williams Coll., 1969; MA in Writing, Johns Hopkins U., 1973; postgrad., Am. Univ., 1973-75; MBA in Strategic Mgmt., Boston Coll., 1988. Researcher Interpub. Group, N.Y.C., 1969-70; cons. NEH, Washington, 1975, Robert Snyder Prodns., Westwood, Calif., 1975-76; lectr. Northeastern U., Boston, 1976-79; educator Martha's Vineyard, Mass., 1980-81; programmer, mgr. dir. data adminstrn. John Hancock, Boston, 1981-86; mgr. Fidelity Investments, Boston, 1986-88; sr. mgr. Apple Computer, Cupertino, Calif., 1988-91; program dir. software engring. strategies Gartner Group, Stamford, Conn., 1991—; lectr. MBA program sch. mgmt. Boston Coll., 1988. Author: (book) Wire Wind, 1970, Eye Quilt, 1971, Roger Wilcoe, 1974, (play) Tivoli, 1980; editor: (jour.) Island, 1980-81. Mem. Jr. Achievement, Boston, 1983; vol. Lindsay for Mayor, N.Y.C., 1969, Harris for Pres., Boston. Mem. IEEE, Assn. for Computing Machinery, Boston Data Adminstrn. Mgmt. Assn. (founder, pres. 1986-88), Boston Computer Soc., Soc. for Info. Mgmt., Nat. Writers Union, Dramatists Guild, Amnesty Internat. Home: 24 Thomes St Rowayton CT 06853 Office: Gartner Group 56 Top Gallant Rd Stamford CT 06904

WEST, PETER DONALD, artist, educator, consultant; b. Washington, Pa., July 14, 1953; s. Donald Peter and Helen Muriel (Roth) W.; m. Elizabeth Lee Brown, Jan. 25, 1980. BFA, Temple U., 1975; MFA, Ohio U., 1977. Artist-in-residence Pa. Coun. on the Arts/Trinity High Sch., Washington, 1979-81; asst. prof. Bethany (W.Va.) Coll., 1981-84; lectr., cons. Learn Shops/Badger Air Brush Co., Franklin Park, Ill., 1984—; gallery artist Gallery G., Pitts., 1980-91, Foster Goldstrom Gallery, N.Y.C., 1990-91. Author: Airbrushing, Tools, Techniques and Materials, 1986; inventor airbrush guidance system. Recipient award Buncher Family Found., 1990, achievement award for excellence in acrylic Am. Artist mag., 1992; resident artist grantee Pa. Coun. on Arts, 1980, fellow, 1992. Mem. Assoc. Artists Pitts., Pitts. Ctr. for Arts, Grap A. Roman Catholic. Home and Studio: RD 2 Box 294 West Alexander PA 15376

WEST, STEPHEN FRANCIS, mathematics educator; b. Oswego, N.Y., Nov. 29, 1946; s. Emmett J. and Louise Wheeler (Johnson) W.; m. Kristine Elizabeth Metroka, Jan. 28, 1967; children: Michelle, Jennifer, Holly, Stephen J. BS, SUNY, Oswego, 1968; MST, Rutgers U., 1974; PhD, U. Tex., 1979. Tchr. math. Pulaski (N.Y.) Acad., 1968-79; asst. instr. U. Tex., Austin, 1976-78; assoc. prof. SUNY, Geneseo, 1979—; speaker in field. Author: Roads to Geometry, 1991; contbr. articles to profl. jours. Recipient Chancellor's Excellence in Teaching award SUNY, 1991. Mem. Math. Assn. Am., Nat. Coun. Tchrs. Maths., Assn. Math. Tchrs. N.Y. State (pres. 1988-89, jour. editor 1991—). Home: 17 Maryknoll Cir Livonia NY 14487-9729 Office: SUNY Math Dept Geneseo NY 14454

WEST, WARREN HENRY, securities trader; b. Chgo., Sept. 18, 1956; s. Wiley and Naomi (Coleman) W.; m. Laraine Capobianco, Feb. 23, 1985; children: Jake, Lee. V.p. Drexel Burnham Lambert, N.Y.C., 1981-83; pres. Strategic Investors Inc., Phila., 1983—. Trustee Betse Nemser Fund, Cherry Hill, N.J., 1989. Mem. Phila. Stock Exchange (mktg. com. 1982-84, options com. 1988-89). Unitarian.

WESTBROOK, NICHOLAS KILMER, museum administrator, historian; b. Boston, July 10, 1948; s. Jack Hall and Elizabeth (Kirkland) W.; m. Virginia Lee Macleod, June 12, 1971; children: Benjamin Macoun, Samuel Farley. AB cum laude, Amherst Coll., 1971; MA, U. Conn., 1973; postgrad., U. Pa., 1973-76. Seasonal ranger-historian Nat. Park Svc., Stillwater, N.Y., 1969-71; asst. to v.p. for interpretation Old Sturbridge Village, Sturbridge, Mass., 1972-75; ednl. materials developer Uni-Coll Corp., Phila., 1975-76; exhibits coord. Minn. Hist. Soc., St. Paul, 1976-78, curator of exhibits, 1978-88; exec. dir. Ft. Ticonderoga, Ticonderoga, N.Y., 1989—; panelist NEH, Washington, 1985—, Inst. Mus. Scis., Washington, 1991—. Editor: Industrial Archeology of the Twin Cities, 1983, Bull. Ft. Ticonderoga Mus., 1991—; book rev. editor Indsl. Archeology, 1983-89; curator several exhibits. Trustee Fedn. for Hist. Svcs., 1990—. Winston Churchill travelling fellow, Gt. Britain, 1981. Mem. Soc. for Indsl. Archeology (bd. dirs. 1983-85, sec. 1986-91), Am. Assn. for State and Local History, Am. Assn. Museums, Soc. for Indsl. Archeology, Soc. for History of Tech., Am. Printing History Assn., Ticonderoga C. of C. (v.p. 1989—), Kiwanis. Presbyterian. Home: Creek Rd Box 8 Crown Point NY 12928 Office: Ft Ticonderoga Fort Rd Ticonderoga NY 12883

WESTCOTT, JEFFREY HOWARD, telecommunications manager; b. North Tonawanda, N.Y., Mar. 6, 1956; s. Paul W. and Barbara H. (Milliman) W.; m. Katherine A. Wein, Jan. 5, 1980; children: Jonathan D., Carolyn A. BS, SUNY, Fredonia, 1978; postgrad., Villanova U., 1978-81. Programmer Sperry Univac, Blue Bell, Pa., 1978-81; systems analyst Sperry, Buffalo, 1981-82, specialist-presales, 1982-84; sr. systems analyst Graphic Controls Corp., Buffalo, 1984-85, sr. info. ctr. cons., 1985-89, mgr. telecommunications, 1989—; instr. North Tonawanda (N.Y.) Community Edn., 1986-88. Dist. commr. Boy Scouts Am., Greater Niagara Frontier Coun., 1991—, asst. dist. commr., 1989-91; v.p. Nine Mile Island Youth Camp, Inc., Amherst, N.Y., 1988—. Recipient Dist. award of merit Polaris Dist. GNFC, Boy Scouts Am., 1991. Mem. Western N.Y., SL1 Users Assn. (bd. dirs. 1990-91). Office: Graphic Controls Corp 189 Van Rensselaer St Buffalo NY 14210-1345

WESTCOTT, KATHLEEN MOTEL, alcoholism counselor; b. New Brunswick, N.J., Nov. 8, 1960; d. Theodore Robert and Jean Marie (Olaski) Motel; m. David A. Westcott, Aug. 16, 1986. BA, U. Denver, 1983; MS, U. Scranton, 1990. Cert. alcoholism counselor, N.Y. Compensation analyst E. F. Hutton, Inc., N.Y.C., 1984-85; benefits asst. Midlantic Nat. Bank, Edison, N.J., 1985-86; grad. asst. U. Scranton (Pa.), 1987-89; alcoholism counseling intern Alcoholism Ctr. Broome County, Binghamton, N.Y., 1989; alcoholism counselor Vol. Family Counseling Svcs., Cortland, N.Y., 1989—. Recipient Hornbeck Scholar award, U. Denver, 1982. Mem. AACD, Assn. Specialists Group Work, Golden Key Nat. Honor Soc. Office: Vol Family Counseling Svcs 10 N Main St Cortland NY 13045-2171

WESTCOTT, RUSSELL THRASHER, management consultant, quality improvement; b. Boston, Mar. 12, 1927; s. Earl Russell and Esther (Thrasher) W.; m. Jeanne Marie Couture, June 11, 1949; children: Edward Allan, Linda Marie. BBA in Indsl. Mgmt., Boston U., 1952. Data processing mgmt. Gen. Elec. Co., Mass., Va., N.Y., Conn., 1952-65; data processing mgr. C.I.T. Fin., N.Y.C., 1965-67; cons. Systems Group of TRW, Redondo Beach, Calif., 1967-69, Consol. Edison of N.Y.C., 1969-73; dir. human resources Consol. Edison of N.Y.C., White Plains, N.Y., 1973-80; pres., owner R.T. Westcott & Assocs., Old Saybrook, Conn., 1979—; pres., co-owner Offerjost-Westcott Group, Old Saybrook, Conn., 1990—. Author: Human resource Management and Development Handbook, 1985. Recipient Pres. award Data Processing Mgmt. Assn., Stamford, Conn., 1965, Am. Soc. for Training & Devel., Southern Conn. Chpt., 1982-83. Mem. ASTD, Nat. Soc. for Performance & Instrn. (treas. Fairchester chpt.), Am. Soc. for

Quality Control, Bus. Adv. Resources, Stamford Mineral Soc., Old Saybrook (Conn.) C. of C. (dir. 1989-91, treas. 1991—). Home: 10 Cricket Ct Old Saybrook CT 06475-2406 Office: RT Westcott & Assoc 263 Main St Old Saybrook CT 06475-2326

WESTERBERG, ARTHUR WILLIAM, chemical engineering educator; b. St. Paul, Oct. 9, 1938; s. Kenneth Waldorf and Marjorie Claire (Darling) W.; m. Barbara Ann Dyson, July 14, 1963; children: Kenneth, Karl. B.S., U. Minn., 1960; M.S., Princeton U., 1961; Ph.D., Imperial Coll., London, 1964. Pres. Farm Engring. Sales Inc., Savage, Minn., 1964-65; sr. analyst Control Data Corp., San Diego, Calif., 1965-67; asst. prof., assoc. prof., prof. U. Fla., Gainesville, 1967-76; prof. chem. engring. Carnegie-Mellon U., Pitts., 1976—, chmn. dept., 1980-83, Swearingen prof., 1982—, dir. Design Research Ctr., 1978-80; dir. Engring. Design Research Ctr., 1986-89. Co-author: Process Flowsheeting, 1979. Mem. NAE, Am. Inst. Chem. Engrs. (lectr. 1989, Computers and Systems Tech. div. award 1983, Walker award 1987, McAfee award 1990), Am. Soc. Engring. Edn. (chem. engring. div. lectr. 1981). Home: 5564 Beacon St Pittsburgh PA 15217-1972 Office: Carnegie-Mellon U Pittsburgh PA 15213

WESTERFIELD, CAROLYN ELIZABETH HESS, city planner; b. New Haven, Conn., May 3, 1933; d. Orvan Walter and Carol Woodruff (Maurer) Hess; m. Holt Bradford Westerfield, Dec. 17, 1960; children: Pamela Bradford, Leland Avery. BA, Wellesley Coll., 1954; postgrad., Yale U., 1954-55, M of City Planning, 1959. Planner, officer mgr. Tech. Planning Assocs., New Haven, Conn., 1955-57, 61-62; assoc. planner City Plan Dept., New Haven, Conn., 1956-59; planner, editor State of Conn. Devel. Commn., 1959-61; cons., 1962—; prin. planner South Cen. Conn. Planning Region, 1979-87; asst. plan dir. Town of Fairfield (Conn.), 1987; planning and zoning adminstr. Town of North Branford (Conn.), 1987-89; devel. vol. programs New Haven Hosp.-Boston City Hosp., 1952-54; del. Assn. Yale Alumni, New Haven, 1969-76, mem., 1969—; alumni bd. Yale U. Sch. Architecture, 1964-76, 85—; lectr. city planning U. New Haven, 1988—. Bd. dirs. Alumni Orgns. Prospect Hill Sch., New Haven, St. Thomas Day Sch., Wellesley Coll. (class officer), Econ. Devel. Commn. Consortium, Hamden, Conn., Design Review Com. clk., Ethics Commn., Conn Child Welfare Assn. Mem. Am. Planning Assn., Am. Inst. Cert. Planners, Conn. Women in Planning & Devel. (co-chmn. program 1987-89, co-chmn. future of Comm. 1989-91), New Haven Colony Hist. Soc., Jr. League New Haven (various exec. positions), Watch Hill Improvement Soc. (pres. 1971-73), Yale U. Womens Orgn. (various exec. positions). Home and office: 115 Rogers Rd Hamden CT 06517-3533

WESTERMAN, JEWELL G., management consultant; b. Malvern, Ark., June 28, 1934; s. Jewell A. and Evelyn (Hunnicut) W.; m. Cassandra Clark, Oct. 14, 1961; children: Amy E., Douglas Clark. BA in Econs. and Psychology, Henderson State U., 1956. V.p. Mitchell & Co., Cambridge, Mass., 1978-81, Mercer Mgmt. Cons., Lexington, Mass., 1981—; adv. bd. Russell Gibson Von Dolen Architects, Hartford, Conn., 1976—, Pioneer Med. Systems, Bedford, Mass., 1988—. Researcher on job enrichment, Library of Congress, 1971. Recipient Presdl. citation (locating jobs for Vietnam vets.), Washington, 1977. Mem. Assn. Internal Mgmt. Cons. (dir. 1990—), Assn. Mgmt. of Organization Design (dir. 1989—), Wellesley Country Club, Wellesley Club, Eastward Ho! Country Club. Republican. Congregationalist. Home: 330 Sea Pine Rd North Chatham MA 02650-1078 Office: Mercer Mgmt Cons 33 Hayden Ave Lexington MA 02173-7934

WESTFRIED, ALEX HUXLEY, anthropology and sociology educator, researcher; b. N.Y.C., Dec. 17, 1919; s. Ernest and Yvonne (Mason) W.; m. Caroline Tears, Apr. 20, 1968 (div. Feb. 1990); children: Eric, Maria; m. Maria Betania Guaranys, July 24, 1990. BA, Williams Coll., 1943; MA in Internat. Rels., U. Pa., 1957; PhD in Social Sci., U. Syracuse, N.Y., 1978. Internat. trade economist U.S. Dept. Commerce, Washington, 1957-58; asst. to pres. Huxley-Westfried Corp., N.Y.C., 1959-62; collaborator books on Mid. East Human Rels. Area Files, Washington, 1958; tchr. social sci. Friends Cen. High Sch., Phila., 1962-67; prof. Western Conn. State U., Danbury, 1967-92, prof. emeritus, 1992—; presenter video on Brazil, Syracuse U., 1987; lectr. N.E. Anthropol. Assn., Mont., Que., Can., 1988; cons. Office of Pastoral Rsch., Archdiocese of N.Y., N.Y.C., 1982; workshop presenter teaching multi-cultural students Danbury High Sch., 1991. Author: Three Puerto Rican Families, 1985; writer, collaborator: Jordan, 1959; dir., editor (video) Racial Democracy in Brazil, 1985. Bd. dirs. Spanish Learning Soc., Danbury, 1980-81. Penfield fellow U. Pa., 1955-56; U.S. Dept. of Def. grantee Bucknell U., 1965, NEH, 1981, Western Conn. State U. grantee, 1985, 86. Fellow Am. Anthropol. Assn.; mem. Am. Sociol. Assn., Northeastern Anthropol. Assn. (contbr.), Clin. Sociol. Assn., Humanist Soc. Democrat. Home: PO Box 97 Southbury CT 06488-0097

WESTHEIMER, FRANK HENRY, chemist, educator; b. Balt., Jan. 15, 1912; s. Henry Ferdinand and Carrie (Burgunder) W.; m. Jeanne Friedmann, Aug. 31, 1937; children: Ruth Susan, Ellen. AB, Dartmouth Coll., 1932, ScD (hon.), 1961; MA, Harvard U., 1933, PhD, 1935; ScD (hon.), U. Chgo., 1973, U. Cin., 1976, Tufts U., 1978, U. N.C., 1983, Bard Coll., 1983, Weizmann Inst., 1987, U. Ill. at Chgo., 1988. Rsch. assoc. U. Chgo., 1936-37, asst. prof., 1941-44, assoc. prof., 1946-48, prof. chemistry, 1948-53; vis. prof. Harvard U., 1953-54, prof. chemistry, 1954-83, prof. emeritus, 1983—, chmn. dept., 1959-62; Overseas fellow Churchill Coll., U. Cambridge, Eng., 1962-63; mem. Pres.'s Sci. Adv. Com., 1967-70; research supr. Explosives Research Lab., Nat. Def. Research Com., 1944-45; chmn. com. survey chemistry Nat. Acad. Scis., 1964-65. Assoc. editor Jour. Chem. Physics, 1942-44, 52-54; editorial bd. Jour. Am. Chem. Soc., 1960-69, Procs. Nat. Acad. Scis., 1983-89; contbr. articles to profl. jours. Recipient Naval Ordnance Development award, 1946, Army-Navy cert. of appreciation, 1946, James Flack Norris award in phys.-organic chemistry, 1970, Willard Gibbs medal, 1970, Theodore W. Richards medal, 1976; award in chem. scis. Nat. Acad. Sci., 1980, Richard Kokes award, 1980, Charles Frederick Chandler medal, 1980, Rosenstiel award, 1981, Nichols medal, 1982, Robert A. Welch award, 1982, Ingold medal, 1983, Cope award, 1982, Nat. Medal of Sci., 1986, Paracelsus medal, 1988, Priestley medal, 1988; fellow Columbia U. NRC, 1935-36, Guggenheim Found., 1962-63, Fulbright-Hays Found., 1974; Repligen award, 1992. Mem. Nat. Acad. Sci. (council 1971-75, 76-79), Am. Philos. Soc. (council 1981-84), Am. Acad. Arts and Scis. (sec. 1985-90), Royal Soc. (fgn. mem.). Home: 3 Berkeley St Cambridge MA 02138-3409

WESTLEY, JOHN WILLIAM, research chemist; b. Cambridge, Eng., Feb. 5, 1936; came to U.S., 1961; s. Harold Sidney and Daisy Victoria (Sorrel) W.; divorced; children: Nicholas John, Peter Miles. BSc, Nottingham, Eng., 1958, PhD, 1961. Rsch. scientist Stanford U., Palo Alto, Calif., 1961-78; asst. dir. Hoffmann-LaRoche, Nutley, N.J., 1968-85; assoc. dir. Smithkline Beecham, Phila., 1985—; ACS lectr. U. Wis., Madison. Editor: Polyether Antibiotics, vol. I and II, 1983, Naturally Occuring Inonophores; mem. editorial bd. Jour. Antibiotics, 1982—; contbr. numerous articles to profl. jours. Mem. AAAS, Am. Chem. Soc., Am. Soc. Pharmacognosy. Episcopalian. Home: B302 Summit Dr Bryn Mawr PA 19010-3206 Office: Smithkline Beecham PO Box 1539 King Of Prussia PA 19010-2237

WESTMAN, JAMES EDWARD, lawyer; b. Jamestown, N.Y., June 7, 1950; s. Edward William and May (Swift) W.; m. Bernadette Mary Duckett, Aug. 3, 1974; children: Beth Anne, John James. BA, SUNY, Albany, 1973; JD, Capital U., 1976. Bar: Ohio 1976, N.Y. 1977. Legis. aide Assemblyman John Beckman, Albany, N.Y., 1970-72; aide Speaker of N.Y. State Assembly, Albany, N.Y., 1972; staff legal asst. Ohio State Med. Bd., Columbus, Ohio, 1975-76; assoc. DeMambro, Donovan & Laurita, Mayville, N.Y., 1977-79; prin. Law Offices of James E. Westman, Jamestown, N.Y., 1979—. Author note Capital Univ. Law Rev., 1975; editor's asst. Jaws of Victory, 1973. City chmn. rep. com. City of Jamestown, 1978-79, councilman, 1982-87; mem. state com. N.Y. State Rep. Party, 1987—. Mem. Comml. Law League Am., Jamestown Bar Assn., Lions (1st v.p. Jamestown chpt. 1985). Republican. Home: 41 Chestnut St Jamestown NY 14701 Office: 300 E 6th St Jamestown NY 14701

WESTMORELAND, SAMUEL DOUGLASS, sociology educator; b. Westchester, Pa., May 29, 1944; s. Nip Thorton and Ella Dee (Ingram) W.; m. Mary Elizabeth Hampton, June 14, 1977; children: Lesia Annetra, Samara Elizabeth. BS, Kutztown U., 1966, MEd, 1971; MA, Lehigh U., 1978. Detached worker YMCA, Reading, Pa., 1966-67; tchr. Coatesville (Pa.) Area Sch. Dist., 1967-71; assoc. prof. sociology Kutztown (Pa.) U., 1971—. Editor: Readings in the Social Sciences, 3d edit., 1980. Mem. Pa. Sociol. Soc., Am. Sociol. Assn., Ea. Sociol. Soc., Assn. Social and Behavioral Scis. (pres. 1990-91), Kutztown Alumni Bd. (bd. dirs. 1991—). Baptist. Office: Kutztown Univ D 21 Kutztown PA 19607

WESTON, ELISABETH ANNE, history educator; b. N.Y.C., July 31, 1947; d. Samuel and Annette (Herkus) W.; m. James Morrill Swan, May 30, 1982; 1 child, Nicholas Alexander Weston-Swan. BA, Sarah Lawrence Coll., 1969; MA, SUNY, Buffalo, 1972, PhD, 1979. Instr. Sweet Briar (Va.) Coll., 1975-76; lectr. SUNY Coll. at Buffalo, 1977-78, SUNY Coll. at Brockport, 1978-79; vis. asst. prof. SUNY, Buffalo, 1979-80; Mellon fellow Washington Univ., St. Louis, Mo., 1981-82; lectr. Canisius Coll., Buffalo, 1977-79, 83-85; asst. prof. SUNY Coll. at Fredonia, 1986—; founder, mem. Buffalo (N.Y.) Feminist Study Group, 1982-91; cons. N.Y. Coun. on the Humanities, 1988, pub. speaker. Contbr. articles to profl. jours. Founding mem. Coalition for Abortion Rights and Against Sterilization Abuse, Buffalo, 1977-91; mem. Erie County Dem. Com., 1984-88. Recipient NDEA grad. fellowship SUNY at Buffalo, 1971-73, Mellon postdoctoral fellowship Washington Univ., St. Louis, 1981-82. Mem. NOW, Am. Hist. Assn., Dem. Socialists of Am. (nat. exec. com. 1981-83). Jewish. Home: 407 Ashland Ave Buffalo NY 14222-1542 Office: Dept History SUNY Coll at Fredonia Fredonia NY 14063

WESTON, FRANCINE EVANS, secondary education educator; b. Mt. Vernon, N.Y., Oct. 8, 1946; d. John Joseph and Frances (Fantino) Pisaniello. BA, Hunter Coll., 1968; MA, Lehman Coll., 1973; cert., Am. Acad. Dramatic Arts, N.Y.C., 1976; PhD, NYU, 1991. Cert. elem., secondary tchr., N.Y. Tchr. Yonkers (N.Y.) Bd. Edn., 1968—; aquatic dir. Woodlane Day Camp, Irvington-on-Hudson, N.Y., 1967-70, Yonkers Jewish Community Ctr., 1971-75; creative drama tchr. John Burroughs Jr. High Sch., Yonkers, 1971-77; stage lighting designer Iona Summer Theatre Festial, New Rochelle, N.Y., 1980-81, Yonkers Male Glee Club, 1981-89, Roosevelt High Sch., 1980-91; rsch. specialist Scholarship Rsch. Svcs., 1992—; master electrician NYU Summer Musical Theatre, 1979-80. Actress in numerous community theatre plays including A Touch of the Poet, 1979; dir. stage prodns. including I Remember Mama, 1973, The Man Who Came to Dinner, 1975; author: A Descriptive Comparison of Computerized Stage Lighting Memory Systems With Non-Computerized Systems, 1991, (short stories) A Hat for Louise, 1984, Old Memories: Beautiful and Otherwise, 1984; lit. editor: (story and poetry collection) Beautifully Old, 1984. Steering com. chairperson Roosevelt High Sch.-Middle States Assn. of Schs. and Colls. Self-Evaluation, 1985-88. Named Tchr. of Excellence, N.Y. State English Coun., 1990, Arrid Tchrs.', 1992; scholar Carter Products, 1992. Mem. U.S. Inst. for Theatre Tech., Nat. Coun. Tchrs. English, N.Y. State Coun. PTAs, N.Y. State United Tchrs. Assn., Yonkers Fedn. Tchrs., Kappa Delta Pi. Republican. Roman Catholic. Office: Roosevelt High Sch Tuckahoe Rd Yonkers NY 10710-5319

WESTURA, WARREN S., photographer; b. N.Y.C., Dec. 29, 1951; s. Stephen J. and Anne W. (Buis) W.; m. Sandra Gayle Ganci, July 29, 1990. BA, Trenton State Coll., 1973. Sales mgr. Boonton (N.J.) Photo, 1973-75; photographer Daily Advance, Dover, N.J., 1975-78; prodn. contr. Howmet Austenal, Dover, N.J., 1984-89; freelance photographer Stanhope, N.J., 1989-90; photographer N.J. Newsphotos, Newark, 1990—. Treas. Barn Theatre, Montville, N.J., 1986-87. Lt. comdr. USNR 1978-87. Mem. Nat. Press Photographers Assn., Naval Intelligence Profls., Naval Res. Assn., Naval Inst., N.J. Press Photographers Assn. Roman Catholic. Home: 9-163 Ashland Ct Stanhope NJ 07874 Office: NJ Newsphotos Rts 1 and 9 S Hemisphere Ctr Newark NJ 07114

WETHE, CHRISTIAN-ANDREW, civil engineer, planner; b. Bklyn., Dec. 19, 1942; s. Christen Christensen and Solveig Ruth (Hessen) W.; m. Barbara Gail Donaldson, June 7, 1969; 1 child, Karl. ScB in Engring., Brown U., 1964; MSCE, Tufts U., 1967; MA in Bus. Mgmt., Cen. Mich. U., 1981. Registered profl. engr. Civil engring. instr. Tufts U., Medford, Mass., 1966-67; rsch. engr. U. Del./Coll. of Marine Studies, Lewes, Del., 1971-83; environ. cons. Wethe Engring. Assocs., Lewes, 1983-85; planner Coast Guard, Atlantic Area, N.Y.C., 1985—. Lt. USCG, 1967-71. Mem. ASCE, Res. Officers Assn. (life). Office: Coast Guard Atlantic Area Bldg 125 Governors Island New York NY 10004

WETHERHOLD, ROBERT CAMPBELL, engineering educator; b. Wilmington, Del., Nov. 19, 1951; s. John Moyer and Mildred (Sherley) W.; m. Ellen Marie Beale, Aug. 21, 1976 (dec. 1981). BME, U. Del., 1974, M in Mech. and Aerospace Engring., 1976, PhD, 1983. Research assoc. U. Del., Newark, 1978-80; engr. E.I. Du Pont De Nemours & Co., Wilmington, 1976-78, 80-81; asst. prof. mech. engring. SUNY, Buffalo, 1983-89, assoc. prof. mech. engring., 1989—; vis. scientist Rockwell Internat. Sci. Ctr., 1990. Contbr. articles to profl. jours., chpts. to books. George Laird Merit fellow, 1982, Am. Soc. Engring. Edn. Summer fellow, NASA, 1985, 86, Air Force Summer fellow, 1987, 88. Mem. ASME, AIAA, Am. Soc. Composites, Mensa, Intertel, Sigma Xi, Tau Beta Pi. Office: SUNY Dept Mech & Aero Engring Buffalo NY 14260

WETHERILL, PHYLLIS STEISS, writer, publisher; b. Ft. Wayne, Ind., Aug. 16, 1923; d. Fred Wilhelm and Myrta May (Flightner) Steiss; m. George West Wetherill, June 17, 1950; children: Rachel, George, Sarah. PhB, U. Chgo., 1947, MA, 1950. Lic. marriage, family and child therapist, Calif. Directing tchr. South Side Spl. Play Sch., Chgo., 1950-51; tchr. spl. edn. Montgomery County Schs., Rockville, Md., 1954-57; tchr. Calvery Luth. Sch., Silver Spring, Md., 1957-59; marriage, family and child therapist Am. Inst. Family Rels., L.A., 1960-68, assoc. dir. Child Guildance Clinic, 1964-68; marriage, family and child therapist in pvt. practice L.A., 1968-75; pub. Cookie Cutter Collectors Club Newsletter, L.A., also Washington, 1972-84; pub. newsletter Cookies, Washington, 1984—; ptnr. Elegant Bouquets. Author: Identifying Your Cookie Cutters, 1978, Encyclopedia of Cookie Shaping, 1981, Cookie Cutters and Cookie Molds, 1985. Fellow Calif. Assn. Marriage and Family Therapists (pres. 1974-75); mem. Bead Soc. Washington, Needlechasers, Assn. for Gravestone Studies, Cookie Cutter Collectors Club (founder). Episcopalian. Home and Office: 5426 27th St NW Washington DC 20015

WETLAUFER, DONALD BURTON, biochemist, educator; b. New Berlin, N.Y., Apr. 4, 1925; s George C. and Olga (Kirckhoff) W.; m. Lucille D. Croce, May 5, 1950; children—Lise, Eric. B.S. in Chemistry, U. Wis., Madison, 1946, M.S. in Biochemistry, 1952, Ph.D., 1954. Chemist Argonne (Ill.) Nat. Lab., 1944, 46-47, Bjorksten Lab., Madison, 1948-50; Carlsberg Lab., Copenhagen, 1955-56; research asso. Harvard U., 1956-61, tutor biochem. sci., 1958-61; asst. prof. biochemistry Ind. U. Med. Sch., 1961-62; asso. prof., then prof. biochemistry U. Minn. Med. Sch., 1962-75; DuPont prof. chemistry U. Del., Newark, 1975—, chmn. dept., 1975-85; vis. investigator Max Planck Inst. Ernahrungsphy., 1974-78; mem. fellowship rev. com. NATO, 1970; cons. Nat. Inst. Gen. Med. Sci., 1964—, NSF, 1980—. Author research papers in field of protein biochemistry, protein folding and high performance protein purification; indsl. cons. NSF predoctoral fellow, 1952-54; Nat. Found. Infantile Paralysis postdoctoral fellow, 1955-56; Am. Heart Assn. postdoctoral fellow, 1956-58; grantee USPHS, 1961—; grantee NATO, 1974-77; grantee NSF, 1977—; grantee AEC, 1962; recipient Career Devel. award USPHS, 1961-62. Mem. AAAS, Am. Chem. Soc. (councilor, alt. councilor div. biol. chemistry 1975-87), Am. Soc. Biochemistry and Molecular Biology, The Protein Soc., Phi Beta Kappa. Office: U Del Dept Chemistry & Biochemistry Newark DE 19716

WETMUR, JAMES GERARD, microbiology educator, consultant; b. New Castle, Pa., July 1, 1941; s. Leon Gerard and Wilma Aileen (Lostetter) W.; m. Brigid Mary Long, Sept. 4, 1965; children: Katherine, John, Tara. BS, Yale U., 1963; PhD, Calif. Inst. Tech., 1967. Chief biochemist U.S. Army Aeromed. Rsch. Lab, Ft. Rucker, Ala., 1967-69; asst. prof. chemistry and biochemistry U. Ill., Urbana, 1969-74; assoc. prof. microbiology Mt. Sinai Sch. Medicine, N.Y.C., 1974-82, prof., 1982—; cons. NIH study sect., Bethesda, Md., 1987-90, Enzo Biochem, N.Y.C., 1983—. Contbr. over 60 articles to profl. publs. Active Town Club, Scarsdale, N.Y., 1975—. Capt. U.S. Army, 1967-69. Recipient Eastman Kodak award Calif. Inst. Tech., Pasadena, Calif., 1967, Career Scientist award N.Y.C. Health Rsch. Coun., 1975; grantee NIH, 1969—, Enzo Biochem, 1987—. Fellow N.Y. Acad. of Scientists (v.p. 1986-88); mem. Am. Soc. for Biochem. and Molecular Biology, N.Y. Sci. Policy Assn. Republican. Home: 994 Post Rd Scarsdale NY 10583-5647 Office: Microbiology Dept Mt Sinai Sch Medicine New York NY 10029

WETSTONE, HOWARD JEROME, physician, administrator; b. Hartford, Conn., Apr. 27, 1926; s. Murray and Natalie (Tonkonow) W.; m. Roan Joy Horowitz, May 8, 1947; children—Robin Lee Wendehack, Mark Lawrence, Scott Lewis, Jeffrey Bennett. BA, Wesleyan U., 1946; MD, Tufts U., 1951. Intern New Eng. Med. Ctr. Hosp., 1951-52, resident, 1952-53; resident Hartford Hosp., 1953-55, dir. med. rsch., 1958-65, asst. dir. dept. medicine, 1965-72, dir. ambulatory svcs., 1972-84, v.p. corp. med. affairs, 1984-87; v.p. med. affairs Conn. Health System, Hartford, 1987-92; med. dir., MEDSPAN Conn. Health System, 1990—; assoc. prof. U. Conn. Med. Sch., Farmington, 1975—; chmn. Med. Delivery Svcs., Inc., 1985-91; mem. Bloomfield Ethics Commn.; chmn. profl. adv. com. Capitol Area Health Consortium. Contbr. articles to profl. jours. Mem. Bloomfield Bd. Edn., Conn., 1955-69, chmn. 1961-69; pres. Conn. Assn. Bds. Edn., 1961-63; exec. com. Conn. Pub. TV Corp., Hartford, 1963-87 , chmn., 1970-74; pres. Capitol Region Edn. Council, Hartford, 1965-66; chmn. Govtl. Rels. Com. Served with USAAF, 1946-47. Mem. AMA, Am. Coll. Emergency Physicians, Conn. Hosp. Assn. (hon.), Conn. State Med. Soc. (pres. elect, chmn. legis. com.), Hartford County Med. Assn. (bd. dirs. 1978—, pres. 1985-86). Republican. Jewish. Home: 77 Kenwood Cir Bloomfield CT 06002-3435 Office: Conn Health System 55 Farmington Ave Hartford CT 06105-3711

WETTEREAU, RICHARD BRADWAY, editor, writer; b. N.Y.C., Jan. 21, 1932; s. James Oswald and Elizabeth Saeger Bradway W.; BA, Columbia U., 1954; m. Cynthia Fairhurst Parks, Oct. 1, 1972; 1 stepdaughter, Catherine Elston Parks. Reporter, asst. mng. editor L.I. Press, 1959-77; L.I. editor, editor Sunday edit., editor, writer Week-in-Rev., editor-at-large N.Y. Post, 1977—. Active, Central Manhasset Civic Assn. Served as 2d lt. U.S. Army. Decorated Purple Heart. Mem. Nat. Ry. Hist. Soc., N. Hempstead Hist. Soc., L.I. Press Club, N.Y. Press Club, Sigma Delta Chi, The Salurians. Quaker. Editor: Homes of the Signers of the Declaration, 1976, The Pennsy Era on Long Island, 1987; co-author: Victorian Railroad Stations on Long Island, 1988. Home: 195 Thompson Shore Rd PO Box 189 Manhasset NY 11030

WETTERHAHN, KAREN ELIZABETH, chemistry educator; b. Plattsburgh, N.Y., Oct. 16, 1948; d. Gustave George and Mary Elizabeth (Thibault) W.; m. Leon H. Webb, June 19, 1982; children—Leon Ashley, Charlotte Elizabeth. B.S., St. Lawrence U., 1970; Ph.D., Columbia U., 1975. Chemist, Mearl Corp., Ossining, N.Y., 1970-71; research fellow Columbia U., N.Y.C., 1971-75, postdoctoral fellow, 1975-76; asst. prof. chemistry Dartmouth Coll., Hanover, N.H., 1976-82, assoc. prof., 1982-86, prof., 1986—; assoc. dean faculty scis., 1990—. Contbr. articles to profl. jours. A.P. Sloan fellow, 1981. Mem. Am. Chem. Soc., Am. Assn. Cancer Research, AAAS, N.Y. Acad. Scis. Office: Dartmouth Coll Dept Chemistry Hanover NH 03755

WETZEL, EDWARD THOMAS, publishing company executive; b. Indpls., Apr. 16, 1937; s. Edward George and Sarah Catherine Wetzel; divorced; children: Raymond, Cynthia. BA, Bethany (W.Va.) Coll., 1959; MBA, U. Mass., Amherst, 1963. Market research analyst Gen. Electric Co., Pittsfield, Mass., 1960-63; editor, spl. projects dir., asst. v.p. DMS, Inc., Greenwich, Conn., 1964-70; pres. Industry News Service, Inc., Wilton, Conn., 1970-92; v.p. Wright Investor's Svc., Bridgeport, Conn., 1992—. Wilton Vol. Ambulance Corps, 1976-81, 83-87. Served to 2d lt. USAFR, 1959-65. Recipient Disting. Citizen award Town of Wilton, 1986. Mem. Planning Forum, Info. Industry Assn., Newsletter Pub. Assn., Kiwanis (pres. bd. dirs. Wilton chpt. 1991-92). Pub. various info. products and svcs. Office: Wright Investor's Svc 1000 Lafayette Blvd Bridgeport CT 06604

WETZEL, GLORIA MAE HIPPS, school principal; b. Clearfield, Pa., May 31, 1941; d. Clifford Charles and Jane O. (Williams) Hipps; m. Ralph Foster Wetzel II; 1 child, Ralph Foster III. BS in Edn., Lock Haven (Pa.) U., 1963; MS in Edn., Beaver Coll., 1985; cert. prin., Temple U., 1988, EdD, 1990. English instr. Clearfield Sch. Dist., 1963-68, Upper Dublin Sch. Dist., Oreland, Pa., 1968-72; tchr. elem. Bryn Athyn (Pa.) Ch. Sch., 1980-84, middle sch. tchr., 1984-86; prin. Acad. of the New Ch., Bryn Athyn, 1986—. Mem. Lit. Rev. Com., Bryn Athyn, 1980-84, Bishop's Coun., Bryn Athyn, 1985—. Fellow Pa. Writing Project; mem. Nat. Coun. Tchrs. of English, Pa. Coun. Tchrs. English, Phi Delta Gamma, Alpha Psi Omega. Republican. Office: Acad of the New Ch 2815 Huntingdon Pike # 278 Bryn Athyn PA 19009-9999

WETZEL, JANICE WOOD, dean, researcher, educator; b. East Orange, N.J., Nov. 30, 1931; d. John and Lynn Fullarton (Murty) Wood; divorced; children: Richard Alan, Kathryn Lynn Robyn, Robert Stuart. Student, U. Mo., 1949-51; BS with honors, Washington U., St. Louis, 1972, MSW, 1973, PhD, 1976. Lic. ind. clin. social worker, Mass. Dir. program planning dept. Mayor's Council on Youth, St. Louis, 1968-74; asst. prof, rsch. assoc. U. Tex. Sch. Social Work, Austin, 1976-80; assoc. prof., chair rsch. Smith Coll. Sch. Social Work, Northampton, Mass., 1980-83; dir., prof. U. Iowa Sch. Social Work, Iowa City, 1983-88; Moses disting. vis. prof. social work Hunter Coll., N.Y.C., 1988-89; dean, prof. Adelphi U. Sch. Social Work, Garden City, N.Y., 1989—; rsch. cons. Barnes Hosp. Complex, St. Louis, 1974-76, San Antonio Health Scis. Ctr., Bexar County Hosp., 1976-78, Austin State Hosp., 1978-79, Northampton State Hosp., 1982-83, McLean Hosp., Belmont, Mass., 1982-89, U. Iowa Sch. Medicine Dept. Psychiatry, 1986-92; presenter in field; mem. nat. exec. com. Ctr. for Understanding Aging, 1983-86. Author: (books) Clinical Handbook of Depression, 1984 (featured selection Behavior Sci. Book Club 1984), 2d edit., 1991, The World of Women: In Pursuit of Human Rights, 1992; (video prodn.) Women of the World (award winning narrated slide presentation), 1985; book reviewer, 1977-89; contbr. articles to profl. publs. Mem. N.Y. Housing Commn., 1991—. Recipient Continuing Edn. award Bus. and Profl. Women of St. Louis, Inc., 1973-74, N.Y.C. Nat. Rehab. Studies award Kappa Kappa Gamma, 1974-75, St. Louis Nat. Rehab. Studies award, 1975-76; grad. fellow George Warren Brown Sch. Social Work Washington U., St. Louis, 1973-76; named Outstanding Alumni Washington U., St. Louis, 1987. Fellow Am. Orthopsychiat. Assn., Gerontol. Soc. Am.; mem. Nat. Assn. Deans and Dirs. Schs. of Social Work (exec. bd., treas. 1991—), Am. Assn. Internat. Aging, Internat. Assn. Schs. of Social Work (UN rep.), Internat. Coun. Social Welfare, World Fedn. Mental Health, Soc. Study Social Problems, Inter-Univ. Consortium Internat. Social Devel. Nat. Com. Gerontology in Social Work Edn. (rsch., planning and practice sect.), Nat. Assn. Social Workers (ho. of dels. 1983-88, internat. com. 1990—, edn. policy & planning com. 1989-90, Coun. on Social Word Edn. Office: Adelphi U Sch Social Work Garden City NY 11530

WETZEL, ROLAND HERMAN, engineer, retired; b. Hartford, Wis., Apr. 29, 1923; s. William George and Bertha Anna (Uber) W.; m. Muriel Evelyn Auler, June 13, 1945; children: Peter, James. BS, U. Wis., 1945, PhD, 1951. Teaching asst. Univ. Wis., Madison, 1946-50; rsch. engr. E.I. du Pont de Nemours & Co., Inc., Wilmington, Del., 1951-53; rsch. supr. E.I. du Pont de Nemours & Co., Inc., Wilmington, 1954-66, rsch. mgr., 1966-68, asst. lab. dir., 1969-73, tech. supt., 1973-75, engring. assoc., 1976-77, ret., 1978. Judge of elections Franklin Twp., Pa., 1981-89. Ensign USN, 1943-46. Mem. Sigma Xi., Tau Beta Pi, Phi Lambda Upsilon. Presbyterian.

WEWER, WILLIAM PAUL, lawyer; b. San Diego, May 27, 1947; s. William P. and Helen E. (Helm) Wewer; m. Katheleen Marquardt, Dec. 6, 1987. BA with honors, Pomona Coll., 1970; JD with high honors, George Washington U., 1977. Bar: D.C. 1977, U.S. Ct. Appeals (D.C. cir.) 1977, Calif. 1980, U.S. Ct. Appeals (9th cir.) 1980, U.S. Dist. Ct. D.C. 1981, U.S. Dist. Ct. (no. dist.) Calif. 1982, U.S. Supreme Ct. 1982, Colo. 1989. Legisl. asst. U.S. Senator Howard W. Cannon, Washington, 1970-74; prof. staff mem. Rules Com. U.S. Senate, Washington, 1974-77; assoc. Sutherland, Asbill & Brennan, Washington, 1977-79; ptnr. Wewer & Mann, P.C., Washington, 1979-83; sole practice Washington and L.A., 1983—; ptnr. Bleak House Publishing Co., Bethesda, Md., 1988-89; cons. various candidates nationwide, 1966-76. Contbr. articles to profl. jours. and nationally syndicated newspaper column. Bd. dirs. Am. Tax Reduction movement, Washington, 1980-89, pres., 1989-91; bd. dirs. Howard Jarvis Taxpayers Assn., L.A., 1980-89, Am. Tax Reduction Found., Washington, 1983-90, Nat. Com.

to Preserve Social Security and Medicare, Washington, 1982-87, various non-profit groups nationwide; sec. Subscription TV Assn., Washington, 1979-83, Calif. Apt. Law Info. Found., L.A., 1989—. Mem. ABA. Republican. Home: 6302 30th St NW Washington DC 20015-2238 Office: 6302 30th St NW Washington DC 20015 also: 621 S Westmoreland Ave Ste 200 Los Angeles CA 90005

WEXELBAUM, MICHAEL, lawyer; b. Bklyn., Aug. 12, 1946; s. Joseph and Beatrice (Skurnick) W.; m. Cynthia Debra Schorr, Apr. 15, 1973 (dec. 1984); children: Joshua David, Stephanie Faye. BA in Econs., Bucknell U., 1968; JD, NYU, 1971. Bar: N.Y. 1972, U.S. Dist. Ct. (so. and ea. dists.) N.Y. 1973. Assoc. Sherman, Citron & Karasik, P.C., N.Y.C., 1972-80; ptnr., head litigation dept. Sherman, Citron & Karasik, P.C., 1980—. Arbitrator Am. Arbitration Assn. and Gen. Arbitration Coun. of Textile and Apparel Industries, N.Y.C., 1982—. Mem. Bankruptcy Lawyers Bar Assn., Lawyers Assn. Textile and Apparel Industries (bd. govs.), Am. Arbitration Assn. (arbitrator). Democratic. Jewish. Home: 408 Club Ct Oceanside NY 11572-5605 Office: Sherman Citron & Karasik PC 900 3d Ave New York NY 10022

WEXLER, DAVID MARK, lawyer; b. Buffalo, N.Y., Sept. 9, 1938; s. Morris Wexler and Tillie (Goldberg) Rovner; m. Roslynn Weinstein. BA, U. Buffalo, 1960, JD, 1963. Pvt. practice Buffalo, 1965—. Contbr. articles to profl. jours. Sgt. USAF Res., 1963-69. Recipient Labor Law award Lawyer's Coop Publishing, 1962-63. Fellow Am. Acad. Forensic Scis.; mem. Am. Coll. Legal Medicine (assoc. in law), Am. Soc. Law and Medicine, Am. Soc. Pharmacy Law, N.Y. State Bar Assn. (mem. com. on med. malpractice), Erie County Bar Assn., N.Y. Acad. Scis., Pitts. Inst. Legal Medicine. Republican. Jewish. Home and Office: 88 Lexington Ave Buffalo NY 14222

WEXLER, LEONARD D., federal judge; b. Bklyn., Nov. 11, 1924; s. Jacob and Bessie (Herman) W.; m. Barbara Blum, Mar. 1953; children: Allison Wexler Smeitanka, Robert, William. BS, Ind. U., 1947; JD, NYU, 1950. Bar: N.Y. 1983, U.S. Dist. Ct. (ea. dist.) N.Y. 1983. Assoc. Siben & Siben Esqs., Bay Shore, N.Y., 1950-56; ptnr. Meyer & Wexler Esqs., Smithtown, N.Y., 1956-83; judge U.S. Dist. Ct. (eastern dist.) N.Y., 1983—; atty. Suffolk County Police Conf., 1956-83; 1st atty. Suffolk County Patrolmen's Benevolent Assn., 1960-75; 1st atty. Suffolk County Detectives Assn., 1964-70; temporary state chmn., legal counsel Com. for Rev. Juvenile Justice System, N.Y. State Bar Assn.; speaker, lectr.; 1st adminstr. Assigned Counsel Plan N.Y. State, 1966-83. Served with U.S. Army, 1943-45. Mem. Suffolk County Criminal Bar Assn. (founder 1965, dir. 1956-60). Republican. Jewish. Home: 94 W Bayberry Rd Islip NY 11751-4905 Office: US Dist Ct 300 Rabro Dr Hauppauge NY 11788-4245

WEXLER, MICHAEL, psychologist; b. N.Y.C., Apr. 30, 1944; s. Leo and Evelyn (Braun) W. BS, Pa. State U., 1966, MS, 1970, DEd, 1972. Diplomate in family psychology Am. Bd. Profl. Psychology; lic. psychologist, marriage counselor, N.J.; cert. sch. psychologist. Intern in psychology NIMH Tng. Program, Long Beach, N.Y., 1969-70; psychologist Bancroft Sch. and Clinic, Haddonfield, N.J., 1972-74; cons. psychologist Junction Drug Clinic, North Wildwood, N.J., 1974-75, Haddon Twp. (N.J.) Pub. Schs., 1982—; pvt. practice Marlton, N.J., 1975—; adj. prof. Community Coll. Phila., 1976-81. Contbr. articles to profl. jours. Mem. S.J. Campaign for Peace and Justice, Moorestown, 1982—. Mem. World Federalists Assn. Amnesty Internat., Greenpeace, N.J. Acad. Psychology (pres. 1990-91), N.J. Psychol. Assn. (exec. bd.), South Jersey Psychol. Assn. (pres. 1982-84), Internat. Coun. of Psychologists, Am. Psychol. Assn., Phila. Soc. Clin. Psychology, Psychologists for Social Responsibility. Home: 132B Cherry Parke Cherry Hill NJ 08002-4061 Office: 526 Lippincott Dr Marlton NJ 08053-4805

WEYR, THOMAS HECTOR, editor; b. Vienna, Austria, Sept. 9, 1927; s. Siegfried Hugo Maria and Helen (Merdinger) W.; m. Carrie Louise McLeod, Apr. 5, 1935 (div. 1961); 1 child, Teodora Dominique; m. Rhoda Ann Ackerson, July 27, 1937; children: Rhoda Garret, Lydia Alexandra, Tamara Nicole. BA, Columbia U., 1948; PhD, U. Vienna, 1952. Reporter UPI, Vienna, 1953-55; diplomatic reporter UPI, Washington, 1955-59; freelance reporter various publs. and networks, Europe, 1959-63; news writer ABC Radio Network, N.Y.C., 1964-66; acct. exec. Curtis Hoxter Inc. Pub. Relations, N.Y.C., 1966-68; mng. editor Rsch. Inst. Am., N.Y.C., 1968-87; directing editor Nat. Inst. Bus. Mgmt., N.Y.C., 1987—. Author: World War II, 1969, Reaching for Paradise, 1978, Hispanic USA, 1988; editor Exec. Strategies, 1990—; translator various books and newspaper articles. Mem. Nat. Press Club, The Players. Democrat. Roman Catholic. Home: 6 Wildway Bronxville NY 10708-5918 Office: Nat Inst Bus Mgmt 1328 Broadway New York NY 10001-2121

WHALEN, JOHN MICHAEL, electrical engineer; b. Derby, Conn., Feb. 27, 1945; s. John Joseph and Mary June (Foley) W. AS in Elec. Engring., U. S.C., 1967; BEE, U. New Haven, 1977, postgrad., 1987; postgrad., U. Conn., 1982. Lic. profl. engr., Conn. Electronics tech. Sikorsky Aircraft div. U. Aircraft, Stratford, 1967-71; sr. engr., rsch. scientist brass div. Olin Corp., New Haven, 1971-85; cons. engr. Ansonia, Conn., 1985-91; MTC supt. U.S. Surg. Corp.; cons. Dresser Industries, Stratford, 1979-80, Quantum Corp., Wallingford, Conn., 1980, Century Brass Products, Waterbury, Conn., 1980-81, Miller Co., Meriden, Conn., 1980-81; owner, operator Video Ctr., Ansonia. Patentee in field. With USMC, 1963-67. Mem. Internat. Maintenance Inst., Am. Inst. Profl. Engrs., Mensa Am., NRA, Titanic Hist. Soc., U.S. Chess Fedn., Mill Order Purple Heart (nat. aide de camp 1982-90, state comdr. 1987-88), VFW (life), Am. Legion, Rotary. Roman Catholic. Home: 161 Pulaski Hwy Ansonia CT 06401-2961

WHALEN, THOMAS M., III, mayor, lawyer; b. Albany, N.Y., Jan. 6, 1934. Student Vincentian Inst., 1951; B.B.A., Manhattan Coll., 1955; LL.B., Albany Law Sch., 1958. Bar: N.Y. 1959. With law firm Cooper Erving Savage, Albany, N.Y., 1963-88; judge City of Albany, 1969-75, pres. Common Council, 1982-83, mayor, 1983—; chmn. Albany Urban Renewal Agy., 1982-88. Served to 1st lt. U.S. Army, 1958-59; served with Army N.G., 1959-65. Fellow ABA, N.Y. State Bar Found.; mem. N.Y. State Bar Assn., Albany County Bar Assn., Am. Arbitration Assn. (arbitrator N.Y. state 1969—). Clubs: University (bd. dirs. 1970-71), Hudson River (bd. govs. 1969—, chmn. 1973-75). Avocations: rowing; cross country skiing; squash; golf. Office: City Hall Eagle St Rm 102 Albany NY 12207-1004

WHALEN, TIMOTHY JOHN, child and adolescent psychiatrist; b. Columbus, Ohio, May 29, 1960; s. John M. and Nana Lee (Richard) W.; m. Barbara Rhoads, June 18, 1983; children: Elizabeth Anne, Thomas Christopher. BS, Davidson (N.C.) Coll., 1982; MD, Ohio State U., 1986. Resident in family practice Riverside Meth. Hosp., Columbus, 1986-87; resident in psychiatry Johns Hopkins Hosp., Balt., 1987-89, resident child and adolescent psychiat., 1989-90, chief resident child and adolescent psychiat., 1990-91; dir. child and adolescent psychiatry Francis Scott Key Med. Ctr., Balt., 1991—; instr. dept. of psychiatry and behavioral scis., dept. pediatrics Johns Hopkins U., Balt., 1991—. Mem. AMA, Am. Psychiat. Soc., Am. Acad. Child and Adolescent Psychiatry, Md. Psychiat. Soc. Democrat. Office: Francis Scott Key Med Ctr B3 S 4940 Eastern Ave Baltimore MD 21224

WHALEY, CHARLES HENRY, IV, communications company executive; b. Elmhurst, N.Y., Jan. 15, 1958; s. Charles Henry III and Edna Mae (Squire) W.; m. Jeanette Marie Smith, Sept. 26, 1987. AAS in Electrical Tech., Queensborough Community Coll., Bayside, N.Y., 1979. Testing engr. GTE/Telenet, Mount Laurel, N.J., 1979-81; field service engr. Gen. Dynamics Communications Co., St. Louis, 1981-82; ops. engr. United Techs. Communications Co., Pine Brook, N.J., 1982-84; sr. ops. engr. United Techs. Communications Co., N.Y.C., 1984-85, ops. supr., 1985-86; project mgr. Telex Computer Products, N.Y.C., 1986; pres. Pertel Communications Corp., Queens Village, N.Y., 1986-90. Democrat. Presbyterian. Office: Pertel Communications NY Inc 221-10 Jamaica Ave Jamaica NY 11428-2198 also: Pertel Communications N/E Inc 5 National Dr Windsor Locks CT 06096

WHALEY, DEBRA T., small business owner, accountant; b. Kilmarnock, Va., June 15, 1954; d. Randolph J. and Ollie May (Hutchings) Thrift; m. Carvel H. Whaley, Feb. 2, 1983. Acctg. Deg., Hesser Coll., 1989. Cert. fin. paraplanner; enrolled agt.; accredited tax advisor. Staff acct. Charles E. Moffat, Acct., Reedville, Va., 1976-83; comptroller The Whistling Oyster, Ogunquit, Maine, 1983-86; prin. Whaley Acctg. Svcs., Wells, Maine, 1986—; tchr. adult edn. Wells-Ogunquit Sch. Dist., 1991—. Mem. Nat. Soc. Pub. Accts., Nat. Assn. Tax Practitioners, Maine Assn. Profl. Accts., Nat. Soc. Tax Profls., Wells C. of C., Wells Rotary (asst. to treas. 1991). Republican. Baptist. Office: Whaley Acctg Svcs RR 1 Wells ME 04090-9801

WHALEY, ROSS SAMUEL, college president; b. Detroit, Nov. 7, 1937; s. Lyle John and Margaret Nielson (Semple) W.; m. Beverly Mae Heemstra, June 14, 1958; children—Heather Jean, Susan Lesli, Lindsay John. B.S., U. Mich., 1959, Ph.D., 1969; M.S., Colo. State U., 1961. Asst. prof., assoc. prof., prof. Utah State U., Logan, 1965-70, dept. head, 1967-70; assoc. dean Colo. State U., Ft. Collins, 1970-73; dept. head U. Mass., Amherst, 1973-76, dean, 1976-78; dir. econ. research USDA Forest Service, Washington, 1978-84; pres. SUNY Coll. Environ. Scis. and Forestry, Syracuse, 1984—; cons. UN FAO, Rome, 1983-84, UN, Budapest, Hungary, 1974, U.S. Peace Corps., South Am., 1972, Geddes, Brecher, Qualls & Cunningham, Denver, 1971-72. Contbr. articles to profl. jours. Bd. dirs. Hiawatha coun. Boy Scouts Am., 1985—; sec. bd. Ausable Inst. Mem. Soc. Am. Foresters (pres. 1991). Mem. Christian Ref. Ch. Home: 2 Bradford Heights Rd Syracuse NY 13224-2158 Office: SUNY Office of Pres Coll Environ Sci & Forestry Syracuse NY 13210

WHARTON, CLIFTON REGINALD, JR., insurance company executive, former academic administrator; b. Boston, Sept. 13, 1926; m. Dolores Duncan, 1950; children: Clifton, Bruce. BA, Harvard U., 1947; MA, Johns Hopkins U., 1948, LLD (hon.), 1970; MA, U. Chgo., 1956, PhD in Econs., 1958; LLD (hon.), U. Mich., 1970, Wayne State U., 1970, Hahneman Med. Sch., 1975, Georgetown U., 1976, Va. State U., 1977, CCNY, 1978, Wright State U., 1979, Lincoln U., 1979, Albany Law Sch., 1980, Duke U., 1981, Amherst Coll., 1983, U. Ill., 1984, U. Vt., 1987, Colgate U., 1987, Tuskegee U., 1987, Tufts U., 1988, Mich. State U., 1988, Claremont U. Ctr. and Grad. Sch., 1989, U. Notre Dame, 1989, Clark Atlanta U., 1990, Howard U., 1991, Shippensburg U., 1991, Miami U., Ohio, 1991, Washington U., 1991; DPS (hon.), Cen. Mich. U., 1970, U. Pitts., 1989; LittD (hon.), N.C. Agrl. and Tech. State U., 1986; LHD (hon.), Oakland U., 1971, No. Mich. U., 1975, Columbia U., 1978, Brandeis U., 1981, NYU, 1981, U. Conn., 1983, U. Mass., Boston, 1985, So. Ill. U., 1987, George Mason U., 1988, L.I. U., 1989, U. Ala., Birmingham, 1989, Va. Commonwealth U., 1990, SUNY, 1990; DSc (hon.), Mercy Coll., 1989, Bryant Coll., 1990; LHD (hon.), St. Paul's Coll., 1992. Exec. trainee Am. Internat. Assn. Econ. and Social Devel., 1948-49, program analyst, 1949-51, head reports and analysis, 1951-53; rsch. asst. econs. U. Chgo., 1953-56, rsch. assoc., 1956-57; exec. assoc. Agrl. Devel. Coun., 1957-58, assoc., 1958-64, dir. Am. univs. rsch., 1964-67, v.p., 1967-69; pres. Mich. State U., 1970-78; chancellor SUNY System, 1978-87; chmn., chief exec. officer Tchrs. Ins. & Annuity Assn. Coll. Retirement Equities Fund, N.Y.C., 1987—; bd. dirs. Ford Motor Co., N.Y. Stock Exch., Tchrs. Ins. and Annuity Assn and Coll. Retirement Equities Fund.; past bd. dirs., dep. chmn. Fed. Res. Bank N.Y., 1985-86. Co-author: Patterns for Lifelong Learning, 1973; editor: Subsistence Agriculture and Economic Development, 1969; contbr. articles to profl. jours. Trustee Rockefeller Found., 1970-87, chmn., 1982-87; trustee Asia Soc., 1967-77, Overseas Devel. Coun., 1969-79, Carnegie Found., 1970-79, Agrl. Devel. Coun., 1973-80, Aspen Inst., 1980—, Com. Econ. Devel., 1980—, Coun. Fin. Aid to Edn., 1983-86, Coun. Fgn. Rels., 1983—, Fgn. Policy Assn., 1983-87, MIT Corp., 1984-86, Acad. Ednl. Devel., 1985-86, Clark Found., 1991—; mem. Commn. on Intercollegiate Athletics, Knight Found., 1990—, N.Y.C. Mayor's Coun. Econ. Advisors, 1990—, Adv. Commn. on Trade Policy and Negotiations, 1990—. Mem. Am. Agrl. Econs. Assn., Assn. Asian Studies, Nat. Acad. Edn., Bus.-Higher Edn. Forum, Univ. Club (N.Y.C.), Country Club (Cooperstown, N.Y.). Office: Tchrs Ins & Annuity Assn & Coll Retirement Equities 730 3d Ave New York NY 10017-3206

WHARTON, RALPH NATHANIEL, psychiatrist, educator; b. Boston, June 15, 1932; s. Nathaniel Philip and Deeda (Levine) W.; AB cum laude, Harvard U., 1953; MD, Columbia U., 1957, degree in psychoanalysis, 1970; children: Naida, Philip, Laura. Intern, Cornell div. Bellevue Hosp., N.Y.C., 1957-58; resident Columbia-Presbyn. Med. Center, N.Y.C., 1961-64; practice medicine, specializing in psychiatry and psychopharmacology, N.Y.C., 1964—; assoc. psychiatry Coll. Physicians and Surgeons, N.Y.C., 1964-69, asst. prof. clin. psychiatry, 1969-72, assoc. prof., 1972-83, prof., 1984—; sr. research psychiatrist N.Y. State Psychiat. Inst., N.Y.C., 1964-70; assoc. attending in psychiatry Columbia-Presbyn. Hosp., 1970—, ex-officio mem. bd. trustees, pres. Soc. Practitioners Columbia-Presbyn. Med. Center, 1980-82; attending psychiatrist Columbia-Presbyterian Med. Ctr., 1984—. Mem. bd. regent, chmn. Wharton Fund for Brain Rsch. Served with M.C., U.S. Army, 1958-61. Named one of Best Drs., N.Y. mag. Fellow N.Y. Acad. Medicine, Am. Psychiat. Assn., Am. Coll. Psychoanalysts (bd. regents 1989—, rsch. trust chmn. dept. psychiatry 1985—); mem. AMA (mem. legis. action com.), Soc. Biol. Psychiatry, Royal Soc. Medicine, Lotos Club (bd. dirs.), Salon De Uirtuosi, Harvard Club (bd. dirs.). Author numerous publs. in field. Office: Columbia Presbyn Med Ctr 1070 Park Ave Ste 1D New York NY 10128-1000

WHARTON, ROBERT MICHAEL, statistics educator; b. Phila., July 26, 1943; s. Joseph Harry and Sarah Marie (Prendergast) W.; m. Florence Ellen Harrison, Sept. 10, 1966; 1 child, Robert Michael Jr. BA, Temple U., 1965, MA, 1968, PhD, 1973. System analyst Gen. Electric Co., Valley Forge, Pa., 1966-68; assoc. prof. Trenten (N.J.) State Coll., 1968-77; div. mgr., corp. planning div. ATT, N.Y.C., 1977-81; prof. stats., dept. chair Grad. Sch. Bus. Grad. Sch. Bus., Fordham Univ., N.Y.C., 1981—; cons. U.S. Dept. Def., Washington, 1981-86. Contbr. articles to profl. jours. Chmn. Hist. Archtl. Review Bd., Langhorne, Pa., 1976—. Mem. Am. Stats. Assn., Prodn. and Ops. Mgmt. Soc. Republican. Roman Catholic. Home: 301 N Bellevue Ave Langhorne PA 19047-2103 Office: Fordham U 113 W 60th St New York NY 10023-7404

WHAYLAND, WILLIAM MATTHEW, III, clergyman; b. Wilmington, Del., June 13, 1957; s. William Matthew Jr. and Mary Louise (Hurd) W.; m. Pamela Sue Meily, May 21, 1988; 1 child, Erin Elizabeth. Student, Pa. State U., Media, 1975-77; BA, Ea. Coll., St. Davids, Pa., 1979; MDiv, Ea. Bapt. Theol. Sem., Phila., 1982; postgrad., Moravian Theol. Sem., Bethlehem, Pa., 1989—. Ordained to ministry United Meth. Ch., 1982. Pastor United Meth. chs., Pa., 1982—, Avondale United Meth. Ch., 1982-85, Minersville United Meth. Ch., 1983-85, Llewellyn United Meth. Ch., 1983-85, Gladwyn United Meth. Ch., 1985-86, Belmont Hills United Meth. Ch., 1985-86, Mountville United Meth. Ch., Lebanon, 1986—, Meml. United Meth. Ch., 1986—; mem. libr. com., Minersville, 1983-85; mem. Camp Innabah site com., Pughtown, 1984-90; sec. Mt. Lebanon Campmeeting Assn., Lebanon, 1988—. Mem. Order of St. Luke, Pi Gamma Mu. Republican.

WHEATLEY, GARY FRANCIS, policy research company executive; b. Cleve., Oct. 11, 1937; s. Donley C. and Eleanor (Tatulinski) W.; m. Maureen F. Mitchell, Dec. 17, 1960; children: Gary Jr., Guy, Gale. BS, U.S. Naval Acad., 1959; MSA, George Washington U., 1973; postgrad., Harvard U., 1982. Ensign USN, 1955, test pilot, 1965; advanced through grades to rear adm., 1989; v.p. Burdeshaw Assoc. Ltd., Bethesda, Md., 1989-90; sr. fellow Hudson Inst., Washington, 1990—. Pres. Colecroft Homeowners Assn., Alexandria, 1990-91. Decorated Legion of Merit; recipient John Paul Jones award for Inspirational Leadership, Navy League of the U.S., 1984. Mem. Soc. of Exptl. Test Pilots. Home: 1401 Laurel View Dr Virginia Beach VA 23451 Office: Hudson Inst 1015 18th St NW Washington DC 20036-5203

WHEELER, CAMILLE BAUDOT, social services executive; b. Richmond, Va., Mar. 9, 1941; d. Frank Wirtley and Camille (Baudot) W.; m. William Hughes Marshall, Aug. 15, 1979. BA, Goucher Coll., 1963; MSW, U. Md., 1968. Lic. cert. social worker. Libr. Birmingham (Ala.) Pub. Libr., 1963-64; social caseworker Balt. (Md.) Dept. Social Svcs., 1964-68, social work supr., 1968-73, mgr. Hampden dist., 1973-79; dir. Balt. County Dept. Social Svcs., Towson, Md., 1979—; pres. Md. Assn. Social Svc. Dirs., Balt., 1987-88; dir., pres. Fund for Social Welfare, Towson, 1990—; mem. grad. adv. coun. Notre Dame Coll. Bd. mem. Community Action Network, Inc., Dundalk, Md., 1978-89; mem. Balt. County Women's Commn., Towson, 1982-85, Pvt. Industry Coun., Towson, 1989—, Govs. Workforce Improvement Coun., Balt., 1990—. Mem. NASW (pres. Md. chpt. 1991—), Am. Pub. Welfare Assn., Child Welfare League Am., Walters Art Gallery, Balt. Mus. Art, LWV. Office: Balt County Dept Social Svc 620 York Rd Baltimore MD 21204-4150

WHEELER, DONALD ALSOP, biology educator; b. Phila., Aug. 16, 1931; s. Clarence Oliver and Margaret (Alsop) W.; m. Dorothy Jean Grezeszak, June 7, 1953; children: Jean, David, Micheal, John. BS, Mich. State U., 1953, MS, 1956; PhD, Cornell U., 1961. Instr. dept. biology Delta Coll., University Center, Mich., 1961-65, chmn. dept. biology, 1963-65; prof. Edinboro Univ. Pa., 1965—, asst. chmn. dept. biology and health svcs., 1970-73; visiting assoc. Calif. Inst. Tech., 1992. Author lab. manuals; lectr. on birth defects. Mem. Erie (Pa.) Philharmonic Chorus, 1982—, Univ. Singers, Edinboro U., 1966-90. Johns Hopkins U. fellow, 1976. Mem. AAAS, Assn. Pa. State Coll. and Univ. Faculty, Johns Hopkins Med. and Surg. Assn., Pa. State Edn. Assn., Sigma Xi. Episcopalian. Home: 5471 Sherrod Hill Rd Edinboro PA 16412-1864 Office: Edinboro U Pa Dept Biology Edinboro PA 16444

WHEELER, DOUGLAS MICHAEL, scriptwriter; b. Palo Alto, Calif., Dec. 21, 1960; s. Joan Christine (Harvey) Wheeler. BS in Computer Sci., Pa. State U., 1984. Computer programmer Kinney Svc. Corp., Camp Hill, Pa., 1984-89, programmer, analyst, 1990—. Contbg. writer Alien Encounters, Eclipse Comics, 1986-87, Cheval Noir, Dark Horse Comics, 1991-92, Twilight Zone, Taboo, DHP, Dr. Strange, Plastron Cafe, 1992; creator/writer Comico Christmas Special, Comico The Comic Co., 1988, Starchild, Grafitti, Arianne, Cockroach Dreams, Aesop's Desecrated Morals, Santa's Desecrated Christmas Stories, Psychotic Hero-Man Goes BERSERK!!!; writer Swamp Thing, DC Comics, 1989-91, Classics Desecrated, 1991-92; creator, writer, editor April Horrors, Rip Off Press, 1992. Mem. The Frying Pan, Cen. Pa. Writers Orgn., Amnesty Internat.

WHEELER, EDWARD STUBBS, technology consultant; b. Phila., June 3, 1927; s. Edward Ezekiel and Margaret Elizabeth (Stubbs) W.; m. Joan Marie Petersen, June 28, 1952; children: Joan B., Edward P., Paul T., Anne M. AB, Haverford Coll., 1948; PhD, Cornell U., 1952. Mgr. agrichems. R&D Atlantic Refining Co., Phila., 1952-59; mgr. adhesive products div. Amchem Products, Inc., Ambler, Pa., 1959-62; mgr. thermosetting polymers Gen. Electric Co., Schenectady, N.Y., 1963-66; mgr. engring. Gen. Electric Co., Balt., 1966-71; cons. corp. exec. staff Gen. Electric Co., Fairfield, Conn., 1971-75; v.p. tech. Lapp Insulator Co., LeRoy, N.Y., 1975-85, v.p., gen. mgr. organic div., 1985-86; pvt. practice Clinton, Conn., 1987—. Patentee in field. With USN, 1945-46. Fellow AAAS; mem. IEEE (sr.), Am. Chem. Soc., Corp. Haverford Coll., Sigma Xi. Mem. Soc. of Friends. Home and Office: 33 Longate Rd Clinton CT 06413-1343

WHEELER, GEORGE CHARLES, consulting company executive; b. Balt., Oct. 9, 1923; s. George Charles and Julia-Elizabeth (Watrous) W.; m. Dorothy W. Whittemore, Sept. 13, 1947 (div. 1977); children: Scott, Craig, Mark, Matthew, Tracy, Bruce; m. Clare Frances Weiner, Jan. 21, 1978. BS in Metall. Engring., Lehigh U., 1944. Various engring. and supervisory positions GE, Mass. and N.Y., 1944-62; mgr. materials, welding and nondestructive testing Knolls Atomic Power Lab., G.E., Schenectady, N.Y., 1962-68, mgr. nondestructive testing, 1968-85; pres., chief exec. officer Wheeler Nondestructive Testing, Inc., Schenectady, 1985—; cons. UN, N.Y.C., 1985—, Internat. Atomic Energy Agy., Vienna, Austria, 1985—; guest lectr. Rensselaer Poly. Inst., Troy, N.Y., Union Coll., Schenectady, 1978-87; mem. math. sci. and tech. com. Schenectady County Community Coll., 1978-85, adj. prof., 1987—. Author: Guide to NDT Personnel Certification, 1990, Guide to Developing Certification Exams, 1992. Troop leader Schenectady area Boy Scouts Am., 1957-64. Mem. ASTM (com. internat. standards), NRA (life), Am. Soc. Nondestructive Testing (hon. life, bd. dirs. 1976-85, pres. 1983-84), Brit. Inst. Nondestructive Testing, Am. Soc. Metals, Nature Conservancy (life). Office: Wheeler Nondestructive Testing Inc 29 Front St Schenectady NY 12305-1301

WHEELER, JEFFREY ALLAN, management consultant; b. Bklyn., Apr. 4, 1944; s. Robert Saunders and Lottie (Neubauer) W.; m. Leslie Ford, Sept. 30, 1969; children: Cecily Almira Ford, Hallie Victoria Ford. AB, Dartmouth Coll., 1966; PhD, Columbia U., 1973. Instr. Dartmouth Coll., Hanover, N.H., 1970-73; v.p. Chase Investment Bank, Rio de Janeiro, 1975-79, Chase Manhattan Bank, Rio de Janeiro, 1981-84; mng. dir. Chase Manhattan Bank, N.Y.C., 1986-88, also bd. dirs.; assoc. Booz Allen & Hamilton, Rio de Janeiro, 1979-81; cons. Oliver Wyman & Co., N.Y.C., 1989—; participant Brookings Inst. Sem., Washington, 1987, Euromoney Sem., Manila, 1987. Home: Village Rd Box 531 New Vernon NJ 07976 Office: Chase Manhattan Bank 1 Chase Plaza 13th Fl New York NY 10081

WHEELER, KATHERINE WELLS, state legislator; b. St. Louis, Feb. 8, 1940; d. Benjamin Harris and Katherine (Gladney) Wells; m. Douglas Lanphier Wheeler, June 13, 1964; children: Katherine Gladney, Lucille Lanphier. BA, Smith Coll., 1961; MA, Washington U., St. Louis, 1966. Founder auction N.H. Pub. TV, Durham, 1973-76; pub. mem. N.H. Pub. Broadcasting Council, Durham, 1975-80; founding mem. bd. govs. N.H. Pub. TV, 1980-88; mem. N.H. Ho. of Reps., Concord, 1988—; coord. internat. visitors program N.H. Coun. World Affairs, 1981—; bd. dirs. Planned Parenthood No. New Eng., Gt. Bay Sch. and Tng. Ctr., Newington, N.H. Active Commn. on Health, Human Svcs. and Elderly Affairs N.H. Ho. of Reps., Concord, 1988; bd. dirs. Devel. Svcs. Strafford County, Inc., 1991—. Named Woman of Yr. Union Leader Newspaper, 1984, Citizen of Yr. Homemakers of Strafford County, 1990; recipient Elizabeth Cambell Outstanding Pub. TV Vol. award Nat. Friends of Pub. Broadcasting, 1984, Meritorious Svc. award N.H. Womnen's Lobby, 1992. Mem. AAUW, AARP, LWV, Order of Women Legis., N.H. Smith Coll. Club (v.p. 1974-76, pres. 1976-78). Democrat. United Ch. Christ. Home and Office: 27 Mill Rd Durham NH 03824-3098

WHEELER, MARILYN GARNSEY, psychotherapist, director; b. Mt. Vernon, N.Y., Sept. 22, 1943; d. Raymond Darwin and Mary (Pavelchek) Garnsey; m. Dan J. Wheeler, Sept. 8, 1962; children: Danny Jr., Maryn Beth, Jennifer Anne. BA magna cum laude, Coll. of St. Rose, 1980; MS and EdS, SUNY, Albany, 1983. Pvt. practice psychotherapist Amsterdam, N.Y., 1981—; exec. dir., therapist Counseling Care & Svcs., Inc., Cohoes, N.Y., 1983—; founder Counseling Care & Svcs., Inc., 1983; mem. adj. faculty SUNY, Albany, 1985—, Antioch/New Eng. Grad. Sch., Keene, N.H., 1991—; cons. Cohoes City Sch. Dist., 1985—. Pres. bd. Rensselaer (N.Y.) Girls Club, 1980-83; elder Second Presbyn. Ch., 1986—, moderator christian edn. com.; bd. dirs. Suburban Albany County Family Self Sufficiency Task Force, 1991—. Mem. AACD, Mental Health Counselors Assn., Kappa Gamma Pi, Delta Epsilon Sigma. Office: Counseling Care & Svcs Inc 22-40 Remsen St Cohoes NY 12047

WHEELER, MARVIN DWAIN, psychologist, mental health director; b. Smithfield, Pa., June 4, 1940; s. Ewing Mackroy and Blanche Olive (Humbert) W.; m. Jean Ann Pasikowski, Aug. 2, 1969; 1 child, Jenene Autumn. BA in Psychology, Waynesburg Coll., 1965; MEd in Rehab., U. Pitts., 1967; PhD in Rehab. and Psychology, U. of Pitts., 1976. Lic. psychologist, Pa.; diplomate Soc. for Behavioral Medicine. Mental health coord. Vocat. Rehab. Ctr., Pitts., 1967-73; dir. mental retardation svcs. Mon-Yough Mental Health and Mental Retardation Svcs., McKeesport, Pa., 1973-78, dir. mental health svcs., 1978—; pvt. practice Glenshaw, Pa., 1982—; cons. psychologist Monongahela (Pa.) Valley Hosp., 1978—, Substance Abuse Svcs., Monessen, Pa., 1980—; lectr. community coll., 1980-83. Co-chmn. steering com. United Mental Health, Pitts, 1969-70; bd. dirs. Children's Svc. Coun., McKeesport, 1974-77; deacon-elder, Glenshaw (Pa.) Presbyn. Ch., 1980—. Mem. APA, Nat. Rehab. Assn., Am. Soc. Behavioral Medicine, Pa. Psychol. Assn. (mem. com. 1974-75, handbook directory com. 1978). Home: 8225 Thompson Run Rd Pittsburgh PA 15237-6347 Office: Mon-Yough MH/MR Svcs 335 Shaw Ave Mc Keesport PA 15132-2988

WHEELER, MARY HARRISON (MARDY WHEELER), human resource development specialist, consultant; b. Easton, Md., May 9, 1938; d. Robert Butler and Elizabeth (Fontaine) Harrison; m. David Weymouth Wheeler, May 9, 1962; children—Paul Harrison, Marjory Butler. B.A. in English, U. Maine-Orono, 1968, cert. in mgmt., 1976; M.S. in Human Resource Devel., Am. U., 1982. Counselor/coordinator Neighborhood Youth Corps, Lewiston, Maine, 1967-69; adminstr. Foruma, U. Maine-Augusta, 1973; tng. supr. Liberty Mutual Ins. Co., Lewiston, 1974-78, asst. dir., supervisory tng.,

Boston, 1978-80, dir. edn., 1980-83, dir. career devel., 1983-85, dir. edn., 1985-89, mgr. orgn. devel., 1989-90, dir. internal tng. U.C. Loss Prevention, 1991—; cons. in field; mem. faculty Middlesex Community Coll., Bedford, Maine, 1981-84, Worcester State Coll., 1985, Bentley Coll., 1987-92, Bryant Coll., 1989-90, U. N.H., 1991—. Author: (with Christine Bingaman and Ralph Graham) Communication Skills for Managers, 1983; (with J. Marshall) Training Type Inventory, 1986; (with R. Leeper) When it's Time to Say Goodbye, Northeast Training News, 1985, Whose Objectives Are They Anyway, Training Magazine, 1988. State bd. dirs. Maine League Women Voters, 1972-74; mem. Monmouth Sch. Bd. (Maine), 1974; mem. Androscoggin County Com. to Hire the Handicapped, Lewiston, 1975-78; mem. adv. bd. Bryant Coll. Ctr. for Mgmt. Devel., 1987-89. Mem. ASTD (mem. at large, chmn. career devel. subm com. Mass. chpt. 1984, bd. dirs. 1987-89, chmn. spring conf. 1988), Am. Personnel & Guidance Assn., Orgn. Devel. Network. Democrat. Episcopalian. Office: Liberty Mut Ins Co 175 Berkeley St Newton MA 02165-2637

WHEELER, PORTER KING, economic consultant; b. Emory, Ga., July 10, 1940; s. Raymond Parks Wheeler and Evelyn (King) Terhune; m. Carolyn V. Wood (div.); m. Mary R. Tietz; 1 child, Mark Henry. BA, Amherst Coll., 1962; MA, Harvard U., 1965, PhD, 1969. Asst. prof. Wesleyan U., Middletown, Conn., 1964-74; sr. economist U.S. Ry. Assn., Washington, 1974-75; sr. analyst Congl. Budget Office, Washington, 1975-78; group dir. com. on budget U.S. Senate, Washington, 1978-81; pvt. practice econs. cons. Washington, 1981—; Bd. dirs. Canton Devel. Co., Balt.; chmn. Canton R.R. Co.; cons. Office Tech. Assessment U.S. Congress, Washington, 1985—, Investment Program Assn., Washington, 1986—. Author: Performance of Initial Public Offerings, 1990; contbr. articles to profl. jours. Treas. Bravo! The Washington Opera, 1983-85, vice chmn. 1986-88. Econ. policy fellow Brookings Instn., Washington, 1975-76; vis. scholar U. Cambridge, 1973. Mem. Transp. Rsch. Bd. (regulatory com. 1991—), Am. Econs. Assn., Soc. Govt. Economists, Transp. Rsch. Forum (pres. 1987-88), Univ. Club Washington, Henlopen Acres Beach Club, Harvard Club, Les Ambassadeurs Club. Democrat. Episcopalian. Home: 6921 Armat Dr Bethesda MD 20817-2101 Office: The Jefferson Group 1341 G St NW Ste 1100 Washington DC 20005-3105

WHEELER, WESLEY DREER, marine engineer, naval architect, consultant; b. N.Y.C., Aug. 3, 1933; s. Wesley Lunn and Rosalie (Smith) W.; m. Dolores Janes-Wheeler, May 27, 1989; children: Wesley P., Jonathan H., Deborah B. BS in Mech. Engring., Worcester Poly. Inst., 1954; MSE in Naval Architecture and Marine Engring., U. Mich., 1958. Naval architect Am. Bulk Carriers, N.Y.C., 1966-68; port engr. Am. Trade and Prodn. Co., N.Y.C., 1968-69; pres. Techmarine, Inc., N.Y.C., 1969-71; asesor tecnico Astilleros Espanoles SA, Cadiz, Spain, 1971-72; tech. dir. Am. Bulk Carriers, N.Y.C., 1972-74; pres. Wesley D. Wheeler Assoc., Ltd., N.Y.C., 1974-83; v.p. J.J. Henry Co. Inc., N.Y.C., 1983; pres. Wheeler Assocs., N.Y.C., 1983—. Elder Fifth Ave Presbyn. Ch., N.Y.C., 1987-92, treas.; dir. Sutton Area Community, N.Y.C., 1987-92, Soc. Naval Architects and Marine Engrs., N.Y.C., 1990-92, treas.; chmn. Soc. Marine Cons., N.Y.C., 1987-92. Mem. Maritime Assn. Port of N.Y./N.J., Soc. Marine Port Engrs. N.Y., Soc. Maritime Arbitrators Inc., Royal Inst. Naval Architects, Inst. Marine Engrs., Asociacion Ingenieros Navales Madrid. Presbyterian. Home: 60 Sutton Pl S New York NY 10022-4168 Office: Wheeler Assocs FDR Sta PO Box 8183 New York NY 10150-8183

WHEELER, W(ILLIAM) SCOTT, composer, conductor, music educator; b. Washington, Feb. 24, 1952; s. Malcolm Frederick and Aurora Dorothy (Anas) W.; m. Christen Struthers Frothingham, Jan. 5, 1985; children: Margaret Lee, Catherine Elizabeth. BA, Amherst Coll., 1973; MFA, Brandeis U., 1978, PhD, 1984. Artistic dir. Dinosaur Annex Music Ensemble, Boston, 1975—; dir. Cambridge (Mass.) Chorale, 1976-78; tchr. music, condr. Emerson Coll., Boston, 1978—; staff reviewer Fanfare mag. Composer (choral) A Babe Is Born, 1979, (theater) A Happy Fellow, 1986 (Ronlin Foreman commn.), Winter Hills, 1987 (Somerville Arts Council commn.), (symphony) Northern Lights, 1987 (Koussevitzky commn.), (opera) The Construction of Boston (libretto by Kenneth Koch), 1989. Guggenheim fellow, 1988-89. Mem. Am. Music Ctr., ASCAP. Episcopalian. Home: 85 Haverhill St North Reading MA 01864-2816 Office: Emerson Coll Div Performing Arts 100 Beacon St Boston MA 02116

WHEELOCK, KEITH WARD, consulting company executive; b. Phila., Oct. 17, 1933; s. Ward and Margot Trevor (Williams) W.; m. Susan Bowen Kimball, June 15, 1956 (div. Nov. 1975); children: Helen Fraser, James Voorhees; m. Bente Lorentzen Ott, July 1978 (div. June 1988). BA, Yale U., 1955; MA, U. Pa., 1957; MS, MIT, 1972. Fgn. svc. officer Dept. State, Washington, 1960-69; dir. programs and policy div. N.Y.C. Housing and Devel. Adminstrn., 1970-71; devel. officer Moody's Investors Svc., Inc., N.Y.C., 1972-74, v.p. internat. ops., 1974-75, exec. v.p., 1975-76; pres. The Fantus Co., Millburn, N.J., 1976-83; mem. Sr. Direct Bradstreet Mgmt. Group, 1979-83; prin. Wheelock Cons., 1983-88; project dir. Mng. Growth in N.J., 1986-90. Mem. Montgomery (N.J.) Twp. Com., 1986-88; initiator, facilitator Century 21 & John Hay Fellows Program, 1991—. Author: Nasser's New Egypt, A Critical Analysis, 1960, New Jersey Growth Management, 1989. Sloan fellow MIT, 1972. Home: PO Box 339 Skillman NJ 08558-0339

WHELAN, JOHN MICHAEL, retired chemist; b. Lyndhurst, N.J., Sept. 12, 1921; s. John Michael and Clara Lillian (Dickel) W.; m. Helen Claire Keckeisen, Oct. 2, 1943; children: Kathleen, Dennis, Kerry. ME, Stevens Inst. Tech., 1941, MS, 1943; PhD, Poly. Inst., Bklyn., 1959. Rsch. chemist Union Carbide Corp., Bloomfield, N.J., 1941-53, group leader, 1953-55; sect. head Union Carbide Corp., Bound Brook, N.J., 1955-63, asst. dir. R&D, 1963-78, rsch. assoc., 1978-83, ret., 1983; Author: The Wooden Plane, 1992; contbr. articles to profl. publs.; patentee in field. Sec. Crestview Swim Club, Murray Hill, N.J., 1960-65. Mem. Collectors of Rare and Familiar Tools Soc. N.J. (treas., pres. 1990—). Home: 38 Colony Ct New Providence NJ 07974-2332

WHELAN, ROGER MICHAEL, lawyer, educator; b. Montclair, N.J., Nov. 12, 1936; s. John Leslie and Helen Louise (Callahan) W.; m. Rosemary Bogdan, Aug. 26, 1961; children: Helen, Theresa, John, James, Kathleen (dec.), Julie, Jennifer. AB cum laude, Georgetown U., 1959, JD, 1962. Bar: D.C. 1962, U.S. Dist. Ct. D.C. 1962, U.S. Ct. Appeals (D.C. cir.) 1962, U.S. Supreme Ct. 1968, U.S. Dist. Ct. Md. 1985. Assoc. Fried, Rogers & Ritz, Washington, 1961-66; ptnr. Doctor & Whelan, Washington, 1967-72; judge U.S. Bankruptcy Ct., Washington, 1972-83; sr. mem. Verner, Liipfert, Bernhard, McPherson & Hand, Chartered, Washington, 1984-89; ptnr. Shaw, Pittman, Potts & Trowbridge, Washington, 1989—; dir. Lincoln Ctr. for Legal Studies, Arlington, Va., 1974-84; disting. lectr. Columbus Sch. Law, Cath. U. Am., Washington, 1975—. Sec. local campaign com., Alexandria, Va., 1964; trustee YMCAA, Silver Spring, Md., 1972-74. Recipient award D.C. Cir. Jud. Conf., 1984. Fellow Am. Coll. Bankruptcy (bd. regents 1990—); mem. Fed. Bar Assn. (chmn. bankruptcy subcom. 1988), Am. Bankruptcy Inst. (bd. dirs. 1991—, chmn. legis. com. 1991—). Republican. Roman Catholic. Home: 17908 Ednor View Ter Ashton MD 20861-9757 Office: Shaw Pittman Potts & Trowbridge 2300 N St NW Washington DC 20037-1122

WHELDEN, MARK MCGILL, engineering technician; b. Hartford, Conn., Dec. 9, 1950; s. Kenneth Richard and Eleanor Marie (McGill) W.; m. Maria Margarete Comeau, May 26, 1979; 1 child, Emily Elizabeth. A in Civil Engring., Hartford State Tech. Coll., 1971. With Conn. Natural Gas Corp., Hartford, 1971—, now engring. technician, 1989—; engring. technician; v.p. CNG Employees Fed. Credit Union, Hartford, 1981-91, pres., 1987, chief steward, 1988-91, Conn. Ind. Utility Workers Local 12924, 1988—. Vol. United Way Greater Hartford, 1975, 90; group mem., facilitator Small Christian Communities, Broad Brook, 1989-91; contbr. Adopt-a-Child Christmas Orgn., Hartford, 1991. Mem. CNG Sportsmen Assn. Republican. Roman Catholic. Home: 32 Rolocut Rd Broad Brook CT 06016-9611 Office: Conn Natural Gas Corp 100 Columbus Blvd Hartford CT 06103-2805

WHELLEY, PETER TINDALE, school psychologist; b. Saranac Lake, N.Y., Feb. 22, 1954; s. John Gerard and Martha Evelyn (Jaquet) W.; m. Sarah Ann Chaplain, Aug. 6, 1977; children: Kathleen Meghan, Patrick Liam, Collin Jaquet. BA, Boston U., 1972; MS, U. Dayton, 1981. Videotape operator, tchr. Boston U. Playgroup, 1974-76; hosp. aide surp. Dayton (Ohio) Children's Psychiat. Hosp., 1976-78; outreach counselor, asst. dir. urban svcs., then supr. YMCA, Dayton, 1978-80; supr. outreach counselors City of Dayton, 1980-81; sch. psychologist Madison County Schs., London, Ohio, 1981-82; emergency rm. mental health therapist Madison County Hosp., London, 1981; sch. psychologist Jefferson County Sch. Dist., Charles Town, W.Va., 1982-88; sch. psychologist, guidance counselor Moultonborough (N.H.) Sch. Dist., 1988—; adj. faculty mem. Shepherd Coll., Shepherdstown, W.Va., 1983-88; mem. selection com. for dir. of Sch. Psychology, U. Dayton, 1981. Bd. dirs. Teen Inst., Corona, N.H., 1989. Mem. Am. Psychol. Assn., Nat. Assn. Sch. Psychologists, N.H. Assn. Sch. Psychologists. Home: PO Box 500 Moultonborough NH 03254-0500 Office: Sch Adminstrv Unit 45 PO Box 149 Moultonborough NH 03254-0149

WHETZEL, JOSHUA CLYDE, JR., museum executive, conservationist; b. Pitts., Mar. 8, 1921; s. Joshua Clyde and Gladys May (Porter) W.; m. Ann Farley Walton, Sept. 27, 1947; children: Joshua C., William M., Rachel W., Thomas P. B.S. in Chemistry, Va. Mil. Inst., 1943; postgrad., U. Pitts., 1963-66. Research assoc. Mellon Inst., Pitts., 1945-48; ptnr. Allegheny Refining Co., Verona, Pa., 1948-63; sec., treas. Conservation Found., Washington, 1967-69; pres. Western Pa. Conservancy, Pitts., 1969-80, chmn., 1980—; pres. Buhl Sci. Ctr., Pitts., 1982-87; bd. dirs. Student Conservation Assn., Charlestown, N.H., 1978-85, 88, chmn., 1985-87; trustee Carnegie Inst., Pitts., 1983-87; chmn. sci. ctr. com. Carnegie Inst. Bd. Trustees, 1987—; dir. Met. Pitts. Pub. Broadcasting, Inc., 1984-90. Mem. citizens adv. council Pa. Environ. Resources, Harrisburg, 1976-83; chmn. Park Commn. Fox Chapel Borough, Pa., 1970-79; elder Shadyside Presbyterian Ch., Pitts., 1973-79; treas. Three Rivers Arts Festival, 1961-67, Ellis Sch., 1963-67; co-chmn. Gov's Garden Commn., Harrisburg, Pa., 1979-81. Served to 1st lt. AUS, 1943-45, ETO. Named Man of Yr. in Conservation Pitts. Jaycees, 1974, Pa. Conservationist of Yr., Pa. Wildlife Fedn., 1986; recipient W.E. Clyde Todd award Audubon Soc. of W. Pa., 1980, Western Pa. Conservation award, 1985. Mem. Duquesne Club, Pitts. Golf Club, Rolling Rock Club (Ligonier, Pa.). Home and Office: 5036 Castleman St Pittsburgh PA 15232-2107

WHIPPLE, BEVERLY, nursing educator, researcher; b. Jersey City, June 30, 1941; d. Howard and Beatrice (Bodei) Hoehne; m. James Whipple, Sept. 15, 1962; children: Allen James, Susan Jane. BS, Wagner Coll., S.I., N.Y., 1962; MEd, Rutgers U., 1967, PhD, 1986, MSN, 1987. RN, N.J., N.Y.; diplomate Am. Bd. Sexologists; cert. sex educator, counselor and rschr., sexologist. Instr. Helene Field Sch. of Nursing, Camden, N.J.; assoc. prof. nursing Gloucester County Coll., Sewell, N.J.; assoc. prof. Rutgers Coll. of Nursing, Newark, N.J.; researcher in field. Co-author: G Spot, Safe Encounters; contbr. numerous articles to profl. jours. Recipient Hugo Beigel award for Rsch. Excellence, Excellence in Rsch. award N.J. State Nurses Assn. Felllow Am. Acad. Nursing, Soc. for Sci. Study Sex.; mem. ANA, AAAS, Am. Pain Soc., Am. Assn. Sex Educators, Counselors and Therapists, Soc. for Sex. Therapy and Rsch., Sex. Info. and Edn. Coun. U.S. Home: 31 NW Lakeside Dr Medford NJ 08055-9589

WHIPPLE, FRED LAWRENCE, astronomer; b. Red Oak, Iowa, Nov. 5, 1906; s. Harry Lawrence and Celestia (MacFarl) W.; m. Dorothy Woods, 1928 (div. 1935); 1 son, Earle Raymond; m. Babette F. Samelson, Aug. 20, 1946; children: Dorothy Sandra, Laura. Student, Occidental Coll., 1923-24; AB, UCLA, 1927, PhD, 1931; AM (hon.), Harvard, 1945; ScD, Am. Internat. Coll., 1958; DLitt (hon.), Northeastern U., 1961; DSc (hon.), Temple U., 1961, U. Ariz., 1979; LLD (hon.), C.W. Post Coll., L.I. U., 1962. Teaching fellow U. Calif. at Berkeley, 1927-29, Lick Obs. fellow, 1930-31; instr. Stanford U., summer 1929, U. Calif., summer 1931; staff mem. Harvard Obs., 1931-77; instr. Harvard U., 1932-38, lectr., 1938-45; research asso. Radio Research Lab., 1942-45, asso. prof. astronomy, 1945-50, prof. astronomy, 1950-77, chmn. dept., 1949-56, Phillips prof. astronomy, 1968-77; dir. Smithsonian Astrophys. Obs., 1955-73, sr. scientist, 1973—; mem. Rocket Research Panel U.S., 1946-57; U.S. subcom NASA, 1946-52, U.S. Research and Devel. Bd. Panel, 1947-52; chmn. Tech. Panel on Rocketry; mem. Tech. Panel on Earth Satellite Program; other coms. Internat. Geophys. Year, 1955-59; mem., past officer Internat. Astron. Union; cons. missions to U.K. and MTO, 1944; del. Inter-Am. Astrophys. Congress, Mexico, 1942; active leader project on Upper-Atmospheric Research via Meteor Photog. sponsored by Bur. Ordnance, U.S. Navy, 1946-51; by Bur. Ordnance, U.S. Navy (Office Naval Research), 1951-57, USAF, 1948-62; mem. com. meteorology, space sci. bd., com. on atmospheric scis. Nat. Acad. Scis.-NRC, 1958-65; project dir. Harvard Radio Meteor Project, 1957-65; adviser Sci. Adv. Bd., USAF, 1963-67; spl. cons. com. Sci. and Astronautics U.S. Ho. Reps., 1960-73; chmn. Gordon Research Confs., 1963; dir. Optical Satellite Tracking Project, NASA, 1958-73; project dir. Orbiting Astron. Obs., 1958-72; dir. Meteorite Photography and Recovery Program, 1962-73, cons. planetary atmospheres, 1962-69; mem. space scis. working group on Orbiting Astron. Observatories, 1959-70; chmn. sci. council geodetic uses artifical satellites Com. Space Research, 1965-70. Author: Earth, Moon and Planets, rev. edit, 1968, Orbiting The Sun: Planets and Satellites of The Solar System, The Mystery of Comets, 1985; co-author: Survey of the Universe; Contbr.: sci. papers on astron. and upper atmosphere to Ency. Brit; mags., other publs.; Asso. editor: Astronomical Jour, 1954-56, 64-71; editor: Smithsonian Contributions to Astrophysics, 1956-73, Planetary and Space Science, 1958-83, hon. editor, 1983—, Science Revs, 1961-70; editorial bd.: Earth and Planetary Sci. Letters, 1966-73; inventor tanometer, meteor bumper; a developer window as radar countermeasure, 1944. Decorated comdr. Order of Merit for research and invention, Esnault-Pelterie award France; recipient Donohue medals for ind. discovery of 6 new comets; Presdl. Cert. of Merit for sci. work during World War II; J. Lawrence Smith medal Nat. Acad. Scis. for research on meteors, 1949; medal for astron. research U. Liege, 1960; Space Flight award Am. Astronautical Soc., 1961; Disting. Fed. Civilian Service award, 1963; Space Pioneers medallion for contbns. to fed. space program, 1968; Public Service award for contbns. to OAO2 devel. NASA, 1969; Leonard medal Meteoritical Soc., 1970; Kepler medal AAAS, 1971; Career Service award Nat. Civil Service League, 1972; Henry medal Smithsonian Instn., 1973; Alumnus of Yr. Achievement award UCLA, 1976; Golden Plate award Am. Acad. Achievement, 1981; Gold medal Royal Astron. Soc., 1983; Bruce Medal, Astron. Soc. Pacific, 1986; Benjamin Franklin fellow Royal Soc. Arts, London, 1968—; depicted on postal stamp of Mauritania, 1986. Fellow Am. Astron. Soc. (v.p. 1962-64, 1987 Russell lecturer), Am. Rocket Soc., Am. Geophys. Union (Fred L. Whipple yearly lectr. estab. in honor planetary div. 1990), Royal Astron. Soc. (assoc.); mem. AAAS, Nat. Acad. Scis., AIAA Astronautics (aerospace tech. panel space physics 1960-63), Astronautical Soc. Pacific, Solar Assos., Internat. Sci. Radio Union (U.S.A. nat. com. 1949-61), Am. Meteoritical Soc., Am. Standards Assn., Am. Acad. Arts and Scis., Am. Philos. Soc. (councillor sect. astronomy and earth scis. 1966-70), Royal Soc. Scis. Belgium (corr.), Internat. Acad. Astronautics (sci. advisory com. 1962-65), Internat. Astronautical Fedn., Am. Meteorol. Soc., Royal Astron. Soc. (assoc.), Phi Beta Kappa, Sigma Xi, Pi Mu Epsilon. Clubs: Examiner (Boston); Cosmos (Washington). Office: 60 Garden St Cambridge MA 02138-1596

WHISHER, BRADLEY EDWARD, insurance company executive; b. Plattsburg, N.Y., Nov. 4, 1954; s. Floyd Edward and Angeline (Molinero) W.; m. Dorinda Laurel Chase, Feb. 12, 1977; children: Lindsay L., Kimberly A., Bradley E. Jr. BSBA, Ithaca Coll., 1976; student, Am. Coll., Bryn Mawr, Pa., 1991—. CLU, chartered fin. cons. Asst. mgr., sales rep. Prudential Ins. Co., Albany, N.Y., 1976-80; asst. mgr., cons. Home Life Ins. Co., Albany, N.Y., 1980-86; mgr. life and fin. svcs. Jardine Ins. Brokers Inc., Schenectady, N.Y., 1986—; cons. St. Clare's Hosp., Schenectady, 1988—, active pension adv. com. Bd. dirs. St. Clare's Hosp. Found., Schenectady, 1989—, Am. Cancer Soc., 1992. Mem. Nat. Assn. Life Underwriters, Am. Soc. CLU, Internat. Assn. Fin. Planners, Million Dollar Round Table, Rotary (dir. track meet Niskayuna club 1987—). Home: 481 Stage Rd Charlton NY 12019 Office: Jardine Ins Brokers Inc 433 State St Schenectady NY 12305

WHITAKER, A(LBERT) DUNCAN, lawyer; b. Ft. Wayne, Ind., Jan. 3, 1932; s. Robert Lynn and Rhoda Irene (Duncan) W.; m. Adelaide B. Saccone, Aug. 13, 1955; children: Brent Robert, Alene G., Karen E. B.A., Yale U., 1954; J.D., U. Mich., 1957. Bar: Mich. 1957, U.S. Ct. Appeals D.C. 1959, U.S. Supreme Ct. 1961. Atty. antitrust div. U.S. Dept. Justice, 1957-59; assoc. Howrey & Simon, Washington, 1959-65, ptnr., 1965—; lectr. George Washington U., George Mason U. Law Sch. Contbr. articles to profl. jours. Mem. ABA, Fed. Bar Assn., D.C. Bar Assn., Order of Coif, Phi Beta Kappa. Clubs: Metropolitan, Nat. Lawyers (Washington). Office: Howrey & Simon 1730 Pennsylvania Ave NW Washington DC 20006-4792

WHITAKER, JOEL, publisher; b. Indpls., May 27, 1942; s. Quincy Myers and Sigur Elizabeth (Moore) W.; m. Donna Kay, Apr. 27, 1985. BS in Bus. Journalism, Ind. U., 1964, MA in Journalism, 1971; JD, Temple U., 1979. Reporter St. Petersburg (Fla.) Times, 1964, copy editor, 1966-68; copy editor Wall St. Journal, N.Y.C., 1968-73; bus. news editor Phila. Evening and Sunday Bull., 1973-78; law clk. Fellheimer, Krakower & Eicen, Phila., 1978-79; mng. editor Bank Letter, N.Y.C., 1979-80; editor, pres. Whitaker Newsletter Inc., Fanwood, N.J., 1980—. Chmn. Fanwood Planning Bd., 1981-85; mem. Downtown Redevel. Commn., Fanwood, 1983-85. With USAR, 1964-85. Mem. Newsletter Assn. (bd. dirs. 1983—, found. trustee 1986—, treas. 1989—), Soc. Profl. Journalists, Nat. Press Club (Washington). Republican. Roman Catholic. Office: Whitaker Newsletters Inc 313 South Ave Fanwood NJ 07023-1350

WHITAKER, JOHN SCOTT, physics educator; b. Oroville, Calif., Nov. 10, 1948; s. Walter Ralph and Barbara (Brittain) W.; m. Bohn Buechner, Sept. 24, 1983; children: Amelia, Elizabeth. BA, U. Calif., Berkeley, 1970, PhD, 1976. Sci. assoc. CERN, Geneva, 1977-78; from asst. prof. to assoc. prof. MIT, Cambridge, Mass., 1978-85; from assoc. prof. to prof. physics Boston U., 1985—. Contbr. articles to profl. publs. U.S. Dept. Energy grantee, 1985—; named Outstanding Jr. Investigator, U.S. Dept. Energy, 1984-85. Office: Boston U Physics Dept 590 Commonwealth Ave Boston MA 02215-2507

WHITBY, OWEN, statistician; b. Luton, Eng., Feb. 24, 1942. BS in Math. with honors, McMaster U., Hamilton, Ont., Can., 1964; MS in Stats., Stanford U., 1966, PhD in Stats., 1972. From instr. to assoc. prof. Columbia U., N.Y.C., 1969-78; from actuarial assoc. to sec. SwissRe Holding (NA) Inc., N.Y.C., 1979-80; from sec. to v.p. North Am. Reins. Corp., N.Y.C., 1980-89; from v.p. to exec. v.p. Atrium Corp., N.Y.C., 1984—; v.p. European Internat. Reins. Co. Ltd., Bridgetown, Barbados, 1987—; sr. v.p. European Atlantic Reassurance Co. Ltd., Bridgetown, 1990—. Mem. AAAS, Am. Statis. Assn., Assn. for Computing Machinery, Biometric Soc., Inst. Math. Statistics, Internat. Actuarial Assn., Soc. Actuaries (assoc.), Soc. CPCU. Office: Atrium Corp 200 Park Ave 16th Fl New York NY 10166-0005

WHITCOMB, JAMES STUART, videographer, photographer, production company; b. Buffalo, May 7, 1957; s. C. Stuart and Helen Nancy (O'Reilly) W. BA in Journalism/Broadcasting, SUNY, Buffalo, 1983. Pres., owner Ad Astra Prodns., Williamsville, N.Y., 1987—; co-owner, videographer, photographer STB Prodns., Williamsville, N.Y., 1989—. Videographer, editor (nature/stress-reduction video) A Celebration of the Four Seasons, 1991; videographer, writer (promotion video) Internat. Modeling and Talent Assn., 1990; videographer numerous prodns. for modeling, fashion, and spl. interst. Home: 71 Rinewalt St Williamsville NY 14221 Office: Ad Astra and STB Prodns PO Box 1725 Williamsville NY 14221

WHITE, A. BURTON, orthopedist; b. N.Y.C., June 2, 1927; s. Louis I. and Jessie (Levinson) W.; m. Hannabelle Lee Shenkin, June 24, 1956; children: Jonathan Richard, Randolph Ellis, Liane Rachel. BA, Cornell U., 1945; MD, Hahnemann U., Phila., 1949. Diplomate Am. Bd. Orthopedic Surgery. Cons. orthopedic surgeon Winthrop U. Hosp., Mineola, N.Y., 1957-87; assoc. attending orthopedic surgeon North Shore U. Hosp., Manhasset, N.Y., 1959—; cons. St. Francis Hosp., Roslyn, N.Y., 1992—; chmn. Nassau County Bd. Health, Mineola, N.Y., 1973-74; dir. Med. Lab. Mut. Ins. Co., N.Y.C., 1975-81; councilor Bd. Coun. Acad. Orthopedic Surgeons, 1982-89. Contbr. articles to profl. jours. Pres. Great Neck (N.Y.) Dem. Club, 1963, 64; del. Nat. Dem. Conv., N.Y.C., 1976. Fellow ACS, Am. Acad. Orthopedic Surgeons, Nassau Acad. Medicine; mem. Nassau County Med. Soc. (pres. 1976-77), N.Y. State Soc. Orthopaedic Surgeons (pres. 1987-88, profl. liability com.), Med. Soc. State N.Y., Ea. Orthopedic Assn. Jewish. Office: 1 Barstow Rd Great Neck NY 11021

WHITE, ADRIAN MICHAEL STEPHEN, mining executive; b. nr. Kent, Eng., Aug. 15, 1940; s. Malcolm Royston and Joan May (Richards) W.; m. Elaine M. Dorion, 1966; children: Malcolm, Catherine. Grad., McGill U., Montreal, 1964. Chartered accountant, Que., Ont. With Coopers & Lybrand, chartered accountants, 1962-66; acting treas. Rothesay Paper Corp., 1965; asst. treas. Genstar Ltd., 1967-71; treas. Brinco Ltd.; also Churchill Falls (Labrador) Corp., 1971-75; treas. Algoma Steel Corp., Ltd., Sault Ste. Marie, Ont., 1975-80; v.p., chief fin. officer Little Long Lac Gold Mines Ltd., Toronto, Ont., 1980-81; v.p. Bank of Montreal, Toronto, 1981-88; exec. v.p., chief fin. officer, bd. dirs. Curragh Resources Group, Toronto, 1988—, also bd. dirs.; fin. columnist Indsl. Mgmt. mag. Bd. dirs. Drs. Hosp. Found., 1986. Mem. Fin. Execs. Inst. (chmn. Can. internat. fin. com.), Internat. Fiscal Assn., Canadian Tax Found. Address: 72 Sir Williams Ln, Islington, ON Canada M9A 1V3 also: 95 Wellington Ste 1900, Toronto, ON Canada M5J 2N7

WHITE, BARBARA EHRLICH, art history educator; b. N.Y.C., Oct. 20, 1936; d. Stanley Ehrlich and Ruth (Krimsky) Ehrlich; m. Leon S. White, Aug. 6, 1961; children: Joel, David. BA, Smith Coll., 1958; MA, Columbia U., 1960, PhD, 1965. Lectr. Queens (N.Y.) Coll., 1959-61, Boston U., summer 1965; lectr. Tufts U., Medford, Mass., 1965-66, asst. prof., 1966-87, adj. prof. art history, 1987—. Author: Renoir: His Life, Art and Letters, 1984, French edit., 1985; editor: Impressionism in Perspective, 1978; contbr. articles to profl. jours. NEH younger scholar fellow, 1969-70; Samuel Kress grantee, 1969-70. Mem. Coll. Art Assn., 19th Century Scholar's Collaborative, Women's Caucus for Art. Office: Tufts U Dept Art History 11 Talbot Ave Medford MA 02155-5812

WHITE, BERTRAM MILTON, chemical executive; b. Boston, Nov. 17, 1923; s. Samuel Louis and Jennie Anne (Cohen) W.; m. Bernice Hannah Ginns; children: Mark Alan, Leland Jeffrey. BS, Lowell Inst. Tech., Cambridge, Mass., 1943. Product mgr. Philipps Bros. Chems. Inc., Holbrook, Mass., 1952-65, Sobin Chems. Inc., South Boston, 1965-69; pres. Solvent Chems. Co., Inc., Malden, Mass., 1969-73; v.p. I.C.C. Chems. Inc., N.Y.C., 1973-80; sr. v.p. Asoma Chems. Inc., Boston, 1980-83, Laporte Chems. USA, Hackensack, N.J., 1983-84; pres. Gen. Plastics and Chems. Co., Natick, Mass., 1984-91, GFI Chems. Inc., Sudbury, Mass., 1991—; bd. dirs. Sudexco N.V., Brussels, Recochem Inc., Montreal, Que., Can.; treas. U.S. Antimony Sales Corp.; pres. Tech. Exporters of Am., Miami, Fla. Served with Corps of Engring. U.S Army, 1943-46, ETO. Decorated Purple Heart. Mem. Drug Chem. and Allied Trades Assn., New Eng. Chemists Club, N.Y.C. Chemists Club, Salesmen's Assn. of Am. Chem. Industry. Jewish. Office: GFI Chems Inc 111 Boston Post Rd PO Box 777 Sudbury MA 01776

WHITE, BONNIE HAVANA, federal agency official; b. Trammel, Va., Nov. 18, 1926; d. John Clark and Cordella (Burke) H.; m. Bonnie Havana Holbrook, Sept. 6, 1958; children: Jonnie, James, Sheila. BS, U. Md., 1988; postgrad., U. D.C., 1990. From libr. aide to examiner SEC, Washington, 1981—. Art docent Hirshborn Mus., 1990; tutor D.C. Pub. Libr. Project for the Deaf, 1991, trainer, 1991. Mem. U. Md. Alumni Assn. Republican. Presbyterian. Home: 1708 Merrimac Dr Adelphi MD 20783

WHITE, BREN DOUGLAS, international business consultant, writer; b. Lafayette, Ind., July 30, 1957; s. Joe Lloyd and Wanita Irene (Robertson) W.; m. Cheryl Lynn Nolan, Aug. 6, 1978; children: Stresa Laren, Trieste Keehan, Bjorn Carrick. BS, Purdue U., 1982; postgrad., Johns Hopkins U., 1987-91. Prodn. supr. GM, Pontiac, Mich., 1979; assoc. cons. AMS Inst., Inc., West Lafayette, Ind., 1980; pers. dir. The Sherwin-Williams Co., Deshler, Ohio, 1981-83; dir. human resources The Sherwin-Williams Co., Balt., 1983-86; corp. dir. pers. and tng. Gen. Physics Corp., Columbia, Md., 1986-88; corp. dir. tng. Case Group, Watford, Eng., and Columbia, Md., 1988; corp. tng. mgr. COMSAT Corp., Washington, 1988-91; pres., chief operating officer The WORLD Group, Inc., Bethesda, Md., 1991—; mem. adv. bd. Internat. Christian U.; mem. global exec. program Georgetown U., Washington; lectr. Johns Hopkins U., Balt., 1987-91, U. Md., College Park, 1990, Purdue U., West Lafayette, 1991, U. Pa., 1992. Author: World Class

Leaders, 1992, (video) Human Performance at its Best, 1987. Deacon Ch. of Christ, Columbia, 1990—. Mem. ASTD (bd. dirs., internat. exec. com. 1991, svc. award 1986, Internat. Tng. award 1990), Soc. Intercultural Edn., Tng. and Rsch., Nat. Soc. Performance and Instrn., Assn. Quality and Participation, Performance Mgmt. Inst. (past. pres.), U.S. Coun. for Internat. Bus. (sponsor rep.), State of Md. Tng. & Edn. Task Force/Telecommunications Industry (high tech. coun.). Office: The WORLD Group Inc 6701 Democracy Blvd Ste 300 Bethesda MD 20817-1574

WHITE, BRUCE DEANE, advertising executive; b. Fall River, Mass., May 20, 1930; s. James Tec and Louise Andros (Deane) W.; m. Sandra Lawton, June 22, 1964; children: Bruce Deane Miller, Lawton Dana Ian. Student, Bryant Coll., Yale Sch. Photography, USN Sch. Photography. Registered emergency med. technician. Dir. pub. relations Sta. WNET-TV, Providence, 1953-54; lighting dir. Sta. WPRO-TV, Providence, 1954-55; TV producer MIT Sta. WGBH-TV, Boston, 1955-57; TV producer Sta. WTEV-TV, Providence, 1957-66, host children's program, 1966-71; agy. exec., treas. Mediaconcepts Corp., Boston, 1969—; pres., chmn. bd. dirs. Ferretworld, Inc., Assonet; hon. chmn. Black-footed Ferret Recovery program Wyo. Dept. Fish and Game; bd. dirs. Michael G. Alfonso Ferret Rescue Ctr. Pres. Greater Fall River Art Assn., 1960-61; chmn. bd. deacons United Ch. Assonet, Mass., 1980—. Served with USN, 1950-52, Korea. Mem. Mass. Soc. Prevention Cruelty to Animals, USS Constitution Mus., Colonial Navy of Mass., SAR (life), Soc. Mayflower Descendents (life), Alden Kindred of Am. (life), Animal Rescue League of Fall River (bd. dirs.), Nat. Wildlife Fedn., United Ferret Orgn. (nat. pres.), Boston Animal Rescue League. Congregationalist. Home: 6 Water St Assonet MA 02702-1114 Office: Mediaconcepts Corp 25 N Main St Assonet MA 02702-1136

WHITE, BYRON R., U.S. Supreme Court justice; b. Ft. Collins, Colo., June 8, 1917; m. Marion Stearns; children: Charles, Nancy. Grad., U. Colo., 1938; Rhodes scholar, Oxford (Eng.) U.; grad., Yale Law Sch. Clk. to chief justice U.S., 1946-47; atty. firm Lewis, Grant & Davis, Denver, 1947-60; dep. atty. gen. U.S., 1961-62; assoc. justice Supreme Ct., U.S., 1962—. Served with USNR, World War II, Pacific. Mem. Phi Beta Kappa, Phi Gamma Delta, Order of Coif. Office: US Supreme Ct Supreme Ct Bldg 1 First St NE Washington DC 20543

WHITE, CATHERINE FRIEND, investment manager; b. Bronxville, N.Y., June 29, 1956; d. Robert Arthur Friend and Alice Haven (Harvey) Newman; m. Richard Edward White, July 1, 1978. BA, Dickinson Coll., 1978; MBA, Babson Coll., 1986. Portfolio acct. Pioneer Group, Inc., Boston, 1980-82; ops. adminstr. Hellman, Jordan Mgmt., Boston, 1982-84; portfolio mgr. Internat. Heritage, Boston, 1986-88; cons. Medford, Mass., 1988-90; pres., portfolio mgr. Fin. Architects, Lexington, 1990—. Editor newsletter Babson Entrepreneurial Exchange Newsletter, 1985. Mem. steering com. Medford Recycles, 1989—; vol. McLean Hosp., Belmont, Mass., 1989—. Mem. NAFE, Assn. for Investment Mgmt. and Rsch., Women on Corp. Bds. (chair 1988—), New Eng. Women Bus. Owners, Social Investment Forum, Internat. Alliance, Am. Assn. Individual Investors (bd. dirs.), Winchester C. of C., Medford C. of C., Toastmasters Internat. Office: Fin Architects 5 Militia Dr Lexington MA 02173-4737

WHITE, CHRISTINE, educator; b. Taunton, Mass., Apr. 1, 1905; d. Peregrine Hastings and Sara (Lawrence) W. Cert., Boston Sch. Phys. Edn.; BS, Boston U., 1935, MEd, 1939. Instr. Winthrop Coll., Rock Hill, S.C., 1927-29; instr., asst. prof. The Woman's Coll. U. N.C., Greensboro, N.C., 1929-41; assoc. prof., head dept. physical edn. Meredith Coll., Raleigh, N.C., 1941-43; assoc. prof., prof. chair dept. physical edn. Wheaton Coll., Norton, Mass., 1943-70, prof. emerita, 1970—. co-editor Taunton Architecture: A Reflection of the City's History, 1981, 89. Chmn. Hist. Dist. Study Com., 1975-78, Recreation Commn., 1972-81; mem. Hist. Dist. Commn., 1979—, sec., 1979-86; mem. Park and Recreation Commn., 1982—. Fellow AAHPERD; mem. AAUP (pres. Wheaton Coll. chpt. 1960-61), AAUW, LWV, Eastern Assn. Phys. Edn. for Coll. Women (bd. dirs. 1950-52, 61-62), Nat. Assn. Phys. Edn. in Higher Edn., Pi Lambda Theta. Home: 40 Highland Ter Taunton MA 02780-4729

WHITE, DENNIS ALLEN, research company executive, science administrator; b. Fairbanks, Alaska, Aug. 2, 1946; s. James Andrew and Mariana Rebecca (Truman) W.; m. Patricia Ann Zagorski, May 1, 1967; children: John Truman, Pamela Rebecca. Student, Fla. State U., 1964-66, RCA Sch. Electronics, 1970-72, Manchester Community Coll., 1969-70. Cert. in nondestructive testing, level III. Computer operator Travelers Ins. Co., Hartford, Conn., 1970-71, First Nat. Stores, East Hartford, Conn., 1971-72; field engr. Scan Optics, East Hartford, 1972-73; research and devel. technician Litton Industries, Hartford, 1973-74; with combat systems support dept. Electric Boat, Groton, Conn., 1974-78; applications and research engr. Hartford Steam Boiler, Hartford, 1978-83; regional mgr. Dunegan Corp., Irvine, Calif., 1983-85; applications specialist Phys. Acoustics Corp., Lawrenceville, N.J., 1985-87; pres. Measurement Services Internat., Inc., Stafford Springs, Conn., 1983—. Patentee in field. Mem. ASTM (chmn. glossary com. 1987—), ASME (chmn. subgroup on acoustic emission 1982—), Am. Soc. Metals, TAPPI, Acoustic Emission Working Group, Am. Soc. Non-destructive Testing (bd. dirs. Conn. Yankee 1987). Home: PO Box 90 Stafford Springs CT 06076-0090 Office: Measurement Svcs Internat PO Box 35 Stafford Springs CT 06076-0035

WHITE, DONALD HAMILTON, JR., engineer; b. Richmond, Va., Nov. 13, 1942; s. Donald Hamilton Sr. and Marian Louise (Garthright) W.; m. Barbara Noël Buckman, Aug. 13, 1966; children: Cherilyn, Donald III, Jonathan, Daniel. BS Nuclear, SUNY Maritime, Bronx, 1964; postgrad., Cornell U., 1986-87. Cert. third asst. marine engr. Engr. AMF-Beaird, Shreveport, La., 1971-72; program mgr. Aqua-Chem div. Coca-Cola, Milw., 1972-74; mgr. Pall Corp., Cortland, N.Y., 1974-88, sr. mgr., 1988—; cons. and speaker in field. Patentee in field; contbr. articles to profl. jours. Mem. ASME, ASTM, Am. Inst. Chem. Engrs., Am. Chem. Soc., Nat. Assn. Corrosion Engrs., Masons (master Homer, N.Y. 1978, 85, past masters assoc. sec. 1985), Order Ea. Star (patron 1983, 88, 90, dist. grand lectr. 1987, 91, comdr. Cortland Commandery 1991). Home: 923 Alfred Ln Homer NY 13077-9350 Office: Pall Corp Rte 281 Cortland NY 13045

WHITE, ERIC JOSEPH JAMES, small business owner; b. Lancaster, Pa., Jan. 7, 1965; s. Elwood Martin and Margot Jane (Snyder) W. Grad. high sch., Landisville, Pa., 1983. Owner White Enterprises, Columbia, Pa., 1983-85, Movie Man, Columbia, 1985—; pres. White Enterprises, Corp., Columbia, 1987—; owner Print Man, 1990—, White Ent. Vending Group, 1990—, Photo Man, 1992—. Recipient Silver medals Pa. Keystone State Games, 1989. Mem. Nat. Arbor Day Found. Republican. Home: 4049 Columbia Ave Columbia PA 17512-9569 Office: White Enterprises Corp 14 Lancaster Ave Columbia PA 17512-1536

WHITE, FRANK, III, university administrator; b. San Antonio, Jan. 13, 1955; s. Frank White Jr. and Dolores Maxine (Woods) Lott. BA in English summa cum laude, Prairie View A&M U., 1975; MA in Journalism, Ohio State U., 1977. Pub. info. asst. Prairie View (Tex.) A&M U., 1978-80; staff writer San Antonio Express-News, 1980-82; asst. editor, assoc. editor Ebony Mag., Chgo., 1982-87; dir. university rels. U. Md. Ea. Shore, Princess Anne, 1987—, lectr. feature writing, 1988; lectr. feature writing, 1988-92. Contbr. articles to jours. Mem. Chesapeake Bay Area Girl Scouts U.S., Wilmington, Del., 1988-89. Fellow Ohio State U., 1976-77. Mem. Sigma Tau Delta. Office: U Md Ea Shore Office U Rels Princess Anne MD 21853

WHITE, GEORGE EDWARD, pedodontist; b. Jamestown, N.Y., July 31, 1941; s. Gordon Ennis and Margaret (Appleyard) W. AB, Colgate U., 1963; DDS, SUNY, Buffalo, 1967; PhD, MIT, 1973; DBA, Century U., 1982. Intern, then resident Children's Hosp., Buffalo, 1967-69; prof., chmn. dept. pediatric dentistry Tufts U. Sch. Dental Medicine, Boston, 1973—; chief dept. oral pediatrics New Eng. Med. Center Hosp., Boston, 1973-80; pvt. practice pedodontics, Boston, 1974—; lectr. MIT, 1975-80; cons. Abcor, Inc.; nat., internat. lectr. Nat. Inst. Dental Rsch. grantee, 1973—. Author: Dental Caries: A Multifactorial Disease, 1975, To Stand Alone, 1979; co-author: Maxillofacial Orthopedics: For the Growing Child, 1983; founder, editor-in-chief Jour. Pedodontics, 1976; editor: Clin. Oral Pediatrics, 1979; contbr. articles to profl. jours. Fellow Am. Acad. Pediatric Dentistry, Acad. Gen. Denistry, Internat. Coll. Dentistry, Internat. Coll. Dentists, Am. Coll. Dentist; mem. Internat. Assn. Dental Rsch., Fedn. Dentaire Internationale, Sigma Xi, Omicron Kappa Upsilon. Office: Tufts U Sch Dental Medicine Dept Pediatric Dentistry 1 Kneeland St Boston MA 02111-1527

WHITE, GEORGE MALCOLM, architect; b. Cleve., Nov. 1, 1920; m. Susanne Neiley Daniels, Apr. 21, 1973; children: Stephanie, Jocelyn, Geoffrey, Pamela. B.S., MIT, 1942, M.S., 1942; M.B.A., Harvard, 1948; LL.B., Case Western Res. U., 1959. Design engr. Gen. Electric Co., Schenectady, 1942-47; practice architecture and law Cleve., 1948-71; Architect of Capitol, Washington, 1971—; Mem. D.C. Zoning Commn.; acting dir. U.S. Bot. Garden; mem. U.S. Capitol Police Bd., U.S. Capitol Guide Bd., U.S. Ho. of Reps. Page Bd., Adv. Council on Hist. Preservation, Internat. Centre Com., Nat. Conservation Adv. Council, Nat. Capital Meml. Commn.; bd. dirs., chmn. design com. Pennsylvania Ave. Devel. Corp.; bd. dirs. Nat. Building Mus.; trustee Federal City Council; mem. art adv. com. Washington Met. Area Transit Authority; bd. regents Am. Archtl. Found.; former chmn. archtl. adv. com. Restoration of Statue of Liberty; chmn. com. for Statue of Liberty Mus.; mem. nat. panel arbitrators Am. Arbitration Assn.; former mem. vis. com. dept. architecture and planning MIT; mem. bd. cons. Nubian monuments at Philae, Egypt.; mem. internat. com. cons. for Egyptian Mus., Cairo; chmn. rev. com. Nat. Capital Devel. Commn. for Canberra, Australia. Works include First Unitarian Ch., Cleve., 1959, Preformed Line Products Co. Office Bldg., Cleve., 1960, Mentor Harbor Yacht Club, 1968, restoration, Old Senate and Supreme Ct. Chambers, U.S. Capitol, 1975, Library of Congress James Madison Meml. Bldg., 1979, U.S. Capitol Power Plant Extension, 1979, master plan for U.S. Capitol, 1981, Hart Senate Office Bldg., 1982, restoration of the west cen. front U.S. Capitol Bldg., 1987. Recipient Gold medal Archtl. Soc. Ohio, 1971, Burton award for Disting. Pub. Svc. Cleve. Club, 1991. Fellow AIA (Thomas Jefferson award 1992), Nat. Soc. Profl. Engrs., ASCE (hon. fellow); mem. Sigma Xi, Eta Kappa Nu, Lambda Alpha, Tau Beta Pi. Office: US Capitol Architect Capitol Washington DC 20515

WHITE, GEORGE WENDELL, JR., lawyer; b. Washington, Nov. 9, 1915; s. George Wendell and Blanche E. (Berry) W.; m. Elnor L. Musson, Apr. 5, 1940; children: Randall C., Wendy Lou Gibson, Cynthia Lee Miller. AB, U. Md., College Park, 1937; LLB, U. Md., Balt., 1939. Bar: Md. 1939. Assoc. Weinberg & Green, Balt., 1940-50; sr. ptnr. White, Mindel, Clarke & Foard, Towson, Md., 1950—. Nat. campaign mgr. Nixon-Agnew, 1972, 76. Sgt. U.S. Army, 1942-45. Mem. ABA, Am. Coll. Trial Lawyers, Md. Trial Lawyers Assn. (pres. 1988—), Elks, Optimists, Gamma Eta Gamma (nat. pres. 1939-42). Democrat. Methodist. Home: 5 Coldwater Ct Baltimore MD 21204-2044 Office: 210 W Pennsylvania Ave Ste 500 Baltimore MD 21204-5332

WHITE, HAROLD TREDWAY, III, management consultant; b. Stamford, Conn., Nov. 3, 1947; m. Elizabeth Phillips. BA in History, Northwestern U., 1970; MBA, Darmouth U., 1974. Asst. to dir. urban affairs Am. Bankers Assn., Washington, 1972-73; sr. assoc. Cresap, McCormick & Paget Cons., 1974-75; dir. planning and devel. Tilton (N.H.) Sch., 1975-78; dir. alumni affairs Amos Tuck Sch. Dartmouth U., Hanover, N.H., 1978-82; chief devel. officer Manhattanville Coll., Purchase, N.Y., 1982-84; cons., 1985; pres. Resource Dynamics Group, White Plains, N.Y., 1987—; adj. asst. prof. Iona Coll., New Rochelle, N.Y., 1989—; assoc. mem. cons. bd. Nat. Ctr. Nonprofit Bds., Washington, 1991—. Contbr. articles to profl. jours. Founder Northwestern U. Sailing Club; v.p., trustee, chmn. planning, devel. and mktg. coms. Tilton Sch., 1978—, pres. bd., 1992—; dir. Legal Awareness of Westchester, 1990—; pres. bd. Sci. Ctr. N.H., 1979-82, Nat. Coun. Alcoholism and Other Drug Addictions/Westchester, 1985-89, Mid. Patent Assn., 1988—; trustee Millbrook (N.Y.) Sch., 1981-87. Office: Resource Dynamics Group 701 Westchester Ave Ste 308W White Plains NY 10604-3076

WHITE, HARRY ROBERT, education educator; b. Albermarle, N.C., Sept. 28, 1933; s. Harry Lemuel and Otelia (Morgan) W.; m. Muriel Bertha Breit, June 25, 1960; children: Bradley Robert, Kevin Charles. BA, Yale U., 1955; MEd, SUNY, 1961; EdD, Stanford U., 1964; MSW, SUNY, 1986. Rsch. asst. Stanford U. Sch. Edn., Stanford, Calif., 1962-63; assoc. prof. edn. SUNY, New Paltz, 1964-69, prof. edn., 1969—; rsch. specialist SUNY/USAID, Rio de Janeiro, 1966-68; elem. edn. adv. SUNY/USAID, Recife, Brazil, 1969-71; chair Dept. Edn. Studies SUNY New Paltz, 1976-81, 85-91. Author: Foundations of Education, 1968. With U.S. Army, 1956-58. Mem. N.Y. State Found. Edn. Assn. (jour. editor 1983-87). Republican. Mem. Reformed Ch. of Am. Home: 119 Plains Rd Wallkill NY 12589-3903 Office: SUNY New Paltz NY 12561

WHITE, HUGH CLAYTON, religion educator; b. Columbus, Ga., Dec. 2, 1936; s. Otis Clayton and Marjorie Louise (Hines) W.; m. Ann McDonnel Shepard, Dec. 28, 1960; children: Lisa Mathews, Jessica Hines. AB, Asbury Coll., 1958; BD, Candler Sch. Theology, Atlanta, 1961; PhD, Drew U., 1967. Prof. religion Rutgers U., Camden, N.J., 1970—. Author: Narration and Discourse in the Book of Genesis, 1991. Mem. Zoning Bd. Adjustment, City of Haddonfield, 1988—. Mem. Soc. Bibl. Lit. (sect. co-chair 1989-92), Am. Acad. Religion. Methodist. Home: 47 Truman Ave Haddonfield NJ 08033-2529 Office: Rutgers U Camden Coll 5th and Pennsylvania Camden NJ 08102

WHITE, JAMEELA ADAMS, nurse; b. Rochester, Pa., Oct. 19, 1954; d. Elie James Adams and Alease Rebecca (Waldron) Adams Curry; m. William Harrison White Jr., June 5, 1982; children: William Maurice, Jamel John. BS in Nursing, Hampton U., 1976. RN, Ohio, N.Y. Pvt. duty nurse Cleve., 1976-78; asst. head nurse ICU, coronary care unit Brentwood Hosp., Cleve., 1978-79; asst. dir. nursing Astor Gardens Nursing Home, Bronx, N.Y., 1983-84; pub. health nurse Westchester County Health Dept., White Plains, N.Y., 1979-86; mgr. patient service VNS-Home Care, Bronx, 1986-90; home care nurse coord., asst. dir. patient svcs. Wartburg Home LTHHCP, Mt. Vernon, N.Y., 1990—. Chairperson policy com. Union Child Day Care, Greenburgh, N.Y., 1991—, mem. edn. com., 1987; bd. dirs. Union Child Day Care, 1991—; pres. nurses unit 1st Bapt. Ch., Elmsford, N.Y., 1987—; mem. North Elmsford Civic Assn., 1988—, TransAfrica, 1989—. Mem. NAACP, Am. Nurses Assn., N.Y. State Nurses Assn., Nat. Black Child Devel. Inst., Black Nurses Assn., Hampton Alumni Assn. (bd. dirs. 1986—), North Elmsford Civic Assn., Chi Eta Phi. Democrat.

WHITE, JAN TUTTLE (MRS. BENJAMIN WINTHROP WHITE), computer company executive; b. Bridgeport, Conn., Nov. 5, 1943; d. Michael and Jennie Agnes (Leko) Soltis; m. David Dustin Tuttle, Oct. 7, 1972 (div. 1988); m. Benjamin Winthrop White, May 6, 1989. BS in Math., Bates Coll., 1965; MBA in Mktg. and Ops. Rsch., Columbia U., 1967. With corp. staff IBM Corp., Armonk, N.Y., 1966; systems engr. IBM Corp., N.Y.C., 1967-69; mktg. rep. to Harvard U. IBM Corp., Cambridge, Mass., 1969-72; asst. to dir. info. processing svcs. MIT, Cambridge, Mass., 1972-75; mng. dir. Tuttle Family Trust, Cambridge, Mass., 1975-81; VAX product mktg. mgr., then sr. product mgr. Digital Equipment Corp., Marlborough, Mass., 1981-86, artificial intelligence market devel. mgr., 1986-87, fin. systems group market devel. mgr., 1987—, market devel. mgr. banking/investments group, 1990—; program mgr. MIT Internat. Fin. Svc. Rsch. Ctr.; Speaker in field. Appeared in Disney channel documentary film Silver Men, 1987. Chmn. Concord Coun. Boston Symphony Orch., assoc. assn. vols., supporter Tanglewood scholarship programs, capt. Centennial Major Gifts campaign; active guild bd. Opera Co. Boston, patron Fledrmaus Ball; life mem., chmn. Emerson Hosp. Aux.; bd. trustees mgmt. rev. com. Women's Ednl. and Indsl. Union; active ladies assn. bd. Concord Antiquarian Mus., bd. advisors Boston Mus. Sci., Sci. Mus. Exhibit Collaborative, Garden Club Concord; life mem. Mus. of Fine Arts, Boston, Nat. Trust for Scotland, Friends of Loch Lomond, Mus. Fine Arts, Boston; mem. fin. com. Trinitarian Congl. Ch.; trustee, life mem. Women's Ednl. and Indsl. Union; bd. dirs., life mem. Hannah Duston Garrison House Assn., Mus. Fine Arts, Boston; patron mem. Friends of Music at the Mus. Fellow Internat. Biog. Ctr. (life); mem. NAFE, Am. Assn. Artificial Intelligence, Am. Biog. Inst. Rsch. Assn. (dep. gov., hon. advisor, nat. rsch. bd. advisors), Harwich Hist. Assn. (life), Stratford Hist. Soc. (life), Internat. Platform Assn., Bates Coll. Class 1965 (sec., treas., reunion chmn., com. chmn. 25th reunion major gifts), Columbia U. Grad. Sch. Bus. Alumni Assn. (nat. chmn. membership, bd. dirs.), Hurrican Island Outward Bound Sch. Invitational Alumni, Columbia Bus. Club Boston (founding dir., bd. dirs.), Columbia Club New Eng. (founding dir.), Columbia Club N.Y., Concord Country Club, Harvard Club, Stone Horse Yacht Club, Women's City Club (com. membership), Royal Scottish Automobile Club, Mass. Hort. Soc., So. Mass. Yacht Racing Assn. Republican. Home: 77 Francis Ave Cambridge MA 02138-1911 Office: Digital Equipment Corp 200 Forest St Marlborough MA 01752-3085

WHITE, JOHN DAVID, retired microbiology researcher; b. Newark, Feb. 14, 1928; s. John Moran and Lily (Levin) W.; m. Irene Ginsberg, Jan. 6, 1950; 1 child, Jonathan L. BA, SUNY, Buffalo, 1948, MA, 1950; PhD in Med. Microbiology, Vanderbilt U., 1953. Microbiologist U.S. Army Biol. Labs., Frederick, Md., 1956-60, chief clin. pathology br., 1961-71; chief ultrastructural pathology U.S. Army Med. Inst. Infectious Dieseases, Frederick, 1972-91; ret., 1991. Contbr. over 50 articles to sci. jours. Bd. dirs. Am. Lung Assn., N.Y.C., 1980—, pres., 1991-92; bd. dirs. Am. Lung Assn. Md., Timonium, 1968—, pres., 1972-73. 1st lt. Med. Svc. Corps, U.S. Army, 1953-56.

WHITE, JOHN JOSEPH, III, lawyer; b. Darby, Pa., Nov. 23, 1948; s. John J. Jr. and Catherine (Lafferty) W.; m. Catherine M Staley, Dec. 9, 1983. BS, U. Scranton, 1970; MPA, Marywood Coll., 1977; JD, Loyola U., New Orleans, 1983. Bar: Pa. 1983, U.S. Dist. Ct. (ea. dist.) Pa. 1983, N.J. 1984, U.S. Ct. Appeals (3d cir.) 1983, U.S. Dist. Ct. N.J. 1984, U.S. Tax Ct. 1984, D.C. 1985, U.S. Supreme Ct. 1987. Exec. dir. Scranton Theatre Libre, Inc., Scranton, Pa., 1973-77; pub. Libre Press Inc., Scranton, 1977-83; pvt. practice Phila., 1983—; owner Mercury Transp. Co., Inc., Lansdowne, Pa., 1987—. Founder, pub. Metro Mag., 1977-83. Founder, Scranton Pub. Theatre, 1976; dir. Scranton Theatre Libre, Inc., 1973. Capt. USAF, 1970-73; lt. col. Res., 1973—. Mem. ABA, Pa. Trial Lawyers Assn., Phila. Bar Assn., Phila. Trial Lawyers Assn., Air Force Assn. (chpt. pres. 1975—), Phi Delta Phi Internat. Legal Frat. Democrat. Roman Catholic. Office: 1334 Walnut St Fl 5 Philadelphia PA 19107-5304

WHITE, LAWRENCE J., economics educator; b. N.Y.C., June 1, 1943; s. Martin H. and Florence M. (Meiman) W. AB, Harvard U., 1964, PhD, 1969; MS in Econs., London Sch. Econs., 1965. Econ. adviser Harvard Devel. Adv. Svc., Pakistan and Indonesia, 1969-70; asst. prof. econs. Princeton U., N.J., 1970-76; mem. faculty Stern Sch. Bus., NYU., 1976—; prof. econs. Stern Sch. Bus., NYU, 1979—, chmn. dept., 1990—; sr. staff economist U.S. Council Econ. Advisers, 1978-79; dir. econ. policy office, antitrust div. Dept. Justice, Washington, 1982-83; mem. Fed. Home Loan Bank Bd., 1986-89; cons. in field. Author: The Automobile Industry Since 1945, 1971, Industrial Concentration and Economic Power in Pakistan, 1974, Reforming Regulation: Processes and Problems, 1981, The Regulation of Air Pollutant Emission from Motor Vehicles, 1982, The Public Library in the 1980s: The Problems of Choice, 1983, International Trade in Ocean Shipping Services: The U.S. and the World, 1988, The S&L Debacle: Public Policy Lessons for Bank and Thrift Regulation, 1991; N.Am. editor Jour. Indsl. Econs., 1984-87, 90—. NSF fellow, 1965-69. Mem. Am. Econ. Assn., Phi Beta Kappa. Office: NYU 90 Trinity Pl New York NY 10006-1594

WHITE, LAWRENCE KEITH, physical chemist; b. Lafayette, Ind., Sept. 16, 1948; s. Harold Keith and Gwendolyn (Brock) W.; m. Patricia Lee Cavender, Jan. 8, 1977; children: Katherine, Andrew, Daniel. BA, Earlham Coll., 1970; PhD, U. Ill., 1975. Rsch. scientist Union Camp Corp., Princeton, N.J., 1977-78; mem. tech. staff RCA Labs.-David Sarnoff Rsch. Ctr., Princeton, 1978-88, sr. mem. tech. staff, 1988—. Contbr. over 50 articles to profl. publs.; patentee in field. Presbyterian.

WHITE, LELAND JENNINGS, priest, theologian, lawyer; b. Charleston, S.C., July 25, 1940; s. Leland S. and Rose Winifred (Budds) W. BA, St. Mary's Sem., Balt., 1962; STB, STL, Gregorian U., Rome, 1966; MA, U. Mich., 1972; PhD, Duke U., 1974; JD, Seton Hall U., 1992. Ordained priest Roman Cath. Ch., 1965. Instr. theology St. Thomas Sem., Kenmore, Wash., 1968-69, St. John's Sem., Plymouth, Mich., 1969-70; asst. prof. religious studies Nazareth Coll., Kalamazoo, Mich., 1974-76, Siena Coll., Loudonville, N.Y., 1976-82; assoc. prof. theology St. John's U., N.Y.C., 1982-89, prof. theology and culture, 1989—; mem. editoral bd. Biblical Theology Bulletin, 1979-82. Author: Act in Theology, 1974, Christ and the Christian Movement, 1985, Jesus the Christ, 1988; asst. editor: Biblical Theology Bulletin, 1982-84, editor 1984—. Mem. ACLU, ABA, Am. Acad. Religion, N.J. Assn. Trial Lawyers of Am., Cath. Theol. Soc. Am., Coll. Theology Soc. Democrat. Office: St John's U Dept Theology Jamaica NY 11439

WHITE, LYNN TOWNSEND, III, political science educator; b. Stanford, Calif., Sept. 16, 1941; s. Lynn Townsend Jr. and Maude (McArthur) W.; m. Barbara Sue White, May 30, 1965; children: Jeremy Townsend, Kevin McArthur. BA in Polit. Economy, Williams Coll., 1963; MA in Polit. Sci., U. Calif., Berkeley, 1965, PhD in Polit. Sci., 1972. With legis. rsch. div. Dem. Study Group, Washington, 1962; instr. New Asia Coll., Hong Kong, 1963; rsch. assoc. Ctr. for S.E. Asian Studies Kyoto U., Japan, 1970-71; instr. polit. sci. dept. U. Calif., Berkeley, 1972-73, 88—; prof. Woodrow Wilson Sch. Politics and East Asian Studies Princeton (N.J.) U., 1973—; vis. scholar U. Hong Kong Ctr. for Asian Studies, 1988-89. Author: Careers in Shanghai, 1978, Policies of Chaos: Causes of Violence in the Cultural Revolution, 1989, (with others) The Modernization of China, 1981. Master Forbes Coll., 1987-88; trustee Princeton-in-Asia, 1982—. U. Calif. fellow, 1963-67, Harry Frank Guggenheim Found. fellow, 1988-89. Mem. Assn. for Asian Studies, Am. Polit. Sci. Assn. Democrat. Presbyterian. Office: Princeton U Woodrow Wilson Sch Princeton NJ 08544

WHITE, MERIT PENNIMAN, engineering educator; b. Whately, Mass., Oct. 25, 1908; s. Henry and Jessie (Penniman) W.; m. Jarmila Jaskova, 1965; children—Mary Jessie, Irene Helen, Elisabeth Cecelia, Ellen Patricia. A.B. cum laude, Dartmouth Coll., 1930, C.E., 1931; M.S., Calif. Inst. Tech., 1932, Ph.D. magna cum laude, 1935. With U.S. Dept. Agr., 1935-37; postdoctoral fellow Harvard U., 1937-38; research asso. Calif. Inst. Tech., 1938-39; asst. prof. Ill. Inst. Tech., 1939-42; cons. OSRD, 1942-45, War and Navy Depts., 1945-47; prof., head civil engring. dept. U. Mass., 1948—, Commonwealth head of dept., 1961-77, Commonwealth prof., 1977—. Contbr. articles to engring. jours. Recipient Pres.'s certificate of merit, 1948. Fellow ASME; mem. ASCE (hon.), Instn. Mech. Engrs. (chartered), Réunion Internat. Laboratoires d'Essais et Recherches sur Matériaux (founding), Boston Soc. Civil Engrs. (hon.), Phi Beta Kappa, Sigma Xi, Tau Beta Pi. Home: Whately MA 01093 Office: U Mass Amherst MA 01003

WHITE, MICHAEL HARLAN, military officer; b. Oak Ridge, Tenn., Jan. 28, 1963; s. Earl Harlan and Linda Phyllis (Booker) W.; m. Suzanne Marie Griffin, Apr. 27, 1991. BA in Psychology, The Citadel, 1986. Commd. ensign USN, 1986, advanced through grades to lt., 1988; primary flight student Naval Air Sta., Pensacola, Fla., 1986-87; in advanced navigator tng. Naval Air Tng. Unit, Sacramento, Calif., 1987-88; in fleet replacement tng. Patrol Squadron 30, Jacksonville, Fla., 1988; asst. ops. officer Patrol Squadron 91, San Francisco, 1988; in legal officer tng. Naval Justice Sch., Newport, R.I., 1988; tactical naviagor, sensor coord. Patrol Squadron Spl. Projects Unit 2, Honolulu, 1988-90; with commandant's staff U.S. Naval Acad., Annapolis, Md., 1991—; officer rep. U.S. Navy Acad. Brigade Activities com., Annapolis, 1991—; cons. U.S. Naval Acad. Budget for Activities Bd., Annapolis, 1991—. Asst. coord. Spl. Olympics, 1991; asst. coord. Big Bros./Big Sisters, Annapolis, 1991. Mem. Assn. of Citadel Men, U.S. Naval Inst. (Outstanding Midshipman 1985), Nat. Georgraphic Assn., Citadel Devel. Found. Republican. Baptist. Home: 5 Cathedral St Annapolis MD 21401 Office: Office of the Commandant US Naval Acad Annapolis MD 21402

WHITE, NANCY, fashion consultant; b. Bklyn., July 25, 1916; d. Thomas J. and Virginia (Gillette) W.; student pvt. schs.; m. Ralph Delahaye Paine, Jr., July 25, 1947 (div. Dec. 1977); m. Clarence J. Dauphinot; children—Gillette Dauphinot Piper, Katharine Delahaye Paine; m. George Keys Thompson, Nov. 1978. Fashion editor Pictorial Rev. mag., 1936-40; asst. fashion editor Good Housekeeping mag., 1940-47, fashion editor, 1947-57; asst. editor Harper's Bazaar, N.Y.C., 1957-58, editor-in-chief, 1958-71; fashion dir. Bergdorf Goodman, N.Y.C., 1972-74; dir. Gen. Mills; fashion cons., N.Y.C., 1974—; cons. fashion design Channel 13 Pub. TV; cons. spl. events Nat. Found. March of Dimes. Former mem. Nat. Coun. of Arts; mem. women's bd. Lighthouse for the Blind. Decorated Knight Order Merit (Italy), Silver

medal Merit (Spain); recipient N.Y. Designers award. Mem. Fashion Group (past pres.). Address: 3 E 77th St Apt 5C New York NY 10021

WHITE, NANCY ANN, educator; b. Acushnet, Mass., Mar. 15, 1949; d. Edward and Marion (Jarvis) Seed; m. Thomas Alexander White; children: Douglas, Alex. Student, Fitchburg (Mass.) State Coll., 1967-69; BA in Edn., Notre Dame Coll., Manchester, N.H., 1984. Cert. tchr., N.H. Tchr. Dame Elem. Sch., Concord, N.H., 1985—. Mem. NEA, Internat. Reading Assn. (Granite State coun.), Concord Edn. Assn., N.H. Assn. Readiness Tchrs., Tchrs. Applying Whole Lang. (Concord chpt.). Office: Concord Sch Dist 16 Rumford St Concord NH 03301-3999

WHITE, RALPH BRADSHAW, cinematographer, explorer; b. San Bernardino, Calif., Aug. 28, 1941; s. Ralph Marion and Helyn Grace (Bradshaw) W.; m. Barbara L. Pixley, June 26, 1966 (div. 1973); children: Randolph Blair, Christabeth Blair. AA, L.A. City Coll., 1963; postgrad., U. So. Calif., 1964. Photo technician North Am. Flight Test Div., L.A., 1962; cameraman NBC Sports in Action, Washington, 1963, ABC Wide World of Sports, N.Y.C., 1964-66; field producer Bill Burrud Prodns., L.A., 1966-71; owner White-Pix Prodns., Hollywood, Calif., 1970—; cinematographer Nat. Geog. Soc., Washington, 1974—; bd. dirs. Editors Guild, Internat. Alliance Theatrical Stage Employees, Hollywood; co-expedition leader The 1987 Titanic Expetition, North Atlantic; mem. The 1985 Titanic Expedition, U.S. Parachute Team (world competition), 1964-65; vis. scientist Soviet Acad. Scis. (World Record Dual Sub Dive 1989). Photographer, author Titanic articles, 1985, Soviet Submersibles articles, 1989; photographer, sky diving book and mags., 1960. Capt. L.A. County Sheriff's Res. Forces, 1974—. With USMC, 1959-62. Recipient Meritorious Svc. medal L.A. County Sheriff's Dept., 1988, The EMMY award Acad. of TV Art & Scis., 1978; named Vol. of Yr., L.A. County, 1988. Fellow Explorers Club (vice chmn. 1985-87); mem. Adventurers Club (bd. dirs. 1985), Deep Submergence Pilots Assn., Force Recon Assn., Masons (sr. warden 1970), Order of Constantine (Knight 1989), Order of St. Lazarus (Knight companion 1988). Republican. Episcopalian. Office: Nat Geographic Soc 17th & M Sts NW Washington DC 20036

WHITE, RICHARD EARL, research scientist; b. Akron, Ohio, Aug. 23, 1933; s. Watson Reedy and Musie Zela (Shanafelt) W.; m. Janice Foster, Jan. 1968 (div. June 1973); 1 child, Bonnie May; m. Pun-Ye Kim, July 15, 1977; 1 child, Daniel Roy. BS, Akron U., 1957; MSc, Ohio State U., 1959, PhD, 1963. Asst. prof. Union Coll., Barbourville, Ky., 1964-65; rsch. scientist U.S. Dept. Agr., Washington, 1965—. Author: A Field Guide to the Insects, 1970, A Field Guide to the Beetles, 1983. Mem. Entomol. Soc. Am. (com. on common names), Entom. Soc. Washington, Coleopterists Soc., Guild Natural Sci. Illustrators. Home: 10103 Quince Apple Ct Upper Marlboro MD 20772-3871

WHITE, RICHARD EDMUND, marketing executive; b. Reading, Pa., June 8, 1944; s. Carl Marshall and Miriam Elizabeth (Curry) W.; m. Kristen Margaret Lloyd, June 17, 1967; children: Ross, Peter, Andrew. BS in Econs., U. Pa., 1967; MBA with distinction, U. Mich., 1968. Gen. mgr. mktg. H. J. Heinz Co., Pitts., 1970-81; dir. mktg. Seven Up Co., St. Louis, 1981-83; v.p. mktg. & sales Herr Foods, Inc., Nottingham, Pa., 1984—. Chmn. fin. com. Sewickley Borough Coun., Pa., 1977-81; pres. So. Chester County Devel. Found., Jennersville, Pa., 1988—; vice chmn., mem. bd. govs. So. Chester County Med. Ctr., 1988—; pres., bd. mgrs. So. Chester County YMCA, West Grove, Pa., Avon Grove United Way, 1988—. Mem. Am. Mgmt. Assn. (mktg. coun.). Republican. Home: 425 Ewing Rd West Grove PA 19390-9166 Office: Herr Foods Inc PO Box 300 Nottingham PA 19362-0300

WHITE, ROBERT CHARLES, JR., music educator; b. Trenton, N.J., Nov. 2, 1936; s. Robert Charles and Emma Elizabeth(Wylie) W. BS, Susquehanna U., Pa., 1958; MA, Columbia U., 1963, EdD, 1968. Dir. vocal music Bloomfield (N.J.) Jr. High Sch., 1959-63, Flagstaff (Ariz.) pub. schs., 1963-65; interim instr. Columbia U., N.Y.C., 1965-67; prof. Queens Coll., CUNY, Flushing, 1966—; prof. music grad. ctr. CUNY, 1988—. Co-author: Italian Art Song, 1989; contbr. articles to profl. jours. With U.S. Army, 1959-61. Fellow Am. Acad. Tchrs. of Singing; mem. N.Y. Singing Tchrs. Assn. (bd. dirs. 1978-88), Nat. Assn. Tchrs. Singing, Am. Choral Dirs. Assn. Democrat. Roman Catholic.

WHITE, ROBERT GANNON, food products executive; b. Boston, Nov. 30, 1930; s. Allan Richard and Esther Mary (Kelley) W.; married; children: Julia, Jennifer, Sarah, Robert Gannon. BS, Georgetown U., 1952; MBA, U. Pa., 1957. Pres. Hendrie's Ice Cream, Milton, Mass., 1960-89, New Eng. Frozen Foods, Southborough, Mass., 1983—; bd. dirs. Baybank South, Dedham, Mass.; pres., dir. Internat. Ice Cream Assn., Washington; pres. Am. Star Dairy, Lexington, Ky.. Past bd. dirs. Milton Hosp.; mem. town meetings, Milton, 1970—; past dir. South Shore C. of C., Quincy, Mass. Lt. comdr. USN, 1952-57, Korea. Mem. Longwood Cricket Club, University Club, Wardroom Club. Republican. Office: New Eng Frozen Foods 1 Harvest Ln Southborough MA 01772

WHITE, STANLEY EVERETT, telecommunications executive, mathematics educator; b. East Orange, N.J., Aug. 19, 1951; s. William E. and Eleanor (Mason) W. BA, U. Wis., 1973; MA, Stanford U., 1974. Asst. editor math. Holt, Reinhart & Winston, N.Y.C., 1975-76; tchr. high sch. math. Madison (N.J.) Bd. Edn., 1976-78, Metuchen (N.J.) Bd. Edn., 1978-79; programmer, instr., developer AT&T, Piscataway, N.J., 1979—; adj. faculty math. Passaic County Community Coll., Paterson, N.J., 1977-79, Essex County Community Coll., Newark, 1979-85. Mem. Nat. Coun. Tchrs. Math. Home: 439 Orange Rd Montclair NJ 07042-4330

WHITE, THOMAS, hospital administrator; b. Sharon, Pa., May 30, 1943; s. Frank and Elizabeth W.; m. Rose Marie Taylor, June 28, 1968. BBA, Youngstown State U., 1970; MSHA, U. Pitts., 1972. With Sharon (Pa.) Gen. Hosp., 1964-70, adminstrv. asst. bldg. svcs., 1969-70; adminstrv. resident Albany (N.Y.) Med. Ctr., 1971-72; asst. exec. dir. Jameson Meml. Hosp., New Castle, Pa., 1972-73; pres., chief exec. officer Jameson Meml. Hosp., 1973—, Jameson Health Sys., Inc., New Castle, 1987—. Mem. Lawrence County Econ. Devel. Corp., Lawrence County Caring Found., Lawrence County United Way; bd. dirs. First Nat. Bank of Wester Pa. Fellow/regent Am. Coll. Healthcare Execs.; mem. Am. Hosp. Assn., Hosp. Assn. Pa. (bd. dirs.), Hosp. Council We. Pa. (bd. dirs.). Office: Jameson Meml Hosp 1211 Wilmington Ave New Castle PA 16105-2595

WHITE, THOMAS CLARENCE, public relations executive, consultant; b. Pitman, N.J., June 10, 1934; s. Edgar Eugene and Dorothy (Mulford) W.; m. Eleanor Koegler, Aug., 1955 (dec. June, 1966); children: Thomas Charles, Jeffrey Robert; m. Indrea Kintisch, Aug. 20, 1967; children: Adam Douglas, Marchel Edgar. BSChemE, Bucknell U., 1956; MBA, Fairleigh Dickinson U., 1977. Chem. process engr. M.W. Kellogg Co., N.Y.C., 1956-60, sales promotion supr., 1960-64, mgr. advt., 1964-65, mgr. pub. rels., 1965-68; dir. pub. rels. Mutch Haberman Joyce, Inc., N.Y.C., 1968-69; dir. pub. info. Am. Fedn. Info. Processing Socs., Montvale, N.J., 1969-79; pub. rels. planning rep. Bell Tel. Labs, Short Hills, N.J., 1979-82; staff dir. pub. rels. IEEE, N.Y.C., 1982-92; cons. Joel Assocs., Teaneck, N.J., 1991—, Engring. Found., N.Y.C., 1992—. Contbr. articles to Datamation, Computerworld, others; patentee in field. Named one of Outstanding Young Men Am., 1970. Mem. IEEE (sr. Centenniel medal 1984), AICE (voting), Pub. Rels. Soc. Am. (voting, v.p. tech. sect. 1980), Assn. for Computing Machinery, Coun. Engring. and Sci. Soc. Execs., Alpha Chi Sigma (chmistry). Home and Office: 377 River Rd Bogota NJ 07603

WHITE, THOMAS DAVID, II, academic administrator; b. Pittsburg, Kans., Sept. 19, 1946; s. Thomas David and Audrey Marie (Parrish) W.; children: Thomas David III, Phillip Edward. AA, Valley Forge Mil. Jr. Coll., 1967; BA, North Ga. Coll., 1969; postgrad., Pa. State U., 1978-82. Cert. adminstr., Vol. Svcs., Assn. Vol. Adminstrs., 1976. Dist. scout exec. Boy Scouts Am., Phila., 1969-72; vol. resource coord. Norristown (Pa.) State Hosp., 1972-74; assoc. dir. vol. resources Pennhurst Ctr., Spring City, Pa., 1974-79; dir. vol. resources Embreeville State Hosp., Coatesville, Pa., 1979-81; dir. alumni affairs and constituent rels. Valley Forge Mil. Acad., Wayne, Pa., 1981-85; assoc. univ. dir. alumni rels. Rutgers, The State Univ. N.J., Newark, 1985-90; exec. dir. alumni rels. George Washington U., Washington, 1990—; adj. faculty Pa. State U., 1975-76; sr. cons., co-founder Cons. Community, Phila., 1976-82; founder, pres. AADM Assocs., Wayne, Pa., 1983-90. Contbr. articles to profl. publs.; author profl. manuals. Sec., Roboda Community Assn., Royersford, Pa., 1981-83. Mem. Internat. Platform Assn., Coun. for Advancement and Support of Edn., Assn. Vol. Adminstrn., Nat. Assn. Ind. Schs., Assn. Vocat. Action Scholars, S.E. Region Vol. Coords. Assn., Valley Forge Mil. Acad. Alumni Assn. (bd. dirs. exec. com.), VFMA Soc. of the Golden Sword (knight), Rutgers Club (bd. trustees), George Washington U. Club (adv. com.). Republican. Home: 500 S Park Ave Audubon PA 19403 Office: George Washington U Alumni House 714 21st St NW Washington DC 20052-0001

WHITE, TIMOTHY OLIVER, newspaper editor; b. Albany, N.Y., June 29, 1948; s. Oliver C. and Yvonne (Letourneau) W.; 1 child, Eric B. BA in English, Siena Coll., 1971. Reporter Cape Cod Times, Hyannis, Mass., 1971-72, asst. Sunday editor, 1972-75, news editor, 1975-79, asst. editor, 1979-83, mng. editor, 1983—. Mem. AP Mng. Editors, New England AP News Exec. Assn. (v.p. 1992), New England Soc. Newspaper Editors. Home: 46 Maple Ln Brewster MA 02631 Office: Cape Cod Times 319 Main St Hyannis MA 02601

WHITE, WENDEL ALBERICK, art educator, artist, photographer; b. Newark, Sept. 2, 1956; s. Howard Alberick and Symera (Hoggard) W.; m. Carmela Colon, May 23, 1981; 1 child, Amanda Rachel. BFA, Sch. Visual Arts, N.Y.C., 1980; MFA, U. Tex., 1982. Teaching asst. U. Tex., Austin, 1980-82; instr. photography Bellevue Hosp. High Sch., N.Y.C., 1983-84; photog. archivist Essence Mag., N.Y.C., 1986; workshop instr. Internat. Ctr. for Photography, N.Y.C., 1984-86; asst. prof. art Stockton State Coll., Pomona, N.J., 986—; adj. instr. art Sch. Visual Arts, 1985-88, Cooper Union Sch. Art, N.Y.C., 1989-90; bd. dirs. Kodak Ednl. Adv. Coun., Rochester, N.Y., 1991—. Works include photog. images Indsl. Lamdscapes, 1988, Afro-Am. Communities in So. N.J., 1992; contbr. editor ICP Ency. of Photography, 1984; author exhbn. catalog. Bd. dirs. Atlantic City Hist. Mus., 1989—. U. Tex. fellow, Austin, 1990-81. Mem. Soc. Photog. Educators (multicultural caucus 1991—, advocacy com. 1991—), Photog. Resource Ctr., Lightwork. Democrat. Office: Stockton State Coll Div Arts and Humanities Pomona NJ 08240

WHITE, WILLIAM NELSON, lawyer; b. Balt., Sept. 8, 1938; s. Nelson Cardwell and Ellen Atwell (Zoller) W.; m. Mary Kathleen Bitzel, Sept. 2, 1960 (div. 1971); children: Craig William, Jeffrey Alan, Colin Christopher; m. Christine Lewin Hanna, July 8, 1978. LLB, U. Md., 1968, JD, 1969. Bar: Md. 1972, U.S. Ct. Appeals (4th cir.) 1975, U.S. Dist. Ct. Md. 1976, U.S. Spreme Ct. 1976. Asst. state's atty. Balt., 1972; assoc. Brooks & Turnbull, Balt., 1973-76; pvt. practice Balt., 1977—; counsel St. Andrews Soc. Balt., 1989—. Pres. deacons Roland Park Presbyn. Ch., Balt., 1987. Mem. ABA, Md. Bar Assn., Baltimore County Bar Assn., U. Md. Alumni Assn. for Greater Balt. (pres. 1977), Baltimore County C. of C., St. George's Soc. Balt. (counsel). Office: 305 W Chesapeake Ave Ste L-3 Baltimore MD 21204-4421

WHITEHAIR, LEO ANTHONY, health science administrator; b. Abilene, Kans., June 13, 1929; s. John Leo and Mary Agnes (Morgan) W.; m. Gloria Mary Vezza, Aug. 9, 1958; children: Kirsten, Robert, Courtney. BS and DVM, Kans. State U., 1953; MS, U. Wis., 1954, PhD, 1962. Diplomate Am. Coll. Vet. Preventive Medicine. Commd. 2d lt. USAF, 1954, advanced through grades to lt. col.; vet. officer Aeromed. Lab. Wright-Patterson AFB, Dayton, Ohio, 1954-58; vet. officer nutrition br. Food Inst. of Amerd Forces, Chgo., 1961-62; vet. officer, food scientist biology and medicine div. AEC, Germantown, Md., 1967; health scientist adminstr. animal resources br. div. rsch. resources NIH, Bethesda, Md., 1968-75, dir. regional primate rsch. ctr. program, 1975-85; adminstr. biomed. rsch. lab. ARC, Rockville, Md., 1985-87; dir. comparative med. program Nat. Ctr. for Rsch. Resources, NIH, Bethesda, 1987—. Contbr. articles to profl. jours. Capt. USPHS, 1967-85. Recipient Helwig-Jennings award Am. Coll. Vet. Preventive Medicine, 1981. Mem. AVMA, D.C. Vet. Medicine Assn. (pres. 1992). Office: NIH Bethesda MD 20892

WHITEHEAD, JENNIFER, computer information scientist; b. Coventry, Eng., Mar. 21, 1950; came to U.S., 1975; d. Charles William and Mildred (Jackson) W.; m. Michael Joseph Maller, Dec. 20, 1977; children: Julian Benjamin, Abigail Esther. BS, U. London, Eng., 1971; MS, U. Warwick, Eng., 1972, PhD, 1975. Asst. prof. Tex. A&M U., College Station, 1975-79; lectr. Northwestern U., Evanston, Ill., 1979-80; asst. prof. Queens Coll., CUNY, Flushing, 1980-89, assoc. prof., 1989—. Contbr. articles to profl. jours. Mem. Am. Math. Soc., Assn. Computing Machinery. Home: 26 Croyden Ave Great Neck NY 11023 Office: CUNY Queens Coll Dept Computer Sci Flushing NY 11367

WHITEHEAD, LOIS KOSINSKI, public relations consultant; b. Bayonne, N.J., Jan. 17, 1947; d. Walter and Frances (Kubiak) Kosinski; divorced; children: Heather, Christopher, Ashley. B Mktg., Pace U.; cert. pub. rels. mgmt., NYU. Staff asst. mktg. Paine Webber, N.Y.C., 1969-76; mgr. press rels. Am. Soc. Travel Agts., N.Y.C., 1976-77; communications mgr. ADP Fin. Data Svcs., N.Y.C., 1977-81; pub. rels. account exec. William Hetherington & Co., Newark, 1981-86; investor rels. assoc. Hal Smith Assocs., Saddle River, N.J., 1985-87; v.p. pub. rels. Brett Assocs., Little Falls, N.J., 1990-91; pres. LKW Assocs., Edison, N.J., 1986—; cons. Passaic County Bar Assn., Paterson, 1988-90, SHARE, Newark, 1988—. Author: In the Works, 1991. Active Bush Campaign for Pres., Cary Edwards Campaign for Gov. Named Diamond Dozen Pres., N.J. Fedn. Women's Clubs, Bayonne, N.J., 1972, Hon. Cert., N.J. Ending Hunger Now, 1991. Mem. Pub. Rels. Soc. Am., Nat. Investor Rels. Inst., Govs. Club N.J., Publicity Club N.Y. Republican. Roman Catholic. Office: LKW Assocs 205 Merrywood Dr Edison NJ 08817-2504

WHITEHURST, WILLIAM WILFRED, JR., management consultant; b. Balt., Mar. 4, 1937; s. William Wilfred and Elizabeth (Hogg) W.; B.A., Princeton, 1958; M.S., Carnegie Inst. Tech., 1963; m. Linda Joan Potter, July 1, 1961; children—Catherine Elizabeth, William Wilfred, III. Mathematician Nat. Security Agy., Fort George G. Meade, Md., 1961-63; mgmt. cons. McKinsey & Co., Inc., Washington, 1963-66; partner L.E. Peabody & Assos., Washington, 1966-69, exec. v.p., dir. L.E. Peabody & Assos., Inc., Lanham, Md., 1969-82, pres., dir., 1983-86, pres. W.W. Whitehurst & Assoc., Inc., Cockeysville, Md., 1986—. Contbr. to Code of Fed. Regulations 49 C.F.R. Sect. 1157. Served to lt. comd. USNR, 1958-61. Recipient Diploma De Honor 14th Pan Am. Rwy. Congress. Mem. Am. Railway Engring. Assn., Transportation Rsch. Forum, Assn. for Investment Mgmt. and Rsch., Ops. Rsch. Soc. Am., Inst. Mgmt. Scis., Washington Soc. Investment Analysts. Episcopalian. Clubs: University, Princeton (Washington); Princeton (N.J.) Quadrangle. Home and Office: 12421 Happy Hollow Rd Cockeysville Hunt Valley MD 21030-1711

WHITEMAN, GILBERT LEE, management consultant; b. Guilford, Conn., Dec. 17, 1931; s. Clifford Thomas and Dorothy Eleanor (Swift) W.; m. Betty Jane Hlavaty, Nov. 17, 1952 (div. Oct. 1973); children: Jana Lynn, Brian Lee, Jeffrey Craig; m. Jean Ellen Thomas, June 21, 1975. AA, Los Angeles Valley Jr. Coll., 1957; BGEd, U. Nebr., 1960; MA, U. Okla., 1965; PhD, Mich. State U., 1972. Enlisted USAF, 1949, commd. 2nd lt., 1957; advanced through grades to lt. col., 1972; sr. spokesman U.S. Command, Vietnam, 1972-73; ret. USAF, 1974; assoc. dean Grad. Sch., U. New Haven, 1974-81; pres. Interdependence Assocs. Inc., Guilford, Conn., 1977—; owner The Whiteman Resource, Guilford, 1981—. Author: Effective Managerial Communication, 1983, Management Skills for Supervisors, 1984, Managing Time and Stress, 1985, Listening Skills for Supervisors, 1986. Mem. Internat. Listening Assn. (life), Speech Communication Assn. (life), Am. Soc. Profl. Cons., Sigma Delta Chi, Alpha Epsilon Rho. Republican. Congregationalist. Home: PO Box 224 Guilford CT 06437-0224 Office: The Whiteman Resource 280 Durham Rd Guilford CT 06437-2006

WHITENER, JEAN VERONICA, psychotherapist; b. Bklyn.; d. Alexander and Zenobia A. (Mann) W. BA, Cen. State U., Wilberforce, Ohio, 1960; MSW, Howard U., 1966. Diplomate in Clin. Social Work. Clinic administr. Bklyn. Psychiat. Ctrs., 1970-77; cons. D.H.M.H., State of Md., Balt., 1978-79; psychotherapist D.C. Inst. Mental Hygiene, Washington, 1979-81, Community Mental Health Activity, Ft. Meade, Md., 1981-83; pvt. practice psychotherapy Columbia, Md., 1984-87; exec. dir., owner Columbia Inst. Psychotherapy, 1987—; v.p. Howard County Mental Health Assn., Columbia, 1989-91. Mem. NASW, Assn. Mental Health Adminstrs., Md. Register Clin. Social Workers, Am. Orthopsychiat. Assn., Acad. Cert. Social Workers, Howard County Mental Health Assn., Alpha Kappa Alpha. Democrat. Episcopalian. Office: Columbia Inst Psychotherapy Oakland Mills Profl Bldg Ste 220 Columbia MD 21045

WHITESEL, CANDICE GAIL, non-profit organization funding consultant; b. Akron, Ohio, Jan. 11, 1954; d. Walter Frank and Daisy Nell (Carpenter) Krueger; m. Richard Lynn Whitesel, Apr. 1, 1982. AAS in Data Processing, U. Akron, 1978; BA in Psychology, River Coll., 1991. Sr. sales and export rep. Ohio Sci., Inc., Bedford Heights, 1978-81; corp. sales adminstr. Ohio Sci., Inc., Bedford, Mass., 1982-83; prof. Buckeye Coll., Mogadore, Ohio, 1980-81; dir. sales and mktg. Quasar Data Products, Inc., Brecksville, Ohio, 1981-82; receiving supr. Bierce Libr., U. Akron, 1983-87; cons. Iconoclastic Enterprises, Nashua, N.H., 1983—. Contbr. articles to various publs. Mem. CHild Care Svcs. Study Com., Nashua, 1986, Foster Parent Adv. Com., Nashua, 1990; vol. Info. and Referral, Nashua, 1988-90, John Glenn Presdl. Com., Nashua, 1988-90; bd. dirs. Nashua Soup Kitchen and Shelter, 1988—; bd. dirs., chair pub. rels. com. Nashua Vis. Nurse Assn., 1988-90; v.p. Nashua Foster Parents Assn., 1986-90; mem. Nashua Inter-Agy. Coun., 1988—. Mem. N.H. Children's Lobby, Network Child Abuse Orgn. Democrat. Office: Iconoclastic Enterprises 22 Shingle Mill Rd Nashua NH 03062-2101

WHITESIDE, DUNCAN, disabilities foundation executive; b. Boston, Nov. 30, 1935; s. Frederick Shattuck and Caroline Freeman (Lawrence) W.; m. Elena Scott, June 11, 1960 (div. 1975); children: Nicholas, Michael, Sylvia; m. Sandra Gates, 1976; stepchildren: Todd, Tim, Keith, Wendy. AB, Harvard U., 1961; MBA, NYU, 1971; cert. in non-profit mgmt., Columbia U. Internat. lending mktg. officer Chase Manhattan Bank, N.Y.C., Frankfurt, Fed. Republic Germany, 1961-72; asst. to exec. dir. Moblzn. for Youth, N.Y.C., 1973-74; adminstrv. dir. Transitional Svcs. N.Y., N.Y.C., 1975-77; dir. tech. assistance program One to One Found., N.Y.C., 1978-80, exec. dir., 1981-82; dir. Resource Ctr. for Devel. Disabilities, N.Y.C., 1983-90; pres. Maidstone Found., N.Y.C., 1984—; bd. dirs. New Alternatives for Children, Nassau Suffolk Autism Soc., Cow Bay Housing. Treas. Coun. on Adoptable Children, Lakeside, Family and Children's Svc.; v.p. Russian Ethnic Bilingual Cultural and Ednl. Assn.; exec. com. N.Y. State Gov.'s Planning Coun. on Devel. Disabilities; chair Veatch Com., North Shore Unitarian Universalist Soc., Plandome, N.Y., 1991—, bd. dirs. Unitarian Universalist UN Office; pres. Port Washington (N.Y.) Community Chest, 1992—. Recipient Merit awards U.S. Info. Agy., 1959; named Adv. of Yr., N.Y. Assn. Community Residence Adminstrs., 1983, Advs. for Svcs. for Blind Multihandicapped, 1985, Chase Manhattan Citizen of Yr., 1972. Mem. Assn. for People with Severe Handicaps, Nat. Network Grantmakers, Soviet Am. Sail Found., Internat. League of Soc. for Persons with Mental Handicaps. Office: Maidstone Found 1225 Broadway 9th Fl New York NY 10001

WHITE-SMITH, RICHARD, state conservation executive; b. Yonkers, N.Y., Jan. 26, 1945; s. Charles A. and Margaret (Ryan) S.; m. Joan Elizabeth White, Apr. 24, 1982; 1 child, Morgen. BA, U. Notre Dame, 1966. Pub. health specialist U.S. Peaces Corps, Malawi, Africa, 1966-68; asst. dir. DEROS Vets. Program, Yonkers, 1971-73; vets. counselor N.Y.S. Div. of Vets. Affairs, Bklyn., 1973-77; exec. dir. Vets. Upgrade Ctr. of N.Y., Bklyn., 1977-81, Hudson Mohawk Urban Cultural Pk. Commn., Cohoes, N.Y., 1981-87, N.Y. Pks and Conservation Assn., Albany, 1987—. Active Urban Cultural Pk Adv. Coun., Schenectady, 1990—. Cpl. USMC, 1969-71. Recipient Presdl. citation for Outstanding Community Svc. by Vietnam Era Vet. U.S. Pres., 1979. Home: 32 Surrey Rd Glenville NY 12302 Office: NY Pks and Conservation Assn 35 Maiden Ln Albany NY 12207

WHITFIELD, STEPHEN JACK, history educator; b. Houston, Dec. 3, 1942; s. Bert and Joan (Schwarz) W.; m. Donna Elaine Arzt, Aug. 21, 1977 (div. 1983); m. Lee Cone, Dec. 15, 1984; children: Kimberly, Andrea. BA, Tulane U., 1964; MA, Yale U., 1966; PhD, Brandeis U., 1972. Instr. So. U., New Orleans, 1966-68; from asst. prof. to assoc. prof. Brandeis U., Waltham, Mass., 72-85, prof., 1985—; vis. prof. Hebrew U., Jerusalem, Israel, 1983-84. Author: Scott Nearing: Apostle of American Radicalism, 1974, Into the Dark: Hannah Arendt and Totalitarianism, 1980, Voices of Jacob, Hands of Esau, 1984, A Critical American: The Politics of Dwight Macdonald, 1984, A Death in the Delta: The Story of Emmett Till, 1988, American Space, Jewish Time, 1988, The Culture of the Cold War, 1991; rev. editor Am. Jewish History, 1979-86. Recipient Kayden prize U. Colo., Boulder, 1981, Fulbright Found. professorship, 1983-84. Mem. Am. Jewish Hist. Soc. (mem. academic coun.). Home: 3 Ewell Ave Lexington MA 02173-7507 Office: Brandeis U 415 South St Waltham MA 02154-2700

WHITING, ANNE MARGARET, biology educator; b. Morrisville, Vt., May 17, 1941; d. Roland Wesley and Ruby Viola (Davis) W.; children: Vani Grace, Vara Joy. BA, Eastern Nazarene Coll., 1963; MS, U. Ill., 1965; PhD, Penn State U., 1969. Prof. biology Houghton (N.Y.) Coll., 1968—. Mem. Am. Inst. Biol. Sci., Am. Sci. Affiliation, Sigma Xi. Wesleyan. Office: Houghton Coll Houghton NY 14744

WHITLA, DEAN KAY, academic director; b. Butte, Nebr., Sept. 19, 1925; s. William Kenneth and Flora (Fleming) W.; m. Janet Parker, Aug. 2, 1975. BS, U. Nebr., 1949, MA, 1950, PhD, 1957; postgrad., Harvard U., 1959. Instr. U. Nebr., Lincoln, 1951; rsch. psychologist USAF, Washington, 1952-53; dir. rsch. and evaluation Harvard U., Cambridge, Mass., 1954—, instr., 1957-59, assoc. dir. adminstrn., 1957—, asst. prof., 1960-68, dir. Inst. Coll. Adminstrn., 1960—, lectr., 1968—; founder, dir. Danforth Ctr. Teaching, Cambridge, 1957-87; cons. Bush Found., St. Paul, 1972—; cons. Ford Found., N.Y.C., 1975-80; evaluator United Negro Coll. Fund Colls., 1989—; statistician Risk Mgmt. Found., Cambridge, 1986—. Co-author: Cognitive Aging, 1991; editor: Handbook on Assessment, 1968; editor jour. On Teaching and Learning, 1969-68, College Teaching, 1965-75; contbr. articles to profl. publs. Mem. Am. Psychol. Assn., Am. Statis. Assn. (v.p., treas. Boston chpt. 1957-68), Boston Harvard Club. Office: Harvard U OIRE Shannon Hall 25 Francis Ave Cambridge MA 02138-2009

WHITLEY, SANDRA ANN, training consultant, educator; b. Pitts., Oct. 30, 1951; d. Frank J. and Maryann (Juran) Lynch; m. Dan E. Whitley, Mar. 10, 1973; children: Dan II, W. Brian. AA, Allegheny Community Coll., 1971; student, U. Pitts., 1972-73; BS, BA magna cum laude, Robert Morris Coll., 1991. Acctg. clk. Gen. Electric Credit, Charlotte, N.C., 1971-76; corp. acct. Mellon Bank, N.A., Pitts., 1976-79, investment analyst, 1979-80, asst. officer, 1980, capital mkts. acctg. supr., 1980-82, acctg. officer, 1982, mgr., 1983-86, cons./specialist, 1986—; acct./cons. Whitley's Hair Design, Coraopolis, Pa., 1979; instr. Allegheny C.C., 1992—; substitute tchr. Moon Area Sr. High, 1992. Mem. Springhill Civic League, Pitts., 1980-86. Recipient Outstanding Achievement award Credit Mgrs. Assn., 1971. Mem. Pa. Assn. Notaries, Alpha Kappa, Alpha Tau Sigma. Office: 220 Glenmore Dr Coraopolis PA 15108-9653

WHITLOW, CHARLES GLENN, librarian, researcher; b. Jackson, Tenn., Nov. 24, 1954; s. Glenn H. and Blonnie Isabella (Hill) W. BS in Liberal Arts, U. Tenn., 1976, BA in Liberal Arts, 1978; MLS, Columbia U., 1982, cert. in advanced librarianship, 1991. Profl. pianist and organist, 1966—; cons., acad. researcher Libr. of Congress, Washington, 1978; asst. reference libr. AT&T Corp. Librs., N.Y.C., 1979-83; head libr. pers. ATT-IS, Morristown, N.J., 1984-85; systems libr. ATT-IS/ATT-Techs., Morristown, 1985-89; tax libr. AT&T Corp. Hdqrs., Morristown, 1989. Author: McNairy County History, 1973, Marcus Wright Bibliography, 1980; editor: AnteBellum Poetry, 1978. Friend N.Y.C. Pub. Libr., 1988—; vol. Glenlora Nursing Home, Chester, N.J., 1989—; chncellor K.C., Flanders, N.Y., 1990-91. Recipient Community Svc. award McNairy County C. of C., 1972, Young Gentlemen's award Jaycees, 1972. Mem. ALA, Am. Guild Organists, Music Libr. Assn., Columbia U. Alumni Assn. (sec. N.Y.C. chpt. 1988-90, v.p. 1990-91, pres. 1991—), Phi Kappa Phi, Phi Eta Sigma, Psi Chi. Roman Catholic. Home: 202 Monroe St Boonton NJ 07005-2164 Office: AT&T 412 Mount Kemple Ave C190/W18 Morristown NJ 07960-6617

WHITMORE, KAY REX, photographic company executive; b. Salt Lake City, July 24, 1932; s. Rex Grange and Ferrol Terry (Smith) W.; m. Yvonne Schofield, June 6, 1956; children: Richard, Kimberly, Michele, Cynthia, Suzanne, Scott. Student, U. Utah, 1950-53, BS, 1957; MS, MIT, 1975. With Eastman Kodak Co., Rochester, N.Y., 1957—, engr. film mfg., 1957-67; with factory start-up Eastman Kodak Co., Guadalajara, Mex., 1967-71; various mgmt. positions film mfg. Eastman Kodak Co., Rochester, 1971-74, asst. v.p., gen. mgr. Latin Am. Region, 1975-79, v.p., asst. gen. mgr. U.S. and Can. Photog. Div., 1979-80, exec. v.p. and gen. mgr., 1981-83, pres., 1983-90, chmn. bd., pres., chief exec. officer, 1990—, also bd. dirs.; bd. dirs. The Chase Manhattan Corp., New Am. Schs. Devel. Corp. Trustee U. Rochester. With U.S. Army, 1953-55. Mem. Am. Soc. for Quality Control, Bus. Roundtable, Bus. Coun. Mem. LDS Ch. Office: Eastman Kodak Co 343 State St Rochester NY 14650-0229

WHITMORE, MENANDRA M., librarian; b. Ancash, Peru; d. Rafael and Jacinta (Moreno) Mosquera; m. Jacob L. Whitmore III, Jan. 7, 1965; children: Jacqueline Grace, Michelle Jacinta. Degree in social work, U. Catolica del Peru, 1967; MLS, U. P.R., 1974, Catholic U. Am., 1984. Social worker Cornell U., Vicos, Peru, 1960-62, Servicio de Extension Agricola del Peru, 1962-63, Am. Friends Svc. Com., Mex. and Peru, 1963-65; libr. Colegio Maria Auxiliadora, P.R., 1971, Country Day Sch., San Jose, Costa Rica, 1975-76, Colegio San Ignacio, P.R., 1976-77; dir. libs. Am. Coll. P.R., 1977-80; libr. Lib. Gov. Printing Office, 1981-84; chief acquisitions sect., mgr. Hispanic employment program Pentagon Lib., Washington, 1984—. Author: (all pub. under name Menandra Mosquera) Bibliography on Hypsipyla, 1976, Bibliography of Forestry of Puerto Rico, 1984, Useful Trees of Tropical North America, 1988. Recipient commendation Dept. Def., 1987-90. Mem. ALA, Soc. for Acquisition Latin Am. Libr. Materials, Reforma (treas. Washington chpt. 1988, pres. 1989-91, nat. ways and means chair 1991—).

WHITNEY, CAROL MARIE, securities sales professional; b. Torrington, Conn., Mar. 31, 1946; d. Charles Lester and Emily Mae (Orr) W.; divorced 1976; 1 child, Lydia Michelle Wiston. BA in French, Wells Coll., 1968; 5th yr. cert., So. Conn. Coll., 1971; postgrad., N.Y. Inst. Fin., 1976, Hartford U. Grad. Ctr., 1990. Trainee/investment exec. Blyth-Eastman Dillon, Hartford, Conn., 1976-77; account exec./registered rep. Bache Halsey-Stuart Shields, Hartford, Danbury, Conn., 1977-81, Advest, Inc., Hartford, 1981-88; registered securities rep. West Hartford, Conn., 1988-91; fin. con., investment analyst, pres. Ask My Assoc., Collinsville, Conn., 1988—; v.p. registered rep. E.T. Andrews & Co. Inc., Hartford, Conn., 1991—; v.p. Conn. Fin. Network, 1991—; sec. Internat. Assn. for Fin. Planning, Hartford, 1982-83, pub. rels. Conn. chpt., Hartford, 1983-85, ethics chairperson Conn. chpt., Hartford, 1985-86. Performing mem. Farmington Valley chpt. Sweet Adelines, Simsbury, Conn., 1976-82. Named for Effective Speaking and Human Rels., Dale Carnegie, West Hartford, 1985. Mem. Hartford Stockbrokers Club. Republican. Episcopalian. Home: PO Box 462 Collinsville CT 06022-0462

WHITNEY, DANIEL EUGENE, engineer, consultant; b. Chgo., June 8, 1938; s. Alan David and Ruth (Flesch) W.; m. Cynthia Lee Kolb, June 15, 1963; children: David, Karl. SB, MIT, 1960, SM, 1965, PhD, 1968. Cons. C.S. Draper Lab., Cambridge, Mass., 1966-74, staff engr., 1974-89, sect. chief, 1989-91; from asst. to assoc. prof. MIT, Cambridge, 1968-74. Author, editor: Concurrent Design of Products & Processes, 1989; inventor in field. Lt. USNR, 1961-66. Fellow ASME (awards com. 1988—); sr. mem. IEEE, Robot Inst. Am. Home: 141 Rhinecliff St Arlington MA 02174-7331 Office: CS Draper Lab 555 Technology Sq Cambridge MA 02139-3563

WHITNEY, LESTER FRANK, agricultural sciences educator; b. New Bedford, Mass., Mar. 21, 1928; s. Walter Elisha and Orasie (Lapointe) W.; m. Phyllis Marian Burrill; children: Marcia, Mark, Scott, Dean, David, John, Steven. BS in Agrl. Engring., U. Maine, 1949; MS in Agrl. Engring., Mich. State U., 1951, PhD, 1964. Registered profl. engr., Mass. Cons. engr. Jack H. Kelly Onion Farms, Inc., Parma, Mich., 1950-51; design, proj. engr. Ariens Co., Brillion, Wis., 1951-53; agrl. engr. Maine Potato Growers, Inc., Presque Isle, Maine, 1953-54; plant engr., chief engr., plant supt. Wirthmore Feed Div., CPC Internat., Brattleboro, Vt., 1954-59; asst. prof. agrl. engring. dept. U. Mass., Amherst, 1959-63, assoc. prof. food and agrl. engring. dept., 1963-67, prof. food engring. dept., 1977-91; consulting machine designer, Douglas G. Peterson Assocs., Greenfield, Mass., 1981—. Patentee in field; contbr. articles to profl. jours. Chmn. Amherst Planning Bd., 1965-71; mem. Amherst Sch. Bldg. Com., 1965-67, Lake Amherst Com., 1966-69; elected town meeting mem. Amherst, 1964-69. Recipient NSF sci. faculty fellowship, E. Lansing, Mich., 1963, Hood Found. award, NSF, East Lansing, 1962, Mass. Soc. of Agr. award, 1962. Mem. Am. Soc. Agrl. Engrs., Inst. Food Tech., Sigma Xi. Republican. Protestant. Home: 48 Jeffrey Ave Amherst MA 01002-2532

WHITNEY, PHILIP MATHER, manufacturing company executive; b. Bridgeport, Conn., Dec. 20, 1941; s. Philip M. and Eva (Trotter) W.; m. Louise Marie Hubbard, Oct. 28, 1977; children: John, Cherie, Stephanie. BS in Acctg., U. Bridgeport, 1963. CPA, Conn. Sr. acct. Deloitte & Touche, New Haven, 1963-67; cost acctg. mgr. Bullard Co., Bridgeport, 1967-72; contr. Bullard Castings Inc., Bridgeport, 1973; staff contr. White Consol. Industries, Cleve., 1974-76; v.p. fin. ATF-Davidson Co., Whitinsville, Mass., 1976-89; chief fin. officer Riverdale Mills Corp., Northbridge, Mass., 1989—. Mem. AICPA, Nat. Assn. Accts., Lions, Beta Gamma Sigma. Home: 7 Dudley Ln Sutton MA 01590 Office: Riverdale Mills Corp 130 Riverdale St Northbridge MA 01534

WHITNEY, RALPH ROYAL, JR., financial executive; b. Phila., Dec. 10, 1934; s. Ralph Royal and Florence Elizabeth (Whitney) W.; m. Fay Wadsworth, Apr. 4, 1959; children: Lynn Marie, Paula Sue, Brian Ralph. BA, U. Rochester, 1957, MBA, 1972. Spl. agt. Prudential Ins. Co., Rochester, N.Y., 1958-59, divsn. mgr., 1959-63; gen. agt. Nat. Life Vt., Syracuse, 1963-64; contr. Wadsworth Mfg. Assocs. Inc., Syracuse, 1964-65, v.p., 1965-68, pres., 1968-71; pres. Warren (Pa.) Components Corp., 1968-72; pres., mng. prin. ptnr. Hammond Kennedy Whitney & Co., N.Y.C., 1972—; chmn. IFR Systems Inc.; chmn., CEO Holbrook Patterson Inc., Globe Ticket & Label Co., Grobot File Co. Am., Maine Rubber Co.; bd. dirs. Excel Industries Corp., Baldwin Tech. Corp., Unistrut Corp. Am., Selas Corp. Am., D.M. Mossberg & Son Inc., Keene Corp., Adage Inc. Mem. N.Y. Yacht Club, Lotus Club (N.Y.C.), Century Club (Syracuse), Merion Cricket Club, Princeton Club. Episcopalian. Home: 100 Grays Ln Apt 108 Haverford PA 19041-1753

WHITNEY, THOMAS PORTER, writer, translator; b. Toledo, Jan. 26, 1917; s. Herbert Porter and Louise (Metzger) W.; m. Marguerite Carusone, Sept. 21, 1974; children by previous marriages: John Herbert, Louise Whitney Christofferson, Julia Forrestel. Grad., Phillips Exeter Acad., 1934; AB summa cum laude, Amherst Coll., 1937; MA, Columbia U., 1940. Instr. social scis. Bennett Coll., 1940-41; social sci. analyst OSS, Washington, 1941-44; attache, chief econ. sect. U.S. Embassy, Moscow, USSR, 1944-47; staff corr. AP of Am., Moscow, USSR, 1947-53; fgn. news analyst AP of Am., N.Y.C., 1953-59; propr. Whitney Book Shops Conn., 1975—; pres. Book Call, New Canaan, Conn., 1982—. Author: Has Russia Changed, 1960, Russia in My Life, 1962; editor: The Communist Blueprint for the Future, 1962, Khrushchev Speaks, 1963; editor, translator: The New Writing in Russia, 1964, In a Certain Kingdom, Twelve Russian Fairy Tales, 1972, The Young Russians, A Collection of Stories About Them, 1972; translator: One Day in the Life of Ivan Denisovich, 1963, Scarlet Sails, 1967, Prince Ivan, The Firebird and the Gray Wolf, 1968, The First Circle, 1968, Vasilisa the Beautiful, 1970, Forever Flowing, 1972, The Nobel Lecture on Literature, 1972, The Foundation Pit, 1973, The Gulag Archipelago, Vol. I, 1973, Vol. II, 1975, Children of the Street, 1979, Memoirs of General Peter Grigorenko, 1982, The Month Brothers, 1982, Dangerous Thoughts, 1990, No Return, 1990; contbr. articles to popular mags. including Wall Street Jour., N.Y. Times. Trustee Julia A. Whitney Found., Washington, Conn., Saratoga Performing Arts Ctr., 1989—. Mem. Overseas Press Club Am. (pres. 1958-59), ASCAP, PEN Am. Ctr., Thoroughbred Owners and Breeders Assn. (trustee 1984—), Nat. Mus. Racing, Yaddo Corp. (corp. mem.), Phi Beta Kappa, Alpha Delta Phi. Clubs: The Brook (N.Y.); Century Assn., Thoroughbred of Am., Saratoga Reading Rooms. Office: 901 Georgia St Key West FL 33040

WHITNEY, WILLIAM GORDON, investment management company executive; b. Rochester, N.Y., Oct. 12, 1922; s. William and Marguerite (Gordon) W.; m. Margaret M. Deis, Mar. 16, 1971; children: Carol Joy, Lance A., Valerie A., Fredericka A., William A. BS in Adminstrv. Engring., Cornell U., 1943; MBA with distinction, Harvard U., 1951. Field engr. Norma Hoffman Bearings Corp., Stanford, Conn., 1946-49; cons. McKinsey & Co., N.Y.C., 1951-54; v.p. Am. Airlines, Inc., N.Y.C., 1954-62; gen. mgr. Martin Marietta Corp., Balt., 1963-68; pres. Whitney & Co., Inc., Rochester, 1969—; chmn. Whitney Holdings, Ltd., N.Y.C., 1984—. With USN, 1944-46. Mem. Delta Upsilon. Office: Whitney and Co Inc 102 Panorama Rochester NY 14625-2315

WHITSELL, JOHN CRAWFORD, II, general surgeon; b. St. Joseph, Mo., Dec. 21, 1929; s. Ora Earl and Lorena (Spratt) W. AB, Grinnell Coll., 1950; MD, Washington U., St. Louis, 1954. Diplomate Am. Bd. Surgery, Am. Bd. Thoracic Surgery. From instr. to clin. prof. surgery Cornell U. Med. Ctr., N.Y.C., 1963-70; from asst. attending to attending in surgery N.Y. Hosp., N.Y.C., 1964-70; surg. dir. Rogosin Kidney Ctr. N.Y. Hosp.-Cornell Med. Ctr., N.Y.C., 1973-75; attending in surgery N.Y. Hosp., 1970—; clin. prof. surgery Cornell Med. Coll., 1970—; surg. cons. Rogosin Kidney Ctr., 1975—, Sharon (Conn.) Hosp., 1976—. Contbr. articles to profl. jours. Capt. USAF, 1961-63, Eng. Fellow ACS; mem. Transplantation Soc., N.Y. Surg. Soc., Am. Soc. Transplant Surgeons, N.Y. Soc. for Thoracic Surgery, Soc. Thoracic Surgeons, N.Y. Acad. Medicine, N.Y. Soc. Cardiovascular Surgery, Harvey Soc., Union Club of N.Y., Phi Beta Kappa. Office: 449 E 68th St New York NY 10021

WHITSON, EDWARD RICHARD, psychologist, educator; b. Jersey City, N.J., Sept. 27, 1944; s. Edward Kenneth and Erna Faye (Haubold) W.; m. Debbie Ann Lewis, July 12, 1980; children: Rebecca Ann Lewis-Whitson, Kristin Sara Lewis-Whitson, Tessa Elizabeth Lewis-Whitson. BS in Psychology, Math., Pa. State U., 1967; MEd, Antioch Grad. Sch. New Eng., 1974; MA, SUNY, Buffalo, 1980, PhD, 1983. Lic. psychologist, N.Y. Tchr. Glassboro (N.J.) Intermediate Sch., 1968-69; tchr., sch. adminstr. The Barlow Sch., Amenia, N.Y., 1969-73; exec. dir. Ashland (Mass.) Ednl. Community Ctr., 1974-75; grad. asst. psychology dept. SUNY, Buffalo, 1975-79; sch. psychologist Cleveland Hill Union Free Sch. Dist., Cheektowaga, N.Y., 1979-82; clin. intern Erie County Med. Ctr., Buffalo, 1982-83; asst. prof. psychology SUNY, Geneseo, 1983-91, assoc. prof., assoc. dean coll., 1991—. Co-author: Paraprofessionals in Mental Health, 1979; author book rev.; co-author chpt. in book. Bd. dirs. Mental Health Assn. Livingston County, N.Y., 1986—, Community Svcs. Bd., Livingston County, 1988—, Integrated Mental Health, Monroe and Livingston Counties, N.Y., 1990—. Mem. Am. Psychol. Assn., Ea. Psychol. Assn., Soc. for Psychol. Study of Social Issues. Home: 65 Highland Pky Rochester NY 14620-2503 Office: Dept Psychology SUNY-Geneseo Geneseo NY 14454

WHITTAKER, RICHARD PAWLING, orthopedic surgeon; b. Upper Darby, Pa., June 12, 1940; s. Robert Lincoln and Helen (Rudolph) W.; m. Margaret Michael, June 27, 1964; children: Laura, Susan, Keith, Scott. BA, U. Pa., Phila., 1962, MD, 1966. Diplomate Am. Bd. Orthopedic Surgery. Intern Pa. Hosp., Phila., 1967, resident, 1968; resident in orthopedic surgery Hosp. of U. Pa., Phila., 1971; ptnr. Pottstown (Pa.) Fracture Ctr., 1974-77, Orthopedic Specialists of Pottstown, Ltd., 1977—; staff Montgomery Hosp., Norristown, Pa., 1983—; asst. clin. prof. U. Pa. Sch. Medicine, Phila., 1978—; visiting orthopedic cons. Makere U., Kampala, Uganda, 1984; sec. Pottstown Hosp. Bd. Dirs., 1989-90. Contbr. articles to profl. jours. Bd. dirs. Presbyn. Ch., Pottstown, 1976-79; mem. sch. bd. Pottsgrove Sch., Pottstown. Maj. U.S. Army, 1971-74, lt. col., 1991, Saudi Arabia. Recipient Gold Crest award Salvation Army, 1985. Mem. Phila. Orthopedic Soc. (program chmn. 1982-83, bd. dirs. 1983-84), Pa. Orthopedic Soc. (bd. dirs., pres. 1990-91), Pottstown Meml. Med. Ctr. (exec. com.), Rotary. Republican. Office: Orthopedic Specialists of Pottstown 1603 E High St Pottstown PA 19464

WHITTEMORE, FRANK BOWEN, environmental, energy and management consultant; b. Worcester, Mass., Dec. 16, 1916; s. Frank Bowen and Blanche (Barney) W.; m. Marjorie Usher, Jan. 24, 1943; children: Suzanne Blanche, David Chandler. Student, Roanoke Coll., 1937-38, Franklin Tech. Coll., 1941, Worcester Polytech. Inst., 1942. Various positions Norton Co., Worcester, 1942-79; exec. dir. Providence Engring. Soc., 1978-79; pres. Rhode Islanders Saving Energy office of Gov., Providence, 1979-81; vice chmn. Narragansett Bay Commn., Providence, 1980-86; mgmt. cons. Barrington, R.I., 1980—. Contbr. numerous articles to mags., newspapers. Vice chmn. Barrington Zoning Bd., 1964-65; founder, exec. dir. Bar-Zap Litter Program, Barrington, 1966—; founder, chmn., trustee Save the Bay, Providence, 1973—; mem. Gov's. Task Force for Clean Water, Providence, 1981-82, Justice Assistance Corp., Providence, 1982-83; mem. Common Cause (coord. Nat. Issues), Providence, 1980—; dir. mktg. R.I. Parks Assn., 1985-86, Barrington Juvenile Hearing Bd., 1988—, Barrington Substance Abuse Task Force, 1988—, R.I. Earth Day State Com.; chair State Fund Raising; chmn. bd. dirs. Bristo County (R.I.) Citizens for Better Water Mgmt., 1990; mem. Save the Running River Task Force Barrington Land Conservancy. With USAF, 1943. Recipient citations from R.I. Senate, 1978, Ho. Reps., 1979, Gov., 1981, N.E. Environ. Network Leadership award Tufts U., Medford, Mass., 1984, Outstanding Environmentalist award Save The Bay, Providence, 1983. Mem. Audubon Soc. of R.I. (Runins River chpt. bd. dirs.). Unitarian. Home and Office: 11 Devonshire Dr Barrington RI 02806-4015

WHITTEN, STEVEN DAVID, career services director, educator; b. Lynn, Mass., Jan. 4, 1950; s. Philip Mason and Marion (Leonard) W.; m. Marie Catherine Volo, Apr. 7, 1974; children: Kathryn, Sarah. BA in English, Salem (Mass.) State Coll., 1973, MEd in Counseling, 1984. Dir. guidance Landmark Sch., Prides Crossing, Mass., 1974-86; dir. career svcs. R.I. Sch. of Design, Providence, 1986—. Author brochures. Mem. Nat. Soc. Exptl. Edn., Mid. Atlantic Mus. Assn., Eastern Coll. Placement Officers (program com. 1988-91), Coll. Placement Coun., R.I. Career Counselors (bd. dirs. 1991—), Coll. Art Assn., New Eng. Mus. Assn. Home: 45 Cady Rd Barrington RI 02806-3537 Office: RI Sch of Design 2 College St Providence RI 02903-2707

WHITTINGHAM, M(ICHAEL) STANLEY, chemist; b. Nottingham, Eng., Dec. 22, 1941; came to U.S., 1968, naturalized, 1980; s. William Stanley and Dorothy Mary (Findlay) W.; B.A. in Chemistry, Oxford U., 1964, M.A. (Gas Council scholar 1964-67), D.Phil., 1968; m. Georgina Judith Andai, Mar. 23, 1969; children: Jenniffer Judith, Michael Stanley. Rsch. asso., head solid state electrochemistry group Materials Center, Stanford U., 1968-72; mem. staff Exxon Research Co., Linden, N.J., 1972—, group head solid state chem. physics, 1975-78, dir. solid state scis., 1978-80, mgr. chem. engring. tech., 1980-84; dir. phys. scis. Schlumberger Co., Ridgefield, Conn., 1984-88; prof. chemistry, dir. The Inst. for Materials Rsch., SUNY, 1988—; cons., lectr. in field. Mem. Electrochem. Soc. (Young Author award 1971), Am. Chem. Soc. (chmn. solid state sect. 1987, chmn. Binghampton sect. 1991), Am. Phys. Soc., N.Y. Electrochem. Soc. (chmn. 1980-81). Author, editor papers in field; author 5 books. Home: 396 Meeker Rd Vestal NY 13850-3230 Office: SUNY Dept Chemistry Binghamton NY 13902-6000

WHITTINGTON, CONSTANCE VICTORIA, communications executive; b. Balt., Oct. 12, 1954; d. Philippa I. W. BS, U. Md., 1978; MBA, Loyola Coll., Balt., 1984. Editor Port Balt. Mag. Md. Port Adminstrn., Balt., 1978-80, asst. dir. port promotion, 1980-82; mgr. pub. rels. and advt. Comml. Credit Co., Balt., 1982-84; dir. mktg. and devel. YMCA Greater Balt., 1984-85; v.p. RM&D Pub. Rels., Balt., 1985-87; v.p., gen. mgr. Earle Palmer Brown Pub. Rels., Phila., 1987-89; v.p. corp. communications Earle Palmer Brown Cos., Bethesda, Md., 1989—. Mem. Pub. Rels. Soc. Am. (past pres. Md. chpt., cert.), Balt. Pub. Rels. Coun., Pub. Rels. Soc. Am. Phila., Counselor's Acad. Pub. Rels. Soc. Am. Republican. Office: Earle Palmer Brown Cos Arlington Rd Bethesda MD 20814-5206

WHITTINGTON, HARRISON DEWAYNE, superintendent, consultant; b. Crisfield, Md., June 9, 1931; s. Alfonza Cottman and Maryland Louvetta Whittington; m. Louise Eva Holden. BS, Morgan State U., 1948; MEd, Pa. State U., 1961; EdD, Nova U., 1980. Tchr. Woodson Sch., 1954-62, prin., 1962-68; title I coord. Somerset County Pub. Schs., Princess Anne, Md., 1968-70; dir. fed. programs Somerset County Pub. Schs., Princess Anne, 1970-74, 74-76, coord. spl. programs, 1976-80, coord. supr. supporting svcs., 1980-81, asst. supt., 1981-88, supt. of schs., 1988—; coord. human rels. Md. State Dept. Edn., 1974; cons. Univ. Md. Eastern Shore and Salisbury State Coll.; trustee Coun. on Econ. Edn. in Md.; mem. adv. com. for Ednl. Block Grants; presenter in field; many others. Bd. dirs. Somerset County Head Start Inc., Somerset County Am. Red Cross, McCready Meml. Hosp., Somerset County Heart Asns., Somerset County Recreation Commn., Shore-Up, Inc.; active Md. adv. coun. Community Coordinated Child Care, Md. Coun. on Family Rels., Somerset County Social Svcs., Somerset County Commn. on Mental Health and Planning Com., Somerset County Phys. Fitness Commn. and many others. Named Community Leader of Am., 1969, Citizen of the Yr., Omega Psi Phi, 1971, Outstanding Educator in Am., 1973-74, Outstanding Black Community Leader, Salisbury State Coll., 1974, Outstanding Black Community Leader, UMES, 1976, others. Mem. NEA (state del. 1968, 69, 70), Nat. Alliance Black Educators, Internat. Reading Assn., Nat. Assn. Adminstrs. State and Fed. Edn. Programs, Md. State Tchrs. Assn., Md. Assn. Supervision and Curriculum Devel., Md. Coun. Adminstrs. of Compensatory Edn., Md. Assn. for Publicly Supported Continuing Edn., Md. Assn. Affirmative Action Officers, Md. Assn. for Adult Community Continuing Edn., Md. Negotiating Svc. (v.p.), Tchrs. Assn. Somerset County (pres. 1968) and many others. Republican. Methodist. Home: 28767 Hudsons Rd Marion Station MD 21838 Office: Somerset County Pub Schs Prince William St Princess Anne MD 21853-1227

WHITTINGTON, RONALD FREDERICK, educational administrator; b. Marion, Md., July 26, 1949; s. Frederick Hubbard and Naomi (Archie) W.; m. Marilyn Elaine Portlock, June 3, 1972; 1 child, Colby. BSEd, U. Del., 1971; MBA, Cen. Mich. U., 1983. Tchr. Newark Sch. Dist., 1971-73; asst. headmaster St. Croix (V.I.) Country Day Sch., 1973-75, Goud Hope Sch., St. Croix, 1975-78; asst. dir. admissions U. Del., Newark, 1978-86, asst. dean Coll. of Bus., 1986-88, asst. to pres., 1988—. Exec. coun. Del Marva Boy Scout Coun., Wilmington, Del., 1990; exec. bd. Del. ACLU, Wilmington, 1990; com. mem. United Way of Del., Wilmington, 1986. Mem. Am. Coun. on Edn., Alpha Phi Alpha. Office: U Del 104 Hullihen Ct Newark DE 19716-0001

WHITTINGTON, VANESSA ELIZABETH, educator; b. Boston, Apr. 15, 1960; d. Samuel Wall and Ernestine (Brazand Hundley) W. BS, Bridgewater State U., 1978; postgrad., Cambridge Coll., 1992—. Elem. tchr. Boston (Mass.) Pub. Schs., 1983—, Pauline A. Shaw, Dorchester, Mass., 1987—; adult edn. sec. Boston Pub. Schs., 1982, 83, mem. graphic learning com., 1983, impact II tchr. adaptor; musician cable TV program Gospel Expressions Prodns.; tutor Metco (after sch. program); mem. Primary Summer Source Inst., 1991. Mem. local Sunshine Band, 1985, state pres., 1989—. Tutor Metco (after sch. program); mem. Children's Mus. and the Mus. Sci., Women's HEritage Trail, 3 Regent St. Young Adult Choir, Women's Choir. with USAR, 1979—. Mem. Assn. Supervision and Curriculum Devel., Greater Boston Reading Coun., Boston Tchrs. Union, Black Educators Alliance of Mass., Nat. Coun. Tchrs. English, Women's Heritage Trail, African Meeting House. Democrat.

WHITTLE, DAVID BRIAN, marketing professional; b. Hollywood, Calif., Nov. 12, 1953; s. Lavar E. Whittle and Arlene (Larsen) Bascom; m. Serena Laree Robins, Nov. 26, 1982; children: Jared, Nicia, Michael, Andrew. BS cum laude with highest honors, Brigham Young U., 1979, MBA, 1984. Missionary The Ch. of Jesus Christ of LDS, Tokyo, 1973-75; sales intern Gen. Mills, Dallas, 1978; auditor Price Waterhouse, San Jose, Calif., 1979-80; contr. Zeda Computers Internat., Provo, Utah, 1981; ptnr. Lloyds Computers, Orem, Utah, 1982; fin. analyst IBM, Boca Raton, Fla., 1984-86; mktg. rep. IBM, Bethesda, Md., 1986-88; adv. mktg. rep. IBM, Gaithersburg, Md., 1989—; mem. field adv. coun. IBM Entry Systems, 1990, IBM 0S/2 Evangelist, 1992—. Hinckley scholar Brigham Young U., 1978. Mem. Brigham Young U. Mgmt. Soc. (stake rep. 1987—). Republican. Home: 9424 Bethany Pl Gaithersburg MD 20879-1262 Office: IBM 100 Lakeforest Blvd Gaithersburg MD 20879-3395

WHITTLESEY, JUDITH H., public relations executive; b. Bartlesville, Okla., Dec. 28, 1942; d. Harry Haynes and Suzanne (Arnote) Holloway; m. Dennis Jeffrey Whittlesey, Aug. 3, 1968; children: Kristin Arnote, Kevin Jeffrey. BA, U. Okla., 1964; postgrad., Tulsa U., 1965, U. Va., 1971-72. Staff aide Office of the V.P. of U.S., Washington, 1979-81, Com. for Future of Am., Washington, 1981-82; dep. dir. scheduling in advance Mondale-Ferraro Campaign, Washington, 1982-84; dir. media rels. The Susan Davis Cos., Washington, 1986-87, v.p., 1987-88, exec. v.p., 1988—. Bd. dirs. Cultural Alliance of Greater Washington, 1983—, Washington Project for the Arts, 1987—; elder Chevy Chase Presbyn. Ch., Washington, 1985-88. Recipient numerous Mercury and Anvil awards, 1988-91. Office: The Susan Davis Cos 1146-19th St NW Washington DC 20036

WHITTY, GERARD CHARLES, bank executive; b. Rochester, N.Y., May 11, 1950; s. Frank Walter and Florence (Edelman) W.; 1 child, Michelle Lynn. BA in Math., St. John Fisher Coll., Rochester, N.Y., 1974. Collection supr. Lincoln First Bank, Rochester, N.Y., 1975-77; asst. v.p. 1st Fed. Savings & Loan, Rochester, 1977-82; v.p. Citizens Savings Bank, Ithaca, N.Y., 1982-90; cons. to mortgage banking industry Charleston, S.C., 1990—; owner, pres. J.W. Enterprises, Fairport, N.Y., 1991—; ptnr. Whibergrand Assocs., Ithaca, 1989. Author: Effective Transfers of Servicing, 1987; contbr. article to profl. publ. Bd. dirs. Rochester C. of C., 1980. With USAR, 1970-76. Home: PO Box 12763 Charleston SC 29422-2763 Office: JW Enterprises Greatwood Ct Ste 25-4 Fairport NY 14450

WHITWORTH, WILLIAM A., magazine editor; b. Hot Springs, Ark., Feb. 13, 1937; s. William C. and Lois Virginia (McNabb) W.; m. Carolyn Hubbard, Dec. 27, 1969; children—Matthew, Katherine. B.A., U. Okla., 1960. Reporter Ark. Gazette, Little Rock, 1960-63; reporter N.Y. Herald Tribune, 1963-65; staff writer The New Yorker, 1966-72, assoc. editor, 1973-80; editor-in-chief The Atlantic Monthly, Boston, 1981—. Office: Atlantic Monthly 745 Boylston St Boston MA 02116-2636

WHYBROW, PETER CHARLES, medical educator, medical college dean; b. Hertforshire, Eng., June 13, 1939; came to U.S., 1964, naturalized, 1975; s. Charles Ernest and Doris Beatrice (Abbott) W.; m. Margaret Ruth Steele, Dec. 11, 1962 (div. 1988); children: Katherine, Helen. Student, Univ. Coll., London, 1956-59; M.B., B.S., Univ. Coll. Hosp. Med. Sch., 1962; diploma psychol. medicine, Conjoint Bd., London, 1968; M.A. (hon.), Dartmouth Coll., 1974, U. Pa., 1984. House officer endocrinology Univ. Coll. Hosp., 1962, sr. house physician psychiatry, 1963-64; house surgeon St. Helier Hosp., Surrey, Eng., 1963; house officer pediatrics Prince of Wales Hosp., London, 1964; resident psychiatry U. N.C. Hosp., 1965-67, instr., research fellow, 1967-68; mem. sci. staff neuropsychiat. research unit Charshalton, Surrey, 1968-69; dir. residency tng. psychiatry Dartmouth Med. Sch., Hanover, N.H., 1969-71; prof. psychiatry Dartmouth Med. Sch., 1970-84, chmn. dept., 1970-78, exec. dean, 1980-83; prof., chmn. dept. psychiatry U. Pa., Phila., 1984—, Ruth Meltzer prof. psychiatry, 1992; psychiatrist-in-chief Hosp. U. Pa., 1984—; dir. psychiatry Dartmouth Hitchock Affiliated Hosp., 1970-78; vis. scientist NIMH, 1978-79; cons. VA, 1970—, NIMH, 1972— ; chmn. test com. Nat. Bd. Med. Examiners, 1977-84; researcher psychoendrocrinology. Author: Mood Disorders: Toward a New Psychobiology, 1984, The Hibernation Response, 1988; Editor: Psychosomatic Medicine, 1977; mem. editorial bd.: Community Psychiatry, Psychiat. Times, Directions in Psychiatry; contbr. articles to profl. jours. Recipient Anclote Manor award psychiat. rsch. U. N.C., 1967, Sr. Investigator award Nat. Alliance for Rsch. into Schizophrenia and Depression, 1989; Josiah Macy Jr. Found. scholar, 1978-79. Fellow Am. Psychiat. Assn., Royal Coll. Psychiatrists (founding mem.), Am. Coll. Psychiatrists; mem. Assn. Am. Med. Colls., Soc. Psychosomatic Research, Am. Assn. Chmn. Depts. Psychiatry (pres. 1977-78), Royal Soc. Medicine, AAAS, Am. Psychopath. Assn., Soc. Biol. Psychiatry, N.Y. Acad. Scis., Soc. Neurosci., Sigma Xi, Alpha Omega Alpha. Club: Cosmos (Washington). Address: 135 S 19th St Philadelphia PA 19103 Office: U Pa Dept Psychiatry 305 Blockley Hall Philadelphia PA 19104-6021

WHYTE, BRUCE LINCOLN, management executive, marketing professional; b. N.Y.C., Mar. 13, 1941; s. Lincoln Dodge and Louise (Connor) W.; m. Judith McCarthy. BS, Fordham U., N.Y., 1962; MS, NYU, 1963. Editor corp. planning Am. Airlines, N.Y.C., 1963-65; sr. mktg. analyst Ea.

Airlines, N.Y.C., 1965-67; v.p. Deckcraft Corp., N.Y.C., 1967-69; founder & pres. Original Print Collectors Group, N.Y.C., 1972; chmn. bd. OPCG (Sub. Reader's Digest), N.Y.C., 1980-84; pres. Bruce Whyte Enterprises, internat. fine arts bus., N.Y.C., 1984—; cons. mktg. The Prudential Co., N.Y.C., 1986, Am Express, N.Y.C. 1987; sr. mktg. cons. A.R.T. Corp., N.Y.C., 1988; bus. cons. Mystic Seaport Mus. 1990—; Am. art liaison Doctors of the World, Paris, 1992; registered expert witness U.S. Treasury Dept., 1983—. Editor: Art Newsletter OPCG Newsletter, 1972-84 (Best award in U.S.A. 1983-84). Sr. Advisor U.S. Congl. Adv. Bd., Wash. 1981-83; chmn. Com. U.S. Senatorial Bus. Adv. Bd., Wash. 1981-83; trustee, v.p. Hist. Preservation Soc., N.Y.C. 1986—; U.S. art liaison Found. Mitterand (The Universal Declaration of Human Rights) on behalf of Amnesty Internat., U.N., UNESCO, High Commn. on Refugees, Nat. Mus., Heads of State, Paris, N.Y.C., 1989.; consumer art protection legis. advisor, atty. gen. N.Y. State Senate and Assembly, 1981. Recipient Best of Art Catalogues award, Sroge Colorado Springs, 1983; Artist fellow, 1988—. Mem. Fine Arts Publ. Assn. (bd. dirs. 1984—), The Nat. Arts Club (gov., treas. 1972-74, 86—).

WIBLE, CLARENCE EDWARD, accountant; b. Greensburg, Pa., Jan. 24, 1946; s. Clarence Edward and Marie (Bard) W.; m. Deborah Kay Johnson, Apr. 21, 1972; children: Rachel Sue, Mark Edward. BS in Edn., Ind. U. of Pa., 1967, postgrad., 1970; postgrad., St. Vincent Coll., 1972. CPA, Pa. Enforcement examiner Pa. Liquor Control Bd., Pitts., 1967-68; acct. H & T Sales, Inc., Greensburg, 1970-71, Richard Patterson, CPA, Greensburg, 1972-73, Francis O. Cramer, CPA, Greensburg, 1973-75; owner C. Edward Wible P.A., Greensburg, 1971-72, C. Edward Wible, CPA, Mt. Pleasant, Pa., 1975-83; prin. Horner, Wible & Assocs., Greensburg, 1983—, Horner-Wible, Inc., Greensburg, 1990—; mem. adv. bd. Comml. Nat. Bank, Latrobe, Pa., 1991—. Treas. 1st United Meth. Ch., Greensburg, 1986-90; sec.-treas. Westmoreland County Community Coll., Youngwood, Pa., 1978-86; chmn. vacancy bd. Mt. Pleasant Twp., 1991—. With U.S. Army, 1968-70. Mem. Pa. Inst. CPAs, Mt. Pleasant C. of C. (dir.), Elks. Republican. Home: 2451 Route 819 N Mount Pleasant PA 15666-9161 Office: Horner Wible & Assocs 415 S Main St PO Box 915 Greensburg PA 15601

WICK, TAMARA, artist, writer; b. July 15, 1961; d. James Alan and Maxine Evelyn (Tankersley) W.; m. John E. Kulukundis, 1986. BA in Comm./Broadcasting, Ariz. State U., 1984. Adminstrv. asst. to sr. v.p. Altschiller Reitzfeld Advtg., N.Y.C., 1984-86; asst. to exec. prodr. video devel. Columbia Pictures Industries, N.Y.C., 1986-87; pub. rels. coord., asst. to Estée Lauder and Ida Stewart Estée Lauder Cos., N.Y.C., 1987-89. Active Met. Mus. Art, N.Y.C. Recipient Scholastic award Nat. Conf. Tchrs. English 1976, nominee writing award; Merit scholar U. Ariz., 1976. Mem. NAFE, U.S. Equestrian Team, N.Y. Women in Comm., N.Y. Zool. Soc., N.Y. Young Reps. Club, Ariz. State U. Alumni, Kappa Kappa Gamma Alumnae. Episcopalian. Home: 150 W 56th St New York NY 10019

WICKER, ROBERT KIRK, chemistry educator, consultant; b. Altoona, Pa., Mar. 4, 1939; s. Robert Kirk and Ethel May (Bowers) W.; m. Helen May Notopoulos, Mar. 3, 1961; children: Robert K., Katharine M., Kirk N. BS, Juniata Coll., Huntingdon, Pa., 1960; MS, U. Del., 1963, PhD, 1966. Asst. prof. chemistry Davis and Elkins (W.Va.) Coll., 1965-66; prof. Washington (Pa.) and Jefferson Coll., 1967—; cons. on edn. and chemistry to numerous indsl. cos., State of Pa., Dept. Energy, NSF, 1980—. Author: (manual) Physical Chemistry, 1985; also articles. Pres. Assn. for Retarded Citizens, Washington, 1984-86; tutor Washington Literacy Coun., 1990—. Mem. Am. Chem. Soc., Sigma Xi. Republican. Lutheran. Home: RR 1 Box 126 Washington PA 15301-8201 Office: Washington & Jefferson Coll Lincoln St Washington PA 15301-6720

WICKER, THOMAS GREY, retired journalist; b. Hamlet, N.C., June 18, 1926; s. Delancey David and Esta (Cameron) W.; m. Neva Jewett McLean, Aug. 20, 1949 (div. 1973); children: Cameron McLean, Thomas Grey; m. Pamela Abel Hill, Mar. 9, 1974. A.B. in Journalism, U. N.C., 1948; Nieman fellow, Harvard, 1957-58. Exec dir. Southern Pines (N.C.) C. of C., 1948-49; editor Sandhill Citizen, Aberdeen, N.C., 1949; mng. editor The Robesonian, Lumberton, N.C., 1949-50; pub. info. dir. N.C. Bd. Pub. Welfare, 1950-51; copy editor Winston-Salem (N.C.) Jour., 1951-52, sports editor, 1954-55, Sunday feature editor, 1955-56, Washington corr., 1957, editorial writer, city hall corr., 1958-59; assoc. editor Nashville Tennesseean, 1959-60; mem. staff Washington bur. N.Y. Times, 1960-71, chief bur., 1964-68; assoc. editor N.Y. Times, 1968-85, columnist, 1966-91. Author: (pseudonym Paul Connolly): novels Get Out of Town, 1951, Tears Are For Angels, 1952, So Fair, So Evil, 1955; under own name: novels The Kingpin, 1953, The Devil Must, 1957, The Judgment, 1961, Facing the Lions, 1973, Unto this Hour, 1984; non-fiction Kennedy Without Tears, 1964, JFK and LBJ: The Influence of Personality Upon Politics, 1968, A Time to Die, 1975, On Press, 1978, One of Us: Richard Nixon and the American Dream, 1991; contbr. articles to nat. mags., chpts. to books. Served to lt. (j.g.) USNR, 1952-54. Mem. Soc. Nieman Fellows, Century Assn. Office: care NY Times Co 229 W 43d St New York NY 10036

WICKERSHAM, JOHN MOORE, classical studies, educator; b. Phila., Aug. 12, 1943; s. John H. and Margaret Virginia (Stuart) W.; m. Annabel Caldwell Lee, Aug. 13, 1963 (div. Mar. 4, 1980); 1 child, Ellen Grover; m. Erlis Ann Tropea, Jan. 5, 1985. AB, U. Pa., 1964, MA, 1965; BA, Oxford U., 1972; PhD, Princeton U., 1972. Instr. in classical studies U. Pa., Phila., 1969-72; asst. prof. classical studies Ursinus Coll., Collegeville, Pa., 1972-80, assoc. prof. classical studies, 1980-87, prof. classical studies, 1987—. Editor: Greek Historical Documents: The Fourth Century BC, 1973; author and editor: Myth and the Polis, 1991. Participant spl. seminar Nat. Endowment for the Humanities, U. Pa., 1976-77, summer seminar, Harvard U., 1985. Mem. Am. Phil. Assn., Classical Assn. of the Atlantic States (Hahn scholarship com. 1987—), Soc. for Promotion of Hellenic Studies. Presbyterian. Office: Ursinus Coll Collegeville PA 19426

WICKFIELD, ERIC NELSON, investment company executive; b. Bryn Mawr, Pa., Feb. 14, 1953; s. Paul Gilbert Jacobs and Patricia Ruth (Nelson) Davies; m. Kristine Margaret Erickson, June 21, 1974 (div. 1976); m. Sara Lou Datt, July 23, 1977 (div. 1990); 1 child, Eric N. Jr.; m. Leslie Walsh Willingham, June 8, 1990. BS, Rochester Inst. Tech., 1974; MBA, Boston U., 1990. Project mgr. Flight Safety Internat., Wichita, Kans., 1976-82; v.p. Aufleger-Garrett, Stillwater, Okla., 1982-86; demonstration pilot citation div. Gen. Dynamics, Wichita, 1986-87; pres. Prompt Fin. Inc., Concord, Mass., 1987—; bd. dirs. Prompt Fin. Inc., Concord; bd. dirs. Phorum Re Investment Corp., N.Y.C., The Cleaning Solution, Inc., Boston. Co-author: Sustaining High Performance, 1990; editor: 421 Pilot's Training Manual, 1981. Mem. Internat. Operator's Coun., Aircraft Owner's & Pilot's Assn. Republican. Methodist. Office: Prompt Fin Inc 30 Monument Sq Concord MA 01742-1857

WICKHAM, ROBERT DEAN, physician; b. Sayre, Pa., Aug. 11, 1923; s. Darley Jenkins and Anna (Dell) W.; m. Louise Jullien, Sept. 24, 1955; children: Louise, Lisa, Leslie, Robert Jr. AB, Drew U., 1947; MD, Albany Med. Soc., 1952. Diplomate Am. Bd. Urology, Nat. Bd. Med. Examiners. Intern Northwestern Med. Ctr., Chgo., 1952-53, surgical resident, 1953-54; resident and chief urology Squire Clinic, Columbia Presbyn., N.Y.C., 1955-57; attending urologist St. Luke's Roosevelt Med. Ctr., N.Y.C., 1958—; mem. tech. expert panel RBRVS, Harvard Sch. Pub. Health; bd. dirs. Trivest Corp.; presenter, lectr. in field. Editorial bd.: Internat. Jour. Urology and Nephrology; contbr. articles to profl. jours. With U.S. Army, 1943-46, WWII, ETO. Decorated Bronze Star with two oak leaf clusters. Mem. AMA, Am. Urol. Soc. (sec., pres. N.Y. sect. 1988-91, recipient commendation 1991), Am. Assn. Clin. Urologists (pres.-elect to pres. 1991-93), Hungarian Soc. Urology (hon. medal 1991), N.Y. State Urol. Soc., N.Y. State Med. Soc., N.Y. County Med. Soc., N.Y. Acad. Medicine, Soc. for Urology and Engring., Hosp. Grads. Soc., Am. Guild Organists, others. Republican. Office: 425 W 59th St New York NY 10019

WICKRAMANAYAKE, SANDHYA RUKMAL (KARUNARATNE), accountant; b. Colombo, Western, Sri Lanka, Apr. 27, 1958; d. Kankanamalage Mahinda and Dolly Winifred (Wettasinghe) Karunaratne; m. Godage Bandula Wickramanayake, Dec. 1, 1983. ACA, Inst. Chartered Accts., Colombo, Sri Lanka, 1983. CPA, Ohio. Staff acct. Ernst & Whinney, Colombo, Sri Lanka, 1978-79, sr. acct., 1980-83, supr., 1983; sr. acct. Parms & Co., Columbus, Ohio, 1986-88; sr. acct. Ohio State U., Columbus, 1988-89, chief acct., 1990; contr. George Sch., Newtown, Pa., 1991—. Mem. Am. Inst. CPA's, Pa. Inst. CPA's, Inst. Chartered Accts. Sri Lanka (assoc.). Buddhist. Home: 4 Woodland Ct Cranbury NJ 08512 Office: George Sch Newtown PA 18940

WIDGOFF, MILDRED, physicist, educator; b. Buffalo, Aug. 24, 1924; d. Leo Widgoff and Rebecca Shulimson; children—Eve Widgoff Shapiro, Jonathan Bernard Widgoff Shapiro. B.A., U. Buffalo, 1944; Ph.D., Cornell U., 1952. Rsch. assoc. Brookhaven Nat. Lab., Yaphank, N.Y., 1952-54; rsch. fellow Harvard U., Cambridge, Mass., 1955-58; asst. prof. rsch. Brown U., Providence, 1959-66, assoc. prof. rsch., 1966-74, prof. physics, 1974—. Fellow Am. Phys. Soc.; mem. Sigma Xi, Phi Beta Kappa, Phi Kappa Phi. Office: Brown U Dept Physics PO Box 1843 Providence RI 02912-0001

WIDMAN, SARAH ELIZABETH, public relations executive, writer; b. Cin., Apr. 26, 1945; d. Robert Benjamin and Edith Elizabeth (Slimp) Howard.; m. George Parker Widman, Oct. 17, 1970; children: Robert Duncan, James Parker. BA, U. Cin., 1967. Copy editor The Evening Press, Binghamton, N.Y., 1967-68, feature writer, 1968-69; reporter The Daily Press, Utica, N.Y., 1969-70, reporter, photographer Rome (N.Y.) bur., 1972-73; reporter The Sun Bull., Binghamton, 1970-72; pub. rels. cons. Oneida Co. Bd. of Coop. Ednl. Svcs., New Hartford, N.Y., 1979-82; editor Alumni Mag. Ursinus Coll., Collegeville, Pa., 1983-90, asst. dir. communications, 1988-90, dir. communications, 1990—. Contbr. articles to Redbook, C.S. Monitor, others. Coord. Concerned Citizens for Utica Pub. Libr., 1975-77; sec. Troop 113 Boy Scouts Am., Trappe, Pa., 1989—; chair com. on communication Pa. S.E. Conf. United Ch. Christ, Collegeville, 1988-90; mem. long range planning com. Perkiomen Valley High Sch., Graterford, Pa., 1989; active Coun. for Advancement and Support of Edn. Mem. Coll. and Univ. Pub. Rels. Assn. Pa., Pi Delta Epsilon. Democrat. Office: Ursinus Coll PO Box 1000 Collegeville PA 19426

WIDMER, WILBUR JAMES, civil engineering educator; b. West New York, N.J., Oct. 20, 1918; s. Gottfried and Louisa Marie (Ringeisen) W.; m. Pearl Adell Gilmore, Sept. 4, 1950; children: Frederick James, Wilbur Warren, Mark Thomas. BCE, The Cooper Union, N.Y.C., 1946; SM, MIT, 1948, postgrad., 1956-57; postgrad., U.R.I., 1964-65. Registered engr., Conn.; diplomate Am. Acad. Environ. Engrs. Hull design technician Gibbs & Cox Naval Architecture, N.Y.C., 1943-47; instr. U. Conn., Storrs, 1948-50, asst. prof., 1950-58, assoc. prof., 1958-72, prof. civil engring., 1972-88; sanitary engr. WHO, Lahore, Pakistan, 1968-70; prof. emeritus U. Conn., Storrs, 1988—; cons. C.W. Riva Co., Providence, 1950-64, J.S. Minges, Farmington, Conn., 1958-67, WHO, Brazil/Saudi Arabia, 1972, 79, Ptnrs. of the Americas, Brazil, 1986. Author tech. papers in field. Recipient Arthur Sidney Bedell award Water Pollution Control Assn., New Eng. Sect., 1972, Pres.'s award Conn. Treatment Plant Operators Assn., Hartford, 1975. Fellow Am. Soc. Civil Engrs. (recipient Robert Ridgeway award 1946, Benjamin Wright award 1987), Royal Soc. Health/United Kingdom (emeritus); mem. Am. Water Works Assn., Water Pollution Control Fedn., Am. Soc. Limnology and Oceanography (emeritus), Astron. Soc. Greater Hartford. Republican. Roman Catholic. Office: U Conn Dept Civil Engring PO Box U-37 Storrs CT 06269

WIDNALL, SHEILA EVANS, university administrator; b. Tacoma, Wash., July 13, 1938; d. Rolland John and Genievieve Alice (Krause) Evans; m. William Soule Widnall, June 11, 1960; children: William, Ann. BS, MIT, 1960, MS, 1961, PhD, 1964; PhD (hon.), New Eng. Coll., 1975, Lawrence U., 1987, Cedar Crest Coll., 1988, Smith Coll., 1990, Mt. Holyoke Coll., 1991, Ill. Inst. Tech., 1991. Asst. prof. aero. Astronautics MIT, Cambridge, 1964-70, assoc. prof., 1970-74, prof., 1974—, assoc. provost, 1992—; dir. univ. research U.S. Dept. Transp., Washington, 1974-75; bd. dirs. Chemfab Inc., Bennington, Vt., Aerospace Corp., L.A., Draper Labs., Cambridge; trustee Carnegie Corp., 1984-92. Contbr. articles to profl. jours.; patentee in field; assoc. editor AIAA Jour. Aircraft, 1972-75, Physics of Fluids, 1981-88, Jour. Applied Mechanics, 1983-87; mem. editorial bd. Sci., 1984-86. Chmn. faculty MIT, Cambridge, 1970-81, com. on undergrad. admission and fin. aid, 1982-84; bd. visitors U.S. Air Force Acad., Colorado Springs, Colo., 1978-83. Fellow AAAS (bd. dirs. 1982-89, pres. 1987-88, chmn. 1988-89), AIAA (bd. dirs. 1975-77, Lawrence Spery award 1972), Am. Phys. Soc. (exec. com. 1979-82); mem. Boston Mus. Sci. (trustee 1989—, Washburn award 1988), ASME, Am. Acad. Arts and Scis., Soc. Women Engrs. (outstanding achievement award 1975), Nat. Acad. Engring. (coun. 1992—), Seattle Mountaineers. Office: MIT 77 Massachusetts Ave Rm 33218 Cambridge MA 02139-4307

WIEBE, DONALD, mechanical engineer, consultant; b. Indicot, Nebr., June 30, 1923; s. Henry H. and Elizabeth (Thiesen) W.; m. Thora Kathern Merritt, Apr. 20, 1945; children: Charles Marion, John Merritt. BSEM, W.Va. U., 1949, MSEM, 1959; postgrad., U. Pitts., 1954-64. Lic. profl. engr., Pa., W.Va. Rsch. engr. Joy Mfg. Co., Franklin, Pa., 1949-51; mgr. exptl. sta. Joy Mfg. Co., Pitts., 1953-62; asst. prof. W.Va. U., Morgantown, 1951-53; mgr. engring. mechanics Westinghouse Astronuclear Lab., Pitts., 1962-65; mgr. rsch. and engring. A. Stucki Co., Pitts., 1965-76, v.p. rsch. and engring., 1976-86; cons. rail transp. Sewickley, Pa., 1986—; mem. vis. com. Sch. Mines W. Va. U., 1960-64, mem. adv. com. Mech. and Aerospace Engring., 1981—; lectr. NSF, Greensburg, Pa., 1960-72. Granted 30 U.S. and 49 fgn. patents relating to mining, indsl. and transp. systems and equipment. Pres. Tanglewood Civic Assn., Greensburg, 1965-67, Witherow Civic Assn., Sewickley, 1971-73. 1st lt. U.S. Army, 1943-46. Named Disting. Alumni W.Va. U. Fellow ASME (Arnold Stucki award); mem. AIME, Soc. Exptl. Mechanics, Instrument Soc. Am. (life).

WIEDEFELD, MARCIA FENCHAK, program director; b. Norwich, N.Y., Mar. 28, 1964; d. Paul and Ellen Marie (Bohochick) Fenchak; m. Paul Jerome Wiedefeld, Jan. 2, 1988. BS, Towson (Md.) State U., 1986; MA, George Washington U., 1989. Cert. rehab. counselor. Mental health intern Sheppard-Pratt Hosp., Towson, 1985; child life intern Johns Hopkins Hosp., Balt., 1986; employment tng. specialist The Schapiro Tng. Employment Prog., Balt., 1986-87; acting prog. dir. The Schapiro Tng. Employment Prog., 1987, employment placement specialist, 1987-89; program mgr. The Schapiro Tng. Employment Program, Balt., 1989-90; coord. coop. edn. Baltimore City Community Coll., 1990; cons. Greater Balt. Com., 1991; coord. cooperative edn. New Community Coll. Balt., 1991—; lectr. in field; cons. in field. Contbr. articles to profl. jours. Scholar, George Washington U., 1987-89, Ukrainian Nat. Assn., 1982, State of Md., 1982-86. Democrat. Home: 713 Morningside Dr Towson MD 21204

WIEDEMAN, RICHARD LAWRENCE, electronics executive; b. Oneonta, N.Y., Mar. 13, 1945; s. Richard and Lena (Carnicelli) W.; m. Patricia A. Rose, Aug. 30, 1965; children: Kimberly Ann, Michelle Sarah. BSEE, Clarkson U., 1967. Design engr. Raytheon Corp., Sudbury, Mass., 1967-71; project engr. Fenwal, Inc., Ashland, Mass., 1971-77; prin. engr. Waters Assocs., Milford, Mass., 1977-80; pres. Serial Lab. Products, Inc., Marlboro, Mass., 1980—; co-founder Test Site Svc. Co., Marlboro, Mass., 1991—; cons. electro-magnetic compatibility and product safety for electronic products; presenter seminars in field. Contbr. articles to profl. jours.; inventor dual smoke detector system; co-inventor conductive monomer coating for metals. Mem. IEEE, VMEbus Internat. Trade Assn., Omicron Pi Omicron. Republican. Roman Catholic. Lodge: Elks. Home: 265 Kings Grant Rd Marlborough MA 01752-2319 Office: Serial Lab Products Inc PO Box 766 Marlborough MA 01752-0766

WIEDEMANN, CHARLES LOUIS, dentist; b. Belvidere, N.J., May 6, 1936; s. Charles and Clothilde Paulina (Fischer) W.; m. Jacqueline Burdzy, June 11, 1960; children: Lorraine Carol, Julie Patricia. B.A., Rutgers U., 1957; DDS with honors, Fairleigh Dickinson U., 1962; postgrad. student Inst. for Grad. Dentists, 1968-69, U. Pa., 1974-75. Pvt. practice dentistry, Hackettstown, N.J., 1966—; mem., founder dental sect. staff Hackettstown Community Hosp., chief of dentistry, 1973-75, 77-78; dental health dir. Clarence W. Sickles Med. Ctr., Hackettstown, N.J., 1970—; pres. Rexxcom Systems Computer Software, Co., 1990—; columnist Hackettstown Gazette, 1983-85; co-dir. Stargazer, Board of Ed, Online Mag. telecommunications systems, 1985-86; lectr. Morris County Coll., dental socs. Chmn. Bd. Health, Washington Twp., Morris County, N.J., 1975-78; co-dir. telecommunication system Hunterdon Cen. Regional High Sch., 1989—; presentations to Morris, Warren, and Sussex Counties, N.J. elem. schs. ann., 1966—. Designer giant talking toothbrush, talking molar. Capt. Dental Corps, AUS, 1962-65. Recipient cert. Stuart L. Isler Found. for Preventive Dentistry, 1986. Fellow Acad. Gen. Dentistry, Am. Endodontic Soc. (Communicator of Yr. award 1983); mem. ADA (panel on quarterly survey of pvt. practitioners 1990—), Am. Analgesia Soc., Internat. Analgesia Soc., N.J. Dental Assn. Warren-Sussex Dental Soc., Tri-County Dental Soc., Hackettstown Dental Study Group (co-founder 1974—). Republican. Author: The Now Philosophy for Dentistry, 1972, Fantastic Facts About Dental Health, 1975; (computer software) The Format Machine, 1987, Autofont, 1990, rev. edit. 91, The Magic Font Machine (Magifont, Magivue, Magishow), 1990, News 1, 1991; co-author: (computer software) Autodoc, 1990, rev. edit., 1991; author, designer (computer software Rexxcom, 1992. Editorial adv. panel Dental Econs. Jour., 1979-80; contbr. articles to profl. jours. and mags. Mem. Found. for Motivation in Dentistry (founder, chmn., bd. dirs. 1973—). Office: 110 Mill St Hackettstown NJ 07840

WIEDEMANN, DOUGLAS HENRY, mathematician; b. Milw., Oct. 10, 1953; s. Herbert Paul and Henrietta (Pfeil) W. BSEE, Princeton U., 1975; MSEE, Carnegie-Mellon U., 1977; PhD, Waterloo U., 1986. Mem. rsch. staff IDA-CCR, Princeton, N.J., 1978-91; sr. scientist Thinking Machines Corp., Cambridge, Mass., 1991—. Office: Thinking Machines Corp 245 1st St Cambridge MA 02142-1292

WIEDER, BRUCE TERRILL, law clerk, electrical engineer; b. Cleve., Dec. 9, 1955; s. Ira J. and Judith M. (Marx) W. BSEE, Cornell U., 1978; MBA, U. Tex., 1980, JD with honors, 1988. Bar: Tex. 1988, U.S. Dist. Ct. (we. dist.) Tex. 1989, U.S. Patent and Trademark Office 1989, U.S. Ct. Appeals (fed. cir.) 1990, D.C. 1991. Engr. Motorola, Inc., Austin, Tex., 1979-85; assoc. Arnold, White & Durkee, Austin, 1988-90; law clk. U.S. Ct. Appeals (Fed. cir.), Washington, 1990-91; assoc. Burns, Doane, Swecker & Mathis, Alexandria, Va., 1991—. Mem. IEEE, ABA, Am. Intellectual Property Law Assn., Alpha Phi Omega (life), Beta Gamma Sigma (life). Office: Burns Doane Swecker & Mathis 699 Prince St Alexandria VA 22313

WIEGAND, DONALD ARTHUR, research physicist; b. Rochester, N.Y., July 21, 1927; s. Arthur Francis and Mildred Julia (Fox) W.; m. Apr. 11, 1959 (div. July 1971); children: Caryn Wiegand Neidhold, Kim. BEE, Cornell U., 1952, MEE, 1953, PhD, 1956. Rsch. assoc. Cornell U., Ithaca, N.Y., 1955-56; rsch. physicist Carnegie Inst. Tech., Pitts., 1956-59, asst. prof., 1959-64, assoc. prof., 1964-68; rsch. physicist Armament Rsch. Devedl. and Engring. Ctr., Picatinny Arsenal, N.J., 1968-79, 90—; supervisor rsch. physicist ARDEC, Picatinny Arsenal, N.J., 1979-90. Contbr. over 30 articles to sci. jours.; patentee in field. With USMC, 1945-46. Fulbright grantee Technische Hochschule, Darmstadt, Fed. Republic Germany, 1960-61. Mem. Am. Phys. Soc., Materials Rsch. Soc., Sigma Xi, Tau Beta Pi, Eta Kappa Nu, Phi Delta Phi, Gamma Alpha. Home: 44 Center Grove Rd Apt F8 Randolph NJ 07869-4450 Office: ARDEC Picatinny Arsenal NJ 07806-5000

WIEHL, JOHN JACK, foundry executive; b. Bklyn., May 4, 1920; s. Ferdinand and Theresa (Kogut) W.; m. Ruth Dorothy Anderson, May 11, 1946; children: John R., Edward, Robert, Fred. Grad. high sch., Elmhurst, N.Y. Cert. molder. Pres. Wiehl Bros. Brass Foundry, Bklyn., 1946-53, Hoboken (N.J.) Bronze Foundry, 1968-72, Franklin (N.H.) Non-Ferrous Foundry, 1981—; owner Wiehl Dairy Farm, Milford, N.Y., 1954-67; foundry mgr. Perkins Marine, Miami, Fla., 1973-74, Watts Regulator, Lawrence, Mass., 1974-76, Samuel Eastman, Concord, N.H., 1976-78, Hayes Fluid Control, Gastonia, N.C., 1978-79, Jenkins Bros., Bridgeport, Conn., 1979-81. With USN, 1944-46, ETO, PTO. Mem. Am. Legion, Elks (brother). Office: Franklin Non-Ferrous Foundry PO Box 35 Calef Hill Rd Franklin NH 03235

WIEMER, ROBERT ANTHONY, columnist; b. N.Y.C., June 11, 1931; s. George Charles and Alice Elizabeth (Johnson) W.; m. Doris Marguerite Potts, Jan. 17, 1953; children: Dolris, Robert Anton. BA in English, Hofstra U., 1957. Reporter Newsday, L.I., 1957-59, copy editor, 1959-61, UN corr., 1961-63, news editor, 1963-65, editorial writer, 1965—, columnist, 1972—; book reviewer Newsday, 1972—. Author: (with others) Naked Came the Stranger, 1969. Staff sgt. USMC, 1948-52, with USCG Aux., 1989—. Recipient Disting. Editorial Writing award N.Y. State Pubs. Assn., 1969, Best Editorial award Press Club L.I., 1986. Mem. Nat. Conf. Editorial Writers, Nat. Soc. Newspaper Columnists, Ketewomoke Yacht Club, Am. Motorcyclist Assn., Pi Delta Epsilon. Office: Newsday Inc Long Island NY 11747

WIENER, HARRY, pharmaceutical company executive, physician; b. Vienna, Austria, Oct. 29, 1924; s. Joseph and Beile W.; m. Charlotte Baran, May 1, 1982. BS, Bklyn. Coll., 1945; MD, L.I. Coll. Medicine, 1949. With Pfizer Inc., N.Y.C., 1958—, dir. profl. info., 1958—. Author: Generic Drugs—Safety and Effectiveness, 1973, Schizophrenia and Anti-Schizophrenia, 1977, Findings in Computed Tomography, 1979. Served with M.C., AUS, 1953-55, Korea. Mem. AMA, N.Y. Acad. Medicine, Am. Med. Writers Assn. Developer Wiener numbers for calculation of phys. properties of hydrocarbons, 1947, proposer theory of human pheromones, 1966, genetics-environment symmetry in schizophrenia, 1976. Home: 429 E 52d St New York NY 10022 Office: 235 E 42d St New York NY 10017

WIENER, LEONARD, news journalist; b. N.Y.C., Sept. 23, 1940; s. Isidore and Ethel (Berkowitz) W.; m. Edith Herman, June 16, 1974. BA, U. Mich., 1962, MA, 1964. Reporter Milw. Jour., 1964-67; reporter bus. news Chgo. Daily News, 1967-71, Chgo. Tribune, 1971-79; assoc. editor U.S. News and World Report, Washington, 1979-88, sr. editor taxes/personal fin., 1988—. Home: 5501 Burling Ct Bethesda MD 20817 Office: U S News and World Report 2400 N St NW Washington DC 20037

WIENER, MORTON, psychologist; b. N.Y.C., July 13, 1920; s. Aaron and Eva (Schwartz) W.; m. Beatrice Newman, Nov. 8, 1941; children: Meryl Ann Bertenthal, Craig, Roberta. BS in Social Scis., CCNY, 1949, MS in Edn., 1950; PhD, U. Rochester, 1953. Lic. psychologist, Mass.; diplomate Am. Bd. Profl. Psychology. Clin. psychologist, asst. chief Carter Meml. Hosp., Indpls., 1953-54; chief psychologist Cen. State Hosp., Indpls., 1954-56; asst. prof. U. Rochester, 1956-57; assoc. prof. Clark U., Worcester, Mass., 1957-64, prof., 1964-90, dir./co-dir. clin. tng. prog., 1957-73, 77-91, assoc. chair psychology, 1973-74, acting chair psychology, 1978-79, prof. emeritus psychology, 1991—; cons. VA Psychology Tng. Program, 1956—; mem. personality and cognition sect. NIMH, 1968-70. Cons. editor Jour. Nonverbal Behavior, 1980-89, Psychol. Assessment, 1989-91; co-author: Language Within Language, 1968; co-editor: What is Schizophrenia?, 1991; contbr 59 articles to profl. jours., chpts. to books. Bd. dirs. Community Ctr., Worcester, 1964-66. With Signal Corps, U.S. Army, 1943-46. Rsch. grantee USPHS, 1958-77, Office Edn., Nat. Inst. Edn., 1970-77. Fellow Am. Psychol. Assn., Am. Psychol. Soc.; mem. AAUP, Ea. Psychol. Assn., Phi Beta Kappa. Office: Clark U Dept Psychology 950 Main St Worcester MA 01610

WIENER, SOLOMON, author, consultant, former city official; b. N.Y.C., Mar. 5, 1915; s. Morris David and Anna (Pinchuk) W.; m. Gertrude Klings, Feb. 24, 1946; children: Marjorie Diane Wein, Willa Kay Ehrlich. BS, Cornell, 1936; MPA, NYU, 1946. Exam. asst. N.Y.C. Dept. Personnel, 1937-42, civil service examiner, 1946-55, asst. div. chief, 1955-59, div. chief, 1959-67, asst. dir. exams., 1967-70, dir. exams., 1970-72, asst. personnel dir. exams., 1972-75; author, cons., 1975—; tchr. Washington Irving Evening Adult Sch., N.Y.C., 1949-60, tchr.-in-charge, 1960-67. Served with AUS, 1942-46, PTO. Decorated Bronze Star. Mem. Am. Soc. Pub. Adminstrn., Internat. Personnel Mgmt. Assn., Authors Guild, Res. Officers Assn., Ret. Officers Assn., Assn. of U.S. Army, Am. Def. Preparedness Assn. Author: A Handy Book of Commonly Used American Idioms, rev. edit., 1981, Manual de Modismos Americanos Más Comunes, rev. edit., 1981, A Handy Guide to Irregular Verbs and the Use and Formation of Tenses, 1959, Guía Completa de Los Verbos Irregulares en Inglés y el Uso y Formación de los Tiempos, 1959, Questions and Answers on American Citizenship, rev. edit., 1982, Clear and Simple Guide to Business Letter Writing, rev. edit., 1978, The College Graduate Guide for Scoring High on Employment Tests, 1981, The High School Graduate Guide for Scoring High on Civil Service Tests, 1981, How to Take and Pass Simple Tests for Civil Service Jobs, 1981, Officer Candidate Tests, 2d edit., 1990, Military Flight Aptitude Tests, 1989;

co-author Practice for the Armed Forces Test, ASVAB, 1988, Practica para el Examen de las Fuerzas Armadas, ASVAB En Español, 1989; contbr. to ARCO ROTC Coll. Guide, 1988. Home: 523 E 14th St New York NY 10009-2927

WIERMAN, JOHN CHARLES, mathematician, educator; b. Prosser, Wash., June 30, 1949; s. John Nathaniel and Edith Elizabeth (Ashley) W.; m. Susan Shelley Graupmann, Aug. 13, 1971; 1 child, Adam Christopher. BS in Math., U. Wash., 1971, PhD in Math., 1976. Asst. prof. math. U. Minn., Mpls., 1976-81; asst. prof. Johns Hopkins U., Balt., 1981-82, assoc. prof., 1982-87, prof., 1987—, chmn. math. scis. dept., 1988—; sr. rsch. fellow Inst. Applied Math. and its Applications, Mpls., 1987-88. Co-author: First-Passage Percolation on the Square Lattice, 1978; contbr. articles to profl. jours. Grad. fellow NSF, 1971-74; NSF rsch. grantee, 1976—. Fellow Inst. Math. Stats.; mem. Bernoulli Soc., Am. Math. Soc., Am. Statis. Assn., Math. Assn. Am., AAAS, Phi Beta Kappa. Office: Johns Hopkins U Dept of Scis. Math 34th & Charles Sts Baltimore MD 21218

WIESEL, ELIE, writer, educator; b. Sighet, Romania, Sept. 30, 1928; arrived in Paris, 1945; came to U.S., 1956, naturalized, 1963; s. Shlomo and Sarah (Feig) W.; m. Marion Erster Rose, 1969; 1 child, Shlomo Elisha. Student, The Sorbonne, Paris, 1948-51; LittD (hon.), Jewish Theol. Sem., N.Y.C., 1967, Marquette U., 1975, Simmons Coll., 1976, Anna Maria Coll., 1980, Yale U., 1981, Wake Forest U., 1985, Haverford Coll., 1985, Capital U., 1986, L.I. U., 1986, U. Paris, 1987, U. Conn., 1988, U. Cen. Fla., 1988, Wittenberg U., 1989, Wheeling Jesuit Coll., 1989; LHD (hon.), Hebrew Union Coll., 1968, Manhattanville Coll., 1972, Yeshiva U., 1973, Boston U., 1974, Coll. of St. Scholastica, 1978, Wesleyan U., 1979, Brandeis U., 1980, Kenyon Coll., 1982, Hobart/William Smith Coll., 1982, Emory U., 1983, Fla. Internat. U., 1983, Siena Heights Coll., 1983, Fairfield U., 1983, Dropsie Coll., 1983, Moravian Coll., 1983, Colgate U., 1984, SUNY, Binghamton, 1985, Lehigh U., 1985, Coll. of New Rochelle, 1986, Tufts U., 1986, Georgetown U., 1986, Hamilton Coll., 1986, Rockford Coll., 1986, Villanova U., 1987, Coll. of St. Thomas, 1987, U. Denver, 1987, Walsh Coll., 1987, Loyola Coll., 1987, Ohio U., 1988, Concordia Coll., 1990, N.Y.U., 1990, Fordham U., 1990, Conn. Coll., 1990, Upsala Coll., 1991, Duquesne U., 1991, Roosevelt U., 1991; PhD (hon.), Bar-Ilan U., 1973, U. Haifa, 1986, Ben Gurion U., 1988; LLD (hon.), Hofstra U., 1975, Talmudic U. Fla., 1979, U. Notre Dame, 1980, La Salle U., 1988; HHD (hon.), U. Hartford, 1985, Lycoming Coll., 1987, U. Miami, 1988, Brigham Young U., 1989; D of Hebrew Letters, Spertus Coll. Judaica, 1973; DSc (hon.), U. Health Scis./Chgo. Med. Sch., 1989; ThD, U. Åbo Akadem, 1990; Doctor of Humane Letters, Hunter Coll., 1992; Doctor of Humane Letters (honoris causa), Susquehanna U., 1992, Am. u., 1992. Disting. prof. Judaic studies CCNY, 1972-76; prof. religious studies and univ. prof. Boston U., 1976—, prof. philosophy, 1988—; Henry Luce vis. scholar in humanites and social thought Whitney Humanities Ctr. Yale U., 1982-83; dist. vis. prof. lit and philosophy Fla. Internat. U., 1982; Henry Luce vis. scholar in Humanities and Social Thought, Whitney Humanities Ctr., Yale U., 1982-83; Disting. vis. prof. Lit. and Philosophy, Fla. Internat. U., 1982; chmn. U.S. Pres.'s Commn. on the Holocaust, 1979-80, U.S. Holocaust Meml. Council, 1980-86; hon. chmn. Nat. Jewish Resource Ctr., U.S. Com. to Free Vladimir Slepak, N.Y.C. Holocaust Meml. Commn., Am. Friends of Ghetto Fighter's House; hon. pres. Am. Gathering of Jewish Holocaust Survivors; bd. dirs. Nat. Com. on Am. Fgn. Policy, 1983—, Hebrew Arts Sch., HUMANITAS, Am. Assocs. Ben-Gurion U. of the Negev, Mut. of Am., France Libertés; v.p. Internat. Rescue Com., 1985—; bd. govs. Oxford Ctr. for Postgrad. Hebrew studies, Haifa U., Tel-Aviv U.; bd. trustees Yeshiva U., 1977—; colleague Cathedral St. John the Divine, 1975—; mem. adv. bd. Boston U. Inst. for Philosophy & Religion, Nat. Inst. Against Prejudice & Violence, Internat. Ctr. in N.Y., Friends of Akim USA, Friends of LeChambon; mem. jury Neustadt Internat. Prize Lit., 1984; lectr. Andrew W. Mellon Ann. Lecture Series Boston U., 92d St. YMHA, YWHA Ann. Lectr. Series, ann. radio broadcast series Eternal Light for Jewish Theol. Sem. Am. Author: Night, 1960, Dawn, 1961, The Accident, 1962, The Town Beyond the Wall, 1964, The Gates of the Forest, 1966, The Jews of Silence, 1966, Legends of Our Time, 1968, A Beggar in Jerusalem, 1970, One Generation After, 1971, Souls on Fire, 1972, The Oath, 1973, Ani Maamin, 1973, Zalmen, or the Madness of God, 1975, Messengers of God, 1976, A Jew Today, 1978, Four Hasidic Masters, 1978, The Trial of God, 1979, Le Testament D'Un Poète Juif Assassiné (France's Prix Livre-Inter 1980, Bourse Goncourt, 1980, Prix des Bibliothécaires, 1981), 1985, Images from the Bible, 1980, Five Biblical Portraits, 1981, Somewhere A Master, 1982, Paroles d'Étranger, 1982, The Golem, 1983, The Fifth Son (Grand Prix de la Littérature, City of Paris), 1985, Signes d'Exode, 1985, Against Silence (3 vols., ed. Irving Abrahamson), 1985, Job ou Dieu dans la Tempête, 1986, A Song for Hope, 1987, The Nobel Address, 1987, Twilight, 1988; (essays) Silences et Mémoire d'hommes, 1989, L'Oublié, 1989, From the Kingdom of Memory, 1990, Célébration Talmudique, 1991, Sages and Dreamers, 1991, The Forgotten, 1992, (with John Cardinal O'Connor) A Journey of Faith, 1990, (with Albert Friedlander) The Six Days of Destruction, 1988, (dialogues with Philippe-Michaël Saint-Cheron) Evil and Exile, 1990; editorial and adv. bds. Midstream, Religion and Lit. (U. Notre Dame), Sh'ma: Jour. of Responsibility, Forthcoming: Jewish Imaginative Writing, Hadassah Mag., Acad. of the Air for Jewish Studies, Holocaust and Genocide Studies: An Internat. Jour.; subject of 17 books; journalist Israeli, French and Am. newspapers. Chmn. adv. bd. World Union Jewish Students, 1985—; comité d'Honneur Ligue International Contre le Racisme et l'Antisemitisme, 1985—; founder Nat. Jewish Ctr. Learning and Leadership; mem. adv. bd. Andrei Sakharov Inst.; mem. soc. fellows Ctr. Judaic Studies, U. Denver; bd. overseer Bar-Ilan U., 1970—. Recipient Prix Rivarol, 1963, Jewish Heritage award, Haifa U., 1975, Remembrance award, 1965, Prix du Souvenir, 1965, Nat. Jewish Book Council award, 1965, 73, Prix Médicis, 1968, Prix Bordin French Acad., 1972, Eleanor Roosevelt Meml. award, N.Y. United Jewish Appeal, 1972, Am. Liberties medallion Am. Jewish Com., 1972, Martin Luther King Jr. medallion, CCNY, 1973, Annual award for Disting. Service to Am. Jewry, Nat. Fedn. of Jewish Men's Clubs, 1973, Faculty Disting. Scholar award Hofstra U., 1974, Rambam award Am. Mizrachi Women, 1974, Meml. award N.Y. Soc. Clin. Psychologists, 1975, First Spertus Internat. award, 1976, Myrtle Wreath award Hadassah, 1977, King Solomon award, 1977, Liberty award HIAS, 1977, Jewish Heritage award, B'nai B'rith, 1966, Avodah award, Jewish Tchrs. Assn., 1972, Humanitarian award, B'rith Sholom, 1978, Joseph Prize for Human Rights, Anti-Defamation League, 1978, Zalman Shazar award State of Israel, 1979, Presdl. Citation, NYU, 1979, Inaugural award for Lit., Israel Bonds Prime Minister's Com., 1979, Jabotinsky medal, State of Israel, 1980, Rabbanit Sarah Herzog award Emunah Women of Am., 1981, Le Grand Prix Littéraire du Festival Internat. Deauville, 1983, Internat. Lit. prize for Peace, Royal Acad. Belgium, 1983, Lit. Lions award N.Y. Pub. Library, 1983, Jordan Davidson Humanitarian award Fla. Internat. U., 1983, Anatoly Scharansky Humanitarian award, 1983, Grand Officer, Legion of Honor, France, Congressional gold medal, 1984, Voice of Conscience award Am. Jewish Congress, 1985, Remembrance award, Israel Bonds, 1985, Anne Frank award, 1985, Freedom of Worship medal FDR 4 Freedoms Found., 1985, Medal of Liberty award Statue of Liberty Presentation, 1986, Nobel Peace Prize, 1986, First Herzl Lit. award, First David Ben-Gurion award, Nat. UJA, Gov.'s award, Shaarei Tzedek, Internat. Kaplun Found. award Hebrew U. Jerusalem, Scopus award, 1974, Am.-Israeli Friendship award, Disting. Writers award Lincolnwood Library, 1984, First Chancellor Joseph H. Lookstein award Bar-Ilan U., 1984, Sam Levenson Meml. award Jewish Community Relations Council, 1985, Comenius award Moravian Coll., 1985, Henrietta Szold award Hadassah, 1985, Disting. Community Service award Mut. Am., 1985, Covenant Peace award Synagogue Council Am., 1985, Jacob Pat award World Congress Jewish Culture, 1985, Humanitarian award Internat. League Human Rights, 1985, Disting. Foreign-Born Am. award Internat. Ctr. N.Y., Inc., 1986, Freedom Cup award Women's League Israel, 1986, First Jacob Javits Humanitarian award UJA Young Leadership, 1986, Freedom award Internat. Rescue Com., 1987, Achievement award Artist and Writers for Peace in the Middle East, 1987, La Grande Médaille de Vermeil de la Ville de Paris, 1987, La Médaille de la Chancellerie de l'Université de Paris, 1987, La Médaille de l'Université de Paris, 1987, First Eitinger Prize, U. Oslo, 1987, Lifetime Achievment award Present Tense mag., 1987, Spl. Christopher award The Christophers, 1987, Achievement award State Israel, 1987, Sem. medal Jewish Theol. Sem. Am., 1987, Metcalf Cup and Prize for Excellence in Teaching, Boston U., 1987, Spl. award Nat. Com. on Am. Fgn. Policy, 1987, Grã-Cruz da Ordem Nacional do Cruzeiro do Sul, Brazil's highest distinction, 1987, Profiles of Courage award B'nai B'rith, 1987, Centennial medal U. Scranton, 1987, Citation from Religious Edn. Assn., 1987, Golda Meir Sr. Humanitarian award, 1987, Presdl. medal Hofstra U., 1988, Human Rights Law award Internat. Human Rights Law Group, 1988, Bicentennial medal Georgetown U., 1988, Janus Korczak Humanitarian award NAHE, Kent State U., 1989, Count Sforza award in Philanthropy Interphil, 1989, Lily Edelman award for Excellence in Continuing Jewish Edn. B'nai B'rith Internat., 1989, George Washington award Am. Hungarian Found., 1989, Bicentennial medal N.Y.U., 1989, Internat. Brotherhood award C.O.R.E., 1990, Frank Weil award for Disting. Contbn. to Adv. of N.Am. Jewish Culture Jewish Community Ctrs. Assn. N.Am., 1990, 1st Raoul Wallenberg medal U. Mich., 1990, Award of Highest Honor Soka U., 1991, Facing History and Ourselves Humanity award, 1991, 5th Centennial Christopher Columbus medal City of Genoa, 1992, 1st Primo Levi award, 1992, Lit. Arts award Nat. Found. for Jewish Culture, 1992, Ellis Island Medal of Honor, 1992; Beth Hatefutsoth hon. fellow, 1988; honors established in his name: Elie Wiesel award for Holocaust Rsch., U. Haifa, Elie Wiesel Chair in Holocaust Studies, Bar-Ilan U., Elie Wiesel Endowment Fund for Jewish Culture, U. Denver, 1987, Elie Wiesel Disting. Svc. award, U. Fla., 1988, Elie Wiesel awards for Jewish Arts and Culture B'nai B'rith Hillel Founds., 1988, Elie Wiesel Chair in Judaic Studies Conn. Coll., 1990. Fellow Jewish Acad. Arts and Scis., Am. Acad. Arts

WIESEL, TORSTEN NILS, neurobiologist, educator; b. Upsala, Sweden, June 3, 1924; came to U.S., 1955; s. Fritz Samuel and Anna-Lisa Elisabet (Bentzer) W.; 1 dau., Sara Elisabet. MD, Karolinska Inst., Stockholm, 1954; D Medicine (hon.), Karolinska Inst, Stockholm, 1989; AM (hon.), Harvard U., 1967; ScD (hon.), NYU, 1987, U. Bergen, 1987. Instr. physiology Karolinska Inst., 1954-55; asst. dept. child psychiatry Karolinska Hosp., 1954-55; fellow in ophthalmology Johns Hopkins U., 1955-58, asst. prof. ophthalmic physiology, 1958-59; assoc. in neurophysiology and neuropharmacology Harvard U. Med. Sch., Boston, 1959-60; asst. prof. neurophysiology and neuropharmacology Harvard U. Med. Sch., 1960-64, asst. prof. neurophysiology, dept. psychiatry, 1964-67, prof. physiology, 1967-68, prof. neurobiology, 1968-74, Robert Winthrop prof. neurobiology, 1974-83, chmn. dept. neurobiology, 1973-82; Vincent and Brooke Astor prof. neurobiology, head lab. Rockefeller U., N.Y.C., 1983—, pres., 1992—; Ferrier lectr. Royal Soc. London, 1972; NIH lectr., 1975; Grass lectr. Soc. Neurosci., 1976; lectr. Coll. de France, 1977; Hitchcock prof. U. Calif.-Berkeley, 1980; Sharpey-Schafer lectr. Phys. Soc. London; George Cotzias lectr. Am. Acad. Neurology, 1983. Contbr. numerous articles to profl. jours. Recipient Jules Stein award Trustees for Prevention of Blindness, 1971, Lewis S. Rosenstiel prize Brandeis U., 1972, Friedenwald award Assn. Rsch. in Vision and Ophthalmology, 1975, Karl Spencer Lashley prize Am. Philos. Soc., 1977, Louisa Gross Horwitz prize Columbia U., 1978, Dickson prize U. Pitts., 1979, Nobel prize in physiology and medicine, 1981, W.H. Helmerich III award 1989. Mem. Am. Physiol. Soc., Am. Philos. Soc., AAAS, Am. Acad. Arts and Scis., Nat. Acad. Arts and Scis., Swedish Physiol. Soc., Soc. Neurosci. (pres. 1978-79), Royal Soc. (fgn. mem.), Physiol. Soc. (Eng.) (hon. mem.). Office: Rockefeller U York Ave & 66th St New York NY 10021

WIESEN, DAVID LIPMAN, managment consultant; b. N.Y.C., Feb. 23, 1932; s. Nissan and Norma (Lipman) W.; m. Muriel B. Lechter, Sept. 25, 1966; 1 child, Sloan Chase. BS, Mass. Inst. Tech., 1954; MBA, N.Y. U., 1964. Pres. ADEC Inc., Fairfield, N.J., 1957-84, Tacrad Corp., Fairfield, N.J., 1971-85, Wiesen Assocs., Newark, 1984—; sec. MIT of No. N.J., N.Y.C., 1980—; chmn. N.J. Entrepreneurial Network, Princeton, 1988—; treas. MIT Ent. Forum of N.Y., 1991—. Vice chmn. MIT Ednl. Coun., Cambridge, 1980—. Capt. Signal Corps, U.S. Army, 1954-57. Mem. Quarter Century Wireless Assn. (pres. 1990—). Home: 18 Wilbur Ave Newark NJ 07112 Office: Wiesen Assocs PO Box 536 Fairfield NJ 07007

WIESENBERG, JACQUELINE LEONARDI, lecturer; b. West Haven, Conn., May 4, 1928; d. Curzio and Filomena Olga (Turrinziani) Leonardi; m. Russel John Wiesenberg, Nov. 23; children: James Wynne, Deborann Donna. BA, SUNY, Buffalo, 1970, postgrad., 1970-73, 80—. Interviewer, examiner U.S. Dept. Labor, New Haven, 1948-52; sec. W.I. Clark Co., Hamden, Conn., 1952-55; acct. VA Hosp., West Haven, 1956-60; acct.-commissary U.S. Air Force Missle Site, Niagara Falls, N.Y., 1961-62; tchr. Buffalo City Schs., 1970-73, 79; acct. Erie County Social Svcs., Buffalo, 1971-73; lectr., 1973—. Contbr. articles to CAP, U.S. Air Force mag., 1954—. Capt., Nat. Found. March of Dimes, 1969—, com. mem. telethon, 1983-86; den mother Boy Scouts Am., 1961-68; chmn. Meals on Wheels, Town of Amherst, 1975-76; leader, travel chmn. Girl Scouts Am., 1968-77; mem. Nat. Congress Parents and Tchrs., 1957—; heart fund vol. Heart Assn., 1960-86. Mem. AAUW, NAFE, Internat. Platform Assn., Am. Astrol. Assn., Western N.Y. Conf. Aging, Nat. Geographic Soc., Nat. Trust for Hist. Preservation, Epsilon Delta Chi, Alpha Iota. Home: 14 Norman Pl Amherst NY 14226-4233

WIESENBERG, RUSSEL JOHN, statistician; b. Kaukauna, Wis., Apr. 9, 1924; s. Emil Martin and Josephine (Appelbaker) W.; m. Jacqueline Leonardi, Nov. 23; children: James Wynne, Deborann Donna. BS, U. Wis., 1951; postgrad. Cornell U., 1960-61, U. Mich., 1969, George Washington U., 1976. Analyst, Gen. Electric Co., West Lynn, Mass., 1951-56; specialist Internat. Gen. Electric Co., Rio de Janeiro, Brazil, 1956-59; statistician Gen. Motors Corp., Lockport, N.Y., 1959-65, sr. statistician, Harrison Radiator div., 1965-78, sr. reliability engr., 1978-82, sr. reliability statistician, 1982-87. Auditor, Community Chest Fund, 1952-55; umpire Little League Baseball, 1962-65; committeeman Buffalo Area council Boy Scouts Am., 1962—, Cub Scout committeeman, 1962-64, Webelos cubmaster, 1963-64; mem. Nat. Congress Parents and Tchrs., 1963—; heart fund Vol. Heart Assn., 1968; tournament dir. Am. Legion Baseball, 1975; vol. United Way campaign, 1983, nat. telethon March of Dimes, 1983-84. Served with AUS, 1943-46. Decorated Bronze Star. Mem. AAAS, Am. Statis. Assn., Nat. Register Sci. and Tech. Pers., U. Wis. Alumni Assn., Artus, Internat. Platform Assn., Phi Kappa Phi. Lutheran. com.). Contbr. articles to profl. jours. Home: 14 Norman Pl Buffalo NY 14226-4233

WIESNER, JEROME BERT, engineering educator, researcher; b. Detroit, May 30, 1915; s. Joseph and Ida (Friedman) W.; m. Laya Wainger, Sept. 1, 1940; children: Stephen Jay, Zachary Kurt, Elizabeth Ann, Joshua A. B.S., U. Mich., 1937, M.S., 1938, Ph.D., 1950. Assoc. dir. U. Mich. Broadcasting Service, 1937-40; chief engr. Acoustical Record Lab., Library of Congress, 1940-42; staff MIT Radiation Lab., Cambridge, Mass., 1942-45, U. of Calif. Los Alamos Lab., 1945-46; mem. faculty MIT, Cambridge, 1946-71, dir. research lab. of electronics, 1952-61, head dept. elec. engring., 1959-60, dean of sci., 1964-66, provost, 1966-71, pres., 1971-80, inst. researcher and prof., 1980—; spl. asst. to Pres. on sci. and tech., 1961-64; chmn. Pres.'s Sci. Adv. Com., 1961-64; chmn. tech. assessment adv. coun. Office Tech. Assessment, U.S. Congress, 1976-79; bd. dirs. Cons. for Mgmt., Inc., The Faxon Co., Magnascreen, Rothko Chapel. Author: Where Science and Politics Meet, 1965, ABM—An Evaluation, 1969. Bd. govs. Weizman Inst. Sci.; trustee Woods Hole Oceanographic Inst., Kennedy Meml. Trust; bd. of overseers Harvard U., 1987—; bd. dirs. Internat. Found. for Survival and Devel. of Humanity, MacArthur Found.; life mem. MIT Corp., Cambridge. Fellow IEEE, Am. Acad. Arts and Scis.; mem. Am. Philos. Soc., AAUP, Am. Geophys. Union, Acoustical Soc. Am., Nat. Acad. Engring., Nat. Acad. Scis., MIT Corp. (life), Sigma Xi, Phi Kappa Phi, Eta Kappa Nu, Tau Beta Pi. Home: 61 Shattuck Rd Watertown MA 02172-1310 Office: MIT 20 Ames St # 15207 Cambridge MA 02142-1308

WIETING, GARY LEE, federal agency executive; b. Huron, S.D., Apr. 24, 1937; s. LeRoy Charles and Edna Lorraine (Crawley) W.; m. Nancy Lou Clark, July 9, 1961 (div. 1991); children: Kevin Clark, Brian David. BA, U. Ill., 1961; MBA, Lake Forest Sch. Mgmt., 1983. Logistics mgr. U.S. Army, Vietnam, 1967-68, NATO/Shape Support Group, Belgium, 1968-72, 8th U.S. Army, Korea, 1972-73, U.S. Army Readiness Region, Ft. Sheridan, Ill., 1973-77, U.S. Army Recruiting Command, Ft. Sheridan, Ill., 1977-83; rsch. and devel. logistics mgr. Belvoir Rsch. and Devel. Ctr., Ft. Belvoir, Va., 1983-85, 88-90; personal svcs. logistics mgr. Hdqrs. Dept. of Army, Washington, 1985-88; logistics mgr., assoc. program mgr. for adv. automation FAA, Washington, 1990—. Capt. U.S. Army, 1957-77. Decorated Army Commendation medal, Bronze Star medal; recipient Comdr. Award for Civilian Svc., U.S. Army, 1988. Home: 2646 Redcoat Dr Alexandria VA 22303 Office: FAA 800 Independence Ave SW Washington DC 20591

WIGAL, DONALD WAYNE, management consultant; b. Indpls., Jan. 16, 1933; s. Wayne Wendel and Louise (Eder) W. BS, U. Dayton, 1955; MA, U. Notre Dame, 1965; PhD, Columbia Pacific U., 1981. Instr. Dayton (Ohio) U., 1952-69; info. specialist Grey Advt., N.Y.C., 1970-75; exec. editor Dell Pub., N.Y.C., 1975-80, Lakewood Books, Clearwater, Fla., 1980-85; sr. cons. Mainstream Access, N.Y.C., 1985-90, LoBue Assocs., Fairlawn, N.J., 1990; sr. cons., owner TransKey, Atlanta, Ga., 1991; prof. Columbia Pacific U., San Rafael, Calif., 1982—; dir. Inst. Independent Studies, N.Y.C., 1975—; indexer The N.Y. Times Encyclopedia of Film, 1985, The Acad. Am. Encyclopedia, Princeton, N.J., 1980. Author: Experiences in Faith, 1969, General Knowledge, 1981: co-author: Screen Experience, 1968, New Age Encyclopedia of Mysticism, 1990. Cons. Govs. Conf. Children of Alcoholics, N.Y.C., 1982. Ecumenical fellow Danforth Found., Antioch Coll., 1968; recipient Disting. Alumnus award U. Dayton, 1985. Mem. Am. Soc. Composers Authors & Publishers, Am. Soc. Journalists & Authors, Williams Club, Ankylosing Spondylitis Assn. (life). Democrat. Home: 4 Park Ave New York NY 10016-5339 Office: Alternative Rsch PO Box 432 New York NY 10156-0432

WIGGANS, SAMUEL CLAUDE, horticulturist, consultant, agronomist; b. Lincoln, Nebr., Sept. 2, 1922; s. Cleo Claude and Martha (Chinn) W.; m. Ruth Evelyn Littlefield, Sept. 7, 1957; children: James Claude, Thomas Claude. BS, U. Nebr., 1947, MS, 1948; MS, U. Wis., 1948, PhD, 1951. Asst. prof. agronomy and botany Iowa State U., Ames, 1951-58; assoc. prof. horticulture Okla. State U., Stillwater, 1958-63; prof., chair dept. hort. sci. U. Vt., Burlington, 1963-65, prof., chair plant and soil sci. dept., 1965-80; prin. horticulturist USDA/Coop. State Rsch. Svc., Washington, 1980—. Contbr. over 95 articles to profl. jours. Deacon 1st Congl. Ch., Burlington, 1973-77; chmn. Boy Scouts Am., Shelburne, Vt., 1974-75. With U.S. Army, 1942-46, col. USAR. Fellow Am. Soc. Hort. Sci. (bd. dirs. Alexandria chpt. 1973-75, AAAS; mem. Am. Hort. Therapy Assn. (bd. dirs., treas. Gaithersburg, Md. chpt. 1984-86), Am. Soc. Agronomy (bd. dirs. Madison, Wis. chpt. 1975-76), N.E. Am. Soc. Hort. Sci. (pres. 1973-75). Home: 4610 Duncan Dr Annandale VA 22003-4612

WIGGINS, GUY ARTHUR, artist; b. New London, Conn.; s. Guy Carleton and Dorothy Stuart (Johnson) W.; m. Dorothy Palmer, Sept. 26, 1959; children: Guy Stuart, Noel Carleton. Student, Stanford U., 1939-40; BA magna cum laude, UCLA, 1950; MA, Harvard U., 1951; MS in Econs. with mark of distinction, London Sch. Econs., 1956. Polit. analyst Supreme Comdr. Allied Powers, Tokyo, 1945-48; program officer Econ. Coop. Adminstrn., Djakarta, Indonesia, 1951-52; desk officer Econ. Coop. Adminstrn., Washington, 1952-53; econ. analyst Fgn. Econ. Policy Coun., Washington, 1956-57; economist U.S. Dept. of State, Washington, 1957-59, fgn. svc. officer, 1959-75; sr. adviser U.S. Mission to UN, N.Y.C., 1973-75; freelance artist N.Y.C., 1975—; cons. Friends in the West, N.Y.C., 1975-78. Editor: The Political Reorganization of Japan, 1948; contbr. articles to profl. publs.. Exhibited in one-man shows at Optique Gallery, Lambertsville, N.J., 1987, Old Lyme (Conn.) Acad. Fine Arts, 1988; in group shows at New Britain Mus. Am. Art, 1979-80, Marbella Gallery, N.Y.C., 1981, Trenton (N.J.) Mus., 1988. Spl. agt. CIC, 1942-46. Mem. Art Students League (life), Harvard Club, Salmagundi Club, Phi Beta Kappa. Episcopalian.

WIGGINS, JAMES BRYAN, religion educator; b. Mexia, Tex., Aug. 24, 1935; m. Kay Wiggins, Aug. 15, 1956; children: Bryan, Karis. BA, Tex. Wesleyan U., 1957; BD, So. Meth. U., 1959; PhD, Drew U., 1963; postgrad., Tübingen U., Fed. Republic Germany, 1968-69. Ordained to ministry Meth. Ch., 1959. Instr. humanities Union Jr. Coll., Cranford, N.J., 1960-63; asst. prof. religion Syracuse (N.Y.) U., 1963-69, assoc. prof., 1969-75, prof., 1975—, dir. grad. studies, 1975-80, chair dept. 1980—; exec. dir. Am. Acad. Religion, 1983-91, dir., 1973-75, 83-91; cons. in field. Author: The Embattled Saint, 1966, Foundations of Christianity, 1970; editor: Religion as Story, 1975, Christianity: A Cultural Perspective, 1987; contbr. articles to profl. jours. Trustee Scholars Press, Atlanta, 1983-91, chmn., 1986-91. Rockefeller Found. fellow, 1962-63. Fellow Soc. for Arts (bd. dirs. 1976—), Religion and Culture; mem. AAUP, Am. Acad. Religion, Am. Soc. Ch. History, Am. Hist. Assn. Democrat. Home: 308 Kimber Rd Syracuse NY 13224-1834 Office: Syracuse U Dept Religion 501 Hall of Langs Syracuse NY 13244

WIGNER, EUGENE PAUL, physicist, educator; b. Budapest, Hungary, Nov. 17, 1902; came to U.S., 1930, naturalized, 1937; s. Anthony and Elisabeth (Einhorn) W.; m. Amelia Z. Frank, Dec. 23, 1936 (dec. 1937); m. Mary Annette Wheeler, June 4, 1941 (dec. Nov. 1977); m. Eileen C.P. Hamilton, Dec. 29, 1979. Chem. Engr. and Dr. Engring., Technische Hochschule, Berlin, 1925; hon. D.Sc., U. Wis., 1949, Washington U., 1950, Case Inst. Tech., 1956, U. Chgo., 1957, Colby Coll., 1959, U. Pa., 1961, Thiel Coll., 1964, U. Notre Dame, 1965; D.Sc. (hon.), Technische Universität Berlin, 1966, Swarthmore Coll., 1966, Université de Louvain, Belgium, 1967; Dr.Jr., U. Alta., 1957; L.H.D. (hon.), Yeshiva U., 1963; hon. degrees, U. Liège, 1967, U. Ill., 1968, Seton Hall U., 1969, Cath. U., 1969, Rockefeller U., 1970, Israel Inst. Tech., 1973, Lowell U., 1976, Princeton U., 1976, U. Tex., 1978, Clarkson Coll., 1979, Allegheny Coll., 1979, Gustav Adolphus Coll., 1981, Stevens Inst. Tech., 1982, SUNY, 1982, La. State U., 1985. Asst. Technische Hochschule, Berlin, 1926-27, asst. prof., 1928-33; asst. U. Göttingen, 1927-28; lectr. Princeton U., 1930, part-time prof. math. physics, 1931-36; prof. physics U. Wis., 1936-38; Thomas D. Jones prof. theoretical physics Princeton U., 1938-71; on leave of absence, 1942-45; with Metall. Lab., U. Chgo., 1946-47; as dir. research and devel. Clinton Labs.; dir. CD Rsch. Project, Oak Ridge, 1964-65; Lorentz lectr. Inst. Lorentz, Leiden, 1957; cons. prof. La. State U., 1971-85, ret., 1985; mem. gen. adv. com. AEC, 1952-57, 59-64; mem. math. panel NRC, 1952-54; physics panel NSF, 1953-56; vis. com. Nat. Bur. Standards, 1947-51; mem. adv. bd. Fed. Emergency Mgmt. Agy., 1982-91. Author: (with L. Eisenbud) Nuclear Structure, 1958, The Physical Theory of Neutron Chain Reactors (with A.M. Weinberg), 1958, Group Theory and its Applications to the Quantum Mechanics of Atomic Spectra, 1931, English translation, 1959, Symmetries and Reflections, 1967, Survival and the Bomb, 1969. Decorated medal of Merit, 1946, Order of Banner of Republic of Hungary, Rubies, 1990; recipient Franklin medal Franklin Inst., 1950, citation N.J. Tchrs. Assn., 1951, Enrico Fermi award AEC, 1958, Atoms for Peace award, 1960, Max Planck medal German Phys. Soc., 1961, Nobel prize for physics, 1963, George Washington award Am. Hungarian Studies Found., 1964, Semmelweiss medal Am. Hungarian Med. Assn., 1965, Nat. Sci. medal, 1969, Pfizer award, 1971, Albert Einstein award, 1972, Golden Plate medal Am. Acad. Achievement, 1974, Disting. Achievement award La. State U., 1977, Wigner medal, 1978, Founders medal Internat. Cultural Found., 1982, Medal of the Hungarian Central Rsch. Inst., Medal of the Autonomous Univ. Barcelona, Am. Preparedness award, 1985, Lord Found. award, 1989; named Nuclear Pioneer, Soc. Nuclear Medicine, 1977, Colonel Gov. of La., 1983. Mem. AAAS, Royal Soc. Eng. (fgn.), Royal Netherlands Acad. Sci. and Letters, Am. Nuclear Soc. (first recipient Eugene P. Wigner award 1990), Am. Phys. Soc. (v.p. 1955, pres. 1956), Am. Math. Soc., Am. Assn. Physics Tchrs., Am. Acad. Arts and Scis., Am. Philos. Soc., Nat. Acad. Scis., N.Y. Acad. Scis. (hon. life mem.), Austrian Acad. Scis., German Phys Soc., Franklin Inst., Acad. Sci., Gottingen, Germany (corr.), Hungarian Acad. Sci. (hon.), Austrian Acad. Scis. (hon.), Hungarian L. Eötvös Phys. Soc. (hon.), Sigma Xi. Office: Princeton U Jadwin Hall Princeton NJ 08540

WIKERD, PAUL HUBERT, chemical company executive; b. Lancaster, Pa., Sept. 14, 1947; s. Paul Huber and Loretta Mae (Hufford) W.; m. Marjorie Ann Roland, Oct. 25, 1947. BS in Chem. Engring., U. Pitts., 1970. Lic. AKC judge. Devel. engr. Western Elec., Lisle, Ill., 1970-73; engr. Buckbee-Mears Co., St. Paul, 1973-76; engring. mgr. Buckbee-Mears Co., Cortland, N.Y., 1976-80, tech. svcs. mgr., 1980-81, ops. mgr., 1981-82, gen. mgr., 1982-89, v.p., 1989-90; v.p. J.M. Murray Ctr., 1990—; v.p. worldwide sales and mktg. BMC Industries, N.Y.C., 1991—; chair bd. dirs. J.M. Murray Ctr., Cortland. Bd. dirs. Baden-Powell coun. Boy Scouts Am., Dryden, 1983-87; exec. devel. U. Mich., 1990. Mem. Soc. Info. Display, Photo Chem. Machining Inst., Corland County C. of C. (bd. dirs. 1983-86), Basset Hound Club Am. (pres. 1991—). Republican. Home: 5667 W Scott Rd Homer NY 13077-9336 Office: BMC Industries Inc Kellogg Rd # 189 Cortland NY 13045-3135

WIKOFF, HOWARD ELY, county park administrator; b. Trenton, N.J., Oct. 26, 1949; s. Peter and Alice (Ely) W.; m. Nancy Helen Powell, May 20, 1972; children: Jeremy P., Rebecca E. Student, Monmouth Coll., 1967-69; BS in Forestry, W.Va. U., 1972. Naturalist Monmouth County Park System,

Lincroft, N.Y., 1973-74, park mgr., 1974-76, sr. park mgr. for historic sites, 1976—; cons. Howard E. Wikoff, Allentown, N.J., 1980—. Pres. trustees Presbyn. Ch., Allentown, 1989. Mem. Soc. Preservation of Old Mills (advt. mgr. 1983-90), Assn. Living Hist. Farms and Agrl. Museums, Assn. Preservation Tech. Office: Monmouth County Park System Newman Springs Rd Lincroft NJ 07738-1329

WILBERGER, JAMES ELDRIDGE (JACK WILBERGER), neurosurgeon; b. Richmond, Va., May 5, 1952; s. James Eldridge and Florence Belle (Galloway) W.; m. Mary Ellen Tormey, July 21, 1981; children: Matthew, Adam, Melanie. BA, U. Richmond, 1974; MD, Med. Coll. Va., 1978. Diplomate Am. Bd. Neurol. Surgery. Intern, then resident U. Pitts., Pitts., 1978-84; dir. neurotrauma, co-dir. comprehensive epilepsy svc. Med. Coll. Pa., Pitts., 1989—; c-chmn. Nat. Com. on Neurotrauma, 1990—; med. dir. Sch. Health Scis. Physician Asst. program Duquesne U., 1991—. Author: Spinal Cord Injury in Children, 1988; contbr. articles to profl. jours. Bd. dirs. Washington Head Injury Project, Pitts., 1991; v.p. Pitts. Neurosci. Found., 1991; dir. Think First Program, Pitts., 1991. Recipient Wakeman Neurosci. Rsch. award Duke U., 1990, Nat. Rehab. Week award, 1990. Fellow ACS, Am. Coll. Sports Medicine; mem. Am. Assn. Neurol. Surgeons (sec.-treas. joint sects. neurotrauma and critical care, 1990-92), Congress of Neurol. Surgeons, Am. Assn. for the Surgery of Trauma, Am. Spinal Injury Assn. Office: Dept Neurosurgery 420 E North Ave Ste 302 Sewickley PA 15212-4746

WILBORN, THOMAS LOCKART, national security affairs analyst; b. Louisville, July 10, 1930; s. Earl D. and Verna Elizabeth (Lockart) W.; m. Sally Clair Cornell, Aug. 20, 1955; children: Sally Elizabeth, Susan Cornell. AB, U. Ky., 1952, MA, 1955, PhD, 1965; diploma, U.S. Army War Coll., Carlisle Barracks, Pa., 1991. Asst. coord. Ky. Rsch. Found., Lexington, 1959-60; adminstrv. officer U. Ky., Bandung, Indonesia, 1960-62; from asst. prof. to assoc. prof. Cen. Mo. State U., Warrensburg, 1963-70; assoc. prof. James Madison U., Harrisonburg, Va., 1970-74; nat. security affairs analyst U.S. Army War Coll., Carlisle Barracks, Pa., 1974—; mem. adv. com. Coun. on U.S.-Korean Security Studies, Pulham, Wash., 1987—. Author: How Northeast Asians View Their Society, 1991; mem. editorial bd. Parameters, 1980-83; contbr. chpts. to books, articles to profl. jours. 1st lt. U.S. Air Force, 1952-54. Mem. Internat. Studies Assn., Assn. Asian Studies, Coun. on U.S.-Korean Security Studies. Office: US Army War Coll Strategic Studies Inst Carlisle Barracks PA 17013

WILBUR, MELISSA ELLEN, educator; b. N.Y.C., Apr. 11, 1944; d. Maxwell Stanley and Cecille Rebecca (Schoenfeld) Symon; m. Barry Stephen Wilbur, Mar. 31, 1968; children: Adam Mathew, Shoshanna Beth. BS, NYU, 1965; MS, CCNY, 1970. Tchr. N.Y.C. Bd. Edn., 1966-90; tech. ctr. specialist, 1990—; adj. Fordham U., 1991—; treas. mem. basic skills com. Community Sch. Improvement Program, N.Y.C., 1989—; workshop condr.; trainer tchr.-to-tchr. substance abuse prevention N.Y. State Resource Ctr.; mem. adv. bd. N.Y. State Drug Free Schs. Tng. Grant; adjunct Fordham U., Bklyn. Coll. Mem. sch. bd. Free Synagogue Westchester, Mt. Vernon, N.Y., 1986—, trustee, 1988—; past pres. Rena Hadassah; chairperson Young Leaders for Westchester Region, Hadassah, v.p. Westchester Region Hadassah. Grantee Parent Improvement Program, Impact II-channel 13. Home: 30 Ascot Rd Yonkers NY 10710-1404 Office: Pub Sch 86 2756 Reservoir Ave Bronx NY 10468-2702

WILBUR, RICHARD PURDY, educator, writer; b. N.Y.C., Mar. 1, 1921; s. Lawrence L. and Helen (Purdy) W.; m. Mary Charlotte Hayes Ward, June 20, 1942; children: Ellen Dickinson, Christopher Hayes, Nathan Lord, Aaron Hammond. AB, Amherst Coll., 1942, AM, 1952, DLitt (hon.), 1967; AM, Harvard U., 1947; LHD (hon.), Lawrence Coll., Washington U., Williams Coll., U. Rochester, SUNY, Potsdam, 1986, Skidmore Coll., 1987, U. Lowell, 1990; DLitt (hon.), Clark U.; D.Litt., Am. Internat. Coll., Marquette U., Wesleyan U., Carnegie-Mellon U.; D.Litt. (hon.), Lake Forest Coll., 1982. Jr. fellow Harvard U., Cambridge, Mass., 1947-50; Asst. prof. English Harvard U., 1950-54; asso. prof. Wellesley Coll., 1955-57; prof. Wesleyan U., 1957-77; writer in residence Smith Coll., 1977-86. Author: The Beautiful Changes, 1947, Ceremony, 1950, A Bestiary, 1955, Things of This World, 1956, Poems 1943-56, 1957, Advice to a Prophet, 1961, Poems of Richard Wilbur, 1963, Walking to Sleep, 1969, The Mind-Reader, 1976, Seven Poems, 1981, The Whale, 1982, New and Collected Poems, 1988 (Pulitzer prize for poetry), (children's books) Loudmouse, 1963, Opposites, 1973, More Opposites, 1991, (criticism) Responses, 1976; co-author: (comic opera, with Lillian Hellman) Candide, 1957, (cantata, with William Schuman) On Freedom's Ground, 1986; translator: (Moliere) The Misanthrope, 1955, Tartuffe, 1963 (co-recipient Bollingen Translation prize 1963), The School for Wives, 1971, The Learned Ladies, 1978, Four Comedies, 1982, (Racine) Andromache, 1982, Phaedra, 1986, Molière's The School for Husbands, 1992; editor: Complete Poems of Poe, 1959, Poems of Shakespeare, 1966, Selected Poems of Witter Bynner, 1978. Decorated chevalier Ordre des Palmes Academiques; recipient Harriet Monroe prize Poetry mag., 1948; Oscar Blumenthal prize, 1950; Edna St. Vincent Millay Meml. award, 1957; Nat. Book award, 1957; Pulitzer prize, 1957; Prix de Rome Am. Acad. Arts and Letters, 1954; Sarah Josepha Hale award, 1968; Bollingen prize, 1971; Brandeis U. Creative Arts award, 1971; Prix Henri Desfeuilles, 1971; Shelley Meml. award, 1973; Harriet Monroe Poetry award, 1978; St. Botolph's Club Found. award 1983; Drama Desk award, 1983, PEN transl. award, 1983; Aiken-Taylor award, 1988; Bunn award, 1988; Washington Coll. Lit. award, 1988, St. Louis Lit. award, 1989, Grand Master Award Birmingham-So. Coll., 1989, Gold medal for Poetry Am. Acad. Inst. arts and Letters, 1991; Guggenheim fellow, 1952-53, 63, Edward MacDowell medal, 1992; Ford fellow, 1960-61, Camargo Found. fellow, 1985, named U.S. Poet Laureate, Libr. Congress, 1987. Fellow MLA (hon.); mem. Am. Acad. Arts and Scis., Nat. Inst. Arts and Letters, Am. Acad. Arts and Letters (pres. 1974-76, chancellor 1976-78, 80-81), Acad. Am. Poets (chancellor), Dramatists Guild, ASCAP, PEN. Club: Century. Home: RR1 Box 82 Dodwells Rd Cummington MA 01026 also: 715R Windsor Ln Key West FL 33040

WILBURN, ADOLPH YARBROUGH, foreign service officer; b. Wauwatosa, Wis., Sept. 17, 1932; s. Adolph and Kizzie Mae (Yarbrough) W.; m. Mary E. Nelson, Mar. 5, 1957; children: Adolph II, Jason David. BS, U. Wis., 1956; MS, Marquette U., 1959; EdD, Harvard U., 1968. Lectr. in chem. Fed. Sci. Sch., Lagos, Nigeria, 1960-61; sci. edn. specialist Nat. Sci. Found., Washington, 1962-65; research assoc. Harvard U., Ciudad Guayana, Venezuela, 1966-68; ednl. planner UNESCO/ Internat. Inst. of Ednl. Planning, Paris, 1968-69; staff assoc. Nat. Acad. of Scis., Washington, 1971-73; assoc. v.p. for academic affairs. U. Wis. System, Madison, 1973-76; dir. Council for Internat. Exchange of Scholars, Washington, 1976-81; career foreign svc. officer U.S. Agy. for Internat. Devel., Washington, 1981—; Mem. Carver Rsch. Found., Tuskeegee, Ala., 1973-81. Co-author: article in The Encyclopedia of Education. Bd. dirs., Madison (Wis.) Urban League, 1974, D.C. Community Humanities Council, 1979, Nat. Council for Internat. Visitors, Washington, 1980; commr. U.S. Commn. to UNESCO, 1979. Mem. AAAS (life), Cosmos Club. Republican. Baptist. Home: 1438 Iris St NW Washington DC 20012-1410

WILBURN, MARY NELSON, lawyer, writer; b. Balt., Feb. 18, 1932; d. David Alfred and Phoebe Blanche (Novotny) Nelson; m. Adolph Yarbrough Wilburn, Mar. 5, 1957; children: Adolph II, Jason David. AB cum laude, Howard U., 1952; MA, U. Wis., 1955, JD, 1975. Bar: Wis. 1975, U.S. Supreme Ct 1981. Lectr. U. Wis. Law Sch., 1975-77, 83, 84, 85; atty. adv. Bur. Prisons, Dept. Justice, 1977-82; chmn. Wis. State Parole Bd., Madison, 1986-87; gen. counsel D.C. Bd. Parole, 1987-89; commr. The Commn. to Restructure the Interstate Compact, 1988-89; mgr. Bethune Mus.-Archives, Inc., 1990; asst. regional counsel mid-atlantic region Fed. Bur. Prisons, 1990—; mem. Wis. Sentencing Commn., 1986-87; adj. lectr. seminar on parole Washington Coll. Law Am. U., 1991. Mem. Madison Met. Sch. Dist. Bd. Edn., 1975-77; assoc. mem. Schutz Am. Sch. Bd., Alexandria, Egypt, 1983-85; commr. Nat. Coun. of Negro Women Commn. on Edn., 1986—; treas. Women's Strategies for 21st Century, Inc. Mem. Internat. Assn. Paroling Authorities (exec. v.p. 1987-89), Nat. Assn. Black Women Attorneys (pres. Rolark chpt. 1989—), Fedn. Nat. de Abogadas, Howard U. Alumni Assn., Links, Inc., Leadership (Am. Class 1991, bd. dirs. Greater Washington 1992), Alpha Kappa Alpha. Office: 10010 Junction Dr Ste # 100 N Annapolis Junction MD 20701

WILCHER, SHIRLEY J., lawyer; b. Erie, Pa., July 28, 1951; d. James S. Wilcher and Jeanne (Evans) Cheatham. AB cum laude, Mt. Holyoke Coll., 1973; MA, New Sch. Social Research, 1976; JD, Harvard U., 1979. Bar: N.Y. 1980. Assoc. Proskauer Rose Goetz and Mendelsohn, N.Y.C., 1979-80; staff atty. Nat. Women's Law Ctr., Washington, 1980-85; assoc. counsel Com. on Edn. and Labor U.S. Ho. Reps., Washington, 1985-90; dir. state rels., gen. counsel Nat. Assn. Ind. Colls. and Univs., Washington, 1990—. Editor Harvard U. Civil Rights/Civil Liberties Law Rev., 1978-79; contbr. articles to profl. jours. Nat. bd. dirs. Nat. Polit. Congress of Black Women, Washington, 1985-87; convenor Black Women's Roundtable on Voter Participation, Washington, 1984-85. Mem. ABA, Nat. Bar Assn., Nat. Conf. Black Lawyers (local bd. dirs. 1980-87, nat. bd. dirs. 1986-87). Democrat. Buddhist. Office: Nat Assn Ind Colls and Univs 500 N Capitol St NW # 800 Washington DC 20001-1531

WILCHINS, HOWARD MARTIN, lawyer; b. Paterson, N.J., Mar. 6, 1945; s. Philip Aaron and Esther (Blake) W.; m. Margaret Mandon, Sept. 6, 1970; children—Julie, Daniel. AB, Mich. State U., 1966; JD, U. Chgo., 1969. BAR: D.C. 1969, U.S. Supreme Ct. 1975. Trial atty. FPC, Washington, 1969-70; spl. asst. to N.Y. Public Service Commn., Albany, 1970-72; dep. sect. chief AEC, Washington, 1972-75; dep. gen. counsel-litigation U.S. Ry. Assn., Washington, 1975-81, gen. counsel, 1981-84; dep. chief enforcement div. FCC Common Carrier Bur., Washington, 1984-90; v.p. Arnold S. Tesh Advisors, Washington, 1990—; mem. faculty Trial Practice Inst., U.S. CSC, 1977-79. Bd. dirs. United Jewish Appeal Greater Washington, 1984-90, Charles E. Smith Jewish Day Sch., 1983—, v.p. 1986-88, pres., 1988-90; mem. Jewish Campus Activities Bd., 1990—; bd. dirs., mem. Capital Camps, 1990—. Mem. ABA, D.C. Bar Assn., Fed. Communications Bar Assn., Am. Arbitration Assn. Home: 5 Feather Rock Pl Rockville MD 20850-3114 Office: 2025 M St NW 1000 Connecticut Ave NW Ste 600 Washington DC 20036-5302

WILCHUSKY, BERNARD LEONARD, radiologist; b. Port Carbon, Pa., Sept. 9, 1932; s. William Joseph and Helen Anne (Kiselis) W.; m. Leann Cecelia Bartok, July 17, 1959; children: Shari, Mark, Dennis, Jayce; m. Luana Best, June 26, 1988; 1 child, Bernard Jr. BS, U. Pitts., 1955, MD, 1958. Diplomate Am Bd. Radiology. Intern Mercy Hosp., Pitts., 1958-59, resident, 1962-65, staff radiologist, 1965—; pres. Diagnostic Imaging Assocs., Pitts., 1990—; cons. staff Braddock Hosp, Pitts., 1980—; clin asst. radiology prof. Sch. Medicine, U. Pitts., 1984-90. V.P. Med. Staff Mercy Hosp., 1984-84. Mem. Am. Coll. of Radiology, Radiol. SOc. of N.Am., Pa. Radiol. Soc., Diagnostic Imaging Assocs. Roman Catholic. Home: 3466 Palomino Dr Gibsonia PA 15044-8964 Office: Diagnostic Imaging Assocs 2041 Blvd Of The Allies Pittsburgh PA 15219-5801

WILCOX, DAVID ERIC, consultant; b. Cortland, N.Y., Sept. 4, 1939; s. James A. and Lucille (Fiske) C.; B.S. in Elec. Engring., U. Buffalo, 1961; postgrad. Syracuse U., 1965, Marist Coll.; M.S., U. Bridgeport, 1977; Ed.D. candidate Rutgers U.; m. Phyllipa Ann Wilcox, Jan. 23, 1977; children: Terri L., Cindy A., Jana L. Research engring. mgr. input/output devices Rome (N.Y.) Air Devel. Center, 1966-70; dir. sales Mercon Inc., Winsooki, Vt., 1970-73, dir., 1972—; pres. Wilcox Tng. Systems, Newburgh, N.Y., 1973—; prin. Exec. Effectiveness, Inc., N.Y.C.; instr. Dale Carnegie courses. Pres. N.Y. State Jaycees, 1972-73, chmn. bd., 1973-74; dir. U.S. Jaycees, 1970-71; bd. dirs., v.p. N.Y. State Spl. Olympics, 1972-73; bd. dirs., treas. Family Counseling Service, Inc. Served to lt. USAF, 1961-65. Registered profl. engr., N.Y. Mem. Soc. Info. Display, IEEE, N.Y., State Soc. Profl. Engrs., Internat. Transactional Analysis Assn., Internat. Platform Assn., Am. Soc. Quality Control. Methodist. Author: Information System Sciences, 1965; also articles. Patentee in field. Home: 511 River Rd Newburgh NY 12550-1304 Office: Rock Cut Rd Newburgh NY 12550 also: 30 W 60th St New York NY 10023

WILCOX, JOHN RICHARD, ethics educator; b. N.Y.C., Jan. 1, 1939; s. Herbert Richard and Margaret M. (Lally) W.; m. Suzanne Loretta Dale, Jan. 5, 1974; children: Kenneth, Lillian, Christopher. BA magna cum laude, Marist Coll., 1961; MA, Fordham U., 1965; PhD, Union Theol. Sem., 1977. High sch. and coll. tchr. Marist Bros. Schs., N.Y., Conn. and Mass., 1961-73; prof. Manhattan Coll., Bronx, N.Y., 1974—, dir. Ctr. for Profl. Ethics, 1984—. Author: Taking Time Seriously, 1978, The Leadership Compass: Values and Ethics in Higher Education, 1992; editor: Internationalization of American Business: Ethical Issues and Cases, 1992; contbr. articles to profl. publs. Chair Westchester County Bd. Ethics, White Plains, N.Y., 1988-92. Fulbright fellow, 1968, Dyson fellow Pace U., 1986. Fellow Soc. for Values in Higher Edn.; mem. Soc. Christian Ethics, Am. Assn. Univ. Adminstrs. (bd. dirs. 1990—). Democrat. Roman Catholic. Home: Hunts Ln Cross River NY 10518-9716 Office: Manhattan Coll Bronx NY 10471

WILCOX, MARSHA ANN, market research executive; b. Summit, N.J., Dec. 25, 1956; d. Marshal L. Wilcox Jr. and Ann H. Conover. MusB, SUNY, Postsdam, 1979; MA, Columbia U., 1982, MEd, 1983, MS, EdD, 1985. Cert. elem. music edn., spl. edn. Research exec. Young & Rubicam, N.Y.C., 1985—; research supr. Young & Rubicam, 1987; staff supr. research AT&T, Basking Ridge, N.J., 1987-88; assoc. research dir. HDM Advt., N.Y.C., 1988-89; assoc. tech. dir. Decision Research Corp., Lexington, Mass., 1989-91; sr. assoc. Applied Mktg. Sci., Inc., Waltham, Mass., 1991—; cons. various orgns. and individuals, met. N.Y.C., 1983—; presenter in field. Contbr. articles to profl. jours. Elder Grace Presbyterian Ch., Montclair, N.J., 1986—. Recipient fed. traineeship in behavior Analysis U.S. Govt., Columbia U., 1983-85. Mem. Assn. for Behavior Analysis, Christian Assn. for Psychol. Studies, Am. Mktg. Assn., Phi Delta Kappa, Kappa Delta Pi. Office: Applied Mktg Sci Inc 303 Wyman St Waltham MA 02154-1217

WILDE, PATRICIA, artistic director; b. Ottawa, Ont., Can., July 16, 1928; m. George Bardyguine; children: Anya, Youri. Dancer Am. Concert Ballet, Marquis de Cuevas Ballet Internat., N.Y.C., 1944-45, Ballet Russe de Monte Carlo, N.Y.C., 1945-49, Roland Petit's Ballet Paris, Met. Ballet Britain, London, 1949-50; prin. ballerina N.Y.C. Ballet, 1950-65; dir. Harkness Sch. Ballet, N.Y.C., 1965-67; ballet mistress, tchr. Am. Ballet Theatre, N.Y.C., 1969-77; dir. Am. Ballet Theatre Sch., N.Y.C., 1977-82; artistic dir. Pitts. Ballet Theatre, 1982—; tchr. Am. Ballet Theatre, 1969-77, Joffrey scholarship program, N.Y.C. Ballet, 1968-69; established Sch. of Grand Theatre of Geneva, 1968-69; adjudicator Regional Ballet in Am. S.E. and S.W., 1969-82; choreographer N.Y. Philharmonic; guest tchr. various ballet cos. and colls.; trustee Dance U.S.A.; panelist Nat. Choreographic Project. Recipient Leadership award in Arts and Letters, 1990. Office: Pitts Ballet Theatre 2900 Liberty Ave Pittsburgh PA 15201-1511

WILDEBUSH, JOSEPH FREDERICK, economist; b. Bklyn., July 18, 1910; s. Harry Frederick and Elizabeth (Stolzenberg) W.; A.B., Columbia, 1931, postgrad Law Sch., 1932; LL.B., Bklyn. Law Sch., 1934, J.D., 1967; m. Martha Janssens, July 18, 1935; children—Diane Elaine (Mrs. Solon Finkelstein), Joan Marilyn (Mrs. Bobby Sanford Berry); m. Edith Sorensen, May 30, 1964. Admitted to N.Y. State bar, 1934, Fed. bar, 1935; practice law, N.Y.C., 1934-41; labor relations dir. Botany Mills, Passaic, N.J., 1945-48; exec. v.p. Silk and Rayon Printers and Dyers Assn. Am., Inc., Paterson, N.J., 1948-70; exec. v.p. Textile Printers and Dyers Labor Relations Inst., Paterson, 1954-70; mem. panel labor arbitrators Fed. Mediation and Conciliation Service, N.Y. State Mediation Bd., N.J. State Mediation Bd., N.J. Pub. Employment Relations Commn., Am. Arbitration Assn.; co-adj. faculty Rutgers U., 1948—; lectr. Pres. Pascack Valley Hosp., Westwood, N.J., 1950-64, chmn. bd., 1964-67, chmn. emeritus, 1967—; dir. Group Health Ins. N.Y., 1950—. Served as maj. Engrs. Corps, AUS, 1941-43. Mem. N.Y. County Lawyers Assn., Am. Acad. Polit. and Social Sci., Indsl. Rels. Rsch. Assn., Ret. Officers Assn., Nat. Geog. Soc. Lutheran. Contbr. articles profl. jours. Home and Office: 37 James Ter Pompton Lakes NJ 07442-1921

WILDER, AMOS TAPPAN, urban studies specialist; b. Boston, Feb. 6, 1940; s. Amos Niven and Catharine (Kerlin) W.; m. Robin Gibbs, June 15, 1968; children: Amos Todd, Jenney Gibbs Wilder. BA, Yale U., 1962, M in Philosophy, 1976; MA, U. Wis., 1967. Adminstr. Yale U., New Haven, 1968-79; sr. assoc. Ptnr. for Livable Pls., Washington, 1979-81; freelance cons. Washington, 1982-84; dir. corp. planning and communications Capital Care, Inc., Vienna, Va., 1984-90; cons. Chevy Chase, Md., 1991—. Bd. dirs. Long Wharf Theater, New Haven, 1970-79, Student Conservation Assn., Charlestown, N.H., 1980-88, Yale Glee Club Assocs., New Haven, 1987—, Christmas in Apr.-USA. Rockefeller Bros. Found. fellow, 1962-63. Mem. Yale Club of N.Y.C., Elizabethan Club, Delta Psi. Home: 5535 Warwick Pl Chevy Chase MD 20815-5505

WILDER, ROBERT DAVID, publishing executive; b. New Brunswick, N.J., June 4, 1948; s. Louis K. Wilder and Shirley (Schwartz) Pratt; m. Dorothy Corenna Slivocka, June 29, 1969; children: Paul Louis, Lauren Beth. BA in Econs., Rutgers U., 1970; MBA in Acctg., Fordham U., 1977. Cert. Internal Auditor. Sect. chief Western Electric, Kearny, N.J., 1970-74; sr. audit supr. Joseph E. Seagram & Sons, N.Y.C., 1974-77, mgmt. cons., 1977-79; audit dir. John Wiley & Sons, N.Y.C., 1979-85, gen. mgr., fin. adminstr., 1985-87, chief fin. officer, 1987-88, v.p. pub. fin. adminstr., 1987-90, sr. v.p., chief fin. officer, 1990—. With U.S. Army Reserves, 1970. Mem. Inst. Internal Auditors. Home: 10 Cobblestone Ct Howell NJ 07731-1604 Office: John Wiley & Sons 605 3rd Ave New York NY 10158

WILDER, RONALD LYNN, rheumatologist, biomedical researcher; b. Long Beach, Calif., Feb. 10, 1947; m. Deborah L. Souter, Dec. 20, 1969; children: Wendy L., Jason M. BS, UCLA, 1969, MD, PhD, 1974. Diplomate Am. Bd. Internal Medicine, Am. Bd. Rheumatology. Intern in medicine U. Calif., San Diego, 1974-75, resident, 1975-76; rsch. assoc. Nat. Inst. Allergy and Infectious Disease, NIH, Bethesda, Md., 1976-79; clin. assoc. Nat. Inst. Arthritis, Musculoskeletal and Skin Diseases, NIH, Bethesda, 1979-81, sr. investigator, attending physician, 1981—. Contbr. numerous articles to med. jours. Office: NIH ARB NIAMS Bethesda MD 20892

WILDER, WILBURETTA (MICKI), nursing consultant; b. Orwell, N.Y., July 10, 1927; d. William James and Grace Irene (Loucks) McDonald; m. John Richard Wilder, Apr. 7, 1951; children: Susan, Carol. Diploma in nursing, U. Rochester, 1948; BS, Syracuse U., 1962; MS, SUNY, Brockport, 1978. RN, N.Y. Dir. health svcs., sch. nurse, tchr. West Genesee Schs., Camillus, N.Y.; pvt. practice sch. health cons. Syracuse, N.Y.; Robert Wood Johnson Found. grantee, project dir. Nat. Assn. Sch. Nurses; cons. N.Y. State Edn. Dept., Bur. Helath Edn. and Svcs.; mem. editorial bd. Pediatric Nursing Update Series. Mem. N.Y. State Nurses Assn. (past chmn. sch. nurse clin. practice unit), Nat. Assn. Sch. Nurses (past bd. dirs. N.Y.), Am. Sch. Health Assn., Sigma Theta Tau. Home: 119 Garland Rd Syracuse NY 13219-1217

WILDEROTTER, PETER THOMAS, non profit executive; b. Newark, N.J., May 24, 1954; s. Arthur W. and Dorothy (King) T.; m. Nancy Ann Lanza, Apr. 27, 1985; 1 child, Peter Arthur. BA in English, Marist Coll., 1976. Area dir. Am. Cancer Soc. N.J. Div., North Brunswick, 1976-86; v.p. resources Planned Parenthood Fedn. Am., N.Y.C., 1987-90; dir. devel. NAACP Legal Defense Fund, N.Y.C., 1991; v.p. devel. NCCJ, N.Y.C., 1992—; bd. dirs. Cath.'s for Choice, Washington, Nat. Unified Svc. Agys.; govt. rels. com. Ind. Sector, Washington, 1990. Mem. Nat. Soc. Fund Raising Execs. Democrat. Roman Catholic. Home: 12 Edgewood Pl Maplewood NJ 07040 Office: NCCJ 71 Fifth Ave New York NY 10003

WILDERSON, SAMUEL FRANCIS, metrologist; b. Balt., Nov. 19, 1946; s. Stewart Worthington and Barbara Wilhelmina (Miller) W.; m. Annette Catherine Leaf, Oct. 2, 1971; 1 child, Sarah Elizabeth. Degree in Elec. Engring., Catonsville Community Coll., Md., 1982. Calibration technician Westinghouse, Landsdown, Md., 1966-70; data technician Johns Hopkins U. Applied Physics Lab., Silver Spring, Md., 1971-72; customer engr. computer div. Hewlett Packard, Rockville, Md., 1972-80; standards metrologist Johns Hopkins U. Applied Physics Lab., Laurel, Md., 1980—. Roman Catholic. Home: 7922 Nottingham Way Ellicott City MD 21043-6761 Office: Johns Hopkins U Applied Physics Lab Johns Hopkins Rd Laurel MD 20723-6099

WILDISH, KAT, ballerina de monde, choreographer, cultural ambassador; b. Sept. 21; d. Leroy Franklin Wildish; m. Christopher Greene Covell. Grad., Sch. Am. Ballet, N.Y.C. With Ballet Who Inc., N.Y.C.; with Am Ballet Theatre, Ballett der Deutschen Oper Am Rhein, Eglevsky Ballet Co., Hamburg Ballet, Joffrey Ballet, Met. Opera Ballet, N.Y.C. Ballet, La Scala Opera Ballet, Zuerich Opern Ballet, others. Appeared in Apparitions, Brigadoon, Concerto Barocco, Le Corsaire, Cortege Hongrois, Daphnis and Chloé, Dying Swan, Giselle, A Midsummer Night's Dream, The Nutcracker, Rhapsody in Blue, Romeo and Juliet, Serenade, Swan Lake, West Side Story, others; performed with Dick Andros, George Balanchine, Mikhail Baryshnikov, Nanette Charisse, Alexandra Danilova, Agnes De Mille, Placido Domingo, Sir Kenneth MacMillian, Rudolf Nureyev, Franco Zefferelli, others. Counselor, speaker, cultural ambassador against child abuse. Recipient Ford Found. Dance scholarships. Address: care Ballet Who Inc PO Box 20174 Cherokee St New York NY 10028

WILDMAN, GEORGE THOMAS, pharmaceutical company executive; b. Grasmere, N.H., Nov. 14, 1935; s. Arthur Stephen and Beatrice Alice (Parkinson) W. BS in Chem. Engring., U. N.H., 1957; MS in Chem. Engring., NYU, 1962; ScD in Chem. Engring., MIT, 1973. Rsch. chem. engr. Merck & Co., Inc., Rahway, N.J., 1957-62; sr. chem. engr. Merck & Co., Inc., Rahway, 1962-65, engring. assoc., 1965-68, rsch. fellow, 1968-72, sect. mgr., 1972-77, mgr. tech. svcs., 1977-80, mfg. mgr., 1980-84, dir. tech. ops., 1984-90, dir. tech. ops. and engring. adminstrn., 1990—; mem. tech. steering com. Ctr. for Chem. Process Safety, N.Y.C., 1988—; mem. adv. com. dept. chem. engring., chemistry and environ. scis., N.J. Inst. Tech., Newark, 1991—. Co-editor: Chemical Reactivitiy and Application to Process Design, 1991; patentee in field. Ednl. councilor MIT, Scotch Plains, N.J., 1975-90. Mem. Am. Inst. Chem. Engrs., Am. Chem. Soc. Home: 2068 Old Raritan Rd Westfield NJ 07090

WILDRICK, CATHERINE RUTH, psychotherapist; b. Morristown, N.J., Sept. 4, 1962; d. Kenyon Jones and Nancy (Mersfelder) W. BA summa cum laude, Wake Forest U., 1985; MA, Montclair State Coll., 1987; postgrad., NYU, 1988—. Grad. asst., acad. counselor Montclair State Coll. Equal Opportunity Fund, Upper Montclair, N.J., 1986-87; acad. advisor Montclair State Coll., Upper Montclair, 1988; family therapist Porject Community Pride, Madison, N.J., 1988-90; mental health counselor II St. Clares-Riverside Med. Ctr., Denville, N.J., 1986—; staff psychologist Fairleigh Dickinson U. Student Counseling Ctr., Madison, 1990—; psychotherapist Family and Children's Svcs. of North Essex, Caldwell, N.J., 1991—; adj. teaching asst. NYU, 1989-90; instr. Fairleigh Dickinson U., Madison, 1990. Mem. Fair Oaks Hosp. Adult Psychiat. Adv. Bd., Summit, N.J., 1990-91; featured guest Suburban Cablevision talk show, East Orange, N.J., 1991; discussant community sponsored panel presentation on "date rape," Madison, 1991. Mem. AACD, Am. Psychol. Assn. (student affiliate), Phi Beta Kappa, Omicron Delta Kappa (pres. chpt. 1984-85), Alpha Kappa Delta. Home: 264 Fairmount Ave Chatham NJ 07928-1825 Office: Fairleigh Dickinson U Student Counseling Ctr 285 Madison Ave Madison NJ 07940-1099

WILE, TIMOTHY SPAULDING, mental health counselor; b. Willimantic, Conn., June 18, 1956; s. John David and Mary Elizabeth (White) W.; m. Mary Beth Glowka, July 20, 1985; children: Charlotte Elizabeth, Cooper Carens. BS in Edn., U. Vt., 1979, MS in Counseling, 1983. Cert. clin. mental health counselor, Vt. Tchr. math. Escuela Bilingue Valle de Sula, San Pedro Sula, Honduras, 1979-80; residential counselor Pine Ridge Sch., Williston, Vt., 1982-84, cons., 1990-91; pvt. practice mental health counseling, Burlington, Vt., 1984—; exec. dir. Green Mountain Prevention Projects, Burlington, 1989—; trainer Vt. 4-H Congress, Burlington, 1989-90. Mem. AACD, Am. Mental Health Counselors Assn., Vt. Mental Health Counselors Assn. (negotiator 1988), Vt. Assn. for Counseling and Devel. (editor, bd. dirs. 1987-89). Office: Dolan House 96 S Union St Burlington VT 05401-3827

WILEN, SAMUEL HENRY, organic chemist, educator; b. Brussels, Mar. 6, 1931; came to U.S., 1942; s. Benjamin Elie and Helen (Spinner) W.; m. Rosamond Lewis, Aug. 28, 1960; children: Robert Marc, Elizabeth. BS cum laude, CCNY, 1951; PhD, U. Kans., 1956. Postdoctoral rsch. assoc. U. Notre Dame, Ind., 1955-57; sci. assoc. U. Groningen, The Netherlands, 1968-69; guest researcher Univ. Libre de Bruxelles, Brussels, 1975-76; vis. prof. U. N.C., Chapel Hill, 1984, 90; from. instr. to assoc. prof. City Coll., CUNY, 1957-70; prof. CUNY, 1971—, chmn. chemistry dept., 1984-87. Co-author: (monograph) Enantiomers, Racemates and Reolutions, 1981; co-editor: (rev. monograph series) Topics in Stereochemistry, 1983—; contbr.

articles to profl. jours. Mem. City Coll. Alumni Assn. (dir., Alumni Svc. award 1980), City Coll. Chemistry Alumni Assn. (pres. 1990—). Office: CUNY City Coll Dept Chemistry New York NY 10031

WILENSKY, JULIUS M., publishing company executive; b. Stamford, Conn., Oct. 10, 1916; s. Joseph and Mary (Wainstein) W.; m. Dorothy T. Jobrack, July 2, 1939; children—Joseph L. (dec.), Nancy L. Jamie, Martha J. Hansen. Student, Rensselaer Poly. Inst., 1934-36. Methods engr. Yale & Towne Mfg. Co., Stamford, 1939-49; prodn. mgr. Yale & Towne Mfg. Co., 1953-57; dir. purchasing lock and hardware div. Eaton Yale & Towne, Rye, N.Y., 1957-67; mayor of Stamford, 1969-73; dir. materials, arms operations Winchester div. Olin Corp., New Haven, 1973-78; pres. Wescott Cove Pub. Co., 1978—; lectr. in field. Author guide books on cruising L.I. Sound, Cape Cod, Windward Islands, Bay Islands of Honduras and Abacos; contbr. articles to boating mags. and newspapers; contbg. editor: Rudder, 1970-77; author cruising columns Ea. and So. edits. Sea mag., 1978-80, Rudder mag., 1981-83; editor cruising guides to Tahiti, French Soc. Islands, Maine (2 vols.), Turkey, Belize, Mexico's Caribbean Coast, I Don't Do Portholes, Lights and Legends, Beachcombing and Beachcrafting, Pacific Wanderer, Irma Quarterdeck Reports, Inside American Paradise. Bd. dirs. Stamford Ctr. for Arts, 1981-90; treas. Lifeline, 1983-85; first v.p. Met. Regional Coun., 1973; mem. Tri-State Regional Planning Commn., 1971-73, Stamford Bd. Fin., 1965-69, Stamford Planning Bd., 1963-65; chmn. Coun. Rep. Clubs, Stamford, 1961-62. With USAAF, 1943-46. Named Republican of Yr. Stamford Reps., 1962. Mem. Am. Mgmt. Assn., Stamford Power Squadron, Stamford Good Govt. Assn. (dir., treas. 1949-57), Stamford Chamber Residences (pres. 1953-55). Home: 51 Barrett Ave Stamford CT 06905-3212

WILENTZ, ROBERT SEAN, history educator, author; b. N.Y.C., Feb. 20, 1951; s. Elias and Jeanne Marie (Campbell) W.; m. Mary Christine Stansell, Jan. 30, 1980; children: James Thomas Farrell, Hannah Cady Rose. BA, Columbia U., 1972, Oxford U., 1974; PhD, Yale U., 1980. Asst. prof. history Princeton (N.J.) U., 1979-85, assoc. prof., 1985-87, prof., 1987—. Author: Chants Democratic, 1984; editor: Rites of Power, 1985. John Simon Guggenheim Meml. Found. fellow, 1990; recipient A.J. Beveridge award Am. Hist. Assn., 1984, Ann. Book award Soc. for History of Early Republic, 1984, F.J. Turner award Orgn. Am. Historians, 1985. Home: 7 Edgehill St Princeton NJ 08540-6801 Office: Princeton U Dept History Princeton NJ 08544

WILES, DAVID KIMBALL, educator; b. Tuscaloosa, Ala., Feb. 23, 1942; s. Kimball and Hilda (Long) W.; m. Marilyn McCall, Jan. 31, 1964; children—Corey, Matthew. B.S. in Edn., Fla. State U., 1964; M.S. in Polit. Sci., U. Fla., 1967, Ed.D. in Adminstrn., 1969. Asst. prof. U. Toronto, Ont., Can., 1969-72; assoc. prof. Va. Poly. Inst., Blacksburg, 1972-74; prof. edn. Miami U., Oxford, Ohio, 1974-78, prof. edn. and pub. policy, SUNY-Albany, 1978—, Rockefeller Coll., U. Albany. Author: (with others) Practical Politics, 1981; Energy, Winter and Schools, 1979; Perspectives on Educational Research, 1971. With U.S. Army, 1965-66, with Res. 1967-68. Grantee N.Y. State Edn. Dept., 1983, Spencer Found., 1982. Fellow Internat. Biblog. Ctr., Am. Coun. Edn. Avocations: body surfing, cross country skiing, reading, microcomputing. Home: PO Box 8220 Saint Augustine FL 32086-0001 Office: SUNY Albany 1400 Washington Ave Albany NY 12222-0001

WILES, MARILYN MCCALL, management consultant; b. Miami, Fla., Aug. 21, 1944; d. Alexander Charles and Dorothy (Peeples) McC.; m. David Kimball Wiles, Jan. 311, 1964; children: Corey, Matthew. BS, Fla. State U., 1966; MEd, U. Fla., 1968; D. of Edn., Va. Poly. Inst., 1974; Postdoctoral Assoc. (hon.), Scripps Found. Gerontology Ctr., 1977. Tchr. Ft. Knox (Ky.) High Sch., 1966-67, Westwood Jr. High Sch., Gainesville, Fla., 1967-69; asst prof. Miami U., Oxford, Ohio, 1975-77; sr. policy analyst N.Y. State Senate, Albany, 1978-85; curriculum coord. NEA, Albany, 1983-84; pres. Alert, Albany, 1984—. Columnist Capital Dist. Bus. Review, Albany, 1990—; author: (policy reports) Old Age and Ruralism, 1980, Energy Conservation and Schs., 1982; Educational Partnership, 1983. Cons. Kettering (Ohio) Found., 1974-77; bd. dirs. Am. Heart Assn., Albany, 1992, Albany Symphony, 1992—; v.p. bd. Sr. Citizens Found., Albany, 1992, Jr. Achievement, Albany, 1992, Cultural Vistas for Youth, Albany, 1992, Tri-County Coun. of Women. Mem. Bus. and Profl. Women's Assn., Bus. Coun. N.Y. State, Women's Bus. Devel. Ctr. (founder, chmn. bd. dirs. 1985-89), Enterprising Women's Leadership Inst. (exec. dir., founder 1991), Capital Dist. Women's Polit. Caucus, Soroptimists, Bethlehem C. of C., Rotary Internat., Albany-Colonie C. of C., Zeta Tau Alpha. Home and Office: Alert RR 1 Box 322 Delmar NY 12054

WILEY, JASON LARUE, JR., neurosurgeon; b. Canandaigua, N.Y., Dec. 2, 1917; s. Jason LaRue and Eva Althea (Moore) W.; m. Alma Williams, Jan. 4, 1944 (div. Feb. 1956); children: Robert W., Richard L.; m. Ann Valentine Gerrish, Apr. 14, 1956 (div. July 1979); children: Martha V., Pamela M., Catherine A. Student, Antioch Coll., 1934-37; MD, Harvard U., 1941. Diplomate Am. Bd. Surgery, Am. Bd. Neurol. Surgery. Intern Kings County Hosp., Bklyn., 1941-42; asst. resident surgery Ellis Hosp., Schenectady, N.Y., 1948-49; from asst. to assoc. resident surgery Rochester (N.Y.) Gen. Hosp., 1949-51; from asst. to assoc. to chief resident neurosurgery Yale U. and Hartford Hosp., New Haven and Hartford Conn., 1951-54; practice medicine specializing in neurosurgery Kansa City, Mo., 1954-56, Rochester, 1956—; chief neurosurgery Rochester Gen. Hosp., 1959-71, emeritus neurosurgeon, 1989—; clin. asst. prof. neurosurgery U. Rochester, 1961-88. Mem. bd. for Profl. Med. Conduct, N.Y. State Dept. Health, Albany, N.Y., 1985—. Served to lt. comdr. USN, 1942-47, PTO. Mem. Med. Soc. County Monroe, Med. Soc. State N.Y., N.Y. State Neurosurg. Soc. (bd. dirs. 1974-77), Congress Neurol. Surgeons, Am. Assn. Neurol. Surgeons. Republican. Club: Canandaigua Yacht. Office: 1445 Portland Ave Rochester NY 14621-3008

WILEY, JOHN PRESTON, JR., magazine editor; b. Rahway, N.J., May 22, 1936; s. John P. and Arabella (Bassett) W.; m. Barbara Hick, Aug. 5, 1961 (div. Oct. 1988); children: John F., Peter C., Catherine A., James P. BS, Fordham Coll., 1958; Cert. Journalism, Columbia U., 1967. Salesman Texaco, Westville, N.J., 1959-60; mng. editor Orange County Post, Washingtonville, N.Y., 1960-62; county editor Times-Herald Record, Middletown, N.Y., 1962-66; deskman UPI, N.Y.C., 1967-68; assoc. editor Physics Today, N.Y.C., 1968-69; sr. editor Natural History mag., N.Y.C., 1969-72; bd. editors Smithsonian mag., Washington, 1973—. Contbg. author: (anthology) Editor's Choice: Smithsonian, 1990. County com. Dem. party, Westchester County, N.Y., 1968-72. Mem. Audubon Naturalist Soc. of Cen. Atlantic States (bd. dirs. 1990—), Nat. Assn. Sci. Writers. Office: Smithsonian Mag MRC 406 900 Jefferson Dr Washington DC 20560

WILF, FREDERIC MARSHAL, lawyer; b. Phila., Mar. 3, 1959; s. Leonard R. and Phyllis Hope (Zabludoff) W. BA, Rutgers U., 1982; JD, Case Western Res. U., 1985. Bar: Pa. 1985, N.J. 1985, U.S. Dist. Ct. N.J. 1985, U.S. Dist. Ct. (ea. dist.) Pa. 1986, U.S. Dist. Ct. (middle dist.) Pa. 1992, U.S. Ct. Appeals (3d cir.) 1986, U.S. Ct. Appeals (Fed. cir.) 1989, U.S. Supreme Ct. 1989. Cons. atty. Bell Telephone Co. of Pa., Phila., 1985-86; assoc. Rapp, White, Janssen & German, Phila., 1986, Elman Assocs., Phila., 1986-88, Lipton, Famiglio & Elman, Media, Pa., 1988-89; ptnr. Elman & Wilf, Media, 1990—. Mem. ABA (ABA/net, corp. law cong. organizer), Pa. Bar Assn., N.J. Bar Assn. Camden County (N.J.) Bar Assn., Phila. Bar Assn., Computer Law Assn., Assn. for Computing Machinery. Democrat. Jewish. Office: Elman & Wilf 20 W 3d St Media PA 19063-2824

WILHELM, JIM, theatrical agent; b. El Paso, Tex., Sept. 6, 1954; s. James Edward and Patricia Ann (Walter) W. BA, Gannon U., 1979. Mgr. bus. Pitts. Playhouse, 1977-79; mng. dir. City Theatre Co., Pitts., 1979; coordinator prodn. Pitts. Civil Light Opera, 1980; sub-agt. Lionel Larner Ltd., N.Y.C., 1982-84; head theatrical Bob Waters Agy., Inc., N.Y.C., 1984-86; v.p. Barry Douglas Talent Agy., N.Y.C., 1986-88, Douglas, Gorman, Rothacker and Wilhelm Inc.-A Talent Agy., N.Y.C., 1988—. Mem. adv. bd. State Theatre of Ky., Bowling Green, Erie Playhouse, Pa. Mem. Am. Film Inst., Nat. Assn. Talent Reps. Roman Catholic. Office: 1501 Broadway Ste 703 New York NY 10036-5503

WILHELMI, HENRY PAUL, landscape architect, community planning consultant; b. Syracuse, N.Y., Oct. 3, 1930; s. William and Caroline Albertine (Spingler) W.; m. Mary Louise Weil, July 24, 1954 (dec. 1971); m. Eleanor Guilfoyle Jerome, Aug. 4, 1973; children: Lauren, Eric, Lisa; stepchildren: Timothy, James, Kathleen, Karen. BS, Syracuse U., 1953, postgrad., 1956-63. Landscape architect Nat. Park Service, Richmond, Va., 1955-56; planner Wheelwright Stevenson & Langran, Phila., 1957; prin. city planner dept. urban improvement City of Syracuse, 1958-64; ptnr. Duryea and Wilhelmi, Syracuse, 1965-75; v.p. Duryea and Wilhelmi P.C., Syracuse, 1975-81; pvt. practice landscape architecture Syracuse, 1981—; pres. Limehill Devel. Corp., Syracuse, 1984—; Adj. lectr., critic Syracuse U., 1959—. Mem. Onondaga County Environ. Mgmt. Coun., Onondaga County Planning Fedn.; bd. govs. Citizens Found. Served with AUS, 1953-55. Recipient various mcpl. and profl. soc. design awards. Mem. Am. Soc. Landscape Architects. Home: 7476 Elmcrest Rd Liverpool NY 13090-2847 Office: 221 Walton St Syracuse NY 13202-2129

WILHITE, CLAYTON EDWARD, advertising executive; b. Saginaw, Mich., Aug. 9, 1945; s. Clayton Robson and Ruth Margaret (Westendorf) W.; m. Ann Denise Douglass, June 27, 1970. BA in Polit. Sci., U. Mich., 1967, MBA, 1969. Account exec., account supr. Foote, Cone & Belding, Chgo. and Sydney, Australia, 1969-75; v.p., account supr. McCann-Erickson, N.Y.C., 1975-77; exec. v.p., dir. Ammirati & Puris Inc., N.Y.C., 1977-83; mktg. dir. Young & Rubicam Ltd., London, 1983-85; chief exec., mng. dir. D'Arcy, Masius, Benton & Bowles (formerly D'Arcy, MacManus, Masius, Inc.), St. Louis, 1985-88; pres. D'Arcy, Masius, Benton & Bowles/USA, N.Y.C., 1988-91, DMB&B/N.Am., N.Y.C., 1991—; bd. dirs. DMB&B Inc. Mem. Exec. Campaign 1976 In-House Advt. Agy. for Pres. Ford Re-election Com., Washington; bd. dirs. Young Pres. Orgn.; mem. vis. com. White Burkett Miller Ctr., U.Va.; mem. pres.'s adv. group U. Mich. Mem. River Club (N.Y.C.), Phi Beta Kappa. Republican. Lutheran. Office: D'Arcy Masius Benton & Bowles Inc 1675 Broadway New York NY 10019-5820

WILK, LEONARD STEPHEN, electrical engineer, educator; b. Adams, Mass., Sept. 29, 1927; s. John Stanley and Julia (Galushka) W.; children: Stephen J., Justin S., Katherine E. SBEE, SMEE, MIT, 1955. Registered profl. engr., Mass. Group leader Missile Guidance Instrumentation Lab., MIT, Cambridge, 1955-60, asst. dir. space guidance, 1960-67; assoc. dir for engring. Measurement Systems Lab., MIT, Cambridge, 1967-74; staff engr. C.S. Draper Lab., Inc., Cambridge, 1974-83, configuratin mgr., 1983-88, prin. mem. tech. staff, 1988—; lectr. dept. aero. and astro. MIT, 1984—; guidance cons. 1st Polaris patrol USN, 1960, Trident II blue ribbon com., 1987; gradiometer cons. MX workshop USAF, 1978. Contbr. articles to sci. jours.; patentee gravity gradiometer, pseudo-diamagnetic suspension, alignment transfer, fluid accelerometer. Petty officer USN, 1945-48. Recipient Polaris commendation USN, 1960, letter of appreciation, 1984; Apollo achievement award NASA, 1969, cert. of recognition, 1976; Apollo commendation MIT, 1969, letter of appreciation USAF, 1978, Lockheed, 1987. Home: 5 Swan Rd Winchester MA 01890-3719 Office: CS Draper Lab Inc 555 Tech Sq MS 37 Cambridge MA 02139

WILKENS, CHRISTOPHER WILLIAM, educator; b. Corvallis, Oreg., July 27, 1947; s. William Wilhelm and Dorthy Ann (Coe) W.; m. Helen L. Reinert, June 28, 1969; children: Lorraine Marie, Christopher George. BA in Secondary Edn., U. Md., 1973; MA in History, Montclair State Coll., 1976, MA in Student Personnel, 1983; student honors program, Holocaust Inst., Hebrew U., Jerusalem, 1988; MA in Ednl. Adminstrn. and Leadership, Montclair State Coll., 1990; MA in Adminstrn. and Leadership, 1991; postgrad., Rutgers U., 1991. Instr., tutor HEW/D.C. Schs., Washington, 1969-73; tchr. Nutley (N.J.) Pub. Schs., 1973-80, Roxbury (N.J.) Pub. Schs., 1980-89; counselor Roxbury Pub. Schs., Succasunna, N.J., 1989—; instr., cons., N.J. Holocaust Commn., N.J. Dept. Edn., 1983—, Vietnam Studies Ctr. Social Studies, Pitts., 1985—; dir. Vietnam studies curriculum coun. Walt Whitman Ctr., Rutgers U.; adj. instr. issues 20th century Upsala Coll., 1992—. Contbg. author: Unit Six: When War Becomes a Crime, 1988; editor reading anthology: The Vietnam Generation-A Time of Turmoil and Change, 1988. Coach Little League, Hopatcong, N.J., 1980—; Sunday sch. tchr., elder, trustee 1st Presbyn. Ch., Stanhope, N.J., 1982—. Sgt. U.S. Army, 1966-69, Vietnam. Geraldine R. Dodge Found. grantee, 1987, N.J. Gov.'s Holocaust Commn. grantee, 1988. Mem. NEA, Nat. Coun. Social Studies, N.J. Edn. Assn., N.J. Coun. Social Studies, Assn. Supervision and Curriculum Devel., Vietnam Vets. Am. (sec. 1987), Am. Legion. Democrat. Home: 13 Morris Rd # 1 Stanhope NJ 07874-2420 Office: Roxbury High Sch 1 Bryant Dr Succasunna NJ 07876-1640

WILKER, NACHAMA LAYA, non-profit organization administrator; b. Bristol, Pa., July 6, 1961; d. Morris David and Paulina Joan (Brownie) W.; m. Robert Jonathan Weiner, Aug. 12, 1990. BA, Hampshire Coll., 1984. Project mgr. Solar Office Mass. Office Energy Resources, Boston, 1983; asst. project mgr. Cambridge (Mass.) Energy Rsch. Assocs., 1984-85; exec. dir. Coun. for Responsible Genetics, Cambridge, 1985—; cons. Greenpeace Internat., Washington, 1990, Studen Pugwash, Atlanta, 1992. Editor Gene Watch Bull., 1985-88; contbr. articles to profl. jours. Mem. Sci. for the People, Cambridge, 1982-91, Nat. Abortion Rights Action League, Washington, 1989—. Threshold grantee Hampshire Coll., 1984. Mem. AAAS, UN (non-govtl. rep.). Office: Coun Responsible Genetics 19 Garden St Cambridge MA 02138-3622

WILKES, HILBERT GARRISON, plant science educator; b. L.A., Oct. 2, 1937; s. Hibert Garrison Sr. and Margret Lee (Boggs) W.; m. Marie Dalton Gibby, Apr. 7, 1978; children: Nathan G., Jennifer E., Andrew D., Katharan G. BA cum laude, Pomona Coll., 1959; PhD, Harvard U., 1966. Asst. prof. Tulane U., New Orleans, 1966-70; asst. prof. U. Mass., Boston, 1970-73, assoc. prof. dept. biology, 1974-84, prof., 1984—; Mem. maize germaplasm com. Rockefeller Found., N.Y.C., 1970-90; mem. life sci. assembly NRC/Nat. Acad. Scis., 1973-77, mem. bd. agrl. genetic resources com., Washington, 1987-91. Mem. editorial bd. Jour. Econ. Botany, 1974-91; contbr. over 78 articles to profl. jours. Fulbright scholar Andhra U., India, 1959-60; Indo-Am. Fulbright scholar, India, 1978-79, CIMMYT fellow, Mex., 1985-86. Mem. AAAS, Am. Agronomy Soc., Am. Bot. Soc., Soc. for Econ. Botany (sec. 1973-78, coun. 1978-86, pres. 1985), Conservation Biology Soc. Home: 263 Main St Hingham MA 02043-1935 Office: U Mass Dept Biology Boston MA 02125

WILKINS, ROBERT EUGENE, school counselor; b. Lima, Ohio, May 11, 1944; s. John Absulum and Paulene Faye (Griffiths) W.; m. Gloria Ruth Brown, Dec. 21, 1968; children: Heather, Melissa, Melinda. BS, Ohio State U., 1966; MS, Syracuse U., 1970. Tchr. Mt. Vernon (Ohio) Schs., 1966-69, Oneida (N.Y.) City Schs., 1969-70; sch. counselor Rome (N.Y.) City Schs., 1971—; dir. counseling office Strough Sch./Rome Sch. System, 1990—. Vestry mem. Oneida-St. John's Episc. Ch., 1983, 90, 91; warden St. John's Episc. Ch., Oneida, 1984; treas. Oneida Area Episc. Consortium, 1985-91. Mem. ACA (region treas. 1987-91, conv. bd. 1991—), N.Y. State Assn. Counseling and Devel. (senate 1981-91, fin com. 1987-92, membership chair 1988-92, coord., editor membership directory 1990-92, v.p. profl. svcs. 1992—). Office: Strough Jr High Sch 801 Laurel St Rome NY 13440-3299

WILKINSON, CHRISTOPHER FOSTER, toxicologist, educator; b. Driffield, Yorkshire, Eng., Feb. 9, 1938; came to U.S., 1961; s. Joseph Kemp and Winifred Margaret (Foster) W.; m. Maria Luisa, Aug. 6, 1976; 1 son, Paul Christopher. B.S., U. Reading, 1961; Ph.D., U. Calif.-Riverside, 1965. Sr. research fellow Agrl. Research Council, Pest Infestation Lab., Slough, Bucks, Eng., 1965-66; asst. prof. Cornell U., Ithaca, N.Y., 1966-71, assoc. prof., 1971-78, prof. insecticide chemistry and toxicology, 1978-88; dir. Inst. Comparative and Environ. Toxicology, Cornell U., 1982-85; toxicology cons. Versar, Inc., Springfield, Va., 1988-91; dir. div. toxicology, v.p. Tech. Scis. Group, Inc., Washington, 1991—; mem. adv. com. NIH, Nat. Acad. Sci.; mem. Fed. Insecticide, Fungicide and Rodenticide Act sci. adv. panel EPA, 1983-85. Editor: Insecticide Biochemistry and Physiology, 1976, Effect of Pesticides on Human Health; contbr. 120 articles to profl. publs. Mem. AAAS, Am. Chem. Soc., Soc. Toxicology. Office: Tech Scis Group Inc 1101 17th St NW Washington DC 20036-4704

WILKINSON, JAMES HOWLAND, controller; b. N.Y.C., May 25, 1942; s. James Salmon and Lois Brown (Westerberg) W.; m. Susan Elaine Hayes, May 2, 1964 (div. 1986); m. Karleen Hope Angeli, May 1, 1987; children: Donal, Thea. Student, Brown U., 1960-62; BSBA, Bryant Coll., Smithfield, R.I., 1967. Controller Cooper Labs., Wayne, N.J., 1975, Bairnco, Union, N.J., 1976-80, Knoll Pharm. Co., Whippany, N.J., 1980-83, Am. Health, Mahway, N.J., 1983-87; dir. fin. New Horizon for the Retarded, 1987; controller Union Theol. Sem., N.Y.C., 1987—. Mem. Nat. Assn. Accts., Nat. Assn. Coll. Bus. Officers. Office: 3041 Broadway New York NY 10027-5710

WILL, JAMES FREDRICK, steel company executive; b. Pitts., Oct. 12, 1938; s. Fred F. and Mary Agnes (Ganter) W.; m. Mary Ellen Bowser, Dec. 19, 1964; children: Mary Beth, Kerry Ann. BSEE, Pa. State U., 1961; MBA, Duquesne U., 1972. Works mgr. Kaiser Steel Corp., Fontana, Calif., 1976-78, v.p. ops., 1978-80, v.p. planning, 1980-81, exec. v.p., 1981, pres., 1981-82; exec. v.p., pres. indsl. group Cyclops Corp., Pitts, 1982-86; pres., chief operating officer Cyclops Corp., Pitts., 1986-88, pres., chief exec. officer, 1989—. Home: 1521 Candlewood Dr Pittsburgh PA 15241-2909 Office: Cyclops Corp 650 Washington Rd Pittsburgh PA 15228-2702

WILLAMAN, ROGERT GLENN, business owner; b. Phila., Nov. 30, 1951; s. Robert G. and Mary E. (Fischer) W.; m. Ann H. Thompson, Nov. 18, 1978. BS in Bus. Mgmt., Johnson & Wales Coll., 1980. Asst. credit mgr. A.T. Cross Co., Lincoln, R.I., 1982-85; pres. A.T. Cross Credit Union, Lincoln, 1983-85; credit mgr. Roger Williams Foods, Providence, 1985-89; owner Creditech, Inc., Providence, 1989—. Mem. S.E. Assn. Credit Mgrs (bd. dirs. 1984-90), N.E. Credit Assn. (chmn. Wholesale Meat Dealers sect. 1987-89). Home: 117 Wollaston St Cranston RI 02910-2728 Office: Creditech Inc 6 Blackstone Valley Pl Ste 206 Lincoln RI 02865-1145

WILLARD, THEODORE ELWOOD, occupational safety/health educator; b. Northumberland, N.H., Dec. 14, 1924; s. Arthur O. and Alice C. (Hammanne) W.; m. Linda A. Petris, Aug. 26, 1945; children: Carol A., Eric J., Steven V. BS in Indsl. Tech. summa cum laude, U. So. Maine, 1986. Master electrician, Maine, N.H. Supr. radiol. control Portsmouth Naval Shipyard, Kittery, Maine, 1963-68, radiol. instr., 1968-72, br. head, 1972-78, nuclear engring. technician, 1978-81, div. head, 1981-85; occupational safety/health specialist Lawrence Paige, Inc., Dover, N.H., 1986; occupational safety/health educator Cen. Tex. Coll., Kittery, 1987-88, Hesser Coll., Kittery, 1990—; notary pub. State of Mass., 1950-57; justice of the peace State of Maine, 1955-62, also notary pub. Dir. Civil Def., Lebanon, Maine, 1959; vol. ARC, Rochester, N.H., 1988; pres. Naval Civilian Adm. Assn., Portsmouth Naval Shipyard, 1985; chmn. combined fed. campaign Kittery, 1984-85; chmn. Family Day, 1982. Recipient cert. Appreciation Supt. of Schs., Kittery, 1985, Am. Red Cross, Rochester, 1988. Mem. Am. Soc. Safety Engrs., Am. Safety Coun., Am. Indsl. Hygiene Assn., Am. Congress of Govt. Indsl. Hygienists. Home and Office: 454 Salmon Falls Rd Rochester NH 03868-5705

WILLARD, WANDA ANN, college programs director; b. Ogdensburg, N.Y., Jan. 25, 1962; d. William Floyd and Eleanor Mary (Cardinal) W. BS, St. Lawrence U., 1984, MEd, 1985. Instr. Mater Dei Coll., Ogdensburg, 1985-86, career counselor, 1985-86; dir. field period and career devel. Keuka Coll, Keuka Park, N.Y., 1986-90, dir. experiential programs, 1990—; presenter Rochester Area Colls., Keuka Park, 1989. Instr. ARC, Penn Yan, N.Y., 1990—; facilitator Challenge Ropes Course, Keuka Park, 1990. Named Yates County Career Woman of Yr., Bus. and Profl. Woman's Club, Penn Yan, 1990. Mem. N.Y. State Coop. Experiential Edn. Assn. (nominating com., presenter 1988, 91), Coll. Placement Coun., Nat. Soc. for Internships and Experiential Edn., Coun. for Adult and Experiential Learning, Kiwanis Club Penn Yan (pres. 1989-90).

WILLAUER, GEORGE JACOB, English language educator; b. Phila., Oct. 30, 1935; s. George Jacob and Mary Catherine (Eshleman) W.; m. Cynthia Cameron Thun, June 11, 1966; children: George Jacob III, Elizabeth Christian. BA, Wesleyan U., 1957; MA, U. Pa., 1959, Ph.D., 1965. Asst. instr. U. Pa., Phila., 1958-62; instr. history Conn. Coll., New London, 1962-66, asst. prof., 1966-72, assoc. prof., 1972-78, prof., 1978—; instr. mystic seaport program in maritime studies Williams Coll., 1986-88; chair Dept. English Conn. Coll., 1972-77, 91—. Author: A Lyme Miscellany: 1776-1976, 1977; contbr. articles to profl. jours. Active MacCurdy-Salisbury Ednl. Found., Old Lyme, Conn.; trustee Lyme Hist. Soc., Florence Griswold Mus.; pres. Century Assn., 1983-88. English-Speaking Union fellow, 1969, 72. Mem. AAUP, MLA. Home: 55-1 Beaver Brook Rd Lyme CT 06371 Office: Conn Coll New London CT 06320

WILLCOX, FREDERICK PRESTON, inventor; b. L.A., Aug. 1, 1910; s. Frederick William and Kate Lillian (Preston) W.; m. Velma Rose Gander, 1935; 1 child, Ann Louise. Grad. high sch. Pvt. practice rsch. and devel. engr. and cons., 1939-51, govt. cons., 1949-50, 61-65; tech. v.p. Fairchild Camera & Instrument Corp., 1951-60; inventor R&D lab. New Canaan, Conn., 1960—. Patentee in field of photog. sci. and data communications; photography work exhibited Smithsonian Gallery. Maj. U.S. Army, 1940-45. Recipient Sherman Fairchild Photogrammetric award Am. Soc. Photogrammetry, 1951. Fellow AAAS; mem. ASME, AIAA, Am. Soc. Photogrammetry and Remote Sensing, Soc. Photog. Scientists and Engrs., Optical Soc. Am., Am. Def. Preparedness Assn. Home and Office: 565 Oenoke Rd New Canaan CT 06840-3613

WILLENBECHER, JAMES FREDERIC, engineering executive; b. N.Y.C., Sept. 22, 1943; s. James Frederic and Catherine Anne (Carroll) W.; m. Judith Lorraine Kreyssig, Aug. 26, 1972. BEE, Villanova U., 1966. Engr. Hamilton Stardard, Windsor Locks, Conn., 1966-82; v.p. engring. Crossfire Engring., Inc., East Windsor, Conn., 1982—; cons. in field. Author: (reference book) Concoction of a Beer Engineer, 1990, (software) Master Winemaker, 1988, Master Brewer, 1990; patentee in field. Supr. altar svcs. All Saints Ch., Somersville, Conn., 1988—. Republican. Roman Catholic.

WILLETT, WALTER CHURCHILL, epidemiologist, educator; b. Hart, Mich., June 20, 1945; s. Elwin Lintin and Lawain (Churchill) W.; m. Gail Valerae Pettiford, June 11, 1973; children: Amani, Kamali. Student, Mich. State U., 1963-66; MD, U. Mich., 1970; MPH, Harvard U., 1973, PhD, 1980. Diplomate Am. Bd. Internal Medicine. Lectr. in medicine U. Dar es Salaam, Tanzania, 1974-75, head community health dept., 1975-77; fellow clin. epidemiology Channing Lab. Med. Sch., Harvard U., Boston, 1977-80; asst. prof. epidemiology Sch. Pub. Health, Harvard U., Boston, 1980-84, assoc. prof. epidemiology, 1984-88, prof. epidemiology and nutrition, 1988—, chmn. dept. nutrition, 1991—; statis. cons. New Eng. Jour. Medicine, Boston, 1987—. Author: Nutritional Epidemiology, 1989; contbr. articles to sci. publs. Mem. Am. Epidemiol. Soc., Soc. for Epidemiol. Rsch., Am. Inst. Nutrition, Alpha Omega Alpha. Office: Harvard Sch Pub Health Dept Nutrition 677 Huntington Ave Boston MA 02115-6023

WILLIAMS, ALEXANDER GEORGE, financial analyst, consultant; b. Freetown, Sierra Leone, West Africa, Feb. 6, 1952; came to U.S., 1980; s. Ivan Harold and Muriel Tunde (Refell) W.; m. Daphne M. Newman-Smart, Sept. 10, 1987; 1 child, Avery Harold. BBA, Howard U., 1987; MBA, Morgan State U., 1989; grad., Nat. Coll. Real Estate Appraisal, 1991. Acct. Barclays Bank Internat., Freetown, 1972-80; fin. mgr. Beefstead Charlie's, Washington, 1980-83; investment specialist Crestar Bank N.A., Washington, 1983-89; fin. cons. SJA Assocs., Silver Spring, Md., 1989—; fin. analyst NASW Inc., Capitol Hill, D.C., 1989—. Mem. Cross Road Transafrica, Freetown, 1973. Mem. Fin. Mgmt. Assn. (v.p. 1989-90).

WILLIAMS, ALICE NOEL TUCKERMAN, foundation administrator; b. Bethesda, Md., Dec. 21, 1918; d. Walter Rupert and Edith (Abercrombie-Miller) Tuckerman; m. Robert High Williams, June 21, 1939 (dec. 1983); children: Sarah Fenno Williams Lord, Edith Tuckerman Williams Ward. Ladies bd. St. John's Child Devel. Ctr., Washington, 1960—; pres. ladies bd. St. John's Devel. Ctr., Washington, 1969-72, v.p., bd. of trustees, 1970-72. Mem. The Colonial Dames of Am. (pres. Washington chpt. 1970-74), Sulgrave. Republican. Episcopalian.

WILLIAMS, AUSTIN BEATTY, zoologist; b. Plattsburg, Mo., Oct. 17, 1919; married; 1 child. AB, McPherson Coll., 1943; PhD in Zoology, U. Kans., 1951. Asst. genetics U. Wis., Madison, 1943-44; tchr. pub. sch., Kans., 1944-46; shrimp investigator Inst. Fisheries Rsch., U. N.C., 1951-52, asst. prof., 1952-55, assoc. prof. Inst. Marine Sci., 1956-63; prof. U. N.C.,

1964-71; asst. prof. U. Ill., Urbana, 1955-56; systematic zoologist Nat. Systems Lab., Nat. Marine Fisheries Svc., Washington, 1971—; researcher in field. Fellow AAAS; mem. Am. Soc. Zoologists, Ecol. Soc. Am., Soc. Systematic Biology (sec. 1985-88), Estuarine Rsch. Fedn. (sec. 1972-73, v.p. 1980-81, pres. 1983-85), Biol. Soc. Washington (editor 1974-77, v.p. 1984-86, pres. 1986-88), Am. Soc. Zool. Nomenclature (v.p. 1989-90, pres. 1990-91). Office: Systematics Lab US Nat Mus Natural History Nat Marine Fisheries Svc Washington DC 20560

WILLIAMS, BABETTE DEANNA, lawyer; b. Washington, July 12, 1960; d. Robert N. Williams and B. Brenda (Lewis) Joyce. BA, Vassar Coll., 1982; JD, Howard U., 1985. Bar: Md. 1986. Treas. BeJay Enterprises, Washington, 1980—; asst. dir. BeJay Learning Ctr., Washington, 1984-86; intern Securities Exch. Commn., Washington, 1984-85; atty. advisor, Benefits Rev. Bd. Dept. Labor, Washington, 1987-88, dep. assoc. chief counsel, 1988—. Mem. Martin Luther King D.C. Support Group, 1985—. Recipient Am. Jurisprudence award Howard Univ. Sch. Law, Washington, 1983. Mem. ABA, Md. Bar Assn., NAACP, Vassar Coll. Student Assn. (chmn. bd. elections 1981-82, class rep. master planning com. 1982), Phi Delta Phi, Zeta Phi Beta (phylacter Eta Pi Zeta chpt. 1990—, Scholastic Achievement awards 1978). Baptist. Home: 701 Winhall Way PO Box 4195 Silver Spring MD 20914-0195 Office: Benefits Review Board Dept Labor 800 K St NW Ste 500 Washington DC 20001-8001

WILLIAMS, BARBARA IVORY, educational researcher; b. Detroit, Apr. 28, 1936; d. Henry Oliver and Willa Mae (Frazier) I.; m. Alney Elliott Whitener, Jan. 1, 1987. BS, Wayne State U., 1957, MEd, 1960; PhD, U. Washington, 1973. Tchr. Detroit Pub. Schs., 1957-68; program assoc. Mich.-Ohio Regional Lab., Detroit, 1968-70; lectr. predoctoral U. Wash., Seattle, 1970-73; sr. program assoc. Far West Lab. for Ednl. Research and Devel., San Francisco, 1973-76; sr. cons. E.H. White & Co., San Francisco, 1976-77; sr. program assoc. Northwest Regional Lab., Portland, Oreg., 1977-84; area coord. Ednl. Testing Service, Washington, 1984-85; edn. group dir. Research and Evaluation Assocs., Washington, 1985-87; ind. cons. Washington, 1987-89; sr. rsch. assoc. Westat, Rockville, Md., 1989—. Mem. Am. Ednl. Research Assn., Am. Psychol. Assn., Nat. Assn. Black Sch. Educators, Phi Delta Kappa, Alpha Kappa Alpha (pres. Portland chpt. 1980-84). Democrat. Baptist. Home: 408 Crittenden St NW Washington DC 20011-4741

WILLIAMS, BRUCE DAVID, financial consultant; b. Washington, June 15, 1932; s. Leo Nicholas and Ruth (Hager) W.; m. Deirdre O'Brien; children: Katherine, Nicole. AB, Harvard U., 1954; MBA, Stanford U., 1956. V.p., treas. Ingersoll-Rand Co., Woodcliff Lake, N.J., 1961-83; mng. dir. Corp. Fin. Assocs., Englewood, N.J., 1984—. Bd. dirs. Englewood (N.J.) Hosp., 1981—; bd. dirs., pres. YMCA Greater Bergen County, Hackensack, N.J., 1989—. Home: 391 Johnson Ave Englewood NJ 07631-2017 Office: Corp Fin Assocs 391 Johnson Ave Englewood NJ 07631-2017

WILLIAMS, BRUCE EDWARD, education educator, consultant; b. St. Paul, Sept. 2, 1931; s. Charles and Mildred (Vance) W.; m. Wilma Elizabeth Lowe, Dec. 21, 1962; children: Deborah Lynn, Lisa Marie. BS, Mankato State U., 1956, MS, 1970; PhD, Union Grad. Sch., Yellow Springs, Ohio, 1977. Juvenile detention officer Hennepin County Detention Ctr., Mpls., 1959-61; tchr. Mpls. Pub. Schs., 1961-68, asst. prin., 1968-70, asst. supt., 1971-72; intern supt. Balt. and Trenton, N.J., 1970-71; asst. dir. Rockfeller Found., N.Y.C., 1972-88; dep. chancellor N.Y.C. Pub. Schs., 1988-89; prof. edn. Hunter Coll., CUNY, 1989—; mem. adv. coun. Coll. Bd., N.Y.C., 1988. Mem. editorial bd. Urban Rev. Pres., trustee Gen. Edn. Bd., N.Y.C., 1980—; trustee Macalester Coll., St. Paul, 1979—, Freedom House, N.Y.C.; mem. adv. com. Nat. Urban League; mem. N.Y. State Gov.'s Adv. Commn. With U.S. Army, 1957-59. Rockefeller Found. fellow, 1970. Mem. Am. Assn. Sch. Adminstrs., Assn. Black Found. Execs. Home: 601 Brook St Mamaroneck NY 10543 Office: CUNY Hunter Coll 695 Park Ave New York NY 10021-5085

WILLIAMS, CARL CHANSON, publishing company executive; b. Cin., Oct. 16, 1937; s. Charles J. and Alcie (Brazile) W.; m. Clare Bathé, May 26, 1985; 1 child, Michelle. A.S., U. Cin., 1965; B.S., SUNY-Brockport, 1974; M.B.A., U. Rochester, 1975. Mgr. fin. systems Xerox Corp., Rochester, N.Y., 1972-77; dir. info. mgmt. Am. Can Co., Greenwich, Conn., 1977-79, mng. dir. info. mgmt., 1979-80, mng. dir. ops. control, 1980-82; sr. v.p., dir. mgmt. info. systems DDB Needham Worldwide, N.Y.C., 1982-90; pres. The Intertechnology Group, Inc., N.Y.C., 1990-91; v.p. infosystems and tech. Macmillian Pub. Co., N.Y.C., 1991—; cons. Stamford Bd. Edn., Conn., 1981-82; lectr. U. Rochester, N.Y., 1975-77; adj. prof. Fordham U., 1991. Exec. dir. Concerned Assn. Rochester, N.Y., 1971-75 bd. dirs. Stamford Community Arts Council, 1983-84. Mem. Soc. Info. Mgmt. (exec. council 1980-83, pres. 1985, pres. coun. 1986—). Office: Macmillan Pub Co 866 3rd Ave New York NY 10022-6221

WILLIAMS, CAROL JORGENSEN, social work educator; b. New Brunswick, N.J., Aug. 12, 1944; d. Einar Arthur and Mildred Estelle (Clayton) Jorgensen; m. Oneal Alexander Williams, July 4, 1980. BA, Douglass Coll., 1966; MS in Computer Sci., Stevens Inst. Tech., 1986; MSW, Rutgers U., 1971, PhD in Social Policy, 1981. Child welfare worker Bur. Children's Svcs., Jersey City, 1966-67, Outagamie County Dept. Social Svcs., Appleton, Wis., 1967-69; supr. WIN N.J. Div. Youth and Family Svcs., New Brunswick, 1969-70; coord. Outreach Plainfield (N.J.) Pub. Libr., 1972-76; rsch. project dir. County and Mcpl. Govt. Study Commn., N.J. State Legislature, 1976-79; assoc. prof. social work Kean Coll. of N.J., Union, 1979—; assessment liaison social work program Kean Coll. of N.J., Union, 1987—; cons. N.J. Div. Youth and Family Svcs., 1979—, Assn. for Children N.J., 1985-88; cons., evaluator Thomas A. Edison Coll., 1977—, mem. acad. coun., others; chair gen. edn. com. Kean Coll. of N.J. Mem. NAFE, NOW, Council on Social Work Edn., Nat. Assn. Social Workers, Assn. for Computing Machinery, Am. Evaluators' Assn., Kean Coll. Fedn. Tchrs. Democrat. Clubs: Good Sam (Agoura, Calif.); Outdoor World (Bushkill, Pa.). Home: 32 Halstead Rd New Brunswick NJ 08901-1619 Office: Social Work Program Kean Coll of NJ Morris Ave Union NJ 07083-7117

WILLIAMS, CLARENCE LEON, management, sociology and public policy company executive, educator; b. Longview, Tex., Aug. 9, 1937; s. Ruby Marlene (McLemore) W.; m. Kathleen Susan Robbins, June 7, 1975; children: Clarence Leon 2d, Thomas Chatterton. BA, Prairie View A&M U., 1959; MA in Sociology, Calif. State U., 1973; postgrad., U. Oreg., 1973-75. Exec. dir. Galveston County (Tex.) Community Action Coun., 1966-68, San Diego County (Calif.) Econ. Opportunity Commn., 1969-70; from assoc. dep. dir. program and contract dept. to dir. budgeting, planning, rsch. and evaluation dept. Econ. and Youth Opportunities Agy., Inc., L.A., 1970-71; dir. Rocky Mtn. Forum Internat. Issues, Denver, 1976-77; cons., adminstr. Regional Ctr. for Health Planning and Rsch. Svcs., Inc., Phila., 1977-78; with Albany (N.Y.) Interracial Coun., Inc., 1978-80; pres. Williams Academic and Pub. Policy Svcs., Fanwood, N.J., 1981—; vis. asst. prof., assoc. prof. Grad. Sch. Internat. Studies, U. Denver, 1976-77; asst. prof., dir. Black Edn. Program Ea. Wash. State Coll., 1975-76; policy analyst, speaker, guest panelist various colls., univs., instns. nationally and internationally including U. Iowa, U. Krakow (Poland), U. Lodz (Poland), Warsaw (Poland) U., U. Erlangen (Fed. Republic Germany), Polish Inst. Sociology, Bergen County (N.J.) Ethical Culture Soc., 1965-92; policy analyst, mgmt. cons. Nat. Rural Ctr., Washington, 1976-79, Computerland and Computer Showcase Inc., N.J., 1987-88. Policy analyst, adv. mem. numerous task forces, govtl. confs. including Kettering Found. programs and confs. on econ. devel. in Asia, Africa, Latin Am., on trans-national dialog in Senegal, Mali, West Africa, 1976-80, Nat. Alliance of Businessmen, 1973-75, White House Conf. on Aging, 1967, White House Conf. on Hunger, Nutrition, Health and Poverty, 1969, Pres.' Adv. Coun. on Reorganization of OEO, 1971; regional race rels./intergroup rels. officer Home and Housing Fin. Agy., Washington, 1964-66; mem. Citizen Amb. Program, Russia and Ea. Europe, 1992. With USAF, 1961-64. Recipient Das Family Acad. Rsch. award, 1992; rsch. grantee Woodrow Wilson Nat. Found.; fellow Ford Found., Martin Luther King, Jr., Woodrow Wilson Found., U. Oreg., 1973-75; named U.S. Rep. to U.N. Human Rights 30th Anniversary Commemorative Programs, Europe, 1979-80. Mem. Alpha Kappa Delta, Phi Kappa Phi. Home and Office: 222 N Martine Ave Fanwood NJ 07023

WILLIAMS, CURTIS ALVIN, JR., biology educator, researcher; b. Moorestown, N.J., June 26, 1927; s. Curtis Alvin and Nola (Johnson) W.; m. Marjorie King, Jan. 20, 1960; children: Jennifer, Scott, Elisabeth. BS, Pa. State U., 1950; PhD, Rutgers U., 1954. Postdoctoral fellow USPHS Pasteur Inst., Paris, 1953-54, Carlsberg Lab., Copenhagen, 1954-55; successively rsch. assoc., asst. prof., assoc. prof. Rockefeller U., N.Y.C., 1955-78; scientist NIH, Bethesda, Md., 1957-60; prof. in biology SUNY, Purchase, 1970—, also dean div. Natural Scis., 1970-80; adj. prof. N.Y.U. Sch. Medicine, N.Y.C., 1976-88; vis. prof. Univ Coll., London, 1978-79, U. So. Calif., L.A., 1985-86; trustee Wenner-Gren Found., N.Y.C., 1991—. Editor: Methods in Immunology and Immunochemistry Vols I through V, 1967-70; contbr. more than 100 articles, reports and revs. to profl. jours. Dir. Friends Neuberger Mus. Art, Purchase, 1986—. With USNR, 1945. Recipient Founders award Internat. Electrophoresis Soc., 1982; fellow NSF, 1978,rsch. grantee, NIH and other orgns., 1959—. Office: SUNY Div Natural Sci Purchase NY 10577

WILLIAMS, DAVID KEITH, software engineer; b. Exeter, N.H., Mar. 4, 1965; s. Horace Robert and Arlene Emily (Locke) W. BS, U. N.H., 1987. Software engr. Micro-Integration, Newmarket, N.H., 1988-89, Alloy Computer Products, Marlboro, Mass., 1989-90, Cableton Systems, Inc., Rochester, N.H., 1990—; cons. in field. Asst. scoutmaster Boy Scouts Am., Newton Junction, N.H., 1986-91. Republican. Baptist.

WILLIAMS, DAVID LLOYD, research chemist, consultant; b. Springfield, Mass., Aug. 15, 1935; s. Lloyd George and Gladys (Danes) W.; m. Virginia Tingley, Oct. 18, 1964. BS in Chemistry and Physics, Trinity Coll., Hartford, Conn., 1957; PhD in Chemistry, Northwestern U., 1962. Sr. rsch. chemist Monsanto Co., Everett, Mass., 1961-69, Am. Hosp. Supply Corp., Everett, 1969-70; program mgr. Abcor Inc., Wilmington, Mass., 1971-80; dir. rsch. Biotek, Inc., Woburn, Mass., 1980-84; staff cons. Arthur D. Little Inc., Cambridge, Mass., 1984-85; sr. scientist Giner, Inc., Waltham, Mass., 1985-88, Copley Pharm. Inc., Canton, Mass., 1988-92, Genetics Inst., Andover, Mass., 1992—; vis. lectr. Salem (Mass.) State Coll., 1990. Contbr. articles to profl. jours.; patentee in field. Rsch. grantee NIH, 1985-91. Mem. Internat. Assn. Dental Rsch., Am. Chem. Soc., Sigma Xi. Home: 258 Haverhill St Reading MA 01867-1808 Office: Genetics Inst 1 Burtt Rd Andover MA 01810

WILLIAMS, DAVID ROYAL, high school basketball coach; b. New Castle, Pa., Aug. 10, 1937; s. Albert and Helen Cronin (Schley) W.; m. Margaret Rose Grieve, May 23, 1959; children: Douglas, Daniel. BS in Edn., Slippery Rock U., 1961; MEd in Counseling, Duquesne U., 1964, MEd in Adminstrn., 1972. Cert. secondary Eng. tchr., history tchr., guidance counselor, prin., Pa. Basketball coach Avonworth High Sch., 1965-77, 89—; coach U.S. Roundball Classic, Pitts., 1972. Deacon, Woodland U.P. Ch., Pitts., 1972-75; sec. Avonworth Mcpl. Authority, Pitts., 1974-77; elder Emsworth (Pa.) U.P. Ch., 1985-88. With U.S. Army, 1955-57. Named Coach of Yr. Western Pa. Interscholastic Athletic League, 1967, '68,'69, '70' '71, '72, '74, '75, '77, '90, '91. Mem. Masons. Home: 426 Walnut Rd Pittsburgh PA 15202-2028 Office: Avonworth High Sch Joseph's Ln Pittsburgh PA 15237

WILLIAMS, DAVID VANDERGRIFT, organizational psychologist; b. Balt., Feb. 5, 1943; s. Laurence Leighton and Mary Duke (Warfield) W.; m. Diane M. Gayeski, Aug. 23, 1980; 1 child, Evan David Williams. BA, Gettysburg (Pa.) Coll., 1965; MA, Temple U., 1967; PhD, U. Pa., 1971. Asst. prof. psychology Ithaca (N.Y.) Coll., 1970-75, assoc. prof. psychology, 1975—; ptnr. OmniCom Assocs., Ithaca, 1979—; Cons. and speaker in field. Co-author: Interactive Media, 1985, (computer based tng.), interactive video software, 1979—; contbr. to books and articles to profl. jours. Bd. dirs. McCormick Ctr., Brooktondale, N.Y., 1988—, Ctr. for Religion, Ethics and Social Policy, Cornell U., 1975-77, Eco-Justice Task Force, Ithaca, 1975-78. Rsch. fellow U.S. Office of Edn., 1967-70; recipient various grants. Mem. ASTD, Am. Psychol. Soc., Nat. Soc. for Performance and Instrn., Am. Correctional Assn., Am. Montessori Soc., Ithaca Yacht Club. Office: OmniCom Assocs 407 Coddington Rd Ithaca NY 14850

WILLIAMS, DENNIS VAUGHN, lawyer, educator; b. Wilkinsburg, Pa., June 3, 1946; s. Thomas Ulysses and Margaret Louise (Pfefferman) W.; m. Shirley Ann Kramer, July 26, 1979; children: Kristin Elizabeth, Katrina Alexandra, Leah Nicole, Shaun Leighton. BBA, Ohio U., 1968; JD, Duquesne U., 1973. Par: Pa. 1973, U.S. Dist. Ct. (we. dist.) Pa. 1973, U.S. Ct. Appeals (3d cir.) 1982, U.S. Supreme Ct. 1987. Gen. counsel Domestic Abuse Office-Women's Shelter, Erie, Pa., 1977-81, Hospitality House-Women's Shelter, Erie, 1981—; instr. Mercyhurst Coll., Erie, 1984—; pvt. practice Erie, 1973—; bd. dirs. Lakeview Devel., Inc., Erie, 1975—; instr. Pa. Dep. Sheriff Tng. Act. Bd. dirs. Am. Cancer Soc., 1986—. With U.S. Army, 1968-70, res. 1970-74. Mem. ABA, Pa. Bar Assn., Pa. Trial Lawyers Assn., Am. Legion. Democrat. Greek Orthodox. Lodge: Elks. Home: 3845 Beech Ave Erie PA 16508-3112 Office: Williams & Adair 332 E 6th St Erie PA 16507-1696

WILLIAMS, DEXTER BRADFORD, controller, financial consultant; b. Boston, Dec. 19, 1950; s. Frederick Washington and Ruth Edith (Crowe) W.; m. Eleanor Louise Dolan, Apr. 12, 1980; children: Bradford Andrew, Cory Brandon. BS in Acctg., Bentley Coll., 1972; MBA, Babson Coll., 1975. Staff auditor Arthur Andersen and Co., Boston, 1972-73; treas. Williams Bus. Products Inc., Boston, 1974-79; acctg. supr. Parker Bros., Beverly, Mass., 1979-80; acctg. mgr. Nat. Med. Care, Inc., Waltham, Mass., 1981-84; asst. contr. Ingalls, Quinn and Johnson, Inc., Boston, 1984-87; contr. Campbell & Assocs., P.C., Cambridge, Mass., 1988—; mng. dir. DBW Tax Preparation Svc., Belmont, Mass., 1976—. Trustee Plymouth Congl. Ch., Belmont, 1990—. Republican.

WILLIAMS, DIANE THERESA, utilities executive; b. Pittston, Pa., Mar. 1, 1955; d. Edward Joseph and Mary Jane (Messitt) Gilroy; m. Joseph Patrick Williams, Jan. 28, 1978. BS, Pa. State U., 1977. Lic. comml. pesticide applicator, Pa. Forest fire patrolman Pa. Bur. Forestry, Scranton, 1977, fire warden, youth leader, 1976-77; city arborist City of Lancaster, Pa., 1978-80; line clearance insp. Pa. Power & Light Co., Honesdale, 1980—. Mem. Am. Horse Show Assn., Soc. Am. Foresters, Internat. Soc. Arborculture. Republican. Roman Catholic. Home: PO Box 367A Lake Ariel PA 18436-0367 Office: Pa Power & Light Co RR 4 Lake Ariel PA 18436-9804

WILLIAMS, DONALD JOHN, research physicist; b. Fitchburg, Mass., Dec. 25, 1933; s. Toivo John and Ina (Kokkinen) W.; m. Priscilla Mary Gagnon, July 4, 1953; children: Steven John, Craig Mitchell, Eino Stenroos. B.S., Yale U., 1955, M.S., 1958, Ph.D., 1962. Sr. staff physicist Applied Physics Lab., Johns Hopkins U., 1961-65; head particle physics br. Goddard Space Flight Center, NASA, 1965-70; dir. Space Environ. Lab., NOAA, Boulder, Colo., 1970-82; prin. investigator Energetic Particles expt. NASA Galileo Mission, 1977—; prin. staff physicist Johns Hopkins U. Applied Physics Lab., 1982-89, dir. Milton S. Eisenhower Rsch. Ctr., 1990—; mem. nat. and internat. sci. planning coms.; chmn. NAS com. on solar-terrestrial rsch., 1989—. Author: (with L.R. Lyons) Quantitative Aspects of Magnetospheric Physics, 1983; assoc. editor: Jour. Geophys. Research, 1967-69, Revs. of Geophysics and Space Research, 1984-86; editor: (with G.D. Mead) Physics of the Magnetosphere, 1969, Physics of Solar-Planetary Environments, 1976; mem. editorial bd.: Space Sci. Revs., 1975-85; contbr. articles to profl. jours. Served to lt. USAF, 1955-57. Recipient Sci. Research award, 1974; Disting. Authorship award, 1976, 85. Fellow Am. Geophys. Soc.; mem. Am. Phys. Soc., Internat. Assn. Geomagnetism and Aeronomy (pres. 1991—), Sigma Xi. Home: 14870 Triadelphia Rd Glenelg MD 21737-9408

WILLIAMS, DUANE EDWARD, military officer; b. Santa Rosa, Calif., Feb. 6, 1944; s. Bernard Edward and Florence Jane (McCleaf) W.; m. Donna Rae Marzetta, Dec. 21, 1969; 1 child, Nicole Elaine. BSEE, Va. Mil. Inst., 1966; MA in Mgmt., Webster U., 1980. Commd. lt. U.S. Army, 1966, advanced through grades to col., 1989; area commdr. U.S. Army Recruiting Command, Pitts., 1975-77; exec. officer 1st battalion 319th Field Artillery, Ft. Bragg, N.C., 1977-79; G-3 team chief XVIII ABN Corps, Ft. Bragg, 1979; ops. officer Carribean Cont Joint Task Force, Key West, Fla., 1979-81; county dir. Office of Sec. of Def., Washington, 1981-83; comdr 1st Bn. 320th Field Arty., Ft. Bragg, 1983-85; div. chief Combined Arms Div., Ft. Benning, Ga., 1985-88; pres., chief exec. officer Growers Equipment Ctr., Biglerville, Pa., 1991—; dir. mil. requirements and capabilities Dept. of Command, Leadership and Mgmt., U.S. Army War Coll., Carlisle Barracks, 1988—. Co-author: Department of Command Leadership & Management Textbook/Army Command and Management: Theory and Practice, 1989—. Vestry mem. Episcopal Ch., N.C., Pa., 1979-81, Pa., 1988—; pres. VMI Alumni Assn. Chpt., Ga., Pa., 1987—. Decorated Bronze Star medal and various other mil. awards U.S. Govt., 1966—. Mem. IEEE, Assn. of U.S. Army, NRA (life.). Office: U S Army War Coll Carlisle Barracks Carlisle PA 17013

WILLIAMS, EARL PATRICK, JR., editor, freelance writer; b. Washington, May 14, 1950; s. Earl Patrick Sr. and Charlie Mae (Wright) W.; m. Susan Miller Day, July 20, 1985. BA, U. Md., 1973; postgrad., Cath. U., 1974. Duplication machine operator Applied Physics Lab. Johns Hopkins U., Silver Spring, Md., 1968-75; substitute tchr. Fairfax County Va. Schs., 1974-75; clk. U.S. Govt. Printing Office, Washington, 1975-76, editor, 1976—; freelance writer, Washington, 1974—. Author: Amtrak's Washington-New York Corridor, 1977, What You Should Know About the American Flag, 1987, What You Should Know About Flags of the Confederacy, 1992; contbr. articles to mags. and newspapers. Active in efforts to achieve recognition of Francis Hopkinson, the designer of first ofcl. U.S. flag; lectr. to sch. groups and civic orgns. on the history of the U.S. flag; mem. N.J. Coun. for Social Studies. Nat. Cathedral Assn., N.Am. Vexillological Assn. Democrat. Presbyterian. Home: 2323 40th Pl NW Apt 201 Washington DC 20007-1617

WILLIAMS, EDWARD DAVID, data processing executive; b. Scranton, Pa., June 20, 1932; s. David Thomas and Mabel (Sims) W. m. Natalie Imnadze, Oct. 18, 1952; children: Denise, Claudia. BBA, Hofstra U., 1960; postgrad. in Bus. Adminstrn., Fairleigh Dickenson U., 1979. Cons. Cresap, McCormick and Paget, N.Y.C., 1964-65; sr. mgmt. cons. Union Carbide Corp., N.Y.C., 1965-67; asst. contr. data processing Western Union, N.Y.C., 1967-69; v.p. mgmt. info. systems ABC, Hackensack, N.J., 1970-86; v.p., chief info. officer Blue Cross Blue Shield of N.J., Newark, 1986-88; v.p. Chantico Pub. Co., Carrellton, Tex., 1989-90; pres. SMC-BIS Inc., Basking Ridge, N.J., 1990—. Speaker in field. Mem. adv. bd. YMCA. With U.S. Army, 1948-52. Decorated Silver Star with oak leaf cluster, Bronze Star with V, Purple Heart with 2 oak leaf clusters. Mem. Soc. Mgmt. Info. Systems, N.J. C. of C., Profit Oriented Systems Planning Bd. (bd. dirs.), Masons. Republican. Office: Science Management Corp PO Box 0600 12 Vreeland Rd Basking Ridge NJ 07920

WILLIAMS, ELLWOOD ELIJAH (ELLWOODSON WILLIAMS), drama educator; b. Jacksonville, N.C., June 17, 1937; s. James Ivy and Vallie (Rhodes) W. BA, Tenn. State U., 1965, MA, 1966. Tchr. aid Tenn. State U., Nashville, 1964-65; tchr. Lincoln U., Jefferson City, Mo., 1966-68; assoc. prof. drama and speech Manhattan Community Coll., N.Y.C., 1969—; playwright Bed-Sty Community Theatre, 1970-72, Harlem Community Workshop, 1978-81, Silvera Writers Workshop, 1980-91. Actor Broadway plays Murderous Angels, 1972-73, Two Gentlemen of Verona, 1973-74; played prin. role in Tony award winning musical on Broadway, 1973; co-author: Speech Communication Workbook, 1989. Recipient Best Actor award Nat. Assn. Dramatic and Speech Arts, Tuskegee, Ala., 1961. Mem. SAG, Actors Equity Assn. Democrat. Baptist. Home: 176 W 87th St New York NY 10024-2902 Office: Manhattan Community Ctr 199 Chambers St #N675 New York NY 10007

WILLIAMS, FRANK J., lawyer, judge; b. Providence, Aug. 24, 1940; s. Frank and Natalie L. (Corelli) W.; m. Virginia E. Miller, Aug. 24, 1966. BA, Boston U., 1962, JD, 1970, MS in Taxation, Bryant Coll., 1986, LHD Lincoln Coll., 1987. Bar: R.I. 1970, U.S. Dist. Ct. R.I. 1970, U.S. Supreme Ct. 1976. Assoc. Tillinghast, Collins & Graham, Providence, 1970-75, Leonard Decof Ltd., Providence, 1976-78; law clk. Graham, Reid, Ewing & Stapleton, Providence, 1969; law clk., adminstrv. asst. R.I. atty. gen., Providence, 1967-68; pres. Frank J. Williams Ltd., attys.-at-law, Providence, 1978—; judge of probate Town of Hopkinton (R.I.), 1978-82, 84-90, solicitor, 1978-82, 84-87; judge of probate Town of West Greenwich, R.I., 1984-86, solicitor, 1984—; dep. judge of probate, 1987—; solicitor Town of Coventry, R.I., 1972-74, 76-78; past spl. counsel Towns of Westerly, Bristol, Hopkinton; atty. Town of Smithfield Sewer Authority, 1974-90; legis. Counsel R.I. Retail Fedn., R.I. Chain Drugstore Comm., R.I. Credit Reporting Alliance, R.I. Mortgage Bankers Assn.; lectr. bus. and legal practices R.I. Sch. Design, Providence, 1976-80; mem. panel of arbitrators Am. Arbitration Assn.; mem. R.I. Bd. of Bar Examiners, 1987—. Pres. Lincoln Group of Boston, 1976-88; pres. Abraham Lincoln Assn. Springfield, Ill. 1986—, Ulysses S. Grant Assn., 1990—; del. R.I. Constitutional Conv., 1986; bd. dirs., sec. John E. Fogarty Found. for Mentally Retarded; mem. corp. Roger Williams Coll.; bd. dirs. Narragansett council Boy Scouts Am., 1969-80; chmn. Lincoln adv. com. Brown U.; mem. Lincoln prize adv. com. Gettysburg Coll. Served to capt. U.S. Army, 1962-67; Vietnam. Decorated Bronze Star, Republic of Vietnam Gallantry Cross with silver star, combat infantryman's badge, Air medal with 2 oak cleaf clusters. Mem. ABA, R.I. Bar Assn. (ho. of dels. 1986—, chmn. new lawyers adv. com. 1976-87), Am. Judicature Soc., Nat. Coll. Probate Judges. Roman Catholic. also: 1111 Main St Hope Valley RI 02903

WILLIAMS, FREDERICK BOYD, priest; b. Chattanooga, Apr. 23, 1939; s. Walter Howard and Matlyn (Goodman) W. BA, Morehouse Coll., 1959; MS, Howard U., 1960; STB, Gen. Theo. Sem., 1963; DMin, Colgate-Rochester Divinity Sch, 1975. Rsch. mathematician NASA, Greenbelt, Md., 1959-60; curate St. Luke's Episc. Ch., Washington, 1963-65; rector St. Clement's Episc. Ch., Inkster, Mich., 1966-72, Church of the Intercession, N.Y.C., 1972—; hon. canon Diocese of Botswana, Gabarone, Africa, 1979—. Contbr. articles to profl. jours. Com. mem. HIV curriculum N.Y.C. Bd. Edn., 1991—; chmn. Harlem Churches for Community Improvement, Inc., N.Y.C., 1991—, Nat. Conf. on AIDS, N.Y.C., 1992—; commr. Black Leadership Commn. on AIDS, N.Y.C., 1991—; mem. adv. bd. Anglican Rep. to UN, N.Y.C., 1992—; founder, treas. Conf. on Afro-Anglicanism, London, 1984—. Recipient scholarship Ford Found. 1955-59, Merrill fellow Harvard U. 1984. Mem. Kappa Alpha Psi, Pi Mu Epsilon, Delta Sigma Rho, Alpha Phi Gamma. Office: 550 West 155th St New York NY 10032

WILLIAMS, GARY MICHAEL, English educator; b. S.I., N.Y., Nov. 17, 1964; s. Gary and Dolores (Giordano) W. BA in Elem. Edn., BA in ESL, St. John's U., S.I., 1986; MS in Elem. Edn., MS in ESL, Coll. S.I., 1990. Tchr. ESL Pub. Sch. 95, Bklyn., 1986—. Mem. Lions (sec. 1987—). Home: 417 Canterbury Ave Staten Island NY 10314

WILLIAMS, GARY MURRAY, medical researcher, pathology educator; b. Regina, Sask., Can., May 7, 1940; s. Murray Austin and Selma Ruby (Domstad) W.; m. Christine Julia Lundberg; children: Walter, Jeffrey, Ingrid. BA, Washington and Jefferson Coll., 1963; MD, U. Pitts, 1967. Diplomate Am. Bd. Pathology, Am. Bd. Toxicology. Assoc. prof. pathology Temple U., Phila., 1971-75; mem. Fels Rsch. Inst., Phila., 1971-75; rsch. prof. N.Y. Med. Coll., Valhalla, 1975—; dir. med. scis., chief. pathology and toxicology div. Am. Health Found., Valhalla, 1975—; mem. toxicology study sect. NIH, Bethesda, Md., 1985-87; mem. working groups Internat. Agy. Rsch. on Cancer, Lyon, France, 1986, 87, 89, 91. Editor: Sweeteners: Health Effects, 1988; co-editor: Cellular Systems for Toxicity Testing, 1983; editor in chief Cell Biology and Toxicology, 1984—; author 320 sci. papers. Lt. comdr. USPHS, 1969-71. Recipient Sheard-Sanford award Am. Soc. Clin. Pathologists U. Pitts., 1967. Mem. Am. Assn. Cancer Rsch., Am. Assn. Pathologists, Soc. Toxicology (Arnold J. Lehman award 1982), Luth. Brotherhood Fraternal Soc. (dist. pres. 1988-90), Phi Beta Kappa, Alpha Omega Alpha. Home: 8 Elm Rd Scarsdale NY 10583-1410 Office: Am Health Found 1 Dana Rd Valhalla NY 10595-1549

WILLIAMS, GEORGE LEO, retired educator; b. N.Y.C., June 29, 1931; s. Leo Dominick and Cathryn Margaret (Schellderfer) W.; m. Adelia Gilda Musa, Feb. 26, 1958; children: Adelia, Marina, Gilda. BA, CUNY, 1953, MA, 1955; PhD, NYU, 1966. Tchr. Port Washington (N.Y.) Pub. Schs., 1953, chairperson integrated studies, 1960-65, coord. Amherst project, 1968-69, chairperson English dept., 1970-90; adminstrv. asst. secondary and higher edn. dept. NYU, N.Y.C., 1965-66; adj. prof. NYU, 1966-74, Adelphi U., Garden City, N.Y. 1967-69, Hofstra U., Hempstead, N.Y., 1967-74; chmn.

profl. growth and devel. com. Port Washington Pub. Schs., 1973-90, chmn. bicentennial com. 1989-90, mem. policy bd. Port Washington Tchr. Ctr., 1987-90. Author: (with others) (play) The Triumph of the Constitution, 1988; contbg. editor L.I. Forum, 1982—; editor Port Arrow Community Newsletter, 1973-84, Cow Neck Peninsula Hist. Soc. Newsletter, 1974-77. Chairperson landmarks com. Cow Neck Peninsula Hist. Soc., Port Washington, 1980—, trustee, 1974-77; commr. landmarks com. Village of Port Washington North, 1983—, chmn., 1991; chair Hist. Landmark Preservation Commn., North Hempstead, N.Y., 1984—; mem. Port Washington Continuing Edn. Adv. Coun. Fulbright grantee, 1959. Mem. ASCD, Nat. Coun. Tchrs. English, Soc. for Presrvation L.I. Antiquities, Port Washington Tchrs. Assn. (v.p. 1963-64, bd. dirs. 1966-74, founder ret. tchrs. chpt. 1991, mewsletter editor 1990-92), Am. Hist. Assn. (cert. of recognition 1988), Friends for L.I.'s Heritage, Roslyn Landmark Soc., N.Y. Geneal. and Biog. Soc., N.Y. State Hist. Assn., Phi Beta Kappa, Phi Alpha Theta, Pi Sigma Alpha. Home: 84 Radcliff Ave Port Washington NY 11050-1600

WILLIAMS, HARRIET CLARKE, retired academic administrator, artist; b. Bklyn., Sept. 5, 1922; d. Herbert Edward and Emma Clarke (Gibbs) W. AA, Bklyn. Coll., 1958; student, Art Career Sch., N.Y.C., 1960; cert., Hunter Coll., 1965, CPU Inst. Data Processing, 1967; student, Chineses Cultural Ctr., N.Y.C., 1973; hon. certs., St. Labre Sch./St. Joseph's, Ind. Sch., Mont., 1990. Adminstr. Baruch Coll., N.Y.C., 1959-85; mktg. researcher 1st Presbyn. Arts and Crafts Shop, Jamaica, N.Y., 1986—; tutor in art St. John's U., Jamaica, 1986—; founder, curator Internat. Art Gallery, Queens, N.Y., 1991—. Exhibited in group shows at Union Carbide Art Exhibit, N.Y.C., 1975, Queens Day Exhbn., N.Y.C., 1980, 1st Presbyn. Arts and Crafts Shop, N.Y.C., 1986, others; contbr. articles to profl. publs. Vol. reading tchr. Mabel Dean Vocat. High Sch., N.Y.C., 1965-67; mem. polit. action com. dist. council 37, N.Y.C., 1973-77; mem. negotiating team adminstrv. contracts, N.Y.C., 1975-78; mem. Com. To Save CCNY, 1976-77, Statue Liberty Ellis Island Found., Woodrow Wilson Internat. Ctr. Scholars, Wilson Ctr. Assocs., Washington, St. Labre Indian Sch., Ashland, Mont. Appreciation award Dist. Coun. 37, 1979; recipient Plaque Appreciation Svcs., Baruch Coll., Key award St. Joseph's Indian Sch., 1990, Key award in Edn. and Art, 1990, others. Mem. Artist Equity Assn. N.Y., NAFE, Lakota Devel. Coun., Am. Film Inst., Bklyn. Coll. Alumni, Nat. Geographic Soc., Nat. Mus. Woman in the Arts (Washington), Statue of Liberty Ellis Island Found., Inc., Alliance of Queens Artists, U.S. Naval Inst., El Museo Del Barrio (N.Y.), Am. Mus. Natural History, Internat. Ctr. for Scholars-Wilson Ctr. Assocs., Arrow Club-St. Labre Indian Sch., others. Roman Catholic. Office: Baruch Coll 17 Lexington Ave New York NY 10010-5526

WILLIAMS, HEATHER NILES, jewelry designer; b. Worchester, Mass., May 8, 1962; d. Norman Briscoe and Cynthia (Fulton) W. BFA, Phila. Coll. of Art, 1984. Jewerly designer Trifari, Krussman & Fishel, N.Y.C., 1984—. Mem. Cooper Hewitt Mus. Mem. U. of Arts Alumni Assn., U.S. Yacht Racing Union. Republican.

WILLIAMS, HENRY WARD, JR., lawyer; b. Rochester, N.Y., Jan. 12, 1930; s. Henry Ward and Margaret Elizabeth (Simpson) W.; m. Linda Leon; children: Edith French, Margaret Williams Warren, Sarah Williams Farrand, Ann Williams Treacy, Elizabeth DeLancey, Victoria Maureen. AB, Dartmouth Coll., 1952; LLB, U.Va., 1958. Bar: N.Y. 1959, U.S. Dist. Ct. (we. dist.) N.Y. 1959, U.S. Dist. Ct. (so. dist.) Mich. 1982, U.S. Ct. Appeals (2d cir.) 1963, U.S. Tax Ct. 1960, U.S. Supreme Ct. 1968, D.C. 1978. Ptnr. Harris, Beach & Wilcox, Rochester, 1958-78, Robinson, Williams, Angeloff & Frank, Rochester, 1978-82, Weidman, Williams, Jordon, Angeloff & Frank, Rochester, 1982-83, Henry Williams & Assocs., Rochester, 1983-89, Williams, Sciortino & Donsky, Rochester, 1990—; bd. dirs. Voplex Corp. Bd. dirs. Presbyn. Residence Ctr. Corp., Geva, chmn.; Ctr. for Environ. Info.; chmn. Genesee Finger/Lakes Regional Planning Coun., 1973-89, maj. leader Monroe County Legislature, 1967-73. Lt. (j.g.) USN, 1952-55. Mem. ABA, N.Y. State Bar Assn., Monroe County Bar Assn. (trustee 1982-85), Raven Soc., Va. Law Rev., Order of Coif, Rochester Yacht Club, Royal Can. Yacht Club, Lake Yacht Racing Assn. (pres. 1985-87, hon. pres. 1988-90), Royal Ocean Racing Club, Omicron Delta Kappa. Home: 69 S Main St Pittsford NY 14534-1903 Office: Williams Sciortino & Donsky 10 Grove St Pittsford NY 14534-1327

WILLIAMS, IRVING LAURENCE, physics educator; b. Newport, R.I., Dec. 3, 1935; s. Leroy Payton and Alberta Helen (Troy) W.; m. Carrie Mae Graves, Aug. 26, 1967; children: Cheryl Anita, Carla Chantrase. EdB, R.I. Coll., 1957; MA in Teaching, Brown U., 1962; PhD, NYU, 1975. Cert. teaching, R.I. Classroom tchr. Newport (R.I.) Sch. Dept., 1962-63; prof. physics Morgan State U., Balt., 1963-67; prof. physics Nassau Community Coll., Garden City, N.Y., 1967—, asst. to pres., 1980-85; adj. prof. Hofstra U., Hempstead, N.Y., 1980-87; dist. clk. Roosevelt (N.Y.) Sch. Bd., 1989-91. Co-author: (lab. workbook) Meterology Lab. Exercises, 1975, 76. Treas. Econ. Opportunity Commn., Nassau County, N.Y., 1984; trustee Grace Lutheran Ch., Malverne, N.Y., 1987, Roosevelt Bd. Edn., 1988; active Roosevelt Rep. Club, 1989; mem. sch. bd. Grace Lutheran Sch., Malverne, 1991. With U.S. Army, 1957-60. Recipient Chancellor's award SUNY, 1975, Citzen's award EOC Nassau County, Hempstead, 1987, Roosevelt Educator's award, Roosevelt Coun., 1989; NSF Weather Svc. grantee, Washington, 1989. Mem. AAUP, Nat. Sci. Tchrs. Assn., Am. Assn. Physics Tchrs., Soc. Coll. Sci. Tchrs., N.Y. Acad. Sci., Am. Assn. Higher Edn., N.Y. Assn. Two Yr. Colls. Republican. Home: 220 Beechwood Ave Roosevelt NY 11575-1634 Office: Phys Scis Dept Nassau Community Coll Garden City NY 11530

WILLIAMS, JAMES B., wholesale distribution company executive; b. Toronto, Ont., Can., Oct. 16, 1945; s. Norman James and Marie (McBride) W.; m. Kathleen Mary Fitzgerald, May 10, 1969; children: Jason Lawrence, Laura Marie. BA, U. Toronto, Ont., Can., 1967; MBA, U. Toronto, 1969. Sr. v.p. fin. and adminstrn., chief fin. officer Dominion Stores Ltd., Toronto, 1969-85; exec. v.p. fin. and adminstrn., chief fin. officer Gt. Atlantic & Pacific Tea Co. Can. Inc., Toronto, 1985-86; exec. v.p. fin. and adminstrn., chief fin. officer Can. Tire Corp. Ltd., Toronto, 1986-88, exec. v.p. mktg., real estate, constrn. and distbn., 1988-91, pres. mdse. bus. group, corp. exec. v.p. dealer rels., 1991—. Office: Can Tire Corp Ltd, 2180 Yonge St, Toronto, ON Canada M4P 2V8

WILLIAMS, JAMES CASE, metallurgist; b. Salina, Kans., Dec. 7, 1938; s. Luther Owen and Clarice (Case) W.; m. Joanne Rufener, Sept. 17, 1960; children: Teresa A., Patrick J. B.S. in Metall. Engring, U. Wash., 1962, M.S., 1964, Ph.D., 1968. Rsch. engr., lead engr. Boeing Co., Seattle, 1961-67; tech. staff N.Am. Rockwell Corp., Thousand Oaks, Calif., 1968-74; mgr. interdivisional tech. program N.Am. Aerospace group, 1974, program devel. mgr. structural materials, 1974-75; prof. metallurgy, co-dir. Ctr. for Joining of Materials, Carnegie-Mellon U., Pitts., 1975-81; pres. Mellon Inst., Pitts., 1981-83; dean Carnegie Inst. Tech., Carnegie-Mellon U., Pitts., 1983-88; gen. mgr. materials dept. GE Aircraft Engines, 1988—; chmn. Nat. Materials Adv. Bd.; mem. Materials Sci. and Engr. Study; mem. adv. bd. Engring. Sch. U. Va.; bd. dirs. Minorities in Math., Sci. and Engring., Wheeling-Pitts. Steel, 1987-91; chmn. vis. com. materials dept. U. Cin. Co-editor: Scientific and Technological Aspects of Titanium and Titanium Alloys, 1976; contbr. numerous articles to tech. jours. Trustee Oreg. Grad. Ctr.; cons. Cubmaster Boy Scouts Am., 1976-77. Recipient Ladd award Carnegie Inst. Tech.; Adams award Am. Welding Soc.; Boeing doctoral fellow. Fellow Am. Soc. Metals (Gold medal 1992); mem. NAE, AIME, ASM, DARPA Materials Rsch. Coun., Alpha Sigma Mu. Republican. Episcopalian. Home: 3307 Brinton Trl Cincinnati OH 45241-4814 Office: GE Aircraft Engines MD H85 Cincinnati OH 45215-6301

WILLIAMS, JAMES EUGENE, construction company executive; b. Gettysburg, Pa., June 20, 1953; s. Clyde Eugene and Mildred A. (Stover) W.; m. Debra Gene Geesey, June 21, 1975; children: Jason, Jennifer. Student, Pa. State U., 1971-73. V.p. C.E. Williams Sons, Inc., Gettysburg, Pa., 1973—. Pres. Gettysburg Teener Baseball League; bd. dirs. Adams County Babe Ruth League, Gettysburg; com. mem. Gettysburg Coll./Community Affairs Com., 1988—. Mem. Gettysburg Optimist Club, Elks, Builders Assn. of Adams County (pres. 1988-89, bd. dirs. 1981—). Republican. Lutheran. Home: 120 Ridgewood Dr Gettysburg PA 17325-8502 Office: CE Williams Sons Inc 36 S 5th St Gettysburg PA 17325-1999

WILLIAMS, JAMES KAY, photography company executive; b. Long Beach, Calif., Mar. 19, 1931; s. Carl T. and Myrtle Mary (Daly) W.; m. Shirley Ann Bench, May 10, 1953 (div. 1973); children: Michael J., Robert D., Kent R., Steven D.; m. Diane Louise Guertin, Aug. 17, 1974; children: Richard A. Benson, Douglas S. Benson. Student, U. Alaska, 1952. Photographer L.B. Stevens Co., Inc., Bangor, Maine, 1953-54, sales mgr., 1956-59, v.p., 1959-62, pres., 1977-79; 1st v.p. L.B. Stevens Co., Inc., Concord, N.H., 1962-77; v.p. Sch. Pictures, Jackson, Miss., 1977-79; dir. sales Yearbook Assocs., Turners Falls, Mass., 1979-81, pres., 1982—; cons., speaker, Associated Collegiate Press, Western Assn. Univ. Publ. Mgrs. Pres. Canterbury (N.H.) PTA, 1968; chmn. N.H. Democrats for Romney for Pres., 1970; com. person, Canterbury Sch. Bd., 1970; coord. Western Mass. Spl. Olympics, Northfield, 1981. With USAF, 1950-53. Mem. Profl. Photographers Am., U.S. Pony Club, Outing Club, Jaycees Bangor, Kiwanis. Republican. Office: Yearbook Assocs PO Box 91 Turners Falls MA 01349-0091

WILLIAMS, JAMES RICHARD, human factors engineering psychologist; b. Chgo., Apr. 16, 1932; s. James Henry and Margaret Lucille (Keefer) W.; m. Jonetta Rae Gilbert, Dec. 19, 1959; children: Janise Rebecca, Jason Richard. BS in Psychology, Purdue U., 1958, MS in Human Factors/Indsl. Psychology, 1960; PhD in Edn., NYU, 1971. Technical asst. Sci. Rsch. Assocs., Chgo., 1960-61; sr. systems cons. System Devel. Corp., Paramus, N.J., 1961-64; human factors engr. Kollsman Instrument Corp., Elmhurst, N.Y., 1964-66; project mgr. System Devel. Corp., Paramus, 1966-69; supr. tng. and standards Bell Labs., Piscataway, N.J., 1969-74; dist. mgr. AT&T, Basking Ridge, N.J., 1975-80; mem. technical staff Bell Labs., Piscataway, 1981-83; human factors curriculum mgr. Bell Communications Rsch., Piscataway, 1984—; cons. NYU, N.Y.C., 1968-70; chair U.S. Tech. Adv. Group on Internat. Standards Orgn. for Ergonomics/Signals and Controls, 1988—. Editor: International Standard for Menu Dialogues with Computer Systems. Cub master Boy Scouts, Watchung, N.Y., 1973-74, asst. scout master, 1975-78. With USAF, 1951-55. Mem. Am. Psychol. Soc. (charter), Assn. for Computing Machinery (spl. interest group computer-human interaction), Human Factors Soc. (rep. 1986—), Delta Rho Kappa, Kappa Delta Pi. Home: RR 1 Box 84 Frenchtown NJ 08825-9705 Office: Bell Communications Rsch 6 Corporate Pl Piscataway NJ 08854-4120

WILLIAMS, JAMES THOMAS, physician, educator; b. Martinsville, Va., Nov. 10, 1933; s. Harry Pemberton and Ruth Ellen (Thomas) W.; m. Jacqueline Cecile Shepard, Apr. 21, 1962; children: Lawrence Dudley, Laurie Cecile. BS, Howard U., 1954, MD, 1958. Diplomate Am. Bd. Internal Medicine, Am. Bd. Endocrinology and Metabolism. Intern Phila. Gen. Hosp., 1958-59; resident in medicine D.C. Gen. Hosp., 1959-60, Freedmen's Hosp., Washington, 1960-62, 64-65; fellow in endocrinology Howard U., Washington, 1965-67, asst. prof. medicine, 1967-74, chief endocrine sect. dept. medicine, 1973-76, assoc. prof. medicine, 1974-85, prof. medicine, 1985—. Capt. U.S. Army, 1962-64. Fellow ACP; mem. Endocrine Soc., Am. Diabetes Assn., Nat. Med. Assn. Democrat. Home: 13414 Tamarack Rd Silver Spring MD 20904-1469 Office: Howard U Hosp 2041 Georgia Ave NW Washington DC 20060-0002

WILLIAMS, JOHN CHAMBERLIN, infosystems engineer, consultant; b. Ridgway, Pa., Aug. 23, 1919; s. R.P. Dean and Wilma E. (Chamberlin) W.; m. Gloria Bradley, Feb. 24, 1951; children: Douglas Bradley, Kathryn Joanne. BEE, Pa. State Coll., 1941; MS in Engring. Scis. and Applied Physics, Harvard U., 1948, PhD in Applied Physics, 1959. Engr., AT&T Long Lines, Phila., 1941-42; staff Radiation Lab., MIT, Cambridge, 1942-45; rsch. asst. Cruft Lab., Harvard U., 1945-59; electronic instrumentation cons., 1945-55; asst. v.p. rsch. Pickard & Burns Electronics, Waltham, Mass., 1959-63, dir. radio sci. dept., 1963-67, dir. rsch. and systems, 1967-68; staff engr. RCA Govt. and Comml. Systems, Camden, N.J., 1968-74; mgr. advanced radiation systems RCA missile & surface radar div., Moorestown, N.J., 1974-80, staff engr. govt. communications systems, Camden, 1980-85, staff engr. communication and info. systems div., 1985-88, cons. 1988—; mem. long wave propagation discussion group U.S. Navy, 1961-69; alternate mem. submarine communications panel Nat. Security Indsl. Assn., 1969-70; assoc. mem. sci. adv. com. Def. Intelligence Agy., 1974-77; mem. U.S. Commn. E on Interference Environment, Internat. Union Radio Sci., 1975—. Troop com. chmn. Boy Scouts Am., 1970-74. Mem. Am. Meteorol. Soc., Am. Geophys. Union, N.Y. Acad. Sci., Sigma Xi, Tau Beta Pi, Eta Kappa Nu. Republican. Presbyterian. Contbg. author: LORAN, 1948, Recent Advances in Atmospheric Electricity, 1959, Industrial Electronics, 1960; patentee in field (4). Home and Office: PO Box 3164 151 Tiffany Ln Gettysburg PA 17325

WILLIAMS, JON EDWARD, clinical psychologist, minister; b. McComb, Miss., May 20, 1937; s. Lloyd Cruise and Pearl (Burris) W.; m. Harley Harris, Dec. 27, 1963; 1 child James Edward. BA cum laude, Millsaps Coll., 1959; MDiv, Union Theol. Sem., 1964; MS, U. Md., 1969, PhD in Clin. Psychology, 1970. Exec. dir. Psychol. Svcs. Inc., Annapolis, Md., 1973—; dir. Inst. for Short-term Therapies, Annapolis, 1987—; speaker in field. Recipient Disting. Svc. award Md. Psychol. Assn., 1985. Fellow Am. Bd. Med. Psychotherapists (diplomate); mem. Am. Acad. Behavioral Medicine (diplomate), Am. Bd. Family Psychologists (diplomate), Am. Bd. Vocat. Experts (diplomate), Am. Bd. Sexology (diplomate). Office: Psychol Svcs Inc 111 Annapolis St Annapolis MD 21401-1397

WILLIAMS, JOSEPH DALTON, pharmaceutical company executive; b. Washington, Pa., Aug. 15, 1926; s. Joseph Dalton and Jane (Day) W.; m. Mildred E. Bellaire, June 28, 1973; children: Terri, Daniel. BS in Pharmacy, U. Nebr., 1950; DSc (hon.), Union U., 1991, U. Nebr., 1989; LHD (hon.), Albany Coll. Pharmacy, Union U., 1980, Rutgers U., 1987, Long Island U., 1988; DSc (hon.), Phila. Coll. Pharmacy and Sci., 1988, Long Island U., 1988, Albany Coll. Pharmacy of Union U., 1991; D Human Svcs. (hon.), Caldwell Coll., 1989; LLD (hon.), Bethune-Cookman Coll., 1990, Coll. St. Elizabeth, 1990, Seton Hall U., 1990, U. Md., 1991, St. Augustine Coll., 1992. Pres. Parke-Davis Co., Detroit, 1973-76; pres. pharm. group Warner-Lambert Co., Morris Plains, N.J., 1976-77; pres. Internat. Group, 1977-79; pres., dir. Warner-Lambert Corp., 1979-80, pres., chief operating officer, 1980-84, chmn. exec. com., 1985-91, 1991—; bd. dirs. AT&T, J.C. Penney & Co., Exxon Corp., Rockefeller Fin. Svcs., Inc. Bd. dirs. People to People Health Found., United Negro Coll. Fund; trustee Columbia U. Served with USNR, 1943-46. Mem. Am. Pharm. Assn., N.J. Pharm. Assn., Somerset Hills Country Club, Links Club, Pine Valley Golf Club, Baltusrol Golf Club, Mid Ocean Club, Robert Trent Jones Internat. Golf Club. Office: Warner-Lambert Co 201 Tabor Rd Morris Plains NJ 07950-2693

WILLIAMS, JOSEPH RICHARD, marketing professional; b. N.Y.C., Jan. 9, 1955; s. Arthur Richard and Grace Lucille (Denon) W. BS in Biology, St. John's U., 1977; MS in Med. Biology, L.I. U., 1983. Quality control technician Pall Biomedical Products, Glen Cove, N.Y., 1977-78, quality control mgr., 1978-81; quality control inspector Merck, Sharp & Dohme, West Point, Pa., 1981, lab. mgr., 1981; product devel. engr. Deknatel div. Pfizer Hosp. Products, Lake Success, N.Y., 1981-82, product devel. mgr., 1982-86; product devel. mgr. Olympus Corp., Lake Success, 1986—. Patentee in field. Home: 25 Willow St Floral Park NY 11001-3407

WILLIAMS, LAWRENCE SOPER, photographer; b. Balt., July 8, 1917; s. Lawrence S. and Ida (Exall) W.; m. Avilda Leyshon Williams, Nov. 21, 1940; children: Jay Stephen, Wendy Lauren. Student, Md. Inst. Wirephoto operator AP, Balt., 1937-38; news photographer Balt. Sun Papers, 1938-40, Harris and Ewing News Photos, Washington, 1940-41; war corr., photographer Bur. Info. U.S. War Dept., Washington, 1941-45; picture editor Holiday mag., Phila., 1945-48; freelance photographer Havertown, Pa., 1949-59; pres. Lawrence S. Williams, Inc., Upper Darby, Pa., 1959-83, chmn., 1983—. Pres. Archtl. Photographers Assn., N.Y.C., 1968-70, Paoli (Pa.) Woods Homeowner's Assn., 1985-86. Recipient Gold medal Artist Guild of Phila., 1965, Silver medal Artist Guild of Pa., 1964, George W. Berry trophy Soc. Comml. Photographers Del. Valley, 1961, 66, 78, 79, 82, Best of Show trophy Am. Mus. Photography, Phila., 1966, 71, 77, 79, 82, Best Comml. Print trophy Guild of Profl. Photographers Del. Valley, 1971, 70, Award of Excellence Am. Advtg. Assn. Pa., 1978, Pres.'s Cup Profl. Photographers Assn. Pa., 1971, numerous archtl., comml., indsl., pictorial awards. Fellow Am. Soc. Photographers; mem. Soc. Comml. Photographers Del. Valley (life)., Profl. Photographers Assn. of Pa. (life), Profl. Photographers Am., Inc. (life), master photography degree 1966, craftsman photography degree, 1968). Republican. Episcopalian. Club: Overbrook Golf (Bryn Mawr, Pa.). Lodge: Shriners. Home: 305 Paoli Woods Paoli PA 19301-1538 Office: 9101 W Chester Pike Upper Darby PA 19082-1192

WILLIAMS, LELAND HENDRY, computer scientist; b. Columbia, S.C., Feb. 24, 1930; s. Wyman Loren and Carolyn Lorraine (Hendry) W.; m. Cornelia Ann Burnett, June 18, 1952; children: Carolyn Leone Williams James, Leland Hendry. BS in Math., U. S.C., 1950; MS in Math., U. Ga., 1951; PhD in Applied Math., Duke U., 1961. Mathematician Redstone Arsenal, Huntsville, Ala., 1951-53, Naval Proving Ground, Dahlgren, Va., 1957; rsch. assoc., lectr. dept. math. Duke U., Durham, N.C., 1960-62; asst. dir., asst. prof. Computer Ctr., Fla. State U., Tallahassee, 1962-66; dir., assoc. prof. Computer Ctr., Auburn (Ala.) U., 1966-70; assoc. prof., prof. computer sci. Duke U., U. N.C., N.C. State U., 1970-88; pres., dir. Triangle Univs. Computation Ctr., Research Triangle Park, N.C., 1970-88; computer resources architect Naval Rsch. Lab., Washington, 1989—; vis. lectr. Math. Assn. Am., 1971-79; cons., vis. prof. U. Edinburgh, Scotland, 1976-77; chmn. peer rev. SIGUCCS, 1983-88; mem. exec. com. BITNET, Inc., Washington, 1984-88; tech. rev. com. adv. sci. computing NSF, Washington, 1984-88. Contbr. articles to profl. jours. Fellow Am. Sci. Affiliation; mem. ACM (nat. coun. 1968-71, 73-74, reg. conf. chmn., mem. and chmn. elect of Disting. Svc. Awards com.), Sigma Xi, Phi Beta Kappa. Baptist. Home: 8432 Porter Ln Alexandria VA 22308-2139 Office: Naval Rsch Lab Code 1003.9 4555 Overlook Ave SW Washington DC 20375-5000

WILLIAMS, LEWIS EDMUND, cardiovascular surgeon; b. Hazleton, Pa., Oct. 21, 1939; s.Lewis Charles and Madelyn Rose (Koehler) W.; m. Maria Therese Curcio, June 27, 1964; children: Dawn Maria, Alison Paige. BS, Fordham U., 1961; MD, N.J. Coll. Medicine, 1965. Diplomate, Am. Bd. Surgery, Am. Bd. Thoracic Surgery. Intern Bellevue Med. Ctr., N.Y.C., 1965-66; resident Tufts New Eng. Med. Ctr., Boston, 1966-71; fellow in thoracic and cardiovascular surgery U. N.C., Chapel Hill, 1973-75; cardiovascular surgeon Nassau Thoracic Cardiovascular Group, Mineola, N.Y.; attenging cardiovascular surgeon Winthrop U. Hosp., Mineola, N.Y.; cons. thoracic surgeon Mercy Hosp., Rockville Center, N.Y., Northport (N.Y.) VA Hosp.; attending surgeon Syosset Community Hosp., Univ. Hosp. Stony Brook, Cardiac Ctr.; dir. thoracic surgery Nassau County Med. Ctr., 1978—; asst. prof. surgery SUNY-Stony Brook, 1976—. Maj. USAF, 1971-73. Fellow ACS, Am. Coll. Cardiology; mem. AMA, Soc. Thoracic Surgery. Republican. Roman Catholic. Office: Nassau Thoracic Group 173 Mineola Blvd Mineola NY 11501-2528

WILLIAMS, MARK TRAVIS, research chemist; b. Sinton, Tex., May 18, 1952; s. Robert Dee and Ruby Louise (Williamson) W. BS in Chemistry, U. So. Miss., 1980. Rsch. asst. U. So. Miss., Hattiesburg, 1980-82, Catalyst Rsch., Balt., 1982-89, SAFT Am., Cockeysville, Md., 1989—. Contbr. articles to profl. jours.; patentee for thrmal battery. With U.S. Army, 1972-74. Mem. Am. Chem. Soc., Am. Soc. for Metals, Electrochem. Soc. Office: SAFT Am 109 Beaver Ct Cockeysville Hunt Valley MD 21030-2166

WILLIAMS, MARSHALL HENRY, JR., physician, educator; b. New Haven, July 15, 1924; s. Marshall Henry and Henrietta (English) W.; m. Mary Butler, Aug. 27, 1948; children: Stuart, Patricia, Marshall, Frances, Richard. Grad., Pomfret Sch., 1942; B.S., Yale, 1945, M.D., 1947. Diplomate Nat. Bd. Med. Examiners, Am. Bd. Internal Medicine. Intern Presbyn. Hosp., N.Y.C., 1947-48; asst. resident medicine Presbyn. Hosp., 1948-49; asst. resident medicine New Haven Hosp., 1949-50, asst. in medicine, 1950; trainee Nat. Heart Inst., 1950; practice medicine, specializing in internal medicine Bronx, N.Y.; chief respiratory sect., dept. cardiorespiratory diseases Army Med. Service Grad. Sch., Walter Reed Army Med. Center, 1953-55; dir. cardiorespiratory lab. Grasslands Hosp., Valhalla, N.Y., 1955-59; dir. chest service Bronx Municipal Hosp. Center, 1959—; vis. asst. prof. physiology Albert Einstein Coll. Medicine, Bronx, N.Y., 1955-59, assoc. prof. medicine and physiology, 1959-66, prof. medicine, 1966—; dir. pulmonary div. Albert Einstein Coll. Medicine—Montefiore Med. Ctr., 1981—. Author: Clinical Applications of Cardiopulmonary Physiology, 1960, Essentials of Pulmonary Medicine, 1982, Consultation in Chest Medicine, 1985; contbr. articles to profl. jours. Served from 1st lt. to capt. U.S. Army, 1950-52. Mem. Am. Physiol. Soc., AAAS, Am. Heart Assn., Westchester Heart Assn (past pres.)., Am. Thoracic Soc., Am. Fedn. Clin. Research, N.Y. Acad. Sci., N.Y. Trudeau Soc. (past pres.), Am. Soc. Clin. Investigation, Soc. Urban Physicians (past pres.), N.Y. Tb. and Health Assn. (past dir.), Alpha Omega Alpha. Home: 103 Fox Meadow Rd Scarsdale NY 10583-2301 Office: Albert Einstein Coll Medicine Bronx NY 10461

WILLIAMS, MARTIN BERRY, fundraiser; b. Pompton Plains, N.J., Oct. 18, 1956; s. Henry Robert and Harryette Jane (Berry) W.; m. Jill Christine Fenske, Apr. 15, 1981; children: Albert Berry. BA, Montclair State Coll., 1979; MA, NYU, 1987. Curator Allaire Village, Farmingdale, N.J., 1979-81, N.J. Hist. Soc., Newark, 1981-82, Staten Island Hist. Soc., 1982-86; planner Middlesex County Cultural & Heritage Commn., New Brunswick, N.J., 1987; interim asst. dir. N.J. Com. for the Humanities, New Brunswick, 1987-88; devel. assoc. Newark Pub. Libr., 1988; devel. officer Found. U.M.D.N.J., Newark, 1989-90; sr. grants officer Newark Pub. Libr., 1990—; v.p., trustee Greater Newark Conservancy, 1990—; trustee Friends of the Newark Pub. Libr., 1990—. Author: Sealed by Brooks, 1980. Trustee Community Nursery Sch., Nutley, N.J.; mem. Pequannock Township Hist. Commn. Mem. VASA Order of Am. Democrat. Mem. Reformed Ch. in Am. Home: 55 Ramapo Rd Pompton Plains NJ 07444-1334 Office: Newark Pub Libr 5 Washington St # 630 Newark NJ 07102-3175

WILLIAMS, MARY BEARDEN, philosophy of biology educator; b. Lexington, Ky., Aug. 29, 1936; d. Edwin Gantt and Walter Harnesbarger (Dallas) W. BA in Math., Reed Coll., 1958; MA in Math., U. Pa., 1961; PhD in Math. Biology, U. London, 1967. Asst. prof. N.C. State U., Raleigh, 1967-73; vis. asst. prof. Ind. U., Bloomington, 1973-74; asst. prof. Ohio State U., Columbus, 1974-76; honors faculty U. Del., Newark, 1976-78, dir. ctr. sci. and culture, 1985-89, assoc. prof., 1978—. Editor: Computers, Ethics, and Society, 1990; contbr. articles in math. biology, philosophy of biology, biology to profl. jours. Fellow NIH, 1964-67; grantee NSF, 1974-75, 75-76, 76-78, 79-80, 82-83, NEH, 1986-90. Mem. Math. Assn. Am. (gov. 1975-78), Philosophy of Sci. Assn. (gov. 1977-79), Soc. for Study of Evolution, Am. Philos. Assn. Office: U Del Ctr Sci & Culture Newark DE 19716

WILLIAMS, NEVILLE, non-profit organization executive; b. Muncie, Ind., Mar. 28, 1943; s. Donald Charles and Rose Eileen (Boughton) W.; m. Robin Baker, Oct. 23, 1981 (div. 1983). Student, U. Colo., 1964-66, U. Neuchatel, Switzerland, 1967. Freelance corr. Vietnam, 1968-69; freelance journalist Montreal, Que., Can., 1970-71, London, 1971-73; writer, producer Sta. WNBC-TV News, N.Y.C., 1973-74; freelance writer Telluride, Colo., 1975-79; media liaison Office of Solar Energy U.S. Dept. Energy, Washington, 1979-80; dir. of mktg. Telluride Ski Resort, Inc., 1981-83; pres., chief exec. officer Picture Show Corp., Telluride, 1983-85; nat. media dir. Greenpeace U.S.A., Washington, 1987-89; pres., chmn. Solar Electric Light Fund, Washington, 1990—; also, bd. dirs.; location mgr. Twentieth Century-Fox, Telluride, 1978; cons. Solarex Corp., Rockville, Md., 1989-90, UN Devel. Programme, N.Y.C., 1991-92; cons., pres. Williams & Assocs., Telluride and Washington, 1983-90. Author: The New Exiles, 1971, (monograph) Great Telluride Strike, 1977; contbr. articles to N.Y. Times mag., Boston Globe mag., Penthouse, Denver mag., others. Apptd. mem. Adv. Com. for Commerce and Devel., State of Colo., 1980-85; apptd. mem. Gov.'s Motion Picture & TV Commn., 1981-85; owner, operator Historic Sheridan Opera House, Telluride, 1982-85; bd. dirs. Radio Sta. KOTO-FM, Telluride, 1977-80. Fellow Am. Solar Energy Soc., Internat. Solar Energy Soc., Solar Energy Industries Assn., Self Realization Fellowship. Office: Solar Electric Light Fund 1739 Connecticut Ave NW Washington DC 20009

WILLIAMS, NORMAN, legal educator, city planner; b. Chgo., Dec. 26, 1915; s. Norman and Joan (Chalmers) W.; m. Jeanne Tedesche, Nov. 27, 1947; children: Norman Jr., Joan Chalmers, Roger Sidney, Sarah Dorothy. BA, Yale U., 1938, LLB, 1943; postgrad., Corpus Christi Coll., Eng., 1938-39, Yale U., 1939-40. Bar: N.Y. 1944. Practice N.Y.C., 1943-48; sr. analyst The Plan for Rezoning N.Y., N.Y.C., 1948-50; from acting dir. to dir. div. of planning, acting chief to chief office of master planning N.Y.C. Dept. of Planning, 1950-60; cons. Outdoor Recreation Resources Rev.

Commn., 1961; dir. Guyana Project Joint Ctr. for Urban Studies, Caracas, Venezuela, 1961-62; exec. dir. Gov.'s adv. commn. on transp. State of N.J., 1964-65; mem., vice chmn. Princeton (N.J.) Borough Planning Bd. and Princeton Regional Planning Bd., 1965-75; prof. Vt. Law Sch., 1976—; prof. urban planning and law U. Ariz., 1978-86; vis. lectr. city planning Columbia U. Architecture Sch., 1951-61, Yale U. Architecture Sch., 1952-61; vis. prof. city planning MIT, 1960, U. Va., 1973; vis. prof. law Rutgers-Newark U., 1965-75, U. Ariz., 1976-78, 87-91, Vt. Law Sch., 1975; prof. urban planning Rutgers U., 1969-75. Note editor, editor-in-chief Yale U. Law Jour., 1942; author: (with others) Vermont Townscape, 1986, American Land Planning Law, 5 vols., 1974-75, 2d edit., 8 vols., 1984-88; contbr. numerous articles to profl. jours. Pres. Citizens Housing and Planning Council N.Y., N.Y.C., 1950; mem. Billings Park Commn., Woodstock, Vt., 1985—. Mem. Am. Planning Assn. (Disting. Leadership award 1991), Am. Inst. of Cons. Planners. Democrat. Unitarian. Clubs: Yale (N.Y.C.); Lakota (Barnard, Vt.) (bd. dirs. 1977-80, 82-85), Elizabethan, Yale U. (bd. govs. 1937-38). Home: 26 River St Woodstock VT 05091-1022 Office: Vt Law Sch South Royalton VT 05068

WILLIAMS, PAUL ALAN, artist; b. Detroit, Sept. 10, 1934; s. Archie Theodore and Alva (Constance) W.; m. Sandi Oliver Simoni, May 2, 1982; children: John Mortimer Wilson, Melissa Anne Wilson, Philip Keith Wilson. Student, Chadsey Art Sch., Detroit, 1948-49, Meinzinger, Detroit, 1950-51; BPA, Art Ctr., L.A., 1959. Illustrator self-employed Weston, Conn., 1962-84, fine artist, oil painter self-employed, 1982—; art tchr. Hampton, Va., 1960-61. Prin. works include 3 major internat. calendars Scot Paper Co., 1972-79 (Gold Medal); space coordinator artist for major promotions Nordon-Unit-Tech., 1982-85 (12 awards), Radio City Music Hall, 1980-83. With U.S. Army, 1959-61. Recipient Bravo Advt. award Detroit Art Dirs., 1960-80, Award of Excellence, Soc. of Illustrators, 1967-71, Gold Medal cert., 1972-82. Mem. Soc. Am. Impressionists, Allied Artists of Am. Inc., Am. Fedn. Artists, New Eng. Appraisers Assn., Soc. of Illustrators, Carriage Barn of Waverly Pk. Home: 11 Tubbs Spring Dr Weston CT 06883-1413 Office: Sandi Oliver Fine Art PO Box 1203 Weston CT 06883-0203

WILLIAMS, PETER CHARLES, mathematician, educator; b. Detroit, Dec. 24, 1933; s. William Brown and Martha Chlotilde (Palms) W.; m. Marija Laima Gilvydis, June 11, 1966; children: Maria Elena, Peter Albert. BChE, U. Detroit, 1958, ABT-Chem.Engring., 1960-63; MA in Math., Wayne State U., 1965; ABD-Math., U. Wis., 1965-69. Asst. prof. math. U. Wis., LaCrosse, 1969-72; project leader/amb. advanced engring. staff/air program GMC Tech. Ctr., Warren, Mich., 1972-74; rsch. chem. engr. BASF-Wyandotte (Mich.) Chem. Co., 1976-77; aerospace/environ. engr. Hamilton Std., United Tech., Windsor Locks, Conn., 1977-86; faculty math. U. Conn., Storrs, 1987-89; author Don Quixote Ent., East Longmeadow, Mass., 1990—; head math. lab. U. Wis., LaCrosse, 1969-71; head math. dept. Math. High Sch., Detroit, 1963-64. Author computer program: Sizing Program for Freedom Space Station, 1986; contbr. articles to profl. jours.; author: Manual for Handling Air Pollution Data, 1973. Usher Tanglewood-Boston Symphony Orch., 1985; head bass sect. Springfield (Mass.) Symphony Orch., 1985-86. Mem. Fellow Tugboat-AMS; mem. Air Pollution Control Assn. (hon. mem.). Roman Catholic. Home: 509 Chestnut St East Longmeadow MA 01028

WILLIAMS, PETER MACLELLAN, nuclear engineer; b. N.Y.C., Aug. 30, 1931; s. Gilbert Harris and Evelyn (Buss) W.; m. Lois Crane, Oct. 6, 1956; children: Jane, Gilbert, Katherine, Anne, Louise, Robert. B in Chem. Engring., Cornell U., 1954; MS in Nuclear Engring., MIT, 1957; PhD in Nuclear Engring., U. Md., 1971. Engr. DuPont Savannah River, Aiken, S.C., 1954-55; task engr. AGN, San Ramon, Calif., 1957-60; project mgr. Am. Machine & Fdry., Greenwich, Conn., 1960-62; research staff Princeton U., N.J., 1962-67; sr. project mgr., specialist in high temperature gas cooled reactors U.S. Nuclear Regulatory Commn., Washington, 1967-91; dir. div. high temperature gas cooled reactors U.S. Dept. of Energy, Washington, 1991—; mem. Chernobyl Tracking Team, 1986; U.S. del. to gas-cooled reactors working group, Internat. Atomic Energy Agy., 1991; steering com. mem. U.S.-Japan Implementing Agreement on gas-cooled reactors, 1991. Contbr. articles to profl. jours.; author various reports. Scoutmaster Boy Scouts Am., Potomac, Md., 1972, cubmaster, 1983-86; pres. PTA Winston Churchill High Sch., Potomac, 1981. Assoc. fellow AIAA; mem. Am. Nuclear Soc., Sigma Xi. Democrat. Unitarian. Home: 9418 Thrush Ln Rockville MD 20854-3991 Office: US Dept Energy Adv Reactors Div HTGRS NE-451 Mail Stop Washington DC 20585

WILLIAMS, PHILIP NEEDLES, manufacturing company executive; b. Summit, n.J., Jan. 22, 1953; s. Herbert Philip and Margaret (Needles) W.; m. Laura E.O. Herrlin, June 26, 1976. BS in Acctg., Lehigh U., 1975. CPA, N.Y. Mem. audit staff Arthur Young & Co., N.Y.C., 1975-79, audit mgr., 1980; v.p. Dusenbery Engring. Co., Inc., Morristown, N.J., 1980-84, pres., 1984—. Republican. Office: Dusenbery Engring Co Inc 309 E Hanover Ave Morristown NJ 07960-4077

WILLIAMS, RALPH J., immuno-hematologist; b. N.Y.C., May 3, 1954; s. Ralph and Connie (Branca) W.; m. Felicia Romeo, Oct. 1, 1977; children: Jennifer, Stefanie, Jessica. BS, Mercy Coll., 1982; postgrad., NIH, 1978-79. Sr. technologist Bronx (N.Y.) VA Med. Ctr., 1980-88; supr. Montefiori Med. Ctr., Bronx, 1988-89; sr. technologist NYU Med. Ctr., N.Y.C., 1988-90; sect. chief blood bank Bronx VA Med. Ctr., 1990—. With U.S. Army, 1972-74. Mem. Am. Assn. Blood Banks, Am. Soc. Clin. Pathologists, City of N.Y. Dept. Health, N.Y. Blood Ctr., Disable Am. Vet., Am. Legion. Home: 2411 Dorsey St Bronx NY 10461-2903 Office: Bronx VA Med Ctr 130 W Kingsbridge Rd Bronx NY 10468-3992

WILLIAMS, ROBERT JOSEPH, museum director, educator; b. Bennington, Vt., June 21, 1944; s. Joseph and Ruthe Allison (Moody) W. BS in Edn., U. Vt., 1970; MA in Interdisciplinary Social Sci., San Francisco State U., 1981. Tchr. adult edn. Mt. Anthony Union High Sch., Bennington, Vt., 1972-74; columnist Bennington Banner, 1972-77; tchr. San Francisco State U., 1976-79; founder, dir. NORRAD Drug Rehab. Ctr., San Francisco, 1986-88; museum curator Shaftsbury (Vt.) Historical Soc., 1989—; founder, dir. Bennington Tutorial Ctr., 1971-74. Author: Toward Humanness in Education, 1981, Chalice of Leaves: Selected Essays and Poems, 1988; author: (with others) Intimacy, 1985. Recipient Edmunds Essay medal Vt. Historical Soc., Montpelier, 1961, award of the League of Vt. Writers, 1972, Golden Poet award World of Poetry, Sacramento, Calif., 1990. Democrat. Home: 102 Putnam St Bennington VT 05201-2348 Office: Shaftsbury Hist Soc PO Box 401 Shaftsbury VT 05262-0401

WILLIAMS, RONALD DOHERTY, lawyer; b. New Haven, Apr. 6, 1927; s. Richard Hugh and Ethel W. (Nelson) W.; m. Laura Costarelli, Aug. 25, 1951; children: Craig F., Ronald D., Ellen A., Jane E. B.A., U. Va., 1951, LL.B., 1954. Bar: Conn. 1954. Assoc., Pullman, Comley, Bradley & Reeves, Bridgeport, Conn., 1954-60, ptnr., 1960-88, Williams, Cooney & Sheehy, 1989—; mem. Fed. Jud. Com., 1988—, com. unauthorized practice law, 1988—, com. to study rules civil practice & procedure, 1984-86; atty. state trial referee, 1984-90. Selectman Town of Easton (Conn.), 1975-85, justice of the peace, 1977—, town atty., 1985—; v.p. Bridgeport Area Found.; mem. adv. com. U. Bridgeport Law Sch., 1982—; mem. statewide Grievance Com., 1985-91, chmn., 1989-91. Served with AC, U.S. Army, 1945-46. Fellow Am. Coll. Trial Lawyers; mem. ABA, Conn. Bar Assn. (bd. govs. 1975-78), Bridgeport Bar Assn. (pres. 1975), Conn. Def. Lawyers Assn. (pres. 1984-85), Trial Attys. Am., Am. Bd. Trial Advs. Republican. Roman Catholic. Club: Algonquin (Bridgeport). Home: 14 Newman Dr Easton CT 06612-1915 Office: 1 Lafayette Cir Bridgeport CT 06604-6021

WILLIAMS, RONALD N., adult education educator; b. Bklyn., Apr. 17, 1951; s. Racine and Annie (Thompson) W.; m. Isabel Parrilla, Feb. 14, 1990; 1 child, Victor. BS in Health Sci., L.I. U., 1974, MS in Edn. Counseling Psychology, 1977. Asst. dir., coord. Medgar Evers Coll. CUNY, Bklyn., 1977-81; adj. lectr. Bernard Baruch Coll. CUNY, N.Y.C., 1981-88, coord., mgr. student activities Bernard Baruch Coll., 1983-88; coord. student activities N.Y. Tech. Coll. CUNY, Bklyn., 1988-90, counselor adult basic edn. N.Y. Tech. Coll., 1991—; adj. lectr. Borough of Manhattan Community Coll. CUNY, N.Y.C., 1991—; instr. N.Y.C. Bd. of Edn., Bklyn., 1974, 76, 83-84, 90; cons. counselor N.Y.C. area policy bd. #13, 1979. V.p. Grymes Hill Neighbors for Neighbors, S.I., N.Y., 1991—. Mem. Assn. Student Personnel Adminstrs. Home: 610 Victory Blvd Staten Island NY 10301 Office: NYC Tech Coll CUNY 250 Jay St Brooklyn NY 11201

WILLIAMS, ROY HENRY, software engineer; b. Pensacola, Fla., Jan. 19, 1936; s. Frank B. and Rebecca (Mullens) W.; m. Nancy Gail Truitt, May 31, 1958; children: Julie, Trudy, Roy Jr. BS in Engring. Physics, U. Tenn., 1959; MS in Advanced Tech., SUNY, Binghamton, 1988. Co-op. programmer Union Carbide Nuclear Co., Oak, Tenn., 1957-58; engr. programmer N.Am. Rockwell, L.A., 1959-62; sr. assoc. programmer IBM Corp., Houston, 1962-70; adv. programmer IBM Corp., Morris Plains, N.J., 1970-74, Cape Canaveral, Fla., 1974-76, Owego, N.Y., 1976-85, Gaithersburg, Md., 1985—; adj. prof. computer sci. dept. Montgomery Coll., Rockville, Md., 1988—. Mem. AAAS, Internat. Soc. Parametric Analysts, Internat. Platform Assn., N.Y. Acad. Scis. Home: 8608 Oak Bluff Ct Gaithersburg MD 20879-4337 Office: IBM Fed Systems Co 18100 N Frederick Ave Gaithersburg MD 20879-3395

WILLIAMS, RUSSELL EUGENE, economist, administrator, educator; b. Lansing, Mich., May 24, 1951; s. Russell Eugene and Alma Westine (Stone) W.; m. Deborah Anne Carter, Apr. 26, 1987. BA, Amherst Coll., 1972; postgrad., Boston U., 1977-79, U. Mass., 1991—. Program analyst U.S. Dept. Labor, Washington, 1972-73; unit coordinator Peter Bent Brigham Hosp., Boston, 1974-77; research asst. Regional Inst. for Employment Policy, Boston, 1977-79; analyst Abt Assocs., Cambridge, Mass., 1980-81; budget analyst Mass. Dept. Social Svcs., Boston, 1982; assoc. dir. Met. Coun. Ednl. Opportunity, Boston, 1982-91. Mem. bd. mgrs. New Eng. Home for Little Wanderers, Boston, 1987—; mem. av. bd. Mass. Advanced Studies program, 1989—; mem. social svc. allocations rev. com. United Way Massachusetts Bay, 1988-91, mem. child care initiative task force, 1988-89; mem. Boston Black Polit. Task Force, 1981-84; chairperson Boston Operation Big Vote, 1982-84. Ford Found. Predoctoral fellow, 1991—, Nat. Achievement scholar, 1968-72, Cert. of Appreciation, Fenway Neighborhood, Boston, 1982. Home: 360 Thacher St Milton MA 02186-3230

WILLIAMS, S. LLOYD, psychologist; b. L.A., Nov. 20, 1948; s. Jonathan Frampton W. and Marguerite Marshall. BA, Antioch Coll./West, 1975; PhD, Stanford U., 1983. Lic. psychologist, Pa. Postdoctoral fellow in clin. rsch. dept. psychiatry U. Pitts., 1982-84; asst. prof. psychology Lehigh U., Bethlehem, Pa., 1984-89, assoc. prof. psychology, 1989—; dir. Lehigh Phobia Program, Bethlehem, 1984—. Contbr. articles to profl. jours. Recipient Nat. Rsch. Svcs. and FIRST awards NIMH. Mem. Am. Psychol. Assn., Am. Psychol. Soc., Assn. for Advancement of Behavior Therapy. Home: 525 S Bishopthorpe St Bethlehem PA 18015-2754 Office: Lehigh U Psychology Bldg 17 Bethlehem PA 18015

WILLIAMS, STEPHEN FAIN, federal judge; b. N.Y.C., Sept. 23, 1936; s. Charles Dickerman and Virginia (Fain) W.; m. Faith Morrow, June 11, 1966; children: Susan, Geoffrey Fain, Sarah Margot Nu, Timothy Dwight, Nicholas Morrow. B.A., Yale U., 1958; J.D., Harvard U., 1961. Bar: N.Y. 1962, Colo. 1977. Assoc. Debevoise, Plimpton, Lyons & Gates, N.Y.C., 1962-66; asst. U.S. atty. So. Dist. N.Y., 1966-69; asst. prof. law U. Colo., Boulder, 1969-77; prof. U. Colo., 1977-86; judge U.S. Ct. Appeals (D.C. cir.), Washington, 1986—; vis. prof. UCLA, 1975-76; vis. prof., fellow in law and econs. U. Chgo., 1979-80; vis. William L. Hutchison prof. energy law So. Meth. U., 1983-84; cons. Adminstrv. Conf. U.S., 1974-76, FTC, 1983-85; mem. Boulder Area Growth Study Commn., 1972-73. Contbr. articles to law revs., mags. Served with U.S. Army, 1961-62. Mem. Am. Law Inst. Office: US Courthouse 3rd & Constitution Aves NW Washington DC 20001

WILLIAMS, THOMAS ALLISON, lawyer; b. Port Chester, N.Y., Dec. 19, 1936; s. Howard Hunter and Mary Katharine (Covell) W.; m. Anne Lamson Bell, Sept. 7, 1961; children: Thomas Allison, Laura L., James C., David D. BA in Econs., Yale U., 1959, LLB, 1962. Bar: N.Y. 1963. Assoc. Milbank, Tweed, Hadley & McCloy, N.Y.C., 1962-70, ptnr., 1971—. Trustee Rye Free Reading Room (N.Y.), 1965-85, pres., 1978-85; trustee Rye Presbyn. Ch., 1972-75; trustee, chmn. planning com. United Hosp., Port Chester, N.Y., 1978-86, chmn. bd., 1986—; trustee Westchester Libr. System, Westchester, N.Y., 1968-73, pres., 1972-73. Mem. ABA, N.Y. State Bar Assn., Assn. of Bar of City of N.Y., Am. Yacht Club, Manursing Island Club. Republican. Presbyterian. Office: Milbank Tweed Hadley & McCloy 1 Chase Manhattan Plz New York NY 10005-1401

WILLIAMS, TONDA, entrepreneur, consultant; b. N.Y.C., Nov. 21, 1949; d. William and Juanita (Rainey) W.; 1 child, Tywana. Student, Collegiate Inst., N.Y.C., 1975-78, C.W. Post Coll., 1981-83; BA in Bus. Mgmt., Am. Nat. U., Phoenix, 1983. Notary pub. N.Y. Asst. controller Acad. Ednl. Devel., N.Y.C., 1971-81; mgr. office Chapman-Apex Constrn. Co., Bayshore, N.Y., 1982-84; specialist computer RGM Liquid Waste Removal, Deerpark, N.Y., 1985-87; contr. LaMar Lighting Co., Freeport, N.Y., 1987—; owner, pres. Omni-Star, Bklyn., 1981—. Author: Tonda's Songs in Poetry, 1978, The Magic of Life, 1991; co-author: Computer Management of Liquid Waste Industry, 1986. Recipient Golden Poet award World of Poetry, 1992. Mem. Am. Mus. Natural History, Am. Soc. Notary Pubs. Home: 74 Cedar Dr Bay Shore NY 11706-2419

WILLIAMS, VERONICA ANN, management information systems marketing manager; b. Washington, Feb. 8, 1956; d. Vernon and Shirley Ann (Felton) W. BA, Brandeis U., 1977; MBA, Northwestern U., 1979. Systems mktg. rep. Control Data Corp., Chgo., 1979-81, mktg. rep., 1981-82; staff mgr. AT&T, Basking Ridge, N.J., 1982-84; nat. account exec. AT&T, N.Y.C., 1984-86; mgr. bus. planning AT&T, Berkeley Heights, N.J., 1986-87; product mgr. AT&T, Morristown, N.J., 1987-88; dist. mgr. Unisoft Corp., N.Y.C., 1988-89; acct. mgr. Lotus Devel. Corp., N.Y.C., 1989-90; dir. bus. devel., 1990-91, Software Corp. of Am., Stamford, Conn., 1990-91; pres. Absolute Computer Techs., Inc., N.J., 1985—. Mem. South Orange Planning Bd., 1985-87, South Orange Citizens Budget Adv. Com., 1983—. Mem. Nat. Black MBA Assn. (fin. chmn. Chgo. br. 1979-81, Performance award 1981). Home: 541 Scotland Rd South Orange NJ 07079-3009 Office: ACT Computer PO Box 978 South Orange NJ 07079-0978

WILLIAMS, WARREN REED, JR., consulting company executive; b. Candor, N.Y., Oct. 17, 1927; s. Warren Reed and Pauline Alma (Hover) W.; m. Betty Ruth Lowe, July 14, 1950; children: Warren Reed III, Carol Lynn Williams Nasser. BA, SUNY, Binghamton, 1952; postgrad., Pa. State U., 1952-53; SUNY, 1977-78. Sr. metall. chemist Bendix Corp., South Montrose, Pa., 1953-72; staff engr. Allied Signal Corp., Sidney, N.Y., 1972-87; pres. WRW Cons., Montrose, 1986—. Counselman, pres. Montrose Borough Coun., 1969-87; rep. committeeman Ward 1, 1970-78; chmn. Susquehanna County Bd. of Commr., 1992—. Mem. Soc. Aero. Engrs., Soc. Plastics Engrs. (pres. elect 1990—), Masons (past master 1961), KC (past grand commdr. Pa. 1976-77), Royal Arch Masons (past high priest 1964), Royal and Select Master Masons (past illustrious master), Toastmasters (past pres.). Republican. Methodist. Home: 14 Griffis St Montrose PA 18801-1008

WILLIAMS, WILLIAM GORDON, public information officer; b. Scranton, Pa., Aug. 18, 1935; s. William D. and Norah L. (Evans) W.; m. Mary Jane Sayers, June 13, 1959; children: David B., Jonathan G., Johanna B. Student, Pa. State U., 1953-55, 58-59. Reporter Reading (Pa.) Times, 1959; news editor The Progress, Clearfield, Pa, 1959-71; editor AP, Phila., 1971-74; corr. in charge AP, Harrisburg, Pa., 1974-77; press sec. Rep. State Com, Harrisburg, 1978; dir. pub. info. Pa. Ho. of Reps., Harrisburg, 1978—; vice chmn. Nat. Conf. State Legislators Leadership Staff Sect., 1986. Author: Days of Darkness: The Gettysburg Civilians, 1986. Pres. Clearfield Area United Fund, 1970; bd. dirs. AID for Clearfield Inc., 1960; Clearfield County Devel. Coun., 1960, Clearfield County Beautification Com., 1960. With USN, 1955-57. Recipient 1st Place Spot News award Pa. Newspapers Pubs. Assn., Clearfield, 1960, Young Man of Yr. award The Clearfield Area Jaycees, 1960. Mem. Harrisburg Area Civil War Roundtable (pres. 1985). Republican. Methodist. Home: 100 Fairway Dr Camp Hill PA 17011-2066

WILLIAMS, WILLIAM HENRY, history educator, liberal arts coordinator; b. Port Jervis, N.Y., June 9, 1936; s. Henry and Esther Marcy (Crooker) W.; m. Helen Garrett, June 28, 1959; children: Dawn, Mark. BA, Drew U., 1958; MS in Edn., Yeshiva U., 1959; PhD, U. Del., 1971. Tchr. social studies Pawling (n.Y.) Cen. High Sch., 1959-63; instr. U. Del., Georgetown, 1967-71, asst. prof., 1971-77, assoc. prof., 1977-86, prof., 1986—, Southern coord. MALS program, 1990—; cons. Pa. Hosp., Phila., 1975; mem. bd. archives and history Peninsula Conf. United Meth. Ch., Dover, Del., 1988—; cons. Smith Island Project, State of Md., Annapolis, 1991—. Author: America's First Hospital, 1976, Garden of American Methodism, 1984, The First State: An Illustrated History of Delaware, 1985. Chair Del. Humanities Coun., Wilmington, 1976-77, Georgetown Bicentennial Com., 1975-76, Sussex County Magna Carta Com., Georgetown, 1986-87; cons. scholarship com. Del. Heritage Commn., Wilmington, 1985-87. U. Del. fellow, 1976, 80, 90-91, Am. Philos. Soc. fellow, 1972, NEH fellow, 1973, 85; recipient Joseph P. del Tufo award Del. Humanities Forum, 1980. Mem. Orgn. Am. Historians, Hist. Soc. Del. (bd. editors 1988—), Soc. Historian of the Early Am. Rep. Methodist. Home: 238 W Pine St Georgetown DE 19947-1830

WILLIAMS, WILLIAM HENRY, II, publisher; b. Birmingham, Ala., Oct. 21, 1931; s. Calvin Thomas and Lillian Elizabeth (Levey) W.; m. Lewis Mozelle Hensley, Feb. 28, 1959; 1 child, William Henry III. Student, Baylor U., 1952-55. Printer Waco (Tex.) Tribune-Herald, 1950-59; internat. rep. Internat. Typog. Union, Colorado Springs, Colo., 1960-68; editor, gen. mgr. Colorado Springs Free Press, 1969-70; dir. labor relations The Morning Telegraph, N.Y.C., 1970-72; gen. mgr. Daily Racing Form, Hightstown, N.J., 1972-89, nat. gen. mgr. for U.S. and Can., 1990-91, pub., 1991—; mem. adv. council journalism dept. Baylor U., Waco, 1970-72. Chmn. CentraState Med. Ctr., Freehold, N.J., 1982-83, CentraState Health Affiliates, Freehold, 1987—; vice chmn. Ctr. for Aging, Inc., Freehold, 1985-90; dep. mayor Freehold Tsp. Com., 1987, mayor 1989-90, committeeman, 1985—; chmn. Freehold Mayor's Task Force on Substance Abuse, 1987-91. Named an Hon. Trustee Freehold Area Hosp., 1985—. Mem. Am. Newspaper Pubs. Assn., Newspaper Personnel Relations Assn., N.J. Press Assn., NCCJ (Brotherhood award 1986). Republican. Lutheran. Club: Exchange (Hightstown) (charter pres.). Lodges: Masons (32 degree), Shriners, Optimists (charter mem. Freehold chpt.). Home: 45 Kettle Creek Rd Freehold NJ 07728-3023 Office: Daily Racing Form Div 10 Lake Dr Hightstown NJ 08520-5321

WILLIAMS, WILLIAM JOSEPH, physician, educator; b. Bridgeton, N.J., Dec. 8, 1926; s. Edward Carlaw and Mary Hood (English) W.; m. Margaret Myrick Lyman, Aug. 12, 1950 (dec. Aug., 1985) ; children: Susan Lyman, William Prescott, Sarah Robb; m. Karen A. Hughes, Feb. 18, 1989. Student, Bucknell U., 1943-45; MD, U. Pa., 1949. Diplomate: Am. Bd. Internal Medicine. (hematology com. 1976-80). Intern U. Pa., 1949-50, Am. Cancer Soc. research fellow in Biochemistry, 1950-52, resident medicine, 1954-55, assoc. to asst. prof. medicine, 1955-58, assoc. prof. to prof. medicine, chief hematology, 1961-69; sr. instr. microbiology Case Western Res. U., 1952; asst. prof. medicine Washington U., St. Louis, 1959-60; research fellow Oxford U., Eng., 1960-61; mem. hematology tng. com. Nat. Inst. Arthritis and Metabolic Disease, 1964-68, research career program com., 1968-72; prof., chmn. dept. medicine SUNY Health Sci. Ctr., Syracuse, 1969—, interim dean Coll. Medicine, 1991—; vis. scientist Walter and Eliza Hall Inst., Melbourne, Australia, 1980; vis. prof. Monash U., Melbourne, 1980; mem. thrombosis adv. com. Nat. Heart and Lung Inst., 1969-73, chmn., 1971-73; adv. coun. Nat. Arthritis, Metabolism and Digestive Diseases, 1975-79; mem. residency rev. com. internal medicine Accreditation Coun. Grad. Med. Edn., 1983-89, mem. bd. appeals panel for internal medicine, 1989; mem. N.Y. State Coun. Grad. Med. Edn., 1987-89. Editor-in-chief: Hematology, 1972, 3d edit., 1983, 4th edit., 1989; contbr. articles to med. lit. Trustee Everson Mus. Art, 1975-81, 83-89. With USNR, 1944-46, 52-54. Recipient Research Career Devel. award Nat. Heart Inst., 1963-68; Daland fellow Am. Philos. Soc., 1955-57; Markle scholar, 1957-62. Mem. AMA, ACP (gov. Upstate N.Y. 1976-81), Am. Soc. Biol. Chemists, Am. Soc. Clin. Investigation, Assn. Am. Physicians, Am. Clin. and Climatol. Assn., Am. Heart Assn. (council on thrombosis exec. com. 1977-81), Internat. Soc. Thrombosis and Haemostasis, Assn. Profs. Medicine, Am. Soc. Hematology, Interurban Clin. Club (sec. 1964-70), Internat. Hematology Soc., Alpha Omega Alpha. Mem. Soc. Friends. Home: 5160 Peck Hill Rd Jamesville NY 13078-9724 Office: 750 E Adams St Syracuse NY 13210-2306

WILLIAMS, WILLIAM ROBERT, naval officer; b. Syracuse, N.Y., Jan. 2, 1949; s. Edward Myron and Mary Agnes (Blank) W.; m. Karen Ann Halsey; children: Rebecca Ann, Sarah Jane, William Matthew. BS, U.S. Naval Acad., 1971; Masters Gen. Adminstrn., U. Md., 1982; grad., Nat. War Coll., 1987. Commd. ensign USN, 1971, advanced through grades to capt., 1986, various assignments, 1976-80; instr. U.S. Naval Acad. USN, Annapolis, Md., 1980-82; exec. officer U.S.S. Aubrey Fitch USN, Mayport, Fla., 1982-84; mil. pers. policy coord. Office of the Chief of Naval Ops. USN, Washington, 1984-86; staff mem. Directorate for Joint Support Joint Chiefs of Staff, Washington, 1987-89; commdg. officer USS Conyngham (DDG-17), Norfolk, Va., 1989-90, USS Arthur W. Radford, 1990-91; staff comdr. 2d Fleet, 1992—. Mem. Surface Naval Assn., U.S. Naval Inst., Nat. War Coll. Alumni Assn., U.S. Naval Acad. Alumni Assn., VFW. Home: 2108 Turnstone Quay Virginia Beach VA 23454-1338

WILLIAMS, WILLIE, JR., physicist, educator; b. Independence, La., Mar. 24, 1947; s. Willie Sr. and Lee Anner (Booker) W. B.S., So. U., 1970; M.S., Iowa State U., 1972, Ph.D., 1974. Mem. faculty Lincoln U., Lincoln University, Pa., 1974—, assoc. prof. physics, 1979-84; prof. physics Lincoln U., Lincoln University, 1984—, chmn. dept., 1976—, chmn. sci. and math. div., 1978-80, 83—, founder, dir. Lincoln Advance Sci. and Engring. Reinforcement (LASER) Program, 1980—, dir. pre-engring., 1976—; bd. dirs. women tech. program Lincoln U. Urban Ctr., Phila.; vis. prof. Ctr. for Teaching Innovation, Drexel U., 1975; liaison officer Nat. Assn. for Equal Opportunity in Higher Edn., Dept. Def. Program., 1987—; mem. steering com. NSF Comprehensive Ctr. for Minorities, Phila.; bd. dirs. Prime Inc., Phila. Contbr. articles to profl. jours. Chmn. Cheyney Lincoln Temple Cluster, 1974-78; pres. The Men Fedn., So. U., 1968-69. Recipient Lindback award for Outstanding Teaching, 1976, Outstanding Scientist award White House Initiative, 1988; named one of Outstanding Young Men of Am., 1979; fellow NASA, 1979, Mobil Oil Corp., 1977, Nat. Bur. Standards, 1979, Dept. Def., 1980-81, Navy fellow, 1982. Mem. AAAS, AAUP, Am. Assn. Physics, N.Y. Acad. Scis., Math. Assn. Am., Am. Phys. Soc., Nat. Soc. Black Physicists, Nat. Geog. Soc., Iowa State Alumna Assn., Sigma Xi, Sigma Pi Sigma. Baptist. Home: 1454 Church Hill Pl Reston VA 22094-1228 Office: Lincoln U Dept Physics Lincoln University PA 19352

WILLIAMSON, CRAIG EDWARD, ecology educator; b. Boston, July 20, 1953; s. John William and Marion Elizabeth (Haines) W.; m. Gail Anne Lindsay, Oct. 5, 1974; children: Evan David, Trevor John. AB, Dartmouth Coll., 1975, PhD, 1981; MA, Mt. Holyoke Coll., 1977. Asst. prof. ecology Lehigh U., Bethlehem, Pa., 1981-87, assoc. prof., 1987—; dir. Pocono Comparative Lakes Program, Bethlehem, 1989—. Contbr. over 25 articles to profl. publs. Grantee NSF, 1983, 90, 91, Andrew Mellon Found., 1989, 91, Geraldine Dodge Found., 1989, 90. Mem. Am. Soc. Limnology and Oceanography, Ecol. Soc. Am., N.Am. Lake Mgmt. Soc., Sigma Xi. Office: Lehigh U Dept Earth/Environ Sci Williams Hall 31 Bethlehem PA 18015

WILLIAMSON, FLETCHER PHILLIPS, real estate broker; b. Cambridge, Md., Dec. 16, 1923; s. William Fletcher and Florence M. (Phillips) W.; student U. Md., 1941, 42; m. Betty June (Stoker), Apr. 6, 1943; 1 son, Jeffrey Phillips; m. 2d, Helen M. Stumberg, Aug. 28, 1972. Test engr. Engring. Lab., Glen Martin Co., 1942-43; salesman Corkran Ice Cream Co., Cambridge, 1946-50; real estate broker, 1950—; chmn. bd. Williamson Real Estate, Dorchester Corp., 1963-72; bd. dirs. WCEM, Inc., 1966-75; vice chmn. bd., dir. Nat. Bank of Cambridge, 1979—; dir. Cam-Storage Inc., Dorchester Indsl. Devel. Corp., Delmarva Bank Data Processing Ctr.; co-receiver White & Nelson, Inc. Bd. dirs. Delmarva council Boy Scouts Am.; past pres. Cambridge Hosp., United Fund of Dorchester County; bd. dirs. Del. Mus. Natural History, Dorchester County Pub. Library; bd. dirs., v.p. Game Conservation Internat.; v.p. Del. Mus. Natural History. Served as ordnance tech. intelligence engr. AUS, 1943-46; ETO. Mem. Md. Real Estate Assn. (gov. 1956-66), Outdoor Writers Assn., Nat. Rifle Assn., Nat. Def. Preparedness Assn., Cambridge Dorchester C. of C. (dir. 1955—), Power Squadron (comdr. 1954-56), Dorchester County Bd. Realtors (pres.),

Scandinavian Atlantic Salmon Group, Explorers Club, Soc. of S. Pole. Methodist. Clubs: Rolling Rock, Shikar Safari, Anglers, Chesapeake Bay Yacht, Camp Fire, Md., Georgetown. Lodges: Masons, Shriners.

WILLIAMSON, HELEN THORWORTH, clinical psychologist; b. Irvington, N.J., Dec. 15, 1927; d. John Andrew and Hazel Sayre (Tichenor) Thorworth; m. Donald Henry Williamson, Sept. 4, 1948; children: Diane, Steven, Nina, David, Lisa Crane. BA, William Smith Coll., 1949; MA, Fairfield U., 1965; PhD, NYU, 1971; DSc (hon.), Hobart, 1976. Lic. clin. psychologist. Psychologist Lincoln Inst., N.Y.C., 1970-72; prof. psychology Manhattanville Coll., Purchase, N.Y., 1972-80; pvt. practice N.Y.C., 1971—; cons. in field. Author: Teaching Tolerance for Ambiguity, 1971. Bd. trustees Stamford Hosp., 1960-66; pres. Stamford Hosp. Aux., 1960-66. Recipient Outstanding Civic Leader Stamford Advocate, 1966, Trustee Scholarship, Scholarship Hobart and William Smith Colls., 1945, Founder's Day award NYU, 1971. Mem. APA (mem. clin. div., mem. psychotherapy div.), Psychologists in Ind. Practice, N.Y. Clin. Psychologists, N.Y. State Psychol. Assn., Am. Acad. Psychotherapists, Soc. for Personality Assessment. Presbyterian. Home: 218 Russet Rd Stamford CT 06903-1810 Office: 111 E 85th St New York NY 10028-0958

WILLIAMSON, JEFFREY PHILLIPS, consultant; b. Cambridge, Md., Sept. 30, 1945; s. Fletcher Phillips Williamson and Betty June (Stoker) Deissler; m. Susan Elizabeth Polaski, May 9, 1975; 1 child, Mary Elizabeth. BA in Econs., Washington Coll., Chestertown, Md., 1967. Cert. rev. appraiser. Property mgr. Nat. Savs. & Trust Co., Washington, 1966-67; real estate broker Williamson Real Estate, Cambridge, Md., 1968-71; farmer Eccleston's Hill, Cambridge, 1969—; cons. J. Williamson, Cons., Cambridge, 1971—. Vestryman's warden Christ Episcopal Ch., Cambridge, 1981-83, vestryman, 1989-92, chmn. endowment com., 1984-88, chmn. fin. com., 1989-92; trustee Md. Hist. Trust, Balt., 1983-86. Mem. Dorchester County Bd. Realtors (MLS com. 1988-89), Henryville (Pa.) Fly Fishers (sec.-treas. 1987—), Phila. Gun Club, Masons. Republican. Episcopalian. Office: 3905 Bestpitch Ferry Rd Cambridge MD 21613

WILLIAMSON, JOHN, economist; b. Hereford, Eng., June 7, 1937; s. Harry and Eileen (Heap) W.; m. Denise Rausch de Souza, Mar. 30, 1974; children: Andre, Daniel, Theresa. BSc in Econs., London Sch. of Econ., 1958; PhD, Princeton U., 1963. Lectr. U. of York, Eng., 1963-68; cons. UK Treasury, London, 1968-70; prof. U. Warwick, Eng., 1970-77; advisor IMF, Washington, 1972-74; prof. Pontificia Universidade Catolica, Rio de Janeiro, Brazil, 1978-81; sr. fellow Inst. for Internat. Econs., Washington, 1981—; specialist advisor House of Commons Select Com. on Treasury, London, 1982-83. Author: Failure of World Monetary Reform, 1977; Political Economy and International Money, 1987. Pres. U. London Liberal Fedn., London, 1957-58. Mem. Royal Econ. Soc. (coun. 1976-77), Am. Econ. Assn. Home: 3919 Oliver St Bethesda MD 20815-3434 Office: Inst for Internat Econ 11 Dupont Cir NW Washington DC 20036-1207

WILLIAMSON, LIZ (ELIZABETH ANNE RAY WILLIAMSON), dancer, choreographer, educator; b. Winston-Salem, N.C.; d. Alexander Hamilton and Maude E. (Young) Ray; m. William Elliott Williamson; 1 child, Wonza Williamson Sinclair. AB, Radcliffe Coll.; MA, NYU. Tchr., Howard U., Tuskegee Inst., Bennett Coll., Greensboro, N.C., Ethical Culture Sch., N.Y.C., The Dalton Sch., N.Y.C.; artist-in-residence Talladega Coll., Ala.; master tchr. in jazz 1st Statewide Dance Conf., Nashville; prof. dance Hostos Community Coll., CUNY, 1972-73; master tchr. modern and jazz Fla. chpt. Dance Masters Am., Miami Beach, 1971, 1st N.Y. State Coll. and U. Dance Festival, 1971; master tchr. in jazz U. Alta., Edmonton, Can., 1972, Colony Club, N.Y.C., Brick Parish House, N.Y.C.; tchr. Philadanco, Phila., 1988, Internat. Ballet Competition, Jackson, Miss., 1986, 90, Kuopo (Finland) Music and Dance Festival, 1991, Am. Dance Festival Duke U., Durham, N.C., 1989; jazz artist-in-residence Jacob's Pillow, Mass., summer, 1973; chmn. performing and visual arts dept., head dance dept. Dalton Sch., N.Y.C., 1971-74; numerous master classes and workshops; choregrapher Jazz Ballet for Skeel Dancers, Oak Ridge, 1970, Mass. Jazz Ballet, 1970; master tchr. Palucca Sch., Dresden, German Dem. Republic, 1978, Bonn, Fed. Republic Germany, 1978, Les Ballet Jazz, Montreal, Que., Can., 1982; choreographer Dallas Black Dance Co., 1980, Juneau Dance Unltd., Alaska, 1980; vis. tchr. jazz ballet Moderno Enid Sauer Studio, Rio De Janeiro, Brazil, 1977, N.C. Sch. Arts, Winston-Salem, 1973, 74; dancer with Donald McKayle and Alvin Ailey cos., Merry-Go-Rounders, N.Y.C. Appeared in N.Y. City Center's Finian's Rainbow, Carmen Jones; in summer stock The Boy Friend, Show Boat, Follies of 1910, Carnegie Hall, 1960; appeared on Jackie Gleason TV show; films Edge of the City, A Man Called Adam, 1960; rec. artist Hoctor Records. Recipient Elsa Heilich Kempe award Dance Masters Am., 1976, Recognition Achievement award Radcliffe Coll., 1989, Oak Ridge Commemorative medal, 1970, Plaudit award, 1981. Mem. Nat. Assn. Regional Ballet (bd. dirs. 1977-78), New Dance Group (bd. dirs. 1977-78), Soc. Stage Dirs. and Choreographers. Author: Fundamentals of Teaching Modern Dance and Modern Jazz, 1956; editor article on jazz dance Dance mag., 1978, Jazz Gymnastics, Jazz Dance including Aerobic, 1983; contbr. articles to mags. Address: Wonza Prodns 1270 Fifth Ave Apt 5T New York NY 10029

WILLIAMSON, LORI ANN, advertising professional; b. Staten Island, N.Y., Mar. 5, 1966; d. Donald Ray and Helen Clair (Lawler) W. BBA, Pace U., 1989. Asst. coord. advt. Pace U., N.Y.C., 1989—.

WILLIAMSON, MAYNARD BURDEN, university official; b. Englewood, N.J., Mar. 12, 1922; s. James Maynard and Ethel (Burden) W.; m. Joan Brewer (div. 1973); m. Taeko Yasuda, Apr. 16; children: Christopher B., James M. AB, Princeton U., 1943; MPA, Shippensburg U. Pa., 1991. V.p. Quimica Hercules Hercules Internat., Mexico, 1961-64; mktg. mgr. Latin Am. Hercules Inc., Wilmington, Del., 1964-66, internat. mgr. terephthalates, 1966-69, area dir. Far East, 1969-85; exec. dir. Princeton (N.J)-in-Asia, 1986-89, pres., 1989—; mem. East Asian studies adv. coun. Princeton U., 1989—. Chmn. Asian Pacific Coun., 1980-81; trustee Summer Festival, Shippensburg U. Pa., 1987—. Lt. (j.g.) USN, 1943-47, ETO. Mem. Am. C. of C. Japan (pres. 1975-77), Princeton Club N.Y., Carlisle Country Club, Nassau Club. Democrat. Episcopalian. Home: 300 Walnut Bottom Rd Carlisle PA 17013-3741 Office: Princeton in Asia 224 Palmer Hall Princeton U Princeton NJ 08544

WILLIAMSON, PATRICK LESLIE, biology educator; b. Dickinson, N.D., Apr. 15, 1948; s. Willard and Eunice Williamson; m. Anne Theresia Kirkpatrick, Apr. 18, 1970; children: Adam, Eleanor. BA, Beloit (Wis.) Coll., 1970; MA and PhD, Harvard U., 1974; MA, Amherst (Mass.) Coll., 1990. Staff fellow NIH, Bethesda, Md., 1974-77; prof. Amherst Coll., 1977—. Contbr. articles to profl. jours. Fogarty fellow, 1990. Mem. Am. Soc. Cell Biology. Office: Amherst Coll Dept of Biology Amherst MA 01002

WILLIAMSON, RAY ADDISON, federal agency administrator; b. Cleve., Sept. 6, 1938; s. Paul J. and Lois V. (Burt) W.; m. Abigail F. Harrison, July 1, 1961 (div. 1980); children: Ethan D., Sarah A.H.; m. Carol L. Carnett, Oct. 18, 1986. BA in Physics, Johns Hopkins U., 1961; PhD in Astronomy, U. Md., 1968. Asst. prof. U. Hawaii, Honolulu, 1967-69; tutor St. John's Coll., Annapolis, Md., 1969-74, asst. dean, 1974-79; sr. analyst Office Tech. Assessment U.S. Congress, Washington, 1979-88, sr. assoc., 1988—; pres. Scientific Manpower Commn., Washington, 1983. Author: Living the Sky, 1984, (with others) They Dance in the Sky, 1987; co-editor: Earth and Sky, 1992; cons. editor Archaeastronomy Bull., 1979—, Space Policy, 1985—, Space Power, 1989—. Fellow Smithsonian Instn., 1977-78. Mem. AAAS, AIAA, Soc. for Am. Archaeology, Am. Folklore Soc., Western Writers Am. Office: Office Tech Assessment US Congress Washington DC 20510

WILLIAMSON, RICHARD DALE, photographer, designer electronic imagery; b. DeQueen, Ark., Jan. 10, 1947; s. James Richard and Dorothy Marie (Dale) W. BFA, U. Tex., 1969. Ptnr. Aerographics, N.Y.C., 1975—; scenic designer Studio 54, N.Y.C., 1978-89; assoc. editor Details mag., N.Y.C., 1985-90. Home and Office: 514 W 24th St New York NY 10011-1103

WILLIAMSON, ROBERT THOMAS, university official; b. Detroit, Nov. 6, 1946; s. Robert Thomas and Sarah (Simmons) W.; m. Jean Simmonds; children: Robert, Jodie, Katherine, Rebecca. BA, Coll. Wooster, 1968; JD, U. Balt., 1975. With new products dept. McCormick and Co., Hunt Valley, Md., 1970-72, with corp. legal dept., 1974-76; mktg. administr. McCormick Properties, Hunt Valley, 1972-74; dir. tech. assistance ctr. Plattsburgh State U., N.Y., 1976-82; chief officer external affairs Clarkson U., Potsdam, N.Y., 1982-85, v.p. external affairs, 1985-88; exec. v.p. Clarkson U., Potsdam, 1988—; bd. dirs. Devel. Authority North Country, Watertown, N.Y., J.R. Westons, Inc.; adv. bd. No. Advanced Techs. Corp., Potsdam. Bd. dirs. United Way Clinton and St. Lawrence Counties, N.Y., 1979-87, Adirondack North Country Assn., 1977-87; chmn. Canton Potsdam Hosp. Found.; exec. bd. Seaway Valley coun. Boy Scouts Am. Lt. USN, 1968-70. Mem. Am. Soc. Engring. Edn., Nat. Assn. Mgmt. and Tech. Assistance Ctrs. (pres. 1979-81), Coun. Advancement and Support Edn., Univ. Club. Presbyterian. Office: Clarkson U Snell Hall Potsdam NY 13676

WILLIAMSON, RUSHTON MAROT, JR., communications/project manager; b. Evanston, Ill., Aug. 4, 1948; s. Rushton Marot and Marjorie Adelaide (Woods) W.; m. Katherine Calvert Watson, Dec. 17, 1977; children: Marot Roelker, Alec Armstrong. BS, Utah State U., 1971; MS, U. So. Calif., 1982. Project mgmt. profl., 1987. Commd. 2d lt. USMCR, 1971, advanced to capt., 1976; mem. tech. staff Electrospace Systems Inc., Arlington, Va., 1982-86; project mgr. Def. Info. Systems Agy., Washington, 1986—. Editor: PMP Certification Workbook, 1989. Vice chmn. Nat. Debutante Cotillion, Washington, 1976-77, mem. married com., 1980-85, chmn. married com., 1985-92; mem.-at-large Potomac Woods Citizens Assn., Rockville, Md., 1984-87, 90-92, v.p., 1988-89; mem. Traffic Action Com., Rockville, 1987-88, Armed Forces Inaugural Com., 1977. Mem. Project Mgmt. Inst. (chpt. pres. 1984, v.p. 1985, pres. 1988-89; internat. chmn. cert. rev. com. 1988-91, cert. test com. 1988-90, chmn. mktg. com. 1990-91, advisor cert. bd. 1992, disting. contbn. award 1991), Armed Forces Communications and Electronics Assn., Nat. Contract Mgmt. Assn., Canoe Cruisers Assn. Washington, Blue Ridge Voyageurs (bd. dirs. 1988). Republican. Methodist. Home: 1583 Kimblewick Rd Rockville MD 20854-6152 Office: Def Info Systems Agy Washington DC 20305

WILLIAMSON, RUTH, actress; b. Balt., Jan. 25, 1954; d. Frank Thomas and Hazel Grace (Wheeler) W. BA, U. Md., 1976. mem. adv. bd. Shakespeare on Wheels, U. Md., 1990—. Appeared in Broadway plays Annie, 1980-82, Smile, 1986-87, Musical Comedy Murders of 1940, 1987, Guys & Dolls, 1992; appeared on TV (soap opera) Loving, 1990; films include Malcolm X, 1991; appeared in over 200 commls.; author: (play) Send Up a Flair, 1990, (children's book) Foo's Purple Spot, 1991. Sponsor Save the Children, Westport, Conn., 1982—; benefactor GMHC, N.Y.C., 1984—, Southern Poverty Law Ctr., Birmingham, Ala., 1985—, Greenpeace, 1989—. Recipient Amoco award of Excellence, 1976. Mem. SAG, AFTRA, Actor's Equity Assn., Actor's Fund (life). Democrat.

WILLIAMSON, WILLIAM OWEN, geological and chemical educator, consultant; b. Luton County, Eng., Jan. 30, 1911; came to U.S., 1959; s. Owen and Susan Winifred (Pollock) W.; m. Olive Zoe Tucket, Aug. 5, 1958. BSc in Chemistry with honors, London U., 1931, BSC in Geology with honors, 1932, PhD in Geology, 1934, DSc in Geology and Chemistry, 1958. Chief asst. in ceramics North Staffordshire Tech. Coll., Stoke-on-Trent, Eng., 1934-42; rsch. officer Ministry of Supply, Birmingham, Eng., 1942-45; profl. officer Govt. Metall. Lab., Johannesburg, South Africa, 1945-47; prin. rsch. officer Commonwealth Sci. and Indsl. Rsch. Orgn., Melbourne, Australia, 1947-59; prof. Pa. State U., University Park, 1959-76, emeritus prof., 1976—. Contbr. chpts. to books, numerous articles to profl. jours. Fellow Royal Chem. Soc., Am. Ceramic Soc.; mem. Mineral. Soc. (U.K.), Geologists Assn. (U.K.), Archaeol. Inst. Am. Office: Pa State U 116 Steidle University Park PA 16802

WILLIER, STEPHEN ACE, music educator; b. Centerville, Iowa, Sept. 7, 1952; s. Charles John and Janet (Gerard) W. BM, U. Iowa, 1974, MA, 1976; PhD, U. Ill., 1987. Asst. prof. music Temple U., Phila., 1989—; lectr. music Ariz. State U., Tempe, 1981-82, U. Ill., Urbana, 1983-87, vis. asst. prof. music, 1988-89; program annotator Opera Co. Phila., 1990—; series lectr., opera handbook annotator Pa. Opera Theater, 1991—. Contbr. articles to profl. jours. and encys. Mem. Musical Fund Soc., Am. Musicol. soc., Pi Kappa Lambda, Eta Eta (sec.-treas. 1991—). Office: Temple U Boyer Coll Music Philadelphia PA 19122

WILLIG, SIDNEY HENRY, lawyer, legal educator; b. N.Y.C., July 2, 1919; s. Wilhelm Wolf and Jean Leah (Levine) W.; m. Eleanor Frances Huss, May 22, 1943; children: Steven Elliott (dec.), Kenneth Charles, Randi Debra. AB, Bklyn. Coll., 1938; JD, Bklyn. Law Sch., 1958; BS in Pharmacy, St. Johns U., Queens, N.Y., 1947; MA, CUNY, 1952. Bar: N.Y. 1950, Pa. 1969, U.S. Supreme Ct. 1973; cert. tchr.; lic. pharmacist. Sales rep. Winthrop Chem. Co., N.Y.C., 1947-52; regional sales mgr. Winthrop Breon Inc., N.Y.C., 1952-54; dir. regulatory affairs Winthrop Labs., N.Y.C., 1954-67; prof. Law Sch. Temple U., Phila., 1967-87, prof. Sch. of Dentistry and Pharmacy, 1967-85; of counsel Sterling Drug Inc., N.Y.C., 1967-86, assoc. gen. counsel, dir. litigation, 1987—; adj. prof. law St. John's U. Coll. Pharmacology and Nursing, Queens, 1958-64; prof. Pa. Coll. Podiatric Medicine, Phila., 1977-86; cons. HEW, Washington, 1973-78; advisor to asst. sec. Health Med. Malpractice Ins., Washington, 1975; dep. atty. gen. Atty. Gen.'s Office, State of N.Y., 1957, 58. Author: Nurses Guide to the Law, 1970, Legal Aspect of Dentistry, 1972, Drug Abuse in Industry, 1972, Current Good Manufacturing Practices of Pharmaceuticals, 1973. Pres. St. John's U. Alumni Fedn., Queens, 1954-60; co-chair S.I. Beautification Com., 1962-65. 1st lt. USAF, 1943-49, ETO. Recipient Pres.'s award Am. Soc. for Pharmacy Law, 1991, Pres.'s medal to outstanding alumnus St. Johns U., 1990; grantee Nat. Pharm. Coun. of Washington, 1970-75, U.S. Dept. Health and Human Resources, 1971, Am. Assn. Podiatry, 1980. Mem. ABA, N.Y. State Bar Assn., Pa. Bar Assn., Del. Valley Coll. Consortium (co-bd. dirs.), Assn. of Food and Drug Ofcls. (assoc.), Def. Rsch. Inst. (chair com. 1990-91), Am. Assn. Law Schs., Nat. Assn. Bd. of Pharmacy (bd. dirs. edn. com. 1970-75), Fedn. of Med. Bds. (dir. continuing edn. com. 1972-75), Nat. Assn. Bds. of Acctg. (bd. dirs. edn. com. 1972-75). Office: Sterling Winthrop Inc 90 Park Ave Staten Island NY 10302-1440

WILLING, ROBERT NELSON, archdeacon; b. N.Y.C., June 15, 1934; s. Robert Nelson and Anne (Steinmetz) W.; divorced 1987; children: Theresa, Robert III, Catherine, Laura. BA in Philosophy, Hobart Coll., 1957; MDiv, Nashotah House, 1960; postgrad., NYU, 1962-68. Ordained to ministry Episcopal Ch. as deacon and priest, 1960. Curate St. Margaret's Ch., Bronx, N.Y., 1960-63; rector Trinity Ch., Mt. Vernon, N.Y., 1963-70, St. John's and St. Clement's, Mt. Vernon, 1967-70; vicar St. Paul's, Eastchester, N.Y., 1967-70; bd. dirs. Hudson Area Housing Authority, Tarrytown, N.Y., Mid-Hudson Rural Migrant Com., New Paltz, N.Y.; dep. Gen. Conv., Episcopal Ch., 1973—; del. N.Y. State Coun. Chs., Syracuse, 1978-88; adj. prof. Union Theol. Sem., N.Y.C., 1984-86, Gen. Theol. Sem., N.Y.C., 1988—. Editor regional newsletter; contbr. articles to profl. jours. Mem. adv. com. to Supt. Schs. on race, religion, teaching history, Mt. Vernon, 1965-66, Mayor's Commn. on Housing, Mt. Vernon, 1967-69, Upward Bound, Sarah Lawrence Coll., 1968-70. Recipient Key to City of Mt. Vernon City Legislature, 1970, Bishop N.Y. Cross Right Rev. Paul Moore Jr., 1985. Mem. Am. Mgmt. Assn., Alban Inst., Episcopal Peace Fellowship, Order of Holy Cross, Am. Philatelic Soc., Kappa Alpha. Home and Office: Upper Boiceville Rd Boiceville NY 12412

WILLIS, BARBARA FLORENCE, artist; b. Bronx, N.Y., Dec. 17, 1932; d. Gerard and Anna Barbara (Schelmeyer) Ossman; m. Sidney Frank Willis, 1955; children: Jerry Dale, Frank Larkworthy. Grad., Vesper George Sch. Art, 1955. One-woman shows include Jackson Weatherbee, Newburyport, Mass., 1986-87, Am. Artists Profl. League, 1987, 88, 89, Audubon Soc., N.Y.C., 1988, Springfield (Mass.) Art League, 1989, Springfield Acad. Artists, 1989-90, 91, Pastel Soc. Am., N.Y.C., 1989, Copley Soc. Am., 1990, RH Love Gallery, Chgo., 1990, Cape Code Artists Assn., 1990, 91; one-woman show Peel Gallery, Danby, Vt., 1988, joint one-man show, 1992. Recipient hon. mention Am. Artists Profl. League, 1987, Springfield Acad. Aartists, 1989, 90, Salamagundi Show,1990, Cape Code Artists Assn.,1991, Realistic Artist award Pastel Soc. Am., 1989; 1st prize Winter Mem. Show, Copley Artists Soc., 1991, Spring Mems. Show Jurors award, 1991; award Acad. Artists Assn., 1992. Home and Office: Old Stagecoach Rd Bennington NH 03442-4325

WILLIS, CRAIG DEAN, university president; b. Cambridge, Ohio, Mar. 21, 1935; s. John Russell and Glenna (Stevens) W.; m. Marilyn Elaine Foster, June 9, 1956; Mark Craig, Bruce Dean, Todd Laine, Garth John. B.A., Ohio Wesleyan U, 1957; M.A., Ohio State U., 1960, Ph.D., 1969. Registrar Ohio Wesleyan U., 1964-69; dir. admissions Wright State U., 1970-72, dean, 1971-77; v.p. acad. affairs Concord Coll., 1977-82; pres. Lock Haven U. Pa., 1982—; vice chmn. Clinton region Mellon Bank Cen., 1987, chmn., 1988, also bd. dirs.; bd. dirs. Lock Haven U., Lock Haven Hosp.; chmn. Lock Haven Hosp. Health Fund; cons. Ellis Assocs., Princeton, W.Va., 1980-82. Chmn. bd. Kirkmont Preschool, Beavercreek, Ohio, 1974-77, Beavercreek Library, 1976-77, Regional Edn. Service Agy., Beckley, W.Va., 1978-82; mem. N.E.-Midwest leadership Coun., 1989—. Recipient Disting. Alumnus award dept. edn. Ohio Wesleyan U., 1991; scholar Sohio Oil, 1953, Govt. of France, Paris, 1964, Shell Oil Co, 1967. Mem. Commn. State Coll. and Univ. Pres., Assn. State Colls. and Univs., Rotary (Citizen of Yr. award Lock Haven 1989), Ohio Wesleyan U. Alumni Assn. (Disting. Sesquicentennial Alumnus of the Edn. 1992), Phi Kappa Phi, Kappa Kappa Psi, Phi Delta Kappa, Kappa Delta Pi. Presbyterian. Office: Lock Haven U North Fairview St Lock Haven PA 17745

WILLIS, JAKIE ARLETA, educator; b. Richland, Ga.; d. Jacob C.W. and Ardella (Alford) Williams; m. Frank A. Willis (dec.); children: Beverly Donita, Reginald Tyronne. BS, Albany State Coll., 1951; MA, NYU, 1957. Cert. elem. edn. Tchr. Stewart County, Lumpkin, Ga., 1951-63; tchr. Stratford Bd. Edn., Stratford, Conn., 1963—. Named Outstanding Tchr. Am., Fuller & Dees, Washington, 1975. Mem. Assn. for Supervision and Curriculum Devel., NEA, Stratford Edn. Assn. (sec. 1965-77, pres. 1980-81), Conn. Edn. Assn., Alpha Kappa Alpha (pres. Bridgeport, Conn. chpt. 1985-89). Democrat. Methodist. Home: 1361 South Ave Stratford CT 06497-6619

WILLIS, PATRICIA CANNON, curator, researcher; b. Chgo., Sept. 21, 1938; d. Charles Bernard and Blanche Alice (Reardon) Cannon, m. Robert J. Willis, July 4, 1972. BA, Barat Coll., 1964; AM, U. Chgo., 1966, PhD, 1972. Curator Rosenbach Mus. and Libr., Phila., 1975-87; curator Am. lit. Beinecke Rare Book and Manuscript Libr. Yale Univ., New Haven, 1987—; advisor Jour. Modern Lit., Phila., 1987—; fellow U.S. Army War Coll., Carlisle, Pa., 1990; cons. Rsch. Libr. Group, Stanford, Calif., 1991—. Author: Marianne Moore: Vision into Verse, 1987 (ALA award 1988); editor: Complete Prose of Marianne Moore, 1986, Marianne Moore: Woman and Poet, 1991. Media coord. Common Cause, Trenton, N.J., 1973-78. Dissertation fellow AAUW, 1970; Jr. Humanist fellow NEH, 1973. Mem. MLA, Am. Lit. Assn., Elizabethan Club, Soc. for Textual Scholarship. Office: Yale Univ Beinecke Rare Book and Manuscript Libr 1603A Yale Station New Haven CT 06520

WILLIS, SID FRANK, artist, educator; b. Newark, Dec. 14, 1930; s. Frank Larkworthy and Venita Pearl (Dupree) W.; m. Barbara Florence Ossman; children: Jerry Dale, Frank Larkworthy II. Grad., Vesper George Sch. of Art, Boston, 1956; student, Atelier Robert Douglas Hunter, 1956-59. Tchr. Sharon Art Ctr., Sharon, N.H., 1965-81; painting instr. Franklin Pierce Coll., Rindge, N.H., 1972-73; tchr. Vesper George Sch. of Art, Boston, 1970-74. Contbr. pictures to N.Y. Graphic Soc. and Yankee Mag. Recipient four Gold Medals Jordan Show, Vayana Meml. Grand Prize Oqunquit Art Ctrs., Stillife Prize Ellsworth Gallery, Acrylic Prize Cape Cod Art Assn., Gold Medal Best In Show Boston Guild, Gold Medal Popular Prize Heritage Salon. Mem. Guild of Boston Artists, Pastel Soc. of Am., So. Vt. Art Assn., Copely Soc. Am. Artists Profl. League, New Am. Acad. of Art, N.H. Art Assn. Home: 7 Old Stage Coach Rd Bennington NH 03447

WILLKIE, WENDELL LEWIS, II, lawyer; b. Indpls., Oct. 29, 1951; s. Philip Herman Willkie and Rosalie (Heffelfinger) Hall; m. Carlotta Fendig, June 27, 1987; children: Alexandra Elizabeth, Diana Fendig. AB, Harvard U., 1973; BA, Oxford (Eng.) U., 1975, MA, 1983; JD, U. Chgo., 1978. Bar: N.Y. 1979. Assoc. Simpson Thacher and Bartlett, N.Y.C., 1978-82; gen. counsel NEH, Washington, 1982-84; assoc. counsel to Pres. The White House, Washington, 1984-85; chief of staff, counselor to Sec. U.S. Dept. Edn., Washington, 1985, gen. counsel, 1985-88; spl. counsel Bush-Quayle, 1988; counsel Office of the Pres.-elect, Washington, 1988-89; spl. advisor to the Sec. Dept. of Commerce, Washington, 1989, gen. counsel, 1989—. Harvard U. scholar, 1969-73, Rhodes scholar, 1973. Republican. Episcopalian. Home: 4826 Drummond Ave Bethesda MD 20815-5429 Office: Dept Commerce 14th Constitution Ave NE Washington DC 20230-0001

WILLOUGHBY, MICHAEL JAMES, banker; b. Washington, Nov. 2, 1945; s. Jesse Deaderick and Dorma Laverne (Herzog) W.; m. Ruth Marie Birchett, June 21, 1975; children: Susanne Marie, M. Andrew, Christopher Daniel. BA, U. Oreg., 1966; MBA, Tex. Tech U., 1972. Asst. sec. Chem. Bank, N.Y.C., 1975-78; v.p. Bank New Eng., N.A., Boston, 1978-85; exec. v.p. Riggs Nat. Bank, Washington, 1985—. Contbr. chpt. to banking book. Mem. Corp. for Boston, 1984-85, Mass. Gov.'s Energy Adv. Bd., 1984-85; elder Fairfax Presbyn. Ch.; dir. D.C. chpt. Am. Red Cross. Capt. U.S. Army, Vietnam. Decorated Bronze Star, Air medal. Mem. Robert Morris Assocs.-Chesapeake (sr. assoc.), Greater Washington Bd. Trade, The County Club of Fairfax, Rotary (Washington chpt.), Sigma Iota Epsilon. Presbyterian. Home: 6305 Pebblebrook Trce Centreville VA 22020-4907 Office: Riggs Nat Bank 800 17th St NW Washington DC 20006-3944

WILLOW, JUDITH ANN LOYE, tax preparer; b. Harrisburg, Pa., Oct. 2, 1939; d. John Steve and Mary Grace (Bergstresser) Loye; m. Robert Glenn Willow, June 14, 1957; 1 child, Robert Allen. Grad. high sch., Harrisburg. Cert. tax preparation, Pa. Legal sec. McNees, Wallace & Nurick, Harrisburg, 1957-58; tax preparer H&R Block, Harrisburg, 1967—; tax info. source TV interviews, Sta. WHP-TV 21, Harrisburg, 1982—, Sta. WHTM-TV 27, Harrisburg, 1988-89. Dir. Dauphin (Pa.) Recreation Assn., 1970-80; water safety instr. ARC, Harrisburg, 1970-80; v.p. PTA, Dauphin, 1966, sec., 1968. Mem. Nat. Honor Soc. Democrat. Mormon. Home: 704 Charles Rd PO Box 171 Dauphin PA 17018 Office: Exec Tax Svc H&R Block Olde Liberty Sq Harrisburg PA 17109

WILLS, JEAN MARIE, nursing educator; b. Greensburg, Pa., Nov. 17, 1939; d. Arthur J. and Eleanor M. (Eisaman) Miller; m. David W. Wills, June 10, 1960; children: Donna, Diane. Cert., Shadyside Hosp., Pitts., 1960; BS in Nursing, BS in Edn., U. Pitts., 1980, MSN in Nursing Care of Children, 1982, PhD in Nursing, 1991. Staff nurse Citizen's Gen. Hosp., New Kensington, 1961, 62-80; staff nurse ICU Children's Hosp., Pitts.; asst. instr. affiliate program U. Pitts., 1981-82, asst. prof., 1982—. Contbr. articles to profl. jours. Univ. scholar U. Pitts., 1983, scholarship NIH, 1980-81. Mem. ANA, Pa. Nurses Assn. (Area #6), Tri-State Nursing Computer Network, Soc. Otorhinolaryngology and Head/Neck Nurses, Sigma Theta Tau, Pi Lambda Theta.

WILMOTH, GREGORY HICKS, psychologist; b. Louisville, Feb. 15, 1947; s. Leslie Hicks and Eileen (O'Doherty) W.; m. Cynthia May Cohen, May 6, 1984; 1 child, Rebecca Lee. BA, U. Ky., 1969; MA, SUNY, Binghamton, 1975, Western Ky. U., 1977; PhD, U. Fla., 1980. Instr. Edison State Coll., Pigua, Ohio, 1975-77; NIMH predoctoral fellow U. Fla., Gainesville, 1977-79, project mgr., 1979-80; asst. prof. U. Md., College Park, 1980-87; pub. policy analyst Am. Psychol. Assn., Washington, 1987-89; analyst-in-charge U.S. Gen. Acctg. Office, Washington, 1989—; cons. U. Md., 1983-84, Quincy Co., Landham, Md., 1983-84. Editor: Psychological Perspectives on Abortion, 1992; mem. editorial bd.: Jour. of Social Issues, 1990-93; contbg. author: Family Policy and Abortion, 1991, Moral Reasoning, 1980; contbr. articles to profl. jours. Mem. Am. Psychol. Assn., Coalition for Psychology in the Pub. Interest (pres. 1990-91), Soc. for Population and Environ. Psychology (coun. mem. 1990-93), Soc. for Psychol. Study of Social Issues (coun. mem. 1992-93). Office: US General Acctg Office 441 G St NW Washington DC 20548-0002

WILNER, MILTON, psychologist, educator; b. N.Y.C., Aug. 12, 1924; s. Philip and Rebecca (Pollack) W.; m. Dorothy Harriet Levine, Apr. 10, 1949; children: Deborah Sue Wilner Hoffman, Judith Anne Wilner Lawrence. BA,

NYU, 1949, PhD, 1955. Psychol. intern VA, Denver and N.Y.C., 1951-55; staff psychologist VA, N.Y.C., 1955-66; pvt. practice N.Y.C., 1955—; field selection officer Peace Corps, U.S., Africa, Malasia, 1966-71; chief of svc. South Beach Psychiat. Ctr., N.Y.C., 1972-89; clin. prof. Downstate Med. Ctr., Bklyn., 1974—. With Signal Corps, U.S. Army, 1942-45, PTO. Mem. Am. Assn. for Partial Hospitalization (pres. 1986-88, editor newsletter 1986—). Home: 21-50 33d Rd #14A Long Island City NY 11106 Office: 1070 Park Ave # 1B New York NY 10128-1000

WILNER, PETER JON, civil engineer; b. Bklyn., Mar. 13, 1945; s. Gabriel and Roslyn (Schwartz) W.; children: Rachael, Matthew. BS, Cornell U., 1967, ME, 1968. Registered profl. engr. N.Y., N.J., Fla., Va., Ind. Asst. soils engr. Soil Mechanics Bur. N.Y. State Dept. Transp., Albany, 1968-72; project engr. Site Engrs., P.A., Montclair, N.J., 1972-77; soils engr. Stone & Webster Engrng. Co., N.Y.C., 1977-78; v.p. Thor Engrs., P.A., Livingston, N.J., 1978—. Pres. Roxbury Twp. (N.J.) Soccer Club, 1986. Mem. Am. Soc. Civil Engrs., Builders Assn. Met. N.J., Cornell Soc. Engrs. (regional v.p. Ithaca, N.Y. chpt. 1974-76), Northern N.J. Assn. Soccer Referees, Trout Unltd. Office: Thor Engrs PA 513 W Mt Pleasant Ave Livingston NJ 07039-1721

WILSON, ABRAHAM, lawyer; b. Zhitomir, Ukraine, Nov. 19, 1922; came to U.S., 1923; s. Isaac and Katie (Garshoig) W.; m. Gloria Bachman, July 26, 1949 (div. Dec. 1965); 1 child, Chana; m. Christine Haftkowycz, July 23, 1966; children: Marko A., Raissa. BS, Rutgers U., 1947, MS in Chemistry, 1950, PhD in Chemistry, 1951; JD cum laude, Seton Hall U., 1974. Bar: N.J. 1974, U.S. Dist. Ct. N.J. 1974, U.S. Dist. Ct. (so. and ea. dists.) N.Y. 1974, U.S. Patent Office 1974, U.S. Supreme Ct. 1984. Sr. scientist Colgate Palmolive Co., Jersey City, 1951-55; sr. chemist Am. Cyanamid Co., Bound Brook, N.J., 1955-62, group leader phys. chemistry rsch., 1962-72, sr. scientist, 1972-74; counsel, asst. to pres. Triangle-Price Co., Inc., South Brunswick, N.J., 1974-76; pvt. practice Piscataway, N.J., 1976-86; ptnr. Sherman, Kuhn, Justin, Wilson & Spadoro, P.A., Piscataway, 1986-89, Rubin, Rubin, Malgran & Kuhn, Piscataway, 1989-90, Smith & Schechter, Piscataway, 1990—; instr. phys. chemistry Rutgers U., 1951-56; gen. counsel Enzon, Inc., South Plainfield, N.J., 1981-87, outside counsel, 1987—. Patentee in field. Councilman Borough of Millstone, N.J., 1959-61, mayor, 1962-64; bd. dirs. Piscataway Community TV Authority, 1986—, chmn. bd. dirs., 1986-88; bd. dirs. Raritan Valley ARC, 1986—; mem. environ. commn. Twp. of Piscataway, 1988—. 2nd lt. USAF, 1943-46, PTO. Vis. fellow Imperial Coll. Sci. Tech., London, 1961-62. Mem. Am. Chem. Soc., N.J. Bar Assn., N.J. Patent Bar Assn., Middlesex County Bar Assn., Am. Intellectual Property Assn. Democrat. Jewish. Office: Smith & Schechter 216 Stelton Rd Piscataway NJ 08854-3284

WILSON, ALICE BLAND, real estate consultant; b. Rainelle, W.Va., Apr. 1, 1938; d. Brady Floyd and Mildred Martha (George) Bland; m. Louis William Groves, Jr., Apr. 20, 1957 (div. 1981); children: Martha Rachel, Leonora Jayne; m. Glen Parten Wilson, Dec. 11, 1982. AB, W.Va. U., 1959, postgrad. in microbiology, 1975-78. Contract adminstr. Washington Plate Glass Co., Washington, 1979-80; mem. acctg. staff Forbes Co., Washington, 1981; customer relations rep. Stern's Co., Washington, 1982; real estate assoc. Prudential Preferred Properties, Washington, 1985—. Contbr. articles to Jour. Parasitology. Vol. coord. John Glenn for Pres. campaign, Washington, 1983-84; co-chmn. hospitality com. Women's Nat. Dem. Club, Washington, 1985—; mem. internat. adv. coun. ARC, Washington, 1985—; mem. exec. com. Nat. Symphony Orch., 1990—. Mem. Washington Assn. Realtors (mem. residential sales com. 1985—), Leading Edge Soc., Million Dollar Club. Avocations: flying, aerobatics, nature study. Home: 433 New Jersey Ave SE Washington DC 20003-4034 Office: Prudential Preferred Properties 2550 M St NW Washington DC 20037

WILSON, ARTHUR WILLIAM, computer and communications consultant; b. Balt., Mar. 4, 1961; s. Charles Robert and Elizabeth Ann W.; m. Jennifer Drebing, Aug. 11, 1984; children: Zachary William, Adam Arthur. BSME, Drexel U., 1983; MS in Computer Sci., The Johns Hopkins U., 1986. Gen. engr. Ballistic Rsch. Lab., U.S. Army, Aberdeen Proving Ground, Md., 1980-85; mem. tech. staff System Planning Corp., Arlington, Va., 1985-86, GTE Govt. Systems, Rockville, Md., 1986—; ind. computer cons., Olney, Md., 1988—. I.R. Dunlop scholar Drexel U., 1982; acad. scholar W.Va. U., 1978. Mem. Capital PC Users Group. Home: 17520 Gallagher Way Olney MD 20832-2065 Office: GTE Govt Systems 1700 Research Blvd Rockville MD 20850-3156

WILSON, BRUCE ALLAN, mechanical engineer; b. Kinston, N.C., Nov. 17, 1957; s. Roger Allan and Helen Phyllis (McKee) W.; m. Jacqueline Aldine Golden, Aug. 6, 1988; 1 child, Matthew Curtis. BS in Engring., Duke U., 1981; postgrad., Johns Hopkins U. Engr. AAI Corp., Hunt Valley, Md., 1980-84, sr. engr., 1984-88, design engr., 1988—. Mem. AIAA, Balt. Ski Club (past bd. dirs.). Office: AAI Corp PO Box 126 Cockeysville Hunt Valley MD 21030-0126

WILSON, CHARLES ALDEN, manufacturing executive; b. Washington County, Ind., Oct. 8, 1943; s. Alden H. and Betty Ann (Kay) W.; m. Sandra Kay Hart, June 7, 1965; children: James, Jonathan, Christopher. BS in Acctg., Miami U. of Ohio, 1965; postgrad., U. Ga., 1973; MBA, U. Pa., 1977. CPA Pa., N.J. Advanced through grades to Capt. USN, 1965-81; mng. ptnr. Precison Sheeting Svc., Pennsauken, N.J., 1980-88; pres. Precison Sheeting Svc., Camden, N.J., 1989—; v.p. Graphic Arts Credit Union, Phila., 1984-91. Dir. The Kings Christian Sch., Haddon Heights, N.J., 1982-91; trustee Bapt. Sunday Sch. Bd., Nashville, 1988—. Mem. Tech. Assn. of Pulp and Paper Industry (com. officer 1986-88), Am. Inst. CPA's, N.J. Soc. CPA's, Pa. Inst. CPA's, Beta Alpha Psi, Lambda Chi Alpha. Republican. Baptist. Office: Precision Sheeting Svc North 2d and Erie Sts Camden NJ 08102

WILSON, CHARLES ELMER, mechanical engineering educator, consultant; b. Passaic, N.J., Aug. 2, 1931; s. Charles Elmer Paul and Carrie Mildred (MacNab) W.; m. Elizabeth Frieda Weisenbacher, Aug. 17, 1958; children: Susan, Laura, Jennifer. BSME, N.J. Inst. Tech., 1953, MSME, 1958; MS in Engring. Mechanics, NYU, 1962; PhD in Mech. Engring., Poly. U., 1970. Registered profl. engr., N.J. Engr. Otis Elevator Co., N.Y.C., 1953-54, Bendix Corp., Teterboro, N.J., 1956; prof. N.J. Inst. Tech., Newark, 1956—; cons. in field; expert witness various cts. and bds., N.J., 1975—. 1st author: Mechanism, 1969, Kinematics and Dynamics, 1983; author: Noise Control, 1989; co-author: Machine Design, 1975. Mem., past chair adv. com. Natural Resources Environ. Commn., Cedar Grove, N.J., 1971—. With USAF, 1954-56. AEC fellow Cornell U., 1959, NASA fellow Stanford U., 1964, 65, NSF fellow Poly. U., 1978-79. Mem. AAUP, Inst. Noise Control Engrs., Acoustical Soc. Am., Montclair Soc. Engrs. Democrat. Presbyterian. Home: 19 Highview Ter Cedar Grove NJ 07009-1505 Office: NJ Inst Tech University Heights Newark NJ 07009

WILSON, CHRISTINE DALPHIN, title examination company executive; b. Fall River, Mass., Jan. 11, 1946; d. Richard Stephen and Rose Marie (DeGrace) Dalphin; m. Donald Alfred Wilson, Aug. 20, 1967; children: Richard David, Stephen James. BS, U. N.H., 1968. Restaurant mgr. W.T. Grants, Old Town, N.H., 1968-70; bus. office mgr. Wilsons on Moosehead (Maine) Lake, 1970-74; v.p. Land & Boundary Cons. Inc., Newfields, N.H., 1974—; cons. and lectr. in field. Vol. March of Dimes, Kensington, N.H., 1977, Jerry Lewis Telethon, Exeter, N.H., 1978, 79; organizer troop 189 and pack 197 Boy Scouts Am., Kensington and Newfields, 1984, 90, dist. commr., 1984-88, chmn. dist. com., 1988—, chmn. scouting for food, 1989-92. Recipient Wood Badge Daniel Webster coun. Boy Scouts Am., 1984, Dist. Merit award, 1989, Silver Beaver award, 1990. Mem. AAUW, Order of the Arrow, Delta Zeta (Panhellenic advisor U. N.H. 1976-78). Republican. Home: 84 Main St Newfields NH 03856-9999 Office: Land & Boundary Cons Inc PO Box 446 Exeter NH 03856-0322

WILSON, CYNTHIA LINDSAY, artist; b. Washington, May 3, 1945; d. Mark Childress Jr. and Anne Ruth (Jones) Lindsay; m. Gregory K. Wilson, Nov. 10, 1973. BFA, Auburn U., 1967. Exhibited in one-person shows at Ga. Tech. Gallery, Atlanta, Spaces Gallery, Mt. Dora, Fla., 1988, Fairfield (Ct.) U. Ctr. for Fin. Studies, 1991, Atelier Gallery, New Milford, Conn., 1991; group shows include Am. Artists Profl. League, N.Y.C., 1989, 90, Allied Artists Ann., N.Y.C., 1990, 91, Catharine Lorillard Wolfe Ann., N.Y.C., 1987, 90, 91, Salamagundi Non-Men. Ann., N.Y.C., 1990, 91, Knickerbocker Artists Ann., N.Y.C., 1990, New Eng. Watercolor Soc. N.Am. Open, Boston, 1990,. Tutor in English as 2d lang. Literacy Vols., Westport, Conn., 1989—; art tchr. Adolescent Shelter for Abused Teens, Baton Rouge, 1982-83. Recipient 1st prize-watercolor Spectrum 1991, New Canaan, Conn., Dick Blick award Pa. Watercolor Soc., 1989, others. Mem. Pa. Watercolor Soc., Am. Artists Profl. League, Nat. Assn. Women Artists, Nat. League Am. Pen Women (award of merit 1989), Oil Pastel Assn., Artists Equity, Catherine Lorillard Wolfe Art Club. Republican. Congregationalist. Home and Studio: 2 Side Hill Rd Westport CT 06880

WILSON, DANA LYNN BARTLETT, marketing director; b. San Francisco; s. Albert Bartlett and Ruth Evelyn (Erickson) W. BA in English, U. Houston, 1968; MA in Am. Studies, U. Tex., 1970; postgrad., U. Paris-Sorbonne, 1972; Faculte des Letters, U. Nice, France, 1973. Advt. agy. D.B.& B., Inc., Boston, 1970-71; with Wilson & Assocs., 1974-83; dir. mktg. Boston Mus. of Sci., 1983—. Author: Boston English Illustrated, Moa Boston English; contbr. articles to profl. jours.; producer, writer film Ramesses the Great, 1988; videos include Kenya, 1987, India, 1987, Herod's Harbor, 1989 Special Effects, 1989, Gold!, 1989, Soviet Space, 1990, Great Barrier Reef, 1990. Mem. Am. Film Inst. Episcopalian. Office: Boston Mus of Sci Sci Park Boston MA 02114

WILSON, DANIEL DONALD, engineering executive; b. Pitts., Oct. 28, 1958; s. Howard Raymond and Eleanor Hinsdale (Clark) W.; m. Jean Basia Sitko, Oct. 26, 1991. BS in Math., U. Vt., 1979; MS in Ops. Rsch., Stanford U., 1988. Systems analyst Raytheon System Design Lab., Bedford, Mass., 1979-83; software engr. Raytheon Svc. Co., Huntsville, Ala., 1983-85; sr. engr. Raytheon System Design Lab., Bedford, 1986-88; mgr. analytical models Raytheon System Design Lab., Tewksbury, Mass., 1988—. Mem. AIAA (treas. 1990-92, sec. 1992—), Ops. Rsch. Soc. Am. (sec. 1976-79), Vt. Astron. Soc. (sec. 1976-80). Home: 19 Rutland St Cambridge MA 02138-2512 Office: Raytheon Systems Design Lab PO Box 1201 m/s T3TGG Tewksbury MA 01876-0901

WILSON, DAVID BUCKINGHAM, biochemistry educator; b. Cambridge, Mass., Jan. 15, 1940; s. E. Bright and Emily (Buckingham) W.; m. Nancy Jane Heffelfinger, Dec. 20, 1962; children: Allison Kay, Ashley Linn, Laurie Elizabeth. BA, Harvard U., 1961; PhD, Stanford U., Palo Alto, Calif., 1966. Postdoctoral fellow Med. Sch. Johns Hopkins U., Balt., 1966-67; asst. prof. Cornell U., Ithaca, N.Y., 1967-73, assoc. prof., 1973-84, prof., 1984—. Editor, author: Enzymatic Hydrolysis of Cellulose, 1991. Bd. dirs. Tompkins Community Hosp., 1982-92. Mem. AAAS, Am. Soc. Microbiology, Am. Soc. Biol. Chemists. Democrat. Home: 232 Troy Rd Ithaca NY 14850-9473 Office: Cornell U 458 Biotechnology Blvd Ithaca NY 14853

WILSON, DAVID RICHARD, foreign exchange executive; b. Chillocothe, Ohio, Mar. 9, 1948; s. David William and Hellen Elizabeth (Moore) W.; m. Marcia Ann Clasgens, Oct. 8, 1977; children: Emily, Seth, Catherine. BA in Econs., Miami U., Oxford, Ohio, 1970; MBA in Fin., NYU, 1984. Fgn. exch. trader Bank Leumi Trust Co. of N.Y., N.Y.C., 1979-80; trader Bank of Montreal, N.Y.C., 1980-86; v.p. internat. sales Chase Manhattan Bank, N.Y.C., 1986-88; v.p. Girozentrale Vienna, N.Y.C., 1988—. Co-author: Corporate Financial Risk Management, 1992. Vol. Peace Corps, Ecuador, 1970-73, Deak Perera Group, San Juan, P.R., 1975-78; treas. Cold Spring (N.Y.) Fire Co., 1985—; mem. adv. com. Philipstown Community Coun., 1992—; active Cold Spring Fire Co. Named Fireman of Yr., Cold Spring Fire Co., 1991. Mem. Nat. Assn. Bus. Economists, Forex Assn. North Am., Treasury Mgmt. Assn.

WILSON, DON WHITMAN, archivist, historian; b. Clay Center, Kans., Dec. 17, 1942; s. Donald J. Wilson and Lois M. (Sutton) Walker; m. Patricia Ann Sherrod, July 9, 1983; children—Todd, Jeffrey, Michael, Denise. AB, Washburn U., Topeka, 1964; MA, U. Cin., 1965, PhD, 1972, LittD (hon.), 1988. Archivist Kans. State Hist. Soc., Topeka, 1967-69; instr. history Washburn U., 1967-69; historian, dept. dir. Dwight D. Eisenhower Library, Abilene, Kans., 1969-78; assoc. dir. State Hist. Soc. Wis., Madison, 1978-81; dir. Gerald R. Ford Library and Mus., Ann Arbor, Mich., 1981-87; lectr. history U. Mich., 1982-87; Archivist of the U.S. Washington, 1987—. Author: Governor Charles Robinson of Kansas, 1975; editor: D-Day: The Normandy Invasion, 1971; bd. editors: Teaching History Jour., 1975—. Mem. Abilene Library Bd., 1973-76; mem. Abilene City Commn., 1976-78; pres. Dickinson County Hist. Soc., Abilene, 1976-77. NDEA fellow, 1964-67; recipient Pub. Service award Gen. Services Adminstrn., 1973. Mem. Am. Hist. Assn. (mem. Beveridge Book Prize com. 1979-82), Am. Assn. State and Local History, Kans. Hist. Soc. (bd. dirs. 1987—), Am. Antiquarian Soc., Soc. Am. Archivists, Cosmos Club. Republican. Baptist. Home: 316 E Beverley St Staunton VA 24401 Office: Nat Archives Pennsylvania Ave & 8th St NW Washington DC 20408

WILSON, DONALD ALFRED, land boundary consultant, surveyor; b. Greenville, Me., Mar. 31, 1941; s. Donald Henry and Ada Robinson (Lawler) W.; m. Christine Marie Dalphin, Aug. 20, 1967; children: Richard David, Stephen James. BS, U. Maine, 1965; MS, U. N.H., 1967. Registered land surveyor, profl. forester, N.H., Maine. Instr. U.N.H., Durham, 1967-68, U. Maine, Orono, 1968-74; pres. Border Land Consultants, Inc., Ossipee, N.H., 1974-76, Land & Boundary Consultants, Inc., Exeter, N.H., 1976—; cons. Ga. Power Co., Fla. Dept. Transportation, Allegheny Power Authority, and others; lectr. to surveying assns. throughout the U.S. Author: Deed Descriptions I Have Known But Could Have Done Without, 1982, A Selection of Massachusetts Laws Pertaining to Surveying and Real Property; co-author Evidence and Procedures for Boundary Location, 2d edit. 1981, Boundary Control and Legal Principles, 3d edit., 1986, Alabama Law: Land Surveying and Boundaries, 1990, Easements and Reversions, 1992; contbr. over 100 articles to tech. manuals and pubs. on surveying and boundaries. Lectr. to many environ. groups, hist. socs., geneal. socs., univs., boy scouts and real estate groups on surveying and boundary law. Numerous honors for his work in fields of surveying and boundaries. Fellow Am. Congress on Surveying and Mapping, N.H. Land Surveyors Assn. (v.p. 1976, pres.-elect 1977, pres. 1978, bd. dirs. 1979-86); mem. Nat. Forensic Ctr., Am. Forestry Assn. (life), Can. Inst. Surveying and Mapping, Am. Soc. Photogrammetry and Remote Sensing, Maine Soc. Land Surveyors (bd. dirs. 1974-75, 78, v.p. 1976, pres. 1977), Vt. Soc. Land Surveyors, Natural Resources Coun. Maine, Soc. for Protection N.H. Forests, N.H. Old Graveyards Assn., N.H. Hist. Soc., Land Info. Assembly, New Eng. Hist. Geneal. Soc., N.E. Land Title Assn. Republican. Congregationalist. Office: Land & Boundary Cons 69 Main St Newfields NH 03856-0179

WILSON, DONALD RICHARD, small business executive; b. Plaistow, N.H., Feb. 8, 1936; s. Harold Maxwell and Evelyn Dorothy (Shaw) W.; m. Carol Mae Anderson, June 30, 1956; children: Jeffrey Dale, Brenda Lee, Thomas Brian. BS, U. Wash., 1958; PhD, UCLA, 1962. Mgr. protein adhesives Am. Marietta Co., Seattle, 1958; sr. rsch. chemist textile fibers DuPont Co., Wilmington, Del., 1961-67; rsch. mgr. Xerox Corp., Webster, N.Y., 1967-75; rsch. dir. Celanese Rsch. Co., Summit, N.J., 1975-82, Pennalt Corp., King of Prussia, Pa., 1983; v.p. R&D Chem. Systems Rsch., Inc., Fairfield, N.J., 1983-84; pres. Advanced Polymer Tech., Inc., Landing, N.J., 1985—. Contbr. articles to profl. jours. Rsch. fellow NSF, 1959-60, 60-61. Mem. Am. Chem. Soc. (polymer div.), Assn. Rsch. Dirs. (pres. 1984-85), N.Am. Membrane Soc., Sigma Xi, Phi Lambda Upsilon. Home: PO Box 6 Glasser NJ 07837-0006 Office: Adv Polymer Tech Inc PO Box 221 Landing NJ 07850-0221

WILSON, DORIS FANUZZI, educator; b. N.Y.C., Oct. 17, 1935; d. Vitoantonio and Rose (Colavito) Panzarino; children: James Douglas Fanuzzi, Robert Alan Fanuzzi; m. Richard Gerard Wilson, Aug. 21, 1977 (div. 1987). BA cum laude, Hunter Coll., 1956; MA, Montclair State Coll., 1978. With Tri-County Ednl. Vocat. High Sch., Totowa, N.J., 1979-80; learning disabilities tchr., cons. Fairlawn (N.J.) Bd. Edn., 1980-82, Somerville (N.J.) Bd. Edn., 1982-83, Regional Child Study Team, Franklin, N.J., 1983-84; cons. curriculum and instrn. div. devel. disabilities N.J. Dept. Human Svcs., Trenton, 1984-91. Active Rep. Women of 90's, Nat. Women's Polit. Caucus, Mercer County Rep. Task force. Mem. AAUW, N.J. Assn. Learning Cons., Learning Disabilities Assn., Internat. Platform Assn., Trenton Hist. Soc. Office: Dept Human Svcs Arthur Brisbane Child Treatment Ctr PO Box 625 Deal NJ 07723

WILSON, EDWARD OSBORNE, biologist, educator; b. Birmingham, Ala., June 10, 1929; s. Edward Osborne and Inez (Freeman) W.; m. Irene Kelley, Oct. 30, 1955; 1 dau., Catherine Irene. BS, U. Ala., 1949, MS, 1950; PhD, Harvard U., 1955; DS (hon.), Duke U., Grinnell Coll., Lawrence U., U. West Fla., Fitchburg State Coll., Macalester Coll.; DPhil, Uppsala U.; LHD (hon.), U. Ala., Hofstra U.; LLD (hon.), Simon Fraser U. Jr. fellow Soc. Fellows, Harvard U., 1953-56, mem. faculty, 1956—, Baird prof. sci., 1976—, Mellon prof. sci., 1990—, curator entomology, 1971—; fellow Guggenheim Found., 1978, mem. selection com., 1982-89; bd. dirs. World Wildlife Fund, 1983—, Orgn. Tropical Studies, 1984—. Author: The Insect Societies, 1971, Sociobiology: The New Synthesis, 1975, On Human Nature, 1978 (Pulitzer prize of nonfiction), Promethean Fire, 1983, Biophilia, 1984, (with Bert Holldobler) The Ants, 1990 (Pulitzer prize for nonfiction), Success and Dominance in Ecosystems, 1990, The Diversity of Life, 1992. Recipient Cleve.-AAAS rsch. prize, 1967, Nat. Medal Sci., 1976, Leidy medal Acad. Natural Sci., Phila., 1979, Disting. Service award Am. Inst. Biol. Scis., 1976, Mercer award Ecol. Soc. Am., 1971, Founders Meml. award and L.O. Howard award Entomol. Soc. Am., 1972, 85, Archie Carr medal U. Fla., 1978, Disting. Svc. award Am. Humanist Soc., 1982, Tyler ecology prize, 1984, Silver medal Nat. Zool. Park, German Ecol. Inst. prize, 1987, Weaver award scholarly letters Ingersoll Found., 1989, Crafoord prize Royal Swedish Acad. Scis., 1990, Prix d'Inst. de la Vie, Paris, 1990, Revelle medal, 1990, Gold medal Worldwide Fund for Nature, 1990, Achievement award Nat. Wildlife Fedn., 1992, others. Fellow Am. Acad. Arts and Scis., Am. Phil. Soc., Deutsche Akad. Naturforsch.; mem. NAS, Am. Genetics Assn. (hon. life), Brit. Ecol. Soc. (hon. life), Entomol. Soc. Am. (hon. life), Zool. Soc. London (hon. life), Am. Humanist Soc. (hon. life), Royal Soc. London, Finnish Acad. Sci. and Letters, Royal Soc. Sci. Uppsala (Sweden). Home: 9 Foster Rd Lexington MA 02173-5505 Office: Mus Comparative Zoology Harvard U Cambridge MA 02138

WILSON, ELIZABETH WEISENBACHER, nursing educator, consultant; b. Irvington, N.J., Nov. 21, 1938; d. Alfred and Frieda (Erhardt) Weisenbacher; m. Charles E. Wilson, Aug. 17, 1958; children: Susan Wilson Cuthbert, Laura Wilson Porter, Jennifer Wilson Chrysson. BS, Upsala Coll., East Orange, N.J., 1960; MA, Montclair State Coll., 1972; EdD, Rutgers U., 1984. RN. Prof. Bergen Community Coll., Paramus, N.J., 1972—; nursing and legal cons., 1991—. Author: (with others) Guide for Industrial Noise Control, 1982; contbr. articles to profl. jours. Commr. N.J. State Commn. on Smoking or Health, 1986-91; mem. N.J. Interagency Coun. on Smoking or Health, 1986-91; mem. Cedar Grove Advisory Health Coun., 1989—. Mem. Am. Cancer Soc. (Bergen unit exec. com. chmn. 1986-87, pub. edn. chmn. 1986-87, bd. of mgrs. 1985-89, faculty and grant reviewer 1988—, facilitator trainer of 1990), Oncology Nursing Soc., N.J. Nurses Assn. (resolution author 1984). Presbyterian. Home: 19 Highview Ter Cedar Grove NJ 07009-1505 Office: Bergen C C 400 Paramus Rd Paramus NJ 07652-1508

WILSON, EWEN MACLELLAN, government executive; b. Nairobi, Kenya, July 29, 1944; came to U.S., 1969; s. Walter Maclellan and Barbara (Gange) Maclellan W.; m. Kay Stephens, May 31, 1969; children: Libby, Cindy, Riara. BS, U. London, 1965; MS, W.Va. U., 1970; PhD, N.C. State U., 1973. With conservation and extension dept. Ministry of Agrl., Banket, Rhodesia, 1965-68; research fellow U. Rhodesia, Salisbury, 1973-74; asst. prof. Va. Tech. Inst., Blacksburg, 1975-77; dir. econs. and stats. Am. Meat Inst., Arlington, Va., 1977-83, v.p., 1983-85; apptd. dep. asst. sec. U.S. Dept. Agrl., Washington, 1985-87, asst. sec., 1987-89; pres. Wilson Agribus. Analysis, 1989-90; exec. dir. Commodity Futures Trading Commn., Washington, 1990—; mem. Chgo. Mercantile Exchange Live Cattle Adv. Com., Chgo., 1979-81; mem. USDA-USTR Agrl. Tech. Adv. Com. on Livestock, Washington, 1982-85. Mem. Am. Agrl. Econs. Assn. Republican. Episcopalian. Office: Commodity Futures Trading Commn 2033 K St NW Washington DC 20581-0002

WILSON, FRED LEE, technical educator, consultant; b. Detroit, Sept. 5, 1938; s. Greene Osborne and Adele (Simmons) W.; m. Jimmie Joan Bennett, Sept. 2, 1967; children: Joel F., Robert B. BA, Murray State U., 1959; PhD, U. Kans., 1964. Sr. rsch. engr. Exxon Rsch. Corp., Houston, 1966-69; prof. Rochester (N.Y.) Inst. Tech., 1969—; cons. Wilson Assocs., Pittsford, N.Y., 1969-91. Mem. Boces Sch. Bd., Fairport, N.Y., 1983-88, Pittsford Sch. Bd., 1984-89. Capt. U.S. Army, 1964-66. Mem. Am. Phys. Soc. (N.Y. state sect. sec., treas. 1978—). Home: 496 Thornell Rd Pittsford NY 14534-9741 Office: Rochester Inst Tech 1 Lomb Memorial Dr Rochester NY 14623-5603

WILSON, FREDERICK, science administrator; b. Sharon, Pa., Aug. 6, 1941; s. Walter Kenneth and Delores B. (Christensen) W.; m. Patsy Ann Shurtleff, June 27, 1970; children: Kevin Andrew, Craig Alan, Lara Glenn. BS, Westminster Coll., 1963; MS, SUNY Health Ctr., Syracuse, 1973. Tech. specialist SUNY/Health Sci. Ctr., Syracuse, 1968-72; supr., spl. chemistry Smith Kline Clin. Labs., Boston, 1972-73; clin. chemist Pathologists Assocs. Med. Labs., Muncie, Ind., 1973-78, The Saratoga Hosp., Saratoga Springs, N.Y., 1978-85; lab. dir. Equine Drug Testing/Cornell Univ., Saratoga Springs, 1985-91; dir. lab. ops. equine drug testing Cornell U., Ithaca, N.Y., 1991—; cons. in field, 1985-87. Author: Cost Control in Clinical Laboratory, 1985; contbr. articles to profl. jours. Mem. Am. Assn. for Clin. Chemistry (affiliate). Republican. Presbyterian. Office: Cornell U Equine Drug Testing 925 Warren Dr Ithaca NY 14850-9772

WILSON, GLEN PARTEN, association administrator; b. Waco, Tex., Dec. 10, 1922; s. Glen P. and Hazel (Parnell) W.; m. Alice B. Groves, Dec. 11, 1982. BS in Aero. Engring., U. Tex., Austin, 1943, MA in Psychology, 1948, PhD in Psychology, 1952. Engr. Lockheed Aircraft Co., Burbank, Calif., 1943-44; teaching fellow, rsch. asst., instr. U. Tex., Austin, 1946-52; rsch. psychologist USAF, Lackland AFB, Tex., 1952-53; gen. mgr. Tex. Ednl. Devices Co., Austin, 1953-54; asst. to Senator Lyndon B. Johnson Washington, 1955-57; staff Senate Preparedness Investigating Subcom. and Senate Spl. Com. on Space and Astronautics, Washington, 1957-59; chief clk., profl. staff mem. Senate Com. on Aero. and Space Scis., Washington, 1959-77; cons. Washington, 1977-79; spl. asst. for student activities NASA, Washington, 1979-80, acting dir. acad. affairs div., 1980-82; pres. Marie D. and Glen P. Wilson Found., Washington, 1982-87; exec. dir. Nat. Space Soc., Washington, 1984-88, exec. dir. emeritus, 1988—; lectr. on aero. and space programs, Senate orgn., sci. policy, tech. assessment, student activities, space activism. Participant as staff passage of Nat. Aeros. and Space Act, 1958, Communications Satellite Act, 1962, NASA Authorization Acts, 1958-77; editor Policy Planning for Aeronautical Rsch. and Devel., Senate Document 90, 89th Congress, 1966; developer NASA shuttle student involvement program, 1980, space edn. orgn., 1984—. With USN, 1944-46. Recipient Exceptional Svc. medal NASA, 1981; Nat. Space Soc. Hdqrs. renamed The Glen P. Wilson Internat. Space Ctr., 1988. Mem. AIAA (spl. presdl. citation 1976), Am. Astro. Soc., AAAS, Nat. Space Soc., Internat. Acad. of Astronautics, Sigma Xi, Nat. Space Club, Cosmos Club. Home: 433 New Jersey Ave SE Washington DC 20003-4034 Office: 922 Pennsylvania Ave SE Washington DC 20003-2197

WILSON, GLENN SHAW, quality engineer; b. Pitts., Oct. 25, 1932; s. Claude Weikert and Sarah Dorothy (Shaw) W.; m. Mildred Henrietta Wilson, Dec. 10, 1955 (dec. June 1984); children: Rebecca Wang, Ruth Shidner, Wade; m. Carol Anne Burton, Sept. 28, 1985; 1 stepson, Matthew Elwell. BS in Indsl. Mgmt., Carnegie Mellon U., 1955; postgrad., Alfred U., 1982; MBA, Wilmington Coll., 1988. Cert. quality engr. Sr. indsl. engr. Wallingford (Conn.) Steel Co., 1957-61; glass plant ind. engr. Hartford divsn. Emhart Corp., Bloomfield, Conn., 1961-69; mgr. finished prodn. Pierce Glass divsn. Indian Head, Port Allegany, Pa., 1969-75; asst. corp. quality mgr. Nat. Bottle Corp., Bala Cynwydd, Pa., 1975-77; dir. quality/productivity improvement Wheaton Glass Co., Millville, N.J., 1977-92; mgr. quality assurance Carr-Lowery Glass Co., Balt., 1992—; instr. U. Del., Newark, 1979; adj. mgmt. faculty Glassboro (N.J.) State Coll., 1980—; cons. Wingwalker Quality Concepts, Woodstown, N.J., 1989—. Co-author: (pamphlets) Chemical Specialties Manufacturers Assn. Guidelines for Glass Container Aerosol Testing, 1984, Parenteral Drug Assn. Model for Supplier Certification, 1990. Bd. dirs. McKean County Solid Waste Authority, Smethport, Pa., 1965-69; v.p. Port Allegany Sch. Bd., 1965-69; mem. Seneca Highlands Dist. Sch. Bd., Smethport, 1966-69; recycling com. mem. Borough of Woodstown, 1989—. 1st Lt. U.S. Army, 1955-57. Scholar Buhl Found., 1950-51, Carnegie Inst. Tech., 1950-51. Mem. Am. Soc. Quality Control (cert., sect.

chmn. 1988-90, examining and auditing com. chmn. 1990—, Svc. Appreciation award 1990, Food, Drug, Cosmetic divsn., Stats. divsn., Chem. & Process Industries divsn.). Republican. Presbyterian.

WILSON, JOHN FLETCHER, speech professional; b. Keyser, W.Va., June 1, 1923; s. James Vincent and Susan May (Patton) W. BA, Wayne State U., 1947, MA, 1948; PhD, U. Wis., 1955. Instr. speech Monmouth (Ill.) Coll., 1948-50; instr. to asso. prof. Cornell U., Ithaca, N.Y., 1953-67; assoc. prof. speech Herbert H. Lehman Coll., CUNY, Bronx, 1967-71, prof., 1971-89, ret., 1989, chmn. dept. speech and theatre, 1979-85; cons. in field. Author: (with Carroll C. Arnold) Public Speaking as a Liberal Art, 1964, 6th edit. (with Molly Meijer Wertheimer), 1990. Served with USAAF, 1943-46, USAF, 1950-51. Mem. AAUP, Speech Communication Assn., Am. Forensic Assn., Eastern Communication Assn. (pres. 1977-78), N.Y. State Speech Communication Assn. (pres. 1968-69), N.Y. State Forensic Assn. (pres. 1956-57), Rhetoric Soc. Am., Tau Kappa Epsilon. Republican. Presbyterian. Home: 201 E 21st St Apt 3K New York NY 10010-6405

WILSON, JOHN LEO, marketing executive; b. Cambridge, Mass.; s. Leo F. and Barbara A. (Farrell) W.; m. Mary Collins, June 14, 1973; children: Megan Elizabeth, Anne Marie. BS, Boston Coll., 1971; MBA, Boston U., 1976. Sr. acct. rep. Lever Bros. Co., N.Y.C., 1971-76; product planner Ford Motor Co., Dearborn, Mich., 1976-81; nat. mktg. mgr. Adolph Coors Co., Golden, Colo., 1981-83; dir. mktg. and sales Bose Corp., Framingham, Mass., 1983—. With U.S. Army, 1971-76. Home: 52 Myrick Ln Harvard MA 01451 Office: Bose Corp. The Mountain Framingham MA 01701

WILSON, JOHN RANDOLPH, cardiologist; b. Boston, Oct. 29, 1948; m. Marguerite, 1977; children: Marisa Lauren, Jonathan Wyndham, Julie Elisabeth. Student, Pomona Coll., 1967-68; BA in History, Stanford U., 1970; MD, Harvard U., 1974; MS, U. Pa., 1989. Intern Cleve. Met. Gen. Hosp., 1974-75, resident, 1975-77; fellow cardiology Hosp. U. Pa., Phila., 1977-79, rsch. fellow cardiology, 1979-80, dir. heart failure program, 1982-91, dir. cardiac exercise and heart failure program, 1986—; asst. prof. medicine U. Pa. Sch. Medicine, Phila., 1980-89, assoc. prof., 1989. Mem. editorial bd. Internat. Jour. Cardiology, 1984—, Am. Jour. Cardiology, 1984—, Index and Revs. in Cong Heart Failure, 1988—; editorial cons. Circulation and Annals of Internal Medicine, 1982, 88. Recipient Rsch. Career Devel. award NIH, 1986-91; merit rev. grantee VA, 1991-94; grantee-in-aid Am. Heart Assn., Southeastern Pa. chpt., 1990-91, Nat. Am. Heart Assn., 1990-93. Fellow Am. Coll. Cardiology; mem. Am. Fedn. Clin. Rsch. (assoc.), Am. Heart Assn. Office: Hosp U Pa 3400 Spruce St 3 White Bldg Philadelphia PA 19104

WILSON, JOSEPH DENNIS, risk manager; b. Pitts., Dec. 31, 1949; s. Joseph B. and Eileen (Deller) W.; m. Christine Marie Petras, Aug. 20, 1977; children: Jessica Leigh, Joshua Luke, Jacob John. BBA in Acctg., Robert Morris Coll., 1974; Assoc. in Risk Mgmt., Ins. Inst. Am., 1988. Office mgr. Eichleay Corp., Pitts., 1974-75, project office mgr., 1975-79, asst. to v.p., 1979-80, mgr. adminstrv. svcs., 1980-85; mgr. adminstrv. svcs. Eichleay Holdings Inc., Pitts., 1985—; Penn Profl. Indemnity Ltd., Hamilton, Bermuda, 1989—, Am. Risk Transfer Ins. Co., Hamilton, 1988—, RIMS-Pitts., 1989—; chmn. Constrn. Industry Inst. Ins. Task Force, Austin, Tex., 1988—. Editor Eichleay Corporation Manual, 1984. Treas. Pitts. Northstars Boosters Assn., Wildwood, Pa., 1988-91. Mem. Risk Ins. Mgmt. Soc., Constrn. Fin. Mgmt. Assn., Constrn. Industry Inst., Rotary, Masonic Temple. Methodist. Home: 8565 Peters Rd Mars PA 16046-9330 Office: Eichleay Holdings Inc Fifth and Penn Aves Pittsburgh PA 15206-4407

WILSON, KARL A., biochemistry and molecular biology educator; b. Buffalo, Jan. 19, 1947; s. Raymond A. and Rosella M. (Feinen) W.; m. Anna Li Tan, Dec. 28, 1974; 1 child, Kathleen Ann. BA in Biology, SUNY, Buffalo, 1969, PhD in Biochemistry, 1973. Postdoctoral assoc. Roswell Park Meml. Inst., Buffalo, 1973-74; postdoctoral assoc. dept. chemistry Purdue U., West Lafayette, Ind., 1974-76; asst. prof. SUNY, Binghamton, 1976-83, assoc. prof., 1983-91, prof., 1991—, dir. biochemistry, 1984—. Contbr. articles to Jour. Biol. Chemistry, Protides of the Biol. Fluids, Plant Physiology, Phytochemistry, and others; contbr. numerous articles to profl. publs. Grantee NSF, Amideast, SUNY. Mem. AAAS, Am. Soc. Plant Physiologist, Am Chem. Soc., Am. Soc. Biochem. Molecular Biology. Office: SUNY Dept Biol Scis Binghamton NY 13902-6000

WILSON, KENNETH GEORGE, language professional, English; b. Akron, Ohio, Apr. 21, 1923; s. Herbert George and Margaret Marie (Johns) W.; m. Marilynn Jane Clarke, Aug. 31, 1946; children: Derek George, Stephanie Clarke Wilson Haas. AB in English, Albion Coll., 1943; MA, U. Mich., 1948, PhD, 1951. Instr. in English U. Conn., Storrs, 1951-55, asst. prof. English, 1955-60, assoc. prof. English, 1960-63, prof. English, 1963-81, head dept. English, 1965-66, dean Coll. Liberal Arts & Scis., 1966-70, v.p. acad. programs, 1970-74, v.p. acad. affairs, 1974-81, prof. English emeritus, 1981-88; younger humanist fellowship panel NEH, Washington, 1970, 71, program project site panelist, 1972-74, nat. bd. cons., 1974—; mem. exec. com. Conf. on Coll. Composition and Communication, 1967-69. Author, editor: Essays on Language & Usage, 1959, 63, 71, (monograph) MIE Complaynt Against Hope, 1957, (book) Van Winkle's Return, 1987; editor: Harbrace Guide to Dictionaries, 1963. Mem. Commr. of Ednl. Task Force, Conn., 1982-83; commr. Commn. for Instns. of Higher Edn. 1985-91; mem. Conn. Humanities Coun., 1977-83. Recipient Rackham Pre-Doctoral fellow U. Mich., 1950-51, Disting. Faculty award U. Conn., 1961, Univ. Professorship, 1981. Mem. MLA of Am., Medieval Acad. Am., Linguistic Soc. of Am., Nat. Coun. Tchrs. English, Conn. Acad. Arts & Scis., Phi Beta Kappa, Phi Kappa Phi. Home and Office: 3B Sycamore Dr Storrs Mansfield CT 06268-2000

WILSON, LEWIS LANSING, insurance executive; b. Cobleskill, N.Y., Jan. 26, 1932; s. Clarence A. and Ordella (Walker) W.; m. Barbara Jane Kathan, June 7, 1952; children: Susan W. Coleman, Joan, Peter L. (dec.). Grad. high sch., Cobleskill. Cert. profl. ins. agt., ins. cons. Mgr. claims Sterling Ins. Co., Cobleskill, 1950-57; ins. agt. State Farm Ins. Co., Cobleskill, 1957-59; pres. Lewis L. Wilson, Inc., Cobleskill, 1959—; owner Wilson Tel. Exch., Cobleskill, 1978-86, Wilson Security, Inc., Cobleskill, 1981-86; rep. N.Y. Mapp Program, 1985-88. Town chmn. Cobleskill Rep. Party, 1978-83; chmn. Schoharie County Rep. Com., N.Y., 1983—, Cobleskill SUNY Found. Fund Drive; commr. Schoharie County Bd. Elections, 1983—; pres. Cobleskill Cen. Sch. Bd., Community Hosp. Schoharie County, Cobleskill; dir. Schoharie Colonial Heritage. Mem. Profl. Ins. Agts. (pres. 1989, bd. dirs. 1984—, v.p. 1987, 1st v.p. 1988, pres. 1989—, Ins. Agt. of Yr. 1986), N.Y. Ind. Ins. Agts. (regional v.p.), N.Y. Life Underwriters, Rotary (pres. Cobleskill chpt., gov. dist. 719 1982, Paul Harris fellow 1985-86), Elks (exalted ruler, hon. founder nat. found. 1980). Republican. Methodist. Home: 31 Grandview Dr Cobleskill NY 12043-1321 Office: PO Box 39 Cobleskill NY 12043-0039

WILSON, LINDA SMITH, university administrator; b. Washington, Nov. 10, 1936; d. Fred M. and Virginia D. (Thompson) Smith; m. Paul A. Wilson, Jan. 22, 1970; 1 dau. by previous marriage: Helen K. Whatley, a stepdau., Beth A. Wilson. B.A., Newcomb Coll., Tulane U., 1957; Ph.D., U. Wis., 1962. Postdoctoral rsch. assoc. U. Md., College Park, 1962-64, rsch. asst. prof., 1964-67; vis. asst. prof. U. Mo.-St. Louis, 1967-68; asst. to vice chancellor for rsch., asst. vice chancellor for rsch., assoc. vice chancellor for rsch. Washington U., St. Louis, 1968-75; assoc. vice chancellor for rsch. U. Ill., Urbana, 1975-85; assoc. dean Grad. Coll., U. Ill., Urbana, 1978-85; v.p. for rsch. U. Mich., Ann Arbor, 1985-89; pres. Radcliffe Coll., Cambridge, Mass., 1989—; chmn. adv. com. office sci. and engring. pers. NRC, 1990—; mem. dir.'s adv. coun. NSF, Washington, 1980-89, adv. com. sci. edn., 1990—, adv. com. edn. & human resources, 1990—; mem. Nat. Commn. on Rsch., Washington, 1978-80; mem. com. on govt.-univ. relationships NAS, 1981-83, mem. coun. for govt.-univ.-industry rsch. roundtable, 1984-89; mem. rsch. resources adv. coun. NIH, Bethesda, Md., 1978-82, energy rsch. adv. bd. DOE, 1987-90; mem. sci., tech. and the states task force Carnegie Commn. on Sci., Tech. and Govt., 1991—. Author book chpts.; contbr. articles to profl. jours. Bd. govs. YMCA, Champaign-Urbana, Ill., 1980-83; mem. adv. bd. Nat. Coalition for Sci. and Tech., Washington, 1983-87. Recipient Centennial award Newcomb Coll., 1986; named One of 100 Emerging Leaders Am. Coun. Edn. and Change, 1978. Fellow AAAS (bd. dirs. 1984-88); mem. Am. Chem. Soc. (bd. coun. com. on chemistry and pub. affairs 1978-80), Soc. Rsch. Adminstrs. (Disting. Contbn. to Rsch. Adminstrn. award 1984), Nat. Coun. Univ. Rsch. Adminstrs., Assn. for Biomed. rsch. (bd. dirs. 1983-86), Inst. Medicine (mem. coun. 1986-89), Nat. Acad. Scis. (coordinating coun. for edn. 1991—), Am. Coun. on Edn. (commn. on women in higher edn. 1991-93), Phi Beta Kappa, Sigma Xi, Alpha Lambda Delta, Phi Delta Kappa, Phi Kappa Phi. Home: 76 Brattle St Cambridge MA 02138-3452 Office: Radcliffe Coll Office of Pres Fay House 10 Garden St Cambridge MA 02138

WILSON, LISA, marketing executive; b. Belville, N.J., Sept. 6, 1959; d. John and Rita (Hughes) Wilson. BS, Ithaca Coll., 1981; MPH, Yale U., 1988. Phys. therapist Human Performance Ctr., Milford, Conn., 1983-86; dir. personnel Health Care Assocs., Avon, Conn., 1987-88; dir. mktg. Athena Health Care Assocs., Waterbury, Conn., 1988-89; pres. Health Market, Inc., Simsbury, Conn., 1989—. Preceptor Senate Majority Office, Hartford, 1989; student advisor Yale U., New Haven, 1989. Mem. APHA, Nat. Spinal Cord Injury Assn. (bd. dirs. 1988-89), Am. Mktg. Assn. (bd. dirs.), Conn. Assn. Women in Health Care Mgmt., Conn. Assn. Health Care Mktg. Office: Health Market Inc 76 Hartford Rd Simsbury CT 06070

WILSON, LOUISE ASTELL MORSE, educator, home economist; b. Corning, N.Y., Oct. 26, 1937; d. James Leland and Hazel Irene (Bratt) Morse; m. Robert Louis Wilson, Dec. 26, 1965 (dec. June 1981); 1 child, Patricia Louise. BS, SUNY, Buffalo, 1960; MS, Elmira Coll., 1971. Cert. home economist, N.Y. Tchr. Corning City Sch. Dist., 1960—; com. mem. Corning Sch. Dist., 1991—. Mem. Internat. Fed. Home Econs. (area rep. 1991—), Am Home Econs. Assn., Am. Vocat. Assn., N.Y. Home Econs. Assn. (treas. 1989-91), N.Y. State Home Econs. Tchrs. Assn. (area coord. 1988-89), Corning Tchrs. Assn. (exec. coun. 1981-91), Order Ea. Star (past matron), Corning Country Club. Republican. Methodist. Home: PO Box 2 Coopers Plains NY 14827-0002

WILSON, LOWELL LEWIS, animal science educator, researcher; b. Egan, Ill., Jan. 3, 1936; s. Clifford Earl and Vernie Mae (Schreiber) W.; m. Mary Eleanor Crea, Feb. 29, 1956; children: Joan Marie, Jon Clifford, Richard Lowell. BS, Wis. State U., Platteville, 1958; MS, S.D. State U., 1961, PhD, 1964. Research asst. S.D. State U., Brookings, 1960-64; extension animal scientist Purdue U., Lafayette, Ind., 1964-67; assoc. prof. animal sci. Pa. State U., University Park, 1967-71, prof., 1971—; sec.-treas., v.p, pres. N.E. Am. Dairy Sci. Assn./Am. Animal Soc., 1984-88. Contbr. chpts. and numerous articles to profl. publs. Served as sgt. U.S. Army, 1955-58. Recipient Edn. award Am. Polled Hereford Assn., 1974, Merit award Am. Forage and Grassland Council, 1978, Research award Gamma Sigma Delta, 1979. Mem. Am. Soc. Animal Sci. (Livestock Mgmt. award 1974), Am. Genetic Soc., Council Agrl. Sci. and Tech., Am. Meat Sci. Soc., Pa. Beef Council (sec., treas., bd. dirs. 1979—), Pa. Cattlemen's Assn. (sec., v.p., pres., bd. dirs. 1977—). Republican. Methodist. Office: 324 Henning Bldg Pa State U Dept Dairy and Animal Sci University Park PA 16802

WILSON, MALCOLM CAMPBELL, banker; b. Phila., Dec. 9, 1942; s. James Murray and Janet (Haines) W.; m. Barbara Ann Bahmermann, June 10, 1989; children from previous marriage:Jennifer Marie, David Campbell, Andrew Russel. B.S. in Bus. Adminstrn., Drexel U., 1966; M.B.A. in Fin., 1968. Chartered fin. analyst. Research analyst Provident Nat. Bank, Phila., 1971-77, co-mgr. research dept., 1977-78, dir. equity research, 1978-84, dir. econ. and investment research, 1984-88; chief investment officer PNC Fin. div. Provident Nat. Bank , Phila., 1986-88, sr. v.p., mgr. personal svcs. group, 1989—. Served with U.S. Navy, 1968-71. Fellow Fin. Analysts Fedn.; mem. Mayflower Soc., Pa. Soc. Sons of Revolution, N.Y. Soc. Security Analysts. Republican. Episcopalian. Advocations: hunting; fishing; golf. Office: Provident Nat Bank 17th and Chestnut Sts Philadelphia PA 19103

WILSON, MARGARET ELIZABETH, educator; b. New Haven, Conn., Apr. 11, 1935; d. Burriss Gahan and Margaret Henrietta (Shove) W. BS, Syracuse U., 1958, MS in sci. edn., 1962; MA in Biology, Hofstra U., 1973. Biology tchr. Homer (N.Y.) Cen. High Sch., 1958-60; gen. sci. tchr. Manhassett (N.Y.) Jr. High Sch., 1960-61; biology tchr. Bellmore-Merrick (N.Y.) Cen. High Sch. Dist., 1961-90; ret., 1990. Vol. marine ecology div. Nassau County Health Dept., Mineola, N.Y., 1984-89, N.Y. Aquarium, Bklyn., 1971-90, curriculum writing team, 1989; sec. PTA, J.F. Kennedy High Sch., 1967-90. NSF scholar, 1969. Fellow Sci. Tchrs. Assn. N.Y. Stte (bd. dirs. 1962-90), N.Y. State Marine Edn. Assn. (bd. dirs. 1978-90), Conn. Sci. Tchrs. Assn. (bd. dirs. 1992—), Am. Inst. Biol. Scis. Home: 6 Eagle Ridge Dr Gales Ferry CT 06335-1904

WILSON, MELISSA ANNE, sculptor; b. New Rochelle, N.Y., July 9, 1968; d. Paul Alan Williams and Sandra Oliver Simondi. Degree in art, Silvermine Sch. Art, 1989, Wooster Art Ctr., 1990. Art asst. Sandi Oliver, Weston, Conn., 1987—. Asst. editor catalogue, 1991; exhibited in group exhibition Lever House, N.Y.C., 1990 (1st in show). Mem. Internat. Sculpture Assn., Stanley Bleifeld Assn. Fairfield (asst. sculptor). Home: 11 Tubbs Spring Dr Box 1203 Weston CT 06883-0203 Office: Sandi Oliver Fine Art Box 1203 Weston CT 06883

WILSON, MICHAEL HOLCOMBE, Canadian government official; b. Toronto, Ont., Can., Nov. 4, 1937; s. Harry Holcombe and Constance L. (Davies) W.; m. Margaret Catherine Smellie, Oct. 17, 1964; children: Cameron, Geoffrey, Lara. Student, Upper Can. Coll.; B. Comm., U. Toronto, 1959. With Harris & Partners Ltd., Toronto, 1961-63, 65-73; v.p. Harris & Partners Ltd., 1972; exec. v.p. following merger with Dominion Securities Ltd., 1973-79; mem. Can. Ho. of Commons, Ottawa, 1979—; minister of state for internat. trade Govt. Can., Ottawa, 1979-80; minister of fin. Govt. Can., 1984-91, min. of industry, sci. & tech., min. internat. trade, 1991—. Campaign chmn. Can. Cancer Soc., 1972-75, pres., 1977-79; bd. dirs. Dellcrest Children's Home. Mem. Investment Dealers Assn. (chmn. Ont. dist. 1975-76), Kappa Alpha. Progressive Conservative. Anglican. Clubs: Toronto, Toronto Golf, Badminton and Racquet, Osler Bluff Ski, Can. of Toronto (dir. 1972-78, v.p. 1976-78). Office: House of Commons, Rm 515-S, Ottawa, ON Canada K1A 0A6

WILSON, NEIL ERNEST, college administrator, career counselor; b. Quincy, Mass., Mar. 6, 1955; s. Norman Lee and Ruth Shirley (Bloch) W. BS in Psychology, Syracuse (N.Y.) U., 1977; MA in Counseling Psychology, Boston Coll., 1987. Coord. placement svcs./coop. edn. Merrimack Coll., North Andover, Mass., 1988—; adj. faculty in continuing edn. U. Mass., Lowell, 1987—. Mem. young leadership div. Combined Jewish Philanthropies, Boston. Mem. AACD, Ea. Coll. Pers. Officers, New England Assn. for Coop. Edn. and Field Experience, Nat. Career Devel. Assn., Greater Boston/Syracuse U. Alumni Club (bd. mem. 1978—), Appalachian Mountain Club, Career Counselors Consortium Boston (steering com., treas. 1989—). Home: 282 Highland Ave Somerville MA 02143 Office: Merrimack Coll 300 Turnpike St North Andover MA 01845-5800

WILSON, PATRICK ELLIOTT, insurance company executive; b. Greenvile, S.C., Nov. 16, 1934; s. Broadus Patterson Wilson and Georgia Lee (Gibson) Blackwell; m. Amelia Ray Dossett, Mar. 25, 1961. Student, Duke U., 1953-54; BS, Presbyn. Coll., 1958. CLU. Mgmt. trainee Travelers Ins. Co., Charlotte, N.C., 1959-60; field supr. Travelers Ins. Co., Columbia, S.C., 1960-62, asst. mgr., 1962-64; advanced underwriting cons. Travelers Ins. Co., Atlanta, 1964-65; asst. dir. Travelers Ins. Co., Hartford, Conn., 1965-69; dir. tng. Travelers Ins. Co., Hartford, 1969-74, 2d v.p., 1974-79; asst. v.p. GEICO, Washington, 1979-82, v.p., 1982—. With U.S. Army, 1958. Mem. Am. Soc. CLU and ChFC, Nat. Assn. Life Underwriters. Republican. Episcopalian. Office: GEICO Geico Pla Washington DC 20076

WILSON, RICHARD PHILIP, ophthalmologist, researcher; b. Frankfurt, Germany, May 22, 1947; came to U.S., 1948; s. Philip Murray and Neva Pearl (Cornelius) W.; m. Karen Lynn Kraus, May 9, 1981; 1 child, Philip Rylan. AB, The Johns Hopkins U., 1969; MD, U. Mo., 1979. Clerkship Community Psychiatry Queens Cliff Mental Health Ctr., North Ryde, Australia, 1973, Psychiatric Hosp., Sidney, Australia, 1973; internal med. clerkship U.S.S. Hope, Maceio, Brazil, 1973; surgery internship U. Va. Hosp., Charlotteville, 1973-74; psychiatry residency Vanderbilt U. Hosp., Nashville, 1974-75; opthalmology residency, than fellowship The Wills Eye Hosp., Phila., 1975-78, 78-79; asst. surgeon, than assoc. surgeon Wills Eye Hosp. Glaucoma Svc., 1979-84, 84-88; dir. Glaucoma Svc. Rsch. Lab., Wills Eye Hosp., 1979—; assoc. surgeon, dir. Lankenau Hosp. Glaucoma Svc., Phila., 1984—, 1979—; opthalmologist TumuTumu Hosp., Presbyn. Ch. of East Africa, Keratina, Kenya, 1979; vis. prof. Kenyatta U. Hosp., Nairobi, Kenya, 1979; asst. prof., than assoc. prof. Thomas Jefferson U. Sch. of Med., Phila., 1979—, 88—; dir. Resident Edn., Lankenau Hosp., 1980-87; cons. Saudi Arabian Govt. for King Khaled Eye Spl. Hosp., Ryiad, 1982, Am. Acad. of Opthalmology, 1985-86; course dir. 14th Annual Wills Eye Hosp. Glaucoma Conf., 1990. Sect. editor (Glaucoma) Yr. Book of Opthalmology and Key Opthalmology, Chgo., 1988—; author (video-tape) The Management of Combined Cataract and Glaucoma, 1989;reviewer: Archives of Opthalmology, Archives of Internal Medicine, Am. Jour. of Opthalmology, Jour. of the AMA Opthalmology, 1989; contbr. numerous articles to profl. jours. and books. Dir. Outreach Program to Kenya Vol. Opthalmology Staff Wills Eye Hosp., 1978—; bd. dirs. Assoc. Svcs. for the Blind, Phila. 1982-84. Mem. AMA (appointed Diagnostic and Therapeutic Tech. Assessment Reference Panel 1990), Am. Acad. of Opthalmology, Am. Glaucoma Soc. (chmn. Profl. Terminology and Codes, 1989-90, rep. to Am. Acad. of Opthalmology CPT Task Force, 1989—), ACS, Pa. Med. Assn., Montgomery County Med. Assn., Opthalmology Club of Phila., Phila. Coll. Physicians, Assn. for Rsch. in Vision and Opthalmology. Democrat. Presbyterian. Home: 243 Beech Hill Road Wynnewood PA 19096 Office: Opthalmic Subspeciality Cons Will Eye Hospital 9th and Walnut Sts Philadelphia PA 19107

WILSON, ROBERT ALBERT, pharmaceutical company executive; b. Jamestown, N.Y., Dec. 20, 1936; s. Albert C. and Minnie M. (Leroy) W.; m. Marcia K. Milton, Aug. 22, 1959; children: Jonathan, Kathryn. BA magna cum laude, Colgate U., 1959; diploma, Sch. Advanced Internat Studies, Bologna, Italy, 1960; MA, Johns Hopkins, 1961. News editor/announcer Sta. WJOC, Jamestown, 1953-57; staff reporter Post-Jour., Jamestown, 1958-61; intelligence research specialist U.S. Info. Agy., Washington, 1963-66, sr. editor, 1966-72; sr. assoc. pub. affairs Pfizer, Inc., N.Y.C., 1972-78, assoc. dir. pub. affairs, 1978-81, v.p. pub. affairs, 1981—; pres. Pfizer Found., Inc., N.Y.C., 1981—; bd. dirs. Nat. Health Coun., Washington, steering com. Pharm. Mfg. Assn. Pub. Affairs, Washington, 1979—; chmn. adv. com. Found. for Higher Edn., Stamford, Conn., 1988—. Exec. com. Religion ikn Am. Life, N.Y.C., 1988—. With U.S. Army, 1961-63. Named Outstanding Young Man in Am. U.S. Jaycees, 1971. Mem. Pub. Relations Soc. of Am., Am. Acad. Polit. Sci., Riverside Yacht Club, Colgate Club (bd. dirs. 1982-87), Phi Beta Kappa. Office: Pfizer Inc 235 E 42nd St New York NY 10017-5703

WILSON, ROBERT ARTHUR, urban studies educator; b. Danville, Pa., Apr. 1, 1937; s. William Reynold and Mildred Irene (Paul) W.; m. Lynn Dockety; 1 child, Andrew Paul. BA, Temple U., 1963, MA, 1965, PhD, 1971. Dir. rsch. Del. Dept. of Pub. Welfare, Wilmington, 1964-65, Community Svcs. Coun. of Del., Wilmington, 1965-67; assoc. prof. urban affairs U. Del., Newark, 1973—; cons. in field. Author: Urban Sociology, 1977. Mem. Am. Sociol. Assn., Ea. Sociol. Assn., Am. Mktg. Assn. Office: U Del Coll Urban Affairs Newark DE 19716

WILSON, ROBERT CRAIG, association executive; b. Paterson, N.J., Jan. 16, 1941; s. Robert Baer and Katherine Ann (Greiner) W.; m. Nancy Dorothy Howatt, Sept. 23, 1972; children: Craig Ryan, Alexander Robert. BA in Econs., Fairleigh Dickinson U., 1964; Cert., San Diego Golf Acad., 1984. Supr. vets. benefits U.S. VA, San Diego, 1975-84; exec. dir. Nat. Amputee Golf Assn., Amherst, N.H., 1981—; cons. OSI, Inc., King of Prussia, Pa., 1991—; consumer advocate a.f.i. ENDOLITE, Miami, Fla., 1988-91./. Assoc. editor Amputee Golfer, 1987—, author, 1987—; contbr. articles to profl. jours. Lt. comdr. USN, 1964-74. Decorated Navy Air Medal (2). Mem. Ea. Amputee Golf Assn. (v.p. 1989-92), DAV (life). Republican. Episcopalian. Home: 11 Walnut Hill Rd Amherst NH 03031 Office: Nat Amputee Golf Assn PO Box 1228 Amherst NH 03031

WILSON, ROBERT HENRY, psychologist, educator; b. Abington, Pa., May 18, 1945; s. Robert Henry and Eleanore Mae (Whitaker) W.; m. Karen Bofinger, Dec. 22, 1973. BS in Edn., Shippensburg U., 1967, MS in Counseling Psychology, 1972; MA in Psychology, Lehigh U., 1975. Tchr. Neshaminy Sch. Dist., Langhorne, Pa., 1967—, student assistance program dir., 1985—; pres. RHW Counseling/Consulting, Newtown, Pa., 1983—; mem. state-wide student assistance program com. Dept. Edn., 1988—. Editor: Program and Practices Manual, 1988, 2d edit., 1991. Recipient citation Pa. Ho. of Reps., 1986, 87, 88, 90, U.S. Ho. or Reps., 1988, Presdl. award U.S. Dept. Edn., 1990. Mem. Am. Fedn. Tchrs. (exec. sec. 1980-89), Am. Psychol. Assn. Office: Neshaminy Sch Dist 2001 Old Lincoln Hwy Langhorne PA 19047-3295

WILSON, ROBERT HOWELL, pension fund executive; b. Columbia, S.C., Nov. 23, 1928; s. Alex Wilson and Marian M. (Howell) Sumpter Wilson; m. Margaret Wilson, Oct. 1948 (dec.); children Robert, James, Margaret, Beverly, Marian; m. Elizabeth Spotwood, Mar. 6, 1954; children: James, Ronald, Dorissa, Timothy. Student, Benedict Coll., 1947. Bus. agt. United Food & Comml. Workers Local 174, N.Y.C., 1963-83, pres., 1983—; chmn. bd. trustees United Food Comml. Workers Local 174 Pension Fund, 1983—, Health CARe Fund., Comml. Fund. V.p. Queens labor Coun., 1984; commr. Plainfield Housing Authority, 1985—; trustee Calvary Bapt. Ch., 1976, Benedict Coll., 1968-74, BIC, N.J.; mem. adv. bd. N.Y.C. Bd. Vocat. Edn., 1972—, Myopia Rsch. Found., 1976—, Assn. Children with Retarded Mental Devel., 1984; nat. bd. dirs. Coalition of Black Trade Unionists, Washington, 1972—. Recipient award Deborah Hosp. Found., 1977, award Easter Seals, 1981, award Angel Guardians of Elderly, 1984, award State of Israel Bond, 1984, Assn. CHildren with Retarded Mental Devel., 1985, United Way, 1990, proclamation City of Newark, 1990, N.Y.C., proclamation Consumer Assembly, 1990. Mem. NAACP (life). Democrat. Baptist. Home: 903 Central Ave Plainfield NJ 07060-2310 Office: United Food & Comml Workers 120 E 16th St New York NY 10003-2113

WILSON, ROBERT WOODROW, radio astronomer; b. Houston, Jan. 10, 1936; s. Ralph Woodrow and Fannie May (Willis) W.; m. Elizabeth Rhoads Sawin, Sept. 4, 1958; children—Philip Garrett, Suzanne Katherine, Randal Woodrow. B.A. with honors in Physics, Rice U., 1957; Ph.D., Calif. Inst. Tech., 1962. Research fellow Calif. Inst. Tech., Pasadena, 1962-63; mem. tech. staff AT&T Bell Labs., Holmdel, N.J., 1963-76; head radio physics research dept. AT&T Bell Labs., 1976—. Discoverer 3 deg. k microwave background radiation, 1965; discoverer CO and other molecules in interstellar space using their millimeter wavelength radiation. Recipient Henry Draper medal Royal Astron. Soc., London, 1977, Herschel medal Nat. Acad. Scis., 1977; Nobel prize in physics, 1978; NSF fellow, 1958-61; Cole fellow, 1957-58. Mem. Am. Astron. Soc., Internat. Astron. Union, Am. Phys. Soc., Internat. Sci. Radio Union, Nat. Acad. Scis., Phi Beta Kappa, Sigma Xi. Home: 9 Valley Point Dr Holmdel NJ 07733-1320 Office: AT&T Bell Labs HOH L239 PO Box 400 Holmdel NJ 07733

WILSON, SULE GREG C., archivist, writer, folklorist, educator; b. Washington, Mar. 9, 1957; s. Ernest James and Mignon (Gregory) W.; m. Vanessa Gale Thomas, Aug. 1, 1981; 1 child, Shepsut Kemkem. Student, Oberlin Coll., 1975-77; BFA in TV Prodn., NYU, 1980, MA in History, cert. in archives mgmt., hist. editing & manuscript conservation, 1984. Researcher, performer Internat. Afrikan-Am. Ballet, N.Y.C., 1977-82; archives cons. N.Y. Stock Exch., N.Y.C., 1982-85; archivist YMCA of Greater N.Y., N.Y.C., 1984-86; archives specialist Schomburg Ctr. Rsch. in Black Culture, N.Y. Pub. Libr., N.Y.C., 1986-89; pedagogue in spl. edn. and social studies N.Y. Bd. Edn., 1989-90; A-V archives cons. The World Bank, 1990-91; project specialist African Am. Index Project, Nat. Mus. Am. History, Smithsonian Inst., 1991—; lectr., vis. prof. Yale U., Touro Coll., Cornell U., Jersey City State Coll., African Heritage Ctr., numerous others; cons. Sphinx, Inc., N.Y.C., 1986-90. Author: The Drummer's Path: Moving the Spirit with Ritual and Traditional Drumming Inner Traditions International, 1992, also producer companion audio program The Drummers Path: African and Diaspora Percussive Music, 1992; contbr. articles, revs., photographs to numerous pubs. Mem. Soc. Am. Archivists, Mid-Atlantic Region Archives Conf., Am. Soc. Curriculum Devel., Acad. Cert. Archivists, Auser Auset Soc. Office: PO Box 5643 Silver Spring MD 20913-5643 also: 7003 Westmoreland Ave Takoma Park MD 20912-4405

WILSON, THOMAS MATTHEW, III, lawyer; b. Ware, Mass., Feb. 22, 1936; s. Thomas Matthew Jr. and Ann Veronica (Shea) W.; m. Deborah Ord Lockhart, Feb. 10, 1962; children: Deborah Veronica, Leslie Lockhart, Thomas Matthew IV. BA, Brown U., 1958; JD, U. Md., 1971. Bar: Md. 1972, U.S. Ct. Appeals (4th cir.) 1976, U.S. Supreme Ct. 1977. Sales mgr. Mid-Eastern Box Mfg. Co., Balt., 1966-74; asst. atty. gen., chief antitrust div. State of Md., Balt., 1974-79; ptnr. Tydings & Rosenberg, Balt., 1979—. Mem. editorial adv. bd. Bur. of Nat. Affairs Antitrust and Trade Regulation Report, 1979—; patentee in field. Mem. ABA (sect. on antitrust law 1974—, chmn. state antitrust enforcement com. 1986-89, mem. antitrust sect. coun. 1990-93), Md. Bar Assn. (antitrust subcom. 1975-78), Internat. Bar Assn. (sect. on bus. law, antitrust law and monopolies com. 1983—), Merchants Club, Churchwarden's Chess Club. Republican. Home: Baobab Farm Hampstead MD 21074 Office: Tydings & Rosenberg 100 E Pratt St Baltimore MD 21202-1009

WILSON, TIMOTHY KENNETH, manufacturing executive; b. Detroit, Aug. 28, 1960; s. Kenneth A. and Bernice T. (Jessick) W.; m. Teresa Sue Bergerstock, Sept. 23, 1989. BS in Indsl. Engring., U. Mich., 1982; MBA, Syracuse U., 1987. Cert. prodn. and inventory mgmt., APICS, 1990. Mfg. engr. Welch Allyn, Skaneateles Falls, N.Y., 1982-84; mfg. engr. mgr. Welch Allyn, Skaneateles Falls, 1984-88, prodn. mgr., 1988—; membership dir. APICS, Syracuse, N.Y., 1989-91, treas., 1991—. Inventor in field. Mem. Purchasing Mgmt. Assn., Adirondak Mt. Club, Am. Prodn. and Inventory Control Soc. Home: 512 Walberta Rd Syracuse NY 13219-2238

WILSON, VALERIE, singer; b. Bronxville, N.Y., Nov. 17; d. William Burnett and Rose Marie (Rendinell) W.; m. Emil Mosbacher III, Nov. 6, 1984 (div. 1985); m. Paul David Weinberg, July 10, 1988. MusB, Juilliard, 1976, MusM, 1977. Solo vocalist in Benjamin Britten's Les Illuminations, 1977, Bob Hope Spl. Fight for Sight, 1977; singer appearing in Saturday Night Live, 1986-87, Comic Relief, 1990; soloist and group singer for numerous TV and radio commls., 1977—; background singer for recordings including The Wall, Lost in Love, A Chorus Line; singer and songwriter Band of Angels. Recipient Grant Merwyn Daughtry Found., 1973, Scholarship The Juilliard Sch., 1972-77.

WILSON, VINCENT JOSEPH, JR., writer, historian, publisher; b. Cleve., Apr. 24, 1921; s. Vincent Joseph and Genevieve Margaret (Vleck) W.; m. Mary Jo Cavender, Sept. 30, 1944; children: Nicholas Cavender, Liza Jane. Student, Georgetown U., 1939-41; AB with honors, Ariz. State U., 1948; MA, Claremont Grad. Sch., 1949; postgrad., Harvard U., 1949-50. Instr. English dept. Mitchell Coll., New London, Conn., 1950-53, chmn. English dept., 1953-55; corr. New London Day, 1952-55; editor Nat. Security Agy., Fort Meade, Md., 1956-62, sr. staff writer, 1963-71, chief historian, sr. editor, 1972-81; pub. Am. History Rsch. Assn., 1962—; lectr. English, U. Md., 1959-67, George Washington U., 1963-65. 1st lt. USAAF, 1943-46. Author: The Book of the Presidents, 1962, 10th edit., 1985; The Book of Great American Documents, 1967, 76, 87; The Book of States, 1972, 79, 3d edit., 1992; The Book of the Founding Fathers, 1974, 86; The Book of Distinguished American Women, 1983, 2d edit., 1992; contbr. articles in field to various publs. Recipient Freedoms Found. at Valley Forge Washington medal, 1968, Honor award, 1974, Nat. Security Agy. Meritorious Svc. award, 1975. Mem. Cosmos Club (Washington). Home and Office: 1711 Gold Mine Rd PO Box 140 Brookeville MD 20833

WILSON, WANDA LEE, entertainment promotions professional; b. Pitts., May 15, 1950; d. James A. Davis, Jr. and Dorothy (Love) Davis Anselmi; m. Kirby L. Wilson Sr., Apr. 23, 1976 (div. July 1984); children: Le Chon Kirb, Lia Shawnyea. Student, Connelly Tech. Sch., Pitts., 1968-71, Allegheny Community Coll., Pitts., 1968-71, U. Pitts., 1984, 86. Stand-in co-host The Together Show Sta. KDKA-TV, CBS, Pitts., 1971; adminstrv. sec. GE, Pitts., 1971-78; sec., notary public Sta. WPCB-TV, Wall, Pa., 1979-80; producer, host The Wanda Wilson Show Am. Cablevision Co., Monroeville, Pa., 1981-84, Warner Cable Co. and Pitts. Telecommunications, Inc., 1984-87; mktg. mgr. The Informer newspaper Homewood Brushton Revitalization and Devel., Pitts., 1984-87; pres. local, nat. internat. pub. rels. W-W Prodns./Wanda Wilson Enterprises, Pitts., 1984—; sr. clk./chemical monitor Gencorp Aerojet Tech. Systems, Rancho Cordova, Calif., 1987-90; publicist, cons. Easy Internat., Pitts., 1990—; studio camera operator Sta. WPXI-TV, Pitts., 1990—; occasional writer, copywriter, announcer local radio shows, Pitts., 1972-85; radio show co-host, announcer Internat. People's Radio and TV, Sacramento, 1987; promoter concerts, screen plays, sound tracks Wan Mar Prodns., 1991—. Author (poetry) Love Traces on My Mind, 1972, (songs lyrics) The First Time I Saw You, 1982; performer poetry recitals, Pitts., 1973, (TV movies) $10,000,000 Getaway, 1990, Bump in the Night, 1990, Dead and Alive, 1991, (feature film) Lorenzo's Oil, 1991; producer, hostess WanMar Info. and Talent Showcase Cable TV, Pitts., 1991—. Active Citizen Action for Reduction of Toxic Chems. in Product Packaging, 1990; organizer civic and community events, energy conservation, 1984-87; mem. Pitts. History and Landmarks Found., Smithsonian Assocs., 1991. Mem. NAFE, AFTRA, Smithsonian Assocs., Pitts. Model's Assn., Pitts. Media Fedn. Democrat. Office: 716 Beltzhoover Ave # 1 Pittsburgh PA 15210 also: W-W Prodns, Wanmar Prodns PO Box 100061 Pittsburgh PA 15233

WILSON, WILLIAM STANLEY, oceanographer; b. Alexander City, Ala., June 5, 1938; s. Norman W. and Helen C. (Hackemack) W.; m. Anne M. Stout; 1 child, Lauren. BS, William & Mary Coll., 1959, MA, 1965; PhD, Johns Hopkins U., 1972. Marine biol. collector Va. Inst. Marine Sci., Gloucester Point, 1959-62, computer systems analyst, 1964-65; computer systems analyst Chesapeake Bay Inst., Balt., 1965-66; phys. oceanography program mgr. Office of Naval Rsch., Washington, 1972-78; chief oceanic processes program NASA, Washington, 1979-89, program scientist earth observing system, 1989-92; asst. adminstr. for ocean svcs. and coastal zone mgmt. NOAA, Washington, 1992—. Recipient Antarctica Svc. medal NSF, 1961, Superior Civilian Svc. award USN, 1979, Exceptional Sci. Achievement medal NASA, 1981, Disting. Achievement award MTS and Compass Publs., 1989. Mem. Am. Meteorol. Soc., Am. Geophys. Union (Ocean Scientist award 1984), Oceanography Soc. (com. chmn. 1989—), Sigma Xi. Home: 219 Tunbridge Rd Baltimore MD 21212-3423 Office: NOAA/NOS 1825 Connecticut Ave NW Ste 611 Washington DC 20235

WILTON, ROBERT FREDERICK, software engineer; b. Meriden, Conn., Apr. 8, 1953; s. Joseph William and Dorothy Amelia (Vollmer) W.; m. Olga Rita Fernandez, May 18, 1985. Diploma, Computer Processing Inst., Bridgeport, Conn., 1983. Profl. musician, 1972-80; mgr. Fairgraphics Custom Photo Lab., New Haven, 1980-82, Color and Design Exchange, Newington, Conn., 1982-83; programmer Gen. Reinsurance Corp., Stamford, Conn., 1983-84; systems engr. Mgmt. Sci. America, Inc., Hamden, Conn., 1984-86; project leader Mgmt. Sci. America, Inc., Hamden, 1986-88, application software cons., 1987-88, project mgr., 1988-90; project mgr. Dun & Bradstreet Software Svcs., Inc., Hamden, 1990—. Home: 20 Brookdale Rd Meriden CT 06450-5920 Office: Dun & Bradstreet Software 2750 Dixwell Ave Hamden CT 06518-3320

WILTRAUT, DOUGLAS SCOTT, artist; b. Allentown, Pa., July 12, 1951; s. Richard Walter and Dorothy Elda (Prinz) W.; m. Elizabeth Jane Sewalls, Oct. 25, 1975; children: Laura, Jonathan. BFA in Painting, Kutztown U., 1973. One-man shows include Retrospective: Moravian Coll., Bethlehem, Pa., 1973-83, Douglas Wiltraut: Select Works, Whitehall Twp. Pub. Libr., 1989; group shows include Butler Inst. Am. Art, 1977, 86, Nat. Acad. Design 163rd, 1988, Nat. ARts Club 94th Open Watercolor Exhibition, 1984, Adirondacks Nat. Exhibition of Am. Watercolors, 1988, 89, 90, 91, Nat. Soc. Painters in Casein & Acrylic, 1974—, Allied Artist of Am., 1974—, Audubon Artists, Inc., 1974—. Recipient award Butler Inst. Am. Art, 1986. Mem. Nat. Soc. Painters in Casein and Acrylic (bd. dirs. 1977-86, v.p. 1980, pres. 1989—, Today's Art medal 1974), Audubon Artists, Inc. (v.p. 1989—, Silver Medal 1986), Allied Artists Am. (Ralph Fabri medal 1985-87), Pa. Watercolor Soc., Knickerbocker Artists (Silver medal 1988, Gold medal 1989). Home: 969 Catasauqua Rd Whitehall PA 18052-5501

WILTSE, JON FREDERICK, marketing professional; b. Fulton, N.Y., July 3, 1950; s. John Henry and Helen (Malone) W.; m. Sharon Elizabeth Dennis, Aug. 3, 1974 (div.); children: Shawn, Brendan. BSEE, SUNY, Buffalo, 1972; MBA, U. Rochester, 1980. Sales engr. Northland div. Scott Fetzer Co., Watertown, N.Y., 1973-74, sales mgr., 1974-80; dir. mktg. Northland div. Scott Fetzer Co., Watertown, 1980-82; v.p., gen. mgr. Northland div. Scott Fetzer Co., Mt. Juliet, Tenn., 1982-84; v.p. mktg. and engring. Northland div. Scott Fetzer Co., Watertown, 1984-90, gen. mgr., 1990—. Patentee motor for rotary brush. Mem. Growth Club, Beta Gamma Sigma. Republican. Roman Catholic. Office: Northland Scott Fetzer Co 968 Bradley St Watertown NY 13601-1295

WINAWER, GAIL TRIFFLEMAN, accountant; b. Syracuse, N.Y., Oct. 18, 1939; d. David and Betty (Cantor) Triffleman; m. Joel M. Winawer, Apr. 3, 1960 (dec. 1990); children: Stephen, Robert. BS in Acctg., NYU, 1961; MBA in Tax., Pace U., 1982. CPA, N.Y. Staff mgr. Oppenheim, Appel, Dixon & Co., N.Y.C., 1961-81; ptnr. Spicer & Oppenheim, N.Y.C., 1981-90, Goldstein Golub Kessler, N.Y.C., 1990—. Bd. dirs. Goldstein Found., N.Y.C., 1991—, Crames Found., 1991—. Mem. AICPAs, N.Y. State Soc. CPAs (dir. 1988-91), Accts. Club of N.Y. Office: Goldstein Golub Kessler 1185 Ave Of The Americas New York NY 10036-2601

WINBIGLER, LEON FRANCIS, retail executive; b. Brookfield, Mo., 1926. Grad., U. Mo., 1948. Pres. Root Dry Goods Co., 1954-55, MacDougall Southwick Co., 1955-62, Lion Dry Goods Co., 1962-74; v.p. Mercantile Stores Co. Inc., Wilmington, Del., 1968-74, now chmn., chief exec. officer, also bd. dirs. Office: care Merc Stores Co Inc 1100 N Market St Wilmington DE 19801-1246

WINBUSH, WANDA GAIL, federal program administrator; b. Washington, Aug. 18, 1958; d. Walter Winbush and Velma Ruth (Johnson) W. BS, Norfolk State U., 1980; MA in Counseling, U. D.C., 1991. Word processor Treasury Dept. U.S. Govt., Washington, 1980, supr., 1980-82, acct. technician, 1982-83; councelor PGARC, Bowie, Md., 1980-82; program analyst Dept. Navy U.S. Govt., Washington, 1984-88, NASA, Washington, 1988—; socialization coord. Anchor House, Washington, 1991—. Mem. Delta Sigma Theta. Office: NASA 600 Independence Ave SW Washington DC 20546-0002

WINCE-SMITH, DEBORAH L., federal agency administrator; m. Michael B. Smith; 2 children. Grad. magna cum laude, Vassar Coll., 1972; Master's, Cambridge (Eng.) U., 1974. Former program mgr. internat. programs NSF; asst. dir. internat. affairs and global competitiveness Office of Sci. and Tech. Policy The White House, 1984-89; asst. sec. tech. policy Dept. Commerce, Washington, 1989—. Office: Dept Commerce Tech Policy 14th & Constitution Ave NW Washington DC 20230-0001

WINCHESTER, ALICE, periodical editor, writer; b. Chgo., July 26, 1907; d. Benjamin Severance and Pearl Adair (Gunn) W. AB, Smith Coll., 1929; LHD (hon.), Russell Sage Coll., 1966; LittD (hon.), Hobart & William Smith Colls., 1973. Assoc. editor The Mag. Antiques, N.Y.C., 1934-38, editor, 1938-72; guest curator Whitney Mus. Am. Art, N.Y.C., 1973-74. Author: How to Know American Antiques, 1951, Versatile Yankee: The Art of Jonathan Fisher, 1973; co-author: Primitive Painters in America, 1750-1950, 1950, (exhbn. catalogue) The Flowering of American Folk Art Whitney Mus., 1973; editor: The Antiques Book, 1950, Living With Antiques, 1941, 1968, The Antiques Treasury, 1959, Collectors and Collections, 1961. Trustee N.Y. State Hist. Assn., Cooperstown, 1955-86, Old Sturbridge (Mass.) Village, 1955-65, Shakertown at Pleasant Hill, Harrodsburg, Ky., 1974-90; adv. com. Gov.'s Com. on Historic Sites, N.Y., 1956-63, hon. mem.; mem. Friends of Am. Wing Met. Mus. of Art, N.Y.C., 1972—. Recipient Smith Coll. medal, 1968, Louise du Pont Crowninshield award Nat. Trust for Hist. Preservation, 1972, Henry Francis du Pont award Winterthur (Del.) Mus., 1990. Mem. Am. Soc. Interior Designers (hon.), Nat. Soc. Colonial Dames in Am., The Cosmopolitan Club. Home: 4 Currituck Rd Glen Crest Glen Hill Rd Danbury CT 06811-4976

WINCHESTER, BONNIE POSICK, public information officer, consultant; b. Derby, Conn., Aug. 15, 1960; d. Steven Michael and Theresa Yvonne (Gagne) Posick; m. Charles Eric Winchester, Nov. 24, 1984; 1 child, Cristina Elizabeth; 1 stepchild, Eric Matthew. Student, U. Bridgeport, 1978-79; BS in Journalism, So. Conn. State U., 1984. From copy person to editorial asst. The Jackson Newspapers, Inc., New Haven, Conn., 1984-85; mgmt. trainee Brian Alden, Inc., Milford, Conn., 1985; asst. mgr. Brian Alden, Inc., New Haven, 1985-86; billing clerk Bob Thomas Ford, Inc., Hamden, Conn., 1986-87; info. officer Hamden (Conn.) Pub. Schs., 1987-88; pub. info. officer New Haven Pub. Schs., 1988—. Contbr. articles to newspapers. Mem. Earth Day 20 Com., New Haven, 1990, Household Hazardous Waste Com., New Haven, 1990; sec. edn. com. chmn. We Mean Clean! Citizens and Business for a Clean New Haven, 1990—. Mem. Nat. Sch. Pub. Rels. Assn. (Conn. chpt. chmn. special events). Republican. Roman Catholic. Office: New Haven Pub Schs 54 Meadow St New Haven CT 06519-1743

WINCHESTER, JAMES FRANK, medicine educator; b. Glasgow, Mar. 24, 1944; came to U.S., 1976; s. Alexander Graham and Elizabeth Mary (McKillop) W.; m. Patricia Jane, May 16, 1968; children: J. Craig, Jane E. MB, ChB, Glasgow U., 1969, MD, 1981. Sr. registrar Royal Infirmary, Glasgow, 1974-76; asst. prof. medicine Georgetown U., Washington, 1976-82, assoc. prof., 1982-87, prof., 1987—, acting. dir. divsn. nephrology, 1988—; attending physician Georgetown U. Med. Ctr., 1976—. Editor: Clinical Management of Poisoning and Drug Overdose, 1990. Chmn. Nat. Kidney Found. of Nat. Capital Area, Washington, 1989. Mem. Internat. Soc. Peritoneal Dialysis (sec.-treas. 1984—), Am. Soc. Artificial Internal Organs (mem. exec. com. 1990), Nat. Kidney Found. (regional pres. 1991—), Am. Fedn. Clin. Rsch., Am. Clin. Climatol. Assn., Am. Soc. Transplant Physicians, Am. Soc. Nephrology, Internat. Soc. Nephrology. Office: Georgetown U 3800 Reservoir Rd NW Washington DC 20007-2196

WINCOR, RICHARD, lawyer, author; b. N.Y.C., Aug. 18, 1921; s. Henry George and Mildred (Freund) W.; m. Margaret Reber, Apr. 19, 1949 (dec. Oct. 1971); m. Daisy Maria Pollak, Oct. 9, 1972. AB, Harvard U., 1942, JD, 1948. Bar: N.Y., 1949. Assoc. Hays St. John, N.Y.C., 1949-50, Lewis & Mound, N.Y.C., 1950-55; v.p. Shellric Corp., N.Y.C., 1955-60; ptnr. Stern, Wincor & Burns, N.Y.C., 1960-71; of counsel Coudert Bros., London, also N.Y.C., 1971—; guest lectr. U. Amsterdam, 1974, Cath. U., Washington, 1989. Author: Copyrights in the World Marketplace, 1990, 9 others. 2d lt. U.S. Army, 1942-45. Recipient prize ASCAP, 1948. Mem. Harvard Club of N.Y.C., Landsdowne Club (London). Office: Coudert Bros 200 Park Ave New York NY 10166

WINDELEV, CLAUS, engine manufacturing company executive; b. Goerlev, Denmark, Sept. 17, 1943; came to U.S., 1966; s. Jens Peder and Grethe Oline (Jensen) W.; m. Alis Larsen (div. Mar. 1988); children: Tena, Lisa; m. Kathleen Gutzan Nelson, Nov. 25, 1989 (div. Mar. 1992). MSME, Tech. U., Copenhagen, 1966. Engr. Boeing Co., Seattle, 1966-70, Messerschmitt-Boelkow-Blohm, Munich, 1970-72; engr. Burmeister & Wain, Copenhagen, 1972-74, mgr. design, 1972-77, mgr. R&D, 1975-77; sales mgr. Burmeister & Wain Am. Corp., N.Y.C., 1977-78, v.p., 1978-80; pres. B&W Diesel Inc., N.Y.C., 1980-84; exec. v.p., gen. mgr. Man GHH Corp., N.Y.C., 1984-89; pres. Man B&W Diesel Inc., N.Y.C., 1989—. Contbr. articles on diesel engines to profl. publs.; exhibited in group shows, 1988—. Mem. Govt. Com. on Future Denmark Engring. Studies, 1975-77. Fellow Inst. Marine Engrs.; mem. ASTM, ASME, Soc. Naval Architects and Marine Engrs., Danish C. of C., Danish Club (Princeton, N.J.). Republican. Home: 64 Cooper Rd Denville NJ 07834-3402 Office: MAN B&W Diesel Inc 17 State St New York NY 10004-1501

WINDHAGER, ERICH ERNST, physiologist, educator; b. Vienna, Austria, Nov. 11, 1928; came to U.S., 1954; s. Maximilian and Bertha (Feitzinger) W.; m. Helga A. Rapant, June 18, 1956; children: Evelyn Ann, Karen Alice. MD, U. Vienna, 1954. Research fellow in biophysics Harvard Med. Sch., Boston, 1956-58; instr. in physiology Cornell U. Med. Coll., N.Y.C., 1958-61; vis. scientist U. Copenhagen, 1961-63; asst. to prof. physiology Cornell U. Med. Coll., N.Y.C., 1963—, Maxwell M. Upson prof. physiology and biophysics, 1978—, chmn. dept. physiology, 1973—. Recipient Homer W. Smith award N.Y. Heart Assn., 1978. Office: Cornell U Med Coll Dept Physiology 1300 York Ave New York NY 10021-4896

WINDHAM-BANNISTER, SUSAN RICHARDS, business consultant; b. St. Louis, July 9, 1951; d. Frank Oliver and Ruth Allen (Gordon) Richards; m. Daniel J. Windham, Sept. 2, 1972 (div. 1977); m. Leonard Gordon Bannister, June 30, 1990. BA, Wellesley Coll., 1972; PhD, Brandeis U., 1977; postdoctoral, Harvard U., 1980. Dir. social svcs. Model Cities Family Life Ctr., Boston, 1972-73; sr. assoc. Abt Assocs., Inc., Cambridge, Mass., 1977-80; ind. cons. Boston, 1980-85; v.p., dir. health cons. svcs. Abt Assocs., Inc., Cambridge, 1985—; bd. dirs. Resthaven Nursing Home Corp., Boston, Nat. Register Health Svc. Providers in Psychology, Washington. Co-author: Competive Strategys for Health Care Organizations, 1983, Medicaid and Other Public Policy Experiments, 1984. Mem. NAACP, chmn. health com., 1987; mem. Urban League, Boston, Mass. Pub. Health Coun., Boston, 1983-86. Recipient Ford Found. fellowship, 1975-77. Mem. 100 Black Women (charter mem.). Democrat. Episcopalian. Office: Abt Assocs Inc 55 Wheeler St Somerville MA 02145-3405

WINDHAUSEN, JOHN DANIEL, history educator; b. Syracuse, N.Y.; m. Janet Flewelling; children: John, Charles, Thomas, Brenda, Lisa. Prof. history, chmn. Soviet studies com. St. Anselm Coll., Manchester, N.H., 1959—; teaching fellow Citizen Exchange Corps in USSR, 1966-75, acad. council, 1972-75; research assoc. Ill. Summer Lab. on Russia, 1974. Editor, translator: The Reign of Ivan III, 1978, The Great Russian Society in the Age of Ivan III, 1979; editor: Sports Ency. N.Am., vol. I, 1987, vol. II, 1988, vol. III, 1989, vol. IV, 1990; USSR regional editor Internat. Jour. Sport History; contbr. articles on edn., athletics in Russia, history to profl. jours. Mem. NAACP, AAUP, N.H. Council for Humanities, Manchester Inst. Arts and Scis. (trustee), Am. Assn. for Advancement Slavic Studies, N.Am. Soc. Study Sports History. Democrat. Roman Catholic. Home: 3 Gold St Manchester NH 03102-1202 Office: St Anselm Coll Manchester NH 03102

WINEGARD, WILLIAM CHARLES, Canadian legislator; b. Hamilton, Ont., Can., Sept. 17, 1924; s. William and Hilda (Yaxley) W.; m. Elizabeth Jaques, Jan. 9, 1947; children: William, Charles, Kathryn. B.A.Sc. in Metall. Engring. (honours), U. Toronto, 1949, M.A.Sc. in Metall. Engring., 1950, Ph.D. in Phys. Metallurgy, 1952. Pres. W. C. Winegard & Assocs., U. Guelph; mem. Ho. of Commons, Guelph, Ont., 1984—; min. of state (sci. and tech.) Ho. of Commons, Ottawa, Ont., Can., 1989, min. for sci., 1990. With Royal Can. Navy, 1942-45. Fellow Am. Soc. for Metals. Progressive Conservative. Anglican. Office: Ho of Commons, Parliament Bldgs Rm 256, Ottawa, ON Canada K1A 0A6

WINEGRAD, GERALD WILLIAM, lawyer, state senator, educator; b. Balt., Sept. 9, 1944; s. Benjamin Bernard and Eleanor D. (Messick) W.; m. Madeline Frost Powers, Dec. 10, 1970; children: Pamela Leah, Susan Frost, Rebecca Ann. B.A., Western Md. Coll., 1966; J.D., U. Md., 1969. Bar: Md. 1969. Assoc. revisor Gov.'s Commn. to revise the code, Annapolis, Md., 1974-78; cons. Friends of the Earth, Washington; mem. Md. Senate, 1982—; instr. pub. policy, environ. Grad. Sch. U. Md., 1988. Bd. dirs. Md. Environ. Trust, Balt., 1983—; mem. Chesapeake Bay Commn.; mem. Md. Ho. of Dels., 1978-82; del. Dem. Nat. Conv., 1984. Lt. JAGC, USN, 1970-74, comdr. Res. Recipient Outstanding Conservation Legislator award Md. Wildlife Fedn., 1981, Cert. of Merit, Common Cause of Md., 1984, Outstanding Conservation Legislator award Clean Water Action Project, 1985, Outstanding Environmentalist award Sierra Club, 1985. Mem. Nat. Conf. State Legislators (energy com.), Sierra Club, of Md., Am. Legion, Optimists. Democrat. Roman Catholic. Office: Md State Senate Capitol Bldg Annapolis MD 21401

WINETT, JOEL M., information systems specialist; b. Boston, Mar. 1, 1938; s. Charles and Freda (Rubin) W.; m. Ruth Schiff, July 8, 1965; children: Barbara, Rachel, Carol. BSEE, MIT, 1960, postgrad., 1965; MSEE, Columbia U., 1961. Mem. tech. staff Lincoln Lab. MIT, Lexington, Mass., 1961-73; dir. computer scis. TASC, Reading, Mass., 1973-79; mgr. sci. applications Sanders Assoc., Nashua, N.H., 1979-81; product mgr. BGS Systems, Waltham, Mass., 1981-83, systems mgr., 1983-89, dir. quality assurance, 1989—. Mem. govt. study com. Town Meeting, Framingham, Mass., 1969—. Mem. Assn. Computing Machinery. Home: 10 Berkeley Rd Framingham MA 01701-2821 Office: BGS Systems 128 Technology Dr Waltham MA 02254-9111

WINGATE, CATHARINE LOUISE, health science administrator; b. Boston. BS, Simmons Coll., 1943; MA, Radcliffe-Harvard Grad. Sch., 1948; PhD, Columbia U., 1961. Rsch. scientist Columbia Univ., N.Y.C., 1954-63; radiol. physicist Naval Radiol. Def. Lab., San Francisco, 1963-66; sr. rsch. scientist, assoc. prof. N.Y.U., N.Y.C., 1966-67; assoc. radiol. physicist Brookhaven Nat. Lab., Upton, N.Y., 1967-70; rsch. asst. prof. to rsch. assoc. prof. SUNY, Stony Brook, N.Y., 1970-78; health sci. adminstr. NIH, Bethesda, Md., 1978—; med. physicist dosimetrist Nassau County Med. Ctr., East Meadow, N.Y., 1974-78. Assoc. editor: Medical Physics Jour., 1979-85; contbr. articles to profl. jours. Mem. N.Y. Acad. Scis., Am. Assn. Physicists in Medicine, Radiation Rsch., Soc. Nuclear Medicine, Soc. Maquetic Resources in Medicine. Office: NIH Westwood Bldg Rm 357 Bethesda MD 20892

WINGATE, GEORGE BRADBURY, artist; b. Mt. Holly, N.J., Oct. 13, 1941; s. Francis A. and Helen (Abbot) W.; m. Penny Wingate, Sept. 12, 1981; 1 child, Anne. BA, U. Rochester, 1963; postgrad., Syracuse U. Sch. Architecture, 1964; student, New Sch., N.Y.C., 1972-77, Art Students League, 1973-78. Instr. Parsons Sch. Design, N.Y.C., 1987-89, Gordon Coll., Wenham, Mass., 1989—. One-man shows at John Pence Gallery, San Francisco, 1983, 85, Joseph Keiffer Gallery, N.Y.C., 1989, Five Points Gallery, East Chatham, N.Y., 1989, Foxhall Gallery, Washington, 1984-87, 90; exhibited in group shows at Virginia Lynch Gallery, Tiverton, R.I., 1991, Cooley Gallery, Old Lyme, Conn., 1990-91, Pence Gallery, San Francisco, 1987-92, others. Mem. Art Students League (life), N.Y. Arts Group. Home: Dameys Way Marblehead MA 01945-3232

WINGATE, JOHN BARNUM, human services administrator, mechanical engineer; b. Elizabeth, N.J., June 12, 1937; s. John Williams and Isabel (Barnum) W.; m. Judith Wagner, Dec. 5, 1959; children: Jennifer R. Wingate Schott, John Williams II, Jeffrey Bennett. BSME, Lehigh U., 1958; MBA, CCNY, 1964. Lic. nursing home adminstrs., N.Y. Engr., mgr. Western Electric Co., Inc., N.Y.C. and Kearny, N.J., 1959-73; 1st deputy dir. L.I. Coll. Hosp., Bklyn., 1973-77; owner, mgr. Westtown (N.Y.) Market, 1977-78; commr. Dept. Social Svcs., Orange County, Goshen, N.Y., 1978-81; adminstr. Burke Rehab. Ctr., White Plains, N.Y., 1981-84; exec. dir. Internat. Ctr. for Disabled, N.Y.C., 1984—; bd. dirs., chmn. med. com. N.Y. State Assn. Rehab. Facilities, Albany; pres. U.S. Coun. for Internat. Rehab., Washington, 1991—; mem. President's Com. on Employment People with Disabilities, Washington, 1984—; mem. adv. coun. for occupational edn. N.Y.C. Bd. Edn., 1989—. Pres., prin. officer L.I. Coll. Hosp., Bklyn., 1970-73; mem. fin. com. Jack Kemp for Pres., N.Y., 1987-88; v.p. Greenwich House, Inc., N.Y.C., 1988—; chmn. Open Congregation, N.Y.C., 1988-90. 1st lt. U.S. Army, 1958-59, 61-62. Recipient Pres.'s Com. on Employment of Handicapped, 1986, Private Sector award BIPED Corp., 1985, Achievement award N.Y. State Dept. Edn., 1989. Mem. Am. Congress of Rehab. Medicine, N.Y. Pub. Welfare Assn. (assoc.), N.Y. State Head Injury Assn. (1st chmn. Provicers coun.), Am. Hosp. Assn., Nat. Rehab. Assn., United Way (Key Agy. mem.), 60 East Club. Republican. Congregational. Office: Internat Ctr for Disabled 340 E 24th St New York NY 10010-4097

WINGATE, VIVA LOUISE, computer science educator; b. Flushing, N.Y., Jan. 23, 1940; d. David Robert and Helen Agnes (Busch) W. BA in Chemistry magna cum laude, St. John's U., 1971; MS in Computer Sci., N.Y. Inst. Tech., 1981; PhD in Computer Sci., U. Cen. Fla., 1989. Elem. tchr. various parochial schs. L.I., N.Y., 1959-69; tchr. sci. St. Michael's High Sch., Bklyn., 1969-71; programmer analyst Diocese of Rockville Centre (N.Y.), 1971-80; instr. computer sci. N.Y. Inst. Tech., Westbury, 1980-82; instr. computer sci. Molloy Coll., Rockville Centre, 1981-82, asst. prof. computer sci., 1988—; dir. Dominican Data Systems, Amityville, N.Y., 1982-83; grad. teaching asst. U. Cen. Fla., 1983-88. Mem. chorale St. Agnes Cathedral. Fellow U. Cen. Fla., Orlando, 1983. Mem. AAUP, Computer Soc. of IEEE, Assn. Computing Machinery, Kappa Delta Pi. Roman Catholic. Home: 1 Quealy Pl Rockville Centre NY 11570-4035 Office: Molloy Coll 1000 Hempstead Ave Rockville Centre NY 11570-1199

WINGERT, HANNELORE CHRISTIANE, real estate sales executive, chemicals executive; b. Karlsbad, Czechoslavakia; came to U.S., 1962, naturalized, 1967; d. Andreas and Gisela Maria (Ciharz) Zwickel; m. Rudolf Wingert, Feb. 9, 1963; children: Angela, Helene, Christopher, Rudolf. I.B.A., Stadt. Berufsschule, Fed. Republic Germany, 1961; postgrad. in mgmt., Bergen Community Coll., 1983. Lic. real estate, N.J. Clk. various cos., N.J., 1963, bilingual sec., 1963-78; exec. sec., adminstrv. asst. Lurgi Corp., Hasbrouck Heights, N.J., 1978-81; sr. exec. sec. Degussa Corp., Teterboro, N.J., 1981-83, asst. product mgr. silica, 1983-85, asst. product mgr. H202, 1985-87, sales promotion coord., 1987; sales assoc. Schlott Realtors, Kinnelon, N.J., 1987—. Author community newsletter, 1977-79. Mem. Bd. Realtors Morris and Passaic (N.J.) Counties; chmn. master planning com. High Crest Lake, West Milford, N.J., 1974-75; advisor Jr. Woman's Club Kinnelon-Butler, Butler, N.J., 1973-74; tchr. computer classes Bd of Realtors, Passaic County, 1989-90. Mem. N.J. Fed. of Woman's Clubs (past pres.), High Crest Lake Woman's Club (pres. 1972-73) (West Milford, N.J.). Republican. Roman Catholic. Home: 204 High Crest Dr West Milford NJ 07480-3710 Office: Coldwell Banker Schlott Kinnelon 1450 State Route 23 Butler NJ 07405-1624

WINGERTER, JOHN PARKER, artist, photographer; b. N.Y.C., July 27, 1940; s. William and Catherine (Parker) W.; m. Joan Aleen Patiky; 1 child, Janet. Student, Columbia U., 1958-61; LLB, LaSalle U., 1968; postgrad., Arts Student League, 1970-72. Dir. Noho Gallery, N.Y.C., 1982-84; One man shows include Nomo Gallery, 1978, 79, 80, 81, 82, 83, 84, 85, 86, 87, 88; exhibitions in group shows at Adelphi U., 1983, LeSalon Des Nations Centre for Contemporary Arts, 1984. Home: 58 Meadow Glen Rd Northport NY 11768-2711 Studio: Main St Huntington NY 11743-6903

WINIARSKI, MARK GREGORY, clinical psychologist; b. Buffalo, June 2, 1950; s. Albin Walter and Rose (Dudynic) W.; m. Loretto Kenny, Nov. 20, 1974 (div. 1977); m. Diane Lynn Sturm, May 29, 1988. BS in Journalism, Northwestern U., 1972; MS in Journalism, Columbia U., 1973; PhD, Fla. State U., 1988. Lic. psychologist, N.Y. Newspaper reporter various newspapers, 1973-81; psychology intern NYU Med. Ctr.-Bellevue Hosp., 1987-88; psychologist Spellman Ctr. for HIV Disease, St. Clare's Hosp., N.Y.C., 1987-90, Blanton-Peale Counseling Ctr., Forest Hills, N.Y., 1988—; psychologist in pvt. practice Forest Hills, N.Y., 1989—; asst. prof. epidemiology and social medicine Albert Einstein Coll. Medicine, Bronx, 1991—; psychosocial coord. Primary Care & Substance Abuse Project Dept. Family Medicine, Montefiore Med. Ctr., Bronx, 1990—, project dir. AIDS Mental Health and Primary Care Integration Project, 1991—. Author: AIDS-Related Psychotherapy, 1991; contbr. articles to profl. jours. Mem. Am. Psychol. Assn., Soc. of Behavioral Medicine, N.Y. State Psychol. Assn., Queens County Psychol. Assn. Office: Montefiore Med Ctr 111 E 210th St Bronx NY 10467-2490

WINICK, CALVIN PHILLIP, employee benefits consultant; b. N.Y.C., Sept. 18, 1931; s. Leonard D. and Beatrice (Silverman) W.; m. Lorraine Adler, Dec. 25, 1957; children: Bruce Howard, Adam Bryan. BS in Mgmt. cum laude, Rutgers U., 1960. Supr., group Prudential Ins. Co., Newark, 1953-59; account exec. Pension Planning Co., N.Y.C., 1959-62; asst. mgr., group Hartford Ins. Co., N.Y.C., 1962-63; group ins. mgr. Hamilton Life Ins. Co., N.Y.C., 1963-65; v.p., dir. Thomas Jefferson Life Ins. Co., N.Y.C., 1965-70; pres., dir. Serv-Co Adminstrs., N.Y.C., 1970-84; pres. Winick Associates, Matawan, N.J., 1969—. Cpl. U.S. Army, 1952-54, Korea. Mem. Knights of Pythias. Home: 40 Appletree Dr Matawan NJ 07747-3746

WINKELJOHANN, ROSEMARY JOSEPHINE, English educator; b. Cin., Nov. 6, 1929; d. Henry J. Winkeljohann and Johanna (Kenning) Diekman. BA, Edgecliff Coll., 1958; MEd, Xavier U., 1966; MA in Psychology, U. Ill., 1976, PhD, 1979; MA in Theology, U. Toronto, 1985. Cert. reading specialist, supr., teaching, Ohio. Reading curriculum coord. Archdiocese Cons. Bd. Edn.; asst. prof. edn. Xavier U., 1965-72; dir. mem. svcs. Nat. Coun. Tchrs. English, 1972-78; assoc. prof. edn. N.D. U., 1978-80; prin. St. Ursula Villa, Cin., 1980-84; sabbatical study U. Toronto, 1984-85; prof. Millersville U., 1985—. Contbr. articles to profl. jours. Mem. Nat. Coun. Tchrs. English (exec. bd. 1985-87), Internat. Reading Assn., Assn. Childhood Edn. Internat., Nat. Coun. Rsch. English, U.S. Bd. Books for Young (bd. dirs.), Lancaster-Lebanon Reading Coun. (exec. bd. 1987-92), Phi Delta Kappa, Pi Lambda Theta. Roman Catholic. Office: U Pa Millersville Ctr for Edn Millersville PA 17551

WINKELMAN, JOHN, health association executive; b. Highland Park, Ill., Nov. 25, 1953; s. Howard and Ethel (Landsberg) W.; 1 child, Sarah. BS in Econs., U. Pa., 1975; MBA, Wharton U., 1980. Quality assurance specialist Def. Logistics Agy., Phila., 1975-78; v.p. Health Rsch. & Ednl. Trust, Princeton, N.J., 1980-84; owner Winkelman Assocs., Trenton, N.J., 1984-88; exec. dir. Hosp. Data Resources, Sea Girt, N.J., 1988-91; div. dir. Healthcare Design Systems, Sea Girt, 1991—. Com. sec. E. Windsor (N.J.) Econ. Devel. Com., 1990. Mem. Healthcare Fin. Mgmt. Assn. (com. mem. 1984—), Wharton Healthcare Alumni Assn. (bd. dirs. 1988—). Office: Healthcare Design Systems 2164 Rte 35 North Sea Girt NJ 08750

WINKELSTEIN, JERRY ALLEN, pediatrician, educator; b. Syracuse, N.Y., Sept. 5, 1940; s. Warren W. and Lillian (Sirkin) W.; m. Marilyn Link, June 21, 1969; children: Beth, Amy. BA, Syracuse U., 1961; MD, Einstein Med. Sch., 1965. Diplomate Am. Bd. Pediatrics. Asst. prof. pediatrics Johns Hopkins U., Balt., 1973-76, assoc. prof., 1976-82, prof., 1982—, prof. immunology, 1990—; dir. div. immunology, dept. pediatrics Johns Hopkins Hosp., Balt., 1981—. Contbr. articles to sci. jours. Chmn. med. adv. com. Immuno Deficiency Found., 1982—. Lt. comdr. USPHS, 1968-70. Recipient Mead-Johnson award Am. Acad. Pediatrics, 1982. Mem. Am. Pediatric Soc., Soc. Pediatric Rsch., Am. Soc. Clin. Investigation, Infectious Disease Soc. Home: 109 Deepdene Rd Baltimore MD 21210-1911 Office: Johns Hopkins Hosp CMSC 1103 Baltimore MD 21205

WINKLER, KATHERINE MAURINE, technological company executive; b. Louisville, Nov. 29, 1940; d. Myrick and Maurine (Holland) W. Cert. in foreign studies, Inst. for Am. Univs., 1961; BA, Transylvania U., 1963. Market rsch. field supr. Procter & Gamble, Cin., 1963-65; Eng. tchr. Louisville Ky. Sch. System, 1967-68; mgmt. and staff positions in mktg., human resources and edn. IBM, Louisville, Lexington, Ky., Mpls. and Westchester, N.Y., 1968—; indsl. sector div. quality mgr. IBM, Milford, Conn., 1990—. Author: Leadership, 1982. Com. mem. Mpls. Cultural Affairs Com., 1970; com. mem. Village of Tarrytown (N.Y.) Main St. com., 1981-82; trustee Westchester County Hist. Soc., Elmsford, N.Y., 1989—. Named Outstanding Young Woman of Am., 1972. Mem. Am. Soc. Quality Control, Ky. Col. Home: 74 Drake Rd Scarsdale NY 10583-6447

WINKLER, LEONARD P., electrical engineering educator; b. N.Y.C., Dec. 29, 1944; s. Abraham I. and Myrna (Levy) W. BSEE, Poly. U. Bklyn., 1965, MSEE, 1967, PhD in Elec. Engring., 1970. Asst. prof. Coll. of S.I., N.Y.C., 1970-76, assoc. prof. elec. engring., 1977—. Contbr. articles to profl. jours. Grantee, Intel Corp., 1982, NSF, 1973. Mem. IEEE, Eta Kappa Nu (chpt. v.p. 1965), Tau Beta Pi (chpt. sec. 1965), Sigma Xi. Office: Coll S I Staten Island New York NY 10301

WINN, STEWART DOWSE, JR., engineer, construction management consultant; b. Newcastle-Upon-Tyne, Eng., Apr. 8, 1936; s. Stewart Dowse and Frances (Faust) W.; m. Elizabeth Dial Gray, Feb. 2, 1963; 1 child, Michael Stewart. BS in Indsl. Engring., Ga. Inst. Tech., 1958, MS in Indsl. Engring., 1963. Registered profl. engr., Tex., Calif., Ala. Engr. Brown Engring. Co., Cape Canaveral, Fla., 1963-64, Dow Chem. Co., Cape Canaveral, Fla., 1964-66; sr. engr. Tex. Instruments, Dallas, 1966-68; owner Winn & Assocs., Dallas, 1968-76; control mgr. Wash. Pub. Power Supply System, Olympia, 1976-83; v.p. O'Brien-Kreitzberg & Assocs., Merchantville, N.J., 1983—. Lt. USN, 1958-63. Mem. ASCE, Am. Inst. Indsl. Engrs. (pres. Dallas chpt. 1967-68), Am. Soc. Cost Engrs., Project Mgmt. Inst., Nat. Soc. Profl. Engrs., St. George's Club. Republican. Presbyterian. Home: 3 Oak Ter Merchantville NJ 08109-2033 Office: O'Brien Kreitzberg & Assocs 4350 Haddonfield Rd Ste 300 Merchantville NJ 08109-5596

WINNEGRAD, MARK HARRIS, municipal investigator; b. Bronx, N.Y., Nov. 11, 1948; s. Joseph and Bella Ruth (Polivy) W. BA, CUNY, Bronx, 1971, MA, 1976, MLS, 1973. Investigator N.Y.C. Dept. of Finance, 1977-80; investigator N.Y.C. Dept. of Transp., 1980-84, sr. investigator, 1984—. Author: (monograph) Highlights of the History of Printing on Stamps, 1973, (handbook) Spirits of the Revolution, 1974, Printing on Stamps, 3d edit., 1989. Mem. Graphics Philately Assn. (pres. 1978—), Am. Topical Assn. (life), Am. Philatelic Soc. (mem. Journalists, Authors, Poets on Stamps study group). Office: NYC Dept Transp 34-02 Queens Blvd Long Island NY 11101

WINNETT, MICHAEL DAVID, mechanical engineer; b. Waukegan, Ill., Dec. 17, 1955; s. David Melton and Winnie Mae (Browning) W.; m. Kim Elaine Rethmeier, Aug. 6, 1977; children: Daniel Michael, Christopher Ryan. BSME magna cum laude, U. Mo., Rolla, 1978. Engr. Olin Corp., E. Alton, Ill., 1976-78; project engr. Anheuser-Busch Inc., St. Louis, 1978-80, constrn. mgr., 1981-84; project mgr. Pepsi-Cola Co., Somers, N.Y., 1984-88, mgr. tech. devel., 1989-90, project mgr. for new plants/offices/whses., 1988-90. Co-inventor air rinser, 1991. NSF grantee, 1977. Mem. ASME, Tau Beta Pi. Office: Pepsi-Cola Co 1 Pepsi Way Somers NY 10589-2200

WINOGRAD, AUDREY LESSER, advertising executive; b. N.Y.C., Oct. 6, 1933; d. Jack J. and Theresa Lorraine (Elkind) Lesser; m. Melvin H. Winograd, Apr. 29, 1956; 1 child, Hope Elise. Student, U. Conn., 1950-53. Asst. advt. mgr. T. Baumritter Co., Inc., N.Y.C., 1953-54; asst. dir. pub. relations and creative merchandising Kirby, Block & Co., Inc., N.Y.C., 1954-56; div. mdse. mgr., dir. advt. and sales promotion Winograd's Dept. Store, Inc., Point Pleasant, N.J., 1956-73, v.p., 1960-73, exec. v.p., 1973-86; pres. AMW Assocs., Ocean Twp., N.J., 1976—. Editor bus. newsletters. Bd. dirs. Temple Beth Am, Lakewood, N.J., 1970-72. Mem. NAFE, Jersey Pub. Rels. and Advt. Assn. (past pres., bd. dirs.), Retail Advt. and Mktg. Assn. Internat., Monmouth Ocean Devel. Coun., Monmouth County Bus. Assn. (bd. dirs. 1985—, pres. 1988-90), N.J. Assn. Women Bus. Owners, Am. Soc. Advt. and Promotion, Ocean C. of C., Soc. Prevention Cruelty to Animals, Humane Soc., United Animal Nation U.S., Internat. Fund Animal Welfare, World Wildlife Fund, Friends of Animals, Animal Protection Inst., Retail Advt. Conf. Office: AMW Assocs 10 Pine Ln Asbury Park NJ 07712-7242

WINSHIP, M. DOUGLAS, pharmaceutical company executive; b. Glen Ridge, N.J., Jan. 8, 1949; s. Marvin Jay and Lou Ellen (Leech) W.; m. Denise Marie Schedeman, Feb. 12, 1977 (div. Aug. 1990); children: Matthew Douglas, Megan Deanna; m. Mary Evans Harmon, Jan. 1, 1991. BS in Chemistry, Upsala Coll., 1971; postgrad., Rutgers U., 1973-77. Asst. scientist Schering Corp., Bloomfield, N.J., 1971-73, assoc. scientist, 1973-76; tech. data assoc.-drug regulatory affairs USV Pharm. Corp., Tuckahoe, N.Y., 1976-79; mgr.-drug regulatory affairs Revlon Health Care Research & Devel., Tuckahoe, 1979-83, asst. dir.-drug regulatory affairs, 1983-85; assoc. dir.-drug regulatory affairs Oxford Research Internat. Corp., Clifton, N.J., 1985, dir.-drug regulatory affairs, 1986-87; mgr. regulatory affairs Sea Pharm, Inc., Princeton, N.J., 1987-88; dir. drug regulatory affairs, quality assurance Curative Techs., Inc., Setauket, N.Y., 1988-91, v.p. drug regulatory affairs and quality assurance, 1991—. Asst. coach, referee Parsippany Soccer Club, N.J., 1983-89; asst. coach Par-Troy West Little League, Parsippany, 1987. Mem. Regulatory Affairs Profl. Soc., Drug Info. Assn., Tissue Techology (v.p. regulatory affairs 1991-92). Episcopalian. Office: Curative Techs Inc Box 9052 14 Research Way 25 Boxwood Dr Morristown NJ 07960

WINSKI, LOUISE FLORENCE, quality assurance professional; b. Phila., June 20, 1950; d. Walter Joseph and Florence Helen (Hejnar) W. BSc, Phila. Coll. Pharmacy & Sci., 1972; MA, LaSalle U., 1991. Med. technologist Lower Bucks Hosp., Bristol, Pa., 1972-75; staff biologist Merck, Sharp & Dohme Pharm. Co., West Point, Pa., 1975-88, quality assurance auditor, 1988-90, quality assurance assoc., 1990—. Mem. AACD, Am. Soc. Clin. Pathologists, Am. Mental Health Counselors Assn., Nat. Career Devel. Assn. Home: 1090 Bayless Pl Norristown PA 19403-1464 Office: Merck Sharp & Dohme Pharm Co Sumneytown Pike West Point PA 19486

WINSLADE, THOMAS EDWIN, lawyer; b. Omaha, May 30, 1952; s. George Edwin and H.I. (Lockhart) W. BA, Claremont Men's Coll., 1974; JD, Columbia U., 1976. Bar: N.Y. 1977, Pa. 1985. Assoc. Shearman & Sterling, N.Y.C., 1976-83; assoc. counsel Mellon Bank, Pitts., 1984-87; v.p., asst. resident counsel Morgan Guaranty Trust Co., N.Y.C., 1987—. Mem. Emerging Markets Traders Assn. (chair Brazil com.). Office: Morgan Guaranty Trust Co 60 Wall St New York NY 10260-0001

WINSLOW, JULIAN DALLAS, retired lawyer, historian; b. Elizabeth City, N.C., Oct. 10, 1914; s. Joseph D. and Mary Anne (Cooper) W.; m. Jean Littell, Dec. 27, 1941; children: Julian Dallas, Mary P. Winslow Reddick, Helen L. BS in Commerce, U. N.C., 1935, JD, 1941; MA in History, U. Del., 1988. Bar: N.C. 1941, Del. 1949, U.S. Dist. Ct. Del. 1952, U.S. Ct. Appeals (3d cir.) 1982. Assoc. J.H. LeRoy Jr., Elizabeth City, 1941-42; pvt. practice Elizabeth City, 1945-48, Wilmington, Del., 1949-89; ret. Wilmington, 1989; ptnr. Winslow Realty Co., 1974—; solicitor Currituck County (N.C.) Ct. 1946-47; chief of enforcement heavy machinery and indsl. materials sect. Office Price Stablzn., Del. dist. 1952; arbitrator Am. Arbitration Assn. Lt. USCG, 1942-45. Decorated Philippine Liberation medal. Mem. Del. State Bar Assn. (com. labor and employment law). Republican. Episcopalian.

WINSOR, ELEANOR WEBSTER, conflict management/dispute resolution consultant; b. Champaign, Ill., Dec. 1, 1941; d. Chauncey Wilson and Eleanor (Litschauer) Webster; m. Curtin Winsor, May 6, 1972; 1 child, Ellen. AB, Hollins Coll., 1963; MS, U. Pa., 1966; DSc, Wilkes Coll., 1986. Mng. dir. Nat. and Hist. Resource Assn., Phila., 1967-74; exec. v.p. Pa. Environ. Coun., Phila., 1974-86, Pa. Environ. Rshc. Fedn., Phila., 1974-86; pres. Winsor Assocs., Ardmore, Pa., 1984—; bd. dirs. community Dispute Settlement Program Del. County, 1987-90; bd. dirs. Pa. Coun. Mediators, 1988—, chairperson, 1989-90; adj. prof. Wilkes U., Wilkes Barre, Pa. Mem. citizens adv. coun. Pa. Dept. Environ. Resources, 1979-88, mem. environ. quality bd., 1980-83, 84-88; mem. Lower Merion Twp. Planning Commn., Ardmore, 1974—, chairperson, 1990—; bd. dirs. Pa. Resources Coun., Media, 1969-86; chairperson Pa. Solid Waste Adv. Com., Harrisburg, 1984-86; mem. exec. com. Earth Conservancy, Wilkes Barre, Pa.; chairperson bd. trustees West Hill Sch., Rosemont, Pa., 1985-91; trustee Agnes Irwin Sch., Rosemont, 1985-91. Recipient Conservationist of Yr., North Area Environ. Coun., 1984. Mem. Soc. of Profls. in Dispute Resolution (sec. Del. Valley chpt. 1990—), Earth Conservancy Wilkes-Barre (exec. com.). Episcopalian. Office: Winsor Assocs PO Box 432 Ardmore PA 19003-0432

WINSTEAD, CAROL JACKSON, mathematics educator; b. Balt., Dec. 23, 1947; d. John Jay and Patricia (Murnaghan) Jackson;m. Thomas Williamson Jr., June 28, 1969; children: Troy, Peter. AA, Pine Manor, Boston, 1967; BA, Goucher Coll., 1969; MS in Edn. with honors, Johns Hopkins U., 1991. 3d grade tchr. Bryn Mawr Sch., Balt., 1972-73, 5th grade tchr., 1973-75, math. tchr., 1975-77; prin. C.J. Enterprises, Balt., 1986-87; math. tchr. St. Pauls Sch. for Girls, Brooklandville, Md., 1988-90; community counselor, Au Pair Care, 1991. Fundraiser Boys Latin Sch. and Gilman Sch., Balt., 1990-92. Mem. St. George's Garden Club (treas., admissions com. 1985-91, Horticulture award 1981), Chi Sigma Iota. Home and Office: 901 Malvern Ave Baltimore MD 21204-6713

WINSTEN, ROYCE L., real estate executive; b. Providence, Nov. 18, 1957; s. Harold H. and Anita (Horowitz) W.; m. Dorothy Malone, Dec. 17, 1989; children: Vanessa, Jesse, Hannah. BA in Econs., Conn. Coll., 1980; MBA, Duke U., 1985. Vice pres. Atel, Inc., San Francisco, 1980-83, Planned Residential Communities, Inc., West Long Branch, N.J., 1985-91; pres. Axiom Property Mgmt. Corp., West Long Branch, 1991—; bd. dirs. Met. Savs. Bank, Mayfield Heights, Ohio, Met. Fin. Corp., Mayfield Heights. Alumni interviewer Duke U., 1985—. Mem. Inst. Real Estate Mgmt., Nat. Assn. Indsl. and Office Parks, West Long branch Rep. Club. Office: Axiom Property Mgmt Corp 60 Hwy 36 West Long Branch NJ 07764

WINSTON, BRIAN NORMAN, university dean, media educator; b. Evesham, Worcestershire, Eng., Nov. 7, 1941; came to U.S., 1979; s. Reuben and Anita (Salamons) W.; m. Adele Muriel Jackson, Sept. 5, 1978; children: Jessica, Matthew. BA in Laws, Oxford U., 1963, MA, 1971. Researcher, producer, dir. Granada TV, Manchester, Eng., 1963-66, producer, dir., 1969-72; producer, dir. BBC TV, London, 1966-69; prof. Bradford (Eng.) Coll. Art, 1972-73; head gen. studies Nat. Film Sch., Beaconsfield, Eng., 1973-79; program dir. Glasgow (Scotland) U., 1974-76; prof., dept. head NYU, N.Y.C., 1979-86; dean Sch. Communications, Pa. State U., State College, 1986—; bd. mem. 1st Amendment Coalition Pa., Phila., 1987—, Pa. Humanities Coun., Phila., 1989—. Author: Misunderstanding Media, 1986 (Choice award 1986); scriptwriter TV documentary Civilization and the Jews, 1984; columnist The Listener, 1975-91; pub. Pub. Mag., London, 1985; contbr. articles to profl. jours. Bd. mem. United Way Center County, Pa., 1990—. Recipient Emmy award NATAS, L.A., 1985. Mem. Writers Guild, English Speaker Union (v.p. Cen. Pa. br. 1987—). Home: 909 W Fairmount State College PA 10801 Office: Pa State U Sch Communication Carnegie Bldg University Park PA 16802

WINSTON, KRISHNA RICARDA, language professional, translator; b. Greenfield, Mass., June 7, 1944; d. Richard and Clara (Brussel) W.; 1 child, Danielle Billingsley. BA, Smith Coll., 1965; MPhil, Yale U., 1969, PhD, 1974. Instr. Wesleyan U., Middletown, Conn., 1970-74, asst. prof., 1974-77; assoc. prof. Wesleyan U., Middletown, 1977-84, prof., 1984—. Author: O. v. Horvath: Close Readings of Six Plays, 1975; translator: O. Schlemmer, Letters and Diaries, 1972, S. Lenz, The Heritage, 1981, G. Grass, Two States, One Nation, 1990, C. Hein, The Distant Lover, 1989, G. Mann, Reminiscences and Reflections, 1990, J.W. v. Goethe, Wilhelm Meister's Journeyman Years, 1989, C. v. Krockow, The Hour of the Women, 1991, E. Heller, With the Next Man Everything Will be Different, 1992, R.W. Fassbinder, The Anarchy of the Imagination, 1992. Vol. Planned Parenthood, Middletown, 1972-77; mem. Recycling Task Force, Middletown, 1986-87; chmn. Resource Recycling Adv. Coun., Middletown, 1989—. Recipient Fellowship, German Acad. Exchange Svc. Mem. MLA, N.E. MLA, Soc. for Exile Studies, Am. Lit. Translators' Assn., Am. Assn. Tchrs. German, Phi Beta Kappa (pres. Wesleyan chpt. 1987-90). Home: 655 Bow Ln Middletown CT 06457-4808 Office: Wesleyan Univ German Dept Middletown CT 06459

WINSTON, ROBERT T., psychologist; b. Aug. 14, 1937. BA in Psychology, Hofstra U., 1960; MS in Clin. and Counseling Psychology, North Tex. State U., 1962; PhD, St. Andrews Coll., London, 1966; EdD in Adminstrn. and Supervision, Rutgers U., 1976. Lic. psychologist, sch. psychologist, guidance counselor, sch. social worker, N.J.; cert. sch. adminstr., supr., bus. mgr., prin., N.J., sch. dist. adminstr., sch. adminstr., supr., N.Y. Clin./ednl. dir. Diagnostic Ctrs., Watchung, N.J., 1965—; supr. spl. edn. Belleville (N.J.) Pub. Schs., 1970-72; asst. to supt. South Plainfield (N.J.) Pub. Schs., 1967-70; sch. psychologist Lincoln High Sch., Jersey City, 1988-92; chief evaluator Police Testing and Tng. Ctr., N.J. Fellow Internat. Coun. Sex. Edn. and Parenthood; mem. Am. Assn. Sex Educators, Counselors & Therapists (cert.), Am. Soc. for Clin. Hypnosis, Assn. for Advancement Ethical Hypnosis, Internat. Soc. for Profl. Hypnosis, Internat. Soc. Stress Analysts, Biofeedback Soc. Am. Home and Office: 20 Stanie Glen Rd Watchung NJ 07060

WINTER, FRED JOSEPH, dentist; b. N.Y.C., May 25, 1950; s. Paul and Helen (Weissfeld) W.; m. Pamela Marlene Satz, June 10, 1973; children: Dayle Michelle, Stacy Debra. BA in CHemistry, NYU, 1972; DMD in Oral Medicine with Honors, U. Pa., 1976. Pvt. practice dentistry Elm Ct. Dental Assn., Metuchen, N.J., 1976—; active John F. Kennedy Med. Ctr., 1977—; team dentist St. Peter's Orofacial Anomalies Team, 1982—. Contbr. articles to profl. jours. Mem. ADA, Acad. Gen. Dentistry, Acad. for Sports Dentistry, N.J. Dental Assn. (rep. jud. council 1979-85, ho. of dels. 1976—, council on legis. 1984—), Am. Cleft Palate Assn., Metuchen C. of C. (pres. 1986—). Democrat. Jewish. Office: Elm Ct Dental Assocs 1 Elm Ct Metuchen NJ 08840-1300

WINTER, NICHOLAS RADFORD, management consultant; b. Beckenham, Kent, Eng., Feb. 3, 1966; came to U.S., 1990; s. Donald Thomas and Maureen Janis (Sharp) W. 1st class honors in elec. & info. scis., Cambridge U., Eng., 1987. Mgmt. trainee British Telecom, London, Eng., 1983-87; mgmt. cons. Strategic Planning Assocs., London, 1987-90, N.Y.C., 1990—; cons. Computer One, Cambridge, Eng., 1985; bus. planner Echo Hill Outdoor Sch., Worton, Md., 1990. Mem. IEEE (assoc.). Office: Mercer Mgmt Cons Inc 375 Park Ave New York NY 10152

WINTER, RALPH KARL, JR., federal judge; b. Waterbury, Conn., July 30, 1935; married. B.A., Yale U., 1957, J.D., 1960. Bar: Conn. 1973. Research assoc., lectr. Yale U., 1962-64, asst. prof. to assoc. prof. law, 1964-68, prof. law, 1968-82; judge U.S. Ct. Appeals (2d cir.), New Haven, 1982—; spl. cons. subcom. on separation of powers U.S. Senate Com. on Judiciary, 1968-72; sr. fellow Brookings Inst., 1968-70; adj. scholar Am. Enterprise Inst., 1972-82; vis. prof. law U. Chgo., 1966. Contbr. articles to profl. jours. Office: US Ct Appeals 55 Whitney Ave New Haven CT 06510-1300

WINTER, ROBERT, aerospace executive and engineer; b. N.Y.C., Aug. 27, 1938; s. Harry and Ida Sarah (Lenny) W.; m. Linda Waldgeir, Aug. 20, 1960; 1 child, Jeffrey Michael. B Aero. Engring., NYU, 1960, MS in Aeros. and Astronautics, 1963; postgrad., Harvard U., 1963-64. Asst. research scientist NYU, 1960-63; sr. scientist Avco Corp., Wilmington, Mass., 1963-65; group head structural scis. Allied Research Assocs., Concord, Mass., 1965-68; research scientist Grumman Corp. Research Ctr., Bethpage, N.Y., 1969-81, sr. staff scientist, 1981-88, dir. engring. ops., 1988—. Contbr. articles to tech. jours., chpts. to books; patentee in field. Fellow (assoc.) AIAA; mem. Soc. Experimental Mechanics, Sigma Xi. Office: Grumman Corp Rsch Ctr A08-035 Bethpage NY 11714

WINTERER, WILLIAM G., hotel executive; b. St. Louis, July 7, 1934; s. Herbert O. and Dorothy (Sprengnether) W.; m. Victoria Thompson, Sept. 2, 1967; children: William, Andrew, Britton, Mark. BA, U. Fla., 1956; MBA, Harvard U., 1962. Mgr. corp. fin. dept., ptnr. Goodbody & Co., 1966-69; pres. Fla. Capital Corp., Greenwich, Conn., 1969-72; owner Griswold Inn, Essex, Conn., 1972—, Town Farms Inn, Middletown, Conn., 1978-85, Dock N' Dine at Saybrook Point, Old Saybrook, Conn., 1981-86; bd. dirs. Custom Marine, Inc.; mem. adv. bd. United Bank and Trust, 1972-89. Life trustee, founding pres. Conn. River Found. at Steamboat Dock; trustee Ivoryton Playhouse Found., 1979-82; corporator Middlesex Hosp.; trustee Nat. Maritime Hist. Soc.; mem. Goodspeed Opera Bd. of Advisors; commr. Conn. Hist. Commn., 1979-82; mem. bd. advisors USS Constitution Mus.; bd. dirs. Gov.'s Vacation Travel Coun., 1976-79, chmn., bd. trustees Conn. River Mus. at Steamboat Dock. Officer USCGR. Mem. Conn. Restaurant Assn. (dir. 1973-77), English Speaking Union, N.Y. Yacht Club, Seawanhaka Corinthian Yacht Club, Essex Yacht Club (bd. govs.), Pettipaug Yacht Club, Ocean Cruising Club, Harvard Club, Williams Club, Hartford Club, Old Lyme Beach Club, Poly. Club, Old Lyme Country Club, Essex Platform Tennis Club, St. George's Soc. Republican. Roman Catholic. Home: Turtle Bay Essex CT 06426

WINTERLING, MARY ANN, educational administrator; b. Balt., Mar. 15, 1943; d. Leo George and Loretta Catherine (Novak) W. BA, Coll. Notre Dame, 1965; M in Edn., Johns Hopkins U., 1971, cert. in advanced study in edn., 1980. Tchr. Balt. City Pub. Sch. No. 47, Hampstead Hill, 1965-74; asst. prin. Balt. City Pub. Sch. No. 150, Bentalou Elem. Sch., 1974-80, prin., 1980—, asst. prin. sr. tchrs., 1978-79. Sec. S.E. Civic Orgn., 1972-73; mem. Adminstrs. Adv. Coun., 1976-79; mem. City Wide Chpt. I, adv. com., 1987—, chmn. so. dist., 1987—. Mem. Assn. for Supervision and Curriculum Devel., Nat. Assn. Elem. Sch. Tchrs., Nat. Assn. Elem. Sch. Prins., Md. Assn. Elem. Sch. Prins., Assn. Tchr. Educators, Johns Hopkins U. Alumni Assn., Pub. Sch. Adminstrs. and Suprs. Assn., Pi Lambda Theta, Phi Delta Kappa, Johns Hopkins Club. Democrat. Roman Catholic. Office: 220 N Bentalou St Baltimore MD 21223-1440

WINTERMANS, JOSEPH JACK GERARD FRANCIS, financial services executive; b. Eindhoven, North Brabant, The Netherlands, Oct. 4, 1946; arrived in Canada, 1974; s. Joseph J.F.G. and Catherine (Van Dijk) W.; m. Eileen Simon, Oct. 30, 1972. LLB, Leyden, The Netherlands, 1967, LLM, 1972; MBA, Queens, Kingston, Ont., Can., 1972. V.p. Bristol Myers Can., Toronto, Ont., 1981-82; sr. v.p. Am. Express Can., Markham, Ont., 1982-87; pres. Can. Tire Acceptance Ltd., Welland, Ont., 1988—. Mem. Am. Mktg. Assn. (pres. Toronto chpt. 1981-82). Office: Can Tire Acceptance Ltd, 555 Prince Charles Dr, Welland, ON Canada 23C 6BS

WINTERS, LAURENCE HOWARD, sales executive; b. Montclair, N.J., June 18, 1947; s. Frank Foote and Shirley (Brown) W.; m. Pamela G. Winters, Sept. 13, 1981; 1 child, Laurence Howard Jr. BA in Philosophy, Bucknell U., 1969; MBA in Fin., Columbia U., 1972. Fin. analyst Pepsi Co., Purchase, N.Y., 1973-75; sr. fin. analyst Ladies Home Jour., Downe Communications, N.Y.C., 1975-76; v.p. security sales Loeb Rhoades Inc., N.Y.C., 1976-79, Thomson McKinnon Inc., N.Y.C., 1979-84, Dillon Read Inc., N.Y.C., 1984-86, Kidder Peabody, N.Y.C., 1986-91, Dillon Read Inc., N.Y.C., 1991—; pres., chief exec. officer Library Inc., Westhampton, N.Y., 1989-91. Advisor Southampton (N.Y.) party, 1991. Capt. U.S. Army, 1969-71. Mem. Univ. Club, Westhampton Country Club, La Ronde Club, Williamsport Country Club. Republican. Episcopalian. Home: 122 Country Rd Remsenburg NY 11960-9999 Office: Dillon Read Inc 535 Madison Ave New York NY 10022

WINTERS, MATTHEW LITTLETON, minister; b. Chare, Mich., Sept. 23, 1926; s. Matthew Littleton and Bertha Alexsandra (Ruthven) W.; m. Elizabeth Wiegand, Oct. 16, 1954; children: Deborah Anne, Matthew IV. BA, Wittenberg U., 1950; MDiv, Hamma Divinity Sch., 1954; DD (hon.), Gettysburg Coll., 1972. Ordained to ministry Evang. Luth. Ch. in Am., 1954. Assoc. pastor Holy Trinity Luth. Ch., Buffalo, 1954-60; sr. pastor Trinity Luth. Ch., Camp Hill, Pa., 1960-75, Holy Trinity Luth. Ch., Buffalo, 1975—; pres. Luth. Co-ordinated Ministry Buffalo, 1984-89; bd. dirs. Concerned Ecumenical Ministry, Buffalo. Pres. Lothlorien Therapeutic Riding Ctr., E. Aurora, N.Y., 1989—. Mem. Rotary. Republican. Home: 16 Huntington Ct Buffalo NY 14221-5310 Office: Holy Trinity Luth Ch 1080 Main St Buffalo NY 14209-2389

WINTERS, ROBERT CUSHING, insurance company executive; b. Hartford, Conn., Dec. 8, 1931; s. George Warren and Hazel Keith (Cushing) W.; m. Patricia Ann Martini, Feb. 10, 1962; children: Sally, Beth. BA, Yale U., 1953; MBA, Boston U., 1963. With Prudential Ins. Co. Am., 1953—, v.p. actuary, 1969-75, sr. v.p. Cen. Atlantic home office, 1975-78, exec. v.p., Newark, 1978-84, vice chmn., 1984-86, chmn., chief exec. officer, 1987—; pres. Pruco Inc.; bd. dirs. Allied-Signal Inc. Served with AUS, 1954-56. Fellow Soc. Actuaries; mem. Am. Acad. Actuaries (past pres.), Partnership for N.J., N.J. C. of C. (bd. dirs.), Greater Newark C. of C. (chmn. bd. 1985-87), Am. Coun. Life Ins. (chmn. bd. dirs.), Bus. Coun., Bus. Roundtable, Sigma Xi. Office: Prudential Ins Co Am 751 Broad St Newark NJ 07102-3777

WINTERTON, JOSEPH HENRY, computer software executive; b. Oneida, N.Y., July 22, 1948; s. Stewart Grant and Margaret (Durant) W.; m. Susan Marie Briggs, May 29, 1971; children: Tamara Leigh, Danielle Marie, Derek James. AAS, Canton (N.Y.) Coll., 1968; BA, SUNY, Potsdam, 1970. Adv. programmer IBM Corp., Poughkeepsie, N.Y., 1970-81; mgr. R & D Candle Corp., L.A., 1981-83; dir. R & D Candle Corp., White Plains, N.Y., 1983—. Coach Yorktown (N.Y.) Athletic Club, 1988—; treas. Hudson Valley Christian Acad., Mahopac, N.Y., 1986-87, Yorktown Theatre Workshop, Yorktown Heights, N.Y., 1989-92; bd. dirs. Yorktown Theatre Co.; trustee Calvary Bapt. Ch., Ossining, N.Y., 1986. Republican. Mem. Christian Ch. Home: 1521 Hanover St Yorktown Heights NY 10598-4709 Office: Candle Corp 925 Westchester Ave White Plains NY 10604-3507

WINTHROP, ELIZABETH AMORY, horse trainer; b. N.Y.C., Dec. 14, 1931; d. Robert and Theodora (Ayer) W.; m. Malcolm P. Ripley, Apr. 21, 1958 (div. 1974). Student, Bradford Jr. Coll., 1952, Columbia U., 1956. Horse trainer Morley Farms, Millbrook, N.Y., 1955-67, Millbrook, 1967—. Bd. dirs. Fund for Animals, N.Y.C., 1974—, N.Y. State Humane Assn., New Paltz, N.Y., 1975—; pres. Winley Found., N.Y.C., 1967—; judge Am. Horseshow Assn., N.Y.C., 1966-88. Mem. Defenders of Wildlife (life), Nat. Audubon Soc. (life), Wild Horse Organized Assistance (life), World Wildlife Fund, African Wildlife Found., Human Soc. of the U.S., Nat. Inst. of Social Scis., Colony Club. Republican. Episcopalian. Home: RR 1 Box 40 Millbrook NY 12545-9720

WINTON, CALHOUN, literature educator; b. Ft. Benning, Ga., Jan. 21, 1927; s. George Peterson and Dorothy (Calhoun) W.; m. Elizabeth Jefferys Myers, June 30, 1948; children: Jefferys Hobart, William Calhoun. Student, Ga. Inst. Tech., 1944-46; BA, U. of the South, 1948; MA, Vanderbilt U., 1950, Princeton U., 1954; PhD, Princeton U., 1955. Instr. Dartmouth Coll., Hanover, N.H., 1954-57; asst. prof. U. Va., Charlottesville, 1957-60; asst. prof. then assoc. prof., asst. dean Grad. Sch. U. Del., 1960-67; prof. dept. English U. S.C., Columbia, 1967-75, chmn. dept., 1970-73; prof. U. Md., College Park, 1975—, dir. Rsch. Ctr. for Humanities, 1988-90; del. Jt. Nat. Com. on Langs., Washington, 1986-90. Author: (biography) Captain Steele, 1964, Sir Richard Steele, 1970; editor: Plays of Aaron Hill, 1981. Pres. faculty guild U. Md., 1986-89; bd. dirs. Md. Fedn. Tchrs., Balt., 1986-89. Capt. USN, 1944-47, 50-52. Am. Philos. Soc. grantee, 1960; Guggenheim Found. fellow, 1965-66, Folger fellow Folger Shakespeare Libr., Washington, 1970; Fulbright lectureship Fulbright Commn., Ankara, Turkey, 1979-80. Mem. MLA (exec. com. South Atlantic chpt. 1977-80), Am. Soc. 18th-Century Studies (founder 1970—), East Cen. Soc. 18th Century Studies (pres. 1987), Assn. Princeton Grad. Alumni (exec. bd. 1986-90), Cosmos Club Washington, Princeton Club (N.Y. and Washington). Democrat. Episcopalian. Home: 4403 Van Buren St Hyattsville MD 20782-1122 Office: U Md Dept English College Park MD 20742

WINTON, CRAIG BREWSTER, electronics engineer; b. Montclair, N.J., Nov. 25, 1951; s. William Brewster and Ruth (Seller) W.; m. Michele Lynn Angiletta, Apr. 4, 1981; children: William Brewster II, Alexander David. BSEE, N.J. Inst. Tech., 1974, MSEE, 1979. Test equipment engr. Wagner Electric Corp., Livingston, N.J., 1974-77; instrument engr. Crawford & Russell, Inc., South Plainfield, N.J., 1977-80; M.T.S. AT&T Bell Labs., Murray Hill, N.J., 1980-85; supr. AT&T Bell Labs., Whippany, N.J., 1985-90, Murray Hill, 1990—. Mem. IEEE, Tau Beta Pi, Eta Kappa Nu. Episcopalian. Home: 308 Stirling Rd Plainfield NJ 07060-5942 Office: AT&T Bell Labs 3A-314B 600 Mountain Ave Murray Hill NJ 07974

WIPPEL, JOHN FRANCIS, philosophy educator; b. Pomeroy, Ohio, Aug. 21, 1933; s. Joseph Edward and Mary Josephine (Andrews) W. BA in Philosophy, Cath. U. Am., 1955, MA in Philosophy, 1956, STL in Theology, 1960; PhD in Philosophy, Louvain, Belgium, 1965; Maitre agrégé in Philosophy, Louvain, 1981. Ordained priest Roman Cath. Ch., 1960. Instr. philosophy Cath. U., Washington, 1960-61, 63-65, asst. prof. philosophy, 1965-67, assoc. prof. philosophy, 1967-72, ord. prof. philosophy, 1972—, acad. v.p., 1989—; vis. assoc. prof. U. Calif., San Diego, 1969. Assoc. editor Yale Libr. of Medieval Philosophy; author: Godfrey of Fontaines, 1981 (Mercier prize 1981), Metaphysical Themes in Thomas Aquinas, 1984, Boethius of Dacia, 1987; co-author: Medieval Philosophy, 1969; editor: Studies in Medieval Philosophy, 1987; contbr. articles to profl. jours. Basselin scholar, 1953-56, Penfield fellow, 1961-63; NEH fellow, 1970-71, 84-85. Mem. Medieval Acad. Am., Metaphys. Soc. Am., Am. Cath. Philos. Assn. (pres. 1986-87), Soc. Medieval and Renaissance Philosophy (pres. 1982-84), Societe international pour l'etude de la philosophie medievale. Office: Cath Univ of Am 620 Michigan Ave NE Washington DC 20064-0001

WIPPERN, RONALD FRANK, financial and corporate consultant; b. Huntington, W.Va., June 28, 1933; s. Virgil V. and Lucille (Hotzfield) W.; m. Jill Kathleen Nelson, June 20, 1982; children: Christopher, Mitchell, Stacy, Joscelyn. BS, U. Colo., 1955, MBA, 1961; PhD, Stanford U., 1964; MA (hon.), Yale U., 1979. Asst. prof. U. Minn., Mpls., 1964-66; assoc. dean, assoc. prof. Dartmouth Coll., Hanover, N.H., 1966-71; prof. IMEDE Mgmt. Devel. Inst., Lausanne, Switzerland, 1971-73; assoc. prof. Harvard U. Bus. Sch., Boston, 1973-76; prof. Yale U., New Haven, 1976-87; pres. Ronald F. Wippern, Inc., New Canaan, Conn., 1987—; bd. dirs. Super D Corp., N.Y.C., Big V Holdings, Inc., N.Y.C.; cons. McKinsey & Co., Inc., N.Y.C., 1973—, 1st Boston Corp., N.Y.C., 1986—, Bankers Trust Co., N.Y.C., 1985—, Toronto Dominino Bank, 1988—. Author: Shipping Investments, 1975, Cases in Modern Financial Management, 1980; contbr. numerous articles in profl. jours. Expert witness U.S. Ho. of Reps., 1975; cons. Ford Found., N.Y.C. and Latin Am., 1967-71. Served to lt. USN, 1956-59. Ford Found. fellow, 1961-64. Mem. Am. Econ. Assn., Am. Fin. Assn. Democrat. Office: 815 Silvermine Rd New Canaan CT 06840-4330

WIRONEN, ROBERT ALAN, semiconductor equipment company executive; b. Gardner, Mass., June 26, 1955; s. Francis Albert and Jeanne Rita (Gariepy) W.; m. Susan Jane Bishop; children: Michael, Thomas, Gregory. AS in Engring., Wentworth Coll., 1975; BArch, Boston Arch. Ctr., 1981. Registered architect, Mass. Facilities planner Simplex Time Recorder, Gardner, 1975-80; mgr. facilities engring. GCA Corp., Bedford, 1980-83; dir. engring. Med. Sch. Harvard U., Boston, 1983-87; dir. mfg. MRS Tech., Inc., Chelmsford, 1987—; adb. bd. Am. Inst., Plant Engrs., Cin., 1984-87; pres. Tyngsboro Community Playscape, Inc., 1989—. Active Tyngsboro (Mass.) Hist. Commn., 1983—. Mem. Am. Prodn. and Inventory Control. Republican. Roman Catholic. Office: MRS Tech Inc 10 Elizabeth Dr Chelmsford MA 01824-4112

WIRT, GARY LAUCK, education administrator, consultant; b. Wilmington, Del., May 29, 1948; s. Richard William and Naomi (Lauck) W. BA, U. N.C., 1970; MA, Washington Coll., Chestertown, Md., 1975. Dir. Bennett Halfway House, Wilmington, 1970-85; asst. dir. New Castle (Del.) Community Mental Health Ctr., 1985-87; exec. dir. Mental Health Assn. Del., Wilmington, 1987-88; dean of students Goldey-Beacom Coll., Wilmington, 1988-89, v.p. student affairs, 1989—; mem. Gov.'s Adv. Coun. on Alcoholism, Drug Abuse, and Mental Health, 1987; cons. in stress mgmt. field. Mem. State of Del. Human Rights Com., 1987; mem. children's com. State Bar Assn., 1988-90; co-chmn. Coun. United Way Agy. Execs., Wilmington, 1988. Recipient People to Watch award Delaware Today Mag., 1988. Mem. Alliance for the Mentally Ill, Iota Kappa chpt. Alpha Tau Omega. Home: 37 W 6th St New Castle DE 19720-5068 Office: Goldey-Beacom Coll 4701 Limestone Rd Wilmington DE 19808-1927

WIRTH, HAROLD EDWARD, small business owner; b. New Orleans, Mar. 10, 1905; s. Louis Charles and Caroline (Lindermann) W.; m. Maria Zichichi. Student, Internat. Accts. Soc. and Jefferson Coll., 1922-25, George Washington U., 1954, Naval War Coll., 1962. V.p., gen. mgr. Brown-Wirth Motor Co., Gulfport, Miss., 1928-30; zone mgr. Ford Motor Co., Arabi, La., 1930-33; various mgmt. positions Firestone Tire and Rubber Co., Akron, Ohio, 1933-70; owner Wirth Investment Adv. Service, Kensington, Md., 1970—; founder and dir. Washington Rubber Group, 1941—, Montgomery County Taxpayers League Inc., Bethesda, Md., 1975—; D.C. Metro. Area Transp. Fedn., Washington, 1956—. Bd. dirs., v.p. Allied Civic Group, Silver Springs, Md., 1950—; former v.p., dir. Rock Creek Hills Citizen's Assn., Kensington, Md., 1950—; bd. dirs., legis. com. Montgomery County Taxpayer's League, Inc., 1979—; nat. v.p. Navy League of U.S., Washington, 1960-67. Recipient 3 Cawton awards Allied Civic Group, Navy Sec. Disting. and Meritorious Svc. awards. Mem. Navy League U.S. (hon. asst. treas. 1968—, commodore 1977, Hall of Fame 1989), Am. Def. Preparedness Assn. (life), Am. Logistics Assn. (life), Assn. U.S. Army, Air Force Assn., Nat. Assn. Execs., Internat. Club, Nat. Press Club, Capitol Hill Club, Nat. Economists Club, Nat. Aviation Club, World Trade Ctr. Club (New Orleans), Congl. Country Club. Republican. Roman Catholic. Home: 9515 E Bexhill Dr Kensington MD 20895-3164

WISCH, BILL, magician; b. Englewood, N.J., Apr. 30, 1947; s. William Richard and Margaret (O'Connell) W.; m. Lois C., Feb. 12, 1972; children: Kevin, Cheryl. Freelance musician Montvale, N.J., 1971-76; lectr., magic Wisch-Craft, Montvale, 1977-81; trainer, sales various locations throughout North America, 1981-86; br. mgr., sales Minolta, N.J., 1985-87; pres. Wisch-Craft, Inc., Hackettstown, N.J., 1987-89, performer, inventor, salesman, 1989—; tchr. in field of magic; cons. Chicopee/Johnson & Johnson, New Brunswick, N.J., 1991. Inventor Official Magic Dust (voted one of top new products by Party and Paper Retailer mag. 1987); author seminar "How to Navigate Your Showmanship". With USN, 1967-71, Europe. Recipient Hall of Fame scholarship Downbeat Mag., 1966, Master of Magic award Magic Townhouse, N.Y.C., 1983—; sponsored student of Tony Slydini, N.Y.C., 1976, others. Fellow So. Am. Magicians, Internat. Brotherhood of Magicians; mem. IBM-Ring 113 (pres. Paterson, N.J. br. 1975-76), Toastmasters (ednl. v.p. Ridgewood, N.J., 1983). Home: 810 Mansfield Vlg Hackettstown NJ 07840-3526 Office: Wisch-Craft Inc 810 Mansfield Vlg Hackettstown NJ 07840-3526

WISDOM, GRAHAM JOHN, software engineer; b. Woking, Surrey, England, Apr. 23, 1949; came to U.S., 1978; s. LEslie Arthur and Dorothy (Christine) W.; m. Pamela Mary Harper, May 13, 1972; children: Andrew, Nicholas, Phillip. BSc in Electronic Engring., U. Southampton, England, 1970. Prin. engr. Plessey Co., Poole, England, 1970-77; software designer Internat. Computers Ltd., Bracknell, England, 1977-78; dept. mgr. ITT Corp., Shelton, Conn., 1978-85; integration mgr. ITT Corp., Brussels, 1985-87; dir. software engring. Avanti Corp., Newport, R.I., 1988-89; dir. product devel. Timeplex Corp., Woodcliff Lake, N.J., 1989—. Patentee memory feature. Mem. IEEE. Home: 46 Wyndham Hill Middletown RI 02840 Office: Timeplex 470 Chestnut Ridge Rd Woodcliff Lake NJ 07675

WISE, BEVERLY DENISE, psychologist, health care administrator; b. Pitts., Feb. 28, 1954; d. Norman Edward and Dorothy Arlene (Fretwell) W. BA, Mt. Holyoke Coll., 1976; MA, U. Pa., 1979; PhD, U. Pitts., 1987. Lic. psychologist, N.Y. Intern East Orange (N.J.) VA Med. Ctr., 1983-84; crisis intervention counselor East Orange Gen. Hosp., 1984-85; sr. clinician St. Clare's Hosp.-Community Mental Health Ctr., Denville, N.J., 1985; rsch. assoc. Pitts. Cancer Inst., 1985-87; neuropsychologist Bronx (N.Y.) Psychiatric Ctr., 1988-90; coord. mental health svcs. Spellman Ctr. HIV-Related Disease St. Clare's Hosp., N.Y.C., 1990—; pvt. practice N.Y.C., 1989—. Author: (with others) Stress and Breast Cancer, 1988; contbr. articles to profl. jours. Mem. APA, N.Y. State Psychol. Assn. (mem. AIDS task force 1991—), Soc. Behavioral Medicine, N.Y. Neuropsychology Group, Sigma Xi. Home: 3440 Amboy Rd 329 W 108th St Apt 5B Staten Island NY 10306 Office: 27 W 96th St Ste 16 New York NY 10025-6515

WISE, HARRY H., securities industry executive; b. Cambridge, Mass., Oct. 1, 1938; s. Robert and Ethel (Pastan) W.; m. Dorothy Kalins, Feb. 11, 1968 (div. 1970); m. Katherine Erlandson, June 12, 1983 (div. 1989); m. Ruth Lindenaum, June 16, 1991. BA, Harvard U., 1960, MBA, 1966; postgrad., Yale U., 1960-61. Assoc. McKinsey & Co. Inc., N.Y.C., 1966-68; v.p. Carl Marks & Co. Inc., N.Y.C., 1968-72, Source Capital, Inc., Los Angeles, 1972-74; mgr. pvt. investments Citibank N.A., N.Y.C., 1974-76; exec. v.p. Am. Capital Ptnrs., N.Y.C., 1976-81; pres. Madison Equity Capital Corp., N.Y.C., 1981—; chmn. HW Assocs., Inc., N.Y.C., 1981-89; mng. dir. Portfolio Strategy Group, 1990—; bd. dirs. Empire Inst. Group, N.Y.C. Author HW Petroleum Newsletter, 1986—. Bd. dirs., v.p. Assoc. Camps, Inc., N.Y.C., 1982—; bd. dirs. YM and YWHA's Greater N.Y., N.Y.C., 1982-92; commencement marshal, aide Harvard U., Cambridge, Mass., 1984-85. Capt. USAFR, 1961-64. Mem. Nat. Assn. Corp. Dirs., Harvard U. Alumni Assn. (com. 1981-90), Econ. Round Table San Francisco, Harvard Club N.Y. (house com.), Harvard Bus. Sch. Club Greater N.Y. (exec. v.p., bd. dirs. 1975-83, Achievement award 1972, 82), East Hampton Tennis Club, Harvard Club Boston, Army and Navy Club. Jewish. Home: 1010 5th Ave New York NY 10028 Office: HW Assocs Inc 505 Park 20th Ave New York NY 10022-1106

WISE, JOE ROBERT, JR., cardiologist; b. Ft. Worth, July 11, 1939; s. Joe Robert and Madge (Brelsford) W.; m. Katherine Hudson, 1957; children: Robert, Elizabeth, Jonathan, Johanna. BS, Tex. Christian U., 1960; MD, U. Tex., Dallas, 1964. Intern in edicine Parkland Meml. Hosp., Dallas, 1964-65, resident, 1967-69; fellow in cardiology Royal Postgrad. Med. Sch., Hammersmith Hosp., London, 1969-70; intern in medicine Ea. Maine Med. Ctr., Bangor, 1973—, head cardiology sect., 1979—; pvt. practice, N.E. Cardiology Assocs., Bangor, 1977—; mem. govt. rels. com. Am. Coll. of Cardiology, Bethesda, Md., 1987—. Contbr. articles to profl. jours. Capt. M.C., USAF, 1965-67. Named Mead Johnson Residency scholar, 1970; grantee Bingham Fund, 1973. Fellow Am. Coll. Cardiology (govt. rels. com. 1987—), ACP; mem. Am. Heart Assn. (fellow coun. on clin. cardiology), Am. Coll. Phys. Execs., Med. Group Mgmt. Assn., Am. Group Practice Assn. Office: NE Cardiology Assocs 1 Evergreen Woods Bangor ME 04401-5600

WISE, JOHN PERRY, natural resources consultant; b. Boston, Feb. 9, 1924; s. John P. and Mary A. (Sheehan) W.; m. Beatrice M. Donnelly, Jan. 9, 1960; children: John P., Charles W., Beatrice M. AB, Suffolk U., 1950; MS, U. N.H., 1953. Biologist Bur. Comml. Fisheries, Woods Hole, Mass., 1953-60; tech. assistance officer FAO of UN, Rome, 1960-65; biologist Nat. Marine Fisheries Svc., Miami, Fla., 1965-73; sr. specialist Nat. Marine Fisheries Svc., Washington, 1973-75; div. chief Nat. Marine Fisheries Svc., 1975-81; biostatistician Internat. Commn. For Conservation of Atlantic Tunas, Madrid, 1981-86; pvt. practice cons. Washington, 1987—. Author numerous books; contbr. articles to publs. With USMC, 1942-45, 50-51. Recipient Disting. Svc. medal U.S. Dept. Interior. Home and office: 4545 Connecticut Ave NW Washington DC 20008-6042

WISE, KENNETH KELLY, English educator, photographer, critic; b. New Castle, Ind., Dec. 1, 1932; s. John Kenneth W. and Geraldine (Kelly) Edwards Wise; m. Sybil Anahid Zulalian, Aug. 15, 1959; children: Jocelyn Anne, Adam Kelly, Lydia Louise. B.S., Purdue U., 1955; M.A., Columbia U., 1959. Instr. English Mt. Hermon Sch., Gill, Mass., 1960-66; instr. English Phillips Acad., Andover, Mass., 1966—, chmn. dept., 1978-82, acting dean faculty, 1982-83, dean faculty, 1985-90; founder, dir. Andover Woodrow Wilson Inst. for Recruitment of Tchrs., Andover, Mass., 1989—; photography critic The Boston Globe, 1982—; art commentator Nat. Pub. Radio, 1987-89; photography and English cons. Nat. Humanities Faculty, Concord, Mass., 1970-83; mem. Pub. Art Adv. Bd. of Mass. Coun.; cons. editor Addison House Pubs., Danbury, N.J., 1974-79. Author: (with Kalkstein and Regan) English Competence Handbook, 1972; editor: The Photographers' Choice, 1975, Lotte Jacobi, 1978, Portrait: Theory, 1981, Photo Facts and Opinions, 1981; author, photographer: Still Points, 1977, A Church, A People, 1979; editor photographer: City Limits, 1987; assoc. editor: Views, Jour. Photography, 1980-81; works included in anthologies, one-man shows, Portland Museum Art, Maine, 1974, Silver Image Gallery, Columbus, Ohio, 1975, Canon Photo Gallery, Amsterdam, Holland, 1977, Focus Gallery, San Francisco, 1977, Art Mus., U. Mass., Amherst, 1978, Neikrug Gallery, N.Y.C., 1979, Sheldon Gallery, U. Nebr., Lincoln, 1980, Yuen Lui Gallery, Seattle, 1980, Rose Art Mus., Brandeis U., Waltham, Mass., 1981, Blixt Gallery, Ann Arbor, Mich., 1981, Snite Art Gallery, U. Notre Dame, 1981, Jeb Gallery, Providence, 1981, Currier Gallery Art, Manchester, N.H., 1985, Addison Gallery Am. Art, Andover, Mass., 1985, Art Ctr., DePauw U., 1986, Art Gallery, Conn. Coll., 1986, Yuen Lui Gallery, Seattle, 1986, Kresge Art Mus., Mich. State U., 1987, Brockton Art Mus., 1987; group shows include Inst. Contemporary Art, Boston, 1972, Mus. Fine Arts, Boston, 1974, Fogg Art Mus., Cambridge, 1976, Sidney Janis Gallery, N.Y.C., 1977, The Photographer's Gallery, London, 1979, Il Diaframma, Milan, Italy, 1979, Iisalmen Kamera, Helsinki, Finland, 1984, Archive Gallery, N.Y., 1987, Mass. Coll. Art, 1988, Martin Schweig Gallery, St. Louis, 1988, Satellite Gallery, Cultural Affairs Dept., Los Angeles. Served with USN, 1955-57, PTO. Office: Phillips Acad Andover MA 01810

WISE, RICHARD EVANS, insurance company executive; b. Lancaster, Pa., Sept. 24, 1947; s. William Edmund and Dorothy Christelle (Evans) W.; m. Kathrine Suzanne Keller, Jan. 2, 1971; 1 child, Thomas Edmund. BS, West Chester (Pa.) U., 1970; MEd, Pa. State U., 1976, PhD, 1980. Project adminstrn. mgr. Hartford Ins. Group, 1977-80; v.p., tng. mgr. Conn. Nat. Bank, 1980-83; corp. tng. and devel. dir. Travelers Corp., Hartford, 1983-89; dir. corp. strategy and rsch. Travelers Corp., 1989—; cons. R.E. Wise and Assocs., Hartford, 1982—; adj. prof. Hartford Grad. Ctr.; pres. Am. Inst. Banking; editorial bd. mem. Internat. Jour. of Instrnl. Media. Contbr. articles to various profl. jours.; designer Travelers Management Development Continuum, 1984-86. Mem. Hartford Mgmt. Devel. adv. bd., Greater Hartford Arts Coun.; vice chmn. Windsor Govt. Study Commn., 1992—. Named Outstanding Alumnus Pa. State U., 1987; Chapter of Excellence Am. Inst. of Banking, 1983. Mem. Assn. for Ednl. Communications and Tech. (cert. of Merit, 1986, 88, Outstanding Practice award, 1983, div. coun. pres. 1990—), Am. Soc. for Tng. and Devel., Phi Delta Kappa. Democrat. Methodist. Lodge: Masons. Home: 8 Cobblestone Way Windsor CT 06095-2224 Office: Travelers Corp One Tower Square Hartford CT 06183

WISE, ROBERT PHILIP, biopharmacoepidemiologist, clinical pharmacologist; b. Chgo., Oct. 13, 1949; s. Wilfred and Harriet Frances (Traub) W.; m. Izione Santos Silva, Mar. 8, 1980; children: Matthew Raymond, Andrea Louise. BA, Carleton Coll., 1971; MD, Northwestern U., Chgo., 1975; MPH, Harvard U., 1977. Diplomate Am. Bd. Preventive Medicine, Am. Bd. Clin. Pharmacology, Epidemic Intelligence Svc. Student fellow in tropical medicine La. State U., Medellin, Colombia, 1975; med. intern Northwestern Meml. Hosp., Chgo., 1975-76; resident in internat. health Pan Am. Health Orgn., Guatemala, 1977-78; course asst. Harvard Sch. Pub. Health, Boston, 1979-81; cons. pub. health Pragma Corp., Bamako, Mali, 1982; cons. preventive medicine Aurora Assocs., Guinea, Bissau, 1982; cons. Ronco Cons., Guinea, Bissau, 1983; physician, Spanish Clinic Brigham & Women's Hosp., Boston, 1979-83; epidemiologist Ctrs. for Disease Control, Atlanta, 1983-85; pharmacoepidemiologist FDA Ctr. for Drug Evaluation and Rsch., Rockville, Md., 1985-90, FDA Ctr. for Biologics Evaluation and Rsch., Rockville, 1991—; part-time physician Fed. Employee Occupational Health Clinic, Rockville, 1989—. Contbr. articles to profl. jours. Bd. dirs. Community Clinic, Inc., Rockville, 1991—. Comdr. USPHS, 1983—. Recipient Citation, Pub. Health Svc., 1990, Achievement medal, 1989. Fellow Am. Coll. Preventive Medicine (Recognition award 1986, 89); mem. APHA, Nat. Coun. Internat. Health, Internat. Soc. Pharmacoepidemiology, Commd. Officers Assn. of USPHS. Jewish. Home: 1612 Auburn Ave Rockville MD 20850-1144 Office: FDA CBER HFB 265 8800 Rockville Pike Bethesda MD 20892-0001

WISE, SAMUEL PAUL, III, psychiatrist; b. Plains, Ga., May 8, 1921; s. Burr Thaddeus and Lundie Louise (Lamar) W.; m. Ruth Sturgeon, 1947 (div. 1966); children: Samuel P., Blake B., Frank Lamar, Sarah; m. Kathleen Hughes, Nov. 25, 1966; 1 child, Melissa Marshall. BA, Emory U., 1941; MD, Tulane U., 1946. Diplomate Am. Bd. Internal Medicine. Internist Casey Clinic, San Benito, Tex., 1955-60; asst. prof. medicine Baylor U., Houston, 1960-61; research asso. Inst. Psychiatry & Human Behavior U.Md., Balt., 1961-68; resident in psychiatry Springfield Hosp. Ctr., Sykesville, Md., 1964-67; psychiatrist-in-chief Dorchester unit Ea. Shore Hosp.Ctr., Cambridge, Md., 1967-77; med. dir. Dorchester County Mental Health Clinic, Cambridge, 1967-92; clin. instr. Dept. Psychiatry, U. Md., Balt., 1968—; cons. in field; lectr. in field. Contbr. articles to profl. jours. Maj. U.S. Army, 1952-55. Fellow Acad. Psychosomatic Medicine; mem. Am. Psychiat. Assn. (life), Md. Psychiat. Soc. (life), Med.-Chiurtical Faculty of Md., Alpha Omega Alpha. Democrat. Episcopalian. Home: 103 High St Cambridge MD 21613-1814 Office: Dorchester County Mental Health 103 High St Cambridge MD 21613

WISE, SYBIL ZULALIAN, educator; b. Malden, Mass., Apr. 15, 1935; d. Badrig Barsam and Elmon (Jivelekian) Zulalian; m. Kenneth Kelly Wise, Aug. 15, 1959; children: Jocelyn Anne, Adam Kelly, Lydia Louise. BS in Early Childhood Edn, Wheelock Coll., Boston, 1957. Tchr. The Pike Sch., Andover, Mass., 1980—; mem. Kindergarten Curriculum Adv. Com. for Highreach Learning. Office: The Pike Sch Sunset Rock Rd Andover MA 01810-4898

WISE, WILLIAM HARVEY, IV, community service executive; b. Alexandria, Va., Apr. 28, 1948; s. William Harvey III and Emily Virginia (Miller) W.; m. Susana Andrea Joublanc, July 28, 1973; children: Adam J., Andrea Susana, Virginia Elizabeth. BS, Washington & Lee U., 1970; postgrad, George Washington U., 1972. Acct. Arthur Andersen & Co., Washington, 1970-71; contr. Joint Action in Community Svc., Inc., Washington, 1971-79, dep. dir., 1979-87, exec. dir., 1987—; mem. Ind. Sector, Washington, 1987—, Nat. Assembly of Nat. Voluntary Health and Social Welfare Orgns., Washington, 1989—. V.p. Whittier Woods Civic Assn., Bethesda, Md., 1983-86; cubmaster Boy Scouts Am., Bethesda, 1984-85; fin. com. chmn. Concord-St.-Andrew's United Meth. Ch., Bethesda, 1983-86; bd. dirs. Ridgeleigh Homes Assn., Potomac, Md., 1988—. Mem. Mensa, Kenwood Golf and Country Club. Home: 8229 Gainsborough Ct Potomac MD 20854 Office: Joint Action Community Svc 5225 Wisconsin Ave Washington DC 20015

WISEMAN, DOUGLAS CARL, education educator; b. Nashua, N.H., Feb. 28, 1935; s. Howard W. and Ruth D. (Aiken) W.; m. Bonnie Lou Berry, Oct. 8, 1960; children: Mark, Lori, Kathleen. BEd, Plymouth (N.H.) State Coll., 1961; MS, Ind. U., 1962, PED, 1970. Cert. tchr. health, math., phys. edn., sci. Tchr. high sch. Nashua (N.H.) Pub. Schs., 1960-61, tchr. jr. high, 1962-63; teaching asst. Ind. U., Bloomington, 1961-62; tchr. high sch. Portage (Mich.) High Sch., 1963-64; instr., asst. prof. Plymouth (N.H.) State Coll.,

1964-69; asst. prof. Northeastern U., Boston, 1969-71; dir. athletics, chmn. dept. Plymouth State Coll., 1971-80, prof., chair dept. edn., 1980—; cons. Am./Nat. Red Cross, Laconia, N.H., 1971—, State Dept. Edn., Concord, 1980—. Author: Adapted Physical Education, 1982; contbr.: Practical Research, 1989; contbr. articles to profl. jours. Spl. police officer Grafton County Underwater Search and Rescue Squad, Ashland, N.H., 1986—; chair sch. bd. Plymouth Regional Sch. Dist., 1989-91. Cpl. U.S. Army, 1953-56. AHPER and Dance Eastern Dist. scholar, 1990-91. Republican. Office: Plymouth State Coll Rounds 035 Plymouth NH 03264

WISEMAN, WILLIAM FENTON, museum administrator; b. Chgo., July 16, 1939; s. William Parr and Mary Louise (Fenton) W.; m. Linda Faitoute White, June 25, 1962; children: Claire, Christopher. BA, Cornell U., 1961; MBA, Babson Coll., Wellesley, Mass., 1977. Adminstrv. asst. Little, Brown & Co., Boston, 1964-72; chief fin. officer Godine Pubs., Boston, 1972-80; bus. mgr. The Children's Mus., Boston, 1980—. With U.S. Army, 1961-63. Mem. Union Boat Club. Republican. Episcopalian. Home: 48 Oxbow Rd Needham MA 02192-1016

WISHNER, STEVEN R., retail executive; b. N.Y.C., Mar. 21, 1950; s. Jerome and Florence (Wanger) W.; m. Lauri Ruth Berkson, June 5, 1977; children: Andrew R., Sara M. BA, Colgate U., 1972; MBA, Cornell U., 1976. 2nd v.p. Chase Manhattan Bank, N.Y.C., 1976-78; functional v.p. Chase Manhattan Bank, 1978; dir. fin. svcs. Gen. Instrument Corp., Clifton, N.J., 1978-79; asst. to treas. Gen. Instrument Corp., 1979-81; dir. fin. svcs. Viacom Internat. Inc., N.Y.C., 1981-82; asst. treas. Viacom Internat. Inc., 1982-86; v.p., treas. Zayre Corp., Framingham, Mass., 1987-89; v.p. fin., treas. The TJX Cos., Inc., Framingham, 1987—; bd. dirs. Tech. Communications Corp.; mem. ea. adv. bd. Protection Mut. Ins. Co., 1987-91. Mem. Fin. Execs. Inst., Nat. Assn. Corp. Treas., Nat. Investor Rels. Inst., Cornell U. Alumni Assn. (co-chmn. admissions com., alumni exec. coun. 1987-90), Masons. Home: 92 Fox Run Rd Sudbury MA 01776-2768 Office: The TJX Cos Inc 770 Cochituate Rd Framingham MA 01701-4630

WISHNIE, PETER ALLAN, podiatrist; b. N.Y.C., July 18, 1960; s. Seymour and Judith (Rosenbaum) W.; m. Robin Jill Freedman, May 29, 1988. BS, SUNY, Stony Brook, 1982; BS in Med. Scis., Calif. Coll. Podiatric Medicine, 1985, D Podiatric Medicine, 1987. Resident in podiatric medicine and surgery Parson's Hosp., Flushing, N.Y., 1987-88; resident in foot and ankle surgery Hadassah Med. Ctr., Jerusalem, 1988-89; pres. Affiliated Podiatry, Piscataway, N.J., 1989—; lectr. in field, Bound Brook, N.J., 1991; assoc. Somerset Med. Ctr., 1990—, St. Peter's Med. Ctr., 1990—, SurgiCare-Surgery Ctr., 1990—. Contbr. articles to profl. pubs. Vol. March of Dimes, Middlesex County, N.J., 1989-91, Am. Heart Assn., Middlesex County, 1991. Mem. Am. Coll. Foot Surgeons (assoc.), Am. Acad. Podiatric Sports Medicine (assoc.). Office: 84 Stelton Rd Piscataway NJ 08854

WISLOCKI, PETER GREGORY, metabolism and environmental chemist; b. Derby, Conn., Jan. 21, 1947; s. Peter Daniel and Eva (Lechus) W.; m. Mary Kay Anderson, Aug. 5, 1972; children: Daniel, Andrew. BS in Chemistry, Fairfield U., 1968; PhD in Oncology, U. Wis., 1974. Postdoctoral fellow Hoffmann LaRoche, Nutley, N.J., 1974-76, vis. scientist, 1976-77; asst. prof. U. Nebr., Omaha, 1977-78; rsch. fellow Merck & Co., Rahway, N.J., 1978-83, sr. rsch. fellow, 1983-87, dir., 1988—. Author numerous chpts. in books; contbr. articles to profl. jours. Mem. Am. Chem. Soc. (chmn. drug metabolism discussion group 1984-85), Am. Soc. Pharmacology and Exptl. Therapeutics, Am. Assn. for Cancer Rsch. Office: Merck & Co PO Box 2000 Rahway NJ 07065-0900

WISNEFSKY, WALTER, utility rate specialist, educator; b. Norwich, Conn., Jan. 5, 1944; s. Benjamin and Arline Helen (Slitt) W.; m. Barbara Ina Sack, June 11, 1966; children: Sheryl Esther, Eric Craig, Judy Faye. AS in Bus. Adminstr., Mitchell Coll., 1964; BSBA, Am. Internat. Coll., 1966; MBA, U. Hartford, 1979. Acct. Siskin Shapiro & Co., Hartford, Conn., 1966; various acctg. positions N.E. Utilities Svc. Co., Berlin, Conn., 1968-84; sr. rate specialist State of Conn. Dept. Pub. Utility Control, New Britain, Conn., 1984—; adjunct faculty Cen. Conn. State U., New Britain, 1979—, Tunxis Community Coll., Farmington, Conn., 1987—; tutor, pvt. practice, Newington, Conn., 1988—. Basketball and soccer coach Newington Parks and Recreation, 1979-84; bd. dirs. Hartford chpt. Juvenile Diabetes Found., Bloomfield Conn., 1986-90. Jewish. Home: 6 Clarendon Ter Newington CT 06111-4309 Office: Dept Pub Utility Control 1 Central Park Plz New Britain CT 06051-2227

WISNER, BENJAMIN GOODWIN, food and environmental policy educator; b. Sanford, Fla., Sept. 27, 1943; s. Benjamin Goodwin and Patricia (McCoy) W.; m. Sonia Ruth Kruks, Feb. 9, 1978; 1 child, Gabrielle Kaya Kruks-Wisner. BA, U. Calif., Davis, 1965; MA, U. Chgo., 1966; PhD, Clark U., 1978. Devel. vol. Am. Friends Svc. Com., Mbambara Village, Tanzania, 1966-68; rsch. asst. Hazards Rsch. Group, Clark U., Worcester, Mass., 1968-71; rsch. assoc. U. Nairobi, Kenya, 1971-72; lectr. community health U. Dar es Salaam, Tanzania, 1972-74; lectr. geography Sheffield (U.K.) U., 1976-77; assoc. prof. U. Eduardo Mondlane, Maputo, Mozambique, 1978-80; asst. prof. U. Wis., Madison, 1980-81; cons. UN Univ. Food-Energy Nexus, Paris, 1982-86; Henry R. Luce prof. Hampshire Coll., Amherst, Mass., 1987—; vis. prof. Rutgers U., New Brunswick, N.J., 1981-87, Swiss Fed. Tech. Inst., Zurich, 1983-84; dir. Luce Food Program, Amherst, 1987—; cons. WHO, Geneva, 1991—, UN Econ. Commn. on Africa, Addis Ababa, 1989-90; health sector coord. Task Force on African Devel., Atlanta, 1990—; cons. World Works Found., Bridgewater, 1986-88, Western Mass. Food Bank, Hatfield, 1987—, Bread for the World Inst., Washington, 1989—. Author: Power and Need in Africa, 1988; editor: Geography & Human Ecology, 1986, Landuse and Development in Africa, 1977; editor Social Sci. and Medicine Jour., 1989; contbr. articles to profl. jours. NSF rsch. grantee, 1969-71, Internat. Geog. Union (Paris) travel grantee, 1978, Swedish Acad. Scis. rsch. grantee, 1982-83, UNESCO travel grantee, 1984. Fellow Soc. for Applied Anthropology (sr. fellow); mem. Assn. Am. geographers, Rural Sociol. Soc., Internat. Peace Rsch. Assn., African Studies Assn. Democrat. Religious Soc. Friends. Office: Hampshire Coll Social Studies West St Amherst MA 01002-2954

WISNER, ROSCOE WILLIAM, JR., human resources executive; b. Beatrice, Nebr., Mar. 17, 1926; s. Roscoe William Sr. and Genevieve M. (McVey) W.; m. Louise Jackson, Mar. 15, 1952; children: Jacqueline Louise, Valerie Joyce. BA, Lincoln U., Oxford, Pa., 1950; MEd, Temple U., 1963. Accredited profl. in human resource mgmt. Sr. personnel examiner Phila. Personnel Dept., 1954-64; supr. testing and rsch. Port Authority of N.Y. and N.J., N.Y.C., 1964-76, coord. spl. programs for people with disabilities, 1976-91; ret.; instr., adj. faculty LaGuardia Community Coll. Author: Performance Test Procedures and Problems, 1964; contbr. articles to profl. jours. Adv. coun. Industry-Labor Coun., Albertson, N.Y., 1976—, N.Y.C. Bd. Edn. Spl. Edn. Project Future, 1986—, Rusk Rehab. Inst., N.Y.C., 1980—, Kessler Rehab. Inst., East and West Orange, N.J., 1979—, Mayor's Office People with Disabilities, N.Y.C., 1980—; exec. dir. Community Action Program, Westbury, 1965; mem. Watchful Eye Civic Assn., Roosevelt, N.Y., 1983—. Recipient Disting. Svc. award Port Authority of N.Y. and N.J., 1990, Profl. Achievement award Ea. Region/Pub. Personnel Assn. Conf., 1969. Mem. Am. Psychol. Assn. (assoc.), Internat. Pers. Mgmt. Assn., Soc. Human Resource Mgmt., Am. Soc. Pub. Adminstrn. Home: 266 E Greenwich Ave Roosevelt NY 11575-1205

WISSEMANN-WIDRIG, NANCY, artist; b. Jamestown, N.Y., Mar. 19, 1929; d. Ross Frank and M. Gertrude (Peck) Widrig; m. John Joseph Wissemann, July 25, 1953; children: Melanie Wissemann Essex, Christopher, Timothy. BA, Syracuse U., 1951; MFA, Ohio U., 1952. One woman shows include Tibor de Nagy Gallery, N.Y.C., 1974, 77, 80, 81, 83, Hobe Sound North, Brunswick, Maine, 1984, Tatistcheff Gallery, N.Y.C., 1987, 92, Caldbeck Gallery, Rockland, Maine, 1989; group exhibitions include Mus. at Stony Brook, N.Y., 1990, Farnsworth Mus., Rockland, 1990, ABC Hdqrs., 1991; represented in permanent collections including Mut. N.Y. Hdqrs., Amerada Hess Corp., AT&T Co., Bank of Boston, Canton Art Inst., Conde Nast Publs., Inc., Port Authority N.Y., U. Kans. Mus. Fine Arts, U. Tulsa, Lloyd's Bank Calif., C. Carey Ellis & Assocs., Owens-Corning Fiberglass. Mem. adv. bd. East End Arts and Humanities Coun., Riverhead, N.Y., 1979-85. Recipient Oustanding Realist award Western N.Y. Artists, 1964, purchase award Childe Hassam Fund, AAAL, 1969. Democrat. Unitarian. Home and Studio: Box 524 Southold NY 11971

WISSER, LAWRENCE, advertising agency executive; b. Ft. Leavenworth, Kans., Aug. 14, 1922; m. Virginia Boyle, Aug. 20, 1967; children: William, Tracy, Andrea. BA, U. Ga., 1942; PhD, U. Chgo., 1949. Creative dir. Storm and Klein, 1955-58; v.p., copy chief Emil Mogul Inc., 1958-60; from v.p. to pres. Weiss and Geller, 1960-66; pres., creative dir. Wisser and Sanchez Inc., 1965-79; pres. Lawrence Wisser & Co., Inc., Ossining, N.Y., 1982—. Author: Motivation in Advertising; contbr. Advt. Age, Media Decisions. Named Time Mag. Ad Man of Yr.; recipient CLIO and EFFIE awards, 1972, 73, 77. Office: Lawrence Wisser & Co Inc Quaker Bridge Rd PO Box 942 Ossining NY 10562-4719

WIST, GREGORY JOHN, college registrar; b. Jamaica, N.Y., Feb. 28, 1947; s. John Francis and Lucille (Lott) W.; m. Helen Agnes McMorrow, Oct. 21, 1972; children: Jennifer, Megan, Elizabeth. BA, SUNY, Stony Brook, 1969, MA, 1972; MBA, Baruch Coll., 1985. Cert. secondary social studies, N.Y. Tchr. Brentwood (N.Y.) Pub. Schs., 1969-70; resource agt. N.Y. State Dept. Mental Hygiene, Queens Village, 1970-72; asst. registrar La Guardia Community Coll., L.I. City, N.Y., 1972-77, assoc. registrar, 1977-79; registrar Borough of Manhattan Community Coll., N.Y.C., 1979-82, sr. registrar, 1982—; prof. Borough of Manhattan Community Coll., N.Y.C., 1979—. Pres. St. Philip Neri Sch. Bd., Northport, N.Y., 1989—, v.p., 1987-89; mem. steering com. Regional Sch. Bd., East Northport, N.Y., 1990—. Mem. N.J./N.Y. Assn. Coll. Registrars (steering com. 1979—), Am. Assn. Coll. Registrars, Mid. States Assn. Coll. Registrars, Am. Records Mgrs. Assn., Assn. Fgn. Student Advisors. Office: Borough of Manhattan Community Coll 199 Chambers St New York NY 10007-1006

WIST, PAUL GABRIEL, accountant; b. Balt., July 25, 1929; s. George John and Regina Marie (Ward) W.; m. Mary Lee Vaeth, Oct. 23, 1954; children: Paul Gabriel, Timothy V., Matthew W., Ami A. ABA, U. Balt. 1951. CPA; cert. fin. planner. Assoc. C.W. Amos & Co., Balt., 1952-56, partner, 1956-69, mng. partner, 1969-85, sr. partner, 1985—. Bd. dirs. Md. Blue Cross, 1965-73; bd. dirs. Assoc. Cath. Charities, 1976-88, pres., 1985-88; mem. adv. bd. St. Joseph Hosp., 1964-88, Stella Maris Hospice, 1969-73; trustee Cardinal Shehan Center for Aging, 1977—, Marian House, Inc., 1982-89, McAuley Inst., Inc., 1987—, St. Joseph Hosp. Found., 1988—; trustee Am. Inst. CPAs Benevolent Fund, 1977-83, pres., 1980-83; bd. visitors U. Balt., 1984-88, trustee ednl. found., 1984—; trustee Children's Fund, Inc., 1986—, pres., 1987—. Served with USNR, 1948-49. Recipient Cardinal Gibbons medal, 1973, Papal medal, 1982, U. Balt. Disting. Svc. award, 1990; named Alumnus of Yr., U. Balt., 1982. Mem. AICPAs (coun. 1974-75, 77-80), Md. Assn. CPAs (pres. 1975-76, Pub. Svc. award 1990), Internat. Assn. Fin. Planners, Nat. Assn. Accts., Internat. Exec. Svc. Corps, Ctr. Club Balt., Towson (Md.) Golf and Country Club, Rotary (pres. 1986-87). Roman Catholic. Home: 523 St Francis Rd Baltimore MD 21204-1327 Office: 2 N Charles St Suite 210 Baltimore MD 21201

WIT, DAVID EDMUND, software company executive; b. N.Y.C., Feb. 25, 1962; s. Harold Maurice W. and Joan Leta (Rosenthal) Sovern; m. Kathleen Mary Bentley, Sept. 9, 1989. BA summa cum laude, Hamilton Coll., 1985. Rsch. assoc. E.M. Warburg Pincus and CO., N.Y.C., 1985-86; co-chief exec. officer Logicat Inc., N.Y.C., 1986—; bd. dirs. Calif. Energy Co., Omaha, 1987—, chmn. audit com., 1992—. Mem. N.Y. Software Industry Assn. (steering com. 1991—), Univ. Club, Phi Beta Kappa. Home: 736 W End Ave New York NY 10025 Office: Logicat Inc 201 E 16th St New York NY 10003

WITBECK, ROBERT WILLIAM, SR., financial executive; b. Big Rapids, Mich., Sept. 7, 1952; s. Teddy B. and Dorothy Jean (Gillett) W.; m. Lois Joslin Kingsbury, June 12, 1972 (div. Feb. 1981); children: Katherine, Michael; m. Sharon Elizabeth Tufts, Oct. 12, 1985; 1 child, Robert William. BA, New Coll., Sarasota, Fla., 1974; MS, Bentley Coll., 1980. CPA, Mass. Mgmt. trainee Eckerd Drug Stores, Sarasota, 1972-74; mgr. Elliot Drug Stores, Savannah, Ga., 1974-77, Revco Drug Stores, Savannah, 1977-78; supr. Donald B. Hilton & Co. CPA, Newton, Mass., 1980-84; contr. New Eng. Copy Specialists, Woburn, Mass., 1984-87, v.p. fin., 1987—. Treas. Christ Ch., Waltham, Mass., 1982—, jr. warden, 1991, Eucharist minister, 1988—. Mem. AICPA, Inst. Mgmt. Accts., Mass. Soc. CPAs. Home: 659 South St Waltham MA 02154-1403 Office: New Eng Copy Specialists 39 6th Rd Woburn MA 01801-1757

WITCHER, ROBERT CAMPBELL, bishop; b. New Orleans, Oct. 5, 1926; s. Charles Swanson and Lily Sebastian (Campbell) W.; m. Elisabeth Alice Cole, June 4, 1957; 2 children. BA, Tulane U., 1949; MDiv, Seabury-Western Theol. Sem., 1952, DD, 1974; MA, La. State U., 1960, PhD, 1968; DCL (hon.), Nashotah House, 1989. Ordained priest Episcopal Ch., 1953; consecrated bishop, 1975; priest-in-charge St. Andrew Ch., Linton, La. and St. Patrick Ch., Zachary, La., 1953-56; priest-in-charge St. Augustine Ch., Baton Rouge, La., 1953-54; rector St. Augustine Ch., 1954-61; canon pastor Christ Ch. Cathedral, New Orleans, 1961-62; rector St. James Ch., Baton Rouge, 1962-75; coadjutor bishop L.I., 1975-77; bishop, 1977-91; prof. ch. history Mercer Sch. Theology, 1975-91; interim bishop of Armed Forces, 1989-90; bishop in residence Baton Rouge, New Orleans, 1991-92; pres. Mercer Scholarship Fund; trustee Ch. Pension Fund, 1991-92; pres. bd. trustees estate belonging to Diocese of L.I., 1975-91; pres. Anglican Soc. N.Am., 1980-83; sec. pastoral com. House of Bishops; chmn. Com. To Revise Title III, 1980-90; chmn. Com. on Developing Guidelines for Theol. Edn. Author: The Episcopal Church in Louisiana, 1801-1861. Trustee U. of South, 1963-69, Seabury-Western Theol. Sem., 1963-82, Gen. Theol. Sem., 1979-88, Ch. Pension Fund, 1985—; pres. Episcopal Health Svcs.; bd. dirs. Nat. Coun. Alcoholism, L.I. Coun. Alcoholism, St. Mary's Hosp. for Children. Capt. USNR, ret. Mem. N.Y. State Council Chs., L.I. Council Chs. (com. social justice). Address: 1934 Steele Blvd Baton Rouge LA 70808

WITHERELL, JAMES LESTON, vocational rehabilitation counselor; b. Rumford, Maine, June 19, 1953; s. Earle Roy and Lucille May (Dermody) W. BA in English, U. Maine, 1981, BA in Psychology, 1982; MS in Edn., U. So. Maine, 1990. Group mgr. Zayre Corp., Rumford, 1983-84; adminstr. Seven Elms Boarding Home, Washington, Maine, 1984-88; pvt. practice rehab. counseling Lewiston, Maine, 1990—. Vol. Am. Lung Assn. Maine, Augusta, 1988—. With U.S. Army, 1974-77. Mem. AACD, Penobscot Wheelmen. Office: Jim Witherell Rehab 11 Ventura St Lewiston ME 04240-4636

WITHERELL, PETER CHARLES, regulatory entomologist; b. Athol, Mass., Sept. 23, 1943; s. Charles Emerson and Ruth Eva (Dodge) W.; m. Beatriz Alicia Plaza Gonzales, Nov. 9, 1981; children: Tina, Philamer. B.S., U. Mass., 1965; M.S., U. Calif., Davis, 1970, Ph.D., 1973. Registered profl. entomologist. Asst. area supr. Aedes aegypti mosquito eradication program USPHS, Fla., 1965-68; grad. rsch. asst. entomology U. Calif., Davis, 1969-72, postdoctoral rsch. entomologist, 1973-74; asst. dir. rsch. Dadant & Sons, Inc., Hamilton, Ill., 1975-76; grain insp. U.S. Dept. Agr., Balt., 1977-78; plant protection and quarantine officer U.S. Dept. Agr., Laredo, Tex., 1978-81; sta. supr. Miami Methods Devel. Sta. U.S. Dept. Agr., 1981-85; asst. dir. Methods Devel. Ctr., Hoboken, N.J., 1985—. Contbr. articles to profl. jours. Mem. Entomol. Soc. Am. (bd. cert.), Orgn. Profl. Employees Dept. Agr., Sigma Xi. Home: 16 Willis Rd North Arlington NJ 07031-5810 Office: Methods Devel Ctr PPQ APHIS USDA 209 River St 209 River St Hoboken NJ 07030-5899

WITHERS, BARBARA ANN, editor; b. Wichita, Kans., June 23, 1939; d. Robert R. and Mary (Stryker) W. BA, Whitman Coll., Walla Walla, Wash., 1961; MRE, Union Theol. Sem., N.Y.C., 1964; EdD, Columbia U., 1975. Dir. children's wk. Winnetka (Ill.) Congl. Ch., 1964-66; dir. middle sch. Riverside Ch., N.Y.C., 1966-72; interim dir. Christian edn., 1973; freelance ednl. cons. N.Y.C., 1973-75; editor ednl. resources Presbyn. Ch. U.S.A., N.Y.C., 1975-90; editor The Pilgrim Press, 1990-91; freelance editor and writer, 1989—; Editor: The Pilgrim Press, 1990—; editor, writer: Language about God in Liturgy and Scripture: A Study Guide, 1980, Language and the Church: Articles and Designs for Workshops, 1984, others; contbr. articles to profl. jours. Editor, writer: Language about God in Liturgy and Scripture: A Study Guide, 1980, Language and the Church: Articles and Designs for Workshops, 1984, others; contbr. articles to profl. jours. Mem. Religious Edn. Assn., Assn. United Ch. Educators, Orgn. for Study of Communication, Lang. and Gender. Home: 380 Riverside Dr Apt 7E New York NY 10025-1821

WITHUHN, WILLIAM LAWRENCE, museum administrator and curator, railroad economics consultant; b. Portland, Oreg., Aug. 12, 1941; s. Vernon Lawrence and Ruth Eleanor (Ferguson) W.; m. Gail Joy Hartman, Nov. 22, 1964; children: James, Thomas, Harold. BA, U. Calif.-Berkeley, 1963; MBA with distinction, Cornell U., 1977, MA, 1980, postgrad., 1980-82. Commd. regular 2d lt. USAF, 1963, advanced through grades to capt., 1967; indsl. engr., asst. dir. manpower and orgn. USAF, Travis AFB, Calif., 1964-65; global, polar, tactical, and instr. navigator worldwide USAF, 1965-72; spl. ops. navigator USAF, Vietnam; select lead navigator Mil. Airlift Command USAF, 1970-72; ret., 1972; intern, then staff asst. U.S. Ho. of Reps., 1973-74; v.p. Va. & Md. R.R. Co., Cape Charles, Va., 1977-81, Md. & Del. R.R., Federalsburg, Md., 1977-81; sr. v.p. Ont. Midland R.R., Ont. Cent. R.R., Sodus, N.Y., 1979-83; v.p. Rail Mgmt. Svcs., Inc., Syracuse, N.Y., 1979-83, RSA Leasing Co., Syracuse, 1980-83; exec. v.p. Am. Coal Enterprises, Inc., Akron, Ohio, 1980-82; v.p., gen. mgr. Allegheny So. Ry., Martinsburg, Pa., 1982-83; acting dir. R.R. Mus. of Pa., 1982-83; curator transp. Nat. Mus. Am. History Smithsonian Inst., Washington, 1983—, dep. chmn. dept. sci. and tech., 1984-91, spl. asst. to dir., 1990—; bd. dirs., chmn., transp. cons. The Waring Group Inc., Salisbury, Md., 1983-89. Contbr. articles to profl. jours. Decorated D.F.C. with cluster, Bronze Star, Air medal with 11 clusters, Antarctic Svc. medal; De Karman fellow, 1979-80, Smithsonian fellow, 1980-81. Mem. Am. Inst. Indsl. Engrs., Soc. for History of Tech., Ry. and Locomotive Hist. Soc. (dir., v.p.), Internat. Assn. Ry. Operating Officers, Cornell Club Washington, Theta Chi. Home: 6311 Barrs Ln Lanham Seabrook MD 20706-2841 Office: Nat Mus Am History Smithsonian Instn Rm 5010 Washington DC 20560

WITKIN, ARTHUR AARON, psychologist; b. N.Y.C., Aug. 17, 1921; s. Jack and Sadye (Leibowitz) W.; m. Ethel Greenblatt, Feb. 3, 1945 (dec. 1986); children: Jill, Richard, Jeannie. BS, CCNY, 1941, MS, 1943; PhD, NYU, 1956. Lic. psychologist N.Y. State. Chief psychologist Personnel Scis. Ctr., N.Y.C., 1956—; prof. psychology Queens Coll.-CUNY, 1956—. Author: A Business Executives Guide to Interviewing, 1960. With U.S. Army, 1943-46. Mem. Am. sychol. Soc., N.Y. State Psychol. Assn. (pres. personnel div. 1980-82, coun. rep. 1988—, McClelland award 1987). Home: 1418 The Colony Hartsdale NY 10530-1727 Office: Personnel Scis Ctr 41 E 42nd St Rm 805 New York NY 10017-5303

WITKIN, MILDRED HOPE FISHER, psychotherapist, educator; b. N.Y.C.; d. Samuel and Sadie (Goldschmidt) Fisher; children: Georgia Hope, Roy Thomas, Laurie Phillips; m. Jorge Radovic, Aug. 26, 1983. AB, Hunter Coll., MA, Columbia U., 1968; PhD, NYU, 1973. Diplomate Am. Bd. Sexology, Am. Bd. Sexuality; cert. supr. Head counselor Camp White Lake, Camp Emanuel, Long Beach, N.J.; tchr. econs., polit. sci. Hunter Coll. High Sch.; dir., group leader follow-up program Jewish Vacation Assn., N.Y.C.; investigator N.Y.C. Housing Authority; psychol. counselor Montclair State Coll., Upper Montclair, N.J., 1967-68; mem., lectr. Creative Problem-Solving Inst., U. Buffalo, 1968; psychol. counselor Fairleigh Dickinson U., Teaneck, N.J., 1968, dir. Counseling Center, 1969-74; pvt. practice psychotherapy, N.Y.C., also Westport, Conn.; sr. faculty supr., family therapist and psychotherapist Payne Whitney Psychiat. Clinic, N.Y. Hosp., 1973—; clin. asst. prof. dept. psychiatry Cornell U. Med. Coll., 1974—; assoc. dir. sex therapy and edn. program Cornell-N.Y. Hosp. Med. Ctr., 1974—; sr. cons. Kaplan Inst. for Evaluation and Treatment of Sexual Disorders, 1981—; supr. master's and doctoral candidates, NYU, 1975-82; pvt. practice psychotherapy and sex therapy, N.Y.C., also Westport, Conn.; cons. counselor edn. tng. programs N.Y.C. Bd. Edn., 1971-75; cons. Health Info. Systems, 1972-79; vis. prof. numerous colls. and univs.; chmn. sci. com. 1st Internat. Symposium on Female Sexuality, Buenos Aires, 1984. Exhibited in group shows at Scarsdale (N.Y.) Art Show, 1959, Red Shutter Art Studio, Long Beach, 1968. Edn. legislation chmn. PTA, Yonkers, 1955; publicity chmn. United Jewish Appeal, Scarsdale, 1959-65; Scarsdale chmn. mothers com. Boy Scouts Am., 1961-64; mem. Morrow Assn. on Correction N.J., 1969-91. Recipient Bronze medal for svcs. Hunter Coll.; United Jewish Appeal plaque, 1962; Founders Day award N.Y. U., 1973, citation N.Y. Hosp./Cornell U. Med. Ctr., 1990. Fellow Internat. Coun. Sex Edn. and Parenthood of Am. U., Am. Acad. Clin. Sexologists; mem. AAUW, APA, AACD, Internat. Assn. Marriage and Family Counselors, Am. Coll. Sexuality (cert.), Women's Med. Assn. N.Y.C., N.Y. Acad. Sci., Am. Coll. Pers. Assn. (nat. mem. commn. II 1973-76), Nat. Assn. Women Deans and Counselors, Am. Assn. Sex Educators, Counselors and Therapists (regional bd., nat. accreditation bd., cert. internat. supr.), Soc. for Sci. Study Sex Therapy and Rsch., Eastern Assn. Sex Therapists, Am. Assn. Marriage and Family Counselors, N.J. Assn. Marriage and Family Counselors, Ackerman Family Inst., Am. Personnel and Guidance Assn., Am., N.Y., N.J. psychol. assns., Creative Edn. Found., Am. Assn. Higher Edn., Assn. Counselor Supervision and Edn., Profl. Women's Caucus, LWV, Am. Assn. counseling and Devel., Am. Women's Med. Assn., Nat. Coun. on Women in Medicine, Argentine Soc. Human Sexuality (hon.), Am. Assn. Sexology (diplomate), Pi Lambda Theta, Kappa Delta Pi, Alpha Chi Alpha. Author: 45-And Single Again, 1985; contbr. articles to profl. jours. and textbooks; lectr. internat. workshops, radio and TV. Home: 9 Sturges Commons Westport CT 06880-2832 Office: 35 Park Ave New York NY 10016-3838

WITMAN, GEORGE BODO, III, cell biologist, researcher; b. Upland, Calif., July 19, 1945; s. George Bodo Jr. and Alwilda Marion (Cochran) W.; m. Rita Louise Ricciuti, June 14, 1969; children: George B., Anthony R., Andrew J. BA, U. Calif., Riverside, 1967; PhD, Yale U., 1972. Postdoctoral fellow U. Chgo., 1972-73, U. Wis., Madison, 1973-74; asst. prof. Princeton (N.J.) U., 1974-81; staff scientist Worcester Found. for Exptl. Biology, Shrewsbury, Mass., 1981-82, sr. scientist, 1983-90, prin. scientist, 1990—, dir. male fertility program, 1985—; adj. assoc. prof. dept. cell biology U. Mass. Med. Ctr., Worcester, 1985—. Contbr. articles to profl. jours. Mem. AAAS, Am. Soc. for Cell Biology, Am. Soc. for Biochemistry and Molecular Biology, Genetics Soc. Am., Protein Soc., Electron Microscopy Soc. Am. Office: Worcester Found Exptl Biol 222 Maple Ave Shrewsbury MA 01545-2732

WITMER, JOHN E., JR., newswriter, editor; b. Lancaster, Pa., May 28, 1935; s. J. Elwood and Florence Dorothy (Howry) W. BS in Speech, Emerson Coll., 1963. Reporter Sta. WORK, York, Pa., 1959; reporter, editor Sta. WBZ, Boston, 1960-63; writer, editor ABC News, N.Y.C., 1964—. With USAF, 1955-59. Mem. Radio TV News Dirs. Assn., Soc. Profl. Journalists. Democrat. Congregationalist. Home: 195 Adams St Apt 15F Brooklyn NY 11201-1854 Office: ABC News 125 West End Ave New York NY 10023-6345

WITMEYER, JOHN JACOB, III, lawyer; b. New Orleans, Dec. 18, 1946; s. John J. and Thais Audrey (Dolese) W. B.S., Tulane U., 1968; J.D. with distinction, Duke U., 1971. Bar: N.Y. Assoc. Mudge Rose Guthrie & Alexander, N.Y.C., 1971-76; ptnr. Ford Marrin Esposito & Witmeyer, N.Y.C., 1976—. Col. USAR. Office: 120 Wall St New York NY 10005

WITMEYER, STANLEY HERBERT, retired art educator, dean; b. Palmyra, Pa., Feb. 14, 1913; s. Harry George and Carrie May (Himmelberger) W.; m. Marian Hebing, June 22, 1940 (dec.); children: Gail, Donald, Robert, Anne, Paul; m. Helen Ickes, Dec. 13, 1979. Diploma, Rochester Inst. Tech., 1936; BS, SUNY, Buffalo, 1939; cert., U. Hawaii, Hilo, 1945; MFA, Syracuse U., 1946. With dept. paper emulsion Eastman Kodak, Rochester, N.Y., 1936-37; tchr. Park Sch., Amherst, N.Y., 1937; designer Rochester Gas and Electric, 1937-49, Rochester Telephone Co., Bradford, N.Y., 1937-49, Elmer Lapp Assoc., Rochester, 1937-49; instr. art Cuba (N.Y.) Schs., 1939-43; prof. art. Sch. Art, Rochester Inst. Tech., 1946-78, assoc. dean, dir., 1946-78; cons. Genesee Community Coll., Batavia, N.Y., 1988—. Graphic designer; watercolor artist; contbr. articles to profl. jours. Assoc. dir. Vt. Boys Camp, Plymouth; pres. Arts Coun. Rochester, 1955-58. 1st sgt. U.S Army, 1943-46. Named Disting. Alumni SUNY, 1962. Mem. Rochester Inst. Tech. Alumni Assn. (pres. 1955, Disting. Alumni award 1952-53), Nathaniel Rochester Soc. of Rochester Inst. Tech., Stadium Club (bd. dirs.), Torch Club (pres. 1954, bd. dirs.). Home: 54 Clarkes Xing Fairport NY 14450-3029

WITT, CHRISTOPHER JOHN, engineering executive; b. Flushing, N.Y., Dec. 24, 1931; s. Christopher Willie Arthur and Marie Louise (Roth) W.; m. Clara Elsie Scheuing, July 5, 1958; children: Erika Lynn Witt-Seiden, Christopher Frank. BEE, Poly. U., Bklyn., 1953, MEE, 1954; postgrad., Cornell U., 1985. Registered profl. engr., N.Y. Rsch. fellow Microwave Rsch. Inst., Bklyn., 1953-54; sr. engr. guidance and control Sperry Gyroscope Co., Lake Success, N.Y., 1956-63; lunar module guidance and control project engr. Grumman Corp., Bethpage, N.Y., 1963-68, sect. chief guidance and control, 1966-68, mgr. orbiting astron. obs., 1968-70, mgr. system engring., 1970-73, dir. Schwendler Devel. Ctr., 1973-87, dir. corp. devel. labs., 1987—. Mem. zoning bd. appeals Village of Laurel Hollow, N.Y., 1968—; troop com. chmn. and asm. troop 360 Boy Scouts Am., Huntington, N.Y., 1975—; pres. Poly. U. Alumni Assn., Bklyn., 1989-91; tchr. Sunday sch. Oyster Bay Presbyn. Ch., 1983-86. 1st lt. U.S. Army, 1954-56. Named Dedicated Alumnus, Poly. U. Alumni Assn., Bklyn., 1989. Mem. IEEE (sr., chmn. audit com.), Aircraft Industry Assn. (ad-hoc com. on ultra reliable electronics), Nat. Security Industry Assn. (exec. com. mem. rsch. and engring. com. 1991—, chmn. internat. tech. subcom. rsch. and engring. com. 1991—), Grumman Flying Club (pilot), Sigma Xi. Home: 8 White Oak Tree Rd Laurel Hollow NY 11791

WITTE, CARLTON ROYAL VINCENT, health facility administrator; b. Point Pleasant, N.J., Aug. 29, 1946; s. Carl George and Marion Ida (Pollock) W.; m. Barbara Ann Koontz, Aug. 30, 1969 (div. Mar. 1977); children: Michelle Darlene, Carl Joseph; m. Joyce Ann Smith, Dec. 4, 1977; children: Brett Jonathan, Bryan Christopher, Kristin Ann-Marie. BA in Psychology, U. Tex., 1969; MA in Pub. Adminstrn., U. Okla., 1977; postgrad., Command and Gen. Staff Coll., 1985. Commd. 2d lt. U.S. Army, 1969, advanced through grades to lt. col.; chief patient svcs. Rader Army Health Clinic, Ft. Myer, Va., 1972-73; asst. adminstr. dept. of clinics Forrestal Army Health Clinic, Washington, 1972-74; asst. adminstr. Walter Reed Army Inst. of Rsch., Washington, 1975-78; adminstr. Office of Div. Surgeon, 3d Armored Div., Fed. Republic Germany, 1979-81; assoc. adminstr. Walter Reed Army Med. Ctr., Washington, 1981-84; chief adminstr. Pentagon Health Clinic, Washington, 1984-86; chief patient adminstrn. Walson Army Community Hosp., Ft. Dix, N.J., 1986-90; ret. U.S. Army, 1990; dir. adminstrn. dept. ob-gyn Hershey Med. Ctr., Pa. State U., 1990-92; regional adminstr. ARA Svcs. Correctional Med. Systems, Balt., 1992—; cons. Witte Investment Adv. Svc., Odenton, Md., 1984—; chmn. Joint Commn. on Accreditation of Healthcare Orgns. steering com., Walson Hosp., Ft. Dix, 1986-90. Author booklet: Patient Administration Guide-Physicians, 1988; co-author: Patient Administration for Commanders, 1988. Mem. rescue squad, tng. officer Dale City (Va.) Vol. Fire and Rescue, 1975-77; bd. dirs. Pheasant Run, Laurel, Md., 1982-84; charter mem., chmn. liturgy com. St. Joseph's Parish, Ft. Dix, 1988, mem. parish coun., 1988-89; coach Little League, Ft. Dix and South Hanover, Pa., 1989-91. Decorated Legion of Merit. Mem. Am. Coll. Health Care Execs., Med. Group Mgmt. Assn., Mil. Order of World Wars (perpetual mem), Mil. Order of Med. Merit. Roman Catholic. Home: 1191 Hillcrest Rd Odenton MD 02113-4932 Office: Balt City Detention Ctr Correctional Med Systems 401 E Eagan St Baltimore MD 21202

WITTE, MARVIN EDWIN, retired elementary school principal; b. Bklyn., June 18, 1929; s. Martin and Esther (Samuels) W.; m. Phoebe Carol Lipson, July 15, 1962; children: Marc, Marlene. BA in Liberal Arts, NYU, 1950, MA in Elem. Edn., 1953; EdD, Nova U., 1975. Cert. sch. adminstr./supr., N.Y. Elem. tchr. East Meadow (N.Y.) Sch. Dist., 1953-57, Plainview-Old Beth Sch. Dist., Plainview, N.Y., 1957-59; asst. elem. prin. Old Bethpage Sch. Dist., Plainview, N.Y., 1959-60, elem. prin., 1960-88; interim prin. Merrick (N.Y.) Sch. Dist., 1989-90; field supr., adj. prof. Bowling Coll., Oakdale, N.Y., 1988—; adj. prof. C. W. Post Coll., L.I. U., 1981-83, Hofstra U., Hempstead, N.Y., 1967-68; speaker in field. Composer sch. songs. Entertainer/accordionist Around the Corner-Sq. Dancing-Jones Beach, CBS-TV, Cen. Island Nursing Home, Plainview; life mem. Plainview-Old Bethpage PTA. Mem. Nassau County Elem. Sch. Prin. Assn. (pres. 1983-84, Educator of Yr. 1984), L.I. Assn. Supervision and Curriculum Devel. (pres. 1985-86), Coun. of Adminstrs. and Suprs., N.Y. State Retired Adminstrs. Assn., Arts and Scis. Masons (London), Phi Delta Kappa. Home: 26 Hollywood Dr Plainview NY 11803

WITTERHOLT, VINCENT GERARD, chemist; b. N.Y.C., Sept. 24, 1932; s. Joseph and Helen (Merkel) W.; m. Alice E. Zaborowski, Sept. 11, 1954; children: Diane, Mark, Valerie, Kenneth, Alison, Monica. BS, Queens Coll., 1953; PhD, Purdue U., 1958. Rsch. chemist E.I. Dupont De Nemours & Co., Inc., Deepwater Pt., N.J., 1958-68, rsch. supr. organic chemicals dept., 1968-72, chief supr., 1973-74, div. head dyes, 1975-80; from rsch. fellow to departmental fellow agrl. products E.I. Dupont De Nemours & Co., Inc., Wilmington, Del., 1983-91, Dupont fellow agrl. products, 1991—; chmn. Dupont Fellows Forum, 1992. Author: (with others) Kirk-Othmer: Encyclopedia of Chemical Technology, 1969. Mem. Am. Chem. Soc., Alpha Chi Sigma. Home: 334 Spalding Rd Wilmington DE 19803 Office: EI Dupont De Nemours Co Inc Experimental Sta E402 Wilmington DE 19898

WITTIG, RAYMOND SHAFFER, lawyer; b. Allentown, Pa., Dec. 13, 1944; s. Raymond Baety and Alice (Shaffer) W.; m. Beth Glover, June 21, 1975; children: Meaghan G., Allison G. BA, Pa. State U., 1966, MEd, 1968; JD, Dickinson Sch. Law, 1974. Bar: Pa. 1974, U.S. Ct. Appeals (D.C. cir.) 1978. Rsch. psychologist Intext Corp., Scranton, Pa., 1968; minority counsel, procurement subcom. and gen. oversight subcom. Small Bus. Com., U.S. Ho. of Reps., Washington, 1975-76, 77-78; minority staff dir. full Ho. Small Bus. Com. U.S. Ho. of Reps., Washington, 1979-84; pvt. practice, 1984—. Capt. U.S. Army, 1969-71. Mem. Nat. Order Barristers, Capitol Hill Club.

WITTING, LLOYD ALLEN, chemicals executive; b. Chgo., May 18, 1930; s. Theodore Allen and Elsie Martha (Korinek) W.; m. Lucille Ruth Gerches, Aug. 9, 1956; children: Sandra, Cynthia, Michael. BS, U. Ill., 1952, MS, 1953, PhD, 1956; postdoctoral, U. Wis., 1957-59. Assoc. biochemist Am. Meat Inst. Found./U. Chgo., 1955-57; med. rsch. assoc. III and IV Ill. Dept. of Mental Health, Elgin, 1959-67, acting dir. rsch., 1967-72; asst. prof. Coll. of Medicine U. Ill., Chgo., 1962-73; assoc. prof. Tex. Women's U., Denton, 1972-74; cons. North Tex. Edn. & Tng. Coop., Gainesville, 1975-76; sr. chemist Supelco, Inc., Bellefonte, Pa., 1976-77, tech. dir., 1977-90, dir. regulatory compliance, 1990—; cons. Matreya, Inc., Pleasant Gap, Pa., 1989—. Editor: Glycolipid Method, 1976; co-editor: Modif of Lipid Metabolism, 1975; contbr. numerous articles to profl. jours. Grantee NIH, 1967-72. Mem. Am. Oil Chemists Soc. (assoc. editor 1972-86, Merit award 1986), Am. Chem. Soc., Am. Inst. Nutrition, Am. Assn. Chem. Labeling, Am. Soc. Biol. Chemists. Lutheran. Home: 249 Oakley Dr State College PA 16803-1349 Office: Supelco Inc Supelco Park Bellefonte PA 16823

WITTMANN, HORST RICHARD, physicist, electronics engineer; b. Worms, Germany, Jan. 31, 1936; came to U.S., 1966; s. Richard and Herta (Fiegelmullner) W.; divorced; children: Ute, Thomas, Michael. PhD in Physics, U. Graz, Austria, 1964. Elec. systems engr. Bolkow, Munich, 1964-66; team leader Physics Lab., Missile Command, Redstone Arsenal, Ala., 1966-70; program mgr. for electronics Army Rsch. Office, Durham, N.C., 1970-73; assoc. dir. for electronics Army Rsch. Office, Research Triangle Park, N.C., 1973-84; dir. electronics Air Force Office Sci. Rsch., Washington, 1984-91, dir. physics and electronics, 1991—; mem. accreditation com. Accreditation Bd. for Engring. and Tech. Contbr. articles to sci. jours.; patentee on laser spectroscopy. Fulbright-Hays fellow U. Vienna, Austria, 1977-78. Mem. IEEE (sr., editorial bd. Proc.), Am. Phys. Soc. Home: 1109 Palmer Rd Apt 8 Fort Washington MD 20744-7112 Office: Air Force Office Sci Rsch NE Bldg 410 Bolling AFB Washington DC 20332-6448

WIXOM, WILLIAM DAVID, art historian, museum administrator, educator; b. Phila., July 17, 1929; s. Clinton Wood and Beatrice Rachel (Hunt) W.; BA, Haverford (Pa.) Coll., 1951; MA, Inst. Fine Arts NYU, 1963; m. Nancy Coe, Aug. 8, 1959; 3 children. Asst. curator to curator medieval and renaissance decorative arts Cleve. Mus. Art, 1958-78, chief curator early western art, 1979; chmn. dept. medieval art and The Cloisters, Met. Mus. Art, N.Y.C., 1979—; adj. assoc. prof. history of art Case Western Res. U., Cleve., 1967-78, adj. prof., 1978; adj. prof. N.Y.U., 1981-82; mem. adv. council for Snite Mus. Art Notre Dame U., 1974—. Bd. dirs. Internat. Ctr. Medieval Art, N.Y.C., 1971-82, pres., 1971-74. Belgium-Am. Ednl. Found. fellow, 1962; Nat. Endowment Arts grantee, 1973; fellow Pierpont Morgan Library, 1979—. Fellow Soc. of Antiquaries of London; mem. Coll. Art Assn. (dir. 1979-83), Medieval Acad. Am., Internat. Center Medieval Art. Quaker. Author: Treasures from Medieval France, 1967; Renaissance Bronzes from Ohio Collections, 1975; contbg. author The Royal Abbey of Saint Denis in the Time of Abbot Suger, 1981, The Treasury of San Marco, 1985; Gothic and Renaissance Art in Nuremberg, 1986, Festschrift Gerhard Bott, 1987, Hommage à Hubert Landais, 1987; contbr. articles in field to profl. jours. Office: Cloisters Fort Tryon Pk New York NY 10040

WLAZELEK, BRIAN GENE, psychologist; b. Allentown, Pa., Nov. 12, 1957; s. Joseph Wlazelek and Virginia (Gardner) Marone; m. Jeanne Marie Werner, June 21, 1980; children: Kristen Michelle, Sara Renee. BA in Psychology, Temple U., 1979, MEd in Counseling Psychology, 1980; PhD in Counseling Psychology, Lehigh U., 1990. Lic. psychologist, Pa. Therapist Cumberland County Guidance Ctr., Millville, N.J., 1980-81; staff psychologist Atlantic Mental Health Ctr., Atlantic City, N.J., 1981-83, First Hosp. Wyo. Valley, Wilkes-Barre, Pa., 1983-85, Pocono Med. Ctr., East Stroudsburg, Pa., 1985-88; counseling psychologist, asst. prof. Kutztown (Pa.) Univ., 1988—; adj. prof. Allentown Coll. of St. Francis de Sales, Center Valley, Pa., 1990—. sr. cons. Family Life Svcs., Topton, Pa., 1989—; consulting psychologist First Hosp., Wilkes-Barre, Pa., 1989—, Pocono Med. Ctr., East Stroudsburg, 1988—. Named Temple Univ. Pres.'s Scholar, 1980. Mem. AACD, APA, Masons, Rotary (pres. 1992—), Assn. Counseling Ctr. (sec.-treas. 1991-92), Phi Beta Kappa, Psi Chi, Chi Sigma Iota. Lutheran. Home: RR 1 Box 860E Lenhartsville PA 19534-9656 Office: Kutztown Univ Stratton Adminstrn Bldg Kutztown PA 19530

WLUKA, DAVID, land developer and planner, marketing consultant; b. Salzburg, Austria, Aug. 18, 1946; came to U.S., 1948; s. Icek and Bronia (Patashnik) W.; m. Nancy Berger, Jan. 6, 1968; children: Aaron, Jordana. BA in Sociology, Boston U., 1967, MA in Urban Sociology, 1970. Planning aide Boston Redevel. Authority, Boston, 1965-66; prin. planner, v.p. CPS Planners, Boston, 1969—; mng. broker Lee Gold, Realtors, Sharon, Mass., 1977-79, C-21 Homes by Sunrise, Sharon, 1980-83; pres. David Wluka Real Estate, Sharon, 1984—; ptnr. Skanska USA, 1985—, Brown-Wluka Realty Assocs., 1989—; dir. devel. Simeone Corp., 1988—. Mem. Sharon Comprehensive Plan Com., 1973; chmn. Mass. Local Growth Policy Com., Sharon, 1977. Mem. Am. Planning Assn., Urban Land Inst., Greater Boston Real Estate Bd. (bd. dirs. Multi-List Svc. 1986—, v.p. Multi-List Svc. 1991-92, mem. exec. bd. 1987, 90-92, housing prodn. task force). Democrat. Jewish. Home: 19 Pond View Cir Sharon MA 02067-1136 Office: 65 Pond St PO Box 333 Sharon MA 02067

WOEHLING, MARY-PATRICE, English educator; b. N.Y.C., 1959; d. Henry F. and Cecil (Griffin) W. BA, St. John's U., 1981, MA, 1983; PhD, CUNY, 1991. Tchr. Katharine Gibbs Sch., N.Y.C., 1984-90, 91—; adj. instr. St. John's U., Jamaica, N.Y., 1983-84. Home: 16016 12th Rd Flushing NY 11357-1926

WOELFLEIN, ANN BUCKLEY, investment company official; b. Boston, July 2, 1933; d. Arthur Jerome and Ann Louise (Dorgan) Buckley; m. Kevin Gerard Woelflein, Sept. 9, 1957; children: Karl, Luise, Drew, Peter. BA, Regis Coll., 1955; MS, Drexel U., 1963. Literature chemist Arthur D. Little, Cambridge, Mass., 1955-57; chem. librarian Allied Chem., Glenoldes, Pa., 1957-59; bus. ref. librarian U. Pa., Phila., 1961-68; cons. Cath. Library Assn., Haverford, Pa., 1965-68, Northwestern Union, Evanston, Ill., 1968-72, Link, Inc., N.Y.C., 1976-78, Bd. Edn. Greenwich (Conn.) Schs., 1979-82; v.p. U.S. Capital Investment Co., Greenwich, 1983—. Vice chmn. Friends of Music, Smithsonian Instn., Washington, 1982—; mem. women's bd. Am. Heart AAssn., 1983—. Cath. Libr. Assn. scholar, 1962. Mem. Spl. Librs. Assn. Home: 33 Club Rd Riverside CT 06878-2002 Office: US Capital Investments Co 2 Greenwich Pla Greenwich CT 06830

WOFFORD, HARRIS LLEWELLYN, lawyer, senator; b. N.Y.C., Apr. 9, 1926; s. Harris Llewellyn and Estelle (Gardner) W.; m. Emmy Lou Clare Lindgren, Aug. 14, 1948; children: Susanne, Daniel, David. B.A., U. Chgo., 1948; study fellow, India, 1949, Israel, 1950; LL.B., Yale U., 1954, Howard U., 1954. Bar: D.C. 1954, U.S. Supreme Ct. 1958, Pa. 1978. Asst. to Chester Bowles, 1953-54; law assoc. Covington & Burling, Washington, 1954-58; legal asst. to Rev. Theodore Hesburgh, Commn. on Civil Rights, 1958-59; assoc. prof. Notre Dame Law Sch., 1959-60, on leave, 1961-66; asst. to Sen. Kennedy, 1960; spl. asst. to Pres. Kennedy, 1961-62; spl. rep. for Africa, dir. Ethiopian program U.S. Peace Corps, 1962-64; assoc. dir. Peace Corps, Washington, 1964-66; pres. Coll. at Old Westbury, SUNY, 1966-70, Bryn Mawr (Pa.) Coll., 1970-78; counsel firm Schnader, Harrison, Segal and Lewis, Phila. and Washington, 1979-86; chmn. Pa. Dem. State Com., 1986; sec. labor and industry Commonwealth of Pa., 1987-91; U.S. senator from Pa., 1991—; vis. lectr. Howard Law Sch., 1956. Author: It's Up to Us, 1946, (with Clare Wofford) India Afire, 1951, Of Kennedys and Kings, 1980; editor: Embers of the World, 1970; co-editor: Report of the U.S. Commission on Civil Rights, 1959. Mem. Coun. Fgn. Rels., 1968—; co-chmn. Com. for Study of Nat. Svc., 1977-80; mem. U.S. Adv. Com. on Nat. Growth Policy Processes, 1975-76; trustee The Am. Coll., Bryn Mawr, 1975-83; mem. coun. U.S.-South Africa Leader Exch. Programk 1971-87; bd. dirs. Internat. League for Human Rights, 1979—, pres., 1980; bd. dirs. Pub. Interest Law Ctr. Phila., 1978-87; trustee Martin Luther King Ctr. for Nonviolent Social Change, 1983-87; governing coun. Wilderness Soc., 1983-87. Served with USAF, 1944-45. Mem. ABA. Roman Catholic. Office: U S Senate Office of Senate Members Washington DC 20510

WOFSY, STEVEN CHARLES, astrophysicist; b. N.Y.C., June 24, 1946. BS in Chemistry with honors, U. Chgo., 1966; MA in Chemistry, Harvard U., 1967, PhD in Chemistry, 1971. Rsch. assoc. Smithsonian Astrophysical Obs., Cambridge, Mass., 1971-73; lectr. on atmosphere Harvard Univ., Div. Applied Scis., Cambridge, 1973-77, chemistry and rsch. fellow, assoc. prof., 1977-82, sr. rsch. fellow, 1982—. Contbr. numerous articles to profl. jours. Mem. AAAS, Am. Geophysical Union (James B. MacIlwane award 1982), Am. Soc. Limnology and Oceanography.

WOGRIN, CONRAD ANTHONY, university administrator, computer science educator; b. Denver, Apr. 16, 1924; s. Conrad and Rosina (Hassler) W.; m. Lois Barbara Yohans, June 2, 1951; children: Sandra Ellen Wogrin Warren, Carol Ann, Nancy Elizabeth. Student, Mich. Coll Mine and Technology, 1943-44; B in Engring., Yale U., 1948, M in Engring., 1951, DEng, 1955. Asst. prof. elec. engring. Yale U., New Haven, 1955-61, assoc. prof. applied sci., 1961-67, assoc. dir. computer rsch., 1966-67; prof. computer sci. U. Mass., Amherst, 1967—, dir. univ. computing, 1967-85, head computer sci. program, 1969-71, chmn. computer & info. sci. dept., 1985-87, assoc. vice chancellor rsch. and grad. studies, 1988—; cons. Mitre Corp., New Bedford, Mass., 1963-65, NASA, Goddard Space Flight Ctr., Md., 1965-68; pres. VIM Inc., Mpls., 1982-84. Chmn. Bd. Edn., Cheshire, Conn., 1958-64; active Planning Bd., Amherst, 1989-90. Sgt. U.S. Army, 1942-46. Mem. AAAS, IEEE, Am. Assn. Computing Machines. Episcopalian. Home: 121 Aubinwood Rd Amherst MA 01002-1625 Office: Univ Mass Assoc Vice Chancellor Rsch Amherst MA 01003

WOH, EDGAR AUGUSTO, architect; b. Lima, Peru, Dec. 31, 1955; came to U.S., 1980, naturalized, 1985; s. Shui Kee and Zoila (Tang) W. BArch, Nat. U. Engring., Lima, 1980; MArch, SUNY, Buffalo, 1985. Registered architect, N.Y.; cert. Nat. Coun. Archtl. Registration Bds. Intern architect Papp Architects, White Plains, N.Y., 1980-83; project architect Gibbons Heidtmann Salvador, White Plains, 1985-89; architect Daniel Mann Johnson & Mendenhall, N.Y.C., 1989—. Mem. AIA, Nat. Arbor Day Found., World Wildlife Fund, U. Buffalo Alumni Assn., N.Y. State Assn. Architects. Democrat. Roman Catholic. Home: 201 Mayflower Ave New Rochelle NY 10801 Office: DMJM 300 E 42d St New York NY 10017

WOHL, RONALD GENE, lawyer; b. N.Y.C., Dec. 10, 1934; s. Arthur and Bernice (Deutch) W.; m. Linda Susan Meltsner, May 2, 1965; children: Allison Brooke Wohl George, Arthur Evan, Amanda Kate. AB, Syracuse U., 1956, LLB, 1961; LLM, Bklyn. Law Sch., 1967. Bar: N.Y. 1962, U.S. Dist. Ct. (so. and ea. dists.) N.Y. 1963, U.S. Ct. Appeals (2d cir.) 1964, U.S. Supreme Ct. 1965, U.S. Dist. Ct. (no. dist.) N.Y. 1977, U.S. Dist. Ct. Conn. 1980, U.S. Tax Ct. 1986. Law clk. to judge Jacob Mishler U.S. Dist. Ct. (ea. dist.) N.Y., N.Y.C., 1963-64; assoc. Edward Gettinger & Peter Gettinger, N.Y.C., 1962-63, 68-70; asst. U.S. atty. U.S. Dept. of Justice, N.Y.C., 1964-68; ptnr. Squadron, Gartenberg, Ellenoff & Pleasant, N.Y.C., 1970-71; pvt. practice N.Y.C., 1971-74; sr. ptnr. Finkelstein, Bruckman, Wohl, Most & Rothman, N.Y.C., 1974—. Trustee Roslyn (N.Y.) Union Free Sch. Dist., 1981-92. Lt. U.S. Army, 1957. Mem. N.Y. Bar Assn., N.Y. Dist. Attys. Assn., Assn. of Bar of City of N.Y., Nassau County Bar, Fed. Bar Coun., Soc. of Med. Jurisprudence. Home: 70 The Intervale Roslyn Estates NY 11576 Office: Finkelstein Bruckman Wohl Most & Rothman 575 Lexington Ave New York NY 10022

WOHLERT, EARL ROSS, academic administrator, marketing and management consultant; b. Phila., Oct. 19, 1963; s. Anton Emil and Dona Lee (Zimmerman) W. BA, Hawaii Loa Coll., Kaneohe, 1986; MBA, U. New Haven, 1992. Acct. Sch. of Medicine, Yale U., New Haven, 1987-88, fin. analyst, 1988-90, assoc. adminstr. fin., 1990—; chief exec. officer Enigma Devel. Group, Branford, Conn., 1991—. Ensign USNR, 1992. Mem. Adminstrs. Internal Medicine, Med. Group Mgmt. Assn. (acad. practice assembly, fin. mgmt. soc., internal medicine assembly). Home: 25 Farm River Rd Branford CT 06405 Office: Yale U Sch of Medicine 333 Cedar St New Haven CT 06510

WOHLGELERNTER, BETH, organization executive; b. N.Y.C., Jan. 30, 1956; d. Maurice Nathaniel and Esther Rachel (Feinerman) W. BA, Barnard Coll., 1977. Exec. aide to pres. Barnard Coll., N.Y.C., 1977-80; spl. asst. to pres. The Commonwealth Fund, N.Y.C., 1980-81; asst. to chief exec. officer/pres. Mary McFadden, Inc., N.Y.C., 1981-84; exec. adminstr. The Donna Karan Co., N.Y.C., 1984-90; exec. dir. Hadassah, The Women's Zionist Orgn. Am., Inc., N.Y.C., 1990—. Bd. dirs., v.p. N.Am. Conf. on Ethiopian Jewry, N.Y.C., 1981-85, bd. advisors, 1985—; bd. govs. Lincoln Sq. Synagogue, N.Y.C., 1988—. Office: Hadassah The Women's Zionist Orgn Am Inc 50 W 58th St New York NY 10019

WOHLGELERNTER, MAURICE, English educator; b. Serotsk, Poland, Feb. 13, 1921; came to U.S., 1936; s. Jacob Isaac and Devorah (Wallerstein) W.; m. Esther Feinerman, Feb. 1, 1948; children: Debra, Elli, Beth. BA, Yeshiva U., N.Y.C., 1941; MA, Columbia U., 1946, PhD, 1961. Ordained rabbi, 1944. Rabbi Inwood Jewish Ctr., N.Y.C., 1946-78; asst. prof. Yeshiva U., N.Y.C., 1955-70; prof. Baruch Coll., N.Y.C., 1972—, N.Y. Inst. Tech., Old Westbury, 1968-72; vis. prof. Yeshiva U., 1986—, New Sch., N.Y., 1966-68, 1991—, Bar-Ilan U., Ramat-Gan, Israel, summer, 1966-68. Author: Israel Zangwill: A study, 1964, Frank O'Connor: An Introduction, 1977; editor: The King of Schnorrers, 1964, History, Religion and Spiritual Democracy, 1980, The Great Hatred, 1988. NEH rsch. grantee, 1980; Creative Writing fellow Va. Ctr. for the Creative Arts, 1982, Meml. Found., 1982-83. Mem. MLA, New Eng. MLA, James Joyce Soc., Am. Coun. for Irish Studies. Home: 181 E 73rd St New York NY 10021-3514

WOHLSTEIN, SCOTT DAVID, corporate executive; b. Cleve., Dec. 12, 1963; s. Richard Ivon and Barbara Joan (Cirin) W. AAS, Camden County Coll., Blackwood, N.J., 1983; BS, SUNY, N.Y.C., 1992. Technician Transistor Devices, Inc., Dover, N.J., 1983-85; sr. engring. technician UNC Inc., Naval Products, Uncasville, Conn., 1985-89; photonics specialist SD Labs., inc., Convent Station, N.J., 1980—, pres., 1980—. Consulting editor: Measurements and Controls, 1990—; author: (textbook) Lasers: A Practical Guide, 1992; contbr. articles to profl. jours. and textbooks. Selected to attend Accelerated Physics, Astronomy and Laser Sci. Workshop, Ball State U., 1980. Mem. Am. Inst. Physics, Optical Soc., Am., Laser Inst. Am., Internat. Soc. Optical Engring., N.Y. Acad. Scis.

WOLCOTT, DAVID RITTENHOUSE, state official; b. Mt. Holly, N.J., Dec. 17, 1949; s. John and Margaret (Pearce) W.; m. Caroline Elizabeth Leising, July 16, 1983. AB, Dartmouth Coll., 1978. Project assoc. Syracuse (N.Y.) Rsch. Corp., 1978; project mgr. Internat. Bus. Svcs., Inc., Washington, 1978-81; sr. project mgr. N.Y. State Energy R & D Authority, Albany, 1981—, dir. integrated resources rsch. program, 1989—; adv. bd. Nat. Assn. Energy Svc. Cos. 1984—, chmn., 1984-85; pres. bd. trustees Demand-Side Mgmt. Tng. Inst., 1991—; tech. adv. com. N.Y. State Inst. in Superconductivity, 1988-90; speaker in field. Contbr. articles to tech. jours. Recipient spl. recognition U.S. Dept. Energy, 1984, 86, nat. award Coun. State Govts., 1986. Mem. Am. Solar Energy Soc., Assn. Energy Engrs., Assn. Demand-Side Mgmt. Profls., Appalachian Mountain Club (Boston). Office: NY State Energy R&D Auth Two Rockefeller Pl Albany NY 12223

WOLD, PATRICIA NEELY, psychiatrist; b. Lincoln, Nebr., Jan. 1, 1927; d. John Marshall and Edna (Perry) Neely; m. Aaron Wold; children: Marshall, Leo, Miriam. BA, U. Nebr., 1948, MD, 1952. Intern E.J. Meyer Meml. Hosp., Buffalo; resident in psychiatry Mass. Mental Health Ctr., Boston, 1953-55, chief svcs., 1955-56, mem. staff, 1955-56; mem. staff Southard Clinic, Boston, 1956-57, R.I. Mental Hygiene, Providence, 1963-65; med. dir. Farley Community Mental Health Ctr., East Providence, 1965-80; pvt. practice psychiatry Providence, 1965—. Mem. Am. Psychiat. Assn., R.I. Med. Soc., R.I. Med. Women's Assn., R.I. Psychiat. Assn. Office: 355 Thayer St Providence RI 02906-1589

WOLF, ALICE K., city councillor; b. Vienna, Austria, Dec. 24, 1933; d. Frederick Koerner and Renee (Engel) K.; m. Robert A. Wolf, 1955; children: Eric Jeffrey, Adam Nathaniel. BS, Simmons Coll., 1955; MPA, Harvard U., 1978. Residence staff MIT, Lincoln Lab, 1955-62; residence staff Computer Corp Am., 1967-71, pers. dir., 1971-76; mem. Cambridge Sch. Com., 1974-81, vicechairwoman, 1976-77, 80-81; chairwoman Ward 7 Dem. Com., 1976-85; committeewoman Mass. State Dem. Com.; former vice-mayor City of Cambridge, Mass., mayor, 1990-91. Del. Dem. Nat. Conv., 1980, 88, 92, State Conv., 1979, 81, 83, 85, 87, 89. Mem. NOW, Mass. Women's Polit. Caucas Cambridge Mental Health Assn., Am. for Dem. Action, Nat. Orgn. Women Am. Civil Liberties Union, Nat. Office: 795 Massachusetts Ave Cambridge MA 02139-3219

WOLF, BARBARA ANNE, research administrator, biologist; b. N.Y.C., July 24, 1947; d. Boris and Molly (Gruberg) W.; B.A. magna cum laude (N.Y. State Regents scholar, Stanley Koncal award 1968), Queens Coll., City U. N.Y., 1968; Ph.D. in Biology, M.I.T., 1973; m. Robert Stanley Spiel, Aug. 25, 1973; children—Melissa Heather, Seth Brandon. Research asst. chem. synthesis Sloan-Kettering Inst. for Cancer Research, Rye, N.Y., 1967; teaching asst. cell biology M.I.T., Cambridge, 1969-70, supr. grad seminars, 1972-73; research asst. virology Rockefeller U., N.Y.C., 1973-75, fellow Nat. Cancer Inst., 1975-77, research assoc., oncological studies, summer, 1977; mgr. biol. services Revlon Research Center, Bronx, N.Y., 1977-80, dir. biol. svcs., 1981-87, dir. cosmetic rsch., 1987—; assoc. prof. Coll. Pharmacy St. John's U., Queens, N.Y., 1981. Mem. Am. Soc. Microbiologists, Soc. Toxicology, Am. Coll. Toxicology, Soc. Invest Dermatology, Soc. of Cosmetic Chemists, Genetic Toxicology Assn., Environ. Mutagen Soc., AAAS, N.Y. Acad. Scis., Sigma Xi, Phi Beta Kappa, Beta Delta Chi. Contbr. articles on cell biology and oncology to sci. jours.; patentee in field. Office: 2121 State Rt 27 Edison NJ 08817-3370

WOLF, BRIAN GEORGE, paramedic, emergency preparedness consultant; b. Hershey, Pa., Oct. 4, 1962; s. George Lamar and Pearl Rebecca (Deppen) W. Paramedic cert., Davenport Coll., 1981; student, Harrisburg Area Community Coll., 1986—. Cert. Pa. EMT. Instr. Harrisburg (Pa.) Inst. Emergency Med. Services, 1983-88; paramedic Community Gen. Osteopathic Hosp., Harrisburg, Pa., 1983-88; emergency preparedness consultant SE Techs., Harrisburg, 1987-; adminstrv. internship Emergency Health Services Fedn., Lemoyne, Pa., 1987—, York-Adams Emergency Med. Resource Ctr., York, Pa., 1987—. Mem. Pa. Paramedic Assn., Emergency Health Services Fedn. Republican. Home: PO Box 92 Campbelltown PA 17010-0092

WOLF, CAROL EUWEMA, computer science educator; b. New Castle, Pa., June 11, 1936; d. Ben and Catherine (Michmerhuizen) Euwema; m. Edward Lincoln Wolf, June 15, 1958. BA, Swarthmore (Pa.) Coll., 1958; MA, Cornell U., 1962, PhD, 1964. Asst. prof. SUNY, Brockport, 1968-75; adj. asst. prof. Iowa State U., Ames, 1975-86; assoc. prof. Pace U., N.Y.C., 1986—, chmn. computer sci., 1988—. Mem. Assn. for Computing Machinery, IEEE Computer Soc., N.Y. Acad. Scis., Math. Assn. Am., Assn. for Women in Math., Upsilon Pi Epsilon. Home: 34 Plaza St E Apt 607 Brooklyn NY 11238-5058 Office: Pace U Computer Sci Dept Pace Pla New York NY 10038

WOLF, DALE EDWARD, state official; b. Kearney, Nebr., Sept. 6, 1924; s. Harry E. and Mabel Irene (Moss) W.; m. Clarice Elaine Marshall, Dec. 31, 1945; children: Janet Lynn, Glenda Elaine, Thomas Marshall, James Dale. BSc, U. Nebr., 1945; PhD in Agronomy and Weed Control, Rutgers U., 1949. With Dept. Agr., 1946; assoc. prof. agronomy Rutgers U., 1949; with E.I. duPont de Nemours & Co., Inc., from 1950, dir. agrichem. mktg., then gen. mgr. biochem. dept., 1972-79; v.p. biochems., also chmn. bd. subs. Endo Labs., Inc., Wilmington, Del., from 1979; group v.p. Agrl. Products, Wilmington, Del., from 1983; dir. Del. Devel. Office, Dover, 1987-89; lt. gov. of Del. Dover, 1989—. Co-author: Principles of Weed Control, 1951. Bd. dirs. Del. chpt. ARC, 1975; gen. campaign chmn. United Way Del., 1978, also bd. dirs.; gen. campaign chmn. Girls Club Del., 1987. Served to 1st. lt. AUS, 1943-46. Decorated Bronze Star, Purple Heart. Mem. Nat. Agrl. Chem. Assn. (chmn. 1981-83), Pharm. Mfrs. Assn. (dir.), Sigma Xi, Alpha Zeta. Lutheran. Club: Masons. Office: Office of Lt Gov Legis Hall Dover DE 19901

WOLF, ERICK GUENTHER, pharmaceutical company executive; b. Cin., Nov. 9, 1953; s. P.C. and Amalie (Weiss) W.; m. Arliss Ridgway, May 15, 1982; children: Kyle, Natalie, Daniella. BS, Pa. State U., 1977, MBA, 1979. Sales rep. Am. Cyanamid Co., Wayne, N.J., 1979-81, product mgr., 1981-83; product mgr. Am. Hosp. Supply, Irvine, Calif., 1983-85; bus. mgr. Cyanmid Internat., Munich, 1985-89; dir. ops. Cyanmid Internat., Wayne, 1990—; v.p. A.A. Wolf & Assocs., Laguna Beach, Calif., 1983-85. Office: Cyanamid Internat 1 Cyanamid Pla Wayne NJ 07470

WOLF, EVAN WILLIAMS, management consultant; b. Logan, Ohio, Jan. 2, 1947; s. Joseph Thomas Wolf and Inez Elaine (McKiddie) Cogswell; m. Trudy Lynn Schmidt, Sept. 6, 1969 (div. Jan. 1981). BS in Chemistry, Cleve. State U., 1970; MBA in Gen. Mgmt., Rutgers U., 1980. Plant chemist Jamestown (N.Y.) Electro Plating Works, 1971-73; quality assurance supr. Johnson & Johnson Baby Products Co., Park Forest, Ill., 1973-76; quality assurance mgr. Johnson & Johnson Baby Products Co., Skillman, N.J., 1976-78; sr. tech. svc. scientist Surgikos, Inc., Piscataway, N.J., 1978-79; sr. buyer Surgikos, Inc., Arlington, Tex., 1979-85; dir. quality GP Plastics, Inc., Dallas, 1985-86, Omega Optical Co., Dallas, 1986-87; mgmt. cons. Chimitt Gilman Homchick, Inc., Radnor, Pa., 1987—; quality cons. Omega Optical, Dallas, 1987. Lt. U.S. Army, 1970-76. Mem. Soc. for Advancement of Mgmt. (pres. 1986-87), MENSA (regional coord. 1978-79), Am. Legion. Home: 402 Bradshaw St Cedar Hill TX 75104-1981 Office: Chimitt Gilman Homchick Inc 1111 W Dekalb Pike Ste 101 Wayne PA 19087-2179

WOLF, HARRY, utilities company executive; b. Newton, Mass., Oct. 18, 1947; s. Bernard and Ann (Elkins) W.; m. Carol Ruth Bloom, May 17, 1987. BSEE, Carnegie Mellon U., 1969; MSEE, Northea. U., Boston, Mass., 1974; MBA, MIT, 1978. Engr. Raytheon Co., Bedford, Mass., 1969-77; assoc., treas. J. Makowski Assocs., Inc., Boston, 1978-85; treas. Essex Power Svcs., Inc., Boston, 1985—; also bd. dirs.; bd. dirs. Merrimack Valley Energy Inc., Essex Devel. Assocs., Inc. Pres. Pepper Hill Estates Condominium Trust, Winchester, Mass., 1987—. Home: 38 Edward Dr Winchester MA 01890-3601 Office: Essex Power Svcs Inc 1 State St Boston MA 02109-3507

WOLF, JAMES RICHARD, association executive, lawyer; b. N.Y.C., Apr. 17, 1930; s. Rudolf and Janet Natalie (Selig) W. BA, Yale U., 1952, JD, 1956. Bar: N.Y., 1957, Pa., 1975. Atty. U.S. Atomic Energy Commn., Washington, 1956-59; assoc. dir. atomic energy law rsch. project U. Mich. Law Sch., Ann Arbor, 1959-60; v.p., sec. Nuclear Sci. & Engring. Corp., Pitts., 1960-67; univ. counsel U. Pitts., 1967-75; atty. U.S. Nuclear Regulatory Commn., Rockville, Md., 1976—; dir. Continental Divide Trail Soc., Bethesda, Md., 1978—; mem. Continental Divide Nat. Scenic Trail Adv. Coun., Denver, 1980-86. Author: (5 book series) Guide to the Continental Divide Trail, 1976-91; author (essay) Annals of Wyo., 1988, 91. Pres. Audubon Soc. Western Pa., Pitts., 1967-69. With USN, 1952. Recipient Fulbright scholarship, 1952-53. Home: 10201 Grosvenor Pl # 510 Rockville MD 20852 Office: Continental Divide Trail Soc PO Box 30002 Bethesda MD 20824

WOLF, LEWIS ISIDORE, lawyer; b. Bklyn., June 8, 1933; s. Ephraim and Rachel (Dunajevsky) W.; m. Ruth Ullmann; children: Sara S., Joseph J. BA, Bklyn. Coll., 1954; JD cum laude, Bklyn. Law Sch., 1957; LLM, NYU, 1967. Bar: N.Y. 1958, U.S. Dist. Ct. (so. and ea. dists.) N.Y. 1961, U.S. Ct. Appeals (2d cir.) 1964, U.S. Supreme Ct. 1964. Pvt. practice law, N.Y.C., 1958—; atty. and mng. atty. Cosmopolitan Mut. Ins. Co., 1958-77, atty. of record, 1977-81; mem. firm Smith, Mazure, Director & Wilkins, P.C., N.Y.C., 1981—; arbitrator N.Y. County Civil Ct. With Army NG, 1957-63. Mem. ABA, N.Y. State Bar Assn., N.Y. County Lawyers Assn., Am. Arbitration Assn. (arbitrator accident claims tribunal). Office: 111 John St New York NY 10038-3001

WOLF, REVA JUNE, art historian; b. Denver, June 17, 1956; d. Abraham and Ruth (Smith) W. BA summa cum laude, Brandeis U., 1978; MA, NYU, 1981, PhD, 1987. Gallery lectr., course instr. Mus. Modern Art, N.Y.C., 1984-88; lectr. SUNY, Purchase, 1987-88; asst. prof. fine arts Boston Coll., Chestnut Hill, Mass., 1988—; Mellon Faculty Fellow Harvard U., Cambridge, Mass., 1990-91; vis. fellow Yale Ctr. for Brit. Art, New Haven, 1989. Author: (book/exhibit/catalogue) Goya and the Satirical Print, 1991 (NEA grant 1990-91); contbr. articles, essays, books revs. to profl. publs. Recipient faculty rsch. incentive grant Boston Coll., 1989, J. Clawson Mills fellowship Met. Mus. Art, N.Y.C., 1985-86. Mem. MLA, Am. Soc. Eighteenth Century Studies, Am. Soc. Hispanic Art Hist. Studies, Coll. Art Assn. Am. Office: Fine Arts Dept/Boston Coll 885 Centre St Newton MA 02159-1164

WOLF, ROBERT FARKAS, systems avionics company executive, environmental planning consultant; b. N.Y.C., Feb. 19, 1932; s. Desidar Farkas and Christina (Hodosy) Wolf; m. Victoire M. Cullerot, Oct. 8, 1960. BS in Liberal Studies, SUNY, Albany, 1981; MBA in Econs., Rivier Coll., Nashua, N.H., 1987. Engring. designer Mpls. Honeywell Co., Manchester, N.H., 1956-63; design engr. Sanders Assocs., Nashua, 1963-79; systems analyst Kollsman Instruments Co., Merrimack, N.H., 1979—. Bd. dirs. Webster House Children's Home, Manchester, 1975-80; chmn. Mont Vernon (N.H.) Planning Bd., 1981—, N.H. Regional Planning Commn., Nashua, 1984—. Mem. Nat. Assn. Regional Couns., N.H. Planners Assn. Republican. Home: 15 S Main St Mont Vernon NH 03057 Office: Kollsman Co 220 Daniel Webster Hwy Merrimack NH 03054-4844

WOLF, STUART ALAN, physicist; b. Bklyn., Sept. 15, 1943; s. Irving and Evelyn (Kaiser) W.; m. Iris Tabachnick, June 26, 1965; children: Alyssa Robin, Dori Ilana. AB, Columbia Coll., N.Y.C., 1964; MS, Rutgers U., 1966, PhD, 1969. Rsch. assoc. Case Western Res. U., Cleve., 1969-72; rsch. physicist Naval Rsch. Lab., Washington, 1972-81, supervisory rsch. physicist, 1982—; vis. scholar UCLA, 1981-82; chmn. materials subcom. Applied Superconductivity Conf., 1990. Editor Jour. Superconductivity, 1987—, Novel Superconductivity, 1987, Percolation, Localization and Superconductivity, 1983, Inhomogeneous Superconductivity, 1979; author: Fundamentals of Superconductivity, 1990. Pres. Chelsea Woods Owners Soc., Greenbelt, Mo., 1985-86. Recipient Meritorious Civilian Svc. award USN., 1984. Fellow Am. Phys. Soc. (divisional councillor condensed matter div. 1992); mem. AIME, Sigma Xi. Jewish. Home: 13303 Katrinka Dr Bowie MD 20720-4734 Office: Naval Rsch Lab 4555 Overlook Ave SW Washington DC 20375-5000

WOLF, THOMAS WALTER, marketing professional; b. Bklyn., Oct. 12, 1954; s. Gerhard O. and Norma Ann (Hofacker) W.; m. Barbara J. Kahrs, July 19, 1980; children: Matthew Carl, Daniel Peter. BS in Acctg., Susquehanne U., 1976; MS in Acctg., L.I. U., 1979. Owner Printronix, Bklyn., 1977; tax acct. Jaffe & Waxberg, Bklyn., 1977-78; budget analyst Hearst Mags., N.Y.C., 1977-79, asst. acctg. mgr., 1979-80, bus. mgr., 1980-81, exec. asst. v.p., 1982-85, pub., 1985-89, gen. mgr. new products devel., 1989-91, gen. mgr. mag. devel., 1992—. Tribute com. co-chmn. Inner-City Scholarship Fund, N.Y.C., 1987; mem. Nat. Trust for Hist. Preservation, Whitney Mus. of Am. Art, Smithsonian Assocs. Mem. Internat. Furnishing and Design Assn., N.Y. Athletic Club. Office: Hearst Mags 959 8th Ave # 411 New York NY 10019-3737

WOLF, TIMOTHY GRIFFING, lawyer; b. Balt., July 22, 1946; s. G. Van Velsor and Alice Roberts (Kimberly) W.; m. Veronica Marie Clarke, Apr. 28, 1984; 1 child, Zachary Clarke. BA, Columbia U., 1974; JD with honors, U. Md., Balt., 1982. Bar: Md. 1982, D.C. 1983. Assoc. Hyatt & Rhodes, Washington, 1982-83; sr. asst. state's atty. for Howard County, Md. State's Atty.'s Office, Ellicott City, Md., 1983-92; pvt. practice law Ellicott City, Md., 1992—. Pres. bd. dirs. Handel Choir Balt., 1990—. With U.S. Army, 1967-70. Mem. ABA, Md. Bar Assn., Howard County Bar Assn., Phi Beta Kappa. Democrat. Episcopalian. Office: Office of State's Atty 9050 A Frederick Rd Ellicott City MD 21042

WOLF, WAYNE HENDRIX, electrical engineering educator; b. Washington, Aug. 12, 1958; s. Jesse David and Carolyn Josephine (Cunningham) W.; m. Nancy Jane Porter, Aug. 12, 1989. BS with distinction, Stanford U., 1980, MS, 1981, PhD, 1984. Lectr. Stanford (Calif.) U., 1984; staff mem. AT&T Bell Labs., Murray Hill, N.J., 1984-89; asst. prof. elec. engring. Princeton (N.J.) U., 1989—. Co-editor: High-Level VLSI Synthesis, 1991; contbr. Physical Design Automation of VLSI Systems, 1989. Mem. IEEE, Assn. Computing Machinery, Phi Beta Kappa, Tau Beta Pi. Office: Princeton U Dept Elec Engring Princeton NJ 08544

WOLF, WILLIAM MARTIN, computer company executive, consultant; b. Watertown, N.Y., Aug. 29, 1928; s. John and Rose (Emrich) W.; m. Eileen Marie Jolly, Aug. 19, 1952 (div. 1974); children: Rose, Sylvia, William. BS, St. Lawrence U., 1950; MS, U. N.H., 1951; postgrad., U. Pa., 1951-52, MIT, 1952-55. Programmer digital computer lab. MIT, Cambridge, Mass., 1952-54; pres. Wolf R & D Corp., Boston, 1954-69, Wolf Computer Corp., Boston, 1969-76, Planning Systems Internat., Boston, 1976-81, Micro Computer Software Inc., Cambridge, 1981-88, Tech. Acquisition Corp., Boston, 1989-91, Planning Internat., Inc., Boston, 1989-91, Wolfsort Corp., Boston, 1989—; co-founder, pres. Assn. Ind. Software Cos., Washington, 1965-67, Design Sci. Inst., Phila., 1969-73, Nat. Coun. Profl. Svc. Firms, Washington, 1970-75; seminar leader MIT Sloan Sch., Cambridge, 1970; co-founder, bd. dirs. Harbor Nat. Bank, Boston. Author computer program; inventor management system, orbit calculator, sorting method. Co-founder X-10 Orgn., Boston, 1962; trustee Addison Gilbert Hosp., Gloucester, Mass., 1963; v.p. Young Pres. Orgn., Boston, 1970; overseer Mus. Sci., Boston, 1989—; mem. Computer Mus. Named Outstanding Young Man in Boston, Jaycees, 1982; recipient Speaker's award Data Processing Mgmt. Assn., 1966. Mem. World Bus. Coun., MIT Club (Alumni award 1991), Boston Computer Soc., Forty-Niners. Office: Wolfsort Corp 1 Longfellow Pl Apt 3123 Boston MA 02114-2429

WOLFE, ALLAN, physicist; b. Bklyn., Dec. 19, 1942; s. Isidor Irving and Florence (Rosenfeld) W.; m. Marta Elias Boneta, Dec. 30, 1967; 1 child, Daniel Duchaune. BS, Poly. Inst. Bklyn., 1964; MS, U. N.H., 1969, PhD, 1971. Physics chmn. Nasson Coll., Springvale, Maine, 1973-74; prof. physics N.Y.C. Tech. Coll., Bklyn., 1974—; physicist, visitor AT&T Bell Labs., Murray Hill, N.J., 1977—; physics researcher U. L'Aquila, Italy, 1989, Indian Inst. Sci., Bangalore, India, 1990, Japan Soc. Promotion Sci., Tokyo, 1990. Contbr. articles to profl. jours. Office: NYC Tech Coll 300 Jay St # 812N Brooklyn NY 11201-2902

WOLFE, HARVEY EDWARD, rehabilitation consultant; b. Lebanon, Pa., Dec. 10, 1924; s. Harvey Edward and Edna Emma (Swanger) W.; m. Mary Elizabeth Moyer, Aug. 6, 1946. BS, Xavier U., 1949, MEd, 1951; postgrad. in rehab. counseling, Columbia U., Boston U. and U. So. Ill., 1958-59; ScD (hon.), Cen. Christian, 1965. State rehab. svcs. State of Ohio, 1952-61; program cons. Am. Found. for Blind, APHA, Arthritis Found., Ministry Def., Saudi Arabia, 1961-75; sr. assoc. Greenleigh Assocs., Inc., N.Y.C., 1966-81; cons. Forest Hills, N.Y., 1981—; cons. to fed. and state agys., 1962—; mem. rev. panel Applied Rsch. Grants, U.S. Dept. Edn., Grants for Surveys of Facilities for Handicapped; lectr. Xavier U., Cin., 1956-61. Contbr. articles to profl. jours. Project dir. Internat. Survey, Sheltered Employment, Easter Seal Found., World Commn. Vocat. Rehab., U.S. Rehab. Svc. Adminstrn., Internat. Prosthetics Info. Svc., Youth Health Risk Factors, CDC, 1964-80. Fellow Royal Soc. of Health. Home & Office: 104-40 Queens Blvd # 16T Flushing NY 11375-6147

WOLFE, J. MATTHEW, lawyer; b. Pitts., Mar. 29, 1956; s. James Michael and Mary Evangeline (Andrews) W.; m. Deborah Ann Smith, Oct. 2, 1982; children: James M., Ross M. BA, U. Pa., 1978; JD, Villanova U., 1981. Bar: Pa. 1981, U.S. Dist. Ct. (ea. dist.) Pa. 1985, U.S. Ct. Appeals (3rd cir.) 1985. Atty. Community Legal Svcs., Phila., 1979-80; pvt. practice Phila., 1981-82, 89—; asst. counsel Pa. Dept. of Transp., Phila, 1983-86; spl. prosecutor various counties Pa., 1984-86; spl. asst. dist. atty. Berks County, Reading, Pa., 1984-86; dep. atty. gen. Commonwealth of Pa., Phila., 1986-89; spl. asst. dist. atty. Phila., 1991—; gen. counsel Univ. Bus. Machines, Inc., Upper Darby, Pa.; instr. Pa. Bar Inst., Harrisburg, 1984. Assoc. editor The Docket newspaper, 1980-81; contbr. articles to The Trumpet newspaper, 1981—. Leader 27th Ward Rep. Com., Phila., 1979—; bd. dirs. Univ. City Town Watch, 1983-85, Spruce Hill Community Assn., Phila., 1980—; chmn. Univ. City Rep. Com., 1990—; mem. Sch. Bd. Task Force on Scholastics and Sports, Phila., 1986—, Cedar Park Neighbors, 1986—; mem. neighborhood adv. coun. 18th Police Dist., Phila., 1987—; vice chmn. Woodland Dist. Phila. coun. Boy Scouts Am., 1989-91. Mem. ABA, Pa. Bar Assn., West Phila. C. of C. (bd. dirs. 1989—), Pi Sigma Alpha, Phi Delta Theta (editor Phi Oracle newsletter). Roman Catholic. Home: 4256 Regent Sq Philadelphia PA 19104-4439 Office: 4529 Baltimore Ave Philadelphia PA 19143-2192

WOLFE, JAMES RONALD, lawyer; b. Pitts., Dec. 10, 1932; s. James Thaddeus and Helen Matilda (Corey) W.; m. Anne Lisbeth Dahle Eriksen, May 28, 1960; children: Ronald, Christopher, Geoffrey. B.A. summa cum laude, Duquesne U., 1954; LL.B. cum laude, NYU, 1959. Bar: N.Y. 1959. Assoc. Simpson Thacher & Bartlett, N.Y.C., 1959-69, ptnr., 1969—. Co-editor: West's McKinney's Forms, Uniform Commercial Code, 1965. Served to 1st lt. U.S. Army, 1955-57. Mem. ABA, N.Y. State Bar Assn., Assn. of Bar of City of N.Y., Am. Judicature Soc., N.Y. Law Inst. Republican. Roman Catholic. Home: 641 King St Chappaqua NY 10514-3807 Office: Simpson Thacher & Bartlett 425 Lexington Ave New York NY 10017-3903

WOLFE, JAMES WILLARD, company executive; b. Decatur, Ill., Aug. 7, 1955; s. Dudley Anderson and Barbara (Lampe) W.; m. Bonnie Heineman, Apr. 14, 1984. BS, Ind. U., 1977, MBA, 1979, JD, 1981. Legis. dir. Sen. Dan Quayle, Washington, 1981-83; corp. counsel Finalco Capital Corp., McLean, Va., 1983-85; dir. New Venture Devel. Corp., Washington, 1985-87, v.p., 1989—; v.p. Ind. U. Found., Bloomington, 1987-89; dir Nat. Entrepreneurship Found., Indpls., 1988—, Nat. Supercomputing Found., Washington, 1985-89; guest lectr. Ind. Exec. Program, Washington, 1982, Nat. Entrepreneurship Acad., 1987—; lectr. on fed. govt. procurement Cert. Auctioneers Inst., 1988—; pres. The Georgetown Bus. Ctr., Washington, 1985-87; dir. New Venture Devel. Corp., VentureLease, Inc., Bloomington, Ind., Bristol Capital Mgmt., Inc., N.Y.C.; pres., dir. Interlink Ent., Inc., 1989—; cons. in field. Trustee Ind. U., 1977-79; counselor NIH Adv. Rsch. Resources Coun., Washington, 1987—. Mem. ABA, Ind. Bar Assn., U.S. Tax Ct. Bar Assn., Nat. Assn. of Coll. and Univ. Bus. Officers, Coun. for Advancement and Support of Edn., Nat. Bus. Incubation Assn. (founding dir.), Sigma Phi Epsilon, University Club of Bloomington, Skyline Club of Indpls. Republican. Presbyterian. Home: 210 N Oakland St Arlington VA 22203 Office: New Venture Devel Corp 733 15th St NW Washington DC 20005

WOLFE, JEAN ELIZABETH, medical illustrator; b. Newark, N.J., Oct. 3, 1925; d. Arthur Howard and Ethel (Harper) Wolfe; B.S., Russell Sage Coll., 1947; student Pratt Inst., 1949-50; diploma U. Rochester Sch. Medicine and Dentistry, 1955; postgrad. (W.B. Saunders fellow), U. Pa., 1955-56, U. Pa., 1980; M.F.A., U. Pa., 1973, M.A. (hon.), 1973. Exhibitor, Pratt Inst. Galleries, Bklyn., 1958, N.Y. Med. Coll., 1958, Assn. Med. Illustrators, 1961-86, 90, AMA, N.Y.C., 1965, Phila., 1965, A.C.S., Atlantic City, 1965, Rsch. Study Club L.A., 1966, Phila. Art Alliance, 1967, 73, U. Pa. Ophthal. Soc., 1967-68, N.J. Med. Soc., 1968, Cayuga Mus. History and Art, 1968, Pensacola Art Ctr., 1969, FAA Aero. Center, Oklahoma City, 1970, Scheie Eye Inst., 1972-75, Assn. Med. Illustrators Traveling Salon, 1978, Moore Coll. Art, 1985, Mus. of Am. Illustration Soc. of Illustrators, 1986, Mutter Mus., Phila. Coll. of Physicians, 1990—, Axis Gallery, Phila., 1992; represented in permanent collections Archives of Med. Visual Resources, Francis A. Countway-Harvard Med. Library, Boston, Mutter Mus., Phila. Coll. Physicians, comprehensive collection of major work donated by Scheie Eye Inst., life history and momentos housed in The Arthur and Elizabeth Schlesinger Libr. on the History of Women in Am., Radcliffe Coll.; contbg. illustrator Adler's Textbook Ophthalmology, 8th edit., 1969; illustrations in med. books, jours., pharm. house pubs.; instr. Pembroke Coll. Brown U., 1947-49; mem. faculty Kimberley Sch., Upper Montclair, N.J., 1950-52; free lance med. illustration Studio N.Y. Med. Coll., 1956-60; instr. Pratt Inst., 1958-59; assoc. in med. illustration U. Pa. Sch. Medicine, 1960-72, research asst. prof. med. art in ophthalmology, 1972-85; independent studio (fine art) painting and medical illustration, 1985—; guest lectr. Johns Hopkins Med. Sch., 1973, NIH; guest artist USAF, Air Force Acad. and NORAD, 1971. Recipient Merit certificate AMA; Appreciation certificate ACS; 1st prize Pensacola Art Center, Am. Heart Assn., 1969, Gold medal Graphic Arts Soc. of Del. Valley, 1973. Fellow Assn. Med. Illustrators (emeritus); mem. Phila. Art Alliance, Assn. Med. Illustrators (Ralph Sweet, Tom Jones awards, gov. 1970—, chmn. nominating com. 1972-73, vice chmn. bd. govs. 1973-74, chmn. bd. 1974-75, nominating com., Lifetime Achievement award 1989—, adv. coun. Vesalius Trust 1990—), Soc. Illustrators (cert. merit 1986), Coll. Art Assn., Women's Caucus for Art.

WOLFE, JOEL WILLIAM, history educator; b. Phila., May 22, 1960; s. Donald Bernard and Barbara Jane (Greenberg) W. BS in Fgn. Svc., Georgetown U., 1982; MA in Latin Am. Studies, U. N.Mex., Albuquerque, 1984; PhD in History, U. Wis., 1990. Asst. prof. Williams Coll., Williamstown, Mass., 1989—. Campaign aide Dem. Party, N.Mex., 1982. Mellon Found. fellow, 1983, Tinker Found. fellow, 1985, U.S. Dept. of Edn. fellow, 1984-86, Fulbright-Hays fellow, 1986-87. Mem. Am. Hist. Assn., Latin-Am. States Assn. Jewish. Office: Williams Coll Dept of History Williamstown MA 01267

WOLFE, RAYMOND, physicist, researcher; b. Hamilton, Ontario, Canada, Apr. 8, 1927; came to U.S. 1950; s. William and Ethel (Starkman) W.; m. Ursula Kaufmann, Mar. 26, 1954; children: Jeremy M., Nicola Wolfe Tuchow, Jacqueline Wolfe Pierce. BA, U. Toronto, 1949, MA, 1950; PhD, U. Bristol, Bristol, England, 1955. Physicist Kodak Rsch. Labs., Rochester, N.Y., 1950-52, General Electric Co. Rsch., Wembley, England, 1954-57, AT&T Bell Labs., Murray Hill, N.J., 1957--. Editor Applied Solid State Science, 1969-85; contrib. articles to jours. Fellow Am. Phys. Soc. Home: 21 Walker Dr Nw Providence NJ 07974-1742 Office: AT&T Bell Labs Murray Hill NJ 07974

WOLFE, RUSSELL SIMMONS, JR., management consultant; b. Orangeburg, S.C., Sept. 2, 1952; s. Russell Simmons and Myrtle (Huntley) W.; m. Diana Fae Rariden, Sept. 6, 1986. BS in Gen. Engring., U.S. Mil. Acad., West Point, N.Y., 1974; MBA, Vanderbilt U., 1986. Sr. engr. Westinghouse Electric Corp., Idaho Falls, Idaho, 1979-82; project mgr. Energy Consultants, Inc., Harrisburg, Pa., 1982-84; mgr. MIS and credit Am. Tea and Coffee Co., Inc., Nashville, Pa., 1986-88; project mgr. EG&G Svcs., Inc., Idaho Falls, 1988—. Capt. U.S. Army, 1974-79. Recipient Jones scholarship Vanderbilt U., Nashville, 1984, 85. Mem. Beta Gamma Sigma. Republican. Home and Office: 16 Pheasant Run Ln Stratham NH 03885-2268

WOLFE, THOMAS KENNERLY, JR., writer, journalist; b. Richmond, Va., Mar. 2, 1931; s. Thomas Kennerly and Helen (Hughes) W.; m. Sheila Wolfe; children—Alexandra, Thomas. AB, Washington and Lee U., 1951, LittD (hon.), 1974; PhD in Am. Studies, Yale U., 1957; DFA (hon.), Mpls. Coll. Art, 1971; LHD (hon.), Va. Commonwealth U., 1983, Southampton Coll. (N.Y.), 1984, Longwood Coll., 1989; LittD (hon.), St. Andrews Presbyn. Coll., 1990. Reporter Springfield (Mass.) Union, 1956-59; reporter, Latin Am. corr. Washington Post, 1959-62; reporter, mag. writer N.Y. Herald Tribune, 1962-66; mag. writer N.Y. World Jour. Tribune, 1966-67; contbg. editor New York mag., 1968-76, Esquire Mag., from 1977. Contbg. artist: Harper's Mag, 1978-81; exhibited one-man show of drawings, Maynard Walker Gallery, N.Y.C., 1965, Tunnel Gallery, N.Y.C., 1974; Author: The Kandy-Kolored Tangerine-Flake Streamline Baby, 1965, The Electric Kool-Aid Acid Test, 1968, The Pump House Gang, 1968, Radical Chic and Mau-mauing the Flak Catchers, 1970, The New Journalism, 1973, The Painted Word, 1975, Mauve Gloves and Madmen, Clutter and Vine, 1976, The Right Stuff, 1979, In Our Time, 1980, From Bauhaus to Our House, 1981, The Purple Decades: A Reader, 1982, The Bonfire of the Vanities, 1987; contbr. articles to Esquire Mag; others. Recipient Front Page awards for humor and fgn. news reporting Washington Newspaper Guild, 1961; award of excellence Soc. Mag. Writers, 1970; Frank Luther Mott Rsch. award, 1973; Va. laureate for lit., 1977; Harold D. Vursell Meml. award Am. Acad. and Inst. Arts and Letters, 1980; Am. Book award for gen. nonfiction, 1980; Columbia Journalism award, 1980; citation for art history Nat. Sculpture Soc., 1980; John Dos Passos award, 1984; Gari Melchers Medal, 1986, Benjamin Pierce Cheney Medal Ea. Wash. U., 1986, Washington Irving Medal St. Nicholas Soc., 1986, Theodore Roosevelt medal Theodore Roosevelt Assn., 1990, Wilbur Cross medal Yale Grad. Sch. Alumni Assn., 1990. Office: care Farrar Straus & Giroux Inc 19 Union Sq W New York NY 10003-3304*

WOLFENSBERGER, WOLF PEREGRINE JOACHIM, education educator; b. Mannheim, Germany, July 26, 1934; came to U.S., 1950; s. Friedrich and Helene (Löwit) W.; m. Nancy Artz, Feb. 13, 1960; children: Margaret, Joan, Paul. BA in Philosophy, Siena Coll., 1955; MA in Psychology, St. Louis U., 1957; PhD in Psychology and Spl. Edn., Peabody Coll., 1962. Staff psychologist Muscatatuck State Sch., Butlerville, Ind., 1958-59; dir. human devel. Greene Valley Hosp. and Sch., Greeneville, Tenn., 1960-62; dir. rsch. and tng. Plymouth State Home and Tng. Sch., Northville, Mich., 1963-64; asst. prof., then assoc. prof. Nebr. Psychiat. Inst., Omaha, 1964-71; vis. scholar Nat. Inst. on Mental Retardation, Toronto, Ont., Can., 1971-73; prof. spl. edn. Syracuse (N.Y.) U., 1973—, dir. Tng. Inst. Human Svc. Planning, Leadership & Change Agy, 1973—; cons. Nat. Inst. Mental Retardation, Toronto, 1973-86. Editor, author newsletter TIPS, 1981—; author books in field; contbr. articles to profl. publs. Co-founder, bd. dirs. Friends of L'Arche of Syracuse, 1974-90; founder, mem. various civic and svc. groups; Cath. worker Base Community of Unity Kitchen, 1979—. Recipient Jubilee Silver medallion Queen Elizabeth II of Eng., 1978. Fellow AAAS, Am. Assn. Mental Deficiency (life, Leadership award 1978); mem. Onondaga County Assn. Retarded Citizens, Greater Omaha Assn. Retarded Citizens (life), U.S. Chess Fedn. (expert), Grey Panthers, Sigma Xi. Home: 301 Scottholm Blvd Syracuse NY 13224-1731 Office: Syracuse U Tng Inst 805 S Crouse Ave Syracuse NY 13244-2280

WOLFENSOHN, JAMES DAVID, bank executive; b. Sydney, Australia, Dec. 1, 1933; naturalized, 1980.; s. Hyman and Dora (Weinbaum) W.; m. Elaine Ruth Botwinick, Nov. 26, 1961; children: Sara, Naomi, Adam. BA, U. Sydney, 1954, LLB, 1957; MBA, Harvard U., 1959. Bar: Supreme Ct. of Australia 1957. Ptnr. Ord Minnett (brokers), Australia, 1963-65; mng. dir. Darling & Co. (investment bankers), Australia, 1965-67, J. Henry Schroder Wagg, London, 1967-69; pres. J. Henry Schroder Banking Corp., N.Y.C., 1970-76; exec. dep. chmn., dir. Schroders Ltd., London; prin. exec. officer Schroder Group, London, 1974-77; gen. ptnr. Salomon Bros., N.Y.C., 1977-81; chmn. Salomon Bros. Internat., London, 1977-81; pres., owner James D. Wolfensohn, Inc., 1981—; chmn. Kennedy Ctr. for Performing Arts, N.Y.C., 1990—; vis. lectr. fin. U. New South Wales, 1963-66; bd. dirs. CBS Inc.; Continental Grain Co. Contbr. articles to profl. jours. Mem. Australian Olympic team, 1956; chmn. bd. dirs. John F. Kennedy Ctr. for the Performing Arts, Washington; bd. dirs. Met. Opera Assn., Joint Ctr. for Polit. Studies; trustee Rockefeller Found., 1979-85, Population Council, 1977-84; chmn., trustee Inst. for Advanced Study, Princeton, N.J.; hon. trustee Brookings Inst., 1991; trustee Rockefeller U., 1985—, Howard Hughes Med. Inst., 1987—; mem. bd. and steering com. Am. Friends of Bilderberg, Inc., 1985—; dir. Internat. Fedn. Multiple Sclerosis Socs.; chmn. emeritus Carnegie Hall, 1991. Served as aviator Royal Australian Air Force, 1954-60. Mem. Council on Fgn. Relations, Inc. Clubs: Century Assn., Harvard (N.Y.C.). Office: James D Wolfensohn Inc 599 Lexington Ave New York NY 10022-6030 also: John F Kennedy Ctr for the Performing Arts New Hampshire Ave & F St NW Washington DC 20566

WOLFERT, RUTH, Gestalt therapist; b. N.Y.C., Nov. 10, 1933; d. Ira and Helen (Herschdorfer) W. BS summa cum laude, Columbia U., 1967, post-grad., 1966-68. Pvt. practice N.Y.C., 1972—; dir. Action Groups, N.Y.C., 1974-76, Gestalt Groups, N.Y.C., 1976—; adv. faculty, mem. coordinating bd. Women's Interart Ctr., N.Y.C., 1971-75, also bd. dirs.; mem. faculty Inst. for Experiential Learning and Devel., 1988—, Woodstock U., 1989—, Gestalt Inst. Atlanta, 1989—; presenter Stockton (N.J.) State Coll., 1974-75; presenter in field. Contbg. author: (booklet) A Consumer's Guide to Non-Sexist Therapy, 1978. Mem. Assn. Humanistic Psychology (bd. dirs. ea. regional network 1981-87, pres. 1985-87), N.Y. Inst. Gestalt Therapy (trainer 1979—, chair workshops program 1979-83, co-chair conf. 1983-85, interim exec. com. 1988-90, conf. com. 1989-91, brochure com. 1987—), Assn. Transpersonal Psychology (co-chair N.Y. discussion group 1983-85), N.Y. Acad. Scis. Office: Gestalt Groups 161 E 91st St New York NY 10128-2436

WOLFF, EDWARD NATHAN, economics educator; b. Long Branch, N.J., Apr. 10, 1946; s. Arthur Seymour and Ethel (Kalmenoff) W.; m. Jane Zandra Forman, Nov. 27, 1977; children: Spencer, Ashley. BA, Harvard U., 1968; PhD, Yale U., 1974. Rsch. assoc. Nat. Bur. Econ. Rsch., N.Y.C., 1974-77; asst. prof. NYU, 1974-79, assoc. prof., 1979-84, prof., 1984—; mng. editor Rev. of Income and Wealth, 1987—; cons. UN, 1981-82, Com. Econ. Dev., N.Y.C., 1981-82, Inst. Rsch. Poverty, Madison, Wis., 1984-88, Inst. Social Rsch., Ann Arbor, Mich., 1982-85, Jerome Levy Econs. Inst., 1989-91. Author: Growth, Accumulation and Unproductive Activity, 1987; editor: International Comparisons of Household Wealth Distribution, 1987; co-author: Productivity and American Leadership: The Long View, 1989; co-editor: International Perspectives on Profitability and Accumulation, 1991; contbr. articles to profl. jours. Grantee NSF, 1984-90, Exxon Found., 1984-88, Fishman-Davidson Ctr. U. Pa., 1987-89, Sloan Found., 1990—, Mellon Found, 1991—. Mem. Am. Econ. Assn., Internat. Assn. Rsch. Income and Wealth (coun. 1987—), Internat. Inst. Pub. Fin., European Soc. Population Economists. Office: NYU Dept Econs 269 Mercer St Rm 700 New York NY 10003-6633

WOLFF, GREGORY STEVEN, insurance company executive; b. Manchester, Conn., Dec. 10, 1951; s. Thomas J. and M. Elizabeth (Grandburg) W.; m. Elizabeth Mae Heppenstall, June 3, 1971; children: Keith J., James T., Kyle M. BA in Edn., U. Conn., 1974. Cert. fin. planner. Insurance salesman Northwestern Mut. Life, Glastonbury, Conn., 1974-76, Wolff-Zackin & Assocs., Inc., Vernon, Conn., 1976—; lectr. in field; bd. dirs. Manchester Meml. Hosp.; mem. bd. of incorporators Savs. Bank of Manchester. Contbr. articles to profl. jours.; co-author: Financial Need Analysis I, cassette prog. Bd. dirs., sec., v.p. Transitional Living Ctr.; co-founder Manchester Soccer Camp, 1981. Mem. Nat. Assn. Life Underwriters, Conn. Assn. Life Underwriters, Hartford Assn. Life Underwriters (past pres.), Million Dollar Round Table, Ct. of Table. Methodist. Home: 361 Timrod Rd Manchester CT 06040-6751 Office: Wolff-Zackin & Assocs PO Box H Vernon Rockville CT 06066-1369

WOLFF, IVAN A., management consultant; b. Louisville, Feb. 10, 1917; s. Harry J. and Hermine Wolff; m. Mary Strawitz, Mar. 2, 1941; children: Martin, Ronald, Harold, James. BA, U. Louisville, 1937; MA, U. Wis., 1938, PhD, 1940, postgrad., 1940-41. Rsch. scientist No. Regional Rsch. Ctr. USDA, Peoria, Ill., 1941-58; lab. chief No. Regional Rsch. Ctr. USDA, Peoria, 1958-69; dir. Ea. Regional Rsch. Ctr. USDA, Phila., 1969-80; cons. Oreland, Pa., 1980—; mem. Fed. Exec. Bd., Phila., 1970-80; dir. emeritus U.S. Dept. Agr. Ea. Regional Rsch. Ctr., Phila., 1982—; mem. Presdl. Task Force on Use of Agrl. Products, 1956; mem. com. on natural toxicants in foods NRC, 1970-73. Editor: Handbook of Processing and Utilization in Agriculture, 3 vols., 1982-83; co-editor: Toxicants Occurring Naturally in Foods, 1973; contbr. articles to profl. jours., chpts. to books; patentee in field. Bd. chmn. Ea. Montgomery County Bd., ARC, Abington, Pa., 1990-92. Recipient Best Article of Yr. in Soc. Jour., Agronomy Soc., 1967. Mem. German Roundtable of Jewish Geneaol. Soc. Phila. (chmn. 1990—), Retired Execs. and Profls., Am. Chem. Soc. (chmn. Peoria sect. 1959-60), Am. Oil Chemists Soc. (assoc. editor jour. 1970-82), Inst. Food Technologists, B'nai B'rith (treas. Maimonides unit 1986-89). Home and Office: 124 Weldy Ave Oreland PA 19075-1244

WOLFF, KENNETH JOHN, insurance agent; b. Pitts., May 4, 1956; s. James F. and Callista A. (Pottmeyer) W.; m. Nancy J. Hickey, Nov. 8, 1986; 1 child, Callista M. Student, Allegheny Coll., 1974-76; BSBA, Duquesne U., 1978. Prin. K.J. Wolff Enterprises, Pitts., 1975-86; agt. Heck Agy., Inc., Pitts., 1979-84; owner, broker Forest Park Realty, Pitts., 1984—; owner Heck Ins. Svc., Pitts., 1986—. Patron Forest Hills (Pa.) Civic Assn., 1989-91; Sunday driver coord. Forest Hills Community Svc., 1984—; active Forest Hills Planning Commn., 1986—. Mem. Young Agts. Pitts. (pres., dir. 1986-88), Ins. Club Pitts., Rotary (bd. dirs. Forest Hills chpt. 1986—, pres. 1988-89, dist. rep. 1989-90). Republican. Office: Heck Ins Svc 2209 Ardmore Blvd Pittsburgh PA 15221-4851

WOLFF, KURT JAKOB, lawyer; b. Mannheim, Fed. Republic of Germany, Mar. 7, 1936; s. Ernest and Florence (Marx) W.; m. Sanda Lynn Dobrick, Dec. 28, 1958; children: Tracy Ellin, Brett Harris. AB, NYU, 1955; JD, U. Mich., 1958. Bar: N.Y. 1958, U.S. Supreme Ct. 1974, Hawaii 1985, Calif. 1988. Sole practice, N.Y.C., 1958—; assoc. Hays, Sklar & Herzberg, 1958-60; sr. assoc. Nathan, Mannheimer, Asche, Winer and Friedman, 1960-65; sr. assoc. Otterbourg, Steindler, Houston & Rosen, 1965-68, sr. ptnr., 1968-70, dir., treas. 1970—, chmn. bd., 1978-82, chief exec. officer, 1982— ; spl. master N.Y. Supreme Ct., 1977-85; vol. master U.S. Dist. Ct. (so. dist.) N.Y., 1978-82. Lectr., U. Mich. Law Sch.; mediator dept. Desciplinary com., mem. com. legal edn. and bar admission, 1991—). Mem. N.Y. State Bar Assn. (lectr.), Am. Arbitration Assn. (arbitrator), N.Y.C. Bar Assn. (arbitration com. 1979-83, state cts. of superior jurisdiction com. 1983-86, appellate div. first judicial dept., spl. mediator for the departmental disciplinary com., mem. com. on legal edn. and admission to the bar, 1991—), ABA (chmn. ins. com. econs. sect. 1980-82, editor arbitration newsletter, arbitration com. sect. of litigation), Hawaii State Bar Assn., Calif. State Bar Assn., Gen. Arbitration Council Textile Industry N.Y.C., Fed. Bar Council. Contbr. articles to legal jours. Home: 9 Sunset Dr N Chappaqua NY 10514-1633 also: 48-641 Torrito Ct Palm Desert CA 92260 Office: 230 Park Ave New York NY 10169-0005

WOLFF, RICHARD CARL, financial planner, insurance agency and pension planning company executive; b. Boston, July 17, 1933. Student, Boston U., 1957-60. CLU. Pres. Richard C. Wolff Ins. Agy., Lynnfield, Mass., 1960—, Fiscal Planning Corp., Lynnfield, Mass., 1978—, Multi Pension Planning Co., Lynnfield, Mass., 1979—; mem. adv. bd. para-acturay program Benly Coll., Waltham, Mass., 1982—; past chmn. adv. bd. Elite Club of Western Life, St. Paul; lectr. on fringe benefits. Author: Measure of Success, 1987. Pres. Temple Israel, Swampscott, 1981-83, pres. Bortherhood, 1987-89. Recipient Legion of Honor, DeMolay, 1978, Man of Yr. award, Temple Israel, 1989. Mem. Top of Table (charter), Million Dollar Round Table (life), Mass. Assn. Accident/Health Underwriters (pres. 1965-66), Essex County Estate Planning Assn. (founder, pres. 1975-76), Boston Life Underwriters Assn. (founder, pres. North Shore br. 1979-80), Swampscott Bus. Council (pres. 1980), Lynn C. of C. (v.p. 1982-85, disting. svc. award 1984, community leader award 1985), Peabody C. of C. (bd. dirs. 1985-86), Masons (master 1974), K.P., Rotary (Peabody award, Paul Harris fellow, pres. 1975-76), B'nai B'rith (pres. 1962-63, bd. dirs. 1991, Jewish family svc.). Office: Fiscal Planning Corp 5 Broadway Saugus MA 01906

WOLFF, STANLEY B., financial company executive; b. N.Y.C., July 22, 1919; s. Max and Lillian (Baumohl) W.; m. Helen Kotcher, 1947 (div. 1956); 1 child, Mark; m. Joan Rita Sukloff, Mar. 25, 1962; children: Nancy, Robert. BA, NYU, 1939, MA, 1946. Fgn. svc. officer U.S. Dept. of State, Washington, 1946-55; asst. to pres. Olivetti Corp. Am., N.Y.C., 1955-60; mgr. govt. sales Xerox Corp., Rochester and Washington, 1960-66; mgr. govt. sales div. Litton Industries, Washington, 1966-68; v.p. Paine Webber, Washington, 1968—. Sgt. U.S. Army, 1942-45. Mem. lNat. Press Club, Legal and Fin. Group. Home: 8400 Magruder Mill Ct Bethesda MD 20817 Office: Paine Webber 1300 I St NW Washington DC 20005

WOLFF, STEVEN ALEXANDER, arts and entertainment consultant; b. N.Y.C., July 18, 1957; s. Joel Charles and Joan (Mittlemark) W.; m. Gail English Loflin, June 12, 1988; 1 child, Jessica Sadye. BA in Econs., SUNY, Brockport, 1978; MFA in Theatre Adminstrn., Yale U., 1981. Cert. mgmt. cons. Cons. Artec Cons., N.Y.C., 1981-83; mgr. Theatre Projects Cons., N.Y.C., 1983-88; sr. v.p., prin. Hill Arts & Entertainment/AMS/ArtSoft Mgmt. Svcs., Guilford, Conn., 1988-91; pres. AMS Planning & Rsch. Corp., Southport, Conn., 1991—; Lectr. in field. Contbr. articles to profl. jours. Recipient Cert. of Honor, Am. Nat. Red Cross, 1978. Mem. Internat. Downtown Assn., Assn. Performing Arts Presenters, Urban Land Inst. (full mem.). Office: AMS Planning & Rsch Corp 2507 Post Rd PO Box 423 Southport CT 06490-0423

WOLFF, STUART IRA, financial executive; b. N.Y.C., May 21, 1940; s. Kieve C. and Beatrice (Horowitz) W.; m. B. Bonney Green, May 26, 1974; children: Lakey S., Duv T. BS, NYU, 1962. Asst. mgr. Beneficial Fin. Co., N.Y.C., 1963-64; credit supr. Am. Express Co., N.Y.C., 1964-72; fin. systems analyst Trans Union Systems Corp., N.Y.C., 1973-74; v.p. ops. and pers. Nandy Knits, Inc., Greenvale, N.Y., 1974-81; controller, adminstrv. and pers. dir. Corp. Knitting, Inc., Passaic, N.J., 1981-85; chief fin. officer Windjammer Fashions, Inc., N.Y.C., 1985—. Coach St. Matthews Youth Group, Dix Hills, N.Y.; mgr. Half Hollow Little League, Dix Hills. Mem. Am. Mgmt. Assn., Nat. Knitwear and Sportswear Assn., NYU Alumni Assn. Democrat. Jewish. Home: 30 Manchester Blvd Wheatley Heights NY 11798 Office: Windjammer Fashions Inc 1333 Broadway New York NY 10018

WOLFF-SALIN, MARY RIETTA HELEN, psychotherapist; b. July 30, 1932; d. Bernard O. Wolff-Salin and Helen V. Wolff. BA, Stanford U., 1956; MA, San Diego Coll. for Women, 1962, Sophia U., Tokyo, 1969; STD, Louvain U., Belgium, 1973; Grad., Emmanuel College, Boston, 1984. Joined Soc. of Sacred Heart; nat. cert. counselor; lic. counselor, Mass. Instr., counselor Internat. U. Sacred Heart, Tokyo, 1962-69; pastoral psychotherapist LaSalette Pastoral Counseling, Attleborough, Mass., 1984-86, Monadnock Area Pastoral Counseling Svcs., Keene, N.H., 1985-86, Founds. Ctr. for Pastoral Counseling/Psychotherapy, Newton, Mass., 1986-88; pvt. practice psychotherapy Cohasset/Newton, 1984—; Jungian analyst-in-tng. C.G. Jung Inst., Boston. Author: No Other Light: Points of Convergence in Psychology and Spirituality, 1986, The Shadow Side of Community and the Growth of the Self, 1988. Fellow Am. Assn. Pastoral Counselors; mem. AACD, Am. Mental Health Counselors Assn. Roman Catholic. Home and Office: 136 Border St Cohasset MA 02025-2044

WOLFGANG, JERALD IRA, economic development educator; b. Niagara Falls, N.Y., Apr. 8, 1938; s. Louis and Rose (Jochnowitz) W.; m. Joan Barbara Winter, Aug. 18, 1968; l child, Lynn Jessica. BS in Edn., SUNY, Buffalo, 1962, MS in Adminstrn., 1966. Tchr. Niagara Falls Schs., 1962-68; asst. to Gov. Rockefeller Albany, N.Y., 1968-71, dep. commr. for State of N.Y. Dept. Motor Vehicles, 1971-75; with N.Y. State Senate, Buffalo, 1976; spl. asst. to minority leader N.Y. State Assembly Office of Minority Leader, Buffalo, 1977-83; dir. Western N.Y. Edn. Ctr. for Econ. Devel., Buffalo, 1983—; bd. dirs., Southern Tier West Regional Planning and Devel.; adv. bd., State of N.Y. Small Bus. Assn., Western N.Y. Council for Edn. and Employment Equity, Western N.Y. Economic Devel. Corp., N.Y. State Economic. Devel. Corp., Western N.Y. Internat. Trade Council, Inc. Active in Niagara Community Ctr. & Girls Club, Niagara County Am. Cancer Soc., YMCA, Niagara Univ. Council, Mt. St. Mary's Hosp., Lewiston, Native Am. Ctr. for the Living Arts, Inc., Camp Nia-Y, Lewiston-Porter All Sports Scholarship Dinner; chmn. Niagara County Republican Com, 1978-86; sec. N.Y. Republican State Com, 1982-88; chmn. Town of Lewiston Environmental & Coastal Zone Com. 1989. Named Republican of Year 1977, Man of Year Niagara Taxpayers League, Inc., 1987; recipient: Top Hat Award Outstanding Svc. to Community, WHLD Radio and Niagara Frontier Svcs., 1978, Distinguished Achievement award, SUNY Buffalo United Univ . Professions, Pres.'s award for outstanding club leadership, Lewiston Kiwanis, 1979, Outstanding svc. award, YMCA, 1982, and numerous similar awards. Mem. Am. Vocational Assn., Assn. of Vocational Edn. Administrators of N.Y. State, Greater Buffalo C. of C., Help and Instruct Residents in Edn., Nat. Assn. of Small Bus. Internat. Trade Educators., N.Y. Assn. for Continuing Community Edn., N.Y. Council for Edn. and Employment Equity, N.Y. State Council on Vocational Edn., N.Y. State Economic Devel. Council, Niagara County Labor Mgmt. Council, Niagara Frontier Industry Edn. Council, Lewiston Kiwanis, Niagara Falls County Club. Republican. Jewish. Home: 4267 Lower River Rd Youngstown NY 14174-9702 Office: NY Edn Ctr Econ Devel 2 Pleasant Ave W Lancaster NY 14086-2108

WOLFMAN, BRUNETTA REID, education administrator, educator; b. Clarksdale, Miss., Sept. 4, 1931; d. Willie Orlando and Belle Victoria (Allen) Reid Griffin; m. Burton Wolfman, Oct. 4, 1952; children: Andrea, Jeffrey. BA, U. Calif., Berkeley, 1957, MA, 1968, PhD, 1971; DHL (hon.), Boston U., 1983; DP (hon.), Northeastern U., 1983; DL (hon.), Regis Coll., 1984, Stonehill Coll., 1985; DHL, Suffolk U., 1985; DET (hon.), Wentworth Inst., 1987; AA (hon.), Roxbury Community Coll., 1988. Asst. dean faculty Dartmouth Coll., Hanover, N.H., 1972-74; asst. v.p. acad. affairs U. Mass., Boston, 1974-76; acad. dean Wheelock Coll., Boston, 1976-78; cons. Arthur D. Little, Cambridge, Mass., 1978; dir. policy planning Dept. Edn., Boston, 1978-82; pres. Roxbury Community Coll., Boston, 1983-88, ACE sr. fellow, 1988-89; assoc. v.p. acad. affairs George Washington U., Washington, 1989-92, prof. edn., 1992—; pres. bd. dirs. Literacy Vols. of Capitol Region; bd. dirs. Am. Coun. Edn., Harvard Community Health Plan. Author: Roles, 1983. Bd. overseers Wellesley (Mass.) Coll., 1981; bd. dirs. Boston-Fenway Program, 1977, Freedom House, Boston, 1983, Boston Pvt. Industry Coun., 1983, NCCJ, Boston, 1983, co-chmn.; bd. overseers Boston Symphony Orch.; trustee Mus. Fine Arts, Boston; councilor Coun. on Edn. for Pub. Health. Recipient Freedom award NAACP No. Calif., 1971; Amelia Earhart award Women's Edn. and Indsl. Union, Boston, 1983. Mem. Am. Sociol. Assn., Assn. Black Women in Higher Edn., D.C. Sociol. Soc., Greater Boston C. of C. (edn. com. 1982), Cosmos Club (Washington), Pi Lambda Theta, Alpha Kappa Alpha (Humanitarian award 1984), Phi Delta Kappa. Home: 2022 Columbia Rd NW Washington DC 20009-1352 Office: George Washington U 2121 I St NW Washington DC 20052-0001

WOLFMAN, BURTON I., financial planning company executive; b. Chgo., Sept. 10, 1930; s. Jack and Lillian (Chalet) W.; m. Brunetta Reid, Oct. 4, 1952; children: Andrea, Jeffrey. BA, U. Calif., Berkeley, 1951, MA, 1961. Teen age dir. Jewish Community Ctr., San Francisco, 1952; union officer Internat. Harverster UAW, Oakland, Calif., 1952-57; rsch. economist Inst. Indsl. Rels. U. Calif., Berkeley, 1957-61, assoc. dir. analytical studies, 1961=72; dir. instnl. rsch. Dartmouth Coll., Hanover, N.H., 1972-73; under sec. edn. Commonwealth of Mass., Boston, 1973-76; v.p. adminstrn. Radcliffe Coll., Cambridge, Mass., 1976-80; v.p. fin. Brandeis U., Waltham, Mass., 1980-84; pres. Wolfman assocs., Boston, 1985—; ct. receiver Avalon Schs., Lenox, Mass., 1984-89; mem. task force Nat. Ctr. Higher Edn. Mgmt., Boulder, Colo., 1972-75; invited speaker OECD, Paris, 1976, 78; aj. faculty Harvard Grad. Sch. Edn., Cambridge, Mass., 1980-82; keynote speaker Assn. Instnl. Rsch., Kansas City, Mo. Pres. Community Coun., Kensington, Calif., 1968; chmn. bd. Fine Arts Work Ctr., Provincetown, Mass., 1982—; bd. dirs. Urban Arts, Boston, 1987-89, Evergreen Sch., 1991—. Democrat. Jewish. Office: Wolfman Assocs 2022 Columbia Rd NW Washington DC 20009

WOLFORD, CLYDE RICHARD, academic administrator, consultant; b. Tyler, Tex., May 12, 1951; s. Clyde Leroy and Edna Mae (Schreiner) W.; m. Karen Anne Berry, Aug. 23, 1980; children: Michelle Anne, Michael Richard. BA, Baylor U., 1973; MA, Stephen F. Austin State U., 1975; postgrad., Okla. State U., 1975-77. Asst. prof. SUNY, Oswego, 1977-81; dir. computer svcs. Le Moyne Coll., Syracuse, N.Y., 1981-90, dir. info. systems, 1991—; cons. Wolford and Assocs., Syracuse, 1979—. Author: Introduction to Psychology, 1977, (manual) Research Grants and Accounting, 1978. Trustee Onondaga Hill United Meth. Ch., Syracuse, 1992—. Teaching Program grantee NSF, 1979. Mem. Coll. and Univ. Systems Exchange, Interuniv. Comm. Coun. Home: 4347 Olympus Heights Syracuse NY 13215 Office: Le Moyne Coll Le Moyne Heights Syracuse NY 13214

WOLFORD, LARRY EUGENE, library director; b. Three Churches, W.Va., Dec. 20, 1952; s. Max Neeley and Catherine Rebecca (McBride) W.; m. Janice Jessup, Nov. 27, 1976; children: Eric Jessup, Caitlin Ruth. BS, Trenton State Coll., 1976; MLS, Rutgers U., 1983. Tchr., librarian Delanco (N.J.) Twp. Pub. Schs., 1976-77; researcher narcotics New Hanover (N.J.) Twp. Police Dept., 1977-78; prin. librarian Burlington County Library, Mt. Holly, N.J., 1978-85; library dir. Middletown (N.J.) Twp. Pub. Library, 1985-88; cons. Delanco, N.J., 1978—; libr. dir. Holy Family Coll., Phila., 1989-91; rsch. analyst State of N.J. Dept. Community Affairs, 1991—. Mem. ALA, N.J. Libr. Assn. (exec. com., pub. rels. com., acad. rsch. com., libr. devel. com.), Pa. Libr. Assn. Home and Office: 2841 Burlington Ave Riverside NJ 08075-5037

WOLFSON, ROBERT JOSEPH, economics educator; b. Buffalo, N.Y., Feb. 9, 1925; s. Jacob and Rose (Ladinsky) W.; m. Betty Bunes, 1954; children: Paul J., Anne R., Laura E. Wolfson-Hvichia. BS in Math. and Physics, U. Chgo., 1947, MA in Econs., 1950, PhD in Econs., 1956. Asst. study dir. Survey Rsch. Ctr., Univ. Mich., Ann Arbor, Mich., 1951-53; instr., social sci. Univ. Chgo., Ill., 1953-56; asst. prof., econs. Mich. State Univ., East Lansing, Mich., 1956-60; asst. prof. mgmt., dir. mgmt. scis. rsch. project UCLA, L.A., 1960-61; sr. project dir. C-E-I-R, Inc., Beverly Hills, Calif., 1961-63; economist Rand Corp., Santa Monica, Calif., 1963-65; prin. scientist System Devel. Corp., Santa Monica, 1965-66; prof., econs. Syracuse (N.Y.) Univ., 1966—; cons. N.Y. Met. Region Study, Regional Plan Assn., N.Y.C., 1957-58; cons., assistant commr. edn. U.S. Office of Edn., Washington, 1967-69; vis. prof. econs. and philosophy Washington Univ., St. Louis, 1976-77. Author: A Formal Lexicon for the Social Sciences, 1990; contbr. chpt. to book and articles to profl. jours. With USN, 1943-46. Recipient Undergrad. honor scholarship U. Chgo., 1941-43, Walgreen Found. scholarship Walgreen Found., U. Chgo., 1948-49, Ford Faculty Rsch. fellowship Ford Found., 1959-60. Mem. Am. Econs. Assn., AAUP (nat. coun., standing com. 1971—, state and local exec. com., chpt. officer Syracuse 1968—). Office: Syracuse U Dept Econs 316 A Maxwell Hall Syracuse NY 13244-1090

WOLIN, ALFRED M., district judge; b. Orange, N.J., Sept. 17, 1932; s. George and Juliet (Rosenstock) W.; m. Jane Zapiekov, Mar. 27, 1960; children: Roger, Marc. BA, U. Mich., 1954; LLB, JD, Rutgers U., 1959. Pvt. practice Elizabeth, N.J., 1960-80; judge Union County Dist. Ct., Elizabeth, N.J., 1980-85, Union County Superior Ct., Elizabeth, N.J., 1985-88, U.S. Dist. Ct., Newark, N.J., 1988—; atty. Roselle Bd. Adjustment, 1965-74; legis. aide to Senator Matthew J. Rinaldo, N.J. Senate, 1970-72; spl. asst. prosecutor Union County, 1970; congl. field rep. 12th congl. dist., 1972-79; mcpl. prosecutor Town of Westfield, N.J., 1973-74. Chief staff atty. Union County Legal Aid Soc., 1964-74; mem. Union County Ethics Com., sec., 1970-78, exec. com. Statewide Speedy Trial Com., Conf. Presiding Criminal Judges, Criminal Practice Com.; active Temple Emanuel, Jewish Fedn. Cen. N.J. SPC 2 U.S. Army, 1954-56, Germany. Mem. ABA, Am. Judicature Soc., N.J. Bar Assn. (judicial selection, discipline of the bar, lawyer referral coms.), Union County Bar Assn. (sec. 1970-74, pres. elect 1975, pres. 1976, judicial appointments com.), Fed. Judges Assn. Jewish. Office: US Dist Ct 367 US Courthouse & PO Bldg Newark NJ 07101

WOLIN, DORIS DIAMOND, psychologist; b. N.Y.C., Oct. 18, 1929; d. Philip Charles and Hattie (Bentley) Diamond; m. Gero Diels (div.); m. Sidney Wolin; children: Laurie, James; m. Frank Norris, Sept. 20, 1986. BA, NYU, 1951, MA, 1957; postgrad., Yeshiva U., 1958—; PhD, Heed U., 1988. Sch. psychologist Lawrence Sch. Systems, L.I., N.Y., 1959-60, New Hope Clinic, 1959-60, Jamaica Ctr. for Psychotherapy, 1960-61; instr. in psychology Bklyn. Coll., 1961-62; therapist Bklyn. Community Counseling Ctr., 1961-66; psychotherapist Testing and Advisement Ctr., NYU, 1951; pvt. practice clin. psychology N.Y.C., 1951—; theapist N. Jersey Mental Health Assocs., Oakland, N.J., 1979-81; cons. Bd. of Edn., L.I., N.Y., 1987—; instr. L.I. U. Bklyn. Ctr., 1971—; adj. prof. psychology L.I. U., 1971, Coll. New Rochelle, 1989; psychologist Save A Marriage, N.Y.C., 1977—; cons. Ctr. Psychotherapy and Counseling, Fairlawn, N.J., 1988-90, Astoria Blue Feather Presch. Intervention Program, 1989-90, Kingsbrook Jewish Med. Ctr., 1990-91, East River Child Devel. Ctr., 1991. Member Rose Garden Bklyn., Botanic Garden, Hort. Soc. of N.Y.; mem. aux. Bklyn. Botanic Gardens. Mem. N.Y. Soc. of Clin. Psychologists, Am. Psychol. Assn., Am. Group Psychotherapy Assn., Bklyn. Psychol. Assn., N.Y. State Psychol. Assn., Soc. for the Sci. Study of Sex, Psychologists in Pvt. Practice. Home: 90 8th Ave Brooklyn NY 11215-1553 Office: 60 Franklin St Morristown NJ 07960-5398

WOLIN, JAMES MICHAEL, budget analyst; b. Bklyn., Apr. 1, 1955; s. Sidney Harry and Doris (Diamond) W. BS in Bus. and Econs., Hofstra U., 1977, MBA in Fin., 1981. Analyst Aspen Systems, Inc., N.Y.C., 1979-80; prodn. coord. Hudson's Bay Co., N.Y.C., 1980-85; systems coord. Morgan Guaranty Trust Co., N.Y.C., 1985-86; info. mgr. Prudential-Bache Securities, N.Y.C., 1986-88; acting unit head Office of Mgmt. and Budget, City of New York, 1988—. Mem. jr. com. Nat. Ctr. Learning Disabilities. Mem. Am. Mgmt. Assn. Home: 240 Waverly Pl New York NY 10014-2213

WOLIN, MEYER JEROME, microbiologist; b. Bronx, N.Y., Nov. 10, 1930; s. Harry and Reba (Bien) W.; m. Eileen A. Felton, June 19, 1955; children: Benjamin L., Hayley A. BA, Cornell U., 1951; PhD, U. Chgo., 1954. Asst. prof. U. Ill., Urbana, 1956-62, assoc. prof., 1962-66, prof., 1966-74; chief rsch. scientist Wadsworth Ctr. Labs & Rsch., N.Y. State Dept. Health, Albany, 1974—; prof. SUNY, Albany, 1985—, chmn. dept. environ. health and toxicology, 1985-87; chief lab. environ. biology Wadsworth Ctr. Labs. & Rsch., N.Y. State Dept. Health, Albany, 1985—. Mem. editorial bd. Jour. Bacteriology, 1968-74, Microbiol. Revs., 1978-85, Infection & Immunity, 1978-84; contbr. 82 articles to sci. jours.; author 23 sci. revs. and book chpts. Alderman City Coun., Urbana, 1961-65; mem. Zoning Bd. Appeals, Urbana, 1965-73. Postdoctoral fellow USPHS, U. Minn., U. Ill., 1954-56, sr. post-doctoral fellow NSF, U. Newcastle upon Tyne, Eng., 1964-65. Mem. ACS, AAAS, Am. Soc. Microbiology (vis. prof. Tucuman U., Argentina 1980), N.Y. Acad. Sci., Am. Soc. for Molecular Biology and Biochemistry. Office: Wadsworth Ctr for Labs & Rsch Empire State Pla Albany NY 12201-0509

WOLIN, MICHAEL STUART, physiology educator; b. Bklyn., Sept. 11, 1953; s. Emanuel and Anita (Klein) W.; m. Theresa Marie Burke, Oct. 25, 1987; 1 child, Joshua Mark. BA in Chemistry, SUNY, Binghamton, 1975; MS, Yale U., 1977, MPhil, 1978, PhD, 1981. NIH Nat. Rsch. Svc. fellow Tulane U. Sch. Medicine, New Orleans, 1981-82, instr. pharmacology, 1982-83; asst. prof. physiology N.Y. Med. Coll., Valhalla, 1983-89, assoc. prof., 1989—; prin. investigator NIH, 1984—. Mem. editorial bd. Am. Jour. Physiology; contbr. articles to Jour. Biol. Chemistry, Am. Jour. Physiology, Jour. Pharmacology, also others. Biomed. rsch. scholar C.H. Revson Found., 1983-85. Mem. AAAS, Am. Thoracic Soc. (sci. program com. 1990—), Am. Heart Assn. (cardiopulmonary coun. 1984—, sci. program com. 1986—, established investigator 1987—, prin. investigator 1983—, Albert Hyman award La. chpt. 1983), Am. Physiol. Soc., Oxygen Soc., Microcirculatory Soc. Democrat. Jewish. Home: 40 Goodwin Ave White Plains NY 10607-1014 Office: NY Med Coll Dept Physiology Valhalla NY 10595

WOLINS, JOSEPH, artist; b. Atlantic City, Mar. 26, 1915; s. Morris and Rebecca (Katerinska) W.; m. Selma Polikoff Lazaar, Dec. 7, 1957; children: Richard Lazaar, David Lazaar, John Wolins, Sarah Wolins. Student, Nat. Acad. Design, 1931-35. Painter with Fed. art projects, 1934-41; tchr. South Shore Art Sch., Rockville Center, N.Y., 1950-55, 92d St. YMHA, N.Y.C., 1960, Bklyn. Mus. Art Sch., 1961-62, Long Beach (N.Y.) High Sch., 1962-68; pvt. classes, 1961—. One-man exhbns. include, Contemporary Arts Gallery, N.Y.C., Bodley Gallery, N.Y.C., Silvermine Guild, Norwalk, Conn., Slater Mus., Norwich, Conn., Agra Gallery, Washington, Everson Mus., Syracuse, N.Y.; group exhbns. include, World's Fair, N.Y.C., 1939, J.B. Neumann Gallery, N.Y.C., Toledo Mus., Corcoran Art Gallery, U. Ill. Mus., Pa. Acad. Fine Art, Whitney Mus., Sao Paolo Mus. Modern Art, Norfolk (Va.) Mus., Smithsonian Instn., Butler Art Inst., Youngstown, Ohio, Met. Mus. Art, N.Y.C.; rep. permanent collections, Met. Mus. Art, Norfolk Mus., Albert Gallery at St. Joseph's (Mo.) U., Fiske U. Art Gallery, Mobile, Mus. in Ein Horod, Israel, Butler Art Inst., Nat. Mus. Am. Art, Washington, Slater Mem. Mus., Norwich, Conn., Wichita (Kans.) Art Mus., Everson Mus. of Art, Syracuse, N.Y., New Brit. Mus. Art (Conn.), Boca Raton Art Mus., Fla., also pvt. collections. Grantee Mark Rothko Found., 1971; recipient Painting award Audubon Artists, 1976, Painting award Nat. Inst. Arts and Letters, 1976, Painting award Am. Soc. Contemporary Artists,

1976. Mem. Audubon Artists, Am. Soc. Contemporary Artists. Address: 463 West St New York NY 10014

WOLINSKY, CARY SOL, photographer; b. Pitts., Oct. 14, 1947; s. Mayer and Rosalyn (Levin) W.; m. Barbara Ware Emmel, Nov. 24, 1979; 1 child, Yari Emmel. BS in Pub. Communications, Boston U., 1969. Photographer Boston Globe, 1969-72; freelance photographer Boston, 1972—; contract photographer Nat. Geographic, Washington, 1980—; founder, ptnr. Trillium Studios, Norwell, Mass., 1983, Electric Book Co., Washington, 1990—. Exhibited in group shows Babson Coll., Wellesley, Mass., 1980-81, Corcoran Gallery Art, Washington, 1988-90, Pucker Gallery, Boston, 1988, Art Complex Mus., Duxbury, Mass., 1991, Wawrzonek Gallery, Worcester, Mass., 1919; also others; represented in permanent collections Boston U., Beth Israel Hosp., Boston, DeCordova Art Mus., Lincoln, Mass., Nat. Geog. Soc., also others; contbr. photographs to numerous mags. and books. Office: Nat Geog Soc 17th and M Sts NW Washington DC 20036

WOLKO, HOWARD STEPHEN, mechanical engineer; b. Buffalo, Apr. 30, 1925; s. Stephen and Jennie (Herman) W.; m. Ruth Allene Westphal, Sept. 7, 1950; children: Leslie, Kurt, Lindsey, Nels. BS, U. Buffalo, 1949, MS, 1953; DSc, George Washington U., 1967. Design engr. scientific instruments div. Am. Optical Co., Buffalo, 1950-52; rsch. assoc. Cornell Aero. Lab., Buffalo, 1952-55; chief structures rsch. Bell Aircraft Corp., Niagara Falls, N.Y., 1955-59; head solid mechanics engring. sci. directorate Air Force Office Sci. Rsch., Washington, 1959-62; chief structural mechanics office advanced rsch. and tech. NASA, Washington, 1962-67; prof. mech. engring. Tex. A&M U., College Station, 1967-72; prof., dept. chmn. mech. engring. Memphis (Tenn.) State U., 1972-73; asst. dir. sci. and tech. Nat. Air and Space Mus. Smithsonian Instn., Washington, 1973-80, advisor for tech. aeronautics, 1980—; cons. Va. Air & Space Ctr., Hampton, 1990—, Mus. Flight, Seattle, 1987. Author: In the Cause of Flight, 1981; editor: The Wright Flyer: An Engineering Perspective, 1987. With USN, 1943-46, ETO. Home: 1561 Evers Dr Mc Lean VA 22101-5006 Office: Nat Air and Space Mus Washington DC 20560

WOLKSTEIN, DIANE, storyteller; b. N.J., Nov. 11, 1942; d. Harry Wolf and Ruth Barenboim; 1 child, Rachel Cloudstone. BA, Smith Coll., Northampton, Mass., 1964; MA, Bank St. Coll., 1967. Official storyteller City of N.Y.; tchr. storytelling to grad. students Bank St. Coll., N.Y.C.; storyteller bi-weekly radio program Sta. WNYC-FM Radio; pres. N.Y.C. Storytelling Ctr., 1982-89. Author: 8,000 Stones, 1972, The Cool Ride in the Sky, 1973, The Visit, 1974, Squirrel's Song, 1975, Lazy Stories, 1976, The Red Lion, 1977, The Magic Orange Tree and Other Haitian Folk Tales, 1978, White Wave, 1979, The Banza, 1980, Ihanna, Queen of Heaven and Earth: Her Stories and Hymns from Sumer, 1983, The Magic Wings, 1985, The Legend of Sleepy Hollow, 1987, DreamSongs: Abulafia, Part of My Heart, 1991, The First Love Stories: From Isis and Osiris to Tristan and Iseult, 1991, Oom Razoom: Go I Know Not Where, Bring Back I Know Not What, 1991, Little Mouse's Painting, 1992, (audiocassettes) Tales of Hopi Indians, 1974, Eskimo Stories: Tales of Magic, 1975, California Fairy Tales, 1975, Hans Christian Andersen in Central Park, 1984, Romping, 1985, Fairy Tales from Estonia, 1986, Epic of Inanna, 1987, Joseph, 1987, Psyche and Eros, 1988. Home: 10 Patchin Pl New York NY 10011-8342

WOLLER, RICHARD LEE, entrepreneur; b. Newark, Mar. 3, 1957; s. Myron and June (Zeckendorf) W.; m. Nancy Tara Stoll, Oct. 16, 1988. BA, Syracuse U., 1979; MPA, NYU, 1986. Lab technician U. Medicine and Dentistry N.J., Piscataway, 1979-81; rsch. asst. Meml. Sloan-Kettering Cancer Ctr., N.Y.C., 1982-85; adminstrv. resident Med. Coll. Cornell U., N.Y.C., 1985-86; assoc. dir. clin practice plan Health Sci. Ctr. SUNY, Bklyn., 1986-87, dir. ops. Dean's office, 1987-89; entrepreneur Speed of Light Printing, Bklyn., 1987-89, Berkshire Hiking Holidays, Lenox, Mass., 1989—. Contbr. articles to profl. jours. Home and Office: PO Box 2231 Lenox MA 01240-5231

WOLLMAN, ERIC, administrative manager; b. Bklyn., May 26, 1951; s. Harry and Lillian (Levine) W. AA, Kingsborough Community Coll., 1970; BA, Bklyn. Coll., 1973; postgrad., Bklyn. Law Sch., 1989—. Exec. asst. to treas. Dept. Fin., N.Y.C., 1973-76; supervising investment analyst Office of Comptroller, N.Y.C., 1976-85, project mgr., 1985-90, adminstrv. mgr.proxy unit, 1990—. V.P. com. to preserve Brighton Beach, Bklyn., 1988; aux. lt. N.Y.C. Police Dept., 1973—; mem. Public Works Forum, 1991—; commr. of deeds, 1992-94. Recipient award of valor N.Y.C. Police Dept., award of merit United Fund of Greater N.Y. Mem. ABA (law student divsn.), NRA, N.Y. State Bar Assn. (law student divsn.), Student Bar Assn. (v.p. evening divsn. 1991-92), Bklyn. Coll. Alumni Assn., Aux. Police Benevolent Assn. (exec. bd.), Phi Delta Phi. Democrat. Jewish. Home: 2222 E 18th St Brooklyn NY 11229-4454 Office: NYC Office of Comptroller One Centre St Rm 736 New York NY 10007

WOLLMAN, HARRY, medical educator; b. Bklyn., Sept. 26, 1932; s. Jacob and Florence Roslyn (Hoffman) W.; m. Anne Carolyn Hamel, Feb. 16, 1957; children—Julie Ellen, Emily Jane, Diana Leigh. A.B. summa cum laude (hon. John Harvard scholar 1950-53, hon. Harvard Coll. scholar 1953-54, Detur award 1951), Harvard, 1954, M.D., 1958. Diplomate: Am. Bd. Anesthesiology. Intern U. Chgo. Clinics, 1958-59; resident U. Pa., 1959-63, assoc. in anesthesia, 1963-65, mem. faculty, 1965-87, prof. anesthesia, 1970-87, prof. pharmacology, 1971-87, Robert Dunning Dripps prof., chmn. dept. anesthesia, 1972-87; prin. investigator Anesthesia Rsch. Ctr., 1972-78; program dir. Anesthesia Rsch. Tng. Grant, 1972-87; sr. v.p., chief acad. officer, dean Sch. Medicine Hahnemann U., Phila., 1987—, prof. anesthesiology, 1987—, prof. pharmacology, 1987—; Mem. anesthesia drug panel, drug efficacy study, com. on anesthesia Nat. Acad. Scis.-NRC, 1970-71, com. on adverse reactions to anesthesia drugs, 1971-72; mem. pharm. and toxicology tng. grants com. NIH, 1966-68, anesthesia tng. grants com., 1971-73, surgery, anesthesia and trauma study sect., 1974-78; chmn. com. on studies involving human beings U. Pa., 1972-76, chmn. clin. practice exec. com., 1976-80. Assoc. editor for revs.: Anesthesiology, 1970-75; Contbr. and editor books. NIH research traineeship fellow, 1959-63; Pharm. Mfg. Assn. fellow, 1960-61. Mem. Pa. Soc. Anesthesiologists (pres. 1972-73), Am. Physiol. Soc., Assn. U. Anesthetists (exec. council 1971-74, chmn. sci. adv. bd. 1975-77), Soc. Acad. Anesthesia Chairmen (chmn. com. on financial resources 1973-77, pres.-elect 1976-77, pres. 1977-78), Am. Soc. Anesthesiologists, Phila. Soc. Anesthesiologists, AMA, Pa. Med. Soc., Phila. County Med. Soc., Am. Dental Soc. Anesthesiology (adv. bd. 1985—), John Morgan Soc., Coll. Physicians Phila., Phi Beta Kappa, Sigma Xi. Republican. Unitarian. Home: 2203 Delancey Pl Philadelphia PA 19103-6501 Office: Hahnemann U Broad And Vine St Philadelphia PA 19102-1178

WOLLMAN, JUNE ROSE, clothing executive; b. Bklyn., June 14, 1929; d. Louis and Ella (Klein) Nierenberg; m. Howard Louis Wollman, Sept. 29, 1922; children: Jodi Ann (dec.), Randi Sue. Interior designer June Rose Decors Ltd., Valley Stream, N.Y., 1951—; with Louella Realty, N.Y.C., 1956-85; designer Lou Nierenberg Corp., N.Y.C., 1956-80; with Lou Nierenberg Internat., N.Y.C., 1974-85; with Lou Nierenberg Ltd., N.Y.C., 1985—, real estate pres., 1985—; cons. fake furs, jackets, coats, N.Y.C., 1985—. Trustee Green Acres Civic Cos., Valley Stream, 1951—; presenter scholarship South High Sch., Valley Stream, 1969—, Temple Emanuel, Lynbook, N.Y., 1969—; founding sponsor Mt. Sinai Med. Ctr., past v.p.; pres. Sam & Rose Klein Family; pres. Jodi Ann Wollman Glioblastomn Rsch. Fund, 1970-90. Recipient L.I.J.H. Med. Ctr. award Ladies Svc. Guild, New Hyde Park, N.Y., 1965-85, Mt. Sinai Med. Ctr. award, N.Y.C., 1969-89. Mem. Am. Jewish Congress (pres. South Shore chpt. 1957-63). Republican. Jewish. Home: 13 Cloverfield Rd Valley Stream NY 11581-2421 Office: June Decors Ltd 13 Cloverfield Rd Valley Stream NY 11581-2421

WOLLMAN, LEO, physician; b. N.Y.C., Mar. 14, 1914; s. Joseph and Sara (Samrick) W.; m. Eleanor Rakow, Aug. 16, 1936 (dec. Sept. 1953); children: Arthur Lee, Bryant Lee; m. Charlotte Kornberg Seidman, Oct. 6, 1954 (dec. May 1984); m. Ellen Hahn, Mar. 25, 1985. BS, Columbia U., 1934; MS, NYU, 1938; MD, Royal Coll. Edinburgh, 1942; PhD (hon.), Rochdale, 1972; DSc (hon.), U. Mich., 1973. Diplomate Am. Bd. Hypnosis in Ob-Gyn, Nat. Bd. Acupuncture Medicine, Am. Acad. Pain Mgmt., Am. Bd. Psychiatry and Neurology, Am. Bd. Sexology. Intern Cumberland Hosp., Bklyn., 1942-43; resident Leith Gen. Hosp., 1942; practice medicine specializing in ob-gyn Bklyn., 1944-72; in psychiatry, 1972—; mem. staff Maimonides, Coney Island, Caledonian hosps., Bklyn., Park East, Mt. Sinai hosps., N.Y.C. Author: Write Yourself Slim, 1976, Eating Your Way to a Better Sex Life, 1983, numerous articles in profl. jours.; editor-in-chief: Jour. Am. Soc. Psychosomatic Dentistry and Medicine, 1968-83; editor newsletter: Soc. Sci. Study Sex; editor: News Bull. of Inst. for Comprehensive Medicine; assoc. editor: Jour. Sex Research; internat. editor: Latin Am. Jour. Clin. Hypnosis; films I Am Not This Body, 1970, StrangeHer, 1971, Let Me Die a Woman, 1978. Pres. Jewish Com. Coun. Greater Coney Island, 1989—. Recipient Jules Weinstein Ann. Pioneer in Modern Hypnosis award, 1964. Fellow Am. Geriatrics Soc., N.Y. Acad. Scis. (life), Acad. Psychosomatic Medicine (sec. 1965), Soc. Clin. and Exptl. Hypnosis (life), Am. Soc. Clin. Hypnosis (life), Soc. Sci. Study Sex (pres. Eastern region 1979-81), Am. Soc. Psychical Research (life), Am. Med. Writers Assn. (life), Internat. Soc. Comprehensive Medicine, Am. Acad. Psychiatry and Neurology, Am. Coll. Sexology; mem. Nat. Geog. Soc. (life), AAAS (council 1971-73), Am. Assn. Social Psychiatry, Am. Soc. Abdominal Surgeons, Internat. Soc. Nonverbal Psychotherapy, N.Y. State Soc. Med. Research, Royal Medico-Psychol. Assn. (Eng.), N.Y. Soc. for Gen. Semantics, Nat. Assn. on Standard Med. Vocabulary (sec. 1964—), Am. Assn. History Medicine, Am. Assn. Study Headache, Am. Acad. Dental Medicine, Am. Assn. Marriage Counselors, Soc. Med. Jurisprudence, Bklyn. Psychol. Assn., Canadian Soc. for Study Fertility, Am. Fertility Soc. (life), Internat. Fertility Assn., Internat. Soc. for Clin. and Exptl. Hypnosis (life), Am. Soc. Psychosomatic Dentistry and Medicine (pres. 1969-72, exec. dir. 1973-83), Assn. Advancement Psychotherapy, Pan-Am. Med. Assn., Andalusian Soc. Sophrology and Psychosomatic Medicine, Brit. Med. Assn., Bklyn. Acad. Medicine, Internat. Soc. Psychoneuroendocrinology, L.I. Hist. Soc.; also hon. mem. numerous fgn. orgns. Address: 3813 Poplar Ave Brooklyn NY 11224-1301

WOLLNER, BARRY STUART, state government official; b. Bridgeport, Conn., Aug. 2, 1953; s. Martin and Gloria (Wexler) W.; m. Ronnie Hochberg, July 6, 1986. BS, Rider Coll., 1975; MSW, Yeshiva U., 1977. Housing dir. West Bronx (N.Y.) Housing and Neighborhood Resource Ctr., 1978-81, Midwood Devel. Corp., Bklyn., 1981-84; mortgage analyst dept. housing preservation and devel. City of N.Y., 1984-87; housing and community devel. rep. div. housing renewal State of N.Y., N.Y.C., 1987—. Mem. True Potential Toastmasters Club (edn. v.p. 1988—, pres. 1990, Toastmaster of Yr. 1988), B'nai Brith (sec. Manhattan coun. 1988, pres. B.A.S.I.C. unit 1982-84, 88, adv. bd. career and counseling services N.Y. 1989—, 1st place dist. membership award 1980-81). Democrat. Jewish. Office: NY State Div Housing Community Renewal 1 Fordham Pla E221 Bronx NY 10458

WOLMAN, M. GORDON, geography educator; b. Balt., Aug. 16, 1924; s. Abel and Anna (Gordon) W.; m. Elaine Mielke, June 20, 1951; children: Elsa Anne, Abel Gordon, Abby Lucille, Fredericka Jeannette. Student, Haverford Coll.; A.B. in Geology, Johns Hopkins U., 1949; M.A. in Geology, Harvard U., 1951, Ph.D., 1953. Geologist U.S. Geol. Survey, 1951-58, part-time, 1958—; assoc. prof. geography Johns Hopkins U., Balt., 1958-62; prof. Johns Hopkins, 1962—; chmn. dept. geography and environ. engring., 1958-90, Interim Provost, 1987, 1990; Mem. adv. com. geography U.S. Office Naval Rsch.; mem. exec. com. Div. Earth Sci. NRC; mem. com. internat. environ. programs, mem. environ. studies bd.; mem. com. water, mem. exec. com. Earth Sci. div., mem. com. mineral resources and environment, chmn. nat. commn. water quality policy NAS; chmn. NRC Com. Adv. U.S. Geol. Survey; chmn. NAS Commn. Geoscis., Environment and Resources; cons. in field to City of Balt., Baltimor County, State of Md., fed. govt. and industry. Author: Fluvial Processes in Geomorphology, 1964; Editorial bd.: Science mag. Pres. bd. trustees Park Sch., Balt., Md. Acad. Scis., Sinai Hosp., Balt.; pres. bd. dirs. Resources for Future, 1980-87; mem. adv. com. Inst. Nuclear Power Ops., 1982-85; mem. Balt. City Charter Revision Commn., Community Action Com., Balt. With USNR, 1943-46. Recipient Meritorious Contribution award Assn. Am. Geographers, 1972. Fellow Am. Acad. Arts and Scis.; mem. Nat. Acad. Scis., Am. Geophys. Union (chmn. subcom. sedimentation, pres. hydrol. sect.), Geol. Soc. Am. (v.p. 1983, pres. 1984), Washington Geol. Soc., ASCE, Agrl. Hist. Soc., Am. Geog. Soc. (councilor 1965-70, Cullum Geog. medal 1989), Assn. Am. Geographers, Phi Beta Kappa, Sigma Xi, Md. Acad. Scis. (mem. exec. com. 1970-75). Home: 2104 W Rogers Ave Baltimore MD 21209-4553

WOLMAN, STEPHEN ROBERT, executive search company executive; b. Bklyn., Jan. 10, 1943; s. Norman Paul and Helen (Schenkelbach) W.; m. Ann Ellen Fonfa, Nov. 27, 1987. BA, Hunter Coll., 1965; MBA, Bernard M. Baruch Coll., 1973. Pers. mgr. Diamond Shamrock, Bklyn., 1967-70; pers. dir. Park Electrochem. Corp., Queens, N.Y., 1970-74, Topps Chewing Gum Inc., Bklyn., 1974-77, Revlon, N.Y.C., 1977-81; pres. S.R. Wolman Assocs. Inc., N.Y.C., 1981—. Contbr. articles to profl. jours. Office: S R Wolman Assocs Inc 133 E 35th St New York NY 10016-3886

WOLMAN, WILLIAM, economist, journalist; b. Montreal, Que., Can.; s. Nathan and Toba (Wexler) W.; m. Ann Livia Colamosca, Jan. 7, 1982; children: John, Flora. BA, McGill U., 1948; PhD, Stanford U., 1957. Asst. prof. econs. Wash. State U., Pullman, 1954-60, sr. editor, 1974-83, chief economist, 1989—; econs. editor Bus. Week, N.Y.C., 1960-69; v.p. Citicorp, N.Y.C., 1969-71, Argus Rsch. corp., N.Y.C., 1971-74; exec. editor Bus. Times, N.Y.C., 1983-84; chief economist CNBC, Ft. Lee, N.J., 1989—. Office: Bus Week 1221 Ave of the Americas New York NY 10020

WOLOTSKY, HYMAN, retired college dean; b. N.Y.C., Nov. 27, 1918; s. Max and Bessie (Davis) W.; m. Ruth Schaffel, Mar. 31, 1946; children: Eugene, Paul. BA, CCNY, 1947; MA, Columbia U., 1948, doctoral studies, 1975-80. Cert. social worker. Program dir. Jewish Community Ctr., Portland, Maine, 1949-51; asst. exec. dir. Montgomery County Jewish Community, Chevy Chase, Md., 1951-53; exec. dir. Jewish Community Ctr. of Revere, Mass., 1953-59, YM-YWHA of Brockton, Mass., 1959-61, Mid-Westchester YM & YWHA, Eastchester, N.Y., 1961-65; exec. dir. early childhood ctr. Bank St. Coll. of Edn., N.Y.C., 1965-70, assoc. to provost, 1970-81, assoc. dean, 1981-84; cons. Assn. Mgmt. Svcs., New Rochelle, N.Y., 1984—; field instr. U. Md., College Pk., 1951-53, Boston U. Sch. Social Work, 1954-56, NYU Sch. Social Work, 1965-66, Hunter Coll. Sch. of Social Work, N.Y.C., 1967-70. Co-author: Career Development in Head Start, 1970, Brace Program of Systematic Observation, 1976; producer of videotapes including Experiencias Pre-escolares en Venezuela, 1978; contbr. articles to profl. jours. Trustee Fleetwood Synagogue, Mount Vernon, N.Y., 1963—, Clinton Child Care Assn., N.Y.C., 1970-80, Eastchester Youth Bd., 1961-64. Corp. U.S. Army, 1941-46. Mem. AAUP, Faculty Club Columbia U., Fleetwood Synagogue (pres. 1971-74). Democrat. Jewish. Office: Assn Mgmt Svcs 1270 North Ave New Rochelle NY 10804-2629

WOLOWITZ, STEVEN, lawyer; b. Chgo., June 27, 1952; s. Myron and Rose (Gaines) W.; m. Allison Josephy, June 15, 1974; children: Ashley Rose, Jordan Michael. BA with distinction, George Washington U., 1974, JD with honors, 1977. Bar: N.Y. 1978, U.S. Dist. Ct. (so. and ea. dists.) N.Y. 1979, U.S. Ct. Appeals (2d and 7th cirs.) 1984, U.S. Ct. Appeals (5th cir.) 1988, U.S. Supreme Ct. 1988. Assoc. Rosenman & Colin, N.Y.C., 1977-85, ptnr., 1986-88; ptnr. Mayer, Brown & Platt, N.Y.C., 1988—; arbitrator Nat. Futures Assn., 1988—. Contbr. articles to profl. jours. Mem. Phi Eta Sigma, Phi Beta Kappa. Office: Mayer Brown & Platt 787 7th Ave Ste 2400 New York NY 10019-6018

WOLOWNIK, STEPHEN MICHAEL, librarian; b. Chester, Pa., July 22, 1946; s. Dmytro and Mary (Harasym) W. BA, U. Pa., 1968; MS, Drexel U., 1989. Dir., founder U. Pa. Balalaika Orch., Phila., 1966-72, 81—, Odessa Balalaikas, L.A., 1973-76; founding mem. Great Am. Gypsy Band, Atlanta, 1977-80; libr. Lippincott Libr., U. Pa., Phila., 1983—. Writer: (film) Discovering Russian Folk Music, 1975. Fulbright grantee, 1969. Mem. Balalaika & Domra Assn. Am. (exec. dir. 1978—, cons., 1978—). Libertarian. Eastern Orthodox. Home: 2225 Madison Square Philadelphia PA 19146 Office: Lippincott Libr Wharton Sch 3420 Walnut St Philadelphia PA 19104

WOLPER, ALLAN L., journalist, educator; b. N.Y.C.; s. Sydelle Wolper; m. Joanna Birnbaum; children: Jill, Richard, Kim. BS, NYU, 1965. Reporter Providence Jour., 1965-67; polit. writer, contbg. writer campus journalism, editor and pub. mag. AP, N.Y.C., 1967-69; polit. writer N.Y. Post, N.Y.C., 1970-63; writer, producer WABC Eyewitness News, N.Y.C., 1974-75; editor, columnist Soho Weekly News, N.Y.C., 1974-82; host, writer, producer of Right to Know Suburban Cablevision and N.J. Network, Sta. WNYC-TV, N.Y.C., Newark and Avenel, N.J., 1982-89; host, producer series on media Right to Know Right to Know syndicated pub. radio series on the media, Newark, 1989—; dir. journalism Rutgers U., Newark, 1978—. Host, producer, writer documentary The Marielitos, 1984, Hillside: Desegration, 1985, Impact, 1988, TV spl. The First Amendment, 1989; contbr. articles to profl. jours. With U.S. Army, 1961-63. Recipient best pub. affairs program award Internat. TV and Video Festival, 1985, Nat. Cable TV Assn., 1986, award for cable excellence, 1986, 3 Ace awards Nat. Cable TV, 1985, 86, Lowell Mellett award Pa. State U., 1985, Alfred I. duPont award Columbia U., 1985, award in broadcast journalism N.J. Press Assn., 1987. Mem. AAUP, Soc. Profl. Journalists (chmn. freedom of info. com. Deadline Club N.Y.C. br. 1980, Outstanding Broadcast Journalism award 1984, 87, Disting. Svc. award bicentennial broadcast competition 1989, spl. award N.J. chpt. 1990, spl. award N.J. chpt. media criticism 1991). Home: 327 Central Park W New York NY 10025-7631 Office: Rutgers U Hill Hall Newark NJ 07102

WOLPERT, ETTA, artist, poet; b. Mpls., Dec. 6, 1930; d. Garrett and Gertrude G. (Gruenberg) W. BA, U. Minn., 1952, MA, 1954. Asst. to Allen Tate U. Minn., Mpls., 1952; tutor Harvard U. Bur. of Study Counsel, Cambridge, Mass., 1955-59; instr. English Emerson Coll., Boston, 1955-58; workshop leader in poetry Cambridge Ctr. for Adult Edn., Boston, 1956; asst. prof. English & Art No. Essex Community Coll., Haverhill, Mass., 1964-66; leader art history workshop Brandeis Study Group, Lexington, Mass., 1962; social worker Welfare Dept., Lowell, Mass., 1969-71; artist, poet freelance Lexington, Mass., 1975—. One-woman show includes Cary Meml. Libr., 1962; exhibited in shows at Habit Inst., 1991, Cambridge Art Assn., 1992, 4th Ann. Internat. Exhibit, 1989; author: (poems) Selections, 1973. Recipient Hon. Mention, World of Poetry, 1991, Hon. Mention in Poetry Contest, Harvard Summer Sch., 1965, Two First prizes New Eng. Poets Club, 1969. Mem. Ariel Gallery, Gallery of Art Investment, Cambridge Art Assn., New Eng. Poetry Club. Home: 4 Revere St Lexington MA 02173-4420

WOLPIN, ALAN DAVID, computer company executive; b. N.Y.C., Jan. 30, 1940; s. Samuel M. and Gertrude (Spector) W.; children: Ginny, Michelle Wolpin Adams, Steven. BS, Rochester Inst. Tech., 1961. Sr. devel. engr. Nat. Cash Register, Dayton, Ohio, 1967-73; mgr. software Raytheon Data Systems, Norwood, Mass., 1973-78; program mgr. Codex Corp., Mansfield, Mass., 1978-81; sr. product engr. Datachecker, Maynard, Mass., 1982-86; v.p. software devel. Advanced Video Products, Littleton, Mass., 1987—. Fin. com. mem. Sharon, Mass., 1981-83. Home: 1 Seminole Cir Sharon MA 02067-2943 Office: Advanced Video Products PO Box 1450 Littleton MA 01460-4450

WOLSKI, DONNA CATHERINE, computer graphics executive; b. Buffalo; d. Arthur B. and Althea (Kranz) Wittmer; m. Arthur W. Wolski, Aug. 23, 1969; children: Darren, John. AAS in Mgmt. acad. excellence, Erie Community Coll., Buffalo, 1982; cert. computer sci., SUNY at Buffalo. Data analyst Am. Standard, Cheektowaga, N.Y., 1978-82; mktg. systems coord. Automotive Parts div. ITT, Tonawanda, N.Y., 1982-86; adminstrv. asst. to pres. Arcata Graphics/Buffalo, Depew, N.Y., 1986—; instr. mktg. decision making Evening div. Bryant and Stratton. Mem. NAFE, Bus. Tchr.'s Assn. of N.Y., D-E-L C. of C. (chmn.). Office: Arcata Graphics/Buffalo Tc Industrial Park Depew NY 14043-2015

WOLSLAYER, VALERIE ANN, public relations executive; b. Pitts., Nov. 4, 1966; d. Jerry Edward Wolslayer and Paula (Harvey) Snyder. BA in Communications, Am. U., 1989. Asst. mgr. Edmonson & Gallagher, McLean, Va., 1986-87; bldg. adminstr. Milbard Assoc./The Barlow Corp., Chevy Chase, Md., 1987; jr. pension cons. Phoenix Mut. Life Ins. Co., Bethesda, Md., 1987-88; account exec. Griffin & Co., Washington, 1989—. Mem. Internat. Assn. Bus. Communications (Silver Inkwell excellence award 1990, Silver Inkwell merit award 1990), Pub. Rels. Soc. Am. Republican. Episcopalian. Office: Griffin & Co 1000 Potomac St NW # 206 Washington DC 20007-3501

WOLSON, CRAIG ALAN, lawyer; b. Toledo, Feb. 20, 1949; s. Max A. and Elaine B. (Cohn) W.; m. Janis Nan Braun, July 30, 1972 (div. Mar. 1986); m. Ellen Carol Schulgasser, Oct. 26, 1986; children: Lindsey, Michael and Geoffrey (triplets). BA, U. Mich., 1971, JD, 1974. Bar: N.Y. 1975, U.S. Dist. Ct. (so. and ea. dists.) N.Y. 1975, U.S. Ct. Appeals (2d cir.) 1975, U.S. Supreme Ct. 1978. Assoc. Shearman & Sterling, N.Y.C., 1974-81; v.p., asst. gen. counsel Thomson McKinnon Securities Inc., N.Y.C., 1981-85; v.p., sec., gen. counsel J.D. Mattus Co., Inc., Greenwich, Conn., 1985-88; also bd. dirs. J.D. Mattus Co., Inc. and affiliated cos., Greenwich; v.p., asst. gen. counsel Chem. Bank, N.Y.C., 1988—; dep. clk. Lucas County Courthouse, Toledo, 1968-69, 71-72. Articles and adminstrv. editor U. Mich. Law Rev., 1973-74. Mem. ABA, N.Y. State Bar Assn., Assn. of Bar of City of N.Y., Corp. Bar Assn. of Westchester and Fairfield, Phi Beta Kappa, Phi Eta Sigma, Pi Sigma Alpha. Home: 15 Dingletown Rd Greenwich CT 06830 Office: Chem Bank 380 Madison Ave New York NY 10017-2513

WOLTERS, CURT CORNELIS FREDERIK, foreign service officer; b. Nymegen, The Netherlands, Mar. 13, 1938; came to U.S., 1957; s. Frederik and Cornelia Johanna (Jansen) W.; m. Sara J. Daughters, June 10, 1962 (div. 1980); children: Gwyneth, Chad; m. Charlotte Cooper, Sept. 22, 1980 (div. 1988); children: Lottena, Cicely; m. Sylvana K. Perry, Apr. 1989; 1 child, Roger. Student, Wash. State U., 1958-61, U. Bonn, Fed. Republic Germany, 1962-63; BA, U. Oreg., 1964, MA, 1966; MBA, U. Washington, 1976; PhD, Pacific Western U., 1989. Asst. sec. Rep. Botswana Govt., Gaborone, 1966-68; program advisor The Ford Found., N.Y.C., 1968-74; sr. rsch. analyst Seattle C. of C., 1974-76; sr. assoc. Inst. Pub. Adminstrn. N.Y., N.Y.C., 1976-78; freelance economist Africa, 1978-79; econ. program officer, diplomat (AID) Dept. State, Washington, 1979—; cons. Inst. for Puget Sound Needs, Seattle, 1975-76, Pacific Cons., Washington, 1976. Contbr. numerous articles to profl. jours.; author project evaluations. Mem. civic action com. Congress of Racial Equality, Eugene, Oreg., 1965-66; vol. campaign Dixie Lee Ray Gubernatorial Campaign, Seattle, 1976; treas., chmn. fin. com. Internat. Sch. Islamabad, 1989-92. Carnegie Found. fellow, 1964-65, Africa-Asia Pub. Service fellow Maxwell Sch., 1966-68; recipient Air Defense Command Outstanding Ednl. Achievement award USAF, 1960. Mem. Am. Econ. Assn., U.S. Govt. Employees Assn. (Islamabad), Wilson Ctr. (assoc. of Smithsonian Instn.), Am. Fgn. Svc. Assn., Holland Am. Club (treas. Greater Seattle Area 1975-76). Office: O/AID/REP US Embassy APO AE 09812-2203

WOLTERSDORF, OTTO WILLIAM, JR., chemist, researcher; b. Phila., June 19, 1935; s. Otto William Sr. and Grace (Hook) W.; m. Ruth Eveline Plomgren, June 29, 1957; children: Lisa, Erik. BA, Gettysburg (Pa.) Coll., 1956; MS, Pa. State U., 1959. Rsch. asst. Merck & Co. Inc., West Point, Pa., 1959-65, rsch. chemist, 1965-67, sr. rsch. chemist, 1967-73, rsch. fellow, 1973-83, sr. rsch. fellow, 1983—. Inventee, co-inventee numerous patents in field. Republican. Lutheran. Home: 200 Dorset Way Chalfont PA 18914-2322 Office: Merck & Co Inc West Point PA 19486

WOMACK, IDALAH DEMINA, social services administrator; b. Phila., Aug. 2, 1943; d. Floyd Joseph and Gertrude Mary (Chappell) W.; divorced. Student, William Penn Bus. Inst., 1963-65; BS in Social Work, Temple U., 1977, MSW, 1979; postgrad., Glassboro State Coll., 1983. Control clk. U.S. Treasury Dept., Phila., 1964-69; tech. decoder U.S. Dept. Def., Phila., 1969-73; social worker Camden (N.J.) Bd. Edn., 1979—; dir. Higher Edn. Resource Service, Phila., 1983—; cons. Ctr. Social Policy, Phila., 1978, 88; lectr. Coun. for Exceptional Children, Phila., 1980, Temple U., Phila., 1982—, Dresel U., Phila., 1984, U. Pa., Phila., 1985—; owner U.S. Higher Edn. Resources, 1992—. Author: Over 500 Financial Aid Resources, 1983, Womack's Guide to Getting Free College Money, 1991; playwright Blueberry, 1990; contbr. articles to newspapers, mags. Former mem. exec. bd. NAACP, Phila., 1958-65; tech. advisor Resident's Adv. Bd., Phila., 1977-82, Welfare Rights Orgn., 1979; pres. Family Ednl. Resource Svc. Ctr., Inc., Phila., 1984-86; bd. dirs. Tenants' Action Group, 1988-91. Recipient J.F. Kennedy Sportsmanship award U.S. Treasury Dept., 1964, Disting. Service award Pre-Sch. for Handicapped, Camden, N.J., 1980, Maple Leaf

award Internat. Congress for Sci. Study Mental Deficiencies, 1982, Outstanding Service to Youth award Juvenile Resource Ctr. Inc., Camden, 1988. Mem. Chi Rho (pres. Greensboro, S.C. chpt. 1962-65). Democrat.

WONG, AMY ANMEI, chiropractor; b. Shanghai, China, Dec. 3, 1941; came to U.S., 1963; d. Kai Pang; m. Pak Kuen Wong, June 11, 1966; 1 child, Kevin Chi Ming. BA, Sydney (Australia) U., 1962; MA, Mich. U., 1965; PhD, U. Wis., 1970; D of Chiropractic, N.Y. Chiropractic Coll., 1986. Cert. secondary teaching. Assoc. prof. Nassau Community Coll., Garden City, N.Y., 1974—; chiropractic doctor Ea. Chiro Health, N.Y.C., 1987—; mem. intercultural com. Nassau Community Coll., Garden City, 1990-91, vol. asst. Spl. Olympics for the Physically Challenged, Nassau, N.Y., 1985. Author, poet: Fifty Five to the Nth Possiblities, 1991; editor: (newsletter) Parents and Tchrs. Assn., Oceanside, N.Y., 1975-80; contbr. articles and poems to jours. Adjustor, writer, vol. People with AIDS Coalition, Lindenhurst, N.Y., 1990-91; active Chinese Ctr. of L.I., West Hempstead, N.Y.; sponsor Mini League Baseball, 1990-92, Girls Softball, 1991. Mem. Am. Chiropractic Assn., N.Y. Chiropractic Assn., Acad. Am. Poets, Internat. Women Writers Guild, Asian Am. Alliance, Kiwanis Club (chair health com. 1989-90). Republican. Office: 2089 Kodma Pl East Meadow NY 11554-2519

WONG, BING KUEN, mathematics educator; b. Shanghai, China, Oct. 4, 1938; s. Cheng Shing and Lai Ming (Chan) Huang; m. Joyce S. K. Chan, June 1966; children: Szu Van, Szu Kay. AB in Math., Pittsburg (Kans.) State U., 1961; MA in Math., U. Ill., 1963, PhD, 1966. Asst. prof. math. Western Ill. U., Macomb, Ill., 1965-66, Rochester Inst. Tech., 1966-68; prof., chmn. math. and computer sci. Wilkes U., Wilkes-Barre, Pa., 1968-85, prof. math. and computer sci., 1985-91, prof. and chmn. math. and computer sci., 1991—; vis. prof. Jinan U., People's Republic China, 1982, U. Pa., Phila., 1985-86. Councilman, Laurel Run, Pa., 1985-91. Mem. Assn. for Computing Machinery, Am. Math. Soc., Math. Assn. Am. (pres. Ea. Pa. and Del. sect. 1985-86), Sigma Xi (pres. 1985-86). Office: Dept Math and Computer Sci Wilkes Univ Wilkes Barre PA 18766

WONG, DENNIS KA-CHEONG, physician, physical therapist; b. Hong Kong, Hong Kong, Jan. 23, 1954. BA, Columbia U., 1977, cert. in phys. therapy, 1978, MS in Phys. Therapy, 1982; MD, Am. U. of the Caribbean, Montserrat, Brit. West Indies, 1988. Intern internal medicine dept. SUNY Health Sci. Ctr., Bklyn., 1988-89; Nat. Inst. on Disability and Rehab. Rsch. fellow Harvard-MIT Rehab. Engring. Ctr., Cambridge, Mass., 1989-90; resident rehab. medicine dept Kingsbrook Jewish Med. Ctr., Bklyn., 1990-92, chief resident rehab. medicine dept., 1992—. Mem. Am. Acad. Phys. Medicine and Rehab.

WONG, ELIZABETH ANN, playwright, journalist; b. South Gate, Calif., June 6, 1958; d. James King and Ruth Tsui (Kwan) W. BA, U. So. Calif., 1980; MFA, NYU, 1991. Reporter KNXT Channel 2 News, L.A., 1980-82, The San Bernardino (Calif.) Sun, 1981-82, The San Diego Tribune, 1982-86, The Hartford (Conn.) Courant, 1986-88; resident Yaddo, Saratoga Springs, N.Y., 1991, Ucross Found., Clearmont, Wyo., 1992. Author: (plays) Letters to a Student Revolutionary, 1991, Kimchee and Chitlins, 1992, China Doll, 1992. Mem. The Dramatist Guild, Circle Repertory Playwrights' Lab., Asian Pacific Alliance for Creative Equality. Home: Greenwich Village New York NY 10012

WONG, LAN KAN, chemistry educator; b. Hong Kong, Sept. 10, 1950; came to U.S. 1970; s. Kwok Hung and Pui (Ho) W.; m. Deborah Chung, May 29, 1976. BS in Chemistry, Calif. State U., Northridge, 1973; PhD in Chemistry, MIT, 1977. Assoc. prof. pharm. sci. U. Pitts., 1979—; asst. prof. Ohio State U., Columbus, 1977-79; bd. dirs. Pharmakon Inc., Pitts., 1982—; cons. Extrel Corp., Pitts., 1985—, Hoffman LaRoche, Nutley, N.J., 1983—; prog. reviewer Nat. Inst. Environ. Health Sci., Research Triangle Park, N.C., 1987—. Inventor in field. Coordinator U.S.-China Pharm. Exchange Prog., Pitts., 1984—. Recipient Outstanding Teaching award, Pharmacology dept. Ohio State U., 1978; Research Recognition award, Cen. Ohio Heart Assn., 1979; NSF fellow, 1972. Mem. Spectroscopy Soc. Pitts., Pitts. Conf., ACS, Am. Soc. Mass Spectrometry. Home: 3812 Henley Dr Pittsburgh PA 15235-5041 Office: U Pitts Sch Pharmacy Pittsburgh PA 15261

WONG, MARIE LISA, accountant; b. Fall River, Mass., Aug. 25, 1965; d. Theodore Joseph and Marie Blanche (Simonne) Bernier; m. John Paul Wong, June 25, 1988; children: Marisa Alysson, John Paul Jr., Jason Michael. BS in Acctg., Southeastern Mass. U., 1987. Acct. Profl. Mgmt. Service, Fall River, 1987—; with Fleet Bank, Fall River, Mass., 1991—. Roman Catholic. Home: 148 Horton St Fall River MA 02723-3108 Office: Fleet Bank 1001 Pleasant St Fall River MA 02723

WONG, WAI MING, financial analyst; b. Hong Kong, July 4, 1966; came to U.S., 1971; s. Pak Sum and Shim Goon (Cheung) W. Student, Norman Thomas High Sch. Bookkeeper Handy & Harman, N.Y.C., 1984-89; cashier Waldbaums, N.Y.C., 1988-89; fin. analyst Chem. Bank, N.Y.C., 1989—. Republican. Home: 25-19 81st St Jackson Heights NY 11370

WOO, JAMES TSUAN-WEN, electronics research and development executive; b. Shanghai, China, Sept. 28, 1936; came to U.S., 1955; m. Sybil K.H. Wong, Aug. 26, 1961; children: Jason, Damon, Rima. BES, U. Portland, 1959; MS, Stevens Inst. Tech., Hoboken, N.J., 1961; ScD, MIT, 1966. Staff scientist Mt. Auburn Rsch. Assocs., Cambridge, Mass., 1966-69; sr. scientist United Tech. Rsch. Lab., East Hartford, Conn., 1969-75; vis. assoc. prof. MIT, 1975-77; assoc. prof. Rensselaer Poly. Inst., Troy, N.Y., 1977-83; pres. InterScience, Inc., Hartford/Troy/Germantown, Md., 1983—. Office: InterScience Inc 105 Jordan Rd Troy NY 12180-8343

WOOD, ALEXANDER WALLACE, biochemist; b. Newburgh, N.Y., Nov. 2, 1944; s. Arnold and Gertrude (Barrowman) W.; m. Barbara Marie Curry, Aug. 24, 1968; children: Caroline Wallace, Emily Boswell. BS, Bates Coll., Lewiston, Maine, 1966; PhD, NYU, 1971. Postdoctoral fellow U. Calif., San Diego, 1970-72; sr. scientist Hoffmann LaRoche, Inc., Nutley, N.J., 1973-80, group chief, 1981-87, rsch. leader, 1987-90, disting. rsch. leader, 1990-91, dir. Dept. Oncology, 1991—; adj. assoc. prof. NYU Sch. Medicine, N.Y.C., 1981-89, adj. prof., 1990—; adv. com. Aspen Cancer Conf., 1992—. Contbr. 135 peer-reviewed articles and 62 abstracts to profl. publs. Pres. Ho-Ho-Kus (N.J.) Bd. Edn., 1988-90. Recipient Founder's Day award NYU Med. Sch., 1971. Mem. Am. Assn. Cancer Rsch., Am. Soc. Pharmacology and Exptl. Therapy, Am. Soc. Biochemistry and Molecular Biology, Joe Jefferson Club. Home: 35 Gilbert Rd Ho Ho Kus NJ 07423-1405 Office: Hoffmann LaRoche Inc Bldg 86 Nutley NJ 07110

WOOD, BERENICE HOWLAND, educator; b. Newport, R.I., Oct. 21, 1910; d. Horatio Gates and Margaret Lorraine (Doyle) W. AB, Vassar Coll., 1934; MA, Columbia U., 1936; postgrad., U. R.I., 1961-65. Clk. 1st Dist. Ct. R.I., Newport, 1942-50; home service dir. ARC, Newport, 1950-61; tchr. Cranston, R.I., 1961-62, Elmhurst Sch., Portsmouth, R.I., 1962-64, Newport, 1964-82; sec. to mayor City of Newport, 1941. Pres. Coun. Social Agys., Newport, 1955-57; active Hist. Soc. Newport, Art Mus. Newport, Redwood Library, Newport, Preservation Soc. Newport. Mem. Point Assn. Newport. Roman Catholic. Home: 82 Mill St Newport RI 02840-3146

WOOD, BRENDA SUE, banker; b. New Castle, Pa., Nov. 7, 1961; d. James Henry and Helen Louise (Stanley) Wilson; m. Geoffrey C. Wood, July 27, 1991. BA in Internat. Relations, Am. U., 1983, MBA in Fin., 1988. Bus. devel. officer Overseas Pvt. Investment Corp., Washington, 1983-84; comml. mgmt. trainee Md. Nat. Bank, Balt., 1984-85; comml. acct. rep. Md. Nat. Bank, Rockville, 1985-86, comml. bank officer, 1986-87, asst. v.p., 1987-89; v.p. Md. Nat. Bank, Greenbelt, Md., 1989—; v.p., group mgr. real estate spl. assets MNC Fin.; task force panelist on professionalism alumnae rels. workshop Am. U. Contbr., editor: Washington's Best Kept Secrets: A U.S. Government Guide to International Business, 1984; co-editor The Rostrom, 1982. Mem. Urban Land Inst., Nat. Assn. Indsl. Office Parks. Republican. Roman Catholic. Home: 3900 Alton Pl NW Washington DC 20016-2210 Office: Md Nat Bank 10 Light St Baltimore MD 21201

WOOD, BRISON ROBERT, investment counselor, retired; b. Pasadena, Calif., Nov. 14, 1931; s. Brison Jarvis and Pamilla (Clarke) W.; m. Constance Craig, Apr. 2, 1955; children: Peter Craig, Wendy Wood Schlosser. BS, Yale U., 1954; MBA with distinction, Harvard U., 1958. Chartered investment counselor. Portfolio mgr. DeVegh & Co., N.Y.C., 1959-65; v.p. DeVegh Mutual Fund, N.Y.C., 1963-65; exec. v.p., chief fin. officer Yeager, Wood & Marshall, N.Y.C., 1965-90; bd. dirs. Yeager, Wood & Marshall, N.Y.C. Author (booklet) Why Not the Best, 1975. 1st lt. USAF, 1956-58. Mem. N.Y. Soc. Security Analysts, Morris County Golf Club, Bent Pine Golf Club, Mendham Valley Gun Club (pres. 1982-85), Grace Episcopal Ch. (vestry, chmn. investment com. 1989—), Family Svc. of Morris County (chmn. investment com. 1991—, bd. dirs.), Tau Beta Pi. Republican. Home: Box 263 Tall Pines Rd New Vernon NJ 07976

WOOD, CATHERINE THERESA, rehabilitation counselor; b. Scranton, Pa., Nov. 5, 1961; d. John J. and Angeline (Liberatori) Garzarella; m. Nelson J. Wood, Aug. 9, 1986; 1 child, Jacqueline. AS, Keystone Jr. Coll., 1985; BA in Psychology, Wilkes Coll., 1987; MS in Rehab. Counseling, U. Scranton, 1990. Cert. rehabilitation counselor. Job devel. specialist United Rehab. Svcs., Wilkes-Barre, Pa., 1990-91; counselor, now on-call counselor Diabetes Treatment Ctr., Scranton, Pa., 1990—; drug and alcohol treatment specialist Cath. Social Svcs., Wilkes-Barre, 1991—. Mem. AACD, Am. Psychol. Assn., Am. Rehab. Counselor Assn. Roman Catholic. Home: 1122 Swetland St Scranton PA 18504-1861 Office: Cath Soc Svcs 33 E Northampton St Wilkes Barre PA 18701-2406

WOOD, DIANE SHARP, educator; b. Rockville, Conn., Aug. 30, 1946; d. Holdsworth Harrison and Ruth Mary (Rosenberg) Sharp; m. Ronald Robert Wood, Feb. 13, 1971; children: Todd Harrison, Derek Kyle. BS in Edn., Cen. Conn. U., 1968, MS in Edn., 1974; 6th yr. adminstrn. cert., U. Conn., 1990. Educator Eli Terry Sch., South Windsor, Conn., 1968-75, Pleasant Valley Sch., South Windsor, 1975—; cons. Soc. for Devel. Edn., Peterborough, N.H., 1991; presenter Inst. for Teaching and Learning, Conn. Dept. Edn., Hartford, 1990. Author: (curriculum texts) Simply Wonderful South Windsor, 1989, Suburban Ways South Windsor, 1990. Mem. ASCD, Conn. Assn. for Supervision & Curriculum Devel., Nat. Edn. Assn., Conn. Edn. Assn., South Windsor Edn. Assn., Nat. Staff Devel. Coun. Home: 141 Woodmont Dr East Hartford CT 06118-3340 Office: Pleasant Valley Sch 591 Ellington Rd South Windsor CT 06074-4198

WOOD, JAMES, supermarket executive; b. Newcastle-upon-Tyne, Eng., Jan. 19, 1930; came to U.S., 1974; s. Edward and Catherine Wilhelmina (Parker) W.; m. Colleen Margaret Taylor, Aug. 14, 1954; children: Julie, Sarah. Grad., Loughborough Coll., Leicestershire, England; hon. LHD, St. Peter's Coll., N.J. Chief food chain Newport Coop. Soc., S. Wales, U.K., 1959-62, Grays Food Coop. Soc., Eng., 1962-66; dir., joint dep. mng. dir. charge retailing Cavenham, Ttd., Hayes, Eng., 1966-80; pres. Grand Union Co., Elmwood Park, N.J., 1973-79; chief exec. officer, dir. Grand Union Co., from 1973, chmn. bd., 1979-80; chmn. bd., chief exec. officer, pres. Gt. Atlantic & Pacific Tea Co., Inc., 1980—; bd. dirs. Asarco, Inc., Irma Fabrikerne A/S, Denmark, Schering-Plough Corp. Active World USO, UNICEF, United Jersey Bank. With Brit. Army, 1948-50. Mem. Food Mktg. Inst. (bd. dirs.). Roman Catholic. Office: Gt Atlantic & Pacific Tea Co 2 Paragon Dr Montvale NJ 07645-1718

WOOD, JEREMY SCOTT, architect, urban designer; b. Glen Ridge, N.J., Oct. 23, 1941; s. William Gamble and Alice-Marguerite (Scott) W.; m. Robin Benensohn-Rosefsky, June 14, 1970; children: Alexis, Jonas, Augusta. AB, Yale U., 1964, M in Architecture, 1970. Registered architect, Ma. Sr. assoc. TAC/The Architects Collaborative, Inc., Cambridge, Mass., 1970—; instr. Boston Archtl. Ctr., 1970-76; head tutor Dept. of Art History and History of Modern Architecture Yale U., 1969-70. Author: (section and chpt. in books) Adaptive reuse: Issues and Case Studies in Building Preservation, 1988, Office Buildings, 1989; prin. works include Health Care Internat. Hosp. and Hotel, Clydebank, Glasgow, Scotland, Copley Pl., Boston, The Westin Hotel at Copley Pl., Boston, Liberty Ctr. and Vista Internat. Hotel, Pitts., Wellington Bus. Ctr. Offices, Medford, Mass., Two Portland (Maine) Sq. Office Bldg., One Mifflin Pl., Cambridge, Groton (Mass.) Sch. Dormitories; asst. editor Perspecta 11; corr. Architecture and Urbanism, 1976; contbr. articles to profl. jours. Recipient award of Excellence Assn. of Sch. Bus. Offcls., Coun. of Ednl. Facilities Planners, AIA, 1976, Concrete Industry Bd. Spl. Recognition award The Westin Hotel, Boston, 1983, Prestressed Concrete Inst. award, 1983, Honor award Associated Gen. Contractors of Mass., 1985. Mem. AIA, Boston Soc. Architects, Mass. State Assn. of Architects, Am. Planning Assn., Soc. of Archtl. Hists. (life, New Eng. chpt.), Boston Inst. of Contemporary Art, The Archtl. League of N.Y. Home: 10 Pigeon Hill Rd Weston MA 02193-1620 Office: TAC The Architects Collaborative Inc 46 Brattle St Cambridge MA 02138-3700

WOOD, NORMAN DWIGHT, collections administrator; b. Rockville Centre, N.Y., Sept. 29, 1941; s. Robert Linden and Coralyn (Karpen) W.; m. Katherine Ann Huegel Wood, June 19, 1941; children: Douglas, Jennifer, Nicole. Grad. high sch., Bogota, N.J. Credit mgr. E.J. Korvete, S.I., N.Y., 1964-66; installment loan officer E.J. Korvete (purchased by NAC Credit Corp.), Newark, 1966-68; authorization mgr. NAC Credit Corp., Balt., 1968-70, operations mgr., 1970-73; credit cycle mgr. CHoice, Towson, Md., 1973-78; collection mgr. Choice, Towson, 1978-81; process mgr. Citicorp MidAtlantic, Towson, 1981-84; regional credit mgr. Citicorp MidAtlantic, McLean, Va., 1984-87; sr. credit mgr., v.p. Citicorp Mortgage Inc., Woodcliff Lake, N.J., 1987-90; v.p. consumer credit collections Chase, Rochester, N.Y., 1991—. With USN, 1962-64, USNR, 1964-67. Mem. Internat. Consumer Credit Assn., Mortgage Bankers Assn., Balt. Consumer Credit Assn. (bd. dirs. 1983-86, v.p. 1984, pres. 1985, Exec. of Yr. 1985), Soc. Cert. Consumer Credit Execs. (cert.), Md. Jaycees (maj. Md. Militia 1976, state dir. 1977), Jaycees Internat. (senator 1977). Republican. Roman Catholic. Home: 38 St Andrews Dr Washington NJ 07882-9056

WOOD, PETER JOHN, non-profit housing executive; b. Hagerstown, Md., Jan. 4, 1953; s. Eugene Field Wood Jr. and Grace Creeger Cook; m. Janice Marie Andersen, Apr. 23, 1983; children: Alisson Marie, Lauren Andersen. BA, Wake Forest U., 1974; postgrad., Pratt Inst., 1990—. Regional dir. Carolina Action, Durham, N.C., 1975-78, Ga. Action, Atlanta, 1978-80; nat. dir. ACORN, New Orleans, 1980-84; exec. dir. Mass. ACORN Housing Corp., Boston, 1984-86, Mutual Housing Assn. N.Y., N.Y.C., 1987-90, Mutual Housing Assn. Southwestern Conn., Stamford, 1990—. Dir. Chem. Community Devel. adv. bd., N.Y.C., 1988-90. Revson fellow, 1990-91. Mem. Am. Planning Assn. Unitarian Universalist. Office: Mutual Housing Assn SW Conn 800 Summer St # 330 Stamford CT 06901-1023

WOOD, SUSAN YARDLEY, non-profit organization administrator, Latin American affairs specialist; b. Phila., July 13, 1957; d. John Henry and Jean Robertson (Brown) W. BA in Polit. Sci., Tufts U., 1979; MA in Internat. Affairs, Columbia U., 1988. Assoc. Am. Friends Svc. Com., San Francisco, 1979-84; rsch. assoc. Rockefeller Found., N.Y.C., 1988-89; exec. dir. N.Am. Congress on Latin Am., N.Y.C., 1990—; cons. Northern Calif. Ecumenical Coun., San Francisco, 1985-86; leader Mexican Friends Workshop, Sonora, Mex., 1986; intern Ford Found., N.Y.C., 1987. Columbia U. fellow, 1986-88. Mem. Latin Am. Studies Assn., Nat. Soc. Fund Raising Execs., Phi Beta Kappa. Mem. Soc. of Friends. Office: NAm Congress on Latin Am 475 Riverside Dr Ste 454 New York NY 10115-0095

WOOD, WENDY DEBORAH, filmmaker; b. N.Y.C., Oct. 4, 1940; d. John Meyer and Marion Emily (Peters) W.; m. William Dismore Chapple, Dec. 7, 1963; 1 son, Samuel Eliot. BA cum laude, Vassar Coll., 1962; MA, Stanford U., 1964. Teaching asst. Stanford U., 1962-64; photographer, film editor Bristol (Eng.) U., 1964-66, asst. dir. Internat. Conf. Film Schs., 1966; research asst. biology dept. U. Conn., Storrs, 1970-72; sr. media specialist Aetna Life & Casualty Co., Hartford, Conn., 1972-89; media writer, producer, dir. U. Conn. Ctr. for Media and Tech., Storrs., 1989—; pres. Chapple Films, Inc., 1972—; films include: Yankee Craftsman, 1972; Alcoholism, Industry's Costly Hangover, 1974; Draggerman's Haul, 1975; Flight Without Wings, 1977; Auto Insurance Affordability (2 awards), 1981; Where Rivers Run to the Sea (award), 1981; Our Town is Burning Down (6 awards), 1982; Wellness at the Worksite, 1984 (4 awards); Welcome to the Aetna Institute, 1985 (4 awards); Aenhance, 1989 (3 awards). Recipient CINE Golden Eagle award Council on Internat. Non-theatrical Events, 1972, 76, 84, 1st Place award Indsl. Photography, 1974, cert. Outstanding Creativity U.S. TV Commls. Festival, 1974, EFLA award Am. Film Festival, 1974, 76, Dir's. Choice award Sinking Creek Film Festival, 1975, award Columbus Film Festival, 1975, award Excellence Life Ins. Advtrs. Assn., 1975, Silver Screen award U.S. Indsl. Film Festival, 1976, 81, 1st place award Conn. Film Festival, 1977, 1st prize Nat. Outdoor Travel Film Festival, 1978, 1st pl. Houston Film Festival, 1982, CINE Golden Eagle, 1982, 84, award Am. Film Festival, 1982, N.Y. Film Festival, 1982, 83, Silver CINDY award Assn. Visual Communicators, 1985, others. Bd. dirs. Windham Regional Arts Council, 1987, 88, 89; mem. jury N.Y. Internat. Video and Film Festival. Mem. Info. Film Producers Am. (nat. dir., pres. chpt. 1981-82, Cindy award 1971, 72, 81, 82, 85, 87), Internat. Quorum Motion Picture Producers, Audio Visual Communicators (pres. Conn. chpt. 1985, treas. 1988). Democrat. Quaker. Home: 604 Phoenixville Rd Chaplin CT 06235-2211 Office: U Conn Media Ctr U-1 Storrs CT 06269

WOOD, WENDY LLOYD, English educator; b. North Tonawanda, N.Y., Jan. 22, 1944; d. Edward Franklin and Margaret (Lloyd) Messing; 1 child, Christopher Lloyd Wood. BS in Edn. summa cum laude, Buffalo State U., 1973, MS in Edn., 1975; MS in Edn. and Community Counseling, St. Bonaventure U., Olean, N.Y., 1991. Reading tchr. Evelyn Wood Reading Dynamics, Buffalo, 1967-73, office mgr., 1969-73; English tchr. Pioneer Cen. High Sch., Yorkshire, N.Y., 1978—; children's program dir. Holimont Ski Sch., Ellicottville, N.Y., 1985—; advisor Literary Club, Nat. Honor Soc., others. Author/editor: Self Esteem for Middle School Students, 1991; contbr. articles to profl. jours. Named Tchr. of the Yr. Pioneer Cen. High Sch. Mem. Am. Assn. Counseling and Devel., Profl. Ski Instrs. Am. (region V children's rep. 1989—), Kappa Delta Pi. Home: PO Box 333 Yorkshire NY 14173-0333

WOODALL, SAMUEL ROY, JR., trade association executive; b. July 8, 1936; s. Samuel Roy W.; m. Jane Marvin Brock, Aug. 5, 1958; children—Samuel Roy III, Lawrence B., Claiborne A., George G. B.A., U. Ky., 1958, LL.B., 1962; postgrad. (Woodrow Wilson fellow), Yale U., 1959. Bar: Ky. bar 1962. Atty. Ky. Dept. Ins., 1962-64, gen. counsel, 1965-66; commr. ins. Commonwealth Ky., 1966-68; assoc. firm Wyatt, Grafton and Sloss, Louisville, 1968-69; ptnr. Wyatt, Grafton and Sloss, 1969-72; pres. Western Pioneer Life Ins. Co. (and predecessors), Louisville, 1972-76; asst. to pres. Am. Life & Accident Ins. Co., Louisville, 1976-80; pres. Nat. Assn. Life Cos., Washington, 1980—; guest instr. ins. law U. Louisville, 1968-69. Note editor: U. Ky. Law Rev, 1961-62. Pres. Citizen's Met. Planning Council, Louisville, 1970-71; chmn. City of Louisville Riverfront Commn., 1970-75, Ky. Heritage Commn., 1964-77; bd. dirs. Bingham Child Guidance Clinic, Louisville, 1969-76, Youth Performing Arts Council, 1979-80. Recipient Sullivan medallion U. Ky., 1958; named 1 of Ky.'s 3 Outstanding Young Men Ky. Jr. C. of C., 1968. Mem. Louisville Bar Assn., Ky. Bar Assn., D.C. Bar Assn., Fedn. Ins. Counsel, Phi Beta Kappa, Phi Alpha Delta (pres. chpt. 1961-62). Home: 2851 29th St NW Washington DC 20008-4111 Office: Nat Assn Life Cos 1455 Pennsylvania Ave NW Suite 1250 Washington DC 20004

WOODARD, RICHARD CHARLES, college administrator; b. Utica, N.Y., Feb. 13, 1939; s. Albert Richard and Margaret Olwen (Williams) W.; m. Elizabeth Dorothy Vanderpool, Sept. 10, 1965; children: Lisa, Jennifer. BA, Utica Coll., 1961; MA, Syracuse U., 1966. With Peace Corps, Venezuela, 1962-64; high sch. tchr. N.Y. and Mich. pub. schs., 1966-71; teaching asst. Calif. State U., Chico, 1971-73; dir. rsch. United Way of Greater Rochester, N.Y., 1974-83; dir. prospect rsch. Hobart and William Smith Colls., Geneva, N.Y., 1983-87, dir. devel. ops., 1989—; assoc. dir. major gifts U. Rochester, 1987-88; dir. major gifts Utica (N.Y.) Coll., 1988-89. Mem. APHA, Am. Prospect Rsch. Assn. (bd. dirs. Upstate N.Y. chpt. 1991—), Coun. Advancement and Support of Edn. Presbyterian. Home: 1 Mountain Rd Rochester NY 14625-1816 Office: Hobart & William Smith Colls Alumni House 615 S Main St Geneva NY 14456-3108

WOODBRIDGE, JOSEPH ELIOT, company executive; b. Phila., July 15, 1921; s. Donald Eliot and Helen J. (McFarland) W.; m. Barbara Elizabeth Laquer, 1945 (dec. 1946); 1 child, Barbara Patricia; m. Carol Macy Coburn, Oct. 8, 1949; children: Stephen Eliot, Carol Jean, Margaret Elizabeth, Dudley Alan, Katherine Helen. BA with honors, Princeton U., 1943, MS, 1944, PhD, 1946. Chemist Ruber Reserve Project Princeton U., 1943-44, chemist Manhattan project, 1944-46; group leader Atlantic Refining Co., Phila., 1946-60; v.p., dir. rsch. Harleco, Phila., 1960-66; dir rsch. Sadtler Rsch. Labs., Phila., 1966-68; dir. clin. products Worthington Biochem., Freehold, N.J., 1968-71; rsch. dir. Princeton Biomed., 1971-81; pres. Alladin Diagnostics, Inc., Princeton, N.J., 1981—. Contbr. articles to profl. jours.; patentee in field. Fellow AAAS; mem. Am. Assn. for Clin. Chemistry, Am. Soc. Clin. Pathology. Republican. Unitarian.

WOODBURN, FRANK CRAIG (FURY WOODBURN), musician, woodworker; b. Endicott, N.Y., May 7, 1959; s. Vern Dickson Woodburn and Barbra Louise (Nickles) Simmons; m. Tina Lee Reese, May 22, 1982 (div. Sept. 1990); children: Ian Andrew, Emily Elizabeth; m. Karen Mae Johnson, Apr. 1992; children: Craig Mikeal, Pat Metheny; stepchildren: Charity, Cheyanne. Student, Thompkins Cortland Coll., 1981, 82. With Hadco Printed Circuits, Oswego, N.Y., 1980-81; temporary material handler IBM, Oswego, N.Y., 1982; floor controller Universal Instruments, Binghamton, Ny, 1984; inventory controller Endicott Rsch Group, 1986; production expeditor GE, Johnson City, N.Y., 1987; asbestos handler Sunstream Constrn., Endicott, N.Y., 1988, Modern Techniques, Johnson City, 1989; with IBM, Endicott, 1990, Simmons Cable TV, Oswego, 1990. Lead vocals-guitar Chance, Smithboro, N.Y., 1980-81, North Ave, Owego, N.Y., 1981-82, Electric Forces, Newfield, N.Y., 1983-84, Bad Boy, Binghamton, N.Y., 1985; composer music and lyrics: Par La Furer, 1988, I Wanna Rock You, 1990. Mem. Sons of the Am. Legion, Moose. Home and Office: The Woodster Woodworking Box 410E Swartlick Rd Owego NY 13827

WOODBURN, SCOTT EDWARD, podiatrist; b. Glendale, Calif., July 12, 1958; s. Robert Thomas and Rosalie Gladys (Walker) W. AA in Natural Scis., Pasadena City Coll., 1979; BS in Psychobiology, Loma Linda U., 1981; D of Podiatric Medicine, Calif. Coll. Podiatric Medicine, 1986. Diplomate Am. Bd. Podiatric Surgery, Am. Bd. Podiatric Orthopedics. Resident in podiatric surgery Md. Podiatry Residency Program, Balt., 1986-88, dir. edn., 1990—; podiatrist Podiatry Assocs., P.A., Balt., 1988—; mem. com. Nat. Bd. Podiatric Med. Examiners, 1991, Podiatric Medicine Exam. Bd., 1989—, also mem. exam. com.; mem. credentials com. Am. Bd. Podiatric Surgery, Balt., 1990-91. Author: (with others) Podiatry for the Assistant, 1989. Fellow Am. Coll. Foot Surgeons (adv. panel 1991); mem. Am. Podiatric Med. Assn., Md. Podiatric Med. Assn., Pi Delta. Office: Podiatry Assocs 300 E Joppa Rd Ste 21B Baltimore MD 21204-3020

WOODBURY, FRANKLIN BENNETT WESSLER, metallurgical engineer; b. Joplin, Mo., Dec. 11, 1937; s. Samuel and Pauline Patricia (Bennett) W. AS, Joplin Jr. Coll., 1963; BS in Metall. Engring., U. Mo., Rolla, 1966. Registered profl. engr., Mo., Minn. Assoc. engr. Uranium div. Mallingckrodt Chem., St. Charles, Mo., 1964; rsch. fellow GM Rsch. Lab., Warren, Mich., 1966; asst. instr. metall. engring. U. Mo., Rolla, 1968-71; rsch. metallurgist Twin Cities Rsch. Ctr., Bur. Mines Dept. Interior, Minn., 1971-80; staff engr. office of dir., div. mineral resources tech. Dept. Interior, Washington, 1980-81, participant deptl. exec. managerial devel. program, 1980-81, mgr. substitute materials rsch., 1981-82, mgr. advanced mining tech. div. conservation and devel. mining rsch., 1982-87, sr. staff engr. for minerals and metals, 1987-91, asst. chief div. policy and regulatory analysis, 1991—. Contbr. papers to profl. publs. and confs. Mem. sci. and tech. resource coun. Minn. Legislature, 1977-80. With USAF, 1957-61. Named Engr. of Yr., Minn., 1978; NDEA grad. fellow, 1967-70. Mem. AIME (sec.-treas. Washington sect. 1984-85, 2d v.p. 1986-87, 1st v.p. 1989-90, pres. 1990-91), Nat. Soc. Profl. Engrs. (chmn. nat. task group on engring. mgmt. 1977-80, bd. govs. profl. engrs. in govt. 1976-86, rep. to organizing com. internat. conf. engring. mgmt. 1986—, res. fund com. 1988-89, audit com. 1989-90, budget com. 1989-90, bd. dirs. 1989-90), Nat. Inst. for Engring. Mgt. and Systems (bd. dirs. 1989—), Minn. Soc. Profl. Engrs. (exec. com. at-large 1978-80, chmn., vice chmn. coms.), Minn. Engring. Socs. Joint Task Com. on Engring. Edn. (chmn. 1977-80), Mo. Soc. Profl. Engrs., Va. Soc. Profl. Engrs. (pres. George Washington chpt. 1983-84, bd. dirs. 1982-86, v.p. for govt. 1984-86, state pres. 1988-89), Washington Soc. Engrs., Scientists and Engrs. Tech. Assessment Coun. Minn. (AIME rep. to bd. dirs. 1976-78, v.p. 1978-80), Am. Soc. Engring. Mgmt. (chmn. Nat. Capitol Area sect. 1985-86, nat. membership chmn. 1985-86 dir.-at.-large, bd. dirs. 1986-88,

nat. pres. elect 1988-90, nat. pres. 1990-92), Am. Soc. for Metals, KC, Nat. Capital Inter Fraternity Forum (bd. dirs. 1990—), Sigma Xi, Sigma Pi (chmn. edn. and scholarship com. 1989—, internat. chmn. edn. and acad. com., expansion com., province archon Mo., Ark. 1968-70, Va. 1988—), Tau Beta Pi, Alpha Sigma Mu. Roman Catholic.

WOODBURY, ROBERT LOUIS, university chancellor; b. Dover, N.J., Apr. 6, 1938; s. Glen P. and Barbara Carr W.; m. Anne Pelletreau, Aug. 29, 1959; children: Richard G., Mark P., John M. B.A., Amherst Coll., 1960; M.A., Yale U., 1962, Ph.D. in Am. Studies, 1966; DHL (hon.), Bowdoin Coll., 1988, Westfield State Coll., 1989; LLD (hon.), Amherst Coll., 1990. Instr. history Calif. Inst. Tech., Pasadena, 1964-66; asst. prof. Calif. Inst. Tech., 1966-68; assoc. prof. edn. U. Mass., Amherst, 1968-71; prof. U. Mass., 1971-79, assoc. dean of edn., 1969-71, assoc. provost, 1971-76, vice chancellor for student affairs, 1976-78; pres. U. So. Maine, Portland, 1979-86; chancellor U. Maine System, Bangor, 1986—; chmn. bd. Coun. on Internat. Ednl. Exch.; chmn. New Eng. Bd. Higher Edn.; bd. dirs. Coll. Constrn. Loan Ins. Assn., Am. Assn. State Colls. and Univs., Am. Univ. Bulgaria, Edn. Commn. of States; vis. scholar U. London, 1974-75. Bd. dirs. Bangor Edn. Found., East Maine Med. Ctr. Woodrow Wilson fellow, 1960-61; Danforth fellow, 1960-64. Mem. NAACP, Am. Assn. Higher Edn. Home: 166 Broadway Bangor ME 04401-5208 Office: U Maine System Office 107 Maine Ave Bangor ME 04401-4380

WOODBURY, RONALD GLEN, academic affairs director; b. Glen Ridge, N.J., Apr. 3, 1943; s. Glen Pride and Barbara (Carr) W.; m. Melissa Teele, June 26, 1965; children: Sarah, Deborah. BA, Amherst Coll., 1965; MA, Columbia U., 1967, PhD, 1971. Instr., asst. prof. U. Calif., Irvine, 1969-72; prof. Evergreen State Coll., Olympia, Wash., 1972-87, program coord., 1981-82, Core program convener, 1978-79, acad. dean, dir., 1982-86; v.p. for acad. affairs Lock Haven (Pa.) U., 1987-90, Potsdam (N.Y.) Coll., 1990—; mem. instl. devel. team Alaska Pacific U., 1980-81; cons. on computing and liberal arts. Author: Assumptions and the Social Sciences, 1977, (with others) Teaching? Research? Service, 1990. Mem. Tumwater (Wash.) Sch. Bd., 1974-78, pres., 1976; mem. Thurston (Wash.) Regional Planning Coun., 1974-78; advisor Tumwater High Sch. Honors Program, 1975-85; mem. Tumwater United Meth. Ch., 1973-87, chair parish rels., social com., pastor parish rels.; translator, historian for ch.-community group vis. Nicaragua, 1987. Recipient Citizen Achievement award Tumwater United Meth. Ch., 1986. Mem. ACLU, Am. Assn. Higher Edn., Consumers Union. Presbyterian. Office: Potsdam Coll Pierrepont Ave Potsdam NY 13676-2027

WOODCOCK, D. JOHN, clergyman; b. Phila., Nov. 15, 1945; s. Samuel Elwood and Bernice Marie (O'Donnell) W.; m. Mary Louise Emerson, Feb. 10, 1977; children: Emily Jann, Brendan Neale. BA, Temple U., 1968; STB, Phila. Div. Sch., 1971; MA, Temple U., 1982. Pastor Ch. of Loving Shepherd, West Chester, Pa., 1971—; mem. adj. faculty Temple U., St. Joseph's U., La Salle U., Swarthmore Coll., 1975-90; co-founder Bournelyf Spl Camp, Westtown, Pa., 1980, moderator, 1989—. Organizing mem. Chester County (Pa.) Ecumenical Group, 1990, Chester County Housing Coalition, Lionville, Pa., 1991. Mem. Religious Coun. of West Chester (pres. 1989-91). Home: PO Box 72 Westtown PA 19395-0072

WOODCOCK, LES, editorial director; b. Amityville, N.Y., June 30, 1927; s. Horace Henry and Carol (Reimenschneider) W.; m. Mary Theresa Gill, Aug. 16, 1953; children: Mark, Kathleen Lopes, Susan, Brian, Kevin, Maria Schiavello. BS, Columbia U., 1954. Writer/editor Sports Illustrated, N.Y.C., 1954-68; corres. Time Inc. News Bur., Rome, Italy, 1968-69; ME/v.p. Sportsworld Communications Corp., N.Y.C., 1969-70; editor/v.p. Sports Guide, Inc., N.Y.C., 1970-71; editor, pubr., v.p. Turf & Sport Internat., Ltd., Balt., 1972-75; asst. editor, pubr. Classic, N.Y.C., 1975-79; editor L.I. Life, Manhasset, N.Y., 1980-82; pres. Edit Aids, Douglaston and N.Y.C., 1983-88; editorial dir. Major League Mktg., N.Y.C., 1985—, Westport, Conn., 1985—. Contbr. articles to profl. jours. Pres. Plandome Civic Assn., 1967-68. With U.S. Army, 1946-47. Mem. Soc. of the Silarians. Democrat. Home and Office: 100 W 57th St New York NY 10019-3327

WOODFIN, PAUL BEVERLY, II, accountant; b. Roanoke, Va., Mar. 2, 1928; s. Paul Beverly and Florence Margaret (Crute) W.; m. Joanne Lewis Stewart, Sept. 27, 1952; children: Paul Beverly III, Sarah Linda, Mary Stewart, David Phillips. BS, U. Richmond, Va., 1950; postgrad., Columbia U., 1951, NYU, 1952-53. CPA, N.Y., D.C. Acct. Price Waterhouse, N.Y.C., 1951-78; prin. Paul B. Woodfin, CPA, N.Y.C., 1978—. Mem. AICPAs, N.Y. State Soc. CPAs, Phi Beta Kappa. Republican. Office: 633 2nd St Brooklyn NY 11215-2601

WOODLOCK, DAVID JEROME, mental health administrator, management consultant; b. St. Louis, Aug. 18, 1947; s. David J. and Joanne (Huffington) W.; m. Nancy Perkins, Aug. 21, 1982; children: David Payne, Kathleen, Emma E., Maggie E. BS, Syracuse U., 1970, MS, 1974. Dir. residential svcs. Cath. Charities, Syracuse, N.Y., 1978-82; dir. ops. N.Y. State Regional Office of Mental Health, Syracuse, 1982—; bd. dirs. Syracuse (N.Y.) Cath. Charities; cons. Cornell U., 1990, Mut. of N.Y., 1991. Co-author: Psycho Educational Services for Children, 1982; contbr. Jour. Adminstrn. in Mental Health: Interactive Planning Models, 1992. Home: 207 Thornton Circle S Camillus NY 13031 Office: NYS Office Mental Health 545 Cedar St Syracuse NY 13210

WOODLOCK, DOUGLAS PRESTON, federal judge; b. Hartford, Conn., Feb. 27, 1947; s. Preston and Kathryn (Ropp) W.; m. Patricia Mathilde Powers, Aug. 30, 1969; children: Pamela, Benjamin. BA, Yale U., 1969; JD, Georgetown U., 1975. Bar: Mass. 1975. Reporter Chgo. Sun-Times, 1969-73; staff mem. SEC, Washington, 1973-75; law clk. to Judge F.J. Murray, U.S. Dist. Ct. Mass., Boston, 1975-76; assoc. Goodwin, Procter & Hoar, Boston, 1976-79, 83-84, ptnr., 1984-86; asst. U.S. atty., Boston, 1979-83; judge U.S. Dist. Ct., Boston, 1986—; instr. Harvard U. Law Sch., 1981, 82; mem. U.S. Jud. Conf. Com. on Space and Facilities, 1987—. Contbr. articles to profl. jours. Articles editor Georgetown Law Jour., 1973-75. Chmn. Commonwealth of Mass. Com. for Pub. Counsel Services, 1984-86, Town of Hamilton Bd. Appeals, 1978-79. Recipient Dir.'s award U.S. Dept. Justice, 1982. Mem. ABA, Mass. Bar Assn., Boston Bar Assn., Am. Law Inst., Am. Judicature Soc., Am. Bar Found. Office: US Dist Ct McCormack PO & Courthouse Rm 1502 Boston MA 02109

WOODMAN, JEAN WILSON, educator, consultant; b. New Brunswick, N.J., June 3, 1949; d. Richard and Doris (Pappa) Wilson; m. G. Roger Woodman; 1 child, Kevin. BA in English, St. Mary-of-the-Woods Coll., Terre Haute, Ind., 1971; MA in Teaching magna cum laude, Monmouth Coll., West Long Branch, N.J., 1981. Cert. tchr., N.J. Tchr., chmn. English dept. St. Peter Sch., Point Pleasant, N.J., 1973-77, 80-85, Holy Family Sch., Lakewood, N.J., 1985-89; tchr. ESL and supplemental instrn. Lakewood Prep. Sch., Howell, N.J., 1991—; ednl. cons. J.W. Woodman Assocs., Lakewood, 1982—; sr. v.p. Cynosure Cons., Inc., Lakewood, 1987—. Contbr. poems to profl. publs. Judge Voice of Democracy Contest, VFW, Point Pleasant, 1984—; committeewoman Ocean County Reps., 1990—; mem. Lakewood Rep. Club. Mem. Lakewood Soccer Club.

WOODRING, JOHN OLMER, JR., financial planner and advisor; b. York, Pa., Feb. 4, 1947; s. John Olmer and Louise Romaine (Mummert) W.; Ph.D., Am. U., 1982; m. Carolyn Sue Henry, Mar. 30, 1969; children—John A., Rachel Sue. Sec., Govt. Employees Assn., Inc., Washington, 1971-76; pres. N.Am. Mint, Bird-in-Hand, Pa., 1973-76, Keystone Mint, Bird-in-Hand, 1973-76; adminstr. Little People Day Care Schs., York, 1976-85; mem. accreditation com. United Pvt. Acad. Schs. Assn. Pa., 1979-85; mem. founders group Luth. Ednl. Assn. York County, 1979-85; with Fin. & Managerial Services of York, 1972—, MONY Fin. Services, 1985—. Served with USMC, 1966-70. Decorated Navy Achievement medal; recipient Letter of Appreciation for United Fund dr., Nat. Assn. Public Accts., 1973. Registered fin. planner. Mem. York C. of C., U.S. Pvt. Acad. Schs. Assn. Pa., Nat. Assn. Public Accts., Internat. Assn. Registered Fin. Planners, Inc., VFW, Nat. Rifle Assn., York Hist. Soc. Democrat. Lutheran. Home: 221 Silver Spur Dr York PA 17402-2732 Office: 871 Clare Ln York PA 17402 also: 5007 Carlisle Pike Mechanicsburg PA 17055

WOODRING, THOMAS JOSEPH, publisher; b. Bronx, Dec. 23, 1953; s. Thomas and Margaret (Conway) W.; m. Joanne B. Urban, Apr. 24, 1955. BA in Sociology, Iona Coll., New Rochelle, N.Y., 1975. Sales dir. Middle East Econ. Digest, London, 1981-83; advt. sales dir., pub. Multi-Housing News Mag., N.Y.C., 1983-89; pub. Kitchen & Bath Bus. Mag., N.Y.C., 1989—, group pub. Bldg. Group, 1991—; profl. basketball player European Pro League, 1975-80. Mem. mktg. com. Nat. Coun. Housing Industry, 1985-89; mem. Nat. Multi-Housing Coun., 1988-89; with exec. pub. program Johnson Sch. Mgmt., Cornell U., 1989. Republican. Roman Catholic. Office: Miller Freeman Inc 1515 Broadway New York NY 10036-5702

WOODRUFF, PAUL HARRISON, civil engineer, consultant; b. Harbor Springs, Mich., Oct. 10, 1937; s. Leon A. and Nelda (Harrison) W.; m. Marcia Jane Misteli, June 27, 1959; children: Paula, Daniel, Janet, Mark, Joy, Tama. BSCE, Mich. State U., 1959, MSCE, 1961. Diplomate Am. Acad. Environ. Engr.; registered profl. engr. Del., Fla., Ill., Ind., Iowa, Ky., Mich., Minn., N.J., Ohio, Pa., R.I., Wis., Mo. Waste control engr. Dow Chem. Co., Midland, Mich., 1961-64; project engr., project mgr. Roy F. Weston, West Chester, Pa., 1964-67, v.p., 1967-71, pres., 1971-77; pres., chief exec. officer, chmn. bd. Environ. Resources Mgmt., Inc., West Chester, 1977—; bd. dirs. Core States Bank, N.A. Author more than 30 papers on environ. mgmt., waste control and resource recovery. Div. chmn. United Way Chester county, 1981-82, vice chmn., 1988, chmn., 1989; bd. dirs. YMCA West Chester, 1988—, pres. 1991—; chmn. Water Quality 2000; mem. Del. Valley Earth Week Coalition Adv. Bd.; mem. adv. bd. Chester County Citizens to Save Open Space; founder, chmn. Chester County Youth Exposition, 1990-91. Named Entrepreneur of Yr., Delaware Valley Svcs. Category, 1989. Mem. ASCE, ASME, Water Environment Fedn. (Willem Rudolphs medal 1967), Water Pollution Control Assn. Pa., Air and Waste Mgmt. Assn., World Pres.'s Assn., Am. Pub. Works Assn., TAPPI, Rotary (past pres. West Chester club). Republican. Presbyterian. Home: 774 S Warren Ave Malvern PA 19355 Office: Environ Resources Mgmt Inc 855 Springdale Dr Exton PA 19341

WOODS, CHARLES G., architectural designer, author; b. Chgo., June 24, 1953; s. Sid Woods and Barbara (Poklacki) Meisner; m. Julie Kettle Gundlach. Student, St. Johns Coll., Annapolis, Md., 1971; BA, Campus Free Coll., Boston, 1979; MA in Philosophy, Beacon Coll., Boston, 1981; postgrad., Union Grad. Sch. Head design Natural Architecture, Honesdale, Pa., 1979—; tchr. philosophy Harper Jr. Coll., Palatine, Ill., 1980; cons. editor Popular Sci., N.Y.C., 1989—. Author: Natural Architecture, 1984, Complete Each Sheltered House, 1986; contbr. articles to over 60 mags. including Popular Sci., Archtl. Record, Better Homes and Garden. Winner Nat. Contest Solar Age Mag.; recipient Solar House Contest award. Mem. Neo-Platonic Soc. Democrat. Roman Catholic. Home: Sugar St RD 3 PO Box 538 Honesdale PA 18431-0541 Office: Natural Architecture 65 Commercial St Honesdale PA 18431-1873

WOODS, J. P., pharmaceutical company executive; b. Houston, June 22, 1950; s. William Oliver and Lilly Virginia (Hetherington) W. Student, Blinn Coll., Brenham, Tex., 1968-69; BA, Ft. Lewis Coll., Durango, Colo., 1971. Div. mgr. Gateway Sporting Goods, Denver, 1971-74; dist. mgr. Super X Drug, Inc., Cin., 1974-77; v.p. sales Bon Ton, Inc., Dallas, 1977-80; regional sales mgr. John O. Butler Co., Chgo., 1980-81; sales mgr. Fox Meyer, Inc., Oklahoma City, 1981-82; sales cons., trainer Rugby Labs., Inc., N.Y.C., 1982-83; nat. dir. key accounts United Rsch. Labs., Inc., Mut. Pharm., Inc., Phila., 1983-88; v.p. Western div. Barr Labs., Pomona, N.Y., 1988—; elected to Tex. State Bd. Pharmacy, 1992. Author, editor: Sales and Marketing Techniques, 1984. Mem. Rep. Presdl. Task Force, Washington, 1982—, life membership honor roll; mem. Presdl. Commn., 1988; sustaining mem. Rep. Nat. Com., Washington, 1983—, cert. recognition, 1991-92; preferred mem. Nat. Conservative Polit. Action Com., Washington, 1983—; elected mem. Rep. Campaign Coun. Com., 1992—; elected del. State Tex. Rep. Party, 1992; founding mem. CBN Founders, Virginia Beach, Va., 1986—; active Christian Coalition, 1992, Kenneth Copeland Ptnrs. Ministries, 1992. Recipient Medal of Merit, Ronald Reagan, Pres., Washington, 1985, Presdl. Commn. from Ronald Reagan, 1986, Cert. of Recognition Rep. Nat. Com., 1991-92; named to Rep. Presdl. Task Force Life Membership Honor Roll. Mem. Nat. Assn. Chain Druggists, Nat. Wholesale Drug Assn., Nat. Assn. Retail Druggists, Tex. Pharm. Assn. (com. mem. 1991-92), DAV Comdrs., U.S. Senatorial Club (founder). Mem. Full Gospel Ch.

WOODS, JOHN WILLIAM, electrical, computer and systems engineering educator, consultant; b. Washington, Dec. 5, 1943; s. John Gill and Margaret (McHugh) W.; m. Harriet Hemmerich, June 17, 1972; children: Anne, Christopher. BSEE, MIT, 1965, MSEE, 1967, PhD, 1970. Sr. rsch. engr. Lawrence Livermore (Calif.) Nat. Lab., 1973-76; asst. prof. Rensselaer Poly. Inst., Troy, N.Y., 1976-78, assoc. prof., 1978-84, prof., 1985—; vis. prof. Delft Tech. U., The Netherlands, 1985; program dir. NSF, Washington, 1987-88; cons. Schlumberger, Ridgefield, Conn., 1981-83, Codex Corp., Canton, Mass., 1983-84, Kodak, Rochester, N.Y., 1985-86, John Hopkins Applied Physics Lab., Laurel, Md., 1987, Calian Communications Ltd., 1990—. Co-author: Probability and Random Processes for Engineers, 1986; editor Subband Image Coding, 1991; mem. editorial bd. Graphical Models and Image Processing, 1989—; contbg. author book chpts., numerous rsch. papers. Mem. Com. Acad. Excellence, Clifton Park, N.Y., 1984. Capt. USAF, 1969-73. Grantee NSF, Air Force Office Sci. Rsch., Dept. Def., Ctr. Advanced TV Studies, Washington, 1978—. Fellow IEEE (mem. editorial bd. Transactions on Video Tech. 1990—); mem. IEEE Signal Processing Soc. (com. chair 1983-85, ednl. com. com. chair 1987—, ad com. mem. 1986-88, assoc. editor jour. 1979-82, Best Paper award 1977, 86, Meritorious Svc. award 1989). Roman Catholic. Home: 43 Longview Dr Clifton Park NY 12065-2318 Office: Rensselaer Poly Inst ECSE Dept Troy NY 12180-3590

WOODS, JOHN WILLIAM, JR., restaurant owner and operator; b. Sisseton, S.D., Mar. 1, 1963; s. John William Sr. and Alva Verna (Sheppard) W.; m. Lisa Anne Mattern, Oct. 28, 1989. BA, Grove City (Pa.) Coll., 1986. Registered rep. John Hancock Fin. Svcs., Trevose, Pa., 1986-87; mgr. Chick-Fil-A of the Gallery Market East, Phila., 1988-89; owner, operator Chik-Fil-A of Burlington Ctr., Burlington, N.J., 1989—; bd. dirs. Burlington Ctr. Mchts. Assn., 1989, 91—, pres., 1990. Republican. Methodist. Home: 307B Hastings Way Mount Laurel NJ 08054-1809 Office: Chick-Fil-A Burlington Ctr 256 Burlington Ctr Burlington NJ 08016

WOODS, JUDITH FELL, special education educator, speech/language pathologist; b. Columbus, Ind., Oct. 1, 1946; d. Robert Leo and Pheriba Jane (Dolen) Fell; m. Merton Gerard Woods, Dec. 18, 1971; 1 child, Samuel Alexander. BS, Purdue U., 1968; MA, Fairfield U., 1975. Cert. spl. edn. tchr.; cert. speech/lang. pathologist. Speech/lang. pathologist Stamford (Conn.) Pub. Sch., 1968-71, Worcester (Vt.) Pub. Sch., 1972, Greenwich (Conn.) Pub. Sch., 1972-78, Norwalk (Conn.) Hosp., summer 1976-78; spl. edn. tchr. Greenwich Pub. Sch., 1988—; cons. J & J Books, New Orleans, 1991—. Co-author (series of 108 books) J & J Lang. Readers, 1992. Treas. Greenwich Tchrs. Fed. Credit Union, 1978-84; coach, vol. Conn. Spl. Olympics, Greenwich, 1972-84; vol. Bartlett Arboretum, Stamford, 1988—. Recipient Vol. award U.S. Spl. Olympics, 1988. Mem. Conn. Speech/Lang. Assn., Internat. Orton Dyslexia Soc., Tracey Sch. PTO (vol. 1989—). Roman Catholic. Home: 84 Newtown Ave Norwalk CT 06851 Office: CC Parkway Sch Lower Cross Rd Greenwich CT 06830

WOODS, MARY KAY, accountant; b. Herkimer, N.Y., Aug. 30, 1960; d. Edward Wallis and Teresa Emily (Dygert) Woods; m. Robert Canfield Wolcott, Sept. 21, 1985. BS, Clarkson U., Potsdam, N.Y., 1982. CPA, Conn. Mem. staff KPMG Peat Marwick, Stamford, Conn., 1982-87, tax mgr., tax, 1987-89, sr. mgr., tax, 1989—; sec. KPMG Peat Marwick-Stamford Mgmt. Coun., 1990—. Mem. com. Greenwich (Conn.) YMCA, 1990—; treas. Bartlett Arboretum Assn., Inc., Stamford, 1987-90; instr. individual tax Greenwich High Sch. Adult Edn., 1987. Mem. AICPA, N.Y. State Soc. CPAs, Am. Soc. Women Accts. (pres. Chpt. 133 1990-91). Office: KPMG Peat Marwick 3001 Summer St Stamford CT 06905-4317

WOODS, MERILYN BARON, psychologist, consultant; b. Bklyn., July 8, 1927; d. David Theodore and Helen (Mintz) Baron; m. John Galloway Woods, Sept. 15, 1948; children: Anne Helen, Elizabeth Ruth. BS, Cornell U., 1948; MEd, Temple U., 1957; PhD, Bryn Mawr Coll., 1968. Lic. psychologist, Pa. Rsch. asst. psychiatry Temple U., Phila., 1958-59, instr., counselor students, 1960-64; clin. psychologist Gloucester County Guidance Ctr., Woodbury, N.J., 1959-60; seminar coord. Bryn Mawr Coll., 1966-67, lectr., 1968-70, asst. prof., 1970-73; dir. counseling and placement Jewish Employment and Vocat. Svc., 1973-75; assoc. dean students Rider Coll., 1975-77; dir. student svcs., clin. asst. prof. mental health scis. Hahnemann Med. U., Phila., 1978-83; dir. Ctr. for Pers. and Profl. Devel. Pa. Coll. Optometry, Phila., 1983—; pvt. practice psychologist Phila., 1983-86; pres. pvt. practice, 1986—. Mem., pres. bd. mgrs. Sr. Employment and Ednl. Svc., Phila., 1983—; bd. dirs. Awbury Arboretum Assn., 1986—; mem. Mayor's Sci. and Tech. Adv. Coun.-div. Urban Affairs City of Phila., 1973-76. Tuition scholar Bryn Mawr Coll. Fellow Nat. Vocat. Guidance Assn., Pa. Psychol. Assn., Behavior Therapy and Rsch. Soc. (clin.); mem. APA, ACA, Ea. Psychol. Assn., Am. Assn. Pers. Assn., Phila. Soc. Clin. Psychologists (bd. dirs. 1981-91), Nat. Bd. Cert. Counselor (cert. career counselor), Cornell Alumni Club of Phila. (co-pres. 1989-91, bd. dirs. 1985—). Office: 5928 Devon Pl Philadelphia PA 19138-1510

WOODS, RAYMOND GEORGE, JR., financial advisor; b. Wilkes-Barre, Pa., Mar. 23, 1958; s. Raymond G. and Mary Ellen (McCabe) W.; m. Sandra Lee Keech, Nov. 27, 1982; children: Eric R., Alan L. BSBA, Shippensburg U., 1980. With sales and mgmt. div. Burroughs Corp., Harrisburg, Pa., 1980-84; salesperson Gen. DataComm, Camp Hill, Pa., 1984-86; fin. cons. Shearson Lehman Bros., Harrisburg, 1986-90; fin. advisor Prudential Securities, Harrisburg, 1990—. Mem. Venture Investment Forum, West Shore Jaycees (pres. 1989-90, Jaycee of the Yr. 1988-89). Republican. Roman Catholic. Home: 135 Ewe Rd Mechanicsburg PA 17055 Office: Prudential Securities 1011 Mumma Rd Wormsleysburg PA 17043

WOODS, WALTER EARL, biomedical manufacturing executive; b. Phila., Sept. 26, 1944; s. Walter Earl and Janet I. (Ferguson) W.; m. Anna Maria Gianfreda, Dec. 4, 1975; children: Jeffrey, Elaine, Roberto, Carlo. BS in Biology, Del. Valley Coll. Sci. and Agr., 1966. Pilot plant operator Shell Chem., Woodbury, N.J., 1966-67; virologist, tissue culturist 1st U.S. Med. Lab., N.Y.C. and Ft. Meade, Md., 1967-69; virologist Mercke, Sharpe & Dohme, West Point, Pa., 1969-70; quality control and assurance supr. Richardson-Merrell Inc., Swiftwater, Pa., 1970-74; cons., dir. influenza vaccine mfg. Richardson-Merrell Inc., Naples, Italy, 1974-75; mgr. biol. prodn. Richardson-Merrell Inc., Swiftwater, 1976-81; dir. vaccine mfg. Connaught Labs., Inc., Swiftwater, 1982-84; dir. mfg. resource planning, class A rating Richardson-Merrell Inc., Swiftwater, 1984-88, dir. product devel. and mgmt., 1989-91; dir. project mgmt., chmn. bus. groups Pasteur Mérieux Connaught, 1991—; bd. dirs. Connaught-Daiichi Joint Venture, Tokyo. Bd. dirs. Northeastern Pa. Indsl. Resource Ctr., Wilkes-Barre, Pa., 1988-91. Mem. Pharm. Mfr.'s. Home: 53 Deerfield Way Scotrun PA 18355 Office: Connaught Labs Inc Box 187 Swiftwater PA 18370

WOODSIDE, LISA NICOLE, academic administrator; b. Portland, Oreg., Sept. 7, 1944; d. Lee and Emma (Wenstrom) W. Student Reed Coll., 1962-65; MA, U. Chgo., 1968; PhD, Bryn Mawr Coll., 1972; cert. Harvard U. Inst. for Ednl. Mgmt., 1979; postgrad. West Chester U., 1988—. Mem. dean's staff Bryn Mawr Coll., 1970-72; asst. prof. Widener U., Chester, Pa., 1972-77, asso. prof. humanities, 1978-83, asst. dean student services, 1972-76, asso. dean, 1976-79, dean, 1979-83; acad. dean, prof. of humanities Holy Family Coll., Phila., 1983—, v.p., dean acad. affairs, prof. humanities, 1990—; cons. State N.J. Edn. Dept., 1990; accreditor Commn. on Higher Edn., Middle States Assn., 1979-83. Co-author: New Age Spirituality: An Assessment. City commr. for community rels. Chester, 1980-83; mem. Adult Edn. Council Phila. Am. Assn. Papyrology grantee Bryn Mawr Coll.; S. Maude Kaemmerling fellow Bryn Mawr Coll. Mem. Am. Assn. Higher Edn., Coun. Ind. Colls., Eastern Assn. Coll. Deans, Pa. Assn. Colls. and Tchr. Educators, AAUW (univ. rep. 1975-83), Nat. Assn. Women in C. of C., Chester County Hiking Club, Del. Valley Orienteering, Phi Eta Sigma, Alpha Sigma Lambda, Psi Chi. Home: 360 Saybrook Ln # A Media PA 19086-6761 Office: Holy Family Coll Torresdale Philadelphia PA 19114

WOODSON-CORLEY, SHELLEY CECILE, mental health therapist; b. Detroit, July 20, 1961; d. Johnnie and Dewey Etta (Smith) Woodson; m. Richard Steven Corley, May 24, 1986; children: Taylor Cecile Corley, Richard Steven Corley II. BS, Howard U., 1983; MA, U. D.C., 1988. Nationally cert. counselor; cert. marriage and family therapist. Congrl. intern Senator Carl Levin from Mich., Washington, 1982; sch. counselor D.C. Pub. Schs., Washington, 1986, pupil personnel, ednl. counselor, 1988—; therapist, pub. speaker Charleston (S.C.) Women's Med. Ctr., 1986-88; marriage and family therapist Counseling Cons., Inc., Washington, 1989—; dir., mentor program D.C. Pub. Schs.-Pupil Personnel Svcs., Washington, 1990—; cons. in field. Author: Whatever You Envision, 1991. Mem. Ward 5 Coun. on Edn., Washington, 1991. Mem. AACD, NAACP, Am. Sch. Counselor's Assn., Am. Assn. for Multi-cultural Counseling, Nat. Coun. of Negro Women, Delta Sigma Theta. Methodist. Home: 3839 26th St NE Washington DC 20018-3126 Office: Counseling Cons Inc 2707 12th St NE Washington DC 20018-1715

WOODSWORTH, ANNE, librarian, university official; b. Fredericia, Denmark, Feb. 10, 1941; d. Thorvald Ernst and Roma Yrsa (Jensen) Lindner; 1 child, Yrsa Anne. BFA, U. Man., Can., 1962; BLS, U. Toronto, Ont., Can., 1964, MLS, 1969; PhD, U. Pitts., 1987. Edn. libr. U. Man., 1964-65; reference libr. Winnipeg Pub. Library, 1965-67; reference libr. sci. and medicine dept. U. Toronto, 1967-68; med. librarian Toronto Western Hosp., 1969-70; research asst. to chief librarian U. Toronto, 1970-71, head reference dept., 1971-74; personnel dir. Toronto Pub. Library, 1975-78; dir. librs. York U., Toronto, 1978-83; assoc. provost for librs. U. Pitts., 1983-88, assoc. prof., 1988-91; dean Palmer Sch. Libr. and Info. Sci. L.I. U., 1991—; pres. Anne Lindner Ltd., 1974-83; bd. dirs. Population Rsch. Found., Toronto, 1980-83, Ctr. for Rsch. Libraries, 1987-88; mem. rsch. libraries adv. coun. OCLC, 1984-87. Author: The Alternative Press in Canada, 1972, Leadership and Research Libraries, 1988, Patterns and Options for Managing Information Technology on Campus, 1990, Library Cooperation and Networks, 1991, Managing the Economics of Leasing and Contracting Out Information Services, 1992. Can. Coun. grantee, 1974, Ont. Arts Coun. grantee, 1974, Coun. on Libr. Resources grantee, 1986, 88, 91; UCLA sr. fellow, 1985. Mem. ALA (com. on accreditation 1990-94), Can. Assn. Rsch. Librs. (pres. 1981-83), Assn. Rsch. Librs. (bd. dirs. 1981-84, v.p. 1984-85, pres. 1985-86), Pa. Libr. Assn., N.Y. Libr. Assn., Internet Soc., Am. Soc. Info. Sci., Soc. Scholarly Pub. Office: Long Island U CW Post Campus LI U Brookville NY 11548

WOODWARD, AARON ALPHONSO, III, corporate professional; b. Jamaica, N.Y., Feb. 19, 1947; m. Joan Juanita Kemp, June 13, 1970; children: Aaron IV, Allen, Darnell, Kelvin. BS in Acctg., Cen. State U., Wilber Force, Ohio, 1971. Brake assembler Delco Moraine, Dayton, Ohio, 1967-69; supr. ops. Citibank, N.Y.C., 1970-72; budget and fin. aid. officer Medgar Evers Coll., Bklyn., 1972-75; salesman N.Y. Life Ins. Co., Bklyn., 1975-83; ins. broker MONY, Happauge, N.Y., 1982, Allstate Ins. Co., Farmingdale, N.Y., 1982-83; bus. mgr. Count Basie Enterprises, N.Y.C., 1983-84, corp. sec., 1984, chief exec. officer and treas., 1984—; co-trustee Diane Basie Trust, N.Y.C., 1983—; co-trustee and executor Estate of William J. Basie, N.Y.C.; co-guardian Diane Basie, N.Y.C. and The Bahamas, 1984—; chairperson Nat. Alliance Bus., 1979-84. Co-producer (album) The Legend, The Legacy, The Count (3 Grammy nominations), 1990, Count Basie Orch. Live at the El Morocco; union contractor (album) Big Boss Band (Grammy recipient), 1991. Chmn. bd. trustees Christ Bapt. Ch., Coram, N.Y., 1984-86; deacon and Sunday sch. tchr., 1983-87; bd. dirs. Brookhaven NAACP, Suffolk County, L.I., 1980-83, Internat. Jazz Hall of Fame, Kansas City, Mo. Recipient U.S. Presdl. Commendation award President of U.S., 1981; named Black Achiever in Industry Harlem YMCA, 1980; various sales achievement awards. Mem. NAACP (life), NARAS, Nat. Assn. Jazz Educators, Nat. Jazz Svc. Orgn., Am. Fedn. Musicians, 100 Black Men of N.Y., Cen. State U. Alumni Assn. (pres. metro. chpt. 1980-81), Omega Psi Phi., Nu Omicron. Democrat. Office: Count Basie Enterprises Inc 111 8th Ave Ste 1501A New York NY 10011-5201

WOODWARD, GILBERT LEAVITT, hospital public relations administrator; b. Portland, Maine, Apr. 19, 1917; s. Louis Burton and Edna (Leavitt) W.; m. Ruth K. Pehrson, Apr. 14, 1951 (dec. Feb. 1988); children: Deborah, Gilbert Leavitt Jr., Cynthia, Robert, John. BA, Bates Coll., 1939.

Copy writer Charles Sheldon Advt. Agy., Springfield, Mass., 1947-55; asst. advt. mgr. Stanley Home Products, Inc., East Hampton, Mass., 1955-66; assoc. campaign dir. Marts and Lundy, N.Y.C., 1966-68; pub. rels. dir. Ketchum Inc., Pitts., 1968-70; asst. devel. dir. Luth. Med. Ctr., Bklyn., 1970-72; adj. prof. community rels. St. Francis Coll., Bklyn., 1975-78; dir. pub. rels. and devel. Wyckoff Heights Hosp., Bklyn., 1972-80; dir. pub. affairs Met. Hosp. Ctr., N.Y.C., 1980—; publicity dir. Advt. Club Springfield, 1948-55. Editor newsletters for 3 major hosps. in N.Y.C., 1972-91. Chmn. fundraising campaign for Suffolk County Coun., Boy Scouts Am., L.I., N.Y., 1972. Capt., C.E., AUS, 1941-46. Recipient Citation for newsletter Maceachern Awards Competition, Milw., 1983. Mem. Profl. Communicators N.Y., Health Care Pub. Rels. and Mktg. Soc. Greater N.Y., Greater N.Y. Hosp. Assn. (vice-chmn. pub. rels. agy. com. 1973-79). Republican.

WOODWARD, JOHN TAYLOR, III, lawyer; b. N.Y.C., Sept. 10, 1940; s. John Taylor Jr. and Helen (Ashbrook) W.; divorced; children: John Taylor IV, Seth Warner, Anne Dulles. BA cum laude, Princeton U., 1962; JD, Harvard U., 1965. Bar: N.Y. 1966. Assoc. Cadwalader, Wickersham & Taft, N.Y.C., 1965-68; gen. atty. Johnson & Johnson, New Brunswick, N.J., 1969-78, internat. counsel, asst. gen. counsel, 1978-86, corp. sec., 1986—. Mem. ABA, Assn. of Bar of City of N.Y., Am. Soc. Corp. Secs., Stockholder Rels. Soc. of N.Y., Princeton Charter Club (gov. 1969—), Phillips Exeter Acad. Alumni Coun., Bedens Brook Club, Princeton Club (N.Y.C.). Republican. Office: Johnson & Johnson One Johnson & Johnson Pla New Brunswick NJ 08933

WOODWARD, KIRK, theater director; b. Louisville, Nov. 22, 1947; s. Ernest and Mary Hardin (Morris) W.; m. Patricia Ann Woodward, June 23, 1984; children: Erin, Heather, Craig. BA, Washington and Lee U., 1969. Acting instr. N.Y.C. Housing Authority, 1975; dir. acting studies Pushcart Players, Verona, N.J., 1979-82; dir. New Scripts Project, N.Y.C., 1986; pres. The Attic Ensemble, Jersey City, 1982-85; programmer analyst Time Warner Inc., N.Y.C., 1985—; instr. Performers Theater Workshop, West Orange, N.J., 1989—; mng. dir. Stage Left, Inc., N.Y.C., 1986—. Author: (play) Who's Who in Murder, 1990 (1st pl. award Harding County Playwriting Competition). Elder Presbyn. Ch. Upper Montclair. 1st lt. USAR, 1970-72, Korea. Mem. Dramatists Guild Am., Delta Upsilon. Home: 517 Upper Mountain Ave Upper Montclair NJ 07043 Office: Stage Left Inc PO Box 3251 New York NY 10185

WOODWARD, ROBERT A., radio broadcasting executive; b. Lakewood, Ohio, Aug. 29, 1947; s. Roy and Mamie (Brady) W.; m. Nancy R. Woodward, June 20, 1970; children: Kelly, Christian, Tom. BS in Mktg., U. Dayton, 1969. Intern Sta. WMAL TV/Radio, Washington, 1972-73; acct. exec. Sta. WMOD/Sonderling Broadcasting, Washington, 1973, Sta. WASH/Metromedia, Washington, 1973-80; gen. sales mgr. Sta. WCXR/Metroplex, Washington, 1980-86; ptnr., oper. officer U.S. Radio, Washington, 1987—. Recipient Master Strategist award Rsch. Group, 1988. Mem. Potomac Woods Swim and Tennis Club (v.p. 1988—). Home: 6 Monterra Ct Rockville MD 20853 Address: WWIN(AM) 200 S President St 6th flr Baltimore MD 21202

WOODWARD, ROBERT UPSHUR, newspaperman; b. Geneva, Ill., Mar. 26, 1943; s. Alfred E. and Jane (Upshur) W.; m. Elsa Walsh, Nov. 25, 1989; 1 child, Tali. B.A., Yale U., 1965. Reporter Montgomery County (Md.) Sentinel, 1970-71; reporter Washington Post, 1971-78, met. editor, 1979-81, asst. mng. editor, 1981—. Author: (with Carl Bernstein) All the President's Men, 1974, The Final Days, 1976, (with Scott Armstrong) The Brethren, 1979, Wired, 1984, Veil: The Secret Wars of the CIA, 1987, The Commanders, 1991, (with David S. Broder) The Man Who Would Be President, 1992. Served with USN, 1965-70. Office: Washington Post Co 1150 15th St NW Washington DC 20071-0002

WOODWELL, MARGOT BELL, broadcasting executive; b. Pitts., Mar. 5, 1936; d. Davitt Stranahan and Marian (Whieldon) Bell; m. William Herron Woodwell, June 24, 1960; children: Davitt Bell, William Herron, James Ross. A.B., Vassar Coll., 1957. Dir. community support Sta. WQED, Pitts., 1978-84, v.p., sta. mgr., from 1984, now v.p., gen. mgr. Pres. bd. trustees St. Edmunds Acad., Pitts., 1972-75; pres. bd. trustees Episcopal Diocese Pitts., 1975-78; bd. dirs. Union Nat. Bank of Pitts., Cen. Blood Bank, County Bd. of Health, Lemington Home for Aged, Greater Pitts. Literacy Coun., Pitts. Literacy Initiative; mem. standing com., 1982—; chmn. Episcopal Diocese Renewal Fund, Pitts., 1980—; trustee Vassar Coll., Poughkeepsie, N.Y., 1982—, chmn. devel. com.; mem. Allegheny County Bd. of Health, Health Edn. Ctr. adv. com., steering com. co-chmn. program com. Leadership Pitts., The Mayor's Commn. on Families, women's com. Mus. of Art of the Carnegie, community adv. bd. Jr. League of Pitts., adv. bd. Pa. State Coalition for Literacy, adv. coun. Pa. Dept. Edn. Workplace; bd. dirs. Greater Pitts. Literacy Coun., Pitts. Salvation Army; mktg. com. United Way of Allegheny County. Recipient A Celebration of Excellence award for Media Mgmt. Triangle Corner Ltd., 1986, Outstanding Svc. award Pa. Assn. Adult and Continuing Edn., 1987; named YWCA Woman of Yr. in Communications, 1988, Bishop's award Episcopal Diocese of Pitts., 1988. Office: Sta WQED 4802 5th Ave Pittsburgh PA 15213-2956

WOODWORTH, DONALD DURYEA, hotel executive; b. Troy, N.Y., June 3, 1935; s. Lemuel William and Elizabeth Maude (Duryea) W.; m. Kerry Pendleton, Sept. 5, 1964 (dec. Aug. 1983); children: Bronwyn, Dandridge; m. Barbara Martin, May 16, 1990; children: Chresten, Kenneth, Glenn. BS, Cornell U., 1957; postgrad., Emory U., 1965. Vice pres. Club Cons., Inc., Atlanta, 1963-71; pres. Equity Svcs, Corp., Atlanta, 1972-87; pres., mng. dir. Wequassett Inn, East Harwich, Mass., 1978-86; pres. Mohonk Mountain House, 1988-91, Penwood Corp., Canton, Mass., 1991—; lectr. resort mgmt. seminar Aruba Hotel and Tourism Assn., Caribbean Hospitality Tng. Inst.; bd. dirs. Cayuga Hospitlity Advisors, Inc. Author: Principles of Financial Management for Tennis Clubs, 1973. Mem. facilities com. U.S. Tennis Assn., 1974-86; mem. coun. Cornell U., TRIAD, Cornell Sch. Hotel Adminstrn., 1982-87; bd. dirs. Cayuga Hospitality Advisors, Inc., 1990—, Cape Cod Cornellians, 1983-86, Fedn. of Cornell Clubs, 1985-88, Cornell Alumni Assn., 1986-87. Served to capt. U.S. Army, 1958-62. Fellow Culinary Inst. Am.; mem. Vice Chancellor's and Trustees' Soc. U. of the South, Cornell Soc. Hotelmen (life, dir., pres., exec. com.), Chatham Yacht Club. Office: Penwood Corp care Beaumont Trust 1017 Turnpike St # 11A Canton MA 02021-2828

WOODY, CRAIG L., physicist; b. Balt., Mar. 26, 1951; s. Earl L. and Cordelia D. Woody; m. Margaret Claire Schapperle, May 28, 1973; 1 child, Gregory L. BA, Johns Hopkins U., 1973, MA, 1974, PhD, 1979. Rsch. trainee Argonne (Ill.) Nat. Lab., summer 1972; rsch. assoc. Los Alamos (N.Mex.) Sci. Lab., summer 1973, Johns Hopkins U., Balt., 1973-78; postdoctoral assoc. Stanford (Calif.) Linear Accelerator Ctr., 1978-79; asst. physicist Brookhaven Nat. Lab., Upton, N.Y., 1979-81, assoc. physicist, 1981-83, staff physicist, 1983—. Contbr. articles to profl. jours. Mem. Am. Phys. Soc., Phi Beta Kappa. Office: Brookhaven Nat Lab Physics Dept Bldg # 510C Upton NY 11973

WOODYARD, JEFFREY LYNN, communications educator; b. York, Pa., Jan. 26, 1957; s. Janet Louise (Sweeney) W. BS in Secondary Edn., Shippensburg U., 1978; MA in Theol. Studies, Gordon Conwell Theol. Sem., 1983; doctoral student, Temple U., 1988—. Cert. tchr., Pa. Community theatre producer York (Pa.) Recreation Commn., 1978; tchr. lang. arts Sch. Dist. of York, 1978-81, coord. of pers., 1983-84, tchr. lang. arts, 1984-85; asst. prof. Shippensburg U. Pa., 1985—. Mem., worship leader, preacher African Meth. Episcopal Ch., Carlisle, Pa., 1985-89, York, 1978-80, Balt., 1987-89. Republican. Home: 73 Bard Dr Shippensburg PA 17257-9134 Office: Shippensburg U of Pa Dept Speech/Theatre Arts Shippensburg PA 17257

WOODYSHEK, J. DANIEL, lawyer; b. Englewood, N.J., May 27, 1948; s. Joseph John and Marjorie (Leahy) W.; m. Alice Ann Murphy; children: David Daniel, Michael Patrick, Danielle. BS cum laude, Marywood Coll., Scranton, Pa., 1976; JD, Boston U., 1979. Bar: Mass. 1980, U.S. Dist. Ct. Mass. 1980. Assoc. Roche, Carens & DeGiacomo, Boston, 1980-83, Shocket, Dockser & Assocs., Boston, 1983-85; ptnr., head real estate dept. Shocket & Dockser, Natick, Mass., 1985—. Active local polit. campaigns. Mem. ABA, (conveyance com. 1988—), Mass Bar Assn. (real property sec.), Mass. Conveyancers Assn., Pi Gamma Mu, Lambda Iota Tau, Delta Epsilon Sigma. Democrat. Roman Catholic. Home: 12 Kings Rd Canton MA 02021-1706 Office: Shocket & Dockser PO Box 8007 Natick MA 01760-0050

WOOLARD, EDGAR S., JR., chemical company executive; b. Washington, N.C., Apr. 15, 1934; s. Edgar Smith and Mamie (Boone) W.; m. Peggy Harrell, June 9, 1956; children: Annette, Lynda. BS, N.C. State U., 1956. Indsl. engr. Du Pont, Kinston, N.C., 1957-59, group supr. indsl. engring., 1959-62, supr. mfg. sect., 1962-64, planning supr., 1964-65; staff asst. to prodn. mgr. Du Pont, Wilmington, Del., 1965-66; product supr. Du Pont, Old Hickory, Tenn., 1966-69; engring. supt. Du Pont, Hickory, Tenn., 1969-70; asst. plant mgr. Du Pont, Camden, S.C., 1970-71, plant mgr., 1972-73; dir. products mktg. div. Du Pont, Wilmington, Del., 1973-75, mng. dir. textile mktg. div., 1975-76, mgr. corp. plans dept., 1976-77, gen. dir. products and planning div., 1977-78, gen. mgr. textile fibers, 1978-81, v.p. textile fibers, 1981-83, exec. v.p., 1983-85, vice chmn., 1985-87, pres., chief oper. officer, 1987-89, chmn., 1989—, also bd. dirs.; Du Pont; bd. dirs. Wilmington Textile Found., Citicorp., IBM Corp., Joint Coun. on Econ. Edn., Seagram Co. Ltd. Trustee Med. Ctr. Del., N.C. State U., Winterthur Mus. Lt. U.S. Army. Office: Du Pont 1007 N Market St Wilmington DE 19898-0001

WOOLEY, ALLAN DELMAS, classics educator; b. Rumford, Maine, Jan. 24, 1936; s. Allan Delmas and Margaret Elizabeth (Beddow) W.; m. Ann Elizabeth Welch, Aug. 31, 1963; 1 child, Helena. BA, Bowdoin Coll., 1958; MA, Princeton U., 1960, PhD, 1962; postgrad., U. Hamburg, Fed. Republic Germany, 1960-61. Teaching asst. Princeton (N.J.) U., 1959-60; instr. Duke U., Durham, N.C., 1962-65, asst. prof., 1965-67; chair classics Gould Acad., Bethel, Maine, 1967-68; instr. in Greek and Latin Phillips Exeter (N.J.) Acad., 1968-90, acad. computer coord., 1983-88, chair classics dept., 1990—; mem. faculty NEH Summer Inst., Bowdoin Coll., 1987. Co-author: Fabulae Graecae, 1990; contbr. articles to profl. publs.; copyright computer programs. Mem. N.H. Classical Assn., Classical Assn. New Eng. (pres. 1989-90, chair computer com.), Boston Computer Soc., Portsmouth Users Group (shareware libr. 1990-91). Home: 10 Whitley Rd Exeter NH 03833-1511 Office: Phillips Exeter Acad Exeter NH 03833

WOOLEY, RICHARD EARL, personnel company executive; b. Peoria, Ill., Apr. 2, 1965; s. Donald Roy and Teresa Marie (Hunt) W. Student, Columbia U., 1983-84. Intern-constituent corr. U.S. Senator Joseph R. Biden Jr., 1982; speechwriter EEOC, Washington, 1983-84; pres., chief exec. officer Metroproof Inc., N.Y.C., 1986-91; pres. Metroproof, Inc., N.Y.C., 1990—; v.p. Compuword, Inc., N.Y.C., 1989—. Author: The Inelegance of Essentials, 1984-85; editor numerous articles, manuscripts. Mem. Am. Mgmt. Assn., Internat. Platform Orgn., CDO Club (sec. 1984-88). Democrat. Office: Metroproof Inc 1776 Broadway Ste 702 #1931 New York NY 10019

WOOLF, HARRY, historian, educator; b. N.Y.C., Aug. 12, 1923; s. Abraham and Anna (Frankman) W.; children: Susan Deborah, Alan, Aaron, Sara Anna. BS, U. Chgo., 1948, MA, 1949; PhD, Cornell U., 1955; DSc (hon.), Whitman Coll., 1979, Am. U., 1982; LHD (hon.), Johns Hopkins U., 1983, St. Lawrence U., 1986. Instr. physics Boston U., 1953-55; instr. history Brandeis U., 1954-55; asst. prof. history U. Wash., 1955-58, assoc. prof., 1958-59, prof. history of sci., 1959-61; Willis K. Shepard prof. history of sci. Johns Hopkins U., 1961-76, chmn. dept. history of sci., 1961-72, provost, 1972-76; dir. Inst. for Advanced Study, Princeton, N.J., 1976-87, prof., 1987—; trustee Cluster C Funds Merrill Lynch, 1982—; mem. adv. coun. Sch. Advanced Internat. Studies, Washington, 1973-76; adv. bd. Smithsonian Rsch. awards, 1975-79; trustee Assoc. Univs., Inc., Brookhaven Nat. Labs., 1972-82; mem. vis. com. student affairs MIT, 1973-77, mem. corp. vis. com. dept. linguistics and philosophy, 1977-83, mem. corp. vis. com. dept. physics, 1979-85; mem. Nat. Adv. Child Health and Human Devel. Coun. NIH, 1977-80; mem. vis. com. Rsch. Ctr. for Lang. Scis., Ind. U., 1977-80; com. visitors Vanderbilt Grad. Sch., Nashville, 1977-79; adv. coun. dept. philosophy Princeton U., 1980-84, adv. coun. dept. comparative lit., 1982—; mem. adv. panel WGBH, NOVA, 1979—; bd. dirs. Westmark Internat., 1987—; mem. adv. coun. NSF, 1984-89. Author: Transits of Venus, 1959, 81, Quantification, 1961, Science as a Cultural Force, 1964, Some Strangeness in the Proportion, 1980, The Analytic Spirit, 1981; contbr. articles, revs. to profl. publs.; editor: Isis Internat., rev. devoted to history of sci. and its cultural influences, 1958-64; series editor The Sources of Sci., 1964—; assoc. editor: Dictionary of Scientific Biography, 1970-80; editorial bd. Interdisciplinary Sci. Revs, 1975—; editorial adv. bd. The Writings of Albert Einstein, 1977—. Trustee Hampshire Coll., Amherst, Mass., 1977-79, Winterthur Mus., 1978-83; bd. govs. Tel-Aviv U., 1977—; trustee-at-large Univs. Rsch. Assn., Inc., 1978-89, chmn. bd., 1979-89; mem. adv. coun. John F. Kennedy Inst. for Handicapped Children, 1979—; mem. Internat. Rsch. and Exchs. Bd., 1980—; chmn. MX Missile basing adv. panel Office Tech. Assessment U.S. Congress, 1980-81; trustee Rockefeller Found., 1984—; bd. dirs. Alex. Brown Mut. Funds, Balt., 1981—; dir. at large Am. Cancer Soc., 1982-86; mem. sci. adv. bd. Wissenschaftskolleg zu Berlin, 1981-87; mem. adv. bd. Stanford Humanities Ctr., 1981-87; bd. dirs. W. Alton Jones Cell Sci. Ctr., 1982-85. NSF sr. postdoctoral fellow, Europe, 1961-62. Fellow AAAS (v.p. 1960), Acad. Internat. d'Histoire des Scis.; mem. History of Sci. Soc., Am. Philos. Soc., Coun. on Fgn. Rels., Am. Acad. Arts and Scis., Phi Beta Kappa, Sigma Xi, Phi Alpha Theta. Office: Inst for Advanced Study Olden Ln Princeton NJ 08540-4920

WOOLF, HOWARD, marketing professional; b. N.Y.C., Jan. 24, 1947; s. William and Sylvia (Chernok) W.; m. Karen Sara Kagel, July 17, 1971; 1 child, Samantha. BSCE, Clarkson U., 1968; MBA, Boston Coll., 1977. Mfg. mgr. GE Co., Lynn, Mass., 1968-74; sales mgr. Digital Equipment Corp., Boston, 1974-81, Meriden, Conn., 1981-86; mktg. mgr. Digital Equipment Corp., Nashua, N.H., 1986—. Home: 84 Crestwood Dr Hollis NH 03049 Office: Digital Equipment Corp 10 Tara Blvd Nashua NH 03062

WOOLF, PAUL DANIEL, physician, educator, researcher; b. N.Y.C., Aug. 14, 1942; s. Irwin and Paula (Cohen) W.; m. Nancy Susan Slater, Dec. 25, 1965; children: David Jeffrey, Karen Elizabeth. BA with honors, U. Pa., 1964; MD, NYU, 1968. Diplomate in endocrinology Am. Bd. Internal Medicine. Intern, resident NYU Med. Ctr./Bellevue Hosp., N.Y.C., 1968-71; instr., fellow U. Rochester (N.Y.) Med. Ctr., 1971-73; asst. prof. medicine U. Rochester, 1975-81, assoc. prof., 1981-89, prof., 1989—, prof. pediatrics, 1992—, acting head endocrine/metabolism unit, 1992—; dir. ambulatory programs, dept. medicine U. Rochester, 1986—. Contbr. more than 70 articles to profl. jours. Lt. comdr. USN, 1971-73. Mellon fellow U. Rochester, 1985-88, Buswell fellow U. Rochester, 1977; recipient Rochester Regional Diabetes award, 1977. Fellow ACP; mem. Am. Fedn. Cin. Rsch. (chair eastern sect. 1981-82), Am. Soc. Clin. Investigation, Am. Thyroid Assn. Office: U Rochester Med Ctr PO Box 693 Rochester NY 14642-0001

WOOLLEY, JOHN EDWARD, trade association executive; b. Jersey City, July 17, 1935; s. Ogden Price and Catherine Hildegard (Tanney) W.; m. Sandra Marina Turtzo, Oct. 23, 1984. BA, Rutgers U., 1957; MBA, U. Ala., 1970. Commd. U.S. Army, 1957-82, advanced through grades to col.; co. comdr. 1st Inf. Divsn. U.S. Army, Vietnam, 1965-66; ops. staff officer, exec. officer Office of Dep. Chief of Staff, Ops., U.S. Army, Washington, 1967-69; ops. staff officer, White House briefer Orgn. of Joint Chiefs of Staff, Washington, 1970-73; bn. comdr. and chief of staff 1st Inf. div. U.S. Army, Germany, 1973-76; chief ops. officer III US Corps, U.S. Army, Ft. Hood, Tex., 1977-78; comdr. 2nd Brigade, 2nd Armored div. U.S. Army, Ft. Hood, Tex., 1978-79; planner Office of Dep. Chief of Staff Ops., U.S. Army, Washington, 1979-82; v.p. and sr. v.p. United Coal Co., Bristol, Va., 1982-86; dir. Food Mktg. Inst., Washington, 1988—. Contbr. articles to profl. jours. Bd. dirs. Jr. Achievement, Bristol, Va., 1984-86. Decorated Legion of Merit (3), Bronze Star medals (2), Army Commendation medal. Mem. Ret. Officers Assn., Am. Soc. Assn. Execs., Country Club of Bristol (bd. dirs. 1983-86), Army Navy Country Club, Tau Kappa Epsilon (chpt. pres. 1956-57). Republican. Roman Catholic. Home: 214 Skyline Dr Bristol TN 37620 Office: Food Mktg Inst Ste 500 800 Connecticut Ave NW Washington DC 20006

WOOLLEY, STEVEN E., business association executive; b. Amarillo, Tex., Feb. 24, 1943; s. Eugene E. and Frances O. W.; m. Dianna Stevens; children: Jennifer, Sarah, Kari, Jeff. BA, U. Minn., 1965. Asst. city mgr. City of Hopkins, Minn., 1965-68; community planner State Planning Agy., St. Paul, 1968-70; dir. orgn. & program analysis State of Minn., St. Paul, 1970-73; assoc. dir. The Mgmt. Ctr. Coll. of St. Thomas, St. Paul, 1973-74; program mgr. U.S. C. of C., Mpls., 1974-75; regional mgr. N.W. Region U.S. C. of C., Mpls., 1975-82; exec. mgr. Ea. Region U.S. C. of C., N.Y.C., 1982—; adj. faculty Baruch Coll., N.Y.C., 1987—; faculty Inst. for Orgn. Mgmt., Washington, 1980—. Contbr. articles to various jours. Mem. Dist. Export Council, N.Y.C., 1984—, Regional Plan Assn., N.Y.C., 1986—. Named Man of the Year Hennepin County Review, 1968, 70, Outstanding Young Man Jaycees, 1971. Mem. Am. C. of C. Execs., Am. Soc. Assn. Execs., N.Y. Soc. Assn. Exedcs. (bd. dirs.), Union League. Episcopalian. Home: 49 Summit Rd Riverside CT 06878-2104 Office: US C of C 711 3rd Ave New York NY 10017-4014

WOOLSTON-CATLIN, MARIAN, psychiatrist; b. Seattle, Jan. 20, 1931; d. Howard Brown and Katharine Nichols (Dally) Woolston; m. Randolph Catlin Jr., July 5, 1959; children: Laura Louise, Jennifer Woolston, Randolph III. BA cum laude, Vassar Coll., 1951; MD, Harvard U., 1955. Diplomate Nat. Bd. Medicine. Intern and resident in medicine Children's Hosp., Boston, 1956; resident in psychiatry Mass. Mental Health Ctr., Boston, 1957-59; fellow in child psychiatry Tavistock Clin., London, 1961; commonwealth fellow in child psychiatry Harvard U. at Gaebler Children's Unit, Waltham, Mass., 1975-78, clin. instr. psychiatry, 1978-79; pvt. practice Wellesley Hills, Mass., 1978-91, Medfield, Mass., 1991—; clin. instr. psychiatry Harvard U. at Mass. Mental Health Ctr., Boston, 1957-59, 78-82, Tufts U. at Mass. Mental Health Ctr., 1957-59; mem. exec. bd. Parents' and Children's Svcs., Boston, 1983-86. Designer H.H. Hunnewell Meml. Garden for New England Flower Show Mass. Hort. Soc., 1975 (Ames Cup award). Mem. exec. bd. Ext. Div. New England Conservatory Music, 1972-75. Fellow Am. Acad. Child and Adolescent Psychiatry; mem. AMA, Am. Psychiat. Assn., Mass. Psychiat. Assn., Mass. Med. Soc., Boston Vassar Club (exec. bd. 1963-75), Hills Garden Club Wellesley (exec. bd. adn design chief 1973-75). Episcopalian. Home and Office: 314 North St Medfield MA 02052-1204

WOOLVERTON, PAUL, protective services official; b. Trenton, N.J., Nov. 15, 1930; s. Norman Nelson and Euphemia Elizabeth (Keegan) W.; m. Rita Lucy Debonis, Apr. 19, 1959; children: Christopher Jude, Timothy Paul, David Edward, Paul Jr. AA, Rider Coll.; BS, Trenton State Coll. Patrolman Pub. Safety Dept. City of Trenton, 1958-67; detective then capt. of county detectives Prosecutors Office Mercer County, Trenton, 1967—. With USN, 1949-54. Mem. Patrolmen Assn., Detectives Assn. of N.J., Delaware Valley Radio Assn., Masons, Colonial Sportsmens club. Democrat. Anglican. Home: 347 Hewitt St Trenton NJ 08611-1125 Office: Mercer County Prosecutors O PO Box 8068 Trenton NJ 08650-0068

WOOLWICH, ELLIOTT WILLIAM, educator; b. Hartford, Conn., Mar. 11, 1939; s. Albert Joseph Woolwich and Ida (Rubin) Weiner; m. Rosemary R. Ring, Dec. 28, 1963; children: Alan James, Ellen Mary, Jennifer Jane. BS, Cen. Conn. State U., 1963; MS, U. Hartford, 1968, 6th yr. degree, 1970. Cert. elem. edn. tchr., Conn. Spl. edn. tchr. Hartford Sch. Dist., 1963-71, Bloomfield (Conn.) Sch. Dist., 1971-73; supr. spl. edn. dept. Danbury (Conn.) Sch. Dist., 1973-83; dir. pupil svcs. Bethel (Conn.) Sch. Dist., 1983-88, supr. spl. edn., 1987-88, asst. prin., 1988-89; tchr. 2d grade Berry Sch., Bethel, 1989—; pres. Western Conn. Chpt. 873 Coun. for Exceptional Children, Danbury, 1977-80, membership chmn., 1980-89; exec. dir. Lead Ednl. Resources, Bridgewater, Conn., 1986—; chmn. Conn. State Fedn. Coun. for Ex-Children. Mem. Bridgewater Planning and Zoning Commn., 1977-87, chmn., 1985-87. Hartford Assn. Retarded Citizens scholar, 1966-67; named Man of Yr. Mid-Western Conn. Coun. on Alcholism, 1988; recipient Mental Health award New Britain (Conn.) Jr. Women's Club, 1968. Mem. Western Conn. Chpt. Coun. for Exceptional Children (chmn. 1982—), Conn. State Fedn. Coun. for Exceptional Children (Amy Phillips award 1988), Assn. for Supervision and Curriculum Devel., Conn. Cons. Network (bd. dirs. 1986—), Phi Delta Kappa. Democrat. Home: 144 Main St N Bridgewater CT 06752-1222 Office: Frank A Berry Sch Ednl Park Bethel CT 06801

WOOSNAM, RICHARD EDWARD, venture capitalist, lawyer; b. Anderson, Ind., June 27, 1942; s. Richard Wendell and Ruth (Cleveland) W.; children: Cynthia S., Elizabeth C. BS, Ind. U., 1964, JD, 1967, MBA, 1968. Bar: Ind. 1967, U.S. Dist. Ct. (so. dist.) Ind. 1967. Instr. bus. law Ind. U., Bloomington, 1966-68; assoc. Ferguson, Ferguson & Lloyd, Bloomington, 1967-68; dep. prosecutor Monroe County (Ind.), Bloomington, 1967-68; tax acct. Price Waterhouse, Phila., 1968-69; v.p., treas. Innovest Group, Inc., Phila., 1969-82, chmn., pres., 1983—, also dir.; guest lectr. Wharton Sch. Bus., U. Pa., Ind. U., Bloomington, 1975—; bd. dirs. Capital Mgmt. Corp., Mass Microsystems, Inc., Skyworks, Inc., Pearce Perrone & Co., Inc.; adv. coun. Nat. Entrepreneurship Found. Mem. ABA, Ind. Bar Assn., World Affairs Coun., Union League of Phila. Republican. Methodist. Home: 429 Leopard Rd Berwyn PA 19312-1925 Office: 1600 Market St Fl 2601 Philadelphia PA 19103-7226

WOOSTER, ANN-SARGENT, writer, art instructor; b. Chgo.; d. Harold Abbot and Marcia (Wright) W. AB, Bard Coll., 1968; MA, Hunter Coll., 1972, Hunter Coll., 1976. Instr. Queens Coll., N.Y.C., 1973-75; instr. history of architecture and furniture interiors Kean Coll., Union, N.J., 1979-83; instr. Advanced TV Workshop, Phila. Coll. of Art, 1982, NYU, N.Y.C., 1985-86; artist-in-residence Godard Jr. High Sch., 1988; lectr. N.Y. Sch. of Interior Design, N.Y.C., 1989—; instr. history of art and architecture Sch. Visual Arts, N.Y.C., 1975—. Appeared in Need to Know, Roller Skates for Christmas, 1977, Meditations on the Alphabet, 1977, Breathing: The Word Passes Through You, 1977, Morpheme's Vacation, 1977, Star Station, 1977, Do You Believe in Water, 1976, Emily Likes the TV, 1976, The Dollar Value of Man, 1975, Airport, 1975; contbg. editor Cover, Express; writer for various art mags. in field; producer, performer of video art. Recipient Helena Rubenstein fellowship Whitney Mus. Art, 1975, N.Y. State Coun. of Arts Critics grant, 1982, Artist in Residence grant Visual Studies Workshop, Artist in Residence grant P.A.S.S., 1983, Artist in Residence grant Global Village, 1984-85, N.Y. State Coun. Media Prodns. grant, 1985, Artists' fellowship in Video, N.Y. Found. for Arts, 1988, Best Script award, Best Direction and Best Overall Prodn. award Rose City Video Festival. Mem. Internat. Assn. Art Critics (sec. Am. chpt.). Home: 170 2nd Ave New York NY 10003-5779

WORDEMAN, ANN MARIE, school counselor; b. Middletown, Ohio, Oct. 6, 1947; d. Carlton Daniel and Mary Dorothy (Dauphinee) Hammond; m. Matthew Robert Wordeman, Aug. 4, 1978. BA, U. Cin., 1976; MA, Western Conn. State U., 1983; postgrad., L.I. U. Acctg. clk. Champion Internat., Hamilton, Ohio, 1967-73; media teaching asst. Tarryton Cen. Schs., North Tarrytown, N.Y., 1980-81, in sch. suspension, 1981-82, guidance intern, 1982; sch. counselor Mahopac (N.Y.) Cen. Schs., 1983—; trainer adv. cons. Peerleadership, Mahopac, 1984—; presenter programs sexual abuse for teens, Mahopac, 1985—; family group leader Teen Inst., Putnam County, N.Y., 1989-81. Trainer DARE Program, Mahopac Cen. Schs., 1984—; advisor Boy Scouts Am., Cin., 1970-78; counselor Women Helping Women, 1973-77; founding mem. Putnam Coalition for Youth, Mahopac, 1984-87. Mem. Nat. Coun. Alcoholism, Nat. Peer Helpers, Am. Sch. Counselors Assn., N.Y. State Counselors Assn., Am. Assn. Counseling and Devel. Office: Mahopac Cen Schs Baldwin Place Rd Mahopac NY 10541

WORDEN, KATHARINE COLE, sculptor; b. N.Y.C., May 4, 1925; d. Philip Gillette and Katharine (Pyle) Cole; m. Frederic G. Worden, Jan. 8, 1944; children: Rick, Dwight, Philip, Barbara, Katharine. Student Potters Sch., Tucson, 1940-42, Sarah Lawrence Coll., 1942-44. Sculptor; works exhibited Royce Galleries, Galerie Francoise Besnard (Paris), Cooling Gallery (London), Galerie Schumacher (Munich), Selected Artists Gallery, N.Y.C., Art Inst. Boston, Reid Gallery, Nashville, Weiner Gallery, N.Y.C., Boston Athanaeum, House of Humor and Satire, Gabrovo, Bulgaria, 1983, Newport Bay Club, 1984; pvt. collections Grand Palais (Paris), Dakar and Bathurst, Africa; dir. Stride Rite Corp., 1980-85; occupational therapist psychopathic ward Los Angeles County Gen. Hosp., 1953-57; Headstart vol., Watts, Calif., 1965-67; tchr. sculpture Watts Towers Art Center, 1967-69; participant White House Women Doers Luncheon meeting, 1968; dir. Cambridgeport Problem Center, Cambridge, Mass., 1969-71; mem. Jud. Nominating Commn., 1976-79; bd. overseers Boston Mus. Fine Arts, 1980-

83; bd. govs. Newport Seamens Ch. Inst., 1989-91; trustee Communication Research Inst., Miami, Fla., 1960-69, chmn. bd., 1966-69; trustee Newport Art Mus., 1984-86, 92—, Newport Health Found., 1986-91, Hawthorne Sea Fund, 1990—; bd. dirs. Boston Center for Arts, 1976-80, Child and Family Svcs. of Newport County, 1983-90, 91—. Mem. Common Cause (Mass. adv. bd. 1971-72, dir. 1974-75), Mass. Civil Liberties Union (exec. bd. 1973-74, dir. 1976-77). Home: 24 Ft Wethrill Rd Jamestown RI 02835-2908

WORK, CLYDE EVERETTE, retired mechanical engineering educator; b. Bridgeport, Nebr., Jan. 31, 1924; s. Guy Horton and Mary Ethel (Warnock) W.; m. Elizabeth Ann, June 21, 1948; children: Cathleen, Janice, Richard, Steven. BS, U. Ill., Urbana, 1945, MS, 1948, PhD, 1952. Rsch. asst., assoc. U. Ill., Urbana, Ill., 1946-50, instr., asst. prof., 1950-53; assoc. prof. Rensselaer Poly. Inst., Troy, N.Y., 1953-57; prof., head engr. mech. Mich. Technol. U., Houghton, 1957-68, assoc. dean engring., 1969-84; UNESCO vis. prof. Maulana Azad Coll. Tech., Bhopal, India, 1968-69; vis. prof. mech. engring. U. Ilorin, Ilorin, Nigeria, 1978-79; dean engring. Western New Eng. Coll., Springfield, Mass., 1984-91; cons. Engstrom Helicopter Co., Menominee, Mich., 1960-62; tech. advisor Soc. for Exptl. Mechanics, Bethel, Conn., 1975—. Author: Mechanics and Materials, 1968, Introduction to Dynamics, 1976, Introduction to Statics, 1978. Pres. Portage Lake Coun. of Chs., Houghton, 1963-64, Portage Lake United Fund, 1965-66; treas. bd. Portage Lake Libr., 1964-68; bd. dirs. Habitat for Humanity, 1987-91,. Recipient Disting. Tchr. award Mich. Technol. U., 1965. Mem. Am. Soc. Engring. Edn. Mechanics Div., Am. Soc. Testing & Materials, Rotary Internat.; fellow Soc. for Experimental Mechanics, Phi Kappa Phi, Sigma Xi, Tau Beta Pi. Presbyterian.

WORK, JANE ALLEN, psychologist; b. Phila., May 17, 1916; d. Robert Louis and Lois (McKinney) Allen; m. Homer R. Allen (dec. 1963); children: Robert M., Emily Allen Berg, Homer G.; m. William McClean Work, 1979. BA, Westminster Coll., 1965; MA, Case Western Res. U., 1967, PhD, 1973. Lic. psychologist, Penn. Sch. psychologist City of Cleve., 1968-70; psychologist spl. edn. dist. Lake County, Ill., 1970-73, Coop. Ednl. Svc. Agy. 18, Burlington, Wis., 1974-76; dir. psychol. svcs. Marion (Ohio) Area Counseling Ctr., 1976-78; pvt. practice psychology Pitts., 1978-87; freelance writer Pittsburgh, 1987—; instr. Loyola U., Chgo., Roosevelt U., Chgo., 1973-74, Nat. Sch. Edn., Evanston, Ill., 1974. Mem. Pa. Task Force for Women, Harrisburg, 1986. Mem. Am. Psychol. Assn., Nat. Writers Club, NOW (pres. South Hills chpt. 1987-88, editor newsletter 1990—), Alumni Coun. Case Western Res. U. (sec.), Sylvania Hills Hound and Hunt Club, Entre Nous Club. Democrat. Presbyterian. Home and Office: 718 Robinwood Dr Pittsburgh PA 15220-1009

WORK, WILLIAM H(ENRY), architect, consultant; b. Lynn, Mass., Mar. 15, 1948; s. William Worthington and Dorothy Frances (Nash) W.; m. Jennie Young, Nov. 25, 1971; children: Wesley Ann, Grace Meiching. B.Arch., Pratt Inst., 1971. Registered architect, N.Y. Design drafter Welton Becket Assocs., N.Y.C., 1973-76; sr. designer Gruzen & Ptnrs., N.Y.C., 1977-79; project mgr. Environ. Research and Devel. Inc., N.Y.C., 1979-81; mgr. cons. services Resource Dynamics, Inc., N.Y.C., 1981-82; project mgr. The Gruzen Partnership, N.Y.C., 1982-85; v.p. cons. services MiCAD Systems, Inc., N.Y.C., 1985-88; dir. computer resources Kohn Pedersen Fox Conway Assocs., Inc., N.Y.C., 1988—; cons. architect Paolo Riani Assocs., Florence, Italy, 1976-78; adj. asst. prof. constrn. tech. NYU, 1989—. Designer, producer mag. cover Interiors, 1981 (Art Dirs. Club merit award 1982, Soc. Pub. Design merit award 1982). Mem. AIA. Home: 531 Main St New York NY 10044-0105 Office: Kohn Pedersen Fox Conway Assoc Inc 251 W 57th St New York NY 10019-1802

WORKLEY, IDA, real estate executive; b. Ellwood, Pa., Jan. 30, 1934; d. Anthony and Mary Grace (Laurito) Joseph; m. Donald E. Workley, Sept. 5, 1952 (div. 1980); children: Patti Jean, David Mark. Grad. high sch., Ellwood City, Pa., 1951. Realtor assoc. Bob Garvin Agy., Inc., Beaver, Pa., 1978—. Mem. Pa. Assn. Realtors, Beaver County Bd. Realtors, Am. Inst. Real Estate Appraisers (cand.), Par Excellence Club (life), Million Dollar Sales Club. Republican. Home: 825 Chateau Dr Ellwood City PA 16117-3006 Office: Bob Garvin Agy Inc 877 Mcintosh Sq Beaver PA 15009-2623

WORKMAN, DOUGLAS ALEX, business manager; b. Balt., June 12, 1963; s. Jerry R. and Judy Mary (Davis) W.; m. Joan C. Barry, Nov. 11, 1990. BA in Fin. and Mktg., Loyola Coll., Balt., 1985, MBA in Fin., 1992. Mktg. analyst Filterite/Brunswick, Balt., 1984-86, product mgr., 1986-89; fin. analyst Memtec Am. Corp., Balt., 1990—, bus. mgr., 1991—. Mem. Am. Mktg. Assn., Balt. Coun. Fgn. Affairs. Home: 6243 Bellona Ave Baltimore MD 21212 Office: Memtec Am Corp 2033 Greenspring Dr Timonium MD 21085

WORKS, JOHN HAMILTON, JR., lawyer; b. Kansas City, Mo., July 13, 1954; s. John Hamilton and Ellen (Johnson) W.; m. Angela DeMeo, Oct. 15, 1983. BA, U. Kans., 1977; cert. Langue Francaise Degre Superieur, Sorbonne U. Paris IV, 1977; cert. d'Etudes Politiques avec mention, Inst. d'Etudes Politiques, Paris, 1978; JD, U. Denver, 1982. Bar: N.Y. 1983. Mgmt. assoc. Marine Midland Bank, N.Y.C., 1978-79; assoc. Sage Gray Todd & Sims, 1982-83, Shearman & Sterling, N.Y.C., 1983-84, Hawkins, Delafield & Wood, N.Y.C., 1984-85, Cahill Gordon & Reindel, N.Y.C., 1985-90; v.p., asst. gen. counsel J.P. Morgan & Co. Inc., N.Y.C., 1990—; mgr. Phil Neal Group, Kansas City, Mo., 1984—. Editor-in-chief Denver Jour. Internat. Law and Policy, 1982. President Monticello Assn., Charlottesville, Va., 1987-89; pres., bd. dirs. 111 Condominium, N.Y.C., 1989-90; chancellor Episcopal Diocese of L.I., 1991—. Mem. ABA, Descs. Signers Declaration Indepedence (bd. dirs. 1987—), Candlewood Lake Club (bd. dirs., sec. 1988-90), Sons of the Revolution in N.Y. State (asst. sec. 1991—). Republican. Home: 25 Underhill Rd Locust Valley NY 11560-2224 Office: JP Morgan & Co Inc 60 Wall St New York NY 10260-0001

WORLEY, ROBERT WILLIAM, JR., lawyer; b. Anderson, Ind., June 13, 1935; s. Robert William and Dorothy Mayhew (Hayler) W.; m. Diana Lynn Matthews, Aug. 22, 1959; children—Nathanael, Hope. B.S. in Chem. Engring., Lehigh U., 1956; LL.B., Harvard U., 1960. Bar: Conn. 1960, Fla. 1977, U.S. Supreme Ct. 1966. Assoc. then ptnr. Cummings & Lockwood, Stamford, Conn., 1960-91; gen. counsel Consol. Asset Recovery Corp. sub. Chase Manhattan Corp., Bridgeport, Conn., 1991—. Mem. trustees com. on bequests and trusts Lehigh U., 1979—; chmn. Greenwich Arts Council, 1981-82; v.p., bd. dirs. Greenwich Choral Soc., 1962-77, 80, mem., 1960—; bd. dirs. Greenwich Ctr. for Chamber Music, 1981-85, Greenwich Symphony, 1986-89; commr. Greenwich Housing Authority, 1972-77; past mem. Republican Town Com. Greenwich; mem. bldg. com. for sr. ctr. Greenwich Bd. Selectmen, 1980-81; mem. Conn. Legis. Task Force on the Probate System, 1991—. Served to capt. JAGC, AUS, 1965. Mem. ABA, Conn. Bar Assn. (exec. com. probate sect. 1980), Fla. Bar Assn., Stamford Bar Assn. (sec.), Greenwich Bar Assn., Palm Beach County Bar Assn., Am. Arbitration Assn. Republican. Christian Scientist. Club: Landmark. Home: 258 Riverside Ave Riverside CT 06878-2315 Office: Consol Asset Recovery Corp 961 Main St B-7 Bridgeport CT 06604

WORMAN, HOWARD JAY, physician, educator; b. Paterson, N.J., May 21, 1959; s. Louis and Dora (Rubin) W. BA, Cornell U., 1981; MD, U. Chgo., 1985. Diplomate Am. Bd. Internal Medicine. Intern The N.Y. Hosp., N.Y.C., 1985-86, resident, 1986-87; guest investigator The Rockefeller U., N.Y.C., 1987-90; asst. prof. The Mt. Sinai Sch. Medicine, N.Y.C., 1990—; asst. attending physician The Mt. Sinai Hosp., N.Y.C., 1990—. Contbr. articles to profl. jours. Recipient Physician-Scientist award NIH, 1987-92. Mem. AAAS, Am. CHem. Soc., Am. Fedn. Clin. Rsch. (Trainee award in clin. rsch. 1989, Henry Christian award 1990), Am. Coll. Physicians, Am. Soc. Cell Biology, Am. Assn. Study of Liver Diseases, N.Y. Acad. Scis., Hon. Order Ky. Cols., Phi Beta Kappa. Democrat. Jewish. Office: The Mt Sinai Sch Medicine One Gustave L Levy Pla New York NY 10029

WORMSER, ERIC M(AX), engineering manager, consultant; b. Frankfurt, Fed. Republic of Germany, Apr. 30, 1921; came to U.S., 1938; s. Martin and Anna I. (Meyer) W.; m. Margot Haas, Feb. 15, 1948 (dec. 1987); children: Peter D., Thomas M.; m. Linda Birnbaum, Feb. 20, 1989. BS, MIT, 1942; postgrad., NYU, 1946-48. Registered profl. engr., Conn. Exec. v.p. Barnes Engring., Stamford, Conn., 1952-73; prin. Wormser Sci. Assocs., Stamford, 1973—. Inventor electro optics. Sgt. U.S. Army, 1944-46. Mem. Cosmos Club. Home and Office: 66 Doral Farms Rd Stamford CT 06902-1235

WORONICK, CHARLES LOUIS, research analyst; b. Meriden, Conn., Dec. 4, 1930; s. Peter Walter and Pauline Catherine (Kajrys) W. BS, U. Conn., 1953; MS, U. Calif., Berkeley, 1955; PhD, U. Wis., 1959. NSF postdoctoral fellow Nobel Med. Inst., Stockholm, 1959-61, NIH postdoctoral fellow, 1961-62; asst. prof. chemistry Brown U., Providence, R.I., 1962-66; assoc. non-clin. investigator Pa. Hosp., Phila., 1966-68; assoc. in pathology U. Pa., Phila., 1966-68; biochemist Hartford (Conn.) Hosp., 1968-92; rsch. analyst Hartford Hosp., 1992—; asst. prof. lab. medicine U. Conn. Health Ctr., Farmington, 1973—; cons. staff John Demsey Hosp., Farmington, 1975—, Hartford Hosp., 1968—; mem. subcom. Internat. Union Pure and Applied Chemistry, 1976-81; mem. review panelist nominee NRC, 1984—. Contbr. over 70 articles to profl. jours. Recipient Susman award Infection Disease Soc., 1987. Fellow Nat. Acad. Clin. Biochemists, Assn. Clin. Scientists; mem. Am. Assn. Clin. Chemistry (chmn. Conn. Valley sect. 1978), Sigma Xi (pres. Hartford chpt. 1976-77). Office: Hartford Hosp 80 Seymour St Hartford CT 06115-2700

WORST, SUSAN GAIL, lay worker, editor; b. Chgo., Mar. 29, 1964; d. Raymond John and Karen Ann (Wolff) W.; m. Laurence Cohen, May 26, 1991. BA, Washington U., 1986; postgrad., Harvard U., 1986-87. Deacon U. Luth. Ch., Cambridge, Mass., 1988—; edit. asst. to dir. Beacon Press, Boston, 1988—; mem. bd. worship, U. Luth. Ch., 1990—, mem. Ch. coun., 1991-92, pres. Ch. coun., 1992—. Mem. Women Scholary Publishing (publicist 1990-92), Phi Beta Kappa. Office: Beacon Press 25 Beacon St Boston MA 02108-2824

WORTH, IRENE, actress; b. Nebr., June 23, 1916. B.Edn., U. Calif. at Los Angeles, 1937; pupil, Elsie Fogarty, London, 1944-45. Formerly tchr. Debut as Fenella in: Escape Me Never, N.Y.C., 1942; Broadway debut as Cecily Harden in: The Two Mrs. Carrolls, 1943; London debut in The Time of Your Life, 1946; following roles, mostly on London stage, include Anabelle Jones in Love Goes to Press, 1946; Ilona Szabo in: The Play's The Thing, 1947; as Eileen Perry in: Edward my Son, 1948; as Lady Fortrose in: Home is Tomorrow, 1948; as Mary Dalton in: Native Son, 1948; title role in: LaCrece, 1948; as Olivia Raines in: Champagne for Delilah, 1949; as Celia Coplestone in: The Cocktail Party, 1949, 50; various roles with Old Vic Repertory Co., London, including Desdemona in Othello; Helena in Midsummer Night's Dream and Lady Macbeth in Macbeth; also Catherine de Vausselles in: on tours The Other Heart, S. Africa, 1952; as Portia in: The Merchant of Venice, 1953; joined, Shakespeare Festival Theatre, Stratford, Ont., Can., 1953; as Helena in: All's Well That Ends Well; Queen Margaret in: Richard III; appeared as Frances Farrar in: A Day by the Sea, 1953-54; leading roles in: The Queen and the Rebels, 1955, Hotel Paradiso, 1956; as Mary Stuart, 1957, The Potting Shed, 1958; appeared as Albertine Prine in: Toys in the Attic, 1960 (Page One award); mem., Royal Shakespeare Co., 1962-64; including world tour King Lear, 1964; star: including world tour Tiny Alice, N.Y.C., 1964, Aldwych, 1970; appeared in: Noel Coward trilogy Shadows of the Evening; also appeared as Hilde in: A Song at Twilight; Anna-Mary in: Come into the Garden Maud (Evening Standard award); Hesione Hushabye in: Heartbreak House (Variety Club Gt. Britain award 1967); Jocasta in: Oedipus, 1968; Hedda in: Hedda Gabler, 1970; with internat. Co., Theatre Research, Paris and Iran, 1971; leading role in: Notes on a Love Affair, 1972; Mme. Arkadina in: The Seagull, 1973; Gertrude in: Hamlet; Mrs. Alving in: Ghosts, 1974; Princess Kosmonopolis in: Sweet Bird of Youth, 1975-76 (Jefferson award, Tony award); Lina in: Misalliance, 1976; Mme. Ranevskaya in: The Cherry Orchard, 1977 (Drama Desk award); Kate in: Old Times, 1977, After the Season, 1978, Happy Days, 1979, Eyewitness, 1980, Coriolanus, 1988, Lost In Yonkers, (Tony award, 1991); films include; role of Leonie in: Orders to Kill, 1958 (Brit. Film Acad. award), The Scapegoat, 1958, King Lear, 1970, Nicholas and Alexandra, 1971, Rich Kids, 1979, Eyewitness, 1981, Fast Forward, 1985, Death Trap, also numerous radio, TV appearances, Eng., Can., U.S., including; Stella in: The Lake; Ellida Wangel in: The Lady from the Sea (Daily Mail Nat. TV award), also Candida, Duchess of Malfi, Antigone, Prince Orestes, Variations on a Theme, The Way of the World, The Displaced Person; (with Brit. Broadcasting Co.) Coriolanus, 1984; poetry recitals, recs.; (recipient Whitbread Anglo-Am. award outstanding actress 1967). Decorated comdr. Brit. Empire (hon.). Address: Internat Creative Mgmt care Milton Goldman 40 W 57th St 6th Fl New York NY 10019*

WORTH, MARY PAGE, mayor; b. Balt., Jan. 23, 1924; d. Christian Allen and Margaret Pennington (Holbein) Schwarzwaelder; m. William James Worth, Nov. 4, 1947 (dec. May 1986); children: Margaret Page, William Allen, John David III. Student, Ladycliff Coll., Highland Falls, N.Y., 1941-42, Abbott Sch. Art, Washington, 1942-44. Selectman Town of Searsport, Maine, 1973-75; mayor City of Belfast, Maine, 1986—; recreation chmn. Town of Searsport, 1970-72. Del. Rep. State Conv., Maine, 1970-88; pres. Searsport Reps., 1974-76; active Am. Overseas Assn., 1976—; pres. Searsport C. of C., 1976-79; mem. exec. bd. Waldo County Com. for Social Action, Belfast, 1986—; mem. Abnacki coun. Girl Scouts U.S.; tutor Literacy Vols. Am.; recreation specialist ARC, Camp Haugen, Japan, 1946-47; bd. dirs. RSVP-Waldo County, Head Start Waldo County; vol. tchr. Sch. for Blind, Cholon, Republic Vietnam, 1959-61, Am. School at Saigon, Republic Vietnam, 1959-61; club dir. USAF Spl. Services, Fort Belvoir, Va., 1962-63, U.S. Army Spl. Services, Fort Belvoir, Va., 1963-64. Mem. DAR (Maine officer 1986—), Internat. Platform Assn., Retired Officers Assn., Belfast Garden Club (parliamentarian 1984—), Waldo County Human Soc. (pres. 1990—), Waldo County Law Enforcement (v.p. 1990—), Rotary (gov.'s com. Maine St. '90), VFW Aux., Am. Legion Aux. Home: 58 Bayview St Belfast ME 04915-1661 Office: City of Belfast Mayor's Office 71 Church St Belfast ME 04915-1796

WORTH, MICHAEL JOHN, university administrator; b. Wilkes-Barre, Pa., Mar. 16, 1946; s. Joseph Henry and Meta C. (Gehlken) W.; children: Shane Michael, Lindsey Dugan. AB, Wilkes Coll., 1968; MA, Am. U., 1970; PhD, U. Md., 1982. Asst. to pres. Wilkes Coll., Wilkes-Barre, 1971-74; dir. devel. and pub. rels. Allentown Coll., Pa., 1974-77; dir. devel. U. Md., College Park, 1977-83; v.p. devel., alumni affairs George Washington U., Washington, 1983—. Gen. editor: Public College and University Development, 1985. Contbr. articles to profl. jours. Mem. Coun. Advancement and Support of Edn., Am. Assn. Higher Edn., Assn. Study of Higher Edn. Democrat. Office: George Washington U 805 Rice Hall Washington DC 20052

WORTHINGTON, BARRY K., national association executive director; b. Sayre, Pa., July 24, 1954; s. Foster Gale and Moneta (Kast) W.; m. Louise J. Latella, Nov. 28, 1986; children: Barry K., Kerry L. BS, Pa. State U., 1979; MS, U. Houston, 1984. Supr. Houston Lighting and Power Co., 1980-87; v.p. Thomas A. Edison Found., Southfield, Mich., 1987-88; exec. dir. U.S. Energy Assn., Washington, 1988—; mem. adv. bd. Leadership Inst. for Sci. Edn., Glastonbury, Conn., 1989—; mem. Natural Gas Roundtable, Washington, 1989—. Co-author Energy-Nat. Wildlife Fedn., 1978; editor Energy-1990 USEA, 1990, Global Climate Change, 1990. Dir. architecture com. Homeowners Assn., Olney, Md., 1989-90. Mem. Nat. Energy Resources Assn., Nat. Sci. Suprs. Assn. (award judge 1989-91), Assn. Energy Economists. Office: US Energy Assn 1620 I St NW Washington DC 20006

WORTHINGTON, CHARLES ROY, physics educator; b. Australia, May 17, 1925; came to U.S., 1956; s. Thomas Charles and Mary Ivy (Hodge) W.; m. Alma Rose Burnier, Dec. 12, 1959; children—Laurie Alma, Keith Charles, Ian Roy. B.S., Adelaide U., 1950, Ph.D., 1955. Mem. MRC Biophysics Rsch. unit Kings Coll., London, 1958-61; asst. prof., assoc. prof. physics dept. U. Mich., 1961-69; prof. biol. scis. and physics Carnegie-Mellon U., Pitts., 1969—. Contbr. articles to profl. jours. Served with Royal Australian Air Force, 1944-45. Mem. Biophys. Soc. Home: 3024 Sturbridge Ct Allison Park PA 15101-1538 Office: 4400 5th Ave Pittsburgh PA 15213-2683

WORTHINGTON, GEORGE MARSHALL, public relations and marketing consultant; b. Houston, Dec. 15, 1953; s. Thomas Eugene and Nancy Ann (Willis) W. BA, Trinity U., San Antonio, 1972; M in Internat. Affairs, Columbia U., 1978, cert. in mgmt., 1983, postgrad., 1992—. Writer, analyst Planned Parenthood of N.Y.C., 1978-79, spl. projects coord., 1979-80, mgr., trainer African Family Planning Nurse Practitioner Tng. program, 1980-83; pres. Worthington Assocs. Worldwide, N.Y.C., 1983—. Author: International Compendium of AIDS Programs and Policies, 1989. Alt. rep., mem. numerous non-govtl. orgns. UN, UNICEF, UNESCO, WHO, ECOSOC; rep. Internat. Coun. on Disability; bd. dirs. Ednl. Equity Concepts, Ctr. for Independence of Disabled, N.Y.; founder, mem. working group on AIDS, Non-Govtl. Orgns. Com. on UNICEF, Coun. World Orgns. Concerned About AIDS. Named one of Outstanding Young Men in Am., 1985, 87; recipient Outstanding Nat. Project award Nat. Inst. Justice, 1984; Jesse Smith Noyes Found. scholar, 1985, Health and Child Survival fellow USAID/Johns Hopkins U., 1991, Charles Revson fellow Columbia U., 1991-92. Mem. Soc. for Internat. Devel. (sec., bd. dirs. 1982-85), Soc. for Ethical Culture (numerous coms.), Am. Pub. Health Assn., Nat. Coun. Internat. Health, Internat. AIDS Soc., Internat. Soc. for AIDS Edn. Democrat. Home and Office: 3D-345 W 21st St New York NY 10011-3059

WORTHINGTON, ROBERT MELVIN, educational consultant; b. Roulean/Saskatchewan, Can., May 31, 1922; naturalized citizen, 1943; BS, Ea. Ky. U., 1948, LLD, 1972; MA, U. Minn., 1949, PhD, 1958; DHL (hon.), Lincoln U., 1973. Supr. vets. tng. and indsl. edn. Minn. State Dept. Edn.; asst. state commr. edn., state dir. Vocat. Tech. and Adult Edn. N.J.; assoc. U.S. Commr. Edn.; dir. Bur. Adult, Vocat. and Tech. Edn.; chmn. sr. rsch. assoc. Career Devel. Assocs. Inc., Princeton, N.J.; assoc. commr. higher edn. Utah System Higher Edn.; mem Joint Com. on Edn. and Tgn. for Nat. Security; asst. sec. vocat. and adult edn. U.S. Dept. Edn., 1981-86; cons. edn. and tng.; cons. edn. and tgn. Edgewater Park, N.J., 1990—; apptd. by Pres. Bush White House Commn. on Presdl. Scholars, 1990; mem. Met. Lit. Task Force; mem. Mgmt. Systems Devel. Coun., Edn. Credit Mgmt. Policy Oversight Bd., Sec.'s Com. on Fraud Waste and Mismanagement, Nat. Commn. Employment Policy; Gov.'s Manpower Planning Coun., Utah State Adv. Coun. on Sci. and Tech.; acting pres. Coll. Ea. Utah.; head U.S. delegation UNESCO World Conf. on Adult Edn. and Lifelong Learning, Tokyo; U.S. del. OECD, Paris; prof., chmn. dept., indsl. edn. and tech. Trenton State Coll.; vis. prof. end. Rutgers U., Boston U. Author 8 books; contbr. articles to profl. jours.; editoral bd. Edn. Digest; editor Jour. Indsl. Tech. Tchr. Edn. 1st lt. U.S. Army Air Corps, 1943-47. Home: 315 Edgewater Ave Beverly NJ 08010-1417

WORTHMAN, MOSES, artist; b. Bklyn., Feb. 16, 1911; s. Louis and Mary (Connor) W.; m. Bernice Fine, Sept. 19, 1940; children: Joan Iris, Bonnie Rachel Worthman Goodman. Student, Art Students League N.Y., 1928-33. Art dir. Culver Glassware Co. Inc., Rahway, N.J., 1975. One man shows include Albany (N.Y.) Inst. of History & Art, 1970, Belanthi Gallery, Bklyn., 1980, State Bank of Albany, 1981, Francesca Anderson Gallery, Boston, 1986; group exhibition shows include Nat. Acad. Design, N.Y.C., 1987, Salmagundi Club, N.Y.C., 1987 (Salmagundi award 1987), Art U.S.A., Grand Junction, Colo., 1987, Am. Watercolor Soc., N.Y.C., 1986, 87, 88, 89, Allied Artists of Am., 1989, Nat. Arts Club, Gramercy Park, N.Y., 1989, San Diego Watercolor Soc., 1989, Museo De La Acuarella, Mexico City, 1989, others.; pvt. collections include Museo De La Acuarella, Alabany Inst. of History & Art. Recipient spl. tribute Knickerbocker Artists, 1985, silver medal, 1987, silver medal of honor, Allied Artists of Am., 1989, Liquitex award Ga. Watercolor Soc., 1989, Munford award, 1989, Nat. Arts Club Heydenryk award 1990, also over 60 other awards and medals. Mem. Am. Watercolor Soc. (signature mem., treas., 3d v.p., Barse Miller award 1988, High Winds award and medal 1989), Allied Artists Am. (treas., v.p., chmn. demonstrations), Artists Fellowship (rec. sec.), Hudson Valley Art Assn. (juror, numerous awards, spl. tribute 1989), North Shore Arts Assn. Gloucester (A.T. Hibbard award 1984, numerous others), Nat. Arts Club (exhbns. com. 1978-87, chmn. watercolor exhbn.). Democrat. Jewish. Home: 3027 Brighton 5th St Brooklyn NY 11235-6407 Office: Culver Glassware Co Inc 1905 Elizabeth Ave Rahway NJ 07065-4037

WORTIS, JOSEPH, psychiatrist; b. N.Y.C., Oct. 2, 1906; s. Harry and Selina (Brunswick) W.; widowed 1986; children: Henry, Avi, Emily Wortis Leider. BA, NYU, 1927; MD, U. Vienna, Austria, 1932. Diplomate, Am. Bd. Psychiatry. Resident Bellevue Hosp., 1932-34, Johns Hopkins Hosp., 1938-39; prof. SUNY, Stony Brook, 1972—. Author: Tricky Dick and His Pals, 1949, Soviet Psychiatry, 1950, Fragments of Analysis with Freud, 1952; editor Biol. Psychiatry Jour., 1966—, Mental Retardation and Devel. Disabilities Rev., 1970—. Lt. comdr. USPHS, 1943-45. Mem. Soc. Biol. Psychiatry (pres. 1966-67, Gold medal 1976, Disting. Svc. award 1982), Am. Assn. Mental Deficiency (v.p. 1960-61), Am. Acad. Mental Retardation (pres. 1962-63), Am. Psychiat. Assn., Am. Pub. Health Assn., Internat. Coll. Higher Nervous Activity (sec. 1987—). Home and Office: 152 Hicks St Brooklyn NY 11201-2303

WORTMAN, RICHARD S., historian, educator; b. N.Y.C., Mar. 24, 1938; s. Joseph R. and Ruth (Nacht) W.; m. Marlene Stein, June 14, 1960; 1 child, Leonie. B.A., Cornell U., 1958; M.A., U. Chgo., 1960, Ph.D., 1964. Instr. history U. Chgo., 1963-64, asst. prof., 1964-69, asso. prof., 1969-76, prof., 1976-77; prof. history Princeton U., 1977-88, dir. Russian studies, 1982-88; prof. history Columbia U., 1988—; trustee Nat. Council for Soviet and Eastern European Research, 1983-89; sr. fellow Harriman Inst., 1985-86. Author: The Crisis of Russian Populism, 1967, The Development of a Russian Legal Consciousness, 1976, (with Leopold Haimson and Ziva Galilli) The Making of Three Russian Revolutionaries: Voices from the Menshevik Past, 1987. Social Sci. Research Council grantee, 1975-76; Guggenheim fellow, 1981-82. Mem. Am. Assn. Advancement Slavic Studies (pres. Mid-Atlantic Slavic Conf. 1982-83), AAUP., Am. Hist. Assn. Home: Apt 91 410 Riverside Dr New York NY 10025-7924

WORTMAN, THOMAS ILDEPHONSE, director residences, consultant; b. St. Marys, Pa., Sept. 2, 1965; s. Ivan W. and Ruby A. (Goodreau) W. BA, Edinboro (Pa.) U., 1987; MA, Indiana U. of Pa., 1989. Residence dir. IUP, Indiana, Pa., 1987-89; resident dir. Duquesne U., Pitts., 1989-90; residence dir. Indiana U. of Pa., 1990—; cons. Elite Metal Products, St. Marys, 1987—. Mem. AACD, NEA, Pa. State Edn. Assn., Am. Coll. Pers. Assn., Pa. Coll. Pers. Assn., Nat. Assn. Student Pers. Adminstrs. Home and Office: Indiana U of Pa Housing & Residence Life G-14 Sutton Indiana PA 15705

WORTZEL, LAWRENCE HERBERT, marketing educator; b. Newark, Sept. 28, 1932; s. Charles and Sadie (Bornstein) W.; m. Heidi Pamela Vernon, Dec. 23, 1956; children: Joshua Charles, Jennifer Rachel. BS, Rutgers U., 1954; MBA with distinction, Harvard U., 1963, D.B.A., 1967. Ptnr., owner two pharmacies N.J., 1957-61; rsch. asst., then rsch. assoc. Harvard U., 1963-65; mem. faculty Boston U., 1965—, prof. mktg., 1969—, chmn. dept., 1968-72, 73-75; faculty assoc. Mgmt. Analysis Ctr., Group/Gemini, 1978—; faculty assoc. in residence Mgmt. Analysis Ctr., 1982-83, 89-90; vis. rsch. prof. Mktg. Sci. Inst., 1976; cons. World Bank, 1978—, Inst. for Internat. Econ. Mgmt., Beijing and Shanghai, People's Republic of China, 1981—. Co-author: The Development of Financial Managers, 1971; co-editor: Marketing to the Changing Household, 1984, Strategic Management of Multinational Corporations: The Essentials, 1984, Global Strategic Management: The Essentials, 1991. Bd. dirs. Boston Concert Opera Assn., 1981-87; pres. Boston U. Hillel Found., 1985-87. Served with U.S. Army, 1956-57. Mem. Am. Mktg. Assn., Assn. Consumer Rsch. Acad., Acad. Internat. Bus., Am. Econ. Assn., Strategic Mgmt. Soc., Acad. Mgmt. Jewish. Home: 39 Stafford Rd Newton MA 02159-1818 Office: 704 Commonwealth Ave Boston MA 02215-2404

WORTZEL, MURRAY N., library consultant, educator; b. Bklyn., July 1, 1923; s. Alex and Anna (Weintraub) W. AB, Stanford U., 1946; MLS, Columbia U., 1963, cert., 1974. Cashier, bookstore mgr. Sch. Social Work Columbia U., NYC, 1950-63; asst. to social sci. libr. Hunter Coll., NYC, 1963-64; social sci. libr., instr. Hunter Coll., Bronx, 1964-66; reference libr. Herbert H. Lehman Coll. CUNY, Bronx, 1967-79, asst. prof., 1970-80, periodicals libr., assoc. prof., 1981-89; ret., 1989; guest lectr. Baruch Coll. CUNY, 1979; libr. U.S. Ops. CUNY/Lehman-Hiroshima Coll., 1990-91. Referee articles in social scis. for Spl. Librs. Jour., N.Y., 1970—; contbr. articles to profl. jours. Co-planner, moderator program on The Homeless: On the Streets, in Transit and in Statistics, Spl. Librs. Assn., N.Y.C., 1989; vol. Kurt Weill Found. for Music Archives, 1989—; planner, participant Spl. Libr. Assn. program on the history and future of the Social Sci. Div.'s Health and Human Svcs. Roundtable, Pitts., 1990. With U.S. Army, 1942-

45. Faculty fellow Lehman Coll., CUNY, Bronx, 1965-66. Mem. ALA (numerous coms.), AAAS, Spl. Librs. Assn. (chmn. social sci. div. 1974-75, book rev. editor 1982—, Disting. Svc. award 1987, sec.-treas. social sci. div. 1988—, Hall of Fame inductee 1989), Soc. Work Librs. Group (coord., Coun.l Social Work Edn. (presenter of paper 1989, co-planner author forums 1990-92), Social Welfare History Group (co-chair), N.Y. Acad. Sci., Sigma Xi, Kappa Delta Pi. Home: 401 1st Ave Apt 11C New York NY 10010-4009

WORZBYT, JOHN CHARLES, counseling education educator; b. Auburn, N.Y., Sept. 9, 1943; s. John and Audrey (Loomis) W.; m. Jean Ann Vogelsperger, Mar. 26, 1967; children: Jason, Janeen. BS in Elem. Edn., SUNY, Oswego, 1965; EdM, U. Rochester, 1968, EdD in Counselor Edn., 1971. Cert. grades K-8 and common br. subjects, N.Y., cert. guidance, N.Y., nat. cert. counselor. Tchr. Union Springs (N.Y.) Bd. Edn., 1965-67; elem. guidance counselor West Genesee Bd. Edn., Carmillas, N.Y., 1970-72; prof. Indiana (Pa.) Univ. of Pa., 1972—; coord. of doctoral studies Dept. of Counselor Edn., Indiana Univ. Pa., 1986—; project coord. U.S. Dept. Edn. Rsch., Washington, 1989-91; cons. R. J. S. Films, Inc., Altoona, Pa., 1989—, T.E.A.M. Fight Against Drugs, Phila., 1990—. Author: Beating the Odds, 1991, 3R's Decision Making, 1991; co-author: Assessment and Behavior Problem Children, 1983, Elementary School Counseling, 1989. Pres. bd. YMCA, Indiana, 1991; bd. mem. Indiana (Pa.) County Child Care, 1991; chairperson Pastor Parish Rels.-Meth. Ch., Marion Center, Pa., 1991. Recipient U.S. Dept. Edn. grant Drug Free Schs. & Communities grant, 1989. Mem. AACD (Nat. Disting. Svc. registery 1989), Am. Sch. Counselors Assn. (Rsch. award 1990), Assn. for Counselor Edn. & Supervision, Nat. Bd. for Cert. Counselors, Nat. Ctr. for Self Esteem, Nat. Assn. for Humor and Creativity, Phi Delta Kappa. Home: 193 Route 119 Home PA 15747-9438 Office: Indiana Univ Pa Indiana PA 15705

WOSNITZER, MOREY, urologist; b. Passaic, N.J., Sept. 4, 1929; s. Morris and Ethel (Saltzman) W.; m. Nancy Joell Coplin, Sept. 18, 1978; children: Matthew, Brian. BS, Rutgers U., 1951, MS, 1952; MD, Columbia U., 1956. Diplomate Am. Bd. Urology, Am. Bd. Sexology. Intern in surgery Mt. Sinai Med. Ctr., N.Y.C., 1956-57, asst. resident in surgery, 1957-58; asst. resident in urology Columbia Presbyn. Med. Ctr., N.Y.C., 1958-59, Mass. Gen. Hosp., Boston, 1959-60; resident in urology Peter Bent Brigham Hosp., Boston, 1962-63; pvt. practice Springfield, N.J., 1964—; assoc. in Clin. Urology Columbia U., N.Y.C., 1975—; clin. instr. in Urology Cornell U., N.Y.C., 1989—. Lt. Comdr. USN, 1960-62. Fellow ACS, Internat. Coll. of Surgeons. Office: 420 Morris Ave Springfield NJ 07081

WOZNIAK, EDWARD JOSEPH, accountant; b. Buffalo, July 16, 1955; s. John Joseph and Frances (Malachowski) W. BS, SUNY, Buffalo, 1977. Adminstrv. asst. U. N.Y. Libr. Resources Coun., Buffalo, 1974-80; corp. acct. mgr. Tops Markets, Inc., Buffalo, 1980—. Mem. Hallwalls Art Gallery; vol. Albright-Knox Art Gallery, 1975; pres. Buffalo Pub. Libr. Credit Union, 1978-82; treas. Burchfield Art Ctr; bd. dirs. Polish Arts Club Buffalo; mem. fin. com. Buffalo State Coll. Found., 1991—. Named Credit Union Vol. of Yr. Nat. Assn. Fed. Credit Unions, Denver, 1981, Young Leader of Yr. YMCA, Buffalo, 1986. Republican. Roman Catholic. Office: Tops Markets Inc 60 Dingens St Buffalo NY 14206-2308

WOZNIAK, ROBERT HOWARD, psychology educator; b. San Antonio, Tex., Nov. 1, 1944; s. John Michael and Mary Agnes (Flood) W.; m. Nora Lynn Ashinhurst, Sept. 23, 1967; children: Robert Joel, John Keith. AB, Coll. of Holy Cross, Worcester, Mass., 1966; PhD, U. Mich., 1971. Asst. prof. Inst. Child Devel. U. Minn., Mpls., 1971-76, rsch. assoc., project dir. Rsch., Devel. & Demonstration Ctr. in Edn. Handicapped Children, 1976-78; visiting asst. prof. psychology dept. Tchrs. Coll. Columbia U., N.Y.C., 1979-80; assoc. to full prof., chmn. dept. human devel. Bryn Mawr (Pa.) Coll., 1980—; dir. Child Study Inst., Bryn Mawr Coll.; cons. Nat. Libr. Medicine, Bethesda, Md., 1990—, Childhood, Sta. WNET-TV, N.Y.C., 1989—. Author: (booklet) Childhood: A Viewer's Guide, 1991; co-compiler: A Century of Serial Publications in Psychology, 1984; contbr. articles to profl. jours. J. McKeen Cattell Found. fellow, 1986-87. Mem. Jean Piaget Soc. for Study of Cognitive Devel. (pres. 1985-87, bd. dirs. 1981-90), Cheiron Soc. for History of Behavioral Scis. (chmn. exec. com. 1990—), Soc. for Rsch. in Child Devel. (archivist 1986—). Office: Bryn Mawr Coll Dept Human Devel Bryn Mawr PA 19010

WOZNIUK, VLADIMIR, educator, consultant; b. Munich, Sept. 19, 1950. BA, U. Conn., 1975; MA, George Washington U., 1978, Yale U., 1982; PhD, U. Va., 1984. Asst. prof. U. Ga., Athens, 1984-85, North Ky. U., Highland Heights, 1985-86, Lafayette Coll., Easton, Pa., 1986-90; assoc. prof. Western New England Coll., Springfield, Mass., 1990—. Author: From Crisis to Crisis: Soviet-Polish Relations, 1987; author, editor: Understanding Soviet Foreign Policy, 1990; author revs. and OP-ED procs.; contbr. articles to profl. jours. and newspapers. NEH summer grantee, 1986, 91, Sloan Found. grantee, 1987-88. Mem. Yale Russian Chorus (alumnus 1981-82). Office: Western New England Coll Box 2119 Springfield MA 01119

WRAGG, LAISHLEY PALMER, JR., lawyer; b. Pitts., Oct. 11, 1933; s. Laishley Palmer and Irma Grace (Hill) W.; m. Marilyn Jean Smith, Apr. 26, 1957; children: Laishley P., Peter M.B. BBA, U. Mich., 1955; LLB cum laude, Harvard U., 1960; diploma in comparative legal studies, Trinity Hall Coll., Cambridge U., Eng., 1961. Bar: N.Y. 1962, U.S. Supreme Ct. 1974, Conseil Juridique, France 1977, Avocat France, 1992. Assoc. Cravath, Swaine & Moore, N.Y.C., 1961-62, 1965-69, Paris, 1963-65; assoc. Curtis, Mallet-Prevost, Colt & Mosle, N.Y.C., 1969-70, ptnr., 1970—. Contbr. articles to profl. jours. Mem. U.S. Dept. State ad hoc com. on large constrn. projects; U.S. del. to 15th-20th sessions of UNCITRAL. Lt. USN, 1955-57. Mem. ABA (chmn. subcom. on regional orgns. of com. on internat. instns. law of sect. internat. law and practice), Assn. Bar of City of N.Y., U.S. Coun. Internat. C. of C. (com. on restrictive bus. practices), Inter-Am. Bar Assn., French Am. C. of C., Am. Yacht Club, N.Y. Yacht Club, Royal Ocean Racing Club, Hawks Club, Ekwanok Country Club, Automobile Club France, Duquesne Club, N.Y. Croquet Club. Republican. Presbyterian. Home: 123 E 75th St New York NY 10021-2851 Office: Curtis Mallet-Prevost Colt & Mosle 101 Park Ave New York NY 10178-0002

WRAY, GILBERT ANDREW, mechanical and civil engineer; b. Montreal, Que., Can., Aug. 5, 1940; s. Aage and Laurette (Pilote) W.; m. Nicole Patricia Flynn, Feb. 11, 1989; 1 child, Jon. BS in Engring., U. Montreal, 1963; MME, Stevens Inst. Tech., Hoboken, N.J., 1967; CE, Stevens Inst. of Tech., Hoboken, N.J., 1990. Registered profl. engr., Que. Instr. Loyola Coll., Montreal, 1963-64; rsch. asst. Stevens Inst. Tech., Hoboken, 1964-65, rsch. engr. Davidson Lab., 1965-72, chief vehicle mech. and devel. div. Davidson Lab., 1972-87, group mgr. transp. rsch. Davidson Lab., 1987-89, rsch. prof. civil engring. dept., 1988-92, adj. prof. mech. engring. dept., 1988—; pres. Mech. Design and Inst. Cons. Inc., West Caldwell, N.J., 1981—; liability cons. Mech. Design and Inst. Cons., West Caldwell, 1981—; subcom. chmn. CUNY, Transp. Rsch. Consortium, N.Y.C., 1989—. Contbr. articles to profl. jours. Mem. Soc. Automotive Engrs., Am. Soc. for Testing and Materials, Am. Acad. Forensic Sci., Internat. Soc. Terrain Vehicle Systems, N.Y. Acad. Sci., Internat. Swift Assn., Sigma Xi. Roman Catholic. Office: Mech Design and Inst Cons 280 Passaic Ave West Caldwell NJ 07006-8206

WREAN, WILLIAM HAMILTON, economist; b. Ft. Sheridan, Ill., Apr. 7, 1935; s. Joy Thomas and Jean Hamilton (Kinsella) W.; m. Elisabeth Wendy Kurth, June 28, 1957; children: Katherine Hunter, Jeanne Hamilton, Jennifer Wendy, William Hamilton, Jr. BA, Yale U., 1957; MS, U. Wis., 1962, PhD, 1967. Exec. trainee Citibank, N.A., N.Y.C., 1957-58; jr. security analyst and jr. portfolio mgr. Brown Bros. Harriman and Co., N.Y.C., 1960-61; from instr. to asst. prof. Dartmouth Coll., Hanover, N.H., 1965-69; assoc. prof. Boston U., 1969-71; hon. fellow Harvard U., Cambridge, Mass., 1971-72; ptnr. Sacajawea & Co., Wellesley, Mass., 1972—; bd. dirs. Masco Corp., Boston; cons. Fed. Res. Bank Boston, 1975. Author: The Demand for Business Loan Credit, 1974. Mem. Weston (Mass.) Fin. Com., 1979-85, chmn., 1984-85; gov. Hazel Hotchkiss Wightman Tennis Ctr., Weston, 1973-75; trustee Weston Metco Scholarship Trust, 1978—, Wheelock Coll., Brookline, Mass., 1981—. 2d lt. U.S. Army, 1957-58. Mem. Am. Econs. Assn., Am. Fin. Assn., Boston Econ. Club, Country Club (Brookline), Norfolk Hunt Club (Dover, Mass.), Hillsboro Club (Hillsboro Beach, Fla.), Appalachian Mountain Club. Unitarian. Office: Sacajawea & Co 148 Linden St Ste 204 Wellesley MA 02181-7900

WREGE, CHARLES DECK, management educator; b. Newark, Mar. 11, 1924; s. Carl and Louise (Deck) W.; m. Beulah Marion Cippel, May 28, 1950. BA, Upsala Coll., 1952; MA, New Sch. for Social Rsch., 1955; MBA, NYU, 1956, PhD, 1961. Owner, operator Yearound Display Co., N.Y.C., 1946-50; indsl. engr. Weston Elec. Instruments, Newark, 1952-56; instr. in mgmt. Sch. Commerce NYU, 1956-61; asst. prof. mgmt. Univ. Coll. Rutgers U., New Brunswick, N.J., 1961-80; assoc. prof. mgmt. Sch. Adminstrv. Scis. Rutgers U., New Brunswick, 1980-85, assoc. prof. mgmt. Sch. Bus., 1985-91; adj. prof. Cornell U., Ithaca, N.Y., 1991—; vis. prof. Cornell U., 1980, vis. researcher, 1981. Author: Spring Lake: An Early History, 1976, Facts and Fallacies of Hawthorne: Historical Analysis of the Hawthorne Illumination Tests and their Influence on the Hawthorne Studies, 1986, Trolley Treasures, vol. 1, 1987, vol. 2, 1988, Frederick W. Taylor, Father of Scientific Management; Myth and Reality, 1991. Active Spring Lake (N.J.) Bicentennial Com., 1975-76; hist. advisor Labor-Mgmt. Documentation Ctr. Cornell U., Ithaca, N.Y., 1980—, vis. researcher, 1980-81; advisor bus. history archives GMI Engring. and Mgmt. Inst., Flint, Mich., 1989—; active, cons. archivist Friends of N.J. R.R. and Transp. Mus., Inc., 1992—. With USAAF, 1943-46. Recipient Disting. Paper award So. Mgmt. Assn., 1985, Midwest Case Writers Assn., 1986. Mem. Acad. Mgmt. (historian 1979—, editor history div. newsletter 1979-86, chmn. history div. 1985, chmn. centennial com. 1979-85, feature editor acad. news 1988—), Am. Inst. Hist. Tech. (v.p. 1987—), Ctr. for Canal History and Tech. Home: 23 Worthington Ave Spring Lake NJ 07762-1659

WRIGHT, ALAN CARL, chemist, educator; b. Bangor, Maine, Aug. 16, 1939; s. Frank Harding and Gladys Ellen (Dearborn) W.; m. Olga Kokinos, Aug. 16, 1964; children: Mary K., Marlena E. BS, U. Maine, 1961; PhD, U. Fla., 1966. Rsch. chemist Am. Cyanamid Co., Stamford, Conn., 1966-69; asst. prof. Ea. Conn. State U., Willimantic, 1970-76, assoc. prof., 1976-82, prof., 1982—. Mem. Am. Chem. Soc., AAAS, AAUP, Sigma Xi, Tau Beta Pi. Office: Ea Conn State U Willimantic CT 06226

WRIGHT, ALBERT JAY, III, foundation executive; b. Buffalo, Sept. 3, 1927; s. Albert Jay and Doris (Crooker) W.; m. Jane Morgan, Apr. 22, 1950; children: Albert Jay IV, Jane Wright Spohn. BA in Econs., Hamilton Coll., 1949; BSBA, U. Buffalo, 1953. CPA, N.Y. Mgmt. trainee Mfrs. and Traders Trust Co., Buffalo, 1949-51; sr. acct. R. P. Schermerhorn & Co., Buffalo, 1951-56; ptnr. Peat, Marwick Mitchell & Co. and predecessor firm, Buffalo and Chgo., 1956-83; exec. v.p. adminstrn., treas. Med. Found. Buffalo, Inc., 1984—. Chmn. bd. trustees Westminster Ch., 1958; chmn. bd. dirs. Met. YMCA, 1980-81, Crippled Children's Guild, 1987-90, Goodwill Industries of Buffalo, 1985-87; bd. dirs. NCCJ, Shea's Buffalo Ctr. for Performing Arts. With USN, 1945-46. Recipient Gold Key award for community svc. Buffalo YMCA, 1984, Community Leader award Goodwill Industries of Western N.Y., 1990. Mem. SAR (pres. Buffalo chpt. 1992), N.Y. State Soc. CPAs (pres. Buffalo chpt. 1978-79), Am. Legion, Automobile Club Western N.Y. (chmn. bd. dirs. 1988), Country Club Buffalo (treas. 1977, 78, 83), Saturn Club (bursar 1988, dean 1989), Mid-Day Club Buffalo (treas. 1974, v.p. 1975), Masons (Grand Rep. Panama to State of N.Y. 1987-91). Office: Med Found Buffalo Inc 73 High St Buffalo NY 14203-1196

WRIGHT, B. ANN, dean; b. Arkansas City, Kans.; d. Leroy Dale Hines and Dorothy Belle (Probst) Griffith; m. Willard Alan Wright; children: Randolph Alan, Rebecca Ann. BS, U. Rochester, N.Y., 1963, MA, 1966, PhD, 1977. Cert. secondary edn. tchr., N.Y. Tchr. English Irondequoit High Sch., Rochester, 1963-70, Geneseo (N.Y.) High Sch., 1973-77; asst. dir. undergrad. admissions U. Rochester, 1977-79, assoc. dir. undergrad. admissions, 1979-82, dir. undergrad. recruitment, 1982-84, dir. admissions, 1984-91; dean of enrollment mgmt. Smith Coll., Northampton, Mass., 1991—; mem. scholarship rev. com. Ednl. Testing Svc., Princeton, N.J., 1988-91; mem. faculty Snowmass Inst., 1989; steering com. The Common Application, Reston, Va., 1989—, chmn. nat. steering com., 1991—; mem. SAT com., membership com. The Coll. Bd.; commencement speaker Allendale-Columbia Sch., Rochester, N.Y. Contbr. articles to profl. jours. Mem. alumni bd. U. Rochester, 1975-78; trustee The Harley Sch., 1989-91, com. on excellence, 1991; mem. com. Pittsford (N.Y.) Sch. Tech. Adv. Bd., 1991. Mem. N.Y. State Assn. Coll. Admissions Counselors (pres. 1989, Disting. Svc. award 1989), Nat. Assn. Coll. Admissions Counselors (Editor's award 1991). Office: Smith Coll Northampton MA 01063

WRIGHT, CALEB MERRILL, federal judge; b. Georgetown, Del., Oct. 7, 1908; s. William Elwood and Mary Ann (Lynch) W.; m. Katherine McAfee, Nov. 29, 1937; children: Thomas Merrill, William Elwood, Scott McAfee, Victoria. BA, Del. U.; LLB, Yale U., 1933. Bar: Del. 1933. Solo practice Georgetown, 1933-55; U.S. dist. judge Del. Dist., 1955-57, chief judge, 1957-73, sr. judge, 1973—. Mem. Del., Sussex County bar assns., Am. Judicature Soc., Am. Law Inst., Kappa Alpha. Republican. Presbyterian. Club: Wilmington. Home: 2401 Pennsylvania Ave #806 The Devon Wilmington DE 19806 Office: US Dist Ct 844 N King St # 34 Wilmington DE 19801-3519

WRIGHT, CHARLES JOSEPH, chemist; b. Montour Falls, N.Y., May 27, 1938; s. Grant and Sarah Ellen (Withiam) W. BS, U. Rochester, 1960; MS, MIT, 1962. Rsch. chemist, then sr. rsch. chemist, chem. div. Kodak Rsch. Labs., Rochester, N.Y., 1964-78, sr. rsch. chemist, rsch. assoc. analytical sci. div., 1978-86; tech. assoc. analytical tech. div. Eastman Kodak Co., Rochester, 1986-91. Patentee in field. Mem. Am. Soc. for Mass Spectrometry, Phi Beta Kappa. Presbyterian. Home: 1210 Majestic Way Webster NY 14580-9539

WRIGHT, DENNIS EARL, telephone company researcher; b. Camden, N.J., July 31, 1951; s. James Evertt and Rita Dolores (Genovese) W.; m. Donna Maria Rowan, Feb. 12, 1972; children: Christine Denise, Steven Anthony. BS, U. Ill., Chgo., 1977; MS, Carnegie Mellon U., 1979. Mem. R & D staff AT&T Bell Labs., Holmdel, N.J., 1977—. With USN, 1969-75. Edmund James scholar U. Ill., 1975-77, Indsl. scholar, 1976. Mem. IEEE (sr.), AIAA, Armed Forces Communications and Electronic Assn., Assn. for Computing Machinery, Phi Kappa Phi. Home: 103 Statesir Pl Red Bank NJ 07701-6141 Office: AT&T Bell Labs Rm 4M 311 Crawfords Corner Holmdel NJ 07733-1988

WRIGHT, DONALD WILLIAM, JR., wholesale distribution executive; b. Pitts., Apr. 26, 1947; s. Donald William and Jane (Nelson) W.; m. Linda Marie Sunseri, Feb. 14, 1976; children: Natalie Marie, Juston Donald. BA, Washington & Jefferson, 1969. With sales H. C. Harrington Co., Pitts., 1971-74, pres., chief exec. officer, 1974—; pres. Nat. Spa & Pool Inst., Alexandria, Va., 1989. Mem. safety com. Consumer Product Safety Coun., Washington, 1987-88; mem. coun. Red Cross, Pitts., 1988—; dir. Cystic Fibrosis, Pitts., 1988—. 1st lt. U.S. Army, 1969-71. Decorated bronze star U.S. Army, Vietnam, 1970, bronze star with one oak leaf cluster U.S. Army, Vietnam, 1971. Office: H C Harrington Co 3201 Smallman St Pittsburgh PA 15201-1492

WRIGHT, FAITH-DORIAN, artist; b. Bklyn., Feb. 9, 1934; d. Abraham and Molly (Janoff) J.; m. Jordan Merritt, Igrid-beth. BS, NYU, 1955, MA, 1958; postgrad., Pratt and Parsons Sch. of Design. Works exhibited in Kathryn Markel Gallery, N.Y.C., 1981, 82, Cumberland Gallery, Nashville, 1981, 82, Barbara Gillman Gallery, Miami, 1982, Hand and Hand Gallery, 1985, 86, Suzanne Gross, Phila., 1986, 87, Gallery Four, Alexandria, Va., 1986, 87, 88, Henri Gallery, Washington, 1986, 87, 88, 89, 90, 91, Benton Gallery, Southampton, N.Y., 1986, 87, 88, 89, 91, King Stephen Mus., Hungary, 1987, Nat. Gallery Women in the Arts, 1987, 88, 90, 90, 91, 92Ruth Volid Gallery, Chgo., 1990, James Gallery, Pitts., 1990, Aart Vark Gallery, Phila., 1990, Merrill Chase Gallery, Chgo., 1990, 91, 92, Guild Hall Mus., East Hampton, N.Y., 1991. Joy Berman Gallery, Phila., 1992, Ctr. for Book Arts, N.Y.C., 1992; permanent exhbitions including Nat. Postal Art Mus., Ottawa, Can., Nat. Inst. Design, Ahmedabad, India, Fine Arts Acad., New Dehli, India, Mus. Modern Art, N.Y.C., Nat. Mus. Women in the Arts, Washington, D.C., Israel Mus., Jerusalem, Brenau Coll., Grainsville, Ga., Blue Cross, Blue Shield, Phila., Mc Donald's, Oakbrook, Ill., The Hyatt Collection, Chgo.; contbr. critical essays to various periodicals. Mem. Women in Arts, Women's Caucus for Arts, Artists Equity. Address: 300 E 74th St New York NY 10021

WRIGHT, JAMES PHILIP, science administrator; b. St. Petersburg, Fla., Apr. 10, 1934; s. James Grady and Amanda Christina (Mickelson) W.; m. Barbara Jean Douglas, Aug. 18, 1956; children: James, Lee, Kirsten, Karen. AA, St. Petersburg (Fla.) Jr. Coll, 1954; BS, U. Fla., 1956; PhD, U. Chgo., 1961. Rsch. assoc. NASA Inst. for Space Studies, N.Y.C., 1961-63; vis. prof. Math. Rsch. Ctr., Madison, Wis., 1963-64; lectr., rsch. assoc. Harvard U., Cambridge, Mass., 1964-70; physicist Smithsonian Astrophysical Obs., Cambridge, Mass., 1964-70; staff assoc. NSF, Washington, 1970-71, program dir., 1971—. Author scientific papers. Mem. Am. Astron. Soc., Internat. Astron. Union, Phi Theta Kappa, Phi Beta Kappa. Office: NSF 1800 G St NW Washington DC 20550-0002

WRIGHT, JAY BROWN, public communications educator; b. Miami Beach, Fla., Dec. 20, 1940; s. Harold Estle and Josephine (Brown) W.; m. Yolanda Tamburrino, Oct. 10, 1970. BS in Journalism, Northwestern U., Evanston, Ill., 1962, MS in Journalism, 1963; PhD in Mass Communication, Syracuse U., 1977; M of Studies in Law, Yale U., 1979. Advt. copywriter Caldwell, Larkin & Sidener-VanRiper, Inc., Indpls., 1963-64; prof. S.I. Newhouse Sch. Pub. Communications, Syracuse (N.Y.) U., 1967—; exec. dir. N.Y. Fair Trial Free Press Conf., Syracuse, 1972—. Author: The First Amendment and the Fourth Estate, 1985, The First Amendment and the Fifth Estate, 1986; editor: The Legal Handbook for New York State Journalists, 1986; scriptwriter "Assignment: Courthouse", 1990. Vice-chmn. Historic Review Commn., Fayetteville, N.Y., 1986—. With U.S. Army, 1964-67. Recipient Bastian Meml. award Northwestern U., 1963, Pres.'s award Syracuse Press Club, 1985. Mem. Assn. for Edn. in Journalism and Mass Communications (law div. head 1982-83), Media Law Com. of N.Y. State Bar Assn. Home: 416 Brooklea Dr Fayetteville NY 13066-1404 Office: Syracuse U 215 University Pl Syracuse NY 13244-2100

WRIGHT, JEANNE ELIZABETH JASON, advertising executive; b. Washington, June 24, 1934; d. Robert Stewart and Elizabeth (Gaddis) Jason; m. Benjamin Hickman Wright, Oct. 30, 1965; stepchildren: Benjamin, Deborah, David, Patricia. B.A., Radcliffe Coll., 1956; M.A., U. Chgo., 1958. Psychiat. social worker Lake County Mental Health Clinic, Gary, Ind., Psychiat. and Psychosomatic Inst., Michael Reese Hosp., Chgo., Jewish Child Care Assn., N.Y.C., 1958-70; gen. mgr. Black Media, Inc. (advt. rep. co.), N.Y.C., 1970-74; pres. Black Media, Inc. (advt. rep. co.), 1974-75; pres., exec. editor, syndicator weekly editorial features Black Resources, Inc., N.Y.C., 1975—. Mem. planning com. First Black Power Conf., Newark, 1966, Second Black Power Conf., Phila., 1967, First Internat. Black Cultural & Bus. Expn., N.Y.C., 1971; nat. bd. dirs. Afro-Am. Family & Community Svcs., Inc., Chgo., 1971-75; founding coun. mem. Nat. Assault on Illiteracy Program, 1980—; pres. Metro-N.Y. chpt. Nat. Assn. Media Women, Inc., 1986-89. Recipient Pres.' award Nat. Assn. Black Women Attys., 1977, 2d ann. Freedom's Jour. award Journalism Students and Faculty of U. D.C. Dept. Communicative and Performing Arts, 1979, Communication award Harlem Svc. Ctr., ARC, 1988, Spl. award Beta Omicron chpt. Phi Delta Kappa, 1982; named Disting. Black Woman in Industry, Nat. Coun. Negro Women, 1981. Mem. AAAS, Nat. Assn. Social Workers, Acad. Cert. Social Workers, Nat. Assn. Media Women (pres. Met. N.Y. chpt. 1986-89, Nat. Media Woman of Yr. award 1984, 86, Founders award 1986), Newswomen's Club N.Y., U. Chgo. Alumni Assn., NAACP, Radcliffe Club, Harvard Club, Alpha Kappa Alpha. Democrat. Office: 410 Central Park W Penthouse C New York NY 10025 also: 231 W 29th St Ste 1205 New York NY 10001-5209

WRIGHT, JOHN PARDEE, investment company executive; b. Hong Kong, May 9, 1957; s. William Bigelow and Polly (Pardee) W.; m. Mary Porter, Nov. 24, 1979; children: Heather Marie, Justin Pardee. Cert., L'Institut De Sci. Politique, Paris, 1978; BA, Middlebury (Vt.) Coll., 1979; MBA, Amos Tuck Sch., 1984. Fin. trainee Gen. Mills, Inc., Mpls., 1979-80, asst. mgr., 1980-81, mgr., 1981-82; fin. analyst Keefe, Bruyette & Woods, Inc., Hartford, Conn., 1984-86, v.p., 1986—; tchr. New Eng. Sch. of Banking, Williamstown, Mass., 1987—. Treas. local chpt. Phillips Exeter Acad., Hartford, 1987—; off campus interviewer Middlebury Coll., Simsbury, Conn., 1981-86. Republican. Congregationalist.

WRIGHT, KEVIN NEIL, criminal justice educator; b. Childress, Tex., Apr. 9, 1951; s. William Neil and Beth (Jackson) W.; m. Karen Elizabeth Stoeckel, Oct. 25, 1975; children: April Eve, William Neil II. BS, Sam Houston State U., 1972, MA, 1973; PhD, Pa. State U., 1977. Asst. prof. pub. policy Lamar U., Beaumont, Tex., 1976-78; asst. prof. criminal justice U. Tenn., Chattanooga, 1978-80; assoc. prof. criminal justice SUNY, Binghamton, 1980-92, prof., 1992—; vis. fellow Fed. Bur. Prisons, Washington, 1989-90, 91-92; cons. KPMG Peat Marwick, Washington, 1990. Author: The Great American Crime Myth, 1985; editor: Crime and Criminal Justice in a Declining Economy, 1981; contbr. articles to profl. jours. Bd. dirs. Transitional Opportunities Corp., Binghamton, 1991—, Crime Victims Assistance Ctr., Binghamton, 1990—; mem. Conditional Release Commn., Broome County, N.Y., 1990—. Fellowship W.K. Kellogg Found., 1986-90; prin. investigator Nat. Inst. Justice, 1983-85. Mem. Am. Soc. Criminology, Acad. Criminal Justice. Democrat. Office: SUNY Sch Edn and Human Devel Binghamton NY 13902-6000

WRIGHT, KEVIN W., historic preservation specialist; b. Newton, N.J., Jan. 26, 1952; s. John Ivan and Teresa Marie (Mullen) W.; m. Deborah S. Powell, Aug. 21, 1976; children: Ivan, Benjamin, Anna. BA in History, Rutgers U., 1974. Sr. historic preservation specialist N.J. Div. Parks and Forestry, River Edge, 1981—; lectr. in field; researcher Hackensack Meadowlands, De Korte State Park, 1989; mem. Newton (N.J.) Historic Preservation adv. commn., 1987—. Author: Around the Green, Newton, N.J., 1991; co-author: High Point of the Blue Mountains, 1990; co-author exhibit catalogue. Grantee N.J. Hist. Commn., 1990, Office N.J. Heritage, 1988-90. Mem. Sussex County Hist. Soc. (pres. 1987-90, trustee 1978—), Bergen County Hist. Soc., Soc. Preservation Old Mills, Canal Soc. N.J. (bd. dirs. 1979-89). Home: 1209 Main St River Edge NJ 07661-2026

WRIGHT, MAX, data processing executive, consultant; b. Windsor, England, June 14, 1954; came to the U.S., 1989; s. Harold Edwin and Sheila Doreen (Young) W.; m. Linda Marion Levin, Nov. 26, 1984 (div. 1989); m. Catherine Jean Chawner, Jan. 18, 1991. Electronics tech. Electricity Supply Commn., Germiston, South Africa, 1972-74, R. Muller, Johannesburg, South Africa, 1974-75; svc. mgr., sr. technician OKTV, George, South Africa, 1975-77; field engr. Burroughs Machines, Johannesburg, 1978-79; systems analyst Sidha Assocs. (Pty.) Ltd., Johannesburg, 1980-84, mng. dir., 1984—; v.p. Arisoft, Inc., N.Y.C., 1989—; dir. Arisoft (Pty.) Ltd., Johannesburg. Contbr. articles to profl. jours. Tchr. Transcendental meditation, 1979—; treas. South African Assn. Age of Enlightenment, 1980-87. Recipient Nat. Leader's award for outstanding contbn. South African Assn. Age of Enlightenment, 1981. Mem. FUSE, Inc., L.I. Capital Age of Enlightenment, Mensa, Inertel. Office: Arisoft Software 717 E Jericho Tpke Ste 223 Huntington Station NY 11746-7517

WRIGHT, MICHAEL FRANK, advertising copywriter; b. Mishawaka, Ind., Oct. 1, 1947; s. Frank Ruhl and Mary Salome (Klopfenstein) W.; m. Peggy Mary Schnorr, Dec. 21, 1970; 1 child, Benjamin Francis. BA with distinction, U. Wis., Madison, 1972, MA in English, 1974, ABD in English, 1978. Dir., instr. Wis. Sch. Music, Madison, 1972-78; account exec. WFMR-FM Radio/Milw. Mag., 1978-79; dir. mktg. and pub. rels. Milw. Ballet Co., 1979-80; copywriter The Brady Co., Menomonee Falls, Wis., 1980-82; sr. advt. specialist SMS Corp., Malvern, Pa., 1983-88; sr. copywriter Earle Palmer Brown & Spiro, Phila., 1988-91, Ted Thomas Assocs., Phila., 1991—. Contbr. music critiques, feature articles, featured columns to various publs.; programmer, announcer Guitaromania, Sta. WPEB-FM, 1985-89. Mem. Phila. Advt. Club, Phila. Classical Guitar Soc., Guitar Found. Am. Home: 1010 S 47th St Philadelphia PA 19143-3602 Office: Ted Thomas Assocs 210 W Washington Sq Philadelphia PA 19106

WRIGHT, MICHAEL KEARNEY, public relations executive; b. Durham, N.C., Apr. 23, 1928; s. Wilburn Kearney and Roberta Audrey (Lee) W. BS, N.C. Cen. U., 1951; MS, Columbia U., 1954. Actor, singer, dancer

Broadway and TV, 1951-60; dir. edn. Am. Cancer Soc., N.Y.C., 1960-69; dir. audio/visual edn. Media Medica, Inc., N.Y.C., 1969; dir. N.Y. office McFadden, Strauss & Irwin Inc., N.Y.C., 1970-75; v.p. ICPR, N.Y.C., 1975-77; sr. v.p. Stone Assocs., N.Y.C., 1977-85; pres. The Wright Co., N.Y.C., 1985; v.p. The Lippin Group, N.Y.C., 1985—; pub. rels. cons. Nuclear Rsch. Assocs., New Hyde Park, N.Y., 1967-69. Bd. dirs. CSC Repertory Co., N.Y.C., 1988-89; counsellor 1st Ch. of Religious Sci., N.Y.C., 1981—, Alcoholics Anonymous, N.Y.C., 1970—; lectr. Sci. of Mind, N.Y.C., 1988—; supporter ASPCA, Humane Soc., Morris Dees and others. With U.S. Army, 1946-47. Mem. NATVAS, Am. Film Inst., Smithsonian Assocs., Nat. Geog. Soc., Actor's Equity Assn., Alpha Kappa Mu, Beta Kappa Chi. Home: 200 E 36th St # 11G New York NY 10016

WRIGHT, MILTON, artist, educator; b. Dayton, Ohio, July 3, 1920; s. Milton and Ann Margaret (Grosvenor) W.; m. Mary Breene Loughridge, Nov. 16, 1946; children: Martha Ann Crouch, Lorin. BFA, Miami U., Oxford, Ohio, 1942; cert., Sch. Art Studies, N.Y.C., 1948, Academie Julian, Paris, 1950. Tchr. Bklyn. Mus. Art Sch., 1950-75, Queens Coll., N.Y.C., 1960-65; asst. prof. L.I. U., Bklyn., 1965-75; tchr. Poly Prep Country Day Sch., Bklyn., 1953-77. Paintings included in exhbns., Denver Art Mus., 1944, Galerie Ariel, Paris, 1950, Dayton Art Inst., 1945-51, Washington Irving Gallery, N.Y.C., 1960, Saltpeter Gallery, N.Y.C., 1965, 68, Cove Gallery, Wellfleet, Mass., 1991; represented in permanent collections including Town Hall, Truro, Mass., Truro Hist. Soc., Town Hall, Truro, Eng., L.I. U., Miami U., Dayton Art Inst. Mem. Truro Hist. Commn. Sgt. USAF, 1942-46. Mem. Truro Hist. Soc. (v.p.). Democrat. Home: Great Hollow Rd PO Box 314 North Truro MA 02652-0314

WRIGHT, OTIS CLARENCE, JR., consultant; b. Ft. Fairfield, Maine, Nov. 24, 1940; s. Otis Clarence and Charlotte (Morrell) W.; m. Linda J. Oak; children: Otis Clarence III, Jonathan Douglas. BS, MIT, 1964. Group leader MIT, Cambridge, Mass., 1962-65; product support staff Electronic Assocs., Inc., West Long Branch, N.J., 1965-66; ops. mgr. Electronic Assocs., Inc., El Segundo, Calif., 1966-68; product mgr. Electronic Assocs., Inc., West Long Branch, 1968-71, mgr., advanced planning, 1971-74; mng. dir. EAI-Electronic Assocs. PTY., Ltd., St. Leonards, N.S.W., Australia, 1974-84; v.p. Electronic Assocs., Inc., West Long Branch, 1984-91; pres. Real Time Initiatives, Ocean, N.J., 1990—; tech. adv. com. U.S. Dept. Commerce, Washington, 1988—. Trustee Wayside (N.J.) United Meth. Ch., 1986. Mem. Australian Inst. Dirs., Australian Pioneers Club (Sydney). Republican. Home: 9 High Ridge Rd Asbury Park NJ 07712-3460 Office: Electronic Assocs Inc 185 Monmouth Rd West Long Branch NJ 07764-1019

WRIGHT, PATRICIA DILLIN, psychiatrist; b. Vincennes, Ind., Mar. 7, 1951. BA, Smith Coll., 1972; MD, Ind. U. Med. Ctr., Indpls., 1977. Intern, then resident in psychiatry U. N.Mex. Med. Ctr., Albuquerque, 1980-82; child psychiatry fellow Harvard U. Med. Sch.-Cambridge (Mass.) Hosp., 1982; pvt. practice psychiatry Cambridge, 1982—; staff psychiatrist New Eng. Meml. Hosp., Stoneham, Mass., 1982-83, Hampstead (N.H.) Hosp., 1983-87; psychoanalytic candidate, Boston Psychoanalytic Soc. and Inst., 1981—; cons., New Eng. Human Resource Ctr., Chelmsford, Mass., 1981-87; supr. child psychiatry, Beth Israel Hosp.-Harvard U. Med. Sch., Boston, 1989—. Mem. Am. Psychiat. Assn., Mass. Psychiat. Soc., Am. Psychoanalytic Assn., Am. Med. Women's Assn., Smith Coll. Club. Office: 124 Mt Auburn St # 258 Cambridge MA 02138-5758

WRIGHT, PAUL COMBE, auditor; b. Ogden, Utah, Sept. 18, 1954; s. Lew and Carol (Combe) W.; children: Natalie, Sandra, Robert; m. Trudie Toussaint, June 1992. BA in Polit. Sci., Brigham Young U., 1978; MA in Urban Studies/Pub. Adminstrn., U. Md., 1979. Program analyst USFDA, Rockville, Md., 1979-80; price monitor Coun. on Wage and Price Stability, Exec. Office of the Pres., Washington, 1980-81; auditor, evaluator Washington Regional Office, GAO, Washington, 1981-88; auditor, evaluator human resources div. Washington, 1988—. Vice pres. Parents without Ptnrs., Washington, 1989-90, 92. Mem. LDS Ch. Home: 5642 Hogenhill Terrace Rockville MD 20853 Office: U S Gen Acctg Office NGB-441 G St NW Ste 5022 Washington DC 20548-0002

WRIGHT, PAUL MICHAEL, editor; b. Ashland, Maine, Oct. 8, 1939; s. Wesley Wilson and Phyllis Arlene (Moode) W.; m. Judith Anne Kelley, June 13, 1964; children: Paul David, Joshua Lloyd. AB in Comparative Lit., Boston U., 1963, ABD in Am. Studies, 1980; MA in English, U. Mass., 1972. Editor Addison-Wesley Publ., Reading, Mass., 1966-67, U. Mass. Press, Amherst, 1967-72, 88—; teaching fellow Boston U., 1972-74; program dir. Boston Pub. Libr., 1974-77; editor G.K. Hall & Co., Boston, 1978-79, Garland Pub., Cambridge, Mass., 1979-81; freelance editor, writer Boston, 1981-88. Author: John W. McCormack, 1985; co-author: Boston: A State of Mind, 1977; (script) Going Down To Boston, 1975; contbr. articles to profl. jours. Mem. community dist. adv. coun. Boston Pub. Schs., 1978-79; bd. dirs. Learning Project, Boston, 1982-88; dir. pub. rels. Hayes for City Coun. campaign, Boston, 1983; treas. Troop 3, Boy Scouts Am., Boston, 1984—. With U.S. Army, 1963-65. Fellow McCormack Inst., U. Mass., Boston. Mem. N.E. Am. Studies Assn., Orgn. Am. Historians, Am. Studies Assn. (mem. coun., 1977-78), Alliance of Ind. Schs. Democrat. Office: U Press U Mass Boston MA 02125-3393

WRIGHT, RICHARD DONALD, financial executive; b. Chester, Pa., Mar. 18, 1936; s. Richard H. and Anita C. (Howery) W.; m. Joan Cooke, Oct. 24, 1959; children: Richard, Paul, Susan. BBA, Pa. State U., 1963. Trainee, corp. fin. mgmt., internal auditor, corp. staff auditor RCA, Cherry Hill, N.J., 1963-66; with Smith Kline French Labs. div. Smith Kline Beckman Corp., Phila., 1966-83, mgr. budget, 1966-69, mgr. planning and control, 1969-70, mgr. fin. ops., 1970-72, contr. mfg. ops., 1972-73, dir. fin. planning, 1973-74, contr. pharm. ops. U.S., 1974-79; v.p., dir. Franklin Town Corp.; pres. F.T. Mgmt. Corp. affiliate Smith Kline Corp., 1979-83; with Henkels & McCoy, Inc., Blue Bell, Pa., 1983—; contr. Henkels and McCoy, Inc., Blue Bell, Pa., 1983-85, v.p., dir., 1985-88, v.p., dir. chief fin. officer, 1988—; lectr. in field. Mem. Fin. Execs. Inst. (cert.), Planning Execs. Inst., Inst. Mgmt. Accts., Sigma Tau Gamma. Home: 104 Shadow Lake Dr Vincentown NJ 08088-8950

WRIGHT, ROBERT C., broadcasting executive; b. Rockville Center, N.Y., Apr. 23, 1943; m. Suzanne Werner, Aug. 26, 1967; children: Kate, Christopher, Maggie. A.B. in History, Coll. Holy Cross, 1965; LL.B., U. Va., 1968. Bar: N.Y. 1968, Va. 1968, Mass. 1970, N.J. 1971. With Gen. Electric Co., 1969-70, 73-80, gen. mgr. plastics sales dept., 1978-80; law sec. to chief judge U.S. Dist. Ct., N.J., 1970-73; pres. Cox Cable Communications, Atlanta, 1980-83; exec. v.p. Cox Communications, 1980-83; v.p., gen. mgr. housewares, audio and cable TV ops. GE, 1983-84; pres., chief exec. officer GE Fin. Svcs. Inc., 1984-86, NBC, N.Y.C., 1986—. Office: NBC 30 Rockefeller Pla New York NY 10112

WRIGHT, STEPHEN LEE, sales executive; b. Charleston, W.Va., Oct. 20, 1957; s. Glen L. and Lois J. (Fisher) W. BS, Clemson U., 1979. Mgmt. trainee Internat. Harvester, Atlanta, 1979-80; dist. sales mgr. Internat. Harvester, Raleigh, N.C., 1980-81; sales rep. Smith, Kline and French Labs., Raleigh, 1981-83; sales specialist Technicare Corp., Raleigh, 1983-86; sales rep. Siemens Med. Systems, Raleigh, 1986-87; nat. accounts mgr. Siemens Med. Systems, Charlotte, N.C., 1987-89; dir., nat. accounts Siemens Med. Systems, Iselin, N.J., 1989—. Mem. Nat. Account Mgrs. Assn., Fedn. Am. Healthcare Systems (exhibits com. 1990-92). Republican. Baptist. Home: 16 Angelica Ct Princeton NJ 08540-9420

WRIGHT, WILLIAM COOK, archivist, researcher; b. Jersey City, July 11, 1939; s. Harry Cook and Edna Margarita (Tompkins) W. BA, Gettysburg Coll., 1961; MA, U. Del., 1965, PhD, 1971. Tchr. Salem (N.J.) High Sch., 1961-65; adj. instr. U. Del., Newark, 1968-70; assoc. dir. N.J. Hist. Commn., Trenton, 1970-76; head Bur. Archives and History N.J. State Libr., Trenton, 1976-83; dir. Div. Archives and Records Mgmt., N.J. State Dept., Trenton, 1983-85; chief Bur. Records Mgmt., Trenton, 1985-89, ret., 1989; coord. state hist. records adv. bd. Nat. Hist. Publs. and Records Commn. 1976-87; mem. adv. com. for papers of William Livingston; sec. N.J. State Records Com., 1976-85, chmn., 1985; mem. adv. bd. dirs. N.J. Archives Series, 1971-86; mem. region 2 adv. coun. Nat. Archives and Records Svc., 1976-77; mem. adv. com. N.J. Newspaper Project, 1983-85, state rev. com. for hist. sites, 1976-79; mem. implementation and planning com. N.J. Supreme Ct., 1982. Author monograph: The Secession Movement in the Middle Atlantic States, 1972; compiler Directory of N.J. Newspapers, 1765-1970; contbr. articles and book revs to profl. jours. Mem. Lawrence Township Cultural and Heritage Adv. Com., 1989—, chmn., 1991. Mem. Acad. Cert. Archivists (cert.), Soc. Am. Archivists, N.J. Hist. Soc. Home: 10 Windsor Ct Sewell NJ 08080

WRIGHT, WILLIAM WYNN, chemist; b. Balt., Aug. 13, 1923; s. Andrew Wynn and Margaret Mary (Peters) W.; m. Mary Theresa Mead, Feb. 10, 1945; children: Ann Wynn, Jane Frances, Stephen William, Kathleen Theresa, Drew Edward. BS magna cum laude, Loyola Coll., Balt., 1944; MS, Georgetown U., 1946, PhD, 1948. Rsch. fellow Georgetown U. Grad. Sch., Washington, 1944; chemist Nat. Bur. Standards, Washington, 1945, FDA, Washington, 1945-79; sr. scientist U.S. Pharmacopeia, Rockville, Md., 1979—; cons., advisor WHO, Geneva, 1960—. Recipient Superior Svc. award U.S. Dept. Health, Edn. and Welfare, Washington, 1964, USPHS, Washington, 1979. Fellow AAAS (life), Assn. Ofcl. Analytical Chemists (life, pres. 1967); mem. Am. Chem. Soc., N.Y. Acad. of Sci. (life), Sigma Xi. Roman Catholic.

WRIGHTON, MARK STEPHEN, chemistry educator; b. Jacksonville, Fla., June 11, 1949; s. Robert D. and Doris (Cutler) W.; m. Deborah Ann Wiseman, Aug. 10, 1968; children: James Joseph, Rebecca Ann. B.S., Fla. State U., 1969; Ph.D., Calif. Inst. Tech., 1972; D.Sc. (hon.), U. West Fla., 1983. Asst. prof. chemistry MIT, Cambridge, 1972-76, assoc. prof., 1976-77, prof., 1977—, Frederick G. Keyes prof. chemistry, 1981-89, head dept. chemistry, 1987-90, Ciba-Geigy prof. chemistry, 1989—, provost, 1990—; Alfred P. Sloan fellow, 1974-76. Author: Organometallic Photochemistry, 1979; editor books in field; cons. editor, Houghton-Mifflin. Recipient Herbert Newby McCoy award Calif. Inst. Tech., 1972, Disting. Alumni award, 1992, E.D. Lawrence award Dept. Energy, 1983, Halpern award in photochemistry, N.Y. Acad. Scis., 1983, Fresenius award Phi Lambda Upsilon, 1984, Dreyfus tchr.-scholar, 1975-80; Alfred P. Sloan fellow, 1974-76, MacArthur fellow, 1983-88. Fellow AAAS; mem. Am. Acad. Arts and Scis., Am. Chem. Soc. (award in pure chemistry 1981, award in inorganic chemistry 1988), Electrochem. Soc. Office: MIT Office of the Provost Dept Chemistry 77 Massachusetts Ave Cambridge MA 02139-4307

WRIGHT-STEVENSON, LINDA MAE, marketing professional; b. Bridgeport, Conn., Dec. 19, 1948; d. Bernard Frank and Mafalda Rose (Hippolitus) Gigliotti; m. David Fraser Wright, Mar. 28, 1974 (div. Aug. 1984); 1 child, Vanessa Thorburn; m. William John Stevenson, Aug. 20, 1988. BA in Sociology, Marymount Coll., 1970; MBA in Mktg., Rochester Inst. Tech., 1984. Mgmt. assoc. Citibank, N.A., Rochester, N.Y., 1983-84; mgr. direct mktg. 1st Fed. Savs. and Loan Assn., Rochester, 1984-86; account mgr. CMS Direct Inc., Rochester, 1986-88, Direct Mktg. Cons., Rochester, 1988—. Mem. steering com. Urbanarium, Rochester, 1980-81; bd. dirs. Greater Rochester Citizens for Action, 1981-82; exec. dir. Greater Rochester Ptnrs. of Ams./Antiqua Barbuda, 1982-83, Rochester Women's Network (steering com. mem. pub. policy issues). Mem. Rochester Women's Network. Republican. Roman Catholic. Club: Toastmasters (Rochester) (bd. dirs., treas. 1985-86). Home: 12 Creekdale Ln Rochester NY 14618-3424 Office: 90 Linden Oaks Rochester NY 14625-2830

WROTH, L(AWRENCE) KINVIN, lawyer, educator; b. Providence, July 9, 1932; s. Lawrence Counselman and Barbara (Pease) W.; m. Susan Collins, May 2, 1958 (div. 1972); children: Ann K., Caroline D., Eliza H.; m. Deborah Bethell, Aug. 10, 1972; 1 dau., Katharine L.; stepchildren—John H., David H., Elizabeth T. and Sarah B. Zobel. B.A., Yale U., 1954; LL.B., Harvard U., 1960. Bar: Mass. 1960, Maine 1974. Teaching fellow, asst. prof. law Dickinson Sch. Law, 1960-62; research assoc. Harvard U., 1962-64; asso. prof. law U. Maine Sch. Law, Portland, 1964-66; prof. U. Maine Sch. Law, 1966—; assoc. dean Sch. Law U. Maine, 1977-78, acting dean, 1978-80, dean, 1980-90; rsch. fellow Charles Warren Center Studies in Am. History, Harvard U., 1968-74; cons. civil and probate procedure, profl. and jud. responsibility, and ct.-bar rels. Maine Supreme Jud. Ct., 1967—; cons. civil and criminal procedure and evidence Vt. Supreme Ct., 1969—. Author: (with R.H. Field and V.L. McKusick) Maine Civil Practice, 2d edit, 1970; editor-in-chief: Province in Rebellion, 1975; editor: (with H.B. Zobel) Legal Papers of John Adams, 1965; reporter: Vermont Rules of Civil Procedure, 1971, Vermont Rules of Criminal Procedure, 1974, Maine Rules of Probate Procedure, 1980, (with J. Dooley) Vermont Rules of Evidence, 1982. Pres. Greater Portland Landmarks, Inc., 1966-69, adv. trustee, 1969-85; adv. coun. Nat. Trust Hist. Preservation, 1967-70; bd. dirs. Maine Bar Found., 1983-89, sec., 1983-86, v.p., 1987, pres. 1988; bd. dirs. Pine Tree Legal Assistance Inc., 1985—; mem. bd. dirs. Nat. Assn. IOLTA Programs, Inc., 1988-90; bd. dirs. Portland Symphony Orch., 1990, v.p. for ops. and resources, 1991—; mem. Maine Commn. on Legal Needs, 1989-90, Commn. to Study Future of Maine's Cts., 1991—. Recipient Littleton-Griswold prize Am. Hist. Assn., 1966, Howard H. Dana award Maine Bar Found., 1991. Mem. Maine Bar Assn. (Disting. Svc. award 1990), ABA, Am. Law Inst., Colonial Soc. Mass., Mass. Hist. Soc. Home: Cobbs Bridge Rd RR 2 Box 575 New Gloucester ME 04260 Office: U Maine Sch Law 246 Deering Ave Portland ME 04102-2837

WROTNIAK, CHESTER MICHAEL, biologist, consultant; b. Kenmore, N.Y., Feb. 2, 1956; s. Chester Richard and Irene Alice (Jenczeski) W.; m. Jamie Therese Perri, Aug. 4, 1984; 1 child, Jennifer Nicole. BA in Life Scis., Niagara U., 1981, MS in Biology, 1983; postgrad., Temple U., 1985-88. Field technician Niagara U., N.Y., 1983-84; lab mgr. Eberline Analytical Corp., Youngstown, N.Y., 1984-85; systems mgr. Becquerel Labs., Buffalo, N.Y., 1988-90; group leader Dames & Moore, West Valley, N.Y., 1990—; chem. hygiene officer West Valley Demonstration Project Environ. Lab, 1990—; cons. in field, Niagara Falls, N.Y., 1989—. Supporter Rep. Candidate City Coun., Niagara Falls, 1990, Niagara Univ. Alumni Assn., 1991. Recipient scholarship Monsanto Rsch., Niagara U., 1981-83. Mem. Health Physics Soc., Am. Chem. Soc. Roman Catholic. Home: 3603 Ferry Ave Niagara Falls NY 14301-2707

WRUCKE, LOWELL THOMAS, information systems executive; b. Minnesota lake, Minn., Jan. 16, 1936; s. Lowell Oscar and Mary Loyola (Chada) W.; m. Sandra Jean Bennett, May 12, 1962 (dec. 1977); 1 child, Douglas; m. Judith Anne Koenig Maher, June 23, 1979; children: Catherine, Margaret, John, Patrick. Student, Hamline U., 1954-56, U. Minn., 1966. Cert. office automation specialist. Systems analyst Census Bur., Suitland, Md., 1967-72, info. systems mgr., 1972-88; info. systems mgr. Census Bur., Balt., 1988-91; dir. systems staff Iverson Mall, Hillcrest Heights, Md., 1991—; cons. Candlelight Soc., Columbia, Md., 1985-89. Dir. Trinity Sch. Athletic Club, Ilchester, Md., 1983-87; vol. Project Literacy, Columbia, 1985-87. With U.S. Army, 1956-59. Recipient Spl. Achievement award Census Bur., 1971, 75, Quality award, 1972, Spl. Cert., 1987, 91. Mem. DEC User Soc., Internat. Statis. Inst. Repubican. Home: 10170 Pasture Gate Ln Columbia MD 21044-1708 Office: Iverson Mall Hillcrest Heights MD 21737

WU, CARL CHERNG-MIIN, ceramic engineer; b. Taiwan, Republic of China, July 10, 1938; s. Sung-Pai and Yueh-Oh (Lin) W.; m. Lisa Cheng, Aug. 1, 1970; 1 child, Priscilla Pei-i. BS, Nat. Taiwan U., 1962; ScM, Brown U., 1967, PhD, 1970. Postdoctoral fellow U. Md., College Park, 1970-73, vis. asst. prof., 1973-77; ceramic engr. Naval Rsch. Lab., Washington, 1977-86, supv. ceramic engr., 1986—. Contbr. papers to profl. pubs. Pres. Washington China Post, 1987-88. Mem. Am. Ceramic Soc., Nat. Inst. Ceramic Engrs., Assn. Chinese Schs. (pres. 1984-85), Chinese-Am. Profl. Assn. (pres. 1984-85), Chinese-Am. Soc. (v.p. 1988—), Chinese Consol. Benevolent Assn. (vice chmn. 1992—). Home: 9605 Newbridge Dr Potomac MD 20854-4435 Office: Naval Rsch Lab Code 6373 Washington DC 20375

WU, DAISY YEN, nutritional biochemist, researcher, consultant; b. Shanghai, Kiangsu, People's Republic China, June 12, 1902; came to U.S., 1949; d. Tse-King and Li-Feng (Yang) Yen; m. Hsien Wu, Dec. 20, 1924 (dec. 1959); children: Evelyn Wan-hsien, Dorothea Wan-lien, Ray Jui, Christine Wan-ming, Ying Victor. BA, Ginling Coll., Nanking, Kiangsu, China, 1921; postgrad., Smith Coll., 1921-22, U. Chgo., summer 1922; MA, Columbia U., 1923; diploma in French, L'Academie Sino Francaise, Beijing, 1944, UN. Lang. Tng. Course, N.Y.C., 1963. Asst. biochemistry Peking Union Med. Coll., 1923-24; rsch. assoc. biochemistry Med. Coll. Ala., Birmingham, 1950-53; tech. assoc. nutrition UN Children's Fund, Food Conservation Div., N.Y.C., 1960-64; assoc. nutrition Columbia U. Inst. Human Nutrition, N.Y.C., 1964-70; sci. assoc. and cons., nutrition and metabolic rsch. unit St. Luke's Hosp., N.Y.C., 1971-86; spl. lectr. Columbia U. Inst. Human Nutrition, N.Y.C., 1970-71. Editor: Hsien Wu 1893-59, 1959, A Guide to Sci. Living, 1963; author: Supplement to Hsien Wu's Principles of Nutrition, 1974; compiler: Wan-lien Dorothea Wu, 1927-1990, In Loving Memory; contbr. articles to profl. jours. Founder The Ming Ming Sch., Peking, pres. bd. and treas, 1934-45. Trustees' Scholarship grantee Ginling Coll., 1918. Fellow APHA, Royal Soc. Health London; mem. Am. Inst. Nutrition, Ginling Assn. in Am. (nat. pres. 1958-60), N.Y. Acad. Scis., Sigma Xi.

WU, STEPHEN S., consultant; b. Hong Kong, Mar. 22, 1922; m. Grace W. Ing, June 23, 1951; children: Norman Nash, Charles Fairman. BA, St. John's U., 1943; MA, Stanford, 1948, Columbia, 1950; MBA, Boston U., 1957; CFA, U. Va., 1965. Various positions with Bank Boston, 1951-88; mem. exec. com. Petroleum Analysts Boston, 1964—. Lectr. Am. Inst. Banking, 1953-72, Northeastern U., 1959-70. Mem. commn. on ministry Episcopal Diocese Mass., 1970-75; trustee Family Service Assn. Greater Boston, 1973-78. Served with AUS, 1945. Recipient Award of Appreciation, U.S. Treasury, 1963. Mem. Fin. Mgmt. Assn. (life). Episcopalian. Office: PO Box 505 Newton MA 02159-0004

WUENSCH, MARC COURTNEY, accountant; b. Jersey City, Jan. 7, 1952; s. John Henry and Dorothy (Pysarchyk) W.; m. Patricia Louise Uhlig, June 24, 1978; children: Jennifer, Allyson. BA, Rutgers Coll., 1974; MBA, Rutgers U., Newark, 1975. CPA, N.J. Staff acct. H.N. Frankel & Co., Ft. Lee, N.J., 1976-78; ptnr. Dorfman, Abrams, Music & Co., Glen Rock, N.J., 1978—. Treas. Make A Wish Found. of N.J., Elizabeth, 1989—, North Haledon (N.J.) Rep. Club, 1990—; mem. North Haledon Bd. Adjustment, 1991—. Fellow N.J. Soc. CPAs (com. on fed. taxation 1989—); mem. AICPA (tax div.). Roman Catholic. Office: Dorfman Abrams Music & Co 11 Harristown Rd Glen Rock NJ 07452-3300

WUERL, DONALD W., bishop; b. Pittsburgh, Nov. 12, 1940; s. Francis J. and Mary A. (Schiffhauer) W. BA, Cath. U. Am., 1962; MA, Cath. U. Am., Rome, 1963; ThM, Pontifical Gregorian U., Rome, 1967; ThD, Pontifical U. St. Thomas, Rome, 1974. Ord. priest, Roman Cath. Ch., Dec. 17, 1966, Rome. Asst. pastor, parochial vicar St. Rosalia Ch., Pitts., 1967-69; sec. to Cardinal John Wright Congregation for Clergy, Rome, 1969-79; vice-rector St. Paul Sem., Pitts., 1980-81, rector, 1981-85; Ord. aux. bishop of Seattle, titular bishop of Rosmarkaeum, 1986, bishop of Pittsburgh, 1988—; sec. to Bishop of Pitts., 1967-69; lectr. Duquesne U., Pitts., 1968-69, 80-85, Pontifical U. St. Thomas, 1975-79; lectr. adult theology program Diocese of Pitts., 1967-69, dir. Inst. Continuing Edn. for Priests, 1982-84, assoc. gen. sec., 1985; ofcl. Congregation for Clergy, Rome, 1969-79; mem. alumni bd. govts. Cath. U. Am., 1977-84, vice-pres. for religious, 1981-82; exec. sec. to Papal rep. for Study of Sems. in U.S., 1982-85. Author: The Forty Martyrs, 1971, Fathers of the Church, 1975, The Catholic Priesthood Today, 1976, The Teaching of Christ: Study Guide, 1977, A Visit to the Vatican, 1981, The Church and Her Sacraments: Making Christ Visible, 1990; co-author: The Teaching of Christ: A Catholic Catechism for Adults, 1976, 3d edit., 1991, A Catholic Catechism, 1986; editor: The Church: Hope of the World, 1972; contbg. author New Cath. Encyc.; contbr. articles to theol. publs. DD (hon.) Duquesne U., 1989, Washington and Jefferson Coll., 1990; HDL (hon.) La Roche Coll., 1990; recipient Disting. Pennsylvanian award Gannon U., 1989; named Vectors/Pitts. 1988 Man of Yr. in Religion. Mem. Fellowship Cath. Scholars, Cath. Theol. Soc. Am., Academia Romana Universale, Am. Cath. Hist. Assn., Phi Kappa Theta. Office: Diocese of Pitts 111 Blvd Of The Allies Pittsburgh PA 15222-1618

WUHL, CHARLES MICHAEL, psychiatrist; b. N.Y.C., Sept. 24, 1943; s. Isadore and Sali (Ackner) W.; m. Gail; children—Elise, Amy. M.D., U. Bologna, 1973. Diplomate Am. Bd. Psychiatry and Neurology. Intern, N.Y. Med. Coll., 1975-76, resident in psychiatry, 1976-77; fellow in child psychiatry Columbia Presbyn. Med. Center, 1977-78; practice medicine specializing in psychiatry and child psychiatry, Englewood, N.J., 1978—; attending staff, mem. faculty N.Y. Med. Coll.; psychiatrist NYU, also asst. clin. prof. psychiatry NYU Sch. Medicine. Contbr. to Psychosocial Aspects of Pediatric Care, 1978, World Book Ency., 1980—. Mem. Am. Psychiat. Assn., AMA, Am. Acad. Child Psychiatry. Office: 163 Engle St Englewood NJ 07631-2530

WUJCIAK, SANDRA CRISCUOLO, personnel executive; b. Newark, Nov. 26, 1949; d. Salvatore Michael Criscuolo and Maria (Agliata) Ventura; m. Alfred J. Wujciak Jr., Oct. 11, 1969; children: Kimberly, Joseph. Student, Morris County Coll., 1979-81. Parental cons. Lake Dr. Sch. Hearing Impaired, Mountain Lakes, N.J., 1975-83; mktg. rep. Accts. On Call, Livingston, N.J., 1981-84, Edison, N.J., 1984-85; br. mgr. Accts. On Call, Edison, 1985-87; area mgr. Accts. On Call, Edison, Princeton, N.J., Mpls., 1987-88; area v.p. Accts. On Call, Edison, Princeton, Atlanta, Cin., Miami, Fla., Mpls., 1988-90, Mpls., Edison, Princeton, N.J., 1990—; area v.p. Accts. on Call, Edison, Princeton, Mpls., 1988—. Pres. ad hoc com. Dodge Tract, Parsippany, N.J., 1979-80. Mem. N.J. Assn. Pers. Cons., Edison C. of C., Rockaway River Country Club (Denville, N.J.). Republican. Roman Catholic.

WULF, RONALD JAMES, biological research director; b. Davenport, Iowa, July 24, 1928; s. Herman F. and Amelia Wulf; m. Barbara Hesselgrave, July 10, 1960; children: James, David, John. BS, U. Iowa, 1950, MS, 1957; PhD, Purdue U., 1964. Chemist John Deere Co., Moline, Ill., 1950-52; pharmacologist rsch. Am. Cyanamid, Pearl River, N.Y., 1957-61; assoc. prof. pharmacology U. Conn., Storrs, 1964-70; dir. biol. rsch. Carter-Wallace Inc., Cranbury, N.J., 1970—. Mem. AAAS, Am. Chem. Soc., Dermal Clin. Evaluation Soc., N.Y. Acad. Sci., Soc. Cosmetic Chemists, Am. Coll. Toxicology, Soc. of Toxicology, Cosmetic Toiletries Fragrances Assn. (chmn. pharmacology-toxicology com. 1988-90). Home: 207 Varsity Ave Princeton NJ 08540 Office: Carter-Wallace Inc Half Acre Rd Cranbury NJ 08512

WULFF, ROGER LAVERN, museum administrator; b. Olean, N.Y., Nov. 16, 1940; s. LaVern Theodore and Marjorie (Perkins) W.; m. Geraldine Schepker, July 3, 1970. AA, Montgomery Jr. Coll., Rockville, Md., 1968; BA, U. Md., 1970; postgrad., Pa. State U., 1971-73, The George Washington U., 1975-79. Pres., chmn. bd. dirs. Mus. Svcs. Internat., Washington, 1980—; founder Mus. Svcs. Internat., 1980—; speaker at various mus. confs. Contbr. articles to profl. jours. Chmn. The Internat. Com. on Mus. Security, editor, 1986—. With U.S. Army, 1959-62. Recipient Excellence in Leadership Svcs. award, Smithsonian Inst., Washington, 1989, Cert. Appreciation, African Am. Mus. Assn., Washington, 1988. Mem. U.S. Com. of the Internat. Coun. of Mus., Internat. Com. for Mus. Security, Internat. Coun. of Mus. (chmn. internat. com. on mus. security), Internat. Com. on Exhbn. Exch., U.S./Internat. Coun. on Monuments and Sites (steering com.), Internat. Cultural Assistance Network, Am. Assn. Mus., Nat. Assn. Mus. Exhbn., Com. on Mil. Mus. in Am., Mus. Assn. Security Com., Com. on Mus. Evaluation and Rsch., Washington Mus. Collaborative. Office: Mus Svcs Internat 1100 16th St NW Washington DC 20036

WUNDERLICH, HERMANN, diversified corporation executive. Vice chmn. bd. mgmt. Bayer AG, Leverkusen, Fed. Republic Germany; chmn. bd. Bayer USA, Inc. (subs. Bayer AG), Pitts. Office: Miles Inc 500 Grant St Pittsburgh PA 15219-2502

WURMSER, JEANNE HAHN, behavioral healthcare company executive; b. Bellefontaine, Ohio, Aug. 6, 1932; d. Donald Randolph and Anna Lucille (Kreglow) Hahn; m. Eric Alan Wurmser, June 7, 1965 (div. July, 1979); 1 child, Kurt. BA, Miami U., 1965; PhD, Columbia U., 1974. Counselor in residence Rutgers U., New Brunswick, N.J., 1966-68; psychologist CPC Mental Health Svcs., Inc., Eatontown, N.J., 1971-74, dir. evaluation and rsch., 1974-79, asst. exec. dir., 1979-80, exec. dir., 1981—; pres. CPC Human Svcs., Inc., Eatontown, 1984—; tech. asst. project dir. region II Pub. Health Svc., N.Y.C., 1976-81; mem. adv. group biometry and epidemiology NIMH, Washington, 1979; bd. dirs. Nat. Coun. of CMHC, Washington, 1986-88; cons. Head Start region II Pub. Health Svc., N.Y.C., 1989—. Author: (with others) Emerging Development in Mental Health Program Evaluation, 1976, Evaluation in Practice, 1979, Assessment for Decision, 1987; editorial bd. mem. Child Behavior Therapy, 1978-81. Alliance mem. Holmdel (N.J.) Alliance for Substance Abuse Prevention, 1991-92; mem. Monmouth Ocean

Devel. Coun., Monmouth County, N.J., 1991. Mem. APA (accreditation site visitor 1978—), N.J. Psychol. Assn., N.J. Assn. Mental Health Agys. (pres. 1982-83. '84-86), Mental Health Corp. Am. (bd. trustees, sec. 1985-89, vice-chair 1990-92, chmn. 1992—). Office: CPC Mental Health Svcs Inc One High Point Center Way Morganville NJ 07751

WURTZ, ROBERT HENRY, scientist; b. St. Louis, Mar. 28, 1936; s. Robert Henry and Alice Edith (Popplwell) W.; m. Sally Smith, Dec. 20, 1958 (div.); children: William, Erica; m. Emily Otis, Apr. 23, 1983. AB, Oberlin Coll., 1958; PhD, U. Mich., 1962. Rsch. assoc. Com. for Nuclear Info., St. Louis, 1962-63; fellow Sch. Medicine, Washington U., 1962-65; rsch. psychologist NIH, Bethesda, Md., 1965-66, physiologist, 1966-78, chief lab. sensorimotor rsch., 1978—; vis. scientist Cambridge U., Eng., 1975-76. Editor: Neurobiology of Saccadic Eye Movement, 1989. Fellow AAAS; mem. NAS, Am. Acad. Arts and Scis., Soc. Neurosci. (pres. 1991), Am. Physiol. Soc., Assn. for Rsch. in Vision and Opthalmology, Soc. Exptl. Psychologists. Office: 9000 Rockville Pike Bethesda MD 20892-0001

WURZBERGER, BEZALEL, psychiatrist; b. Medias, Romania, June 28, 1945; came to U.S., 1967; s. Joshua and Isabella (Fulop) W.; m. Gladys Schmidt, Mar. 19, 1971; children: Tamar, David. BA, Columbia U., 1972; MD, Nat. U., Tegucigalpa, Honduras, 1982. Diplomate, Am. Bd. Psychiatry and Neurology. Intern North Gen. Hosp., N.Y.C., 1982-83; resident in psychiatry Creedmoor Psychiat. Ctr., Queens Village, N.Y., 1983-86; clin. psychiat. fellow N.Y. Med. Coll., Valhala, N.Y., 1986-87; staff psychiatrist Glens Falls (N.Y.) Hosp., 1987—; med. dir., Samaritan Counseling Ctr., Keene, N.Y., 1987—; psychiat. cons., Uihlein Mercy Ctr., Lake Placid, N.Y., 1988—. V.P., Jewish Community Tegucigalpa, 1978-80; bd. dirs., Congregation Shaarey Tefila, Glens Falls, 1989—. Sgt. Israeli Air Force, 1964-67. Mem. AMA, Am. Psychiat. Assn., Soc. Liaison Psychiatry, Honduran Coll. Physicians. Office: Glens Falls Hosp 80 Park St Glens Falls NY 12801-4486

WURZBURGER, WALTER SAMUEL, rabbi, philosophy educator; b. Munich, Germany, Mar. 29, 1920; s. Adolf W. and Hedwig (Tannenwald) W.; m. Naomi C. Rabinovitz, Aug. 19, 1947; children—Benjamin W., Myron I., Joshua J. BA, Yeshiva U., 1944, DD (hon.), 1987; MA, Harvard U., 1946, PhD, 1951. Ordained rabbi, 1944. Rabbi Congregation Chai Odom, Boston, 1944-53, Shaarei Shomayim Congregation, Toronto, Ont., Can., 1953-67, Shaaray Tefila Congregation, Lawrence, N.Y., 1967—; editor Tradition, N.Y.C., 1961-87; columnist Toronto Telegram, 1957-67; adj. assoc. prof. philosophy Yeshiva U., 1967-80, adj. prof., 1980—; bd. dirs. Union Orthodox Jewish Congregations Am. Editor: A Treasury of Tradition, 1967; contbg. editor Sh'ma; contbr. articles to profl. jours., chpts. to books, Ency. Judaica, Ency. of Religion, Ency of Bioethics. Mem. exec. com. United Jewish Welfare Funds of Toronto, 1965-67; past chmn. commn. on adoptions, synagogue commn., trustee Fedn. Jewish Philanthropies N.Y.; bd. dirs. Union Orthodox Jewish Congregations Am.; chmn. com. on interreligious affairs Synagogue Coun. Am., 1973-75, 83-87, pres., 1981-83, hon. pres., 1983-85; mem. interfaith com. United Community Funds of Toronto, 1960-67; v.p. synagogue commn. Fedn. Philanthropies, 1973-75; mem. nat. adv. com. United Jewish Appeal Am., 1971-78. Recipient Nat. Rabbinic Leadership award Union Orth. Jewish Congregations Am., 1983. Mem. Rabbinical Coun. Am. (past pres.), Rabbinical Coun. Can. (past pres.). Home: 138 Hards Ln Lawrence NY 11559-1315 Office: Congregation Shaaray Tefila 25 Central Ave Lawrence NY 11559-1342

WYATT, GREG ALAN, sculptor, educator; b. Grand View, N.Y., Oct. 16, 1949; s. Stanley and Alice (Morrissey) W. BA in Art History, Columbia Coll., 1971, MA in Ceramic Arts, 1974. Art instr. NYU, N.Y.C., 1974-75, Finch Coll., N.Y.C. and San Marino, Italy, 1974-76; asst. prof. Jersey City State Coll., 1974-75; sculptor-in-residence Cathedral of St. John the Divine, N.Y.C., 1983—; dir. Acad. Art-Newington-Cropsey Found., Hastings, N.Y., 1989—. Prin. works include fountains Gramercy Park, 1983, Cathedral of St. John the Divine, 1985, sculpture Am. Bur. Shipping, 1978, Newington-Cropsey Found., 1991, J.C. Penney Portrait monument, 1992, Am. Cyanamid monument, 1992, Princeton Country Day Sch. sculpture, 1992. V.p. Dudley House Arts Com., Harvard U., 1991—; pres. Fantasy Fountain Fund, Inc., N.Y.C., 1984—. Recipient Helen Foster Barnett award Nat. Acad. Sculptors, 1979, Congl. citation, 1992. Mem. Nat. Sculpture Soc., Nat. Arts Club. Studio: Cathedral of St John Divine 1047 Amsterdam Ave New York NY 10025

WYATT, HARRY JOEL, vision science educator; b. Chgo., Apr. 13, 1942; s. Saul Henry and Sophia (Edelman) W. BA magna cum laude, Pomona Coll., 1964; PhD, U. Calif., Berkeley, 1971. Rsch. fellow in biophysics Washington U., St. Louis, 1971-75; asst. prof. Coll. Optometry SUNY, N.Y.C., 1975-77, assoc. prof., 1977-84, prof., 1984—, chair biology, 1988—. Author: Manual of Visual Anatomy and Physiology, 1988; contbr. articles to profl. publs., chpts. to books. Mem. Assn. for Rsch. in Vision and Ophthalmology, Soc. for Neurosci. Office: SUNY Coll Optometry Dept Biology 100 E 24th St New York NY 10010-3610

WYATT, LORETTA SHARON, Latin American studies educator; b. Rocky Ford, Colo., Feb. 27, 1940. Student, Universidade de Coimbra, Coimbra, Portugal, 1960, Universidade do Rio Grande, Brazil, 1962-63; BA, MA, U. N. Mex., 1961,64; PhD, U. Fla., 1969. Asst. prof. dept. history Dept. History U. Wis., 1969-71; assoc. prof. dept. history Dept. History Montclair State Coll., 1972—. Contbg. author: Dwight D. Eisenhower, Soldier, President, Statesman, 1987, others; contbr. numerous articles to profl. jours. Fulbright-Hays scholar, Brazil, 1961-62; NDEA fellow U. Fla., 1965-69; Ford Travel grantee, Brazil, 1968; Am. Philos. Soc. rsch. grantee, Portugal, 1972. Mem. MLA, Am. Hist. Assn., Cath. Hist. Assn., Am. Assn. Tchrs. Spanish and Portuguese, Phi Beta Kappa, Phi Kappa Phi, Phi Summa Iota, Phi Alpha Theta. Office: Dept of History Montclair State Coll Upper Montclair NJ 07043

WYATT, WILSON WATKINS, JR., finance company and public relations executive; b. Louisville, Dec. 3, 1943; s. Wilson Watkins Sr. and Anne (Duncan) W.; m. Jane Clay, Aug. 15, 1964 (dec. 1975); m. Jacqueline Anne Kayrouz, Dec. 29, 1978; children: Carol, Wilson III, Sarah Wyatt, Sarah Bealmear, Jordan Bealmear. Student, U. of the South, 1961-65. Reporter The Courier-Jour., Louisville, 1965-67; pub. rels. account exec. Doe-Anderson Advt., Louisville, 1967-68; account exec. Zimmer-McClaskey-Lewis, Louisville, 1968-70; ptnr. Bennett & Wyatt Pub. Rels., Louisville, 1970-71; state rep., vice chair appropriations and revenue com. Ky. Gen. Assembly, Frankfort, 1969-71; exec. dir. Louisville Cen. Area Inc., 1971-77; dir. corp. affairs and communications Brown & Williamson Tobacco Corp., Louisville, 1977-82; v.p. pub. policy BATUS Inc., Washington, 1982-86; v.p. corp. affairs BATUS Inc., Louisville, 1986-90; sr. v.p. corp. affairs PNC Fin. Corp., Pitts., 1990—; lead U.S. def. pub. rels. activities against hostile take-over for B.A.T. Industries, U.K., 1989-90. Mem. youth adv. com. Atlantic Inst., 1967-68; del. North Atlantic Treaty Assn. Young Leaders Conf., 1967; chmn. Leadership Effort for All Dems., Ky., 1967-68; regional campaign coord. for Robert F. Kennedy, Ky.-Ind., 1968; mem. Pres.'s Forum, Washington, 1990—. Named one of Outstanding Young Men in Am., Ky. Jaycees, 1973. Mem. Pub. Rels. Seminar, Pub. Affairs Rsch. Coun. (conf. bd. 1986—), Pub. Affairs Coun. (bd. dirs. 1982—, exec. com. 1982-86), Speaker's Club (Washington). Home: Poplar Hill Country Club Rd Sewickley PA 15143-9402 Office: PNC Fin Corp Pitts Nat Bank 5th Avenue St Pittsburgh PA 15265-0001

WYCKOFF, JAMES MARSHAL, management consultant; b. Niagara Falls, N.Y., July 3, 1924; s. Lewis Benjamin and Florence Lenore (Wilbur) W.; m. Alice Marjorie Allen, Mar. 29, 1947 (div. Nov. 1, 1968); children: Janis L., Julia V. Darling, David C., Wendy C., Maurice D.; m. Betty Irene Bowler, Nov. 17, 1968. AA, Oreg. State Coll., 1944; BS in Physics, Antioch Coll., 1948; M in Physics, U. Rochester, 1952. Draftsman Gannett, Eastman, Flemming, Greenville, Pa., 1942; electronics lab. tech. Airborne Instruments Lab., Mineola, L.I., 1946-47; physics lab. asst. Antioch Coll., Yellow Springs, Ohio, 1947-48; rsch. asst., teaching asst. Univ. Rochester, N.Y., 1948-51; physicist Nat. Bur. of Standards, Washington, 1951-89; nuclear physicist, gen. phys. scientist Nat. Inst. Sci. and Tech., Gaithersburg, Md., 1951-89; health physicist Stanford (Calif.) Linear Accelerator Ctr., 1967-68; cons. in tech. transfer Gaithersburg, 1990—; editor in chief US2U Technology Exch., Gaithersburg, 1991—; exec. sec. Com. on Fed. Labs, OSTP, Gaithersburg, 1977-78. Editor: Directory of Federal Laboratories, 1982; contbr. articles to profl. jours. 2nd lt. U.S. Army Signal Corps, 1943-46. Recipient Bronze medal U.S. Dept. Commerce, Washington, 1980, Silver medal, 1983, Harold Metcalf award Fed. Lab. Consortium, Washington, 1982, 90. Fellow Tech. Transfer Soc. (bd. dirs., chmn. 1990-92, Pres.'s Gavel 1984, pres. Washington chpt. 1981-87, pres. 1988-90), Standards Alumni Assn. (mem. chmn. 1990-91), Fedn. Am. Scientist, Am. Phys. Soc., Scientific Rsch. Soc. Sigma Xi. Unitarian Universalist. Home and Office: 24300 Hanson Rd Gaithersburg MD 20882-3501

WYCKOFF, RICHARD DARREL, SR., utility industry supplier executive; b. Newport, R.I., Aug. 26, 1944; s. William Darrel and Ruth Francis (Winn) W.; m. Katherine Ellen Partridge; children: Richard Jr., Elizabeth Jane. Student, Miami U., Oxford, Ohio, 1963. Enlisted USN, 1964, reactor operator, 1964-71; engr. officer USN, Windsor, Conn., 1971-73; resigned USN, 1973; instrumentation engr. Maine Yankee Atomic Power Co., Wiscasset, 1973-81; nuclear market mgr. Indsl. Controls div. Simmonds Precision, Vergennes, Vt., 1981-82; northeast accounts mgr. Tech. for Energy Corp., Knoxville, 1982-84; pres. WYTEK Corp., Portland, Maine, 1984—; pres. WYTEK Corp., Portland, Maine, 1984—; developer redundant instrument monitoring system So. Calif. Edison Co., San Clemente, 1988—; dir. rsch. & devel. CANUS Corp., Laguna Hills, Calif., 1989—; cons. The Snowsquall Restoration Project, South Portland, 1988, Waynflete Sch., Portland, 1986, The Bridge Sch., Middlebury, 1982. Patentee in field. Mem. Am. Nuclear Soc., Instrumentation Soc. of Am. Republican.

WYDLER, HANS ULRICH, lawyer, banker, accountant; b. Hamburg, Germany, Nov. 11, 1923; came to U.S., 1927, naturalized, 1932; s. John Joseph and Grethe Adolfine (Heitmann) W.; B.S., Ohio State U., 1944, B.M.E. with honors, 1947; B.I.E. with honors, 1949; M.S., M.I.T., 1948; LL.B., Harvard U., 1951; m. Susan Gail Hart, Sept. 1, 1965; children: Hans Laurence, Steven Courtney. Bar Mass. 1951. Atty., systems engr., trustee Louis J. Hunter Assocs., Boston, 1951-57; asst. v.p. Chem. Bank, N.Y.C., 1958-64; v.p. Mfrs. Nat. Bank Detroit, 1964-65; sr. v.p. Security Nat. Bank, Huntington, N.Y., 1973-74; internat. and tax atty., acct. Hans U. Wydler, N.Y.C., 1966—; dir. Volume Mdse., Inc., Buning Internat. Inc., 1977-84. With USN, 1944-46. Registered profl. engr., Mass. Mem. Acad. Polit. Sci. (life), ABA, N.Y. County Lawyers Assn., ASME. Home and Office: 945 5th Ave New York NY 10021-2655

WYER, JEAN CONOVER, educator, accountant; b. Louisville, Sept. 12, 1950; d. Ramon and Becky (Hutchinson) W. AB, Vassar Coll., 1970; MBA, U. of N. Fla., 1973; postgrad., Northwestern U., 1975; EdD, Coll. of William and Mary, 1980. CPA, Fla. Field staff ARC, Mayport, Fla., 1971-72; research asst. U. of N. Fla., Jacksonville, 1972-73; research asst. Northwestern U., Evanston, Ill., 1973-75, lectr., 1975-76; from asst. prof. to prof. Coll. of William and Mary, Williamsburg, Va., 1977-88; dir. Coopers & Lybrand, N.Y.C., 1988—; cons. Vassar Coll., Poughkeepsie, N.Y., 1983-87, and various orgns.; territorial vice chmn. ARC, Chester, Va., 1986-87. Co-author: Liberal Education in Transition, 1980; contbr. numerous articles to profl. jours. Recipient Mid-Atlantic Finalist award White House Fellows, 1981, Thomas Jefferson Teaching award Coll. of William and Mary, 1982; alumni fellow, 1980, Bredin fellow, 1985, Coll. of William and Mary. Mem. Am. Acctg. Assn. (Innovation in Acctg. Edn. award 1991), AICPA, Am. Ednl. Rsch. Assn. Office: Coopers & Lybrand 1251 Ave Of The Americas New York NY 10020-1104

WYKA, KENNETH ANDREW, respiratory care educator; b. Passaic, N.J., Sept. 18, 1948; s. Andrew Charles and Claire (Bartman) W.; children: Kenneth Andrew Jr., Rebecca Ann, Christine Marie; m. Kathleen Ann McComb, June 3, 1984. BS, Fairleigh Dickinson U., 1970; diploma, Lenox Hill Hosp., 1972; MS, Fairleigh Dickinston U., 1980. Registered respiratory therapist; cert. respiratory therapy technician. Staff respiratory technician Hackensack (N.J.) Med. Ctr., 1971-72; dir. respiratory program Passaic County Community Coll., Paterson, N.J., 1972-76; dir. respiratory dept. Valley Hosp., Ridgewood, N.J., 1976-81; dir. staff devel. Valley Hosp., Ridgewood, 1981-83; exec. dir. The Breathing Ctr., Morristown, N.J., 1984-86; asst. prof. Passaic County Community Coll., Paterson, 1986-88; dir. cardiopulmonary scis., asst. prof. UMDNJ-SHRP, Newark, 1988—, clin. coord. respiratory care program, 1988—; adj. prof. Montclair State Coll., Upper Montclair, N.J., 1986—; cons. in field. Contbr. articles to profl. jours. Chmn. Am. Cancer Soc., Hackensack, 1990-92; bd. dirs. Am. Lung Assn. of N.J., Union, 1978—, past pres. No. region, 1984-86. Recipient Corning Med. Achievement award N.J. Soc. for Respiratory Care, 1978, Presdl. award N.J. Soc. for Respiratory Care, 1976-78, N.J. Chtp. Nat. Soc. for Cardiopulmonary Technology, 1979. Mem. N.J. Soc. for Respiratory Care (del. 1987-95, pres. 1979-83), N.J. Thoracic Soc., Am. Assn. for Respiratory Care, N.J. Soc. for Healthcare, Edn. & Tng. Roman Catholic. Home: 16 Wyckoff Ter Fair Lawn NJ 07410-5520 Office: UMDNJ-SHRP Dept Cardiopulmonary Scis Newark NJ 07107

WYLD, LIONEL DARCY, publications director, consultant, writer, historian; b. Colonie, N.Y., Apr. 25, 1925; s. Fred Herbert and Lillie Grace (Hayford) W.; m. Norma Marian Scherer, Sept. 11, 1954; children: Janet Marian, Kimberley Ellen. AB, Hamilton Coll., 1949; AM, U. Pa., 1950, PhD, 1959. From instr. to prof. U. Notre Dame, Rensselaer Poly. Inst., U. Buffalo, SUNY, 1954-66; dir. rsch. info. Syracuse (N.Y.) U., 1966-67, prof. Am. studies, acting dir., 1967-68; adj. prof. Am. studies Cazenovia Coll., 1968-71; spl. projects staff, student internship program developer and coordinator Navy Dept., 1972-76, editorial mgmt., 1976—; exec. editor, dir. Darcy Assocs. Ltd., 1985—; cons. Cornell Aero. Lab., 1962-67; adminstrv. dir., cons. INDOX Systems Rsch., Syracuse, 1968-70; mem. project rsch. staff U. Pa., 1956-57. Author: Low Bridge! Folklore and the Erie Canal, 1967 (N.Y. State Coun. on Arts award 1970), Preparing Effective Reports, 1967, Walter D. Edmonds, Storyteller, 1982, Boaters and Broomsticks, 1987; co-author: New Directions in Technical Writing, 1978, Your Brand of Communication, 1983, Upstate Literature, 1985 (Ms. prize John Ben Snow Found.); editor, co-author: American Civilization, 1975; contbr. articles to profl. jours.; mem. exec. bd. Jour. Tech. Writing and Communication, 1974-85; author various poems. Served with U.S. Army, 1943-46, ETO, PTO. Grantee Rensselaer Rsch. Fund, 1959-61, State Univ. Rsch. Found., 1964, Coll. Ctr. Finger Lakes, 1970-71; recipient Poet Finalist award New Eng. Assn. Tchrs. English, 1983, 89. Fellow Soc. for Tech. Communication; mem. Orgn. Am. Historians (book reviewer), N.Y. Am. Studies Assn. (v.p. 1970-71, pres. 1971-72, founding editor 1957-72), N.Y. Folklore Soc. (pres. 1964-67), Assn. for Bus. Communication (sr., chmn. various panels), Canal Soc. N.Y. State (chmn. publs. com. 1985—, bd. dirs.). Home: 20 Countryside Dr Cumberland RI 02864-2602

WYLER, DAVID JOHN, physician, scientist; b. N.Y.C., Dec. 21, 1944; s. Paul and Friedel (Weil) W.; m. Bonnie Jean Hughes (div.); children: Jonathan Michael, Benjamin Aaron; m. Deborah Beth Alport, May 17, 1987; 1 child, Samuel Alport. AB cum laude, Brown U., 1966; MD, Harvard U., 1970. Sr. investigator Nat. Inst. Allergy and Infectious Diseases, NIH, Bethesda, Md., 1976-79; asst. prof. medicine Sch. Medicine, Johns Hopkins U., Balt., 1978-79; prof. medicine, molecular biology and microbiology Tufts U. and New Eng. Med. Ctr. Hosp., Boston, 1985—; dir. travelers' health svc. New Eng. Med. Ctr. Hosp., 1989—; cons. NIH, Bethesda, 1975—, Nat. Acad. Scis., Washington, 1991, NSF, Washington, 1982—. Editor (book) Modern Parasite Biology, 1990; contbr. more than 100 sci. articles to profl. jours. Trustee Stoney Hill Farms Homeowners Assn., West Tisbury, Mass., 1989—. Grantee USPHS, 1981—. Fellow ACP, Infectious Diseases Soc. Am.; mem. Am. Soc. Clin. Investigators, Am. Fedn. Clin. Rsch., Am. Soc. Tropical Medicine and Hygiene (councillor 1985-87), Am. Soc. Microbiology, Reticuloendothelial Soc., Am. Assn. Immunologists. Democrat. Jewish. Office: New Eng Med Ctr Hosp 750 Washington St Boston MA 02111-1533

WYLER, STEPHEN MARC WOHLFEILER, veterinarian, administrator; b. Bklyn., June 28, 1945; s. Robert and Jessie Carol (Granat) Wohlfeiler. BS, U. Ga., 1967; DVM, U. Bologna, Italy, 1974. Dir. Animal Med. Hosp., Hempstead, N.Y., 1977—. Bd. dirs. Nassau Animal Emergency Clinic, Westbury, N.Y., 1979-88. Mem. AVMA, L.I. Vet. Med. Assn. Jewish. Office: Animal Med Hosp 779 Peninsula Blvd Hempstead NY 11550

WYLLIE, MICHAEL EUGENE, meteorologist; b. Ft. Dix, N.J., Feb. 23, 1953; s. Joseph Gerard and Helen Frances (Feeney) W. BS, SUNY, 1975; MS, Fla. State U., 1977. Meteorol. intern Nat. Weather Svc., Des Moines, 1978-82; meteorologist Nat. Weather Svc., N.Y.C., 1982-85; regional aviation meteorologist Nat. Weather Svc., Garden City, N.Y., 1985-87; dep. meteorologist-in-charge Nat. Weather Svc., Boston, 1987-90; meteorologist-in-charge Nat. Weather Svc., N.Y.C., 1990—. Office: Nat Weather Svc 30 Rockefeller Pla Mezzanine Rm 9 New York NY 10112

WYMAN, JAMES VERNON, newspaper executive; b. Brockton, Mass., Nov. 17, 1923; s. George Dewey and Christine Laverne (Skinner) W.; m. Viola Marie Bousquet, June 24, 1950; children—J. Vernon, Douglas Phillip, Carolyn Anne. Student, Northeastern U., Boston, 1946-48; B.S. in Journalism, Boston U., 1951. With Providence Jour.-Bull., 1951—, asst. city editor, 1960-63, city editor, 1963-74, exec. city editor, 1974, metro mng. editor, 1974-79, exec. news editor, 1979-85, dep. exec. editor, 1985-88, v.p., exec. editor, 1989—. Served with AUS, 1942-46, PTO. Recipient Yankee Quill award, 1989. Mem. New Eng. AP News Execs. Assn. (past pres.), AP Mng. Editors Assn., New Eng. Soc. Newspaper Editors, Acad. New Eng. Journalists (past dir.), New Eng. Newspaper Assn., Sigma Delta Chi (past pres. New Eng. chpt.). Roman Catholic. Home: 6 Barway Ln Cumberland RI 02864-4914 Office: 75 Fountain St Providence RI 02902-0050

WYMAN, JOEL WENTWORTH, JR., management consultant; b. Florence, S.C., Apr. 13, 1943; s. Joel Wentworth and Mildred (Gwinner) W.; m. Dona Elizabeth Hallum, Jan. 23, 1965; children: Joel Wentworth III, Chadwick Holbrook. BA, Clemson U., 1966. Mgr. NCR Corp., Dayton, Ohio, 1967-79; v.p. The Chase Manhattan Bank, N.Y.C., 1979-83, Na Banco, Melville, N.Y., 1983; sr. cons. Deloitte, Haskins & Sells, N.Y.C., 1984-87; prin. Joel W. Wyman Jr. & Assocs., Huntington, N.Y., 1987-91; ptnr. ISYS Consulting Group Ltd., Huntington, N.Y., 1991—. Home and Office: 19 Royal Oak Dr Huntington NY 11743-4438

WYNN, CHARLES MARTIN, SR., chemistry educator; b. N.Y.C., May 8, 1939; s. Arthur Elias and Bertha (Rehfeld) W.; m. Jean Marie Boris, July 9, 1966; children: Charles, Jr., Joseph, Michelle, Andrew. B Chem. Engring., CCNY, 1960; MS, U. Mich., 1963, PhD, 1965. Instr. of chemistry U. Mich., Ann Arbor, 1965-66; vol. U.S. Peace Corps, Penang, Malaysia, 1966-68; prof. phys. sci. Oakland Community Coll., Farmington Hills, Mich., 1969-79; prof. chemistry Ea. Conn. State U., Willimantic, Conn., 1979—; vis. scholar Wesleyan Univ., Middletown, Conn., 1986; bd. advisors Visual Edn. Assn., Springfield, Ohio, 1982—. Author: (textbooks) Natural Science: Bridging the Gaps, 3d edit., 1991, Laboratory Experiments for Chemistry, 4th edit., 1987, (teacher's manual) Teacher's Manual for Higher School Chemistry, 1967; contbr. numerous articles to profl. jours. Pres. Am. Cancer Soc., Willimantic, 1986-88, Saxton B. Little Free Libr., Columbia, Conn., 1987—; bd. dirs. Camp Horizons, Inc., South Windham, Conn., 1989—, Spl. Olympics Swim Meet, Willimantic, 1985—. Named DuPont Outstanding Teaching fellow U. Mich., 1963, Dist. Faculty Mem., 1992; rsch. Coppers Found., 1962, fellow Union Carbide, 1964, fellow USPHS, 1965. Mem. Am. Chem. Soc., Conn. Scis. Tchrs. Assn., New Eng. Assn. Chemistry Tchrs., AAUP. Office: Eastern Conn State Univ 83 Windham St Willimantic CT 06226-2295

WYNN, MATTHEW DAVID, scientific programmer-analyst, aerospace engineer; b. White Plains, N.Y., Jan. 8, 1964; s. David Fredrick and Mildred Jean (Gogel) W. BS in Aerospace Engring., SUNY, Buffalo, 1986; MEngring. in Aerospace Engring., Cornell U., 1988. Cons. programmer and analyst GE Corp. R & D, Schenectady, 1988; programmer, analyst programmable automation Cornell U., Ithaca, N.Y., 1988; programmer, analyst M.W.E., Hartsdale, N.Y., 1988-89, cons., 1989—; systems analyst Precision Nesting Systems Inc., Cresskill, N.J., 1989—. Mem. AIAA, Acad. Model Aeros., Profl. Ski Instrs. Am. (registered, instr. disabled skiing 1987—), Nat. Handicapped Sports Assn. Home: 100 Pinewood Rd Apt 3A Hartsdale NY 10530-1634

WYNNE, JOHN BOYCE, performing company executive; b. Norfolk, Va., Nov. 5, 1945; s. John Fleming and Mary Boyce (Gwaltney) W.; m. Nadinka Szaksz, May 13, 1968 (div. Aug. 1972). BFA, Va. Commonwealth U., 1968; MFA, Calif. Inst. Arts, 1973. Scene design asst. Va. Mus. Fine Arts Theatre, Richmond, 1968; designer, scenic artist Merle Oberon Theatre, Actors Studio W., Hollywood, Calif., 1973; asst. art dir., scenic artist NBC Studios and CBS Studios, L.A. and Burbank, Calif., 1973-76; guest artist, theatre designer Christopher Newport Coll., Newport News, Va., 1976-78; art dir., designer N. Lee Lacey & Assocs., Calif., 1978-80; guest artistic dir. Danville (Va.) Mus. Fine Arts Theatre, 1980-81; producer, dir. Ancient Arts Films, Smithfield, Va., 1981-82; adminstrv. cons. Tidewater Studio for Performing Arts, Hampton, Va., 1983-84; art dir. Benton, Fisher & Pile, Hampton, 1983-84. Dir., designer: (plays) Hair, 1987, One Flew Over the Cuckoo's Nest, 1989 (Virtuosic Prodn. award), (video documentaries) The Tredegar Ironworks ARchaeology, 1985, The Stridh's 1200, 1985, Bacon's Castle Garden Archaeology, 1985; actor Marat/Sade, Maryland Stage Co., UMBC. Playwright, artistic dir. Carroll County Hist. Soc., Westminster, Md., 1989; actor The Md. Stage Co., 1992. Capt. U.S. Army, 1968-77. Mem. U.S. Inst. Theatre Tech. Methodist. Home: 7437 Clifton Ln Smithfield VA 23430-2929 Office: Catonsville C C 800 S Rolling Rd Baltimore MD 21228-5317

WYON, JOHN BENJAMIN, public health physician, scientist, consultant; b. London, May 3, 1918; s. Guy Alfred and Emma Mildred (Hitchock) W.; m. Elizabeth Glynne Granmer, JUly 10, 1946 (dec. 1989); children: Rachel Margaret, Thomas Cranmer; m. Joan Litchard Kittredge, Feb. 15, 1992. BA, Cambridge U., 1940, MB, 1942, BChir, 1942; MPH, Harvard U., 1953. Med. officer Friends Ambulance Unit, Adua, Ethiopia, 1943-45; med. missionary Ch. Missionary Soc., U.P., India, 1947-52; field dir. Harvard U. Population Study, Punjab, India, 1953-60; from lectr. to sr. lectr. Harvard Sch. Pub. Health Dept. Population Scis., Boston, 1960-88; cons. Andean Rural Health Care, Lake Junaluska, N.C., Sarvodaya Shramadana Movement, Moratuwa Sri Lanka, 1978-89. Author: The Khanna Study, 1971. Mem. Am. Pub. Health Assn., Royal Coll. Physicians. Episcopalian. Office: Dept Population 165 Huntington Ave Boston MA 02115-3117

WYSE, BONNIE L., advertising executive; b. Rochester, N.Y., May 2, 1953; d. Edward J. and Merel (Quigley) W.; divorced; 1 child, Chad Vinke. A in Acctg., Monroe Community Coll., Rochester, 1986; student, St. John Fisher Coll., 1988—. Various office mgmt. positions Rochester, 1971-81; asst. acct. William T. Sirianni CPA, Rochester, 1981-84; contr. Univ. Club, Rochester, 1984-86; v.p. fin. Hart-Conway Co. Inc., Rochester, 1986—. Mem. Rochester Women's Network, Webster Art Club. Republican. Office: Hart-Conway Co Inc 387 Main St E Ste 400 Rochester NY 14604-2107

WYSOCKI, BOLESLAW A(NTONI), psychologist, educator; b. Poland, June 10, 1912; s. Wladyslaw and Wiktoria (Mizia) Wysocki; student U. Cracow, U. Edinburgh (Scotland), Cambridge (Eng.) U., Oxford (Eng.) U., 1932-48; Ph.D., U. London (Eng.), 1954. Came to U.S., 1952, naturalized, 1958. Dir. edn. Ministry Edn., Gt. Britain, 1948-52; counselor, tchr. Marquette U., Milw., 1952-55; asso. prof. psychology Alliance (Pa.) Coll., 1955-57, Merrimack (Mass.) Coll., 1957-60, Regis (Mass.) Coll., 1960-62; prof. psychology Newton (Mass.) Coll., 1962-75, Boston Coll., 1975—. Clin. work mental instns., 1952—. Served as mil. psychologist Polish Army, 1943-48. Mem. Am., Mass., Brit. psychol. socs., Polish Inst. Arts and Scis. in Am., AAUP. Contbr. articles to profl. jours. Home: 240 Brattle St Cambridge MA 02138-4628 Office: Boston Coll Dept Psychology 885 Centre St Newton MA 02159-1156

WYSZKOWSKI, JEFFREY PAUL, communications company professional; b. Somerville, N.J., Mar. 29, 1953; s. Edward Paul and Bertha (Czaplicki) W.; m. Lauren A. Lee, July 16, 1988. BFA, U. Notre Dame, 1971-75; MFA, Syracuse U., 1991. Designer AT&T Bell Labs., Murray Hill, N.J., 1979-88; supr. AT&T Bell Labs., Whippany, N.J., 1988—; mem. graphic design degree adv. com. County Coll. Morris, N.J., 1991. Drawings included in exhibits N.J. Ctr. Visual Arts, 1982, St. Hubert's Giralda Animal Imagery Show, 1985. Mem. Assn. Computing Machinery, Nat. Computer Graphics Assn., Somerset Art Assn., Nat. Assn. Desktop Pubs., Internat. Design by

Electronics Assn. Office: AT&T Bell Labs Rm 2C 243A 1 Whippany Rd Whippany NJ 07981-1500

WYSZKOWSKI, STANISLAW WLADYSLAW PAUL, technology marketing executive; b. Lodz, Poland, June 19, 1934; came to U.S., 1978; s. Wladyslaw Anthony and Halina Anna (Sawicka) W.; m. Burnice Faye Love, Apr. 30, 1952 (div. 1974); 1 child, Moneca Blackwell. BSC in Chem. Engring., U. Toronto, 1958. Rsch. engr. Brit. Am. Bank Note, Ottawa, Can., 1960-69; tech. dir. Sinclair & Valentine Can. Ltd., Toronto, 1969-73; quality assurance mgr. Maclean-Hunter Ltd., Toronto, 1974-78; sr. tech. dir. Am. Bank Note, Bronx, 1980-83; tech. dir. Am. Bank Note Holographics, Elmsford, N.Y., 1983-90, Holografx Div. Crown Roll Leaf, Inc., Paterson, N.J., 1991—. Developer holographic products and applications; contbr. articles to profl. jours. Recipient Recognition Svc. award Mag. Assn. Can., 1978. Office: Holografx Div Crown Roll Leaf Inc 12 Columbia Ave Paterson NJ 07503

WYTOCK, DALE HARRISON, gastroenterologist; b. Chalfont St. Peter, Eng., Dec. 28, 1952; came to U.S., 1954; s. Harry Louis and Florence Ima (Patrick) W.; m. Mary Ann Francis, June 12, 1982; children: Julie, Thomas, Michael. Student, U. Oreg., 1970-73; MD, Creighton U., 1977. Diplomate Am. Bd. Internal Medicine. Internand resident Mayo Clinic, Rochester, Minn., 1977-80, fellow in gastroenterology, 1980-82; cons. gastroenterologist USAF Wilford Hall Med. Ctr., San Antonio, 1982-86; assoc. prof. medicine Uniformed Svcs. U. Health Scis., Bethesda, Md., 1982-86; assoc. in gastroenterology Geisinger CliniC, Danville, Pa., 1986—, dir. gastrointestinal fellowship program, 1991—; clin. assoc. prof. medicine Jefferson Med. Coll., Phila., 1986—. Contbr. articles to profl. jours. Coach Am. Youth Soccer Orgn., Danville, 1990-92. Maj. USAF, 1982-86. Fellow ACP; mem. AMA, Am. Soc. Gastrointestinal Endoscopy, Pa. Med. Soc., Montour County Med. Soc., Am. Gastroenterological Assn. Roman Catholic. Office: Geisinger Med Ctr N Academy Ave Danville PA 17822

WYZANSKI, CHARLES MAX, lawyer, educator; b. Cambridge, Mass., Nov. 26, 1944; s. Charles Edward Jr. and Gisela (Warburg) W.; m. Nilgün Gökgür, Sept. 25, 1982; children: Talya G., Tamara G. AB, Harvard U., 1966, postgrad., 1988; JD, Columbia U., 1971. Bar: Mass. 1972, Pa. 1972. Vol. Peace Corps, Nigeria and Senegal, 1966-68; staff and mng. atty. Community Legal Svcs., Phila., 1972-76; asst. dir. Salzburg (Austria) Seminar, 1977-78; instr. Harvard U. Law Sch., Cambridge, 1978-81; asst. dist. atty. Middlesex County, Cambridge, 1982-85; sr. assoc. Peabody & Brown, Boston, 1986-88; sr. litigation counsel Mass. Dept. Correction, Boston, 1988—; adj. prof. Boston U. Sch. Mgmt., 1988—; chmn. grievance panel Cambridge Housing Authority, 1988—. Bd. dirs. Cambridge Adult Edn. Ctr. Fellow Salzburg Seminar, 1976. Mem. Boston Bar Assn., Am. Arbitration Assn. (arbitrator 1986—). Jewish. Home: 75 Francis Ave Cambridge MA 02138-1911 Office: Mass Dept Correction 100 Cambridge St Cambridge MA 02141-1819

XAVIER, SISTER FRANCIS, nun; b. Watertown, N.Y., Sept. 21, 1916; d. Sarah Emma Nicholson. BS in Nursing, Cath. U. Am., 1944, MS in Adminstrn., Biol., 1948, postgrad. in philosophy, chemistry, 1949-51; LDH (hon.), L.I. Univ., 1967. Registered nurse. Tchr. St. Leo Sch., Bklyn., 1939-40, Holy Angles Sch., Buffalo, 1940-41; oper. room supr. Champlain Valley Hosp., Plattsburgh, N.Y., 1941-42; instr. biology D'Youville Coll., Buffalo, 1944-48, head dept. biology, 1948-51, dean sch. nursing, 1951-62, pres., 1962-68; establisher of expansion program Motherhouse of Grey Nuns, Yardley, Pa., 1969-71; dir. devel. Grey Nuns of the Sacred Heart, Yardley, 1972-92; ind. cons., 1992—; cons. in field; regent N.Y. State Bd. Nurse Examiners, 1952-64; lectr. in field; bd. dirs. A. Barton Hepburn Hosp., Ogensburg, N.Y., chmn. devel. planning, 1976-84. Mem. AAUW, Nat. Cath. Devel. Conf. (v.p. 3 terms, Disting. Svc. award 1986), Ctr. for Study of the Presidency, Am. Acad. Polit. Sci., Nat. Soc. Fund Raising Execs., World Affairs Coun., Phila. Mus. Art, Lower Bucks C. of C., Cath. U. Del. VAlley Alumni (chpt.). Republican. Home and Office: Grey Nuns of the Sacred Heart 1750 Quarry Rd Morrisville PA 19067-3998

YABLON, JEFFERY LEE, lawyer; b. Chgo., June 28, 1948; s. Robert R. and Faye I. (Goldberg) Y.; m. Jean C. LaPrade, Apr. 17, 1983. BA with honors, U. Wis., 1970; JD, Stanford U., 1973. Bar: Calif. 1974, D.C. 1975. Law clk. to Judge Cynthia Holcomb Hall, U.S. Tax Ct., Washington, 1973-75; Fulbright scholar U. Florence, Italy, 1975-76; assoc. Covington & Burling, Washington, 1976-80, Lee, Toomey & Kent, Washington, 1980-82; ptnr. Shaw, Pittman, Potts & Trowbridge, Washington, 1984—; mem. bd. advisors Corp. Taxation mag., N.Y.C., 1988—. Contbr. articles to legal jours. Bd. dirs. Am. Friends Hebrew U., Washington, 1991—. Mem. ABA, State Bar Calif., D.C. Bar. Jewish. Home: 800 25th St NW Washington DC 20037 Office: Shaw Pittman Potts & Trowbridge 2300 N St NW Washington DC 20037

YABLONSKI, JOSEPH JOHN, insurance services company principal; b. Worcester, Mass., July 10, 1944; s. Joseph and Florence Mary (Simonavich) Y.; m. Faith Ann Citroni, Nov. 12, 1983; children: Eric Joseph, Caitlin Ruth. AA, Worcester Jr. Coll., 1968; BBA, Nichols Coll., 1970. Claims supr. Liberty Mutual Ins. Co., Lexington, Mass., 1970-76; asst. sec. Cameron and Colby Co., Inc., Boston, 1976-80; claims dir. Am. Reinsurance Co., Chgo., 1980-81; asst. v.p. Trenwick Reinsurance Group, Stamford, Conn., 1981-85, Palange & Assocs., Inc., Boston, 1985-88; v.p., prin. Northshore Internat. Ins. Svcs., Inc., Salem, Mass., 1988—. Sgt. USAF, 1962-66. Office: Northshore Internat Ins 76 Lafayette St Salem MA 01970-3624

YACHER, LEON ISAAC, geography educator; b. Lima, Peru, Jan. 23, 1950; came to U.S., 1964; s. Jose Vacher and Ethel (Roiter) Greenblott; children: Rebekah, Minah, Aaron. AA, Norwalk (Conn.) Community Coll, 1970; BA, U. N.Mex., 1972, MA, 1974. Asst. prof. SUNY, Oswego, 1977-78; asst. prof. So. Conn. State U., New Haven, 1978-87, assoc. prof., 1987—; cons. Conn. State Dept. Edn., Hartford, Conn., Woodbridge (Conn.) Pub. Schs., 1990—, City of Bridgeport, Conn., 1982-83. Cartographer Systematic Political Geography, 1980; contbr. more than 17 articles to profl. jours., more than 147 maps to books and jours. Vol. lectr. K-12 schs., Conn. Rsch. grantee State Con., 1986-91; Watson fellow Syracuse U., 1974-77. Mem. Assn. Am. Geographers, Am. Congress Surveying and Mapping, Can. Cartographic Assn., New Eng.-St. Lawrence Valley Geog. Soc. (v.p. 1990-91, 91-93), Conn. Geog. Alliance, Geog. Soc. Lima. Office: So Conn State U 501 Crescent St New Haven CT 06515-1330

YAGER, JAMES DONALD, JR., toxicologist, educator; b. Milw., Dec. 29, 1943; s. James D. and Virginia Ruth (Disch) Y.; m. Joanne Zurlo, July 18, 1981; children: Nicholas T., Christopher J., Allison M. BS, Marquette U., 1965; PhD, U. Conn., 1971. Asst. prof. biology Dartmouth Coll., Hanover, N.H., 1974-77; asst. prof. anatomy, pathology Dartmouth Med. Sch., Hanover, 1977-81, assoc. prof. anatomy, 1983-86; assoc. dir. Norris Cotton Cancer Ctr. Dartmouth Med. Sch., Hanover, 1983-89; prof. Dartmouth Med. Sch., Hanover, 1986-89, acting chair dept. pharmacology/toxicology, 1987-89; assoc. prof. environ. medicine NYU Med. Sch., 1981-83; prof., dir. toxicological sci. Johns Hopkins U. Sch. Hygiene and Pub. Health, Balt., 1989—. Active Govs. Coun. on Toxic Substances, Md., 1991. Mem. AAAS, Am. Assn. Cancer Rsch., Fedn. Am. Soc. Experimental Biology, Soc. Toxicology, Am. Soc. Cell Biology.

YAGHJIAN, ARTHUR DAVID, research electrical engineer; b. Providence, Jan. 1, 1943; s. Nubar and Lilly Katherine (Mortenson) Y.; m. Lucretia Bailey, June 30, 1973. ScB, Brown U., 1964, ScM, 1966, PhD, 1969. Asst. prof. Tougaloo (Miss.) Coll., 1967; assoc. prof. Hampton (Va.) Inst., 1969-70; faculty fellow NASA Langley Field, Hampton, 1970; rsch. engr. Nat. Bur. Standards, Boulder, Colo., 1971-82, Rome Lab., Bedford, Mass., 1983—; guest lectr. Indian Inst. Tech., Kharagpur, 1987, Tech. U. Denmark, Lyngby, 1989. Contbr. numerous articles to profl. jours. Recipient 4 spl. achievement awards Nat. Bur. Standards, 1978-83, Bronze medal, 1981, 15 sci. achievement awards Rome Lab., 1983-91; advanced study grantee NATO, Norwich, Eng., 1979. Mem. IEEE (sr., assoc. editor 1983-86), Union Radio Sci. (assoc. editor 1987-88), Electromagnetics Soc., Sigma Xi. Home: 115 Wright Rd Concord MA 01742-2036 Office: Rome Lab/ERCT Hanscom AFB MA 01742-5000

YAGO, GLENN HARVEY, economist, educator, entrepreneur; b. Shreveport, La., Nov. 6, 1950; s. Lawrence J. and Sylvia (Zelinsky) Y.; m. Yudit Jung, Oct. 8, 1972; children: Noah, Gideon, Dena. BA, Tulane U., 1971; MA, Hebrew U., 1976; PhD, U. Wis., 1980. Rsch. asst. Eshkol Inst. Social and Econ. Rsch., Jerusalem, 1971-73; instr. Volkshochschule, Frankfurt, Fed. Republic Germany, 1974; rsch. asst. Inst. Rsch. on Poverty U. Wis., Madison, 1976-77; lectr. dept. sociology U. Wis., 1978-80; assoc. Coact Rsch. Assocs., Madison, 1977-80; asst. prof. dept. sociology SUNY, Stony Brook, 1980-86; dir. Econ. Rsch. Bur. SUNY, 1985—, assoc. prof. Harriman Sch. mgmt. and Policy, 1986—; faculty fellow, Rockefeller Inst., Govt., Albany, N.Y., 1985—; bd. dirs. Barnwell Industries, Inc., Lavalco Industries, Inc., Am. Passage Media Corp.; mem. Lt. Gov.'s Task Force on Plant Closings and Task Force on Workers Equity, State of N.Y., 1984; chmn. N.Y. State Network for Econ. Rsch., Albany, 1988—; mem. Gov.'s Project 2000, 1986. Author: The Decline of Transit, 1984, New York State in the Year 2000 (with others), 1988, Junk Bonds: How High Yield Securities Restructured Corporate America, 1991; contbr. articles to profl. jours. Mem. overall econ. devel. com., Suffolk County Planning Dept., L.I., N.Y. Grantee, Calif. Humanities Coun., 1981, NSF, 1985, 86, 87, N.Y. State Dept. Commerce, 1984, N.Y. State Legislature, 1987; grantee, recipient fellowship, German Marshall Fund of U.S., 1984. Mem. Acad. Mgmt., Assn. Pub. Policy Analysis and Mgmt. Jewish. Office: Am Passage 1114 Ave Of The Americas New York NY 10036-7703

YAHR, MELVIN DAVID, physician; b. N.Y.C., Nov. 18, 1917; s. Isaac and Sarah (Reigelhaupt) Y.; m. Felice Turtz, May 9, 1948; children—Carol, Nina, Laura, Barbara Anne. A.B., N.Y. U., 1939, M.D., 1943. Diplomate: Am. Bd. Psychiatry and Neurology (pres.). Intern Lenox Hill Hosp., N.Y.C., 1943-44; resident Lenox Hill Hosp., also Montefiore Hosp., Bronx, N.Y., 1947-48; staff Columbia, 1948-73, asso. prof. clin. neurology, 1957-62, prof. neurology, 1962-70, H.H. Merritt prof. neurology, 1970-73, asst. dean grad. medicine, 1959-67, assoc. dean, 1967-73; asst. neurologist N.Y. Neurol. Inst., 1948-53, assoc. attending neurologist, 1953-60, attending neurologist, 1960-73; Goldschmidt prof. neurology, chmn. dept. neurology Mt. Sinai Med. Center, 1973-92; Aidekman Family Prof. Neurological Rsch., 1992—; exec. dir. Parkinson's Disease Found., 1957-73; panel neurologist N.Y.C. Bd. Edn., 1958-59; mem. com. evalutation drugs in neurology NIH, 1959-60, panel mem. neurol. study sect., 1959-80; mem. com. revisions U.S. Pharmacopea. Assoc. editor: Internat. Jour. Neurology; editor-in-chief Jour. Neural Transmission, 1989—; Archives Neurology, 1964-89. Fellow Am. Acad. Neurology, N.Y. Acad. Medicine, Harvey Soc.; mem. A.M.A. (chmn. com. neurol. disorders in industry), Am. Neurol. Assn. (sec.-treas. 1959-68, pres. 1969), Assn. Research Nervous and Mental Disease, N.Y. State Neurol. Soc., New York County Med. Soc., Am. Epilepsy Soc., Eastern Assn. Electroencephalographers. Office: Mt Sinai Med Ctr 1 Gustave L Levy Pl New York NY 10029-6504

YALE, JEFFREY FRANKLIN, podiatrist; b. Derby, Conn., Jan. 18, 1943; s. Irving and Bernice (Blume) Y.; m. Lenore Bernsley, Apr. 23, 1987; children: Brian Joseph, Andrew Malcolm. U. Fla., 1960-62; D of Podiatric Medicine, Ill. Coll. Podiatric Medicine, 1966. Diplomate Am. Bd. Podiatric Surgery, Am. Bd. Podiatric Orthopedics, Am. Bd. Med. Quality Assurance and Utilization Rev. Surg. resident Highland Gen. Hosp., Oakland, Calif., 1966-67; capt. U.S. Army Med. Svc., Fort Ord, Calif., 1967-71; instr. masters level Quinnipiac Coll., Hamden, Conn., 1981; cons. surgeon VA Med. Ctr., West Haven, Conn., 1982—; chmn. podiatric surgery Griffin Hosp., Derby, Conn., 1974—; assoc. clin. prof. U. Osteo. Health Scis., Des Moines, 1982—; chmn. Podiatric Medicine Test Com. Nat. Bd. Podiatric Med. Examiners, 1977—; pres. Ct. Examining Bd. in Podiatry, 1979, Am. Acad. Podiatric Sports Medicine, 1986. Author: Firm Footings For the Athlete, 1984, The Arthritic Foot, 1984, Yale's Podiatric Medicine, 3d edit., 1987; contbr. numerous sci. articles to profl. jours. Pres. Yale Podiatry Group, P.C., Ansonia, Conn., 1976—; dir. Podiatry Ins. Co. of Am., Brentwood, Tenn., 1987—; corporator The Savs. Bank of Ansonia, 1982, Griffin Hosp., Derby, Conn., 1982. Capt. U.S. Army, 1967-71. Fellow Am. Acad. Podiatric Sports Medicine, Am. Assn. Hosp. Podiatrists, Am. Coll. Foot Surgeons; mem. New Haven County Podiatric Med. Assn., Conn. Podiatric Med. Assn., Am. Podiatric Med. Assn., Conn. Pub. Health Assn., Am. Pub. HealthAssn., Conn. Examining Bd. in Podiatry. Jewish. Home: 18 Inwood Rd Woodbridge CT 06525-2558 Office: Yale Podiatry Group PC 364 E Main St Ansonia CT 06401-1995

YALKOVSKY, RAFAEL, science writer; b. Chgo., Oct. 11, 1917. BS in Vertebrae Paleontology, U. Chgo., 1946, MS in Marine Geology, 1955, PhD, 1956. Assoc. engr. Crane Co., 1955-56; asst. prof. marine geology U. Mont., 1956-61; prof. geology and oceanography SUNY, Buffalo, 1961-83; sci. reporter Sta. WBFO-FM, 1975-78; vis. scholar Inst. Marine Studies, U. Wash., 1974, U. London Law Sch., 1975. Contbr. articles to profl. jours.; several TV appearances. With U.S. Army, 1942-45, ETO, Atlantic Theatre Ops. 9 NSF grants, Woods Hole Ocean Inst. grantee, 1959. Fellow AAAS, N.Y. Acad. Scis. (life); mem. Am. Geophys. Union (life), U.S. Naval Inst. (life), Nat. Assn. Geology Tchrs., Nat. Assn. Sci. Writers, Internat. Sci. Writers Assn., Sigma Xi (pres. SUNY-Buffalo chpt. 1970-72). Democrat. Jewish. Home: 2397 Bush Rd # 398 Grand Island NY 14072-0398

YAMADA, T(OMOHIKO) ALBERT, public affairs consultant; b. Kamakura, Japan, Sept. 29, 1938; came to U.S., 1958, naturalized, 1969; s. Chisaburoh F. and Edith (Whitworth) Y.; m. Helen J. Washburn, June 6, 1964; children: James W., Sarah W. BA, Elizabethtown Coll., 1962; postgrad., Millersville State Coll., 1962-63, U. N.C., 1963-64. Asst. editor Elizabethtown Chronicle, 1961-63, 64-65; researcher Commerce Clearinghouse, Washington, 1965-66; publs. editor Campbell Soup Co., Camden, N.J., 1966-67; pub. rels. specialist Phila. Gas Works, Div. UGI, Phila., 1967-70; account exec. Mike Masaoka Assocs., Washington, 1970-82, exec. v.p., 1982-86, pres., 1986—; pres. IMPAC&T Inc., 1986—; cons. Nihon Keizai Shimbun, Tokyo, 1981-84. Bd. dirs. Reston Commuter Bus. Inc., Va., 1977-81, Romeo Kojyo Co., Inc., 1983-89. Named Alumni fellow Elizabethtown Coll., 1988. Mem. Pub. Rels. Soc. Am., Soc. Automotive Engrs., Wash. Automotive Press Assn., Am. Assn. Polit. Cons., Am. Mgmt. Assn., Am. League Lobbyists, Internat. Club Wash. Roman Catholic. Home: 11745 Indian Ridge Rd Reston VA 22091-3529 Office: Masaoka & Assocs Inc 900 17th St NW Washington DC 20006-2501

YAMAMOTO, WILLIAM SHIGERU, physiologist, educator; b. Cleve., Sept. 22, 1924; s. Soichi T. and Toyo (Sanada) Y.; m. Mary Ann Stevens, June 19, 1954; children: Kathryn, Polly, Ruth. AB, Park Coll., 1945; MD, U. Pa., 1949, MS (hon.), 1971. Diplomate Nat. Bd. Med. Examiners. Intern Hosp. of U. Pa., Phila., 1951-52; instr. physiology U. Pa. Sch. Medicine, Phila., 1950-51, asst. prof., 1957-62, assoc. prof., 1962-66, prof., 1966-71; prof. biomath. UCLA Sch. Medicine, 1970-71; prof. and chmn. computer medicine George Washington U., Washington, 1971—, dir. Robert Wood Johnson clin. scholars, 1975-79; chmn. Computer Rsch. Study sect., NIH, Betesda, Md. 1963-67; mem. Nat. Adv. Rsch. Resources Coun. NIH, Bethesda, 1971-75; cons. Am. Coll. Ob.-Gyn., Washington, 1989—. Author: (book) Physiological Control and Regulation, 1962, Ay's Neuroanatomy of Celegans, 1991; contbr. over 50 papers to profl. jours., 1988—. Cons. Nat. Ctr. Health Svcs. Rsch., Arlington, Va., 1969-74; active NAS-NAE com. Health Care Tech., Washington, 1976-77. Capt. U.S. Army Med. Corps, 1953-55. Mem. APA, AAAS, Am. Coll. Preventive Medicine, Assn. Computing Machinery, Am. Coll. Med. Informatics, Biomed. Engring. Soc. (bd. dirs. 1978-81), D.C. Columbia Med. Soc. (parliamentarian 1972). Office: George Washington U Med Ctr 2300 K St NW Washington DC 20037-1700

YAMANE, GEORGE MITSUYOSHI, oral diagnosis and radiology educator; b. Honolulu, Aug. 9, 1924; s. Seigi and Tsuta (Moriwaki) Y.; m. Alice Matsuko Nemoto, July 6, 1951; children: Wende Michiko, Linda Keiko, David Kiyoshi. Student, U. Hawaii, 1944; A.B., Haverford Coll., 1946; D.D.S., U. Minn., 1950, Ph.D., 1962. Teaching, research asst. U. Hawaii, Honolulu, 1943-44; teaching asst. div. oral pathology, oral diagnosis Sch. Dentistry, U. Minn., Mpls., 1951-53; asst. prof. oral pathology Coll. Dentistry U. Ill., Chgo., 1957-59; dir. tissue lab. Sch. Dentistry U. Wash., Seattle, 1960-63; asst. prof. oral pathology Sch. Dentistry U. Wash., 1959-63; grad. faculty mem. U. Minn., Mpls., 1963-70; prof., chmn. div. oral diagnosis, oral medicine and oral roentgenology U. Minn., 1963-70; prof., chmn. dept. oral diagnosis and radiology Dental Sch. Coll. of Medicine and Dentistry of N.J., 1970-83, prof. dept. biodental sci., 1983-89, assoc. dean research and post-grad. programs, 1976-79, dir. div. oral and pathobiology, 1988—; cons. Children's Orthopedic Hosp. and Med. Ctr., Seattle, 1960-63, VA Hosp., American Lake, Wash., 1961-63, Mpls., 1964-70; cons. Minn. State Dept. Health, 1965-70, Wyo. State Bd. Health, 1966-70. Contbr. articles to med. and dental jours. Served with AUS. USPHS fellow, 1953-55; recipient Nell S. Talbot Instructorship award Coll. Dentistry U. Ill., 1958; Excellence in Teaching award U. Medicine and Dentistry N.J., 1984, Exceptional Merit award U. Medicine and Dentistry N.J., 1986. Fellow Am. Acad. Oral Pathology, AAAS, Am., Internat. colls. dentists, N.J. Acad. Medicine; mem. Am. Dental Assn., Orgn. Tchrs. Oral Diagnosis (sec.-treas. 1970-73, pres. 1974-75), Am. Acad. Periodontology, Internat. Assn. Dental Research, Am. Assn. Dental Schs., Sigma Xi (pres. Newark chpt. 1985), Omicron Kappa Upsilon, Xi Psi Phi. Office: 100 Bergen St Newark NJ 07103-2407

YAMIN, MICHAEL GEOFFREY, lawyer; b. N.Y.C., Nov. 10, 1931; s. Michael and Ethel Y.; m. Martina Schaap, Apr. 16, 1961; children: Michael Jeremy, Katrina. AB magna cum laude, Harvard U., 1953, LLB, 1958. Bar: N.Y. 1959, U.S. Dist. Ct. (so. dist.) N.Y., U.S. Dist. Ct. (ea. dist.) N.Y., U.S. Ct. Appeals (2d cir.) 1966, U.S. Supreme Ct. 1967. Assoc. Weil, Gotshal & Manges, N.Y.C., 1958-65; sr. ptnr. Colton, Hartnick, Yamin & Sheresky, N.Y.C., 1966—. Bd. trustees Gov.'s Com. Scholastic Achievement, 1976—; chmn. Manhattan Community Bd. 6, 1986-88, mem., 1974-88; mem. Mahattan Borough Bd., 1986-88; bd. trustees Rockland County Soc. Prevention of Cruelty to Children, 1979—. Served as lt. USNR, 1953-55, Korea. Mem. ABA, N.Y. State Bar Assn., Assn. Bar City N.Y., Fed. Bar Coun., Am. Fgn. Law Assn., Internat. Law Assn., Societe de Legislation Comparee, Internat. Bar Assn. Clubs: Harvard Faculty (Cambridge, Mass.); Harmonie, Harvard (N.Y.C.) (trustee N.Y. Found. 1981—, sub-chmn. schs. and scholarships com. 1972—, bd. mgrs. 1985-88, chair house com. 1992—). Home: 206 E 30th St New York NY 10016-8298 Office: 79 Madison Ave New York NY 10016-7802

YAMMARINO, FRANCIS JOSEPH, management educator, consultant; b. Buffalo, Dec. 25, 1954; s. Peter Anthony and Helen Ann (Giangrisostomi) Y.; m. Cathy Ann Apa, July 4, 1982; 1 child, Kayla M., 1989. BS, SUNY-Buffalo, 1976, MBA, 1979, PhD, 1983. Services coordinator Buffalo Savs. Bank, 1972-76; research assoc., instr. SUNY-Buffalo, 1977-79, research fellow, 1979-81, project dir., 1980-81; asst. prof. mgmt. U. Ky., Lexington, 1982-85, SUNY-Binghamton, 1985-90, assoc. prof., 1990— ; mgmt. cons. Fortune 500 cos., several orgs. and agys. Author: (with F. Dansereau and J.A. Alutto) Theory Testing in Organizational Behavior: The Varient Approach, 1984; exec. editor Leadership Quarterly; contbr. articles to profl. jours. Fellow Ctr. for Leadership Studies SUNY-Binghamton (rsch. grantee); mem. Am. Psychol. Assn., Am. Psychological Soc., Soc. Indsl. and Organizational Psychology, Soc. for Human Resources Mgmt., N.Y. Acad. Scis., Acad. Mgmt., Internat. Assn. Applied Psychology, Beta Gamma Sigma. Democrat. Office: SUNY-Binghamton Sch Mgmt Vestal Ave # 6000 Binghamton NY 13903-1317

YAN, XUAN, lawyer; b. Nanyang, Henan, Peoples Republic of China, June 14, 1962; came to U.S., 1984; s. Shaoling and Fongbin (Sun) Y.; m. Delphine Kung. BA, Beijing Inst. Fgn. Langs., 1984; JD, Duke U., 1987. Bar: Pa. 1988. Assoc. Dechert Price & Rhoads, Phila., 1987-89; assoc. corp. counsel Inductotherm Industries, Inc., Rancocas, N.J., 1989-91; div. counsel, asst. sec. Crompton & Knowles Corp., Green Hills, Pa., 1991—. Mem. ABA. Office: Crompton & Knowles Corp Rte 10 Green Hills Corp Ctr Green Hills PA 19607

YANAGIHARA, RICHARD, pediatrician, researcher; b. Honolulu, Aug. 3, 1946; s. Masuo and Tomoyo (Kimura) Y.; m. Angel Anne Smith, Apr. 16, 1988; children: Kaede, John. BA, U. Hawaii, 1968; MD, U. Cin., 1972; MPH, Johns Hopkins U., 1985. Diplomate Am. Bd. Pediatrics. Intern, resident U. Colo. Med. Ctr., Denver, 1972-74; rsch. assoc. NIH, Bethesda, Md., 1974-76; resident U. Calif., San Francisco, 1976-77; fellow health scis. ctr. U. Colo., Denver, 1977-79; rsch. physician NINDS Rsch. Ctr., Tamuning, Guam, 1979-82; special expert NIH, Bethesda, 1982-84, sr. investigator, 1986-90, section chief, 1990—. Cap. USPHS, 1974. Recipient Outstanding Svc. medal USPHS, Bethesda, 1990. Fellow Soc. Pediatric Rsch., Infectious Diseases Soc. Am.; mem. Am. Soc. Tropical Medicine and Hygiene (Bailey K. Ashford medal), Am. Soc. Virology, Am. Pediatric Soc. Office: NIH Bldg 36 Rm 5B-21 Bethesda MD 20892

YANAWAY, DANA EVAN, records manager; b. New London, Conn., July 7, 1967; s. Philip E. Yanaway and Mary E. (Johnson) Robinson; m. Terry Anne O'Neill, Oct. 12, 1991. BA in Polit. Sci., U. Conn., 1989. Constrn. laborer La Porte Fence Co., Glastonbury, Conn., 1988-89; file clk. Day, Berry & Howard Law Firm, Hartford, Conn., 1990—; cons. Legal Assistance, Mystic, Conn., 1991. Intern Conn. Legis., Hartford, 1989. Sgt. USAR, 1985—. Decorated Army Achievement medal U.S. Army, 1989, Drill Sgt. Identification badge, U.S. Army, 1990. Mem. Nat. Space Soc., NRA, Lambda Chi Alpha (v.p. 1988-89), Kappa Kappa Psi (corr. sec. 1988). Republican. Home: 87 Ruby Rd Apt 39 West Willington CT 06279-1326 2: Day Berry & Howard 92 Weston St # 37 Hartford CT 06120-1510

YANCEY, FREDERICK DALTON, III, food products executive; b. Lakeland, Fla., June 18, 1944; s. Frederick Dalton Jr. and Margaret Louise (Johnson) Y.; m. Barbara Cooper, June 14, 1975; children: Mary Elizabeth, Benjamin Cooper. BS in Advt. and Pub. Rels., U. Fla., 1967. Asst. mgr. Quality Ct. Restaurant, Gainesville, Fla., 1965-67; exec. v.p., gen. mgr. Lake County Boy's Ranch Found., Inc., Altoona, Fla., 1970-72; field rep. Fla. Citrus Mut., Lakeland, Fla., 1972-76; dir., industry rels. Citrus Cen., Orlando, Fla., 1976-78; chief exec. officer Fla. Sugar Cane League, Clewiston, 1978-82, exec. vp., 1982-87; exec. v.p. Fla. Sugar Cane League, Washington, 1987—; rep. Rio Grande Valley Sugar Growers, Washington, 1987—. Producer film Everglades Harvest, 1983 (Golden Image award). past pres. Kiwanis, Umatilla, Fla., C. of C., Umatilla; past bd. dirs. Fla. Citrus Processor Assn., Lakeland, Fla. Agrl. Hall of Fame. Capt. U.S. Army, 1967-70, Vietnam. Decorated Bronze Star; recipient Gold Quill award of Excellence, IABC, 1984, Gold Camera award U.S. Indsl. Film Festival, 1984. Mem. Am. Sugar Alliance (exec. com), Fla. House (exec. com.), Greater Washington Soc. Assn. Execs. Methodist. Office: Fla & Tex Sugar Growers 910 16th St NW S-402 Washington DC 20006

YANCEY, KIM BRUCE, dermatology educator; b. Atlanta, Nov. 25, 1952; s. Andrew Jackson and Edrie Mae (Johnson) Y. BS, U. Ga., 1974; MD, Med. Coll. Ga., 1978. Diplomate Am. Bd. Dermatology. Intern dept. internal medicine Med. Coll. Ga., Augusta, 1978-79, resident dept. dermatology, 1979-81; med. staff fellow dermatology br. NIH, Bethesda, Md., 1981-84, sr. staff fellow dermatology br., 1984-85; asst. prof. dept. dermatology Uniformed Svcs. U. Health Scis., Bethesda, 1985-87, assoc. prof. dept. dermatology, 1987—; cons. dermatology br. NIH, Bethesda, 1985—, Nat. Naval Med. Ctr., Bethesda, 1985—, Walter Reed Army Med. Ctr., Washington, 1985—. Author monographs and scientific manuscripts; contbr. articles to profl. jours. Rsch. grantee NIH, 1986—, collaborative rsch. grantee NATO, 1988—. Fellow Am. Acad. Dermatology (editorial bd. 1986—); mem. AMA, Am. Dermatol. Assn. (Young Leadership award 1986), Soc. Investigative Dermatology (bd. dirs. 1982-84, co-chmn. Eastern region 1990—), Am. Fedn. Clin. Rsch., Dermatology Found., Washington Dermatol. Soc. Methodist. Office: Uniformed Svcs U Health Sci 4301 Jones Bridge Rd Bethesda MD 20814-4799

YANDLE, WILLIAM MILES, pharmaceutical executive; b. Aberdeen, Wash., Nov. 24, 1952; s. Herbert William and Evelyn (Miles) Y. BS, U. Oreg., 1977, MBA, 1982. Juvenile counselor Lane County Youth Care, Eugene, Oreg., 1977-80; profl. rep. Merck Sharp & Dohme, Palo Alto, Calif., 1983-85; mktg. analyst Merck Sharp & Dohme, West Point, Pa., 1985-86, media mgr., 1986-87, product mgr., 1987-90, assoc. dir. market rsch., 1990-91, assoc. dir. promotion mgmt., 1991-92, dir. sales info., 1992—. With U.S. Army, 1972-74. Mem. Pharm. Advt. Coun., Port Indian Ski Club. Republican. Episcopalian. Office: Merck Human Health Divsn WP35-251 Sumneytown Pike West Point PA 19486

YANEZ, NIDIA DE, pediatric psychiatrist; b. Ibague, Colombia, Oct. 23, 1936; came to U.S., 1964; d. Teodoro Quarin Soto and Clema (Echeverri) DeGuarin; m. J. Rafael Yanez; children: Eric, Nelson, Loretta. MD, Nat. U., Bogota, Colombia, 1961. Intern Univ. Hosp. San Juan de Dios, Bogota,

1961-62; rotating intern Evengelical Deaconess Hosp., Cleve., 1965-66; resident in pediatrics Hahnemann Med. Coll., Phila., 1966-67; resident in pediatrics Med. Coll. Pa., Phila., 1967-68, resident in child psychiatry Ea. Pa. Psychiat. Inst., 1969-71, resident in adult psychiatry, 1972-74; pvt. practice Wilmington, Del., 1975—; asst. psychiatry dept., sr. pediatric dept. Wilmington Med. Ctr., 1975—, instr. child psychiatry to pediatric residents, 1975—, chief child and adolescent psychiatry, 1983—; staff Terry Children's Psychiat. Ctr., New Castle, Del., 1975-76; mem. Adv. Com. on Mental Health Svcs. to Children and Youth. Mem. Am. Acad. Pediatrics (chmn. mental health com.), Psychiat. Med. Assn., Am. Acad. Child Psychiatry, Child Psychiat. Med. Assn., Am. Pediatric Assn., Am. Med. Women's Assn., Am. Psychiat. Assn., World Psychiat. Assn., Fedn. State Med. Bds., Med. Soc. Del., New Castle County Med. Soc., Colombian Med. Assn. Office: 2401 Pennsylvania Ave Ste 110 Wilmington DE 19804

YANG, CHEN NING, physicist, educator; b. Hofei, Anhwei, People's Republic of China, Sept. 22, 1922; naturalized, 1964; s. Ke Chuan and Meng Hwa Lo; m. Chih Li Tu, Aug. 26, 1950; children: Franklin, Gilbert, Eulee. BS, Nat. S.W. Assoc. U., China, 1942; PhD, U. Chgo., 1948; DSc (hon.), Princeton U., 1958, Bklyn. Poly. Inst., 1965, U. Wroclaw, Poland, 1974, Gustavus Adolphus Coll., 1975, U. Md., 1979, U. Durham, Eng., 1979, Fudan U., 1984, Eldg. Technische Hochschule, Switzerland, 1987. Instr., U. Chgo., 1948-49; mem. Inst. Advanced Study, Princeton U., 1949-55, prof., 1955-66; Albert Einstein prof. SUNY, Stony Brook, 1966—; dir. Inst. Theoretical Physics SUNY, 1966—. Trustee Rockefeller U., 1970-76, Salk Inst., 1978—, Ben Gurion U., 1980—. Recipient Albert Einstein Commemorative award in sci., 1957, Nobel prize for physics, 1957, Rumford prize, 1980, Nat. medal of sci., 1986, Liberty award, 1986. Mem. Am. Phys. Soc., Nat. Acad. Scis., Brazilian Acad. Scis., Venezuelan Acad. Scis., Royal Spanish Acad. Scis., Polish Acad. Scis., Am. Philos. Soc., AAAS (bd. dirs. 1975-79), Sigma Xi. Office: SUNY Dept Physics Stony Brook NY 11794*

YANG, CHUNG SHU, pharmacy educator; b. Beijing, Aug. 8, 1941; s. Shu Chun and Shu Fen (Li) Y.; m. Sue Pai Y. Yang; 1 child, Arlene Ray, Jenny rae. BS, Nat. Taiwan U., 1962; MS, Cornell U., 1965, PhD, 1967. Asst. prof. U. Medicine-Dentistry N.J., Newark, 1971-75, assoc. prof., 1975-79, prof., 1979-87; prof., assoc. chair dept. chem. biology-pharmacognosy Rutgers U., Piscataway, N.J., 1988—; cons., collaborator U.S. Nat. Cancer Inst., Chinese Acad. med. Sci., Henan, China, 1980—; cons. Beijing Cancer Inst., 1987—, Shanghai Cancer Inst., 1985—. Recipient Merit award for cancer rsch. Nat. Cancer Inst., 1987, First Disting. Researcher award N.J. Assn. for Biomed. Rsch. Office: Rutgers Univ Coll Pharmacy Lab Cancer Rsch Frelinghuysen Rd Piscataway NJ 08855-0789

YANG, DAVID CHIH-HSIN, chemistry educator; b. Hsin-Chiang, People's Republic China, Jan. 8, 1947; came to U.S., 1969; s. Warren Ming-Shih and Susi (Chang) Y.; m. Linda Yang, June 12, 1971; children: Stephen J., Alan D. BS, Nat. Taiwan U., Taipei, 1968; PhD, Yale U., 1973. Rsch. assoc. Rockefller U., N.Y.C., 1973-75; asst. prof. chemistry Georgetown U., Washington, 1975-81, assoc. prof., 1981-90, prof., 1990—; vis. prof. Sinica Academia, Taipei, 1991. Grantee NIH, 1977-93, NSF, 1978-90. Mem. AAAS, Am. Soc. Biochemistry and Molecular Biology. Office: Georgetown U Dept Chemistry 37th and O Sts NW Washington DC 20057

YANG, JULIE CHI-SUN, industrial chemist, researcher, consultant; b. Beijing, June 10, 1928; came to U.S., 1951; d. Shao T. and Chung-Yu (Liu) Y. BS, Nat. Tsing-Hua U., Beijing, 1949; MS, Ind. U., 1952; PhD, U. Ill., 1955; postgrad., MIT, 1979. Teaching asst. dept. chemistry Ind. U., Bloomington, 1951-52; rsch. asst. U. Ill., Urbana, 1952-53, Univ. fellow, 1953-55; x-ray chemist Babcock & Wilcox Rsch. Ctr., Alliance, Ohio, 1953; sr. rsch. chemist, rsch. assoc. basic rsch. sect. Johns-Manville (N.J.) Rsch. Ctr., 1955-72; sr. group leader, rsch. mgr. constrn. product div. W.R. Grace & Co., Cambridge, Mass., 1972-91; cons. W.R. Grace & Co., 1991—; cons. Nat. Inst. Standards and Tech., Gaithersburg, Md., 1988—. Patentee in field in U.S. and fgn. countries. Mem. ASTM (com. D-22), Am. Chem. Soc., Am. Mineral. Soc., Brit. Mineralogists Soc., Clay Mineral Soc., Sigma Xi, Iota Sigma Pi, Pi Mu Epsilon. Home: 6 Foster Rd Lexington MA 02173-5506 Office: WR Grace & Co 62 Whittemore Ave Cambridge MA 02140-1692

YANG, RALPH TZU-BOW, chemical engineering educator, researcher; b. Chung King, China, Sept. 18, 1942; came to U.S., 1965, naturalized, 1976; s. Chen Pei and Wei (Gee) Y.; m. Frances H. Chang, Dec. 23, 1972; children—Michael, Robert. B.S., Nat. Taiwan U., 1964; M.S., Yale U., 1968, Ph.D., 1971. Research assoc. Argonne Nat. Lab., Ill., 1972-73; sci. Aluminum Co. of Am., Pitts., 1973-74; group leader Brookhaven Nat. Lab., Upton, N.Y., 1974-78; assoc. prof. SUNY-Buffalo, 1978-82, prof., 1982—, chmn. chem. engring. dept., 1990—; cons. in field. Author: Gas Separation by Adsorption Processes, 1986. Contbr. articles to profl. jours. Patentee in field. Research grantee NSF, 1980—, Dept. Energy, 1980—, Alcoa Found., 1979-81. Mem. Am. Inst. Chem. Engring. (William H. Walker award for excellence in contbn. to chem. engring. lit., 1991), Am. Chem. Soc. (Ind. Engring. Chem. Rsch. jour. 1991—), Am. Carbon Soc. (adv. bd. 1985—).

YANG, TSU-JU (THOMAS YANG), veterinary medicine educator; b. Fengshang, Taiwan, Aug. 14, 1932; came to U.S., 1964; s. Fu-Su and Mon-Tau (Hsu) Y.; m. Sue N. Chou, July 2, 1961; children: Kai H., Andrew T., Michael B. BVM, Nat. Taiwan U., 1955; DVM, Ministry of Exam., Taiwan, 1959; PhD, McGill U., Mont., Can., 1971. Lic. veterinarian, Taiwan. Assoc. mem. Academia Sinica, Taipei, Taiwan, 1961-64; rsch. assoc. U. Pa., Phila., 1964-66; rsch. fellow U. Minn., Mpls., 1966-67; demonstrator McGill U., 1968-71; asst. prof. U. Tenn., Knoxville, 1971-75; assoc. prof. U. Conn., Storrs, 1975-78, prof., asst. head, 1978—; cons. Maine Biotech. Svcs., Inc., 1991—; editorial participant CRC Press, Boca Raton, Fla., 1980—. Contbr. over 105 articles to profl. jours. Grantee NIH, USDA, Nat. Dairy Coun., Am. Kennel Club; recipient Animal Rsch. award Ralston Purina Co., 1988. Office: U Conn Dept Pathobiology 89U 61 N Eagleville Rd Storrs Mansfield CT 06268

YANG, WILLIAM, pediatrician, researcher; b. Qingdao, Shandong, China, Mar. 13, 1948; came to U.S., 1962; s. Maurice and Xing-Qing (Wang) Y.; m. Susan Terozito Depoliti, May 5, 1985; children: Adrienne C., Stephen C. BA in Math., Chemistry, U. Calif., Irvine, 1969; PhD in Chemistry, U. Ill., Chgo., 1973; MD, U. Chgo., 1976. Diplomate Nat. Bd. Med. Examiners, Am. Bd. Pediatrics. Intern in pediatrics Children's Hosp., Phila., 1976-77, resident in pediatrics, 1977-78, fellow in pediatric endocrinology and metabolism, 1978-81; asst. prof. pediatrics U. Pa., Phila., 1981-82; assoc. dir. clin. investigations research and devel. div. Smith Kline & French, Phila., 1982-84, med. dir. Far East, China, 1985-87; clin. assoc. Childrens Hosp. of Phila., 1982—; assoc. med. dir. research and devel. div. Berlex Labs., Cedar Knolls, N.J., 1984-85; med. dir. Ams., Far East, South Africa internat. div. Smith, Kline & French Labs., Phila., 1988-89; area med. dir. Japan, East Asia Smith Kline Beecham Pharms., Phila., 1989—. Contbr. articles to profl. jours. Recipient Young Investigator award NIH, 1982. Mem. AMA, Am. Chem. Soc. Home: 370 Sycamore Ave Merion Station PA 19066-1539 Office: Smith Kline Beecham Pharms 1500 Spring Gardens St Philadelphia PA 19130-4009

YANG, WILLIAM NORMAN, physician, occupational health specialist; b. N.Y.C., Nov. 29, 1948; s. Yih-Chang and Cynthia Norma (Allum-Poon) Y.; m. Nancy Berry Moran, Nov. 28, 1981. BA in Biology, The Univ. of the South, 1970; MD, Emory U., 1974; MPH, The John Hopkins U., 1984. Cert. in Occupational Medicine by Am. Bd. Preventive Medicine. Intern Albany (N.Y.) Med. Ctr., 1974-75; gen. med. officer Marine Corps Recruit Depot, San Diego, 1975-76; resident family practice Camp Pendleton, Calif., 1977-80, staff physician, 1980-83; fellow occupational medicine The John Hopkins Sch. Hygiene and Pub. Health, Balt., 1983-85; staff physician Navy Environ. Health Ctr., Norfolk, Va., 1985-86, head occupational medicine div., 1986-87; head occupational medicine dept. Naval Med. Clinic Norfolk, Norfolk, Va., 1987-89, head environ. preventive medicine unit, 1989-90; dir. occupational medicine residency Uniformed Svcs., U. Health Scis., Bethesda, Md., 1990—. Contbr. articles to profl. jours. on occupational medicine. Mem. AMA, Am. Coll. Occupational and Environ. Medicine, Am. Govtl. Indsl. Hygienists. Episcopalian. Home: 11014 Wickshire Way Rockville MD 20852-3223 Office: USUHS A1039 4301 Jones Bridge Rd Bethesda MD 20814-4799

YANKAUER, ALFRED, physician, educator; b. N.Y.C., Oct. 12, 1913; s. Alfred Sr. and Teresa (Loewy) Y.; m. Marian Wynn, May 22, 1948; children: Kenneth and Douglas (twins). BA, Dartmouth Coll., 1934; MD, Harvard U., 1938; MPH, Columbia U., 1947. Diplomate Am. Bd. Pediatrics, Am. Bd. Preventive Medicine and Pub. Health. Health officer N.Y.C. Dept. Health, 1947-50; asst. commr. of health Rochester (N.Y.) Health Bur., 1950-52; dir. MCH Bur. N.Y. State Dept. Health, Albany, 1952-61; WHO prof. child health Madras (India) Med. Sch., 1957-59; regional advisor Pan-Am. Health Orgn./WHO, Washington, 1961-66; sr. rsch. assoc. Sch. of Pub. Health Harvard U., Boston, 1966-73; prof. family and community health Med. Sch. U. Mass., Worcester, 1973—; asst. prof. health Cornell U. Med. Coll., N.Y.C., 1947-50; med. dir. pediatric nurse practitioner program Gen.Hosp./Northeastern U. Coll. of Nursing, Boston, 1972-79. Editor Am. Jour. Pub. Health, 1975-90; contbr. over 200 articles to profl. jours. Mem. health adv. com. Pub. Affairs Commn., N.Y.C., 1980-88; bd. dirs. Am. Social Health Commn., Research Triangle Park, N.C., 1984-90, chmn. rsch. adv. com., 1990—. Maj., M.C., U.S. Army, 1941-45, ETO. Fellow Am. Acad. Pediatrics; mem. APHA (Excellence award 1990). Democrat. Office: U Mass Med Ctr 55 Lake Ave N Worcester MA 01655-0001

YANKLOWITZ, STEPHEN MICHAEL, consumer products company executive; b. Glens Falls, N.Y., May 15, 1944; s. Harold and E. Beulah (Slater) Y.; m. Sandra Lee Janowski, Aug. 17, 1969; children: Scott Justin, Shawn Mitchell. Grad., Valley Forge Mil. Acad., 1962; AB, Franklin Marshall Coll., 1966; MBA, Am. U., 1968. Various positions Richardson-Vicks Inc., Wilton, Conn., 1968-79; v.p. mktg. and sales Richardson-Vicks Ltd., Toronto, 1979-82, pres., mng. dir., 1982-85; v.p., gen. mgr. crayola prods. div. Binney & Smith subs. Hallmark Cards, Easton, Pa., 1985-89, mem. pub. affairs com., 1987; with Lenox Collections, Langhorne, Pa., 1989-92. Class agt. Franklin and Marshall Coll., Lancaster, 1977; mem. Westport (Conn.) Planning and Zoning Commn., 1978-79, rep. Town Meeting; bd. dirs. Weller Health Ctr., Easton, 1987-89, Wiley House, Bethlehem, Pa., 1988-89. With USAR, 1967-73. Named one of Outstanding Young Men Am. U.S. Jaycees, 1978. Republican. Home: 235 Arreton Rd Princeton NJ 08540

YANNAS, IOANNIS VASSILIOS, polymer science and engineering educator; b. Athens, Apr. 14, 1935; s. Vassilios Pavlos and Thalia (Sarafoglou) Y.; m. Stamatia Frondistou (div. Oct. 1984); children: Tania, Alexis. AB, Harvard U., 1957; SM, MIT, 1959; MS, Princeton U., 1965, PhD, 1966. Asst. prof. mech. engring. MIT, Cambridge, 1966-68, duPont asst. prof., 1968-69, assoc. prof., 1969-78, prof. polymer sci. and engring. dept. mech. engring., 1978—, prof., dept. materials sci. and engring., 1983—; prof. Harvard-MIT Div. Health Scis. and Tech., Cambridge, 1978—; vis. prof. Royal Inst. Tech., Stockholm, 1974. Mem. editorial bd. Jour. Biomed. Materials Research, 1986—, Jour. Materials Sci. Materials Medicine, 1990—; contbr. over 100 tech. articles; 13 patents in field. Recipient Founders award Soc. for Biomaterials, 1982, Clemson award Soc. for Biomaterials, 1992, Fred O. Conley award Soc. Plastics Engrs., 1982, award in medicine and genetics Sci. Digest/Cutty Sark, 1982, Doolittle award Am. Chem. Soc., 1988; fellow Pub. Health Svc., Princeton U., 1963, Shriners Burns Inst., Mass. Gen. Hosp., Boston, 1980-81. Fellow Am. Inst. Chemists; mem. Inst. Medicine of Nat. Acad. Scis. Office: MIT Bldg 3-334 77 Massachusetts Ave Cambridge MA 02139-4307

YANNUZZI, MIGUEL M., bank executive; b. Florida, Camaguey, Cuba, Sept. 4, 1941; came to U.S., 1962; s. Miguel and Juana Adolfina (Cisneros) Y.; m. Miriam Garcia, July 1971; children: Miguel E., David F. BS, Mercy Coll., Dobbs Ferry, N.Y., 1976. Official asst. Citibank N.A., N.Y.C., 1966-70; asst. cashier The Amalgamated Bank of N.Y., N.Y.C., 1970-79; officer Bank Hapoalim B.M., N.Y.c., 1979-80; v.p. Bank of Boston Internat. N.Y., N.Y.C., 1980-87; v.p. internat. pvt. banking S.Am. div. BankAmerica Internat. N.Y., N.Y.C., 1987—. Mem. Lions. Roman Catholic. Home: 55 Pine St New City NY 10956-6239 Office: BankAmerica Internat NY 335 Madison Ave New York NY 10017-4605

YAO, ALICE C., pediatrician; b. Iloilo, The Philippines, Jan. 3; came to U.S. 1959; d. Prudencio and Giok (Co) Y. AA, Far Eastern U., Manila, 1953; MD, Inst. Medicine, Far Ea. Univ., Manila, 1958. Diplomate Am. Bd. Pediatrics, Am. Bd. Pediatric Cardiology, Am. Bd. Neonatal-Perinatal Medicine. Intern in pediatrics Bellevue-NYU Med. Ctr., N.Y.C., 1959-60, resident in pediatrics, 1960-61; fellow in pediatric cardiology SUNY Univ. Hosp., Bklyn., 1961-62, Johns Hopkins Hosp., Balt., 1962-63; rsch. fellow in neonatalogy Karolinska Inst. and Hosp., Stockholm, 1965-68; asst. prof. pediatrics SUNY-Health Sci. Ctr., Bklyn., 1968-73, assoc. prof. pediatrics, 1973-77, prof. pediatrics, 1977—; attending pediatrician Univ. Hosp. Bklyn., 1968—; cons. pediatrician Kings County Hosp., 1968—. Contbr. articles to profl. jours., chpts. to books; author: Placental Transfusion: A Physiological and Clinical Study, 1982. Health Rsch. Coun. Career Scientist, 1969-74; N.Y. Heart Assn. trainee, 1961-62; named Most Outstanding Alumnus, Far Eastern U., 1981; Winthrop Stern's Internship award, 1958. Fellow Am. Coll. Cardiology, Am. Acad. Pediatrics, Am. Physiol. Soc.; mem. Am. Pediatric Soc., Soc. for Pediatric Rsch., Royal Soc. Medicine, Sigma Xi Rsch. Soc. Office: SUNY Health Sci Ctr 450 Clarkson Ave Brooklyn NY 11203-2098

YAO, FUN-SUN FRANK, anesthesiologist; b. Changhwa, Taiwan, Feb. 23, 1942; came to U.S., 1972; s. Sui-Lin and Ju-Hsiang (Ko) Y.; m. Baw-Chyr Yao, Nov. 11, 1969; children: Tong-Yi, Ning-Yen, Titania. MD, Nat. Taiwan U. Med. Coll., 1968. Am. Coll. Anesthesiologists, 1975. Resident in surgery Nat. Taiwan U. Hosp., Taipei, 1969-72; surgical intern Maimonides Hosp., Bklyn., 1972-73; resident anesthesia Cornell Med. Ctr. N.Y. Hosp., N.Y.C., 1973-75, fellow anesthesia, 1975-76; instr. anesthesiology Cornell U. Med. Coll., N.Y.C., 1976-77, asst. prof. anesthesiology, 1977-85, assoc. prof. anesthesiology, 1985—; atending anesthesiologist The N.Y. Hosp., N.Y.C., 1983—. Editor: Anesthesiology, 1983, 88. Fellow Am. Coll. Anesthesiologists, N.Y. Acad. Medicine, N.Y. Acad. Sci.; mem. Am. Soc. Anesthesiology, N.Y. Soc. Anesthesiologists, Soc. Cardiovascular Anesthesiologists, Internat. Anesthesia Rsch. Soc. Buddhist. Office: 525 E 68 St New York NY 10021

YARBOROUGH, WILLIAM GLENN, JR., retired military officer, forest farmer, defense and international business executive; b. Rock Hill, S.C., June 21, 1940; s. William Glenn and Bessie (Rainsford) Y.; m. Betsy Gibson, Jan. 24, 1969; children: Bill, Clinton, Frank, Elizabeth. BS, U. S.C., 1961, MBA, 1969; postgrad. Command and Gen. Staff Coll., 1970, Naval War Coll., 1979, Colgate-Darden Grad. Bus. Sch., U. Va., 1983. Commd. to U.S. Army, advanced through grades to col., 1980; co. and troop comdr. and squadron staff officer, Vietnam, Europe, 1961-71, strategist, Washington, 1971-73, chief of assignments, Office Personnel Mgmt., Mil. Personnel Ctr., Washington, 1973-76; comdr. 1st Squadron, 1st Cavalry, Europe, 1976-78; chief of staff and spl. asst. to chief of staff 1st Armored Div., Europe, 1978; br. chief Office of Chief of Staff, Washington, 1979-80; exec. to dep. commanding gen. Material Devel. and Readiness Command, Washington, 1980-81; exec. asst. sec. for research, devel. and acquisition, Washington, 1981-85; army mktg. dir. Grumman Corp., Bethpage, N.Y., 1990—. Decorated Silver Star, Bronze Star medal with 4 oak leaf clusters and V device, Purple Heart. Mem. Assn. U.S. Army (pres. George Washington chpt., v.p. membership), Am. Legion, Armed Forces Communications and Electronics Assn., U.S. Army Armor Assn., SAR, Am. Def. Preparedness Assn. (bd. dirs. N.Y. chpt.), Purple Heart VFW Soc., Army-Navy Club, Army Navy Country Club, Belle-Meade Country Club.

YARDIS, PAMELA HINTZ, computer consulting company executive; b. N.Y.C., Sept. 23, 1944; d. Edward F. and Isabella (Sawers) Hintz; m. J.A. Yardis, Apr. 2, 1966 (div. July 1980); children: Bradley, Brent, Tricia, Todd, Ryan, Kara, Melissa. BA, Bethany Coll., 1966; MA, Columbia U., 1983, MEd, 1983. Cert. mgmt. cons. Tchr. Yonkers (N.Y.) Pub. Schs., 1966-68; cons. PHY, Inc., Stamford, Conn., 1978-83; account exec. Mgmt. Systems, Stamford, 1982-84; sr. account exec., cons. Mgmt. Dynamics, Yonkers, 1984-86; v.p. GMW Assn., Inc., N.Y.C., 1986-87; pres. Chestnut Hill Cons. Group, Inc., Stamford, 1987—. Chmn. Mayor's Commn. Prevention Youth Drug and Alcohol Abuse, Stamford, 1986-91; mem. Dem. Cen. Com., Stamford, 1984—; bd. dirs., pres. Alcohol and Drug Coun., Inc., Conn. Communities for Drug Free Youth, Childcare, Inc., Youth Shelter. Recipient Gov.'s Community Svc. award, 1988, Golden Rule award J.C. Penney, Bravo award YWCA, 1992. Mem. Women in Mgmt. (v.p. 1986-88, Ann. Recognition award), Data Processing Mgmt. Assn., Advt. Rsch. Found., Inst. Mgmt. Cons. (pres. Fairfield Westchester chpt. 1990—, nat. bd. dirs.), Sales and Mktg. Execs. (bd. dirs.). Presbyterian. Home: 125 Chestnut Hill Rd Stamford CT 06903-4029 Office: Chestnut Hill Cons Group PO Box 15755 Stamford CT 06901-0755

YARDLEY, JONATHAN, journalist, columnist; b. Pitts., Oct. 27, 1939; s. William Woolsey and Helen (Gregory) Y.; m. Rosemary Roberts, June 14, 1961 (div. 1975); children: James Barrett, William W. II.; m. Susan L. Hartt, Mar. 23, 1975. AB, U. N.C., Chapel Hill, 1961; DHL (hon.), George Washington U., 1987. Writer N.Y. Times, 1961-64; editorial writer, book editor Greensboro (N.C.) Daily News, 1964-74; book editor Miami (Fla.) Herald, 1974-78, Washington Star, 1978-81; book critic, columnist Washington Post, 1981—. Author: Ring: A Biography of Ring Lardner, 1977, Our Kind of People: The Story of an American Family, 1989, Out of Step: Notes from a Purple Decade, 1991. Recipient Pulitzer prize for criticism, 1981, Disting. Alumnus award U. N.C., 1989; Nieman fellow in journalism Harvard U., 1968-69. Episcopalian. Home: 223 Hawthorne Rd Baltimore MD 21210-2503 Office: Washington Post 1150 15th St NW Washington DC 20071-0002

YARMOLINSKY, MICHAEL BEZALEL, molecular biologist, microbiologist; b. N.Y.C., Jan. 18, 1929; s. Avrahm Yarmolinsky and Babette Deutsch; m. Sirpa Tuhkanen, June 22, 1962; 1 child, Miriam. AB, Harvard Coll., 1950; PhD, Johns Hopkins U., 1954. Rsch. assoc., instr. NYU Coll. Medicine, N.Y.C., 1954-55; officer USPHS NIMH, NIH, Bethesda, Md., 1955-58; rsch. assoc., asst. prof. biology dept. Johns Hopkins U., Balt., 1958-63; NSF fellow Pasteur Inst., Paris, 1963-64; rsch. chemist Nat. Inst. Arthritis and Metabolic Diseases/NIH, Bethesda, Md., 1964-71; rsch. dir. CNRS Inst. Molecular Biology, Paris, 1971-76; sect. chief rsch. program Frederick (Md.) Cancer Rsch. Facility, 1976-84, sci. coord. rsch. program, 1983-84; sect. chief Nat. Cancer Inst., NIH, Bethesda, 1984—; bd. dirs. Am. Type Culture Collection, Rockville, Md. Assoc. editor: The New Biologist, 1989—. Fellow AAAS; mem. Phi Beta Kappa.

YARMUS, JAMES J., civil engineer; b. Havana, Cuba, Aug. 11, 1941; came to U.S., 1960; s. Leon and Pola (Nieman) Y.; m. Helen Flaster; children: Andrew, Michelle. BCE, CCNY, 1965, M Engring., 1969, MBA, 1973, D Engring., 1983. Registered profl. engr., N.Y., Fla., Mass, Ky., Ark., Pa. Conn., N.J. Pres. J. Yarmus Engring., P.C., N.Y.C., 1974—; chmn. ABL Inspections, Inc., N.Y.C., 1974—, Sumray Environ. Consultants, N.Y.C., 1974—; chmn. uniform code N.Y. State Bd. Appeals and Variances, 1984-92; v.p., N.Y. State Bldg. Ofcls. Conf., Rockland. Contbr. articles to profl. publs. Pres. Clarkstown Band Parents, 1987, New City Jewish Ctr., 1990-92; chmn. Rockland County Jewish Conf. Named Engr./Mgr. of Yr., N.Y. State Soc. Profl. Engrs., 1992. Fellow ASCE; mem. Nat. Acad. Forensic Engrs. (diplomate), Rotary (pres. 1990-91), KP (life). Office: J Yarmus Engring PC 230 N Main St New City NY 10956-5300

YAROS, CONSTANCE LENORE GREENBERG, painter, sculptor; b. Phila., Aug. 3; d. Harry William and Dorothy (Hofberg) Greenberg; m. Irvin Yaros, June 17, 1950 (dec. Nov. 6, 1983); children: Michael J. Yaros, Aimee Y. Silverman, Nancy S. Yaros. Student, Temple U., Tyler Sch. of Art, 1957-60, Blai Studio, 1976-81, Pa. Acad. Fine Arts, 1978-79, 87, Schuler Sch. of Art, 1990. Com. mem. Art at the Armory, Phila., 1990-92; bd. dirs. Artists Equity Assn., Phila., 1976-90. Pvt. collections include Meg and Lynn Strawbridge, 1989, Mary Austin Phipps Fox, 1986, Boris Blai, 1985, 83, Jack Weinstein, 1978; exhibited in group shows including Artists Equity Assn. Triennial, 1984, 88, 91, Allied Artists of Am., 1988, Catherine Loriliard Wolfe Art Club, 1988, Salmagundi Art Club, 1988, Tyler Alumni, 1987, Phila. Sketch Club, 1987, Old York Rd. Art Guild, 1975. Mem. Am. Technion Assn., 1958—; mem. Greenpeace. Mem. Phila. Mus. Art, Allied Artists Am., Am. Soc. Portrait Artists, Am. ARtist Profl. League, Knickerbocher Artists, Pa. Acad. Fine Arts, Artists Equity Assn. Home and Office: 2401 Pennsylvania Ave Apt 4A5 Philadelphia PA 19130-3018

YARRA, NIRMALA KARNAM, psychiatrist; b. Chirala, India, July 15, 1944; came to U.S., 1976; s. Rao H. and Thulesamma V. Yarra; m. Raja Karnam, Apr. 24, 1975. SSLC, St. Joseph's Coll., Guntur, India, 1960; MD, Guntur Med. Coll., 1966; DGO, Med. Coll., Vaizag, India, 1968. Diplomate Am. Bd. Psychiatry and Neurology. Resident Hahnemann U., Phila., 1976-79; psychiatrist Trenton State Hosp., West Trenton, N.J., 1980—; dir. drug treatment program St. Lukes Hosp., Phila., 1988-89; staff psychiatrist Woods Schs., Langhorn, Pa., 1985—. Mem. Am. Psychiatry Assn., Am. Soc. on Alcoholism and Drug Dependencies (diplomate bd.), Am. Bd. Utilization Review (diplomate). Home: 1094 Dixon Ln Jenkintown PA 19046-2431

YASHAD See GORDON, IRWIN GLENN

YASKULKA, LOUISE KATHERINE, executive secretary; b. Bklyn., Feb. 13, 1966; d. Joseph Frank and Julia Katherine (Earl) D. Bus. cert., Katharine Gibbs Sch., N.Y.C., 1985; student, Middlesex County Coll., Edison, N.J., 1986. Art finisher The Enchanted Pen, Staten Island, N.Y., 1983-86; exec. sec. Consumers Distributing, Edison, N.J., 1984-86, Global Union Bank, N.Y.C., 1986, Hongkong and Shanghai Banking Corp., N.Y.C., 1986-87, Salomon Bros., Inc., N.Y.C., 1987—. Mem. Boro-Wide Chorus. Republican. Roman Catholic.

YASLOWITZ, LAWRENCE PHILIP, school counselor; b. N.Y.C., July 28, 1945; s. Joseph and Bernice (Rackler) Y.; m. Ufuk Özbudak; children: Kemal, Yashar David. BA in Spanish, SUNY, Albany, 1968, MS in Teaching ESL, 1972; MS in Counseling, CCNY, 1975; cert. in Psychology, Alfred Adler Inst., 1977. Vol. Peace Corps, Ecuador, 1968-69; Spanish tchr. Ockawamick Cen. Sch., Philmont, N.Y., 1969-70; ESL tchr. Manuela Toro High Sch., Caguas, P.R., 1970-71, Darussafaka Sch., Istanbul, Turkey, 1971-72; bilingual counselor N.Y.C. Bd. Edn., 1972-86; counselor East Ramapo Sch. Dist., Spring Valley, N.Y., 1986—; bd. dirs. Ramapo Youth Counseling Ctr., Suffern, N.Y.; adult edn. instr. Nyack (N.Y.) Sch. Dist., 1986-88; counselor, therapist, pvt. practice, Spring Valley, 1990—; supr. Matol Botanicals, Quebec, Can., 1987. Committeeman Dem. Party, Rockland County, N.Y., 1989—. Recipient trophy Martial Arts Inst. Am., 1987. Fellow Jerrahi Dervish Order; mem. AACD, Zen Community of N.Y. Home: 3410 Paul Ave Apt 15 Bronx NY 10468-1043

YASSA, GUIRGUIS FAHMY, Egyptian photogrammetrist, infosystems specialist; b. Khartoum, Sudan, Oct. 1, 1930; came to U.S., 1969, naturalized, 1976; s. Fahmy and Brinsa Bissada (Nakhla) Y.; m. Laila Naguib Nosseir, Sept. 6, 1959; children: Elham, Medhat, Magdi, Laura. B.Engring. with distinction, Cairo U., 1951, M.Sc. in Surveying, 1964, diploma stats., 1966; Ph.D., Cornell U., 1973. From topographic engr. to photogrammetric engr. to head photogrammetric sect. Survey of Egypt, 1951-67; sr. lectr. Internat. Inst. Aerial Survey, 1967-69; teaching asst. Cornell U., 1969-72; systems analyst, dir. mapping Robinson Aerial Surveys Co., Newton, N.J., 1973-79; tech. analyst Warner Computer Systems Co., Teaneck, N.J., 1979-80; sr. analyst ops. Chase Manhattan Bank, N.Y.C., 1980—. Author papers in field. Govt. of The Netherlands fellow Internat. Inst. Aerial Survey, Delft, 1956. Mem. ASCE, Am. Soc. Photogrammetry, Sigma Xi. Home: 86 Lott Rd Sussex NJ 07461-3907 Office: Chase Manhattan Bank 1 New York Plaza New York NY

YATES, JOHN ROBERT, JR., engineer, educator; b. Boston, Feb. 9, 1930; s. John Robert and Rosemary Natalie (Logue) Y.; m. Virginia Dianne Finocchio, July 3, 1954 (dec. Feb. 1988); children: Deborah A., John Robert, Thomas F., Catherine I.; m. Barbara Marandola, Dec. 28, 1990. A.B., Northeastern U., 1954. Commd. 2d lt. USMC, 1954, advanced through grades to lt. col.; action officer, constrn. team, joint logistics rev. bd. Office Sec. Def., 1969-70; engr. III Marine Amphibious Force, Fleet Marine Force, Okinawa, 1970-71; comdg. officer, marine barracks U.S. Naval Base, Boston, 1971-74, ret., 1974; dir. engring. Soldiers' Home, Chelsea, Mass., 1974-85; energy conservation coord. Exec. Office of Human Svcs., Commonwealth of Mass.; faculty Energy Mgmt. in Healthcare Instns., HEW, 1977. Mem. exec. bd. USO Coun. New Eng., 1971—, pres., 1988—; trustee Charlestown YMCA, 1974—, pres. 1988, vice chmn., 1977-79, chmn., 1980-82. Decorated Joint Svc. Commendation medal, Navy Commendation medal, Army Commendation medal. Mem. Soc. Am. Mil. Engrs. (dir. Boston post), Am., New Eng. hosp. engrs. socs., Navy League U.S. (v.p. Mass. Bay coun.),

Am. Legion, VFW, Bostonian Soc., Wardroom Club (Boston), Army-Navy Club (Washington). Roman Catholic. Home and Office: 37 Chapman Rd Boxford MA 01921-2330

YATES, MARYPAUL, textile company executive; b. Knoxville, Tenn., Nov. 24, 1957; d. Paul and Peggy Adelle (Bryan) Y.; m. Benjamin H. Weisgal, Jan. 1, 1960; 1 child, Bryan Asher Weisgal. Student, U. Ga., 1973-75; BFA magna cum laude, Syracuse U., 1977; AAS, Fashion Inst. Tech., N.Y.C., 1979. Designer, studio mgr. Jeffrey Aronoff Inc., N.Y.C., 1978-81; designer, cons. N.Y.C., 1981-82; stylist Gerli & Co., N.Y.C., 1982-83; dir. design Maharam, Hauppauge, N.Y., 1983-87; prin. Yates Weisgal Inc., N.Y.C., 1987—; adj. instr. Hunter Coll. CUNY, 1978-82, Fashion Inst. Tech. SUNY, N.Y.C., 1985, Parsons Sch. Design, N.Y.C., 1988—; guest speaker various groups, 1980—; lectr., condr. workshops in field, 1980—. Author: Textiles, A Handbook for Designers, 1986; group exhibits include The Galleries, Fashion Inst. Tech., 1984, R.I. Sch. Design, 1985. Mem. Textile Mus., Washington, industry adv. coun. Fashion Inst. Tech., 1984—. Designer products awarded Coty award Fashion Critics Circle, 1980, Roscoe award Resource Coun., 1982, Product award Inst. Bus. Designers, 1986; grantee Ford Found., 1976. Mem. Assn. for Contract Textiles (industry standards com. 1986-88), Color Assn. U.S. (interior forecasting com. 1988—), Color Mktg. Group (color projections com. 1983—), Textile Study Group N.Y., Am. Craft Coun., Surface Design Assn. Office: 185 E 85th St Apt 20F New York NY 10028-2149

YATES, MICHAEL FRANCIS, management consultant; b. N.Y.C., Feb. 9, 1946; s. John Berchmans and Jane Ann (Gretz) Y.; student Canisius Coll., 1963-64; B.A., U. Buffalo, 1968; m. Christine Mary Dallos, Jan. 14, 1967; children—Erik Michael, Alison. Mgmt. trainee, dept. mgr. Sears, Roebuck & Co., Buffalo, 1968-69; cons. Rothman & D'Alessandro, Inc., N.Y.C., 1969-71; sr. cons. Martin & Segal & Co., Inc., N.Y.C., 1971-75, A.S. Hansen, Inc., N.Y.C., 1975-78; exec. v.p. A.M. D'Alessandro & Co., Inc., North Haledon, N.J., 1978-81; mng. dir., nat. practice dir., mgmt. cons. svcs. Alexander & Alexander, Lyndhurst, N.J., 1981—. Pres. Lincoln Sch. PTA, 1975-77; chmn. Bethlehem Twp. Econ. and Indsl. Devel. Bd., 1980-83; pres. Bethlehem Twp. Republican Club; mem. Republican Nat. Com. Mem. Am. Mgmt. Assn., Am. Compensation Assn., Am. Soc. Personnel Adminstrn., Adminstrv. Mgmt. Soc., Aircraft Owners and Pilots Assn. Home: RD 2 Box 38A Glen Gardner NJ 08826 Office: 125 Chubb Ave Lyndhurst NJ 07071-3504

YATES, WILLIAM ALBERT, physician, hospital administrator; b. Ottawa, Ont., Can., Nov. 16, 1929; came to U.S., 1954; s. John Frederick and Mary Edna Irene (Stedman) Y.; m. Patricia Eileen Ellis, Aug. 23, 1953; children: Jeffrey, Donald, Cynthia, Scott. MDCM, Queen's Coll., Kingston, Ont., 1954. Diplomate Am. Bd. Surgery. Internship Conemaugh Valley Meml. Hosp., Johnstown, Pa., 1954-55; residency in gen. surgery Mercy Hosp., Pitts., 1955-59; chmn. dept. surgery Lee Hosp., Johnstown, Pa., 1959-88, v.p. med. affairs, 1988—, med. dir. occupational health, 1990—. Chmn. United Fund, Johnstown, 1976. Flight lt. RCAF, 1950-53. Fellow ACS. Republican. Home: 305 Resty Ct Johnstown PA 15905-1643 Office: Lee Hosp 320 Main St Johnstown PA 15901-1601

YATES-BUCKLES, JEANNETTE KEBER, dentist, prosthodontics educator; b. Hackensack, N.J., Dec. 22, 1942; d. Richard Sigmund and Jeannette Ida (Zweil) Keber; m. Edward Scott Yates, Mar. 18, 1961 (div. June 1979); m. Kenneth Peter Buckles, Oct. 17, 1987; children: Darlene Denise, Edward Scott Jr. A. Applied Sci., Union Coll., 1972; student, Fairleigh Dickinson U., 1972-74; DMD, U. Dentistry and Medicine N.J., Newark, 1977. Postgrad. resident Mt. Sinai Hosp., N.Y.C., 1977-78; assoc. dentist Wayne (N.J.) Dental Group, 1978, Fairfield (N.J.) Dental Group, 1978-79; pvt. practice dentistry Hackensack, 1979—; assoc. prof. prosthodontics Fairleigh Dickinson U. Dental Sch., Teaneck, N.J., 1979-90; attending dentist Hackensack Med. Ctr., 1979-89. Fellow Acad. Gen. Dentistry (award 1987); mem. N.J. Women Dentists Study Group (v.p. 1980-82), N.J. Network Bus. and Profl. Women (v.p. 1985-87, bd. dirs. 1984—). Republican. Scientologist. Office: 67 Summit Ave Hackensack NJ 07601-1290

YATRON, GUS, congressman; b. Reading, Pa., Oct. 16, 1927; s. George H. and Theano (Lazos) Y.; m. Millie Menzies; children: George, Theana. Grad., Kutztown State Tchrs. Coll., 1950. Mem. Reading Sch. Bd., 1955-61, Pa. Ho. of Reps., 1956-60, Pa. Senate, 1960-68, 91st-102nd Congresses from 6th Dist. Pa., 1969—, fgn. affairs com., chmn. subcom. on human rights and internat. orgns.; vice chmn. Am. del. to Mex.-U.S. Interparliamentary Conf., 1979-83. Bd. mgrs. Reading Hosp. Democrat. Office: 2205 Rayburn House Office Bldg Washington DC 20515

YATSEVITCH, GRATIAN MICHAEL, retired army officer, diplomat, engineer; b. Kiev, Russia, Nov. 16, 1911; s. Michael Gratian and Margaret (Thomas) Y.; A.B., Harvard U., 1933, M.A., 1934, postgrad. (J.B. Woodworth fellow), 1935-40; m. Barbara Stewart Franks, July 2, 1973; children by previous marriage—Gael Yatsevitch McKibben, Peter, Kara, Gratian. Mining engr. Zlot Mines Ltd., also Beshina Gold Mines Ltd. of London in Yugoslavia, 1935-40, mgr. gold mine, 1936-40; commd. 2d lt. field arty.-U.S. Army, 1933, advanced through grades to col., 1951; chief cannon and aircraft armament br. devel. prodn. cannon, Office of Chief of Ordnance, 1940-45; mil. attache, Moscow, 1945-46; U.S. del. Allied Control Commn., Sofia, Bulgaria, 1946-47; mil. attache, Sofia, 1947-49; attache and spl. asst. to U.S. Ambassador, Turkey, 1952-53, Iran, 1957-63; sr. staff officer, Washington, 1950-52, 53-57; ret., 1969; hon. chmn. Star Trading and Marine Co., Washington; econ. cons. Middle E. Decorated Legion of Merit with oak leaf cluster. Clubs: Met. (Washington); Carlton, Lansdowne (London); Camden Yacht. Contbr. articles on arty. and mineral. subjects to mags. Home: Easterly Shermans Point Camden ME 04843 Office: Suite 450 1050 17th St NW Washington DC 20036

YAWORSKI, JOANN, reading skills educator; b. Phillipsburg, N.J., Oct. 11, 1956; d. Michael and Cecilia (Ruchala) Y. BA, Pa. State U., 1977; MEd, Millersville U., 1982; postgrad., Lehigh U., 1988-90, SUNY, Albany, 1991—. Cert. tchr. Russian lang., Russian area studies, reading specialist, elem. edn., Tex., N.J., Pa. Reading tutor Ephrata (Pa.) Sr. High Sch., 1980-81; tchr. Am. History/World Cultures Linden Hall Sch., Lititz, Pa., 1981-82; tchr., Russian lang. Spring Branch Sch. Dist., Houston, Tex., 1982-85; dir. devel. reading Green Mountain Coll., Poultney, Vt., 1989—. Mem. Profl. Ski Instrs. of Am., U.S. Figure Skating Assn. Democrat. Roman Catholic. Home: 31 York St Poultney VT 05764-1024 Office: Green Mountain Coll 16 College St Poultney VT 05764-1199

YAZBAK, EUGENE PAUL, engineering company executive; b. Providence, Aug. 6, 1960; s. Fouad Edward and Maureen Fabienne (Moynahan) Y. B-ChemE, McGill U., Montreal, Que., Can., 1982. Tech. tnr.-instrumentation The Foxboro (Mass.) Co., 1982-83, systems analyst, 1983-84; product line mgr., process infrared spectrometers Analytical div. The Foxboro Co., Plymouth, Mass., 1984-85, applied composition measurement systems devel. engr., 1985-86; prin. systems engr. Pilot Corp., Pocasset, Mass., 1986; pres., chief exec. officer, prin. Yazbak Engring. Inc., Monument Beach, Mass., 1986-90; v.p. product devel. Sensonix, Wellesley, Mass., 1987-89; editor Ea. region Control mag., Chgo., 1989-90; sr. engr. MetriCor, Woodinville, Wash., 1990-91, mgr. applied systems engring., 1991—; mktg. mgr. Temperature Products, Dynisco Inc., Sharon, Mass. Roman Catholic. Office: MetriCor PO Box 1007 Monument Beach MA 02553-1007

YAZULLA, STEPHEN, neurobiology educator; b. Jersey City, Sept. 3, 1945; s. Stephen Sr. and Elsie Alvina (Smith) Y.; m. Margaret Ann Stanley, Apr. 23, 1983; children: Lisa, Debra; stepchildren: Caroline, Marie. BS in Psychology, U. Scranton, Pa., 1967; MA in Psychology, U. Del., 1969, PhD in Psychology, 1971. Postdoctoral fellow U. Del., Newark, 1971-72, Harvard U., Cambridge, Mass., 1972-74; asst. prof. SUNY, Stony Brook, 1974-79, assoc. prof., 1979-86, prof., 1986—; mem. study sect. div. rsch. grants NIH, Bethesda, Md., 1985-90, mem. res. rev. bd., 1990—; dir. Electron Microscopy Facilities, SUNY, 1986—. Author chpts. in books; mem. editorial bd. Visual Neurosci., 1990—, Jour. Neurocytology, 1992—; contbr. numerous articles to profl. jours. NIH fellow U. Del./Harvard U., 1971-74; grantee SUNY, 1976—, NSF, 1990-92. Mem. Assn. Rsch. in Vision and Ophthalmology, Internat. Brain Rsch. Orgn., N.Y. Acad. SCis., Soc. for Neurosci., Sigma Xi. Republican. Roman Catholic. Office: SUNY Stony Brook Dept Neurobiology/Behavior Stony Brook NY 11794-5230

YEAGER, DENNIS RANDALL, lawyer; b. Dallas, Jan. 10, 1941; s. William C. and Katherine (Bell) Y.; m. Jere Jones, Aug. 31, 1963; children: Stephanie Ann O'Donnell, Karen Elizabeth, Brenda Marie. BSS, Loyola U. of South, 1964; LLB, Columbia U., 1967. Bar: N.Y. 1967, D.C. 1979, U.S. Supreme Ct. 1971, U.S. Ct. Appeals (2d cir.) 1972, U.S. Ct. Appeals (4th cir.) 1971, U.S. Ct. Appeals (5th cir.) 1970, U.S. Dist. Ct. (so. dist.) N.Y. 1969, U.S. Dist. Ct. Md. 1974, U.S. Dist. Ct. (we. dist.) N.Y. 1975. Dir. law intern program Columbia U., 1967; assoc. Willkie Farr & Gallagher, N.Y.C., 1967-69; dir., chief exec. officer Nat. Employment Law Project, N.Y.C., 1969-75; from assoc. to ptnr. Tufo, Johnston & Allegaert, N.Y.C., 1975-80; ptnr. Yeager & Barrett, N.Y.C., 1980—; chmn. program on bus. errors and omissions ins. Practicing Law Inst., 1983, program on role of outside counsel in bus. investigation, 1985; panelist program on dirs. and officers liabilities, 1988. Mem. ABA, N.Y. State Bar Assn., Assn. of Bar of City of N.Y., Blue Key, Alpha Sigma Nu. Roman Catholic. Home: 70 W 95th St New York NY 10025-6721 Office: Yeager & Barrett 888 7th Ave New York NY 10106-0001

YEAGER, JOSEPH CORNELIUS, consulting psychologist, behavioral researcher; b. Pitts., Jan. 5, 1940; s. Joseph Jacob and Elizabeth Zane (Singleton) Y.; m. Linda Dianne Sommer, Sept. 1, 1983; children: Rachel, Benjamin, Jerimiah. BA, Thiel Coll., 1963; MS, U. Pitts., 1967, PhD, 1969. Dir. human resource devel. USAIR, Pitts., 1964-70; dir. profl. pers. ETS, Princeton, N.J., 1970-74; internal cons. Pfizer Co., N.Y.C., 1974-84; pres. Linguistechs, New Hope, Pa., 1981—. Author: Thinking about Thinking, 1985, The Goal Strategy Book, 1990, What They Didn't Teach: Sales 101, 1990, (video) Psychology of Friendly Persuasion, 1984. Recipient Martin Luther King award Music and Arts Soc., Pitts., 1974. Mem. APA, Am. Psychol. Soc., Human Factors Soc. Office: Linguistechs 111 Pheasant Run Newtown PA 18940-1820

YEAZEL, NICHOLAS JOHN (NICK YOUNG), broadcast news reporter; b. Princeton, Ill., Dec. 12, 1948; s. James William and Elizabeth Victoria (Patronia) Y.; m. Marsha Lynn Browne, Aug. 21, 1971 (div. 1982); m. Deborah Ann Dinoto, Nov. 2, 1982; 1 child, Christopher. AA, Ill. Valley Community Coll., 1969; B Journalism, U. Mo., 1971. Disc jockey WZOE-AM, Princeton, 1968-70, KTGR-FM, Columbia, Mo., 1970-72; talk show host WLW-AM, Cin., 1972-75; anchorman WEEI-AM, Boston, 1975-79, WHDH-AM, Boston, 1979-83; corr. RKO Radio Networks, N.Y.C., 1983-90; reporter CBS News, N.Y.C., 1990—.

YEE, ALBERT HOY, psychologist, educator; b. Santa Barbara, Calif., June 14, 1929; m. Daisy Li King-Ying; children: Lisa Diane, Hoyt Brian, Cynthia Rae. B.A., U. Calif., Berkeley, 1952; M.A., San Francisco State U., 1959; Ed.D., Stanford U., 1965. Post-doctoral research fellow U. Oreg., Eugene, 1966-67; assoc. prof. edn. U. Wis., Madison, 1967-70, prof., 1970-73; prof. ednl. psychology, dean grad. studies and research Calif. State U., Long Beach, 1973-79, originating founder Grad. Ctr., 1974; prof. edn. U. Mont., 1979-83, dean Sch. Edn., 1979-82; sr. lectr. psychology Chinese U. of Hong Kong, 1985-89; dean, prof. psychology Am. Coll., Singapore, 1989-90; sr. lectr. psychology Nat. U., Singapore; dir. program U. Md., Hongkong, 1990; disting. vis. prof. ednl. psychology spl. adviser coll. grad. studies and internat. programs Marist Coll., 1990—; chmn. 1st Fed. Adv. Com. for Asian and Pacific Island Ams., Bur. Census, 1976-81; chair task force on sci. conception of "Race," Soc. for the Psychol. Study of Social Issues, 1991—, . Author: Man, Society and the World, 1968; co-author: Comprehensive Spelling Instruction: Theory, Research and Application, 1971; editor: Social Interaction in Educational Settings, 1971; (with others) Perspectives on Management Systems Approaches to Education: A Symposium, 1973, Search for Meaning, 1984, A Study on Possible Future Developments for Hong Kong: Strategic Planning and Innovations, 1985, A People Misruled: Hong Kong and the Chinese Stepping-Stone Syndrome, 1989, 2d edit., 1992. Mem.legal compliance com. Calif. State Dept. Edn., 1975-79. With AUS, 1952-55, Korea, Japan. Recipient Civic Commendation Madison, 1973; sr. Fulbright lectr. Tokyo and Tamagawa Univs., Japan; also 1st Fulbright scholar to People's Republic China, 1972. Fellow AAAS, Nat. Conf. Research in English, Am. Psychol. Assn. , Am. Psychol. Soc.; mem. Calif. Coll. and Univ. Faculty Assn. (founder 1961), Am. Ednl. Research Assn., Chinese Hist. Soc. Am. and Orgn. of Chinese Americans (Bicentennial speaker), Asian-Am. Psychol. Assn. (pres. 1979-82, jour. editor 1981-82), Brit. Psychol. Soc., Hong Kong Psychol. Soc., Phi Delta Kappa. Office: Marist Coll Soc Behavioral Sci Poughkeepsie NY 12601-1387

YEFIMOV, IGOR MARKOVICH (IGOR MARKOVICH EFIMOV), writer; b. Moscow, Aug. 8, 1937; came to U.S., 1978; s. Mark Y. and Anna (Melnikoval) Y.; m. Marina Rachko, May 29, 1959; children: Leana, Natasha. Dir. Hermitage Publs., Tenafly, N.J., 1981—. Author: (in Russian) Metapolitics, 1978, Practical Metaphysics, 1980, Without Bourgeoises, 1979, As One Flesh (novel), 1981, (as Moscovit) The Judgement Day Archives, 1982, English edit., 1988, Kennedy, Oswald, Castro, Krushchev, 1987, (novel) The Seventh Wife, 1990; (in English) Our Choice and History, 1985; contbr. articles to Mich. Quar. Rev. Geo, Russian Lit. Tri Quar., Kontinent, Russia, others; edn.: Moscow Inst. Lit., Leningrad Poly. Inst.; writer Writer's Union, Leningrade, 1965-78; editor ARdis Pub. House, Ann Arbor, Mich., 1978-81. Mem. Am. Assn. for Advancement of Slavic Studies, Am. Assn. of Tchrs. of Slavic and East European Langs., Internat. Platform Assn. Office: PO Box 410 Tenafly NJ 07670-0410

YEH, JAMES KUEN-JANN, nutritionist; b. Kuen-Ming, Yuen Nang, China, June 27, 1942; came to U.S., 1967; s. Jin Gee-shan Yeh and Shing (Lan) Tsao; m. Jenny Ming, Feb. 1, 1969; children: Berhan S., Bervan Y. BS, Nat. Taiwan U., 1965; MS, U. Wis., 1968, PhD, 1974. Rsch. asst. U. Wis., Madison, 1969-74; rsch. assoc. Brookhaven Nat. Lab., Upton, N.Y., 1974-76; rsch. biochemist Nassau County Med. Ctr., East Meadow, N.Y., 1976-78; dir. metabolism lab. Winthrop-Univ. Hosp., Mineola, N.Y., 1978—; asst. prof. SUNY, Stony Brook, 1980-87; assoc. prof. SUNY, 1988—; adj. prof. L.I. U., Brookville, N.Y., 1980-83; nutrition cons. Life Health Ctr., West Babylon, N.Y., 1986-88; dir. metabolism lab. Winthrop-Univ. Hosp., Mineola, 1978—. Contbr. articles to profl. jours. Grantee NIH, 1975, Retirement Rsch. Found., 1986. Fellow Am. Coll. Nutrition; mem. Am. Soc. of Bone Mineral Rsch., Internat. Conf. on Calcium Regulating Hormones, Am. Coll. Sports Medicine, N.Y. Acad. Sci., Soc. Chinese Bioscientists in Am. Home: 10 Wisteria Pl Syosset NY 11791 Office: Winthrop-Univ Hosp 259 First St Mineola NY 11501

YENCIK, ROBERT JOHN, public relations executive; b. Pitts., May 21, 1960; s. Richard Joseph Yencik and Mathilda (Lustri) Flannery. BJ, U. Mo., 1982. Fin. writer Weiser Group, Chgo., 1982-83; dir. communications Mo. Bankers Assn., Jefferson City, 1983-86; account exec. and supr. Dudreck, DePaul, Ficco & Morgan, Pitts., 1986-88; account supr. Mangus/Catanzano, Pitts., 1988-89; mng. ptnr. YBS Communications, Pitts., 1990—. Mem. Pub. Rels. Soc. Am. (chmn. young profls. com. 1989-90). Republican. Roman Catholic. Home: 7801 Lloyd St Apt 114 Pittsburgh PA 15218-1944 Office: YBS Communications 1600 Three Gateway Ctr Pittsburgh PA 15222-1006

YENISCAVICH, WILLIAM, nuclear scientist; b. Girardville, Pa., June 30, 1934; s. Alexander and Helen (Hencosky) Y.; m. Marlyn June Rakita, Dec. 31, 1955; children: William Walter, David Alexander. BS in Metall. Engring., Drexel U., 1957; MS in Metall. Engring., Carnegie-Mellon U., 1962, PhD in Metall. Engring., 1963. Registered profl. engr., Pa. Nuclear engring. Bettis Atomic Power Lab, Pitts., 1957-66, welding mgr., 1971-76, 80-84, quality assurance mgr., 1976-80; Navy rep. Bettis Atomic Power Lab, Lynchburg, Va., 1984-87; spl. assignment Bettis Atomic Power Lab, Pitts., 1987—; welding rsch. mgr. Cabot Corp., Kokomo, Ind., 1966-71. Contbg. author: Superalloys, 1987; contbg. editor: Welding Handbook, 1981; author tech. papers in field. Office: Bettis Atomic Power Lab PO Box 79 West Mifflin PA 15122-0079

YERACARIS, BERNICE LEVENFELD, psychologist; b. Detroit, Sept. 16, 1920; d. Mitchell Abe and Florence Berman Levenfeld; m. Constantine A. Yeracaris, Sept. 12, 1949; children—Flora, Yoryos, Panos, Anthony. Student Roosevelt U., 1940-42; B.A., U. Chgo., 1944, postgrad. 1947-49. Pvt. practice psychol. therapy, Buffalo, 1951—; instr. Cornell Extension Sch. Labor and Mgmt., 1949-50, U. Buffalo, 1949-50. Diplomate Am. Bd. Psychotherapy. Mem. Am. Psychol. Assn., N.Y. State Psychol. Assn., Psychol. Assn. Western N.Y., Council Advancement Profl. Psychology, Nat. Register Health Service Providers in Psychology, Mental Health Assn. Erie County, Sex, Info. and Edn. Council. Home and Office: 485 Norwood Ave Buffalo NY 14222-1599

YERGANIAN, GEORGE, cell biologist, cytogeneticist; b. N.Y.C., June 14, 1923; s. Charles and Miriam (Krishjian) Y.; m. Sona Arzomanian, Sept. 3, 1950; children: Arra, Athena. BS in Botany, Mich. State U., 1947; PhD in Biology, Harvard U., 1951. Instr. in botany (cytology) U. Minn., Mpls., 1950-51; AEC Postdoctoral fellow Brookhaven Nat. Lab., Upton, N.Y., 1951-52; postdoctoral fellow Boston U., 1952-53; NIH postdoctoral fellow Boston U. and Children's Hosp., 1953-54; chief lab. cytogenetics Dana-Farber Cancer Ctr., Boston, 1954-78; sr. rsch. assoc. Sch. Pub. Health, Harvard U., Boston, 1983—, Cytogen Rsch. and Devel., Inc., West Roxbury, Mass., 1983—; mem.-del. U.S.-USSR genetics com. NIH, 1973, 75; mem. rev. panel for health rsch. U.S. EPA, 1981-90. Contbr. articles to Am. Jour. Human Genetics, Jour. Nat. Cancer Inst.; contbg. author: Pathology of Hamsters, 1972, Molecular Cell Genetics, 1989. Coun. mem. Bellevue Hill Assn., West Roxbury, 1990—. Recipient Prof. Kabakjian Sci. award Armenian Students Assn., 1977. Mem. Tissue Culture Assn. (sec. 1976-80), Soc. for Leukocyte Biology, Venezuelan Tissue Culture Assn. (hon.), Knights of Vartan. Home: 89 Bellevue Hill Rd West Roxbury MA 02132-6423 Office: Harvard U Sch Pub Health 665 Huntington Ave Boston MA 02115-6021

YERGIN, DANIEL HOWARD, writer, consultant; b. Los Angeles, Feb. 6, 1947; s. Irving H. and Naomi Y.; m. Angela Stent, Aug. 10, 1975; children:, Alexander George, Rebecca Isabella. BA, Yale U., 1968; MA, Cambridge U., Eng., 1970, PhD, 1974; PhD (hon.), U. Mo., 1980. Contbg. editor New York mag., 1968-70; research fellow Harvard U., Cambridge, Mass., 1974-76; lectr. bus. sch. Harvard U., 1976-79, lectr. Kennedy Sch. Govt., 1979-83; research assoc. Harvard U., Cambridge, 1983—; pres. Cambridge Energy Research Assoc., Cambridge, 1982—; mem. policy adv. com. Program on U.S.-Japan Rels., Harvard U.; mem. bd. energy experts Dallas Morning News. Author: Shattered Peace, 1977, rev. edit., 1990; co-author: Cold War, 1977, Energy Future, 1979, 3d edit., 1982, Global Insecurity, 1982, Future of Oil Prices: Perils of Prophecy, 1984, The Prize: The Epic Quest for Oil, Money and Power, 1991; contbg. editor Atlantic Monthly, 1977-83. Mem. adv. bd. Solar Energy Research Inst., Golden, Colo., 1979-81. Recipient Best Book award Nat. Hist. Soc., 1977, Eccles Prize for best book on econ. themes, 1992, Pulitzer Prize for gen. non-fiction, 1992; fellow Univ. Consortium for World Order Studies, 1974-75, Rockefeller Found., 1975-79, German Marshall Fund, 1980-81; Marshall scholar Cambridge U., 1974. Fellow Atlantic Inst. Internat. Affairs; mem. Lehrman Inst. (assoc.), Coun. on Fgn. Rels., Nat. Petroleum Coun., Internat. Assn. for Energy Econs., Am. Hist. Assn., Am. Polit. Assn., Royal Inst. Internat. Affairs, Assn. Marshall Scholars (bd. dirs. 1988—), Offshore No. Seas Found. Internat. Coun., The Nature Conservancy (Last Great Places com.), Yale Club (N.Y.C.), Harvard Club (N.Y.C.). Office: Cambridge Energy Rsch Assocs 20 University Rd Ste 450 Charles Sq Cambridge MA 02138

YEROW, MARA H., health administrator; b. Worcester, Mass., Sept. 5, 1951; d. Leonard and Gertrude (Hilfer) Y. BS, U. Mass., 1973; MPH, U. Pitts., 1975. Prog. dir. Council House Inc., Pitts., 1975-78; sr. planner Cen. Mass. Health Sys. Agy., Shrewsbury, Mass., 1978-81; asst. dir. Cen. Mass. Health Sys. Agy., 1981-83; cons. prog. analyst Mass. Dept. Pub. Health, Boston, 1982-86; exec. dir. Cen. Mass. Health Sys. Agy., Shrewsbury, 1983-88; health care cons. Worcester, Mass., 1988—; v.p. corp. svcs. AdCare Hosp. of Worcester, 1988-91; cons. Mara H. Yerow and Assocs., Worcester, 1991—; mem. adv. bd. Clark U. Master's Prog. in Health Adminstrn., Worcester, 1987-89; preceptor U. Mass. Sch. Pub. Health, 1985-87. Mem. Soc. Health Care Planning and Mktg., Mass. Health Care Mgmt. Assn., Mass. Pub. Health Assn., Am. Pub. Health Assn., Am. Health Planning Assn. (bd. dirs., sec. 1988—), Worcester Area C. of C. (pub. affairs com. 1983-91). Jewish. Office: Mara H Yerow & Assocs 55 Camelot Dr Worcester MA 01602

YESNER, RAYMOND, pathologist, consultant; b. Columbus, Ga., Apr. 18, 1914; s. Benjamin Nabrisky and Anna (Tolbert) Y.; m. Bernice Lieberman, Feb. 16, 1947; children: David, Donna, Steven. AB, Harvard U., 1935; MD, Tufts U., 1941; MA (hon.), Yale U., 1969. Chief lab. svc. VA Hosp., Newington, Conn., 1947-53; chief lab. svc. VA Med. Ctr., West Haven, Conn., 1953-74, chief pathologist, 1974-77, dir. electron microscope lab., 1974-80, dir. pathology, 1977-87, chief of staff, 1968-74; dir. autopsy svc. Yale Med. Ctr., New Haven, 1987—; prof. pathology Yale Med. Ctr., 1972-84, prof. emeritus, 1984—, sr. rsch. scientist, 1984—, assoc. dean, 1972-84. Author: (chpt.) Pulmonary Diseases and Disorders, 1988, Clinics in Chest Medicine, 1982; editor: Histological Typing of Lung Tumours, 1981. Pres. Am. Cancer Soc. Conn. div., Wallingford, 1986-88, chmn. Pub. Issues, 1988-91; chmn. Lung Cancer com. WHO, Geneva, 1977-81. Capt. U.S. Army, 1944-47. Recipient Health Meml. award, U. Tex., 1984, St. George medal, Am. Cancer Soc., 1989. Founding mem. Internat. Assn. for Study of Lung Cancer (pathology com. 1983-91); mem. Arthur P. Stout Surgical Pathology Soc., Radiation Therapy Oncology Group (pathology com. 1985-91), Sigma Xi. Home: 16 Sunbrook Rd Woodbridge CT 06525-1833

YEUTTER, CLAYTON KEITH, political organization executive, counsellor to President of U.S.; b. Eustis, Nebr., Dec. 10, 1930; s. Reinhold F. and Laura P. Y.; m. Lillian Jeanne Vierk; children—Brad, Gregg, Kim, Van. BS, U. Nebr., 1952, JD, 1963, PhD in Agrl. Econs., 1966, hon. doctorate; hon. doctorate, Clemson U., Georgetown U., Santa Clara U., Nebr. Wesleyan U., U. Md., DePaul U. Bar: Nebr. 1963, D.C. 1977. Farmer, rancher Nebr., 1957-75; mem. faculty dept. agrl. econs. U. Nebr., Lincoln, 1960-66; dir. Mission in Colombia U. Nebr. Mission in Colombia, Lincoln, 1968-70; exec. asst. Gov. Nebr., 1966-68; adminstr. consumer and mktg. svcs. USDA, Washington, 1970-71; regional dir. Com. for Reelection of Pres., 1972; asst. sec. Agr. for Mktg. and Consumer Svcs., Washington, 1973-74, Agr. for Internat. Affairs and Commodity Programs, Washington, 1974-75; dep. spl. trade rep. Exec. Office of Pres., Washington, 1975-77; sr. ptnr. Nelson, Harding, Yeutter & Leonard, Lincoln, Nebr., 1977-78; pres., chief exec. officer Chgo. Mercantile Exchange, 1978-85; U.S. trade rep., 1985-89; sec. U.S. Dept. Agriculture, 1989-91; chmn. Rep. Nat. Com., Washington, 1991-92; counsellor to the President for domestic policy The White House, Washington, 1992—; bd. dirs. Caterpillar, FMC Corp., Oppenheimer Funds. Contbr. numerous articles to profl. jours. Former trustee Garrett-Evangelical Theol. Sem., Evanston, Ill.; past bd. dirs. Chgo. Coun. on Fgn. Rels.; past bd. visitors Sch. Bus. Adminstrn. Georgetown U.; former trustee, mem. exec. com. Farm Found., Oak Brook, Ill. Served with USAF, 1952-57, USAFR, 1957-87. Recipient Israel Prime Minister's medal, Master Builder of Men award FarmHouse, Leadership award Fowler-McCracken Commn., Consumers for World Trade award. Mem. Nebr. Bar Assn. Republican. Methodist.

YEZZO, DOMINICK, language and literature educator; b. N.Y.C., June 21, 1947; s. Frank and Josephine (Gaspro) Y.; m. Anne Kelly, Jan 16, 1978; children: Emily, John Paul. BA, CUNY, 1975, MA, 1977, JD, 1988. Prof. Nassau Community Coll., Garden City, N.Y., 1980—; adj. prof. Queens Coll., Flushing, N.Y., 1978-80. Author: A G.I.'s Vietnam Day, 1974. With U.S. Army, 1967-69, Vietnam. Mem. Vietnam Vets Am. (sec. Queens chpt. 1984-86). Roman Catholic. Office: Nassau Community Coll Stewart Ave Garden City NY 11530-2200

YGLESIAS, RICARDO ANDRES, JR., chemist; b. Arlington, Va., Feb. 2, 1968; s. Ricardo Andres Sr. and Rita Elizabeth (Johnston) Y. Student, Rutgers State U., 1990—. Salesman Ypsilon 2000 Crafts, El Salvador, 1989-90; lab. tech. J&J Snack Foods Corp., Pennsauken, N.J., 1990—. Roman Catholic. Office: J&J Snack Foods Corp 6000 Central Hwy Merchantville NJ 08109-4607

YI, GYOSEOB, economics educator; b. Namwon, Korea, Oct. 19, 1952; s. Donghwan Yi and Jongwon Song; m. Myungsun Yi, Feb. 1, 1978; children: Jaeheon, Jaeyoung. BA, Seoul (Korea) Nat. U., 1975, MA, 1977; PhD, U. Rochester (N.Y.), 1987. Asst. prof. econs. SUNY, Buffalo, 1985—. Mem.

Am. Econ. Assn., Econometric Soc. Home: 156 Glenhaven Dr Buffalo NY 14228-1854 Office: SUNY at Buffalo Buffalo NY 14260

YIANNES, (IORDANIDES), sculptor, ceramist, educator; b. Athens, Greece, Dec. 16, 1943; came to U.S., 1967; d. Gregory Iordanides and Maria Katsiotis; 1 child, Joshua. Cert., Bklyn. Mus. Arts Sch., 1972; student, New Sch. Social Rsch., 1970-71. Instr. Bklyn. Mus. Art Sch., 1971-78, Bklyn. Coll. CUNY, 1972-82, Greenwich House Pottery, N.Y.C., 1984-85, Queens Coll. CUNY, 1985-88. Recipient 1st prize in Ceramics Alfred Parker award, 1972, Lucile Blanch award for Sculpture Woodstock artist Assn., 1989, Max Beckman scholarship, Bklyn. Mus. N.Y., 1971-72; CETA grantee visual arts program Queens Coun. Arts, 1980. Mem. Am. Crafts Coun. Democrat. Home and Office: 20-41 Shore Blvd Long Island City NY 11105

YIENGPRUKSAWAN, ANUSAK, surgical oncologist; came to U.S., 1984; m. Melanie Hall. MD, Tohoku U., Sendai, Japan, 1978. Diplomate Am. Bd. Surgery. Resident Columbia U. Affiliate Harlem Hosp., N.Y.C., 1984-89; surg. oncology fellow Meml. Sloan-Kettering Cancer Ctr., N.Y.C., 1989-91; attending surgeon, chief div. surg. oncology Meth. Hosp., Bklyn., 1991—; dir. endoscopic ultrasound lab The Meth. Hosp., Bklyn., 1991—. Author: Ultrasound, Endoscopic Ultrasound, Cancer Surgery. Japanese Min. Edn. scholar, 1972-82; Japanese Coun. for Med. Tng. Fellowship Program grantee, Tokyo, 1982-84. Fellow Am. Soc. Gastrointestinal Endoscopy, Soc. Am. Gastrointertinal Endoscopic Surgeons; mem. AMA, Am. Inst. Ultrasonic Med., Bklyn. Surg. Soc. Office: Methodist Hosp Dept Surgery 506 Sixth St Brooklyn NY 11215

YIM, CHARLIE, marketing professional; b. Seoul, Republic of Korea, Apr. 24, 1959; came to U.S., 1974; s. Tal Yong and Myeo Nam (Lee) Y.; m. Chang Suk Han, Apr. 28, 1980; children: Lori Jean, Sylvia Crystal. AS, Pikespeak Coll., Colorado Springs, Colo., 1981; MBA, U. Md., 1985. Mktg. mgr. Gotham Wholesale Beer Corp., Queens, N.Y., 1986-87; sec., treas. S.K.I. Wholesale Beer Corp., Bklyn., 1987—. Pres. Korean Youth Club, Tocoma, Wash., 1983-84, Korean-U.S. Vets. Group, Bklyn., 1990—. Staff sgt. U.S. Army, 1980-86;. Recipient Merit award N.J. gov., 1977, cert. of achievement, 1980. Mem. NRA. Republican. Home: 283 Avenue B Ronkonkoma NY 11779-1915

YIN, FRANK CHI-PONG, medicine educator, biomedical engineering educator; b. Kunming, Yunnan, China, June 21, 1943; came to U.S., 1948; s. Peter Yi-Ming and Nancy Hua-Nien (Chien) Y.; m. Grace Lu-Chi Chen, Apr. 19, 1975; children: Gregory, Jeffrey. BS, MIT, 1965, MS, 1967; PhD, U. Calif. San Diego, La Jolla, 1970, MD, 1973. Intern Univ. Hosp. San Diego, Calif., 1973-74; asst. resident Univ. Hosp. San Diego, 1974-75; clin. assoc. Nat. Inst. on Aging, Balt., 1975-77; fellow cardiology Johns Hopkins Hosp., Balt., 1977-78, staff physician, attending physician, 1978—, asst. prof. medicine and physiology, 1978-83, assoc. prof. medicine, 1983-88, assoc. prof. physiology, 1985—, prof. medicine and biomed. engring., 1988—; mem. cardiovascular and pulmonary study sect. Nat. Heart, Lung and Blood Inst., Bethesda, Md., 1983-87; mem. Frank T. McClure Fellowship Com., Balt., 1990—. Editor: Ventricular/Vascular Coupling, 1987; assoc. editor: Jour. Biomechanical Engring., ASME, 1990—. Chmn. Chinese Lang. Sch. Balt., 1983-90. Y. T. Li Aeronautical Engring. scholar, 1961-65. Fellow Am. Physiol. Soc.; mem. Am. Soc. for Clin. Investigation, Am. Heart Assn., Biomed. Engring. Soc., Biophys. Soc., Cardiovascular Systems Dynamics Soc. Office: Johns Hopkins Med Inst 538 Carnegie Bldg 600 N Wolfe St Baltimore MD 21205-2104

YOBURN, BYRON CROCKER, pharmacologist, educator, researcher; b. Danbury, Conn., Nov. 26, 1950; s. Michael Myer and Irene R. (Crocker) Y. BA, Boston U., 1973; MA, Hollins Coll., 1976; PhD, Northeastern U., 1979. Postdoctoral fellow Columbia U. Med. Sch., N.Y.C., 1979-81; rsch. scientist N.Y. State Psychiat. Inst., N.Y.C., 1981-82; postdoctoral fellow Cornell U. Med. Sch., N.Y.C., 1982-83, instr., 1983-87; asst. prof. Coll. Pharmacy St. Johns U., Queens, N.Y., 1987-89, assoc. prof., 1990—. Office: St Johns U Grand Cen and Utopia Pkwy Queens NY 11439

YOCHELSON, KATHRYN MERSEY, art researcher; b. N.Y.C., Oct. 22, 1910; d. Nathan and Esther Mary Mersey; m. Samuel Yochelson, June 21, 1930 (dec. Nov. 1976); children: John Norman, Bonnie Ellen. BA in Art Edn., New Haven Tchrs. Coll., 1930; postgrad., Yale U., Columbia U., Albright Art Sch., Am. U., U. Md. Tchr. art New Haven Sch. System, 1930-39; lectr. on Israeli art Am. U. Inst. for Learning in Retirement, Washington, 1991. Researcher on artistic roots of Jewish people, 1940—. Organized permanent art collection at Buffalo Jewish Ctr., 1952; chmn. Seven Painters of Israel exhibition, Albright-Knox Art Gallery, 1953, 20 Artists for Israel, George Washington U., Washington, 1968, Personal Vision: Yochelson Collection of Israeli Art, George Washington U., 1987; author: Israeli Art: Golden Threads; lectr. and contbr. articles in field; reviewed books in field. Vol. edn. dept. Albright-Knox Art Gallery, Buffalo, 1940-60; internat. bd. govs. Tel Aviv Mus. Art, 1977; established Dr. Samuel and Kathryn Yochelson meml. lectr. Yale U. Sch. Psychiatry, 1980. Mem. Sunday Scholar Series Com., Albright-Knox Art Glllery (life), Brandeis Women's Com., Hadassah (life), Washington Watercolor Soc. (sec. 1971-72), Nat. Am. Pen Women. Home: 4201 Cathedral Ave NW Apt 824 Washington DC 20016-4901

YOCUM, RONALD HARRIS, chemical company executive; b. Darby, Pa., June 2, 1939; s. Jacob Harris and Gladys (Phillips) Y.; m. Martha Virginia Meitzner, July 6, 1963; children—Beth Ann, James Eric. B.A., Gettysburg Coll., Pa., 1961; Ph.D., U. Pa., 1965. With Dow Chem. Co., 1965—; dir. research and devel. Dow Latin Am. Coral Gables, Fla., 1973-77; dir. research and devel. designed products dept. Midland, Mich., 1977-78, dir. product research Dow USA, 1978-80, dir. research Mich. div., 1980-85; group v.p. Norchem, Rolling Meadows, Ill., 1985-87; group v.p. Quantum Chem. Corp., Cin., 1987-89, pres. USI div., 1989-90, exec. v.p., 1990—. Editor: (with others) Functional Monomers, Vols. I and II, 1974. Active Boy Scouts Am. Mem. Am. Chem. Soc., Chem. Industry Inst. of Tech. (bd. dirs. 1985-86). Republican. Episcopalian. Office: Quantum Chem Corp 11500 Northlake Dr PO Box 429550 Cincinnati OH 45249-1619

YODER, MYRON EUGENE, secondary social studies educator; b. Reading, Pa., Oct. 28, 1953; s. Robert W. and Carmen D. (Keinard) Y.; m. Debra Kuper, Dec. 27, 1975; children: Joshua B., Rebecca A. BE cum laude, Kutztown U., 1976; Masters Equavalency, Pa. Dept. Edn., 1979; MEd cum laude, Kutztown U., 1981. Cert. secondary social studies tchr., Pa. With maintenance ride repair Dorney Pk, Allentown, Pa., 1968-72; postal asst. Lehigh County U.S. P.O. SCF180, Allentown, 1972-73; insp. Fairtex Mills, Allentown, 1973-74; correctional officer Lehigh County Prison, Allentown, 1974-76; emergency prison counselor Lehigh County Prison, 1979-84; mgr., supr. Hosp. Cen. Svcs., Allentown, 1976; tchr., dept. chmn., curriculum coord. Allentown Sch. Dist., 1976—; tchr. trainer Ctr. for Civic Edn., Bicentennial Commn., Callabasas, Calif., 1987—, Temple U. LEAP, 1987—; sch. coord. Boy Scouts Am. Awareness Post, Allentown, 1989—; scholar Pa. Humanities Coun., Phila., 1991—. Photographer (Kinisa Local award 1980, 83); computer programmer Class Dues Record Keeper, 1987-88 (1st dist., 2nd regional runner-up computer learning award), Study Hall Record Keeper, 1988 (1st dist., 2nd regional award). Chmn. Borough of Emmaus Operation Homecoming, 1991; discussion leader Pa. Humanities Coun., Emmaus, 1992; com. mem. Allentown Columbus Quincentenary, 1991, Allentown Black History Month Com., 1990-91. Recipient Applied Econs. Tchr. of the Yr. award Jr. Achievement of Lehigh Valley, 1990; recipient Jr. Achievement Applied Econs. Tchr. of the Yr. for Pa., 1991; selected by Jr. Achievement to travel to Soviet Union to train Soviet tchrs. in using Jr. Achievement applied econs., 1991. Mem. NEA, Nat. Coun. Social Studies, Pa. Coun. Social Studies, Pa. State Edn. Assn. (internat. rels. com. region chmn. 1987—), Lehigh Valley Coun. Social Studies, Allentown Edn. Assn. (v.p. 1991—), Kiwanis. Republican. Lutheran. Office: Louis E Dieruff High Sch 815 N Irving St Allentown PA 18103-1894

YOHAY, STEVEN JACOB, health care company executive, consultant; b. N.Y.C., Nov. 28, 1950; s. Nathan and Natalie (Modlinger) Y.; children: Charlotte, Paige. BS in Psychology, SUNY-Empire State Coll., N.Y.C., 1977. Cert. addiction specialist. Staff counselor-trainee AREBA Casriel Inst., N.Y.C., 1971-72, asst. resident dir., 1972-73, resident dir., 1973-75, exec. dir., 1975-82, pres., chief exec. officer, 1982—; cons. Long Lane Sch., Middletown Conn., Brookside Acad., Mt. Freedom, N.J., The Key, Ghent, Belgium, New Ctr. for Psychotherapies, Boston, Psychiat. Engring. Standards Assn. Contbr. articles to profl. jours. Bd. dirs. N.Y. Regional Therapeutic Communities of Am. Recipient Community Svc. award Bronx Borough Pres.'s Officer, 1966; Regents scholar N.Y. State Bd. Regents, 1966. Fellow Am. Soc. New Identity Process; mem. Am. Coll. Healthcare Adminstrs., Nat. Assn. Alcoholism and Drug Abuse Counselors, Alcohol and Drug Problems Assn. N.Am., Nat. Assn. Addiction Treatment Providers, N.Y. State Assn. Practicing Psychotherapists. Jewish. Home: 96 Savannah Walk Oak Beach NY 11702 Office: AREBA Casriel Inst 500 W 57th St New York NY 10019-2902

YOHE, GARY W., economics educator; b. Abington, Conn., May 10, 1948; s. Jack Wensel and Dorothy June (Hall) Y.; m. Linda Rosemary Citrano, Sept. 21, 1974; children: Marielle Elizabeth, Courtney Jeanne. BA, U. Pa., 1970; MA, SUNY, Stonybrook, 1971; M. Philosophy, Yale U., 1974, PhD, 1975. Asst. prof. SUNY, Albany, 1975-77; assoc. prof. Wesleyan U., Middletown, Conn., 1977-82, prof., 1982—; chair Wesleyan U., 1991—; vis. prof., fellow Yale U., New Haven, 1983, 85, 88—; rsch. cons. NAS, Washington, 1982-83, U.S. EPA, U.S. Dept. Energy, Washington, 1985—; project leader Sigma Xi Program on Climate Change, Research Triangle, N.C., 1988—. Author: Study Guide to Economics, 1985, 88, 91; contbr. articles to profl. jours. Pres. 1st Congregational Ch., Portland, Conn., 1989—; policy cons. Rep. Samuel Gejdenson, Washington, 1980—; chair Gov.'s Commn. on Conn.'s Future, Hartford, 1985-88; chair working group on econ. data Internat. Social Sci. Coun. Mem. Am. Econ. Assn., Assn. Environ. & Resource Economists, Conn. Acad. Sci. and Engring. (elected mem.), AAAS, Sigma Xi (elected mem.). Home: 84 High St Portland CT 06480-1638 Office: Wesleyan U Dept Econs Middletown CT 06459

YOKEN, MEL B., French educator, author; b. Fall River, Mass., June 25, 1939; s. Albert Benjamin and Sylvia Sarah (White) Y.; m. Cynthia Stein, June 20, 1976; children: Andrew Brett, David Ryan, Jonathan Barry. B.A., U. Mass., 1960, Ph.D., 1972; M.A.T., Brown U., 1961. Instr. French U. Mass., Dartmouth, 1966-72, asst. prof., 1972-76, assoc. prof., 1976-81 prof., 1981—, dir. French summer study program French Inst., 1981—; vis. prof. Wheaton Coll., 1987, U. of Montreal, 1981-88, translator New Bedford Superior Ct., New Bedford, Mass., 1985—, Fall River Superior Ct., Fall River, Mass., 1985—; mem. nominating com. Nobel prize for lit., 1972—. Pres. Friends of Fall River Pub. Libr., 1972-80, pres. bd. dirs., 1972-80; pres. New Bedford Pub. Libr., 1980-82, Am. Field Svc., 1985—. Recipient Disting. Svc. award City Fall River, 1974, 80, Excellence in Teaching French award, 1984, 85, Gov.'s citation, 1986, Nat. Disting. Leadership award, 1990; Mel Yoken Day proclaimed by Mayor of New Bedford, 1990; Govt. of Que. grantee, 1981-85, 87-89, Can. Embassy grantee, 1986,87, Southeastern Mass. U. grantee, 1985, 89, 90. Mem. MLA (life), Am. Assn. Tchrs. French (life), Am. Coun. Tchrs. Fgn. Langs., Middlebury Amicale (life), N.E. MLA (coord. 1987—), New Eng. Fgn. Lang. Assn., Mass. Fgn. Lang. Assn. (bd. dir. 1985—), N.Y. State Assn. Fgn. Lang. Tchrs., Internat. Platform Assn., Francophone Assn. (v.p. 1990—), Fall River C. of C., Brown U. Alumni Assn. (rep.), Richelieu Internat. Author: Claude Tillier, 1976, Speech is Plurality, 1978, Claude Tillier (1801-44): Fame and Fortune in His Novelistic Work, 1978, Entretiens Quebecois I, 1986, Entretiens Quebecois II, 1989, Letters of Robert Molloy, 1989, Festschrift in Honor of Stowell Goding, 1992; contbr. articles to profl. jours. Avocations: traveling, languages, baseball, postcards, meteorology books. Home: 261 Carroll St New Bedford MA 02740-1412 Office: U Mass Dartmouth Lang Dept Old Westport Rd North Dartmouth MA 02747-2512

YONDA, ALFRED WILLIAM, mathematician; b. Cambridge, Mass., Aug. 10, 1919; s. Walter and Theophelia (Naruscewicz) Y.; B.S., U. Ala., 1952, M.A. in Math., 1954; m. Mary Jane McManus, Dec. 19, 1949 (dec.); children—Nancy, Kathryn, Elizabeth, John; m. Peggy A. Terrel, June 22, 1975. Mathematician rocket research Redstone Arsenal, Huntsville, Ala., 1953, U.S. Army Ballistic Research Labs., Aberdeen (Md.) Proving Grounds, 1954-56; instr. math. U. Ala., Tuscaloosa, 1954, Temple U., Phila., 1956-57; asso. scientist, research and devel. div. Avco Corp., Wilmington, Mass., 1957-59; sr. mem. tech. staff RCA, Camden, N.J., 1959-66; mgr. computer analysis and programming dept. Raytheon Co. space and information systems div., Sudbury, Mass., 1966-70, mgr. software systems lab., 1969-70, prin. engr. missiles systems div., 1970-73; mgr. systems analysis and programming GTE Govt. Systems Corp., 1973-77, mgr. software engring. Atlantic ops., 1977-82, sr. mem. tech. staff Command Control & Communications Sector, 1983-91; software systems engr. Yonda Software Systems Cons., 1991—. Pres., Milford Area Assn. Retarded Children, 1970-74; vice-chmn. fin. com. Town of Medway, 1973; bd. dirs. Blackstone Valley Mental Health and Retardation Area Bd., 1970-76; trustee Medway Libraries, 1973-82, chmn., 1974-81. Served with USAAF, 1943-46. Hon. fellow Advanced Level Telecommunications Tng. Center, New Delhi, India, 1981. Registered profl. engr. Mem. AAAS, IEEE, Math. Assn. Am., N.Y. Acad. Scis., Sigma Xi, Phi Eta Sigma, Pi Mu Epsilon (pres. Ala. chpt. 1953-54), Sigma Pi Sigma. Contbr. articles to profl. jours. Office: 12 Sunset Dr Medway MA 02053-2008

YONG, YOOK-KONG, civil engineering educator, researcher. BS, Lafayette Coll., 1979; PhD, Princeton U., 1984. Cert. engr.-in-tng. Asst. prof. Rutgers U., Piscataway, N.J., 1983-89, assoc. prof., 1989—; grad. dir. dept. civil engring. Rutgers U., Piscataway, 1992—. Mem. IEEE, ASCE, Acoustical Soc. Am., Tau Beta Pi, Chi Epsilon. Office: Rutgers U Dept Civil Engring PO Box 909 Piscataway NJ 08855-0909

YONKERS, WINIFRED FRANCES, reading specialist; b. Pitts., Sept. 30, 1939; d. Wilfred Lawrence and Mary Frances (Johnson) Haddock; m. Mervyn Leroy, Sept. 14, 1963; children: Pamela Marie, Vernon Lee. BS, U. Pitts., 1961; MA, George Washington U., 1967. Tchr. Pitts. Pub. Schs., 1961-63; tchr. Washington Pub. Schs., 1963-67, reading specialist, 1967—. Treas. Lewisdale Boys and Girls Club, Hyattsville, Md., 1981-86. Mem. Assn. for Supervision and Curriculum Devel., Internat. Reading Assn., D.C. Reading Coun., NAACP, Pi Lambda Theta (treas. 1969-71), Alpha Kappa Alpha (treas. U. Pitts. chpt. 1960-61). Democrat. Baptist. Home: 504 Maestro Ter Silver Spring MD 20901-5034 Office: 2525 17th St NW Washington DC 20009-2801

YORK, HARVEY LEFFERT, lawyer; b. Neptune, N.J., Jan. 27, 1946; s. Herman and Frances York; m. Barbara Miller, July 19, 1970; children: Michael B., David M. BA, Lehigh U., 1967; JD, Am. U., 1970. Bar: N.J. Jud. clk. Ocean County, Toms River, N.J., 1970-71; ptnr. Novins, York, DeVincens & Pentony, Toms River, 1971—; bd. dirs. Garden State Bank, Jackson, N.J.; chmn. N.J. Supreme Ct. Com. on Ethics, 1987. Pres. Ocean County United Way, Toms River, 1991—, Toms River YMCA, 1984-85; v.p. Ocean County UJA, 1984—. Named Man of Yr. Temple Beth Shalom, 1988, Citizen of Yr. Toms River YMCA, 1985; recipient Brotherhood award Nat. Conf. Christians and Jews, 1987. Mem. Kiwanis (pres. Toms River chpt. 1979-80), Toms River Country Club (pres. 1988). Jewish. Home: 460 Madison Ave Toms River NJ 08753-6725 Office: Novins York & Pentony 202 Main St CN2032 Toms River NJ 08753-7497

YORK, JAMES LESTER, research scientist; b. Peoria, Ill., Nov. 12, 1942; s. Wayne Mills and Lucy (Aupperle) Y.; m. Patricia Mary Stanton, Aug. 22, 1970; children: Benjamin, Nora. AB, Bradley U., 1965; PhD, U. Ill., Chgo., 1972. Postdoctoral trainee SUNY, Buffalo, 1972-74, rsch. assoc. prof. psychology, 1981—; rsch. scientist Rsch. Inst. on Alcoholism, Buffalo, 1974—; referee for sci. jours. Psychopharmacology, Alcohol, Alcoholism, Pharmacology, Biochemistry and Behavior, Physiology and Behavior, Behavioral Pharmacology; contbr. articles to profl. publs. Grantee Nat. Inst. Alcohol Abuse and Alcoholism, 1976, 87, 90, 91, N.Y. State Health Rsch. Coun., 1978, 80. Mem. Rsch. Soc. Alcoholism, Soc. Stimulus Properties of Drugs, Am. Soc. Pharmacology and Exptl. Therapeutics, Internat. Soc. Biomed. Rsch. on Alcoholism, Gerontology Soc. Am. Home: 783 Chestnut Hill Rd East Aurora NY 14052-2603 Office: Rsch Inst on Alcoholism 1021 Main St Buffalo NY 14203-1016

YORK, JANET BREWSTER, nurse, family and sex therapist, sculptor; b. N.Y.C., Mar. 5, 1941; d. Edward Cox and Janet Stone Brewster; AA with honors, Briarclif Coll., 1961; RN with highest honors, U. Iowa, 1965; BA summa cum laude, Marymount Manhattan Coll., 1975; MA with honors, N.Y. U., 1978; m. Albert Thompson York, Mar. 31, 1962 (dec.); children: Clifton Gaston, Torrance Brewster; 1 adopted child, Justin Brigham. Nurse, Manhattan Eye, Ear and Throat Hosp., N.Y.C., 1966-74; nurse, counselor Washington Free Clinic, 1969-71; family therapist Ackerman Family Inst., N.Y.C., 1976-80; sex therapist N.Y. Med. Coll., Flower Fifth Ave Hosp., N.Y.C., 1976-80; individual practice family and sex therapy, N.Y.C., 1978—; supervisory staff grad. edn. program in human sexuality N.Y.U. Med. Ctr., 1982—; sculptor, 1988—. Bd. dirs. Spence/Chapin Adoption Agy., Manhattan Eye, Ear and Throat Hosp. Vita fellow Internat. Coun. of Sex Edn. and Parenthood, Am. U., 1981; recipient Evelyn Monte Sculpture award, 1988, Ellsworth Howell Art Sculpture award, 1991. Mem. Am. Soc. for Sex Therapy and Research, Am. Assn. Sex Edn., Counseling and Therapy, Soc. for Sci. Study Sex, Sex Info. and Edn. Council U.S., Am. Assn. Marriage and Family Therapists. Clubs: Lawrence Beach, Rockaway Hunting, N.Y.U, Millbrook, Sandanona. Represented in permanent collection The Dog Mus. of Am., St. Louis; contbr. articles to profl. jours.; also videotape Death as a Part of Life. Home: 155 E 72d St New York NY 10021

YOSHIDA, ROLAND KIYOSHI, academic dean, special education educator; b. L.A., May 3, 1948; s. Robert and Yoshi (Kuniyuki) Y.; m. Sharon A. Stirler, Oct. 13, 1984. BA, U. So. Calif., 1970, MS, 1971, PhD, 1974. Specialist edn. program U.S. Dept. Edn., Washington, 1975-82; assoc. prof. spl. edn. Fordham U., N.Y.C., 1982-84, prof., 1985-87; prof. Queens Coll. CUNY, Flushing, 1987—, dean, 1990—. Contbr. articles to profl. jours. Fellow APA; mem. Phi Beta Kappa. Home: 429 Clinton Ave Apt 52 Brooklyn NY 11238-1663 Office: CUNY Queens Coll 65-30 Kissena Blvd Flushing NY 11367

YOSHIUCHI, ELLEN HAVEN, childbirth educator; b. Newark, Apr. 15, 1949; d. Michael Joseph and Adeline V. (Lindblom) Haven; m. Takeshi Yoshiuchi, Dec. 1, 1973; children: Teri Takumi, Niki Noboru. BA summa cum laude, CUNY, 1980; M Profl. Studies in Human Rels., N.Y. Inst. Tech., 1991. Pvt. practice childbirth edn., 1983-89; program asst. parent/family edn. St. Luke's/Roosevelt Hosp. Ctr., N.Y.C., 1989—. Editor ASPO/N.Y.C. News, 1983-86; contbr. articles to profl. jours. Mem. AACD, Internat. Childbirth Edn. Assn., Assn. Specialists in Group Work, Assn. Multicultural Counseling and Devel., Am. Soc. for Psychoprophylaxis in Obstetrics/Lamaze (cert. tchr., pres. N.Y.C. chpt. 1987-91, nominating com. 1991—, dir. ednl. program approval com. 1991—).

YOST, DAVID JOHN, electrical engineer; b. Martins Ferry, Ohio, Oct. 19, 1938; s. John Marshall and Gladys Marie (Leggett) Y.; m. Wilma Jean Fielding, Mar. 6, 1960; children: Shelly, Michael, Melinda. BSEE, Ohio State U., 1966, MSEE, 1966. Assoc. engr. applied physics lab. Johns Hopkins U., Laurel, Md., 1966-70, sr. engr. applied physics lab., 1970-73, sect. supr. applied physics lab., 1973-77, prin. profl. staff applied physics lab., 1976—, asst. group supr. applied physics lab., 1977-81, group supr. applied physics lab., 1981—. Contbr. articles to profl. jours.; inventor high angle-of-attack missile control system for aerodynamically controlled missiles. With USN, 1957-61. Mem. AIAA (sec. 1990, treas. 1991), IEEE, Soc. Automotive Engrs. (guidance and control com., chmn. B missile and space system subcom. 1987—). Home: 3405 Jennings Chapel Rd Woodbine MD 21797-7509 Office: Johns Hopkins U Applied Physics Lab Johns Hopkins Rd Laurel MD 20707

YOST, DEBORAH SPILLANE, educational consultant, learning disability specialist; b. Tulsa, Mar. 28, 1953; d. Harold Harvey and Evelyn Frances (Dube) Spillane; m. Byron Paul Yost, June 5, 1983. AA, Northwestern Conn. Coll., 1974; BA, St. Joseph Coll., 1978; MA, U. Conn., 1982, postgrad., 1992—. Asst. dir. Calvary Ch. Day Care Ctr., Suffield, Conn., 1974-76; ednl. support specialist Simsbury (Conn.) Pub. Schs., 1979-83; ednl. diagnostician Newington (Conn.) Children's Hosp., 1982; lectr. Cen. Conn. State U., New Britain, 1985-86; coll. advisor Ednl. Counseling & Placement, Inc., N.Y.C., 1983-88; ednl. cons. Frankenberger Assocs., New Haven, 1988—; grad. asst. U. Conn., Storrs, 1991-92; speaker nat. conf. Coun. Exceptional Children, Detroit, 1982; asst. U. Conn., Storrs, 1991. Mem. ACA, Orton Dyslexia Soc. (steering com. New Eng. br. 1990-91), Ind. Ednl. Cons. Assn. (program com. 1989—), Learning Disability Assn. (speaker confs. 1991), Assn. on Handicapped Student Svcs. in Postsecondary Edn., Learning Disability Network (speaker confs. 1988-92), Conn. Assn. for Children with Learning Disabilities (speaker confs. 1989-92). Office: Frankenberger Assocs 88 Prospect St New Haven CT 06511-3797

YOUMAN, ROGER JACOB, editor, writer; b. N.Y.C., Feb. 25, 1932; s. Robert Harold and Ida (Kellner) Y.; m. Lillian Frank, June 22, 1958; children: Nancy, Laura, Joshua, Andrew. B.A., Swarthmore Coll., 1953. Desk asst. CBS News, N.Y.C., 1953; program editor TV Guide, N.Y.C., 1956; regional editor TV Guide, Memphis, 1956-57, Houston, 1957; asst. programming editor TV Guide, N.Y.C., 1957-60; assoc. editor TV Guide, Radnor, Pa., 1960-65, asst. mng. editor, 1965-72, mng. editor, 1972-76, exec. editor, 1976-79, 80-81, co-editor, 1981-90, editor, 1990—; editor Panorama, 1979-80; del. U.S.-Soviet Bilateral Info. Talks, 1988, 90. Author: (with Arthur Shulman) How Sweet It Was, 1966, The Television Years, 1973; contbr. articles to various publs. Served with AUS, 1954-55. Mem. NATAS, Am. Soc. Mag. Editors. Home: 752 Mancill Rd Wayne PA 19087-2043 Office: TV Guide 4 Corporate Ctr Radnor PA 19087

YOUNG, A. THOMAS, defense, aerospace, energy and information systems company executive; b. Wachapreague, Va., Apr. 19, 1938; s. William Thomas and Margaret (Colonna) Y.; m. Page Carter Hayden, June 24, 1961; children: Anne Blair, Thomas Carter. BMechE, B in Aero. Engring., U. Va., 1961; M in Mgmt., MIT, 1972. Designer Newport News (Va.) Shipbldg. & Drycock Co., 1961; with NASA, 1961-82; various positions Langley Research Ctr., Hampton, Va., 1961-69; staff mem. and mission dir. Viking Project Hampton, 1969-76; dir. Hdqrs. Planetary Program Washington, 1976-79; dep. dir. Ames Research Ctr., Moffett Field, Calif., 1979-80; dir. Goddard Space Flight Ctr., Greenbelt, Md., 1980-82; with Martin Marietta Corp., 1982—; v.p. aerospace rsch. and engring. Bethesda, Md., 1982-83; v.p., gen. mgr. Balt. Aerospace, 1983-84, pres., 1984-85; exec. v.p., then. pres. Orlando (Fla.) Aerospace, 1985-87; pres. Electronics & Missiles Group, Orlando, 1987-89; sr. exec. v.p. Martin Marietta Corp., 1989-90, pres., chief operating officer, 1990—; bd. dirs. Cooper Industries, Inc., Dial Corp.; chmn. Gov.'s Space Commn., Tallahassee, Fla., 1987-88. Bd. dirs. Va. Engring. Found. of U. Va. Sch. Engring. and Applied Scis.; prin. Ctr. for Excellence in Govt., Washington, 1987; trustee U. Cen. Fla., 1987-89; mem. Orange County (Fla.) Sch. Bd. Found., 1987-89. Sloan fellow MIT, 1971-72; decorated DSM Viking Project NASA, 1977; recipient Outstanding Leadership medal Voyager Program NASA, 1980, Meritorious Exec. Presdl. Rank award Pres. Jimmy Carter, 1980, Disting. Exec. award Pres. Ronald Reagan, 1981. Fellow AIAA, Am. Astronautical Soc.; mem. Nat. Assn. Engrs. Republican. Methodist. Office: Martin Marietta Corp 6801 Rockledge Dr Bethesda MD 20817-1836

YOUNG, ALLEN, public relations executive; b. Liberty, N.Y., June 30, 1941; s. Louis and Rae (Goldfarb) Y. AB, Columbia U., 1962, MS, 1964; MA, Stanford U., 1963. Reporter Middletown (N.Y.) Times-Herald-Record, 1963; freelance writer S.Am., 1964-67; tchr. Escola Americana, Rio de Janiero, 1966-67; mem. staff Liberation News Svc., N.Y.C., 1967-70; freelance writer N.Y.C., and Mass., 1970-79; reporter, asst. editor Athol (Mass.) Daily News, 1979-89; pub. rels. dir. Athol Meml. Hosp., 1989—; bd. dirs. Mt. Grace Land Conservation Trust. Author: Allen Ginsberg: Gay Sunshine Interview, 1981, Gays Under the Cuban Revolution, 1981, North of Quabbin: A Guide to Nine Massachusetts Towns, 1983; (with Karla Jay) The Gay Report, 1978; editor: More Than Sand and Sea: Images of Cape Cod, 1984, The Millers River Reader, 1988; (with Jay) Out of the Closests, 1972, (with others) After You're Out, 1974, Lavender Cultures, 1977. Mem. Royalston (Mass.) Conservation Commn., 1976-77, 92—, Royalston Bd. Health, 1978-80; chmn. Royalston Zoning Bd. Appeals, 1989—. Fulbright scholar, 1964-65; recipient scholarship Inter.-Am. Press Assn., 1965-66. Home: RR 2 Butterworth Rd Orange MA 01364 Office: Athol Meml Hosp 2033 Main St Athol MA 01331-3598

YOUNG, ANDERSON BRIGGS, park and recreation educator, administrator; b. Rochester, N.Y., Dec. 2, 1949; s. Lawrence E. and Annette (Briggs) Y.; m. Mary Susan Quinby, July 28, 1990. BA, Ohio Wesleyan U., 1971; MDiv, Union Theol. Sem., N.Y.C., 1975; PhD, Ohio State U., 1981.

Living learning programs coord. Capital Univ., Columbus, Ohio, 1976-79; teaching assoc. Ohio State Univ., 1979-81; asst. prof. SUNY Coll., Cortland, N.Y., 1981-84; assoc. prof. SUNY Coll., 1984-88, prof., 1988—, recreation & leisure studies dept. chair, 1985—; bd. chair Coalition for Edn. in Outdoors, Cortland, 1987—; trustee Ohio WesleyanUniv., Delaware, 1971-74, 83-86; mem. Curriculum Adv. Bd., Tompkins-Cortland Community Coll., Dryden, N.Y., 1986—. Contbr. over 20 articles to profl. pubs.; assoc. editor Schole Jour., 1989—.; presenter over 50 profl. meetings, 1981—. Dir. Ohio Wesleyan Univ. Alumni, 1975-81. Mem. Nat. Coun. on Outdoor Edn. (chair 1987-88), Soc. of Park & Recreation Educators, Nat. Recreation & Park Assn., Am. Assn. for Leisure and Recreation (com. chair 1989-91), NYS Outdoor Edn. Assn. Nat. Parks & Conservation Assn., Phi KappaPhi (chpt. treas. 1983-85). Democrat. Home: 561 Lime Hollow Rd Cortland NY 13045-9346 Office: SUNY Coll Park Center Cortland NY 13045

YOUNG, CORNELIUS BRYANT, JR. (C. B. YOUNG), electronics engineer; b. Sardis, Miss., Sept. 2, 1926; s. Cornelius Bryant Sr. and Ethel (Dorr) Y.; m. Marguerite Esther Grosso, May 27, 1950; children: Mark Joseph, Roy Neil, Annette Georgette, Neil Bryant. BEE, Ga. Inst. Tech., 1948; MEE, Bklyn. Poly. Inst., 1954; MS in Computer Sci., Stevens Inst. Tech., 1981. From jr. engr. to dir. applications engring. Western Union, N.Y.C., Upper Saddle River, N.J., 1948-84; sr. engring. specialist ITT Fed. Electric Corp., Paramus, N.J., 1985-89; mgr. commns. and comptrs. The BARC Group, Totawa, N.J., 1990—; cons. C2 Systems Engrings., Ramsey, N.J., 1990—. Contbr. articles to profl. jours.; inventor microwave lens. Pres. Ramsey (N.J.) Ambulance Corps., 1987-89, 90-91; chmn. Ramapo Valley ARC, Ramsey, 1987-88; chmn. troop 31, Boy Scouts of Am., Ramsey, 1968-76; vol. emergency room Valley Hosp., Ridgewood, N.J., 1980—; mem. Ramsey Bd. Health, 1987—, Soc. of Valley Hosp., 1990—; vol. FISH Network, N.W. Bergen County, 1970—. Lt. (j.g.) USNR, 1944-46, with res. 46-64, ret., 1964. Recipient Citizen of Yr. award Troop 31 Boy Scouts of Am., 1987. Mem. IEEE (life, sr.), Assn. for Computing Machinery, Sigma XI (assoc.). Republican. Baptist. Home: 68 Deer Trl Ramsey NJ 07446-2110

YOUNG, DAVID MAYNARD, performing arts organization administrator, theater arts educator, director; b. N.Y.C., May 1, 1928; s. Irving and Mildred (Burns) Y.; m. Faith Barrett, Jan. 10, 1961 (div. 1969); m. Elizabeth Adams, May 22, 1986; children: Michael Charles, Melissa Constance. PhD, Columbia Pacific U. Profl. stage and TV actor NBC's Medallion Theatre, N.Y.C.; producing dir. John F. Kennedy Ctr. for Performing Arts (Am. Coll. Theatre Festival), Washington; tchr. Nat. Conservatory Dramatic Arts, Washington, Smithsonian Instn. Author: Audience Development and Services; contbr. articls to profl. jours. Fellow Coll. Am. Theatre; mem. Am. Community Theatre Assn. (past pres.), Soc. Stage Dirs. and Choreographers, Actors Equity Assn., Assn. for Theatre in Higher Edn. Home: 1249 Derbyshire Rd Rockville MD 20854-6160 Office: Am Coll Theatre Festival Kennedy Ctr Washington DC 20566

YOUNG, DAVID WILLIAM, accounting educator; b. L.A., Feb. 8, 1942; s. William Albert and Hilda Mary (Cook) Y.; m. Ernestine M.L. Van Schaik, Oct. 4, 1968 (div. 1975); m. Francesca Michela Larson, Jan. 28, 1984; children: Christian William, Anthony Edwin. BA, Occidental Coll., 1963; MA, UCLA, 1966; D in Bus. Adminstrn., Harvard U., 1977. Systems engr. IBM, Glendale, Calif., 1963-64; asst. to pres. Lundberg Survey, Inc., Hollywood, Calif., 1964-66; program economist U.S. Agy. Internat. Devel., El Salvador, 1966-69; cons. Thomas Goldsmith & Assoc., Cambridge, Mass., 1969-71; pres. Commonwealth Mgmt. Systems, Cambridge, 1971—; assoc. prof. mgmt. Harvard U. Sch. Pub. Health, Boston, 1976-85; prof. acctg. and control Boston U. Sch. Mgmt., 1985—, chmn. dept. acctg., 1986-91, dir. acctg. MBA program, dir. Inst. Acctg. Rsch. and Edn., 1989—, dir. health care mgmt. program, 1991—; cons. Ctr. for Health Policy Studies Georgetown U., 1988—; vis. prof. mgmt. control Instituto de Estudios Superiores de la Empresa, Barcelona, Spain, 1984. Author: The Managerial Process in Human Service Agencies, 1979, Financial Control in Health Care, 1984, The Hospital Power Equilibrium, 1985, Management Control in Nonprofit Organizations, 1984, 88; contbr. articles to profl. jours. Trustee Mass Eye & Ear Infirmary, Boston, 1989—, Art Inst. Boston, 1990—. Milton Fund fellow Harvard Med. Sch., 1984. Mem. Am. Acctg. Assn., Am. Econ. Assn. Democrat. Office: Boston U Sch Mgmt 704 Commonwealth Ave Boston MA 02215-2404

YOUNG, DEBORAH NELSON, account representative; b. Camden, N.J., July 24, 1961; d. J. Bruce and Joyce H. (Kolody) N. BA, Rutgers U., 1984. Dir. ops. Campus Vacations Assns., Bklyn., 1981-85; asst. mgr. Haddon Travel, Voorhees, N.J., 1985-88; account mgr. Xerox Corp., Marlton, N.J., 1988—; mem. Xerox Community Involvement Program, Marlton, 1988—. Home: 42 Broadacre Dr Mount Laurel NJ 08054

YOUNG, DELANO VICTOR, cell biologist; b. Honolulu, Nov. 17, 1945; s. Lum Fai and Gladys Sau Pung (Wong) Y.; m. Chin-Yi Caroline Yang, Jan. 31, 1970; 1 child, Heather Tien. BS, Stanford U., 1967; PhD, Columbia U., 1973. Postdoctoral fellow Salk Inst. for Biol. Studies, San Diego, 1973-75; asst. prof. dept. chemistry Boston U., 1975-83; asst. dir. Bioassay Systems Rsch. Corp., Woburn, Mass., 1984-86; sr. scientist Damon Biotech, Inc., Needham Heights, Mass., 1986-88, dir., 1988-90; head cell biology Abbott Biotech, Inc. (formerly Damon Biotech, Inc.), Needham Heights, 1990—; group leader tissue culture Transkaryotic Therapies, Inc., Cambridge, Mass., 1992—; cons. D. Van Nostrand Pub., Boston, 1975-83, Allyn and Bacon Pub., Boston, 1975-83; reviewer Sci. Jour. in Biochemistry, 1973—. Author: (chpt.) Inverted Microcarriers: Using Microencapsulation to Grow Anchorage-Dependent Cells, 1991; contbr. over 20 articles to profl. jours. Eugene Higgins fellow Columbia U., 1967-68, Jane Coffin Childs fellow Salk Inst., 1973-75; GM scholar Stanford U., 1963-67. Mem. AAAS, Am. Soc. Cell Biology, Am. Soc. Biochemistry and Molecular Biology, Am. Chem. Soc. (biochem. tech. div.), N.Y. Acad. Scis., Sigma Xi, Phi Beta Kappa, Phi Lambda Upsilon. Roman Catholic. Home: 12 Dennis Rd Wellesley MA 02181-1616 Office: Transkaryotic Therapies Inc 195 Albany St Cambridge MA 02139

YOUNG, DONALD RICHARD, writer, photographer; b. Indpls., June 29, 1933; s. Thomas Fay and Lucile (Boston) Y. BA, Ind. U., 1955; MA, Butler U., 1964. Copy editor Indpls. Star, 1955-56, 58-63; staff editor, sr. editor Encyclopedia Americana, N.Y.C., 1963-77; free-lance editor, writer, photographer N.Y.C., 1977—. Author: American Roulette: The History and Dilemma of the Vice Presidency, 1965, 74, Natural Monuments of America, 1990, Historic Monuments of America; author, photographer: The Great American Desert, 1980; co-author: The Sierra Club Book of Our National Parks, 1990; editor: Adventure in Politics: The Memoirs of Philip LaFollette, 1970, The Sierra Club Guides to the National Parks, Vols. 3, 4, 5, 1984-86; contbr. articles and photographs to many publs. With U.S. Army, 1956-58. Mem. Sierra Club (chmn. N.Y. chpt. 1991—). Republican. Home and Office: 166 E 61st St New York NY 10021-8509

YOUNG, DONALD ROY, pharmacist; b. Belfast, Pa., Oct. 7, 1935; s. Roy Clifford and Gladys Nicholas (Ealer) Y.; m. Joyce Anne Waldridge; children: Donald, Lynda, David. BS in Pharmacy, U. Md., Balt., 1957. Pharmacist Brookside Rhodes Drugs Co., Newark, Del., 1956-57; pharmacist, mgr. Newark Rhodes Drugs Co., 1957-64; pharmacist, owner, mgr. Hudson's Pharmacy, St. Michaels, Md., 1964—; bd. dirs., officer St. Michaels Bank; treas. Calvert Drug Co. Balt., 1970-76. Pres. St. Michaels Improvement Corp., 1966—. Mem. Nat. Assn. Retail Druggists, Ea. Shore Pharm. Assn. (pres. 1967-68, 82-86), Talbot County C. of C. (Outstanding Small Bus. Man of Yr. award 1989), St. Michaels Bus. Assn. (pres.), U. Md. Sch. Pharmacy Alumni Assn. (life), Isaac Walton League, Miles River Yacht Club, Rotary (pres. St. Michaels 1970, Most Outstanding Mem. award 1988), Elks, Masons (32 degree, master 1969-70, apptd. jr. grand deacon of Grand Line 1989-90). Republican. Methodist. Home: 8118 Tricefields Rd PO Box 130 Saint Michaels MD 21663 Office: Hudson's Pharmacy PO Box 130 Saint Michaels MD 21663

YOUNG, DOUGLAS ALAN, physiologist, research scientist; b. Mpls., Sept. 1, 1955; s. LeRoy and Lovie (Jackson) Y.; m. Leslie Henderson, Aug. 9, 1980; children: Paige, Blair. BA, St. Olaf Coll., 1977; PhD, Washington U., 1983. Postdoctoral fellow Washington U. Med. Sch., St. Louis, 1983-86, rsch. asst. prof., 1986-87; asst. fellow Sandoz Rsch. Inst., Sandoz Phram. Corp., East Hanover, N.J., 1987-89, assoc. fellow, 1989-91, sr. assoc. fellow, 1991-92, fellow, sect. head, 1992—. Contbr. over 25 sci. articles to profl. jours. Recipient Feasibility award Am. Diabetes Assn., 1986. Mem. AAAS, Am. Diabetes Assn., Am. Physiol. Soc. Office: Sandoz Pharms 59 Rte 10 East Hanover NJ 07936

YOUNG, DOUGLAS EARLE, systems programmer; b. Cleve., Oct. 23, 1957; s. Bruce Cully and Joan McKenzie Y.; m. Bernadette Marie Bertoty, May 17, 1986; children: Catherine, Colette. BS, W.Va. Wesleyan Coll., 1980; MBA in Info., George Washington U., 1990. Asst. store mgr. F. W. Woolworth, Pitts., 1980-81; asst. sales mgr. Original Arts Co., Pitts., 1981-82; operation support analyst Genix, Pitts., 1983-85; programmer analyst Pepco, Washington, 1985-89, systems programmer, 1989-91; systems programmer Computer Task Group, Washington, 1991—. Mem. KC (youth chmn. Dale City, Va. 1990, Knight of Month Dec., 1990), Beta Gamma Sigma, Phi Sigma Epsilon. Republican. Roman Catholic. Home: 4240 Jonathan Ct Dumfries VA 22026-1130 Office: CT6 1120 Vermont Ave NW Washington DC 20003

YOUNG, EDMOND GROVE, consultant; b. Govans, Md., Oct. 29, 1917; s. Robert E. Lee and Lottie Gertrude (Grove) Y.; m. Jean Elizabeth Auwetter, Sept. 14, 1946; children: Stephen Edmond, Janet Louise Russell, Timothy Alan. BS, U. Md., 1938, PhD, 1943. Chemist Sharples Chems., Wyandotte, Mich., 1943-44; rsch. chemist E.I. DuPont de Nemours & Co., Wilmington, Del., 1944-48, tech. sales rep., 1948-50, mgr. propellant sales, 1950-52, mgr. sales devel., 1952-57, mgr. devel. confs., 1957-68, from mgr. devel. confs., govt. liaison to mgr. bus. devel., 1968-82; cons. NASA, Washington, 1983-85, Jet Propulsion Lab., Pasadena, Calif., 1985-88, U. Del., Newark, 1988—. Chmn. East Greenwich Bd. Zoning Adjustment, Clarksboro, N.J., 1974—. Recipient Silver Medal for Outstanding Svc., Am. Def. Preparedness Assn., 1984. Fellow AAAS; mem. Am. Chem. Soc., Comml. Devel. Assn., Soc. of the Sigma Xi, Phi Kappa Phi, Alpha Chi Sigma. Republican. Methodist. Home and Office: PO Box 67 Mickleton NJ 08056-0067

YOUNG, ELAINE CLAIRE, communications company executive; b. N.Y.C., May 21, 1931; d. Solomon and Anna (Rosenberg) Frumberg; m. Abraham R. Young, Feb. 9, 1958; children: Jeffrey Charles, Benjamin Joseph. BA, Queens Coll., 1952; MS, SUNY, New Paltz, 1960. Cert. elem. tchr., elem. edn. supr., N.Y. Tchr. Bayshore (N.Y.) Elem. Sch., 1952-55, Scarsdale (N.Y.) Sch. Dist., 1956-62; asst. prof. SUNY, New Paltz, 1955-56; resource tchr. Harrison (N.Y.) Cen. Sch. Dist., 1970-72, tchr., 1972-88; producer, moderator Westchester Classroom, Sta. WFAS, White Plains, N.Y., 1980—; owner, mgr. Young Communications, Purchase, N.Y., 1988—; juror Am. Children's TV Festival, 1989, The 1989 Ollie awards, Chgo. Author: I Am a Blade of Grass, 1989. Mem. Congresswoman Nita Lowey's Ednl. Adv. Bd., 1989—; design team mem. Mid-City/Young Minds Project, L.A., 1992. Recipient Svc. Above Self award Rotary Club, Hartsdale, N.Y., 1980. Mem. Am. Fedn. Tchrs., Harrison Assn. Tchrs. Jewish. Home and Office: 178 Duxbury Rd Purchase NY 10577

YOUNG, ELIZABETH BELL, consultant; b. Franklinton, N.C., July 2, 1929; d. Joseph H. and Eulalia V. (Miller) B.; m. Charles A. Young, Nov. 27, 1964. BA, N.C. Cen. U., 1948, MA, 1950; PhD, Ohio State U., 1959. Cert. speech pathologist; cert. audiologist. Chairperson dept. English Barber Scotia Coll., Concord, N.C., 1949-52; dir. speech area, prof. Talladega (Ala.) Coll., 1954-56; dir. speech clinic, prof. Va. State U., Petersburg, 1956-57; prof. Fla. A&M U., Tallahassee, 1959; chmn. dept. English Fayetteville (N.C.) State U., 1959-63; speech pathologist, rsch. asst. Howard U. Sch. Dentistry, Washington, 1963-64; prof., chairperson dept. English U. Md.-East Shore, Princess Anne, Md., 1965-66; prof., supr. Speech Clinic Cath. U. Am., Washington, 1966-79; congl. staff aide U.S. Ho. of Reps., Washington, 1981-82, 88-90; prof. speech U. D.C., Washington, 1983-84; cons. nat. and local orgns. Washington, 1985-88, 90—; lectr. over 250 speeches, seminars and workshops; speechwriter, cons. Nat. Assn. Equal Opportunity in Higher Edn., Washington, 1990. Contbr. articles to profl. jours. Fundraiser, pub. rels. polit. candidates, 1963-90; mem. bd. United Negro Coll. Fund, 1970-80, D.C. Gen. Hosp. Handicapped Intervention Program, 1970-91. Recipient Citations and Certs. of Achievement community and nat. orgns., 1959-90. Fellow Am. Speech-Lang.-Hearing Assn.; mem. Pub. Mems. Assn. (bd. mem. 1980-91), Ohio State U. Alumni Assn., N.C. Cen. U. Alumni Assn. Democrat. Baptist.

YOUNG, FRANKLIN, nutritional biochemistry educator, researcher; b. Beijing, China, Feb. 1, 1928; came to U.S., 1950, naturalized, 1967; s. An-drew On-Yin and Helen (Loh) Y.; m. Kathlina Patanella. Student U. Shanghai, 1946-48; A.B., Mercer U., 1951; B.S., U. Fla., 1952, M. Agr., 1954, Ph.D., 1960. Grad. research fellow U. Fla., Gainesville, 1958-60; post doctoral research fellow, 1960-61; research assoc. Bowman Gray Sch. Medicine, Winston-Salem, N.C., 1961-65, research instr., 1965-66; assoc. prof. U. Hawaii, Honolulu, 1968-83; prof. nutritional biochemistry, chmn. and researcher cardiovascular diseases and hypertension U. Utah, Salt Lake City, 1983-85; prof. nutritional biochemistry West Chester U., Pa., 1985—. Contbr. articles to profl. jours. Mem. Am. Inst. Nutrition, Sigma Xi, Gamma Sigma Delta (charter mem., treas. 1970-71), Phi Kappa Phi, Phi Sigma. Office: West Chester U Dept Health West Chester PA 19383

YOUNG, FREDERICK JOHN, electrical engineering executive, consultant; b. Buffalo, May 19, 1931; s. Frederick J. Young and Mary (Nichol) Brown; m. Beverly Mae Hall, June 5, 1954; children: John Frederick, James Richard, Jeffrey Karl. BS, Carnegie Inst. Tech., 1953, MS, 1954, PhD, 1956. Registered profl. engr., land surveyor, Pa. Asst. prof. elec. engring. Carnegie Inst. Tech., Pitts., 1956-60, assoc. prof. elec. engring., 1960-65, prof. elec. engring., 1965-71; cons. Westinghouse Rsch. Lab., Pitts., 1957-83, DuPont Corp., Wilmington, Del., 1983—; pres. Frontier Tech., Inc., Bradford, Pa., 1976—. 2d tubist Pitts. Symphony, 1950-72; inventor, builder full double tuba, 1990; contbr. articles to profl. jours. Scoutmaster Allegheny Trails coun. Boy Scouts Am., 1968—; mem. SO2 subcom. of adv. com. Allegheny County Pollution Control Bd., 1970—; intervenor for Group Against Smog and Pollution. Grantee NSF, Ford Found., NASA; recipient Engring. Accomplishment award DuPont Corp., Wilmington, Del., 1989. Mem. IEEE (guest editor proc. 1968, chmn. Allegheny Mountain sect., 1989—), Acoustical Soc. Am., Am. Astronautical Soc., Am. Soc. Engring. Edn., AAUP, Sigma Xi, Phi Kappa Phi, Phi Mu Alpha Sinfonia, Alpha Tau Omega, Beta Theta Pi, Eta Kappa Nu. Home and Office: Frontier Tech Inc 800 Minard Run Rd Bradford PA 16701-3718

YOUNG, GENEVIEVE MARIE, lawyer; b. Rochester, N.Y., May 17, 1963; d. David Valentine and Martha Helen (Sullivan) Y. BA, Wellesley Coll., 1985; JD, Georgetown U., 1989; student, Oxford U., Eng., 1983-84. Law clk. Fed. Judicial Ctr., Washington, 1987-88; assoc. Reed Smith Shaw & McClay, Washington, 1989—. Republican. Roman Catholic. Office: Reed Smith Shaw & McClay 1200 18th St NW Ste 1000 Washington DC 20036-2596

YOUNG, GLENN, publisher; b. Chgo., Jan. 28, 1953; s. Michael K. and Julie (Reppert) Y. BA, Yale U., 1975, MFA, 1977; PhD, CUNY, 1982. Prof. NYU, N.Y.C., 1979-80, Wesleyan U., Middletown, Conn., 1980-85, Columbia U., N.Y.C., 1985—; publisher Applause Theatre Books, N.Y.C., 1980—. Office: Applause 211 W 71st St New York NY 10023-3766

YOUNG, HOBART PEYTON, economist, educator; b. Evanston, Ill., Mar. 9, 1945; s. Hobart Paul and Louise (Buchwalter) Y.; m. Fernanda Toueg, Mar. 27, 1982; children: Hobart Patrick, Benjamin Morris Chandler. BA, Harvard Coll., 1966; PhD, U. Mich., 1970. Econ. Nat. Water Commn., Arlington, Va., 1971; from asst. to assoc. prof. CUNY, 1971-75; rsch. scholar, dep. chmn. systems and decision scis. Internat. Inst. for Applied Systems Analysis, Laxenburg, Austria, 1975-81; prof. pub. policy U. Md., College Park, 1981—. Author: Fair Representation, 1982; editor: Cost Allocation, 1985, Fair Allocation, 1985, Negotiation Analysis, 1991, Games and Economic Behavior, 1989—, Social Choice and Welfare, 1990—. NSF grantee, 1975-86, Office Naval Rsch. grantee, 1986-89, Russell Sage Found. grantee, 1989-91; Erskine Fellow in Econs., 1990; recipient Lester R. Ford award Math. Assn. Am., 1976. Mem. Am. Econ. Assn., Am. Polit. Sci. Assn., Econometric Soc., Ops. Rsch. Soc. Am., Internat. Inst. for Applied Systems Analysis (U.S. adv. com.), Cosmos Club. Episcopalian. Office: U Md Sch Pub Affairs College Park MD 20742

YOUNG, IRVING GUSTAV, chemist; b. Bklyn., Dec. 10, 1919; s. Morris and Rebecca (Besner) Yarmush; m. Rosalyn Shanken, Oct. 4, 1941; children: Arlene Linda, Jeffrey Michael. BS, CCNY, 1939; MS, Poly. Inst. of Bklyn., 1950; PhD, Temple U., 1967. Rsch. asst. Bellevue Hosp., N.Y.C., 1939-42; asst. chemist Picatinny Arsenal, Dover, N.J., 1942-44; battery engr. U.S. Electric Mfg. Co., N.Y.C., 1944-51; sr. rsch. chemist Internat. Resistance Co., Phila., 1951-56; chief chemist Transition Metals and Chems., Wallkill, N.Y., 1956-57; asst. rsch. scientist Leeds and Northrup, North Wales, Pa., 1957-59; sr. rsch. scientist Internat. Resistance Co., Phila., 1959-64; rsch. fellow Temple U., Phila., 1964-65; sr. prin. chemist Honeywell Inc., Ft. Washington, 1965-76; program mgr. Solar and Nuclear Standards, N.Y.C., 1976-83. Co-author: Systems Approach to Air Pollution Control, 1974; contbr. articles to profl. jours. Mem. Phi Beta Kappa, Sigma Xi. Home: 22 Four Leaf Rd Levittown PA 19056-1923

YOUNG, JEFFREY THOMAS, economics educator; b. Madison, Wis., Apr. 21, 1948; s. William Henry and Sara Elizabeth (Reish) Y.; m. Cheryl Eileen Merrifield, Aug. 23, 1969; children: Christopher, Janet. BA, U. Maine, 1971; PhD, U. Colo., 1975. Vis. asst. prof. U. Colo., Denver, 1975-76; asst. prof. Marshall U., Huntington, W.Va., 1976-80; asst. prof. econs. St. Lawrence U., Canton, N.Y., 1980-85, assoc. prof., 1985-91, prof., 1991—. Author: Classical Theories of Value, 1978; contbr. articles to profl. jours. Deacon Calvary Bapt. Ch., Canton, 1984-86, Christian Fellowship Ctr., Madrid, N.Y., 1991—. Mem. Am. Econs. Assn., History of Econs. Soc., Assn. for Social Econs., Assn. of Christian Economists. Office: St Lawrence U Dept Econs Canton NY 13617

YOUNG, JOHN DING-E, medical researcher, petrochemical executive; b. Taipei, Taiwan, Dec. 27, 1958; came to the U.S., 1980; s. Tsen Men and Pei Lan (Liv) Y.; m. Susan Ruey-Hwa Wang, July 20, 1985; children: Lena, David. MD, Nat. U. Brasilia, Brazil, 1979; PhD, Rockefeller U., 1983. Intern Nat. U. Brazil, 1979-80; postdoctoral fellow Rockefeller U., N.Y.C., 1983-85, scholar, asst. prof., 1985-90, head lab., 1991—; exec. v.p. Inteplast Corp., Livingston, N.J., 1991—; bd. dirs. Polymer S.A., Cartagena, Colombia; mem. adv. coun. NIH, Bethesda, Md., 1989—; investigator Cancer Rsch. Inst., 1987-90. Adv. editor: Jour. Experimental Medicine, 1990—; contbr. articles to profl. jours.; patentee in field. Lucille P. Markey scholar, 1985-91, Leukemia Soc. Am. scholar, 1991—; Jane Coffin Childs fellow, 1983-85; named Corp. Citizen City of Wharton, Tex., 1990. Home: 890 S Orange Ave Short Hills NJ 07078-1729 Office: Rockefeller U 1230 York Ave New York NY 10021-6341

YOUNG, JOHN KARL, anatomist, educator; b. Mpls., Aug. 15, 1951; s. Lloyd William and Pearl Johanna (Newstrom) Y.; m. Paula Jean Spesock, July 2, 1977; children: Michael Christian, Matthew Thomas. Student, U. So. Calif., L.A., 1968; BS, Cornell U., 1972; PhD, UCLA, 1977. Postdoctoral fellow U. Minn., Mpls., 1977-79; asst. prof. Howard U., Washington, 1979-85, assoc. prof., 1985—. Author: Cells, 1990; contbr. articles to profl. jours. Mem. Am. Assn. Anatomists, Am. Physiol. Assn. Office: Howard U Dept Anatomy 520 W St NW Washington DC 20059-0001

YOUNG, JOHN LANE, history educator; b. Phila., May 11, 1930; s. Charles Nelson and Eva Elda (Lane) Y. BA, U. Tex., 1951; DB, U. Chgo., 1954; MS in Libr. Sci., Columbia U., 1957, PhD, 1970. Ref. libr. Union Theol. Sem., N.Y.C., 1961-67; asst. and assoc. prof. Jersey City State Coll., 1970—; dir. Humanities Media Ctr. N.J., Jersey City, 1989—. Author: American Reference Genealogy, 2d edit., 1986, College Families of Early New England, 1990. Trustee A.J. Muste Meml. Inst., N.Y.C., 1981-84, N.Y. Quar. Meeting, N.Y.C., 1991—; bd. mem. Friends Sem., N.Y.C., 1990—. Pres. fellow Columbia U., N.Y.C., 1966. Mem. Union Concerned Scientists, Planned Parenthood Fedn., N.Y. Geneal. and Biog. Soc. (life). Office: Jersey City State Coll 2039 Kennedy Blvd Jersey City NJ 07305

YOUNG, JOHN LEONARD, psychiatrist, educator; b. Huntington, Ind., Apr. 26, 1943; s. Jay Alfred and Anne Elizabeth (Neff) Y. BA, Stonehill Coll., 1966; ThM, U. Notre Dame, 1970, MS, 1974; MD, Stanford U., 1977. Diplomate Am. Bd. Psychiatry and Neurology; joined Congregation of Holy Cross, ordained priest Roman Cath. Ch., 1971. Resident in medicine Norwalk (Conn.) Hosp., 1977-78; resident in psychiatry Yale U. Med. Sch., New Haven, 1978-81, postdoctoral fellow, 1981-82, asst. prof. psychiatry, 1982-88, asst. clin. prof., 1989—; unit chief Whiting Forensic Inst., Middletown, Conn., 1988—; supr. Pastoral Ctr., New Haven, 1979-86; mem. ethics com. Hosp. of St. Raphael, New Haven, 1982—; jour. reviewer Hosp. and Community Psychiatry, 1988—. Contbr. articles to med. jours. Trustee Stonehill Coll., North Easton, Mass., 1972—; bd. dirs. King's Coll., Wilkes-Barre, Pa., 1983—, Hill Health Ctr., New Haven, 1983-85; cons. law revision com. Conn. Ho. of Reps., Hartford, 1983-85. Recipient President's medal Stonehill Coll., 1980; Stanford U. Med. Alumni Assn. scholar, 1976. Mem. Am. Psychiat. Assn., Am. Acad. Psychiatry and Law, Am. Chem. Soc., Assn. for Clin. Pastoral Edn., Soc. for Sci. Study Religion. Home: 203 Maple St New Haven CT 06511-4048 Office: Whiting Forensic Inst PO Box 70 Middletown CT 06457-0070

YOUNG, JOSEPH H., federal judge; b. Hagerstown, Md., July 18, 1922; s. J. Edgar and Mabel K. (Koser) Y.; m. Doris Oliver, Sept. 6, 1947; children: Stephen A., William O., J. Harrison. A.B., Dartmouth Coll., 1948; LL.B., U. Va., 1951. Bar: Md. 1951. Assoc. firm Marbury Miller & Evans, Balt., 1951-52; assoc. firm Piper & Marbury, Balt., 1952-58, ptnr., 1958-68, mng. ptnr., 1968-71; judge U.S. Dist. Ct. Md., from 1971, now sr. judge; instr. Johns Hopkins U. (McCoy Coll.), 1954-62. Bd. dirs. Legal Aid Soc. Balt., 1958-71, CICHA (Health Appeal), 1964-71; bd. dirs. exec. com. Md. div. Am. Cancer Soc., 1958—, chmn. div. bd. dirs. 1969-71, bd. dirs. 1966—, chmn. nat. svcs. com. 1970-73, chmn. exec. com. 1976-77, dir.-at-large 1973-83, vice-chmn. nat. bd. dirs. 1975-77, chmn. nat. bd. 1977-80, chmn. pub. issues com. 1981-83, past officer dir. 1983-90, hon. life mem. 1990—, chmn. world-wide fight com. 1987-90, also mem. trust adv. bd.; mem. oncology adv. coun. Johns Hopkins U.; chmn. com. on campaign orgn. & pub. edn. Internat. Union Coaha Cancer, Geneva, Switzerland, 1981-90, mem. fin. com., 1990—. Decorated Bronze Star, Purple Heart. Recipient Disting. Service Award Am. Cancer Soc., 1983; Dartmouth Coll. Alumni award, 1983; James Ewing Soc. award, 1983. Mem. 4th Circuit Jud. Conf., Assn. Alumni Dartmouth Coll. (pres. 1984-85). Republican. Presbyterian (elder, deacon, trustee). Clubs: Hamilton Street, Rule Day, Lawyers Round Table. Office: US Dist Ct 101 W Lombard St Baltimore MD 21201-2626

YOUNG, JOSEPH LESLIE, psychologist, government official; b. Chgo., July 26, 1940; s. Harry Israel and Rena (Lipschitz) Y; m. Leila Rosen, Dec. 27, 1964 (dec. Mar. 1986); children: Michal, Avigayl; m. Ina Weinstein Halperin, Mar. 19, 1988. BA, Yale U., 1962; PhD, Stanford U., 1966. Asst. prof. psychology SUNY, Stony Brook, 1966-72; asst. dir. personnel and tng. research programs Office of Naval Research, Arlington, Va., 1972-76; program dir. for human cognition and perception NSF, Washington, 1976—. Contrb. articles to profl. jours. Recipient various acad. awards and grad. fellowships. Mem. AAAS, Am. Psychol. Assn., Am. Psychol. Soc., Ea. Psychol. Assn., Psychonomic Soc., Am. Ednl. Rsch. Assn., Soc. Math. Psychology, Soc. for Computers in Psychology, Cognitive Sci. Soc., Sigma Xi. Jewish. Office: Human Cognition/Perception NSF Washington DC 20550

YOUNG, LEONARD JOSEPH, SR., retired vocational education educator; b. Wilmington, Del., May 25, 1920; s. William Sampson and Alethia Beatrice (Cooper) Y.; m. Vivian Leonora Bridgeforth, Sept. 26, 1942; 1 child, Leonard J. Jr. BS, Hampton Univ., 1947; MEd, Wayne State Univ., 1952; postgrad., Univ. Minn., 1955-56. Cabinetmaker Hampton (Va.) Inst., 1941-43, 46-47; indsl. arts tchr. Ariz. Pub. Schs., Tucson, 1947-48; vocat. edn. tchr. Tenn. A & I State Univ., Nashville, 1948-50, Fla. A & M Univ., Tallahassee, 1951-54; prin. Jacksonville (Fla.) Pub. Sch., 1954-55; vocat. edn. specialist UN ILO, Geneva, 1956-80; vocat. edn. tchr. tng. Temple U., Phila., 1980-90. Pub. mem. Del. State Bd. Nursing, Dover, 1991-93; mem. United Way Com., Wilmington, Del., 1986—, Goodwill Industries Com., Wilmington, 1990—; bd. dirs. UN Assn., Wilmington, 1980—. Sgt. Quartermaster Corps, U.S. Army, 1943-45, ETO. Recipient World Citizen award YMCA North East Region, 1989. Mem. UN Assn. (Del. chpt., bd. dirs. 1980—, pres. 1983-84),

Am. Vocat. Assn. (life), ASTD, Soc. for Internat. Devel., Assn. of Former Internat. Civil Servants, People to People (charter mem. Del. chpt.), Hampton Alumni Assn. (treas. 1988—), Phi Delta Kappa (emeritus), Omicron Tau Theta. Democrat. Home: 302 W 14th St Wilmington DE 19801

YOUNG, LINDA WILCOX, economics educator; b. Greenville, S.C., Feb. 3, 1954; d. Witmer Boyd and Patricia Amelia (Strauss) Wilcox; m. David Gary Young, Sept. 29, 1985; 1 stepchild, Rachael; 1 child, Abigail. AB in Applied Math., U. Calif., Berkeley, 1976, PhD in Agrl. and Resource Econs., 1987. Asst. prof. econs. U. Vt., Burlington, 1986—. Contbr. articles to profl. jours. Trustee Richmond (Vt.) Land Trust, 1989—. Rsch. fellow Doherty Found., 1980, Social Sci. Rsch. Coun., 1982, Kroepsch-Maurice rsch. fellow, 1988. Mem. Am. Econ. Assn., Assn. for Evolutionary Econs., Union Radical Polit. Econs., Latin Am. Studies Assn. Office: U Vt 479 Main St Burlington VT 05405-0078

YOUNG, MARGARET BUCKNER, civic worker, author; b. Campbellsville, Ky.; d. Frank W. and Eva (Carter) Buckner; m. Whitney M. Young, Jr., Jan. 2, 1944 (dec. Mar. 1971); children: Marcia Elaine, Lauren Lee. BA, Ky. State Coll., 1942, MA, U. Minn., 1946. Instr. Ky. State Coll., 1942-44; instr. edn. and psychology Spelman Coll., Atlanta, 1957-60; dir. emeritus N.Y. Life Ins. Co.; alt. del. UN Gen. Assembly, 1973. Mem. pub. policy com. Advt. Coun. Trustee emerita Lincoln Ctr. for Performing Arts; chmn. Whitney M. Young, Jr. Meml. Found., 1971-92; trustee Met. Mus. Art, 1976-90; bd. govs. UN Assn., 1975-82; bd. visitors U.S. Mil. Acad., 1978-80. Author: The First Book of American Negroes, 1966, The Picture Life of Martin Luther King, Jr., 1968, The Picture Life of Ralph J. Bunche, 1968, Black American Leaders-Watts, 1969, The Picture Life of Thurgood Marshall, 1970, pub. affairs pamphlet. Home: 111 Emerson St Apt 1243 Denver CO 80218

YOUNG, NANCY, lawyer; b. Washington, Dec. 3, 1954; d. John Young and Byounghye Chang; m. Paul Brendan Ford Jr., May 28, 1983; children: Paul Brendan Ford III, Ian A. Ford. BA, Yale U., 1975, MA, 1976; JD, Columbia U., 1979. Bar: N.Y. 1981. Assoc. Simpson Thacher & Bartlett, N.Y.C., 1979-82, Richards O'Neil & Allegaert, N.Y.C., 1982-86; ptnr. Richards & O'Neil, N.Y.C., 1986—; lectr. Am. law Gakushuin U., Tokyo, 1990-91, Rikkyo U., Tokyo, 1990-91; lectr. Am. securities law Tokyo U., 1992. Contbr. articles to legal publs. Mem. ABA, Assn. Bar City N.Y., Internat. Bar Assn., Am. Fgn. Law Assn., Internat. Lawyers Cub, Coun. on Fgn. Rels., Yale Alumni Assn. (bd. govs.), Columbia Law Sch. Assn. (bd. dirs.), Columbia U. Alumni Assn. Japan (bd. dirs.), Yale Club Japan (bd. dirs.). Home: 945 5th Ave New York NY 10021-2655 Office: Richards & O'Neil 885 3d Ave New York NY 10022-4802

YOUNG, NICK See **YEAZEL, NICHOLAS JOHN**

YOUNG, PAUL FRANCIS, financial consultant; b. Orange, N.J., July 7, 1921; s. Francis Wayland and Ethel Mae (Gibert) Y.; m. Ruth Crocker, July 10, 1948; children: Sarah C. Manning, Lawrence Renwick, Arthur Lincoln, Charles Jensen. AB, Dartmouth Coll., 1943, MA, 1970; student, MIT Sch. Architecture, 1946-47, U. Calif. Sch. Edn., Berkeley, 1948-51. Instr. bus. adminstrn. New Eng. Coll., Henniker, N.H., 1947-48; adminstrv. asst. U. Calif., Berkeley, 1948-51; asst. then assoc. treas. Dartmouth Coll., Hanover, N.H., 1951-70, treas., 1970-72; treas., sec., trustee Dartmouth Savs. Bank, Hanover, 1972-75, pres., trustee, 1975-83; fin. planner IDS Fin. Svcs., Hanover, 1984-87; fin. cons. Hanover, 1988—; chmn. Hanover Fin. Com., 1960-61; mem. Hanover Adv. Bd. Assessors, 1990—, chmn., 1992—. Trustee Mary Hitchcock Meml. Hosp., Hanover, 1972—, treas., 1974—; trustee Lebanon (N.H.) Coll., 1973-76; treas., bd. dirs. Hanover Improvement Soc., 1972—; bd. dirs. Hanover Conservation Coun., 1989—; treas. Hanover Consumer Coop. Soc., 1953-55; vol. Am. Assn. Ret. Persons/VOTE, Hanover, 1990—; pres., bd. dirs. Eastman Community Assn., Grantham, N.H., 1971-81; pres. Union Ch. of Meredith Neck, 1985-91. Lt. USNR, 1942-46. Mem. Howe Libr. Corp., Dartmouth Class of 1943 (exec. com., treas. 1972-77, pres. 1977-83), Hanover Rotary (Hanover Citizen of Yr. 1992). Republican. Episcopalian.

YOUNG, RICHARD ROBERT, logistics and transportation educator; b. Passaic, N.J., July 18, 1946; s. William Frederick and Helen Mae (Smith) Y.; m. Mary Frances Braccio, Nov. 27, 1971. BS in Commerce, Rider Coll., 1968; MBA, SUNY, Albany, 1971; postgrad., U. Mass., 1973-77, Pa. State U., 1989—. Admitted to practice FMC. Materials handling engr. Thatcher Glass Mfg. Co., Elmira, N.Y., 1969-69; mgr. customer svc. Cooper Labs., Wayne, N.J., 1971; materials mgr. of contracts Sprague Electric Co., North Adams, Mass., 1971-75, mgr. corp. purchasing, 1975-77; mgr. purchasing adminstrn. Am. Hoechst Corp., Somerville, N.J., 1977-80, mgr. group purchasing, 1980-84; mgr. group distbn. Hoechst Celanese Corp., Somerville, 1984-89; lectr. logistics and transp., program dir. purchasing cert. Pa. State U., University Park, 1989—; bd. dirs. Guildcraft Inc., York, Pa.; mem. adv. com. World Trade Inst., N.Y.C., 1985—; cons. Interesource Corp., York, 1978—; participant Logistics Resource Forum, 1985. Contbr. articles to logistics jours. Bd. dirs. No. Berkshire Child Care Commn., North Adams, Mass., 1972-76; mem. Union Twp. (N.J.) Zoning Bd., 1985-89, vice chmn., 1989; v.p. Union Twp. Rep. Club, 1983-87; alt. mem. Hunterdon County (N.J.) Rep. Com., 1987. With USAF, 1968. Mem. Coun. Logistics Mgmt., Nat. Assn. Purchasing Mgmt. (cert.), Am. Soc. Transp. and Logistics (sustaining, assoc. examiner 1989—), Phillipsburg R.R. Historians (co-founder), Masons. Presbyterian. Home: 222 Heatherstone Way Lancaster PA 17601 Office: Pa State U 509 Bus Adminstrn Bldg University Park PA 16802

YOUNG, ROBERT CRAIG, banker; b. N.Y.C., Mar. 15, 1960; s. Robert J. and Gloria L. (Sandhop) Y.; m. Amy S. Trapp. BS cum laude, NYU, 1982, MBA, 1985. Asst. v.p. Chem. Bank, N.Y.C., 1982-86; project mgr. GE Credit Corp., Stamford, Conn., 1986-87; dir. Merrill Lynch & Co., N.Y.C., 1987—. Home: 98 Revere Rd Manhasset NY 11030-2733 Office: Merrill Lynch & Co 250 Vesey St New York NY 10281-1315

YOUNG, ROBERT THOMAS, clinical psychologist, consultant, educator; b. Tucson, Aug. 6, 1945; s. Thomas Carrick and Jean (Stover) Y.; m. Christine L. Young, Dec. 19, 1970; children: Michael R., Sarah Anne. BA, Hanover Coll., 1968; MA, Ohio State U., 1971, PhD, 1974. Cert., lic. psychologist, N.Y. Rsch. dir. Children's Hosp., Columbus, Ohio, 1972-75; staff psychologist Astor Home, Rhinebeck, N.Y., 1975-78, sr. psychologist, 1978-87; clin. dir. Astor Day Treatment, Poughkeepsie, N.Y., 1987—; chief psychologist Astor Clinics, Poughkeepsie, N.Y., 1989—; pvt. practice Hopewell Junction, N.Y., 1977—; cons. Dutchess County Dept. Probation, Poughkeepsie, N.Y., 1988—, Head Start, Beacon, N.Y., 1977-87. Contbr. numerous articles to profl. jours. Coach East Fishkill Soccer Club, N.Y., 1980—. With USAR, 1968-71. Mem. APA, NSAC, Hudson Valley Psychol. Assn. Office: Astor Home and Clinics 230 North Rd Poughkeepsie NY 12601-1328

YOUNG, RUSSELL DAWSON, physics consultant; b. Huntington, N.Y., Aug. 17, 1923; s. C. Halsey and Edna (Dawson) Y.; m. Carol Vaughn Jones, Aug. 14, 1954; children: Bessmarie, Gale, Janet, Shari. BS in Physics, Rensselaer Poly. Inst., Troy, N.Y., 1953; PhD in Physics, Pa. State U., 1959. Rsch. assoc. Pa. State U., State College, 1959-61; project leader Nat. Bur. Stds., Gaithersburg, Md., 1961-73, chief optics and micrometrology, 1973-78; chief mech. processing div. Nat. Bur. Stds., Gaithersburg, 1975-80, ind. sys. div. chief, 1980-81, chief mech. prodn. div., 1980-81; pres. R.D. Young Cons., Pasadena, Md., 1981—; mem. tech. bd. Quanscann, Pasadena, 1988—. Contbr. articles to profl. jours.; inventor in field of instrumentation. 1st lt. Signal Corps, U.S. Army, 1943-46. Recipient Edward V. Condon award Dept. Commerce, 1974, Silver medal, 1979; Presdl. citation, 1986; Wash. Acad. Scis. award, 1988. Fellow Internat. Inst. Prodn. Engring. Rsch., Nat. Inst. Standards and Tech.; mem. Inst. Physics. Home: 852 Riverside Dr Pasadena MD 21122-1730

YOUNG, STEPHANIE CLARK, administrative assistant; b. Ridgewood, N.J., Jan. 16, 1940; d. Melvin Henry and Tress (Clark) Y. BA, Conn. Coll., 1961; postgrad., U. Geneva, 1961-62. Bus. mgr. Finch Coll. Internat. Study Program in Europe, Madrid, Rome, Paris, London, 1969-70; adminstrv. asst. to assoc. dean MBA program Harvard U. Bus. Sch., Boston, 1970-75, alumni reunion coord., 1975-77; asst. sec. Penn Cen. Corp., N.Y., Conn., Ohio, 1980-89; asst. to the v.p. (legal) Allegheny Power System, Inc., N.Y.C., 1989—. Mem. Am. Soc. Corp. Secs., Nat. Parks and Conservation Assn., DAR. Home: 345 E 69th St New York NY 10021-5583 Office: Allegheny Power System Inc 12 E 49th St New York NY 10017-1028

YOUNG, STEPHEN BLASE, computer engineer; b. Schenectady, N.Y., May 19, 1949; s. Thaddeus Bronislaw and Corinne Jill (Young) Lewkowicz; m. Jin Hong, May 3, 1987. BA summa cum laude, Syracuse U., 1971; MA, Harvard U., 1973, PhD, 1978. Rsch. analyst computer sci. lab. Mass. Gen. Hosp., Boston, 1971-72; rsch. asst. Hague Internat., South Portland, Maine, 1978-81, mgr. corp. adminstrn., 1983-85; fgn. expert Chengdu (Peoples Republic of China) U. Sci. and Tech., 1981-83, 85-87; exec. NYGene Corp., Yonkers, N.Y., 1987-88; software specialist Digital Equipment Corp., Boston, 1988—; adj. prof. Poly. U., Farmingdale, N.Y., 1987-88. Author: Oral English for Chinese Scientists, 1985; contbr. articles to profl. jours. Woodrow Wilson fellow, 1972-73. Mem. Phi Beta Kappa.

YOUNG, STEVEN GEORGE, keyboard musician; b. Medford, Mass., July 24, 1960; s. George Waterman and Marjorie Claire (Savage) Y. BMus, Barrington (R.I.) Coll., 1982; MMus, New Eng. Conservatory, Boston, 1985; DMA, Boston U.; AAGO Cert., New Eng. Conservatory, Boston, 1991. Lectr. in music Bridgewater (Mass.) State Coll., 1987—; dir. music St. Catherine of Siena Ch., Norwood, Mass., 1988—; music dir. Braintree (Mass.) Choral Soc., 1989—; accompanist Jubilate Choral, Brockton, 1986—. Operation Bach scholar, Barrington Coll., 1979-81. Mem. Coll. Music Soc., Am. Guild Organists, Nat. Assn. Pastoral Musicians, Am. choral Dirs. Assn. Office: Bridgewater State Coll Music Dept Bridgewater MA 02324

YOUNG, VENUS DEMILO, entrepreneur; b. N.Y.C., June 29, 1959; d. Robert Jackson Darden and Joanna (McIntosh) Foster; m. Aubrey Bernard Young, Sept. 9, 1985; 1 child, Venus DeMilo. BS, Montclair State U., 1983; postgrad., New Sch., N.Y.C., 1983-84, Cen. Tex. Coll., 1985, Am. Sch. Real Estate & Ins., 1989. Clk. Montclair (N.J.) State Coll., 1977-78, coord., 1978-82; adminstrv. asst. Filtered Water Svcs., Inc., N.Y.C., 1983; computer operator Am. Leprosy Missions, Bloomfield, N.J., 1983; substitute tchr. Killeen (Tex.) Ind. Schs., 1985-87, East Orange (N.J.) Bd. of Edn., 1987—; salesperson Water Resources Internat., Temple, Tex., 1986; adminstr. Carpets Galore Co., East Orange, 1991; salesperson Cross Roads Ford, East Orange, 1991. Contbr. articles to profl. jours. Panelist 9 Broadcast Plaza TV Show, Secaucus, N.J., 1992—. Montclair State Coll. scholar, 1979, 80. Mem. Am. Mgmt. Assn. (affiliate), Am. Bus. Seminars, Daimerica, Phi Beta Sigma (1st Runner Up 1978). Home: 25 N Harrison St # 107 East Orange NJ 07017

YOUNG, WILLIAM EDMUND, packaging systems and engineering consultant; b. Ridgewood, N.J., Mar. 22, 1916; s. O. Walter and May Isabelle (Donahue) Junge; m. Julia Edith Copello, May 15, 1939 (div. 1957); children: Paula A., David W.; m. Barbara Lucile Shultz, June 16, 1974. ME, Stevens Inst. Tech., 1937. Registered profl. engr., N.J. Dir. engring. Standard Pkg. Corp., 1951-57; founder, ptnr. Mahaffy Engring. Co., 1957; founder William E. Young Co., Inc., 1961; chmn. bd., ret. William E. Young Co.; mem. container com., adv. bd. mil. pers. supplies, NAS; emeritus mem. Nat. Def. Exec. Res. Over 30 patents in field; contbr. articles to profl. jours. Ret. bd. mem. Shore Area YMCA, Jersey Shore Med. Ctr., Freedoms Found. at Valley Forge, Rsch. & Devel. Assocs. for Mil. and Food Pkg. Mem. ASME, Am. Chem. Soc., Edwin A. Stevens Soc., Newcomen Soc., U.S. Navy League, Stamford Yacht Club, Masons. Republican. Episcopalian. Home: 380 Milford Point Dr Merritt Island FL 32952 Office: 906 Sewall Ave Asbury Park NJ 07712

YOUNG, WILLIAM LEWIS, retired mathematics educator; b. Buffalo, July 27, 1929; s. Charles William Young and Ada Laura (Lynch) Stremble. BS, Hartwick Coll., 1951; MA, Pa. State U., 1962; MSEE SUNY-Buffalo, 1978, M.L.S., 1979. Instr. SUNY-Buffalo, 1960-65; asst. prof. State Coll., Fredonia, N.Y., 1965-67; ops. analyst Calspan, Buffalo, 1967-69; prof. math. dept. Erie Community Coll., Orchard Park, N.Y., 1969-91, coord. math. and computer sci., 1982-84; v.p. faculty fedn., 1974-77. Pres. Aurora Hist. Soc., East Aurora, N.Y., 1975-79, 90—, trustee, 1974-82, 90—; trustee Scheide Mantel bd. Elbert Hubbard Mus., 1990-91; chmn. Millard Fillmore House Council, East Aurora, 1976-81. Served to 1st lt. USAF, 1951-57. Ohio Coll. On-Line Computer Library Ctr. research fellow, 1979. Home: 806 Luther Rd East Aurora NY 14052-9713 Office: Erie Community Coll 4140 Southwestern Blvd Orchard Park NY 14127-2199

YOUNGELMAN, DAVID ROY, psychologist; b. N.Y.C., June 13, 1959; s. Sid and Vicki (Marmon) Y.; m. Sandra Lynn Koznetski, May 22, 1991. BA in Psychology and Philosophy, Bucknell U., 1981; MA in Clin. Psychology, Fairleigh Diskinson U., 1983; D of Psychology, Yeshiva U., 1988. Resident in psychhology VA Med. Ctr., Lyons, N.J., 1987-88, staff psychologist, 1988-89, dir. psychology tng., 1990—, asst., chief psychology svc., 1991—; cons. in field; presenter in field. Mem. APA. Office: VA Med Ctr Dept Psychology 116B Lyons NJ 07939

YOUNG-MALLIN, JUDITH, author; b. Mt. Vernon, N.Y., Aug. 10, 1937; d. Milton and Marion Ethel (Peterfreund) Young; m. Joel Mallin, Aug. 8, 1957 (div. 1985); children: Jennifer Young, Adam Young, Noah Young. Student, Syracuse U., 1955, NYU, 1956, NYU, 1986. Researcher Conde-Nast, N.Y.C., 1957-58; lectr. Am. Crafts Mus., N.Y.C., 1986; ind. lectr. N.Y.C., 1986—; cons., innovator Surreal Eye Series, N.Y.C., 1986-87; lectr. London-Courtauld Inst. Surrealism in N.Y., 1991, Art Inst. Chgo., 1992, Sch. for Visual Arts, N.Y.C., 1992; cons. Am. Masters, N.Y.C., 1991; established Young-Mallin Archives. Author: M.F.K. Fisher, Virgil Thomson, 1990, Juliet Man Ray, 1991, Surrealism and Women, Eileen Agar, 1991, View Anth. Index Edn., 1991, Edward James, 1991. Mem. James Beard Soc. (profl. mem.). Home: 983 Park Ave New York NY 10028-0808

YOUNGS-ANDERSEN, MARIE ALICE, non-profit organization executive director; b. Berkeley, Calif., June 11, 1958; d. Joseph Patrick Jr. and Mary (Stone) Y.; m. Craig R. Andersen, Nov. 30, 1985; children: Jens Patrick, Colin Youngs. BA, Holy Cross Coll., 1980; postgrad., George Washington U., 1981-82. Group tour coord. Prince of Fundy Cruises, Portland, Maine, 1983-86; exec. dir. Physicians for Social Responsibility, Bangor, Maine, 1987-89; adminstrv. dir. Bangor-Brewer YWCA, 1989-90; exec. dir. N.H. Trial Lawyers Assn., Concord, 1990—; bd. dirs. Physicians for Social Responsibility Ea. Maine, 1989-91; cons./dir. Fair Access to the Courts, Concord, 1990—, L.E.G.A.L., Concord, 1990—. Bd. dirs. Bangor Jr. League, 1988-90; legis com. St. Joseph's Hosp., Bangor, 1988-90; mem. Bangor Hist. Preservation Commn., 1988. Mem. Rotary. Democrat. Office: NH Trial Lawyers Assn 1 Tremont St Concord NH 03301-4423

YOUNIE, WILLIAM JOHN, special education educator, researcher; b. Boston, July 25, 1932; s. Edward Younie; m. Anne Marie Ring, Sept. 8, 1956; children: Anne Elizabeth, John William. BS in Edn., Boston Tchr.'s Coll., 1953; MEd, Tufts U., 1954; EdD, Columbia U., 1959. Cert. elem. edn., handicapped and learning disabilities tchr., sch. counselor, N.J. Tchr. elem. Delmar (N.Y.) Pub. Schs., 1954-55, Deer Park (N.Y.) Schs., 1955-56; children's libr. Agnes Russel Columbia U., N.Y.C., 1956-57; tchr. Yonkers (N.Y.) Pub. Schs., 1957-59; dir. edn. Southbury (Conn.) Tng. Sch., 1959-63; assoc. prof. Tchr.'s Coll. Columbia U., N.Y.C., 1963-70; dpet. chair, prof. William Paterson Coll., Wayne, N.J., 1970—; cons. Fedn. of the Handicapped, N.Y.C., 1965-70, Abilities Inc., Albertson, N.Y., 1967-70, Elwyn (Pa.) Inst., 1968-84, Vineland (N.J.) Tng. Sch., 1985-89. Author: Introduction to Work Study Programs, 1965; Instructional Approaches to the Slow Learner, 1966, (with others) The World of Rehabilitation, 1970, Basic Speech Improvement, 1975. Chmn. com. Boy Scouts Am., Southbury, 1959-63; bd. dirs. State Gov.'s Coun. on Mental Retardation, Trenton, N.J., 1970-71, N.J. Spl. Edn. Instnl. Med. Ctr., Clifton, N.J., 1975-76; mem. adv. bd. Edison State Coll., 1990-91. Named Educator of the Yr., Morris chpt. ARC, 1990, N.J. State Assn. for Retarded Citizens, 1990; Fulbright fellow People's Republic of China, 1988. Fellow Am. Assn. on Mental Retardation; mem. ASCD, Coun. for Exceptional Children (pres. Featherstown chpt. 1978), Am. Pers. and Guidance Assn., Assn. for Edn., Communication and Tech. Home: 307 South Dr Paramus NJ 07652-4812 Office: William Paterson Coll 300 Pompton Rd Wayne NJ 07470-2103

YOURON, MICHAEL ROBERT, psychologist; b. Kingston, Pa., Dec. 19, 1955; s. Robert Thomas and Nan Marie (Nixon) Y.; m. Laurie Ann Fulton, Sept. 3, 1977; children: Justin Michael, Christopher Michael. BS in Human Svcs., U. Scranton, 1977; MA in Psychology, Marywood Coll., Scranton, Pa., 1984. Lic. psychologist, Pa. Student intern Scraonton Mental Health/Mental Retardation, 1976-77; mental retardation worker day devel. program Lizerne/Wyoming County Mental Health Ctr. #1, Wilkes-Barre, Pa., 1977-79; counselor The Bridge, Wilkes-Barre, 1979-80; resident counselor Step-by-Step, Inc., Wilkes-Barre, 1982, intake counselor, 1982-83; mental health tech. adolescent unit Wyoming Valley Clinic, 1983-84; staff psychologist, therapist First Hosp. Wyoming Valley, 1984-90, clin. resource cons., 1990—; psychologist Counseling & Learning Assn., Kingston, Pa., 1991—; resident advisor Human Svc. Cons., Wilkes-Barre, 1979; lectr. MMI Prep. Sch., Freeland, Pa., Susquehanna Valley Cen. Sch. Dist., Kirkwood, N.Y., St. Maria Goretti Ch., Plains, Pa.; student assistance presenter Berwick (Pa.) Area Sch. Dist. Coach Kingston Youth Soccer Assn., 1988—. Mem. Am. Psychol. Assn., Pa. Psychol. Assn., Northeastern Pa. Psychol. Assn., Pa. Assn. Student Assistance Profls. Republican. Roman Catholic. Home: 84 Virginia Ter Wilkes Barre PA 18704-4930 Office: Counseling & Learning Assn 230 Wyoming Ave Wilkes Barre PA 18704-3534

YOWELL, LINDA MIRIAM, architect; b. Montclair, N.J., Sept. 8, 1951; d. Daniel and Gilberte (Cazes) Y.; m. Richard M. Zuckerman, Dec. 26, 1976; children: Julia, Emily. AB cum laude, Vassar Coll., 1973; MArch, Columbia U., 1976. Registered architect, N.Y., Conn., N.J. Archtl. designer Collins, Uhl, Hoisington, Anderson, Azmy, Princeton, N.J., 1976-78; architect Smotrich & Platt Architects, N.Y.C., 1978-83; ptnr. Meyer, Yowell & Gifford Architects, N.Y.C., 1983-90; prin. Linda Yowell Architect, N.Y.C., 1990—; v.p. Alliance of Women in Architecture, 1979-81. Co-author, project dir.: (guidebook) Built By Women: A Guide to Architecture in the New York Area, 1981; architect: East Hampton Airport, 1989 (finalist competition Beaux Arch, 1989). Mem. benefit com. Doing Art Together, N.Y.C., 1989—; mem. Nat. Environ. Leadership Coun., Washington, 1990—. Recipient Best Residential Renovation award Beaux Arch 1989, East Hampton, N.Y.;HUD Urban design fellow, William Kinne fellow. Mem. AIA (chair com. Learning by Design: NY), Archtl. League N.Y., Soc. Archtl. Historians.

YPHANTIS, DAVID ANDREW, biology educator; b. Boston, July 14, 1930; s. Kyriakos Paul and Beatrice Bertha (Hansen) Y.; m. Lorna Ruth Nickerson, June 4, 1953; children: Sandra, Peter (dec.), Susan, Kim, Diana. AB, Harvard U., 1952; PhD, MIT, 1955. Rsch. assoc., fellow Am. Cancer Soc. MIT, Cambridge, Mass., 1955-56; asst. biophysicist Argonne (Ill.) Nat. Lab., 1956-58, assoc. biophysicist, 1958-65; asst. prof. Rockefeller U., N.Y.C., 1958-64, assoc. prof., 1964-65; prof. biology SUNY, Buffalo, 1965-68, chmn. dept., 1967-68; instr. physiology Marine Biol. Lab., Woods Hole, 1968-73; prof. molecular and cell biology U. Conn., Storrs, 1968—; vis. prof. U. Crete, Iraklion, 1986—; cons. and vis. investigator Argonne Nat. Lab., 1958-62, 66-67; vis. investigator Brookhaven Nat. Lab., Upton, N.Y., 1962; cons. div. computer rsch. NIH, Bethesda, Md., 1967-80, Xenogen, Mansfield, Conn., 1980-87. Mem. editorial bd. Biophys. Jour., 1962-68, Analytical Biochemistry, 1978-80, Archives Biochemistry and Biophysics, 1974-86. Mem. Biophys. Soc., Am. Chem. Soc., Am. Soc. for Biochemistry and Molecular Biology. Home: 99 River Rd Mansfield Center CT 06250-1018 Office: U Conn 75 S Eagleville Road Ext Storrs Mansfield CT 06269-0001

YU, VICTOR LIN-KAI, physician, educator; b. Mpls., Jan. 9, 1943; s. Robert S.H. and Victoria (Hsiao) Y.; m. Deborah Lin, June 19, 1971; children: Chen Ming, Kwan Ting. BA, Carleton Coll., 1965; MD, U. Minn., 1970. Internship and residency U. Colo., Denver, 1970-72; residency Stanford U., Palo Alto, Calif., 1974, postdoctoral fellow, 1975-77; prof. medicine U. Pitts., 1978—; chmn. bd. sci. counselors NIH, 1986—; chief infectious disease sect. VA Med. Ctr., Pitts., 1981—; disting. lectr., Am. Soc. Microbiology, 1988. Contbr. rsch. on Legionnaires' disease to sci. publs. Recipient Disting. Rsch. award Am. Legion, 1982, Health Svcs. Rsch. Found., 1984; named disting. scientist Chinese Med. Soc., Taipei, Taiwan, 1988. Fellow ACP; mem. Orgn. Chinese Ams. (officer Pitts. sect. 1978—). Home: 87 Longue Vue Dr Pittsburgh PA 15228-1538 Office: U Pitts Scaife Sch Medicine 968 Pittsburgh Pittsburgh PA 15261

YU, YONG MING, physiological biochemist, surgeon; b. Beijing, China, June 20, 1945; came to U.S., 1980; s. Dah-Piao and Hwa-Tzi Hsu Y.; m. Pei-Ra (Bei-Lei) Ling, Sept. 10, 1971; 1 child, Yi-Qian. MD, Peking Union Med. Coll., Beijing, 1970; PhD, MIT, 1987. Surg. resident Minhe County Hosp., Qinghai, China, 1970-78; resident, rsch. student Peking Union Med. Coll. Hosp., Beijing, 1978-80; rsch. fellow, surgery Harvard U. at Mass. Gen. Hosp. and Shriners Hosp., Boston, 1980-88; asst. biochemist Mass. Gen. Hosp. and Shriners Hosp. for Crippled Children, Boston, 1988—; instr. in surgery Harvard U., 1990—; instr. surgery Harvard U., 1990—. Contbr. articles to profl. jours. Named Co-prin. Investigator med. rsch. program Shriners Hosp., 1985-88, 89-91, Prin. Investigator, 1992—. Mem. Am. Burn Assn., N.Y. Acad. Scis., Am. Inst. Nutrition, Sigma Xi. Office: Shriners Hosp 51 Blossom St Boston MA 02114-2623

YUCELT, UGUR, marketing professional, educator; b. Bursa, Turkey, Dec. 15, 1937; came to the U.S., 1965; s. Nazim and Zisan Yucelt; m. Suna Kuli, Aug. 10, 1967; children: Baris, Onur. Diploma, Istanbul U., 1961; MBA, NYU, 1969; PhD, New Sch., N.Y.C., 1980. Instr. Salem (Mass.) State Coll., Salem, Mass., 1974-78; asst. prof. Norwich U., Northfield, Vt., 1978-82, assoc. profc., 1982-84; assoc. prof. Pa. State U.-Harrisburg, Middletown, Pa., 1984—; vis. prof. Oslo Bus. Sch., 1990-91; rsch. assoc. Office Systems Devel., N.Y.C., 1972-74; book reviewer Macmillan Book Pub., N.Y.C., 1989-90. Contbr. articles to profl. jours. Lt. Turkish Army, 1962-64. Fellow Advt. Found., 1990, Direct Mktg. Assn., 1989. Mem. Am. Mktg. Assn., Acad. Mktg. Sci., Inst. Mgmt. Scis., Decision Scis., So. Mktg. Assn. Home: 610 Cardinal Dr Harrisburg PA 17111-5011 Office: Pa State U Harrisburg Sch Bus Adminstrn Middletown PA 17057

YUDAIN, CAROLE GEWIRTZ, public relations executive, writer, photojournalist, audio-visual producer; b. Bronx, N.Y.; d. Sam. I. and Helen (Greenberg) Gewirtz; m. Arthur S. Rosenthal, June 28, 1953 (div. 1963); 1 child, Marc Ian; m. Theodore Yudain, Dec. 28, 1966 (dec. 1970); 1 stepson, Ted Yudain. Student, Bennington (Vt.) Coll., 1950-53; BA, Sarah Lawrence Coll., 1972. Cert. pub. health educator; registered Securities & Exch. Commn. II. With sales tng. program Saks Fifth Ave., N.Y.C., 1952-53; with display advt. dept. Binghamton (N.Y.) Press, 1954-55; advt. copywriter, fashion commentator Fowler, Dick & Walker, Binghamton, 1955-56; promotion TV writer, TV model, on-air guest talk show host Sta. WNBF-AM/TV, Binghamton, N.Y., 1956; feature writer Slenderella Internat., 1957-58; pub. rels. dir. United Fund, Stamford, Conn., 1964-66; newspaper columnist The Daily Item, Port Chester, N.Y., 1973-77, The Conn. Sunday Herald, Bridgeport, 1973-77; pub. affairs and news editor United Hosp., Port Chester, NY, 1973-74; prin. Carol Yudain Pub. Relations, Greenwich, Conn., 1974-78; pub. health educator Bd. of Health, Stamford, 1977; pub. relations dir. Fedn. Jewish Philanthropies of N.Y.C., 1978-79, The Lighthouse, N.Y.C., 1980-81; pub. rels. writer Devel. Corp. for Israel/State of Israel Bonds, N.Y.C., 1983-90; bd. contbrs. Op-Ed news Greenwich Time, 1984—; mem. faculty NYU, 1991—; cons. in field. Contbr. articles to profl. jours. and newspapers. State del. White House Conf. on Children, 1970; chmn. pub. rels. Child Guidance Clinic Greater Stamford, Conn., 1970-76; sec. Greenwich Emergency Med. Svc. Adv. Coun., 1977-79; mem. pub. info. com. S.W. Conn. H.S.A., 1979-80; co-pres. Sisterhood of Temple Shalom, 1983-84; bd. dirs. Gateway Communities, Inc., Stamford, 1987—, spl. events chmn., 1989; mem. pub. rels. com. United Way of Greenwich, 1988-89. Recipient WICI Matrix award, 1982, 83, 87, Internat. Radio Festival of N.Y. award., 1985, 86, 2 prizes Conn. Press Women, 1977, several hon. mentions. Mem. Nat. Acad. Television Arts & Scis., N.Y. Writrs & Artists Peace in Mid East, N.Y. Press Club, Soc. Profl. Journalists, Conn. and Deadline Club N.Y., Am. Med. Writers Assn., Women in Communications, Inc., Conn. Press. Club, Pen Women Internat. Home: 25 Forest St Stamford CT 06901

YUDELSON, JOSEPH SAMUEL, chemist, researcher; b. Philadelphia, N.Y., July 20, 1925; s. Louis and Freda (Dolphman) Y.; m. Tanya Bernstein, Sept. 27, 1952; children: Aline, Michael, Leslie, Margot. BS in Chemistry, U. Pitts., 1950; PhD in Chemistry, Ill. Inst. Tech., 1955. Rsch. chemist

Eastman Kodak Co., Rochester, N.Y., 1954-58, sr. rsch. chemist, 1958-62, rsch. assoc., 1962-69, lab. head, 1970-80, sr. rsch. assoc., 1980-90; contractor Eastman Kodak/TAD Corp., Rochester, N.Y., 1990—. Patentee in field; contbr. articles to profl. jours. Ward leader Monroe County Dem. Orgn., Rochester, 1965. With USN, 1943-46. Recipient Phillips award U. Pitts., 1950, IR-100 award IR-100, Chgo., 1984; NSF scholar Ill. Inst. Tech., Chgo., 1952, Eastman fellow, Rochester, 1953. Mem. Am. Chem. Soc. Democrat. Jewish. Home: 77 Calumet St Rochester NY 14610-1505 Office: Eastman Kodak Co Rsch Lab Rochester NY 14650-2158

YUDIS, MELVIN, physician; b. Phila., May 11, 1937; s. George and Sylvia (Chernoff) Y.; divorced; children: David, Heidi Jo, Jonathan. AB, Temple U., 1959; MD, Jefferson Med. Coll., 1963. Diplomate Am. Bd. Internal Medicine in internal medicine and nephrology, NAt. Bd. Med. Examiners. Intern straight med. Jefferson Med. Coll. Hosp., Phila., 1963-64; resident internal medicine Hahnemann Med. Coll. and Hosp., Phila., 1964-66, NIH postdoctoral fellow in renology and vascular diseases, 1966-67; physician-in-chief sect. nephrology dept. medicine Abington Meml. Hosp., 1969—; clin. assoc. prof. medicine, dept. medicine sect. nephrology Hahnemann Med. Coll. and Hosp., 1969—; attending nephrologist dept. medicine Holy Redeemer Hosp., Meadowbrook, Pa., 1969—; attending physician dept. medicine subsect. nephrology Nazareth Hosp., Phila., 1969—; coun. rep. End Stage Renal Disease Network, 1978—, sec.-treas., 1985, 86, 87; chmn. water purity com, network rep. to State of Pa. presciption drug com. Contbr. articles to profl. jours. Lt. comdr. M.C., USN, 1967-69. Mem. AMA, ACP, Am. Soc. Nephrology, Am. Soc. Artificial and Internal Organs, Am. Soc. Internal Medicine, Internal Soc. Nephrology, Nat. Kidney Found., Am. Coll. Cardiology, Pan Am. Med. Assn., Am. Heart Assn. (mem. exec. com. Montgomery County br. 1974—), Renal Physicians Assn., Internat. Soc. Peritoneal Dialysis, Montgomery County Med. Soc., J. Marion Sims Soc., Pa. Soc. Internal Medicine, Greater Del. Valley Kidney Adv. Coun., Del. Valley Soc. Nephrologists, Pa. Soc. Nephrology (councilor). Office: Hypertension-Nephrology Assocs 1738 Old York Rd Abington PA 19001

YUDKIN, JOSHUA PETER, musician, composer; b. Phila., May 5, 1957; s. I. A. and Janet (Arinsberg) Y. Sr. music cert., Settlement Music Sch., 1974; student, Pa. State U., 1975-76, Phila. Coll. Performing Arts, 1978-81. Dir. music Ctrl. Frate Sound Investment Band, Phila., 1976-78, Joshua Yudkin Band, Phila., 1978-80; keyboardsit The Pedestrians Rock Bank, N.Y., N.J., Pa., 1981-83; keyboardist Pat Martino Band, N.J., Pa., 1983; leader Joshua Yudkin Trio, Phila., 1985-86; composer, leader Joshua Yudkin and the Out Come, N.Y., N.J., Pa., 1987—; keyboardist Red Rodney, Khan Jammal, Ruts Harley Band, N.Y., N.J., Pa., 1988—; pres., owner Out Come Prodns., Phila., 1990—; studio musician various producers, N.Y., N.J., Pa., 1984—. Author numerous mus. compositions in jazz and pop music. Mem. Am. Fedn. Musicians (local 77).

YUEH, NORMA N., library director; b. Beijing, Jan. 21, 1928; came to U.S., 1948; d. C. F. and M. (Sun) Yu; children: Brenda, Dara. BS, St. Joseph's Coll., West Hartford, Conn., 1950; MLS, U. So. Calif., L.A., 1955; DLS, Columbia U., 1974. Adminstrv. asst. to libr. U. So. Calif., 1955-57; asst. br. libr. adult svcs. N.Y.C. Pub. Libr., 1958-60; sch. libr. Yonkers (N.Y.) Sch. System, 1960-63; assoc. libr. William Paterson Coll. of N.J., Wayne, 1963-74; libr. dir. Ramapo Coll. of N.J., Mahwah, 1974—. Contbr. articles to profl. jours. Member multi-ethnic task force Community Resource Coun. Bergen County, N.J., 1990—; mem. exec. bd. Orgn. Chinese Ams., N.J., 1989-91. Mem. ALA, Am. Soc. Info. Sci., Chinese-Am. Librs. Assn. (pres. 1983-84, Disting. Svc. award 1991), N.J. Libr. Assn. (pres. 1988-89, Disting. Svc. award coll. and univ. sect. 1990), N.J. Coll. and Univ. Coalition on Women's Edn. (exec. bd. 1990—), Mid. States Assn. Colls. and Secondary Schs. (accreditation visitor 1974—), LWV (bd. dirs. fin. com. Wayne chpt. 1984-86), Archons of Colophon, Zonta, Beta Phi Mu. Office: Ramapo Coll of NJ 505 Ramapo Valley Rd Mahwah NJ 07430-1623

YUN, DANIEL DUWHAN, physician, foundation administrator; b. Chinjoo, Korea, Jan. 20, 1933; came to U.S., 1959, naturalized, 1972; s. Kapryong and Woo Im Yun; m. Rebecca Sungja Choi, Apr. 13, 1959; children: Samuel, Lois, Caroline, Judith. BS, Coll. Sci. and Engring., Yon-Sei U., 1954, MD, 1958; student U. Pa., 1963. Intern, Quincy (Mass.) City Hosp., 1960; resident and fellow Presbyn.-U. Pa. Med. Ctr., Phila., 1961-65; med. dir. Paddon Meml. Hosp., Nfld., Labrador, Can., 1965-66; dir. spl. care unit Rolling Hill Hosp., Elkins Park, Pa., 1967-79; founder, pres. Philip Jaisohn Meml. Found., Inc., Elkins Park, Pa., 1975-85, also med. dir., trustee; clin. prof. medicine U. Xochicalco, 1978. Mem. Bd. Asian Studies Found., U.S. Senatorial Bus. Adv. Bd.; mem. home safety com. Mayor's Commn. on Svcs. to Aging, Phila.; trustee United Way of Southeastern Pa., co-founder Rep. Presdl. Task Force; mem. U.S. Congl. Adv. Bd.; cons. on Korean affairs Phila. City Coun.; hon. mem. adv. coun. Peaceful Unification Policy of Korea; chmn. bd. Korean-Am. Christian Broadcasting of Phila.; mem. Phila. Internat. City Coord. Com.; commr. Pa. Human Rels. Commn., 1991—; founder, pres. Korean Heritage Found., 1991—; amb. City of Phila., 1991. Recipient Phila. award-Human Rights award, 1981, Disting. Community Svc. award Phila. Dist. Atty., 1981, medal of Merit Presdl. Task Force, 1981, Medal of Nat. Order, Republic of Korea, 1984, Nat. Dong Baek medal Republic of Korea, 1987, award City Coun. Phila., 1987, Gov.'s Pa. Heritage awards, 1990, commendation award Pa. Senate, 1991, award Asian Law Ctr., 1991; named to Legion of Honor, The Chapel of Four Chaplains, named Amb. City of Phila., 1991. Mem. AMA, Am. Soc. Internal Medicine, Am. Coll. Cardiology, Am. Heart Assn. (mem. council on clin. cardiology), Pa. Med. Soc., Phila. County Med. Soc., Royal Soc. Health, Am. Coll. Internat. Physicians, World Med. Assn., Fedn. State Med. Bds., Am. Law Enforcement Officers' Assn., Am. Fedn. Police, Internat. Culture Soc. Korea (hon.), Am. Soc. Contemporary Medicine and Surgery. Home: 3903 Somers Dr Huntingdon Valley PA 19006-1913 Office: 60 Township Line Rd Philadelphia PA 19117-2249

YUN, JAMES MYUNG JU, international business executive; b. Kyungpuk, Korea, Sept. 28, 1938; s. Ungpal and Kwanjo (Hong) Y.; B.A., SUNY, New Paltz, 1963; postgrad. Cornell U., 1964; M.B.A., Fairleigh Dickinson U., 1973; postgrad. Harvard U. Bus. Sch.; m. Susan M. Acker, Dec. 18, 1965; children—Jamie, Cheryl, Adrienne, David. Asst. dir. pharmacology USV Pharms., Yonkers, N.Y., 1965-67; mgr. tech. documentation Schering Corp., Bloomfield, N.J., 1967-74; dir. project mgmt. Hoechst Roussel Co., Sommerville, N.J., 1974-76; dir. sci. communications, dir. research adminstrn. and planning Purdue Frederick Co., Norwalk, Conn., 1976-79, dir. sci. communication, 1976-79, exec. dir. research and devel., 1979-82, new product mktg. dir., 1982-85, mktg. v.p., 1985-86; chmn. Wilton Internat. Group, 1987—. Sec.-treas. Glenwood Terr. Homeowner's Assn., 1974; pres. Wilton Assn. Gifted Children, 1979-81; fin chmn. Black Rock Congregated Ch., 1980—, elder, 1988. Served to 2d lt. Republic of Korea Army, 1959-60. Mem. Am. Chem. Soc., Am. Soc. Info. Sci., Drug Info. Assn., Project Mgmt. Inst., Pharm. Mfrs. Assn., N.Am. Soc. Strategic Planning, Soc. Research Adminstrn., Kyungpuk High Sch. Assn. (pres. 1972) Republican. Home: 79 Sturges Ridge Rd Wilton CT 06897-3231 Office: Wilton Internat Group Wilton CT 06897

YUNKER, PHILIP L., employee relations consultant; b. Greenville, Pa., Apr. 8, 1944; s. Philip A. and Helen Virginia (Valentine) Y.; m. Lois A. DuPont, Sept. 1, 1965; children: Jennifer, Jason, Jonathan. BS, Ind. State U., 1966, MS, 1967. Rsch. psychologist Allstate Ins. Cos., Northbrook, Ill., 1967-69; supr. pers. testing Quaker Oats Co., Chgo., 1969-71, mgr. manpower assessment, 1971-72, mgr. orgnl. devel. and assessment, 1972-73; v.p. human resources Restaurants div. Quaker Oats Co., San Francisco, 1974-84; v.p. human resources Child World, Inc., Aron, Mass., 1985-86; v.p. Adams Nash and Haskell, Cin., 1986—; dir. pledge campaign Chgo. Area Nat. Alliance Businessmen, 1973-74. Exec. bd. Marin coun. Boy Scouts Am., 1978-84, Old Colony coun., 1985-90. Mem. Nat. Food Svc. and Lodging Inst. (bd. dirs. 1976-84). Office: Adams Nash and Haskell 7 Mast Hill Rd Hingham MA 02043-3422

YURCHAK, METRO, education educator; b. Nesquehoning, Pa., July 14, 1928; s. Metro J. and Anna (Thear) Y.; m. Gail A., Nov. 11, 1956; children: Gregory, Carole, Heather, Susan, Jonathan. BS, Lock Haven Univ., 1952; MEd, Pa. State U., 1956, EdD, 1973. Tchr., history Brookville (Pa.) High Sch., 1952-54, Lehighton (Pa.) High Sch., 1954-57, Pennridge High Sch., Perkasie, Pa., 1957-62; guidance counselor, prin. Quakertown (Pa.) High Sch., 1962-68; dir. of student teaching Pa. State U., University Park, 1968-76; dir. of curriculum Bucks County Schs., Doylestown, Pa., 1976-85; dean of acad. Pinebrook Jr. Coll., Coopersburg, Pa., 1985-86, prof. of edn., 1986—; cons. Bucks County Sch., 1976-85, Pinebrook Jr. Coll., 1985—; coord. All Bucks County Effective Teaching Prog., 1980, developer In-Sch. Tng. Progs., 1981—. With USN, 1946-48, ATO. Mem. ASCD (state rep. 1979), Assn. Secondary Sch. Prins. (pres. Bucks County chpt. 1977-79). Am. Orthodox Ch. Home: 2605 Mill Rd Quakertown PA 18951-2297 Office: Pinebrook Jr Coll 600 S Main St Coopersburg PA 18036-2499

YUSPEH, ALAN RALPH, lawyer; b. New Orleans, June 13, 1949; s. Michel and Rose Fay (Rabenovitz) Y.; m. Janet Horn, June 8, 1975. B.A., Yale U., 1971; M.B.A., Harvard U., 1973; J.D., Georgetown U., 1978. Bar: D.C. 1978. Mgmt. cons. McKinsey & Co., Washington, 1973-74; adminstrv. asst., legis. asst. Office of U.S. Senator J. Bennett Johnston, Washington, 1974-78; atty. Shaw, Pittman, Potts & Trowbridge, Washington, 1978-79, Ginsburg, Feldman, Weil and Bress, Washington, 1979-82; gen. counsel Com. on Armed Services-U.S. Senate, Washington, 1982-85; ptnr. Preston, Thorgrimson, Ellis & Holman, Washington, 1985-88, Miller & Chevalier, Washington, 1988-91, Howrey & Simon, Washington, 1991—. Editor Law and Policy in Internat. Business jour., 1978-79, Nat. Contract Mgmt. Jour., 1988-92; assoc. editor Pub. Contract Law jour., 1987-91. Chmn. bd. of ethics, City of Balt., 1988—. Served to 1st lt. USAR, 1971-77. Mem. ABA (vice chmn. com. data and patent rights sect. pub. contract law 1989—). Home: 1812 South Rd Baltimore MD 21209-4506 Office: Howrey & Simon 1730 Pennsylvania Ave NW Washington DC 20006-4706

YUSTER, LEIGH CAROL, publishing company executive; b. Trenton, N.J., July 23, 1949; d. Leon Carl and Helen Loretta (Wisniewski) Markiewicz; m. Charles Yuster (div. Apr. 1985); stepchildren: Sarah, Elizabeth, Jared, Alexandra. Editor R.R. Bowker, N.Y.C., 1971-72, ISBN agy. editorial coord., 1972-78, editorial coord., 1978-79, mgr., AV svcs., 1979-81, mgr., data sources, 1981-83, sr. product mgr., 1983-85, exec. editor, mng. editor, 1985-87, dir. product enhancements, 1987-88, dir. product devel., pub. Ulrich's Database, 1990-91; assoc. pub. Bowker Bus. Rsch., A&I Pub. R.R. Bowker, New Providence, N.J., 1990-91, also pub. Ulrich's Database, 1990-91, pub. Broadcasting & Cable Market Place, 1991—; ptnr. Eagle Bakery, New Providence, 1991—. Recipient Climate of Excellence award, Cahners Pub. Co., Newton, Mass., 1987, Cert. of Appreciation, Consortium of Univ. Film Ctrs., Kent, Ohio, 1986. Mem. ALA, Nat. Fedn. of Abstracting and Info. Svcs., Consortium of Coll. and Univ. Media Ctrs., Actors Equity Assn., Am. Rose Soc., Mercer County Bd. Realtors. Democrat. Jewish. Home: 129 Western Ave Trenton NJ 08618-1713

YVON, BERNARD RENE, educator; b. Chicopee, Mass., Nov. 23, 1935; s. Victor and Alma (DesLisle) Y.; m. Gail Frances Curry, Dec. 26, 1960; children: JoAnn Yvon Eberle, Renee Yvon Napolitano, Bernard George. BS in Edn., Westfield State Tchrs. Coll., 1960; MEd, Westfield State Coll., 1963; EdD in Curriculum Devel., Tchr. Edn., Wayne State U., 1970; postgrad., U. Mass., Smith Coll., Springfield Coll., Laval U., Can. Tchr., prin. Russell H. Conwell Sch., 1960-63; dir. guidance Gateway Regional Jr.-Sr. High Sch., 1963-67; asst. dir. admissions, instr. Westfield (Mass.) State Coll., 1967-68; asst. to dir. undergrad. program elem. edn., instr. Wayne State U., Detroit, 1968-70; asst. prof., edn., dir. student tng. U. Maine, Orono, 1970-75; assoc. prof. U. Maine, 1975-79, prof. math. edn., 1979—, campus coord., student exchange programs Great Britain, 1980—, coord., Canadian student teaching intern program, 1975—, coord., Bangor, Maine schs., undergrad. tchr. edn. students, 1982-90; vis. prof. math. edn. U. Prince Edward Island, Western Wash. U., Bellingham, 1986; vis. sr. lectr. U. East Anglia, Norwich, Eng., 1976-77, 82—; researcher and cons. in field. Contbr. articles to profl. jours. Mem. Nat. Coun. Tchrs. Math., Assn. Can. Studies in U.S., Assn. Tchrs. Math. Lancashire Eng., Math. Assn. Leicester, Eng., Assn. Tchrs. Math. New Eng., Assn. Tchr. Educators Maine (exec. com., chmn. credentials com. 1975-76, rep. collegiate educators Maine nat. ann. del. assembly 1973-76), Phi Delta Kappa, Phi Kappa Phi.

ZABARA, JACOB, neuroscientist; b. Phila., May 8, 1932; s. Joseph and Manya (Cohen) Z.; children: Joseph, Daniel. BS, Johns Hopkins U., Balt., 1953; MS, U. Pa., 1958, PhD, 1959. Instr. Dartmouth Coll., Hanover, N.H., 1960-61; assoc. U. Pa., 1961-66; assoc. prof. Temple U., Phila., 1967—; visiting prof. Stanford U., 1984-86, Hebreu U., Jerusalem, 1974. Inventor: The Neurocybernetic, 1987, Prosthesis, 1989. Fellow NIH, 1960, Lilly Found., Inst. Neurological Sics., 1955-59, Nat. Acad. Scis., 1984-86. Mem. Biophysical Soc., Am. Physiologial Soc., Soc. Neurocsience, Am. Epilepsy Soc. Office: Temple U 3223 N Broad St Philadelphia PA 19140-5096

ZABEL, WILLIAM DAVID, lawyer; b. Omaha, Dec. 14, 1936; s. Louis J. and Anne I. Z.; m. Deborah M. Miller, Oct. 31, 1979; children by previous marriage: Richard, David. AB summa cum laude, Princeton U., 1958; LLB cum laude, Harvard U., 1961. Bar: N.Y. 1961, U.S. Supreme Ct. 1966, Fla. 1975. Ptnr. firm Schulte, Roth & Zabel, N.Y.C., 1969—, Palm Beach, Fla., 1975—; lectr. Cornell Law Sch., So. Fed. Tax Inst., U. Miami Inst. Estate Planning, Great Plains Tax Inst., profl. orgns.; N.Y. State adv. com. U.S. Civil Rights Commn., 1969-73; vol. civil rights litigator Lawyers Constl. Def. Com., Miss., summer 1965; bd. dirs. Del. Mgmt. Holdings Inc. Author: Estate Planning for the Large Estate, 1976, Domicile, Wills and Tax Problems of Migrating Clients Transplanted to Florida, 1976, Income, Estate and Gift Tax Consequences of Marital Settlements, 1979, Estate Planning for Interests in a Closely Held Business, 1981, Use of Trusts in Connection with Marital Dissolutions, 1983, Thy Will Be Done?, 1991; Am. editor: The Lawyer, Eng., 1963-66; mem. editorial adv. bd. Trusts & Estates mag.); contbr. articles to periodicals. Pres. Merlin Found.; mem. Lymphoma Found., Open Soc. Fund, Inc., Soros Founds. (Hungary, former Soviet Union and Central European U., Iris), Ottinger Found., David H. Cogan Found., Picower Med. Rsch. Inst., Samuel Waxman Cancer Rsch. Found., Lawson Valentine Found., Am. Friends of the Israel Mus.; legal counsel Internat. Confedn. Art Dealers; active Princeton U. Resources Coun., 1988—, chmn. planned giving com., 1991—; bd. dirs. Tauber Inst., Brandeis U. Recipient Disting. Community Service award, Brandeis U., 1986; fellow Brandeis U., 1987—. Fellow Am. Coll. Trust and Estate Counsel, Internat. Acad. Estate and Trust Law; mem. ABA, Am. Law Inst., N.Y. State Bar Assn., Assn. of Bar of City of N.Y. (internat. human rights com.), Lawyers Com. for Human Rights (bd. dirs.), Estate Planning Coun. N.Y.C. (bd. dirs. 1975-79), Fla. Bar Assn., Harmonie Club (pres. 1989—92, Phi Beta Kappa. Home: 850 Park Ave New York NY 10021-1845 Office: 900 3d Ave New York NY 10022 also: Phillips Point W Tower 10th Fl 777 S Flagler Dr West Palm Beach FL 33401

ZACCONE, ROBERT MICHAEL, architect; b. Jersey City, Jan. 4, 1946; s. Fabian and Phyllis (Tagliareni) Z.; m. Paula Maria Scarano, Nov. 28, 1944; children: Gregory, Justin. BA in Art, C.W. Post Coll., 1967; BArch, Pratt Inst., 1971; MArch, Columbia U., 1972. Cert. Nat. Coun. Archtl. Registration Bds.; registered architect, N.Y., N.J., N.C.; lic. profl. planner. Designer J.R. Stevenson Corp., Hempstead, N.Y., 1972-76; chief designer Schuman, Lichtenstein, Claman, N.Y.C., 1976-79; assoc. Haines Lundberg Waehler, N.Y.C. and N.J., 1979-88; pres. Robert Zaccone & Assocs., P.C., Old Tappan, N.J., 1988—; vis. assoc. prof. Pratt Inst. Sch. Architecture, Bklyn., 1979—. Executed mural Manhattan Coll. Bus. Sch., 1986; contbg. artist to N.J. State Artists' Handbook, 1986-87; cover artist N.J. Soc. Architects Handbook, 1986-87, Architectural Rendering, 1988; author: Alb't Halse, 1988. Mem. Architects League No. N.J. (treas. 1986-87, pres.-elect 1989-90, Dir.'s award), N.J. Soc. Architects (bd. dirs.), AIA, Columbians. Republican. Roman Catholic. Home: 212 White Ave Westwood NJ 07675-7411

ZACCONE-TZANNETAKIS, PAULA ROSE, health and physical education educator; b. Montclair, N.J., Sept. 6, 1946; d. Joseph J. and Caroline A. (Pico) Zaccone; m. George Tzannetakis, July 19, 1986. BA, Trenton (N.J.) State Coll., 1968; MA, Montclair State Coll., Upper Montclair, N.J., 1972; EdD, Rutgers U., 1979. Cert. health edn. specialist, health, phys, edn. tchr. psychology. Tchr. health and phys. edn. Glen Ridge (N.J.) Pub. Schs., 1968-74; assoc. prof., coord. Seton Hall U. Coll. Edn. and Human Svcs., South Orange, N.J., 1974—; insvc. tchr. for schs. and cons., N.J., 1991. Mem. AAHPERD (health merit award Ea. Dist. Assn. 1990), Assn. for Advancement Health Edn., N.J. Soc. Pub. Health Edn., N.J. Assn. Health, Phys. Edn., Recreation and Dance (v.p. health 1982, pres. 1992), N.J. Health Edn. Coun. (pres. 1986-90, honor award 1990). Office: Seton Hall U McQuaid Hall 218 South Orange NJ 07079

ZACHARIAS, THOMAS ELLING, real estate executive; b. Morristown, N.J., Feb. 19, 1954; s. John Elling and Muriel (Eckes) Z.; m. Clelia LeBoutillier, June 22, 1985; children: Clelia Delafield, John Livingston. BArch and Urban Planning, Princeton U., 1976; M in Pub. and Pvt. Mgmt., Yale U., 1979. Project dir. N.Y. State Urban Devel. Corp., N.Y.C., 1979-81; assoc. Corp. Property Investors, N.Y.C., 1981-83, asst. v.p., 1983-86, v.p., 1987—; v.p. Corp. Realty Cons., N.Y.C., 1989—. Chmn. Mus. Modern Art Adv. Svc., N.Y.C., 1981-87; mem. steering com. Whitney Mus. Lobby Gallery Assocs., N.Y.C., 1985—; bd. dirs. Creative Time, N.Y.C., 1982-88, Nat. Acad. Design, 1988-90. Fgn. Study grantee McConnel Found., London, 1975. Mem. Internat. Coun. Shopping Ctrs., Urban Land Inst., Yale Club, Meadow Club. Home: 1215 5th Ave New York NY 10029-5209 also: 65 Post Crossing Southampton NY 11968 Office: Corp Property Investors 305 E 47th St New York NY 10017

ZACK, SAMUEL ALAN, counselor; b. Hammond, Ind., Jan. 10, 1951; s. Steve and Sally Sue (Zehner) Z.; m. Judith Lorraine Smith, June 9, 1973; children: Stephen Lynn, Jonathan Andrew, Benjamin Martin. BA, U. Mo., 1973; postgrad., U. Md., 1988—. Teaching parent United Meth. Children's Home, Tuscaloosa, Ala., 1974-80, Cummings Agy., Toledo, Ohio, 1980-82, Maryville Acad., Des Plaines, Ill., 1982; residential coord. Community Svcs. for Autistic Adults and Children, Rockville, Md., 1983-85; teaching parent Luth. Children's Home, Salem, Va., 1985-86; shelter mgr., counselor Community Ministries of Rockville, 1987-91, shelter dir., 1992—. Active Montgomery County Coalition for Homeless, Rockville, 1987—. Mem. AACD. Democrat. Office: Community Ministries 114 W Montgomery Ave Rockville MD 20850-4213

ZACK, TIMOTHY EDWIN, corporate executive; b. Buffalo, Jan. 15, 1959. AAS in Bus. Adminstrn., Erie Community Coll., Buffalo, 1980; BS in Bus. Studies, Medaille Coll., 1981; MS in Geo Politics, SUNY, Buffalo, 1988; postgrad., U. London. Enlisted U.S. Army, 1982, advanced through grades to 1st lt., 1990; intern U. Oreg., Eugene, 1979-80; officer U.S. Army, 1988-92; ops. mgr. L.E. Best & Assocs., Buffalo, 1983-84; mktg. mgr. Panagraphics, Buffalo, 1984-86; pres. Unicon Systems, Ltd., Buffalo, 1985—; mem. faculty Intercollegiate Studies Inst., 1988—, Jefferson Community Coll., 1989—. Recipient Polish Medal of Merit; decorated with Bronze Star, 1985, Silver Star, 1987; Genorate Rsch. scholar. Mem. Polish-Am. Vets. Assn., Internat. Cons. Assn., Profl. Businessmen Assn., Assn. of U.S. Army, SUNY Alumni Assn., Medaille Alumni Assn., Gov. Gen.'s Horse Guards, Buffalo Internat. Bus. Assn., Am. Legion, VFW, Polish Singer's Found., Polish Freedom Found., Knights of Malta (Knight Comdrs. of Grace 1991). Home: 269 N Meadowbrook Pky Buffalo NY 14206-2424 Office: Unicon Systems Ltd 2316 Delaware Ave # 150 Buffalo NY 14216-2687

ZADJEIKA, DOLORES MARIE, real estate company officer; b. Phila., Nov. 15, 1934; m. Thomas V. Zadjeika, May 4, 1957; children: Denise, Brenda, Vincent, Karen, Holly. Student, Temple U., 1954-56, Holy Family Coll., 1959-60, Camden County Coll., 1976-79. Cert. grad. real estate inst., cert. real estate brokerage mgr. Steno-clk. Geo. K. Garrett Co., Inc., Phila., 1950-53; exec. sec. Hollingshead Corp., Camden, N.J., 1954-58; suburban dir. YWCA, Stratford, N.J., 1967-77; real estate salesperson Coolidge Realty Agy., Westmont, N.J., 1977-80; broker, owner Applewood Inc., Realtors, Stratford, 1981—. Chairperson Econ. Devel. Com., Stratford, 1987-89, sec., 1989—. Mem. Camden County Bd. Realtors, Sterling Kiwanis (2d v.p. 1990-91). Office: Applewood Inc Realtors 64 Warwick Rd Stratford NJ 08084-1729

ZADROZNY, ARTHUR JOHN, chemical company executive, engineer; b. Newark, Apr. 21, 1954; s. Alexander Henry Zadrozny and Stephanie Helen (Lukas) Grabon; m. Gloria M. Apostol, Aug. 21, 1976; children: Arthur, Kristina, Stephen. BSChemE, N.J. Inst. Tech., 1976; MBA, Ind. U., Gary, 1981. Process engr. ARCO Products Co., Harvey, Ill., 1976-78, environ. egr., 1978-80; sr. environ. engr. ARCO Chem. Co., Phila., 1980-81, sr. bus. analyst, 1981-83, sr. coord. mgr., 1983-86; mgr. petroleum futures ARCO Chem. Co., Newtown Sq., Pa., 1986-87, dir. govt. issues, 1987—; bd. dirs. Pa. Resources Coun., Media, Coun. on Plastics and Packaging in the Environment, Washington. Bd. dirs. West Chester (Pa.) Area Sch. Dist., 1987—. Home: 1229 Gail Rd West Chester PA 19380-4028 Office: ARCO Chem Co 3801 W Chester Pike Newtown Square PA 19073-2387

ZADUNAISKY, JOSE ATILIO, physiology educator; b. Rosario, Litoral, Argentina, July 15, 1932; came to U.S., 1964; s. Abraham and Juana (Lande) Z.; m. Maria F. Dabini, Apr. 12, 1954; children: Laura J., Edward P. BA, Colegio Rivadavia, Buenos Aires, 1949; MD, U. Buenos Aires, 1956, PhD in Physiology, 1958. Postdoctoral fellow U. Dublin, Ireland, 1958-59, U. Copenhagen, Denmark, 1959-60; assoc. prof. U. Louisville, 1964-67, Yale U., New Haven, 1967-73, NYU, N.Y.C., 1973—; prof. NYU, 1976—, dir. Sackler Inst., 1981—; vis. prof. Atomic Energy Commn., Nice, France, 1971, Univ. of Nice, 1988; investigator Mount Desert Island Biol. Lab, Bar Harbor, Maine, 1975—; scholar-in-residence Fogarty Internat. Ctrs./NIH, Bethesda, Md., 1990—, mem. study sect. Visual Sci./NIH, Bethesda, 1976-80. Exec. editor: Experiment Eye Research, 1970-92; editor: Chloride Transport in Membranes, 1982, Toxin Drugs and Pollutants in Marine Animals, 1984. Rsch. grantee NIH, 1960—, tng. grantee, 1960-84; recipient award for Oustanding Contbn. to Vision Rsch., Alcon Rsch. Inst., Tex., 1986. Fellow N.Y. Acad. Scis.; mem. Assn. for Rsch. in Vision and Ophthalmology (sect. chmn., 1971-72, pres. 1980), Internat. Soc. Eye Rsch. (sec. 1978-83, pres. 1984-88). Democrat. Jewish. Office: NYU Med Ctr 550 1st Ave Rm MSB 435 New York NY 10016

ZAFERIOU, PAUL JOHN, retail owner; b. Bronx, N.Y., Apr. 9, 1934; s. John A. and Julia A. (Gorgey) Z.; m. Phyllis K. Stephanou, July 12, 1959; children: Julie, Stephanie, Diane. AAS in Hort., Cornell U., 1954; AAS in Acctg., Westchester Community Coll., 1970; BA in Mgmt., Pace U., 1974; postgrad., NYU, 1986—. Chmn. bd. Colony Flower Shop Inc., White Plains, N.Y., 1957—; pres. Viz-A-Viz Inc., White Plains, 1973—; v.p. White Plains Wholesale Inc., 1986—; pres. NYCONN Bus. Sales/Consulting Inc., 1989—. Trustee Greek Orthodox Ch. of Savier, Rye, N.Y., 1969-71; pres. Good Counsel Acad. Fathers Club, White Plains, 1977-79, pres. United Way, White Plains, 1980-81; dist. chmn. Boy Scouts Am., Westchester County, 1981-82; bd. dirs. Cen. Westchester YMCA, White Plains, 1985—, Rep. City Com. Exec. Bd., White Plains, 1983—, U.S. Selective Svc., 1984—; mem. White Plains Vol. Fire Dept., Keep White Plains Clean Com., 1981, Citizens Budget Rev. Com. City Rep. City Com., 1980. Recipient award for bus. ethics Westchester Regional C. of C. Westchester Regional C. of C. Mem. White Plains C. of C. (founder retail coun. 1967, chmn. civic and beautification com. 1963), Univ. Club (pres. 1980-81), N.Y. Teleflora Internat. (bd. dirs. 1986-90), Lions, Sigma Alpha Epsilon, Rotary (bd. dirs. 1985-90, Merit award 1988), Shriner 320 Mason. Republican. Home: 17 Richbell Rd White Plains NY 10605-4110 Office: 55 Church St White Plains NY 10601-1905

ZAGANO, PHYLLIS, educator; b. N.Y.C., Aug. 25, 1947; d. Paul L. and Elizabeth (Kerwick) Z. BA in English, Marymount Coll., 1969; MS in Pub. Rels., Boston U., 1970; MA in English, L.I. U., 1972; PhD in English, SUNY, Stony Brook, 1979; MA in Theology, St. John's U., Jamaica, N.Y., 1990. Program officer Nat. Humanities Ctr., N.Y.C., 1979-80; asst. prof. Fordham U., Bronx, N.Y., 1980-84; ind. researcher N.Y.C., 1984-88; assoc. prof. communications Boston U., 1988—, dir. instr. for democratic communication, 1992—. Author: Religion and Public Affairs, 1987. Lector, lay minister Ch. of Vincent Ferrer, N.Y.C., 1980—. Lt. comdr. USNR, 1976—. Faculty Rsch. grantee Fordham U., 1983, Rsch. grantee Nat. Inst. Peace, 1984; Coolidge fellow Episcopal Divinity Sch., 1987. Mem. MLA, Am. Journalism Historians Assn., Am. Acad. Religion, Am. Cath. Philos. Assn., Assn. for Edn. in Journalism and Mass Communication, Naval Res. Assn. Roman Catholic. Office: Boston U 640 Commonwealth Ave Boston MA 02215-2422

ZAGARE, FRANK COSMO, political science educator; b. Bklyn., June 7, 1947; s. Domenick Joseph and Josephine Ann (Stager) Z.; m. Patricia M. Sclafani, May 26, 1974; children: Catherine, Ann, Elizabeth. BA, Fordham U., 1969; MA, NYU, 1972, PhD, 1977. Asst. prof. Boston U., 1978-87;

assoc. prof. SUNY, Buffalo, 1987-91, prof., chmn. dept. polit. sci., 1991—. Author: Game Theory, 1984, Dynamics of Deterrence, 1987; contbr. articles to profl. publs. MIT/Harvard fellow 1984; grantee U.S. Inst. Peace, 1989-90, NSF, 1992-94. Mem. Am. Polit. Sci. Assn. (coun. mem. conflict processes sect. 1986-89), Internat. Studies Assn., Midwest Polit. Sci. Assn. Home: 123 Morris Ave Buffalo NY 14214-1609 Office: SUNY Buffalo 520 Park Hall Buffalo NY 14260

ZAGER, RONALD I., chemist, consultant; b. N.Y.C., Dec. 27, 1934; s. Joseph and Theodora (Court) Z; m. Judith Ellen Bilt, Dec. 24, 1961 (div. July 1975); children: Scott Lawrence, Joseph Daniel. BS, Bklyn. Coll., 1955; MS in Chemistry, Stevens Inst. Tech., 1969. Chemist Charles Pfizer & Co., N.Y.C., 1956-58, Halocarbon Products, Hackensack, N.J., 1958-66; devel. chemist Tenneco Chems., Garfield, N.J., 1966-71; sr. chemist Givaudan Corp., Clifton, N.J., 1971-77; tech. dir. Internat. Flavors and Fragrances, Union Beach, N.J., 1977-88; cons. Highlands, N.J., 1988—. Mem. Am. Chem. Soc., Assn. Cons. Chemists and Chem. Engrs. (v.p. 1990-92). Office: Ronald Zager Assocs 1 Scenic Dr Highlands NJ 07732-1329

ZAGON, IAN STUART, neuroscience and anatomy educator, researcher; b. N.Y.C., Mar. 28, 1943; s. Benjamin and Beatrice (Shaffer) Z.; m. Eileen Kostel, Nov. 26, 1964. BS, U. Wis., 1965; MS, U. Ill., 1969; PhD, U. Colo., 1972. Asst. prof. biol. structure U. Miami, Fla., 1972-74; asst. prof. anatomy Pa. State U., Hershey, 1974-78, prof. genetics, 1975—, assoc. prof., 1978-85, prof., 1985-91, prof. cell and molecular biology and neurosci., 1984—, prof. neurosci. and anatomy, 1991—; cons. Nat. Inst. on Drug Abuse, Rockville, Md., 1980—; cons., reviewer NIH, Bethesda, Md., 1984—; grant reviewer Am. Heart Assn. of Pa., 1985—, mem. rsch. coun., 1988—. Author: Maternal Substance Abuse and the Developing Nervous System, Receptors and the Developing Nervous System; mem. editorial bd. Brain Rsch. Bull., 1980—, Physiology and Behavior, 1987—, Pharmacology, Biochemistry and Behavior, 1989—, Advances in Neuroimmunology, 1990—, Internat. Jour. Devel. Neurosci., 1987-89, Brain Rsch., 1992—, Devel. Brain Rsch., 1992—. Mem. Am. Soc. Cell. Biology, Soc. for Neurosci., Assn. for Rsch. in Vision and Ophthalmology.

ZAGOREN, JOY CARROLL, health facility director, researcher; b. N.Y.C., Oct. 31, 1933; d. Murray Morris and Celia (Donner) Rossman; m. Robert H. Zagoren, June 29, 1958 (div. 1988); children: Glenn, Robin; m. Robert Henry Chester, Apr. 1, 1988; children: Peter, Lisabeth, Melinda, Cecily, Kate. BS, NYU, 1957; MS, Adelphi U., 1969; PhD with distinction, NYU, 1981. Sec. sch. faculty Great Neck (N.Y.) Pub. Schs., 1957-71; rsch. scientist Inst. Psychobiol. Studies, Queens Village, N.Y., 1968-71; rsch. assoc. Albert Einstein Coll. Medicine, Bronx, N.Y., 1971-84; asst. prof. SUNY, Stony Brook, 1984-86; dir. Seriatum, N.Y.C., 1991—. Editor: The Node of Ranvier, 1984; contbr. articles to profl. jours. Chairperson Peace Corps Svc. Coun., Tri-State, 1965-75; pres. Kidney Found., L.I., N.Y., 1965-77; v.p. United Community Fund, L.I., 1970-83; bd. dirs. Jerusalem Mental Health Ctr., N.Y.C., 1986—. Recipient post doctoral fellowship NIH, 1982-84, svc. awards Kidney Found., Kiwanis, and others, 1970-87; named Disting. Alumnus of Yr., Adelphi U., 1986. Mem. Am. Assn. Neuropathologists, Am. Assn. Counseling, Esrath Nashim Hosp. (chairperson 1986—), Kappa Delta Epsilon. Democrat. Jewish. Home: 405 E 82d St New York NY 10028 Office: Seriatum PO Box 371 Livingston Manor NY 12758

ZAGORSKY, CAROL LACCI, information systems project director; b. N.Y.C., Nov. 19, 1942; d. Arthur Attilio and Evelyn Marie (Strang) Lacci; m. Eugene Dennis Zagorsky Jr., May 21, 1983. BBA in Econs., St. John's U., Jamaica, N.Y., 1968. Cert. data processor, quality analyst. Programmer info. systems and services dept. N.Y. Life Ins. Co., N.Y.C., 1967-71, programmer analyst, 1971-74, project leader, 1974-78, project mgr., 1978—, div. head, 1988-89, project dir., 1989—; conf. speaker Managing Computer Aided Software Engring. Implementation; lectr. NYU, Info. Technols. Inst., 1990—. Trustee Murray Hill Com., N.Y.C., 1977-79, 85-86, v.p. 1979-85. Mem. Women in Data Processing, Quality Mgmt. Assn. N.Y. (pres. 1991—), Nat. Excelerator Users Group (profl. devel. com.), Met. N.Y. Computer Aided Software Engring. Users Group. Democrat. Episcopalian. Office: NY Life Ins Co 51 Madison Ave New York NY 10010-1603

ZAHAVY, REUVAIN, mathematics educator; b. N.Y.C., July 14, 1953; s. Zev and Edith Doris (Medine) Z. BA, Yeshiva U., 1975, MA, 1977; MS, Adelphi U., 1980, student, 1980—. Instr. St. Peter's Coll., Jersey City, 1981-83; instr. math., com. mem. Queensboro Community Coll./CUNY, Queens, N.Y., 1983—; lectr. CUNY, Queens, 1980-81; adj. lectr. Marymount Manhattan Coll., N.Y.C., 1983; instr. Bd. of Edn. Recertification Progrm, N.Y.C., 1984-85; cons. in field. Author computer software. Judge, Metro. N.Y. Math. Fair, N.Y.C., 1984-85. Scholar, N.Y. Bd. Regents, 1971-75, faculty Yeshiva U., 1975-77, faculty Adelphi U., 1977-80. Mem. Math. Assn. Am., Am. Math Soc., N.Y. Acad. Scis., N.Y. Math. Assn., Pi Mus Epsilon (treas. 1979). Home: 210 E 68th St New York NY 10021-6047 Office: CUNY Queensboro C C 56th Ave and Springfield Blvd Bayside NY 11364

ZAHED, ISMAIL, physics educator; b. Algiers, Algeria, May 22, 1956; came to U.S. 1979.; s. Ali and Baya Z. BSc, U. Algiers, 1979; MSc, MIT, 1981, PhD, 1983. Postdoctoral fellow Niels Bohr Inst., Copenhagen, 1983-84; rsch. assoc. SUNY, Stony Brook, 1984-87, asst. prof. physics, 1987-90, assoc. prof. physics, 1990—. NSF fellow, 1983-84. Office: SUNY Dept Physics Stony Brook NY 11794

ZAHLER, STANLEY ARNOLD, microbial genetics educator; b. N.Y.C., May 28, 1926; s. Irving and Clara (Heimowitz) Z.; m. Eleanor Janette Haugness, Nov. 1, 1952; children: Kathy Ann, Diane Louise, Peter Irving. Student, CCNY, 1941-44; AB, NYU, 1948; MS, U. Chgo., 1950, PhD, 1952. Postdoctoral fellow USPHS, Urbana, Ill., 1952-54; asst. prof. U. Wash., Seattle, 1954-59; from asst. prof. to prof. Cornell U., Ithaca, N.Y., 1959—, chair sect. genetics and devel., 1990—; cons. in field. Ens. USNR, 1944-46. Mem. Am. Soc. Microbiology (various offices 1960-85). Office: Cornell U Biotech Bldg Ithaca NY 14853

ZAHN, MARKUS, electrical engineering educator; b. Bergen-Belsen, Germany, Dec. 3, 1946; s. Irving and Maria (Fischer) Z.; m. Linda Ruth Jasen, June 1, 1969; children: Laura Michelle, Daniel Jacob, Jeffrey David, Amy Elizabeth. BSEE, MSEE, MIT, 1968, cert. in Elec. Engring., 1969, DS, 1970. Prof. Elec. Engring. U. Fla., Gainesville, 1970-80, MIT, Cambridge, 1980—. Author (book) Electromagnetic Field Theory: A Problem Solving Approach, 1979; co-author (videotapes) Demonstrations of Electromagnetic Fields and Energy, 1989. Sr. mem. IEEE. Office: MIT Rm 10-174 Cambridge MA 02135

ZAIK, CAROL FORD, museum director, art historian, educator; b. Springfield, Mass., Aug. 11, 1955; d. Edward William and Margaret (Ford) Z. BA, U. Mass., 1978; MA in Art Edn., Springfield Coll., 1979; PhD, NYU, 1984. Docent, adminstr. Currier Mus., Manchester, N.H., 1984-88; creating one-man sch. house into fine arts mus., West Issipee, N.H., 1988—; actor Mt. Tom Playhouse, Holyoke, Mass., 1965-68. Active Smithsonian Assn., 1965-87, Acad. Polit. Sci., 1983-92, Audibon Soc., 1986-92. Mem. Nat. Art Edn. Assn. (chmn. mus. div. 1987-90), Mass. Art Edn. Assn., Internat. Soc. Edn., Nat. Mus. Women in Arts, Amherst Fine Arts Assn., U.S. Soc. Edn. Through Art, Smithsonian Assocs., Acad. Polit. Sci., Audubon Soc. Democrat. Roman Catholic. Home: 1062 Worthington St Springfield MA 01109-4021

ZAJONC, ARTHUR GUY, physicist; b. Boston, Oct. 11, 1949; s. Fred H. and Margaret (Shelton) Z.; m. B. Heide Knemeyer, Nov. 24, 1974; children: August C., M. Tristan. BS in Engring., U. Mich., 1971, MS, 1973, PhD, 1976; MA, Amherst Coll., 1991. Postdoctoral fellow Joint Inst. Lab. Astrophysics, Boulder, Colo., 1976-78; asst. prof. Amherst (Mass.) Coll., 1978-84, assoc. prof., 1984-91, prof. physics, 1991—; vis. prof. Ecole Normale Superieure, Paris, 1981-82; vis. scientist Max Planck Inst. Quantum Optics, Garching, Germany, 1984, Inst. for Quantum Optics of U. Hanover, Germany, 1986; fellow Fetzer Inst., Kalamazoo, 1990—, Lindisfarne Assocs., N.Y.C., 1985—; advisor Boston Children's Mus., 1990—. Author: Catching the Light, 1992; adv. editor Orion mag., 1990, Re Vision mag., 1991, Holistic Edn. Rev., 1991. Pres. Hartsbrook Waldorf Sch., Hadley, Mass., 1980-90; dir. Camphill Village, Copake, N.Y., 1988—, BD Farmland Conservation Trust, Amherst, 1986—. Lt. USAF, 1971-76. NSF fellow, 1980-83; Rsch. Corp. fellow, 1980-84; Rockfeller grantee, 1990; Fulbright scholar, U. Innsbruck, 1993. Mem. Am. Assn. Physics Tchrs., Anthroposophical Soc. (dir. 1987-89). Office: Physics Dept Amherst Coll Amherst MA 01002

ZAK, DOROTHY ZERYKIER, psychologist; b. Katowice, Poland, Jan. 11, 1950; came to U.S., 1969; d. Mieczystaw and Helena (Stahl) Zerykier; m. Jesse Cooper Brake (dec.); m. Sheldon Jerry Zak, July 6, 1986. BA, Queens Coll., 1973; MA, New Sch. Social Research, 1975. Clin. intern Bergen Pines Hosp., Paramus, N.J., 1976-77; psychologist State Sch. Mentally Retarded, Kinston, N.C., 1977-78, Dorothea Dix Hosp., Raleigh, N.C., 1978-83; pvt. practice cons. N.Y.C., 1983-84; psychologist Fed. Employment and Guidance Services, N.Y.C., 1984-85; vocat. counselor N.Y. Assn. for New Ams. Inc., N.Y.C., 1985-88; ednl. counselor B'nai Brith Career and Counseling Services, N.Y.C., 1988-90; career acad. counselor Touro Coll., N.Y.C., 1990—; part-time cons. St. John's Hosp.-Cath. Med. Ctr. Bklyn. and Queens Weight Loss Program, 1987—. Mem. Am. Psychol. Assn., Polish Inst. Arts and Scis., Am. Assn. for Counseling and Devel., N.Y. Acad. Scis. Office: Touro Coll 844 6th Ave New York NY 10001-4103

ZAK, STEVEN ALLEN, import-export company executive; b. N.Y.C., Sept. 19, 1947; s. Maurice Lawrence and Selma A.; m. Gloria Brady, May 18, 1989; 1 child, Hope. BBA, U. Miami, 1969; M, New Sch. Social Rsch., 1970. Mgr. ops. Visual Graphics Co., Tamarac, Fla., 1971-79; dir. ops. Unit Rig Equipment Co., Tulsa, 1979-82; v.p. ops. Murray Corp., Hunt Valley, Md., 1982-91; pres. S and G Trading Co., Columbia, Md., 1991—; pres. Pacific Rim Imports, Columbia, 1991—; v.p. Melbourne Ltd., Reistertown, Md., 1991—. Mem. Am. Prodn. and Invetnory Control Soc., Purchasing MGrs. Assn., Logistics Coun.

ZAK, VICTORIA JO, writer; b. Perth Amboy, N.J.; d. Joseph Robert and Leona Evelyn (Lembcke) Z.; m. James Michael Keenaghan (div. 1977). BA in English, Douglass Coll., 1966; postgrad., Boston U., 1970-71. Oil painter New England, N.Y., 1969-74; editor, writer various mags., advt. agys., and publishers Boston, 1971-76, designer, craft bus. owner, 1976-80; mng. editor Physician E. Mag., Boston, 1978-81; editor, publisher Outpost Mag., New England, 1980; communications mgr. Nutritional Mgmt. Inc., Boston, 1981-85; writer, author, cons. for various cos. N.J., 1985—. Author: The Fat to Muscle Diet, 1987, The Dieter's Dictionary, 1991; author poetry; Contbr. articles to profl. jours. Tchr. Cambridge (Mass.) Adult Ctr., 1980's; rep. various fund drives. Recipient Patron's Choice award De Cordova Mus., 1983; named finalist in fiction Mass. Artists Found., 1986. Mem. Nat. Writer's Union.

ZAKAIB, LORNE, industrial technology executive; b. Montreal, Que., Can., June 11, 1932; s. Jesse Charles Zakaib and Rea Yvonne Brodeur; m. Viola Kouri, Sept. 3, 1961; children: Janice, Jay. B in Engring., McGill U., Montreal, 1956, diploma in bus., 1974. Program mgr. FIIID Navigation Systems Canadian Marconi, oper. mgr. Marine and Land Communications, 1956-73; exec. v.p. S.N.C. Group, Montreal, 1989—; pres., chief oper. officer S.N.C. Indsl. Techs. Inc., Le Gardeur, Que., Can. Past pres. Assn. for Mentally Retarded. Named Nouveau Performant, City of Montreal, 1986; recipient 3 Mercuriades awards. Mem. IEEE, Order Engrs., Montreal C. of C. Home: 421 Saint Thomas Circle, Saint Lambert, PQ Canada J4R 1Y3 Office: SNC Defence Products Ltd, 2 Pl Felix-Martin, Montreal, PQ Canada H2Z 1Z4 also: SNC Indsl Tech Inc, 5 montée des Arsenaux, Le Gardeur, PQ Canada J5Z 2P4

ZAKHEIM, BARBARA JANE, international business company consulting executive; b. London, Jan. 31, 1953; d. David Sloma and Sarah Frances (Leifer) Portnoi; m. Dov Solomon Zakheim, Aug. 20, 1972 (div. 1990); children: Keith Samuel, Roger Israel, Scott Elisha. BA, Oxford U., Eng., 1974, MA, 1978. Economist Maxima Corp., Silver Spring, Md., 1979, U.S. Dept. Energy, Washington, 1979-80; sr. project analyst Applied Mgmt. Scis., Silver Spring, 1980-83, staff assoc., 1983-85; prin. analyst NUS Corp., Gaithersburg, Md., 1985-87, cons. analyst, 1987-89; pres. Keith R. Scott Assocs., Inc., 1989—, African Treasures, Inc., 1990—; U.S. rep. Coll. Petroleum Studies, Oxford, 1984—; N.Am. rep. Twirltrade Ltd., London, 1985—; mem. adv. com. on women in bus. Theodore Roosevelt Nat. Bank, Washington, 1991-92; profl. team mem. Venture Ptnrs. Internat. Inc., N.Y.C., 1990—. Contbr. articles to profl. jours. Bd. dirs. SE Hebrew Congregation, Silver Spring, 1977-78. Mem. NAFE, Nat. Assn. Environ. Profls., Internat. Network for Women in Enterprise and Trade, Inc. Republican. Home and Office: 911 Kenbrook Dr Silver Spring MD 20902-3228

ZAKRZEWSKI, VLADIMIR JAN, artist; b. Lodz, Poland, Nov. 22, 1946; came to U.S., 1981; s. Wlodzimierz and Elzbieta (Owsepian) Z.; m. Magda Wojcicki, Aug. 8, 1975; 1 child, Sever Titus. MFA, Acad. Fine Arts, Warsaw, Poland, 1970. Artist in residence Stedelijk Mus., Amsterdam, The Netherlands, 1978-79, '82. Represented in permanent collections, Nat. Mus., Warsaw, Poland, Stedelijk Mus., Amsterdam, The Netherlands, Haags Gementemuseum, The Hague, The Netherlands; The Bklyn. Mus.; author: Drawing, 1983. Home and Studio: 52 Chardavoyne Rd Warwick NY 10990

ZAKS, JERRY, theatrical director, actor; b. Stuttgart, Fed. Republic of Germany, Sept. 7, 1946; came to U.S., 1948, naturalized, 1954; s. Sy and Lily (Gliksman) Z.; m. Jill P. Rose, Jan. 14, 1979; children: Emma Rose, Hannah Lily. AB, Dartmouth Coll., 1967; MFA, Smith Coll., 1969. Guest artist, vis. prof. Dartmouth Coll., 1977, 83-84. Actor: (Broadway plays) Grease, 1974, Once in a Lifetime, 1977, 1940's Radio Hour, 1978, Tintypes, 1980, (off-Broadway plays) including Ensemble Studio Theatre, 1971-81, O'Neill Center, Conn., 1975, Phoenix Theatre, 1976-78, Arena Stage, Washington, 1978, N.Y. Shakespeare Festival, 1975, Manhattan Theatre Club, 1980, Roundabout Theatre, (TV and/or films) including Tuscaloosa's Calling Me, 1979, Attica, 1979; star: (CBS-TV movie) Gentleman Bandit, 1981; appeared in: (TV spl.) Yankee Doodle Dandy, Kennedy Center Tribute to James Cagney, 1980; dir.: (plays, musicals) The Foreigner, 1984 (Obie award 1985), The Marriage of Bette and Boo, 1985 (Obie award 1985, Drama Desk award 1985), (nat. tour) Tintypes, Tap Dance Kid, 1985 (Dramalogue award 1985), Beyond Therapy, Sister Mary Ignatius, Baby with the Bathwater, 1984, House of Blue Leaves, 1986 (Antoinette Perry award), Anything Goes, 1987, Lend Me A Tenor, 1989 (Antoinette Perry award), Six Degrees of Separation, 1990 (Antoinette Perry award), Guys and Dolls, 1992 (Tony award); dir. Ensemble Studio, 1978-80, Phoenix Theatre, N.Y.C., 1980-81, Playwrights Horizons, 1981, Phila. Drama Guild, 1981, Denver Ctr. Theater, 1984, N.Y. Pub. Theater, 1984, Assassins, 1990. Bd. dirs. Ensemble Studio Theatre, N.Y.C., 1976—. Mem. AFTRA, Actors Equity Assn., Screen Actors Guild, Soc. Stage Dirs. and Choreographers. Office: Jujamcyn Theatres 246 W 44th St New York NY 10036-3910

ZALACAIN, DANIEL, Spanish educator; b. Havana, Cuba, Dec. 15, 1948; s. Fernando and Alidia (Garxia) A.; m. Gloria Zalacain, June 16, 1974; 1 child, Ana. MA, U. N.C., 1973, PhD, 1976. Asst. prof. Spanish No. Ill. U., DeKalb, 1977-80; asst. prof. Spanish Seton Hall U., South Orange, N.J., 1980-85, assoc. prof. Spanish, 1986—, chmn. Dept. Modern Langs., 1987—. Editor: New Beats: 7 One-Act Hispanic American Plays, 1950; author: Teatro Absurdista Hispanamericano, 1985; contbr. articles to profl. jours. Mem. Am. Assn. Tchrs. of Spanish and Portuguese. Home: 29 Harding Dr South Orange NJ 07079-1202 Office: Seton Hall U Dept Modern Langs South Orange NJ 07079

ZALDASTANI, GUIVY, small business owner; b. Tbilisi, Republic of Ga., Nov. 1, 1919; came to U.S., 1948, naturalized 1953; s. Soliko and Mariam (Hirsely) Z.; m. Meredeth Fowler, Mar. 24, 1933 (div. Jan. 1982); children: Nicholas, Tamara, Nina; m. Micheline de Bievre, May 12, 1984. License en Droit, Sorbonne U., Paris, 1945, Diplome d'Etudes Superieures en Droit, 1946; MBA, Harvard U., 1951. Dept. mgr., buyer Federated Dept. Stores, Boston, 1957-62; pres. Finishing Touch, Boston, 1962-80, Ryan & Elliott Internat. Real Estate, Boston, 1980-83, Zaldastani Cons., Boston, 1982—; bd. dirs. Zaldastani Assocs., Boston. Editor Voice of Free Georgia, 1951-65, Iveria, 1970. Cons. Ho. of Reps. crimes of Krushchev, 1960; pres. Georgian Youth Assn., Paris, 1942-47; charter mem. Rep. Presdl. Task Force, Washington, 1980; co-chmn. Harvard Bus. Sch. Reunion, Cambridge, 1961, 76, 86. Served to lt. French Marines, 1940-41. Mem. Georgian Assn. in U.S. (pres. N.Y. chpt. 1966-74). Republican. Clubs: Harvard (N.Y., Boston); Sommerset (Boston); Cercle de l'Union Interalliée (Paris). Home: The Ridge Orford NH 03777

ZALDASTANI, OTHAR, structural engineer; b. Tbilisi, Georgia, USSR, Aug. 10, 1922; came to U.S., 1946; naturalized, 1956; s. Soliko Nicholas and Mariam Vachnadze (Hirsely) Z.; m. Elizabeth Reily Bailey, June 22, 1963; children: Elizabeth, Anne, Alexander. Diplome D'Ingenieur, Ecole Nationale des Ponts et Chaussees, Paris, 1945; Licencie es Scis., Sorbonne, Paris, 1946; MS in Geotech. Engring., Harvard U., 1947, DSc in Aerodynamics, 1950. Registered profl. engr., Mass., R.I., Tenn., Mo., N.H. Mem. faculty Harvard U., Cambridge, Mass., 1947-50; ptnr. Nichols, Norton and Zaldastani, Boston, 1952-63; pres. Nichols, Norton and Zaldastani, Inc., Boston, 1964-76, Zaldastani Assocs., Inc., Boston, 1976-88, chmn., 1988—; Gordon McKay vis. lectr. structural mechanics Harvard U., 1961; trustee, 1st v.p. Mass. Constrn. Industry Bd., 1973-76; mem. Mass. Designer Selection Bd., 1976-80. Contbg. author: Advances in Applied Mechanics, vol. 3, 1953. Patentee sound absorbing block, prestressed concrete beam and deck system. Trustee Wheelock Coll., Boston, 1975-81, mem. corp., 1984—; trustee Boston U. Med. Ctr., 1976—; trustee Brooks Sch., North Andover, Mass., 1986—. Recipient awards from various orgns. and agys. including Prestressed Concrete Inst., Cons. Engrs. Coun. New Eng., Am. Inst. Steel Constrn., Concrete Reinforcing Steel Inst., Dept. Transp., Am. Concrete Inst. Fellow ASCE (Ralph W. Horne award), AIAA (assoc.), Am. Concrete Inst.; mem. Georgian Assn. in the U.S. (pres. 1958-65), Sigma Xi, Harvard Club, Harvard Faculty Club (Cambridge), Somerset Club (Boston), Country Club (Brookline, Mass.), Rolling Rock Club (Ligonier, Pa.). Home: 5440 31st St NW Washington DC 20015-1346 Office: Zaldastani Assocs Inc 7 Water St Boston MA 02109-4511

ZALLIE, JAMES PAUL, food ingredients company marketing executive; b. Phila., Apr. 22, 1961; s. Peter and Helen Zallie. BS in Food Sci., Pa. State U., 1983; MS in Food Sci., Rutgers U., 1988, MBA in Fin., 1991. Chemist Nat. Starch and Chem. Co., Bridgewater, N.J., 1983-85; devel. chemist Nat. Starch and Chem. Corp., Bridgeport, N.J., 1985-87, project supr., 1987-89, tech. mgr., 1989-92, mng. mktg., 1992—. Contbr. articles to profl. jours.; patentee in field food ingredients. Mem. Inst. Food Technologists, Am. Assn. Cereal Chemists, Am. Assn. Candy Technologists, Am. Soc. Bakery Engrs. Office: Nat Starch and Chem Co 10 Finderne Ave Bridgewater NJ 08807

ZALLINGER, RUDOLPH FRANZ, artist, educator; b. Irkutsk, Siberia, Nov. 12, 1919; came to U.S., 1924; s. Franz Xavier and Marie (Koncheravich) Z.; m. Jean Farquharson Day, Sept. 27, 1941; children: Peter Franz, Kristina, Lisa Day. BFA, Yale U., 1942, MFA, 1971; D Fine Art, U. New Haven, 1980. Instr. painting Yale Sch. Fine Arts, New Haven, 1942-47, asst. prof. painting, 1948-50; artist-in-residence Yale Peabody Mus./Yale U., New Haven, 1953—; faculty Hartford Art Sch. U. Hartford, West Hartford, Conn., 1961-72, prof. drawing and painting, 1972-89; fellow Davenport Coll., Yale U., 1964—, vis. prof., 1989—; bd. dirs. Paier Coll. Art, Hamden, Conn.; adv. com. Sanford Low Meml. Collection Am. Illustration, New Britain (Conn.) Mus. Am. Art. Solo exhbns. include Mystic (Conn.) Seaport Galleries, 1967, Ctr. Gallery, New Haven Jewish Community Ctr., 1975, Dorsky Galleries, N.Y.C., 1981, GE Corp. Hdqrs., Fairfield, Conn., 1981, Davenport Coll., Yale U., 1989; group exhbns. include Cleve. Art Inst., 1977, Joseloff Gallery, U. Hartford, 1964-89; represented in permanent collections Seattle Art Mus., New Britain Mus. Am. Art, N.Y. Times Dist. Hdqrs., Atlanta, Yeshiva U., Tel Aviv, numerous others and pvt. collections. Bd. dirs. Conn. Hospice, 1982, vice-chmn., 1988, co-chmn., 1990. Winner Pulitzer award for painting, 1949; recipient Addison Emery Verrill medal Yale U., 1980, Rudolph F. Zallinger fellowship, 1989; recipient James and Frances Bent award for creativity U. Hartford, 1988. Mem. Nat. Soc. Mural Painters, Conn. Acad. Arts and Scis., Puget Sound Group Northwest Painters, New Haven Paint and Clay Club (bd. dirs., past pres.). Home: 5060 Ridge Rd North Haven CT 06473-1026 Office: Yale Peabody Mus 170 Whitney Ave New Haven CT 06511-3748

ZAMLOWSKI, PETER STEVEN, nature center director; b. New Haven, Aug. 19, 1958; s. Joseph Paul and Helen Sophie (Lukaszewski) Z.; m. Lori Ann Zamlowski; children: Joshua, Jessica. Student, SUNY, Morrisville, 1980. Dir. Westmoreland Sanctuary, Bedford, N.Y., 1980—; bird bander Fish and Wildlife Svc., Washington, 1985—; state hunter safety instr. N.Y. State Dept. Environ. Conservation, Albany, 1984—; bd. dirs. The Manus River Watershed Adv. Coun., 1990—. Leader 4-H Club, Westchester, N.Y., 1980—; adv. bd. Westchester Land Trust Mianus River Watershed Project., 1990—. Recipient Silver Clover award 4-H Coop. Extension, 1986, Gold Clover award, 1991. Mem. Federated Conservationists Westchester County, Sportsmen's Club (pres. No. Westchester chpt. 1984—). Roman Catholic. Home: RR 2 Mount Kisco NY 10549-9802 Office: Westmoreland Sanctuary RR 2 Mount Kisco NY 10549-9802

ZAMORA, ANTONIO, computational linguist; b. Nuevo Laredo, Mex., Dec. 6, 1942; arrived in U.S., 1957; s. Antonio and Clementina (Garza) Z.; m. Marla Faye Cales, Dec. 22, 1967 (div. Mar. 1981); 1 child, Antonio Martin; m. Elena Michelle Pesin, June 26, 1981. BS in Chemistry, U. Tex., 1962; MS in Computer Sci., Ohio State U., 1969. Sr. info. scientist Chem. Abstracts Svc., Columbus, Ohio, 1965-82; sr. programmer IBM Corp., Bethesda, Md., 1982—; mem. adv. bd. Jour. Chem. Info. and Computer Scis., Washington, 1977-84. Contbr. articles to profl. jours., chpt. to book Managing Artificial Intelligence Systems, 1990; patentee natural lang. processing programs. With U.S. Army, 1962-65. Mem. Am. Chem. Soc., Am. Soc. Info. Sci. (Best Paper of Yr. award 1971), Assn. Computational Linguistics. Home: 4601 N Park Ave Apt 411 Bethesda MD 20815-4521 Office: IBM Corp 6905 Rockledge Dr Bethesda MD 20817-1828

ZAMORA, RICARDO MESINAS, management consultant; b. Mexico City, July 13, 1963; came to U.S., 1985; s. Ricardo Laurent Zamora and Maria de Lourdes (Mesinas) Z.; m. Annemarie Binderberger, Jan. 5, 1990; 1 child, Annemarie. BSChemE, U. Iberoamericana, Mexico City, 1984; MSChemE, Rensselaer Poly. Inst., 1987; M in Pub. and Pvt. Mgmt., Yale U., 1991. Registered profl. engr., Mexico. Sales/distbn. analyst The Procter & Gamble Co., Mexico City, 1985; intern, assoc. Booz, Allen & Hamilton, Inc., N.Y.C., 1987-89; intern, project mgr. Booz, Allen & Hamilton, Inc., The Hague, Netherlands, 1990; ops. assoc. Booz, Allen & Hamilton, Inc., N.Y.C., 1991—; teaching asst. Yale Sch. of Orgn. & Mgmt., New Haven, 1990-91; rsch. asst. Rensselaer Poly. Inst., Troy, N.Y., 1986-87; cons. in field Germany, The Netherlands, venezuela, and Mexico. Co-author: Spouting II Hydrodynamics, 1992; author: Geo-Politics vs. Geo-Economics. Mem. Am. Inst. Chem. Engrs., Yale Mfg. Interest Group. Roman Catholic. Home: 446 N Corona Ave Valley Stream NY 11580

ZAMPELLA, ARTHUR DANTE LOUIS, health care facility administrator, physician; b. Jersey City, May 15, 1917; s. Erminio and Filomena (Lettieri) Z.; m. Alice Christine Seely, Aug. 29, 1964; children: Robert, Susan, Clark, Richard, Michael. AB, Columbia Coll., 1938; MD, Boston U., 1943; postgrad., NYU, 1947. Diplomate Nat. Bd. Med. Examiners. Med. dir. Idylease Med. Group, Newfoundland, N.J., 1947—; lab. dir. Idylease Clin. Labs., Newfoundland, 1947—; rsch. analyst Armstrong Engring., Inc., Kinnelon, N.J., 1961-70; med. and exec. dir. Idylease Nursing & Convalescent Home, Newfoundland, 1954-72; med. dir. Nat. Inst. for Rehab. Engring., Butler, N.J., 1970—, Idylease Guidance Ctr., Newfoundland, 1975—; adminstr. West Milford Day Ctr. at Idylease, Inc., Newfoundland, 1977—; aviation med. examiner FAA, Washington, 1964—; preceptor dept. medicine U. Medicine and Dentistry of N.J., Newark, 1973—. Author: General Preparedness Plan for Your Hospital, 1954; editor: The Stork Didn't Bring You, 1964. Police and fire surgeon Twp. of West Milford, N.J., 1954—; team physician West Milford Bd. of Edn., 1971-81; chmn. Crop Walk for Hunger, West Milford, 1981—; pres. Twp. of West Milford Bd. of Health, 1981—; bd. dirs., v.p. West Milford Youth and Family Counseling Bd., 1981-90; chmn. bd. Three Rivers Boy Scouts Am., Wayne, N.J., 1985-88; bd. dirs. Passaic Community Coll.; pres. Shoestring Prodns., 1987-91. Lt. USN, 1944-48, PTO. Recipient Merit award Boy Scouts Am., 1988, Silver Beaver award, 1988, P.A.L. Community Svc. award Police Benevolent Assn., 1989; named Citizen of the Yr., West Milford Rep. Club, 1990; inducted into William L. Dickinson High Sch. Hall of Fame, 1989. Fellow Am. Coll. Sports Medicine, Am. Acad. Family Practice (v.p. 1988-91), Am. Assn. Med. Adminstrs. (v.p. 1976); mem. Allied Health Adv. Coun. (bd. dirs.), N.J.

Cultural Heritage Coun., Mensa, N.Y. Athletic Club (sr.), Rotary. Methodist. Home and Office: 124 Union Valley Rd Newfoundland NJ 07435-1600

ZAMPIELLO, RICHARD SIDNEY, metals and trading company executive; b. New Haven, May 7, 1933; s. Sidney Nickolas and Louise Z.; B.A., Trinity Coll., 1955; M.B.A., U. Bridgeport, 1961; m. Helen Shirley Palsa, Oct. 10, 1961; 1 son, Geoffrey Richard. With Westinghouse Elec. Corp., Pitts., 1955-64; exec. v.p. Ullrich Copper Corp., subs. Foster Wheeler, Kenilworth, N.J., 1964-71; sr. v.p. Gerald Metals, Inc., Stamford, Conn., 1971-85; group v.p. Diversified Industries Corp., St. Louis, 1985-90; pres. Plume and Atwood Brass Mill div. Diversified Industries Corp., Thomaston, Conn., 1985-90; pres. Upstate Metals Corp., Canastota, N.Y., 1990—. Mem. ASME, Soc. Mfg. Engrs., AIME. Clubs: Yale, Mining (N.Y.C.); Lake Waramug Country (Washington, Conn.), Washington Country. Home: Woodbury Rd Washington CT 06793-1814 Office: 20 E Main St Waterbury CT 06702-2302

ZANARDELLI, JOHN JOSEPH, executive director; b. Monongahela, Pa., July 27, 1950; s. John and Linda (Lazzari) Z.; m. Suzanne King, Jan. 29, 1972; children: Brandon John, Stephen William, Robyn Lynn. AA, Community Coll. Allegheny Cty, Pitts., 1970; AS in Acctg., Community Coll. Allegheny Cty., Pitts., 1991; BS in Edn., California U. Pa., 1972; MPH, U. Pitts., 1979. Rsch. asst. grad. sch. pub. health U. Pitts., 1973-78; adminstrv. resident Cen. Med. Ctr. & Hosp., Pitts., 1978-79; vice chmn., sec., dir. Allegheny Mountain Health Enterprises, Inc., Oil City, Pa., 1985-88; exec. v.p. Oil City Area Health Ctr., Inc., 1979-88; exec. v.p., chief oper. officer Grane Healthcare, Inc., Pitts., 1988-90; adminstr., chief oper. officer Southwood Psychiat. Hosp., Inc., Pitts., 1990-91; exec. dir. Allegheny Sr. Care, Pitts., Pa., 1991—; preceptor, health adminstrn. program grad. schs. pub. health & bus. U. Pitts., 1980—; pres. Healthcare Properties, Inc., Pitts., 1983—. Fellow Am. Coll. Healthcare Execs., Am. Hosp. Assn., Young Adminstrs. Group Met. Pitts. Home: 2997 Greenwald Rd Bethel Park PA 15102-1615 Office: Presbyn Assn on Aging Allegheny Div 1215 Hulton Rd Oakmont PA 15139-1196

ZANE, RAYMOND J., lawyer, state senator; b. Woodbury, N.J., July 23, 1939; s. Clarence R. and Veronica (Murphy) Z.; children—Marybeth, Raymond II, Kenneth. B.S. in Bus. Adminstrn., St. Joseph's U., 1965; J.D., Rutger's U., 1974. Bar: N.J. 1974, N.Y. 1989. Freeholder, Gloucester County, Woodbury, N.J., 1971-73; mem. N.J. Senate, 1973—, dep. asst. minority leader. Mem. N.J. Bar Assn., Gloucester County Bar Assn. Home: 509 Sharp Dr Mickleton NJ 08056-1441 Office: 39 S Broad St Woodbury NJ 08096-4609 Other: NJ State Senate State Capitol Trenton NJ 08625

ZANETTI, RICHARD JOSEPH, editor; b. Weehawken, N.J., Mar. 22, 1939; s. Mario and Lucille (Coco) Z.; m. Norma Diane Nesheim, June 28, 1969; children: Joseph, Michael. BSChemE, Bucknell U., Lewisburg, Pa., 1961, MSChemE, 1964. Technologist Mobil Oil Corp., Bklyn., 1964-66; co-founder ASD Arts, Boston, 1979; dept. editor Chem. Wk. Mag., N.Y.C., 1980-84; assoc. editor Chem. Engrng. Mag., N.Y.C., 1984-88, editor-in-chief, 1988—; editorial dir. Chem. and Plastics Info. Svcs., N.Y.C., 1991—; lectr. in field. Producer, dir. documentary film: Standups, 1979; editor Feature Report, Plant Safety, 1988. Cons. Manhattan Coll., Riverdale, N.Y., 1989—. 1st lt. U.S. Army, 1964-65. Mem. Chem. Communications Assn., Drug Chem. and Allied Trade Assn., Tau Beta Pi, Omicron Delta Kappa. Office: McGraw Hill 1221 Ave Of The Americas New York NY 10020-1001

ZANGRILLI, JOHN ANTHONY, insurance executive, pastor; b. Providence, July 26, 1939; s. Antonio and Carmela (Masiami) Z.; m. Beverly E. Zangrilli, July 26, 1958; children: Dianne, Debra, Donna. A, Johnson and Wales Coll., 1977; student, Berean Coll., 1985-88, U. Bibl. Studies, 1988-89; M, Barean Coll., 1990. Lic. fraternal ins. counselor, R.I. Owner Zangrilli & Assocs., West Warwick, R.I., 1972—; pastor Bread of Life Ministries, West Warwick, 1987—, counselor, 1988—; chair Agts. Adv. Com., West Warwick, 1987—. Host TV and radio show Outreach, R.I., Mass., 1988—. Organizer Lord's Pl. Soup Kitchen, West Warwick, 1985. Petty officer USNR, 1956-62. Named Man of Yr. CYO, West Warwick, 1985. Mem. Inst. Christian Counseling (cert.), KC. Home: 146 Burlingame Rd West Warwick RI 02893-2408 Office: Zangrilli & Assocs Bread of Life Ministries PO Box 91 Fiskeville RI 02823-0091

ZANKOWSKI, DOREEN M., lawyer, finance executive; b. Revere, Mass., June 29, 1959; d. Anthony Alfonse and Dolores Ann (Cecere) Z. BA in History and Polit. Sci., Regis Coll., 1981; MS in Econs. and Environ. Planning, Boston U., 1984, M in City Planning, 1986; JD, Suffolk U., 1991. Bar: Mass., Washington, U.S. Ct. Appeals, U.S. Dist. Ct., 1991. Environ. planner Metcalf & Eddy, Inc., Boston, 1981-84; program mgr. Boston Harbor cleanup Camp Dresser & McKee, Inc., Boston, 1985-88, mgr. fin. & strategic planning Hazardous & Indsl. Waste div., 1988-89, asst. to pres. and the office of the chmn., 1989—; assoc. gen. counsel, asst. risk mgr. Mem. ABA (liaison to environ. values com. 1989—, natural resources, constrn. 1987—, adminstrv. fin. subcom. 1987—), Mass. Bar Assn., Boston Bar Assn., Assn. Trial Lawyers Am., Project Mgmt. Inst., Am. Cons. Engrs. Coun., Hazardous Waste Action Coalition, Legal Forum Com., Dante Alighiere Soc., Regis Coll. Alumni Assn. (fund agt. 1987—), Boston U. Alumni Assn., Suffolk U. Law Sch. Alumni Assn., Justinian Law Soc. Democrat. Roman Catholic. Home: 28 Kingman Ave Revere MA 02151-2323 Office: Camp Dresser & McKee Inc One Cambridge Ctr Cambridge MA 02143

ZANN, NICHOLAS T., artist; b. N.Y.C., June 7, 1943; s. Ernest Luke and Ellen Rita (Mihalis) Z.; m. Mary Jo Quay, Dec. 27, 1970 (div. 1983). Student, Sch. of Visual Arts, Manhattan, N.Y., 1967-69. Artist covers for Psychology Today; illustrations for Time, Newsweek, N.Y. Times, Esquire, NBC, ABC, CBS, also covers for books, Broadway posters and corp. clients, 1964—; art work appears in books, mags., TV and advt. campaigns; writer, creator design concepts MAD Mag., Esquire, Scholastic, Grey Advt., others. Recipient Funny Bone award Soc. of Illustrators, 1986. Office: 155 W 68th St Ste 1114 New York NY 10023

ZANOWIAK, PAUL, pharmacy educator; b. Little Falls, N.J., July 11, 1933; s. Harry and Susan (Kreel) Z.; m. Elizabeth Adele Bertsch, Nov. 19, 1957; children: Matthew Gregory, Jennifer Anne, Tamara Joan, Patricia Elizabeth. BS in Pharmacy, Rutgers U., 1954, MS, 1957; PhD, U. Fla., 1959. Registerd pharmacist, Pa. Instr. pharmacy U. Fla., Gainesville, 1958-59; R&D chemist Noxzema Corp., Balt., 1959-64; asst. then assoc. prof. W.Va. U., Morgantown, 1964-71; prof. pharmaceutics Temple U., Phila., 1971—, asst. to dean, 1971-72, actin dean pharmacy, 1972-74, chair dept., 1971-81, dir. div. continuing edn., 1981—. Me. bd. edn. Jenkintown (Pa.) Sch. Dist., 1974—, pres., 1987-88. Mem. Am. Pharm. Assn., Am. Soc. Hosp. Pharmacists, Am. Assn. Colls. Pharmacy (bd. dirs. 1978-80), Am. Assn. Pharm. Scientists, Pa. Pharm. Assn. (pres. 1989-90), Nat. Assn. Retail Druggists, Montgomery County Pharm. Assn., Phila. Pharmacy Forum, Sigma Xi, Rho Chi (pres. 1986-88). Office: Temple U Sch Pharmacy 3307 N Broad St Philadelphia PA 19140-5193

ZAPALA, ROBIN MILLER, alcohol/drug abuse services professional; b. S.I., N.Y., Mar. 24, 1952; d. Paul and Maxine (Lawch) Miller; m. Leonard Joseph Zapala, Aug. 29, 1982. BA, Coll. S.I., 1975, MS in Edn., 1980. Cert. alcoholism counselor, N.Y., 1986. Vocat. edn. therapist United Cerebral Palsy, S.I., 1975-78; project dir. for spl. svcs. grant Kingsborough Community Coll.-CUNY, Bklyn., 1980-83; team coord. Bridgeway House Psychiat. Rehab. Partial Care Facility, N.J., 1983-84; sr. alcoholism counselor St. Vincents/Bayley Seton Hosp., S.I., 1984-88; sr. alcoholism therapist AL-CARE, Albany, N.Y., 1988—. Author, editor: The Teacher and the Disabled Student, 1983. Mem. N.Y. Fedn. Alcoholism Counselors. Home: 318 LaFayette St Schenectady NY 12305 Office: AL-CARE New Karner Rd Albany NY 12205

ZAPOROWSKI, MARK PAUL, economics educator; b. Buffalo, Jan. 25, 1957; s. Edward P. and Jane M. (Juszkiewicz) Z.; m. Stephanie Stabb, Aug. 23, 1986. BS, SUNY, Oswego, 1978; MA, SUNY, Albany, 1981, PhD, 1985. Lectr. SUNY, Albany, 1981-84; asst. prof. Econs. and Fin. Canisius Coll., Buffalo, 1984-90, assoc. prof. Econs. and Fin., 1990—; econ. loss legal cons., 1990—. Contbr. articles profl. jours. Recipient Canisius Coll. rsch. grants, 1985, 86, 88, 90. Mem. Am. Econs. Assn., Am. Stats. Assn. Office: Canisius Coll Dept Econs and Fin 2001 Main St Buffalo NY 14208-1098

ZAPPA, CHARLES R., marketing consultant; b. Balt., Aug. 29, 1943; s. Francis Vincent and Rosemarie (Colimore) Z.; m. Marcia Ann Lesheski, Jan. 30, 1965; 1 child, Stanley Jason. BS, Calif. Poly. U., Pomona, 1969. Rsch. fellow U. Stockholm, 1969-70; fin. analyst TransAmerica, L.A., 1970-71; sales rep. coll. div. McGraw-Hill, L.A., 1971-75; sponsoring editor coll. div. McGraw-Hill, N.Y.C., 1975-74; sr. mktg. mgr. McGraw-Hill Internat., N.Y.C., 1984-86; v.p. Datapro/McGraw-Hill, Delran, N.J., 1986-87, Macmillan Healthcare Info., Morristown, N.J., 1987-88; pres. Future Potential, Inc., mktg. cons., Ridgewood, N.J., 1988—. Contbg. author: (anthology) Rock Giants, 1967; guest columnist N.Y. Times, 1975, Bergen Record, 1991. With USMC, 1961-64, Vietnam. Mem. Textbook Authors Assn., Assn. Am. Pubs. (chmn. mktg. com. coll. div. 1982-84), Am.-Okinawan Karate Assn. Democrat. Unitarian.

ZARA, GERARD JOSEPH, painting contractor and owner; b. Newark, Mar. 4, 1939; s. Gerard Zara and Mildred (Simonsen) Maytidu; m. Carol Scabet, July 23, 1960; children: Richard, Kathleen, John. Grad. high sch., Bloomfield, N.J. Painting contractor pvt. practice, Point Pleasant, N.J., 1964—. Co-author: Prison Money: The Media of Exchange of our Penal Institutions, 1981; author: Prison Tokens and Medals of the United States, 1992. Pres. ann. charity auction Deborah Heart and Lung Ctr., Browns Mills, N.J., 1981—. With U.S. Army, 1958-66. Mem. Ocean County Coin Club (life, pres. 1979-80, 80-81, sec. 1978-79, treas. 1981-85), Garden State Numis. Assn. (pres. 1985-87, treas. 1980-83), Great Eastern Numis. Assn. (bd. mem. 1992—), N.J. Exonumia Soc. (pres. 1989-90). Roman Catholic. Home: 2414 Mark Pl Point Pleasant NJ 08742

ZARB, FRANK GUSTAVE, investment company executive; b. N.Y.C., Feb. 17, 1935; s. Gustave and Rosemary (Antinora) Z.; m. Patricia Koster, Mar. 31, 1957; children: Krista Ann, Frank, Jr. B.B.A., Hofstra U., 1957, M.B.A., 1962, L.H.D., 1975. Trainee Cities Service Oil Co., N.Y.C., 1957-62; gen. partner Goodbody & Co., N.Y.C., 1962-69; exec. v.p. CBWL-Hayden Stone, Inc. (investment banking), N.Y.C., 1969-71; asst. sec. U.S. Dept. Labor, Washington, 1971-72; exec. v.p. Hayden Stone, Inc., N.Y.C., 1972-73; assoc. dir. Office of Mgmt. and Budget, Washington, 1973-74; asst. to Pres., U.S., 1974-77; adminstr. Fed. Energy Adminstrn., Washington, 1974-77; adv. U.S. Congress, 1977-78; gen. ptnr. Lazard Freres & Co., N.Y.C., 1977-88; chmn., pres. chief exec. officer Smith, Barney, Harris, Upham & Co., Inc., N.Y.C., 1988—; bd. dirs. Primerica Corp., BDM Holdings, Inc.,; ty I; mem. adv bd. market oversign and fin. svcs. adv. com. SEC; bd. coun. U.S. and Italy. Author: The Stockmarket Handbook, 1969, Handbook of Financial Markets, The Municipal Bond Handbook. Trustee Hofstra U., Gerald R. Ford Found. Recipient Disting. Scholar award Hofstra U., 1974. Mem. Am. Soc. Pub. Adminstrn. (hon. life), Securities Industry Assn., Coun. Fgn. Rels., Bd. of Securities Investor Protection Corp. Office: Smith Barney Harris Upham & Co 1345 Ave Of The Americas New York NY 10105-0099

ZARCHAN, PAUL, electrical engineer; b. N.Y.C., Oct. 12, 1944; s. Louis and Minnie (Schneiderman) Z.; m. Maxine Ina Sands, Aug. 27, 1967; children: Adina, Ari, Ronit. BSEE, CCNY, 1966; MSEE, Columbia U., 1967. Sr. engr. Raytheon Co., Bedford, Mass., 1967-73, prin. engr., 1975-85; rsch. engr. Israel Ministry Defense, Haifa, 1973-75; staff engr. C.S. Draper Lab. Inc., Cambridge, Mass., 1985—. Author: Tactical and Strategic Missile Guidance, 1990 (C.S. Draper Lab. Inc. award 1990). Fellow AIAA (assoc., guidance control tech. com. 1984-86, publ. com. 1988—). Office: C S Draper Lab Inc 555 Technology Sq Cambridge MA 02139-3563

ZAREMBA, ALAN JAY, communication educator; b. Bklyn., Oct. 22, 1949; s. Meyer and Helen (Reich) Z. BA, SUNY, Albany, 1971; MS, SUNY, 1972; PhD, U. Buffalo, 1977. Tchr., English Colonie (N.Y.) Sch. System, 1972-73; lectr. U. Buffalo, N.Y., 1973-76; prof. SUNY, Fredonia, 1976-81, Northeastern U., Boston, 1981—. Author: Management in New Key, 1989, Mass Communication and International Politics, 1988; contbg. editor: Quality Observer Jour., 1991—; contbr. articles to profl. jours. Recipient Chancellor's award for Excellence in Teaching, SUNY, Albany, 1980, Northeastern Excellence in Teaching award Northeastern U., Boston, 1984, Ed Press award for Excellence in Ednl. Journalism, Edn. Press. Am., 1987. Mem. Internat. Assn. Bus. Communicators. Home: PO Box 262 Weston MA 02193-0001 Office: Northeastern U 360 Huntington Ave Boston MA 02115-5096

ZAREMBA-TYMIENIECKA, ANNA-TERESA, philosophy educator; b. Marianowo, Poland; came to U.S., 1954; d. Zaremba and Maria-Ludwika (de Lanval) Tymieniecki; m. Hendrik S. Hothakker, Sept. 8, 1955; children: Louis, Isabel, Jan. A, U. Krakow, Poland, 1946; MA, U. Paris, 1950; PhD, U. Fribourg, Switzerland, 1951. Teaching asst. U. Calif., Berkeley, 1954-55; instr. Oreg. State U., Corvalis, 1955-56; teacher philosophy several univs., 1956-76; prof., pres., founder World Phenomenology Inst., Belmont, Mass., 1976—. Author: Essence et Existence, 1957, Phenomenology and Science in Contemporary European Thought, 1961, Leibniz's Cosmological Synthesis, 1966, Why Is There Something Rather Than Nothing?, 1966, Eros and Logos, 1972, Logos and Life: Creative Experience and the Critique of Reason, 1988, Logos and Life: The Three Movements of the Soul, The Spontaneous and the Creative in Man's Self Interpretation in the Sacred, 1989, Logos and Life: The Passions of the Soul and the Elements in the Onto-Poiesis of Culture, 1990, (monographs) Beyond Ingarten's Realism, Poetica Nova: At the Creative Crucibles, The Moral Sense in the Foundations of the Social World, The Moral Sense, the Person and the Human Significance of Life, Tractatus Brevis: First Principles of the Metaphysics of Life Charting the Human Condition: Man's Creative Act and the Origin of Rationalities; co-author, editor 46 books; editor-in-chief Analecia Husserliana, Phenomenological Inquiry. Mem. Internat. Fedn. Philos. Socs. (mem. steering com. 1988—). Roman Catholic. Home and Office: World Phenomenology Inst 348 Payson Rd Belmont MA 02178

ZARET, BARRY LEWIS, cardiologist, medical educator; b. N.Y.C., Oct. 3, 1940; s. Irving Z. and Beatrice (Fader) Zaret; m. Myrna Zimmerman, June 23, 1963; children: Adam L., Elliot C., Owen M. B.S., Queens Coll., 1962; M.D., NYU, 1966; M.A., Yale U., 1982. Diplomate: Am. Bd. Internal Medicine. Intern Bellevue Hosp., N.Y.C., 1966-67, resident, 1967-79; research fellow John Hopkins U., Balt., 1969-71; asst. prof. medicine Yale U., New Haven, 1973-76, assoc. prof. medicine and diagnostic radiology, 1976, chief sect. cardiology, 1978—, assoc. prof. medicine and diagnostic radiology, 1980-82, prof. medicine and diagnostic radiology, 1982-84; Robert W. Berliner prof. medicine Yale U., 1984—; mem. staff Yale-New Haven Med. Ctr. Mem. editorial bd.: Am. Jour. Cardiology, 1977—, Jour. Cardiovascular Medicine, 1979—, Jour. Am. Coll. Cardiology, 1986-91, Jour. Cardiac Imaging, 1986—; assoc. editor: Yearbook of Nuclear Medicine, 1980—; contbr. articles to various publs. Recipient Casimir Funk award Soc. Mil. Surgeons, 1973; recipient Herrman Blumgart Pioneer award New Eng. chpt. Soc. Nuclear Medicine, 1978. Fellow Am. Coll. Cardiology, Council Clin. Cardiology, Am. Heart Assn. Council Circulation, Am. Heart Assn., Am. Physiology Soc.; mem. Am. Soc. Clin. Investigation, Am. Fedn. Clin. Research, Soc. Nuclear Medicine, Assn. Univ. Cardiologists, Assn. Profs. Cardiology (pres. 1992), Assn. Am. Physicians, Phi Beta Kappa, Alpha Omega Alpha. Jewish. Club: Interurban Clin. Home: 15 Cassway Rd Woodbridge CT 06525-1214 Office: Yale U Sch Medicine 333 Cedar St # 3fmp New Haven CT 06510-3289

ZARGAJ, TOMISLAV, psychiatrist; b. Novomesto, Slovenia, Yugoslavia, June 19, 1933; came to U.S., 1964; s. Thomas and Maria (Okorn) Z.; m. Paula Maria Malesic, Nov. 17, 1956; children: Paula, Tommy, Michael. MD, U. Loubloana, Slovenia, 1956. Diplomate Am. Bd. Psychiatry and Neurology; lic. physician, Mass., Pa., N.H. Intern U. Hosp., Celje (Yugoslavia) Gen. Hosp., 1956-59; physician Community Health Ctr., Velenje, Slovenia, 1959-64; resident in psychiatry R.I. Med. Ctr., Cranston, 1964-67; fellow Mass. Gen. Hosp., Harvard Med. Sch., Boston, 1967-68; from clin. dir. to asst. supt. Danvers (Mass.) State Hosp., 1968-73; pvt. practice Salem, Mass., 1970—; assoc. chief psychiatry Salem Hosp., 1972—, pres. med. staff, 1991—; cons. Action Profile, Salem, 1987—. Active St. Lukes Guild Cath. Physicians, Boston, 1990—. With Yugoslav Army Med. Corp., 1957-58. Fellow Am. Psychiat. Assn., Mass. Psychiat. Soc.; mem. AMA, Am. Assn. Gen. Hosp. Psychiatrists, Soc. for Exptl. and Clin. Hypnosis, North Shore Psychiat. Assn., Inc. (pres. 1973—), Essex South Mass. Med. Soc. (councellor 1990—, asst. sec. 1992—), Aircraft Owners and Pilots Assn., Danvers Fish & Game Club. Roman Catholic. Home: 10 Fairview Rd Salem MA 01970 Office: North Shore Psychiat Assn 100 Highland Ave Salem MA 01970

ZATKINS, SISTER KAREN MARIE (SUSAN LEONA), pharmacist; b. Phila., May 30, 1950; d. John Joseph and Leona Sophie (Wolski) Z. BS summa cum laude, Temple U., 1981, MS, 1986. Lic. pharmacist. Tchr. St. John Cantius Sch., Phila., 1971-72, St. Stanislaus Sch., Phila., 1972-73, Nazareth Acad., Phila., 1973-76; tchr. sci. Visitation, Norristown, Pa., 1976-78; pharmacist Nazareth Hosp., Phila., 1981-86, dir. pharmacy, 1986—. Mem. Am. Soc. Hosp. Pharmacists, Am. Pharm. Assn., Rho Chi. Democrat. Roman Catholic. Office: Nazareth Hosp 2601 Holme Ave Philadelphia PA 19152-2096

ZATUCHNI, JACOB, internal medicine educator; b. Phila., Oct. 8, 1920. AB in Chemistry, Temple U., 1941, MD, 1944. Cert. cardiovascular diseases Am. Bd. Internal Medicine. Intern Jewish Hosp., Phila., 1944-45; resident diseases of the chest Eagleville (Pa.) Sanatorium, 1945-47; resident internal medicine Temple U. Hosp., Phila., 1947-50; internist Temple U. Sch. Medicine, Phila., 1950; insr. medicine Temple U. Sch. Medicine and Hosp., Phila., 1950-54, asst. prof. medicine, 1954-58, assoc. prof. medicine, 1958-61, chief cardiac clinic B, 1959-60, prof. clin. medicine, 1962-66, prof. medicine, 1966-87, prof. emeritus, 1987—; clin. asst. medicine Episcopal Hosp., 1950-53, assoc. in medicine, 1953-59, teaching chief medicine, 1959-67, head sect. cardiovascular disease, 1967-82, dir. dept. medicine, 1974-82, head heart sta., 1982-87, attending physician, 1982-87; sr. diagnostician Pa. Hosp., 1987—, dir. clin. svcs. cardiovascular sect., 1987—; clin. prof. medicine U. Pa. Sch. Medicine, 1988—. Author: Notes on Physical Diagnosis, 1964; contbr. articles to profl. jours. Fellow Am. Coll. Chest Physicians, Am. Coll. Cardiology, Am. Coll. Physicians, Coun. Clin. Cardiology Am. Heart Assn.; mem. Phila. Coll. Physicians, N.Y. Acad. Scis., Am. Fedn. for Clin. Rsch., Heart Assn. Southeastern Pa., Am. Thoracic Soc., Phila. County Med. Soc., Pa. State Med. Soc., AMA, So. Med. Assn., Am. Soc. Nuclear Medicine, Am. Soc. Echocardiography, Pyramid Honor Soc., Alpha Omega Alpha, Sigma Xi. Office: Pa Cardiol Assn Ltd 801 Spruce St Philadelphia PA 19107-5701

ZATZ, IRVING J., structural engineer; b. N.Y.C., May 27, 1953; s. Hyman and Frances Zatz; m. Janet Gwen Share, Aug. 15, 1976; children: Jonathan, Eric. BS, Cornell U., 1975, M in Engring., 1976. Structural engr. Goodkind & O'Dea, Inc., Clifton, N.J., 1976-77, Grumman Aerospace Corp., Bethpage, N.Y., 1977-80; project engr. engring. analysis div. Princeton (N.J.) U. Plasma Physics Lab., 1980—. Contbr. articles to profl. jours. Bd. dirs., v.p. Princeton Oaks Homeowners Assn.; mgr. West Windsor Little League. Univ. fellow Cornell U., 1975-76; recipient 1st place award James F. Lincoln Engrng. Design Competition, 1975. Mem. AIAA, ASCE (exec. com. met. sect. 1978-80), Am. Concrete Inst., Tau Beta Pi, Chi Epsilon (chpt. treas. 1974-75, pres. 1975-76). Home: 8 Huntington Dr Princeton Junction NJ 08550-2122 Office: Princeton Plasma Physics Lab PO Box 451 Princeton NJ 08543-0451

ZATZ, MARVIN, insurance company executive; b. N.Y.C., Oct. 23, 1932; s. Max and Helen (Lillianthal) Z.; m. Lynne Riederman, Dec. 21, 1952; children: Steven, Kenneth. BA, Bklyn. Coll., 1954; DDS, NYU, 1956; MPH, Harvard U., 1981, MS, 1982. Pvt. practice South Bound Brook, N.J., 1958-80; assoc. dental dir. Brookdale Hosp. Med. Ctr., N.Y.C., 1982-83; dental dir. Empire Blue Cross, N.Y.C., 1983-85; v.p. The Prudential, Roseland, N.J.; dental cons. Delta Dental of Mass., 1980-82. Author: (chpt.) Dental Clinics, 1987. Pres. Middlebrook Regional Bd. of Health, Middlesex, N.J., 1975-78, Bound Brook Bd. of Health, 1978-80. Mem. ADA, Am. Assn. Dental Cons., N.Y. State Dental Soc., N.J. Dental Soc., Nat. Academies of Practice. Office: The Prudential 56 N Livingston Ave Roseland NJ 07068

ZATZKIS, HENRY, retired mathematician; b. Holzminden, Germany, Apr. 7, 1915; came to the U.S., 1940; s. Markus and Lifscha (Eber) Z.; m. Natalie Florence Serlin, July 1, 1951; children: Mark, David. BS, Ohio State U., 1941; MS, Ind. U., 1943; PhD, Syracuse U., 1950. Instr. Ind. U., Bloomington, U. N.C., Chapel Hill, Syracuse (N.Y.) U.; asst. prof. U. Conn., Storrs; assoc. prof. N.J. Inst. Tech., Newark, prof., prof. emeritus. Contbr. articles to profl. jours. Mem. Phi Beta Kappa, Sigma Xi. Jewish. Home: 5 Elliott Pl West Orange NJ 07052-4512

ZAUSNER, MARTIN, investor relations consultant; b. N.Y.C., Aug. 9, 1929; s. Hy and Teddy (Rose) Z.; m. Adrienne Taylor Becker, Jan. 16, 1959. BS, Syracuse U., 1950; MS, Columbia U., 1951; MBA, NYU, 1953. Chmn. bd. dirs. Arthur Schmidt & Assocs., Inc., N.Y.C., 1956—. Author: Corporate Policy and the Investment Community; cons. editor: The Stock Market Handbook; contbr. to Strategy of Corporate Financing. Bd. dirs. Lymphoma Found. Clubs: Sky, Princeton. Office: 342 Madison Ave New York NY 10173

ZAVITSAS, ANDREAS ATHANASIOS, chemistry educator, researcher; b. Athens, Greece, July 14, 1937; came to U.S., 1954; s. Athanasios A. and Catherine K. Zavitsas; m. Lourdes Romanacce, Apr. 17, 1959; 1 child, Athanasios. BS magna cum laude, CCNY, 1959; MS, Columbia U., 1961, PhD, 1962. Rsch. assoc. Brookhaven Nat. Lab., Upton, N.Y., 1962-64; rsch. chemist Monsanto Chem. Co., Springfield, Mass., 1964-67; prof. L.I. U., Bklyn., 1967—, grad. dean, 1975-80; cons. in field. Contbr. articles to Jour. Polymer Sci., Jour. Am. Chem. Soc., Jour. Phys. Chemistry. Chmn. sch. bd. Holy Cross Sch., Bklyn., 1980-87. Mem. Am. Chem. Soc., N.Y. Acad. Scis., Phi Beta Kappa. Greek Orthodox. Office: LI U University Pla Brooklyn NY 11201

ZAVRACKY, PAUL, physics educator; b. Poughkeepsie, N.Y., July 28, 1948; s. Martin Joseph and Mary (Amato) Z.; children: Jacob, Alex, Gregory. Bs in Physics, Northeastern U., 1971, MS in Physics, 1975; PhD in Physics, Tufts U., 1984. Spl. staff MIT Lincoln Lab., Lexington, Mass., 1972-76; mgr. processing dept. Coulter Systems Corp., Bedford, Mass., 1976-80; tech. group leader microsensor program Foxboro (Mass.) Co., 1980-86; v.p. SOI tech. Kopin Corp., Taunton, Mass., 1986-90, chief operating officer, 1990-91; assoc. prof. ECE Northeastern U., Boston, 1991—. Contbr. articles to profl. jours.; patentee in field. Mem. IEEE, Am. Vacuum Soc. Office: Northeastern U 327 Dana Rsch Bldg Boston MA 02115

ZAWISTOWSKI, STEPHEN LOUIS, psychologist, educator; b. Lackawanna, N.Y., July 28, 1955; s. Louis Henry and Alice Theresa (Bartus) Z.; m. Jane Elaine Clark, May 26, 1979; 1 child, Matthew. BA, Canisius Coll., 1977; AM, U. Ill., 1979, PhD, 1983. Vis. asst. prof. Ind. U., Bloomington, 1983-84, postdoctoral fellow, 1984-85; asst. prof. St. John's U., N.Y.C., 1985-88; sr. v.p. ASPCA, N.Y.C., 1988—. Co-author: Animal Rights Handbook, 1990; co-exec. producer (film) Question of Respect, 1990 (Silver Apple award 1990); bd. editors Psychologists for the Ethical Treatment of Animals, 1988—; contbr. articles to profl. jours. Cubmaster Boy Scouts Am., S.I., 1988—; asst. coach S.I. Youth Soccer, 1986—. Recipient Stan Lesny scholarship Kosciuszki Found., 1977, U. Ill. Grad. fellowship, 1977, Postdoctoral fellowship NSF, 1984; named Psychologist of Yr., Psychologists for Ethical Treatment of Animals, 1989. Mem. APA, Behavior Genetics Assn., Animal Behavior Soc., Order of Arrow, Sigma Xi. Office: ASPCA 424 E 92nd St New York NY 10128-6803

ZAX, MELVIN, psychologist, educator; b. Cambridge, Mass., Apr. 14, 1928; s. Joseph and Sadie (Kirshner) Z.; m. Ruth Leah Vogel, Apr. 23, 1977; children: Jeffrey S., David B., Jonathan B. A.B., Boston U., 1951, A.M., 1952; Ph.D., U. Tenn., 1955. Clin. psychologist U. Tenn., Knoxville, 1955-56; staff psychologist St. Elizabeths Hosp., Washington, 1956-57; asst. prof. psychology U. Rochester, N.Y., 1957-62; asso. prof. U. Rochester, 1962-67, prof., 1967—; chmn. exptl. and spl. tng. rev. com. NIMH, 1970-71. Author: (with G. Stricker) Patterns of Psychopathology, 1963, (with E.L. Cowen) Abnormal Psychology: Changing Conceptions, 1972, (with G.A. Specter) An Introduction to Community Psychology, 1974, (with M. Nichols) Catharsis in Psychotherapy, 1977; editor: (with Stricker) The Study of Abnormal

Behavior: Selected Readings, 1964, (with Cowen and E.A. Gardner) Emergent Approaches to Mental Health Problems, 1967, (with D. Dorr and J. Bonner) The Psychology of Discipline, 1983; adv. editor Jour. Cons. and Clin. Psychology, 1965-81; contbr. articles to profl. jours. Served with AUS, 1946-47. NIMH spl. research fellow Psykologisk Inst., Copenhagen, 1966-67. Fellow Am. Psychol. Assn.; mem. Eastern Psychol. Assn., AAUP, Phi Beta Kappa, Sigma Xi, Phi Kappa Phi. Home: 27 Sky Ridge Dr Rochester NY 14625-2167 Office: Dept Psychology Univ Rochester Rochester NY 14627

ZBIEK, PAUL JOHN, history educator; b. Kingston, Pa., Jan. 10, 1952; s. Edward P. and Anne Sophie (Basta) Z.; m. Donna Mae Ide, Nov. 28, 1986; stepchildren: Jason Case, Brandon Case. BA, King's Coll., 1973; MA, East Stroudsburg U., 1982; PhD, Kent State U., 1987. Social worker Vols. In Svc. to America, Wilkes-Barre, Pa., 1974-75, Cath. Social Svcs., Norristown, Pa., 1978-80; prof., history King's Coll., Wilkes-Barre, 1988—; adj. prof. history Keystone Jr. Coll., La Plume, Pa., 1986-88; speaker King's Coll Speakers Bur.; steering com. Northeast Pa. Regional Historians. Contbr. articles to profl. jours. Recipient Univ. Fellowship, Kent State U., 1986, Dissertation Rsch. award, 1986, Pa. Hist. and Mus. Commn. Rsch. Stipend, 1988. Mem. Orgn. Am. Historians, N. Am. Soc. for Sport History, Phi Alpha Theta. Home: RR 1 Box 183 Harveys Lake PA 18618-9753 Office: Kings Coll N River St Wilkes Barre PA 18711

ZDEB, LORRAINE MARIE LOUISE, entrepreneur; b. Somerville, N.J., Mar. 6, 1954; d. Eugene George Nicholas and Mary Joan (Yarosz) Viscione; m. Edward Stanley Zdeb Jr., Oct. 28, 1973. Grad. cosmetology, Tru-Art Beauty Sch., 1972. Asst. mgr. Shepards Inc., Manville, N.J., 1971-73; mgr. operator A&B Factory Outlet, Chester, N.J., 1973-76; pub. rels. and promotion rep. Mad Charles, Inc., Somerville, N.J., 1976-78; asst. mgr. Hit or Miss, Somerville, 1978-80; mgr. Eugena Fashions, Somerville, 1980-90; ptnr. frozen food corp. Universal Cuisine Inc., Bridgewater, N.J., 1984-86; pub. rels. coord., ptnr. The Phoenix Ensemble, Bridgewater, 1985-89; real estate agt. (part-time) Weidel Realtors, Bridgewater, 1989—; pres. Love Your Pet, Somerville, 1991—. Author: Woodland Whispers, 1990. Recipient Golden Poet award World of Poetry, 1987. Roman Catholic. Home: 126 Huff Ave Manville NJ 08835-2216 Office: Love Your Pet PO Box 416 Somerville NJ 08876-0416

ZEBLEY, JOSEPH WILDMAN, JR., management consultant; b. Appleton, Md., July 9, 1914; s. Joseph Wildman and Annie May (Benjamin) Z.; m. Edith Sophie Schubel, July 4, 1947 (dec. Sept. 1972); children: Joseph Wildman III, Charles Schubel. AA, U. Balt., 1947, LLB, 1949; BS in Mil. Studies, U. Md., 1963; BS in Indsl. Mgmt., U. Balt., 1964, JD, 1970; MEd, Johns Hopkins U., 1973; PhD in Human Behavior, Newport U., 1984; cert. advanced study in edn., Johns Hopkins U., 1978. Cert. tchr. supr./administrator edn., Md. Operator Nat. Vulcanized Fibre Co., Newark, Del., 1934-36; owner, operator Clover Valley Produce, Elkton, Md., 1936-39; engring. asst. E.I. duPont de Nemours & Co., Seaford, Del., 1939-41; owner, operator Clover Valley Farms and Zebley Assocs., Balt. and Elkton, Md., 1946—; coord., bd. dir. Balt. Met. Area Manpower Tng. Skills Ctr., 1965-82; adj. prof. Balt. Coll. Commerce (now U. Balt. U. Md. System), 1966-70; exec. sec. Coun. Affiliate Orgns., Am. Assn. Adult Continuing Edn., Washington, 1983—; co-chmn., mem. Avd. Coun. Adult and Community Svcs., Md. State Dept. Edn., 1976—; chmn., mem. Adv. Com. Apprenticeship Info., Md. State Employment Svc., 1978—; com. chmn. Adv. Coun. Adult Continuing Edn. Community Coll. Balt., 1987—; cons. Adv. Com. Adult Literacy, Cecil C.C., 1987—. Author: Battlefield Tour of Metz, France Area, 1961 (Citation 1961), Family Zublin ou Zobel in America, 1736-1976, 1976, Scribbling With My Pen, 1980. Mem. exec. com., dist. chmn. Balt. area coun. Boy Scouts Am., 1970—; chmn., mem. devel. com. Balt. Sherwood Gardens in Guilford, 1970—. Maj. U.S. Army, 1941-46, ETO, ret. Recipient Silver Beaver award Boy Scout Am., 1979, Meritorious Svc. award Am. Assn. Adult and Continuing Edn., Washington, 1984; named Outstanding Adult Educator Lit. Tng. Office Mayor, Balt., 1986. Mem. ASTD, Soc. Advancement Mgmt. (pres. Greater Balt. chpt. 1974-75, Leadership award 1975), Md. Assn. Adult Community and Continuing Edn. (pres. 1982-83, Outstanding Svc. award 1987), Cecil County C. of C., Internat. Platform Assn., Sigma Delta Kappa, Phi Delta Gamma, Advt. and Profl. Club of Balt., Ea. Shore Soc. of City of Balt. (pres. 1989-91), Horticulturists/Foresters, Phi Delta Gamma (pres. Gamma chpt. 1990—), Phi Delta Kappa, Masons, Shriners. Democrat. Home: 3810 Juniper Rd Baltimore MD 21218-1827 Office: Clover Valley Farms 239 Jackson Hall School Rd Elkton MD 21921-2992

ZEBROWITZ, LESLIE ANN, psychology educator; b. Detroit, Nov. 8, 1944; d. Aaron Harry and Esther (Milgrom) Z.; m. A. Verne McArthur (div. July 1988); children: Caleb Jonathan McArthur, Loren Zachary McArthur. BA, U. Wis., 1966; MS, Yale U., 1968, PhD, 1970. Asst. prof. psychology Brandeis U., Waltham, Mass., 1970-76, assoc. prof., 1976-82, prof., 1982—, chmn. dept., 1986-91; Manuel Yellen prof. social rels. Brandeis U., Waltham, 1989—; vis. scholar Henry Murray Rsch. Ctr. Radcliffe Coll., Waltham, 1991-92. Author: Social Perception, 1991; contbr. numerous articles to sci. jours. Ford. Found. faculty fellow, 1973-74; NIMH rsch. grantee, 1975-81, 87—. Fellow Am. Psychol. Assn.; mem. Am. Psychol. Soc. (charter), Soc. for Exptl. Social Psychology, Ea. Psychol. Assn., Phi Beta Kappa. Office: Brandeis U Dept of Psychology Waltham MA 02254

ZEBROWSKI, ERNEST, JR., physics educator, author; b. Sewickley, Pa., Dec. 18, 1944; s. Ernest Thomas and Jozefa (Zajac) Z.; m. Susan Marie Loncar, July 3, 1970 (div. July 1980); 1 child, David Casimir; m. Bonita Gene Ramer, Mar. 10, 1986; children: Elke and Cassandra Kummerow. Student, Providence Coll., 1962-64; BS, Duquesne U., 1966; MS, Carnegie-Mellon U., 1968; PhD, U. Pitts., 1982. Rsch. physicist Jones & Laughlin Steel Corp., Pitts., 1967-68; prof. physics Community Coll. of Beaver County, Monaca, Pa., 1969-89; dir. integrated studies Pa. Coll. Tech., Williamsport, 1989-91, prof. physics, 1991—; cons. ITEC, Inc., Beaver, Pa., 1980-84; ind. cons., 1984—. Author: Fisica un Enfoque para Tecnicos, 1984, Practical Physics, 1980, Fundamentals of Physical Measurement, 1979, Physics for Technicians, 1974; contbr. articles to profl. jours. Bd. dirs. Hopewell Credit Union, Aliquippa, Pa., 1978-88; mem. Bridgewater (Pa.) Planning Commn., 1971-73. Recipient Hist. Rsch. award Nat. Sci. Tchrs. Assn., 1982; NSF grantee, 1991. Mem. Am. Assn. Physics Tchrs. (com. on sci. edn. for the pub. 1990—), Textbook Authors Assn. Office: Pa Coll Tech One College Ave Williamsport PA 17701

ZEBROWSKI, MARILYN FRANCES, psychologist; b. Perth Amboy, N.J., Nov. 14; d. Stephan Charles and Louise Mary (Kowalski) Dobranski; m. Leonard T. Zebrowski, Jan. 28, 1951; children: Diane, Leonard S. Degree in Oral Hygiene, Temple U., 1951, BA in Psychology, 1980; MEd, Antioch U., 1983; PhD, Union Grad Sch. (name changed to The Union Inst.), Cin., 1991. Nat. cert. counselor; cert. gambling counselor, hypnotherapist, dental hygienist. Tchr. bus. Drake Coll., Perth Amboy, 1942-46; tchr., counselor Pub. Sch. 9, Perth Amboy, 1947-49; dental hygienist Dr. Leonard T. Zebrowski, Camden, N.J., 1951-74; editor, writer for syndicated columnist Balt., 1974—; counselor, tchr., hypnotherapist Haddonfield, N.J., 1979—; psychology intern Camden County Health Svcs., Blackwood, N.J., 1981-83, 88-89; psychologist Haddonfield, 1983—. Bd. dirs. Maryville Inc., Glassboro, N.J., 1984-89; apptd. advisor to Gov. William Donald Schaefer of Md. on the Drug and Alcohol Commn., 1992—. Recipient svc. award Maryville Inc., 1987. Mem. Am. Psychol. Assn., Alcohol Counselors Assn., N.J. Compulsive Gambling Assn., Nat. Assn. Compulsive Gamblers, Dental Hygiene Assn., Colwick Women's Club (Cherry Hill, N.J., treas. 1968-72), Zonta, Cherry Hill Gourmet Club. Roman Catholic.

ZEBROWSKI, SISTER MARY THEODORETTE, religious educator, artist; b. South River, N.J., Aug. 30, 1916; d. Charles W. and Emily (Rawa) Z. Tchr. diploma, Cath. U. Am., 1940; BA in Fine Arts, Phila. Coll. Art, 1954; MA in Edn., Seton Hall U., 1974. Joined Bernardine Sisters of St. Francis, 1934. Tchr., missionary, prin. various schs., Pa. and Brazil, 1937-69; tchr. St. Dominic's Sch., Bricktown, N.J., 1969-70; tchr., prin. Sacred Heart Sch., Manville, N.J., 1970-75; prof. Alvernia Coll., Reading, Pa., 1975—, chmn. dept., 1975-88, freelance sculptor, 1989. Exhibited in group shows in U.S., South Am. Recipient svc. award Alvernia Coll., 1985; named Prof. (Artist) Emeritus, Artist-in-Residence, Alvernia Coll., 1989. Mem. Nat. Conf. Adminstrv. Artists, Archives Am. Art, Nat. Art Adminstrs. Assn., Smithsonian Assocs. Home: Alvernia Coll Reading PA 19607 Office: Bernardine Sisters OSF 647 N Spring Mill Rd Villanova PA 19085-2099

ZEDECK, MORRIS SAMUEL, pharmacologist, educator; b. Bklyn., Jan. 25, 1940; s. Hyman and Judith (Yakula) Z.; m. Ellen Lieberman, Mar. 4, 1989; children from previous marriage: Sharon, Beth, Deborah. BS in Pharmacy, Bklyn. Coll. Pharmacy, 1961; PhD in Pharmacology, U. Mich., 1965; MBA, Baruch Coll., 1987. Postdoctoral fellow, dept. pharmacology Yale U., New Haven, Conn., 1965-67; asst. prof. pharmacology Yale U. Sch. of Medicine, New Haven, 1967-68; assoc. mem. Meml. Sloan-Kettering Cancer Ctr., N.Y.C., 1968-83; assoc. prof. Cornell U. Grad. Sch. Med. Sci., N.Y.C., 1969-83; pres. Zedeck Adv. Group, Inc., N.Y.C., 1988—; adj. assoc. prof. John Jay Coll. Criminal Justice, N.Y.C., 1990—. Contbr. articles to profl. jours. Mem. Soc. Toxicology, Am. Coll. Toxicology, Am. Assn. Cancer Rsch., Am. Soc. Pharmacology and Exptl. Therapeutics, AAAS, Soc. Med. Jurisprudence. Home: 245 E 80th St New York NY 10021-0506

ZEDEKER, DANIEL LEE, dentist, educator; b. Dayton, Ohio, Oct. 5, 1956; s. Edward Furay Zedeker and Wanda Elizabeth (Bomholt) Davis; m. Roberta Ann Schaber; 1 child, Lauren Ann. BS, Fla. State U., 1979; DDS, Columbia U., 1983. Pvt. practice Huntington, N.Y., 1983, N.Y.C., 1984—; instr. Columbia U., N.Y.C., 1983-89, asst. clin. prof., 1989—; dir. dental svcs. Childrens Village, Dobbs Ferry, N.Y., 1989-90; com. mem. Greater N.Y. Dental Meeting, N.Y.C., 1988—, clinician, lectr., 1991—. Active Hastings Creative Arts Coun., Hastings on Hudson, N.Y., 1990. Pediatric dental grantee Columbia U., 1984. Mem. ADA, N.Y. Acad. Dentistry, Am. Soc. Dentistry Children, Fedn. Dentaire Internat., First Dist. Dental Soc. N.Y., Carnegie Study Club (v.p. 1988—), Omicron Kappa Upsilon. Office: 30 Central Park S New York NY 10019

ZEDROSSER, JOSEPH JOHN, lawyer; b. Milw., Jan. 24, 1938; s. Joseph and Rose (Zollner) Z. AB, Marquette U., 1959; LLB, Harvard U., 1963. Bar: N.Y. 1964, U.S. Dist. Ct. (so. dist.) N.Y. 1966, U.S. Dist. Ct. (ea. dist.) N.Y. 1971, U.S. Ct. Appeals (2d cir.) 1971, U.S. Ct. Appeals (D.C. Cir.) 1975, U.S. Supreme Ct. 1975. Assoc. William G. Mulligan, N.Y.C., 1964-67, Christy, Bauman, Frey and Christy and successors, N.Y.C., 1967-71; dir. community devel. unit Bedford-Stuyvesant Community Legal Svcs. Corp., N.Y.C., 1971-73; assoc. atty. fed. defender svcs. unit Legal Aid Soc., N.Y.C., 1973-74; asst. atty. gen. Environ. Protection Bur., N.Y. State Dept. Law, N.Y.C., 1974-80; regional counsel EPA, N.Y.C., 1980-82; assoc. prof. St. John's U. Sch. Law, N.Y.C., 1982-86; ptnr. Rivkin, Radler, Dunne & Bayh, Uniondale, N.Y., 1986-89, Breed, Abbott & Morgan, N.Y.C., 1989—. Lectr., contbr. to course handbooks for courses sponsored by Practicing Law Inst. and other assns. Lt. USNR, 1965-74, USAR, 1963-65. Mem. ABA, Assn. of Bar of City of N.Y., N.Y. State Bar Assn. (mem. Environ. Law Sect. Exec. Com.), Alpha Sigma Nu. Roman Catholic. Home: 115 E 34th St Apt 10D New York NY 10016-4629 Office: Breed Abbott & Morgan 153 E 53d St New York NY 10022

ZEGER, STEVEN A., physician; b. Newburgh, N.Y., Jan. 16, 1954; s. Emil and Seren (Schwartz) Z.; m. Eileen Barbara Warren, June 5, 1977; children: Sandra, Allison, Deborah. BS in Biology, Rensselaer Poly. Inst., 1976; MD, U. Cen. del Este Sch. Medicine, 1983. Resident in ob-gyn. Robert Wood Johnson Med. Sch. U.M.D.N.J., 1988; pvt. practice ob-gyn. Havertown, Pa., 1988—. Jr. fellow Am. Coll. Ob-Gyns. Jewish. Home: 1512 Fairview Ave Upper Darby PA 19083-4225

ZEHE, THERESA MARIE, lawyer; b. Cleve., May 31, 1963; d. Daniel Anthony and Loretta Ann (Levan) Z. BA, Quincy (Ill.) Coll., 1985; JD, Cath. U. Am., 1988. Bar: N.Y., 1989, D.C., 1990. Law clk. to hon. judge Richard J. Clark Charles County Cir. Ct., La Plata, Md., 1988-89; atty. Juvenile Rights Div./Criminal Def. Div. Legal Aid Soc. of N.Y., N.Y.C., 1989-90; atty. Pub. Defender's Office County of Monroe, Rochester, N.Y., 1990—. Receptionist Dem. Nat. Com., Washington, 1988. Mem. ABA, N.Y. Bar Assn. Democrat. Roman Catholic. Home: 126-5 Green Moor Way Henrietta NY 14467-8853

ZEHLER, EDWARD JOSEPH, occupational safety and health consultant; b. Phila., Jan. 20, 1940; s. Emil Joseph and Catharine Mary (Gleeson) Z.; m. Joanne Elizabeth Capek, May 25, 1963; children: Andrew M., David J. BS in Chemistry, Villanova (Pa.) U., 1961; postgrad., U. Pa., 1968, Drexel U., 1968-70, N.J. Inst. Tech., 1973-74. Indsl. hygienist Pa. Dept. of Health, Phila., 1964-65; quality control chemist Merck, Sharp and Dohme, Inc., Westpoint, Pa., 1965-66, asst. safety coord., 1966-70; assoc. safety engr. Merck and Co., Inc., Rahway, N.J., 1970-71, safety engr., 1971-73; corp. safety mgr. Am. Hoechst Corp., Somerville, N.J., 1973-81; safety mgr. L.I. Coll. Hosp., Bklyn., 1981-84; corp. safety dir. Alcolac, Balt., 1984-89; sr. scientist Gen. Physics Corp., Columbia, Md., 1989—; mgr. environ. safety tng. and svcs. Gen Physics Corp., Columbia, Md., 1991—. Exhibit guide Nat. Aquarium in Balt., 1987—. With U.S. Army, 1961-64. Mem. Am. Soc. Safety Engrs. (profl.), Md. Chem. Industry Coun. (legis. com. 1985). Democrat. Roman Catholic. Home: 728 S Charles St Baltimore MD 21230-3840 Office: Gen Physics Corp 6700 Alexander Bell Dr Columbia MD 21046-2190

ZEHNER, LEE RANDALL, environmental services executive, research director; b. Darby, Pa., Mar. 15, 1947; s. Warren L. and Alycia G. (Van Riper) Z.; m. Susan D. Hovland, June 23, 1973; children: Adam, Erica. BS in Chemistry, U. Pa., 1968; PhD in Organic Chemistry, U. Minn., 1973. Sr. rsch. chemist Arco Chem. Co., Glenolden, Pa., 1973-78; rsch. group leader Ashland Chem. Co., Dublin, Ohio, 1978-82; mgr. organic rsch. W.R. Grace & Co., Clarksville, Md., 1982-85; dir. biotech. programs Biospherics Inc., Rockville, Md., 1985—, v.p. sci. svcs., 1991—. Author various tech. publs.; patentee in field. Mem. AICE, Am. Chem. Soc., Inst. Food Technologists, Am. Mgmt. Assn. Home: 131 Brinkwood Rd Brookeville MD 20833 Office: Biospherics Inc 12051 Indian Creek Ct Beltsville MD 20705

ZEHNER, MARSHA LOUISE, school system administrator; b. Johnstown, Pa., May 20, 1951; d. Robert and Dorothy Mae (Weaver) Edwards; m. Glenn W. Zehner; 1 child, Greg Edward. BS, Lebanon Valley Coll., 1973; MEd, Millersville (Pa.) U., 1978, cert. in sch. psychology, 1982; PhD in Edn, Pa. State U., 1991. Cert. prin., Pa.; supt.'s letter eligibility, Pa. With Annville (Pa.) Cleona Sch. Dist., 1973—, asst. high sch. prin., 1987-88, asst. to supt., 1988—; spl. edn. auditor Pa. Bur. Spl. Edn., Harrisburg, 1987—. Mem. Am. Psychol. Assn., Pa. Assn. for Supervision and Curriculum Devel., Delta Kappa Gamma, Phi Alpha Epsilon. Republican. Home: 3 Charisma Dr Camp Hill PA 17011-1010

ZEHNER, THOMAS HENRY, aerospace executive; b. Bklyn., Aug. 22, 1944; s. Henry Bernard and Josephine Mary (White) Z.; m. Teresa A. Donegan, Sept. 11, 1965; children: Thomas Jr., Susann. BS in System Sci., Poly. Inst., 1966, MS in Math., Systems, 1969; MBA, Adelphi U., 1976; cert. in program for mgmt. devel., Harvard U., 1987. Systems engr. Grumman Aerospace, Bethpage, N.Y., 1966-71, mgr. engring., 1971-75, program/project mgr., 1975-81, program dir., 1981-89; gen. mgr. Grumman Space Systems, Irvine, Calif., 1989-90, program v.p., gen. mgr., 1990-91; program v.p. Grumman Aircraft Systems Div., Bethpage, 1991—. Mem. AIAA, Am. Defense Preparedness Assn., Am. Mgmt. Assn., Marine Corps Aviation Assn., Tailhook Assn. Republican. Roman Catholic. Home: 35 Osborne Ave Mount Sinai NY 11766-3134 Office: Grumman Aircraft Systems Div Mail Sta # 110 Bethpage NY 11714

ZEHRING, JOHN WILLIAM, academic administrator; b. Phila., Sept. 9, 1947; m. Donna Taber, Aug. 3, 1968; children: Micaela, Jeremiah. BA, Eastern Coll., St. Davids, Pa., 1969; MA, Rider Coll., Lawrenceville, N.J., 1971; MA in Religious Edn., Princeton Theol. Seminary, 1971; MDiv, Earlham Sch. Religion, Richmond, Ind., 1981. Ordained, 1981. Asst. dean Barrington (R.I.) Coll., 1971-75; spl. asst. to pres. Earlham Coll., 1975-83; v.p. for devel. Bangor (Maine) Theol. Seminary, 1983-90; v.p. for instnl. advancement New England Coll., N.H., 1990—; cons. to higher edn., nonprofit orgns. and chs., Lilly Endowment, Inc. Author: You Can Run A Capital Campaign, 1989, Working Smart: A Handbook for Managers, 1985, Making Your Life Count, 1980, Careers in State and Local Government, 1980; editor: Seminary Development News. Mem. Assn. Theol. Schs. (workshop leader), United Ch. Christ (chair ch. and ministry com.), Coun. for Advancement and Support Edn. (exceptional achievement award for pub. rels.). Home: PO Box 455 Henniker NH 03242-0455 Office: New Eng Coll 7 Main St Henniker NH 03242-3244

ZEHRING, KAREN, publishing executive; b. Washington, Dec. 5, 1945; d. Robert William Zehring and Gretchen (Lorenz) Proos; m. George Lang, 1970 (div. 1979); m. Peter Frank Davis, June 10, 1979; children: Timothy, Nicholas, Jesse, Antonia. BA, U. Denver, 1967; postgrad., Yale U., 1967-68. Assoc. pub. mktg. and sales Instl. Investor Systems, Inc., N.Y.C., 1968-74; owner, pub. The Corp. Fin. Letter, N.Y.C., 1976-78; group dir. planning and devel. Bus. Week mag., N.Y.C., 1977-78; owner, pub., exec. editor Corp. Fin. Sourcebook The Corp. Fin. Bluebook, N.Y.C., 1979-84; chmn., pres., pub., editor-in-chief Corp. Fin. mag., N.Y.C., 1986-90; ptnr. Zehring Assocs., Castine, Maine, 1990—. Mem. The Women's Forum, Am. Soc. Mag. Editors, Overseas Press Club. Unitarian. Office: Zehring Assocs PO Box 600 Castine ME 04421-0600

ZEIBER, LINDA MARIE, English educator, writer; b. Lancaster, Pa., July 30, 1948; d. William Joseph and Clara Louise (Allen) Covert; m. Gerald Owen Zeiber, Apr. 3, 1982. BA, Susquehanna U., 1970; edn. cert., Kutztown U., 1971. Tchr. English Reading (Pa.) Sch. Dist., 1972—; contbg. writer The County Mag., Reading, 1978; lectr. Albright Coll., Reading, 1988; freelance writer. Mem. Pa. Coun. Tchrs. English, Green Valley Country Club (Women's Aux.). Republican. Lutheran. Home: 739 Brownsville Rd Reading PA 19608-9799 Office: Reading Sch Dist 8th & Washington Sts Reading PA 19601

ZEICHNER, MARK, lawyer; b. N.Y.C., June 6, 1949; s. Lester and Rosalind (Schulman) Z.; m. Judy Ann Koenig; children: Eric Benjamin, Jessica Dori. AB, Hamilton Coll., 1971; JD cum laude, Syracuse U., 1974. Bar: N.Y. 1975, U.S. Dist. Ct. (so. and ea. dists.) N.Y. 1976, U.S. Ct. Appeals (2d cir.) 1976, U.S. Ct. Appeals (5th cir.) 1978. Assoc. Shearman & Sterling, N.Y.C., 1974-78, Harvis, Pomerantz & Rosenbluth, N.Y.C., 1978-79; ptnr. Harvis & Zeichner, N.Y.C., 1979-89; sr. & mng. ptnr. Zeichner Ellman & Krause, N.Y.C., 1989—. Mem. ABA (uniform comml. code com., letter of credit subcom.), Order of Coif. Office: Zeichner Ellman & Krause 757 3d Ave New York NY 10017

ZEICHNER, SAUL, nursing home administrator; b. Jersey City, Oct. 6, 1935; s. Joseph and Sally (Divock) Z.; m. Janice Louise Kadlec, Dec. 30, 1960; children: Reva Levin, Leah Hedrick, Joel. AB in Sociology, U. Pa., 1957, cert. in supervising, 1964; MSW, Rutgers U., 1962. Lic. nursing home adminstr., R.I. Staff social worker VA Hosp., Lyons, N.J., 1962-66; staff social worker Somerset County Guidance Ctr., Somerville, N.J., 1966-68, supr., 1968-74; dir. social work Morristown (N.J.) Meml. Hosp., 1974-80, asst. v.p., 1980-85, v.p., 1985-88; pres., chief exec. officer Jewish Home for the Aged, Providence, 1988—; dir. Social Club for Mental Health, Somerville, 1964-78; lectr. in field. Author: Social Work Transition from Practice to Administration, 1985. Mayor, Borough of Califon, N.J., 1968-71; chmn. Hunterdon County Mental Health Assn., Flemington, N.J., 1980-84. With U.S. Army, 1957-59. Recipient Cert. for Outstanding Svc., Am. Cancer Soc., 1987, Cert. of Appreciation, Bd. Dialysis Ctr., 1988. Mem. NASW, R.I. Assn. for Facilities for Aging (chmn. com. 1990—). Democrat. Jewish. Office: Jewish Home for Aged 99 Hillside Ave Providence RI 02906-2999

ZEIEN, ALFRED M., consumer products company executive; b. N.Y.C., Feb. 25, 1930; s. Alphonse and Betty (Barthelemy) Z.; m. Joyce Valerie Lawrence, Dec. 26, 1952; children—Scott, Grey, Claudia. B.S., Webb Inst.; M.B.A. postgrad., Harvard U. Group v.p. Gillette Co., Boston, 1973-74, sr. v.p., 1978-81, vice chmn., 1981-90, pres., 1990-91, chmn., chief exec. officer, 1991—; div. gen. mgr. Braun AG, Frankfurt, Federal Republic of Germany, 1974-76, chmn. bd., 1976-78; bd. dirs. Polaroid Corp., Cambridge, Mass., Repligen Corp., Cambridge, Bank of Boston, Mass. Mut. Ins. Co., Springfield. trustee Univ. Hosp., Boston, 1983—. Home: 300 Boylston St Boston MA 02116-3923 Office: Gillette Co Prudential Tower Bldg Boston MA 02199

ZEIGER, DIANE MARY, guidance counselor, educator; b. Harrisburg, Pa., Nov. 6, 1956. Student, St. Joseph's U., Phila., 1976-78; BS in Social Sci., Pa. State U., 1979, early childhood edn. teaching cert., 1981; MS in Edn., U. So. Calif., 1986; state cert. in elem. and secondary sch. guidance counseling, Millersville U., 1990. Cert. early childhood tchr., elem. and secondary sch. guidance counselor, Pa. Math instr. Tri-County Opportunities Industrialization Ctr., Harrisburg, 1980; presch. tchr. Hansel and Gretel Montessori Sch., Harrisburg, 1981; guidance counselor Wodk Edn. Ctr., Nürnberg, West Germany, 1983-87; edn. svcs. specialist, dir. Monteith Edn. Ctr., Nünberg, 1987; edn. specialist Navy Campus, Phila., 1988; guidance counselor Fort Indiantown Gap Edn. Ctr., Annville, Pa., 1988—. Mem. Pa. Adv. Coun. Mil. Educators (com. woman 1990—), Pa. Adv. Coun. Mil. Vets. Edn. Republican. Roman Catholic. Home: 6567 Stanford Ct Mechanicsburg PA 17055

ZEIGLER, JOSEPH WESLEY, arts consultant; b. Bethlehem, Pa., Oct. 11, 1938; s. Wesley Henry and Margaret Elizabeth (Brenner) Z.; m. Alison Damon, Oct. 24, 1964; children: Damon Wesley, Abraham Ives. AB magna cum laude, Harvard Coll., 1960. Managing dir. Ithaca (N.Y.) Festival, 1965-66; from assoc. dir. to exec. dir. Theatre Communications Group, N.Y.C., 1966-69; v.p. Arts Devel. Assocs., N.Y.C., 1972-76; pvt. practice, 1969—; adjunct prof. Brooklyn Coll, CUNY, N.Y. U., Adelphi, SUNY; cons. editor Jour. Arts Mgmt. & Law, Washington, 1980—. Author: Regional Theatre: The Revolutionary Stage, 1973. Bd. dirs. Collegiate Ch., N.Y., 1974—, Collegiate Sch., N.Y. C., 1987—. Arts Adminstrn. Intern Program Grantee Ford Found., N.Y.C., 1962-64. Home and Office: 62 Tuxedo Rd Montclair NJ 07042-5042

ZEIS, JOHN FRANCIS, philosophy educator; b. Buffalo, N.Y., Dec. 6, 1950; s. Frank Joseph and Eleanor (Janson) Z.; m. Pamela Ann Bellus, Sept. 3, 1971; children: John Paul, Benjamin, Michael, Thomas. BA, U. Notre Dame, 1973; MA, Niagara U., 1976; PhD, U. Pa., 1980. Instr. Manhattanville Coll., Purchase, N.Y., 1979-80; asst. prof. Erie Community Coll., Buffalo, 1980-89, Canisius Coll., Buffalo, 1989—. Contbr. articles to profl. jours. Mem. Am. Cath. Philos. Assn. Office: Canisius Coll 2001 Main St Buffalo NY 14208-1098

ZEISE, INGO, safety management consultant; b. Wilmington, Del., Feb. 20, 1932; s. Kurt Siegried and Ilse (Ahlemann) Z.; m. Carol Novak, Oct. 15, 1955; children: Kim Zeise Neel, Lisa Zeise. BS, U. Del., 1953. Cert. safety profl.; PE in safety, Calif. With DuPont Co., 1956-85, safety trainee, safety supr., safety mgr.; pres. Zcon, Inc., Elkton, Md., 1985—; bd. dirs. Del. Safety Coun., Wilmington, 1982—; gen. chmn. Nat. Safety Coun., Chgo., 1978-79. Alumni bd. U. del., Newark, 1984-87; mem. Bd. Licensing Commrs. Cecil County, Md., 1991—. Mem. Am. nat. Standards Inst. (mem. subgroup chmn. 1974—), Cecil County C. of C. (bd. dirs. 1985—), HSC (hon. life mem. constrn. sect. 1986), ASSE. Republican. Office: Zcon Inc 20 Duck Hollow Dr Elkton MD 21921-7610

ZEISS, CLIFFORD JOHN, psychiatrist; b. Bklyn., Apr. 24, 1920; s. John Philip Rudolph and Elizabeth (Monell) Z.; B.S., N.Y. U., 1941; M.D., N.Y. Med. Coll., 1944; postgrad. N.Y. Sch. Psychiatry, 1969-72; m. Ethel May Naughton, May 12, 1944; 1 dau., Holly Elizabeth Zeiss Bruce. Intern, Nassau Hosp., Mineola, N.Y., 1944-45, rotating resident, 1945-46; physician Republic Aviation Corp., Farmingdale, N.Y., 1948-50; practice medicine, specializing in family practice, Valley Stream, N.Y., 1949-69; resident in psychiatry Nassau County (N.Y.) Med. Center, 1969-72; practice medicine, specializing in psychiatry, Valley Stream, 1972-85; Highland, N.Y., 1985—; mem. staff N.E. Nassau Psychiat. Center, Kings Park, N.Y. Vestryman, Holy Trinity Episcopal Ch., Valley Stream, 1954-60. Served to capt. M.C., AUS, 1943-44, 46-47. NIMH grantee, 1969-72. Mem. AMA (Physician's Recognition award 1969, 72, 75, 79, 83, 86), N.Y. State, Ulster County med. socs., Nassau Physicians Guild, Am., Ulster County, Nassau psychiat. socs. Republican. Club: Lions. Home and Office: 8 Pine Ter Highland NY 12528-2710

ZEITLIN, JIDE JAMES, investment banker; b. Ibadan, Nigeria; came to U.S., 1976; s. Arnold S. and Marian E. (Frank) Z. BA, Amherst Coll., 1985; MBA, Harvard U., 1987. V.p. Goldman, Sachs & Co., N.Y.C., 1987—. Office: Goldman Sachs & Co 85 Broad St New York NY 10004

ZEITLIN, ROBERT NORMAN, archaeologist, engineer, packaging industry executive; b. N.Y.C., Sept. 16, 1935; s. Edward Joseph and Bessie (Wolsk) Z.; m. Judith Ann Francis, May 24, 1970; children: Andrew Forrest, Jeremy Edward. BA in Psychology, Cornell U., 1957; BS in Aero. Engring., Boston U., 1959; MA in Anthropology, CUNY, 1969; MPhil, PhD, Yale U., 1972, 79. Dir. tech. publs. Standard Instrument Corp., 1964-65, v.p., 1966-67; teaching asst. CUNY, N.Y.C., 1967-69; teaching asst. Yale U., 1970-71, instr., 1974; instr. Brandeis U., Waltham, Mass., 1976-78; asst. prof. Brandeis U., Waltham, 1979-84, assoc. prof., 1985—; chmn. Key Packageing Industries, Salem, N.H., 1983—, also bd. dirs.; archaeol. excavations; archaeol. cons.; mem. Hist. Commn. Town of Stow, Mass., 1978-81, 85—; trustee Stow Conservation Trust, 1988—; grant reviewer NSF, Ctr. for Field Rsch., Wenner Gren Found., Nat. Geog. Soc.; mem. Rsch. Coun. Can. Contbr. articles to profl. jours. Lt. (j.g.) USN, 1959-64. NSF grantee, 1973-75, 90-9—; Sigma Xi Soc. grantee, 1976; Yale U. fellow, 1969-71, 74; NDEA Title VI fellow, 1971-73; Yale Coun. on Latin Am. Studies grantee, 1970; CUNY fellow, 1967-69. Fellow Sigma Xi; mem. Am. Anthropol. Assn., Northeastern Anthorpol. Assn., Soc. for Am. Archaeology, Soc. for Econ. Anthropology, Soc. for Latin Am. Anthropology, Soc. for Archaeol. Scis. Home: PO Box 352 Friendship ME 04547-0352 Office: Brandeis U Dept Anthropology Waltham MA 02254

ZEITZ, BAILA, psychologist; b. N.Y.C., May 17, 1943; d. David and Tillie Weinstein; m. William A. Zeitz, Sept. 4, 1962; 2 children. B.A. magna cum laude, Bklyn. Coll., 1964; Ph.D., NYU, 1979. Research scientist Rockland Research Inst., N.Y. State Dept. Mental Hygiene, 1974-76; teaching asst. NYU, 1977-78, research asst., 1978-79; fellow Inst. for Rational Emotive Therapy, N.Y.C., 1979-81, mem. staff, 1981-82; dir. research Catalyst Co., N.Y.C., 1979-81; pres. Baila Zeitz & Assocs., N.Y.C., 1981—; dir. Center for Stress and Self Mgmt., N.Y.C., 1982-84; pvt. practice psychotherapy, N.Y.C., 1982—, Teaneck, N.J., 1984-89. Author: Problem Solving for Managers, 1981; co-author: The Best Companies for Women, 1988. Contbr. articles to jours. in psychology, medicine and computer sci. Mem. Am. Psychol. Assn., N.Y. State Psychol. Assn., N.J. State Psychol. Assn., Soc. for Psychol. Study of Social Issues, Met. Assn. Applied Psychology. Jewish. Office: Ste 34 171 E 84th St New York NY 10028-2029

ZELDIS, STEPHEN MARTIN, cardiologist; b. Bklyn., June 11, 1946; s. Milton E. and Norma (Gratz) Z.; m. Roberta L. Weiss, June 8, 1974; children: Mark, Beth. BA, U. Rochester, 1968; MD, Yale U., 1972. Diplomate Am. Bd. Internal Medicine, Am. Bd. Cardiovascular Diseases. Intern Yale-New Haven (Conn.) Hosp., 1972-73, resident, 1973-75; cardiology fellow U. Pa., Phila., 1975-77; dir. non-invasive cardiology Long Island Jewish Med. Ctr., New Hyde Park, N.Y., 1977-81; asst. prof. medicine SUNY, Stony Brook, 1977-87, assoc. prof. medicine, 1987—; acting chief cardiology Nassau Hosp., Mineola, N.Y., 1981-84; chief cardiology Winthrop U. Hosp., Mineola, 1981—, dir. med. edn., 1991. Recipient Leadership award, Am. Heart Assn., Nassau, N.Y., Long Island Heart Coun. Fellow Clin. Coun. Am. Heart Assn., Am. Coll. of Physicians, Am. Coll. Cardiology (key contact com. 1991), Am. Coll. Chest Physicians. Office: Winthrop U Hosp Div Cardiology Mineola NY 11577

ZELEN, HERBERT JACK, engineer; b. N.Y.C., Mar. 16, 1931; s. Max and Eva (Sloan) Zelenko; m. Roberta Marilyn Goldstein, Sept. 7, 1952; children: Beth H., Melissa P. BEE, CCNY, 1952; MSEE, Polytech. Inst. Bklyn., 1960. Devel. engr. ITT Fed. Labs., Nutley, N.J., 1952-61; engring. dir. GE Astrospace Div., Princeton, N.J., 1961-92; cons. A.H. Assocs., Princeton, N.J., 1992—. Fellow AIAA (assoc.); mem. AIAA Communication Satellite Conf. (session chmn. 1986), Kiwanis (sec., v.p. 1971-73). Jewish. Office: AH Assocs 123 Sayre Dr PO Box 800 Princeton NJ 08540

ZELEN, MARVIN, statistics educator; b. N.Y.C., June 21, 1927; m. Thelma Geier, Sept. 10, 1950; children: Deborah, Sandra. BS, CCNY, 1949; MS, U. N.C., 1951; PhD, Am. U., 1957; MA (hon.), Harvard U., 1977. Pres. Frontier Sci. and Tech. Rsch. Found., Boston, 1975—; chief div. biostats. and epidemiology Dana Farber Cancer Inst., Boston, 1977—; prof. Harvard U. Sch. Pub. Health, Boston, 1977—. Sgt. U.S. Army, 1945-46. Fulbright scholar, 1965-66. Fellow Am. Acad. Arts and Sci., AAAS, Inst. Math. Stats., Am. Statis. Assn.; mem. Internat. Stats. Inst. Home: 230 Eliot St Chestnut Hill MA 02167-1447 Office: Harvard Sch Pub Health 677 Huntington Ave Boston MA 02115-6023

ZELENY, ANN DOUGLAS, sculptor; b. Tucson, Dec. 7, 1955; d. Charles Ellingson and Marjorie Ann (Pfeiffer) Zeleny; m. Arthur Jeffrey Munson, Dec. 22, 1974 (div. 1985); 1 child, Frederick Michael Munson Zeleny; m. Carl Douglas Anderson, Nov. 3, 1985; 1 child, Gwyneth Violet Zeleny Anderson. BFA, Va. Commonwealth U., 1977. Songwriter/vocalist Seventh Dawn, Richmond, Washington, 1973-80; archtl. sculptor Monumental Constrn. and Moulding Co., Washington, 1981-86; freelance sculptor, 1986—; co-creator, set designer, propmaster, puppeteer The Mondo Breakfast Show, Arlington, 1984-86; graphics cons. Animator Graphics, Washington, 1991—. Sr. sculptor sites of installation include: The National Theatre, The Washington Times Bldg., The Hay-Adams Hotel, The Phoenix Park Hotel, The Phillips Collection Gallery; songwriter/perform record album: Sunrise, 1976, Dreams, 1978; designer, sculptor, mouldmaker and painter gypsum or cement sculptures including: Green Man, Salamander, Reflection, Release, Eve; cameraperson Arlington Weekly News, 1980-85. Vol. graphics The Greens, 1989—, The Common Mkt. Food Coop., Frederick, Md., 1990—. Recipient "Ammy" Craft Award for set design Arlington Community TV, 1985, Ammy for best variety program, 1985, Ammy for humor, 1986. Mem. Internat. Sculpture Ctr. Office: PO Box 13 Boonsboro MD 21713

ZELIFF, WILLIAM, congressman; b. June 12, 1936; m. Sydna Zeliff. BS, Univ. Conn. Exec. DuPont Co., 1959-76; innkeeper; mem. U.S. Congress from 1st dist. N.H., 1991—. Served U.S. Army. Protestant. Office: US House of Reps 512 Cannon Washington DC 20515-2901*

ZELL, HOWARD CHARLES, chemist; b. Phila., Feb. 11, 1922; s. Howard Elmer Zell and Angeline Marie Salvey; m. Tatiana Elizabeth Kopal, Nov. 22, 1952. BS in Chemistry, St. Joseph's U., Phila., 1943; MS in Organic Chemistry, U. Del., 1951; PhD in Organic Chemistry, U. Pa., 1964. Dir. regulatory affairs Marsam Pharm., Inc., Cherry Hill, N.J., 1987—; br. chief U.S. FDA, Rockville, Md., 1981-87, chemist, 1974-81; prin. scientist Ethicon, Inc., Somerville, N.J., 1965-74; analytical chemist Publicker Ind., Inc., Phila., 1943-44, 46-48; rsch. assoc. Merck, Sharp and Dohme, West Point, Pa., 1948-65. Co-patentee in field; contbr. articles to profl. jours. Pvt. U.S. Army, 1944-46. Mem. Am. Chem. Soc., AAAS, Regulatory Affairs Profls. Soc.

ZELLERS, GEORGE, III, insurance agent; b. Millville, N.J., May 16, 1925; s. George Jr. and Elsie Mae (Gandy) Z.; married, Nov. 7, 1981; children: George, Jay Carole. Grad. high sch., Millville. Administrv. asst., adj. gen. USA Pentagon, Washington, 1942-48; ptnr. svc. sta. bus., Millville, 1948-58; owner, agt. State Farm Ins., Millville, 1958—. Chmn. traffic safety com. Cumberland-Gloucester-Salom Counties, 1967—. With U.S. Army, 1943-46. Mem. Millville Bus. and Profl. Assn. (bd. dirs.). Baptist. Office: State Farm Ins 400 N High St Millville NJ 08332-3000

ZELNER, LAWRENCE, management consultant, mechanical engineer; b. Bklyn., Sept. 5, 1941; s. Hyman and Anna (Parnes) Z.; m. Marjorie Anne Swirsky, Nov. 2, 1975; 1 child, Jonathan. BSME, Poly. Inst. Bklyn., 1962. Engr. Burndy Corp., Norwalk, Conn., 1962-63; project engr. Nabisco, N.Y.C., 1963-68, Revlon, Edison, N.J., 1968-69; v.p. Zelner and Badner, Inc., Englewood, N.J., 1969—; pres. Medinvent, Inc., Englewood, 1983—; cons. to various hosps. and indsl. cos., U.S. and Can., 1969—. Co-author: Hospital Special Care Facilities, 1981; also articles. Pres. 161 Henry Street Coop. Corp., Bklyn., 1976-85; vol. Closter (N.J.) Pub. Sch. System, 1987—. Mem. Inst. Mgmt. Cons. (cert.), Am. Assn. Hosp. Planners. Home: 296 Durie Ave Closter NJ 07624-2431 Office: Zelner and Badner Inc 163 Engle St Englewood NJ 07631-2530

ZELNIO, ROBERT NORMAN, marketing professional; b. Moline, Ill., Apr. 12, 1950; s. Anthony and Norma Lillian (Dendooven) Z.; m. Barbara Jane Gibbons, Aug. 12, 1972 (div. May 1988); children: Christopher Robert, Erin Nicole; m. Janet Smiley Burgoon, May 26, 1989. BS, U. Iowa, 1973, MS, 1975; PhD, U. N.C., 1978. Staff pharmacist, asst. mgr. Walgreens Drug Store, Iowa City, Iowa, 1973, U. Iowa Hosps. and Clinics, Iowa City, 1974, Drug Fair, Washington, Iowa, 1974, VA Hosp., Iowa City, 1975; project dir. Strategic Mktg. Corp., Bala Cynwyd, Pa., 1982-84, dir. rsch., 1984, v.p., 1985-89; v.p. Intersearch Corp., Horsham, Pa., 1989-91; pres., prin. Paragon Rsch. and Cons., Inc., Paoli, Pa., 1991—; adj. asst. prof. Wharton Sch., U. Pa., Phila., 1986; adj. prof. Phila. Coll. Pharmacy and Sci., 1983; asst. prof. Coll. Pharmacy, U. Iowa, 1979, Coll. Pharmacy, U. S.C., 1978; active numerous seminars and workshops in field; mem. editorial Jour. Pharm. Mktg. and Mgmt.; referee Am. Jour. Hosp. Phamacy; cons. in field. Contbr. articles to profl. publs., chpts. to books. Mem. Pharm. Mgmt. Sci. Assn., Pharm. Mktg. Rsch. Group, Internat. Pharm. Mktg. Rsch. Group, Am. Mktg. Assn., Rho Chi, Kappa Psi. Home: 22 Buckwalter Rd Phoenixville PA 19460-2915 Office: Paragon Rsch & Cons Inc 43 Leopard Rd Ste 301 Paoli PA 19301-1552

ZEMANIAN, ARMEN HUMPARTSOUM, electrical engineer, mathematician; b. Bridgewater, Mass., Apr. 16, 1925; s. Parsegh and Filor (Paparian) Z.; m. Edna Odell Williamson Zemanian, July 12, 1958; children: Peter, Thomas, Lewis, Susan. BEE, CCNY, 1947; ScD in Engring., NYU, 1953. Registered profl. engr., N.Y. Tutor CCNY, 1947-48; engr. The Maintenance Co., N.Y.C., 1948-52; from asst. to assoc. prof. NYU, 1952-62; prof. SUNY, Stony Brook, 1962-83, leading prof., 1983--. Author: Distribution Theory and Transform Analysis, 1965, Generalized Integral Transformations, 1968, Realizability Theory for Continuous Linear Systems, 1972, Infinite Electrical Networks, 1991; co-author: Electronics, 1961; co-editor and co-founder: (rsch. jour.) Circuits, Systems and Signal Processing, 1982—. NSF faculty fellow in sci., 1975-76; recipient Science award Armenian Students Assn. Am., 1982; foreign mem. Armenian Acad. of Sciences, 1990. Fellow IEEE; mem. Am. Math. Soc., Soc. for Indsl. and Applied Math. (v.p. publs. 1974-75), Tau Beta Pi, Eta Kappa Nu, Sigma Xi. Democrat. Presbyterian. Office: SUNY Stony Brook NY 11794-2350

ZEMOJTEL, ALEXANDER MICHAEL, business owner; b. Ware, Mass., Apr. 11, 1952; s. Alexander Michael Sr. and Ruth Helen (Lamay) Z. AA in Biology, Holyoke Community Coll., 1974; AS in Nuclear Medicine, George Washington U., 1984. Nuclear medicine technologist South Shore Hosp., South Weymouth, Mass., 1986-87; supr. nuclear medicine dept. Kent County Meml. Hosp., Warwick, R.I., 1987-89; chief fin. officer, ptnr. Apollo Imaging, Inc., Abington, Mass., 1989-91; pres. AMZ Nuclear, Providence, 1991—; mem. adj. faculty George Washington U., 1984; v.p. St Ze Real Estate, Greenville, R.I., 1986—. Sgt. AUS, 1980-86, res., 1986—. Decorated Overseas ribbon, Ary Achievement medal, Good Conduct medal, Res. Overseas medal. Home and Office: 19 Stone St Unit 8 Providence RI 02904-2400

ZEMON, VANCE MARC, neuroscientist; b. Bklyn., Nov. 23, 1951; s. Jerome Richard and Ruth (Cohen) Z.; m. Jane Louise Vadeboncoeur, July 21, 1979; children: Rebecca Mara, Aaron Michael, Jacob Robert. BS in Physics, Clarkson Coll. of Tech., 1973; MA in Exptl. Psychology, Northeastern U., 1976, PhD in Exptl. Psychology, 1979. Postdoctoral fellow The Rockefeller U., N.Y.C., 1979-82, rsch. assoc., 1982, adj. asst. prof. biophysics, 1983-85, asst. prof. biophysics, 1985—; adj. asst. prof. psychology CUNY, 1983, 85; vis. assoc. rsch. scientist Columbia U., N.Y.C., 1985—; adj. faculty New Sch. for Social Rsch., N.Y.C., 1988—; cons. scientist N.Y. Assn. for the Blind, N.Y.C., 1980-85; cons. Neurosci. Corp., Farmingdale, N.Y., 1987—. Sect. editor Internat. Jour. Neurosci., 1990—; contbr. articles to profl. jours. Recipient USPHS Rsch. Svc. award, 1979; NIH grantee, 1986. Mem. Internat. Soc. for Clin. Electrophysiology of Vision, Assn. for Rsch. in Vision and Ophthalmology, Optical Soc. Am., Sigma Xi. Jewish. Home: 30 East St West Nyack NY 10994-2410 Office: The Rockefeller U 1230 York Ave New York NY 10021-6341

ZENDLE, HOWARD MARK, software development researcher; b. Binghamton, N.Y., June 8, 1949; s. Abraham and Evelyn (Hershowitz) Z. BA in Physics summa cum laude, SUNY, Binghamton, 1972, MA in Physics, 1976; MSEE, Syracuse U., 1987. With IBM, Owego, N.Y., 1974—, staff programmer, 1978-83, mgr. microprocessor applications software, 1979-81, mgr. tactical avionics software, 1981-82, adv. programmer, 1983-86, sr. programmer, 1986—; mem. Fed. Sector div. Mktg. Conf. IBM, 1991. Sec. Men's Club Beth David Synagogue, Binghamton, 1984-85, v.p., 1986-88; bd. dirs. Jewish Community Ctr., Binghamton, 1983-86. Recipient Informal awards IBM, 1975, 78, 81, 83, 91. Mem. IEEE, Assn. for Computing Machinery, Cen. Electric Railfan's Assn., Masons, Phi Beta Kappa, Sigma Pi Sigma. Republican. Avocations: railfanning, research into history of industrial development in America.

ZENGULIS, SHERRY LEE, behavioral therapist; b. Easton, Pa., Aug. 27, 1952; d. Melvin Claude and Jacqueline Fay (Shook) Bellis; m. Mark Joseph Zengulis, Mar. 9, 1985; 1 child, Jody Christopher. Assoc. Degree, NCACC, Bethlehem, Pa., 1974; BA in Psychology cum laude, East Stroudsburg U., 1979; postgrad., Moravian Coll., 1990-91; MBA, Fairleigh Dickinson U. Tutor, proctor Psychology Dept. East Stroudsburg (Pa.) U., 1979; therapy asst. Hunterdon Devel. Ctr., Clinton, N.J., 1980-84; behavior therapist Hunterdon Devel. Ctr., Clinton, 1984—; tutor, counselor Project Upward Bound, Bangor, Pa., 1978. Vol. N.J. Spl. Olympics, Hunterdon County, 1981-83; on-site co-coord. Boy Scouts Am., Clinton, 1982. Mem. Inst. Mgmt. Accts. Republican. Methodist. Home: 1001 Butler St Easton PA 18042 Office: Hunterdon Devel Ctr Cn 4220 Pittstown Rd Clinton NJ 08809-4220

ZENKER, GARY, marketing executive; b. Wilmington, Del., Jan. 25, 1962. BA in Econs., Franklin and Marshall Coll., 1984. Mktg. dir. Mid Penn Bank, Millersburg, Pa., 1984-86; mktg. dir., asst. v.p. Progress Fed. Savs. Bank, Plymouth Meeting, Pa., 1986-91; mktg. dir. EVSCO Pharm., Buena, N.J., 1991—; featured speaker Bank Mktg. Advt. Conf., 1990; judge Bank Mktg. Best of Advt., Chgo., 1989-91. Contbr. articles to profl. jours. Recipient First Prize Humor Writing, Harrisburg Writers Assn., 1985. Mem. Bank Mktg. Assn., Lions. Office: EVSCO Pharm 711 S Harding Hwy Buena NJ 08310

ZEO, FRANK JAMES, technology company executive; b. Springfield, Mass., Jan. 9, 1910; s. Michael and Jennie (Acquavella) Z.; m. Dorothea Louise Duncan, June 27, 1942; children: Virginia D. Coate, Cynthia J. Newell. AB, Yale U., 1932; postgrad., Syracuse U., 1935-37. Cons. Pub. Adminstrn. Svc., Chgo. and Boston, 1938-40; cons. Mass. Taxpayers Found., Boston, 1940-58, exec. v.p., 1959-71; cons. mgmt./pub. affairs Boston, 1971—; co-founder, dir. corp. devel. Lexington Power Mgmt. Corp., Wakefield, Mass., 1989—. Member Marblehead (Mass.) Task Force Against Drug and Alcohol Abuse, 1988—; bd. dirs. Greater Boston Salvation Army Bd., 1970—, Exec. Svc. Corps of New Eng., Boston, 1982—, Treble Chorus of New Eng.; co-founder, bd. dirs. Careers for Later Yrs./Operation ABLE of Greater Boston, 1982—, USO Coun. of New Eng., 1985—; chmn. Nat. Taxpayers Conf., Boston, 1970-71; trustee John Hancock Variable Series Trust I, Boston, 1968—; New Eng. peer support coord. Elizabeth Campbell Peer Support Program, Manly, N.S.W., Australia; hon. trustee East Boston Savs. Bank, 1971—, Mass. Taxpayers Found., Boston, 1985—. Lt. Col. USAF, 1942-45. Decorated Legion of Merit. Mem. Govtl. Rsch. Assn. (hon.), Coun. Mem. Yale Club of Boston, Rotary (past pres. Boston club). Congregationalist. Home: 90 Naugus Ave Marblehead MA 01945-1552 Office: Lexington Power Mgmt Corp 271 Edgewater Dr Wakefield MA 01880-6215

ZEPLOWITZ, FRANKLIN, surgeon; b. Buffalo, Sept. 30, 1933; s. Abraham and Ida (Shapiro) Z.; m. Piera Esther SaLama, June 17, 1962; children: David M., Lynn F. Grad., SUNY, Buffalo, 1954, MD, 1958. Diplomate Am. Bd. Surgery. Intern Buffalo Gen. Hosp., 1958-59, resident surgery, 1959-62; chief resident surgery Youngstown (Ohio) Hosp., 1962-63; commd. USNG, 1959, advanced through grades to capt., resigned, 1970; pvt. practice in general surgery Buffalo, 1963—. Fellow ACS; mem. Buffalo Surg. Soc. (pres. 1991—), SUNY at Buffalo Sch. Medicine Alumni Assn. (former pres.), Erie County Med. Soc. (chmn. legis. com., exec. bd.). Office: 2083 S Park Ave Buffalo NY 14220

ZEPPETELLA, ANTHONY JOHN, actuary; b. Bklyn., Dec. 26, 1949; s. Michael Lucio and Filomena (Peluso) Z.; m. Barbara Bahna, July 9, 1972; children: Peter, Thomas. BA in Maths., Bklyn. Coll., 1971; MA in Maths., NYU, 1973, PhD in Maths., 1976. Adj. asst. prof. NYU, 1976; asst. prof. Clarkson U., Potsdam, N.Y., 1976-80; asst. actuarial dir. Mut. Life Ins. Co. of N.Y., N.Y.C., 1980-83, asst. v.p., 1983-86; cons. actuary McKay Barlow Co., Butler, N.J., 1983; v.p., actuary Home Life Ins. Co., N.Y.C., 1986-92; v.p. portfolio mgmt. Phoenix Home Life Ins. Co., Hartford, Conn., 1992—. Author: Practice Exams for Course 151, 1988. N.Y. State Regents scholar, 1966-71; NSF and NIH grantee, 1979-81. Fellow Soc. Actuaries; mem. Am. Acad. Actuaries, Am. Risk and Ins. Assn., Soc. for Indsl. and Applied Maths. Roman Catholic. Office: Phoenix Home Life Mutual Ins Inc One American Row Hartford CT 06115

ZERBY, SANDRA LOIS, college administrator; b. Sunbury, Pa., Oct. 22, 1947; d. John Richard and Lois Laverna (Smith) Z. BS, Millersville (Pa.) U., 1969, MEd, 1975; postgrad., NYU, 1990—. Asst. edn. supr. Community Action Program, Lancaster, Pa., 1971-77; asst. dir. admissions Elizabethtown (Pa.) Coll., 1978-79, dir. admissions, 1979-84; dean admissions and enrollment devel. Westbrook Coll., Portland, Maine, 1984-85; dir. enrollment planning, recruitment and admissions Pa. State U.-Harrisburg, Middletown, 1985-88, asst. to provost for planning, 1990—; cons. Westbrook Coll., 1983-84, Maryville Coll., 1986. Singer Lancaster (Pa.) Symphony Chorus, 1982—; vol. Big Bros./Big Sisters, Millersville, 1965-71; singer, performer for elderly homes, hosps., chs., etc. Home: 241 N Mary St Lancaster PA 17603-3424

ZERMAN, MELVYN BERNARD, publishing company executive, author; b. N.Y.C., July 10, 1930; s. Abraham and Ida (Belsky) Zirman; m. Miriam Baron, Jan. 2, 1985 (dec.); children: Andrew, Jared, Lenore. BA, U. Mich., 1952; MA, Columbia U., 1953. With Oxford Book Co., N.Y.C., 1953-55; asst. editor Abelard-Schuman, Pubs., N.Y.C., 1955-57; office mgr., salesman Harper & Row, N.Y.C., 1957-61, sales rep., 1961-69, sales mgr., 1969-79; sales mgr. Random House, Inc., N.Y.C., 1979-83, sales cons., 1983-87; pres., pub. Limelight Edits., N.Y.C., 1983—; mem. exec. com. N.Y.Is Book Country, N.Y.C., 1985—. Author: Call the Final Witness, 1977, Beyond a Reasonable Doubt, 1981 (Freedoms Found. medal 1981), Taking on the Press, 1986. Mem. Authors Guild, Phi Beta Kappa. Democrat. Office: Limelight Edits 118 E 30th St New York NY 10016-7303

ZEROKA, DANIEL, chemistry educator; b. Plymouth, Pa., June 22, 1941; s. Michael and Mary (Klimchak) Z.; m. Alexandra S. Kotulak, May 27, 1967; children: Daniel Michael, Andrea Marie. BS, Wilkes Coll., 1963; PhD, U. Pa., 1966. Asst. prof., chemistry Lehigh U., Bethlehem, Pa., 1967-74; assoc. prof., chemistry Lehigh U., Bethlehem, 1974-90, prof., chemistry, 1990—; vis. rsch. scientist duPont Cen. R & D, Wilmington, Del., summer 1984; sabbatical leave Cornell U., Ithaca, N.Y., spring 1985; U.S. Army summer rsch. faculty Edgewood (Md.) Area of Aberdeen Proving Ground, summers 1989, 90, 91. Contbr. articles to Jour. Chem. Physics, Jour. Phys. Chemistry, Langmuir, Internat. Jour. Quantum Chemistry, Jour. Am. Chem. Soc. Named NASA Predoctoral fellow, U. Pa., 1964-66, NSF Postdoctoral fellow, Yale U., 1966-67. Mem. Am. Chem. Soc. (sec. Lehigh Valley sect. sec. 1989-90), Am. Phys. Soc., Sigma Xi. Home: 7617 Tilghman St PO Box 14 Fogelsville PA 18015-0014 Office: Lehigh U Dept Chemistry # Bethlehem PA 18015-3172

ZERWEKH-LEE, ZOE, public relations executive; b. Sept. 22, 1957. BSN, Russell Sage Coll. Oncology nurse So. Tier Regional Cancer Program, Binghamton, N.Y., 1981-83, oncology nurse coord., 1983-84; pub. rels. asst. Lourdes Hosp., Binghamton, N.Y., 1984-86, dir. pub. rels., 1986—; bd. dirs. Lourdes Hosp. Aux., co-chair Rehab. and Support Com., Community Hosp. Oncology Program, Lourdes Hosp., 1981, exec. com., 1984. Editor: District 5 Nursing Newsletter, 1988; contbr. numerous workshops and confs. in field. Mem. publ rels. com. Active Am. Heart Assn., 1990—; active United Way Broome County, pub. rels. div., 1990, media/advt. sub-com., 1988-90; mem. mktg./communications sub-com. Am. Red Cross Broome County, 1988-90; mem. pub. edn. com. Am. Cancer Soc. N.Y. State Div., 1982, 83, profl. edn. com., 1982, 83, bd. dirs., 1982, 83; mem. edn. and review com. Broome County Health Fair, 1984, 85. Recipient Cert. of Recognition award Am. Cancer Soc., 1982; Kellas scholar Nat. Honor Soc. of Nursing, 1979. Mem. Am. Soc. for Healthcare Mktg. Pub. Rels., Cen. N.Y. Hosp. Assn. (pub. rels. adv. group, 1988—, nominating com., 1990, by-laws com., 1988), Pub. Rels. Soc. of So. Tier (bd. dirs. membership chmn., 1990, member-at-large, 1987, 88, cert. of recognition, 1989, 90), Empire Communicators Healthcare Orgn. (sec. 1989, treas. 1990, v.p. 1991, pres. 1992), ASHCMPR (touchstone com. 1991). Office: Lourdes Hosp 169 Riverside Dr Binghamton NY 13905-4198

ZEVON TSCHACBASOV, IRENE ANN, artist, consultant, art historian; b. N.Y.C., Nov. 24, 1918; d. Joseph and Minnie (Saslowsky) Zivitofsky; m. Murray Barton, Apr. 28, 1943 (div. 1960); 1 child, Leonard; m. Nahum Tschacbasov, Aug. 30, 1966 (dec. 1984). Pres. Am. Libr. Color Slide Co., Inc., N.Y.C., 1960—. Exhibited in group shows at Glassboro (N.J.) State Coll., Ga. Mus. Art, Athens, Calif. State Libr., Sacramento, Miss. State Coll. for Women, Columbus, Neville Pub. Mus., Green Bay, Wis., Williamantic (Conn.) State Coll., Monmouth (Ill.) Coll., Stetson U., DeLand, Fla., Columbus (Ga.) Mus. Arts and Crafts, Gulf Coast Jr. Coll., Panama City, Fla.; oil paintings on display at numerous museums and ednl. instns. Mem. Nat. Assn. Women Artists. Office: Am Libr Color Slide Co Inc 121 W 27th St New York NY 10001-6207

ZEWIEY, MARK ANTHONY, insurance agent; b. Boston, Sept. 9, 1961; s. Richard Lawrence and Mary Theresa (Sommers) Z.; m. Kathleen Marie Keenan, Nov. 11, 1989; 1 child, Jordane Ashley. AA in Bus. Adminstrn., Massasoit C.C., Brockton, Mass., 1986; student, Suffolk U., 1986-87. Contractor M.A.Z. Constrn., Mass., 1983-86; field agt. KC, New Haven, 1987-90, gen. agt., 1990—; v.p. New England Fraternal Ins. Counselors, Springfield, Mass., 1989-90. With USMC, 1980-83. Roman Catholic. Home: 41 Oregon St East Bridgewater MA 02333 Office: MAZ Agy K of C Ste 5 36 N Bedford St East Bridgewater MA 02333

ZGRODNIK, KIMBERLY ANN, marketing executive; b. Ft. Dix, N.J., July 25, 1967; d. Joseph Frank and Carol (Tudryn) Z. BA, Amherst Coll., 1989. Corp. intern Merrill Lynch, N.Y.C., 1989-91, mktg. assoc., 1989-91, mktg. mgr., 1991—. Mem. benefit com. Vis. Nurse Svcs., N.Y.C., 1989—. Mem. NAFE. Republican. Roman Catholic. Office: Merrill Lynch 717 5th Ave 9th Fl One Financial Ctr New York NY 10022

ZHANG, CHI, education educator; b. Jiaxing, Peoples Republic China, Nov. 19, 1963; came to U.S., 1987; s. Shizheng Zhang and Yayu Toa; m. Dongmei Han, Dec. 31, 1986. BS, Hangzhou U., 1984; MS, La. State U., 1989, PhD, 1991. Instr. Zhejiang Ag. U., Hangzhou, 1984-87; rsch. asst. La. State U., Baton Rouge, 1987-91; asst. prof. U. Del., Newark, 1991—. Mem. Am. Vocat. Assn. Office: U Del Dept Edn Willard Hall Newark DE 19702

ZHAO, ZIJUN, electrical engineer, mathematical scientist; b. Xian, Shanxi, People's Republic China, Jan. 28, 1962; came to U.S., 1986; s. Deyin and Ping (Mann) Z.; m. Yang Cao. BS, Beijing Inst. Aeronautics/Ast., China, 1982, MS, 1983; PhD, Academia Sinica, Beijing, 1986; MA in Math., Temple U., 1987. Rsch. asst. Beijing Inst. Aeronautics and Astronautics, 1982-84, Academia Sinica, 1984-86; instr. Temple U., Phila., 1986-88; postdoct. fellow U. Pa., Phila., 1988-89, rsch. assoc., cons., 1990-91; sr. scientist CTA, Inc., McKee, N.J., 1992—. Contbr. articles to profl. jours. Mem. IEEE, Soc. Indsl. and Applied Math., Soc. Am. Math., Optical Soc. Am. Office: 2500 English Creek Ave Ste 1000 Pleasantville NJ 08232

ZHOU, JIAZU, mathematician, researcher; b. Guiyang, Guizhou, China, Feb. 2, 1954; came to U.S., 1988; s. Zhenyu Zhou and Zhiying Tan; m. Lanping Li, Dec. 12, 1980 (div. Feb. 1991); 1 child, Taosheng. BS, Wuhan U., Hubei, People's Republic of China, 1977, MS, 1986; MA, Temple U., 1990, postgrad., 1990—. Tchr. Rongjiang (Gizhou) Mid. Sch., 1972-74; teaching asst. Wuhan U., 1977-85, lectr., 1985-87; lectr. Wuhan Iron & Steel

U., 1984-88; lectr. Guizhou Normal U., Guiyang, 1984-87, assoc. prof., 1988—; instr. Temple U., Phila., 1988—. Mem. Am. Math. Soc., Guizhou Province Math. Assn., Guizhou Province Scis. Assn., Hubei Province Math. Assn., Hubei Province Scis. Assn. Home: 614 E Willard St Philadelphia PA 19134-1818 Office: Temple U Math Dept Philadelphia PA 19122

ZHU, KEHE, mathematician; b. Miluo, Hunan, People's Republic of China, July 8, 1961; arrived in U.S., 1983; s. Guiqing and Mowen (Feng) Z.; m. Peijia Tan, Aug. 2, 1985; 1 child, Peter F. BS, Nat. U. Def. Tech., Changsha, People's Republic of China, 1981; PhD, SUNY, Buffalo, 1986. Asst. prof. math. U. Wash., Seattle, 1986-88, U. Waterloo, Can., 1988, SUNY, Albany, 1989—. Author: Operator Theory in Function Spaces, 1990; contbr. articles to publs. NSF grantee, 1987—. Mem. Am. Math. Soc. Home: 131 Hillcrest Ave Albany NY 12203-2712 Office: SUNY Math Dept Albany NY 12222

ZIEGLER, DONALD EMIL, federal judge; b. Pitts., Oct. 1, 1936; s. Emil Nicholas and Elizabeth (Barclay) Z.; m. Claudia J. Chermak, May 1, 1965; 1 son, Scott Emil. B.A., Duquesne U., 1958; LL.B., Georgetown U., 1961. Bar: Pa. 1962, U.S. Supreme Ct. 1967. Practice law Pitts., 1962-74; judge Ct. of Common Pleas of Allegheny County, Pa., 1974-78, U.S. Dist. Ct. (we. dist.) Pa., Pitts., 1978—. Treas. Big Bros. of Allegheny County, 1969-71. Mem. ABA, Pa. Bar Assn., Allegheny County Bar Assn., Am. Judicature Soc., St. Thomas More Soc. Democrat. Roman Catholic. Club: Oakmont Country. Office: US Post Office & Courthouse 7th & Grant Sts 6th Fl Courtroom 12 Pittsburgh PA 15219

ZIEGLER, HANS KONRAD, retired electronics engineer; b. Munich, Mar. 1, 1911; came to U.S., 1947, naturalized, 1954; s. Konrad Ludwig and Therese (Schnellinger) Z.; m. Friederika Groenbold, May 14, 1937; children: Friederike Therese, Hans Peter, Christine Maria. BS, Tech. U. Munich, 1932, MS with distinction, 1934, PhD summa cum laude, 1936. Asst. prof. elec. engring. Tech. U. Munich, 1934-36; chief R & D, Rosenthal Isolatoren, Selb, Germany, 1936-47; sci. cons. U.S. Army Electronics R & D Lab., Ft. Monmouth, N.J., 1947-56, asst. dir. rsch., 1956-58, dir. astro electronic div., 1958-59, chief scientist, 1959-62; chief scientist U.S. Army Electronics Command, Ft. Monmouth, 1962-71, dep. for sci., 1967-71; dir. U.S. Army Electronics Tech. and Devices Lab., Ft. Monmouth, 1971-77; ret., 1977; past mem. com. on bio-astronautics Armed Forces and NRC. Co-editor: Handbook of Astronautical Engineering, 1961; patentee in electronic cirs. field. Recipient Meritorious Civil Svc. award Dept. Army, 1962-69, Sec. of Army's Exceptional Civil Svc. award, 1977, Antarctica Svc. medal, 1964. Fellow IEEE (life), Am. Astron. Soc.; mem. Armed Forces Communications and Electronics Assn. (disting. life, former bd. dirs.). Home: 32 E Larchmont Dr Colts Neck NJ 07722-1107

ZIEGLER, JOHN BENJAMIN, chemist lepidopterist; b. Rochester, N.Y., Jan. 2, 1917; s. John Benjamin Sr. and Sarah Jeanette (Murrell) Z.; m. Dorothy Mary Zucker, June 29, 1946 (dec. July 1985); children: Katherine Lois, Jeffrey Benjamin, Conrad Lawrence. BS in Chemistry, U. Rochester, 1939; MS in Chemistry, U. Ill., 1940, PhD in Organic Chemistry, 1946. Cert. chemist. Jr. chemist Merck & Co., Inc., Rahway, N.J., 1940-43; spl. rsch. asst. U. Ill., Urbana, 1943-46; chemist J.T. Baker Chem. Co., Phillipsburg, N.J., 1946-48; assoc. chemist CIBA Pharm. Co., Summit, N.J., 1948-51, sr. chemist, 1951-53, supr. labs., 1953-64, mgr. process rsch. lab., 1964-69; dir. chem. devel. CIBA-GEIGY Pharm. Co., Summit, 1969-75, sr. staff scientist, 1975-80; ret.; bus. adminstr. sci. dept. Seton Hall U., South Orange, N.J., 1980-82. Contbr. articles to profl. jours.; patentee in field. Chmn. com. Union county Tech. inst., 1963; mem. N.J. Coun. R & D. Mem. Am. Chem. Soc., Lepidoptera Rsch. Found., Lepidopterists' Soc., Assn. for Tropical Lepidoptera, Alpha Chi Sigma (pres. Zeta chpt. 1945-46), Sigma Xi. Republican. Home: 64 Canoe Brook Pky Summit NJ 07901-1434

ZIEGLER, LAURENE LOUISE, education educator; b. Roslindale, Mass., Apr. 6, 1951; d. Edward Warren and Jeannette L. (Lozier) Z. BS, North Adams State Coll., 1973; MEd, Boston U., 1977; C.A.G.S., Lesley Coll., 1981; PhD, Mich. State U., 1985. Tchr. 1st grade Rockland (Mass.) Pub. Schs., 1973-82; instr. reading and study skills Mass. Bay Community Coll., Wellesley, 1978-82, U. Lowell (Mass.), 1978-82; supr. student tchrs. Mich. State U., East Lansing, 1982-85; instr. study skills Lansing (Mich.) Community Coll., 1983-85; asst. prof. Pitts. (Kans.) State U., 1985-87; asst. prof., dir. student teaching, dir. profl. devel. ctr. U. Maine, Presque Isle, 1987—; univ. rep. Aroostook (Maine) Right to Read, 1987-91; dir. Project Explore: Gifted and Talented Prog., Presque Isle, 1990-91. Judge U.S. Figure Skating Assn.; trustee Helen P. Knight Sch., 1990—. Recipient Apple award NEA, Kans., 1987; fellow Mich. State U., East Lansing, 1983. Mem. Am. Assn. Colls. and Tchrs. Edn., Internat. Reading Assn., Assn. Bus. and Profl. Women, Am. Assn. U. Women, Delta Kappa Gamma, Phi Delta Kappa (historian liaison 1987-91). Home: 21 State Street Pl Apt 3 Presque Isle ME 04769-2323 Office: U Maine at Presque Isle 181 Main St Presque Isle ME 04769-2888

ZIEGLER, MANDELL STANLEY, composite sheet manufacturing executive; b. Niles, Mich., Dec. 11, 1921; s. Benjamin M. and Frances Maria (Fox) Z.; m. Marjorie Carolyn Klyne, Aug. 19, 1951; children: Thomas, John. BS in Chemistry, U. Notre Dame, 1943; PhD in Organic Chemistry, Mich. State U., 1950. Chemist E. I. DuPont de Nemours & Co., Wilmington, Del., 1950-60, Russell Reinforced Plastics Corop., Lindenhurst, N.Y., 1960-64; chief exec. officer Am. Acrylic Corp., West Babylon, N.Y., 1964—. Patentee in field. Pres. South Bay Jewish Community Coun., Massapequa, N.Y., 1982-90. Lt. (j.g.) USN, 1944-46. Mem. Am. Chem. Soc. Office: Am Acrylic Corp 400 Sheffield Ave West Babylon NY 11704-5399

ZIEGLER, WILLIAM JOHN, JR., podiatrist, retired; b. Phila., July 19, 1922; s. William John and Louisa S. Ziegler; m. Marion Edythe Dotter, Sept. 8, 1943. D of Podiatric Medicine, Temple U., 1948; D of Humane Letters, Pa. Coll. Podiatric Medicine, 1988; hon. fellowship degree, Soc. Chiropodists, 1991. Instr. anatomy dept. Temple U., Podiatry Sch., Phila., 1948-60; assoc. med. staff Am. Oncological Hosp., Phila., 1972-88; assoc. profl. staff Jeanes Hosp., Phila., 1964-88, chief podiatry sect., 1980-88; ret., 1988—; bd. trustees Pa. Coll. Podiatric Medicine, Phila., 1960—; pres. podiatry alumni assn. Temple U., Phila., 1953-55. With U.S. Army Med. Corps, 1943-45. Fellow Am. Assn. Hosp. Podiatrist, Am. Assn. Podiatric Radiologists; mem. Am. Podiatric Med. Assn., Pa. Podiatric Med. Assn., Bucks-Montgomery Podiatric Med. Assn. (past pres. 1951), Scottish Rite, Blue Lodge 646. Republican. Lutheran. Home: 357 Levick St Philadelphia PA 19111-5638

ZIELINSKI, PAUL BERNARD, grant program administrator, civil engineer; b. West Allis, Wis., Sept. 9, 1932; s. Stanley Charles and Lottie Charlotte (Pliskiewicz) Z.; m. Monica Theresa Beres, July 13, 1957; children: Daniel Paul, Gregory John, Robert Mathias, Sarah Anne. BSCE, Marquette U., 1956; MS, U. Wis., 1961, PhD, 1965. Registered profl. engr., Wis., S.C. Asst. instr. engring. mechanics Marquette U., Milw., 1956-59, asst. prof., 1964-67; instr. civil engring. U. Wis., Madison, 1959-64; from asst. prof. to prof. Clemson (S.C.) U., 1967-78, prof. environ. and systems engring., 1982-90, prof. civil engring., 1982-90, prof. emeritus, 1991—; dir. S.C. Water Resources Rsch. Inst., Clemson, 1978-90; assoc. dir. associateship grant program Nat. Rsch. Coun., Washington, 1990—; cons. Am. Pub. Works Assn., Chgo., 1973-76, Nat. Coun. Examiners of Engring. and Surveying, Clemson, 1973—. Chmn. Clemson City Planning Commn., 1971-74; ex-officio mem. S.C. Water Resources Commn., Columbia, 1978-90. Mem. ASCE, Am. Soc. for Engring. Edn., Sigma Xi. Roman Catholic. Home: 2111 Wisconsin Ave NW # 717 Washington DC 20007 Office: Nat Rsch Coun 2201 Constitution Ave NW Washington DC 20418

ZIEMBA, MARK VINCENT, military officer; b. Meriden, Conn., Jan. 26, 1950; s. Theodore T. Ziemba and Anne Marie (Cannatelli) Hamelin; m. Ricki Ann Smith, Feb. 11, 1970; children: Jennifer L., Matthew James. AAS in Indsl. Tech., Community Coll. Air Force, Maxwell AFB, Ala., 1981; AS in Computer Sci. magna cum laude, Burlington County Coll., Pemberton, N.J., 1982; BS in Computer Sci. and Math. cum laude, Angelo State U., San Angelo, Tex., 1984; postgrad., Western New Eng. Coll., Springfield, Mass., 1987-89. Enlisted man USAF, 1969, commd. 2d lt., 1984, advanced through grades to capt., 1988, aerospace ground equipment repair technician, 1969-84; project mgr. software engring. tools and methods Electronic Systems Div., Hanscom AFB, Mass., 1984-88; program mgr. Granite Sentry Electronic Systems Div., Hanscom AFB, 1988-89; lab. program mgr. Rome Lab., Griffiss AFB, N.Y., 1989—; bd. dirs. Up State Fed. Credit Union, Rome; system engr. NETCAP prog. USAF, Operation Desert Storm, 1990-91. Co-author: Welcome to Our Town, 1986, Program Office Guide to Ada, 1986; author: DNSIX Intelligence Network Evaluation, 1991; inventor software Expert Missile Maintenance Aid, 1987. Com. mem. McGuire AFB coun. Girl Scouts U.S.A., 1980-82; coach Boston Spl. Olympics, 1985-86. Mem. Am. Assn. for Artificial Intelligence, Rome Lab. Co. Grade Officer Coun., Mensa (cons. Edn. Rsch. Found. 1988—), Toastmasters (sec. Hanscom AFB 1988-89), Masons, Am. Legion, Epsilon Delta Pi, Phi Theta Kappa. Roman Catholic. Home: RR 1 Box 1874B Ava NY 13303-9718

ZIENTARA, JEFFREY RAYMOND, printing company executive; b. Buffalo, Dec. 18, 1967; s. Raymond W. and Marcia (Gesicki) Z. AS in Printing, Erie Community Coll., Orchard Park, N.Y., 1989. Account exec. Aim Corrugated Container Corp., Buffalo, 1989-91; pres. Perfect Bus. Forms, Cheektowaga, N.Y., 1991—. Mem. Buffalo PC User Group. Roman Catholic. Office: Perfect Bus Forms PO Box 561 Cheektowaga NY 14225-0561

ZIENTS, STEVEN JEFFREY, financial services executive; b. Orange, N.J., Nov. 17, 1954; s. Herbert J. and Judith (Noll) Z.; m. Deborah Tyler, Dec. 27, 1980; children: Samuel Tyler, Alice Noll. BA, Colgate U., 1976; MBA, U. Va., 1980. Asst. v.p. Citicorp, N.Y.C., 1980-85; sr. v.p. T. Rowe Price Retirement Plan Svcs., Balt., 1986—. Office: T Rowe Price 100 E Pratt St Baltimore MD 21202

ZIERDT, CHARLES HENRY, microbiologist; b. Pitts., Apr. 24, 1922; s. Conrad Henry and Nancy Leora (Harshberger) Z.; m. Margaret May Wise, June 1, 1942 (div. 1962); children—Charles Henry, Jr., Carolyn, Douglas, Richard; m. Willadene Smith, Sept. 30, 1967. B.S., Pa. State U., 1943; M.S., U. Mich., 1945; Ph.D., George Washington U., 1967. Rsch. assoc. Parke-Davis & Co., Detroit, 1945-48; microbiologist Henry Ford Hosp., Detroit, 1948-53, USPHS, Detroit, 1953-56; rsch. microbiologist NIH, Bethesda, Md., 1956—. Scientist sponsor U. Md., 1975—; instr. Found. Advanced Edn. Scis., Bethesda, 1978—. Author: Glucose Nonfermenting Gram Negative Bacteria in Clinical Microbiology, 1978; Non-fermentative Gram Negative Rods: Laboratory Identification and Clinical Aspects, 1985; McGraw-Hill Yearbook of Science and Technology, 1986; Diagnostic Procedures for Bacterial Infections, 1987; contbr. over 100 articles to profl. jours. Patentee in field. Active PTA. Fellow Am. Acad. Microbiology; mem. Am. Soc. Microbiology (chpt. pres. 1976), U.S. Fedn. Culture Collections (membership chmn. 1985), Mensa, Model A Ford Club of Am. (Fairfax, Va. chpt. pres. 1985), Sigma Xi. Republican. Avocations: gardening; antique car restoration. Home: 4100 Norbeck Rd Rockville MD 20853-1869 Office: NIH Bethesda MD 20892

ZIERLER, KENNETH, physiologist, physician, educator; b. Balt., Sept. 5, 1917; s. Joseph and Betsey (Levie) Z.; m. Margery Shapiro, June 8, 1941; children: Peggy Zierler Rosenthal, Linda Zierler Jucovy, Sally, Amy, Michael K. AB, Johns Hopkins U., 1936, postgrad., 1936-37; MD, U. Md., 1941. Intern medicine Sinai Hosp., Balt., 1941-42; asst. resident, resident NYU div. Goldwater Meml. Hosp., N.Y.C., 1942-43; fellow, prof. medicine Johns Hopkins U. Med. Sch., Balt., 1946-72, prof. physiology, medicine, 1969-72, 73—; assoc. prof. environ. medicine Johns Hopkins Sch. Hygiene and Pub. Health, Balt., 1956-64; asst. physician to physician Johns Hopkins Hosp., Balt., 1946-72, physician-in-charge dept. phys. therapy, 1950-57, chemist-in-charge, 1957-68, physician, 1973—; dir. Inst. for Muscle Disease, N.Y.C., 1972-73; adj. prof. Rockefeller U., N.Y., 1972-73, Cornell Med. Sch., N.Y., 1972-73; mem. adv. com. on physiology, Office of Naval Rsch., Am. Inst. Biol. Scis., 1964-76, chmn., 1964-72; mem. panel of space biology and medicine Pres.'s Sci. Adv. Com., 1967; cons. task group on tracer kinetics Internat. Commn. on Radiol. Units and Measurements, 1966; mem. cardiovascular B study sect. NIH, 1972-76; co-chmn. rating com. rev. of doctoral programs in biol. scis. N.Y. State Commr. Edn., 1983—. contbr. 234 sci. papers to profl. jours.; mem. editorial bd. Johns Hopkins Hosp. bull., 1956-67, Johns Hopkins Med. Jour., 1967-70, Jour. Clin. Investigations, 1959-64; mem. editorial bd. Circulation Rsch., 1962-67, co-editor, 1966, substitute editor, 1968, assoc. editor, 1968-77; mem. editorial com. Ann. Rev. Physiology, 1971-75; assoc. editor Medicine, 1963-72. Capt. med. corps U.S. Army, 1943-46, ETO, MTO. Decorated Bronze Star; Career scholar Muscular Dystrophy Assn., 1973-91. Mem. Am. Soc. for Clin. Investigations, Assn. Am. Physicians, Endocrine Soc., Am. Diabetes Assn. Office: Johns Hopkins Med Sch 720 Rutland Ave Bldg 918 Baltimore MD 21205-2109

ZIETZ, KARYL LYNN KOPELMAN, author, television reporter, producer, documentary filmmaker; b. N.Y.C., Oct. 11, 1943; d. Bernard and Vera Jean (Wantman) Kopelman; m. Neil J. Stone, Aug. 16, 1970 (div. 1975); m. Joachim Zietz, July 19, 1978. BA in Chemistry, U. Pa., 1965; MA in Film and Broadcast Journalism, Am. U., 1980; spl. cert., Goettinger U., Germany, 1976. Researcher Columbia Coll. Physicians and Surgeons, N.Y.C., 1967-70, NIH, Bethesda, Md., 1971-72; producer, writer Am. Chem. Soc., Washington, 1976-78; producer,researcher Zweites Deutsches Fernsehen, Mainz, Germany, 1978-89; producer, reporter European Television Svc., Cologne, Germany, 1985-88; producer, dir., reporter KOPE Prodns., Washington, 1985—. Author: Opera! Guide to Western Europe's Greatest Houses, 1991, Eastern Europe's and USSR's Great Opera Houses, North America's Opera Companies, Festivals, and Theaters, Opera-Going in South America; producer An Amish Portrait for USIA; producer, dir., writer, interviewer documentary films; contbr. articles to Opera News, La Rivista Illustrata del Museo Teatrale alla Scala. Mem. Music Critics Assn., Coun. Internat. Nontheatrical Events, Internat. Platform Assn., Am. Women in Radio and TV, Assn. Ind. Video and Filmmakers, Cosmos Club. Office: KOPE Prodns 3916 47th St NW Washington DC 20016-5612

ZIFF, JOEL DAVID, psychologist; b. Mpls., June 19, 1947; s. Samuel J. and Helen (Geffen) Z.; m. Elizabeth Rosenzweig, Jan. 1, 1992. BA, Columbia U., 1969; MAT, Harvard U., 1971; EdD, U. Mass., 1979. Lic. psychologist, Mass. Pvt. practice Newton, Mass., 1975—; faculty Mass. Sch. Profl. Psychology, Dedham, Mass., 1987-88; adj. faculty Lesley Coll., Cambridge, Mass., 1986—. Author: The Classroom Meeting: An Alternative Approach to Management and Discipline, 1979, Everyone's Picking On Me!, 1978; contbr. articles to profl. jours. Mem. APA, Mass. Psychol. Assn., Internat. Transactional Analysis Assn., Am. Soc. for Clin. Hypnosis, Soc. for Clin. And Exptl. Hypnosis.

ZIGUN, SYLVIA HELENE, psychotherapist, health educator; b. N.Y.C., July 28, 1934; d. David J. and Anna (Felenstein) Moscovitz; m. Charles Zigun, June 9, 1957; children: Jeffrey, Benjamin. BA, Brown U., 1954; MN, Yale U., 1957; MS, U. Bridgeport, 1980; PhD, The Union Inst., 1989. R.N., Conn. Psychotherapist Psychotherapy Assocs. Fairfield, Conn., 1979—; cons. State of Conn. div. ARC health nursing programs, 1974-75; chmn. nursing svcs. Southeastern Fairfield chpt. ARC, 1974-76, childbirth educator, 1974-76. Mem. ANA, Internat. Acad. Nutrition and Preventive Medicine, N.Y. Acad. Scis., Conn. Nurses Assn., Sigma Xi, Phi Beta Kappa. Home and Office: Psychotherapy Assocs Fairfield 400 Post Rd Fairfield CT 06430-6220

ZILCZER, JUDITH KATY, museum curator, art historian, writer; b. Waterbury, Conn., Nov. 6, 1948; d. Paul and Rose (Merkler) Z. B.A. with distinction, George Washington U., 1969, M.A., 1971; Ph.D., U. Del., 1975. Teaching fellow George Washington U., 1969-71; Smithsonian fellow Nat. Mus. of Am. Art, Washington, 1973-74; research asst. Hirshhorn Mus., Washington, 1974-75, historian, 1976-88; assoc. curator painting, 1988—; asst. professorial lectr. George Washington U., 1976, assoc. professorial lectr., 1979-80; guest curator Phila. Mus. Art, 1979-80; acting chief curator Hirschhorn Mus., 1991-92; assoc. prof., lectr. George Washington U., 1991; cons. High Mus. Art, Atlanta, 1985-86. Author: The Noble Buyer, 1978, Joseph Stella, 1983; co-author: The Advent of Modernism, 1986;contbr. articles to profl. jour. Recipient Spl. Commendation David Lloyd Kreeger Art History Competition, 1970; Fluid Research award Smithsonian Instn., 1977; Unidel fellow U. Del., 1971-73, Smithsonian fellow, 1973-74; Penrose grantee Philos. Soc. Phila. Am. Philos. Soc. grantee, 1976-77. Mem. Coll. Art Assn. Am., Women's Caucus for Art, Nat. Trust Historic Preservation, Am. Assn. Mus., Archives of Am. Art, Assn. Historians of Am. Art., Am. Studies Assn. Democrat. Jewish. Office: Hirshhorn Mus and Sculpture Garden 8th Street Ave SW Washington DC 20560-0001

ZILG, ROBERT JOHN, insurance company executive; b. Plainfield, N.J., May 25, 1954; s. George L. and Mary V. (Denny) Z.; m. Mary B. Schindler, Aug. 4, 1990. BA in English, St. Joseph's Coll., 1976; MA in English, Seton Hall U., 1979; MS in Health Svcs. Mgmt., New Sch. for Social Rsch., N.Y.C., 1991. Dir. product devel., competitive and mktg. rsch. Group div. Met. Life Ins. Co., N.Y.C., 1991—. Contbr. articles to profl. jours. Mem. Group Health Assn. of Am. Office: Met Life Ins Co One Madison Ave Area 24-VW New York NY 10010

ZILKHA, DONALD ELIAS, banker; b. N.Y.C., Apr. 8, 1951; s. Ezra Khedouri and Cecile (Iny) Z.; m. Valerie Kleinprintz. BA, Wesleyan U., Middletown, Conn., 1973. With Morgan Bank, N.Y.C., 1973-80; ptnr. Cofina, N.Y.C., 1980-82; assoc. James D. Wolfensohn, Inc., N.Y.C., 1982-86; mng. ptnr. Donald Zilkha & Co., N.Y.C., 1986—; treas. ZG Holdings, N.Y.C., 1984-90. Active Mt. Sinai Hosp. Bd., bus. coun. Met. Mus. Art. Democrat. Jewish. Clubs: Knickerbocker; Meadow (Southampton); Travellers (France). Office: Donald Zilkha & Co 135 E 57th St 24th Fl New York NY 10022

ZIMBELMAN, DARRELL FRANK, aerospace engineer; b. Denver, Dec. 2, 1963; s. Harold Frank and Karen Lucille (McNassor) Z.; m. Mary Ellen Gumina, Oct. 1, 1988; 1 child, Nicole Marie. BS in Aerospace Engring., U. Colo., 1986, MS in Aerospace Engring., 1987, PhD in Aerospace Engring., 1990. Laborer City of Lakewood, Colo., summers 1982-84; engr. Martin Marietta Astronautics Group, Denver, summer 1985; researcher U. Md., College Park, summers 1986-88; programmer analyst STX/ST Systems Corp., Lanham, Md., 1988; altitude control system engr. Fairchild Space and Def. Corp., Germantown, Md., 1989-91, Ithaco, Inc., Lanham, Md., 1991—; tech. svcs. contractor Goddard Space Flight Ctr., Greenbelt, Md., 1991—. Contbr. articles to profl. jours. Bd. dirs. Flower Hill Homeowners Assn., Gaithersburg, Md., 1991-93. Recipient grad. fellowship NASA, Washington, 1986-88, Regents scholarship U. Colo., Boulder, 1982, 83, Royce J. Tipton scholarship, 1984, 85. Mem. AIAA, Am. Astronautical Soc., Tau Beta Pi, Sigma Gamma Tau (pres. 1985-86). Republican. Office: Ithaco Inc 10123 Senate Dr Lanham MD 20706

ZIMMAR, GEORGE PETER, publishing executive, psychology educator; b. Chgo., Dec. 31, 1937; s. Peter George and Sofia (Kanellis) Z.; m. Doulie J. Pappas; children: Sofia Corrine, Peter David George. BS in Psychology, Roosevelt U., 1960, MS in Exptl. Psychology, 1961; PhD in Neurosci., SUNY, Buffalo, 1966; postgrad., MIT, 1968. Rsch. assoc. Northwestern U. Med. Sch., Chgo., 1960-61; instr. psychology SUNY, Buffalo, 1962-64; asst. prof. Grinnell (Iowa) Coll., 1965-69; prof., chmn. dept. Briarcliff Coll., Briarcliff Manor, N.Y., 1970-77; editor Praeger Pubs., N.Y.C., 1978-81; sr. editor CBS Pub. Group/Elsevier, N.Y.C., 1981-88; editor-in-chief Rowman & Littlefield Pubs., Totowa, N.J., 1988-89; sr. editor Springer-Verlag, N.Y.C., 1989-92; pres. Youth Edn. Systems, Inc., Scarborough, N.Y., 1985—, also chmn. bd. dirs.; adj. prof. Pace U., Pleasantville, N.Y., 1977—, NYU, 1991—; v.p., bd. dirs. McGraw Learning Labs. Inc., Dobbs Ferry, N.Y., 1970-74. Author: Chronology of Wars, 1989; contbr. articles to profl. jours. Pres. Ch. of Our Saviour, Rye, N.Y., 1981-82, bd. dirs., 1973-91; capital campaign officer Hackley Sch., Tarrytown, N.Y., 1988. Hillman fellow Roosevelt U., 1961, Sloan Found. fellow, 1968; Cattell grantee Grinnell Coll., 1967. Mem. Am. Psychol. Assn., Am. Psychol. Soc., Cognite Sci. Soc., Sigma Xi. Greek Orthodox. Office: Youth Edn Systems Inc Scarborough Sation 223 Briarcliff Manor NY 10510

ZIMMER, DAVID ARTHUR, business owner, marketing and computer consultant; b. Pitts., Sept. 10, 1956; s. James Milton and Annamarie (DeSanza) Z. AD in Bus. Adminstrn., Pa. State U., 1976, AD in Computer Sci., 1977; BS in Computer Sci., Rutgers U., 1980; MS, Purdue U., 1981. Jr. systems analyst AT&T Bell Labs., Holmdel, N.J., 1977-80, software systems analyst, 1981-84, system analyst, 1984-86, product devel. mgr., 1986-89; product mgr. AT&T, Morristown, N.J., 1989-90, solution architect, 1990-91; in product mgmt. and mktg. Soft-Switch, Inc., Wayne, Pa., 1991-92; pres. Am. Eagle Entities, Jeffersonville, Pa., 1992—; ind. cons., Ocean, N.J., 1988-91. Tech. dir. software manual AT&T Access Plus, 1987. Office: Am Eagle Entities 450 Forrest Ave Jeffersonville PA 19401

ZIMMER, JAY ALAN, health care executive; b. Newark, May 5, 1952; s. Herbert Forman and Ruth (Tucker) Z.; m. Catherine Marie Krzywicki, Mar. 31, 1973; children: Rebecca, Benjamin, Alison. BA, Ramapo Coll. N.J., Mahwah, 1974; MA, New Sch. Social Research, N.Y.C., 1981; MBA, CUNY, 1990. Asst. dir. Community Svcs., Inc., Toms River, N.J., 1974-81; sr. cons. Community Nutrition Inst., Washington, 1981-82; exec. dir. City of Falls Ch. (Va.), Dept. Social Svcs., 1982-83; adminstr. Atlantic City Med. Ctr., 1983—; cons. in field. Editor workbook/manual: Accounting for the Non-Accountant, 1981. Active United Way of Atlantic County; mem. Dover Twp. Bd. Health, Toms River, 1978-79; mem. Galloway Twp. Sr. Citizens Adv. Com., 1987-. Mem. Gerontol. Soc. N.J. (pres. 1985-87), Northeastern Gerontol. Soc., Am. Mgmt. Assn., Am. Soc. Healthcare Educators, N.Y. Roadrunners, Am. Coll. Healthcare Execs. Home: 414 Camelback Ln Absecon NJ 08201-9655 Office: Atlantic City Med Ctr Jim Leeds Rd Pomona NJ 08240

ZIMMER, RICHARD ALAN, congressman, lawyer; b. Newark, Aug. 16, 1944; s. William and Evelyn (Schlank Rader) Z.; m. Marfy Goodspeed, Dec. 27, 1965; children: Carl William, Benjamin Goodspeed. BA, Yale U., 1966, LLB, 1969. Bar: N.Y. 1971, U.S. Dist. Ct. (so. and ea. dists.) N.Y. 1974, N.J. 1975, U.S. Dist. Ct. N.J. 1975, U.S. Supreme Ct. 1980. Assoc. Cravath, Swaine and Moore, N.Y.C., 1969-75; gen. atty. Johnson & Johnson, New Brunswick, N.J., 1976-91; mem. N.J. Gen. Assembly, 1982-87, chmn. state govt. com., 1986-87; mem. N.J. Senate, 1987-91, 102d U.S. Congress from 12th N.J. dist., 1991—. Chmn. March of Dimes WalkAmerica, Hunterdon County, N.J., 1984-86; treas. Hunterdon Hospice, Flemington, N.J., 1984-86; chmn. Nat. Council for Clean Indoor Air, Washington, 1986—. Mem. ABA, N.J. State Bar Assn., Hunterdon County Bar Assn. Republican. Home: RR 2 Box 391 Flemington NJ 08822-9541 Office: US House of Reps Offices of House Members Washington DC 20515*

ZIMMER-LONG, JANIE LOUISE, mathematics educator; b. Balt., Sept. 25, 1943; d. Joseph Max and Anna Margaret (Vogtmann) Zimmer; m. Gordon Henry Stills, Jan. 7, 1972 (div. May 1978); 1 child, Sanova Stills; m. William Broaddus Long, Jr., Nov. 17, 1984; 1 child, W. Michael. BA in Math., Trinity Coll., Washington, 1966; MEd, Loyola Coll., Balt., 1973; postgrad., U. Md., 1982—. Math. tchr. Norfolk (Va.) Catholic High Sch., 1966-69; math. tchr. Balt. City Pub. Schs., 1969-73, math. specialist, 1980-83; math. dept. chmn. Edmondson High Sch., Balt., 1973-80; math. supr. Howard County Pub. Schs., Ellicott City, Md., 1983-91, exec. supr. math., 1991-92, curriculum coord., 1992—; cons. Md. Math. League, 1987—; prof. U. Md., Balt. County, 1989—; clown/mathemagician Md., 1981—. Columnist in math. jour., 1986—; editor: State Functional Math Guide, 1984. Recipient Outstanding Math. Educator award Md. Coun. Tchrs. of Math., 1991, Outstanding Svc. award Md. Coun. Tchrs. Math., 1985, United Cerebral Palsy, 1974, Citizenship award K.C., 1961, Outstanding Alumna of Yr. award Maryvale Trinity Coll. Prep Sch., 1983. Mem. Md. Coun. Tchrs. Math. (rep. 1986—, pres. 1984-85), Nat. Coun. Tchrs. Math., Nat. Coun. Suprs. of Math., Md. Coun. Suprs. of Math., Cowns of Am. Internat., PSTA (v.p. 1989-90), Freestate Clown Alley, Phi Delta Kappa. Democrat. Roman Catholic. Home: 1749 Heatherwood Way Sykesville MD 21784-5648 Office: Howard County Pub Sch Dist 10910 State Rt 108 Ellicott City MD 21042

ZIMMERMAN, BARRY JOSEPH, educational psychology educator, researcher; b. Sheboygan, Wis., Nov. 23, 1942; s. Victor J. and Ida M. (Dekeyser) Z.; m. Diana J. Conley, Aug. 6, 1966; children: Kristin L., Shana M. BA, U. Ariz., 1965, PhD, 1969; MA, N.Mex. State U., 1966. Lic. psychologist, Ariz. Asst. prof. U. Ariz., Tucson, 1970-72, assoc. prof., 1972-74; assoc. prof. grad. sch. CUNY, N.Y.C., 1974-78, prof. grad. sch., 1978—; vis. scholar Stanford (Calif.) U., 1991; co-investigator Columbia Coll. Physicians and Surgeons, N.Y.C., 1987—. Co-author: Social Learning and Cognition, 1978, Functions of Language and Cognition, 1979, Self-regulated Learning, 1989; mem. editorial bd. Devel. Rev., 1980—, Merrill-Palmer Quar., 1979-80, Contemporary Ednl. Psychology, 1975-90, Jour. of Applied

Devel. Psychology, 1983-90, Am. Ednl. Rsch. Jour., 1992—; editor jour. issue Self-regulated Learning, 1990. Bd. dirs. Am. Lung Assn., 1988-90, coun. mem., 1991—, chair sch. health com., 1988—, rsch. coordinating com., 1989—. Rsch. Support grantee Nat. Inst. Heart, Lung and Blood, 1987-91, 90-95. Fellow APA (divs. 7, 15, 16), Am. Psychol. Soc.; mem. Am. Ednl. Rsch. Assn. (asst. chair div. C 1991-92), Am. Thoracic Soc. (chair behavioral sci. assembly 1991—), Soc. for Rsch. in Child Devel., AAUP, Leonia Tennis Club. Office: CUNY Grad Sch 33 W 42nd St New York NY 10036-8099

ZIMMERMAN, BERNARD, investment banker; b. Bklyn., Dec. 7, 1932; s. Jacob and Pearl (Schechner) Z.; BBA, City Coll. N.Y., 1954; MBA, NYU, 1957; m. Joyce M. Singer, Dec. 24, 1960; children: Wayne Jay, Ellen Holly. CPA, N.Y. Fin. exec. consumer products Spartans Industries, Inc., N.Y.C., 1961-65; sr. v.p. Scheinman, Hochstin, and Trotta, Inc., N.Y.C., 1965-72; pres. Bernard Zimmerman and Co., Inc., 1972—; sr. v.p. corp. fin. Gruntal & Co., Inc., 1983-84; pres., chmn. bd. St. Lawrence Seaway Corp., Indpls., 1985—; sr. v.p. The Zimmerman Group, Inc., 1991—; liquidating trustee Unity Buying Svc. Co. Liquidating Trust, Hicksville, N.Y.; bd. dirs. Sbarro, Inc., Commack, N.Y.; fin. cons. Beautiful Visions-U.S.A., Ltd., Hicksville, N.Y., StairMaster Sports, Kirkland, Wash.; adv. dir. McFrank & Williams, N.Y.C., Citadel Motivation, Inc., Metuchen, N.J. With AUS, 1955-57. Mem. N.Y. State Soc. CPAs, Am. Arbitration Assn., N.Y. Road Runners Club. Home and Office: 18 High Meadow Rd Weston CT 06883-2903

ZIMMERMAN, CAROLE LEE, public relations professional; b. Roxboro, N.C., Aug. 28, 1948; d. Ray Richard and Annie Theresa (O'Briant) Z.; m. Richard A. Hoehn, Oct. 26, 1991; 1 child, Kristin Nicole Sizemore. BS in Edn., Fla. State U., 1970; publs. specialist cert., George Washington U., 1980; postgrad., Am. U., 1992—. Tchr. Gadsden County Pub. Schs., Quincy, Fla., 1971-72, Am. schs., Kaiserslautern and Darmstadt, Germany, 1975-76; editor, writer U.S. Life Cos., Arlington, Va., 1980-84; dir. communications Bread for the World, Washington, 1984—. vol. homeless women's shelter Luther Pl. Meml. Ch., Washington, 1983—. Mem. Am. Soc. Assn. Execs., Internat. Assn. Bus. Communicators, Pub. Rels. Soc. Am., Washington Women in Comm., Washington Women in Pub. Rels. Democrat. Lutheran. Office: Bread for the World 802 Rhode Island Ave NE Washington DC 20018-1763

ZIMMERMAN, D(ONALD) PATRICK, lawyer; b. Albany, N.Y., Mar. 20, 1942; s. Bernard M. and Helen M. (Eshelman) Z. Student Lawrenceville Sch., 1960; BA, Rollins Coll., 1964; JD, Dickinson Sch. Law, 1967. Bars: Pa. 1968, U.S. Supreme Ct. 1971. Atty., Legal Aid, 1968-69; pub. defender, Lancaster County, Pa., 1969-72; sole practice, Lancaster, Pa., 1974—; instr. Ct. Common Pleas for Constables, 1976—; solicitor Lancaster County Dep. Sheriff Assn., 1977—, Lancaster County Constable Assn., 1975—; instr. sheriff's dept. Lancaster County for Dep. Sheriffs, 1978—; of counsel to Dep. Sheriff Assn. Pa., 1979-81; spl. counsel Pa. State Constables Assn., 1981; chmn. Bd. Arbitrators Lancaster County, 1975-81; spl. counsel Legislative Com. to Constable Assn. Pa., 1982. Recipient Ofcl. Commendation of Merit, Lancaster County Sheriff's Dept., 1979, Ofcl. Commendation of Merit Fraternal Order Police State Lodge 66, 1985, Outstanding Svc. award, 1987, Disting. Service award Fraternal Order State Police Pa., 1987, Outstanding Leadership award, 1988. Mem. ABA, Am. Trial Lawyers Assn., Pa. Bar Assn., Lancaster County Bar Assn. Author: The Pennsylvania Landlord and Tenant Handbook, 1982; contbr. articles to profl. jours. Office: 214 E King St Lancaster PA 17602-2977

ZIMMERMAN, FLORENCE ARLINE, nurse; b. New Holland, Pa., Dec. 2, 1924; d. Milton Burkhart and Florence Marie (Jackson) Z. BSN, Goshen Coll., 1954; MS, U. Pa., 1962; EdD, Temple U., 1980. Nurse advisor Pusan Children Charity Hosp., Korea, 1957-62; with WHO, SEARO, Project India 114.1, 1963-64; instr. Lankenau Sch of Nursing, Phila., 1964-65; nurse Sch. Dist. of Phila., 1965-66; asst. prof. Goshen (Ind.) Coll., Goshen (Ind.) Coll., Ea. Mennonite Sch. Nursing, Harrisonburg, Va., 1967-68; nursing supr. Sch. Dist of Phila., 1968-88; v.p. Rambo Com Sight for Blind, Media, Pa., 1980-; advisor Diamond St. Health Ctr., Phila. 1985-86, Primary Health Care Nurse Role, Mungeli India, 1981-87. Author: Pediatric Nurse Manual-India, 1964, Relationship Between Health Factors and Academic Performance, 1979, School Nurse Manual, 1982; contbr. chpt. to The Gift of Presence, 1991. Sch. nurse Child Abuse Task Force Hall Mercer, Phila., 1976-80; mem. Presdl. Task Force, Washington, 1980-87; sch. nurse cons. Strawberry Mansion Task Force, Phila. 1986-87. Mem. Mennonite Nurses Assn., Mennonite Health Assn., Nat Coun. Internat. Health, Am. Nurses Assn., Phila. Assn. Sch. Adminstrs., Lancaster Mennonite Nurse Assn. (pres. 1991—). Home: 108 Hill Rd New Holland PA 17557-9339 Office: Rambo Com Sight for Curable Blind 411 Old Forge Rd Media PA 19063-5510

ZIMMERMAN, JAMES LOUIS, real estate broker, appraiser; b. Upper Darby, Pa., Apr. 7, 1936; s. Louis E. and Amelia (Grosso) Z.; m. Vera P. Fegan, June 11, 1960 (div. 1970); 1 child, James L. II. BS, NYU, 1965; MPA, CUNY, 1972. Lic. real estate broker and appraiser. With Port Authority of NY & NJ, N.Y.C., 1956-81; real property appraiser Town of Ramapo, Suffern, N.Y., 1986-91; pvt. practice real estate broker Suffern, N.Y., 1982—; small clains assessment rev. hearing officer 9th Jud. Dist., White Plains, N.Y.; cons. Town of Ramapo, Suffern. Chmn. local bd. 101 U.S. Selective Svc. System, Rockland County, N.Y.; mem. nat. coun. Am. Soc. for Pub. Adminstrn., Washington, 1976-78. Howard S. Cullman fellow Port Authority of NY & NJ, 1979. Mem. N.Y. State Assessor's Assn., Rockland County Bd. Realtors (profl. standards com., dir. comml. and investment div.). Home and office: 107 Somerset Dr Suffern NY 10901-6905

ZIMMERMAN, JAY JAMES, mathematics educator; b. Evanston, Ill., Aug. 10, 1954; s. William Robert and Elsie Lorraine (Fairaizl) Z.; m. Rebecca Louise Alderson, Dec. 10, 1988. BA, Knox Coll., 1976; MS, U. Ill., 1979, PhD, 1983. Instr. Mich. State Univ., East Lansing, 1983-86; asst. prof. Univ. Ala., Tuscaloosa, 1986-89, Towson (Md.) State Univ., 1989—. Contbr. articles to profl. jours. Mem. Am. Math. Soc., Math. Assn. Am. Office: Towson State U Towson MD 21204

ZIMMERMAN, JEAN, lawyer; b. Berkeley, Calif., Dec. 3, 1947; d. Donald Scheel Zimmerman and Phebe Jean (Reed) Doan; m. Gilson Berryman Gray III, Nov. 25, 1982; children: Charles Donald Buffum, Catherine Elisabeth Phebe (twins); stepchildren: Alison Travis, Laura Rebecca, Gilson Berryman. BSBA, U. Md., 1970; JD, Emory U., 1975. Bar: Ga. 1975, D.C. 1976, N.Y. 1980. Asst. mgr. investments FNMA, Washington, 1970-73; assoc. counsel Fuqua Industries Inc., Atlanta, 1976-79; assoc. Sage Gray Todd & Sims, N.Y.C., 1979-84; assoc. counsel J. Henry Schroder Bank & Trust Co., N.Y.C., 1984-85, asst. gen. counsel, 1986, assoc. gen. counsel, 1987; assoc. gen. counsel, asst. sec. IBJ Schroder Bank & Trust Co., N.Y.C., 1988-90, chief counsel, sec., 1991—; asst. sec. IBJ Schroder Leasing Corp., N.Y.C., 1987-90, dir., sec., 1991—; asst. sec. IBJ Schroder Banking Corp., N.Y.C., 1989-90, chief counsel, sec., 1991—; asst. sec. IBJ Schroder Internat. Bank, Miami, Fla., 1989-90, sec., 1991—; asst. sec. IBJS Capital Corp., N.Y.C., 1989-90, sec., 1991—; sec. Bonaght Corp., N.Y.C., 1991—; chief legal officer, sec. Execution Svcs. Inc., N.Y.C., 1991—. Founder, officer ERA Ga., Atlanta, 1977-79; bd. dirs. Ct. Apptd. Spl. Advs., 1988—. Named one of Outstanding Atlantans, 1978-79. Mem. ABA, Assn. Bar of City of N.Y., Ga. Assn. Women Lawyers (bd. dirs. 1977-79), Am. Soc. Corp. Secs., Inc., LWV, DAR. Democrat. Office: IBJ Schroder Bank & Trust Co 1 State St New York NY 10004-1505

ZIMMERMAN, JEFFREY, psychologist; b. N.Y.C., Jan. 19, 1954. BS in Psychology, Am. U., Washington, 1975; MA in Clin. Psychology, U. Miss., 1978, PhD in Clin. Psychology, 1980. Diplomate Am. Bd. Med. Psychotherapists. Staff therapist United Social & Mental Health Svcs., Willamantic, Conn., 1980-81; psychologist, chief psychologist dept. rehab. medicine Mt. Sinai Hosp., Hartford, Conn., 1981-85; dir. Conn. Psychol. Group, P.C., Avon, Conn., 1985—. Mem. Am. Psychol. Assn., Conn. Psychol. Assn. (coun. rep. 1988-90). Office: Conn Psychol Group 40 Dale Rd Avon CT 06001-3612

ZIMMERMAN, JUDITH ELIN, history educator; b. Chgo., Sept. 13, 1939; d. Leo M. and Sara F. (Radoff) Z. BA, Swarthmore (Pa.) Coll., 1960; MA, Russian Inst. cert., Columbia U., 1963, PhD, 1967. Lectr. Sir George Williams U., Mont., Que., Can., 1965-67; asst. prof. Carnegie-Mellon U., Pitts., 1967-71; from assoc. prof. to prof. U. Pitts., Greensburg, 1972—. Author: Midpassage, 1989; co-trans., editor: Landmarks, 1986. Vice pres. regional campuses United Faculty, Pitts., 1985-87. Harvard U. fellow, 1972-73; NEH grantee, 1990-91. Mem. Am. Hist. Assn., Am. Assn. Advancement of Slavic Studies. Democrat. Home: 5432 Kipling Rd Pittsburgh PA 15217-1038 Office: U Pitts Greensburg Campus Greensburg PA 15601

ZIMMERMAN, LEONARD NORMAN, microbiologist; b. N.Y.C., Sept. 13, 1923; s. Harry and Mae (Coplin) Z.; m. Rima Grossman, Nov. 26, 1946; children: Erik E., Raul L., Leda E. BS, Cornell U., 1948, PhD, 1951. Asst. prof. Pa. State U., University Park, 1951-56, assoc. prof., 1956-61, prof., 1961—, head dept. microbiology, 1973-78, assoc. dean Coll. Sci., 1978-87, dean Coll. Sci., 1987-89, dean emeritus, 1989. Co-author: Basic Bacteriology, 1979; contbr. articles to profl. jours. Sgt. U.S. Army, 1943-46. Recipient rsch. awards NIH, NSF. Mem. NSF, Nat. Cancer Inst. (site visit com. 1986). Office: Pa State U Frear Lab Rm 306 University Park PA 16802

ZIMMERMAN, MAURICE JACOB, gastroenterologist, educator, consultant; b. N.Y.C., May 27, 1932; s. Louis and Ethel (Rogovoy) Z.; m. Carol Lois Volk, Mar. 23, 1958; children: Lori Beth Benson, Susan Hollis Weil. BS cum laude, CCNY, 1953; MD, SUNY, Bklyn., 1958. Intern Mt. Sinai Hosp., N.Y.C., 1958, fellow in gastroenterology, 1963-65, assoc. attending physician, 1958—; resident Bronx VA Hosp., N.Y.C., 1959-60; asst. resident in medicine Mt. Sinai Hosp., N.Y.C., 1962-63; pvt. practice gastroenterology N.Y.C., 1965—; cons. in gastroenterology Mt. Sinai Hosp., N.Y.C., 1965—; assoc. clin. prof. medicine Mt. Sinai Sch. Medicine, 1986—. Co-author: The Secretin Test, 1973, The Crohn's Disease and Ulcerative Colitis Fact Book, 1983, People...Not Patients, The Exocrine Pancreas: Basic and Clinical Aspects, 1986; contbr. articles to profl. jours. Capt. USAF, 1960-62. Fellow ACP, Am. Coll. Gastroenterology; mem. Am. Gastroent. Assn., Crohns and Colitis Found. Am. (Achievement award N.Y. chpt. 1982), Phi Beta Kappa, Phi Beta Kappa Assocs. Jewish. Office: 68 E 86th St New York NY 10028-1012

ZIMMERMAN, TODD JONES-FOSTER VOLNEY, consultant; b. Atlanta, June 22, 1946; s. Harold F. and Edythe F. (Disbrow) Z.; m. Laura Volk, June 4, 1969; children: Brian Alexander, Christopher Scott. Student, Duke U., 1965-69. Dir. violation cert. office of rent control City of N.Y., 1972-74; exec. dir. N.Y. Realty Owners, 1975-76; editor Real Estate Weekly, N.Y.C., 1976-77; exec. editor Multi-Housing News, N.Y.C., 1978-81, editor, pub., 1981-88; chmn. Multi-Housing World Conf., N.Y.C., 1981—; co-mng. dir. Zimmerman Assocs., Inc., Clinton, N.J., 1988—; editor, pub. Real Estate Times (now Comml. Property News), N.Y.C., 1986-88; co-editor Multi-Family Investment Outlook, Denville, N.J., 1990—. Contbr. articles to profl. jours. Bd. dirs. Maturity Market Perspectives, Santa Barbara, Calif., 1989—; Nat. Assn. Sr. Living Industries, Annapolis, Md., 1986—, sr. v.p., 1987-88; pres. North County Conservancy, Annandale, N.J., 1990—. Mem. Inst. Residential Mktg. Office: Zimmerman Assocs Inc 51 Main St Clinton NJ 08809-1313

ZIMMON, DAVID SAMUEL, physician; b. Bklyn., Dec. 2, 1933; s. Louis Harold and Sylvia (Zimmerman) Z.; m. Anita Adelhardt, Sept. 11, 1962; children: Daniel, Rachel, Julian Adam. Student, Emory U., 1951-53; MD, Harvard U., 1958. Diplomate Am. Bd. Internal Medicine and Gastroenterology. Intern Bellevue Hosp. (Cornell II div.), N.Y.C., 1958-59; resident Meml. Ctr. for Cancer, N.Y.C., 1959-61; fellow gastroenterology Bellevue Hosp., N.Y.C., 1961-62; rsch. asst. Royal Free Hosp., London, 1962-63, liver disease rsch. fellow, 1963-64; chief gastroenterology Vets. Hosp., N.Y.C., 1965-84; asst. prof. to prof. clin. medicine NYU Sch. of Medicine, N.Y.C., 1965-91; attending physician Bellevue Hosp., N.Y.C., 1965-89; attending physician in medicine, radiology and surgery St. Vincent's Hosp., N.Y.C., 1974-91; vis. prof. Australian Soc. for Gastrointestinal Endoscopy, 1980; pres. N.Y. Soc. for Gastrointestinal Endoscopy, 1976; chmn. Symposium Endoscopic Biliary Surgery, World Congress Gastrointestinal Endoscopy, Stockholm, 1982; chmn. sect. of biliary and pancreatic endoscopy European Soc. for Digestive Endoscopy, Barcelona, Spain, 1984. Editor: Surgical Endoscopy of the Gastrointestinal Tract, 1982; inventor in field; contbr. over 100 articles to profl. jours. Recipient Palmer award William Beaumont Gastrointestinal Soc., 1977. Fellow Am. Coll. Physicians; mem. Internat. Assn. for Study of the Liver, Internat. Biliary Assn., Am. Assn. for the Study of Liver Disease, Am. Gastrointestinal Assn., Am. Soc. for Gastrointestinal Endoscopy. Office: 36 7th Ave Ste 516 New York NY 10011-6609

ZINBERG, STANLEY, physician, educator; b. N.Y.C., Aug. 18, 1934; s. Phillip M. and Etta (Beck) Z.; m. Margaret R. Wright (div. 1981); children: Lloyd M., Randi Ellen, Gregory A. BA, Columbia Coll., 1955; MD, SUNY, 1959; MS, NYU, 1990. Diplomate Am. Bd. Obstetrics and Gynecology. Intern Cornell Med. div. Bellevue Hosp., N.Y.C., 1959-60; resident in ob-gyn. NYU Bellevue Med. Ctr., N.Y.C., 1960-64; assoc. prof. ob-gyn. NYU Sch. Medicine, N.Y.C., 1966—; chief gynecology Bellevue Hosp., N.Y.C., 1975-81; chief ob-gyn. N.Y. Downtown Hosp., N.Y.C., 1981—; mem. staff NYU Hosp.; examiner Am. Bd. Ob-gyn., 1976—; mem. Residency Rev. Com. for Ob.-gyn., 1987—; chmn. faculty coun. NYU Sch. Medicine, N.Y.C., 1978-79; pres. med. staff N.Y. Downtown Hosp., N.Y.C., 1991—. Contbr. articles to profl. jours. Capt. U.S. Army, 1964-66. Fellow Am. Coll. Obstetricians and Gynecologists (Manhattan sect. chmn. 1979-82), N.Y. Obstet. Soc. (pres. 1989-90), N.Y. Acad. Medicine (chmn. sect. on ob-gyn. 1985-86), N.Y. Gynecol. Soc.; mem. Assn. Profs. of Gynecology and Obstetrics (affiliate), Soc. Alumni Bellevue Hosp., Bellevue Obstet. and Gynecol. Soc. (pres. 1988-92). Home: 1365 York Ave 33K New York NY 10021 Office: NY Downtown Hosp 170 William St New York NY 10038

ZINDELL, PAUL J., newspaper publisher, investment executive; b. Catskill, N.Y., Mar. 22, 1948; s. Frederick Clark and Arlene (Clark) Z.; m. Deborah Joan Taylor, May 27, 1973; 1 child, Meghan Kelly. Editor, reporter Register-Star Newspapers, Hudson, N.Y., 1966-70, prodn. mgr., 1970-77, gen. mgr., 1977-80, pres., 1980-85; pres., pub. Californian Pub. Co., El Cajon, Calif., 1989—, also bd. dirs., 1989—; pres. Kendell Holdings Inc., Hudson, 1985—; bd. dirs. Empire Info. Svcs., Schenectady, N.Y., Sun Coast Media Group, Venice, Fla., T.H.A. Inc., Albany, N.Y. Pres. Columbia County United Way, Hudson, 1979; bd. dirs. N.Y. State United Way, Albany, 1980-82; trustee Siena Coll., Albany, 1985—; mem. bd. edn. St. Patrick's High Sch., Catskill, 1982-86. Recipient Disting. Svc. award Hudson Jaycees, 1980, Citizens award Columbia County. Mem. N.Y. State Pubs. Assn. (pres. 1984), Columbia Golf and Country Club (v.p. 1980-82), Hudson Elks. Roman Catholic. Home: Star Rte Box 106C Claverack NY 12513 also: 5220 Fiore Terr San Diego CA 92122 Office: Kendell Holdings Inc 745 Warren St Hudson NY 12534 also: Californian Pub Co 1000 Pioneer Way El Cajon CA 92022

ZINGERLINE, ARTHUR WILLIAM, metallurgist; b. Rome, N.Y., Sept. 18, 1950; s. Harold James and Mazie (Kells) Z.; m. Bonnie Lee Lauri, Dec. 27, 1972; children: Craig Arthur, Julie Lauri. BS in Geology, Rensselaer Poly. Inst., 1972. Rsch. geologist Revere Copper & Brass Co., Rome, N.Y., 1972-80; metall. technician GE AESD Aerospace, Utica, N.Y., 1980; plant metallurgist, SPC coord. Rome (N.Y.) Strip Steel Co., 1980—. Trustee Rome Acad. Scis., 1973—; mem. AAU/Athletic Congress, 1974—; mem. Mohawk Valley Quality Improvement Coun.; ski league coach Woods Valley Alpine Tng. Ctr. Mem. Am. Soc. Metals, Am. Soc. Quality Control (cert. quality engr.), Steuben Striders, U.S. Ski Assn., N.Y. State Ski Racing Assn. Republican. Lutheran. Home: 1313 N George St Rome NY 13440-2701 Office: Rome Strip Steel Co 530 Henry St Rome NY 13440-5608

ZINK, LUBOR JAN, journalist, author; b. Klapy, Czechoslovakia, Sept. 20, 1920; s. Vilem and Bozena (Wohl) Z.; naturalized Brit. citizen, 1949, Can. citizen, 1963; grad. Prague Sch. Econs., 1939, 1945-48; m. Zora Nechvile, Apr. 1, 1942; 1 son, Alec Guy. Info. Officer Ministry Fgn. Affairs, Prague, Czechoslovakia, 1945-48; monitor, broadcaster BBC, Eng., 1948-51; polit. and econ. analyst Allied Authorities, W. Europe, 1951-57; editorial page editor Brandon (Man., Can.) Sun, 1958-62; polit. columnist Toronto (Ont., Can.) Telegram, 1962-71; syndicated columnist Toronto Sun, 1971—; radio and TV commentaries. Progressive Conservative candidate Parliament, 1972, 74. Served to 1st lt. (present rank Lt. Col.) Czechoslovak Brigade, Brit. Army, 1940-45. Decorated Mil. Cross, medal for Bravery; recipient Can. Nat. Newspaper award, 1961, Bowater award for Journalism, 1962, Colin M. Brown Freedom medal and award, 1989. Mem. Parliamentary Press Gallery (life), Royal Can. Legion, Masaryk Meml. Inst. Toronto (hon.). Author: The Uprooted, 1962; Under the Mushroom Cloud, 1962; Trudeaucracy, 1972; Viva Chairman Pierre, 1977; What Price Freedom?, 1981; also novels (2) and books of poetry (4) in Czech. Home: 47 Queensline Dr, Nepean, ON Canada K2H 7J3 Office: Parliamentary Press Gallery, Ho of Commons, Ottawa, ON Canada K1A 0A6

ZINMAN, DAVID JOEL, conductor; b. N.Y.C., July 9, 1936; s. Samuel and Rachel Ilo (Samuels) Z.; m. Leslie Heyman (dec.); children: Paul Pierre, Rachel Linda, Raphael; m. Mary Ingham, May 19, 1974. B.Mus., Oberlin (Ohio) Conservatory, 1958; M.A., U. Minn., 1961. Asst. to Pierre Monteux, 1961-64; guest condr. U.S. and Europe; music dir. Netherlands Chamber Orch., 1964-77, Rochester (N.Y.) Philharm. Orch., 1974-85; prin. guest condr. Rotterdam Philharm. Orch., 1977-79, chief condr., 1979-82; prin. guest condr., music dir. designate Balt. Symphony Orch., 1983-85, music dir., 1985—; adj. prof. Eastman Sch. Music, Rochester. Rec. artist Phillips, Nonesuch, Decca/London, Decca/Argo, Angel/EMI, Telarc, Sony Classical. Recipient Grand Prix du Disque, 1967, 82, Edison award, 1967, 3 Grammy awards, 1990. Office: Balt Symphony Orch 1212 Cathedral St Baltimore MD 21201-5545*

ZINN, DAVID BENJAMIN, composer, pianist, author, music publisher; b. N.Y.C., Dec. 20, 1953; s. William and Sophia (Kalish) Z. BA, NYU, 1982, MA in Music Theory and Composition, 1984. Co-founder Excelsior Music Pub. Co., N.Y.C., 1979—, Visionary Music Pub. Co., 1980—, Nat. Music Promotion Agy., 1980—; exec. mgr. Peace Libr. of Internat. Symphony for World Peace, Inc., 1981—; adj. prof. N.Y. U., 1986—; co-founder Excelsior Typographers and Engravers, 1985, Krazy Klassics Kompany, New Age Publs., Missing Link Pubs., Imperial Pubs., 1986, Zinn Pub. Group, Zinn Comm., Innovation Records, Krazy Klassic Records, Empco Recordings Internat., Associated Sci. Press, Hanover House; concert pianist, rec. artist; composer songs, works for piano, arranger for bands; electronic music synthesist; innovator new systems of music theory; lectr. U.S., Can.; asst. dir. pub. rels. Vitametrics of Am., Planetary Telecommunication Svcs., 1978-80; composer in residnece NYU, 1991—, Earlhour Coll., 1992. Author: The Structure & Analysis of the Modern Improvised Line, 1978, The Structure & Analysis of Modern Harmony, 1981, The Structure & Analysis of the Modern Bass Line for Keyboard and All Bass Instruments, 1982, Chromaticon, 1990, The Hanon Companion's, vols. 1-4, 1990; composer for piano: New Age Portfolio (Quantum Mist, Sonic Serenade, Cosmic Canons, Buddha Blues, Etude Equals Musical Canon Squared, Irish Tales, Sonata Americana, Hebraic Suite, Jazz a la Paganini, Medatation Waltz); The Awakening; Transformation; Fusion Sonata; Scottish Trilogy; Metacosmos; Turkey Cookin' in the Straw; Concert Jazz Rag; Jazzmin, Be-Bach; Jazz Chopsticks (6 hands-1 piano), Spanish Sojourn, Metatations, Mindframes, French Impressions, China Fantasy, The Looney Sonata, Digital Blues, Simplexity, Waltzamatron, Willows Passing, Save the Earth, Chromatic Boggie, Minimalisms, Tremelondo, The Ice-Cream Suite, Mozart's Jive, Stompin' at the White House, Poison Ivories, The Quaker/Shaker Peace, Chopin in Blue, Jazz Impromtu, Boptata and Jazz Fugue, Ludwig's Out, Christmas Bash, Gonna Salsalido, Swingin' Hanon, Pictures by an Exhibitionist. Mem. ASCAP. Contbr. article to publ. in field. Home: 35-19 215th Pl Bayside NY 11361

ZINRAM, STEPHEN JOSEPH, alumni affairs director; b. Erie, Pa., Apr. 5, 1963; s. Robert C. and Carol (Moran) Z.; m. Cynthia Ann Ricke, Aug. 30, 1986. BS in Communications, Clarion (Pa.) U., 1985, MS in Communications, 1988. Asst. gen. mgr. Erie Cardinals Baseball Club, 1985-86; asst. sports info. dir. Clarion U., 1986-88; asst. alumni dir. Robert Morris Coll., Coraopolis, Pa., 1988-89, dir. alumni affairs, 1989—. Volunteer employee's campaign United Way, Coraopolis, 1989, 90; vol., cons. strenghth tng. program Sewickley (Pa.) YMCA, 1990. Mem. Nat. Soc. Fund Raising Execs., Coun. for Advancement and Support Edn., Clarion U. Alumni Assn. (bd. dirs. Pitts. chpt. 1990—). Democrat. Roman Catholic. Home: 320 Ohio Blvd # 8D Sewickley PA 15143 Office: Robert Morris Coll Narrows Run Rd Coraopolis PA 15108-1189

ZIRPOLO, RICHARD A., sales executive; b. Bklyn., Sept. 22, 1946; s. Nicholas John and Rita (Manguso) Z.; m. M. Pat Kelley, Dec. 12, 1969; children: Kathryn, Sarah. BA, U. Detroit, 1969; MA, John Jay CUNY, 1972. Field sales person Gillette Corp, Detroit and Chgo., 1972-74; sales trainer Gillette Corp, Chgo., 1974-75; sales mgr. Gillette Corp, N.Y.C., 1976-86; sales mgr. Corp. Ventures Group Gillette Corp., Boston, 1986-88; v.p. sales Misco Inc., N.J., 1988—; Bd. dirs. Misco Inc., Holmdel, N.J., 1988—. Democrat. Roman Catholic.

ZITO, ALLISON ANN, textile weaver, museum staff member; b. Elizabeth, N.J., Oct. 26, 1960; d. Robert Joseph Zito and Kathleen Marie (Carriere) Mazzaccaro. Student, Moore Coll. Art, 1978-80; BFA, Phila. Coll. Art, 1984. Weaver illustrator Hoch Studios, Glenmore, Pa., 1975-85; tchr.fashion illustration Taylor Bus. Inst., Pomona, N.J., 1981; artist handweaver A.R. Textiles, Phila., 1984—; gallery dir. Mill Brook Art Gallery, Brownsville, Vt., 1986-88; exhibit preparator Balch Inst. for Ethnic Studies, Phila., 1988—, Mutter Mus., Phila., 1989-91, Nat. Mus. Am. Jewish History, Phila., 1990—; computer operator Neveling Card Stamping Co., Phila., 1989; conservator Carli Restorations, Phila., 1991; art handler Phila. Mus. Art, 1992. Exhibited in group shows Del. Art Mus., Wilmington, 1989, Berkshire Mus., Pittsfield, Mass., 1990, Phila. Mus. Art, 1990, Nat. Mus. of Am. Jewish History, 1992, numerous juried and invitational exhibits, 1984—; contbg. artist Contemporary Phila. Artists, 1990. Pa. Coun. on Arts fellow, 1991. Mem. Am. Craft Coun. Home: 337 S 7th St Philadelphia PA 19106 Office: A R Textiles 2d Fl 915 Spring Garden St Philadelphia PA 19123-2605

ZITO, ROSS ALAN, environmental educator; b. N.Y.C., July 12, 1952; s. William and Estelle Nora Z.; m. Rose Mina Feiler; 1 child, Elon. BA, SUNY, 1974; MS in Environ. Studies, Antioch Coll., 1977. Cert. recreation adminstr., N.J. Curator Westchester Dept. of Parks, Recreation and Conservation, White Plains, N.Y., 1977-78, Museum of Arts and Scis., Macon, Ga., 1978-81; nature ops. mgr. City of Gainesville (Fla.), 1981-86; supr. environ. svcs., dir. environ. edn. ctr. Somerset County Park Commn., Basking Ridge, N.J., 1986—; project mgr. and designer Bivens Arm Nature Park, Gainesville, 1985. Sec. Somerset County Environ. Stewardship Coun., 1990—. Mem. Nat. Assn. Interpretation (regional dir. 1987-89, nat. treas. 1989-91), Alliance for N.J. Environ. Edn. (v.p. 1987-92, editor 1992—), Environ. Stewardship Coun. of Somerset County (sec. 1990—). Jewish. Office: Somerset County Pk Commn 190 Lord Stirling Rd Basking Ridge NJ 07920-1399

ZITOMER, SHELDON BARRY, lawyer; b. Phila., Dec. 23, 1948; s. Donald and Norma (Faermann) Z.; m. Barbara Jane Cohen Zitomer, June 8, 1969; children: Benjamin, Nicholas. AB, Temple U., 1970; JD, Hastings Coll. of Law, 1974. Bar: Pa. U.S. Dist. Ct. (ea. dist.). Atty. Joseph Boardman, Esq., PC, Phila., 1974-79, Bernard L. Kubert, PC, Phila., 1978-79; atty. pvt. practice, Phila., 1979—, Warminster, Pa., 1988—; cons. atty. Bikers Against Manslaughter, 1979—. Mem. Warminster (Pa.) C. of C., 1990—, Harley Owners Group. Home and Office: 570 Newtown Rd Warminster PA 18974-5212

ZITTEL, JOHN DAVID, acoustical engineer; b. Oklahoma City, Oct. 4, 1953; s. Robert James and Alice Lou (Kahlor) Z.; m. Sheila Marie Barry, June 4, 1988. BS, Pa. State U., 1975; Ocean Engr., MIT, 1979. Sr. oceanographer Applied Physics Lab. Johns Hopkins U., Laurel, Md., 1979-85; sr. engr. Bolt, Beranek and Newman Inc., New London, Conn., 1985-88; v.p. Marine Acoustics Inc., Mystic, Conn., 1988-91; asst. program mgr. Applied Physics Lab., Johns Hopkins U., Laurel, Md., 1991—. Mem. Conservation Commn., Town of Groton, 1987; vol. Mystic Seaport Mus., 1989. Mem. Acoustical Soc. Am., Sigma Xi, Tau Beta Pi. Office: Johns Hopkins U Applied Physics Lab Johns Hopkins Rd Laurel MD 20723

ZIVIELLO, ALFRED GERALD, surgeon; b. N.Y.C., June 4, 1930; s. Alfred Alphonse and Lylia (Marquette) Z.; m. Cecilia Garber, Feb. 11, 1961; children: Alfred Gerald Jr., David, Lee, Charles. BA, Dartmouth Coll., 1952; MD, U. Ottawa, Ont., Can., 1957. Diplomate Am. Bd. Surgery. Intern Med. Coll. Va., Richmond, 1957-58, gen. surg. resident, 1958-62; attending surgeon St. Charles Hosp., Point Jefferson, N.Y., 1962—; dir.

surgery John T. Mather Hosp., Port Jefferson, 1984—; asst. prof. Stony Brook (N.Y.) Hosp., 1986—. Fellow ACS. Home: 5 W Gate Ln East Setauket NY 11733-1645 Office: 251 E Oakland Ave Port Jefferson NY 11777

ZLOTCHEW, CLARK MICHAEL, Spanish educator; b. Jersey City, N.J., Oct. 14, 1932; s. Harry and Francine (Granoff) Z.; m. Marilyn Barbara Kocin, Dec. 26, 1965; children: Philip, Ethan, David. BS, NYU, 1957; MA, Middlebury Coll., 1966; PhD, SUNY, BInghamton, 1974. Instr. Spanish SUNY, Geneseo, 1970-74; asst. prof. SUNY, Fredonia, 1975-78, assoc. prof., 1978-82, prof., 1982—; project coord. program for Hispanic seasonal workers Bd. Cooperative Ednl. Svcs., Batavia, N.Y., 1974-75. Translator: Seven Conversatations with Jorge Luis Borges, 1982, Falling Through the Cracks: Stories of Julio Ricci, 1989; (with others): Light and Shadows: Selected Poems of Juan Ramon Jimenez, 1987, The House in the Sand: Prose Poems by Pablo Neruda, 1990; contbr. articles to profl. jours. Mem. MLA, Am. Assn. Tchrs. Spanish and Portuguese, N.E. MLA, Academia Portena del Lunfardo (corr.), Inst. Internat. de Lit. y Cultura Hispanica, N.Y. State Coun. on Linguistics (sec. 1979), No. Chautaqua Torch Club (pres. 1990-91). Home: 18 Westerly Dr Fredonia NY 14063-1606 Office: SUNY Fredonia NY 14063

ZLOTNITSKY, MICHAEL JACOB, educator, consultant, translator; b. Charkov, Ukraine, USSR, June 12, 1945; arrived in Israel, 1958; s. Jacob and Sarah (Schneiderman) Z.; m. Leah Kaufman, Aug. 30, 1965; children: Ephraim, Chanan, Tal. Diploma in engring., Technion, Israel, 1967, diploma in vocat. edn., 1971. Educator in engring. Vocat. Network, Israel, 1971-82; owner, gen. contractor Tel Aviv, 1982-86; educator in engring. Md. Drafting Inst., Langley Park, Md., 1987-90. Author: Memory Absentees, 1973. With Israel Army Res. Home: 13837 Dowlais Dr Rockville MD 20853-2630

ZLOTOLOW-STAMBLER, ERNEST, real estate executive, architectural executive; b. Buenos Aires, Sept. 27, 1943; came to U.S., 1981; m. Laura I. Chotti; children: Dan A., Vanessa E., Paul J. BA, Buenos Aires Nat. Coll., 1960; cert. architecture, U. Buenos Aires, 1968. Lic. architect; registered profl. engr., Argentina. Prof. U. Buenos Aires, 1964-81; mng. ptnr. Zlotolow, Chotti & Assocs., Buenos Aires, 1968-81; pres. Imparsa Corp., Buenos Aires, 1970-86; mng. ptnr. Archeting Assocs., Buenos Aires, 1970-81; prof. U. Belgrano, Buenos Aires, 1976-80; v.p. Playa de la Gruta Corp., Montevideo, Uruguay, 1976-78; project mgr. Kravco Corp., King of Prussia, Pa., 1981-84; chmn. Zlotolow-Evantash-Reider Ltd., Southeastern, Pa., 1985—; pres. Meridian Devel. Corp., Wayne, Pa., 1985—, U.S.E.S. Corp., 1989—; gen. ptnr., One Jenkintown (Pa.) Sta. Assocs., 1984-89. Contbr. articles to profl. publs. Paul Harris fellow, 1987, Guy Gundaker fellow, 1990, Paul Vaughan fellow, 1991. Mem. AIA, Urban Land Inst., Nat. trust Historic Preservation, Pa. Soc. Architects, Rotary (pres. 1990-91, chmn. charitable found. 1990-91). Office: Meridian Devel Corp PO Box 623 Southeastern PA 19399-0623

ZLOTOWSKI, MARTIN, psychologist; b. Lodz, Poland, Aug. 10, 1934; s. Pawel and Helen Z.; m. Judith Ann Lifschitz, May 17, 1974; children: David, Steven, Laura. BA, NYU, 1955; MA, Mich. State U., 1958, PhD, 1960. Research assoc. Grad. Sch. Public Health, U. Pitts., 1960-61; research assoc., lectr. Boston U., 1961-62; staff psychologist VA Hosp., Coatesville, Pa., 1962-65, unit chief, 1965-73; clin. dir. St. Mary Providence, 1966-70; assoc. prof. spl. edn. West Chester (Pa.) U., 1973—, grad. coord., 1987—; dir. Counseling Assocs., Paoli, Pa., 1973-85, exec. dir., 1985—. V.p. Victim Witness Services Chester County, 1976-77. Fellow Phila. Soc. Clin. Psychologists (pres. 1978-79, sec. human services ctr. 1982), Phila. Psychol. Assn., Am. Orthopsychiat. Assn.; mem. Am. Psychol. Assn., Mental Health Assn. S.E. Pa. Democrat. Jewish. Home: 605 Eagle Rd Wayne PA 19087-3437

ZMIJEWSKI, CHESTER MICHAEL, pathology educator; b. Buffalo, June 3, 1932; s. Francis Albert and Sophia Josephine Z.; m. Helen Elizabeth Borkowski, June 2, 1954; children: Michael P., Christopher M., Robert J., David N. BA, U. Buffalo, 1955, MA, 1957, PhD, 1960; MA (hon.), U. Pa., 1978. Instr. bacteriology, immunology U. Buffalo, N.Y., 1961; asst. prof. pathology Med. Coll. Va., Richmond, 1961-63; asst. prof. immunology Duke U., Durham, N.C., 1963-67, assoc. prof. immunology, 1967-70; dir. immunology Ortho Rsch. Found., Raritan, N.J., 1970-73; assoc. prof. pathology U. Pa., Phila., 1975-84, prof. pathology, 1984—; cons. Pa. Jersey Red Cross, Phila., 1978—; assoc. dir. William Pepper Labs., Hosp. Univ. Pa., Phila., 1983—. Author three text books and numerous book chpts.; contbr. over 100 articles to profl. jours. Mem. Am. Assn. Blood Banks, Am. Assn. Immunologists, Am. Soc. Histocompatibility and Immunogenetics (pres. 1978), Acad. Clin. Lab. Physicians and Scientists, Am. Soc. Transplant Physicians, United Network for Organ Sharing (chmn. histocompatibility com. 1990—). Roman Catholic.

ZOBEL, RYA W., federal judge; b. Germany, Dec. 18, 1931. A.B., Radcliffe Coll., 1953; LL.B., Harvard U., 1956. Bar: Mass. 1956, U.S. Dist. Ct., Mass., 1956, U.S. Ct. Appeals (1st cir.) 1967. Mem. Hill & Barlow, Boston, 1967-73; mem. Goodwin, Procter & Hoar, Boston, 1973-79; U.S. dist. judge of Mass. Boston, 1979—. Mem. ABA, Boston Bar Assn., Am. Bar Found., Mass. Bar Assn., Am. Law Inst. Office: US Dist Ct McCormack PO & Courthouse Rm 1802 Boston MA 02109*

ZOCCO, JOY MARIE, systems analyst; b. Elizabeth, N.J., Aug. 3, 1942; d. John and Georgette (Fongemie) Stimpson; m. Joseph Zocco, June 20, 1964 (div. July 1976); children: Eric Paul, Corina Beth. AS, Charter Oak Coll., 1989. Programmer Datek Cons., Newington, Conn., 1978-80; programmer I Conn. Dept. Mental Health, Middletown, 1980-82, programmer II, 1982-84, programmer analyst, 1984-88; data processing systems analyst Conn. Dept. Health Svcs., Hartford, 1989—; project mgr. Drinking Water Supplies Sect., Conn., 1988-91. Office: Conn Dept Health Svcs 150 Washington St Hartford CT 06106-4476

ZODIKOFF, DAVID HYMAN, social studies educator; b. Binghamton, N.Y., Mar. 31, 1933; s. Ellen (Meier-Rothschild) Zodikoff; m. Christina Golashevski, June 9, 1957; 1 child, Michele. BS, SUNY, Cortland, 1957; MA, Columbia U., 1960; EdD, Syracuse (N.Y.) U., 1967. Cert. elem. edn. and social studies tchr., N.Y. Tchr. elem. Islip (N.Y.) Pub. Schs., 1957-65; prof. SUNY, 1967-89, adj. prof., 1989—; cons. book reviewer ALA, Chgo., 1970-88. Author 3 books and poems; contbr. articles to profl. jours. President B'nai B'rith, 1976-80. With USN, 1950-54. Mem. Nat. Coun. Social Studies, Phi Delta Kappa. Office: SUNY Edn Dept Cortland NY 13045

ZOELLER, BETTY ANN, secondary school guidance director; b. Elizabeth, N.J., Aug. 2, 1931; d. Joseph Patrick and Anne Marie (McNamara) Murphy; m. R. Peter Zoeller, Dec. 18, 1971. BA in English, Pace U., 1954; M in Counseling, Fairfield (Conn.) U., 1966, CAS in Psychol. Examining, 1969. Cert. counselor, N.J. Guidance dir. Preston High Sch., Bronx, N.Y., 1966-68, Lacoudaire Acad., Upper Montclair, N.J., 1969-71, Paul VI Regional High Sch., Clifton, N.J., 1971-90; pvt. practice as psychol. examiner Upper Montclair, 1978-79; guidance dir. Paterson (N.J.) Cath. High Sch., 1991—. Mem. Fieldstone Assn., Upper Montclair, 1978—, Zonta Internat., 1983-87; vol. Am. Cancer Soc.; presenter Diocesan Profl. Day, 1991. Mem. AACD, Passaic County Counselors Assn. (exec. bd., program chmn. 1978-84, Recognition award), N.J. Profl. Counselors Assn. Roman Catholic. Home: 28 Marquette Rd Montclair NJ 07043-2635 Office: Paterson Cath High Sch 764 11th Ave Paterson NJ 07514-1099

ZOELLER, JACK CARL, financial executive; b. Buffalo, Feb. 26, 1949; s. Ronald Carl and Margaret Lillian (Wademan) Z.; m. Kathryn Louise Helmke, Apr. 25, 1981; children: Andrew, Alexander. BS, U.S. Mil. Acad., 1970; M of Pub. Policy, Harvard U., 1972; M of Letters, Oxford (Eng.) U., 1974. Program budget officer Army Chief of Staff's Office, Pentagon, Washington, 1978-80; v.p. E.F. Hutton & Co., Inc., N.Y.C., 1982; pres. E.F. Hutton Indemnity Group, N.Y.C., 1983-85, Capital Risk Mgmt., Iselin, N.J., 1985-87; exec. v.p. Comfed Mortgage Co., Lowell, Mass., 1987-88; also bd. dirs. Comfed Mortgage Co., Cambridge, Mass., pres., 1988-91; pres. ComFed Savs. Bank, Lowell, 1990-91; chmn. chief exec. officer ComFed Bancorp., Cambridge, Mass., 1990—. Mem. exec. com. Lowell Devel. and Fin. Corp., 1989-91. Capt. U.S. Army, 1970-80. Decorated Meritorious Svc. medals; Rhodes cholar Oxford U., 1972. Mem. West Point Soc. N.Y. (bd. govs. 1985-87), Fed. Nat. Mortgage Assn. (N.E. regional adv. bd. 1990-91), New Eng. Hist. Geneal. Soc. Home: 5 Hampton Rd Lexington MA 02173-8038 Office: ComFed Bancorp 124 Mt Auburn St Cambridge MA 02138-5758

ZOFFER, H. JEROME, educator, university dean; b. Pitts., July 23, 1930; s. William and Sarah Leah (Fisher) Z.; m. Maye Rattner, July 19, 1959; children: Gayle Risa, William Michael. B.B.A., U. Pitts., 1952, M.A., 1953, Ph.D., 1956; C.P.C.U., Am. Inst., Phila., 1954. Sales and mgmt. cons., 1952-60; instr. Sch. Bus. Adminstrn., U. Pitts., 1953-56, asst. prof., 1956-59; assoc. prof. Sch. Bus. Adminstrn., U. Pitts. (Joseph M. Katz Grad. Sch. Bus.), 1959-66; prof. Sch. Bus. Adminstrn., U. Pitts. (Grad. Sch. Bus.), 1966—, chmn. dept. real estate and ins., 1958-60, dir. spl. studies, 1960-62, asst. dean for acad. affairs, 1962-65, assoc. dean for adminstrn., 1965-68, dean Grad. Sch. Bus., 1968—; dir. Red Bull Inns of Am., Inc., 1978-86, Penn. Traffic Co., 1977-87, Oliver Realty Co., 1980-87, Pennwood Savs., 1991—; Ford Found. fellow in applied math. U. Pa., Phila., 1961-62; mem. visitation com. Am. Assembly Collegiate Schs. of Bus., 1972-75, mem. standards com., 1974-78, mem. exec. com., 1975-87, chmn. accreditation rsch. com., 1974-84, v.p. bd. dirs., 1984-85, pres., 1985-86, chmn. Mid. States Evaluation Accrediting Teams, 1967—. Author: The History of Automobile Liability Insurance Rating: 1900-1958, 1959; also monographs.; contbr. articles to profl. jours. Bd. dirs., v.p. Leadership Inst. for Community Devel., 1968-73, Allegheny chpt. Epilepsy Found. Am., 1971-77; bd. dirs. Pitts. Dist. Export Coun., 1974-77; bd. govs. Internat. Ins. Seminars, Inc., 1968-77; mem. festival bd. Three Rivers Art Festival, 1988—; mem. steering com. Leadership Pitts., 1986-91; bd. dirs. Student Cons. Project, U. Pitts., 1970—, Consortium for Coop. and Competitiveness, 1986—, Moral Force in the Workplace, 1986—. Named Man of Yr. in Edn., Vectors Pitts., 1986, Disting. Alumnus, 1989, U. Pitts. Alumni Assn. Mem. AAUP, Soc. CPCU, Am. Econ. Assn., Soc. Psychol. Study Social Issues, Inst. Mgmt. Scis., Mid. Atlantic Assn. Colls. Bus. Adminstrn. (pres. 1972-73), Am. Assn. Univ. Adminstrs. (exec. com. 1971-79, pres. 1975-77, dir. 1980-83, pres. found. 1983—), Univ. Club (bd. dirs. 1988—, sec. 1990-91, v.p. 1991-92), Omicron Delta Gamma, Beta Gamma Sigma (pres. Beta chpt. 1964-68). Home: 5620 Aylesboro Ave Pittsburgh PA 15217-1402 Office: U Pitts Katz Grad Sch Bus Pittsburgh PA 15260

ZOGBY, JAMES JOSEPH, organization executive; b. Utica, N.Y., Nov. 19, 1945; s. Joseph and Celia Zogby; m. Eileen Patricia McMahon, Aug. 3, 1964; children: Joseph Roy, Elizabeth Ann, Sara Hope, Matthew Thomas, Mary-Margaret. BA, LeMoyne Coll., 1967; Arabic lang. cert., U. Pa., 1969; PhD in Religion, Temple U., 1975. Assoc. prof. history and philosophy Shippensburg (Pa.) Coll., 1972-80; fellow-in-residence Princeton (N.J.) U., 1976-77; founder and dir. nat. office Palestine Human Rights Campaign, Washington, 1978-80; exec. dir., co-founder Am.-Arab Anti-Discrimination Com., Washington, 1984; dep. campaign mgr. Jesse Jackson for Pres. Campaign, Washington, 1984; pres., founder Arab Am. Inst., Washington, 1985—; instr. Rosemont (Pa.) Coll., 1969-71; part-time instr. religion Temple U., Phila., 1969-72; adj. prof. polit. sci. Dickinson Coll., Carlisle, Pa., 1975; dir. faculty seminar Gettysburg (Pa.) Coll., 1976. Author: Palestinians: Invisible Victims, 1981; editor Rising Sun Monthly, 1969-70, Taking Root, Bearing Fruit: Arabs in Am., 1984. V.p. Nat. Rainbow Coalition, Washington, 1989—; adv. bd. Washington Com. on Haiti, Washington, 1989—; active DC-Martin Luther King Commn., Washington, 1987—. Mem. Assn. Arab Am. Univ. Grads (v.p. 1976-77), Nat. Assn. Arab Ams. (bd. dirs. 1975—), Coun. on Fgn. Rels., UN Assn. Nat. Capital Area (bd. dirs. 1991—). Democrat. Roman Catholic.

ZOGBY, JOANN HELEN, vocational school educator; b. Shenandoah, Pa., May 9, 1943; d. Benjamin and Helen I. (Gardinsky) Mays; m. Faris C. Zogby, Dec. 27, 1970 (dec. Aug. 1985); 1 child, Mark R. BS, Bloomsburg (Pa.) U., 1963, MEd, 1967; postgrad., Temple U., 1988. Cert. lead tchr., vocat. dir., secondary prin., supr., Pa. Tchr. Pottsville (Pa.) Area High Sch., 1963-68; tchr. Schuylkill County Area Vocat. Tech. Sch., Marlin, Pa., 1968-74, 86-91, coord. tech., 1991—, lead tchr., 1988—. Sec. Ringtown (Pa.) Valley Med. Ctr., 1985-88; pres. Ringtown Area Pub. Libr., 1988—; auditor Ringtown Boro, 1988—. Named Outstanding Tchr., Schuylkill County Area Vocat. Tech. Sch., 1972. Mem. NEA, ASCD, Am. Vocat. Assn., Pa. Vocat. Assn., Nat. Staff Devel. Coun., Pa. Edn. Assn., Am. Legion Aux., Lionesses (pres. Ringtown 1987-88, treas. 1988-91, 100% Pres. award 1988), Delta Pi Epsilon, Omicron Tau Theta. Roman Catholic. Home: PO Box 45 Ringtown PA 17967-0045 Office: Schuylkill County Area Vocat Tech Sch PO Box 130 Mar Lin PA 17951-0110

ZOGHBI, HABIB GEORGE, real estate developer, investment banker; b. Lebanon, May 16, 1955; came to U.S., 1974; s. George Zoghbi and Mary Baklini. BS, Boston Coll., Chestnut Hill, Mass., 1977; MBA, Harvard U., 1980. Banker Morgan Bank, N.Y.C., 1979-85; chmn. Trading and Capital Strategies, N.Y.C., 1986-89; pres. 1st Fin. Corp., N.Y.C., 1985—; pres., chmn. 1st Investment Corp., N.Y.C., Paris, 1988—; asst. prof. NYU Grad. Sch. Bus., 1981-90; cons. New Eng. Telephone, Am. Press, Recats Internat., Baii Banking Corp.; bd. dirs. 1st Investment Corp., Travel Network, N.Y.C. Home: 320 E 46th St New York NY 10017-3042 Office: 1st Fin Corp 425 Madison Ave New York NY 10017-1110

ZOIDIS, MARILYN AMELIA, historian, educator; b. Bangor, Maine, Aug. 8, 1949; d. Peter Gregory and Eleanor Christine (Mallios) Z. BS in Edn., U. Maine, 1971, MEd, 1978; MA in History, Carnegie Mellon U., 1991, postgrad., 1991—. Exec. dir. Bangor Hist. Soc., 1984-87, Freeport (Maine) Hist. Soc., 1988-90; instr. history Carnegie Mellon U., Pitts., 1990—; asst. dir. collections Hist. Soc. Western Pa., Pitts., 1992—; mem. museum adv. panel Maine Arts Commn., Augusta, 1985-87. Co-author: Woodsmen and Whigs, 1991; contbr. articles and book rev. to Maine Hist. Quar. Office: Hist Soc Western Pa 1212 Smellmen St Pittsburgh PA 15222

ZOLBERG, ARISTIDE RODOLPHE, political science educator, researcher; b. Brussels, Belgium, June 14, 1931; came to U.S., 1948; s. Samuel and Sabina (Fiszhaut) Z.; m. Vera Lenchner, Feb. 1, 1953; children: Erica Wendy, Daniel Robert. B.A., Columbia U., 1953; M.A., Boston U., 1956; Ph.D., U. Chgo., 1961. Lectr. Northwestern U., Evanston, Ill., 1960-61; asst. prof. U. Wis.-Madison, 1961-63; asst. prof. U. Chgo., 1963-66, assoc. prof., 1966-69, prof., 1969-83, chmn. dept. polit. sci., 1969-72; Univ.-in-Exile prof. Grad. Faculty New Sch. Social Research, N.Y.C., 1983—; cons. Dept. State, Washington, 1965-68; vis. prof. Princeton U., 1972, U. Paris, 1978, 79, 80, Collège de France, 1986; mem. adv. bd. Nat. Conf. Cath. Bishops' Com. on Migration, 1990—; mem. Comité de Rédaction Internationale, Actes de la Recherche en Sciences Sociales, Paris, 1990. Author: One Party Government in the Ivory Coast, 1964, Creating Political Order, 1966; co-author: Escape from Violence: Conflict and the Refugee Crisis in the Developing World, 1989; editor: Ghana and Ivory Coast: Patterns of Modernization,, 1971, Working Class Formation: Historical Patterns in Western Europe and North America, 1986; mem. internat. editorial adv. bd. Jour. Refugee Studies, 1990—; editorial bd. Internat. Migration Rev. Chair com. on Western Europe, New Sch., 1991. Served with U.S. Army, 1954-55. Inst. for Advanced Study fellow, Princeton, 1972; fellow Social Sci. Research Council, 1964, 68; vis. fellow N.Y.U. Soc. Fellows, 1992; chevalier Ordre des Palmes Académiques (France), 1982. Mem. Am. Polit. Sci. Assn., Francaise de Sc. Politique, Internat. Polit. Sci. Assn., Coun. on Fgn. Rels. Office: New Sch Social Rsch Grad Faculty 65 Fifth Ave New York NY 10003-3003

ZOLBERG, VERA LENCHNER, sociology educator; b. Vienna, Austria, Sept. 22, 1932; came to U.S., 1935; d. David and Gisa (Karp) Lenchner; m. Artistide R. Zolberg, Feb. 1, 1953; children: Erica W., Daniel R. AB, Hunter Coll., 1953; MA in Sociology Anthropology, Boston U., 1956; PhD in Sociology, U. Chgo., 1974. Instr. sociology Edgewood Coll., Madison, Wis., 1962-64; From instr. to asst. prof. St. Xavier Coll., Chgo., 1964-67; vis. prof. Ecole Des Hautes Etudes, Paris, 1979-80; From asst. prof. to assoc. prof. Purdue U., Hammond, Ind., 1974-83; sr. lectr. New Sch. for Social Rsch., N.Y.C., 1983—. Author: Constructing A Sociology of the Arts, 1990; contbr. articles to profl. jours. Mem. Am. Sociol. Assn. (travel grant 1982, 90, fellowship 1991, chmn. culture sect. 1990-91), Sociology of Art of the Internat. Sociol. Assn. (pres. 1990—). Office: Grad Faculty New Sch Social Rsch 65 Fifth Ave 65 Fifth Ave New York NY 10003

ZOLLER, RICHARD EUGENE, manufacturing company executive, real estate agent; b. Cleve., Feb. 15, 1931; s. John Henry and Grace Marie Z.; m. Joanne Ellen Beechinor, Feb. 27, 1954 (div. Sept. 1982); children: Richard Eugene Jr., Martin J., James M., Raymond E.; m. Denise Pierette Maurice, Oct. 20, 1990. BSBA, John Carroll U., 1953; MBA, Case Western Reserve U., 1958. Supt. assembly Euclid div. GMC, Hudson, Ohio, 1955-60; mktg. cons. IBM Corp., Boca Raton, Fla., 1960-88, ret., 1988; ind. contractor cons., facilitator in mfg. and process engring. Boynton Beach, Fla., 1989—; broker, salesman The Keyes Co. Realtors, Lake Worth, Fla., 1989—. Coach little league baseball N.E. Ohio league, 1966-68; mgr. little league baseball, Pepper Pike, Ohio, 1973-79; coach pee wee football, Pepper Pike, 1978-80; bd. dirs. Pepper Pike Civic League, 1976-77. 1st lt. U.S. Army, 1953-55, Korea. Mem. West Palm Beach Golf Assn. Home and Office: 649 Las Palmas Park Boynton Beach FL 33435-2405

ZOLTON, GREGORY MICHAEL, veterinary surgeon; b. Homestead, Pa., Dec. 27, 1948; s. Michael William and Pauline V. (Kuban) Z.; m. Mary Anne, May 22, 1977; children: Gregory II, Alexandra, Justine. BS, W.Va. U., 1970; VMD, U. Pa., 1974. Intern AMC, N.Y.C., 1976-78, resident, 1978; owner, dir. Round Valley Vet. Referral Group, Lebanon, N.J., 1978—; sec. Animerage Corp., N.J., 1988—; gen. ptnr. Animerge Reality Partnership, 1991—. Mem. AVMA, Met. N.J. Vet. Med. Assn., Pa. Vet. Med. Assn., N.W. N.J. Vet. Med. Assn., Nat. Vet. Orthopedic Soc. (bd. dirs. 1987-89), Ea. Vet. Orthopedic Soc. (pres. 1988-90). Republican. Roman Catholic. Office: Round Valley Vet Ref Group 1170 Route 22 W Lebanon NJ 08833

ZOMPANIS, THOMAS ANASTASIOS, substance abuse program director; b. N.Y.C., Feb. 21, 1942; s. Michael and Despina (Mandakis) Z.; children: Emily, Tessa. M of Human Svcs., Lincoln U., 1979; MS in Mgmt., NYU, 1992. Cert. high impact incarceration trainer; state cert. instr., N.Y. Dir. Gaudenzia Inc., Phila., 1970-79; sr. counselor Oxford Project, N.Y.C., 1980-81; dir. Samaritan Village, N.Y.C., 1981-83; acting dir. Substance Abuse Intervention div. N.Y.C. Dept. Corrections, 1986; instr. L.I. U.; trainer N.Y.C. Dept. Corrections. Contbr. articles to profl. jours. Mem. Office of Drug Abuse Policy, N.Y.C. Grantee Med. and Health Rsch. Assn. of N.Y.C., 1992. Fellow Am. Jail Assn., Am. Correctional Assn., N.Y. Fedn. of Alcohol and Chem. Dependency Counselors, Lincoln U. Alumni. Greek Orthodox. Home: 21-39 23d St Astoria NY 11105 Office: NYC Dept Corrections SAID Trailer 12 Shore Rd Rikers Island Flushing NY 11370

ZOOK, BERNARD CHARLES, pathology educator, administrator, researcher; b. Beach, N.D., Nov. 1, 1935; s. Frank N. and Elizabeth Fern (Kramer) Z.; m. Elinore A. (Schillo), Oct. 1, 1955; children—Bernita, Melinda, Andrew. B.S., Colo. State U., 1962, D.V.M., 1963; postgrad. Harvard Med. Sch., 1963-68, Northeastern U., Boston, 1966. Diplomate Am. Coll. Veterinary Pathologists. From research fellow to asst. in pathology Harvard Med. Sch., Boston, 1963-68; from research fellow to assoc. pathologist Angell Meml. Animal Hosp., Boston, 1963-69; asst. prof. George Washington U., Washington, 1969-74, assoc. prof., 1974-83, prof. pathology, 1983—; cons. comml. orgns. Contbr. articles on heart disease, poisoning, radiation injury and other med. conditions to profl. jours. Vol. Seneca council Boy Scouts Am., 1981-84. Research fellow Smithsonian Instn., 1969—, NIH, 1967-68; grantee Murray Corp., 1981-85, Nat. Cancer Inst., 1975-86, Population Council, 1981-85, Motorola Corp., 1991—. Mem. AVMA, AAAS, Radiation Research Soc., Soc. Toxicologic Pathologists, Nat. Soc. Med. Research (bd. dirs. 1981-86), Beta Beta Beta, Phi Zeta. Republican. Roman Catholic. Club: Bridge. Lodge: K.C. Avocations: music; painting. Office: George Washington U Med Ctr 2300 I St NW Washington DC 20037-2337

ZORAIAN, JOHN PAUL, securities trader; b. Bklyn., Aug. 11, 1955; s. Paul and Rose (Ohanian) Z.; m. Kathleen Zoraian, Oct. 21, 1979; children: Jacqueline, John. BBA, Hofstra U., 1977. CPA, N.Y. Examiner Nat. Assn. Securities Dealers, N.Y.C., 1977-78; sr. acct. Peat Marwick Mitchell, N.Y.C., 1978-80; chief fin. officer Junction Advisors Inc., N.Y.C., 1980—. Mem. Rep. Nat. Com., Washington, 1989. Mem. AICPA, Nat. Assn. of Accts., Securities Industry Assn. Republican. Armenian Orthodox. Home: 45 Eastover Dr East Northport NY 11731-4330 Office: Junction Advisors 9 W 57th St New York NY 10019-2600

ZORN, GUS TOM, physics educator; b. Ada, Okla., June 18, 1924; s. Charles August and Nell (McLachlan) Z.; widowed. BSEE, Okla. A&M, 1948; MS in Physics, U. N.Mex., 1953; Dott. in Fisica, Padua U., 1954. Asst. in physics Inst. di Fisica, Padua, Italy, 1951-54; rsch. assoc. Brookhaven Nat. Lab., Upton, N.Y., 1954-56, assoc. physicist, 1956-62; assoc. prof. physics U. Md., College Park, 1962-72, prof., 1972—; vis. scientist Max Planck Inst. Physics, Munich, Fed. Republic Germany, 1958; vis. physicist Desy Lab., Hamburg, Fed. Republic Germany, 1984. Contbr. 150 articles to profl. jours. With inf. U.S. Army, 1943-45. Rsch. Bd. grantee U. Md., 1978, 88. Fellow Am. Phys. Soc.; mem. N.Y. Acad. Sci. Home: 8722 23d Ave Adelphi MD 20783 Office: Physics Dept U Md College Park MD 20742

ZORNOW, DAVID M., lawyer; b. N.Y.C., Mar. 31, 1955; s. Jack and Marion (Gilden) Z.; m. Martha Malkin, July 21, 1985; children: Samuel Morris, Hannah Jane. AB summa cum laude, Harvard U., 1976; JD, Yale U., 1980. Bar: N.Y. 1981, U.S. Ct. Appeals (3rd cir.) 1982, U.S. Dist. Ct. (so. dist. N.Y.) 1983, U.S. Ct. Appeals (2d cir.) 1984, U.S. Dist. Ct. (D.C.) 1989, U.S. Ct. Appeals (D.C. cir.) 1989, U.S. Dist. Ct. (Ariz.) 1990. Law clerk to Judge Herbert J. Stern U.S. Dist. Ct. N.J., Newark, 1980-82; assoc. Kramer Levin Kamin Nessen & Frankel, N.Y.C., 1982-83; asst. U.S. atty. so. dist. N.Y. U.S. Atty.'s Office, N.Y.C., 1983-87; assoc. counsel Office Ind. Counsel-Iran/Contra Investigation, Washington, 1987-89; ptnr. Skadden Arps Slate Meagher & Flom, N.Y.C., 1989—; vis. faculty Trial Advocacy Workshop Harvard Law Sch., Cambridge, Mass., 1988. Mem. ABA (com. on white collar crime), Fed. Bar Coun., Assn. of Bar of City of N.Y., N.Y. Assn. Criminal Def. Lawyers, N.Y. Coun. Def. Lawyers. Office: Skadden Arps Slate Meagher & Flom 919 3d Ave New York NY 10022

ZOSS, ABRAHAM OSCAR, chemical company executive; b. South Bend, Ind., Feb. 17, 1917; s. Harry and Fannie (Friedman) Z.; B.S. in Chem. Engring., U. Notre Dame, 1938, M.S., 1939, Ph.D., 1941; m. Betty Jane Hurwich, Dec. 24, 1939; children—Roger, Joel, Hope Zoss Schladen; m. 2d, Magda Szanto, May 26, 1978. With Gen. Aniline & Film Corp., Easton, Pa., 1941-47, tech. mgr., Linden, N.J., 1947-55, plant mgr., 1955-57; mgr. mfg. adminstrn., chem. div. Minn. Mining & Mfg. Co., St. Paul, 1957-58, prodn. mgr. chem. div., 1958-60; v.p. Photek Inc., West Kingston, R.I., 1960-62; asst. corp. tech. dir. Celanese Corp., N.Y.C., 1962-65, corp. tech. dir., 1965-66, corp. dir. comml. devel., 1966-69; v.p. corp. devel. Tenneco Chems., Inc., N.Y.C., 1969-71, Universal Oil Products Co., Des Plaines, Ill., 1971-72; group v.p. Engelhard Industries div. Engelhard Minerals & Chem. Corp., Murray Hill, N.J., 1972-74, v.p. bus. devel., 1974-77; v.p. corp. devel. CPS Chem. Co., Inc., Old Bridge, N.J., 1977, dir., v.p., chief adminstrv. officer, 1978-84; pres. Bus. Devel. Internat., Verona, N.J., 1984—; mem. field info. agy. Office Tech. Svc., Commerce Dept., Europe, 1946; teaching asst. U. Notre Dame, 1939-41. Mem. Met. Mus. Art, N.Y.C., Mus. Modern Art, N.Y.C. Recipient Centennial Sci. award U. Notre Dame, 1965. Fellow Am. Inst. Chemists, AAAS; mem. Am. Chem. Soc., Am. Inst. Chem. Engring., N.Y. Acad. Scis., Comml. Devel Assn., Soc. Chem. Industry, Tech. Transfer Soc. Societe de Chimie Industrielle (pres. Am. sect.), Chemists Club (N.Y.C.). Contbr. articles to profl. publs. Patentee in field. Home and Office: One Claridge Dr Ste 904 Verona NJ 07044

ZOTTER, JEFFREY LEE, health facility administrator; b. Allentown, Pa., Dec. 4, 1954; s. Alfred Norman and Margaret Sarah (Himmelberger) Z.; m. Michelle Stephanie Buss, May 25, 1984 (div. Mar. 1987); m. Patricia Ann Crelli, Sept. 20, 1991. BA, Muhlenberg Coll., 1978; MBA, Widener U., 1984. Lic. nursing home adminstr., Pa. Acctg. mgr. Lehigh Valley Hosp. Ctr., Allentown, 1974-84; dir. fin. planning med. Coll. Pa., Phila., 1984-85; chief fin. officer Slate Belt Nursing & Rehab. Ctr., Bangor, Pa., 1985-89; adminstr. New Medico Rehab. Ctr. Phila., Lafayette Hill, Pa., 1989-91; dir. fin. Ridgaway Philips Co., Springhouse, Pa., 1991—; instr. Cedar Crest Coll., Allentown, 1988-89. Big brother Big Brothers & Big Sisters of Lehigh

County, Allentown, 1980-89; vol. Cystic Fibrosis Found., Allentown, 1980-85. Mem. Am. Hosp. Assn. Republican. Lutheran. Home: 135 Meadowbrook Dr Huntingdon Valley PA 19006-6842

ZOUARY, MAURICE H., film and television producer; b. Bklyn., July 17, 1921; s. Ellie Louis and Marie Louise Z.; student N.Y. Sch. of Indsl. Art and Design, 1937-39; m. Edith Brueckner, Feb. 3, 1959. Gen. asst. Randforce Amusement Theatre, N.Y.C., 1936-39, Translux Theatre, Circuit, N.Y.C., 1940-42; arts and media Buchanan Advt., N.Y.C., 1944-47; designer Egmont Arens Indsl. Design, N.Y.C., 1947-49; writer of film commls. Grey Advt. Agy., N.Y.C., N.Y., 1951-54; producer TV programs for various TV shows, N.Y. and Hollywood, 1949-51; producer: (semi-documentary film) Martin Luther—Rebel Priest; founder Filmvideo Releasing Corp., N.Y.C., 1957, producer, 1957—; cons. to NBC and CBS, 1960—; pres. TV Nat. Releasing Corp., 1976—; exec. v.p. Movietronics Corp. Am., Inc.; Author: Kids Eye Views of the News, Destruction of a Genius; also producer/writer documentary Destruction of a Genius; co-author First Sound of Movies; lectr. on history of motion picture sound to various colls., 1968—. With USNR, 1942-43, C.E., U.S. Army, 1942-44. Named to Honorable Order of Ky. Colonels. Fellow Radio Club Am. (life, Lee DeForest award); mem. NATAS, Internat. Radio and TV Soc., Nat. Assn. of TV Program Execs., The DeForest Pioneers (award 1976), The Motion Picture Pioneers, Nat. Soc. of Scribes (named Master Calligraphic Artist), Art Students League of N.Y. (life). Republican. Contbr. articles on pioneering of DeForest's synchronized sound on film, on history of entertainment as relates to communication media; subject of books including The Silent Clowns (Walker Kerr), The Birth of the Talkies (Geduld), Reminiscing with Sissle and Blake (Robert Kimball), The Fleischer Story (Leslie Cabarga). Home: 56 Marlborough Rd Brooklyn NY 11226-2606 Office: 1650 Broadway Rm 710 New York NY 10019

ZREBIEC, LOUIS, JR., educational researcher; b. Niagara Falls, N.Y., June 19, 1936; s. Louis Odrowaz and Helen (Zajac) Z. BA in Math., SUNY, Buffalo, 1960, PhD in Ednl. Psychology, 1975; MS in Math. Edn., Canisius Coll., 1965. Cert. tchr., N.Y. Tchr. math. Buffalo Bd. Edn., 1961-65; instr. math. Millard Fillmore Coll., Buffalo, 1966-67; asst. to dir. admissions and records SUNY, Buffalo, 1967-68, lectr. psychology, 1975-76, assoc. dir. instl. studies, 1979-86; cancer rsch. scientist Roswell Park Meml. Inst., Buffalo, 1968-69; assoc. dir. stas. Fla. Regional Med. Program, Tampa, 1969-70; pvt. endl. cons. Niagara Falls, N.Y., 1986—; reader Ednl. Stas. Author: A Rationale of Statistics for the Behavioral Sciences, 1978, Letters Concerning Change (from Louis Zrebiec Jr.) to Change Agents: Some Thoughts, 1990, Some Currents and Dynamics Basic to the Next Decade and the Next Century, 1991, Fulfillment in Lifelong Learning and Development, 1991. SUNY-Buffalo Rsch. Found. grantee, 1971. Mem. IEEE, ACM, N.Y. Acad. Sci., Am. Mgmt. Assn., Assn. for Instl. Rsch., Northeastern Assn. for Instl. Rsch., Am. Math. Soc., Am. Assn. Higher Edn. Home and Office: PO Box 2164 Niagara Falls NY 14302

ZUBER, RICHARD ARTHUR, information services executive; b. Rochester, N.Y., Nov. 27, 1951; s. Richard Arnold and Jeanette (Gugliotta) Z.; m. Jacqueline Duane, Sept. 22, 1973; children: Jeffrey, Laura. AAS, SUNY, Alfred, 1971; BA in Computer Sci., SUNY, Potsdam, 1973; MS, Rochester Inst. Tech., 1976. Programmer asst. Rochester Telephone, 1973-74, programmer, 1974-78, systems analyst, 1978-80, applications mgr., 1980-90, dir., 1990—. Mem. Assn. for Systems Mgmt.

ZUBROW, SIDNEY N., internist; b. Phila., Aug. 30, 1913; s. Nathan and Sara (Kantrowitz) Z.; m. Molly Cohen; m. Betzy Zubrow Cohen, Diane Zubrow Sand. BA, U. Pa., 1934; MD, Hahnemann Med. Coll., 1938. Diplomate am. Bd. Internal Medicine. Intern Mt. Sinai Hosp., Phila., 1938-39; pvt. practice, 1956—; assoc. prof. medicine Med. Sch. U. Pa., Phila., 1973—; cons. to dept. internal medicine Pa. Hosp., Phila., 1973. Maj. U.S. Army, 1941-46. Named Physician of Yr. Phila. County Med. Soc., 1981. Fellow ACP, Phila. Coll. Physicians; mem. AMA, Phila. County Med. Soc., Pa. Med. Soc., Jewish Acad. Arts and Scis. Republican. Jewish. Home: 1820 Rittenhouse Sq Philadelphia PA 19103-5832 Office: 301 S 8th St Philadelphia PA 19106-4014

ZUCCO, CATHLEEN MARIA, mathematics educator; b. Syracuse, N.Y., Apr. 10, 1954; d. Joseph James and Mary Louise (Vinciguerra) Z. BA in Math. magna cum laude, Le Moyne Coll., 1976; MS in Math., Syracuse U., 1979. Cert. secondary math. tchr., N.Y. Tchr. math. Franciscan Acad., Syracuse, 1976-78, Skaneateles (N.Y.) High Sch., 1980-82; instr. math., computer programming higher edn. program Le Moyne Coll., Syracuse, summer 1977-86, instr. math., 1982—, dir. math. ctr., 1987—; reviewer coll. math. textbooks West Ednl. Pub., Addison Wesley, Richard D. Irwin, Macmillan. Le Moyne Coll. acad. scholar, 1972-76; summer fellow Syracuse U., 1980. Mem. Nat. Coun. Tchrs. Math., Math. Assn. Am., Assn. Math. Tchrs. N.Y. State, Super Math. Computer Sci. Com., Pi Mu Epsilon. Home: 351 N Edwards Ave Syracuse NY 13206-2208 Office: Le Moyne Coll Le Moyne Heights Syracuse NY 13214

ZUCK, ALFRED MILLER, association executive; b. East Petersburg, Pa., Aug. 27, 1934; s. Walter Newton and Mary (Miller) Z.; m. Geraldine Connelly, July 21, 1957; children: Susan, David. BA, Franklin and Marshall Coll., 1957; MPA, Syracuse U., 1958. Dir evaluation Employment and Tng. Adminstrn., Dept. Labor, Washington, 1968-70, dir adminstrn. and mgmt., 1970-75; comptroller U.S. Dept. Labor, Washington, 1975-77; exec. dir. Commn. on Exec., Legis. and Jud. Salaries, Washington, 1980; asst. sec. Dept. Labor, Washington, 1977-83, acting sec., 1981; asst. adminstr. EPA, Washington, 1983; exec. dir. Nat. Assn. Schs. of Pub. Affairs and Adminstrn., Washington, 1983—; dir. fed. program Presdl. Commn. on Youth Opportunities, Washington, 1967-68; pres. Internat. Inst. Adminstrv. Scis., Brussels, 1989—, Am. Consortium for Internat. Pub. Adminstrn., Washington, 1984-89; bd. dirs. Pub./Pvt. Venture, Inc., Phila., 1984—. Recipient Presdl. Disting. Exec. award Pres. of U.S., 1980; Disting. Alumni award Franklin and Marshall Coll., 1980. Fellow Nat. Acad. Pub. Adminstrn. (trustee 1989—); mem. Phi Beta Kappa. Office: NASPAA 1120 G St NW Ste 730 Washington DC 20005-3801

ZUCKER, HERBERT, publishing executive; b. N.Y.C., July 7, 1928; s. Reuben and Bess E. (Kolber) Z.; m. Nancy E. Fine, Nov. 26, 1953; children: Bradley Charles, Eileen Sherri, Amy Diane. BA, NYU, 1950; MS, UCLA, 1953. Regional mgr. TV Guide, Miami, Fla., 1954-61; mgr. nat. merchandising TV Guide, Radnor, Pa., 1961-66; nat. mgr. regional sales TV Guide, Radnor, 1966-75, dir. pub. relations, 1975-80, dir. mktg., broadcast and cable, 1980—; lectr. to trade assns., colls., univs., 1965—. Contbr. articles to TV Guide. Served with U.S. Army, 1951-53. Mem. Advt. Club (v.p. 1957-59). Office: TV Guide 4 Corporate Ctr Radnor PA 19087

ZUCKER, JERRY M., producer; b. Buffalo, Jan. 3, 1960; s. William and Judith Clara (Balassa) Z. BA in Advt., Syracuse U., 1982. Publicity asst. 21st Century Films, N.Y.C., 1981-82; writer pub. rels. Studio Arena Theatre, Buffalo, 1982-83; writer pub. rels., greeting cards Recycled Paper Products, Chgo., 1983-85; mgr. prodn. Fred Sider Advt., Chgo., 1984-85, Stern Walters Advt. Agy., Chgo., 1985-87; writer greeting cards Calif. Dreamers, Chgo., 1985-87; photographer M & W Color Lab., Buffalo, 1987—. Producer of 60-minute comedy video Bad Films, 1989; producer music video Will Powe,r 1990 (Silver medal Hiroshima Film Festival 1991); writer, photographer trading card set Assassin Trading Cards, 1992, Old Time Outlaws Trading Cards, 1992. Mem. Toy Mfrs. Am., Hallwalls Gallery. Home: 95 Inwood Pl Buffalo NY 14209

ZUCKER, STEFAN, tenor, writer, editor, radio broadcaster; b. N.Y.C. BS, Columbia U., 1967; postgrad., NYU, 1967-72. Freelance tenor concerts and operas in U.S. and Europe, 1965—; tenor RCA Records, N.Y.C., 1972-77; guest singer radio and TV programs, U.S. and Europe, 1975—; radio producer, host WKCR-FM, N.Y.C., 1980—; opera critic N.Y. Tribune, 1983-84; producer, adminstr. Harlem Civic Opera, N.Y.C., 1967; philosophy lectr. Coll. Ins., N.Y.C., 1972. Record producer including Rossini's Rivals: Music By Then-Famous, Now-Obscure, Italian Composers, 1984; singer, producer, stage dir., adminstr. various operas; editor Opera Fanatic mag., 1986—; contbr. articles to Internat. Dictionary of Opera, Opera News, The Opera Quar., Am. Record Guide, Opera Fanatic, News World, Professione Musica, others. Pres. Bel Canto Soc., Inc., 1985—. Named Worlds Highest Tenor by Guinness Book of World Records, 1979—; subject of record Stefan Zucker: The World's Highest Tenor, 1981. Mem. NYU Philosophy Assn. (pres. 1969-72, v.p. 1968), Music Critics Assn., Assn. Furtherment Bel Canto (pres. 1967-80). Office: Bel Canto Soc Inc 11 Riverside Dr New York NY 10023-2504

ZUCKER-FRANKLIN, DOROTHEA, medical scientist, educator; b. Berlin, Aug. 9, 1930; came to U.S., 1949; d. Julian and Gertrude (Feige) Zucker; m. Edward C. Franklin, May 15, 1956 (dec. 1982); 1 child, Deborah Julie. BA, Hunter Coll., 1952; MD, NYU, 1956. Diplomate Am. Bd. Internal Medicine. Intern Phila. Gen. Hosp., 1956-57; resident in internal medicine Montefiore Hosp., N.Y.C., 1957-59, postdoctoral fellow in hematology, 1959-61; with Med. Sch. NYU, N.Y.C., 1962—, prof. Med. Sch., 1974—, dir. lab., 1966—; asst. attending physician Montefiore Hosp., 1961-65; assoc. attending physician Univ. Hosp., 1968-74, attending physician, 1974—; assoc. attending physician Bellevue Hosp., 1968-74, attending physician, 1974—; cons. physician Manhattan (N.Y.) VA Hosp., 1970—, PHS Agy. for Healthcare Policy and Rsch., 1992—; sci. adv. bd., rev. panel Israel Cancer Rsch. Fund, 1982—; mem. U.S.-Israel Binat. Sci. Found., 1980—; bd. dirs. Henry M. and Lillian Stratton Found., Inc., 1987—; AID related Rsch. Rev. Com. NIHLB, 1986-90; mem. allergy immunol. com. NIH, 1974-80, pathological tng. com. NIH, 1971-74, Health Resource Coun., N.Y.C., 1971-74, blood products com. FDA, 1981-87. Mem. editorial bd. Blood, 1973-76, 80-86, Jour. Reticuloendothelial Soc., 1964-74, 80—, Am. Jour. Pathology, 1979—, Blood Cells, 1980—, Ultrastructural Pathology, 1979, Am. Jour. Medicine, 1981—, Hematology Oncology, 1982—, Jour. Immunology, 1986—; author: (with others) The Physiology and Pathology of Leukocytes, 1962, Atlas of Blood Cells, Function and Pathology, 1981, 2d edit., 1989, Amyloidosis, 1990. Recipient Career Devel. award NIH, 1965-70; NIH Rsch. grantee, 1970—. Fellow N.Y. Acad. Scis.; mem. Am. Fedn. Clin. Rsch., Am. Soc. Clin. Investigation, Am. Assn. Physicians, Am. Soc. Hematology (chairperson subcom on leukocyte physiology 1977, chairperson subcom. on immunohematology 1984, exec. coun. 1985—, advanced learning resources com. 1987—), Soc. Exptl. Biology and Medicine, Am. Soc. Exptl. Biology, Am. Soc. Immunologists, Am. Soc. Cell Biology, Reticuloendothelial Soc. (pres. program and nominatingcoms. 1984-85), N.Y. Soc. Electron Microscopists (pres. 1962, 84-85), N.Y. Soc. for Study Blood. Office: NYU Med Ctr 550 1st Ave New York NY 10016-6402

ZUCKERMAN, EDWARD PAUL, editor, publisher; b. Chgo., Oct. 31, 1942; s. Joseph and Rose (Ferber) Z. Reporter Chgo. Heights (Ill.) Star, 1963-64, Kankakee (Ill.) Daily Jour., 1964-67, Gary (Ind.) Post-Tribune, 1967-70; corr. Knight-Ridder Newspapers, Washington, 1970-80; editor, pub. Amward Publs., Inc., Washington, 1980—; exec. dir. Project for Investigative Reporting on Money in Politics, Washington, 1985-86; lectr. Am. U., Washington, 1987-88, George Washington U., 1987-88, U. Miami, 1987-88. Editor: Almanac of Federal PACs, 1986, 88, 90, 92, PACs and Lobbies, 1980—. Recipient Media award for advancement of econ. understanding Amos Tuck Sch. Bus. Adminstrn. Dartmouth Coll., 1977. Mem. Nat. Press Club, Investigative Reporters and Editors Assn. Office: Amward Publs Inc 2000 National Press Bldg Washington DC 20045

ZUCKERMAN, JEFFREY IRA, lawyer; b. N.Y.C., Jan. 15, 1950; s. Sidney Harold and Beatrice (Rosenthal) Z.; m. Miriam Emily Sternberg, June 25, 1978; children: Aron Meir, Lea Bayla, Yitzhak Chaim, Eliezer Moshe, Daniel Yishayahu. BA with honors in Econs. cum laude, CCNY, 1969; JD, Yale U., 1972. Bar: N.Y. 1973, U.S. Ct. Appeals (2nd cir.) 1973, U.S. Dist. Ct. (so. and ea. dist.) N.Y. 1974, U.S. Supreme Ct. 1976, U.S. Dist. Ct. (no. dist.) N.Y. 1978, U.S. Ct. Appeals (D.C. cir.) 1978, U.S. Ct. Appeals (10th cir.) 1981, D.C. 1983, U.S. Dist. Ct. D.C. 1983. Law clk. for judge U.S. Ct. Appeals (2d cir.), N.Y.C., 1972-73; assoc. Sullivan & Cromwell, N.Y.C., 1974-81; spl. asst. to asst. atty. gen. antitrust div. U.S. Dept. of Justice, Washington, 1981-84; chief of staff U.S. EEOC, Washington, 1984-86; dir. Bur. Competition FTC, Washington, 1986-89; ptnr. Curtis, Mallet-Prevost, Colt & Mosle, Washington, 1989—. Chmn. bd., pres. Nat. Jewish Outreach Program, N.Y.C., 1978—, Fund for Jewish Future, N.Y.C., 1990—; v.p., bd. dir. Silver Spring Eruv Assn., 1985-89; bd. dirs. Capital Legal Coun., B'nai B'rith, 1987-90, Hebrew Day Sch. of Montgomery County, 1986, Met. Comm. on Torah Edn., N.Y.C., 1979-81, Jewish Advs. of the West Side, N.Y.C., 1979-81, Be'er Hagolah Insts., Bklyn., 1980-81, Internat. Assn. of Jewish Lawyers and Jurists Am. sect., Washington, 1991—. Mem. ABA, N.Y. State Bar Assn., N.Y. County Lawyers Assn., Assn. of Bar of City of N.Y., D.C. Bar (co-chair antitrust law com.), Yale Law Sch. Assn. D.C. (pres. 1983-84), Internat. Assn. Jewish Lawyers and Jurists (bd. dirs. Am. sect. 1992—), Internat. C. of C. (commn. on law and practices relating to competition), U.S. Coun. for Internat. Bus. (com. on competition law and policy), Phi Beta Kappa. Republican. Home: 1217 N Belgrade Rd Silver Spring MD 20902

ZUCKERMAN, LINDA DIX, health facility administrator; b. Syracuse, N.Y., Mar. 18, 1956; d. William Ernest and Betty Ann (Geandreau) Dix; m. Alan Michael Zuckerman, May 27, 1978. BS, Upstate Med. Ctr., 1978; MBA, Ga. State U., 1982, MHA, 1983. Cytotechnologist Biomed. Ref. Labs., Burlington, N.C., 1978-81; fin. svcs. coord. Health S.E., Atlanta, 1983-84; sr. mgmt. cons. Laventhol & Horwath, Phila., 1984-85; sr. mgt. cons. ECRI, Plymouth Meeting, Pa., 1985-87; lab. mgr. St. Francis Hosp., Wilmington, Del., 1987-88, adminstrv. dir., 1988—. Contbr. articles to profl. jours. Mem. Am. Coll. Healthcare Execx., Healthcare Fin. Mgmt. Assn., Clin. Lab. Mgmt. Assn. Home: 343 Blackbird Station Rd Townsend DE 19734

ZUCKERMAN, MARY ELLEN WALLER, marketing educator; b. Gainesville, Fla., Jan. 10, 1954; d. David Allen and Ruth Barbera (Ergood) Waller; m. Miron Zuckerman, Sept. 3, 1988; children: David Benjamin, Jonathan Michael. BA, Simmons Coll., 1976; MBA, Columbia U., 1982, PhD, 1987. Fgn. svc. officer U.S. Dept. of State, Washington and N.Y.C., 1982-83; assoc. prof. SUNY, Geneseo, 1985—; rsch. fellow Gannett Found. Media Ctr., N.Y.C., 1989-90; vis. assoc. prof. McGill U., Montreal, Can., 1990-91. Author: Sources on the History of Women's Magazines 1792-1960, 1991, (with others) The Magazine in America, 1991; contbr. articles to profl. jours. NEH grantee, 1987; Spencer Found. fellow, 1992-95. Mem. Am. Mktg. Assn. (pres. Rochester, N.Y. chpt. 1991—, Eastern rep. 1989—), Am. Hist. Assn., Assn. for Consumer Rsch., Econ. and Bus. History Orgn., Orgn. of Am. Historians, Bus. History Conf., Berkshire Conf. on Women's History. Office: SUNY 206C Welles Geneseo NY 14454

ZUCKERMAN, PHILIP WARREN, publishing executive; b. Roslyn, N.Y., Mar. 21, 1951; s. Irvin and Selma (Apple) Z.; m. Dorothy D. Pearson, May 13, 1978; children: Andrew P., Charles H. P. BA, U. Denver, 1973. Pres. Applewood Books, Bedford, Mass., 1976—; bd. dirs. Franklins' Insight, Boston, Franklin R & D Co., Boston. Trustee Bedford (Mass.) Pub. Libr., 1989—. mem. N.E. Harbor Swim Club. Office: Applewood Books 18 North Rd Bedford MA 01730-1051

ZUCKER-SEEMAN, HELENE, art program director. BS, Boston U., 1971; MLS, Queens Coll., 1973; postgrad., NYU, 1976, Columbia U., 1977. Rep. U.S. Maitre Binoche Auction House, Paris, 1973-74; dir. Louis K. Meisel Gallery, N.Y.C., 1973-80; dir. art program The Prudential Ins. Co. of Am., Newark, 1980—. Contbr. articles to profl. jours.; lectr. in field; curated group shows including Robeson Ctr. Gallery, Rutgers U., 1984, City Without Walls Gallery, Newark, 1982, 83, James St. Art Festival, Newark, 1982; lectr. Norton Gallery of Art, 1990, Johnson Atelier, 1991, N.Y.U.. Home: 176 Broadway New York NY 10038-2511

ZUEHLKE, CARL WILLIAM, retired chemist; b. Bonduel, Wis., Oct. 28, 1916; s. Albert and Minnie Wilamina (Dehn) Z.; m. Cecelia Orlando Rago, Aug. 11, 1977 (dec. 1987); m. Hildegard Rose Koepf, Feb. 4, 1989. BS, U. Wis., 1938; MS, U. Mich., 1940, PhD, 1942. Chemist in charge methods lab. Allied Chem. and Dye Corp., Edgewater, N.J., 1942-45; chief chemist East St. Louis (Ill.) works Allied Chem. and Dye Corp., 1945-46; asst. mgr. control div. Allied Chem. and Dye Corp., N.Y.C., 1946-48; rsch. chemist Eastman Kodak Rsch. Labs., Rochester, N.Y., 1948-52, rsch. assoc., 1952-61, sr. rsch. assoc., 1961, asst. head chem. div., 1961-68, head analytical sci. div., 1968-79; chmn. Gordon Rsch. Conf. Analytical Chemistry, New Hamton, N.H., 1967. Contbr. chpts. to books: Silver Treatise on Analytical Chemistry, 1966, 75 Years of Kodak Research, 1989; contbr. articles to profl. jours.; patentee in field. Pres. Rochester Orthoptic Ctr., 1954; chmn. Rochester Assn. for United Nations, 1965, United Nations Week Monroe County, Rochester, 1962; dep. chief radiol. div. Monroe County CD, 1962. Home: 92 Skyview Ln Rochester NY 14625-1626

ZUGBY, ROBERT COURY, educator; b. Washington, Jan. 13, 1941; s. Emile and Lillian Genevieve (Coury) Z.; m. Cecilia Ann Nedeff; 1 child, Kristina Elizabeth. AB in Biology, Cath. U. Am., 1963. Cert. Secondary Sci. Educator, Md. Tchr. St. Martin's High Sch., Balt., 1965-66, Overbrook Children's Ctr., Arlington, Va., 1966-67, Northwestern High Sch., Hyattsville, Md., 1968-69, Arundel Sr. High Sch., Severna Park, Md., 1968-69; researcher, writer AAAS, Washington, 1969-71; writer Flow Labs., Inc., Rockville, Md., 1971-73; ptnr., mgr. Elpro Assocs., Takoma Park, Md., 1973-87; tchr. Our Lady of Sorrows Sch., Takoma Park, Md., 1987-88, Acad. of Notre Dame, Washington, 1988-89, Elizabeth Seton High SCh., Bladensburg, Md., 1989-90, Prince George's County Pub. Schs., 1990—. Mem. Prince George's County Bd. Appeals, Upper Marlboro, Md., 1987—; chair Coalition of Greenbelt (Md.) East Communities, 1985-90; pres. Greenbelt Access TV, Inc., 1987—; pres. Parish Coun. Our Lady of Lebanon Ch., Washington, 1985-87; city councilperson City of Greenbelt, 1983. Democrat. Maronite Catholic. Home: 94 Ridge Rd Greenbelt MD 20770-0741 Office: DuVal High Sch Lanham MD 20770

ZUKERMAN, MICHAEL, lawyer; b. Bklyn., Oct. 3, 1940; s. Charles Morris and Gertrude Ethel Zukerman; m. Claire J. Goldsmith, June 25, 1961 (div. 1986); children: Steven, Amy; m. Elaine DeMasi, Nov. 21, 1986; children: Jaclyn, Laura. BS, U. Fla., 1961; LLB, St. John's U., 1964; LLM, NYU, 1966. Bar: N.Y. 1965, Pa. 1983, U.S. Tax Ct. 1984. Credit analyst, loan officer Franklin Nat. Bank, 1964-66; assoc. Jaffin, Schneider, Kimmel & Galpeer, N.Y.C., 1966-67; ptnr. Zukerman, Licht & Friedman and predecessors, N.Y.C., 1967-79, Baskin & Sears, P.C., N.Y.C., 1979-85, Graubard, Moskowitz, Dannett, Horowitz & Mollen, 1985-86, Gersten, Savage, Kaplowitz & Zukerman, 1986-89; of counsel Olshan, Grundman, Frome & Rosenzweig, 1990—; pres. First Ptnrs. Credit Corp., N.Y.C., 1988—, exec. v.p. Brookhill Group, 1986-88; mem. bd. dirs. Interjurist LTD, internat. law firm. Contbg. editor Real Estate Taxation and Acctg., 1988—; lectr. on various subjects, 1986—. Trustee Temple Beth Torah, Melville, N.Y., 1972-80; bd. dirs. Suffolk Jewish Community Planning Bd., Hauppague, N.Y., 1982-85, WATSCO, Inc., Am. Vending Assocs., Dayton Mgmt. Corp.; trustee, treas. YMHA Suffolk County, Hauppague, 1980-85; bd. dir. Anti Defamation League of Westchester; co-chmn. bus. adv. counsel Town of Greenburgh. Mem. ABA. Home: 6 Thomas St Scarsdale NY 10583-1031 Office: Olshan Grundman Frome & Rosenzweig 505 Park Ave New York NY 10022-1106

ZUKIN, STEPHEN RANDOLPH, psychiatrist; b. Phila., Aug. 15, 1948; s. Solomon G. and Rose (Katz) Z.; children: Valerie Anne, Heather Nicole. BA, Haverford Coll., 1970; MD, Johns Hopkins U., 1974. Diplomate Am. Bd. Psychiatry and Neurology. Intern and resident in psychiatry Mt. Zion Med. Ctr., San Francisco, 1974-77; asst. prof. of psychiatry SUNY - Downstate, Bklyn., 1977-79, Mt. Sinai Sch. Medicine, N.Y.C., 1979-82; assoc. prof. psychiatry Albert Einstein Coll. Medicine, Bronx, N.Y., 1982-87, assoc. prof. neuroscience, 1984-87, prof. psychiatry and neuroscience, 1987—. Author more than 75 scientific publs., 1974—; co-discoverer Phencyclidine receptor of brain, 1979. Rsch. grantee Nat. Inst. on Drug Abuse, 1980—; recipient Kempf Fund award for R&D in Psychol. Psychiatry, 1992. Mem. Am. Psychiatric Assn., Soc. for Neuroscience, Am. Coll. Neuropsychopharmacology, Am. Soc. Pharmacology and Exptl. Therapeutics.

ZUKOWSKI, KIMBERLY JOAN, university housing director; b. Buffalo, Aug. 29, 1962; d. Lawrence John and Diane Evelyn (Adams) Z. BA, Alfred U., 1984, MS in Edn., 1986. Cert. elem. tchr., math., N.Y. Residence hall dir. Alfred Univ., Alfred, N.Y., 1984-86; admissions counselor Alfred Univ., 1985-86; housing dir. Daemen Coll., Amherst, 1986-88; univ. housing dir. Niagara Univ., Niagara Falls, 1988—. Mem. Assn. Coll. & Univ. Housing Officers, Coll. Student Pers. Assn., Phi Kappa Phi, Psi Chi, Alpha Phi Omega. Office: Niagara U Housing Office O'Shea Hall Niagara University NY 14109

ZUKOWSKI, WALTER HENRY, emeritus administrative science educator; b. Worcester, Mass., Sept. 28, 1914; s. Frank B. and Helen (Jankowska) Z.; m. Lucille Kathryn Pinette, Dec. 26, 1955; 1 dau., Mary L.A. B.B.A., Clark U., 1948, A.M., 1949, Ph.D., 1956. Instr. Worcester Poly. Inst., 1949-50, Clark U., 1951-52; mem. faculty Colby Coll., Waterville, Maine, 1952—; prof. adminstrv. sci. Colby Coll., 1965-73, Wadsworth prof. adminstrv. sci., 1973-82; emeritus Wadsworth prof. adminstrv. sci., 1982—; chmn. dept. adminstrv. sci. Colby Coll., 1958-80; asst. prof. La. State U. (C.Z. br.), summers 1952-54; vis. prof. Rockefeller Found. grantee Al-Hikma, U., Baghdad, Iraq, 1958-59, Robert Coll., Instanbul, Turkey, 1965-66; vis. prof., cons. ednl. policy Iranzamin Coll., Tehran, Iran, 1972-73; cons. in field, 1956—. Mem. platform com. Maine Republican Party, 1964. Served with USAAF, 1942-46. Mem. Am. Finance Assn., Am. Econ. Assn., Am. Accounting Assn. Home: PO Box 402 Waterville ME 04903-0402

ZUMOFF, BARNETT, endocrinologist; b. Bklyn., June 1, 1926; s. Abraham and Stella (Zumoff) Z.; m. Selma Silver, Nov. 11, 1951; children: Janine, Francine, Linda. AB, Columbia U., 1945; postgrad., Albany Med. Coll., 1945-47; MD, L.I. Coll. Medicine, 1949. Diplomate Am. Bd. Internal Medicine, Am. Bd. Endocrinology and Metabolism; cert. in endocrinology; lic. physician, N.Y. Rotating intern, med. resident Bklyn. Jewish Hosp., 1949-50, 51; straight med. intern Mass. Meml. Hosp., 1950-51; resident pathology Bklyn. VA Hosp., 1954-55; resident medicine univ. svc. Kings County Hosp., 1954-55; spl. fellow medicine, clin. asst. medicine Meml. Ctr., 1955-57; clin. asst. medicine Kings County Hosp., 1957-62; asst. Sloan-Kettering Inst., 1957-60, assoc., 1960-62; asst. medicine James Ewing Hosp., 1959-62, assoc. attending physician div. neoplastic medicine, 1961-63; attending physician dept. oncology, 1963-82; attending physician dept. medicine James Ewing Hosp., 1977-82, 87—, Hosp. for Joint Diseases-Orthopedic Inst., 1981—; attending physician and chief div. endocrinolog and metabolism dept. medicine Beth Israel Med. Ctr., N.Y.C., 1981—; instr. in medicine Cornell U. Med. Coll., 1958-62; asst. prof. Albert Einstein Coll. Medicine, 1965-71, assoc. prof., 1971-78, prof., 1978-82; vis. prof., 1987—; prof. Mt. Sinai Sch. Medicine, 1982—; asst. dir. Clin. Rsch. Ctr., Montefiore Hosp., 1961-76, dir. 1976-81, dir. cancer endocrinology, 1976-84, sr. investigator Inst. Steroid Rsch., 1963-81; vis. physician Rockefeller U. Hosp., 1978-84; adj. attending physician Mt. Sinai Med. Ctr., 1988—. Editorial bd. Jour. Clin. Endocrinology and Metabolism, 1971-76, Anticancer Rsch., 1981—, Breast Disease-An Internat. Jour., 1987—; translator Yiddish poetry. Pres. Workmen's Circle, 1984-88, 92—, The Forward Assn., 1991—; co-pres. Congress for Jewish Culture, 1989—; active Atran Found., 1987—. With M.C., USAF, 1951-82, brig. gen. Res. ret. Decorated Legion of Merit, Combat Readiness medal, Meritorious Svc. medal, Air Force Commendation medal. Fellow ACP; mem. AMA, AAAS, Am. Heart Assn. (coun. on arteriosclerosis), Am. Soc. Clin. Investigation, Endocrine Soc., Aerospace Med. Assn., Am. Diabetes Assn. (profl. sect.), Am. Fedn. Clin. Rsch., Assn. Mil. Surgeons U.S., Soc. Med. Cons. Armed Forces, Soc. USAF Flight Surgeons, N.Y. Diabetes Assn. Home: 3710 Bedford Ave Brooklyn NY 11229-1704 Office: Beth Israel Med Ctr Div Endocrinolgy Metabolism 1st Ave at 16th St New York NY 10003

ZUNICK, FRANKLIN HARVEY, store planner, sales executive; b. Boston, Apr. 16, 1939; s. Isadore and Miriam (Lamkin) Z.; m. Roberta Eleanor Cordette, May 12, 1963; children: Mark, Jeffrey. BS in Bus. Adminstrn., Suffolk U., Boston, 1961. Dept. mgr. Marrud Inc., Saugus, Mass., 1962-63, Bradlees Dept. Stores, Woburn, Mass., 1964-65; asst. store mgr. Bradlees Dept. Stores, Somerville, Mass., 1965-66; dir. store ops. Bradlees Dept. Stores, Braintree, Mass., 1967-69, dir. store planning, 1969-73; store planner, sales mgr. DeStafano Studios Inc., Woburn, 1973—. With U.S. Army, 1961-69. Mem. Nat. Assn. Display Industries, Inst. Store Planners. Jewish. Home: 21 Nancy Ave Peabody MA 01960-2612

ZUNINO, NATALIA, psychologist; b. N.Y.C., Nov. 23, 1937; d. Frank Anthony and Elizabeth (Delafield) Zunino; m. Philip Puschel, June 29, 1974 (div. 1978). BA, Mt. Holyoke Coll., Mass., 1959; MA, Columbia U., 1962,

NYU, 1975; PhD, NYU, 1982. Researcher Time-Life Books, N.Y.C., 1962-67; sr. editor Harcourt Brace Jovanovich, N.Y.C., 1967-80; staff psychotherapist Met. Ctr. for Mental Health, N.Y.C., 1983-85; adj. asst. prof. Coll. Staten Island, N.Y.C., 1984-86; staff psychotherapist Washington Sq. Inst., N.Y.C., 1984-87; faculty/staff psychotherapist Ctr. for Study of Anorexia & Bulimia, N.Y.C., 1984—; supr. Met. Inst. Tng. in Psychoanalytic Psychotherapy, N.Y.C., 1985—; supr. staff psychotherapist Bulimia Treatment Assocs., N.Y.C., 1986—; psychotherapist family and couple treatment Inst. Contemporary Psychotherapy, N.Y.C., 1988-92; extern Family Inst. of Westchester, Mt. Vernon, N.Y., 1990-91; psychotherapist family and couple treatment, Inst. for Contemporary Psychotherapy, N.Y.C., 1988-92; extern Family Inst. of Westchester, Mt. Vernon, N.Y., 1990-91; cons. in field. Editor: Psychology: Its Principles and Applications, 1969, 8th edit. 1984, Sociology: The Study of Human Relationships, 1972, 2nd edit. 1977; contbr. articles to profl. jours. Mem. APA. Home: 115 4th Ave New York NY 10003-4900

ZUPSIC, MATTHEW MICHAEL, insurance company executive; b. Pitts., Aug. 30, 1950; s. Joseph Matthew and Antoinette (Birsic) Z.; m. Vicki Jean Quinn, Oct. 8, 1982; children: Tina Elizabeth, Matthew Quay. BA, Marietta Coll., 1972. Mktg. rep. Hartford Ins., Pitts., 1972-76; ins. agt. Githens Ins. Ctr., Belle Vernon, Pa., 1976-77; v.p.; ptnr. Burchill Ins. Agy., Inc., Pitts., Pa., 1977-88; pres. Harte, Hawke & Zupsic Ins. Agy., Pitts., Pa., 1989—. Mem. Pa. Assn. Ind. Ins. Agts. (bd. dirs. 1980-88), Ind. Ins. Agts. Pitts. (treas. 1983, 1st v.p. 1984-86, pres. 1986-88), B&S Investment Club (pres 1985-87). Democrat. Roman Catholic.

ZURAV, EDWARD H., lawyer; b. Newark, Sept. 19, 1956; s. David B. and Frances S. (Stalford) Z. BS, Seton Hall U., 1979, JD, 1986. Bar: N.J. 1986, U.S. Ct. Appeals (3d cir.) 1987. Pres., founder E-Z Way Tutoring, Union, N.J., 1984—; pvt. practice Union, 1987—; one-on-one tutor for Scholastic Aptitude Test, Law Sch. Admission Test, Grad. Record Exam., 1984—. Mem. ABA, N.J. Bar Assn., Union County Bar Assn., Essex County Bar Assn. Republican. Jewish. Home: 28 Woodland Dr Roselle NJ 07203-2461 Office: E-Z Way Tutoring 1460 Morris Ave Union NJ 07083-3313

ZURICK, JACK, engineer; b. Bklyn., May 28, 1952; s. Joseph and Edelgard (Wendland) Z.; m. Nenita Cardinal, Apr. 28, 1990. Pre-engring student, Queensborough Community Coll., 1969-71, AAS, 1971-73. Cert. Assoc. Engring. Technician. Elec. designer Ebasco Svcs., Inc., N.Y.C., 1973-76; design engr. Gibbs & Cox, Inc., N.Y.C., 1976-78; elec. designer Sci. Design Co., Inc., N.Y.C., 1978-85; design engr. Vikonics, Inc., Secaucus, N.J., 1985-87; sr. elec. designer H-R Internat., Inc., Edison, N.J., 1988—; cons. Sherman Svcs., Inc., Somerset, N.J., 1988, Gen. Indsl. Techs., Inc., Valleystream, N.Y., 1987-88. Mem. Nat. Inst. for Cert. Engring. Technols. Assn. (assoc. engring. technician), Tau Alpha Pi (v.p. 1972-73). Home: 59 Pheasant Run Freehold NJ 07728 Office: H-R Internat Inc 2045 Lincoln Hwy Edison NJ 08817

ZURIER, ROBERT BURTON, medical educator, clinical investigator; b. Passaic, N.J., Feb. 19, 1934; s. Milton and Lillian (Matzner) Z.; m. Catherine Elizabeth Miers, June 3, 1962; 1 child, Adam Wheaton. BS, Rutgers U., 1955; MD, U. Tex. Southwestern Med. Ctr., Dallas, 1962; MA (hon.), U. Pa., 1981. Intern, then resident in medicine Boston City Hosp., 1962-64; fellow in medicine St. Lukes Hosp., N.Y.C., 1964-66; fellow in rheumatology NYU, 1970-73; asst. prof. medicine U. Conn., Farmington, 1973-76; pvt. practice internal medicine Holden, Mass., 1967-70; assoc. prof. U. Conn., Farmington, 1976-80; prof., chief. rheumatology U. Pa., Phila., 1980-91; prof. medicine, dir. rheumatology div. U. Mass. Med. Ctr., Worcester, 1991—. Served to capt. USAR, 1956-68. Guggenheim Found. fellow, 1986. Mem. AAAS, Am. Coll. Rheumatology, Am. Soc. Clin. Investigation, Interurban Clin. Club (pres. 1989-90). Office: Univ Mass Med Ctr 55 Lake Ave N Worcester MA 01655-0001

ZUZOV, JANICE CLAIRE, occupational therapist; b. Trenton, N.J., Sept. 8, 1963; d. Michael and Ann (Sakowski) Z.; m. Jeffrey Mershon, June 1, 1991. BS in Occupational Therapy, Kean Coll., 1986; postgrad., Trenton State Coll., 1990—. Cert. pediatric therapist. Staff therapist St. Lawrence Rehab. Ctr., Lawrenceville, N.J., 1986-87; chief of therapy Somerset Med. Ctr., Somerville, N.J., 1987-90; therapist Princeton (N.J.) Med. Ctr., 1991—; chair N.J. Occupational Therapy SIG Adminstrn., 1991, N.J. Occupational Therapy High Sch. Awareness, Somerset County. Mem. AACD, Am. Occupational Therapy Assn., N.J. Occupational Therapy Assn. (spl. svc. award 1990), Princeton Holistic Health Assn., Greenpeace.

ZUZZIO, ELIZABETH ANN, nurse; b. Glen Ridge, N.J., July 7, 1946; d. George Ramond and Bertha Elizabeth (Young) Beck; children: Paul Albert, Joy Ann. BSN, Rutgers Coll. Nursing, 1968; MA in Counseling, Seton Hall U., 1991. RN, N.J. Staff nurse babies unit United Hosp., Newark, N.J., 1968; pub. health nurse East Orange (N.J.) Health Dept., 1968-70; sch. nurse Franklin Sch., Kearny, N.J., 1970-72; staff nurse, instr. Columbus Hosp., Newark, 1971-75; extern Newton (N.J.) Meml. Hosp. Rehab. Unit, 1990-91. Vol. Domestic Abuse Hotline, Newton, 1986—, Sunrise House, Lafayette, N.J., 1986; lamaze instr., Kearny, 1973-75; vol. Andover Intermediate Care, 1988-89, Byram (N.J.) Day Com., 1988. Mem. Am. Mental Health Counselors Assn., Am. Assn. for Counseling and Devel., Sigma Theta Tau (treas. 1967-68), Kappa Delta Phi. Methodist. Home: 16 Allamuchy Trl Andover NJ 07821-9422

ZWANZIGER, DANIEL, physicist; b. N.Y.C., May 20, 1935; s. David and Frances (Murstein) Z.; m. Dana Levor, Sept. 6, 1977; children: Jenny Daisy, Emily Rose. AB, Columbia U., 1955, PhD, 1960. Lectr. U. Calif., Berkeley, 1960-62; ricercatore U. Rome, 1962-63; chercheur etranger Commissariat Energie Atomique, Saclay, France, 1963-65; vis. scientist Weizmann Inst., Rehovoth, Israel, 1969-70; assoc. Cern, Geneva, Switzerland, 1980; vis. prof. Ecole Nomale Superieure, Paris, 1980; prof. NYU, 1965—. Contbr. articles to profl. jours. Rsch. grantee NSF, 1966—. Fellow Am. Phys. Soc. Home: 37 Hemlock Dr North Tarrytown NY 10591 Office: Physics Dept NYU 4 Washington Pl New York NY 10003

ZWEIER, RICHARD JOSEPH, JR., secondary school educator, education supervisor; b. Lebanon, Pa., Jan. 5, 1951; s. Richard Joseph and Verna Ruth (Leedy) Z.; m. Deborah Ann Troxel, Aug. 11, 1973 (div. 1985); 1 child, David Richard; m. Nancy Patricia Baylock, Mar. 3, 1985. BS in Music Edn., Lebanon Valley Coll., Annville, Pa., 1972; MMus, Manhattan Sch. Music, 1980. Tchr. Franklin (N.J.) Pub. Schs., 1973-75; tchr., choral dir. Vernon (N.J.) Twp. High Sch., 1975—, music supr. 9-12, 1985—; music supr. K-12 Vernon Twp. Pub. Schs., 1991—; pvt. voice instr., Vernon, 1977—; condr. N.J. All-State Chorus, Atlantic City, 1984, N.J. All-State Opera Festival Chorus, East Orange, 1989, Miss. State Music Camp Chorus, Starkville, summers 1988, 89. Artistic dir., prin. condr. Community Choral Soc., Vernon, 1989—. Mem. NEA, Music Educators Nat. Conf., N.J. Music Educators Assn. (state bd. dirs. 1980-83, 87-90, chmn. choral procedures com. 1988-90), Assn. for Supervision and Curriculum Devel., Prins. and Suprs. Assn., North Jersey Sch. Music Assn., Am. Choral Dirs. Assn. Home: 31 Woodland Dr Vernon NJ 07462 Office: Vernon Twp High Sch PO Box 800 Vernon NJ 07462-0800

ZWIEP, DONALD NELSON, mechanical engineering educator; b. Hull, Iowa, Mar. 18, 1924; s. Daniel and Nellie (De Stigter) Z.; m. Marcia J. Hubers, Sept. 3, 1948; children: Donna J., Mary N., Joan L., Helen D. BS in Mech. Engring., Iowa State Coll., 1948, MS in Mech. Engring, 1951; DEng (hon.), Worcester Polytech. Inst., 1965. Registered profl. engr., Mass. Design engr. Boeing Airplane Co., 1948-50, sr. tool engr., summer 1953, summer faculty asso., 1955; asst. prof. Colo. State U., 1951-56, assoc. prof., 1956-57; cons. engr. aviation div. Forney Mfg. Co., 1956-57; prof., head dept. mech. engring. Worcester Polytech. Inst., 1957-88, acting head mgmt. engring., 1974-76, chmn. Mfg. Engring. Application Ctr., 1981-88, acting provost, v.p. acad. affairs, 1988-90, prof., dept. head emeritus, 1990—; constrn. engr. U.S. C.E., summer 1954; cons. engr., acting chief engr. J.J. Malir, Inc., summer 1956. Chmn. bd. trustees James F. Lincoln Arc Welding Found., 1976—. Served as pilot USAAF, World War II, CBI; lt. col. USAFR; cons. and ednl. specialist Res. Fellow ASME (v.p. edn. 1972—, pres. 1979-80); mem. Am. Soc. Engring. Edn. (pres. Colo. State U. chpt. 1954-55, treas. Rocky Mountain sect. 1955, dir. 1974-75), Soc. Mfg. Engrs., Am. Welding Soc., Sigma Xi, Omicron Delta Kappa, Tau Beta Bi, Sigma Tau, Pi Tau Sigma. Methodist. Club: Torch. Home: 47 Birchwood Dr Holden MA 01520-1937 Office: Worcester Poly Inst 100 Institute Rd Worcester MA 01609-2276

ZYSBLAT, WILLIAM LARRY, accountant; b. Fair Lawn, N.J., Nov. 20, 1950; s. Morris and Joan (Stern) Z. BS, Syracuse U., 1972. CPA, N.Y. Acctg. supr. Peat Marwick Main; chief fin. officer Sir Prodns., 1976-78; prin. Sound Advice, Inc., 1978-87; ptnr. Rascoff/Zysblat Orgn., L.A., N.Y.C., 1988—; bus. mgr. to performing artists including The Rolling Stones, David Bowie, Pink Floyd, Duran Duran, Paul Simon, The Estate of Elvis Presley, David Brenner, others. TV producer spls. including The Ann. Internat. Rock Awards, David Bowie's Glass Spider, and others; tour producer including David Bowie, 1983, 87, 90, Rolling Stones, 1975, 76, 78, 81, 82, 89, 90, Pink Floyd, 1988, 89, Paul Simon, 1991. Recipient numerous gold and platinum record awards, medal N.Y. Internat. Film and TV Festival. Mem. N.Y. State Soc. CPAs, AICPA.